The New York Times

CROSSWORD PUZZLE

DICTIONARY

The New York Times

CROSSWORD PUZZLE DICTIONARY

• Third Edition •

By Tom Pulliam and Clare Grundman

A HUDSON GROUP BOOK

Random House
Puzzles & Games

Produced in association with Morningside Editorial Associates, Inc.

Designed by Martin Connell

Originally published in hardcover in 1995 and in trade paperback in 1997 by Times Books, a division of Random House, Inc., as *The New York Times Crossword Puzzle Dictionary, 3rd Edition*.

Library of Congress Cataloging in Publication Data

Pulliam, Tom.
    The New York Times crossword puzzle dictionary.

    "A Hudson Group book."
    1. Crossword puzzles—Glossaries, vocabularies, etc.
I. Grundman, Clare, 1913–   . II. New York Times.
III. Title
GV1507.C7P83 1984   793.73'2'03   84-40108
ISBN: 0-8129-3122-X

Random House Puzzles & Games Website address:
www.puzzlesatrandom.com

Printed in the United States of America

19   18   17   16   15   14   13   12   11   10

PREFACE to the First Edition

THE NEW YORK TIMES CROSSWORD PUZZLE DICTIONARY exceeds in completeness and scope all other puzzle dictionaries. No useful word has been omitted. Not only have puzzles themselves been combed for synonyms that are used over and over, but also a word-for-word reading of major unabridged dictionaries, both current and old, has produced a thoroughly complete and extensive checklist.

Each of us has been solving and compiling puzzles for many years, and our chief purpose has been to design a practical and easy-to-use dictionary, in the belief that your needs and requirements for such a volume closely reflect our own. For example, the synonyms are arranged by the number of letters, and then alphabetized so you can quickly find the very word that fills the spaces in the puzzle. Another feature, one that seems obvious for a crossword puzzle dictionary but is not found in most of them, is that all words are printed in easy-to-read capital letters. The type has been chosen with great care for its legibility, and the three-column format not only provides a short line of type to scan but also enables us to get a very large number of words on each page.

Synonyms of great length have been omitted to give room for the shorter, more useful words. The puzzler can always "fill in" the very long words provided he has a good supply of short common synonyms. We have placed, therefore, an arbitrary ceiling of eight-letter word-lengths, knowing this will satisfy almost all needs. Here and there, however, you will find occasional exceptions to this rule. These are synonyms of such frequent, interesting, and normal usage that their omission might handicap the puzzler.

The "shaded boxes" scattered through the book are a notable and unique feature of THE NEW YORK TIMES CROSSWORD PUZZLE DICTIONARY. They collect under one heading a variety of categories and synonyms that you would have a hard time finding in other dictionaries. For example, when you are confronted by the clue "Brazilian river" merely turn to the shaded area marked BRAZIL, where you will find several excellent possibilities. Similarly, look for a "Philippine native" under PHILIPPINES, or a "Scottish measure" under SCOTLAND.

Another useful feature is the lavish listing of phrases. For instance, instead of being confronted by the simple clue "Sword," you may run up against "Double-edged sword." Under the entry word SWORD in this dictionary you will find ample phrases that qualify the entry word or more sharply specify its meaning. Also, given the definition "Turn aside," simply look under TURN and find that phrase, along with many others.

THE NEW YORK TIMES CROSSWORD PUZZLE DICTIONARY is a versatile reference book that you will want to keep on your desk or next to your chair for help, not only with crossword puzzles, but also for a large variety of other puzzles and contests. In addition, it will be invaluable for writers, speakers, and the like, for (with more than one-half million words) it is one of the largest books of synonyms ever published. Its simple arrangement makes it far easier to use than the standard thesauri.

Our hope is that you will come to use this new word book as we might. Get to know it and be adventuresome! If the first entry you consult does not corner the exact word you are seeking, let any listing at that spot lead you to a cross-reference. Follow this track until you have the right word "treed."

A project of this scope may well have been beyond the ability of only two to accomplish. We have required and welcomed top-flight support during our work. Although many might be named, special note must be given to the efforts of Richard Martz and David House of Dartmouth College, who were responsible for much of the computerization; also, to Gorton Carruth and Robert O'Brien of Morningside Associates. Each made his individual contributions, which we gratefully acknowledge.

Happy word hunting!

Tom Pulliam
Clare Grundman

1974

PREFACE to the Second Edition

This Second Edition of THE NEW YORK TIMES CROSSWORD PUZZLE DICTIONARY greatly augments the First Edition. We have added approximately 100,000 new entry words and synonyms into a new four-column format, which maintains the same easy-to-read features and the large numbers of words per page, including many new longer words. An outstanding innovation of this Second Edition is the inclusion of the titles of major works of literature and music, as well as their authors and composers, and the names of characters in books, plays, operas, etc. Another very important addition is the listing of famous people from various walks of life—painters,

physicians, playwrights, botanists, etc.—as well as
those men and women who have won Nobel Prizes
and who have been inducted into the Hall of Fame.
We have also assembled what we believe to be the
most comprehensive listing of prefixes, suffixes, and
combining forms, which are †listed by meaning,ê
and the largest list of biblical, mythological, and literary relationships ever to appear in a crossword
puzzle dictionary. And, of course, we have retained
from the First Edition the unique "shaded boxes"
that feature pertinent facts about geographical locations.

We would like to acknowledge once more the excellent assistance of Gorton Carruth and Robert
O'Brien of Morningside Editorial Associates and to
thank the many puzzlers who have sent us their compliments and suggestions.

Again, we wish you happy word hunting!

T.P.
C.G.

1984

Preface to the Third Edition

In the decade since the Second Edition of THE
NEW YORK TIMES CROSSWORD PUZZLE DICTIO-
NARY was published, the nature of crossword puzzles has changed in several ways, some obvious and
some subtle. These changes, which we determined
several years ago would require a Third Edition in
order to have an up-to-date dictionary, are reflected
in the many alterations and additions you will find in
the text. In the last few years writers of crossword

puzzles have made the clues less obvious, thus making the puzzles more difficult to solve. We believe that the average solver appreciates this additional challenge. You will discover in this Third Edition, therefore, many alternate and uncommon synonyms of finding words. You will also discover many synonyms consisting of phrases of two or more words unaccompanied by qualifying explanations, such as "two words." For example, under the finding word "succeed" you will find MAKEIT. Consider, AT HOME under "in," SHOOIN under "winner (easy)," the slangy GOAPE under "flip," and the three-word phrase INARUT under "stuck." Please remember that all phrases are listed, just as they are written in puzzles, as one word. This use of phrases makes solving crossword puzzles more interesting, as does the use of "gimmicks" or unifying themes, slang, and words and phrases associated with the space age and the drug culture. You will find a more extensive coverage of these kinds of subjects in this new edition. We have also included a list of "partners," a category that has come into increasing use. For example, the clue asks for the "partner of hither," intending you to fill in YON. These pairings are all listed under the finding word "partners" and written in the dictionary as one word: HITHERYON, KITHKIN, YINYANG, etc. You will find a similar listing under "alternatives," which suggests the use of tore instead of tand,ê as in "alternative of hit" is MISS and is entered as HITMISS. Particularly useful new categories of finding words are those dealing with sports teams and players. For example, under "hockey" or "football" you will find lists of players and teams. Other similar finding words include baseball, golf, and tennis. Finally, we have updated many lists, such as Nobel Prize winners and persons who are well-known for their achievements in their professions, such as "author," "playwright," and "statesman." In short, all these additions confirm that this Third Edition of THE NEW YORK TIMES CROSSWORD PUZZLE DICTIONARY remains the most comprehensive and current puzzle dictionary available.

Once again we would like to acknowledge the excellent and necessary assistance of Gorton Carruth of Morningside Editorial Associates. For this Third Edition we are grateful for the contributions of Edmund Yee, who guided us through the intricacies of the computer, and Bruce Wetterau, who updated the geographical boxes and expanded the categories of occupations. Our thanks also go to Henry Griffin for much of the keyboarding. We are especially grateful to the many puzzlers who have written us over the years with their suggestions and well wishes.

Happy word hunting!

T.P.
C.G.

1995

The New York Times

CROSSWORD PUZZLE

DICTIONARY

A

A AY HA AIR ARY PER ALFA EACH
ALPHA
  (EVER —) ARROW
AA LAVA
AAL AL MULBERRY
AARDVARK ANTEATER EARTHHOG
EDENTATE
AARDWOLF HYAENID
AARON (BROTHER OF —) MOSES
  (BURIAL PLACE OF —) HOR
  (FATHER OF —) AMRAM
  (MOTHER OF —) JOCHEBED
  (SISTER OF —) MIRIAM
  (SON OF —) ABIHU NADAB ELEAZAR
ITHAMAR
  (WIFE OF —) ELISHEBA
AARONIC LEVITIC LEVITICAL
AARON'S ROD MULLEIN
AB HATI
ABA ABAYAH
ABACA HEMP FIBER LUPIS LINAGA
MANILA
ABACK SHORT
ABACUS SOROBAN SHWANPAN
ABADDON PIT HELL ABYSS SATAN
APOLLYON
ABAFT AFT BACK BAFT ABAFF
ASTERN BEHIND REARWARD
  (— THE BEAM) LARGE
ABALONE EAR PAUA AWABI NACRE
ORMER UHLLO ASSEIR MOLLUSK
ABANDON EGO CAST DROP FLEE
JUNK QUIT SINK ABAND ALLAY
CHUCK DITCH EXPEL LEAVE PLANT
REMIT SCRAP WAIVE YIELD ABJURE
BANISH BETRAY DESERT DEVEST
DISUSE DIVEST EXPOSE FOREGO
FORHOO FORLET FORSAKE RECANT
REFUSE REJECT RELENT RESIGN
SLOUGH STRAND VACATE DEPLORE
DISCARD FORFEIT FORSAKE
SCUTTLE ABDICATE FORHOOIE
FORSWEAR JETTISON RASHNESS
RENOUNCE SURCEASE RELINQUISH
  (— EVIL WAYS) REFORM
  (WITH —) DESPERATELY
ABANDONED BAD LEFT LORN LOST
VACANT WICKED CORRUPT FORLORN
PROJECT DEPRAVED DERELICT
DESERTED DESOLATE FLAGRANT
FORSAKEN
ABANDONING
  (PREF.) LIPO
ABANDONMENT BURIAL DUNKIRK
APOSTASY ABATEMENT
  (— OF RESTRAINT) LETUP
ABANGA ADY

ABAS (FATHER OF —) CELEUS
LYNCEUS
  (MOTHER OF —) METANIRA
HYPERMNESTRA
  (SON OF —) PROETUS ACRISIUS
ABASE SINK VAIL VALE AVALE AVILE
BLAME DEMIT DIMIT LOWER SHAME
ABJECT BEMEAN DEBASE DEFAME
DEJECT DEMEAN DEPOSE GROVEL
HUMBLE LESSEN MEEKEN REDUCE
DEGRADE DEPRESS MORTIFY
DIMINISH DISGRACE DISHONOR
ABASED ABAISSE DEJECTED
ABASH AWE COW BASH BAZE DASH
AVALE ESBAY SHAME HUMBLE
AFFRONT CONFUSE MORTIFY
BEWILDER BROWBEAT CONFOUND
ABASHED BLANK CHEAP SHAMED
ASHAMED FOOLISH SHEEPISH
ABASHMENT VERGOYNE
ABATE EBB END LOW CALM CURB
FAIR FALL MEND OMIT SLOW SOFT
VAIL VOID WANE ALLAY ALLOW
ANNUL APPAL BREAK CHECK LOWER
QUASH RELAX REMIT SLAKE SWAGE
ASLAKE DEDUCT LESSEN PACIFY
REBATE REDUCE RELENT ABOLISH
ASSUAGE CASSARE CHANCER
NULLIFY QUALIFY SLACKEN SUBSIDE
DECREASE DIMINISH MITIGATE
MODERATE OVERBLOW PALLIATE
ABATEMENT DELF FALL ALLAY
DELFT DELPH LETUP GUSSET MIOSIS
RABATE DECREASE DISCOUNT
PROSTRATION
  (— OF DISEASE) LYSIS
ABATIS OBSTACLE SLASHING
ABAXIAL DORSAL
ABBA FATHER
ABBAY ABBACY
ABBE MONK CLERIC CURATE PRIEST
ABBESS AMMA VICARESS
ABBEY ABADIA ABBAYE PRIORY
CONVENT NUNNERY CLOISTER
ABBOT ABBAS COARB
ARCHIMANDRITE
  (— OF MISRULE) BISHOP
ABBREVIATE CUT CLIP DOCK PRUNE
DIGEST ABRIDGE BOBTAIL CURTAIL
SHORTEN CONDENSE CONTRACT
TRUNCATE
ABBREVIATED SHORT BOBTAIL
CRYPTIC MUTILATE
ABBREVIATION LAPSE SIGLUM
SYMBOL
  (PL.) CIGLA
ABC ALPHABET

ABDA (FATHER OF —) SHAMMUA
(SON OF) ADONIRAM
ABDEEL (SON OF —) SHELEMIAH
ABDERITE FOOL SCOFFER
SIMPLETON
ABDI (SON OF —) KISHI
ABDICATE CEDE QUIT DEMIT EXPEL
LEAVE REMIT DEPOSE DISOWN
FOREGO RESIGN RETIRE VACATE
ABANDON DISCLAIM RENOUNCE
ABDICATION DRIFT
ABDIEL (FATHER OF —) GUNI
(SON OF —) AHI
ABDOMEN BOUK WOMB ALVUS
APRON BELLY MELON MIRAC PLEON
THARM PAUNCH VENTER STOMACH
(PREF.) CELI COELI VENTR(I)(O)
ABDOMINAL BELLY HEMAL CELIAC
COELIAC VENTRAL VISCERAL
ABDON (FATHER OF —) MICAH HILLEL
JEHIEL SHASHAK
ABDUCT LURE TAKE STEAL ABDUCE
KIDNAP RAVISH SPIRIT CAPTURE
ABDUCTED RAPT
ABDUCTION APAGOGE RAPTURE
**ABDUCTION FROM THE
SERAGLIO** (CHARACTER IN —)
OSMIN PASHA BLONDE BELMONTE
PEDRILLO CONSTANZE
(COMPOSER OF —) MOZART
ABDUCTOR SPIRIT
ABEAM ABREAST
ABECEDARIAN TYRO NOVICE
LEARNER BEGINNER
ABECEDARIUS ABC
ABED SICK RESTING RETIRED
SLEEPING
ABEL (BROTHER OF —) CAIN SETH
(FATHER OF —) ADAM
(MOTHER OF —) EVE
(PARENT OF —) ADAM
ABE LINCOLN IN ILLINOIS
(AUTHOR OF —) SHERWOOD
(CHARACTER IN —) ABE ANN GALE
MARY SETH TODD GREEN SPEED
GRAHAM JIMMIE MENTOR NINIAN
BOWLING DOUGLAS EDWARDS
HERNDON RUTLEDGE
ABELMOSK MUSK MALLOW
ABENCERAGES (CHARACTER IN —)
ALMANSOR
(COMPOSER OF —) CHERUBINI
ABENCERRAJE (AUTHOR OF —)
VILLEGAS
(CHARACTER IN —) JARIFA NARVAEZ
RODRIGO ABINDARRAEZ
ABERDEEN ANGUS BLACK DODDY
DODDIE
ABERRANT WILD CLAMMY DEVIANT
ABNORMAL STRAYING VARIABLE
ABERRATION SLIP WARP ERROR
FAULT LAPSE MANIA DELIRIUM
DELUSION INSANITY

ABESSIVE CARITIVE
ABET AID EGG BACK HELP BOOST
COACH ASSIST FOMENT INCITE
SECOND SUCCOR UPHOLD COMFORT
CONNIVE ESPOUSE FORWARD
FURTHER SUPPORT SUSTAIN
ADVOCATE BEFRIEND
ABETO ACXOYATL
ABETTING CONFEDERATE
ABETTOR FAUTOR ADVOCATE
PROMOTER
ABEYANCE ABEYANCY DORMANCY
(IN —) ONICE
ABEYANT LATENT
ABHIMANYU (FATHER OF —)
ARJUNA
(VICTIM OF —) LAKSHMANA
ABHOR UG IRK HATE SHUN AGRISE
DETEST LOATHE DESPISE DISLIKE
EXECRATE ABOMINATE
ABHORRENCE HATE ODIUM
HATRED HORROR DISGUST DISLIKE
SCUNNER AVERSION LOATHING
ABHORRENT ODIOUS UGSOME
HATEFUL ABSONANT INFAMOUS
REPUGNANT
ABI (SON OF —) HEZEKIAH
ABIA (FATHER OF —) BECHER SAMUEL
JEROBOAM REHOBOAM
(HUSBAND OF —) HEZRON
ABIATHAR (FATHER OF —)
AHIMELECH
ABIDA
(FATHER OF —) MIDIAN
ABIDE BE WIN WON BEAR BIDE KEEP
LAST LEND LENG LIVE REST STAY
WAIT ABEAR AWAIT DELAY EXIST
HABIT PAUSE STAND SWELL TARRY
ENDURE HARBOR LINGER REMAIN
RESIDE SUBMIT INHABIT SOJOURN
SUBSIST SUSTAIN CONTINUE
TOLERATE
(— BY) HOLD
ABIDING ABY FAST STABLE LASTING
ABIDINGNESS PERMANENCE
ABIEL (SON OF —) KISH
ABIES FIRS CONIFERS
ABIETATE SYLVATE
ABIEZER (FATHER OF —) GILEAD
ABIGAIL MAID
(HUSBAND OF —) DAVID NABAL
JETHER
(SON OF —) AMASA DANIEL
CHILEAB
ABIGEUS ABACTOR
ABIHAIL (DAUGHTER OF —) ESTHER
(FATHER OF —) HURI ELIAB
(HUSBAND OF —) ABISHUR
REHOBOAM
(SON OF —) ZURIEL
ABIHU (BROTHER OF —) NADAB
(FATHER OF —) AARON
(MOTHER OF —) ELISHEBA

ABIHUD (FATHER OF —) BELA
ABIJAH (FATHER OF —) DAVID
SAMUEL JEROBOAM REHOBOAM
(SON OF —) ASA HEZEKIAH
ABILITY G CAN MAY CLAY EASE
FORM HAND CLASS FLAIR FORCE
MIGHT POWER SKILL STUFF VERVE
ENERGY ENGINE INGINE MAUGHT
STROKE TALENT CALIBER CUNNING
FACULTY POTENCY APTITUDE
CAPACITY STRENGTH
(— TO ENTER) ACCESS
(— TO THROW) ARM
(BATTING —) STICKWORK
(CREATIVE —) IMAGINATION
(FIELDING —) GLOVE
(INVENTIVE —) CONTRIVANCE
(MENTAL —) INGENY BRAINPOWER
ABIMELECH (BROTHER OF —)
JOTHAM
(FATHER OF —) GIDEON ABIATHA
ABINADAB (FATHER OF —) SAUL
JESSE
ABINOAM (SON OF —) BARAK
ABIPON CORONADO
ABIRAM (FATHER OF —) HIEL ELIAB
ABISHAI (BROTHER OF —) JOAB
ASAHEL
(MOTHER OF —) ZERUIAH
ABISHALOM (DAUGHTER OF —)
MAACHAH
ABISHUA (FATHER OF —) BELA
PHINEHAS
(SON OF —) BUKKI
ABISHUR (FATHER OF —) SHAMMAI
ABITAL (HUSBAND OF —) DAVID
ABITUB (FATHER OF —) SHAHARAIM
(MOTHER OF —) HUSHIM
ABJECT LOW BASE MEAN POOR
SUNK VILE HELOT PRONE SORRY
CRAVEN MENIAL PALTRY SORDID
SUPINE FAWNING FORLORN
IGNOBLE SERVILE SLAVISH
BEGGARLY CRINGING DEGRADED
DOWNCAST LISTLESS WRETCHED
ABJOINT ABSTRICT
ABJURE DENY NITTE SPURN
ESCHEW RECALL RECANT REJECT
RESIGN REVOKE ABANDON
DISAVOW EJURATE RETRACT
ABNEGATE DISCLAIM FORSWEAR
RENOUNCE
ABLAUT APOPHONY
ABLAZE ALOW AFIRE ALOWE
ABLEEZE BURNING GLOWING
RADIANT GLEAMING INFLAMED
ABLE APT BIG CAN FIT FERE ADEPT
HABIL SMART THERE CLEVER EXPERT
FACILE FITTED HABILE POTENT
STRONG BASTANT CAPABLE
DOUGHTY DEXTROUS POSSIBLE
POWERFUL SKILLFUL SUITABLE
TALENTED VIGOROUS

(— TO WALK) FEERIE FEIRIE
(SUFF.) (— TO) FUL
ABLE-BODIED YAL YALD YAULD
ABLENESS
(SUFF.) ABILITY IBILITY
ABLUTION BATH WIDU WUDU
WUZU LOTION BAPTISM BATHING
WASHING
ABNAKI WABANAKI
ABNEGATE DENY ABJURE FOREGO
REFUSE REJECT DISAVOW DISCLAIM
FORSWEAR IMMOLATE RENOUNCE
ABNER (BROTHER OF —) KISH
(FATHER OF —) NER
(SLAYER OF —) JOAB
(SON OF —) JAASIEL
(WIFE OF —) RIZPAH
ABNORMAL ENORM QUEER UTTER
ERRATIC UNUSUAL VICIOUS
ABERRANT ATYPICAL FREAKISH
TERATOID ANOMALOUS
MONSTROUS
(PREF.) ANOM(O) DYS MAL PARA
POLY PSEUD(O)
ABNORMALITY ATAXY ATAXIA
LETHAL ANOMALY BROWNING
DEMENTIA ENORMITY
(CATTLE —) SAWDUST
ABOARD ON ONTO ACROSS
ATHWART
ABODE COT DAR HUT INN WON
BODE CELL FLAT HALL HOME NEST
OMEN REST SEAT TENT WOON
BEING BOWER DELAY HAUNT HOUSE
MANOR PITCH RESET SIEGE SUITE
ABIDAL BIDING ESTATE ADDRESS
COTTAGE HABITAT LODGING
MANSION SITTING CUNABULA
DOMICILE DWELLING RESIANCE
TENEMENT
(— OF DEAD) DAR AARU HELL ARALU
HADES ORCUS SHEOL HEAVEN
SHADES XIBALBA NIFLHEIM
(— OF DELIGHT) ELYSIUM
(— OF EVIL POWERS) ABYSS
(— OF GIANTS) UTGARD
(— OF GODS) MERU ASGARD
OLYMPUS
(— OF LOST SOULS) ABADDON
(— OF MEN) MIDGARD
(— OF SOULS) LIMBO
(— OF SPIRITS) HELL
(ANIMAL —) ZOO MENAGERIE
(CELESTIAL —) HEAVEN
(FILTHY —) STY STYE
(MISERABLE —) DOGHOLE
(SHELTERED —) SHADE
ABOLISH END BLOT KILL ABATE
ANNUL ERASE FORDO QUASH
CANCEL EFFACE FOREDO RECALL
REPEAL REVOKE VACATE DESTROY
NULLIFY RESCIND REVERSE
ABROGATE

ABOLITION EXTINCTION

ABOMA BOA BOM BOMA

ABOMASUM READ REED

ABOMINABLE VILE NASTY RUSTY CURSED ODIOUS ROTTEN BEASTLY HATEFUL HEINOUS MALEDICT NEFANDOUS

ABOMINABLY BEASTLY

ABOMINATE HATE ABHOR DETEST LOATHE EXECRATE

ABOMINATION EVIL CRIME CURSE HORROR PLAGUE DISGUST AVERSION

ABONGO BABONGO

ABORAL DORSAL ABACTINAL

ABORIGINAL ABO YAO FIRST NATAL BINGHI NATIVE SAVAGE NATURAL PRIMARY ORIGINAL
(— WOMAN) GIN

ABORIGINE KA KHA AINU TODA ALFUR BAIGA BLACK BOONG DASYU MAORI MYALL ALFURO ARANDA ARANTA ARUNTA BINGHI INDIAN KIPPER KODAGA NATIVE SAVAGE ADIBASI CHINHWAN WARRAGAL WARRIGAL
(AUSTRALIAN —) ABO

ABORT SLIP

ABORTION ABORT FAILURE CASTLING FETICIDE MISBIRTH

ABORTIVE IDLE VAIN BLIND FUTILE BOOTLESS

ABOUND SNY FLOW SNEE TEEM COVER FLEET SWARM REDOUND OVERFLOW
(SUFF.) ULENT

ABOUNDING RIFE FLUSH ROUTH COPIOUS REPLETE TEEMING UBEROUS ABUNDANT AFFLUENT PROLIFIC
(— IN POSSESSIONS) RICH
(SUFF.) IOUS OSE OUS

ABOUT BY IN OF ON RE SAY ASTO AWAY NEAR SOME UMBE UPON ANENT ASTIR CIRCA ABROAD ACTIVE ALMOST ANENST AROUND CIRCUM TOWARD ENVIRON CIRCITER
(PREF.) AMB(I) AMPH(I)(O) CIRCUM HYPER PERI

ABOUT-FACE FLOP

ABOVE ON UP OER SUP ATOP OVER PAST UPON ABEEN ABOON ABUNE ALOFT SUPRA BEFORE BEYOND HIGHER THEREUP OVERHEAD SUPERIOR
(— GENERAL LEVEL) APART
(PREF.) EP EPH EPI HYPER OVER SUPER SUPRA SUR

ABOVEBOARD HONEST

ABRADE RAW RUB BARK FILE FRET GALL RASP SAND WEAR CHAFE ERASE GRATE GRAZE GRIND SCORE SCUFF TOUCH SCOTCH SCRAPE IRRITATE

ABRADER FILE RASP EMERY SANDER ABRASER GRINDER SCRAPER

ABRAHAM (BIRTHPLACE OF —) UR
(BROTHER OF —) HARAN NAHOR
(CONCUBINE OF —) HAGAR
(FATHER OF —) TERAH
(GRANDFATHER OF —) NAHOR
(GRANDSON OF —) ESAU
(NEPHEW OF —) LOT
(SON OF —) ISAAC MEDAN SHUAH MIDIAN ZIMRAN ISHMAEL JOKSHAN
(WIFE OF —) SARAH KETURAH

ABRASION BURN GALL OUCH SCAR SORE GRAZE BRUISE BLASTING

ABRASIVE SAND EMERY PUMICE QUARTZ SILICA ALUNDUM BORAZON ERODENT ABRADANT CORUNDUM PUMICITE SCRUBBER

ABRAXAS GEM STONE AMULET ABRASAX

ABREAST EVEN AFRONT BESIDE HANGING

ABRET BREAD WAFER

ABRI SHED COVER DUGOUT SHELTER

ABRIDGE CUT DOCK LASK BRIEF ELIDE LIMIT RASEE RAZEE BRIDGE REDUCE SHRINK CURTAIL DEPRIVE REWRITE SHORTEN ABSTRACT BREVIATE COMPRESS CONDENSE CONTRACT DIMINISH RETRENCH SIMPLIFY ABBREVIATE

ABRIDGED TAIL

ABRIDGEMENT BRIEF ABREGE DIGEST PRECIS RESUME SKETCH COMPEND EPITOME PANDECT SUMMARY SUMMULA ABSTRACT BOILDOWN BREVIARY SYNOPSIS ABBREVIATION ABBREVIATURE

ABROAD OFF ASEA AWAY ABOUT ASTIR FORTH ABREED AFIELD ASTRAY WIDELY DISTANT OUTWARD OVERSEA OFFSHORE

ABROGATE ANNUL QUASH REMIT CANCEL REPEAL REVOKE VACATE ABOLISH NULLIFY RESCIND RETRACT DISSOLVE OVERRULE

ABROGATION REPEAL

ABRUPT BOLD CURT DEAD FAST RUDE BLUFF BLUNT BRIEF BRUSK HASTY ICTIC PLUMP QUICK ROUGH SHARP SHEER SHORT STEEP STUNT SURLY TERSE TOTAL CHOPPY CRAGGY CRUSTY PROMPT RUGGED SUDDEN ANGULAR BRUSQUE PRERUPT VIOLENT HEADLONG VERTICAL PRECIPITATE
(NOT —) SOFT

ABRUPTLY BANG SHARP SHORT STEEPLY SUDDENLY

ABSALOM (FATHER OF —) DAVID
(MOTHER OF —) MAACHAH
(SISTER OF —) TAMAR
(SLAYER OF —) JOAB

ABSALOM, ABSALOM (AUTHOR OF —) FAULKNER
(CHARACTER IN —) BON ROSA ELLEN HENRY JUDITH SHREVE SUTPEN THOMAS CHARLES COMPSON GOODHUE QUENTIN MCCANNON COLDFIELD
ABSAROKA CROW
ABSCESS BOIL MORO SORE ULCER FESTER INCOME LESION QUINSY VOMICA EXITURE GUMBOIL PARULIS APOSTEME SQUINACY
ABSCISIC ACID DORMIN
ABSCISSA X COSINE
ABSCISSION APOCOPE
ABSCOND GO FLY RUN BOLT FLEE HIDE QUIT ELOPE SCRAM SMOKE DECAMP DEPART DESERT ELOINE ESCAPE LEVANT WITHDRAW
ABSEILING RAPPEL
ABSENCE CUT LACK VOID WANT BLANK LEAVE DEFECT REMOVE VACUUM DEFAULT FAILURE VACANCY FURLOUGH
(— FROM DUTY) LIBERTY
(— FROM ONE'S COUNTRY) EXILE
(— OF AN ORGAN) AGENESIA AGENESIS
(— OF BIAS) DETACHMENT
(— OF CEREMONY) FAMILIARITY
(— OF FAMILIARITY) DISTANCE
(— OF FEELING) APATHY
(— OF FEVER) APYREXY APYREXIA
(— OF FORM) ENTROPY
(— OF GOVERNMENT) ANARCHY
(— OF INHIBITIONS) ANIMALITY
(— OF LIGHT) BLACK DARKNESS
(— OF MARRIAGE) AGAMY
(— OF MIND) ABSTRACTION
(— OF NAILS) ANONYCHIA
(— OF PAIN) ANODYNIA
(— OF PIGMENTATION) ACHROMA ACHROMIA
(— OF SKULL) ACRANIA
(— OF TAIL) ANURY
(— OF TASTE) AGEUSIA
(— OF TRUMPS) CHICANE
(— OF TRUTH) FALSEHOOD
(PERMITTED —) LEAVE
(PREF.) DYS ECTRO NON
ABSENT CUT OFF OUT AWAY AWOL GONE LOST WANE DESERT MUSING LACKING MISSING NOTHERE WANTING ABSORBED DREAMING
(— IN MIND) ABSTRACT
(PREF.) ECTRO
ABSENTMINDED FLAKY MUSED MUSING DISTRAIT DREAMING ABSTRACTED
ABSENTMINDEDNESS STARGAZING
ABSINTHE AJENJO GENIPI

ABSOLUTE GOD ONE TAO TAT DEAD DOWN FAIR FINE FREE MEAR MEER MERE PLAT PLUM PURE RANK REAL SELF TRUE VERY BLANK CLEAR FIXED PLUMB SHEER STARK STONE TOTAL UTTER WHOLE ENTIRE PROPER SEVERE SIMPLE SQUARE BRAHMAN CERTAIN PERFECT PLENARY ABSTRACT COMPLETE DESPOTIC EVENDOWN EXPLICIT IMPLICIT POSITIVE
(— TEMPERATURE) T
(NOT —) NISI FINITE CONDITIONAL
ABSOLUTELY YEA YES AMEN BONE COLD DEAD FAIR JUST PLAT SLAP PLAIN PLUMB STARK BARELY FAIRLY FLATLY SIMPLY WHOLLY SHEERLY ENTIRELY EVENDOWN
ABSOLUTION EXCUSE PARDON SHRIFT LOOSING SHRIVING
ABSOLUTISM CAESARISM DESPOTISM
ABSOLVE FREE QUIT CLEAR LOOSE REMIT ACQUIT ASSOIL EXCUSE EXEMPT FINISH PARDON SHRIVE UNBIND CLEANSE FORGIVE JUSTIFY RELEASE DISPENSE LIBERATE OVERLOOK
ABSORB EAT FIX SOP SUP BLOT SOAK SUCK TAKE AMUSE DRINK MERGE RIVET UNITE DEVOUR ENGAGE ENGULF ENWRAP IMBIBE INGEST INSORB INWRAP OCCUPY SPONGE STIFLE COMBINE CONSUME ENGROSS IMMERSE INVOLVE OCCLUDE SWALLOW
(— GRADUALLY) OSMOSE
ABSORBED DEEP GONE LOST RAPT SUNK FIXED ABSENT BURIED ENRAPT HIPPED INTENT PLUNGED RIVETED WRAPPED IMMERSED ABSTRACTED
(— BY) ALL
ABSORBENT BASE DOPE FOMES BARYTA SPONGY ANTACID SORBENT ANTIACID BIBULOUS DRINKING
ABSORBER SNUBBER
(— OF MONEY) LICKPENNY
(SHOCK —) BUFFER DAMPER
ABSORPTION AUTISM PREOCCUPATION
(— UNIT) SABIN
ABSORPTIVE SPONGY
ABSQUATULATE DECAMP ABSCOND
ABSTAIN DENY FAST KEEP STAY AVOID CEASE SPARE SPURN WAIVE DESIST DISUSE ESCHEW FOREGO REFUSE REJECT FORBEAR REFRAIN RESTRAIN TEETOTAL WITHHOLD
(— FROM) FAST FORGO LEAVE ADJURE ESCHEW FOREGO REFRAIN
ABSTAINER TOTE RECHABITE

ABSTEMIOUS SOBER ACETIC
SLENDER MODERATE
ABSTENTION CELIBACY CHASTITY
ABSTERGE WIPE BATHE CLEAN
PURGE RINSE
ABSTINENCE ENCRATY
ABSTINENT SOBER ABSTEMIOUS
ABSTRACT CULL DEED DRAW NOTE
PART PURE TAKE BRIEF IDEAL STEAL
ABSORB DEDUCT DETACH DIGEST
DIVERT DOCKET NOETIC PRECIS
REMOVE ABRIDGE COMPEND
EPITOME EXCERPT ISOLATE PURLOIN
SECRETE SUMMARY VIDIMUS
ABSTRUSE ACADEMIC ARGUMENT
BREVIATE DISCRETE PRESCIND
SEPARATE SYLLABUS SYNOPSIS
TABLEITY WITHDRAW
METAPHYSICAL
(— SECRETLY) SUBDUCT
(NOT —) CONCRETE
(PL.) PARATITLA PARATITLES
ABSTRACTED REMOTE
ABSTRACTION STUDY ENTITY
ABSENCE REVERIE ABSTRACT
QUODDITY
(MENTAL —) REVERY REVERIE
ABSTRUSE DARK DEEP HIGH
HIDDEN MYSTIC REMOTE SECRET
SUBTLE CURIOUS OBSCURE RETIRED
ABSTRACT ACROATIC ESOTERIC
PROFOUND METAPHYSICAL
ABSTRUSENESS DEPTH
ABSURD HOT RICH WILD DOTTY
DROLL FALSE INANE INEPT SILLY
SCREWY STUPID ASININE FATUOUS
FOOLISH LAPUTAN ABSONANT
DOGGEREL FABULOUS COCKAMAMY
MONSTROUS RIDICULOUS
PREPOSTEROUS
ABSURDITY BETISE FATUITY
FOOLERY FOPPERY WALTROT
MAGGOTRY NONSENSE UNREASON
ABUNA METRAN
ABUNDANCE WON COPY FLOW
MORT SONS WONE CHEAP DEPTH
FLUSH FOUTH POWER RIVER ROUTH
ROWTH SCADS SONSE STORE
WRECK BOUNTY FOISON GALORE
LAVISH OODLES PLENTY POWDER
RICHES TALENT UBERTY WEALTH
FLUENCY LASHINS PLEROMA
SATIETY BELLYFUL FULLNESS
LASHINGS OPULENCE PLEURISY
RIMPTION PLENITUDE REDUNDANCY
(IN —) APLENTY
ABUNDANT FAT OLD FREE LUSH
MUCH RANK RICH RIFE AMPLE
FLUSH HEFTY LARGE OPIME ROUTH
ROWTH STORE DEMOID GALORE
HEARTY ROUTHY APLENTY COPIOUS
FERTILE FULSOME LIBERAL OPULENT

PROFUSE REPLETE TEEMING
UBERANT UBEROUS WEALTHY
AFFLUENT FRUITFUL GENEROUS
NUMEROUS PLENTIFUL
(NOT —) LIGHT SPARE
(PREF.) HADR(O) LARGI
ABUNDANTLY RIFE WELL FREELY
PLENTY LARGELY HEARTILY
ABUSE MAR MOB TAX BUSE CALL
DRUB FLAY GAFF HARM HURT LACK
MAUL RAIL RUIN SLAM TEEN VAIN
BASTE BLAST CRIME CURSE FAULT
GRIEF SCOLD SLANG SNASH SPOIL
BERATE DEFILE INJURE INSULT
MALIGN MISSAY MISUSE MUMBLE
PUNISH RAVISH REVILE TANCEL
TANSEL VILIFY YATTER AFFRONT
BACKJAW BEDEVIL DECEIVE DESPITE
FALSIFY MISBEDE MISCALL
MISNAME OBLOQUY OUTRAGE
PERVERT PROFANE SLANDER
TRADUCE UPBRAID VIOLATE
BALLARAG BUSINESS DISHONOR
FRUMPERY LANGUAGE MALTREAT
MISAPPLY MISTREAT REPROACH
SLAPDASH
(— OF FREEDOM) LICENCE LICENSE
ABUSED DOWNTROD
DOWNTRODDEN
ABUSIVE FOUL DIRTY SHREWD
CORRUPT SATIRIC CHEATING
INSOLENT LIBELOUS
ABUT BUTT JOIN REST TOUCH
ADJOIN BORDER BUTTAL PROJECT
ABUTILON MALLOW
ABUTMENT CRIB PIER ALETTE
BUTTRESS
ABUTTING FLUSH ADJACENT
ABY ABIDING
ABYSM ABIME BISME DOWNFALL
ABYSMAL DEEP DREARY PROFOUND
UNENDING WRETCHED
ABYSS PIT POT DEEP GULF HELL
HOLE VOID ABYSM CHAOS CHASM
DEPTH GORGE ABRUPT BOTTOM
VORAGO ABADDON AVERNUS
GEHENNA SWALLOW DOWNFALL
INTERVAL
ABYSSAL ABYSMAL BASSALIAN
ABYSSINIA
(SEE ETHIOPIA)
ABYSSINIAN SIDI ABASSIN
(— BANANA) ENSETE
ACACALLIS (FATHER OF) MINOS
(MOTHER OF —) PASIPHAE
(SON OF —) GARAMAS
AMPHITHEMIS
ACACIA GUM JAM KOA WELD WOLD
BABUL GIDYA MULGA MYALL SIRIS
THORN TIMBE VEREK WOALD
WOULD ARABIC BABLAH BINDER
GIDGEA GIDGEE GIDYEA HASHAB

LEGUME LOCUST MIMOSA SALLEE
WATTLE YARRAN BLUEBUSH
BRIGALOW CHAPARRO IRONWOOD
ROSEWOOD

ACADEMIC IVY MOOT RIGID
FORMAL ACADEME CLASSIC
DONNISH ERUDITE LEARNED
POMPIER PEDANTIC PLATONIC
(— HEAD) DEAN

ACADEMY LYCEE CRUSCA LYCEUM
MANEGE SCHOOL ACADEME
COLLEGE SOCIETY YESHIVA
SEMINARY
(FRENCH —) FORTY
(RIDING —) MANAGE MANEGE

ACADIAN CAJUN

ACAJOU CAJU CAJOO CAJOU

ACALEPH MEDUSA MEDUSAN

ACAMAS (BROTHER OF —)
ARCHELOCHUS
(FATHER OF —) ANTENOR THESEUS
EUSSORUS
(MOTHER OF —) THEANO PHAEDRA
(SLAYER OF —) AJAX MERIONES
(SON OF —) MUNITUS

ACANA ALMIQUE

ACANTHA FIN SPINE THORN
PRICKLE ACANTHON

ACAPU WALNUT WACAPOU
CHAPERNO

ACARID MITE NYMPH NYMPHA
OCTOPOD DIBRANCH PROTONYMPH

ACARNAN (BROTHER OF —)
AMPHOTERUS
(FATHER OF —) ALCMAEON
(MOTHER OF —) CALLIRRHOE

ACASTUS (FATHER OF —) PELIAS
(SLAYER OF —) PELEUS
(WIFE OF —) HIPPOLYTE

ACAUDAL BOBBED ANUROUS
ECAUDATE TAILLESS

ACAULESCENT STEMLESS

ACCEDE LET AGREE ALLOW ENTER
GRANT YIELD ACCORD ASSENT
ATTAIN COMPLY CONCUR CONCEDE
CONFORM CONSENT

ACCELERATE GUN REV RUN HYPO
JAZZ RACE SPUR URGE DRIVE FAVOR
FORCE HURRY LINAC SPEED HASTEN
ADVANCE FORWARD FURTHER
QUICKEN ANTEDATE DISPATCH
EXPEDITE INCREASE THROTTLE

ACCELERATED
(PREF.) TACHY

ACCELERATING
(PREF.) AUXO

ACCELERATION PICKUP SPEEDUP
(— OF REACTION) CATALYSIS
(— UNIT) STAPP

ACCELERATOR GAS GUN SPEEDER
BETATRON BEVATRON THROTTLE
(LINEAR —) LINAC

ACCENT BEAT BIRR BLAS BURR
MARK TONE ACUTE GRAVE ICTUS
PITCH PULSE SOUND THROB VERGE
BROGUE LENGTH RHYTHM STRESS
THESIS EMPHASIS
(DORIC —) PLATEASM
(IRISH —) BROGUE
(MUSICAL —) BEAT
(WITHOUT AN —) ATONIC

ACCENTED FZ SFZ TONIC STRONG
MARCATO MARCANDO SFORZATO

ACCENTUATE ACCENT

ACCENTUATION DECLAMATION
ENHANCEMENT

ACCEPT BUY EAT BEAR FANG HAVE
HOLD JUMP TAKE ADMIT ADOPT
AGREE ALLOW HONOR INFER MARRY
ASSENT ASSUME AVOUCH POCKET
RATIFY AGREEON AGREETO
APPROVE BELIEVE CONCEDE
EMBRACE ESPOUSE RECEIVE
SETTLEFOR
(— AS ONE'S OWN) NOSTRIFICATE
(— AS TRUE) ACCREDIT
(— AT RANDOM) DRAW
(— BETS) BOOK
(— EAGERLY) LEAP
(— INHERITANCE) ADIATE
(— READILY) SWALLOW
(— WITHOUT QUESTION) ABIDE

ACCEPTABLE LIEF VALID SIGHTLY
WELCOME GRACIOUS PASSABLE
PLEASANT

ACCEPTANCE PASS SNAFF ADITIO
TAQLID PASSAGE CREDENCE
CURRENCY
(— OF INHERITANCE) CERNITURE
(— OF ORDER) ALLOTMENT

ACCEPTATION MEANING
ACCEPTANCE

ACCEPTED GOING VULGAR
POPULAR APPROVED CREDITED
ORTHODOX STANDARD
(NOT —) OUT
(WIDELY —) INVETERATE

ACCEPTOR BASE

ACCESS FIT WAY ADIT DOOR GATE
PATH ROAD ENTRY GOING ROUTE
ACCOST AVENUE COMING ENTREE
PORTAL STREET ADVANCE
APPROACH ENTRANCE PAROXYSM
RECOURSE
(— OF DISEASE) ATTACK

ACCESSIBILITY EXPOSURE

ACCESSIBLE NEAR OPEN HANDY
PATENT AFFABLE PRESENT FAMILIAR
PERVIOUS SOCIABLE GETATABLE

ACCESSION ENTER ACCESS AFFLUX
ALLUVIO ILLAPSE ADDITION
ALLUVION ENTRANCE INCREASE

ACCESSORY HAT AIDE ALLY DOME
TOOL EXTRA SCARF HELPER

ABETTOR ADAPTER ADAPTOR ADJUNCT ANCILLA ENCLAVE FITTING FIXTURE ADDITIVE HATSTAND ORNAMENT
(PL.) ADDENDA FIXINGS STAFFAGE

ACCIACCATURA MORDENT

ACCIDENT HAP CASE LUCK EVENT GRIEF PRANG SHUNT CHANCE HAZARD INJURY MISHAP FORTUNE QUALITY CALAMITY CASUALTY DISASTER FORTUITY INCIDENT ROLLOVER
(— IN CAR RACING) SHUNT
(AUTOMOBILE —) FATAL
(EUCHARISTIC —S) SPECIES
(HAVE — WITH) PRANG

ACCIDENTAL ODD CASUAL CHANCE RANDOM EXTERNAL

ACCIPITER ERNE HAWK

ACCLAIM CRY CLAP FAME HAIL LAUD ROOT CHEER CLAIM ECLAT EXTOL SHOUT PRAISE APPLAUD HOSANNA OVATION PLAUDIT RECLAME WELCOME APPLAUSE
(NOISY —) RIOT

ACCLAMATION CRY VOTE CHEER SHOUT ACCLAIM HOSANNA PLAUDIT APPLAUSE

ACCLIMATE ENURE INURE HARDEN SEASON ACCUSTOM

ACCLIMATIZE SALT ADAPT HARDEN ORIENT SEASON

ACCLIVITY BANK BROW HILL RISE GRADE PITCH SLANT SLOPE TALUS ASCENT HEIGHT INCLINE

ACCOLADE EMMY KISS RITE SIGN AWARD HONOR KUDOS MEDAL OSCAR TOKEN EULOGY SYMBOL EMBRACE GARLAND CEREMONY

ACCOMMODATE AID BED BOW FIT CAMP GIVE HELP HOLD LEND SORT SUIT ADAPT BOARD DEFER FAVOR HOUSE LODGE SERVE YIELD ADJUST COMPLY FAVOUR OBLIGE SETTLE CONFORM CONTAIN FASHION ATTEMPER GARRISON

ACCOMMODATING OBLIGING

ACCOMMODATION LOAN BERTH CLASS BERTHAGE GIFFGAFF
(— BILL) KITE
(PL.) PASSAGE

ACCOMPANIED FRAUGHT

ACCOMPANIMENT SON ALBA BACKUP BURDEN ESCORT OOMPAH ADJUNCT DESCANT SUPPORT OBLIGATO
(IMPROVISED —) VAMP
(PLAY JAZZ —) COMP
(PL.) FIXINGS

ACCOMPANIST JONGLEUR

ACCOMPANY SEE BACK FARE FERE JOIN LEAD TEND WAIT BRING PILOT ASSIST ATTEND CONCUR CONVEY CONVOY ESCORT FOLLOW SECOND SQUIRE COEXIST CONDUCT CONSORT SUPPORT CHAPERON

ACCOMPANYING FELLOW ADJUNCT
(PREF.) SYMPHORI

ACCOMPLICE PAL AIDE ALLY CHUM BUDDY CRONY LOUKE SHILL TILER BONNET COHORT FELLOW HELPER ABETTOR FEODARY FEUDARY HUSTLER PARTNER STEERER

ACCOMPLISH DO GO END WIN CHAR FILL WORK ENACT EQUIP FETCH FORTH SWING AFFORD ATTAIN EFFECT FINISH FULFIL MANAGE VIRTUE ABSOLVE ACHIEVE CHEVISE COMPASS EXECUTE EXPLETE FULFILL FURNISH OPERATE PERFECT PERFORM REALIZE SUCCEED COMPLETE CONTRIVE DISPATCH ENGINEER OUTCARRY NEGOTIATE

ACCOMPLISHED APT ABLE ARCH DONE ADEPT ENDED GREAT TERSE BESEEN EXPERT HANDSOME TALENTED

ACCOMPLISHMENT ART END DEED FEAT PASS CRAFT SKILL EFFECT TALENT VIRTUE EARNING QUALITY FRUITION LEARNING
(PRIOR —) ANTICIPATION

ACCORD GIVE JIBE JUMP SUIT UNIT AGREE ALLOW ATONE AWARD BEFIT CHIME CHORD CORDE GRANT LEVEL STAND TALLY UNITY ACCEDE ADJUST ASSENT BESTOW BETEEM COMPLY CONCUR SETTLE UNISON COMPORT COMPOSE CONCEDE CONCERT CONCORD CONGREE CONSENT CONSORT HARMONY RAPPORT RESPOND UNANIME DIAPASON SYMPATHY
(— WITH) SUIT
(IN —) ALONG

ACCORDANCE CONCERT CONSENT
(IN —) ALONG

ACCORDANT EVEN ATTUNED AGREEING COHERENT SUITABLE

ACCORDING
(— TO) AD BY AUX SEC EMFORTH ENFORTH PURSUANT SECUNDUM
(— TO ART) SA
(— TO LAW) SL

ACCORDINGLY SO ERGO THEN THUS HENCE IGITUR

ACCORDION LANTUM FLUTINA FLAUTINO

ACCOST BAIL HAIL MASH MEET ABORD ASSAY BOARD GREET SPEAK ACCESS BROACH HALLOO SALUTE ACCOAST ADDRESS SOLICIT APPROACH GREETING

ACCOUCHEUR OBSTETRICIAN

ACCOUCHEUSE MIDWIFE
ACCOUNT TAB BILL BOOK DEEM
DRAW ITEM NICK NOTE RATE REDE
SAKE TAIL TALE TELL TEXT WORD
AUDIT BLAME CHALK COUNT JUDGE
SCORE STATE STORY VALUE WORTH
BATTEL CREDIT DETAIL ESTEEM
HORARY LEGEND NOTICE PROFIT
REASON RECKON RECORD REGARD
RELATE RENDER REPORT REPUTE
TREATY ACCOMPT COMPOST
COMPUTE EXPLAIN JOURNAL
LEXICON NARRATE PROCESS
RECITAL TAILZIE BREVIARY
CONSIDER ESTIMATE RELATION
TREATISE BORDEREAU
MONOGRAPH RECKONING
PRESENTATION
(— FOR) SAVE EXPLAIN
(—S FOR PROVISIONS) BATTELS
(ACCURATE —) GRIFF GRIFFIN
(CREDIT —) TICK
(KIND OF —) IRA NOW
(LONG —) ILIAD MEGILLAH
(LONG, INVOLVED —) MEGILLA
MEGILLAH
(OFFICIAL —) PROTOCOL
(SAVINGS —) IRA
(SHORT —) KETCH
(TRAVEL —) ITINERARY
(PL.) BATTELS
ACCOUNTABILITY DETAIL
LIABILITY
ACCOUNTABLE LIABLE AMENABLE
ACCOUNTANT CLERK SIRCAR
SIRKAR AUDITOR PESHKAR
PUTWARI KULKARNI MUTSUDDY
RECKONER
ACCOUNTANT-GENERAL
DAFTARDAR DEFTERDAR
ACCOUNTING TASK REASON
COSTING
ACCOUTER ARM RIG GIRD ARRAY
DRESS EQUIP ATTIRE CLOTHE OUTFIT
BEDIGHT FURNISH HARNESS
PROVIDE
ACCOUTERMENTS GEAR TIRE
DRESS ATTIRE GRAITH
ACCREDIT ALLOT VOUCH CREDIT
DEPUTE APPOINT APPROVE ASCRIBE
BELIEVE CERTIFY CONFIRM ENDORSE
LICENSE SANCTION
ACCRETION SUM GAIN GROWTH
DEPOSIT EXUDATE ADDITION
ADHESION INCREASE
(INJURIOUS —) RUST
ACCRUAL ACCRUE DEMERIT
ACCRUE ADD WIN EARN GAIN GROW
PILE ARISE ENSUE ENURE INCUR
INURE ISSUE MATURE RESULT
SPRING ACQUIRE COLLECT
REDOUND ACCRESCE CUMULATE
INCREASE

ACCUMULATE DRAW FUND GROW
HEAP HIVE MASS PILE SAVE AMASS
DRIFT HOARD STACK STORE TOTAL
ACCRUE GARNER GATHER MUSTER
RACKUP SCRAPE COLLECT CONGEST
HARVEST INCREASE
ACCUMULATION DRIP DUMP FUND
GAIN HEAP MASS PILE LODGE STACK
STORE ANLAGE BACKUP BUDGET
COLUMN DEBRIS GARNER BACKLOG
CUMULUS DEPOSIT DOSSIER
MORAINE DIVIDEND INTEREST
(— OF FLUID) EDEMA OEDEMA
ASCITES
(— OF FORCE) CHARGE
(— OF SNOW) ALIMENTATION
(— OF TRIFLES) FLOTSAM
(— ON CONCRETE) LAITANCE
ACCURACY NICETY FIDELITY
JUSTNESS PRECISION
(— OF ADJUSTMENT) TRAM
(HISTORICAL —) SYNCHRONISM
ACCURATE JUST LEAL NICE TRUE
CLOSE EXACT FLUSH RIGHT DEADON
NARROW PROPER SEVERE STRICT
CAREFUL CORRECT CURIOUS
PRECISE FAITHFUL PERQUEER
PUNCTUAL RIGOROUS TRUTHFUL
(NOT —) IMPURE
(UNPLEASANTLY —) BRUTAL
ACCURATELY JUST FAIRLY JUSTLY
CLOSELY EXACTLY INSOOTH
ACCURSED FEY CURSED DAMNED
DOOMED FORBID SACRED WARIED
BLASTED MALEDICT
ACCUSATION BEEF WITE BLAME
CAUSE CRIME POINT WHITE APPEAL
ATTACK CHARGE THREAP THREEP
ACCUSAL SCANDAL DELATION
(FALSE —) SUGGESTION
ACCUSATORY WRAYFUL
ACCUSE TAX WRY CALL FILE NOTE
SHOW SLUR TASK WITE WRAY
ACOUP ARGUE BLAME PEACH TAINT
TOUCH WHITE APPEAL ATTACH
ATTACK BECALL BEWRAY CHARGE
DEFAME DELATE DETECT INDICT
INTENT MURMUR APPEACH
ARRAIGN ATTAINT CENSURE
IMPEACH IMPLEAD TRADUCE
CHASTISE COMPLAIN DENOUNCE
QUESTION REDARGUE REPROACH
(— UNJUSTLY) SLANDER
ACCUSER CHARGER DELATOR
LIBELANT
ACCUSING CULPATORY
DENUNCIATORY
ACCUSTOM URE USE WIN WON
HAFT WONT ADAPT BREAK DRILL
ENURE FLESH HABIT HAUNT INURE
TRAIN ADDICT ADJUST CUSTOM
INDUCE ORIENT SEASON CONSORT
EDUCATE TOUGHEN ACQUAINT

(— **HORSE TO BIT**) MOUTH
(— **TO PASTURE**) HAFT
ACCUSTOMED TAME USED WONE
WONT USANT USUAL INURED
CHRONIC CURRENT HABITED
CONSUETE
ACCUSTOMEDNESS HABIT
ACE AS ALS JOT ONE PIP TIB ATOM
CARD HERO MARK TOPS UNIT WHIZ
ADEPT BASTO FLYER POINT BULLET
EXPERT AVIATOR BRISQUE PARTICLE
(— **OF CLUBS**) BASTA BASTO
(— **OF SPADES**) SPADILLE SPADILLO
(— **OF TRUMPS**) TIB HONOR PUNTO
(**THREE —S**) GLEEK
ACEDIA SLOTH ACCIDIA ACCIDIE
ACEPHALOUS HEADLESS
ACER NEGUNDO
ACERB ACID HARD SOUR TART ACRID
HARSH SHARP BITTER SEVERE
ACERBAS (**WIFE OF —**) ELISSA
ACERBATE EMBITTER IRRITATE
ACERBITY ACRIMONY ASPERITY
CYNICISM SEVERITY TARTNESS
ACESTES (**FATHER OF —**) CRIMISUS
(**MOTHER OF —**) EGESTA
(**WIFE OF —**) ENTELLA
ACETABULUM PAN PYXIS CUPULE
ACETABLE HOLDFAST
ACETAL KETAL FORMAL KETATE
BUTYRAL
ACETALDEHYDE ETHYL ETHANAL
ALDEHYDE
ACETIC SOUR SHARP ZOONIC
ACETOPHENETIDIN PHENACETIN
ACETYLENE TOLAN ALKINE ALKYNE
ETHINE ETHYNE TOLANE
ACHAEMENES (**BROTHER OF —**)
XERXES
(**FATHER OF —**) DARIUS
(**SLAYER OF —**) INARUS
ACHAEUS
(**FATHER OF —**) XUTHUS
(**MOTHER OF —**) CREUSA
ACHBOR (**FATHER OF —**) MICHAIAH
(**SON OF —**) BAALHANAN
ACHE AKE NAG NIP ECHE GELL HURT
LONG PAIN PANG PINE RACK WARK
WERK HACHE SMART STANG STOUN
THROB THROE WARCH YEARN
DESIRE MISERY STITCH STOUND
TWINGE TWITCH ANGUISH EARACHE
SORENESS
ACHENE CYPSELA UTRICLE
ACHIEVE DO END GET WIN EARN
GAIN HACK HAVE MAKE FETCH
FORCE NOTCH REACH SCORE
AFFORD ARRIVE ATTAIN EFFECT
FINISH OBTAIN CHEVISE COMPASS
EXPLOIT FULFILL PERFORM PROCURE
PRODUCE REALIZE SUCCEED
TRIUMPH COMPLETE CONCLUDE
CONTRIVE ACCOMPLISH

(— **HARMONY**) AGREE
(— **ORIENTATION**) ADJUST
ACHIEVED (**SOMETHING EASILY —**)
GIMME
ACHIEVEMENT ACT JOB DEED FEAT
WORK ACTION CAREER RESULT
STROKE EXPLOIT HARVEST
PROWESS SUCCESS FELICITY
(**COMPLETE —**) TRIUMPH
ACHILLEA PTARMICA
ACHILLES PELIDES
(**COMPANION OF —**) PATROCLUS
(**FATHER OF —**) PELEUS
(**FRIEND OF —**) PATROCLUS
(**GRANDFATHER OF —**) AEACUS
(**HORSE OF —**) XANTHUS
(**MOTHER OF —**) THETIS
(**SLAYER OF —**) PARIS
ACHIM (**FATHER OF —**) SADOC
(**SON OF —**) ELIUD
ACHING SORE
ACHIOTE OLEANA ACHUETE
ANNATTO ARNATTA ARNATTO
ACHRAS SAPOTA
ACHROMACYTE SHADOW
ACHROMATIC GRAY GREY
NEUTRAL
ACHSAH (**FATHER OF —**) CALEB
(**HUSBAND OF —**) OTHNIEL
ACICULAR SPLINTERY
ACID DRY LSD YAR DIAL DOPA KEEN
PABA SOUR TART ACERB ACRID
ALGIN AMINO CERIN EAGER HARSH
LYSIN MALIC OLEUM RHEIN SHARP
ULMIC ABRINE ALLIIN BITING BITTER
DORMIN FOLATE GLYCIN LYSINE
NIACIN PROLIN SERINE TWEAKY
VALINE ACERBIC ACETOSE CERASIN
FILICIN GLYCINE PROLINE STEARIN
VINEGAR ORNITHINE PENICILLIN
(**CRYSTALLINE —**) EDTA
(**KIND OF —**) MALIC ADIPIC KAINIC
MURAMIC
(**NITRIC —**) AQUAFORTIS
(**NUCLEIC —**) DNA RNA
(**SEQUENCE OF NUCLEIC —**) INTRON
(**PREF.**) ACETO OXY
(**SUFF.**) (— **RADICAL**) OYL
ACID HYDROGEN
(**SUFF.**) HYDRIC
ACIDITY ACOR VERDURE ACERBITY
SOURNESS VERJUICE
ACIDULOUS TART
ACIS (**FATHER OF —**) FAUNUS
(**LOVER OF —**) GALATEA
(**MOTHER OF —**) SYMAETHIS
(**SLAYER OF —**) POLYPHEMUS
ACIS & GALATEA (**CHARACTER IN
—**) ACIS GALATEA POLYPHEMUS
(**COMPOSER OF —**) HANDEL
ACKNOWLEDGE NOD OWN AVER
AVOW SIGN ADMIT ADOPT ALLOW
GRANT KITHE KYTHE THANK YIELD

ACCEDE ACCEPT AGNIZE ANSWER
ASSENT AVOUCH BEKNOW COUTHE
FATHER REWARD CONCEDE CONFESS
DECLARE OBSERVE PROFESS
DISCLOSE RECOGNIZE
ACKNOWLEDGEMENT GRANT
THANK AVOWAL CREDIT SHRIFT
APOLOGY AGNITION COGNOVIT
COGNISANCE COGNIZANCE
RECOGNITION
(— OF MISTAKE) JEOFAIL
(— OF SERVICE) GRAVITY
(— OF SIN) PECCAVI
(WRITTEN —) RECEIPT
ACLE AKLE IRUL JAMBA IRONWOOD
PYENGADU
ACLYS HURLBAT
ACME IT ACE CAP TOP APEX CULM
HIGH PEAK CREST PITCH POINT
STATE APOGEE CLIMAX COMBLE
CRISIS CULMEN HEIGHT HEYDAY
SUMMIT ZENITH CUMULUS SUBLIME
CAPSHEAF CAPSTONE PINNACLE
ACNE WHELK ROSACEA
ACOLYTE BOY HELPER NOVICE
SERVER LEARNER PATENER
THURIFER
ACOMIA BALDNESS
ACONITE BIKH ACONITUM ·
NAPELLUS
ACORN NUT MAST GLAND OVEST
BALANUS BELLOTA BELLOTE
(— CUPS) VALONIA
(PL.) MAST CAMATA PANNAGE
CAMATINA
(PREF.) BALAN(I)(O) GLANDI
GLANDULI
ACORN-SHAPED BALANOID
ACOUSTICS SONICS PHONICS
ACQUAINT KNOW TELL TEACH
VERSE ADVISE INFORM NOTIFY
SCHOOL APPRISE APPRIZE POSSESS
RESOLVE
ACQUAINTANCE KITH HABIT
COUSIN FRIEND GOSSIP PICKUP
AFFINITY FAMILIAR INTIMATE
(CLOSE —) HABIT INWARDNESS
(PRACTICAL —) PRACTICE PRACTISE
(PL.) KITH SOCIETY
ACQUAINTED VERSED ACQUENT
VERSANT
(CLOSELY —) INTIMATE
ACQUIESCE BOW ABIDE AGREE
CHIME YIELD ACCEDE ACCEPT
ASSENT COMPLY CONCUR SUBMIT
CONCEDE CONFIRM CONFORM
CONSENT
ACQUIESCENCE ASSENT
ACQUIRABLE
(PREF.) CTETO
ACQUIRE ADD BAG BUY GET WIN
EARN FORM GAIN GRAB HAVE MAKE
REAP ADOPT AMASS ANNEX BEGET

CHEVY CHIVY GLEAN INCUR LEARN
REACH SEIZE STEAL ATTAIN CHIVEY
CHIVVY DERIVE EFFECT GARNER
OBTAIN SECURE SNATCH COLLECT
CONQUER DEVELOP PROCURE
RECEIVE CONTRACT
(— DESIRABLE QUALITY) AGE
(— KNOWLEDGE) LERE
ACQUIRED (NOT —) NATURAL
ACQUIREMENT (— OF CONTROL)
TAKEOVER
ACQUISITION WIN GAIN LUCRE
ACQUEST ACQUIST GETTING
CONQUEST ACCESSION
(DISHONEST —) GRAFT
(VALUED —) PRIZE
ACQUISITIVE GRABBY
ACQUIT PAY FREE QUIT CLEAR QUIET
ASSOIL BEHAVE BESTOW EXCUSE
PARDON ABSOLVE COMPORT
CONDUCT RELEASE REQUITE
LIBERATE OVERLOOK UNCHARGE
ASSOILZIE
ACQUITTAL EXCUSE DISCHARGE
ABSOLUTION
ACQUITTANCE QUIETUS RELEASE
ACRE AKER LAND ACKER FIELD
STANG ARPENT COLLOP FARMHOLD
(QUARTER —) ROOD
(120 —S) HIDE
(2-3RDS —) COVER
(PL.) ACREAGE
ACREMAN CARUCARIUS
ACRID HOT ACID BASK KEEN SOUR
HARSH ROUGH SHARP SURLY BITING
BITTER CAUSTIC PUNGENT REEKING
UNSAVORY VIRULENT
ACRIMONIOUS MAD ACID KEEN
ACRID ANGRY GRUFF HARSH IRATE
SHARP SNELL SURLY BITTER
CAUSTIC STINGING VIRULENT
ACRIMONY VIRUS ACERBITY
ASPERITY PUNGENCY SOURNESS
ANIMOSITY
ACRISIUS (BROTHER OF —)
PROETUS
(DAUGHTER OF —) DANAE
(FATHER OF —) ABAS
(MOTHER OF —) AGLAIA
(SLAYER OF —) PERSEUS
(WIFE OF —) AGANIPPE EURYDICE
ACROBAT ZANY KINKER GYMNAST
TOPPLER TUMBLER BALANCER
AERIALIST ROPEWALKER
ACRONYM INITIALISM
ACROPOLIS FORT HILL POLIS
CADMEA CITADEL LARISSA
ACROSOME IDIOSOME IDIOZOME
ACROSS OVER SPAN YOND CROSS
ABOARD THWART ATHWART
OPPOSITE TRAVERSE
(CLEAN —) SHONT
(PREF.) DIA OVER TRANS

ACROSTIC ABC AGLA DORA GAME
POEM TANAK PHRASE PUZZLE
TANACH
ACRYLIC PROPENOIC
ACT BE DO GO APE LAW LET ACTU
AUTO BILL COME DEAL DEED DORA
FACT FEAT HOCK JEST MAKE MOVE
PART PASS PLAY SKIT SLIM TAKE
TURN WORK ACTUS DRAMA EDICT
EMOTE ENTRY EXERT FEIGN GRACE
KARMA MODEL SCENE SHIFT SHTIK
STUNT ACTION BEHAVE BESTIR
DECREE DEMEAN FACTUM MANAGE
RAGMAN SHTICK COMPORT
EXECUTE EXPLOIT PERFORM
PORTRAY PRETEND STATUTE
FUNCTION PRETENSE SIMULATE
(— AFFECTEDLY) MIMP POSTURE
(— AGGRESSIVELY) HUSTLE
(— AS WANTON) RIG
(— AWKWARDLY) HOCKER
(— BADLY) HAMFATTER
(— BEFORE) ANTICIPATE
(— BLUNDERINGLY) BULL
(— DECEITFULLY) DOUBLE
(— DISHONESTLY) FUDGE
(— FIRST) LEAD
(— FOOLISHLY) FON FONNE FOLEYE
FOOTER FOOTLE
(— FRIVOLOUSLY) FRIVOL FRIBBLE
(— IN A NERVOUS WAY) JITTER
(— INDECISIVELY) DITHER
(— INDEPENDENTLY) SEVER
(— IN THEATER) GAFF
(— OF APPROVAL) EUGE
(— OF BEGGING) CADGE
(— OF CIVILITY) CURTSY DEVOIR
CURTSEY
(— OF KINDNESS) CARESS BENEFIT
(— OF LABOR) DILIGENCE
(— OF PRAYER) DEVOTION
(— OF STUPIDITY) BETISE
(— OF TRICKERY) COG
(— OF UNKINDNESS) CUT
(— OUT) ENACT DRAMATIZE
(— PLAYFULLY) DALLY BANTER
(— QUICKLY) GIRD
(— RASHLY) RACKLE
(— SLOWLY) DAWDLE
(— SPORTIVELY) DAFF
(— SUDDENLY) FLASH
(— TIMIDLY) NESH
(— TOGETHER) AGREE COACT
CONCUR CONCORD
(— TRIFLINGLY) JANK
(— UPON) TOUCH AFFECT HANDLE
(— UP TO) EVEN
(— VIGOROUSLY) TWIG TURNTO
(— WITHOUT RESTRAINT)
FREEWHEEL
(COMICAL —) JIG
(CONVENTIONAL —) AMENITY

(CORRUPT —) DEPRAVITY
(CRIMINAL —) INFAMY
(DARING —) ESCAPADE
(DECEITFUL —) ABUSE
(DECEPTIVE —) FEINT
(ECCENTRIC —) CANTRIP
(EVIL —) MALEFICENCE
(FAULTY —) PARAPRAXIS
(FOOLISH —) DIDO IDIOTISM
(FORBIDDEN —) CRIME
(FORMAL —) CEREMONY
(FRAUDULENT—) SCAM
(HABITUAL —) EXERCISE
(HASTY —) FLING
(HOSTILE —) BLOW
(INJURIOUS —) SPOIL
(KIND OF —) RIOT
(LAUDATORY —) COUP
(LITURGICAL —) LAVABO
(LIVELY —) JIG
(MERITORIOUS —) MITZVAH
(MISCHIEVOUS —) DIDO CANTRAP
CANTRIP
(OFFENSIVE —) AFFRONT
(OFFICIAL —S) ACTA
(PLAYFUL —) RALLERY RAILLERY
(PRAISEWORTHY —) DEMERIT
(RUDE —) INCIVILITY
(SUDDEN VIOLENT —) BENSEL BENSIL
(THOUGHTLESS —) FOLLY
(UNMANNERLY —) SOLECISM
(UNUSUAL —) STUNT
(VALOROUS —) WORSHIP
(VARIETY —) SKETCH
(WRONG —) DERELICT DERELICTUM
(PL.) DOINGS
(SUFF.) ADE ATE CY ICE ION ISM TH
ACTAEON (FATHER OF —)
ARISTAEUS
(MOTHER OF —) AUTONOE
ACTINAL ORAL
ACTING AGENT SERVING HISTRIONIC
(— AGAINST) ADVERSE
(— BY TURN) ALTERN
(— IN RETURN) RECIPROCAL
(— ODDLY) HAYWIRE
(— RAPIDLY) DRASTIC
(UNSKILLFUL —) BUNGLING
ACTINIAN OPELET VESTLET
ACTINOST RADIAL RADIALE
ACTINOZOAN SEAFLOWER
ACTION ACT AIR DAP JOB PAS ACTO
CASE DEED FACT FRAY GEST PLAY
PLOY PUSH SHOW STEP SUIT WORK
ACTIO DOING EDICT FIGHT FLING
GESTE ISSUE THING TREAD VENUE
AFFAIR AGENCY BATTLE BEFOOT
COMBAT PRAXIS CONDUCT FACTION
GESTURE MEASURE PROCESS
TANQUAM ACTIVITY BEHAVIOR
BUSINESS CONFLICT FUNCTION
PRACTICE PRACTISE

(— BETWEEN HORSE AND RIDER)
APPUI
(— OF DRAMA) EPITASIS
(— OF WIND) EOLATION
(— PAINTING) TACHISM
(— POTENTIAL) SPIKE
(ABSURD —S) BOSH
(ANTAGONISTIC —) ATOMISM
(BLAMEWORTHY —) WITE
(CAPRICIOUS —) FREAK
(CHEMICAL —) ACTINISM
(COARSE —) HARLOTRY
(CONCLUDING —) MOPUP
(CONVULSIVE —) SPASM
(COOPERATIVE —) SYNERGISM
(COURT —) LAW SUIT ASSIZE
LAWSUIT QUERELA QUERELE
(CRUEL —) RUTH
(CUSTOMARY —) COURSE
(DIVINE —) THEURGY
(DUE —) ORDER
(EXAGGERATED —) PRODUCTION
(EXTEMPORE —) SCHEDIASM
(FANTASTIC —) ABTIC
(FINAL —) CATASTROPHE
(FOOLISH —) FOPPERY INEPTITUDE
(FRISKY —) FRISKIN
(FRIVOLOUS —) DALLIANCE
(HOSTILE —) OPPOSITION
(IMPULSIVE —) STAMPEDE
(INDIRECT —) WINDLASS
(INITIAL —) LEADOFF INDUCTION
(INTRODUCTORY —) PROLOGUE
(JOINT —) COACTION
(LEGAL —) DEBT SUIT ACCOUNT
DETINET DETINUE PROCEEDING
(MEAN —S) DOGGERY
(MILITARY —) SWEEP OPERATION
(ODD —S) JIMJAMS
(PLAYFUL —) FUN FROLIC
(RASH —) HASTE
(REPEATED —) DRUM DOUBLE
(SUDDEN —) FLISK
(SYMBOLIC —) CHARADE
(TACTLESS —) GAUCHERIE
(UNAVOIDABLE —) FORCEPUT
(UNINTERMITTED —) HEAT
(VIOLENT —) AFFRAY
(WHIMSICAL —S) HUMORS
HUMOURS
(WILY —) WRINKLE
(PREF.) CIN(O) CINET(O) KIN(O) KINESI
KINET(O)
(SUFF.) ADE AL ANCE ANT ARD ATION
CY ENCE ESIS ING ISATION IVE
IZATION MENT OSIS PRACTIC PRAXIA
PRAXIS SIS SOME LE LING
ACTIS (FATHER OF —) RHODE
(MOTHER OF —) HELIUS
ACTIVATE SPARK ACTIFY ELICIT
(— BY MIXING WITH WATER)
PROOF

ACTIVATION
(SUFF.) KINESIS
ACTIVATOR GOAD
ACTIVE UP YAL YAP YEP BUSY GAIN
LISH LIST PERT RASH SPRY TRIG
WHAT YALD YARE YEPE YERN ABOUT
AGILE ALERT ALIVE ASTIR BRISK
DEEDY FRESH LIGHT LINGY LUSTY
NIPPY PEART QUICK READY SMART
SNELL SPILY SPRIG STOUT SWANK
VIVID WIGHT YAULD YERNE ACTUAL
BOUNCY CLEVER DIRECT FEERIE
FEIRIE FIERCE HEARTY LIVELY LIVING
MOVING NIMBLE PROMPT QUIVER
SEMMIT SPEEDY SPRACK SPROIL
SPRUCE SPRUNT SWANKY WIMBLE
DASHING DEEDFUL DELIVER
DYNAMIC HOPPING HUMMING
KINETIC STHENIC THRODDY
YANKING ANIMATED ATHLETIC
BRAWLING DILIGENT SPIRITED
VIGOROUS
(EXCESSIVELY —) MANIC
(NORMALLY —) ABOUT
ACTIVELY DOWN BUSILY DEEDILY
HEARTILY
ACTIVITIES
(PL.) DOINGS
ACTIVITY ACT ADO GOG VIR FIZZ
LIFE PLAY PUSH STIR BLAST CAPER
EVENT HEART RAJAS RALLY TRADE
VIGOR ACTION AGENCY BUSTLE
ENERGY HUSTLE SATTVA SPROIL
AGILITY CALLING BUSINESS
EXERCISE FUNCTION MOVEMENT
PARERGON STIRRING OCCUPATION
(— OF INTELLECT) NOESIS
(BUSTLING —) RUSH
(CHOICE OF —) THING
(FRENZIED —) HUSTLE
(FUNCTIONAL —) SHOP
(GAY —) MERRYMAKING
(MENTAL —) CONCEIT BRAINWORK
MENTATION
(SHARED —) COMMUNITY
(SPHERE OF —) SCENE
(STORMY —) RAGE
(TEACHING —) REALIA
(TROUBLESOME —) COIL
(PL.) GOINGSON
(SUFF.) OR
(OUTBURST OF —) FEST
ACTON HOGTON HAQUETON
ACTOR HAM DOER HERO LEAD MIME
STAR AGENT BUFFO COMIC DROLL
EXTRA HEAVY MIMIC PLANT SERIO
SUPER ARTIST BUSKER COWBOY
DISEUR FEEDER FIDDLE MUMMER
PLAYER PUPPET STAGER TOMMER
ARTISTE CABOTIN DISEUSE HISTRIO
PRIMOMO ROSCIUS STORMER
TROUPER AISTEOIR COMEDIAN

HISTRION JUVENILE STROLLER
THESPIAN
(BROTHER OF —) AUGEAS
(DAUGHTER OF —) POLYMELA
(FATHER OF —) DIOMEDES
MYRMIDON
(INDIFFERENT —) JAY
(INEPT —) HAM
(INFERIOR —) SHINE
(MOTHER OF —) DEION PASIDICE
(SON OF —) CTEATUS EURYTUS
MENOETIUS
(PREF.) HISTRIO

ACTRESS DIVA STAR INGENUE
STARLET FARCEUSE PREMIERE
THESPIAN

ACTUAL GOOD HARD REAL TRUE
VERY POSIT RIGHT BODILY FACTUAL
GENUINE CONCRETE DEFINITE
EXISTING MATERIAL POSITIVE
TANGIBLE

ACTUALITY ACT FACT BEING VERITY
REALITY ENERGEIA REALNESS

ACTUALLY BUT DONE TRULY FAIRLY
ITSELF REALLY
(NOT —) NOMINALLY

ACTUATE ACT EGG RUN DRAW
MOVE URGE ENACT IMPEL ROUSE
START AROUSE COMPEL EXCITE
INCITE INDUCE AGITATE ANIMATE
ENLIVEN INSPIRE POINTED SHARPEN
MOTIVATE PERSUADE

ACUITY FINENESS

ACUMEN WIT INSIGHT CAPACITY
KEENNESS SAGACITY

ACUMINATE TAPE

ACUTE ACID FINE HIGH KEEN TART
HEAVY QUICK SHARP SMART SNACK
SNELL ARGUTE ASTUTE CRYING
SHREWD SHRILL SUBTLE TREBLE
URGENT CRUCIAL FEELING INTENSE
POINTED VIOLENT CRITICAL INCISIVE
POIGNANT ACUMINATE
PENETRATING PENETRATIVE
(MOST —) DIRE
(NOT —) SLOW GRAVE CHRONIC
(PREF.) OXY

ACUTENESS DEPTH SENSE ACUITY
ACUMEN NOSTRIL INCISION
SAGACITY SUBTLETY
(— OF SMELL) HYPEROSMIA

ACYCLIC SPIRAL ALIPHATIC

ACYLOIN
(SUFF.) OIN

ADA (BROTHER OF —) PIXODARUS
(HUSBAND & BROTHER OF —)
IDRIEUS

ADAD RAMMAN

ADAGE SAW DICT REDE TEXT WORD
AXIOM MAXIM MOTTO HOMILY
SAYING TRUISM WHEEZE BROMIDE
PRECEPT PROVERB APHORISM
APOTHEGM PAROEMIA

ADAGIO ADAGE ADAGIETTO

ADAH (HUSBAND OF —) ESAU LAMECH
(SON OF —) JABAL JUBAL ELIPHAZ

ADAIAH (FATHER OF —) SHIMHI
JEROHAM

ADALIA (FATHER OF —) HAMAN

ADAM ADE EDIE ADKIN
(GRANDSON OF —) ENOS ENOCH
(SON OF —) ABEL CAIN SETH
(TEACHER OF —) RAISEL
(WIFE OF —) EVE LILITH

ADAM-AND-EVE CRAWFOOT

ADAMANT FIRM GRIM HARD SOLID
STONY ADAMAS DIAMOND
UNMOVED OBDURATE SOLIDITY
STUBBORN

ADAMANTINE FIRM HARD BORON
STONE VAJRA ADAMANT

ADAM BEDE (AUTHOR OF —) ELIOT
(CHARACTER IN —) ADAM SETH
DINAH HETTY ARTHUR BARTLE
IRVINE MARTIN MASSEY MORRIS
POYSER SORREL DONNITHORNE

ADAMITE NUDIST PICARD

ADAMS ANSEL

ADAM'S APPLE GUZZLE
THROATBOLL

ADAM'S FLANNEL MULLEIN

ADAM'S NEEDLE YUCCA

ADAPT APT FIT PLY PUT EDIT MOLD
SORT SUIT AGREE HUMOR INURE
SHAPE TALLY ADJUST CHANGE
COMPLY DERIVE DOCTOR HUMOUR
TEMPER ARRANGE CONFORM
CONVERT FASHION PREPARE
QUALIFY ATTEMPER CONTRIVE
EQUALIZE MODULATE REGULATE
ACCOMMODATE

ADAPTABILITY FLUIDITY
ELASTICITY

ADAPTABLE LABILE ELASTIC
PLASTIC PLIABLE FLEXUOUS

ADAPTATION CONSERTION
(— TO MUSIC) SETTING

ADAPTED FIT FOR FITTED SUITED
CONGENIAL

ADAPTER KIT ARRANGER

ADAXIAL SUPERIOR POSTERIOR

ADBEEL (FATHER OF —) ISHMAEL

ADD AD EIK EKE SAY SUM TOT CAST
FOOT GAIN JOIN LEND PLUS TOTE
AFFIX ANNEX GIVEN PUTON TOTAL
UNITE ACCRUE ADJECT APPEND
ATTACH CONFER FIGURE RECKON
SUPPLY ACCRETE AUGMENT
COMBINE COMPILE COMPUTE
ENLARGE SUBJOIN SUMMATE
INCREASE
(— ALCOHOL) SPIKE
(— AN ENTRY) RUNON
(— FUEL) BEET
(— IN WRITING) ASCRIBE
(— ON) AFFIX ANNEX

(— STRENGTH) HEARTEN
(— TO) ADORN ENRICH AUGMENT
ENHANCE
(— UP) SUM TOT COUNT TALLY
TOTAL AMOUNT
(— WORT TO BEER) KRAUSEN
ADDA SCINK SKINK LIZARD
ADDAR (FATHER OF —) BELA
ADDAX PYGARG PYGARGUS
ADDED AND EKE PLUS ADJUNCT
(— SOMETHING) TILLY
(RECENTLY —) FRESH
ADDEND SUMMAND
ADDENDUM RIDER
ADDER ATHER KRAIT VIPER ELAPID
NADDER NEDDER CRIBBER ELAPOID
HAGWORM HOGNOSE HYPNALE
(KIND OF —) MILK
ADDERING (KIND OF —) CRIB
ADDER'S-TONGUE LILY LILIUM
COXCOMB ROOSTERS
ADDERWORT BISTORT
ADDI (FATHER OF —) COSAM
(SON OF —) MELCHI
ADDICT FAN BUFF DOPE DOPY HYPE
USER WINO COKEY COKIE FIEND
HOPPY HOUND JUNKY SLAVE
DOTARY DEVOTE JUNKER JUNKIE
DELIVER DEVOTEE HABITUE
HOPHEAD SNIFTER ACCUSTOM
DOPEHEAD SNOWBIRD
ADDICTED GIVEN PRONE HOOKED
BIBULOUS
ADDICTION HABIT JONES MONKEY
BIBACITY
ADDITION AND EIK EKE ELL TAB TOO
ALSO ELSE GAIN PLUS AFFIX ICING
RIDER ACCESS ACCRUE AUGEND
ENCORE GANSEL INCOME PREFIX
ADJUNCT ADVANCE AUCTARY
CODICIL JOINING PENDANT UNITING
ADDENDUM INCREASE MANTISSA
ACCESSION
(— TO ARTICLE) SHIRTTAIL
(— TO BEEHIVE) IMP
(— TO CALENDAR) EPACT
(— TO MASS) FARCE FARSE
(— TO PRICE) ADVANCE
(— TO WORD) PARAGOGE
(EXTRANEOUS —) ACCRETION
(TRIVIAL —) FILIP FILLIP
(PREF.) IN —) SUPER
ADDITIONAL NEW ELSE MORE
ADDED EXTRA FRESH OTHER TIDDER
TOTHER ANOTHER BESIDES
FURTHER ACCESSORY PIGGYBACK
ADDITIVE CUMOL CUMENE
PRESERVATIVE
(HAND-CREAM —) ALOE
ADDLE EARN HOME IDLE MIRE
AMAZE FILTH RIPEN SPOIL CURDLE
MUDDLE THRIVE AGITATE CONFUSE
BEFUDDLE BEWILDER

ADDLED ASEA EMPTY PUTRID
MUDDLED UNSOUND
ADDRA DAMA NANGER
ADDRESS AIM SUE WOO BACK CALL
EASE HAIL HOME MINT PRAY TACT
TALK TULK TURN ABODE APPLY
BOARD COURT DRESS ELOGE GREET
POISE SKILL SPEAK TREAT ACCOST
ADJUST APPEAL BOUNCE CHARGE
DEVOTE DIRECT EULOGY MANNER
PARLEY SALUTE SERMON SPEECH
BEHIGHT CONDUCT CONSIGN
ENTRUST LECTURE ORATION
TUTOYER APPROACH DEDICATE
DELIVERY DISPATCH FACILITY
HARANGUE INSCRIBE PETITION
(— FAMILIARLY) TOM TUTOYER
(— FOR GI) APO
(— SAUCILY) CHYAK CHYACK
(METHOD OF —) TONE
(PART OF —) ZIP
(PULPIT —) KHUTBA KHUTBAH
ADDUCE BEAR CITE GIVE NAME
ALLAY ARGUE BRING INFER OFFER
QUOTE ALLEGE ASSIGN OBJECT
ADVANCE COUNTER MENTION
PRESENT
ADE SQUASH
ADELIE PENGUIN
ADEPS FAT LARD
ADEPT ACE APT DON ABLE HANDY
ADROIT ARTIST CRAFTY DEACON
EXPERT MASTER VERSED ANCIENT
ARTISTE CAPABLE DABSTER
MAHATMA DEXTROUS SKILLFUL
PROFICIENT
ADEQUATE DUE FIT ABLE ENOW
FAIR FULL GOOD MEET WELL AMPLE
DIGNE EQUAL COMMON DECENT
ENOUGH PROPER CONDIGN
PASSABLE SUITABLE
COMMENSURATE SATISFACTORY
(BARELY —) BRIEF
ADER (FATHER OF —) BERIAH
ADHERE HEW HUG CLAG CLAM
CLOG GLUE HOLD JOIN KEEP LINK
ABIDE AFFIX APPLY CLEAM CLING
STICK UNITE ATTACH CEMENT
CLEAVE COHERE FREEZE ACCRETE
ANNERRE PERSIST
ADHERENCE CLING ABIDANCE
ADHESION ARIANISM FIDELITY
ADHERENT IST ITE AIDE ALLY JAIN
SIKH ADEPT BAHAI BLACK BONPA
DEIST JAINA SIDER SPIKE STOOP
FACTOR KIRKER VOTARY APRISTA
BAHAIST CHANIST FASCIST FLACIAN
GNOSTIC NICAEAN OWENIAN
SECTARY SEQUELA THOMIST
AGATHIST BELIEVER BUDDHIST
CABALIST DISCIPLE FAITHFUL
FATALIST FOLLOWER HUMANIST
HYLICIST IMPERIAL PARTISAN

RETAINER SERVITOR SOCINIAN
UPHOLDER MONTANIST
(PL.) FOLD FOLLOWING
(SUFF.) ITE
ADHERING PERTINACIOUS
ADHESION BLOCKING STICKAGE
SYNECHIA
ADHESIVE GUM WAX BOND CLAM
GLUE SIZE TAPE DABBY DAUBY
PASTE TACKY BINDER CEMENT
CLINGY GLUTEN MASTIC PLUCKY
SMEARY STICKY HOTMELT
MOUNTANT MUCILAGE TENACIOUS
(PREF.) GLUT
ADHESIVENESS STICK
ADHIBIT USE ADMIT AFFIX APPLY
ATTACH
ADIANTUM MAIDENHAIR
ADIEL (SON OF —) AZMAVETH
ADIEU ADEW CIAO ADDIO ADIOS
LEAVE FAREWELL
AD INFINITUM EVER
ADIPOCERE GRAVEWAX
ADIPOSE FAT HARD SUET FATTY
OBESE PURSY SQUAT TALLOW
ADIT DOOK DOOR ENTRY SOUGH
STULM ACCESS TUNNEL PASSAGE
APPROACH ENTRANCE
ADJACENT NEAR NIGH CLOSE
FLUSH HANDY BESIDE NEARBY
MEETING VICINAL ABUTTING
TOUCHING CONTIGUOUS
(PREF.) (— TO) AC AD AF AG AL AP AS
AT
ADJECTIVE ADNOUN DIPTOTE
EPITHET NOMINAL MODIFIER
ADJOIN ADD ABUT BUTT JOIN LINE
TACK COAST MARCH TOUCH UNITE
ACCOST APPEND ATTACH BORDER
CONTACT NEIGHBOR
ADJOINING VICINAL
ADJOURN END MOVE RISE STAY
ARISE CLOSE DEFER DELAY RECESS
SUSPEND DISSOLVE POSTPONE
PROROGUE
ADJUDGE TRY ARET DEEM FIND
GIVE HOLD RATE ALLOT AREAD
AREED ARETT AWARD GRANT JUDGE
ORDER ADDEEM ADDICT ADDOOM
ASSIGN DECERN DECIDE DECREE
ORDAIN REGARD BEHIGHT
CONDEMN SENTENCE
(— GUILTY) DAMN
(— NOT GUILTY) ABSOLVE
ADJUDICATE ACT TRY HEAR PASS
RULE JUDGE DECIDE ESTEEM
RECKON REGARD SETTLE ADJUDGE
CONSIDER SENTENCE
ADJUNCT AID HELP PART WORD
ANNEX DEVICE PHRASE ADJOINT
ANCILLA APENAGE EPITHET FITTING
GARNISH PERTAIN TEACHER

ADDITION ADDITIVE APPANAGE
APPENDIX ORNAMENT
ADJURATION OATH APPEAL
SWEARING
ADJURE ASK BEG BID BIND ETHE
PRAY CRAVE PLEAD SWEAR APPEAL
CHARGE OBTEST BESEECH
COMMAND CONJURE CONTEST
ENTREAT REQUEST UNSWEAR
ADJUST FIT FIX KEY SET CAST EASE
FORM FREE GEAR JUST LINE PARE
RATE SIZE SORT SUIT TRAM TRIM
TRUE TUNE ADAPT ADMIT ALIGN
ALINE ALTER ANGLE COAPT EQUAL
FRAME PATCH RANGE RIGHT SHAPE
ACCORD ATTUNE HAMMER JUSTEN
ORIENT SETTLE SQUARE TEMPER
WANGLE ADDRESS ARRANGE
BALANCE CHANCER COMPOSE
CONCERT CONFORM CORRECT
DISPOSE JUSTIFY PREPARE RECTIFY
COMPOUND REGULATE CALIBRATE
ACCOMMODATE
(— A LOOM) GATE
(— DULY) CONCENT
(— SAIL) FLATTEN
(PREF.) CO
ADJUSTABLE ELASTIC
ADJUSTED KEYED
(ACCURATELY —) TRUE
ADJUSTER FIXER FITTER ASSESSOR
ADJUSTMENT FIT GEAR MISE TRIM
FITNESS FITTING CHANCERY
(— OF DISPUTE) MISE
(COST —) COLA
(HARMONIOUS —) TUNE
ADJUTANT AIDE ALLY STORK
ARGALA HELPER HURGILA
MARABOU OFFICER
ADJUVANT AIDE HELPER ADJUNCT
HELPFUL
ADLAI (SON OF —) SHAPHAT
AD-LIB FAKE
ADMAN HUCKSTER
ADMEASURE METE
ADMETUS (FATHER OF —) PHERES
(WIFE OF —) ALCESTIS
ADMINISTER DO RUN DEAL DEEM
DOSE GIVE MOVE RULE APPLY SERVE
TREAT DIRECT GOVERN MANAGE
SETTLE SUPPLY TENDER ADHIBIT
CONDUCE CONDUCT CONTROL
EXECUTE EXHIBIT FURNISH
HUSBAND DISPENSE MINISTER
(— FORCIBLY) HAND
(— SACRAMENT) BISHOP HOUSEL
ADMINISTRATION HELM RULE
SWAY POLICY TAHSIL CONDUCT
DIOCESE ECONOMY RECTORY
REGIMEN CARRIAGE DISPOSAL
MINISTRY
(— OF OATH) JURATION

(CORRUPT —) MALVERSATION
(REVENUE —) HACIENDA
ADMINISTRATOR CAID HELM QAID
GABBAI ALCAIDE MANAGER
TRUSTEE DIRECTOR EXECUTOR
MINISTER PROVICAR PROCONSUL
(— OF COMPUTER BOARD) SYSOP
(INCA —) CURACA
(MORMON —) APOSTLE
ADMIRABLE FINE GOOD HIGH NEAT
GRAND GREAT LUMMY PROUD
DIVINE AMIABLE CAPITAL ELEGANT
MIRANDA RIPPING
ADMIRAL (ALSO SEE NAVAL OFFICER)
FLAG AMREL AMRELLE CAPITAN
FLAGMAN GENERAL NAVARCH
(KIND OF —) RED REAR VICE
ADMIRATION CULT FUROR GLORY
ESTEEM LIKING WONDER CONCEIT
WORSHIP ADULATION
(— FOR BIGNESS) JUMBOISM
(EXTRAVAGANT —) FUREUR
ADMIRE DIG LIKE LOVE ADORE
EXTOL HONOR PRIZE VALUE ESTEEM
MARVEL REGARD REVERE WONDER
ADULATE APPROVE DELIGHT IDOLIZE
RESPECT VENERATE
ADMIRER FAN BEAU LOVER SWAIN
AMATEUR DEVOTEE FOLLOWER
IDOLATER
(PL.) FOLLOWING
ADMISSION FEE ADIT CALL ENTRY
ACCESS CHARGE ENTREE TICKET
APOLOGY CONSENT INGRESS
ENTRANCE RECEPTION CONCESSION
(— TO BAR) CALL
(— TO MINISTRY) ORDINATION
(CONCLUSIVE —) ESTOPPEL
ADMIT COP KEN LET OWN AVER
AVOW BEAR TAKE AGREE ALLOW
ENTER GRANT IMMIT INLET ACCEDE
ACCEPT ADJUST ASSENT AVOUCH
ENROLL INDUCT PERMIT SUFFER
ADHIBIT CONCEDE CONFESS
INCLUDE PROFESS RECEIVE SUFFICE
INITIATE
(— AS MEMBER) INDUCT
(— AS VALID) SUSTAIN
(— OPENLY) OWNUPTO
(— TO HOLY ORDERS) ORDAIN
ADMITTANCE ACCESS ADMITTY
ENTRANCE
ADMITTED GIVEN GRANTED
ADMITTING THOUGH
(REGRETFULLY —) AFRAID
ADMIX DALLOP DOLLOP
ADMIXTURE DASH ALLOY BLEND
SHADE SPICE TINGE DALLOP DOLLOP
FLAVOR LEAVEN STREAK MIXTURE
SOUPCON COMPOUND INFUSION
ADMONISH WARN CHIDE SCOLD
ADVISE ENJOIN EXHORT NOTIFY

REBUKE REMIND SCHOOL CAUTION
COUNSEL MONITOR REPROVE
ADMONITION ITEM ADVICE CAVEAT
HOMILY CAUTION LECTURE REPROOF
WARNING DOCUMENT REMINDER
ADNATE ADHERENT EPIGYNOUS
(— TO CALYX) INFERIOR
ADO DO COIL DEED FLAP FUSS ROUT
STIR TODO WORK HOOHA HURRY
TOUSE TOWSE BOTHER BUSTLE
EFFORT FLURRY HUBBUB POTHER
RUCKUS BLATHER BLETHER
SPUTTER TROUBLE TURMOIL
BUSINESS FOOFARAW
ADOBE MUD CLAY DOBE DOBY SILT
BRICK DOBIE TAPIA MUDCAP
ADOLESCENCE TEENS YOUTH
NONAGE PUBERTY MINORITY
ADOLESCENT LAD TEEN YOUNG
YOUTH TEENER IMMATURE
TEENAGER
(DISRUPTIVE —) NED
(PROSPECTIVE —) PRETEEN
ADONIJAH (BROTHER OF —) AMNON
ABSALOM CHILEAB
(FATHER OF —) DAVID
(MOTHER OF —) HAGGITH
(SLAYER OF —) BENAIAH
ADONIS ADON
(FATHER OF —) CINYRAS
(MOTHER OF —) MYRRH MYRRHA
ADOPT TAKE STEAL ACCEPT ASSUME
ATTACH BORROW CHOOSE FATHER
FOLLOW FOSTER MOTHER TAKEON
ACQUIRE EMBRACE ESPOUSE
RECEIVE WELCOME ADVOCATE
ARROGATE MAINTAIN
ADOPTION ESPOUSAL
(— OF DEBTS) ASSUMPTION
ADORABLE LOVELY LOVABLE
CHARMING
ADORATION HOMAGE WORSHIP
DEVOTION
(— OF GOD) LOVE
ADORE DOTE LAUD LOVE EXALT
EXTOL HONOR WURTH ADMIRE
ESTEEM PRAISE REVERE GLORIFY
IDOLIZE WORSHIP VENERATE
ADORN DUB FIG GEM ORN SET BEAD
BUSK DECK DILL DINK FOIL GAUD
GILD LACE OUCH PICK PINK POSH
STUD SWAG TRIM ADORE ANORN
ARRAY BEDUB BEGEM BELAY BESEE
BRAVE CROWN DIGHT DRAPE DRESS
FRONT GRACE HIGHT INLAY JEWEL
MENSK PRANK PRICK PRIDE PRIMP
PRINK ROUGE SPLAY SPRIG TRICK
AGUISE ATTIRE ATTRAP BECOME
BEDECK BETRIM BLAZON BROOCH
CLOTHE COLLAR DAMASK DIADEM
EMBOSS ENAMEL ENRICH ENROBE
FIGURE FINIFY FRIEZE FRINGE

GRAITH INSTAL INVEST ORNIFY
POUNCE PURFLE QUAINT STATUE
SUBORN TASSEL ADONISE APPAREL
BEDIGHT BEDIZEN COMMEND
CORONET DEPAINT DIGNIFY
EMPEARL FEATHER FOLIAGE
FURNISH GARNISH GLORIFY GRATIFY
IMPLUME SPANGLE VARNISH
BEAUTIFY DECORATE EMBLAZON
FLOURISH ORNAMENT SPLENDOR
(— WITH MOSAIC) TESSELLATE

ADORNED CLAD BESEEN DAEDAL
ORNATE PICKED BRAIDED CLOTHED
COLORED DAISIED FIGURED
OVERHUNG
(GAUDILY —) TAWDRY
(SHOWILY —) BEPRANKED

ADORNMENT TIRE ADORN DRESS
PRIDE BEAUTY DECORE TAHALI
TINSEL DECKING OUNDING
PRANKING TIREMENT

ADOXY TENET

ADRAMMELECH (BROTHER OF —)
SHAREZER
(FATHER OF —) SENNACHERIB

ADRASTUS (BROTHER OF —)
MECISTEUS
(DAUGHTER OF —) AEGIA DEIPYLE
(FATHER OF —) TALAUS GORDIUS
(MOTHER OF —) LYSIMACHE
(SISTER OF —) ERIPHYLE

ADRESTUS (BROTHER OF —)
AMPHIUS
(FATHER OF —) MENOPS
(SLAYER OF —) DIOMEDES

ADRIANA LECOUVREUR
(CHARACTER IN —) ADRIANA
MAURICE BOUILLON MICHONNET
(COMPOSER OF —) CILEA

ADRIEL (FATHER OF —) BARZILLAI
(WIFE OF —) MERAB

ADRIFT ASEA LOST AWAFT LIGAN
LOOSE AFLOAT DERELICT FLOATING
UNMOORED

ADROIT DEFT EASY FEAT GOOD NEAT
SLIM ADEPT HANDY READY SMART
SNACK TIGHT TRICK ARTFUL CLEVER
EXPERT HABILE NIMBLE CUNNING
DEXTROUS HANDSOME SKILLFUL

ADROITNESS ART EASE TACT
KNACK SKILL ADDRESS FACILITY

ADSORBENT BASE EARTH SILICA

ADULATE FAWN LAUD GLOSS GLOZE
PRAISE REVERE FLATTER

ADULATION GLOSE GLOZE PRAISE
INCENSE FLATTERY

ADULT MAN FULL MANLY MATURE
EPHEBIC GROWNUP THRIVEN
(SCIENCE OF TEACHING —S)
ANDRAGOGY
(YOUNG COLLEGE-EDUCATED —)
YUP YUPPIE

ADULTERANT DOPE MULTUM
ALMEIDINA

ADULTERATE CUT MIX CARD DASH
LOAD ABUSE ALLOY HOCUS TAINT
DEACON DEBASE DEFILE DILUTE
EXTEND MANAGE WEAKEN
BASTARD CORRUPT FALSIFY VITIATE
DENATURE IMPURIFY SPURIOUS
(— WINE) LIME

ADULTERATED CUT SHAM IMPURE
CORRUPT SPURIOUS

ADULTEROUS ERRING

ADULTERY AVOUTRY CUCKOLDOM
CUCKOLDRY MISCONDUCT

ADUMBRATE IMAGE SHADE VAGUE
OBSCURE SUGGEST INTIMATE

ADUMBRATION SHADE SHADOW
PHANTASM

ADUNCOUS BENT HOOKED

ADUST BURNT FIERY GLOOMY
SALLOW PARCHED SCORCHED
SUNBURNT

ADVANCE GO AID PAY SOP WAY
BULL CITE COME DASH GAIN HELP
INCH LAUD LEND LIFT LOAN MARK
MOVE NEAR NOSE PASS PUSH RISE
SHOW STEP WORM AVANT BOOST
BRING CREEP ENTER EXALT EXTOL
FAVOR FORGE MARCH OFFER PLACE
PREST RAISE SERVE SPEED STAIR
STAKE THROW ADDUCE ADMOVE
ALLEGE AMOUNT ASSIGN ASSIST
AVAUNT BETTER DEGREE EXTEND
FAVOUR GROWTH HASTEN INCEDE
INROAD PREFER PREPAY SCHOOL
STRIDE STRIKE THRIVE TRAVEL
VAUNCE BENEFIT DEVELOP ELEVATE
ENHANCE FORTHGO FORWARD
FURTHER HEADWAY IMPREST
IMPROVE PROCEED PROCESS
PROMOTE PROMOVE PROPOSE
PROSPER PROVECT SUCCEED
ADDITION DEVELOPE HEIGHTEN
INCREASE PROGRESS PROGRESSION
(— BY CUTTING) DRIVE
(— BY LEAPS) SALTATION
(— IN LIFE) WAY
(— LABORIOUSLY) STRIVE
(— OBLIQUELY) SIDLE
(— OF MONEY) IMPREST
(— ONE'S POINT) TAKE
(— RUDELY) ELBOW
(— SLOWLY) INCH WORM CRAWL
CREEP
(— WAVERINGLY) HOBBLE
(— WITH EFFORT) DRAG
(DIFFICULT —) SLOG
(GRADUAL —) ILLAPSE
(STEADY —) SWING
(SUDDEN —) SHOOT
(VIGOROUS —) SWING
(PL.) APPROACHES

ADVANCED FAR DEEP GONE HIGH
LATE AHEAD OUTER FORWARD
IMPREST LIBERAL VANWARD
FOREMOST
(— IN AGE) DEEP ANTIQUATED
(— IN YEARS) SENIOR AGEABLE
ELDERLY
(MOST —) EXTREME FARTHEST
FOREMOST HEADMOST
(WELL —) AGED

ADVANCEMENT UP GOOD ASCENT
INCREASE

ADVANCING RISING
(— BY DEGREES) GRADUAL
(— RAPIDLY) RAKING

ADVANTAGE AD BOT USE VAN BEST
BOOT BOTE DRAW DROP EDGE GAIN
GOOD HANK JUMP MEND NOTE
ODDS PULL SAKE VAIL ASSET AVAIL
BULGE BUNCE FAVOR FRAME FRUIT
KINCH LAUGH POINT SPEED START
STEAD USAGE BEHALF BEHOOF
BETTER CARROT EFFECT PROFIT
ACCOUNT BENEFIT CAPITAL EXPLOIT
FORDEAL FURTHER PROMOTE
PURPOSE UTILITY VANTAGE
HANDICAP INTEREST LEVERAGE
OVERHAND OVERPLUS PERCENTAGE
(ACCIDENTAL —) FLUKE
(UNDUE —) ABUSE
(UNEXPECTED —) WINDFALL

ADVANTAGEOUS GOOD JOLI WELL
JOLIE GOLDEN PLUMMY SPEEDY
USEFUL ELIGIBLE BEHOVEFUL
PROPITIOUS
(PREF.) EU

ADVENT DAWN COMING INCOME
ARRIVAL APPROACH PAROUSIA

ADVENTITIOUS CASUAL FOREIGN
STRANGE ACQUIRED EPISODIC
ACCESSORY

ADVENTURE GEST LARK RISK SEEK
WAGE EVENT GESTE PERIL QUEST
AUNTER AUNTRE CHANCE DANGER
HAZARD EMPRISE EMPRIZE FORTUNE
VENTURE ESCAPADE JEOPARDY
(TALE OF —) CONTE

ADVENTURER ROUTIER ARGONAUT
PICAROON

ADVENTURESS DEMIREP
DEMIMONDAINE

ADVENTUROUS BOLD RASH
DARING ERRANT AUNTROUS
RECKLESS

ADVERSARY FOE ENEMY RIVAL
SATAN FOEMAN OPPONENT
(— OF GOD) DEVIL
(PREF.) ENSTATO

ADVERSE FOE ILL EVIL CROSS
LOATH THRAW AVERSE INFEST
WITHER AWKWARD COUNTER
DIVERSE FROWARD HOSTILE

OPPOSED CONTRARY INIMICAL
OPPOSING OPPOSITE OVERWART
THRAWART
(PREF.) COUNTER

ADVERSITY ILL WOE CROSS DECAY
NIGHT MISERY SORROW WITHER
ILLNESS TROUBLE CALAMITY
DISTRESS MISFORTUNE

ADVERT HEED AVERT RECUR REFER
ALLUDE ATTEND RETURN REVERT
OBSERVE CONSIDER

ADVERTISE CRY BARK BILL CALL
PLUG PUFF STAR WARN BLURB
INFORM NOTIFY PARADE DECLARE
DISPLAY OBSERVE PLACARD
PUBLISH ANNOUNCE PROCLAIM

ADVERTISED AFFICHE

ADVERTISEMENT AD BILL SIGN
BLURB CHANT PITCH PROMO
ADVERT CACHET DODGER NOTICE
POSTER TEASER AFFICHE PLACARD
STUFFER CIRCULAR HANDBILL

ADVERTISING BUSH BILLING
PUFFERY
(EXTRAVAGANT —) HYPE
(MASS-MEDIA —) ADMASS
(RADIO OR TV —) PLUGOLA

ADVICE AVIS AVYS LORE NEWS REDE
AVYSE INPUT STEER ADVISO DEVICE
NOTICE CAUTION CONSEIL COUNSEL
OPINION TIDINGS GUIDANCE
MONITION
(PL.) INFORMATION

ADVICE-BOAT AVISO

ADVISABLE BOOK PROPER PRUDENT

ADVISE SAY READ REDE TELL VISE
WARN WISE AREAD AREED COACH
GUIDE WEISE WEIZE ADJURE ADVISO
BEREDE CONFER DEVISE EXHORT
INFORM PONDER REVEAL APPRISE
APPRIZE COUNSEL ACQUAINT
ADMONISH CONSIDER RECOMMEND
(— AGAINST) DISSUADE
(— STRONGLY) URGE
(— WRONGLY) MISCOUNSEL

ADVISED DELIBERATE

ADVISER AIDE TOUT COACH COMES
TUTOR DOCTOR EGERIA LAWYER
NESTOR ADVISOR MONITOR
STARETS TEACHER ATTORNEY
CROUPIER DIRECTOR FIELDMAN
PREACHER

ADVISORY URGING PRUDENT

ADVOCACY BOOM FAVOR AVOWRY
FAVOUR ARIANISM

ADVOCATE PRO ABET BACK PUSH
URGE VOGT ACTOR ADOPT FAVOR
PLEAD ASSERT AVOWRY BACKER
DEFEND IDEIST LAWYER PATRON
SYNDIC ABETTOR APOSTLE DECLAIM
ENDORSE ESPOUSE EXPOUND
FASCIST GOLDBUG PATRIOT

PLEADER PROCTOR PROMOTE
SCHOLAR SUPPORT ATTORNEY
CHAMPION CLUBBIST DEFENSOR
EXPONENT HUMANIST PARTISAN
PREACHER PARACLETE PROPONENT
(— FAVORED BY JUDGE) PEAT
(— OF REVOLT) ANARCH
(SUFF.) ARIAN CRAT
ADVOWSON ADVOCACY TENEMENT
PATRONAGE
ADZ AX AXE ADZE EDGE ADDIS
ADDICE EATCHE THIXLE HATCHET
AEACUS (FATHER OF —) ZEUS
JUPITER
(MOTHER OF —) AEGINA
(SON OF —) PELEUS PHOCUS
TELAMON
(WIFE OF —) ENDEIS
AECHMAGORAS (FATHER OF —)
HERCULES
(MOTHER OF —) PHIALO
AECIUM CAEOMA
AEDON (BROTHER OF —) AMPHION
(FATHER OF —) PANDAREUS
(HUSBAND OF —) ZETHUS
POLYTECHNUS
(MOTHER OF —) HARMOTHOE
(SON OF —) ITYLUS
AEETES (DAUGHTER OF —) MEDEA
(FATHER OF —) HELIOS
(MOTHER OF —) PERSA PERSEIS
(SON OF —) APSYRTUS
AEGAEON (BROTHER OF —) GYGES
COTTUS
(FATHER OF —) URANUS
(MOTHER OF —) GE GAEA
(WIFE OF —) AEMILIA
AEGEAN SEA (ANCIENT PEOPLE
OF —) PSARA PSYRA SAMIAN
LELEGES SAMIOTE
(GULF OF —) SAROS
(ISLAND OF —) COS IOS KEOS NIOS
RODI SCIO CHIOS LEROS MELOS
NAXOS PAROS PATMO SAMOS
SIROS TENOS THERA ANDROS
IKARIA IMBROS LEMNOS LESBOS
RHODES SKYROS
(RIVER INTO —) STRUMA VARDAR
MARISTA
(TOWN ON —) CHIOS VATHY
MYTILENE
AEGEON (WIFE OF —) AEMILIA
AEGEUS (BROTHER OF —) LYCUS
NISUS PALLAS
(FATHER OF —) PANDION
(SON OF —) THESEUS
(WIFE OF —) PYLIA
AEGIA (FATHER OF —) ADRASTUS
(HUSBAND OF —) POLYNICES
(SON OF —) THERSANDER
AEGINA (FATHER OF —) ASOPUS
(MOTHER OF —) METOPE
(SON OF —) AEACUS

AEGIR HLER GYMIR
(WIFE OF —) RAN
AEGIRITE ACMITE
AEGIS EGIS SHIELD AUSPICE
DEFENCE DEFENSE
AEGISTHUS (FATHER OF —)
THYESTES
(MOTHER OF —) PELOPIA
(SLAYER OF —) ORESTES
AEGLE (BROTHER OF —) PHAETHON
(FATHER OF —) HELIUS
(MOTHER OF —) CLYMENE
AEGYPTUS (BROTHER OF —)
DANAUS
(FATHER OF —) BELUS
(MOTHER OF —) ANCHINOE
(SON OF —) LYNCEUS
AENEAS (COMPANION OF —)
ACHATES
(FATHER OF —) ANCHISES
(GREAT-GRANDSON OF —) BRUT
(MOTHER OF —) VENUS
APHRODITE
(SON OF —) IULUS ASCANIUS
(WIFE OF —) CREUSA LAVINIA
AENEID (AUTHOR OF —) VIRGIL
(CHARACTER IN —) ANNA DIDO
JUNO VENUS AENEAS PALLAS
TURNUS EVANDER LATINUS LAVINIA
ANCHISES ASCANIUS
AENGUS (MOTHER OF —) BOANN
AEOLUS (BROTHER OF —) DORUS
XUTHUS
(DAUGHTER OF —) ARNE CANACE
ALCYONE HALCYONE
(FATHER OF —) HELLEN HIPPOTES
(MOTHER OF —) ARNE ORSEIS
(SON OF —) ATHAMAS CRETHEUS
SISYPHUS SALMONEUS
AEON AGE EON ERA AION AEVUM
CYCLE KALPA PERIOD
(PAIR OF —S) SYZYGY
AEPYTUS (FATHER OF —)
CRESPHONTES
(MOTHER OF —) MEROPE
AERATE AERIFY CHARGE INFLATE
AERIAL AERY AIRY TWIN AERIE
LOFTY DIPOLE UNREAL AEOLIAN
ANTENNA ETHEREAL
(ROTATING —) SCANNER
(WIRELESS —) RADIATOR
AERIALIST FLIER FLYER
AERIE AERY AIRE AYRE EYRY NEST
AIERY BROOD EYRIE
AERIFORM UNREAL GASEOUS
AEROBE BACTERIUM
AERODROME AIRPORT AIRFIELD
AEROEMBOLISM BENDS
AEROFOIL FOIL SLAT ROTOR
CONTROL SURFACE
AEROLITE AEROLITH
AERONAUT PILOT SKYMAN
AERONAUTICS AVIATION

AEROPE (DAUGHTER OF —)
ANAXIBIA
(FATHER OF —) CATREUS CERHEUS
(HUSBAND OF —) ATREUS
PLISTHENES
(LOVER OF —) THYRESTES
(SISTER OF —) CLYMENE
(SON OF —) MENELAUS
AGAMEMNON
AEROPLANE (SEE AIRPLANE)
FANJET JALOPY RAIDER PARASOL
PROPJET SOCIABLE SPITFIRE
AEROSE BRASSY
AEROSTAT AIRSHIP BALLOON
AIRCRAFT
AERUGO RUST PATINA
AESACUS (FATHER OF —) PRIAM
(LOVER OF —) HESPERIA
(MOTHER OF —) ARISBE ALEXIRRHOE
AESEPUS (BROTHER OF —)
PEDASUS
(FATHER OF —) BUCOLION
(MOTHER OF —) ABARBAREA
(SLAYER OF —) EURYALUS
AESON (BROTHER OF —) PELIAS
(FATHER OF —) CRETHEUS
(MOTHER OF —) TYRO
(SON OF —) JASON
(WIFE OF —) ALCIMEDA
AESTHETIC ARTISTIC ESTHETIC
TASTEFUL
AETA ITA
AETHALIDES (FATHER OF —)
HERMES MERCURY
(MOTHER OF —) EUPOLEMIA
AETHRA (FATHER OF —) OCEANUS
PITTHEUS
(MOTHER OF —) TETHYS
(SON OF —) HYAS THESEUS
AETOLUS (FATHER OF —) ENDYMION
(SON OF —) CALYDON PLEURON
(WIFE OF —) PRONOE
AFAR OFF AWAY SAHO FERNE
FERREN REMOTE YFERRE DANAKIL
DANKALI DISTANT
AFARA LIMBA
AFFABLE FAIR OPEN BLAND CIVIL
FRANK SUAVE BENIGN FACILE
FORTHY GENIAL SOCIAL URBANE
AMIABLE CORDIAL GENERAL
LIKABLE CHARMING FAMILIAR
FRIENDLY GRACIOUS PLEASANT
SOCIABLE TOWARDLY CONVERSABLE
AFFAIR DO JOB PIE BLOW CASE DEAL
DUEL GEAR PLOY BRAWL CAUSE
EVENT FIGHT LEVEE PARTY THING
ACTION BATTLE BEHALF BEMENT
EFFFIR MATTER SETOUT SHAURI
BLOWOUT CONCERN FUNERAL
HOEDOWN JOURNEY LIAISON
PALAVER SHEBANG BUSINESS
COMETHER ENDEAVOR HYPOTHEC
INTRIGUE OCCASION PROCEEDING

(CONFUSED —) SCHEMOZZLE
(CRITICAL —) KANKEDORT
(LOVE —) LOVE AMOUR INTRIGUE
(SOCIAL —) FORMAL JUNKET SUPPER
(STATE —S) ESTATE
(PL.) SQUARES OCCASIONS
AFFECT AIL AIR HIT BEAR MELT
MOVE POSE RINE SHAM STIR SWAY
ALLOT ALTER ANNOY ASSAY COLOR
DRIVE FANCY FEIGN HAUNT IMPEL
MINCE SHOCK TOUCH ASPIRE
ASSIGN ASSUME CHANGE DESIRE
MOLEST SOFTEN STRIKE THRILL
ATTAINT ATTINGE BEWITCH
CONCERN EMOTION FEELING
IMPRESS OPERATE PASSION
PRETEND PROFESS ALLOCATE
DISPOSED FREQUENT INTEREST
SIMULATE
(— BY HANDLING) TOUCH
(— DEEPLY) CUT
(— FAVORABLY) LIKE
(— INJURIOUSLY) INTERESS
(— STRONGLY) HIT HOLD SURPRISE
(— WITH EXCITEMENT) BLOW
(— WITH FEELING) SMITE
AFFECTATION AIR AIRS POSE SHAM
FRILL GRACE MINCE CHICII CONCEIT
DISPLAY FOPPERY FROUNCE
GRIMACE PIETISM FONDNESS
PRETENSE PUPPYISM
(PL.) LUGS
AFFECTED MOY AIRY CAMP FEAT
AILED APISH MOVED POSEY CHICHI
FALLAL FEISTY FORMAL PRETTY
QUAINT SEIZED FEIGNED MINIKIN
MISSISH REACHED SMITTEN STILTED
TAFFETA TAFFETY TOUCHED
INVOLVED PRECIEUX PRECIOUS
RECHERCHE
(— BY DECAY) DOTY
(— WITH RABIES) MAD
(EASILY —) SENSIBLE
(SOMETHING —) CAMP
(SUFF.) IC ICAL PATH(IA)(IC)(Y)
AFFECTING AIRIFIED FRAPPANT
POIGNANT TOUCHING
AFFECTION LOVE WAFF ALOHA
AMOUR BOTCH FLAME HEART
CHERTE DOTAGE ESTEEM HYDROA
MALADY REGARD THRUSH AILMENT
CHARITY EMOTION FEELING
PASSION SYMPTOM CHLOASMA
DEARNESS DEVOTION FONDNESS
KINDNESS MELICERA TENDENCY
(LASTING —) WARMSPOT
(MORBID —) SEQUELA
(PARENTAL —) STORGE
(PROFOUND —) WORSHIP
(PL.) HEART HEARTSTRING
(SUFF.) OMA PATHY
AFFECTIONATE DEAR FOND WARM
ARDENT DOTING LOVING TENDER

AMOROUS CORDIAL DEVOTED EARNEST ZEALOUS ATTACHED PARENTAL SISTERLY

AFFECTIVE SENSIBLE

AFFERENT BEAR ESODIC SENSORY ADVEHENT INFERENT

AFFIANCE AFFY FAITH TRUST ASSURE ENGAGE ENSURE FIANCE PLEDGE PLIGHT SPOUSE BETROTH PROMISE CONTRACT RELIANCE

AFFIANCED INTENDED

AFFIANT DEPONENT AFFIDAVIT

AFFIDAVIT DAVY OATH AFFIANT AFFIDAVY AFFYDAVY

AFFILIATE ALLY UNIT ADOPT MERGE UNITE ATTACH BRANCH RELATE ASCRIBE CHAPTER CONNECT FILIATE

AFFINITY KIN TELE FAMILY LIKING AVIDITY CHEMISM KINDRED KINSHIP RAPPORT ALLIANCE GOSSIPRY HOMOLOGY RELATION SYMPATHY COGNATION
(PREF.) (— **FOR**) TROP(IDO)(O)
(SUFF.) (— **FOR**) PHIL(A)(AE)(E)(IA) (ISM)(IST)(OUS)(US) TROPE TROPISM

AFFIRM PUT AFFY AVER AVOW TAKE POSIT STATE SWEAR TRUTH VOUCH ADHERE ALLEGE ASSERT ATTEST AVOUCH DEPOSE RATIFY SUBMIT THREAP THREEP VERIFY ASSEVER CONFIRM DECLARE PROFESS PROTEST TESTIFY MAINTAIN PREDICATE

AFFIRMATION SAY VOW YES AMEN OATH WORD DIXIT PONENT THESIS AVERRAL AVERMENT

AFFIRMATIVE AY AYE NOD YAH YEA YEP YES AMEN ATEN YEAH PONENT DOGMATIC POSITIVE

AFFIX ADD FIX PEN PIN SET CASE CLIP FAST JOIN NAIL SEAL SIGN ADDON ANNEX INFIX STAMP UNITE ANCHOR APPEND ATTACH FASTEN SETTLE STAPLE ADHIRIT CONNECT ENTITLE FORMANT IMPRESS PLASTER SUBJOIN

AFFLATUS FURY FUROR FRENZY VISION IMPULSE

AFFLICT AIL RUE TRY VEX COMB FIRE HOLD HURT PAIN PINE RACK TUKE ARRAY ASSAY BESET CURSE GRILL GRIPE HARRY PINCH PRESS SEIZE SMITE TRYST VISIT WOUND WRING BURDEN GRIEVE HARASS HUMBLE INFECT MOLEST PESTER REMORD SCORCH STRAIN STRESS STRIKE CHASTEN INFLICT OPPRESS SCOURGE TORMENT TROUBLE DISTRESS LACERATE STRAITEN

AFFLICTED JOB SAD SORRY AILING WOEFUL GRIEVED HAUNTED SMITTEN IMPAIRED STRICKEN TROUBLED

AFFLICTION WOE EVIL LOSS PAIN SORE TEEN TINE TRAY ASSAY CROSS GRIEF PRESS SMART STOUR BUFFET DURESS MISERY PATHOS PLAGUE SORROW STRESS THRONG AILMENT DISEASE ILLNESS PASSION PURSUIT SCOURGE TORTURE TROUBLE CALAMITY DISTRESS HARDSHIP SEVERITY SICKNESS VEXATION MARTYRDOM
(**SECRET** —) HAIRSHIRT
(PL.) CUP
(SUFF.) (— **WITH**) ITIS

AFFLICTIVE SAD DIRE SORE SOUR HEAVY SEVERE

AFFLUENCE EASE AFFLUX INFLUX PLENTY RICHES WEALTH FORTUNE OPULENCE

AFFLUENT FAT RICH FLUSH RIVER BRANCH SPRUIT STREAM COPIOUS FLOWING HALCYON OPULENT WEALTHY ABUNDANT INFLUENT

AFFORD GO BEAR GIVE LEND GRANT INCUR OFFER STAND THOLE YIELD CONFER ENDURE MANAGE SUPPLY ACHIEVE FORWARD FURNISH FURTHER PRODUCE PROVIDE MINISTER

AFFRAY FEUD FRAY RIOT ALARM BRAWL BROIL CLASH FIGHT MELEE SCARE SPURN ATTACK BATTLE COMBAT EFFRAY ENFRAI FRIGHT STRIFE TERROR TUMULT ASSAULT CONTEST QUARREL SCUFFLE STARTLE FRIGHTEN STRUGGLE

AFFRIGHT COW FEAR AGAST ALARM DAUNT DOUBT DREAD SCARE AGRISE APPALL DISMAY CONFUSE STARTLE TERRIFY FRIGHTEN

AFFRONT CUT DEFY SLAP ABUSE BEARD PEEVE HARASS INJURE INSULT NETTLE OFFEND SLIGHT STRUNT ASSAULT OFFENCE OFFENSE OUTRAGE PROVOKE CONFRONT DISGRACE ILLTREAT IRRITATE CONTUMELY

AFFUSION POURING INFUSION

AFGHAN RUG GHAN COVER DURANI HASARA HAZARA PATHAN BLANKET PAKHTUN PUKHTUN ACHAKZAI COVERLET

AFGHAN FOX CORSAC CORSAK

AFGHANISTAN
CAPITAL: KABUL
COIN: PUL ABBASI AMANIA AFGHANI
LAKE: HELMAND
LANGUAGE: DARI PASHTO PUSHTU BALOCHI BALUCHI
MEASURE: JERIB KAROH
MOUNTAIN: KOH SAFEO CHAGAI PAMIRS SULAIMAN HIMALAYAS
NATIVE: SISTANI

PARLIAMENT: SHURA
PROVINCE: GHOR FARAH HERAT
KABUL KUNAR KUNUZ LOGAR
MAZAR ZABUL GHAZNI KAPISA
PARWAN WARDAK
RIVER: LORA OXUS CABUL FARAH
HARUT INDUS KABUL KHASH
KUNAR KOKCHA KUNDUZ HELMAND
MURGHAB AMUDARYA
SEA: DARYA
TOWN: RUI JURM NANI WAMA ASMAR
BALKH DOSHI HERAT KABUL KUNAR
MARUF MATUN MUKUR PAHRA
TULAK URGAN CHAMAN GHAZNI
KUNDUZ NAUZAD PANJAO RUSTAK
SANGAN SAROBI TUKZAR WASHIR
BAGHLAN BAMIYAN DILARAM
KANDAHAR MAZARESHARIF
TRIBE: SAFI TURK ULUS KAFIR TAJIK
UZBEK BALOCH BALUCH HAZARA
KIRGIZ PATHAN
WEIGHT: PAU PAW SER SIR KARWAR
KHURDS

AFICIONADO FAN AMATEUR
DEVOTEE GROUPIE FOLLOWER
AFIELD ABROAD ASTRAY
AFIRE ALOW ALOWE EAGER ABLAZE
AFLAME ARDENT BURNING FLAMING
A-FLAT AS AIS
AFLOAT ASEA ASWIM AWAFT
AWASH ADRIFT BUOYED NATANT
ABROACH FLOODED UNFIXED
FLOATING
AFOOT ABOUT AGATE ASTIR
ABROAD TOWARD WALKING
AFORE ERE
AFOREMENTIONED SAID SUCH
AFORESAID SAME DITTO NAMED
PRIOR PREVIOUS
AFORETIME ERE FORMER FORMERLY
AFRAID RAD REDE ADRAD FRAID
PAVID REDDE TIMID AGHAST CRAVEN
FEARED SCARED WROTHE AFEARED
ALARMED ANXIOUS ASCARED
CHICKEN FEARFUL GASTFUL
COWARDLY GHASTFUL TIMOROUS
AFREET JINN AFRIT DEMON GIANT
IFRIT JINNI AFRITE EFREET
AFRESH ANEW ANON OVER AGAIN
NEWLY DENOVO ENCORE REPEATED

AFRICA
(ALSO SEE SPECIFIC COUNTRIES)
DESERT: NAMIB NEFUD NUBIAN
SAHARA ARABIAN KALAHARI
LAKE: CHAD CONGO NYASA VOLTA
ALBERT KARIBA MALAWI RUDOLF
TURKANA VICTORIA TANGANYIKA
MOUNTAIN: MERU ATLAS ELGON
KENYA TEIDE TOUBKAL KARISIMBI
RASDASHAN RUWENZORI
DRAKENSBERG KILIMANJARO

NATION: CHAD MALI TOGO BENIN
CONGO EGYPT GABON GHANA
KENYA LIBYA NIGER SUDAN ZAIRE
ANGOLA GAMBIA GUINEA MALAWI
RWANDA UGANDA ZAMBIA ALGERIA
BURUNDI LESOTHO LIBERIA
MOROCCO NAMIBIA NIGERIA
SENEGAL SOMALIA TUNISIA
BOTSWANA CAMEROON DJIBOUTI
ETHIOPIA TANZANIA ZIMBABWE
SWAZILAND IVORYCOAST
MADAGASCAR MAURITANIA
MOZAMBIQUE UPPERVOLTA
BURKINAFASO SIERRALEONE
SOUTHAFRICA GUINEABISSAU
RIVER: NILE ORANGE LIMPOPO
SENEGAL ZAMBEZI
WATERFALL: FINCHA TUGELA
KALAMBO RUACANA TESSISAT
VICTORIA

AFRICAINE, L' (CHARACTER IN —)
INEZ DAGAMA SELIKA NELUSKO
(COMPOSER OF —) MEYERBEER
AFRICAN BOER AFRIC
AFRICAN MARIGOLD KHAKIBOS
AFRIKAANS TAAL DUTCH
AFRO NATURAL
AFT BACK REAR ABAFT AFTER
ASTERN BEHIND
(FARTHEST —) AFTERMOST
AFTER A AB BY TO AFT EFT FOR SIN
ANON NEXT PAST POST SYNE ABAFT
APRES ARTER EFTER INFRA LATER
SINCE ASTERN BEHIND BEYOND
FOLLOW HINDER
(— MEALS) PC
(PREF.) EPH EPI INFRA META POST
AFTERBIRTH HEAM SECUNDINE
SOOTERKIN
AFTERBODY TONNEAU
AFTERBURNER AUGMENTER
AFTEREFFECT SEQUEL SEQUELA
(PL.) HANGOVER
AFTERGRASS FOG AFTERFEED
AFTERIMAGE SPECTRUM
PHOTOGENE SENSATION
(KIND OF —) PURKINJE
AFTERMATH FOG ETCH LOSS ISSUE
ROWEN ROWET TRAIL TRAIN ARRISH
EDDISH EDGREW EDGROW EFFECT
PROFIT RESULT SEQUEL UPSHOT
EAGRASS STUBBLE BACKWASH
AFTERMOST LAST HINDMOST
AFTERNOON AFTER TARDE
UNDERN EVENING TEATIME
AFTERPIECE JIG EPODE EXODE
EXODIUM POSTLUDE
AFTERSONG EPODE
AFTERSWARM CAST SPEW SPUE
CASTLING
AFTERTASTE TWANG FAREWELL
AFTERTHOUGHT FOOTNOTE

AFTERWARD EFT POST SITH THEN
APRES LATER INABIT EFTSOON
EFTSOONS
AFTERWARDS SYNE
AGA AGHA LORD CHIEF
(WIFE OF —) BEGUM
AGAIN OR TO BIS EFT YET AGIN
ANEW ANON AYEN AYIN BACK MORE
OVER NEWLY AFRESH DENOVO
ENCORE ITERUM EFTSOON FRESHLY
FURTHER EFTSOONS MOREOVER
(— AND AGAIN) AND
(PREF.) ANA OVER PALI RE
AGAINST BY IN UP CON GIN NON
AGIN ANTI GAIN INTO WITH AGAIN
ANENT AYENS UNTIL ANENST
AVERSE AYENST CONTRA GAINST
UPTILL VERSUS FERNENT FORNENT
OPPOSED ADVERSUS CONTRAIR
FORENENT FORNENST FORNINST
(— HOPE) AGLEE AGLEY
(PREF.) ANTH ANTI CAT(A) CATH
CONTRA ENANTIO GAIN OB
AGAL HEADROPE
AGALLOCH AGGUR ALOES GAROO
GARROO GARROW TAMBAC LINALOE
AGALWOOD CALAMBAC
AGAMA AGA AGHA GUANA AGAMID
IGUANA LIZARD AGAMIAN
AGAMEDE (FATHER OF —) AUGEAS
(HUSBAND OF —) MULIUS
AGAMEMNON (BROTHER OF —)
MENELAUS
(DAUGHTER OF —) ELECTRA
IPHIGENIA
(FATHER OF —) PLISTHENES
(GRANDFATHER OF —) ATREUS
(MOTHER OF —) AEROPE
(SON OF —) ORESTES
(WIFE OF —) CLYTEMNESTRA
AGAMETE SPORE
AGAMID AGA AGHA BALETE BALITI
AGAPANTHUS TULBAGHIA
LOVEFLOWER
AGAPE LOVE OPEN FEAST GAPING
YAWNING
AGAR MOSS GELOSE KANTEN
GELOSIN GELOSINE
AGARIC BLEWITS BLUSHER FLYBANE
LEPIOTA
AGASP EAGER GASPING
AGATE TAW ONYX RUBY SARD
ACHATE GAGATE MARBLE PEBBLE
QUARTZ
(KIND OF —) MOSS
AGATI SESBANIA
AGAVE ALOE LILY PITA AGAUE
AMOLE DATIL SISAL LILIUM MAGUEY
MESCAL PULQUE ZAPUPE CANTALA
KARATTO KERATTO TEQUILA
HENEQUEN HENIQUEN JINIQUEN
SOAPWEED

(BROTHER OF —) POLYDORUS
(FATHER OF —) CADMUS
(HUSBAND OF —) ECHION
(MOTHER OF —) HARMONIA
(SISTER OF —) INO SEMELE AUTONOE
(SON OF —) PENTHEUS
AGE ALD BIN DAY ELD EON ERA AEON
EDGE GRAY OLAM TIME YUGA AETAT
CYCLE EPOCH GETON OLDEN RIPEN
SECLE WORLD YEARS MATURE
MELLOW PERIOD SIECLE WITHER
CENTURY DEVELOP GLACIAL
OLDNESS SECULUM SENESCE
VORHAND ANCIENTY DURATION
ETERNITY LIFETIME MAJORITY
MATURITY
(— OF MOON) EPACT
(— OF 100 YEARS) CENTENARY
(ADVANCED —) DOTAGE
(BEING UNDER 13 YEARS OF —)
PRETEEN
(EARLY MIDDLE —) SUMMER
(FULL —) MAJORITY
(GREAT —) ANTIQUITY GRANDEVITY
(OLD —) CRUTCH SENIUM VETUSTY
SENILITY
(PREF.) (OLD —) GERONT(O)
PRESBY(O)
(SUFF.) AEVAL EVAL
(HAVING APPROXIMATE — OF) ISH
ISTIC
AGED AE AET AGY OLD RIPE ANILE
HOARY OLDEN PASSE FEEBLE INFIRM
MATURE SENILE WINTRY YEARED
ANCIENT ELDERLY OGYGIAN
WINTERED
(NOT —) GREEN
(WELL —) STALE
AGEE AJEE AWRY AGLEY ASKEW
(SON OF —) SHAMMAH
AGELESS ETERNAL TIMELESS
AGELONG SECULAR SAECULAR
AGENCY DINT HAND CHECK FORCE
LEVER MEANS MOYEN ORGAN
PROXY ACTION BUREAU MEDIUM
OFFICE ARBITER BENEFIT BROKERY
FACULTY LIBRARY MACHINE
ACTIVITY COMPTOIR COURTESY
MINISTRY
(PUBLIC —) AUTHORITY
(REGULATORY —) QUANGO
(RESTORATIVE —) BALM
(SUPPOSITITIOUS —) ENTELECHY
(THERAPEUTIC —) MODALITY
(WORLD WAR II —) WPA
AGENDA LIST PLAN ROTA OUTLINE
AGENDUM ITEM SLATE DOCKET
RECORD RITUAL PROGRAM
AGENOR (BROTHER OF —) BELUS
(DAUGHTER OF —) EUROPA
(FATHER OF —) ANTENOR NEPTUNE
(MOTHER OF —) LIBYA

(SON OF —) CILIX CADMUS PHOENIX
(WIFE OF —) TELEPHASSA
AGENT SPY AMIN DOER ETCH GENE
ACTOR AMEEN BUYER CAUSE
ENVOY MEANS ORGAN PROXY
REEVE RIDER VAKIL WALLA ADUROL
ASSIGN ATOPEN BROKER BURSAR
COMMIS DEALER DEPUTY ENGINE
FACTOR FILER KEHAYA LEDGER
MEDIUM MINION MUKTAR PESKAR
SELLER SYNDIC VAKEEL WALLAH
BAILIFF BLISTER CHANNEL COUCHER
DRASTIC FACIENT FEDERAL
HUSBAND LEAGUER MOOKTAR
MOUNTAR MUKTEAR MUTAGEN
OFFICER PESHKAR PROCTOR
SCALPER APPROVER ATTORNEY
AUMILDAR CATALYST EMISSARY
EXECUTOR GOMASHTA GOMASTAH
IMPROVER INCITANT INSTITOR
MINISTER MITICIDE MOOKHTAR
OPERATOR PROMOTER QUAESTOR
RESIDENT SALESMAN VIRUCIDE
MIDDLEMAN OPERATIVE SATELLITE
SENESCHAL MAINSPRING
PROCURATOR PLENIPOTENTIARY
(— AGAINST LEPROSY) DAPSONE
(— INVESTIGATING DRUG
VIOLATIONS) NARC NARK
(— OF CROMWELL) AGITATOR
(ANTIKNOCK —) ADDITIVE AI KYLATE
(BINDING —) CHELATOR
(CLEANSING —) SOAP
(CONFIDENTIAL —) AMIN AMEEN
(DESTRUCTIVE —) DEVOURER
(EMPLOYMENT —) PADRONE
(ENFORCEMENT —) LAW
(ENVIRONMENTAL —) ZEITGEBER
(ESPIONAGE —) COURIER
(FISCAL —) STEWARD
(FIXING —) HYPO
(GOVERNMENT —) NARC NARCO
(HEALING —) BALSAM
(LIGHTLY-VALUED —) PAWN
(MEDICINAL —) DRASTIC
(MILK-CURDLING —) RENNET
(NARCOTIC —) NARC NARK GAZER
(OXIDIZING —) NINHYDRIN
(PRESS —) FLACK
(PUBLICITY —) BEATER
(PURCHASING —) CIRCAR SIRCAR
SIRKAR
(SECRET —) SBIRRO OPERATIVE
(SPECIAL —) TMAN
(SPIRITUAL —) POWER
(STIMULATING —) FILIP FILLIP
(SUBVERSIVE —) STOOGE
(SWEETENING —) DULCIN
(UNDERCOVER —) SPOOK
(VOLATILE —) SPIRIT
(WETTING —) SPREADER
(SUFF.) ANT FIER STAT(IC)(ICS)

AGE-OLD TIMEWORN
AGESILAUS (BROTHER OF —) AGIS
(FATHER OF —) ARCHIDAMUS
(MOTHER OF —) EUPOLIA
AGGLOMERATE HEAP LUMP MASS
PILE SELF SLAG WIND CHAOS
GATHER CLUSTER COLLECT
AGGLOMERATION HORDE
CONGERY FAVELLA CONGERIE
AGGRANDIZE LIFT BOOST EXALT
RAISE ADVANCE AUGMENT DIGNIFY
ELEVATE ENLARGE MAGNIFY
PROMOTE INCREASE
AGGRAVATE IRK NAG VEX FEED
LOAD TWIT ANGER ANNOY TAUNT
TEASE BURDEN PESTER WORSEN
AGGREGE BEDEVIL ENHANCE
ENLARGE MAGNIFY PROVOKE
AGGRIEVE HEIGHTEN INCREASE
IRRITATE
AGGRAVATED ACUTE
AGGREEABLE ACCEPTABLE
AGGREGATE ADD ALL SUM
AUGE BAND BULK CLON CLUB COMB
DEME FLOC GOUT LATH MASS
BLOCK BUNCH CLASS CLONE COVER
CROWD FIELD GROSS SHOOT SMEAR
TOTAL UNITE WHOLE AMOUNT
BALLAS DOMAIN PLUREL VOLUME
ASBOLAN COLLECT SCHMEAR
SCHMEER ARCULITE ASBOLANE
ASBOLITE AXIOLITE COMPOUND
COVERAGE CUMULITE ENSEMBLE
MANIFOLD MULTEITY TOTALITY
(— OF CELLS) TISSUE
(— OF CRYSTALS) TREE
(— OF MICA) BOOK
(— OF MINERALS) EYE
(— OF ORE) KIDNEY
(— OF POINTS) CELL
(— OF RELATED THINGS) SHMEAR
SCHMEAR
(— OF STATEMENTS) AUTHORITY
(— OF TISSUES) BODY
(MATHEMATICAL —) FIELD
SEQUENCE
(MOLECULAR —) MICELLE
(SOIL —) PED
(SUFF.) ERY
AGGREGATION HEAD HERD NEST
CLUMP CUTIN FLOCK GORGE GROUP
LURRY SWARM COLONY FAMILY
NATION SYSTEM CLUSTER CONGERY
GALLERY SORITES CONGERIE
EUMERISM
AGGRESSION WAR RAID ATTACK
INJURY ASSAULT OFFENSE
INVASION
AGGRESSIVE BUTCH PUSHY
PUSHING AGONISTIC TRUCULENT
AGGRESSIVENESS CRUST
DEFIANCE BELLICOSITY

AGGRIEVE TRY HARM HURT PAIN HARRY WRONG INJURE AFFLICT OPPRESS TROUBLE DISTRESS

AGGRIEVED SORE OFFENDED

AGHAST AGAST AFRAID

AGHRERATH (FATHER OF —) PESHENG
(SLAYER OF —) AFRASIAB

AGILAWOOD AGALLOCH AGALLOCHUM

AGILE DEFT FAST LISH SPRY WIRY ADEPT ALERT BRISK CATTY ELFIN FLEET LITHE NIFTY NIPPY QUICK WANLE WITHY ACTIVE ADROIT FEERIE FEIRIE LIMBER LISSOM LITHER LIVELY LUTHER NIMBLE QUIVER SUPPLE WANDLE LISSOME SALIENT SPRINGE SPRINGY ATHLETIC

AGILITY LEVITY SPROIL SLEIGHT ACTIVITY LEGERITY SALIENCE

AGING BINNING
(PREMATURE —) GERODERMA GERODERMIA

AGIO BATTA DISAGIO PREMIUM DISCOUNT EXCHANGE

AGIST TAX FEED RATE GRAZE PASTURE

AGITATE FAN IRK JAR VEX WEY FRET FUSS MOVE PLOT RILE ROCK ROIL SEEK STIR TEEM ALARM ALTER BREAK BROIL CHURN DRIVE HARRY IMPEL QUAKE ROUSE SHAKE AROUSE BETOSS BUSKLE DEBATE DEVISE EXCITE FOMENT HARASS INCITE JABBLE JOSTLE JUMBLE JUSTLE LATHER MANAGE RATTLE RUFFLE SEETHE ACTUATE CANVASS COMMOVE CONCUSS DISCUSS DISTURB PERTURB REVOLVE TEMPEST TORMENT TROUBLE ACTIVATE CONTRIVE CONVULSE DISQUIET DISTRACT TRANSACT
(— A LIQUID) SPARGE

AGITATED WILD HECTIC STEWED STORMY YEASTY AGITATO ESTUOUS UNQUIET AESTUOUS FEVERISH FLURRIED SEETHING OVERWROUGHT

AGITATION GOG JAR JOG BOIL FEAR FLAP FRET FURY GUST HEAT ITCH JERK JOLT SNIT STEW ALARM DANCE HURRY QUAKE SHAKE STORM STOUR TWEAK YEAST BREEZE BUSTLE DITHER ENERGY FIZZLE FLIGHT FLURRY FRENZY JABBLE MOTION PUCKER QUIVER RIPPLE SHAKES TAKING TREMOR TUMULT UNREST WELTER EMOTION FERMENT FLUSTER FLUTTER MADNESS RAMPAGE STICKLE SWITHER TEMPEST TURMOIL DISQUIET PAROXYSM UPHEAVAL COMMOTION

(— AND PROPAGANDA) AGITPROP
(— IN LIQUID) JABBLE
(BODILY —) JACTATION
(MENTAL —) STEW

AGITATOR HOG TREATER

AGLAIA (FATHER OF —) JUPITER
(MOTHER OF —) EURYNOME
(SISTER OF —) THALIA EUPHROSYNE

AGLET TAB TAG LACE STUD PLATE AIGLET PENDANT SPANGLE HAWTHORN STAYLACE

AGLEY AWRY AGLEE ASIDE ASKEW WRONG

AGLYCON GENIN NONSUGAR SAPOGENIN

AGNATE AKIN ALLIED COGNATE KINDRED

AGNEL MOUTON

AGNOETE THEMISTIAN

AGNOMEN NAME ALIAS EPITHET SURNAME COGNOMEN NICKNAME

AGNOSTIC ATHEIST DOUBTER SKEPTIC NESCIENT

AGO BY SIN BACK ERST GONE PAST SENS SYNE YGOE YORE ABACK AGONE SINCE YGONE SINSYNE BACKWARD
(LONG —) ANCIENTLY

AGOG AVID KEEN ASTIR EAGER LIVELY EXCITED VIGILANT

AGOING AGATE

AGONIZE BEAR RACK STRAIN WRITHE

AGONIZING GRINDING HARROWING

AGONY ACHE PAIN PANG DOLOR GRIEF GRIPE PANIC STOUR THRAW THROE TRIAL ACHING ANGUISH ANXIETY EMOTION TORMENT TORTURE TRAVAIL DISTRESS PAROXYSM

AGOUTI CAPA CAVY PACA ACUCHI AGOUTY ACOUCHI ACOUCHY

AGRAFFE CLASP

AGRARIAN RURAL PASTORAL PRAEDIAL

AGRAULOS (DAUGHTER OF —) HERSE PANDROSOS
(FATHER OF —) ACTAEUS
(HUSBAND OF —) CECROPS

AGREE FAY FIT GEE HIT PAN YES GIBE GREE JIBE JUMP MEET SIDE SORT SUIT ADMIT ALLOW ATONE BLEND CHECK CLICK CLOSE FADGE GRANT HITCH JUTTY LEVEL MATCH PIECE STAND TALLY UNITE YIELD ACCEDE ACCEPT ACCORD ADHERE ASSENT ASSORT COMPLY CONCUR CONDOG COTTON ENGAGE REWARD SETTLE SQUARE SUBMIT ARRANGE BARGAIN COMPORT CONCEDE CONFORM CONGREE CONGRUE CONSENT CONSIGN DARESAY PACTION PROMISE COINCIDE

COMPOUND CONTRACT COVENANT
QUADRATE
(— **MUTUALLY**) STIPULATE
(— **TO**) ACCEPT
(— **TO JOIN**) ADHERE
(— **UPON**) TAILYE TAILZEE TAILZIE
(— **WITH**) SIT LIKE SIDE TAIL
ANSWER

AGREEABLE AMEN EASY FAIR FINE
GOOD KIND LIEF NICE SOFT WEME
AMENE CANNY DULCE GRATE JOLIE
JOLLY LITHE LUSTY QUEME READY
SAPID SMIRK SUANT SUAVE SUENT
SWEET COMELY COWDIE DAINTY
DULCET KINDLY LIKELY MELLOW
SAVORY SMOOTH SUITED ADAPTED
AMABILE AMIABLE COUTHIE
DOUCEUR TUNABLE WELCOME
WILLING WINSOME AMENABLE
CHARMING DELICATE GRATEFUL
LIKESOME LOVESOME OBLIGING
PLACABLE PLAUSIVE PLEASANT
PLEASING PURSUANT SOCIABLE
SUITABLE THANKFUL CONGENIAL
PALATABLE
(**NOT** —) ABHORRENT
(**UNPLEASANTLY** —) SACCHARINE

AGREED ON DONE CONTENT

AGREEING CONNATE CONTENT
ACCORDANT ACCORDING

AGREEMENT GO FIT NOD AXIS
BOND DEAL FINE LINE MISE PACT
TACK TAIL TRUE MISE ATONE COVIN
LEASE MATCH TERMS TOUCH TRUTH
TRYST UNITY WHIZZ ACCORD
ACTION ASSENT CARTEL CAUTIO
COMART COMITY COVINE DICKER
LEAGUE PACTUM PLEDGE TREATY
UNISON ANALOGY BARGAIN
CLOSING CLOSURE COMPACT
CONCERT CONSENT CONSORT
CONSULT ENTENTE HARMONY
ONENESS PACTION RAPPORT
CONTRACT DIAPASON SANCTION
SORTANCE SYMPATHY ACCEPTANCE
ACCORDANCE
(— **OF SOUND**) CHIME
(— **TO JOIN**) ADHESION
(**GRAMMATICAL** —) ATTRACTION
(**IN** —) ASONE
(**REPURCHASE** —) REPO
(**SECRET** —) CAHOOT CAHOOTS
COLLUSION

AGRICANE (**SLAYER OF** —) ORLANDO

AGRICULTURAL ARABLE GEOPONIC
GEOPONICAL

AGRICULTURE FARMING GAINAGE
TILLAGE AGRONOMY
(— **SYSTEM**) KOLKHOZ
(**PREF.**) AGRO

AGRICULTURIST THO FARMER
GROWER SANTAL PLANTER
RANCHER

AMERICAN REID MORTON RUFFIN
TAYLOR THOMAS WATSON
BORLAUG
CANADIAN MACKAY SAUNDERS
ENGLISH TULL YOUNG
GERMAN NAUMANN
SWISS SAUSSURE

AGRIMONY CLIVE BONESET
BORWORT HEMPWEED

AGRIPPINA (**SON OF** —) NERO

AGRITO AGARITA MAHONIA
ALGERITO ASHBERRY

AGRIUS (**BROTHER OF** —) LATINUS
TELEGONUS
(**FATHER OF** —) ULYSSES ODYSSEUS
PORTHAON
(**MOTHER OF** —) GAEA CIRCE EURYTE
(**SON OF** —) THERSITES

AGRONOMIST (**ALSO SEE**
AGRICULTURIST)

AGROUND SEWED ASHORE
BEACHED STRANDED

AGRYPHA LOGION

AGRYPNIA INSOMNIA
SLEEPLESSNESS

AGUACATE AHUACA AVOCADO

AGUAMAS PINGUIN

AGUE CHILL EXIES FEVER MALARIA
QUARTAN SHAKING SHIVERS

AGUE TREE SASSAFRAS

AGUEWEED BONESET

AGUR (**FATHER OF** —) JAKEH

AH AY ACH

AHAB (**FATHER OF** —) OMRI
(**NEIGHBOR OF** —) NABOTH
(**WIFE OF** —) JEZEBEL

AHAR AGEE AJEE

AHARAH (**FATHER OF** —) BENJAMIN

AHARTALAV YARROW MILFOIL

AHASBAI (**SON OF** —) ELIPHELET

AHAZ (**FATHER OF** —) MICAH JOTHAM

AHAZIAH (**FATHER OF** —) AHAB
JEHORAM
(**MOTHER OF** —) JEZEBEL ATHALIAH

AHBAN (**FATHER OF** —) ABISUR
(**MOTHER OF** —) ABIHAIL

AHEAD ON UP ALEE FORE AFORE
ALONG DORMY BEFORE DORMIE
ONWARD ALREADY ENDWAYS
ENDWISE FORWARD LEADING
ADELANTE ADVANCED ANTERIOR
(— **OF TIME**) FAST
(**STRAIGHT** —) FORERIGHT

AHEM HUM

AHIAH (**FATHER OF** —) AHITUB
JERAHMEEL
(**SON OF** —) BAASHA

AHIAM (**FATHER OF** —) SHARAR

AHIEZER (**FATHER OF** —)
AMMISHADDAI

AHIHUD (**FATHER OF** —) SHELOMI

AHIKAM (**FATHER OF**) SHAPHAN
(**SON OF** —) GEDALIAH

AHILUD (SON OF —) BAANA JEHOSHAPHAT

AHIMAAZ (DAUGHTER OF —) AHINOAM
(FATHER OF —) ZADOK

AHIMELECH (FATHER OF —) AHITUB

AHINADAB (FATHER OF —) IDDO

AHINOAM (FATHER OF —) AHIMAAZ
(HUSBAND OF —) SAUL DAVID
(SON OF —) AMNON

AHIO (FATHER OF —) BERIAH JEHIEL ABINADAB

AHIRAM (FATHER OF —) BENJAMIN

AHISAMACH (SON OF —) AHOLIAB

AHISHAHAR (FATHER OF —) BILHAN

AHITUB (FATHER OF —) AMARIAH PHINEHAS
(SON OF —) ZADOK AHIJAH AHIMELECH

AHLAI (FATHER OF —) SHESHAN
(HUSBAND OF —) JARHA
(SON OF —) ZABAD

AHOAH (FATHER OF —) BENJAMIN

AHOLIBAMAH (FATHER OF —) ANAH
(HUSBAND OF —) ESAU

AHOY AVAST

AHUEHUETE CEDAR SABINO CYPRESS

AHURA MAZDA ORMAZD

AHUZAM (FATHER OF —) ASHUR
(MOTHER OF —) NAARAH

AH WILDERNESS
(AUTHOR OF —) ONEILL
(CHARACTER IN —) BELLE DAVID MILLER MURIEL RICHARD MCCOMBER

AIAH (BROTHER OF —) ANAH
(DAUGHTER OF —) RIZPAH
(FATHER OF —) ZIBEON

AID KEY ABET BACK BEET HAND HELP PONY REDE ALLAY BOOST COACH FAVOR GRANT SERVE SPEED TREAT ASSIST CRUTCH FAVOUR FRIEND PROFIT RELIEF REMEDY RESCUE SECOND SUCCOR SUPPLY UPHOLD ADVANCE AIDANCE ANCILLA BACKING BENEFIT COMFORT ENDORSE FORWARD FURTHER INDORSE RELIEVE SECOURS SERVICE SUBSIDY SUPPORT ADJUVATE AUXILIUM BEFRIEND SUFFRAGE
(— A VESSEL) HOVEL
(— A WAITER) BUS
(— IN MONEY) SUBSIDY
(— SECRETLY) SUBAID
(COMPLEXION —) FUCUS
(FAMILY —) AFDC
(MORMON —) COUNSELOR COUNSELLOR

AIDA (CHARACTER IN —) AIDA AMNERIS RADAMES AMONASRO
(COMPOSER OF —) VERDI

AIDAN (FATHER OF —) GABRAN

AIDE AID BEAGLE DEPUTY SECOND OFFICER ORDERLY ADJUTANT GALLOPER PARAPROFESSIONAL
(BULLFIGHTER'S —) CAPEADOR

AIDS (— VIRUS) HIV

AIGRETTE EGRET HERON PLUME SPRAY AIGRET FEATHERS

AIL ILE AILD EILE EYLE FAIL PAIN PINE AFFECT BOTHER FALTER SUFFER AFFLICT DECLINE TROUBLE COMPLAIN DISTRESS

AILANTHUS SUMAC SUMACH

AILING SICK CRAZY CRONK DONCY DONSY SOBER DONSIE SICKLY UNWELL CRAICHY CREACHY

AILMENT AIL ILL PIP COUGH MALADY DISEASE ILLNESS DISORDER SICKNESS WEAKNESS
(SUDDEN —) WAFF
(WINTER —) STREP

AIM END LAY TRY BEAD BEAM BEND BENT BUTT FINE GLEE GOAL HEAD HOLD LEAD MARK MINT PLAN SAKE SEEK TEMP VIEW VIZY WINK ACIES BLANK DRIVE ESSAY ETTLE GUESS LEVEL POINT PRICK SCOPE SIGHT TRAIN VISIE VIZZY ASPIRE DESIGN DIRECT ESTEEM INTEND INTENT OBJECT SCHEME STRIVE ADDRESS ATTEMPT CHIMERA MEANING PRETEND PURPOSE RESPECT STAGGER CHIMAERA CONSIDER ENDEAVOR ESTIMATE PRETENSE STEERING TENTAMEN
(— A BROADCAST) NARROWCAST
(— A KICK) FLING
(— AT) EYE AFFECT
(— FURTIVELY) STEAL
(— HIGH) LOB
(— INDIRECTLY) GLANCE

AIMED FAST
(— AT) AFFECTED

AIMING LEVEL GUNLAYING

AIMLESS IDLE BLIND CHANCE RANDOM DRIFTING

AIMLESSNESS FLANERIE

AIR AER PEW SKY AERE ARIA AURA AYRE BROW DIRT FEEL LILT LOFT MIEN PORT POSE SONG TELL TUNE VENT WIND AVION ETHER FRILL OZONE UTTER VOICE AERATE AETHER ALLURE ASPECT BROACH CACHET MANNER MELODY OSTENT PIAFFE REGARD REGION STRAIN VANITY WELKIN WITHER BEARING DISPLAY EXHIBIT EXPRESS FANFARE MALARIA NEPHELE PIAFFER ATTITUDE BEHAVIOR CARRIAGE PRESENCE
(— COOLED) WATERLESS
(— EXHALED) BLAST
(— IN MOTION) BREATH
(— OUT) VENT

(— PLANT) LIFELEAF
(AFFECTED —S) FRILLS
(BOASTFUL —) PARADO
(CHEERFUL —) LILT
(CONFIDENT —) BRAVURA
(COOL —) FRESCO
(COQUETTISH —) MINAUDERIE
(FETID —) REEK
(FOUL —) DIRT
(HAUGHTY —S) ALTITUDES
(MUSICAL —) ARIA SOLO TUNE
BRAWL MELODY ARIETTA ARIETTE
BRAVURA CANZONE MUSETTE
CAVATINE
(OPEN —) OUTDOORS OUTOF
DOORS
(POISONOUS —) MALARIA
(POMPOUS —) SWELL
(PRETENTIOUS —) SIDE
(PURE —) SERENE
(PUT ON —S) PROSS
(PUT ON —) TELEVISE
BROADCAST
(STALE —) STEAM
(STIFLING —) SMORE
(THE —) GATE
(WARM —) OAM
(PL.) LUGS FRONT
(PREF.) AER(O) ATM(O) PNEO
PNEUM(A)(ATA)(O)(ON)(ONO)
PNEUSTA
AIRBORNE ALOFT
AIRCRAFT KITE ABORT BLIMP CRAFT
FLYER PLANE GLIDER TRIJET
AEROBUS AERONEF AIRSHIP
BALLOON AEROBOAT AERODYNE
AEROSTAT AIRLINER AIRPLANE
AUTOGIRO AUTOGYRO GYRODYNE
TILTROTOR GYROCOPTER
ROTORCRAFT ORNITHOPTER
(— DESIGN) STEALTH
(— WAITING TO LAND) STACK
(ARMED —) GUNSHIP
(LARGE JET —) WIDEBODY
(SMALL —) STOL
(UNIDENTIFIED —) UFO BOGY BOGEY
BOGIE
(UNMANNED —) RPV
AIRCRAFTSMAN ERK
AIRCREWMAN KICKER AIREDALE
AIRFARE (CLASS OF —) APEX
AIRFIELD AERODROME SATELLITE
AIRFOIL FIN FLAP SLAT BLADE
CANARD SURFACE AEROFOIL
ELEVATOR
**AIR FORCE (WOMEN COMPONENTS
OF —)** WAF
AIRHEAD SAP
AIRILY JAUNTILY
AIRING OUTING
AIRLESS STUFFY STIFLING
AIRLINE KLM SAS TWA BWIA ELAL
ALOHA DELTA USAIR FEEDER IBERIA

QANTAS SABENA SKYWAY UNITED
NONSKED LUFTHANSA
AIRMAN ACE FLIER FLYER BIRDMAN
WARBIRD AERONAUT WASTEMAN
AIRPLANE BUS CUB JET MIG SST
BAKA GYRO KILL KITE SHIP ZERO
AVION CAMEL CRATE FLIER FLYER
FRITZ GOTHA HEINE JENNY LINER
PLANE SCOUT SNOOP AIRBUS
BOMBER CANARD CESSNA CHASER
COPTER FANJET FERRET FESSEL
FOKKER GLIDER JENNIE PUSHER
SMOKER TANDEM VESSEL VIMANA
AERONEF AVIATIK AVIETTE BIPLANE
CLIPPER FIGHTER FLIVVER FLYAWAY
HOTSHOT PENGUIN SNOOPER
SPOTTER STINSON TRACTOR
WARBIRD AEROSTAT ALBATROS
KAMIKAZE SEAPLANE SKYCOACH
SKYCRAFT SOCIABLE STRUTTER
TRIPLANE TURBOJET WARPLANE
AEROPLANE MONOPLANE
(— ENGINE) RAMJET
(COMMANDEER —) SKYJACK
(JET —) AIRBUS
(JUMPING FROM —) SKYDIVING
(PART OF —) FIN POD TAB FLAP WING
BLADE CABIN PYLON RADAR ENGINE
RUDDER AILERON COCKPIT
COWLING SPOILER ELEVATOR
REVERSER STABILIZER SUPPRESSOR
(REMOTE-CONTROLLED —) DRONE
(TYPE OF —) TRIJET
AIR PLANT LIFELEAF LIVELEAF
AIRPORT DROME AIRPARK JETPORT
SCUTTLE AIRDROME AIRFIELD
AIRSCREW PUSHER
AIRSHIP (SEE ALSO AIRPLANE AND
AIRCRAFT) SHIP BLIMP GASBAG
AERONAT AEROSTAT PARSEVAL
ZEPPELIN
AIRSTREAM PEW DOWNWASH
AIRSTRIP LILY
AIRTIGHT SEALED AIRPROOF
HERMETIC
AIRWAY MONKEY RETURN SKYWAY
AIRWAVE WINDWAY WINDROAD
AIRY GAY COOL RARE THIN EMPTY
HUFFY LIGHT MERRY WINDY AERIAL
BLITHE BREEZY FLUFFY JAUNTY
JOCUND LIVELY STARRY AIRLIKE
AIRSOME HAUGHTY JOCULAR
SFOGATO AFFECTED ANIMATED
DEBONAIR DELICATE ETHEREAL
FLIPPANT GRACEFUL SPARKISH
TRIFLING VOLATILE
AISLE WAY YLE AILE LANE NAVE
WALK ALLEE ALLEY FEEDWAY
GANGWAY PASSAGE CORRIDOR
AIT OAT EYOT HOLM ILOT ISLE EIGHT
ISLET ISLOT
AITCH ACHE
AITCHBONE ICEBONE EDGEBONE

AJA (FATHER OF —) RAGHU DILIPA
AJAR OPEN DISCORDANT
AJAX AIAS
  (FATHER OF —) OILEUS TELAMON
  (MOTHER OF —) ERIBOEA PERIBOEA
AJIGARTA (SON OF —) SUNAHSEPA
AJONJOLI SESAME
AJOWAN AJAVA AIWAIN
AKALI SHAHIDI
AKAN (FATHER OF —) EZER
AKEAKE AKE HOPBUSH IRONWOOD
AKHA KAW
AKIMBO ANGLED AKEMBOLL
  AKENBOLD
AKIN SIB LIKE NEAR NIGH ALIKE
  CLOSE AGNATE ALLIED COUSIN
  SIBBED TENDER COGNATE CONNATE
  GERMANE RELATED SIMILAR
  (— ON MALE SIDE) AGNATIC
  (NOT —) UNSIB
AKKUB
  (FATHER OF —) ELIOENAI
AKRA ACCRA INKRA
AKU VICTORFISH
AL AAL AWL MULBERRY
ALA AXIL DRUM WING AXILLA
  RECESS NOSEWING

ALABAMA

CAPITAL: MONTGOMERY
COUNTY: LEE BIBB CLAY DALE PIKE
  COOSA HENRY LAMAR MACON
  PERRY BLOUNT BUTLER COFFEE
  DALLAS ELMORE ETOWAH GENEVA
  GREENE MARION MONROE
  MORGAN SHELBY SUMTER WILCOX
  CHILTON
LAKE: MARTIN
MOUNTAIN: CHEAHA LOOKOUT
  RACCOON
NATIVE: LIZARD
RIVER: PEA COOSA CAHABA MOBILE
  SIPSEY TENSAW CONECUH PERDIDO
  SEPULGA WARRIOR TOMBIGBEE
  TALLAPOOSA
STATE BIRD: YELLOWHAMMER
STATE FISH: TARPON
STATE FLOWER: CAMELLIA
STATE TREE: PINE LONGLEAF
TOWN: OPP PIPER SELMA ATHENS
  CORONA HEFLIN JASPER LANETT
  LINDEN MARION MOBILE SAMSON
  BREWTON FLORALA GADSDEN
  ANNISTON SYLACAUGA
  TUSCALOOSA

ALABASTER GYPSUM TECALI
  ONYCHITE
ALACK ALAS ALAKE
ALACRITY HASTE SPEED CELERITY
  RAPIDITY
ALAMEDA MALL WALK

ALAMETH (FATHER OF —) BECHER
ALAN ALAND ALANT ALAUNT
ALANG-ALANG COGON KOGON
ALANS GHUZ OGHUZ
ALANTIN INULIN
ALAR PTERIC WINGED AXILLARY
  WINGLIKE
ALARBUS (MOTHER OF —) TAMORA
ALARDO (BROTHER OF —)
  BRADAMANT
ALARM COW DIN BELL FEAR FRAY
  GAST LARM ALERT BROIL CLOCK
  DAUNT FEEZE LARUM NOISE PANIC
  ROUSE SCARE SIREN START STILL
  UPSET AFFRAY ALARUM APPALL
  AROUSE ATTACK BUZZER DISMAY
  EXCITE FRIGHT OUTCRY SIGNAL
  TERROR TOCSIN DISTURB GLOPNEN
  GLOPPEN MOUNTEE STARTLE
  TERRIFY TORPEDO WARNING
  AFFRIGHT DISQUIET FRIGHTEN
  SURPRISE CONSTERNATION
  (FIRE —) STILL FIREBOX
ALARMED SCARY SCAREY FEARFUL
  GASTFUL AFFRAYED GHASTFUL
  SCAREFUL STREAKED
ALARMER HUER
ALARMING SCARY SCAREY
  FEARFUL SCAREFUL
ALARMIST JITTERBUG
ALAS AY ACH HEU LAS OCH TSK VAE
  WOE EHEU HECH OIME WALY ALACK
  HALAS HELAS OIMEE SOSAD
  HARROW OCHONE OTOTOI
  WAESUCK ULLAGONE WAESUCKS
  WELLADAY WELLAWAY

ALASKA

CAPITAL: JUNEAU
GLACIER: MUIR
ISLAND: ADAK ATKA ATTU UMNAK
  KODIAK UNIMAK AFOGNAK
  DIOMEDE NUNIVAK
ISLAND GROUP: RAT ALEUTIAN
  PRIBILOF ANDREANOF
LAKE: NAKNEK ILIAMNA
MOUNTAIN: BONA VETA SPURR
  KATMAI PAVLOF FORAKER
  MCKINLEY
MOUNTAIN RANGE: CRAZY BROOKS
  KAIYUH CHUGACH KILBUCK
  WRANGELL
NATIVE: ALEUT AHTENA ESKIMO
  INGALIK KOYUKON TLINGIT
PENINSULA: KENAI SEWARD
PURCHASER: SEWARD
RIVER: CHENA KOBUK YUKON COPPER
  NOATAK TANANA KOYUKUK
  SUSITNA CHULITNA COLVILLE
  KUSKOKWIM PORCUPINE
STATE BIRD: PTARMIGAN
STATE FLOWER: FORGETMENOT

STATE TREE: SPRUCE
TOWN: EEK NOME RUBY KENAI SITKA
  UMIAT BARROW JUNEAU KODIAK
  NENANA SKAGWAY KOTZEBUE
  ANCHORAGE FAIRBANKS
  KETCHIKAN
VOLCANO: KUKAK SPURR GRIGGS
  KATMAI MAGEIK MARTIN PAVLOF
  DOUGLAS ILIAMNA REDOUBT
  TORBERT TRIDENT WRANGELL

ALASTRIM AMAAS
ALATE WINGY
ALB ALBE AUBE CAMISIA CHRISOM
  VESTMENT
ALBACORE TUNA TUNNY GERMAN
  GERMON LONGFIN ALALONGA
  ALALUNGA MACKEREL SCOMBRID

ALBANIA

ANCIENT PEOPLE: ILLYRIAN
CAPITAL: TIRANA TIRAND
COIN: LEK FRANC QINTAR QINTARKA
KING: ZOG
LAKE: ULZE OHRID PRESPA SCUTARI
  OHRIDSKO
MOUNTAIN: KORAB SHALA PINDUS
  KORITNIK
REGION: EPIRUS
RIVER: MAT DRIN OSUM SEMAN
  BOJANA ERZENI SEMENI VIJOSE
  SHKUMBI
TOWN: LIN FIER KLOS LESH BERAT
  CROIA DUKAT KORCE KRUJE PECIN
  PEQIN QUKES RUBIC SPASH VLONE
  VLORE AVLONA BERATI BITSAN
  DARDHE DURRES KORRCE PERMET
  PRESHE TIRANA VALONA ALESSIO
  DURAZZO KORITZA SCUTARI
  SHKODER
TRIBE: GEG CHAM GHEG TOSK

ALBANIAN GEG GHEG GUEG
  ARNAUT SKIPETAR
ALBATROSS GONY GOON GONEY
  GOONY NELLY FABRIC GOONEY
  GOONIE QUAKER SEABIRD
  ALCATRAS BLUEBIRD STINKPOT
ALBEIT ALL ALBE ALBEE ALLBE
  THOUGH HOWBEIT
ALBERIC (WIFE OF —) MAROZIA
ALBERTA (CAPITAL OF —)
  EDMONTON
  (LAKE OF —) BANFF JASPER
  WATERTON
  (RIVER OF —) BOW OLDMAN WAPITI
  ATHABASCA
  (TOWN OF —) CALGARY REDDEER
  LETHBRIDGE MEDICINEHAT
ALBIGENSIANS CATHARI
ALBINISM ALPHOSIS
ALBINO LEUCAETHIOP

ALBITE PERICLINE
ALBIZZIA SIRIS
ALBOIN (FATHER OF —) ALDUIN
  (SLAYER OF —) HELMICHIS
  (WIFE OF —) ROSAMUNDA
ALBUM ALBE BOOK RECORD
  VOLUME REGISTER
ALBUMEN WHITE
ALBUMIN ALBUMEN PHASELIN
  SYNTONIN
ALBUMINOID ELASTIN FIBROIN
  KERATIN PROTEIN SERICIN
  COLLAGEN GORGONIN
ALBURNUM SAP BLEA SPLINT
  SAPWOOD
ALBUS BLANCO
ALCAEUS (DAUGHTER OF —) ANAXO
  (FATHER OF —) PERSEUS
  ANDROGEUS
  (MOTHER OF —) ANDROMEDA
  (SON OF —) AMPHITRYON
ALCAIDE CADE CAID QAID JUDGE
  ALCADE
ALCATHOUS (FATHER OF —) PELOPS
  (MOTHER OF —) HIPPODAMIA
  (SLAYER OF —) OENOMAUS
  IDOMENEUS
  (WIFE OF —) EUAECHME
ALCESTIS (AUTHOR OF —)
  EURIPIDES
  (CHARACTER IN —) APOLLO
  ADMETUS ALCESTIS HERCULES
  THANATOS
  (FATHER OF —) PELIAS
  (HUSBAND OF —) ADMETUS
ALCHEMIST ADEPT ARTIST CHEMIC
  CHEMICK CHEMIST HERMETIC
  (AUTHOR OF —) JONSON
  (CHARACTER IN —) DOL ABEL FACE
  SURLY COMMON DAPPER MAMMON
  PLIANT SUBTLE ANANIAS DRUGGER
  EPICURE KASTRIL LOVEWIT
  WHOLESOME TRIBULATION
ALCHEMY ART MAGIC ALCUMY
  CHYMIA SPAGYRIC
  (GOD OF —) HERMES
ALCHFRITH (FATHER OF —) OSWIU
  (MOTHER OF —) EANFLAED
  (WIFE OF —) CYNEBURH
ALCHORNEA DOVEWOOD
ALCIBIADES (FATHER OF —) CLINIAS
  (MOTHER OF —) DINOMACHE
ALCIMEDE (FATHER OF —)
  PHYLACUS
  (HUSBAND OF —) AESON
  (MOTHER OF —) CLYMENE
  (SON OF —) JASON
ALCIMEDES (BROTHER OF —)
  ARGUS MEDEUS PHERES
  MERMERUS TISANDER THESSALUS
  (FATHER OF —) JASON
  (MOTHER OF —) MEDEA

ALCINA (SISTER OF —) MORGANA
LOGISTILLA
(VICTIM OF —) RUGGIERO
ALCINOUS (DAUGHTER OF —)
NAUSICAA
(FATHER OF —) NAUSITHOUS
(MOTHER OF —) PERIBOEA
(WIFE OF —) ARETE
ALCIPPE (DAUGHTER OF —)
MARPESSA
(HUSBAND OF —) EVENUS METION
(SON OF —) DAEDALUS
ALCIS (FATHER OF —) ANTIPOENUS
(SISTER OF —) ANDROCLEA
ALCITHOE (FATHER OF —) MINYAS
(SISTER OF —) ARSIPPE LEUCIPPE
ALCMAEON (FATHER OF —)
AMPHIARAUS
(MOTHER OF —) ERIPHYLE
(WIFE OF —) CALLIRRHOE
ALPHESIBOEA
ALCMENE (FATHER OF —)
ELECTRYON
(HUSBAND OF —) AMPHITRYON
(SON OF —) HERCULES IPHICLES
ALCOHOL ALKY ETHAL ETHYL IDITE
LEDOL NEROL VINYL AMYROL
ANDROL CEDROL ELEMOL GLYCOL
GUAIOL HYDROL IDITOL LUPEOL
LUTEIN METHYL PHYTOL SPIRIT
STERIN STERNO STEROL TALITE
ACRITOL ADONITE ALDITOL
ALKANOL ANISOIN BORNEOL
BUTANOL CAROTOL DECANOL
ETHANOL FENCHOL HEPTITE
HEXITOL INOSITE MANNITE
MENTHOL PHORBOL PULEGOL
QUINITE SCOPINE SORBITE STETHAL
STYRONE TAGETOL TALITOL
TROPINE XYLITOL CATECHOL
LINALOOL MANNITOL METHANOL
GLYCERINE PYRIDOXINE
(ETHYL —) METHS
(NOT USING —) STRAIGHT
ALCOHOLATE SPIRIT ESSENCE
ALCOHOLIC ALKY
(HERBAL — DRINK) SNAPS
(NOT —) SOFT
ALCOHOLOMETER GENOMETER
VINOMETER
ALCOVE BAY NOOK BOWER NICHE
ORIEL STALL CARREL RECESS
CARRELL CUBICLE DINETTE RETREAT
SERVERY ALHACENA SNUGGERY
TABLINUM
ALCYONARIAN SEAPEN
ALCYONE (BROTHER OF —)
EURYSTHEUS
(FATHER OF —) ATLAS AEOLUS
(HUSBAND OF —) CEYX
(MOTHER OF —) ENARETE PLEIONE
(SON OF —) ANTHAS HYRIEUS

ALDABELLA (BROTHER OF —)
OLIVIERO BRANDIMARTE
(FATHER OF —) MONODANTES
(HUSBAND OF —) ORLANDO
ALDEHYDE ALDOL CITRAL ALKANAL
CHLORAL COGENER DECANAL
GLYOXAL HEXANAL RETINAL
RETINEL ACROLEIN CONGENER
FURFURAL PIPERONAL PYRIDOXINE
ALDER ARN OLER ALNUS ELDER
OWLER SAGEROSE
(PREF.) ALNI
ALDERMAN BAILIE SENIOR
HEADMAN
ALDFRITH (BROTHER OF —)
ECGFRITH
(FATHER OF —) OSWIU
ALE MUM NOG BASS BEER BOCK
BREW FLIP MILD NOGG PURL SCUD
YELL AUDIT CLINK DARBY JOUGH
KVASS LAGER NAPPY STOUT
ALEGAR PORTER STINGO SWANKY
BITTERS MOROCCO OCTOBER
PHARAOH HUGMATEE
(— BREWED WITH BRACKISH WATER)
TIPPER
(— MIXED WITH SWEETENER)
BRAGGET
(INFERIOR —) SWANKY SWANKEY
(NEW —) SWATS
(SOUR —) ALEGAR
(SPICED —) SWIG
(STRONG —) MUM HUFF BURTON
STINGO HUFFCAP
(WEAK —) TWOPENNY
ALEATORY HAZARDOUS
ALEBION (BROTHER OF —) BERGION
DERCYNUS
(FATHER OF —) NEPTUNE POSEIDON
(SLAYER OF —) HERCULES
ALECOST COSTMARY
ALECTRYON TITOKI
ALEE AHEAD LEEWARD
ALEHOUSE PUB TAVERN BARROOM
MUGHOUSE POTHOUSE
ALEKO (CHARACTER IN —) ALEKO
ARENSKY ZEMFIRA
(COMPOSER OF —) RACHMANINOFF
ALEMBIC LIMBEC LIMBECK
CUCURBIT
(PART OF —) HEAD LAMP CUCURBIT
RECEIVER
ALERT APT GAY HEP HIP YAL YEP
FOXY GLEG KEEN LIVE PERT SNAP
TRIG WAKE WARN WARY YALD YEPE
ACUTE AGILE ALARM ALIVE AWAKE
AWARE BREME BRISK EAGER ERECT
LEERY MERRY NIPPY PEART PEERT
QUICK READY SHACK SHARP SIREN
SLICK SWIFT TIGHT WAKER YAULD
ACTIVE ALARUM ARRECT BRIGHT
DAPPER LIVELY NIMBLE PROMPT

SLIPPY SPRACK SUDDEN TIPTOE
TOCSIN WACKER CAREFUL
KNOWING WAKEFUL WORKING
PREPARED THOUGHTY VIGILANT
WAKERIFE WATCHFUL
ALERTNESS NOUS SNAP ANTENNA
APTNESS APTITUDE
(MENTAL —) WIT
ALETES (FATHER OF —) HIPPOTES
AEGISTHUS
(MOTHER OF —) CLYTEMNESTRA
(SLAYER OF —) ORESTES
ALETTE WING ABUTMENT
ALEUT ATKA ORARIAN UNALASKA
ALEUTIANS (ISLANDS AND ISLAND
GROUPS OF —) FOX RAT ADAK ATKA
ATTU NEAR KISKA UMNAK KODIAK
(TOWN OF —) UNALASKA
(VOLCANO ON —) SHISHALDIN
ALEWIFE BANG ALLICE ALOOFE
BUCKIE ALEWHAP HERRING OLDWIFE
POMPANO WALLEYE GRAYBACK
GREYBACK SAWBELLY SKIPJACK
ALEXANDER ALEX PARIS SAWNY
ELLICK SAWNEY SAWNIE ISKANDER
(BIRTHPLACE OF —) PELLA
(FATHER OF —) SIMON
(HORSE OF —) BUCEPHALUS
ALEXIARES (FATHER OF —)
HERCULES
(MOTHER OF —) HEBE
ALFA HALFA ESPARTO
ALFALFA HAY MEDIC FODDER
LEGUME LUCERN LUCERNE
ALFILARIA ERODIUM FILAREE
FILARIA PINWEED PINGRASS
ALFORJA BAG POUCH WALLET
ALFARGA ALFORGE
ALGA NORI ALGAL BROWN FUCUS
JELLY SLAKE SLOAK SLOKE DESMID
DIATOM FUNORI NOSTOC AMANORI
GULAMAN HAITSAI OARWEED
SEAWEED ANABAENA FERNLEAF
GELIDIUM HAIRWEED ROCKWEED
SEABEARD SILKWEED SPOROGEN
WHIPCORD ZOOGLOEA
ALGAE
(PREF.) PHYC(O)
(SUFF.) PHYCEAE
ALGARROBA CAROB CALDEN
ALGEBRA LOGISTIC
(KIND OF —) LIE LINEAR BOOLEAN
ALGEBRAIC COSSIC
ALGENIB MIRFAK

ALGERINE COOLOOLY KOOLOOLY
ALGID COLD COOL CHILLY CLAMMY
ALGOLOGY VERATRIN PHYCOLOGY
ALGONKIAN CREE EOZOIC
(— ROCKS) UNKAR
ALIAS AKA ELSE OTHER ANONYM
AYLESS ASSUMED EPITHET
PSEUDONYM
(UNDER AN —) INCOGNITO
ALIBI PLEA EXCUSE APOLOGY
PRETEXT
ALIDADE INDEX DIOPTER
ALIEN ET GER DEED FREMD METIC
ALAUNT ALLTUD AUBAIN CONVEY
EXOTIC INMATE REMOTE ADVERSE
DENIZEN FOREIGN FRAMMIT
INVADER OUTLAND STRANGE
DETAINEE STRANGER TRANSFER
ALIENATE PART WEAN ALIEN AVERT
ANNALY CONVEY DEMISE DEVEST
FREEZE FORFEIT SUBVERT AMORTIZE
DISUNITE ESTRANGE MORTMAIN
SEPARATE STRANGER TRANSFER
WITHDRAW
ALIENATION GIFT DISTASTE
DISUNION DISUNITY DIVISION
DONATION INSANITY
ALIENIST PSYCHOPATH
PSYCHIATRIST
ALIGHT DROP LAND LEND REST STOP
AVALE LATCH LIGHT LODGE PERCH
ROOST STOOP SWOOP ARRIVE
SETTLE BURNING DESCEND

ALIGN LINE TRAM TRUE ALINE
ARRAY DRESS RANGE ADJUST
ARRANGE MARSHAL
(— PAPER) JOG
ALIGNED FAIR COLORED
COLLINEAR
ALIGNMENT KELTER KILTER
GROUPING ORIENTATION
ALII ARIKI
ALIKE AKIN BOTH LIKE SAME EQUAL
INLIKE SQUARE YLICHE EQUALLY
SIMILAR UNIFORM
(PREF.) HOM(O) ISO
ALIMENT PAP FOOD FUEL BROMA
MANNA VIANDS ALIMONY PABULUM
RATIONS
ALIMONY ALIMENT
ALINDA (FATHER OF —) ALPHONSO
ALIPHATIC FATTY ACYCLIC
ALIVE VIF BUSY KEEN SPRY VIVE
AGILE ALERT ALIFE ASTIR AWARE
BEING BRISK FRESH GREEN QUICK
VITAL AROUND EXTANT LIVING
SLIPPY ANIMATE VIBRANT
ANIMATED EXISTENT SENSIBLE
SWARMING
(PREF.) VIVI
ALKALI LYE REH BASE BRAK KALI
SALT SODA USAR BRACK CAUSTIC
(PREF.) KALI
ALKALINITY (REDUCED —) ACIDOSIS
ALKALOID BASE ERGOT ESERE
ARICIN BRUCIN CEVINE CODEIN
CONINE CURINE ESERIN QUINIA
QUININ ACONINE ARABINE ARICINE
ATROPIA BOGAINE BOLDINE
BRUCINE CAFFEIN COCAINE CODEINE
CONIINE EMETINE HARMINE
HYGRINE JERVINE KAIRINE NARCEIN
NEOPINE OUABAIN PTOMAIN
QUININE SCOPINE SINAPIN SOLANIN
SOPHORA VIOLINE CURARINE
CYTISINE PIPERINE MESCALINE
QUINIDINE YOHIMBINE PAPAVERINE
PILOCARPINE VINBLASTINE
VINCRISTINE CAMPTOTHECIN
ALKANE BUTANE PARAFFIN
ALKANET BUGLOSS PUCCOON
REDROOT
ALKANNIN ORCANET ANCHUSIN
ORCHANET
ALKENE OLEFIN
ALKYD GLYPTAL
ALL A AL ANY SUM EACH FULL TOTE
AUGHT EVERY GROSS OMNES
OUGHT QUITE TOTAL TOTUM TUTTA
TUTTO WHOLE ENTIRE SOLELY
WHOLLY PLENARY ENTIRELY
EVERYONE TOTALITY
(— BUT ABSOLUTELY) ALMOST
(— IN) ALTOGETHER
(— TOGETHER) COLLECTEDLY
(AND —) ANA

(AT —) AVA ANYWISE ANYTHING
ANYWHERE
(OF —) AVA
(PREF.) CUNCTI OMN(I) PAM PAN
PANT(A)(O) PASI
ALLANITE CERINE CERITE ORTHITE
ALLAY AID LAY CALM CITE COOL
EASE HELP HUSH STAY ABATE
AGATE ALLOY CHARM CHECK DELAY
QUELL QUIET SALVE SLAKE STILL
ADDUCE LESSEN PACIFY QUENCH
REDUCE SOFTEN SOLACE SOOTHE
STANCH SUBDUE TEMPER APPEASE
ASSUAGE COMFORT COMPOSE
LIGHTEN MOLLIFY RELIEVE REPRESS
STAUNCH MITIGATE PALLIATE
ALLAYED DEFERRED
ALL-CREATING OMNIFIC
ALLEGATION PLEA COUNT VOUCH
CHARGE ESSOIN AVERRAL FICTION
PROFERT SCANDAL SURMISE
AVERMENT SCIENTER PRETENSION
ALLEGE LAY SAY AVER AVOW CITE
SHOW URGE ALLAY CLAIM FEIGN
INFER LEDGE OFFER PLEAD QUOTE
STATE SWEAR TRUMP VOUCH
ADDUCE AFFIRM ASSERT ASSIGN
CHARGE DEPOSE ESSOIN OBTEND
RECITE ADVANCE ASCRIBE DECLARE
LIGHTEN PRESENT PROFESS
PROPOSE MAINTAIN
ALLEGED SUPPOSED SURMISED
ALLEGIANCE FOY TIE DUTY FAITH
HONOR FEALTY HOMAGE LYANCE
LOYALTY SERVAGE SERVICE TRIBUTE
CIVILITY DEVOTION FIDELITY
LIGEANCE
ALLEGORICAL PARABOLIC
SYMBOLICAL
ALLEGORICALLY SECRETLY
ALLEGORIZE TALMUDIZE
ALLEGORY MYTH TALE FABLE
STORY EMBLEM PARABLE
APOLOGUE METAPHOR
ALLELE GENE
ALLELOMORPH GENE
ALLELUIA AEVIA LAUDS
ALL-EMBRACING INFINITE
SWEEPING
ALLERGEN INHALANT GOLDENROD
ALLERGY ATOPY IDIOBLAPSIS
ALLEVIATE AID BALM CALM CURE
EASE HELP ABATE ALLAY QUIET
ALIGHT ALLEGE LENIFY LESSEN
PACIFY SOFTEN SOLACE SOOTHE
SUCCOR SUPPLE TEMPER ASSUAGE
COMPOSE CONSOLE CORRECT
LENIATE LIGHTEN MOLLIFY RELEASE
RELIEVE DIMINISH MITIGATE
MODERATE PALLIATE
ALLEVIATION ALAY SOLACE
ALLEY MIG ROW WAY CHAR LANE
LEAD MALL MEWS PASS PATH VENT

WALK-WENT WIND WYND AISLE
ALLEE BLIND BYWAY CHARE ENTRY
TEWER WEENT ALLEGE PEEWFF
SMOOTH TRANCE VENNEL PASSAGE
(BLIND —) LOKE STOP CLOSE
POCKET RUELLE IMPASSE

ALL FOR LOVE (AUTHOR OF —)
DRYDEN
(CHARACTER IN —) ANTONY
OCTAVIA OCTAVIUS CLEOPATRA
DOLABELLA VENTIDIUS

ALLHALLOWTIDE HOLLANTIDE

ALLHEAL PANACEA VALERIAN
WOUNDWORT

ALL-HOLY PANAGIA PANHAGIA

ALLIANCE AXIS PACT UNION
ACCORD FUSION LEAGUE LYANCE
TREATY COMPACT ENTENTE SOCIETY
AFFINITY AGNATION CACTALES
COVENANT DREIBUND FEDERACY
FUNGALES LILIALES TRIPLICE
CONSOCIATION
(— IN WAR) SYMMACHY

ALLICE SHAD ALEWIFE POMPANO

ALLIED SIB AKIN AGNATE COUSIN
JOINED LINKED UNITED COGNATE
CONNATE FEDERAL GERMANE
KINDRED RELATED SIMILAR
RELATIVE

ALLIGATOR GATOR NIGER CAIMAN
CAYMAN CROTCH JACARE LIZARD
TRAVOY YACARE CRAWLER CREEPER
LAGARTO TRAVOIS ALAGARTO
LORICATE
(— PEAR) ZABOCA AVOCADO
AGUACATE
(— TURTLE) LOGGERHEAD
(MALE —) BULL

ALLIGATORING WEBBING

ALLIGATOR PEAR AVOCADO

ALL-INCLUSIVE WIDE GLOBAL

ALLITERATION RHYME LETTER

ALLITERATIVE LITERAL

ALLIUM LILY ONION GARLIC

ALLNESS OMNEITY OMNITUDE

ALLOCATE DEAL DOLE METE RATE
ALLOT AWARD SHARE AFFECT
ASSIGN DEVOTE OUTPLACE

ALLOCATION DRAW DESIGNATION

ALLODIAL UDAL

ALLODIUM ESTATE

ALLONGE RIDER

ALLOT FIX SET ARET BILL CAST DEAL
DOLE GIVE MARK METE PART RATE
SORT ALLOW ARETT AWARD CAVEL
GRANT SHARE ACCORD AFFECT
ASSIGN BESTOW DEPUTE DESIGN
DIRECT INTEND ORDAIN RATION
ACCOUNT APPOINT DESTINE
PRORATE QUARTER SPECIFY
TRIBUTE ALLOCATE PROPORTION
(— QUARTERS) CANTON

ALLOTHEIST PAGAN

ALLOTMENT CUT LOT DOLE CAVEL
SHARE RATION SIZING LOTMENT
LOTTERY PORTION DIVISION
PITTANCE

ALL-OUT DEAD

ALLOW LET LOW BEAR GIVE HAVE
LEND LOAN ADMIT DEFER GRANT
LEAVE STAND THOLE YIELD ACCEPT
ACCORD ASSIGN BESTOW BETEEM
ENABLE ENDURE PERMIT SUFFER
APPROVE CONCEDE CONFESS
LICENCE LICENSE SUFFICE SUPPOSE
SUSTAIN CONSIDER DISPENSE
SANCTION TOLERATE
(— UNWILLINGLY) GRUDGE

ALLOWABLE FREE LICIT LAWFUL
PERMISSIBLE

ALLOWANCE BOT FEE ICE AGIO
BOTE DOLE EASE EDGE GIFT HIRE
ODDS RATE SALT SIZE ARRAS BATTA
CLOFF GRANT LEAVE RATIO SHARE
STENT STINT BOUCHE BOUNTY
CORODY FODDER MARGIN RATING
REGAIN SALARY SEQUEL TANTUM
ALIMENT ALIMONY CORODY
DIETARY DIOBELY LEAKAGE
LOWANCE PENSION PORTION
PREBEND SCALAGE STIPEND
TEARAGE APPENAGE APPROVAL
BREAKAGE DISCOUNT DRAFTAGE
ORDINARY QUANTITY SANCTION
SOLATIUM VIATICUM
(— FOR EXPENSES) DIET
(— FOR MAINTENANCE) ALIMENT
(— FOR THICKNESS) BOXING
(— FOR WASTE) TARE TRET
(— FOR WEIGHT) BUG TARE DRAFT
DRAUGHT
(— OF ARROWS) SHEAF
(— OF FOOD) DIET BOUCHE DIETARY
(— OF TIME OR DISTANCE) LAW
(— TO WORKER'S) MAGS MAGGS
(CLOTHING —) INLAY
(CORRECTIVE —) SALT
(EXTRA —) BUCKSHEE
(NEGATIVE —) INTERFERENCE
(SERVANT'S —) LIVERY

ALLOWED VENIAL LICENTIATE
(NOT —) ILLICIT FORBIDDEN

ALLOWING THOUGH

ALLOY LAY LOY MIX AICH ASEM
AI PAX BIDRI BIDRY BRASS CALIN
DURAL FLINT INVAR MOKUM MONEL
TERNE ALBATA ALNICO ALUMEL
BIDREE BILLON BRONZE CERMET
GARBLE ILLIUM LATTEN LEAVEN
NEOGEN NIELLO OCCAMY OREIDE
OROIDE PEWTER SOLDER TAMBAC
TOMBAC TOMBAK ACIERAL
ALCHEMY AMALGAM BABBITT
BIDDERY ELINVAR INCONEL MIXTURE
NITINOL PAKTONG PERLITE
RHEOTAN RHODITE SEMILOR

SIMILOR TAENITE TUTANIA TUTENAG
ALFENIDE ARGENTON ARSEDINE
AWARUITE CALAMINE CARACOLI
CARACOLY DORALIUM ELECTRUM
EUTECTIC GUNMETAL HARDENER
KAMACITE METALINE NICHROME
ORICHALC ROMANIUM STELLITE
ZIRCALOY PINCHBECK PORPORINO

ALL-PERVADING UNIVERSAL
ALL-PURPOSE VERSATILE
**ALL QUIET ON WESTERN
FRONT** (AUTHOR OF —) REMARQUE
(CHARACTER IN —) PAUL KROPP
ALBERT BAUMER MULLER TJADENS
KEMMERICH STANILAUS
KATCYINSKY

ALL RIGHT OK YES OKAY AGREED
OKEYDOKE
ALL-ROUND OVERALL OVERHEAD
ALLSEED FLAXSEED BURSTWORT
ALL SOULS' DAY SOULMASS
ALLSPICE BUBBY PIMENTO
ALL'S WELL THAT ENDS WELL
(AUTHOR OF —) SHAKESPEARE
(CHARACTER IN —) DIANA LAFEU
HELENA BERTRAM LAVACHE
MARIANA PAROLLES VIOLENTA

ALLTHORN JUNCO
ALLUDE HINT IMPLY POINT REFER
ADVERT GLANCE RELATE CONNOTE
MENTION SUGGEST INDICATE
INTIMATE
ALLURE IT AIR COY WIN WOO BAIT
DRAW LEAD LURE MOVE SWAY WILE
ANGLE BRIBE CHARM COURT DECOY
SNARE TEMPT ALLECT ENTICE
ENTRAP ILLURE INDUCE INVITE
SEDUCE ATTRACT BEGUILE
ENSNARE BLANDISH INESCATE
INVEIGLE PERSUADE SIRENING
ALLUREMENT BAIT CORD LURE
SNARE ALLURE GLAMOR GUDGEON
AGACERIE SOLICITATION
ALLURING GREEN TAKING AGACANT
SIRENIC SUGARED TAKEFUL
CATCHING CHARMING ENTICING
FETCHING TEMPTING
ALLUSION HINT TWIT TOUCH
GLANCE REFLEX INKLING MENTION
INNUENDO INSTANCE REFERENCE
ALLUSIVE CANTING
ALLUVIUM WASH
ALLY PAL AIDE JOIN RANGE UNION
UNITE BACKER COHORT COXCOX
FRIEND HELPER LEAGUE ALLIANT
CONNECT PARTNER ADHERENT
CONFEDER FEDERATE
(PL.) FOEDERATI
ALMANAC ORDO PADDY CALENDAR
ALMANDINE GARNET CARBUNCLE
ALMEMAR BEMA BIMA BIMAH
ALMIGHTY GOD GREAT MAKER
CREATOR EXTREME JEHOVAH

INFINITE POWERFUL PUISSANT
OMNIPOTENT
ALMOND DOE PILI BADAM CHUFA
JORDAN KAMANI KANARI AMYGDAL
BISCUIT TALISAY ALMANDER
ALMENDRO AMYGDALA ROSACEAN
VALENCIA
(— BROWN) WOOD
(— SHAPED OBJECT) MANDORLA
(PREF.) AMYGDAL(O) MANDEL(O)
ALMONRY AMBRY
ALMOST JUST LIKE MOST MUCH
NEAR NIGH ABOUT ANEAR CLOSE
AMAIST FECKLY MOSTLY NEARLY
NIGHLY MUCHWHAT WELLMOST
WELLNEAR WELLNIGH PRACTICALLY
(PREF.) PARA PEN(E)
ALMS DOLE GIFT ALMOIN AUMOUS
AWMOUS BOUNTY CORBAN
MAUNDY RELIEF ALMOIGN CHARITY
HANDOUT PASSADE DEVOTION
DONATION GRATUITY OFFERING
PITTANCE BENEFACTION
(GIVER OF —) ALMONER
ALMSHOUSE POORHOUSE
WORKHOUSE
ALMSMAN BLUECOAT
ALMUCE HOOD AMICE VAGAS
TIPPET VAKASS VARKAS
ALODIUM ODAL ODEL ODHAL
ESTATE PROPERTY
ALOE PITA AGAVE
(— EXTRACT) ORCIN ORCINAL
ALOEUS (FATHER OF —) NEPTUNE
POSEIDON
(MOTHER OF —) CANACE
(SON OF —) OTUS EPHIALTES
(WIFE OF —) IPHIMEDIA
ALOFT UP HIGH ABOVE AHIGH
UPWARD AHEIGHT SKYWARD
OVERHEAD
(PREF.) HYPS(I)(O)
ALONE ALL ONE BARE LANE LORN
ONLY SOLE SOLO ALOOF APART
SOLUS SIMPLY SINGLE SOLEIN
SOLELY SULLEN UNIQUE ALONELY
FORLORN UNAIDED DESOLATE
DETACHED ISOLATED SEPARATE
SOLITARY
(ALL —) LEELANE LEELONE
(PREF.) MANI MON(O) SOLI
(SUFF.) MONAS
ALONG ON UP VIA AWAY LANG WITH
YOND AHEAD LONGS BESIDE
FORBYE FOREBY ONWARD ALONGST
ENDLONG FORWARD PARALLEL
TOGETHER
(— THE MARGIN) DOWN
(— WITH) AND
(WELL —) ENDWAYS ENDWISE
(PREF.) (— WITH) SYM
ALONGSIDE AT BY ASIDE CLOSE
ABOARD BESIDE ABREAST FORNENT

SIDLINS FORNENST PARALLEL
(PREF.) PAR(A)
ALONSOA MASKFLOWER
ALOOF DRY ICY SHY COLD COOL
ABACK ALONE APART PROUD
ABEIGH FROSTY OTIOSE REMOTE
SILENT SKEIGH DISTANT REMOVED
STUCKUP RESERVED
ALOPECIA PELADE ATRICHIA
BALDNESS
ALOPECIC BALD
ALOPECURUS FOXTAIL
ALOT SLEW
ALOUD OUT
ALPACA PACO
ALPENGLOW AFTERGLOW
ALPENSTOCK STOCK BERGSTOCK
ALPHABET ABC ABCEE ABSEY CUFIC
KUFIC LATIN ONMUN ORDER BISAYA
BRAHMI CIPHER GLAGOL HANGUL
HANKUL KAITHI NAGARI PRIMER
ROMAJI SARADA SCRIPT TAGALA
VISAYA ALJAMIA FUTHARK KALEKAH
LETTERS PESHITO ALJAMIAH
CROSSROW GUJARATI GURMUKHI
(— SQUARE) TABLEAU
(ARABIC —) BA FA HA RA TA YA ZA
AYN DAD DAL JIM KAF KHA LAM MIM
NUN QAF SAD SIN THA WAW ZAY
ALIF DHAL SHIN GHAYN
(CELTIC —) OGAM OGHAM
(GREEK —) MU NU PI XI CHI ETA PHI
PSI RHO TAU BETA IOTA ZETA ALPHA
DELTA GAMMA KAPPA OMEGA
SIGMA THETA LAMBDA EPSILON
OMICRON UPSILON
(HEBREW —) HE PE MEM NUN SIN
TAW VAV WAW AYIN BETH HETH
KAPH QOPH RESH SHIN TETH YODH
ALEPH GIMEL SADHE ZAYIN DALETH
LAMEDH SAMEKH
(OLD IRISH —) OGAM OGHAM
ALPHAEUS (SON OF —) JAMES
MATTHEW
ALPHESIBOEA (FATHER OF —) BIAS
PHEGEUS
(HUSBAND OF —) ALCMAEON
(SON OF —) ADONIS
ALPS (LAKE IN —) ZUG COMO ISEO
THUN GARDA BRIENZ GENEVA
ZURICH LUCERNE MAGGIORE
CONSTANCE
(PASS IN —) SPLUGA ARLBERG
BRENNER SIMPLON SPLUGEN
SEMPIONE
(PEAK IN —) ROSA VISO BLANC
LEONE TRIGLAV VOLJNAC EISENHUT
PARADISO HOCHSTUHL
MARMOLADA MONTBLANC
KELLERWAND SACCARELLO
(VALLEY IN —) ZERMATT CHAMONIX
ENGADINE INTERLAKEN
GRINDELWALD LAUTERBRUNNEN

ALREADY EEN NOW DONE EVEN
SINCE BEFORE
ALSACE-LORRAINE REICHSLAND
ALSINE ALLBONE
ALSO SO ALS AND EKE TOO YET
ERST ITEM MORE PLUS ALONG
DITTO BESIDES FURTHER THERETO
LIKEWISE MOREOVER
(— KNOWN AS) AKA
ALSO-RAN SLOWPOKE
BACKMARKER
ALTAMONT (WIFE OF —) CALISTA
ALTAR ARA BEMA BOMOS TABLE
WEVED ACERRA AUTERE HAIKAL
SHRINE TRIPOD VEDIKA CHANCEL
CHANTRY ESCHARA SCROBIS
THYMELE OMPHALOS REPOSOIR
REPOSITORY
(— BACK) TABLE
(— TOP) MENSA
ALTARPIECE ANCONA DIPTYCH
TRIPTYCH
ALTAZIMUTH ABA
ALTER COOK DRAW EDIT GELD MOVE
RASE TURN VARY VEER WEND
ADAPT AMEND BREAK ELIDE EMEND
FORGE RESET SHAPE SHIFT ADJUST
BUSHEL CENSOR CHANGE DEFORM
IMMUTE JIGGER MODIFY MUTATE
NEUTER REVISE TEMPER UNSAME
CHAFFER COMMUTE CONVERT
CORRECT CORRUPT DISTORT
FASHION QUALIFY RECYCLE
STRANGE ACTIVATE EXCHANGE
REJIGGER
(— APPEARANCE) WRY
(— BOUNDARIES) DEACON
(— BRANDS) DUFF
(— DIRECTION) BREAK
(— FRAUDULENTLY) FIDDLE
(— STANCE) CLOSE
ALTERATION DOWN CROSS ACTION
CHANGE JANGLE DISEASE HEMIOLA
MUTATION UPHEAVAL
(— OF BOUNDARY) ERUB ERUV
ALTERATIVE LAPPA FUMARIA
ALTERCATE JANGLE STICKLE
WRANGLE
ALTERCATION SPAT TIFF TILT
BRAWL BROIL CRASH CROSS FIGHT
BARNEY BICKER FRACAS JANGLE
STRIFE BRABBLE CONTEST DISPUTE
PASSAGE QUARREL WRANGLE
SQUABBLE
ALTERED BURNT BROKEN VARIED
ANOTHER FEIGNED ADJUSTED
(— BY AGE) STALE
(PREF.) EPH EPI META
ALTERNATE ELSE SWAY VARY
OTHER RECUR SHIFT ALTERN
CHANGE RINGER ROTATE SECOND
SEESAW SPIRAL EXCHANGE
INTERMIT TRAVERSE

(— LEAPS AND DIVES) GREYHOUND
(— PLAYERS) PLATOON
(PREF.) CO COUNTER
ALTERNATELY ABOUT
RECIPROCALLY
ALTERNATION ADDITION
(— OF GENERATIONS) METAGENESIS
ALTERNATIVE OR FORK HORN
BACKUP CHOICE EITHER OPTION
DISJUNCT ELECTION
(PREF.) ALLELO
ALTERNATIVES (SEE PARTNERS)
DODIE INOUT ONOFF HITMISS
WINLOSE FISHFOWL HIDEHAIR
ONEOTHER SINKSWIM WHITERYE
FACTFANCY HERETHERE
WHEREWHEN ALLNOTHING
TRICKTREAT
ALTERNATOR MAGNETO
ALTHAEA MALLOW
(FATHER OF —) THESTIUS
(HUSBAND OF —) OENEUS
(SON OF —) MELEAGER
ALTHAEMENES (FATHER OF —)
CATREUS
(SISTER OF —) AEROPE CLYMENE
APEMOSYNE
ALTHORN SAX ALTO ALTUS
SAXHORN
ALTHOUGH ALL EEN SET ALBE ALIF
EVEN THAT WHEN WHILE ALBEIT
THOUGH WHENAS DESPITE HOWBEIT
WHEREAS
ALTITUDE APEX PEAK HIGHT LEVEL
PITCH HEIGHT STATURE
(SUN'S GREATEST —) APOGEE
ALTO MEAN ALTUS ALTHORN
SAXHORN
ALTOGETHER ALL NUDE QUITE
SHEER STICK AGREAT ALGATE
BODILY FREELY WHOLLY EXACTLY
TOTALLY UTTERLY ALLTHING
ENTIRELY
ALTRUISM OTHERISM
ALTRUISTIC HEROIC HEROICAL
ALUDEL POT LUDEL UDELL
ALULA LOBE WING ALULET SQUAMA
TEGULA LOBULUS WINGLET
CALYPTER
ALULIM ALOROS
ALUM AUM ALME GRAD ALUMEN
MIGITE TSCHER STYPTIC HARDENER
KALINITE
(FEATHER —) ALUNOGEN
ALUMINA ARGIL ALOXITE
ALUMNUS GRAD PUPIL GRADUATE
ALUMROOT HEUCHERA
ALUR LUR LURI
ALVAN (FATHER OF —) SHOBAL
ALVEARY HIVE BEEHIVE
ALVELOZ SAP
ALVEOLA FAVEOLUS
ALVEOLAR SPUMOID GINGIVAL

ALVEOLATE FAVOSE FAVOUS
PITTED
ALWAYS O AY AYE EEN EER EVER
SIMLE STILL ALWISE SEMPRE
ALGATES FOREVER EVERMORE
ALYSSUM ALISON MADWORT
ALZIRA (CHARACTER IN —) ALZIRA
GUSMAN ZAMORO
(COMPOSER OF —) VERDI
AM M AM HAM
(— NOT) NAM AINT AMNT
(I —) CHAM CHYM
AMA CUP AMULA CRUET DIVER
VESSEL CHALICE
AMABILE GENTLE TENDER
AMACRATIC AMASTHENIC
AMADAVAT WAXBILL TIGERBIRD
AMADIS (COMPOSER OF —) LULLY
AMADOU PUNK TINDER
AMAH NURSE SERVANT
**AMAHL AND THE NIGHT
VISITORS** (COMPOSER OF —)
MENOTTI
AMAIN GREATLY FORCIBLY
AMAL (FATHER OF —) HELEM
AMALA AMLAH
AMALASONTHA (FATHER OF —)
THEODORIC
AMALEK (FATHER OF —) ELIPHAZ
(MOTHER OF —) TIMNAH
AMALGAM ALLOY MAGNESIA
ARQUERITE
AMALGAMATE MIX FUSE JOIN
- ALLOY BLEND MARRY MERGE UNITE
BLUNGE MINGLE COMBINE
COALESCE COMPOUND
AMALGAMATION MERGER
ADDITION
AMALGAMATOR PLATEMAN
AMANORI NORI LAVER
AMANUENSIS PENMAN SCRIBE
TYPIST RECORDER
AMARANTA (HUSBAND OF —)
BARTOLUS
AMARANTH JATACO PIGWEED
FLORAMOR
(PL.) LIGHTHOUSES
AMARETTO LIQUEUR MACAROON
AMARIAH (FATHER OF —) BANI
MERAIOTH
(SON OF —) AHITUB
AMARILLO FUSTIC
AMARYLLIS LILY AGAVE CRINUM
SNOWFLAKE
AMASA (FATHER OF —) ITHRA
HADLAI JETHER
(MOTHER OF —) ABIGAIL
AMASAI (SON OF —) MAHATH
AMASHAI (FATHER OF —) AZAREEL
AMASIAH (FATHER OF —) ZICHRI
AMASS HEAP HILL MASS PILE SAVE
GROSS HOARD STACK STORE
GATHER COLLECT COMPILE

CONGEST ENGROSS ASSEMBLE
OVERHEAP ACCUMULATE

AMASSMENT HEAP

AMATA (DAUGHTER OF —) LAVINIA
(HUSBAND OF —) LATINUS

AMATEUR HAM LAY TIRO TYRO
NOVICE SUNDAY VOTARY ADMIRER
DABBLER DEVOTEE FANCIER
JACKLEG PATRIOT VARMENT
VARMINT BEGINNER
(GOLF —) DUFFER

AMATEURISH BUSH TYRONIC

AMATORY EROTIC LOVING TENDER
AMOROUS GALLANT ANACREONTIC

AMAZE AWE WOW MAZE STAM
STUN ALARM FERLY FLOOR ASTONY
AWHAPE WONDER ASTOUND
CONFUSE IMPRESS PERPLEX
STAGGER STUPEFY ASTONISH
BEWILDER CONFOUND DUMFOUND
FRIGHTEN SURPRISE

AMAZED AGAPE INAWE AGAZED
BUSHED ASTONIED

AMAZEMENT STAM AMAZE FERLY
GHAST FERLIE FRENZY WONDER
MADNESS SURPRISE
CONSTERNATION
(INTERJECTION TO EXPRESS —)
YIKES

AMAZIAH (FATHER OF —) JOASH

AMAZON VIRAGO

AMBARI KANAF KENAF KANAFF

AMBASSADOR AGENT ELCHI
ENVOY VAKIL DEPUTY ELCHEE
LEDGER LEGATE NUNCIO VAKEEL
EMBASSY LEAGUER CAPUCIUS
DIPLOMAT MINISTER

AMBASSADORIAL FECIAL FETIAL

AMBASSADORS (AUTHOR OF —)
JAMES
(CHARACTER IN —) JIM MAMIE
MARIA SARAH JEANNE POCOCK
GOSTREY LAMBERT NEWSOME
CHADWICK STRETHER WAYMARSH

AMBER GRIS LIME AWMER RESIN
FUSTIC LAMMER SUCCIN YELLOW
BURMITE AMBEROID ELECTRUM
SUNSTONE
(PREF.) ELECTRO SUCCIN(I)(O)

AMBERFISH JUREL CARANX
KAHALA RUNNER CARANGID
CARANGIN KINGFISH MACKEREL
MEDREGAL

AMBERGRIS AMBER AMBRACAN

AMBERINA (KIND OF —) PLATED

AMBERJACK ALMICORE
CORONADO

AMBIENCE MILIEU AMBIANCE

AMBIGUITY AMBAGE PARADOX

AMBIGUOUS DARK VAGUE DOUBLE
FORKED LOOSE CRYPTIC DUBIOUS
DOUBTFUL SLIPPERY SPURIOUS
(NOT —) EXPRESS

AMBIT LIMIT SCOPE SPACE BOUNDS
EXTENT SPHERE CIRCUIT COMPASS
BOUNDARY PRECINCT

AMBITION ATE GOAL HOPE WISH
GLORY DESIRE PURPOSE
PRETENSION

AMBITIONLESS DRIFTING

AMBITIOUS AVID BOLD HIGH KEEN
EAGER ETTLE SHOWY EMULOUS
ASPIRANT ASPIRING

AMBITUS TENOR

AMBIVALENCE BIPOLARITY

AMBIVALENT EQUIVOCAL

AMBLE FOOL GAIT MOOCH PADNAG
MEANDER SAUNTER TRIPPLE

AMBLING TOLUTATION

AMBLYOPIA SNOWBLINDNESS

AMBO DESK PULPIT

AMBOCEPTOR COPULA
MEDIATOR

AMBOYNA LINGOA KIABOOCA

AMBROSIA AMRITA AMBROSE
HONEYDEW KINGWEED

AMBROSIAL DIVINE FRAGRANT

AMBRY SAFE CHEST NICHE AUMRIE
CLOSET PANTRY RECESS ALMONRY
ARMOIRE ARMARIUM CUPBOARD

AMBULANCE PANNIER AUXILIUM
BRANCARD
(— ATTENDANT) EMT

AMBULATE GAD HIKE MOVE WALK

AMBULATORY ALURE GALLERY
PORTICO CLOISTER PERAMBLE

AMBUSCADE WATCH WAYLAY
BUSHMENT

AMBUSH NAB LURE LURK TRAP
WAIT AWAIT BLIND BUSSE CATCH
COVER LUNCH SHOMA SNARE STALE
TRAIN WATCH INBUSH THREAT
WAYLAY FORELAY SCUPPER
DISGUISE ENBUSSHE AMBUSCADE
(SUFF.) (ONE IN —) DOLOPS

AMCHOOR AMHAR

AMELIA (AUTHOR OF —) FIELDING
(CHARACTER IN —) BOOTH JAMES
TRENT AMELIA HARRIS ATKINSON
HARRISON MATTHEWS ELIZABETH

AMELIORATE EASE HELP MEND
AMEND EMEND BETTER REFORM
IMPROVE PROMOTE

AMEN YEA TRULY ASSENT SOBEIT
VERILY APPROVAL SANCTION

AMENABLE GAME OPEN LIABLE
PLIANT SUBJECT OBEDIENT
MALLEABLE

AMEND END BEET HEAL MEND
ALTER ATONE BEETE EMEND REDUB
BETTER CHANGE DOCTOR REFORM
REMEDY REPAIR REPEAL REVISE
CONVERT CORRECT ENLARGE
IMPROVE RECOVER RECTIFY
REDRESS RESTORE CHASTISE

AMENDING COMPENSATION

AMENDMENT RIDER AMENDS
REFORM SLEEPER
AMENDS BOOT MEND ASSETH
ASSYTH REWARD APOLOGY
REDRESS
AMENITY JOY COMITY FEATURE
SUAVITY CIVILITY COURTESY
MILDNESS
(PL.) AGREMENS FROUFROU
NICETIES
AMENT JUL CHAT IDIOT IULUS
MORON CATKIN CACHRYS CATTAIL
GOSLING IMBECILE NUCAMENT
AMERCE FINE MERCE MULCT TREAT
AFFEER PUNISH SCONCE CONDEMN
FORFEIT
AMERCEMENT MULCT UNLAW
BLOODWIT
AMERICA INDIA
AMERICAN YANK GRINGO YANKEE
YANQUI AMERICA WESTERN
JONATHAN COLUMBIAN
(— OF EUROPEAN STOCK) WASP
(— OF MEXICAN DESCENT) CHICANA
CHICANO
(AUTHOR OF —) JAMES
(CHARACTER IN —) BREAD CINTRE
CLAIRE NEWMAN NIOCHE TRISTRAM
VALENTIN BELLEGARDE
CHRISTOPHER
AMERICAN GRAY JAKO
AMERICANISM HECKERISM
AMERICAN TRAGEDY
(AUTHOR OF —) DREISER
(CHARACTER IN —) ALDEN CLYDE
SAMUEL SONDRA ROBERTA
FINCHLEY GRIFFITHS
AMESTRIS (FATHER OF —) OTANES
ONOPHAS
(WIFE OF —) XERXES
AMETHYST ONEGITE CORUNDUM
AMIABILITY DOUCEUR
AMIABLE GOOD KIND WARM SWEET
CLEVER GENIAL GENTLE LOVING
MELLOW SMOOTH TENDER AFFABLE
LOVABLE WINSOME CHARMING
ENGAGING FRIENDLY OBLIGING
PLEASING
AMICABLE KIND FRIENDLY
NEIGHBORLY
AMICE AMIT AMYS CAPE COWL
HOOD EPHOD ALMUCE DOMINO
TIPPET VAKASS AMICTUS VESTMENT
AMID IN OMEL AMELL AMONG
AMIDST DURING IMELLE AMONGST
BETWEEN
AMIDAS (BROTHER OF —) BRACIDAS
AMIDE LACTAM SULTAM ANILIDE
ARYLIDE PEPTIDE
AMIDST AMONG AMONGST
AMILDAR AUMIL
AMIN IDI
AMINE ANILIN ANILINE PSILOCIN

AMINO ALANINE
AMINO-ACID LYSINE
AMISS ILL MIS AWRY BIAS AGATE
AGLEY ASKEW WONKY WRONG
ACROSS AGRIEF ASTRAY FAULTY
MISTAKE IMPROPER
(PREF.) MIS PAR(A)
AMITRIPTYLINE ELAVIL
AMITTAI (SON OF —) JONAH
AMITY PEACE ACCORD CONCORD
HARMONY
AMMA ABBESS MOTHER
AMMIEL (DAUGHTER OF —)
BATHSHEBA
(FATHER OF —) OBEDEDOM
(SON OF —) MACHIR
AMMIHUD (SON OF —) TALMAI
PEDAHEL SHEMUEL ELISHAMA
AMMINADAB (FATHER OF —) RAM
ARAM KOHATH UZZIEL
(SON OF —) NAASSON
AMMISHADDAI (SON OF —)
AHIEZER
AMMIZABAD (FATHER OF —)
BENAIAH
AMMO BBS
(— FOR TOY GUN) CAP CAPS
AMMONIA HARTSHORN
AMMONIAC OSHAC
AMMONITE POLYPOD AMMONOID
BACULITE CACULOID CERATITE
SALIGRAM
AMMONIUM CARBONATE
HARTSHORN
AMMOPHILA STAR STARR
AMMUNITION AMMO AMMU ARMS
SHOT BOMBS FODDER POWDER
SHELLS BULLETS BUCKSHOT
GRENADES MATERIAL MATERIEL
ORDNANCE SHRAPNEL
AMNESIA LAPSE FORGETFULNESS
AMNESTY COWLE PARDON
OBLIVION
AMNION SAC CAUL SEROSA
INDUSIUM MEMBRANE
AMNON (FATHER OF —) DAVID
(HALF-SISTER OF —) TAMAR
AMOBARBITAL AMYTAL
AMOEBA AMEBA AMEBULA
PROTEUS AMOEBULA RHIZOPOD
AMOK MAD AMUCK CRAZY CRAZED
VIOLENT FRENZIED
(RUNNING —) ARIOT
AMOLE EMOL AMOULI AMOLILLA
MANFREDA
AMON (FATHER OF —) MANASSEH
(SON OF —) JOSIAH
AMONG IN MID AMID INTO MANG
MONG OMEL WITH AMANG AMELL
MIDST AMIDST BIMONG IMELLE
WITHIN BETWEEN
(— OTHER THINGS) IA
(PREF.) EPH EPI INTER

AMOR EROS LOVE CUPID AMOROSO
AMORAL NEUTRAL NONMORAL
AMORET (HUSBAND OF —)
SCUDAMORE
  (SISTER OF —) BELPHOEBE
AMORINO CUPID
AMORITE CANAANITE
AMOROUS FOND GAMY SOFT
WARM CADGY JOLLY MUSHY NUTTY
ARDENT COQUET EROTIC LOVELY
LOVING SPOONY TENDER WANTON
AMATIVE AMATORY AMIABLE
FERVENT GALLANT JEALOUS
SMICKER LOVESOME VENEREAN
AMOROUSLY SMICKLY
AMORPHOUS VAGUE ATELENE
HYALINE DEFORMED FORMLESS
INCHOATE RESINOUS
AMORT ALAMORT DEJECTED
LIFELESS
AMORTIZE DESTROY MORTISE
ALIENATE
AMOUNT GO GOB LOT SUM SUP TOT
ANTE BODY COME DOSE DRAW FECK
KIND LEVY MESS REAM RISE SOUD
SOWD TALE UNIT WARE ADDUP
CHUNK COUNT GROSS MOUNT PRICE
REACH STACK STORE STUFF TOTAL
WHOLE BUDGET DEGREE DOLLOP
DOSAGE EFFECT EXTENT FIGURE
MATTER NUMBER SUPPLY ADVANCE
FOOTING QUANTUM SCRUPLE
SIGNIFY SLATHER TODDICK
INCREASE QUANTITY SPOONFUL
SURMOUNT VALIDOM
(— BORNE BY BEAST) SEAM
(— CARRIED AT ONE TIME) GANG
(— DUE) BILL SCORE
(— HELD) CAPACITY
(— LEFT IN VESSEL) ULLAGE
(— OF BASS) BOOMINESS
(— OF CONCRETE) LIFT
(— OF DYE) STRIKE
(— OF FLOW) STRENGTH
(— OF FREIGHT) CARLOAD
(— OF GAS) BREATH
(— OF HERRINGS) CRANNAGE
(— OF LEAKAGE) SLIP
(— OF LIQUOR) SLUG
(— OF MEDICINE) DOSAGE
(— OF MONEY) BEAN BOND CASH
SCOT
(— OF OIL) ALLOWABLE
(— OF PAYMENT) FOOTAGE
(— OF POWDER) INCREMENT
(— OF SOIL) INTHROW
(— OF WATER) CATCHMENT
(— OF WORK) ASSIGNMENT
(— OWED) LIABILITY OBLIGATION
(PAID) COST
(— PROVIDED) SUPPLY
(— TURNED BY SPADE) GRAFT
(APPRECIABLE —) BEANS

(COMPLETE —) FULL
(CONSIDERABLE —) MIGHT HANTLE
HATFUL
(EXACT —) NICK
(EXTRA —) BONUS
(GREAT —) MICKLE INFINITY
MOUNTAIN
(GREATEST —) MAXIMUM
(GROSS —) SLUMP
(INADEQUATE —) DEFICIENCY
(INDEFINITE —) BAIT SNAG SOME
(INFINITESIMAL —) IOTA
(INSIGNIFICANT —) SCRAT PEANUTS
PEPPERCORN
(LARGE —) GOB LOB JUNT LUMP
MINT RAFT SNAG SWAG SIEGE
SLASH SPATE BOODLE SOMDEL
BONANZA SOMDIEL CARTLOAD
MUCHNESS SOMEDEAL
(LAVISH —) SLATHER
(LEAST —) DIDDLY
(LEAST POSSIBLE —) GRAIN
AMBSACE
(LIMITED —) SPRINKLING
(MEDICINAL —) DOSAGE
(MINUTE —) HAIR FLEABITE
(RENT —) GALE
(SIZABLE —) CHUNK SMART
(SLIGHT —) ADDED SNACK TILLY
TINGE
(SLIGHTEST —) BEANS
(SMALL —) ACE BIT DAB TAD DITE
DOIT DRAB DRAM DRIB FLOW HAET
HINT HOOT INCH LICK MITE SNAP
SONG SPOT SKOSH SPECK SPURT
TRACE DRAPPY PICKLE SMIDGE
TICKET CAPSULE DRAPPIE GLIMMER
KENNING SMIDGEN SMIDGIN
THOUGHT
(SMALLEST —) JOT STIVER MINIMUM
STEEVER STUIVER
(SMALLEST —S) MINIMA
(TENFOLD —) DECUPLE
(USUAL —) GRIST
(WHOLE —) ALL SUBSTANCE
(YEARLY —) ANNUITY
(SUFF.) ANCE ANT ENCE
AMOUR DRURY DRUERY AMOURET
INTRIGUE PARAMOUR
AMOZ (SON OF —) ISAIAH
AMPERSAND AND ALSO PLUS
AMPASSY IPSEAND
AMPHETAMINE SPEED UPPER
BENZEDRINE
AMPHIALUS (MOTHER OF —)
CECROPIA
AMPHIARAUS (DAUGHTER OF —)
EURYDICE DEMONASSA
(FATHER OF —) OICLES
(MOTHER OF —) HYPERMNESTRA
(SON OF —) ALCMAEON
AMPHILOCHUS
(WIFE OF —) ERIPHYLE

AMPHIBIA BATRACHIA
AMPHIBIAN EFT OLM FROG HYLA
NEWT RANA TOAD ANURA SIREN
SNAKE AMPHIB AXOLOTL CAUDATE
ERYOPID PROTEUS TADPOLE
AISTOPOD SALAMANDER
AMPHIBOLE EDENITE ORALITE
URALITE ASBESTOS CROSSITE
TREMOLITE SMARAGDITE
AMPHICARPA FALCATA
AMPHICTYON (FATHER OF —)
DEUCALION
(MOTHER OF —) PYRRHA
AMPHIGASTRIUM UNDERLEAF
AMPHIGORIC INANE
AMPHILOCHUS (FATHER OF —)
AMPHIARAUS
(MOTHER OF —) ERIPHYLE
AMPHION (BROTHER OF —) ZETHUS
(FATHER OF —) ZEUS IASUS JUPITER
(MOTHER OF —) ANTIOPE
(WIFE OF —) NIOBE
AMPHIOXUS LANCELET
AMPHIPOD SHRIMP
AMPHISSA (FATHER OF —) ECHETUS
MACAREUS
(MOTHER OF —) CANACHE
AMPHISSUS (FATHER OF —)
APOLLO
(MOTHER OF —) DRYOPE
AMPHITHEA (DAUGHTER OF —)
ANTICLEA
(HUSBAND OF —) AUTOLYCUS
AMPHITHEATER BOWL OVAL
ARENA CAVEA CIRCUS CIRQUE
STADIUM THEATER
AMPHITRITE (FATHER OF —)
NEREUS OCEANUS
(HUSBAND OF —) NEPTUNE
POSEIDON
(MOTHER OF —) TETHYS
(SON OF —) TRITON
AMPHITRYON (AUTHOR OF —)
PLAUTUS
(CHARACTER IN —) SOSIA ALCMENA
JUPITER MERCURY AMPHITRYON
(DOG OF —) LAELAPS
(FATHER OF —) ALCAEUS
(MOTHER OF —) HIPPONOME
(WIFE OF —) ALCMENE
AMPHORA JUG URN VASE CADUS
DIOTA PELIKE
AMPHOTERUS (BROTHER OF —)
ACARNAN
(FATHER OF —) ALCMAEON
(MOTHER OF —) CALLIRRHOE
AMPLE BIG FAIR FULL GOOD MUCH
RICH SIDE WIDE BROAD GREAT
LARGE LUCKY PLUMP ROOMY
ROUND SONSY WALLY ENOUGH
HEARTY PLENTY PROLIX COPIOUS
LIBERAL OPULENT WEALTHY
ABUNDANT ADEQUATE BARONIAL

GENEROUS HANDSOME SPACIOUS
PLENTIFUL
AMPLIFICATION GAIN
AMPLIFIED EXTENDED
AMPLIFIER BOOSTER REPEATER
AMPLIFY PAD FARCE FARSE SWELL
WIDEN DILATE EXPAND EXTEND
STRESS AUGMENT ENLARGE
STRETCH AMPLIATE HEIGHTEN
INCREASE LENGTHEN MULTIPLY
AMPLITUDE BULK BREADTH
LATITUDE OPULENCE
AMPLY LARGE
AMPUTATE CUT LOP PRUNE SEVER
CURTAIL
AMPUTATION APOCOPE ABLATION
AMPYCUS (FATHER OF —) PELIAS
(MOTHER OF —) CHLORIS
(SON OF —) MOPSUS
AMRAM (FATHER OF —) BANI DISHON
(SON OF —) MOSES
AMRITA RASA
AMULA AMA VESSEL
AMULET GEM MET ANKH HAND
JUJU MOJO PLUM CHARM IMAGE
MENAT SAFFI SAFIE TOKEN FETISH
GRIGRI MASCOT SAPHIE SCROLL
TABLET ABRAXAS AMALETT
ICHTHUS ICHTHYS PERIAPT
CHURINGA GREEGREE HAGSTONE
LIGATURE ORNAMENT TALISMAN
PHYLACTERY
AMULIUS (BROTHER OF —)
NUMITOR
(FATHER OF —) PROCAS
(NEPHEW OF —) LAUSUS
AMURRU MARTU
AMUSE GAME LAKE ENJOY MIRTH
SHORT SPORT ABSORB DELUDE
DIVERT ENGAGE FROLIC PLEASE
POPJOY SOLACE TICKLE BEGUILE
DISPORT GRATIFY PASTIME
BEWILDER DISTRACT RECREATE
(— IMMENSELY) SLAY
(— ONESELF) POPJOY
(— VERY MUCH) SLAY
AMUSEMENT FAD FUN JEU GAME
JEST LAKE PLAY MIRTH SPORT
LAKING MUSERY PASTIME
COTTABUS LAUGHTER PLEASURE
(PL.) MIDWAY
AMUSING RICH COMIC DROLL
FUNNY MERRY WITTY COMICAL
FOOLISH KILLING RISIBLE FARCICAL
HUMOROUS PLEASANT SPORTFUL
(SOMEONE —) GIGGLE
(SOMETHING OR SOMEONE —) HOOT
AMYCLAS (FATHER OF —)
LACEDAEMON
(MOTHER OF —) SPARTE
(SON OF —) HYACINTHUS
AMYCUS (FATHER OF —) NEPTUNE
POSEIDON

(MOTHER OF —) MELIA
(SLAYER OF —) POLLUX
AMYGDALA TONSIL
AMYL AMYDON PENTYL ISOAMYL
AMYLASE PTYALIN DIASTASE
AMYMONE (FATHER OF —) DANAUS
(HUSBAND OF —) ENCELADUS
(SON OF —) NAUPLIUS
AMYNTOR (FATHER OF —)
ORMENUS
(SON OF —) PHOENIX
(WIFE OF —) CLEOBULE
AMYTHAON (BROTHER OF —)
AESON PHERES
(FATHER OF —) CRETHEUS
(MOTHER OF —) TYRO
(SON OF —) BIAS MELAMPUS
(WIFE OF —) IDOMENE
AN ONE ARTICLE
ANA EVENTS OMNIANA SAYINGS
ANABAPTIST DIPPER ABECEDARIAN
ANABAS MARTINICO
ANABATIC DESCENDING
ANABLEPS FOUREYES
ANABO NABO ANABONG
ANABRANCH BRANCH TALLYWALKA
ANACAONA (BROTHER OF —)
BEHECHIO
(HUSBAND OF —) CAONABO
ANACHARSIS (BROTHER OF —)
SAULIUS
ANACHRONISM SOLECISM
ANACONDA BOA ABOLLA SUCURI
SUCURY CAMOUDIE SUCURUJU
ANACREONTIC TEIAN
ANACRUSIS UPBEAT
ANADEM CROWN DIADEM FILLET
WREATH CHAPLET CORONET
GARLAND
ANAGNOST LECTOR READER
ANAGOGICAL MYSTICAL
ANAGRAM REBUS PUZZLE
METAGRAM LOGOGRIPH
(PL.) VERBARIUM
ANAGUA KNACKAWAY KNOCKAWAY
ANAH (DAUGHTER OF —)
AHOLIBAMAH
(FATHER OF —) ZIBEON
ANAL PODICAL
ANALABOS CLOAK
ANALGESIC ANODYNE CODEINE
QUININE ANTIPYRIN PHENALGIN
ANALOGICAL NORMAL
ANALOGOUS LIKE SIMILAR
ANALOGUE DFDT ANALOG
ANALOGY QIYAS PARALLEL
PREDISONE
(CLOSE —) PARITY
ANALYSIS TEST INDEX STUDY
ANATOMY AUTOPSY SCANSION
SOLUTION
(BLOWPIPE —) PYROLOGY
(CHARACTER —) PSYCHOGRAPH

(ECONOMIC —) DYNAMICS
(LOGICAL —) SYLLOGISM
ANALYST SHRINK
ANALYTIC SUBTLE REGULAR
(NOT —) SYNTHETIC SYNTHETICAL
ANALYTICAL CLINICAL DIVISIVE
ANALYZE RUN PART SIFT ASSAY
BREAK PARSE SENSE STUDY WEIGH
ASSESS DIVIDE REDUCE DISSECT
EXAMINE ITEMIZE RESOLVE TITRATE
UNPIECE APPRAISE CONSTRUE
DIAGNOSE SEPARATE
(— ACCOUNT) AGE
(— VERSE) SCAN
ANAMITE TWINE
ANANAS ANANA PINGUIN
ANANI (FATHER OF —) ELIOENAI
ANANIAS LIAR SIDRACH
(FATHER OF —) NEDEBAEUS
(WIFE OF —) SAPPHIRA
ANANSI NANCY
ANAPEST ANTIDACTYL
ANARCHIST RED PROVO REBEL
ANARCH NIHILIST REDSHIRT
SOLECIST
ANARCHY RIOT CHAOS REVOLT
LICENSE MISRULE DISORDER
ANASARCA EDEMA DROPSY
ANASAZI PUEBLO PLATEAU
ANASCHISTIC EUMITOTIC
ANASTOMOSIS GLOMUS
ANASTROPHE INVERSION
ANATASE OCTAHEDRITE
ANATH (SON OF —) SHAMGAR
ANATHEMA WO BAN MUD WOE
OATH CURSE CENSURE
ANATHEMATIZE BAN CURSE
ACCURSE EXECRATE
ANATHOTH (FATHER OF —) BECHER
ANATOMIST
AMERICAN TODD ALLEN EVANS
SABIN WYMAN DWIGHT KNOWER
COGHILL HERRICK STOCKARD
AUSTRIAN HYRTL
BELGIAN VESALIUS
DANISH STENO
DUTCH TULP GRAAF CAMPER COITER
DUBOIS
ENGLISH GRAY OWEN JONES QUAIN
COWPER HARVEY HAVERS HILTON
HUNTER WILLIS
FRENCH ROBIN DUVERNEY
DUPUYTREN POISEUILLE
CRUVEILHIER
GERMAN HIS FICK ROUX HENLE
MEYER BRAUNE EBERTH KRAUSE
MECKEL MULLER RATHKE WAGNER
FRORIEP SIEBOLD ANDERSCH
BISCHOFF HARTMANN MEISSNER
SCHULTZE SCHWALBE WRISBERG
GEGENBAUR HELMHOLTZ
LIEBERKUHN SOEMMERRING
WEIDENREICH

GREEK RUFUS HEROPHILUS ERASISTRATUS
ITALIAN CORTI ASELLI PACINI SCARPA VAROLI CALDANI COLOMBO COTUGNO ROLANDO MALPIGHI EUSTACHIO FALLOPIUS PACCHIONI
SCOTTISH BELL MONRO FERRIER GOODSIR PETTIGREW MACALISTER
SWEDISH KEY
SWISS BAUHIN HALLER HARDER BRUNNER

ANATOMIZE ANALYZE DISSECT

ANATOMY TOPOLOGY
(— OF HORSE) HIPPOTOMY
(MICROSCOPIC —) HISTOLOGY
(VEGETABLE —) PHYTOTOMY

ANAX (FATHER OF —) URANUS
(MOTHER OF —) GE GAEA
(SON OF —) ASTERIUS

ANAXARETE (LOVER OF —) IPHIS

ANAXIBIA (DAUGHTER OF —) PELOPEA ALCESTIS PISIDICE
(FATHER OF —) BIAS
(HUSBAND OF —) PELIAS
(SON OF —) ACASTUS

ANAXO (BROTHER OF —) AMPHITRYON
(DAUGHTER OF —) ALCMENE
(FATHER OF —) ALCAEUS
(HUSBAND OF —) ELECTRYON

ANCAEUS (FATHER OF —) ALEUS NEPTUNE LYCURGUS POSEIDON
(MOTHER OF —) ASTYPALAEA
(SON OF —) AGAPENOR

ANCESTOR ION MIL ADAM EBER HETH ROOT SIRE DORUS ELDER STOCK APETUS ATAVUS AUTHOR BELDAM EPONYM FATHER MANNUS MILEDH PARENT STIPES ANCIENT BELDAME BELSIRE EPAPHUS FLEANCE FORBEAR IAPETUS ISHMAEL KACHINA SAKULYA DARDANUS FOREBEAR FOREGOER MILESIUS MYRMIDON RELATIVE PREDECESSOR PRIMOGENITOR
(— CULT) MANISM
(—S OF GOTLANDERS) GEAT
(MAORI —) TIKI TUPUNA
(PL.) OLDERS ANCESTY

ANCESTRAL AVAL AVITAL AVITIC LINEAL FAMILIAL

ANCESTRY KIN RACE SEED ATHEL FAMILY ORIGIN PEOPLE SOURCE STRAIN DESCENT KINDRED LINEAGE BREEDING PEDIGREE

ANCHINOE (FATHER OF —) NILUS
(HUSBAND OF —) BELUS
(SON OF —) DANAUS AEGYPTUS

ANCHISES (FATHER OF —) CAPYS
(MOTHER OF —) THEMIS
(SON OF —) AENEAS

ANCHOR FIX BIND DRAG DRUG HOOK MOOR REST SLUG SPUD STOP AFFIX BERTH BOWER KEDGE RIVET SHEET STOCK ATTACH DROGUE FASTEN HERMIT KEDGER KELLEG SECURE STREAM CHAPLET CONNECT DEADMAN GRAPNEL GROUSER KILLICK MUDHOOK SUPPORT COCKBILL
(— IN PLACE) ACOCKBILL
(— RING) TORUS
(AT —) ASTAY
(BEAM —) WALL
(PART OF —) ARM EYE KEY PEE PIN BALL BILL HEAD HOOP PALM RING CROWN FLUKE STOCK TREND THROAT

ANCHORAGE DOCK STAY HARBOR REFUGE RIDING MOORAGE ABUTMENT BERTHAGE ROOTHOLD

ANCHORITE MONK LONER HERMIT ASCETIC EREMITE RECLUSE STYLITE ANCHORET

ANCHOVY NEHU BOCON SPRAT HERRING SARDINE
(— SAUCE) ALEC
(PL.) ALICI

ANCHUSA OXTONGUE

ANCHUSIN ALKANET

ANCIENT ELD OLD AGED AULD FERN HIGH HOAR IAGO YORE EARLY ELDER HOARY OLDEN BYGONE ENSIGN FORMER NOETIC PISTOL PRIMAL VETUST ANTIENT ANTIQUE ARCHAIC ARCHEAN CLASSIC OGYGEAN OGYGIAN HISTORIC NOACHIAN OBSOLETE PRIMEVAL PRISTINE TIMEWORN
(MOST —) ELDEST
(PREF.) ARCHAE PALAE(O) PALE(O)
(PREF.) PALE PALE(O)

ANCIENTLY OLD HIGH

ANCILLA HELPER ADJUNCT SERVANT

ANCON ELBOW CORBEL CONSOLE

AND N U AN ET SO ANT TOO ALSO PLUS BESIDES FURTHER MOREOVER AMPERSAND
(— SO FORTH) ETC USW
(SYMBOL OF —) AMPERSAND

ANDAMAN MINCOPI MINKOPI MINCOPIE

ANDESITE BONINITE TIMAZITE PROPYLITE

ANDHAKA (FATHER OF —) KASYAPA
(MOTHER OF —) DITI
(SLAYER OF —) SHIVA

ANDIRON DOG CHENET COBIRON FIREDOG HESSIAN HANDIRON LANDIRON

ANDORRA (LANGUAGE OF —) CATALAN
(NATIVE OF —) ANDOSIAN
(RIVER OF —) VALIRA

ANDRADITE APLOME GARNET

ANDRAEMON (FATHER OF —)
OXYLUS
(MOTHER OF —) GORGE DRYOPE
(SON OF —) THOAS
ANDREA CHENIER (CHARACTER IN
—) ANDREA COIGNY GERARD
CHENIER MADELEINE
(COMPOSER OF —) GIORDANO
ANDROCLES AND THE LION
(AUTHOR OF —) SHAW
(CHARACTER IN —) LAVINIA
MEGAERA ANDROCLES FERROVIUS
ANDROCONIUM STIGMA PLUMULE
ANDROGEUS (FATHER OF —)
MINOS
(MOTHER OF —) PASIPHAE
ANDROID ROBOT AUTOMATON
ANDROMACHE (AUTHOR OF —)
EURIPIDES
(CHARACTER IN —) PELEUS THETIS
ORESTES PYRRHUS HERMIONE
MENELAUS MOLOSSUS
ANDROMACHE NEOPTOLEMUS
(FATHER OF —) EETION
(HUSBAND OF —) HECTOR HELENUS
NEOPTOLEMUS
(SON OF —) PIELUS ASTYANAX
MOLOSSUS PERGAMUS
ANDROMEDA (FATHER OF —)
CEPHEUS
(MOTHER OF —) CASSIOPEA
(RESCUER OF —) PERSEUS
ANDROMEDE BIELID
ANDRON (FATHER OF —) ANIUS
(SISTER OF —) OENO ELAIS SPERMO
ANECDOTAL LITERARY
ANECDOTE GAG TOY JOKE TALE
YARN EVENT STORY SKETCH
HAGGADA EXEMPLUM HAGGADAH
(COLLECTION OF —S) ANA
ANECHOIC DEAD
ANEMIA SURRA SURRAH ANAEMIA
HYPAEMA HYPHEMA HYPHEMIA
ISCHEMIA SPANEMIA CHLOROSIS
ANEMIC LOW PALE WEAK MEALY
WATERY LIFELESS
(PREF.) CHLOR(O)
ANEMONE LILY CRASS EMONY
POLYP OPELET ACTINIA BOWBELLS
SNOWDROP
(KIND OF —) RUE
ANENT ON RE ASTO ABOUT ANENST
BESIDE TOWARD AGAINST OPPOSITE
ANESTHESIA BLOCK CORYL
SPINAL
ANESTHETIC GAS CRNA ETHER
ACOINE EVIPAN OBTUSE OPIATE
COCAINE DULLING MENTHOL
METOPRYL PARAFORM PROCAINE
SEDATIVE PHENOCAIN
METHOXYFLURANE
(SUFF.) CAINE
ANESTHETIST CRNA

ANESTHETIZE FREEZE ETHERIZE
ANEW OVER AGAIN NEWLY AFRESH
ITERUM NEWLINS NEWLINGS
RECENTLY
(PREF.) RE
ANFRACTUOUS SPIRAL BENDING
SINUOUS WINDING TORTUOUS
ANGEL MAH DEVA EBUS ANGLE
ARDOR ARIEL DAEVA DULIA NAKIR
YAKSA ABDIEL ARIOCH BACKER
BELIAL CHERUB MONKIR MUNKAR
NEKKAR SERAPH SPIRIT THRONE
UZZIEL YAKSHA ANGELET EGREGOR
ISRAFEL RAPHAEL SPONSOR
WATCHER ZADKIEL ZOPHIEL
APOLLYON GUARDIAN ITHURIEL
SUPERNAL
(— OF DEATH) AZRAEL SAMMAEL
(DESTROYING —) ABADDON
(FALLEN —) SATAN
(FALLEN —S) HELL
(GUARDIAN —) YAKSA YAKSHA
VAKOTII
(RECORDING —) SIJIL SIJILL
(PL.) HOST FRAVASHI SERAPHIM
ANGELFISH MONK MUNK ANGEL
QUOTT RHINA SQUAT MONACH
CICHLID FLATFISH KINGSTON
MONKFISH SQUATINA
ANGELIC SAINTLY BEATIFIC
CHERUBIC HEAVENLY SERAPHIC
ANGELICA JELLICA ARCHANGEL
(FATHER OF —) GALAPHRON
(LOVER OF —) ORLANDO
ANGELIN PACAY ANGELEEN
ANGELIQUE (CHARACTER IN —)
CHARLOT BONIFACE ANGELIQUE
(COMPOSER OF —) IBERT
ANGER ARR IRE IRK MAD VEX BATE
BILE BURN CRAB FELL FUME FURY
GALL GRIM HUFF MOOD RAGE RILE
ROIL RUFF TEEN TIFF ANNOY BIRSE
ONAME GRIPE HATEI IRISH PIQUE
SPONK SPUNK STURT THRAW
WRATH BOTHER CHOLER DANDER
ENRAGE EXCITE GRIEVE MADDEN
MONKEY NETTLE OFFEND RANCOR
SPLEEN TALENT TEMPER WARMTH
BURNING DESPITE DUDGEON
EMOTION INCENSE INFLAME
PASSION PROVOKE STOMACH
ACRIMONY DISTRESS EBENEZER
IRRITATE VEXATION
ANGERED SORE AGRAMED PELTISH
INCENSED
ANGICO CURUPAY
ANGINA PRUNELLA
ANGIOSPERM HARDWOOD
METASPERM
ANGLE IN BOB DIP ELL OUT TEE WRO
CANT COIN COOK DRAW FISH FORK
HADE KEEN KNEE LEAD NOOK PEAK
SITE WICK ANCON ARRIS AXIAL

BEVEL BIGHT CHOIL COIGN DRAFT
DRIFT ELBOW FLEAM GROIN GUISE
INGLE PHASE POINT QUOIN SLANT
SLOPE ALLURE ANGULE ASPECT
CANTON CORNEL CORNER DIRECT
ENGHLE EPAULE HADING LAGGEN
LAGGIN OCTANT SCHEME SQUARE
TORNUS ANGLIAN ANGULUS
ANOMALY AZIMUTH BASTION
DRAUGHT GIMMICK KNUCKLE
PERIGON RAVELIN SALIENT
ARGUMENT DECALAGE DIHEDRAL
FISHHOOK INTRIGUE SHOULDER
OBLIQUITY
(— OF BEVEL) FLEAM FLEEM
(— OF BOWSPRIT) STEEVE STEEVING
(— OF CLUB HEAD) LIE
(— OF EYELIDS) CANTHUS
(— OFF) JAG
(— OF HAT BRIM) BREAK
(— OF HIPBONE) HOOK
(— OF LEAF) AXIL
(— OF RAFTER) HEEL
(— OF TIMBER KNEE) BREECH
(DRIFT —) LEEWAY
(OBTUSE —) HEEL BULLNOSE
(ROCK —) DIEDRE
(ROOF —) HIP FASTIGIUM
(ROUND —) PERIGON
(SALIENT —) ARIS ARRIS PIEND
(PREF.) ANGULO GON(I)(IO)(Y)(YO)
(SUFF.) GON
ANGLED CANTED NOOKED
ANGULATE
(PREF.) ACUTI
ANGLER MONK FRIAR THIEF SLIMER
LOPHIID RODSTER SPINNER
WIDEGAB WIDEGAP ALLMOUTH
FROGFISH MONKFISH PISCATOR
TOADFISH WALTONIAN
ANGLESMITH SLABMAN
ANGLEWORM ESS WORM
FISHWORM
ANGLICAN EPISCOPAL
ANGLO CAUCASIAN

ANGOLA
CAPITAL: LUANDA
COIN: LWEI KWANZA MACUTA
  MACUTE
DISTRICT: CABINDA
KINGDOM: BAKONGO
LANGUAGE: BANTU KIMBUNDU
MONEY: KWANZA LWEI
MOUNTAIN: LOVITI
PLATEAU: PLANALTO
PORT: LOBITO LUANDA
RIVER: CONGO CUITO KASAI CUANDO
  CUANZA CUNENE KUNENE
  KWANDO KWANZA CUBANGO
TOWN: LOBITO LUANDA LUBANGO
  BENGUELA MOSSAMEDES
  NOVALISBOA
TRIBE: BANTU KIKONGO
WATERFALL: RUACANA

ANGORA CAT GOAT ANGOLA RABBIT
ANGRILY ANGERLY IRATELY
FUMINGLY
ANGRY MAD ASHY EVIL GRIM GRUM
HIGH RILY ROID ROSY SORE WARM
WAXY WILD WRAW CROOK CROSS
GRAME HUFFY IRATE IROUS MOODY
RATTY RILEY SNAKY STUNT VEXED
WEMOD WROTH BIRSIT CHAFED
CROUSE FRENZY FUMING FUMOUS
HEATED IREFUL LOADED SHIRTY
SNAKEY STUFFY TICKED ENRAGED
FRETFUL FURIOUS HOPPING
IRACUND PAINFUL RILEDUP ROPABLE
SNAKISH SPLEENY TEEDOFF
UPTIGHT CHOLERIC INFLAMED
RIGOROUS SEETHING SPITFIRE
TEMPERED VEHEMENT WREAKFUL
INDIGNANT PASSIONATE
(BE —) STEAM
(MAKE —) FROST
ANGRY-LOOKING THUNDERY
ANGUISH WOE ACHE HARM HURT
PAIN PANG RACK TRAY AGONY
ANGST ANGUS DOLOR GRIEF THROE
MISERY REGRET SORROW ANGOISE
ANGWICH REMORSE TORMENT
TORTURE TRAVAIL DISTRESS
(CHRIST'S —) AGONY
ANGUISHED GRIEFFUL
ANGULAR BONE BONY EDGY LEAN
SLIM THIN GAUNT SHARP ABRUPT
POINTED SCRAWNY CORNERED
(NOT —) SOFT
(PREF.) ANG
ANGULARITY EDGINESS
ANGUS FORFAR FORFARSHIRE
ANHYDRIDE LACTAM SULTAM
FULGIDE LACTIDE SULTONE
GLUCOSAN MANNITAN SORBITAN
ANHYDRITE VULPINITE
ANHYDROUS DRY DESICCATED
ANI WITCH CUCKOO JEWBIRD
KEELBILL KEELBIRD TICKBIRD
ANIAM (FATHER OF —) SHEMIDAH
ANIARA (COMPOSER OF —)
BLOMDAHL
ANIMADVERSION BLAME REMARK
CENSURE COMMENT REPROOF
WARNING MONITION REPROACH
REFLECTION
**ANIMAL (ALSO SEE UNDER SPECIFIC
HEADINGS)** FAT DEER BEAST BIPED
BLACK BRUTE GRADE GROSS LUSTY
STORE STRAY BRUTAL CARNAL
DAPPLE DESPOT FLESHY KICKER
MAMMAL RODENT SILVAN SORREL
SPONGE SYLVAN BEASTIE BREEDER
CARRION CRITTER EPIZOON FATLING
LINSANG SENSUAL BURROWER

CREATURE EMIGRANT ORGANISM
PREDATOR
(— COLLECTION) LARDER
(— FOR MARKET) STOCKER
(— INHABITED BY SPIRIT) GUACA
HUACA
(— LIVING IN CAVES) TROGLOBITE
(— OF LITTLE VALUE) SCALAWAG
SKALAWAG
(— RESEMBLING MAN) HOMINOID
(—S AS RENT) CAIN
(— SHOT) KILL
(— VICTIM OF MOTOR VEHICLE)
ROADKILL
(— WITH BLACK COAT AND
MARKINGS) PARSON
(— WITH DOCKED TAIL) CURTAL
(BEEF —) BONER GRASSER
(BOVINE —) BOSS BRUTE
(BROKEN-DOWN —) CROCK
(CARNIVOROUS —) GENET GENETTE
SARCOPHILE
(CASTRATED —) SEG SEGG SPAY
SPADO GELDING
(COLD-BLOODED —) ECTOTHERM
(CREATED —) BARAMIN
(DECOY —) COACH
(DOMESTIC —) DOER SCRUB BESTIAL
FOLLOWER SCRUBBER
(DRAFT —) AVER AIVER
(EMACIATED —) FRAME SKELETON
(FABULOUS —) KYLIN BUNYIP
DRAGON ACEPHAL GRIFFIN GRIFFON
GRYPHON UNICORN SEMITAUR
TRAGELAPH
(FARM —S) STOCK
(FEMALE —) HEN SHE LADY JENNY
SHEDER
(FERAL —) CIMAROON CIMARRON
CIMMARON
(FLEA-RIDDEN —) FLEABAG
(FOOTLESS —) APOD APODE
(FOSSIL —) ZOOLITE
(FREAKISH —) FERLY FERLIE
(GRASSHOPPER-EATING —)
WHANGAM
(GRAY —) GRIZZLE
(GRAZING —) HERBAGER
(GREEDY —) GORB
(HORNED —) HORN REEM
(HORNLESS —) POLLARD
(HUNTED —) QUARRY
(HYPOTHETICAL —) PROAVIS
(IMAGINARY —) WHANGAM
CATAWAMPUS
(LOWER —) BEAST CREATURE
(LUSTY OR PLUMP —) BILCH BILSH
(MALE —) HE TOM BUCK BULL JACK
STAG JOHNNY BACHELOR
(MARINE —) LANCELET
(MATURE —) SENIOR
(MEAT —) CHOPPER
(MISCHIEVOUS —) ELF

(MYTHICAL —) HODAG KYLIN
MOONACK
(ODD —) SPLACKNUCK
(PACK —) HUNIA SUMPTER
(PARTY —) STAG
(PET —) CADL
(PREMATURE —) SLINK
(PURSUED —S) GAME
(ROASTED —) BARBECUE BARBEQUE
(SADDLE —) LOPER
(SCRAWNY —) SCRAG
(SHORN —) SHEAR
(SKINNY —) SCRAE
(SLUGGISH —) DRUMBLE
(SOLID-HOOFED —) SOLIPED
(SPOTTED —) CALICO
(STOCKY —) BLOCK
(STUNTED —) SHARGAR SHARGER
(THICKSET —) NUGGET
(TOTEM —) EPONYM
(UNBRANDED —) SLICK
(UNCASTRATED —) ENTIRE
(UNDERSIZED —) DURGAN DURGEN
SCALAWAG SCALLYWAG
(UNHOUSED —) OUTLER OUTLIER
(UNMANAGEABLE —) OUTLAW
(UNWEANED —) SUCKER
(WANDERING —) STRAY ESTRAY
(WARM-BLOODED —) ENDOTHERM
HAEMATHERM
(WATER —) AQUATIC AQUATILE
(WEAK —) DRAG DOWNER
(WILD —) SAVAGE WILDLING
(WING-FOOTED —) ALIPED
(WORNOUT —) KANCKER
(WORTHLESS —) CARRION
(YOUNG —) HOG BIRD HOGG JOEY
SHOT TOTO STORE JUNIOR PULLUS
FATLING LITTLIN KINDLING LITTLING
SUCKLING YOUNGLET
(2-HORNED —) BICORN BICORNE
(4-FOOTED —) TETRAPOD
(PL.) ZOA FAUNA NECTON NEKTON
(PREF.) ZO(E)(IDIO)(IDO)(O)
ZOOLOGICO
(RUMINATING —) MERYC(O)
(SUFF.) ACEA AD THERE THERIA
THERIUM ZOA ZOIC ZOON

ANIMALCULISM SPERMISM
ANIMALITY HOGGERY
ANIMALS
(SUFF.) ATA IDA IDEA INI
ANIMA MUNDI WELTGEIST
ANIMATE ACT PEP FIRE MOVE PERK
STIR URGE ALIVE BRISK CHEER DRIVE
FLUSH IMBUE IMPEL LIGHT LIVEN
QUICK ROUSE VITAL AROUSE BRIGHT
ENSOUL EXCITE INCITE INDUCE
INFORM KINDLE LIVING PROMPT
SPIRIT VIVIFY ACTUATE COMFORT
ENLIVEN INSPIRE QUICKEN ACTIVATE
ENERGIZE INSPIRIT VITALIZE
(NOT —) BRUTE

ANIMATED UP GAY VIF GLAD VIVE ALIVE ANIME BRISK QUICK VITAL VIVID ACTIVE ARDENT BLITHE BOUNCY BRISKY LIVELY LIVING SPARKY SPUNKY BUOYANT JOCULAR STHENIC BOUNCING INSTINCT LIFESOME SPIRITED VIGOROUS

ANIMATION BRIO ELAN FIRE HEAT LIFE VERVE SPIRIT SPARKLE

ANIMATOR INFORMER

ANIME COPAL ELEMI RESIN ROSIN ANIMATO

ANIMIKEAN LAWSON

ANIMISM NATURISM

ANIMOSITY HATE PIQUE SPITE ANIMUS ENMITY HATRED MALICE RANCOR DISLIKE ACRIMONY

ANIMUS MIND ONDE WILL EFFORT ENMITY SPIRIT TEMPER ATTITUDE

ANIRUDDHA (FATHER OF —) PRADYUMNA

ANISE ANET DILL CUMEN UMBEL FENNEL SIKIMI SHIKIMI

ANIUS (DAUGHTER OF —) OENO ELAIS SPERMO
(FATHER OF —) APOLLO
(MOTHER OF —) RHOEO CREUSA
(SON OF —) ANDRON
(WIFE OF —) DORIPPE

ANKH TAU

ANKLE COOT CUIT HOCK QUIT ANCLE QUEET TALUS WRIST TARSUS SHACKLE
(COCKED —S) KNUCKLING
(PREF.) TAL(I)(O) TARS(I)(O)

ANKLEBONE TALUS ASTRAGAL

ANKLET SHOE SOCK BANGLE FETTER SHACKLE

ANLAGE INCEPT PROTON INITIAL BLASTEMA

ANNA (FATHER OF —) BELUS
(SISTER OF —) DIDO

ANNA BOLENA (CHARACTER IN —) ANNE JANE HENRY PERCY BOLEYN SEYMOUR
(COMPOSER OF —) DONIZETTI

ANNA KARENINA (AUTHOR OF —) TOLSTOY
(CHARACTER IN —) ANNA KITTY LEVIN ALEXEI STEPAN KARENIN VRONSKY OBLONSKY KONSTANTINE SHTCHERBATSKY

ANNALIST WRITER RECORDER

ANNALS FASTI NIHONGI REGISTER

ANNAM (ALSO SEE VIETNAM) VIETNAM
(BOAT OF —) GAYYOU GAYDIANG
(MEASURE OF —) LY GON NGU QUO SAO TAT PHAN THAT SHITA THUOC TRUONG
(TOWN OF —) HUE VINH TOURANE QUANGTRI
(WEIGHT OF —) CAN BINH DONG

ANNAS (FATHER OF —) SETHI

ANNATTO OTTER URUCU ORLEAN ROUCOU SALMON ACHIOTE ACHUETE ANNOTTO ARNATTO ORLEANS

ANNEAL BAKE FUSE HEAT SMELT TEMPER INFLAME TOUGHEN GRAPHITE

ANNEALER TUBER HEATER

ANNEALING LIGHTING

ANNELID NAID WORM LUGWORM SERPULA ANNULATE SANDWORM SERPULAN OLIGOCHAETE

ANNEX ADD ELL LAY JOIN WING AFFIX SEIZE UNITE ADJECT ANNECT APPEND ATTACH FASTEN ACQUIRE CONNECT FIXTURE POSTFIX SUBJOIN ADDITION ANNEXURE DOCUMENT PENTHOUSE

ANNIE OAKLEY PASS TICKET FREEBEE FREEBIE

ANNIHILATE END OUT KILL RAZE RUIN SLAY ABATE ANNUL ERASE WRECK DELETE DEVOUR NOUGHT QUENCH REDUCE ABOLISH DESTROY EXPUNGE DECIMATE UNCREATE DISCREATE PULVERIZE

ANNIHILATION FANA NEGATION

ANNIVERSARY FETE MASS EMBER FEAST ANNUAL JUBILEE YEARDAY BIRTHDAY FESTIVAL YAHRZEIT
(100TH —) CENTENNIAL
(1000TH —) MILLENIUM
(150TH —) SESQUICENTENNIAL
(200TH —) BIMILLENARY BIMILLENIUM
(25TH —) SEMIJUBILEE
(50TH —) SEMICENTENNIAL

ANNONA ATIS ATTA ATEES

ANNOTATE EDIT NOTE STET GLOSS BENOTE NOTIFY POSTIL REMARK APOSTIL COMMENT EXPLAIN FOOTNOTE

ANNOTATION APOSTIL COMMENT SCHOLION SCHOLIUM

ANNOTATOR NOTIST SCHOLIAST

ANNOUNCE BID CRY BODE CALL DEEM MAKE SCRY SHOW SING TELL BRUIT CLAIM KNELL STATE VOICE ASSERT BLAZON BROACH DENOTE HERALD INFORM PREACH REPORT REVEAL SIGNAL SPRING STEVEN DECLARE DIVULGE FORERUN GAZETTE PUBLISH SIGNIFY DENOUNCE FORETELL INTIMATE PROCLAIM RENOUNCE SENTENCE

ANNOUNCEMENT BID CRY HAT BILL CALL LEAD ALARM BANCO BANNS BLURB EDICT ALARUM DECREE DICTUM NOTICE GAZETTE SENSING BULLETIN CIRCULAR DECISION RESCRIPT PROCLAMATION
(— OF DAWN) AUBADE
(STAGE —) SENNET

ANNOUNCER NEBO PAGE CRIER
EMCEE CALLER DEEJAY HERALD
NUNCIO VEEJAY GONGMAN
GRINDER SPIELER NUNCIATE
SPRUIKER
ANNOY ARR BUG DUN EAT EGG GET
GIG HOX IRE IRK NAG NOY NYE TRY
VEX BAIT BORE BURN FASH FRET
FUSS GALL GRIG HALE HARM HAZE
HUFF HUMP MIFF NARK PAIN RILE
ROIL CHAFF CHASE CHEVY CHIVY
DEVIL GRAMY GRATE HARRY PEEVE
PIQUE SPITE STURT TEASE THORN
UPSET WEARY WORRY BADGER
BOTHER CADDLE CHIVEY CHIVVY
EARWIG ENRAGE GRAVEL HAGGLE
HARASS HATTER HECKLE HECTOR
INFECT INJURE MADDEN MOLEST
NEEDLE NETTLE OFFEND PESTER
POTTER PUTOUT RATTLE REHETE
RUFFLE TICKLE BEDEVIL DISTURB
HOTFOOT JACKSON TERRIFY
TROUBLE ACERBATE CONTRARY
DISTRESS IRRITATE PERSECUTE
ANNOYANCE VEX DRAG FASH PEST
WEED CROSS GRIEF LOATH SPITE
STALL THORN INSECT PESTER
DISGUST FASHERY NOYANCE
TROUBLE UMBRAGE FASHERIE
FLEABITE NOISANCE NUISANCE
PINPRICK
ANNOYED SORE TEEDOFF INSULTED
ANNOYING TARE PESKY NOYOUS
DISEASY HATEFUL IRKSOME
NOISOME PAINFUL TARSOME
FASHIOUS FRETSOME NIGGLING
SPITEFUL TIRESOME PROVOKING
PESTIFEROUS
ANNOYINGLY CONFOUNDED
CONFOUNDEDLY
ANNUAL BOOK BUGLE PLANT
FLOWER YEARLY ANNUARY
BUGSEED BUGWEED ETESIAN
GIFTBOOK PERIODIC YEARBOOK
(OLD WORLD —) WELD
ANNUITY CENSO CONSOL INCOME
PENSION TONTINE PERPETUITY
ANNUL TOL CASS NULL TOLL UNDO
VOID ADNUL AVOID BLANK ELIDE
ERASE QUASH REMIT RETEX UNLAW
CANCEL FRIVOL NEGATE RECALL
REPEAL REVERT REVOKE UNLIVE
VACATE ABOLISH CASHIER CASSARE
CASSATE DESTROY NULLIFY
RESCIND RETRACT REVERSE
VACUATE ABROGATE ARROGATE
DEROGATE DISANNUL DISSOLVE
IMBECILE OVERRIDE OVERRULE
ANNULAR BANDED CYCLIC RINGED
ANNULATE CINGULAR CIRCULAR
ANNULARLY RINGWISE
ANNULET RING RIDGE FILLET
ANNULUS MOLDING

ANNULLING VACATUR
ANNULMENT UNDOING
ABATEMENT
ANNULUS RING ANNULE COLLAR
GYROMA INDUSIUM
ANNUNCIATION MARYMASS
ANNUNCIATOR TELLER INDICATOR
ANOA BUFFALO SAPIUTAN
ANODE PLATE ZINCOID
ANODIC ASCENDING
ANODYNE BALM ACOPON BROMAL
OPIATE REMEDY EUGENOL SOOTHER
NARCOTIC SEDATIVE CHLORODYNE
ANOINT FAT OIL RUB BALM BEAT
CERE NARD ANELE ANOIL CREAM
CROWN ENOIL LATCH NUNCT PRUNE
SALVE SMARM SMEAR SMERL
CHRIEM GREASE INUNCT SPREAD
THRASH MOISTEN UNGUENT
ANOINTMENT CHRISMATORY
ANOMALOUS ODD DIFFORM
STRANGE UNUSUAL ABERRANT
ABNORMAL ATYPICAL PECULIAR
ANOMALY CREEPER CYCLOPY
EPILOIA PARADOX CYCLOPIA
ANON NAN ANEW ONCE SOON
AGAIN LATER AFRESH BEDEEN
BEDENE THENCE SHORTLY
ANONYMITY NOBODYNESS
ANONYMOUS UNKNOWN
NAMELESS UNAVOWED UNSIGNED
ANOPLURA PARASITA PEDICULINA
ANORAK CAGOUL KAGOOL KAGOUL
KAGOULE
ANOTHER NEW THAT ALIAS FRESH
SECOND TIDDER TOTHER ANITHER
FURTHER
(PREF.) ALTERO
(ONE —) ALLELO
ANOXIA ASPHYXIA
ANSHUMANT (FATHER OF —)
ASAMANJAS
(GRANDFATHER OF —) SAGARA
ANSWER DO IT SAY SIT ECHO MEET
PLEA REIN SUIT ATONE AVAIL COMES
COVER JAWAB REACT REPLY SERVE
LETTER REJOIN RESULT RETORT
RETURN RIPOST ACCOUNT COUNTER
DEFENCE DEFENSE FULFILL
RESPOND SATISFY ANTIPHON
COMEBACK PLEADING REBUTTAL
REPARTEE RESPONSE SOLUTION
(— BACK) CHOP
(— FOR) FORM VANG
(— IN FUGUE) COMES
(— OF POPE) RESCRIPT
(— SHARPLY) SNAP
(— THE PURPOSE) DO FIT SUIT AVAIL
SERVE
(— TO CHARGE) PLEA
(DECISIVE —) SOCKDOLAGER
SOCKDOLOGER
(EXAM —) TRUE FALSE

(GIVE IMPROMPTU —) FIELD
(LEGAL —) DUPLY
ANSWERABLE EQUAL LIABLE
FITTING ADEQUATE AMENABLE
ANSWERER USHABTI
ANSWERING
(PREF.) COUNTER
ANT ANAI ANAY ANER ATTA GYNE
MIRE AMPTE EMMET KELEP MAXIM
MINIM NURSE SAUBA SIAFU SLAVE
AMAZON DRIVER ERGATE NASUTE
NEUTER WORKER BULLDOG
FORAGER FORMICE OUVRIER
PISMIRE PISSANT PONERID REPLETE
SOLDIER TERMITE ACULEATA
DORYLINE FORMICID GYNECOID
HONEYPOT MACRANER MICRANER
MYRMICID TAPINOMA
(— LION) DOODLEBUG
(— SHRIKE) BATARA
(— STUDY) MYRMECOLOGY
(— THRUSH) PITTA
(— TREE) WORMIGO
(PART OF —) EYE WAIST GASTER
ANTENNA MANDIBLE
(WINGED —) ALATE
(WORKER —) ERGATE
(PREF.) FORMI(CI) MYRMECO MYRMO
TERMITO
(SUFF.) MYRMEX
ANTA PIER PARASTAS PEDESTAL
PILASTER
ANTACID SATURANT
ANTAEUS (FATHER OF —) NEPTUNE
POSEIDON
(MOTHER OF —) GE GAEA
ANTAGONISM WAR ANIMUS
ENMITY QUARREL AVERSION
CONFLICT
(IN —) COUNTER
ANTAGONIST FOE ENEMY PARTY
RIVAL FOEMAN BATTLER WARRIOR
COPEMATE OPPONENT OPPOSITE
WRANGLER
(— OF DRUGS) NALAXONE
NALOXONE
ANTAGONISTIC ADVERSE
COUNTER HOSTILE ANTERGIC
CONTRARY INIMICAL OPPONENT
OPPOSITE
(— TO GROWTH) ANTIBLASTIC
(NOT —) SYMPATHETIC
(PREF.) ENANTIO
ANTAGONIZE OPPOSE CONTEST
ANTARCTICA (— CAPE) ADARE
(MOUNTAIN ON —) TYREE GARDNER
KIRKPATRICK
(VOLCANO ON —) EREBUS
MELBOURNE
ANT BEAR BEAR ERDVARK
AARDVARK ANTEATER EDENTATE
TAMANOIR

ANTE PAY STAKE
(— UP) KICKIN
ANTEATER TAPIR NUMBAT ECHIDNA
TAMANDU AARDVARK AARDWOLF
DASYURID EDENTATE PANGOLIN
TAMANDUA TAMANOIR
ANTEBRACHIUM CUBIT CUBITAL
CUBITUS FOREARM
ANTECEDENT FORE CAUSE PRIOR
FORMER REASON WHENCE PREMISE
ANTERIOR PREVIOUS PRECEDING
PRECEDENCE PREVENIENT
(— OF CANON) GUIDA
ANTECHAMBER LIWAN
ANTEDATE PRECEDE PREDATE
FOREDATE PREEXIST
ANTEDATED FORETIMED
ANTELOPE GNU GOA KID KOB RAM
SUS ASTE BISA BUCK DODA DUST
GUIB IBEX KOBA KUDU ORYX PALA
PUKU ROAN SUNI TOPI TORA ADDAX
BAIRA BEIRA BEISA BEKRA BOHOR
BONGO BOVID BUBAL CHIRU ELAND
GORAL GUIBA IPETE LICHI NAGOR
NYALA ORIBI PEELE PERON SABLE
SAIGA SASIN SEROW TAKIN YAKIN
BAGWYN BHOKRA BUBALE CABREE
CABRET CABRIE CABRIT CHOUKA
DIKDIK DUIKER DUYKER DZEREN
DZERIN DZERON GOORAL GRIMME
HEROLA IMPALA INYALA KOODOO
LECHWE LELWEL NAKONG NILGAI
NILGAU PALLAH POOKOO PYGARG
RHEBOK ALGAZEL BLAUBOK
BLESBOK BUBALIS CHAMOIS
CHIKARA DEFASSA GAZELLE
GEMSBOK GERENUK GREENUK
GRYSBOK MADOQUA REDBUCK
RHEEBOK SASSABY STEMBOK
AGACELLA BLEEKBOK BLESBUCK
BONTEBOK BOSCHBOK BUSHBUCK
KORRIGUM LEUCORYX REEDBUCK
STEENBOK PRONGHORN
HARTEBEEST
(YOUNG —) KID LAMB
ANTEMERIDIEM ACKEMMA
ANTENNA DISH HORN LOOP PALP
TIER YAGI AERIAL DIPOLE FEELER
TACTOR DOUBLET WHISKER
MONOPOLE PARABOLA RADIATOR
(SHORTWAVE —) YAGI
ANTENNATA INSECTA
ANTENOR (FATHER OF —) AESYETES
(MOTHER OF —) CLEOMESTRA
(WIFE OF —) THEANO
ANTERIOR FORNE FRONT PRIOR
ATLOID BEFORE FORMER ANTICUS
PRORSAL VENTRAL ATLANTAL
INFERIOR PREVIOUS PRECEDING
(PREF.) ANTER(O) EPH EPI PRE PRO
ANTEROOM HALL FOYER LOBBY
ENTRANCE

ANTEROS (BROTHER OF —) EROS
　(FATHER OF —) ARES MARS
　(MOTHER OF —) APHRODITE
ANTEWAR PREBELLUM
ANTHAS (FATHER OF —) NEPTUNE
　POSEIDON
　(MOTHER OF —) ALCYONE
ANTHELION HALO NIMBUS
　ANTISUN AUREOLE
ANTHELMINTIC CUNIC BRAYERA
　EMBELIN PINKROOT SCAMMONY
　SANTONICA PIPERAZINE
　PHENOTHIAZINE
ANTHEM HYMN SONG AGNUS
　MOTET PAEAN PSALM INTROIT
　RESPOND ASPERGES ISODICON
　(JAPANESE —) KIMIGAYO
ANTHEMIUS (FATHER OF —)
　PROCOPIUS
ANTHER TIP AGLET CHIVE THECA
ANTHESIS BLOOM BLOSSOM
ANTHILL BANK TUMP
ANTHOCYANIN ENIN OENIN
　BETANIN PUNICIN VIOLANIN
ANTHOLOGIST RHAPSODE
　RHAPSODIST
ANTHOLOGY ANA POSY
　ALBUM SYLVA CORPUS READER
　GARLAND SYNTAGMA
　CHRESTOMATHY
ANTHOZOAN CORAL POLYP
　ANEMONE GULINULA
ANTHRACITE CULM
ANTHRACITIC HARD
ANTHRACONITE STINKSTONE
　SWINESTONE
ANTHRAX SANG CHARBON
　BLACKLEG
ANTHROPOLOGIST TOTEMIST
　CULTURALIST
　AMERICAN BIRD BOAS COON MEAD
　BEALS DIXON HOUGH JENKS LEWIS
　SAPIR STARR BUTLER DORSEY
　GEERTE HOLMES HOOTON LAUFER
　LINTON MERCER POWELL PUTNAM
　RIPLEY WEAVER BATESON BRINTON
　FOLKMAR KROEBER LAFARGE
　MONTAGU SPINDEN WISSLER
　BENEDICT GWALTNEY HRDLICKA
　MACCURDY KLUCKHORN
　MACDONALD HERSKOVITS
　GOLDENWEISER
　AUSTRALIAN DART
　AUSTRIAN LUSCHAN
　BELGIAN BIEBUYCK
　ENGLISH HODGE KEITH PERRY SMITH
　TYLER BEDDOE HADDON HOWITT
　LEAKEY MARETT RIVERS GOODALL
　TURNBULL MALINOWSKI
　FINNISH WESTERMARCK
　FRENCH HAMY BROCA DENIKER
　LAPOUGE TOPINARD DUCHAILLU

　MORTILLET HOVELACQUE
　MANOUVRIER
　GERMAN WAITZ GUNTHER
　HARTMANN SCHWALBE
　BLUMENBACH WEIDENREICH
　SCHOETENSACK
　ITALIAN SERGI MANTEGAZZA
　NORWEGIAN HEYERDAHL
　SCOTTISH FRAZER MONBODDO
ANTHROPOPHAGITE CANNIBAL
ANTIA (BELOVED OF —)
　BELLEROPHON
　(FATHER OF —) IOBATES
　(HUSBAND OF —) PROETUS
ANTIAIRCRAFT ARCHIE
ANTIANEIRA (FATHER OF —)
　MENETES
　(SON OF —) ECHION ERYTUS
ANTIBALLOONER SEPARATOR
ANTIBIOTIC BIOTIC ABIOTIC FILIPIN
　HUMULON TYLOSIN CIRCULIN
　CITRININ CLAVACIN CLAVATIN
　COLISTIN FRADICIN HUMULONE
　NEOMYCIN NYSTATIN RIFAMPIN
　SUBTILIN VIOMYCIN POLYMYCIN
　PUROMYCIN RIFAMICIN GENTAMICIN
　OLIGOMYCIN PENICILLIN RIFAMPICIN
ANTIBODY LYSIN REAGIN BLOCKER
　GLUTININ PRECIPITIN
ANTIC TOY DIDO FOOL LARK WILD
　CAPER CLOWN COMIC DROLL MERRY
　PRANK STUNT GAMBOL BUFFOON
　CAPRICE GAMBADE GAMBADO
ANTICHRIST BEAST
ANTICIPATE BALK BEAT HOPE JUMP
　WISH ALLOT AUGUR AWAIT DREAD
　PSYCH SENSE STALL DIVINE EXPECT
　PSYCHE THWART DEVANCE
　FORERUN FORESEE OBVIATE
　PORTEND PREPARE PREVENE
　PREVENT PROPOSE RESPECT
　SUPPOSE ANTEDATE FORECAST
　FOREFEEL FORETAKE PROSPECT
ANTICIPATION TYPE ODIUM
　AUGURY OPINION THOUGHT
　PROSPECT PROLEPSIS PRESCIENCE
　PREMONITION
ANTICIPATORY PREVENIENT
ANTICLEA (FATHER OF —)
　AUTOLYCUS
　(HUSBAND OF —) LAERTES
　(SON OF —) ULYSSES ODYSSEUS
ANTICLIMAX BATHOS
ANTICLINE ARCH DOME NAPPE
　ISOCLINE OVERFOLD
ANTICOAGULANT WARFARIN
ANTICYCLONE HIGH
ANTIDEPRESSANT DOXEPIN
　NIALAMIDE PARGYLINE
　NORTRIPTYLINE
ANTIDOTE GUACO BEZOAR EMETIC
　GALENA REMEDY THERIAC

DELETERY THERIACA BEZOARDIC
MITHRIDATE BLEXIPHARMIC
(— TO POISON) ORVIETAN
ANTIGEN N LYSOGEN BIOLOGIC
PRECIPITINOGEN
ANTIGERMANISM VANSITTARTISM
ANTIGONE (AUTHOR OF —)
SOPHOCLES
(BROTHER OF —) POLYNICES
(CHARACTER IN —) CREON HAEMON
ISMENE ANTIGONE TIRESIAS
(FATHER OF —) OEDIPUS
(MOTHER OF —) JOCASTA
(SISTER OF —) ISMENE
ANTIGORITE SERPENTINE
ANTIGUA & BARBUDA
(CAPITAL:) SAINTJOHNS
(COIN:) DOLLAR
(ISLAND:) ANTIGUA BARBUDA
REDONDA
(LANGUAGE:) ENGLISH
(TOWN:) CODRINGTON
ANTILOCHUS (FATHER OF —)
NESTOR
(MOTHER OF —) ANAXIBIA
(SLAYER OF —) MEMNON
ANTIMALARIAL PENTAQUIN
PENTAQUINE
ANTIMASK ANTIC ANTICK
ANTIMONIAL STIBIAL
ANTIMONY SB KOHL REGULUS
STIBIUM
(PREF.) STIB(IO)
ANTIMONY SULFIDE SURMA
SOORMA
ANTINOMIAN FIDUCIARY
ANTINOMY PARADOX
ANTIOPE (FATHER OF —) NYCTEUS
(HUSBAND OF —) LYCUS THESEUS
(SISTER OF —) HIPPOLYTE
(SON OF —) ZETHUS AMPHION
HIPPOLYTUS
ANTIOXIDANT BHA SESAMOL
ANTIPATHY HATE ODIUM ENMITY
NAUSEA RANCOR ALLERGY DISGUST
DISLIKE AVERSION DISTASTE
DYSPATHY LOATHING
ANTIPHON SALVE GRADUAL
PLACEBO GRADUALE
ANTIPHONALLY CHOIRWISE
ANTHEMWISE
ANTIPHONARY LEDGER
ANTIPHUS (BROTHER OF —)
MESTHLES
(FATHER OF —) PRIAM
TALAEMENES
(HALF-BROTHER OF —) ISUS
(MOTHER OF —) HECUBA
ANTIPODAL ANTARCTIC
ANTIPYRETIC SALOL MALARIN
THALLIN THALLINE
ANTIQUARY ARCHAIST
ANTIQUARIAN

ANTIQUATED OLD AGED FUSTY
MOSSY PASSE FOGRAM FOSSIL
VOIDED ANCIENT ARCHAIC FOGYISH
NOACHIAN OBSOLETE OUTDATED
OUTMODED TIMEWORN
ANTIQUE ANTIC RELIC SIRUP SYRUP
VIRTU ANTICK NOETIC ANCIENT
ARCHAIC NOACHIC NOACHIAN
OUTMODED ARCHAICAL
(PERSON WHO LOCATES —S) PICKER
ANTIQUITY ELD OLD PAST YORE
RELIC OLDNESS ANCIENCE
ANCIENCY
(PL.) ARCHEOLOGY ARCHAEOLOGY
ANTIRED WHITE
ANTI-SEMITISM JUDOPHOBIA
ANTISEPTIC CAVA EGOL KAVA SALT
AMIDO AMINE EUPAD EUSOL IODOL
SALOL AMADOL IATROL IODINE
KRELOS PHENOL PICROL ALCOHOL
ALUMNOL ARBUTIN ASEPTIC
COLYTIC LORETIN STERILE TACHIOL
TEUCRIN THALLIN CREOSOTE
ICHTHYOL KAVAKAVA METAPHEN
TEREBENE THALLINE MERBROMIN
ACRIFLAVINE
(SUFF.) IOM
ANTISOCIAL HOSTILE ANARCHIST
ANTISPASMODIC KELLIN SAMBUL
SUMBAL SUMBUL KHELLIN
PAPAVERINE STRAMONIUM
PENTOBARBITAL
ANTISTROPHE REVERT
COUNTERTURN
ANTITHESIS AND CONTRAST
ANTITHETICAL OPPOSITE
ANTITOXIN SERUM BIOLOGIC
ANTIVIVISECTIONIST BESTIARIAN
ANTIWAR (— GROUP) DOVES
ANTLER DAG HORN KNOB RIAL TRAY
DAGUE RIGHT ROYAL SHOOT SPIKE
BOSSET SHOVEL TROCHE SPELLER
DEERHORN SURROYAL TROCHING
(— POINT) TROCHING
(BRANCH OF —) TINE PRONG
(PL.) HEAD ATTIRE
ANT LION LACEWING DOODLEBUG
NEUROPTERAN
ANTONINA (HUSBAND OF —)
BELISARIUS
ANTONY AND CLEOPATRA
(AUTHOR OF —) SHAKESPEARE
(CHARACTER IN —) EROS IRAS
MENAS PHILO ALEXAS ANTONY
GALLUS SCARUS SEXTUS SILIUS
TAURUS AGRIPPA LEPIDUS MARDIAN
OCTAVIA THYREUS VARRIUS
CANIDIUS CHARMIAN DERCETAS
DIOMEDES DOMITIUS MECAENAS
OCTAVIUS SELEUCUS CLEOPATRA
DEMETRIUS DOLABELLA VENTIDIUS
EUPHRONIUS MENECRATES
PROCULEIUS

ANTONYM OPP OPPOSITE
ANTOTHIJAH (FATHER OF —)
  JEROHAM
ANTSHRIKE BATARA
ANTSY EDGY FUSSY TENSE FIDGETY
ANT THRUSH PITTA
ANT TREE HORMIGO
ANUB (FATHER OF —) COZ
ANUS ASS ARSE BUNG VENT SIEGE
  TEWEL
  (PREF.) ANO PROCT(O)
  (SUFF.) PROCTA
ANVIL BLOCK INCUS SNARL STAKE
  STITH TEEST STETHY STITHY
  ANDVILE ANFEELD BICKERN
  BEAKIRON
  (— SUPPORT) STOCK
  (MINIATURE —) STAKE STUMP
  (PREF.) INCUD(O)
ANXIETY HOW CARE CARK FEAR
  FRAY PAIN ALARM ANGOR ANGST
  DOUBT DREAD PANIC WORRY
  KIAUGH NERVES PUCKER ANGUISH
  CAUTION CHAGRIN CONCERN
  SCRUPLE TENSION THOUGHT
  TROUBLE DISQUIET SUSPENSE
  SOLICITUDE
  (— ABOUT HEALTH) HYPOCHONDRIA
  (EXTREME —) RACK
ANXIOUS AGOG BUSY FOND TOEY
  EAGER FIRST UPSET AFRAID UNEASY
  ANGUISH CAREFUL CARKING
  EARNFUL FORWARD TIDIOSE
  UNQUIET DESIROUS RESTLESS
  THOUGHTY WATCHFUL CONCERNED
ANY A AN AY AIR ALL ARY ONI ONY
  AIRY EVER PART SOME WHAT
  (— WHATEVER) ALL
  (NOT —) NARY
ANYBODY ANY ONE ANYONE
  SOMEONE
ANYHOW HOW NOHOW NOWAY
  ALWAYS ANYWAY
ANYONE HE MAN ANYBODY
ANYTHING THAT AUGHT OUGHT
ANYWAY NOHOW ALWAYS
ANYWHERE EIHWER OWHERE
  UBIQUE ANYPLACE
ANYWISE ANYHOW ANYWAY
  ANYWAYS
AOUDAD ARUI UDAD AUDAD SHEEP
  CHAMOIS
APACE FAST QUICK QUICKLY RAPIDLY
  SPEEDILY
APACHE YUMA PADUCA CIBECUE
  VAQUERO QUERECHO MESCALERO
APAGOGE ABDUCTION
APAP EPIPHI
APAR APARA BOLITA MATACO
APART BY OFF AWAY BOUT ELSE
  ALONE ALOOF ABROOM ASIDE RIVEN
  SOLUS SPLIT YTWYN ABREID
  ATWAIN LONELY SUNDRY ASUNDER

  ENISLED REMOVED SEVERAL
  SEVERED SEPARATE PIECEMEAL
  (— FROM) BARRING
  (TAKE —) UNRIG
  (WIDE —) ASPAR
  (WIDELY —) ABROAD
  (PREF.) CHORI DI DICH
APARTMENT BUT PAD WON DIGS
  FLAT HALL LOFT ROOM STEW WENE
  WONE WOON ABODE BOWER OECUS
  ORIEL ROOMS SALON SOLAR SUITE
  ANDRON CLOSET DECKER DINGLE
  DUPLEX GROTTO LYCEUM SALOON
  SINGLE SOLLAR SPENCE STANZA
  BUTTERY CHAMBER COCKPIT
  GALLERY MANSION PRIVACY
  BUILDING EPHEBEUM SHOWROOM
  SOLARIUM TENEMENT THALAMUS
  MAISONETTE
  (— FOR IDOL) TING
  (— IN CASTLE) BOWER
  (— IN CHURCH) SACRISTY
  (— OF WARSHIP) COCKPIT
  (BACHELOR —) GARCONNIERE
  (OUTER —) BUT
  (PRIVATE —) MAHAL PARADISE
  (RENTED —) LET
  (PL.) GYNAECEUM
APATHETIC CALM COLD COOL DEAD
  DOWF DULL BLASE DOWFF INERT
  STOIC GLASSY SUPINE TORPID
  ADENOID PASSIVE UNMOVED
  LISTLESS SLUGGISH LETHARGIC
  PERFUNCTORY
APATHY SLOTH ACEDIA CAFARD
  PHLEGM TORPOR LANGUOR
  DOLDRUMS DULLNESS LETHARGY
  OMISSION STOICISM STOLIDITY
  (EXTREME —) STUPOR
APATITE IJOLITE MOROXITE
  PHOSPHORITE
APAYAO ISNEG
APE KRA LAR PAN BOOR COPY DUPE
  FOOL MAHA MIME MOCK SHAM
  WILD BEROK CLOWN CRAZY MAGOT
  MIMIC ORANG PONGO PYGMY
  APELET BABOON GELADA GIBBON
  LANGUR MARTEN MARTIN MIRROR
  MONKEY OURANG PARROT PONGID
  SIMIAN SIMIID BUFFOON COPYCAT
  EMULATE GORILLA IMITATE PORTRAY
  PRIMATE SATYRUS SIAMANG
  DURUKULI IMITATOR MANTEGAR
  SIMULATE ORANGUTAN
  (— STUDY) PITHECOLOGY
  (GO —) FLIP FLIPOUT
  (PREF.) PITHEC(O)
  (SUFF.) PITHECUS
APEAK VERTICAL
APEIRON MATTER
APELIKE SIMIAN
APER BOAR MIME SNOB CLOWN
  MOCKER BUFFOON COPYCAT

APERCU DIGEST GLANCE PRECIS
SKETCH INSIGHT OUTLINE
APERIENT LAX OPENER CASCARA
APERIODIC DEADBEAT
APERITIF KIR WHET CINZANO
DUBONNET
APERTURE F EYE GAP OPE VUE
BOLE BORE HOLE LEAK PASS PORE
RENT RIMA SLIT SLOT VENT BREAK
CHASM CLEFT CRACK LIGHT MOUTH
PUPIL STOMA CUTOUT HIATUS
KEYWAY LOUVER WINDOW FISSURE
KEYHOLE OPENING ORIFICE OSTIOLE
PINHOLE PUNCTUM SWALLOW
TROMPIL APERTION FENESTRA
LOOPHOLE OVERTURE SPIRACLE
(— OF CORROLLA) RICTUS
APEX EPI PIN TIP TOP ACME AUGE
CONE CUSP NOON PEAK RUFF CREST
HIGHT PITCH POINT SPIRE APOGEE
CLIMAX CRISIS CUPULA GENION
HEIGHT SUMMIT TITLE VERTEX
ZENITH CACUMEN EVEREST PAPILLA
PUNCTUM PINNACLE
(— OF HELMET) CREST
(— OF OBELISK) PYRAMIDION
(PREF.) APIC(O)
(SUFF.) ACE
APHAREUS (BROTHER OF —)
LEUCIPPUS
(FATHER OF —) PERIERES
(MOTHER OF —) GORGOPHONE
(SON OF —) IDAS LYNCEUS
(WIFE OF —) ARENE
APHASIA ALALIA ALEXIA JARGON
APHEMIA ASYMBOLIA
APHID APHIS LOUSE APTERA BLIGHT
COLLIER DIMERAN MIGRANS
PUCERON BLACKFLY GREENFLY
GYNOPARA HOMOPTER
APHIDAS (DAUGHTER OF —) ANTIA
(FATHER OF —) ARCAS
(MOTHER OF —) ERATO MEGANIRA
CHRYSOPELIA
(SON OF —) ALEUS
APHIS ANTCOW GREENFLY
APHORISM SAW ADAGE AXIOM
GNOME MAXIM MOTTO SUTRA
SUTTA CLICHE DICTUM SAYING
WISDOM EPIGRAM PRECEPT
PROVERB APOTHEGM PISHOGUE
APHORISTIC GNOMIC
APHRODISIAC DEWTRY DAMIANA
VENEREAL VENEREOUS
APHRODITE VENUS CYPRIS URANIA
ANTHEIA MYLITTA CYTHEREA
PANDEMOS
(FATHER OF —) ZEUS JUPITER
(HUSBAND OF —) VULCAN
(LOVER OF —) ARES
(MOTHER OF —) DIONE
(SON OF —) EROS CUPID AENEAS
APIARIST SKEPPIST

APIARY HIVE SKEP BEEYARD
BEEHOUSE
APICULTURE BEEKEEPING
APIECE UP ALL PER APOP EACH
SERIATIM
APIKORES BECORESH
APIO ARRACACH ARRACACHA
APIOS SOIA SOJA GLYCINE
APIS HAPI
(FATHER OF —) APOLLO PHORONEUS
(MOTHER OF —) LAODICE
APISH SILLY FOPPISH AFFECTED
APITONG BAGAC HAPITON KERUING
APIUM UMBEL
APLENTY GALORE
APLITE HAPLITE
APLOMB TACT NERVE POISE SURETY
COOLNESS
APOCALYPSE DOOM SHOWING
REVELATION
APOCRISIARY RESPONSAL
APOCRYPHA (— BOOK) BEL EZRA
ABGAR ENOCH TOBIT BARUCH
DANIEL ESDRAS JUDITH AERAPHA
JUBILEES MANASSES MACCABEES
ECCLESIASTICUS
APOCRYPHAL SHAM FALSE UNREAL
DOUBTFUL FABULOUS FICTIOUS
APODAL FOOTLESS
APODE EEL
APOGEE ACME APEX AUGE PEAK
CLIMAX ZENITH
APOGON AMIA CARDINAL
APOLLO SUN PAEAN DELIUS
AGYIEUS APOLLON LYKEIOS
PATROUS PHOEBUS PYTHIUS
CYNTHIUS PYTHAEUS
(FATHER OF —) ZEUS JUPITER
(MOTHER OF —) LETO LATONA
(SISTER OF —) DIANA ARTEMIS
APOLLYON DEVIL SATAN ABADDON
APOLOGETIC SORRY
APOLOGUE MYTH FABLE STORY
APOLOGY PARABLE ALLEGORY
APOLOGY PLEA ALIBI AMENDS
EXCUSE PARDON REGRET PRETEXT
SCRUPLE APOLOGIA
(INTERJECTION EXPRESSING —)
OOPS WOOPS
APOPHONY ABLAUT
APOPHYGE SCAPE ESCAPE
APOPLEXY ESCA SHOCK STROKE
POPLESIE
APOSTASY FALL LAPSE
APOSTATE RAT LAPSED CONVERT
HERETIC PERVERT SECEDER
DEFECTOR DESERTER DISLOYAL
RECREANT RENEGADE TURNCOAT
APOSTATIZE DESERT
APOSTLE ESCAPE TEACHER DISCIPLE
FOLLOWER PREACHER
(BIBLICAL —) JOHN JUDE LEVI PAUL
DENIS JAMES JUDAS PETER SIMON

ANDREW PHILIP THOMAS DIDYMUS
MATTHEW BARNABAS MATTHIAS
APOSTLE BIRD CATBIRD
APOSTROPHE TUISM TURNWAY
TURNTALE
APOTHECARY CHEMIC SPICER
CHEMICK DRUGGIST
APOTHECIUM CUP PELTA TRICA
SHIELD ARDELLA LIRELLA PATELLA
APOTHEGM SAW DICT ADAGE
AXIOM GNOME MAXIM SUTRA
DICTUM SAYING SUTTAH PROVERB
APHORISM SENTENCE
APOTHEOSIS DEIFICATION
CONSECRATION
APOTHEOSIZE DEIFY EXALT
ELEVATE GLORIFY CANONIZE
APPAIM (FATHER OF —) NADAB
APPALL STUN APPAL DAUNT SHOCK
DISMAY REDUCE REVOLT WEAKEN
ASTOUND DEPRESS DISGUST
DISMISS HORRIFY PETRIFY TERRIFY
AFFRIGHT ASTONISH ENFEEBLE
FRIGHTEN OVERCOME
APPALLING AWFUL AWESOME
FEARFUL TERRIBLE TERRIFIC
APPANAGE GRANT ADJUNCT
APANAGE
APPARATUS AID BOX GUN LOG SET
ADON DRAG ETNA FAKE GEAR GRIP
HECK HELM LAMP LIFT STOW TIRE
TOOL BURET GANCH HOIST HORSE
LEECH RELAY SCUBA SHEAR SIREN
SONAR SPRAY STILL STOVE SWING
BUDDLE BUFFER COILER COOKER
DEVICE DINGUS ENGINE FEEDER
FILTER FOGGER GADGET GEYSER
GRAITH LADDER LIFTER MILKER
ORRERY OUTFIT REFLUX RUDDER
SEESAW SHEARS SMOKER SMUDGE
TACKLE TIPPLE TREMIE TROMPE
AERATOR AIRBATH ALEMBIC
APPAREL AUTOMAT BAGGAGE
BALANCE BASCULE BURETTE
DERRICK ECHELON FURNACE
GASOGEN GRILLER HOISTER
INHALER ISOTRON MACHINE
MEGAFOG PINCERS PRESSER
SOUNDER SOXHLET SPRAYER
STEAMER STIRRER TELEPIX
TREMOLO TRIMMER UTENSIL
AGITATOR AQUALUNG BLOWDOWN
CALUTRON CONVEYER CONVEYOR
CRYOSTAT DIALYZER DIAPHOTE
DIGESTER DRENCHER DUMBBELL
EOLIPILE EQUIPAGE ERGOSTAT
GASIFIER GAZOGENE INJECTOR
ISOSCOPE JACQUARD OSMOGENE
OZONIZER PULMOTOR PURIFIER
RECORDER REDUCTOR REHEATER
SCRUBBER SOFTENER STRIPPER
HANGLIDER ABSORPTIOMETER
(— IN STOMACH OF LOBSTER) LADY

(SEGMENTAL —) BRAINSTEM
(SWIMMING —) SCUBA
(SUFF.) STAT(IC)(ICS)
APPAREL DECK FARE GARB GEAR
ROBE SECT TIRE WEAR WEDE ADORN
ARRAY BESEE CLOTH DRESS EQUIP
HABIT MITER TUNIC ATTIRE CLOTHE
GRAITH INFULA OUTFIT PARURE
ROBING CLOBBER COSTUME
FURNISH GARMENT HARNESS
PREPARE RAIMENT VESTURE
CLOTHING FOOTWEAR HEADWEAR
WARDROBE
(ECCLESIASTIC —) FANON ORALE
MANIPLE CHASUBLE CORPORAL
(HEAD —) MILLINERY
(MILITARY —) WARENTMENT
(MOURNING —) WEEDS
(RICH —) ARRAY
APPARENT OPEN BREEM BREME
CLEAR OVERT PLAIN FORMAL
PARENT PATENT PHANIC CERTAIN
EVIDENT GLARING OBVIOUS
SEEMING SHALLOW VISIBLE
DISTINCT ILLUSORY MANIFEST
PALPABLE PROBABLE SEMBLANT
SEMBLABLE OSTENSIBLE
APPARENTLY
(PREF.) QUASI
APPARITION HUE HANT SHOW
DREAM FANCY FETCH GHOST HAUNT
IMAGE LARVA PHASM SHADE SHAPE
SPOOK ASPECT DOUBLE IDOLUM
SOWLTH SPIRIT SPRITE STOUND
SWARTH TAISCH THURSE VISION
WRAITH DISPLAY EIDOLON FANTASY
FEATURE PHANTOM SPECTER
SPECTRE EPIPHANY ILLUSION
PHANTASM PRESENCE REVENANT
SPECTRUM SEMBLANCE
APPARITOR BEADLE PARURE
PARITOR SUMMONER
APPEAL ASK BEG BID CRY CALL CASE
PLEA SEEK SUIT APPLY CHARM
CLEPE REFER SPEAK ACCUSE
ADJURE AVOUCH INVOKE PRAYER
SUMMON ADDRESS CONJURE
ENTREAT IMPLORE REQUEST SOLICIT
APPROACH ENTREATY PETITION
ADJURATION
(— FOR CONTRIBUTIONS) WHIP
(— FOR HELP) SOS
(— FOR QUARTER) KAMERAD
(— TO) APPLY AVOUCH INVOKE
ARRAIGN
(SEX —) IT OOMPH
(SOLEMN —) OATH
APPEALING CUTE NICE CATCHY
CLEVER NELLOW CUNNING
SUGARED PLEASANT
(STRIKINGLY —) ZINGY
APPEAR BID CAR EYE GET COME
DAWN FARE LOOK LOOM MAKE

MEET PEER REAR RISE SEEM WALK
ARISE ENTER ISSUE KITHE KYTHE
OCCUR SOUND THINK ARRIVE
BESEEM EMERGE INFORM REGARD
SPRING BLOSSOM COMPEAR
DEVELOP OUTCROP RESEMBLE
(— ABOVE GROUND) BREER BRAIRD
(— AND DISAPPEAR) COOK
(— BETTER) GAIN
(— BRIEFLY) GLINT
(— DIRECTLY BEFORE) AFFRONT
(— FAINTLY) GLIMMER
(— SUDDENLY) BURST
(— UNEXPECTEDLY) BLOOM IRRUPT
(PREF.) PHANER(O) PHANTA PHANTO

APPEARANCE AIR CUT HUE CAST
FARE FORM GARB IDEA LATE LEEN
LOOK MIEN SHOW VIEW BLUSH
COLOR EIDOS FAVOR FRONT GUISE
HABIT LOOKS PHASE PHASM SHAPE
SIGHT SOUND SPICE-ASPECT EFFECT
FACIES FAVOUR MANNER OBJECT
OSTENT REGARD VISAGE ARRIVAL
DISPLAY FARRAND FASHION
FEATURE GLIMPSE OUTSIDE
RESPECT SHOWING SPECIES
ARTEFACT ARTIFACT EPIPHANY
ILLUSION LIKENESS PRESENCE
PRETENSE SEMBLANCE
(— OF LIGHT ON HAIR) HAG
(BRILLANT —) SHINE
(CLOUDED —) HAZE CHILL
(CONSPICUOUS —) FIGURE
(DISTINCTIVE —) AURA
(FIRST —) DAWN DEBUT SPRING
(GENERAL —) RIG
(GUEST —) CAMEO
(IMPOVERISHED —) BEGGARY
(MERE —) INTENTIONAL
(MOCK —) SIMULACRUM
(MOTTLED —) ROE DAPPLE
(MOTTLED SKY —) BLINK
(OF NEAT —) PREPPY PREPPIE
(OUTWARD —) FACE SEEM SHOW
FACADE APPAREL BALLOON
SEEMING SURFACE
(PERSONAL —) PRESENCE
(SERIES OF —S) ROAD
(STRIPED —) ROE
(SUPERNATURAL —) APPARITION
(SURFACE —) TOUR BLOOM
(UNGAINLY —) ANGULARITY
(VAGUE —) BLUR
(PREF.) SPECTRO
(SUFF.) OPSIA OPSIO OPSIS OPSY
PHANE PHANOUS PHANT PHANY

APPEASE LAY PAY CALM EASE HUSH
SATE ALLAY ALONE ATONE MEASE
PEACE PEASE QUIET SLAKE STILL
DEFRAY GENTLE MEEKEN MODIFY
PACIFY PLEASE SOFTEN SOOTHE
ASSUAGE CONTENT DULCIFY

GRATIFY MOLLIFY PLACATE SATISFY
STICKLE SUFFICE SWEETEN
MITIGATE PROPITIATE
(— APPETITE) STAY

APPEASEMENT MUNICHISM

APPELLATION NAME TERM GODDY
STYLE TITLE APPEAL CALLING
EPITHET GOODMAN SURNAME
COGNOMEN METRONYM NICKNAME

APPEND ADD PIN TAG CLIP HANG
JOIN TACK AFFIX ANNEX ADJOIN
ATTACH FASTEN AUGMENT POSTFIX
SUBJOIN

APPENDAGE ARM AWN FIN LEG TAB
TAG ARIL BARB CAUD FLAP HOOK
HORN LIMB LOBE SPUR TAIL AFFIX
BEARD CAUDA CERAS EXITE RIDER
SCALE TROLL WHISK CERCUS
CIRRUS CORONA ELATER ENDITE
LAGENA LIGULE PALPUS PAPPUS
STIPEL STYLET SUFFIX UROPOD
ADJUNCT ANTENNA AURICLE
CODICIL EARLOBE EMBLAST FIXTURE
FURCULA GONOPOD HOUSING
MALELLA PENDANT STIPULE
SWIMMER THIMBLE TRAILER
WINGLET ADDITION ADHERENT
ASCIDIUM BRACHIUM EMPODIUM
FILAMENT GNATHITE PEDIPALP
PENDICLE PHYLLOID PREDELLA
RHABDITE SYNTROPE MAXILLIPED
(— ON MOCCASIN) TRAILER
(EAR-SHAPED —) AURICLE
(PL.) ADNEXA ANNEXA FORCEPS

APPENDIX EKE ANNEX LABEL
APPEND VERMIX AURICLE CODICIL
PENDANT ADDENDUM AURICULA
EPILOGUE

APPERCEPTION RECOGNITION

APPERTAIN LIE FALL REFER BELONG
EFFEIR RELATE CONCERN PERTAIN

APPETITE MAW YEN LUST PICA
TUCK URGE WILL ZEST BELLY BLOOD
GORGE GREED GUSTO TASTE TWIST
BULIMY DESIRE FAMINE GENIUS
GODOWN HUNGER LIKING OREXIS
RELISH STROKE TALENT BULIMIA
CRAVING EDACITY LONGING
PASSION STOMACH SWALLOW
WANTING CUPIDITY FONDNESS
GULOSITY TENDENCY
(— LOSS) ANOREXIA
(ANIMAL —) BLOOD
(CANINE —) PHAGEDENA
(EXCESSIVE —) LIMOSIS GULOSITY
POLYPHAGIA
(PERVERTED —) MALACIA
(RAVENOUS —) LIMOSIS
(SUFF.) OREXIA PHIL(A)(AE)(E)(IA)
(ISM)(IST)(OUS)(US)

APPETIZER WET WHET SAUCE
CANAPE RAMAKI RELISH RUMAKI

SAVORY CEVICHE SASHIMI APERITIF COCKTAIL DUBONNET
(CHICKEN LIVER —) RUMAKI
APPETIZING NICE GUSTY SAVORY GUSTFUL GUSTABLE PALATABLE
APPLAUD HUM CLAP LAUD RISE ROOT RUFF CHEER EXTOL HUZZA PRAISE ACCLAIM APPROVE COMMENT ENDORSE HOSANNA PLAUDIT
(GROUP HIRED TO —) CLAQUE
APPLAUDER
(PL.) CLAQUE
APPLAUSE CLAP HAND BRAVO CHEER ECLAT HUZZA SALVO HURRAH PRAISE ACCLAIM OVATION CLAPPING
(— WITH THE FEET) RUFF
APPLE MAC PIP CRAB OHIA POME COPEI JAMBO BEEFIN BIFFIN CODLIN DOUCIN ESOPUS GOLDIN KARELA KAVIKA MACUPA MAKOPA PIPPIN PUFFIN RENNET RUSSET BALDWIN BEAUFIN CODLING COSTARD FAMEUSE GOLDING PEELING POMEROY RAMBURE RIBSTON RUDDOCK WAGENER WEALTHY WINESAP AMPALAYA COCCAGEE CORTLAND GREENING JONATHAN MCINTOSH NONESUCH PARADISE PEARMAIN POMANDER POROPORO QUEENING REINETTE ROSACEAN SWEETING WHITSOUR QUARENDEN QUARANTINE
(— OF PERU) JIMSON JIMPSON SHOOFLY
(— OF THE EYE) PUPIL
(BITTER —) COLOCYNTH
(CRAB —) CRAB SCRAB WHARRE POWITCH
(CRUSHED —) POMACE
(EMU —) COLANE
(GOLDEN —) BEL BAEL
(LIKE AN —) POMACEOUS
(PEARLIKE —) SORB
(PEELED —) DUMPLING
(SHRIVELED —) CRUMPLING
(SLICED DRIED —S) SNITS SNITZ SCHNITZ
(SMALL —) CODLIN CODLING
(SMALL —S) GRIGGLES
(STUNTED —) SCRUNT
(THORN —) MAD METEL
(PREF.) POMI POMO
APPLEBERRY DUMPLING
APPLEJOHN DEUSAN DEUZAN
APPLE-POLISH BROWNNOSE
APPLIANCE GEAR GRAB IRON TOOL BRACE CLAMP DEVIL FLIER FLYER GLOBE SHADE BONNET BREWER DEVICE ENGINE FABRIC GADGET GAITER JUICER SPLINT WINDLE CHANGER MACHINE SCRAPER

STOPPER UTENSIL BALANCER DEVIATOR
(PL.) FURNITURE
APPLICABLE APT FIT MEET PROPER USEFUL FITTING PLIABLE APPOSITE RELATIVE RELEVANT SUITABLE
(STRICTLY —) PROPER
(UNIVERSALLY —) CATHOLIC
(WIDELY —) BROAD
APPLICANT PROSPECT
APPLICATION USE DAUB FORM BLANK TOPIC APPEAL EFFORT ADDRESS EPITHEM REQUEST EPITHEME LENITIVE PETITION PRACTICE SEDULITY
(— OF KNOWLEDGE) PRACTICE PRACTISE
(— OF TESTS) DOCIMASY
(— OF THE MIND) STUDY
(— TO WRONG PURPOSE) ABUSE
(MEDICINAL —) PLASTER DRESSING FRONTING LENITIVE
(MENTAL —) INTENTION
APPLICATOR COLPOSTAT
APPLIED (CLOSELY —) ACCUMBENT
(PREF.) TECHNO
APPLIQUE DAG DAGGE ATTACH DESIGN ORNAMENT
APPLY ASK LAY PLY PUT RUB SET USE BEAR BEND CLAP DAUB GIVE HOLD MOVE SEEK TOIL TURN WORK ADAPT GRIND IMPLY LABOR LIKEN REFER SMEAR ADDICT APPEAL APPOSE BESTOW BETAKE BUCKLE COMPLY DEVOTE DIRECT EMPLOY EXTEND RESORT ADHIBIT COMPARE CONFORM IMPRESS OVERLAY PERTAIN REQUEST SOLICIT UTILIZE DEDICATE DISPENSE MINISTER PETITION
(— BRAKE) BUR
(— COSMETICS) DO POP
(— GRAPHITE) BLACKLEAD
(— GREASE) ARM
(— HOT CLOTHS) FOMENT
(— IMPROPERLY) ABUSE
(— ONESELF) ATTEND INTEND MUCKLE ADDRESS
(— PIGMENT) DRAG
(— TO) CONSULT CONTACT
APPOGGIATURA BACKFALL ACCIACCATURA
(DOUBLE —) FALL
APPOINT ARM FIX SET CALL DECK GIVE MAKE NAME ALLOT ARRAY AWARD COOPT CREST DIGHT ELECT ENACT EQUIP INSET PITCH PLACE POINT SHAPE SLATE ASSIGN ASSIZE ATTACH CREATE DECREE DEPUTE DETAIL DEVISE DIRECT ENTAIL ORDAIN OUTFIT SETTLE STEVEN TAILYE ARRAIGN CONFIRM DESTINE

DISPOSE FURNISH GAZETTE
RESOLVE TAILZIE DELEGATE
DEPUTIZE INDICATE NOMINATE
ORDINATE
(— A CLERIC) COLLATE
(— BEFOREHAND) STALL
(— TO BENEFICE) PRESENT
APPOINTED DUE DATIVE
APPOINTEE PLACEMAN
APPOINTMENT SET DATE BERTH
ORDER TRYST BILLET OFFICE STEVEN
COMMAND STATION CREATION
DELEGACY POSITION
(— OF HEIR) INSTITUTION
APPORTION LOT DEAL DOLE MARK
METE PART RATE ALLOT AWARD
CAVEL GRANT PARAL SHARE SHIFT
WEIGH APPLOT ASSESS ASSIGN
DIVIDE PARCEL RATION TAVERN
ARRANGE BALANCE QUARTER
ALLOCATE DESCRIBE ADMEASURE
PROPORTION
APPORTIONMENT DIVISION
APPOSITE APT PAT COGENT TIMELY
GERMANE INCIDENT RELATIVE
RELEVANT SUITABLE
APPRAISAL APPRIZAL
APPRAISE GAGE LOVE METE RATE
ASSAY GAUGE JUDGE PRICE PRIZE
VALUE ASSESS ESTEEM EVALUE
PONDER PRAISE SIZEUP SURVEY
ADJUDGE ANALYZE COMMEND
ESTIMATE EVALUATE
APPRECIABLE ANY SENSIBLE
PERCEPTIBLE
APPRECIATE DIG FEEL LOVE JUDGE
PRIZE RAISE SAVOR TASTE VALUE
ADMIRE ESTEEM SAVOUR ADVANCE
APPRIZE APPROVE CHERISH REALIZE
INCREASE TREASURE
APPRECIATION EYE GUSTO SENSE
CONCEIT PERCEPTION
APPRECIATIVE AWAKE GRATEFUL
(— OF BEAUTY) ESTHETIC AESTHETIC
APPREHEND COP GET LAG NAB SEE
FEAR HEAR KNOW NOTE SCAN TAKE
VIEW CATCH DREAD GRASP GRIPE
INTUE SEIZE ARREST BEHOLD
DETAIN INTEND INTUIT BELIEVE
CAPTURE CONCEIT ENDOUTE
FORESEE IMAGINE REALIZE RECEIVE
SENSATE SUPPOSE CONCEIVE
DISCOVER OVERTAKE PERCEIVE
APPREHENDED GRIPPIT
APPREHENSIBLE NOETIC SENSATE
SENSIBLE
APPREHENSION CARE FEAR FRAY
PAIN PANG SCAN WERE ALARM
DOUBT DREAD FANCY WORRY
ARREST DISMAY NOESIS ANXIETY
CAPTURE CONCERN PRESAGE
SUSPECT DISTRUST MISTRUST
SUSPENSE COGNITION PREHENSION

APPREHENSIVE APT ANTSY JUMPY
FEARED MORBID ANXIOUS FEARFUL
JEALOUS NERVOUS STREAKY
UPTIGHT DOUBTFUL SOLICITOUS
APPRENTICE CUB BIND BOOT SNOB
TYRO CADET DEVIL BURSCH HELPER
JOCKEY NOVICE BANKMAN
GROMMET LEARNER TRAINEE
WAISTER APRENDIZ BEGINNER
JACKAROO PRENTICE SERVITOR
TURNOVER
(— ON SHIP) BRASSBOUNDER
(LONDON —) FLATCAP
(SHOEMAKER'S —) SNOB
APPRENTICESHIP SERVITUDE
APPRISE WARN LEARN TEACH
ADVISE INFORM NOTIFY REVEAL
APPRIZE ACQUAINT DISCLOSE
INSTRUCT
APPROACH TRY ADIT BUMP BURN
CHAT COME COST DRAW NEAR NERE
NIGH ROAD ABORD BOARD CLOSE
COAST ESSAY STALK VERGE ACCEDE
ACCESS ACCOST ADVENT ANIMUS
APPEAL BORDER BREAST BROACH
COMING GATHER GONEAR IMPEND
PROACH TRENCH ADVANCE
AGGRESS APPULSE CONTACT
PREFACE SEAGATE SUCCEED
CONVERGE NEIGHBOR ONCOMING
(— FROM WINDWARD) BEAR
(— GAME) DRAW
(— HOSTILELY) SWAY
(— NEAR) TOUCH
(— OF DEATH) FIT
(— OF NIGHT) FALL
(— TENDENCY) ADIENCE
(GOLF —) SHIPSHOT
(INDIRECT —) FEELER
(INVITING —) PASS
APPROACHABLE COMMON
AFFABLE ACCESSIBLE
APPROACHING LIKE COMING
TOWARD ONCOMING
APPROBATION TEST FAVOR
PROOF TRIAL ASSENT FAVOUR
LOANGE PRAISE REGARD REPUTE
PLAUDIT APPLAUSE APPROVAL
SANCTION
APPROPRIATELY APROPOS
APPROPRIATE ADD APT DUE FIT
LAY PAT AKIN CRIB FEAT GOOD GRAB
GRIP HELP JUST MEET SINK SUIT
TAKE ALLOT ANNEX FITTY HAPPY
RIGHT STEAL USURP ASSELF
ASSIGN ASSUME BORROW DECENT
DEVOTE DEVOUR DIGEST GATHER
GENTIL KINDLY PILFER PIRATE
POCKET PROPER TIMELY WORTHY
APPROVE APROPOS CABBAGE
CONDIGN CONVERT FITTING
GERMANE GRABBLE GRADELY
IMPOUND PREEMPT PURLOIN

RELATED SECRETE SWALLOW
ACCROACH APPOSITE ARROGATE
BECOMING DESERVED EMBEZZLE
GRACEFUL HANDSOME IDONEOUS
PECULIAR PROPERTY RELEVANT
RIGHTFUL SUITABLE
(— UNLAWFULLY) HEIST STEAL
(MOST —) CHOICE
APPROPRIATED ASSUMED
PECULIAR
APPROPRIATENESS APTNESS
DECENCY FITNESS APTITUDE
(NICE —) ELEGANCE
APPROPRIATION FUND VOTE
DEVOTION
(FRAUDULENT —) CON
EMBEZZLEMENT
APPROVAL AMEN ECLAT ASSENT
ESTEEM APPROOF CONSENT
PLAUDIT SUPPORT APPLAUSE
BLESSING SANCTION SUFFRAGE
AGREEMENT
(EXPRESSION OF —) VOILA
(FLIGHT —) AOK
APPROVE DO OK BUY DIG TRY
AMEN HAVE LIKE OKAY OKEH PASS
TEST VOTE ALLOW BLESS CLEAR
FAVOR PROVE VALUE ACCEPT
ADMIRE BISHOP CONCUR RATIFY
AGREEON APPLAUD CERTIFY
COMMEND CONFIRM CONSENT
ENDORSE EXHIBIT INDORSE
SUPPORT ACCREDIT MANIFEST
SANCTION
APPROVED TRYE EXPERT PROBAL
ACCEPTED ORTHODOX
(NOT —) OUT
APPROVING HEARTY
APPROXIMATE NEAR ABOUT CIRCA
CLOSE COAST ROUGH COARSE
GENERAL NOMINAL APPROACH
ESTIMATE
APPROXIMATELY SAY AWAY GAIN
MUCH NIGH SOME ABOUT CIRCA
ALMOST AROUND NEARLY TOWARD
CRUDELY ROUGHLY
APPROXIMATING COMPARATIVE
APPROXIMATION CIRCA
COUNTERFEIT
APPURTENANCE GEAR ANNEX
ASSIGN EFFEIR ADJUNCT COMFORT
APPANAGE PENDICLE
(PL.) ADDENDA
APRICOT COT UME ANSU MUME
ABRICOCK BLENHEIM
(DRIED —S) MEBOS MEEBOS
APRIORI PURE
APRON BIB CAP BASE BOOT BRAT
DICK RAMP SLOP TAYO TIER COVER
EPHOD BARVEL BISHOP CANVAS
DAIDLE DICKEY NAPRON RUNWAY
SHIELD TARMAC TOUSER BRATTLE
CANVASS DAIDLIE GREMIAL TABLIER

LAMBSKIN PINAFORE PRASKEEN
BARMCLOTH
(— OF FURNITURE) PETTICOAT
(— OF SEAT) FALL
(CHILD'S —) TIER BISWOP SLIPPER
(LEATHER —) DICK DICKY BARVEL
DICKEY BARMFEL BARVELL
BARMSKIN
(MASON'S —) LAMBSKIN
(SILKEN —) GREMIAL
(PL.) ARMITAS
APROPOS APT FIT PAT MEET TIMELY
RELEVANT SUITABLE
APSE BEMA APSIS NICHE CHEVET
CONCHA EXEDRA RECESS EXHEDRA
PROTHESIS
APSIS APSE AUGE
APSYRTUS (FATHER OF —) AEETES
(MOTHER OF —) IDYIA ASTERODIA
(SISTER OF —) MEDEA
APT FIT PAT YAP ABLE DEFT FAIN FEAT
GLEG KEEN VAIN WONT ADEPT
ALERT HAPPY PRONE QUICK READY
ASPERT CLEVER DOCILE KITTLE
LIABLE LIKELY PRETTY SUITED
TOWARD APROPOS CAPABLE FITTING
IDONEAL WILLING APPOSITE
DEXTROUS DISPOSED HANDSOME
IDONEOUS INCLINED POIGNANT
PRACTIVE PREPARED SKILLFUL
SUITABLE
(— TO CHANGE) LABILE
(— TO TURN) WALT
APTERYX KIWI RATITE KIVIKIVI
KIWIKIWI
APTITUDE ART BENT GIFT HEAD
TURN CRAFT FLAIR HABIT KNACK
SKILL VERVE GENIUS TALENT
ABILITY CONDUCI FACULTY FITNESS
LEANING CAPACITY INSTINCT
TENDENCY
APTLY PAT
APTNESS GIFT KNACK SKILL
APTITUDE FELICITY
APUS CYPSELUS MICROPUS
AQUARIUS SKINKER
AQUATIC (RARE —) MONKSEAL
AQUEDUCT AQUA DUCT CANAL
AQUAGE SPECUS CHANNEL
CONDUIT PASSAGE
(— OF SILVIUS) ITER
AQUEOUS HYDATOID WATERISH
AQUILA (WIFE OF —) PRISCILLA
AQUILANT (BROTHER OF —)
GRYPHON
ARA MACAW
(FATHER OF —) JETHER
ARAB AHL AUS IBAD OMAN SLEB
WAIF ARABY GAMIN NOMAD SAUDI
TATAR SEMITE SLUBBI URCHIN
ARABIAN BEDOUIN SARACEN
SOLUBBI AZZAZAME KABABISH
LARRIKIN SLOUBBIE YEMENITE

ARABELLA (CHARACTER IN —)
MATTEO ZDENKA WALDNER
ARABELLA MANDRYKA
(COMPOSER OF —) STRAUSS
ARABESQUE ORNATE MORISCO

ARABIA

COIN: LARI CARAT DINAR KABIK
RIYAL
DESERT: NYD ANKAF DEHNA NAFUD
NEFUD
DISTRICT: ASIR
GARMENT: ABA HAIK CABAAN
BURNOUS
GODDESS: ALLAT
HOLY CITY: MECCA MEDINA
HOLY LAND: HEJAZ
ISLAND: SOCOTRA
JUDGE: CADI
KINGDOM: NEJD
MEASURE: DEN SAA FERK KIST ACHIR
BARID CABDA CAFIZ COVID CUDDY
MAKUK QASAB TEMAN WOIBE
ZUDDA ARTABA ASSBAA COVIDO
FEDDAN GARIBA GHALVA CAPHITE
FARSAKH FARSANG KILADJA
MARHALE NUSFIAH
MOUNTAIN: NEBO HOREB SINAI
PORT: ADEN
RULER: AMIR EMIR AMEER EMEER
STATE: ASIR OMAN YEMEN KUWAIT
TOWN: ABHA ADEN BEDA BERA HAIL
RIAD SANA TAIF DUBAI HAUTA
HOFUF JIDDA MECCA MOCHA QATIF
TAIZZ YENBO ANAIZA MANAMA
MATRAH MEDINA RIYADH SALALA
SHAQRA BURAIDA HODEIDA
MUKALLA ONEIZAH SHARJAH
TRIBE: AUS ASIR IRAD TEMA KEDAR
DIENDEL SHUKRIA
WEIGHT: ROTL BAHAR CHEKI KELLA
MAUND NASCH NEVAT OCQUE
OUKIA RATEL TOMAN VAKIA
BOKARD DIRHEM MISKAL FARSALAH

ARABIC CARSHUNI GARSHUNI
KARSHUNI THAMUDIC
(— ALPHABET) BA FA HA RA TA YA ZA
AYN DAD DAL JIM KAF KHA LAM MIM
NUN QAF SAD SIN THA WAW ZAY
ALIF DHAL SHIN GHAYN
ARABLE FERTILE PLOWABLE
TILLABLE
ARACHNID CRAB MITE TICK TAINT
ACARID ACARUS CARTER SPIDER
CARTARE OCTOPOD PEDIPALP
SCORPION SOLPUGID
PSEUDOSCORPION
ARACHNOID KINGCRAB
ARAD (FATHER OF —) BERIAH
ARAGONITE ALABASTER
ARAIN ARRAND
ARAKANESE MAGHI

ARAM (FATHER OF —) ESROM
HEZRON KEMUEL SHAMER
ARAMAIC SYRIAC MANDAEAN
(— TRANSLATION) TARGUM
ARAN (BROTHER OF —) UZ
(FATHER OF —) DISHAN
ARANEA EPEIRA
ARAPAIMA PIRARUCU
ARAPONGA BELLBIRD
ARAROBA ZEBRAWOOD
ARAROS (FATHER OF —)
ARISTOPHANES
ARAUCANIAN AUCA PAMPA
MAPOCHE MOLUCHE PAMPERO
PICUNCHE
ARAWA AOTEA MATATUA
ARAWAK ARUA BARE URAN ARAUA
BAURE CAMPA CHANE GUANA INERI
SIUSI BAINOA BANIVA GUINAU
IGNERI GOAJIRO IPURINA CAQUETIO
CUSTENAU
ARBALEST BALISTER CROSSBOW
ARBITER REF UMP JUDGE CRITIC
ODDMAN UMPIRE ADVISER
DAYSMAN ODDSMAN OVERMAN
REFEREE DICTATOR STICKLER
ARBITRAGE SHUNTING
ARBITRARY SEVERE THETIC
WILLFUL ABSOLUTE DESPOTIC
MASTERLY
(NOT —) FREE
ARBITRATE DECIDE MEDIATE
ARBITRATION DAYMENT
ARBITRATOR ARB REF JUDGE
UMPIRE ARBITER MUNSIFF REFEREE
MEDIATOR
ARBOR BAR AXLE BEAM ABODE
BOWER SHAFT STAFF STALK TRAIL
ARBOUR BOWERY GARDEN HERBER
PANDAL RAMADA VOIDER BERCEAU
HARBOUR MANDREL MANDRIL
ORCHARD PERGOLA RETREAT
SPINDLE TRELLIS FRESCADE
TONNELLE
ARBORVITAE AKEKI ALERCE
ARBUTUS IVY MAYFLOWER
ARC BOW ARCH BEND FOIL HALO
CURVE HANCE ORBIT SPARK SWING
FOGBOW FOLIUM OCTANT RADIAN
COMPASS RAINBOW FROSTBOW
(— OF HORIZON) AZIMUTH
AMPLITUDE
(ELECTRIC —) SPARK
ARCA BOX CHEST PATEN ARCULA
ARCADE ORB AVENUE LOGGIA
STREET GALLERY PORTICO
ARCATURE CLOISTER
ARCADIAN CAJUN
ARCANE RUNIC HIDDEN SECRET
MYSTERIOUS
ARCAS (FATHER OF —) ZEUS
JUPITER
(MOTHER OF —) CALLISTO

ARCESIUS (FATHER OF —) ZEUS
JUPITER CEPHALUS
(MOTHER OF —) PROCRIS EURYODIA
(SON OF —) LAERTES
ARCH ARC BOW COY SET SLY BACK
BEND COPE COVE DOME HARP HOOP
IRIS LEER OGEE PASS PEND PERT
SPAN ARCUS CHIEF CURVE FAULD
GREAT HANCE HUNCH INBOW
JOWEL OGIVE PAUKY PAWKY POKEY
PRIME ROACH SAUCY SWEEP VAULT
ARCADE BRIDGE CALCAR CAMBER
CLEVER DIADEM FOGBOW FORNIX
GIRDLE IMPISH INVERT LANCET
MANTEL SPRING SUNBOW WICKET
ZYGOMA ARCHWAY CONCAVE
CUNNING EMINENT GATEWAY
ROGUISH SEGMENT SQUINCH
SUPPORT TESTUDO TRIUMPH
WAGGISH ALVEOLAR ESPIEGLE
FOGEATER OVERCAST SCUNCHEON
(— OF FIREPLACE) MANTEL
MANTELTREE
(— OF SKY) FIRMAMENT
(— OF WATER) CURL TUBE TUNNEL
(DENTAL —) ARCADE
(LOGGING —) SULKY
(PART OF —) PIER CHORD IMPOST
PILLAR ABUTMENT EXTRADOS
INTRADOS KEYSTONE SKEWBACK
SPANDREL SPRINGER VOUSSOIR
(POINTED —) OGIVE
(PL.) SUBARARCUATION
ARCHAEOCYTE SORITE
ARCHAEOLOGIST POTHUNTER
PREHISTORIAN
AMERICAN CLAY LOVE DAVIS EVANS
HAWES SHEAR SOREN BARBER
BUTLER GLUECK GORDON GORMAN
HAYNES HEWETT HOLMES KIDDER
MORELY PARKER PORTER SNYDER
SQUIER MERRIAM NUTTALL REISNER
SAVILLE SPEISER ALBRIGHT
BREASTED CUMMINGS HANFMANN
ROBINSON STERRETT THOMPSON
BANDELIER CARPENTER
MOOREHEAD RICHARDSON
FROTHINGHAM
AUSTRALIAN CHILDE
AUSTRIAN ARNETH STUDNICZKA
CANADIAN CURRELLY
CZECH HROZNY
DANISH ZOEGA MULLER POULSEN
WORSAAE BRONDSTED
MATHIASSEN STEENSTRUP
DUTCH GRUYTERE
ENGLISH BELL COOK GANN GELL
HALL BIBBY BUDGE EVANS RYMER
STEIN CARTER CHILDE LAYARD
MURRAY NEWTON PETRIE WARREN
BEAZLEY BRAYLEY BURROWS
DAWKINS DODWELL FELLOWS
GARDNER HERBERT HOGARTH
PENROSE WHEELER WOOLLEY
GARSTANG HAMILTON LAWRENCE
MALLOWAN RIDGEWAY STEPHENS
THOMPSON BABINGTON
FRENCH LEBAS MAURY PUGIN
VOGUE BORDES BREUIL CAGNAT
CHOISY CLARAC COCHET FORBIN
GAIDOZ LARTET MORGAN PERROT
SAULCY BABELON CHANTRE
CHARNAY DELATRE HOMOLLE
LEBLANT PEIRESC POTTIER
BERTRAND DIEULAFOY LENORMANT
DECHELETTE QUATREMERE
WADDINGTON LECHEVALIER
GERMAN MAU ROSS TREU ADLER
BRAUN BRUNN CONZE SARRE
ANDRAE BECKER HELBIG HILLER
MULLER NISSEN SCHOLL CURTIUS
GERHARD LASAULX WELCKER
WIEGAND BENNDORF BOTTIGER
KOLDEWEY KOSSINNA PETERSEN
ESSENWEIN LOESCHCKE MICHAELIS
SCHLIEMANN FURTWANGLER
WINCKELMANN
GREEK TSOUNTAS
ICELANDIC MAGNUSSON
IRISH STOKES ODONOVAN
MACALISTER
ISRAELI YADIN SUKENIK
ITALIAN BONI LANZI ROSSI CANINA
CESNOLA FIORELLI LANCIANI
MARUCCHI VISCONTI
POLISH MICHALOWSKI
RUSSIAN KOPPEN POGODIN
CHWOLSON
SCOTTISH RAMSAY BURGESS
SWEDISH BRENNER MONTELIUS
SWISS KELLER
ARCHAIC OLD ANCIENT ANTIQUE
HISTORIC OBSOLETE
(PREF.) PALE
ARCHAISM (USE OF —S)
GADZOOKERY
ARCHANGEL SATAN URIEL GABRIEL
MICHAEL RAPHAEL HIERARCH
ARCHBISHOP HATTO PRELATE
PRIMATE ORDINARY
ARCHDEMON BELFAGOR
BELFAZOR
ARCHDIOCESE EPARCHY
ARCHDUKE ERZHERZOG
ARCHEAN EOZOIC
ARCHED ARCHY CONVEX ARCUATE
EMBOWED VAULTED HOOPLIKE
CAMERATED
(— IN) CONCAVE
(PREF.) TOXIC(O) TOX(I)(O)
ARCHEGONIUM CALYPTRA
OOANGIUM
ARCHELAUS (BROTHER OF —)
PHILIP ANTIPAS
(FATHER OF —) HEROD
(MOTHER OF —) MALTHAKE

ARCHEMORUS (FATHER OF —)
LYCURGUS
(MOTHER OF —) EURYDICE
(NURSE OF —) HYPSIPYLE
ARCHER BOW CLIM CLYM BOWER
BUTTY CUPID ROVER BOWBOY
BOWMAN BOWYER SHOOTER
PANDARUS
(EQUIPMENT OF —) TACKLE
ARCHER-FISH DARTER
ARCHERY TOXOLOGY ARTILLERY
(— SPACE) PETTICOAT
(PREF.) TOX(I)(O) TOXIC(O)'
ARCHETYPE IDEA MODEL FIGURE
SAMPLE ESSENCE EXAMPLE
PARAGON PATTERN EXEMPLAR
FRAVASHI ORIGINAL PARADIGM
PROTOTYPE
ARCHIL CORKE CORCIR CORKER
PERSIS CUDBEAR LECANORA
ORCHILLA ORSEILLE
ARCHING CAMBER
ARCHITECT MAKER ARTIST ARTISAN
BUILDER CREATOR PLANNER
BEZALEEL DESIGNER SURVEYOR
AMERICAN DAY ORR PEI COBB COPE
CRAM CRET HOOD HOWE HUNT
JAHN KAHN MIES PELZ POPE POST
SERT TOWN VAUX WANK WARE
YEON ADLER ALLEN BACON BAYER
BUTTS CASEY CRAMP DAVIS FLAGG
GEHRY GOULD HEINS HOBAN
MAHER MCKIM MILLS OBATA PELLI
PRICE RODIA TANGE WAUGH WHITE
BARBER BREUER GEDDES GILMAN
GRAHAM HAIGHT HEJDUK HOWARD
ITTNER JENNEY KASKEY MIZNER
NEUTRA OWINGS ROGERS UPJOHN
WALKER WALTER WARREN WRIGHT
BRAGDON BRUNNER BURNHAM
CARRERE CORBETT EIDLITZ GILBERT
GOODHUE GRIFFIN HOWELLS
KENDALL KIESLER KIMBALL LAFARGE
LATROBE LESCAZE PARSONS
PEABODY PEREIRA PLOWMAN
RAYMOND STURGIS TUTHILL
BENJAMIN BOGARDUS BOSWORTH
BULFINCH COOLIDGE DINKELOO
HARRISON HASTINGS HOLABIRD
MCINTIRE SULLIVAN THOMPSON
THORNTON VANBRUNT YAMASAKI
MAGONIGLE RICHARDSON
STEWARDSON STRICKLAND
HARDENBERGH WHEELWRIGHT
AUSTRIAN NULL URBAN GRAVES
WAGNER FERSTEL HASENAUER
HOLZMEISTER
BELGIAN VELDE POELAERT
BRAZILIAN COSTA NIEMEYER
CZECH ZITEK
DANISH NYROP UTZON HANSEN
JACOBSEN

DUTCH OUD KEYSER BERLAGE
CUYPERS LOMBARD MOREELSE
EGYPTIAN CALLINICUS
ENGLISH KENT NASH SHAW TITE
WEBB WREN ADAMS BAKER BARRY
BLORE DANCE GLOAG GOTCH GWILT
JONES MOULD SCOTT SOANE
STONE WYATT BODLEY CLARKE
COOPER HANSOM HUSSEY PAXTON
STREET STUART BECKETT BENTLEY
GIBBERD JACKSON KNOWLES
LUTYENS PEARSON PENROSE
RICKMAN ATKINSON CHAMBERS
COCKERAM FLETCHER NESFIELD
VANBRUGH CHAMPNEYS
HAWKSMOOR NICHOLSON
WILKINSON CATHERWOOD
LANCHESTER WATERHOUSE
ABERCROMBIE BUTTERFIELD
PENNETHORNE
FINNISH EERO AALTO SAARINEN
GESELLIUS
FRENCH DUC ETEX COTTE DUBAN
LEVAU MAROT PUGET BENARD
BERAIN BROSSE LEDOUX LEFUEL
LESCOT NEPVEU ANTOINE BALTARD
BLONDEL BULLANT DAVIOUD
DELORME FORMIGE GABRIEL
GARDNER GARNIER LENOTRE
MANSART PERCIER PEVSNER
VIOLLET ANDROUET CHALGRIN
CUVILLES FELIBIEN FONTAINE
HITTORFF LEPAUTRE PERRAULT
SOUFFLOT LEMERCIER
LECORBUSIER
GERMAN HOLL LENZ ADLER ERWIN
GEDON LENNE SPEER KLENZE
MESSEL MOLLER SEMPER STULER
BEHRENS FRIESEN GROPIUS
HOLBEIN NEUMANN OLBRICH
POELZIG HEGEMANN LANGHANS
SCHINKEL SCHLUTER ALTDORFER
ESSENWEIN MENDELSOHN
POPPELMANN KNOBELSDORFF
GREEK ICTINUS DOXIADIS
MNESICLES SOSTRATOS
DINOCRATES HIPPODAMUS
POLYCLITUS CALLICRATES
HUNGARIAN STEINDL
IRISH MAGINNIS
ISRAELI SAFDIE
ITALIAN BONI DANTI DOLCI GENGA
NERVI PONTI PORTA POZZO VINCI
AGNOLO ALESSI BONOMI CIGOLI
COSIMO GIOTTO IUVARA PISANO
ROMANO SERING SOLARI SUARDI
VASARI ALBERTI ALGARDI BELLINI
BERNINI BIBIENA CAGNOLA
CONTINO CORTONA FONTANA
GIORGIO GUARINI LAURANA
MADERNA PERUZZI TIBALDI TRIBOLO
VIGNOLA AGOSTINO AMMANATI

BRAMANTE CIVITALI GIOCONDO
LOMBARDO PALLADIO PALLASIO
PIRANESI SCAMOZZI BORROMINI
PIERMARINI SANMICHELI
SERVANDONI VANVITELLI
PRIMATICCIO BRUNELLESCHI
MICHELANGELO
JAPANESE ISOZAKI
MEXICAN BARRAGAN
POLISH NOWICKI SPYCHALSKI
ROMAN COSMATI COSSUTIUS
RUSSIAN BRYULOV
SCOTTISH ADAM ROSS GIBBS
STIRLING MACKINTOSH
SPANISH CANO GAUDI CANDELA
HERRERA VILLANUEVA
SWEDISH TESSIN ASPLUND
OSTBERG TENGBOM
SWISS FRISCH LECORBUSIER
TURKISH SINAN
ARCHITECTURAL TECTONIC
OECODOMIC
ARCHITECTURE DRAVIDA
ARCHITRAVE EPISTYLE PLATBAND
ARCHIVES TABULARY TABULARIUM
ARCHIVOLT RING ARCHBAND
HEADBAND
ARCHLUTE THEORBO
ARCHON RULER DIRECTOR OFFICIAL
THESMOTHETE
ARCHWAY ARCH PEND ARCUS
PAILOO PAILOU
ARC LAMP MONOPHOTE
ARCOGRAPH BOW
ARCO SALTANDO SPICCATO
ARCTIC ICY COLD COOL GELID POLAR
BOREAL CHILLY FRIGID GALOSH
NORTHERN OVERSHOE
(— VEHICLE) SNOCAT
ARCTIUM LAPPA
ARCTOID URSINE
ARD (FATHER OF —) BELA
ARDENT HOT AVID FOND KEEN LIVE
WARM EAGER FIERY GLEDY RETHE
SHARP ABLAZE FERVID FIERCE
IGNITE STRONG TORRID AMOROUS
BURNING CORDIAL DEVOTED
EARNEST FEELING FERVENT
FLAMING FORWARD GLOWING
INTENSE SHINING ZEALOUS
DESIROUS EMPRESSE FEVERISH
FLAGRANT ROMANTIC SANGUINE
SCALDING SPORTIVE VEHEMENT
PERFERVID
ARDON (FATHER OF —) CALEB
(MOTHER OF —) AZUBAH
ARDOR DASH EDGE ELAN FIRE GLOW
HEAT LOVE ZEAL ZEST ESTRO FLAME
GUSTO HEART TAPAS VERVE WRATH
DESIRE FERVOR FOUGUE METTLE
SPIRIT SPLEEN WARMTH ARDENCY
EARNEST ENTRAIN PASSION

DEVOTION FEROCITY VIOLENCE
VIVACITY
ARDUOUS HARD LOFTY STEEP STIFF
SEVERE TRYING ONEROUS
EXACTING TIRESOME TOILSOME
ARDYS (FATHER OF —) GYGES
ARE MU RE AIR ARN ARUN HARE
AREA BELT PALE SIZE TREF ZONE
BASIN COAST COURT FIELD PLACE
RANGE REALM SCENE SCOPE SPACE
TRACT ACCENT AREOLA EXTENT
GROUND LOCALE MOARIA REGION
SECTOR SPHERE SPREAD VOLUME
ACREAGE AMENITY AREAWAY
CIRCUIT COMPASS CONTENT
COUNTRY EXPANSE EXPANSE
KINGDOM PURLIEU SURFACE
CAPACITY DISTRICT ENCEINTE
PLOTTAGE PROVINCE
(— ALONG HIGHWAY) STRIP
(— AROUND MOUTH) DELTA
PERISTOME
(— AT INTERSECTION) CIRCUS
(— BETWEEN FILLETS) CANALIS
(— IN BACTERIAL CULTURE) PLAQUE
(— IN CARTOON) BALLOON
(— IN CULTURE) PLAQUE
(— IN FRONT OF HOCKEY GOAL)
CREASE
(— IN HOSTILE TERRITORY) AIRHEAD
(— OF ACTIVITY) METIER
(— OF EXPERIENCE) BOOK
(— OF FLAG) CANTON
(— OF INTEREST) SCENE
(— OF OLDER LAND) KIPUKA
(— OF OPEN WATER AMID ICE)
POLYNYA
(— OF RIDGES) BILO
(— OF TIMBERLAND) CHENA
(— ON MOON) MARE WANE TERRA
(— OVER GATE) PORTAL
(— RELATE) SPACIAL SPATIAL
(—UNIT) TAN YOKE LABOR VIRGATE
PLETHRON PLOWGANG PLOWGATE
(BLANK —) BITE HOLE
(BORDER —) OUTSKIRT OUTSKIRTS
(BORDERED —) PANEL
(COMBAT —) GLACIS
(CONTINENTAL —) MOARIA
(CULTURAL —) HORIZON
(CURLING —) PARISH
(DARK — OF MOON) MARE MARIA
(DENUDED —) BURN
(DIKED —) SLUSHPIT
(DISEASED —) PLAQUE
(ELONGATED —) BELT
(ENCLOSED —) FOLD SEPT
(EXTRAMURAL —) BANLIEUE
(FENCED —) CAGE COMPOUND
(FERTILE —) HAMMOCK
(FLOORING —) SQUARE
(FORTIFIED —) BASTION ENCEINTE

(GATHERING —) MANDAPA
(HOCKEY —) GOALMOUTH
(HOSPITAL —) ICU
(HUNTING —) SURROUND
(IMMOBILE - OF EARTH'S CRUST)
CRATON
(INFESTED —) FLYBELT
(ISOLATED —) POCKET
(LARGE —) LANDMASS
(LIMITED —) SPOT
(LOW-LYING —) GLADE SWALE
COULEE COULIE GUTTER
(LUMINOUS —) AUREOLA AUREOLE
(MINE —) SQUEEZE
(NUCLEAR —) HEARTH ECUMENE
(OPEN —) COURT LAUND PLAZA
CAMPUS SQUARE HAGGARD
(OVERGROWN —) COGONAL
(PASTURE —) SOUM
(PAVED —) CAUSEY
(PLOWED —) BREAK
(RAISED —) TRIBUNE
(RESIDENTIAL —) BANLIEU BANLIEUE
(RURAL —) STICKS BOONIES
BOONDOCKS
(SHOPPING —) MALL MART ARCADE
EMPORIUM
(SLUM —) STEW
(SMALL —) AREOLA
(SMOKING —) BULLPEN
(STERN —) AFTERPART
(STORAGE —) STACK
(SUBURBAN —) ADDITION
FAUBOURG
(SUNKEN —) SAG
(SWAMPY —) SLASH
(TEST —) MILACRE
(TIDAL —) CLAMFLAT
(TRANSITION —) ECOTONE
(TREELESS —) SLICK
(TUMID —) CERE
(UNCLEARED —) BUSH
(UPLAND —) COTEAU
(VOLCANIC —) SOLFATARA
(WASTE —) FOREST
(WOODED —) HAG BOSK BOSQUE
(SUFF.) (GEOGRAPHIC —) GAEA GEA
ARECA ARAK ARCHA BETEL
ARELI (FATHER OF —) GAD
ARENA AREA LIST OVAL RING RINK
COURT FIELD SCENE SCOPE SPACE
STAGE CIRCUS CIRQUE REGION
SPHERE COCKPIT STADIUM TERRAIN
THEATER BULLRING
(ATLANTA —) OMNI
(JAI ALAI —) FRONTON
ARENACEOUS SANDY GRITTY
SABULOUS
AREOLA PIT AREA RING SPOT SPACE
CAVITY
ARES MARS ENYALIUS GRADIVUS
QUIRINUS
(FATHER OF —) ZEUS JUPITER

(MOTHER OF —) ENYO HERA JUNO
(SON OF —) REMUS CYCNUS
ROMULUS
ARETE CREST
(FATHER OF —) DIONYSIUS
(HUSBAND OF —) DION ALCINOUS
(MOTHER OF —) ARISTOMACHE
AREUS (BROTHER OF —) TALAUS
LEODOCUS
(FATHER OF —) BIAS
(MOTHER OF —) PERO
ARGALA STORK MARABOU
ARGALI AMMON ARKAR AOUDAD
ARGAN IRONWOOD
ARGANTE (DAUGHTER OF —)
OCTAVIA ZERBINETTE
ARGENT LUNA MOON PEARL WHITE
BLANCH SILVER CRYSTAL SHINING
SILVERY

ARGENTINA
CAPITAL: BUENOSAIRES
COIN: PESO CENTAVO ARGENTINO
DANCE: TANGO CUANDO GAUCHO
FALLS: GRANDE IGUAZU
INDIAN: LULE GUARANI
LAKE: VIEDMA CARDIEL FAGNANO
MUSTERS
MEASURE: SINO VARA LEGUA
CUADRA FANEGA LASTRE
MANZANA
MONEY: AUSTRAL
MOUNTAIN: TORO ANDES CHATO
LAUDO MAIPU POTRO CONICO
PISSIS RINCON FAMATINA
MURALLON OLIVARES TRONADOR
ZAPALERI ACONCAGUA INCAHUASI
TUPUNGATO MERCEDARIO
LLULLAILLACO
PLAIN: PAMPA PAMPAS
PORT: ROSARIO
PROVINCE: CHACO JUJUY SALTA
CHUBUT CORDOBA FORMOSA
LARIOJA MENDOZA NEUQUEN
TUCUMAN MISIONES PATAGONIA
REGION: CHACO PATAGONIA
RIVER: SALI ATUEL CHICO COYLE
DULCE LIMAY NEGRO PLATA TEUCO
BLANCO CHUBUT CUARTO FLORES
GRANDE PARANA QUINTO SALADO
BERMEJO DESEADO MENDOZA
TERCERO TUNUYAN SENGUERR
TOWN: AZUL GOYA ORAN PUAN
BAHIA JUNIN LANUS LUJAN METAN
SALTA PARANA RAWSON RUFINO
VIEDMA ZARATE BOLIVAR CORDOBA
DOLORES FORMOSA LABANDA
MENDOZA NEUQUEN POSADAS
RAFAELA ROSARIO TUCUMAN
USHUAIA GALLEGOS CATAMARCA
VOLCANO: LANIN MAIPU DOMUYO
PETEROA TUPUNGATO
WATERFALL: IGUAZU

WEIGHT: LAST GRANO LIBRA QUINTAL TONELADA

ARGES (BROTHER OF —) BRONTES STEROPES
(FATHER OF —) URANUS
(MOTHER OF —) GE GAEA
ARGIA (FATHER OF —) OCEANUS ADRASTUS
(HUSBAND OF —) INACHUS POLYBUS POLYNICES ARISTODEMUS
(MOTHER OF —) TETHYS AMPHITHEA
(SON OF —) ARGUS PROCLES EURYSTHENES
ARGIL CLAY ALUMINA
ARGIOPE (DAUGHTER OF —) EUROPA
(HUSBAND OF —) AGENOR
(SON OF —) CILIX CADMUS THASUS CERCYON PHINEUS PHOENIX
ARGOL TARTAR
ARGOSY SHIP FLEET GALLEON RAGUSYE
ARGOT CALO CANT FLASH LINGO SLANG JARGON PATOIS PATTER DIALECT
ARGUE JAW ARGY CHOP FUSS MEAN MOOT MOVE SPAR TIFF WORD ARGIE CAVIL ORATE PLEAD PROVE TREAT ACCUSE ADDUCE CAFFLE DEBATE EVINCE HASSLE REASON ARRAIGN CONTEND CONTEST COUNTER DISCUSS DISPUTE WRANGLE ERGOTIZE INDICATE MAINTAIN PERSUADE QUESTION TRAVERSE
(— DEDUCTIVELY) SYLLOGIZE
(— SNAPPISHLY) YAFF
(— SUBTLY) DISTINGUISH
ARGUEBUS HAGBUT HACKBUT
ARGUER JAW
ARGUMENT ROW AGON BEEF BLUE CASE FUSS MOOT PLEA SPAR SPAT TEXT TIFF CLASH DEBAT INDEX KNIFE LEMMA PROOF THEME TOPIC BARNEY COMBAT CORKER DEBATE DUSTUP ELENCH HASSLE MATTER TUSSLE APAGOGE CLAMPER DEFENCE DEFENSE DILEMMA DISPUTE ESSENCE FLUDDUB POLEMIC RHUBARB SOPHISM SORITES SUMMARY ABSTRACT CLINCHER COURSING EVIDENCE SPARRING TRILEMMA REASONING PARALOGISM PERSUASION
(— FOR) PRO
(— IN FAVOR) PRO
(ART OF —) POLEMICS
(CONSLUSIVE —) SOCKDOLAGER SOCKDOLAGER
(DECISIVE —) SETTLER
(ILLOGICAL —) FALLACY
(INVALID —) SOPHISM
(SCHOLASTIC —) QUODLIBET
(THEORETICAL —) ACADEMICS

ARGUMENTATION DEBATE DISPUTE ERGOTISM CHOPLOGIC
ARGUMENTATIVE ERISTIC FRATCHY FORENSIC
ARGUS (FATHER OF —) ZEUS JUPITER PHRIXUS
(MOTHER OF —) ARGIA NIOBE CHALCIOPE
(SLAYER OF —) HERMES MERCURY
ARGUSFISH SCAT
ARHAT MONK LOHAN RAKAN SAINT ARAHANT
ARIA AIR SOLO SONG TUNE MELODY SORTIE ARIETTA ARIETTE SORTITA
ARIADNE (FATHER OF —) MINOS
(HUSBAND OF —) THESEUS
(MOTHER OF —) PASIPHAE
ARIADNE AUF NAXOS
(CHARACTER IN —) ARIADNE BACCHUS ZERBINETTA
(COMPOSER OF —) STRAUSS
ARIAN AGNOETE AGNOITE HOMOEAN ANOMOEAN EUSERIAN
ARID DRY BALD BARE DULL LEAN BARREN DESERT JEJUNE MEAGER DROUTHY PARCHED STERILE THIRSTY DROUGHTY WITHERED
ARIDAI (FATHER OF —) HAMAN
ARIDATHA (FATHER OF —) HAMAN
ARIDITY DROUTH DROUGHT SICCITY
ARIES RAM
ARIKARA REE
ARIL POD ARILLUS COATING ARILLODE
ARIODANTE (COMPOSER OF —) HANDEL
ARIODANTES (LOVER OF —) GENEURA
ARISAI (FATHER OF —) HAMAN
ARISBE (FATHER OF —) MEROPS
(HUSBAND OF —) PRIAM DARDANUS HYRTACUS
(SON OF —) ASIUS NISUS AESACUS
ARISE WAX COME FLOW FORM GROW LIFT REAR RISE SOAR STEM AWAKE BEGIN BUILD EXIST ISSUE MOUNT RAISE SPRAY STAND START SURGE TOWER WAKEN ACCRUE AMOUNT APPEAR ASCEND ATTAIN DERIVE EMERGE HAPPEN KITTLE SPRING DEVELOP EMANATE EXSURGE PROCEED REDOUND SOURDRE
(— FROM) STEM
ARISING LEVEE EMERGENT
(PREF.) (— WITHIN) IDIO
ARISTAEUS (DAUGHTER OF —) MACRIS
(FATHER OF —) APOLLO
(MOTHER OF —) CYRENE
(SON OF —) ACTAEON
(WIFE OF —) AUTONOE
ARISTE (BROTHER OF —) CHRYSALE

ARISTO (BROTHER OF —)
SGANARELLE
ARISTOCRACY CLASS ELITE
GENTRY ARISTOI SAMURAI NOBILITY
OPTIMACY
ARISTOCRAT LORD NOBLE ARISTO
JUNKER GRANDEE PARVENU
EUPATRID OPTIMATE PATRICIAN
(RUSSIAN —) BOIAR BOYAR
BOYARD
(PL.) ARISTOI
ARISTOCRATIC HIGH TONY NOBLE
QUALITY CAVALIER BELGRAVIAN
ARISTODEMUS (BROTHER OF —)
TEMENUS CRESPHONTES
(FATHER OF —) ARISTOMACHUS
(SON OF —) PROCLES EURYSTHENES
(WIFE OF —) ARGEIA
ARISTOTELIAN PERIPATETIC
ARITHMETIC SUM AUGRIM
ALGORISM
(— FIGURE) ADDEND
ARITHMOMETER MULTIPLIER

ARIZONA

CAPITAL: PHOENIX
COUNTY: GILA PIMA YUMA PINAL
APACHE MOHAVE NAVAJO COCHISE
YAVAPAI COCONINO GREENLEE
MARICOPA SANTACRUZ
INDIAN: HOPI PIMA YUMA NAVAHO
NAVAJO PAPAGO HUALPAI
MOUNTAIN: BANGS GROOM LEMMON
TURRET HUALPAI PASTORA
MERIDIAN
MOUNTAIN RANGE: GILA KOFA
MOHAWK GALIURO HUALPAI
AQUARIUS BUCKSKIN
PEAK: HUMPHREYS
RIVER: GILA SALT ZUNI VERDE
PUERCO COLORADO
STATE BIRD: CACTUSWREN
STATE FLOWER: SAGUARO
STATE NICKNAME: OCOTILLO
STATE TREE: PALOVERDE
TOWN: AJO ELOY MESA NACO YUMA
GLOBE LEUPP TEMPE BISBEE
JEROME MCNARY SALOME TOLTEC
TUCSON CLIFTON CORTARO
KINGMAN MORENCI NOGALES
PHOENIX SAFFORD FREDONIA
PRESCOTT FLAGSTAFF
TOMBSTONE

ARJUN KUMBUK
ARJUNA (FATHER OF —) PANDU
(SON OF —) ABHIMANYU
ARK BIN BOX BOAT SHIP BARGE
CHEST HUTCH BASKET COFFER
REFUGE WANGAN WANGAN RETREAT SHELTER
WANIGAN FLATBOAT
ARKANSAN ARKANSAWYER

ARKANSAS

CAPITAL: LITTLEROCK
COUNTY: LEE CLAY DREW PIKE POLK
POPE YELL BOONE CROSS DESHA
IZARD LOGAN SHARP STONE
BAXTER CHICOT LONOKE SEARCY
CALHOUN PRAIRIE PULASKI
OUACHITA
INDIAN: CADDO OSAGE QUAPAW
CHOCTAW CHEROKEE
LAKE: CONWAY NIMROD GREESON
NORFOLK OUACHITA
MOUNTAIN: RICH GAYLOR MAGAZINE
MOUNTAIN RANGE: OZARK OUACHITA
NATIVE: TOOTHPICK
NICKNAME: WONDER
PRESIDENT: CLINTON
RIVER: RED WHITE SALINE BUFFALO
CURRENT COSSATOT OUACHITA
STATE BIRD: MOCKINGBIRD
STATE FLOWER: APPLE BLOSSOM
STATE TREE: SHORTLEAFPINE
TOWN: COY CUY KEO OLA ROE ULM
ALMA BONO CASA DELL DIAZ MORO
ENOLA PERLA RISON RONDO
WYNNE ALICIA JASPER PIGGOTT

ARKOSE ARENITE SANDSTONE
ARLECCHINO (CHARACTER IN —)
LEANDRO BOMBASTO COLUMBINE
HARLEQUIN
(COMPOSER OF —) BUSONI
ARLESIANA, L' (CHARACTER IN —)
ROSA MAMMAI METIFIO VIVETTE
FEDERICO
(COMPOSER OF —) CILEA
ARM FIN OAR TOE BOOM HEEL LIMB
WING BLADE BOUGH CRANE EQUIP
FENCE FIORD FIRTH FJORD FORCE
GARDY INLET MIGHT OXTER POWER
RIFLE SNORD STOCK BRANCH
CRUTCH ENERGY FRETUM GIBBET
MEMBER OUTFIT PINION RADIAL
SLEEVE TAPPET WEAPON CATCHER
DERRICK DRAWARM FLIPPER
FOREARM FORTIFY FURNISH
GARNISH HARNESS OCKSTER
PREPARE PROTECT PROVIDE
QUILLON SUPPORT ARMORIAL
CROSSARM FOLLOWER FORELIMB
PULLDOWN SOUPBONE STRENGTH
TRANSEPT
(— FORCES) MIRV
(— HOLDING FLINT) HAMMER
(— OF BARNACLE) CIRRUS CIRRHUS
(— OF CHAIR) ELBOW
(— OF CRANE) JIB GIBBET
RAMHEAD
(— OF GIN) START
(— OF PROPELLER) BLADE
(— OF RECORD PLAYER) PICKUP

(— OF SEA) COVE FLOW MEER MERE BRACE CANAL FIRTH FRITH GRAIN FRETUM ESTUARY EURIPUS
(— OF SPINNING MULE) SICKLE
(— OF WINDMILL) VANE WHIP
(— WITH GAFF) HEEL
(INDEX —) DIOPTER
(IRON —) CRANE
(KIND OF —) BOSTON
(LEVER —) SWEEP
(PITCHING —) SOUPBONE
(WINDMILL —) VANE
(PL.) ARMORY ARMAMENT
(PREF.) BRACHI
ARMADA NAVY FLEET FLOTILLA
ARMADILLO APAR PEBA TATU APARA POYOU TATOU BOLITA MATACO MATICO MULITA PELUDO DASYPOD TATQUAY TATUASU EDENTATE KABASSOU LORICATE PANGOLIN
(SMALL —) PICHI PICHICIAGO
ARMAMENT ARMADA BATTERY
ARMATURE ARMING KEEPER LIFTER
ARMBAND BRASSARD
ARMCHAIR CHAIR ELBOW BERGERE FAUTEUIL LOVESEAT
ARMED FLUTE HEELED DAGGERED WEAPONED

ARMENIA

ANCIENT CAPITAL: ANI ARTASHAT ARTAXATA
ANCIENT NAME: MINNI
CAPITAL: EREVAN ERIVAN YEREVAN
COIN: RURLE
FORTRESS: EREBUNI
HERO: ARA ARAM HAIK ARAME VARTAN
KING: ASHOT GAGIK TIDAT ZAREH DIKRAN ARTAKIAS ARTASHES TIGRANES ZARIADES
KINGDOM: URARTU VANNIC CILICIA SOPHENE ARDSRUNI
LAKE: VAN SEVAN URMIA
LANGUAGE: ARMENIAN
MOUNTAIN: ARA ALAGEZ ARARAT TAURUS ALADAGH ARAGATS KARABAKH
NATIVE: ARMEN GOMER
PLAIN: ARARAT
RIVER: KUR ARAS KURA ARAKS CYRUS DEBET HALYS ZANGA AGSTEV ARAXES RAZDAN TIGRIS HRAZDAN VOROTAN AKHURYAN EUPHRATES
SAINT: SAHAK MESROP
TOWN: NVAN SIVAS BITLIS EREVAN KUMAYN SPITAK ERZURUM KUMAIRI TRABZON LENINAKAN

ARMENIAN ERMYN HADJI HAIKH
ARMFUL LOCK YAFFLE

ARMHOLE MAIL SCYE OXTER ARMSCYE ARMSEYE ARMSIZE
ARMIDE (CHARACTER IN —) ARMIDA RINALDO
(COMPOSER OF —) GLUCK
ARMINIO (COMPOSER OF —) HANDEL
ARMISTICE LULL PEACE TRUCE INDUCIAE
ARMLET BANGLE TABLET TORQUE ARMHOOP
ARMONI (FATHER OF —) SAUL
(MOTHER OF —) RIZPAH
ARMOR (AND SPECIFIC PIECES THEREOF) ARMS BACK BOOT EGIS JAMB MAIL TACE WEED ACTON AMURE BARDS BRACE CUISH CULET DORON GUARD GUIGE JAMBE PIECE PLATE PROOF SCALE STEEL TAPUL TASSE TRUSS ARMLET ARMOUR BEAVER BRINIE BRUNIE BYRNIE CAMAIL CORIUM COUTER CRANET CUISSE GORGET GRAITH GREAVE JAMBER POLEYN RONDEL SECRET SHIELD TASSET THORAX TONLET TUILLE VOIDER AILETTE ARMHOOP BESAGNE BROIGNE CORSLET CUIRASS DEFENSE EPAULET HARNESS HAUBERK JAZERAN KNEELET LAMBOYS PALETTE PANOPLY PLACATE POITRIL REREDOS ROUNDEL SABATON VENTAIL BRASSARD PAULDRON RAMENTUM VAMBRACE BAINBERGS RONDACHEPALLETTE
(— ON TREE) TROPHY
(— PLATE) TUILLE
(ELBOW —) CUBITIERE
(FOOT —) SABATON SABBATON SOLLERET
(HEAD —) ARMET CASQUE HELMET PALLET SCONCE VENTAIL AVENTAIL
(HORSE —) BARB BARD BARDE CRINET CHAMFRON CRINIERE CHAMFRAIN
(LEATHER —) CORIUM
(LEG —) BOOT JAMB CUISH JAMBE CUISSE GREAVE JAMBER TUILLE JAMBEAU CHAUSSES
(NECK —) COLLAR GORGET
(PADDED —) GAMBESON
(SUIT OF —) CAST STAND
(PREF.) HOPL(O)
ARMOR-BEARER SQUIRE ARMIGER CUSTREL
ARMORED PANZER
ARMORER GUNSMITH ARTIFICER
ARMORICAN BRETON
ARMORY ARSENAL HERALDRY
ARMPIT ALA OXTER AXILLA ARMHOLE

ARMS TACKLE
(PREF.) HOPL(O)
ARMS AND THE MAN (AUTHOR
OF —) SHAW
(CHARACTER IN —) LOUKA RAINA
NICOLA PETKOFF SERGIUS
CATHERINE BLUNTSCHLI
ARMY FERD HERE HOST IMPI LEVY
MAIN ARRAY CROWD FORCE HERSE
HORDE POWER RANKS ZOMBI
COHORT HONVED LEGION NUMBER
THRONG TROOPS MILITIA BATTALIA
CHIVALRY MILITARY
(HOSTILE —) FOE
(MEMBER OF IRISH REPUBLICAN —)
PROVO
(VOLUNTEER —) VOLAR
(PL.) SABAOTH
(PREF.) STRATO
ARMY OFFICER (ALSO SEE
SOLDIER)
ARMYWORM GRASSWORM
ARNE (FATHER OF —) AEOLUS
(HUSBAND OF —) METAPONTUS
(MOTHER OF —) THEA
(SON OF —) AEOLUS BOEOTUS
ARNOTTO ROUCOU
AROAR REBOANT
AROD (FATHER OF —) GAD
AROID APII ARAD TARO APIUM
KRUBI TANIA KONJAK TANIER
YAUTIA PINUELA CALADIUM
CUNJEVOI MOCOMOCO
CUCKOOPINT
AROMA AURA NOSE ODOR NIDOR
SAVOR SCENT SMELL SNUFF SPICE
FLAVOR BOUQUET PERFUME
REDOLENCE
(— OF WINE) BLOOM
AROMATIC BALMY SPICY SWEET
MASTIC ODOROUS PIQUANT
PUNGENT FRAGRANT REDOLENT
SPICEFUL
AROUND NEAR UMBE ABOUT CIRCA
CIRCUM ENVIRON
(PREF.) AMBI AMPHI CIRCUM PERI
AROUSAL INDUCTION
AROUSE SOW CALL CITE FIRE GAIN
HEAT MOVE REAR SPUR STIR WAKE
WHET ADAWE ALARM ALERT AWAKE
EVOKE FLESH PIQUE RAISE RALLY
ROUSE ROUST SHAKE STEER
WAKEN ABRAID AWAKEN ELICIT
EXCITE FOMENT INCITE INDUCE
KINDLE REVIVE STIRUP SUMMON
THRILL TURNON ACTUATE
AGITATE CONNOTE INCENSE
INFLAME INSPIRE PROVOKE
STEAMUP SUGGEST WHOMPUP
INSPIRIT
(— DISPLEASURE) AGGRAVATE
(— ENMITY) ESTRANGE
(— WRATH) SPLEEN

ARPEGGIATE BREAK
ARPEGGIO SWEEP ROULADE
FLOURISH
(— EFFECT) RASGADO
ARPHAXAD (FATHER OF —) SHEM
ARRACACHA APIO ARRA
ARRACK ARAK RACK ARAKI
RACKAPEE
ARRAIGN TRY CITE ARGUE PEACH
ACCUSE CHARGE IMPUTE INDICT
INDITE SUMMON APPOINT IMPEACH
DENOUNCE
ARRANGE DO FIX LAY RAY SET CAST
COMB EDIT FILE FORM PLAN PLAT
RAIL RULE SIDE SIZE SORT TIER TIFT
WORK ADAPT AGREE ALIGN ALINE
ARRAY BESEE CURRY DRAPE DRESS
ETTLE FANCY FRAME GRADE ORDER
PITCH RANGE SCORE SHAPE SHIFT
SPACE STALL TRICK ADJUST
BRANCH CODIFY DAIKER DESIGN
DEVISE FETTLE FORMAT INFORM
ORDAIN SETTLE SOLUTE TAILYE
ADDRESS APPOINT BESPEAK
CATALOG COLLATE COMPONE
COMPOSE CONCERT DISPOSE
ENRANGE GRADATE MARSHAL
PERMUTE PREPARE REDRESS
SERIATE TAILZEE TAILZIE ALPHABET
CLASSIFY CONCLUDE ORGANIZE
REGULATE TABULATE COLLOCATE
CONJOBBLE NEGOTIATE STIPULATE
ORCHESTRATE
(— BEFOREHAND) FORLAY FORELAY
(— FANTASTICALLY) HARLEQUINIZE
(— FASTIDIOUSLY) PREEN
(— HAIR) SET TED COIF TRUSS
COIFFE
(— HARMONIOUSLY) GRADATE
(— IN FLOCKS) HIRSEL HIRSLE
(— IN FOLDS) DRAPE
(— IN LAYERS) DESS TIER
(— IN ROW) RACE
(— STRAW) HAULM
(— SYSTEMATICALLY) DIGEST
(— WITH BEST AT TOP) DEACON
ARRANGEMENT FIX FLY LAY RAY
DEAL FLOW PLAT RANK TIFF ARRAY
BUILD DRAPE INDEX ORDER SETUP
BORDER DESIGN HOOKUP LAYOUT
SCHEME SETOUT SYNTAX SYSTEM
TREATY BLEEDER INTERIM POSTURE
TONTINE ATTITUDE CONTRACT
DISPOSAL GROUPING POSITURE
SEQUENCE ORDONNANCE
ORIENTATION BANDSTRATION
ORCHESTRATION
(— IN LINE) RANK SERIES
(— IN LOCK) DETECTOR
(— OF BRISTLES) CHAETOTAXY
(— OF CHESS PAWNS) CHAIN
(— OF COMPUTER ELEMENTS)
ARRAY

(— OF DRAPERIES) CAST
(— OF FLOWERS) CASCADE
CORSAGE IKEBANA PARTERRE
(— OF GRADES) CURVE
(— OF GUNS) ARMADA
(— OF HAIRDO) FORETOP
(— OF HAIRS) SCOPA
(— OF HOOKS) GIG
(— OF LOOM BARS) GRIFF GRIFFE
(— OF PARTS) STRUCTURE
(— OF ROCKS) BEDDING
(— OF TACKLE) BURTON
(— OF TIMBER) ANCHOR
(— OF TROOPS) ECHELON
(BETTING —) PERM
(CIRCULAR —) CYCLE
(DISHONEST —) CROSS
(GEOMETRICAL —) LATTICE
(MUSICAL —) CHART
(ORDERED —) PERMUTATION
(SECRET —) PACK
(TRADITIONAL —) AKOLUTHIA
AKOLOUTHIA
(TRAVEL —) CHARTER
(PREF.) TAX(EO)(I)(O)
(LACK OF —) ATAXO
(SUFF.) OSIS TACTIC TAXIS TAXY
ARRANGEMNET (SECRET —)
PACKK
ARRANGING ORDONNANT
(JAPANESE ART OF FLOWER —)
IKEBANA
ARRANNGEMENT (MUSICAL—)
SCORE INSTRUMENTATION
ARRANT BAD THIEF OUTLAW
ROBBER VAGRANT OUTRIGHT
PRECIOUS RASCALLY
ARRAS ORRIS ARISTE DRAPERY
TAPESTRY
ARRASTRA TAHONA
ARRAU JURARA
ARRAY DON DUB FIG ARMY BUSK
DECK DOLL FYRD GALA GARB HOST
POMP RAIL RANK ROBE VEST ADORN
ALIGN ALINE ATOUR DRESS EQUIP
HABIT HARKA HEDGE ORDER ADIGHT
AGUISE ATTIRE ATTRAP BEDECK
CLOTHE DEVICE FETTLE FINERY
GRAITH INVEST LAYOUT MUSTER
PLIGHT SERIES SETOUT SHROUD
ADDRESS AFFAITE AFFLICT APPAREL
ARRANGE BATTERY BEDIGHT
COMPANY DISPLAY DISPOSE
ENVELOP FURNISH FYRDUNG
MARSHAL PANOPLY REPAREL
ACCOUTER
(— OF CHEMICALS) ARA
(— OF GUNS) BROADSIDE
(— OF TROOPS) PAREL
(— OF WEAPONS) ARMORY
(— TASTELESSLY) DAUB
(BATTLE —) ACIES HERSE BATTALIA
(MATHEMATICAL —) MATRIX

ARRAYED HABITED ABULYEIT
ARREAR DEBT BEHIND UNPAID
ARRIERE
(IN —S) BACK BEHIND
ARREST CAP COP FIX FOB LAG NAB
NIP VAG BALK BUST CURB FALL
GLOM GRAB HALT HOLD JAIL KEEP
NAIL NICK PULL REST SHOP SIST
STAY STEM STOP ARRET CATCH
CHECK DELAY PINCH REEST SEIZE
STILL STUNT ATTACH BRIDLE
COLLAR DECREE DETAIN ENGAGE
FINGER HAULIN HINDER PLEDGE
PULLIN RETARD SLOUGH SNEEZE
THWART CAPTION CAPTURE
CUSTODY SUSPEND IMPRISON
OBSTRUCT RESTRAIN
(— DEVELOPMENT) FIXATE
(— OF BLEEDING) HEMOSTASIS
(— OF DEVELOPMENT) ABORTION
(— OF GROWTH) STASIS
(PUT UNDER —) BUST
ARRESTER (SPARK —) BONNET
ARRESTING DOLD OEIZING
MAGNETIC PLEASING STRIKING
ARRET EDICT ARREST DECREE
DECISION JUDGMENT
ARRHA HANDGELD
ARRIGANTLY HIGH
ARRIS PIEN ANGLE PIEND ARRIDGE
ARRIVAL COMER IKBAL VENUE
ADVENT COMING INCOMING
REACHING
(— TIME) TOUCHDOWN
(— TIME RECORD) OS
(NEW —) ROOINEK
(UNTIMELY —) LATECOMER
ARRIVE GO SEY COME FALL FLOW
GAIN LAND LEND ROVE GETIN LIGHT
OCCUR REACH WORTH ACCEDE
APPEAR ATTAIN HAPPEN OBTAIN
UPCOME CHECKIN COMPASS
(— AT) GET HIT FIND GAIN HENT
MAKE BRING EDUCE FETCH GUESS
SEIZE ATTAIN DERIVE ESTIMATE
(— AT LAST) ROLLIN
ARRIVED-IN DONE
ARROBA ROVE
ARROGANCE PRIDE SWANK TUMOR
BOWWOW HUBRIS BOBANCE
CONCEIT DISDAIN EGOTISM
HAUTEUR STOMACH BOLDNESS
SUCCUDRY SURQUIDY
ARROGANT BOLD COXY HIGH
MOOD COBBY COCKY GREAT HUFFY
JOLLY LOFTY PROUD STOUT SURLY
WLONK ASSUME CHESTY FIERCE
LORDLY UPPISH UPPITY WANTON
FORWARD FROSTED HAUGHTY
HAUTAIN HUFFISH POMPOUS
STATELY TOPPING AFFECTED
ASSUMING CAVALIER FASTUOUS
IMPUDENT SNUFFING SUPERIOR

TUMOROUS OVERBEARING
OVERWEENING

ARROGATE GRAB TAKE CLAIM SEIZE
USURP ASSUME ADROGATE

ARROW FLO PIN ROD SEL BOLT
DART REED SELF SELL SHOT VIRE
BLUNT DEATH FLANE ROVER SHAFT
ARCHER FLIGHT GANYIE GARROT
QUARRY SPRITE TACKLE WEAPON
BOBTAIL DOGBOLT MISSILE
POINTER PROJECT QUARREL
SAGITTA SPINNER FISHTAIL
FORKHEAD
(— ARUM) TUCKAHOE
(— IN GRASS) GREEN SNAKE
(— IN LEG OF STAND) FOOT
(FIRE —) MALLEOLUS
(PART OF —) TIP BUTT HEAD NOCK
PILE POINT SHAFT FEATHER
FLETCHING
(POISONED —) DERRID SUMPIT
(WOBBLING —) FISHTAIL
(PREF.) BELO(NO) HASTATO SAGITTI
SAGITTO TOX(I)(ICO)(O)

ARROWHEAD BUNT FORK HEAD
PILE FLUKE POINT NEOLITH ARTIFACT
CROWBILL FORKHEAD SPICULUM

ARROWROOT PIA ARUM MUSA
SAGU ARARU CANNA TACCA TIKOR
ARARAO CURCUMA

ARROWSMITH (AUTHOR OF —)
LEWIS
(CHARACTER IN —) MAX ALMUS
JOYCE LEORA SILVA TERRY LANYON
MARTIN GUSTAVE WICKETT
GOTTLIEB SONDELIUS ARROWSMITH
PICKERBAUGH

ARROWWORM SAGITTA
CHAETOGNATH

ARROYO DRAW WADI BROOK CREEK
GULCH GULLY HONDO ZANJA
COULEE RAVINE STREAM CHANNEL
BARRANCA BARRANCO

ARRRANGED (— IN BUNDLES)
DESMOID

ARSENAL ARMORY SUPPLY
MAGAZINE

ARSENOPYRITE MISPICKEL

ARSHIN ARCHIN ALTSCHIN
(ONE-24TH OF —) PARMAK PARMACK

ARSINOE (DAUGHTER OF —) ERIOPIS
(FATHER OF —) PHEGEUS LEUCIPPUS
(HUSBAND OF —) ALCMAEON
(MOTHER OF —) PHILODICE
(SISTER OF —) PHOEBE HILAIRA

ARSIS BEAT ICTUS ACCENT RHYTHM
UPBEAT DOWNBEAT

ARSON FIRE CRIME FELONY
BURNING

ARSONIST ARSONITE

ARSPHENAMINE SIX SALVARSAN

ART WILE CRAFT KNACK KUNST
MAGIC SKILL TRADE MISTER TECHNE
ARTWORK CALLING CUNNING
DESCANT DISCANT FACULTY
FINESSE MYSTERY SCIENCE
APTITUDE ARTIFICE BUSINESS
LEARNING PRACTICE PRACTISE
(— OF APPLYING TESTS) DOCIMASY
(— OF BLAZONING) ARMORY
(— OF CALCULATING) ALGORISM
ALGORITHM
(— OF DEFENSE) SKIRMISH
(— OF FLOWER ARRANGEMENT)
IKEBANA
(— OF FLOWER ARRANGING)
IKEBANA
(— OF HEALING) LEECHCRAFT
(– OF HORSEMANSHIP) MANEGE
(— OF PREPARING COLORS)
GUMPTION
(— OF SELF-DEFENSE) AIKIDO
(— OF SPEECH) RHETORIC
(— OF TYING KNOTS IN PATTERN)
MACRAME
(— SUPPLIES) OILS
(DIABOLIC —) DEVILRY DEVILTRY
(DRAMATIC —) STAGE
(IRRATIONAL —) DADA
(JAPANESE — MOVEMENT) YAMATO
YAMATOE
(JUNK —) NEODADA
(KIND OF —) OP POP CLIP JUNK
MARTIAL OPTICAL
(LEG —) CHEESECAKE
(MAGIC —) WITHERCRAFT
(MYSTERIOUS —) CABALA KABALA
CABBALA KABBALA QABBALA
CABBALAH KABBALAH QABBALAH
(NOT —) SHLOCK
(OCCULT —) THEURGY
(RUN AN — SHOW) CURATE
(SHODDY —) BONDIEUSERIE
(TYPE OF —) STREETSCAPE
(PREF.) TECHNI TECHNO TYP(I)(O)
(SUFF.) ERY SHIP TECHNICS TECHNY
TYPAL TYPE TYPIC TYPY
(RELATING TO —) METRIC

ARTAXERXES (COMPOSER OF —)
ARNE

ART DECO DECO MODERNE
(— MASTER) ERTE
(— PAINTER) ERTE

ARTEMIS UPIS DELIA DIANA PHOEBE
CYNTHIA AMARYSIA

ARTERY WAY PATH ROAD AORTA
PULSE ROUTE COURSE DENTAL
FACIAL RADIAL STREET VESSEL
ANONYMA CAROTID COELIAC
CONDUIT HIGHWAY SCIATIC
VAGINAL CEREBRAL CERVICAL
CORONARY DORSALIS EMULGENT
PROFUNDA
(NECK —) CAROTID

ARTFUL APT FLY SLY FOXY WILY
AGILE DOWNY PAWKY SUAVE

ADROIT CLEVER CRAFTY FACILE
PRETTY QUAINT SCHEMY SHREWD
SMOOTH TRICKY CROOKED
CUNNING KNOWING PLAITED
POLITIC PRACTIC SUBTILE VULPINE
DEXTROUS SCHEMING STEALTHY
ARTFULNESS CUNNING ARTIFICE
SUBTLETY
ART GRAY QUAKER SEAMIST
ARTHRITIS GOUT CARPITIS
ARTHROPOD GOLACH GOLOCH
SPIDER CHILOPOD DIPLOPOD
PERIPATUS
ARTHUR (FATHER OF —) UTHER
ARTICHOKE BUR CANADA CYNARA
CARDOON CHOROGI CROSNES
KNOTROOT
ARTICLE A AN YE LOT ONE THE
BOOK ITEM TERM BRIEF CHEAT
ESSAY GEANE PAPER PIECE PLANK
POINT STORY THEME THING CLAUSE
DETAIL LEADER NOTICE OBJECT
REPORT FEATURE BROCHURE
CAUSERIE DOCTRINE PARTICLE
POSTFACE TREATISE
(— OF CLOTHING) DUD DIDO APRON
CLOUT DICKY FANCY THING CASUAL
DICKEY GARMENT COINTISE
CREATION
(— OF FOOD) CATE KNACK
(— OF FURNITURE) STICK
(— OF LITTLE WORTH) DIDO
(— OF SILK) SQUEEZE
(— OF TRADE) PADNAG
(— OF UNUSUAL SIZE) IMPERIAL
(—S OF FAITH) CREDENDA
(—S OF MERCHANDISE) CHAFFER
(CAST-IRON —S) KENTLEDGE
(CHEAP —) CAMELOT
(CHOICE —) VALUABLE
(CONTERFEIT —) DUMMY
(DECORATIVE —) LACKER LACQUER
(FANCY —) CONCEIT
(FIVE —S) HAND
(GENUINE —) GOODS
(HANDICRAFT —) BOONDOGGLE
(INFERIOR —S) SHODDY
(METAL —S) BATTERY
(MISCELLANEOUS —S) SUNDRIES
(NESWPAPER —) STORY LEADER
FEATURE
(NONDESCRIPT —) DODAD DOODAB
DOODAD WHATNOT
(PALTRY —) GIMCRACK JIMCRACK
(PERSONAL —) CHOSE
(SECONDHAND —) JUNK
(SHOWY —) FRIPPERY
(TRIFLING —) KNICKKNACK
(VALUABLE —S) SWAG
(WORTHLESS —) TRANGAM
(PL.) WARES
ARTICULAATE (INDISTINCTLY —)
THICK

ARTICULATE BACK JOIN CLEAR
FRAME JOINT SPEAK UNITE UTTER
VOCAL ACCENT FLUENT VERBAL
EXPRESS JOINTED PHONATE
DISTINCT SYLLABLE
(— ASCHILD) LISP
(— CONFUSEDLY) SPUTTER
ARTICULATED BACK BLADE DENTAL
DORSAL LABIAL JOINTED ALVEOLAR
CEREBRAL VERTEBRATE
ARTICULATION NODE JOINT VOICE
SUTURE ARTHRON JUNCTURE
SYNTAXIS
(DEFECTIVE —) LALLATION
LAMBDACISM
ARTIFACT CELT DISC DISK BATON
GUACA HUACA AMGARN BRONZE
EOLITH FABRIC GORGET REJECT
RONDEL SAGAIE SKEWER ABRADER
ARTEFAC DISCOID RACLOIR SCRAPER
ARTEFACT DATEMARK RONDELLE
TRANCHET
(JAPANESE — S) HANIWA
(PL.) CACHE CERAUNIA
ARTIFICE ART GIN JET GAUD HOAX
JOUK PLAN PLOT RUSE TURN WILE
BLIND CHEAT COVIN CRAFT CROCK
CROOK DODGE DRAFT FEINT FETCH
FRAUD GUILE SHIFT SKILL STALL
TRAIN TRICK CAUTEL DECEIT DEVICE
DOUBLE ENGINE CHICANE COMPASS
CUNNING DODGERY DRAUGHT
EVASION FINESSE SHUFFLE SLEIGHT
COZENAGE DISGUISE DOUBLING
INTRIGUE MANAGERY MANEUVER
PRACTICE PRACTISE PRETENCE
STRATEGY TRICKERY WINDLASS
(PL.) CABAL CRANS
ARTIFICER WRIGHT ARTIFEX
WORKMAN DAEDALUS LAPIDARY
MECHANIC OPIFICER TVASHTAR
TVASHTRI
ARTIFICIAL CUTE SHAM BOGUS
DUMMY FAKED FALSE ARTFUL
ERSATZ FORCED FORGED STAGEY
UNREAL ASSUMED BASTARD
FEIGNED PLASTIC AFFECTED
FABULOUS FALSETTO POSTICHE
POSTIQUE SPURIOUS
(NOT —) REAL NATURAL
(OVERLY —) ALEXANDRIAN
(SOMETHING —) CAMP
ARTIFICIALITY MANNERISM
ARTILLERY (OR PIECE THEREOF)
ARMS GUNS DRAKE SAKER CANNON
MINION HEAVIES LANTACA LANTAKA
CANNONRY ORDNANCE
(— FIRE) STONK RAFALE
ARTILLERYMAN GUN GUNNER
LASCAR REDLEG LASHKAR
ENGINEER TOPECHEE
ARTISAN FEVER SMITH ARTIST
COOPER ARTIFEX TARKHAN

WORKMAN KAMMALAN LETTERER
MECHANIC OPIFICER OPERATIVE
SILVERSMITH
ARTISANSHIP FOLKCRAFT
ARTIST (ALSO SEE PAINTER) DAB
NABI POET ACTOR ADEPT BRUSH
HILDA RAPIN DANCER ETCHER
EXPERT FICTOR MASTER SINGER
WIZARD ARTISAN ARTISTE ARTSMAN
FAUVIST OPERANT PAINTER PONTIST
SCHEMER ANIMATOR COLORIST
FUSINIST IDEALIST LADISLAW
LETTERER MAGICIAN MUSICIAN
SCULPTOR SKETCHER STIPPLER
PASTELIST PRIMITIVE MINIMALIST
PASTELLIST
(— **SCHOOL**) LUMINISM
(**SIDEWALK** —) SCREEVER
(PL.) SCHOOL
ARTISTIC ARTLY DAEDAL EXPERT
ESTHETIC PAINTERLY
(— **MATERIAL**) KITSCH
(— **QUALITY**) VERTU VIRTU
ARTISTRY FOLKCRAFT
ARTLESS NAIF OPEN FRANK NAIVE
PLAIN SEELY CANDID RUSTIC SIMPLE
GIRLISH NATURAL INNOCENT
ARTS TRIVIUM
(**MARTIAL** —) BUDO
ART-SONG LIED
ARTY CHICHI
ARUGULA RUGOLA
ARUM ARAD TARO AROID CALALU
DRAGON TAWKEE WAMPEE
MANDRAKE TUCKAHOE
ARVIRAGUS CADWAL
(**FATHER OF** —) CYMBELINE
(**WIFE OF** —) DORIGEN
ARYAN MEDE SLAV OSSET NORDIC
OSSETE
(**NOT** —) ANARYA
ARZA (**SLAYER OF** —) ZIMRI
AS S SO ALS FOR HOW QUA ALSO
INTO LIKE SOME THAT THUS TILL
WHEN EQUAL QUOAD SINCE WHILE
BRONZE THEWAY WHENAS BECAUSE
EQUALLY SIMILAR QUATENUS
(— **FAR AS**) TO INTO QUATENUS
(— **IT WERE**) FAIRLY
(— **LONG AS**) SOBEIT
(— **MUCH**) ALSMEKILL
(— **SOON**) ALSOON ASTITE ALSWITH
DIRECTLY
(— **TO**) QUOAD
(— **WELL**) EVEN
(— **WELL AS**) FORBY FORBYE
(— **YET**) HITHERTO
ASA (**FATHER OF** —) ABIJAH
ASAFETIDA HING LASER FERULA
ASAHEL (**BROTHER OF** —) JOAB
(**MOTHER OF** —) ZERUIAH
(**SLAYER OF** —) ABNER

(**SON OF** —) JONATHAN
(**UNCLE OF** —) DAVID
ASANDER (**BROTHER OF** —)
PARMENION
(**FATHER OF** —) PHILOTAS
ASAPH (**FATHER OF** —) BECHERIAH
(**SON OF** —) JOAH ASARELAH
ASARABACCA HAZEL FOALFOOT
ASAREEL (**FATHER OF** —)
JEHALELEEL
ASARELAH (**FATHER OF** —) ASAPH
ASBESTOS ABBEST XYLITE
AMIANTH ABSISTOS ALBESTON
AMIANTUS WOODROCK EARTHFLAX
(**BLUE** —) CROCIDOLITE
ASCALAPHUS (**BROTHER OF** —)
IALMENUS
(**FATHER OF** —) ARES MARS
ACHERON
(**MOTHER OF** —) ORPHNE GORGYRA
ASTYOCHE
(**SLAYER OF** —) DEIPHOBUS
ASCEND UP STY RISE SOAR STYE
UPGO ARISE CLIMB MOUNT SCALE
STAIR TOWER AMOUNT ASPIRE
BREAST CLIMAX UPRISE CLAMBER
UPCLIMB ESCALATE PROGRESS
ASCENDANCY SWAY POWER
CONTROL MASTERY SUCCESS
DOMINION OWERANCE PRESTIGE
ASCENDANT ARISING MOUNTANT
ASSURGENT
ASCENDING ANODAL ANODIC
ORIENT UPHILL UPWARD ANABATIC
ASPIRANT SUBERECT
(— **WITHOUT A TURN**) FLYING
ASCENSION APOTHEOSIS
ASCENT STY HILL RAMP RISE RIST
UPGO CLIMB GLORY GRADE MOUNT
RAISE SCEND SLOPE STEEP STEPS
STILL UPWAY SOURCE STAIRS
UPCOME UPGANG UPHILL UPRISE
UPWITH INCLINE SCALING UPGRADE
UPSWING EMINENCE GRADIENT
ASCERTAIN GET SEE SET TRY FEEL
FIND TELL COUNT GLEAN LEARN
PITCH PROVE ASSURE ATTAIN
FIGURE ANALYSE ANALYZE APPRISE
APPRIZE COMPUTE MEASURE
UNEARTH DISCOVER
ASCETIC NUN MONK SOFI SUFI YATI
YOGI DANDY FAKIR FRIAR SADHU
SOFEE STOIC YOGIN CHASTE
ESSENE HERMIT SADDHU SEVERE
SOOFEE STRICT ADAMITE AUSTERE
BHIKSHU DEVOTEE EREMITE
RECLUSE SRAMANA STYLITE
TAPASVI AVADHUTA MARABOUT
NAZARITE SANNYASI
(PL.) THERAPEUTAE
ASCIDIAN POLYP CUNGEBOI
CUNGEVOI TETHYDAN TUNICATE

ASCIDIUM PITCHER VASCULUM
ASCOCARP ASCOMA
ASCOGONIUM ARCHICARP
ASCOMA CUPULE
ASCRIBABLE DUE
ASCRIBE LAY ARET EVEN GIVE APPLY
BLAME COUNT GUESS IMPLY INFER
PLACE REFER TITLE ACCUSE ALLEGE
ARETTE ASSIGN ATTACH CHARGE
CREDIT IMPUTE PREFER RECKON
RELATE ASCRIVE ENTITLE ACCREDIT
ARROGATE DEDICATE INSCRIBE
INTITULE
ASCRIPTION LAUD CREDIT
ADDITION
ASCUS BAG SAC THECA ASCELLUS
ASEA LOST ADDLED ADRIFT PUZZLED
SAILING CONFUSED
ASEMIA ASYMBOLIA
ASENATH (FATHER OF —)
POTIPHERAH
(HUSBAND OF —) JOSEPH
(SON OF —) EPHRAIM MANASSEH
ASEXUAL AGAMIC NEUTER
AGAMOUS
(PREF.) AGAM(O)
ASGARD (GODS OF —) AESIR
ASH AS ALS ASE ASS FIG RON COKE
SORB ARTAR ASHEN EMBER FRAIN
ROWAN CINDER CORPSE DOTTEL
DOTTLE TEPHRA WICKEN CLINKER
RESIDUE DOGBERRY FRAXINUS
HOOPWOOD WINETREE
(BARILLA —) PULVERINE
(FRUIT OF —) SAMARA
(SILKY —) CEDAR
(PL.) ASE AXAN KELP SOIL ASHEN
VAREC WASTE BREEZE CINDERS
CREMAINS PULVERIN
ASHAMED MEAN NACE NAIS
ABASHED HANGDOG HONTOUS
SHAMEFACED
ASHBEL (FATHER OF —) BENJAMIN
ASH-BLOND CENDRE
ASH-COLORED CINEREAL
CINEREOUS
ASHEN WAN GRAY GREY PALE
WAXEN WHITE PALLID GHASTLY
BLANCHED CINEREAL
ASHER (FATHER OF —) JACOB
(MOTHER OF —) ZILPAH
ASHES (— OF CREMATED BODY)
CREMAINS
(HUMAN—) CREMAINS
(PREF.) CINE SPODO TEPHRA TEPHRO
ASHKENAZ (FATHER OF —) GOMER
ASHKOKO CONY DAMAN HYRAX
ASHLAR ASELAR RANGEWORK
ASHORE ACOST ALAND AGROUND
BEACHED STRANDED
ASHTAVAKRA (FATHER OF —)
KAHODA

ASHTRAY SPITKID SPITKIT
ASHUR FEROHER
(FATHER OF —) HEZRON
(MOTHER OF —) ABIAH
(WIFE OF —) HELAH
ASHVATH (FATHER OF —) JAPHLET
ASHY WAN CINEREAL
ASIA (FATHER OF —) OCEANUS
(HUSBAND OF —) IAPETUS
(MOTHER OF —) TETHYS
(SON OF —) ATLAS EPIMETHEUS
PROMETHEUS

ASIA
(ALSO SEE SPECIFIC COUNTRIES)
DESERT: GOBI TAKLAMAKAN
LAKE: ARAL URMIA BAYKAL CASPIAN BALKHASH
MOUNTAIN: FUJI DJAJA JANNU KAMET PAMIR ARARAT KUNGUR KUNLUN LHOTSE MAKALU MUZTAG NOSHAQ NUPTSE SEMERU TRIVOR EVEREST RATHONG ANNAPURNA
NATION: IRAN IRAQ LAOS OMAN BURMA CHINA INDIA JAPAN NEPAL QATAR SYRIA TIBET YEMEN BHUTAN ISRAEL JORDAN RUSSIA TAIWAN TURKEY ARMENIA BAHRAIN CROATIA LEBANON VIETNAM CAMBODIA HONGKONG MALAYSIA MONGOLIA PAKISTAN THAILAND INDONESIA KAMPUCHEA SINGAPORE AZERBAIJAN BANGLADESH NORTHKOREA SOUTHKOREA AFGHANISTAN SAUDIARABIA
RANGE: ALTAI KOLYMA HIMALAYA
RIVER: OB SI AMUR LENA URAL INDUS GANGES MEKONG TIGRIS HWANGHO SALWEEN TANGTZE YENISEI EUPHRATES IRRAWADDY
VOLCANO: APO USU FUGI GEDE TAAL AGUNG ALAID DEMPO MAYON RAUNG MARAPI MERAPI SEMERU SINILA SLAMET ULAWUN TAMBORA TJAREME GAMALAMA KERINTJE RINDJANI TOLBACHIK BULOSANSUNDORO
WATERFALL: JOG GOKAK KEGON MEKONG CAUVERY

ASIA MINOR (ANCIENT REGION
OF —) IONIA
ASIAN LAO THAI
ASIDE BY BYE OFF AGEE AWAY GONE
NEAR PAST AGLEY ALOOF APART
ASKEW FORBY ASLANT ASTRAY
BESIDE BEYOND BYHAND FORBYE
FORTHBY LATERAL PRIVATE WHISPER
OVERHAND RESERVED SECRETLY
SEPARATE SIDEWISE OVERBOARD
TOTHEWIND

ASININE DULL CRASS DENSE INEPT SILLY ABSURD ASSISH OBTUSE SIMPLE STUPID DOLTISH FATUOUS FOOLISH IDIOTIC MORONIC

ASIUS (FATHER OF —) DYMAS HYRTACUS
(SISTER OF —) HECUBA
(SLAYER OF —) AJAX IDOMENUS

ASK BEG SPY SUE FAND PRAY QUIZ CLAIM CRAVE EXACT FRAYN PLEAD QUERY SPEAK SPEER SPEIR SPELL SPERE ADJURE DEMAND DESIRE EXAMIN EXPECT FRAIST FRAYNE INVITE BESEECH BESPEAK CONSULT ENTREAT IMPLORE INQUIRE REQUEST REQUIRE SOLICIT PETITION QUESTION
(— ALMS) CANT THIG
(— FOR) BEG BID CRY DUN LAIT SEEK BESPEAK INQUIRE REQUEST
(— PAYMENT) CHARGE

ASKANCE AWRY ASKEW ASKILE CROOKED SIDEWAYS

ASKEW CAM AGEE ALOP AWRY AZEW AGLEE AGLEY AMISS ATILT CRAZY GLEED TIPSY ASKANT ASLANT ATWIST FLOOEY SKEWED SKIVIE ASQUINT CROOKED OBLIQUE BIASWISE COCKEYED SIDELING

ASKING ROGATION ROGATORY

ASKWARD HAMHANDED

ASLANT ASIDE SLOPE
(PREF.) PLAGI(O)

ASLEEP DEAD FAST IDLE LATENT NUMBED DORMANT NAPPING

ASOCIAL EGREGIOUS

ASOKA (FATHER OF —) BINDUSARA

ASOPUS (DAUGHTER OF —) ORNIA THEBE AEGINA ASOPIS CLEONE PIRENE SINOPE CHALCIS CORCYRA SALAMIS TANAGRA THESPEIA
(SON OF —) ISMENUS PELASGUS
(WIFE OF —) METOPE

ASP ESP ASPIC COBRA SNAKE VIPER ASPIDE URAEUS CERASTES

ASPAR (FATHER OF —) ARDABURIUS

ASPARAGUS LILY GRASS SPRUE ASPERGE SPARAGE SPERAGE
(— GARNISH) PRINCESS
(— UNIT) SPEAR
(INFERIOR —) SPRUE

ASPATHA (FATHER OF —) HAMAN

ASPECT AIR HUE WAY AURA BROW FACE HAND KIND LEER LOOK MIEN SIDE VIEW VULT ANGLE COLOR DECIL FACET GUISE IMAGE NORMA PHASE SIGHT STAGE TRINE VISOR VIZOR DECILE FACIES FIGURE GLANCE MANNER PHASIS REGARD VISAGE APPAREL BEARING ESSENCE FEATURE MALEFIC OUTLOOK

RESPECT RETRAIT SEXTILE SHOWING SPECIES CARRIAGE CONSPECT FOREHEAD OUTSIGHT PROSPECT QUINTILE CHARACTER SEMBLANCE
(— OF CURVE) INSIDE
(— OF EMOTION) AFFECT
(— OF MOON) CRESCENT
(— OF MUSICAL NUANCES) AGOGICS
(BALEFUL —) DISASTER
(CULTURAL —) EMANATION
(DETERMINING —) HEART
(DORSAL —) NOTUM
(EXTERNAL —) PHYSIOGNOMY
(FACIAL —) EXPRESSION
(LANGUAGE —) DURATIVE
(OF PLANETS) QUARTILE
(OF STARS) QUINCUNX
(PRIMARY —) HIGHWAY
(QUARTILE —) SQUARE
(SECONDARY —) BYWAY

ASPEN APS ASP ALAMO NITHER POPLAR POPPLE QUAKER QUAKING TREMBLE

ASPER AKCHA AKCHEH OTHMANY

ASPERGILLUM HYSSOP SPRINKLE STRINKLE

ASPERITY IRE RIGOR ACERBITY ACRIMONY TARTNESS ANIMOSITY

ASPERSE SKIT SLUR SPOT ABUSE DECRY LIBEL SPRAY DEFAME DEFILE MALIGN REVILE SHOWER VILIFY APPEACH BLACKEN DETRACT LAMPOON SLANDER TARNISH TRADUCE BESMIRCH FORSPEAK SPRINKLE

ASPERSION SLUR BAPTISM CALUMNY INNUENDO

ASPHALT BREA PITCH SLIME FILLER MANJAK BITUMEN CUTBACK MANJACK BYERLITE UINTAITE GILSONITE

ASPHALTUM CONGO

ASPHODEL KNAVERY AFFODILL

ASPHYXIA APNEA APNOEA ACROTISM SUFFOCATION

ASPIC JELLY GELATIN GELATINE LAVENDER

ASPIRANT (— TO KNIGHTHOOD) DONZEL SQUIRE

ASPIRATE ROUGH SPIRITUS

ASPIRATION GOAL IDEAL DESIRE RECOIL SIGHTS AMBITION PRETENSION

ASPIRE AIM STY HOPE LONG MINT RISE SEEK SOAR WISH ETTLE MOUNT TOWER YEARN ASCEND ATTAIN DESIRE PRETEND

ASPIRIN FEBRIFUGE

ASPIRING ASPIRANT

ASRIEL (FATHER OF —) GILEAD

ASS DOLT FOOL JADE KHUR MOKE BURRO CHUMP CUDDY DICKY

DUNCE EQUID GUDDA HINNY NINNY
CUDDIE DAPPLE DICKEY DONKEY
ONAGER ASINEGO ASSHEAD
JACKASS LONGEAR MALTESE
SOLIPED IMBECILE
(FEMALE —) JENNY JENNET
(MALE — S) JACKSTOCK
(WILD —) KIANG KULAN KYANG
KIYANG KOULAN ONAGER HEMIPPE
CHIGETAI GHORKHAR HEMIONUS
(PL.) JACKSTOCK
(PREF.) ONISCI ONO
ASSAI MANICOLE
ASSAIL WOO BASH BEAT FRAY HOOT
JUMP PELT SAIL ASSAY BESET FLYAT
PRESS SETAT SHOCK STONE WHACK
WHANG ACCUSE ATTACK BATTER
BICKER BULLET HURTLE IMPUGN
INFEST INSULT INVADE MALIGN
MOLEST OFFEND OPPUGN RAGEAT
RATTLE SAILYE SCATHE STRIKE
ASSAULT ATTEMPT BELABOR
BESEIGE BOMBARD CATCALL
ENFORCE ASSEMBLE BLUDGEON
TOMAHAWK
(— WITH DIN) PEAL
(— WITH LANGUAGE) REVILE
BULLYRAG BALLLYRAG
(— WITH RAILLERY) BANTER
(— WITH WORDS) TONGUE
ASSAILANT ONSETTER
ASSAM (MOUNTAIN OF —) JAPVO
(STATE OF —) KHASI MANIPUR
(TOWN OF —) IMPHAL SADIYA
GAUHATI SHILLONG
(TRIBE OF —) AO AKA AOR AHOM
GARO NAGA
ASSARACUS (BROTHER OF —) ILUS
GANYMEDE
(FATHER OF —) TROS
(MOTHER OF —) CALLIRRHOE
(SISTER OF —) CLEOPATRA
(SON OF —) CAPYS
ASSART SART THWAITE
ASSASSIN THAG THUG BRAVE
BRAVO FEDAI FIDAI NINJA CUTTLE
FIDAWI HITMAN KILLER SLAYER
RUFFIAN STABBER TORPEDO
HACKSTER MURDERER SICARIUS
ASSASSINATE KILL SLAY MURDER
REMOVE
ASSASSINATION THUGGEE
ASSAULT MUG BEAT BLOW COSH
FRAY RAID SLUG ABUSE ALARM
ASSAY BRUNT HARRY ONSET POISE
POUND SHOCK SMITE STORM STOUR
VENUE AFFRAY ALARUM ASSAIL
ATTACK BREACH BUFFET CHARGE
ENGINE EXTENT HOLDUP INSULT
INVADE NAPALM ONFALL STOUND
STOUSH THRUST YOKING ATTEMPT
BOMBARD DESCENT LAMBAST

PURSUIT RUNNING VIOLATE
INVASION OUTBURST BUSHWHACK
ASSAY RUN SAY TRY TEST ESSAY
PROOF PROVE TOUCH TRIAL ASSAIL
ATTACK EFFORT ANALYZE ATTEMPT
EXAMINE TASTING ANALYSIS
APPRAISE ENDEAVOR ESTIMATE
HARDSHIP
ASSAYER POTDAR TESTER
(CONTAINER OF —) CUPEL
ASSAYING DOCIMASY
ASSEMBLAGE ARMY BODY CAMP
CLOT COMA CREW HERD HOST
MASS PACK RUCK BUNCH CHOIR
COURT CROWD DRIFT DROVE FLOCK
GROUP LEVEE POSSE QUIRE SALON
SHOCK SWARM TRIBE CONVOY
GALAXY HOOKUP RESORT SPREAD
SYSTEM THRONG CIRCUIT CLUSTER
COLLEGE COMPANY COMPLEX
CONVENT CULTURE SOCIETY
STATION STATUTE TABAGIE
ASSEMBLY AUDITORY CONGRESS
MULTIPLE PARLIAMENT
(— OF FOSSILS) COLONY
(— OF INTEGERS) IDEAL
(CONFUSED —) FARRAGO
ASSEMBLE FIT LAY POD SAM BULK
CALL HERD HOST KNOT MASS MEET
ROUT SAMM AMASS ASAME FLOCK
GROUP PIECE RALLY TROOP UNITE
COUPLE GATHER HUDDLE MUSTER
SUMMON COLLATE COLLECT
COMPILE CONDUCE CONVENE
CONVOKE RECRUIT CONGRESS
CONGREGATE
(— CARDS) BUNCH
ASSEMBLED ACCOYLD
ASSEMBLER BONDER
ASSEMBLING MUSTER PARADE
ROUNDUP
ASSEMBLY HUI SUM BAUD BEVY
BOGY DIET DRUM DUMA FEIS HUEY
MALL MOOT RAAD ROUT SEJM
SEYM TING AGORA BOGEY BOULE
COURT COVEN CURIA DOUMA
FORUM GROUP JUNTA LEVEE PARTY
PRESS SABHA SETUP SOBOR SYNOD
THING TROOP AENACH AONACH
ASSIZE BOBBIN BUSING CHAPEL
COETUS COVINE GEMOTE MAJLIS
PARADE PLENUM POWWOW SEIMAS
SENATE STEVEN CHAMBER CHAPTER
COLLEGE COMITIA COMMAND
COMPANY CONCION CONSORT
CONVENT COUNCIL DIETINE
EOTATES FOLKMOT HUSTING
LANDTAG MEETING PENSION
SERVICE SESSION SOCIETY
SYNAGOG SYNAXIS TEMPEST
TYNWALD ZEMOTVO AUDIENCE
CONCLAVE CONGRESS ECCLESIA

FOLKMOOT PLACITUM PORTMOTE
PRESENCE SEDERUNT SOBRANJE
TINEWALD TRIBUNAL VOLKSTAG
WARDMOTE CONCOURSE
(— HOUSE) KASHIM
(— OF BLESSED) HEAVEN
(— OF CONDUCTORS) BUS
(— OF DEPUTIES) AMPHICTYONA
(— OF ELDERS) KGOTLA
(— OF WITCHES) COVEN SABBAT
SABBATH
(AFTERNOON —) LEVEE
(BOY SCOUT —) JAMBOREE
(CLOSED —) CONCLAVE
(CROWDED —) SQUEEZE
(EVENING —) ROUT
(FASTENER —) SEMS
(FULL —) PLENUM
(GRENADE —) BOUCHON
(IRELAND —) DAIL SEANAD
(IRISH —) DAIL
(RIOTOUS —) MOB DONNYBROOK
(PL.) PLENA COMITIA
ASSENT AYE BOW NOD YEA YES
AMEN SEAL SENT ADMIT AGREE
GRANT YIELD ACCEDE ACCEPT
ACCORD BELIEF CHORUS COMPLY
CONCUR SUBMIT UNISON APPROVE
CONCEDE CONFESS CONFORM
CONSENT ADHESION CONSTATE
OKEYDOKE SANCTION SUFFRAGE
ACCESSION OKEYDOKEY
(— TO) GOWITH
ASSERT LAY BRAG SHOW POSIT
VOICE AFFIRM ALLEGE ASSURE
AVOUCH DEFEND DEPONE DEPOSE
INTEND INTENT THREAP UPHOLD
ADVANCE BETOKEN CONFIRM
CONTEND DECLARE PROTEST
SUPPORT ADVOCATE CHAMPION
CONSTATE MAINTAIN OUTSTAND
POSITIVE PREDICATE
ASSERTING (POSITIVELY —) THETIC
ASSERTION VOW FACT HOTI CLAIM
VOUCH AVERMENT
(— OF MASCULINITY) MACHISMO
(BOASTFUL —) JACTATION
(DUBIOUS —) PLINYISM
ASSERTIVE BRASH DOGMATIC
POSITIVE
ASSESS LAY TAX CESS DOOM LEVY
MISE RATE SCOT TOLL AGIST CENSE
PRICE STENT SUMUP TEIND VALUE
AFFEER ASSIZE CHARGE EXTEND
IMPOSE SAMPLE MEASURE
APPRAISE ESTIMATE
ASSESSMENT FEE LUG TAX CESS
DUTY LEVY SCOT TOLL CULET
JUMMA PRICE RATAL STENT TITHE
WORTH EXTENT IMPOST PURVEY
SURTAX TARIFF SCUTAGE BRIGBOTE
TAXATION

ASSESSOR JUDGE MUFTI RATER
TAXER CESSOR LISTER TASKER
AUDITOR STENTOR TAXATOR
(PL.) FINTADORES
ASSET PLUS HONOR GETPENNY
PROPERTY RESOURCE STRENGTH
ASSETS GOODS MEANS MONEY
STOCK CREDIT WEALTH CAPITAL
EFFECTS ACCOUNTS PROPERTY
RESOURCE
ASSEVERATE SAY VOW AVER AVOW
STATE SWEAR AFFIRM ALLEGE
ASSERT ASSURE DECLARE PROTEST
ASSEVERATION VOW OATH
STATING
ASSHUR (FATHER OF —) SHEM
ASSIDUOUS BUSY GREAT ACTIVE
DEVOTED PENIBLE STUDIED
DILIGENT FREQUENT SEDULOUS
STUDIOUS
ASSIGN FIX LET PUT SET ARET CAST
CEDE DEAL DOLE DRAW GIVE METE
RATE SEAL SHOW SIGN ALLOT
ALLOW APPLY ARETT AWARD DIGHT
ENDOW REFER SHIFT TITLE ADDUCE
AFFECT ALLEGE ATTACH CHARGE
CONVEY DESIGN DIRECT ENTAIL
ORDAIN ACCOUNT ADJUDGE
APPOINT ASCRIBE CONSIGN
DISPOSE ENTITLE SPECIFY STATION
TRIBUTE ALLOCATE ANTEDATE
ARROGATE DELEGATE INSCRIBE
TRANSFER
(— QUARTERS) BILLET
(— TASK) STINT
ASSIGNATION DATE MEET TRYST
MEETING
ASSIGNMENT DECK DUTY TASK
CHORE GRIND STENT STINT TUNCA
CESSIO LESSON CESSION BUSINESS
HOMEWORK PLACEMENT
(FOREIGN —) POST
ASSIGNOR CEDOR CEDENS CEDENT
ASSIMILATE MIX ONE FUSE ADAPT
ALTER BLEND LEARN MERGE
ABSORB DIGEST IMBIBE COMPARE
CONCOCT RESEMBLE
ASSIMILATION ECHOISM
HOMEOSIS RECOGNITION
(— OF FOOD) CONCOCTION
ASSINIBOIN HOHE
ASSIR (FATHER OF —) KORAH
EBIASAPH JECONIAH
ASSIST AID ABET BACK HELP JOIN
AVAIL BOOST COACH FAVOR NURSE
SERVE SPEED STEAD ATTEND
ESCORT PROMPT SECOND SQUIRE
SUCCOR BENEFIT COMFORT
FURTHER RELIEVE SUPPORT
SUSTAIN ADJUVATE BEFRIEND
(— A READER) FESCUE
(— AT) STAY

ASSISTANCE AID ALMS CAST GIFT
HAND HELP LIFT BOOST FAVOR
HEEZE RELIEF REMEDY SUCCOR
SUPPLY ADJUTOR COMFORT
SECOURS SUBSIDY SUPPORT
AUXILIUM EASEMENT GIFFGAFF
LARGESSE

ASSISTANT CAD AIDE ALLY HAND
HELP MAID MATE PUNK SOUS ZANY
CLERK GROOM USHER VALET
AIDANT BUMPER COMMIS CURATE
DEPUTY FLUNKY HELPER LEGATE
NIPPER SECOND TULTUL YEOMAN
ABETTOR ACOLYTE ADJOINT
ADJUNCT DOORMAN DRESSER
HOGGLER PADRINO PARTNER
PROVOST RUBBLER SHIFTER
STRIKER SWAMPER ADJUTANT
ADJUVANT FELDSCHER GOMASHTA
LECTURER MINISTER OFFSIDER
PARASITE SERVITOR SIDESMAN
SUBPRIOR
(— TO ANIMAL SHOW JUDGE)
STEWARD
(AUCTIONEER'S —) SPOTTER
(BOY —) NIPPER
(DOCTOR'S —) FELDSHER
(DYEING —) CARRIER
(GUNNER'S —) MATROSS
(MASON'S —) GOUJAT
(MATADOR'S —) CHULO
(POLICE —) CORPORAL
(SURVEYOR'S —) CHAINMAN
(WAITER'S —) BUSBOY OMNIBUS

ASSOCIATE MIX PAL AIDE ALLY
BAND CHUM HERD JOIN LINK MATE
MOOP MOUP PEER WALK WIFE YOKE
BLEND BUDDY CRONY HABER
MATCH TRAIN TROOP ASSORT
ATTACH ATTEND CHABER COHORT
COUSIN FASTEN FELLOW FRIEND
HELPER HOBNOB MARROW MEDDLE
MEMBER MINGLE PUISNE PUISNY
RELATE SOCIUS SPOUSE TRAVEL
ADJUNCT ASSOCIÉ BRACKET
COALITE COMMUNE COMPANY
COMPEER COMRADE CONNECT
CONSORT HUSBAND PARTNER
PEWMATE SOCIATE COMPLICE
CONFRERE CONJOINT CONVERSE
COPEMATE FAMILIAR FEDERATE
FOLLOWER FREQUENT GADSHILL
IDENTIFY INTIMATE PARTAKER
ACCOMPANY ACCOMPLICE
(— WITH) FRAT MOOP MOUP
(DEMON —) FLY
(PL.) ENTOURAGE

ASSOCIATED
(PREF.) SYM
(SUFF.) (— WITH) IC(AL)

ASSOCIATION HUI BODY BOND
BUND CLUB GILD HONG HUNT TONG
ARTEL BOARD GUILD HANSA HANSE
SANGH TRUCK UNION CARTEL
CERCLE CHAPEL COMITY CONGER
GRANGE LEAGUE LEGION LYCEUM
PLEDGE SANGHA SCHOLA VERLIN
CIRCUIT COMBINE COMPANY
CONSORT CONTACT CONVENT
COUNCIL SOCIETY SOROSIS
SYNOECY AFFINITY ALLIANCE
ASSEMBLY ATHENEUM CONVERSE
HABITUDE INTIMACY SODALITY
SYNOMOSY TAALBOND
ORGANIZATION
(— OF FOSSILS) FAUNULA FAUNULE
(ANTAGONISTIC —) ANTIBIOSIS
(BANK —) SANDL
(BOOK-SELLERS' —) CONGER
(CLOSE —) HARNESS INTIMACY
(EMPLOYERS' —) GREMIO
(FARMERS' —) GRANGE
(IN —) ALONG
(LABOR —) ARTEL UNION
(RELIGIOUS —) SAMAJ
(SECRET —) CABAL
(STUDENTS' —) CORPS
(SYMBIOTIC —) ACAROPHILY

ASSOIL RID SOIL ATONE CLEAR
SOLVE ACQUIT PARDON REFUTE
ABSOLVE DELIVER EXPIATE FORGIVE
RELEASE RESOLVE

ASSONANCE PUN RHYME
PARAGRAM

ASSORT BOLT CULL SUIT WINNOW
(— COINS) SHROFF

ASSORTED CHOW CHOWCHOW

ASSORTER FEEDER LOOKER

ASSORTMENT BAG LOT SET OLIO
BATCH BUNCH GROUP SUITE
RAGBAG MIXTURE
(— OF COLORS) PALETTE
(— OF TYPE) BILL FONT
(COMPLETE —) STANDARD

ASSUAGE REET CALM EASE LIOS
LISS ABATE ALLAY CHARM DELAY
LISSE MEASE SALVE SLAKE STILL
SWAGE LENIFY LESSEN MODIFY
PACIFY QUENCH REDUCE SOFTEN
SOLACE SOOTHE TEMPER APPEASE
COMFORT MOLLIFY QUALIFY RELIEVE
SATISFY DIMINISH MITIGATE
MODERATE

ASSUASIVE MILD LENIENT LENITIVE
SOOTHING

ASSUME DON PUT SAY SET BEAR
DARE FANG GIVE MASK PULL SHAM
SHIP TAKE ADOPT ANNEX CLOAK
ELECT ENDUE FEIGN GUESS INDUE
INFER RAISE USURP ACCEPT AFFECT
BETAKE CLOTHE FIGURE ASSUMPT
BELIEVE PREMISE PRESUME
PRETEND RECEIVE SUBSUME
SUPPOSE SURMISE ACCROACH

ARROGATE SIMULATE PERSONATE
POSTULATE UNDERTAKE
(— CHARACTER) ACT AFFECT
(— FORM) ENGENDER
(— OFFICE) ACCEDE
(— PAINTING STANCE) BACK
ASSUMED ALIAS FALSE GIVEN
FEIGNED AFFECTED BORROWED
ASSUMING LOFTY UPPISH UPPITY
AFFECTED ARROGANT SUPERIOR
ASSUMPTION ALSOB DONNEE
THESIS BALLOON FICTION SURMISE
HOMEOSIS MARYMASS PRETENCE
PRETENSE PRESUMPTION
(BASIC —) BEGINNING
(EMPTY —) IMAGINATION
ASSURANCE FACE GALL SEAL
BRASS CHEEK FAITH NERVE POISE
TRUST APLOMB AVOUCH BELIEF
CAUTIO CREDIT PLEVIN PLIGHT
SAFETY COURAGE PROMISE
WARRANT AUDACITY BOLDNESS
COOLNESS FIRMANCE FOREHEAD
SECURITY SUREMENT
ASSURE AFFY AVER SURE TELL
CINCH HIGHT SEWUP VOUCH AFFEER
ASSERT ENSURE ENSURE INSURE
PLEDGE SECURE SEKERE SICCAR
SICKER WITTER BETROTH CERTIFY
CONFIRM DECLARE HEARTEN
PROMISE PROTEST RESOLVE
WARRANT AFFIANCE CONVINCE
EMBOLDEN PERSUADE
ASSURED BOLD CALM COLD FIRM
PERT SURE BOUND SIKER SLUSH
FACILE PROBAL SECURE SICCAR
SICKER CERTAIN POSITIVE
(— OF SUCCESS) MADE
(BLUNTLY —) KNOCKDOWN
ASSUREDLY AMEN SOON INDEED
PERDIE REDELY SICCAR SICKER
SURELY VERILY HARDILY WITTERLY
ASSYRIA ASHUR ASSUR ASSHUR
(CAPITAL OF —) CALAH NINEVEH
ASSYRIAN NESTORIAN
(— PLUM) SEBESTEN
ASTER ARNICA COCASH AMELLUS
BEEWEED BONESET EUASTER
ASTROFEL COMPOSIT CYTASTER
MONASTER STARWORT STOKESIA
ASTERIA (DAUGHTER OF —) HECATE
(FATHER OF —) COEUS
(HUSBAND OF —) PERSES
(MOTHER OF —) PHOEBE
(SISTER OF —) LETO LATONA
ASTERISK MARK STAR ASTER
ASTERISM WINDMILL
(THREE —S) ASTERISM
ASTERIUS (BROTHER OF —) AMPHION
(FATHER OF —) ANAX HYPERASIUS
(SLAYER OF —) MILETUS
ASTERN AFT BAFT HIND REAR ABAFT
APOOP BEHIND OCCIPUT BACKWARD

ASTEROID EROS HEBE IRIS JUNO
CERES DIONE FLORA IRENE METIS
VESTA ASTREA EGERIA EUROPA
HYGEIA PALLAS PLANET PSYCHE
THALIA THEMIS THETIS ELECTRA
EUNOMIA FORTUNA LUTETIA
CALLIOPE MASSALIA PLANTOID
STARFISH STARLIKE VICTORIA
ASTHMA PHTHISIC
ASTHMATIC POUCY PURSY POUCEY
WHEEZY PANTING PUFFING
ASTIR UP AGOG ABOUT AFOOT
AGATE ALERT GOING ACTIVE
AROUND ASTEER MOVING ROUSED
ABROACH EXCITED STIRRING
VIGILANT
ASTONISH AWE DAZE STAM AMAZE
KNOCK SHOCK DAMMER MARVEL
STOUND ASTOUND GLOPPEN
IMPRESS STARTLE AMERVEIL
BEWILDER CONFOUND SURPRISE
ASTONISHING AMAZING
FABULOUS MARVELOUS
MARVELLOUS MINDBOGGLING
ASTONISHMENT MUSE FERLY
DISMAY FARLEY MARVEL STOUND
WONDER SURPRISE
ASTOUND BEAT STUN ABASH
AMAZE APPAL SHOCK STOUN
APPALL STOUND STAGGER STUPEFY
STUPEND TERRIFY ASTONISH
CONFOUND SURPRISE
ASTOUNDED STUPENT
ASTOUNDING STUNNING
ASTRAEA (FATHER OF —) ZEUS
JUPITER
(MOTHER OF —) THEMIS
(SISTER OF —) PUDICITIA
ASTRAEUS (BROTHER OF —) PALLAS
PERSES
(FATHER OF —) CRIUS
(MOTHER OF —) EURYBIA
ASTRAGAL TALUS CHAPLET
CORNICE BAGUETTE
ASTRAGALAR
(PREF.) TALO
ASTRAGALUS TALUS VETCH
HUCKLEBONE
ASTRAKHAN BOKHARA
ASTRAL REMOTE STARRY STELLAR
ASTRAEAN SIDEREAL STARLIKE
ASTRAY AWRY LOST WILL ABORD
AGATE AGLEE AGLEY AMISS ASIDE
GLEED WRONG ABROAD AFIELD
ERRANT ERRING FAULTY DEPAYSE
DEVIOUS FORLORN SINNING
WILSOME MISTAKEN STRAYING
ASTRIDE ATOP ABOARD ACHEVAL
SPANNING
ASTRINGENCY ACERBITY
ACRIMONY
ASTRINGENT ACID ALUM COTO
SOUR TART ACERB HARSH ROUGH

SAPAN STERN TONER CORNUS MAOTIC PONTIC SEVERE TANNIN ALUMNOL AUSTERE BINDING CATECHU PUCKERY RHATANY STYPTIC GERANIUM TRILLIUM (NOT —) SOFT

ASTROLOGER JOTI JOSHI ARTIST JOTISI MERLIN ZADKIEL SCHEMIST

ASTROLOGY STARCRAFT MATHEMATICALS

ASTRONAUT (— ACTIVITY) SPACEWALK

ASTRONOMER JOTI JOSHI JOTISI
AMERICAN BOK SEE BOND BOSS HALE HALL HILL POOR REES TODD VERY ABELL ADAMS BAADE BAUER BOWEN CHASE ELKIN FROST HOUGH HYNEK MAURY PEASE SAGAN SWIFT YOUNG AITKEN BAILEY CANNON DRAPER HOLDEN HUBBLE HUSSEY JACOBY KEELER KUIPER LOOMIS LOWELL PEIRCE PETERS PORTER RENIZE ROGERS SEARES STRUVE WALKER WATSON WILSON BARNARD BURNHAM EASTMAN FLEMING GILLIES JASTROW LANGLEY LITTELL MERRILL MITCHEL MOULTON NEWCOMB PERRINE RITCHEY RUSSELL SAFFORD SHAPLEY SLIPHER WHITNEY ASHBROOK BOWDITCH CAMPBELL CHANDLER COMSTOCK DOUGLASS HARKNESS STEBBINS TOMBAUGH WINTHROP WOODWARD ALEXANDER DOOLITTLE LEUSCHNER MOREHOUSE PICKERING PRITCHETT HARRINGTON RUTHERFURD SCHAEBERLE RITTENHOUSE SCHLESINGER FICHELBERGER
AUSTRIAN FALB HAGEN LITTROW PURBACH
BELGIAN QUETELET
CANADIAN KLOTZ PLASKETT
CZECH KOHOUTEK
DANISH BRAHE DREYER HANSEN ROEMER SCHUMACHER LONGOMONTANUS
DUTCH BLAEU SITTER HUYGENS KAPTEYN
EGYPTIAN PTOLEMY
ENGLISH AIRY HIND POND RYLE TODD WARD ADAMS BAILY DIXON DYSON INNES JEANS JONES MASON MILNE MURIS WALES CLERKE DARWIN HALLEY LOVELL BRADLEY CHALLIS CLAXTON DELARUE GREGORY HUGGINS LOCKYER LUBBOCK MICHELL PARSONS PENROSE PROCTOR BRISBANE COPELAND EDDINTON GLAISHER GOMPERTZ HERSCHEL HORROCKS EDDINGTON FLAMSTEED MASKELYNE PRITCHARD

CARRINGTON GELLIBRAND GROOMBRIDGE SHEEPSHANKS FINNISH STONE
FRENCH BIOT FAYE LYOT PONS WOLF HENRY LOEWY RAYET BAILLY FERNEL MOREUX PICARD VALLOT BORELLY BOUVARD CASSINI DELISLE JANSSEN LALANDE LAPLACE MARALDI MESSIER MOUCHEZ PUISEUX DELAMBRE DELAUNAY LACAILLE LAGRANGE BIGOURDAN CHACORNAC LEMONNIER LEVERRIER TISSERAND BURCKHARDT FLAMMARION MAUPERTUIS
GERMAN BEER BODE WOLF ZACH BAYER BIELA ENCKE GALLE GAUSS GRAFF KEMPF KNOPF MAYER ARNOLD ARREST AUWERS BESSEL BRUHNS HANSEN HARZER IDELER KEPLER LAMONT MADLER MARIUS MOBIUS MULLER OLBERS PETERS RUMKER SPORER STRUYE TEMPEL AMBRONN APIANUS BRENDEL BRUNNOW LAMBERT SCHONER SCHWABE FOERSTER GUTHNICK HARTMANN HERSCHEL HEVELIUS LINDENAU MERCATOR RHATICUS SCHEINER WINNECKE FABRICIUS PALITZSCH SCHONFELD
GREEK CONON METON PTOLEMY AUTOLYCUS CALLIPPUS CLEOMEDES OENOPIDES SOSIGENES HIPPARCHUS THEODOSIUS ANAXIMANDER ARISTARCHUS CLEOSTRATUS ERATOSTHENES
INDIAN AHWADHATA BRAHM AGUPTA
IRISH BALL PARSONS HAMILTON MOLYNEUX
ITALIAN AMICI FRISI DONATI ORIANI PIAZZI SECCHI BORELLI GALILEI GALILEO RICCIOLI TACCHINI BIANCHINI BOSCOVICH FRACASTORO SCHIAPARELLI
NORWEGIAN HANSTEEN
POLISH COPERNICUS
RUSSIAN BREDICHIN SHKLOVSKY
SCOTTISH GILL NICHOL WILSON GREGORY ANDERSON FERGUSON HENDERSON
SWEDISH DUNER BOHLIN GYLDEN CELSIUS ANGSTROM BACKLUND BRANTING STROMGREN
SWISS ZWICKY
ASTRONOMICAL FAR HUGE GREAT URANIC DISTANT IMMENSE URANIAN COLOSSAL INFINITE (— INSTRUMENT) ARMILL
ASTRONOMY WAGON WAGONER WAGGONER
ASTROPHEL PENTHIA STARLIGHT
ASTUTE SLY FOXY KEEN WILY ACUTE CANNY QUICK SHARP SMART

CLEVER CRAFTY NASUTE SHREWD
CUNNING KNOWING SKILLED
ASTYAGES (FATHER OF —)
CYAXARES
ASTYANAX (FATHER OF —) HECTOR
(MOTHER OF —) ANDROMACHE
ASTYDAMIA (FATHER OF —) PELOPS
(MOTHER OF —) HIPPODAMIA
(SON OF —) AMPHITRYON
ASTYOCHE (DAUGHTER OF —)
PHYLEUS
(LOVER OF —) HERCULES
(SON OF —) TLEPOLEMUS
ASUNDER ATWO APART SPLIT
ATWAIN SUNDER SUNDRY DIVIDED
DIVORCED YSOWNDIR
(PREF.) AP(H) DI DICH(O)
ASURA VARUNA
ASVATTHAMAN (FATHER OF —)
DRONA
(MOTHER OF —) KRIPA
ASYLUM ARK HOME JAIL ALTAR
COVER GRITH HAVEN BEDLAM
HARBOR REFUGE ALSATIA COLLEGE
HOSPICE RETREAT SHELTER
BUGHOUSE MADHOUSE NUTHOUSE
ASYMMETRIC PEDIAL
AS YOU LIKE IT (AUTHOR OF —)
SHAKESPEARE
CHARACTER IN — ADAM CELIA
CORIN PHEBE AMIENS AUDREY
DENNIS JAQUES LEBEAU OLIVER
CHARLES MARTEXT ORLANDO
SILVIUS WILLIAM ROSALIND
FREDERICK TOUCHSTONE
AT A AL AU BY IN TO ALS TIL TILL
UNTO ATTEN THERE HEREAT
(— ALL) ANY AVA EVER HALF
OUGHT SOEVER HOWEVER
ATABAL DRUM TABOR ATTABAL
ATALANTA (CHARACTER IN —)
MERCURY ATALANTA MELEAGER
(COMPOSER OF —) HANDEL
(FATHER OF —) IASUS
(HUSBAND OF —) MELANION
HIPPOMENES
(MOTHER OF —) CLYMENE
ATAMAN CHIEF JUDGE HETMAN
HEADMAN
ATARAH (HUSBAND OF —)
JERAHMEEL
(SON OF —) ONAM
ATAVISM REVERSION
ATELIER SHOP STUDIO BOTTEGA
WORKSHOP
ATEO WAKEA
ATES SWEETSOP
ATHALARIC (FATHER OF —)
EUTHELRIC
(MOTHER OF —) AMALASUINTHA
ATHALIAH (FATHER OF —) AHAB
(HUSBAND OF —) JEHORAM
(MOTHER OF —) JEZEBEL

ATHAMAS (DAUGHTER OF —) HELLE
(FATHER OF —) AEOLUS
(MOTHER OF —) ENARETE
(SON OF —) PHRIXUS LEARCHUS
PALAEMON
(WIFE OF —) INO NEPHELE
ATHANAGILD (DAUGHTER OF —)
BRUNEHILDE GALESWINTHA
ATHANOR OVEN ATHENOR FURNACE
ATHAPASKAN HAW HARE HUPA
KATO KASKA AHTENA BEAVER
CHETCO GILENO LASSIK SARCEE
SEKANI CARRIER CHILULA KOYUKON
KUTCHIN
ATHEIST ZENDIK DOUBTER INFIDEL
NASTIKA AGNOSTIC APIKOROS
NETHEIST
ATHENA ALEA AUGE NIKE ALERA
AREIA ERGANE HIPPIA HYGEIA
ITONIA PALLAS POLIAS AIANTIS
MINERVA APATURIA
ATHENIAN ATTIC CHORAGUS
CHOREGUS
ATHLAI (FATHER OF —) BEBAI
ATHLETE PRO BLUE JOCK KEMP
STAR BOXER COLOR CRACK CUTEY
CUTIE TURNER ACROBAT AMATEUR
GYMNAST STICKER TUMBLER
VARMINT GAMESTER REPEATER
WRESTLER PENTATHLETE
(COLLEGE —) REDSHIRT
ATHLETIC AGILE BURLY LUSTY VITAL
BRAWNY GYMNIC ROBUST SINEWY
STRONG BOARDLY BOORDLY
MUSCULAR POWERFUL VIGOROUS
ATHLETICS GAMES SPORT EXERCISE
AT-HOME ASSEMBLY
ATHWART CROSS ABOARD ACROSS
ASLANT OBLIQUE SIDEWISE
TRAVERSE
ATLANTIC CROAKER HARDHEAD
ATLANTIC OCEAN POND
MILLPOND
ATLAS BOOK LIST MAPS TOME TITAN
TELAMON MAINSTAY
(DAUGHTERS OF —) ATLANTIDES
(FATHER OF —) IAPETUS
(MOTHER OF —) CLYMENE
(WIFE OF —) PLEIONE
ATLE ETHEL
ATMAN ATMA ATTA SELF
ATMOSPHERE AIR SKY AURA FEEL
LIFT MOOD TONE AROMA CLIME
DECOR ETHER PLACE SMELL
FROWST MIASMA NIMBUS SPHERE
WELKIN FEELING HYALINE QUALIFY
AMBIANCE AMBIENCE
(— OF DISCOURAGEMENT) CHILL
(CHARACTERISTIC —) VIBE
(EMOTIONAL —) VIBE VIBES
(NOXIOUS —) MIASMA
(OUTERMOST PART OF —)
GEOCORONA

(SECTION OF —) SOLENOID
(SENSED —) KARMA
(STALE —) FROUST FROWST
(STUFFY —) FUG
(SUFFOCATING —) STIFLE
ATMOSPHERIC AERIAL METEORIC
ATMOSPHERICS STATIC STRAYS
  SFERICS SPHERICS
ATOLL LAGOON
ATOM ACE BIT ION JOT DIAD DYAD
  HAET HATE IOTA MITE MOTE WHIT
  ATOMY HENAD LABEL MONAD
  SHADE SPECK TINGE ADATOM
  BRIDGE CARBYL HEPTAD ISOBAR
  TETRAD ATOMIZE BODIKIN IONOGEN
  ISOTOPE NUCLIDE RADICAL SPECIES
  FUNCTION ISOSTERE MOLECULE
  PARTICLE PERISSAD QUANTITY
  CORPUSCLE SCINTILLA
  (— TOTALITY) MATTER
  (COMBINING —) ACCEPTOR
  (TAGGED —) TRACER
  (PL.) SMITHERS SMITHEREENS
ATOMIC TINY MINUTE NUCLEAR
  (— PARTICLE) MUON
ATOMIZE PULVERIZE
ATOMIZER SPRAY SPARGE SCENTER
  SPRAYER AIRBRUSH ODORATOR
  PERFUMER
  (CONTENTS OF —) SCENTS
ATOMS
  (PREF.) (CONTAINING 20 —) EICOS
  (CONTAINING 4 CARBON —) BUT
  (HAVING ARRANGEMENT OF —)
  GALA GALACTO
  (PRESENCE OF 2 NITROGEN —) DIAZ
ATONE AGREE AMEND ACCORD
  ANSWER ASSOIL RANSOM REDEEM
  REPENT APPEASE EXPIATE RESTORE
  SATISFY
  (— FOR) ABY BYE ABYE MEND ABIDE
  ABEGGE
ATONEMENT MEND RANSOM
  MICHTAM PENANCE SATISFACTION
  ACCEPTILATION
ATOP ACOR OVER UPON
ATORAI DAURI
ATOSSA (FATHER OF —) CYRUS
  (HUSBAND OF —) DARIUS SMERDIS
  CAMBYSES
ATRABILIOUS SAD GLUM ADUST
  GLOOMY MOROSE SULLEN
ATRAMENTOUS INKY
ATRAX (DAUGHTER OF —) CAENIS
  HIPPODAMIA
  (FATHER OF —) PENEUS
  (MOTHER OF —) BURA
ATREUS (BROTHER OF —) THYESTES
  (FATHER OF —) PELOPS
  (HALF-BROTHER OF —) THYESTES
  (MOTHER OF —) HIPPODAMIA
  (SON OF —) MENELAUS
  (WIFE OF —) AEROPE

ATRIP AWEIGH
ATRIUM HALL ATRIO COURT CAVITY
  AURICLE CHAMBER PASSAGE
ATROCIOUS BAD DARK RANK VILE
  AWFUL BLACK CRUEL GROSS
  ATROCE BRUTAL ODIOUS SAVAGE
  WICKED HEINOUS UNGODLY
  VIOLENT FLAGRANT GRIEVOUS
  HORRIBLE TERRIBLE MONSTROUS
ATROPHIC AUANTIC
ATROPHY RUST STUNT TABES
  MACIES MOLDER SHRINK STARVE
  SWEENY WITHER SWINNEY
  WASTING STULTIFY
  (PREF.) NECR(O)
ATROPINE DATURINE
ATTACH ADD FIX PUT SET SEW TAG
  TIE BIND BOLT GLUE HANG JOIN
  LINK NAIL SPAN TAKE VEST WELD
  ADOPT AFFIX ANNEX BEWED CLING
  FOUND HINGE HITCH LATCH PASTE
  SCREW SEIZE SPEND STICK TACHE
  TATCH UNITE ACCUSE ADDICT
  ADHERE ADJOIN APPEND ARREST
  CEMENT DEVOTE ENGAGE ENTAIL
  ENTIRE FASTEN FATHER INDICT
  SPLINE ADHIBIT APPOINT ASCRIBE
  CONNECT ESPOUSE SUBJOIN
  (— TEMPORARILY) SECOND
ATTACHED FAST FOND ADNATE
  DOTING ADJUNCT BIGOTED SESSILE
  ADSCRIPT INSERTED
ATTACHING INCIDENT ALLIGATION
ATTACHMENT ARM GAG BAIL BALE
  DRUM FLAY HEAD HECK LOVE MOTE
  SHIM SHOE AMOUR CHUCK CRUSH
  DOBBY DODAD FENCE GUARD STRIG
  AFFAIR BEATER BINDER BUMPER
  DAMSEL DOBBIE DOCTOR DOODAD
  DREDGE FELLER FETICH FETISH
  HEMMER HILLER LAPPET LAYBOY
  MARKER PACKER PICKUP SECTOR
  SHIELD SIDING ADAPTOR AFFAIRE
  BIGOTRY BRAIDER CREASER
  DROPPER FASTGER FITTING
  GIGBACK HEADSET HOLDING
  JOINTER KNOCKUP LEVELER
  SPANNER SPRAYER DEVOTION
  DINGDONG FASTNESS FIXATION
  FONDNESS GOVERNOR HEADREST
ATTACK FIT HIT HOP MUG SIC BAIT
  BOMB BOUT CLAW COSH DINT FAKE
  FANG FORK FRAY GANG GIVE HOOK
  JUMP MACE PAIL PANG RAID RISE
  RUSH SAIL SICK SLOW TACK TURN
  WADE YOKE ABUSE ALARM ASSAY
  BEGIN BESET BLAST BLITZ BOARD
  BRASH BRUNT CATCH CHECK DRIVE
  FIGHT FLUSH FORAY FORCE GLIDE
  HARRY HOUND ICTUS ONSET POISE
  PULSE SALLY SCUFF SETON SMITE
  SOUSE SPASM SPELL STORM
  ACCESS ACCUSE ACTION AFFRAY

AFFRET ASSAIL ATTAME BATTLE
BICKER BODRAG CHARGE CRISIS
DOUBLE ENVAYE EXPUGN EXTENT
GRUDGE INDICT INFEST INSULT
INVADE OFFEND ONFALL ONRUSH
POUNCE RUFFLE SAVAGE SHOWER
SORTIE STOUND STRIKE STROKE
TACKLE TAKING THRUST AGGRESS
ASPERSE ASSAULT ATTEMPT
BARRAGE BELABOR BELIBEL
BESEIGE BOMBARD CENSURE
CRUSADE DESCENT OFFENSE
PICKOUT POTSHOT RUNNING
SCALING SEIZURE STACKER
CAMISADE CAMISADO ENDEAVOR
ESCALADE PAROXYSM SKIRMISH
SURPRISE TOMAHAWK OFFENSIVE
ONSLAUGHT PENETRATION
(— FEEDBAG) TIEIN
(— IN COCKFIGHT) SHUFFLE
(— OF ILLNESS) GO
(— OFILLNESS) FIT
(— OF ILLNESS) DWAM DWALM
ACCESS
(— OFILLNESS) ONFALL SEIZURE
(— OF SICKNESS) WHIP SEIZURE
(— TO ROB) THUG
(— WITH SHOUTS) HUE
(— WITH WORDS) STOUSH
(— ZEALOUSLY) CRUSADE
(BOMBING —) PRANG
(CHESS —) FORK
(CRITICAL —) SLATING
(FENCING —) GLIDE
(LIGHT —) TOUCH
(NIGHT —) CAMISADO
(PROLONGED —) SIEGE
(SLIGHT —) WAFF
(SUDDEN —) ICTUS RAPTUS
SURPRISE
(SUICIDAL —) KAMIKAZE
(SURPRISE —) ALARM ALARUM
(VERBAL —) FIRE SALVO BLUDGEON
(SUFF.) LEPSIA LEPSIS LEPSY LEPT(IC)
ATTACKER AGGRESSOR
OFFENDANT
(SUFF.) MASTIX
ATTACK ON THE MILL
(CHARACTER IN —) MERLIER
DOMINIQUE FRANCOISE
MARCELLINE
(COMPOSER OF —) BRUNEAU
ATTAI (FATHER OF —) REHOBOAM
(MOTHER OF —) AHLAI MAACHAH
ATTAIN GO GET HIT WIN BUMP COME
EARN GAIN RISE SORT ARISE CATCH
COVER CROSS FETCH PROVE REACH
TOUCH ACCEDE AMOUNT ARRIVE
ASPIRE EFFECT OBTAIN SECURE
STRIKE ACHIEVE ACQUIRE COMPASS
PROCURE SUCCEED OVERTAKE
(— TO ACCOMPLISH) FIND FORCE

ATTAINMENT ARRIVAL ADEPTION
ENERGEIA PURCHASE
(— OF NIRVANA) MOKSHA
(SCHOLARLY —) LETTERS
ATTAR ITR OIL ATAR OTTO ATHAK
OTTAR ESSENCE PERFUME
ATTEMPT GO PUT SAY SHY TRY
BASH BOUT BURL DARE DASH FAND
FIST FOND HACK JUMP MIND MINT
MIRD OSSE SEEK SHOT SLAP STAB
WAGE WORK ASSAY BEGIN ESSAY
ETTLE FLING FRAME OFFER ONSET
PRESS PROOF PROVE START TEMPT
TRIAL WHACK ASSAIL ATTACK
EFFORT FRAIST STRIVE ENFORCE
IMITATE PRETEND PROFFER
STAGGER VENTURE CONATION
ENDEAVOR EXERTION PURCHASE
TENTAMEN
(— TO AROUSE) AGITATE
(— TO BRIBE) APPROACH
(— TO INFLUENCE) AGITATION
(— TO THROW RIDER) ESTRAPADE
(ABORTIVE —) FUTILITY
(FIRST —) DEBUT
(PREF.) PEIRA
ATTEND GO HO HOA HOO SEE BEAT
FAND HARK HEAR HEED LIST MIND
OYES OYEZ STAY TEND WAIT WALK
APPLY AUDIT AWAIT GUARD NURSE
SERVE TREAT VISIT WATCH ASSIST
CONVEY ESCORT FOLLOW HARKEN
INTEND LACKEY LISTEN SECOND
SHADOW SQUIRE CONDUCT
CONSORT ESQUIRE HEARKEN
LACQUEY PERPEND RETINUE
ACCOMPANY
(— A LADY) WAIT
(— FUNERAL) FOLLOW
(— REGULARLY) KEEP
(— TO) MIND TREAT FETTLE INTEND
(— UPON) TENT CHASE CHAPERON
ATTENDANCE GATE SUIT CHAPEL
NUMBER OFFICE REGARD SERVICE
PRESENCE
ATTENDANT BOY FLY LAD JACK
MAID MUTE PAGE PEON SYCE ZANY
CADDY COMES GILLY GROOM GUIDE
JAGER USHER VALET ALEXAS
CADDIE DACTYL DAMSEL EMILIA
ESCORT FRIEND GESITH GILLIE
HAIDUK HOGMAN JAEGER KAVASS
MINION PORTER SQUIRE STOCAH
TUBMAN VARLET VERGER WAITER
YEOMAN ALIPTES ARMORER
BULLDOG CHOBDAR COURIER
CROSSER DAMOSEL FAMULUS
FENELLA FOOTBOY GHILLIE
HALLMAN HOSTESS JACKMAN
LINKMAN ORDERLY PAGEBOY
PIQUEUR PRESSER SEQUENT
SERVANT SHIPBOY SPOUTER

TRABANT TRESSEL ATTENDEE
BEACHBOY CHASSEUR CORYBANT
CRUTCHER FEWTERER FOLLOWER
GATHERER HANDMAID HENCHBOY
HENCHMAN HOUSEMAN MINISTER
MYRMIDON OBSERVER OUTRIDER
ROSALINE SERGEANT SERJEANT
STAFFIER TIPSTAFF WATERMAN
OBSERVANT PURSUIVANT
CHAMBERLAIN
(— OF CYBELE) CORYBANT
(ARMED —) CAVASS KAVASS
(CROSSING —) GATEMAN
(FLIGHT —) STEW STEWARD
STEWARDESS
(FUNERAL —) MUTE
(KNIGHT'S —) SWAIN CUSTREL
ESQUIRE
(PALACE —S) BOSTANGI
(PROCTOR'S —) BULLDOG
(SHIP'S —) STEWARD
(YOUNG —) BOY LAD JACK PAGE
KNIGHT
(PL.) MEINY STAFF CORTEGE
RETINUE
ATTENDED FRAUGHT
ATTENDER (HABITUAL —) PATRON
ATTENTION EAR CARE GAUM HEED
HIST MARK MIND NOTE RUSH SHUN
TENT COURT FLOOR GUARD STUDY
TASTE DETAIL FAVORS NOTICE
REGARD ACCOUNT ACHTUNG
ADDRESS EARNEST HEARING
RESPECT THOUGHT AUDIENCE
(— FROM SUPERIOR) TASHRIF
TASHREEF
(— TO PETTY ITEMS) MICROLOGY
(AMOROUS —) GALLANTRY
(FIXED —) DHARANA
(FLATTERING —) HOMAGE
(INTERJECTION TO ATTRACT —)
YOOHOO
(PLEASING —) INCENSE
(SPECIAL —) ACCENT
(PL.) FUSS
ATTENTIVE WARY ALERT AWAKE
CIVIL CLOSE SHARP TENTY ARRECT
INTENT POLITE ALLEARS CAREFUL
GALLANT HEEDFUL LISTFUL
MINDFUL PRESENT DILIGENT
OBEDIENT STUDIOUS THOUGHTY
VIGILANT WATCHFUL
(— TO) IMMINENT
ATTENUATE SAP DRAW FINE THIN
WATER DILUTE LESSEN RAREFY
REDUCE WEAKEN SLENDER AVIANIZE
DECREASE DIMINISH EMACIATE
ENFEEBLE TAPERING
ATTENUATED RARE THIN GAUNT
AERIAL DILUTED SPINDLY FINESPUN
SMORZATO
ATTENUATION LOSS

ATTENUATOR PAD
ATTEST CHOP SEAL SIGN PROVE
STATE SWEAR VOUCH ADJURE
AFFIRM INVOKE RECORD WITTEN
CERTIFY CONFESS CONFIRM
CONSIGN TESTIFY WARRANT
WITNESS EVIDENCE INDICATE
MANIFEST
ATTESTATION VOUCH DOCKET
RECORD
ATTESTED SWORN CERTIFIED
ATTIC LOFT CELER SOLAR SOLER
GARRET TALLET GRENIER COCKLOFT
(— SIDE) SKEELING
ATTILA (BROTHER OF —) BLEDA
(CHARACTER IN —) LEO EZIO ATTILA
FORESTO ODABELLA
(COMPOSER OF —) VERDI
(FATHER OF —) MUNDZUK
(WIFE OF —) HILDA ILDICO
ATTIRE (ALSO SEE DRESS) BEGO
BUSK GARB SUIT TIRE ADORN
ARRAY BIGAN DRESS GETUP HABIT
AGUISE ENROBE PLIGHT REVEST
TOILET ADDRESS APPAREL DUBBING
PANOPLY ACCOUTER CLEADING
EQUIPAGE FEATHERS
(EPISCOPAL —) PONTIFICAL
(FORMAL —) BALLDRESS
(SHINING —) SHEEN
ATTIRED TRICKSY
(— IN FINERY) BRAW
ATTITUDE AIR CUE SET BIAS MIEN
MOOD POSE SIDE ANGLE FRAME
HEART PHASE SHAPE SHELL SIGHT
SLANT STAND ACTION ANIMUS
ASPECT MANNER SPIRIT STANCE
BEARING FEELING GESTURE
POSTURE STATION STOMACH
BEHAVIOR CARAPACE CROTCHET
HABITUDE POSITION
PREPOSSESSION
(— OF HUNTING DOG) POINT
(HABITUAL —) SONG
(MENTAL —) SENSE
(PREVAILING —) STREAM
ATTITUDINIZE POSE POSTURE
ATTORNEY DOER AGENT AVOUE
PROXY VAKIL DEPUTY FACTOR
FISCAL LAWYER LEGIST MUKTAR
SYNDIC VAKEEL PROCTOR
ADVOCATE PROSECUTOR
ATTRACT BAIT CALL DRAW LURE
PULL TILL WIND BRING CATCH
CHARM COURT FETCH TEMPT
ALLURE ATTACH ENGAGE ENLIST
ENTICE GATHER INVITE SEDUCE
STRIKE BEWITCH PROCURE
INTEREST MAGNETIZE
(— FISH) CHUM
ATTRACTANT (MOTH SEX —)
GYPLURE

ATTRACTION TUG BAIT CALL CARD CLOU DRAW PULL CHARM DRAFT FAVOR SPELL TRACT APPEAL DESIRE FAVOUR MAGNET BLOWOFF COITION DRAUGHT GRAVITY INDRAFT ADHESION AFFINITY COHESION CONTRACT PENCHANT SIDESHOW WITCHERY
(KIND OF —) ADDED
(SEX —) GYPLURE

ATTRACTIVE FLY BRAW CHIC CUTE FAIR FOXY GOOD NICE BONNY DISHY FATAL JOLLY NIFTY QUEME SONSY SWEET COMELY FLASHY FRUITY HEPPEN LOVELY LURING PRETTY SAVORY SEEMLY SNAZZY TAKING TRICKY AMIABLE CIRCEAN CUNNING EYEABLE EYESOME GRADELY LIKABLE WINNING WINSOME ALLURING CHARMING ENGAGING ENTICING FEATURED FETCHING GRACEFUL GRACIOUS HANDSOME INVITING SPECIOUS TEMPTING VENEREAN PERSONABLE PREPOSSESSING
(— TO OPPOSITE SEX) EPIGAMIC
(FALSELY —) MERETRICIOUS
(NOT —) FOUL INCURIOUS
(STRIKINGLY —) ZINGY

ATTRACTIVENESS CHARM GRACE LOOKS BEAUTY GLAMOR AMENITY GLITTER AFFINITY HARLOTRY

ATTRIBUTABLE DUE

ATTRIBUTE FOX OWE PUT GIVE MARK SIGN TYPE ALLOT BADGE BLAME CHARM PLACE POWER REFER TRAIT ALLEGE ALLUDE ARRECT ASSERT ASSIGN BESTOW CHARGE CREDIT IMPUTE PREFER REPUTE SYMBOL ADJUNCT APANAGE ASCRIBE COUNTER ESSENCE PERTAIN QUALITY ACCREDIT APPANAGE ARROGATE GRANDITY INTITULE PROPERTY PROPRIUM STRENGTH
(—S OF ROCKS) GEOLOGY
(— WRONGFULLY) FOIST
(PL.) SARIRA SHARIRA

ATTRIBUTION ACCENT THEORY ANIMISM ETIOLOGY

ATTRITION WEAR GRIEF REGRET SORROW ANGUISH ABRASION BLASTING FRICTION

ATTUNE KEY TUNE ADAPT AGREE ACCORD ADJUST TEMPER PREPARE

ATUA AKUA DEMON SPIRIT

ATYPICAL RARE BIZARRE ABERRANT GROTESQUE

AUBADE ALBA

AUBERGE INN ALBERGO

AUBERGINE EGGPLANT

AUBURN ABRAM BLOND CACHA CUTCH BLONDE CACHOU CATECHU GOREVAN TULIPWOOD

AU COURANT CONTEMPORARY

AUCTION CANT ROUP SALE SELL VEND COKER TRADE BARTER BRIDGE HAMMER OUTCRY TROVER VENDUE OUTROOP UNCTION DISPOSAL KNOCKOUT PORTSALE

AUCTIONEER CRIER CRYER OUTCRIER

AUDACIOUS BOLD BRASH BRAVE FRACK HARDY SAUCY AUDACE BRAZEN CHEEKY DARING FORWARD ARROGANT FEARLESS IMPUDENT INSOLENT INTREPID SPIRITED BAREFACED DEVILMAYCARE
(NOT —) CIVIL
(PIQUANTLY —) SASSY SAUCY

AUDACITY CHEEK NERVE COURAGE BOLDNESS TEMERITY HARDIHOOD PRESUMPTION

AUDIBLE RIFE ALOUD CLEAR HEARD AUTOMATIC

AUDIBLY ALOUD

AUDIENCE EAR PIT FANS AUDIT COURT FLOOR HOUSE PUBLIC GALLERY HEARING ASSEMBLY AUDITORY TRIBUNAL

AUDIT SCAN CHECK PROBE APPOSE RECKON VERIFY ACCOUNT EXAMINE INQUIRE INSPECT ESTIMATE

AUDITION READ HEARING

AUDITOR CENSOR HEARER APPOSER AUDIENT PITTITE COUNTOUR DISCIPLE LISTENER

AUDITORIUM HALL ROOM CAVEA FRONT ODEUM THEATER AUDITORY

AUDITORY ORAL OTIC AURAL AUDILE ACOUSTIC AUDITIVE

AUGE
(FATHER OF —) ALEUS
(HUSBAND OF —) TEUTHRAS
(MOTHER OF —) NAERA
(SON OF —) TELEPHUS

AUGER BIT POD BORE BORAL BORER GRILL BORING GIMLET NAUGER WIMBLE PIERCER TEREBRA
(PREF.) TRYPAN(O)

AUGHT ACHT EAWT AUCHT OWNED CIPHER NAUGHT WORTHY NOTHING VALIANT ANYTHING

AUGMENT ADD EKE FEED GROW HELP URGE BOOST EXALT SWELL APPEND DILATE EXPAND EXTEND AMPLIFY BALLOON ENHANCE ENLARGE IMPROVE INFLAME MAGNIFY COMPOUND HEIGHTEN INCREASE MAJORATE MULTIPLY
(— IN STRENGTH) INGROSS

AUGMENTATION RISE EKING SWELL GROWTH AUCTARY ADDITION

AUGMENTED SHARP EXTREME
AUGUR BODE OMEN SEER SPEAK
AUSPEX DIVINE BETOKEN CONJECT
FORESEE OMINATE PORTEND
PREDICT PRESAGE PROMISE
PROPHET SIGNIFY DENOUNCE
FOREBODE FORESHOW FORETELL
FOREWARN INDICATE PROPHESY
AUGURY ORE OMEN RITE SIGN
SOOTH TOKEN HANSEL RITUAL
AUSPICE HANDSEL PRESAGE
CEREMONY
AUGUST AWFUL GRAND NOBLE
KINGLY SERENE SOLEMN EXALTED
STATELY IMPOSING MAJESTIC
(FIRST DAY OF —) LAMMAS LUGNAS
LUGHNAS LUGNASAD
(PREF.) SEBASTO
AUGUSTINIAN AUSTIN
ASSUMPTIONIST
AUHUHU HOLA
AUK FALK LOOM ARRIE DIVER LEMOT
MURRE NODDY SCOOT SCOUT
SKOUT MARROT PUFFIN ROTCHE
STARIK TINKER DOVEKEY DOVEKIE
PENGUIN PYGOPOD SEAFOWL
WILLOCK GAIRFOWL GAREFOWL
ROCKBIRD RAZORBILL
AULA HALL COURT EMBLIC
AUNT TIA BAWD AUNTY NAUNT
TANTA TANTE AUNTIE GOSSIP
(— SALLY) STICKS
AURA AIR HALO ODOR PUFF AROMA
NUMEN SAVOR SMELL BREEZE
NIMBUS BUZZARD ESSENCE
FEELING
(CHARACTERISTIC —) VIBE
(SENSED —) KARMA
(VITALIZING —) VIBE VIBES
AURAL OTIC AUDIAL
AUREATE GOLDEN ORNATE ROCOCO
YELLOW
AUREOLE HALO CROWN GLORY
LIGHT AREOLA CORONA GLORIA
NIMBUS VESICA GLORIOLE
MANDORLA
AUREUS (HALF —) SEMIS
AURICLE EAR PINNA ATRIUM EARLET
TRUMPET PAVILION
AURICULAR OTIC
AURICULATE EARED
AURIGA WAGONER WAGGONER
AURIST OTOLOGIST
AUROCHS TUR UROX URUS BISON
WISENT BONASUS
AURORA EOS DAWN DRAPERY
MORNING
AURORA BOREALIS DANCERS
STREAMERS
AUSPICE CARE OMEN SIGN AUGURY
PORTENT GUIDANCE
(PL.) EGIS AEGIS

AUSPICIOUS FAIR GOOD TWINE
WHITE BRIGHT CHANCY DEXTER
CHANCEY FAVORING PROPITIOUS
PROSPEROUS
AUSTERE BARE COLD HARD SOUR
BLEAK BUDGE GRAVE GRUFF HARSH
RIGID ROUGH SHARP STERN STIFF
STOUR BITTER CHASTE FORMAL
RUGGED SEVERE SIMPLE SOMBER
STRICT SULLEN TETRIC ASCETIC
CRABBED DANTEAN EARNEST
SERIOUS GRANITIC RIGOROUS
TETRICAL ASTRINGENT PURITANICAL
AUSTERITY RIGOR CATOISM
RIGORISM SIMPLICITY
AUSTRAL SOUTHERN

STRAIT: TORRES
TOWN: AYR YASS DUBBO PERTH WAGGA ALBURY AUBURN CAIRNS CASINO COBURG DARWIN HOBART MACKAY SYDNEY BENDIGO GEELONG KOGARAH MILDURA MITCHAM ADELAIDE BRISBANE ESSENDON RANDWICK RINGWOOD MELBOURNE TOOWOOMBA
VALLEY: GROSE JAMIESON MEGALONG
WATERFALL: TULLY COOMERA WALLAMAN WENTWORTH WOLLOMOMBI
WATER HOLE BILLABONG
WOMAN: LUBRA

AUSTRALIAN ANZAC AUSSIE DIGGER AUSTRAL CURRENCY KANGAROO WARRAGAL WARRIGAL (— GIRL) LUBRA

AUSTRIA

ANCIENT PEOPLE: HUNS AVARS RAETIANS SLOVENES BAVARIANS
CAPITAL: WIEN VIENNA
CELTIC KINGDOM: NORICUM
COIN: DUCAT KRONE FLORIN HELLER ZEHNER GROSCHEN SCHILLING
DUCHY: STYRIA CARNIOLA CARINTHIA
EMPEROR: CHARLES FRANCIS FERDINAND
LAKE: ALMSEE FERTOTO MONDSEE BODENSEE TRAUNSEE CONSTANCE NEUSIEDLER
MEASURE: FASS FUSS JOCH MASS MUTH YOKE HALBE LINIE MEILE METZE PFIFF PUNKT ACHTEL BECHER SEIDEL DLAFTER VIERTEL DREILING
MOUNTAIN: STUBAI EISENERZ RHATIKON KITZBUHEL
NATIVE: STYRIAN TYROLEAN
NOBILITY: RITTER
PASS: LOIBL ARLBERG BRENNER PLOCKEN
PROVINCE: TIROL TYROL STYRIA VIENNA SALZBURG CARINTHIA VORARLBERG
RIVER: INN MUR DRAU ENNS KAMP LECH MURZ RAAB DONAU MARCH SALZA THAYA TRAUN DANUBE SALZACH
RIVER PORT: LINZ KREMS VIENNA
ROMAN PROVINCE: RAETIA NORICUM PANNONIA
TOWN: ENNS GRAZ LECH LINZ RIED WELS WIEN GMUND LIENZ STEYR TRAUN LEOBEN VIENNA BREGENZ MODLING SPITTAL VILLACH DORNBIRN SALZBURG INNSBRUCK
WATERFALL: KRIMML GASTEIN GOLLING

WEIGHT: MARC SAUM UNZE DENAT KARCH PFUND STEIN CENTNER PFENNIG VIERLING

AUTACOID HORMONE INCRETION
AUTARCHIC FREE
AUTHENTIC ECHT PURE REAL SURE TRUE EXACT PUCCA PUCKA PUKKA RIGHT VALID ACTUAL DINKUM PROPER CORRECT CURRENT GENUINE SINCERE CREDIBLE OFFICIAL ORIGINAL RELIABLE
AUTHENTICATE SEAL PROVE VOUCH ATTEST SIGNET VERIFY APPROVE CONFIRM LEGALIZE
AUTHOR DOER JUDE SIRE JUDAS MAKER RULER AUCTOR FACTOR FORGER LOKMAN PARENT PENMAN SCRIBE SOURCE WRITER ANCIENT CLASSIC CREATOR ELOHIST FOUNDER LOLLIUS ANCESTOR BEGETTER COMPILER COMPOSER IDEALIST IMMORTAL INVENTOR JEHOVIST ORIGINAL PAYYETAN PRODUCER
(BAD —) BLOTTER
(PL.) SS
AMERICAN ADE BOK GAY ILG LEA LEE NIN NYE POE ZIM AGAR AGEE AUEL BABB BATE BAUM BEER BELL BODE BOVA BOYD BUCK BURT CAIN CARO CARR COIT COOK DANA DAHL DYER EDDY EDEL ERTE EWEN FARB GALE GANN GASS GRAU GREY HALL HAHN HUIE HUME HUNT JONG KEMP KREY KYNE LANE LASH LONG LOOS LUCE MACY MAYO NASH PAUL POST POHL PUZO RAND ROTH SHAW SUHL URIS WARD WATT WEBB WEST WOOD WOUK AARON ADAMS ADLER AIKEN ALBEE ALGER ALSOP AMORY ANSON ANTIN ARNOW BACON BARTH BASSO BATES BAUGH BEACH BEEBZ BENET BINNS BOLES BOYLE BRITT BROWN BRUSH CABLE CAHAN CANBY CHILD CLAPP COOKE CORLE CRANE CREWS CUPPY DAVIS DEISS DIETZ DOBIE DODGE DRURY DUNNE EARLE EATON ELLIS EVANS FAUST FOESS FOOTE GATES GOYEN GRAFF GREEN HARTE HECHT HOBAN HORAN HULME HURST HYAMS IRWIN JAFFE JAKES KELLY KESEY KEYES KIELY KOVEL LAPPE LEECH LEWIS LILLY LODGE LORTZ LYNES LYTLE MABEE MAJOR MARCH MASON MASUR MCFEE MERTZ NIZER OATES ODELL OGDEN OHARA PAINE PANEK POOLE POTOK PUSEY QUEEN RAINE RECHY REESE REEVE RIVES ROARK SELBY SEUSS SIMAK SIMMS SMITH STEIN STONE STONG STOUT STOWE TEALE TEVIS THANE THARP TRINE

TRYON TUDOR TULLY TWAIN UHNAK
VANCE VIDAL VORSE WALSH WATTS
WELTY WEEMS WELLS WHITE
WHYTE WILEY WOLFE WYLIE YERBY
ADAMIC ALCOTT ALGREN ANGELL
ARTHUR ASIMOV AUSTIN BAILEY
BARNES BECKER BELLOW BESSIE
BISHOP BOWLES BRALEY BRINIG
BROWNE BURMAN BURNET CABELL
CAPOTE CARMER CARSON CATHER
CATLIN CATTON CHIANG CLARKE
COLTON COOPER CORBIN CORLEY
CROUSE DANNAY DARGAN DAVIES
DELAND DEVOTO DIDION DILLON
DOWNEY ELLROY EVARTS FARSON
FERBER FIELDS FINLEY FISHER
FLAVIN FLEBBE FORBES FULLER
GADDIS GILMAN GINOTT GORMAN
GUNTER HALPER HARRIS HAWKES
HERBST HOBART HOLMES HOLZER
HOOKER HORGAN HOSMER HOWARD
HUGHES IRVING JACKSON JEWETT
KELLER KESTER KUMMER LAIKEN
LARCOM LEGUIN LIDDEY LONDON
LOVETT LUDLUM LUMMIS MAILER
MANNES MARCUM MARTIN MCEVOY
MILLAY MILLER MORLEY MORROW
MUNSON NATHAN NORRIS PARKER
PITKIN POLITI PORTER POWELL
PROUTY RHODES RIFKIN RIPLEY
ROURKE RUNYON SALTUS SENDAK
SEVERN SHEEHY SONTAG STEELE
STREET STRONG STYRON SUCKOW
SWADOS TALESE TAYLOR TERKEL
THAYER THOMAS TOLAND TOOMER
TRUMAN TUTTLE UPDIKE VERLEN
WALLOP WARNER WATKIN WERNER
WILDER WILLIS WILSON WINTER
WINWAR WISTER WRIGHT YERKES
ALDRICH ANDREWS BABBITT
BANNING BELLAMY BENNETT
BIGELOW BIGGERS BOYESEN
BOYNTON BURGESS BURNETT
CALKINS CARROLL CHEEVER
CHILTON CLEMENS COMFORT
COURNOS COZZENS CUMMINS
CURWOOD DERLETH DREISER
EDMONDS ELLIOTT ELLISON
ERSKINE FARRELL FAWCETT
FERNALD FINEMAN FOLLETT
FRANKEN FREEMAN GALLICO
GARLAND GIFFORD GLASGOW
GRATTAN GUNTHER HAMMETT
HEYWARD HOLDING HOPKINS
JANIFER JOHNSON KAILLOR
KELLAND KEROUAC KILVERT
KOMROFF LAFARGE LARDNER
LINCOLN LINDSAY LOSSING
MASTERS MULFORD MUMFORD
MURFREE NABOKOV OSTENSO
OURSLER PARRISH PARROTT PEATTIE
PRESTON PRUETTE ROBERTS
ROLVAAG SAMPSON SAROYAN

SEIFERT SKINNER TARBELL TERHUNE
THEROUX THOREAU THURBER
TRAUBEL VANDINE VANDYKE
VANLOON VOELKER VOLLMER
WAKEMAN WEBSTER WESCOTT
WHARTON WHITNEY WINSLOW
WOOLSEY WOOLSON YOUMANS
ATHERTON ATKINSON AYSCOUGH
BAKELESS BARRETTO BENCHLEY
BILLINGS BRADFORD BURDETTE
CALDWELL CANTWELL CHAMBERS
CLEGHORN COLLISON CONNOLLY
CONVERSE CRAWFORD DONNELLY
FAULKNER FERGUSON FREDERIC
GELLHORN GLASPELL GOODRICH
HAGEDORN HARRISON HEINLEIN
JOHNSTON KEMELMAN KIRKLAND
KOSINSKI KRUMGOLD LATHBURY
MACAULAY MACGRATH MARQUAND
MELVILLE MICHENER MITCHELL
NORDHOFF PERELMAN PETERKIN
PHILLIPS PROKOSCH RAWLINGS
REPPLIER RICHARDO RINEHART
SALINGER SANDBURG SEDGWICK
SINCLAIR SPILLANE SPINGARN
SPOFFORD STANFORD STARRETT
STEPHENS STOCKTON STODDARD
TIETJENS TOLEDANO TORRENCE
TURNBULL VANDOREN VONNEGUT
WESTCOTT WIDDEMER WILLIAMS
ALTSHELER BACHELLER BERCOVICI
BODENHEIM BROMFIELD
BURROUGHS CARPENTER
CHURCHILL DOSPASSOS
EGGLESTON GRANBERRY
HAWTHORNE HEMINGWAY
ISHERWOOD KORZYBSKI LANCASTER
LOCKRIDGE MCCULLERS NICHOLSON
OSULLIVAN SANTAYANA
SCHULBERG SIGOURNEY STALLINGS
STEINBECK STEVENSON STRIBLING
WOOLLCOTT CLENDENING
FITZGERALD MCCUTCHEON
SOUTHWORTH TARKINGTON
TROWBRIDGE UNTERMEYER
VANVECHTEN CANTACUZENE
CHAMBERLAIN GERSTENBERG
MINNIGERODE SCHLESINGER
STRATEMEYER HERGESHEIMER
ARGENTINIAN PUIG BORGES GALVEZ
MARMOL SABATO CANDIOTI
TIMERMAN CAPDEVILA
AUSTRALIAN STOW WEST BECKE
COWAN GREER WHITE BROWNE
CLARKE LAWSON PORTER POWELL
CALVERT COLLINS DAVISON
EGERTON TRAVERS PRICHARD
SOUTHALL VILLIERS BRINSMEAD
CAMBRIDGE MOOREHEAD
RICHARDSON
AUSTRIAN LIND ADLER BAYER
KAFKA PRAED ZWEIG WERFEL
BARTSCH COLERUS NEUMANN

PICHLER ROSEGGER SCHREKER
ALTENBERG BURCKHARD SCHREIBER
SCHNITZLER VONDODERER
BELGIAN COSTER HYMANS PICARD
EEKHOUD SIMENON DECOSTER
LEMONNIER
BRAZILIAN AMADO CUNHA MORAES
TAUNAY GUIMARAES LISPECTOR
VERISSIMO
BULGARIAN VAZOV CANETTI
CANADIAN COX ROY CARR GROVE
MOWAT SETON SULTE ATWOOD
BIRNEY BRIAND ERDMAN HAILEY
LEVINE MILLAR MOODIE PARKER
CAMERON GLASSCO LEACOCK
MCLUHAN NEUHAUS RICHLER
SERVICE TRUDEAU CHAMBERS
LAURENCE MCDOWELL STRINGER
SULLIVAN CALLAGHAN DELAROCHE
MACDONALD MACLENNAN
PICKTHALL VANPAASEN
CHILEAN CORTES ALLENDE
COLOMBIAN CARO REYES CUERVO
CARRASQUILLA
CZECH HASEK MUCHA LANGER
HOLECEK JIRASEK KUNDERA
COMENIUS VANCURRA
DANISH BANG NEXO HERTZ KIDDE
SKRAM BLIXEN LARSEN RORDAM
BAUDITZ CLAUSEN DINESEN
PALUDAN TANDRUP ANDERSEN
FREUCHEN INGEMANN JACOBSEN
BUCHHOLTZ COUPERIUS
DRACHMANN GJELLERUP
JORGENSEN MICHAELIS
BREGENDAHL KIERKEGAAD
DUTCH LOOY EEDEN BEKKER
CREMER DEJONG EMANTS JENSEN
LENNEP DEVRIES ERAMUS
DEHARTOG MAARTENS
ENGLISH DAY LEE PYM AMIS AYER
BECK BEHN BELL BRAY COLE DANE
ERTZ FENN FORD GLYN HONE HULL
HUME KOPS LAMB LEEK LEON LEVY
LONG LYLY MORE MUIR PAUL PAYN
REED REID PHYS RICE SAKI SHAW
SNOW WAIN WARD WEBB WEST
WOOD WREN ADAMS AMORY AYRES
BARRY BATES BAYLY BERRY BLOOM
BRETT BRYCE BURKE CAINE COMBE
CORVO CRABB CRAIK CRISP CROWE
DAVIE DEFOE DIGBY DIXON DOYLE
ELIOT ELLIS EWING FRAYN GIBBS
HARDY HEAD HEVER HINDE HOLME
INNES JAMES JEANS KEOWN LEVER
LEWIS LOCKE LOFTS LOWRY LUCAS
MASON MAYNE MCFEE MILNE
MOORE MUNRO MURRY ORCZY
OUIDA POWYS RAMEE READE ROPES
SCOTT SHARP SHIEL SHUTE SMITH
STEEL STERN SWIFT WAUGH WELLS
WOOLF WYLIE YONGE YOUNG
ALDISS ALLSOP AMBLER ANGELL

ASCHAM ASHTON ASTELL AUBREY
AUSTEN AUSTIN BARING BARRIE
BAWDEN BELLOC BENSON BESANT
BLOUNT BLYTON BORROW BRAINE
BRIDGE BRONTE BROPHY BULLEN
BUNYAN BURGIN BURTON CALDER
CANNAN CASTLE CHURCH CONRAD
CRONIN ESSLIN FARNOL FELKIN
FOSTER GODWIN GOUDGE GRAHAM
GRAVES GREENE HILTON HOBBES
HOLTBY HORLER HOWELL HOWITT
HUDSON HUGHES HUXLEY JEROME
LANDON LANDOR LYTTON MACHEN
MORGAN MORTON MOSLEY
MURRAY NESBIT NORTON ONIONS
ORMSBY ORWELL PALMER PORTER
POWELL PUDNEY REEVES RUSKIN
SANDYS SANSOM SAYERS SEWELL
SHANKS SOUTAR SPRING STERNE
SYMONS TAYLOR WALTON WARNER
WARREN WARTON WATSON
WEYMAN WRIGHT AGUILAR
ASHFORD BAGNOLD BALCHIN
BALDWIN BARCLAY BENNETT
BENTLEY BERNERS BIRRELL BOLITHO
BOTTOME BULLETT BUNBURY
CHAMIER CHATWIN CLELAND
COCKTON COLLINS CORELLI CRISPIN
DAICHES DEEPING DICKENS
DODGSON DOUGLAS DUDENEY
EDWARDS FARJEON FIRBANK
FORSTER FORSYTH FREEMAN
GARNETT GASKELL GIBBONS
GISSING GOLDING GUTHRIE
HAGGARD HASSALL HAWKINS
HAZLITT HEWLETT HICHENS
HORNUNG HOUSMAN JACKSON
JOHNSON KENNEDY KIPLING
LAMBURN LECARRE LEHMANN
LESSING LOVESEY LOWNDES
MARRYAT MAUGHAM MAXWELL
MCKENNA MITFORD MONTAGU
MORISON NICHOLS OXENHAM
PEACOCK PERTWEE RANSOME
RITCHIE ROBERTS SASSOON
SHELLEY SITWELL SMEDLEY
SOWERBY SPENDER SURTEES
TOLKIEN TOYNBEE VACHELL
WADDELL WALLACE WALPOLE
ZIMMERN BARBAULD BARTLETT
BEERBOHM BRITTAIN CHRISTIE
DASHWOOD DEIGHTON FIELDING
FLETCHER FORESTER HAMILTON
HARRADEN KERNAHAN KINGSLEY
KNOBLOCK KOESTLER LAWRENCE
LEIGHTON MACAULAY MARRIOTT
MEREDITH MORDAUNT OLIPHANT
OLLIVANT PATTISON SINCLAIR
SMOLLETT STANNARD STOPPARD
STRETTON THIRKELL TROLLOPE
WALMSLEY ZANGWILL AINSWORTH
ALDINGTON BERESFORD
BLACKMORE BLACKWOOD

BROUGHTON CARPENTER
CHURCHILL DEQUINCEY DUMAURIER
GERHARDIE GOLDSMITH
GREENWELL GREENWOOD
HENRIQUES KINGSMILL LINKLATER
LITVINOFF LLEWELLYN MANSFIELD
MITCHISON MONKHOUSE
OPPENHEIM PEMBERTON PHILLPOTS
PICKTHALL PRIESTLEY PRITCHETT
RADCLIFFE ROBERTSON SCHREINER
SOUTHWOLD STACPOOLE
STAPLEDON THACKERAY TREVELYAN
WHITEHEAD WILKINSON WILLCOCKS
WODEHOUSE FOTHERGILL
GALSWORTHY HUTCHINSON
MEYERSTEIN MUGGERIDGE
RICHARDSON SHORTHOUSE
SWINNERTON WILLIAMSON
DANGERFIELD YOUNGHUSBAND
ESTONIAN TAMMSAARE
FINNISH AHO KIVI CANTH KALLAS
CYGNAEUS SALMINEN SILLANPAA
TAVASTSTJERNA
FRENCH FOA GAY NAU SUE AIDE
ARON AYME BLOY GIDE HUGO KARR
MAEL SADE SAND UZES ZOLA
ABOUT BAZIN BEDEL BLOCH BOVET
BUTOR CAMUS CARCO CEARD
COLET DUMAS DURAS FABRE GENET
GIONO HEMON LOUYS OHNET PEYRE
ROSNY SAGAN VERNE ACHARD
AGOULT ARAGON ARGENS ARLAND
AULNOY AVENEL BALZAC BEDIER
BENOIT BERAUD BISSON BIYIDI
BLOUET BODARD BOULLE BRUEYS
BUFFON CASSOU CLADEL CRAVEN
DAUDET DONIOL EPINAY ELUARD
FAYARD FRANCE HALEVY HUZARD
IMBERT JAMMES LACLOS LEROUX
LESAGE MOULIE PROUST REBOUX
SARTRE SCHURE TROYAT VERCEL
VOLNEY ANCELOT ARNAULT
BAUMANN BEHAINE BERNARD
BERQUIN BONNARD BOSSUET
BOURGET BOUVIER CAZOTTE
COCTEAU COLETTE DEBERLY DELTEIL
DURTAIN FEYDEAU FONTANE
GAUTIER HERMANT HERVIEU
HOFFMAN IONESCU LAVEDAN
LEBLANC LERMINA MALRAUX
MAURIAC MAUROIS MERIMEE
MONNIER PREVOST REGNIER
ROLLAND ROMAINS SANDEAU
SARASIN SIMENON TENDRON
ASSOLANT BANVILLE BARBUSSE
BEAUVOIR BENJAMIN BERENGER
BERNANOS BERTRAND BONVALOT
BORDEAUX BOYLESVE BRUNHOFF
CENDRARS CHARTIER CLARETIE
DORGELES DUFRESNY ESTAUNIE
FEUILLET FLAUBERT FOUCAULT
GENEVOIX GONCOURT GREVILLE
HOUSSAYE HUYSMANS KOCKLOTI

LATAILLE MALHERBE MARIETON
MARIVAUX MONTEPIN MONTFORT
PERRAULT RABELAIS ROUSSEAU
SAVIGNON SCHOPFER SOUPAULT
STENDHAL VALLETTE VOLTAIRE
BEAUCHAMP BOUHELIER CHERVILLE
COULEVAIN DESCHANEL FONTAINAS
MARMONTEL MIOMANDRE
POURTALES SENANCOUR
BAZANCOURT CHARLEVOIX
DESJARDINS FAUCONNIER
MAUPASSANT APOLLINAIRE
MARGUERITTE
GERMAN APEL BALL BAUM BOLL
BURG HEYM HOLZ HUCH KURZ
MANN ARNDT BULOW BUSSE EBERS
ERNST GRASS GROTH HAGEN HALBE
HAUFF HESSE HEYSE HUBER KUHNE
LANGE LAUBE MAREK MUGGE
MUNDT RAABE UNRUH ZESEN
ZWEIG BECKER BEREND BINZER
BLUNCK BUICKE CONRAD DAUMER
DEWOHL DREYER HAUSER HEYDEN
JENSEN JOHNCT KLEIST KNIGGE
LEWALD LUDWIG MILLER MORIKE
MUSAUS REUTER SCHMID VIEBIG
WERNER BERTUCH BRONNEN
CONRADI DAUBLER FALLADA
FREYTAG GLAESER GUTZKOW
HEIBERG KASTNER KRETZER
LAROCHE NEUMANN OSTWALD
REDWITZ RICHTER SEGHERS
VULPIUS AUERBACH BORKENAU
BRENTANO ECKSTEIN FRAENKEL
HAUSMANN HOCHHUTH HOFFMANN
KOTZEBUE LIENHARD MEISSNER
REMARQUE ROQUETTE WOLZOGEN
ZSCHOKKE BEYERLEIN GANGHOFER
IMMERMANN SCHUCKING
SIODMAKK SUDERMANN UECHTRITZ
WILBRANDT WITZLEBEN ZERKAULEN
ZOBELTITZ FLAISCHLEN
GERSTACKER KELLERMANN
SPIELHAGEN WASSERMANN
WILDERMUTH HASENCLEVER
FEUCHTWANGER SCHOPENHAUER
GREEK AESOP HOMER BARDIS
IOPHON LONGUS LUCIAN BABRIUS
PLUTARCH ARISTOTLE ONOSANDER
KAZANTZAKIS
GUATEMALAN ASTRUIAS
HUNGARIAN FAY BIRO JOKAI
DOBOZY FARAGO FOLDES JOSIKA
KARMAN SALTEN HEGEDUS
VAMBERY HARSANYI KOESTLER
KORMENDI
ICELANDIC KAMBAN ARNASON
LAXNESS SAEMUND GUNNARSSON
THORODDSEN GUDMUNDSSON
INDIAN ALI ABBAS ANAND GHOSE
MEHTA RUSHDIE SORABJI
CHATTERJI SHRIDHARANI
KRISHNAMURTI

IRISH DALY WEST BEHAN BOWEN COYLE CROLY DOYLE GWYNN JOYCE KEANE LECKY LETTS LOVER MOORE MOYES STERN TYNAN WILDE BARLOW BROOKE CROFTS ERVINE GRAVES LEFANU LESLIE MARTIN OBRIEN OGRADY OKELLY PEARSE STOKER TREVOR BECKETT CCOGARTY ORKERY DUNSANY LARDNER LAWLESS MACGILL MATURIN MAXWELL MURDOCH OCONNER STARKIE CARELTON CHILDERS KAVANAGH ODONNELL OFAOLAIN ORIORDAN STEPHENS OFLAHERTY TODHUNTER WARBURTON WIBBERLEY BARRINGTON MCALLISTER SOMERVILLE **ISRAELI** OZ BROD AGNON BUBER **ITALIAN** VARE BRUNO PULCI SERAO TASSO AMICIS FARINA MAFFEI PAPINI PAVESE SILONE ALBERTI BARRILI BARZINI BONATTI CARCANO DELEDDA GALIANI GIACOMO MANZONI MOHAVIA PELLICO ALBRIZZI BERSEZIO SABATINI BOCCACCIO CHIARELLI CORRADINI DANNUNZIO FOGAZZARO GUERRAZZI BELGIOIOSO BERTINELLI PREZZOLINI CASTELNUOVO PIRANDELLO **JAPANESE** ENDO BAKIN NAGAI OZAKI TAMAI MISHIMA FUKUZAWA KAWABATA MURASAKI **LATVIAN** RAINIS **MEXICAN** AZUELA GAMBOA TRAVEN FUENTES **NEW ZEALAND** EDEN ADAMS MARSH DUGGAN BOLITHO LYTTLETON MANSFIELD RUSSELL **NIGERIAN** ALUKO ACHEBE DELANO SOYINKA TUTUOLA **NORWEGIAN** LIE BULL BOJER FONHUS HAMSUN UNDSET COLLETT GARBORG INGSTAD ELVESTAD KIELLAND ASBJORNSEN **PERUVIAN** PALMA URETA ALEGRIA CACERES **POLISH** REJ ASCH PRUS STRUG ANCZYC BERENT CONRAD GOETEL BALUCKI REYMONT WITTLIN ZAPOLSKA ZELENSKI ZEROMSKI ZULAWSKI MILKOWSKI NALKOWSKA DANILOWSKI KONOPNICKA KRASZEWSKI CHMIELOWSKI OSSENDOWSKI SIENKIEWICZ KORZENIOWSKI ANDREZEJEWSKI **PORTUGUESE** LOBO BRAGA SOUSA DANTAS MORAES **ROMAN** LUCAN APULEIUS PHAEDRUS VELLEIUS PETRONIUS **RUMANIAN** BEIN GOGA NEGRUZZI CARAGIALE RADULESCU

RUSSIAN BLOK BABEL BUNIN FEDIN GOGOL GORKI FADEEV GLINKA HERZEN KRYLOV KUPRIN LEONOV LESKOV AKSAKOV ALDANOV AMALRIK ANDREEV CHEKHOV GARSHIN GLADKOV KATAYEV PILNYAK PUSHKIN ROMANOV TOLSTOI BULGAKOV KARAMZIN POTEKHIN SHALAMOV SHUKSHIN TURGENEV USPENSKI VERESAEY BESTUZHEV EHRENBURG GONCHAROV KOROLENKO LERMONTOV PASTERNAK SHOLOKHOV SUMAROKOV USPENSKII DOSTOEVSKI YUSHKEVICH ZOSHCHENKO AMFITEATROV ARTSYBASHEV GRIGOROVICH LAZHECHNIKOV SOLZHENITSYN **SCOTTISH** TEY DENT GALT GUNN HOGG LANG BEITH BROWN COMBE JACOB MUNRO SCOTT SHARP SPARK YOUNG AYTOUN BARRIE BROGAN BUCHAN GIBBON SHAIRP WATSON BALFOUR CHESNEY FERRIER HERRIOT MACLEAN MACLEOD BUCHANAN CRAUFURD CROCKETT LOCKHART MAITLAND MARSHALL OLIPHANT URQUHART FINDLATER MACDONALD MACKENZIE MITCHISON MOLESWORTH **SOUTH AFRICA** HEAD SEED PATON CLOETE MILLIN PLOMER **SOUTH AFRICAN** BLOOM COETZEE GORDIMER BALLINGER **SPANISH** ALAS BAREA PEREZ RIVAS ROJAS TRIGO ALEMAN BAROJA ESPRIU PEREDA SENDER AGUILAR ALARCON ESPINEL MACHADO CABALLERO CERVANTES **SWEDISH** AURELL CARLEN EDGREN MOBERG MWRDAL WAHLOO AHLGREN LIDGREN SJOWALL ALMQVIST LAGERLOF SCHWARTZ BACKSTROM LUNDEGARD LAGERKVIST STRINDBERG STREINDBERG WETTERBERGH **SWISS** ROD FREY HEER KING HESSE WYSS SPYRI FRISCH FUSELI KAISER BITZIUS FEDERER KERLLER OLIVIER DURRENMATT **WELSH** MAP EVANS PRYCE WYNNE DAVIES THOMAS ARUNDEL POLLETT LLEWELLYN **YUGOSLAVIAN** ANDRIC DJILAS DEDIJER **AUTHORITATIVE** GRAVE CLASSIC OFFICIAL ORACULAR POSITIVE TEXTUARY MAGISTERIAL (PREF.) CURIO **AUTHORITY** LAW ROD SEE BALL RULE SWAY ADEPT BOARD FAITH POWER RICHE RIGHT SAYSO STAMP

SWING TITLE ARTIST AUTHOR
CREDIT DANGER EMPERY EXPERT
FASCES PUNDIT REGENT REGIME
SWINGE WEIGHT AMITATE
COMMAND CONTROL DYNASTY
FACULTY LEADING LICENCE LICENSE
POTENCY SCEPTER WARRANT
DISPOSAL DOMINION DOMINIUM
HEGEMONY LORDSHIP PRESTIGE
SANCTION STRENGTH
PROCURATION
(— OF SWITZERLAND) BUNDESRAT
(ARBITRARY —) ABOVE
(CHALLENGE —) REBEL
(COLLEGE —) DON
(MORAL —) MANA
(ONE HIGHEST IN —) SUPREMO
(PAPAL —) VATICAN
(ROYAL —) SCEPTRE SOVRANTY
(SPIRITUAL —) KEYS KHILAFAT
(SUPREME —) SAY SIRCAR SIRKAR
(TEACHING —) MAGISTERIUM
(UNLIMITED —) AUTOCRACY
(PL.) ISNAD SIRCAR
(SUFF.) CRACY CRAT(IC)
AUTHORIZATION FIAT BARAT
BERAT PASSPORT SANCTION
WARRANTY PERMISSION
AUTHORIZE LET LEAL VEST ALLOW
CLEAR CLOTHE PERMIT RATIFY
APPROVE EMPOWER ENDORSE
ENTITLE INDORSE JUSTIFY LICENSE
WARRANT ACCREDIT DELEGATE
LEGALIZE SANCTION
AUTHORIZED LEGAL OFFICIAL
AUTHORSHIP PENCRAFT PATERNITY
AUTO (ALSO SEE AUTOMOBILE)
CRATE CHUMMY LIZZIE
(— RACING MANEUVER) SLINGSHOT
(— RACING PROBLEM) SPINOUT
(CONVERTIBLE —) RAGTOP
(UNSATISFACTORY —) LEMON
AUTOBIOGRAPHY VITA MEMOIR
AUTOCHTHONOUS NATIVE
EDAPHIC ENDEMIC
AUTOCLAVE DIGESTER DIGESTOR
AUTOCRACY MONARCHY
AUTOCRAT CHAM CZAR TSAR
TZAR MOGUL CAESAR DESPOT
AUTARCH MONARCH DICTATOR
MONOCRAT
AUTOCRATIC ABSOLUTE
AUTO-DA-FE AUTO SERMO
AUTOGRAPH NAME SIGN MANUAL
INSCRIBE
AUTOLYCUS (DAUGHTER OF —)
ANTICLEA
(FATHER OF —) HERMES MERCURY
(HALF-BROTHER OF —) PHILAMMON
(MOTHER OF —) CHIONE
AUTOMATIC REFLEX MACHINE
MECHANICAL
(PREF.) SELF

AUTOMATON GOLEM ROBOT
AUTOMA ANDROID MACHINE
AUTOMOBILE BUG BUS CAR SIX
AUTO FOUR HEAP JEEP PONY TRAP
BUGGY COACH COUPE CRATE
EDSEL EIGHT MOTOR PONEY RACER
SEDAN BUCKET CHUMMY CUSTOM
JALOPY JUNKER SALOON WHEELS
AUTOCAR COMPACT FLIVVER
HACKNEY HARDTOP MACHINE
MINICAR MINIVAN PHAETON
STEAMER TORPEDO VOITURE
CARRYALL DRAGSTER ELECTRIC
FASTBACK ROADSTER SQUADROL
SUBURBAN VICTORIA HATCHBACK
NOTCHBACK
(CONVERTIBLE —) RAGTOP
DROPHEAD
(DEMONSTRATOR —) DEMO
(KIND OF —) RENTACAR
(MIDGET —) DOODLEBUG
(NOISY —) BANGER
(SMALL —) MINI
AUTONOE (FATHER OF —) CADMUS
(HUSBAND OF) ARISTAEUS
(MOTHER OF —) HARMONIA
(SISTER OF —) AGAVE
(SON OF —) ACTAEON
AUTONOMOUS FREE SEPARATE
AUTONOMY SOVEREIGNTY
SEPARATENESS
(— OF GOD) ASEITY ASEITAS
AUTOPSY NECROPSY
AUTUMN FALL KHARIF AUTOMPNE
FALLTIME MATURITY
AUXILIARY AID YOU AIDE ALLY
ANSAR AIDING BRANCH DONKEY
HELPER ABETTER ABETTOR
ADJUNCT HELPING PARTNER
ADJUTANT ANCILLARY PERIPHERAL
(PL.) FOEDERATI
AVAIL DO AID DOW USE BOOT HELP
FADGE SERVE SKILL STEAD VALUE
MOMENT PROFIT BENEFIT BESTEAD
PREVAIL SERVICE SUCCEED SUFFICE
UTILIZE SUBSERVE
(— ONESELF) EMBRACE IMPROVE
SUBSERVE
AVAILABLE FIT FREE OPEN FLUSH
HANDY LOOSE ONTAP READY
PATENT USABLE PRESENT VISIBLE
ATSTORES
AVALANCHE SLIDE LAWINE
VOLLENGE
AVANT-COURIER HERALD
SCURRIER
AVANT-GARDE LITERATI
AVARICE GREED MAMMON MISERY
AVIDITY CUPIDITY RAPACITY
AVARICIOUS CLOSE SLOAN GREEDY
HAVING HUNGRY SORDID STINGY
GRIPING GRIPPLE ITCHING MISERLY
COVETOUS GRASPING

AVATAR BALARAMA EPIPHANY
AVELLANEOUS HAZEL
AVENGE REPAY RIGHT VISIT WRACK
WREAK AWREAK PUNISH BEWREAK
REQUITE REVENGE SATISFY
CHASTISE
AVENGER KANAIMA NEMESIS
WREAKER
AVENS GEUM BENNET BAREFOOT
AVENTURINE SUNSTONE
GOLDSTONE
AVENUE RUE WAY GATE MALL PIKE
ROAD ALLEE ALLEY DRIVE ENTRY
ACCESS ARCADE ARTERY DROMOS
RIDING STREET AVENIDA OPENING
PASSAGE
AVER SAY AIVER CLAIM PROVE STATE
SWEAR AFFIRM ALLEGE ASSERT
ASSURE AVOUCH DEPOSE VERIFY
DECLARE JUSTIFY PROFESS
PROTEST
AVERAGE PAR SUM DUTY FAIR
MEAN NORM RULE SOSO RATIO
USUAL VALUE CHARGE MEDIAL
MEDIAN MEDIUM MIDDLE NORMAL
TARIFF ARRIAGE ESTIMATE
MEDIOCRE MIDDLING MODERATE
ORDINARY OVERHEAD QUANTITY
STANDARD
(DOW-JONES —) DOW
(NOT —) BORDERLINE
AVERNAL HELLISH INFERNAL
AVERSE LOTH BALKY LOATH AFRAID
ADVERSE AWREAK AGAINST OPPOSED
BACKWARD INIMICAL OPPOSITE
PERVERSE RELUCTANT
(— TO) ABOVE
AVERSION TOY HATE DERRY ODIUM
ENMITY HATRED HORROR PHOBIA
REGRET DESPITE DISDAIN DISGUST
DISLIKE MISLIKE DISTASTE
ABOMINATION
(— TO FOOD) APOSITIA
(— TO WORK) ERGOPHOBIA
AVERT WRY BEND FEND MOVE SHUN
TURN WARD AVOID DETER DODGE
EVADE PARRY SHEER TWIST DEFRAY
DIVERT RETARD SHIELD DECLINE
DEFLECT EXPIATE PREVENT
ALIENATE ESTRANGE FOREFEND
WITHTURN
AVESTA ZEND
AVIARY CAGE HOUSE VOLARY
ORNITHON
AVIATOR ACE FLIER FLYER PILOT
AIRMAN FLYING ICARUS BIRDMAN
LOOPIST LUFBERY MANBIRD
SOLOIST
AVID LSD AGOG KEEN WARM EAGER
ARDENT GREEDY HUNGRY JEJUNE
ANXIOUS ATHIRST CRAVING
LONGING THIRSTY DESIROUS
GRASPING

AVIDITY AVARICE CUPIDITY
AVIFAUNA BIRDS ORNIS BIRDLIFE
AVIKOM JACKS
AVOCADO COYO PEAR PALTA
AHUACA CHININ MARROW PERSEA
ZABOCA ABACATE ABBOGADA
AGUACATE ALLIGATO
AVOCET BARKER TILTER YELPER
SCOOPER
AVOID FLY SHY BALK FLEE HELP MISS
PASS QUIT SAVE SHUN VOID WARE
ABHOR ANNUL AVERT BURKE DITCH
DODGE ELUDE EVADE EVITE FEIGN
HEDGE PARRY SHIFT SHIRK SKIRT
SKULK SLACK SPAIR SPARE START
WANDE WONDE ABJURE BLENCH
BYPASS DETOUR ESCAPE ESCHEW
REFUTE REMOVE VACATE ABSTAIN
DECLINE EVITATE FORBEAR FORSAKE
REFRAIN
(— A PUNCH) SLIP
(— COMMITMENT) FUDGE
(— EXPENSE) HELP MISS SKIVE
(— OVERWORKING) FAVOR
(— RESPONSIBILITY) BLUDGE
(— SUPERHIGHWAY) SHUNPIKE
(PREF.) PHYGO
AVOIDANCE DODGE OUTLET
EVASION ESCHEWAL
(— OF RISK) CAUTION
(PREF.) PHOB(O)
AVOIDING (— BATTLE) FABIAN
AVOIRDUPOIS HEFT
AVOUCH AVER ASSERT
AVOW OWN BIND WARE ADMIT
STATE AFFIRM ASSERT AVOUCH
DEPONE DEPOSE DEVOTE CONFESS
DECLARE JUSTIFY PROFESS
MAINTAIN
AVOWAL OATH WORD AVOURE
PROTEST
AVOWED FRANK SWORN STATED
DECLARED
AWAIT BIDE HEED KEEP PEND STAY
TEND WAIT ABIDE TARRY WATCH
ATTEND EXPECT IMPEND REMAIN
WAYLAY
(— PAYMENT) CARRY
AWAITING BEFORE BIDING
AWAKE DAW STIR WAKE ADAWE
ALERT ALIVE AWARE ROUSE ABRADE
ABRAID ACTIVE AROUSE AWAKEN
EXCITE CAREFUL HEEDFUL STARTLE
VIGILANT
AWAKEN DAW STIR ALERT AROUSE
BESTIR EXCITE KINDLE
AWAKENER
(ARMY —) BUGLE
AWAKENING REVIVAL WAKEFUL
AWARD LAW ARET CLIO GIVE HUGO
KUDO MARK MEED METE OBIE
TONY WARD ALLOT ARETT EDGAR
GRANT MEDAL PRICE PRIZE

ACCORD ACTION ADDEEM ADDOOM
ADWARD ASSIGN BESTOW BOUNTY
CONFER DECIDE GRAMMY MODIFY
ADJUDGE APPOINT CONSIGN
CUSTODY KEEPING ACCOLADE
SENTENCE
(ATHLETIC —) LETTER
(DETECTIVE FICTION —) EDGAR
(MOVIE —) OSCAR
(MYSTERY-NOVEL WRITING —)
EDGAR
(RADIO OR TELEVISION —) CLIO
(RECORDING —) GRAMMIE
(STATUETTE —) GRAMMY REUBEN
(TELEVISION —) EMMY
(THEATER —) OBIE
(THEATRICAL —) TONY
(WRITING —) HUGO
(PL.) DESERTS

AWARE HEP HIP RECK SURE WARE
WARY WISE ALERT ALIVE AWAKE
JERRY BEWARE KNOWING
MINDFUL APPRISED INFORMED
SENSIBLE SENTIENT VIGILANT
WATCHFUL
(— OF) ONTO
(KEENLY —) HIP

AWARENESS EAR FEEL SENSE
FEELING INSIGHT COGNITION
SENSATION PERCEPTION
(— OF SUPERNATURAL) VISION
(— OF WORTH) APPRECIATION

AWASH ASEA ADRIFT AFLOAT
FLOODED SWAMPED FLOATING

AWAY BY TO AWA FRO OFF OUT VIA
WAY AFAR GONE PAST SCAT YOND
ALONG APART ASIDE FORTH HENCE
ABROAD ABSENT BEGONE ONWARD
THENCE DISTANT FROWARD
FAREWELL TOTHEWIND
(— FROM) DOWN WITH ALONE
ALOOF APART BESIDE
(— FROM HOME) AFIELD OUTLAND
(— FROM MOUTH) ABORAL
(— FROM PORT) AFLOAT
(FARTHER —) BEYOND
(PREF.) DE E
(— FROM) APH APO

AWE COW WOW FEAR AMAZE DAUNT
DREAD SCARE FRIGHT HORROR
REGARD TERROR WONDER BUFFALO
RESPECT ASTONISH BEWILDER
OVERCOME RELIGION

AWED SOLEMN
AWEIGH ATRIP
AWE-INSPIRING GODFUL SOLEMN
AWESOME RELIGIO FEARSOME
OLYMPIAN

AWESOME EERY FELL HOLY AWFUL
EERIE WEIRD SOLEMN DREADED
GHOSTLY

AWESTRUCK SILENT
AWETO WERI

AWFUL DIRE FINE UGLY DREAD
GHAST AUGUST HORRID AWESOME
FEARFUL HIDEOUS SATANIC
DREADFUL SHOCKING TERRIBLE

AWFULLY AWFUL FIERCE
AWHILE FORABIT
AWKWARD AWK CAR GAUM UNCO
BLATE CRANK DODGY FALSE FUDGY
GAUMY GAWKY GOATY INAPT INEPT
SPLAY STIFF UNCOW UNKED UNKID
CLUMSY GAUCHE RUSTIC STICKY
THUMBY UNEASY WOODEN
ADVERSE BOORISH CUBBISH
FROWARD HALTING LOUTISH
LUMPISH STILTED UNCANNY
UNCOUTH UNHANDY UNREADY
BUNGLING CLOWNISH FECKLESS
LUBBERLY PERVERSE UNGAINLY
UNTOWARD UNWIELDY CLOUTERLY
GRACELESS MALADROIT
(— LOOKING) HORSY
(— PERSON) CLOUT KLUTZ TAWPY
TUMFIE
(NOT —) FACILE

AWKWARD PERSON GALOOT
AWL BROD BROG NAIL NALL PROD
PROG ALENE BRODE ELSEN NALLE
BROACH DRIVER ELSHIN FIBULA
GIMLET BRADAWL SCRIBER
STABBER

AWN AIL EAR JAG BARB BEAK JAGG
PILE ARISTA BRISTLE
(— OF BARLEY) HORN
(— OF OATS) JAG JAGG
(PL.) BEARD

AWNED BARBATE
AWNING TILT BLIND SHADE VELUM
CANOPY SEMIAN SHADER TIENDA
TENTORY SEMIANNA SUNBLIND
SUNSHADE VELARIUM

AWNLESS NOT NOTT HUMBLE
HUMMEL POLLARD MUTICOUS

AWRY CAM WRY AGEE BIAS SKEW
AGLEY AMISS ASKEW GLEED GLEYD
SNAFU WONKY WRONG ACROSS
ASIDEN BLOOEY BLOOIE CAMMED
FLOOEY SKIVIE THRAWN ASKANCE
ASQUINT ATHWART CROOKED
OBLIQUE PERVERSE

AX ADZ AXE CAN ADZE EAWT FIRE
HACHE MATAX BIFACE CANCEL
CUTOUT PICKEL PIOLET POLEAX
THIXLE TWIBIL BESAGUE BOUCHER
BROADAX CHOPPER CLEAVER
HATCHET JEDDING PULASKI TWIBILL
FRANCISC PALSTAVE SUNDERER
TOMAHAWK
(DOUBLE —) LABRYS
(HEADSMAN'S —) MANNAIA
(MASON'S —) CAVEL
(PART OF —) EAR EYE BUTT FACE
HAFT HEAD POLL BLADE HELVE
HANDLE

(WOODEN —) MACANA
(PREF.) SECURI
AXENIC GERMFREE
AXHAMMER CAVEL CAVIL KEVEL
KNAPPER
AXIAL VENTRAL
AXIL ALA
AXILLA AXIS ARMPIT SHOULDER
AXILLARY ALAR
AXIOM SAW ADAGE MAXIM MOTTO
BYWORD DICTUM SAYING TRUISM
DIGNITY PRECEPT PROVERB
APHORISM APOTHEGM DIGNITAS
PETITION SENTENCE POSTULATE
AXIOMATIC PRIMITIVE
AXIS AXE NUT AXLE STEM ARBOR
HINGE STALK ARBOUR CAUDEX
CENTER CHITRA RACHIS CAULOME
CORNCOB DENTATA POLAXIS
SPINDLE SUCCULA SYMPODE
TENDRIL AXLETREE MONOPODE
(— OF A FLOWER) CYME SPIKE
UMBEL CORYMB RACEME PANICLE
(— OF COCHLEA) MODIOLUS
(PREF.) AX(I)(IO)(O)(ONO)
AXLE EX BAR COD PIN AXIS BOGY
ARBOR BOGEY BOGIE EXTRE SHAFT
AXTREE SLEEVE MANDREL SPINDLE
SUCCULA
AXOLOTL SIREDON
AXON PROCESS
AYAH IYA CHAY EYAH MAID NURSE
AYE I AY EY EYE PRO YEA YES EVER
ALWAYS ASSENT FOREVER
AYESHA (HUSBAND OF —)
MOHAMMED
AYU AI SWEETFISH
AZALEA ERICA MINERVA CARDINAL
AZALIAH (SON OF —) SHAPHAN
AZANIAH (SON OF —) JESHUA
AZAREEL (FATHER OF —) BANI
JEROHAM
(SON OF —) AMASHAI MAASIAI
AZARIAH (FATHER OF —) JEHU ODED
ETHAN NATHAN AHIMAAZ JEROHAM

JOHANAN MAASEIAH JEHALELEL
ZEPHANIAH JEHOSHAPHAT
(SON OF —) JOEL
AZAZ (SON OF —) BELA
AZAZEL EBLIS
AZAZIAH (SON OF —) HOSHEA
AZERBAIJAN (ALSO SEE RUSSIA)
(CAPITAL OF —) BAKU
(CAPITOL OF —) BAKU
AUTONOMOUS REGION:
NAGORNOKARABAKH
AUTONOMOUS REPUBLIC:
NAKHICHEVAN
CANAL: SHIRVAN KARABAKH
CAPITAL: BAKU BAKY
COIN: MANAT
LAKE: GEYGYOL
LANGUAGE: AZERI
MOUNTAIN: TUFAN SHAKHDAG
BAZARDYUZYU KYUMYURKYOY
MOUNTAIN RANGE: TALISH TALYSH
CAUCASUS MUROVDAG SHAKHDAG
ZANGEZUR
PLAIN: MUGAN SHIRVAN LENKORAN
MILSKAYA
RIVER: ARAS KURA ARAKS
TOWN: GANJA SUMGAIT KIROVABAD
AZIMUTH ZN ARC BEARING
AZMAVETH (SON OF —) PELET JEZIEL
AZOLE PYRROLE
AZOR (FATHER OF —) ELIAKIM
AZRIEL (SON OF —) SERAIAH
AZRIKAM (FATHER OF —) AZEL
NEARIAH
(SLAYER OF —) ZICHRI
AZTEC AZTECA MEXICA MEXICAN
TENOCHCA
AZUBAH (HUSBAND OF —) CALEB
(SON OF —) JEHOSHAPHAT
AZUR (SON OF —) HANANIAH
JAAZANIAH
AZURE BICE BLUE HURT JOVE
COBALT JOVIAL JUPITER CERULEAN
SAPPHIRE
AZZAN (SON OF —) PALTIEL

B

B SI BEE BAKER BRAVO
(— FLAT) ZA BEMOL
BA TRIPOS
BAA MAA MAE BLEAT
BAAL BEEZEBUB
BAANA (FATHER OF —) AHILUD
(SON OF —) ZADOK
BAANAH (BROTHER OF —) RECHAB
(FATHER OF —) HUSHAI RIMMON
(SLAYER OF —) DAVID
(SON OF —) HELEB HELED
BAARA (HUSBAND OF —)
SHAHARAIM
BAASHA (FATHER OF —) AHIJAH
BABBAR UTU UTUO
BABBITT PHILISTINE
(AUTHOR OF —) LEWIS
(CHARACTER IN —) TED MYRA PAUL
TANIS ZILLA GEORGE VERONA
BABBITT JUDIQUE REISLING
BABBLE CHAT GASH KNAP PURL
TOVE BABIL BLATE CLACK CLYDE
GLOCK HAVER PRATE TAVER WLAFF
CACKLE DITHER GABBLE GAGGLE
GLAVER GOSSIP JANGLE MURMUR
PALTER PIFFLE RABBLE TAIVER
TUMULT BLABBER BLATHER
BLETHER BLUSTER BRADDLE
CHATTER CHIPPER CLATTER PRATTLE
SMATTER TWADDLE TWATTLE
GLAISTER
RABBLER CACKLER BLATEROON
STIPITURE
BABBLING LALLATION
(PREF.) LALO
BABE NAIF INFANT
BABEL DIN MEDLEY TUMULT
CHARIVARI CONFUSION
BABESIA APIOSOMA NUTTALIA
PIROPLASMA
BABOON APE PAP PAPA DRILL
ADONIS BAVIAN CHACMA GIRRIT
PAPION SPHINX RABUINA MANDRILL
HAMADRYAD
BABUL SANT SUNT ACACIA BABOOT
GARRAT GONAKE NEBNEB ATTALEH
GONAKIE
BABUSHKA SCARF KERCHIEF
BABY MOP BABA BABE CHAP DOLL
JOEY NENE TOTO WEAN BAIRN
CHILD HUMOR SPOIL WAYNE CHRISM
CODDLE FONDLE INFANT MOPPET
PAMPER POUPEE PUPPET SQUALL
WEANIE BAMBINO CHRISOM
INDULGE PAPOOSE PREEMIE
WADDLER PAPPOOSE
(— FOOD) PAP

BABY CARRIAGE PRAM BUGGY
WAGON GOCART STROLLER
PERAMBULATOR
BABYISH TIDDY PULING SIMPLE
PUERILE CHILDISH
BABYLONIA CHALDEA
BABYLONIAN
(— CYCLE) SAROS
BABY'S BREATH GYP GYPSOPHILA
BACALAO MURRE SCAMP ABADEJO
CODFISH GROUPER GUILLEMOT
BACCATE BERRIED
BACCHANAL DEVOTEE REVELER
CAROUSER
BACCHANTE FROW MAENAD
BACCHUS LIBER LYAEUS BROMIUS
DIONYSUS
(AUNT OF —) INO
(FATHER OF —) ZEUS JUPITER
(MOTHER OF —) SEMELE
BACHELOR BACH SEAL BATCH
GARCON WANTER BACULERE
BENEDICT CELIBATE
BACILLUS GERM VIRUS MICROBE
BACK AID FRO TUB VAT ABET BAKE
BECK FULL HIND HINT NAPE NATA
REAR TAIL ABACK AGAIN ANGEL
BOOST BROAD CHINE DORSE FAVOR
NOTUM SPINE SPLAT STERN VOUCH
ASSIST DORSUM HINDER RETRAL
SECOND SOOTHE TERGUM TROUGH
UPHOLD VERIFY CISTERN ENDORSE
FINANCE POSTERN RIGGING
SPONSOR SUPPORT SUSTAIN
BACKWARD FULLBACK HALFBACK
MAINTAIN
(— A ROWBOAT) STERN
(— OF ANIMAL) RIG TERGUM
(— OF ARCHERY TARGET) BOSS
(— OF AWNING) RIDGEROPE
(— OF BOOK) DORSE SPINE
(— OF DULL) ROOF
(— OF HAND) OPISTHENAR
(— OF HEAD) INION NODDLE NIDDICK
OCCIPUT
(— OF INSECT) NOTUM
(— OF NECK) NAPE NUQUE SCRUFF
(— OF PAGE) FV
(— OUT) BEG JIB DUCK FLUNK
CRAWFISH
(— TO BACK) ADDORSED
(— UP) ABET PROVE VERIFY
(— WATER) STERN SHEAVE
(ANIMALS' —S) DORSA
(BROUGHT —) REDUX
(SHOWING —) TERGANT
(PREF.) ANA DORSI DORSO NOT(O)

OPISTH(O) POST RE RETRO TERGI
TERGO
(AT THE — OF) OPISTH(O) POSTERO
(BENT —) POSTERO RECURVI
RECURVO
(SUFF.) NOTUS
BACKACHE NOTALGIA
BACKBAND RIGWIDDIE RIGWOODIE
BACKBITING CATTY DETRACTION
BACKBOARD BANK MONITOR
BACKBONE BACK GRIT GUTS CHINE
NERVE PLUCK RIDGE SPINA SPINE
LADDER METTLE SPIRIT GRISTLE
RIGBANE SPINULE STAMINA
VERTEBRA
(— OF FISH) GRATE
BACKCHAT MOUTH CROSSTALK
BACK-COMB TEASE
BACKCOUNTRY BUSH STICKS
BOONIES BACKLAND BACKVELD
BOONDOCKS
BACKDROP OLEO SCENERY SETTING
BACKER ANGEL
BACKFIELD SECONDARY
BACKFIRE BOOMERANG
BACKFLASH GUTTER
BACKGAMMON IRISH LURCH
TABLE FAYLES GAMMON TABLES
BACKGAME TICKTACK VERQUERE
(— MAN) BLOT TABLEMAN
BACKGROUND FOND REAR
GROUND OFFING LINEAGE SETTING
BACKDROP DISTANCE EXTERIOR
OFFSCAPE TRAINING EDUCATION
(— OF FLOWERS) BOCAGE
(MUSICAL —) SUPPORT
BACKHANDED AWKWARD
BACKHOE PULLSHOVEL
BACKHOUSE PRIVY OUTHOUSE
BACKING AID EGIS AEGIS BACKUP
BEHIND LINING MUSLIN REFUSE
SUPPORT HEARTING FINANCING
(LEGAL —) STRENGTH
BACKLASH LASH SHAKE SLACK
BACKLOG RESERVE SURPLUS
BACKBRAND
BACKPACK GEAR LOAD
BACKPIECE DOSSIERE
BACKPLATE REREDOS
BACKREST LAZYBACK
BACKROPE GOBLINE
BACKSEY SEY SIRLOIN
BACKSLIDE FALL LAPSE DESERT
REVERT RELAPSE
BACKSPIN DRAG UNDERCUT
UNDERSPIN
BACKSTITCH PURL PEARL
BACKSTOP BUTT
BACK TALK LIP SASS
BACKWARD FRO JAY LAX YON
BACK CRAB DARK DULL LOTH ABACK
AREAR BLATE INAPT LOATH THRAW

UNAPT ARREAR ASTERN AVERSE
BYGONE POSTIC RETRAD RETRAL
STUPID ARRIERE BASHFUL LAGGARD
LAGGING REVERSE UPSTAGE
DILATORY IGNORANT LATEWARD
PERVERSE REARWARD RINKYDINK
TAILFIRST
(PREF.) OPISTH(O) RE RETRO
BACKWARDNESS DARKNESS
BARBARISM
BACKWARDS YON ABACK AROUND
(PREF.) OPISO PALI(M)(N)
BACKWASH SLIPSTREAM
BACKWATER EBB COVE SLEW SLUE
SNYE BAYOU BOGAN SHEAVE
SLOUGH RETRACT RETREAT
BACKWASH BILLABONG
BACKWOODS BRUSH
BACKWOODSMAN HICK WOODSY
BUCKSKIN HILLBILLY
BACKWORT COMFREY
BACON PIG BARD MEAT PORK BARDE
JAMON PRIZE SPECK FLITCH
GAMMON RUSTIC SAWNEY
GAMBONE SOWBELLY
(UNSMOKED —) PANCETTA
BACOPA BRAMIA
BACTERIOLOGIST
AMERICAN GAY KAHN NOVY PARK
BURKE CRAIG ERNST MOORE PLOTZ
BERGEY ENDERS JORDAN FRANCIS
KENDALL NOGUCHI THEILER
ZINSSER
BELGIAN BORDET
BRAZILIAN CHAGAS
CANADIAN WESBROOK
CUBAN AGRAMONTE
ENGLISH TWORT FLEMING
FRENCH ROUX RAMON MARTIN
LAVERAN NICOLLE CHAMBERLAND
GERMAN KOCH FLUGGE GAFFKY
GRUBER HUEPPE BEHRING EHRLICH
GARTNER LOFFLER FRAENKEL
PFEIFFER UHLENHUTH
WASSERMANN
JAPANESE HATA SHIGA KITAZATO
RUMANIAN BABES
RUSSIAN METCHNIKOFF
SPANISH FERRAN
SWISS YERSIN
BACTERIUM ROD COLI GERM
AEROBE COCCUS CYTODE ANTHRAX
CHOLERA LYSOGEN MICROBE
PROTEUS SARCINA VIBRION
BACILLUS LISTERIA PATHOGEN
SHIGELLA BOTULINUS CYTOPHAGA
HEMOPHILE INFECTANT INFECTION
SPIRILLUM MICROCOCCUS
PNEUMOCOCCUS SCHIZOMYCETE
PNEUMOBACILLUS
BAD BIG DUD ILL SAD EVIL FULL HARD
LEWD POOR PUNK QUED SICK SOUR

VILE WICK ADDLE GAMMY LOUSY
NASTY SORRY WEARY WORST
WRONG ARRANT FAULTY LITHER
LUTHER NOUGHT ROTTEN SEVERE
SHREWD SINFUL UNGOOD UNKIND
WICKED BALEFUL BANEFUL CHRONIC
CORRUPT FEARFUL HARMFUL
HEINOUS HURTFUL IMMORAL
INUTILE NAUGHTY SPOILED TAINTED
UNLUCKY UNMORAL UNSOUND
VICIOUS ANNOYING CRIMINAL
DEPRAVED DOGGEREL FIENDISH
FLAGRANT INFERIOR PRECIOUS
SINISTER UNSUITED
(— MANNERS) TROLLOPE
(ASTROCIOUSLY —) PIACULAR
(OUTRAGEOUSLY —) GRIEVOUS
(OUTSTANDINGLY —) ARRANT
PIACULAR
(RATHER —) INDIFFERENT
(VERY —) FEARFUL ALMIGHTY
GODAWFUL EXECRABLE
(PREF.) CAC(O) CACH DYS KAK(O)
MAL(F) MIS
(SUFF.) CACE
BADDERLOCKS MURLIN PURSES
HENWARE SEAWEED HONEYWARE
BADEBEC (HUSBAND OF —)
GARGANTUA
(SON OF —) PANTAGRUEL
BADGE PIN BLUE MARK SIGN STAR
COLOR CREST CROSS FAVOR HONOR
ORDER PATCH TOKEN WINGS
BUTTON BUZZER COLLAR EMBLEM
ENSIGN FASCES GARTER GIGLIO
PLAQUE SHIELD SYMBOL TIPONI
WEEPER CHEVRON EPAULET
FEATHER BRASSARD EPISEMON
INSIGNIA SCAPULAR VERNICLE
EPAULETTE COGNISANCE
(— OF VIRGINITY) SNOOD
(JAPANESE —) MON KIRIMON
(PILGRIM —) SCALLOP
(RUSSIAN —) ZNAK
(PL.) INSIGNIA
BADGER NAG PAT BAIT GRAY GREY
GRIS MELE PATE ANNOY BRACE
BROCK BRUSH CHEVY CHIVY HURON
MELES PAHMI RATED RATEL TAXEL
TAXUS TEASE WORRY BAUSON
BAWSON BOTHER BRAROW CHIVVY
HAGGLE HARASS HAWKER HECKLE
KIDDER MELINE PESTER TELEDU
WOMBAT BAUSOND GRISARD
TORMENT BRAIREAU BULLYRAG
CARCAJOU HUCKSTER IRRITATE
STINKARD MISTONUSK
(— STATE) WISCONSIN
(AUSTRALIAN —) WOMBAT
(BURROW OF —) SET SETT
(COMPANY OF —S) CETE
(LIKE A —) MELINE

BADGER-DOG DACHSHUND
BADINAGE FOOL CHAFF JOKER
BANTER RAILLERY TRIFLING
BADLANDS MALPAIS
BADLY BAD ILL EVIL HARD ILLY SICK
SADLY EVILLY HARDLY POORLY
UNWELL FAULTILY WICKEDLY
VICIOUSLY
(PREF.) MAL
BADMINTON POONA
BADNESS MALICE PRAVITY
UNVALUE EVILNESS
(SUFF.) CACE
BADROULBOUDOUR
(HUSBAND OF —) ALADDIN
BAD-TEMPERED CRANKY STROPPY
CROTCHETY FOUL ANGRY STINGY
CRABBED GROUCHY
BAFF LOFT
BAFFLE FOX GET BALK BEAT FOIL
LICK MATE POSE STOP UNDO CHEAT
CHECK ELUDE EVADE FLING STICK
STUMP BLENCH BOGGLE DEFFAT
DELUDE FICKLE HUMBUG OUTWIT
PUZZLE RESIST THWART BUFFALO
CONFUSE DECEIVE QUIBBLE
STONKER BEWILDER CONFOUND
DISGRACE JUGGLING
BAFFLED FOXED BEATEN
BAFFLING SHREWD ELUSIVE
BAG COD KIT LOT MAT NET PAD POD
POT SAC CELL DRAG GRIP HOBO KILL
LAND LOBE MAIL POCK POKE SACK
TOOT TOTE TRAP WOMB BELLY
BOUGE BULSE CATCH DILLI DILLY
EMERY FLOAT HUODY PETER POUCH
PURSE SCRIP SEIZE SHOOT SNARE
STEAL BLOUSE BUDGET CAVITY
ENTRAP FOLLIS GASBAG MATAPI
PAGGLE POCKET POUNCE SACHET
SEABAG VALISE WALLET ALFORJA
BALLOON BEANBAG BLISTER
BUCKRAM CANTINA CAPCASE
CAPTURE CUSHION DESTROY
GAMEBAG GOMUKHI HANDBAG
HOLDALL RETICLE SANDBAG
SARPLER SATCHEL TRAVOIS
BALLONET CARRYALL CORNSACK
ENTRAILS ENVELOPE FOLLICLE
KNAPSACK MONEYBAG OVERSLIP
POCHETTE RETICULE RUCKSACK
SUITCASE WINESKIN MULTIWALL
WEEKENDER PORTMANTEAU
(— BULGING) SWAG
(— FOR DIAMONDS) BULSE
(— FOR LETTERS) MAIL POUCH
KAREETA MAILBAG POSTBAG
(— FOR TOOLS) WALLET
(— OF ANISEED) DRAG
(— OF PERFUME) SACHET
(— OF WOOL) POCKET
(— WITH POCKETS) TIDE TIDY

(ANATOMICAL —) CECUM CAECUM STOMACH
(AUSTRALIAN —) SWAG DILLI SHIRT SHAMMY
(GAS —) CELL
(GRAB —) FISHPOND
(HAWSE —) JACKASS
(KIND OF —) DOGGY DOUGLAS
(LEATHER —) JAG JAGG ASKOS BUDGE BOUGET MUSSUK
(NET —) SNOOD GARLAND
(SEWING —) HUSSY
(SLEEPING —) FUMBA FLEABAG SLEEPER
(WATER —) CHAGAL CHAGEN CHAGUL
(PREF.) UTRI
(SUFF.) SACCATE SACCI SACCO
BAGASSE BEGASS LINAGA MEGASS
BAGATELLE CANON TRUNK VERSE CANNON TRIFLE NOTHING
BAGEL ROLL BIALY
(PARTNER OF —) LOX
BAGGAGE ARMS GEAR MINX SWAG CUTTY HUZZY NASTY SAMAN STUFF TENTS TRASH WENCH HARLOT REFUSE TRASHY TRUNKS CLOTHES DUNNAGE EFFECTS FARDAGE PLUNDER RUBBISH SALMARY SUMPTER VALISES CARRIAGE HARLOTRY RUBBISHY UTENSILS
BAGGAGE CAR WAGON FOURGON
BAGGER SACKER BATCHER
BAGGING SOUTAGE
BAGGY LOOSE POCKY PURSY FLABBY PUFFED PURSIVE SACCATE
BAGNIO BAIN BATH BAGNE PRISON BROTHEL HOTHOUSE
BAGPIPE MUSE PIPE PIVA DRONE TITTY BIGNOU BINIOU CHORUS GEWGAW MUSETTE PIFFERO SAMBUKE DULCIMER SYMPHONY ZAMPOGNA CORNAMUTE CORNEMUSE SYMPHONIA
(PART OF —) BAG CORD PIPE DRONE MOUNT STOCK TASSEL CHANTER WINDBAG BLOWPIPE
BAGUETTE CHAPLET
BAH PO FIE FOH PAH POH ROT RATS FAUGH PSHAW NONSENSE
BAHAMAS (CAPITAL OF —) NASSAU
(ISLAND OF —) ABACO EXUMA ANDROS BIMINI
(TOWN IN —) FREEPORT
BAHIA (CAPITAL OF —) SALVADOR
BAHRAIN (CAPITAL OF —) MANAMA
(MONEY OF —) FILS DINAR
(TOWN OF —) RIFAA JIDHAFS
BAIL BOW DIP BALE BOND HOOP LADE LAVE RING RYND YOKE LADLE SCOOP THROW VOUCH BUCKET HANDLE PLEDGE SECURE SURETY

VADIUM CAUTION CUSTODY DELIVER RELEASE REPLEVY BAILSMAN BULWARKS SECURITY GUARANTEE
(— OUT) ABANDON
BAILEE LESSEE POSITOR CONDUCTOR
BAILER SPOUCHER
BAILIFF FOUD GRAB HIND AGENT REEVE SAFFO SCULT STAFF BAILIE BAILLI BEADLE BEAGLE DEPUTY FACTOR GRIEVE LOOKER OFFICE PORTER PREVOT SCHOUT VARLET BUMTRAP GRIPPER PROVOST PUTTOCK SHERIFF STEWARD APPROVER HUISSIER OVERSEER TIPSTAFF CATCHPOLE CATCHPOLL CONSTABLE HUNDREDER PORTREEVE SENESCHAL WAPENTAKE
BAILIWICK AREA FIELD DOMAIN OFFICE SPHERE PROVINCE
BAILMENT MUTUUM
BAILOR LESSOR
BAIN NEAR LITHE READY SHORT DIRECT LIMBER SUPPLE FORWARD WILLING
BAIRN WEAN
BAIT BAD BOB COG DAP LUG BITE CAST CHUM FEED HALT HANK LURE PLUG TAIL DECOY HOUND LEGER SHACK SLATE SQUID STALE TEMPT TRAIN WORRY ALLURE APPAST ATTACK BADGER BERLEY ENTICE HARASS HECKLE HECTOR KILLER LEDGER REPAST SHRAPE SLIVER FULCRUM GUDGEON PROVOKE TAGTAIL TOLLING TORMENT BRANLING CUNGEBOI BRANDLING
(— FOR BIRDS) SHRAP SHRAPE
(— FOR COD) CAPELIN
(— WITH DOGS) SLATE
(GREASY —) ROGUE
(GROUND —) BERLEY
(MAGGOT —) GENTLE
(SCENTED —) DRAG
(SPINNING —) PROPELLER
BAITING HANK
BAIZE BAY BAYES BAYETA DOMETT BOCKING
BAKE DRY BURN FIRER COCT COOK FIRE BATCH BROIL GRILL PARCH ROAST ANNEAL HARDEN BISCUIT PISTATE SCALLOP CLAMBAKE ESCALLOP
(— EGGS) SHIRR
(— THOROUGHLY) SOAK
BAKED CASINO COCTILE
(— IN EARTH OVEN) KALUA
(— PRODUCT) KICHEL
BAKER OVEN FIRER BAXTER BURNER FURNER PISTOR FURNACE OVENMAN ROASTER
BAKER BIRD HORNERO

BAKERY PIZZERIA
BAKING CUIT DATCH COCTION
  FURNAGE ASSATION
BAKONGO FIOT
BALAAM (FATHER OF —) BEOR
BALACHONG NGAPI
BALAK (FATHER OF —) ZIPPOR
BALANCE BEAM EVEN PEIS REST
  SWAY TRIM COVER ERASE PEISE
  POISE SCALE TRONE WEIGH WEIHE
  ADJUST AUNCEL CANCEL EMBLEM
  EQUATE KELTER KELVIN KILTER
  LAUNCE OFFSET SANITY SQUARE
  STRIKE DESEMER LIBRATE OVERRUN
  RESIDUE TRABUCH TRUTINE
  EQUALITY EQUALIZE EQUATION
  SERENITY WESTPHAL TREBUCHET
  PROPORTION
  (— DUE) ARREAR
  (— IN ACCOUNT) CREDIT
  (— OF SAILS) ATRY
  (MAKE —) EQUATE
  (MENTAL —) HEAD
  (PREF.) STATO
BALANCED EVEN EQUAL LEVEL
  TRUED APOISE KITTLE WEIGHED
  COMPLETE QUADRATE TOGETHER
  (PREF.) SYM
BALANCER HALTER ACROBAT
  GYMNAST HALTERE
BALATA ICICA BULLACE BEEFWOOD
  BORRACHA
BALCONY POY ORIEL PORCH STOOP
  CIRCLE GAZEBO PIAZZA PODIUM
  SOLLAR BALAGAN GALLERY
  MIRADOR PERGOLA TERRACE
  BRATTICE CANTORIA VERANDAH
  MEZZANINE
BALD RAW BARE BASE BOLD CRUDE
  DODDY NAKED PLAIN CALLOW
  PALTRY PEELED PILLED SIMPLE
  CALVOUS EPILOSE LITERAL POLLARD
  GLABROUS HAIRLESS TONSURED
  (— HEAD) PILGARLIC
  (— SPOT) TONSURE
  (PREF.) PHALACRO
BALDACHIN CANOPY CIBORIUM
BALDER BALDR BALDUR BAELDAEG
  (CHILD OF —) FORSETE FORSETI
  (FATHER OF —) ODIN
  (SLAYER OF —) HOTH LOKE LOKI
  HOTHR
  (WIFE OF —) NANNA
BALDERDASH ROT GUFF PUNK
  GOOEY TRASH TRIPE DRIVEL
  JARGON FLUBDUB NONSENSE
  BALDUCTUM RIGMAROLE
BALDMONEY MEU SPIGNEL
  SPICKNEL
BALDNESS ACOMIA CALVITY
  ALOPECIA ATRICHIA OPHIASIS
  CALVITIES

BALDPATE ZUISIN POACHER
BALDRIC BELT LACE GIRDLE ZODIAC
  BALTEUS SUPPORT NECKLACE
BALE NO GIB NOT WOE EVIL FIRE
  HARM LAVE PACK PYRE BLOCK
  CRATE DEATH FARDO SERON BALLOT
  BUNDLE EMBALE SEROON SORROW
  PACKAGE SARPLER
BALEARIC ISLANDS
  (ISLAND OF —) IBIZA CABRERA
  MAJORCA MINORCA CONEJERA
  (MEASURE OF —) PALMO MISURA
  QUARTA QUARTIN BARCELLA
  (TOWN OF —) IBIZA MAHON PALMA
  (WEIGHT OF —) CARGO CORTA
  QUARTANO
BALEEN WHALEBONE
BALEFUL BAD EVIL DEADLY MALIGN
  SACRED SULLEN MALEFIC NOXIOUS
  RUINOUS SIDERAL SINISTER
  WRETCHED MALEFICENT
BALI (CAPITAL OF —) DENPASAR
  (DANCE OF —) LANDJA DARIS KRISS
  BARONG KETJAK MONKEY DJANGER
  (MOUNTAIN OF —) AGOENG
  (MUSICAL INSTRUMENT OF —)
  GAMELAN
  (RICE FIELD OF —) SAWAII
  (STRAIT OF —) LOMBOK
  (TOWN OF —) SINGARADJA
BALIN (BROTHER OF —) SUGRIVA
  (SLAYER OF —) RAMA
BALINGHASAY ANAM ANAN
BALK GAG HEN HUE JIB JUB SHY
  BEAM BILK BUCK BULL COND FOIL
  CORM HADE HEAP LICK LOFT MISS
  OMIT PROP SHUN SKIP SLIP STAY
  STOP AVOID BAULK BLOCK CHECK
  CLAMP DEMUR HUNCH MOUND
  REBEL REEST RIDGE STAKE STICK
  WAVER BAFFLE DEFEAT FALTER
  HINDER IMPEDE OUTWIT RAFTER
  REFUSE STRAIN THWART BLUNDER
  CODLING GALLOWS ISTHMUS
  MISTAKE
  (— IN FISHING) HUE COND
  (HALF —) FLITCH
  (PL.) MIDDLES
BALKAN (— COIN) NOVCIC
  (— COUNTRY) GREECE SERBIA
  ALBANIA RUMANIA BULGARIA
  (— INSTRUMENT) GUSLA
  (— RIVER) JIU OLT IBAR JIUL SAVA
  TISA OLTUL DANUBE MORAVA
  (— SEA) BLACK AEGEAN IONIAN
  ADRIATIC
BALKER HUER CONNER
BALKY NAPPY STICK MULISH REESTY
  RESTIVE CONTRARY STUBBORN
  OBSTINATE
BALL IN BAL BOB FLY HOP NOB ORB
  PEA TOY BEAD BOWL CLEW CLUE

KNOB KNOP KNUR PICK PILL POME
PROM TRAP DANCE EDGER FAULT
FLOAT GLOBE GLOME HURLY ORBIT
PEARL PUPPY SHAPE SNACK SPORT
TRUCK BULLET BUTTON HOOKER
HURLEY MOONIE MUDDLE PEELEE
PELLET PELOTA POMMEL POMPON
RONDEL RUNDLE SPHERE SQUASH
BALLOON CONFUSE FLOATER
GLOBULE INCURVE INSHOOT
KNAPPAN LEATHER MANDREL
PELOTON RIDOTTO SLITTER
ASSEMBLY BASEBALL BISCAYEN
FANDANGO FOOTBALL GROUNDER
HANDBALL QUENELLE SOFTBALL
SPHEROID TRAPBALL
(— AS SHIP'S SIGNAL) SHAPE
(— FOR MUSKET) GOLI SLUG
(— OF CLAY) KNICKER
(— OF FIRE) DYNAMO
(— OF RICE OR MEAT) PINDA
(— OF THREAD) COP CLEW CLUE
GOME BOTTOM COPPIN WHARROW
(— OF THUMB) THENAR CUSHION
(— OF WASTE IRON) COBBLE
(—S OF MEDICI FAMILY) PALLE
(— USED IN SHINTY) PEG
(BILLIARD —) SPOT IVORY SNOOKER
(BOWLED —) TICE CURVE SKYER
BAILER BUMPER FIZZER GOOGLY
KICKER POODLE SEAMER YORKER
CREEPER SNORTER SPINNER
BREAKBACK CROSSOVER
INSWINGER
(BOWLING —) DODO JACK
(CORK —) PLUMBER
(CRICKET —) SNICK SHOOTER
(CROQUET —) ROVER
(DECORATIVE —) DRAGEE
(FIVES —) SNACK
(FORCEMEAT —) QUENELLE
(FRIED —) RISSOLE
(GOLF —) PUTTY
(HARD —) SNUG
(HOCKEY —) NUN NUR ORR
(INK —) PUMPET
(JAI ALAI —) PELOTA
(KIND OF —) MINIE
(MEAT —S) CECILS
(PLASTIC —) WIFFLE
(SKITTLE —) CHEESE
(SPONGE —) NERF
(TENNIS —) PALM
(WOODEN —) KNUR
(PREF.) GLOBI GLOBO SPHAER(O)
SPHER(O)
(SUFF.) SPHAERA SPHERE
SPHERIC(AL)
BALLAD JIG LAI LAY LILT·MELE POEM
SONG CAROL DERRY FANCY BALLET
BYLINA CARVAL SONNET BALLANT
CANZONE CORRIDO GWERZIOU
SINGSONG

BALLAST BED CRIB LOAD TRIM
METAL POISE STONE BOTTOM
BURDEN GRAVEL WEIGHT BALANCE
LASTAGE SANDBAG DRAGROPE
KENTLEDGE SABURRATE
BALLERINA DANCER DANSEUSE
BALLET BALLAD MASQUE BOURREE
PANTOMIME
(— COACH) REPETITEUR
(— LEAP) CABRIOLE ENTRECHAT
(— MOVEMENT) VOLE FERME TEMPS
APLOMB CHASSE OUVERT POINTE
RELEVE RETIRE ALLONGE ARRONDI
ASSEMBLE ATTITUDE ARABESQUE
(— POSE) ARABESQUE
(— PROP) BARRE
(— SPIN) PIROUETTE
BALLHOOTER BRUTTER
BALLISTA SWEEP MANGONEL
BALLOON BAG BALL BLIMP EXPAND
GASBAG AIRSHIP DISTEND DRACHEN
INFLATE SAUSAGE SKYHOOK
AEROSTAT ENVELOPE DIRIGIBLE
(TRIAL —) KITE
BALLOONING BOSOMY
BALLOONIST AERONAUT
AEROSTAT
BALLOON VINE FAROLITO
HEARTPEA HEARTSEED
BALLOT BALE POLL PROX VOTE
ELECT PROXY VOICE BILLET CHOICE
POLICY TICKET SUFFRAGE
BALLROOM SALOON
BALLYHOO BALLY HOOPLA
BALM OIL BEEB BITO DAUB ODOR
SALVE ANOINT BALSAM EMBALM
LOTION RELIEF SOLACE SOOTHE
ANODYNE BESMEAR COMFORT
PERFUME UNGUENT OINTMENT
(— OF GILEAD) CANADA
OPOBALSAM
(BURN —) ALOE
BALMORAL CAP BOOT SHOE
BALMY DAFT MILD SOFT BLAND
DAFFY MOONY SPICY SUNNY SWEET
GENTLE INSANE SERENE HEALING
LENIENT AROMATIC BALSAMIC
DRESSING FRAGRANT SOOTHING
BALONEY BULL BUNK CROCK
HOOEY BUNKUM BUSHWA
BUSHWAH
BALSA RAFT FLOAT GUANO POLAK
POLACK BOBWOOD CORKWOOD
BALSAM FIR RIGA TOLU UMIRI
COPALM GURJAN GURJUN STORAX
AMPALEA COPAIBA CREEPER
AMPALAYA BDELLIUM BENJAMIN
OINTMENT
BALSAM APPLE KARELA
AMARGOSA AMPALAYA BALSAMINE
BALSAM FIR SAPIN BAUMIER
BALSAM POPLAR TACAMAHAC
BALSAMROOT SUNFLOWER

BALSAMWEED MOONSHINE
FEATHERWEED
BALT YOD ESTH LETT ESTONIAN
BALTIC (— GULF) RIGA DANZIG
BOTHNIA FINLAND
(— ISLAND) AERO DAGO FARO OSEL
ALAND ALSEN OESEL OLAND
GOTLAND HIIUMAA BORNHOLM
(— PORT) KIEL RIGA MEMEL REVAL
DANZIG GDANSK TALINN LEIPAJA
(— RIVER) ODER ODRA DVINA
VIADUA
(— TOWN) MEMEL DANZIG GDANSK
LEIPAJA
BALUCHISTAN (— CULTURE)
QUETTA
BALUSTER SPOKE COLUMEL
BANISTER COLUMELLA
BALUSTRADE BARRER PARAPET
RAILING BALCONET BANISTER
BAMBI (AUNT OF —) ENA
BAMBOO DHA CANE REED BATAK
GLUMAL GUADUA TONKIN BATAKAN
WANGHEE WHANGEE
(SACRED —) NANDIN
(WOVEN —) SAWALI
BAMBOOZLE DUPE HAVE CHEAT
COZEN GRILL CAJOLE HUMBUG
BUFFALO BUMBAZE DECEIVE
DEFRAUD MYSTIFY PERPLEX
BAN BAR WOE TABU VETO BANAL
BANUS BLOCK CURSE EDICT ORDER
TABOO BANISH CENSOR ENJOIN
FORBID HINDER INVOKE NOTICE
OUTLAW CONDEMN EXCLUDE
ANATHEMA DENOUNCE EXECRATE
PROHIBIT
(— ON NEWS) BLACKOUT
(LEGAL —) ESTOP
BANA (DAUGHTER OF —) USHA
BANAK UCUUBA
BANAL FLAT CORNY INANE SILLY
STALE TRITE VAPID JEJUNE INSIPID
MUNDANE TRIVIAL
BANANA FEI FIG MUSA SABA BERRY
ENSETE FINGER SAGING LACATAN
PLATANO SAGUING SUNBEAM
PLANTAIN
(KIND OF —) TOP
BANANAS BALMY BATTY DAFFY
BAND BAR GAD HUB TIE TUB ZON
BEAD BELT BEND BOND CAME CASH
CORD CREW CUFF FALL FERD FESS
GANG GATE GIRT HOOD HOOP KNOT
LACE LIST RING SASH SHOE TAPE
WISP ZONA ZONE AMPYX BANDY
BRAID CHOIR CLAMP CORSE COVEY
COVIN CRAPE CROWN FEMUR FLOCK
FRAME GIRTH GORGE GUARD JATHA
LABEL MEINY NOISE PANEL PATTE
PRIDE QUIRE SABOT SNOOD STRAP
STRIP STROP TAPIS TORSE TRACK
TRIBE UNITE WERED WITHE ARMLET

BENDEL BINDER BORDER BOYANG
BRIDGE BUNDLE CIMBIA CLAVUS
COHORT COLLAR COLLET COPULA
COVINE CRANCE CRAVAT DECKLE
FASCIA FETTER FILLET FRIEZE FRINGE
FUNNEL GAMMON GARTER GASKET
GIRDLE HYPHEN LEGLET MATRIX
NIPPER NORSEL PLEDGE RADULA
REGULA ROLLER SCREED STRAKE
STRING STRIPE SWATHE TAENIA
TETHER TISSUE WEEPER BINDING
BLANKET CHAMBUL CIRCLET
COMPANY ENOMOTY FERRULE
FRONTAL GARLAND HATBAND
HEADING NECKTIE ORPHREY
PALLIUM PIGTAIL PROMISE SEQUELA
SHACKLE SHOEING SWADDLE
VINCULUM
(— ACROSS SUNSPOT) BRIDGE
(— AROUND MAST) PARREL
(— AT BOTTOM OF WALL) PLINTH
(— FOR HEAD) VITTA
(— IN BRAIN) LIGULA FRENULUM
FUNICULUS
(— IN ROCKS) FAHLBAND
(— OF CLAY) COTTLE
(— OF COLOR) SOCK SLASH STRIA
LACING FASCIOLE SPECTRUM
(— OF CRAPE) WEED SCARF
(— OF FUR) TIPPET
(— OF INDIANS) SHIVWITS
(— OF LIGHT) STREAMER
(— OF PILLAGERS) SKINNERS
(— OF PIPERS) POVERTY
(— OF PLASTER) SCREED
(— OF PURPLE) CLAVUS
(— OF STARS) GALAXY
(— OF STRAW) GAD SIMMON
(— OF TISSUE) TENDON TISSUE
(— OF 13 WITCHES) COVEN
(— ON HORSE'S HOOF) FROG
(— ON SHIELD) ENDORSE
(— TO COMPRESS CHEEKS)
CAPISTRUM
(— TOGETHER) BANDY
(— UNDER TONGUE) LYTTA
(ARMED —) JATHA POSSE
(ARMOR —) TONLET
(CIRCULAR —) HOOP RING ANNULE
WREATH
(DANCE —) CHORO COMBO
(DECORATIVE —) PATTE LEGLET
CORNICE ARCHIVOLT
(DIVIDING —) CLOISON
(EUCHARISTIC —) MANIPLE
(FOREHEAD —) INFULA
(HEAD —) BANDEAU
(IRON —) FRET GATE TRUSS FUNNEL
STRAKE
(LACE —) SCALLOP
(MUSICIANS —) CONCERT
(NOISY —) CALLITHUMP
(RADIO —) CHANNEL

(RAISED —) RIB
(RESONANCE —) FORMANT
(STREET —) MARIACHI
(TRIBAL —) AIMAK
(PL.) GRIPES INTERLACERY
(PREF.) TAENI(A)(O) ZON(I)(O)
(SUFF.) (CILIATED —) TROCH(A)(AL)
(OUS)(US)
BANDAGE BAND BELT BIND TAPE
BLIND BRACE CLOUT DRESS GALEA
LINEN SLING SPICA SWARF SWATH
TRUSS BINDER COLLAR CRAVAT
FASCIA FETTLE FILLET LIGATE NIPPER
ROLLER SWARTH SWATHE SWEATH
REVERSE ROLLING SWADDLE
TRUSSER ACCIPTER CAPELINE
CINCTURE GAUNTLET LIGAMENT
LIGATURE SCAPULAR STOCKING
CAPISTRUM
(— FOR NOSE) ACCIPITER
(EYE —) MUFFLER
(FINGER —) HOVEL
(JAW —) FUNDA
(PL.) SWADDLING
BANDALORE QUIZ
BANDANNA WEB TURBAN
BANDANA PULICAT PULICATE
PULLICAT
BANDAR RHESUS
BANDEAU BRA BAND STRIP FILLET
BRASSIERE
BANDICOOT RAT MARL BILBI BILBY
BADGER BIELBY PINKIE QUENDA
BANDIT CACA TORY BRAVO THIEF
BANISH HAIDUK HEYDUK OUTLAW
ROBBER BANDIDO BRIGAND
LADRONE TULISAN BUSHWACK
MARAUDER MIQUELET PICAROON
RAPPAREE BANDOLERO
(PL.) MANZAS
BANDLEADER MASTER MAESTRO
CHORAGUS CONDUCTOR
BANDORE PANDORA PANDURA
(PREF.) PANDURI
BANDSMAN WINDJAMMER
BANDSTAND KIOSK STAND
BANDY VIE BAND CART CHOP SWAP
TRADE LEAGUE RACKET STRIVE
CHAFFER CONTEND DISCUSS
CARRIAGE EXCHANGE
SHUTTLECOCK
(— WORDS) REVIE GIFFGAFF
BANE BAN WOE BONE EVIL HARM
KILL PEST RUIN CURSE DEATH
VENOM INJURY MURDER POISON
SLAYER NEMESIS SCOURGE
MISCHIEF MURDERER NUISANCE
BANEBERRY COHOSH REDBERRY
TOADROOT GRAPEWORT
BANEFUL BAD ILL EVIL VILE SWART
HARMFUL HURTFUL NOXIOUS
RUINOUS VENOMOUS SINISTRAL
PERNICIOUS

BANG POM RAP BAFF BEAT BLOW
BOOT DASH DOCK DRUB POUF RUSH
SCAT SLAM SWAP SWOP TANK
BLAFF CLASH CRACK DRIVE EXCEL
FORCE IMPEL POUND SLAKE SLUMP
SOUND SPANG STRAM THUMP
WHACK WHANG WHUMP BOUNCE
CUDGEL ENERGY FRINGE STRIKE
THRASH THUNGE THWACK SARDINE
SURPASS THUNDER FORELOCK
(— ON HEAD) BRAIN
BANGLADESH (CAPITAL OF —)
DACCA
(MONEY OF —) TAKA
(NATIVE OF —) BENGALI
(PAISA OF —) POISHA
(RIVER OF —) GANGES
(TOWN IN —) KHULNA CHITTAGONG
COIN: TAKA
BANGLE ORNAMENT
BANGTAIL NAG
BANG-UP SLAP CRACK TIPTOP
BANISH BAN FREE ABAND EJECT
EXILE EXPEL FLEME WAIVE WREAK
BANDIT DEPORT DISPEL DISTER
FORSAY OUTLAW ABANDON
CONDEMN CONFINE DISMISS
DIVORCE EXCLUDE DISPLACE
RELEGATE EXPATRIATE
BANISHED FUGITIVE
BANISHMENT EXILE BANNIMUS
OUTLAWRY XENELASY OSTRACISM
XENELASIA
BANISTER RAILING BALUSTER
BANJO BOX BANJORE BANJORINE
(— SITE) KNEE
BANK BAR BAY COP JUG RIM ROW
BINK BRAE BREW BUTT CAJA DIKE
DUNE DYKE EDGE HEAD HILL LINK
MASS PILE RAKE RAMP RELY RIPA
RIVE SAND SCAR SEAT SIDE TIER
WEIR BANCO BENCH BLUFF BRINK
COAST DITCH EARTH FENCE HOVER
HURST LEVEE MARGE MOUND
MOUNT RIDGE SAVER SHARE SHELF
SHOAL SHORE SLOPE STACK STAGE
TRUST BANQUE BORROW CAISSE
CAUSEY CRADGE DEGREE DEPEND
DOUBLE MARGIN RANDOM RECKON
RIVAGE STRAND ANTHILL BANKING
CUSHION DEPOSIT LOMBARD
POTTERY SANDBAG SHALLOW
WINDROW BARRANCA PLATFORM
TRAVERSE
(— A FIRE) REST
(— ASSOCIATION) SANDL
(— FOR DRYING BRICKS) HACK
(— OF CANAL) BERM BERME
HEELPATH
(— OF EARTH) COP DAM DITCH
(— OF RIVER) RIPA WHARF STRAND
(— OF SAND OR MUD) BAR SCALP
(— OF SNOW) WREATH SNOWDRIFT

(— OF TURF) SUNK
(KIND OF —) STILL
(OVERHANGING —) BREW HOVER
(RUSSIAN —) CHAPETTE
(SAVINGS —) THRIFT
(STEEP —) HEUCH HEUGH WOUGH
BARRANCA BARRANCO
(PREF.) RIPI
BANKER BOOK SETH SETT FACTOR
FINDER SAHKAR SHROFF SOUCAR
SOWCAR LOMBARD MARWARI
MONEYER SPONSOR TAILLEUR
BANQUETER FINANCIER
BANKNOTE CRISP FLIMSY SCREEN
(FORGED —) STUMER
(PL.) CABBAGE
BANKRUPT SAP BONG BUNG BUST
DUCK RUMP BREAK BROKE DRAIN
SMASH STRIP BROKEN BUSTED
DYVOUR QUISBY CRACKED
DEPLETE
BANKRUPTCY SMASH FAILURE
SMASHUP
BANKSMAN LANDER HILLMAN
BANLIEUE LOWY ENVIRONS
BANNER FANE FLAG JACK SIGN
COLOR BUMPER ENSIGN FANNON
PENNON LABARUM LEADING
PENNANT SALIENT BANDEROL
BRATTACH FOREMOST GONFALON
ORIFLAMB STANDARD STREAMER
VEXILLUM BEAUSEANT ORIFLAMME
(— ON TRUMPET) TABARD
(FUNERAL —) BANNEROL
GUMPHEON GUMPHION
(PL.) ENSIGNRY
BANNOCK PANAK DIGGER JANNOCK
BANNS CRY BANS CRIES NOTICE
SIBRET SIBRIT SIBREDE SPURRINGS
BANQUET FETE MEAL DIFFA FEAST
DINNER JUNKET MANGER REGALE
REGALO REPAST SEUDAH SPREAD
AHAAINA CONVITO CONVIVE
NAMGERY REGALIO CAROUSAL
FESTIVAL SYMPOSIUM SYSSITION
BANQUETER CONVIVE SYMPOSIAST
BANQUETING EPULATION
TRENCHERING
BANQUETTE FIRESTEP
BANSHEE BOW SIDHE TROLL
BANTAM COCK GRIG BANTY DANDY
SAUCY CHICKEN SEBRIGHT
COMBATIVE
BANTENG OX TSINE BANTIN
TEMADAU
BANTER COD KID RAG ROT CHIP
FOOL JEST JOKE JOSH MOCK QUIZ
RAIL RAZZ BORAK CHAFF DRAPE
JOLLY QUEER RALLY ROAST TAUNT
TRICK DELUDE DERIDE HAGGLE
SATIRE BADINER STASHIE RADINAGE
CHAFFING GIFFGAFF RAILLERY
RIDICULE

BANTING DIET DUGOUT
BANTU ILA BULU GOGO GUHA HEHE
YAKA ZULU DUALA KAFIR KAMBA
KIOKO KONDE KONGO LAMBA
SHONA SWAZI BANYAI BASUTO
DAMARA HERERO KAFFIR NATIVE
THONGA WAGUHA YAKALA CABINDA
MASHONA SWAHILI WACHAGA
(— LANGUAGE) ILA RONGA NYANJA
THONGA KIRUNDI NYAMWEZI
BANTUSTAN HOMELAND
BANYAN BUR BURR BANIYA BUNNIA
JAGUEY
BAOBAB MOWANA IMBONDO
TEBELDI CALABASH ADANSONIA
BAPTISM CLEANSING IMMERSION
PALINGENY PERFUSION
BAPTISMAL FONTAL
BAPTIST DIPPER DOPPER DIDAPPER
SEPARATE TRASKITE
BAPTIZE DIP DEPE FULL NAME
HEAVE VOLOW PLUNGE PURIFY
ASPERSE CLEANSE IMMERSE
CHRISTEN SPRINKLE
BAPTIZED ILLUMINATE
BAR BAN DAM FID FOX GAD INN LAW
LEG RIB ROD TAP AXLE BALK BAND
BANK BAUR BEAM BOLT BOOM BULL
CAKE CHAR CORE CROW DRAG FLAT
GATE HIDE JOKE LOCK MAKE OUST
POLE RACK RAIL REEF SAVE SETT
SHUT SKID SLAB SLAT SLIP SLOT
SNIB STOP TREE YARD ARBOR
BAULK BENCH BETTY BILBO BLOCK
BLOOM BRACE CATCH CLASP CLOSE
COURT CRAMP CREEL DEDAN DETER
DOLLY EASER EMBAR ESTOP FENCE
FORCE GEMEL HEDGE HORSE HUMET
LEVER PERCH PILOT PINCH PITCH
RANCE RATCH SHADE SHAFT SHAPE
SIGHT SLOTE SNEEK SPELL SPOON
SPRAG STAFF STANG STAVE STEEK
STRAP STRIP STRUT SWIPE TRACE
YAIRD ANCONY BARRET BATTEN
BILLET BISTRO BODEGA BROOCH
BUMPER CRUTCH DOFFER DOLLEY
DOLLIE EVENER EXCEPT EYEBAR
FASTEN FORBAR FORBID FORCER
FORSET GRILLE HEAVER HINDER
LADDER MEAGRE NORMAN PEELER
RABBLE RADIAL RETURN RIFFLE
SALOON SHADES SHANTY STOWER
STRIPE TABLET TANGLE TILLER
TOGGLE BARRACE BARRAGE
BARRIER BOBSTAY BOLSTER
BUVETTE CHANNEL CHARIOT
CONFINE COUNTER DRAWBAR
EXCLUDE GALLOWS MANDREL
MANDRIL OVERARM PREVENT
SCRATCH SIDEBAR SNIBBLE SPINDLE
STEMMER TOMBOLO TOPRAIL
TRUNDLE WIREBAR ASTRAGAL
KNIFEWAY MURDERER PESSULUS

(— FOR TAPPING FURNACE) LANCET
(— IN CHIMNEY) SWEE
(— IN FABRIC) BARRE
(— IN RIVER) CHAR SANDBAR
(— IN SEA) SWASH
(— OF CULTIVATOR) ARCH
(— OF DOOR) SLOT STANG
(— OF ELECTRIC SWITCH) BLADE
(— OF GATE) SPAR LEDGE
(— OF HARROW) BULL
(— OF LOOM) EASER SWORD BATTEN
BACKSTAY
(— OF METAL) ZED
(— OF RAYS) SHOOT
(— OF SAND) TOMBOLO
(— OF STEEL) BLOOM BILLET
STIRRUP
(— OF WAGON) SHETH
(— OF WHEEL) SPOKE
(— ON BOWSPRIT) WHISKER
(— ON SIDE OF BOWSPRIT) WHISKER
(— ON WINDMILL) UPLONG
(— SUPPORTING MILLSTONE)
MOLINE
(— WITH SHACKLES) BILBOES
(— WITH SPIKES) HERISSON
(CAST IRON —) SOW
(CONNECTING —) ZYGON
(HERALDIC —) FESS FESSE HUMET
LABEL
(JOINTED —) CHILL
(KIND OF —) RAW WET CASH FERN
NERF OPEN SWAY SALAD DATING
OYSTER SINGLES
(MINING —) MOIL
(NOTCHED —) RISP SKEY
(PAIR OF —S) GEMEL GEMMEL
(REFRESHMENT —) BUFFET CANTEEN
(SOAP FRAME —) SESS
(STIRRING —) CRUTCH
(TAMPING —) STEMMER
(TYPEWRITER —) BAIL BALE SPACER
SHUTTLE
(UNSAVORY —) DIVE
(WEAVING —) TEMPLE
(WHEEL —) AXLE SPOKE
BARABARA HUT
BARACHEL (SON OF —) ELIHU
BARAK (FATHER OF —) ABINOAM
BARANI BRANDY
BARB AWN BUR JAG MOW BURR CLIP
FILE FLUE HAIR HERL HOOK JAGG
BEARD HORSE POINT RIDGE SHAFT
SPEAR PIGEON STRAIN TIPPET
WITTER BARBARY BARBULE BRISTLE
FILAMENT KINGFISH
(— OF ANCHOR) FLUKE
(— OF ARROW) HOOK WING BEARD
WITTER
(— OF FEATHER) HARL HERL RAMUS
PINNULA FILAMENT
(— OF HARPOON) FLUE FLUKE
(THROW —S AT) ZING

(PREF.) ONC(O)
BARBADOS (CAPITAL OF —)
BRIDGETOWN
(MOUNTAIN OF —) HILLABY
(NATIVE OF —) BIM BAJAN
BARBADOS CHERRY ACEROLA
BARBADOS PRIDE SANDALWOOD
BARBAREA CAMPE
BARBARIAN HUN BOOR GOTH RUDE
WILD ALIEN BRUTE SAVAGE VANDAL
RUFFIAN FOREIGNER HOTTENTOT
UNTUTORED TRAMONTANE
BARBARIC GROSS ATROCIOUS
BARBARISM CANT DATISM
SAVAGISM SOLECISM
BARBARITY FERITY CRUELTY
FELLNESS FEROCITY RUDENESS
SAVAGERY BRUTALITY
BARBAROUS FELL RUDE WILD
CRUEL BRUTAL FIERCE GOTHIC
BESTIAL FOREIGN HUNNISH
INHUMAN SLAVISH UNCIVIL
IGNORANT CUTTHROAT FEROCIOUS
PRIMITIVE
BARBARY MAGOT MAGHRIB
MOGHRIB
(— STATE) TUNIS ALGIERS
MOROCCO TRIPOLI
BARBASCO CUBE JOEWOOD
BARBECUE ASADO BOCAN BUCCAN
(— ITEM) KABOB
BARBEL BEARD CIRRUS WATTLE
BARBLET CYPRINID
BARBER NAI FIGARO POLLER SHAVER
TONSOR SCRAPER TONSURE
(— FISH) TANG
BARBER OF BAGDAD
(CHARACTER IN —) ABUL BEKAR
CALIPH MARGIANA NUREDDIN
(COMPOSER OF —) CORNELIUS
**BARBER OF SEVILLE (CHARACTER
IN —)** BERTHA FIGARO ROSINA
BARTOLO LINDORO ALMAVIVA
(COMPOSER OF —) ROSSINI
BARBERRY MAHONIA
BARBET BARBION BARMKIN
DREAMER BARBICAN PUFFBIRD
WATERRUG IRONSMITH PEARLBIRD
THICKHEAD TIGERBIRD
BARBITAL VERONAL
BARBITURATE DOWNER SECONAL
GOOFBALL SECOBARBITAL
PENTOBARBITAL PHENOBARBITAL
BARBULE RADIUS RADIOLUS
**BARCHESTER TOWERS (AUTHOR
OF —)** TROLLOPE
(CHARACTER IN —) BOLD SLOPE
ARABIN BERTIE NERONI ELEANOR
GRANTLY HARDING OBADIAH
PROUDIE SEPTIMUS STANHOPE
CHARLOTTE ETHELBERT QUIVERFUL
BARD BHAT MUSE POET SCOP SWAN
DRUID OVATE RUNER SCALD SKALD

OSSIAN SHAPER SINGER BARDING PENBARD MINSTREL MUSICIAN TALIESEN DEMODOCUS SEANNACHIE

BARE DRY BALD LEAN MERE NUDE POOR THIN ALONE BLEAK CRUDE EMPTY NAKED PLAIN PLUME SCANT STARK STRIP WASTE BARISH BARREN CALLOW DENUDE DIVERT DIVEST EXPOSE HISTIE MARGIN MEAGER MEAGRE PALTRY PILLED REVEAL SCARRY SIMPLE DIVULGE EXPOSED UNARMED UNCOVER DENUDATE DESOLATE DISCLOSE STRIPPED DESTITUTE
(— SKIN) BUFF
(— TEETH) TUCK
(NOT —) COOL
(PREF.) GYMN NUDI PSIL(O)

BAREFACED GLARING IMPUDENT AUDACIOUS SHAMELESS

BAREFOOT UNSHOD

BARELY JIMP JUST ONLY FANIT HARDLY MERELY POORLY SIMPLY UNEATH UNNETH NAKEDLY UNNETHE EDGEWAYS SCANTILY SCARCELY SLIGHTLY

BARER NAVVY DELVER FEIGHER MUCKMAN CALLOWER

BARFISH DORAB

BARFLY SOT TOSSPOT

BARGAIN GO BUY RUG WOD COPE DEAL HUCK KOOP MART MISE PACT PICK RUGG SALE SELL SNIP SONG TROG WHIZ CHEAP FIGHT PRICE STEAL TROKE TRUCK WHACK WHIZZ BARTER DICKER HAGGLE HIGGLE INDENT NIFFER PALTER CHAFFER CHEAPEN COMPACT CONTEND CONTEST DISPOSE PACTION TRAFFIC CONTRACT COVENANT PENNORTH PURCHASE STRUGGLE WANWORTH PENNYWORTH
(— HARD) PRIG
(— IN MINING) STURT

BARGAINER NIP KITE COPER COWPER CHAFFERER
(SHARP —) SCREW

BARGAINING MART ACHATE CHAFFER CHEAPING HUCKSTERY
(KIND OF —) PLEA

BARGE ARK BOX BOY HOY TOW TUB BARK BOAT FUST LUMP PRAM RAFT SCOW TROW BARCA CASCO DUMMY FOIST LUNGE LURCH PRAAM SCOLD SHREW VIXEN BARQUE BERATE BUGERO DREDGE GALLEY GYASSA PRAHAM REBUKE STUMPY TENDER THRUST WHERRY BALLOON BIRLING BIRLINN CHALANA DROGHER GABBARD GABBART GONDOLA LIGHTER OMNIBUS TOWBOAT TUMBLER TUMBRIL BILLYBOY

BUDGEROW CARRIAGE BUCENTAUR MOORPUNKY
(COAL —) KEEL
(FRENCH —) TOUE
(TOWED —) BUTTY

BARGEMAN PUG BARGEE BARGER HOYMAN HUFFLER

BARGHEST PADFOOT

BARITE CAUK CAWK TIFF CAULK BARYTES BARYTINE HEPATITE

BARITONE DEEP

BARK AGO BAG BAY OUF RUB TAN WAP YAP YIP BAFF BOAT BOOF COAT COTO DITA HOWL HUSK OPEN PEEL PELT PILL REND RIND ROSS SKIN SNAP TAPA WAFF YAFF YAWP YELP YIPE AABEC BALAT BARCA BARGE COUGH MOCHA NIEPA SHELL SHOUT SPEAK STRIP TIMBE YAMPH YOUFF ABRADE AGAMID AVARAM BARKEY BOWWOW CASSIA CORNUS CORTEX GIRDLE MASSOY SINTOC TRANKY WAFFLE YAFFLE CASCARA MALAMBO MESENNA PEREIRA PHLOEUM SOLICIT TANBARK DOUNDAKE EUONYMUS FRANGULA GRANATUM MEZEREUM WOODSKIN RHYTIDOME QUERCITEON
(AROMATIC —) CANELLA CULILAWAN
(EXTERIOR OF —) ROSS
(INNER —) BAST
(LAVER OF —) HAT
(PREF.) CORTICI CORTICO PHELLO PHLO(E)(EO) QUIN(O)

BARKER BUFFER DOORMAN GRINDER SPIELER SPUDDER SPRUIKER CHARLATAN

BARKING BAY SPUD QUEST LATRANT LATRATION

BARLEY BIG BEAR BENT BERE BIGG GRAIN SPRAT LICORN HORDEUM WHITECORN
(AWN OF —) HORN
(GROUND —) TSAMBA
(HULLED —) PTISAN
(REFUSE —) SHAG FLINTS
(PREF.) ALPHITO CRITHO

BARLEY CAKE
(PREF.) MAZO

BARN BYRE AMBAR LATHE STALL GRANGE STABLE SKIPPER COWHOUSE
(— OWL) LULU MADGE
(COW —) SAUR SHIPPON
(PART OF —) BAY HIP DOOR EAVE APRON GABLE RIDGE VERGE AWNING CUPOLA DORMER PENTHOUSE VENTILATOR WEATHERVANE

BARNACLE BRAY BREY ACORN LEPAS CYPRIS ANATIFA BALANID LEPADID CIRRIPED GNATHOPOD SACCULINA

BARNBURNER SOFT
BARNSTORM TOUR
BARNYARD PIGHTLE BACKSIDE
FARMYARD STRAWYARD
BAROMETER GLASS ANEROID
OROMETER STATOSCOPE
BARON THANE DAIMIO BARONET
FREEMAN FREIHERR
(COURT —) HALLMOOT
BARONET SIR
BARONY HAN DOMAIN
BAROQUE GOTHIC ORNATE ROCOCO
GROTESQUE IRREGULAR
BAROTO VINTA
BARRACK CAMP BOTHY CASERN
CANNABA CUARTEL
BARRACKS HOOCH HOOTCH
(DETENTION —) GLASSHOUSE
BARRACUDA CUDA KAKU SPET
BARRY PELON SNAKE SNOEK SNOOK
BECUNA PICUDA SCOOTS SENNET
VICUDA KATONKEL SCOOTERS
BARRAGE BAR SALVO ATTACK
VOLLEY BARRIER DRUMBEAT
DRUMFIRE UMBRELLA CANNONADE
FUSILLADE
BARRAMUNDA SALMON CYCLOID
DIPNOAN FLATHEAD CERATODUS
BARRED CUCKOO RIBBED STRIPED
BARREL FAT HUB KEG TUN VAT BUTT
CADE CASK DRUM KANG TREE
WOOD BOWIE QUILL SHELL STAND
UNION FESSEL GIRNAL GIRNEL
HOGGET RUMBLE RUNLET TIERCE
TUMBLE VESSEL CALAMUS CISTERN
PACKAGE RATTLER RUNDLET
TUMBLER CYLINDER HOGSHEAD
KILDERKIN
(— OF FEATHER) CALAMUS
(— OF REVOLVER) CHAMBER
(— ROW) LONGER
(— WITH CRANKS) VANGEE
(CAPSTAN —) SPOOL
(CORE —) LANTERN
(HERRING —) CADE CRAN
(PART OF —) HEAD HOOP CHIME
STAVE BOTTOM
(SMALL —) KEG KIT CADE KNAG
RUNLET BARRICO RUNDLET
(TAR —) CLAVIE
(PL.) ALOT
BARRELHOUSE GUTBUCKET
BARREN DRY ARID BARE BOWY
DEAD DEAF DOUR DULL EILD GAST
GELD LEAN NUDE POOR SALT SECK
YELD YELL ADDLE BLEAK BLUNT
BOWEY DRAPE DUSTY EMPTY
GAUNT GHAST GUESS NAKED
STARK STERN WASTE YEILD DESERT
EFFETE FALLOW HISTIE HUNGRY
JEJUNE MEAGER STUPID SAPLESS
STERILE DESOLATE IMPOTENT

TEEMLESS TREELESS
(NOT —) FACILE FECUND
(PL.) LANDES
(PREF.) STEIRO
BARREN GROUND
(AUTHOR OF —) GLASGOW
(CHARACTER IN —) JASON RUFUS
GENEVA JOSIAH NATHAN OAKLEY
PEDLAR DORINDA ELLGOOD
GREYLOCK
BARRENNESS DEARTH VACANCY
EMPTINESS
BARRICADE BAR STOP BLOCK
CLOSE FENCE ABATIS PRISON
BARRAGE BARRIER DEFENSE
FORTIFY OBSTRUCT RAMFORCE
REVETMENT ROADBLOCK
(— OF TREES) ABATIS
BARRIER ALP BAR DAM BALK BOMA
BOOM CRIB CROY DIKE DOOR DYKE
FOSS GATE LINE LOCK PALE STOP
WALL WEIR BAULK BOUND CHAIN
FENCE FOSSE GRILL HEDGE LIMIT
STILE STUMP CORDON GLACIS
GRILLE HURDLE SCREEN TREBLE
BARRAGE CEILING CHICANE CURTAIN
GALLERY PARAPET RAILING
RAMPART BOUNDARY FORTRESS
FRONTIER STOCKADE STRENGTH
TRAVERSE
(— ACROSS RIVER) STILL KIDDLE
(— IN TRUCK) HEADER
(— OF STAKES) STOCKKADE
(— OF TREES) SHELTERBELT
(ARTIFICIAL —) FOSS FOSSE
(OIL SPILL —) BOOM
(PROTECTIVE —) REDOUBT
(RACECOURSE —) RAILS
(SPIKED —) TURNPIKE
(TRAFFIC —) SEPARATOR
(PL.) BAIL
(PREF.) HERCO
BARRING BUT SAVE CLOSED
BARRISTER COLT BARMAN JUNIOR
LAWYER TUBMAN COUNSEL
POSTMAN TEMPLAR ADVOCATE
ATTORNEY SERJEANT
(PL.) BAR
BARROOM PUB CAFE HOUSE
BISTRO SALOON CANTINA DOGGERY
GROCERY TAPROOM DRAMSHOP
DRINKERY EXCHANGE GROGGERY
GROGSHOP
BARROW HOD HOG BANK BIER
DUNE GALT HILL MOTE TUMP CARRY
GRAVE GURRY HURLY MOUND
SEDAN TRUCK BURROW GALGAL
KURGAN NAVETA HILLOCK TROLLEY
TUMULUS MOUNTAIN PUSHCART
BARRULET VIVRE
BARTENDER MIXER BARMAN
BARMAID SKINKER TAPSTER

BARTER CHAP CHOP COPE COUP
HAWK MANG MONG SELL SWAP
TROG VEND CORSE TRADE TROKE
TRUCK DICKER NIFFER SCORSE
BARGAIN CAMBIUM CHAFFER
PERMUTE TRAFFIC TRUCKLE
COMMERCE EXCHANGE TRUCKAGE

**BARTERED BRIDE (CHARACTER
IN —)** JASEK JENIK KECAL MICHA
TOBIAS MARENKA ESMERALDA
(COMPOSER OF —) SMETANA

BARTERER COPER COWPER
TRUCKER

BARUCH (FATHER OF —) NERIAH
ZABBAI COLHOZEH

BARYTES CAUK CAWK HEPATITE

BARZILLAI (SON OF —) ADRIEL

BASAL BASIC BASILAR RADICAL

BASALT MARBLE NAVITE DIABASE
GHIZITE KULAITE POTTERY
AUGANITE BANDAITE BASANITE
DOLERITE ANAMESITE ARAPAHITE
MELAPHYRE SUDBURITE VARIOLITE
(DECOMPOSED —) WACKE

BASE BED DEN HUB LOW TUT ANIL
CLAM EVIL FOOT FOUL HUBB HUNK
LEWD MEAN POOR RELY REST ROOT
SACK STAY STEM STEP VILE BASIS
BLOCK CHEAP DIRTY FIRST FLOOR
FOUND LACHE MUDDY PETTY SNIDE
SOCLE STAND STOOL WORSE
ABJECT BOTTOM BRASSY COARSE
COMMON DEMISS GROUND
GRUBBY HARLOT HUMBLE MENIAL
NOUGHT PALTRY PATAND PATTEN
PERRON PODIUM RASCAL SECOND
SHABBY SORDID VULGAR
BASTARD CAITIFF COMICAL
CURRISH DEBASED FOOTING
HANGDOG HILDING HOUSING
IGNOBLE OUTPOST PEASANT
ROINISH SERVILE SLAVISH STADDLE
STANDER SUBBASE SUPPORT
CHURLISH COISTREL COISTRIL
DEGRADED DRAWHEAD HARLOTRY
HOLDFAST INFAMOUS INFERIOR
MECHANIC MESCHANT PEDESTAL
PEDIMENT RASCALLY SCULLION
SHAMEFUL STANDARD STEPPING
SUBSTRAT UNWORTHY WRETCHED
NIDDERING
(— IN GAME) HOME
(— IN QUALITY) LEADEN
(— OF BRANCH) KNOT
(— OF CANNON) SOUL
(— OF OPERATIONS) BOOK HOME
(— OF OVULE) CHALAZA
(— OF PETAL) CLAW
(— OF PILLAR) PATTEN
(— OF PLANT) CAUDEX
(— OF POLLINIUM) DISC DISK
(— OF ROCK) MAGMA MAGMU

(— OF TUBER) HEEL
(— OF WORD) STEM
(CHEMICAL —) ALKALI ACRIDAN
ADENINE ANSERIN CHOLINE
GUANINE ACRIDANE ACTININE
AGMATINE ALDIMINE ALKALOID
ANSERINE CONYRINE GALEGINE
KETIMINE LEPIDINE SEMIDINE
(HIDDEN —) LAIR
(HOME —) DEN
(LEAF —) FOVEA
(LOGARITHM —) E RADIX
(OFF —) AWOL
(PROJECTING —) PLINTH
(SECOND —) KEYSTONE
(STALKLIKE —) CNIDOPOD
(PREF.) BASI TAPIN(O)
(SUFF.) HEDRAL

BASEBALL PILL APPLE DUSTER
FLOATER INSHOOT LEATHER
BEANBALL HARDBALL HORSEHIDE
STICKBALL
(— DOUBLEHEADER) TWINIGHT
(— FLY) POPUP
(— PLAYER) OTT COBB DEAN FORD
MAYS ROSE RUTH RYAN AARON
BANKS BENCH BERRA BROCK
CAREW EVERS LYONS PAIGE REESE
SPAHN YOUNG FELLER GEHRIG
GOSLIN KEELER KOUFAX MANTLE
MUSIAL SEAVER CARLTON DYKSTRA
HORNSBY JACKSON JOHNSON
CLEMENTE DIMAGGIO DRYSDALE
ROBINSON STARGELL WILLIAMS
YANNIGAN BOTTOMLEY KILLEBREW
CAMPANELLA STRAWBERRY
YASTRZEMSKI
(— PRACTICE) FUNGO
(— TEAM) CUBS METS REDS EXPOS
TWINS ANGELS ASTROS BRAVES
GIANTS PADRES REDSOX ROYALS
TIGERS BREWERS DODGERS
INDIANS MARLINS ORIOLES PIRATES
RANGERS ROCKIES YANKEES
BLUEJAYS ANGELS PHILLIES
WHITESOX ATHLETICS CARDINALS
(— THROW) PEG TOSS
(HIGH-BOUNCING —) CHOPPER
(MODIFIED —) TBALL

BASEBOARD GRIN SKIRT PLINTH
EASEMENT MOPBOARD SKIRTING
WASHBOARD

BASE-DEALING BROKING

BASELESS IDLE UNFOUNDED

BASEMAN SACKER

BASEMENT BASE CELLAR
TAHKHANA

BASENESS FELONY VILITY
BEGGARY SQUALOR TURPITUDE

BASH BAT LAM TRY BEAT BLOW
DENT GALA MASH SWAT WHAM
WHOP ABASH BEANO PARTY SLOSH

SMASH ASSAIL BRUISE STRIKE
ATTEMPT BLOWOUT JAMBOREE
BASHEMATH (FATHER OF —)
ISHMAEL
(HUSBAND OF —) ESAU
BASHFUL COY SHY HELO SHAN
BLATE HELOE TIMID MODEST
PUDENT ASHAMED DAUNTED
BACKWARD BLUSHING DAPHNEAN
DISMAYED LOATHFUL PUDIBUND
RETIRING SACKLESS SHAMEFUL
SHEEPISH SKITTISH VERECUND
SHAMEFACED
BASHFULNESS PUDOR SHYNESS
BASIC NET BASE BASAL VITAL
BOTTOM BEDROCK CANONIC
CENTRAL CLASSIC PRIMARY
ZINCOUS CARDINAL ULTIMATE
ELEMENTAL ESSENTIAL SUBSTRATE
BASIL TULASI
BASILICA (PART OF —) APSE BEMA
NAVE AISLE ALTAR NARTHEX
TRANSEPT
BASIN DOP PAN BOWL COMB COVE
DISH DOCK EWER FLOW FONT GULF
LAKE PARK SINK SLAD TALA TANK
COMBE LAVER SLAKE STOUP
BASSON BULLAN CHAFER CIRQUE
HOLLOW LAVABO LEKANE LOUTER
MARINA VALLEY VESSEL CUVETTE
PISCINA RECEIPT URCEOLE
BIRDBATH CESSPOOL LAVATORY
RECEPTOR VANITORY WASHBOWL
GEMELLION
(— FOR RAINWATER) IMPLUVIUM
(DESERT —) PLAYA
(GEOLOGICAL —) BOLSON
(MOUNTAIN —) HOYA PUNA
(OYSTER —) PISCINA
(ROCK —) KEEVE KIEVE
(SEA —) FLOW
(PREF.) LECAN(O)
BASIS BASE FOND FOOT FORM FUND
ROOT SILL AXIOM RADIX STOCK
ANLAGE BOTTOM GROUND
ACCOUNT BEDROCK FOOTING
PREMISE SUPPORT GRAVAMEN
STRENGTH AUTHORITY CRITERION
FUNDAMENT GROUNDSEL
SUBSTANCE
BASK SUN BEEK LAZE WARM ACRID
BATHE ENJOY REVEL BITTER REJOICE
APRICATE
BASKET IE ARK COB FAN HOT KIT
LUG PAD PED PEG POT RIP TAP TOP
BUCK CAUL COBB COOP CORB CORF
CRIB FLAT GOAL HOTT IEIE KIPE KISH
KIST KITT LEAP MAND MAUN SKEP
TAPE TILL TOUR TRUG WEEL CABAS
CASSY CESTA CHEST CRAIL CRASH
CRATE CREEL DEVIL DILLI DILLY FRAIL
GRATE MAUND MOLLY NATTE RUSKY

SCULL SWILL WILLY BEACON
BOKARK CASSIE CLEAVE COFFIN
COURGE CRADLE DORSEL DORSER
DOSSER FANNER FASCET GABION
HAMPER HOBBET HOBBIT HOPPET
JICARA JUNKET KIBSEY KIPSEY
MOCOCK MOLLIE MURLIN PEGALL
PETARA POTTLE PUNNET SEQUIN
SERPET TAPPET TEANAL TOPNET
VOIDER WINDEL WINDLE WISKET
ZEQUIN CANASTA CORBEIL CRESSET
FLASKET HANAPER MURLAIN
PANNIER PATTARA PITARAH PRICKLE
SCUTTLE SEEDLIP SHALLOW
SKEOUGH SKIPPET WATTAPE
WHISKET CALATHUS CANISTER
CHEQUEEN ZECCHINO
(— BOTTOM) SLATH
(— FOR CRUMBS) VOIDER
(— FOR EELS) BUCK COURGE
(— FOR FIGS) TAP CABAS FRAIL
TAPNET
(— FOR FISH) CREEL
(— FOR FRUIT) CALA MOLLY
CALATHOS
(FISH —) CRAN HASK
(JAI ALAI —) CESTA
(PART OF —) RIB RIM FOOT JOIN
RAND SLEW WALE FITCH STAKE
UPSET BORDER HANDLE
(REFUSE —) SIEVE
(WICKER —) RIP
BASKETBALL HOOP
(— ATTEMPT) SETSHOT
(— FOUL) HACK
(— GOAL) TIPIN
(— PLAYER) BIRD REED WEST EWING
ONEAL PIVOT BAYLOR ERVING
JABBAR JORDAN MALONE MCHALE
PARISH PETTIT THOMAS UNSELD
WALTON WORTHY BARKLEY FRAZIER
GRUENIG JOHNSON RUSSELL
ALCINDOR HAVLICEK OLAJUWON
PIVOTMAN SWINGMAN ROBERTSON
STEINMETZ DEBUSSCHERE
(— SHOT) JAM DUNKSHOT
SLAMDUNK
(— TEAM) BING HEAT JAZZ NETS
SUNS BARRY BUCKS BULLS COUSY
HAWKS KINGS MAGIC SPURS
LAKERS PACERS BRADLEY BULLETS
CELTICS HORNETS NUGGETS
PISTONS ROCKETS CLIPPERS
WARRIORS CAVALIERS MAVERICKS
CHAMBERLAIN SUPERSONICS
TIMBERWOLVES TRAILBLAZERS
SEVENTYSIXERS KNICKERBOCKERS
(DUNK SHOT) JAM
(FREE-THROW LANE IN —) PAINT
(KIND OF — PASS) SPOT OUTLET
BASKET MAKER ANASAZI
BASKETRY UPSET

BASKETWORK TEE SLEW WALE
SLATH STAKE SLATHE STROKE
SLEWING
BASMATH (FATHER OF —) SOLOMON
(HUSBAND OF —) AHIMAAZ
BASQUE VASCON EUSCARA
EUSCARO IBERIAN BISCAYAN
(— DIALECT) LABOURDIN
(PL.) VASCONA VASCONES
BAS-RELIEF PLAQUETTE
BASS LOW PES CHUB DEEP DRUM
FOOT ROCK BASSO DRONE HURON
ROCHE SWEGO VOICE BORDUN
BRASSE BURDEN CHERNA GROUND
JUMPER REDEYE SINGER STRIPE
ACHIGAN BARFISH BOURDON
BROWNIE GROWLER JEWFISH
STRIPER BACHELOR BIGMOUTH
BLUEFISH CABRILLA CONTINUO
ROCKFISH SPOTTAIL STREAKER
TALLYWAG WELSHMAN LINESIDES
(— DRUM) TAMBURONE
(— PART) ALBERTI
(DRONE —) BOURDON
(GROUND —) OSTINATO
(LEADING —) SUCCENTOR
(THOROUGH —) BC
BASSOON REED CURTAL FAGOTT
BOMBARD FAGOTTE FAGOTTO
WOODWIND
(PART OF —) BELL BOOT BUTT WING
CROOK JOINT
BASSWOOD LIN BASS WAHOO
LINDEN WICOPY DADDYNUT
WHITEWOOD
BAST LIBER RAMIE PHLOEM
NODEBURN
BASTARD GET SOB BASE FALSE
CANNON COWSON GALLEY HYBRID
IMPURE MAMZER BYSPELL GETLING
LOWBRED MONGREL WOSBIRD
BANTLING BASEBORN MISBEGET
NAMELESS SPURIOUS WHORESON
(PREF.) NOTH(O)
BASTE SEW BEAT CANE COOK DRUB
LARD TACK FLAMB SAUCE CUDGEL
JIPPER PUNISH STITCH THRASH
BASTION JETTY BULWARK LUNETTE
MOINEAU
(PART OF —) FACE RAMP ANGLE
FLANK GORGE CURTAIN BANQUETTE
BAT CAT HIT WAD BACK BAKE BATE
BEAT CLUB FOWL GAIT JACK LUMP
MASS SWAT TRAP WINK BANDY
BATON BRICK CHUCK FUNGO HARPY
PIECE SPREE STICK ALIPED BACKIE
BASTON BEETLE CUDGEL DRIVER
KALONG PADDLE POMMEL RACKET
STRIKE STROKE WILLOW BAUCKIE
FLUTTER JAVELIN MORMOPS
NOCTULE VAMPIRE BLUDGEON
ROUSETTE SEROTINE BARBASTEL

REARMOUSE REREMOUSE
CHEIROPTER
(GO TO — FOR) AID
(PART OF —) KNOB MEAT LABEL
BARREL HANDLE SIGNATURE
(PREF.) NYCTERI
(SUFF.) NYCTERIS
BATAK (— DIALECT) TOBA
BATCH LOT BAKE BREW CAST CROP
FINE MASS MESS RAFT SORT BUNCH
FLOOR GROUP BAKING CHEESE
MAKING BOILING BREWING
FORMULA MIXTURE RAISING
QUANTITY
(— OF EGGS) SETTING
(— OF GRAIN) GRIST
(— OF MAIL) SEPARATION
BATCHER BAGGER
BATE BAIT BEET PARE PUER PURE
GRAIN
BATELEUR BERGHAAN
BATEMAN DRENCHER
BATFISH ANGLER FR DIABLO MALTHE
DEVILFISH
BATH DIP TUB BAIN BATE LOSS PERT
TOSH BATHE LAVER STEEP THERM
BAGNIO DOUCHE LIQUOR MIKVAH
PICKLE PLUNGE SHOWER SPONGE
BALNEUM LAVACRE ABLUTION
BALNEARY
(FOOT —) PEDILUVIUM
(HOT —) STEW SCALD STUFE THERM
STUPHE THERME
(HOT-AIR —) STOVE
(MUD —) ILLUTATION
(PHOTOGRAPHIC —) FIXER
(SITZ —) BIDET SITZBAD SEMICUPE
INSESSION
(SPINNING —) DOPE
(STEAM —) SAUNA
(TANNING —) BATE SOAK
(TURKISH —) HAMMAM HUMMUM
HOTHOUSE
(WHIRLPOOL —) JACUZZI
(PREF.) BALNE(O)
BATHE BAY TUB BAIN BASK DOOK
LAVE STEW WASH CLEAN DOUSE
DOWSE EMBAY SOUSE STEEP
ENWRAP FOMENT SHOWER SPLASH
EMBATHE IMMERSE PERVADE
SUFFUSE PERMEATE
BATHHOUSE SEW STEW SAUNA
STUFE BAGNIO CABANA HAMMAM
STUPHE BALNEARY
BATHING LAVACRE LAVEMENT
(— SUIT) SLIP TOGS MAILLOT
(SAND —) SABURRATION
BATHROBE PEIGNOIR
BATHROOM BILLY BALNEARY
BATHSHEBA (FATHER OF —) ELIAM
AMMIEL
(HUSBAND OF —) DAVID URIAH

(SON OF —) NATHAN SHIMEA
SHOBAB SOLOMON
BATHTUB TUB TOSH LAVACRE
BATIA (FATHER OF —) TEUCER
(HUSBAND OF —) DARDANUS
(SON OF —) HIPPOCOON
ERICHTHONIUS
BATON ROD BEND BURN WAND
STAFF STICK BAGUET BASTON
CUDGEL BOURDON SCEPTER
SCEPTRE BAGUETTE CROSSBAR
TRUNCHEON
BATSMAN BAT BATTER HITTER
SLOGGER SLUGGER STRIKER
BATTALION WARD CONREY
BATTEN END LAY RIB SLAT SLEY
CLEAT LEDGE BATTON BEATER
ENRICH FATTEN REEPER THRIVE
FERTILIZE
(PL.) SPARRING
BATTER RAM BEAT DENT MAIM
MAUL PELT CLOUR DINGE FRUSH
PASTE POUND SMASH BALLER
BRUISE BUFFET HAMMER HATTER
HITTER PUMMEL THRING TUMBLE
BATSMAN BOMBARD CRIPPLE
DESTROY FRITTER SHATTER
SLUGGER STRIKER DEMOLISH
BATTERCAKE WAFFLE CRUMPET
BATTERING BLAST LACING
BATTERY PILE SINK TIRE TROOP
RADEAU EXCITER SINKBOX
SINKBOAT ACCUMULATOR
(GUN —) SWINGER
BATTLE WAR CAMP DUEL FEUD FRAY
MART MEET TILT TOIL UNDO BRUSH
FIELD FIGHT JOUST STOUR ACTION
AFFAIR AFFRAY CAMLAN COMBAT
SHOWER STRIVE CONTEND CONTEST
HOSTING JOURNAL JOURNEY
WARFARE CONFLICT SKIRMISH
STRUGGLE ENCOUNTER
NAUMACHIA THEOMACHY
(PREF.) MACHO
(SUFF.) MACHIA MACHY
BATTLE-AX WIFLE POLEAX SPARTH
TWIBIL BROADAX HALBERD TWIBILL
WHIFFLE FAUCHARD FRANCISC
BATTLE CRY CRY BANZAI ENSIGN
GERONIMO SLUGHORN
BEAUSEANT
BATTLEFIELD ARENA BLAIR CHAMP
TAHUA CHAMPAIGN
BATTLEGROUND COCKPIT
TERRAIN
BATTLEMENT KERNEL MERION
PINION BARMKIN CORNELLE
MURDRESS
(PART OF —) CRENEL MERLON
MACHIOLATION
BATTLE OF LEGNANO
(CHARACTER IN —) LIDA ARRIGO

ROLANDO FREDERICK BARBAROSSA
(COMPOSER OF —) VERDI
BATTLESHIP MAINE CARRIER
BATTOLOGIZE ITERATE
BATTUS (FATHER OF —)
POLYMNESTUS
(MOTHER OF —) PHRONIMA
BATTY BATS BUGGY CRAZY SILLY
BANANAS BATLIKE FOOLISH
BAUBLE BOW TOY BEAD GAUD
BUTTON GEWGAW TRIFLE MAROTTE
TRINKET GIMCRACK PLAYTHING
BAWD AUNT HARE DIRTY MADAM
DEFILE MADAME PANDER COMMODE
MACKEREL PROCURER PURVEYOR
BAWDINESS RAUNCH
BAWDRY SCULDUDDERY
BAWDY LEWD DIRTY SCARLET
SKULDUGGERY
BAWL CRY HOWL ROAR ROUT YAUP
YAWP BLORE GOLLY SHOUT BELLOW
BOOHOO GOLLAR OUTCRY GLAISTER
(— OUT) JUMP CRACK SCOLD
BAY ARM COD DAM RIA VOE BANK
BARK CHOP COVE GULF HOLE HOPE
HOWL LOCH ROAN TREE WICK YAUP
YAWP BAHIA BASIN BAYOU BERRY
BIGHT COLOR CREEK FIORD FJORD
FLEET HAVEN HORSE INLET LOUGH
MOUTH ORIEL QUEST SINUS SPEAK
TRAVE BABBLE HARBOR LAUREL
RECESS SEVERY TONGUE WINDOW
BADIOUS BAYGALL ENCLOSE
ESTUARY MALABAR SILANGA
ULULATE BREWSTER CHESTNUT
(— OF BARN) GOAF SKEELING
SKILLING SKILLION
(— OF LIBRARY) CLASSIS
(— OF STATE) MASSACHUSETTS
(SWEET —) BREWSTER
BEAVERWOOD
BAYBERRY AUSU PIMIENTA
WAXBERRY
BAYOU SLEW SLOO SLUE BROOK
CREEK INLET RIVER OUTLET
SLOUGH STREAM RIVULET
BACKWATER
BAY WINDOW ORIEL MIRADOR
BAZAAR FAIR FETE SALE AGORA
BURSE CHAWK CHOWK MARKET
ALCAZAR CANTEEN BOOKFAIR
EMPORIUM BEZESTEEN
BDELLIUM GUGAL GUGUL GOOGUL
BE ABE ARE BES BEEN BETH BIST LIVE
ABIDE EXIST OCCUR WORTH REMAIN
BREATHE CONSIST SUBSIST
CONTINUE
(TO —) SER ETRE SEIN
BEACH AIR BANK CHIP MOOR NARD
RIPA SAND SLIP COAST PLAGE PLAYA
PRAYA SHORE GROUND SHILLA
STRAND HARDWAY SEASIDE

SHINGLE LAKESHORE
(— **PROTECTOR**) SEAWALL
(— **RIDGE**) FULL
(**PROJECTING** —) CUSP
(**SANDY** —) MACHAIR
(PREF.) THIN(O)
BEACH APPLE CANAJONG
BEACHCOMBER SEASONER
  STRANDLOOPER
BEACHED AGROUND
BEACH FLEA SCUD SCREW
  SANDBOY
BEACH GRASS STAR SPIRE
  MARRAM BENTSTAR
BEACON MARK PIKE SIGN BAKEN
  FANAL GUIDE PHARE RACON ENSIGN
  PHAROS RAMARK SIGNAL CRESSET
  SEAMARK WARNING BALEFIRE
  NEEDFIRE SIGNPOST STANDARD
  (**RADAR** —) RACON NAVAID
BEAD NIB POT DROP FOAM GAUD
  AGGRI AGGRY BUGLE FILET GRAIN
  KNURL PEARL QUIRK SIGHT STAFF
  ARANGO BAGUET BAUBLE BICONE
  BUBBLE CORNET FILLET HEISHE
  HEISHI PELLET PIPPER POPPET
  PRAYER RONDEL WAMPUM CABLING
  DEWDROP GLOBULE MOLDING
  SPARKLE TRINKET AVEMARIA
  CABOCHON
  (**PREHISTORIC** —) ADDERSTONE
  (**ROSARY** —) GAUD PATERNOSTER
  (**SHELL** —S) SEWAN
BEADING VEINING
  (PL.) TASBIH
BEADLE CRIER MACER POKER USHER
  PEDRAL DUMBLE HAHMAN HERALD
  BAILIFF NUTHOOK OFFICER
  SERVITOR SUMMONER APPARITOR
  MESSENGER
BEADSMAN BEGGAR HERMIT
  BLUEGOWN GOWNSMAN
BEAK NEB NIB BECK BILL CLAP NOSE
  PIKE PROW LORUM SNOUT SWORD
  TUTEL MASTER NOZZLE SPERON
  WEAPON EMBOLON EMBOLUM
  FOREBOW MOLDING ROSTRUM
  BEAKHEAD MANDIBLE CAPITULUM
  (— OF SHELL) UMBO
  (— OF SHIP) SPERON
  (— OF SWORDFISH) SWORD
  (PREF.) RHAMPH(O) RHYNCH(O)
  ROSTR(I)(O)
  (SUFF.) RHYNCHUS RHYNCUS
  ROSTRAL
BEAKED NASUTE
BEAKER CUP HORN TASS BIKER
  BOCAL BOUSE GLASS BARECA
BEAM BAR LEG RAY TIE BALK BEAK
  BOOM EMIT GLOW GRIN PLAT SILE
  SILL SKID SPAR STUD ARBOR BAULK
  CABER FLASH GLEAM GLEED JOIST

LIGHT RAYON SHAFT SHAPE SHINE
SHOOT SMILE SPEAR STANG STOCK
TRAVE BINDER BULKER CAMBER
CHEESE COLLAR FLITCH GIRDER
GLANCE HEADER MANTEL NEEDLE
RAFTER SUMMER TIMBER TRABES
TREVIS WALKER BALANCE BUMPKIN
CATHEAD CHANNEL CHEVRON
DORMANT DRAWBAR FRIJOLE
MADRIER PINRAIL RADIATE SLEEPER
SUPPORT TRANSOM TRIMMER
TYNDALL AXLETREE BROWPOST
HERISSON PADSTONE PLOWHEAD
ROOFTREE STENTREL TEMPLATE
BRESSUMMER
(— OF LIGHT) CHINK GLEED RAYON
SHAFT PENCIL SIGNAL STREAM
SUNBEAM STRICTURE
(**HIGH** —) BRIGHTS
(**LARGE** —) BALK LACE BAULK
SUMMER
(**LOW** —) DIM
(**POWERFUL** —) LASER
(**SANIO'S** —) CRASSULA
(**WEAVER'S** —) TRAM TAVIL
(PL.) CRANEWAY
(PREF.) DOCO
BEAMER SMILER SCUDDER
BEAMING GAY ROSY BRIGHT
  LUCENT MASSIVE RADIANT SHINING
BEAMY BROAD BRIGHT JOYOUS
  LUCENT MASSIVE RADIANT
  MIRTHFUL
BEAN BON NIB URD CHAP FABA FAVA
  GRAM HABA HEAD LIMA POLE SNAP
  TEPE TICK DRAIN CARAT PULSE
  SIEVA SKULL TONKA CACOON
  CASTER COLLAR FELLOW KIDNEY
  LABLAB LENTIL NIPPLE NOGGIN
  RUNNER RUTTEE SEEWEE STRIKE
  TEPARY THRASH TRIFLE CALABAR
  FRIJOLE MAZAGAN PHASEMY
  SNAPPER WINDSOR BONAVIST
  BONNYVIS RAMBUTAN TICKBEAN
  TORNILLO
  (— CURD) TOFU
  (— OF CHINA AND JAPAN) ADZUKI
  (**BROKEN COFFEE** —S) TRIAGE
  (**KIND OF** —) GOA MOTH MUNG
  PINTO TONKA TEPARY WINGED
  (**LOCUST** —) CAROB
  (**MESCAL** —) SOPHORA
  (PL.) NIBS FASELS FESELS PODDER
  PODWARE
  (PREF.) FABI
BEANFEAST BEANO
BEANIE DINK
BEAN-SHAPED FABIFORM
BEANSHOOTER TRUNK
  PEASHOOTER
BEAN TREF BOGUM
BEAN TREFOIL LABURNUM

BEAR GO CUB LUG BALU BERN BORN
CAST DREE DUBB FURE GEST GIVE
HAVE HOLD LIFT TEEM TOTE URSA
WEAR YEAN ABEAR ABIDE ALLOW
BALOO BEGET BHALU BREED BRING
BROOK BROWN BRUIN CARRY DREIE
DRIVE GESTE ISSUE KOALA POLAR
PRESS SPARE STAND STICK THOLE
THROW WEIGH WIELD YIELD AFFORD
BEHAVE BRUANG CONVEY ENDURE
IMPORT INFANT KADIAK KINDLE
KODIAK PIERCE RENDER SUFFER
THRUST UPHOLD URSULA WOMBAT
WOOBUT ABROOKE ARCTOID
BROWNIE COMPORT CONDUCT
EPHRAIM FORBEAR GRIZZLY
MUSQUAW PRODUCE STOMACH
SUPPORT SUSTAIN UNDERGO
FISSIPED SILVERTIP
(— A PART) CONTRIBUTE
(— DOWN) BROWBEAT OVERSWAY
(— EVIDENCE) ASSERT
(— EXPENSES) DEFRAY
(— FLOWERS) FLOURISH
(— FRUIT) FRUCTIFY
(— IN MIND) REMEMBER
(— INVESTIGATION) WASH
(— ON) CONCERN
(— OUT) PROPORT
(— PATIENTLY) DIGEST
(— UP) CAPE ENDURE SUSTAIN
(— WITH CREDIT) TEEM
(— WITNESS) TEEM SPEAK ATTEST
DEPOSE
(— YOUNG) FIND YEAN CALVE CHILD
(MALE —) BOAR
(NYMPH CHANGED TO —) CALLISTO
(SLOTH —) ASWAIL
(STUFFED —) TEDDY
(PREF.) ARCT(O) URSI
(SUFF.) FER(ENCE)(ENT)(OUS) GEN(E)
(ESIA)(ESIS)(ETIC)(IC)(IN)(OUS)(Y)
GER(ENCE)(ENT)(OUS)
BEARBERRY LARB WHORTLE
BILBERRY DOGBERRY FOXBERRY
CREASHAKS
BEARCAT PANDA
BEARD ANE AWN AVEL BARB DEFY
FACE FUZZ NECK NOSE PEAK TUFT
ZIFFS ARISTA BEAVER GOATEE
TASSEL AFFRONT BARBULE
CHARLEY CHARLIE VANDYKE
IMPERIAL STILETTO WHISKERS
BILLYGOAT
(— OF GRAIN) AIL AWN
(— TREATISE) POGONOLOGY
(KIND OF —) GYPSUM
(SMALL —) BARBET
(PREF.) ATHERO POGON(O)
(SUFF.) POGON
BEARDED AWNIE HAIRY BARBED
BARBATE HIRSUTE POGONIATE
WHISKERED

BEARDLESS NOT NOTT IMBERBE
POLLARD
BEARDTONGUE PENSTEMON
BEARER NEWS HAMAL MACER
BEADLE HAMMAL HOLDER PACKER
PORTER ANCIENT CARRIER JAMPANI
PINCERN CHAPRASI ESCUDERO
PORTATOR STANDARD MESSENGER
SUPPORTER
(— OF GREAT BURDEN) ATLAS
(ARMOR —) ESQUIRE
(BURDEN —) HAMAL HAMMAL
(CROZIER —) CROCIARY
(CUP —) SAKI COPPER
(PALANQUIN —) BOY SIRDAR
MUSAHAR
(SHIELD —) SQUIRE ESCUDERO
(STANDARD —) ANCIENT
(STRETCHER —) BRANCARDIER
(SWORD —) PORTGLAVE PORTGLAIVE
(PREF.) PORTE
BEARING AIM AIR COD BALL DUCT
GEST MIEN ORLE PORT RUBY BIRTH
FRONT GESTE HABIT JEWEL POISE
SETUP TENUE TREND ALLURE
APPORT ASPECT BILLET CHARGE
COURSE DEPORT GERENT GIGLIO
MANNER ORIENT SADDLE STANCE
THRUST VOIDER ADDRESS AZIMUTH
CONDUCT FASHION GESTURE
MEANING POSTURE PURPORT
RHODING SUPPORT AMENANCE
ATTITUDE BEHAVIOR BIRTHING
CARRIAGE DELIVERY DEMEANOR
FOOTSTEP PEDESTAL PRESENCE
PRESSURE RELATION STANDARD
TENDENCY TOURNURE YIELDING
REFERENCE
(— AWAY) DEFERENT
(— FRUIT) FRUCTED
(— OUTWARD) EFFERENT
(— UPON) RELEVANT
(ARROGANT —) HUFF
(CONSEQUENTIAL —) POMP
(HERALDIC —) GAD DELF ENTE GORE
MARK ORLE PALL WEEL CROWN
DELFT DELPH FUSIL LAVER PHEON
BILLET DEVICE ENSIGN GOUTTE
CHAPLET CLARION DEMIVOL
PLASQUE QUARTER ORDINARY
QUENTISE TRESSURE
(PERSONAL —) GARB
(PREF.) PHOR(O)
(SUFF.) GEROUS IGEROUS PARA
PAROUS PHORA PHORE(SIS) PHORIA
PHOROUS PHORUS
BEARLIKE URSINE
BEAR'S-EAR AURICULA
BEAR'S-FOOT OXHEAL PEGROOTS
BEARSKIN BUSBY
BEAR STATE ARKANSAS
BEAST BETE HOOF BRUTE VACHE
ANIMAL JUMENT CRITTER MONSTER

MUSIMON VENISON BEHEMOTH BLIGHTER OPINICUS
(— OF BURDEN) JUMENT SUMPTER
(CASTRATED —) SPADO
(DEAD —) MORKIN
(FABULOUS —) YALE THRIS BAGWYN BICORN TRICORN UNICORN DINGMAUL EPIMACUS OPINICUS GYASCUTUS
(HORNED —) RETHER ROTHER
(STURDY —) NUGGET
(WILD —) FERIN FERINE OUTLAW UNDEAST
(WILD —S) ZIIM
(3-HORNED —) TRICORN
(PREF.) THER(A)(IO)(O)
(SUFF.) THERE THERIA THERIUM

BEASTLIKE THEROID
BEASTLY GROSS PRONE ANIMAL BRUTAL WICKED BESTIAL BRUTISH INHUMAN SWINISH OFFENSIVE
BEAT BAT BUM COB DAD FAN FIB LAM PIP PLY PUG PUN RUN TAN TAP TAW TEW TIE WAX BAFF BAIT BANG BASH BATE BELT BEST BLOW BOLT BRAY BUFF BURN CANE CAST CHAP CLAP CLUB COIL COLT COMB CRAB DAUD DING DINT DRUB DUMP DUNT FELL FIRK FLAP FLAX FLOG FRAM FRAP FRAT GROW HAZE JOWL KILL LACE LAMP LASH LICK LOUK LUMP LUSH MAUL MELL MEND MILL PAIK PALE PANT PELT POLT POSS PRAT ROUT SCAT SLAM SLAT SLOG SOCK SOLE SOWL STUB SWAP SWOP TACK TAKD TICK TRIM TUCK TUND TWIG WALK WARP WELT WHIP WHOP WIPE BANDY BASTE BATON BEPAT BERRY BIRCH BLES CHURN CLINK CREAM CURRY DOUSE DRASH DRESS DRIVE FEEZE FIGHT FILCH FLAIL FLANK FORGE ICTUS INLAY KNOCK LABOR NEVEL NOINT PASTE PATCH POUND PULSE PUNCH ROUGH ROUND SCATT SCOOP SCOUR SKELP STAMP STRAP SWACK SWING TARGE THREP THROB THUMP TREAD TRUMP UPEND WADDY WHACK WHANG WORST ACCENT ANOINT BAMBOO BATTER BENSEL BETTLE BOUNCE BUFFET COTTON CUDGEL DEFEAT DOWSEL FEAGUE FETTLE HAMMER HAMPER JACKET KNEVEL LARRUP LATHER NEAVIL NODDLE OUTRUN PUMMEL RADDLE REBUKE REESLE RHYTHM SCUTCH SQUASH STOUND STOUSH STRIKE STRIPE STROKE SUGGIL SWINGE SWITCH TANSEL TEWTAW TEWTER THRASH THREAP THREIP THREPE THRESH TICKLE WAGGLE WALLOP WATTLE WUTHER ASSAULT BATTUTA BELABOR BLATTER BLISTER CADENCE CANVASS CONQUER CONTUSE EXHAUST FATIGUE FLYFLAP KNUCKLE LAMBACK LAMBAST LOBTAIL LOUNDER PULSATE REESHIE SHELLAC SURPASS SWABBLE SWADDLE TROLLOP TROUNCE VIBRATE MALLEATE PALPITATE SPIFLICATE
(— ABOUT) BUSK BANGLE
(— AGAINST) BLAD
(— AGAINST THE WIND) LAVEER
(— BACK) REBUFF
(— BARLEY) PAIL WARM
(— CLOTHES) BATTLE
(— COVERT) TUFT
(— DOWN) LAY FELL FULL ABATE FLASH
(— EGGS) CAST
(— FIBERS) BRUSH
(— FLAX) SCUTCH
(— HIGH) LEAP
(— IT) LAM
(— OF DRUM) RUFF RAPPEL RATTAN
(— OF HEART) DUNT STROKE
(— ON BUTTOCKS) COB
(— OUT) THRESH
(— SEVERELY) DRUB LUMP SOAK BASTE SOUSE LATHER
(— SMALL) CHAP
(— TO AND FRO) BANDY
(— TO WINDWARD) LAVEER
(— UP) WHISK SWITCH WORKOVER
(— VIOLENTLY) WETHER
(— WINGS) BATE FLAP
(— WITH HAMMER) DOLLY
(— WITH WHIP) SJAMBOK
(— WOODS) TUSK
(MUSICAL —) SALSA BOUNCE BATTUTA
(WEAK —) ARSIS
(PREF.) TYPTO

BEATEN BEAT BETE BATTU PARTY TRITE TRADED
BEATER RAB MAUL SEAL CANER LACER STOCK DASHER DRIVER MALLET TRIMMER SCUTCHER THRESHER
BEATIFIC DEIFIC ELYSIAN
BEATIFIED BLEST BLESSED
BEATIFY SAINT HALLOW HEAVEN ENCHANT GLORIFY SANCTIFY
BEATING COB COBB LICK TUND BEANS DOUSE JESSE PULSE STICK HAZING HIDING HOSING ROPAND TATTOO BASHING BATTERY BELTING CLANKER DASHING DUSTING LICKING SKELPIN WELTING WHALING BIRCHING DRESSING DRUBBING RIBROAST SLOSHING WHIPPING JACKETING STRAPPADO PERCUSSION
BEATITUDE JOY BLISS BENISON MACARISM HAPPINESS

BEATRICE DI TENDA (CHARACTER IN —) AGNESE FILIPPO BEATRICE VISCONTI OROMBELLO (COMPOSER OF —) BELLINI

BEATRICE ET BENEDICT (CHARACTER IN —) HERO CLAUDIO BEATRICE BENEDICT SOMARONE (COMPOSER OF —) BERLIOZ

BEAU BEW BOY CHAP BLADE DANDY FLAME LOVER SPARK SWELL ADONIS ESCORT FELLOW GARCON STEADY SUITOR TATTLE ADMIRER AIMWELL BRAVERY COURTER COXCOMB CUPIDON GALLANT SPARKER FOLLOWER

BEAU GREGORY COCKEYE

BEAUISH DOGGY

BEAUT PIP DILLY

BEAUTIFUL FAIR-FINE GLAD GOOD MEAR MEER MERE WALY BELLE BONNY KALON LUSTY SHEEN WLITY WLONK BLITHE BONNIE COMELY DECORE FREELY LOVELY POETIC PRETTY VENUST ANGELIC ELEGANT FORMOSE FORMOUS TEMPEAN TOKALON CHARMING DELICATE ESTHETIC FAIRSOME GORGEOUS GRACEFUL HANDSOME LUCULENT SPECIOUS MAGNIFICENT (PREF.) CALI CALLI CALLO CALO PULCHRI

BEAUTIFY FAIR GILD ADORN GRACE HIGHT PREEN PRIMP PRUNE BEAUTY BEDECK DECORE ENAMEL QUAINT ADONIZE ENHANCE GARNISH GLORIFY DECORATE FAIRHEAD EMBELLISH PULCHRIFY

BEAUTY GEM FACE FAIR FORM GLEE BEAUT BELLE CHARM FAVOR GLORY GRACE PRIDE WLITE FINERY LOOKER LOVELY POLISH DECORUM FEATURE TOKALON SPLENDOR FORMOSITY (— OF FORM) SYMMETRY (— OF STYLE) ELEGANCE (PREF.) CALI CALLI CALLO CALO PULCHRI

BEAVER BOOMER CASTOR RODENT PRALINE MUSHROOM SEWELLEL STARLING (— SKIN) PLEW (— STATE) OREGON (DARK —) NUTMEG

BEBAI (SON OF —) ZECHARIAH

BEBEERINE CURINE

BEBEERU SWEETWOOD GREENHEART

BECAUSE AS SO FOR THAT BEING CAUSE SINCE THERE FORWHY THROUGH INASMUCH

BECCAFICO FIGEATER FIGPECKER

BECHE-DE-MER PIDGIN TREPANG

BECHER (FATHER OF —) EPHRAIM BENJAMIN

BECHORATH (FATHER OF —) APHIAH

BECK RUN VAT BECON BROOK CREEK (— AND CALL) DEVOTION

BECKEN CYMBALS

BECKET SQUILGEE SQUILLGEE

BECKON BOW NOD WAG BECK WAFT WAVE CURTSY SUMMON BIDDING COMMAND CURTSEY GESTURE

BECKONING WAFTURE

BECLOUD HIDE MASK BEDIM DARKEN MUDDLE MYSTIFY OBSCURE OBNUBILATE

BECLOUDED FOGGY

BECOME GO FIT GET RAX SET SIT WAX COME FALL GROW LIKE PASS SUIT TAKE TILL WEAR ADORN BEFIT GRACE PROVE WORTH ACCORD BEFALL BESEEM BETIDE CHANGE IWORTH BEHOOVE FLATTER PROCEED (— A PARTY) ACCEDE (— AUDIBLE) ARISE (— BETTER) GAIN (— BIGGER) SPREAD (— DAMP) EVE (— DAZED) DWAM DWALM (— DIM) DASWEN (— DROWSY) DOW (— EVENTUALLY) ENDUP (— FAT) GRAZE (— FLUID) FLOW FLUX LEACH (— KNOWN) GO KITHE KYTHE SPUNK (— MEMBER) JOIN (— MOLDY) FUST MOUL FINEW (— MOROSE) SOUR (— ROUND) GLOBE (— SOUR) FOX BLINK CARVE (SUFF.) IZE

BECOMING FIT FEAT GOOD BHAVA FITTY RIGHT COMELY DUEFUL GAINLY PROPER DECORUM FARRAND FARRANT DECOROUS HANDSOME SUITABLE WISELIKE (SUFF.) ESCENT ESCENCE ESCENCE

BECOMINGLY TALLY

BED COT HAY KIP LIT PAD PAN TYE BAND BASE BODY BUNK DOSS DOWN FLOP FORM LAIR PLOT SACK VEIN WADI WADY BERTH BOIST COUCH FLASK FLOCK GRATE GROVE LAYER ROOST THORE BORDER BOTTOM COUCHE CRADLE GIRDLE HOTBED LIBKEN LIBKIN LITTER MATRIX OSIERY PALLET STRATA CHANNEL CHARPOY FLEABAG HAMMOCK LODGING QUARTER REPOSAL SEEDBED SETTING STRATUM SUBSOIL TRUCKLE TRUNDLE BASSINET CAPSTONE LENTICLE PLANCHER SHAKEDOWN (— DOWN) DOSS (— IN WAGON) KATEL

(— OF ANIMAL) LAIR KENNEL
(— OF CLAY) CLOD
(— OF COAL) BRAT DELF SEAM
(— OF EMBERS) GRIESHOCH
(— OF FIRE CLAY) THILL
(— OF FURNACE) HEARTH
(— OF GUN-CARRIAGE) FLASK
(— OF HAND PRESS) COFFIN
(— OF OYSTERS) PLANT
(— OF REFUSE) NITRIARY
(— OF ROCK) CAP PLUM
(— OF ROSES) ROSARY
(— OF SEDIMENT) WARP
(— OF SHELLFISH) BANK
(— OF STONES) SHINGLE
(— OF STREAM) DRAW WASH
NULLAH BILLABONG STREAMWAY
(— SIZE) KING TWIN QUEEN DOUBLE
SINGLE
(CREEK —) COULEE COULIE
(DRIED LAKE —) CHOTT SEBKA
SHOTT
(FEATHER —) TIE TYE
(FOLDING —) SLAWBANK
(GO TO —) SACKOUT
(LOW —) LOWBOY
(OYSTER —) STEW LAYER SCALP
CLAIRE LAYING OYSTERAGE
(RUBBLE —) CALLOW
(SEED —) SEMINARY
(WATER-BEARING —) AQUAFER
AQUIFER
(WOODEN —) RUSTBANK
(PREF.) CLIN(O) STRATI STROMATI
STROMATO
(SUFF.) STROMA
BEDAD (SON OF —) HADAD
BEDAN (FATHER OF —) GILEAD
BEDAUB CLAG CLAT DAUB MOIL
SOIL SLAKE SMEAR PARGET
SLUBBER SLAISTER BEPLASTER
BEDBUG BUG CHINK CIMEX CHINCH
CHINTZ COREID PUNESE VERMIN
CIMICID PUNAISE REDCOAT
CONENOSE HEMIPTER HOUSEBUG
BEDCHAMBER RUELLE BEDROOM
CUBICLE
BEDCLOTHES COVER BEDDING
CLOTHES
BEDCOVER COMFORTER
PALAMPORE
BEDDING BEDROLL DOMESTICS
BEDECK GEM BEDO LARD TRAP
ADORN ARRAY DIGHT GRACE PRINK
ORNAMENT EMBELLISH
BEDECKED PRINKY
BEDEGUAR SPONGE
BEDEIAH (FATHER OF —) BANI
BEDEVIL ABUSE ANNOY BESET
WORRY HARASS MUDDLE PESTER
BEWITCH CONFUSE TORMENT
BEDEW DEW DAMPEN SHOWER
EMBATHE IRRORATE

BEDIZEN DAUB ADORN ARRAY DIZEN
BEDAUB
BEDLAM ZOO RIOT NOISE RUDAS
ASYLUM TUMULT UPROAR
MADNESS MADHOUSE BETHLEHEM
BEDLAMITE MADMAN
BEDOUIN ABSI ARAB BEDU MOOR
NOMAD BADAWI BEDAWEE
SHAMMAR HOWEITAT
BEDQUILT POURPOINT
BEDRAGGLE DAG DRABBLE
TRACHLE
BEDRAGGLED FORLORN
SHOPWORN
BEDRAIL RAVE RATHE
BEDRIDDEN ILL AILING BEDFAST
(NOT —) AFOOT
BEDROCK LEDGE NADIR SHELF
BOTTOM HARDPAN STONEHEAD
BEDROLL BINDLE
BEDROOM FLAT BERTH CABIN
BEDDER DORMER BOUDOIR
CHAMBER CUBICULO WARDROBE
GARDEROBE
BEDSORE ANACLISIS DECUBITUS
BEDSPREAD ALEZE STRAIL
BEDCOVER COVERLET COVERLID
BEDSTAFF SLAT
BEDSTEAD BED COT CRIB HATCH
STEAD STAPLE ANGAREP CHARPOY
BEDSTRAW CRUDWORT CURDWORT
FLEAWEED BEDFLOWER
CROSSWORT SCRAMBLER
BED TESTER SPARVER
BEDWARMER CURATE
BEDWEAN FJS
BEE DOR FLY APIS BEVY KING RING
KARBI MASON NOMIA NURSE PARTY
DINGAR DRONEL DRONER FROLIC
INSECT NOTION TORQUE TSETSE
WORKER ANDRENA DEBORAH
KOOTCHA MELISSA RAISING
SERPENT STINGER SWERVER
TRIGONA ANDRENID ANGELITO
HONEYBEE QUILTING SCOPIPED
SHUCKING WAXMAKER GATHERING
(KIND OF —) KILLER
(PERTAINING TO —S) APIAN
(QUEEN —) KING
(PL.) BEEN BONE HIVE SPEW
SOCIALES
(PREF.) API
BEEBREAD CERAGO AMBROSIA
BEECH BUCK BIRCH MYRTLE
FLINDOSA FLINDOSY
(PREF.) FAGI FAGO
BEECHNUT SPLITNUT
(PL.) BUCK MAST PANNAGE
BEEF JERK REEVE BULLY GRIPE JERKY
VIFDA VIVDA CASSON CUTTER
CHARQUI TOPSIDE COMPLAIN
COMPOUND PASTRAMI PIPIKAULA
(— FOR SLAUGHTER) MART

(BOILED —) BOUILLI
(BROILED —) CHURRASCO
(CORN —) BULLY
(CUT OF —) SEY LOIN RUMP SIDE
BARON CHINE CHUCK FLANK ROAST
ROUND SHANK STEAK ALOYAU
CUTLET SADDLE BRISKET KNUCKLE
QUARTER SIRLOIN EDGEBONE
SHOULDER AITCHBONE NINEHOLES
RATTLERAN
(GROUND —) HAMBURGER
(INFERIOR —) COMPOUND
(JERKED —) TASAJO BILTONG
CHARQUE CHARQUI
(LEAN —) LIRE
(PIECE OF —) PAILLARD
(SALTED —) JUNK VIFDA
(STRIPS OF —) FAJITA
BEEF BREAD SWEETBREAD
BEEFEATER OXBIRD BUPHAGA
OXBITER OXPECKER TICKBIRD
BEEFWOOD TOA BELAH BELAR
FILAO
BEEFY HEAVY HEFTY SOLID BRAWNY
FLESHY
BEE GLUE PROPOLIS
BEEHIVE GUM BUTT GUME HIVE
SKEP PYCHE STAND STATE STOCK
SWARM APIARY HAIRDO HOPPET
ALVEARY SWARMER BEEHOUSE
PRAESEPE
(— STATE) UTAH
(— TOMB) TREASURY
BEEKEEPER HIVER BEEMAN
BEEHERD APIARIST SKEPPIST
BEELIADA (FATHER OF —) DAVID
BEELZEBUB DEVIL
BEEN BE BON SEE BONE
BEEPER PAGER
BEE PLANT GUACO STINKWEED
BEER ALE MUM BIER BOCK BREW
FARO GAIL GROG GYLE HOPS KVAS
MALT MILD QUAS SCUD SUDS
BELCH CHANG CHICA GROUT KVASS
LAGER POMBE QUASS SCUDS
STOUT WEISS CHICHA DOUBLE
GATTER LIQUOR PORTER SPRUCE
STINGO SWANKY WEISS WALLOP
ZYTHUM CERVEZA PANGASI
PHARAOH PILSNER TANKARD
TAPLASH TAPWORT CERVISIA
PILSENER
(ADD TO —) KRAUSEN
(BAD —) TACK TAPLASH
(HOT — AND GIN) PURL
(INFERIOR —) BELCH SWANKY
(KIND OF —) NEAR
(SMALL —) TIFF GROUT
(SOUR —) BEEREGAR
(STRONG —) HUFF NAPPY DOUBLE
STINGO
(THIN —) PRITCH SWIPES
(TIBETAN —) CHANG

(WARM — AND OATMEAL) STORRY
(WEAK —) BEVERAGE
BEERA (FATHER OF —) ZOPHAH
BEER-GARDEN BRASSERIE
BEERHOUSE KNEIPE TIDDLYWINK
BEERI (DAUGHTER OF —) JUDITH
(SON OF —) HOSEA
BEESWAX CAPPING
BEET CHARD MANGEL MANGOLD
STECHLING
(SUGAR —) BOLTER
BEETLE BAT BOB BUG DOR JUT RAM
BEAT BUZZ FLEA FOWL GOGA
GOGO IPID MAUL MELL STAG TROX
TURK UANG AMARA ATLAS BORER
BULGE CAROB CHUCK CLOCK DRIVE
FIDIA GOGGA HISPA LYCID MELOE
SAGRA TIGER BATLET CHAFER
CLERID COCUYO CUCUYO ELATER
GOLACH GOLOCH HISTER JUTOUT
KHAPRA LICTUS MALLET MELOID
PESTLE PRUNER PTINID SAWYER
SCARAB WEAVER WEEVIL ADELOPS
BRUCHID BUZZARD CADELLE
CARABID CARABUS CLOCKER
CUCUJID FIDDLER FIREFLY GIRDLER
GOLDBUG HORNBUG LADYBUG
LUCANID PAUSSID PRIONID
PROJECT SILPHID SKIPPER SNAPPER
SOLDIER TANBARK TICKLER
ATEUCHUS CALOSOMA CETONIAN
COCKTAIL CURCULIO DYTISCID
ENGRAVER EROTYLID FIGEATER
GLOWWORM HARDBACK LADYBIRD
LAMPYRID LOWERING OVERHANG
RUTELIAN SCOLYTID SEARCHER
SHARNBUD SHARNBUG SKIPJACK
SPHINDID SQUASHER SQUEAKER
SYMPHILE TOKTOKJE WHIRLWIG
DEDEMERID LONGICORN
OSTOMATID TUMBLEBUG TWIRLIGIG
WHIRLIGIG SCAPHIDIUM
RHYNCHOPHORAN
(KIND OF —) OIL
(RHINOCEROS —) UANG
SCARABAEID
(PL.) XYLOPHAGA
BEEWEED ASTER TONGUE
BEFALL HAP COME LIMP SORT TIDE
TIME CHEFE CHIVE OCCUR SHAPE
ASTART BECOME BETIDE HAPPEN
PERTAIN
BEFIT DOW SIT COME LONG SEEM
SORT SUIT BESET SERVE BECOME
BEHOVE BESEEM BETIDE BEHOOVE
BEFITTING FIT AFTER DECENT
PROPER WORTHY SEEMING
THRIFTY BECOMING DECOROUS
SORTABLE
(PROFESSIONALLY —) ETHICAL
(SUFF.) LY
BEFOG GAUM CLOUD OBSANE
CONFUSE MYSTIFY

BEFOOL BOB FON SOT BURN COLT CRAP DOLT DUPE FODE JADE POOP ASSOT ELUDE FONNE BEFLUM DIDDLE TRIFLE FOULIFY

BEFOOLING BITE

BEFORE OR TO AIR BUT ERE FOR GIN TIL ANTE FORE SAID TILL YORE AFORE AHEAD ANENT AVANT CORAM FIRST FORBY FORNE FRONT PRIOR SOPRA UNTIL ERENOW FORBYE FORMER RATHER SOONER TOFORE WITHIN AGAINST ALREADY EARLIER FORTHBY FORWARD

(— LONG) SOON ERELONG

(JUST —) TOWARD FORMERLY

(PREF.) FORE OB PRAE PRE PRO PROTER(O)

BEFOREHAND AFORE

BEFORE-MENTIONED SAID SUCH

BEFOUL FILE SLUT SOIL BERAY DIRTY GRUFT BEMIRE DAGGLE DARKEN DEFILE DRABBLE FEWMAND POLLUTE SLUTTER BESQUIRT ENTANGLE

BEFOULED SHARNY

BEFRIEND AID ABET HELP FAVOR ASSIST FOSTER FRIEND SUCCOR BENEFIT SUPPORT SUSTAIN

BEFUDDLE BOX GAS ADDLE BESOT MUDDLE BECLOUD CONFUSE FLUSTER MYSTIFY STUPEFY

BEFUDDLED REE MUSED

BEG ASK BID CRY SUE WOO CANT COAX KICK MOVE MUMP PRAY PRIG SEEK SORN SUIT THIG TRAM CADGE CRAVE MAUND MOOCH PLEAD SCAFF SHOOL TEASE YEARN ADJURE FLEECH BESEECH ENTREAT IMPLORE MAUNDER REQUEST SKELDER SOLICIT PETITION OBSECRATE PANHANDLE

BEGET GET WIN BEAR HAVE KIND SIRE BREED YIELD BIGATE CREATE FATHER ACQUIRE ENGRAFF CONCEIVE ENGENDER GENERATE PROCREATE

(PREF.) GONIDIO GONIMO GONIO GON(O)

BEGETTER SIRE AUTHOR FATHER MOTHER PARENT

BEGETTING

(SUFF.) GON(E)(IDIUM)(IMO)(IUM)(Y)

BEGGAR BLOB PROG RUIN ASKER HALFY LAZAR RANDY ROGUE THRUM TRAMP ARMINE BACACH BIDDER CADGER CANTER DYVOUR MUMPER PARIAH PAUPER SORNER WRETCH ABRAHAM ALMSMAN BAIRAGI BEGSTER JARKMAN LAZARUS MAUNDER PARDHAN PROCTOR RUFFLER SCAFFER SORNARI STEMMER THIGGER ABRAMMAN BADGEMAN BEADSMAN BESOGNIO BEZONIAN BLUEGOWN DUMMERER GLASSMAN PALLIARD STROLLER WHIPJACK MENDICANT SCHNORRER

(— DESCRIPTION) PASS

(SWINDLING —) JARKMAN

(VIOLENT —) RANDY RANDIE

(PL.) GUEUX

BEGGARED PEELED

BEGGARLY MEAN POOR CHEAP PETTY SORRY ABJECT PALTRY PILLED PEGRALL BANKRUPT INDIGENT HUNGARIAN

BEGGAR'S-LICE STICKWEED

BEGGARS' OPERA (AUTHOR OF —) GAY

(CHARACTER IN —) LUCY POLLY LOCKIT PEACHUM MACHEATH

BEGGAR-TICK CUCKOLD

(PL.) BOOTJACKS

BEGGARY THIG WANT INDIGENCE PAUPERISM

BEGGING MAUND CRAVING OPENERS MENDICANT THOMASING

(— FOR FOOD) SCRANNING

(FRAUDULENT —) TRUANDISE

BEGHARD PICARD

BEGIN GIN GYN HIT FALL FANG HEAD JUMP LEAD OPEN RISE TAME YOKE ARISE ENTER FRONT START ATTACK ATTAME INSTATE SPRING STREAK TEEOFF INSTATE COMMENCE GETGOING INCHOATE INITIATE

(— AGAIN) RENEW REOPEN RESUME

(— IN EARNEST) SETTO

(— TO APPEAR) PEEP

(— TO MELT) GIVE

(— TO WORK) GEL

BEGINNER BOOT PUNK TIRO TYRO ROOKY SOFTA GINNER NOVICE ROOKIE SOPHTA AMATEUR ENTRANT RECRUIT RUBBLER STUDENT TRAINEE FRESHMAN INCEPTOR NEOPHYTE NEWCOMER NOVELIST ABECEDARIAN

BEGINNING EGG ORD DAWN EDGE GERM HEAD RISE ROOT SEED ALPHA BIRTH DEBUT ENTRY FIRST FRONT ONSET START VAUNT AURORA INCOME INSTIL ONCOME ORIGIN OUTSET SETOUT SOURCE SPRING CALENDS DAWNING GENESIS HANDSEL INCIPIT INFANCY INITIAL INITION KALENDS NASCENT OPENING SUNRISE ENTRANCE EXORDIUM INCHOATE OUTSTART RUDIMENT

(— OF A TRILL) RIBATTUTA

(FROM THE —) ABOVO

(NEW —) EPOCH

(PL.) INCUNABULA

(PREF.) ACR(O)

(SUFF.) ARCH ARCHIC ARCHY ESCENT

BEGONE OFF OUT VIA AWAY SCAT
SHOO SCOOT SCRAM AROINT
AVAUNT DEPART SKIDOO SKIDDOO
VAMOOSE
BEGONIA GAIETY GAYETY
BEGRIME COOM SOIL COLLY DITCH
GRIME BECOOM SMIRCH SMUDGE
BRUCKLE
BEGRIMED DIRTY GRIMY SMUDGY
CINDERY SMIRCHY
BEGRUDGE ENVY GRUDGE MALIGN
JALOUSE
BEGTI NAIR COCKUP
BEGUILE FOX COAX FODE FOIL FOND
GULL LURE VAMP WILE WISE AMUSE
CHARM COZEN ELUDE EVADE
GUILE TEMPT TRICK TROLL TRYST
WEIZE BRIGUE BUTTER DELUDE
DIVERT ENTRAP JUGGLE VAMPEY
DECEIVE ENSNARE FLATTER
FLUMMER MISLEAD MOUNTEBANK
BEHALF HALF PART SAKE SIDE
FAVOR SCORE STEAD AFFAIR
MATTER PROFIT BENEFIT DEFENCE
SUPPORT INTEREST
BEHAVE DO ACT LET BEAR FARE
HAVE KEEP MAKE PLAY WALK WORK
ABEAR CARRY REACT TREAT ACQUIT
DEMEAN DEPORT HANDLE COMPORT
CONDUCT CONTAIN DISPORT
GESTURE MANAGER FUNCTION
REGULATE RESTRAIN
(— AFFECTEDLY) MOP
(— AWKWARDLY) GAUM HOCKER
(— BOLDLY) GAUSTER
(— BRASHLY) HOOK
(— CHURLISHLY) CARL
(— EVASIVELY) DODGE
(— FOOLISHLY) DOLT
(— IRRATIONALLY) FREAK
(— MEANLY) SNEAK
(— MISCHIEVOUSLY) LARK
(— NOISILY) HELL REHAYTE
(— OSTENTATIOUSLY) SWANK
(— RIOTOUSLY) ROLLICK GALRAVAGE
GILRAVAGE
(— VULGARLY) RAMP
BEHAVING
(SUFF.) ANT ENT
BEHAVIOR AIR MIEN PORT RULE
THEW WALK FRONT GUISE HABIT
LATES USAGE ACTION COURSE
GOINGS MANNER ACTIONS BEARING
BIGOTRY COMPORT CONDUCT
DECORUM ERGASIA FACTION
FASHION HAVANCE HAVINGS
AMENANCE ATTITUDE BLINDISM
BREEDING BYRONICS CARRIAGE
FUNCTION MAINTAIN PERFORMANCE
(AMOROUS —) SPORT
(ARROGANT —) SIDE SWAGGER
(COURTEOUS —) COMITY COURTESY

(DECENT —) CIVILITY
(EXCITED —) RAMPAGE RAMPAUGE
(FOOLISH —) SIMPLES SOTTISE
(GOAL-DIRECTED —) HORME
(GOOD —) STRAIGHT
(IMPROPER —) MISCONDUCT
(LIVELY —) TITTUP
(LOUTISH —) BUFFOONERY
(RIOTOUS —) RAMPAGE
(SILLY —) SPOONISM
(SLEAZY —) SMARM
(STUDIED —) ART
(SUSPICIOUS —) SUS
(UNDERHANDED —) SKULLDUGGERY
(VIOLENT —) THUGGERY
BEHEAD NECK
BEHEST BID LAW HEST RULE ORDER
DEMAND BIDDING COMMAND
MANDATE
BEHIND AFT HINT PAST RUMP ABACK
ABAFF ABAFT AFTER AHIND AREAR
LATER PASSE TARDY ARREAR
ASTERN DERERE BACKWARD
DILATORY
(— TIME) OVERDUE
(PREF.) META POST POSTERO
RETRO
BEHINDHAND TARDY LAGGARD
DILATORY HINDERLY
BEHOLD LA LO EYE SEE SPY ECCE
ESPY GAZE HOLD KEEP LOOK SCAN
STOP TOOT VIEW VISE WAIT HOLDE
OCULE SIGHT VOILA WATCH ASPECT
DESCRY MIRROR REGARD RETAIN
DISCERN OBSERVE SURVISE
WITNESS
BEHOLDEN OWING AFFINED
BOUNDEN OBLIGED INDEBTED
BEHOOVE DOW FIT NEED SUIT THAR
BEFIT OUGHT THARF BELONG
PROPER REQUIRE
BEIGE HOP TAN ECRU HOPI GREGE
DORADO GREIGE STRING SUNBURN
BEING ENS ESSE FEAL SELF ENTIA
GNOME HUMAN SHAPE TROLL
ANIMAL ENTITY EXTANT LIVING
MORTAL PERSON SYSTEM ESSENCE
PRESENT REALITY VIVENCY
CREATURE EXISTENT ONTOLOGY
PRESENCE STANDING
(ANIMATE —) LIFE JAGAT
(BIONIC HUMAN —) CYBORG
(CELESTIAL —) ANGEL CHERUB
SERAPH WATCHER DIVINITY
(DIMINUTIVE —) ELF GNOME
(DIVINE —) DEV DEVA DEMIGOD
(ESSENCE OF —) SAT
(ETERNAL —) EON AEON
(EVIL —) DEVIL GHOUL
(FABULOUS —) TENGU TORNIT
(HAVING REAL —) ONTIC
(HUMAN —) BODY BUCK JACK SOUL

BLADE HUMAN SLIME ANIMAL
ADAMITE CREATURE RATIONAL
CHRISTIAN
(IDEAL —) IMMORTAL
(ILL-FAVORED —) BLASTIE
(IMAGINARY —) SYLPH TERMAGANT
(INNER —) INWARD SPRITE INBEING
(INNERMOST —) HEART
(INTRINSIC —) ESSENCE
(LEGENDARY —) GIANT
(LIVING —) BLOOD WIGHT
(MATERIAL —) HYLIC
(PERFECT —) GOD
(PHYSICAL —) FLESH
(SEMIDIVINE —) SHEDU LAMASSU
(SMALL —) INCHLING
(SO —) SAEBEINS
(SUPERNATURAL —) DEV MAN AKUA
ATUA DEVA JANN ZEMI ADARO
BALAM DAEVA DEMON FAIRY TROLL
WIGHT DAEMON GARUDA GODKIN
SPIRIT GODLING FOLLETTO
HAMINGJA
(SUPREME —) DEITY MONAD
NYAMBE NZAMBI CREATOR
(TRUE —) OUSIA
(PREF.) ONT(O) ZO(E)(IDIO)(IDO)(O)
ZOOLOGICO
(HUMAN —) ANTHROP(O)
(SUFF.) IC(AL) ZOA ZOIC ZOON
BELA (FATHER OF —) AZAZ BEOR
BENJAMIN
BELABOR PLY BEAT DRUB LASH
WORK ASSAIL BOUNCE CUDGEL
HAMMER HAMPER THRASH THWACK
BELARUS (ALSO SEE RUSSIA)
CANAL: DNIEPERBUG
CAPITAL: MINSK
COIN· RUBLE
LAKE: NARACH NAROCH DRISVYATY
DRYSVYATY ASVEYSKAYE
OSVEYSKOYE
MARSH: PRIPET PALESSE POLESYE
MOUNTAIN: DZERZHINSKAYA
DZYARZHINSKAYA
NAME: BYELARUS BELORUSSIA
BYELORUSSIA
PEOPLE: BELARUS RUSSIAN
BELORUSSIAN WHITERUSSIAN
PLAIN: BEREZINA
RIVER: BUG DRUT SOZH DISNA DNEPR
DVINA DYSNA NEMAN SLUCH
DNEPRO PRIPET PTITCH DAUGAVA
DNIEPER NEMUNAS PRIPYAT
SHCHARA YASELDA BEREZINA
PRYPYATS SVISLOCH BYAREZINA
MUKHAVETS
TOWN: BREST GOMEL HOMEL PINSK
GRODNO HRODNA BORISOV
MOGILEV VITEBSK ZHODINO
BOBRUISK BOBRUYEK MOGILYOV
MOLODECHNO BRESTLITOVSK

BELAY BESET BELAGE INVEST
WAYLAY BESFIGE
BELCH YEX BOCK BOKE BOLK BURP
GALP RASP RIFT ERUCT FRUCT
REBOKE ERUCTATE
BELCHING BRASH
BELDAM HAG FURY TROT CRONE
RUDAS ALECTO ERINYS RUDOUS
VIRAGO BELDAME JEZEBEL
TISIPHONE
BELEAGUER BELAY BESET INVEST
ASSAULT BESEIGE LEAGUER
BLOCKADE SURROUND
BELEAGUERING SIEGE
BELEM PARA
BELEMNITE ARTIFACT KERAUNION
BELFRY SHED TOWER BEFFROY
CLOCHER CLOGHEAD BELLHOUSE
BELGIAN FLEMING
BELGIAN CONGO
(CAPITAL OF —) LEOPOLDVILLE
(LAKE IN —) KIVU MWERU ALBERT
(PROVINCE OF —) KIVA KASAI
EQUATOR KATANGA ORIENTAL
(RIVER IN —) RUKI KASAI LINDI
LOMAMI LUKUGA UBANGI ARUWIMI
LULONGA
(TOWN IN —) BOMA LULUABOURG

BELGIUM
CANAL: YSER UNION ALBERT
CAMPINE
CAPITAL: BRUSSELS BRUXELLES
GAUL TRIBE: REMI BELGAE NERVII
MEASURE: VAT AUNE LAST PIED
CARAT PERCHE BOISSEAU
MOUNTAIN: BOTRANGE
NAME: BELGIE BELGIQUE
PLATEAU: ARDENNES HOHEVENN
PORT: OSTEND ANTWERP
PROVINCE: LIEGE NAMUR ANTWERP
BRABANT HAINAUT LIMBURG
FLANDERS HAINAULT
RIVER: LYS DYLE LEIE MAAS MARK
YSER BOUCQ DEMER LESSE MEUSE
NETHE RUPEL SENNE DENDER
COCAUT MANJH OURTHE SAMBRE
SEMOIS VESDRE WARCHE AMBLEVE
SCHELDT
TOWN: AS AAT ANS ATH HAL HUY
MOL SPA AATH AMAY ASSE BOOM
BREE DOEL GAND GEEL GENK GENT
HOEI LIER LOOZ MONS VISE WAHA
ZELE AALST ALOST ARLON CINEY
EEKLO ESSEN EUPEN EVERE GENCK
GHENT HEIST IEPER JETTE JUMET
LIEGE NAMUR RONSE TIELT UCCLE
VORST WEZET YNOIR YPRES
AARLEN ANVERS BERGEN BILZEN
BRUGES DEURNE EISENE IZEGEM
LEUVEN LIERRE MERXEM OPWIJK
OSTEND ANTWERP ARDOOIE

BERCHEM DOORWIK HERSTAL
HOBOKEN IXELLES LOUVAIN
MECHLIN ROULERS SERAING
TONGRES TOURNAI BRUSSELS
COURTRAI KORTRIJK MECHELEN
MOUSCRON TONGEREN TURNHOUT
VERVIERS WATERLOO
WEIGHT: LAST CARAT LIVRE POUND
CHARGE CHARIOT ESTERLIN

BELIE BELONG DEFAME BESEIGE
FALSIFY PERTAIN SLANDER TRADUCE
DISGUISE STRUMPET SURROUND
MISREPRESENT
BELIEF CRY FAY ISM LEVE MIND SECT
TAKE TROW VIEW VOTE WEEN
CAUSE CREDO CREED DOGMA FAITH
OBEAH TENET TROTH TRUST CREDIT
GROUND CRIANCE FEELING
HOLDING OPINION TROWING
ARYANISM BITHEISM CREDENCE
DOCTRINE FINALISM HUMANISM
RELIANCE THANATISM
PREPOSSESSION
(— HANDED DOWN) TRADITION
(— IN DEVILS) DIABOLISM
(— IN GHOSTS) EIDOLISM
(— IN GOD) DEISM THEISM
(— IN MAGIC) OBEAH
(CONVENTIONAL —) PIETY
(FALSE —) DELUSION
(GROUNDLESS —) CANARD
(MORTAL —) HALL
(READY —) ACCEPTATION
(SHALLOW —) BALLOON
(SUPERSTITIOUS —) FREET
(TRADITIONAL —) ICON IKON EIKON
(UNFOUNDED —) FICTON
(UNIMPORTANT —) FAD
BELIEVABLE PLAUSIBLE
BELIEVE BUY WIS DEEM FEEL HOLD
TAKE TREW TROW WEEN CREED
FAITH FANCY GUESS JUDGE SEPAD
THINK TRUST ACCEPT CREDIT
ESTEEM EXPECT DARESAY SUPPOSE
ACCREDIT CONSIDER CREDENCE
(— ERRONEOUSLY) FEIGN
(— NAIVELY) SWALLOW
(— UNCRITICALLY) EAT
(HARD TO —) TALL
BELIEVER IST LEVER BOTARY KITABI
CREDENS ADHERENT ARMINIAN
(SUFF.) ARIAN
BELIEVING CREDENT FAITHFUL
BELISARIO (CHARACTER IN —)
ANTONIA EUTRIPIO BELISARIUS
(COMPOSER OF —) DONIZETTI
BELISE (BROTHER OF —) PHILAMINTE
BELITTLE DIS DUMP DECRY DWARF
SNEER BEMEAN DEMEAN MINISH
SLIGHT DETRACT DIMINUE LIGHTLY
MINIMIZE VILIPEND DENIGRATE
DISCREDIT DISPARAGE

BELITTLER ZOILUS
BELIZE (CAPITAL OF —) BELMOPAN
BELL HUB TOM CALL FAIR GONG
HUBB RING ROAR CHIME CLOAK
CLOCK CODON FLARE KNELL SWELL
TENOR BASKET BELLOW BUBBLE
CLOCHE CROTAL CURFEW PHONIC
SOCKET TAPPER TOCSIN TOLLER
TREBLE TRIPLE VESPER ANGELUS
BLOSSOM CAMPANA CAMPANE
COROLLA COWBELL JANGLER
JINGLER LOWBELL SKELLAT SKILLET
TAMBOUR TANTONY TINKLER
CASCABEL COCKBELL DINGDONG
DOORBELL HANDBELL HAWKBELL
MORTBELL PAVILLON STARTLER
TINGTANG
(ALARM —) TOCSIN
(CLOSED —) CROTAL
(EVENING —) CURFEW
(FUNERAL —) TELLER
(HAND —) CLAG
(LARGE —) SIGNUM
(LOWEST —) BORDON BOURDON
(PART OF —) BOW LIP HEAD CROWN
MOUTH WAIST CLAPPER SHOULDER
(PASSING —) KNELL
(SACRING —) SQUILLA
(SLEIGH —) GRELOT CROTALUM
(PREF.) CAMPANI CAMPANO
BELLABELLA HAELTZUK HEILTSUK
BELLADONNA DWALE MANICON
BANEWORT DAFTBERRY
DWAYBERRY MYDRIATIC
NIGHTSHADE
BELLARIA (HUSBAND OF —)
PANDOSTO
BELLARMINE GRAYBEARD
GREYBEARD LONGBEARD
BELLBIRD MAKO SHRIKE COTINGA
ARAPUNGA KORIMAKO MAKOMAKO
CAMPANERO
BELLBOY BUTTONS
BELLE SPARK TOAST
(SPANISH —) MAJA
BELLEEK POTTERY CHAMPAGNE
**BELLE HELENE, LE (COMPOSER OF
—)** OFFENBACH
BELLEROPHON (FATHER OF —)
GLAUCUS
(MOTHER OF —) EURYMEDE
BELLFLOWER LOBELIA RAMPION
BELLWORT HASKWORT IVYBELLS
MILKWORT
BELLHOP PAGE BELLBOY HALLBOY
CHASSEUR
BELLICOSE MAD IRATE WARFUL
HOSTILE WARLIKE MILITANT
BELLIGERENT BRISTLY HOSTILE
SCRAPPY STROPPY WARLIKE
CHOLERIC FIGHTING JINGOIST
COMBATIVE IRASCIBLE LITIGIOUS
WRANGLING PUGNACIOUS

BELLISANT (HUSBAND OF —) ALEXANDER
(SON OF —) ORSON VALENTINE
BELLOW CRY LOW MOO YAP DAWL BEAL BELL GAPE ROAR ROME ROUT YAUP YAWP BELVE BLART BLORE CROON ROUST SHOUT TROAT BULLER CLAMOR RUMMES BLUSTER RUMMISH THUNDER ULULATE
BELLOWING ROUT ROUST BELLING BLATANT BOATION MUGIENT
BELLOWS RELY LUNGS BULIES FEEDER SANDER WINKER SYLPHON WINDBAG EXPELLER
(SMALL —) PLUFF
(STORAGE —) RESERVOIR
(PREF.) PHYSA PHYSALLO PHYSO
BELLOWS FISH BUGLER SNIPEFISH
BELL RINGER TOLL YOUTH TOLLER CLINKUM
BELL-TOWER BELFRY CAMPANILE
BELLWETHER MASTER
BELLY BAG COD GIE GUT MAW POD BOUK BUNT FILL KYTE MARY WAME WEAM WOMB BINGY BOSOM BULGE FRONT GORGE PLEON TABLE THARM THERM TRIPE BAGGIE BINGEE HUNGER PAUNCH VENTER ABDOMEN BALLOON STOMACH TUMBREL APPETITE
(PREF.) CELI COELI(O) GASTER(O) GASTR(I)(O) VENTRI VENTRO
(SUFF.) GASTER GASTRIA
BELLYACHE CARP YAMMER COMPLAIN COLLYWOBBLES
BELLYBAND WANTY
BELLYING BUNTING PREGNANT
BELLY-UP BANKRUPT
BELONE SEAPIKE
BELONG BE GO FIT LIE BEAR FALL RELY APPLY BELIE GROUP AFFEIR INHERE RELATE RETAIN BEHOOVE PERTAIN APPERTAIN SUBSCRIBE
BELONGING
(SUFF.) EAE
(— TO) AR ARY EAN INE ISE ORIUM
BELONGINGS ALLS DUDS FARE GEAR GOODS TRAPS ASSETS DUFFEL DUFFLE ESTATE USINGS BAGGAGE EFFECTS CHATTELS PROPERTY PURPRISE FURNITURE HOUSEHOLD PARAPHERNALIA
BELOVED DEAR IDOL LIEF AIMEE BOSOM CHERI SWEET ADORED CHERIE MINION DARLING PRECIOUS INAMORATA INAMORATO
(MOST —) ALDERLIEFEST
BELOW ALOW BAJO DOWN ABLOW AFTER INFRA NEATH SOTTO UNDER BEHIND BENEATH
(PREF.) INFERO INFRA SUB
BELT LAS AREA BAND BEAT BLOW CEST FELT GIRD LACE LIST MARK

RING SASH SLUG ZONE GIRTH MITER MITRE PATTE STRAP STRIP SWATH TRACT WAIST WHACK ZONAR ZONIC BODICE CENTER CESTUS CINGLE FETTLE GIRDLE INVEST LUNGER REGION STRAIT STRIPE SWATHE ZONNAR ZONULE BALDRIC BALTEUS CIRCUIT PASSAGE BALTHEUS CEINTURE CINCTURE CINGULUM ELEVATOR ENCIRCLE MECHANIC SURROUND CUMBERBUND CUMMERBUND
(— OF FOG) BLANKET
(AMMUNITION —) BANDOLEER BANDOLIER
(ASTROLOGICAL —) CLIMATE
(CONVEYOR —) HAUL
(ENDLESS —) APRON CREEPER
(GREEK —) ZOSTER
(HINDU SWAMP —) TERAI
(KIND OF —) VANALLEN
(MACHINE —) SWIFTER
(MINERAL —) RANGE
(PACKHORSE'S —) WANTY
(PART OF —) TIP HOLE FRAME PANEL PRONG BUCKLE FILLER KEEPER LINING PIPING TONGUE STITCHING
(TREE —) BERM BERME
(PL.) BALTEI
(PREF.) ZON(O)
BELTED ZONATE GIRDLED CINCTURED
(— WITH WHITE) SHELTED
BELUGA HUSE HUSO HAUSEN MARSOON WHITEFISH
BELUS (BROTHER OF —) AGENOR
(FATHER OF —) NEPTUNE POSEIDON
(MOTHER OF —) LIBYA EURYNOME
(SON OF —) DANAUS CEPHEUS AEGYPTUS
BELVEDERE GAZEBO LOOKOUT
BELVIDERA (FATHER OF —) PRIULI
(HUSBAND OF —) JAFFIER
BELVIDERE MIRADOR
BEMIRE DAG SOIL JARRLE
BEMOAN RUE MEAN MOAN SIGH WEEP MOURN PLAIN BEWAIL LAMENT DEPLORE
BEMUSE SOT BULL DAZE AMUSE
BEMUSED DOPY DOPEY PIXILATED MOONSTRUCK
BENAIAH (FATHER OF —) JEHOIADA
(SON OF —) PELATIAH
BENCH PEW BANC BANK BENK BERM BINK DAIS DEAS FORM MESA SEAT SILL STEP TRAM BASIN BASON BERME BREAK CABIN CHAIR FORME JUDGE PLANK STALL STOOL BANCUS BANKER SCONCE SEDILE SETTEE SETTLE SITTER COUNTER DRESSER REPOSAL SHAMBLE SITTING TRESTLE TRIBUNE ALEBENCH
(— FOR DAIRY TUBS) TRAM

(— FOR KNEADING DOUGH) BREAK
(CHURCH —) PEW
(KNEELING —) PRIEDIEU
(OUTDOOR —) EXEDRA EXHEDRA
(PLAYER'S —) WOOD
(ROWER'S —) BANK THOFT ZYGON THWART
(SHOEMAKER'S —) FORME
(TAILOR'S —) SHOPBOARD
(WORKMAN'S —) SIEGE

BEND BOW ESS NID NIP PLY SAG SET
SNY WIN WRY ABOW ARCH BENT
BOOL BUCK COPE CURB DOME FAUD
FLEX FOLD GENU HOOK KINK LEAN
LOUT PLOY RUMP TURN VERT WEEP
ANGLE BATON BIGHT BREAK COUCH
COUDE COURB CRANK CRIMP CRINK
CROOK CULGE CURVE DROOP FLECT
FRESE HINGE HUNCH INBOW KNEEL
PLASH PLICA QUIRL ROUND SCRAG
SKELP SLANT STOOP TREND TWINE
TWIST BOUGHT BUCKLE CAMBER
CONVEX COTICE CROUCH SPRING
COMPASS FLEXURE RECLINE
GENUFLECT
(— IN) INFLECT
(— IN HANDRAIL) RAMP
(— IN PIPE) TRAP DIPTRAP
(— IN REVERENCE) PROSTRATE
(— IN SHIP'S TIMBER) SNY
(— KNEE) KNUCKLE
(RIVER —) OXBOW
(SUFF.) FLECT(ION) FLEX(ION)

BENDER BUM JAG LEG BUST KNEE
TEAR DRUNK SPREE BRIDGE
WHOPPER GUZZLING SIXPENCE
BRANNIGAN INFLECTOR

BENDING BOW SAG KNEE KNOT PLIE
CROOK CURVE LITHE TWIST PLIANT
SUPPLE TWISTY ANFRACT FLEXION
HOGGING SINUOUS BUCKLING
FLECTION
(— DOWNWARD) RECLINATE
(— OF ROCK) DRAG
(BALLET —) PLIE
(PREF.) SPHINGO

BENDLETS FRET
BENDY TREE MIRO MAHOE
BENEATH ALOW ANETH BELOW
LOWER UNDER ANEATH
(PREF.) HYPO INFRA SUB
BENEDICITE BENISON CANTICLE
BENEDICT NEOGAMIST
BENEDICTINE CLUNIAC
CAMALDOLESE TIRONENSIAN
BENEDICTION ABOT AMEN ABOTH
NANDI AMIDAH BROCHO PRAYER
BENISON BERAKAH BLESSING
BENEFACTION ALMS BOON GIFT
PRESENT DONATION GRATUITY
BENEFACTOR AGENT ANGEL
DONOR FRIEND HELPER PATRON
SAVIOR MAECENAS PROMOTER

BENEFICE FEE FEU FEUD FIEF FAVOR
SCARF CURACY LIVING BENEFIT
CANONRY PRELACY RECTORY
TOTQUOT DONATIVE KINDNESS
SINECURE VICARAGE PLURALITY
BENEFICENCE BOON GIFT GRACE
BOUNTY CHARITY GOODNESS
KINDNESS
BENEFICENT KINDLY AMIABLE
BENEFIC GRACIOUS
BENEFICIAL GOOD USEFUL
HEALTHY HELPFUL BONITARY
SALUTARY SANATIVE SINGULAR
AVAILABLE BENIGNANT DESIRABLE
ENJOYABLE HEALTHFUL LUCRATIVE
REWARDING WHOLESOME
PROFITABLE
BENEFICIARY HEIR USER DONEE
CESTUI CESTUY USUARY VASSAL
LEGATEE FEUDATORY
(SUFF.) EE
BENEFIT AID USE BOON BOOT GAIN
GIFT GOOD HELP PERK PROW SAKE
AVAIL BOOST FRUIT SELTH STEAD
VISIT ASSIST BEHALF BEHOOF
BETTER FRINGE PROFIT SALUTE
USANCE ADVANCE BESPEAK
CONCERT DESERVE IMPROVE
SERVICE UTILITY BEFRIEND INTEREST
(— SUCCESSFULLY) FLY
BENEVOLENCE JEN BOUNTY
GOODNESS GOODWILL HUMANITY
BENEVOLENT GOOD KIND BENIGN
KINDLY LOVING AMIABLE LIBERAL
GENEROUS AVUNCULAR BENIGNANT
ALTRUISTIC PROPITIOUS
HUMANITARIAN PHILANTHROPIC
(WEAKLY —) GOODYGOODY
BENHANAN (FATHER OF —) SHIMON
BEN HUR (AUTHOR OF —) WALLACE
(CHARACTER IN —) HUR IRAS JUDAH
ESTHER TIRZAH MESSALA
BALTHASAR SIMONIDES
BENIGN BOON GOOD KIND MILD
BLAND SWEET TRINE GENIAL
GENTLE AFFABLE BENEFIC BENEDICT
GRACIOUS INNOCENT SALUTARY
FAVORABLE WHOLESOME
BENIGNANT KIND BLAND GENIAL
LIBERAL GRACIOUS MERCIFUL
BENIN (CAPITAL OF —) PORTONOVO
(TOWN IN —) COTONOU
BENISON BOON BENEDICTION
BENJAMIN BENZOIN
(FATHER OF —) HARIM JACOB
BILHAN
(MOTHER OF —) RACHEL
(SON OF —) ARD EHI BELA GERA
ROSH ASHBEL BECHER HUPPIM
MUPPIM NAAMAN
BENNET CLOVEWORT
BENNISEED SESAME
BENO TUBA

BENT AIM BOW SET BIAS CAST CURB GIFT TURN BANDY BOUND BOWED BOWLY COUDE COURB CRANK CRUMP FLAIR HUMOR KNACK LURCH PRONE SQUAT SWING TASTE TREND AKIMBO ANLAGE BENNET BIASED BRACED COURBE COURSE CURVED DOGLEG ENERGH GENIUS HOOKED INTENT LIKING NECKED SQUINT SWAYED TALENT ADUNCAL ARCUATE BUCKLED CROOKED CURVANT EMBOWED FLEXION FLEXURE IMPETUS INTENSE LEANING LEVELED PRONATE PURPOSE STOOPED TENSION ADUNCOUS APTITUDE ARCUATED CRUMPLED DECLINED FLECTION IMMINENT INFLEXED PENCHANT REFLEXED TENDENCY
(— AT THE END) HAMATE HOGGED GRYPANIAN
(— DOWNWARD) BOWED DECURVED INCUMBENT RECLINATE
(— IN) INCAVATE
(— INWARD) ADUNC
(— OF MIND) GEME AFFECTION
(EASILY —) LITHY
(NATURAL —) SWING
(SPECIAL —) VERVE
(PREF.) ANKYL(O) CAMPTO CURVI CYPH(O) CYRT(O) SCOLIO
BEN-TEAK NANDI NANAWOOD
BENT-GRASS FIBRIN REDTOP
BENUMB NIP DAZE DUNT NUMB STUN CHILL DAVER DOZEN SCRAM SHRAM CUMBER DEADEN PERISH STOUND BINOMEN FRETISH FRETIZE STIFFEN STUPEFY TORPEDO TORPEFY
BENUMBED CHILL SCRAM ASLEEP CLUMSE CLUMSY FROZEN TORPID CLUMPST SHRAMMED
RENUMBING LEADEN
BENVENUTO CELLINI
(CHARACTER IN —) POMPEO TERESA ASCANIO CELLINI BALDUCCI SALVIATA BENVENUTO FIERAMOSCA
(COMPOSER OF —) BERLIOZ
BENZAYDA
(LOVER OF —) OZWY
BENZENE PHENE BENZIN BENZOL PHENENE
(SUFF.) PHEN(E)
BENZINE
(PREF.) PHEN(O)
BENZOIN BENJOIN LINDERA BENJAMIN FIXATIVE
(SUFF.) OIN
BEOR (SON OF —) BELA BALAAM
BEOWULF (AUTHOR OF —)
UNKNOWN
(CHARACTER IN —) WIGLAF BEOWULF GRENDEL HIGELAC UNFERTH AESCHERE HONDSCIO HROTHGAR

BEQUEATH GIVE WILL ENDOW LEAVE OFFER BESTOW COMMIT DEMISE DEVISE LEGATE QUETHE BEQUEST COMMEND TRANSMIT
BEQUEST GIFT WILL LEGACY BEQUEATH HERITAGE PITTANCE ENDOWMENT BENEFACTION
BERACHIAH (SON OF —) ASAPH
BERAIAH (FATHER OF —) SHIMHI
BERATE JAW NAG DRUB LASH RAIL ABUSE BASTE CHIDE SCOLD SCORE SLATE REVILE CENSURE REPROVE UPBRAID CHASTISE
BERBER RIF RIFF KABYL SHLUH KABYLE SHILHA HARATIN MZABITE SHILLUH HARRATIN MOZABITE
(— CHIEF) CAID
BERCEUSE CRADLESONG WIEGENLIED
BEREAVE ROB STRIP WIDOW DIVEST SADDEN DEPRIVE DESPOIL
BEREAVED ORB BEREFT VIDUOUS WIDOWED DESOLATE
BEREAVEMENT ORBITY ORBITUDE VIDUATION
BERECHIAH (SON OF —) ASAPH MESHULLAM ZECHARIAH
BEREFT ORB LORN LOST POOR QUIT WIDOW ORBATE FORLORN FORFAIRN DESTITUTE
BERG FLOE BARROW ICEBERG FLOEBERG
BERGAMOT BOSE BERGAMA BURGAMOT
BERGERE SEAT
BERGYLT ROCCFISH
BERI (FATHER OF —) ZOPHAH
BERIAH (FATHER OF —) ASHER EPHRAIM
BERIBERI KAKKE
BERITH BRIS BRISS BRITH
BERM BERME LISIERE HEELPATH
BERMUDA PETREL CAHOW
BERNICE (FATHER OF —) HEROD
BERRY BAY DEW HAW ALEY BEAT CRAN POHA RASP BACCA BLACK CUBEB FRUIT GRAIN GRAPE LANSA MOUND SALAL SAVIN BURROW LANSAT LANSEH SABINE THRESH CURRANT ETAERIO HILLOCK ACROSARC ALLSPICE COWBERRY DEWBERRY HAWEBAKE PERSIMMON POKEBERRY SASKATOON PEPPERCORN SHEEPBERRY POMEGRANATE
(ACID —) CURRANT
(COFFEE —) CHERRY
(DRIED —) PASA
(JUMPER —) ABHAL
(LAUREL —) BAY
(POISONOUS —) BANEBERRY
(PREF.) BACCI COCC(I)(O)
BERRY-LIKE BACCATE ACINIFORM

BERTH BED JOB BUNK DOCK SLIP SOPT CABIN PLACE UPPER BILLET OFFICE SECURE LODGING MOORING SLIPWAY POSITION ANCHORAGE

BERTHA (FATHER OF —) CARIBERT (HUSBAND OF —) PEPIN HEREWARD (SON OF —) CHARLES

BERYL EMERALD AEROIDES HELIODOR GOSHENITE MORGANITE AQUAMARINE

BERYLLIA GLUCINA GLUCINE

BERYLLIUM GLUCINUM

BESEECH ASK BEG BID CRY SUE WOO PRAY CRAVE HALSE PLEAD PRESS ADJURE APPEAL OBTEST CONJURE ENTREAT IMPLORE SOLICIT IMPETRATE OBSECRATE

BESET PLY SET SIT BEGO SAIL STUD ALLOT BELAY BIGAN HARRY PRESS SIEGE SPEND STEAD ASSAIL ATTACK HARASS INFEST OBSESS WAYLAY ARRANGE BESIEGE OVERSET PERPLEX BLOCKADE ENCUMBER ENTHRONG OBSTRUCT SURROUND BELEAGUER
(— WITH DIFFICULTIES) SCABROUS

BESHOW SKIL CUDDY CUDDEN CUDDIE BADDOCK COALFISH SKILFISH

BESIDE BY HEAR INBY NEXT ALONG ANENT ASIDE FORBY ABREAST AGAINST FORNENT ADJACENT FORNENST
(— ONE ANOTHER) ABREAST
(— ONESELF) FEY
(PREF.) EPH EPI PAR(A)

BESIDES BY TO AND BUT TOO YET ALSO ELSE MORE OVER PLUS THEN UNTO WITH ABOVE AGAIN FORBY SUPRA BESIDE BEYOND EXCEPT FORBYE WITHAL THERETO WITHOUT LIKEWISE MOREOVER
(PREF.) EPH EPI PROS

BESIEGE GIRD GIRT BELAY BELIE BESET SIEGE STORM ATTACK OBSESS OBSIDE PESTER PLAGUE COMPASS SOLICIT SURROUND BELEAGUER

BESMEAR RAY BALM DAUB SOIL APPLY COVER GRIME GRUFT MUDDY SLAKE SMEAR SULLY TAINT BEDAUB PLATCH BESLIME SMOTHER BESMIRCH BESLUBBER

BESMIRCH TAR DASH SLUR SOIL SMEAR SULLY TAINT SLURRY SMIRCH ASPERSE BLACKEN DRAGGLE TURPIFY DISCOLOR

BESMIRCHED MACULATE MACULATED

BESMUT CROCK

BESOM COW MAP DRAB BISME BROOM SWEEP SLOVEN HEATHER

BESOT DULL ASOTE ASSOT MUDDLE STUPID STUPEFY BEFUDDLE

BESOTTED BEDAZED DRUNKEN INFATUATED

BESPANGLE DOT STAR STUD ADORN JEWEL INVENT SPRINKLE

BESPATTER BLOT DASH JAUP SOIL SPOT MUDDY PLASH STAIN SULLY BEGARY SPARGE ASPERSE SCATTER SMOTTER REPROACH SPRINKLE

BESPEAK CITE HINT SHOW ARGUE IMPLY ORDER SPEAK TRYST ACCOST ATTEST ENGAGE STEVEN ADDRESS ARRANGE BENEFIT BETOKEN DISCUSS EXCLAIM RESERVE FORETELL INDICATE

BESPECKLE DASH

BESPECTACLED SPECCY

BESPRINKLE DROP SHED POWDER ASPERSE BESTREW BESPRING SPRINKLE BEQUIRTLE

BEST O ACE BEAT GOOD LACE MOST PICK TOPS WALE CREAM ELITE EXCEL PRIZE WORST CHOICE DEFEAT FINEST FLOWER OUTWIT SUNDAY TIPTOP UTMOST ARISTOS CONQUER GARLAND LARGEST OPTIMUM PALMARY DAMNDEST GREATEST KOHINOOR OUTMATCH OUTSTRIP POSSIBLE TOPNOTCH VANQUISH
(SUNDAY —) BRAWS
(PREF.) ARIST(O)

BESTIAL LOW VILE WILD BRUTE FERAL PRONE BRUTAL FILTHY BEASTLY BRUTISH INHUMAN SENSUAL BARBARIC BELLUINE DEPRAVED

BESTIR STIR AWAKE SHIFT STEER AROUSE HUSTLE
(— ONESELF) LEG

BEST MAN PARANYMPH

BESTOW ADD PUT USE CAST DEAL DOTE GIVE SEND STOW TAKE WARE ALLOT ALLOW APPLY AWARD BESET GRANT INFER LODGE PLACE SPEND THOLE WREAK ACCORD BETEEM CONFER DEMISE DEVOTE DIVIDE DONATE DOTATE EMPLOY ENTAIL ESTATE EXTEND IMPART IMPOSE RENDER SHOWER COLLATE COMMEND DISPOSE ENLARGE EROGATE INDULGE INSTATE PARTAKE PRESENT QUARTER TRIBUTE BEQUEATH
(— LAVISHLY) HEAP
(— UPON) GIFT

BESTOWAL DOLE DISPOSAL COLLATION LARGITION
(— OF PRAISE) ACCOLADE

BESTOWED GIVEN

BESTRIDE HORSE STRIDE STRADDLE OVERSTRIDE

BET GO UP BAS BOX LAY PUT SET VIE
WAD ANTE BACK BRAG CHIP GAGE
HOLD JACK NOIR PAIR PLAY PLOT
PUNT RISK WAGE BOUND CARRE
HEDGE ROUGE SAVER SPORT STAKE
WAGER GAMBLE HAZARD IMPAIR
MANQUE MILIEU PLEDGE DERNIER
PREMIER ACCUMULATOR
(— AGAINST) MILK COPPER
(— AT LONG ODDS) SKINNER
(— BOLDLY) BLUFF
(— CHIP) CHECK
(FARO —) SLEEPER
(HEDGING —) SAVER
(MULTIPLE —) PARLAY
(POKER —) BLIND
(RACE —) WIN SHOW PLACE DOUBLE
EXACTA PARLAY TRIPLE TRIFECTA
(RACING —) WIN SHOW PLACE
DOUBLE EXACTA PARLAY TRIPLE
PERFECTA QUINELLA TRIFECTA
(UP THE —) RAISE
BETA AND GAMMA GUARDS
BETA-BLOCKER TIMOLOL
BETAKE GO GET HIE MOVE TAKE
APPLY CATCH GRANT ASSUME
COMMIT REMOVE REPAIR RESORT
COMMEND JOURNEY WITHDRAW
(— ONESELF) BUN HIT BOUN MARK
PIKE TEEM AVOID FOUND HAUNT
REFER TRUSS YIELD
(— ONESELF TO MILL) SUE
BETEL PAN IKMO ITMO SERI SIRI
SIRIH PINANG PUPULO
BETEL LEAF PAN BUYO PAUN
PAWNE
BETEL NUT BONGA BONYA BUNGA
SUPARI
BETHABARA NOIBWOOD
GREENHEART
BETHEL BETHESDA
BETHINK TAKE THINK ADVISE DEVISE
RECALL REFLECT CONSIDER
REMEMBER RECOLLECT
(— ONE'S SELF) MIN MINE
UMBETHINK
BETHLEHEM BEDLAM
BETHROOT TRILLIUM
BETHUEL (DAUGHTER OF —)
REBEKAH
(FATHER OF —) NAHOR
(MOTHER OF —) MILCAH
(UNCLE OF —) ABRAHAM
BETHUMP POUND PUMMEL
LOUNDER
BETIDE HAP TIDE BEFIT OCCUR TRITE
WORTH BECOME BEFALL CHANCE
HAPPEN BETOKEN PRESAGE
BETIMES ANON RATH SOON EARLY
HAITHE TIMEOUS SPEEDILY
FORTHWITH
BETOKEN MARK NOTE SHOW SIGN
AUGUR TOKEN ASSERT BETIDE

DENOTE EVINCE IMPORT SHADOW
BESPEAK EXPRESS OBLIQUE
PORTEND PRESAGE SIGNIFY
FOREBODE FORESHOW INDICATE
BETONY BROOMWORT
BETRAY BLAB BLOW BOIL GULL SELL
SHOP SILE SING SPOT TELL TRAY
UNDO WRAY ABUSE CROSS FALSE
PEACH ROUND SPILL SPLIT SWICK
SWIKE ACCUSE BEWRAY DELUDE
DESCRY DESERT QUATCH REVEAL
SEDUCE SNITCH SQUEAL BEGUILE
DECEIVE FALSIFY MISLEAD PROMOTE
TRAITOR DISCLOSE DISCOVER
(— CONFIDENCES) SPILL
BETRAYAL RAP ABUSE ACCUSE
TREASON GIVEAWAY PRODITION
BETRAYER RAT JUDAS SKUNK
SEDUCER TRAITOR DERELICT
RECREANT SQUEALER
BETRAYING TELLTALE
BETROTH AFFY EARL TOKEN TROTH
TRUTH ASSURE ENGAGE ENSURE
PLEDGE PLIGHT ESPOUSE PROMISE
AFFIANCE CONTRACT DESPOUSE
HANDFAST
BETROTHAL ESPOUSAL HANDFAST
BETROTHED SURE VOWED
ASSURED ENGAGED HANDFAST
INTENDED COMBINATE
(AUTHOR OF —) MANZONI
(CHARACTER IN —) LUCIA RENZO
RODRIGO ABBONDIO BORROMEO
CRISTOFORO
BETTA PLAKAT
BETTER AID TOP BEET MEND AMEND
EMEND EXCEL SAFER WISER BIGGER
EXCEED REFORM ADVANCE CHOICER
CORRECT GREATER IMPROVE
PROMOTE RECTIFY RELIEVE
SUPPORT SURPASS EMINENCE
INCREASE SUPERIOR
(— A SCORE) BREAK
(— THAN ORDINARY) EXTRA
BETTING ACTION GAMBLING
(— ARRANGEMENT) PERM
(— SYSTEM) PAROLI ALEMBERT
BETTOR ORALER
BETTY JENNY COTBETTY JOCRISSE
MOLLYCOT WIFECARL
BETWEEN AMID EMEL AMELL
AMONG ENTRE TWEEN YTWYN
ATWEEN ATWIXT TWEESH AVERAGE
BETWIXT
(PREF.) DI INTER INTRA
BEUDANITE CORKITE
BEVEL BLOW CANT CONE EDGE
PUSH REAM ANGLE BEARD BEZEL
MITER MITRE SLANT SLOPE SNAPE
SPLAY ASLANT CIPHER RHYMER
CHAMFER INCLINE OBLIQUE
(— EDGES) BEARD
(WITHOUT —) FLAT

BEVERAGE ADE ALE AVA CUP NOG POP RUM SAP TEA BEER BREW CHIA GROG MABI MATE MEAD MILK NIPA SODA WHIG WINE CHOCA CIDER CLARY COCOA DRAFT DRINK JULEP LAGER LEBAN MORAT MULSE NEGUS PUNCH SHRUB SMASH TREAT TWIST WATER BISHOP COFFEE EGGNOG LIQUID LIQUOR NECTAR PORTER SPRUCE TISWIN BUNNELL CASSINA CORDIAL LIMEADE OENOMEL POTABLE STEPONY TULAPAI ALEBERRY COCKTAIL LEMONADE LIBATION PIQUETTE POTATION SANGAREE SWITCHEL BADMINTON CALIBOGUS CHOCOLATE GINGERADE ORANGEADE POMPERKIN SOMETHING
(— FROM COW'S MILK) KEFIR KEPHIR
(— FROM PEPPERS) KAVA KAVAKAVA
(— FROM SAP) TUBA
(— OF BUTTERMILK AND WATER) BLAND
(— OF CHAMPAGNE) POPE
(— OF GODS) NECTAR
(— OF HONEY AND WATER) HYDROMEL METHEGLIN
(— OF HOT MILK) POSSET
(— OF PORT WINE) BISHOP
(— OF VINEGAR AND WATER) POSCA
(— OF WINE AND WATER) SPRITZER
(ALCOHOLIC —) DEW ARAK SAKE SAKI ARRAK BASIG SHRUB SNAPS STUFF ARRACK FIREWATER STIMULANT
(COLA —) DOPE
(EFFERVESCENT —) FIZZ
(FERMENTED —) BASI KAVA KUMYS KUMISS
(FRUIT —) BEVERAGE
(INSIPID —) WASH
(JAPANESE —) SAKE SAKI
(MEXICAN —) TEPACHE
(POLYNESIAN —) AVA KAVA
(WEAK —) LAP
(PL.) WAIPIRO

BEVY HERD PACK COVEY DROVE FLOCK GROUP SWARM FLIGHT SCHOOL COMPANY

BEWAIL CRY RUE WEY KEEN MOAN RAME SIGH WAIL WEEP MOURN PLAIN BEMOAN GRIEVE LAMENT PLAINT SORROW THROPE DEPLORE COMPLAIN

BEWARE WAR CAVE GARE HEED SHUN TENT WARD AVOID SPEND ESCHEW WARNING

BEWILDER FOG FOX MAR BEAT DAZE FOIL GAUM MAZE STUN ABASH ADDLE AMAZE AMUSE DEAVE DIZZY BAFFLE BEMIST BEMUSE BOTHER DAZZLE DUDDER MOIDER MOMBLE MUDDLE PUZZLE WANDER WILDER BUFFALO BUMBAZE CONFUSE FLASKER MYSTIFY NONPLUS PERPLEX STAGGER STUPEFY ASTONISH CONFOUND DISTRACT ENTANGLE OVERMUSE SQUATTER SURPRISE
(PREF.) PLAZO

BEWILDERED MAR ASEA LOST MANG WILL AGAPE ATSEA DAZED MAZED MUZZY BUSHED MAPPED BEMAZED STUPENT WILSOME CONFUSED HELPLESS WILLYARD PERPLEXED

BEWILDERMENT AWE FOG DAZE MISMAZE STICKLE AMAZEMENT CONFUSION PERPLEXITY

BEWITCH HEX WISH BLINK CHARM MAGIC OBEAH SPELL WITCH ENAMOR ENTICE GLAMOR GRIGRI HOODOO STRIKE THRILL ATTRACT BEDEVIL DELIGHT ENCHANT GLAMOUR ENSORCEL FORSPEAK GREEGREE OVERLOOK

BEWITCHED RAPT ENRAPT HAGGED

BEWITCHING SIREN

BEYOND BY FREE OVER YOND ABOVE ASIDE AYOND FORBY ULTRA BEHIND BEYANT YONDER BENEATH BESIDES FORTHBY FURTHER OUTGATE PASSING WITHOUT OVERMORE SUPERIOR HEREAFTER
(— CONTROL) MASTERLESS
(— DOUBT) ASSURED
(— HOPE) DESPERATE
(— ORDINARY METHODS) AFIELD
(— THE MARK) GONE
(— THE MOUNTAINS) TRAMONTANE
(— THE SEA) ULTRAMARINE
(— THIS) STILL
(GO —) OVERSHOOT
(PREF.) EXTRA HYPER META OVER PARA PERI PRETER SUPER TRANS ULTRA

BEYOND HUMAN POWER
(AUTHOR OF —) BJORNSON
(CHARACTER IN —) SANG CLARA ELIAS HANNA ADOLPH RACHAEL ROBERTS

BEZALEEL (FATHER OF —) URI

BEZANT SOLIDUS

BEZEL RIM TOP EDGE OUCH SEAL BEVIL BEZIL CROWN FACET CHATON FLANGE MARQUISE TEMPLATE

BEZER (FATHER OF —) ZOPHAH

BEZIQUE PENCHANT

BEZOAR GOATSTONE HIPPOLITH

B-GIRL SITTER

BHAKTA BHAGAVATA

BHANG BANG BENG BENJ HEMP HASHISH

BHARAL TUR HALL NAHOOR BURRHEL

BHARTRIHARI (BROTHER OF —) VIKRAMADITYA
BHIKSHU GELONG
BHIMA (FATHER OF —) VAYU PANDU
  (MOTHER OF —) KUNTI PRITHA
BHUTAN (ASSEMBLY OF —) TSONGDU
  (CAPITAL OF —) THIMPHU
  (COIN OF —) CHETRUM
  (CURRENCY OF —) PAISA RUPEE CHETRUM NGULTRUM
  (LANGUAGE OF —) DZONGKHA
  (MONEY OF —) NGULTRUM
  (RIVER OF —) MACHU MANAS AMOCHU
BHUTAN PINE KAIL
BIANCA (HUSBAND OF —) FAZIO LEONTIO
  (SISTER OF —) KATHERINE
BIANNUAL BIYEARLY
BIANOR (FATHER OF —) TIBERIS
  (MOTHER OF —) MANTO
BIAS PLY WRY AWRY BENT CANT SWAY WARP AMISS COLOR FAVOR POISE SLANT SLOPE SWING TWIST BIGOTRY INCLINE OBLIQUE SUGGEST CLINAMEN COLORING DIAGONAL TENDENCY PREJUDICE PROCEDURE SPECTACLE
  (— IN NEWS REPORTING) PLUGOLA
  (BROTHER OF —) MELAMPUS
  (FATHER OF —) AMYTHAON
  (MOTHER OF —) IDOMENE
  (WIFE OF —) PERO IPHIANASSA
BIASED SLANT ANGLED COLORED OBLIQUE PARTIAL SLANTED
  (— ONE) BIGOT
BIB SIP BRAT POUT APRON BLAIN DRINK BRASSY FEEDER TIPPLE TUCKER BAVETTE
  (CHILD'S —) BISHOP
  (LEATHER —) DICK
BIBLE BOOK ITALA VULGATE SCRIPTURE
  (— TEXT) MIKRA MIORA
  (BOOK OF —) EX CHR COL COR DAN EPH GAL GEN HAB HAG HEB HOS IER JOB KIN LAM LEV MAL MIC NAH NEH NUM PET REV ROM SAM TIM ACTS AMOS CANT DEUT EZEK EZRA JOEL JOHN JUDE JUDG LUKE MARK MATT OBAD PHIL PROV RUTH SONG ZECH ZEPH HOSEA JAMES JONAH KINGS MICAH NAHUM PETER THESS TITUS DANIEL ECCLES ESTHER EXODUS HAGGAI ISAIAH JOSHUA JUDGES PHILEM PSALMS ROMANS SAMUEL EZEKIEL GENESIS HEBREWS MALACHI MATTHEW NUMBERS OBADIAH TIMOTHY JEREMIAH NEHEMIAH PHILEMON PROVERBS CANTICLES EPHESIANS GALATIANS LEVITICUS ZECHARIAH ZEPHANIAH CHRONICLES COLOSSIANS REVELATION CORINTHIANS DEUTERONOMY PHILIPPIANS ECCLESIASTES LAMENTATIONS THESSALONIANS
  (SYRIAC VERSION OF —) PESHITO
BIBLE LEAF COSTMARY
BIBULOUS DRINKING BIBACIOUS
BICEPS HAMSTRING
BICKER JAR WAR BOWL SPAR TIFF ARGUE BRAWL CAVIL FIGHT SCRAP ASSAIL ATTACK BATTLE CONTEND DISPUTE PICKEER QUARREL QUIBBLE WRANGLE PETTIFOG SKIRMISH SQUABBLE
BICKERN ANVIL BEAKIRON
BICUSPID PREMOLAR
BICYCLE BIKE QUAD CORGI CORGY CYCLE HOBBY MOUNT STEED WHEEL JIGGER ORNARY SAFETY TANDEM ORDINAR TRIPLET ORDINARY ROADSTER TENSPEED
  (— FOR TWO) TANDEM
  (— MANEUVER) WHEELIE
  (PART OF —) ARM LUG RIM CLIP FORK POST RACK RING SEAT STAY STEM TIRE CHAIN GUARD PEDAL SHIFT SPOKE FENDER HANGER SADDLE DOWNTUBE SPROCKET CHAINWHEEL DERAILLEUR
  (PLACE WHERE —S ARE SERVICED) CYCLERY
  (STATIONARY —) EXERCYCLE
BID GO BEG NAP BEDE BODE CALL GIVE HEST HIST PRAY TELL WISH CHEAP CLEPE FRAGE OFFER ORDER ADJURE CHARGE DIRECT ENJOIN INVITE REVEAL SIMPLE SUMMON TENDER BALANCE CHEAPEN COMMAND DECLARE DROPVIE ENTREAT PROFFER ANNOUNCE PROCLAIM PROPOSAL
  (— ADIEU) TEACH
  (— AT AUCTION) CRY
  (— IN CARDS) CUE FROG JUMP PASS SKIP SOLO FRAGE GRAND NULLO SHIFT BOSTON DEFEND DEMAND DENIAL DOUBLE SMUDGE BLUCHER COMMAND SHUTOUT SUPPORT CONTRACT REDOUBLE SCHMEISS
  (FIRST —) OPENER OPENERS
  (MAKE FIRST —) OPEN
  (SEALED —) TICKET
BIDDING BEHEST AUCTION BIDDANCE DIRECTIVE
BIDE FACE STAY WAIT ABIDE AWAIT DWELL TARRY WATCH ENDURE REMAIN SUFFER SOJOURN CONTINUE TOLERATE
BIDENS CUCKOLD MANZANILLA
BIDET SITZBAD INSESSION
BIDRI VIDRY BIDDERY TUTENAG
BIENNIAL TRIETERIC

BIER BEAR PYRE FRAME GRAVE HANDY HORSE TABUT COFFIN HEARSE LITTER SUPPORT FERETORY FERETRUM

BIFURCATION WYE FORK SPLIT BRANCH CROTCH CRUTCH FORKING DIVISION DICHOTOMY

BIG FAT BARO BOLD HUGE MUCH VAST BULKY CHIEF GAUCY GRAND GREAT GROSS HUSKY LARGE GAUCIE MIGHTY BIGGISH BUMPING EMINENT HUMMING LEADING MASSIVE POMPOUS UPRIGHT VIOLENT BOASTFUL BOUNCING ENORMOUS GENEROUS GIGANTIC IMPOSING PLUMPING PREGNANT SLAPPING SWANKING SWAPPING THUMPING
(— C) CANCER
(— WITH YOUNG) FULL GRAVID
(FAIRLY —) TIDY
(MARVELOUSLY —) TREMENDOUS
(VERY-) SKELPING SLASHING
(PREF.) MAGNI

BIGFOOT SASQUATCH
BIGHORN ARGAL AOUDAD ARGALI CIMARRON
BIGHT BAY BEND BITE COIL GULF LOOP ROVE ANGLE CURVE INLET NOOSE BOUGHT CORNER HOLLOW POCKET
BIGMOUTH BLAB
BIGNESS BULK
BIGOT CAFARD ZEALOT FANATIC MUMPSIMUS
BIGOTED BIASED NARROW HIDEBOUND ILLIBERAL SECTARIAN
BIGOTRY INTOLERANCE
BIGROOT MANROOT BITTERROOT
BIG SHOT HEAVY MUCKAMUCK
BIG SKY COUNTRY MONTANA
BIGWIG SWELL
BIKE (KIND OF —) MOTOR TRAIL
BIKINI TANGA
(TOPLESS —) MONOKINI
BILE BOIL GALL HUMP VENOM CHOLER GROWTH RANCOR ATRABILE MELANCHOLY
(PREF.) BILI CHOL(E)(O)
(SUFF.) CHOLIA CHOLY
BILGE PUMP SCUM BOUGE BULGE BILLAGE THURROCK
BILHAH (SON OF —) DAN NAPHTALI
BILHAN (FATHER OF —) JEDIAEL
BILIMBI CAMIAS KAMIAS CUCUMBER
BILINGUAL DIGLOT
BILIOUS GALLISH LIVERISH
BILIOUSNESS LIVER CHOLER
BILK DO GYP BALK DUPE HOAX CHEAT COZEN TRICK DELUDE FLEECE SWEDGE DECEIVE DEFRAUD SWINDLE

BILL ACT DUN GET LAW NEB NIB TAB BEAK CHIT CLAP GETT KITE NOTE PECK SHOT CHECK ENTRY LIBEL SCORE VISOR CARESS CHARGE DOCKET INDICT LAWING PECKER PICKAX POSTER STRIKE DERTRUM INVOICE LAMPOON MATTOCK PLACARD PROGRAM REMANET STATUTE BILLHOOK DOCUMENT HEADLAND INNOCENT PETITION TREASURY RECKONING ACCEPTANCE
(— OF ANCHOR) PEE PEAK
(— OF COMPLAINT) QUERELA
(— OF CREDIT) ANGEL
(— OF DIVORCE) GET GETT
(— OF EXCHANGE) SOLA HUNDI DEVISE
(— OF FARE) MENU CARTE
(— OF PARCELS) FACTURE
(ACCOMMODATION —) KITE
(COUNTERFEIT —S) STIFF
(DOLLAR —) BUCK SPOT SINGLE FROGSKIN
(POSTPONED —) REMANET
(REVOLUTIONARY —) ASSIGNAT
(TAVERN —) RECKONING
(10-DOLLAR —) TEN TENNER SAWBUCK
(100-DOLLAR —) CENTURY
(2-DOLLAR —) DEUCE
(5-DOLLAR —) FIN VEE FIVE FIVER

BILLET BAR GAD HUT LAY LOG LOOP NOTE PASS POST SPOT BERTH ENROL HOUSE LODGE ORDER SHIDE SPRAG STICK STRAP BALLOT BULLET COUPON ENROLL HARBOR LETTER LIBBET NOTICE TICKET BEARING EPISTLE MISSIVE POLLACK COALFISH DOCUMENT FIREWOOD ORNAMENT POSITION QUARTERS
(— SOLDIERS) CESS
BILLET-DOUX CAPON
BILLETING LIVERY
BILLFISH GAR LONGJAWS SAILFISH SPEARFISH
BILLFOLD WALLET NOTECASE
BILLHOOK BILL DHAW HOOK PAWPAW SLASHER SNAGGER SCIMITAR
BILLIARD
(— STROKE) LAG
(KIND OF — SHOT) BANK CAROM
BILLIARD BALL IVORY
BILLIARD CUE MACE MAST
(TIP OF —) LEATHER
BILLIARDS PILLS TRUCKS
(— SHOT) CAROM
(LAWN —) TROCO
BILLIKEN MASCOT
BILLINGSGATE ABUSE SLAPDASH
BILLION MILLIARD
(PREF.) GIGA

BILLIONTH
(PREF.) BICRO NANO
**BILL OF MARRIAGE (CHARACTER
IN —)** MILL FANNY SLOOK TOBIAS
EDOARDO
(COMPOSER OF —) ROSSINI
BILLON BAIOC VELLON BAJOCCO
BILLOW SEA BLOW WAVE BULGE
CLOUD FLOAT SURGE SWELL
RESACA RIPPLE ROLLER WALLOW
BREAKER UNDULATE
BILLY CAW CHAP CLUB GOAT MACE
MATE BATON FANNY NEDDY
CUDGEL FANNIE FELLOW BROTHER
COMRADE BILLIKIN BILLYCAN
BLUDGEON JACKSHAY BLACKJACK
TRUNCHEON
BILLY BUDD (CHARACTER IN —)
BUDD VERE BILLY CLAGGART
(COMPOSER OF —) BRITTEN
BILLYCOCK DERBY
BILSHAN (COMPANION OF —)
ZERUBBABEL
BIMAH ALMEMAR ALMEMON
BIMHAL (FATHER OF —) JAPHLET
BIN ARK BOX CUB GUM BING BONE
CART CRIB VINA FRAME HUTCH
KENCH PUNGI STALL STORE WAGON
BASKET BUNKER GARNER HAMPER
MANGER POCKET TROUGH WITHIN
BLEACHER
(— FOR CEMENT) SILO
(— FOR FISH) KENCH
(— FOR GRAIN) ARK
BINARY HYDRIDE
BINATE DUAL DOUBLE PAIRED
COUPLED TWOFOLD GEMINATE
BINAURAL DIOTIC
BIND JAM LAP TIE WAP EARL FAST
FRAP GIRD GYVE HOLD HOOP JOIN
KNIT KNOT LASH MAIL NAIL TAPE
YERK BRACE CADGE CHAIN CINCH
EDDER GIRTH SNAKE STICK STRAP
TRUSS ATTACH BUNDLE COMMIT
EMBIND ENGAGE FETTER FREEZE
GARTER GIRDLE LIGATE OBLIGE
PICKLE STRAIN SWATHE TETHER
WRITHE ARTICLE ASTRAIN BANDAGE
CONFINE EMBOUND ENCHAIN
GRAPPLE SHACKLE SWADDLE
ASTRINGE CONCLUDE FLIGHTER
HANDFAST INNODATE LIGATURE
OBLIGATE RESTRAIN
(— A FALCON) MAIL
(— BY LEASE) THIRL
(— BY OATH) SACRAMENT
(— BY PLEDGE) GAGE SWEAR
(— IN BUNDLE) KID BAVIN
(— INTO SHEAVES) GAVEL THRAVE
(— ONESELF) ADHERE
(— ROUND) WHIP
(— TOGETHER) LIME FAGOT SEIZE
CEMENT FAGGOT ASTRINGE

RELIGATE COLLIGATE
(— TO SECRECY) TILE
(— UP) KILT RAVIN TRUSS UPBAND
ASTRICT REVOLVE
(— WINGS) PINION
(— WITH THREAD) OOP
(PREF.) SPHINGO
(SUFF.) SPHINX
BINDER BAND BEAM BOND CORD
ROPE BALER COVER FRAME LEVER
FILLET FOLDER GIRDER HEADER
LIGNIN STAPLE TARMAC HAYBAND
BONDSTONE BOOKMAKER
(— OF SAND-DUNES) MARRAM
MARRUM
BINDING TAG BAND CORD GARD
HARD LEAR ROPE TAPE YAPP COVER
VALID CADDIS EDGING RIBBON
BOUNDEN CADDICE GALLOON
LAPPING MOUSING WEBBING
FAITHFUL LIGATIVE LIGATORY
STRINGENT OBLIGATORY
(— FAST) IRON
(— OF BOOK) DOCK FACE YAPP
(— OF GOLD) BISSET
(— ON DRESS) FENT
(SUFF.) DESIS
BINDLESTIFF BUM
BINDLE STIFF HOBO
BINDWEED BINE WIRE CREEPER
TIEVINE BEARBIND BEARBINE
BELLBINE BINEWEED CORNBIND
HELLWEED MILKMAID WOODBINE
WITHYWIND
BINE WIRE
BINGE BAT BOW HIT BLOW BUST
SOAK TEAR TOOT TOPE BEANO
PARTY SOUSE SPRAY SPREE CRINGE
BLOWOFF CAROUSAL
(ON A —) ONATEAR
BINGO KENO BEANO LOTTO BRANDY
SCREENO TOMBOLA
BINNACLE PYX BITTACLE
BINNUI (FATHER OF —) HENADAD
(SON OF —) NOADIAH
BINOCULARS GLASS
BINOMIAL DIONYM BINOMEN
BIOCHEMIST
AMERICAN LI BERG CORI LOEB
BLOCH BOYER DOISY KAMEN
MOORE OCHOA SHEAR TATUM
ASIMOV BEADLE CORDES SLOTTA
WATSON ALSBERG AXELROD
LIPMANN OSBORNE SCHALLY
SHAFFER KORNBERG NORTHRUP
NIRENBERG
ARGENTINIAN LELOIR
CANADIAN COLLIP
DANISH DAM
ENGLISH CHAIN KREBS PERUTZ
PORTER SANGER HOPKINS
MITCHELL
FRENCH MONOD DUCLAUX

GERMAN LYNEN LIPMANN
SWISS THEORELL
BIODEGRADABLE SOFT
BIOGEOGRAPHY CHOROLOGY
BIOGRAPHER PLUTARCH
  AMERICAN DAY BEER COFFIN
  HENDRICK VANDOREN
  ENGLISH CECIL ROWSE FORSTER
  DRINKWATER
  ROMAN SUETONIUS
  SCOTTISH BOSWELL LOCKHART
BIOGRAPHY BIO LIFE VITA MEMOIR
  ACCOUNT HISTORY RECOUNT
  PSYCHOGRAPH
  (— OF A SORT) OBIT
  (— OF SAINTS) HAGIOGRAPHA
  HAGIOGRAPHY
  (KIND OF —) TELLALL
BIOLOGIST NATURALIST
  AMERICAN EAST JUST LUTZ MAYR
  WALD BRONK CHILD CLARK LURIA
  MINOT PEARL SABIN SAGAN SHULL
  TYLER WOODS BAILEY BEADLE
  BUMPUS CARREL COTTAM FISHER
  JORDAN LITTLE OSBORN PALADE
  SPERRY WELLER CONKLIN EHRLICH
  HERRICK HERSHEY WETMORE
  CHAMBERS DELBRUCK DISABATO
  HARRISON SEDGWICK STOCKARD
  VISHNIAC
  AUSTRALIAN BURNET
  AUSTRIAN STEINACH
  BELGIAN CLAUDE
  CUBAN FINLAY
  ENGLISH CRICK GEDDES HUXLEY
  MIVART SANGER BATESON COBBOLD
  KENDREW MEDAWAR ROMANES
  CUMMINGS MILSTEIN NICHOLSON
  ABERCROMBIE
  FRENCH GIARD CARREL NOCARD
  BOUCHARD LEDANTEC
  GERMAN WOLFF DRIESCH
  EHRLICH HAECKEL SPEMANN
  UEXKULL WEISMANN
  MUCKERMANN
  IRISH ALLMAN
  NORWEGIAN MJOEN
  RUSSIAN BAER GURVICH LYSENKO
  MEDVEDEV METCHNIKOFF
  SCOTTISH GEDDES THOMSON
  SWISS ARBER
BIONIC (— HUMAN BEING) CYBORG
BIOPHORE BIOGEN PLASOME
BIOPLAST MICELLA MICELLE
BIOTITE MICA ANOMITE MEROXENE
  RUBELLAN
BIOTOPE STATION
BIPARTITE
  (PREF.) DIPHY
BIPED DIPODE HINDQUARTERS
BIRCH COW BIRK CANE FLOG WHIP
  ALDER ALNUS CANOE SWISH
  BETULA BIRKEN TAWHAI HICKORY

BIRCHBARK CANOE
BIRD ANI DAW DOG JAY NUN PIE TIT
  TUI CHAT COOT CROW DOVE FOWL
  HERN IBIS JACK KAGU KITE KNOT
  LARK QUIT RUFF TERN TODY WING
  WREN BAKER BRANT CHUCK CLEAR
  COVEY EGRET FINCH FLIER FLYER
  GOOSE HOBBY JUNCO LARID LIVER
  PEWEE PEWIT RAVEN ROBIN SNIPE
  STILT SWIFT TEREK TURCO TWITE
  VIREO BULBUL DICKEY DIPPER
  DRIVER DRONGO DUCKER DUNLIN
  FALCON FINGER GROUSE GUINEA
  HOOPOE HOOTER JACANA JAEGER
  LINNET MARTEN MOCKER NESTER
  ORIOLE OSCINE PHOEBE PLOVER
  SHRIKE SILVAN SINGER SITTER
  SYLVAN THRUSH TROGON TURNIX
  VERDIN YAWPER ANTBIRD BABBLER
  BLUEJAY BUNTING BUSTARD
  BUZZARD CATBIRD CHIRPER
  COTINGA COURLAN FEATHER
  FLAPPER FLICKER FLIGGER FLOPPER
  GRACKLE HALCYON HORNERO
  HURGILA INCOMER IRRISOR
  JACAMAR JACKDAW KINGLET
  MINIVET MOULTER ORTOLAN
  PEACOCK PERCHER QUILLER
  REDWING SCRAPER SKINNER
  SKYLARK SPARROW SUNBIRD
  SWALLOW TANAGER TINAMOU
  TITLARK TOMFOOL WARBLER
  WAXWING WAYBUNG ACCENTOR
  AIRPLANE AMADAVAT ANNOTINE
  BLACKCAP BLACKNEB BLUEBIRD
  BOATBILL BOBOLINK BOBWHITE
  BUBBLING CAGELING CARINATE
  COCKBIRD COCORICO DREPANID
  FERNBIRD FIREBIRD FIRETAIL
  GROSBEAK GRUIFORM IBISBILL
  JUVENILE KILLDEER KINGBIRD
  LOBEFOOT LONGSPUR OXPECKER
  PALMIPED PHEASANT PLUMIPED
  POORWILL PREACHER REDSTART
  SALTATOR SONGBIRD STARLING
  SURFBIRD SWAMPHEN TAPACOLO
  THRASHER THROSTLE TITMOUSE
  TREMBLER UMBRETTE WHINCHAT
  WOODCHAT WOODCOCK YEARBIRD
  COCKYOLLY CROSSBILL
  ROADRUNNER MOCKINGBIRD
  (— CHASED BY HAWK) QUARRY
  (— OF BRILLIANT PLUMAGE) TODY
  JALAP BARBET ORIOLE TROGON
  JACAMAR KIROMBO MINIVET
  TANAGER
  (— OF INDIA) BAYA KALA SHAMA
  (— OF OMEN) WAYBIRD
  (— OF PREY) OWL HAWK KITE EAGLE
  ELANT GLEAD GLEDE STOOP
  EAGLET ELANET BUZZARD
  GOSHAWK STOOPER VULTURE
  ACCIPITER

(AFRICAN —) TAHA QUELEA TOURACO UMBRETTE NAPECREST
(AUSTRALIAN —) EMU ROA LORY ARARA LEIPOA BOOBOOK BUSTARD FIGBIRD WAYBUNG BELLBIRD LORIKEET LYREBIRD MANUCODE
(BIG-BEAKED —) BECARD HORNBILL
(CRESTED —) KAGU COPPY HOATZIN TOPKNOT
(CROCODILE —) TROCHIL
(DECOY —) CALL STOOL
(DIVING —) AUK LOON GREBE DARTER DOPPER DUCKER GRAYLING PLUNGEON
(EUROPEAN —) ANI DAW MEW QUA CIRL DARR KITE MALL MORO QUIS ROOK STAG WHIM YITE AMSEL BOONK GLEDE MAVIS MERLE OUSEL OUZEL SACER SAKER SERIN TARIN TEREK TERIN WHAUP AVOCET CUCKOO CUSHAT GAYLAG GODWIT MARTEN MERLIN MISSEL REDCAP WHEWER WINDLE WINNEL WRANNY BITTERN BUSTARD HAYBIRD KESTREL MOTACIL ORTOLAN SAKERET STARNEL WHISKEY WINNARD WITWALL BARGOOSE CHEPSTER DOTTEREL GARGANEY REDSTART WHEATEAR WHEYBIRD WHIMBREL WRANNOCK YOLDRING
(EXTINCT —) MOA DODO JIBI KIWI MAMO RUKH OFFBIRD
(FABULOUS —) FUM ROC FUNG HALCYON OOFBIRD WHISTLER
(FEMALE —) HEN JENNY
(FICTITIOUS —) JAYHAWK PHOENIX
(FISH-CATCHING —) OSPREY CRABIER
(FLEDGLING —) SQUAB
(FLIGHTLESS —) EMU GOR MOA DODO EYAS GORB GULL KAGU KIWI CALLOW GORLIN APTERYX GORLING NESTLER OSTRICH PENGUIN BUBBLING NESTLING
(FRIGATE —) IOA IWA
(FRUIT-EATING —) COLY
(GALLOWS —) HEMPY HEMPIE
(GAME —) QUAIL SNIPE COLIMA GROUSE INCOME FLAPPER INCOMER PHEASANT PARTRIDGE
(GREEN —) SIRGANG
(HAWAIIAN —) IO OO AVA IOA IWA OOA IIWI JIBI KOAE MAMO MOHO OMAO OOAA KAMAO PALILA
(HORN-HEADED —) KAMICHI
(INJURED —) CRIPPLE
(LARGEST —) LAMMERGEIER
(LIMICOLINE —) PRATINCOLE
(LONG-TOED —) JACANA
(MADAGASCAR —) KIROMBO
(MECHANICAL —) ORTHOPTER
(MYTHICAL —) FUM ROC GANZA SIMURG SIMURGH
(NEW ZEALAND —) KEA MOA OII ROA

HUIA KAKA KIWI KOKO KUKU KULU PEHO RURU TITI WEKA POAKA KAKAPO KOKAKO KUKUPA APTERYX KORIMAKO MOREPORK NOTORNIS
(NIGHT —) OWL OWLET
(NOISY —) PIE MAGPIE
(PASSERINE —) QUIT FINCH SPARROW STARNEL SWALLOW SYLVIID DREPANID FALCONET FERNBIRD GRALLINA JACKBIRD OVENBIRD
(PERTAINING TO —S) OSCINE
(PISCATORY —) ERNE TERN
(RAPACIOUS —) SKUA JAEGER
(RASORIAL —) SCRATCHER
(RUNNING —) COURSER
(SAMOAN —) IAO
(SEA —) AUK ERN ERNE GONY GULL PINK SKUA SMEW TERN EIDER MURRE SOLAN FULMAR GANNET HAGDON OSPREY PETREL PUFFIN PELICAN SEAFOWL MURRELET MALLEMUCK
(SHORE —) REE RAIL SORA SNIPE STILT WADER AVOCET CURLEW PLOVER WILLET WRYBILL SHEATHBILL
(SHORT-TAILED —) BREVE
(SINGING —) LARK WREN PIPIT ROBIN VEERY VIREO CANARY LINNET MOCKER ORIOLE OSCINE SINGER THRUSH WARBLER FAUVETTE REDSTART NIGHTINGALE
(SMALL —) TIT TODY WREN DICKY PEGGY PIPIT TYDIE VIREO DICKEY LINNET SISKIN TOMTIT CREEPER SPARROW TITLARK COCORICO GNATSNAP PERCOLIN STARLING WHEATEAR
(SOUTH AMERICAN —) GUAN MINA MITU MYNA RARA TOCA BAKER CHAJA JOPIM TURCO BARBET BECARD CHUNGA TOUCAN CARIAMA OILBIRD BELLBIRD BOATBILL CARACARA GUACHARO HOACTZIN PUFFBIRD SCREAMER TAPACOLO TAPACOLO TERUTERO
(STYLIZED —) DISTELFINK
(TROPICAL —) ANI GUAN KOAE TODY BOS'N BOSUN JALAP BARBET BECARD MOTMOT TROGON JACAMAR MANAKIN WIGTAIL LONGTAIL SALTATOR
(WADING —) HERN IBIS RAIL SORA CRANE HERON SNIPE STILT STORK ARGALA AVOCET GODWIT JACANA LIMPKIN BOATBILL FLAMINGO SHOEBILL SHOEBIRD SANDERLING
(WILD —S) GALLINAE
(WITCH —) ANI
(YEAR-OLD —) ANNOTINE
(YOUNG —) EYA GULL PIPER CHEEPER FLAPPER NESTLER

BIRDIKIN NESTLING
(PL.) AVIFAUNA POLYMYODI
PRAECOCES
(PREF.) AVI ORNIS ORNITH(I)(O)
(SUFF.) ORNIS ORNITHES
BIRD BOLT BURBOLT QUARREL
BIRDBRAIN SIMP
BIRD CAGE AVIARY PINJRA VOLARY
VOLERY PADDOCK
BIRDCATCHER FOWLER
BIRD CHERRY DOGWOOD
EGGBERRY HACKWOOD HAGBERRY
BIRDLIFE ORNIS
BIRD-LIKE ORNITHOID
BIRDLIME GLUE LIME BELIME
VISCUM BIRDGLUE
BIRD OF PARADISE APUS
MANUCODE RIFLEBIRD
BIRD-REARING AVINCULTURE
BIRDS (AUTHOR OF —)
ARISTOPHANES
(CHARACTER IN —) EPOPS TEREUS
BASILEIA EUELPIDES PISTHETAERUS
BIRD'S-FOOT FOWLFOOT
SERRADELLA
BIRD'S KNEE SUFFRAGO
BIRD'S MANTLE STRAGULUM
BIRDY AVIAN
BIRENO (WIFE OF —) OLIMPIA
BIRETTA SARRET
BIRI BIDI
BIRL ROTATE
BIRTH KIN BEAR FALL YEAN BLOOD
BURDEN GENTRY ORIGIN BEARING
BORNING DESCENT GENESIS
LINEAGE DELIVERY GENITURE
NASCENCY NATALITY NATIVITY
(FALSE —) SOOTERKIN
(GENTLE —) GENTILITY
(GENTLE —)0 GENTRICE
(GIVE —) CALVE
(HIGH —) PARAGE
(HONORABLE —) BLOOD
(OF LOW —) CRESTLESS
(OF NOBLE —) CORONETED
(PREF.) NATI
(SUFF.) (GIVING —) PARA PAROUS
BIRTHMARK MOLE IMAGE NAEVE
NEVUS BLEMISH SPILOMA
SIGNATURE
BIRTHPLACE INCUNABULA
BIRTHRATE NATALITY FERTILITY
BIRTHRIGHT KIND BIRTHDOM
HERITAGE
BIRTHROOT BATHROOT BATHWORT
DEATHROOT DISHCLOTH
SQUAWROOT
BIRTHSTONE (APRIL —) DIAMOND
(AUGUST —) SARDONYX
(DECEMBER —) TURQUOISE
(FEBRUARY —) AMETHYST
(JANUARY —) GARNET
(JULY —) RUBY

(JUNE —) PEARL
(MARCH —) BLOODSTONE
(MAY —) EMERALD
(NOVEMBER —) TOPAZ
(OCTOBER —) OPAL
(SEPTEMBER —) SAPPHIRE
BIRTHWORT GUACO ASARUM
BATHROOT
BISAYAN AKLAN CEBUAN AKLANON
CEBUANO
BISCUIT BUN NUT BAKE ROLL RUSK
SNAP WOOD BREAD COOKY SCONE
WAFER BISQUE COOKIE DODGER
MALLOW MUFFIN PARKIN PERKIN
SIMNEL CRACKER GALETTE PENTILE
PRETZEL RATAFIA RATIFIA CRACKNEL
HARDTACK ZWIEBACK GINGERSNAP
(ALMOND —) RARAFIA
(BROKEN —S) DUNDERFUNK
(COLOR —) DOE PAWNEE
(SHIP —) HARDTACK DANDYFUNK
DUNDERFUNK
BISECT FORK CROSS HALVE SPLIT
CLEAVE DIVIDE MIDDLE SEPARATE
BISECTION MEDIATION
BISEXUAL ACDC
BISHOP EP ABBA EPUS LAWN PAPA
POPE ANGEL COARB DENIS ARCHER
BUSTLE DESPOT EPARCH EXARCH
MAGPIE PRESUL PRIEST PRIMUS
ROCHET ROCKAT PONTIFF PRELATE
PRIMATE TULCHAN ANTISTES
DIOCESAN DIRECTOR ORDINARY
OVERSEER PONTIFEX PATRIARCH
METROPOLITAN
(— AND MARTYR) EM
(ANGLICAN —) MAGPIE
(CHESS —) ALFIN ALPHYN ARCHER
(NEIGHBOR OF —) KING QUEEN
KNIGHT
(PL.) PURPLE
BISHOPRIC SEE
BISHOP'S-WEED AMMI AMMEOS
KHELLA WILLIAM BOLEWORT
BULLWORT GOUTWEED TOOTHPICK
BISHOPWEED GOUTWEED
GOUTWORT
BISKOP BRUSHER STEENBRAS
BISMARK KRAPFE KRAPFEN
BISMUTH WISMUTH TINGLASS
BISON BUGLE BOVINE MITHAN
WISENT AUROCHS BONASUS
BUFFALO
BISTORT PATIENCE ADDERWORT
ASTROLOGE SNAKEWEED
SNAKEWORT
BISTRO BAR CAFE TAVERN
WINESHOP ESTAMINET NIGHTCLUB
BIT ACE FID FIP GAG JOT NIP ORT PIP
TAD WEE ATOM BITE BITT CHIP CROP
CURB DITE DOIT DRIB FLAW FOOD
GRUE HAET HATE HOOT IOTA ITEM
LEVY MITE MOTE PART RIFF SLUT

SNAP SNIP SPOT TOOL WHIT AUGER
BLADE CHECK CRUMB DRILL GROAT
PATCH PEZZO PIECE POINT SCRAP
SHRED SHTIK SKOSH SMACK SNACK
SPECK STEEK TASTE THRUM WIGHT
BITTIE BRIDLE CANNON EATING
MORSEL PELHAM PICKLE SCATCH
SHTICK SIPPET SMIDGE SPLICE
STITCH STIVER TITTLE TRIFLE
BRADOON BRIDOON CHILENO
GLIMMER MODICUM MORCEAU
PALLION PORTION SCHTICK
SMIDGEN SMIDGIN SNAFFLE
THOUGHT TRANEEN FISHTAIL
FRACTION FRAGMENT QUANTITY
SMIDGEON SMITCHIN TWOPENNY
(— OF GOSSIP) HEARING
(— OF INFORMATION) GRIFF GRIFFIN
WRINKLE
(— OF KEY) WEB
(— OF LAND) CROOK
(— OF METAL) FLITTER
(— OF TOAST) SNIPPET
(—S AND PIECES) GUDDINO
GUBBINGS
(—S OF COKE) BREEZE
(—S OF WRITING) EXCERPTA
(— TO EAT) MUNGEY
(A —) SOME
(COMIC —) SIGHTGAG
(CUTTING —) CHASER
(DRILL —) CROWN
(FANCIFUL —) FLAM
(FIPPENY —) SIXPENCE
(FLORID —) FLOURISH
(HORSE'S —) KEVEL SNODE CANNON
PELHAM SCATCH SNAFFLE
BASTONET
(LEAST —) FIG JOT RAP DAMN HANG
LICK GHOST GROAT RIZZOM STITCH
(LITTLE —) PICK TOUCH BITTOCK
REMNANT SOUPCON
(ONE — PER SECOND) BAUD
(ONE QUARTER —) GILL
(ONE BILLION —S) GIGABIT
(SEQUENCE OF —S) BYTE
(SMALL —) BLEB GLIM SPUNK
(SMALL —S) SMATTER
(THEATRICAL —) SHTICK SCHTICK
(TINY —) TAD SPECK DRIBBLE
SCRINCH TODDICK
(PL.) SMITHERS SMITHEREENS
BITCH DO GYP FLUB LAMP SLUT
BRACH BROOD CHEAT GROUSE
COMPLAIN
BITE BIT CUT EAT JAW NIP BAIT CHAM
CHEW ETCH FOOD GASH GNAP
GNAW HOLD KNAP MEAL RIVE SNAP
TAKE CHACK CHAMM CHAMP CHEAT
GNASH PINCH SEIZE SMART SNACK
STING TOOTH TRICK CRUNCH
MORSEL NIBBLE PIERCE SAVAGE
BUGBITE CHEATER CORRODE

FORBITE IMPRESS MORSURE
MUNCHET PARTAKE SHARPER
SLANDER
(— AT) HIT
(— GREEDILY) HANCH
(— REPEATEDLY) CHAMP
BITER
(SUFF.) DECTES
BITHIAH (HUSBAND OF —) MERED
BITING BIT HOT ACID HOAR KEEN
ACRID NIPPY QUICK SHARP SNELL
BITTER RODENT SEVERE SHREWD
STINGY TEETHY TWEAKY CAUSTIC
CUTTING MORDANT MORSURE
NIPPING PUNGENT SUBACID
DRILLING INCISIVE PIERCING
POIGNANT SCALDING SCATHING
STINGING ACIDULOUS MORDACIOUS
BITIS ECHIDNA
BITO BALM HAJILIJ
BITON (BROTHER OF —) CLEOBIS
(MOTHER OF —) CYDIPPE
BITT BLOCK KNIGHT BOLLARD
(PL.) RANGEHEADS
BITTER AWA GAL ACID ACRE ASIM
BASK KEEN MARA RUDE SALT SORE
SOUR TART ACERB ACRID AMARA
ASPER BLEAK EAGER HARSH IRATE
SHARP SNELL BITING PICRIC SEVERE
AUSTERE CAUSTIC CRABBED
CUTTING FERVENT GALLING
GALLISH PAINFUL PUNGENT SATIRIC
POIGNANT SARDONIC STINGING
SUBAMARE VIRULENT ASTRINGENT
ACRIMONIOUS
(NOT —) MILD
(PREF.) PICR(O)
(SUFF.) PICRIN
BITTER APPLE COLOCYNTH
BITTER BIT SMALLPOX
BITTERBUSH SNAKEROOT
BITTER CLOVER YELLOWTOP
BITTERLY SOUR FELLY BITTER
ROUNDLY CURSEDLY
BITTERN BUMP SOCO BOONK
BUTOR EGRET HERON BITORE
BUMBLE BUMMLE BUTTAL KAKKAK
BLITTER BUMMLER FRICIUS
DUNKADOO GRUIFORM LONGNECK
(FLOCK OF —) SEDGE SIEGE
BITTERNESS RUE ACOR BILE FELL
GALL ATTER MARAH ENMITY MALICE
RANCOR AMARITY ACERBITY
ACRIDITY ACRIMONY ASPERITY
FERVENCY SEVERITY WORMWOOD
(EXTREME —) VIRULENCE
(WITH —) AMAREVOLE
BITTER PIT STIPPEN
BITTERROOT LEWISIA
TOBACCOROOT
BITTERS AMER
BITTER SPAR DOLOMITE
BITTERSWEET FELLEN DOGWOOD

LOBSTER SOLANUM WAXWORK
DULCAMARA FELONWOOD
FELONWORT FEVERTWIG
WITHYWIND WOLFBERRY
BITTER VETCH ERS
BITTERWEED RAGWEED
HORSEWEED
BITTERWORT FELWORT DANDELION
BITUMEN TAR CONGO PITCH SLIME
MALTHA ASPHALT CARBENE
ALKITRAN ALCHITRAN ELATERITE
BIVALENT DIATOMIC
BIVALVE HEN CLAM SPAT PINNA
COCKLE DIATOM MUSSEL OYSTER
MOLLUSK NUCULID PANDORA·
SCALLOP TOHEROA
BIVOUAC CAMP ETAPE WATCH
ENCAMP SHELTER
BIZARRE ODD ANTIC DEDAL GONZO
OUTRE QUEER QUAINT ANTICAL
BAROQUE CURIOUS FANCIFUL
ECCENTRIC FANTASTIC GROTESQUE
OUTLANDISH
BLAB LAB CHAT BLART BLATE CHEEP
CLACK PEACH PRATE BABBLE
BETRAY GOSSIP REVEAL SQUEAL
TATTLE BLABBER CHATTER CLATTER
BLABBERMOUTH YENTA
BLACK DHU JET WAN CALO CROW
DARK EBON FOUL INKY NOIR PIKY
SOOT BUGLE COLLY DUSKY DWALE
MURKY NEGRO NOIRE RAVEN SABLE
SOOTY TARRY THICK ATROUS
BRUNET DISMAL ETHIOP GLOOMY
MURREY PITCHY SULLEN ABAISER
AFRICAN BLACKEN DIAMOND
MELANIC NEGRITO NIGRINE
NIGROUS PICEOUS SCHWARZ
SWARTHY UNCLEAN MOURNFUL
(— AND BLUE) LIVID
(— OUT) CONK
(BONE —) SPODIUM
(BROWNISH —) LAVA
(GREENISH —) CORBEAU
(IVORY —) ABAISER
(LIGHT-SKINNED —) BROWN
(RATHER —) DUSKISH
(VIOLET —) CROW
(PREF.) ATRO MAVRO MEL(A)
MELAN(O) NIGRI
(SUFF.) MELANE
BLACKAMOOR BLECK NEGRO
MORIAN NEGRESS ETHIOPIAN
BLACK ARROW
(AUTHOR OF —) STEVENSON
(CHARACTER IN —) DICK ELLIS OATES
DANIEL JOANNA OLIVER SEDLEY
LAWLESS RICHARD SHELTON
BRACKLEY DUCKWORTH
BLACK ASH HOOPWOOD
BLACKBALL PIP PILL BALLOT
EXCLUDE HEEBALL OSTRACIZE

BLACK BASS HURON TROUT
ACHIGAN GROWLER OCHIGAN
BLACKBERRY AGAWAM LAWTON
BRAMBLE DEWBERRY MULBERRY
ROSACEAN
(— BUSH) MORE
BLACKBIRD ANI DAW PIE CROW
MERL AMSEL COLLY MERLE OUSEL
OUZEL RAVEN BLACKY COLLEY
MAIZER BLACKIE COWBIRD GRACKLE
JACKDAW REDWING WOOFELL
TROOPIAL
BLACKBOARD SLATE CHALKBOARD
GREENBOARD
BLACKBREAM TARWHINE
BLACK-BROWED GLOOMY
BLACK BRYONY LILY LILIUM
OXBERRY BINDWEED MANDRAKE
BLACK BUCK SASIN
BLACKCAP GULL JACK PEGGY
HAYBIRD WARBLER JACKSTRAW RASPBERRY
TITMOUSE JACKSTRAW RASPBERRY
BLACKCOCK GROUSE
BLACKDAMP STYTH STYTHE
CHOKEDAMP
BLACKDRINK YAPON YAUPON
BLACKEN INK TAR CHAR CORK SMUT
SOIL SOOT BLECK CLOUD COLLY
JAPAN SMOKE SULLY BEFOUL
BLATCH DARKEN DEFAME MALIGN
SMEETH SMIRCH SMUTCH VILIFY
ASPERSE BENEGRO NIGRIFY
SLANDER SMOLDER TRADUCE
BESMIRCH
BLACKENED REECHY
BLACKENING SWART SWARTH
BLACKEYE COWPEA
BLACKFELLOW BLACKBOY
YAMMADJI
BLACKFIN CISCO SESIS
BLACKFISH GRIND TAUTOG
BORLASE DOGFISH GRAMPUS
POTHEAD HARDHEAD
BLACKFLY GNAT SIMULIID
BLACKFOOT BLOOD KAINAH
PIEGAN SIKSIKA SIHASAPA
BLACK GROUPER MERO AGUAJI
WARSAW GARRUPA
BLACKGUARD CUR SHAG BLECK
CATSO GAMIN GUARD SNUFF SWEEP
ROTTER LADRONE SKELLUM
VAGRANT BLAGGARD CRIMINAL
LARRIKIN VAGABOND SCOUNDREL
BLACK GUILLEMOT CUTTY TYSTE
SCRABE DOVEKEY DOVEKIE
SCRABER PUFFINET
BLACK GUM TUPELO HORNPIPE
STINKWOOD
BLACK HAW SLOE BOOTS ALISIER
STAGBUSH VIBURNUM
BLACKHEAD COMEDO
BLACK HOLE COLLAPSAR

BLACK HOREHOUND HENBIT ARCHANGEL
BLACK HORSE SUCKER SUCKEREL
BLACKING LINK BLECK BLATCH BLEACH ATRAMENT
BLACK IRONWOOD AXMASTER AXEMASTER
BLACKISH DUSKY MOREL SWART BLACKY
BLACKJACK OAK SAP CLUB COSH DUCK FLAG JACK BILLY BEETLE BLENDE JERKIN BOMBARD NATURAL BLUDGEON
BLACKLEG LEG FIRE SCAB SNOB ANTHRAX GAMBLER JACKLEG APOSTATE BLACKNEB BLACKNOB SWINDLER KNOBSTICK
BLACK LETTER GOTHIC
BLACKLY SABLY
BLACK MAGIC VODUN VODOUN DIABLERIE
BLACKMAIL BLEED BRIBE CHOUT COERCE EXTORT RANSOM TRIBUTE CHANTAGE
BLACKMAILER GHOUL BRIBER LEECHER
BLACK MANGROVE COURIDA
BLACK MEDIC HOP TREFOIL NONESUCH SHAMROCK
BLACKNESS GRIME DARKNESS NIGRITUDE
BLACK NIGHTSHADE MOREL DUSCLE SOLANUM BLUEBERRY MOONSHADE TROMPILLO
BLACK OLIVE OXHORN
BLACKOUT SKIT
BLACK PEPPER PIMENTA
BLACK PINE MATAI
BLACK POISON WALNUT
BLACK RHINOCEROS BORELE KEITLOA UPEYGAN
BLACK SALLY SALLEE MUZZLEWOOD
BLACK SANICLE LUNGWORT MASTERWORT
BLACK SHANK LANAS
BLACK SKIMMER CUTWATER SHEARBILL
BLACKSMITH GOW SMUG LOHAR SHOER SMITH PLOVER SMITHY VULCAN BROOKIE FARRIER STRIKER BURNEWIN IRONSMITH
BLACKSNAKE WHIP QUIRT RACER ELAPID RUNNER COLUBRID
BLACK SPECK DARTROSE
BLACK SPURGE FLUXWEED
BLACKTAIL DASSY DASSIE
BLACK TERN DARR STARN
BLACKTHORN HAW SLOE SNAG SCROG GRIBBLE SLOEBUSH SLOETREE SNAGBUSH
BLACKTOP PAVE

BLACK-VARNISH TREE THEETSEE
BLACK VULTURE URUBU CORBIE ZOPILOTE
BLACK WALNUT NOGAL
BLACKWATER STATE NEBRASKA
BLACK WIDOW POKOMOO
BLACK WOLF KARAKURT
BLACKWOOD BITI LIGHTWOOD
BLACKWORT COMFREY
BLADDER SAC VES ASCO VESICA AMPULLA BLATHER BLISTER INFLATE UROCYST UTRICLE VESICLE
(AIR —) POKE SWIM SOUND SINGALLY
(PL.) ASCI
(PREF.) ASC(I)(IDI)(IDIO)(O) CYST(I)(O) PHYSO VESICO
(SUFF.) CYST(IS)
BLADDER-AND-STRING BUMBASS
BLADDER CAMPION BEHN BEHEN SILENE COWBELL SNAPPER RATTLEBOX
BLADDER KETMIE MODESTY
BLADDERNUT BAGNUT
BLADDER-WORM CESTODE
BLADDERWORT POPWEED
BLADDER WRACK CUTWEED KELPWARE
BLADE BIT FIN FOP OAR SAW WEB BLOW BONE BOWL EDGE EPEE FLAG HEAD LEAF LIMB TANG WEAK BLOOD BRAND DANDY FLUKE GRAIN GUIDE HEALD KNIFE LANCE SHEAR SPARK SPEAR SPIRE SWORD BLUNGE BUCKET BUSTER CUTTER DOCTOR FOIBLE HEDDLE LAMINA PAGINA RIPPER ROARER SCYTHE SICKLE TOLEDO BAYONET CHIPPER GALLANT POLESAW SCALPEL SCAPULA SCRAPER SPINNER MOLDBOARD PROPELLER
(— OF FAN) VANE
(— OF GRASS) PILE CHIRE SPEAR SPIRE STRAP TRANEEN
(— OF KNIFE) TANG GRAIN
(— OF LEAF) LIMB LAMINA
(— OF MORION) COMB
(— OF OAR) PALM PEEL PELL WASH
(— OF PROPELLER) FAN
(— OF SCISSORS) BILL
(— OF YOUNG GRAIN) SORAGE
(BROAD —) SPATULA
(CULTIVATOR —) SWEEP DUCKFOOT
(MIXER —) BEATER
(NARROW —) DISC
(SKATE —) RUNNER
(SURGICAL —) LEUCOTOME
(SUFF.) SPATH
BLAES CAM CAN CALM CAUM
BLAFFERT PLAPPERT
BLAGGERMOUTH YENTA GOSSIP

BLAH DRAB DULL MEDIOCRE
BLAIN RUBY SORE BULLA BLISTER
INFLAME PUSTULE
BLAKE MCKAY
BLAMABLE FAULTY CULPABLE
BLAME RAP CALL CHOP HURT LACK
ONUS SAKE SPOT TWIT WITE CHIDE
FAULT GUILT ODIUM PINCH PINON
SHEND SNAPE SWICK SWIKE THANK
TOUCH WHITE ACCUSE ATTASK
BUMBLE BURDEN CHARGE DIRDUM
PLIGHT REBUKE REVILE SCANCE
APPOINT ASCRIBE CENSURE
CONDEMN CULPATE OBLOQUY
REPROOF REPROVE SLANDER
UPBRAID WITHNIM REPROACH
BLAMED BLINDING BLISTERING
BLAMELESS PURE ENTIRE PERFECT
INNOCENT SACKLESS SPOTLESS
WITELESS RIGHTEOUS
BLAMEWORTHY GUILTY CRIMINAL
CULPABLE REPROBATE
BLANCH FADE PALE BLENK CHALK
SCALD WHITE APPALL ARGENT
BIANCA BLEACH BLENCH FALLOW
WHITEN ETIOLATE
BLANCHED ASHEN MEALY ETIOLATE
BLOODLESS COLORLESS
BLANCMANGE FLUMMERY
BLAND COLD KIND MILD OILY OPEN
SOFT SLEEK SUAVE BENIGN BREEZY
GENIAL GENTLE SMOOTH URBANE
AFFABLE AMIABLE LENIENT
VANILLA FAVONIAN GRACIOUS
UNCTUOUS
BLANDISH COAX CHARM ALLURE
BLANCH CAJOLE FONDLE SMOOTH
FLATTER WHEEDLE HONEYFUGLE
BLANDISHMENT SOOTH LISALVE
(PL.) TREACLE
BLANDLY CREAMILY
BLANK BARE BURR FLAN FORM SHOT
VOID ANNUL BLIND BREAK CHASM
CLEAN EMPTY FALSE RANGE SPACE
WASTE WHITE COUPON VACANT
ANTIQUE BRINDLE NONPLUS
UNMIXED VACUOUS UNFILLED
(MAY BE —) STARE
BLANKED BLIND
BLANKET RUG BROT MAUD WRAP
BLUEY COTTA COVER CUMLY LAYER
MANTA PATTU QUILT SHEET SUGAN
THROW AFGHAN COOLER CUMBLY
GLOBAL KAMBAL MANTLE PALLET
PONCHO PUTTOO SERAPE SOOGAN
SPREAD STIFLE STROUD TILPAH
CHIRIPA DOUBLER SMOTHER
WHITTLE COVERLET MACKINAW
(— A VESSEL) WRONG
(— OF SKINS) KAROSS
(— WITH BOMBS) SATURATE
(BUSHMAN'S —) BLUEY
(HORSE —) MANTA

(QUILTED —) BROT
(SADDLE —) CORONA
·(PREF.) REGO
BLANKETING DUFFEL DUFFLE
BLANKNESS VACUITY NEGATION
BLARE PEAL BLART BLAST BLEAR
· NOISE BLAZON SCREAM FANFARE
TANTARA TRUMPET
BLARNEY CON TAFFY BUTTER
CAJOLE SAWDER FLATTER WHEEDLE
BLAS GIL RUY
BLASPHEME ABUSE CURSE DEFAME
REVILE PROFANE
BLASPHEMOUS BAD RIBALD
IMPIOUS PROFANE
BLASPHEMY CALUMNY CURSING
IMPIETY ANATHEMA SWEARING
BLAST BUB NIP WAP BANG BLOW
FRAP GALE GUST RUIN RUST SHOT
TOOT WAFF WIND BLAME BLIST
BLORE SPLIT STUNT TRUMP ATTACK
BLIGHT BUGGER FORBID NIDDER
NITHER REBUFF VOLLEY WITHER
BLUSTER DESPOIL EXPLODE
SHATTER SHRIVEL DYNAMITE
OUTBURST PROCLAIM WHIRLPUFF
(— OFF) START
(— OF WIND) GUST RISE PERRY
PIRRIE VENTOSITY
(— ON HORN) TOOT PRYSE
(— WITH COLD) SNEAP
(FURIOUS —) SNIFTER
(MILITARY —) SALVO
(RAINY —) BLATTER
BLASTED BLAME BLAMED BLIGHTED
BLINDING BLINKING
BLASTER FROSTER SHOOTER
SHOTMAN
BLASTING SCATHING SHOOTING
STELLATION
(— METHOD) MUDCAP
BLASTOMERE MESOMERE
MACROMERE MICROMERE
BLASTULA PLACULA PLANULA
PLANULAN
BLATANT GLIB LOUD BRASH GROSS
NOISY SILLY VOCAL COARSE GARISH
TONANT VULGAR BRAWLING
STRIDENT
BLATHER ADO RAVE STIR BLEAT
BABBLE WAFFLE BLITHER PRATTLE
NONSENSE
BLAUBOK ETAAC BLUEBUCK
BLAZE LOW BURN FIRE GLOW HACK
LEAM LOWE LUNT MARK SHOT SPOT
FLAME FLARE FLASH GLARE GLEAM
GLORY INGLE RATCH SHINE STARE
STEAM TORCH BLAZON BLEEZE
BONFIRE PIONEER SPLENDOR
(— OUT) FLAP
(HEAVENLY —) NOVA
BLAZING AFIRE FIERY FLAMY LIGHT
TORRID FLAMING FLARING

BLAZING STAR LIATRIS GRUBROOT SNAKEROOT

BLAZON DECK SHOW ADORN BLARE BLAZE BOAST DEPICT SHIELD DECLARE DISPLAY EXHIBIT PUBLISH EMBLAZON INSCRIBE

BLAZONED ARMED BANNERED

BLEACH SUN WASH BLEAK CHALK CROFT POACH BLANCH BLENCH CHLORE PURIFY WHITEN DECOLOR LIGHTEN BLONDINE ETIOLATE PEROXIDE
(— PULP) POTCH

BLEACHER WHITSTER

BLEACHERS SCAFFOLD

BLEAK DIM RAW BLAE BLAY COLD DOUR GRAY PALE ABLET OURIE SPRAT STARK SWALE ALBURN BITTER BLEACH DISMAL DREARY FRIGID PALLID CUTTING DESOLATE CHEERLESS

BLEAK HOUSE
(AUTHOR OF —) DICKENS
(CHARACTER IN —) JO ADA JOHN ALLAN CLARE FLITE GUPPY KROOK BUCKET ESTHER RAWDON DEDLOCK JELLYBY RICHARD WILLIAM CARSTONE CHADBAND JARNDYCE SKIMPOLE LEICESTER SUMMERSON WOODCOURT TULKINGHORN

BLEAT BAA MAA BLAT BLEA YARM BLART BLATE BLATHER BLUSTER WHICKER

BLEATING BALANT

BLEB BLOB BULLA BUBBLE BLISTER PUSTULE VESICLE SWELLING

BLEED RUN FLUX MILK WEEP BLOOD LEECH MULCT SWEAT SWINDLE TEICHER PHLEBOTOMIZE

BLEEDER STICKER

BLEEDING BLOODY SANGLANT

BLEEDING HEART EARDROP DICENTRA

BLEMISH MAR BLOT BLUR DENT FLAW GALL LACK MAIM MARK MOIL MOLE RIFT SAKE SCAR SLUR SPOT TASH VICE WANT AMPER BLAME BOTCH BRECK CLOUD CRACK FAULT FLECK MULCT NAEVE SPECK STAIN SULLY TACHE TAINT TOUCH BLOTCH BREACH DEFAME DEFECT IMPAIR INJURE MACULA MACULE MAYHEM SMIRCH STIGMA BUBUKLE CATFACE DEFAULT FAILING FISSURE SUNSPOT MACULATION
(— IN CLOTH) AMPER SULLY
(— IN PAPER) FISHEYE
(PRINTING —) MACKLE

BLEMISHED BAD WEMMY

BLENCH FOIL SHUN WILE AVOID ELUDE EVADE QUAIL SHAKE SHIRK TRICK BAFFLE BLANCH BLEACH FLINCH RECOIL SHRINK DECEIVE

BLEND MIX RUN BLOT FADE FUSE JOIN MELD MELT MENG MOLD ADMIX BLIND CREAM GRADE MERGE MOULD PUREE SHADE SMEAR SPOIL STAIN TINGE UNITE BLUNGE COMMIX CRASIS DAZZLE MINGLE TEMPER COMBINE CONFUSE CORRUPT DECEIVE GRADATE MIXTURE POLLUTE COALESCE CONCRETE IMMINGLE TINCTURE CONTEMPER
(— OF NOISES) CHARM
(— OF SHERRY) SOLERA
(— OF WINES) CUVEE

BLENDE JACK SPHALERITE

BLENDED FONDU FUSED MIXED MERGED MINGLED CONFLATE CONFLUENT

BLENDING FUSION HOTCHPOT

BLENNY GUNNEL SHANNY EELPOUT JUGULAR KELPFISH SENORITA WOLFFISH WRYMOUTH QUILLFISH ROCKSKIPPER

BLESBOK NUNNI BLESBUCK

BLESS KEEP SAIN WAVE ADORE ANELE BENSH CROSS EXTOL FAVOR GUARD THANK VISIT WOUND CROUCH FAVOUR HALLOW PRAISE THRASH APPROVE BEATIFY EMBLISS GLORIFY PROTECT MACARIZE PRESERVE SANCTIFY

BLESSED HOLY BLEST HAPPY SEELY DIVINE JOYFUL SACRED OCCLFUL BENEDICT BHAGAVAT BLISSFUL BLOOMING HALLOWED HEAVENLY CELESTIAL
(— MAN) BEATI
(— WOMAN) BEATA

BLESSEDNESS BLISS FELICITY BEATITUDE HAPPINESS

BLESSING BOON GIFT SAIN BLISS DUKAN GRACE SORRA BARAKA DUCHAN PRAISE BENISON DARSHAN WORSHIP BERACHAH FELICITY MACARISM BEATITUDE
(PL.) CUP

BLEU DE ROI SEVRES

BLIGHT NIP FIRE RUIN RUST SMUT SOKA BLAST BRANT EDEMA FROST SNEAP MILDEW NITHER TAKING WITHER DESTROY
(— OF HOPS) FIREBLAST
(PREF.) UREDO

BLIGHTER GUY SOD FELLOW

BLIND BET POT ANTE BOMA DARK DEAD DULL HIDE HOOD SEEL BISME BLANK BLEND CHICK CLOAK DUNCH SHADE STAKE STALL WAGER AMBUSH BISSON BLENDE DARKEN DAZZLE SCREEN SECRET AIMLESS ANTIQUE BANDAGE BATTERY DENIGHT ECLIPSE EYELESS OBSCURE PRETEXT RAYLESS SHUTTER ABORTIVE ARTIFICE

BAYARDLY BLINDING EXCECATE
HOODWINK IGNORANT INVOLVED
JALOUSIE OUTSHINE PURBLIND
UMBRELLA VENETIAN
(— IN ONE EYE) PEED GLEED GLEYD
(— MAN) MOLE
(HALF —) STARBLIND
(PART OF —) SLAT
(PL.) PERSIENNES
(PREF.) CECO TYPHL(O)
BLIND ALLEY LOKE STOP POCKET
IMPASSE
BLINDER FLAP HOOD BLIND BLUFF
LUNET WINKER BLINKER EYEFLAP
LUNETTE HOODWINK BLINDFOLD
BLINDFOLD MOP DARK BLINK BLUFF
SCARF MUFFLE BANDAGE BLINDER
OBSCURE ENCLOSER HEEDLESS
HOODWINK RECKLESS CONCEALED
BLINDING BISME BISSON
BLINDMAN'S BLUFF POST
HOODWINK
BLINDNESS BISSON CECITY
MYOPSY ABLEPSY ANOPSIA
MEROPIA ABLEPSIA DARKNESS
IGNORANCE
(— TO TRUTH) AVIDYA AVIJJA
(COLOR —) ACHROBIA
MONOCHROMATISM
(DAY —) HEMERALOPIA
(NIGHT —) NYCTALOPIA
(PARTIAL —) MEROPIA HEMIOPSIA
(RED-GREEN —) DALTONISM
(SNOW —) CHIONABLEPSIA
(STUDY OF —) TYPHLOLOGY
(TEMPORARY —) MOONBLINK
BLINDSTITCH FELL
BLINDWORM SLOW ORVET ANGUID
HAGWORM SLOWWORM
BLIND-YOUR-EYES GANGWA
ALIPATA
BLINK BAT PINK SHUN WINK BLUSH
CHEAT FLASH GLEAM SHINE TRICK
GLANCE IGNORE OBTUSE WAPPER
BLINTER CONDONE GLIMMER
GLIMPSE NEGLECT NICTATE SPARKLE
TWINKLE
BLINKER EYE BLINK BLUFF LIGHT
EYELID SIGNAL WAPPER WINKER
BLINDER FLASHER GOGGLES
COQUETTE HOODWINK MACKEREL
BLINKING PINK OWLISH
BLINTZE BLIN BLINTZ PANCAKE
BLIP PIP ECHO
(SONAR —) ECHO
BLISS JOY EDEN KAIF SEEL SEIL
BLESS GLORY ANANDA HEAVEN
DELIGHT ECSTASY GLADDEN
NIRVANA RAPTURE FELICITY
GLADNESS PARADISE PLEASURE
BLISSFUL HOLY SEELY BLITHE
EDENIC BLESSED ELYSIAN UTOPIAN
BEATIFIED GLORIFIED

BLISTER BEAT BLAB BLEB BLOB
BLOW BOIL BURN LASH QUAT APTHA
BLAIN BLIBE BULGE BULLA TOPIC
VESIC APHTHA BUBBLE CUPOLA
SCORCH SOTTER TETTER BLADDER
BLUSTER SCALDER SKELLER VESICLE
VESICATE
(PREF.) PUSTULI VESICUL(O)
BLISTERED BULLATE
BLISTERING VESICANT
BLITHE GAY GLAD BONNY BUXOM
HAPPY JOLLY MERRY BONNIE JOVIAL
JOYOUS LIVELY GAYSOME JOCULAR
WINSOME CHEERFUL GLADSOME
SPRIGHTLY
BLITZ REDDOG
BLIZZARD BLOW GALE WIND BURAN
PURGA RETORT SNIFTER
SQUELCHER
(— STATE) SD SDAK
BLOAT BLOW BLAST BLOWN FLOAT
HOOVE HOVEN PUFFY SWELL
BOWDEN EXPAND TUMEFY DISTEND
FERMENT INFLATE
BLOATED FOZY BLOAT BROSY
CURED FOGGY HOVEN PUFFY TUMID
GOTCHY SODDEN TURGID POMPOUS
REPLETE
BLOATER MOONEYE
BLOB LIP WEN BEAD BLEB BLOT BOIL
CLOT DAUB DROP GLOB GOUT LUMP
MARK MASS BUBBLE DALLOP
DOLLOP PIMPLE SPLASH BLEMISH
BLISTER BLOSSOM GLOBULE
PUSTULE SPLOTCH
BLOC RING BLOCK CABAL PARTY
UNION CLIQUE BENELUX FACTION
BLOCK AME BAR COB COG DAM DIE
DIT DOG FID HOB HUB JAM KEY NOG
ROW TOP VOL BALK BASE BEAR BILK
BLOC BUCK BUNT CAKE CLOG CUBE
DRUM FOIL FOUL FROG GLUT HEAD
JAMB LEAD MASK MASS MOCK
QUAR STAY STEP STOP TRIG BAULK
BRICK CHAIR CHECK CHEEK CHUMP
CLAMP CLEAT CLOSE COVER DETER
DOLLY DUMMY EMBAR FLOAT HEART
HORST JUMBO NUDGE PARRY PATCH
SHAPE SLUMP SPIKE SPOKE STOCK
STUFF STUMP ASSIZE DENTIL
DOLLEY DOMINO FIPPLE FORMER
HAMPER HINDER IMPEDE KIBOSH
MONKEY MUFFLE MUTULE OPPOSE
OUTWIT QUERRE RIPPER SADDLE
SCOTCH SNATCH SQUARE STREET
STYMIE TAPLET THWART TROLLY
WAYLAY BOLLOCK BOLSTER
BUCKLER CONDEMN DEADEYE
ERRATIC INHIBIT OUTLINE PREVENT
QUADREL RAMHEAD STONKER
TRIGGER TROLLEY BLOCKADE
DEADHEAD ELECTRET FOLLOWER
KEYSTONE MONOLITH OBSTACLE

OBSTRUCT STOPPAGE WITHSPAR
BRIQUETTE
(— AT SPAR END) STEEVE
(— A WHEEL) SCOTE
(— FOR SKIDDING LOGS) BICYCLE
(— FOR SLAVE SALES) CATASTA
(— IN SPEAKING) STAMMER
(— OF BUILDINGS) INSULA
(— OF COAL) JUD JUDD
(— OF EARTH'S CRUST) HORST
(— OF GRANITE) SET
(— OF ICE) SERAC
(— OF LAND) FORTY
(— OF SEATS) CUNEUS
(— OF SHARES) TRANCHE
(— OF TIMBER) BOLT JUGGLE
(—S OF STONE) DIMENSION
(— SUPPORTING MAST) STEP
(— THE WAY) SCOAT
(— UP) BAR DAM CLOY QUIRT
CONDEMN OPPILATE FORECLOSE
(— WITH HOLE IN IT) WAPP EUPHROE
(— WITH PROJECTING CORE) SETTLE
(ARCHITECTURAL —) DRUM STONE
DENTIL IMPOST MUTULE PLINTH
DOSSERET
(BUILDING —) MEGALITH
(CHOPPING —) HACKLOG
(CLAY —) DRAWBAR
(FAULT —) MASSIF
(FELTED —) DAMPER
(FOOTBALL —) CRACKBACK
(FULCRUM —) GLUT
(FUSE —) CUTOUT
(HOSPITAL —) PAVILION
(IRON —) USE VOL BITT ANVIL CHAIR
(LOGGING —) LEAD JUMBO
(NAUTICAL —) CHUCK HEART STOCK
SADDLE DEADEYE FAIRLEAD
(ORNAMENTAL —) BOSS MODILLION
(PAVING —) SET CUBE SETT STONE
WHEELER
(PLASTER —) BATTER
(POLISHING —) BUFF FLOAT RABOT
(PRINTING —) CUT QUAD RISER
QUADRAT
(PULLEY —) CRAWL
(SANDSTONE —) SARSEN
(SQUARED —) MITCHEL
(STUMBLING —) HURTING
(TACKLE —) CALO TONGUE
(VAULTING —) BUCK HORSE
BLOCKADE DAM FERM BESET
BLOCK EMBAR SIEGE WHISKY
BESIEGE EMBARGO BLOCKAGE
OBSTRUCT BARRICADE BELEAGUER
BLOCKAGE LOGJAM
BLOCKER CASER BRACER
(CHANNEL —) NIFEDEPINE
BLOCKHEAD ASS LUG OAF SAP
BUST CLOT COOF COOT DAFF DOLT
FOOL MOME NOWT STUR BLOCK
BOOBY CHUMP CUDDY GULEM

GOOSY IDIOT NINNY SNIPE SUMPH
CUDDIE DIMWIT DISARD NITWIT
NOODLE TUMPHY TURNIP ASSHEAD
BUZZARD DIZZARD DULBERT
JACKASS LACKWIT MUDHEAD
NOGHEAD TOMFOOL BEEFHEAD
BONEHEAD CLODPATE CLODPOLL
CODSHEAD DULLHEAD DULLPATE
DUMBHEAD DUMMKOPF GAMPHREL
HARDHEAD JOLTHEAD LUNKHEAD
BLOCKHOUSE SPUR PUNTAL
GARRISON
BLOCKING JAM JAMB DUNNAGE
BLOCKADE CROSSING
BLOCKISH STOLID
BLOKE EGG GUY MAN CHAP COVE
TOFF BLOAK JOKER FELLOW
BLOLLY BEEFWOOD CORKWOOD
PORKWOOD
BLOND BAN FAIR LIGHT BLONDE
FLAXEN GOLDEN YELLOW LEUCOUS
BLONDINE
(AUTUMN —) FAWN
BLOOD KIN SAP GORE LIFE MASS
MOOD RACE SANG SANK BLADE
BLUDE BLUID CRUOR FLESH FLUID
SERUM STOCK CLARET INDRED
KAINAH SLUDGE GALLANT KINSHIP
KINSMAN LINEAGE RELATION
TROPHEMA
(— CONDITION) SICKLEMIA
(— OF GREEK GODS) ICHOR
(— RELATED) HEMAL
(CORRUPT —) YQUSTIR
(HALF —) DEMISANG
(PREF.) HAEM(A)(O) HAEMAT(O)
HEM(A)(O) HEMAT(O) SANGUI
SANGUINO SANO
(SUFF.) AEMIA EMIA HAEMIA HEMIA
BLOOD CLOT
(PREF.) THROMB(O)
BLOODCURDLING GORY HORROR
BLOODFLOWER HIPPO REDHEAD
BLOODWEED
BLOODHOUND LYM LYAM LYME
HOUND LIMER SLOTH BANDOG
LEAMER SLEUTH TIEDOG
LYAMHOUND SLEUTHHOUND
BLOODIED BEBLED
BLOODLESS DEAD ANEMIC
ANAEMIC INHUMAN TURNIPY
LIFELESS UNFEELING
BLOODLETTER BLEEDER
BLOOD-LETTING PHLEBOTOMY
BLOODLIKE HEMATOID HAEMATOID
BLOOD PHEASANT ITHAGINE
BLOOD PUDDING BLUTWURST
BLOOD-RED SANGUINE
BLOODROOT PUCCOON REDROOT
BOLOROOT COONROOT CORNROOT
TURMERIC SANGUINARIA
BLOODSHED DEATH CARNAGE
VIOLENCE SLAUGHTER

BLOODSHOT RED INFLAMED
BLOODSTAINED GORY
BLOODSTONE SANGUINE
HEMACHATE
BLOODSUCKER LEECH SPONGER
VAMPIRE
BLOODTHIRSTINESS
ACHARNEMENT
BLOODTHIRSTY BLOODY CARNAL
SANGUINE TIGERISH FEROCIOUS
MURDEROUS SANGUINARY
BLOOD VESSEL VEIN COMES
HEMAD ARTERY CAPILLARY
(PREF.) ANGIO
BLOODWOOD AJHAR JAROOL
BLOODY GORY RUDE BALLY BLODE
CRUEL RUDDY BLUGGY CRUENT
GRISLY PLUCKY CRIMSON BLEEDING
DEATHFUL HEMATOSE INFAMOUS
SANGLANT BUTCHERLY CRUENTOUS
FEROCIOUS MERCILESS
MURDEROUS SANGUINARY
BLOODY BARK LANCEPOD
BLOOM DEW BLOW CAST HAZE
KNOT BLURT BLUSH CHILL BLOOTH
BLOWTH BLOSSOM BLOWING
ANTHESIS BLOOMING FLOREATE
FLOURISH
(— OF WILLOW) GULL
(— ON INSECT) POLLEN
(— ON SHELL) CUTICLE
(— ON TREE) GOSLING
(FULL —) HEYDAY
(METAL —S) HEAT
(POWDERY —) PRUINA
BLOOMER ERROR BLOWER
BLUNDER FAILURE
BLOOMERS KNICKERS PANTALETS
BLOOMERY FORGE HEARTH
FURNACE
BLOOMING PERT ROSY FLUSH
FRESH GREEN PRIME ABLOOM
FLORID BLOWING FLAMING ROSEATE
BLINKING
BLOOPER BLOOMER
BLOSSOM BUD BELL BLOB BLOW
CHIP SILK BLOOM LEHUA FLOWER
BLOWING BURGEON PROSPER
BOURGEON FLOURISH
(BLIGHTED —) BLAST
(HERALDIC —) FRASE FRAISE
(PL.) SET BLOSSOMRY
BLOSSOMING BLOWTH FLORAISON
FLORULENT
(— AFTER NOON) POMERIDIAN
BLOT MAR BLOB BLUR DAUB SOIL
SPOT BLACK BLANK BLEND BLOTE
ERASE SMEAR SPECK STAIN SULLY
BLOTCH CANCEL DAMAGE EFFACE
IMPAIR MACULA SHADOW SMIRCH
SMOUCH SMUDGE SMUTCH STIGMA
BLEMISH ECLIPSE EXPUNGE

INKBLOT OBSCURE SPLOTCH
TARNISH DISGRACE REPROACH
(— OUT) OUT BURY ANNUL ERASE
CANCEL DELETE EXPUNGE
BLOTCH DAB BLOT DASH GOUT
MONK SPOT AMPER PATCH SMEAR
SPLAT STAIN MACULA MOTTLE
PLOTCH PURPLE SMIRCH SPLASH
STIGMA BLEMISH PUSTULE SPLOTCH
ERUPTION MACULATE
(PL.) BLIBE
(PREF.) MACUL(I)(O)
BLOTCHED SCABBY PIEBALD
MACULATE SCABROUS SPLASHED
MACULATED
(SUFF.) MACULATE
BLOTCHY SCOVY
BLOTTER BLAD
BLOTTO LIT
BLOUSE CHOLI MIDDY SHIRT SMOCK
TUNIC WAIST CAMISA GUIMPE
JUMPER CASAQUE VAREUSE
CAMISOLE CASAQUIN JIRKINET
(ABBREVIATED —) HALTER
(BUSHMAN'S —) BLUEY
(KIND OF —) PEASANT
BLOW BOB COB COP CUT DAB DAD
DUB FAN FIB HIT JAB JAR NAP ONE
PAT PEG POP RAP TAP TIP TIT WAP
ANDE BAFF BASH BEAT BELT
BIFF BIRR BLAD BLAW BRAG BUFF
BULL BUMP BUTT CHAP CHOP CONK
COUP CRIG CUFF DASH DAUD DENT
DING DINT DIRD DOLE DRAW DRUB
DUNT DUSH FLAP FLEG FLIG FUFF
FUNK GALE GOWF GUST HACK HUFF
HURT JOLT KNAP KNEE LASH LEAD
LEFT LICK LOUK LUSH MINT ONER
PAIK PALT PANT PASS PICK PIRR
PLUG POLT PUCK PUFF PUSH SCAT
SCUD SHOT SLAM SLAP SLAT SLUG
SOCK SPAT STOP SWAP SWAT SWOP
SWOT THUD WELT WHAP WHOP
WIND WIPE YANK BINGE BLADE
BLAST BLIZZ BLOOM BOAST BRUNT
BURST CLAUT CLINK CLOUR CLOUT
CLUMP CLUNK CRUMP CRUNT
CURSE DEVEL DOUSE DOWSE
DUNCH FACER FILIP FLACK FLICK
FLIRT GOWFF ICTUS IMPEL KNOCK
OUTER PALMY PANDY PASTE PEISE
PLUMP PLUNK PUNCH RIGHT SHAKE
SHOCK SKELP SKIRL SKITE SLASH
SLIPE SLOSH SMACK SMASH SMITE
SNICK SOUND SOUSE SPANK SPEND
STORM STRIP SURGE SMACK SWEEP
SWIPE THROW THUMP TOUCH TRICE
WHACK WHANG WHIFF WHOOF
WHUFF BELTER BENSEL BENSIL
BETRAY BOUNCE BUFFET CONKER
DEPART DIRDUM DUNDER EXPAND
FILLIP FISTER FLOWER FROLIC

HANDER HUFFLE LARRUP REBUKE
SIFFLE STOUSH STRIPE STROKE
SWITCH THUNGE THWACK WALLOP
WINDER AFFLATE ASSAULT
ATTAINT BELLOWS BENSAIL
BLOSSOM BLOWOUT BLUSTER
BOASTER COUNTER CRUSHER
DESTROY INFLATE KNOCKER
LAMBACK LOUNDER MOUTHER
PUBLISH SHATTER SMACKER
SPANKER SQUELCH WHAMPLE
WHIFFLE WHIRRET WHITHER
CALAMITY DISASTER KNOCKOUT
PASHWAFF SASARARA SICKENER
SIDEWINDER
(— ABRASIVES) BLAST
(— CEMENT) KIBOSH
(— GUSTILY) FLAW TUCK WINNOW
(— IN PUFFS) FAFF
(— NOSE) SNITE
(— OFF STEAM) SNIFT
(— OF WHALE) SPOUT
(— ON CHEEK) ALAPA
(— ON HEAD) NOB CONK CLOUR
CONKER NOBBER TOPPER NOBBLER
(— ON NOSE) NOSER CANKER
NOZZLER SMELLER
(— SMOKE) NOSE
(— SOFTLY) BREATHE
(— UP) BOMB BLAST DYNAMITE
SUFFLATE
(— UPON) WINNOW
(— VIOLENTLY) STORM
(— WITH CUDGEL) DUB DRUB CRUNT
(— WITH FIST) BOP BOX PEG BELT
HOOK CLOUT BUFFET ROUNDHOUSE
(— WITH FOOT) BOOT KICK SPURN
(BOXING —) BLAST FACER
(DECISIVE —) SOCKDOLAGER
SOCKDOLOGER
(FENCING —) MONTANT
(GENTLE —) CHUCK
(GLANCING —) SCUFF
(HARD —) SLOG STOT YANK BEVEL
SWACK TWITCHER
(HEAVY —) DAD DONG DRUB DUNT
ONER SLAM SLUG CLOUT KNOCK
POISE SOUSE SQUAT STAVE SWASH
STOUND PLUMPER REEMISH
(LIGHT —) WAFF
(MOCK —) FEINT
(NOISY —) DUNDER DUNNER
(RESOUNDING —) CLAP CRACK
(SHARP —) BAT NAP CLIP KNAP SLAP
SPAT CLICK FLICK FLEWIT STINGER
(SLIGHT —) SCLAFF
(SMART —) CLIP FLIP SKELP SKITE
YANKER
(SUDDEN —) ZAP
BLOWCASE EGG
BLOWER PAN DRIER DRYER WHALE
FANNER PUFFER BELLOWS BLOOMER

BOOSTER MUMBLER BRAGGART
OUTBURST
(GLASS —) GAFFER
BLOWGUN SUMPIT SUMPITAN
SARBACANE PEASHOOTER
BLOWHOLE BLOW GLOUP SPOUT
SPIRACLE
(— IN STEEL) ROAK
BLOWING ABLOW BLAST BLORE
GUSTY BLUSTER BLUSTERY
(— AT LOW SPEED) SLACK
(— AT RIGHT ANGLES) SIDE
(— OF WHALE) SPOUT
BLOWN STALE TIRED OPENED
WINDED BLOSSOM SWOLLEN
TAINTED BETRAYED FLYBLOWN
INFLATED
BLOWOUT BASH BLOW FEED MEAL
BURST VALLEY FLAMEOUT
WINGDING WHINGDING
BLOWPIPE HOD SUMPIT SUMPITAN
SARBACANE
(PEWTERER'S —) HOD
BLOWSY DOWDY BLOUSY BLOWZY
FROWZY
BLOWY DUSTY
BLUBBER CRY FAT SOB BLUB FOAM
WAIL WEEP BIBLE MELON PIECE
SPECK SPICK SWELL THICK WHINE
BUBBLE FLITCH LIPPER LUBBER
MEDUSA NETTLE SEETHE BLABBER
BLUSTER SLOBBER SWOLLEN
WHIMPER
(— AT WHALE'S NECK) CANT
(CUT WHALE —) FLENSE
(REFUSE —) FENKS FOOTING
FRITTERS
BLUDGEON BAT HIT SAP CLUB
COSH MACE BILLY STICK TOWEL
COERCE COURSE BLACKJACK
TRUNCHEON
BLUE (ALSO SEE COLOR) HAW LOW
SAD SKY AQUA DICE BLAE BLEU
CYAN GLUM SAXE TEAL WOAD
AZURE BERYL LIVID NIKKO PERSE
SMALL WAGET COBALT GLOOMY
INDIGO LUPINE ORIENT PEWTER
RISQUE SEVERE TRYPAN CELESTE
CYANINE GENTIAN GOBELIN HYPPISH
LEARNED LIBERTY LOBELIA MATELOT
MISTBLU MURILLO NATTIER
PEACOCK QUIMPER REGATTA
WATCHET CERULEAN DEJECTED
LABRADOR LARKSPUR LITERARY
MAZARINE MIDNIGHT NATIONAL
SAPPHIRE WEDGWOOD POMPADOUR
(— DYE) METHYL
(BLACKISH —) BLO BLOO
(DEEP —) SMALT
(DULL —) HAW
(ROYAL —) HATHON
(SHADE OF —) INDE COPEN

(PREF.) CYAN(O) INDICO IND(I)(O)
(SUFF.) (— PIGMENT) CYAN(IC)
BLUEBELL CROWBELL HAREBELL
BLUEBERRY OHELO STONER
PALBERRY RABBITEYE VACCINIUM
BLUEBIRD (— GUIDE) LEADER
BLUE-BLACK BLO
BLUEBLOSSOM LILAC
BLUEBONNET CAP SCOT BLUECAP
BLUEBOTTLE BLUET BLAVER
BARBEAU BLAWORT BLOWFLY
BLUECAP BLUECUP BRUSHES
HARDOCK BLUEBLAW HYACINTH
CORNBINKS
BLUE CREEPER LOVE
BLUE CURLS FLEASEED FLEAWEED
BLUE-EYED GRASS PIGROOT
SATINFLOWER
BLUEFIN TUNNY
BLUEFISH ELF BASS ELFT SHAD
TUNA HORSE SAURY DARZEE TAILER
TAILOR FATBACK SKIPJACK
WEAKFISH
(YOUNG OF —) SNAPPER WHITEFISH
BLUEGILL BREAM SUNFISH
PONDFISH PUMPKINSEED
BLUE GOOSE BALDHEAD
BLUEGRASS STATE KENTUCKY
BLUE GREEN VENICE
BLUE GUM FEVERGUM
EUCALYPTUS
BLUE HEN STATE DELAWARE
BLUE HERON CRANE NAILROD
BLUEJACKET SAILOR DRAGMAN
BLUEJOINT REDTOP BLUETOPS
BLUENESS CYANOSIS
(— OF SKIN) CYANOSIS
BLUENOSE PRUDE
BLUE-PENCIL EDIT EMEND
BLUE PETER ASK
BLUE PINE LIM
BLUE POINTER MAKO
BLUEPRINT MAP PLAN PLOT DRAFT
TRACE SKETCH DIAGRAM PROJECT
CYANOTYPE
BLUE RUNNER JUREL
BLUES MARE DUMPS CAFARD
DISMAL GLOOMS DISMALS
HORRORS HUMDRUM MEGRIMS
SADNESS DOLDRUMS DOLEFULS
MULLIGRUBS
BLUE SHEEP BURHEL
BLUE SLATE SKAILLIE
BLUESTOCKING BLUE PEDANT
BASBLEU
BLUE SUCCORY CATNACHE
CUPIDONE
BLUET PISSABED EYEBRIGHT
INNOCENCE
BLUE TIT NUN STONECHAT
BLUE TITMOUSE YAUP TYDIE
TIDIFE BLUECAP
BLUETONGUE THICKHEAD

BLUE VERVAIN IRONWEED
BLUE VINNY DORSET
BLUEWEED ECHIUM IRONWEED
ADDERWORT
BLUFF ALTO BANK BRAG CURT FOOL
RUDE BLUNT BRAVE BURLY CLIFF
FRANK GRUFF SHORT SURLY SWANK
WINDY ABRUPT BOUNCE CRUSTY
BLINDER BLINKER BLUFFER
BRUSQUE DECEIVE UNCIVIL
BARRANCA BARRANCO CHURLISH
HOODWINK IMPOLITE
BLUISH BLEUATRE
BLUISH-GRAY MERLE
BLUISH-GREEN AQUAMARINE
BLUMEA PLACUS
BLUNDER ERR MIX BALK BONE
BOOB BUBU BULL DOLT FLUB GAFF
ROIL SKEW SLIP STIR TRIP BEVUE
BLOOP BONER BOTCH BREAK ERROR
FAULT FLUFF GAFFE LAPSE MISDO
BOGGLE BOOBOO BUMBLE BUMMLE
BUNGLE ESCAPE FUMBLE GAZEBO
HOWLER MAFFLE MINGLE MUDDLE
SLIPUP BLOOMER BLOOPER
CLANGER CONFUSE DERANGE
FAILURE FLOATER MISSTEP MISTAKE
OVERSEE SOTTISE STUMBLE
PRATFALL SOLECISM
((AMUSING —) HOWLER
(— IN LANGUAGE) BULL
(— IN SPEECH) SOLECISM
(HUMILIATING —) PRATFALL
(VERBAL —) SLIPSLAP SLIPSLOP
BLUNDERBUSS TRABU TRABUCO
TRABUCHO TROMBONE ESPINGOLE
BLUNDERER BUMBLER BUMMLER
KNOTHEAD LUMBERER
BLUNDERING AWKWARD
BUMBLING
BLUNT BALD BATE BULL CURT DAMP
DULL FLAT MULL SNUB ABATE BLATE
BLUFF BRUSK DUBBY FRANK INERT
MORNE PLAIN PLUMP STUNT TERSE
CANDID CLUMSY DEADEN DIRECT
OBTUND OBTUSE REBATE RETUND
SHEATH STUBBY STUPID BRUSQUE
DISEDGE HACKNEY SHEATHE
SNUBBED SPADISH STUBBED
STUPEFY HEBETATE
BLUNTED MORNED
(PREF.) OBTUSI
BLUNTLY PLAT PLUMP FLATLY
CRUDELY FRANKLY
BLUR DIM FOG HUM BLOB BLOT FADE
FUZZ MIST SLUR SOIL SPOT BLEAR
CLOUD FUDGE SHAKE SMEAR STAIN
SULLY MACKLE MACULE SMUDGE
STIGMA BLEMISH CONFUSE
FEATHER OBSCURE TAILING
BLURB AD BOLT PUFF RAVE BRIEF
PROMO NOTICE
(PROMOTIONAL —) PROMO

BLURRED FAINT FUZZY MUZZY
VAGUE WOOZY BLEARY BLURRY
CLOUDY SMEARY SMUDGY SWIMMY
WOOLLY CLOUDED COMATIC
EDGELESS FLANNELLY
BLURRING HALATION
BLURT BLAT BOLT PLUMP BLUNDER
EXCLAIM
BLUSH BLUE GLOW BLINK COLOR
FLUSH GLEAM PAINT ROUGE TINGE
CHANGE GLANCE MANTLE REDDEN
CRIMSON FLICKER SCARLET
LIKENESS JOSEPHINE
BLUSHING RED ROSY ABLUSH
ROSEATE FLUSHING ROSACEOUS
BLUSTER GAS BEEF BLOW DING
HUFF RAGE RAIL RANT RAVE BLAST
BLEAT BLORE BOAST BRACE BULLY
NOISE STORM SWANK BABBLE
BELLOW BOUNCE FRAPLE HECTOR
HUFFLE TUMULT WUTHER BLUBBER
BRAVADO FLUSTER GAUSTER
ROISTER SWAGGER WHITHER
BOASTING BULLYING THREATEN
RODOMONTADE
BLUSTERER SWAG FLASH HECTOR
HUFFER FRAPLER HUFFCAP TEARCAT
CACAFOGO FANFARON
BLUSTERING BOG LOUD BLUFF
BRASH BULLY VAPORS HUFFCAP
VAPOURS ARROGANT BULLYING
BLUSTERY RAW
BOA BOM BOID BOMA ABOMA JIBOA
SCARF THROW ABOLLA ADJIGA
GIBOIA JOBOYA PYTHON ADJIGER
CAMOODI EMPEROR PEROPOD
ANACONDA CORALLUS
BOADICEA
(HUSBAND OF —) PRASUTAGUS
BOAR HOG APER SUID BRAWN SWINE
BARROW HOGGET TUSKER
BRAWNER SOUNDER SUIDIAN
VENISON WILRONE BRISTLER
SANGLIER HOGGASTER
(— CRY) FREAM
(— HEAD) HURE
(— IN 2ND YEAR) HOGGET
(— IN 3RD YEAR) HOGSTEER
HOGGASTER
(— STY) FRANK
(YOUNG —) GRISE SOUNDER
(PREF.) SUI
BOARD EAT LAG PAX TOE DAIL DEAL
DECK DIET EATS FARE FLIP HACK
JOIN KEEP LATH MEAT SHIP SIGN
SLAT TRAY TRIP ASTEL BUIRD CHESE
CLEAR COARD COUCH COURT ENTER
FOUND GETIN GETON HOUSE LODGE
MEALS PANEL PLANK RATCH SHIDE
STAGE STALL SWALE TABLE THEAL
ABACUS ACCOST ASTYLL COMMON
PALLET PLANCH RANDOM RIBBON
SHIELD SIDING TUCKER CABINET

CHAMBER COUNCIL CRIMPER
DUOVIRI ENPLANE ENTRAIN
KNEELER PALETTE PENSION
PLANCHE SCRAPER TABLING
TRANSOM WHATMAN APPROACH
ASSEMBLY BOXBOARD CUPBOARD
EXCLUDER FETIALES KEYBOARD
LAPBOARD PEGBOARD TRIBUNAL
PRESSBOARD MORTARBOARD
(— FOR FALCON'S MEAT) HACK
(— OF BRIDGE) CHESS
(— OF LOOM) CARD
(— OF MILL WHEEL) AWE
(— ON CALF'S NOSE) BLAB
(— OVER) BERTH
(— WITH GROOVE) COULISSE
(— WITH HANDLE) CLAPPER
(— WITH NUMBER) SLATE
(— WITH PINS) RIDDLE
(— WITH TEETH) HACKLE RUFFER
(BLOCKHEAD —) DOLL
(CHANNEL —) PAN
(CHESS —) TABLER
(DRAWING —) COQUILLE
(EXHIBITION —) FRAME
(FLOOR —) KEY
(GAME —) HALMA
(HEART-SHAPED —) PLANCHET
(KIND OF —) OUIJA MALIBU
(MORTAR —) HAWK
(NOTCHED —) HORSE
(OTTER —) DOOR
(POLING —) RUNNER
(PRESSED —S) FELT
(PULP-PRESSING —) COUCH
(RABBETED —S) SHIPLAP
(SHEATHING —S) SARKING
(STRIKE —) SCREED
(TANNING —) BEAM
(THIN —) SHIDE SARKING
(THIN —S) SLITWORK
(WARPING —) BARTREE
BOARDED PLANCHED
BOARDER MEALER TABLER GRAINER
PENSIONER SOJOURNER TRANSIENT
BOARDING LIVERY
BOARDINGHOUSE FONDA HOUSE
PENSION
BOARDWALK MARINA DUCKBOARD
BOARWOOD CHEWSTICK
BOAST BOG GAB JET BEEF BLAW
BLOW BRAG CROW POMP PUFF
RAVE VANT WIND WOST YELP BLAST
BRAVE CRACK CRAKE EXTOL EXULT
GLORY PRATE QUACK ROOSE
SCOLD SKITE VAPOR VAUNT VOUST
YOLPE AVAUNT BLAZON BLEEZE
BOUNCE CLAMOR FLAUNT INSULT
MENACE OUTCRY SPLORE BLUSTER
BRAVING CLAMOUR DEVAUNT
DISPLAY GLORIFY SWAGGER
FLOURISH THREATEN VANTERIE
VAUNTERY

BOASTER BLOW HUFF GALAH SKITE
BLOWER CROWER GASCON PEDANT
PRATER SHAKER BLOWOFF
BOUNCER BRAGGER BRAVADO
CRACKER RUFFLER BLOWHARD
BRAGGART CACAFUGO FANFARON
GLORIOSO JINGOIST RODOMONT
TARTARIN WOUSTOUR

BOASTFUL BIG BRAG HIGH COCKY
LARGE BRAGGY PARADO BOBADIL
JACTANT VAUNTIE FANFARON
GLORIOUS GASCONADE THRASONIC

BOASTFULLY SIDE LARGE

BOASTFULNESS GLORY EGOTISM
WINDINESS

BOASTING BLOW HUFF YELP BOAST
CRACK PRATE ROOSE QUACKY
BOBANCE GASSING JACTANCE
JACTANCY QUACKISH VAPORING
VAUNTAGE VENTOSITY
RODOMONTADE
(EMPTY —) GAS

BOAT ARK BUM BUN CAT COG COT
DOW GIG MON TUB ACON BAIT
BARK BOOT BRIG CARV CHOP COCK
DHOW DINK DORY DUMP FLAT FOUZ
JUNK PAIR PLAT PRAM PUNT RAFT
SCOW SHIP SKAG TACK TODE TOPO
TROW WAKA YAWL YOLE ACCON
AVISO BANCA BARCA BARGE BARIS
BATEL BIDAR BOLIA BOYER BULLY
BUYER CANOE COBLE CRAFT DHONI
DINGY FERRY FOIST FORTY FUNNY
JOLLY KETCH LAKER LINER NADIR
OOLAK PIECE PILOT PRAAM RACER
SHELL SHOUT SIKAR SKIFF SKIFT
SMACK TOPPO UMIAK WAAPA WHIFF
XEBEC ZEBEC BAIDAK BANGKA
BATEAU BAWLEY BELLUM BILALO
BORLEY BOTTOM BOUTRE CAIQUE
CARVEL CAYUCO CHEBEC COCKLE
CRUISE CUTTER DINGHY DREDGE
DRIVER DROVER DUGOUT FLATTY
GALLEY GARVEY GAYYOU GLIDER
HOOKER JAGGER JIGGER KEELER
KICKER KUPHAR LATEEN LERRET
MAILER NAGGAR NUGGAR PACKET
PEAPOD PEDULE PICARD PINKIE
PLAYTE PULWAR RANDAN ROCKER
SANDAL SCAPHE SCHOUW SCHUYT
SETTEE SINGLE SKERRY STRUSE
TANKER TENDER TIMBER TOGGER
TORPID TRANKY TROUGH VESSEL
WAFTER WHERRY ZEBECK AIRBOAT
ALMADIA ANGEYOK BALLOEN
BALLOON BAULEAH BUMBOAT
CAISSON CARRIER CATCHER
CORACLE COROLAN CRUISER
CURRACH DOGBODY DRIFTER
DROGHER FLATTIE FLEETER FLYBOAT
FOYBOAT FRIGATE GAIASSA
GASBOAT GEORDIE GONDOLA
HOVELER HUFFLER KELLECK LIGHTER

MACHINE MASOOLA NACELLE
PEARLER PEDIWAK PINNACE
PIRAGUA POOKAWN PUTELEE
SCOOTER SCULLER SHALLOP
SHARPIE SHIKARA SIKHARA SKAFFIE
SKIPPET SPONGER SPYBOAT
STEAMER TRAWLER TUCKNER
TUMBREL TUMBRIL VEDETTE
WHIRREY BALANGAY BARANGAY
BILLYBOY BOOMBOAT BULLBOAT
BUMBARGE CANALLER CHALOUPE
CHEBACCO CHELINGA CHELINGO
COCKBOAT COROCORE DAHABEAH
DUCKBOAT FIREBOAT FLAGBOAT
KEELBOAT LIFEBOAT MACKINAW
MONOXYLE NEWSBOAT OYSTERER
PALANDER PANCHWAY PESSONER
PESSULUS PULLBOAT SAILBOAT
SCHOKKER SCHOONER SURFBOAT
TONGKANG TRANSFER OUTRIGGER
(— OF MALTA) DGHAISA
(— WITH SAILS AND OARS)
LYMPHIAD
(ABANDONED —) DERELICT
(CANAL — OF VENICE) VAPORETTO
(CHEMICAL —) CAPSULE
(CHINESE —) JUNK SAMPAN
(CLUMSY —) HOOKER DROGHER
(COLLEGE —) TORPID
(DISPATCH —) AVISO PACKET
(ESKIMO —) KAMIK UMIAK OOMIAC
UMIACK
(FERRY —) BAC CUTT
(FISHING —) COG BOVO BUSS DONI
CANOA COBLE DHONI NOBBY PYKAR
SMACK VINTA BALDIE BAWLEY
BORLEY DOGGER DROVER FISHER
KUPHAR NICKEY SANDAL SCAFFY
SEINER SEXERN TOSHER VOLYER
WHALER CARAVEL CRABBER
DRAGGER FOLLYER POOKAUN
SHARPIE SKAFFIE TRAWLER
DRAGBOAT GAROOKUH SHRIMPER
(FLAT-BOTTOM —) ARK BAC BUN
DORY FLAT PLAT PRAM PUNT SCOW
BARGE COBLE DOREY FLOAT MOSES
PRAAM SHOUT BATEAU BUGEYE
GAYYOU PUTELI GONDOLA LIGHTER
FLATBOAT GUNDELOW JOHNBOAT
(FLY —) BUSS FLUTE FLIGHT
(GANGES —) PUTELI
(HIGHLAND —) BIRLINN
(INCENSE —) NEF SHIP NAVICULA
(MALAY —) COROCORE GALLIVAT
(MORTAR —) PALANDER
(OPEN —) WHIFF LERRET SHALLOP
(PATROL —) SPITKID SPITKIT
(PLEASURE —) FUNNY PEDALO
(RACING —) SIX FOUR EIGHT SCULL
SHELL SINGLE TORPID SCULLER
(SHIP'S —) GIG MOSES DINGEY
DINGHY LAUNCH TENDER PINNACE
(SKIN —) BIDAR BAIDAR ANGEYOK

BIDARKA BULLBOAT
(SMALL —) CARTOPPER
(WICKER —) KUFA GOOFA GOOFAH
CORACLE
(3-OAR —) RANDAN
(6-OAR —) SEXERN
(8-OAR —) SHIP
(PL.) LIGHTERAGE
(PREF.) CYMBI CYMBO
(SUFF.) SCAPH
BOATBUILDING SETWORK
BOATHOOK STOWER HITCHER
BOATMAN DANDI DANDY PHAON
BARGER BOWMAN CHARON YAWLER
HOBBLER HOVELER HUFFLER
COBLEMAN VOYAGEUR WATERMAN
GONDOLIER
BOAT SEAT TAFT
BOAT-SHAPED NAVICULAR
(PREF.) SCAPH(O)
BOAT SHELL YET SWEETMEAT
BOATSWAIN BOSN BOSUN SERANG
TINDAL
BOAZ (FATHER OF —) SALMA
SALMON
(SON OF —) OBED
(WIFE OF —) RUTH
BOB RAB BOW CUT DAB DIP HOD JOG
POP RAP TAP BALL BLOW BUFF CALF
CLIP CLOD COIN CORK DUCK GRUB
JEER JERK JEST KNOB MOCK WORM
BUNCH CHEAT DANCE FILCH FLOAT
FLOUT SHAKE TAUNT TRICK BINGLE
BOBBER BOBBLE BUFFET CURTSY
DELUDE HOBBLE POMMEL POPPLE
STRIKE WEIGHT BOBSLED BOBTAIL
CLUSTER HAIRCUT PAGEBOY
PENDANT PLUMMET REFRAIN
SHINGLE SHILLING
(— UP) LOLLOP
BOBAC PAHMI TARBAGAN
BOBBER CORK DUCK FLOAT BOBFLY
BOBBIN PIN CONE CORD PIRN REEL
BRAID QUILL SPOOL BROCHE
HANGER SKREEL TAVELL WORKER
RATCHET SPINDLE TARELLE
TORCHON
(PL.) BONES
BOBBINET ILLUSION
BOBBING DOOK
BOBBLE ERROR
BOBOLINK DEER REED SUCKER
BUNTING MAYBIRD ORTOLAN
REEDBIRD RICEBIRD
BOBSLED BOB DRAY BOBLET RIPPER
TRAVERSE
BOBWHITE COLIN QUAIL PARTRIDGE
BOBWIG DALMAHOY
BOCACCIO JACK TOMCOD
BOCCACCIO TRECENTIST
BOCCARELLA NOSEHOLE
BOCCARO YIHSING
BOCE BOGUE OXEYE

BOCHERU (FATHER OF —) AZEL
BODE OMEN SIGN STOP AUGUR
OFFER HERALD MESSAGE PORTEND
PRESAGE FOREBODE FORECAST
FORESHOW FORETELL INDICATE
BODHISATTVA KWANNON
MAITREYA AVALOKITA PADMAPANI
BODICE JUPE CHOLI GILET JUMPS
WAIST RASQUE BOLERO CORSET
JELICK LYFKIE CORSAGE OVERBODY
SLIPBODY
BODIERON BOREGAT
BODILESS MOONSHINE
BODILY SOLID SOMAL ACTUAL
CARNAL FLESHLY SOMATIC
CORPORAL ENTIRELY EXTERNAL
MATERIAL PERSONAL PHYSICAL
SARKICAL VISCERAL CORPOREAL
(NOT —) INTERIOR
BODKIN AWL PIN POINT BROACH
DAGGER NEEDLE POPPER HAIRPIN
PONIARD STILETTO EYELETEER
BODLE TURNER
BODO CACHARI
BODY BOD BAND BELL BOLE BOOK
BOUK BUCK BULK CREW DEHA FORM
HEAD LICH MASS MOLD NAVE RIND
RUPA SOMA STEM ATOMY FLESH
FRAME HABIT MOULD SHANK STIFF
TORSO TRUNK CORMUS CORPSE
CORPUS CUERPO EXTENT FUSEAU
LICHAM PERSON SARIRA AIRFOIL
ANATOMY CADAVER CARCASS
COMPANY ECONOMY QUANTUM
SKINFUL SUPTION TEXTURE
CORSAINT DEMARCHY EXTENSUM
MAJORITY PHYSIQUE QUARROME
TENEMENT PERSONNEL
(— OF ARROW) SHAFT STELE
(— OF BASILICA) NAVE
(— OF BEES) SWARM
(— OF BELIEVERS) FAITH
(— OF CANONS) CHAPTER
(— OF CARDINALS) CONCLAVE
(— OF CEREMONIES) RITUAL
(— OF CHILDREN) INFANTRY
(— OF CHRISTIANS) KOINONIA
COMMUNION
(— OF CONSTABLES) POSSE
(— OF CORINTHIAN CAPITAL) VASE
(— OF DOCTRINES) DOGMA
(— OF ECHINODERM) DISC DISK
(— OF EVIDENCE) CASE CORPUS
(— OF FIBERS) FORNIX
(— OF FOLLOWERS) SECT
(— OF GUARDS) WARD
(— OF HELMET) BELL
(— OF ISLAMIC CUSTOM) SUNNA
SUNNAH
(— OF JUDGES) JUDICIARY
(— OF KNOWLEDGE) STUFF
(— OF LAW) CODE SHAR HALAKA
SHARIA PANDECT SHARIAT

HALACHAH
(— OF LEGEND) SAGA
(— OF MANKIND) HERD
(— OF MUSCLE) BELLY
(— OF NOTIONS) FOLKLORE
(— OF OFFICERS) BUREAU
(— OF ORE) BUNCH MANTO
(— OF PIGMENT) EYESPOT IMPASTO
(— OF POETRY) EPOS
(— OF PRINCIPLES) ORGANON
(— OF ROCK) DIKE DYKE HORSE
STOCK BIOHERM MUDFLOW
INTRUSION
(— OF SINGERS) CHORUS
(— OF STATUTE) PURVIEW
(— OF STUDENTS) CLASS
(— OF TEN) DECURY
(— OF TENANTS) GAVEL HOMAGE
(— OF THIEVES) SCHOOL
(— OF TRADITIONS) HADIT HADITH
(— OF TROOPS) FORCE TAXIS
AMBUSH BATTLE CONREY SCREEN
SQUARE BRIGADE LASHKAR
SUPPORT BATTALIA GARRISON
(— OF TYPE) SHANK
(— OF VASSALS) BAN MANRED
(— OF WARRIORS) IMPI
(— OF WATER) BAY RIP SEA BAHR
FORD HEAD LAKE LAVE POND POOL
WAVE ABYSS BAYOU DRINK FLOOD
OCEAN SHARD SHERD SWASH
LAGOON NYANZA STREAM
FLOWAGE SWALLOW
(— OF WELLBORN MEN) COMITATUS
(— OF WRITINGS) SMRTI SMRITI
(— OF 12 MEN) DOUZAINE
(— POLITIC) ESTATE
(— RIDDLED BY BULLETS) SIEVE
(CAROTID —) GLOMUS
(CART —) SIRPEA
(CELESTIAL —) SUN BALL COMET
PLANET SPHERE ELEMENT ASTEROID
PLANETOID SATELLITE
PLANETESIMAL
(CIRCULAR —) DISC DISK
(COMPACT —) GLOBE
(CONDUCTING —) GROUND
(CORPORATE —) SOCIETY
(DEAD —) LICH MORT GHOST
CADAVER CARCASS CARRION
SUBJECT
(DEFEATED —) ROUT
(ECCLESIASTICAL —) CLASSIS
(ELASTIC —) CUSHION
(EXTENDED) LENGTH
(FAT —) EPIPLOON
(FRUITING —) CONK CLAVA
ASCOCARP MAZAEDIUM
(GALACTIC —) SPINAR
(GLOBULAR —) NOB KNOB
(GOVERNING —) KAHAL SYNOD
DURBAR SENATE DECARCHY

DIRECTORY
(HAT —) HOOD
(HEAVENLY —) SUN LAMP STAR
COMET LIGHT CANDLE
(HOLLOW —) TUBE
(HUMAN —) EARTH
(HYALINE —) DRUSE
(IMMUNE —) DESMON
(JUDICIAL —) FORUM
(KIND OF —) LIFTING
(LEGISLATIVE —) CHAMBER
ASSEMBLY CONGRESS LAGTHING
PARLIAMENT
(MAIN — OF ARMY) BATTLE
(MATHEMATICAL —) FILAMENT
(MORMON —) BISHOPRIC
(MORTAL —) KHET
(POROUS —) MADREPORITE
(PRESBYTERIAN —) SESSION
JUDICATORY
(RELIGIOUS —) SECT CONVENT
(REPRODUCTIVE —) EGG GEMMA
SPORE GEMMULA
(ROUND —) GLOBE
(SONOROUS —) PHONIC
(SPIRITUAL —) SAHU
(SWELLING —) BOSS
(UNICELLUAR —) SPORE
(WAGON —) BED BUCK PUNT
(PREF.) CORPORI SOMAT(O)
SOMATICO SOMI
(SUFF.) CY DEMA SOMA(TO)(TOUS)
SOME SOMIA SOMIC SOMOUS
SOMUS
(— OF A KIND) ID
BODYGUARD THANE ESCORT
INWARD HUSCARL RETINUE
TRABANT THINGMAN WARDCORS
(CRIMINAL'S —) MINDER
BOER TAKHAAR AFRIKANER
BOG BUG CAR DUB FEN GOG HAG
BOLD CARR CESS FLOW HAG
MOOR MOSS OOZE QUAG SINK
SLEW SLUE SPEW STOG SUDS SYRT
WASH LETCH MARSH MIZZY SAUCY
SLADE SLOCK SWAMP MORASS
MUSKEG POLDER SLOUGH CRIPPLE
FORWARD PEATERY TURBARY
QUAGMIRE
(MARSH —) QUAG
(PEAT —) CESS MOSS PETARY
YARPHA
(PREF.) HELO
BOG ASPHODEL KNAVERY
BOGEY BUG COW HAG BOGIE BOGLE
DEVIL GNOME TRUCK BOGGLE
BOOGER GOBLIN BOGGARD
BOGGART BUGABOO BUGBEAR
SPECTER SPECTRE
BOGGED SLOUGHED
BOGGLE JIB SHY BALK FOIL STOP
ALARM BOTCH DEMUR SCARE START

STICK BAFFLE BUNGLE GOBLIN
SHRINK BAUCHLE BLUNDER
PERPLEX SCRUPLE STUMBLE
FRIGHTEN HESITATE

BOGGY WET DEEP MIRY SOFT FENNY
FOGGY GOUTY HAGGY MOSSY
SNAPY SPEWY MARISH MARSHY
QUAGGY SLOBBY SWAMPY WAUGHY
BOGGISH QUEACHY SQUASHY

BOGIER RIDER GEARMAN

BOGLAND SLADE

BOGLE GOBLIN

BOG MANGANESE WAD
LAMPADITE

BOGO ABILO ABILAO

BOGOMILE PATARIN PATARINE

BOGUS FAKE SHAM FALSE PHONY
• SPURIOUS

BOGY GOBLIN

BOHEME, LA (CHARACTER IN —)
MIMI COLLINE MUSETTA RODOLFO
MARCELLO SCHAUNARD
(COMPOSER OF —) PUCCINI

BOHEMIAN ARTY PICARA PICARD
PICARO ARTISTIC
(— RIVER) ELBE VLTAVA LUZNICE
BEROUNKA
(— TOWN) PISEK PLZEN PRAHA
TABOR PILSEN PRAGUE

**BOHEMIAN GIRL (COMPOSER
OF —)** BALFE

BOHOR REEDBUCK

BOIL FRY PET STY BILE BLOB BOLL
BRAN BREW BUCK BUMP COCT
COOK COWL LEEP PLAY PUSH QUAT
RAGE SEED SORE STEW STYE TEEM
WALL WALM WELL BLAIN BOTCH
DREDE STEAM BETRAY BUBBLE
BULDER BULLER BURBLE DECOCT
GALLOP PIMPLE RISING SEETHE
SIMMER TOTTLE WABBLE WOBBLE
ANTHRAX BEALING BREEDER
CATHAIR ELIXATE ESTUATE INFLAME
AESTUATE EBULLATE FURUNCLE
PHLEGMON CARBUNCLE
(— IN LYE) BUCK
(— SYRUP) PEARL
(SAND —) BLOWOUT
(PREF.) COCTO DOTHI(EN)(O) ZEO

BOILED SOD SODDEN
(— WITHOUT SAUCE) ANGLAISE

BOILER YET REEF STILL COPPER
KETTLE RETORT TEACHE ALEMBIC
CALDRON FURNACE
(SALT —) WELLER

BOILERMAKER
(PART OF —) BEER

BOILING WALM ABOIL FERVID
COCTION FERVENT SCALDING
SEETHING ELIXATION

BOILING POINT
(PREF.) COCTO

BOISTERER (MASTER OF —)
FORTUNIO

BOISTEROUS GURL HIGH LOUD
RUDE WILD BURLY GURLY NOISY
RANDY ROARY ROUGH WINDY
COARSE RUGGED SHANDY STOCKY
STORMY STRONG UNRULY FURIOUS
MASSIVE ROARING VIOLENT
BIGMOUTH CUMBROUS LARRIKIN
STRIDENT VEHEMENT ROBUSTIOUS

BOLD BIG BOG MOD YEP DERF HARD
KEEN PERT RASH RUDE TALL WHAT
YEPE APERT BARDY BIELD BRASH
BRAVE BRENT FRACK FREAK FRECK
GALLY HARDY JOLLY LARGE MANLY
NERVY PAWKY PEART POKEY RUDAS
SAUCY STEEP STOUT WLONK
ABRUPT AUDACE BRASSY BRAZEN
CROUSE DARING FIERCE HEROIC
PLUCKY PRETTY STRONG ASSURED
DASHING DEFIANT FORWARD
GRIVOIS HAUGHTY MASSIVE
VALIANT ARROGANT FAMILIAR
FEARLESS IMMODEST IMPUDENT
INTREPID MALAPERT POWERFUL
RESOLUTE TEMEROUS
(NOT —) GENTEEL

BOLDFACE BOLD BLACK FULLFACE

BOLDLY CRANK BARELY CROUSE
HARDLY HARDILY ROUNDLY
STRONGLY

BOLDNESS BROW DARE FACE GALL
BIELD CHEEK NERVE PLUCK VIGOR
DARING BRAVERY COURAGE
FREEDOM AUDACITY TEMERITY
HARDIHOOD
(— OF SPEECH) PARRHESIA

BOLDO NUTMEG

BOLE CLAY DOSE STEM BOLUS
CRYPT TRUNK RUDDLE TIMBER

BOLETUS CEPE

BOLIDE METEOR FIREBALL

BOLIVIA PILE

BOLIVIA
CAPITAL: LAPAZ SUCRE
COIN: TOMIN CENTAVO
DEPARTMENT: LAPAZ ORURO PANDO
ELBENI POTOSI TARIJA
FORMER CAPITAL: ORURO
INDIAN: URO INCA ITEN MOXO URAN
ARAWAK AYMARA CHARCA CHICHA
IXIAMA TACANA PUQUINA
QUECHUA SIRIONE TUMUPASA
LAKE: POOPO COIPASA ROGAGUA
AULLAGAS TITICACA
MEASURE: LEAGUE CELEMIN
MOUNTAIN: JARA CUSCO CUIZCO
PUPUYA SAJAMA SORATA ILLAMPU
ANCOHUMA ILLIMANI ZAPALERI
MOUNTAINS: ANDES CUNSAS
SANSIMON SANTIAGO

PANPIPE: SICU SIKU
PLATEAU: ALTIPLANO
RIVER: BENI YATA ABUNA APERE
  BOOPI LAUCA ORTON BAURES
  GRANDE ICHILO ITENEZ MADIDI
  MAMORE MIZQUE TARIJA YACUMA
  GUAPORE ITONAMA MACHUPO
  BENECITO INAMBARI PARAGUAY
  PARAPETI
SALT DEPOSIT: UYUNI EMPEXA
SWAMP: IZOZOG
TOWN: IVO ICLA ITAU MOJO POJO
  SAYA YACO YATA YURA CLIZA LAPAZ
  LLICA ORURO QUIME SUCRE UNCIA
  UYUNI ZONGO GUAQUI POTOSI
  TARIJA
VOLCANO: OLLAGUE
WEIGHT: LIBRA MARCO

BOLL BOW POD BULB KNOB SNAP
  ONION BUBBLE CAPSULE
  (FOURTH —) FIRLOT
BOLLARD BITT KEVEL DOLPHIN
  DEADHEAD
  (—S AND BITTS) APOSTLES
BOLLER STRIPPER
BOLL WEEVIL PICUDO
BOLO MACHETE SUNDANG
BOLSHEVIK RED MAXIMALIST
BOLSHEVISM COMMUNISM
  SOVIETISM
BOLSHEVIST BOLO
BOLSTER AID PAD JACK PILLOW
  CUSHION HEADING STIFFEN
  SUPPORT BACKSTOP BALUSTER
  COMPRESS MAINTAIN
BOLT BAR JAG KEY LUE PEN PIN ROD
  RUN BEAT BURR CRAM DART DUMP
  FLEE GULP LOCK PAWL SHUT SIFT
  SLOT SNIB SPAR STUD ARROW
  BILBO CLOSE ELOPE FLASH FLOUR
  GORGE LATCH RIVET SETUP SHAFT
  STOCK ASSORT DECAMP DESERT
  FASTEN FLIGHT GANYIE GARBLE
  MOOTER PINTLE PURIFY QUARRY
  REFINE SAFETY SEARCE SECURE
  SNIBEL STREAK STRONG TOGGLE
  WINNOW ABSCOND BAYBOLT
  DOGBOLT EYEBOLT MISSILE
  QUARREL SETBOLT SHACKLE
  SLABBER THUNDER DRAWBOLT
  FASTENER FISHBOLT FLATHEAD
  KINGBOLT RINGBOLT SEPARATE
  SLUMMOCK STAMPEDE
  (— FOOD) SKOFF
  (DOOR —) DRAWBOLT
  (FIERY —) RESHEPH
  (LIGHTNING —) SHAFT
  (THUNDER —) FULMEN
  (PREF.) GOMPHO
BOLTER BOLT SIEVE DRESSER
  MUGWUMP
BOLTHEAD MATRASS

BOLUS BALL PILL
BOMB DUD EGG ROC AZON BOOM
  FRAG BLARE CRUMP PRANG RAZON
  SHELL SQUIB ASHCAN SALUTE
  AEROSOL BALLOON BOMBARD
  GRENADE MARMITE TORPEDO
  AEROBOMB FIREBALL WHIZBANG
  PINEAPPLE INCENDIARY
  (— RELEASE) TOGGLE
  (FLYING —) DOODLEBUG
  (KIND OF —) SKIP
  (TRENCH —) MINNIE
  (UNEXPLODED —) DUD
  (PL.) STICK
BOMBARD BOMB PELT CRUMP
  SHELL ATTACK BATTER BOTTLE
  STRAFE
BOMBARDMENT BLITZ SIEGE
  ATTACK RAFALE STRAFE BATTERY
  SHELLING
BOMBARDON TUBA NICOLO
  POMMER BRUMMER
BOMBAST GAS PAD PUFF RAGE
  RANT RAVE STUFF TUMOR BLUSTER
  FUSTIAN TYMPANY BALLYHOO
  BOASTING RHAPSODY TURGIDITY
BOMBASTIC PUFFY TUMID VOCAL
  WINDY FLUENT HEROIC MOUTHY
  TURGID BLOATED BOMBAST
  FLOWERY FUSTIAN OROTUND
  POMPOUS RANTING STILTED
  SWOLLEN INFLATED SWELLING
  (— STYLE) TYMPANY
BOMBAY DUCK BUMALO
  BUMMALO
BOMBER (TYPE OF —) STEALTH
BOMBINATE HUM BUZZ
BONACE TREE NOSEBURN
BONACI AGUAJI
BONA FIDE LEVEL GENUINE
  AUTHENTIC
BONANZA BUNCH
BONANZA STATE MONTANA
BONBON CANDY CREAM GOODY
  DAINTY CARAMEL COSAQUE
  SNAPPER CONFETTO
  (PL.) CONFETTI
BOND BON DOG TIE VOW ANDI BAIL
  BAND DUTY FIVE FOUR GILT GLUE
  GYVE HOLD KNOT LINK NOTE YOKE
  BOUND CHAIN NEXUS SWATH
  BINDER CEDULA CEMENT CONNEX
  COPULA COUPLE ENGAGE ESCROW
  FETTER LEAGUE PLEDGE SOLDER
  SWATHE FOREIGN HUSBAND
  LIAISON LIBERTY LINKAGE
  MANACLE SHACKLE STATUTE
  ADHESIVE CONTRACT COVENANT
  LIGAMENT LIGATION LIGATURE
  MORTGAGE SECURITY VADIMONY
  VINCULUM
  (EMOTIONAL —) RAPPORT
  (KIND OF —) JUNK

(PL.) IRON KHAKIS SHORTS
(PREF.) DESM(A)(IDI)(IDIO)(O) ETHMO
OSSE(O) OSSI OST(E)(EO)
(SUFF.) (CONTAINING TRIPLE —) OLIC
BONDAGE YOKE THRALL HELOTRY
SERFDOM SLAVERY BONDSHIP
THIRLING CAPTIVITY SERVITUDE
BONDED CATTED ENGAGED
BONDMAN CARL ESNE PEON SERF
CHURL HELOT SLAVE STOOGE
SURETY THRALL VASSAL CHATTEL
PEASANT SERVANT VILLEIN
BONDSMAN
BONDSTONE BINDER BONDER
KEYSTONE
BONE OS DIB HIP LUZ RIB TOT RANE
ULNA BLADE FEMUR HYOID ILIUM
INCUS JUGAL MALAR SLATE STONE
TALUS TIBIA UNION VOMER CANNON
COCCYX CONCHA COPULA CUBOID
EPURAL FIBULA FILLET HAMATE
NUCHAL PECTEN RADIAL SPLINT
STAPES TRIPOD UNGUIS ZYGOMA
DENTARY PALATAL PROOTIC
CORACOID PALATINE PARIETAL
PERIOTIC PISIFORM QUADRATE
TEMPORAL NAVICULAR OPERCULAR
METACARPAL
(— OF ARM) RADIU
(— OF DIGIT) PHALANX
(— OF NOSE) VOMER TURBINAL
(ANKLE —) TALUS
(EAR —) INCUS HAMMER STAPES
MALLEUS TYMPANIC
(HEEL —) CALCANEUM
(HIP —) HUGGIN
(HORSE'S —) RACK
(PELVIC —) PUBIS
(PUBIC —) PECTEN
(SHIN —) CNEMIS
(SKULL —) SQUAMOSAL
(SMALL —) OSSICLE
(THIGH —) FEMUR
(WRIST —) RADIALE SCAPHOID
TRAPEZOID
(PL.) DICE CLAPPERS ETHMO
KNACKERS SKELETON
(PREF.) ETHMO USSE(O) OSSI OST(E)
(EO)
(SUFF.) OST(EON)(EUS)(OSIS)
BONE-BLACK SPODE SPODIUM
BONED
(SUFF.) OSTEUS
BONEFISH OIO MACABI GRUBBER
BONYFISH LADYFISH
BONEHEAD SAP BOOB STUPE
BONER BUBU FLUB ROCK ERROR
BRODIE STAYER STUMER BLOOMER
BLOOPER BLUNDER MISTAKE
STEELER STUMOUR
BONES
(PREF.) (— OF HAND OR FOOT)
PHALANGI(A)

BONESET COMFREY AGUEWEED
EUPATORY HEMPWEEK
BONEYARD STOCK
BONFIRE BLAZE TANDLE TAWNIF
RALEFIRE BURNFIRE NEEDFIRE
BONGO DOR BUNGO CANOE
BONI MUNI
BONIFACE HOST
BONING SAP
BONITO AKU ATU NICE COBIA SARDA
BONITA ROBALO ALBACORE
KATONKEL MACKEREL SCOMBRID
SKIPJACK
BONNET CAP HAT COWL HOOD POKE
POXY SCON COVER DECOY SCONE
SHAPE TOQUE CAPOTE MOBCAP
SLOUCH CHAPEAU COMMODE
CORONET LEGHORN SOWBACK
VOLUPER BALMORAL BONGRACE
HEADGEAR
BONNET MONKEY ZATI MUNGA
TOQUE MACACO RILAWA MACAQUE
BONNY GAY FINE MERRY PLUMP
BLITHE BONNIE PRETTY STRONG
HEALTHY BUDGEREE HANDSOME
BEAUTIFUL
BONTOK IGOROT
BONUS GIN TIP GIFT MEED PLUM
PLUS AWARD BRIBE BUNCE BUNTS
PILON PRIZE SPIFF REGALO REWARD
CUMSHAW DOUCEUR PREMIUM
SUBSIDY BOUNTITH DIVIDEND
TANTIEME LAGNIAPPE
BON VIVANT SPORT EPICURE
GOURMET
BON VIVEUR FLANEUR
BONY HARD LANK THIN LANKY STIFF
TOUGH OSTEAL SKINNY ANGULAR
OSSEOUS SCRAGGY SKELETAL
BONYFISH MENHADEN
BOO FIE HUMBUG
BOOB ASS OAF FOOL GOON GOOP
DUNCE GOONY NEDDY NITWIT
BOOBOOK OWL PEHO RURU
CUCKOO MOPOKE MOPEHAWK
MOREPORK
BOOB TUBE BOX
BOOBY GAWK GONY SULA DUNCE
IDIOT LOSER PATCH PRIZE SILLY
SLEIGH STUPID CAMANAY PIQUERO
GOOSECAP
BOOBYALLA DOGWOOD
WATERBUSH
BOODLE LOOT SWAG CROWD GRAFT
BUDDLE NOODLE PAYOFF PLUNDER
CABOODLE
BOOGEYMAN PADFOOT
TANKERABOGUS
BOOJUM SNARK
BOOK MO LIL LOG CHAP CODE FORM
HEFT OPUS PAGE TEXT TOME
ALBUM ALDUS BIBLE CANON CANTO
CODEX DETUR DIARY DIVAN ENTER

FLETA FOLIO FROST GUIDE KITAB
LIBEL LIBER QUAIR QUIRE RAZEE
ZOHAR ALDINE ANONYM BODONI
CURSUS DOCKET ENGAGE HERBAL
LEDGER MAHZOR MANUAL MISSAL
NUMBER REBIND RECORD RITUAL
SCHOOL TICKET TROPER VOLUME
BLOTTER CATALOG COUCHER
DIETARY DISCARD FEODARY
GARLAND GRAMMAR JOURNAL
LAWBOOK LEXICON MANDALA
OCTAPLA OMNIBUS ORDINAL
OUTBOOK PEERAGE RECITER
SAMHITA SERVICE SLEEPER SPEAKER
SPELLER SYNAXAR TERRIER TICKLER
TRAVAIL TRIGLOT TYPICON TYPICUM
WRITING BANKBOOK BROCHURE
CALCULUS CASEBOOK CASHBOOK
CHAPBOOK COOKBOOK COPYBOOK
DECRETAL DOCUMENT FESTIVAL
GIFTBOOK GOSPELER HANDBOOK
HARDBACK HERDBOOK JESTBOOK
JUVENILE LIBRETTO PASTORAL
POMANDER POSTBOOK REGISTER
SONGBOOK STUDBOOK SYNAXARY
TALEBOOK TRIODION TWENTYMO
VESPERAL PAPERBACK PONTIFICAL
NOMENCLATOR PROCESSIONAL
PHARMACOPOEIA
(— BACK) DORSE
(— FOR HARVARD GRADUATE)
DETUR
(— OF CHARTS) WAGONER
PORTOLAN
(— OF DEVOTIONS) ORARIUM
(— OF HERALDRY) ARMORY
ARMORIAL
(— OF HOMILIES) POSTIL
(— OF MAPS) ATLAS
(— OF PSALMS) PSALTER TEHILLIM
(— OF RULES) HOYLE
(— OF SERVICES) PIE
(— OF SOLUTIONS) KEY
(— OF THE MASS) ORDO
(— SECTION) OCTAVO QUARTO
(—S KEPT IN PRINT) BACKLIST
(— THAT DOESN'T SELL) PLUG
(CHEAP —) BLOOD
(CHINESE —) CHING
(COMIC —) COMIX
(COMMONPLACE —) ADVERSARIA
(ELEMENTARY —) PRIMER
(FIRST READING —) ABC ABCEE
ABSEY
(FOLDED —) ORIHON
(HOLY —) VEDA
(IMPROPER —S) FACETIAE
(INSTRUCTION —) METHOD
(JOKE —) JOE JESTBOOK
(LOST HEBREW —) JASHAR JASHER
(MEMORANDUM —) AGENDA
JOTTER TICKLER
(MINIATURE —) BIBELOT

(PART OF —) CASE FLAP COVER
HINGE JOINT SPINE TITLE JACKET
LINING ENDLEAF BACKBONE
ENDPAPER HEADBAND BACKSTRIP
SHELFBACK
(PRAYER —) PORTAS SIDDUR
PORTASS PORTHORS
(READING —) ABC ABCEE ABSEY
(RECORD —) LIBER TICKLER
(RELIGIOUS —) KITAB KORAN QURAN
GOSPEL HORARY KYRIAL PROSAR
GRADUAL KYRIALE BREVIARY
MEGILLAH ORDINARY SYNAXARY
(SACRED —) KORAN QURAN PURANA
(SERVICE —) COMES GRAIL TEXTUS
(SLOW-SELLING —) PLUG
(STRANGE —S) CURIOSA
(UNBOUND —) CAHIER
(PL.) LIBRI SHELF STUDY EROTICA
SCRIPTURE
(PREF.) BIBLIO LIBRI
BOOKBINDING STUB YAPP STRING
BOOKBINDINNG LAWCALF
BOOKCASE DESK STAGE STALL
SCRINE PLUTEUS CREDENZA
BOOK COVER LID SIDE FOREL
RECTO VERSO FORREL REVERSE
REVERSO
BOOKISH BOOKY ERUDITE INKHORN
PEDANTIC STUDIOUS
BOOKLET FOLDER NOVELET
BROCHURE
BOOK LOUSE PSOCID
BOOKMAKER LAYER BOOKER
BOOKIE
BOOKMARK MARKER TASSEL
REGISTER
BOOK PALM TARA TALIERA
BOOKSELLER STATIONER
BIBLIOPOLE
BOOKSHELF DESK PLUTEUS
(PL.) CLASSIS
BOOKWORM GOME GRUB NERD
TOOL WONK CEREB GNURD GRIND
SQUID SPIDER WEENIE
BOOM JIB BEAM BOMB BUMP CRIB
POLE ROAR SPAR BRAIL CHAIN
CRANE CROON PROBE BUMPKIN
CATHEAD CURTAIN RESOUND
SUPPORT BOWSPRIT FLOURISH
(CRANE —) ARM GIB JIB
BOOMBOX (SOUND FROM —)
BLARE
BOOMER TNT
BOOMERANG KALIE KILEY KYLIE
WANGO ATLATL BOUNCE RECOIL
LEEWILL REBOUND WOMERAH
WOOMERA BACKFIRE HORNERAH
LEEANGLE RICOCHET TROMBASH
BOOMING HUMMING ROARING
BOOM IRON WITHE CRANCE
BOON GAY BENE GIFT GOOD KIND
BOUND FAVOR GRANT MERRY

ORDER BENIGN BOUNTY GOODLY
JOVIAL PRAYER BENEFIT COMMAND
PRESENT BLESSING INTIMATE
PETITION BENEFACTION

BOONDOCKS STICKS BOONIES

BOOR CAD OAF BOER BORE CARL
HICK JACK KERN LOUT PILL RUNT
SLOB CARLE CHUFF CHURL CLOWN
KERNE SLAVE BUMKIN CARLOT
CLUNCH HOBLOB JOBSON JOSKIN
LUBBER LUMMOX RUSTIC BUMPKIN
CAUBOGE GROBIAN PEASANT
VILLAIN BOEOTIAN BOSTHOON
CLODHOPPER

BOORISH ILL RUDE CRASS GAWKY
ROUGH RUNTY SURLY CLUMSY
RUSTIC SAVAGE SULLEN VULGAR
WOOLEN AWKWARD CRABBED
HIRSUTE HOBLIKE KERNISH LOUTISH
PEAKISH ROISTER UNCOUTH VILLAIN
WOOLLEN BOEOTIAN CARTERLY
CHURLISH CLODDISH CLOWNISH
LUBBERLY SWAINISH TACTLESS
UNGAINLY

BOORISHNESS VILLAINY
GROBIANISM

BOOST AID LEG ABET BACK BOOM
HELP LIFT PLUG PUSH COACH EXALT
HOIST HOOSH RAISE ASSIST
ADVANCE COMMEND ELEVATE
ENDORSE PROMOTE INCREASE

BOOT PAC PAD USE CURE GAIN HALF
HELP HOOF KICK PUNT SHOE SOCK
AVAIL BOOTY DERBY EJECT EVICT
JEMMY KAMIK PEWEE SPOIL BOOTEE
BUDGET BUSKIN CASING CHUKKA
CRAKOW ENRICH FUMBLE GAITER
GALOSH INSHOE JEMIMA JOCKEY
MUKLUK PEDULE SHEATH BENEFIT
BOTTINE COTHURN COWHIDE
CRUISER HESSIAN HIGHLOW
SEABOOT SHOEPAC VANTAGE
BALMORAL BOTTEKIN CHASSURE
COVERING FINNESKO JACKBOOT
LARRIGAN NAPOLEON COTHURNUS
WAFFLESTOMPER

(— OF CARRIAGE) FOREBOOT
(— ON SADDLE) GAMBADE
GAMBADO
(CAR —) BUSTLE
(CLIMBING —) SCARPETTO
(HALF —) PAC BUSKIN COCKER
SKILTY BRODEKIN
(HIKING —) WAFFLESTOMPER
(HOB-NAILED —) BAT
(HORSE'S —) SCALPER
(KIND OF —) DENVER
(LUMBERMAN'S —) CRUISER
(MARINE —) SKINHEAD
(RIDING —) JEMMY JIMMY JODHPUR
(SEALSKIN —) KAMIK
(STOUT —) STOGA STOGY
(TO —) ALSO

(TORTURE —) SQUEEZER
(WATERPROOF —) WADER
(PL.) OVERS WADER FINNESKO
HESSIANS

BOOTBLACK SHINER BLACKER
SHOEBOY

BOOTED OCREATE

BOOTES WAINMAN HERDSMAN

BOOTH BOX BULK COOP DESK LOGE
SHED SHOP SOOK BOTHY CABIN
CRAME HOUSE KIOSK LIWAN LODGE
PITCH SLANG STALL STAND BOTHAN
PAGODA PANDAL PAYBOX SUCCAH
SUKKAH TIENDA BALAGAN
COCKSHY TABERNA

BOOTLACE LACET THONG

BOOTLEG SHY SLY ILLEGAL ILLICIT

BOOTY BOOT FANG GAIN LOOT PELF
PREY SACK SWAG BUTIN CHEAT
FORAY GRAFT PRIZE CREAGH FLEECE
SPOILS DESPOIL PILLAGE PLUNDER
SPREAGH SPREATH STEALTH
PURCHASE SPULLZIE STEALAGE

DOOZE BOLL BOUT BUDGE DRINK
HOOCH SPREE FUDDLE LIQUOR

BOOZY TIPPLE LIQUORY

BOP POP JIVE DANCE SHUFFLE

BOPHUTHATSWANA
(CAPITAL OF —) MMABATHO
(TOWN OF —) TEMBA MABOPANE
GARANKUWA

BORAGE ANCHUSA

BORAX FLUX TINCAL
(— SOURCE) KERNITE

BORDER CUT HEM RIM TAB ABUT
BABK BRIM CURB DADO EAVE EDGE
LIMB LINE LIST LOVE MARK NARK
ORLE RAND ROON RUND SIDE TRIM
WELL WELT BOARD BOUND BRAID
BRINK CHEEK COAST COSTA DRAFT
FILET FLANK FOREL FRAME FRILL
GUARD LIMIT MARCH MARGE MARLI
PLAIT SHORE SKIRT STRIP SWAGE
TOUCH VERGE ACCOST ADJOIN
COTISE EDGING FILLET FORREL
FRINGE IMPALE LACING LIMBUS
LISERE MARGIN ORFRAY PURFLE
QUADRA SCREED STRIPE TANIKO
WEEPER CONFINE DRAUGHT FIMBRIA
FLOROON MARGENT SELVAGE
VALANCE BOUNDARY DOUBLING
FRONTIER MARCHESE NEIGHBOR
OUTSKIRT PLATBAND SKIRTING
SURROUND TERMINUS TRESSOUR
TRESSURE
(— OF EXTERNAL EAR) HELIX
(— OF LACE) PICOT
(— OF ROCK) SALBAND
(— OF SAIL) DOUBLING
(— OF SHIELD) BORDURE
(— OF STREAM) RUND
(— ON) ABUT ACCOST AFFRONT
NEIGHBOR

(FLOWERED —) FLOROON
(ORNAMENTAL —) PURL WAGE FRAME FRINGE MATTING DENTELLE TRESSURE
(RIBBON —) FRILAL
(PL.) CONFIN PURLIEU CONFINS
(PREF.) CRASPEDO LIMBI
BORDERED ORLE LIMBATE
BORDERER MARCHMAN
BORDERING MARGENT FRONTIER
BORDERLAND BOUNDS
(— OF HELL) LIMBO
BORE BIT CUT EAT IRK JET TAP DRAG FLAT HOLE JUMP PALL PILL POKE REAM RUSH SINK SIZE TIDE TIRE TOOL ANNOY AUGER CHINK DRILL EAGRE ENNUI GAUGE GOUGE OUGHT PLONK PRICK PUNCH SUGUR TEWEL THIRL TRICK VAPOR WEARY BEFOOL CANNON GIMLET PIERCE THRILL THRUST TUNNEL WIMBLE YAWNER BROMIDE CALIBER CALIBRE CONCAVE CREVICE HUMDRUM NUDNICK OPENING AIGUILLE CAPILLUS DIAMETER DRAWBORE GRATIANO POROROCA
(— OF CANNON) SOUL CHASE
(PREF.) FORAMINI
BOREAL NORTHERN
BOREAS AQUILO AQUILON
(BROTHER OF —) NOTUS HESPERUS ZEPHYRUS
(DAUGHTER OF —) CLEOPATRA
(FATHER OF —) ASTRAEUS
(MOTHER OF —) EOS AURORA
(SON OF —) ZETES CALAIS
BORED BLASE HOHUM WEARY ENNUYE TEDIOUS SATIATED
BOREDOM YAWN BLAHS ENNUI ACEDIA TEDIUM
(FEELING OF —) BLAHS
BORELE KEITLOA UPEYGAN
BORER MOLE BARDEE WIMBLE HAGFISH TANBARK TERMITE TERRIER FLATHEAD SHIPWORM WOODWORM
(PREF.) TRYPAN(O)
BORING DIM DRY FLAT SLOW HOHUM BROACH STODGY STUPID TIRING LUMPISH TEDIOUS PIERCING TIRESOME TEREBRANT
(— TOOL) AUGER GIMLET WIMBLE AIGUILLE
(SOMETHING —) DRAG
BORIS GODUNOV (CHARACTER IN —) BORIS PIMEN DMITRY GRIGORY MISSAIL RANGONI SHUISKY VARLAAM
(COMPOSER OF —) MUSSORGSKY
BORN N NEE NATE INNATE NASCENT NATURAL UTERINE ORIGINAL
(— OUT OF WEDLOCK) BASTARD
(NEWLY —) NEONATE

(NOBLY —) GENEROUS
(PREMATURELY —) SLINK ABORTIVE
(WELL —) FREE EUGENIC
(SUFF.) GEN(E)(ESIA)(ESIS)(ETIC)(IC)(IN)(OUS)(Y)
BORNE RODE NARROW CARRIED ENDURED
(— AFFRONTEE) CABOCHED
(— LOWER THAN USUAL) ABASED
(— ON WATER) AFLOAT
(WIND —) EOLIAN

BORNEO
BAY: ADANG KUMAI SAMPIT
CAPE: ARU DATU LOJAR PUTING SAMBAR SELATAN
MOUNTAIN: RAJA SARAN NIJAAN TEBANG
MOUNTAINS: IRAN MULLER SCHWANER
NAME: KALIMANTAN
NATIVE: DYAK DAJAK
RIVER: ARUT IWAN BAHAU BERAU KAJAN PADAS PAWAN BARITO KAPUAS SEBUKU KAHAJAN MAHAKAM MENDAWI PEMBUANG
TOWN: KUMAI SAMBAS SAMPIT MALINAU PAGATAN SANGGAU SINTANG TARAKAN KETAPANG
TREE: KAPOR KAPUR
WEIGHT: PARA CHAPAH

BORO MARIANA
BORON BORAX ULEXITE
BORORO COROADO
BOROUGH BURG CITY PORT TOWN WICK BORGO BRUSH BURGH CASTLE COUNTY CITADEL FORTESS VILLAGE TOWNSHIP
(SUFF.) BURG
BORROW BOT BITE COPY HIRE KICK LOAN SHIN TAKE THIG ADOPT STEAL TOUCH DESUME DUPLEX PLEDGE STRIKE SURETY CHEVISE HOSTAGE MUTUATE TITHING
BORROWED SECONDHAND
BORROWER BOT CRIB MUTUARY
BORROWING ECLECTIC
BORS (BROTHER OF —) BAN
(UNCLE OF —) LANCELOT
BORSCHT
(— INGREDIENT) BEETS
BOS OX NEAT TAURUS
BOSH END ROT JOKE SHOW TALK TOSH FUDGE TRASH BUSHWA FIGURE FLAUNT HUMBUG TRIVIA HOGWASH TOSHERY GALBANUM NONSENSE POPPYCOCK
BOSKY BUSHY TIPSY WOODY FUDDLED
BOSNIA & HERZEGOVINA (ALSO SEE YUGOSLAVIA)
CAPITAL: SARAJEVO

COIN: DINAR
LANGUAGE: BOSNIAN
  SERBOCROATIAN
MOUNTAIN: MAGLIC
MOUNTAIN RANGE: GRMEC CINCAR
  RADUSA VITOROG KLEKOVACA
  PLJESIVICA
PEOPLE: SERB SLAV CROAT
RIVER: UNA SAVA BOSNA DRINA
  VRBAS NERETVA
SEA: ADRIATIC
TOWN: MOSTAR RAGUSA BANJALUKA
  DUBROVNIK
BOSNIA-HERZEGOVINA (RIVER
  OF —) BOSNA DRINA NERETVA
  (TOWN OF —) TUZLA MAGLAJ
  MOSTAR VISOKO SARAJEVO
BOSOM LAP BARM BUST CLOSE
  DICKY HEART SINUS BREAST CAVITY
  DESIRE DICKEY RECESS BELOVED
  EMBRACE GREMIAL INCLOSE
  INTIMATE POITRINE
  (— OF DRESS) SQUARE
  (FALSE —) PLUMPER
BOSS BUR HUB MOD NOD ORD PAD
  POP BAAS BEAD BOCE BUHR BURR
  CAPO COCK CZAR KNOB KNOP KNOT
  NAIL NAVE NULL STUD TSAR BULLA
  BULLY BWANA CHIEF EMPTY JEWEL
  KNOSP ORDER OWNER PEARL
  ANCHOR BROOCH BUCKRA BUTTON
  CHEESE DIRECT HOLLOW HONCHO
  MANAGE MASTER OCULUS PATERA
  PELLET SHIELD BULLION CACIQUE
  CAPATAZ CAPTAIN CUSHION
  FOREMAN HASSOCK HEADMAN
  HOBNAIL MANAGER PADRONE
  PHALERA SPANGLE SPONSON
  DIRECTOR DOMINATE DOMINEER
  MISERERE OMPHALOS OVERSEER
  UMBILICUS
  (— OF LOGGING CAMP) BULLY
  (— OF SHIELD) UMBO
  (FIRE —) GASMAN
  (LEATHER —) BUTTON
  (MINE —) SHIFTER SHIFTMAN
  (POLITICAL —) CACIQUE CAUDILLO
  (STRAW —) BULL LEADER
  (PREF.) UMBO
BOSSY PUSHY
BOSTONIAN HUBBITE
BOT OESTRUM OESTRUS
BOTANIST HERBALIST HERBARIAN
  AMERICAN AMES BEAL COOK GRAY
  HOWE ROSE BROWN CLUTE GAGER
  HEALD JAMES JONES LOGAN
  MOORE PURSH SEARS SHULL SMALL
  VASEY BAILEY BESSEY CANNON
  CARVER CUTLER DUDLEY DUGGAR
  FARLOW HARRIS HOWELL JEPSON
  LEMMON PEIRCE SHANTZ TAYLOR
  TORREY WATSON BARTRAM
  BIGELOW BRITTON COULTER

CROCKER ELLIOTT FERNALD
GOODALE HOLLICK JOHNSON
MERRILL PEATTIE POLLARD RYDBERG
SWINGLE THURBER CALDWELL
CAMPBELL COPELAND KNOWLTON
MARSHALL TRELEASE BLAKESLEE
FAIRCHILD LONGWORTH
NIEUWLAND OSTERHOUT
SULLIVANT UNDERWOOD
CHAMBERLAIN
  AUSTRIAN UNGER KERNER MENDEL
  JACQUIN HABERLANDT
  BELGIAN LINDEN
  CANADIAN SAUNDERS
  DANISH HANSEN WARMING
  JOHANNSEN RAUNKIAER
  DUTCH TREUB DODOENS
  ENGLISH WARD BOWER BUDDLE
  CLARKE DARWIN GERARD HOOKER
  HUDSON MARTYN PAXTON TURNER
  BENNETT FORSYTH HAWORTH
  HENSLOW JACKSON LINDLEY
  DRYANDER SIBTHORP BABINGTON
  FRENCH BORNET MAGNOL MIRBEL
  THURET TRECUL BONNIER JUSSIEU
  LECLUSE MICHAUX TULASNE
  DECAISNE MILLARDET JACQUEMONT
  TOURNEFORT VANTIEGHEM
  DESFONTAINES
  GERMAN BOCK COHN KOCH LINK
  MOHL ZINN BLUME DRUDE FUCHS
  KUNTH SACHS ENGLER GLOXIN
  GMELIN GOEBEL HEDWIG KUNTZE
  MIGULA REINKE CORRENS EICHLER
  FITTING GARTNER JUNGIUS
  KARSTEN KUTZING MOLISCH
  PFEFFER RIVINUS WARBURG
  BRUNFELS LEDEBOUR LONITZER
  SPRENGEL DILLENIUS GRISEBACH
  KOLREUTER CAMERARIUS
  HOFMEISTER PRINGSHEIM
  REICHENBACH STRASBURGER
  HUNGARIAN ENDLICHER
  IRISH HARVEY
  ITALIAN TONI CORTI ALPINI BECCARI
  CESALPINO
  JAPANESE IKENO
  NORWEGIAN GUNNERUS
  RUSSIAN BUNGE FAMINTSYN
  SCOTTISH AITON BROWN DOUGLAS
  FORTUNE MORISON FALCONER
  SPANISH CAVANILLES
  SWEDISH DAHL KALM FRIES RETZIUS
  ACHARIUS AFZELIUS LINNAEUS
  THUNBERG ANDERSSON
  BROMELIUS
  SWISS BAUHIN VAUCHER CANDOLLE
BOTANY HERBARISM PHYTOLOGY
BOTCH MAR MUX BOIL BOSS FLUB
  MEND MESS MULL SORE BITCH
  BODGE BUTCH FLUFF FUDGE SPOIL
  STICK BOGGLE BOLLIX DUMDLE
  BUNGLE COBBLE JUMBLE MUCKER

REPAIR TINKER BLUNDER BUTCHER
CLAMPER SCAMBLE SCLATCH
SLUBBER SWELLING
BOTCHER GRILSE SALMON TINKER
BUNGLER BUTCHER CLOUTER
COBBLER
BOTCHERY PATCHERY
BOTE KINBOT MAGBOTE CARTBOTE
FRITHBOT PLOWBOTE WAINBOTE
BOTFLY BOTT BREEZE GADBEE
GADFLY NITTER CANOPID OESTRID
TORSALO DIPTERAN OESTRIAN
BOTH BO ALL TWO BAITH EQUALLY
(PREF.) AMBI AMBO AMPH(I)(O) BIS
(— SIDES) AMPHI
BOTHER ADO AIL BUG IRK NAG VEX
FASH FAZE FUSS JADE WORK
ANNOY DEAVE HARRY KNOCK PHASE
TEASE TRADE WORRY BADGER
BUSTLE CUMBER DITHER FLURRY
GRAVEL HARASS HASSLE MEDDLE
MITHER MOIDER MOLEST MUCKLE
PESTER PLAGUE POTHER POTTER
PUTTER PUZZLE TAMPER CONFUSE
DISTURB FASHERY GRIZZLE PERPLEX
TERRIFY TRACHLE TROUBLE
BEWILDER DISTRESS IRRITATE
NUISANCE
BOTOCUDO BORUN AIMORE
AYMORO
BOTONEE TREFLEE FLEURONE
BO TREE PIPAL

BOTSWANA
CAPITAL: GABORONE GABERONES
COIN: PULA RAND THEBE
DESERT: KALAHARI
LAKE: DOW NGAMI
LANGUAGE: BANTU CLICK KHOISAN
  SETSWANA
MONEY: PULA THEBE
MOUNTAIN: TSODILO
NATIVE: BANTU TSWANA BUSHMAN
RIVER: NATA OKWA CHOBE NOSOB
  CUANDO MOLOPO SHASHI
  CUBANGO LIMPOPO OKAVANGO
TOWN: KANYE ORAPA TSANE SEROWE
  LOBOTSI MOCHUDI PALAPYE
  THAMAGA GABERONES

BOTTLE JUG BOSS SKIN VIAL VIOL
AMPUL ASKOS BETTY BOCAL BUIRE
BURET CADUS COOJA CROFT CRUET
CRUSE FIFTH FLASK GIRBA GLASS
GOURD HOUSE PHIAL SPLIT VERRE
ALUDEL BACBUC BUNDLE CARAFE
CARBOY CASTER CASTOR CHAGUL
CHATTY CREWET DORUCK DUBBER
FESSEL FIASCO FLACON FLAGON
GOGLET GUTTUS JORDAN LAGENA
MAGNUM MARINE MATARA NURSER
PACKER SIPHON VESSEL WOULFF
BALLOON BIBERON BOMBARD

BOMBOLA BURETTE CANTEEN
CARAFON COSTREL DEADMAN
FLACKET FLOATER GRENADE
INKHORN BOMBONNE BORACHIO
BUILDING CALABASH DECANTER
DEMIJOHN GARDEVIN JEROBOAM
MARIOTTE PRESERVE REHOBOAM
PEPPERBOX
(— IN WICKER) CARBOY DEMIJOHN
(EGYPTIAN —) DORUCK
(EMPTY —) MARINE
(HOT-WATER —) PIG
(LARGE —) KIT JEROBOAM
(LEATHER —) BOOT JACK DUBBA
BUDGET DUBBER DUPPER MATARA
BOMBARD BORACHIO WHINNOCK
WINESKIN
(MEDICINE —) VIAL PHIAL
(OVERSIZED —) BALTHAZAR
(PAIR OF —S) GEMEL GEMMEL
(PART OF —) LIP CORK KICK NECK
PUNT MOUTH MUZZLE CAPSULE
SHOULDER
(PILGRIM'S —) AMPULLA
(SMALL —) VIAL AMPUL CRUET
PHIAL SPLIT FLACON AMPOULE
TICKLER CRUISKEN CRUISKEEN
(18 —S OF WINE) RIDDLE
(40 —S) KEMPLE
(PREF.) UTRI
BOTTLE CAP CAPSULE
BOTTLE CARRIER FASCET
BOTTLE CASE CELLAR
BOTTLEHEAD DOEGLING
BOTTLER COOPER
BOTTOM ASS BED ARSE BASE DALE
DOUP FLAT FOND FOOT FUND HOLM
LEES REAR ROOT ABYSS BASIS
DREGS FLOOR LAIGH NADIR BATHOS
FOUNCE FUNDUS GROUND GUTTER
LAAGTE LEEGTE BEDROCK LOWLAND
SUPPORT SURFACE BUTTOCKS
INTERVAL SEDIMENT TETRAPOD
(— LINE) NET
(— OF BENCH) TOE
(— OF CUPOLA) HEARTH
(— OF FURROW) SOLE
(— OF GRATE) NIGGARD
(— OF PAGE) TAIL
(— OF PISTOL GRIP) BUTT
(— OF POT) POTSTONE
(— OF PRINTER'S GALLEY) SLICE
(— OF PULLEY BLOCK) BREECH
(— OF SEA) GROUND BENTHOS
(— OF SOLE) NAUMK NAUMKEAG
(— OF STACK) STADDLE
(MARSHY —) SIKE
(ROCK —) HARDPAN
(PL.) HOLM HOLME
BOTTOM-DWELLING DEMERSAL
BOTTOMER FOOTMAN
STATIONMAN
BOTTOMLAND STRATH

BOTTOMLESS ABYSMAL
BOTTOM LINE CRUX UPSHOT
OUTCOME SUMMARY CONCLUSION
BOTULISM I AMSIEKTE LAMZIEKTE
BOUDOIR ROOM BOWER CABIN
BEDROOM CABINET
BOUGH ARM LEG LIMB TWIG CHUCK
SHOOT SPRAY SPRIG BRANCH
RAMAGE SHROUD GALLOWS
PHYLLIS OFFSHOOT SHOULDER
(— ON TAVERN) BUSH
(— USED AS TORCH) ROUGHIE
(DRY —) ROUGHY ROUGHIE
(PL.) RAMAGE DUNNAGE RAMMAGE
BOUGHT KEFT STORE ZEBINA
BOUGIE CANDLE COLLYRIE FILIFORM
BOUILLABAISSE POTPOURRI
BOULDER NOB KELK KNOB ROCK
STONE GIBBER BOOTHER DORNICK
ERRATIC GRAYBACK HARDHEAD
MEGALITH POTSTONE
BOULE BIRNE
BOULEVARD DRIVE PRADO AVENUE
STREET ALAMEDA HIGHWAY
TERRACE CORNICHE
BOULTER TRAWL SPILLER SPILLET
BOUNCE DAP BANG BLOW
BRAG BUMP DING DIRD FIRE GATE
JUMP LEAP OUST SACK STOT BOAST
BOUND BULLY CAROM CHUCK EJECT
KNOCK SCOLD THUMP VERVE
BLAGUE MORGAY SPIRIT SPRING
STRIKE ADDRESS BLUSTER
CHOUNCE DISMISS REBOUND
SWAGGER PINGPONG PROCLAIM
RICOCHET
(— A BABY) DANDLE
(— BACK) RECOVER
BOUNCER BUMPER CHUCKER
SCROUGER
BOUNCING BIG BUXOM LUSTY
STOUT BOUNCY HEALTHY
WALLOPING
(— OF TONGUE) FLAP
BOUNCING BET SOAPWORT
BOUND DAP END HOP LOP BENT
BIND BOND BONE BROW BUTT DART
GIRT JUMP LEAP LIST MERE RAMP
RISE SCUD SKIP STEM STOT SURE
TERM WALL AMBIT BORNE BOURN
FIXED GOING LIMIT READY SALLY
SCOUP SKELP START STEND STING
TILED VAULT VERGE BORDER
BOUNCE BOURNE BUTTAL CAVORT
CURVET DEFINE DOMAIN FINISH
GAMBOL GIRDED HURDLE JETTED
LIABLE LOLLOP OBLIGE PRANCE
SPRING AFFINED BARRIER CERTAIN
CHAINED CLOSURE CONFINE
CONTAIN COSTIVE DELIMIT DRESSED
GAMBADO INCLUDE REBOUND
SALTATE OCCURED SUBSULT
TERMINE TRUSSED BOUNDARY

CONFINED DESTINED ENCLOSED
FASCIATE FRONTIER HANDFAST
LANDMARK LIMITATE OBLIGATE
PINIONED PRECINCT PREPARED
RESTRICT SHACKLED
(— ALONG) SLING
(— BY OATH) SWORN
(— BY OBLIGATION) AFFINED
(— CLUMSILY) LOLLOP
(NOT —) SOLUTE
(RIGIDLY —) STATIC STATICAL
(PL.) PALE AMBIT MOUND CLOSURE
COMPASS CONFINE PURLIEUS
PERIPHERY
BOUNDARY AHU END RIM DOLE
DOOL EDGE FINE FORM LINE LIST
MARK MEAR MEER MERE META
METE PALE SURF TERM TRIG WALL
AMBIT BOURN CLOSE FENCE FRAME
FRONT HEDGE LIMES LIMIT MARCH
MEITH MOUND SHORE VERGE
BORDER COLLET DEFINE OCTROI
OCTROY TROPIC BARRIER BOUNDER
BUTTING COMPASS FURLONG
OUTLINE CURBLINE FRONTIER
LANDLINE LIMITARY PRECINCT
TERMINUS UMSTROKE PERIMETER
PERIPHERY MAGNETOPAUSE
(— OF EARTH'S CRUST-MANTLE)
MOHO
(PL.) ABUTTALS ENVIRONS
(PREF.) HORO LIMI ORI TERMINO
(— OF AIR MASS) FRONTO TERMINO
BOUNDER CAD HARE RAKE ROUE
ROTTER
BOUNDING (— LINE) RUBICON
BOUNDLESS VAST UNTOLD
ENDLESS ETERNAL INFINITE
UNLIMITED
BOUNDLESSNESS INFINITY
BOUNTEOUS BOON CROWNED
LIBERAL PLENTEOUS
BOUNTIFUL GOOD LUSH RICH
AMPLE FREELY LAVISH LIBERAL
PROFUSE ABUNDANT GENEROUS
BOUNTY BOON GIFT MEED AWARD
BONUS GRANT LARGE VALOR
WORTH BONTEE REWARD VIRTUE
LARGESS PREMIUM PRESENT
PROWESS SUBSIDY DONATIVE
GOODNESS GRATUITY KINDNESS
BOUQUET BOB AURA ODOR POSY
AROMA BLOOM CIGAR POSEY SHEAF
SPRAY BOWPOT BUSKET SHOWER
CORSAGE NOSEGAY BOUGHPOT
(— GARNI) FAGOT FAGGOT
(DEVELOP —) BREATHE
BOURDON BURDEN
BOURGEOIS ORGON COMMON
POOTER STUPID BOORISH BURGHER
(KIND OF —) PETIT
BOURGEOIS GENTILHOMME
(AUTHOR OF —) MOLIERE

(CHARACTER IN —) CLEANTE LUCILLE COVIELLE JOURDAIN

BOURSE SALE BOLSA BORSE CAMBIO

BOURTREE ELDER

BOUT GO JOB BOOT FALL PULL TURN BOOZE BRASH CRASH ESSAY FIGHT MATCH PLUCK ROUND SCRAP SIEGE TRIAL VENNY VENUE ATTACK COURSE FRACAS YOKING ASSAULT ATTEMPT CAROUSE CIRCUIT CONTEST DEBAUCH OUTSIDE WITHOUT CONFLICT

(— OF INDULGENCE) JAG

(DRINKING —) BAT BEND BUST TIRL BOOZE SPRAY SPREE RANDAN SCREED SPLORE CAROUSE GAEDOWN WASSAIL POTATION

BOUTONNIERE BOUQUET BUTTONHOLE

BOUW BAHU BAHOE

BOVAARISM EGO

BOVATE OSKEN OXGANG OXGATE OXLAND

(TWO —S) HUSBANDLAND

BOVINE OX BOS COW BOSS BULL CALF DULL NEAT SLOW ZEBU BEAST BISON STEER ANIMAL COWISH HUMLIE HUMMEL OXLIKE ROTHER BULLOCK TAURINE BANGTAIL LEPTOBOS

BOW ARC LEG LUG NOD SAW TIE YEW ARCH BAIL BEAK BECK BEND BENT CURB DUCK FOLD FORE GORA JOUK KNEE KNOT LATH LOUT MOVE PROW SELF STEM SWIM TRUE TURN WEND BINGE CLINE CONGE COQUE COUCH CROOK CRUSH CURVE DEFER GOURA HONOR KNEEL NOEUD SHIKO STICK STOOP VENIE YIELD ARCHER ASSENT BAUBLE BUCKLE CONGEE CRINGE CROUCH CURTSY FIDDLE FOGBOW RIBBON SALAAM SALUTE SCRAPE SUBMIT SWERVE TOURTE WEAPON DEPRESS FOREBOW FORMBOW HANDBOW INCLINE INFLECT LONGBOW NECKTIE RAINBOW ARBALEST COURTESY CRESCENT ENTRANCE FOGEATER GREETING STONEBOW TRUELOVE OBEISANCE

(— DOWN) ALOUT HUMBLE

(— IN ONE PIECE) SELF

(— LOW) BINGE

(— OF PLOW) DRAIL

(— OF VESSEL) HEAD PROW STEM HAWSE ENTRANCE

(— ON SCRAPER) BAIL BALE

(— ON SEA) ATRY

(— OUTWARD) CONVEX

(— SLIGHTLY) ADDRESS

(OVERHANGING —) SWIM

(PART OF —) DIP TIP BACK FACE GRIP

LIMB LOOP NOCK BELLY BRIDGE HANDLE RECURVE SERVING BOWSTRING

(PART OF VIOLIN —) NUT TIP FROG HAIR HEAD POINT SCREW STICK

(WITH THE —) ARCO

(PREF.) ARCI ARCO TOX(I)(ICO)(O)

BOWDLERIZE EDIT

BOWED ARCO BENT BANDY KNEED ARCATE ARCATO CURVED BULGING CURVANT SHAMBLE DOWNBENT

(PREF.) TOX(I)(O)

BOWELS GUT GUTS WOMB BELLY COLON ROPES VISCERA ENTRAILS

(PREF.) VISCER(I)(O)

BOWER RUN BOOR JACK NOOK SALE ABODE ARBOR JOKER KNAVE ANCHOR BOWNY LEFSEL PANDAL BERCEAU CABINET CHAMBER COTTAGE EMBOWER ENCLOSE LEVESEL PERGOLA RETREAT SHELTER TRELLIS THALAMUS

(— FOR SNAKES) KISI

(GARDEN —) ALCOVE

BOWERBIRD CATBIRD COLLARBIRD

BOWFIN AMIA GANOID LAWYER MORGAY SAWYER CHOUPIC DOGFISH GRINDAL GRINDLE GRINNEL MUDFISH

BOWIE STATE ARKANSAS

BOWING CERNUOUS FEATHERING

BOWL CAP CUP PAN TUN COUP ROLL TASS TRAY WOOD ARENA BASIN BOWIE DEPAS GUARD JORUM KITTY LAVER MAZER PHIAL PITCH ROGAN SCALE TANOA TAZZA TREEN TROLL BEAKER BICKER CHAWAN CLOSET COOTIE CRATER FESSEL JICARA KETTLE LEKANE MAZARD MORTAR PIGGIN TROUGH TUREEN VESSEL BRIMMER DITCHER DOUBLER DUGGLER SCYPHOS SKYPHOS SPILLER STADIUM TOUCHER TRINDLE TRUNDLE WHISKIN AQUARIUM BRIDECUP FISHBOWL JEROBOAM LAVATORY MONTEITH REHOBOAM PORRINGER

(— ILLEGALLY) JERK

(— OF PIPE) CHILLUM STUMMEL

(— ON PEDESTAL) TAZZA SALVER

(— OUT) YORK

(— THAT TOUCHED JACK) TOUCHER

(— WITH TWO HANDLES) CAP DEPAS

(DRINKING —) TUN TASS

(MARBLE CUTTER'S —) SEBILLA

(OBLONG —) PITCHI

(PUNCH —) SNEAKER

(SHALLOW —) CAP COUPE WHISKIN

(SMALL —) JACK

(SOUP —) ECUELLE

(SUGAR —) SUGAR SUCRIER

(TOILET —) HOPPER

(WOODEN —) CAP BOWIE COGIE

KITTY ROGAN BASSIE BICKER
COGGIE COOTIE
BOWLEG OUTKNEE
BOWLEGGED BANDY VALGUS
BOWLER HAT POT DERBY KEGLER
PINMAN SPINNER TRUNDLER
(CRICKET —S) ATTACK
BOWLINE BOWLIN FARGOOD
BOWLING BOWLS ATTACK KEGLING
TENPINS
(— GAME) BOCCI
BOWLS RINK BOCCE ROCCIE
BOWMAN ARCHER
BOW-SHAPED ARCATE
BOWSPRIT SPAR
BOWSTRING SERVING
BOWYER BOWER ARTILLER
BOX BED BIN CAR EAR FUR GIG KIT
LOB LUG PIX PYX TYE ARCA BARK
BODY BOOT CAGE CAJA CASE CIST
CRIB CUFF CYST DRAB FLAT HEAD
LOGE MILL PACK PUNG SCOB SEAT
SLAP SLUG SPAR STOW TILL TRAY
ARBOR BARGE BIJOU BOIDT DUIST
BUXUS CADDY CAPSA CHEST CLOUT
CRATE FIGHT FRAME HUTCH LADLE
POUCH PUNCH SHRUB STALL TRUNK
ASCHAM BRUISE BUFFET BUNKER
CARTON CASKET COFFER COFFIN
DRAWER GRILLE HAMPER HATBOX
HAYBOX HOPPER ICEBOX MAROON
MOCUCK PATRON PETARA PILLAR
SAGGER SHRINE STRIKE TARBOX
VANITY ARCANUM BANDBOX
BATTERY BOXTREE BOXWOOD
CABINET CAISSON CARRIER
CASHBOX CASQUET CASSONE
COFFRET CONFINE COREBOX
DICEBOX DREDGER DUSTBOX
ENCLOSE EXHAUST FOSTELL
FREEZER HANAPER JACKBOX
PACKAGE PILLBOX PITARAH PRINTER
SANDBOX SCATULA SHELTER
TRUMMEL WHERRET BOXTHORN
DOVECOTE DRAGEOIR JUNCTION
LAVARIUM MATCHBOX POMANDER
SHOWCASE SLIPCASE SOLANDER
SWEATBOX PEPPERBOX
PHYLACTERY
(— FOR CARRYING COAL) DAN
(— FOR CARRYING ICE) YAKHDAN
(— FOR CLOTHES) PETARA PITARA
PITARAH
(— FOR COSMETICS) PUFFBOX
(— FOR CUTLERY) CANTEEN
(— FOR FIRE) CHAUFFER
(— FOR FISH) CAR NID
(— FOR MONEY OFFERING) ARCA
LADLE
(— FOR SALT) DRAB
(— FOR SEAL) SKIPPET
(— FOR SEED) LEAP
(— FOR TOBACCO) BUTT DOSS

CADDY SARATOGA
(— FOR TROUSSEAU) GLORYBOX
(— IN TIMEPIECE) BARREL
(— IN WHEEL HUB) FUR
(— OF BIRCHBARK) MOCUCK
(— OF CYLINDER) BUSH
(— OF FIRE CLAY) SAGGAR SAGGER
(— OF ORGAN) BOOT SWELL
(— SHAPED LIKE BOOK) SOLANDER
(— TO SHELTER BELL) SCONCE
(— USED AS DARKROOM) TENT
(BALLOT —) URN
(BERRY —) HALLOCK
(BREAD —) BARGE
(CANDLE —) BARK
(CIRCULAR —) THIMBLE
(COLLECTION —) BROD
(COMPASS —) KETTLE BINNACLE
(DICE —) RATTLE
(FANCY —) ETUI ETWEE
(FLOATING —) CAISSON
(FOUNDRY —) FRAME
(IRON —) HANGER
(JAPANESE —) INRO
(JUGGLER'S —) TRANKA
(KIND OF —) FUZZ READY
(MONEY —) CASH SAFE PIRLIE
(ORE —) SKIP
(PERFUME —) CASSOLETTE
(PIVOTING —) TOUR
(PRESENTATION —) COFFRET
(PRINTING —) TURTLE
(REFRIGERATOR —) COOLER
(SHADOW —) SPAR
(SHALLOW —) FLAT BACKET HARBOR
(SNUFF —) MILL MULL
(TEA —) CADDY
(TELEPHONE —) KIOSK
(TIN —) TRUMMEL VASCULUM
(WITNESS —) PETER STAND
(PREF.) CAPSULI CAPSULO CISTO
PYXID(O)
BOX BRIER INDIGO INKBERRY
BOXCAR LOWRY STOCKCAR
BOX ELDER MAPLE NEGUNDO
BOXER PUG CHAMP DARES BANTAM
MILLER NOBBER TANKER WELTER
BRUISER CRUISER FIGHTER
SLUGGER SPARRER BUFFETER
PUGILIST SOUTHPAW
BOXFISH CHAPIN COWFISH
SHELLFISH TRUNKFISH
BOXING PLUG RING FANCY SAVATE
PARINGS SCIENCE SPARRING
(— GLOVE) MUFFLE
(— JAB) LEFT RIGHT
BOXING-GLOVE CESTUS MUFFLE
BOX TORTOISE COOTER
BOXWOOD KNYSNA DUDGEON
BOXY BLOCKY
BOY BO BUB FAG GUY HIM LAD PUR
TAD BOYO CHAP LOON NINO PAGE
PUER BILLY BUBBY BUDDY CHABO

CHILD CRACK GAMIN GILPY GROOM
KNAVE PUTTO ROGUE SWAIN VALET
YOUTH BIRKIE BUTTON CALLAN
CHOKRA GAFFER GARCON MANNIE
MASTER NIPPER RASCAL SHAVER
STIRRA UMFAAN URCHIN BOUCHAL
CALLANT DRAWBOY GLEANER
GOSSOON GRUMMET JACKBOY
RUBBLER SERVANT SPADGER
TRAPPER CLERGION HENCHBOY
MUCHACHO SPALPEEN
(— DRESSED AS WOMAN) MALINCHE
(— IN LIVERY) TIGER
(— NOT YET 13) PRETEEN
(— OF FREE BIRTH) CAMILLUS
(ALTAR —) ACOLYTE THURIFER
(AWKWARD —) CUB CALF GRUMMET
(BABY —) NENE
(BLESSED —) BEATUS
(BOISTEROUS —) GILPY GILPEY
(BOLD —) SPALPEEN
(CHIMNEY SWEEPER'S —) CHUMMY
(CHOIR —) CHILD
(CLEANING —) BUSBOY
(COLLIER'S —) HODDER
(EFFEMINATE —) SISSY
MOLLYCODDLE
(ERRAND —) GALOPIN
(FIRST-YEAR —) GYTE
(FIRST YEAR —) GYTE
(GOOD OLD —) BUBBA
(HEAD —) SENIOR CAPTAIN
(HOMELESS —) ARAB
(ILL-MANNERED —) CUB
(LOVER —) ROMEO
(MESSENGER —) PAGE
(MISCHIEVOUS —) NICKUM
(MY —) AVICK
(NATIVE —) MOWGLI
(NON-JEWISH —) SHEGETZ
(OFFICE —) DUFTRY DUFTERY
(PERT —) CRACK
(POOR —) HERO
(ROGUISH —) CRACK GAMIN URCHIN
(SAUCY —) NACKET
(SERVING —) KNAVE PEDEE CHOKRA
MOUSSE FOOTBOY GOSSOON
(SILLY —) CALF
(SMALL —) BO BUDDY UMFAAN
SPADGER
(SPRIGHTLY —) CRACK
(STABLE —) MAFU MAFOO MEHTAR
(TEDDY —) DUCKTAIL
(TOWN —) CAD
(WINGED —) PUTTO
(YOUNG —) LAD SONNY YOUTH
NIPPER
(PL.) BOYHOOD
(PREF.) PAED(O) PAID(O) PED(O)
BOYCOTT MITE SHUN AVOID DEBAR
BLACKBALL
BOYFRIEND BEAU STEADY
BOYISH GAMIN GAMINE

BRA BANDEAU
BRABANTIO
(DAUGHTER OF —) DESDEMONA
BRACE DUO LEG MAN TIE TWO BEND
BIND CASE FRAP GIRD JACK KNEE
LACE MARK PAIR PROP SPUR STAY
STEM STUD CLAMP CRANK DWANG
GIRTH HOUND NERVE POISE RIDER
SHORE STEEL STOCK STRUT ANKLET
BINDER BRACHE CLENCH COLLAR
COUPLE CRUTCH FASTEN FATHOM
HURTER SPLINT STRING WIMBLE
BOTTINE BRACKET EMBRACE
REFRESH SPANNER STIFFEN
SUPPORT ACCOLADE BITBRACE
BITSTALK BITSTOCK BUTTRESS
CROSSBAR ENCIRCLE ORTHOTIC
(— ACROSS CABLE) STUD
(— AND HALF) LEASH
(— A YARD) TRAVERSE
(— BETWEEN FRAMES) TOM
(— FOR POST) SPUR
(— UP) ACCINGE SHARPEN
(PART OF —) BOW HEAD JAWS PAWL
RING CHUCK CRANK QUILL SHELL
HANDLE RATCHET
(PL.) BRIDGING
BRACED BENT
(— ABACK) ABOX
BRACELET BAND RING ARMIL CHAIN
ARMLET BANGLE GRIVNA ARMILLA
CIRCLET MANACLE POIGNET
RACETTE WRISTER BARRULET
HANDCUFF MUFFETEE WRISTLET
(— USED AS MONEY) MANILLA
(SHELL —) SANKHA
BRACER TONIC SHORER BLOCKER
ARMGUARD STIFFENER STIMULANT
BRACHIAL HUMERAL
BRACHIOPOD ATREMATE ATRYPOID
SPIRIFER
BRACHIUM ARM
BRACHYCEPHALIC ROUNDHEADED
BRACING CRISP QUICK TONIC
DUNNAGE
BRACKEN FERN TARA BRAKE PLAID
BRACKET BIBB COCK CONK FORK
GATE PUNK ANCON BELOW BRACE
CLASS CONCH COUCH CRANE
CRANK CROOK LEVEL SHELF STRUT
TRUSS ANCONE BECKET BRIDGE
CORBEL COUPLE GUSSET HANGER
LADDER MUTULE SADDLE SCONCE
BECKETT CONSOLE DERRICK
FEATHER FIXTURE GATELEG
LOOKOUT POTENCE SPONSON
SPOTTED BRAGWORT CATEGORY
CROTCHET MISERERE SPECKLED
STRADDLE MODILLION CANTILEVER
(PL.) HOOKS CROOKS
BRACKISH YAR FOIST SALTY
BRACKY SALINE BREACHY SALTISH
NAUSEOUS

BRACT HUSK LEAF GLUME LEMMA
PALEA PALET SCALE SPADIX SPATHE
BRACTLET PHYLLARY

DRACTEOLE PROPHYLL

BRAD PIN NAIL PRIG RIVET SPRIG

BRADAMANT
(BROTHER OF —) RINALDO
(HUSBAND OF —) ROGERO

BRAE BANK BRAY BROW HILL CLEVE
SLOPE WOUGH CLEEVE VALLEY

BRAG GAB JET BLAH BLAW BLOW
CROW DEFY FACE HUFF PUFF WIND
WOST YELP BLUFF BOAST CRACK
FLIRD PREEN SKITE STRUT VAUNT
BLEEZE BOUNCE INSULT SPLORE
SPROSE SQUIRT DISPLAY GAUSTER
ROISTER SWAGGER BRAGGART
FLOURISH PRETENSE THREATEN

BRAGGART BRAG PUFF BOAST
FACER BLOWER CROWER GASBAG
GASCON HECTOR POTGUN SKITER
THRASO BLOWOFF BOASTER
BOBADIL BOUNCER CRACKER
RUFFLER SHALLOW VAPORER
BANGSTER BLOWHARD CACAFUGO
FANFARON PAROLLES PUCKFIST
RENOWNER RODOMONT SKIPJACK

BRAGGARTISM COCKALORUM

BRAGGING ROOSE JACTANCE
RODOMONT THRASONIC

BRAHMA KA SELF BRAMAH

BRAHMAN ARYAN HINDU PUNDIT
SMARTA BRAHMIN

BRAID CUE BRAY GIMP JERK LACE
PLAT TAIL TRIM BREDE FANCY FREAK
JIFFY LACET MILAN ONSET ORRIS
PLAIT PLEAT QUEUE START TAGAL
TRACE TRADE TRESS TRICK TWINE
VOMIT WEAVE BOBBIN BORDER
CORDON EDGING GALLON LACING
MOMENT PLIGHT RIBBON RICRAC
SENNET SNATCH STRING BANDING
BULLION CAPRICE ENTWINE
UPBRAID BRANDISH ORNAMENT
REPROACH RICKRACK SOUTACHE
TRIMMING
(— FOR HATS) SENNET SINNET
(— OF WIG) SNAKE
(LINEN —) INKLE

BRAIDER RATCHER

BRAIDING FROG BREDE

BRAIDWORK LACET

BRAIN MAD BEAN HARN MIND PATE
UTAC WITS AXION HAIRN HAURN
SKULL GENIUS NODDLE PSYCHE
FURIOUS SENSORY THINKER
CEREBRUM HEADPIECE
(— WAVE PATTERN) THETA
(IN THE —) UPSTAIRS
(KIND OF —) PEA
(MUDDLED —) SMOKEJACK
(PART OF —) PONS CORTEX FORNIX
THALAMUS VENTRICLE

(PL.) HARN PATE SCONCE HEADPIECE
(PREF.) CEREBELLI CEREBELLO
CEREBR(I)(O) ENCEPHAL(O)
(SUFF.) ENCEPHALIA ENCEPHALUS
ENCEPHALY

BRAINCHILD IDEA

BRAINLESS SILLY STUPID FOOLISH
WITLESS

BRAINPAN PAN HARNPAN PANNICLE

BRAIN SAND SABULUM

BRAIZE BECKER

BRAKE COW BULL BURR CAGE CLOG
CURB DRAG FERN LOCK RACK SKID
SLOW STAY TARA TRAP TRIG BLOCK
CHECK COPSE DELAY DETER GRIPE
SNARE SPOKE SPRAG VOMIT BRIDLE
CONVOY HARROW HINDER REMORA
RETARD STAYER WARABI BRACKEN
DEADMAN DILEMMA SLIPPER
STOPPER THICKET TRIGGER
DRAGROPE RETARDER
(— PART) DISC SHOE

BRAKEMAN GUARD SHACK SHAKE
BRAKIE NIPPER DILLIER SNAPPER
SWAMPER DILLYMAN INCLINER
TRAINMAN

BRAKES ANCHORS

BRAMBLE WHIN BRIER RHAMN THIEF
THORN BUMBLE JAGGER LAWYER
STICKER DEWBERRY MAYBERRY
NESSBERRY
(PREF.) BATO

BRAMBLE BUSH TUTU GRANJENO

BRAMBLING KATE SNOWHAMMER

BRAMBLY DUMAL SPINY THORNY
PRICKLY

BRAN GRIT SEED DARAK TREAT
CEREAL CHESIL CHISEL POLLARD
TOPPING BEESWING
(— AND MEAL) SHORTS
(CORNMEAL —) HUSK
(FINE —) POLLEN
(UNSORTED —) RUBBLES
(PREF.) PITYRO

BRANCH ARM BOW COW KOW LAP
LEG LOP RAY RUN BARB BROG BUSH
CHAT FANG FORK LIMB PALM PART
RAME RICE RISE SNAG SNUG SPUR
STEM STUD TANG TWIG YARD AXITE
BAYOU BOUGH BREAK BRIAR BRIER
CREEK DRUPA GRAIN LAYER LULOV
PLASH PRONG RAMUS REISE SCROG
SHOOT SHRAG SPRAY SPRIG STICK
TWIST VIMEN WITHE BUREAU
CLADUS DIVIDE DRUPKA EXOPOD
GERMEN GREAVE GROWTH LEADER
MEMBER OFFSET OUTLET PHYLUM
PORTIO RADDLE RAMAGE RAMIFY
RUNNER SHROUD SPRANG STOLON
STREAM TAPOUN CHAPTER
CLADODE DIALECT DIVERGE
ENDOPOD FURCATE LATERAL
PHYLLIS RAMULUS TENDRIL

TORRENT ANAPHYTE BRONCHUS
DISTRICT EFFLUENT OFFSHOOT
PEASTICK SCAFFOLD SPRANGLE
TRAILING PHYLLOCLADE
RAMIFICATION
(— OF ANTLER) SPELLER ADVANCER
(— OF COLONY) STIPE
(— OF CRAFT) INDUSTRY
(— OF FAMILY) SEPT
(— OF FEATHER) BARB
(— OF HORN) RIAL ANTLER
(— OF IVY) BUSH
(— OF LEARNING) ART STUDY
FACULTY KNOWLEDGE
(— OF MATHEMATICS) ALGEBRA
CALCULUS
(— OF THALLUS) STICHID
(— OF TREASURY) FISCUS
(DEAD —) FLAG
(EVERGREEN —S) GREENS
(LANGUAGE —) INDIC
(LOCAL —) COURT
(MINE —) LEADER
(PALM —) LULAB
(RAILWAY —) LYE
(SHORT THICK —) STUMP
(SLENDER —) WHIP
(SMALL —) RICE
(YOUNGER —) CADET
(PL.) LOFT RAMI SKIRT SPRAY
RAMAGE CYPRESS DEADWOOD
(PREF.) CLON(O) FRONDI RAMI
RAMOSO RAMULI
(SUFF.) RAMOSE
BRANCHED FORKY FORKED RAMATE
RAMOSE CLADOSE TROCHED
RAMIFORM
(SUFF.) CLADOUS
BRANCHES
(SUFF.) (HAVING —) CLEMA
BRANCHIA GILL
BRANCHING ARMY RAMOSE
FURCATE DICHOTOMY
BRANCHIOPOD SHRIMP
BRANCHLET RAMULUS SPILLER
BRAND BIRN BLOT BURN CHOP FLAW
KIND MARK NOTE SEAR SMIT SMOT
SORT VENT WIPE BUIST INURE LABEL
SCEAR STAIN STAMP SWORD TAINT
TORCH BARREL MARQUE STIGMA
FLAMBEAU NAMEPLATE STIGMATIZE
BRANDED INFAMOUS
BRANDIMART
(SLAYER OF —) GRADASSO
(WIFE OF —) FLORDELIS
BRANDING IRON BRAND CAUTER
SEARER CAUTERY
BRANDISH WAG DART STIR WAVE
WIND BLESS BRAID SHAKE SWING
WIELD FLAUNT HURTLE QUAVER
RUFFLE STRAIN WINNOW FLUTTER
GLITTER SWAGGER VIBRATE
WAMPISH FLOURISH VAMBRASH

BRANDY DOP VSO BOOF FINE JACK
MARC VSOP BINGO MOBBY NANTS
NANTZ PEACH RAKIA VVSOP CINDER
COGNAC GRAPPA KIRSCH PUPELO
RAKIJA VISNEY ANISADO AQUAVIT
QUETSCH ARMAGNAC CALVADOS
SLIVOVIC SLIVOVITZ AGUARDIENTE
(— AND WATER) MAHOGANY
(PLUM —) SLIVOVITZ SLIVOWITZ
(SOUTH AFRICAN —) SMOKE
BRANDYWINE
(VICTOR AT —) HOWE
BRANK MUMPS BRIDLE PILLORY
BRANLE BRAWL
BRAN-LIKE PITYROID
BRANT ROUT ERECT PROUD QUINK
SHEER STEEP ROUGHT
BRASH GAY BOLD FACY RASH HASTY
NERVY SAUCY STORM ATTACK
RUBBLE BRITTLE FORWARD
IMPUDENT TACTLESS BALDFACED
BRASQUE STEEP
BRASS CASH ALLOY CHEEK MONEY
NERVE BRAZEN BRONZE MASLIN
ORMOLU OFFICER ORICHALC
(— PLAYER) WINDJAMMER
(PREF.) CHALC(O) CHALK(O)
BRASSARD ARMBAND
BRASSEY BIB
BRASSICA CABBAGE
BRASSIERE BANDEAU
BRASSWARE DINANDERIE
BRASSY LOUD RUDE BRAZEN
COARSE SHRILL IMPUDENT
STRIDENT OVERBLOWN
BRAT BIB GET IMP BROT FILM SCUM
APRON BAIRN BILSH BROLL CHILD
CLOAK GAITT SCAMP INFANT
MANTLE TERROR URCHIN GARMENT
BANTLING
BRATTICER AIRMAN CANVASMAN
BRAVADO POMP BRAG PRIDE
STORM SWASH HECTOR BLUSTER
BOMBAST BRAVERY SWAGGER
VAUNTERY GASCONISM
BRAVE BOLD BRAW DARE DEFY FACE
FINE GAME GOOD PROW TALL WILD
ADORN BOAST BRAVO BULLY FELON
HARDY JOLLY MANLY MOODY
ORPED ROMAN STIFF STOUT VAUNT
WIGHT BRAWLY BREAST DARING
HEROIC MANFUL PLUCKY SANNUP
STURDY BRAVADO DOUGHTY
GALLANT HAUTAIN SOLDIER
SWAGGER VALIANT VENTURE
WARRIOR CAVALIER DEFIANCE
EMBOLDEN FEARLESS INTREPID
LIONLIKE STALWART SUPERIOR
VALOROUS VIRTUOUS
BRAVELY BIG FINELY
BRAVE NEW WORLD
(AUTHOR OF —) HUXLEY
(CHARACTER IN —) JOHN MARX

MOND CROWNE LENINA WATSON
BERNARD MUSTAPHA HELMHOLTZ

BRAVERY GRIT VALOR SPIRIT VIRTUE
BRAVADO BRAVURA COURAGE
HEROISM JOLLITY MANHEAD
MANHOOD PROWESS BOLDNESS
CHIVALRY

BRAVO OLE RAH EUGE THUG BRAVE
BULLY BANDIT CUTTER BRAVADO
SHABASH VILLAIN APPLAUSE
ASSASSIN

BRAWL DIN ROW BEEF CLEM DUST
FRAY RIOT BLIND BROIL CHIDE
CLASH FIGHT FLYTE MELEE REVEL
RISSA SCOLD SCRAP AFFRAY BICKER
FRACAS FRATCH HABBLE REVILE
RUFFLE RUMPUS SHINDY STOUSH
STRIFE TUMULT UPROAR YATTER
BAGARRE BOBBERY BRABBLE
BRANGLE DISCORD DISPUTE
QUARREL SCUFFLE TUILYIE
WRANGLE COMPLAIN RIXATION
SQUABBLE STRAMASH

BRAWLER FRATCH NICKER SQUARER
FRAMPLER NIGHTCAP OUTCRIER

BRAWLING NOISY BLATANT FLITING
SCAMBLING SHEMOZZLE

BRAWN BEEF BOAR LIRE PORK FLESH
SINEW FATTEN MUSCLE MANPOWER
STRENGTH
(MOCK —) HEADCHEESE

BRAWNY BEEFY FLESHY ROBUST
SINEWY SQUARE STRONG STURDY
CALLOUS MUSCULAR POWERFUL
STALWART

BRAXY BRADSOT

BRAY CRY MIX RUB BEAT ROUT TOOL
CRUSH GRIND NOISE POUND STAMP
BRUISE HEEHAW OUTCRY PESTLE
THRASH WHINNY

BRAYERA KOSO CUSSO KOSSO

BRAZEN BOLD CALM HARD PERT
BRASS HARDY HARSH SASSY
AENEAN BRASSY BLATANT CALLOUS
FORWARD IMMODEST IMPUDENT
INSOLENT METALLIC

BRAZENFACED CHEEKY

BRAZIER HEARTH MANGAL BRASERO
HIBACHI REREDOS SCALDINO

BRAZIL ROSET

BAY: MARAJO IGRANDE SEPETIBA
GUANABARA

BIRD: MITU MITUA

CAPE: FRIO BLANCO BUZIOS GURUPY
ORANGE SAOTOME SAOROQUE

CAPITAL: BRASILIA

COIN: JOE REIS CONTO DOBRA
CENTAVO HALFJOE MILREIS
CRUZEIRO

DAM: FURNAS ITAIPU PEIXOTO

DANCE: SAMBA MAXIXE

ESTUARY: PARA

FALLS: IGUACU IGUASSU

INDIAN: ANTA ACROA ARARA ARAUA
BRAVO CARIB GUANA ARAWAK
CARAJA CARAYAN JAVAHAI
TARIANA BOTOCUDO CHAMBIOA

ISLAND: MARACA MARAJO BANANAL
CARDOSO CAVIANA MEXIANA
COMPRIDA

LAKE: AIMA FEIA MIRIM

MEASURE: PE MOIO PIPA SACK VARA
BRACA FANGA LEGOA MILHA
PALMO PASSO TONEL CANADA
COVADO CUARTA LEAGUE QUARTO
TAREFA ALQUIER GARRAFA
ALQUEIRE

MONETARY UNIT: CRUZADO

MOUNTAIN: URUCUM BANDEIRA
ITATIAIA

MOUNTAINS: MAR GERAL ORGAN
PIAUI ACARAI GURUPI ORGAOS
PARIMA AMAMBAI CARAJAS
GRADAUS RONCADOR TOMBADOR

NATIVE: CABOCLO CURIBOCA
MAMELUCO PAULISTA

PORT: RIO PARA BAHIA BELEM CEARA
NATAL SANTOS PELOTAS SALVADOR

PRESIDENT: BRAS DUTRA FILHO
VARGAS

RIVER: APA ICA DOCE GEIO IVAI JARI
PARA PARU SONO TEFE ABUNA
ANAUA APORE CAPIM CLARO
CORUA ICANA IRIRI ITAPI JURUA
JUTAI MANSO NEGRO PARDO PIAUI
PRETO TIETE TURVO URUBU VERDE
XINGU AJUANA AMAZON ARINOS
BALSAS BRANCO CANUMA CONTAS
CUIABA DEMINI GRAJAU GRANDE
GURUPI IBICUI IGUACU JAPURA
JAVARI MEARIM MORTES MUCURI
PARANA PURPUS RONURO SANGUE
TACUTU TIBAGI UATUMA UAUPES
VELHAS CORUMBA IGUASSU
MADEIRA PARAIBA SUCURIU
TAPAJOS TAQUARI TEODORO
URUGUAI ARAGUAIA PADAUIRI
PARACATU PARAGUAI PARNAIBA
SOLIMOES TARAUACA

STATE: ACRE PARA AMAPA BAHIA
CEARA GOIAS GOYAZ PIAUI PARANA
PIAUHY ALAGOAS GUAPORE
PARAIBA RORAIMA SERGIPE
AMAZONAS MARANHAO PARAHIBA
PARAHYBA RONDONIA SAOPAULO

TOWN: ACU EXU ICO IPU ITU JAU LUZ
RIO UBA BAGE FARO IBIA IJUI ITAI
LAPA LINS PARA PIUI TUPA UNAI
BAHIA BAIAO BAURU BELEM CEARA
NATAL NEVES CAMPOS CUIABA
ILHEUS MACEIO MANAOS MANAUS
OLINDA RECIFE SANTOS ARACAJU
CARUARU CITORIA GOIANIA
ITABUNA JUNDIAI NITEROI PELOTAS
TAUBATE UBERABA ANAPOLIS

BRASILIA CAMPINAS CURITIBA
LONDRINA SALVADOR SOROCABA
TERESINA
TREE: APA ICICA UCUUBA ARARIBA
WALLABA
WATERFALL: GLASS IGUAZU
WEIGHT: BAG ONCA LIBRA ARROBA
OITAVA ARRATEL QUILATE QUINTAL
TONELADA

BRAZIL NUT JUVIA CASTANA
BRAZILWOOD SAPPAN VERZINO
HYPERNIC PEACHWOOD
SAPPANWOOD
BREACH GAP CHAP FLAW GOOL
RENT RIFT SLAP BRACK BRECK
BURST CHASM CLEFT CRACK PAUSE
SPLIT WOUND BRUISE HARBOR
HERNIA HIATUS INROAD SCHISM
SCREED SLUICE ASSAULT BLEMISH
DISPUTE FISSURE OPENING
QUARREL RUPTURE BREAKING
CREVASSE FRACTION FRACTURE
INTERVAL OUTBREAK SOLUTION
TRESPASS
(— IN DIKE) GOOL
(— IN SEAWAY) GOOL
(— OF CHASTITY) SCULDUDDRY
SKULDUDDERY
(— OF CONTINUITY) SALTUS
(— OF DUTY) BARRATRY
(— OF ETIQUETTE) SOLECISM
(— OF FAITH) TREASON
(— OF GRAMMAR) SOLECISM
(— OF MORALITY) SCAPE VAGARY
(— OF PEACE) AFFRAY DISORDER
FRACTION
(— OF RULES) FOUL
(— OF SYNTAX) SOLECISM
(— OF UNITY) SOHISM
BREAD BAP BUN NAN PAN BODY
BRAD DIET FARE FOOD LOAF NAAN
PAIN PITA PONE RIMA ROLL ROTI
RUSH RUSK TOKE AZYME BABKA
BATCH BATON BOXTY CAPER CHEAT
KISRA LIMPA MICHE POORI ROOTY
TOMMY CHALLA CHAPON COCKET
DAMPER DODGER ENZYME HALLAH
KANKIE MASLIN MATZOS PANNAM
SIMNEL TAMMIE WASTEL YANNAM
ALIMENT ANADAMA BANNOCK
CHALLAH EULOGIA MANCHET
POPOVER STOLLEN TOASTER
CORNCAKE FOCACCIA HARDTACK
SOFTTACK TORTILLA ZWIEBACK
PUMPERNICKEL
(— AND MILK) POBS PANADA
POBBIES
(— BOX) PANETIERE
(— QUALITY) PANEITY
(BATCH OF —) CAST
(BUTTERED —) CAPER
(DRY —) TOKE

(EUCHARISTIC —) BODY HOST
AZYME
(FANCY —) BRAID
(INDIAN —) NAN
(ITALIAN —) FOCACCIA
(KIND OF —) FRY PITA POCKET
(MAIZE —) PIKI
(OATMEAL —) ANACK JANNOCK
(POTATO —) FADGE
(QUICK —) SCONE
(S. AFRICAN —) DIKA
(SLICE OF —) TARTINE TRENCHER
(SMALL LOAF OF —) COB
(SMALL PIECE OF —) SIPPET
MEALOCK
(SOPPED —) MISER BREWIS BROWIS
(SWEET —) BUN BROWNIE STOLLEN
(TOASTED —) SIPPET
(TWICE-BAKED —) ZWIEBACK
(UNLEAVENED —) AZYM AZYME
BANNOCK CHAPATTI
(WHEAT —) CHEAT HOVIS COCKET
MANCHET PARATHA
(YEAST-LEAVENED —) SALLYLUNN
(PREF.) ARTO PANI
BREADBOARD PANEL
BREADED ANGLAISE
BREADFRUIT MASI RIMA RIMAS
DUGDUG NANGCA CAMANSI
CASTANA ANTIPOLO BREADNUT
CHESTNUT
BREADNUT RAM
BREADROOT PSORALEA
BREADTH BEAM WIDTH LATITUDE
(— OF PLANK) STRAIK STRAKE
(FINGER'S —) DIGIT
BREADWINNING GAP BOON BUST
DASH HINT KNAP PICK PLOW REND
RENT RIFT RIVE
BREAK GO CUT JAR LOP TEN ABRA
BUST CHIP DRAG FALL FLAW KNAP
PART RUIN RUSH SLIP SNAP STEP
STOP TEAR TURN UNDO WASH
WORK ALTER BLANK BRACK BURST
CHECK CHINK CLEFT COMMA CRACK
CRAZE DAUNT FALSE FRACT FRUSH
LAPSE PAUSE PLUCK ROUGH SEVER
SMASH SOLVE SPAWN SPELT STAVE
SWING WOUND BRUISE CABBLE
CHANGE CLEAVE CRANNY CUTOUT
DEFEAT HIATUS IMPAIR LACUNA
PIERCE SALTUS SHREND SPRING
TEWTAW TEWTER BLUNDER
CAESURA CRACKLE CRANKLE
CREVICE CRUMBLE DESTROY
DISABLE DISPART DISRUPT EXHAUST
FISSURE GRITTLE INFRACT INTERIM
OPENING RESPITE RUPTURE
SHATTER TAILING VARIATE
BREATHER CREVASSE DIERESIS
DIFFRACT FRACTION FRACTURE
FRAGMENT INFRINGE INTERVAL
SEPARATE SOLUTION STRAMASH

(— APART) SUNDER DISRUPT SHATTER
(— AWAY) BOLT PEEL ESCAPE
(— BOULDERS) BULLDOZE
(— DOWN) CONK FAIL GIVE CRAZE CROCK PLASH TRAIK UNMAN BRUISE TUMBLE ANALYZE FOUNDER REFRACT COLLAPSE INFRINGE
(— FORCE) BAFFLE
(— FORTH) BOIL ERUPT EVENT FLASH EXPLODE
(— FROM ICE MASS) CALVE
(— GLASS) SHREND DRAGADE
(— IN) ENTER
(— IN PIECES) CHAP DICE KNAP CRASH CRAZE SMASH SMOKE SHIVER CRUMBLE FRITTER SMATTER DEMOLISH DIFFRACT DISJOINT SPLINTER STRAMASH
(— INTO) BROACH IRRUPT
(— INTO FOAM) COMB
(— INWARD) STAVE
(— IN WAVES) JABBLE
(— IN YARN) SMASH
(— LANCE) TAINT
(— OF CONTINUITY) SALTUS
(— OFF) NUB DROP SNAP CEASE LEAVE ABRUPT DIREMPT INTERMIT PRETERMIT
(— OFF END) SNUB
(— OPEN) BUST CHOP FORCE
(— ORE) COB SPALL SPAWL
(— OUT) ERUPT START ASSURD STRIKE
(— RANKS) DISMISS
(— SHARPLY) KNALY
(— SILENCE) QUATCH QUETCH
(— SKIN) GALL
(— SLATE) SCULP
(— STONE) CAVIL KEVEL
(— THE BACK) CHINE
(— THROUGH) BEAT FORCE BREACH
(— THROUGH SHELL) PIP
(— UP) BUCK FALL MELT FLOUR SEVER SPALE SPLIT STASH INCIDE DEGRADE DIFFUSE DISBAND DISSECT DISTURB REFRACT SCARIFY SCATTER CROSSCUT DISJOINT DISPERSE DISSOLVE DISUNIFY FRAGMENT
(— UP EARTH) HACK FALLOW
(— UP SIEGE) LEVY
(— WATER) FIN
(— WINDOWS) NICK
(INDUSTRY —) SHAKEOUT
(STEM —) BROWNING
(SUFF.) CLASE CLASIA CLAST(IC)
BREAKABLE BRITTLE BRUCKLE FRIABLE DELICATE FRANGIBLE
BREAKAGE GRIEF
BREAKAX IRONWOOD
BREAKDOWN JUBA EDGER BURNOUT DEBACLE HOEDOWN ANALYSIS COLLAPSE DILUTION

(— OF RIND) ADUSTIOSIS
(ELECTRIC —) AVALANCHE
BREAKER JUMP SURF WAVE BARECA BEAKER BILLOW COMBER ROLLER CRACKER SLEDGER LEDGEMAN SCRAPPER
(— OF WORD) WARLOCK
(CIRCUIT —) CUTOUT
(ROCK —) ALLIGATOR
(PL.) BREACH
(SUFF.) CLASTIC
BREAKFAST BRUNCH DEJEUNE DISJUNE DEJEUNER DISJEUNE
(— FOOD) GRANOLA
BREAKING BREACH BREAKUP FRACTION FRACTURE SOLUTION
(— COVER) GETAWAY
(— DOWN) LYSIS
(— FORTH) ERUPTIVE
(— OFF) CHIPPING ABRUPTION
(— OF OATH) PERJURY
(— UP) DEBACLE ANALYSIS DISUNION
(SUFF.) CLASE CLASIA CLAST(IC)
(— INTO SMALL PIECES) THRIPSIS
BREAKSTONE SAXIFRAGE
BREAK-UP DEBACLE
BREAKWATER COB DAM COBB CROY DIKE MOLE PIER PILE QUAY JETTY GROYNE REFUGE BULWARK STOCKADE
BREAM TAI BRIM CARP CHAD SCUP SHAD ZOPE BROOM RUMAN BALEEN BARWIN BRAISE SARGUS OLDWIFE SUNFISH WAREHOU CYPRINID FLATFISH TARWHINE STEENTJIE
BREAST DUG BOOB BUMP CROP FACE BOOBY BOSOM BRAVE BUBBY CHEST HEART MAMMA PETTO STALL BAZOOM PECTUS POMMEL THORAX BRISKET COUNTER KNOCKER FOREBOWS
(— OF HORSE) COUNTER
(PHOTOGRAPH OF —S) MAMMOGRAM
(PL.) BUST
(PREF.) MAMM(I)(ILLI) MAST(O) MAZ(O) PECTORI STERN(O) STETH(O)
BREASTBAND HORSE
BREASTBONE BREAST STERNUM XIPHOID
BREASTHOOK CRUTCH FOREHOOK
BREASTPIECE RABAT RABBI
BREASTPLATE EGIS URIM AEGIS BREAST BYRNIE GORGET LORICA ORACLE SHIELD THORAX CUIRASS PALETTE POITREL PECTORAL PLASTRON RATIONAL
(HIGH PRIEST'S —) RATIONAL
BREASTS
(SUFF.) MASTIA
BREASTWORK FORT REDAN SANGAR SCHANZ SCHERM SCONCE

SUNGAR BRATTLE PARAPET
PLUTEUS RAMPART BARBETTE
BRATTICE
BREATH AIR ANDE GASP HUFF LIFE
ONDE PANT PECH PUFF SIGH WAFT
WIND BLAST PAUSE SCENT SMELL
VAPOR WHIFF WHIFT BREEZE FLATUS
PNEUMA HALITUS INSTANT RESPITE
SUSPIRE SPIRACLE
(— OF WIND) SPIRIT
(BAD —) OZOSTOMIA
(DIVINE —) NEPHESH
(LIFE —) PRANA SPIRIT
(STINKING —) FUMOSITY
(PREF.) PNEO PNEUM(A)(O)
PNEUMATO PNEUMON(O) RESPIRO
SPIRACULI SPIRO
(SUFF.) PNEA PNEUSTA PNOEA
BREATHE ANDE LIVE ONDE PANT
PECH PUFF SIGH VENT EXIST EXUDE
SPEAK SPIRE UTTER ASPIRE EXHALE
INHALE WHEEZE AFFLATE EMANATE
RESPIRE SUSPIRE
(— HEAVILY) FOB PECH FNESE
SOUGH THROTTLE
(— LABORIOUSLY) GASP
(— NOISILY) SOUGH SNOTTER
(— OUT) EXPIRE
(— UPON) FAN
BREATHER PAUSE
BREATHING AIR ALIVE PNEUMA
SPIRIT GASPING AFFLATUS SPIRITUS
SPIRATION
(— HEAVILY) SUSPIRIOUS
(LABORED —) ASTHMA
(ROUGH —) ASPER
(SMOOTH —) LENE LENIS
BREATHING-SPACE BARLEY
RESPIRATION
BREATHLESSNESS TIFT
BREATHY HOLLOW ADENOID
BRECCIA BROCKRAM
BRED (WELL —) FREE
BREECH BORE BUTT DOUP BLOCK
BRICK CULOTTE DRODDUM
BUTTOCKS CYLINDER DERRIERE
(— OF SECURITY) LEAK
BREECHBLOCK BLOCK VENTPIECE
BREECHCLOTH HIPPEN HIPPING
BREECHES HOSE CHAPS JEANS
LEVIS SLOPS STOCK TREWS BRACAE
BRAGAS BREEKS GASKIN SMALLS
TIGHTS TROUSE TRUSSES
BOMBARDS BREEKUMS JODHPURS
KICKSIES KNICKERS LEATHERS
TROUSERS PANTALOON
SMALLCLOTHES
(KNEE —) SMALLS
BREED GET ILK BEAR KIND RACE
REAR SORT BEGET BROOD CASTE
CAUSE CLASS FANCY HATCH ISSUE
RAISE STOCK STORE TRAIN CREATE
GENDER STRAIN EDUCATE NOURISH

PRODUCE PROGENY SPECIES
VARIETY ENGENDER GENERATE
INSTRUCT MULTIPLY PULLULATE
(— OF BEEF CATTLE) BEEFALO
(— OF CATS) RAGDOLL
(— OF SWINE) LACOMBE
(DWARF —) TOY
(DWARF—) TOY
BREEDER RANCHER AURELIAN
HERDSMAN HORSEMAN
(FISH —) MILTER
BREEDING ORIGIN DESCENT
NURTURE TUPPING BEHAVIOR
CIVILITY PREGNANT TRAINING
(— PLACE) NIDUS
(GOOD —) GENTRY
BREEZE AIR AURA BLOW FLAW GALE
GUST PIRR SNAP STIR WIND BLAST
RUMOR SLANT WALTZ BREATH
DOCTOR REPORT SLATCH SPIRIT
ZEPHYR FRESHEN MUZZLER
QUARREL VIRASON WHISPER
(COOL —) DOCTOR
(GENTLE —) AIR AURA ZEPHYR
(LAND —) TERRAL
(SHOOT THE —) GAB JAW
(STIFF—) STOUR TIFTER
BREEZE FLY WHAME
BREEZY AIRY BRISK FRESH WINDY
AIRISH
BRETHREN IKHWAN
BRETON ARMORICAN
BREVE NOTE WRIT BRIEF MINIM
ORDER SHORT PRECEPT
BREVIARY ORDO CURSUS DIGEST
LEDGER PORTAS COUCHER EPITOME
SUMMARY ABSTRACT PORTESSE
PORTHORS
(— CONTENTS) PRAYERS
BREVITY SYNTOMY LACONISM
UNLENGTH BRIEFNESS SHORTNESS
TERSENESS BRACHYLOGY
BREW ALE MIX BEER BOIL MAKE PLOT
POUR DRINK HATCH STEEP STOUT
BROWST DEVISE DILUTE FOMENT
GATHER LIQUOR SEETHE CONCOCT
INCLINE PREPARE CONTRIVE
(HOME —) SAMOGON
BREWER TUNNER
BREWERY BRASSERIE
BREWING GAIL GYLE BROWST
BUMMOCK
BRIBE BUD BUY FEE FIX OIL ROB SOP
TIP BAIT DASH GIFT HAVE HIRE MEED
MOIL PALM VAIL WAGE BONUS
CUDDY GRAFT OFFER STEAL SUGAR
TEMPT TOUCH BOODLE EXTORT
GREASE HAMPER NOBBLE PAYOLA
SQUARE SUBORN CORRUPT
DOUCEUR SWEETEN TICKLER
GRATUITY VENALIZE
(— TO A POLICEMAN) NUT
(— TO POLICEMAN) NUT

BRIBERY MEED
(OPEN TO —) VENAL
BRIC-A-BRAC CURIO VERTU VIRTU
BIBELOT TROCKERY TRUMPERY
BRICK BAT BUR BURR GLUT MARL
PAVE TILE BLOCK GAULT QUARL
SLOPE SPLIT STOCK STONE TOOTH
CUTTER FELLOW HEADER PAMENT
PAVIOR BACKING CLINKER FLETTON
GRIZZLE PERPEND SOLDIER
BURNOVER
(— WALL) NECK
(CRACKED —) CHUFF SHUFF
(FINAL HALF —) JACK
(IMPERFECT —) SHIPPER BURNOVER
(PILE OF —S) HACK CLAMP
(PULVERIZED —) SOORKY SOORKEE
(SECOND-RATE —) GRIZZLE
(SECOND QUALITY —S) BRINDLES
(SOFT —) CUTTER RUBBER PICKING
(SQUARE —) QUADREL
(STACK OF —) LIFT
(SUN-DRIED —) BAT ADOBE
(UNBURNT —) ADOBE
(WOODEN —) DOOK
(PL.) CLAYWARE
(PREF.) PLINTHI
BRICKBAT GIBE
BRICKLAYER BRICKY MASONER
BRICKMAKER MOLDER
BRICKWORK HOB BRICKING
BRIDAL NUPTIAL BRIDALTY
BRIDE KALLAH SPOUSE SHULAMITE
SWEETENER
BRIDE OF LAMMERMOOR
(AUTHOR OF —) SCOTT
(CHARACTER IN —) LUCY CALEB
EDGAR FRANK ASHTON HAYSTON
WILLIAM RAVENSWOOD
BALDERSTONE
BRIDE-PRICE LOBOLD LOBOLO
BRIDESHEAD REVISITED
(AUTHOR OF —) WAUGH
(CHARACTER IN —) ROY REX CARA
KURT BERYL CELIA JULIA RYDER
BRIDEY ANTHONY BLANCHE
CHARLES MOTTRAM CORDELIA
MUSPRATT SAMGRASS MARCHMAIN
MULCASTER SEBASTIAN
BRIDESHEAD
BRIDESMAID PARANYMPH
BRIDEWELL JAIL MILLDOLL
BRIDGE WAY BRIG LINK NOSE PONS
PONT REST SPAN WIEN CROSS
SIRAT TOWIE GANTRY ISLAND
JIGGER RIALTO RUNWAY SANGAR
AUCTION BASCULE BIFROST
CHANNEL CONNECT CULVERT
EXOSTRA PASSAGE PASSING
PINNOCK PONCEAU PONTOON
PROPONS TRAJECT TRESTLE
VIADUCT CONTRACT TRAVERSE
DUPLICATE

(— BID) SPLINTER
(— BUILDER) PONTIFEX
(— HAND) YARBOROUGH
(— HOLDING) HONORS TENACE
YARBOROUGH
(— MARKER) PYLON
(— OF MUSICAL INSTRUMENT)
MAGAS CHEVALET CHEVILLE
(— PLAY) RUFF UPPERCUT
(— SEAT) EAST WEST DUMMY
NORTH SOUTH
(— TO PARADISE) ALSIRAT
(ARCADED —) RIALTO
(BILLIARDS —) JIGGER
(CONTRACT —) CHICAGO GHOULIE
PLAFOND
(FLUE —) ALTAR
(GATEWAY —) GOUT
(HOSE —) JUMPER
(IMPEDANCE —) DIPLEXER
(NATURAL —) ARCH
(PLANK —) LIGGER
(RAISE — BID) JUMP
(ROPE SUSPENSION —) JOOLA
(RUDE —) CLAPPER
(PREF.) GEPHYR(O) PONTI PONTO
BRIDGEMAKER PONTIFEX
BRIDGEMAN EBBMAN
BRIDGE OF SAN LUIS REY
(AUTHOR OF —) WILDER
(CHARACTER IN —) PIO JAIME PILAR
MANUEL PEPITA ESTEBAN JUNIPER
PERICHOLE MONTEMAYOR
BRIDGING ASTRIDE STRUTTING
BRIDLE BIT CURB REIN RULE BRAKE
BRANK BRIDE CHUCK GUARD QUICK
STRUT DIRECT GOVERN HALTER
MASTER SIMPER SUBDUE BLINDER
CONTROL LORMERY REPRESS
SNAFFLE SWAGGER CAVESSON
RESTRAIN SUPPRESS
BRIDLE PATH SPURWAY
BRIEF FEW CURT LIST RIFE WRIT
BLURB BREVE CHARM PITHY QUICK
SHORT TERSE ABRUPT COMMON
CURTAL FLYING HOURLY LETTER
LITTLE SNIPPY SUDDEN ABRIDGE
CAPSULE COMPACT COMPOSE
CONCISE CRYPTIC INVOICE LACONIC
MANDATE OUTLINE PRECEPT
SUMMARY BREVIATE CONDENSE
FLEETING FLITTING SNATCHED
SNIPPETY SUCCINCT SYLLABUS
(PL.) BIKINI
(PREF.) BREVI
BRIEF CASE FOLIO TASHIE
BRIEFED (WELL —) UPON
BRIEFLY BRIEF ENFIN SHORTLY
BRIEFS JOCKEY
BRIER BARB PIPE BRIAR ERICA THORN
SMILAX BRUYERE PRICKER
INKBERRY
BRIER TREE PIPER

BRIG RIG JAIL PRISON GEORDIE
BRIGADE TERZO CAMPOO
BRIGAND THIEF USKOK BANDIT
KLEPHT LATRON PIRATE ROBBER
CATERAN KETTRIN LADRONE
ROUTIER SOLDIER PICAROON
BANDOLERO
(PL.) TCHETNITSI
BRIGANDAGE DACOITY
BRIGANDINE PLACCATE
BRIGHT APT GAY NET FINE GILD
GLAD GLEG HIGH LIVE ROSY ACUTE
AGLOW ALERT ANIME BEAMY BRAVE
CLEAR CRISP EAGLE FLARY FRESH
GEMMY JOLLY LIGHT LUCID NITID
PRINT QUICK RIANT SHARP SHEEN
SHEER SHINY SMART SMOLT STEEP
SUNNY TINNY VIVID WHITE WITTY
BERTHA CHEERY CLEVER FLASHY
FLORID GARISH LIMPID LIVELY
LUCENT ORIENT SERENE SHRILL
SILVER BEAMISH DIAMOND DILUCID
FORWARD FULGENT LAMBENT
RADIANT RINGING SHINING
ANIMATED CHEERFUL FLASHING
GLEAMING LIGHTFUL LUMINOUS
LUSTROUS SPLENDID SPLENDOR
STARLIKE SUNSHINY
(— IN COLOR) NEON
(BLINDINGLY —) GLARING
(NOT —) SOFT
(OFFENSIVELY —) GARISH
(SOFTLY —) LAMBENT
(TOO —) ROARY ROARIE
(VULGARLY —) GAUDY
(PREF.) AETHIO AGLAO LAMPR(O)
BRIGHTEN GILD LAMP BLOOM
CHEER CLEAR FLAME GLOZE LIGHT
LIVEN SHINE SNUFF CANTLE ENGILD
POLISH ANIMATE BURNISH EMBRAVE
ENLIVEN FURBISH LIGHTEN REFRESH
SMARTEN ILLUMINE
BRIGHTENED LITUP
BRIGHTENER FLUOROL
BRIGHTLY GAY CLEAR LIGHT SHEEN
BRIGHT FRESHLY SHEENLY
BRIGHTNESS SUN BLAZE BLOOM
ECLAT FLAME GLARE GLEAM GLINT
GLORY GLOSS LIGHT NITOR SHEEN
SHINE ACUMEN BRIGHT CANDOR
FULGOR LUSTER CLARITY GLISTEN
GLITTER LAMBERT NITENCY
SPARKLE RADIANCE SPLENDOR
BRILLIANCE
(— OF TOBACCO) FLASH
(— UNIT) STILB
(UNIT OF —) NIT
(PREF.) GANO
BRIGUE BLAT
BRILLIANCE FAME BLARE BLAZE
ECLAT FLAME GLARE GLORY SHINE
VALUE KEENNESS RADIANCE
SPLENDOR VIVACITY REFULGENCE

BRILLIANCY FIRE BLARE ECLAT
GLORY REFLET CLARITY GLITTER
ORIENCY RADIANCE SPLENDOR
BRILLIANT GAY GOOD KEEN SAGE
WISE BREME QUICK VIVID BRIGHT
CLEVER GIFTED LIVELY PURPLE
SIGNAL BRAVURA BRITTLE EMINENT
FLAMING GLARING LAMBENT
LAMPING LOZENGE PRISMAL
RADIANT SHINING BLINDING
DAZZLING DIZZYING GLORIOUS
INSPIRED LUCULENT LUMINOUS
SLASHING SPLENDID PRISMATIC
(TRANSIENTLY —) METEORIC
BRIM LIP RIM RUT SEA EDGE TURF
BLUFF BRINK MARGE OCEAN VERGE
WATER BORDER MARGIN TURNUP
COPULATE STRUMPET
(— OF HAT) FLAP LEAF POKE BRINK
TARFE SLOUCH
BRIMFUL TIPFUL TOPFUL CROWNED
BRIMMING BIG FULL ABRIM
BRIMSTONE SULFUR VIRAGO
SULPHUR BRINSTON SPITFIRE
(PREF.) THI(O)
BRIMSTONY LURID
BRINDLED TABBY TAWNY BRANDED
FLECKED STREAKED
BRINE SEA MAIN SALT BRACK LEACH
OCEAN TEARS PICKLE MARINADE
BRINER COBBERER
BRING DO LAY TEE WIN BEAR BUCK
CALL FIRK LEAD STOP TAKE TEEM
CARRY DRIVE ENDUE FETCH INCUR
APPORT ARRIVE CONVEY DEDUCE
CONDUCE CONDUCT EXHIBIT
PROCURE PRODUCE
(— ABOUT) DO SEE BREW MAKE
STAY TEEM CAUSE DIGHT FRAME
INFER MOYEN SETUP SHAPE SWING
CREATE EFFECT INVOKE SECURE
SPIRIT COMPASS CONDUCE INSPIRE
OPERATE PROCURE PRODUCE
CATALYZE OCCASION TRANSACT
PERPETRATE
(— ABOUT CAPTURE) ACCOUNT
(— BACK) REFER EFFECT RECALL
REDUCE REDUCT RELATE RETURN
REVIVE REVOKE PRODUCE RESTORE
OCCASION RETRIEVE TRANSACT
(— BEFORE) HAUL
(— CHARGE) APPEACH
(— DOWN) LAY DROP FALL FELL
STOP ABATE COUCH EMBASE
SOFTEN DECLINE DESCEND
DISMOUNT OVERTHROW
(— DOWN STEER) HOOLIHAN
(— FORTH) CAST FOAL GIVE MAKE
TEEM YEAN EDUCE HATCH ISSUE
SPAWN THROW PROFER DELIVER
TRADUCE ENGENDER PROCREATE
(— FORTH YOUNG) EAN KID YEAN
(— FORWARD) CITE LEAD INFER

ADDUCE ALLEGE ADJOUST
ADVANCE PROPOSE
(— IN) EARN INFER USHER IMPORT
INDUCE INVECT REPORT RETURN
ADHIBIT
(— INTO BATTLE) COMMIT
(— INTO COURT) SIST
(— INTO DISGRACE) FOUL
(— LOW) AVALE DEGRADE SUPPLANT
(— ON) INFER INDUCE
(— ONESELF) GET
(— OUT) DRAW ACCENT ELICIT
DISINTER HEIGHTEN
(— OVER) CONVERT
(— SHIP INTO POSITION) EASE
(— TO A HALT) STICK
(— TO AN END) DO END FIT DOCK
DRAW REDD CEASE FORDO DECIDE
EXPIRE FINISH FOREDO FULFIL
DISJOIN INCLUDE COMPLETE
CONCLUDE DISSOLVE SURCEASE
(— TO BAY) CORNER
(— TO BEAR) EXERT
(— TOGETHER) JOIN AMASS RAISE
UNITE ADDUCT CONFER CORRAL
ENGAGE ENLINK GATHER SUMMON
COLLATE COLLECT COMPILE
COMPORT ASSEMBLE CONFLATE
ENSEMBLE
(— TO HEEL) FACE
(— TO LIFE) EVOKE ANIMATE
(— TO LIGHT) GRUB REAP DREDGE
ELICIT EXPOSE REVEAL UNEARTH
DISCLOSE DISCOVER
(— TO NAUGHT) DASH FOIL UNDO
NEGATE CONFUTE DESTROY
(— TO PERFECTION) RIPEN
(— TO STOP) CURB HALT ARREST
(— TO THE GROUND) GRASS
(— UP) REAR BREED NURSE RAISE
TRAIN NURSLE NUZZLE UPREAR
EDUCATE NOURISH
(SUFF.) FER(ENCE)(ENT)(OUS)
(— ABOUT) FIC(AL)(ATE)(ATION)
(ATIVE)(ATOR)(ATORY)(E)(ENCE)(ENT)
(IAL)(IARY)(IENT) FIQUE
BRING-DOWN LETDOWN
COMEDOWN
BRINGER (OF BABIES) STORK
(— OF BAD LUCK) JINX JONAH
(— OF BAD NEWS) SCREECHOWL
(— OF DREAMS) MAB
(— OF GOOD LUCK) MASCOT
BRINGING-UP BREEDING
EDUCATION
BRINJAL EGGPLANT
BRINK END EVE LIP RIM SEA BANK
BRIM EDGE FOSS MARGE SHORE
VERGE BORDER MARGIN MARGENT
PRECIPICE THRESHOLD
BRINY BRACK SALTY SALINE
BRACKISH MURIATED
BRIOCHE ROLL STICH SAVARIN

BRISE-SOLEIL BLIND SUNBREAK
SUNSHADE
BRISK GAY BRAG BUSY CANT FAST
KEEN PERK PERT RACY RASH SPRY
TRIG VIVE YARE YERN AGILE ALERT
ALIVE BUDGE BUXOM CANTY COBBY
CRANK CRISP FRESH FRISK KEDGE
NIPPY PEART PEPPY PERKY QUICK
ROUND ZIPPY ACTIVE BREEZY
COCKET CROUSE DAPPER FLICKY
LIVELY NIMBLE SNAPPY SPRACK
SPRUNT TROTTY VIVACE ALLEGRO
CHIPPER HUMMING ROUSING
ANIMATED BRUSHING FRISKFUL
GALLIARD RATTLING SMACKING
SPANKING SPIRITED
(SOMEWHAT —) ALLEGRETTO
BRISKLY YERN SHARP YERNE BUSILY
CROUSE ALLEGRO ROUNDLY
BRISKNESS ALACRITY VIRITOOT
BRISTLE AWN JAG RIB BARB HAIR
JAGG SETA TELA BIRSE BRUSH
PARCH PREEN STARE STRUT STYLE
TOAST AVISTA CHAETA PALPUS
RUFFLE SETULA STIVER STRIGA
STYLET GLOCHIS SMELLER STUBBLE
WHISKER ACICULUM FRENULUM
SPICULUM VIBRISSA VIBRACULUM
(PREF.) CHAET(I)(O) CHETO HIRSUTO
HORRI SETI SETULI
(SUFF.) CHAETA CHAETES CHAETUS
BRISTLED HERISSE HORRENT
BRISTLE-SHAPED STYLOID
BRISTLING ROUGH HISPID HORRID
SETOSE THORNY HORRENT
SCRUBBY SPINOUS
BRISTLY BIRSY PENNY SETOSE
STUBBY SCRUBBY STICKLE
BRITAIN
(PREF.) BRITO
BRITISH ENGLISH BRITANNIC
WHITEHALL
BRITISH COLUMBIA (CAPITAL OF
—) VICTORIA
(MOUNTAINS OF —) COAST CARIBOO
CASCADE PURCELL SELKIRK
MONASHEE
(RIVER OF —) NASS LIARD PEACE
FRASER SKEENA STIKINE
(TOWN OF —) KELOWNA KAMLOOPS
VANCOUVER
BRITISH GUM DEXTRIN DEXTRINE
BRITISH HONDURAS (BAY OF —)
CHETUMAL
(CAPITAL OF —) BELMOPAN
(FORMER CAPITAL OF —) BELIZE
(MOUNTAIN RANGE OF —) MAYA
(TOWN OF —) CAYO STANN
COROZAL
BRITOMARTIS (FATHER OF —) ZEUS
JUPITER
(MOTHER OF) CARME
BRITON BRIT CELT SCOT BRYTHON

BRITTANY ARMORICA
(NATIVE OF —) BRETON
BRITTLE DRY FROW WEAK BRASH
CANDY CRIMP CRISP CRUMP EAGER
FRAIL FROWY FRUSH SHORT SPALT
CRISPY CRUMPY FEEBLE FICKLE ·
FROUGH GINGER INFIRM SLIGHT
BRICKLE BRUCKLE CRACKLY FRAGILE
FRIABLE REDSEAR SHIVERY SMOPPLE
BRITCHEL DELICATE SNAPPISH
(— AT HIGH HEAT) REDSHORT
BRITTLEBUSH ENCELIA
BRITTLE STAR OPHIUROID
BROACH AIR AWL CUT PIN ROD TAP
OPEN OUCH SHED SPIT SPUR STAB
TAME VEER VENT BEGIN DRESS DRIFT
PRICK RIMER SPOOL START VOICE
ATTAME BORING BROOCH DRIVER
FIBULA LAUNCH PIERCE REAMER
RHYMER STRIKE ENLARGE EXPRESS
PUBLISH SPINDLE SQUARER VIOLATE
WIDENER APPROACH DEFLOWER
DRIFTPIN INCISION PORPOISE
BROAD DEEP FREE VAST WIDE
AMPLE BEAMY BRAID DORIC GROSS
LARGE LARGO PLAIN ROOMY SPLAY
SQUAB STOUT THICK WOMAN
COARSE GLOBAL BELCHER EVIDENT
GENERAL GRIVOIS LIBERAL OBVIOUS
PLATOID BARNYARD SPACIOUS
TOLERANT
(— AND FLAT) PLATOID
(NOT —) STRAIT
(PREF.) EURY LATI PLAT(Y)
BROADBILL GAYA RAYA GAPER
SCAUP BOATBILL SHOVELER
SWORDFISH
BROADCAST AIR SOW SEED SEND
CARRY RADIO STREW AIRING
SPREAD DECLARE DIFFUSE PUBLISH
SCATTER ANNOUNCE TELEVISE
TRANSMIT
BROADCLOTH CASTOR SUCLAT
TAUNTON
BROADEN BREDE WIDEN DILATE
EXPAND EXTEND SPREAD ENNOBLE
BROADHORN ARK
BROADLOOM CARPET
BROAD-MINDED LIBERAL
BROADNESS BIGNESS LIBERALITY
BROADSIDE RAM TIRE BROAD
GARLAND
BROADSWORD BILL KRIS GLAIVE
HANGER SPATHA CUTLASS FERRARA
CLAYMORE MONTANTO SCIMITAR
BROBDINGNAGIAN HUGE
BROCADE ACCA BROCHE KINCOB
KINKHAB NISHIKI BAUDEKIN
DAMASSIN
BROCADED BROCHE
BROCCOLI ASPARAGUS
BROCCOLI BROWN GOAT LOAM
PLOVER RABBIT

BROCCOLI RABE RAPINI RAPPINI
BROCHURE TRACT BOOKLET
PAMPHLET TREATISE
BROCKET PITA STAG BROCK SPITTER
BRODIAEA GRASSNUT
BROGAN STOGA STOGY BROGUE
STOGIE
BROGUE STOGY STOGIE
BROIL ROW BURN CHAR FEUD FRAY
GRID HEAT TOIL ALARM BRAWL
GRILL MELEE SCRAP SWELT AFFRAY
BIRSLE BRAISE GRILLY SPLORE
SQUEAL TUMULT BRANDER BRULYIE
CARBONE CONTEST DISCORD
DISPUTE EMBROIL FRIZZLE GARBOIL
QUARREL SIMULTY BARBECUE
BLOODWIT CONFLICT GRILLADE
STRAMASH
BROILED CASINO
BROILER GRILL SEARER CHICKEN
POUSSIN
BROKE HOG LOW BUST SKINT
STONY STONEY CHICANE UPTIGHT
BANKRUPT
BROKEN DOWN DUFF RENT RUDE
TORN BLOWN BROKE BURST FRACT
GAPPY HAIRY KAPUT ROMPU ROUGH
TAMED BRASHY HACKLY RUINED
SHAKEN CRACKED CRUSHED .
FRACTED REDUCED SUBDUED
VICIOUS WHIPPED BANKRUPT
CONTRITE OUTLAWED RUPTURED
TATTERED WEAKENED
(— BUT NOT TRAINED) GREEN
(— IN) STOVEN
(— IN HEALTH) CRAZY
(— OFF) ABRUPT
(EASILY —) GINGER
(PREF.) FRACTO
BROKEN-DOWN HAYWIRE .
DISJASKED DISJASKIT
BROKER AGENT CRIMP BANIAN
BANYAN CORSER DEALER FACTOR
JOBBER BROGGER CHANGER
COURSER MONEYER PEDDLER
REALTOR SCALPER HUCKSTER
INSTITOR MERCHANT
BROKERAGE AGIOTAGE
BROMATIUM KOHLRABI
BROME CHEAT
BROMEGRASS CHESS
BROMIA
(HUSBAND OF —) SOSIA
BROMO ACID EOSIN EOSINE
BROMUS DRAWK
BRONCHITIS HUSK HOOSE HOOZE
BRONCO PONY PONEY CAYUSE
BRONCHO MUSTANG
BRONCOBUSTER BUSTER GINETE
BUCKAROO
BRONZE AES TAN BUST ALLOY
BROWN COWBOY ORMOLU STATUE
ASIATIC GUNMETAL

(— AGE CULTURE) UBAID
(ANTIQUE —) CACAO
(GILDED —) VERMEIL
(MEDAL —) CALABASH
(PREF.) CHALC(O) CHALK(O)
BRONZEWING SQUATTER
BROOCH BAR PIN BOSS LACE OUCH
PRIN PROP CAMEO CLASP MORSE
PREEN SLIDE SPRAY SPRIG FIBULA
NOUCHE PLAQUE SHIELD FERMAIL
PETALON CROTCHET ORNAMENT
SUNBURST
BROOD EYE FRY NYE SET SIT MOPE
NEST NIDE RACE STEW TEAM TRIP
WEEP AERIE BREED CLOCK COVER
COVEY FLOCK GLOOM GROUP HATCH
HOVER ISSUE SEDGE STOCK WORRY
YOUNG CLETCH CLUTCH FAMILY
KINDLE LITTER PONDER PROGENY
SPECIES CLECKING COGITATE
(— OF BIRDS) AERY AERIE COVEY
EYRIE SEDGE SIEGE
(— OF PHEASANTS) EYE NID NYE
NIDE
BROODER HOVER MOTHER
NURSERY
BROOK RUN BEAR BECK BURN GHYL
GILL LAKE RILL RUSH SIKE ABIDE
BAYOU BOURN CREEK FLEET GLIDE
STAND STELL TCHAI ARROYO
BRANCH CANADA DIGEST ENDURE
GUTTER RINDLE RIVOSE RUNLET
RUNNEL SICKET STREAM SUFFER
ABROOKE COMPORT CONCOCT
STOMACH QUEBRADA TOLERATE
(RIPPLING —) PURL
(SALT —) LICK
BROOKLET BECK DOKE RILL RILLET
RUNNEL RILLOCK RIVULET
BROOM COW MOP FRAY SWAB WISP
BESOM BISME RREAM BRUSH
SCRUB SPART SWEEP UALIS WHISK
GENISTA HAGWEED WHISKER
HACKWEED SPLINTER
(DYER'S —) GENET DYEWOOD
(NATIVE —) DOGWOOD
(TOPS OF —) SCOPARIUS
(PREF.) SCOPI SCOPULI
BROOMCORN HURL
BROOMCORN MILLET HIRSE
PANIC PANICLE KADIKANE
BROOMRAPE HELLROOT HERBBANE
BROOMROOT SACATON ZACATON
BROSE ATHOLE CROWDIE
BROTH SEW BREE BROO FOND KAIL
KALE SOUP DASHI GLAZE STOCK
BREWIS CULLIS JUSSAL JUSSEL
LIQUOR SKILLY CALDERA POTTAGE
SOUCHIE SUPPING BOUILLON
CONSOMME PISHPASH POSSODIE
POWSOWDY
(FISH —) DASHI

BROTHEL KIP CRIB STEW BAGNE
HOUSE BAGNIO BORDEL CORINTH
LUPANAR SHEBANG BORDELLO
CATHOUSE HOOKSHOP HOTHOUSE
JOYHOUSE SERAGLIO
BROTHER FR BUB FRA KIN PAL SIB
BHAI BRER EGIL FRAY MATE MONK
PEER BILLY BUBBY BUDDY CADET
FRERE FRIAR FELLOW FRAILE FRATER
GERMAN COMRADE SIBLING
FOSTERER
(HUSBAND'S —) LEVIR
(LAY —) SCOLOG
(WIFE'S —) AFFINE
(YOUNGER —) CADET
(PL.) FF ADELPHI BRETHREN CURIATII
HARLUNGEN
(PREF.) ADELPHO FRATRI
(SUFF.) ADELPHIA ADELPHOUS
BROTHERHOOD GILD GUILD LODGE
ORDER PAPEY FRIARY BRATSVO
CHISHTI THIASOS THIASUS
BRODHULL SODALITY
(— OF FREEMASONS) CRAFT
(LITERARY —) FELIBRIGE
BROTHER-IN-LAW MAUGH
BROTHERS KARAMAZOV
(AUTHOR OF —) DOSTOEVSKI
(CHARACTER IN —) IVAN ALEXEY
DMITRI FYODOR ALYOSHA KATRINA
ZOSSIMA GRUSHENKA
SMERDYAKOV
BROUGHAM PILLBOX CARRIAGE
BROUGHT BROCHT
(— FROM ELSEWHERE) DERIVED
(— TO BAY) CORNERED
(— TOGETHER) CONFLATE
(— UP BY HAND) CADE
BROUHAHA SCRAP
BROW TOP BRAE EDGE MIEN SNAB
BOUND BRINK CREST EAVES FRONT
RIDGE SLOPE BOLDNESS FOREHEAD
BROWBEAT BOSS CARP FACE
ABASH BULLY BOUNCE HECTOR
DEPRESS DUMBCOW OUTFACE
SWAGGER
BROWBEATEN HACKED
BROWN (ALSO SEE COLOR) ART DUN
LES TAN ARAB COIN COOK DARK
GOAT LION SEAR ABRAM ACORN
ARGUS BRUNO DUSKY HAZEL KAFFA
MOSUL PABLO PENNY QUAIL SEDGE
SEPIA TAWNY TENNE TOAST UMBER
APACHE BEAVER BRUNET BURNET
GLOOMY MALAGA MANILA MASTIC
MOHAWK PALOMA PLOVER PONGEE
RABBIT RUSSET SENNET TANNED
TURTLE WIGWAM ASPHALT
FUSCOUS HARVEST LIBERIA
MUSCADE OAKWOOD OXBLOOD
POMPEII PRAIRIE REDWOOD
TANBARK TOBACCO VESUVIN
BRUNETTE MOCCASIN MUSHROOM

PHEASANT PERSIMMON PYGMALION
(CONDOR —) TIFFIN
(DARK —) BURNET
(GRAYISH —) DUN
(HAIR —) ARGALI
(LIGHT —) BRAN ALOMA ALESAN
STRING
(OLIVE —) BARK AUTUMN
(REDDISH —) BAY ROAN SORE SEPIA
AUBURN CROTAL GINGER RUSSET
SORREL AMBROSIA
(YELLOWISH —) AZTEC ALMOND
BAMBOO BLONDE BEESWAX
ALDERNEY
(PREF.) AITHO
BROWNBACK DOWITCH
DOWITCHER
BROWNED ADUST
BROWN HEART RAAN
BROWNIE ELF NIS COOKY DOBBY
NISSE URISK DOBBIE GOBLIN
URUISG
BROWNING SCALD SCORCH
SUNTAN
BROWNISH UMBER BURNET
(— BLACK) LAVA
BROWN LUNG DISEASE
BYSSINOSIS
BROWNSTONE CHESTNUT
BROWSE BRUT CROP FEED GRAZE
FORAGE NIBBLE PASTURE
BRUCITE NEMALITE
BRUISE JAM BASH BRAY BUBU DENT
DUNT HURT JAMB MAIM MAUL
SORE STUN TUND BLACK BREAK
BRIZZ CRUSH CURRY DELVE DINGE
FRUSH POUND PUNCH SQUAT
BATTER BREACH HATTER INJURY
INTUSE MANGLE POUNCE SHINER
STOUND SUGGIL BATTERY
CONTUND CROWNER DAMMISH
DISABLE
(— FLAX) BRAKE
BRUISED HURT LIVID FROISSE
BRUIT DIN FAME RALE ROAR TELL
NOISE RUMOR SOUND BLAZON
CLAMOR REPORT DECLARE HEARSAY
BRUNEI (— WEIGHT) PARA CHAPAH
(COIN OF —) SEN
(TOWN OF —) SERIA
BRUNET DARK BLACK BROWN GIPSY
GYPSY MORENA SWARTHY
BRUNETTE MORENITA
BRUNHILD
(HUSBAND OF —) GUNTHER
BRUNT JAR BLOW JOLT CLASH
FORCE ONSET SHOCK ATTACK
EFFORT IMPACT STRAIN STRESS
ASSAULT OUTBURST VIOLENCE
BRUSH DIP DUB PIG TIP BOSH CARD
COMB DUST FLAP FLAT FRAY KIYI
SKIM SWAB BROOM CHAPE CLEAN
COPSE FIGHT FITCH GRAZE LINER

SABLE SCOPA SCRUB SCUFF SWEEP
SWOOP WHISK BADGER BATTLE
BRIGHT BROSSE DABBER DAUBER
DUSTER MOGOTE PALLET PENCIL
PICKUP PUTOIS RIGGER RUBBER
SPONGE STROKE TEASEL CLEANSE
FOXTAIL GRAINER GROOMER
MOTTLER STIPPLE STRIPER THICKET
SCRUBBER SKIRMISH SOFTENER
STIPPLER TARBRUSH NAILBRUSH
PAINTBRUSH
(— ASIDE) SCUFF
(— IN DANCING) SCUFFLE
(— OF HIR) PENCIL
(— OF TWIGS) COW
(— TO CLEAN SHIP BOTTOM) HOG
(BLUNT —) BLENDER
(DENSE —) BUNDOCKS BOONDOCKS
(ELECTRIC —) DOCTOR
(EMPHASIZED —) SLAP
(FLESH —) SCRAPER STRIGIL
(GROWTH OF —) SYLVAGE
(POLLEN —) SCOPA SAROTHRUM
(SMALL —) TOOL FITCH FITCHEW
(PREF.) MUSCARI SCOPI
BRUSHER LIMBER LIPPER
BRUSH MAKER FLIRTY FLICKER
BRUSH SHUNT PIGTAIL
BRUSHWOOD HAG RICE RONE
RUSH BAVIN BRAKE BRUSH COPSE
FRITH REISE SCROG SCRUB SPRAY
COPPET GARSIL MALLEE RAMMEL
SCRAWL SCRUNT SHROGS TINNET
TINSEL COPPICE ROUGHIE TEENAGE
THICKET WOODRIS BUSHWOOD
OVENWOOD
BRUSQUE CURT RUDE BLUFF BLUNT
GRUFF HASTY ROUGH SHORT
ABRUPT VIOLENT CAVALIER
IMPOLITE
BRUT DRY
BRUTAL CRUEL FERAL GROSS
CARNAL COARSE FERINE SAVAGE
BEASTLY BESTIAL BRUTISH CADDISH
DOGGISH INHUMAN BELLUINE
INHUMANE INSOLENT RUTHLESS
BRUTALITY SADISM
BRUTE BETE BEAST GROSS YAHOO
ANIMAL BRUTAL SAVAGE BEASTLY
BESTIAL BRUTISH GORILLA RUFFIAN
BRUTISH FELL CRUEL BRUTAL
CARNAL FIERCE SAVAGE STUPID
BESTIAL INHUMAN SENSUAL
GADARENE
BRYONY HOP NEP ALRAUN
COWBIND MANDRAKE
(— FRUIT) OXBERRY
BRYOPHYTE MOSS ANOPHYTE
LIVERWORT
BRYOPHYTIC MOSSY MOSSED
BRYOZOAN POLYZOAN
BRYTHONIC CYMRIC KYMRIC
BRITTONIC

BUBBLE AIR BUB BEAD BELL BLEB
BLOB BOIL BOLL DUPE FOAM GLOB
SCUM SEED OAPER CHEAT EMPTY
VAPOR BURBLE DELUDE HOTTER
POPPLE SEETHE SOTTER TRIFLE
BLISTER BLUBBER DECLIVE GLOBULE
DELUSIVE
(— IN GLASS) BOIL REAM SEED
BLISTER
(FORMATION OF —S) EBULLISM
(PL.) SUDS
(PREF.) BULLI
BUBBLING GAY BULLER BURBLY
BOILING GASSING EFFUSIVE
BUBINGA KEVAZINGO
BUBO EMEROD
BUCCANEER PIRATE RIFLER ROBBER
VIKING CORSAIR MARINER SPOILER
MAROONER PICAROON
BUCHMANITE GROUPER
BUCHU BUKA DIOSMA
BUCK FOB RAM BOIL BUTT DEER
DUDE MALE PRIG REAR SOAK STAG
TOFF WASH BLOOD DANDY MONEY
PITOII BASIN STEEP BASKET DOLLAR
OPPOSE RESIST STRIVE SAWBUCK
BUCKJUMP BUCKWASH
(— IN 1ST YEAR) FAWN
(— IN 2ND YEAR) PRICKET
(— IN 3RD YEAR) SORREL
(— IN 4TH YEAR) SORE
(— STEADILY) SUNFISH
(— UP) BRACE
BUCKBEAN BOGBEAN THREEFOLD
BUCKER DOLLYMAN
BUCKET SAY TUB BAIL BOOT BOWK
CAGE ORAB MEAL PAIL SKIP BOWIE
CHEAT SCOOP SKEEL STOOP STOUP
BAILER DIPPER DRENCH HOPPET
KIBBLE SITULA SUCKER VESSEL
FERMAIL GRAPPLE SNAPPER
SWINDLE CANNIKIN HEDGEHOG
PAINTPOT
(— ON MILL WHEEL) AW AWE EIE
(— ON WHEELS) SKIP
(GLASS-MAKING —) CUVETTE
(GRAVEL —) GRAB
(HOISTING —) HUDGE
(PART OF —) EAR RIM BAIL BODY
CURL HANDLE
(TWO – S OF WATER) GAIT
BUCKEYE CANOE
BUCKEYE STATE OHIO
BUCKLAW HAYSTON
BUCKLE BOW BEND CURL KINK
OUCH TACK TACK WARP BRACE
CLASP MARRY STRAP TACHE TWIST
FIBULA CONTEND FERMAIL GRAPPLE
FASTENER STRUGGLE
BUCKLER CRAB BLOCK PELTA SCUTE
TARGE SHIELD TAIRGE TARGET
BUCKLUM BUCKRAM ROTELLA
ROUNDEL SHUTTER RONDACHE

BUCKLING KINK UPSET
BUCK RAKE SWEEP
BUCKRAM STIFFENER
BUCKS BREAD DOUGH MONEY
MOOLA DINERO
BUCKTHORN COMA RHAMN SCROG
WAHOO ALATERN CASCARA
BEARWOOD FRANGULA LOTEBUSH
WAYTHORN STINKWOOD
BUCKTHORN BROWN SUMAC
SUMACH
BUCKWHEAT BUCK CRAP BRANK
WRIGHT KNOTWEED SARRAZIN
POLYGONUM
(PL.) FAGOPYRUM
BUCOLIC IDYL LOCAL NAIVE RURAL
FARMER RUSTIC SIMPLE COWHERD
ECLOGUE AGRESTIC HERDSMAN
PASTORAL
BUCOLION (FATHER OF —)
LAOMEDON
(SON OF —) AESEPUS PEDASUS
(WIFE OF —) ABARBAREA
BUD BUR DYE GEM IMP PIP BULB
BURR CION FORM GERM GIRL GROW
KNOP KNOT WORK CAPOT CHILD
CLOVE GEMMA GRAFT SCION SHOOT
SPRIT SPURT YOUTH BUDLET BULBIL
BUTTON FLOWER GERMIN OCULUS
OILLET SPROUT BLOSSOM BROTHER
CABBAGE GEMMULE PLUMULE
ROSEBUD TENDRON BOURGEON
BULBILLA
(BLIGHTED —) BLAST
(BROOD —) SOREDIUM
(UNDERGROUND —) TURION
(UNDEVELOPED —) EYE
(UNOPENED —) KNOSP
(PL.) CAPERS
(PREF.) BLAST(O) GEMMI GEMMO
BUDDENBROOKS (AUTHOR OF —)
MANN
(CHARACTER IN —) TOM JEAN TONI
ERICA GERDA HANNO JOHANN
THOMAS ANTONIE GRUNLICH
CHRISTIAN PERMANEDER
BUDDHA FO FOH BUTSU JATAKA
GAUTAMA SRAMANA DAIBUTSU
(— STORY) JATAKA
(FATHER OF —) SUDDHODANA
(SON OF —) KAHULA
BUDDHISM DAIJO FOISM KEGON
CHANISM LAMAISM HINAYANA
(— CODE) VINAYA
(BRANCH OF —) MAHAYANA
BUDDHIST (— DOCTRINE) ANATTA
TRIKAYA
(— FESTIVAL) WESAK
(— MOUNTAIN) OMEI
(— PATH) VEHICLE
(— SCHOOL) RITSU
(— SECT) SHIN TENDAI
(— TEACHER) GURU

(— WHO ATTAINED NIRVANA) ARHAT ARAHAT

BUDDLE TYE FRAME BODDLE SLIMER STRIPE TROUGH

BUDDY BO BOY BUD DOC PAL JACK MATE COBBER DIGGER BROTHER COMRADE COMPADRE TENTMATE

BUDGE FUR JEE BOGY MOVE STIR BOOZE BRISK MUDGE STIFF THIEF JOCUND LIQUOR SOLEMN AUSTERE POMPOUS MOVEMENT

BUDGET BAG BOGY BOOT PACK PLAN ROLL BATCH BOGEY BOGIE BUNCH STOCK STORE BOTTLE BUNDLE PARCEL SOCKET WALLET PROGRAM

BUFF ASH BOB FAN TAN BLOW COAT CURT FIRM SHINE SNUFF SPARK BUFFET POLISH STURDY DEVOTEE STAMMER STUTTER NAUMKEAG
(TILLEUL —) ALABASTER

BUFFALO OX ANOA ARNA ARNI BUFF STAG ARNEE BISON BUGLE BUFFLE HAMPER KERBAU MURRAH WUNTEE CARABAO CARIBOU GAZELLE OVERAWE TIMARAU ZAMOUSE BEWILDER SAPIUTAN SELADANG
(WATER —) ARNEE

BUFFALO CHIPS BODEWASH

BUFFALO FISH SUCKER BUFFALO BIGMOUTH GOURDHEAD

BUFFER DOG PAD FROG RACK BUMPER FENDER HURTER PISTOL CUSHION

BUFFET BAR BOB BOX BEAT BLAD BLOW BUFF CUFF GOWF PLAT SCAT SLAP TOSS YANK FILIP KNOCK SCUFF SCUFT SMITE STOOL ABACUS BATTER FILLIP FLEWIT SERVER SETOUT STRIKE STRIVE THRASH COLPHEG CONTEND COUNTER HASSOCK SMACKER SQUELCH CREDENCE CREDENZA CUPBOARD SPANGHEW

BUFFETING DIRD SKITE DUSTING

BUFFLEHEAD DUCK FOOL CLOWN BUFFLE DIPPER DOPPER MARIONET WOOLHEAD MERRYWING

BUFFOON DOR WAG WIT APER FOOL JAPE MIME MOME VICE ZANY ACTOR ANTIC BUFFO CLOWN COMIC DROLE DROLL HARLOT JESTER MUMMER STOOGE ANTIQUE BOUFFON FARCEUR JUGGLER PIERROT PLAYBOY SCOGGIN TOMFOOL BALATRON GRACIOSO HUMORIST MACAROON MERRYMAN OWLGLASS PLEASANT RIDICULE PANTALOON SCARAMOUCH PUNCHINELLO

BUFFOONERY JAPERY ZANYISM CLOWNERY TOMFOOLERY

BUFO TOAD

BUG (ALSO SEE INSECT) DOR FLU FLAW GERM IDEA MITE BOGEY BULGE FIEND LYGUS ROACH ARADID BEDBUG BEETLE BUGGER CAPSID CHINCH COREID CORUCO ELATER GLITCH INSECT SALDID SCHEME TINGID BELLIED BOATMAN BUGBEAR CIMICID CORSAIR FORWARD POMPOUS STRIDER ASSASSIN BARBEIRO CONENOSE HEMIPTER HOBBYIST NAUCORID VINCHUCA
(— OFF) LEAVE
(KIND OF —) LYGUS DAMSEL
(RED —) CHIGGA CHIGGER
(SOW —) SLATER
(PREF.) CIMI(CI)
(SUFF.) CORIS

BUGABOO BOGY FEAR GOGA GOGO OGRE TURK ALARM BOGEY BOGIE GOGGA BODACH GOBLIN BUGBEAR SPECTER SPECTRE WORRICOW

BUGANDA
(— KING) KABAKA

BUGBANE COHOSH BUGWORT RICHWEED HELLEBORE

BUGBEAR BUG COW BOGY OGRE BOGEY BOGIE CADDY MORMO POKER BOGGLE BOGGART BUGABOO FEARBABE SCAREBUG

BUGGER SOD CHAP BOOGER FELLOW PERSON RASCAL HERETIC

BUGGY CART NUTS PRAM SHAY TRAP NUTTY CALESA CABOOSE CALESIN FOOLISH VEHICLE DEMENTED INFESTED ROADSTER STANHOPE

BUGLE BEAD HORN AJUGA BLACK BUFFALO BULLOCK CLARION HUTCHET TRUMPET KEYBUGLE
(— CALL) WARISON
(PART OF —) CUP RIM BELL BITE EDGE
(YELLOW —) IVA

BUGLER WINDJAMMER

BUGLEWEED IVA AJUGA

BUGLOSS ALKANET ANCHUSA BLUEWEED OXTONGUE

BUILD BIG SET FORM LEVY MAKE REAR TELD DRIVE EDIFY ERECT FOUND FRAME HOUSE PUTUP RAISE SHAPE THROW CREATE FABRIC GRAITH TAILLE TIMBER COMPILE EXTRUCT FASHION ASSEMBLE PHYSIQUE
(— FIRE) CHUNK
(— HASTILY) CLAP
(— NEST) AERIE NIDIFY
(— UP) AGGRADE
(BODY —) HABITUS STATURE

BUILDER EPEUS MAKER BIGGAR EPEIUS HANGER ERECTOR ENGINEER

TECTONIC
(DAM —) DAMMER
(PREF.) TECTO
(SUFF.) TECT
BUILDING GIN CASA CRIB DOME
FLAT HALL IGLU JAIL LAND PILE
SHED SHOP SLAB SPOT TELD ABBEY
AEDES ARENA BLOCK COURT FOLLY
FRAME HOTEL HOUSE IGLOO JAWAB
STORE STUDY ARMORY BIGGIN
BOTTLE CASING CHAPEL FABRIC
GARAGE HAMMAM INSULA LYCEUM
PALACE SCHOOL SUCCOR BREWERY
BROODER CARBARN COLLEGE
DIORAMA EDIFICE FACTORY FLATTOP
FOUNDRY KURHAUS MANSION
PALAZZO SALTERN STATION
SYNAGOG ATHENEUM BAGHOUSE
BASILICA BROLETTO CHANCERY
DIPTEROS DRYHOUSE DWELLING
DYEHOUSE ELEVATOR EPHEBEUM
FIRETRAP FOURPLEX GASHOUSE
GINHOUSE HOTHOUSE ICEHOUSE
MAGAZINE NYMPHEUM PANORAMA
SERAPEUM STEMMERY TAXPAYER
TENEMENT VELODROME
OBSERVATORY OUTBUILDING
PLANETARIUM MEETINGHOUSE
(— BLOCK) MEGALITH
(— FOR AIRCRAFT) DOCK
(— GROUPS) HAM
(— OF STONE) KAABA CASHEL
TRUDDO TRULLO
(— ON POSTS) PATAKA
(— WITH TRIANGULAR FRONT)
AFRAME
(BUDDHIST —) TOPE
(CIRCULAR —) THOLE THOLOS
ROTUNDA
(CRUDE —) SHANTY
(DILAPIDATED —) FLEAPIT ROOKERY
FIRETRAP
(EXHIBITION —) MUSEUM
(FARM —) BARN STABLE HACIENDA
(FORTIFIED —) CASTLE
(GLOOMY —) MAUSOLEUM
(GRAIN —) GARNER
(GROUP OF —S) CLUSTER
(JAI ALAI —) FRONTON
(MOVABLE —) TURRET
(ORNAMENTAL —) ALCOVE
(PUBLIC —) CASINO THEATER
THEATRE COLISEUM
(QUADRANGULAR —) TETRAGON
(QUARANTINE —) LAZARET
(ROUND —) THOLUS
(SACRED —) CHURCH MOSQUE
TEMPLE SACRARY PANTHEON
SARAPEUM
(SERIES OF —S) SWEEP
(SLIGHT —) SHED
(SMALL —) HUT COOP HOCK EDICULE

(SPORTS —) CAGE
(STATELY —) DOME
(STORAGE —) BARN HORREUM
(SUBSIDIARY —) ANNEX
(TALL —) SKYSCRAPER
(TRADE —) HALL
(UNCOMFORTABLE —) ARK
(PL.) FUNDUS
BUILD-UP GROWTH
BUILT SET BOUKIT STACKED
TIMBERED
(COMPACTLY —) CORKY
(HEAVILY —) BLOCKY
(LOOSELY —) GANGLING
(STRONGLY —) BURLY GROSS
QUARRY
(WELL —) BUIRDLY
BUKIDNON MONTES BINOKID
BUKKI (FATHER OF —) JOGLI
ABISHUA
(SON OF —) UZZI
BULB BUD SET BLUB CORM IXIA
KNOB LAMP ROOT SEED SEGO
CAMAS CHIVE CLOVE FLOAT GLOBE
ONION SWELL TUBER BULBIL
BULBUS CAMASS CROCUS GARLIC
OFFSET SCILLA RABIANA GALTONIA
SPARAXIS TRITONIA PHOTOFLASH
(— OF PERCUSSION) CONCHOID
(CUBICAL —) FLASHCUBE
(LIGHT —) HELION
(ONION —) BUTTON
(PL.) SQUILL
(PREF.) BULBI BULBO
BULBIL CHIVE BULBLET
(PL.) SPAWN
BULBLET CHIVE CORMEL BULBULE
NUCLEUS PROPAGO
BULBUL KALA BUHLBUHL GREENBUL
LEAFBIRD

GABROVO KARLOVO PLOVDIV
SISTOVA TIRNOVO RUSTCHUK
WEIGHT: OKA OKE TOVAR

BULGARIAN POMAK

BULGE BAG BUG JUT SAG BIAS BULB
BUMP CASK HUMP KNOB LUMP PANT
BILGE BLOAT BOUGE FLASK POUCH
START STRUT SWELL BEETLE BILLOW
COCKLE EXTEND PUCKER WALLET
BLISTER PROJECT OVERHANG
PROTRUDE SWELLING PROJECTION
(**— OUT**) TUT BELLY BOWDEN
STRUNT
(**OFFENSIVE —**) SALIENT

BULGING FULL BOMBE BOWED
BUGGY GOUTY PUDGY TUMID
BAGGED BUNCHY CONVEX GOOGLY
TOROSE GAMPISH GIBBOUS
GOUTISH SWOLLEN BOUFFANT
PROPTOSIS

BULK BODY BOUK FECK HEAP HEFT
HOLD HULK HULL LUMP MASS MOLE
PILE SIZE BURLY CARGO GROSS
MIGHT POWER SLUMP STALL SWELL
CORPSE EXPAND EXTENT FIGURE
VOLUME BIGNESS MAJORITY
QUANTITY
(PREF.) ONCO

BULKHEAD CHECK BATTERY
PARTITION

BULKY BIG MAIN BURLY GROSS
LARGE LUSTY PUDGY STOUT
CLUMSY STODGY HULKING
LUMPING MASSIVE VOLUMED
WEIGHTY CUMBROUS UNWIELDY
(PREF.) PYCN(O)

BULL COP SEG APIS BEEF BILL JEST
MALE ROAN SEAL SEGG SLIP STOT
TORO ZEBU BACIS BEEVE BOBBY,
BONER BOVID BRUTE CROCK DRINK
EDICT ERROR ANIMAL BOVINE
BUSHWA LETTER PEELER TAURUS
BULLOCK BUSHWAH CRITTER
CRUSADE NOVILLO TAURINE
CAJOLERY DOCUMENT FLATTERY
IRISHISM
(**— AREA**) QUERENCIA
(**— KILLING**) VOLAPIE
(**HORNLESS —**) DODDY DODDIE
(**HUMAN-HEADED —**) SHEDU
CAMASSU
(**YOUNG —**) STOT BUGLE MICKY
STIRK STOTT BULLOCK
(PL.) BATTERY
(PREF.) TAUR(I)(O)

BULLA BLEB BULL SEAL BLAIN
BLISTER VESICLE

BULL CELL TORIL

BULLDOG BULL BULLER BULLDOZE

BULLDOZE COW RAM BULLY FORCE
SCOOP COERCE BROWBEAT
BULLYRAG RESTRAIN

BULLDOZER (PART OF —) ARM EYE
SHOE TANK BLADE FRAME IDLER
LEVER LIGHT STRUT TRACK
CANOPY FENDER GRILLE ROLLER
CLEANER HOUSING MUFFLER
CYLINDER

BULLET ACE GUN BALL LEAD PILL
SHOT SLUG TOWEL CONOID
DUMDUM PELLET PICKET SINKER
TRACER DINGBAT MISSILE PELLOCK
PROJECT SPITZER BISCAYAN
MUSHROOM WADCUTTER
(**— SIZE**) CALIBER
(**KIND OF —**) MAGIC
(PL.) BALL LEAD STUFF

BULLETIN ITEM MEMO NOTICE
POSTER REPORT SERIAL PROGRAM
NEWSBILL

BULLETIN BOARD (OPERATOR
OF —) SYSOP

BULLFIGHT CORRIDA NOVILLADA

BULLFIGHTER TORERO MATADOR
PICADOR CAPEADOR TOREADOR
NOVILLERO

BULLFIGHTING REJONEO
TAUROMACHY
(**— MOVEMENT**) PASE
(**PASE IN —**) VERONICA

BULLFINCH ALP OLP HOOP MAWP
MONK NOPE OLPH POPE HEDGE
TANNY TAWNY MONACH REDBIRD
REDHOOP SHIRLEY BLOODALP
TONYHOOP

BULLHEAD CUR POUT POGGE
COTTOID

BULLHEADED SET

BULLHORN HAILER LOUDHAILER

BULLIMONG FARRAGE

BULLION BILLOT

BULLISH STIFF

BULLOCK HOG HOGG NEAT NOWT
STOT BUGLE COACH KNOUT STEER
STIRK BOVINE
(**AUSTRALIAN —**) SNAIL
(**BAD-TEMPERED —**) RAGER
(**DECOY —**) COACH

BULL-ROARER BUZZ BUMMER
BUZZER ROARER TUNDUN HUMBUZZ
TURNDUN WHIZZER

BULL'S-EYE EYE BULL DUMP GOLD
BLANK OXEYE WHITE TARGET
ROUNDEL

BULL SNAKE GOPHER

BULL TROUT TRUFF

BULLY COW NUT BOAT BOSS FACE
FINE GOOD HAZE HUFF MATE BRAVE
BRAVO GREAT JOLLY SNOOL TIGER
VAPOR BOUNCE CUTTER CUTTLE
HARASS HECTOR HUFFER JOVIAL
RUFFLE TYRANT BLUSTER BOUNCER
BULLOCK DARLING DASHING
GALLANT GAUSTER HUFFCAP
ROISTER RUFFIAN RUFFLER SLASHER

SOLDIER SWAGGER BANGSTER
BARRATER BLUDGEON BROWBEAT
BULLDOZE DOMINEER FRAMPLER
NIGHTCAP RABIATOR
(MASTIC —) ACOMA

BULLY TREE BALATA BULLACE
GAUSTER BEEFWOOD

BULRUSH REED RISP RUSH TULE
SEDGE BUMBLE GLUMAL AKAAKAI
CATTAIL PAPYRUS SCIRPUS
TUSSOCK

BULWARK BAIL FORT WALL FENCE
JETTY MANTA MOUND TOWER
SCONCE WARDER BASTION DEFENCE
DEFENSE PARAPET PROTECT
RAMPART WEREWALL

BUM BEG DIN BOOM HOBO
DRINK DRONE IDLER MOOCH SHACK
STIFF TRAMP FROLIC GUZZLE
ROTTER SPONGE SQUEEF GUZZLER
LAYABOUT VAGABOND BINDLESTIFF

BUMBERSHOOT GAMP

BUMBLE ERR

BUMBLEBEE DOR CLOCK BUMBEE
BUMBLE CARDER BUMBLER

BUMBLER OAF IDIOT KLUTZ

BUMMER FLOP FAILURE SKIDDER
STINKER

BUMP CRY HIP HIT NOB BANG BLOW
BOOM BUNK DIRD JOLT JOWL KNOB
LUMP NERF WHAP WHOP BARGE
BULGE CLASH CLOUR CLOUT DUNCH
KNOCK ORGAN THUMP BOUNCE
CANNON IMPACT JOUNCE NODULE
STRIKE BITTERN COLLIDE CONFLICT
SWELLING
(— IMPOLITELY) KNEE
(— IN SKI RUN) MOGUL
(— OFF) KILL SCRAG MURDER
(— ON SKI RUN) MOGUL
(— ON WHALE'S HEAD) HOVEL

BUMPER BOWL FINE GOOD FACER
GLASS ROUSE BUFFER CASABE
FENDER GOBLET HURTER KELTIE
BOUNCER BRIMMER DINGMAN
CARANGID
(— GUARD) OVERRIDER

BUMPER CAR DODGEM

BUMPKIN JAY YAP BEAM BOOM
BOOR CHAW CLOD GAWK HICK LOUT
PUTT RUBE SWAB SWAD TIKE TYKE
CHURL CLOWN ROBIN YAHOO YOKEL
FARMER JOSKIN LUMMOX RUSTIC
BUCOLIC CAUBOGE HAWBUCK
CHAWBACON

BUMPTIOUS COXY BRASH COCKSY

BUN PUG CHOU BRICK COOKIE
CRESCENT
(PL.) BUTTOCKS

BUNAH
(FATHER OF —) JERAHMEEL

BUNCH BOB SET WAD BALE BOSS
CHOU CLEW CLOT CLUB CLUE COMA

KICK KNOB KNOT PACK SWAD TUFT
WISP BREAK CLUMP FAGOT FLOCK
KNOLL PAHIL THUMP CLUTCH
GAGGLE HUDDLE CLUSTER
(— OF BANANAS) HAND STEM
(— OF FEATHERS) LURE PLUME
(— OF FLAX) HEAD STRICK
(— OF FLOWERS) POSY BOWPOT
BOUGUET BOUQUET NOSEGAY
BOUGHPOT
(— OF FOLIAGE) FINIAL
(— OF FRUIT) HOG STRAP
(— OF GRAIN) RIP
(— OF GRAPES) RAISIN
(— OF GRASS) WHISK
(— OF HAIR) COB
(— OF HERBS) BOUQUET
(— OF IVY) BUSH
(— OF RAGS) MOP
(— OF TOBACCO LEAVES) HAND
BREAK
(— OF TWIGS) COW KOW ROD
(— UP) SHRUG
(LONG —) OTRING
(SMALL —) WISP

BUNCHER BINDER

BUNCHY TRUSS

BUNCO SCAM CHEAT

BUNCOMBE HOOEY BUNKUM

BUND BAND QUAY PRAYA LEAGUE
SOCIETY

BUNDLE KID LOT PAD TOD WAD WAP
BALE BAND BEAT BOLT BOOK BUNG
DRUG DRUM GARB HANK HAUL
HEAD KNOT LOCK PACK ROLL SWAG
BLUEY BULTO BUNCH FADGE FAGOT
GAVEL GLEAN GROUP LITCH NICKY
PETER SHEAF SKEIN TARRY TRACE
TRUSS TURSE WADGE BARSOM
BATTEN BINDLE BOTTLE BUDGET
DRIVER DUFTER FAGGOT FARDEL
FASCES FUMBLE GATHER KNITCH
LOGGIN NUMBER PACKET PARCEL
SCROLL THRAVE DORLACH FASCINE
GARBAGE MATILDA PACKAGE
FASCICLE TROUSSEAU
(— BARLEY) SHEAVE
(— OF BOARDS) BOLT
(— OF CELLULOSE) MICROFIBRIL
(— OF FASCINES) ROULEAU
(— OF FIBRILS) AXONEME
(— OF FILAMENTS) BYSSUS
(— OF FLAX) BEET HEAD
(— OF HAIR) LEECH
(— OF HAY, STRAW, ETC.) WAP WASE
WISP GAVEL SHEAF BATTEN BOLTIN
BOTTLE TIPPLE WINDLING
(— OF HEATH) KID
(— OF HIDES) KIP
(— OF NERVE FIBERS) TRACT
COLUMN
(— OF PAPERS) DPUR DUFTER
(— OF RODS) FASCES

(— OF SACKS) BADGER
(— OF SACRED TWIGS) BARSOM
(— OF THONGS) KNOUT
(— OF TOBACCO) CARROT
(— OF TWIGS) BIRCH BROOM
FAGGOT
(— OF WOOD) PIMP BAVIN FAGOT
(— OF YARN) HAUL SLIP
(— OF 60 SKINS) TURN
(— UP) EMBALE
(BUSHMAN'S —) DRUM BLUEY
BUNG CORK DOOK PLUG SHIVE SPILE
STOPPER
BUNGEY KIT
BUNGI-BUNGI STAVEWOOD
BUNGLE ERR BOOB DUFF FLUB
GOOF MESS MUCK MUFF MULL
BLUNK BOTCH FAULT FLUFF FUDGE
MISDO SPOIL STICK BOGGLE BOLLIX
BUMBLE FOOZLE FUMBLE MANGLE
MOMBLE MUCKER MUDDLE TAILOR
TOGGLE BAUCHLE BLUNDER
BUTCHERY SHAMMOCK
BUNGLER MUFF LUMMOX PUDDLE
TINKER BLUNKER BUMBLER
BUMMLER FOOZLER DAUBSTER
SCHLEMIEL
BUNGLING FLUFF FUDGY INERT
CLUMSY AWKWARD TINKERLY
MUDDLEHEADED
BUNGO BONGO CANOE
BUNG START FLOGGER
BUNION ONION WYROCK
CARBUNCLE
BUNJI-BUNJI CUDGERIE
BUNK BED CAR BLAA BLAH CASE
JUNK SACK ABIDE BERTH BUNKO
FRAME HOKUM HOOEY LEAVE
LODGE SLEEP TRUCK BUNKUM
TIMBER BALONEY BOLSTER
CHICORY HEMLOCK TWADDLE
BUNCOMBE COBBLERS MALARKEY
NONSENSE
BUNKHOUSE BULLPEN
BUNKUM BLAH BULL BUNK CROCK
FUDGE HOKUM HOOPLA BALONEY
BUNCOMBE MALARKEY
BUNTAL BURI BANGKOK
BUNTING EBB POP CIRL FLAG PAPE
POPE CHINK DUMPY FINCH PLUMP
COTTON STOCKY TOWHEE UNTIDY
COWBIRD ETAMINE GARMENT
OATFOWL ORTOLAN ROUNDED
BELLYING BOBOLINK PRUSIANO
RICEBIRD RINGBIRD SLOVENLY
NONPAREIL
BUNTON DIVIDER
BUNUS (FATHER OF —) HERMES
(MOTHER OF —) ALCIDAMEA
BUOY DAN NUN WAFT BAKEN ELATE
FLOAT LAGAN RAISE BEACON
MARKER DOLPHIN SUSTAIN

DEADHEAD LEVITATE MAKEFAST
SONOBUOY
(KIND OF —) SONOBUOY
BUOYANCY BALON BALLON LEVITY
SPRING ELATION
BUOYANT GAY CORKY HAPPY LIGHT
BLITHE BOUNCY FLOATY LIVELY
ELASTIC HOPEFUL JOCULAR LILTING
SPRINGY ANIMATED CHEERFUL
SANGUINE SPIRITED VOLATILE
BUPHAGUS (FATHER OF —) IAPETUS
(MOTHER OF —) THORNAX
(SLAYER OF —) ARTEMIS
BUR BUZZ TEAZEL STICKER
BURBARK AKONGE BOXBUSH
BURRBARK
BURBOT COD CONY CUSK LING LOTA
CONEY LOCHE LAWYER MORGAY
DOGFISH EELPOUT GUDGEON
BIRDBOLT
BURBUNG BORA
BURDEN TAX VEX BIRN CARE CARK
CLAG CLOG DRAG DUTY FARE FOOT
GANG LADE LOAD MUCK ONUS
PORT SEAM TACK TASK BIRTH
CARGO CROWD CRUSH DRONE
HEAVY LABOR MIDST CHARGE
CUMBER ENTAIL FARDEL HAMPER
IMPOSE LADING SADDLE THRACK
WEIGHT BALLAST BURTHEN
CONVETH FRAUGHT FREIGHT
HAGRIDE ONERATE OPPRESS
REFRAIN REPRISE SUMPTER
TROUBLE CAPACITY CARRIAGE
ENCUMBER ENGREGGE HANDICAP
OVERCOME PRESSURE QUANTITY
RUMBELOW MILLSTONE
RESPONSIBILITY
(— OF SONG) WHEEL FADING
HOLDING OVERTURN OVERWORD
(FINANCIAL —) EXPENSE
BURDENED HEAVY LADEN GRAVID
FRAUGHT HARASSED
BURDENER INCUBUS
BURDENSOME HEAVY IRKSOME
ONEROUS WEIGHTY CUMBROUS
GRIEVOUS GRINDING LOADSOME
BURDOCK DOCK GOBO CLITE CLOTE
CLOTS DRAIN LAPPA BARDANE
BURWEED BUZZIES CADILLO
CLOTBUR HARDOCK HAREBUR
CLEAVERS HAULBACK
BUREAU DESK CHEST AGENCY
EXCISE OFFICE CENTRAL DRESSER
AGITPROP
BUREAUCRAT MANDARIN
BURFISH ATINGA
BURGEON BUD GROW ERUPT
SHOOT SPROUT
BURGESS CITIZEN FREEMAN
PORTMAN COMMONER GORGIBUS
(PL.) BURGWARE

BURG GRASS SANDBUR COCKSPUR
SANDSPUR
BURGH ROYALTY
BURGLAR YEGG CRACK THIEF
GOPHER ROBBER RAFFLES
YEGGMAN PETERMAN PICKLOCK
(— TOOL) LOID
BURGLARY BREAK CRACK THEFT
LARCENY ROBBERY STEALAGE
BURGLE ROB SCREW
BURGUNDY MACON POMMARD
VOUGEOT TONNERRE
BURIAL FUNERARY INTERMENT
(— MOUND) TOLA HUACA
BURIAL PLACE AHU TOMB GRAVE
BURIAL GIGUNU LAYSTOW PYRAMID
CATACOMB CEMETERY GOLGOTHA
LAYSTALL
BURIED HIDDEN HUMATE SEPULT
ABSORBED IMBEDDED
(NOT —) UNRESTED
(RECENTLY —) GREEN
BURIN GRAVER PLASTIC
BURKINA FASO (CAPITAL OF —)
OUAGADOUGOU
(LANGUAGE OF —) BOBO LOBI SAMO
MANDE MOSSI
(MOUNTAIN IN —) TEMA
(NATIVE OF —) BOBO LOBI SAMO
BISSA HAUSA MANDE MARKA
MOSSI PUEHL TUAREG SENOUFO
VOLTAIC YATENGA MANDINGO
(RIVER IN —) VOLTA SOUROU
(TOWN OF —) PO LEO DORI PAMA
YAKO DJIBO GAOUA LAWRA
HOUNDE TOUGAN BANFORA
BURL BURR KNAR KNOT LUMP
KNAUR PIMPLE PUSTULE
BURLAP GUNNY CROCUS BAGGING
HESSIAN SACKING WRAPPING
BURLER LECKER SPILER
BURLESQUE APE ODD COPY JEST
MIME SKIT BURLY DROLL FARCE
REVUE COMEDY OVERDO PARODY
BUFFOON JOCULAR MIMICRY
MOCKERY OVERACT DOGGEREL
RIDICULE TRAVESTY
BURLY BIG FAT BLUFF BULKY GROSS
HEAVY HUSKY LARGE LUSTY NOBLE
OBESE STOUT THICK TRAMP
BOWERLY BUIRDLY MASTIFF
STATELY IMPOSING
BUR MARIGOLD BACLIN CUCKOLD
BURMESE KADU BIRMAN
ARAKANESE
BURN GYP BREN BREW CHAR FIRE
GLOW PLOT RAZE RILL SEAR SERE
TEND TIND ADUST BLAZE BROIL
BROOK CENSE CHARK CLAMP FLAME
FLARE OUTDO PARCH PLOUT QUICK
ROAST SCALD SCAUM SINGE SWEAL
WASTE WATER CLOZLE IGNIFY

SCORCH SIZZLE STREAM CHARPIT
COMBURE COMBUST CONSUME
CREMATE CROZZLE FLICKER FRIZZLE
INCENSE OXIDIZE RIVULET
SCOWDER SMOLDER SWINDLE
FLAGRATE SQUANDER AMBUSTION
(— FEEBLY) GUTTER
(— FITFULLY) FLICKER
(— IN) INURE
(— MIDNIGHT OIL) LUCUBRATE
(— OUT) GUT
(— THOROUGHLY) ASH
(— UP) ADUST EXUST
(— WITH LITTLE FLAME) SMUDGE
(LET —) BISHOP
(PREF.) COMBURI
BURNED ADUST COMBUST
(PREF.) AITHO
BURNER BEAK ETNA KORO BAKER
PILOT ARGAND BUNSEN CENSER
BATSWING CALCINER GASLIGHT
THURIBLE WELSBACH
BURNET SELFHEAL BLOODWORT
BURNING HOT FIRE LIVE ADUST
AFIRE ANGRY BLAZE CALID EAGER
FIERY FLAME GLEDY QUICK SCALD
URENT ABLAZE ARDENT FERVID
FIRING LIVING TORRID USTION
ADURENT CAUSTIC CAUTERY
FERVENT FLAMING GLARING
GLOWING INTENSE MORDANT
SCOWDER SHINING ARDUROUS
EXCITING FLAGRANT INUSTION
MUIRBURN PARCHING SCOUTHER
(— BRIGHTLY) LIGHT
(— OF FORESTS IN INDIA) JHOOM
(MALICIOUS —) ARSON
(NO LONGER —) EXTINCT
(PREF.) IGNI
BURNING BUSH WAHOO
BURNISH RUB GLAZE GLOSS INLAY
POLISH FURBISH
BURNISHED BROWN WHITE
BURNISHER AGATE BUFFER GLAZER
FROTTON POLISHER
BURNT ADUST BRULE COMBUST
BURP BOKE BELCH BUDDLE
BURR NUT PAD RIB BARB BIRR BOSS
BUZZ HALO KNOB PILE RING ROVE
SLUG WHIR BRIAR BURGH CROUP
WHARL WHIRR BANYAN CIRCLE
CORONA TEASEL TUNNEL WASHER
CORONET STICKER PARASITE
(— IN WOOD) GNAR KNAR
(— OF ANTLER) CORONET
(— ON TYPE) RAG
BURRO ASS DONKEY
BURROW BED DEN DIG SET BURY
HEAP HOLE HOWK MINE MOLE PIPE
ROOT TUBE BERRY COUCH EARTH
MOUND FURROW ROOTLE TUNNEL
CLAPPER GALLERY PASSAGE

SHELTER EXCAVATE WORMHOLE
(— AS EEL) MUD
(— IN) MOIL
(— OF BADGER) SET
(— OF OTTER) COUCH
(FOSSIL —) SCOLITE
BURROWS TOWN
BURSA SAC SACK POUCH CAVITY
BURSULA
BURSAR BOWSER PURSER TERRAR
BOUCHER CASHIER
BURSE CASE SHOP FOREL BAZAAR
BOURSE POCKET
BURST FIT FLY POP BLOW BUST
DASH GUSH GUST LOSS LOUP REND
SCAT TILT BLAST BLOUT BREAK
CRACK ERUPT FLAFF FLASH GRAZE
REAVE SALVO SCATT SHOUT SPASM
SPLIT START STAVE BROKEN
DAMAGE INJURY SPROUT EXPLODE
IMPLODE RUPTURE SHATTER
AIRBURST OUTBREAK SUNDERED
(— ASUNDER) OUTRIVE
(— FORTH) ERUPT SALLY EXPIRE
BALLOON
(— IN) IRRUPT IMPLODE
(— INTO FRAGMENTS) FLITTER
(— INTO LAUGHTER) BUFF
(— OF ACTIVITY) BRASH SPURT
SPRINT SPLURGE
(— OF ARTILLERY) GRAZE RAFALE
(— OF CHEERS) SALVO
(— OF ENERGY) BANG
(— OF FIRING) COUGH
(— OF HARMONIOUS SOUND)
DIAPASON
(— OF LIGHT) FLASH GLORY
(— OF SPEED) KICK FLUTTER
(— OF TEARS) BLURT
(— OF TEMPER) FUFF BOUTADE
(— OF WIND) FLAW
(— OPEN) DEHISCE UPBRAST
(— OUT) BUFF PRORUMP
(— THE HEART) RIVE
(SUFF.) RRHAGE RRHAGIA RRHAGY
BURSTER GALE LUGGER CRACKER
BURSTING TUMID ABURST
BLOWOUT RUPTION ERUPTING

BURUNDI
CAPITAL: BUJUMBURA
COIN: FRANC
LAKE: RUGWERO TSHOHOHA
NATIVE: TWA HUTU BANTU PYGMY
TUTSI WATUSI
PEOPLE: WATUSI
RIVER: KAGERA RUVUBU RUZIZI
AKANYARU MALAGARAZI
TOWN: NGOZI BURURI KITEGA
MUYINGA BUJUMBURA

BURY URN CAMP HIDE MOOL RAKE
TURF VEIL CLOAK COVER EARTH
GRAVE INTER INURN PLANT VAULT
WHELM ENTOMB ENWOMB HEARSE
INHUME SEPULT SHROUD BEDELVE
CONCEAL ENGROSS IMMERSE
PITHOLE REPRESS SECRETE
FUNERATE INHEARSE SUBMERGE
SEPULCHER
BUS CLEAR CAMION JITNEY JEEPNEY
MINIBUS DOUBLEDECKER
(PRIVATE —) PIRATE
BUSBOY OMNIBUS PICCOLO
BUSH TOD BUTT BOSCH BURSE
CLUMP GROVE PLASH SCRAY SHRUB
BOUCHE BRANCH BUSKET MAQUIS
TAVERN BOSCAGE BOUCHON
CLUSTER OUTBACK THICKET
BUSHLAND
(— OF HAIR) GLIB
(— SICKNESS) TAURANGA
(BLACKBERRY —) BRAMBLE
(PRICKLY —) GORSE
(ROSE —) ROSIER ROSIERE
(STUNTED —) SCROG
(WILD ROSE —) BRIAR BRIER
(PL.) RUFFMANS
(PREF.) THAMN(O)
BUSHBUCK BONGO
BUSH CLOVER HAGI
BUSH COW ZAMOUSE
BUSHEL FOO FOU GOB LOT MET
EPHA EPHI EPHAH BUCKET MODIUS
STRICK
(1.6 —) FANEGA
(1-HALF —) TOVET
(1-HALF TO 3-4THS —) CABOT
(1-4TH —) PECK
(3-4THS —) SKIPPLE
(3 TO 5 —S) SACK
(4 —S) COMB COOMB
(41.28 —) WEY
(8 —S) SEAM
BUSHER SWAMPER
BUSHGRASS WOODREED
BUSHING BUSH COAK DRILL LINER
BOUCHE COLLET LINING SLEEVE
BOUCHON FERRULE GROMMET
PADDING
(HALF —) STEP
BUSHMAN GUNG BUSHY KHUAI
ABATOA ABATWA WHALER
BUSHBOY SWAGMAN NEGRILLO
(PL.) SAN SAAN
BUSHMASTER CURUCUCU
SURUCUCU
BUSHWHACKER PAPAW PAWPAW
BUSHY BOSKY SHOCK DUMOSE
DUMOUS BUSHMAN QUEACHY
BUSIED VERSANT
BUSILY THRANG
BUSINESS ADO ART BIZ FAT JOB PIE
CARE FEAT FIRM FUSS GAME GEAR
LINE NOTE TASK WORK CAUSE
CRAFT ERGON TRADE TRUCK AFFAIR

CUSTOM EMPLOY ERRAND MATTER
METIER NEGOCE OFFICE PIDGIN
PIGEON RACKET TURKEY ACCOUNT
BEESWAX CALLING CONCERN
JOURNEY PALAVER TRADING
TRAFFIC ACTIVITY AGIOTAGE
BESOIGNE COMMERCE FOLLOWER
INDUSTRY INTEREST VOCATION
OCCASIONS OCCUPATION
(— WITHOUT ASSETS) SHELL
(COMIC —) LAZZO
(MONKEY —) JOUKERY PAWKERY
(STAGE —) BYPLAY

BUSINESSMAN TYCOON POACHER
BOURGEOIS CONVERTER

BUSKIN BOOT SHOE CALIGA
BOTTINE COTHURN BRODEKIN
COTHURNUS

BUSS SMOUCH

BUSSU UBUSSU TROOLIE

BUST BUMP FAIL RUIN TAME BOSOM
BREAK BURST BUSTO CHEST EDGAR
FLUNK SPREE BRONZE DEMOTE
REDUCE STATUE TURKEY DEGRADE
DISMISS FAILURE PROTOME
PORTRAIT
(— SHAPE) TAILLE

BUSTARD KORI OTIS WATO PAAUW
TURKEY BEBILYA HOUBARA
KORHAAN FLORICAN GOMPAAUW
(PREF.) OTIDI

BUSTIC AUSUBO CASSADA

BUSTLE ADO TEW BUZZ FIKE FRAY
FUSS JUMP STIR WHEW WHIR
FRISK HASTE HYPER KNOCK PAVIE
STEER WHIRL WHIRR BISHOP
BUMBLE ENERGY FISSLE FISTLE
FLURRY FUSTLE HUDDLE HUSTLE
POTHER PUDDER RACKET ROMAGE
RUFFLE TATTER THRONG TUMULT
UNREST UPROAR CLATTER CLUTTER
CONTEND LOUSTER SCOWDER
SCUFFLE SCUFTER SPUFFLE
ACTIVITY IMPROVER SPLUTTER
STRUGGLE TOURNURE CRINOLETTE
(—ABOUT) TROT

BUSTLING ADO BUSY FUSSY
SPOFFISH STIRRING

BUST-UP SCUFFLE

BUSY FAST FELL APPLY BRISK QUICK
ACTIVE ATWORK EIDENT EMPLOY
INTENT LIVELY OCCUPY ORNATE
STEERY THRONG UNIDLE ENGAGED
HOPPING HUMMING OPEROSE
TROUBLE WORKING DILIGENT
EMPLOYED EXERCISE OCCUPIED
SEDULOUS TIRELESS UNTIRING
PRAGMATIC PRAGMATICAL
(— ONESELF) STRAP
(— WITH TRIFLES) FIDDLE FIDDLING
(NOT —) SLACK

BUSYBODY BUSY SNOOP YENTA
EARWIG SPOFFY ARDELIO MARPLOT

MEDDLER SNOOPER FACTOTUM
QUIDNUNC PRAGMATIC

BUT AC LO MA BIT SED YEA YET
MERE ONLY SAVE ARRAH STILL
ALWAYS EXCEPT UNLESS BESIDES.
HOWBEIT HOWEVER

BUTCHER KILL SLAY BUTCH SPOIL
BUNGLE KIDDER LEGGER LEMMER
MURDER VENDOR BOTCHER
BRAINER BRITTEN FLESHER
MEATMAN PORKMAN KILLCALF
PIGSTICK SLAUGHTER

BUTCHERBIRD SHRIKE MATAGASSE

BUTCHER'S-BROOM RUSCUS
BRUSCUS

BUTCHERY MURDER CARNAGE
MASSACRE SHAMBLES SLAUGHTER

BUTEA DHAK

BUTEO BUZZARD

BUTES (BROTHER OF —)
ERECHTHEUS
(FATHER OF —) NEPTUNE PANDION
POSEIDON
(SISTER OF—) PROCNE PHILOMELA
(WIFE OF —) CHTHONIA

BUTLER SOMLER YEOMAN BOTELER
SERVANT SPENCER STEWARD
CELLARER CONSUMAH KHANSAMA
STEPHANO MAJORDOMO

BUTT JUR JUT MOT PIT PUT RAM
RUN TOY TUP BUCK BUNT BURT
BUSH CART CASK DISH DOSS FOOL
GOAD GOAL GOAT HORN JOLT JURR
PIPE POLL PUCK PUSH STUB TANG
TOPE TURR BOUND DUNCH HINGE
JOINT MOUND ROACH SCOPE STOCK
STUMP BREECH TARGET THRUST
BEEHIVE BUTTOCK PARAPET
PROJECT REVERSE STUMMEL
ARIETATE FLATFISH FLOUNDER
RIDICULE SACKBUTT
(— FOR RIDICULE) GAME SPORT
STALE COCKSHY
(— OF CIGAR) DOCK SNIPE
(— OF HORSEHIDE) SHELL
(— OF JOKE) JEST SCOGGIN
JESTWORD
(CIGARETTE —) BUMPER
(HALF —) BEND

BUTTE HILL PICACHO

BUTTER RAM GOAT SHEA CLART
COCUM BAMBUK BEURRE CAJOLE
LEKVAR SPREAD BLARNEY FLATTER
(— MEASURE) SPAN
(— SUBSTITUTE) VANASPATI
(ARTIFICIAL —) BOSH OLEO BOSCH
MARGARINE
(ASTRONOMICAL —) ARIES
(BROWNED IN —) NOISETTE
(PRUNE —) LEKVAR
(SEMIFLUID —) GHI GHEE

BUTTER-AND-EGGS RANSTEAD
TOADFLAX

BUTTERBUR CLEAT CLOTE ELDIN GALON GALLON OXWORT GILTCUP FLEADOCK

BUTTERCUP BOLT CYME CRAZY ANEMONE CRAISEY CROWTOE GILTCUP GOLDCUP KINGCOB KINGCUP CRAWFOOT CROWFOOT FROGWORT PASQUEFLOWER

BUTTERFISH GUNNEL POMPANO WHITING PALOMETA SKIPJACK

BUTTERFLY IO BLUE ARGUS COMMA ELFIN GHOST NYMPH QUEEN SATYR SWIFT WHITE ZEBRA ADONIS ALPINE APOLLO CALIGO COPPER DANAID HOPPER IDALIA JUGATE MORPHO PIERID PROGNE PSYCHE SULFUR THECLA URSULA VIOLET YELLOW ADMIRAL BUCKEYE DIURNAL DOLPHIN EMPEROR FRENATE MONARCH PIERINE SATYRID SKIPPER SULPHUR TROILUS TUSSOCK VANESSA VICEROY ARTHEMIS CECROPIA CRESCENT GRAYLING HESPERID ITHOMIID WANDERER METALMARK (— BREEDER) AURELIAN

BUTTERFLY FISH MOJARRA FLATFISH

BUTTERFLY WEED FLUXROOT MILKWEED WINDROOT

BUTTERMILK WHIG JOCOQUE SOURDOOK (— AND WATER) BLAND

BUTTERSCOTCH TOFFY

BUTTERTREE MAHWA

BUTTERWORT BEANWEED ROTGRASS SHEEPWEED

BUTTERY BOTRY LARDER SPENCE BUTLERY SPICERY

BUTTOCK CHEEK

BUTTOCKS ASS BUM BUN CAN FUD HAM ARSE BUNS BUTT CULE DOCK DOUP DUFF LEND MOON POOP PRAT SEAT TAIL TOBY TUSH CROUP FANNY NATES SLATS STERN TOUTE TUSHY BEHIND BOTTOM BREECH CHEEKS CURPIN HEINIE HINDER TUSHIE CROUPON CRUPPER DRODDUM HURDIES KEISTER BACKSIDE DERRIERE NATIFORM POSTERIOR (PRACTICE OF EXPOSING —) MOONING (PREF.) NATI PYG(O) (SUFF.) PROCTA PYGAL PYGE PYGIA(N) PYGOUS PYGUS

BUTTON BUD ZIP BOSS CHIN DOME HOOK KNOB KNOP SPUR TUFT BADGE CATCH GLIDE OLIVE PEARL PRILL BARREL BAUBLE BOUTON BUCKLE GLIDER SHINER TOGGLE TROCHE DEWDROP HORNTIP KNICKER NETSUKE PRESSEL REGULUS DOORBELL FASTENER OLIVETTE (— MAN) SOLDIER (KIND OF —) PANIC

BUTTONBUSH BUCKBRUSH SWAMPWOOD

BUTTONHOLE EYE LOOP SLIT

BUTTON SNAKEROOT LIATRIS SAWWORT

BUTTONWOOD COTONIER

BUTTRESS NOSE PIER PILE PROP SPUR STAY BRACE BRICK ALLETTE OUTCAST OUTSHOT SUPPORT TAMBOUR ABUTMENT (— MEMBER) TIRE

BUTYL TETRYL

BUXOM MILD AMPLE JOLLY PLUMP PRONE SONSY BLITHE CRUMBY CRUMMY FLORID FODGEL HUMBLE PLIANT SONSIE BOWERLY BOUNCING FLEXIBLE OBEDIENT OBLIGING YIELDING JUNOESQUE

BUY CHAP COFF COUP GAIN HAVE SHOP SNIP TAKE BRIBE CLAIM TRADE ABEGGE MARKET RANSOM REDEEM SECURE ACQUIRE CHAFFER PURCHASE (— BACK) REPRISE (— OFF) BRIBE APPEASE (— UP STOCKS) COVER (GOOD —) DEAL

BUYER CHAP AGENT CATER BEGGER EMPTOR PATRON VENDEE CHAPMAN SHOPPER ACHATOUR CUSTOMER PROSPECT (— OF CLOTH) REDUBBER

BUYING ACATE ACHATE EMPTION (— MANIA) ONIOMANIA

BUZ (FATHER OF —) NAHOR (MOTHER OF —) MILCAH

BUZI (SON OF —) EZEKIEL

BUZZ HUM BURR CALL DASH HISS HUSS HUZZ RING WHIR FLAY FLING PHONE RUMOR BUMBLE NOTION WHOOSH WHISPER

BUZZARD AURA FOOL HAWK PERN BUTEO GLADE GLEDE HARPY STOOP BEETLE CURLEW PREYER STUPID PUDDOCK PUTTOCK VULTURE BROMVOEL

BUZZER BEE BELL ALARM HOWLER SIGNAL WHIZZER

BY A P X AB AT OF TO AGO BYE GIN PAR PER TIL ABUT ANON INTO NEAR PAST TILL APART ASIDE CLOSE FORBY BESIDE TOWARD BESIDES THROUGH (— AND —) ANON (— AND BY) BELIVE BIMEBY (— FAR) EASILY (— HEART) PERQUEIR (— HOOK OR CROOK) HABNAB (— MEANS OF) PER MOYENANT (— NO MEANS) NA

(— **REASON OF THIS**) HEREAT
(— **STEALTH**) STOWLINS
(— **SURPRISE**) ABACK
(— **THE DAY**) PD
(— **THE ORDER OF**) O
(— **THE WAY**) APROPOS
(— **THIS TIME**) ALREADY
(— **WAY OF**) VIA
(GONE —) AGO PAST
(NEAR —) GIN
(PREF.) PRETER
BY-BIDDER FUNK CAPPER PUFFER
BYBLIS (BROTHER OF —) CAUNUS
(FATHER OF —) MILETUS
(MOTHER OF —) IDOTHEA
BY-CHANNEL BAYOU BRANCH
BYCOKET ABACOT ABOCOCKET
BYGONE PAST YORE OLDEN BYPAST
FORMER ANCIENT ANTIQUE

ELAPSED BACKWARD DEPARTED
FOREPAST PRETERIT
BYPASS JUMP SHUN AVOID BURKE
EVADE SHUNT CUTOFF DETOUR
CIRCUIT OUTFLANK
BYPATH LANE BYWAY UNDERWALK
BY-PRODUCT SPINOFF SCRAP
SHORTS EFFLUVIUM MIDDLINGS
OUTGROWTH
BYRE SHIPPEN COWHOUSE
BYRNIE ARMOR
BYROAD BOREEN
BYWAY LANE PATH ALLEY BYPATH
BYWALK OUTWAY SIDEWAY
BYWORD ADAGE AXIOM MOTTO
BYNAME DIVERB PHRASE SAYING
NAYWORD PROVERB NICKNAME
REPROACH
BY-WORK PARERGON

C

C DO CEE DOH COCA CHARLIE
HUNDRED
CAAMA FOX ASSE SILVER
CAB FLY KAB HACK TAXI ARABA
ARANA CABIN NODDY GHARRI
CRAWLER HACKNEY SHOWFUL
TAXICAB VETTURA COUPELET
MOTORCAB
(HINDU —) JUDKA
(KIND OF —) GYPSY
(LOW-HUNG —) HERDIC
(2-PONY —) KOSONG
(4-WHEELED —) BOUNDE BOUNDER
DROSHKY GROWLER
CABAL PLOT RING JUNTA JUNTO
PARTY BRIGUE CLIQUE SCHEME
SECRET CHATTER CONSULT COUNCIL
DISPUTE FACTION TALKING
INTRIGUE CAMARILLA
CABALASSOU ARMADILLO
CABALISTIC MYSTIC
CABARET CAFE TAVERN
CABASSOU XENURUS
CABBAGE CAB CHOU CRIB KALE
WORT CROUT FILCH SAVOY STEAL
STOCK PECHAY PILFER TAILOR
BOWKAIL OXHEART PAKCHOI
PALMITO PURLOIN BORECOLE
COLEWORT CRUCIFER CULTIGEN
DRUMHEAD KOHLRABI KERGUELEN
(CHINESE —) BOKCHOY PAKCHOI
(KIND OF —) NAPA
(STUFFED —) HOLISHKES
(PL.) WORTS
CABBAGE BARK ANGELIM
ANGELIN
CABBAGE SOUP SHCHI STCHI
SHTCHEE
CABBAGE STALK CASTOCK
CABBIE HACK
CABDRIVER HACK MUSH CABBY
CABMAN COCHER MUSHER
COCHERO HACKMAN
CABIN BOX CAB COT DEN HUT CAVE
CELL CREW CRIB SHED TILT BOOTH
CHOZA COACH CUDDY FELZE HOVEL
LODGE SHACK BOHAWN CABANA
CASITA LITTER REFUGE SALOON
SHANTY SHELTY WIGWAM
BEDROOM BOUDOIR COTTAGE
HUDDOCK MUDSILL
(— ON SHIP'S DECK) TEXAS
ROUNDHOUSE
(DOUBLE —) SADDLEBAG
(PASSENGER —) VAN
(RUSSIAN LOG —) IZBA
CABIN-BOY GRUMMET

CABINET ARK BOX BUHL CASE FILE
SINK AMBRY BAHUT BOARD CABIN
CHEST BAFFLE BUREAU CLOSET
ICEBOX ALMIRAH BOUDOIR
COMMODE CONSOLE COUNCIL
ETAGERE FREEZER JUKEBOX
WHATNOT CELLARET CUPBOARD
MINISTRY SHOWCASE VARGUENO
MONOCLEID
(FILING —) MORGUE
CABINET-MAKER EBENISTE
CABINETMAKER EBENISTE
CABLE GUY TOW BOOM COAX CORD
FAST JUNK LINK ROPE STAY WIRE
CABLET GANGER STRAND TETHER
COAXIAL GUNLINE SKYLINE
CATENARY HIGHLINE TELEGRAM
UMBILICAL
(— WITH EYE AT EACH END) STRAP
(— WOUND) KECKLING
(CHAIN —) BOOM
(DERRICK —) BACKSTAY
(SPLICED —) SHOT
(SUSPENDED —) ROPEWAY
CABLE CAR TELFER TELPHER
CABLED RUDENTED
CABMAN IZVOZCHIK
CABOCHON CAB SHELL CARBUNCLE
CABOODLE KIT LOT CALABASH
CABOOSE CAB CAR VAN CRIB
HACK BUGGY CRUMMY GALLEY
PALACE BOUNCER COOKROOM
DOGHOUSE
CABRILLA CONY GAPER GROUPER
CABRIOLE LEG
CABSTAND HASARD HAZARD
CABUYA PITEIRA
CACAO BROMA COCOA ARRIBA
COCKER CRIOLLO FORASTERO
CACHARI BODA
CACHE BURY HIDE DEPOT STASH
STORE MEMORY SCREEN CONCEAL
DEPOSIT TREASURE
CACHELOT WHALE
CACHET SEAL STAMP WAFER
ESSENCE KONSEAL
CACIQUE BUNYAH CASSICAN
HANGNEST
CACKEREL MENDOLE
CACK-HANDED CLUMSY AWKWARD
CACKLE CANK CONK CLACK LAUGH
BABBLE GABBLE GAGGLE GIGGLE
GOSSIP KECKLE TITTER CHACKLE
CHATTER SNICKER TWADDLE
LAUGHTER
CACKLING GAGGLING
CACKLING GOOSE GREASER

CACOMISTLE CIVET ARCTOID RINGTAIL BASSARISK
CACOON SEGRA SEQUA
CACOPHONOUS HARSH RAUCOUS JANGLING STRIDENT
CACTUS BLEO DILDO NOPAL RAVOSO CARDON CEREUS CHAUTE CHENDE CHINOA CHOLLA COCHAL MESCAL PEYOTE PEYOTL TASAJO AIRAMPO BISAGRE BISNAGA SAGUARO ALICOCHE CHICHIPE PITAHAYA XEROPHIL
(— FRUIT) MUYUSA
(KIND OF —) RATTAIL
CAD CUR BOOR CHUM HEEL CHURL LOUSE SWEEP BRAKJE MUCKER RASCAL ROTTER BOUNDER BUDMASH DASTARD BLIGHTER ASSISTANT
CADASTRAL UNIT YOKE
CADAVER BODY STIFF CORPSE CARCASS SUBJECT SKELETON
CADAVEROUS PALE GAUNT LIVID PALLID GHASTLY HAGGARD
CADDIE NACKET
CADDIS FLY DUN CADEW SEDGE CADBIT
CADDISWORM PIPER
CADDO ADAI TEXAS EYEISH HAINAI KICHAI HASINAI
CADE LAMB SOCK
CADENAS NEF
CADENCE BEAT FALL IAMB LILT PACE TONE CLOSE METER METRE PULSE SOUND SWING THROB DACTYL IAMBUS JINGLE RHYTHM BACCHIC ANAPAEST CLAUSULA MOVEMENT MEDIATION
(GREGORIAN —) TROPE
CADENZA MELISMA BARIOLAGE
CADET SON DODO GOAT PLEBE YOUTH EMBRYO JUNIOR SERGEANT
CADGE BEG BOT BUM TIE BIND HAWK CARRY MOOCH PEDDLE SPONGE SCROUNGE
CADGER BOT BUM DEALER HAWKER CARRIER PACKMAN SPONGER HUCKSTER SCAMBLER
CADGY KEDGY MERRY WANTON AMOROUS LUSTFUL CHEERFUL MIRTHFUL
CADMUS (DAUGHTER OF —) INO AGAVE SEMELE AUTONOE
(FATHER OF —) AGENOR
(MOTHER OF —) TELEPHASSA
(SISTER OF —) EUROPA
(SON OF —) POLYDORUS
(WIFE OF —) HARMONIA
CADRE CORE FRAME
CADUCEUS WAND STAFF SCEPTER SCEPTRE KERYKEION
CAECUM TYPHLON
(PREF.) ILEO TYPHL(O)

CAESAR (WORDS FROM —) ETTU
CAESURA REST STOP BREAK PAUSE INTERVAL DIAERESIS
CAFE BAR PUB CAFF AGOGO TAVERN BARROOM CABARET TAVERNA ESTAMINET
(— AU LAIT) ALESAN
(ROADSIDE —) BUVETTE
CAFE CREME SUEDE
CAFETERIA AUTOMAT
CAFFEINE THEIN THEINE
CAGAYAN IBANAG
CAGE BOX CAR GIG MEW PEN COOP CORF CRIB GOAL BRAKE CAVEA GRATE HUTCH AVIARY BASKET BUCKET CHAPEL ENCAGE FLIGHT PRISON CHANTRY CONFINE ENCLOSE LANTERN SHELTER TUMBREL TUMBRIL CARRIAGE ELEVATOR IMPRISON LAVARIUM RETAINER SCAFFOLD STRAINER
(— FOR HAWKS) MEW
(— FOR HENS) CAVEY CAVIE
(— FOR MOUTH) MUZZLE
(— OF MINE SHAFT) GIG
(— OF TRAM) CABIN
(BIRD —) AVIARY PINJRA VOLARY BIRDCAGE
(FIRE —) CRESSET
(KIND OF —) RIB
(LOBSTER —) CORF CREEL
(REVOLVING —) TUMBLER
CAGED PENT CAPTIVE
CAGER ONSETTER
CAGEY CAGY WARY GOONY
CAGMAG KEGMEG
CAGOT AGOTE
CAHITA YAQUI
CAHOT PITCHHOLE
CAIMAN CAYMAN JACARE ALLIGATOR
CAIN (BROTHER OF —) ABEL SETH
(FATHER OF —) ADAM
(MOTHER OF —) EVE
(SON OF —) ENOCH
CAINAN (FATHER OF —) ENOS ARPHAXAD
(SON OF —) SALA MAHALALEEL
CAINGANG COROADO AWEIKOMA CORONADO
CAIRN MAN PIKE MOUND RAISE GAL GAL CATSTONE STONEMAN
CAIRNGORM MORION SMOKESTONE
CAISSON BOX PONT CAMEL CHEST WAGON COFFER PONTON SAUCER CAMAILE CHAMBER LACUNAR PONTOON
(— DISEASE) BENDS
CAITIFF BASE MEAN VILE COWARD WICKED CAPTIVE COWARDLY PRISONER WRETCHED
CAJOLE COG CON JIG COAX FLAM FLUM PALP WORD CARNY CHEAT

CURRY DECOY FRAIK INGLE JOLLY
TEASE BEFLUM CARNEY DELUDE
DIDDLE ENTICE FRAISE HUMBUG
WHILLY BEGUILE BEHONEY CUITTLE
FLATTER PALAVER SOOTHER
TWEEDLE WHEEDLE BLANDISH

CAJOLERY FRAIK SOOTH TAFFY
WILES BUTTER FRAISE WHILLY
BLARNEY DAUBERY FLATTERY

CAKE BAR BUN NUT WIG BAKE BALL
FLAE FOOL LUMP MASS MOLE PUFF
TART ARVAL BATTY BLOCK BOXTY
COOKY CRUST CUPID FADGE KYAAK
PATTY SCONE SHIVE TORTE WAFER
WEDGE BARKLE CIMBAL COOKIE
DAMPER ECLAIR GATEAU HALLAH
HARDEN KICHEL KUCHEN NACKET
PARKIN PASTRY POPLIN SIMNEL
TABLET WASTEL ASHCAKE BANBURY
BANNOCK BRIOCHE BROWNIE
CAKETTE CARAWAY CASSATA
CROZZLE CRUMPET CUPCAKE
FAIRING GALETTE GENOISE
HOECAKE MANCHET NUTCAKE
OATCAKE PANCAKE PLASTER
POPADAM CHRIMSEL CLAPCAKE
KUGELHOF MADELINE MARZIPAN
SEEDCAKE SOLIDIFY SOULCAKE
TORTILLA TURNPIKE
(— OF CLAY) PLATTEN
(— OF COCONUT PULP) POONAC
(— OF MEAL) DODGER
(— OF RUBBER) BISCUIT
(ALMOND —) RATAFIA
(CORN —) PONE
(CREOLE RICE —) CALA
(EASTER —) TANSY
(FANCY —) SUNKET
(FLAT —) PLATE BUNUELO GALETTE
PLACENT CHRIMSEL
(FOURTH PART OF —) FARL FARLE
(FRIED —) WONDER CRULLER
DOUGHNUT
(GINGER —) BOLIVAR
(GRIDDLE —) LATKE FLIPPER FRITTER
FLAPJACK
(HOLIDAY —) SIMNEL
(HONEY —) LEKACH
(INDIAN —) PARATHA
(KIND OF —) LANE FUNNEL
(LAMB AND WHEAT —) KIBBE
KIBBEH
(LEAVENED —) BAP
(NEW YEAR'S —) HAGMENA
HOGMANAY
(OATEN —) BANNOCK
(OIL —) GRIT POONAC
(PIECE OF —) CINCH BREEZE
(PLUM —) SIMNEL
(POTATO —) FADGE
(PRESS —) CACHAZA
(RAISIN —) BABA
(RUM —) BABA

(SEED —) WIG SEEDCAKE
(TEA —) LUNN SCONE PIKELET
(THIN —) WAFER JUMBLE BANNOCK
TORTILLA
(UNLEAVENED —) CHAPATI CHAPATTI
(YEAST —) KOJI SAVARIN
(PL.) AMSATH COLYBA

CAKED CLIT
CAKE PULLER KNOCKER
CAKES AND ALE (AUTHOR OF —)
MAUGHAM
(CHARACTER IN —) AMY KEAR KEMP
ALROY ROSIE EDWARD GEORGE
ASHENDEN TRAFFORD DRIFFIELD
CALABA BIRMA GALBA
CALABASH GOURD CURUBA JICARA
CALABASH TREE HIGUERO
CALABOOSE JUG BRIG JAIL STIR
POKEY COOLER PRISON CABOOSE
BASTILLE HOOSEGOW
CALABUR TREE CAPULI CAPULIN
SILKWOOD
CALAIS (BROTHER OF —) ZETES
(FATHER OF —) BOREAS
(MOTHER OF —) ORITHYIA
CALAMANCO MANKIE
CALAMINE CADMIA
CALAMINT BASIL
CALAMITOUS BAD SAD DIRE EVIL
BLACK FATAL BITTER DISMAL TRAGIC
WOEFUL ADVERSE BALEFUL DIREFUL
HAPLESS RUINOUS UNHAPPY
UNLUCKY GRIEVOUS TRAGICAL
WRETCHED
CALAMITY ILL WOE BLOW DOOM
EVIL RUIN RUTH SLAP HYDRA STORM
WRACK MISERY ONCOME PLAGUE
SORROW EXTREME SCOURGE
ACCIDENT DISASTER DISTRESS
FATALITY JUDGMENT MISCHIEF
CALAMONDIN ORANGE
CALAMANSI
CALAMUS PEN CANE REED QUILL
ACORUS RATTAN ROTANG
CALANGAY ABACAY COCKATOO
CALANTHA (FATHER OF —)
AMYCLAS
CALASH CALESA GALECHE
CALCANEUM FIBULARE
HYPOTARSUS
CALCAR OVEN SPUR FURNACE
CALCARIUM PREHALLUX
CALCEOLARIA FAGELIA IONIDIUM
CALCIFY CRETIFY
CALCINING BURNING
CALCINO MUSCADINE
CALCITE APHRITE CALCSPAR
ALABASTER ARAGONITE ARGENTINE
HISLOPITE
CALCIUM LIME
CALCIUM CARBONATE WHITING
DRIPSTONE
CALCIUM HYDROXIDE LIME

CALCIUM SULPHATE PLASTER
CALCULATE AIM SUM CALK CAST
PLAN RATE TELL COUNT FRAME
THINK CIPHER DESIGN EXPECT
FIGURE NUMBER RECKON ACCOUNT
AVERAGE CALLATE COMPUTE
PREPARE CONSIDER ESTIMATE
FORECAST
(— BY ASTROLOGY) ERECT
CALCULATED COLD MEASURED
CALCULATING COLD WISE BRITTLE
CAUTIOUS
CALCULATION CARE SHARE
CALCUL ACCOUNT CAUTION
WORKING CALCULUS FORECAST
HINDCAST PRUDENCE
(PL.) FIGURES
CALCULATOR TABLE ABACUS
ABACIST SOROBAN CALCULER
COMPUTER ISOGRAPH
CALCULUS STONE UROLITH
ANALYSIS
(PREF.) LITH(O)
(SUFF.) LITE LITH(IC) LITIO
CALDRON POT RED VAT LEAD ALFET
BOILER KELDER KETTLE TRIPOD
VESSEL CALDERA CAULDRON
CALEB (DAUGHTER OF —) ACHSAH
(FATHER OF —) HEZRON JEPHUNNEH
(SON OF —) HUR
CALENDAR ORDO DIARY FASTI
ALMANAC CALENDS JOURNAL
KALENDS REGISTER SCHEDULE
(— ADDITION) EPACT
(— OF MARTYRS) MENOLOGY
(— SIGN) ZODIAC
(ADDITION TO —) EPACT
(PL.) FASTI
CALENDER TABBY SCHREINER
CALENDERER CANROYER
SMOOTHER
CALENDS K KAL
CALF CA BOB BOX BOY LEG BOSS
BUSS DOLT VEAL VEAU BOBBY
BOSSY BUNCH DOGIE MOGGY
PODDY RANNY SOOKY YOUTH
MUSCLE VEALER WEANER
BULCHIN FATLING SLEEPER
CALFLING
(LIKE A —) VITULINE
(OF LEG —) SURAL
(PREMATURE —) SLINK
(STRAY —) MAVERICK
(UNBRANDED —) LONGEAR SLEEPER
(YEARLING —) BUD DAIRT
(YOUNG —) DEACON
(PL.) CAURE
CALF'S-FOOT JELLY SULZE
FISNOGA
CALFSKIN OOZE COROVA VELLUM
GRASSER TULCHAN VEALSKIN
CALIBER BORE RANK DEGREE
TALENT ABILITY BREADTH COMPASS

QUALITY CAPACITY DIAMETER
MAGNITUDE
(HIGH —) STATURE
CALIBRATED BRIX BEAUME BALLING
CALICHE CALCRETE TEPETATE
NITRATINE
CALICO BLAY PINTO SALLO CHINTZ
SALLOO CROYDON SPOTTED
DUNGAREE GOLDFISH
CALICO ASTER WISEWEED
CALICOBACK STINKBUG
CALICO BASS CRAPPIE BACHELOR
CALICO-BUSH KALMIA
CALICUT KOZHIKODE

CALIFORNIA

CAPITAL: SACRAMENTO
COLLEGE: MILLS POMONA WHITTIER
COUNTY: INYO KERN MONO NAPA
YOLO YUBA MARIN MODOC
COLUSA LASSEN MERCED PLACER
PLUMAS SHASTA SOLANO SONOMA
SUTTER TEHAMA TULARE ALAMEDA
VENTURA SISKIYOU CALAVERAS
DESERT: MOJAVE COLORADO
INDIAN: HUPA POMO YANA YUKI
KAROK MAIDU MIWOK WAPPO
WIYOT YUROK PATWIN SHASTA
TOLOWA YOKUTS CHUMASH
LUISENO SALINAN SERRANO
DIEGUENO
LAKE: MONO SODA EAGLE OWENS
TAHOE SALTON TULARE ALMANOR
BERRYESSA
MOUNTAIN: MUIR LASSEN SHASTA
WHITNEY
NAME: ELDORADO
PARK: LASSEN SEQUOIA YOSEMITE
PRESIDENT: NIXON
PRISON: ALCATRAZ
RESORT: OJAI
RIVER: EEL MAD PIT KERN OWENS
PUTAH STONY FEATHER KLAMATH
RUBICON TRINITY SACRAMENTO
STATE BIRD: QUAIL
STATE FLOWER: POPPY
STATE NICKNAME: GOLDEN
STATE TREE: REDWOOD
TOWN: LODI AZUSA CHICO CHINO
INDIO BLYTHE CARMEL COVINA
EUREKA FRESNO LOMPOC MERCED
OXNARD POMONA SONOMA
TULARE ALAMEDA BURBANK
GARDENA NEEDLES SALINAS
VALLEJO VISALIA ALTADENA
BERKELEY PASADENA REDLANDS
CUCAMONGA
UNIVERSITY: USC UCLA CALTECH
STANFORD

CALIPER JENNY ODDLEGS CALIPERS
CALIPH ABU ALI BEKR IMAM OMAR
CALIF OTHMAN ABBASID UMAYYAD

CALISTA (HUSBAND OF —)
ALTAMONT CLEANDER
(LOVER OF —) LOTHARIO LYSANDER
CALISTO, LA
(CHARACTER IN —) PAN JOVE JUNO
DIANA LYCAON CALISTO MERCURY
ENDYMION
(COMPOSER OF —) CAVALLI
CALIXTINE UTRAQUIST
CALK (ALSO SEE CAULK) JAG NAP
PAY COPY CORK FILL STOP CAULK
CLOSE HORSE ROUGH CAREEN
CALTROP CHINTZE OCCLUDE
SILENCE
CALKING OAKUM
CALL HO KA BAN BID CRY CUP DUB
HOY SAY SEE CITE COOP DIAL HAIL
JERK NAME NOTE PAGE PIST ROUP
STOP TERM TOOT YELL BEDUB
CHUCK CLAIM CLEPE CLOCK ELECT
HALLO HIGHT HOLLA PHONE ROUSE
SHOUT SPEAK STYLE UTTER VISIT
VOUCH WAKEN YODEL ACCUSE
APPEAL AROUSE BECALL CHANGE
DEMAND HALLOA HALLOO INVITE
INVOKE MUSTER QUETHE SUMMON
TEKIAH TERUAH YELPER ACCLAIM
ADDRESS APPOINT BEHIGHT
BETITLE COLLECT COMMAND
CONVENE CONVOKE DECLARE
ENTITLE IMPEACH INQUIRE
INSTYLE MOUNTEE WHISTLE
ANNOUNCE APPELATE ASSEMBLE
NOMINATE PROCLAIM TRANSFER
VOCATION
(— A BET) STAY
(— ALOUD) COUNT
(— BACK) RSVP RECALL REVOKE
(— COARSELY) ROOP ROUP
(— DOWN) BRAWL DEVOCATE
IMPRECATE
(— FOR) CRY TAKE CLAIM EXACT
DEMAND DESIRE COLLECT SOLICIT
(— FOR HELP) SOS
(— FOR HOGS) SOOK SOOEY
(— FOR PARLEY) CHAMADE
(— FORTH) STIR EVOKE BECKON
ELICIT INDUCE INVOKE ATTRACT
PROVOKE SUGGEST
(— HOUNDS) LIFT
(— IN ANGER) GREET
(— IN CHILDRENS' GAMES) FAN FEN
FIN VENTS
(— IN MARBLES) DUBS
(— INTO QUESTION) IMPUGN
OPPUGN
(— IN WHIST) ABUNDANCE
(— LOUDLY) CRY HAIL ACCLAIM
(— MAN BY MAN) ARRAY
(— ON TELEPHONE) BUZZ
(— OUT) HAIL LURE ASCRY EVOKE
HALLO GOLLAR GOLLER HOLLER
HULLOO

(— THE GAME) UMP
(— TO ACCOUNT) AREASON
CONTROL
(— TO ARMS) ALARM ALARUM
RAPPEL
(— TO BELLBOY) FRONT
(— TO CAT) CHEET
(— TO COURT) ARRAIGN
(— TO COWS) PROO SOOK COBOSS
SOOKIE
(— TO DUTY) TURNOUT
(— TO FOOD) SOSS
(— TO HORSE) HIE HUP WAY PROO
(— TO MIND) CITE MING RECORD
BETHINK RECOLLECT
(— TO PRAYER) ADAN AZAN
(— TO READINESS) ALERT
(— TO SPARROW) PHIP PHIPPE
(— TO WITNESS) APPEAL
(— UPON) ASK SEE CITE GREDE
HALSE BECALL DEPOSE ENGAGE
SUMMON ADDRESS BESEECH
IMPLORE
(BIRD'S —) WEET
(BOATSWAIN'S —) WINDING
(BRIDGE —) DOUBLE
(BUGLE —) POST HALLALI STABLES
(CLOSE —) TOUCH
(DUCK —) SQUAWKER
(FRIENDLY —) CEILIDH
(HUNTING —) MOT RECHATE
RECHEAT
(KIND OF —) ROLL COLLECT
(MORNING —) MATIN
(NAUTICAL —) AHOY
(SHEPHERD'S —) OVEY
(SOCIAL —) VISIT
(SPORTSMAN'S —) HOICKS YOICKS
HALLALI
(SQUARE DANCE —) GEE HAW
(STAGE TRUMPET —) SENNET
SINNET
(TRUMPET —) BERLOQUE
CALLA ARUM LILY DRAGON
MAYFLOWER
CALLBOY FRONT CALLER HALLBOY
CALLED NEMPT
CALLER FLOORMAN
CALLIGRAPHER PENMAN WRITER
COPYIST ENGROSSER
CALLIGRAPHY LETTERING
CHIROGRAPHY
CALLING ART JOB WAY CALL HAIL
RANK TRADE CAREER METIER
NAMING OUTCRY MISSION
MYSTERY PURSUIT STATION
SUMMONS WARNING BUSINESS
FUNCTION POSITION SHOUTING
VOCATION
(— TO ACCOUNT) AUDIT
(— TOGETHER) MUSTER
CALLIOPE (FATHER OF —) ZEUS
JUPITER

(MOTHER OF —) MNEMOSYNE
(SON OF —) ORPHEUS
CALLIRRHOE (FATHER OF —)
OCEANUS
(HUSBAND OF —) TROS ALCMAEON
(SON OF —) ILUS GANYMEDE
ASSARACUS
CALLISTO (FATHER OF —) LYCAON
(SON OF —) ARCAS
CALLITHRIX HAPALE JACCHUS
CALLOP YELLOWBELLY
CALLOSAL TRABAL
CALLOSITY SEG CALLUS SITFAST
TYLOSIS CHESTNUT
CALLOUS HARD HORNY TOUGH
BRAWNY OBTUSE SEARED TORPID
WAUKIT DEDOLENT OBDURATE
HEARTLESS
CALLOUSED BRAWNY
CALLOW BALD BARE CRUDE GREEN
SQUAB JEJUNE MARSHY IMMATURE
UNFORMED YOUTHFUL
CALLUS SEG POROMA TYLOMA
CALLOUS
(— ON HORSE) RINGBONE
(PREF.) PORA PORO
CALM LAY LEE COOL DILL EASY EVEN
FAIN FLAT HUSH LOWN LULL MEES
MILD REST SOFT STAY ABATE ALLAY
CHARM LEVEL LITHE LOUND MEASE
PEACE QUELL QUIET SLEEK SMOLT
SOBER STILL STOIC STREW APLOMB
DEFUSE DOCILE GENTLE GLASSY
IRENIC PACIFY PLACID SEDATE
SERENE SETTLE SILENT SLATCH
SLIGHT SMOOTH SOOTHE STEADY
APPEASE ASSUAGE CALMATO
COMPOSE GLACIAL HALCYON
MOLLIFY PACIFIC PATIENT PLACATE
QUALIFY QUIETEN RESTFUL
UNMOVED CALMNESS COMPOSED
DECOROUS MODERATE PEACEFUL
PLACABLE RESTRAIN SERENITY
TRANQUIL UNRUFFLE POSSESSED
PHILOSOPHIC
(INTERNAL —) HARMONY
(NOT —) BOISTEROUS
CALMING SEDATIVE
CALMLY COOLY COOLLY STILLY
CALMNESS CALM LULL POISE
PHLEGM REPOSE SERENE TEMPER
ATARAXY COOLNESS SERENITY
SOBRIETY STILLNESS
CALNO KULLANI
CALOMEL TURPETH
CALORIC THERMOGEN
CALORIE THERM THERME
CALQUE LOANSHIFT
CALTROP CROWTOE GALTRAP
BULLHEAD CROWFOOT
CALUMET PIPE PEACEPIPE
CALUMNIATE BLOT SLUR TEEN
BELIE LIBEL ACCUSE ATTACK BEFOUL

DEFAME MALIGN REVILE VILIFY
ASPERSE BLACKEN SLANDER
TRADUCE
CALUMNIATION SATIRE
ASPERSION
CALUMNY SLUR ATTACK DEPRAVE
OBLOQUY SLANDER ASPERSION
CALVA CALOTTE SINCIPUT
CALVARIA SKULLCAP
CALVARY GOLGOTHA
CALVE FRESHEN
CALVINIST GENEVAN GOMARIAN
CALYCE (FATHER OF —) AEOLUS
(MOTHER OF —) ENARETE
(SON OF —) ENDYMION
CALYCULUS CELL CALYX
CALYPTER ALULA SQUAMA
CALYPTRA CAP VEIL EPIGONIUM
CALYX CUP POP HULL HUSK LEAF
CULOT SEPAL SHUCK
(PREF.) CALYC(I)(O)
CAM COG AWRY LOBE TRIG ASKEW
CATCH SNAIL WIPER LIFTER TAPPET
CROOKED TRIPPET KNOCKOFF
PERVERSE ROLLBACK
CAMACHILE INGA HUAMUCHIL
CAMAGON MABOLO
CAMAS LOBELIA
CAMBER SET ARCH BEND SWEEP
ROUNDUP CROSSFALL

CAMBODIA

CAPE: SAMIT
CAPITAL: PNOMPENH PHNOMPENH
COIN: SEN RIEL PUTTAN PIASTER
SULE SIAM
LAKE: TONLESAP
MOUNTAIN: PAN AURAL
MOUNTAINS: DANGREK CARDAMOM
ELEPHANT
NAME: CAMBOJA CAMBODGE
KAMPUCHEA
NATIVE: CHAM KHMER
RIVER: SAN SEN BASSAC MEKONG
PORONG SREPOK SEKHONG
TONLESAP
RUINS: ANGKORWAT
TOWN: HEAM TAKEO KAMPOT KRATIE
PURSAT KOHNIEH KRACHEH
ROVIENG SAMRONG PNOMPENH
SISOPHON
WEIGHT: MACE TAEL

CAMBODIAN KHMER
CAMBRIC LAWN BATISTE PERCALE
CAMBUSCAN
(SON OF —) CANACE CAMBALLO
ALGARSIFE
CAME BAND CALM
CAMEL COLT OONT DELOUL DROMED
FENDER HAGEEN MEHARI CAISSON
TYLOPOD BACTRIAN RUMINANT
DROMEDARY

CAMEL GRASS SCHOENANTH
CAMELLIA JAPONICA
CAMEL LIP CHILOMA
CAMELOPARD GIRAFFE
CAMEO GEM GAMAHE CAMAIEU
CARVING PHALERA RELIEVO
ANAGLYPH
(— MATERIAL) ONYX
CAMERA KINO KODAK CHAMBER
MINICAM PANORAM ENLARGER
MINIATURE VERASCOPE
CAMCVORDER
(— AND RECORDER) PORTAFAX
PORTAPACK
(— SHOT) PAN
(— TUBE) VIDICON
(KIND OF —) REFLEX
(PART OF —) LUG BODY DOOR KNOB
LENS LOCK CRANK DRIVE FOCUS
LATCH SCALE STRAP TIMER BUTTON
SENSOR SOCKET WINDOW ADVANCE
BELLOWS LANYARD RELEASE
SHUTTER PHOTOCELL TRANSDUCER
VIEWFINDER
(SHIELD FOR —) GOBO
(VIDEO —) CAMCORDER
CAMERAMAN LENSMAN
CAMEROON (CAPITAL OF —)
YAOUNDE
(RIVER OF —) DJA NYONG SANAGA
(TOWN OF —) EDEA POLI YOKO
BAFIA KRIBI DOUALA
CAMILLA (FATHER OF —) METABUS
(SLAYER OF —) ARUNS
CAMILLE (AUTHOR OF —) DUMAS
(CHARACTER IN —) DUVAL ARMAND
NANINE CAMILLE GAUTIER
PRUDENCE VARVILLE
CAMIRUS (FATHER OF —)
CERCAPHUS
(MOTHER OF —) CYDIPPE
CAMISOLE WAISTCOAT
CAMLET MOHAIR PARAGON
BARRACAN
CAMOMILE OXEYE MORGAN
MAYWEED
CAMOUFLAGE FAKE HIDE DAZZLE
MUFFLE SCREEN CONCEAL DISGUISE
CAMOUFLET STIFLER
CAMP TAN PEST TENT DOUAR ETAPE
HORDE SIEGE TABOR CASTLE
LAAGER SUGARY BIVOUAC
HUTMENT LASHKAR LODGING
MAHALLA PALANKA ZAREEBA
QUARTERS
(— OF INDIAN SOLDIERS) LASHKAR
(— OUT) MAROON OUTLIE
(HOBO —) JUNGLE
(LABOR —) GULAG
(LUMBER —) CHANTIER
(PRISONER —) OFLAG STALAG
(PREF.) CASTRA
(SUFF.) CASTER CESTER CHESTER

CAMPA ANDA ANDI ANTI
CAMPAIGN BLITZ DRIVE PLAIN
WHOOP CANVASS CRUSADE
JOURNEY SERVICE SOLICIT
WARFARE
(STUNT —) JIHAD
CAMPANA GUTTA
CAMPANERO COTINGA ARAPUNGA
BELLBIRD COTINGID
CAMPANILE TOWER BELFRY
CLOCHER STEEPLE CARILLON
CAMPANULA BELLWORT
CAMPESTRAL AGRARIAN
CAMP-FOLLOWER BOY BUMMER
LASCAR
CAMPHOL BORNEOL
CAMPHOR ASARONE BORNEOL
MENTHOL
(ANISE —) ANETHOLE
CAMPHOR TREE KADUR KAPOR
CAMPING BIVOUAC
CAMPION ROBIN COWBELL
CAMPUS GATE QUAD YARD
FIELD
CAN CUP JUG MAY MOW POT TIN
ABLE FIRE JAIL SACK BILLY CADDY
COULD ESHIN OILER PUTUP SHALL
SKILL BOTTLE VESSEL ABILITY
BOMBARD CANIKIN CAPABLE
CREAMER DISMISS GROWLER
PIPETTE BILLYCAN CONSERVE
PRESERVE
(— FOR LIQUOR) JACK
(— ON WHEELS) DANDY
(BULGED —) SWELL FLIPPER
(DEFECTIVE —) SPRINGER
(LEAKY —) LEAKER
(MILK —) CHURN
(SPRAY —) AEROSOL
(TIN —) DESTROYER
(TRASH —) DUSTBIN
(PREF.) SCYPH(I)(O)
CANAAN (FATHER OF —) HAM
CANAANITE ARKITE HIVITE
AMORITE HIVVITE JEBUSITE
CANACE (BROTHER OF —)
MACAREUS
(FATHER OF —) AEOLUS
(MOTHER OF —) ENARETE
(SON OF —) TRIOPAS

CANADA
(ALSO SEE SPECIFIC PROVINCES)
BAY: JAMES HUDSON UNGAVA
GEORGIAN
CAPITAL: OTTAWA
INDIAN: CREE COMOX HAIDA NISKA
SARSI STALO MICMAC NAHANE
NOOTKA SARCEE SEKANE CARRIER
NANAIMO SHUSWAP SONGISH
TAHLTAN ALGONKIN COWICHAN
LILLOOET MALECITE SQUAMISH
TSATTINE

ISLAND: READ BANKS BYLOT COATS DEVON SABLE BAFFIN MANSEL VICTORIA ANTICOSTI VANCOUVER

ISLANDS: PARRY BELCHER BATHURST MAGDALEN

LAKE: BEAR CREE GARRY RAINY SLAVE LOUISE SIMCOE ABITIBI DUBAWNT NIPIGON KOOTENAY OKANAGAN NIPISSING

MEASURE: MINOT PERCH ARPENT CHAINON

MOUNTAIN: LOGAN ROYAL ROBSON TREMBLANT

MOUNTAIN RANGE: SKEENA CARIBOO PEMBINA STELIAS COLUMBIA LAURENTIAN

NATIVE: CANUCK

PARK: YOHO BANFF ACADIA JASPER

PENINSULA: GASPE BOOTHIA MELVILLE

PROVINCE: BC NB NS MAN ONT PEI QUE ALTA SASK QUEBEC ALBERTA ONTARIO MANITOBA NOVASCOTIA NEWBRUNSWICK NEWFOUNDLAND SASKATCHEWAN

PROVINCIAL CAPITAL: QUEBEC REGINA STJOHN HALIFAX TORONTO EDMONTON VICTORIA WINNIPEG CHARLOTTETOWN

RIVER: HAY RED BACK PEEL PEACE SLAVE YUKON FRASER NELSON OTTAWA SKEENA THELON KOKOSAK PEMBINA PETAWAWA SAGUENAY MACKENZIE RICHELIEU

STRAIT: CABOT DEASE HECATE HUDSON GEORGIA

SYMBOL: MAPLELEAF

TERRITORY: YUKON

TOWN: HULL BANFF LAVAL GUELPH OSHAWA REGINA SARNIA CALGARY HALIFAX LACHINE MONCTON NANAIMO SUDBURY TORONTO WELLAND WINDSOR KINGSTON MONTREAL VICTORIA WINNIPEG SASKATOON VANCOUVER

UNIVERSITY: MCGILL DALHOUSIE

WATERFALL: DELLA PANTHER TAKAKKAW

CANADA BLUEBERRY SOURTOP
CANADA GOOSE HONKER BUSTARD OUTARDE
CANADA JAY MEATBIRD MOOSEBIRD
CANADA LYNX PISHU LUCIVEE
CANADA PLUM CHENEY
CANADA VIOLET JUNFFLOWER
CANADIAN CANUCK
CANAILLE MOB FLOUR RABBLE DOGGERY RIFFRAFF
CANAL CUT CANO DUCT LODE PIPE SHAT TUBE BAYOU DITCH DRAIN FOSSA GRAFF KLONG SCALA ZANJA ESTERO GROOVE KENNEL STRAIT TRENCH VAGINA ACEQUIA APHODUS CHANNEL CONDUIT FOREBAY RACEWAY SHIPWAY TOWPATH AQUEDUCT EMISSARY IRRIGANT MILLRACE PROSODUS VOLKMANN
(— LABORER) NAVIGATOR
(ALIMENTARY —) GUT ENTERON INTESTINE
(ANATOMICAL —) SCALA MEATUS
(CARINAL —) LACUNA
(PREF.) MEATO
CANARD DUCK HOAX RUMOR GRAPEVINE
CANARY DICKY FRILL SERIN LIZARD ROLLER CAYENNE CHOPPER JONQUIL SQUEALER
(— HYBRID) MULE

CANARY ISLAND

CAPITAL: SANTACRUZ
ISLAND: ROCA CLARA FERRO LOBOS PALMA ROCCA GOMERA HIERRO INFERNO GRACIOSA TENERIFE LANZAROTE
MEASURE: FANEGADA
MOUNTAIN: TEYDE LACRUZ ELCUMBRE TENERIFE
PROVINCE: LASPALMAS
TOWN: LAGUNA ARRECIFE VALVERDE
VOLCANO: TENEGUIA

CANARY MOSS CORKIR
CANASTA SAMBA BOLIVIA
(— PLAY) MELD
CANCEL AX BLOT DASH DELE OMIT UNDO VENT WIPE ABORT ADEEM ANNUL BELAY CROSS ERASE QUASH REMIT SCORE SCRUB DELETE EFFACE KILLER RECALL REMOVE REVOKE STROKE ABOLISH DESTROY EXPUNGE NULLIFY RESCIND RETRACT SCRATCH SUBLATE UNWRITE ABROGATE OVERRIDE WRITEOFF OBLITERATE
CANCELED OFF NOGO
CANCELER BUMPER STAMPER
CANCELLATION GRID CANCEL REVOKE RECISION SURRENDER
CANCER BIGC WOLF KASHYAPA SCIRRHUS
(PREF.) CARCIN(O)
CANCERWORT FLUELLIN
CANDAREEN FAN FEN
CANDELABRUM PHAROS MENORAH GIRANDOLE
CANDID FAIR JUST OPEN PURE BLUNT CLEAR FRANK NAIVE PLAIN HONEST ARTLESS JANNOCK

SINCERE EVENDOWN INNOCENT
SPLENDID STRAIGHT PLAINSPOKEN
CANDIDA (AUTHOR OF —) SHAW
(CHARACTER IN —) MORELL
CANDIDA MARCHBANKS
CANDIDATE AGREGE LEGACY
ESQUIRE NOMINEE ASPIRANT
GRADUAND ORDINAND PROSPECT
(DOCTORAL) ABD
(DOCTORAL —) ABD
(LIST OF —S) SLATE
(TEACHING —) AGREGE
CANDIDE (AUTHOR OF —) VOLTAIRE
(CHARACTER IN —) CACAMBO
CANDIDE PANGLOSS PAQUETTE
CUNEGONDE
CANDIDIASIS MONILIASIS
CANDIED GLACE
CANDLE DIP WAX GLIM SIZE SLUT
LIGHT SPERM TAPER TOLLY TORCH
BOUGIE CIERGE MORTAR PLANET
SHAMUS SLUSHY TALLOW TORTIS
CANDELA PERCHER PRICKET
SHAMMES AMANDINE
(IMITATION —) JUDAS
(SQUARE —) QUARRIER
CANDLEFISH SKIL EULACHON
HOOLAKIN OOLACHAN SKILFISH
SABLEFISH
CANDLEHOLDER SPIDER
CANDLEMAKER CHANDLER
TALLOWER
CANDLEMAS TERM MARYMASS
CANDLENUT AMA LAMA BIABO
KUKUI IGUAPE KEMIRI LUMBANG
ABURAGIRI
CANDLESNUFFER DOUTER
CANDLESTAND TORCHERE
CANDLESTICK BUGIA DYKER JESSE
STICK CRUSIE LAMPAD MORTAR
SCONCE PASCHAL PRICKET
CHANDLER DICERION FLAMBEAU
STANDARD TORCHERE TRIKERION
(TALL ORNAMENTAL —) TORCHERE
CANDLEWICK MATCH SNAST
SHROUD
(CHARRED PART OF —) SNOT SNUFF
SNUFFING
CANDLEWOOD CIRIO OCOTILLO
TABANUCO
CANDOR PURITY FAIRNESS
KINDNESS INTEGRITY SIMPLICITY
CANDY DROP DUMP KISS PIPE ROCK
CREAM CRISP DULCE FUDGE GLACE
GUNDY LOLLY NABIT SPICE SQUIB
SWEET TAFFY BONBON COMFIT
DRAGEE HUMBUG NOGADA NOUGAT
PATTIE PENIDE BRITTLE CANDIEL
CARAMEL CONGEAL FLATTER
FONDATE GUMDROP SWEETEN
SWEETIE TORRONE ALPHENIC
LOLLIPOP STICKJAW PEPPERMINT

(DECORATIVE —) DRAGEE
(PL.) CUTS CONFETTI
CANDYTUFT CRUCIFER
(PL.) IBERIS
CANE ROD BEAT CRAB DART FLOG
PIPE REED STEM TUBE WAND WHIP
BIRCH GIBBY GUNDY LANCE STAFF
STICK SWISH TOLLY WADDY
BAMBOO JAMBEE KEBBIE PUNISH
RATTAN CALAMUS HICKORY KIPPEEN
MALACCA SCOURGE STADDLE
TICKLER WHANGEE GIBSTAFF
(BLACK —) JAPAN
(END OF —) FRAZE
(SPLIT —) CANEWORK
(TIP OF —) FERRULE
CANELLA CINNAMON WHITEWOOD
CANELO CIXO
CANESCENT HOARY
CANE TREE BEJUCO
CANFIELD KLONDIKE
CANICULA SIRIUS
CANINE CUR DOG FOX PUP FISC
TUSH WOLF DOGLY DOGLIKE
LANIARY EYETOOTH
CANING RATTAN BIRCHING
CANISTEL TIES EGGFRUIT
CANNA ACHIRA GOLDBIRD
CANNABIS BHANG GANJA GUAZA
GUNJA HEMPWORT
(— TOPS) TAKROURI
CANNEL BONE FURCULE
CANNEL COAL AMPELITE
CANNER CANMAN TINNER
CANNIBAL WINDIGO LESTRIGON
THYESTEAN
CANNON BIT EAR GUN BASE SHOT
TUBE ASPIC CAROM CRACK MOYEN
PIECE SACRE SACRI SAKER SHANK
SLING THIEF BARKER BICORN
CURTAL FALCON FOWLER JINGAL
LICORN MORTAR POTGUN BASTARD
BOMBARD BULLDOG CHAMBER
HANDGUN LOMBARD MOYENNE
ROBINET SERPENT STINGER
UNICORN BASILISK CULVERIN
HOWITZER MURDERER OERLIKON
ORDNANCE SPITFIRE CARAMBOLE
CARRONADE ZUMBOORUK
(— OF BELL) EAR
(CARRIAGE OF —) NADRIER
(DISCHARGE OF —) TIRE
(DUMMY —) QUAKER
(PART OF —) BASE BORE FACE KNOB
NECK OGEE RING VENT CHASE FILET
SWELL BREECH BUTTON FILLET
MUZZLE CHAMBER DOLPHIN
GUNLOCK RIMBASE ASTRAGAL
CASCABEL TRUNNION REINFORCE
CANNONBALL GUN PILL TEAR
BULLET GUNSTONE
CANNON BOSS TRUNNION

CANNON PLUG TAMPION
CANNOT CANT CANNA DONNA
DOWNA UNABLE
CANNULA TROCAR
CANNY SLY COZY SNUG WARY WILY
WISE COONY LUCKY PAWKY QUIET
SAVVY CLEVER FRUGAL GENTLE
SHREWD STEADY CAREFUL
CUNNING KNOWING PRUDENT
QUIETLY THRIFTY CAUTIOUS
SKILLFUL WATCHFUL
CANOE AMA KIAK LISI PAHI PROA
WAKA AOTEA ARAWA BANCA BIRCH
BONGO BUNGO CANKA KAYAK
KOLEK PRAHU SKIFF TONEE UMIAK
VINTA WAAPA BAIDAR BALLAM
BAROTO CORIAL CUNNER DUGOUT
OOMIAK PAOPAO PITPAN PUNGEY
TAINUI TROUGH WHERRY ALMADIA
BIDARKA BUCKEYE CANADER
CASCARA CORACLE CURIARA
CURRANE HOROUTA LAKATOI
PIRAGUA PIROGUE BALANGAY
BARANGAY FALTBOAT FOLDBOAT
MONOXYLE MONTARIA TAKITUMU
THAMAKAU TSUKUPIN WOODSKIN
CANON FEN LAW CODE FUGA HYMN
LAUD LIST ROTA RULE SONG AXIOM
GORGE GULCH MODEL NODUS
ROUND TABLE TENET ACTION
DECREE GNOMON BROCARD
LIBRARY PRECEPT STATUTE
DECISION MATHURIN STAGIARY
STANDARD SACRISTAN
PREBENDARY PREMONSTRATENSIAN
(BODY OF —S) CHAPTER
CANONICAL CANONIC ACCEPTED
ORTHODOX
(NOT —) APOCRYPHAL
CANOODLE PET CARESS FONDLE
CAN OPENER CHURCHKEY
CANOPY SKY CEIL COPE DAIS HOOD
TILT CHUPA CROWN HOVEL SHADE
STATE VAULT AWNING BUBBLE
CELURE ESTATE FINIAL GABLET
HUPPAH PELMET SHADOW TESTER
CEILING HEAVENS MARQUEE
SHELTER SPARVER BASILICA
CIBORIUM COVERING OVERWOOD
PAVILION SEMIANNA SHAMIANA
TABERNACLE
(— ABOVE THRONE) STATE
(— FOR LIVESTOCK) HOVEL
(— OF ALTAR) DAIS CIBORIUM
(— OF HEAVEN) VAULT
(— OVER BROODER) HOVER
(BED —) TESTER SPARVER
(HEARSE —) MAJESTY
CANT TIP COAX HEEL LEAN LIST
NOOK SING TILT TURN ARGOT BEVEL
CHANT DRIFT FLASH FIELD LINGO
LUSTY MERRY NICHE PITCH SHARE

SLANG SLANT SLOPE WHINE
CAREEN CASTER CORNER INTONE
JARGON LIVELY PATOIS PATTER
SNIVEL AUCTION DIALECT INCLINE
PORTION SINGING WHEEDLE
CHEERFUL PRETENSE VIGOROUS
CANTABRIGIAN CANTAB
CAMBRIDGE
CANTALA MAGUEY
CANTALOUPE MELON MUSKMELON
CANTANKEROUS ILL CURSED
CUSSED ORNERY KICKISH PIGGISH
CANKERED CONTRARY PERVERSE
CANTATA MOTET SERENATA
PASTORALE VILLANCICO
(CHILDREN'S —) KINDERSPIEL
CANTEEN BAR FLASK BAZAAR
CANTINA
CANTER JOG RUN GAIT LOPE PACE
RACK AUBIN ROGUE BEGGAR
WHINER TRIPPLE SNUFFLER
VAGABOND
CANTERBURY BELL MILKWORT
CAMPANULA
CANTERBURY TALES
(AUTHOR OF —) CHAUCER
(CHARACTER IN —) NUN COOK DYER
HOST MONK WIFE CLERK FRIAR
REEVE DOCTOR KNIGHT MILLER
PARSON PRIEST SQUIRE WEAVER
YEOMAN CHAUCER PLOWMAN
SHIPMAN FRANKLIN MANCIPLE
MERCHANT PARDONER PRIORESS
SERGEANT SUMMONER CARPENTER
HABERDASHER
CANTICLE ODE HYMN LAUD SONG
CANTO ANTHEM CANTIC HIRMOS
BRAVURA MAGNIFICAT
CANTILEVER LOOKOUT SEMIBEAM
CARTOUCHE
CANTING CANT PIOUS SNUFFLING
CANTO AIR FIT BOOK DUAN PACE
RUNE SONG VERSE MELODY PASSUS
CANTICLE
CANTON ANGLE UNION CORNER
VOLOST PORTION QUARTER
SECTION DISTRICT DIVISION
(HALF —) ESQUIRE
CANTOR HAZAN HAZZAN SINGER
CHANTER CHAZZAN SOLOIST
PSALMIST
CANVAS FLY PAT DUCK GLUT PATA
SAIL TARP TENT TEWK CLOTH COAST
SCRIM TOILE VITRY BALINE BURLAP
CATGUT LINING MUSLIN PICTURE
POLDAVY SACKING SCUTAGE
DRABBLER PAINTING VANDELAS
SAILCLOTH
(— COVER) TARP
(— FOR CONVEYING GRAIN) APRON
(OLD CONDEMNED —) RUMBOWLINE
(RUBBERIZED —) TOSH

(STUFFED —) BOLSTER
(TARRED —) COAT
CANVASBACK CAN DIVER CHEVAL
DUCKER POCHARD BULLNECK
CANVASS BEAT CASE DRUM HAWK
POLL SIFT RANDY STUDY DEBATE
PEDDLE SEARCH AGITATE DISCUSS
EXAMINE SOLICIT TROUNCE
CAMPAIGN CONSIDER
CANVASSER AGENT POLLER
ROADMAN
CANYON CAJON CHASM COULE
GORGE GULCH ARROYO CANADA
RAVINE
CANZONE ODE
CAOUTCHOUC RUBBER ELATERITE
CAP CUP FEZ HAT LID PAD POT TAJ
TAM TIP TOP ACME CALL COIF CORK
COWL DINK DOME DOWD ETON
GAGE HOOD HURE JOAN KEEP KEPI
MATE SHOE SHOW TOPI BERET
BOINA BUSBY CHIEF COVER CROWN
EXCEL FANON GALEA HOUVE KULAH
MATCH MUTCH OUTDO PHANO
PUNCH SEIZE SHAKO TOPEE TRUMP
ARREST BARRAD BARRET BEANIE
BIGGIN BIRRUS BONNET CALPAC
CLIMAX COCKUP CORNET GALERA
HELMET HUBCAP JINNAH MOBCAP
PILEUS PINNER PRIMER PUZZLE
SUMMIT TABARD TURBAN ALOPEKE
BIRETTA CALOTTE CAMAURO
CAPITAL CEREVIS CHAPEAU CHECHIA
CLOSURE COMMODE FERRULE
FLATCAP FORAGER HEADCAP
OVERLIE OVERTOP PERPLEX
PETASOS PILLBOX PILLION
SOWBACK SURPASS THIMBLE
TURNCAP ACROSOME BALMORAL
BEARSKIN BYCOCKET CAPELINE
CHAPERON COONSKIN ELECTRIC
FOLLOWER HEADGEAR PHRYGIUM
SKEWBACK SKULLCAP SURPRISE
TARBOOSH
(— FOR PILEDRIVER) PUNCH
(— OF FLAGSTAFF) TRUCK
(— OF FOAM) HOOD
(— OF MUSHROOM) PILEUS
(— OF PIER) CUSHION
(— OF PYXIDIUM) LID
(— OF WATCH) DOME CROWN
(— ON MAST) TRUCK
(ACADEMIC —) MORTARBOARD
(BISHOP'S —) HURA HURE
(CANADIAN —) TUQUE
(CHIMNEY —) GRANNY
(HORSEMAN'S —) MONTERO
(HUNTER'S —) MONTERA MONTERO
(ICE —) BRAE CALOTTE
(JESTER'S —) COXCOMB FOOLSCAP
(MILITARY —) KEPI BUSBY SHAKO
CHAPKA CZAPKA
(MOUNTAIN —) SCALP

(OLD WOMAN'S —) TOY
(PERCUSSION —) AMORCE CAPSULE
(PERUVIAN —) CHULLO
(POPE'S —) CAMAURO
(ROMAN —) PILEUS
(ROOT —) CALYPTRA
(TRIANGULAR —) CALPAC KALPAK
CALPACK
(WOMAN'S —) TOY CAUL DOWD
JOAN KELL MUTCH COMMODE
VOLUPER BIGGONET
(WOOLEN —) BOINA TOQUE TUQUE
(PREF.) PILEI PILEO PILO
CAPABILITY POWER STROIL ABILITY
CONDUCT FACULTY POTENCY
CAPACITY
CAPABLE APT CAN FIT ABLE GOOD
ADEPT CAPAX FENDY TIGHT EXPERT
SKILLED POWERFUL
(— OF BEING DEFENDED) TENABLE
(— OF BEING DRAWN OUT) DUCTILE
(— OF BEING SEVERED) SEVTILE
(— OF BEING THROWN) MISSILE
(— OF BEING UTTERED) EFFABLE
(— OF FLYING) VOLANT
(— OF SUBMISSION) AMENABLE
(NORMALLY —) ABOUT
(SUFF.) ABLE IBLE (— OF) ILE
CAPACIOUS FULL SIDE WIDE AMPLE
BROAD LARGE ROOMY WOMBY
GOODLY ROOMFUL CAPTIOUS
ROOMSOME SPACIOUS
CAPACITOR CONDENSER
CAPACITY BACK BENT BIND DISH
GIFT GIVE SIZE TURN BLAST FLAIR
FORCE KNACK MODEL POWER SKILL
SPACE AGENCY BOTTOM BURDEN
ENERGY ENGINE EXTENT GENIUS
MODULE SPREAD TALENT VOLUME
ABILITY CALIBER CALIBRE CONTENT
FACULTY FITNESS QUALITY
APTITUDE INSTINCT STRENGTH
INFLUENCE
(— FOR EATING) STROKE
(— FOR ENDURANCE) STAY
(— FOR HIGHER KNOWLEDGE)
INTELLECT
(— OF LATHE) SWING
(— OF SHIP) BURDEN
(— TO UNDERSTAND LANGUAGE)
ORACY
(CIVIL —) CAPUT
(INNATE —S) STAMINA
(INTELLECTUAL —) BROW
(LOAD-PULLING —) DRAFT DRAUGHT
(MENTAL —S) BELFRY
(SPECIAL —) KNACK
(UNIT OF —) MUD MUID LAGEN
KISHEN MEDIMNUS KILDERKIN
(UNLIMITED —) INFINITY
CAPANEUS (FATHER OF —)
HIPPONOUS BELLEROPHON
(SLAYER OF —) JUPITER

(SON OF —) STHENELUS
(WIFE OF —) EVADNE
CAPARISON DECK TRAP HOUSE
COVERING TRAPPING
CAPARISONED BARDED
CAPE RAS COPE GAPE HEAD HOOK
LOOK NAZE NECK NESS SKAW TANG
WRIT AMICE CAPPA CLOAK FICHU
ORALE POINT SAGUM STARE STOLE
TALMA BERTHA BYRRUS CABAAN
CHAPEL DOLMAN MANTLE SONTAG
TABARD TIPPET CHLAMYS LEATHER
MANTEEL MOZETTA SALIENT
TANJONG VANDYKE CIRCULAR
COLLARET HEADLAND LAMBSKIN
MANTILLA MOZZETTA PALATINE
PELERINE SEALSKIN INVERNESS
RAINPROOF
(— OF SKINS) KAROSS
(— OF STRAW) MINO
(BULLFIGHTER'S —) CAPA
(CLERGICAL —) ALMUCE
(DRESSING —) TOILET
(FEATHER —) AHUULA
(HOODED —) HUKE DOMINO
(LACE OR SILK —) VISITE
(LOW —) TANG
(PAPAL —) FANO FANON FANUM
ORALE PHANO
(RAIN —) CAPOTE
CAPE ANTEATER AARDVARK
CAPE ARMADILLO PANGOLIN
CAPE DUTCH TAAL
CAPE GOOSEBERRY POHA
CAPE HARTEBEEST CAAMA
CAPE HEN STINKER STINKPOT
CAPEK (— DRAMA) RUR
CAPELIN SMELT ICEFISH
CAPE PIGEON PINTADO
CAPE POLECAT ZORIL MUISHOND
CAPER HOP JET DIDO HOIT JUMP
LEAP ROMP SKIP SKIT ANTIC BRANK
DANCE FLING FLISK FRISK PRANK
SAUCE SCOUP SHRUB CAVORT
CURVET FRISCO FROLIC GAMBOL
GAMOND PRANCE SPRING TITTUP
VAGARY CORSAIR COURANT
FRISCAL GAMBADO PRANKLE
CAPRIOLE MARIGOLD
(— ABOUT) FLING CAVORT
(SILLY —) SHINE
CAPER SPURGE CATEPUCE
CAPE TOWN BOVENLAND
**CAPE VERDE ISLANDS (CAPITAL
OF —)** PRAIA
(TOWN OF —) MINDELO
(VOLCANO ON —) FOGO
CAPHITE KIST
CAPITAL CAP CASH CITY FUND GOOD
LIMA MAIN RARE SEAT BASIC CHIEF
FATAL GREAT MAJOR MONEY
MUANG STOCK VITAL DEADLY
HEADLY IMPOST LETTER LISBON

MORTAL PRIMAL UNCIAL WEALTH
CENTRAL CHATTEL DRESDEN
LEADING RADICAL SERIOUS
WEIGHTY CABECERA CATALLUM
CHAPITER CHAPTREL DOSSERET
SWINGING
(— OF HEAVEN) AMARAVATI
(— OF HELL) PANDEMONIUM
(DIVISION OF —) ABACUS
(GAMBLER'S —) STAKE
(INADEQUATE —) SHOESTRING
CAPITALIST MONEYER
CAPITATUM MAGNUM
CAPITELLUM KNOP
CAPITOL STATEHOUSE
CAPITOLINE SATURNIAN
CAPITULATE DEFER
CAPITULATION MUNICH TREATY
CAPITULUM HEAD KNOP
ANTHODIUM
CAPO DON BOSS HEAD
CAPOTE HOOD CAPPO CLOAK
BONNET MANTLE TOPPER
CAPPED PILEATE PILEATED
CAPPER CORKER SEALER STEERER
CAPPY TALLOWY
CAPRICCIO (CHARACTER IN —)
FLAMAND OLIVIER MADELEINE
(COMPOSER OF —) STRAUSS
CAPRICE FAD TOY KINK MOOD WHIM
ANTIC BRAID CRANK FANCY FREAK
HUMOR QUIRK CHANGE MAGGOT
NOTION SPLEEN TEMPER VAGARY
WHIMSY BOUTADE CONCEIT
CROCHET IMPULSE TANTRUM
WHIMSEY
CAPRICIOUS DIZZY DODDY FLUKY
MOODY CHANCY FICKLE FITFUL
KITTLE PLATTY WANTON COMICAL
ERRATIC FLIGHTY MAGGOTY
MOONISH PEEVISH VAGRANT
WAYWARD EPISODAL FANCIFUL
FREAKISH HUMOROUS PERVERSE
SKITTISH UNSTEADY VARIABLE
VOLATILE CROTCHETY FANTASTIC
VAGARIOUS
CAPRICIOUSNESS FREAK
CAPRICORN GOAT
CAPRIPEDE SATYR
CAPRYL RUTYL DECANOYL
CAPSHEAF CAP HOOD
CAPSICUM AJI PEPPER PAPRIKA
(— SAUCE) TABASCO
CAPSID MIRID
CAPSIZE COUP KEEL PURL UPEND
UPSET WRONG WHEMMLE
OVERTURN
CAPSTAN CRAB DRUM DANDY
HOIST LEVER CYLINDER WINDLASS
CAPSTONE ACME LECH TOPSTONE
CAPSULE CAP POD URN BOLL CASE
CYST PILL SEED PEARL PERLE SHELL
THECA WAFER AMPULE BARROW

CACHET COCOON OOCYST SHEATH
AMPOULE EYEBALL OTOCYST
SEEDBOX SILIQUE VANILLA
PERICARP PYXIDIUM
(— OF LSD) MICRODOT
(DRUG —S) RED REDS
(PERSON WHO TAKES —S) PILLHEAD
(SPACE —) TERRELLA
(PREF.) THEC(A)(I)(O)

CAPTAIN BO BOH CID BAAS HEAD
JOAB RAIS REIS BARAK CHIEF
LEADER MASTER NAAMAN SOTNIK
CAPITAN FOREMAN HEADMAN
MANAGER PATROON SKIPPER
FLUELLEN GOVERNOR SUBAHDAR
(— OF ARAB VESSEL) NACODAR
(— OF CAVALRY) RESSALDAR
RITMASTER
(— OF CRICKET TEAM) SKIPPER
(— OF CURLING TEAM) SKIP
(— OF PRIVATEER) CAPER
(— OF SHIP) WAFTER
(STRICT —) SUNDOWNER

CAPTAINS COURAGEOUS
(AUTHOR OF —) KIPLING
(CHARACTER IN —) DAN JACK DISKO
TROOP CHEYNE HARVEY MANUEL
SALTERS

CAPTAIN'S DAUGHTER (AUTHOR
OF —) PUSHKIN
(CHARACTER IN —) MARIA PETER
ALEXEI ZOURIN EMELYAN GRINEFF
GRINYEV EGOROVNA IVANOVNA
MIRONOFF PUGACHEV SHVABRIN
VASILISA SAVELITCH POUGATCHEFF

CAPTION TITLE LEADER LEGEND
CUTLINE HEADING SUBHEAD
CITATION HEADLINE SUBTITLE

CAPTIOUS CRAFY TESTY CRAFTY
SEVERE CARPING CYNICAL FRETFUL
PEEVISH TETTISH ALLURING
CATCHING CAVILING CONTRARY
CRITICAL

CAPTIOUSLY TUTLY

CAPTIVATE WIN TAKE CATCH
CHARM RIVET ALLURE ENAMOR
PLEASE RAVISH SUBDUE ATTRACT
BEWITCH CAPTIVE CAPTURE
ENCHANT ENTHRALL INTEREST
OVERTAKE SURPRISE

CAPTIVATED EPRIS EPRISE CAPTIVE

CAPTIVATING TAKING KILLING
WINNING WINSOME CATCHING

CAPTIVE SLAVE DANIEL ENAMOR
THRALL BRISEIS CAITIFF CAITIVE
PRISONER
(— OF HERCULES) IOLE

CAPTIVITY BOND IRON BONDS
CHAINS DURESS BONDAGE
SERFDOM SLAVERY
(— OF THE JEWS) EXILE

CAPTOR TAKER VICTOR CATCHER

CAPTURE BAG COP FIX GET NAB NET
WIN FALL FANG GRAB HOOK LAND
PREY SNIB TAKE TRAP TREE CARRY
CATCH FORCE PINCH PRIZE PURSE
RAVEN SEIZE SWOOP ARREST
COLLAR CORRAL ENTRAP GOBBLE
OBTAIN PIRACY REDUCE TAKING
CAPTIVE LOWBELL SEIZURE WINNING
EXCHANGE SURPRISE UNDERNIM
(— BACKGAMMON PIECE) HIT
(— BIRDS) TOODLE
(— GAME) SATCHEL
(— OF ALL PRIZES) SWEEP
(— TROUT) TICKLE

CAPTURED COLLARED

CAPUCHIN MONKEY CAY SAI
CEPID SAJOU WEEPER SAPAJOU
RINGTAIL

CAPULIN CEREZA

CAPYBARA CAVY CARPINCHO

CAPYS (FATHER OF —) ASSARACUS
(SON OF —) ANCHISES
(WIFE OF —) THEMISTE

CAR BOX BUS PIG AUTO BOGY BUNK
DOLL DRAG DUMP GRIP JEEP RATH
TRAM ZULU BOGEY COACH CRATE
DINER DUMMY GURRY HUTCH
JIMMY RATHA SEDAN STOCK TRAIN
TRUCK WRONG BASKET BOXCAR
BUFFET CHIPPY DINGEY DINGHY
DUPLEX HOPPER JIGGER JINGLE
SALOON SETOFF SMOKER TOURER
AWKWARD CARROCH CHARIOT
COMBINE FLATCAR FREEZER GIRAFFE
GONDOLA HANDCAR MINIVAN
SIDECAR TELPHER TRAILER TROLLEY
VEHICLE VETTURA AMPHICAR
DRAGSTER HORSECAR OUTSIDER
QUADRIGA ROADSTER SINISTER
(— FOR TRAIN CREW) CABOOSE
(— ON RAIL) TROLLEY
(BAGGAGE —) BLIND
(BRAND OF —) FORD SAAB CHEVY
DODGE MAZDA VOLVO PLYMOUTH
(CABLE —) GONDOLA
(COAL —) HUTCH JIMMY WAGON
WAGGON
(CONVERTIBLE —) RAGTOP
(DEALER'S —) DEMO
(ELECTRIC —) TELFER TELPHER
(ELEVATOR —) CAB CAGE
(EMPTY —) EMPTY IDLER
(ENCLOSED CABLE —) GONDOLA
(FUNNY —) DRAGSTER
(GO BY —) AUTO MOTOR
(JAUNTING —) SIDECAR
(KIND OF —) PACE PROWL SQUAD
HEARSE MUSCLE
(KIND OF POLICE —) PANDA
(LOG —) BUNK
(LOW-WHEELED —) HUTCH TRUCKLE
(MINE —) SKIP LARRY BARNEY
GIRAFFE GUNBOAT
(MONORAIL —) GYROCAR

(OBSERVATION —) BUGGY
(OLD —) HEAP CRATE JUNKER
(OLD-TIME —) REO NASH EDSEL
ESSEX STUTZ DESOTO HUDSON
MAXWELL
(POLICE —) CRUISER
(POLICE PATROL —) PANDA
(SMALL —) MINICAB ECONOBOX
(STYLE OF —) COUPE SEDAN
(TOURING —) PHAETON
(TOY RACING —) SLOTCAR
(TROLLEY —) SHORT
(USED —) DOG
CARABAO BUFF BUFFALO
CARACAL GORKUN SYAGUSH
CARACARA HAWK CARANCHA
CHIMANGO
CARACOLE FRISK CAREER
CARADOC BALA CRADOCK
CARAFE CROFT BOTTLE
CARAGUATA CHAGUAR
CARAJURA CHICA
CARAMBOLA BLIMBING BALIMBING
CARAMEL BLACKJACK
CARAPA CRAB CRAPPO CRABWOOD
CARAPACE CRUST SHELL LORICA
SHIELD CALAPASH
(SUFF.) STEGE STEGITE
CARAT (HUNDREDTH OF —) POINT
CARATE PINTA
CARATHIS (SON OF —) VATHEK
CARAVAN VAN TREK TRIP FLEET
TRAIN CAFILA COFFLE CONVOY
SAFARI TRAVEL JOURNEY VEHICLE
CONDUCTA
CARAVANSARY INN CHAN KHAN
HOTEL SERAI ZAYAT HOSTEL IMARET
CHOULTRY HOSTELRY SERAGLIO
CARAVEL NINA
CARAWAY CARVY UMBEL
CARBAMATE MEPROBAMATE
CARBAMIDE UREA
CARBINE STEN DRAGON MUSKET
DRAGOON ESCOPET
(BRITISH —) STEN
CARBOHYDRATE SUGAR AMYLAN
GELOSE INULIN STARCH FUCOSAN
GLUCIDE CELLULIN DEXTRINE
DEXTROSE GLYCOGEN GRAMININ
PENTOSAN TRITICIN CELLULOSE
PARAMYLUM POLYSACCHARIDE
CARBON COAL COKE COPY SOOT
NORIT CRAYON DIAMOND REPLICA
CHARCOAL GRAPHITE SCHUNGITE
(PREF.) ANTHRAC(O)
(SUFF.) ANE
CARBONADO BORT BOART BOORT
CARBON
CARBONATE BURN CHAR FIZZ
AERATE ALKALI ENLIVEN ENERGIZER
CARBONATOR GASMAN
CARBON DIOXIDE CHOKEDAMP
(SUFF.) CAPNIA

CARBONIZE CHAR
CARBONIZER PICKLER
CARBORUNDUM EMERY ABRASIVE
SILUNDUM
CARBOXYL
(SUFF.) (CONTAINING —) OIC ONIC
CARBUNCLE RUBY PYROPE
ANTHRAX CHARBOCLE
(PREF.) ANTHRAC(O)
CARBURETOR CARB DIFFUSER
VAPORIZER
CARCASS BEEF BODY BOUK CASE
CULL BLOCK MUMMY CORPSE
CARRION
(— OF WHALE) CRANG KRANG
KRENG
CARCERULE SARCOBASIS
CARD ACE MAP PAM WAG CLUB
COMB DRAW FACE FIVE FOUR JACK
KING MENU PLAN ROVE STOP BALOP
BLANK CARTE CHART CHECK DEUCE
DUMMY EIGHT ENTRY EQUAL FICHE
FLATS GREEN HEART HONOR JOKER
LOSER PIECE QUEEN SPADE STAMP
STIFF TAROT TEASE BENDER CARTEL
CONVEX FILLER KICKER KNIGHT
PIGEON READER SECOND TICKET
TOWSER BRAGGER BRISQUE
DIAMOND PROGRAM RELEASE
STARTER STOPPER TAROCCO
TRIUMPH BOOKMARK COMOQUER
DECKHEAD DRAWCARD SCHEDULE
SCRIBBLE SQUEEZER STRIPPER
TIMECARD
(— GAME) WAR
(— IN OMBRE) MANILLE
(— LAST IN BOX) HOCK HOCKELTY
(— WOOL) TUM ROVE
(ACE OF CLUBS —) BASTA BASTO
MATADOR PUPPYFOOT
(ACE OF SPADES —) MATADOR
SPADILLE
(ACE OF TRUMPS —) TIB
(AVIATOR'S —) CARNET
(CLUB —) OAK
(COMPASS —) FLY ROSE
(CREDIT —) PLASTIC
(CRIBBAGE —) CRIB
(DEAD —) SLEEPER
(DIAMOND —) PICK CARREAU
(DISCARDED —S) CRIB
(DRAWING —) BLOWOFF
(FARO —) SODA
(FOUR —) CATER QUATRE
(FOURTH —) CASE
(HIGHEST UNPLAYED —) COMMAND
(IN THE —S) PROBABLE
(JOKER —) BRAGGER MISTIGRIS
(KIND OF —) PUNCH REPORT
HOLLERITH
(KING, QUEEN OR KNAVE —) COST
FACE
(KNAVE —) PAM TOM JACK BOWER

EQUES MAKER NODDY COQUIN
KNIGHT PICARO VARLET WENZEL
CUSTREL PEASANT VILLAIN
VARLETTO
(LAYOUT OF —S) TABLEAU
(LOW —) GUARD
(MARKED —) STAMP
(POSTAL —) COVER
(PULLING —S) TIRE
(QUEEN AND KNAVE —S) INTRIGO
INTRIGUE
(RUN OF —S) SEQUENCE
(SPADE —) PICK DIGGER
(STOCK —) TALON
(THIRD HIGHEST TRUMP —) BASTA
(THREE —) TREY THREE
(WILD —) FREAK
(3 —S IN SEQUENCE) TIERCE
FOURCHETTE
(3 —S OF KIND) TRIO TRICON PAIRIAL
TRIPLET
(3 ACE —S) CORONA
(3 FACE —S) GLEEK
(4 OF TRUMPS —S) TIDDY
(5 FACE —S) BLAZE
(7, 8 AND 9 —S) VOIDS
CARDAMOM KNOBWOOD
CARDBOARD CARD PALL BLANK
BOGUS CARTON BRISTOL
TAGBOARD PAPERBOARD
(SMALL PIECES OF —) CHAD
(TWO —S) SPHEROGRAPH
CARDER TOZER TEASER TUMMER
CARDIALGIA HEARTBURN
CARDIGAN CORGI WAMUS FABRIC
JACKET WAMPUS SWEATER
CARDINAL RED MAIN BASIC CHIEF
CLOAK VITAL ALEPHA CLERIC
DATARY PRINCE RADICAL ALEFNULL
ALEFZERO CAMPEIUS PENITENTIARY
CARDINALATE PURPLE
CARDINAL BIRD CARNAL REDBIRD
REDLEGS GROSBEAK REDSHANK
CARDINAL FISH FUCINITA
ALFONCINO
CARDSHARP TRAMPOSO
CARDSHARPER GREEK SHARPER
SPIELER
CARE DO DOW HOW CARK CURE
DUTY FASH FRET HEED KEEP KEPE
MIND PASS RECK SOIN TEND TENT
WISH YEME COUNT GRIEF GUARD
NURSE PAINS SORGE TRUST WORRY
BURDEN CARIEN CHARGE CUMBER
DESIRE GRIEVE KIAUGH LAMENT
REGARD SORROW ANXIETY AUSPICE
CAUTION CHERISH CONCERN
CULTURE CUSTODY KEEPING
RESPECT RUNNING SCRUPLE
THOUGHT TUITION BUSINESS
PERIERGY TENDMENT NURTURANCE
PRECAUTION SOLICITUDE
(— FOR) KNOW MIND RECK TEND

WARD FORCE NURSE SAVOR FATHER
MATTER REGARD CHERISH PROCURE
(— FOR ONESELF) BACH
(— OF HOUSEHOLD) HUSBANDRY
(— OF LIVESTOCK) CHORE
(— OF THE OLD) GERIATRY
(GIVE EXCESSIVE — TO) WETNURSE
(JUDICIOUS —) LEISURE
(WATCHFUL —) TENDANCE
OVERSIGHT
CAREEN GIP CANT HEEL KEEL LIST
TILT VEER LURCH SLOPE SWIFT
INCLINE
CAREENING ALIST AREEL
CAREER RUN WAY LIFE ROAD RUSH
SPEED TRADE CHARGE COURSE
GALLOP CALLING CARIERE PURSUIT
(— SUMMARY) BIO VITA
(MILITARY —) ARMS SERVICE
(SELECT A —) GOINTO
CAREFREE EASY FRANK HAPPY
BREEZY DEGAGE HOLIDAY
DEBONAIR
CAREFUL BUSY WARY CANNY
CHARY CLOSE EXACT HOOLY TENTY
CHOICE DAINTY EIDENT EYEFUL
FRUGAL NARROW TENDER ANXIOUS
CURIOUS ENVIOUS GUARDED
HEEDFUL PAINFUL PRUDENT THRIFTY
ACCURATE CAUTIOUS CRITICAL
DILIGENT DISCREET DREADFUL
GINGERLY MOURNFUL PUNCTUAL
TROUBLED VIGILANT WATCHFUL
OBSERVANT METICULOUS
SOLICITOUS PUNCTILIOUS
CAREFULLY HOOLY NARROW
CANNILY CHARILY TENTILY CHOICELY
GINGERLY
CAREFULNESS CAUTION
CARELESS LAX COOL EASY LASH
RASH MESSY SLACK CASUAL
OVERLY RAKISH REMISS SECURE
SLOPPY SUPINE UNTIDY UNWARY
CURSORY LANGUID SLIGHTY
UNCANNY HEEDLESS LISTLESS
MINDLESS RECKLESS SLATTERN
SLIPSHOD SLOVENLY YEMELESS
NEGLECTFUL SLATTERNLY
CARELESSLY SLACK OVERLY
SLACKLY SLIGHTLY
CARELESSNESS LACHES LAXITY
INCAUTION
CARESS COY HUG PAT PET BILL CLAP
DAUT DAWT KISS MUCH NECK INGLE
NURSE CODDLE COSSET CUDDLE
FONDLE PAMPER STROKE CHERISH
EMBRACE FLATTER BLANDISH
CANOODLE LALLYGAG
CARETAKER KEEPER WARDER
JANITOR
CAREWORN HAGGARD
CARGO BULK LAST LOAD BURDEN
LADING FREIGHT PACKAGE PORTAGE

CARGASON PROPERTY SHIPLOAD
SHIPMENT TRAFFICS
CARIAMA CHUNGA SERIEMA
CARIB GALIBI CALINAGO
CARIBBEAN (— GULF) DARIEN
HONDURAS
(— ISLAND) CUBA SABA ARUBA
HAITI NEVIS BEQUIA NASSAU
TOBAGO ANTIGUA BARBUDA
BONAIRE CURACAO GRENADA
JAMAICA TORTOLA ANGUILLA
BARBADOS DOMINICA TRINIDAD
GUADELOUPE MONTSERRAT
(— ISLAND GROUP) TURKS CAICOS
CAYMAN LEEWARD ANTILLES
WINDWARD
CARIBE PIRAI PIRANHA CHARACINE
CARIBOU STAG RANGIFER REINDEER
CARICATURE APE COPY MOCK SKIT
FARCE LIBEL MIMIC SQUIB OVERDO
PARODY SATIRE CARTOON
TRAVESTY BURLESQUE
CARILLON PEAL
CARILLONNEUR CAMPANIST
BELLMASTER
CARINA KEEL
CARIOUS ROTTEN
CARMELITE EXTERN TERESIAN
CARMEN (CHARACTER IN —) JOSE
CARMEN ZUNIGA MICAELA
ESCAMILLO
(COMPOSER OF —) BIZET
CARMI (FATHER OF —) REUBEN
(SON OF —) ACHAN
CARMINATIVE GINGER CALAMUS
CAMPHOR ANETHOLE VALERIAN
CARMINE RED LAKE CRIMSON
SCARLET
CARNAGE WAR MURDER POGROM
STRAGE BUTCHERY MASSACRE
BLOODSHED SLAUGHTER
CARNAL CROW LEWD GROSS
ANIMAL BODILY SEXUAL BESTIAL
BRUTISH EARTHLY FLESHLY
SECULAR SENSUAL WORLDLY
MATERIAL PANDEMIC PHYSICAL
TEMPORAL
CARNATION JACK PINK FLAKE
BIZARRE PICOTEE DAYBREAK
DIANTHUS GRENADINE MALMAISON
CARNELIAN SARD COPPER
(BEAD OF —) ARANGO
CARNIVAL FETE SHOW CARNY
CANVAS APOKREA CANVASS
REVELRY FASCHING FESTIVAL
CARNIVORE CAT DOG FOX BEAR
COON LION LYNX MINK PUMA SEAL
WOLF CIVET GENET HYENA OTTER
PANDA PEKAN RATEL SABLE STOAT
TIGER BADGER COUGAR ERMINE
FELINE FERRET FISHER FOUSSA
JACKAL JAGUAR MARTEN OCELOT
POSSUM SERVAL WEASEL DASYURE
GLUTTON LEOPARD MEERKAT
POLECAT RACCOON TIGRESS
AARDWOLF MONGOOSE OPPOSSUM
PREDACEAN ZOOPHAGAN
(FOSSIL —) CREODONT
CARNIVOROUS SARCOPHAGOUS
CAROB HUSK LOCUST ALGAROBA
CAROL LAY NOEL SING SONG DITTY
YODEL WARBLE WASSAIL MADRIGAL
AGUINALDO
CAROLINA ALLSPICE SHRUB
**CAROLINE ISLANDS (— ISLAND
GROUP)** PALAU
(ISLAND OF —) YAP HALL PALU TRUK
PELEW PULAP OROLUK PONAPE
WOLEAI PELELIU
(TOWN OF —) LOT NIF RUNU KOROR
MUTOK TOMIL PONAPE MALAKAL
GARUSUUN
CAROLINGIAN KARLING
CAROM SHOT BOUNCE CANNON
GLANCE STRIKE REBOUND BILLIARD
CARAMBOLE
CAROUSAL BAT GELL LARK ORGY
RIOT ROMP TOOT BINGE FEAST
RANDY REVEL ROUSE SPRAY SPREE
FROLIC SHINDY SPLORE BANQUET
CAROUSE REVELRY WASSAIL
DRINKING FESTIVAL JAMBOREE
CAROUSE JET BOUT HELL RANT
TEAR TOOT BINGE BIRLE BOUSE
DRINK QUAFF RANDY REVEL ROUSE
SPREE TOAST COURANT JOLLIFY
WASSAIL CAROUSAL
CAROUSER BACCHANT BACCHANAL
CAROUSING REVEL RAFFING
(— OF ICEBOUND SEAMEN) MALLE
MOLLIE
CARP KOI NAG BITE DRUM SING
SNAG TALK YERK CAVIL PINCH PRATE
SCOLD SPEAK CENSOR GROUSE
NIBBLE RECITE TWITCH CENSURE
CHATTER CRUCIAN QUIBBLE
COMPLAIN CYPRINID GOLDFISH
(CRUCIAN —) GIBEL
(LAKE —) DRUM LAKER
(PREF.) CYPRIN(O)
CARPAL ACTINOST
CARPEL ACHENE CARPID COCCUS
MERICARP CARPOPHYL
(PL.) CORE
CARPENTER ANT LOHAR FITTER
FRAMER HOUSER JOINER PINNER
WRIGHT BUILDER HOWSOUR
WOODMAN INDENTER TECTONIC
TIMBERER PITWRIGHT SHIPWRIGHT
(SHIP'S —) CHIPS
(PREF.) TECTO
CARPENTRY WOODWORK
WRIGHTRY
CARPER MOME CRITIC KNOCKER
CARPET MAT RUG AGRA KALI KUBA
HERAT KILIM SARUK SCOLD SUMAK

TAPET TAPIS TEKKE USHAK AFGHAN
FLOSSA FRIEZE KASHAN KIDDER
KIRMAN LAVEHR NAMMAD RUNNER
SAROUK SAXONY SELJUK SMYRNA
TABRIZ VELVET WILTON DHURRIE
GIORDES HAMADAN INGRAIN
ISFAHAN ISPAHAN SHEMAKA
TEHERAN AKHISSAR AMRITSAR
BRUSSELS COVERING FOOTPACE
KARABAGH MOQUETTE TAPESTRY
TURCOMAN VENETIAN AXMINSTER
SITRINGEE
(HOLY —) KISWA
(PILELESS —) KILIM GELEEM
CARPETING FILLING
CARPET SHARK WOBBEGONG
CARPET SHELL EEROCK PULLET
CARPETWEED FICOID FICOIDAL
MESEMBRYANTHEMUM
CARPING CRAB CAPTIOUS CAVILING
CRITICAL
CARPSUCKER QUILLBACK
CARPUS WRIST CARPOPODITE
CARRAGEEN KILLEEN
CARREL STALL CUBICLE
CARRIAGE AIR CAB CAR FLY GIG RIG
RUT SET VIS ARBA BIGA CART CHAR
DRAG DUKE EKKA GAIT GARB HACK
LOAD MIEN PORT RUTH SHAY TEAM
TRAP WYNN ARABA BANDY BRAKE
BREAK BRETT BUGGY CHAIR COACH
COUPE ESSED FRONT JUTKA MIDGE
NODDY PANEL POISE SADOO SETUP
SULKY TENUE TONGA TRUCK
WAGON BURDEN CALASH CHAISE
CHARET CISIUM CONVOY DENNET
DROSKY FIACRE GHARRY GOCART
HANSOM HERDIC KOSONG LANDAU
MANNER MOTION PORTER REMISE
SADDLE SPIDER STANCE SURREY
TANDEM TELEGA TROIKA BAGGAGE
BEARING BERLINE BOUNDER
BRITSKA CALECHE CALESIN
CARAVAN CARIOLE CAROCHE
CHARIOT COACHEE CONDUCT
CROYDON DOGCART DOSADOS
DROSHKY FORECAR GESTURE
HACKMAN HACKNEY MINIBUS
PHAETON POSCHAY SHANDRY
SKYHOOK TALLYHO TARTANA
TILBURY TRANSIT TROLLEY
UNICORN VECTURE VEHICLE
VETTURA VOITURE VOLANTE
WAFTAGE BAROUCHE BEHAVIOR
BROUGHAM CARRIOLE CARRYALL
CLARENCE CURRICLE DEARBORN
DEMEANOR DORMEUSE EQUIPAGE
PORTANCE PRESENCE ROCKAWAY
SOCIABLE STANHOPE TARANTAS
TOURNURE VICTORIA
(— IN PHILIPPINES) CALESA
(— OF HANDPRESS) COFFIN
(— OF HORSE) AIR

(AMMUNITION —) CAISSON
(CEREMONIAL —) RATH
(ELEVATED —) LIFT
(GUN —) CHASSIS
(INDIAN —) RUT EKKA BANDY
GHARRI GHARRY
(JAVANESE —) SADO SADOO
(LIVERY —) REMISE
(LOG —) DRAG
(PUBLIC —) FLY OMNIBUS
CARRIAGE HOUSE REMISE
CARRIAGEWAY SWEE
CARRIED (— AWAY) RAPT ENLEVE
CARRIER HOD BASE JEEP SHIP TRAM
BUGGY HAMAL KAHAR MACER
PLANE SABOT TAMEN TIGER BARKIS
BEARER CADGER COOLIE HAMMAL
HODMAN JAGGER PACKER PORTER
RUNNER TAILER WEASEL DRAYMAN
DROGHER FLATTOP POSTMAN
REMOVER TACULLI TROTTER
VEHICLE CARGADOR CARRYALL
PORTATOR RAILROAD TEAMSTER
SUBSTRATE
(— OF DISEASE) VECTOR
(COAL —) FLATIRON
(COLOR —) LURRIER
(CRANE —) GANTRY
(ENDLESS —) TAILER
(FIRE —) PORTFIRE
(MAIL —) COURIER POSTMAN
(ORE —) BARGE BOXCAR
(WATER —) BHISTI BHEESTY
(PREF.) PORTE
CARRION KET VILE OFFAL CORPSE
HOODIE REFUSE ROTTEN CARCASS
CORRUPT DOGMEAT CROWBAIT
CARRION BIRD SCAVENGER
CARRION CROW DOWP HOODY
URUBU CORBIE HOODIE GERCROW
CARROT UMBEL CONIUM DAUCUS
CACHRYS SECRETE BUPLEVER
HILLTROT
(DEADLY —) DRIAS
(PERUVIAN —) ARRACACH
(PREPARED WITH —S) CRECY
CARROTING SECRETAGE
CARROUSEL RIDE WHIRLGIG
QUADRILLE
CARRY CAR HUG JAG LUG BEAR
BUCK CART DRAY FARE GEST HAUL
HAVE HOLD HUMP LEAD PACK PORT
SHOW TAKE TOTE TUMP BRING
BROOK CADGE CROSS FERRY GESTE
GUIDE POISE WALTZ WEIGH BEHAVE
CONVEY CONVOY DELATE DEPORT
DERIVE EXTEND COMPORT CONDUCT
CONTAIN ENTRAIN PORTAGE
PRODUCE SUPPORT SUSTAIN
UNDERGO BAJULATE CONTINUE
TRANSFER TRANSMIT
(— AWAY) FIRK DRAIN REAVE SWEEP
TRUSS ABLATE ASPORT

(— **CLUBS**) CADDY CADDIE
(— **EFFIGY**) GUY
(— **FORWARD**) EXTEND
(— **IN OXCART**) KURVEY
(— **INTO EFFECT**) FULFIL FULFILL
(— **IN TRIUMPH**) CHAIR
(— **LIQUOR**) BOOTLEG
(— **OFF**) RAP HENT LIFE SACK FETCH
HEAVE RIFLE SCOUR SWOOP
ABDUCT ASPORT BRAZEN KIDNAP
SPIRIT
(— **ON**) DO RUN WAR HAVE LEAD
LEVY WAGE APPLY DRIVE ENSUE
FIGHT TRAIN CREATE DEMEAN
FOLLOW MANAGE OCCUPY
CONDUCT EXERCISE MAINTAIN
TRANSACT
(— **ONESELF**) HOLD
(— **ONWARD**) CONTINUE
(— **OUT**) DO ACT END GIVE LAST
HONOR AFFORD EFFECT ACHIEVE
EXECUTE FULFILL PERFORM SATISFY
PERPETRATE
(— **TOO FAR**) OVERDO
(— **UPWARD**) RAP ESCALATE
(SUFF.) GER(ENCE)(ENT)(OUS) PHER
PHORA PHORE(SIS) PHORIA
PHOROUS PHORUS
(— **ON**) IZE
CARRYALL BUS CASE WAGON
CARRIAGE
CARRY-ALONG TOTE
CARRYING BURDEN GERENT
FRAUGHT
(— **AWAY**) REVEHENT
(— **ON**) GESTION
(— **WEIGHT**) EFFECTIVE
(PREF.) (— **ON**) PHORO
CART CAR JAG POT RUT BUTT CHAR
COOP COUP DRAY HAUL JANG LEAD
LOAD PLOW PUTT RUTH TOTE WAIN
ARABA BANDY BOGEY BOGIE
CADDY CARRY DANDY DILLY DOLLY
SULKY TONGA TRUCK WAGON
BARROW CADDIE CHAISE CHARET
CISIUM CONVEY DOLLIE DUMPER
GHARRI GHARRY JIGGER JINKER
KURUMA LIMBER PLOUGH SPIDER
CARIOLE CARRETA CHARIOT
DOGCART GUJERAT HACKERY
MORFREY SHALLOW SHANDRY
TROLLEY TRUNDLE TUMBLER
TUMBREL TUMBRIL VEHICLE
BUCKCART DUMPCART HANDCART
PUSHCART
(— **WITH TANK**) TUMBLER
(**BULLOCK** —) BANDY HACKERY
(**COSTER'S** —) TROLL
(**COVERED** —) JINGLE CARIOLE
(**FARMER'S** —) PUTT GAMBO
MORPHREY
(**FREIGHT** —) CARRETON
(**LOG** —) TUG BUNK

(**LUMBER** —) GILL BUMMER
(**MILKMAN'S** —) PRAM
(**OX** —) RECKLA
(**PARCELS** —) FLY
(**TIMBER** —) CUTS
(**TIP** —) COOP COUP COUPE
(**UNDERSLUNG** —) FLOAT
(**2-PONY** —) KOSONG
(**2-WHEELED** —) BANDY BUGGY
SULKY CARRETA TUMBREL
(**3-WHEELED** —) PORTER
CARTE MAP CARD LIST MENU CHART
CHARTER DIAGRAM
CARTE BLANCHE BLANK
CARTEL CARD DEFY PACT POOL SHIP
PAPER TRUST CORNER LETTER
TREATY CONTRACT SYNDICATE
CARTER CARMAN JAGGER LEADER
DRAYMAN LADEMAN TRUCKER
HORSEMAN TEAMSTER
CART-HORSE AVER
CARTILAGE COPULA TISSUE
CRICOID EPIURAL GRISTLE RADIALE
STERNUM TARSALE THYROID
CHONDRUS EPIPUBIS HYPOHYAL
SESAMOID TURBINAL
(— **UNDER DOG'S TONGUE**) LYTTA
(PREF.) CHONDR(I)(IO)(O) CRICO
(SUFF.) CHONDRIA CHONDRY
CRINUS
CARTILAGINOUS CHONDRIC
CARTLOAD SEAM FOTHER
CARTOGRAPH MAP PLAT CHART
CARTOGRAPHER CHARTIST
MAPMAKER
AMERICAN GANNETT HUTCHINS
SOUTHACK STEVENSON
ENGLISH SPEED
GERMAN KIEPERT STIELER
PETERMANN WALDSEEMULLER
RUSSIAN KAULBARS
SWISS SIEGFRIED
CARTON BOX CASE SHELL
CARTOON EPURE ANIMATION
CARTOONING (— **AWARD**) REUBEN
CARTOONIST AMERICAN DAY FOX
KEY REA ARNO BAER BALD BODE
CADY CAPP DODD DUNN HELD HESS
LUKS NAST BARKS BLOCK BURCK
CRUMB DARCY DIRKS DUFFY EDSON
ERNST GOULD HATLO KIRBY LANTE
MCCAY NEHER OPPER PLUMB
SAXON STEIG TERRY YATES
YOUNG ADDAMS BERNDT BRIGGS
CANIFF DEITCH DISNEY DORGAN
FISHER KEMBLE KOTSKY MUSIAL
NEWELL NOWLAN POWERS RIPLEY
SCHULZ SOGLOW DARLING GRUELLE
KEPPLER MAULDIN MCMANUS
TRUDEAU WEBSTER GOLDBERG
HERBLOCK OUTCAULT SCHULTZE
WESTOVER WILLIAMS NANKIVELL
STEINBERG HERSHFIELD FITZPATRICK

AUSTRALIAN LINDSAY
BELGIAN CULLIFORD
DUTCH RAEMAEKERS
ENGLISH LOW SPY DYSON LEECH
SMYTHE FURNISS GILLRAY
HAMPSON TENNIEL ROBINSON
LANCASTER BAIRNSFATHER
FRENCH GOSCINNY
GERMAN MEGGENDORFER
MEXICAN ARRIOLA COVARRUBIAS
WELSH BATEMAN ILLINGWORTH
CARTOUCHE MESA OVAL DURANGO
CARTRIDGE
CARTRIDGE BAG CASE HULL BLANK
SHELL SHORT BULLET MAGNUM
PATRON CAPSULE TORPEDO
HANDLOAD SHOTSHELL
(PART OF —) RIM CASE HEAD NOSE
SLUG CRIMP BULLET JACKET
PRIMER
(TAPE —) CASSETTE
(TYPE OF —) POPIN
CARTULARY COUCHER
CARTWHEEL CLOGWHEEL
CARUCATE CARVE PLOWLAND
(ONE EIGHTH —) OXGANG OXGATE
OXLAND
CARUNCLE ARIL COMB
STROPHIOLE
CARVE CUT ALAY SIDE BEHEW
BREAK GRAVE KIRVE MINCE SHEAR
SPLAY SPOIL THIGH INCISE QUINSE
SCULPT THWITE TRENCH UNLACE
ENCHASE ENGRAIL ENGRAVE
DISJOINT MALAHACK SCULLION
(— A BIRD) WING
(— AN EEL) TRUNCHEON
(— CHICKEN) FRUSH
(— GOOSE) REAR
(— HEN) SPOIL
(— PEACOCK) DISFIGURE
(— PLOVER) MINCE
(— SWAN) LIFT
(PREF.) GLYPHO GLYPT(O) SCULPTO
(SUFF.) GLYPH
CARVED CARVEN GLYPHIC INCISED
(PREF.) GLYPT(O)
CARVER BODGER KIRVER CROPPER
FROSTER IVORIST CISELEUR
TRENCHER
CARVING CAMEO GLYPH IVORY
ENTAIL SCRIVE GLYPTIC MASKOID
NICKING APLUSTRE INTAGLIO
TRIPTYCH PETROGLYPH
(— ON MOLDING) GADROON
(— ON TREE) DENDROGLYPH
(CIRCULAR —) TONDO
CARYA HICORIA
CARYATID TELAMON CANEPHORA
(PART OF —) GAINE
CARYOCAR SOUARI
CARYOPHYLLUS JAMBOSA
CARYOPSIS SEED

CASABLANCA (CHARACTER IN —)
ILSA
CASANOVA AMORIST
CASCABEL POMMEL POMMELION
CASCADE LIN FALL LINN FORCE
SPOUT CATARACT
CASCARA BUCKTHORN WAHOO
SHITTIM
CASCARILLA CROTON GOATWEED
SWEETWOOD
CASE BAG BOX CUP HAP LEG POD
POT PYX BIND BOOT BUNK BURR
CASK COPE DEED DESK DOCK DOME
FILE PACK PAIR ROLL SUIT TICK
BRACE BRIEF BULLA BURSE CADDY
CASUS CAUSE CHAPE COVER CRATE
EVENT FOLIO FOREL HUSSY HUTCH
PRESS PYXIS SHELL STATE THECA
THING TRIAL ACTION AFFAIR APPEAL
BARREL BINDER BOXING CARTON
CASING CELLAR CHANCE CHRISM
COFFIN COUPLE LOCKET LORICA
MATTER PATRON PENNER PETARD
POPPET QUIVER RIDDLE SHEATH
SHRINE STATOR SURVEY TASHIE
TWEEZE VALISE VANITY CABINET
CAMISIA CAPCASE CAPSULE
COUNTER CUSHION DIECASE
ENCLOSE ENVELOP EXAMPLE
GEARBOX HOLDALL HOLSTER
HOUSING HUMIDOR INCLOSE
LAWSUIT LUNETTE PACKAGE
REMANET SATCHEL SHIPPER
WARDIAN ACCIDENT ARGUMENT
BOOKCASE CARRYALL CUPBOARD
ENVELOPE EQUIPAGE EXEMPLAR
GARDEVIN INSTANCE KNAPSACK
PACKSACK PORTFIRE SHOWCASE
SITUATED SOLANDER TANTALUS
CARTRIDGE PORTFOLIO
(— CONTAINING ELEVATOR BELT) LEG
(— ENCLOSING CLOCK DIAL) HOOD
(— FOR BOTTLES) CELLARET
(— FOR CARDS) SHOE
(— FOR COMPASS) BINNACLE
(— FOR DECANTERS) TANTALUS
(— FOR EXPLOSIVES) TRUNK
(— FOR JEWELS) TYE
(— FOR MAINSPRING) BARILLET
(— FOR MOLD) COPE CHAPE
(— FOR MONEY) WALLET
(— FOR MUMMY) SLEDGE
(— FOR PISTOL) HOLSTER
(— FOR PULLEY) BLOCK
(— FOR RIFLE) BOOT
(— FOR SEWING ITEMS) HUSSY
(— FOR TOOLS) TROUSSE
(— FOR TWEEZERS) BUBBLEBOW
(— FOR WRITING MATERIALS)
STANDISH
(— IN WATCH) DOME BARREL
(— OF) A
(— OF FLOUR BOLTER) HUTCH

(— OF VENETIAN BLIND) HEADBOX
(— WITH COMPARTMENTS) RIDDLE
(BONY —) CARAPACE
(CARTRIDGE —) DOP CARTOUCHE
(COSMETIC —) COMPACT
(COURT —) LAWSUIT
(EGG —) OVISAC OOTHECA
(EMPTY —) SHELL
(FIREWORKS —) LANCE
(GRAMMATICAL —) DATIVE ESSIVE
LATIVE ELATIVE FACTIVE ABLATIVE
EQUATIVE ERGATIVE GENITIVE
ILLATIVE LOCATIVE VOCATIVE
ACCUSATIVE
(HOPELESS —) GONER
(LARVA —) INDUSIUM
(LUGGAGE —) IMPERIAL
(ORNAMENTAL —) ETUI
(PAPER —) COFFIN
(PILLOW —) SLIP
(SMALL —) MINAUDIERE
(SPORE —) ASCUS
(WICKER —) HASK BARROW
HANAPER
(WING —) SHARD
(WRITING —) KALAMDAN
(PREF.) THEC(A)(I)(O)
(EGG —) OOTHEC(O)
(SUFF.) THECA THECIUM
CASED BOUND
CASEMENT SASH LUKET WINDOW
CASE OF SERGEANT GRISCHA
(AUTHOR OF —) ZWEIG
(CHARACTER IN —) BABKA LYCHOW
GRISCHA WILHELMI WINFRIED
BJUSCHEFF PAPROTKIN PONJANSKI
SCHIEFFENZAHN
CASH (SHORT OF —) STRAPPED
CASHEW ACAJOU ANACARD
CASHEW TREE ACAJOU
CASHIER CASS CAST BREAK DEALER
POTDAR PURSER TELLER CHECKER
DISMISS
CASHIERED BROKEN DEGOMME
CASHMERE KASHMIR PRUNELL
CASH REGISTER DAMPER REGEST
GREFFIER RECORDER REGISTER
CASING BODY BOOT BUNG CASE
CURB HULL SHOE SKIN TIRE APRON
BELLY DERMA EPHOD GAINE LINER
ROUND STOCK TRUNK BOXING
COFFIN COLLET JACKET KISHKE
LINING SCROLL SHEATH VOLUTE
COWLING FEEDBOX HOUSING
MANHEAD OUTCASE STAVING
THIMBLE CACHEPOT COVERING
PLOWSHOE SHIRTING WHEELBOX
(— FOR BRAIN) HARNPAN
(— FOR SHAFT) TUB
(BOILER —) JACKET
CASINO BAKED BROILED
(— CALL) HITME
(— EMPLOYEE) DEALER

CASK KEG PIN TUB TUN VAT BOSS
BUTT CADE COWL DRUM KNAG PIPE
RAPE RIER SLIP TREE WOOD ANKER
BOWIE BULGE FOIST STAND UNION
BARICA BARREL CARDEL CASQUE
DOLIUM FIRKIN FOODER LONGER
OCTAVE TIERCE WINGER BARRICO
BREAKER FOSTELL LEAGUER
RUNDLET SACKBUT CASSETTE
HOGSHEAD PUNCHEON QUARDEEL
ROUNDLET KILDERKIN
(BREWING —) UNION
(LOCKED —) TANTALUS
(PERFORATED —) POT
(SMALL —) KEG TUB KNAG STOOP
STOUP
(WINE —) FAT TUN BOSS BUTT PIPE
TIERCE HOGSHEAD
(PL.) COOPERAGE
CASKET BOX PIX TYE CASE CASK
CIST TILL TOMB BUIST CHEST
ACERRA CHASSE COFFER COFFIN
SHRINE CADENAS FOSTELL
CASSETTE
CASK-STAND STILLAGE STILLION
CASPIAN (— FEEDER) YSER
CASQUE CASK HORN GALEA
HELMET BRASSET
CASSABANANA CURUBA
CASSANDRA SEER
(BROTHER OF —) HELENUS
(FATHER OF) PRIAM
(HUSBAND OF —) AGAMEMNON
(MOTHER OF —) HECUBA
(SLAYER OF —) CLYTEMNESTRA
CASSAREEP CAXIRI
CASSAVA AIPI YUCA AIPIM YUCCA
CASIRI CAZIRI MANIOC TAPIOCA
(— DISH) TAPIOCA
CASSEROLE TUREEN COCOTTE
MARMITE TERRINE TZIMMES
CASSETTE TAPE MAGAZINE
CARTRIDGE
CASSIA KEZIA SENNA SICKLEPOD
CASSIA FISTULA AMALTAS
CASSIMERE ZEPHYR
CASSINI OLEG
CASSITERITE TINSTONE
CASSITES KUSHSHU
CASSOCK GOWN SLOP VEST APRON
GIPPO SIMAR SYMAR PRIEST
PELISSE SIMARRE SOUTANE
ZIMARRA
CASSOWARY EMU MURUP
MOORUP RATITE
CAST MEW PUT SET AURA BILL DART
HURL MOLD MOLT PICK SHED SLAT
SLIP SPEW SWAK TINT TOSS TREE
TURN WHAP WHOP WURP BLOCK
BRAID CHUCK COOST DEUCE DRIVE
EJECT ERECT FLING FLIRT FOUND
FUSIL HEAVE IMAGE KEIST PITCH
SHADE SHAPE SHOOT SLING STAMP

THROW TINGE COLLAR INJECT
NOSING STRIKE STRIND THRILL
AGARWAL CASHIER DEPOSIT
DISCARD MOULAGE VIBRATE
CASTLING CONSPECT OUTSLING
POLYTYPE TINCTURE
(— ASIDE) DICE FLING
(— A SPELL) TAKE HOODOO BESPELL
BEWITCH FORSPEAK
(— ASPERSIONS) SLUR SKLENT
APPEACH
(— AWAY) DUMP SHOVE DEJECT
REJECT
(— DICE) WHIRL
(— DISCREDIT) GLANCE
(— DOWN) DASH DUMP HURL SINK
ABASE AMATE AMORT AWARP
STREW ABATTU ABJECT DECAST
DEJECT DEMISS THRING ECLIPSE
RUINATE DEJECTED
(— FORTH) SPEW SPUE WARP BELCH
BRAID LAUNCH
(— GLOOM) DUSK CLOUD DARKEN
DEPRESS
(— IN A MOLD) STRIKE
(— LOTS) CAVEL
(— METAL) YET
(— OF DICE) COUP DEUCE
(— OFF) DAFF JILT MOLT SHED DITCH
LOSSE SHAKE SLIRT SLUFF WAIVE
CASTEN DEVEST REFUSE REJECT
SLOUGH ABDICATE RENOUNCE
(— OF HERRINGS) WARP
(— OF LANGUAGE) IDIOM
(— OF NET) SHOT SHOOT
(— ON GROUND) TERRE
(— OUT) EGEST EJECT EXPEL BANISH
ABANDON EXTRUDE OSTRACIZE
(— SHADOW) ADUMBRATE
(— UP) SUM LEVY UPBRAID
(FRESHLY —) GREEN
(PLASTER —) CUIRASS
(SUFF.) JECT
CASTANET CLICKER KNACKER
KNOCKER SNAPPER TCHAPAN
CROTALUM
CASTAWAY WAIF WEFT TRAMP
CRUSOE REJECT OUTCAST DERELICT
STRANDED
CASTE (OR CASTE MEMBER) DOM
MEO AHIR BHAR BHAT GOLA JATI
KOLI KORI MALI MINA PASI TELI
BAGDI BANIA DHOBY GOALA IRAVA
KAHAR KUMNI KUNBI KURMI LADHA
LOHAR MAHAR PALLI PUGGI SAMAR
SANSI SINGH SONAR SUDRA TANTI
VARNA ARORAS BAIDYA BALIJA
BANIAN BHANGI CHAMAR CHETTY
CHUHRA DHANUK DHOBIE DOSADH
DURZEE HOLEYA HOLIYA ILAVAN
JAJMAN KALWAR KAMBOH KHATRI
KUMHAR KURUBA LOHANA MADIGA
NATION PALLAR PRABHU PULAYA

PULIAN PURVOE RAJPUT VAISYA
AGARWAL BRAHMAN BRAHMIN
DHANGAR GADARIA HARIJAN
KAYASTH KOMATRI KURUMBA
NISHADA VELLALA KAMMALAN
KHANDAIT PARAIYAN POVINDAH
RAJBANSI VAKKALIGA
(LOWER —S) PANCHAMA
CASTER VIAL CRUET CRUSE PHIAL
CASTOR HORRAL HURLER MASTER
ROLLER FOUNDER PITCHER TRUCKLE
TRUNDLE
(SURF —) SQUIDDER
CASTIGATE LASH EMEND SCARE
SCORE BERATE PUNISH REVISE
STRAFE SUBDUE CANVASS CENSURE
CHASTEN CORRECT LEATHER
REPROVE CHASTISE KEELHAUL
LAMBASTE FUSTIGATE OBJURGATE
CASTIGATION HELL LASHING
DRESSING
CASTILIAN BROWN TANAGRA
CASTING DIE PIG CAST FONT KEEP
MOLD TYMP BLOCK CHOCK CHUCK
FOUND MOULD BILLET BUMPER
MATRIX MISRUN SPIDER COULAGE
DARTING SEGMENT SEPARATOR
SORTILEGE
(— LOTS) SORTITION
(— OF HOROSCOPE) APOTELESM
(— OF NET) SHOT
(— OVERBOARD) JETTISON
(PL.) SPRAY FOUNDRY
CAST IRON YETLING
CASTLE BURY FORT HALL KEEP ROCK
ROOK ABODE BROCH COURT MORRO
PIECE CASBAH BASTILE BOROUGH
CHATEAU CITADEL SCHLOSS
UDOLPHO BASTILLE CASTELET
CASTILLO FASTNESS FORTRESS
STAROSTY TINTAGEL
(— IN CHESS) JUEZ ROOK TOUR
JUDGE TOWER
(PART OF —) KEEP MOAT WARD
MOUNT TOWER WHARF BAILEY
BRIDGE DONJON TURRET BASTION
BULWARK DUNGEON OUTWORK
RAMPART BARBICAN CASEMATE
GATEHOUSE BATTLEMENT
DRAWBRIDGE PORTCULLIS
(SMALL —) PEEL TOWER CASTLET
CHATELET
CASTLE OF OTRANTO (AUTHOR
OF —) WALPOLE
(CHARACTER IN —) CONRAD JEROME
MANFRED MATILDA ISABELLA
THEODORE
CAST-OFF DISCARD
CASTOR BEAVER LEATHER TRUCKLE
TRUNDLE BARKSTONE
(— AND POLLUX) TWINS GEMINI
DIOSCURI
(MOTHER OF —) LEDA

CASTOR AND POLLUX
(CHARACTER IN —) CASTOR PHOEBE
POLLUX JUPITER MERCURY TELAIRA
(COMPOSER OF —) RAMEAU
CASTOR-OIL
(PREF.) RICIN(I)
CASTOR-OIL PLANT KIKI MAMONA
PALMCRIST
CASTRATE CUT FIX GIB LIB GELD
GLIB SPAY SWIG TRIM ALTER CAPON
DESEX PRUNE STEER CHANGE
DOCTOR EUNUCH NEUTER EVIRATE
CAPONIZE MUTILATE SATURNIZE
CASTRATED CUT GIBBED NEUTER
UNPAVED
(NOT —) STONE ENTIRE
CASTRATO EUNUCH EVIRATO
TENORINO
CASUAL GLID ORRA STRAY BLITHE
BYHAND CHANCE FOLKSY RANDOM
CASALTY CURSORY LEISURE
NATURAL OFFHAND RUNNING
GLANCING INFORMAL
PROMISCUOUS
CASUALTY LOSS DEATH CADUAC
CHANCE HAZARD INJURY MISHAP
ACCIDENT DISASTER
CASUARINA BEEFWOOD
CASUIST JESUIT
CAT GIB RAT REX SOW TAB CHAT
EYRA FLOG GATO LION LYNX MANX
MISS PARD PUMA PUSS CHAUS
CIVET FELID GATOL KITTY KORAT
MANUL MEWER MOGGY OUNCE
PUSSY SMOKE TABBY TIGER TILER
WHITE ZIBET ANGORA BIRMAN
BOMBAY COUGAR FELINE JAGUAR
KITTEN KODKOD MALKIN MARGAY
MAWKIN MIAUER MOGGIE MOUSER
MUSION NEUTER OCELOT PAJERO
PURRER SERVAL SOMALI TIBERT
TORTIE BURMESE CARACAL
CATHEAD CATLING CHEETAH KITLING
KUICHUA LEOPARD LINSANG
PANTHER PERSIAN SIAMESE
TIGRESS WILDCAT WRAWLER
BAUDRONS DASYURID FISSIPED
PUSSYCAT RINGTAIL TONKINESE
(— CRY) WAW MEOW MIAOW
(— GROUP) CLOWDER
(BREED OF —) CYMRIC CHARTREUX
(BREED OF —S) RAGDOLL
(FAMOUS —) MORRIS GARFIELD
MEHITABEL HEATHCLIFF
(FEMALE —) QUEEN WHEENCAT
(MALE —) GIB TOM TOMCAT
(PART OF —) EAR EYE PAW TOE HEEL
KNEE LIPS LOIN NAPE NECK RUMP
TAIL BELLY BREAK ELBOW FLANK
SHANK THIGH WRIST FEELER
DEWCLAW FEATHER WHISKER
FOREHEAD SHOULDER VIBRISSA
METATARSUS

(ROOF-PROWLING —) TILER
(TAILLESS —) RUMPY
(PREF.) AELUR(O) AILUR(O) FELIN(O)
CATACHRESIS ABUSION
CATACHRESTICAL ABUSIVE
CATACLYSM FLOOD DELUGE
DEBACLE DISASTER UPHEAVAL
CATACOMB TOMB CRYPT VAULT
CEMETERY HYPOGEUM
(PL.) ARENARIAE
CATADROMOUS SEAGOING
CATAFALQUE BIER COFFIN
CATALECTIC HEMIAMB TRUNCATED
CATALEPSY TRANCE SEIZURE
CATATONY
CATALOG PIE PYE BILL BOOK LIST
ROLL ROTA BRIEF CANON FLIER
FLYER INDEX PINAX AUTHOR
RAGGER RAGMAN RECORD ROSTER
ARRANGE BEADROW DIPTYCH
NOTITIA BEADROLL BULLETIN
CALENDAR CLASSIFY REGISTER
SCHEDULE SYLLABUS CATALOGUE
DIDASCALY INVENTORY
CATALUFA SCAD TORO BIGEYE
CATALYST CARRIER SAUSAGE
ZIEGLER CATALYTE HOPCALITE
(NEGATIVE —) INHIBITER
CATAMARAN NAG RAFT TROW
BALSA FLOAT NAGGER GUNBOAT
JANGADA MONITOR AUNTSARY
CATAMITE INGLE GUNSEL NINGLE
PATHIC BARDASH GANYMEDE
CATAMOUNT LION LYNX PUMA
COUGAR
CATAPLASM PELOID POULTICE
CATAPULT GUN BIBLE SLING SWEEP
THROW HURTLE LAUNCH ONAGER
TREPAN ALACRAN BRICOLE PEDRERO
TORMENT TRABUCH WARWOLF
BALLISTA CROSSBOW DONDAINE
LAUNCHER MANGONEL MARTINET
SCORPION SPRINGAL STONEBOW
CATARACT LIN FALL LINN FALLS
FLOOD PEARL DELUGE CASCADE
NIAGARA CATADUPE OVERFALL
VICTORIA
CATARRH MUR COLD MURR POSE
RHEUM CORYZA NASITIS
CATASTROPHE ACCIDENT
CALAMITY DISASTER CATACLYSM
CATCALL HOOT
CATCH BAG COB COG COP GET GIN
KEP NAB NET NIP DRAW FANG GLOM
HASP HAUL HAWK HENT HOLD HOOK
LAND MAKE MEET MESS NAIL NICK
PAWL SAVE SEAR SNAG SNAP SNIB
STOP TAKE TRAP VANG BENET
CHAPE CLASP CLEEK CREEL FETCH
GLOVE GRASP HITCH KETCH KNACK
LASSO LATCH PLANT SEIZE SNARE
SNICK SWOOP TRICK TROLL ARREST
ATTAIN BUTTON CLUTCH CORNER

CORRAL DETECT DETENT ENGAGE
ENMESH ENTRAP IMMESH LOCKET
NOBBLE NOODLE SNATCH SPRENT
TAIGLE TAKING TURNEL ATTRACT
CAPTURE ENSNARE GIMMICK
GRAPNEL RELEASE SNIGGLE
SPRINGE TRIGGER CONTRACT
CRANNAGE ENTANGLE FASTNESS
HOLDBACK HOLDFAST OVERTAKE
SNAPHAAN SURPRISE
(— A FLYBALL) SHAG
(— AT PROPER TIME) NICK
(— ATTENTION) FLAG
(— BIRDS) BATFOWL BIRDLIME
(— EELS) SNIGGLE
(— FIRE) SPUNK IGNITE KINDLE
(— FISH) JAB JIG GILL HANG GILLNET
(— FISH WITH HANDS) GUDDLE
GRABBLE HANDFAST
(— HOLD OF) GRIP GRASP
(— IN THE ACT) NAB
(— IN VOICE) FETCH
(— OF DOOR) LATCH SNECK SNICK
(— OF FISH) FARE HAUL SHOT TACK
TRIP SHACK
(— ON) GET GETIT
(— ONE'S BREATH) GASP CHINK
(— SIGHT OF) SPY ESPY SPOT
DESCRY
(CRICKET —) DOLLY
(EASY —) POPUP
(RATCHET —) CLICK
(SAFETY —) CLEVIS
CATCHALL RAGBAG
CATCHER TAKER BIRDER FANGER
LARKER RECEIVER
CATCHFLY SILENE FLYBANE
CATCHING CATCHY TAKING
ALLURING ARRESTING
CATCH-PHRASE SLOGAN WHEEZE
CATCHPOLE BAILIFF PUTTOCK
CATCHWEED CLEAVERS
CATCHWORD CUE TAG MOTTO
BYWORD PHRASE SLOGAN STARTER
CATCHCRY SHIBBOLETH
CATCHY CATCHING APPEALING
CATCH-22 DILEMMA
CATECHISE QUIZ
CATECHISM QUIZ GUIDE MANUAL
CARRITCH QUESTIONS
CATECHU COTCH CUTCH KHAIR
GAMBIER
CATECHUMEN PUPIL AUDIENT
AUDITOR CONVERT BEGINNER
NEOPHYTE COMPETENT
CATEGORICAL DIRECT ABSOLUTE
EXPLICIT KNOCKDOWN
CATEGORIZE ZAG CODE HAVE SORT
CATEGORY WAY KING RANK TALE
CLASS FIELD GENRE GENUS ORDER
STYLE FAMILY LEAGUE NUMBER
RUBRIC SERIES SPECIES DIVISION
PIGEONHOLE PREDICAMENT

(— OF TENSES) INFECTUM
(BIOLOGICAL —) TAXON
(HIGHEST —) IDEA
(PRIMARY —) SUBSTANCE
(TAXONOMIC —) FORM FORMA
GENUS TAXON COHORT LEGION
SUBCLASS SUBGENUS SUBFAMILY
CATENARY ARC
CATER CUT FEED HUMOR SERVE
TREAT PANDER PURVEY SUPPLY
PROVIDE
(PREF.) OPSONI OPSONO
CATERCOUSIN PAL FRIEND
CATERER ACATER MANCIPLE
CATERINA CORNARO
(CHARACTER IN —) ANDREAS
GERARDO CATERINA MOCENIGO
LUSIGNANO
(COMPOSER OF —) DONIZETTI
CATERPILLAR CAT MUGA AWETO
ERUCA CANKER LOOPER PALMER
PORINA RISPER TAILOR WOUBIT
CUTWORM TRACTOR WEBWORM
HANGWORM HORNWORM
SILKWORM SKINWORM WORTWORM
PALMERWORM
(PREF.) CAMPO ERUCI
(SUFF.) CAMPA
CATERWAUL CRY HOWL WAIL
MIAUL WRAWL
CATFACE ARR SCAR
CATFISH MUD CUSK ELOD POUT
RAAD SHAL WOOF BAGRE DORAD
RAASH BARBER DOCMAC GLANIS
GOONCH GOUJON HASSAR MADTOM
MUDCAT BARBUDO CANDIRU
COBBLER FIDDLER PYGIDID SILURID
WALLAGO BULLHEAD BULLPOUT
CORYDORA FLATHEAD MATHEMEG
PLOTOSID SQUEAKER STONECAT
CATGUT THARM THAIRM CATLING
WHIPCORD
CATHARI BULGARI PATARINE
CATHARTIC ALOIN BRYONY PHYSIC
CALOMEL RHUBARB SCOURER
EUONYMUS EVACUANT HYDRAGOG
KALADANA LAPACTIC LAXATIVE
SCAMMONY SOLUTIVE SOLUTORY
PURGATIVE PODOPHYLLIN
CATHAYAN KITAN
CATHEDRA SEE
CATHEDRAL DOM SEE DUOMO
SOBOR MARTYRY MEMORIA
MINSTER BASILICA
(PART OF —) ARCH ROOF CROSS
GABLE IMAGE LABEL SPIRE TOWER
BELFRY FINIAL LINTEL LOUVER
PORTAL WINDOW CROCKET GALLERY
LOZENGE MOLDING MULLION
TRACERY TREFOIL PINNACLE
TYMPANUM DRIPSTONE THROATING
TRIFORIUM CINQUEFOIL
CLERESTORY QUATREFOIL

CATHEXIS CHARGE
CATHODE K KA FILAMENT ELECTRODE HYDROGODE
CATHOLIC BROAD GENERAL LIBERAL TOLERANT
(— ORDER) MARIST DOMINICAN FRANCISCAN
CATHOLICISM PAPISM POPERY
CATHOLICON PANACEA
CATKIN RAG TAG CHAT GULL AGLET AMENT IULUS PUSSY CACHRYS CATTAIL GOSLING
(PREF.) AMENTI
CATMINT NEP NIP
CATNAP NAP DOZE
CATNIP NEP CATARIA CATMINT CATWORT
CATREUS (DAUGHTER OF —) AEROPE CLYMENE APEMOSYNE
(FATHER OF —) MINOS
(MOTHER OF —) PASIPHAE
(SON OF —) ALTHAEMENES
CAT'S-CLAW LONGPOD ESCAMBRON
CAT'S CRADLE HEI
CAT'S-EAR GOSMORE CAPEWEED FLATWEED
CAT'S EYE CHATOYANT
CAT'S-FOOT PUSSYTOE
CAT'S-PAW TOOL PROPERTY
CAT'S-TAIL BULRUSH
CATTAIL DOD DODD FLAG MUSK RUSH TULE AMENT BAYON BLECK CLOUD RAUPO REREE WONGA CATKIN GLADEN TOTORA BULRUSH GLADDON MATREED BLACKCAP CANDUNGI FLAXTAIL
CAT THYME HULWORT
CATTLE ZO BOW FEE GIR AVER DHAN GAUR KINE NEAT NOWT OXEN ZEBU ZOBO DEVON STOCK ANKOLI DURHAM GALYAK ONGOLE ROTHER SINDHI SUSSEX BESTIAL NELLORE REDPOLL COMPOUND OUTSIGHT TUBICORN
(— CARRIED OFF) SPREATH
(ASIAN DAIRY —) REDSINDHI
(BREED OF —) ANGUS BORAN DEVON FJALL KERRY KYLOE SANGA SANGU ANGONI ANKOLE ANKOLI DEXTER DURHAM FULANI JERSEY SUSSEX BAROTSE BRAFORD BRAHMAN BRANGUS COASTER CRIOLLA GUZERAT HARIANA SAHIWAL ALDERNEY AYRSHIRE CHARBRAY FRIBOURG FRIESIAN GALLOWAY GUERNSEY HEREFORD HOLSTEIN KANGAYAM LIMOUSIN LONGHORN
(DWARF —) NATA NIATA
(WILD YOUNG —) KANGAROO
(PREF.) BOVI
CATTLE-BREEDER AHIR ALUR

CATTLE DEALER DROVER
CATTLEHIDE BUFF CROUPON
CATTLEMAN FAZENDEIRO
CATTLE MARKET SALEYARD
CATTLE PEN KRAAL
CATTLE RAID SPRAITH SPREAGH
CATTLE RUN STATION
CATTLE STEALER ABACTOR ABIGEUS
CATTLE YARD CANCHA
CATTY KIN KATI SNIDE
CAUCASIAN OSSET WHITE OSSETE IRANIAN EUROPEAN JAPHETIC PALEFACE
(— LANGUAGE) UDI UDIC UDIN
(PL.) MELANOI
CAUCHO ULE RUBBER
CAUCUS BLOC PRIMARY
CAUDAL POSTERIOR
(PREF.) UR(O)
CAUDATA URODELA
CAUDEX STEM STIPE
CAUGHT GRIPPIT ENTANGLED
(— AT FAULT) TARDY
CAUL HOW WEB KEEL KELL TRUG VEIL GALEA HOUVE DORLOT CREPINE KERCHER NETWORK OMENTUM MEMBRANE SILLYHOW TRESSOUR TRESSURE
(PREF.) AMNIO OMENT(O)
CAULDRON KOHUA CALDRON
CAULICLE SCAPEL ROSTELLUM
CAULIFLOWER BROCCOLI SNOWBALL CHOUFLEUR
CAULK CALK CORK FILL FLAG CHINSE
CAUNUS (FATHER OF —) MILETUS
(MOTHER OF —) CYANEE
(SISTER OF —) BYBLIS
CAUSAL GENETIC
CAUSE DO AIM GAR ISM KEY LET WAY CASE CHAT FATE HOTI LEAD MAKE MOVE ROOT SAKE SPUR SUIT AGENT ARCHE BASIS BREED CAUSA FRAME PARTY SETUP SKILL SLAKE WREAK YIELD ADDICT CREATE EFFECT ELICIT GOSSIP GROUND INDUCE INVOKE MALADY MANNER MATTER MOTIVE OBJECT ORIGIN PARENT REASON RESORT SOURCE SPEECH SPRING CHESOUN CONCERN DISEASE LAWSUIT PROCURE PRODUCE PROVOKE QUARREL SUBJECT BUSINESS ENGENDER GENERATE INSTANCE MOVEMENT OCCASION WHEREFORE MAINSPRING
(— A SORE) RANKLE
(— DAMAGE) DAMNIFY
(— FOR COMPLAINT) COMEBACK
(— OF ANXIETY) BUGABOO
(— OF IRRITATION) GALL
(— OF PAIN) DISEASE
(— OF QUARREL) GRUDGE

(— OF RUIN) BANE
(— OF SORROW) GRIEF
(— OF TERROR) AFFRIGHT
(— OF TROUBLE) TRACHLE
(— PAIN) URN
(— TO ARCH) ROACH
(— TO CONTRACT) PUCKER
(— TO CROUCH) COUCH
(— TO DESERT) DEFECT
(— TO END) ACHIEVE
(— TO GO) HAVE
(— TO MOVE RAPIDLY) GIG
(— TO PROJECT) JET
(— TO RESULT) ISSUE
(— TO STICK) MIRE
(— TO SWELL) BINGE EMBOSS
(— TO THICKEN) CURD
(COMMITTED TO A —) ENGAGE
(FINAL —) END
(FORM-GIVING —) IDEA
(IMMEDIATE —) SIGNAL
(PRIMAL —) URGRUND
(PREF.) AETIO AITIO CAUSI ETIO
(SUFF.) FIC(AL)(ATE)(ATION)(ATIVE)
(ATOR)(ATORY)(E)(ENCE)(ENT)(IAL)
(IARY)(IENT) FIQUE

CAUSED
(SUFF.) (— BY) IC(AL)
CAUSER (— OF TROUBLE)
BOLSHEVIK
CAUSERIE CHAT
CAUSEWAY WAY DIKE ROAD
HIGHWAY CHAUSSEE
CAUSING
(SUFF.) ABLE FACIENT FACT(ION)(IVE)
(ORY) FIC IBLE
CAUSTIC LYE ACID TART ACRID QUICK
SALTY SHARP SNELL ACIDIC BITING
BITTER SEVERE BURNING CAUTERY
CUTTING ERODENT MORDANT
NIPPING PUNGENT PYROTIC SATIRIC
ALKALINE DIERETIC SCATHING
SNAPPISH STINGING ACIDULOUS
SARCASTIC MORDACIOUS
CAUSTICITY ACRIMONY
CAUTERIZATION USTION
INUSTION
CAUTERIZE BURN CHAR FIRE SEAR
BRAND INUST SINGE
CAUTERY MOXA
CAUTION CARE FEAR HEED WARN
GUARD ADVICE CAUTEL CAVEAT
EXHORT ANXIETY COUNSEL
PRECEPT PROVISO WARNING
ADMONISH FORECAST FOREWARN
MONITION PRUDENCE WARINESS
CAUTIOUS SHY CAGY SAFE WARE
WARY ALERT CANNY CHARY SIKER
FABIAN HOOLIE SICKER TENDER
TIPTOE CAREFUL CURIOUS ENVIOUS
FEARFUL FERDFUL GUARDED
PRUDENT DISCREET SUSPENSE
VIGILANT CAUTELOUS

CAUTIOUSLY CANNY CANNILY
CHARILY EASYLIKE GINGERLY
TENDERLY
CAVAL
(PREF.) VEN(I)(O)
CAVALCADE RAID RIDE MARCH
TRAIN PARADE SAFARI COMPANY
JOURNEY PAGEANT
CAVALIER GAY CAVY CURT EASY
FINE BOSSY BRAVE FRANK MOUNT
RIDER ESCORT KNIGHT BRUSQUE
GALLANT HAUGHTY OFFHAND
SOLDIER CAVALERO ROYALIST
CHAMBERER CHEVALIER
COMMANDER
CAVALLA CERO JACK TORO ULUA
JUREL CARANX CARANGID
CREVALLE SCOMBRID
CAVALLERIA RUSTICANA
(CHARACTER IN —) LOLA ALFIO
TURIDDU SANTUZZA
(COMPOSER OF —) MASCAGNI
CAVALRY HORSE HEAVIES CHIVALRY
HORSEMEN YEOMANRY
CAVALRYMAN SOWAR SPAHI
SUWAR HUSSAR JINETE LANCER
REITER ARGOLET COURIER
DRAGOON PLUNGER SABREUR
TROOPER GENDARME HORSEMAN
SILLADAR STRADIOT
(PRUSSIAN —) UHLAN
(PL.) FORAGERS
CAVATINA SOLO
CAVE DEN TIP COVE HOLE LAIR MINE
REAR SINK TOSS WEEM ANTAR
ANTRE CABIN CACHE CAVEA
CRYPT DELVE FOGOU SLADE SPEOS
STORE UPSET BEWARE CAVERN
CAVITY CELLAR DUGOUT GROTTO
HOLLOW LARDER LUSTER PANTRY
PLUNGE SHROUD MANSION
RESERVE SPELUNK CASTILLO
COLLAPSE OVERTURN MITHRAEUM
(— IN) COLT
(ANIMAL LIVING IN —) TROGLODYTE
(ONE WHO EXPLORES —S)
SPELUNKER
(PREF.) SPELEO
CAVEAT BEWARE NOTICE CAUTION
WARNING
CAVE-DWELLER HORITE
TROGLODYTE
CAVE-DWELLING NATUFIAN
(PREF.) TROGLO
CAVEMAN NEANDERTHAL
CAVER SPELUNKER
CAVERN DEN CAVE COVE GROT
HOLE LAIR WEEM CROFT VAULT
ANTRUM CAVITY GROTTO HOLLOW
SPELUNK
(PREF.) ANTR(O)
CAVERNOUS ERECTILE
CAVESSON CHAIN

CAVETTO GULA GORGE
CAVIAR OVA ROE IKRA GARUM IKARY
  BELUGA OSETRA OSSETRA SEVRUGA
CAVIL CARK CARP HAFT QUIP
  HAGGLE CAPTION CHICANE
  QUARREL QUIBBLE PETTIFOG
  QUIDDITY FORMALIZE
CAVILER CRITIC GIRDER HAFTER
  ZOILUS
CAVILING CAPTIOUS CRITICAL
  PICAYUNE
CAVITIED
  (SUFF.) COELOUS COELUS
CAVITY BAG CUP PIT SAC ABRI AXIL
  CASE CAVE CELL DALK DENT DUCT
  HOLE MIND MINE VEIN VOID WELL
  WOMB ABYSS BOSOM BURSA CRYPT
  DRUSE FOSSA GEODE GOUGE
  LUMEN MOUTH ORBIT SCOOP SINUS
  ANTRUM AREOLA AREOLE ATRIUM
  AXILLA BORING CAECUM CAMERA
  CAVERN COELIA COELOM COTYLE
  CRATER DEBLAI GROTTO HOLLOW
  LACUNA POCKET RECESS SCAPHA
  SOCKET VACUUM VOMICA
  ABDOMEN CHAMBER CISTERN
  CYATHUS DIOCOEL KYATHOS
  LOCULUS MORTISE VACUITY
  VACUOLE VESICLE ALVEOLUS
  BROODSAC EPICOELE FOLLICLE
  WELLHOLE VESTIBULE
  (— IN BONE) LACUNA
  (— IN CASTING) PIPE
  (— IN FRUIT) VITTA
  (— IN GLASS) TEAR
  (— IN HEAD OF WHALE) CASE
  (— IN HEART) AURICLE
  (— IN HILLSIDE) ABRI
  (— IN LAVA) AMYGDALE AMYGDULE
  (— IN MINE) BAG
  (— IN ROCK) KETTLE
  (— MADE BY SEALS) IGLOO
  (— OF SEA-SHELL) FLUE
  (ALTAR —) TOMB
  (ANATOMICAL —) LUMEN
  (BAKING —) OVEN
  (BODY —) GUT BELLY CLOACA
  THORAX ABDOMEN STOMACH
  PSEUDOCOEL PERICARDIUM
  (CHEST —) THORAX
  (CRYSTAL-LINED —) VUGG DRUSE
  GEODE
  (DEEP —) WOMB
  (EAR —) CONCHA COCHLEA
  (GUN —) BORE
  (NASAL —) CAVUM
  (SUBTERRANEAN —) SLUGGA
  (UNFILLED — IN ROCK) VUG
  (PREF.) CELI(O) ANTR(O) CAEC(I)
  (O) CEC(I)(O) CEL(I)(O) COEL(I)(O)
  (SUFF.) CELE COELE COELUS
CAVORT PLAY BOUND CAPER
  CURVET GAMBOL PRANCE

CAVY PACA PONY AGOUTI APEREA
  CAYUSE CAPYBARA
  (FEMALE —) SOW
CAW KA CRY CALL CROAK QUARK
  QUAWK
CAY ILOT
CAYMAN JACARE
CAYSTER (DAUGHTER OF —)
  SEMIRAMIS
  (FATHER OF —) ACHILLES
  (MOTHER OF —) PENTHESILEA
CAYUSE CAVY PONY BRONCO
  MUSTANG
CEASE HO BOW CUT DIE END LIN
  BALK BLIN DROP FINE HALT HOLD
  LIFT LISS QUIT REST SACE SHUT
  STAY STOP STOW AVAST CLOSE
  DOWSE LEAVE PAUSE PETER STINT
  SWICK WAIVE DESIST DEVALL EXPIRE
  FINISH FORGET ABSTAIN OUTGIVE
  REFRAIN SUSPEND INTERMIT
  OVERGIVE SURCEASE
  (— FIGHTING) YIELD
  (— MILKING COW) SINE
  (— TEMPORARILY) LIFT
  (— TO ASSERT) ABANDON
  (— TO EXIST) VANISH
  (— TO FLOW) STANCH STAUNCH
CEASELESS EVER ENDLESS
  ETERNAL IMMORTAL UNENDING
CEASING CESSER CESSATION
CEBUS SAI
CECILIA SIS SISSU
CECROPS (DAUGHTER OF —) HERSE
  AGLAUROS PANDROSOS
  (WIFE OF —) AGLAUROS
CECUM
  (PREF.) TYPHL(O)
CEDAR SUGI TOON SAVIN AROLLA
  DEODAR SABINA TUMION CYPRESS
  JUNIPER WAXWING CALANTAS
  PAHAUTEA
CEDAR SWAMP GREENING
CEDAR WAXWING RECOLLET
CEDE CESS GIVE AWARD GRANT
  LEAVE WAIVE YIELD ASSIGN RESIGN
  SUBMIT CONCEDE RENOUNCE
  TRANSFER
CEDILLA TITTLE
CEIBA KAPOK BENTANG POCHOTE
CEIL LINE SYLE OVERLAY WAINSCOT
CEILING CAP TOP DOME LACE LOFT
  CHUTT CUPOLA LINING SCREEN
  SOFFIT SYLING CURTAIN LACUNAR
  PLAFOND TESTUDO COVERING
  DECKHAND OVERHEAD PANELING
  PLANCHER SEMIDOME
CELAENO (FATHER OF —) ATLAS
  (MOTHER OF —) PLEIONE
  (SON OF —) LYCUS NYCTEUS
CELANDINE FICARY KILLWORT
  PILEWORT WARTWEED WARTWORT
  FELONWORT JEWELWEED

CELEBES (GULF OF —) BONE TOLO TOMINI
(ISLAND OF —) MUNA BUTUNG PELENG SULAWESI
(PEOPLE OF —) TORAJA
(TOWN OF —) BUOL LUWUK MANADO MAKASAR
CELEBRANT REVELER
CELEBRATE FETE KEEP SING CHANT DITTY EXTOL HONOR REVEL SACRE SOUND SPEAK BESING CHAUNT EXTOLL PRAISE RECORD RENOWN REPEAT ELEGIZE EXECUTE GLORIFY MAFFICK OBSERVE TRUMPET EMBLAZON EULOGIZE PROCLAIM
(— VICTORY) TRIUMPH
(— 2 MASSES) BINATE DUPLICATE
CELEBRATED KEPT FAMED NOTED FAMOUS EMINENT FEASTED RENOMME STORIED FABULOUS GLORIOUS NOTIFIED OBSERVED RENOWNED
CELEBRATION EED FETE GALA POPE RITE FESTA REVEL COOLIN CUSTOM DOMENT EASTER FIESTA HOOPLA POWWOW RENOWN SIMHAH BLOWOUT HAGMENA HOLIDAY JUBILEE PASCHAL SHINDIG SIMCHAH BINATION BIRTHDAY HOGMANAY MAKAHIKI OCCASION OLYMPIAD POTLATCH SHIVAREE FESTIVITY HOOLAULEA JUNKETING MERRIMENT MILLENIUM
(LIVELY —) RAVEUP
(STUDENT —) GAUDEAMUS
(UNRESTRAINED —) ORGY
(WILD —) ORGY SATURNALIA
CELEBRATOR JUBILIST
CELEBRITY FAME LION NAME STAR CELEB ECLAT RENOWN REPUTE
(PL.) GLITTERATI
CELERITY HASTE HURRY SPEED DISPATCH RAPIDITY VELOCITY SWIFTNESS
CELERY SIT ACHE STICK UMBEL KARPAS SALARY CELERIAC SMALLAGE
CELESTIAL HOLY ASTRAL DIVINE HEAVEN URANIC ANGELIC CHINESE ETHERED EMPYREAL ETHEREAL HEAVENLY OLYMPIAN
(— OBJECT) QUASAR
CELESTITE APOTOME
CELEUS (SON OF —) DEMOPHON TRIPTOLEMUS
(WIFE OF —) METANIRA
CELIBACY CHASTITY VIRGINITY
CELIBATE CLERK CHASTE SINGLE BACHELOR SPINSTER
CELL BOX EGG BAND BOOT CAGE CYTE DISC DISK GERM GONE HOLE JAIL KILL ASCUS CABIN CAROL CLINK CRYPT CYTON FIBER FIBRE GHOST GLAND GROUP OOTID TMEMA TORIL VAULT ZOOID ANAXON CEPTOR COCCUS COOLER CYTODE GAMETE GONIUM INAXON NEURON PRISON SHIELD SIPHON SYPHON WESTON ZYGOTE AGAMETE AMEBULA APOCYTE CELLULE CHAMBER CLOCHAN CLOSTER COCCOID CUBICLE DIPLOID DUNGEON ELEMENT EPICYTE EUPLOID HAPLOID HEMATID INITIAL LOCULUS MYOCYTE NEURONE OOBLAST PAPILLA PLASTID RENETTE SEGMENT SPORONT STEREID TRISOME UTRICLE VESICLE AMACRINE BASOCYTE BASOPHIL BIFORINE BIOPLAST CLOGHAUN DIKARYON FAVEOLUS GLIOCYTE GONIDIUM GONOCYTE HEMOCYTE HOLDOVER IDIOSOME LOCELLUS MYOBLAST ORGANULE PROSORUS RECEPTOR SCLEREID SPERMULE SYNERGID TRACHEID TRIPLOID ZOOBLAST MACROCYTE MICROCYTE MYELOCYTE OSTEOCYTE PHAGOCYTE PROGAMETE MELANOCYTE MOTONEURON NEUTROPHIL OSTEOCLAST MELANOBLAST MELANOPHORE ODONTOBLAST
(— CONTAINING LATEX) LATICIFER
(— OF LEADERS) CADRE
(— OF TEMPLE) NAOS
(BEE —) PIPE
(CLUSTER OF —S) MORULA
(DETENTION —) BULLPEN
(DRY —) NICAD
(EGG —) OVUM
(KIND OF —) LIP HELA KILLER MOTHER
(NERVE —) NEURON NEURONE
(PART OF —) SAP NUCLEUS PLASTID VACUOLE MEMBRANE CENTRIOLE ECTOPLASM ENDOPLASM NUCLEOLUS RETICULUM CENTROSOME CHONDRIOSOME
(PHOTOELECTRIC —) EYE PEC PHOTOCELL
(PLANT —) LATICIFER
(PRISON —) BING HOLE CABIN CLINK COOLER JIGGER
(RECLUSE'S —) ANCHORAGE
(STAB —) BAND
(THIN-WALLED —S) STOMIUM
(VOLTAIC —) BATTERY
(PL.) SPOR LAURA POTLINE SWEATBOX
(PREF.) CYT(IO)(O) GAMET(O) GONIDI ONT(O) THYRE(O) THYRO
(SUFF.) BLAST(IC)(Y) CYTE PHAG(A)(E) (O)(OUS)(US)(Y) PLASIA PLASIS

PLASM(A)(IA)(IC) PLAST PLATI(IC)(Y)
SPONGIA(E)(N) SPONGIUM THYRIS
CELLA NAOS
CELLAR CAVE VAULT BODEGA PALACE
FAVISSA HYPOGEE BASEMENT
HYPOGEUM MATAMORO VAULTAGE
(WINE —) BODEGA
CELLARET TANTALUS
CELLARMAN SOMMELIER
CELL-DIVISION MEIOSIS
CELLULAR
(SUFF.) ENCHYMA ENCHYMATA
CELLULOID XYLONITE
CELLULOSE CRUMB AMYLOID
LIGNOSE TAMIDINE
CELT GAEL GAUL KELT MANX IRISH
WELSH BRETON BRITON EOLITH
GADHEL GOIDEL BRYTHON CORNISH
PALSTAFF PALSTAVE
(PL.) CYMRY KYMRY
CELTIC ERSE GAEL SCOTCH
CEMBALO DULCIMER ZIMBALON
CEMENT FIX KIT TIE GLUE HEAL JOIN
KNIT LIME LUTE SLIP BETON GROUT
IMBED PASTE PUTTY SIMON STICK
TABBY UNITE BINDER CHUNAM
COHERE FASTEN FILLER GULGUL
KIBOSH MALTHA MASTIC MORTAR
OOGLEA SOLDER ASPHALT MIXTION
ADHESIVE ALBOLITE ALBOLITH
CEMENTUM HADIGEON SOLIDIFY
SOLUTION
(BEES' —) PROPOLIS
(SUFF.) LITE LITH(IC) LITIC
CEMENTER GLUER GLUEMAN
SMEARER
CEMENT MIXER TEMPERER
CEMETERY HOWF KILL LAIR LITTEN
CHARNEL BONEYARD CATACOMB
GOLGOTHA URNFIELD NECROPOLIS
CENCHRIAS (FATHER OF —)
POSEIDON
(MOTHER OF —) PIRENE
(SLAYER OF —) ARTEMIS
CENCI (AUTHOR OF —) SHELLEY
(CHARACTER IN —) CENCI MARZIO
ORSINO CAMILLO GIACOMO OLIMPIO
SAVELLA BEATRICE BERNARDO
LUCRETIA
CENERENTOLA, LA (CHARACTER
IN —) TISBE RAMIRO ALIDORO
DANDINI ANGELINA CLORINDA
MAGNIFICO CINDERELLA
(COMPOSER OF —) ROSSINI
CENOBITE NUN MONK FRIAR ESSENE
RECLUSE MONASTIC SYNODITE
CENOTAPH TOMB
CENSE THURIFY
CENSER INCENSER THURIBLE
CASSOLETTE
CENSOR CRITIC SCREEN SYNDIC
LAUNDER RESTRICT SUPPRESS

CENSORIOUS SEVERE BLAMING
CARPING BLAMEFUL CAPTIOUS
CRITICAL CULPABLE SLASHING
CENSORSHIP WRAPS ASSIZE
CENSURE
CENSURABLE TAXABLE BLAMABLE
CULPABLE
CENSURE BAN HIT NIP RAP TAP TAX
WIG CALL CARP DEEM DRUB FLAY
HELL LASH RATE SLAP TASK WITE
BEANS BLAME CHIDE CURSE DECRY
FAULT HOKER JUDGE PINCH SCOLD
SLANG SLASH SLATE TAUNT TOUCH
WHITE ACCUSE ATTACK BERATE
CHARGE REBUFF REBUKE REFORM
REMORD STRAFE TARGUE TIRADE
APPEACH BLISTER CHASTEN
CONDEMN CONTROL DECRIAL
DYSLOGY IMPEACH IMPROVE
INVEIGH REPROOF REPROVE SCARIFY
TRADUCE TROUNCE UPBRAID
BACKBITE CHASTISE DISALLOW
JUDGMENT LANGUAGE REPROACH
SATIRIZE SENTENCE STRICTURE
ADMONITION
(GOD OF —) MOMUS
CENSUS LIST POLL CENSE COUNT
LUSTER LUSTRUM CAPITATION
CENT RED DUIT SANT BROWNIE
CENTAVO STUIVER
(FIVE —S) JITNEY NICKEL
(ODD —S) BREAKAGE
(ONE —) PENNY
(TEN —S) DIME
(TWENTY-FIVE —S) QUARTER
(12 1-2 —S) LEVY
CENTAUR CHIRON NESSUS
HORSEMAN BUCENTAUR SAGITTARY
CENTAURUS (FATHER OF —) IXION
(MOTHER OF —) NEPHELE
CENTAURY BEHN BEHEN SABBATIA
EARTHGALL
CENTENNIAL STATE COLORADO
CENTER COR EYE GIG HUB MID AXIS
CORE NAVE SEAT SNAP YOLK FOCUS
FOYER GLOME HEART MIDST NEXUS
PIVOT SPINE BOTTOM CENTRE
MIDDLE PIPPER STAPLE TEMPLE
CENTRUM ESSENCE LINEMAN
NUCLEUS UMBILIC INCENTER
OMPHALOS SNAPBACK
(— FOR SPINDLE) GIG
(— FOR TARGET) EYE PIN PINHOLE
(— OF ACTIVITY) HUB HIVE
(— OF ARCH) COOM
(— OF ASSURANCE) FORTRESS
(— OF ATTRACTION) FOCUS STAGE
CYNOSURE POLESTAR
(— OF BASKET) SLATHER
(— OF CITY) DOWNTOWN
(— OF CULTIVATION) HOME
(— OF CULTURE) ATHENS

(— OF DIAMOND) WELL
(— OF ESCUTCHEON) NOMBRIL
(— OF FIGURE) CENTROID
(— OF FISHING NET) BUNT
(— OF FLOWER) EYE
(— OF HURRICANE) EYE
(— OF OPERATIONS) SHOP
(— OF POPULATION) CITY
(— OF POWER) SEE SIEGE
(— OF STAGE) LIMELIGHT
(— OF STRENGTH) GANGLION
(— PIECE) HUB
(BASKETBALL —) PIVOTMAN
(COLLECTION —) ENTREPOT
(COMMERCIAL —) MALL MART
MACHI EMPORIUM
(HARD —) KNOT
(INTIMATE —) BOSOM
(KIND OF —) NERVE
(LATHE —) PIKE
(NERVOUS —) BRAIN NIDUS
(NEURAL —) APPESTAT
(OFF —) ALOP
(PROPAGANDA —) AGITPUNKT
(RECREATION —) ARCADE
(REHABILITATION —) HOSTEL
(SHOPPING —) MALL
(TOWARD —) ENTAD
(TRADING —) BEACH EXCHANGE
(VITAL —) HEARTH HEARTBEAT
(PREF.) CENTR(I)(O)
(SUFF.) CENTRIC
CENTERING COOM COOMB CENTRY
FANTAIL
CENTERPIECE ROSACE DORMANT
EPERGNE DUCHESSE
CENTETES TENREC
CENTIARE LI
CENTIGRADE CELSIUS
CENTIME RAPPEN
CENTIMETER GAL
CENTIPEDE VEI VERI EARWIG
GOLACH GOLOCH POLYPOD
CHILOPOD MULTIPED MYRIAPOD
SANTAPEE SCUTIGER SCOLOPENDRA
CENTRAL MID AXIAL BASIC CHIEF
FOCAL MIXED POLAR PRIME MEDIAN
MIDDLE CAPITAL CENTRIC LEADING
NUCLEAR PIVOTAL PRIMARY
CARDINAL DOMINANT
(PREF.) CENTR(I)(O)

CENTRAL AFRICAN REPUBLIC
CAPITAL: BANGUI
COIN: FRANC
NATIVE: BAYA SARA BANDA BWAKA
SANGO YAKOMA BANZIRI MANDJIA
RIVER: BOMU NANA CHARI KOTTO
MBARI MPOKO OUAKA OUHAM
CHINKO LOBAYE SANGHA UBANGI
TOWN: OBO IPPY BIRAO BOUAR
KEMBE NDELE NGOTO PAOUA
RAFAI ZEMIO BABOUA BAKALA

BANGUI BOZOUM BAMBARI
GRIMARI ZEMONGO BERBERATI
BOSSANGOA

CENTRAL AMERICAN LADINO
(— NATION) BELIZE PANAMA
HONDURAS COSTARICA
(— TREE) TUNO TUNU
CENTRANTH SPURFLOWER
CENTRIFUGAL EFFERENT
RADIATING
CENTRIFUGE CYCLONE SEPARATOR
CENTRIPETAL AFFERENT
CENTROSOME CENTRUM
CENTRIOLE
CENTRUM CORE
CENTURIED SECULAR
CENTURY AGE TON SECLE SIECLE
(14TH —) TRECENTO
(17TH —) SEICENTO
CENTURY PLANT ALOE PITA
AGAVE MAGUEY CANTALA TEQUILA
MONOCARP
CENWALH (FATHER OF —) CYNEGILS
CEPHALALGIA SODA HEADACHE
CEPHALIC CRANIAL ATLANTAL
CEREBRAL
CEPHALOPOD SQUID CUTTLE
INKFISH OCTOPUS SPIRULA
DIBRANCH SCAPHITE
CEPHALOTHORAX PROSOMA
CEPHALUS (FATHER OF —) DEION
(MOTHER OF —) DIOMEDE
(WIFE OF —) PROCRIS
CEPHEUS (BROTHER OF —) DANAUS
AEGYPTUS AMPHIDAMAS
(DAUGHTER OF —) ANDROMEDA
(FATHER OF —) ALEUS BELUS
(MOTHER OF —) ANCHINOE
(WIFE OF —) CASSIOPEA
CERAMIC (— WARE) WEDGWOOD
CERAMICS TILES POTTERY
CERAMUS (FATHER OF —) BACCHUS
DIONYSUS
(MOTHER OF —) ARIADNE
CERASTES ASP VIPER
CERATE WAX LARD SALVE UNGUENT
OINTMENT
CERCYON (DAUGHTER OF —) ALOPE
(FATHER OF —) NEPTUNE POSEIDON
HEPHAESTUS
(SLAYER OF —) THESEUS
CEREAL RYE BEAN BRAN CORN
MUSH OATS RICE SAMP TEFF ARZUN
GRAIN MAIZE SPELT WHEAT BARLEY
BINDER FARINA HOMINY PABLUM
OATMEAL SOYBEAN PORRIDGE
CEREAL LEAF FLAG
CEREBRAL CEPHALIC INVERTED
(PREF.) PSYCH(O)
CEREBRATION THOUGHT
CEREBROSIDE KERASIN
CEREMENT SHROUD

CEREMONIAL FORM PRIM RITE STIFF FORMAL RIALTY RITUAL SOLEMN PRECISE STUDIED TRIUMPH UPANAYA AVERSION SPLENDOR
(FOOLISH —) MUMMERY

CEREMONIOUS GRAND LOFTY STIFF FORMAL PROPER SOLEMN PRECISE STATELY STUDIED

CEREMONY BRIS FETE FORM GAUD HAKO ORGY POMP RITE SEAL SHOW SIGN SING BERIT DANCE DOSEH STATE ACTION AUGURY BERITH BRIDAL BURIAL EXEQUY GOMBAY HOMAGE KERIAH MALKAH MAUNDY NIPTER OFFICE PARADE POWWOW REVIEW RITUAL SALUTE BAPTISM DISPLAY KIDDUSH MELAVEH OVATION PAGEANT PANAGIA PORTENT PRODIGY TAHARAH ACCOLADE APOLUSIS ASPERGES COEMPTIO CRIOBOLY ENCAENIA EXERCISE FUNCTION HABDALAH HAKAFOTH HERALDRY MARRIAGE OCCASION SKEYTING INAUGURAL INDUCTION ORDINANCE CORONATION OBSERVANCE
(GRADUATION —) CAPPING
(HAZING —) CREELING
(MARRIAGE —) ESPOUSAL
(TEA —) CHANOYU
(PL.) DEGREE HOLIES AGENDUM FERALIA JUSTMENTS

CERES DEMETER
(DAUGHTER OF —) PROSERPINE PHERREPHATTA
(FATHER OF —) SATURN
(MOTHER OF —) VESTA

CERINTHE HONEYWORT

CERO SEARER SIERRA CAVALLA PINTADO KINGFISH

CERTAIN COLD COOL DEAD FAST FIRM FREE REAL SEAL SURE TRUE BOUND CLEAR EXACT FIXED PLAIN SIKER ACTUAL MEMORY SECURE SICKER STATED WITTER ASSURED PERFECT PRECISE SETTLED SRADDHA ABSOLUTE APPARENT CONSTANT DEFINITE OFFICIAL PALPABLE POSITIVE RELIABLE RESOLVED UNERRING CONFIDENT

CERTAINLY AY AYE WIS AMEN IWIS SOON SURE WHAT YWIS TRULY CERTES INDEED PERDIE SICCAR SICKER SURELY VERILY HARDILY EVERMORE FORSOOTH SECURELY NATURALLY
(MOST —) SO

CERTAINTY YEA CERT PIPE SNIP CINCH POLICY SURETY SURENESS CONSTANCY
(LACK OF —) SCRUPLE

CERTIFICATE BOND CHIT CHECK DEMIT JURAT LIBEL SCRIP TALON TITLE AMPARO ATTEST CEDULA COUPON INDENT PATENT POTTAH RETURN TICKET VERIFY CERTIFY CONSTAT DIPLOMA VOUCHER WARRANT WAYBILL AEGROTAT JUDGMENT KABBALAH NAVICERT REGISTER REGISTRY SECURITY TESCARIA TESTAMUR TEZKIRAH NOTARIZATION
(CUSTOMHOUSE —) COCKET
(MARRIAGE —) LINES
(MINER'S —) LICENCE LICENSE
(PILOT'S —) BRANCH
(SERVANT'S —) CHIT

CERTIFICATION PASS STAMP APPROVAL HECHSHER CLEARANCE DISCHARGE

CERTIFIED SWORN

CERTIFY AVOW VISE AUDIT SWEAR AFFIRM ASSURE ATTEST DEPOSE EVINCE VERIFY WITTER APPROVE ENDORSE LICENSE TESTIFY ACCREDIT

CERTITUDE CERTAIN CONFIDENCE

CERULEAN BLUE AZURE COELIN CYANEAN CYANEOUS

CERUMEN WAX EARWAX

CERVIX NECK

CESS BOG TAX CEDE DUTY LEVY LUCK RATE ABWAB SLOPE YIELD IMPOST MEASURE SURRENDER
(BAD —) SORRA

CESSATION HO END HOO BLIN HALT HUSH LISS LULL REST STAY STOP BREAK CEASE CLOUL DEVAL LETUP LISSE PAUSE SLACK STINT TRUCE CUTOFF DEMISE DISUSE OFFSET PERIOD RECESS CEASING CLOSURE RESPITE ABEYANCE BLACKOUT DESITION INTERVAL SHUTDOWN STOPPAGE SURCEASE SUSPENSE
(— OF HOSTILITIES) TRUCE INDUCIAE ARMISTICE
(— OF LIFE) DEATH
(— OF RESPIRATION) APNEA APNOEA
(— OF WAR) PEACE
(— OF WORK) HARTAL
(DECREED —) MORATORIUM
(TEMPORARY —) RESPITE

CESSPOOL SINK SUMP SINKER CISTERN JAWHOLE SINKHOLE SUSPIRAL

CESTODE POLYZOAN TAPEWORM

CESTRUM POISONBERRY

CESTUS CEST CESTON HURLBAT GAUNTLET WHIRLBAT

CETACEAN ORC CETE ORCA SUSU WHALE BELUGA COWFISH DOLPHIN GRAMPUS NARWHAL MUTILATE PORPOISE

CETO (BROTHER OF —) PHORCYS
(DAUGHTERS OF —) GRAEAE GORGONS HESPERIDES

(FATHER OF —) PONTUS
(MOTHER OF —) GAEA
CEYLON (SEE SRI LANKA) SERENDIP
   TAPROBANE
CEYLONESE CEYLON BURGHER
CEYLON MOSS GULAMAN
CGS UNIT STILB STOKE
CHA TSIA CHAIS
CHACMA BAVIAN BOBBEJAAN

CHAD

CAPITAL: NDJAMENA
COIN: FRANC FRANCCFA
LAKE: CHAD
NATIVE: ARAB SARA KREDA MASSA
   TOUBOU KAMADJA MOUNDAN
PLATEAU: ENNEDI
RIVER: CHARI SHARI LOGONE
   BAHRAOUK
TOWN: ATI BOL LAI MAO FADA FAYA
   MONGO ABECHE BOKORO BONGOR
   LARGEAU MOUNDOU FORTLAMY
   MOUSSORO

CHADOR PHULKARI
CHAETA UNCINUS
CHAETOCHLOA SETARIA
CHAETOPOD SCALEBACK
CHAETURA DRAB BEAR
CHAFE IRK RUB VEX FRET FRIG FROT
   FUME GALD GALL HEAT JOSH RAGE
   STEW WARM WEAR ANGER ANNOY
   CHAFF GRIND SCOLD SNUFF WORRY
   WRING ABRADE BANTER EXCITE
   FRIDGE HARASS INJURY NETTLE
   RANKLE INCENSE INFLAME SNUFFLE
   FRICTION IRRITATE RAILLERY
CHAFER CRESSET
CHAFF GUY HAY PUG RAG ROT BRAN
   CAFF CHIP GUFF GUFF JOSH MOCK
   PULU QUIZ RAZZ BORAK CHIAK
   CHYAK DROSS GLUME HULLS HUSKS
   JOLLY RALLY SLACK STOUR STRAW
   TEASE TRASH BANTER BHOOSA
   REFUSE CAVINGS TAILING RAILLERY
   RIDICULE SHELLING
CHAFFER BANDY SIEVE WARES
   BUYING DICKER HAGGLE HIGGLE
   MARKET PALTER BARGAIN CHATTER
   SELLING TRAFFIC EXCHANGE
CHAFFINCH PINK CHINK SPINK
   TWINK ROBERD SCOBBY SHILFA
   SKELLY ROBINET SNABBIE WETBIRD
CHAFFY SCALY ACEROSE ACEROUS
   PALEATE
CHAFING GALLING IMPATIENCE
CHAFING-DISH HEARTH
CHAGRIN ENVY SPITE VEXATION
CHAGRINED SICK ASHAMED
CHAIN FOB GUY NET ROW SET TEW
   TIE TOE TOW TUG TYE BIND BOND
   CURB FALL FAST FILE GYVE JOIN
   LINE LINK SEAL SOAM TEAM BRAIL

CABLE GROUP GUARD LEASH SHANK
SHEET SLANG SLING SUITE TRACE
TRAIN WRASE CARCAN CATENA
COLLAR CORDON FASTEN FETTER
GANGER HANGER HOBBLE JACKER
JIGGER LINKER RACKAN SECURE
SERIES STRING TETHER TOGGLE
BOBSTAY CATFALL CHIGNON
CONNECT EMBRACE ENSLAVE
LASHING MANACLE NETWORK
PAINTER PENDANT SAUTOIR
SHACKLE TACKLER BACKROPE
BRACELET CARCANET GLEIPNIR
LINKWORK NECKLACE RECEPTOR
RESTRAIN RIGWIDDY STROBILA
WOOLDING
(— FOR ANCHOR) CATFALL PAINTER
(— FOR BINDING) JACKER TACKLER
(— FOR WRAPPING MAST)
   WOOLDING
(— OF AUTHORITIES) ISNAD
(— OF DUNES) SAIF SEIF
(— OF MOUNTAINS) RANGE
(— OF ROCKS) REEF
(— ON CONVICT'S LEG) SLANG
(— TO BIND CATTLE) SEAL
(DECORATIVE —) FESTOON
(ENDLESS —) CREEPER
(KIND OF —) MARKOV
(MAGIC —) GLEIPNIR
(SHORT —) SHANK
(SUSPENDED —) CATENARY
(WATCH —) FOB ALBERT
(PL.) IRONS CONVEYOR
(PREF.) HORMO STREPHO STREPSI
   STREPT(O)
CHAIN LINK SHUT COPULA SWIVEL
CHAINMAN CLASHY CLASHEE
   LINEMAN TAPEMAN
CHAIN-SHAPED CATENOID
CHAIR KEEP SEAT SHOP HORSE
   SEDAN STOOL ESTATE OFFICE
   PULPIT ROCKER SADDLE SITTER
   TONJON CACOLET COMMODE
   FANBACK GONDOLA SITTING
   VOYEUSE WINDSOR ARMCHAIR
   CARRIAGE CATHEDRA FAUTEUIL
   KANGAROO SGABELLO VOLTAIRE
(— FOR PRAYING) PRIEDIEU
(— OF SANCTUARY) FRITHSTOOL
(— OF STATE) THRONE
(— SLUNG FROM POLE) KAGO
   TALABON
(— WITH CANOPY) STATE
(BISHOP'S —) CATHEDRA FALDSTOOL
(EASY —) COGSWELL
(GREEK —) KLISMOS
(KIND OF —) EAMES
(LEAVE THE —) ARISE
(MINING —) DOG
(PART OF —) ARM EAR LEG BACK
POST RUNG SEAT SLAT CREST SPLAT
STILE STUMP ROCKER ARMREST

SPINDLE BACKRAIL HEADPIECE
(PORTABLE —) SEDAN
(SEDAN —) NORIMONO
(SPRING —) PERCH
(THRONE —) SHINZA
CHAIRMAN HEAD CHAIR EMCEE
PRESES SPEAKER CONVENER
DIRECTOR MODERATOR
PROLOCUTOR
(PREF.) SYMPOSI
CHAISE GIG SHAY CHAIR CALESIN
CARRIAGE CURRICLE SHANDRYDAN
CHAISE LONGUE DAYBED
DUCHESSE
CHALAZA TREAD TREADLE
GALLATURE
CHALAZION STYE
CHALCEDONY ONYX OPAL SARD
AGATE CHERT PRASE CATEYE
JASPER PLASMA QUARTZ CARNEOL
OPALINE SARDINE SARDIUS
ENHYDROS CORNELIAN
(RED —) CARNELIAN
CHALCIOPE (FATHER OF —) AEETES
(HUSBAND OF —) PHRIXUS
(MOTHER OF —) ASTERODIA
(SISTER OF —) MEDEA
(SON OF —) ARGUS MELAS
PHRONTIS CYTISSORUS
CHALCIS (CHILDREN OF —) CURETES
CORYBANTES
(FATHER OF —) ASOPUS
(MOTHER OF —) METOPE
CHALCOPYRITE RUN
CHALDEAN SEER KALDANI
BABYLONIAN
(— MEASURE) CANE FOOT MAKUK
QASAB ARTADA GARIBA GHALVA
MANSION
(— RIVER) TIGRIS EUPHRATES
(— TOWN) UR
CHALICE AMA CUP BOWL CALIX
GRAIL REGAL GOBLET KRASIS
CHALK CAUK CORK PALE SCAR TALC
TICK CRETA FLOUR SCORE BLANCH
BLEACH CRAYON CREDIT RUBBLE
WHITEN ACCOUNT WHITING
(GREEN —) PRASINE
(HARD —) HURLOCK
(RED —) RUBRIC
(SURVEYOR'S —) KEEL
(PREF.) CALCAREO CALC(I)(IO)(O)
CHALKBOARD GREENBOARD
CHALKSTONE TOPHUS
CHALKY CRETACIC CRETACEOUS
CHALLENGE HEN VIE BRAG CALL
DARE DEFY FACE GAGE ASSAY
BANCO BLAME BRAVE CLAIM QUERY
STUMP ACCUSE APPEAL BANTER
CARTEL CHARGE DACKER DAIKER
DEMAND DESCRY FORBID IMPUGN
INFIRM INVITE RECUSE SERDAB
ARRAIGN CENSURE IMPEACH

PROVOKE REPROVE SOLICIT
SUMMONS CHAMPION DARRAIGN
DEFIANCE GAUNTLET QUESTION
REPROACH
(— A BULL) CITE
CHALLENGING PIQUANT
BLOODSHOT
CHALONE AUTACOID
CHALYBEATE MARTIAL
CHALYBITE SIDERITE
CHAMBER ODA AGER CELL CIST
DOME FLAT FOLD HALL IWAN KIVA
ROOM SALE TOMB BOWER CAVUM
COURT GOMER HOUSE SENAT
SHAFT SOLAR SOLER STOVE ATRIUM
CAMARA CAMERA COFFER HEADER
HOLLOW MIHRAB SENADO SENATE
SOLLAR SPRING STANZA WILSON
BEDROOM CAISSON CHALMER
CHANNEL CHAUMER CONCAVE
CUBICLE FAVISSA FIREBOX GALLERY
GEHENNA MANSION RECEIPT
CASEMATE CYLINDER DIFFUSER
FOUNTAIN GROSSRAT SMOKEBOX
SNEMOVNA THALAMUS
(— FOR MOLTEN GLASS) FONT
(— IN FURNACE) SHAFT DOGHOUSE
(— OF EAR) SACCULE UTRICLE
(— POT) JORDAN JEROBOAM
(AIR —) SPONSON
(AUDIENCE —) DURBAR
(BOMBPROOF —) CASEMATE
(CLIMATE CONTROL —) BIOTRON
(FIRE —) ARCH STOVE COCKLE
FIREBOX
(FORTIFICATION —) BUNKER
(JUDGE'S —) CAMERA
(OPEN —) LANTERN
(ORGAN —) SWELL
(PERTAINING TO —) CAMERAL
(PISTON —) BARREL
(PRIVATE —) CLOSET CONCLAVE
(PUEBLO —) KIVA ESTUFA
(SLEEPING —) BEDROOM WARDROBE
(SMALL —) LOCULUS
(SUPPLY —) MAGAZINE
(UNDERGROUND —) CAVE CRYPT
CAVERN SERDAB HYPOGEE
(WATERTIGHT —) CAISSON
(PREF.) THALAM(I)(O)
(SUFF.) CELE COELE COELUS
CHAMBERLAIN EUNUCH FACTOR
SERVANT STEWARD PALATINE
POLONIUS
CHAMBERPOT POT JERRY POTTY
JORDAN
CHAMELEON ANOLE ANOLI LACERT
SAURIAN
CHAMFER BEVEL CHIMB CHIME
CHINE FLUTE CIPHER FURROW
GROOVE
CHAMOIS GEMS IZARD AOUDAD
SHAMMY ANTELOPE

CHAMOMILE MAYWEED
MARGUERITE
CHAMONT (SISTER OF —) MONIMIA
CHAMP BITE CHAW FIRM HARD
MASH CHANK CHOMP FIELD GNASH
TRAMPLE
CHAMPAGNE AY BUBBLY SIMKIN
BELLEEK SILLERY CHAMPERS
(IMITATION —) GOOSEBERRY
CHAMPAIGN PLAIN
CHAMPION ACE AID FAN ABET
BACK BOSS DEFY HERO KEMP
GHAZI ASSERT ATTEND DEFEND
KEMPER KNIGHT PATRON SQUIRE
VICTOR APOSTLE ESPOUSE
FIGHTER PALADIN PROTECT
ADVOCATE DEFENDER PALMERIN
PROTAGONIST
CHAMPIONING
(PREF.) PRO
CHAMPIONSHIP TITLE LAURELS
ADVOCACY
CHAMPLEVE ENAMEL INLAID
CHANCE DIE HAP LOT CASE CAST
DINT DRAW FATE LINE LUCK ODDS
RISK SHOT SHOW TIDE BREAK ETTLE
STAKE WHACK BETIDE CASUAL
GAMBLE HAPPEN HAZARD MISHAP
RANDOM SQUEAK STRIKE TUMBLE
AIMLESS FORTUNE OPENING
STUMBLE VANTAGE VENTURE
ACCIDENT CASUALTY EVENTUAL
FORTUITY QUESTION ALEATORIC
OPPORTUNITY PERADVENTURE
(— OF LOSS) RISK
(— OF SUCCESS) PROSPECT
(ADVERSE —) HAZARD
(EVEN —) TOSSUP
(HAPPY-) MERCY
(ILL —) MISHAP
(SLIGHT —) PRAYER
(SLIM —) PRAYER
(UNFORTUNATE —) PITY
(PL.) PROSPECTS
(PREF.) TYCH(O)
CHANCEL BEMA CHOIR ADYTUM
CHANCELLOR LOGOTHETE
CHANCY DODGY ALEATORY
CHANDELIER CORONA LUSTER
PHAROS PENDANT CHANDLER
GASELIER GIRANDOLE
CHANDLER TALLOWER
CHANE OREJON
CHANGE MEW CHOP FLOP MOLT
MOVE ODDS PEAL TURN VARY VEER
WARP WEND ADAPT ALTER AMEND
BREAK COINS EMEND MOULT SHIFT
THROW ADJUST BECOME DIFFER
DIGEST IMMUTE MODIFY MUANCE
MUTATE REMOVE REVAMP REVISE
SWITCH WISSEL WRIXLE COMMUTE
CONVERT CUTOVER DEVIATE

FLUXION MORTIFY BECOMING
DENATURE EXCHANGE INNOVATE
LENITION MUTATION REVISION
TRANSFER TRANSUME VARIANCE
PERMUTATION METAMORPHISM
MODIFICATION METAMORPHOSIS
(— APPEARANCE) DISGUISE
(— BACK) REVERT
(— COLOR) TURN
(— COURSE) GYBE JIBE
(— DIRECTION) CUT CANT CHOP
HAUL KNEE VEER ANGLE BREAK
SHIFT
(— FOR BETTER) HELP
(— FORM) DEVELOP
(— FOR WORSE) BEDEVIL
(— GAIT) BREAK
(— GRADUALLY) PASS GRADUATE
(— IN COURSE) SHEER
(— IN DIRECTION) JOG KNEE STEP
(— IN ELEVATION) FORK
(— IN LAKE LEVEL) SEICHE
(— IN SIZE) ASTOGENY
(— INTO VAPOR) FLASH
(— MONEY) WISSEL
(— OF FORM) SET
(— OF FORTUNE) PERIPETY
(— OF GEAR) KICKDOWN
(— OF HABITAT) MIGRATE
(— OF KEY) TRANSITION
(— OF LIFE) MENOPAUSE
(— OF MIND) CAPRICE
(— OF MOOD) VARY
(— OF PITCH) MOTION INFLECT
(— OF POLICY) TACK
(— OF POSITION) KINESIS
(— OF SEA LEVEL) EUSTACY
(— OF SOUND) BREAKING
(— OF WORD) ANAGRAM
(— ONE'S HEART) REPENT
(— PACE) BREAK
(— POSITION) STIR FLEET HOTCH
(— QUICKLY) FLY
(— RESIDENCE) FLIT
(— SHAPE) DRAW CREEP DEFORM
(— SIDES) RAT
(ABNORMAL —) LESION
(ABRUPT —) DOGLEG SALTATION
(GEAR —) KICKDOWN
(GRADUAL —) DRIFT
(MAKE NO —) STANDPAT
(ONE WHO OPPOSES —) AGINNER
(PRESSURE —) ALLOBAR
(SHORT —) FLUFF
(SMALL —) GROCERY
(UNEXPECTED —) SWITCH
(PL.) DOUBLES PLASTIQUE
(PREF.) ALLAGO ALLASSO AMOEBI
AMOEBO MUTA MUTO
(SUFF.) MUTE
CHANGEABLE EEMIS GIDDY IMMIS
LIGHT WINDY CHOPPY FICKLE FITFUL

CERFUL KETCHY LABILE MOBILE MOTLEY MUABLE SHIFTY WANKLE BRUCKLE ERRATIC MUTABLE PROTEAN UNSTAID VARIANT VARIOUS VOLUBLE AMENABLE CATCHING GLIBBERY MOVEABLE SKITTISH TICKLISH UNSTABLE VARIABLE VEERABLE VOLATILE WEATHERY CHAMELEON VERSATILE

CHANGEABLENESS LEVITY CAPRICE VIBRATION

CHANGED VARIED ANOTHER (PREF.) META

CHANGEFUL FICKLE SHIFTY MUTABLE RESTLESS

CHANGELESS CONSISTENT

CHANGELING AUF AWF OAF DOLT FOOL CHILD DUNCE IDIOT WAVERER IMBECILE KILLCROP RENEGADE TURNCOAT

CHANGEOVER SWITCH

CHANGING FLUXIBLE ALTERNATE (— MONEY) AGIO (CONTINUALLY —) FLOATING

CHANK SANK CONCH

CHANNEL CUT GAT POD REE RUT SOW CANO CAVA DEEP DIKE DUCT DYKE FLUE GATE GOOL GOTE GOUT GURT KILL KYLE LAKE LANE PACE PIPE RACE SLEW SLOO VALE VEIN WADI WADY WASH BAYOU CANAL CARRY CHASE COWAL DITCH DRAIN DRILL FLUME FLUTE GLYPH GUIDE INSET LATCH QUIRK RIVER SINUS SLIDE SOUND STOOL STOVE STRIA SWASH AIRWAY ALVEUS ARROYO ARTERY BRANCH COURSE CUTOFF ESTERO FURROW GROOVE GULLET GUTTER HOLLOW KENNEL KEYWAY LAGOON MEDIUM OFFLET OILWAY RABBET RESACA RIVOSE RUNWAY SLOUGH SLUICE SPECUS STRAIT STRAND STREAM THROAT TROUGH CHAMFER CONDUCT CONDUIT CULVERT CUNETTE EURIPUS OFFTAKE PASSAGE RACEWAY RIVULET SHIPWAY SILANGA STRIGIL THALWEG TIDEWAY WASHOUT AQUEDUCT FLOODWAY GUIDEWAY GUNKHOLE RACELINE SCOURWAY SPILLWAY CANNELURE (— FOR MOLTEN METAL) DOW GATE RUNNER (— IN CLOTH) FLUTE (— IN ICE FIELD) LEAD (— IN MOLD) SPRAY (— OF AQUEDUCT) SPECUS (— OF BRAIN) ITER (— ON A DECK) CHIMB CHIME (— ON WHALE) SCARF (ARTIFICIAL —) GAT GOUT (DRAINAGE —) GAW

(ENGLISH —) SLEEVE (INCLINED —) SHOOT (INFORMATION —) PIPELINE (IRRIGATION —) AUWAI DROVE (LYMPH —) CISTERNA (SECONDARY —) BINNACLE (SLOPING —) CHUTE SHUTE (PREF.) CANALI RHYN(O) SOLEN(O) VAS(I)(O)

CHANNELBILL RAINFOWL

CHANNELED FLUTED

CHANT CANT MELE SING SONG TONE CAROL PSALM SOUGH ANTHEM CANTUS INTONE LITANY MANTRA WARBLE CHORTLE INTROIT PROSODE REQUIEM WORSHIP ALLELUIA ANTIPHON CANTICLE INTONATE SINGSONG PLAINSONG CANTILLATE

CHANTER STICK CANTOR SINGER BAGPIPE SONGSTER CHALUMEAU (— OF BAGPIPE) OBOE

CHANTERELLE CANTINO

CHANTING RAP CHARM HAZANUT ANTIPHONY CHAZZANUT

CHANTLATE SPROCKET

CHANTRY CAGE

CHAOS NU NUN PIE APSU GULF HYLE MESS VOID ABYSS BABEL CHASM BEDLAM JUMBLE MATTER TOPHET ANARCHY MIXTURE DISORDER SHAMBLES TAILSPIN TOHUBOHU

CHAOTIC MUDDLED CONFUSED FORMLESS TUMULTUARY

CHAP BOY BUY DOG LAD MAN RAP WAG BEAN BEAT BIRD BLOW CHIP CHOP COVE DICK DUCK HIND JOHN KIBE MASH MATE NABS SNAP BILLY BLOKE BUCKO BULLY BUYER CHAFT CHINK CLEFT CRACK FRUIT KNOCK LOVER RUMMY SCOUT SPLIT SPORT SPRAY SWIPE TRADE YOUTH BARTER BOHUNK BREACH BUGGER CALLAN CHOOSE CODGER CUFFIN FELLOW FOUTER FOUTRA GAFFER GEEZER JOSSER KIPPER SHAVER STRIKE STROKE TURNIP BASTARD BROTHER CALLANT FISSURE HUSBAND ROUGHEN BLIGHTER CUSTOMER DIVISION MERCHANT (— HANDS) RACK SPRAY (— IN SKIN) KIN KIBE (FINE —) BULLY (OLD —) BO GEEZER (PLUCKY —) COCK (QUEER —) GALOOT (S.AFRICAN —) KEREL (YOUNG —) GAFFER (PL.) CHOPS

CHAPARRAL MONTE CHAMISAL BUCKTHORN

CHAPARRO YAYA
CHAPBOOK CHAP GARLAND
CHAPE CRAMPET MORDANT
CHAPEL CAGE CAPE COPE COWL
HOOD CLOAK CRYPT PORCH SALEM
BETHEL BEULAH CHARRE CHURCH
HAIKAL MORADA SHRINE CAPELLA
CHANTRY CHAPLET CHARNEL
CHHATRI GALILEE MARTYRY
MEETING MEMORIA ORATORY
SACRARY SERVICE BETHESDA
DEACONRY DIACONIA FERETORY
FERETRUM PARABEMA SACELLUM
SODALITY
(UNDERGROUND —) SHROUDS
CHAPERON HOOD ATTEND DUENNA
ESCORT MATRON GRIFFIN PROTECT
GUARDIAN SHEEPDOG TRAPPING
CHAPLAIN PADRE LEVITE ALMONER
CONDUCT ALTARIST ORDINARY
CHAPLAINCY SCARF
CHAPLET BEAD ORLE STUD CROWN
ANADEM ANCHOR CIRCLE FILLET
JAMBER JAMMER ROSARY STAPLE
TROPHY WREATH CORONAL
CORONET GARLAND MOULDING
NECKLACE ORNAMENT
(PREF.) STEMMATI
CHAPLIN
(WIFE OF —) OONA
CHAPMAN CHAP BUYER DEALER
HAWKER TRADER COPEMAN
PEDDLER CUSTOMER MERCHANT
CHAPPIE JOCKEY
CHAPS FLEWS BREECHES LEGGINGS
OVERALLS
CHAPTER BODY CELL PACE POST
CAPUT COURT LODGE BRANCH
CABILDO CAPITAL CORRECT COUNCIL
MEETING SECTION ASSEMBLY
(— OF BOOK) CAPITAL
(— OF KORAN) SURA SURAH
(— OF SOCIETY) CAMP CIRCLE
CHAPTER-HOUSE FRATRY
CHAR BURN CART COAL SEAR BROIL
CHARK CHORE SHARD SINGE TROUT
SCORCH BLACKEN CHARIOT
TORGOCH REDBELLY SAIBLING
SALMONID SANDBANK
(PL.) SALVELINI
CHARA MUSKGRASS
CHARACIN DORADO DOURADE
BLOODFIN
CHARACTER AURA BALL BENT
CARD CASE CLAY CLEF DASH ECAD
FLAT FOND FORM HAIR KIND MAKE
MARK MOLD NOTE PART ROLE RUNE
SIGN SORT TONE TRIM TYPE BRAND
COLOR ETHIC ETHOS FIBER HABIT
HEART HUMOR INDEX SAVOR STAMP
TENOR TOKEN TRAIT WRITE CARACT
CIPHER COCKUP DAGGER DIRECT
EMBLEM FIGURE GENIUS HANGER

LETTER MANNER METTLE NATURE
REPUTE SIGLUM SPIRIT STRIPE
SYMBOL CALIBER CLOTHES EDITION
ENGRAVE ESSENCE IMPRESS
QUALITY CAPACITY FRACTION
IDENTITY IDEOGRAM INFERIOR
INSCRIBE LIGATURE SELFHOOD
SYLLABIC DESCENDER PARAGRAPH
PERSONAGE
(— IN DRAMA) CHORUS
(— IN PLAY) DAME BESSY
(— OF SOIL) LAIR
(ASSUMED —) ROLE FIGURE
INCOGNITO
(BAD —) DROLE BUDMASH
(BASIC —) BOTTOM
(CELTIC —) OGAM OGHAM
(CHIEF —) AGONIST
(CHINESE —) SHOU RADICAL
(COMIC —) PIERROT
(COMMON —) COMMUNITY
(ESSENTIAL —) ALLOY
(FICTIONAL —) PERSONA
(FIRM —) BACKBONE
(GIVE — TO) TONE
(GREEK —) SAMPI
(JAPANESE —S) HIBUNCI
(MENDELIAN —) ALLEL ALLELE
(PHYSICAL —) ARMENOID
(PRIME —) ESSENCE
(SHIFTLESS —) BEAT
(STOCK —) BESSY MACCUS
(TESTED —) ASSAY
(TRIED —) TOUCH
(VULGAR —S) ONMUN
(PL.) MANA
(SUFF.) ERY
(HAVING — OF) IC(AL)
CHARACTERISTIC CAST COST
MARK MIEN ANGLE AROMA GRACE
POINT TACHE TOKEN TRAIT TRICK
ACCENT BEAUTY NATURE STIGMA
STROKE ADJUNCT AMENITY
FEATURE IMPRESS QUALITY SPECIES
TYPICAL ACTIVITY HEADMARK
PECULIAR PROPERTY SYMBOLIC
PARAMETER PROPRIETY PECULIARITY
PARTICULARITY QUALIFICATION
(— OF ANTIBODIES) AVIDITY
(— OF PARTICLES) CHARM
(ADVENTITIOUS —) ACCIDENT
(DISTINGUISHING —) SPECIES
HALLMARK BIRTHMARK
(PECULIAR —) IDIOPATHY
(PL.) CORNERS FACULTY
(SUFF.) IC(AL)
(— OF) ISH ISTIC LY
CHARACTERIZATION ELOGY
ELOGIUM
CHARACTERIZE MARK STYLE
DEFINE DEPICT TITULE ENGRAVE
ENTITLE IMPRINT PORTRAY
DESCRIBE INDICATE INSCRIBE

CHARACTERIZED
(SUFF.) (— BY) AL FUL IAL IC(AL) LEW
CHARACTERLESS INANE
CHARADES GAME
CHARCOAL COAL CARBO CHARK
CARBON FUSAIN PENCIL BLACKEN
SPODIUM SCRIBBET
CHARD BEET
CHARGE FEE LAP LAY RAP TAX BEEF
BILL BUCK CALL CARE CARK CAST
COST CURE DUES DUTY FILL GIBE
KEEP LADE LIEN LOAD NICK NOTE
ONUS RACK RATE REST RUSH SHOT
SIZE SOAK SPAR TASK TOLL WARD
WIKE AGIST BLAME CAUSE CHALK
COUNT CRIME DEBIT EXTRA GYRON
ONSET ORDER PRICE REFER SCORE
SHOCK STICK STING THING TRUST
ACCUSE ADJURE ALLEGE APPEAL
ASSESS ATTACK BEHEST BURDEN
CAREER CENSUS COURSE CREDIT
DAMAGE DEFAME DEMAND DITTAY
ENJOIN ENURNY EXCESS IMPOSE
IMPUTE METAGE OBJECT OFFICE
PIPAGE REATUS SURMIT SURTAX
TARIFF TOWAGE WEIGHT ACIDIZE
ANNULET ARRAIGN ARTICLE
ASCRIBE ASSAULT AVERAGE
BOATAGE CARTAGE CENSURE
CHEVRON CLAMPER COMMAND
CONCERN CONJURE CORKAGE
CORNAGE CUSTODY DOCKAGE
DRAYAGE EMBASSY EXPENSE
FLOTAGE HAULAGE IGNITER
IMPEACH KEEPING MANDATE
MILEAGE MISSION MIXTURE
MOORAGE PANNAGE QUAYAGE
REPRISE SIDEAGE SLANDER SLIDAGE
SURMISE WARPAGE BILLBACK
BRASSAGE CASUALTY CHASTISE
CRESCENT DELAYAGE DENOUNCE
LEGATION ORDINARY OVERLOAD
PLANKAGE POUNDAGE PROVINCE
QUESTION SLINGING SPENDING
STANDAGE TUTORAGE VIGORISH
COMPLAINT ACCUSATION
ACCUSEMENT
(— AGAINST) TILT
(— BATTERY) SOAK BOOST
(— EXCESSIVELY) FLEECE
(— FALSELY) SURMISE
(— FOR GRAZING) AGIST
(— OF FIREARM) LOAD AMORCE
(— OF MENTAL ENERGY) CATHEXIS
(— OF METAL) HEAT
(— OF ORE) POST
(— TO BE PAID) LAW
(— UPON PROPERTY) LIEN
(— WITH CRIME) ACCUSE DELATE
INDICT ARTICLE ATTAINT IMPEACH
(— WITH GAS) AERATE
(AGGREGATE — S) BOOK
(CANNON —) GRAPE

(COVER —) COUVERT
(DEPTH —) CAN ASHCAN
(EXPLOSIVE —) CAP BLAST SNAKE
SQUIB TULIP BOOSTER BURSTER
IGNITER
(FALSE —) CALUMNY
(HERALDIC —) DELF DROP GIRON
GYRON LABEL BEZANT BILLET
DRAGON GURGES BEARING ESQUIRE
(MAILING —) FRANKAGE
(POWDER —) GRAIN
(SHAPED —) BEEHIVE
(SPIRITUAL —) CURE
(TEMPORARY —) CARE
(WINE —) CORKAGE
CHARGEABLE GUILTY
CHARGED UP HOT LADEN BELAST
BILLETY BILLETTE ELECTRIC
INSTINCT
(— WITH EMOTION) SWOLLEN
CHARGEHAND CLICKER
CHARGEMAN BLASTER
CHARGER DISH HORSE MOUNT
STEED ACCUSER COURSER PLATTER
TROOPER
CHARILY FRUGALLY GINGERLY
CHARIOT CAR BIGA CART CHAR
RATH WAIN BUGGY CHAIR ESSED
RATHA TRIGA WAGON CHARET
QUADRIGA
CHARIOTEER AURIGA CARTER
DRIVER IOLAUS LEADER CARTARE
WAGONER MYRTILUS AUTOMEDON
CHARITABLE KIND BENIGN HUMANE
LENIENT LIBERAL GENEROUS
CHARITY ALMS DOLE GIFT LOVE PITY
RUTH MERCY BASKET BOUNTY
CARITAS HANDOUT LARGESS
LENIENCE TZEDAKAH
(SYMBOL OF —) PELICAN
CHARIVARI BABEL SHALLAL
SERENADE SHIVAREE
CHARLATAN FAKE CHEAT FAKER
FRAUD QUACK CABOTIN EMPIRIC
IMPOSTER MAGICIAN SYCOPHANT
MOUNTEBANK QUACKSALVER
CHARLES II DAVID
CHARLIE MCCARTHY STOOGE
CHARLOCK KRAUT RUNCH
HARLOCK KEDLOCK KERLOCK
MUSTARD SINAPIS YELLOWS
CHARDOCK CHEDLOCK SKEDLOCK
SKELLOCH
CHARM IT GBO KEY OBI CALM CHIC
HAND JINX JUJU JYNX LUCK MOJO
PLAY RUNE SNOW SONG TAKE TILL
ZOGO ALLAY AROMA BRIEF CATCH
FAVOR FREET FREIT GRACE LAMIN
MAGIC OBEAH OOMPH SAFFI SAFIE
SPELL VENUS WANGA WEIRD
ALLURE AMULET BEAUTY CARACT
DEASIL DISARM ENAMOR ENGAGE
ENTICE FETISH GLAMOR GRIGRI

INCANT MANTRA MELODY PLEASE
SAPHIE SCARAB SOOTHE SUBDUE
SUMMON VOODOO ABRAXAS
ASSUAGE ATTRACT BEGUILE
BEWITCH CANTION CANTRIP
CONJURE CONTROL DELIGHT
ENCHANT ENTHRAL FLATTER HEITIKI
PERIAPT PHILTER PHILTRE SINGING
SORCERY BLESSING BRELOQUE
COMETHER COQUETRY ENTHRALL
ENTRANCE GLAUMRIE GREEGREE
PISHOGUE PRACTICE TALISMAN
CAPTIVATE MAGNETIZE
PATERNOSTER
(MAGNETIC —) CHARISMA
CHARMED CAPTIVE
CHARMER HOURI SIREN EXORCIST
MAGICIAN SORCERER ENCHANTER
CHARMING LEPID SWEET GOLDEN
WIZARD AMIABLE DARLING
EYESOME TEMPEAN WINNING
WINSOME ADORABLE DELICATE
GRACEFUL LOVESOME
PICTURESQUE
CHARNEL GHASTLY CEMETERY
GOLGOTHA
CHARNEL-HOUSE OSSUARY
GOLGOTHA
CHARON (FATHER OF —) EREBUS
(MOTHER OF —) NOX
CHARPOY BED COT
CHARQUI JERKY XARQUE
CHART MAP BILL CARD MARK PLAN
PLAT PLOT ROSE CARTE GRAPH
SCORE STILL RECORD SCHEME
DIAGRAM EMAGRAM EXPLORE
ISOTYPE OUTLINE PROJECT
DOCUMENT DOPEBOOK MERCATOR
PLATFORM
(— BOOK) WAGONER
(— FROM AIR) AEROVIEW
(— MARK) VIGIA
(— OF A COURSE) RUTTER
(MARINER'S —) ROSE RUTTER
(WEATHER —) ANALOGUE
NEPHANALYSIS
CHARTER FIX LET BOND BOOK DEED
HIRE RENT CARTE CHART FUERO
GRANT LEASE SANAD CHARTA
PERMIT SUNNUD DIPLOMA
CONTRACT GRUNDLOV HEIRLOOM
LANDBOOK MONOPOLY PANCHART
CHARTERHOUSE OF PARMA
(AUTHOR OF —) STENDHAL
(CHARACTER IN —) GINA CONTI
DONGO MOSCA CLELIA FAUSTA
GILETTI FABRIZIO FERRANTE
MARIETTA PIETRANERA
CHARWOMAN CHARER CHARLADY
PORTRESS JANITRESS
CHARY SHY DEAR WARY CHERE
SCANT SPARE DAINTY FRUGAL
PRIZED SKIMPY CAREFUL CURIOUS

SPARING CAUTIOUS HESITANT
PRECIOUS RESERVED SPAREFUL
VIGILANT
CHASE FOG SIC SUE FALL HUNT JERL
SHAG SHOO SICK ANNOY CATCH
CHEVY CHIVY DRIVE HARRY HOUND
SCORE SHACK CACCIA CHIVVY
CHOUSE EMBOSS FOLLOW FRIEZE
FURROW GALLOP GROOVE HALLOO
HARASS HOLLOW INDENT PURSUE
QUARRY SCORSE TRENCH CHANNEL
ENGRAVE HUNTING PURSUIT
ORNAMENT PURCHASE
(— GAME) COURSE
(— HARD) RATTLE
CHASER RAM DRINK HOUND
FROGGER
(WOMAN —) SHEEPBITER
CHASING CISELURE
(— OF GAME) DRIVE
CHASM GAP KIN PIT GULF RIFT
YAWN ABYSS BLANK CANON
CHAOS CLEFT GORGE BREACH
CANYON HIATUS FISSURE
MEGARON SWALLOW VACANCY
APERTURE CREVASSE INTERVAL
VACATION
CHASSE SLIP GLIDE SASHAY
CHASSEUR HUNTER BELLBOY
DOORMAN FOOTMAN HUNTSMAN
CHASSIS SASH FRAME FIGURE
CHASTE CAST PURE ATTIC CLEAN
ZONED DECENT HONEST MODEST
PROPER SEVERE VESTAL VIRGIN
CLEANLY PUDICAL REFINED
CELIBATE INNOCENT VIRGINLY
VIRTUOUS CONTINENT
CHASTEN RATE ABASE SMITE
SMOTE SNEAP SOBER HUMBLE
PUNISH REBUKE REFINE SUBDUE
TEMPER AFFLICT CENSURE CORRECT
NURTURE CHASTISE MODERATE
RESTRAIN
CHASTISE BEAT FIRK FLOG LASH
SLAP TRIM WHIP AMEND BLAME
FEEZE SCOLD SPANK SPILL STRAP
TAUNT ACCUSE ANOINT BERATE
CHARGE DISPLE PUNISH PURIFY
REBUKE REFINE STRAFE SWINGE
TEMPER THRASH TICKLE CHASTEN
CORRECT REPROVE SCOURGE
SHINGLE SUSPECT CASTIGATE
CHASTISEMENT ROD HELL TOCO
TOKO CENSURE PAYMENT
FLOGGING
(DIVINE —) WRATH
CHASTITY HONOR PURITY VIRTUE
HONESTY MODESTY PUDENCY
CELIBACY GOODNESS PUDICITY
INNOCENCE
CHASUBLE CASULA DEACON
INFULA PLANET PAENULA PIANETA
VESTMENT

CHAT GAS JAW MAG RAP BIRD CHIN CONE COZE DISH GIST TALK TELL TOVE TWIG YARN AMENT CAUSE COOSE CRACK DALLY PITCH POINT PRATE PROSE PROSS SPEAK SPIKE VISIT BABBLE BRANCH CATKIN CONFAB COURSE DEVICE GABBLE GIBBER GOSSIP GOSTER HOBNOB JABBER NATTER POTATO POTTER SAMARA CHAFFER CHATTER SHMOOZE CAUSERIE CHATTERY CONVERSE SCHMOOZE SPIKELET STROBILE

CHATEAU HOUSE TOWER CASTLE MANSION SCHLOSS CHATELET FORTRESS

CHATON BASIL BEZEL BEZIL STONE COATING SETTING

CHATTEL CATTLE PLEDGE DEODAND FIXTURE CATALLUM PERSONAL (DISTRAINT OF —S) NAAM (PL.) STUFF FARLEU FARLEY COMODATO HOUSEHOLD

CHATTER GAB JAW MAG RAP YAK YAP BLAB CARP CHAT CHIN CLAP CLAT DISH GASH HACK KNAP RICK TALK TEAR YIRR CABAL CLACK CLASH GARRE HAVER PRATE SHAKE BABBLE BRUDGE CACKLE CLAVER GABBLE GIBBER GOSSIP JABBER JANGLE JARGON PALTER RATTLE SHIVER TATTER TATTLE TINKLE YAMMER YATTER BLABBER BRABBLE CHACKLE CHAFFER CHIPPER CHITTER CLACKET CLATTER CLITTER GARNASH NASHGOB PALAVER PRABBLE PRATING PRATTLE SHATTER SMATTER TRATTLE TWATTLE TWITTER TWITTLE WHITTER BABBLING LOLLYGAG SCHMOOSE SCHMOOZE VERBIAGE (SUFF.) LALIA

CHATTERBOX JAY MAG PIET BUCCO CLACK CRYSTE GOSSIP MAGPIE

CHATTERER JAY MAG PIE BLAB CHUET CHEWET GABBER MAGPIE RATTLE HAVERER

CHATTERING PIET BABBLY CHAVISH POPPING TWITTER TWITTERING BABBLING

CHATTY CHIRRUPY GARRULOUS

CHAUFFEUR DRIVER SHOVER TESTER

CHAUVINISM JINGOISM

CHAUVINIST JINGO JINGOIST

CHAW JAW VEX CHEW ENVY MULL GRIND PONDER

CHAYOTE CHOCHO TALLOTE HUISQUIL MIRLITON

CHEAP LOW BASE GAIN POOR VILE BORAX CLOSE FLASH GAUDY GROSS KITCH LIGHT MUCKY NASTY PRICE SNIDE TATTY TIGHT TINNY VALUE ABJECT BRUMMY CHEESY COMMON CRUMBY CRUMMY JITNEY LEADEN PLENTY SHODDY SLEAZY SORDID STINGY TAWDRY TRASHY UNDEAR BARGAIN CHINTZY POPULAR TINHORN INFERIOR PENNORTH SIXPENNY TWOPENNY BRUMMAGEM PINCHBECK (— ITEM) TWOFER (PREF.) VILI

CHEAPEN DOCK STALE VILIFY SMALLEN

CHEAPSKATE PIKER STIFF

CHEAT DO BAM BOB COG CON FOB FOP FUB GIP GUM GYP JIG NIP TOP BEAT BILK BITE BULL BURN CLIP COLT CRIB DISH DUFF DUPE FAKE FIRK FLAM FLUM GECK GULL HAVE HOAX HOSE JILT JINK JOUK KNAP LIAR MACE MUMP NAIL NICK NOSE POOP PULL REAM ROOK SCAM SELL SHAM SILE SKIN SLUR SNAP SWAP SWOP TRIM WEED WIPE BITCH BLINK BOOTY BUNCO BUNKO COZEN CROOK CULLY DODGE FAKER FLING FOIST FOURB FRAUD FUDGE GLEEK GOUGE GREEK GUILE HOCUS KNAVE LURCH MULCT PINCH PLOAT RATON ROGUE SCAMP SCREW SHARP SHORT SLANG SPOIL STICK STIFF STING SWICK SWIKE TOUCH TRICK VERSE WRINK BAFFLE BLANCH BUBBLE BUCKET CHIAUS CHISEL CHOUSE CLOYNE COGGER DADDLE DECEIT DELUDE DERIDE DIDDLE DOODLE DUFFER EMUNGE EUCHRE FIDDLE FLEECE GAZUMP GREASE HUMBUG HUMMER HUSTLE ILLUDE INTAKE JOCKEY NIGGLE NOBBLE NUZZLE OUTWIT RADDLE RENEGE RIPOFF SHAVER SHICER SNUDGE SUCKER TWICER ABUSION BEGUILE BUBBLER CHICANE COZENER CULLION DECEIVE DEFRAUD ESCHEAT FAITOUR FINAGLE FINESSE FOISTER GUDGEON JUGGLER MISLEAD PLUNDER QUIBBLE SHARPER SHIFTER SKELDER SLICKER SWINDLE VERNEUK ARTIFICE BEJUGGLE CHALDESE CHISELER DELUSION HOODWINK IMPOSTOR INTRIGUE OUTREACH OVERTAKE PICAROON SHAMMOCK SWINDLER BAMBOOZLE CIRCUMVENT SHORTCHANGE

CHEATED SOLD

CHEATER BITE GULL SPEC KNAVE BILKER INTAKE TOPPER SHARPER FINAGLER TREACHER

CHEATING HOCUS BARRAT ODLING ABUSIVE FUBBERY MICHERY ROGUERY CHEATERY JUGGLING TRICKERY

CHECH DUD BOUNCER
CHECK BIT DAM HAP LID NAB NIP
SAY SET TAB BAIL BALK BEAT BILK
BILL CHIP CHIT COOK CRIB CURB
DAMP FACE FOIL GAGE HURT ITEM
KITE PAWL REIN SKID SNEB SNIB
SNIP SNUB STAY STEM STOP STUB
TAKE TEST TICK TRIG TURN TWIT
WERE ABORT ALLAY ANNUL BAULK
BLOCK BRAKE CATCH CHIDE CHILL
CHING CHOKE CRACK CROOK DAUNT
DELAY DETER DRAFT EMBAR FACER
FAULT GAUGE LIMIT MODER PAUSE
QUELL REPEL SNAPE SPOKE STALL
STILL STUNT TALLY TAUNT THROW
TOKEN TRASH WAVER ARAYNE
ARREST ATTACK BAFFLE BOTTLE
BRIDLE CHEQUE COUPON DAMPEN
DEFEAT DETAIN DETENT DURESS
GRAVEL HAFFET HAFFIT HINDER
IMPEDE OPPOSE OUTWIT PULLUP
QUENCH RABBET REBATE REBUFF
REBUKE RETURN SCOTCH STANCH
STAYER STIFLE STYMIE TICKET
VERIFY ANSTOSS AWEBAND
BACKSET BECLOUD COMMAND
CONTAIN CONTROL COUNTER
CURTAIN DRAUGHT INHIBIT
MONITOR REFRAIN REPRESS
REPROOF REPROVE REPULSE
REVERSE SETBACK SNAFFLE
STAUNCH STOPPER TRAMMEL
TROUBLE BULKHEAD ENCUMBER
HOLDBACK OBSTRUCT PULLBACK
RESTRAIN WITHHOLD
(— ENTHUSIASM) DISMAY
(— GRADUALLY) CUSHION
(— GROWTH) BLAST STINT STUNT
(— IN) ARRIVE
(— IN GLASS) SPLIT
(— IN TIMBER) STARSHAKE
(— MOTION) SPRAG
(— OF HORSE) SACCADE
(— PASSER) PAPERHANGER
(— PROGRESS) DEFEAT
(FORGED —) STIFF STUMER
(HOLD IN —) COMPESCE
(ILLEGAL — IN HOCKEY) SPEARING
(RESTAURANT —) LAWING
(WORTHLESS —) DUD STUMER
(WRITE A BAD —) BOUNCE
(PREF.) ISCH(O)
CHECKED CHECK BEATEN CLOSED
CAPTIVE STOPPED
CHECKER DAM DICE FRET KING
CHECK FREAK FRECK PIECE WHITE
DAMPER DRAUGHT
CHECKERBERRY JINKS DRUNKARD
TEABERRY
CHECKERBOARD TABLE DAMBROD
DAMBOARD
CHECKERED PIED VAIR DICED PLAID
CHECKY MOTLEY

CHECKERS DRAFTS CHEQUERS
DRAUGHTS
CHECKERWORK TESSEL CHECKER
TESSERA
CHECKING REST BLOCK SETBACK
EBRILLADE
(— OF HEMORRHAGE) TORSION
(SUFF.) SCHESIS SCHETIC
CHECKMATE LICK MATE STOP
UNDO BAFFLE CORNER DEFEAT
OUTWIT STYMIE THWART SUIMATE
CHECKSTONE CHUCK
CHEDDAR CHEESE
CHEEK CHAP CHOP GALL GENA JAMB
JOLE JOWL LEER SASS WANG WANK
BUCCA CHOKE CHYAK CRUST NERVE
SAUCE SHICK CHYACK HAFFET
HAFFIT OXCHEEK AUDACITY
TEMERITY
(— OF SPUR) SHANK
(— OF VISE) CHAP
(PREF.) BUCCO MEL PAREI(A)
CHEEKBONE MALAR ZYGOMA
CHEEK-POUCH
(— OF BABOON) ALFORJA
CHEEKY BOLD FRESH
CHEEP PIP YAP YIP CHIP HINT PEEP
PULE CHIRP CREAK TWEET SQUEAK
TATTLE
CHEER OLE RAH FARE FOOD MIND
ROOT VIVA YELL BRAVO BRISK CHIRK
ELATE ERECT FEAST HEART HUZZA
JOLLY MIRTH SHOUT SPORT TIGER
WHOOP CANTLE CHERRY GAIETY
HOORAY HURRAH HUZZAH REHETE
SOLACE VIANDS ACCLAIM ANIMATE
APPLAUD CHERISH COMFORT
CONSOLE ENCHEER GLADDEN
HEARTEN JOLLITY LIGHTEN REFRESH
REJOICE SUPPORT UPRAISE
APPLAUSE BRIGHTEN HILARITY
INSPIRIT RECREATE VIVACITY
(BURST OF —S) SALVO
(GOOD —) WELFARE
(JAPANESE —) BANZAI
(SORRY —) PENANCE
CHEERFUL GAY CANT GLAD GLEG
GOOD HIGH ROSY BONNY CADGY
CANTY CHIRK DOUCE HAPPY JOLLY
LIGHT MERRY PEART READY RIANT
SAPPY SUNNY VAUDY BLITHE
BRIGHT CHEERY CHIRPY CROUSE
GAWSIE GENIAL HEARTY HILARY
JOCUND LIVELY RIDENT BUOYANT
CHEERLY CHIPPER HOLIDAY
JOCULAR SMILING WINSOME
CHEERING CHIRRUPY EUPEPTIC
FRIENDLY GLADSOME HOMELIKE
SANGUINE SUNBEAMY SUNSHINE
(PREF.) HILARO
CHEERFULLY GLADLY CANTILY
CHEERLY JOLLILY LIGHTLY CHEERILY
GENIALLY

CHEERFULNESS JOY GLEE TAIT
CHEER CHERTE GAIETY GAYETY
LEVITY SPIRIT JOLLITY BUOYANCY
FESTIVAL GLADNESS HILARITY
(MORE THAN —) GLEE
CHEERING GLAD CORDIAL
CHEERFUL CHIRPING
CHEERIO BYE CIAO TATA LATER
HOORAY HOOROO
CHEERLESS SAD BLAE COLD DIRE
DRAB GLUM GRAY BLEAK DREAR
ELYNG WASTE DISMAL DREARY
GLOOMY WINTRY DOLEFUL
FORLORN JOYLESS SUNLESS
DEJECTED DESOLATE LITHLESS
CHEER PINE CHIL
CHEERY BUXOM BRIGHT BOBBISH
GAYSOME
CHEESE OKA BLUE BRIE EDAM FETA
HAND JACK TOME TRIP APPLE BRICK
COLBY CREAM DAISY DERBY GOUDA
GRANA KENNO MAHON QUESO
SWISS TOMME WHEEL ZIEGA ZIGER
ASIAGO BARRIE BONDON BRYNZA
BURGOS CANTAL CASSAN DUNLOP
GLARUS JUNKET MYSOST ROMANO
RONCAL SAANEN SBRINZ TILSIT
ZAMORA ZIEGER ANGELOT CHEDDAR
CHEVRET COTTAGE CROWDIE
FONTINA FROMAGE GJEDOST
GRUYERE KENNO HAVARTI KASSERI
KEBBUCK LASELVA PRIMOST
PROVOLA RICOTTA SAPSAGO
SERRANO STILTON TETILLA TRUCKLE
AMERICAN CABRALES CHESHIRE
EMMENTAL LONGHORN MUENSTER
PARMESAN PECORINO RACLETTE
SANSIMON SLIPCOAT TRONCHON
LEICESTER MOUSETRAP PROVOLONE
ROQUEFORT WILTSHIRE
MOZZARELLA NEUFCHATEL
SERVILLETA
(— COATING) MOLD
(— DISH) RACLETTE
(— FANCIER) TUROPHILE
(— IN OATMEAL) CABOC
(— ROLLED IN OATMEAL) CABOC
(COTTAGE —) CROWDIE
(CREAM —) JUNKET
(DANISH —) HAVARTI
(GOAT —) CHEVRE
(HUNGARIAN —) LIPTAUER
(INCIPIENT —) CURD
(INFERIOR —) DICK
(KIND OF —) RAT RATTRAP
(LARGE —) KEBBOC
(MELTED —) FONDUTA
(MILD FRENCH —) REBLOCHON
(SAY —) SMILE
(SOFT —) STRACCHINO
(STORE —) CHEDDAR
(WELSH —) CAERPHILLY
(PREF.) CASE(O) TURO TYR(O)

CHEESELIKE CASEOUS
CHEESEPARING STINGY
CHEESE VAT CHESSEL CHESSART
CHEESEWOOD BONEWOOD
WHITEWOOD
CHEETAH CAT OUNCE YOUSE YOUZE
GUEPARD
CHEF COOK COMMIS SAUCIER
CUISINIER
(PASTRY —) PATISSIER
CHEFOO YENTAI
CHELA HAND MANUS NIPPER
PINCER
CHELATE COMPLEX
CHELICERA FALX FANG FALCER
MANDIBLE
CHELLIAN ABBEVILLIAN
CHELONIAN TURTLE TURTOISE
CHELUBAI (FATHER OF —) HEZRON
CHEMICAL (ALSO SEE SPECIFIC
HEADINGS) ACID BASE SALT ALKALI
BLEACH CHEMIC DODGER SAFENER
ADDITIVE ALGICIDE CATALYST
DEHORNER
(— FROM HEMP RESIN) THC
(— IN MARIJUANA) THC
(— WARFARE AGENT) SARIN
(PREF.) ACETO ALCO ALDO AMIDO
AMYL(I)(O) AZ(O) BENZ(O) BOR(O)
BROM(O) BUT(YR)(YRO) CADM(I)(O)
CAPRO CARB(O) CHAVI(O) CUMO
DIAZO DIOL DUPLO EKA ESTERI
FORM(O) GLY(O) IDO IMIDO IMINO
KER(O) KET(O) LAUR LIP LYSO LYXO
MAL(O) MENTH(O) MERCUR(O) METH
MOLYBD MURIO NAPHTH NITRATO
NITRILO NITROSO NOR OLEO ORTHO
OSMIO OX OXAL(O) OXIDI OXIDO
OXIMIDO OXO OXY OZO PENT(A)
PERI PHLOR(O) PHTHAL(O) PIPTO
PLUMB(I)(O) POLY PROP PROS
PROTE(O) PYRROL(O) SYN TOL(U)
(SUFF.) AMIN(E)(O) ANE ASE ATE ENE
ID(E) ILE INE INOL INONE ION ITE ITOL
IUM OIC OIN OL OLE OLIC OLID(E)
ON(E) ONIC ONIUM OSAN OSE OSIDE
OUS OYL PHORE RETIN THIN(E) YL
YNE ZYME
CHEMIN-DE-FER SHIMMY
CHEMISE SARK SHIFT SHIRT SIMAR
SMOCK CAMISA SHIMMY LINGERIE
CHEMISETTE SHAM GUIMPE
TUCKER PARTLET
CHEMIST ANALYST ASSAYER
CHEMICK BENCHMAN COLORIST
DRUGGIST
AMERICAN DOW ABEL CADY CRAM
DANA HALE HALL HARE HART HASS
HUNT KING LAMB LIND LOEB LONG
MARK REID UREY WATT CLARK
COOKE CROSS DEBYE DROWN
DUMEZ FLORY GIBBS GOOCH
HAMOR HERTY KRAUS LEWIS LIBBY

MOORE NOYES POWER SEMON
SMITH SNELL STINE WILEY BROWNE
BUCHER BURTON CALVIN CARVER
CLARKE CRAFTS DARKEN DEDUVE
DORSET DUDLEY EGLOFF HOLMES
HOOVER JULIAN LANDIS LEVENE
MENDEL MORGAN MUNROE PALMER
REMSEN ROBLIN ROGERS SHIMER
SUMNER TORREY WARREN WESSON
ALDRICH ANDREWS ATWATER
CASSIDY CASTNER CUSHMAN
DUSHMAN EDELMAN GIAUQUE
GODLOVE GOMBERG GUTHRIE
HARKINS KHORANA MIDGLEY
ONSAGER PAULING SEABORG
SHERMAN SLOSSON WHITNEY
BANCROFT BENEDICT CHANDLER
COOLIDGE COTTRELL DJERASSI
FRANKLIN HORSFORD LANGMUIR
LIPSCOMB MCCOLLUM MCMILLAN
MIDGELEY MULLIKEN RICHARDS
SILLIMAN SPRINGER STODDARD
WILLIAMS WOODWARD ALEXANDER
CAROTHERS HENDERSON
NIEUWLAND PATTERSON
CHITTENDEN HILLEBRAND
ARGENTINE LELOIR
AUSTRIAN KUHN EMICH PREGL
PRECHTL WELSBACH ZSIGMONDY
BELGIAN STAS SOLVAY HELMONT
BAEKELAND PRIGOGINE
CANADIAN HERZBERG MCLAUGHLIN
CZECH BRAUNER HEYROVSKY
DANISH OERSTED THOMSEN
BRONSTED KJELDAHL SORENSEN
DUTCH COHEN MULDER HOMBERG
ENGLISH ABEL BELL DAVY POPE
SWAN TODD ABNEY BOYLE CROSS
DAKIN DEWAR HENRY MARSH
PROUT SODDY SYNGE YOUNG
BARTON BRANDE DALTON DONNAN
GREGOR HARDEN INGOLD MARTIN
MILLER PERKIN PORTER RAMSAY
THORPE TILDEN WATSON ANDREWS
CROOKES DANIELL FARADAY
HAWORTH HODGKIN NORRISH
TENNANT TRAVERS HATCHETT
MITCHELL PLAYFAIR ROBINSON
WILLIAMS ARMSTRONG CAVENDISH
CORNFORTH FRANKLAND
GLADSTONE PRIESTLEY WILKINSON
HINSHELWOOD
FINNISH VIRTANEN
FRENCH LEHN BAUME BEHAL CONTE
CURIE DUFAY DUMAS FREMY LEBEL
LEBON WURTZ BALARD CLAUDE
DARCET DULONG GERNEZ GUIMET
LEMERY NAQUET ORFILA PERRIN
PROUST RAOULT WERNER CHAPTAL
DAUBENY FRIEDEL GLENARD
LAURENT LEBLANC LUMIERE
MACQUER MOISSAN PASTEUR
PELOUZE THENARD BERTRAND

CAVENTOU CHEVREUL COURTOIS
DEBIERNE DEMARCAY FOURCROY
FOURNEAU GERHARDT GRIGNARD
KUHLMANN REGNAULT SABATIER
BERTHELOT LAVOISIER LECLANCHE
LENORMAND PELLETIER VAUQUELIN
BERTHOLLET CHARDONNET
DUBRUNFAUT LECHATELIER
BOUSSINGAULT SCHUTZENBERGER
GERMAN CARO HAHN KOPP KUHN
MOND ADLER ALDER BOSCH DIELS
EIGEN FRANK HABER KNORR KOLBE
LUNGE MEYER STAHL ACHARD
BAEYER BECHER BREDIG BUNSEN
DOMAGK FITTIG GIESEL GRAEBE
KOSSEL LIEBIG MAGNUS NERNST
TRAUBE WOHLER BERGIUS BISCHOF
BORRGER BUCHNER CASSIUS
CURTIUS ERDMANN FEHLING
FISCHER GLAUBER HOFMANN
OSTWALD TIEMANN WALLACH
WIELAND WINDAUS ZIEGLER
KLAPROTH MARGGRAF SPRENGEL
BEILSTEIN BUTENANDT FRESENIUS
LADENBURG LAMPADIUS SCHEIBLER
SCHONBEIN STRASSMAN
WIEDEMANN ZSIGMONDY
BODENSTEIN DOBEREINER
ERLENMEYER LIEBERMANN
STAUDINGER STROHMEYER
WILLSTATER GOLDSCHMIDT
UNVERDORBEN WILLSTATTER
MITSCHERLICH
HUNGARIAN HEVESY
IRISH KIRWAN STEWART
ITALIAN LEVI NATTA SOVET COVELLI
FABRONI SOBRERO AVOGADRO
CIAMICIAN CANNIZZARO
BRUGNATELLI
JAPANESE FUKUI TAKAMINE
NORWEGIAN WAAGE HASSEL
GULDBERG
POLISH CURIE MOSCICKI
RUSSIAN BACH WALDEN SEMENOV
BUTLEROV MENDELEV ZELINSKI
PRIGOGINE
SCOTTISH URE BELL HALL BLACK
BROWN DEWAR YOUNG BEILBY
GRAHAM THOMSON MACINTOSH
SPANISH RODRIGUEZ
SWEDISH GAHN CLEVE BERGMAN
SCHEELE MOSANDER SEFSTROM
SVEDBERG TISELIUS ARRHENIUS
BERZELIUS CRONSTEDT
BLOMSTRAND ABDERHALDEN
SWISS NEF GLASER KARRER MULLER
PICTET PRELOG WERNER RUZICKA
MARIGNAC SAUSSURE REICHSTEIN
CHEMOSTERILANT METEPA
CHENAANAH (FATHER OF —)
BILHAN
CHENDE CHINOA
CHENFISH KINGFISH

CHENILLE SNAIL
CHEQUEEN BASKET SEQUIN
ZEQUIN CECCHINE ZECCHINO
CHEQUER DICE
CHERAN (FATHER OF —) DISHON
CHERAW SARA
CHEREMIS MARI
CHERISH AID HUG PET BEAR DOTE
HAVE HOPE LIKE LOVE SAVE ADORE
BOSOM BROOD CHEER CLING
COWER ENJOY NURSE PRIZE VALUE
CARESS ESTEEM FADDLE FONDLE
FOSTER GRUDGE HARBOR MOTHER
NESTLE NUZZLE PAMPER PETTLE
REVERE COMFORT EMBOSOM
EMBRACE INDULGE NOURISH
NURTURE PROTECT SUPPORT
SUSTAIN ENSHRINE INSPIRIT
PRESERVE TREASURE
CHERISHED PET DEAR BOSOM
DANDILY AFFECTED PRECIOUS
CHEROOT MANILA TRICHI TRICHY
CHERRY BING CHOP DUKE FUJI
GEAN MERRY MOREL CORNEL
MAZARD DURBANK CAPULIN
CHAPMAN LAMBERT MAHALEB
MARASCA MAYDUKE MORELLO
OXHEART PITANGA WINDSOR
AMARELLE DURACINE EGGBERRY
LUKEWARD NAPOLEON ROSACEAN
BIGARREAU MARASCHINO
MONTMORENCY
CHERRY-BLOSSOM HEBE
CHERRY-COLORED CERISE
CHERRY ORCHARD (AUTHOR OF —
) CHEKHOV
(CHARACTER IN —) ANYA GAYEV
VARYA YASHA DUNYASHA LOPAKHIN
RANEVSKY TROFIMOV CHARLOTTE
CHERRY PLUM MYROBALAN
CHERRY STONE PAIP
CHERT BOONE WHINSTONE
CHERUB AMOR EROS ANGEL CUPID
SERAPH SPIRIT AMORINO
AMORETTO CHERUBIM
CHERVIL BUN KECK ARFOIL CERFOIL
COWWEED HONEWORT MILKWEED
RATSBANE
CHESED (FATHER OF —) NAHOR
CHESS CHEAT SHOGI CHECKER
SKITTLES
(— CHAMPION) TAL
(— EXPERT) TAL
(— MOVE) ZUGZWANG
(INEPT — PLAYER) PATZER POTZER
CHESSBOARD CHESS TABLE
CHECKER
CHESSMAN PIN KING PIECE
CHECKER CHEQUER
(— SET) MEINY MEINIE
(ANY — BUT PAWN) OFFICER
(BISHOP —) ALFIN ALPHIN ARCHER
(CASTLE —) JUEZ ROOK TOUR UDGE

JUDGE LEDGE TOWER
(KNIGHT —) HORSE CHEVALIER
(PAWN —) PON POUNE
(QUEEN —) FERS FIERS PHEARSE
CHEST ARK BOX CUB FIX KIT PIX PYX
ARCA BUST CAJA CASH CIST CYST
FUND KIST SAFE SCOB AMBRY
BAHUT BUIST CADDY FRONT HOARD
HUTCH RAZEE SISTA TRUNK ALMOIN
BASKET BREAST BUNKER BUREAU
CAISSE CAJETA CASKET COFFER
COFFIN FORCER GIRNAL GIRNEL
HAMPER JORDAN LARNAX LOCKER
LOWBOY SCRINE SHRINE SPRUCE
STRIPE THORAX WANGAN BRAZIER
BRISKET CAISSON CAPCASE
CASSONE COMMODE DEPOSIT
DRAWERS DRESSER ENCLOSE
HIGHBOY TOOLBOX WINDBAG
WINDBAG CISTVAEN CUPBOARD
FORCELET MANIFOLD STANDARD
TREASURE TREASURY
(— FOR CUTLERY) CANTEEN
(— FOR FISH) CAUF
(— OF ORES) CAXON
(— PROTECTOR) BIB
(FRONT OF —) BREAST
(MEDICINE —) INRO
(SMALL —) COFFRET
(PREF.) STERN(O) STETH(O)
THORAC(I)(O)
CHESTERFIELD COAT SOFA
CHESTNUT GAG JOKE LING RATA
BROWN HORSE STORY CASTOR
MARRON SATIVA CRENATA DENTATA
(HORSE —) CONKER
(POLYNESIAN —) RATA
(WATER —) LING
(PREF.) CASTANO
CHESTNUT-COLORED BAY ROAN
BADIOUS
CHEST PROTECTOR PECTORAL
CHEVAL-DE-FRISE TURNPIKE
CHEVAL GLASS PSYCHE
CHEVALIER CADET NOBLE KNIGHT
GALLANT CAVALIER HORSEMAN
CHEVET APSE
CHEVILLE PEG
CHEVIN CHUB CHEVESNE
CHEVRON BEAM MARK WOUND
RAFTER STRIPE ZIGZAG
CHEVROTAIN MUSK NAPU DEERLET
KANCHIL MEMINNA PLANDOK
TRAGULE ROOMORAH PEESOREH
RUMINANT
CHEVY TEASE
CHEW CUD EAT GUM TAW BITE CHAM
CHAW GNAW NOSH QUID CHAMP
CHONK GRIND MUNCH RUMEN
CRUNCH MUMBLE CHUMBLE
MEDITATE RUMINATE MANDUCATE
(— OUT) SCOLD
(— THE CUD) KUMINATE

(— THE FAT) GAB JAW YAK
(— UP NOISILY) CHANK GROUZE
CHEWING GUM GUM CHICCLE
CHEWINK FINCH JOREE TOWHEE
GRASSET
CHEYENNE DOG
CHIAN SCIAN
CHIANTI FLORENCE
CHIASTOLITE MACLE ANDALUSITE
CHIBCHA MUISCA
CHIC GOGO PERT POSH TRIG TRIM
KIPPY NATTY NIFTY SMART CHICHI
DAPPER GIGOLO JAUNTY MODISH
TRENDY ELEGANT STYLISH
(KIND OF —) RADICAL
(NO LONGER —) OUT
CHICAGO PORKOPOLIS
CHICANE DECEPTION
CHICANERY DIRT RUSE WILE FEINT
TRICK ARTIFICE INTRIGUE TRICKERY
DECEPTION PETTIFOGGERY
CHICHI ARTY TONY
CHICK BIRD GIRL PEEP TICK CHILD
NATTY POULET SCREEN SEQUIN
SPROUT CHICKEN CHUCKIE
CHICKADEE TOMTIT BLACKCAP
TITMOUSE
CHICKAREE BOOMER
CHICKEN HEN KIP COCK FOWL BIDDY
CAPON CHICK CHILD CHOOK CHUCK
DEEDY FRYER LAYER MANOC POULT
SILKY TIMID AFRAID CHICKY PULLET
SULTAN SUSSEX TURKEN ANCOBAR
BOARDER BROILER DIBBLER
LEGHORN POUSSIN ROASTER
ROOSTER SCRATCH ARAUCANA
COCKEREL PHASANID SPRINGER
(— OUT) WIMPOUT
(— PIECES ON SKEWER) YAKITORI
(— SHELTER) MOTHER
(FRIED —) ESCABECHE
(STRIPS OF —) FAJITA
CHICKEN COOP CAVY CAVIE
CHICKEN-FEED PEANUTS
CHICKEN POX SOREHEAD
VARICELLA
CHICK-PEA CHIT GRAM CHICH CICER
COWGRAM SOWGRAM GARBANZO
GARVANCE
(PL.) FASELS
CHICKWEED BLINK BLINKS SPURRY
ALLBONE STARWORT
CHICO SAPODILLA
CHICORY BUNK CREPIS ENDIVE
SUCCORY WITLOOF BLUEWEED
COMPOSIT RADICCHIO
CHIDE BAN FUSS RAIL RATE BLAME
CHECK FLITE FLYTE SCOLD SNEAP
BERATE REBUFF REBUKE SCHOOL
THREAP THREEP THREEP TONGUE
CENSURE REPROVE UPBRAID
WRANGLE ADMONISH BETONGUE
LAMBASTE REPROACH

CHIDING ROW
CHIEF (ALSO SEE CHIEFTAIN) BO AGA
BIG BOH CAP CID COB DUX MIR MOI
TOP AGHA ALII AMIR ARCH ARII BOSS
CAID CHEF COCK DATO DEAN DOEG
DUCE DUKE EMIR HEAD HIER HIGH
INCA JARL JEFE KAID KHAN KING
MAIN MICO MOST NAIK ONLY QAID
RAIS RAJA REIS TYEE ALDER ALPHA
ARIKI DATTO ELDER FIRST GREAT
MAJOR MATAI NAYAK PRIMA PRIME
PRIMO RAJAH RULER THANE TITAN
VITAL ZAQUE ZIPPA ADALID CABEZA
DEPUTY FLAITH HEADLY INKOSI
KEHAYA KUBERA KUVERA LEADER
LULUAI MASTER MIRDHA NAIQUE
PENLOP PRABHU PRIMAL RECTOR
SACHEM SAYYID SHAYKH SHEIKH
SHERIF STAPLE SUDDER TOPMAN
TURNUS CAPITAL CAPTAIN CENTRAL
EMINENT FOREMAN GENERAL
HEADMAN INGOMAR LEADING
LEMPIRA MUGWUMP OVERMAN
PADRONE PALMARY POLYGAR
PRELATE PREMIER PRIMARY SHEREEF
STELLAR SUPREME TOPSMAN
TRIBUNE CABOCEER CAPITANO
CARDINAL DECURION DIRECTOR
DOMINANT ELDORADO ESPECIAL
FOREMOST GOVERNOR HEADSMAN
HIERARCH INTIMATE MOKADDAM
PREMIERE SAGAMORE STAROSTA
SUBCHIEF PENDRAGON
(— IN INDIA) PRABHU SIRDAR
(— OF ADVOCATES) BATONNIER
(— OF RELIGIOUS ORDER) GENERAL
(— OF TITHING) BORSHOLDING
(— OF 10 MEN) DEAN
(CHINOOK —) TYEE
(CLAN —) TOISECH
(INDIAN —) SUNCK SACHEM SUNCKE
CACIQUE MOCUDDUM SAGAMORE
(MALAY —) RAJA RAJAH
(MOHAMMEDAN —) DATO DATTO
SAYID SAYYID
(SCHOOL —) DUX
(SCOTTISH —) MAORMOR
(TIBETAN —) POMBO
(TURKISH —) AGA AGHA
(VIKING —) SEAKING
(PREF.) ARCH(I) PROT(O)
CHIEFLY MAINLY LARGELY
CHIEFTAIN BEG AMIR CHAM EMIR
HEAD JARL KHAN ASTUR CHIEF
EMEER LEADER SIRDAR CAUDILLO
HIAWATHA
CHIEFTAINCY STOOL CHIEFRY
CHIEFTAINESS QUEEN
CHIFFCHAFF PEGGY CHIPCHAP
CHIPCHOP
CHIFFON SHEER
CHIFFONIER BUREAU CABINET
COMMODE

CHIGGER BICHO PIQUE CHIGGA CHIGOE GIGGER JIGGER LEPTUS REDBUG WHEELWORM

CHIGNON COB KNOT COBBE TWIST

CHIGOE FLEA SIKA BICHO NIGUA PIQUE TIKE SCREW CHIGGA ENIGUA JIGGER SANDBOY SANDWORM

CHIH FU PREFECT

CHILBLAIN KIBE MULE BLAIN MOOLS MOULS PERNIO

CHILD BEN BOY BUD ELF GET IMP KID LAD SON SOT TAD TOT WAY BABA BABE BABY BATA BIRD BRAT CHAP CHIT CION FOOD GIRL GYTE PAGE PUSS TIKE TINY TOTO TROT TYKE WEAN BAIRN BIRTH BROLL BROWL CHICK CHIEL COOKY ELFIN GAMIN ISSUE KEIKI OLIVE POULT SCION TIDDY TRICK WAYNE WENCH WHELP CHERUB COLLOP COOKIE ENFANT FILIUS FOSTER INFANT MOPPET NIPPER PLEDGE PROLES SHAVER STUMPY TACKER TODDLE URCHIN BAMBINO CHOOKIE CHOPPER CHRISOM COCKNEY DICKENS GANGREL GYTLING KINCHIN KITLING LAMBKIN PAPOOSE PRETEEN PROGENY STICHEL SUBTEEN TIDDLER TODDLER TROTTIE WRAWLER YOUNKER BANTLING CHISELER DAUGHTER EPIGONUS JUVENILE LITTLING NURSLING PRATTLER RUNABOUT WEANLING WHIMLING PRESCHOOLER
(— AT BAPTISM) CHRISOM CHRISTOM
(— IN THE WOMB) BURDEN
(— OF THE WORLD) WELTKIND
(— UNDER 7 YEARS) INFANS
(ANNOYING —) BRAT
(BAD-MANNERED —) GOOP
(BAPTISMAL —) CHRISOM
(CHUBBY —) CHUNK
(CODDLED —) COCKNEY
(ELF'S —) AUF OAF CHANGELING
(FAVORITE —) BENJAMIN
(FAVORITE —) BENJAMIN
(FORWARD —) JACKANAPES
(FOSTER —) DAULT NORRY NURRY FOSTER REARLING
(ILLEGITIMATE —) MISHAP BASTARD
(INNOCENT —) CHRISOM
(LAST-BORN —) DILLING
(LOVED —) JOY
(MERRY —) SUNBEAM
(MEXICAN —) NINO
(MISCHIEVOUS —) IMP LIMB TIKE DICKENS
(NAKED —) SCUDDY
(NEGLECTED —) WAIF WASTREL
(NEWBORN —) NEONATE STRANGER
(NURSERY —) PREEMIE
(PAUPER —) MINDER

(PLAYFUL —) ELF WANTON
(PLUMP —) FOB FUB
(PRECOCIOUS —) PRODIGY
(PURE —) DOVE
(ROWDY —) HOODLUM
(SMALL —) TAD TOT MITE SPUD GAITT KIDDY TIDDY TOTUM KIDLET PEEWEE TACKER BAIRNIE
(SPOILED —) CADE COSSET WANTON COCKNEY
(STUNTED —) URF
(SWEET —) CHERUB
(TROUBLESOME —) PICKLE STICHEL
(UNMANNERLY —) SMATCHET
(UNWEANED —) SUCKLING
(YOUNG —) BABY JOEY INFANT SQUIRT GANGREL NESTLER TODDLER BANTLING INNOCENT LITTLING SUCKLING
(YOUNGEST —) WRIG DILLING
(PREF.) INFANTI TECNO(O) PAID(O) PED(O) TECHNO TECNO TEKNO

CHILDBED JIZZEN

CHILDBIRTH LABOR CRYING INLYING TRAVAIL OXYTOCIA
(— WOMAN) PUERPERA
(OF A METHOD OF —) LAMAZE
(PREF.) LOCHIO LOCHO TOCO TOKO
(SUFF.) TOCIA TOCO(US) TOKIA TOKO(US)

CHILDHOOD INFANCY CHILDAGE
(2ND —) DOTAGE TWICHILD

CHILDISH TID WEAK DANSY NAIVE PETTY SILLY YOUNG CHITTY PULING SIMPLE WEANLY ASININE BABYISH CHILDLY FOOLISH KIDDISH PEEVISH PROGENY PUERILE UNMANLY BAIRNISH BRATTISH IMMATURE TOOTLING

CHILDISHNESS DOTAGE

CHILDLESS ORBATE

CHILDREN ISSUE PROLES STRAIN PROGENY OFFSPRING
(NUMBER OF —) PARITY
(SUFF.) PAEDES

CHILE SOCOMPA
(— INDIAN) FUEGUAN

GULF: ANCUD GUAFO PENAS ARAUCO
INDIAN: ONA AUCA INCA ONAN
ARAUCA CHANGO YAHGAN
FUEGIAN MAPUCHE MOLUCHE
PAMPEAN PATAGON RANQUEL
ALIKULUF PICUNCHE TSONECAN
ISLAND: LUZ PRAT BYRON GUAFO
HOSTE MOCHA NUEVA NUNEZ
VIDAL CHILOE DAWSON EASTER
LENNOX PIAZZI PICTON QUILAN
RIESCO STOSCH TALCAN ANGAMOS
CAMPANA HANOVER REFUGIO
TRANQUI CLARENCE HUAMBLIN
NALCAYEC NAVARINO TRAIGUEN
ISLANDS: CHONOS HERMITE PAJAROS
CHAUQUES
ISTHMUS: OFQUI
LAKE: TORO RANCO YELCHO
PUYEHUE RUPANCO
MEASURE: VARA LEGUA LINEA
CUADRA FANEGA
MOUNTAIN: MACA TORO CHATO
MAIPO PAINE POTRO PULAR TORRE
YOGAN APIWAN BURNEY CONICO
JERVIS POQUIS RINCON CHALTEL
COPIAPO FITZROY PALPANA
VELLUDA COCHRANE TRONADOR
YANTELES
MOUNTAINS: ANDES DARWIN
ALMEIDA DOMEYKO
NATIVE: PATAGONIAN
PENINSULA: HARDY LACUY TAITAO
TUMBES
POINT: TORO GALLO LILES LOBOS
LOROS MORRO TALCA TETAS VIEJA
CACHOS GALERA MOLLES
ANGAMOS LAVAPIE
PORT: LOTA TOME ARICA COQUIMBO
PROVINCE: AISEN ARICA AYSEN
MAULE NUBLE TALCA ARAUCO
BIOBIO CAUTIN CHILOE CURICO
OSORNO ATACAMA LINARES
MALLECO COQUIMBO OHIGGINS
SANTIAGO TARAPACA VALDIVIA
RIVER: LOA LAJA YALI ALHUE AZAPA
BRAVO BUENO ELQUI ITATA LAUCA
LLUTA MAIPO MAULE PUELO RAHUE
RAPEL VITOR BIOBIO CAMINA
CHOAPA CHOROS CISNES COLINA
HUASCO LIMARI MORADO PALENA
POSCUA TOLTEN COPIAPO VALDIVIA
SHRUB: LITRE
STRAIT: NELSON MAGELLAN
TOWN: BOCO CUYA LEBU LOTA OCOA
TOCO TOME ARICA TALCA ARAUCO
CURICO GATICO OSORNO SERENA
TEMUCO VICUNA YUMBEL YUNGAY
CALDERA CHILLAN COPIAPO
COQUIMBO RANCAGUA SANTIAGO
VALDIVIA
TREE: RAULI
VOLCANO: LANIN MAIPO ANTUCO
LASCAR LLAIMA OSORNO OYAHUE

TACORA LAUTARO PETEROA
SOCOMAP VILLARICA GUALLATIRI
WEIGHT: GRANO LIBRA QUINTAL
WIND: SURES

CHILEAB (FATHER OF —) DAVID
(MOTHER OF —) ABIGAIL
CHILE-BELLS COPIHUE LAPAGERIA
CHI-LIN KYLIN UNICORN
CHILION (DAUGHTER OF —) ORPAH
(MOTHER OF —) NAOMI
CHILL ICE RAW AGUE COLD COOL
DAZY ALGID ALGOR DAVER GELID
OURIE RIGOR SCHEL SHAKE FRAPPE
FREEZE FRIGID FROSTY SHIVER
SNELLY DEPRESS FRETISH FRISSON
MALARIA COLDNESS
(— OUT) RELAX
CHILLED ICED ACOLD CHILL FROZEN
STARVEN
CHILLING ICY COLD EERY BLEAK
EERIE NIPPY CHILLY WINTRY GLACIAL
NIPPING SHIVERY
CHILLNESS COLD
CHILLY ICY RAW COLD COOL LASH
ALGID BLEAK HUNCH NIPPY PARKY
AGUISH AIRISH ARCTIC CRIMMY
FROSTY FROZEN LEEPIT CAULDRIFE
CHIMAERA BELUE DRAGON CATFISH
PLACOID RATFISH RATTAIL
DOODSKOP
CHIME DIN RIM BELL EDGE PEAL
RING SUIT TING TINK AGREE CHIMB
CHINE PRATE ACCORD CLOCHE
CYMBAL JINGLE MELODY CONCORD
HARMONY SINGSONG
(PL.) BELL
CHIMER CYMAR SIMAR CHIMAR
TABARD
CHIMERA FANCY MIRAGE MOSAIC
POMATO ILLUSION
CHIMERE ROBE
CHIMERICAL VAIN WILD INSANE
UTOPIAN DELUSIVE FANCIFUL
ROMANTIC IMAGINARY
CHIMNEY BAG LUM TUN FLUE
LUMM PIPE TUBE VENT GULLY
STACK STALK TEWEL CHIMLA
FUNNEL LOUVER SMOKER TUNNEL
FISSURE OPENING ORIFICE
FUMIDUCT SMOKESTACK
CHIMNEY CAP TURNCAP
CHIMNEY CORNER FIRESIDE
INGLENOOK
CHIMNEY COWL COW
CHIMNEY HOOD JACK
CHIMNEY PIECE PAREL
CHIMNEY PIPE TALLBOY
CHIMNEY POST SPEER
CHIMNEY-POT TOPHAT
CHIMNEY SEAT SCONCE
CHIMNEY SWEEP SWEEP CHUMMY
FLUEMAN RAMONEUR

CHIMP (SPACE —) ENOS
CHIMPANZEE APE CHIMP JACKO
  JOCKO PIGMY PYGMY NCHEGA
  PIGMEW PYGMEAN
CHIN JAW RAP CHAT TSIN MENTUM
  CHOLLER
  (— POINT) MENTON POGONION
  (DOUBLE —) BUCCULA CHOLLER
  (PREF.) GENIO MENTI MENTO
CHINA WARE JAPAN LENOX SPODE
  CATHAY PARIAN SEVRES TEASET
  CERAMIC CHEENEY DRESDEN
  LIMOGES MEISSEN POTTERY
  CINCHONA CROCKERY EGGSHELL
  (BONE —) WEDGWOOD
  (KIND OF —) HOTEL

CHINA

ABORIGINE: YAO MANS MIAO
  MANTZU YAOMIN MIAOTSE
AREA UNIT: MU MOU MOW
BASIN: TARIM
BAY: LAICHOW HANGCHOW
BUDDHA: FO
CAPE: OLWANPI
CAPITAL: PEKING TAIPEI PEIPING
CHANNEL: BASHI
COIN: PU CASH CENT MACE TAEL TIAO
  YUAN CHIAO SYCEE DOLLAR
CURRENCY: RENMINBI
DEPRESSION: TURFAN
DESERT: GOBI ORDOS SHAMO
  ALASHAN TAKLAMAKAN
DIALECT: WU MIN AMOY HAKKA
  CANTON HSIANG SWATOW
  FOOCHOW WENCHOW KANDARRA
  MANDARIN
DRY LAKE: LOPNOR
DYNASTY: WU HAN SHU SUI WEI YIN
  CHIN CHOU HSIA HSIN MING SUNG
  TANG YUAN CHING SHANG
GULF: POHAI CHIHLI TONKIN PECHILI
  LIAOTUNG
ISLAND: AMOY FLAT MACAO MATSU
  NAMKI CHUSAN HAINAN PRATAS
  QUEMOY TAIWAN YUHWAN
  FORMOSA HUNGTOW TUNGSHA
  CHOUCHAN KULANGSU STAUNTON
ISLANDS: PENGHU TACHEN CHUSAN
  MIAOTAO
LAKE: TAI CHAO KAOYU OLING TELLI
  BAMTSO BORNOR EBINOR ERHHAI
  KHANKA LOPNOR NAMTSO POYANG
  CHALING HUNGTSE KARANOR
  KOKONOR HULUNNOR MONTCALM
  TAROKTSO TELLINOR TIENCHIH
  TSINGHAI TUNGTING
MEASURE: HO HU KO LI MU PU TO TU
  FAN FEN PAU TOU YUN YIN CHIH
  FANG KISH PARA QUEI SHIH TSUN
  CHIANG CHING SHENG SHING
  CHUPAK KUNGHO KUNGLI KUNGMU
  KUNGFEN KUNGYIN KUNGCHIH

MOUNTAIN: OMI OMEI SUNG KAILAS
  POBEDA EVEREST MUZTABH
  SUNGSHAN
MOUNTAINS: ALTAY KUNLUN
  ALASHAN KUENLUN MEILING
  MINSHAN NANLING NANSHAN
  TANGLHA BOGDOULA HIMALAYA
  TAPASHAN TAYULING TIENSHAN
  WUYLISHAN
NAME: CATHAY
NATIVE: PAT
PENINSULA: LEICHU LUICHOW
  LIAOTUNG
PORT: AMOY WUHU AIGUN SHASI
  ANTUNG CANTON CHEFOO DAIREN
  ICHANG NINGPO PAKHOI SWATOW
  SZEMAO WUCHOW YOCHOW
  FOOCHOW HUNCHUN MENGTSZ
  NANKING SAMSHUI SANTUAO
  SOOCHOW WENCHOW CHANGSHA
  HANGCHOW KIUKIANG KONGMOON
  LUNGCHOW SHANGHAI TENGYUEH
  TIENTSIN TSINGTAO WANHSIEN
PROVINCE: HONAN HOPEH HOPEI
  HUNAN HUPEI HUPEN JEHOL
  KANSU KIRIN TIBET ANHWEI FUKIEN
  SHANSI SHENSI TAIWAN YUNNAN
  KIANGSI KWANGSI NGANHUI
  CHEKIANG KWEICHOW LIAONING
  MONGOLIA SHANTUNG SZECHWAN
  TSINGHAI MANCHURIA
RELIGION: JU SHINTO TAOISM
  BUDDHISM
RESERVOIR: SUNGARI
RIVER: SI HAN ILI MIN NEN PEI WEI
  AMUR HUAI LIAO LOHO TUNG YALU
  YUAN YUEN ARGUN FENHO MACHU
  PEIHO TARIM TUMEN WEIHO
  CHUMAR DRECHU DZACHU KHOTAN
  KUMARA LIAOHO MANASS
  MEKONG OCHINA URUNGU YELLOW
  HOANGHO HWANGHO KERULEN
  KIALING SALWEEN SIKIANG
  SUNGARI TSANGPO WUKIANG
  YANGTZE YARKAND YUKIANG
  CHERCHEN HANKIANG HUNGSHUI
  MINKIANG
RULER: WANG
SEA: ECHINA SCHINA YELLOW
STRAIT: HAINAN TAIWAN FORMOSA
TOWN: BAI NOH AHPA AMOY ANSI
  ANTA AOSU FUYU GUMA HAMI
  HUMA IPIN KIAN KISI LIN LOHO
  LUTA MOHO MOYU MULI NIYA
  NOHO NURA OMIN OWPU RIMA
  SAKA SIAN TALI TAYU WUHU WUSU
  WUTU YAAN CHIAI FUSIN HOFEI
  ICHUN JEHOL KIRIN KOKLU LHASA
  MACAO PENKI SHASI TAIAN TALAI
  TUTZE TUYUN TZEPO WUHAN
  WUSIH YENKI YULIN YUMEN
  ANSHAN ANTUNG CANTON
  CHENDU DAIREN FUCHAU FUSHUN

HANKOW HANTAN HARBIN HOIHOW
KALGAN LOYANG LUSHUN MUKDEN
NINGPO PAOTOW PEKING PENGPU
SUCHOW SWATOW TAINAN TAIPEI
TALIEN TSINAN YUNNAN CHUNGTU
FATSHAN FOOCHOW HANYANG
HUHEHOT KAIFENG KUNMING
KWEISUI LANCHOW NANKING
PAOTING PEIPING SOOCHOW
TAIYUAN TIANJIN TZEKUNG
URUMCHI WUCHANG YENPING
CHANGSHA CHAOCHOW CHENGTEH
CHINCHOW HANGCHOW KIAOCHOW
KWEIYANG NANCHANG QARAQASH
SHANGHAI SHENYANG SIANGTAN
TANGSHAN TENGCHOW TIENTSIN
TSINGTAO TUNGCHOW CHUNGKING
WEIGHT: LI TA FAN FEN HAO KIN SSU
TAN YIN CHEE CHIN DONG MACE
SHIH TAEL CATTY CHIEN LIANG
PICUL TCHIN HAIKWAN KUNGFEN
KUNGSSU KUNGCHIN

CHINABERRY LILAC AZEDARACH
CHINABALL SOAPBERRY
CHINA BLUE NIKKO
CHINA-GRASS RAMI RAMEE RAMIE
CHINA HAT HAELTZUK HEILTSUK
CHINAMAN CHOW JOHN JOHNNY
CELESTIAL
(PL.) TANKA
CHINA ROSE MANETTI HIBISCUS
CHINA STONE PETUNSE
CHINA TREE LILAC HAGBUSH
CHINAWARE CRACKLE
CHINCHILLA ABROCOME VIZCACHA
CHINE BACK IKAT CHINK CRACK
CREST GORGE RIDGE SPINE CLEAVE
RAVINE SPROUT CREVICE
CHINESE PAT BABA CHOW CERAI
CHINK SERES SERIC SINIC MANZAS
MONGOL ASIATIC CATAIAN CHINOIS
PIGTAIL SANGLEY
(COMMUNIST —) CHICOM
(PREF.) CHINO SINICO SINO
CHINESE ARTICHOKE CROSNE
CHOROGI CROSNES STACHYS
KNOTROOT
CHINESE CABBAGE PECHAY
PAKCHOI
CHINESE DATE BER JUJUBE
CHINESE GELATIN AGAR
CHINESE PARSLEY CILANTRO
CHING TSING
CHINGPAW KACHIN SINGPHO
YAWYINS
CHINIOFON YATREN
CHINK GAP BORE CASH CHAP COIN
JINK KINK RENT RIFT RIME SCAR
BOORE CHECK CHINE CHUNK CLEFT
CRACK GRIKE KNACK MONEY
CRANNY RICTUS SPRAIN CHINKLE
CREVICE FISSURE APERTURE

CHINPIECE BARBEL
CHINQUAPIN OAK BONNET NUTLET
BONNETS CANDOCK CHESTNUT
WANKAPIN YOCKERNUT
CHINTZ PINTADO SALAMPORE
CHIONE (FATHER OF —) BOREAS
DAEDALION
(HUSBAND OF —) NEPTUNE
(MOTHER OF —) ORITHYIA
DAEDALION
(SLAYER OF —) DIANA
(SON OF —) EUMOLPUS AUTOLYCUS
PHILAMMON
CHIOT SCIOT
CHIP BIT CPU CUT DIB GAG HEW NIG
BONE CHAP CLIP HACK KNAP KNOP
NICK PARE SAND SKIN SNIP SNUB
BEACH CHECK CRACK FLAKE PIECE
SCRAP SKELF SLICE SPALE SPALL
SPALT SPAWL SPELL SPOON WASTE
BORING CHISEL GALLET MARKER
NOODLE COUNTER SHAVING
CHIPPING COSSETTE FRAGMENT
SPLINTER WHITLING
(— IN) ANTE
(— OF SOLDER) LINK
(— OF WOOD) SPOON
(— OUT) DESEAM
(BUFFALO —S) BODEWASH
(COMPUTER MEMORY —) DRAM
(CORN —S) FRITOS
(MEMORY —) DRAM
(POTATO —) CRISP
(SUPPLY OF —S) STACK
(TORTILLA —) NACHO
CHIP BASKET PUNNET
CHIPMAN SCRAPMAN
CHIPMUNK CHIPPY GOPHER GRINNY
HACKEE GRINNIE SQUIRREL
CHIPOLATA SAUSAGE
CHIPPENDALE AFGHAN
CHIPPER GAY SPRY CHIRP PERKY
BABBLE COCKEY FIERCE HACKER
KIPPER LIVELY CHATTER CHIRRUP
TWITTER CHEERFUL
CHIPPINGS SWARF
CHIRO BONYFISH FRANCESCA
CHIROGRAPHY WRITING
CHIRON (— AS CONSTELLATION)
SAGITTARIUS
(FATHER OF —) SATURN
(MOTHER OF —) PHILYRA
CHIROPODIST PEDICURE
CORNCUTTER
CHIROPTEROUS BATTY
CHIRP PEW PIP PEEK PEEP PIPE PULE
TWIT WEAK CHEEP CHELP CHIRK
CHIRL CHIRM CHIRT TWEET TWINK
CHIPPER CHIRRUP CHITTER REJOICE
SHATTER TWEEDLE TWITTER
WHEETLE WHITTER
CHIRPPING TWITTER
CHIRR PITTER

CHIRU SUS

CHISEL BUR CUT GAD CHIP ETCH FORM MOIL PARE SEAT SETT TANG TOOL BRUZZ BURIN CARVE CHEAT DROVE GOUGE HARDY POINT SCOOP SLICK STIFF BROACH CHESIL FIRMER FORMER GRAVEL HAGGLE POMMEL QUARRY REAMER TOOLER BARGAIN BOASTER BOLSTER CHIPPER ENGRAVE GRADINE GRUBBER POINTER QUARREL SCOOPER SCORPER SHINGLE CROSSCUT SPLITTER
(BLACKSMITH'S —) HARDY HARDIE
(FLINT —) TRANCHET
(ICE —) SPUD
(JEWELER'S —) SCAUPER SCORPER
(PREHISTORIC —) CELT
(STONEMASON'S —) TOOL DROVE POMMEL TOOLER SPLITTER
(TOOTHED —) GRADINE
(TRIANGULAR —) BUR BURR
(WHEELWRIGHT'S —) BRUZZ
(PREF.) CELTI

CHISELER CHEAT CROOK COYOTE GOUGER

CHISLON (SON OF —) ELIDAD

CHIT DAB IOU TAB BILL NOTE DRAFT LETTER VOUCHER

CHITARRONE ARCHLUTE

CHITCHAT GAD GASH GUFF TALK BANTER GOSSIP GOSSIPRY BAVARDAGE

CHITINOUS SHELLY

CHITON EXOMIS DIPLOIS EXOMION

CHITTAMWOOD IRONWOOD

CHITTERLINGS SOULFOOD

CHIVALROUS BRAVE CIVIL NOBLE PREUX GENTLE POLITE GALLANT GENTEEL VALIANT WARLIKE KNIGHTLY

CHIVE CIVE SIVE CIVET SITHE ALLIUM

CHIVY RUN VEX BAIT HUNT RACE CHASE CHEVY TEASE BADGER CHIVVY FLIGHT HARASS PURSUE PURSUIT SCAMPER TORMENT MANEUVER

CHLAMYDIA BEDSONIA

CHLOASMA MOTH

CHLOR LEMON

CHLORDIAZEPOXIDE LIBRIUM

CHLORIDE BUTTER CALOMEL MURIATE VIOLOGEN ALEMBROTH

CHLORINE OXYGEN

CHLORION SPHEX

CHLORIS (BROTHER OF —) AMYCLAS
(FATHER OF —) AMPHION
(HUSBAND OF —) NELEUS ZEPHYRUS
(MOTHER OF —) NIOBE
(SON OF —) NESTOR

CHLORITE AMESITE

CHOANA COLLAR

CHOBDAR USHER CHOPDAR

CHOCK COG PAD BLOCK BRACE CHUCK CLEAT SPOKE SPRAG WEDGE SCOTCH
(PL.) STOWWOOD

CHOCKABLOCK SOLID

CHOCOLATE BUD CANDY COCOA NORFOLK JACOLATT
(— MIXTURE) GANACHE
(— SNACK) OREO

CHOGAK SHOQ

CHOICE BET ODD TRY BEST FINE FORE GOOD MIND PICK RARE WALE WEAL WILL CREAM ELITE PRIME VOICE CHOSEN DAINTY DESIRE FLOWER OPTION PICKED PLUMMY SELECT DILEMMA ELEGANT EXCERPT PERMISS DELICATE ELECTION EXIMIOUS UNCOMMON VOLITION RECHERCHE PREFERENCE
(FAVORITE —) STANDBY
(FREE —) SWING DRUTHERS
(PARTICULARLY —) RECHERCHE

CHOICEST PICK PRIMROSE

CHOIR KERE QUIRE CHAPEL CHORUS CHORALE CONCERT KAPELLE PSALMODY

CHOIRBOY CLERGEON CHORISTER

CHOIR LEADER CANTOR CHORAGUS CHORISTER PRECENTOR

CHOIRMASTER CHORAGUS

CHOKE DAM GAG GOB CLOG DAMP PLUG QUAR STOP WARP CHECK CHOCK CLOSE GRAIN GRANE SCRAG WORRY ACCLOY HINDER IMPEDE STIFLE SWARVE CONGEST QUACKLE QUEAZEN QUERKEN REPRESS SILENCE SMOLDER SMOTHER OBSTRUCT QUEASOME SCUMFISH STOPPAGE STRANGLE SUPPRESS THROTTLE
(— OFF) BESET
(— UP) CLOY GORGE STUFF

CHOKEBERRY DOGBERRY SOAPBERRY

CHOKED FOUL WOOLY WOOLLY CLOTTED

CHOKEDAMP STYTHE BLACKDAMP

CHOKERMAN CHAINER CHAINMAN

CHOKWE KIOKO

CHOLER IRE BILE FURY RAGE ANGER WRATH SPLEEN TEMPER DISTEMPER

CHOLERIC MAD ANGRY CROSS FIERY HUFFY TESTY FUMISH IREFUL TOUCHY BILIOUS ENRAGED IRACUND PEEVISH PEPPERY WASPISH WRATHFUL IMPATIENT

CHOLIAMB SCAZON

CHONDRIOME CYTOME

CHOOSE OPT TRY CHAP CULL LIKE LIST LOVE LUST PICK TAKE VOTE WALE WEAL ADOPT ELECT PRICK ANOINT DECIDE GOWITH PLEASE PREFER SELECT EMBRACE ESPOUSE

EXTRACT SEPARATE
(— ABRUPTLY) PLUMP
(— A CAREER) GOINTO
(— EASIEST COURSE OF ACTION) WIMPOUT
(— TO WEAR) FAVOR
CHOOSING OPTION ECLECTIC
CHOOSY PICKY CHOICY FINICAL
CHOP AX AXE CUT HAG HEW JAW
LOP CHAP CHIP DICE GASH HACK
HASH HOWL RIVE SLIT CARVE CLEFT
CRACK KNOCK MINCE NOTCH SLASH
STAMP TRADE TRUCK WHANG
BARTER CHANGE CLEAVE INCISE
EXCHANGE
(— OFF) SNIG
(— SMALL) DEVIL MINCE
(— UP) HACKLE
(— WITH DULL AX) BUTTE
(DOG'S —) FLEW
(PORK —) GRISKIN
CHOPINE CIOPPINO PANTOFLE
CHOPPED CUT CHAPPED
CHOPPER SAX MINCER CLEAVER
SLASHER TRANCHET
CHOPPINESS CHOP JABBLE
CHOPPING BLOCK HACKLOG
CHOPPING TOOL
(— CULTURE) SOAN SOHAN
CHOPPY BUMPY LOPPY LUMPY
PECKY ROUGH SHORT POPPLY
CHORAL (— SOCIETY) ORPHEON
CHORD CORD DYAD ROLL TONE
CORDE NERVE TRIAD TRINE ACCORD
STRING TENDON TETRAD CADENCE
CONCORD HARMONY ARPEGGIO
DIAMETER FILAMENT SFORZANDO
(STRIKE A —) RESONATE
(TOUCH A —) RESONATE
CHORDATA VERTEBRA
CHORE JOB JOT CHAR DUTY TASK
CHARE KNACK STINT ERRAND
BUSINESS
CHOREA JUMP JERKS
CHOREOGRAPHY TERPSICHORE
CHORION SEROSA
CHORISTER SINGER CHANTER
CHOIRBOY
CHORTLE TITTER
CHORUS SONG CHOIR DRONE QUIRE
ACCORD ASSENT BURDEN UNISON
CHORALE HOLDING REFRAIN
RESPONSE THYMELICI
(— IN PLAY) GREX
CHOSEN ELECT ELITE SORTED
ELECTED FANCIED AFFECTED
SELECTED
(CAREFULLY —) RECHERCHE
(PREF.) LECTO
CHOUGH COW CHANK CHEWET
CORBIE CHOCARD
CHOWDER BOUILLABAISSE

CHOWRY COWTAIL
CHRISM CREAM CREME MURON
MYRON
CHRIST X KING LORD TRUE JUDGE
RANSOM VERITY MESSIAH SAVIOUR
DRIGHTEN PARAMOUR
(INFANT —) BAMBINO
CHRISTEN DUB NAME KIRSEN
BAPTIZE
CHRISTENING GOSSIPING
CHRISTIAN XN XT XTIAN UNIATE
GENTILE THOMEAN CHRISTEN
EBIONITE GALILEAN MELCHITE
NAZARENE ORIENTAL STONEITE
TRADITOR COLOSSIAN
(— MONOGRAM) IHS
(— VISITOR TO JERUSALEM) HAJI
HADJI HAJII
(EARLY —) COPT
(EASTERN —) UNIAT
(JEWISH —) JUDAIZER
(PL.) FLOCK LAPSED ACEPHALI
FAITHFUL
CHRISTIANIA CRISTY
CHRISTIANITY WAY XTY XNTY
CHRISTMAS NOEL YULE HOLIDAY
NATIVITY YULETIDE MIDWINTER
CHRISTMAS ROSE BEARFOOT
LUNGWORT MELAMPOD PEDELION
CHRISTOPHE COLOMB
(COMPOSER OF —) MILHAUD
CHRIST'S-THORN NABK JUJUBE
ZIZYPHUS
CHROMA COLOR QUALITY
CHROMATIC HUEFUL FLAMING
SEMITONAL
CHROMATOPHORE ALLOPHORE
LIPOPHORE UNIVALENT
RHODOPLAST
CHROMOLITHOGRAPH
OLEOGRAPH
CHROMOSOME DIAD DYAD IDANT
HOMOLOG ALLOSOME AUTOSOME
IDIOSOME MONOSOME
KARYOMERE LEPTONEMA
PLANOSOME
(ENLARGED REGION OF —) PUFF
(PL.) GEMINI
(SUFF.) (HAVING — NUMBER) PLOID
CHROMOSPHERE SIERRA
CHROMOTROPE DYE
CHRONIC FIXED SEVERE INTENSE
CONSTANT STUBBORN
CHRONICLE BRUT ANNAL DIARY
ENACT RECORD ACCOUNT HISTORY
RECITAL CORNICLE REGISTER
(PL.) ANNALS ARCHIVE
PARALIPOMENON
CHRONICLER WRITER CHRONIST
COMPILER RECORDER HISTORIAN
SEANNACHIE
CHRONOLOGICAL TEMPORAL

CHRONOMETER DIAL HACK CLOCK
TIMER WATCH
CHRYSAL FRET
CHRYSALIS KELL PUPA AURELIA
CHRYSANTHEMUM MUM KIKU
OXEYE SPOON BRUTUS POMPON
KIKUMON KIRIMON AZALEAMUM
PYRETHRUM MARGUERITE
CHRYSEIS (FATHER OF —) CHRYSES
CHRYSIN FLAVONE
CHRYSIPPUS (FATHER OF —)
PELOPS
   (MOTHER OF —) ASTYOCHE
   (SLAYER OF —) HIPPODAMIA
CHRYSOBERYL CATEYE
CHRYSOPAL CYMOPHANE
CHRYSOLITE OLIVINE PERIDOT
CHRYSOPAL
CHRYSOTILE ASBESTOS
CHTHONIAN INFERNAL
CHUB DACE DOLT FOOL KIYI LOUT
POLL CHOPA CHEVIN SHINER
CYPRINID FALLFISH MACKEREL
CHAVENDER HORNYHEAD
CHUBBY FAT CHUFF FUBSY PLUMP
PUDGY CHOATY CHUFFY PLUMPY
ROTUND ROLYPOLY
CHUB MACKEREL TINK TINKER
HARDHEAD SCOMBRID
CHUCK HEN LOG PIG CHUG GRUB
HURL JERK LUMP TOSS CHOCK
CLUCK HEAVE PITCH THROW
BOUNCE CHUCKY COLLET CHUCKLE
DISCARD
CHUCK-A-LUCK SWEAT HAZARD
BIRDCAGE
CHUCKER CROZER
CHUCK-FARTHING CHUCK KNICKER
CHUCKHOLE CAHOT CHUGHOLE
CHUCKIE-STANES DIBS
CHUCKLE CHUCK CLUCK EXULT
LAUGH GIGGLE GIZZEN KECKLE
SMUDGE TITTER CHORTLE
CHUCKLEHEAD DIMWIT
CHUD VEPS VEPSE
CHUDDAR PHULKARI
CHUFA SEDGE GLUMAL CYPRESS
EARTHNUT GALANGAL TIGERNUT
GROUNDNUT
CHUM CAD PAL BAIT MATE PARD
TOLE TOLL BUDDY BUTTY CRONY
SPROG AIKANE CHUMMY COBBER
COPAIN FRIEND PARDNER
ROOMMATE
   (— AROUND) HOBNOB
CHUMMY GREAT MATEY PALLY
FAMILIAR
CHUMP ASS DOLT HEAD BLOCK
PUMPKIN ENDPIECE SCHLEMIEL
CHUNCHO CHAMA
CHUNK DAB DAD FID GOB PAT WAD
JUNK JUNT SLUG CHOCK CHUCK

CLAUT PIECE THROW WHANG
WHANK GOBBET DORNICK KNUCKLE
LUNCHEON
CHUNKY LUMPY PLUMP SQUAT
STOUT THICK TRUSS BLOCKY
CHUBBY STOCKY CHUNKED
CHURCH DOM SEE DOME FANE FOLD
HIGH KILL KIRK KURK TERA ABBEY
AUTEM FAITH FLOCK KOVIL SAMAJ
TITLE BETHEL CHAPEL CHARGE
HIERON SPOUSE TEMPLE EDIFICE
FANACLE IGLESIA LATERAN
MEMORIA MINSTER ORATORY
RECTORY STATION TEMPLET
BASILICA EBENEZER ECCLESIA
PECULIAR PROCATHEDRAL
   (— BOOK) TRIODION
   (AREA OF —) APSE BEMA
   (CHRISTIAN —) BODY ISRAEL
HERITAGE
   (EASTERN —) UNIATE
   (KIND OF —) STAVE
   (MEMBER OF UNIFICATION —)
MOONIE
   (PREF.) ECCLESIASTICO ECCLESI(O)
CHURCHMAN ALDER ELDER
DEACON KIRKMAN PRELATE
   (HIGH —) PUSEYITE PRELATIST
   (LOW —) SIM LOWBOY SIMEONITE
CHURCH-OFFICER BEADLE BEDRAL
BEDERAL
CHURCH SERVICE HEARING
TENEBRAE
CHURCHWARDEN PIPE STRAW
WARDEN WARNER
CHURCHYARD HAW LITTEN
CEMETERY KIRKYARD LYNCHGATE
CHURL CAD MAN OAF BOOR CARL
GNOF HIND LOUT SERF CARLE
CEORL CHUFF GNOFF KNAVE MISER
BODACH CARLOT HARLOT LUBBER
RUSTIC VASSAL YEOMAN BONDMAN
FREEMAN HASKARD HUSBAND
NIGGARD PEASANT VILLAIN VILLEIN
CURMUDGEON
CHURLISH MEAN BLUFF GRUFF
ROUGH RUNTY SURLY URSAL
CRADDY RUSTIC SORDID SULLEN
VULGAR BOORISH CARLAGE
CARLISH CRABBED CURRISH
DOGGISH INCIVIL PEEVISH VIOLENT
CHURN BEAT BOIL KIRN MOIL STIR
DRILL SHAKE BUBBLE SEETHE
AGITATE BARATTE TRUNDLE
CHUTE RUSH SLIP TUBE FLUME
HURRY RAPID SHOOT SLIDE HOPPER
TROUGH DECLINE DESCENT
DOWNFALL STAMPEDE TELEGRAPH
   (MINING —) PASS TELEGRAPH
CHUTZPAH CRUST
CHUZA (WIFE OF —) JOANNA
CIBOL SYBO ONION SYBOW SHALLOT

CIBORIUM PIX PYX CANOPY CIVORY
COFFER CIMBORIO
CICADA CAD CIGALE JARFLY LOCUST
TETTIX LYREMAN HOMOPTER
(SOUND OF —) CHIRR
CICATRICE FESTER
CICATRICLE TREAD GALLATURE
CICATRIX EYE MARK SCAB SCAR
SEAM
CICATRIZE FESTER SCARIFY
CICELY MYRRH
CICERO TULLY
CICERONE GUIDE PILOT MENTOR
ORATOR COURIER SIGHTSMAN
CICERONIAN TULLIAN
CICHLID JEWELFISH
CID HERO CAMPEADOR
(AUTHOR OF —) CORNEILLE
(CHARACTER IN —) GOMES DIEGUE
SANCHE CHIMENE FERNAND
URRAQUE RODRIGUE
CID, EL (COMPOSER OF —)
MASSENET
CIDER PERRY PERKIN SWANKY
SYDDIR POMMAGE SCRUMPY
BEVERAGE COCCAGEE
(HARD —) APPLEJACK
(INFERIOR —) SWANKY
CIGAR PURO TOBY WEED BREVA
CLARO SEGAR SHUCK SMOKE
CONCHA CORONA HAVANA MADURA
MADURO MANILA STOGIE TWOFER
BOUQUET CHEROOT CULEBRA
LONDRES REGALIA TRABUCO
COLORADO LOCOFOCO PANATELA
PERFECTO PICKWICK PURITANO
(PART OF —) BAND FOOT HEAD TUCK
FILLER WRAPPER
CIGARETTE CIG FAG BIRI BUTT KING
PILL SKAG CIGGY CUBEB JOINT
SHUCK SMOKE WHIFF CIGGIE
GASPER REEFER CIGARITO
(— BUTT) ROACH
(— SUBSTANCE) TAR
(MARIHUANA —) JOINT STICK
(MARIJUANA —) JAY JOINT SPLIFF
(PART OF —) BAND FOOT PAPER
FILTER
CIGARFISH SCAD QUIAQUIA
CILIATION
(SUFF.) TRICHA TRICHI(A) TRICHOUS
TRICHY
CILIUM HAIR LASH EYELASH
UNCINUS BARBICEL CILIOLUM
(PREF.) BLEPHAR(O)
CILIX (BROTHER OF —) CADMUS
THANUS PHINEUS PHOENIX
(FATHER OF —) AGENOR
(MOTHER OF —) TELEPHASSA
(SISTER OF —) EUROPA
CILLOSIS LIFEBLOOD
CIMBALOM CEMBALON DULCIMER
CIMEX BEDBUG ACANTHIA

CIMON (FATHER OF —) MILTIADES
(MOTHER OF —) HEGESIPYLE
CINCH BELT GIRD PIPE SNAP
GIMME GIRTH GRAVY BREEZE
CINCHA FASTEN WRAPUP PIANOLA
SINECURE
CINCHONA CHINA QUINA
CINCHONA BARK
(PREF.) QUIN(O)
CINCINNATI PORKOPOLIS
CINCTURE BAND BELT GIRD HALO
LIST RING ZONE GIRTH CENTER
CESTUS COLLAR FILLET GIRDLE
BALDRIC COMPASS ENCIRCLE
SURCINGLE
CINDER ASH TAP COAL GRAY SCAR
SLAG CHARK DROSS EMBER
DANDER SCORIA CLINKER FOXTAIL
RESIDUE
(REFUSE —) BREEZE
(VOLCANIC —) LAPILLUS
(PL.) GLEEDS
CINEMA FILMS DRIVEIN THEATER
CINEMATIZE FILMIZE
CINEMATOGRAPH KINO
VERISCOPE VITAGRAPH
CINEPHILE CINEAST
CINERARIA URNS SENECIO
CINGULUM BAND RIDGE GIRDLE
CINNABAR MINIUM
CINNAMON CANEL SPICE CASSIA
SANELA STACTE CANELLA
BARBASCO
(WILD —) BAYBERRY
CINNAMONROOT FLYBANE
FLEAWORT
CINNAMON STONE GARNET
ESSONITE
CINQUEFOIL FRASIER COWBERRY
HARDHACK ROSACEAN QUINTFOIL
SILVERWEED
CINYRAS (DAUGHTER OF —)
MYRRHA
(FATHER OF —) APOLLO
(SON OF —) ADONIS
CION BUD IMP SECT SLIP GRAFT
SCION SHOOT UVULA SARMENT
GRAFTING
CIPHER KEY NIL CODE NULL ZERO
ALBAM AUGHT OUGHT DECODE
DEVICE FIGURE LETTER NAUGHT
NOUGHT NUMBER SYMBOL
ATHBASH NULLITY MONOGRAM
VIGENERE NOTHINGLY
CIRCASSIAN ADIGHE KABARD
CHERKESS KABARDIN
CIRCE SIREN TEMPTER
(BROTHER OF —) AEETES
(FATHER OF —) SOL
(LOVER OF —) ULYSSES ODYSSEUS
(MOTHER OF —) PERSE
(NIECE OF —) MEDEA
(SON OF —) TELEGONUS

CIRCINATE SCORPIOID

CIRCLE DOT LAP ORB RED SET CLUE
CULT DISK GYRE HALO HOOP IRIS
LOOP MARU ORBE RING RINK ROLL
TOUR TURN ZONE BLACK CAROL
CLASS CROWN CYCLE FETCH FRAME
GROUP KREIS MONDE ORBIT PEARL
REALM RHOMB RIGOL ROUND
ROWEL SKIRT SWIRL TWIRL BEZANT
BROUGH CIRCUS CIRQUE CLIQUE
COLLET COLURE CORDON CORONA
DIADEM EQUANT GIRDLE RONDEL
ROTATE RUNDLE SPIRAL SYSTEM
TROPIC AZIMUTH CHUKKAR
CHUKKER CIRCLET CIRCUIT
COMPANY COMPASS CORONET
COTERIE ENCLOSE HORIZON
MONTHON REVOLVE RINGLET
DEFERENT ECLIPTIC FROSTBOW
ROUNDURE SURROUND
(— AROUND ORGAN) ANNULET
(— IN BULL'S-EYE) CARTON
(— OF FRIED DOUGH) POPADUM
(— OF HELL) MALEBOLGE
(— OF MONOLITHS) CROMLECH
(— TRACED BY HORSE) VOLT
(ASTRONOMICAL —) EQUANT
EPICYCLE
(DANCE —) GALLEY
(EIGHTH PART OF —) OCTANT
(FAIRY —) RINGLET
(FULL —) AMBIT
(GREAT —) EQUATOR ECLIPTIC
MERIDIAN
(IMAGINARY —) CYCLE DEFERENT
(INNER —) BOSOM
(MYSTIC —) MANDALA
(PARHELIC —) FROSTBOW
(QUARTER —) ARC
(STONE —) CAROL HURLER
GORSEDD CROMLECH
(TRAVERSE —) RACER
(TWO —S) CACHET
(PREF.) CYCL(O) GYRO

CIRCLET BAND HALO HOOP RING
CROWN RIGOL VERGE BANGLE
CIRQUE CORONA WREATH CIRCUIT
CORONET VALLARY BRACELET
HEADBAND
(PREF.) STEPHAN(O)

CIRCUIT LAP AREA BOUT EYRE ITER
LOOP TOUR WEND ZONE AMBIT
CHAIN CYCLE ORBIT ROUND ROUTE
VIRON AMBAGE BUFFER CIRCLE
DETOUR DOUBLE HOOKUP SPHERE
UMGANG ZODIAC ADAPTER ADDRESS
COMARCA COMPASS COUNTER
DIOCESE ACCEPTER DIPLEXER
DISTRICT PERIPLUS PROGRESS
(BRANCH —) LEG
(COMPUTER —) NOR NAND
(ELECTRIC —) LEG LOOP DOUBLER
SQUELCH SECONDARY

(ELECTRONIC —) GATE
(INTEGRATED —) CHIP MICROCHIP
(JUNCTION —) TRUNK

CIRCUITOUS MAZY CURVED
CROOKED DEVIOUS OBLIQUE
SINUOUS TWISTED VAGRANT
WINDING FLEXUOUS INDIRECT
RAMBLING TORTUOUS AMBAGIOUS
DECEITFUL DEVIATING WANDERING
ROUNDABOUT
(— METHOD) WINDLASS

CIRCUITOUSLY ROUND

CIRCULAR O BILL FLIER FLYER
LIBEL ORBAL ORBED ROUND
DODGER FOLDER RINGED WHEELY
ANNULAR COMPASS CYCLOID
DISCOID DISLIKE HANDOUT PERFECT
RUNDLED COMPLETE DOPEBOOK
ENCYCLIC GLOBULAR INFINITE
NUMMULAR PAMPHLET DOPESHEET
ORBICULAR

CIRCULAR-KNIT SEAMLESS

CIRCULATE GO AIR MIX MOVE PASS
RISE TURN WALK WIND BANDY
TROLL CANARD PURVEY ROTATE
SCURRY SPHERE SPREAD WANDER
CANVASS CONVECT DIFFUSE
PUBLISH CONVOLVE

CIRCULATING WAIF AFLOAT
AMBIENT CURRENT

CIRCULATION ISSUE COURSE
COVERAGE CURRENCY

CIRCUMCISER MOHEL

CIRCUMCISION BRITH PERITOMY

CIRCUMFERENCE ARC AUGE
AMBIT APSIS GIRTH VERGE BORDER
BOUNDS CIRCLE LIMITS COMPASS
BOUNDARY SURROUND
(— OF SHELL) LIMBUS

CIRCUMFERENTOR PLANCHETTE

CIRCUMFLEX DOGHOUSE
(INVERTED —) HACEK

CIRCUMLOCUTION AMBAGE
CIRCUIT WINDING VERBIAGE

CIRCUMLOCUTORY WORDY

CIRCUMNAVIGATION PERIPLUS

CIRCUMSCRIBE BOUND FENCE
LIMIT DEFINE CAPTURE CONFINE
ENCLOSE ENVIRON ENCIRCLE
RESTRAIN RESTRICT SURROUND
CONSCRIBE

CIRCUMSCRIBED NARROW
INSULAR LIMITED
(PREF.) CIRCUM

CIRCUMSPECT SHY WARY WISE
ALERT CHARY CAREFUL GUARDED
PRUDENT CAUTIOUS DISCREET
VIGILANT WATCHFUL

CIRCUMSPECTION RESPECT
PRUDENCE WARINESS

CIRCUMSTANCE GO FIX CASE FACT
ITEM NOTE EVENT PHASE POINT
START STATE THING AFFAIR DETAIL

FACTOR PICKLE CALLING ELEMENT
EPISODE INCIDENT INSTANCE
POSITION OCCURRENCE PARTICULAR
(BAFFLING —) WARK
(CRITICAL —S) EXTREMES
(DIFFICULT —) WANTS
(EXECRABLE —) ATROCITY
(LUDICROUS —) JEST
(PL.) CIRCS STATE TERMS ESTATE
FORTUNE
CIRCUMSTANCED OFF
CIRCUMSTANTIAL EXACT FORMAL
MINUTE PRECISE DETAILED ITEMIZED
PARTICULAR
CIRCUMSTANTIATE SUPPORT
EVIDENCE
CIRCUMVENT BALK BEAT DISH
DUPE FOIL CHEAT CHECK COZEN
EVADE OUTGO TRICK BAFFLE
DELUDE ENTRAP NOBBLE OUTWIT
THWART CAPTURE DECEIVE
DEFRAUD ENSNARE PREVENT
OUTFLANK SURROUND
UNDERFONG
CIRCUS RING SHOW ARENA CANVAS
CIRCLE CIRQUE CARNIVAL
(— LOT) TOBER
(— RING) TAN
CIRQUE CWM CIRC BASIN CIRCLE
CIRCUS CORRIE RECESS CIRCLET
EROSION
CIS SYN NERAL NORMAL
CISCO KIYI BLOAT BLOATER BLUEFIN
LONGJAW MOONEYE BLACKFIN
GRAYBACK TULLIBEE WHITEFIN
CISKEI (CAPITAL OF —) BISHO
(TOWN OF —) ALICE ZWELITSHA
CISSA SIRGANG
CISSEUS (BROTHER OF —) GYAS
(COMPANION OF —) HERCULES
(FATHER OF —) MELAMPUS
(SLAYER OF —) AENEAS
CISSUS TREEBINE
CIST BOX KIST TOMB CHEST CISTA
QUOIT CASKET CHAMBER KISTVAEN
CISTERCIAN TRAPPIST
CISTERN BAC FAT SAC TUB URN VAT
BACK PANT SUMP TANK URNA WELL
LAVER CAVITY CAISSON CHULTUN
CUVETTE STEEPER FEEDHEAD
CITADEL ARX FORT HALL ALAMO
BURSA BYRSA TOWER CASTLE
BOROUGH CHESTER KREMLIN
ALHAMBRA FASTNESS FORTRESS
TOOTHILL ACROPOLIS
CITATION CITAL NOTICE MENTION
SUMMONS EPIGRAPH MONITION
AUTHORITY EVOCATION
CITE CALL NAME SIST TELL ALLAY
EVOKE QUOTE REFER ACCITE
ACCUSE ADDUCE ALLEGE AROUSE
AVOUCH EXCITE INVOKE NOTIFY
RECITE REPEAT SUMMON ADVANCE

ARRAIGN BESPEAK CONVENT
EXCERPT EXTRACT IMPEACH
MENTION INDICATE INSTANCE
REHEARSE
CITHARA CITHER CITOLE PHORMINX
CITHERN ZITTERN LANGSPEL
CITIZEN CIT ALLY VOTER NATIVE
BURGESS BURGHER CITOYEN
CLERUCH DENIZEN ELECTOR
FLATCAP FREEMAN OPPIDAN
SUBJECT TOWNMAN AMERICAN
CIVILIAN COMMONER CONSCIVE
DOMESTIC NATIONAL OCCUPANT
RESIDENT
(— OF SECOND CLASS) KNIGHT
HIPPEUS
(—S OF MEDINA) ANSAR
(FOREIGN-BORN —) ALIEN
(LATIN — OF U.S.) YANQUI
(PL.) SUBJECT PERIOECI CITIZENRY
(SUFF.) ITE
CITIZENRY COUNTRY SUBJECT
CITRAL GERANIAL
CITRON LIME CEDRA LEMON CEDRAT
ETHROG YELLOW BERGAMOT
CITTERN LAUD CITHERN PENORCON
CITY FU WON BURG DORP TOWN
URBS WOON ZION BURGH CALNO
EKRON JEBUS LILLE MANOA PIECE
PLACE POLIS SETTE STEAD VILLE
CALNEH CENTER CIUDAD CUTHAH
GILEAD JAMNIA JEBUSI LAGADO
NAGARA PITHOM STAPLE BABYLON
CAMBALU CHESTER ELLASAR
FREEDOM JABNEEL MECHLIN
CABECERA ELDORADO MAGAZINE
PALENQUE
(— LIFE) ASHCAN
(— OF GOD) SION ZION
(ANCIENT —) PERGAMUM
(CAPITAL —) SEAT
(CATHEDRAL —) SEE
(CHIEF —) CAPITAL CABECERA
MEGAPOLIS
(RICH —) MAGAZINE
(TREASURE —) RAAMSES
(WICKED —) BABYLON
(PREF.) URBI
(SUFF.) GRAD POLE POLIS POLITAN
POLITE
CITY-STATE POLIS CIVITAS
CIVET CAT CIT GENET RASSE ZIBET
BONDAR FOUSSA MUSANG PAGUMA
ZIBETH CIVETTA FOSSANE LINSANG
NANDINE POLECAT ZIBETUM
ZINSANG FANALOKA MONGOOSE
TANGALUNG
CIVIC LAY CIVIL SUAVE URBAN POLITE
URBANE CIVICAL SECULAR
CIVIL FAIR HEND HENDE SUAVE
POLITE URBANE AFFABLE AMIABLE
COURTLY ELEGANT GALLANT
POLITIC REFINED SECULAR DISCREET

GRACIOUS OBLIGING POLISHED
WELLBRED

CIVILIAN CIT CIVIE CIVIL CIVVY PEKIN
MOHAIR CITIZEN TEACHER CIVILIST
GOWNSMAN OUTSIDER
NONCOMBATANT
(— ENTERTAINING SOLDIER) PYKE

CIVILITY BONTE COURT COMITY
NOTICE AMENITY COURTESY
URBANITY GENTILITY
(PL.) HONORS HONOURS

CIVILIZATION ISLAM KULTUR
POLICE CULTURE ECUMENE CIVILITY
(GREEK —) HELLENISM

CIVILIZE TAME TEACH TRAIN POLISH
REFINE EDUCATE HUMANIZE
URBANIZE

CIVILIZED CHRISTIAN

CIVVIES MUFTI

CLABBER LOP MUD MIRE CURDLE
LOPPER CLAUBER

CLACKDISH CLICKET

CLAD DREST ROBED BESEEN CLEDDE
DECKED ADORNED ARRAYED
ATTIRED CLOTHED COVERED
DRESSED SHEATHED
(— IN PURPLE) PORPORATE
(SCANTILY —) SINGLY

CLADOSE RAMOSE CLADINE
BRANCHED

CLAIM ASK DUE AVER AVOW CALL
CASE DIBS LIEN MINE NAME PLEA
COLOR DRAFT EXACT PLEAD RIGHT
SHOUT TITLE ALLEGE ASSERT
DEMAND DECINE ELICIT EQUITY
INTEND RECKON ACCLAIM COLLECT
DERECHO DRAUGHT PRETEND
PRETEXT PROFESS RECLAIM
REQUIRE SOLICIT ARROGATE
DARRAIGN INTEREST MAINTAIN
PRETENCE PRETENSE PROCLAIM
SUBCLAIM CHALLENGE POSTULATE
PRETENSION PRESCRIPTION
(— IN BUSINESS) CAPITAL
(— IN LEASE) REDDENDO
REDDENDUM
(TO BE BELIEVED) AUTHORITY
(FALSE —) JACTATION
(FORESTER'S —) PUTURE
(INDIAN LEGAL —) HAK HAKH
(JUST —) RIGHT
(MINING —) SHICER

CLAIMANT CLAIMER USURPER
PRETENDER

CLAIRE PARK

CLAIRVOYANCE ESP INSIGHT
VOYANCE LUCIDITY SAGACITY
TELOPSIS PRECOGNITION

CLAIRVOYANT FEY SEER OMENER
PROPHET SEERESS

CLAM MYA BASE CLOG DAUB GLAM
HUSH MEAN BLUNT CLAMP CRASH
GAPER GLAUM GRASP GROPE

PAHUA RAZOR SHELL SMEAR SOLEN
SPOUT STICK VENUS ADHERE
CLUTCH GWEDUC QUAHOG STICKY
BIVALVE CLANGOR COQUINA
MOLLUSK STEAMER ADHESIVE
ARROGATE BULLNOSE SHIPWORM
NANNINOSE
(KIND OF —) RAZOR
(PART OF —) BEAK FOOT SHELL
VALVE MANTLE SIPHON UMBONE
ORIFICE

CLAMBAKE BAKE RALLY CLAMAROO
SQUANTUM

CLAMBER CLIMB SCALE CLAVER
SCRAWM SPRAWL RAMMACK
SCRABBLE SCRAMBLE SPRACHLE
STRUGGLE

CLAMMY DAMP DANK SOFT WACK
MOIST SAMMY STICKY WAUGHY
FLACCID SQUIDGY CLAMMISH

CLAMOR CRY DIN HUE BARK BERE
BUNK GAFF RANE RERD ROAR ROUP
ROUT SONG UTAS WAIL BLARE
BOAST BRUIT CHIDE CHIRM NOISE
OUTAS RERDE RUMOR SHOUT
BELLOW BOWWOW HUBBUB
OUTCRY QUETHE RACKET TUMULT
UPROAR YATTER CLAMOUR EXCLAIM
ORATION STASHIE NORATION
PILILLOO PULLALUE SHOUTING
(— AGAINST) DECRY

CLAMOROUS NIP LOUD AROAR
NOISY VOCAL BLATANT CLAMANT
DINSOME YELLING BRAWLING
DECRYING OPENMOUTHED
OBSTREPEROUS

CLAMP DOG HOG LUG NIP PIN SET
BAIL BALE BEND BOLT BURY CLAM
GLAM GRIP JACK MUTE NAIL VISE
YOKE BLOCK BRACE CLASP CRAMP
GLAND GLAUM HORSE CLINCH
FASTEN MOPHEAD STIRRUP
FASTENER HOLDFAST
(— FOR BASS DRUM) SPUR
(— FOR CORK) AGRAFE AGRAFFE
(— FOR FLASK) GLAND
(— ON TUBE) PINCHCOCK
(STORAGE —) GRAVE

CLAMSHELL CLAM GRAB SHUCK

CLAN ATI HAN KIN SET SIB CULT
GENS HAPU NAME RACE SECT SEPT
SIOL UNIT AIMAK AYLLU CLASS
GENOS GROUP HORDE PARTY TRIBE
ABUSUA CLIQUE FAMILY SENAAH
ABIEZER KINDRED PHRATRY
SATSUMA SOCIETY ZADRUGA
CALPULLI DIVISION
(— SUBDIVISION) OBE

CLANDESTINE BYE SLY FOXY
HEDGE PRIVY QUIET SNEAK COVERT
HIDDEN SECRET BOOTLEG FURTIVE
ILLICIT BACKDOOR HIDLINGS
STEALTHY

CLANG DIN DING PEAL RING TONK CLANK CLASH NOISE JANGLE TIMBRE

CLANGER STUMER

CLANGING JANGLE

CLANGOR DIN CLAM ROAR CLANG HUBBUB UPROAR

CLANGOROUS BRAZEN PLANGENT

CLANGULA HARELDA

CLANK RING RACKLE

CLAP BANG CHOP FLAP PEAL SLAP SPAT TACK CHEER CLINK CRACK SMITE POSTER STRIKE STROKE APPLAUD CHATTER CLAPPER PLAUDIT HANDCLAP
(— OF THUNDER) DINT
(— ON) CRACK

CLAPBOARD KNAPPLE CLAPHOLT

CLAPNET DAYNET

CLAPPER CLAP CLACK RATTLE TONGUE JINGLET KNACKER KNOCKER CROTALUM
(— OF BELL) TONGUE
(PL.) BONES

CLAPPING APPLAUSE

CLAPTRAP HOKUM TRASH TRIPE BLAGUE BUNKUM DEVICE EYEWASH FUSTIAN BUNCOMBE NONSENSE TRICKERY

CLARE MINORESS

CLARENCE GROWLER

CLARET TERSE PONTAC LAFITTE BORDEAUX BADMINTON

CLARIAS HARMOOT KARMOUTH

CLARIBEL (HUSBAND OF —) PHAON

CLARICE (BROTHER OF —) HUON
(HUSBAND OF —) RINALDO

CLARIFIED PURED LAUTER

CLARIFY CLAY FINE CLEAN CLEAR PURGE SNUFF PURIFY REFINE RENDER SERENE SETTLE CLEANSE DESPUME EXPLAIN GLORIFY DEFECATE DEPURATE ELIQUATE SIMPLIFY

CLARIN ACOCOTL

CLARINET BEN BIN BON BEEN BONE REED AULOS CLARY PUNGI CLARONE LAUNEDDAS
(PART OF —) KEY PAD BELL CORK REED CLAMP COVER BARREL LIGATURE MOUTHPIECE FINGERPLATE

CLARION REST CLARE CLARY CLEAR CLARINO SUFFLUE TRUMPET

CLARISSA HARLOWE
(AUTHOR OF —) RICHARDSON
(CHARACTER IN —) HOWE JOHN JAMES MORDEN ROBERT SOLMES BELFORD HARLOWE WILLIAM ARABELLA CLARISSA LOVELACE SINCLAIR

CLARITY GLORY SPLENDOR STRENGTH CLEARNESS SIMPLICITY

CLARY ORVAL CLARRE SALVIA

CLASH JAR BANG BOLT BUMP DASH FRAY NEWS SLAM BRAWL BRUNT CHECK CRASH CROSS FIGHT FRUSH KNOCK OCCUR PRATE SHOCK AFFRAY DIFFER GOSSIP HURTLE IMPACT JOSTLE STRIFE STRIKE TATTLE THRUST THWART COLLIDE DISCORD SCANDAL ARGUMENT CONFLICT
(— OF WORDS) BARGE

CLASHING HARSH CONFLICT FRICTION COLLISION

CLASP HUG PIN CLIP DOME FOLD GRAB GRIP HASP HOLD HOOK HOOP KEEP OUCH STAY TACH BRACE CATCH CLING GRASP MORSE PREEN SEIZE SLIDE SPANG TACHE ACCOLL AGRAFE AMPLEX BECLIP BROOCH BUCKLE CLENCH CLUTCH ENFOLD ENWRAP FASTEN FIBULA GIMMER GIMMOR INCLIP INFOLD JIMMER STRAIN TASSEL AGRAFFE AMPLECT EMBRACE ENTWINE FERMAIL HOLDING MOUSING TENDRIL BARRETTE CORSELET FASTENER SURROUND
(— HANDS) SHAKE WRING

CLASPING AMPLECTANT

CLASS ILK BRAN CHOP FORM KIND RACE RANK RATE SECT SORT SUIT TYPE YEAR BREED CASTE GENRE GENUS GRADE GROUP ORDER RANGE TRIBE VARNA VERGE ASSORT CIRCLE CLINIC DECURY FAMILY GENDER LEAGUE MISTER NATION PHYLUM RATING RECKON REMOVE RUBRIC STRAIN STRIPE CATALOG FACTION LECTURE REGIMEN SEMINAR SPECIES VARIETY CATEGORY DESCRIBE DIVISION GENOTYPE GEOMOROI
(— OF BARDS) THULIR
(— OF GOODS) BRAND
(— OF OUTCASTS) ETA
(— OF PEOPLE) FOLK SALARIAT
(— OF SECURITIES) LEGAL
(— OF SHASTRAS) SRUTI SHRUTI
(— OF SLAVES) HELOTRY
(— OF SOUNDS) ENDING
(— OF TEASELS) KINGS
(ARISTOCRATIC —) ARISTOI
(CHOICEST —) ROBUR
(DEPRESSED —) PANCHAMA
(FIRST —) GAY
(HEREDITARY —) CASTE
(INTERMEDIATE —) SHELL REMOVE
(JAPANESE —) HEIMIN KWAZOKU
(LABORING —) PARAIYAN PROLETARIAT
(LEARNED —) VATES CLERISY

(LOWER —) BELOW GENTE
(LOWER —S) MASSES
(LOWEST —) LAG SCUM
(MIDDLE —) BOURGERIS
   BOURGEOISIE
(PEASANT —) JACQUERIE
(PRIVILEGED —) ARISTOCRACY
(SLAVEHOLDING —) CHIVALRY
(SOCIAL —) ESTATE SHIZOKU
(WAGE EARNINNG —) PROLETARIAT
(WEALTHY —) PLUTOCRACY
(WITH —) INTASTE
(WORKING —) TOIL
(PREF.) CRATO
(SUFF.) CY OIDA OIDEA OIDEI

CLASSIC VINTAGE AUGUSTAN
   TEXTBOOK

CLASSICAL PURE ATTIC GREEK
   LATIN ROMAN CHASTE CLASSIC
   ACADEMIC HELLENIC MASTERLY
   (NOT —) BASE

CLASSICALLY IDEALLY

CLASSIFICATION FILE RANK RATE
   SORT CODEN GENRE GENUS GRADE
   ORDER TAXIS RATING SYSTEM
   ANALYSIS CATEGORY DIVISION
   TAXONOMY BREAKDOWN

CLASSIFIED SECRET

CLASSIFIER COUNTER SEPARATOR

CLASSIFY CODE LIST RANK RATE
   SIZE SORT SUIT TAPE TYPE BREAK
   CLASS DRAFT GRADE GROUP LABEL
   RANGE TRIBE ASSORT CODIFY
   DIGEST DIVIDE IMPOST TICKET
   ACCOUNT ARRANGE BRACKET
   BRIGADE CATALOG DISPOSE
   DRAUGHT GRAMMAR MARSHAL
   SUBSUME REGISTER PIGEONHOLE
   (— TOGETHER) SLUMP

CLASSIS CONFERENCE

CLASSY TONY SMOOTH

CLATHRATE LATTICED

CLATTER DIN JAR CLACK NOISE
   RUMOR BABBLE GABBLE GOSSIP
   HOTTER HURTLE RACKLE RATTLE
   TATTLE BLATTER CHATTER CLUNTER
   CLUTTER PRATTLE REESHLE
   SHATTER SLAMBANG

CLATTERING CLATTERY SLITHERING

CLAUSE ITEM PART CLOSE COMMA
   JOKER PLANK RIDER SALVO TROPE
   MEMBER PHRASE ADJUNCT ARTICLE
   COMMATA PASSAGE PROVISO
   SLEEPER APODOSIS CLAUSULA
   PARTICLE PETITION REDDENDO
   SENTENCE TENENDAS TENENDUM
   NOVODAMUS
   (— IN CREED) FILIOQUE
   (— IN WRIT) TESTE
   (— OF DEED) TESTATUM
   (— OF WILL) DEVISE
   (ADDED —) RIDER
   (ADDITIONAL —) RIDER

(CONDITIONAL —) PROTASIS
(SAAVING —) SALVO
(SUBORDINATE —) PROTASIS

CLAVACIN PATULIN

CLAVER PRATE CLOVER GOSSIP
   CHATTER CLABBER CLAIVER
   CLAMBER

CLAVICHORD CLAVIER MANICORD
   UNICHORD CLARIGOLD
   MONOCHORD

CLAVICLE FURCULE COLLARBONE

CLAVICOR HORN

CLAVIER MANUAL KLAVIER

CLAVUS CORN BUNION HELOMA

CLAW DIG PEG CLEE CRAB FANG
   FAWN HAND HOOK NAIL PULL SERE
   TEAR UNCE CHELA CLAUT CLOOF
   CLUFE COURT GRASP GRIFF ONGLE
   SCLAW SEIZE TALON UNCUS
   CLUNCH CLUTCH CRATCH NIPPER
   POUNCE SCRAPE SINGLE UNGUAL
   UNGUIS UNGULA WEAPON
   CRUBEEN FALCULA FLATTER
   SCRATCH SHUTTLE WHEEDLE
   SCRABBLE
   (HAWK'S —) POUNCE
   (LOBSTER —) CHELA
   (PL.) CLUTCH
   (PREF.) CHEL(I)(O) ONYCH(O) UNGUI
   (SUFF.) ONYCHA ONYCHES ONYCHIA
   ONYCHUS ONYX

CLAY BAT COB PUG WAD WAX BASS
   BEND BODY BOLE BOTT GALT GLEY
   LOAM LUTE MARL MIRE PAPA SMIT
   TILL ARGIL BRICK CLOAM EARTH
   GAULT LOESS OCHRE PASTE RABAT
   TASCO BINDER CLEDGE CLUNCH
   KAOLIN PUDDLE SAGGER DAUBING
   MOULDER RASHING CAMSTANE
   CAMSTONE CIMOLITE FIRECLAY
   GUMBOTIL LATERITE LIFELESS
   SINOPITE SMECTITE
   (— FOR MELTING POTS) TASCO
   (— IN GLASS) TEAR
   (— IRON) BULL
   (— LAYER) VARVE
   (— USED MEDICALLY) FANGO
   (COVERED WITH —) LUTOSE
   (HARD —) BEND
   (HARDENED —) METAL
   (INDURATED —) BASS CLUNCH
   (PIECE OF FIRED —) TILE
   (PIPE —) CAMSTANE CAMSTONE
   (POTTER'S —) SLIP ARGIL PETUNTSE
   (REMOVE —) UNLUTE
   (SURPLUS —) SPARE
   (TOUGH —) LECK
   (3-ARMED, HARD-FIRED —) STILT
   (PREF.) ARGILI(O) ARGILLACEO
   PEL(O)

CLAYEY BOLAR HEAVY MALMY
   MARLY CLEDGY LUTOSE ARGILLIC

CLAYMORE FERRARA MORGLAY

CLAY PIGEON BIRD CLAY
CLAYSTONE LECK
CLAYWARE GLOST
CLEADING CLOTHING
CLEAN DO FAY FEY HOE MOP NET
DRUM DUST FAIR NEAT PURE REDD
RIPE SIDE SMUG SWAB TRIM WASH
WIPE CLEAR CURRY EMPTY FEIGH
GRAVE SCOUR SCRUB SMART
SWEEP TERSE TOSHY BARREL
CHASTE CLEVER KOSHER PURIFY
SPANDY APINOID BANDBOX
CHAMOIS CLEANLY CLEANSE
CLEARLY FURBISH PERFECT
SWINGLE ABSTERGE BACKWASH
BRIGHTLY DEXTROUS ENTIRELY
RENOVATE SCAVENGE SPOTLESS
UNSOILED
(— A FUR) DRUM
(— A PIPE) REAM
(— A QUILL) DUTCH
(— BOAT) CAREEN
(— BY SCRAPING) GRAVE
(— BY SMOKE) SMEEK
(— CANNON) SCALE
(— FEATHERS) PREEN
(— FIREARM) WORM
(— FLAX) SWINGLE
(— IN ACID) BLANCH
(— OUT) USH SPEAR
(— SHIP'S BOTTOM) HOG BREAM
GRAVE
(— UP) DISPATCH
(— WITH VACUUM) HOOVER
(COME —) FESSUP
(RITUALLY —) KOSHER
CLEAN-CUT CRISP
CLEANED BRIGHT
CLEANER SOAP BORAX PURER
FOLDER GUMMER RAMROD
FLUEMAN SPOTTER CLEANSER
(AIR —) CAN
(GRAIN —) KICKER
(STREET —) ORDERLY
CLEAN-LIMBED CLEVER
CLEAN-LINED SPRUCE
CLEANLY PURE CLEAN ADROIT
ARTFUL CHASTE FAIRLY SPANDY
CORRECT ELEGANT INNOCENT
SKILLFUL
CLEANNESS PURITY
CLEANSE FAY BRAN CARD COMB
FARM HEAL PICK SOAP WASH
BROOM BRUSH CLEAN CLEAR DIGHT
DRESS FEIGH FLAME FLUSH PURGE
RINSE SCOUR SCRUB SNUFF
BOTTOM CAREEN EMUNGE PICKLE
PURIFY REFINE SPONGE WILLOW
BAPTIZE CLARIFY DEBRIDE DETERGE
EXPIATE LAUNDER MUNDIFY
SWEETEN ABSTERGE DEPURATE
OFFSCOUR RENOVATE SCAVENGE
SPRINKLE

CLEANSER LYE SOAP CLEANER
PURIFIER DETERGENT DETERSIVE
CLEANSING BATH FLUSH ABLUENT
CLYSMIC WASHING ABLUTION
CLEANING LAVATION DETERGENT
MENDATORY PURGATORY
ABSTERGENT
(CEREMONIAL —) LAVABO
PURGATION
CLEANTE (FATHER OF —) HARPAGON
(LOVER OF —) ANGELIQUE
(SISTER OF —) ELMIRE
CLEANTHE (BROTHER OF —) SIPHAX
CLEANTHIS (HUSBAND OF —)
SOSIA
CLEANUP KILLING SWEEPUP
CLEAR HOT JAM NET PEN RID WAY
CAST EASY FAIR FINE FLAT FREE
GAIN GRUB JAIL JUMP NEAT OPEN
OVER PURE PUTE QUIT REDD RIFE
SHUT SLAM VOID ACUTE ATRIP
AZURE BREAK BREME BRENT BROAD
CHUCK CLEAN CRISP DRIVE LIGHT
LUCID RANGE PLAIN PRINT PRUNE
SCOUR SHARP SMOLT SUNNY SUTEL
SWEEP UNTIE VIVID ACQUIT AERIAL
ASSOIL BRIGHT CANDID CLEVER
EXCUSE EXEMPT FLUTED LAUTER
LIMPID LIQUID LUCENT PATENT
PURIFY REMBLE SERENE SETTLE
SHRILL SMOOTH UNSTOP ABSOLVE
CAPITAL CLARIFY CLARION CRYSTAL
DELIVER DILUCID EVIDENT EXPLAIN
EXPRESS GLARING GRAPHIC
LIGHTEN OBVIOUS PERVIAL RELEASE
SILVERY THROUGH ACCREDIT
APPARENT BRIGHTEN BULLDOZE
DEFINITE DISTINCT EXPLICIT
LUCULENT LUMINOUS MANIFEST
PELLUCID REVELANT PERSPICUOUS
(— AWAY) FAY FEY FEIGH BANISH
DISPEL DISCUSS
(— FROM) ALOOF
(— FROM CRITICISM) VINDICATE
(— IN TONE) SILVER
(— LAND) CURE BRUSH SLASH
DEADEN BUSHHOG
(— OF BLAME) QUIT
(— OFF) QUIT
(— OF FINE HAIR) SLATE
(— OF GROUND) ATRIP AWEIGH
(— OF GUILT) PURGE
(— OF MUD) SLUTCH
(— OF SCUM) SKIM
(— OF SEEDS) GIN RIPPLE
(— OF TUFTS) HOB
(— OUT) BLOW HOOK SWAMP
SKIDDOO HIGHTAIL DISCHARGE
(— PATH) FRAY HACK BUSHWACK
(— TABLE) DISSERVE
(— TABLES) BUS
(— THROAT) HOICK HOUGH
HARRUMPH

(— UP) SOLVE ASSOIL RESOLVE DISSOLVE UNSHADOW

(ALL —) COPACETIC COPESETTIC

(NOT —) DULL DUSKY FOGGY INEVIDENT

CLEARANCE CHOP ROOM RUNBY BACKLASH ALLOWANCE

(— FOR SHIP) PRATIQUE

CLEAR-CUT LUCID SHARP DIRECT CONCISE DECIDED CHISELED DEFINITE DISTINCT INCISIVE TRENCHANT

CLEARED (— FOR ACTION) PREDY

CLEARHEADED LUCID

CLEARING SART FIELD FRITH GLADE SHADE TRACT ALCOVE ASSART RIDING RIDDING SLASHING

(FOREST —) SLASH SLASHING

CLEARLY FAIR CLEAR LIGHT REDLY FAIRLY FRANKLY PATENTLY WITTERLY

CLEAR-MINDEDNESS LUCIDITY

CLEARNESS CLARITY FINESSE EVIDENCE FINENESS

CLEAR-SIGHTED SEEING

CLEARWEED RICHWEED

CLEAT BITT STUD BLOCK CHOCK KEVEL LEDGE RANGE WEDGE BATTEN RIFFLE BOLLARD COXCOMB GROUSER SIRMARK SUPPORT SURMARK

CLEAVAGE RIFT CLEFT WASSIE FISSION FISSURE WEDGING DIVISION SCISSION

(PREF.) SCHISTO SCHIZ(O)

(SUFF.) CLASE SCHISIS SCHIST

CLEAVE CUT RIP CHOP HANG HOLD JOIN LINK PART RELY REND RIFT RIVE SLIT TEAR BREAK CARVE CHAWN CHINE CLAVE CLEFT CLING CLOVE CRACK KNIFE SEVER SHALE SHARE SHEAR SLIVE SPLAT STICK ADHERE BISECT COHERE DIVIDE FURROW PIERCE SLEAVE SUNDER DISPART FISSURE SEPARATE

(— OFF) AXE SCIND

CLEAVER CLIVE CLEAVE FROWER PARANG CHOPPER HATCHET PARANGI

CLEAVERS GRIP CLOTE CLOTS CLITHE HAIRIF HAIRUP BURHEAD LOVEMAN PIGTAIL BIRDLIME

CLEAVING DYSTOME FISSION DYSTOMIC

(— READILY) EUTOMOUS

CLECHE URDE URDY URDEE

CLEF KEY CLIVE CHIAVETTA

CLEFT CUT GAP JAG CHAP CHOP FENT FLAW GASH NOCK REFT RIFT RILL RIMA RIVE SLIT BIFID BREAK CHASM CHAWN CHINK CLOFF CLOVE CRACK CREEK CRENA GULCH KLOOF RILLE RIVEN SINUS SPLIT BREACH

CHAPPY CLEAVE CLOUGH CLOVEN CRANNY CROTCH DIVIDE LISSOM PARTED RECESS RICTUS STIGMA BLASTED CHIMNEY CREVICE DIVIDED FISSURE OPENING SLIFTER APERTURE CREVASSE FRACTURE INCISION INCISURA MULTIFID SCISSURA SCISSURE PALMATIFID

(— BETWEEN HILLS) SLACK RAVINE

(— IN HOOF) SEAM

(— IN ROCK) RIVA

(— IN THE POSTERIORS) NOCK

(— OF BUTTOCKS) CREASE

(PREF.) FISSI SCHISTO SCHIZ(O)

(SUFF.) FID FIDATE

CLEMATIS PIPESTEM CURLYHEAD

CLEMENCY ORE PITY GRACE MERCY LENITY QUARTER KINDNESS LENIENCY MILDNESS

CLEMENT MILD SOFT WARM GENTLE LENIENT MERCIFUL

CLEMENZA DI TITO (CHARACTER IN —) TITUS ANNIUS SEXTUS BERENICE SERVILIA VITELLIA

(COMPOSER OF —) MOZART

CLENCH FIST GRIP GRIT HOLD NAIL BRACE CLASP CLENK CLINT CLOSE GRASP CLINCH CLUTCH DOUBLE

(— FIST) GRIPE

CLEONTE (LOVER OF —) LUCILLE

CLEOPATRA (BROTHER OF —) ILUS ZETES CALAIS GANYMEDE ASSARACUS

(FATHER OF —) IDAS TROS BOREAS PTOLEMY

(HUSBAND OF —) PHILIP PHINEUS PTOLEMY MELEAGER

(MOTHER OF —) MARPESSA ORITHYIA CALLIRRHOE

CLEPE CLUPIEN

CLEPSYDRA GURRY GHURRY

CLERGY CLOTH CRAPE CHURCH CLERISY MINISTRY

(BODY OF —) PULPIT

CLERGYMAN ABBA ABBE DEAN PAPA CANON CLERK FROCK PADRE PILOT PRIOR RABBI VICAR BISHOP CLERIC CURATE DEACON DIVINE DOMINE PAROCH PARSON PASTOR PRIEST RECTOR SUPPLY CASSOCK PRELATE CARDINAL CHAPLAIN CLERICAL DIOCESAN EMERITUS LECTURER MINISTER ORDINARY PREACHER REVEREND SQUARSON PRESBYTER PREBENDARY REVIVALIST

CLERIC ABBE CURE CLERK FROCK DEACON GALLAH LEVITE PRIEST ACOLYTE GOLIARD ANAGNOST

(DISREPUTABLE —) GOLIARD

CLERICAL BLACK CLERIC CLERKISH PARSONIC PARSONLY

(NOT —) LAIC

CLERIMOND (BROTHER OF —)
FERRAGUS
(HUSBAND OF —) VALENTINE
CLERIMONT (LOVER OF —)
CLARINDA
CLERK NUN BABU MONK AGENT
AWARD BABOO CLARK FILER RALPH
WRITE BILLER CHASER CLERIC
COMMIS GRADER HERMIT KITMAN
LAYMAN MAPPER MASTER MUNSHI
PANDIT PENMAN PRIEST PUNDIT
RALPHO SCRIBE SIRCAR TELLER
WRITER YEOMAN ACOLYTE
ACTUARY BOOKMAN CARCOON
COMPOSE DOPSTER GOMASTA
PIARIST SCHOLAR SHIPPER
SHOPMAN STUFFER CLERGEON
CLERGION CLERKESS CURSITOR
EMPLOYEE GREFFIER MUTSUDDY
PENCLERK RECORDER SALESMAN
(— OF ST PAUL) BARNABITE
(CHIEF —) PROTHONOTARY
(HOTEL —) DESKMAN
CLERKLY LEARNED SCRIBAL
CLERGIAL SCHOLARLY
CLEVE BRAE CLIFF CLEEVE HILLSIDE
CLEVER APT SLY ABLE CUTE DEFT
FEAT FELL FINE FOXY GLEG GNIB
GOOD HEND KEEN NEAT SLIM SPRY
AGILE ALERT CANNY CLEAN CLEAR
CUNNY FALSE FEATY FENDY HANDY
HEADY HENDE LITHE QUICK SHARP
SLICK SMART SNACK WITTY ACTIVE
ADROIT ARTFUL ASTUTE BRIGHT
CRAFTY EXPERT HABILE HEPPEN
KITTLE KNACKY NEATLY NIMBLE
PRETTY SHREWD SPIFFY STALKY
SUBTLE AMIABLE CUNNING
GNOSTIC PARLISH PARLOUS
VARMENT VARMINT DEXTROUS
HANDSOME OBLIGING SKILLFUL
TALENTED
CLEVERLY SLICK FEATLY TIDELY
SMARTLY ASTUTELY
CLEVERNESS CAN CHIC NOUS TACT
KNACK SKILL ESPRIT INDUSTRY
DEXTERITY
CLEVIS COP DEE HAKE CLEVY COPSE
BRIDGE BRIDLE MUZZLE SHACKLE
PLOWHEAD
CLEW BALL CLUE HINT GLOBE
GLOME SKEIN BOTTOM HURDLE
THREAD
CLICHE COMMONPLACE
CLICK DOG DOT DASH MESH PAWL
SLAP TICK AGREE CATCH FORGE
SNECK SNICK DETENT PALLET
RATCHET
(— HORSE'S SHOES) FORGE
(HEEL —S) BELLS
(TELEGRAPH —) DASH
CLICK BEETLE DOR ELATER
CLICKER CASTANET

CLIENT CEILE JAJMAN PATRON
PATIENT CUSTOMER HENCHMAN
RETAINER
CLIENTELE TRADE PUBLIC CLIENTRY
CLIFF HOE NIP CRAG HILL KLIP ROCK
SCAR BLUFF CLEVE CLINT HEUCH
HEUGH KRANS SCARP SHORE SLOPE
STEEP CLEEVE HEIGHT KRANTZ
PISKUN CLOGWYN HILLSIDE
PALISADE TRAVERSE
(BROKEN —) CRAG
(ICE —) ICEBLINK
(LINE OF —S) PALISADE
(PREF.) CREMNO
CLIFFY SCARRY
CLIMATE SKY SUN MOOD CLIME
HEAVEN REGION TEMPER ATTITUDE
(SCIENCE OF —) PHENOLOGY
(PREF.) METEOR(O)
CLIMAX CAP TOP ACME APEX HEAD
NEAR PEAK SHUT CREST CROWN
MOUNT SCALE TIGHT APOGEE
ASCEND FINISH HEIGHT PAYOFF
SHINNY SUMMIT ZENITH BLOWOFF
EVEREST CAPSHEAF CAPSTONE
EPIPLOCE CULMINATION
CLIMB GAD STY COON RAMP RISE
SHIN SKIN SOAR STYE CREEP GRIMP
MOUNT SCALE SKLIM SPEED SPEEL
SWARM TWINE ASCEND ASCENT
BREAST SCLIMB SCRAWM SHINNY
SWARVE SWERVE CLAMBER
SCRAMBLE TRAVERSE
(— ABOARD) HOP
(— DOWN) LIGHT UNSCALE
(— IN MOUNTAINEERING) CHIMNEY
(— OVER) SURMOUNT
CLIMBER CUBE AKALA AKELA KAIWI
TIMBO RIGGER SCALER COWHAGE
CRAMPON CREEPER
(MOUNTAIN —) ALPINIST
CLIMBING RAMPANT SCANDENT
(MOUNTAIN —) ALPINISM
CLIMBING FERN NITO AGSAM
CLIMBING IRON SPUR PRICK
CRAMPET CRAMPIT CRAMPON
CREEPER PRICKER CRAMPBIT
CLIMBING PALM RATTAN
CLIMBING PEPPER BETEL
CLIMBING ROSE SCRAMBLE
CLINCH FIX GET HUG ICE TOE BIND
GRIP LOCK NAIL SEAL CLAMP CLING
CLINK CLINT GRASP RIVET SEIZE
CLENCH CLUTCH FASTEN SECURE
SNATCH CONFIRM EMBRACE
GRAPPLE SCUFFLE COMPLETE
CONCLUDE HOLDFAST
CLING HUG BANK HANG HOLD RELY
CLASP HITCH STICK TRUST ADHERE
CLEAVE CLINCH COHERE DEPEND
FASTEN SHRINK WITHER CHERISH
EMBRACE SHRIVEL CONTRACT
CLINGER LIMPET

CLINGFISH SUCKER TESTAR TETARD
  SUCKFISH
CLINGING CLUNG HUGGING
  ADHAMANT ADHERENT OSCULANT
CLINK ALE JUG PUT RAP BEAT
  BLOW BRIG CASH CLAP COIN JAIL
  MOVE RING SLAP CHINK KLINK
  LATCH MONEY RHYME SEIZE
  CLINCH JINGLE LOCKUP MOMENT
  PRISON STRIKE TINKLE INSTANT
  JINGLING
CLINKER BUR DUD BUHR BURR SCAR
  SLAG WASTE HOLLANDER
  (PL.) BREEZE
CLINKER-BUILT SHINGLED
  LAPSTRAKE
CLINKSTONE PHONOLITE
CLINOMETER TRIMMER
CLINTONIA BLUEBEAD DOGBERRY
  COWTONGUE
CLIP BAT BOB CUT DOD HUG LIP LOP
  MOW NIG NIP BARB BEAK CHIP COLL
  CROP DOCK DODD FLAG HOLD PACE
  PARE POLL SNIP TRIM BRUSH CLASP
  DRESS FORCE LUNET MINCE PRUNE
  SHAVE SHEAR SHRIP SNICK STEEK
  CLUPPE CLUTCH CRUTCH FASTEN
  GADGET HINDER HOLDER LACING
  CALIPER CURTAIL CURTAIN EMBRACE
  HICKORY LUNETTE SCISSOR
  SHORTEN DIMINISH ENCIRCLE
  RETAINER
  (— A COIN) SHORTEN
  (— OF LEAD) TINGLE
  (— WOOL) CRUTCH
  (CARTRIDGE —) CHARGER
  (HAIR —) BARRETTE
  (SPRING —) JACK
CLIP-FASTENER DOME
CLIPPED SHORN TONSURED
CLIPPER BOAT SHIP DOCKER SLICER
  CHAINER CLAMMER CLEANER
  GRABMAN GRIPPER SHEARER
  SNAPPER
CLIPPING BOB SCROW CUTTING
  SNIPPING
  (—S OF METAL) SCISSEL
  (PL.) BRASH SHORTS EXCERPTA
CLIQUE COT MOB SET BLOC CLAN
  CLUB GANG KNOT PUSH RING
  CABAL CROWD GROUP JUNTO
  MAFIA WRITE CIRCLE CLETCH
  SCHISM COTERIE FACTION
  CONCLAVE SODALITY CAMARILLA
CLISTHENES (FATHER OF —)
  MEGACLES
  (MOTHER OF —) AGARISTA
CLITANDRE (LOVER OF —) LUCINDE
  CELIMENE ANGELIQUE
CLITELLUM GIRDLE SADDLE
  CINGULUM
CLOAK ABA HAP BRAT CAPA CAPE
  COPE HIDE HUKE IZAR MANT MASK

PALL RAIL ROBE VEIL WRAP AMICE
BURKA CAPOT CHOGA COVER
GREGO GUISE JELAB MANTA
MANTO PILCH SAGUM SHUBA
TALAR TALMA TILMA ABOLLA
AHUULA ASSUME BAUTTA CAMAIL
CAPOTE CASTER CHAMMA CHAPEL
CHIMER DOLMAN JOSEPH MANTLE
MANTUA PHAROS PONCHO RHASON
SCREEN SERAPE SHIELD SHROUD
TABARD VISITE ALICULA BAVAROY
CASSOCK CHLAMYS CHUDDAR
CONCEAL COURTBY GARMENT
MANTEAU PAENULA PALLIUM
PELISSE PELLARD PRETEXT
ROKELAY SHELTER SURCOAT
ZIMARRA ALBORNOZ BURNOOSE
CAPUCHIN CARDINAL DISGUISE
INTRIGUE MANTILLA PALLIATE
ROQUELAURE
(— OF FEATHERS) MAMO AHUULA
(— WITH CROSSES) ANALABOS
(ARAB —) GALABIA GALLABIA
  GALABIYAH
(BULLFIGHTER'S —) CAPA
(CORONATION —) SACCOS
(FUR —) PILCH
(HOODED —) HUKE CAPOT BAUTTA
  BIRRUS BAVAROY CARDINAL
  DJELLABA
(INQUISITION —) SANBENITO
(RED —) CAPE
(RUSSIAN —) SARAFAN
(SHORT —) MANTELET
(SOLDIER'S —) SAGUM MANTEEL
(WATERPROOF —) GOSSAMER
(PREF.) PALLIO
CLOAKED PALLIATE
CLOAKROOM VESTRY VESTIARY
CLOAM DAUB CLOMB CROCKERY
CLOCHE BELL
CLOCK NEF BELL CALL DIAL GOER
GONG TIME WRAP BUNDY CLUCK
GURRY HATCH HURRY KNOCK
METER QUIRK STYLE VERGE WATCH
BEETLE CROUCH GHURRY ORLAGE
TICKER SKELPER STRIKER TATTLER
HOROLOGE INCUBATE ORNAMENT
RECORDER SOLARIUM TELLTALE
(— IN FORM OF SHIP) NEF
(— ON STOCKING) QUIRK GUSHET
  GUSSET
(— WITH PENDULUM) PENDULE
(KIND OF —) CESIUM
(PART OF —) BOB ROD BASE DIAL
  DOOR FACE FOOT HAND HOOD RING
  ROPE CHAIN CREST PLATE TRUCK
  FINIAL PLINTH WEIGHT CHAPTER
  NUMERAL PENDULUM SPANDREL
(TIME —) BUNDY
(WATER —) GURRY GHURRY
  SOLARIUM CLEPSYDRA
CLOCKER SIZER TIMER RAILBIRD

CLOCKWISE DEASIL DESSIL SUNWISE POSITIVE

CLOD SOD CLAT CLOT DOLT DULL LOUT LUMP SLOB TURF CLOUT CLOWN DIVOT EARTH GLEBE GROSS KNOLL YOKEL CLATCH GROUND STUPID BUMPKIN

CLODDISH GROSS STUPID BOORISH

CLODDY GLEBY GLEBOUS

CLODHOPPER BOOR CLOD SHOE RUSTIC HOBNAIL PLOWMAN

CLODIA LESBIA

CLODPATE CLOT DOLT FOOL RAMHEAD CLODPOLE CLODPOLL IMBECILE

CLODPOLE BOOR BUMPKIN

CLOG FUR GUM JAM LOG BALL CLAG CLAM CLOY CURB DRAG GAUM GLUB LEAD LOAD LUMP SHOE SKID STOP BLIND BLOCK CHECK CHOKE DANCE SABOT SPOKE TRASH ACCLOY ADHERE BURDEN CHOPIN COBCAB DAGGLE ENCLOG FETTER FREEZE GALOSH HAMPER HOBBLE IMPEDE PATINE PATTEN REMORA SANDAL SECQUE WEIGHT CONGEST CREEPER ENGLEIM FETLOCK PERPLEX SHACKLE SPANCEL TRAMMEL TRIGGER BEDAGGLE COALESCE ENCUMBER OBSTRUCT OVERSHOE RESTRAIN
(— A FILE) PIN
(WOODEN —S) GETA GETAS

CLOG ALMANAC STAFF

CLOGGED FOUL FURRY PINNY FROZEN CLOTTED BEGUMMED

CLOGGING CLOGGY FOULING CUMBROUS

CLOGGY DULL HEAVY LUMPY STICKY

CLOISONNE SHIPPO

CLOISTER HALL STOA ABBEY AISLE ARCADE FRIARY IMMURE PIAZZA PRIORY CLOSTER CONVENT NUNNERY MONASTERY

CLOISTER AND THE HEARTH
(AUTHOR OF —) READE
(CHARACTER IN —) KATE DENYS ELIAS GILES MARIE PETER BRANDT GERARD MARTIN PIETRO ELIASON MARGARET GHYSBRECHT

CLOISTERED RECLUSE

CLONE DESMA REPLICA SPICULE

CLORINDA
(SLAYER OF —) TANCRED

CLOSE BY IN CAP END GUM HAW HOT TYE ZOP AKIN BUNG CHOP CLAP CLIT DAUB FAST FILL FINE FIRM GRIP HARD HIDE LOUK MEET NEAR NIGH QUIT SEAL SHUT SLAM SNUG SPAR STOP TINE WINK WYND ZERO ANEAR BLOCK BOSOM BREAK CEASE CHEAP CHIEF COAPT DENSE FENCE FINIS FLIRT GARTH GROSS ISSUE MUGGY SNECK SOLID STEEK STICK STIVY THICK TIGHT BUCKLE BUTTON CLAUSE CLENCH CLUTCH DOUBLE EFFECT EXPIRY FINALE FINISH INSTOP INWARD NARROW NEARBY PERIOD SECRET SETTLE SILENT STANCH STINGY STITCH STRAIT STRICT STUFFY THRONG ADJOURN BOROUGH CLOSING CLOSISH COMPACT CONDEMN CONTEXT COSTIVE EXTREME GRAPPLE MISERLY OCCLUDE POCKETY PUTHERY RAMPIRE RECLUDE SHUTTER SIMILAR STAUNCH STOPPER ACCURATE ADJACENT BLOCKADE CLAUSULA COMPLETE COMPRESS CONCLUDE ENCEINTE ESPECIAL FAMILIAR FINALIZE HAIRLINE IMMINENT INTIMATE OBTURATE PARCLOSE PRECLUDE STIFLING PROXIMATE
(— BY) FORBY AROUND BESIDE FOREBY HEREBY FORTHBY SISTERING
(— EYES OF HAWK) SEEL
(— IN) BESET ENCLOSE INCLOSE
(— IN ON) TAKE
(— THE MOUTH) STOPPLE
(— TIGHTLY) SEALOFF
(— TO) BY INBY NEAR NIGH ANEAR INBYE ALMOST AGAINST
(— TO BATSMAN) SILLY
(— TO COMMUNICATION) CORDON
(— TOGETHER) COLLAPSE
(— TO QUARRY) HOT
(— TO THE HEART) DEAR
(— TO THE WIND) SHARP
(— UP) DIT CORK DITT FILL FOLD STOP SERRY UPCLOSE
(— WITH) BIND
(— WITH A CLICK) SNECK
(AS — AS POSSIBLE) CHOCK
(NOT —) UNNEAR
(PARTIALLY —) HOOD
(VERY —) CHIEF STINGY
(PREF.) PLESI(O) PYCN(O) STEN(O)
(SUFF.) STENOSIS

CLOSE-COUPLED COMPACT

CLOSE-CUT SHAVEN

CLOSED DARK DOWN SHUT CLOSE LUCKEN UNOPEN BLOCKED COVERED
(— AT ONE END) BLIND
(PREF.) CLEIST CLIST OCCLUSO

CLOSEFISTED MEAN NEAR FISTY TIGHT SNIPPY STINGY MISERLY HANDFAST

CLOSE-FITTING FIT HARD MEET SNUG THEAT THEET TIGHT THIGHT PRINCESS SUCCINCT PRINCESSE

CLOSE-IN SILLY

CLOSE-KNIT TRUSSED

CLOSE-LIPPED SILENT

CLOSELY FAST JUST NEAR WELL
SADLY ALMOST BARELY HARDLY
NARROW NEARLY JUNCTLY
STRICTLY
CLOSEMOUTHED SECRET SILENT
TACITURN
(NOT —) LEAKY
CLOSENESS DENSITY SECRECY
FIDELITY INTIMACY NEARNESS
PARSIMONY
CLOSER VAMPER CLOSURE
CLOSE-SET THICK SERRIED
CLOSE-SMELLING FROWSTY
CLOSEST NEXT NEAREST
CLOSESTOOL STOLE
CLOSET ARK LOO EWRY ROOM SAFE
ZETA AMBRY CUBBY CUDDY PRESS
LOCKER PANTRY SECRET CABINET
CONCLAVE PRIVATE STORAGE
CONCLAVE CUPBOARD GARDEVIN
WARDROBE
CLOSING FLY SLAM SNAP CLINCH
CLOSURE CLOTURE CLAUDENT
PHASEOUT BUTTONING
(— DOWN OF OPERATIONS)
PHASEOUT
(MUSICAL —) CODA
(TEMPORARY —) SHUTDOWN
CLOSURE END GAG BOLT SEAL
BOUND LIMIT POPTOP ATRESIA
CLOTURE FERRULE TENSION
CLAUSURE FINALITY KANGAROO
(FABRIC —) VELCRO
(SUFF.) CLEISIS CLISIS
CLOT DOT GEL CLAG CLAT GOUT JELL
LUMP MASS MOLE SHED CLART
CLUMP GRUME BALTER COTTER
LAPPER LOPPER CLODDEN CONGEAL
EMBOLUS THICKEN CLODPATE
COAGULUM CONCRETE SOLIDIFY
THROMBUS
(— OF BLOOD) THROMBUS
(— OF DIRT) SPLATCH
(PREF.) THROMB(O)
CLOTH DAB RAG BLUE COAT DRAB
DRAP ECRU FELT FILE PALL SEAM
WARE WOOF BEIGE BLUET CABAN
CLOUT DITTO FOULE GOODS GREEN
KENTE LODEN LUNGI MOORY PRINT
STUPE TAMMY TAWNY TIBET TOILE
TWEED TWILL WIGAN ALPACA
AWNING BENGAL BYSSUS CANAMO
CANVAS CHADOR CLAITH CLERGY
COVERT DOMETT DORSEL DOSSAL
DOSSER DRAPET DUSTER FABRIC
LIVERY LONGYI LOWELL MELLAY
MULETA NAPKIN RENGUE REXINE
SARONG SURNAP TILLOT WITNEY
ACETATE BAGGING BOULTEL
CHADDAR CHRISOM COATING
CRIMSON DRAPERY DUSTRAG
FALDING GARMENT JACONET
ORLEANS PANUELO RAIMENT

SACKING SURNAPE TEXTILE
WATCHET WORSTED BATSWING
CHRISMAL COMPRESS CORPORAL
CRAMOISY DWELLING FROCKING
HOMESPUN LAMBSKIN MATERIAL
PHULKARI RADEVORE SHAATNEZ
SHEETING THICKSET TOILINET
(— FOR BELT) SHROUD
(— FOR SWEAT) SUDARY SUDARIUM
(— FOR WIPING TABLE) FILE
(— FOR WRAPPING CHILD) PILCH
(— FOR WRAPPING FABRICS) TILLET
(— FOR WRAPPING THE DEAD)
CEREMENT
(— HANGING FROM WAISTBAND)
LANGOOTY
(— OF GOLD) LAME
(— OF GOLD) SONERI
(— OF GOLD) SONERIE CICLATON
CHECKLATON
(— OF SINGLE WIDTH) STRAITS
(— REMAINING AFTER CUTTING)
CABBAGE
(— TEXTURE) WALE
(— WORN LIKE KILT) LAVALAVA
(ALTAR —) TOWEL PENDLE PALLIUM
VESPERAL CATASARKA
(ARABIAN —) HAIK CABAN CABAAN
(BAPTISMAL —) CHRISOM
(BARK —) TAPA TAPPA
(BED —) COVER SPREAD
(BLACK —) KISWA KISWAH
(BLUE —) PERSE
(COARSE —) KELT DOZEN DUROY
BUDGE BURREL CANGAN DOWLAS
DOZENS FORFAR FRIEZE HODDEN
KERSEY KHARVA KHARWA STAMIN
STROUD TAPALO WADMAL CAMBAYE
COTONIA DRUGGET FORFARS
RAPLOCH RUGGING SARPLER
SOUTAGE FLUSHING RADEVORE
SARCILIS
(COMMUNION —) FANON SINDON
ANIMETTA CORPORAL PURIFICATOR
(CORDED —) REP REPP
(COTTON —) BAFT JEAN TOBE ADATI
BLUET CAFFA CRASH DURRY JEANS
KHADI KHAKI SURAT BEAVER CALICO
CANGAN DOWLAS DURRIE GANZIE
HUMHUM KALMUK NANKIN PENANG
CAMBAYE FUSTIAN GALATEA
GINGHAM JACONET KHADDAR
LASTING NANKEEN REGATTA
BOGOTANA CRETONNE DOMESTIC
MUSLINET
(CRIMSON —) CRAMASIE CRAMOISY
(DECORATIVE —) SCARF
(DRAB —) KHAKI
(DRIVING —) TOWEL
(EMBROIDERED —) SAMPLER
BAUDEKIN
(FINE —) SINDON SCARLET
(FIORE —) PINA

(GLASS —) DORON
(GOAT-WOOL —) ABA ABBA ABAYA SLING
(GREEN —) KENDAL
(GUNNY —) TAT
(HAIR —) ABA ABBA CILICE
(HEMP —) PINAYUSA
(HOMESPUN —) KELT KHADI PATTU PUTTOO HEADING KHADDAR
(INFERIOR —) MOCKADO
(KIND OF —) LOIN PINA
(LAP —) GREMIAL
(LINEN —) BRIN LINE GULIX DOWLAS FORFAR BRABANT LOCKRAM SILESIA BLANCARD CORPORAL DRILLING GAMBROON GHENTING LINCLOTH
(LONG —) LUNGI WHITE LUNGEE
(ORNAMENTAL —) TRAP DOSSAL DOSSEL
(PACK —) MANTA
(PACKING —) SOUTAGE
(PIECE OF —) APRON CLOUT GODET LANGOOTY
(PURLOINED —) CABBAGE
(RICH —) SCARLET
(ROUGH —) PETERSHAM
(ROYAL —) PURPLE
(SADDLE —) PANEL NUMNAH SHABRACK
(SILK —) CAFFA BENGAL PATOLA LUSTRINE LUSTRING
(SOAKED —) BUCK
(SOFT —) RUGINE
(STAGE —) BACKDROP
(STARCHED —) GUIMPE
(STRIPED —) RAY
(STRONG —) CANVAS DURANCE BARRACAN
(TARTAN —) PLAID
(TURBAN —) SASH
(TWILLED —) JANE JEAN BARATHEA GAMBROON
(UNDYED —) HODDEN
(VARI-COLORED —) MEDLEY MOTLEY
(WASHING —) SHAMMY CHAMOIS
(WATERPROOF —) MAC MACK
(WAX —) MUMJUMA
(WET —) DAB
(WOOL —) SAY DRAB PUKE BEIGE BUREL DOZEN DUROY LAINE STARA TAMIS TAMMY BURNET DOZENS DUFFEL HODDEN KENDAL KERSEY MEDLEY MELTON MUSTER SATARA SAXONY STAMIN TAMINY TARTAN BASTARD BLANKET DUNSTER FLANNEL RAPLOCH ROPLOCH RUGGING BEARSKIN BOMBAZET BUCKSKIN FLORENCE SARCILIS VENETIAN PETERSHAM BOMBAZETTE
(WORSTED —) RASH SHAG BOTANY BOMBAZET
(PREF.) HISTI(O)

CLOTHE DON DUB HAP LAP RIG TOG BUSK COAT DECK GARB GIRD GOWN ROBE VEST ADORN ARRAY CLEAD CLEED DRESS ENDOW ENDUE FLESH FROCK HABIT INDUE ATTIRE BEWRAP SHRIDE SHROUD SWATHE ADDRESS APPAREL FEATHER RAIMENT VESTURE ACCOUTER ACCOUTRE
(PLAIN —) MUFTI
CLOTHED CLAD BECLAD HABITED
CLOTHES CASE DUDS GARB GEAR GORE KAPA SUIT TACK TOGS WEAR BRAWS CLAES DUCKS HABIT ATTIRE FARDEL SHROUD THREAD TROGGS APPAREL BAGGAGE COSTUME IRONING RAIMENT REGALIA THREADS TOGGERY VESTURE WEARING CLOTHING FEATHERS FRIPPERY GARMENTS INDUMENT
(CASTOFF —) FRIPPERY
(CIVILIAN —) MUFTI CIVVIES
(COLORFUL —) TRAPPINGS
(DAINTY —) PRETTIES
(DRESS —) WAMPUM
(FINE —) BRAWS
(HANDSOME —) BRAVERY
(MOURNING —) DOLE
(READY-TO-WEAR —) PRETAPORTER
(SHOWY —) LUGS
(SOAKED —) BUCK
(TRACK —) SILKS
CLOTHES DRYER AIRER TUMBLER
CLOTHES-HORSE MAIDEN SCREEN
CLOTHESPIN PEG
CLOTHESPRESS ARMOIRE TALLBOY WARDROBE
CLOTH FOLDER CUTTLER
CLOTHING (ALSO SEE CLOTHES) BACK BLUE BRAT COAT GARB GEAR SEAM WEAR ARRAY BUREL CLOTH DRESS GREEN HABIT JABOT STUFF ATTIRE FARDEL ROBING VESTRY APPAREL CLOBBER CLOTHES CRIMSON DRAPERY FISHNET OUTWALL RAIMENT THREADS VESTURE WEEDERY INDUMENT KNITWEAR MENSWEAR ORNAMENT SLOPWORK VESTIARY VESTMENT BEACHWEAR
(ARTICLE OF —) VINE
(BLACK —) SABLE
(COARSE —) BUREL
(INFORMAL —) PLAYWEAR
(LOWER —) LAP
(MUSLIM —) IHRAM
(NAUTICAL —) SLOPS
(OF CLASSIC —) PREPPY PREPPIE
(SHEER —) FLIMSIES
(SHOWY —) SHEEN FINERY
(WOMEN'S —) FRILLIES
(WORK —) FATIGUES
(SUFF.) ESTHES

CLOTHING DEALER HOSIER
CLOTHWORKER FULLER
CLOTILDA (FATHER OF —) CHILPERIC
(HUSBAND OF —) CLOVIS AMALARIC
(UNCLE OF —) GUNDEBALD
CLOTTED GORY CLOTTY CLOUTED
GARGETY GRUMOUS LIVERED
CLOTURE GAG CLOSURE
CLOUD DOG FOG NUE SKY BLUR
DAMP DARK DUST FOOL HAZE HELM
HIDE MIST PUFF REEK SMUR ARCUS
BEDIM BEFOG BLOOM DRIFT GLOOM
MUDDY NUBIA OXEYE SHADE STAIN
SULLY SWARM TAINT VAPOR CIRRUS
DAMAGE DARKEN DEEPEN DEFAME
FUNNEL MUDDLE NEBULA NIMBUS
PILEUS POTHER SCREEN SHADOW
STIGMA BLACKEN CONFUSE
CUMULUS ECLIPSE FUMULUS
GRANULE OBSCURE POOTHER
STRATUS SUNSPOT TARNISH
CLOUDCAP CLOUDLET COCKTAIL
NIGHTCAP NUBILATE OVERCAST
WOOLPACK
(— BEFORE STORM) MESSENGER
(— OF DROPS) SPRAY
(— OF DUST OR VAPOR) STEW
SMOTHER
(— OF MIST) SOP
(— OVER MOUNTAIN) HELM
(CIRRUS —S) GOATSHAIR
(DRIVINNG —) SCUD
(FLYING —) RACK
(FUNNEL —) TORNADO
(HIGH —) CIRRUS
(HORIZONTAL —) STRATUS
(KIND OF —) OORT
(LAYER OF —S) DECK
(MASS OF HIGH —S) RACK
(MASSY —) CUMULUS
(NUCLEAR —) FIREBALL
(RAIN —) NIMBUS
(PL.) SCUD SOUP CARRY GASHES
(PREF.) CIRR(I)(O) CIRRH(I)(O) NEBULI
NEPHEL(I)(O) NEPHO NIMBI NUBI
CLOUDBERRY AKPEK MOLKA
AVERIN
(FRUIT OF —) NOOP
CLOUDED HAZY DIRTY DUSTY FILMY
JASPE MUCKY SHADY ACLOUD
GLOOMY TURBID INFUMATE
NEBULOUS
CLOUDINESS FAIR HAZE GLOOM
MUDDLE NUBECULA
CLOUDING DAPPLE
(— OF EYE) CATARACT
CLOUDLESS AZURE CLEAR BRIGHT
CLOUDLIKE NEBULOUS NUBIFORM
CLOUDY DIM DARK DULL HAZY
BLEAR FILMY FOGGY MISTY MUDDY
MURKY SHADY GLOOMY LOWERY
OPAQUE SMURRY VEILED BLURRED
CLOUDED NEBULAR OBSCURE

CONFUSED NEBULOSE NUBILOUS
OVERCAST VAPOROUS
CLOUGH CLUF CLEFT CLOES CLEUCH
CLEUGH RAVINE VALLEY
CLOUT BAT BOX DAB HIT LAP BEAT
BLOW BUMP CLOD CLUB CUFF JOIN
MEND NAIL PULL SLAP SLUG SWAT
JUICE PATCH SMITE WHACK KLOWET
STRIKE TACKET TARGET THRASH
WASHER BANDAGE BOSTHOON
INFLUENCE
CLOVE GAP NAIL CHIVE CLEFT GILLY
BUTTON CLEAVE RAVINE SHERRY
GILLIVER
CLOVE BROWN EAGLE
CLOVEN CLEFT SPLIT DIVIDED
BISULCATE
CLOVEN-FOOTED SLIT FISSIPED
CLOVE PINK GELOFER GRENADIN
CLOVER RED HAGI SEED HUBAM
LOTUS MEDIC NARDU PUSSY
ALSIKE BERSIM LADINO LEGUME
LUXURY NARDOO ALFALFA
BERSEEM BERSINE CLAIVER
COMFORT LUCERNE MELILOT
SAPLING TREFOIL TRIFOLY
COWGRASS HAREFOOT NAPOLEON
PUSSYCAT SHAMROCK SUCKLING
YELLOWTOP
(KIND OF —) LADINO
CLOVER DODDER AILWEED
EPITHYME HAILWEED HAIRWEED
HALEWEED
CLOWN HOB OAF PUT APER BOOR
FOOL GAUM GOFF JOEY LOUT
MIME MOME SWAD ZANY ANTIC
BUFFO CHUFF CHURL COMIC FESTE
IDIOT MIMER PATCH PUNCH WAMBA
ZANNI AUGUST BODACH CHOUGH
HOBBIL JESTER JOSKIN LUBBER
RUSTIC STOOGE AUGUSTE
BODDAGH BUFFOON BUMPKIN
CHARLEY COSTARD KOSHARE
LAVACHE LOBSTER MUDHEAD
PEASANT PIERROT PLAYBOY
SCOFFER TOMFOOL COVIELLO
KOYEMSHI MERRYMAN WHITEFACE
PUNCHINELLO
CLOWNISH RAW RUDE ZANY
GAWKY ROUGH BORREL CLUMSY
COARSE RUSTIC AWKWARD
BOORISH BORRELL HOBLIKE
KERNISH LOBBISH LOUTISH UNCIVIL
VILLAIN BOEOTIAN CLUBBISH
SWADDISH UNGAINLY
CLOY CLOG GLUT NAIL PALL SATE
GORGE PRICK ACCLOY PIERCE
SATIATE SATISFY SURFEIT SATURATE
(— WITH ADORATION) BESOT
CLOYED BLASE
CLOYER SNAP
CLOYING GOOEY SWEET VANILLA
CLOYSOME LUSCIOUS SACCHARINE

CLUB BAT DOG HIT HUI SET BEAT
CANE JOIN MACE MALL MAUL MERE
POLT TEAM BAFFY BANDY BATON
BILLY BUNCH CLOUT HURLY KEBBY
LODGE MASHY ORDER STAFF STICK
TOWEL UNITE YOKEL ZONTA BULGER
CERCLE CIRCLE CLIQUE CUDGEL
HURLEY KEBBIE LIBBET MACANA
MASHIE MENAGE MUCKLE NULLAH
PRIEST STRIKE TAIAHA VEREIN
WEAPON WHITES BOURDON
CAMBUCA COLLEGE COUNCIL
HETAERY HETAIRY SOROSIS
ATHENEUM BLUDGEON CATSTICK
SODALITY SORORITY SPONTOON
TERTULIA KNOBKERRY
(— IN PLAYING CARDS) OAK
(— OF ANTENNA) CLAVUS
(BASEBALL —) FARM
(GOLF —) IRON WOOD BAFFY CLEEK
MASHY SPOON STICK WEDGE
BRASSY BULGER DRIVER JIGGER
LOFTER MASHIE PUTTER BLASTER
MIDIRON NIBLICK CLUSTER
(INTERNATIONAL SERVICE —) GYRO
(MAORI —) MERE MERAI MARREE
(MEMBER OF SERVICE —) SERTOMAN
(POLICEMAN'S —) SAP BILLY
PANTOON SPONTON SPONTOON
NIGHTSTICK LATHI
(POLITICAL —) ROTA FASCIO
HETAERY HETAIRY
(SINGERS' —) GLEE
(SPIKED —) ALLIDE
(SPORTS —) BAT
(WAR —) WADDY
(WOMEN'S —) SOROSIS SORORITY
CIRCLE
(PREF.) CLAVI CORDYL(O) RHOPAL(O)
(SUFF.) CORYNUS
CLUB CARRIER CLAVIGER
CLUBFOOT TALUS VARUS VALGUS
TALIPES CYLLOSIS POLTFOOT
CLUB, GOLF
(PART OF —) TOE FACE GRIP HEAD
HEEL NECK NOSE SOLE HOSEL SHAFT
CLUB MOSS MOSS FOFEET
LYCOPOD PILIGAN CROWFOOT
FERNWORT
CLUBROOT CLUB ANBURY ANBERRY
HANBURY CLUBBING CLUBFOOT
CLUB RUSH RUSH SEDGE GLUMAL
DEERHAIR
CLUB-SHAPED CLAVATE
CLUCK HEN FUSS CHUCK CLACK
CLICK CLOCK CLOOK
CLUE KEY TIP BALL CLEW HINT IDEA
LEAD GUIDE TWINE BOTTOM CLAVIS
THREAD INNUENDO
CLUMP SOP TOD BLOW BUSH CLOT
HEAP KNOT LUMP MASS MOSS
MOTT TOPE TUFT TUMP TURB BLUFF
BUNCH CLAMP GROUP GROVE

HOUSE PATCH PLUMP STUMP TREAD
WUDGE CLUNCH DOLLOP LUMPER
BOSCAGE CLUMPER CLUSTER
THICKET
(— OF BRIERS OR ROSES) ROAN
RONE
(— OF CELLS) SLUDGE
(— OF SHRUBS) BUSH
(— OF SPORANGIA) SORUS
(— OF TREES) BLUFF HOUSE HURST
HYRST BOSQUE
CLUMSILY SOUSE GREENLY
GAUCHELY
CLUMSINESS GAUCHERIE
CLUMSY AWK FLOB LEWD NUMB
RUDE BLUNT BULKY GAUMY GAWKY
HOGGY HULKY INAPT INEPT SCRAM
SPLAY STIFF STOGY CLUMPY
CLUNKY GAUCHE LUBBER NOGGEN
THUMBY WOODEN AWKWARD
BOORISH CHUCKLE LOUTISH
LUMPISH UNHANDY UNREADY
BENUMBED BUNGLING CLOWNISH
FOOTLESS GAUMLESS HANDLESS
LUMBERLY TACTLESS UNGAINLY
UNWIELDY CLOUTERLY PONDEROUS
HIPPOPOTAMIC
(— PERSON) KLUTZ
(NOT —) FINE
CLUPEID HERRING
CLUSTER BOB BOG BUSH CLOT
COMA CONE CYME KNOT LUMP TUFT
BUNCH CLUMP DRUSE GROUP
PLUMP SHEAF SORUS CENTER
COLONY GATHER MORULA PLEIAD
REGIME BOUROCK CLUTHER
DOLPHIN ENVIRON FOLIAGE
FASCICLE NUCLEATE SURROUND
(— AS BEES) BALL KNIT
(— OF BANANAS) HAND
(— OF BRANCHES) SPRAY
(— OF CELLS) ROSETTE
(— OF CRYSTALS) DRUSE
(— OF FEATHERS) MUFF
(— OF FIBERS) NEP
(— OF FLOWERS) CYME TRUSS
CORYMB ANTHEMY PANICLE
(— OF HAIRS) MYSTAX
(— OF METAL BALLS) GRAPE
(— OF NODULES) GRAPES
(— OF PILES) DOLPHIN
(— OF PLANTS) BED
(— OF RAYS) AIGRETTE
(— OF SPORES) SORUS
(— OF STARS) PRAESEPE
(— OF TINES) TROCHE
(— OF WOOL) NEP
(CONFUSED —) SPLATTER
(GERM CELL —) MORULA
(SUSPENDED —) SWAG
(PREF.) CORYMBI CYM(I)(O) KYM(I)(O)
RACEMI RACEMO
CLUSTER BEAN GUAR

CLUSTERED TUFTED RACEMOSE AGGREGATE CONGLOMERATE

CLUTCH HUG NAB SET CLAM CLAW CLEM CLIP FIST GLAM GRAB GRIP NEST BROOD CATCH CLASP CLAUT CLEEK CLICK GLAUM GRASP GRIPE GRISP HATCH LEVER POWER SEIZE TALON CLEACH CLENCH CLETCH CLINCH CUTOUT FASTEN RETAIN SNATCH CLAUGHT CONTROL CRAMPON COUPLING
(— OF EGGS) SET LAWTER LAYING SETTING SITTING LAUGHTER

CLUTCHING GRIP GRIPING

CLUTTER MESS STUFF BUSTLE CUMBER LITTER CLATTER DISORDER CONFUSION

CLUTTERED CLATTY CLOTTED

CLYMENE (DAUGHTER OF —) ALCIMEDE
(FATHER OF —) MINYAS CATREUS OCEANUS
(HUSBAND OF —) IAPETUS NAUPLIUS PHYLACUS
(MOTHER OF —) TETHYS
(SON OF —) OEAX ATLAS IPHICLUS PHAETHON MENOETIUS PALAMEDES

CLYPEUS NASUS EPISTOME PRELABRUM

CLYSTER LAVEMENT INJECTION

CLYTEMNESTRA (BROTHER OF —) CASTOR POLLUX POLYDEUCES
(DAUGHTER OF —) ELECTRA LAODICE IPHIGENIA IPHINASSA CHRYSOTHEMIS
(FATHER OF —) TYNDAREUS
(HUSBAND OF —) TANTALUS AGAMEMNON
(LOVER OF —) AEGISTHUS
(MOTHER OF —) LEDA
(SISTER OF —) HELENA
(SON OF —) ORESTES

CLYTIUS (BROTHER OF —) PRIAM
(FATHER OF —) FURYTUS LAOMEDON
(MOTHER OF —) GAEA
(SLAYER OF —) HERCULES
(SON OF —) CALETOR

COACH BUS CAN FLY DRAG HACK HELP ARABA BOGEY BOGIE BRIEF CABIN FLIER FLYER PILOT PRIME STAGE TEACH TRAIN TUTOR ADVISE DIRECT FIACRE JARVEY MENTOR SALOON ADVISER CHARIOT COACHER CONCORD GONDOLA PREPARE RATTLER TALLYHO TRAINER CARRIAGE DORMEUSE PUPILIZE
(BALLET —) REPETITEUR
(FAST —) FLIER FLYER
(HACKNEY) FIACRE JARVEY
(HEAVY —) DRAG
(SLOW —) SLOWPOKE
(3-WHEELED —) TRICYCLE

COACHDOG DALMATIAN

COACH-HOUSE REMISE

COACHMAN FLY FISH JEHU WHIP PILOT COACHY DRIVER COACHEE COACHER YAMSHIK YEMSCHIK

COACTION EXPLOITATION

COADJUTOR PRIOR

COAGULANT CURD RENNET STYPTIC COAGULUM GELATINE

COAGULATE GEL SET CAKE CLOD CLOT CURD JELL QUAIL YEARN COTTER CURDLE LAPPER LOBBER LOPPER POSSET CLABBER CLOTTER CONGEAL PECTIZE THICKEN COAGULUM CONCRETE SOLIDIFY

COAGULATED CRUDY CURDY LIVERED

COAGULATION GOUT CLOTTER

COAGULUM CLOT THROMBUS

COAK-LIKE PHELLOID

COAL RIB BASS DUFF FUEL SWAD BLOCK CHARK EMBER GHOST GLEED STOKE BARING BRAZIL BURGEE CANNEL CARBON CINDER FIRING SPLINT BACKING BOGHEAD BRIGHTS BYERITE COBBLES LIGNITE RATTLER VITRAIN AMPELITE LANDSALE
(— IN PLACE) SOLID
(— MINE) COLLIERY
(— MINER) COLLIER
(— PILLAR) STOOK
(— SLAB) SKIP
(BAD —) SMUT
(BED OF —) SEAM
(BROWN) LIGNITE
(DIRTY —) RASH
(FINE —) DUFF SCREENINGS
(IMPURE —) SWAD
(INFERIOR —) CROW
(LARGE BLOCK OF —) JUD JUDD
(LIVE OR GLOWING —) GLEED GLEYD
(REFUSE —) BREEZE
(SIZE OF —) EGG NUT PEA LUMP RICE SLACK STOVE BARLEY BROKEN CHESTNUT WALLSEND BUCKWHEAT
(SLATY —) BASS BONE BONY
(SMALL LUMP OF —) NUBBLING
(SMALL PORTION OF UNCUT —) PANEL
(PREF.) ANTHRAC(O) CARBONI

COAL BED SEAM

COALBIN BUNKER

COAL BROKER CRIMP

COAL CAR JIMMY

COAL CHUTE DOCK

COAL DUST COOM CULM SMUT COOMB

COALESCE MIX CLOG FUSE JOIN BLEND MERGE UNITE COHERE EMBODY MINGLE SINTER COMBINE

COALESCENCE UNION FUSION LEAGUE CAPTURE SYNANTHY

COAL-FACE BANK

COALFISH SEY PARR COLEY CUDDY SEITH BESHOW BILLET CUDDEN PODLER SAITHE SILLOC BADDOCK GLASHAN GLASSIN PILTOCK POLLACK
(YOUNG —) PODLER PODLEY COMAMIE POODLER SILLOCK GRAYFISH
COALITION FRONT TRUST UNION FUSION LEAGUE MERGER ENTENTE ALLIANCE
COAL OIL KEROSENE
COALRAKE HOE FREGGIN FRUGGAN SCRAPPLE
COAL WORKER GEORDIE HURRIER
COAL YARD REE
COAMING CURB LEDGE COMBING
COARSE FAT LOW RAW BASE BULL DANK FOUL HARD HASK LEWD LOUD RANK RUDE SOUR VILE BAWDY BRASH BROAD CRASS CRUDE DIRTY GREAT GROFF GROSS HARSH HASKY HEAVY LARGE LOOSE PLAIN RANDY ROUGH ROUTH ROWTY RUDAS STOGY STOUR THICK UNORN BLOWSY BRAZEN BRUTAL CALLOW CHUFFY COMMON DUDGEN EARTHY IMPURE INCULT RANDIE RIBALD ROUDAS RUDOUS RUGGED RUSSET RUSTIC SORDID SULTRY UNFELE VULGAR BLATANT CARLAGE CARLISH CRIBBLE FULSOME GOATISH LOUTISH LOWBRED OBSCENE PROFANE RAPLOCH RAUCOUS ROINISH SENSUAL BARBARIC CLOWNISH HOMESPUN IMMODEST INDECENT PLEBEIAN STUBBORN UNCHASTE
COARSE-FIBERED STRONG
COARSE-GRAINED DRY GRUFF
COARSELY BROADLY HARSHLY
COARSEN HACKNEY
COARSENESS RAUNCH HOGGERY
COAST BANK LAND RIPA BEACH BOARD CLIFF SHORE SLIDE WARTH ADJOIN BORDER RIVAGE STRAND BOBSLED SEASIDE APPROACH SEABOARD SEASHORE ROLLALONG
COASTAL ORARIAN
COASTER MAT SLED TILE DOLLY TROUT BARCON CRADLE CREEPER MISTICO TOBOGGAN
COAST GUARD
(U.S. — WOMAN) SPAR
COASTLAND MAREMMA
COAT FUR LAY PEE SAC TOG BARK BLUE BUFF CONY DAUB FOIL FOLD HIDE HUSK JACK JAMA JUPE MIDI PINK RIND SACK SCAB SEAL TOGE ZINC BENNY CLOTH CONEY COVER CRUST FLASH FROCK GLACE GLAZE HABIT JAMAH JEMMY LAYER OILER PAINT PLATE QUYTE SAQUE SHELL

TERVE ALPACA BYRNIE COATEE DUSTER ENAMEL ENROBE EXTIMA GROUND HACKLE INTIMA INVEST JACKET JOSEPH KIRTLE LACKER MANTLE MELOTE PARGET PELAGE RABBIT REEFER SEALER SILVER SLOUGH STUCCO TABARD VENEER BEESWAX BOBTAIL CASSOCK COATING COURTBY CRISPIN CUTAWAY GARMENT GROGRAM INCRUST KARAKUL LACQUER OILCOAT OVERLAY PALETOT PELISSE PLASTER SHELLAC SHOOTER SPENCER STRATUM SUBCOAT SURCOAT SURTOUT SWAGGER TOGEMAN TOPCOAT VESTURE BENJAMIN COURTEPY GRAPHITE INTONACO MACKINAW MEMBRANE OVERCOAT ROCKELAY SEALSKIN SHERWANI SILICATE TEGUMENT TRENCHER OUTERCOAT PETERSHAM REDINGOTE CHESTERFIELD
(— FOOD) DREDGE
(— LENS) BLOOM
(— OF ARMS) CREST BLAZON BEARINGS
(— OF BIRD SKINS) TEMIAK
(— OF BLOOD VESSEL) MEDIA
(— OF CARIBOU SKINS) KOOLETAH
(— OF DEFENSE) JACK
(— OF EYE) CHOROID
(— OF EYEBALL) SCLERA
(— OF GRAVEL) BLOTTER
(— OF INDIA) ACHKAN
(— OF MAIL) FROCK BRINIE BYRNIE SECRET HAUBERK HABERGEON CATAPHRACT
(— OF ORGAN) INTIMA
(— OF OVULE) PRIMINE
(— OF PLASTER) SET ARRICCIO BROWNING INTONACO
(— OF SEED) ARIL BRAN EPISPERM
(— OF WOOL) FLEECE
(— WITH ALLOY) TERNE
(— WITH PITCH) PAY
(— WORN UNDER ARMOR) GAMBESON
(CLOSE-FITTING —) TRUSS
(DEER'S WINTER —) BLUE
(FIRST — OF TIN) LIST
(FUR —) ANARAK ANORAK
(HAIR —) MELOTE
(HERALD'S —) TABARD
(HOODED —) GREGO CAPOTE
(KIND OF —) TRENCH
(LONG —) MAXI JIBBA JIBBAH KAPOTE DJIBBAH MAXICOAT NEWMARKET
(LOOSE —) CASSOCK PALETOT INVERNESS
(MILITARY —) TUNIC BLOUSE BUFFCOAT
(OLD —) MUMMOCK

(RIDING —) JOSEPH
(SACKCLOTH —) SANBENITO
(SEALSKIN —) NETCHA
(SEED —) ARIL
(SHEEPSKIN —) ZAMARRA ZAMARRO
(SHORT —) PEA JUMP MIDI SACK TERNE JERKIN REEFER PEACOAT
(THREE-QUARTER LENGTH —) ACHKAN
(WATERPROOF —) BURSATI SLICKER
(WOMAN'S —) CARACO DOLMAN
(WOOLLY —) LANUGO
COATED GLACE BACKED FURRED LOADED PLATED CANDIED
(— WITH FLOUR AND CRUMBS) MILANESE
COAT HANGER SHOULDER
COATI NASUA TEJON NARICA PISOTE ARCTOID
COATING (ALSO SEE COAT) FUR GUM ARIL DOPE DRAB FILM FLOR HAIR HOAR SKIN BLOOM FLASH GLACE GLAZE ICING SCALE BEAVER CHATON COVERT CRUSTA FINISH JACKET PATINA VENEER BACKING DIPCOAT FURRING GILDING LACQUER OVERLAY PLATING TINNING ACIERAGE CAMBOUIS CLADDING EMULSION FLOODING MUCILAGE OVERCOAT PERIDIUM PLASTERING
(— FOR METAL) SLUSH
(— OF BACTERIA) SLIME
(— OF GLASS) MOILES FOLIATION
(— OF GLUE) ENAMEL
(— OF ICE) GLAZE
(— OF SEED) TESTA
(— OF TONGUE) ATTER
(CHEESE —) MOLD
(CORROSION —) RUST
(METAL —) CLAD CLADDING
(MIRROR —) FOIL
(OUTSIDE —) CRUST
(POWDERY —) DOWN
(PROTECTIVE —) RESIST
(PRUINOUS —) FARINA
(SEED —) TESTA
(WALL —) GROUT
COATLICUE (HUSBAND OF —) MIXCOATL
(SON OF —) HUITZILOPOCHTLI
COATTAIL LABIE LAPPET
COAX BEG COY PET CANT DUPE FAGE FAWN LURE URGE WILE JOLLY TEASE BANTER CAJOLE CUITLE CUTTER ENTICE FLEECH SEDUCE BEGUILE CROODLE CROWDLE CRUDDLE FLATTER IMPLORE SOOTHER WHEEDLE BLANDISH COLLOGUE INVEIGLE PERSUADE
COAXIAL CONCENTRIC

COB EAR LOB MEW COBB
COBALT (— EXPORTER) ZAIRE
COBBERER ROARER ROUSER
COBBLE DARN MEND PAVE SOLE BOTCH PATCH STONE BUNGLE COGGLE REPAIR RESOLE
COBBLER PIE SNOB SHEEP SOLER SUTOR ARTIST COZIER SOUTER BOTCHER CATFISH CRISPIN POMPANO SADDLER CHUCKLER SCORPION SNOBSCAT
COBBLERFISH COBBLER SUNFISH SHOEMAKER
COBBLESTONE COGGLE
COBBY STOUT HEARTY LIVELY STOCKY COMPACT
COBIA SNOEK SNOOK
COBLE MULE KOBIL
COBNUT COB OUABE HOGNUT PIGNUT
COBRA ASP NAG HAJE NAGA NAJA KRAIT VIPER ELAPID URAEUS
COBWEB NET TRAP SNARE WEVET GOSSAMER
COCA CUCA KHOKA TRUXILLO
COCAINE BLOW COKE SNOW TOOT CRACK FLAKE FREEBASE
(— MIXED WITH HEROIN) SPEEDBALL
(— USER) COKEHEAD
(— WITH HEROIN) SPEEDBALL
(TAKE —) SPEEDBALL
COCASH ASTER SWANWEED
COCCOID BERRYLIKE
COCCULUS CEBATHA FISHBERRY
COCCUS COFFEEBUG
COCCYX RUMPBONE
(PREF.) COCCYGEO COCCYG(O)
COCHE MOCOA
COCHINEAL GRAIN BLANCO COCCUS GRANILLA
COCHINEAL FIG NOPAL
COCHINEAL INSECT VERMIL VERMEIL VERMILION
COCK COX TAP BANK BOOT COIL FOWL HEAP KORA PILE RICK SPAN COCKY COQUE FIGHT FUGIE GALLO SHOCK STACK STRUT VALVE YOWLE CRAVEN FAUCET HAMMER HEELER LEADER CONTEND GORCOCK PETCOCK ROOSTER SWAGGER ASTROLOG COCKBIRD COCKEREL COXBONES GAMECOCK JERMONAL STOPCOCK
(— GUNLOCK) NAB
(— OF HAY) HIPPLE
(— OF THE WALK) KINGFISH
(— WITHOUT COURAGE) CRAVEN
(— WITHOUT SPURS) MUCKNA
(FIGHTING —) FUGIE HEELER TURNPOKE
(TURKEY —) STAG
(WATER —) KORA
(WEATHER —) FANE VANE

(PREF.) ALECTORO ALECTRYO GALLI

COCKADE KNOT BADGE COCKARD ROSETTE TRICOLOR

COCKATIEL QUARRION

COCKATOO ARA ARARA COCKY GALAH MACAW ABACAY COCKIE PARROT CORELLA JACATOO CALANGAY GANGGANG

COCKATOO BUSH BLUEBERRY

COCKBOAT COG COCK SCULL COGBOAT

COCKCHAFER MAYBUG OAKWEB BUZZARD HUMBUZZ MAYBEETLE

COCKCROW DAWN

COCKED HAT SCRAPER RAMILLIE

COCKER CODDLE COGGER CUITER QUIVER SPANIEL

COCKEREL COCK SLIP BANTAM

COCKFIGHT MAIN SPAR

COCKINESS BRAVADO SWAGGER

COCKLE COCK GALL GITH KILN OAST BULGE KAKEL SHELL STOVE DARNEL NUCULA PALOUR PUCKER RIPPLE WABBLE ZIZANY CUCKOLD WRINKLE HARDHEAD
(PREF.) CONCH(O)

COCKLEBUR COTS CLOTE COCKLE BURDOCK BURWEED CADILLO CLOTBUR CUCKOLD CLOTWEED DITCHBUR

COCKNEY ARRY ORTHERIS LONDONESE

COCKPIT PIT RING RINK WELL ARENA CABIN FIELD GALLERA

COCKROACH BUG DRUM ROACH BEETLE BLATTID DRUMMER KNOCKER

COCKSCOMB CREST COXCOMB

COCKSFOOT HARDGRASS

COCKSPUR FINGRIGO GARABATO

COCKTAIL SOUR ZOOM BRONX CRUSTA GIBSON GIMLET MAITAI COBBLER MARTINI NEGRONI SAZERAC SIDECAR STINGER SWIZZLE APERITIF DAIQUIRI MARGARITA GRASSHOPPER TEQUILASUNRISE
(— INGREDIENT) SAZERAC
(KIND OF —) MOLOTOV

COCK-UP MESS

COCKY PERK PERT CRANK PERKY CROUSE FARMER JAUNTY COCKING ARROGANT

COCO KOKO BROMA COCOA COKER YUNTIA

COCOA MAHAL TURTLE PATASHTE

COCOA BROWN PUEBLO

COCONUT COCO COCKER NARGIL COCOANUT

COCONUT FIBER COIR KAIR KYAR CAYAR

COCONUT MEAT COPRA

COCONUT PALM KOKO NIOG

COCOON POD CLEW CLUE KELL SCAB SHED SHELL BOTTOM DOUPION FOLLICLE

COCO PLUM ICACO HICACO

COCOWOOD KOKRA

COCOYAM TARO YAUTIA

COCUSWOOD KOKRA

COD BAG BIB COR KID POD AXLE BANK CUSK FOOL GADE HOAX HUSK POOR ROCK BELLY DORSE DROUD GADID POUCH SCROD SHALE SHAUP TORSK BURBOT CODGER CULTUS ESCROD FELLOW MULVEL PILLOW POCKET TOMCOD WACHNA BACALAO CODFISH CODLING CUSHION KEELING KILLING MILWELL MORRHUA SCROTUM CABELIAU DOLEFISH KABBELOW KLIPFISH ROCKLING
(BUFFALO —) LING
(CURED —) DUNFISH
(DRIED —) STOCK
(PILE OF DRIED —) YAFFLE
(SALTED —) COR KLIPFISH HABERDINE
(YOUNG —) SPRAG

CODA END CAUDA RONDO EPILOG FINALE CODETTA EPILOGUE POSTLUDE

CODDLE PET BABY CADE COOK MUCH HUMOR NURSE SMALM SPOIL CARESS COCKER COSSET COTTON FONDLE PAMPER PTISAN QUADLE PARBOIL

CODE BCD LAW FLAG ASCII CANON CODEX DOGMA FUERO CIPHER DIGEST SECRET SIGNAL MULTEKA PRECEPT DOOMBOOK MICROCODE
(— OF CEREMONIES) RITUAL
(— OF CHIVALRY) BUSHIDO
(— OF LAWS) ADA ADAT PANDECT SHERIAT DOOMBOOK
(— OF REGULATIONS) RULE
(— OF RULES) VINAYA
(— OF WHAT IS FITTING) DECORUM PROTOCOL
(— WORD) ALFA XRAY ZULU ROGER ROMEO TANGO SIERRA VICTOR YANKEE WHISKEY
(COMPUTER —) BCD ASCII
(INFORMATION —) EBCDIC
(KIND OF —) ZIP AREA MORSE PENAL
(PUNCHCARD —) HOLLERITH
(PUNCH CARD —) HOLLERITH
(READ BAR —S) SCAN

CODETTA CONDUIT

CODE WORD EUPHEMISM

CODEX ALEF CODE ALEPH ANNAL

CODFISH POOR SPRAG TORSK KEELING

CODGER COD CUFF CHURL CRANK MISER FELLOW NIGGARD

CODICIL ANNEX LABEL SCRIPT

CODIFY INDEX DIGEST CLASSIFY

CODLING HAKE

CODOL RETINOL

CODON TRIPLET

CODSWALLOP TRIPE

COEFFICIENT CUMULANT AUSTAUSCH

COELENTERATE POLYP MEDUSA ACALEPH RADIATE ACALEPHE

COENOBIUM COLONY

COENOCYTE SYMPLASM SYMPLAST SYNCYTIUM

COENZYME NAD NADH NADP NADPH COFACTOR

COERCE COW CURB MAKE BULLY CHECK DRIVE FORCE ORDER COHERT COMPEL HIJACK CONCUSS ENFORCE REPRESS SANDBAG BLUDGEON BULLDOZE DISTRAIN RESTRAIN RESTRICT BLACKJACK

COERCION HEAT FORCE DURESS COMMAND

COEUR D'ALENE SKITSWISH

COEUS (BROTHER OF —) ENCELADUS
(DAUGHTER OF —) LETO LATONA ASTERIA
(FATHER OF —) URANUS
(MOTHER OF —) GAEA
(SISTER OF —) FAMA RUMOR
(WIFE OF —) PHOEBE

COFFEE JO JOE RIO CAFE COHO COHU JAVA MILD DECAF MOCHA BOGOTA BRAZIL CAUFLE CHAQUA JAMOKE SANTOS TRIAGE ARABICA BOURBON MELANGE SUMATRA ESPRESSO MAZAGRAN MEDELLIN TRILLADO CAPUCCINO CAPPUCCINO
(— DISPENSER) URN
(DECAFFEINATED —) DECAF
(KIND OF —) DECAF
(MORNING —) ELEVENS

COFFEE BEAN QUAKER

COFFEEBERRY JOJOBA CASCARA SOYBEAN PEABERRY

COFFEE CAKE KUCHEN

COFFEECAKE (ROUND —) TEARING

COFFEE-CUP FINGAN FINJAN

COFFEEHOUSE INN CAFE CAFENEH CAFENER CAFENET

COFFEEMAKER SILEX

COFFEEPOT PERCOLATOR

COFFEE TREE BONDUC CHICOT VIRGILIA

COFFER ARK BOX DAM PYX CHEST HUTCH TRUNK CASKET FORCER FORCET SPRUCE TRENCH CAISSON CASHBOX CASSOON COFFRET LACUNAR LAQUEAR CIBORIUM STANDARD

COFFIN BIER CASE CIST KIST MOLD PALL SHELL BASKET CASING CASKET COFFER HEARSE TROUGH THROUGH
(LEADEN —) COPE

COG CAM LIE NOG CAUK COCK GEAR JEST CATCH CHEAT CHOCK CHUCK COGUE COZEN TENON TOOTH TRICK WEDGE WHEEL CAJOLE COGGING DECEIVE PRODUCE QUIBBLE WHEEDLE

COGENT GOOD PITHY VALID POTENT STRONG TELLING FORCIBLE POWERFUL PREGNANT

COGITATE MULL MUSE PLAN THINK PONDER CONNATE MEDIATE REFLECT CONSIDER

COGNATE KIN AKIN ALIKE ALLIED COGENER KINDRED RELATED SIMILAR BANDHAVA RELATIVE APOPHONIC

COGNITION GNOSIS NOESIS KENNING KNOWLEDGE PERCEPTION
(SUFF) GNOSIA GNOSIC GNOSTIC GNOSY

COGNITIVE KNOWING EPISTEMIC

COGNIZANCE KEN WIT HEED MARK BADGE CREST EMBLEM NOTICE BEARING COCKADE KNOWING PRIVITY WITTING

COGNIZANT WARE WISE AWAKE AWARE GUILTY KNOWING WITTING ACKNOWNE SENSIBLE
(BE —) DEEM

COGNIZE KNOW

COGNOMEN NAME BYNAME AGNOMEN SURNAME NICKNAME PATRONYM

COGON ILLUK KUNAI LALANG

COGWOOD CERILLO

COHABIT BED LIVE DWELL ADHERE OCCUPY COMPANY ACCUSTOM

CO-HEIR PARCENER

COHERE FIT BOND GLUE SUIT AGREE CLING SEIZE STICK UNITE ADHERE CEMENT CLEAVE CONNECT COINCIDE

COHERENCE UNION CONSENT CONTEXT COHESION STRENGTH

COHERENT SERRIED

COHESION BOND ADHESION HARDNESS STRENGTH

COHESIVE FATTY GLUEY TENACIOUS

COHESIVENESS TENACITY

COHOBA PARICA

COHORT PAL ALLY BUDDY FRIEND PARTNER

COHOSH SQUAWROOT PAPOOSEROOT

COHUNE COROJO COROZO

COIF CAP HOW HOOD HOUVE BEGGIN BIGGIN BURLET HAIRDO QUAIFE

ARRANGE CALOTTE BIGGONET
COIFFURE SKULLCAP
COIFFURE COIF HEAD HAIRDO
TUTULUS TRESSURE
(KIND OF —) BOB BUN AFRO
PAGEBOY
COIL ADO WIN WIP ANSA CLEW CURL
FAKE FANK FURL FUSS HANK LINK
LOOP ROLL TUFT WIND ENROL
FLAKE HELIX QUERL QUILE ROUND
SPIRE TENSE TESLA TWINE TWIRL
TWIST WHORL WRING BOBBIN
BOTTOM BOUGHT DIMMER ENROLL
GLOMUS HEATER RENDER RUNDLE
SPIRAL TEASER TOROID TUMULT
UPWIND VOLUME WINDUP WREATH
ENTRAIL HAYCOCK INVOLVE
PRIMARY RINGLET ROULEAU
SNAKING TICKLER TROUBLE
WREATHE COFUSION CONVOLVE
ENCIRCLE INDUCTOR OVERCOIL
(— IN STILL) SCROLL
(— INTO BALL) WIRE
(— OF CAPILLARIES) TUFT
(— OF HAIR) BUN PUG
(— OF SNAKE) FOLD
(— OF WIRE) BOBBIN SOLENOID
(— OF YARN) SKEIN
(INDUCTION —) JIGGER
(PREF.) SPIRILLO SPIR(I)(O)
COILED GYRATE TORTILE WRITHEN
TURBINAL
COILER FLARER
COILING SPIRY
COIN AS BU PU AVO BAN BIT BOO
COB DAM DIE DUB ECU FIL JOE KIP
LAT LEK LEU LEV LEY ORI PUL SEN
SOL TRA WEN WON ZUZ ABAS
ANNA ATTE BAHT BATZ BESA CASH
CENT CHIP CHON DEMY DIME DOIT
DONG DOTT DUMP DURO FELS FILS
GILL GROS GROT HARP HOON
HWAN JACK JANE KRAN KYAT LEVY
LION MAIL MAKE MERK MILL MINT
MITE MULE OBAN ONZA OORD
PARA PAUL PESA PESO PICE POND
POUL QUAN RAND RIAL ROCK RYAL
SCAD SENT SINK SIZE SLUG TAEL
TARA TARE TARI TARO TIAO TREY
TYPE UNIT ACKEY AGNEL AGORA
AKCHA ALBUS ALTIN ALTUN AMANI
ANGEL ANGLE ASPER BAIOC BAIZA
BATTE BEKAR BELGA BETSO BEZZO
BISTI BLANC BLANK BODLE BROAD
BROWN CHINK CLINK COIGN
CONTO COROA CROSS CROWN
CUNYE DARIC DINAR DISME DOBLA
DUCAT EAGLE EYRIR FANAM FANON
FODDA FRANC GAZET GRANO
GROAT GROSZ HALER HECTE
JACOB JULIO JUSTO KOBAN
KRONA KRONE KROON LIARD LIBRA
LITRA LIVRE LOUIS MEDAL MEDIN

MEDIO MILAN MOHUR MOPUS
NOBLE NOMOS OBANG ORKEY
ORKYN PAISA PAOLO PARDO PENNY
PERAU PESSA PIECE PLACK PLATE
POALI POALO PROOF PRUTA QUART
QUINE RAPPE REBIA RIDER RIYAL
ROYAL RUBLE RUPIA SAGA SAPEK
SCEAT SCUDO SCUTE SEMIS SHAHI
SICCA SMASH SOLDO STAMP
STYCA SUCRE TALER TANGA TANKA
TEMPO THRIP TICAL TRIME UNCIA
UNITE WHITE ABASSI ABBASI
AFGHAN AHMADI ARGENT ASSARY
AUREUS AZTECA BALBOA BAUBEE
BAWBEE BEAVER BEZANT BIANCO
BLANCO BOGACH BRONZE CARLIN
CENTAS CHAISE COBANG CONDOR
COPPER CORONA CUARTO CUNZIE
DECIME DENARY DENIER DERHAM
DINDER DIOBOL DIRHAM DIXAIN
DIZAIN DOBLON DODKIN DOLLAR
DOPPIA DOUBLE ESCUDO FILLER
FLORIN FOLLIS FORINT GEORGE
GIULIO GOURDE GRIVNA GROSSO
GUINEA GULDEN HARPER HELLER
ICHIBU ITZEBU JUSLIK KLIPPE
KOPECK KORONA KORUNA LAUREL
LEPTON MACUTA MAHBUB MAIDEN
MANCUS MEDINO MISKAL NICKEL
NORKYN OCHAVO OCTAVE ONGARO
PADUAN PAGODA PARDAO PATACA
PATART PHILIP PRUTAH QUEZAL
ROSARY SALUNG SALUTE SATANG
SEQUIN SESKIN SHEKEL SHIELD
SIGLOS SINKER SIXAIN SOMALO
SOVRAN STATER STELLA STIVER
TALENT TARGET TESTAO TESTER
TESTON THALER THOMAN TOSTON
TRIENS TUMAIN TUNGAH TURNER
TURNEY TURTLE UNGARO VINTEM
XERIFF YUZLIK ZECHIN ZEHNER
ZEQUIN ALFONSO ALTILIK ANGELET
ANGELOT ANGOLAR ANGSTER
BAIOCCO BAJOCCO BARBONE
BOLIVAR CARDECU CARLINE
CARLINO CAROLIN CAROLUS
CENTAVO CHALCUS CHALKOS
CORDOBA COUNTER CRUSADO
DAMPANG DRACHMA DUCATON
DUPLONE ESCALAN FANTASY
JACOBUS JOANNES KASBEKE
KREUZER LEMPIRA LEONINE
LEOPARD LUIGINO MANGOUR
MARENGO MOIDORE MONARCH
MUZOONA NOUMMOS ONCETTA
PAHLAVI PARISIS PATACAO
PATAGON PATAQUE PENNING
PFENNIG PISTOLE QUADRIN
QUARTER QUATTIE QUETZAL
QUINYIE REDDOCK RUDDOCK
RUSPONE SANTIMS SCRUPLE
SEXTANS SILIQUA SIZEINE SOLIDUS
SPECIES STAMPEE STOOTER

STUIVER SULTANE TALLERO
TEECALL THRYMSA TORNESE
TRIOBOL UNICORN XERAFIN
ALBERTIN AMBROSIN AQUILINO
AUGUSTAL AUKSINAS BAETZNER
BAGATINE BECHTLER BLAFFERT
BLANKEEL BLANKILO BROCKAGE
CAVALIER CHINKERS CHUCKRAM
COLONIAL COURONNE CROCKARD
CRUZEIRO DECUSSIS DENARIUS
DIDRACHM DIOBOLON DOUBLOON
EQUIPAGA FARTHING FILIPPIC
FREDERIK GAZZETTA GENOVINO
GIGLIATO GIUSTINA GROSCHEN
HARDHEAD HYPERPER IMPERIAL
ISABELLA JOHANNES KREUTZER
LUSHBURG MACARONI MAJIDIEH
MARAVEDI MARCELLO METALLIK
MILESIMA PATACOON PAVILION
PICAYUNE PIEDFORT PISTOLET
PLAPPERT PORTAGUE QUADRANS
QUADRINE QUARTINE QUINCUNX
RESTRIKE RIGMAREE RISDALER
RIXDALER SCUDDICK SEMUNCIA
SESTERCE SHILLING SIXPENCE
SKILLING SLEEPING SOLIDARE
STERLING STOTINKA SULTANIN
TENPENNY TETROBOL THIRTEEN
TWOPENCE ZECCHINO BRACTEATE
(— AROUND NECK) TALI
(— FLIP CALL) HEADS TAILS
(— HAVING MINTING ERROR) FIDO
(— IMPERFECTLY MINTED)
BROCKAGE
(— OF TRIFLING VALUE) RAP
(BASE) SHAND GREEN GINKER
(CLAD —) SANDWICH
(COUNTERFEIT —) RAP GRAY GREY
SLIP SHEEN SHOFUL STUMER
STUMOR
(ISRAEL —) AGORA
(ISRAEL —S) AGOROT
(PLUGGED —) PLUG
(SMALL THICK —) DUMP
(PL.) AGOROT CHANGE CHINKS
SERIES COINAGE
(PREF.) NUMISMATO NUMMI
COINAGE FICTION GALUMPH
MINTAGE
COINCIDE FIT GEE JIBE JUMP AGREE
TALLY CONCUR
COINCIDENCE SYNCHRONY
COINCIDENT EVEN TOGETHER
COINCIDING CONGRUENT
CONSILIENT
COINER MONIER MONEYER
SMASHER
COINS CHANGE
COITION SOIL VENERY MEETING
CONGRESS
COKE ASK COAL COLK CORE DOPE
CHARK COCAINE
(BROKEN —) BREEZE

COL GAP NEK HALS JOCH PASS
HALSE SWIRE SADDLE
COLANDER SIEVE STRAINER
COLAXAIS (BROTHER OF —)
ARPOXAIS LIPOXAIS
(FATHER OF —) TARGITAUS
COLCOTHAR SAFFRON TUSCANY
COLD FLU ICY MUR NIP COOL DEAD
DULL FRIO HARD HASK HOAR MURR
ROUP SOUR ACALE ACOLD AGUED
ALGID BLEAK CHILL CRISP FISHY
FROID FRORE GELID GLACE GLARE
OORIE OURIE PARKY POOSE RHEUM
SHARP SNELL STONY VIRUS ARCTIC
BITTER BOREAL CHILLY CLAMMY
CRIMMY FREDDO FRIGID FRIGOR
FROSTY GLASSY MARBLY STECKY
WAIRCH WINTRY BRITTLE CATARRH
CHILLED COLDISH COSTIVE DISTANT
FROSTED GLACIAL INHUMAN
MORFOND SHIVERY STRANGE
FREEZING MORFOUND PIERCING
RESERVED RHIGOSIS STANDOFF
UNHEATED REPULSIVE
(— IN HEAD) POSE POOSE CORYZA
CATARRH GRAVEDO SNIVELS
SNIFFLES SNIFTERS
(BITTER —) ARCTIC
(VERY —) ICY GELID FRIGID PEEVISH
(PREF.) CRY(O) FRIGO FRIGORI KRY(O)
PSYCHRO
COLD-BLOODED BRUTAL LEEPIT
COLD CUTS ASSIETTE
COLD-HEARTED COLD FROZEN
BLOODLESS
COLDLY DAILY DRYLY
COLDNESS COLD FROST STEEL
PHLEGM ALGIDITY ASPERITY
DISTANCE FROIDEUR
COLDONG FRIARBIRD
COLE CALE KAIL KALE COLZA FRIGOR
COLEWORT
COLE-SEED COLZA NAVEW
COLESEED NAVEW
COLEUS KOORKA
COLEWORT COLE KALE RIBE STOCK
CABBAGE
(SPROUT OF —) STOVEN
COLIC BATS FRET BATTS GUTTIE
BELLYACHE
COLICROOT UNICORN ALOEROOT
HUSKROOT HUSKWORT STARWORT
COLIMA TAPA IRONWOOD
COLISEUM HALL STADIUM THEATER
COLOSSEUM
COLL HUG CLIP CULL POLL PRUNE
EMBRACE
COLLABORATE AID ASSIST
COOPERATE
COLLAGEN OSSEIN
COLLAPSE CAVE FALL FLOP FOLD
GIVE SINK WILT CRASH SLUMP
WRECK BUCKLE SHRINK TUMBLE

COLLAPSE CAPSIZE CROPPER CRUMBLE
CRUMPLE DEBACLE DEFLATE
FAILURE FLUMMOX FOUNDER
SMASHUP CONTRACT DOWNFALL
MELTDOWN TAILSPIN PROSTRATION
(— OF NUCLEUS) SYSTOLE
COLLAPSED QUAT CLUNG
COLLAPSIBLE FOLDING
COLLAPSING FAILURE COLLABENT
COLLAR CAP FUR NAB DAB BOSS
ETON FALL FANO GILL GRAB POKE
RING RUFF CHAIN DICKY FANON
FANUM FICHU PHANO RUCHE SEIZE
STOCK TRASH WHISK BERTHA
CARCAN CHOKER COLLET COLLUM
DICKEY GORGET PARRAL PARREL
RABATO REBATO SADDLE SLEEVE
TACKLE TORQUE TUCKER TURNUP
BOBACHE BOBECHE CAPTURE
CHIGNON CIRCLET PANUELO
PARTLET POTHOOK REBATER
SHACKLE STICKUP VANDYKE
CARCANET CINCTURE NECKBAND
NECKLACE RABATINE STARCHER
TURNDOWN
(— FOR HORSE) BARGHAM BRECHAM
(HIGH —) GILLS JAMPOT
(HORSE —) BRECHAM
(IRON —) JOUG JOUGS CARCAN
POTHOOKS
(LACE —) SCALLOP
(MAGISTRATE'S —) GOLILLA
(ROMAN —) RABAT
(WHEEL-SHAPED —) RUFF
(WOODEN —) CANG CANGUE
COLLAR BEAM SPANNER
SPANPIECE
COLLARBONE CLAVICLE
COLL'ARCO ARCATO
COLLARED ACCOLLE ACCOLLEE
TORQUATE
COLLAR PAD AFTERWALE
COLLATE BESTOW CONFER VERIFY
COMPARE
COLLATERAL SIDE ASSETS MARGIN
OBLIQUE INDIRECT PARALLEL
SECURITY
COLLATION TEA MEAL BEVER
LUNCH REPAST SERMON ADDRESS
READING DEJEUNER HOTCHPOT
TREATISE
COLLEAGUE AIDE ALLY UNITE
DEPUTY SOCIUS ADJUNCT COLLEGE
COMPEER CONSORT PARTNER
CONFRERE CONSPIRE
COLLECT JUG SAM TAX CALL CARD
CULL DRAW HEAP LEVY LIFT PICK
PILE POOL REAR SAMM SAVE AMASS
CROWD GLEAN GROUP HOARD
RAISE STORE SWEEP ACCOIL
ACCRUE CENTER CONFER GARNER
GATHER MUSTER PRAYER SEMBLE
SHEAVE UPTAKE ARCHIVE CLUSTER

COMPILE CONGEST ENGROSS
IMPOUND RAMMASS RECUEIL
SCAMBLE SYNAPTE ASSEMBLE
CONFLATE CONTRACT CUPBOARD
INGATHER RESEMBLE SCRAMBLE
SCROUNGE
(— AND DRIVE INTO ENCLOSURE)
WEAR
(— FOOD) FORAGE
(— GRAIN) GAVEL
(— INTO COVEY) JUG
(— MONEY) NOB
(— WAGES) UPLIFT
COLLECTED CALM COOL SOBER
SERENE PRESENT COMPOSED
(PREF.) ATHRO
COLLECTION ANA BAG KIT SET
BAND BEVY BOOK CLAN CROP FILE
HEAD HEAP KNOT LEVY OLIO RAFT
SORT ALBUM ANNEX ARRAY BATCH
BUDGE BUNCH DEPOT FLOCK GLEAN
GROUP HOARD KITTY SHEAF STORE
SUITE SWATH TROVE AFFLUX
BUDGET BUNDLE CONGER CORPUS
FARDEL MISHNA PARCEL RAGBAG
RECULE SORITE SPRING SWATHE
TUMBLE ACCOUNT BOILING
BULLARY CLUSTER COLLECT
CONGERY EXHIBIT FERNERY FISTFUL
FLUTTER GALLERY QUOTITY RECUEIL
SAMHITA SMATTER SMYTRIE
SYLLOGE TERRIER ASSEMBLY
CABOODLE CONGERIE CUSTOMAL
FASCICLE GATHERUM GLOSSARY
JINGBANG ROMESCOT ROMESHOT
SYNTAGMA
(— AT FOX HUNT) CAP
(— OF ALMS) QUEST
(— OF ANIMALS) ZOO HEAD
(— OF BOOKCASES) STACK
(— OF BOOKS) SET BIBLE CANON
LIBRARY
(— OF CONIFERS) PINETUM
(— OF DATA) GROUND
(— OF FORMULAS) CODEX
(— OF FOUR) TETRAD
(— OF HUTS) BUSTEE
(— OF JOKES) SOTTISIER
(— OF LAWS) CODE
(— OF MAPS) ATLAS
(— OF OBJECTS) AFFAIR
(— OF OPINIONS) SYMPOSIUM
(— OF PERSONS) BOODLE
(— OF PLANTS) SERTULE
(— OF POEMS) DIVAN DIWAN SYLVA
ANTHOLOGY
(— OF PUS) ABSCESS HYPOPYON
(— OF REVENUES) TAHSIL TEHSIL
(— OF ROCKS) SUITE
(— OF RULES) SUTRA SUTTA
(— OF SAMPLES) SWATCH
(— OF SAYINGS) ANA SUTRA SUTTA
(— OF SMALL THINGS) SMYTRIE

(— OF SPECIMENS) CABINET
(— OF STAFFS) SYSTEM
(— OF STORIES) LEGEND
(— OF TIPS) TRONC
(— OF TOOLS) LAYOUT
(— OF TREES) SERINGAL
(— OF UNWANTED ANIMALS)
LARDER
(— OF VIEWS) SYMPOSIUM
(— OF WIVES) SERAGLIO
(— OF WRITINGS) CORPUS
(— OF 24 SHEETS) QUIRE
(CHURCH —) PLATE
(CONFUSED —) CLUTTER
(MISCELLANEOUS —) OLIO FARDEL
SMYTRIE
(VALUABLE —) TROVE
(VAST —) CLOUD
(SUFF.) ERY
COLLECTION-BOX LADLE
COLLECTIVE ARTEL GROUP
AGGREGATE
COLLECTIVELY ASONE
COLLECTIVIST COMMUNIST
SOCIALIST
COLLECTOR COMB CAMEIST
CURIOSO DUSTMAN FURIOSO
UPTAKER ANTIQUER COUNTOUR
GATHERER OOLOGIST STAMPMAN
VIRTUOSO ZAMINDAR
(— ITEMS) RARIORA
(— OF BUTTERFLIES) AURELIAN
(— OF HERBS) SIMPLER
(— OF REVENUE) AUMIL AUMILDAR
TALUKDAR ZAMINDAR
(— OF UNNEEDED ITEMS) PACKRAT
(BILL —) DUNNER
(CUSTOMS —) HOPPO CUSTOMER
(INDISCRIMINATE —) MAGPIE
(ITEMS OF —) VIRTU
(TAX —) CAID QAID GABBAI
PUBLICAN TAHSILDAR
COLLECTORATE TALUK
COLLEEN GIRL LASS MISS BELLE
CAILIN DAMSEL
COLLEGE TOL HALL AGGIE HOUSE
LYCEE CAMPUS COLAGE SCHOOL
SIWASH ACADEMY MADRASA
SEMINARY SORBONNE
(KIND OF —) CLUSTER
(MUSLIM —) MADRASA MADRASSAH
COLLEGER TUG
COLLET BAND NECK RING CHUCK
CULET CASING CIRCLE COLLAR
COLLUM FLANGE BUSHING
COLLIDE HIT RAM BUMP DASH FRAY
HURT BARGE CLASH CRASH KNOCK
SHOCK SMITE WRECK CANNON
HURTLE STRIKE THRUST
(— HEAD-ON) RAM
(— WITH) PRANG
(— WITH) IMPINGE
COLLIE KELPIE BEARDIE

COLLIER MINER PLOVER GEORDIE
COILYEAR FLATIRON SCUTCHER
COLLIERY MINE
COLLIMATE ALIGN
COLLINATE ALIGN
COLLIQUATION SYNTEXIS
COLLISION HIT FOUL CLASH CRASH
PRANG SHOCK SHUNT HURTLE
IMPACT JOSTLE PILEUP SMASHUP
CLASHING CONFLICT
COLLOCATE SET PLACE ARRANGE
COLLOID GEL
COLLOP PIECE
COLLOQUIAL FAMILIAR INFORMAL
COLLOQUIUM INDUCEMENT
COLLOQUY CHAT TALK PARLEY
DIALOGUE
COLLOTYPE ARTOTYPE HELIOTYPE
COLLUDE PLOT SCHEME CONNIVE
COLLOGUE CONSPIRE
COLLUM NECK
COLLUSION DECEIT CAHOOTS
SECRECY PRACTICE PRACTISE
COLLUSIVE COVINOUS COLLUSORY

COLOMBIA

CAPE: VELA AGUJA MARZO AUGUSTA
CAPITAL: BOGOTA
CAY: VELA VIGIA RONCADOR
COIN: PESO REAL CONDOR PESETA
CENTAVO
FORMER NAME: DARIEN
NEWGRANADA
GULF: URABA CUPICA DARIEN TIBUGA
TORTUGAS
INDIAN: BORO CUNA HOKA MACU
MUZO PAEZ CARIB CATIO CHOCO
COFAN COGUI CUBEO GUANE PIJAO
SEONA ARAWAK BETOYA CALIMA
INGANO SALIVA TAHAMI TUCANO
TUNEBO YAHUNA ACHAGUA
ANDAQUI CHIBCHA CHIMILA
GUAHIBO GUAJIRO PANCHES
PUINAVE PUITOTO QUECHUA
TAIRONA GUARAUNO MOTILONE
INLET: TUMACO
ISLAND: BARU NAIPO FUERTE
GORGONA CUSACHON
MEASURE: VARA AZUMBRE CELEMIN
MOUNTAIN: CHITA HUILA PURACE
TOLIMA
MOUNTAINS: ABIBE ANDES BAUDO
COCUY AYAPEL PERIJA TUNAHI
CHAMUSA ORIENGAL
PLAINS: LLANOS
POINT: CRUCES LACRUZ SOLANO
CARIBANA GALLINAS
PORT: LORICA CARTAGENA
PROVINCE: META CAUCA CHOCO
HUILA VALLE ARAUCA BOYACA
CALDAS NARINO TOLIMA VAUPES
BOLIVAR CAQUETA GUAJIRE
VICHADA AMAZONAS PUTUMAYO

RIVER: UVA BITA META MUCO SINU TOMO UPIA YARI BAUDO CAUCA CESAR ISANA MESAI NECHI PATIA PAUTO SUCIO AMAZON ARAUCA ARIARI ATRATO CAGUAN VAUPES YAPURA CAQUETA GUAINIA INIRIDA TRUANDO VICHADA APAPORIS CASANARE GUAVIARE PUTUMAYO MAGDALENA
TOWN: TEN ANZA BUGA CALI MITU MUZO PAEZ SIPI TADO TOLU YARI BELLO CHINU GUAPI NEIVA PASTO TUNJA BOGOTA CUCUTA IBAGUE QUIBDO SANGIL CARTAGO LETICIA PALMIRA PEREIRA POPAYAN GIRARDOT MEDELLIN MONTERIA CARTAGENA
TREE: ARBOLOCO
VOLCANO: PURACE
WEIGHT: BAG SACO CARGA LIBRA QUILATE QUINTAL

COLON CROWN POINT HEMISTICH MESYMNION
COLONEL (— OF LIFEGUARDS) GOLDSTICK
COLONIAL OVERSEA OVERSEAS
COLONIST BOOR COLON FATHER CUTHEAN PIONEER PLANTER SETTLER EMIGRANT
(— IN AFRICA) BOER
(— IN SICILY) SIKELIOT
(AUSTRALIAN —) STERLING
(PL.) DEHAITES DEHAVITES
COLONIZE ECIZE FOUND PLANT GATHER SETTLE MIGRATE
COLONIZER OECIST OEKIST
COLONNADE ROW STOA PORCH PARVIS PIAZZA XYSTUS EUSTYLE GALLERY PARVISE PERGOLA PORTICO TERRACE CHOULTRY DIASTYLE PERISTYLE
COLONNETTE COLUMELLA
COLONUS SERF TENANT
COLONY STATE STOCK SWARM CENOBE CORMUS APOIKIA COLONIA CENOBIUM GANNETRY PLANTATION POLYZOARIUM
(— OF BEES) HIVE SKEP SWARM
(BRYOZOAN —) ESCHARA
COLOPHONY ROSIN
COLOR (ALSO SEE SPECIFIC COLOR) DIP DYE HUE BLEE CAST FAKE FLAG PUKE SUIT TINT TONE BADGE BLUSH GLAZE GLOSS GRAIN PAINT SHADE STAIN TAINT TASTE TENNE TINCT TINGE TOUCH BANNER BLEACH BOTTOM BRIDGE CHROMA ENSIGN INFECT LOCKET MANTLE RADDLE REDDEN STREAK TEMPER COULEUR DEPAINT DISTORT ENGRAIN PENNANT PIGMENT SPECKLE

COLORING STANDARD TERTIARY TINCTURE
(— IMPARTED TO HERRINGS) GILDING
(— LOSS) POLIOSIS
(— OF BIRD) SMUT
(— OF BODY) HEAT
(— OF EYES OF FOWLS) DAW
(— OF HONEY) AMBER
(— OF HUMAN FLESH) CARNATION
(— OF REFLECTED LIGHT) OVERTONE
(— OF ROCK) STONE
(AUTUMN —) OCHER
(BLUE —) FOG JAY SKY WAD AQUA BICE CIEL CYAN DELF DUSK IRIS NAVY PAON SAXE WADE WOAD ZINC AZURE BERYL BLUET CADET CAPRI CHING COPEN DELFT DELPH DIANA DRAKE EMAIL GRAPE METAL NIKKO ORION PEARL ROYAL SLATE SMALT SMOKE VANDA CANTON CENDRE COELIN ENSIGN GROTTO HATHOR INDIGO LUPINE MARINE MASCOT MIGNON ORIENT PENSEE ROMANY SEVRES VENICE ZENITH CELESTE CERAMIC CHICORY DUSTBLU GOBELIN HORIZON LIBERTY LOBELIA LOGWOOD MATELOT PEACOCK PETUNIA RAMESES SISTINE SIXTINE ABSINTHE BLUEBIRD BLUEWOOD BRITTANY CAESIOUS CATTLEYA CERULEAN CERULEUM DUCKLING ELECTRIC GENDARME HYACINTH INFANTRY LABRADOR LARKSPUR MASCOTTE MAZARINE MIDNIGHT MOONBEAM NATIONAL SAPPHIRE TWILIGHT WEDGWOOD
(BROWN —) BAY ELK FOX OAK TAN ARAB BARK BOLE BRAN BURE CAIN CLAY CORK CUBA DATE DEER DRAB DUST ECRU FAON FAWN GOAT GOLD HOPI IRON LAMA LION MAST MESA MUSK PUCE SEAL SIAM TEAK ACORN ADUST ALOMA AZTEC BEIGE BISON BLOND BLUSH BOLUS BRIAR BRICK BRIER BROWN BUNNY CACAO CAMEL CANNA CLOVE COCOA CONGO EAGLE FRIAR FUDGE GIPSY GRAIN GYPSY HAZEL HENNA KAFFA KHAKI LIVER MAHAL MALAY MECCA MINIM MUMMY NEGRO OTTER PABLO QUAIL SABEL SEDGE SEPIA SIENA SIRUP SNUFF SUDAN SUEDE SUMAC SYRUP TABAC TAFFY TENNE TOAST TOPAZ AFGHAN ALESAN ALMOND APACHE ARGALI AUBURN BAMBOO BEAVER BISQUE BISTER BISTRE BLONDE BRONCO BRONZE BURNET COCHIN COFFEE CONDOR COOKIE COWBOY CROTAL DORADO ESKIMO FALLOW GINGER GRAVEL GROUSE HAVANA ISABEL LOUTRE

MAROON MERIDA MOHAWK MUFFIN
NUTMEG ORIOLE PAWNEE PLOVER
PUEBLO RABBIT RACKET RUDDLE
RUSSET SAHARA SANTOS SHERRY
SORREL SPHINX SPONGE STRING
STUCCO SUMACH SUNTAN THRUSH
TIFFIN TURTLE ASPHALT BADIOUS
BEESWAX BITUMEN BRACKEN
BRONCHO CALDRON CATTAIL
CIGARET COCONUT COTRINE
CRACKER DOGWOOD DURANGO
FEUILLE FILBERT GAZELLE GOREVAN
HARVEST LEATHER LIBERIA
MALABAR MIRADOR MORDORE
MOROCCO MUSCADE MUSTANG
NORFOLK OAKWOOD PERIQUE
PRALINE RACQUET ROSARIO
SABELLA SUNBURN SUNDOWN
TALLYHO TANBARK TOBACCO
TUSCANY ALDERNEY ALGERIAN
AMBROSIA BISMARCK BOBOLINK
CALABASH CARTOUCH CAULDRON
CINNAMON CLAYBANK CORDOVAN
DOUBLOON ETRUSCAN EUCHROME
HAZELNUT ISABELLA KOLINSKY
LEAFMOLD MANDALAY MOCCASIN
MOLESKIN MOROCCAN MUSHROOM
NOISETTE PHEASANT SAUTERNE
SHAGBARK STARLING TAMARACK
TEAKWOOD TERRAPIN TORTOISE
WOODBARK
(DEAD-LEAF —) FILEMOT
(DEEP —) DARK
(FAST —) GRAIN
(FAWN —) WHEATEN
(GREEN —) BOA FIR IVY ALOE BICE
FERN JADE LEEK MOSS NILE SAGE
ALOES CEDRE CHLOR DRAKE FAIRY
HOLLY KELLY LOVAT OLIVE SPRAY
CANNON EMPIRE HUNTER JASPER
LAUREL LIERRE LIZARD MEADOW
MOUSSE MYRTLE SPRUCE VERDET
CELADON CITRINE CORBEAU
CRESSON CYPRESS EMERALD
INGENUE JADEITE JUNIPER
MESANGE NEPTUNE OLIVINE
PERIDOT SEAFOAM SERPENT
TILLEUL VERDURE BAYBERRY
CHASSEUR COPPERAS EMERAUDE
GLAUCOUS GLOWWORM PARAKEET
PERRUCHE PISTACHE POPINJAY
SHAMROCK TARRAGON VIRIDIAN
WOODLAND
(GRIZZLED —) AGOUTI AGOUTY
(LACK OF —) PALLOR
(LOSE —) FADE
(OF A DARKISH —) SUBFUSE
(OTHER —S) OR ASH BAT DOE DUN
JET TEA CHIP CORN CROW DAWN
DOVE GRAY GREY GULL HEMP LAVA
LEAD MODE MOLE NICE NUDE PLUM
PORT PUKE ROAN RUST SAND SOOT

WOOD AMBER BEACH BLACK CAMEO
CERES CHILE CHILI COPRA CRANE
CRASH CREAM DWALE EBONY FLESH
GRAPE GREBE GREGE MAUVE
MOUSE PANSY PHLOX PLOMB
PRAWN PRUNE PUTTY RIFLE SABLE
SPICE STEEL THYME TWINE ANATTO
AURORA AUTUMN CASTOR CINDER
COLLIE CORCIR DAHLIA DAMSON
DENVER EVEQUE FIESTA FUSTIC
GAMBIA GRIEGE KASPER MALLOW
MODENA NAVAHO NAVAJO NIMBUS
NUTRIA ONDINE ORCHID OXFORD
OYSTER PEANUT PEBBLE PIGEON
QUAKER RAISIN RESEDA ROUCOU
SEASAN SILVER TUSCAN VANITY
VESTAL VIOLET WALNUT ADMIRAL
ANNATTO ARBUTUS ARDOISE
ARNATTA BEGONIA BERMUDA
BLOSSOM BRINDLE CARAIBE
CARAMEL CORBEAU COTRINE
COWSLIP CRACKER CRUISER
MORELLO MURILLO NATURAL
OPHELIA PELICAN PONTIFF POPCORN
PRELATE PUMPKIN QUIMPER
REGATTA ROSEBUD SAKKARA
SANDUST SPARROW SUNBEAM
THISTLE TUSSORE VERVAIN VIOLINE
WEIGELA WHEATEN ALUMINUM
AMARANTH AMETHYST BLONDINE
CARMETTA CHARCOAL CLEMATIS
COCOBOLO COQUETTE CREVETTE
CYCLAMEN EGGPLANT EMINENCE
FELDGRAU FLAMINGO GILLIVER
GRAPHITE GUNMETAL HONEYDEW
IMPERIAL JACINTHE LAVENDER
MARATHON MORILLON MULBERRY
PALMETTO ROSEWOOD SAUTERNE
SQUIRREL SUNBURST WIRELESS
WISTARIA WISTERIA CARNELIAN
(RED —) DAWN FLEA GOLF GOYA
HEBE LAKE MIST PUCE RUBY TULY
WINE AGATE BRASS BRICK CANNA
CANON CEDAR CORAL CUTCH
EMBER FLAME FLASH GULES LILAC
MELON NYMPH PEACH PEONY
POPPY ROSET SIENA SPARK TOTEM
ACAJOU ARCHIL AURORE AUTUMN
AZALEA BRAZIL CANYON CARROT
CATSUP CERISE CHERRY CHERUB
CLARET COGNAC DAMASK FRAISE
GAIETY GARNET GAYETY GRANET
JOCKEY KERMES MADDER MALAGA
MIKADO MURREY NECTAR ORCHIL
PATISE SALMON SANDIX SHRIMP
SIERRA SULTAN TITIAN TOMATO
AFRICAN ANAMITE ANEMONE
BEGONIA BISCUIT BOKHARA
CARMINE CASTORY CATAWBA
CATCHUP CATECHU CRIMSON
CURRANT FIREFLY FUCHSIA FUCHSIN
GRANATE GRANITE HEATHER

INDIANA KETCHUP LACQUER
LOBSTER MAGENTA MASCARA
NACARAT OXBLOOD PAPRIKA
POMPEII PONCEAU REDWOOD
ROSETAN ROSETTE RUBELLE
SAFFLOR SARAVAN SCARLET
SINOPLE STAMMEL SULTANA
VERMEIL ALKERMES AMARANTH
ARCHILLA BISMARCK BORDEAUX
BURGUNDY CAMELLIA CARDINAL
CHAUDRON CHEROKEE CHERUBIM
CHESTNUT COCOANUT CONFETTI
DAMONICO DIANTHUS DUBONNET
EVENGLOW GERANIUM GRENADIN
GRIDELIN MAHOGANY MANDARIN
MAROCAIN NACARINE TOREADOR
(SOLID —) SOLID
(TONE —) TIMBRE
(YELLOW —) HAY RAT WAX BEAR
BUFF CLAY CORN CUIR ECRU FLAX
GOLD LARK LIME MOTH WELD WOLD
ACIER ALOMA AZTEC BEIGE BLAKE
BRASS CRASH CREAM GRAIN HONEY
IVORY LEMON MAIZE MAPLE SHELL
STRAW TAUPE WOULD ACACIA
ALMOND BANANA CANARY CATHAY
CHROME CITRON CITRUS CROCUS
DORADO FALLOW MANILA MASTIC
MIMOSA NANKIN NUGGET OXGALL
SULFUR SUNRAY SUNSET ANTIQUE
APRICOT BISCUIT CAVALRY CHAMOIS
GAMBOGE JASMINE JONQUIL
LEGHORN MEXICAN NANKEEN
PRAIRIE RHUBARB SAFFRON
SULPHUR SUNGLOW ANTELOPE
CALABASH CAPUCINE COCKATOO
DAFFODIL EGGSHELL GENERALL
GOLDMIST MARIGOLD ORPIMENT
PRIMROSE SNOWSHOE
(PL.) FLAG
(PREF.) CHROM(AT)(ATO)(I)(IDIO)(O)
(HAVING DARK —) FUSCO
(SUFF.) CHROIA CHROIC CHROID
CHROMASIA CHROME CHROMIA
CHROMY CHROOUS
COLORABLE SPECIOUS PLAUSIBLE

COLORANT STAIN
COLORATION BLEE PILE FLASH
CLOUDING COLORISM SCHILLER
PIGMENTATION
COLORATURA GORGIA SOPRANO
COLOR-BLIND MONOCHROMATIC
(— TO RED) PROTANOPIC
COLOR-BLINDNESS DALTONISM
COLORED FAW HUED MALE TINCT
BIASED DEPAINT STAINED
(— IN RED) RUBRIC
(— LIKE PIPE BOWL) TROUSERED
(BRILLIANTLY —) SUPERB FLAMING
PSYCHEDELIC
(GORGEOUSLY —) FLAMBOYANT
(HIGHLY —) CHROMATIC PRISMATIC
(PARTI —) PIED PIEBALD
(UNIFORMLY —) HARD
(PREF.) CHROM(AT)(ATO)(I)(IDIO)(O)
(SUFF.) CHROME CHROOUS
COLORFUL GAY BRAVE JUICY VIVID
COLORY GOLDEN FREAKED
GORGEOUS
COLORING DYE BLEE TINT PAINT
TINGE TINGENT BRONZING PAINTING
TINCTURE
(— FOR EYELASHES) MASCARA
(— MATTER) TINCTION
(GARISH —) JAZZ
(SUFF.) CHROMY
COLORING MATTER
(SUFF.) PHYLL(A)(OUS)(UM)(Y)
COLORLESS WAN DRAB DULL PALE
ASHEN BLAKE BLANK PLAIN ANEMIC
MOUSEY PALLID HUELESS NEUTRAL
ACHROMIC ACHROOUS BLANCHED
ETIOLATE LIFELESS
(PREF.) LEUC(O)
COLOSSAL BIG HUGE VAST GREAT
JUMBO LARGE IMMENSE TITANIC
ENORMOUS GIGANTIC MONSTROUS
COLOSSUS GIANT TITAN STATUE
COLOSSO MONOLITH
COLOSTRUM FOREMILK AFTERINGS
COLT FOAL STAG FILLY POTRO STAIG
HOGGET POLEYN STAGGIE
EQUULEUS
COLTER LAVER COOTER COULTER
FOREIRON
COLTSFOOT DOCK CLOTE HOOFS
CLEATS FARFARA LAGWORT
SOWFOOT BULLFOOT CLAYWEED
FOALFOOT
COLUGO COBEGO
COLUMBATE NIOBATE
COLUMBIA SINKIUSE
COLUMBINE AQUILEGE BLUEBELL
CHUCKIES ROCKBELL
COLUMBITE DIANITE NIOBITE

COLUMBUS (BIRTHPLACE OF —) GENOA

COLUMELLA STALACE

COLUMN COG LAT ROW ANTA FILE FUST GOAL LINE POLE POST PROP STUB BAGUE LALLY SHAFT STELA STELE TORSO TRUNK WURTZ ASOKAN CORNER GNOMON PILLAR SCAPUS STAPLE STRING TSWETT COLUMEL SUPPORT VIGREUX CYLINDER PILASTER
(— IN EAR) MODIOLUS
(— OF FIGURES) SUM
(— OF FILAMENTS) SYNEMA
(— OF MOLTEN ROCK) PLUME
(BUDDHIST —) LAT
(FIGURE USED AS —) ATLAS TELAMON
(PART OF —) BASE DADO NECK OVOLO SHAFT TORUS ABACUS PLINTH REGLET SCOTIA CAPITAL ECHINUS FLUTING ASTRAGAL CINCTURE COLARENO PEDESTAL
(PART OF A —) SOCLE
(ROCK —) HOODOO
(ROULETTE —) DERNIER
(SPINAL —) HORN SPINE BACKBONE
(STRUCTURAL —) LALLY
(TWISTED —) TORSO

COLUMNAR TERETE STELENE COLUMNAL VERTICAL

COLUMNIST WRITER ANALYST

COLY MOUSEBIRD

COLZA SARSON

COMA TUFT BUNCH CARUS SLEEP SOPOR STUPOR SUBETH TORPOR TRANCE SEMICOMA CHEVELURE

COMATOSE OUT DROWSY LETHARGIC

COMB CARD GILL KAME LASH PICK RACK RAKE REDD REED SEEK TOZE BREAK BRUSH CAMBE CLEAN CREST CTENE CURRY FLISK RAVEL TEASE HACKLE SMOOTH CUSHION HATCHEL WRAITHE BEATILLE CARUNCLE TORTOISE
(KIND OF —) HOT
(WEAVING —) RADDLE
(PREF.) CTEN(O) LOPH(I)(IO)(O) PECTINATO

COMBAT WAR BLOW BOUT COPE DUEL FRAY MEEK MEET RUSH TILT CLASH FIGHT JOUST REPEL STOUR ACTION AFFRAY BATTLE MEDLEY OPPOSE RESIST SHOWER STRIFE CONTEND CONTEST COUNTER DERAIGN DISPUTE EXPLOIT SCUFFLE SERVICE ARGUMENT CONFLICT STRUGGLE
(— BETWEEN KNIGHTS) JOUST
(FUTILE —) SCIAMACHY
(SHAM —) SCIOMACHY
(SINGLE —) DUOMACHY

COMBATANT DUELER BATTLER FIGHTER CHAMPION GLADIATOR

COMBATIVE BANTAM MILITANT AGONISTIC BELLICOSE DEPENDENT PUGNACIOUS AGONISTICAL

COMBE HOPE

COMBED CRESTED

COMBER WAVE HANDER BREAKER KEMPSTER

COMBINATION KEY BLOC CLUB GANG PACT POOL RING CABAL COMBO GROUP JUNTO PARTY TRUST UNION CARTEL CLIQUE CORNER CRASIS FUSION LEAGUE MEDLEY MERGER AMALGAM BATTERY COMBINE CONSORT COTERIE FACTION HARMONY JOINING MIXTURE ADDITION ALLIANCE ENSEMBLE MONOPOLY GOODLIBET
(— OF CARDS) SET BUILD FLUSH SPREAD STRAIGHT
(— OF CIRCUMSTANCES) ACTION
(— OF COLORS) HARLEQUIN
(— OF FACES) FORM
(— OF FIRMS) TRUST
(— OF INTAGLIO FORMS) GRYLLI
(— OF NUMBERS) GIG SADDLE
(— OF TACKLES) JEERS
(— OF TONES) CHORD
(— OF 10) DECUPLET
(DANCE —) SEQUENCE
(HARMONIOUS —) CONCORD
(NOSE-JAW —) LAYBACK
(SCORING —) IMPERIAL
(PREF.) HAPT(O)

COMBINE ADD FIX MIX WED BIND BLOC CLUB JOIN NICK POOL BLEND GROUP JOINT MARRY MERGE TOTAL UNITE ABSORB CONCUR LEAGUE MEDDLE MERGER MINGLE SPLICE ACCRETE AMALGAM COMPACT CONJOIN CONJURE MACHINE COALESCE COMPOUND CONCRETE CONDENSE CONFLATE CONSTRUE CONTRACT CUMULATE FEDERATE ORCHESTRATE
(— AGAINST) BOYCOTT
(— WITH GAS) AERATE
(— WITH WATER) AQUATE

COMBINED GUM BOUND FIXED JOINT UNITED CONJOINT

COMB-LIKE PECTINAL

COMBO (SMALL —) TRIO

COMBUST START

COMBUSTIBLE FUEL FIERY ARDENT CINDER PICEOUS BURNABLE

COMBUSTION FIRE HEAT FLAME THERM TUMULT BURNING BACKFIRE

COME BE GET LAY COOP DRAW FALL GROW HAUL PASS WHEN ARISE CHIVE FETCH ISSUE LIGHT OCCUR REACH ACCRUE ADVENE APPEAR

ARRIVE BECOME BEFALL EMERGE
HAPPEN OBTAIN SPRING ADVANCE
DEVELOP EMANATE PROCEED
APPROACH PRACTICE
(— ABOUT) ARISE OCCUR CHANCE
(— AFTER) SUE FOLLOW
(— APART) FRAY SHED BREAK STAVE
(— BACK) REVERSE
(— BACK TO LIFE) REVIVE
(— BEFORE) FORERUN PREVENE
ANTECEDE ANTEDATE
(— BETWEEN) INTERPOSE
INTERVENE
(— DOWN) AVALE SWOOP ALIGHT
DESCEND SUCCEED DISMOUNT
(— FORTH) EMIT BREAK ISSUE
ACCEDE FORTHGO FURNACE
(— FORWARD) ACCEDE
(— IN CONTACT) ATTINGE
(— IN SECOND) PLACE
(— IN THIRD) SHOW
(— INTO BLOOM) BURST BLOSSOM
(— INTO COLLISION) MEET CLASH
COLLIDE
(— INTO EXISTENCE) FORM BEGIN
ACCRUE HAPPEN SPRING
(— INTO POSSESSION) ACQUIRE
INHERIT
(— OF AGE) MAJORIZE
(— OFF) HARL PEEL
(— OUT) ISSUE APPEAR EMERGE
EMANATE
(— SUDDENLY) CLAP PLUMP
(— THROUGH) DELIVER
(— TO) TOUCH ADVENE STRIKE
RECOVER REVERSE
(— TO AN END) PASS
(— TO BELIEVE IN) ADOPT
(— TO CONCLUSION) DECIDE
(— TO DIE) DO DIE SET DROP EXPIRE
FINISH SURCEASE
(— TOGETHER) ADD HERD JOIN MEET
AMASS CONCUR COUPLE GATHER
COLLECT COMBINE CONVENE
ASSEMBLE
(— TO GRIEF) FOUNDER
(— TO HAND) OFFER
(— TO LIGHT) SPUNK DEVELOP
(— TO MIND) OCCUR STRIKE
(— TO NOTHING) ABORT
(— TO PASS) SORT BREAK LIGHT
BEFALL BETIDE HAPPEN
(— TO PERFECTION) RIPEN
(— TO REST) LODGE SETTLE
(— TO STAND STILL) STOP
(— TO TERMS) AGREE TRYST
ACCORD BARGAIN COMPOSE
COMPOUND ACCOMMODATE
(— TO THE SURFACE) RISE
(— UNDER) SUBVENE
(— UPON) FIND CROSS INVENT
STRIKE OVERTAKE
(FULLY —) EXPIATE

COMEBACK RALLY ANSWER
RETORT RETURN REBOUND RIPOSTE
HAULBACK RECOVERY REPARTEE
COMECRUDO CARRIZO
COMEDIAN WAG WIT CARD ACTOR
ANTIC CLOWN COMIC GAGMAN
JESTER BUFFOON FUNSTER
COMOEDUS FUNMAKER FUNNYMAN
PATTERER
COMEDO BLACKHEAD
COMEDOWN BATHOS DESCENT
LETDOWN
COMEDY SOCK DRAMA FARCE
LAZZO REVUE SITCOM COMEDIA
TEMACHA COMOEDIA TRAVESTY
BACCHIDES SLAPSTICK
(HEROIC —) NATAKA
(KIND OF —) STANDUP
(SITUATION —) SITCOM
(PREF.) COMICO
COMEDY OF ERRORS
(AUTHOR OF —) SHAKESPEARE
(CHARACTER IN —) LUCE PINCH
AEGEON ANGELO DROMIO ADRIANA
AEMILIA EPHESUS LUCIANA
SOLINUS BALTHAZAR ANTIPHOLUS
COMELINESS GRACE DECORUM
FEATURE VENUSTY PULCHRITUDE
COMELY FAIR GOOD HEND PERT
TALL TIDY WEME BONNY BUXOM
HENDE QUEME SONCY SONSY
TIGHT DECENT FORMAL GOODLY
LIKELY LIKING LOVELY PRETTY
PROPER SEEMLY SONSIE VENUST
FARRANT FORMFUL SIGHTLY
BECOMING DECOROUS FEATURED
GRACEFUL HANDSOME PLEASING
SUITABLE
COME-ON TEASER
COMET STAR METEOR XIPHIAS
SUNGRAZER
(— HEAD) COMA
COMEUPPANCE REBUKE DESERTS
BUSINESS
COMFIT CANDY SUCKLE CONFECT
PRALINE CONSERVE PRESERVE
(PL.) CONFETTI
COMFORT AID EASE REST STAY
BIELD CHEER LIGHT SOOTH VISIT
ENDURE RELIEF REPOSE SOLACE
SOOTHE SUCCOR ANIMATE
ASSUAGE CHERISH CONFIRM
CONSOLE ENLIVEN GLADDEN
REFRESH RELIEVE SUPPORT SUSTAIN
INSPIRIT NEPENTHE PLEASURE
REASSURE GEMUTLICH
COMFORTABLE RUG BEIN BIEN
COSH COSY COZY EASY FEEL FEIL
LIKE SNUG TOSH TRIG CANNY
COMFY COUTH CUSHY LITHE QUEME
QUILT SCARF SONCY COUTHY
HEPPEN PENTIT SONSIE RELAXED
RESTFUL CHEERFUL DELICATE

EUPHORIC HOMELIKE WRISTLET
GEMUTLICH
COMFORTABLE-LOOKING SONSY
SONSIE
COMFORTABLY SWEETLY
COMFORTED CONSOLATE
COMFORTER PUFF COVER DUVET
EIDER NAHUM QUILT SCARF TIPPET
CHEERER PACIFIER
COMFORTING TOSY TOSIE
FRIENDLY
COMFORTLESS DREARY FORLORN
UNCOUTH DESOLATE EITHLESS
COMFREY DAISY BONESET
BACKWORT KNITBACK BRUISEWORT
COMIC WAG CLOWN DROLL FUNNY
STRIP BUFFONE COMIQUE THALIAN
COMEDIAN FARCICAL
COMICAL LOW BASE BUFFO DROLL
FUNNY MERRY QUEER STRIP WITTY
BOUFFE AMUSING CARTOON
JOCULAR RISIBLE STRANGE TRIVIAL
HUMOROUS TICKLISH BURLESQUE
SPLITTING
COMING DUE ANON COME NEXT
VENUE ADVENT FUTURE TOWARD
ARRIVAL FOOTING FORWARD
BECOMING DESERVED NAISSANT
PAROUSIA
(— AFTER) LATTER
(— AND GOING) FITFUL
(— FORTH) NAISSANT
(— INTO BEING) BIRTH GENESIS
(— NEAR) ACCESSION
(— NEXT) FOLLOWING
(— OUT) DEBUT ISSUE EGRESS
(— TO) ADIT
(— TOGETHER) SEANCE CONGRESS
COUPLING GATHERING
(— TO OFFICE) ACCESS ACCESSION
(SECOND —) PAROUSIA
(SECOND — OF CHRIST) PAROUSIA
COMMA POINT VIRGULE
(SCRATCH —) DIAGONAL
COMMAND DO BID SAW SOH BECK
BODE BOON CALL COME EASY FIAT
HEST HETE MAND RATE RULE SWAY
WARN WILL WISH WORD BEKEN
CHECK COVER EDICT EXACT FORCE
HIGHT ORDER POWER SWEEP UKASE
ADJURE BEHEST CHARGE COMPEL
DECREE DEMAND DEVICE DIRECT
ENJOIN GOVERN HOOKUM IMPOSE
MASTER ORACLE ORDAIN STEVEN
SUMMON APPOINT BEHIGHT
BIDDING CONCERN CONTROL
DICTATE JUSSION JUSSIVE LEADING
MANDATE OFFICER PRECEPT
REQUIRE SKIPPER WARRANT
BIDDANCE DOMINEER IMPERATE
INSTRUCT MANDAMUS RESTRAIN
(— EMOTIONS) GRIP
(— OF ARMY) CONDUCT

(— TO COMPUTER TO STORE DATA)
SAVE
(— TO DOGS) MUSH
(— TO HORSE) GEE HAW HUP HUPP
WHOA GIDDAP HUDDUP
(— TO TURN LEFT) HAW
(— TO TURN RIGHT) GEE HUP HUPP
(EXCLUSIVE —) MONOPOLY
(MAGICIAN'S —) PRESTO
(NAUTICAL —) AVAST
(ORGANIC —) PERACID
COMMANDANT GOVERNOR
KILLADAR
COMMANDED IMPERATE
COMMANDEER PRESS HIJACK
(— AIRCRAFT) SKYJACK
(— AN AIRPLANE) SKYJACK
COMMANDER CID CIO DUX DUKE
EMIR HEAD JEFE BLOKE CHIEF
EMEER ADALID LEADER MASTER
RAMMER TARTAN ALCALDE CAPTAIN
CROWNER DECARCH DEKARCH
DRUNGAR EMPEROR GENERAL
KHALIFA MARSHAL NAVARCH
OFFICER VAIVODE HERETOGA
HIPPARCH LOCHAGER LOCHAGUS
MYRIARCH PHYLARCH RISALDAR
SERASKER TAXIARCH TETRARCH
VINTENER PROCONSUL
(— IN CHIEF) SIRDAR TARTAN
TURTAN ADMIRAL GENERAL
(ANGLO-ASIAN) SIRDAR
(CAVALRY —) RISALDAR
COMMANDERY PRECEPTORY
COMMANDING DOMINANT
IMPERANT IMPERIAL IMPOSING
COMMANDMENT LAW RULE
ORDER COMMAND MITZVAH
PRECEPT BODEWORD
(DIVINE —) LAW
(TEN —S) DECALOG DECALOGUE
COMMANDO RAIDER RANGER
CHINDIT FEDAYEE STORMER
(MEMBER OF — GROUP) FEDAYEE
COMMELINA DEWFLOWER
COMMEMORATE FETE KEEP FEAST
REMENE EPITAPH MEMORATE
MONUMENT REMEMBER
MEMORIALIZE
COMMEMORATION AWARD
MEDAL COMMEM PLAQUE JUBILEE
MEMORIA MENTION SERVICE
EBENEZER ENCAENIA MEMORIAL
REMEMBRANCE
COMMEMORATIVE HONORARY
MEMORIAL
COMMENCE FALL FANG FILE MOVE
OPEN ARISE BEGIN FOUND START
ARRAME EMBARK INCEPT LAUNCH
SPRING STREAK STREEK INITIATE
COMMENCEMENT ONSET ORIGIN
OUTSET KICKOFF OPENING
ENTRANCE

COMMENCING INITIAL NASCENT INCIPIENT

COMMEND KEN PAT GIVE LAUD ADORN ALOSE BEKEN BOOST EXTOL GRACE OFFER BESTOW BETAKE COMMIT PRAISE RESIGN APPLAUD APPROVE BESPEAK BETEACH DELIVER ENTRUST INTRUST BEQUEATH

COMMENDABLE GOOD WORTHY LOVABLE LOWABLE LAUDABLE

COMMENDATION LAUD PRAISE CITATION
(**EFFUSIVE —**) SLAVER
(**MARKED —**) APPLAUSE

COMMENSAL EPIZOON MESSMATE

COMMENSALISM SYNOECY SYMPHILY COMMUNISM

COMMENSURATE EVEN EQUAL ENOUGH ADEQUATE RELEVANT

COMMENT BARB BRAG GIBE JIBE NOTE TALK WORD ASIDE BREAK DUNCE GLOSS GLOZE INPUT CUTTER DILATE GAMBIT NOTATE POSTIL REMARK SCANCE CAPTION DESCANT DISCUSS EXPLAIN EXPOUND ADDENDUM SCHOLION SCHOLIUM DISPRAISE
(**— DISAPPROVINGLY**) HARRUMPH
(**BITING —**) BARB
(**CAUSTIC —**) SATIRE
(**ILL-TIMED —**) CLANGER
(**MARGINAL —**) APOSTIL
(**WITTY —**) RIFF

COMMENTARY GLOSS GEMARA MEMOIR SATIRE ACCOUNT COMMENT MEKILTA POSTILS FOOTNOTE GLOSSARY TREATISE
(**RABBINICAL —**) HAKAM AGADAH HAGGADA HAGGADAH
(**PL.**) MIDRASHIM

COMMENTATOR HAKAM CRITIC GLOZER ANALYST GLOSSIST SCHOLIAST

COMMERCE TRADE BARTER CHANGE TRAFFIC BUSINESS EXCHANGE MERCATURE NAVIGATION

COMMERCIAL STORE TRADY TRADAL MERCHANT TRADEFUL
(**— ESTABLISHMENT**) HONG

COMMERCIALISM HUCKSTERISM MERCANTILISM

COMMINGLE MIX FUSE JOIN BLEND IMMIX MERGE UNITE MINGLE COMBINE COMINGE EMBROIL COMEDDLE

COMMINUTE MILL CRUSH GRIND POUND POUNCE POWDER

COMMINUTED FINE

COMMISERATE PITY

COMMISERATION EMPATHY SYMPATHY

COMMISSION PLAT SEND TASK BOARD PRESS TRUST BRANCH BREVET CHARGE DEMAND DEPUTE ERRAND LEGACY OFFICE ORDAIN PERMIT COMMAND CONSIGN DUOVIRI EMPOWER FITTAGE GOSPLAN MANDATE MISSION SQUEEZE WARRANT CORNETCY DELEGATE ENCHARGE INTERPOL OVERRIDE POUNDAGE
(**— AS CAPTAIN**) POST
(**CHARGING NO —**) NOLOAD

COMMISSIONAIRE CADDY CADDIE DUBASH

COMMISSIONER ENVOY TRIER LEDGER ARRAYER OFFICER PRISTAW DELEGATE

COMMISSURE VINCULUM

COMMIT DO GIVE PULL STOW TAKE ALLOT ARRET HIGHT LEAVE REFER TEACH ARETTE ASSIGN BETAKE ENGAGE PERMIT REMAND BEHIGHT BETEACH COMMAND COMMEND COMMISE CONFIDE CONSIGN DELIVER DEPOSIT ENTRUST INTRUST INTRUSE BEQUEATH DEDICATE DELEGATE IMPRISON RELEGATE RECOMMEND PERPETRATE
(**— ERROR**) SNAPPER
(**— MONEY**) INVEST
(**— TO BATTLE**) LAUNCH
(**— TO JAIL**) JUG
(**— TO MEMORY**) CON LEARN MEMORIZE
(**— VIOLENCE**) TOUCH
(**— WASTE**) ESTREPE

COMMITMENT OBLIGATION

COMMITTAL COMPROMISE

COMMITTED ENGAGED
(**— TO**) ENGAGE

COMMITTEE BODY JURY RUMP BOARD GROUP JUNTA TABLE BUREAU SOVIET COUNCIL DELEGACY POLITBURO PRESIDIUM SYNDICATE

COMMIXTURE MIXTURE HOTCHPOT CONFUSION IMMISSION

COMMODE CAP CHEST STOOL TOPKNOT CUPBOARD FONTANGE

COMMODIOUS FIT AMPLE ROOMY PROPER USEFUL SPACIOUS SUITABLE CAVERNOUS

COMMODITY ITEM WARE GOODS STUFF EXPORT FUTURE STAPLE ARTICLE SHIPMENT
(**— SOLD SHORT**) BEAR
(**UNSALABLE —**) DRUG
(**PL.**) KIND SPOTS CHANDLERY

COMMON LAY LOW NOA TYE BASE MEAN RIFE TOWN VILE BANAL BRIEF CHEAP EJIDO EXIDO GREEN GRIMY GROSS JOINT LEASE OFTEN SLACK STALE TACKY TRITE USUAL COARSE

DEMOID FAMOUS MODERN MUTUAL
ORNERY PROPIO PUBLIC SIMPLE
VULGAR AVERAGE CURRENT
DEMOTIC GENERAL GENERIC
IGNOBLE NATURAL POPULAR
PROFANE RAFFISH REGULAR TRIVIAL
UNNOBLE VILLAIN BANAUSIC
EPIDEMIC FAMILIAR FREQUENT
HABITUAL MECHANIC MEDIOCRE
ORDINARY PANDEMIC PLEBEIAN
TRIFLING TRITICAL RECIPROCAL
(— OF ESTOVERS) BOT BOTE
(IN —) ALIKE
(NOT —) UNTRADED
(PL.) COMMUNE
(PREF.) CAEN(O) CEN(O) COEN(O)
HOM(O)

COMMONER SNOB CEORL PLEBE
SIMPLE BURGESS CITIZEN STUDENT
ROTURIER

COMMONLY OFTEN VULGO
FAMILIARLY

COMMONNESS IDIOTISM
COMMUNITY VULGARITY

COMMON PEOPLE VULGUS

COMMONPLACE DULL FADE WORN
BANAL DAILY PLAIN PROSE PROSY
STALE TOPIC TRIPY TRITE USUAL
COMMON DEJAVU GARDEN HOMELY
MODERN TRUISM VULGAR FADAISE
HUMDRUM INSIPID PROSAIC
TEDIOUS TRIVIAL BANALITY
BROMIDIC COPYBOOK EVERYDAY
ORDINARY RUMTYTOO PLATITUDE
PEDESTRIAN

COMMONPLACENESS BATHOS
HUMDRUM

COMMON SENSE WIT NOUS SALT
GUMPTION

COMMONWEAL WEAL REPUBLIC

COMMONWEALTH POLIS STATE
ESTATE PUBLIC WEALTH COMONTE
COUNTRY COMMONTY
(IDEAL —) UTOPIA

**COMMONWEALTH OF
INDEPENDENT STATES** (SEE
RUSSIA)

COMMOTION DO ADO DIN BREE
DUST FLAP FRAY FUSS HEAT HELL
RIOT STIR TODO TOSS WHIR ALARM
FLARE FUROR HURLY HURRY STORM
STOUR WHIRL BUSTLE CATHRO
FISSLE FISTLE FLURRY FRACAS
FRAISE FURORE GARRAY HOOPLA
HOTTER MOTION MUTINY PHRASE
POTHER RUFFLE SHINDY SPLORE
SQUALL STEERY TUMULT UNREST
UPSTIR WELTER BLATHER BLUSTER
CATOUSE CLATTER KIPPAGE SHINDIG
TAMASHA TEMPEST TURMOIL
DISORDER ERUPTION REMOTION
STIRRAGE STRAMASH URRIVEE
UPHEAVAL UPRISING

COMMUNAL EJIDAL

COMMUNE MIR AREA DEME TALK
ARGUE REALM SHARE TREAT ADVISE
CONFER DEBATE IMPORT PARLEY
REVEAL CONSULT DISCUSS DIVULGE
COMMERCE CONVERSE DISTRICT
STANITZA TOWNSHIP
(DUTCH —) EDE

COMMUNICABLE OPEN FRANK
CATCHING SOCIABLE

COMMUNICATE SAY GIVE SHOW
SIGN TELL BREAK DRILL SPEAK
TELEX YIELD BESTOW COMMON
CONVEY IMPART INFECT INFORM
REVEAL SIGNAL ADDRESS BREATHE
DECLARE DICTATE DIVULGE
CONVERSE DESCRIBE INTIMATE
(— BY ALLUSION) IMPLY

COMMUNICATION CALL NOTE
WORD CABLE FAVOR LETTER SPEECH
ADDRESS DIVULGE GALLERY
MESSAGE COMETHER LANGUAGE
TELEGRAM MEMORANDUM
(— SERVICE) TELEX
(— SYSTEM) VOICEMAIL
(ESTABLISH —) LOGIN LOGON

COMMUNICATIVE FREE SOCIABLE
EXPANSIVE

COMMUNION CULT HOST MASS
SECT FAITH CREED FAITH SHARE
UNITY CHURCH HOMILY COMMUNE
CONCORD NAGMAAL SYNAGOG
ANTIPHON COMMERCE CONVERSE
KOINONIA VIATICUM
(— SERVICE) ACTION

COMMUNISM LENINISM SOVIETISM

COMMUNIST RED COMMIE SOVIET
COMRADE

COMMUNITY MIR BODY BURG CITY
CLAN DESA MARK MURA DESSA
FIRCA STATE THORP CENOBY
CLIMAX COLONY FAMILY HAMLET
MILLET NATION POLITY PUBLIC
SOCIES ANTHILL BOHEMIA
COMMUNE COMONTE CONVENT
HERONRY KINGDOM PHALANX
SOCIETY VILLAGE ZADRUGA
AUTONOMY COMMONTY DISTRICT
LIKENESS PRIORATE PROVINCE
SODALITY SWEEPDOM TOWNSHIP
(— OF ANCHORITES) LAURA
(— OF INTERESTS) KINSHIP
(— OF KNIGHTS TEMPLARS)
PRECEPTORY
(— OF NATURE) RACE
(— OF ORGANISMS) GAMODEME
(— OF TURKS) KIZILBASH
(ANCIENT GREEK —) DEME
(CHURCH —) BODY FOLD FLOCK
SYNOD PARISH
(COOPERATIVE —) PHALANSTERY
(ECOLOGICAL —) SERE PROCLIMAX
(JEWISH —) JEWRY KOLEL ALJAMA

SHTETL JUDAISM SHTETEL
SYNAGOG KEHILLAH
(MAORI —) KAIK KAIKA
(PERUVIAN —) AYLLU COMUNIDAD
(PLANT —) HEATH FOREST ALTERNE
ENCLAVE
(RELIGIOUS —) CENOBY SAMGHA
SANGHA CONVENT CENOBIUM
(RUSSIAN —) MIR
(UTOPIAN —) PANTISOCRACY
(VILLAGE —) IKHWAN
COMMUTATE COMMUTE UNDIRECT
COMMUTATIVE ABELIAN
COMMUTATOR BREAK BREAKER
RHEOTROPE
COMMUTE ALTER CHANGE TRAVEL
CONVERT EXCHANGE
COMMUTER
(GROUP OF —S) VANPOOL
COMOROS (CAPITAL OF —) MORONI
(ISLAND OF —) MWALI MOHELI
NZWANI ANJOUAN NJAZIDJA
(VOLCANO OF —) KARTHALA
COMPACT SAD BALL BOND CASE
FAST FIRM HARD KNIT PACK PACT
PLOT SNUG TRIM TRUE BRIEF CLOSE
COVIN CROWD DENSE GROSS
HARDY HORNY MATCH PITHY SOLID
SPISS TERSE THICK TIGHT BEETLE
COMART HARDEN LEAGUE SHRINK
SPISSY STOCKY TREATY VANITY
BARGAIN CONCISE CONCORD
CROWDED NUGGETY PACTION
SERRIED TABLOID ALLIANCE
CONDENSE CONTRACT COVENANT
FLAPJACK HEAVYSET SOLIDIFY
SUCCINCT PELLETIZE
(PREF.) GLOMERO GLOMERULO
PYCN(O) PYKN(O)
COMPACTED SAD CROWDED
(PREF.) PECTO
COMPACTNESS BODY DENSITY
FASTNESS SOLIDITY INTENSITY
COMPANION PAL SOC CHUM FERE
MAKE MATE PEER TWIN WIFE BILLY
BUDDY BULLY BUTTY CHINA COMES
CRONY CULLY DARES GREEK MATCH
MATEY MAUGH RIVAL SPORT
ATTEND BELAMY BILLIE BROLGA
COBBER COHORT COMATE CUMMER
CUPMAN DUENNA EGERIA ESCORT
FELLOW FRIEND GESITH GOSSIP
KIMMER MARROW PANION SHADOW
SPOUSE STEADY TROJAN ACHATES
COMPANY COMPEER COMRADE
CONSORT ELPENOR FRANION
HUSBAND PARTNER SOCIATE
SOCIETY SPECIAL BARNACLE
BEAUPERE COMPADRE CORRIVAL
EPHESIAN EPHESINE FAITHFUL
FAMILIAR HELPMATE PARALLEL
PLAYFERE SYNODITE
(ARCHER'S —) BUTTY

(DRINKING —) CUPMATE
(POT —) ALEKNIGHT
(READING —) LECTRICE
(TABLE —) CONVICTOR
(PL.) SOCIETY
(PREF.) HETAERO
COMPANIONABLE FERE MATEY
SOCIAL CORDIAL FELLOWLY
GRACIOUS SOCIABLE
COMPANION-AT-LARGE BILLY
BILLIE
COMPANIONS (SEE PARTNERS)
COMPANIONSHIP FERE SHIP
HAUNT COMPANY SOCIETY AFFINITY
COMPANY CIE CRY MOB SET BAND
BEVY BODY CORE CREW CRUE FARE
FERE FIRM GANG GEST GING HERD
HOST MANY PUSH ROUT SORT TEAM
TURM AERIE COVEN COVEY CROWD
FLOCK FLOTE GESTE GROUP GUEST
HORDE JATHA MEINY PARTY SQUAD
SUITE TROOP TURMA CIRCLE CLIQUE
COHORT COVINE CURNEY DECURY
LOCHUS OUTFIT RESORT THRAVE
THRONG TROUPE TWENTY VOLLEY
BATTERY COLLEGE CONDUCT
CONSORT HOLDING JIMBANG
MANIPLE SOCIETE SOCIETY THIASOS
THIASUS VISITOR ASSEMBLY
FAISCEAU FOLKMOOT JINGBANG
PRESENCE
(— OF BADGERS) CETE
(— OF BIRDS) BANK
(— OF BOOKSELLERS) CONGER
CONGENER
(— OF DANCERS) COMPARSA
(— OF HERDSMEN) BOOLY BOOLEY
(— OF HERONS) SEDGE SIEGE
(— OF HORSEMEN) TROOP
(— OF LIONS) PRIDE
(— OF MARTENS) RICHESSE
(— OF MUSICIANS) ORCHESTRA
(— OF PEACOCKS) MUSTER
(— OF PERFORMERS) TROUPE
(— OF PLOVERS) STAND
(— OF SINGERS) CHOIR QUIRE
CHORUS
(— OF SWANS) BANK
(— OF TEN) DECURY DECURIA
(— OF THE FAITHFUL) FOLD
(— OF TRAVELERS) CAFILA
CAVALCADE
(— OF WOMEN) GAGGLE
(— OF WORSHIPERS) THIASUS
(— OF WORSHIPPERS) THIASUS
(EXCLUSIVE —) CROWD
(FINANCIAL —) FACTOR
(FIRE —) SQUAD
(MILITARY —) WATCH DECURY
VENLIN PELOTON VEXILLUM
(RECORDING —) LABEL
(SUITABLE —) BESORT
COMPARABLE LIKE SAME SIMILAR

COMPARATIVE
(SUFF.) ER IOR

COMPARE VIE EVEN LIKE SIZE APPLY
EQUAL LIKEN MATCH SCALE TALLY
ALLUDE CONFER PARIFY RELATE
SEMBLE BALANCE BRACKET
COLLATE EXAMINE SENIBLE SIGNIFY
STACKUP ASSEMBLE CONFRONT
CONTRAST ESTIMATE PARALLEL
RESEMBLE SIMILIZE
(— WITH) TO

COMPARISON SIMILE ANALOGY
BALANCE COMPARE PARABLE
PARAGON DISIMILE LIKENESS
LIKENING METAPHOR PARALLEL
(— OF HOROSCOPES) SYNASTRY

COMPARTMENT BAY BIN BOX CAB
POD CELL DECK FLUE PANE PART
SLOT WELL ABODE CABIN HATCH
HUTCH PANEL STALL VOLET ABACUS
ALCOVE BUNKER GARAGE HOPPER
MUFFLE REGION SEVERY SMOKER
ALVEOLE CABINET CAPSULE
CELLULE CHAMBER FIREBOX
HOUSING KITCHEN LOCULUS
MANSION ROTONDE SECTION
ALVEOLUS COALHOLE DIVISION
FOREPEAK GRINTERN LOCELLUS
STEERAGE TRAVERSE PIGEONHOLE
(— FOR COAL) BUNKER
(— FOR TREATING ORE) KITCHEN
(— IN BAR) SNUG SNUGGERY
(— IN BARN) BAY
(— IN CAR) BOOT
(— IN STOVE) BROILER
(— OF COACH) IMPERIAL
(— OF ROOF) SEVERY
(— OF VAULTING) SEVERY
(— OF WINDOW) LIGHT
(— ON GAMEBOARD) STORE
(— ON ROULETTE WHEEL) EAGLE
(— ON TRAIN) COUCHETTE
(CARGO —) HOLD
(DECOMPRESSION —) POD
(DETACHABLE —) POD
(GAS-TIGHT —) BALLONET
(GUNNER'S —) BLISTER
(REFRIGERATOR —) CHILLER
(SCREENED —) TRAVERSE
(SLEEPING —) CUBICLE
(STAGECOACH —) COUPE
(STORAGE —) BOOT

COMPASS BOW AREA DIAL GAIN
ROOM ROSE SIZE TOUR AMBIT FIELD
GAMUT RANGE REACH SCOPE
SWEEP TENOR WHEEL ARRIVE
ATTAIN BOUNDS CIRCLE DEGREE
DEVICE DIACLE EFFECT EXTENT
MERIST MODULE SPHERE SPREAD
VOLUME ACHIEVE AZIMUTH CALIBER
CIRCUIT CONFINE DIVIDER EMBRACE
ENCLOSE ENVIRON HORIZON
IMAGINE PELORUS PURVIEW
TRAMMEL BOUNDARY CINCTURE
CIRCUITY DIAPASON PRACTICE
PRACTISE SURROUND
(— IN SHIP'S CABIN) TELLTALE
(— NEEDLE END) LILY
(— OF MELODY) AMBITUS
(— OF TONES) DIAPASON
(— OF VOICE) GAMUT SCALE
(— POINT) RHUMB
(BELL-MAKING —) CROOK
(PART OF —) PIN CARD DOME HOOD
PIVOT HOUSING BINNACLE

COMPASS BOX KETTLE

COMPASS CARD ROSE PEDRERO
PERRIER

COMPASSION RUE PITY RUTH
GRACE HEART MERCY PIETY SORRY
KARUNA LENITY REMORSE
STOMACH CLEMENCY HUMANITY
KINDNESS SYMPATHY

COMPASSIONATE MEEK RUTH
SOFT HUMAN GENTLE TENDER
CLEMENT PIETOSO PITEOUS PITIFUL
GRACIOUS MERCIFUL

COMPASS PLANT PILOTWEED
ROSINWEED

COMPASS QUARTER PLAGE

COMPASS SIGHT VANE

COMPATIBILITY MATCH

COMPATIBLE AKIN CIVIL ARTISTIC
SUITABLE

COMPATRIOT NATIVE PATRIOT
SYNETHNIC

COMPEL GAR MAKE MOVE URGE
BRING CAUSE COACT DRIVE EXACT
FORCE IMPEL PRESS SHOVE COERCE
ENJOIN EXTORT INCITE OBLIGE
THREAT ACTUATE AFFORCE ATTRACT
COMMAND DRAGOON ENFORCE
NECESSE REQUIRE VIOLENCE
NECESSITATE
(— TO GO) HALE
(— TO PAY) STICK

COMPELLED HAS FAIN MUST
BOUND FORCED ENFORCED

COMPELLING COGENT STRONG
TELLING BRUISING FORCEFUL

COMPELLINGLY BADLY

COMPENDIOUS BRIEF SHORT
TERSE DIRECT COMPACT CONCISE
SUMMARY SUCCINCT

COMPENDIUM LIST BRIEF APERCU
DIGEST PRECIS SKETCH SURVEY
CATALOG COMPEND EPITOME
LEXICON MEDULLA OUTLINE
PANDECT SUMMARY SYLLOGE
ABSTRACT BREVIARY BREVIATE
LANDSKIP SYLLABUS SYNOPSIS
ABRIDGEMENT
(— OF DOCTRINE) SYMBOL

COMPENSATE PAY JIBE AGREE
ATONE COVER REPAY TALLY OFFSET
RECOUP REDEEM REWARD SQUARE

COMMUTE CORRECT PLASTER
REDRESS REPRISE REQUITE
RESTORE SATISFY COMPENSE
DISPENSE EQUALIZE
COMPENSATION BOT FEE PAY UTU
BOOT BOTE HIRE MEND TOLL BONUS
LOWER WAGES AMENDS ANGILD
GERSUM OFFSET REWARD SALARY
SETOFF DAMAGES FREIGHT
PAYMENT REDRESS SALVAGE
STIPEND BREAKAGE DONATIVE
EARNINGS INTEREST OCTOGILD
PILOTAGE PITTANCE REQUITAL
SOLATIUM
(— FOR INJURY) SATISFACTION
(— FOR KILLING MAN) MANBOT
MANBOTE
(MEAGER —) PITTANCE
(WORKER'S —) COMPO
COMPENSATORILY EVEN
COMPETE PIT VIE COPE KEMP TEND
CLASH MATCH RIVAL STRIVE
CONTEND CONTEST EMULATE
CORRIVAL
(— WITH) BUCK
COMPETENCE SKILL ABILITY
FACULTY CAPACITY
COMPETENCY MAY CAPACITY
COMPETENT UP APT CAN FIT ABLE
GOOD HOME MEET SANE ADEPT
CAPAX SMART SWEET TIGHT INTACT
LAWFUL WORTHY CAPABLE
ENDOWED SKILLED ADEQUATE
SUITABLE QUALIFIED
COMPETITION VIE DRAW GAME
HEAT JUMP RACE MATCH PRIZE
TRIAL WAGER CONTEST PARAGON
RIVALRY BIATHLON CONCOURS
CONFLICT
(— AMONG REAPERS) KEMP
(ATHLETIC —) MEET
(DRIVING —) RALLY RALLYE
(VERSE —) TENSON
COMPETITOR FOE ENEMY MATCH
RIVAL WAGER COUSIN PLAYER
AGONIST ENTRANT CORRIVAL
FAVORITE GAMESTER OPPONENT
(FORMIDABLE —) TIGER
COMPILATION ANA BOOK CODE
CENTO DIGEST CASEBOOK
DIRECTORY GATHERING
COMPILE ADD EDIT AMASS GATHER
SELECT ARRANGE COLLECT
COMPOSE PREPARE
COMPILER AUTHOR EDITOR
COLLATOR GATHERER GLOSSIST
SCISSORER
COMPLACENT CALM SMUG PLACID
FATUOUS PRIGGISH
COMPLACENTLY FATLY
COMPLAIN AIL NAG YAP YIP BEEF
CARP CRIB FRET FUSS GREX KEEN
KICK KREX MEAN MOAN MOOT

MUTE RAIL RULE WAIL YELP YIRN
BITCH BLEAT BRAWL CRAKE CROAK
CROON GRIPE GROWL GRUMP
GRUNT PINGE PLAIN WHINE BEWAIL
CHARGE COTTER CREATE GRIEVE
GROUSE GRUTCH HOLLER KVETCH
MURMUR PEENGE REPINE SQUAWK
THREAP THROPE WHINGE YAMMER
CHUNNER DEPLORE GRIZZLE
GRUMBLE INVEIGH NITPICK PROTEST
BELLYACHE
COMPLAINANT ACTOR ASKER
ORATOR ACCUSER PLAINER
QUERENT RELATOR
COMPLAINER CRAB WHINER
CRYBABY KVETCHER
COMPLAINING BRAY PULY WHINY
LATRANT QUERENT DOLEANCE
QUERULOUS
COMPLAINT RAP BEEF CARP FUSS
HOWL MEAN MOAN WAIL BITCH
GRIPE GROWL WHINE CHESON
GROUCH GROUSE GRUDGE GRUTCH
HOLLER KVETCH LAMENT MALADY
NIGGLE PLAINT REPINE SQUAWK
AILMENT DISEASE GRUMBLE
ILLNESS PROTEST QUARREL
QUERELE RECLAMA TRAGEDY
COMPLAIN DISORDER DOLEANCE
GRAVAMEN JEREMIAD
(SUBDUED —) MURMUR
COMPLAISANCE AMENITY
SUAVITY FACILITY URBANITY
COMPLAISANT BON ABLE EASY
KIND BUXOM CIVIL SUAVE BONAIR
POLITE SMOOTH SUPPLE URBANE
AFFABLE AMIABLE BOWABLE
LENIENT GRACIOUS OBLIGING
PLEASING
COMPLEMENT CREW GANG FORCE
TALLY ALEXIN AMOUNT COUSIN
ADJUNCT OBVERSE PENDANT
(MILITARY —) STRENGTH
COMPLEMENTARY OPPOSITE
(PREF.) COUNTER
COMPLETE DO ALL CAP END BLUE
DASH DEAD DEEP DONE FAIR FILL
FINE FULL JUST PASS PURE RANK
VERY CLEAN CLOSE CROWN EVERY
GROSS LARGE PLAIN PLUMB POINT
PUCCA PUKKA QUITE RIPEN ROUND
SOLID SOUND STARK STONE TOTAL
UTTER WHOLE CHOATE DAMPEN
DEADLY EFFECT ENTIRE FINISH
GLOBAL HOLLOW INTACT MATURE
PROPER SINGLE STRICT VESTED
ACHIEVE COMPLEX EXECUTE
EXPLETE FULFILL GERMANE
OUTWORK PERFECT PLENARY
REALIZE REPLETE SPHERAL
ABSOLUTE BLINKING CIRCULAR
CONCLUDE FINALIZE IMPLICIT
INTEGRAL OUTRIGHT OVERCOME

PRECIOUS PROFOUND THOROUGH
BODACIOUS NEGOTIATE
ACCOMPLISH
(— CARELESSLY) HUDDLE
(— IN SYLLABLES) ACATHLECTIC
(REMARKABLY —) SPLENDID
(PREF.) HOL(O) TEL(E)(EO)
COMPLETED PAU OVER CLOSED
SUMMED COMPLETE FINISHED
(NOT —) DURATIVE
COMPLETELY ALL JAM BARE BUCK
FAIR FLAT GOOD SLAM SLAP SPAN
BLACK CLEAN CLOSE FULLY PLUMB
QUITE SHEER SMACK SPANG STARK
STICK STOCK UTTER BODILY ENTIRE
GAINLY HOLLOW PURELY SPANDY
WHOLLY ALGATES BLANKLY
THROUGH CLEVERLY DIRECTLY
ENTIRELY HEARTILY OUTRIGHT
WHOLEHOG
(PREF.) DE DIS OB PAN
COMPLETENESS DEPTH ALLNESS
FULLNESS RIPENESS INTEGRITY
PLENITUDE
COMPLETION END CROWN FINISH
(PREF.) TELEUT(O)
COMPLEX HARD MAZY BEING
ETHOS FIELD HYOID MIXED ADDUCT
DESERT KNOTTY SYSTEM CULTURE
NETWORK SAMKARA SINUOUS
TANGLED TWISTED ABSTRUSE
COMPOUND EQUATION EXCHANGE
INVOLVED MANIFOLD SAMSKARA
SYNDROME CISPLATIN MACROCOSM
(— OF CHARACTERISTICS)
PERSONALITY
(— OF DIALECTS) HINDI
(— OF HORMONES) CALINE
(— OF IDEAS) EGO SYSTEM
(— OF SHOPS) MALL
(BASEMENT —) FLOOR
(NOT —) SIMPLE
COMPLEXION HUE RUD BLEE CAST
LEER LOOK RUDD TINT COLOR
HUMOR STATE TENOR TINGE ASPECT
TEMPER COLORING
(BAD —) DYSCHROA
COMPLEXITY NODUS SCHEME
TANGLE INTRIGUE
COMPLIANCE TRUE ASSENT
MUNICH CESSION CONSENT
HARMONY OBSEQUY ABIDANCE
CIVILITY FACILITY FORMALITY
COMPLIANT EASY MEEK OILY SOFT
BUXOM FACILE PLIANT SUPPLE
COMMODE DUCTILE DUTIFUL
WILLING AMENABLE OBEDIENT
TOWARDLY YIELDING TRACTABLE
COMPLICATE INTORT PUZZLE
TANGLE EMBROIL INVOLVE PERPLEX
BEWILDER INTRIGUE INTRICATE
COMPLICATED HARD KNOTTY
PROLIX COMPLEX GORDIAN

SNARLED TANGLED INVOLVED
PLEXIFORM
COMPLICATION KNOT NODE PLOT
NODUS SNARL TANGLE INTRIGUE
(— IN STORY) NODE
COMPLIMENT GIFT KUDO LAUD
EXTOL EULOGY PRAISE SALAAM
SALUTE ADULATE APPLAUD
BOUQUET COMMEND DOUCEUR
FLATTER TRIBUTE ENCOMIUM
FLUMMERY GRATUITY GREETING
(EMPTY —) FLUMMERY
COMPLY PLY CEDE OBEY ABIDE
ADAPT AGREE APPLY YIELD ACCEDE
ACCORD ASSENT ENFOLD SUBMIT
CONFORM EMBRACE OBSERVE
(— WITH) OBEY SERVE OBSERVE
SATISFY
COMPONE GOBONE GOBONY
COMPONENT KEY DRAG FORM
ITEM PART UNIT GIVEN FACTOR
MEMBER SIMPLE ELEMENT
FORMANT PARTIAL CONJUNCT
INTEGRAL
(— OF ARMY) CAVALRY
(— OF CELL WALLS) CALLOSE
(ELECTRIC —S) CIRCUITRY
(PHYSICAL —S) HARDWARE
(PRINCIPAL —) BASIS
COMPORT ACT BEAR HAVE HOLD
JIBE KEEP SUIT ABEAR AGREE
BROOK CARRY TALLY ACCORD
ACQUIT BEHAVE DEMEAN ENDURE
SQUARE CONDUCT
COMPORTMENT DEALING
BEHAVIOR DEMEANOR
COMPOSE BAT PEN SET CALM COMP
DITE FORM LULL MAKE ALLAY BREVE
BRIEF CLERK CLINK COUCH DIGHT
DRAFT FRAME ORDER PATCH PIECE
SPELL STICK WRITE ACCORD ADJUST
CREATE DESIGN GRAITH INDITE
NOTATE RECITE REDACT SETTLE
SOOTHE STEADY ARRANGE
COMPACT COMPILE COMPONE
CONCOCT CONFORM DICTATE
DISPOSE DRAUGHT FASHION
PATIENT PRODUCE TYPESET
COMPOUND COMPRISE REGULATE
(— POETRY) MAKE SING
COMPOSED SET CALM COOL QUIET
SOBER WROTE DEMURE DIGEST
PLACID SEDATE SERENE COMPACT
WRITTEN COMPOUND DECOROUS
TOGETHER TRANQUIL
(— IN METER) FOOTED
(ILL —) LAME
COMPOSEDNESS SOSSIEGO
COMPOSER BARD POET LYRIC
ODIST AUTHOR LYRIST PENMAN
WRITER CONTEUR ELEGIST FANTAST
MAESTRO COLORIST ELEGIAST
IDYLLIST ILIADIST MELODIST

MONODIST MUSICIAN PHANTAST
TUNESMITH
AMERICAN FRY BIRD BOND CAGE
COLE IVES KERN ROOT BEACH
BLOCH DANKS FOOTE HANDY
HAYDN HOMER LEHAR NEVIN OHARA
PRATT ROREM SCOTT SOUSA WEILL
BARBER CADMAN HARRIS KRENEK
LOOMIS PALMER PARKER PISTON
PORTER SEEGER SPEAKS SUESSE
TAYLOR WINNER ANTHEIL BRISTOW
CHASINS COPLAND DEKOVEN
GILBERT GOLDMAN HAESCHE
HERBERT MENOTTI PARROTT
RODGERS SCHUMAN THOMSON
YOUMANS BARTLETT BROCKWAY
BURLEIGH CHADWICK CONVERSE
GERSHWIN GOODRICH GRAINGER
KREISLER SESSIONS THOMPSON
ARMSTRONG BERNSTEIN
CARPENTER ELLINGTON
MACDOWELL
ARGENTINIAN CASTRO
AUSTRIAN FUX GAL BERG WOLF
BRULL DRDLA MOTTL ZAYTZ BLEYLE
CZERNY EYBLER LANNER MOZART
BITTNER NEUKOMM STRAUSS
BRUCKNER DIABELLI GYROWETZ
KORNGOLD REZNICEK SCHUBERT
HEUBERGER MILLOCKER
SCHONBERG GANSBACHER
ALBRECHTSBERGER
BELGIAN FETIS LEKEU BENOIT
BERIOT BLOCKX BRASIN DUMONT
FRANCK GRISAR JONGEN GEVAERT
HUBERTI LEMMENS MATHIEU
CAMPENHOUT
BRAZILIAN GOMES VILLALOBOS
CANADIAN BRANSCOMB
CZECH BENDL NOVAK DVORAK
FIBICH FORSTER JANACEK KUBELIK
SMETANA DESPAUER NESWADBA
KALLIWODA KOVAROVIC
MYSLIVECEK
DANISH ENNA GADE HAMERIK
NIELSEN HARTMANN
DUTCH FODOR OBRECHT ARCADELT
WAGENAAR SWEELINCK
ENGLISH BAX TYE ARNE BLOW BYRD
CARR CLAY HOOK MONK BACHE
BLISS BOYCE CAREY COOKE COWEN
CROFT ELGAR ELVEY FIELD HOLST
LAWES LOCKE PARRY SCOTT TOVEY
ARNOLD ASHTON AUSTIN AVISON
BARNBY BISHOP BRIDGE COATES
COWARD CRAMER CROTCH CROUCH
CUSINS DAVIES DELIUS DIBDIN
GERMAN GLOVER GREENE HANDEL
LAMOND LINLEY MCEWEN ONEILL
PARKER TALLIS THOMAS WALTON
WILSON ATTWOOD BANTOCK
BARNETT BENNETT CELLIER
COLEMAN DUNHILL FARRANT

GIBBONS HORSLEY IRELAND
JACKSON LATROBE NOVELLO
PURCELL STAINER STORACE
BENJAMIN BOUGHTON SULLIVAN
TYRWHITT ARMSTRONG CALDICOTT
HESELTINE MACFARRNE MACKENZIE
SOMERVELL GOLDSCHMIDT
RAVENSCROFT
FINNISH PACIUS KAJANUS
MADETOJA MELARTIN PALMGREN
SIBELIUS WEGELIUS JARNEFELT
MERIKANTO
FRENCH ERB HUE ADAM INDY LALO
ALARD ALKAN AUBER AURIC BAZIN
BIZET COHEN DAVID DUKAS FAURE
GOUVY HERVE IBERT LULLY MASSE
MEHUL RAVEL REBER REYER SATIE
WIDOR AUBERT AUDRAN CAMPRA
CHOPIN DANCLA DAQUIN DUBOIS
DUPARC GODARD GOSSEC GOUNOD
HALEVY HEROLD LECOCQ LEROUX
PIERNE STRAUS THOMAS BERLIOZ
BERTINI BOESSET BRUNEAU
CAMBERT CHELARD COQUARD
DEBUSSY DELIBES DUCASSE
GUIRAUD LACOMBE LAPARRA
LECLAIR LESUEUR MARTINI
MILHAUD POULENC SCHMITT
CHABRIER CHAUSSON COUPERIN
DALAYRAC ERLANGER GODIMEL
GUILMANT HONEGGER LEFEBVRE
MAILLART MASSENET MESSAGER
MONSIGNY BOELLMANN BOIELDIEU
CHAMINADE OFFENBACH
WECKERLIN BURGMULLER
DESAUGIERS DESTOUCHES
PLANQUETTE WALDTEUFEL
CHARPENTIER
GERMAN ABT ETT AHLE BACH BOHM
BOTT DORN GOTZ HAAS KAUN LOBE
ORFF RAFF ABERT BIBER BLECH
BOEHE BRUCH DANZI EBERS FASCH
FESCA FINCK FRANK GENEE GLUCK
GRAUN GRELL KLEIN LOEWE NEEFE
WEBER ALBERT AMBROS BECKER
BERGER BOHNER BRAHMS COMMER
CRUGER ECKERT EITNER FLOTOW
HILLER JENSEN KOHLER KUCKEN
KUHLAU KUHNAU LINCKE MÄHLER
WAGNER WINTER BARGIEL CONRADI
EBERLIN HASSLER JARNACH
MOLIQUE NAUMANN RICHTER
SILCHER STRAUSS WULLNER
ZOLLNER AGRICOLA BENEDICT
BRAMBACH DIETRICH DRAESEKE
EBERWEIN HOFFMANN HOLSTEIN
KAMINSKI KEUSSLER KIRCHNER
KREUTZER PFITZNER REINECKE
SCHUMANN VOLKMANN AIBLINGER
AMBROSIUS BEETHOVEN
BRAUNFELS BUXTEHUDE
CANNABICH DELLINGER HINDEMITH
KLUGHARDT MARSCHNER

MATTHESON MEYERBEER
NEITHARDT REICHARDT
BELLERMANN BLUMENTHAL
DESTOUCHES PRAETORIUS
SCHARWENKA HUMPERDINCK
MENDELSSOHN FRANCKENSTEIN
LEICHTENTRITT
HUNGARIAN ERKEL HUBAY LEHAR
LISZT BARTOK KODALY KUSSER
JOACHIM ROMBERG DOHNANYI
GOLDMARK
IRISH BALFE OSBORNE WALLACE
ITALIAN LOTI PAER PERI ARAIA BAINI
BOITO BRAGA CESTI CLARI COSTA
VERDI ALFANO ANERIO ARDITI
ARTUSI BUSONI CIAMPI COCCIA
MERULO NANINI PACINI PEROSI
VECCHI ALBERTI ALLEGRI ANFOSSI
ARIOSTI BASSANI BAZZINI BELLINI
BERTONI BIANCHI CACCINI CALDARA
CAMBINI CASELLA CAVALLI
COLONNA CONCONE CORELLI
DURANTE FERRARI FLORIMO PICCINI
PORPORA PUCCINI ROSSINI SALIERI
TARTINI TOSELLI VIADANA VIVALDI
ZACCONI ZARLINO AGOSTINI
ALBINONI BERNABEI CLEMENTI
FIORILLO GABRIELI GAGLIANO
GIORDANI GIORDANO JOMMELLI
LEGRENZI MARCELLO MASCAGNI
PRATELLA RAIMONDI RESPIGHI
SPONTINI ANIMUCCIA BANCHIERI
BONONCINI BOTTESINI BRAMBILLA
CARISSIMI CAVALIERI CHERUBINI
DONIZETTI GUGLIELMI LOCATELLI
MALIPIERO MARCHETTI MORLACCHI
PAISIELLO PERGOLESI SCARLATTI
TOMMASINI VICENTINO BOCCHERINI
CAMPAGNOLI MERCADANTE
MONTEVERDI PALESTRINA
PONCHIELLI ZINGARELLI
LEONCAVALLO
MEXICAN CHAVEZ CARRILLO
NORWEGIAN GRIEG KJERULF
NORDRAAK SVENDSEN
SCHJELDERUP
POLISH KOLBERG FITELBERG
KAMIENSKI KARLOWICZ MONIUSZKO
NOSKOWSKI SZYMANOWSKI
PORTUGUESE ARNEIRO MACHADO
BOMTEMPO PORTOGALLO
RUMANIAN ENESCO OTESCUA
RUSSIAN LVOV SEROV GLINKA
LIADOV ONEGIN TANEEV ARENSKI
BORODIN REBIKOV GODOWSKY
LIPAUNOV SCRIABIN BALAKIREV
CHEREPNIN GLAZOUNOV
KASHPEROV KASTALSKI MUSORGSKI
PROKOFIEV KALINNIKOV
MOUSORGSKY STRAVINSKY
AZANCHEVSKI BORTNYANSKI
TCHAIKOVSKY KHACHATURIAN
RACHMANINOFF SHOSTAKOVICH

SCOTTISH GOW SPOTTISWOODE
SPANISH ARBOS FALLA CASALS
ALBENIZ MARTINI PEDRELL BARBIERI
GUERRERO VICTORIA
SWEDISH ALFVEN HALLEN
ATTERBERG HALLSTROM
WENNERBERG
SWISS EGLI HEGAR HUBER
VENEZUELAN CARRENO
WELSH EVANS PARRY
COMPOSITE HYBRID ITALIC MOTLEY
COMPLEX COMPOSED CONCRETE
INTEGRAL
COMPOSITION ANA DITE MASS
OPUS WORK CENTO DITTY DRAMA
FUGUE GETUP MURKY PIECE POESY
STUCK THEME ACCORD EULOGY
FILLER HAIKAI LESSON MAGGOT
MONODY THESIS THREAD VULGUS
ARTICLE COMPOST CONSIST
DISPLAY EBURINE EPISTLE MIXTURE
PICTURE STOPPER WRITING
ACROSTIC CAUSERIE COMPOUND
DIALOGUE DIAPENTE EXERCISE
FANTASIA FROTTAGE HEELBALL
(— FOR BILLIARD BALLS) COMPO
(— TO BE ACTED) PLAY DRAMA
(— TO FILL LEATHER) STUFF
(AMOROUS —) EROTIC
(ARTISTIC —) COLLAGE
(BAGPIPE —) PORT
(BANKRUPT'S —) COMPO
(BUILDING —) STAFF
(CHORAL —) MOTET CANTATA
ORATORIO
(GUMMY —) GROUND
(HAND —) CASEWORK
(HUMOROUS —) BURLA
(IMPERFECT —) SOOTERKIN
(INSTRUMENTAL —) AIR GATO
FANCY RONDO GROUND SKETCH
SONATA TIENTO BOURREE CANZONE
BERCEUSE CONCERTO FANTASIA
RHAPSODY SYMPHONY
PASSACAGLIA
(LITERARY —) BOOK CENTO DEBAT
ESSAY PIECE COMEDY SATIRE
SKETCH THESIS TREATISE
(MAGIC —) HELLBROTH
(MUSICAL —) DUET GLEE IDYL OPUS
SOLO SONG TRIO BURLA CANON
DANCE ELEGY ETUDE FUGUE GAZEL
IDYLL MESTO MOTET NONET SCORE
STUDY ADAGIO ARIOSO AZIONE
ENTREE GHAZEL HOCKET HOQUET
SEPTET SEXTET BALLADE BOURREE
BOUTADE BRAVURA ORGANUM
QUARTET SCHERZO TOCCATA
CAVATINA CHACONNE CLAUSULA
CONCERTO INNOMINE SERENADE
SINFONIA STANDARD SYMPHONY
ANTIPHONY OFFERTORY
PROCESSIONAL

(NARRATIVE —) BALLAD
(PLASTIC —) CEMENT
(POETIC —) GLOSS KAVYA
(RAMBLING —) SATIRE RHAPSODY
(RELIGIOUS —) MOTET ANTHEM
HYMNIC CANTATA ORATORIO
(RUBBER —) GUM
(VEDIC —) GAYATRI
(VITREOUS —) ENAMEL
(VOCAL —) ARIA SOLO SONG
CANON ANTHEM ELEVATIO
CONDUCTUS
(WORDLESS —) VOCALISE
(PL.) JUVENILIA LITERATURE
COMPOSITOR COMP TYPO ADMAN
SETTER BANKMAN CASEMAN
CLICKER PRINTER STONEMAN
COMPOST PELF SOIL MINGLE
COMPOTE MIXTURE COMPOUND
DRESSING
COMPOSURE BOND MIEN POISE
QUIET UNION REPOSE TEMPER
BALANCE POSTURE CALMNESS
SERENITY
(LOSE —) CHOKE
COMPOTATION SYMPOSIUM
COMPOTE BOWL COMPORT
COMPOST
COMPOUND LSD MIX NTA BASE
DIOL ENOL FILL JOIN MIXT SOUR
TEPA ALKYL ALLOY AMIDE AMINE
BLEND DIENE ESTER FURIL IMIDE
OXIDE UNION ACETAL ADJUST
ALKIDE BORANE COMMIX COPULA
IODIDE JUMBLE KETONE MEDLEY
PHENOL POLYOL PTERIN PYRONE
SETTLE TEMPER URACIL URAMIL
AGATHIN ALCOHOL ALLICIN
ALLOXAN AMALGAM AMIDATE
AMIDINE AMINATE AMMONIA
ARGYROL CARBENE COMBINE
COMPLEX COMPONE COMPOSE
COMPOST DVANDVA KAMPONG
KHELLIN PHORBIN PREPARE SPIRANE
STEROID AGLUCONE AGLYCONE
ALIZARIN ALKOXIDE AMMONATE
ANTIPODE APIGENIN BRAZILIN
CEROMIDE COMPOSED FUCHSONE
GARDENIN GENTISIN GOSSYPOL
IODOFORM ISOLOGUE STYRACIN
CARBORANE YELLOWCAKE
(ADHESIVE —) SALVE
(CHEMICAL —) PCB
(COLORLESS —) FURAN FURANE
(COMBINING —) ACCEPTOR
(CRYSTALLINE —) TEPA
(EXPLOSIVE —) TNT
(HALOCARBON —) DBCP
(OF A CHEMICAL —) ORGANO
(ORGANIC —) ENOL
(POISONOUS —) KETENE CACODYL
GLYCINE HELENIN STIBINE

(SYNTHETIC —) ANDROGEN
SORBITAN
(PREF.) (PARENT —) NOR
(SUFF.) GENIN
(CARBON —) ENE
COMPOUNDED CONCRETE
COMPOSITE
COMPOUNDER TANKER
COMPOUNDING INTIMACY
COMPREHEND GET SEE KNOW
TAKE TWIG COVER GRASP IMPLY
LATCH REACH SAVVY SEIZE SENSE
SKILL SMOKE SPELL ATTAIN
BOTTOM DIGEST EMBODY FATHOM
FOLLOW PIERCE UPTAKE COMPASS
CONTAIN DISCERN EMBRACE
ENCLOSE IMAGINE INCLUDE
INVOLVE REALIZE RECEIVE
SWALLOW COMPRISE CONCEIVE
CONCLUDE PERCEIVE
COMPREHENSIBLE EXOTERIC
INCLUDED SENSABLE SCRUTABLE
COMPREHENSION HOLD SABE
GRASP SAVVY SENSE ESPRIT
FATHOM NOESIS UPTAKE EPITOME
INSIGHT KNOWING SUMMARY
BEARINGS PREHENSION
(OF READING —) CLOZE
COMPREHENSIVE BIG FULL WIDE
BROAD GRAND LARGE GLOBAL
SCOPIC CAPABLE CONCISE GENERAL
GENERIC CATHOLIC ENCYCLIC
SPACIOUS
COMPREHENSIVENESS POWER
SCOPE EXTENT BREADTH WIDENESS
LARGENESS
COMPRESS NIP TIE BALE BIND FIRM
LACE WRAP CLING CRAMP CROWD
CRUSH PINCH PRESS SMASH
BUNDLE DEFORM DIGEST GATHER
SHRINK STRAIN THRONG ABRIDGE
ASTRICT BOLSTER CABBAGE
COMPACT CURTAIL DEFLATE
EMBRACE FLATTEN PLEDGET
REPRESS SQUEEZE SQUINCH
ASTRINGE CONDENSE CONTRACT
LAMINATE PEMMICAN RESTRAIN
SUPPRESS
(— WOOL) DUMP
(HOT —) STUPE
(MEDICAL —) BOLSTER PLEDGET
COMPRESSED STRICT CROWDED
SUCCINCT ANGUSTATE COARCTATE
COMPRESSION CRUSH SQUEEZE
PRESSURE THLIPSIS
(PREF.) SYMPIESO SYMPIEZO
COMPRESSOR PUMP ROTARY
CONDENSER
COMPRISE HOLD COVER IMPLY
SEIZE ATTACH CONFER EMBODY
EMPLOY MUSTER COMPOSE
CONTAIN EMBRACE ENCLOSE

INCLUDE INVOLVE CONCEIVE PERCEIVE

COMPROMISE FINE TRIM COMMIT INTERIM COMPOUND ENDANGER PALLIATE TEMPORIZE

COMPROMISED BRULE

COMPROMISING FALSE

COMPULSION NEED URGE FORCE PRESS DURESS STRESS IMPULSE COACTION COERCION DISTRESS EXACTION PERFORCE NECESSITY

COMPULSORY COERCIVE FORCIBLE NECESSARY

(NOT —) OPTIONAL

COMPUNCTION QUALM REGRET SORROW REMORSE SCRUPLE PENITENCE

COMPURGATOR COJUROR COSWEARER

COMPUTATION COMPOT ACCOUNT COMPUTE CALCULUS COMPUTUS ESTIMATE RECKONING

COMPUTE ADD SUM CAST ITEM RATE COUNT TALLY VALUE ASSESS CIPHER FIGURE NUMBER RECKON ACCOUNT BALANCE SUPPUTE ESTIMATE CALCULATE

COMPUTER HOST MINI ADDER ENIAC LAPTOP MANIAC DESKTOP MAINFRAME PROCESSOR MINICOMPUTER

(— ADD-ON) ESE

(— ALL-PURPOSE CODE) BASIC

(— BINARY DIGIT) BIT

(— CAPACITY) RAM ROM

(— CHIP) CPU

(— CIRCUIT) NOR NAND

(— CIRCUIT BOARD) SIMM

(— CODE) BCD ASCII

(— COLLECTION OF DATA) DATABASE

(— COMPANY) AST IBM NEC ACER DELL APPLE COMPAQ GATEWAY MACINTOSH PACKARDBELL HEWLETTPACKARD

(— COMPONENT) CHIP

(— CORRECTION) PATCH

(— CURSOR MOVER) MOUSE TRACKBALL

(— DATA) FILE PUSHDOWN

(— DEVICE) WAND MOUSE

(— DISK) FLOPPY MINIFLOPPY

(— DISK OPERATING SYSTEM) MSDOS PCDOS

(— FAILURE) CRASH

(— GATE) AND

(— GATEWAY) PORT

(— HARDWARE) PC CPU DRIVE MONITOR PRINTER KEYBOARD

(— INDEX) KWIC

(— INFORMATION) DATA DATABASE

(— INFORMATION UNIT) BYTE MEGABYTE

(— INSERT) DISK

(— INSTRUCTION) MACRO

(— INTERFACE) PORT

(— KEY) ALT END ESC TAB CTRL HOME ENTER

(— LANGUAGE) ADA APL BCD RPG LISP LOGO ALGOL BASIC COBOL PASCAL PROLOG FORTRAN

(— LIST) MENU

(— MEMORY) RAM ROM PAGE CACHE EPROM STACK SCRATCHPAD

(— MEMORY CHIP) DRAM

(— MEMORY MODULE) CHIP SIMM

(— MONITOR) VGA SVGA

(— MOVIE) HAL

(— NERD) WEENIE

(— NETWORK) LAN

(— PRINTED TEXT) HARDCOPY PRINTOUT

(— PROGRAM) WORM VIRUS EDITOR LOADER FORTRAN SPREADSHEET BULLETINBOARD

(— PROGRAMMABLE MEMORY) EPROM

(— PROGRAMS) SOFTWARE

(— SEQUENCE OF BITS) BYTE

(— SOCKET) BANK PORT

(— SOFTWARE) DRIVER MONITOR

(— SOFTWARE NAME) LOTUS

(— SOUND) BEEP

(— STORAGE) FIELD

(— SYMBOL) ICON

(— SYSTEM) KLUGE KLUDGE TRSDOS

(— SYSTEMS COMMUNICATION) GATEWAY

(— UNIT) BIT BYTE ONEK

(— VIDEO DEVICE) MONITOR

(— VIDEO DISPLAY OF TASKS) MENU

(— WHIZ) HACKER

(ADMINISTRATOR OF — BOARD) SYSOP

(COMMAND TO — TO STORE DATA) SAVE

(COPY OF — FILE) BACKUP

(ENTER — DATA INTO MEMORY) WRITE

(ENTER A — PROGRAM) LOAD

(FLASHING — CUE) CURSOR

(FUNCTIONING PERIOD OF —) UPTIME

(HEART OF —) CPU

(HINT ON — TO CONTINUE) PROMPT

(INDICATOR ON — SCREEN) CURSOR

(INTEGRATED — CIRCUIT) CHIP

(KIND OF) ANALOG HYBRID DIGITAL

(KIND OF —) DESKTOP

(LINK FOR TWO —S BY PHONE) MODEM

(MAGNETIC — RECORD) DISK

(MOVE — DISPLAY UP OR DOWN) SCROLL

(NETWORK —) HOST
(OPERATOR OF — PROGRAM) SYSOP
(PARTS OF — SYSTEM) HARDWARE
(PHYSICAL PARTS OF — SYSTEM)
HARDWARE
(PRODUCER OF — SYSTEMS) OEM
(READY A —) BOOT
(RELATING TO — DISK) WINCHESTER
(STORED — MEMORY) FIRMWARE
(STORE OF — DATA) PUSHDOWN
(PL.) CYBER

COMRADE PAL ALLY CHUM MATE
PEER BILLY BUDDY BUTTY CRONY
HABER HAVER TOWNY BURSCH
CHABER CHAVER COPAIN COUSIN
DIGGER ENGIDU FELLOW FRATER
FRIEND GOSSIP HEARTY BROTHER
COMPEER CONVIVE BEAUPERE
CAMARADA CAMARADE COMORADO
CONFRERE COPEMATE TOVARICH
SKAINSMATE
(— AT TABLE) CONVIVE
(PL.) SOCE

COMRADESHIP CAMARADERIE

CON DO RAP ANTI KNOW LEAD LOOK
PORE QUIN READ SCAN CHEAT
CUNNE GUIDE KNOCK LEARN STEER
STUDY DIRECT PERUSE REGARD
VERSUS AGAINST DECEIVE EXAMINE
INSPECT OPPOSED SWINDLE

CONCAVE CAVE VOID CAMUS
MINUS ARCHED DISHED HOLLOW
SIMOUS VAULTY VAULTED
CRESCENT INCURVED
(SUFF.) COELOUS COELUS

CONCAVITY COVE DISH CONCHA
HOLLOW VENTER KNEEPAN

CONCEAL MEW WRY BURY DERN
FEAL HIDE KEEP LENE MASK SCUG
SILE VEIL VEST WRAP BLIND BOSOM
CACHE CLOAK COUCH COVER FEIGN
LAYNE PLANT SHADE BURROW
CLOSET DOCTOR ELOIGN EMBOSS
HUDDLE HUGGER IMBOSK OCCULT
POCKET SCREEN SHADOW SHIELD
SHROUD STIFLE VIZARD ABSCOND
ENVELOP OPPRESS PLASTER
SECRETE SMOTHER BESCREEN
DISGUISE ENSCONCE PALLIATE
PRETENCE PRETENSE WITHHOLD
(— A FUGITIVE) HARBOR
(— A TRAIL) TRASH
(— INFORMATION) LAYNE
(— PROFITS) SKIM
(— TO AVOID TAX) SKIM

CONCEALED DERN SCUG SNUG
BLIND PERDU PRIVY BURROW
COVERT HIDDEN LATENT OCCULT
PERDUE SECRET VEILED COVERED
LARVATE WRAPPED ABSTRUSE
CRYPTOUS HIDEAWAY RECONDITE
(— BY) BENEATH
(PREF.) ADEL(O)

CONCEALING DESIGNING
OBVELATION

CONCEALMENT MEW LAIN COVER
FRAUD NIGHT STALE SECRECY
CELATION VELATION SECRETION
(— OF TREASURE) MISPRISION
(IN —) DOGGO

CONCEDE OWN CEDE GIVE ADMIT
AGREE ALLOW GRANT WAIVE YETTE
YIELD ACCORD ASSENT BETEEM
CONFESS OTTROYE BEGRUDGE
ACKNOWLEDGE
(— AS ADVANTAGE) SPOT

CONCEIT EGO TOY IDEA SIDE WIND
CRANK FANCY KNACK POESY PRIDE
QUIRK BABERY DEVICE NOTION
VAGARY VANITY BIGHEAD CAPRICE
EGOTISM OUTRAGE TYMPANY
CONCETTO FLIMFLAM
(VIVID —) VISION

CONCEITED BUG BRAG COXY FESS
VAIN CHUFF COCKY FLORY HUFFY
PENSY PROUD SAUCY CLEVER
BIGGETY BIGGITY ARROGANT
DOGMATIC NOSEWISE PENSEFUL
PRIGGISH SNOBBISH

CONCEIVABLE EARTHLY POSSIBLE

CONCEIVE FORM HOLD MAKE PLAN
TEEM WEEN BEGIN BRAIN CATCH
DREAM FANCY FRAME GUESS IMAGE
THINK DESIGN DEVISE IDEATE
INTEND PONDER SETTLE GESTATE
IMAGINE REALIZE SUPPOSE
SUSPECT COMPRISE CONTRIVE
ENVISAGE

CONCENTRATE AIM FIX MASS PILE
BUNCH COACT EXALT FOCUS PURSE
UNIFY ARREST ATTEND CENTER
CITRIN DECOCT DISTIL FIXATE
GATHER SINGLE COMPACT CONGEST
DISTILL ENGROSS ESSENCE
EXTRACT THICKEN ABSOLUTE
APPROACH ASSEMBLE CONDENSE
CONTRACT FOCALIZE GRADUATE
(— ORE) STRAKE

CONCENTRATED HARD DENSE
FIXED INTENT STRONG EXALTED
INTENSE
(NOT —) DIFFUSE

CONCENTRATION BRIX TITER
CENTER BALLING SAMADHI ACTIVITY
FIXATION PELMANISM
(— OF ARTILLERY FIRE) STONK
(— OF ENERGY) EXCITON
(— OF GRAPE JUICE) BESHMET
(— OF PLANTS) BED
(— OF SOLUTION) MOLARITY
(EXCESS —) MONOMANIA

CONCEPT GUT GUTS IDEA PLAN
FANCY IMAGE BEGRIFF CONCEIT
OPINION THOUGHT ABSOLUTE
CATEGORY PLURALISM PERCEPTION

CONCEPTION ENS IDEA VIEW EIDOS

FANCY FETUS IMAGE BELIEF DESIGN
EMBRYO ENTITY NOTION CONCEIT
CONCEPT PROJECT PURPOSE
CATEGORY ESTHETIC NOTATION
RATIONAL
(— OF IDEA) HENT
(— OF ONESELF) BOVARISM
BOVARYSM
(ABSTRACT —) ARCHETYPE
(FALSE —) IDOL DELUSION
(QUICKNESS OF —) PREGNANCY
CONCEPTUAL IDEAL NOTIONAL
CONCEPTUALISM SERMONISM
CONCERN BUG BEAR CARE FEAR
FIRM GEAR HAND PART RECK SAKE
APPLY CAUSE CERNE DRIVE EVENT
GRIEF HEART SORGE STAND TOUCH
WORRY AFFAIR AFFECT BEHOLD
CHARGE DIRECT EMPLOY FINGER
IMPORT MATTER REGARD THRUST
ANXIETY ARTICLE BOTTLER
COMPANY DISTURB FUNERAL
INVOLVE PERTAIN RESPECT
SHEBANG SOLICIT TROUBLE
BUSINESS HYPOTHEC INTEREST
JEALOUSY
(— ONESELF) DEAL PASS TOUCH
INTERMIT
(INDUSTRIAL —) COLOSSUS
(PRUDISH —) COMSTOCKERY
(SOMETHING CAUSING —)
ALBATROSS
(SPECIAL —) ACCENT
(WORLDLY —S) EARTH
(SUFF.) (— FOR) ITIS
CONCERNED INTENT ANXIOUS
VERSANT WORRIED ATWITTER
BOTHERED
CONCERNING BY OF ON RE TO FOR
TIL TILL ABOUT ANENT ANENST
APROPOS TOUCHING
CONCERT POP PLAN RECK UNITE
ACCORD DEVISE SMOKER ARRANGE
BENEFIT CONCENT CONCORD
CONSORT CONSULT HARMONY
POPULAR RECITAL NEGOTIATE
CONCERT-HALL ODEON ODEUM
CONCERTINA ORGAN LANTUM
SQUIFFER BANDONION MELOPHONE
CONCESSION BOON FAVOR GRANT
LEASE STOOP ASSENT GAMBIT
OCTROY CESSION EPITROPE
MYNPACHT ADMISSION ALLOWANCE
PRIVILEGE
CONCESSIONAIRE GRIFTER
CONCH CONK PUNK SHELL COCKLE
MUSSEL STROMB STROMBUS
SCUNGILLI
CONCIERGE SUPER PORTER SUISSE
WARDEN DVORNIK JANITOR
CONCILIATE GET CALM EASE GAIN
ATONE HONEY THING ADJUST
PACIFY SOFTEN ACQUIRE APPEASE

CONCILE MOLLIFY PLACATE SATISFY
PROPITIATE
CONCILIATOR ARBITRATOR
CONCILIATORY MILD SOFT GENTLE
GIVING IRENIC LENIENT PACIFIC
WINNING IRENICAL LENITIVE
TREATABLE
CONCISE CURT NEAT TRIG BRIEF
CRISP PITHY SHORT TERSE COGENT
CUTTED COMPACT LACONIC
POINTED PRECISE SERRIED
SUMMARY TABLOID MUTILATE
PREGNANT SUCCINCT
CONCISELY PRESSLY ELLIPTICALLY
CONCISENESS BREVITY ECONOMY
SYNTOMY FASTNESS SYNTOMIA
BRACHYOLOGY
CONCLAMATION SHOUT
CONCLAVE SOBOR CLOSET
CHAMBER MEETING AREOPAGY
ASSEMBLY
CONCLUDE BAR END AMEN FINE
REST TAKE CLOSE DRIVE ESTOP
INFER JUDGE LIMIT CLINCH DECIDE
DEDUCE EXPIRE FIGURE FINISH
GATHER INDUCE PERIOD REASON
RECKON SETTLE ACHIEVE ARRANGE
COLLECT CONFINE EMBRACE
ENCLOSE RESOLVE SUPPOSE
COMPLETE DISPATCH ESTIMATE
GRADUATE PARCLOSE RESTRAIN
CONCLUDED OVER COMPLETE
CONCLUDING LAST DESITIVE
CONCLUSION END AMEN CODA
ERGO FINE LAST TERM CLOSE
ENVOY EVENT FINIS ISSUE LOOSE
OMEGA POINT ENDING FINALE
FINISH PERIOD RESULT SEQUEL
THIRTY UPSHOT CLOSURE CURTAIN
FINDING OUTCOME SEQUELA
VERDICT APODOSIS DECISION
EPILOGUE FINALITY FRUITION
GODSPEED ILLATION ILLATIVE
JUDGMENT PARCLOSE SENTENCE
(— OF ARIA) CABALETTA
(FINAL —) ISSUE
(RANDOM —) SURMISE
(PL.) COLLATION
CONCLUSIVE LAST FINAL VALID
COGENT CERTAIN EVIDENT EXTREME
TELLING DECISIVE DEFINITE
ULTIMATE
CONCOCT MIX BREW COOK FAKE
PLAN PLOT VAMP FRAME HATCH
THINK DECOCT DEVISE DIGEST
INVENT MINGLE REFINE SCHEME
COMPOSE CONFECT DREAMUP
PERFECT PREPARE COMPOUND
INTRIGUE
CONCOCTION PLAN PLOT MUMMY
DEVICE MUMMIA BREWING
MIXTURE SNEEZER BUSINESS
COMPOUND

CONCOMITANT SEQUELA INCIDENT ACCESSORY ASSOCIATE ATTENDANT ATTENDING COMPANION CONJOINED COOPERANT SATELLITE

CONCORD PART AGREE AMITY PEACE TERMS UNION UNITY TREATY UNISON COMPACT CONCENT CONCERT HARMONY ONENESS QUARTER COVENANT SYMPATHY COMMUNITY
(— OF SOUNDS) SYMPHONIA

CONCORDANT UNISON TUNABLE TUNEFUL HARMONIC UNISONAL UNISONOUS

CONCORDE SST

CONCOURSE CROWD HAUNT PLACE POINT REPAIR RESORT THRONG COMPANY ASSEMBLY FREQUENCE
(INFERNAL —) HELL

CONCRESCENCE ADHESION

CONCRETE CLOT FIRM HARD REAL BETON GROUT SOLID UNITE ACTUAL CEMENT GUNITE COMBINE CONGEAL SPECIAL COALESCE COMPOUND POSITIVE TANGIBLE AEROCRETE

CONCRETION CLOT KNOT MESS FLINT FUSIL PEARL STONE BEZOAR DOGGER NODULE TOPHUS LITHITE OTOLITH CALCULUS HAIRBALL POTSTONE SEBOLITH GALLSTONE
(— IN BAMBOO) TABASHIR TABASHEER

CONCUBINAGE KARAO KAREWA HETAERISM

CONCUBINE DASI MOLL HAGAR RIZPAH BEDMATE HETAIRA ODALISK MISTRESS ODALISQUE

CONCUPISCENCE DESIRE

CONCUPISCENT ANTSY

CONCUR HAND JIBE JOIN AGREE CHECK CHIME UNITE ACCEDE ACCORD ASSENT CONDOG APPROVE COMBINE CONSENT CONVENT COINCIDE CONSPIRE CONVERGE
(— IN) SUBSCRIBE

CONCURRENCE UNION ASSENT BESTOW CONSENT CONSORT MEETING ADHESION SYNDROME ADMISSION

CONCURRENT COEVAL UNITED MEETING COPUNCTAL

CONCUSSION BUMP SHOCK IMPACT ICEQUAKE COMMOTION

CONDEMN BAN CAST DAMN DEEM DOOM FILE FINE HISS BLAME BLESS DECRY JUDGE AMERCE ATTAIN AWREAK BANISH DETEST ADJUDGE CENSURE CONVICT DENOUNCE FORJUDGE REPROACH SENTENCE PROSCRIBE
(— AS SPURIOUS) OBELIZE

CONDEMNATION BAN DOOM BLAME CENSURE DECRIAL BRICKBAT

CONDEMNATORY SEVERE ADVERSE

CONDEMNED FATAL DAMNED

CONDENSATION BAN STORY DIGEST CAPSULE BOILDOWN

CONDENSE CUT JIG BRIEF UNITE DECOCT DIGEST HARDEN LESSEN NARROW REDUCE SHRINK ABRIDGE CAPSULE COMBINE COMPACT DEFLATE DENSATE DISTILL SHORTEN SQUEEZE THICKEN COMPRESS CONTRACT DIMINISH PEMMICAN SOLIDIFY

CONDENSED CURT BRIEF CAPSULE COMPACT CONCISE SUMMARY TABLOID ABSORBED

CONDENSER ALUDEL REFLUX BALANCER CAPACITOR

CONDER HUER

CONDESCEND DEIGN FAVOR GRANT SNOOT STOOP ASSENT OBLIGE SUBMIT CONCEDE DESCEND

CONDESCENDING AVUNCULAR

CONDESCENSION STOOP DISDAIN COURTESY DIGNATION

CONDIGN DUE FIT FAIR JUST SEVERE WORTHY ADEQUATE SUITABLE

CONDIMENT SOY HERB KARI MACE SAGE SALT CAPER CURRY DULCE DULSE SAUCE SPICE THYME AIWAIN AJOWAN CATSUP CLOVES GARLIC PEPPER RELISH SAMBAL TAMARA BADIANE CANELLA CHUTNEY KETCHUP MUSTARD OREGANO PAPRIKA VINEGAR ALLSPICE BALACHAN BLATJANG DRESSING SEASONER TURMERIC

CONDITION IF AND FIG PLY WAY CASE FORM HOOD MODE NICK PASS RANK ROTE TERM TIFF TRIM ANGLE BIRTH CAUSE CENSE CLASS COLOR COVIN ESTRE FACET JOKER PLACE POINT SHAPE STAGE STATE THEAT WHACK AGENCY DEGREE DONNEE ESTATE FETTLE GENTRY MORALE MUSCLE PLIGHT STATUS STRING ARTICLE CALLING FEATHER FOOTING PLISKIE PREMISE PREPARE PROVISO STATION SUSPEND COVENANT OCCASION POSITION PROTASIS STANDING PREDICAMENT REQUIREMENT
(— IN LIFE) NICHE SPHERE
(— OF ANXIETY) CARK
(— OF BODY) HEAT AFFECTION
(— OF FATIGUE) FRAZZLE
(— OF FLUCTUATION) EURIPUS
(— STATED BEFOREHAND) PREMISE
(BEING IN DIRTY —) GRUNGY
(CHANCE —) ACCIDENT

(CRUSHED —) MASH
(DEBASED —) CACHEXY CACHEXIA
(DEPRESSED —) DOWNBEAT
(DETERMINING —) GROUND
(DIRTY —) CLAT
(DISEASED —) DIEBACK
(DISGRACEFUL —) IGNOMINY
(DRUNKEN —) BUN
(DUE —) ORDER
(FAULTY —) MALADY
(FLOURISHING —) HEALTH
(GENERAL —) VOGUE
(HABITUAL —) TENOR
(LOW —) NOTHING
(MEAN —) DUST
(MISERABLE —) SQUALOR
(MORBID —) HOLDOVER
(MOST APPROPRIATE —) CHECKER
(NECESSARY —) MEAN
(NEUROTIC —) LATAH
(ORDERLY —) DECENCY
(PAINFUL —) CRICK
(PERMANENT —) HEXIS
(PROPER —) KILTER
(PROTECTIVE —) CALLUS CALLOUS
(SCURFY —) BUCKSKIN
(STATIONARY —) JIB
(SUBLIME —) HEAVEN
(SURROUNDING —) AIR
(TRUE —) SIZE
(UNEQUAL —) ODDS
(UNPROSPEROUS —) ILLTH
(UNWHOLESOME —) MALADY
(WEATHER —S) ELEMENTS
(PL.) HAND TERMS STRINGS
(SUFF.) ACITY ATION DOM ERY ICE
ICITY ILITY ION ISM MENT NESS OR
OSIS SHIP TH TY
(MORBID —) IASIS
CONDITIONAL EVENTUAL
CONNEXIVE PROVISORY QUALIFIED
CONDITIONED FINITE LIMITED
CONDITIONER DEGGER
CONDITIONING EDUCATION
HYPOTHESIS
CONDOLE MOAN
CONDOLENCE PITY RUTH EMPATHY
SYMPATHY
CONDOM JOHNNY RUBBER
JOHNNIE PROPHYLACTIC
CONDONE BLINK REMIT ACQUIT
EXCUSE FORGET IGNORE PARDON
ABSOLVE FORGIVE OVERLOOK
CONDOR TIFFIN BUZZARD VULTURE
CONDUCE GO AID HELP HIRE LEAD
TEND BRING GUIDE CONFER EFFECT
ENGAGE ADVANCE CONDUCT
FURTHER REDOUND
CONDUCT ACT CON RUN USE WIN
BEAR CALL COND CONN DEED
FACT FARE FIRK FORM GARB GEST
HAND KEEP LEAD MIEN PLAY QUIT
RULE SHOW TAKE WAGE WALK

BATON CARRY CHAIR DRESS DRIVE
FETCH GESTE GUARD GUIDE HABIT
MAYNE SITHE TRADE TRAIN USAGE
USHER ACTION ATTEND BEHAVE
COLORS CONVEY CONVOY COURSE
DEDUCE DEMEAN DEPORT DIRECT
ESCORT GOVERN INDUCT MANAGE
MANNER SQUIRE ACTIONS
BEARING CHANNEL COMPERE
COMPORT CONDITE CONDUCE
CONDUIT CONTAIN CONTROL
EXECUTE GALLANT GESTION
OFFICER OPERATE WIREWAY
ARRIVISM BEHAVIOR CARRIAGE
CHAPLAIN COURTESY DEMEANOR
GUIDANCE REGULATE SHEPHERD
TRANSACT
(— AROUND) TROT
(— ONESELF) DO ACT ACQUIT
BEHAVE BESTOW DEMEAN DEPORT
COMPORT CONTAIN DISPORT
ENTREAT MAINTAIN
(APPROPRIATE —) DHARMA
(BRASH —) FACE
(CONVENTIONAL —) PRAXIS
(DISORDERLY —) RANDAN
(DORMANT —) LATENCY
(DUTIFUL —) PIETY
(ETHICAL —) HONOR
(MORAL —) LIFE
(NORMAL —) WAY
(PROPER —) CRICKET
(RECKLESS —) DEVILRY DEVILTRY
(RIGHT —) TE TAO
(RIOTOUS —) RANDAN
(SAFE —) KOWL COWLE
(SEDITIOUS —) MISPRISION
(SHOWY —) BRAVADO
(SLOPPY —) SWASH
(SOCIAL —) MANNERS
(VAINGLORIOUS —) HEROICS
(WANTON —) RUFF
(WEAK —) FOLLY
CONDUCTANCE G
(UNIT OF —) MHO SIEMENS
CONDUCTION COURSING
CONDUCTOR CON BOND CADE
LEAD MAIN BRUSH GUARD SHUNT
SPOUT TRUNK BRIDGE BUSMAN
CARMAN CONVOY COPPER ESCORT
FEEDER LEADER OFFSET RETURN
CAPTAIN CATHODE MAESTRO
MANAGER AQUEDUCT BATONIST
CICERONE CONVEYOR DIRECTOR
EMPLOYEE FILAMENT STICKMAN
ANELECTRIC
(— OF FESTIVAL) SKUDLER
(ELECTRIC —) FILAMENT
(LIGHTNING —) ROD
(OMNIBUS —) CAD
(WOMAN —) CLIPPIE
(PL.) SERVICE
(SUFF.) EER

CONDUIT BOSS DUCT GOUT MAIN
PIPE SINK TUBE WIRE CABLE CANAL
CUNDY SEWER STACK HEADER
SLUICE TROUGH CARRIER CHANNEL
CHIMNEY CONDITE CONDUCT
CULVERT CUNDITE EXHAUST
FOGGARA LATERAL LAUNDER
PASSAGE WIREWAY AQUEDUCT
OLEODUCT PENSTOCK UTILIDOR
WASTEWAY
(PL.) LIMBERS

CONDYLOMA SYCOMA

CONE CAP YOW CHAT KING MOXA
PINA TOOT CONUS CRACK SCREW
SHAPE SPIRE YOWIE BOBBIN CONOID
MONTRE PASTIL CLUSTER CONELET
CONIOLE FISSURE FRUSTUM
PROLONG PYRAMID STROBIL
THIMBLE CANNELON DUMPLING
GALBULUS PASTILLE PINECONE
STROBILE STROBILUS
(— OF CLOTH) VANE
(— OF FIR) YOW YOWIE STROBIL
STROBILE STROBILUS
(— OF GUNPOWDER) PEEOY
(— OF HOP PLANT) BUR BURR
(— OF SILVER AMALGAM) PINA
(— ON LOG END) CAP
(— ON SHOE) CLEAT
(— STRUCTURE) NURAGHE
(HALF —) FORME NAPPE
(ICE CREAM —) ICE CORNET
(INVERTED —) HOPPER
(KIND OF —) NOSE
(PAPER —) SPILL COFFIN
(ROPE-MAKING —) TOP
(TOP CUT FROM —) UNGULA
(TRAFFIC —) PYLON
(VOLCANIC —) PUY MONTICULE
(PL.) HOPS
(PREF.) CON(I)(ICO)(O) STROBILI

CONENOSE BEDBUG BARBEIRO

CONE-SHELL ADMIRAL

CONESTOGA WAGON CARAVAN

CONEY CONY HYRAX HYRACID
GUATIBERO

CONFAB CHAT TALK POWWOW
CONFLAB PRATTLE

CONFABULATE TALK

CONFECTION CHOW MOSS CANDY
DULCE FUDGE MEBOS SWEET
BONBON COCKLE COMFIT DAINTY
DRAGEE HALVAH JUNKET MAJOON
NOUGAT SWEETY TABLET CARAMEL
CONFECT FONDANT MIXTURE
POMFRET PRALINE SEATRON
SUCCADE ANGELICA CHOWCHOW
CODINIAC COMPOUND CONSERVE
DELICACY MARZIPAN PRESERVE
QUIDDANY SUBTLETY
MARSHMALLOW
(TURKISH —) HALVAH

CONFECTIONERY CIMBAL
TUCKSHOP CONFISERIE

CONFEDERACY BUND COVIN
CREEK JUNTA KEDAR UNION COVINE
LEAGUE COMPLOT ALLIANCE
COVENANT FEDERACY ILLINOIS
BLACKFOOT

CONFEDERATE AID PAL REB ALLY
BAND PUFF COVER REBEL STALL
UNITE LEAGUE SANTAR ABETTER
ABETTOR CONJURE FEDARIE
FEDERAL FEODARY PARTNER
STEERER CONSPIRE FEDERARY
FEDERATE
(— SOLDIER) CONFED JOHNNY
GRAYBACK GRAYCOAT GREYBACK
(PICKPOCKET'S —) STALL

CONFEDERATION BODY BUND
ZUPA GUEUX UNION LEAGUE
COMPACT HASINAI SOCIETY
ALLIANCE COVENANT
(— OF VILLAGES) ZUPA

CONFER DUB GIVE MEET TALK
AWARD ENDOW FEOFF GRANT INFER
PARLE SPEND TREAT ADVISE
BESTOW COMMON CONFAB DONATE
ENTAIL HUDDLE IMPARL IMPART
INVEST PARLEY POWWOW COLLATE
COMMUNE COMPARE CONDUCE
CONSULT CONTACT COUNSEL
DISCUSS INSTATE PRESENT
COLLOGUE COMPRISE CONVERGE
NEGOTIATE
(— DEGREE UPON) CAP
(— KNIGHTHOOD UPON) DUB

CONFERENCE DIET TALK SYNOD
TREAT TRUST CAUCUS CONFAB
HUDDLE INDABA KORERO PARLEY
PARVIS POWWOW SUMMIT CIRCUIT
COUNCIL MEETING PALAVER
PARLING SEMINAR COLLOQUE
COLLOQUY CONCLAVE CONGRESS
PRACTICE PRACTISE TUTORIAL
PARLIAMENT
(SCIENCE —) PUGWASH

CONFERRING GRANT DATION

CONFESS OWN AVOW FESS KNOW
SING ADMIT GRANT KITHE ACKNOW
AGNISE ATTEST AVOUCH BEKNOW
COUTHE RENDER REVEAL SHRIFT
SHRIVE SQUEAK CONCEDE DIVULGE
PROFESS WHITTLE DISBOSOM
DISCLOSE DISCOVER MANIFEST
ACKNOWLEDGE

CONFESSION ALHET CREDO CREED
GRANT AVOWAL SHRIFT SHRIVE
VIDDUI ASHAMNU FORMULA
PECCAVI COGNOVIT
(MUTUAL —) SHARING

CONFESSIONAL SHRIFT MALCHUS

CONFESSOR FATHER SHRIFT
SHRIVER

CONFIDANT PRIVY FRIEND INWARD
INSIDER PRIVADO INTIMATE
CONFIDE AFFY RELY TELL TRUST
COMMIT DEPEND LIPPEN BELIEVE
CONSIGN ENTRUST INTRUST
(— IN) VENTURE
CONFIDENCE FACE HARK HOPE
BIELD CHEEK FAITH STOCK TRUST
APLOMB BELIEF CREDIT FIANCE
FIDUCE METTLE MORALE SECRET
SPIRIT SURETY COUNSEL COURAGE
PRIVITY AFFIANCE BOLDNESS
CREDENCE RELIANCE SECURITY
SURENESS
(—GAME) SCAM STING
CONFIDENT BOLD SMUG SURE
COCKY CRANK HARDY SIKER
CROUSE SECURE SICKER TRAIST
ASSURED CERTAIN HOPEFUL
RELIANT CONSTANT FEARLESS
FIDUCIAL IMPUDENT POSITIVE
SANGUINE TRUSTFUL
CONFIDENTIAL PACK BOSOM PRIVY
CLOSET COVERT HUSHED INWARD
SECRET PRIVATE ESOTERIC FAMILIAR
INTIMATE
CONFIDING TRUSTY CREDENT
RELIANT TRUSTFUL CONFIDENT
CONFIGURATION FORM SHAPE
FIGURE BANDING CONTOUR
DIAMOND GESTALT OUTLINE
GEOMETRY POSITURE OPPOSITION
PERSPECTIVE
(CELESTIAL —) SYZYGY
CONFINE BAR BOX CUB DAM HEM
MEW NUN PEN PIN STY TIE BAIL
BIND BOOM CAGE COOP CRIB
FOLD HASP JAIL KEEP LACE LOCK
PEND SEAL SHUT SPAN STEW
STOP STOW BOUND CABIN CHAIN
COART CRAMP CROWD DELAY
FENCE HOUSE LIMIT MARCH PINCH
POUND STICK STINT THIRL BORDER
BOTTLE COARCT CORRAL EMDANK
FETTER FORBAR HAMPER HURDLE
IMMURE IMPALE IMPARK INTERN
KENNEL PINION POCKET PRISON
SHUTIN STRAIN TETHER ASTRICT
CHAMBER COMPASS CONTAIN
IMPOUND INCLUDE MANACLE
PINFOLD POISTER RECLOSE
SECLUDE SHACKLE TRAMMEL
BASTILLE BOUNDARY CLOISTER
CONCLUDE DISTRAIN FOCALIZE
IMPRISON RESTRAIN STRAITEN
WAREHOUSE
(— IN HANDKERCHIEF) MAIL
(PL.) AMBIT PURLIEU PERIPHERY
CONFINED ILL FAST PENT BOUND
CAGED CLOSE CRAMP BEDRID
IMPALE IMPENT PENTIT SEALED
CAPTIVE CRAMPED CRIBBED LIMITED

SQUEEZY IMPENDED IMPLICIT
INTERNED PAROCHIAL
(— TO CERTAIN AREA) ENDEMIC
(—TO ONE) PROPER
(— TO SELECT GROUP) ESOTERIC
CONFINEMENT MEW BOND HOLD
JAIL WARD CRYING GATING
DURANCE INLYING JANKERS
WARDING CLAUSURE FIRMANCE
GROANING LOCKDOWN SOLITARY
CONFINES AMBIT
CONFINING NARROW
CONFIRM FIX SET FIRM SEAL PROVE
VOUCH AFFEER AFFIRM ASSENT
ASSURE ATTEST AVOUCH BISHOP
CLINCH FASTEN HARDEN RATIFY
REABLE SECOND SETTLE STABLE
VERIFY APPROVE COMFORT
COMPACT CONSIGN ENDORSE
FORTIFY JUSTIFY PROPORT SUPPORT
SUSTAIN THICKEN ACCREDIT
CONVINCE CORROBER ENTRENCH
INSTRUCT SANCTION STRENGTH
VALIDATE CORROBORATE
REDETERMINE
CONFIRMATION PROOF CHRISM
SANCTION
CONFIRMED SET FIXED SWORN
ARRANT STABLE CERTAIN CHRONIC
AFFEERED HABITUAL HARDENED
RATIFIED
CONFISCATE GRAB SEIZE USURP
CONDEMN CONFISK ESCHEAT
PUBLISH DISTRAIN
CONFISCATION ESCHEAT
INCENSION
CONFLAGRATION WAR FIRE BLAZE
FEVER BURNING INFERNO
CONFLICT JAR WAR AGON BATE
BOUT BUMP CAMP DUEL FRAY MEET
MUSS RIFT AGONY BROIL BRUSH
CLASH FIGHT GRIPS MIXUP STOUR
ACTION BATTLE COMBAT MUTINY
OPPOSE SCRAPE SHOWER STRIFE
CONTEND CONTEST DISCORD
SCUFFLE WARFARE ANTIMONY
CLASHING DISAGREE MILITATE
SKIRMISH STRIVING STRUGGLE
COLLISION COLLUCTATION
(DRAMATIC —) AGON
(FINAL —) ARMAGEDDON
CONFLICTING ADVERSE
ABHORRENT
CONFLUENCE FORK CROWD INFALL
CONFLUX MEETING JUNCTION
CONFLUENT FORK
CONFORM DO GO FIT HEW BEND
LEAN OBEY SORT SUIT ABIDE ADAPT
AGREE APPLY SHAPE YIELD ACCEDE
ADJUST ASSENT COMPLY CONFER
SETTLE SQUARE SUBMIT COMPOSE
CONFIRM

(**— TO**) KEEP MEET ANSWER BEHAVE
SATISFY
CONFORMABLE DONE SUING
SUITED CONFORM PURSUANT
QUADRANT
CONFORMATION FORM BUILD
(**MENTAL —**) SAMSKARA
CONFORMING FAIR SAME COMELY
DECENT CORRECT CONGRUOUS
CONFORMIST BOY COMPLIER
CONFORMITY FIT ACCORD DHARMA
EQUITY REASON HARMONY JUSTICE
KEEPING ACCURACY AFFINITY
JUSTNESS LIKENESS SYMMETRY
CONGRUITY FORMALITY
ACCORDANCE CONSERTION
(**— TO LAW**) DECENCY LEGALITY
(**— WITH GOOD MANNERS**)
PROPRIETY
CONFOUND MIX BLOW DASH MATE
MAZE ROUT STAM STUN WHIP
ABASH ADDLE AMAZE APPAL BLAST
FOUND SHEND SPOIL STUMP WASTE
AWHAPE BAFFLE BUNKER COMMIT
DISMAY DUDDER MINGLE MUDDLE
RABBIT RATTLE ASTOUND BUMBAZE
CONFUSE CONFUTE CORRUPT
DESTROY FLUMMOX FORLESE
MISTAKE NONPLUS PERPLEX
PETRIFY STUMBLE STUPEFY
ASTONISH BABELIZE BEWILDER
DISTRACT DUMFOUND SURPRISE
SPIFLICATE
CONFOUNDED MATE BALLY BLAME
RUDDY BLAMED DEUCED POCKED
BLASTED BLESSED MURRAIN
PEEVISH DUMMERED JIGGERED
SWITCHED CONSARNED
(**BE —**) ABAVE ABAWE
CONFRATERNITY BODY UNION
SOCIETY CONFRAIRY
CONFRONT DARE DEFY FACE MEET
NOSE BEARD BRACE BRAVE CROSS
FRONT STAND ACCOST ASSAIL
BREAST OPPOSE RESIST VISAGE
AFFRONT COMPARE OUTFACE
PROPOSE ENVISAGE THREATEN
CONFRONTATION FACEOFF
CONFRONTING BEFORE ADVERSE
ABUTTING CONFRONT
CONFUSE BOX FOX MIX BALL DASH
DAZE DOIT DOZE DUST GAUM HARL
MAZE MUSS ROIL ROUT ABASH
ADDLE AMAZE BEFOG BITCH BLEND
CLOUD DEAVE DIZZY MUDDY SHEND
SHENT SNARL STEER TWIST UPSET
BAFFLE BEDAZE BEMUSE BOTHER
BURBLE CADDLE COMMIT CORPSE
DUDDER DUDDLE FLURRY FUDDLE
GRAVEL JUMBLE MADDLE MAFFLE
MAMMER MASKER MIZZLE MOIDER
MOMBLE MUDDLE PUZZLE RAFFLE

RATTLE TWITCH WIMPLE BECLOUD
BEDEVIL BLUNDER BUMBAZE
DERANGE DIFFUSE EMBROIL
FLUSTER GARBOIL GIDDIFY MISTAKE
MYSTIFY NONPLUS PERPLEX
PERTURB SCATTER SHUFFLE
STUPEFY UNRAVEL BEFUDDLE
BEWILDER CONFLATE CONFOUND
DISORDER DISTRACT DUMFOUND
ENTANGLE MISORDER SQUATTER
OBFUSCATE
(**— AN ACTOR**) CORPSE
(**— BY NOISE**) DUDDER
CONFUSED ASEA LOST ADDLE
DIZZY FOGGY FUZZY HEAVY MISTY
MUDDY MUZZY VAGUE WESTY
WOOLY BLOTTO CLOUDY DOILED
DOITED DRUMLY JUMBLY MEDLEY
MOPISH MUSHED SHAGGY TAVERT
WOOLLY BEMUSED BLURRED
CHAOTIC CLOUDED CONFUSE
DIFFUSE MIFFLED OBSCURE RATTLED
STUPENT COCKEYED DERANGED
FLURRIED INVOLVED STREAKED
FLUSTERED INDISTINCT
SCRAMBLING MUDDLEHEADED
(**— IN LANGUAGE**) BABYLONIAN
(**EASILY —**) BASHFUL
CONFUSEDLY PELLMELL
CONFUSING DIZZY MAZEFUL
BAFFLING BLINDING DIZZYING
CONFUSION PI DIN PIE COIL DUST
FLAP FUSS HARL MESS MOIL RIOT
AMAZE ATAXY BABEL CHAOS CHEVY
CHIVY DERAY FRASE HAVOC HURLY
LARRY LURRY SNAFU SNARL STROW
ATAXIA BABBLE BAFFLE BALLUP
BEDLAM BUMBLE CHIVVY DUDDER
FRAISE HABBLE HOBBLE HUBBUB
HUDDLE JABBLE JUMBLE MASTIC
MUCKER MUDDLE POTHER PUCKER
RABBLE RUFFLE RUMPUS THRONG
TOPHET TUMULT UPROAR WELTER
ANARCHY BLUNDER BLUSTER
CLUTTER COBWEBS FARRAGE
FLUTTER GARBOIL HURLING KIPPAGE
LOUSTER MISMAZE MISRULE
ROOKERY RUMMAGE SCADDLE
SCOWDER TOPHETH TURMOIL
WHEMMEL WIDDRIM BABELISM
DISARRAY DISORDER EQUIVOKE
HOOROOSH SCOUTHER SHAMBLES
SPLUTTER STRAMASH TOHUBOHU
CONFUTATION DISPROOF
CONFUTE DENY EVICT REBUT
EVINCE EXPOSE REFUTE FALSIFY
IMPROVE EXPOSE SILENCE SUBVERT
CONCLUDE CONFOUND CONVINCE
DISPROVE INFRINGE OVERCOME
REDARGUE
CONGEAL GEL ICE SET GEAL JELL
CANDY COTTER CURDLE FREEZE

HARDEN STIFFEN STORKEN THICKEN
CONCRETE SOLIDIFY
(— **INTO HOARFROST**) RIME
CONGEALED FROZEN
CONGELATION FROST
CONGENER BEAVER DOTTREL
DOTTEREL
CONGENIAL SIB BOON HAPPY
NATAL NATIVE AMIABLE CONNATE
KINDRED
CONGENITAL INNATE CONNATE
CONNATAL GENETOUS
CONGER SEAEEL
CONGERIES CALCULARY
COLLECTION
CONGEST STUFF IMPACT
CONGESTED INJECTED
CONGESTION JAM HEAP LAMPAS
LAMPERS CROWDING STOPPAGE
CONGLOMERATE HEAP MASS PILE
ROCK STACK BANKET PSEPHITE
NAGELFLUH
(—**S OF JAPAN**) ZAIBATSU
(**JAPANESE** —) ZAIBATSU
CONGLOMERATION HUDDLE
GLOMMOX IMBROGLIO
CONGO MUMMY ASPHALTUM

CONGO

CAPITAL: BRAZZAVILLE
COIN: FRANC FRANCCFA
LAKE: MWERU TUMBA UPEMBA
LEOPOLD
NATIVE: SUSA VILI MANTU PYGMY
BATEKE MBOCHI WABUMA
BAKONGO BANGALA
PLATEAU: BATEKE
RIVER: UELE CONGO KWILU LULUA
NGOKO NIARI SANGA WAMBA
KWENGE LOANGE SANGHA UBANGI
KOUILOU LUBILASH
TOWN: EWO EPENA HOLLE JACOB
OKOYO SEMBE MAKOUA OUESSO
ZANAGA DOLISIE ENYELLE
LOUBOMO SOUANKE DJAMBALA
BRAZZAVILLE
TRIBUTARY: LOMAMI UBANGI
ARUWIMA LUAI ARA LUAPULA
ITIMBIRI

CONGOU KEEMUN
CONGRATULATE HUG JOY LAUD
GREET SALUTE FLATTER MACARIZE
(— **ONESELF**) PREEN
CONGRATULATION PARABIEN
(**PL.**) GRATTERS
CONGREGATE HERD MASS MEET
PACK TEEM GROUP SWARM TROOP
GATHER MUSTER COLLECT CONVENE
ASSEMBLE
CONGREGATION PEW BODY FOLD
HERD HOST MASS FLOCK SAMAJ

SWARM CHURCH PARISH COMPANY
MEETING ORATORY SYNAXIS
ASSEMBLY BRETHREN CHAPELRY
(— **OF WITCHES**) COVEN
(**JEWISH** —) KOLEL ALJAMA
SYNAGOG
(**PL.**) CHARGE
CONGRESS MOD DAIL DIET SYNOD
UYEZD OBLAST OUYEZD POWWOW
COUNCIL GORSEDD MEETING
ASSEMBLY CONCLAVE
(— **OF BARDS**) EISTEDDFOD
CONGRESSMAN SENATOR
DOUGHFACE
CONGRUITY ACCORD CONCORD
FITNESS HARMONY KEEPING
SYMMETRY COHERENCE
CONGRUOUS CONGRUE
HARMONIC SUITABLE ACCORDING
CONICAL CONIC TAPER COPPED
MITRAL COPPLED TAPERING
(**PREF.**) TURBINATO TURBIN(I)(O)
CONICALLY
(**PREF.**) TURBINATO
CONIDIUM CIDIUM ARTHROSPORE
CONIFER FIR YEW PINE CEDAR
LARCH SPRUCE SOFTWOOD
EVERGREEN
CONIFERAE PINALES
CONIUM HEMLOCK
CONJECTURE AIM CAST PLOT ROVE
SHOT VIEW AUGUR ETTLE FANCY
GUESS OPINE THINK BELIEF DIVINE
THEORY CONJECT IMAGINE OPINION
PRESUME SUPPOSE SURMISE
SUSPECT HINDCAST SUPPOSAL
CONJOIN JOIN KNIT ATTEND
EMPALE IMPALE ALLIGATE
CONJOINED JOINED JUGATE
LINKED JUGATED CONJUNCT
TOUCHING
CONJOINTLY JUNCTLY TOGETHER
CONJUGAL SPOUSAL CONNUBIAL
CONJUGATE YOKED JOINED
UNITED COUPLED INFLECT
PARONYMOUS
CONJUGATION SYNGAMY
ZYGOSIS CYTOGAMY ENDOGAMY
SYNOPSIS
CONJUNCTION AS ET IF OR AND
BUT NOR TIE THAN JOINT SINCE
SYNOD UNION UNITY THOUGH
COITION CONSORT JOINDER
CONJUNCT RATIONAL
(**PREF.**) (**IN** —) CO
CONJUNCTIVITIS PINKEYE
CONJUNCTURE SEASON
CONJURATION ART CHARM MAGIC
SPELL VOODOO EXORCISM
CONJURE PRAY WISH CHARM
HALSE ADJURE ENJOIN INVENT
INVOKE SUMMON BESEECH

COMBINE ENTREAT IMAGINE
CONSPIRE CONTRIVE EXORCIZE
(— UP) RAISE
CONJURE MAN CUNJAH CUNJER
GOOFER GUFFER
CONJURER MAGE PELLAR
POWWOW SHAMAN WIZARD
JUGGLER WARLOCK WIELARE
ANGEKKOK JONGLEUR MAGICIAN
PYTHONIC SORCERER
CONJURING JADU JADOO
CONJURY VOODOOISM
CONK FAIL HEAD KONK NOSE FAINT
KNOCK STALL BRACKET
CONNECT COG PUT TIE ALLY BIND
BOND GEAR GLUE JOIN KNIT KNOT
LINK AFFIX CHAIN MARRY NITCH
UNITE ATTACH BRIDGE CEMENT
COHERE COMMIT CONNEX COUPLE
ENLINK FASTEN PLUGIN RELATE
SPLICE COMBINE ENCHAIN INVOLVE
APPARENT CATENATE CONTINUE
DOVETAIL INTERTIE
(— TREADLE) CORD
CONNECTED ALLIED CONNEX
AFFINED COUPLED HANGING
(— WITH) ABOUT
(ELECTRICALLY —) ALIVE
(NOT —) FOREIGN ASYNARTETE
(SYNTACTICALLY —) ABSOLUTE
(SUFF.) (— WITH) ARIA ARIUM AST
ORIAL

CONNECTICUT
CAPITAL: HARTFORD
COLLEGE: TRINITY
COUNTY: TOLLAND WINDHAM
INDIAN: PEQUOT MOHEGAN NIANTIC
STATE BIRD: ROBIN
STATE FLOWER: LAUREL
STATE NICKNAME: NUTMEG
STATE TREE: OAK
TOWN: AVON BETHEL CANAAN
COSCOB DARIEN MYSTIC SHARON
STORRS WILTON DANBURY
MERIDEN NIANTIC NORWALK
NORWICH TOLLAND WINDSOR
NEWHAVEN SIMSBURY WESTPORT
GREENWICH RIDGEFIELD
UNIVERSITY: YALE WESLEYAN

CONNECTING BETWEEN SYNDETIC
CONNECTION Y HUB TAP TIE BOND
LINK HITCH NEXUS UNION BUCKLE
CLEVIS FAMILY GROUND REPORT
SUTURE SWIVEL BEARING BOLSTER
CONTACT DESCENT FERRULE
HOLDING KINSHIP LIAISON LINKAGE
RAPPORT SIAMESE SIBNESS
SOCIETY AFFINITY ALLIANCE
COMMERCE CONNEXUS INTIMACY
JUNCTION LIGATION RELATIVE
SYNDETIC RELATIONSHIP

(— BETWEEN UNIVERSES)
WORMHOLE
(ELECTRICAL —) GROUND
(FISH-LINE —) LEADER
(FORKED —) BRANCH
(MECHANICAL —S) LEADOUT
(WORKING —) GEAR
CONNECTIVE IZAFAT SUTURAL
JUNCTION LIGATIVE SYNDETIC
VINCULAR
CONNECTOR AND
CONNING TOWER SAIL
CONNIVANCE CAHOOT CAHOOTS
CONNIVE ABET PLOT WINK BLINK
CABAL ASSENT FOMENT INCITE
COLLUDE
(— AT MEDICAL TREATMENT) COVER
CONNIVING FOXY
CONNOISSEUR JUDGE CRITIC
EXPERT CAMEIST EPICURE
GOURMET CIDERIST DILETANT
LAPIDARY COGNOSCENTE
MEDIEVALIST
(— OF WINES) OENOPHILE
CONNOTATION DEPTH INTENT
MEANING
CONNOTE MEAN
CONNUBIAL MARITAL CONJUGAL
DOMESTIC
CONQUER GET WIN BEAT BEST
DOWN FIRK GAIN LICK ROUT TAME
WHIP CRUSH DAUNT DEBEL EVICT
DEBELL DEFEAT EVINCE HUMBLE
IMPORT MASTER REDUCE SUBDUE
VICTOR ACQUIRE PREVAIL SUBJECT
SURPASS TRIUMPH OVERCOME
OVERGANG SURMOUNT VANQUISH
CONQUEROR HERO MASTER
VICTOR WINNER TRIUMPHER
CONQUEST MASTERY SCALING
TRIUMPH VICTORY WINNING
CONSANGUINEOUS AKIN CARNAL
KINDRED NATURAL RELATED
CONSANGUINITY BLOOD NASAB
KINSHIP AFFINITY
CONSCIENCE WORD DAENA HEART
INWIT SENSE SCRUPLE THOUGHT
CONSCIENTIOUS FAIR JUST EXACT
RIGID EIDENT HONEST STRICT
DUTIFUL UPRIGHT FAITHFUL
CONSCIENTIOUSNESS RELIGION
CONSCIOUS KEEN WARE ALIVE
AWAKE AWARE JERRY GUILTY
FEELING KNOWING WITTING
RATIONAL SENSIBLE SENTIENT
CONSCIENT
(— OF) ONTO
CONSCIOUSNESS EGO HEART
SENSE SPIRIT ANOESIS FEELING
THOUGHT SENTIENT AWARENESS
PERCEPTION
(HALF —) DOVER
(REGAIN —) COMETO

CONSCRIPT LEVY CHOCO DRAFT ENROL ENLIST MUSTER DRAFTEE DRAUGHT RECRUIT JEANJEAN

CONSCRIPTION LEVY

CONSECRATE VOW FAIN HOLY SAIN SEAL BLESS DEIFY HEAVE SACRE ANOINT DEVOTE HALLOW ORDAIN SACRATE CONSACRE DEDICATE SANCTIFY

CONSECRATED BLEST OBLATE SACRED VOTARY VOTIVE BLESSED SACRATE HALLOWED HIERATIC

CONSECRATION IHRAM SACRE SACRY SACRING DEVOTION HOLINESS

CONSECUTIVELY TOGETHER

CONSECUTIVENESS SEQUENCE

CONSENT HEAR AGREE ALLOW GRANT YIELD ACCEDE ACCORD AFFORD ASSENT BETEEM COMPLY CONCUR PERMIT APPROVE GOODWILL PERMISSION

CONSENTIENT UNANIMOUS

CONSEQUENCE AND END BORE EVENT FORCE FRUIT ISSUE SUITE WORTH BROWST CHARGE EFFECT ENTAIL FIGURE GROWTH IMPORT MOMENT REPUTE RESULT SEQUEL WEIGHT CONCERN OUTCOME PRODUCE PURPOSE SEQUELA SEQUENT BACKLASH INTEREST MISCHIEF OCCASION SEQUITUR COROLLARY OUTGROWTH CONSECTARY RAMIFICATION
(DONE IN —) PURSUANT
(HARMFUL —) EVIL
(ILL —) MISCHIEF
(PERSON OF —) HEAVY
(PL.) AFTERINGS

CONSEQUENT COMES THESIS ADJUNCT

CONSEQUENTIAL HEAVY POMPOUS COROLLARY MOMENTOUS

CONSEQUENTLY SO ERGO THEN THUS HENCE LATER PURSUANT PRESENTLY

CONSERTAL SUTURAL

CONSERVATION HUSBANDRY

CONSERVATISM BOURBONISM

CONSERVATIVE SAFE TORY FUSTY QUIFT STAID FABIAN HUNKER STABLE BOURBON DIEHARD HARDHAT MODERATE UNIONIST

CONSERVATORY STOVE SCHOOL ACADEMY

CONSERVE CAN JAM SAVE GUARD GUMBO JELLY DEFEND SECURE OILFIELD UPHOLD HUSBAND PROTECT SEATRON SUSTAIN MAINTAIN PRESERVE
(GRAPE —) UVATE

CONSIDER AIM BAT LET SEE CALL CAST DEEM GAUM GIVE HASH HEAR HEED HOLD MULL MUSE RATE SEEM TAKE TALE VIEW VISE WISE ALLOW BESEE COUNT ENTER ETTLE JUDGE PANSE POISE SPELL STUDY THINK VERSE VOLVE WEIGH ADVERT ADVISE BEHOLD DEBATE DEVISE DIGEST ESTEEM EXPEND FIGURE IMPUTE PONDER REASON RECKON REGARD REWARD SURVEY ACCOUNT BELIEVE BETHINK CANVASS CONSULT EXAMINE INSPECT PERPEND PREPEND REFLECT RESPECT REVOLVE SUPPOSE COGITATE ESTIMATE MEDITATE PERPENSE RUMINATE
(— FAVORABLY) CREDIT
(— PROS AND CONS) ARGUE
(— SEPARATELY) SPECIALIZE

CONSIDERABLE GAY GEY FAIR GOOD TIDY BONNY CANNY GEYAN GREAT LARGE SMART STARK GOODLY PRETTY GOODISH HEALTHY INTENSE NOTABLE SEVERAL HANDSOME POWERFUL SENSIBLE UNLITTLE

CONSIDERABLY FAR GAY GEY WELL GEYAN PRETTY SMARTLY

CONSIDERATE KIND MILD NICE GENTLE TENDER CAREFUL HEEDFUL PRUDENT SERIOUS TACTFUL DELICATE GRACIOUS ATTENTIVE

CONSIDERATENESS GRACE
(MUTUAL —) SHU

CONSIDERATION GUT GUTS SAKE COUNT PRICE STUDY TOPIC ADVICE ASPECT COMITY DEBATE ESTEEM MOMENT MOTIVE NOTICE REASON REFLEX REGARD SURVEY ACCOUNT INSIGHT PREMIUM RESPECT THOUGHT ALTRUISM COURTESY DELICACY EMINENCE EMPHASIS GRATUITY PROSPECT SANCTION
(BASIC —) BEDROCK
(ETHICAL —) SCRUPLE
(THOUGHTFUL —) THEORIA
(UNDER —) ONTHETAPIS

CONSIDERED ADVISED DELIBERATE

CONSIDERING IF FOR SINCE SEEING

CONSIGN DOOM GIVE MAIL SEND SHIP ALLOT AWARD CHECK DIGHT REMIT SHIFT YIELD ASSIGN COMMIT DESIGN DEVOTE REMAND RESIGN ADDRESS RETEACH CONFIDE DELIVER DEPOSIT ENTRUST INTRUST BEQUEATH DELEGATE RELEGATE TRANSFER
(— FOR DESTRUCTION) ACCURSE
(— TO OBLIVION) BURY EXPUNGE
(— TO PERDITION) DAMN CONDEMN

CONSIGNEE AGENT FACTOR SHIPPER RECEIVER

CONSIGNMENT INVOICE FOREDOOM SHIPMENT
(— OF TEA) BREAK

CONSIST LIE HOLD RELY REST
DWELL EXIST STAND INHERE RESIDE
CONTAIN EMBRACE COMPRISE
CONSISTENCY BODY UNION
DEGREE CONCENT CONCORD
HARMONY KEEPING COMPAGES
EVENNESS FIRMNESS SOLIDITY
SYMMETRY
CONSISTENT EVEN FIRM STEADY
DURABLE LOGICAL REGULAR
UNIFORM COHERENT ENDURING
SUITABLE COMPATIBLE SEQUACIOUS
(— WITH NATURE) KIND KINDLY
(BE —) ACCORD
(MAKE —) CLEAR
CONSISTING
(PREF.) (— OF) DIA
(SUFF.) (— OF) IC(AL)
CONSOCIES
(SUFF.) ETUM
CONSOLATION SOP FINE RELIEF
SOLACE COMFORT SPIRITING
CONSOLE CALM ALLAY ANCON
CHEER ORGAN TABLE SOLACE
SOOTHE BRACKET CABINET
COMFORT RELIEVE SUPPORT
SUSTAIN CARTOUCH
CONSOLER PARACLETE
CONSOLIDATE COG MIX KNIT
MASS POOL WELD BLEND CLOSE
MERGE UNIFY UNITE HARDEN
MINGLE SETTLE COMBINE COMPACT
ANKYLOSE COALESCE COMPRESS
CONDENSE ORGANIZE SOLIDIFY
CONSOLIDATED CONFLATE
CONSOLS GOSCHENS
CONSOMME MADRILENE
CONSONANCE ACCORD UNISON
HARMONY DIAPASON DIAPENTE
SYMPATHY SYMPHONY
CONSONANT WAW MUTE STOP
DENTAL FORTIS LABIAL LETTER
LIQUID SONANT UNISON LATERAL
MUTABLE PALATAL PLOSIVE
SPIRANT UNIFIED ALVEOLAR
ASPIRATA ASPIRATE BILABIAL
EJECTIVE GEMINATE HARMONIC
SUITABLE
(CONSECUTIVE —S) CLUSTER
(SMOOTH —) LENE LENIS
(TENSE AND STRONG —) FORTIS
(VOICELESS —) SURD SPIRATE
CONSORT COT AIDE ALLY JOIN
MATE MOUP WIFE YOKE GROUP
TROOP UNITE ACCORD ATTEND
ESCORT MINGLE SPOUSE COMPANY
COMRADE CONCERT DAMKINA
EMPRESS HUSBAND PARTNER
ACCUSTOM ASSEMBLY PRINCESS
(VISHNU'S —) LAKSHMI
CONSPECTUS LIST APERCU
SURVEY OUTLINE THEATER THEORIC
SPECTRUM SYNOPSIS

CONSPICUOUS BIG BOLD RANK
CLEAR FAMED NOISY PLAIN STARY
EXTANT FAMOUS MARKED PATENT
SIGNAL BLATANT EMINENT GLARING
NOTABLE OBVIOUS POINTED
SALIENT SIGHTLY STARING VISIBLE
APPARENT EMPHATIC FLAGRANT
KENSPECK MANIFEST STRIKING
PROMINENT NOTICEABLE
OUTSTANDING
(— ONE) STANDOUT
CONSPIRACY COUP PLAN PLOT
RING CABAL COVIN JUNTO PARTY
COVINE SCHEME COMPACT
COMPLOT INTRIGUE CATILINISM
CONSPIRATOR PACKER PLOTTER
SCHEMER
CONSPIRE ABET PACK PLOT CABAL
UNITE LEAGUE SCHEME COLLUDE
COMPLOT CONJURE CONNIVE
COLLOGUE CONTRIVE
CONSTABLE COP BULL PEON SLOP
BEADLE BEAGLE HARMAN KAVASS
KEEPER KOTWAL WARDEN BAILIFF
CORONER DOZENER NUTHOOK
OFFICER STALLER SUBASHI
ALGUAZIL DOGBERRY TIPSTAFF
CASTELLAN CATCHPOLE CATCHPOLL
BORSHOLDER
CONSTANCE
(FATHER OF —) FONDLOVE
NONESUCH
(HUSBAND OF —) ALLA
(SON OF —) ARTHUR
CONSTANCY ZEAL ARDOR FAITH
TRUTH FEALTY HONESTY LOYALTY
ONENESS PURPOSE DEVOTION
FIDELITY
CONSTANT K SET EVEN FIRM JUST
LEAL TRUE FIXED LOYAL SOLID STILL
TIGHT TRIED ITHAND STABLE
STEADY CERTAIN CHRONIC DURABLE
FOREVER LASTING REGULAR
STAUNCH UNIFORM DEFINITE
ENDURING FAITHFUL POSITIVE
RESOLUTE SEDULOUS STANDING
PERENNIAL
(KIND OF —) HUBBLE
CONSTANTLY AWAY EVER ALWAYS
THRONG
CONSTANT NYMPH
(AUTHOR OF —) KENNEDY
(CHARACTER IN —) DODD KATE
CARYL LEWIS SUSAN TESSA
ALBERT SANGER TERESA ANTONIA
PAULINA FLORENCE CHURCHILL
SEBASTIAN
CONSTELLATION ARA CUP FLY FOX
LEO APUS ARGO COLT CROW CRUX
DOVE GOAT GRUS HARE HARP LION
LYNX LYRA MAST PAVO PLOW SIGN
SWAN TAUR URSA VELA WAIN WOLF
ALTAR ARIES CAMEL CETUS CLOCK

CRANE DRACO EAGLE GROUP HYDRA
INDUS LEPUS LIBRA LUPUS MALUS
MENSA MUSCA NORMA ORION
PYXIS RAVEN TABLE VIRGO WAGON
WHALE ANTLIA AQUILA AURIGA
BOOTES CAELUM CANCER CARINA
CORVUS CRATER CYGNUS DIPPER
DORADO FORNAX GEMINI HYDRUS
INDIAN LIZARD OBELUS OCTANS
OKNARI PICTOR PISCES PISCIS
PLOUGH PUPPIS SCALES SCUTUM
TAURUS TIGRIS TOUCAN TUCANA
VOLANS ALGEBAR CEPHEUS
CLUSTER COLUMBA COMPASS
DOLPHIN FURNACE GIRAFFE
LACERTA MONARCH OETAEUS
PATTERN PEACOCK PEGASUS
PERSEUS PHOENIX RHOMBUS
SAGITTA SCORPIO SERPENS
SERPENT SEXTANS SEXTANT
XIPHIAS AQUARIUS ASTERISM
CHAMPION CIRCINUS CYNOSURE
EQUULEUS ERIDANUS HERCULES
HERDSMAN KASHYAPA QUADRANS
REINDEER RETICULE SCORPION
SCORPIUS SCULPTOR TRIANGLE
(— OF VEGA) LYRA

CONSTERNATION FEAR ALARM
PANIC DISMAY FRIGHT HORROR
TERROR TREPIDITY

CONSTIPATE BIND ASTRICT

CONSTIPATED BOUND COSTIVE
STENOTIC

CONSTIPATION STENOSIS

CONSTITUENT ATOM ITEM PART
PIECE VOTER DETAIL FACTOR FUSAIN
MATTER MEMBER SIMPLE ELECTOR
ELEMENT FEATURE TAGMEME
INTEGRAL
(— OF BLOOD SERUM) OPSONIN
(— OF CLINKER) ALITE CELITE
(— OF COAL) DURAIN FUSAIN
(— OF DURAIN) ATTRITUS
(— OF MUSCLE) CREATINE
(— OF STEEL) PEARLITE
(—S OF BEER) EXTRACT
(NECESSARY —) ESSENCE
(PL.) MATTER BIOSESTON

CONSTITUTE BE FIX SET FORM
MAKE ENACT ERECT FORGE FOUND
SHAPE SPELL CREATE DEPUTE
GRAITH ORDAIN APPOINT COMPOSE
FASHION STATION COMPOUND
COMPRISE

CONSTITUTION LAW SET CODE
SETT BEING CANON FRAME FUERO
HUMOR SETUP STATE CHARTE
CRASIS CUSTOM DESIGN ESTATE
HEALTH NATURE TEMPER CHARTER
HABITUS SYNODAL GRONDWET
GRUNDLOV HABITUDE PHYSIQUE
POLITEIA

(— STATE) CONNECTICUT
(BODILY —) HABIT SPIRITS
(GERMINAL —) HEREDITY

CONSTITUTIONAL WALK HECTIC
INNATE RIKKEN EXERCISE

CONSTITUTIVE FORMAL

CONSTRAIN ART PUT TIE ARCT
BEND BIND CURB DOOM FAIN HALE
HOLD LEAD URGE CHAIN CHECK
CLASP COART CRAMP DETER DRIVE
FORCE IMPEL LIMIT PRESS COERCE
COMPEL EVINCE OBLIGE RAVISH
SECURE STRAIN THRAST ASTRICT
CONFINE CONJURE ENFORCE
MANACLE OPPRESS REPRESS
VIOLATE COMPRESS CONCLUDE
DISTRESS OBLIGATE PERFORCE
POUNDAGE RELIGATE RESTRAIN

CONSTRAINED FAIN TIED VAIN
BOUND FORCED FORMAL UNEASY
COACTED

CONSTRAINING UNEASY
COMPELLENT

CONSTRAINT BOND CRAMP FORCE
BRIDLE DURESS STRESS RESERVE
STRAINT COERCION DISTRESS
PRESSURE

CONSTRICT TIE BIND CURB GRIP
CHOKE CRAMP LIMIT STRAP HAMPER
SHRINK STRAIN STRAIT ASTRICT
DEFLATE SQUEEZE STIFFEN TIGHTEN
ASTRINGE COMPRESS CONDENSE
CONTRACT DISTRAIN RESTRICT

CONSTRICTED STRAIT STRICT
ADENOID
(— AT INTERVALS) MONILIFORM

CONSTRICTION KNOT CHOKE
ISTHMUS STENOSIS THLIPSIS

CONSTRICTOR BOA ABOMA NOOSE
GUAVINA

CONSTRUCT UP BIG ATOM FORM
IDEA LEVY MAKE REAR BUILD CRAFT
DIGHT EDIFY ERECT FRAME MODEL
WEAVE BURROW DEDUCE DESIGN
DEVISE FABRIC ARRANGE CARPENT
COMBINE COMPILE COMPOSE
CONCEPT CONFECT CONTOUR
EXTRUCT FASHION CONSTRUE
ENGINEER PRACTISE SLIPFORM
(— ARCH) TURN

CONSTRUCTED BUILT EDIFICATE
(CAREFULLY —) CLEVER
(HASTILY —) GIMCRACK JIMCRACK

CONSTRUCTION BOOM ALTAR
FRAME FABRIC MONSTER SYNESIS
APPROACH BUILDING DWELLING
ERECTION
(— OF NAME) ABSTRACTION
(— SET) ERECTOR
(ABSTRACT —) STABILE
(GRAMMATICAL —) SYNESIS
APPOSITION
(POINTED —) BEAK

CONSTRUCTIVE PONENT FACTIVE
HELPFUL VIRTUAL CREATIVE IMPLICIT
INFERRED
CONSTRUCTOR ENGINEER
CONSTRUE INFER PARSE STRUE
INTEND RENDER ANALYZE CONSTER
DISSECT EXPLAIN EXPOUND
RESOLVE
CONSUL SUFFECT
CONSULT LOOK SEEK TALK ADVISE
CONFER EMPARL IMPARL COUNSEL
RESOLVE
CONSULTANT EXPERT ADVISER
COUNSEL
CONSULTATION ADVICE COUNCIL
COUNSEL
CONSUL, THE (CHARACTER IN —)
JOHN MAGDA SOREL
(COMPOSER OF —) MENOTTI
CONSUME EAT SUP USE BOLT BURN
CHEW FANG FARE FEED FRET GULP
IDLE KILL RUST TAKE TUCK WEAR
DALLY DRINK FLAME LURCH RAVEN
SHIFT SPEND TOOTH WASTE
ABSORB BEZZLE BROWSE CANKER
DEVOUR ENGAGE EXPEND FINISH
IMBIBE INHALE PERISH PUNISH
VANISH CORRODE DESTROY
DWINDLE ENGROSS EXHAUST
SWALLOW CONTRIVE SQUANDER
(— IN LARGE QUANTITY) PUNISH
(— TOTALLY) KILL
(— VORACIOUSLY) HOG
CONSUMED ALL PAU DOWN BURNT
SPENT COMBUST OUTWORN
CONSUMER MOUTH
(UNPRODUCTIVE —) CATERPILLAR
CONSUMING EATING SACRED
BURNING FLAMING
CONSUMMATE END FINE FULL RIPE
CLOSE IDEAL SHEER ARRANT EFFECT
FINISH FULFIL RATIFY ACHIEVE
CONSUME CROWNED FULFILL
PERFECT PERFORM ABSOLUTE
COMPLETE MERIDIAN THOROUGH
CONSUMMATION CROWN PERIOD
UPSHOT
CONSUMPTION USE DECAY WASTE
EXPENSE WASTING PHTHISIS
SPENDING
(PREF.) PHTHISIO
CONSUMPTIVE LUNGY HECTIC
PREDATORY
CONTACT ABUT JOIN KISS MEET
SLED CROSS TOUCH TRUCK UNION
ARRIVE IMPACT SYZYGY EPHAPSE
HOLDING MEETING TACTION
JUNCTION TANGENCY TOUCHING
(— BY RADIO) RAISE
(— OF TELEGRAPH KEY) ANVIL
(ELECTRICAL —) HUB HUBB POINT
(EVIL —) CONTAGION
(FLEETING —) BRUSH

(FORCIBLE —) IMPACT
(3-POINT —) OSCNODE
(PREF.) HAPT(O) THIGMO
CONTAGION POX TAINT VIRUS
MIASMA POISON
CONTAGIOUS TAKING NOXIOUS
SMITTLE CATCHING EPIDEMIC
CONTAIN RUN HAVE HOLD KEEP
STEM STOW TAKE CARRY CHECK
CLOSE COVER HOUSE EMBODY
ENFOLD ENSEAM HARBOR RETAIN
COMPILE EMBRACE ENCLOSE
INCLUDE INVOLVE RECEIVE
SUBSUME SUSTAIN COMPRISE
RESTRAIN
(PREF.) CHADA
CONTAINED IN
CONTAINER BAG BOX CAN CUP HAT
JAR JUG KEG LUG NIN PAN POD POT
TIN TUB URN VAT BAIL BOMB CAGE
CASE CASK CRIB DISH DRUM EWER
FILE FLAT JACK SACK SALT SILO
SINK SKIP TANK TUBE VASE VIAL
ALBUM BASIN BILLY CADDY CHEST
CRATE CRUET CRUSE DEWAR EMPTY
FLASK GLASS GOURD POUCH SCOOP
SCRAY STAND STOOP STOUP
BARREL BASKET BOTTLE BUCKET
BUSHEL CARBOY CARTON CASTER
CASTOR COOLER CRADLE DUSTER
HAMPER HATBOX HOLDER INKPOT
MAILER PICNIC RABBIT RIDDLE
SHAKER WITJAR AEROSOL AMPULLA
BANDBOX BLADDER CAPSULE
COASTER COSTREL CRISPER
FEEDBOX HANAPER HOLDALL
INKWELL OILDRUM PACKAGE
SEEDLIP SHIPPER SNIFTER SPOONER
STEEPER CANISTER DECANTER
DEMIJOHN ENVELOPE HOGSHEAD
HONEYPOT INHOLDER KNAPSACK
PENTAGON PUNCHEON SLIPCASE
RELIQUARY POCKETBOOK
(— FOR BEER) GROWLER
(— FOR BOBBINS) BUFFALO
(— FOR BRANDY) SNIFTER
(— FOR COINS) BANK
(— FOR EXPLOSIVE CHARGE) CAP
(— FOR FISH) BASS
(— FOR GOLD DUST) SHAMMY
(— FOR HOLY OIL) STOCK
(— FOR LEFTOVER FOOD)
DOGGYBAG DOGGIEBAG
(— FOR PLANTS) BAND
(— HUNG FROM OBI) INRO
(— IN WHICH TO HEAT DRUGS)
COOKER
(— MADE OF HOLLOW LOG) GUM
(— OF ASSAYER) CUPEL
(COFFEE —) INSET
(DESSERT —) COUPE
(DRINK —) DOP
(EARTHENWARE —) STEAN

(FIRECLAY —) SETTER
(KITCHEN —) CANISTER
(RAILROAD —S) BUNKER
(SHELVED —) CABIN
(SHIPPING —) KIT
(SNUFF —) WEASAND
(TOBACCO —) SARATOGA
(VENTILATED —) CHIP
(5-GALLON —) JERICAN JERRICAN
(PL.) CONVEYER CONVEYOR

CONTAINING
(SUFF.) IC(AL)

CONTAMINATE FOUL HARM SLUR
SMIT SOIL STAIN SULLY TAINT
BEFOUL DEBASE DEFILE INFECT
INJURE POISON ATTAINT CORRUPT
DEBAUCH FLYBLOW POLLUTE
TARNISH VITIATE DISHONOR

CONTAMINATED DIRTY DEGRADED
INFECTED

CONTAMINATION INFECTION
TAINTMENT
(— IN GLASS) STONE

CONTE TALE CRAYON

CONTEMN HATE FLOUT SCORN
SPURN REJECT SLIGHT DESPISE
DISDAIN CONTEMPT INDIGNIFY

CONTEMPLATE FACE MUSE PLAN
SCAN VIEW DEIGN STUDY THINK
WEIGH BEHOLD DESIGN PONDER
REGARD SURVEY CHERISH PROPOSE
REFLECT CONSIDER ENVISAGE
ENVISION MEDITATE

CONTEMPLATION MUSE STUDY
DHYANA MUSING PRAYER REGARD
THEORY INSIGHT MOONING
REQUEST THEORIA PETITION
RECOLLECTION
(OF PACT) RETROSPECT
RETROSPECTION

CONTEMPLATIVE BROODY
PENSIVE THEORIC STUDIOUS

CONTEMPORANEOUS COEVAL
LIVING MODERN CURRENT EXISTING

CONTEMPORARY EQUAL COEVAL
FELLOW CURRENT PRESENT
YEALING EXISTENT SIMULTANEOUS

CONTEMPT PRUT SCORN SHAME
SNEER SLIGHT CONTEMN DESPECT
DESPITE DISDAIN HETHING
MOCKERY DEFIANCE DERISION
DESPISAL DISGRACE MISPRIZE
MISPRISION OPPROBRIUM
(— FOR DANGER) TEMERITY
(— OF OPPOSITION) DEFIANCE
(ONE HELD IN —) FINK

CONTEMPTIBLE LOW BASE MEAN
POOR VILE BALLY CHEAP DIRTY
DUSTY LOUSY MANGY MUCKY
PETTY POCKY RUDDY SCALD SORRY
ABJECT BLOODY CRUDDY GRUDDY
MEASLY PALTRY SCABBY SCUMMY
SCURVY SHABBY SNOTTY SORDID

YELLOW BROKING LIGHTLY PEEVISH
PELTING PITIFUL SCALLED SCORNED
SHITTEN SLAVISH SQUALID
BAUBLING BEGGARLY FRIPPERY
INFAMOUS INFERIOR PICAYUNE
PITIABLE PRECIOUS SNEAKING
UNWORTHY WRETCHED
MISBEGOTTEN
(— PERSON) CRUD
(SUFF.) (— ONE) EEN EER

CONTEMPTIBLENESS BEGGARY

CONTEMPTUOUS SLIGHT SNEERY
SNOOTY HAUGHTY LIGHTLY SLIGHTY
SPITOUS ARROGANT FLOUTING
INSOLENT SCOFFING SCORNFUL

CONTEND TUG VIE WAR WIN CAMP
COCK COPE DEAL FRAB KEMP PLEA
RACE WAGE ARGUE BANDY BRAWL
CHIDE CLAIM FIGHT FLITE PRESS
ASSERT BATTLE BICKER BREAST
BUCKLE BUFFET BUSTLE COMBAT
DEBATE DIFFER JOSTLE JUSTLE
MEDDLE OPPOSE PINGLE REASON
STRIVE BARGAIN COMPETE CONTEST
COUNTER DISPUTE PROPUGN
QUARREL SCUFFLE STICKLE SUSTAIN
WRESTLE CONFLICT CONTRAST
CONTRIVE MAINTAIN MILITATE
SQUABBLE STRUGGLE
(— FOR) SUPPORT

CONTENDER ATHLETE STICKLER

CONTENT PAY CALM EASE GIST
GLAD PAID RATH SATE APPAY HAPPY
HUMOR RATHE SERVE AMOUNT
CUBAGE PLEASE APPEASE CONTENU
GRATIFY PERFECT REPLETE SATIATE
SATISFY SUFFICE WILLING BLISSFUL
CAPACITY CONTINEU WILCWEME
(—3 OF 3ACK) BUDGET
(—S OF STOMACH) COOKIES
(CUBICAL —) VOLUME
(ENERGY —) STRENGTH
(HEAT —) ENTHALPY
(SUPERFICIAL —S) AREA
(PL.) LINING

CONTENTED COZY FAIN VAIN QUIET
SATED CONTENT PLEASED
CHEERFUL

CONTENTION WAR BAIT BATE CASE
FEUD PLEA RIOT TIFF TOIL BROIL
CHEST CLAIM STRUT BICKER
COMBAT DEBATE ESTRIF JANGLE
STRIFE CHIDING CONTEKE CONTEST
DISCORD DISPUTE OPINION
QUARREL RIVALRY WRANGLE
ARGUMENT CONFLICT SQUABBLE
STRUGGLE VARIANCE
COLLUCTATION
(VERBAL —) WORDS

CONTENTIOUS CROSS BATEFUL
PEEVISH PERVERSE BELLICOSE

CONTENTMENT EASE BLISS
HEAVEN PLEASURE SATISFACTION

CONTERMINOUS NEXT ADJACENT FRONTIER PROXIMAL

CONTEST GO IT BEE FIX RUN SUE TRY VIE AGON BOUT CAMP COPE DUEL FEUD FRAY GAME HOLD KEMP LAKE MART PULL RACE SHOW SPAR TIFF TILT TURN YOKE AGONY ARGUE BROIL CLASH DERBY EVENT FIGHT MATCH PLATE PRIZE RODEO ROLEO SCRUB SPORT TRIAL WAGER ACTION ADJURE AFFRAY BATTLE BISLEY COMBAT DEBATE DEFEND FLIGHT OPPOSE RESIST RUBBER SEESAW STRIFE STRIVE TUSSLE YOKING BARGAIN BRABBLE CLASSIC COMPETE CONTECK CONTEND DERAIGN DISPUTE GRAPPLE PROTEST SHUTOUT TOURNEY WARFARE ARGUMENT CONCOURS CONFLICT DOGFIGHT HANDICAP LITIGATE SKIRMISH SLUGFEST STRIVING STRUGGLE WALKAWAY WALKOVER PANCRATIUM PENTATHLON
(— EASILY WON) LAUGHER
(— IN WORDS) SPAR
(— NARROWLY WON) SQUEAKER
(ATHLETIC —) AGON BIATHLON
(AUTOMOBILE — ON FROZEN LAKE) ICEKHANA
(BEAUTY —) PAGEANT
(CLOSE —) DICE
(DRAWN —) TIE DRAW STALEMATE
(MOCK —) SCIAMACHY
(MOST IMPORTANT —) SUPERBOWL
(RACING —) DRAG
(REAPING —) KEMP
(PREF.) MACHO
(SUFF.) AGONIST(IC) MACHIA MACHY

CONTESTANT VIER RIVAL WAGER PLAYER AGONIST ENTRANT SCRATCH FINALIST PROSPECT

CONTIGUITY ADJACENCY CONFINITY IMMEDIACY

CONTIGUOUS NEAR NEXT NIGH NEARBY TANGENT ABUTTING ADJACENT TOUCHING

CONTINENT ASIA MASS PORE SOBER AFRICA CHASTE EUROPE CONTENT CAPACITY MAINLAND MODERATE ABSTINENT
(VANISHED —) LEMURIA

CONTINGENCY BOOK CASE EVENT CHANCE ADJUNCT CONTACT VENTURE ACCIDENT CASUALTY FORTUITY INCIDENT JUNCTURE PROSPECT

CONTINGENT TROOP CASUAL CHANCE DOUBTFUL EVENTUAL INCHOATE POSSIBLE TOUCHING ACCIDENTAL DELEGATION

CONTINUAL STILL HOURLY ABIDING ENDLESS ETERNAL LASTING REGULAR UNDYING UNIFORM CONSTANT ENDURING UNBROKEN

CONTINUALLY AY AYE EVER STILL ALWAYS EVERLY HOURLY STEADY ENDLESS ETERNAL FOREVER MINUTELY

CONTINUANCE STAY WHEN DELAY LEASE SEQUEL ABIDING DURANCE LASTING ABIDANCE DURATION STANDING SURVIVAL

CONTINUANT OPEN LIQUID DURATIVE

CONTINUATION SEQUEL CONTANGO DURATION PROLONGATION PERSEVERATION
(— OF DOUBLET) BASQUE

CONTINUE BE DO ABY SUE ABYE BIDE DURE HOLD JUMP KEEP LAST LIVE STAY TIDE ABIDE CARRY EXIST PERGE STICK UNITE ABEGGE BELEVE ENDURE EXTEND PURSUE REMAIN RESUME BELEAVE CONNECT CONTUNE PERSIST PROCEED PROLONG SUBSIST SURVIVE SUSTAIN PROTRACT
(— UNALTERED) TARRY

CONTINUED STILL SERIAL CHRONIC CONSTANT

CONTINUING ABIDING DURABLE LASTING DURATIVE PERPETUAL PERSISTENT OUTSTANDING
(— FOR LONG TIME) CHRONIC
(— TO BE) YET

CONTINUITY TRACT SCRIPT COHESION SCENARIO CONTINUUM
(PREF.) SYNECHIO

CONTINUOUS RUN EVEN ANEND EIDENT ENTIRE EYDENT STEADY CHRONIC ENDLESS RUNNING UNBROKEN PERENNIAL PERPETUAL

CONTINUOUSLY AWAY EVER FAST ANEND OUTRIGHT

CONTORT WRY BEND COIL CURL TURN WARP GNARL SCREW TWIST WREST CRINGE DEFORM WRITHE DISTORT PERVERT SQUINCH WREATHE OBVOLUTE

CONTORTED WRY WRIED KNOTTY CRISPED KNOTTED SCREWED WRITHEN OBVOLUTE

CONTORTION SCREW STITCH WRITHE MURGEON WORKING

CONTOUR FORM LINE CURVE GRAPH SHAPE SWEEP AMOEBA FIGURE OUTLINE PROFILE CARTOUCH CONTORNO MANDORLA PLANFORM TOURNURE
(— ON SHIP) HANCE

CONTRA CONTRE AGAINST COUNTER OPPOSED

CONTRABAND HOT GOODS ILLEGAL ILLICIT SMUGGLED UNLAWFUL

CONTRABASS BASS OCTOBASS
CONTRACEPTIVE SHEATH MINIPILL
  (ORAL —) PILL
CONTRACT GET BOND DRAW FARM
  FORM HALE KNIT PACT SALE TACK
  CATCH CLOSE COACT COUCH
  CRAMP FEVER INCUR LEASE LIMIT
  NEXUM PINCH SHRUG SNURP
  CARTEL COCKLE COMMIT CRINGE
  ENGAGE FUTURE GATHER HIRING
  INDENT LESSEN MUTUUM NARROW
  PIGNUS PLEDGE POLICY PROMPT
  PUCKER REDUCE SHRIMP SHRINK
  SUBLET TREATY ABRIDGE APPALTO
  BARGAIN BUMMERY CHARTER
  COMPACT CRIMPLE CRUMPLE
  CURTAIL DEFLATE FIDUCIA
  MANDATE PROMISE SCRUNCH
  SHORTEN SHRIVEL SOCIETY
  WRINKLE ASSIENTO BOTTOMRY
  CONDENSE COVENANT HANDFAST
  HARDNESS LOCATION RESTRICT
  STEELBOW STRAITEN SYNGRAPH
  ABBREVIATE OBLIGATION
  (— BROW) FROWN
  (— INTO WRINKLES) KNIT
  (BRIDGE —) SOLO AUCTION
  (MARRIAGE —) KETUBA AFFIANCE
  HANDFAST BETROTHAL SPONSALIA
CONTRACTED BOXY CRAMP
  BOOKED ASTRICT INGROWN
  INSULAR SCREWED CONTRACT
CONTRACTILITY MOTILITY
CONTRACTION HM ANT NIP TIC TIS
  AINT CANT ISNT KNIT MAAM WONT
  CRAMP HADNT HASNT NISUS SPASM
  CRASIS GATHER INTAKE MUSTNT
  SHRINK TWITCH ELISION EPITOME
  WOULDNT APNEUSIS TRACTION
  ABRIDGMENT ABRIDGEMENT
  (— OF HEART) SYSTOLE
  (— OF SYLLABLES) SYNIZESIS
  (PL.) TREPPE
CONTRACTOR KHOT BUTTY
  BUILDER REMOVER SUPPLIER
CONTRADICT DENY BELIE CROSS
  REBUT FORBID IMPUGN NEGATE
  OPPOSE RECANT REFUTE THREAP
  COUNTER GAINSAY REVERSE
  WITHSAY CONTRARY DISPROVE
  DOWNFACE NEGATIVE OUTSTAND
CONTRADICTION CLASH DENIAL
  DEMENTI PARADOX WITHSAW
  ANTILOGY ANTIMONY ANTILOQUY
  (LUDICROUS —) BULL
CONTRADICTORY OPPOSE
  ANTINOME OPPOSITE THWARTING
CONTRAPTION RIG TOOL DEVICE
  DOODAD GADGET JIGGER CONCERN
  MACHINE DOOHICKEY HOOTNANNY
CONTRARIETY DISCORD
CONTRARILY BACKWARD
  CRISSCROSS

CONTRARIWISE CONTRA
  CONTRARY
CONTRARY BALKY CROSS KICKY
  SNIVY AVERSE CONTRA CUSSED
  ORNERY SNIVEY THRAWN ADVERSE
  COUNTER CRABBED FROWARD
  HOSTILE INVERSE OPPOSED PEEVISH
  RESTIVE REVERSE STROPPY
  WAYWARD ABSONANT ANTIPODE
  CAPTIOUS CONTRAIR INIMICAL
  OPPOSITE PERVERSE PETULANT
  SINGULAR ABHORRENT
  (— EXPRESSION) OXYMORON
  (— TO) BESIDE AGAINST ATHWART
  (— TO HAPPINESS) ILL
  (— TO REASON) SILLY ABSONANT
  (PREF.) CONTRA COUNTER DIS RETRO
CONTRAST CLASH STRIFE COMPARE
  CONTEND DISCORD ANTIMONY
  DIVISION DYNAMICS OPPOSITE
CONTRASTING
  (PREF.) CONTRA
CONTRAVENE DEFY DENY HINDER
  OPPOSE THWART DISPUTE VIOLATE
  INFRINGE OBSTRUCT
CONTRAVENTION SIN VICE CRIME
  BREACH OFFENSE
CONTRETEMPS SLIP BONER HITCH
  MISHAP SCRAPE ACCIDENT INCIDENT
CONTRIBUTE AID ANTE FORK GIVE
  HELP MAKE TEND CAUSE ENTER
  GROUT PUTUP SERVE ASSIST
  BESTOW CONCUR CONFER DONATE
  PUNGLE RENDER SUPPLY TENDER
  ANIMATE CONDUCE FURNISH
  FURTHER PROVIDE THROWIN
CONTRIBUTING ACCESSORY
CONTRIBUTION BIT SUM TAX
  ALMS BOON GIFT SCOT SHOT ESSAY
  INPUT SHARE IMPOST SYMBOL
  ARTICLE LARGESS PAYMENT
  PRESENT RENEWAL WRITING
  DONATION EXACTION OFFERING
  ROMESHOT
  (CHURCH —) TITHE
  (LITERARY —) PAPER
  (SMALL —) MITE
CONTRITE WORN SORRY HUMBLE
  RUEFUL PENITENT SORROWFUL
CONTRITION SORE SORROW
  PENANCE PENITENCE
CONTRIVANCE (ALSO SEE DEVICE)
  ART BOW FLY GIN JET JIG LEG DROP
  GEAR HARP JACK KITE LURE PAGE
  PLAN PLOT RASP REED TOOL ALARM
  BRAKE CARRY CHECK DOLLY DRAFT
  FLOAT FRAME GUIDE HICKY KNACK
  MIXER QUIPU SHIFT SNARE STOCK
  ANCHOR DAMPER DECEIT DESIGN
  DEVICE DOCTOR DOLLIE ENGINE
  FABRIC FANGLE GABION GADGET
  GIMBAL HANGER HARROW HEATER
  HICKEY HOLDER JIGGER JINKER

MARKER MORTAR MUZZLE POLICY
RATTLE SCHEME SLUICE SPIDER
TEASEL WEIGHT WHEEZE WINDAS
WRENCH BOLSTER CLEANER
CLEARER CONCERN COUPLER
CUNNING DINGBAT DRAUGHT
FICTION FISHWAY HUMIDOR
KNOCKER MACHINE PAGEANT
PROJECT REDUCER ROASTER
SCRAPER SHEBANG SPANNER
STOPPER TOASTER TRIPPER VOLVELL
ADAPTION ARTIFICE CROTCHET
DUTCHMAN EUPYRION FAKEMENT
FORECAST GOVERNOR INDUSTRY
MOLITION OXIDATOR REGISTER
RESOURCE SCISSORS SQUEEZER
SUBTLETY WITCRAFT

CONTRIVE GET LAY BREW CAST
DRAW FIND FIRK MAKE PLAN PLOT
WORK FRAME FUDGE HATCH SHAPE
STAGE WEAVE AFFORD DESIGN
DEVISE DIVINE ENGINE FIGURE
INVENT MANAGE SCHEME WANGLE
ACHIEVE AGITATE COMMENT
COMPASS CONCOCT CONJURE
CONSULT CONTEND FASHION
IMAGINE MACHINE PROCURE
PROJECT REPAREL CONSPIRE
ENGINEER FORECAST INTRIGUE
PURCHASE

CONTRIVED PAT SLICK STAGED
TIMBERED

CONTRIVER DAEDAL DAEDALUS
ENGINEER

CONTRIVING FASHION SCHEMERY

CONTROL BIT LAP LAW MAN POT
RUN CONN CURB EGIS GRIP HAND
HANK HAVE HOLD REDE REIN RULE
STAY SWAY WIND AEGIS BOOST
CHARM CHECK COACT DAUNT
DUMMY GRASP GUIDE LEASH ORDER
POWER STEER SWING THEAT TREAT
TUTOR VERGE WIELD BANDON
BRIDLE CHARGE CLUTCH COERCE
CORNER DANGER DIRECT EMPERY
GOVERN HANDLE MANAGE POCKET
TEMPER AMENAGE COMMAND
CONDUCT CONTAIN CUSTODY
FORBEAR MASTERY MONITOR
QUALIFY STRINGS COACTION
DOMINATE DOMINIUM IMPERIUM
MODERATE REGULATE SERVOTAB
POSSESSION
(— A BULL) MANDAR
(— OF RESOURCES) HUSBANDRY
(— OVER WIFE) MANUS
(ABSOLUTE —) BECK
(FIRE —) BLANKET
(GET EXCLUSIVE — OF) SEWUP
(GOVERNMENT —) DIRIGISM
SQUADRISM
(MANUAL —) JOYSTICK

(NONCLERICAL —) LAICISM LAICITY
(OUT OF —) RUNAWAY
(VOLUME —) GAIN

CONTROLLED STEADY SERVILE
CONTAINED

CONTROLLER FENCER GERENT
MASTER STARTER
(SPEED —) GOVERNOR RHEOCRAT

CONTROLLING MASTER LEADING
DOMINANT HEGEMONIC

CONTROVERSIAL ERISTIC POLEMIC

CONTROVERSIALIST ERISTIC
POLEMIC DISPUTANT GLADIATOR

CONTROVERSY FLAP PLEA SPAT
SUIT CHEST FUROR BATTLE COMBAT
DEBATE FURORE HASSEL HASSLE
HOORAH HURRAH STRIFE TUSSLE
DISPUTE POLEMIC QUARREL
WRANGLE ARGUMENT TRAVERSE
CONTENTION
(ART OF —) POLEMICS

CONTROVERT DENY FACE MOOT
ARGUE DEBATE DEFEND OPPOSE
OPPUGN REFUTE CONTEST DISPUTE
GAINSAY DISPROVE

CONTUMACIOUS UNRULY
RIOTOUS CONTUMAX INSOLENT
MUTINOUS PERVERSE STUBBORN

CONTUMELY ABUSE SCORN INSULT
CONTECK DISDAIN REPROOF
UPBRAID CONTEMPT RUDENESS

CONTUSE BEAT POUND THUMP
BRUISE INJURE SQUEEZE

CONTUSION POUND BRUISE

CONUNDRUM PUN WHIM GUESS
ENIGMA PUZZLE RIDDLE CONCEIT
CROTCHET

CONURE ARATINGA

CONVALESCE MEND GUARISH
RECOVER

CONVENANCE FORM

CONVENE SIT CALL HOLD MEET
UNITE GATHER MUSTER SUMMON
CONVENT CONVOKE ASSEMBLE
CONVERGE

CONVENIENCE GAIN BEHOOF
URINAL LEISURE COMMODITY

CONVENIENT FIT GAIN HEND NIGH
HANDY HENDE READY ATHAND
CLEVER FITTED PROPER SUITED
USEFUL ADAPTED AVENANT
COMMODE HELPFUL BECOMING
EXPEDITE SUITABLE OPPORTUNE
COMMODIOUS

CONVENIENTLY WELL HANDILY
CLEVERLY

CONVENT ABBEY HOUSE TEKKE
TEKYA CENOBY COVENT FRIARY
PRIORY MEETING RECLUSE CLOISTER
LAMASERY MOTHERHOUSE

CONVENTION DIET FEIS FORM MISE
RULE TABU SYNOD TABOO USAGE

CARTEL CAUCUS CUSTOM TREATY
DECORUM MEETING ASSEMBLY
ASSIENTO CONCLAVE CONGRESS
CONTRACT COVENANT PRACTICE
PRECEDENT
(LONG-ESTABLISHED —) TRADITION
(SET OF —S) PROTOCOL
(STAGE —) ASIDE
(PL.) DECENCIES
CONVENTIONAL MORE NOMIC
RIGHT TRITE USUAL DECENT
FORMAL MODISH PROPER CORRECT
POMPIER REGULAR ACADEMIC
ACCEPTED COPYBOOK ORTHODOX
CUSTOMARY
(RIGIDLY —) UPTIGHT
CONVENTIONALITY FORM
ACADEMISM FORMALITY
GRUNDYISM
CONVENTIONALIZE STYLIZE
CONVERGE JOIN MEET FOCUS
CONCUR CORNER CONNIVE
DESCEND APPROACH FOCALIZE
CONVERSANT ADEPT BUSIED
EXPERT VERSED SKILLED FAMILIAR
OCCUPIED
CONVERSATION RAP SAY CALL
CHAT CHIN RUNE TALE TALK BOARD
CRACK PROSE CACKLE CONFAB
DEVICE GOSSIP PARLEY POWWOW
SPEECH YABBER CEILIDH COMMUNE
CONDUCT PALAVER PURPOSE
BACKCHAT BEHAVIOR CAUSERIE
CHITCHAT COLLOGUE COLLOQUY
DIALOGUE GIFFGAFF HARANGUE
PARLANCE QUESTION COLLOCUTION
(— BETWEEN WHALERS) GAM
(LIGHT —) SMALLTALK
CONVERSATIONALIST TALKER
CAUSEUR
CONVERSE CHAT CHIN LIVE MOVE
TALK DWELL SPEAK CACKLE
COMMON CONFER DEVISE HOMILY
PARLEY REASON COMMUNE
CONVERT DISCUSS OBVERSE
PROPOSE REVERSE COLLOQUE
EXCHANGE OPPOSITE QUESTION
CONVERSION CHANGE EXCHANGE
METRICATION PROSELYTISM
(— INTO VAPOR) FLASH
(— OF IRON) FINING
CONVERT TAW TURN WEND ALTER
AMEND APPLY MAULA RENEW
CHANGE DECODE DETECT DIRECT
MAWALI NOVICE SHAIKH SOUPER
COMMUTE CONCOCT RESOLVE
RESTORE REVERSE ACTIVATE
CONVERSE DISCIPLE NEOPHYTE
PERSUADE PROSELYTE
(— COTTON) LAP
(— INTO CASH) NEGOTIATE
(— INTO LEATHER) TAN TAW

(— INTO LIQUID) BREW
(— INTO MONEY) REALIZE
(— INTO PELLETS) PRILL
(— INTO SOAP) SAPONIFY
(— INTO STEEL) ACIERATE
(— INTO STONE) LAPIDIFY
(— INTO VAPOR) EVAPORATE
(— SOAP) CLOSE
(— TO CARBON) CHAR
(— TO ISLAM) SHEIK
CONVERTER ROTARY SELECTOR
CONVERTIBLE AUTO DROPHEAD
(— CAR) RAGTOP
CONVERTIPLANE STOL
CONVEX BOWED ARCHED CAMBER
CURVED BULGING EMBOWED
GIBBOUS ROUNDED
CONVEXITY CAMBER ARCUATION
CONVEY JAG BEAR BOOK CART
CEDE DEED DUCT HAVE LEAD MEAN
PASS SEND SIGN TAKE TOTE WAIN
WILL BRING CARRY DRIVE FETCH
GRANT GUIDE HURRY STEAL ARRIVE
ASSIGN CONVOY DEDUCE DELATE
DEMISE DEVISE ELOIGN GIGGIT
IMPART IMPORT REMOVE YMMOTE
AUCTION CHANNEL CHARIOT
CHARTER CONDUCT DELIVER
DERRICK DISPONE DISPOSE LIGHTER
RESTORE ALIENATE BEQUEATH
DESCRIBE TRANSFER TRANSMIT
(— AN ESTATE) DEMISE
(— BY ALLUSION) IMPLY
(— FORCIBLY) HUSTLE
(— HORIZONTALLY) ADVECT
(— LEGALLY) DEED GRANT LEASE
DEMISE ELOIGN DISPONE
(— NEARER) BRING
(— SECRETLY) CRIM
CONVEYANCE BUS CAR AUTO
CART DEED DRAG GIFT LOAD SLED
TAXI TRAM GRANT SEDAN STAGE
TAUGA THEFT TRAIN WAGON
DEMISE JINGLE CHARTER CONDUCT
COURIER MACHINE RATTLER TRAILER
TRAJECT TRANSIT TROLLEY
VECTURE VEHICLE WAFTAGE
CARRIAGE CARRYING CONVEYAL
DELATION FERRIAGE STEALING
TRANSFER
CONVEYOR LIFT WORM DRAPER
LADDER SHAKER CARRIER CREEPER
HURRIER SCRAPER CAROUSEL
CONVEYER ELEVATOR
CONVICT LAG CAST FIND STAR
ARGUE EXILE FELON LIFER PROVE
TAINT ATTAIN FORCAT LAGGER
TERMER TRUSTY APPROVE ATTAINT
CAPTIVE CONDEMN CULPRIT
EXPIREE IMPEACH REPROVE
CRIMINAL JAILBIRD PRISONER
REDARGUE SENTENCE

CONVICT FISH MANINI HINALEA
CONVICTION CREDO CREED DOGMA
FAITH HEART SENSE TAINT TENET
BELIEF CREDIT CONCERN OPINION
SENTENCE
CONVINCE SELL EVICT FETCH
ASSURE EVINCE REPROVE RESOLVE
SATISFY CONCLUDE
(— OF ERROR) CONVICT
CONVINCED FIRM SOLD SURE
CERTAIN ABSOLUTE POSITIVE
CONVINCING SOUND VALID
COGENT POTENT EVIDENT TELLING
FORCIBLE LUCULENT POWERFUL
PREGNANT
CONVIVIAL GAY BOON FESTAL
GENIAL JOVIAL SOCIAL FESTIVE
HOLIDAY JOCULAR REVELING
ANACREONTIC
CONVIVIALITY REVEL FESTIVAL
MERRYMAKING
CONVOCATION DIET SYNOD
CALLING COUNCIL MEETING
SUMMONS ASSEMBLY CONGRESS
VOCATION
CONVOKE CALL HOLD GATHER
SUMMON CONVENE ASSEMBLE
CONVOLUTE COIL ROLL WIND
TWIST TANGLE WRITHE CONTORT
INVOLUTE OBVOLUTE
CONVOLUTED GYRATE
CONVOLUTION COIL CURL FOLD
TURN WRAP GYRUS SWIRL TWINE
TWIRL TWIST WHORL CUNEUS
GYROMA VOLUME VOLUTION
CONVOLUTIONAL SNAKY
CONVOLVE TURN WIND TWIST
ENFOLD ENWRAP INFOLD WRITHE
CONVOLVULUS BINDWEED
SCAMMONY
CONVOY LEAD WAFT CARRY GUARD
GUIDE PILOT TRADE WATCH ATTEND
CONVEY ESCORT MANAGE
CONDUCT WAFTAGE SAFEGUARD
CONVULSE ROCK STIR SHAKE
EXCITE AGITATE DISTURB
CONVULSION FIT SHRUG SPASM
THROE ATTACK TUMULT UPROAR
CONVULSE LAUGHTER PAROXYSM
COMMOTION
CONVULSIVE FITFUL EPILEPTIC
CONY DAS HARE PIKA CONEY CUNNY
DAMAN DASSY GANAM HUTIA
HYRAX BURBOT CONEEN DASSIE
GAZABO GAZEBO RABBIT WABBER
ASHKOKO BOOMDAS HYRACID
KLIPDAS HYRACOID KLIPDACH
COO CROO CURR WOOT CHIRR CHIZZ
CROOD MURMUR CROODLE
CRUDDLE
COOEE BIRD KOEL
COOK DO FIX FRY BAKE BOIL CHEF
COCT FAKE MAKE SEAR STEW BROIL

CUIRE CUSIE FRIZZ GRILL POACH
ROAST SCALD SHIRR STEAM SWING
BRAISE CODDLE COOKIE COOPER
DECOCT DIGEST PORTER SAUTEE
SEETHE SIMMER ARTISTE BROILER
FRIZZLE GRIDDLE PASTLER PERCOCT
POTAGER PREPARE PROCESS
SERVANT SMOTHER SWAMPER
BAWARCHI BOBACHEE COCINERO
CUSINERO GRILLADE MAGIRIST
PASTERER MICROWAVE
(— IN BOILING LIQUID) POACH
(— IN MICROWAVE) ZAP NUKE
(— TOO LONG) OVERDO
(— UP) BUILD
(BULL —) FLUNKY FLUNKEY
GREASER
(SHIP'S —) DOCTOR SLUSHY SKILLET
SLUSHER
(PREF.) MAGIRO
COOKED DONE FRIED BOILED
(— BY BOILING) AUBLEU
(— IN CLAY OVEN) TANDOORI
(— IN EARTHENWARE OVEN)
TANDOORI
(— IN EARTHEWARE OVEN)
TANDOORI
(— WITH SUGAR) CANDIED
(PREF.) COCTO
COOKEE FLUNKY HASHER FLUNKEY
COOKER CANNER HAYBOX
DIGESTER
COOKERY CURY CUISINE KITCHEN
MAGIRICS
COOKHOUSE GALLEY
COOKIE CAKE OREO ROCK SNAP
COOKY HERMIT KIPFEL SPRITZ
BISCUIT BROWNIE OATCAKE
PLACENT BISCOTTO CRESCENT
SEEDCAKE
(KIND OF —) FORTUNE
COOKING COCTION
(— UTENSIL) WOK
(INDIAN —) TANDOORI
(STYLE OF —) HUNAN
COOKING KIND OF —) TEXMEX
COOKROOM CUDDY
COOKWARE
(KIND OF —) TEFLON
COOL AIR FAN HEP HIP ICE RAD CALM
COLD DOWN KEEL AKELE ALGID
ALLAY ALOOF CHILL EVENT FRESH
GELID NERVY QUEEL SOBER STAID
WHOLE AIRISH CALLER CHILLY
PLACID QUENCH SEDATE SERENE
TEMPER UNWARM COOLISH DISTANT
RADICAL REFROID UNMOVED
CARELESS CAUTIOUS COMPOSED
MITIGATE MODERATE TRANQUIL
NERVELESS POSSESSED
NONCHALANT UNFLAPPABLE
(— IN WATER) SLACK SLACKEN
(— OF EVENING) SERENE

(— OFF) FAN
(BLOW ONE'S —) LOSEIT
COOLED COLD FRAPPE
COOLER PEN COLA ICER JAIL KEEL
OLLA SINK POKEY ICEBOX LOCKUP
PRISON SINKER KEELFAT ALCOGENE
(WINE —) GLACIER
COOLIE CHANGAR MADRASI
MAZDOOR
COOLING REFRESHING
COOLNESS COOL FROST NERVE
SWALE APLOMB PHLEGM SERENITY
SANGFROID
COOM CULM GAUM SMUT SOOT
COOMB GRIME SLACK
COONTIE SAGO ZAMIA COMPTIE
COOP COT CUB CUP MEW PEN POT
RIP CAGE COOB COTE JAIL CRAMP
HUTCH BASKET CORRAL CONFINE
(— UP) PEN IMMEW INCOUP
(HEN —) CAVEY CAVIE BARTON
COOPER BUNGS COPER COWPER
HEADER HOOPER TUBBER TUBBIE
TUBMAN
COOPERATE HAND TEND AGREE
COACT UNITE CONCUR COMBINE
CONDUCE CONNIVE COADJUTE
CONSPIRE
COOPERATION SOCIETY COURTESY
TEAMWORK
COOPERATIVE COOP ARTEL SOCIAL
SYNERGIC
(RUSSIAN —) ARTEL
(SOVIET—) ARTEL
(SOVIET —) ARTEL
CO-OPT ABSORB
COORDINATE MESH SINE ADAPT
EQUAL ADJUST ARRANGE SYNTONY
ABSCISSA CLASSIFY ENSEMBLE
COORDINATION BOND SKILL
HARMONY LIAISON
COORG KADAGA
COOT CUIT DUCK RAIL QUEET SMYTH
BELTIE GORHEN PELICK SCOTER
HENBILL LOBIPED PULLDOO
LOBEFOOT RAILBIRD SWAMPHEN
COP BAG NAB ROB BANK BLOW BULL
HEAD HEAP JOHN LIFT PILE TRAP
TUBE ADMIT CATCH CREST FILCH
MOUNT QUILL SHOCK SNARE STEAL
STOCK SWIPE BOBBIN COPPIN
PEELER SPIDER STRIKE CAPTURE
(— OUT) EVADE
COPA YAYA COPITA
COPAL BOEA LOBA ANIME CONGO
KAURI KAURY RESIN COWRIE
DAMMAR CHAKAZI
COPE VIE WAR CAPE DUTY FACE LIFT
MEET CAPPA CLOAK COVER DRESS
EQUAL FIGHT MATCH NOTCH RIVAL
VAULT WIELD BARTER CANOPY
CHAPEL COMBAT MANTEL MUZZLE
OPPOSE SEMBLE STRIKE STRIVE

ANABATA CHLAMYS CONTEND
CONTEST GRAPPLE MANDYAS
PLUVIAL COMPLETE EXCHANGE
FACTABLE SEMICOPE STRUGGLE
VESTMENT
COPEHAN WINTUN
COPEPOD CALANID CAYENNE
DIAPTOMID
COPIAPITE MISY MISSY IHLEITE
COPIER COPIST SCRIBE JOHNSONIAN
COPING CAP COPE FLUE SKEW
CORDON CAPSTONE FACTABLE
COPING STONE TABLET TABLING
COPIOUS FREE FULL GOOD LUSH
RANK RICH AMPLE LARGE FLUENT
LAVISH DIFFUSE FLOWING FULSOME
LENGTHY PROFUSE REPLETE
TEEMING UBEROUS ABUNDANT
AFFLUENT FRUITFUL GENEROUS
NUMEROUS PLENTIFUL
COPIOUSNESS COPY PLENTY
COPPER AES COP BULL CENT BOBBY
METAL PENNY VENUS CUPRUM
PEELER VELLON BLISTER CARNELIAN
(GILDED —) VERMEIL
(OF —) AEN
(PREF.) CHALC(O) CHALK(O) CUPR(I)(O)
(SUFF.) CHALCITE
COPPERAS COPEROSE INKSTONE
COQUIMBITE
COPPERHEAD REDEYE MOCCASIN
COPPERSMITH TINKERBIRD
COPPER SULFATE BLUESTONE
COPPER SULFIDE FERRETTO
COVELLINE COVELLITE
COPPERY CUPREOUS
COPPICE COP BROW WOOD COPPY
COPSE FIRTH FRITH GROVE COVERT
FOREST GROWTH SPROUT THICKET
ARBUSTUM
(SUFF.) DRYMIUM
COPREUS (FATHER OF —) PELOPS
(HORSE OF —) ARION
(MOTHER OF —) HIPPODAMIA
COPSE CUT HAG HASP HEWT HOLI
MOTT SHAW TRIM DROKE HURST
CLEVIS SPINNY COPPICE LOWWOOD
SHACKLE SPINNEY ARBUSTUM
COPEWOOD
COPULA BAND LINK UNION
COPULATE RUT BULL LINE RIDE
COVER MOUNT SERVE TREAD
GENDER
COPY APE CALK CAST ECHO EDIT
LOAD MIME MOCK NICK TEXT DITTO
DUMMY GROSS IMAGE MIMIC
MODEL PRINT REVIE STICK STUFF
TRACE XEROX CALQUE DOUBLE
ECTYPE EFFIGY FILLER FLIMSY
FOLLOW MATTER RECORD REFLEX
SAMPLE SHADOW EDITION EMULATE
ENGROSS ESTREAT EXTRACT
IMITATE PATTERN REDRAFT REPLICA

REPRINT RUBBING TRACING
VIDIMUS APOGRAPH AUTOTYPE
EXEMPLAR EXSCRIBE EXSCRIPT
KNOCKOFF LIKENESS MANIFOLD
POROTYPE PORTRAIT RESEMBLE
SPECIMEN MICROCOPY MINIATURE
PHOTOSTAT
(— EDITOR) SLOT
(— ILLEGALLY) PIRATE
(— IN COMPUTER) DUMP
(— OF DOCUMENT) EXTRACT
PROTOCOL
(— OF DRESS) FORD
(DUPLICATE — OF PROGRAM)
BACKUP
(ENLARGED —) MACROCOPY
(EXACT —) TENOR
(FIRST —) DRAFT
(LITERARY —) STUFF
(MAKE A — OF) CLONE
(PRINTING —) KILL BOGUS
(SMALL —) MINATURE
(UNREMUNERATIVE —) LEAN
(WORTHLESS —) BALAAM
(XEROX —) REPRO
COPYING MIMICRY INSINUATION
COPYIST COPIER PENMAN SCRIBE
COPYCAT SCRIVENER
COPYREAD EDIT SUBEDIT
COQUET TOY VAMP COPPY DALLY
FLIRT TRIFLE BLINKER CELIMENE
COQUETRY AGACERIE
COQUETTE TOYER
COQUILLE SHELL
COQUINA DONAX
CORA NAYARIT
(HUSBAND OF —) ALONZO
CORACIIFORM NONPASSERINE
CORACLE SCOW CURAGH CURRACH
CURRANE
CORAL RED PINK AKORI BLOOD
POLYP ALCYON PALULE PORITE
FUNGIAN OCULINA ACROPORE
ASTRAEAN CORALLUM FAVOSITE
POLYPITE STAGHORN TUBIPORE
ZOOPHYTE MADREPORE MILLEPORE
CORAL BEAN SOPHORA FRIJOLILLO
CORAL-BELLS HEUCHERA
CORALBERRY BUCKBUSH
CORALFISH DOLLFISH
CORALROOT ORCHID CRAWLEY
CORAL SNAKE ELAPID ROLLER
ELAPOID SCYTALE
CORAL TREE GABGAB ERYTHRINA
CORBEIL PANNIER
CORBEL KNOT ANCON CORBET
TIMBER BRAGGER RESPOND
CARTOUCH SPRINGER
CORBELING SQUINCH
CORBIESTEP CATSTEP CROWSTEP
CORCIR CORKE ARCHIL CORKER
ORCHIL ARCHILLA

CORD AEA RIB AGAL BAND BIND
BOND FILE LACE LASH LINE ROPE
WELT BRAID CHORD FUNIS GUARD
LEASH LIGNE MATCH NERVE OLONA
TWINE TWIST BINDER BOBBIN
BRIDLE BUNGEE CATGUT CHORDA
CORDON FIADOR GIRDLE LASHER
LISERE RACHIS SENNET STRING
TENDON TOGGLE AMENTUM
BOWYANG BULLION CORDING
FUNICLE LANIARD LANYARD
MACRAME SEAMING SEIZING
SKIRREH TIEBACK URACHUS
BELLPULL CHENILLE DRAWCORD
HAIRLINE SHOELACE WHIPCORD
(— AROUND BOWSTRING) SERVING
(— FOR PIPING) BOBBIN
(— OF CANDLENUT BARK) AEA
(CROCHETING —) CORDE
(ELASTIC —) BUNGEE
(ELECTRIC —) FLEX
(EMBROIDERY —) ARRASENE
(FACE —) RANK
(FRINGED —) LLAUTU
(HAMMOCK —S) CLEW
(HAWK'S —) CREANCE
(KIND OF —) RIP
(MASON'S —) SKIRREH
(ORNAMENTED —) AGLET AIGLET
(PARACHUTE —) SHROUD
(SACRED —) KUSTI
(SPINAL —) EON AEON NUKE
(TWISTED —) TORSADE
(PL.) PANTS
(PREF.) CHORD(O)
CORDAGE DA COIR ERUC FERU
HEMP IMBE JUTE KYAR ROPE
HAMBER SENNIT RIGGING
(LENGTH OF —) CATENARY
CORDATE HEARTED
CORDED TIED JETTED REPPED
RIBBED WELTED TWILLED
CORDELIA
(SISTER OF —) REGAN
COR-DE-NUIT PASTORITA
CORDER RUFFER
CORDIAL REAL WARM CREAM
ARDENT CASSIS CLOVES DEVOUT
ELIXIR GENIAL HEARTY PASTIS
CORDATE DIAMBER LIQUEUR
PERSICO RATAFIA ROSOLIO SINCERE
ZEALOUS ANISETTE FRIENDLY
GRACIOUS PERSICOT VIGOROUS
BENEDICTINE
(NOT —) DISTANT STANDOFF
(PL.) SWEETS
CORDIERITE IOLITE FAHLUNITE
CORDITE
(INVENTOR OF —) ABEL
CORDON BLEU BENGALEE
CORDONNET CRESCENT
CORDUROY DUROY

CORDWOOD BODYWOOD
CORE AME COB HUB NUT BONE COKE
COLK GIST KNOT NAVE PITH BLOCK
FOCUS HEART NOWSE RUMPF
SPOOL BARREL CENTER CENTRE
HEATER KERNEL MATRIX MIDDLE
NODULE POCKET STAPLE CENTRUM
CHEMISE COMPANY CORNCOB
ESSENCE NUCLEUS FILAMENT
HEARTING
(— OF COAL) STOCK
(— OF COLUMN) BELL HEART
(— OF CRICKET BALL) QUILT
(— OF LOG) PITH
(— OF MOLD) NOWEL
(EARTH'S HYPOTHETICAL —) NIFE
(WATER —) GLASSINESS
CORE ARBOR STALK
COREE CORANINE
CORELIGIONIST BROTHER
COREMIUM SYNEMA SYNNEMA
COREOPSIS TICKSEED TICKWEED
LEPTOSYNE
CORF TUB CAGE CAWF COFF CORB
SKIP CREEL BASKET DOSSER
CORFU CORCYRA KERKYRA SCHERIA
CORGI CARDIGAN PEMBROKE
CORIANDER
(— LEAVES) CILANTRO
CORIOLANUS
(AUTHOR OF —) SHAKESPEARE
(CHARACTER IN —) CAIUS TITUS
BRUTUS JUNIUS TULLUS LARTIUS
MARCIUS VALERIA AUFIDIUS
COMINIUS MENENIUS SICINIUS
VIRGILIA VOLUMNIA
CORIUM CUTIS DERMA LAYER
DERMIS
CORK BUNG PLUG FLOAT SHIVE
SUBER BOBBER BOUCHON CRINKLE
PHELLEM SOBERIN STOPPER
STOPPLE
(PREF.) PHELL(O) SUBERI
CORKED BOUCHE
CORKER LULU ONER WHIZ BEAUT
DILLY RAKER WHIZZ CUTTER DOOZER
HUMDINGER
CORKSCREW WORMER
CORKWING CONNER GOLDFINNY
CORKWOOD BALSA GUANO
HAREFOOT
CORM SET BULB SEED CORMEL
CORMUS FREESIA UINTJIE
CORMEL BULBLET
(PL.) SPAWN
CORMORANT SHAG CRANE GORMA
NORIE SCARF SCART DUIKER
DUYKER GORMAW GUANAY SCARFE
SCARTH GLUTTON SHAGLET
CORN ZEA DANA DENT MAIS SALT
SAMP GRAIN MAIZE SPIKE WYROK
AGNAIL CALLUS CLAVUS HELOMA

INDIAN KERNEL MEALIE NOCAKE
NUBBIN POWDER WYROCK FORMITY
FRUMENT FRUMENTY PRESERVE
SAUTERNE
(— SALAD) MACHE
(— SPURREY) YARR
(CROW —) COLICROOT
(CRUSHED —) STAMP
(DECORATED EAR OF —) TIPONI
(EAR OF —) ICKER
(GUINEA —) DURRA DHURRA
(INDIAN —) MAIZE INDIAN NOCAKE
(PARCHED —) ROKEE NOCAKE
PINOLE YOKAGE GRADDAN
ROKEAGE YOKEAGE
(STRING OF —) TRACE
(UNRIPE EAR OF —) TUCKET
CORNAGE HORNGELD
CORN BREAD PONE KANKIE
BANNOCK
CORNCOB COB
CORN COCKLE GITH COCKLE
POPPLE COCKWEED HARDHEAD
MELANTHY
CORNCRACKER STATE KENTUCKY
CORNCRAKE RAIL CORNBIRD
CORN CROWFOOT JOY
GOLDWEED HELLWEED JACKWEED
CORNEL DOGWOOD REDBRUSH
KILLIKINICK KINNIKINICK
CORNEOUS HORNLIKE KERASINE
CORNER IN GET OUT WRO BEND
CANT COIN HALK HERN JAMB NOOK
POOL TRAP TREE WICK ANCON
ANGLE BIGHT CATCH COIGN ELBOW
HERNE INGLE JAMBE NICHE QUOIN
TRUST BOTTLE CANTLE CANTON
COLLAR CORNEL CRANNY RECESS
SQUARE OUTSIDE QUINYIE TURNING
MONOPOLY
(— IN A DRIFT) ARRAGE
(— OF EYE) CANTHUS
(— OF GUNSTOCK) TOE
(— OF MOLDBOARD) SHIN
(— OF SAIL) CLEW CLUE TACK
GOOSEWING
(CHIMNEY —) LUG
(LOWER —) CLEW CLUE
(RE-ENTRANT —) DIEDRE
(ROUNDED —) FILET FILLET
(SECRET —) CREEK
(TIGHT —) BOX
(PREF.) KERAT(O)
(— OF EYE) CANTH(O)
CORNERPIECE BUMPER CANTLE
CORNERSTONE COIN BASIS COIGN
QUOIN HEADSTONE
CORNET CONE HORN ZINK TWIST
ZINKE ZINCKE CORONET CORNETTO
CORNOPEAN
CORNETFISH FLUTEMOUTH
HEMIBRANCH

CORN-FED RUSTIC
CORNFIELD MOW
CORN FLAG LEVERS
CORNFLOWER BLUET BLAVER
BARBEAU BLUECAP BLUECUP
BLAEWORT
CORN GROMWELL SALFERN
CORNHUSK CAP
CORNHUSKER STATE NEBRASKA
CORNHUSKING SHUCKING
CORNICE CAP BAND DRIP EAVE
JOPY ANCON CROWN JOWPY
DETAIL GEISON PELMET ANTEFIX
MOLDING SURBASE ASTRAGAL
SWANNECK
(**UNDER SIDE OF —**) PLANCIER
(**PREF.**) GEISSO
CORNICHON GHERKIN
CORNICLE SIPHON SYPHON
CORNISHMAN CELT KELT
CORN MARIGOLD GOLD GOOLS
BODDLE BOODLE BUDDLE GOWLAN
GOLDING GOLLAND
CORN MEAL MASA SAMP ATOLE
HOECAKE
CORN PARSLEY UMBEL
CORN POPPY BLAVER CANKER
COCKLE COPROSE EARACHE
PONCEAU REDWEED SOLDIER
CORN SALAD MACHE FETTICUS
MILKGRASS
CORN SPURREY YARR
CORN STACK HOVEL
CORNSTALKS KARBI
CORNSTARCH BINDER
CORNU HORN THYROHYAL
CORNUCOPIA HORN CORNU
COFFIN
CORNUS CORNIN REDBRUSH
CORN VIOLET SPECULARIA
CORN WOUNDWORT STACHYS
CORNY BANAL STALE TRITE MICKEY
BUCKEYE
COROADO BORORO
CORODY CONRED
COROEBUS
(**FATHER OF —**) MYGDON
(**SLAYER OF —**) DIOMEDES
COROLLA CUP BELL COROL CUPULE
LIGULE PERIANTH
COROLLARY DOGMA PORISM
RESULT TRUISM ADJUNCT THEOREM
CONSECTARY
COROMANDEL COLCOTHAR
CORONA BUR BURR CIGAR CROWN
GLORY AURORA FILLET ROSARY
WREATH AUREOLE CIRCLET
CORONET GARLAND LARMIER
SCYPHUS
CORONAL CRONET CORONEL
CROWNAL
CORONATION ABHISEKA
CROWNMENT

CORONATION OF POPPAEA
(**CHARACTER IN —**) NERONE OTTONE
SENECA OTTAVIA POPPAEA
DRUSILLA
(**COMPOSER OF —**) MONTEVERDI
CORONER ELISOR CROWNER
EXAMINER SEARCHER
CORONET BAND BURR CROWN
TIARA ANADEM CIRCLE CRONET
DIADEM TIMBRE WREATH CHAPLET
CORONAL CROWNAL CROWNET
GARLAND CROWNLET
CORONIS (**FATHER OF —**) PHLEGYAS
PHORONEUS
(**HUSBAND OF —**) BUTES
(**LOVER OF —**) APOLLO ISCHYS
(**SON OF —**) ASCLEPIUS
CORONOPUS CARARA
CORPORAL NYM FANO NAIG NAIK
PALL FANON FANUM NAYAK PHANO
BODILY EXEMPT GUNNER NAIGUE
NAIQUE SINDON TINDAL
CORPORATE UNITED COMBINED
CORPORATION BODY CITY FIRM
POUCH TRUST SCHOLA BOROUGH
COLLEGE COMMUNE FREEDOM
GUILDRY SOCIETY SPONSOR
CORPOREAL REAL HYLIC SOMAL
ACTUAL BODILY CARNAL FLESHLY
SOMATIC MATERIAL PHYSICAL
TANGIBLE
CORPOSANT HERMO
CORPS CORE ORDU VELITES
SERAGLIO
(**— DE BALLET**) ENSEMBLE
(**MEMBER OF WOMEN'S ARMY —**)
WAC
CORPSE BIER BODY CLAY DUST LICH
MORT GHOST MUMMY RELIC STIFF
TRUCK ZOMBI CORPUS DEADER
ZOMBIE ANATOMY CADAVER
CARCASS CARRION CROAKER
DEADMAN FLOATER
(**— WASHING**) TAHARAH
(**PREF.**) NECR(O)
CORPSELIKE CADAVEROUS
CORPSMAN MEDIC BEARER
CORPULENCE FAT FATNESS
STOUTNESS
CORPULENT FAT BEEFY BULKY
BURLY FATTY GROSS HUSKY OBESE
PLUMP PURSY STOUT TUBBY
FLESHY GREASY PORTLY ROTUND
ADIPOSE BELLIED WEIGHTY
CORPUSCLE CELL GHOST GLOBULE
HEMATID HAEMATID HEMOCYTE
CORRAL PEN STY COOP ATAJO
POUND TAMBO CONFINE ENCLOSE
STOCKAGE SURROUND
(**ELEPHANT —**) KRAAL KEDDAH
CORRECT DUE FIT FIX TIC BEET
BOOK EDIT JAKE JUST LEAL LEAN
MARK MEND NICE OKAY SMUG TRUE

AMEND CHECK CLEAN EMEND
EXACT ORDER RIGHT SOUND SPILL
ADJUST BETTER CHANGE DEADON
INFORM PROPER PUNISH REBUKE
REFORM REMEDY REPAIR REVAMP
REVISE SEEMLY STRICT ADDRESS
CHAPTER CHASTEN CORRIGE
ELEGANT IMPROVE PERFECT PRECISE
RECLAIM RECTIFY REDRESS
REGULAR REPROVE RIGHTON
SINCERE ACCURATE CHASTISE
DEFINITE EMENDATE EQUALIZE
REGULATE RIGOROUS STRAIGHT
TRUTHFUL CASTIGATE
(APPROXIMATELY —) BALLPARK
(GRAMMATICALLY —) CONGRUE
(MATHEMATICALLY —) PURE
(NOT —) INEXACT
(PREF.) ORTH(O)

CORRECTABLE CORRIGIBLE
CORRECTED TRUE
(NOT —) RAW
CORRECTION YARD REFORM
CENSURE FLEXURE IMPRINT
REDRESS SCOURGE FUGACITY
(— IN COMPUTER PROGRAM) PATCH
CORRECTIVE SALT REMEDY
CORRECTLY JUST RIGHT ARIGHT
MEETLY RIGHTLY SOUNDLY
PROPERLY
CORRECTNESS TRUTH DECORUM
FITNESS JUSTICE ACCURACY
JUSTNESS VERACITY
CORREGIDOR, DER (CHARACTER
IN —) TIO LUCAS MERCEDES
FRASQUITA CORREGIDOR
(COMPOSER OF —) WOLF
CORRELATE PARALLEL
HARMONIZE
CORRELATIVE OR NOR THEN
EQUAL STILL EITHER MUTUAL
NEITHER ANALOGUE CONJOINT
REDDITIVE
CORRESPOND FIT GEE JIBE SUIT
AGREE MATCH TALLY WRITE ACCORD
ANSWER CONCUR SQUARE
COMPORT RESPOND COINCIDE
PARALLEL QUADRATE
(— IN SOUND) ASSONATE
(— TO) ENSUE
CORRESPONDENCE MAIL TALLY
ANALOGY CONSENT HARMONY
KEEPING LETTERS TRAFFIC
FUNCTION HOMOGENY HOMOLOGY
SYMMETRY SYMPATHY SIMILARITY
SIMILITUDE PARALLELISM
RESEMBLANCE
(— IN SOUND) RIME RHYME
(INCOMPLETE —) ASSONANCE
(OFFICIAL —) BUMF
CORRESPONDENT NEWSMAN
QUADRATE RELEVANT STRINGER
SUITABLE STRINGMAN

CORRESPONDING LIKE SIMILAR
PARALLEL ACCORDANT CONGRUENT
(PREF.) COUNTER
CORRESPONDINGLY SORTLY
SIMILARLY
CORRIDA BULLFIGHT
CORRIDOR HALL AISLE ORIEL VISTA
ARCADE COULOIR GALLERY
PASSAGE COULISSE HALLCIST
TRESANCE
CORRIE CIRQUE
CORRIGENDUM ERROR ERRATUM
CORROBORATE PROVE SECOND
APPROVE COMFORT CONFIRM
SUPPORT SUSTAIN ROBORATE
CORRODE EAT BITE BURN ETCH
FRET GNAW RUST DECAY ERODE
EXEDE TOUCH WASTE BEGNAW
CANKER IMPAIR CONSUME
GRAPHITE
CORRODING BITE RODENT ESURINE
CORROSION EROSION EMBAYMENT
CORROSIVE ACID ACRID ARDENT
DITING CORSIE EATING CAUSTIC
EROSIVE ESURINE FRETFUL
MORDANT DIERETIC
CORRUGATE GIMP CRIMP CRISP
FURROW RUMPLE CRINKLE
CRUMPLE WRINKLE
CORRUGATED PLAITED WRINKLY
FURROWED WRINKLED
CORRUGATION BAT FOLD GILL
REED RUGA CREASE PUCKER
CRINKLE WRINKLE
CORRUPT BAD ILL LOW ROT WEM
RENT EVIL RANK SICK SOIL VILE
ADDLE BLEND BRIBE FALSE SPOIL
STAIN SULLY TAINT VENOM VENOM
WEMMY AUGEAN CANKER DEBASE
DEFILE FESTER IMPURE INFECT
PALTER POISON PUTRID RAVISH
ROTTEN SEPTIC ABUSIVE ATTAINT
BEDEVIL BEGRIME BESHREW
CARRION CORRUMP CROOKED
DEBAUCH DEFINED DEGRADE
DEPRAVE ENVENOM FALSIFY
IMMORAL PECCANT PERVERT
POLLUTE PUTREFY SUBVERT
TRADING VIOLATE VITIATE
CONFOUND DECADENT DEPRAVED
EMPOISON PERVERSE POLLUTED
PRACTICE PRACTISE SINISTER
VITIATED PERVERTED ADULTERATE
CONTAMINATE PECKSNIFFIAN
CORRUPTED SICK
CORRUPTION DIRT SOIL VICE
DECAY SPOIL TAINT JOBBERY
PRAVITY SQUALOR ADULTERY
BARRATRY INFECTION
MALVERSATION PUTREFACTION
CORSAC ADIVE KARAGAN
CORSAGE WAIST BODICE BOUQUET
CANEZOU

CORSAIR BUG CAPER PIRATE ROBBER CURSARO PICAROON ROCKFISH
CORSAIR, THE (CHARACTER IN —) SEID MEDORA CORRADO GULNARA
(COMPOSER OF —) VERDI
CORSELET LORICA THORAX ALLECRET HALECRET
CORSET BELT BUSK STAY STAYS GIRDLE LORICA SUPPORT
CORSICA (CAPITAL OF —) AJACCIO
(HARBOR OF —) BASTIA
(MOUNTAIN OF —) CINTO ROTONDO
(RIVER OF —) GOLO TARAVO GRAVONE
(TOWERLIKE STRUCTURES OF —) TORRI
(TOWN OF —) CALVI CORTE ALERIA BASTIA AJACCIO SARTENE
(VEGETATION OF —) MAQUIS
CORSICAN PINE LARCH
CORTEGE POMP SUITE TRAIN PARADE RETINUE
CORTEX BARK PEEL RIND MANTLE PALLIUM PERIBLEM PERIDIUM
CORUNDUM RUBY SAND EMERY ADAMAS ALUMINA ABRASIVE AMETHYST CORINDON SAPPHIRE BARKLYITE
(SYNTHETIC —) EMERALD
CORUSCATE BLAZE FLASH GLEAM SHINE GLANCE GLISTEN GLITTER RADIATE SPARKLE BRANDISH
CORVEE POLO
CORVINO (WIFE OF —) CELIA
CORYPHENE DORADO
CORYTHUS
(FATHER OF —) ZEUS PARIS JUPITER
(SON OF —) DARDANUS
(WIFE OF —) ELECTRA
CORYZA COLD
COSAM (FATHER OF —) ELMODAM
COSA RARA, UNA
(CHARACTER IN —) TITA LILLA CORRADO LISARGO GIOVANNI
(COMPOSER OF —) SOLER
COSCET COTTAR COTARIUS COTSETLE
COSETTE (MOTHER OF —) FANTINE
COSH SANDBAG
COSI FAN TUTTE (CHARACTER IN —) ALFONSO DESPINA FERRANDO DORABELLA GUGLIELMO FIORDILIGI
(COMPOSER OF —) MOZART
COSMETIC KOHL WASH CREAM FUCUS HENNA LINER PAINT PETER ROUGE BLANCH CERUSE CRAYON ENAMEL POMADE POWDER BLUSHER BRONZER GLEAMER MASCARA PANCAKE STIBIUM AMANDINE LIPSTICK STIBNITE
(— PREPARATION) TONER

COSMIC VAST MUNDANE ORDERLY CATHOLIC INFINITE
COSMOLABE PANTACOSM
COSMOPOLITAN URBAN ECUMENIC PANDEMIC AMPHIGEAN
COSMOS EARTH GLOBE ORDER REALM WORLD FLOWER HEAVEN HARMONY UNIVERSE
COSSACK TURK TATAR ATAMAN HETMAN TARTAR ZAPOROGUE
COSSET MUD PET LAMB CARESS CODDLE CUDDLE FONDLE PAMPER TIDDLE
COSSETTE CHIP SLICE STRIP SCHNITZEL
COST SIT GAFF LOSS PAIN SOAK BASIS PRICE SPEND STAND VALUE CHARGE DAMAGE OUTLAY SCATHE EXPENSE FREIGHT REPRISE ESTIMATE SPENDING
(LOW —) LOWBALL

COSTA RICA

CAPE: ELENA VELAS BLANCO
CAPITAL: SANJOSE
COIN: COLON CENTIMO
DANCE: PUNTO TORITO
GULF: DULCE NICOYA PAPAGAYO
INDIAN: BORUCA GUAYMI
ISLAND: COCO
LAKE: ARENAL
MEASURE: VARA CAFIZ CAHIZ FANEGA TERCIA CAJUELA CANTARO MANZANA
MOUNTAIN: BLANCO CHIRRIPO
PENINSULA: OSA NICOYA
POINT: QUEPOS CAHUITA GALONOS LLERENA
PORT: LIMON PUNTARENAS
RIVER: POAS IRAZU MATINA SIXAOLA TENORIA TARCOLES
TOWN: CANAS LIMON VESTA BORUCA NICOYA BAGACES CARTAGO GOLFITO HEREDIA LIBERIA NEGRITA ALAJUELA COLORADO GUAPILES
VOLCANO: POAS IRAZU
WEIGHT: BAG CAJA LIBRA

COSTERMONGER COSTER HAWKER NIPPER PEARLY PEDDLER BARROWMAN
COSTIVE BOUND EMPLASTIC
COSTLINESS DEARTH DEARNESS
COSTLY DEAR FINE HIGH RICH SALT PRICY DAINTY LAVISH PRICEY SILVER COSTFUL COSTLEW GORGEOUS PLATINUM PRECIOUS PRODIGAL SPLENDID PRICELESS
COSTMARY TANSY ALECOST MAUDLIN ROSEMARY
COSTREL KEG HEAD FLASK BOTTLE COYSTREL

COSTUME RIG DRAG GARB ROBE SARI SUIT BURKA DRESS GETUP HADIT SHAPE TRUSS ATTIRE DOMINO FORMAL SETOUT TOILET APPAREL BLOOMER CLOTHES POLLERA RAIMENT SCARLET UNIFORM CHARSHAF CLOTHING ENSEMBLE TOILETTE VENETIAN
(ACADEMIC —) GUISE
(JUDO —) JUDOGI
(KARATE —) GI GIE

COSTUSROOT PACHAK PUTCHOCK

COSY FEEL FEIL SNUG INTIME

COT BED HUT MAT PEN BOAT COOP COTE FOLD ABODE BOTHY CABIN COUCH COVER HOUSE STALL COTEEN CRADLE GURNEY PALLET SHEATH TANGLE CHARPAI CHARPOY COTTAGE SHELTER BEDSTEAD COTHOUSE DWELLING STRETCHER

COTERIE SET RING CABAL JUNTO MONDE CIRCLE CLIQUE GALAXY SETOUT CENACLE CIRCUIT COLLEGE PLATOON SOCIETY

COTHURNUS BOOT BUSKIN COTHURN

COTILLION GERMAN

COTINGA CHATTERER

COTO OREJON

COTTA KATHA STOLE MANTLE BLANKET SURPLICE VESTMENT

COTTAGE BOX COT HUT BACH BARI COSH CRIB SHED WALK BOTHY BOWER CABIN HOUSE HOVEL LODGE SHACK BOHAWN BOTHIE CABANA CHALET SHELTER BUNGALOW COTHOUSE SHEELING SHIELING THALTHAN
(RUSSIAN —) DACCA

COTTAGE CHEESE SKYR SMEARCASE SMIERCASE

COTTAGER MAILER

COTTER KEY MAT PIN VEX CLOT BOWPIN COTMAN FASTEN MAILER POTTER PUCKER SHRINK TOGGLE WITHER CONGEAL COTTIER PEASANT SHRIVEL VILLEIN COTARIUS COTTAGER COTTEREL ENTANGLE FORELOCK LINCHPIN

COTTON SAK BEAT DRAB FLOG MALO PIMA AGREE BAYAL BOLLY DERRY MATTA SAKEL SURAT BROACH CODDLE COMBER DHURRY FABRIC MAARAD MALLOW NANKIN PEELER STAPLE ALGODON BENDERS BOMBACE CANTOON DHURRIE GARMENT GINNING SILESIA SUCCEED
(— SQUARE) TZUT TZUTE
(BOLL OF —) SNAP
(NAPPED) LAMBGKIN
(PAINTED —) INDIENNE

(PIECE OF —) SPONGE
(PRINTED —) CHINTZ SARONG
(RAW —) LINT BAYAL
(SILK —) FLOSS
(STOUT —) THICKSET
(STRIPED —) BENGAL
(TREE —) MACO
(TWILLED —) JEAN SALLO SALLOO
(WAD OF —) TAMPON
(WASTE —) GRABBOTS
(PREF.) BYSSI BYSSO

COTTON GRASS CANNA CANNACH DRAWLING

COTTON PLANT LAMB
(— FLOWER) SQUARE

COTTON TREEE SIMAL

COTTONWOOD ALAMO POPLAR

COTTON-WOOL BOMBAST WADDING

COTYLEDON BUTTON PICHURIM SARCOLOBE

COUCAL PHEASANT

COUCH BED COT KIP LAY LIE HIDE LAIR LURK SOFA SUNK DIVAN INLAY LODGE PRESS SKULK SLINK SNEAK SNOOP SQUAB SQUAT UTTER BURROW CLOTHE DAYBED LITTER PALLET PLINTH SETTEE CONCEAL EXPRESS HAMMOCK OTTOMAN OVERLAY RECLINE TRANSOM RECAMIER
(NUPTIAL —) THORE
(WOODEN —) RUSTBANK
(PREF.) CLIN(O) STROMATI STROMATO
(SUFF.) STROMA

COUCH GRASS CUTCH KUTCH QUACK QUICK TWICH QUITCH SCOTCH SCUTCH STROIL QUICKEN WITHVINE

COUGAR CAT PUMA PAINTER PANTHER CARCAJOU

COUGH YEX YOX BAFF BARK HACK HOST KINK CHINK CROUP HOAST HOOSE HOOZE TISICK TUSSIS

COUGH DROP PASTIL TROCHE LOZENGE PASTILLE

COUGH SYRUP LINCTUS

COULEE DRAW GORGE GULCH COOLEY RAVINE

COULOMB WEBER

COUMA SORVA HYAHYA

COUNCIL BODY BULE DAEL DIET DUMA FONO RAAD REDE YUAN BOARD BOULE BUNGA CABAL CAPUT DIVAN DIWAN DOUMA JIRGA JUNTA JUNTO SABHA SOBOR STATE SYNOD THING JIRGAH LUKIKO MAJLIS POWWOW QUORUM SENATE SOVIET TARYBA CABILDO CABINET CHAMBER CONSULT GERUSIA HUSTING MEETING PENSION

WHITLEY ASSEMBLY CONCLAVE
CONGRESS FOLKMOOT FOLKMOTE
HEEMRAAD HEEMRAAT MINISTRY
PLACITUM RIGSRAAD CAMARILLA
PARLIAMENT AMPHICTYONS
(— CHAMBER) DIVAN
(MORMON —) PRESIDENCY

COUNCILLOR RAT VIZIR ENDUNA
INDUNA VIZIER FAIPULE SENATOR
WISEMAN DECURION
(PL.) ANZIANI

COUNSEL RAD LORE REDE RULE
RUNE SILK WARD WARN AREED
CHIDE DEVIL GUIDE ADVICE ADVISE
CONFER LEADER ABOGADO
CAUTION COUNCIL LECTURE
ADMONISH ADVOCATE PRUDENCE
(JUNIOR LEGAL —) DEVIL
(KING'S —) SILK
(SACRED —) TORAH

COUNSELOR RAT SAGE WITE
CONSUL LAWYER MENTOR NESTOR
ADVISER ADVISOR COUNSEL
ECHEVIN GONZALO PROCTOR
STARETS ADVOCATE ATTORNEY
REDESMAN UCALEGON

COUNT ADD GAN SUM TOT BANK
CAST EARL FOOT GANO GRAF NAME
RELY RIME SIZE TALE TELL TOTE
COMES COMPT COMTE GRAVE
JUDGE RHYME SCORE TALLY WEIGH
CENSUS CONSUL COUNTY DEPEND
ESTEEM FIGURE IMPUTE MATTER
NUMBER RECKON TOTTLE ACCOUNT
ARTICLE ASCRIBE COMPUTE
GANELON ADNUMBER NUMERATE
SANCTION CALCULATE PALSGRAVE
(— IN BILLIARDS) DOUBLE
(— OF A FIBER) GRIST
(— OF SHEEP OR CATTLE) BREAK
(— ON) LITE RELY
(— UNIT) WARP

COUNTABLE DISCRETE

COUNTE COMTE

COUNTENANCE AID MUG OWN
RUD ABET BROW FACE GIZZ LEER
MIEN PUSS SHOW VULT CHEER
FAVOR FRONT GRACE ASPECT
ENDURE UPHOLD VISAGE APPROVE
BEARING CONDUCT ENDORSE
FEATURE PROFFER SUPPORT
BEFRIEND DEMEANOR FOREHEAD
SANCTION SEMBLANCE
(PREF.) PROSOP(O)

COUNTER BAR DIB LOT BANK BUCK
CENT CHIP DESK DUMP EDDY FISH
JACK KIST PAWN STOP CAROM
CHECK FORCE HATCH JETON MERIL
PIECE SHELF STALL STAND TABLE
TOTER SHELF COMBAT GEIGER
ISLAND JETTON MARKER OPPOSE
SQUAIL ADVERSE BUTTOCK
CONTEND CURRENT FANTAIL

SHAMBLE CONTRARY MAHOGANY
OPPOSITE TELLTALE
(— TO) AGAINST
(LEADEN —) DUMP
(LUNCH —) PLACE
(PREF.) ANTI GAIN

COUNTERACT CHECK CANCEL
OPPOSE RESIST THWART BALANCE
CORRECT DESTROY NULLIFY
ANTIDOTE NEGATIVE

COUNTERACTION DEADLOCK

COUNTERACTIVE REMEDY
ADVERSE

COUNTERBALANCE COVER WEIGH
CANCEL SETOFF BALANCE

COUNTERCLOCKWISE DIRECT
DIRECTLY

COUNTERCURRENT BACKSET

COUNTEREARTH ANTICHTHON

COUNTERFEIT ACT BASE COIN
COPY DAUB DUFF FAKE IDOL MOCK
SHAM BELIE BOGUS DUMMY FALSE
FEIGN FLASH FORGE FUDGE GAMMY
MIMIC PHONY QUEER SNIDE AFFECT
ASSUME CHEMIC ERSATZ FORGED
PSEUDO TINSEL BASTARD CHEMICK
DUFFING FALSIFY FASHION FEIGNED
FORGERY IMITANT IMITATE SIMULAR
BORROWED DEFORMED PHANTASM
POSTICHE POSTIQUE RESEMBLE
SIMILIZE SIMULATE SPURIOUS
SUPPOSED BRUMMAGEM
(PREF.) PSEUD(O)

COUNTERFEITER COINER
JACKMAN JARKMAN SCRATCHER

COUNTERFEITERS (AUTHOR OF —)
GIDE
(CHARACTER IN —) LAURA VEDEL
ARMAND GEORGE ROBERT BERNARD
EDOUARD LILLIAN OLIVIER VINCENT
DOUVIERS GRIFFITH MOLINIER
PASSAVANT GHERIDANISOL
PROFITENDIEU

COUNTERFEITING COINING
FICTION POSTICHE POSTIQUE

COUNTERFOIL FOIL STUB CHECK

COUNTERFORT SCONCE BUTTRESS

COUNTERION GEGENION

COUNTERIRRITANT MOXA GINGER
IODINE PEPPER MUSTARD
CANTHARIS

COUNTERMAND STOP ANNUL
CANCEL FORBID RECALL REVOKE
ABOLISH RESCIND REVERSE
UNORDER ABROGATE PROHIBIT

COUNTERMOVE DEMARCHE

COUNTERMOVEMENT BACKFIRE

COUNTERPANE PANE QUILT
LIGGER BEDSPREAD

COUNTERPART COPY LIKE MATE
SPIT TWIN FETCH IMAGE MATCH
MORAL SHELL TALLY COUSIN
DOUBLE SHADOW BALANCE

COUNTER OBVERSE PENDANT
SIMILAR ANTIPART PARALLEL
RESCRIPT SIMILITUDE
(SPEECH —) A
COUNTERPOINT FOIL DESCANT
CONTRAST FABURDEN
COUNTERPOISE POISE OFFSET
BALANCE EQUALIZE MAKEWEIGHT
COUNTERPOISON ORVIETAN
COUNTERSIGN BACK MARK SEAL
SIGN SIGNAL CONFIRM ENDORSE
PASSWORD SANCTION
COUNTERSINK DISH REAM BEVEL
CHAMFER
COUNTERSTATEMENT ANSWER
COUNTERSUN ANTHELION
COUNTER-TENOR ALTO
COUNTERTENOR ALTO
COUNTERWEIGHT TARE
MAKEWEIGHT
COUNTERWORD ANIMAL
COUNTER
COUNTESS OLIVIA COMTESSE
CONTESSA
COUNTING ACCOUNT
COUNTLESS INFINITE NUMBERLESS
(PREF.) MYRI(A)(O)
COUNT OF MONTE CRISTO
(AUTHOR OF —) DUMAS
(CHARACTER IN —) FARIA ALBERT
DANTES EDMOND HAIDEE
MONDEGO MORRELL DANGLARS
MERCEDES FERDINAND VALENTINE
VILLEFORT CADEROUSSE
MAXIMILIAN
COUNTRIFIED JAY RURAL BUCOLIC
LOBBISH AGRESTIC CORNPONE
HOBNAILED
COUNTRY SOD DESH EARD HICK
HOME KITH LAND PAIS SOIL ADDLE
CLIME EARTH FAIRY FRITH MARCH
PLAGE REALM STATE TRACT WEALD
GROUND KINTRA KINTRY NATION
PEOPLE REGION STICKS UPLAND
IMAMATE KWINTRA MONKERY
MUFASAL BACKVELD DISTRICT
DOMINION ELDORADO LANDWARD
MAGAZINE MOFUSSIL REGALITY
PRINCIPALITY
(— DANCE) CLOG
(— OF ETHIOPIA) SEBA
(— OF ORIGIN) HOMELAND
(— OF PERFECTION) EUTOPIA
(— ON SEA) SEABOARD
(— STYLE) PAYSANNE
(ANCIENT —) ARAM
(BIBLICAL —) SHEBA
(CABIN —) LOBBY
(FRONTIER —) BORDER
(HOME —) BLIGHTY
(IMAGINARY —) FREWHON LILLIPUT
RURITANIA
(LIMESTONE —) KARST

(MARITIME —) MAREMMA
(MYTHICAL —) UTOPIA LEONNOYS
SVITHIOD SWITHIOD TEUTONIA
(OPEN —) BLED VELD FIELD VELDT
WEALD CAMPAIGN
(PETTY —) TOPARCHY
(ROUGH —) STICKS BOONIES
BOONDOCK BUNDOCKS
BOONDOCKS
(RURAL —) OUTBACK
(PREF.) RURI
(SUFF.) STAN
COUNTRYMAN HOB BOOR HIND
KERN TIKE CHURL CLOWN HODGE
KERNE SWAIN YOKEL GAFFER
GIBARO JIBARO GRANGER HAYSEED
LANDMAN PAESANO PAISANO
PEASANT PLOWMAN LANDSMAN
(PL.) KITH
COUNTRY-ROCK METAL
COUNTRY-SEAT CHATEAU
COUNTRYSIDE BLED BOCAGE
MOFUSSIL
COUNTRY WIFE
(AUTHOR OF —) WYCHERLEY
(CHARACTER IN —) HORNER ALITHEA
HARCOURT SPARKISH PINCHWIFE
COUNTY AMT LAN SEAT FYLKE
SHIRE DOMAIN PARISH BOROUGH
COMITAT NORFOLK DISTRICT
COUP BUY BLOW DEAL PLAN PLAY
COUPE FAULT SCOOP UPSET ATTACK
BARTER PUTSCH REFAIT STRIKE
STROKE CAPSIZE TRAFFIC
OVERTURN
COUP DE POING BOUCHER
HANDSTONE
COUPE CUT CABRIOLET LANDAULET
COUPED HUMETTY HUMETTEE
COUPLE DUO TIE TWO BOND CASE
DYAD JOIN LINK MATE PAIR SPAN
TEAM TWIN YOKE BRACE LEASH
MARRY TWAIN UNITE GEMINI SPLINE
SWINGE BRACKET CONNECT
COUPLER COUPLET DOUBLET
SHACKLE TWOSOME VOLTAIC
ACCOUPLE ASSEMBLE COPULATE
ACCOMPANY
(— OF HAWKS) CAST
(ROMANTIC —) ITEM
COUPLED GEMEL YOKED JOINED
WEDDED GEMELED COPULATE
GEMINATE
COUPLER LINK RING BOBBER
COPULA JANNEY LINKER SUTURE
UNITER DRAGBAR DRAWBAR
REDUCER SHACKLE SNAPPER
TIRASSE DRAGBOLT DRAWBOLT
DRAWGEAR SHACKLER
COUPLET BAIT COPLA ELEGIAC
COUPLING HUB HICKY UNION
CLUTCH HICKEY NIPPLE SHACKLE
SHACKLER

COUPON TWOFER VOUCHER
COURAGE BIEL FIRE GRIT GUTS
MIND MOOD PROW SAND SOUL
BIELD CREST HEART HONOR MOXIE
NERVE PLUCK SPUNK VALOR DARING
DAUBER METTLE PECKER SPIRIT
VIRTUE VIRTUS BRAVERY COJONES
CORAGIO HEROISM MANHEAD
MANHOOD MANSHIP PROWESS
STOMACH VENTURE AUDACITY
BOLDNESS CORRAGIO FIRMNESS
TENACITY
(— OF CONVICTION) STAMINA
(MORAL —) STRENGTH
(PREF.) THYM(O)
(SUFF.) THYMIA
COURAGEOUS BOLD GAME GOOD
TALL BRAVE GUTSY HARDY LUSTY
MANLY STOUT WIGHT DARING
GRITTY HEROIC MANFUL PLUCKY
SPUNKY CORIAUS GALLANT
SPARTAN STAUNCH VALIANT
FEARLESS GENEROUS INTREPID
VALOROUS
COURAGEOUSLY BIG BRAVELY
COURANT ROMP CAPER DANCE
LETTER CORANTO CURRENT
GAZETTE RUNNING
COURBARIL JATOBA LOCUST
GUAPINOL CUAPINOLE
COURGETTE ZUCCHINI
COURIER NEWS POST GUIDE SCOUT
KAVASS NEWING POSTER ESTAFET
ORDERLY PATAMAR POSTBOY
POSTMAN SOILAGE CICERONE
CURSITOR DRAGOMAN HORSEMAN
ORDINARY PATTAMAR
COURLAN LIMPKIN
COURONNE CROWN
COURSE FLY LAP RUN WAY BEAT
BENT FLOW GAGE GAME GANG
GATE HEAT HUNT LANE LINE LODE
MESS MODE PACE PATH RACE RACK
RAIK RAND RILL RING RINK ROAD
ROTA ROTE WENT CLASS COURS
CRUST CURRY CURVE CYCLE DRAFT
DRIFT DRIVE EMBER GAUGE GREAT
LAPSE LAYER LEDGE MARCH MOYEN
ORBIT PLATE POINT ROUTE SENSE
SITHE SPACE STEPS SWELT SWING
TENOR TRACK TRACT TRADE TRAIL
TREND WEENT ARTERY CAREER
COPING CURSUS DROMOS FURROW
GALLOP GIRDER GUTTER HONORS
MANNER METHOD MOTION RESACA
SCHOOL SERIES SPHERE STREAM
STREET SYSTEM TRIPOS ZODIAC
AZIMUTH BEELINE CHANNEL CIRCUIT
CONDUCT DIAULOS DRAUGHT
HIGHWAY LECTURE PASSADE
PASSAGE PATHWAY PROCESS
ROUTINE RUNNING SEMINAR
SERVICE STRETCH SUBJECT

SUCCESS TIDEWAY TRAJECT
TRUNDLE CURRENCY CURRICLE
DIADROME DISTANCE ELECTIVE
PROGRESS RECOURSE SEQUENCE
STEERAGE TENDENCY
MOTORDROME
(— OF ACTION) LARK TACK TROD
VEIN DANCE CUSTOM ROUTINE
DEMARCHE
(— OF ACTIVITY) SIDELINE
(— OF A ROPE) LEAD
(— OF BOAT) LEG
(— OF BRICK) BED ROWLOCK
SCINTLE CREASING
(— OF FEEDING) DIET
(— OF KNITTING) BOUT
(— OF LIFE) GOINGS PILGRIMAGE
(— OF LIGHTNING) STREAK
(— OF LUCK) FORTUNE
(— OF MASONRY) BAHUT STILT
COPING HEADING SKEWBACK
(— OF NATURE) TAO
(— OF PROCEDURE) RULE
(— OF PROCEEDING) FORE
(— OF PURSUIT) SCENT
(— OF ROADBED) SUBCRUST
(— OF STONES) BED PLINTH
(— OF STUDY) DEBATE COLLEGE
LECTURE SEMINAR ELECTIVE
(— OF SUN) JOURNEY
(— OF TREATMENT) CURE
(— OF WALL) CORNICE
(— WITH GREYHOUNDS) GREW
(BELL-RINGING —) HUNT
(CIRCULAR —) SWEEP CHUKKAR
CHUKKER COMPASS
(COLLEGE —) PRECEPTORIAL
(CURVING —) SWING
(CUSTOMARY —) GUISE
(DOWNWARD —) DIP DECLINE
TOBOGGAN
(DUE —) TRAIN
(EASY —) PIPE
(EASY COLLEGE —) GUT
(EXACT —) BEAM
(FIRST —) ANTEPAST
(FIXED —) RUT
(FREE —) FORTH
(HONEST —) UPANDUP
(IRREGULAR —) ERROR
(LAST —) VOID
(MIDDLE —) MIDS TEMPER
(NATURAL —) RITA
(NORMAL —) WAY
(OBLIQUE —) SKEW
(OFF —) ASTRAY
(OVERHANGING —) JET
(PREDETERMINED —) DESTINY
(RACING —) RINK
(REGULAR —) ORBIT ROUTINE
(ROUNDABOUT —) DETOUR
WINDLASS
(SETTLED —) BIAS GROOVE

(SKIING —) SCHUSS
(ZIGZAG —) TACK
(PREF.) DROM(O)
COURSER HORSE RACER STEED
CUSSER CHARGER
COURSING CURSIVE
COURT BAR BID HOF SEE SUE WOO
AREA BAIL BODY CLAW FUSS GATE
GIRL LEET QUAD ROTA SEAT SEEK
SUIT TOWN WALE WARD WYND
YARD ARENA BENCH BUREO CURIA
CURRY DAIRI DIVAN FAVOR FORUM
FUERO GARTH JUDGE PATIO SHIRE
SPACE SPARK SPOON SWEET TEMPT
THING THINK TOURN TRAIN YAMEN
ADALAT ALLURE ATRIUM BAILEY
COUNTY DARGAH DURBAR DURGAH
GEMOTE HOMAGE INVITE PALACE
PARVIS PURSUE SPLUNT SUITOR
TOLSEY ADAWLUT ADDRESS
ASSIZES ATTRACT BARMOTE
DUOVIRI EPHETAE FOREIGN HELIAEA
HUSTING JUSTICE PARVISE RETINUE
SOLICIT TEMENOS TOURNEL
AUDIENCE BURHMOOT CHANCERY
FOUJDARY LAWCOURT MARKMOOT
MARKMOTE QUARANTY SERENADE
SESSIONS SWANMOTE TRIBUNAL
WOODMOTE PERIBOLOS
PARLIAMENT
(— FAVOR) FAWN
(— OF A HUNDRED) MALL MALLUM
MALLUS
(— OF CIRCUIT JUDGES) EYRE
(— OF FORTRESS) PEEL
(— OF MIKADO) DAIRI
(— ORDER) VACATUR
(— THE GREAT) LEVEE
(ECCLESIASTICAL —) ROTA CURIA
SYNOD COLLOQUY AUDIENCIA
(EXERCISE —) EPHEBEUM
(FORTIFIED —) BAWN
(GERMAN —) FEHM VEHM
(INNER —) PATIO
(MUSLIM —) DIVAN DIWAN
(REFORMED —) CLASIS
(SMALL —) WIND WYND CORTILE
(SUPREME —) SUDDER
(TAKE TO —) SUE
(TURKISH —) GATE
COURTEOUS FAIR HEND BUXOM
CIVIL GENTY SUAVE BONAIR GENTLE
POLITE SMOOTH URBANE AFFABLE
CORDIAL GALLANT GENTEEL
GENTILE REFINED DEBONAIR
FAMILIAR GRACIOUS OBLIGING
COURTEOUSLY FAIR FAIRLY
GENTLY KINDLY AFFABLY
COURTEOUSNESS COMITY
COURTESAN MADAM QUAIL THAIS
WHORE COURTY GEISHA LALAGE
MADAME PLOVER AMOROSA
ASPASIA CANIDIA DELILAH LORETTE

PUCELLE DEVADASI
(PL.) DEMIMONDE
COURTESY MENSK COMITY EXTENT
GENTRY MANSHIP TASHRIF
BREEDING CALIDORE CORTEISE
ELEGANCE GENTRICE GRATUITY
URBANITY
(PL.) HONORS
COURTHOUSE CUTCHERY
KACHAHRI
COURTIER CURAN OSRIC WOOER
OSRICK COURTER IACHIMO
COURTMAN DAMOCLES POLONIUS
COURTING SUING SPLUNT
COURTLY HEND AULIC CIVIL HENDE
POLITE AULICAL ELEGANT REFINED
STATELY POLISHED DIGNIFIED
COURT-NOUE RONCET
COURTSHIP SUIT AMOUR DRURY
SPARKING
COURTYARD AREA WYND CLOSE
CURIA PATIO ATRIUM TRANCE
BALLIUM CORTILE TETRAGON
CURTILAGE
COUSIN COZ KIN AKIN HERO ALLIED
NEPHEW
COUSIN BETTE
(AUTHOR OF —) BALZAC
(CHARACTER IN —) HULOT AGATHE
CREVEL MONTES ADELINE LISBETH
HORTENSE MARNEFFE VICTORIN
CELESTINE STEINBOCK
COUSINRY KITH
COVE CO BAY DEN CAVE CHAP FILE
GILL HOLE NOOK PASS SUMP BASIN
BAYOU BIGHT CREEK INLET ARMLET
COVING FELLOW HOLLOW RECESS
VALLEY MOLDING CALANQUE
GUNKHOLE
COVENANT BIND BOND BRIS MISE
PACT TRUE AGREE BERIT BRITH
TOUCH ACCORD BERITH CARTEL
COMART CONAND ENGAGE INDENT
LEAGUE PATISE PLEDGE TREATY
BARGAIN COMPACT CONCORD
PROMISE ALLIANCE CONTRACT
DOCUMENT HANDFAST TREATISE
COVENANTER HILLMAN TRUEBLUE
COVER DO CAP COT HAP LAP LAY LID
NAP TOP TUP WRY BIND CEIL CLAD
COAT COOM CURE DAUB DECK FACE
FADE FALL FURL GARB GATE HEAD
HEAL HEEL HIDE HILL HOOD LATH
LEAD LEAP LINE MASK PAVE ROOF
SILE SPAN TELD TICK TIDE TILT VEIL
WRAP APRON BATHE BOARD CLOAK
CLOUT COPSE CROWN DRAPE DRESS
FENCE FLESH FLOOD GUISE HATCH
KIVER MOUNT RECTO SCARF SERVE
SHADE STREW STUDY THEAK THEEK
TOWEL TREAD VERSO WELME
WHALM AWNING BATTER BINDER
BLAZON CANOPY CHALON CLOTHE

DOUBLE EARLAP ENAMEL ENCASE
ENFOLD ENROBE ENTIRE ENVEIL
FOLDER HACKLE IMMASK INVEST
JACKET KIRTLE MANTLE OVERGO
POTLID RUNNER SCONCE SCREEN
SHADOW SHEATH SHIELD SLEEVE
SPREAD SPRING SWATHE TOILET
TOPPER WHAUVE APPAREL ASPHALT
BANDAGE BESTREW BLANKET
CAPSULE CONCEAL CONTECT
COUVERT ELYTRON EMBRACE
ENCRUST FASCINE HEADCAP
HOUSING INCRUST KNEECAP
MANHEAD OBSCURE OMNIBUS
OVERLAY PRETEXT SHEATHE
SHELTER SHUTTER TAMPION
THIMBLE BEDCOVER COMPRISE
COVERCLE DEBRUISE ENCLOTHE
ENSCONCE HOODWINK IMMANTLE
OVERHAIL OVERSILE OVERWEND
PALLIATE PRETENCE PRETENSE
SLIPOVER SURPOOSE
(— A FIRE) BANK DAMP
(— AROUND FLOWER) CYMBA
(— BRICKS) SCOVE
(— BY EXCUSES) ALIBI PALLIATE
(— DISPERSEDLY) STREW
(— FOR ALEMBIC) HEAD
(— FOR CHAIR BACK) TIDY
(— FOR CHALICE) PALL
(— FOR DIAPER) SOAKER
(— FOR ENGINE) COWLING
(— FOR FOOD) BELL
(— FOR GUN) TAMPION
(— FOR MILITARY CAP) HAVELOCK
(— FOR PISTON) FOLLOWER
(— FOR POWDER PAN) HAMMER
(— FOR REAL PURPOSE) STALE
(— FOR WIRES) BOOTLEG
(— GROUND) HEAT
(— HEARTH) FETTLE
(— OF BALL) CARCASS
(— OF BOILER) VOMIT
(— OF COFFIN) COOM
(— OF HAWSEHOLE) BUCKLER
(— OF MATTRESS) TICK TICKING
(— OF MINE CAGE) BONNET
(— OF RIFLE MAGAZINE) GATE
(— OF SPORANGIUM) EPIGONE
(— OF VEGETATION) GROWTH
(— OPPRESSIVELY) SMOTHER
(— OVER) RAKE WELME WHELM
QUELME SHEUGH BECLOUD
OVERDECK WITHHELE OVERWHELM
(— PLANTS) BAG
(— PROTECTIVELY) SHROUD
SHEATHE
(— ROAD) BLIND
(— SOIL WITH CLAY) GAULT
(— UP) HAP BELY FOLD BELIE SALVE
SLEEK HUDDLE
(— WITH ASHES) SOIL

(— WITH BACON) BARD
(— WITH BOMBS) SATURATE
(— WITH CLAY) CLOAM
(— WITH COWL) MOB
(— WITH CRUMBS) BREAD
(— WITH DOTS) CRIBBLE
(— WITH DROPS) DAG
(— WITH EARTH) BURY HEAL INTER
(— WITH FILM) SKIM
(— WITH FLESH) INCARN
(— WITH FOAM) EMBOSS
(— WITH GOLD) GILD
(— WITH MEAL) MELVIE
(— WITH MUD) BEMUD BELUTE
(— WITH OAKUM) FOTHER
(— WITH PITCH) PAY
(— WITH PLASTER) PARGET
(— WITH SHEATH) GLOVE
(— WITH SOLDER) SPLASH
(— WITH STONE) ASHLAR
(— WITH STRAW) THATCH
(— WITH TIN) BLANCH
(— WITH TOPSOIL) KELLY
(— WITH WATER) DOUSE DOWSE
FLOOD WHELM OVERFLOW
(— WITH WAX) CERE
(— WITH WEAVING) GRAFT
(— WITH WINGS) BROOD
(BED —S) HEALING
(BEEHIVE —) QUILT
(BOOK —) CASE SIDE
(CANVAS —) TARP TARPAULIN
(GLASS —) STRIKE
(KIND OF —) MAIL
(PACK —) MANTA
(PILLOW —) CASE SHAM
(POSTAL —) ENTIRE
(POT —) BRED
(RAIN —) TARP
(SADDLE —) PILCH HOUSING
(SEED —) TESTA
(SLIDING —) BRIDGE
(TABLE —) BAIZE DUCHESSE
(WING — OF BEETLE) SHARD
(PREF.) OPERCULI
COVERAGE PROTECTION
COVERALL GOWN JUMPER
COVERED CLAD FULL SHOD TECT
BLIND MOSSY CLOSED COVERT
HIDDEN ENCASED OBTECTED
SCREENED
(— WITH CRYSTALS) DRUSY
(— WITH FEATHERS) HIRSUTE
(— WITH FOREST) HYLEAN
(— WITH HAIRS) COMATE VILLOUS
(— WITH PROTUBERANCES) HUMPY
(— WITH SCALES) SCUTATE
(— WITH SEAWEED) TANGLY
(— WITH WHITE DUST) PRUINOSE
(THINLY —) BARISH
(PREF.) CALYPT(O) CRYPT(O)
KRYPT(O)

COVERED WAGON WHITETOP
BUCKWAGON
COVERER DECKER
COVERING (ALSO SEE COVER) BOX
COT FUR HAP KEX LAG ARIL BARB
BARK BOOT CASE CAUL COAT CUFF
DECK FILM HAME HEAD HOOD HULL
HUSK KELL MASK OVER PALL PUFF
ROBE ROOF SLIP SPAT TARP TILE TILT
TRAP VEIL APRON ARMOR BRAID
BURSE CRUST DRESS GLOBE GLOVE
HATCH QUILT SCALE SHELL SKIRT
STALL SWARD TESTA TUNIC TWEEL
WREIL ARMING ATTIRE AWNING
BANCAL BANKER CANOPY CANVAS
COVERT DRAPET EMBRYO ENAMEL
FACING FENDER GAITER GANOIN
HACKLE HATCAP HELMET JACKET
MUZZLE PELAGE SADDLE SCREEN
SHEATH SHROUD SINDON TEGMEN
VERNIX BLANKET BUFFONT CAMISIA
CAPPING CAPSULE CEILING COATING
COWLING EARLAP ENVELOP
EXCIPLE GRATING HAPPING HEALING
HEELCAP HOUSING MUFFLER
OVERLAY PURPORT SARPLER
SHADING SHELTER SHOEING SLIPPER
TECTURE TEGMENT VESTURE
WRAPPER ARMGUARD BLAZONRY
BOARDING CASEMENT CLEADING
CLOTHING COMPRESS COVERLET
EGGSHELL EPISPORE INDUMENT
INDUSIUM MANTELET MANTLING
OVERCAST PAVILION PERICARP
SETATION UMBRELLA TECTORIAL
PILLOWCASE
(— FOR ANTENNA) RADOME
(— FOR BENCH) BANKER
(— FOR BOXERS' HANDS) CESTUS
(— FOR CHEST) STOMACHER
(— FOR EGG) COSY
(— FOR FOREHEAD) BONGRACE
(— FOR NECK) TUCKER PARTLET
(— FOR ROOF APEX) EPI
(— FOR SHOULDERS) STOLE
(— FOR SKI) SKIN
(— FOR STIRRUP) HOOD
(— FOR TEAPOT) COSY COZY
(— OF BED) TIKE
(— OF BELL ROPE) GRIP
(— OF BIRD) INDUMENT
(— OF BOW HANDLE) ARMING
(— OF CASH SHORTAGE) LAPPING
(— OF EYEBALL) CORNEA
(— OF FEATHERS) DOWN
(— OF GILLS) OPERCULUM
(— OF MUMMY) CARTONAGE
CARTONNAGE
(— OF NUTMEG) MACE
(— OF PIE) CRUST
(— OF ROOT) CALYPTRA
(— OF ROPE) SERVICE

(— OF VEGETATION) FLEECE
(— OVER DRESS) PINAFORE
(—S FOR NIPPLES) PASTIES
(— WITH IRON) ACIERAGE
(CAST —S) EXUVIAE
(CHIMNEY —) COWL
(CLOTH —) TOILET
(COARSE —) CADDOW TILLET
(DEFENSIVE —) ARMOR KICKER
(EAR —) EARLAP EARFLAP EARMUFF
OREILET
(EYE —S) GOGGLES
(FLOOR —) RUG TILE CRASH CARPET
LINOLEUM OILCLOTH
(FOUL —) SCUM
(HEAD —) CAP HAT WIG HAIR HIVE
HOOD CURCH BONNET HELMET
BIRETTA CHAPEAU CHAPERON
HAVELOCK HEADRAIL TROTCOZY
(LEATHER —) GAMBADO
(LEG —) BOOT HOSE STOCK GAITER
LEGGIN PEDULE KNEELET LEGGING
STOCKING
(LIGHT —) GRIMING
(LINEN —) BARB
(OUTER —) BARK HIDE HULL HUSK
CRUST TESTA JACKET CARAPACE
(PLANT —) PERIDERM
(PROTECTIVE —) APRON ARMOR
SHELL COCOON
(SADDLE —) MOCHILA
(SEED —) PERIGONE
(SHELF —) OILCLOTH
(SLIGHT —) CYMAR
(SOFT —) DOWN
(STAGE —) HEAVENS
(STERILE —) DRAPE
(STICKY DAMP —) GLET
(THIN —) FILM SCRUFF WASHING
(PREF.) CALYPT(O) COLE STEG(O)
STRATI STRATO
(SUFF.) DERM(A)(ATOUS)(IA)(IS)(Y)
(— OF PLATE) STEGE
COVERLET PANE HELER HOUSE
QUILT REZAI THROW AFGHAN
CADDOW CHALON COLCHA LIGGER
SPREAD BLANKET BUFFALO
COVERLID DAGSWAIN
COVER-SHAME SAVIN SAVINE
COVERT DEN LAY LIE SLY LAIR VERT
EARTH NICHE PRIVY ASYLUM
HARBOR HIDDEN LATENT MASKED
MYSTIC REFUGE SECRET COVERED
DEFENSE PRIVATE SHELTER TECTRIX
THICKET DISGUISE INVOLVED
(PL.) CRISSUM
COVERTLY CLOSE CLOSELY
COVET ACHE ENVY PANT WANT
WISH CRAVE YEARN YISSE DESIRE
GRUDGE HANKER
COVETOUS AVID GAIR GARF FAGER
FRUGAL GREEDY SORDID STINGY

ENVIOUS GRIPPLE MISERLY
DESIROUS GRASPING
COVETOUSNESS GREED MISERY
AVARICE YISSING COVETISE
CUPIDITY PLEONEXIA
COVEY BEVY FALL BROOD FLOCK
HATCH COVERT COMPANY
COVIN BAND CREW FRAUD COVINE
COMPANY CONVENE ASSEMBLY
TRICKERY
COW AWE KEY NOT BEEF BOGY BOSS
COWL CURL FAZE MOIL MULL NOTT
ROAN RUNT VACA ABASH ALARM
BEEVE BOSSY BROCK BULLY CUSHA
DAUNT DOMPT DRAPE MOGGY
QUAIL SCARE SNOOL VACHA BOVINE
BULLER COLLOP CRUMMY GOBLIN
HAWKEY HAWKIE HEIFER MAILIE
MILKER MULLEY ROTHER SUBDUE
BOARDER BUGBEAR BULLOCK
CRITTER CRUMMIE DEPRESS
MESTENO MILCHER OVERTOP
SQUELCH TERRIFY ALDERNEY
AUDHUMLA BROWBEAT COWBRUTE
DISPIRIT FRIGHTEN STRIPPER
THREATEN
(— ABOUT 3 FEET HIGH) GYNEE
(— BEFORE CALVING) SPRINGER
(BAD-TEMPERED —) RAGER
(BARREN —) DRAPE BARRENER
(DRY —) KEY SEW
(HORNLESS —) NOT MOIL NOTT
DODDY MULEY DODDIE HUMLIE
MAILIE HUMBLIE POLLARD
MOULLEEN
(NOTED —) ELSIE
(PART OF —) HIP JAW RIB CROP HOCK
HOOF HORN KNEE LOIN NECK POLL
RUMP TAIL TEAT CHEST CHINE
FLANK GIRTH PLATE THIGH THURL
UDDER BARREL BRIDGE DEWLAP
MUZZLE SWITCH THROAT BRISKET
DEWCLAW PASTERN PINBONE
WITHERS FOREHEAD
(PREGNANT —) CALVER INCALVER
(WHITE-FACED —) HAWKEY HAWKIE
(YOUNG —) QUEY STIRK HEIFER
(PL.) KYE KINE DAIRY
(PREF.) VACCI(NI)(NO)
COWARD COW CUR COOF DAFF
FUNK FUGIE LACHE PIKER CRAVEN
FUNKER PIGEON BUZZARD CAITIFF
CHICKEN COUCHER DASTARD
MEACOCK NITHING PANURGE
QUITTER NIDERING POLTROON
RECREANT TURNBACK TURNTAIL
VILLIAGO
COWARDICE DASTARDY LASHNESS
POLTROONERY
COWARDLINESS PUSILLANIMITY
COWARDLY SHY ARGH FAINT LACHE
TIMID AFRAID COWARD COWISH
CRAVEN TURPID YELLOW CAITIFF

CHICKEN GUTLESS HILDING
MEACOCK FACELESS NIDERING
POLTROON RECREANT SNEAKING
POLTROONISH PIGEONHEARTED
COW BARN BYRE SAUR BARTH
SHIPPON VACCARY
COWBIRD BECCO BUNTING
CUCKOLD OXBITER COKEWOLD
LAZYBIRD
COWBOY HAZER RIDER ROPER
SCREW WADDY CHARRO GAUCHO
GINETE HERDER JINETE WADDIE
COWHAND COWHERD COWPOKE
GRAZIER HERDBOY LLANERO
PANIOLO PUNCHER REFUGEE
VAQUERO BUCKAROO DALLYMAN
JACKAROO NEATHERD NOWTHERD
OUTRIDER PASTORAL RANCHERO
SWINGMAN WRANGLER
COWCATCHER GUARD LASSO
PILOT FENDER
COWED HANGDOG DOWNCAST
COWER HUG COUR FAWN RUCK
HOVER QUAIL SHRUG SNOOL SQUAT
STOOP TOADY WINCE COORIE
CRINGE CROUCH HURKLE SHRINK
CROODLE CRUDDLE
COWFISH TORO BECCO CUCKOLD
MANATEE SIRENIA
COWHAGE KIWACH
COWHAND PEELER FLANKER
STOCKMAN
COWHERB COCKLE SOAPWORT
COWHERD HERDSMAN NEATHERD
COWHOUSE BYRE SHIPPEN
SHIPPON
COWL CAP COW LID SOE TUB COUL
HOOD MONK MITER BONNET
CUCULE CAPUCHE SCUTTLE
CAPUCHIN
COW PARSNIP MADNEP CADWEED
HOGWEED PIGWEED BEARWORT
BUNDWEED
COWPEA SITAO FRIJOL FRIJOLE
TOWCOCK BLACKEYE BLACKPEA
COWPEN CUPPEN CUPPIN
COW PILOT PINTANO
COWPOX PAPPOX KINEPOX VACCINA
VACCINIA
COWRIE COWRY VENUS ZIMBI
CYPRAEID
COWSHED STALL
COWSLIP PAIGLE PRIMULA SHOOTER
AURICULA CYCLAMEN MARIGOLD
PRIMROSE
COXA HIP HAUNCH
COXCOMB FOP NOB BUCK DUDE
FOOL PRIG TOFF CLEAT DANDY
HINGE PRINCOX POPINJAY PRINCOCK
COXCOMBRY FOPPERY
COXSWAIN PATROON
COY PAL SHY ARCH COAX NICE
ALOOF CHARY DECOY QUIET SQUAB

STILL ALLURE CARESS DEMURE
MODEST PROPER SKEIGH BASHFUL
DISTANT PEEVISH STRANGE
RESERVED SKITTISH VERECUND
KITTENISH
COYNESS SHYNESS
COYO CHININ
COYOL COROJO COROZO
COYOTE VARMINT
  (— STATE) SOUTHDAKOTA
COYPU DEGU NUTRIA
COZBI
  (FATHER OF —) ZUR
COZEN COG CON BILK FOOL GULL
POOP CHEAT TRICK CHISEL GREASE
BEGUILE DECEIVE DEFRAUD
SWINDLE HOODWINK
COZENER SNAP SNECKDRAW
COZENING SIMILATE
COZIER CADGER CODGER COSIER
COZY RUG BEIN BIEN COSY EASY
HOMY SAFE SNUG BIELD CANNY
COMFY CUSHY HOMEY CHATTY
PENTIT SECURE TOASTY COVERING
FAMILIAR HOMELIKE SOCIABLE
CPU CHIP
CRAB GIN UCA BOCO JUEY MAJA
ZOEA ANGER ARROW AYUYU BLUEY
MAIAN MAIID MAJID RACER SANDY
THIEF WINCH BUSTER CANCER
GROUCH GROUSE HARPER HERMIT
KARURI NIPPER PARTAN PEELER
PUNGAR PUNGER RACING SCRAWL
SPRITE BUCKLER BUCKLUM
BURSTER CABOUCA CANCRID
DECAPOD FIDDLER GRUMBLE
INACHID OCYPODE PANFISH
POLYPOD SHEDDER SOLDIER
SPECTER SPECTRE SURIQUE
ARACHNID CRABFISH DORIPPID
GRAPSOID HORSEMAN IRRITATE
LIMULOID LITHODID OCHIDORE
OXYSTOME PAGURIAN PORTUNID
RANINIAN TRAVELER WINDLASS
BRACHYURA
  (KIND OF —) SNOW PURSE
  (MATING —) DOUBLER
  (PREF.) CANCERI CANCERO CANCRI
  CARCIN(I)(O)
CRAB APPLE CRAB SCRAB SCROG
  COLING
CRABBED SOUR UGLY CABBY
CRANK CROSS SURLY TESTY BITTER
COPPED CROOSE CROUSE CRUSTY
MOROSE RUGGED SULLEN TEETHY
TRYING BOORISH CANKERY CRABBIT
CRAMPED CRONISH CROOKED
FRABBIT GNARLED KNOTTED
OBSCURE PEEVISH CANKERED
CHURLISH CONTRARY CRABBISH
LIVERISH PETULANT VINEGARY
CRABBEDNESS ACRIMONY
ASPERITY

CRABCATCHER CRABIER
CRABER VOLE AGOUARA
CRABGRASS DRAWK FONIO PANIC
DARNEL PANICLE CRABWEED
ELEUSINE
CRAB LOUSE CRAB MORPION
MOREPEON
CRAB PLOVER DROME
CRAB'S-EYE JEQUIRITY
CRAB TREE GRIBBLE
CRABWOOD ANDIROBA
POISONWOOD
CRACK GAG KIN POP BANG BLOW
CHAP CHIP CHOP CLAP CONE DOKE
FENT FLAW GAIG JEST JIBE JOKE
KIBE LEAK LICK QUIP REND RIFT RIME
RIVE SCAR SLAT SNAP YERK BRACK
BREAK CHARK CHECK CHICK CHINE
CHINK CLACK CLEFT CRAKE CRAZE
FLAKE FLANK FLASH GRIKE KNACK
KNICK SCORE SHAKE SLASH SOLVE
SPANG SPLIT CLEAVE CRANNY
SLITER SPIDER SPRING BLEMISH
CRACKLE CREVICE FISSURE SLIFTER
SLITHER FRACTURE HAIRLINE
STRAMASH
  (— A WHIP) YERK FLANK
  (— IN FLESH) KIN CHAP KIBE
  (— IN FLOOR) STRAKE
  (— IN INGOT) SPILL
  (— IN MAST) SPRING
  (— IN ROCK) GRIKE JOINT
  (— IN SEA ICE) RIFTER
  (— IN STEEL) CHECK SPILL
  (— OPEN) SEAM
  (— PETROLEUM) BURN
  (— WHILE FIRING) DUNT
  (FILLER FOR —S) SPACKLE
  (PL.) CRAZE
  (PREF.) RIMI
CRACKAJACK NAILER NAILING
CRACKBRAINED BATS CRAZY
NUTTY CRACKY ERRATIC
CRACKED BATS FLED NECKED
CHAPPED COMICAL TOUCHED
CRACKERS
CRACKER BAKE LIAR WAFER
BONBON POPPER BISCUIT BOASTER
BREAKER BURSTER COSAQUE
REDNECK SALTINE SNAPPER
  (— STATE) GEORGIA
  (BOILED —S) CUSH
  (BROKEN —S) DUNDERFUNK
CRACKERJACK ACE TRUMP
CRACKING CRAZE SHIVERING
  (PL.) SCRAP
CRACKLE SNAP BREAK CRACK CRISP
BRUSTLE CRINKLE SPARKLE
SPUTTER CREPITATE
CRACKLING CRISP GREAVE SNAPPY
CRACKEL CRACKLE CREMANT
GREAVES CRACKNEL CRITLING
CREPITANT

(— OF PAPER) RATTLE
(PL.) SCRAPS GRIEBEN
CRACKNEL SIMNEL CRACKLING
CRACKPOT NUT CRACK ERRATIC
LUNATIC CRANKISH
CRACKSMAN YEGG BURGLAR
PETEMAN
CRADLE BED COT CRIB REST ROCK
WOMB CRATE FRAME CRECHE
MATRIX ROCKER SADDLE TROUGH
BERCEAU SHELTER BASSINET
CUNABULA
(— FOR SHIP) BED SLEE
(— FOR VATS) STILLING STILLION
(— IN ARCHERY) PURSE
(CERAMICS —) CHUM
(GRAIN —) CADAR CADER
(PL.) CHOCKS
CRADLESONG BERCEUSE
CRADLING BRACK
CRAFT ART BARK BOAT SAIL FRAUD
GUILE SKILL TRADE BARQUE BATEAU
CAUTEL DECEIT DROGER METIER
MISTER POLICE ROADER STRUSE
TALENT VESSEL ABILITY CUNNING
DROGHER MYSTERY PANURGY
SLEIGHT APTITUDE ARTIFICE
BASKETRY VOCATION
(ANTIQUATED OR CLUMSY —)
HOOKER
(CLUMSY —) ARK
(LANDING —) DUCK
(PREF.) TECHNI TECHNO
(SUFF.) TECT
CRAFTILY FOXILY
CRAFTINESS DESIGN SLEIGHT
SLYNESS
CRAFTSMAN CARL HAND CARLE
CRAFT NAVVY ARTIST WRITER
ARTISAN TOHUNGA WORKMAN
LETTERER MECHANIC ARTIFICER
MACHINIST
CRAFTY SLY ARCH DEEP DERN FINE
FOXY NOUP SLIM WILY WISE ADEPT
COONY PAWKY SLAPE SLEEK ADROIT
ARTFUL ASTUTE CALLID QUAINT
SHREWD SOLERT SUBTLE TRICKY
CUNNING POLITIC SLEEKIT SLEIGHT
SUBTILE VAFROUS VERSUTE
VULPINE CAPTIOUS DEXTROUS
ENGINOUS FETCHING JESUITIC
SLEIGHTY CAUTELOUS
CRAG TOR CRAW KNEE NECK ROCK
SCAR SPUR ARETE BRACK CLIFF
CLINT CRAIG HEUCH HEUGH THROAT
(PREF.) CREMNO
CRAGGY ROUGH ABRUPT CLIFFY
CLIFTY KNOTTY PAMPER RUGGED
CRAGGED KNAGGED
CRAKE CROW RAIL ROOK RAVEN
CORNBIRD RAILBIRD
CRAKOW BEAKER CRACOWE
POULAINE

CRAM BAG MUG RAM WAD BONE
CRAP FILL GLUT LADE PACK PANG
PORR PURR STOW TRIG TUCK URGE
CROWD CRUSH DRIVE FARCE FORCE
FRANK GORGE GRIND LEARN PRESS
SCRAM STECH STUDY STUFF TEACH
AGROTE BONEUP CROMME PESTER
STEEVE STODGE THRACK
(— WITH RICH FOOD) PAMPER
CRAMMED PANG STODGY
CHOCKFUL JAMPACKED
CRAMMER CRAM FEEDER
CRAMMING GAVAGE
CRAMP ART ARCT COOP CRIB KINK
PAIN TUCK CRICK CRIMP CROWD
DOWEL PINCH STUNT TRAMP
AGRAFE DOGTIE HAMPER HINDER
KNOTTY PESTER CONFINE CRAMPER
CRAMPET COMPRESS CONTRACT
RESTRAIN RESTRICT
CRAMPED POKY CRIMP POKEY
NIGGLY BOUNDED CRIMPED
SQUEEZY NIGGLING
CRAMPFISH TORPEDO
CRAMPING UNEASY
CRAMPON CRAMP CRAMPET
CRAMPOON
CRANBERRY BERRY CRANE ERICAD
BOGWORT PEMBINA ACROSARC
BILBERRY BOGBERRY COWBERRY
FENBERRY FOXBERRY CROWBERRY
(— BUSH) PIMBINA
CRANBERRY TREE PEMBINA
SNOWBALL VIBURNUM
CRANE JOB GRUS HOOK SWAY
CYRUS DAVIT HERON HOIST JENNY
RAISE SARUS TITAN WADER BROLGA
COOLEN JIGGER KULANG SAHRAS
COOLUNG CRAWLER DERRICK
GOLIATH KAIKARA WHOOPER
ADJUTANT GRUIFORM TRAVELER
(— FOR FIREPLACE) COTTREL
COTTEREL
CRANE ARM GIB JIB GIBBET
RAMHEAD COTTEREL
CRANE-FLY LONG-LEGS
CRANESBILL ALUMROOT
DOVEFOOT FLUXWEED
CRANIUM PAN HEAD CRANE CRANY
SKULL BRAINPAN
(PART OF —) INION
CRANK NUT WIT BENT SICK WALT
WEAK WHIM WIND BRACE GRUMP
LOOSE ROGUE SHAKY THROW
WALTY WINCH AILING BOLDLY
CRANKY EVENER GROUCH HANDLE
INFIRM AWKWARD BRACKET
FANATIC LUSTILY
(SOMEWHAT —) TENDER
CRANKCASE SUMP
CRANKINESS ANGULARITY
CRANKY UGLY CRAZY CRONK CROSS
LUSTY SHAKY TESTY AILING

CRANNY FIFISH INFIRM SICKLY CROOKED GROUCHY PERVERSE TORTUOUS

CRANNY HOLE NOOK CHINK CLEFT CRACK CORNER CRANNEL CREVICE FISSURE

CRANTARA TARIE

CRANTS WREATH CORANCE GARLAND

CRAPE BAND CURL FRIZ CREPE CRIMP DRAPE GAUZE SHROUD MOURNING

CRAPE MYRTLE JAPONICA ASTROMEDA

CRAPPIE BACH SHAD BATCH CALICO CROPPIE BACHELOR BACULERE NEWLIGHT SACALAIT TINMOUTH CHINKAPIN

CRAPS CRAP HAZARD

CRASH BASH FAIL FALL RACK BLAST BURST CLOTH CRUSH FRUSH PRANG SHOCK SMASH SOUND FIASCO FRAGOR HURTLE FAILURE SHATTER STENTER COLLAPSE ICEQUAKE SPLINTER STRAMASH
(— OF THUNDER) CLAP

CRASHING ROPAND SMASHING

CRASH-LAND DITCH

CRASS RAW DULL LOUD RUDE CRUDE DENSE GROSS ROUGH THICK COARSE OBTUSE STUPID

CRASSNESS SQUALOR

CRATCH CRIB RACK CRITCH MANGER GRATING

CRATE BOX CAR CASE CRIB FLAT PLANE SERON BASKET CRADLE ENCASE HAMPER HURDLE CACAXTE CANASTA CARRIER PACKAGE VEHICLE
(EMPTY —) EMPTY

CRATER CUP PIT CONE HOLE DINOS FOVEA NICHE CELEBE HOLLOW CALDERA
(— FORMED BY STEAM) MAAR
(LUNAR —) LINNE
(VOLCANIC —) MAAR

CRATUS (FATHER OF —) PALLAS URANUS
(MOTHER OF —) GAEA STYX

CRAUNCH CRANCH SCRANCH

CRAVAT TIE TECK ASCOT FRONT SCARF STOCK CHOKER GRAVAT BANDAGE NECKTIE OVERLAY SOUBISE CRUMPLER

CRAVE ASK BEG GAPE ITCH LONG NEED PINE PRAY SEEK WISH COVET GREED YEARN DESIRE HANKER HUNGER LINGER THIRST YAMMER BESEECH ENTREAT IMPLORE REQUEST REQUIRE SOLICIT APPETITE

CRAVEN AFRAID COWARD SCARED DASTARD COWARDLY DEFEATED OVERCOME POLTROON RECREANT SNEAKING

CRAVING AVID ITCH WANT LETCH DESIRE HUNGER THIRST LONGING APPETITE LIKEROUS TICKLING APPETENCE
(— FOR LIQUOR) DRY
(— FOR UNNATURAL FOOD) PICA
(ABNORMAL —) BULIMY BULIMIA BOULIMIA

CRAW MAW CRAG CROP STOMACH

CRAWFISH KREEF

CRAWL LAG COON DRAG FAWN INCH LOOP RAMP SHUG SWIM CREEP KRAAL SLIDE SLIME SNAKE TRAIL BUSTLE CRINGE GROVEL SCRAWL SCRIDE CLAMBER SLITHER SNIGGLE TRUDGEN INCHWORM SCRABBLE

CRAWLING
(SUFF.) (— CREATURE) ERPETON

CRAWLY CREEPY

CRAYFISH DAD CRAB YABBY YABBIE CAMARON CRAWDAD LOBSTER CAMBARUS CRABFISH CRAWFISH

CRAYON KEEL PLAN CHALK CONTE SAUCE PASTEL PENCIL SKETCH SANGUINE

CRAZE BUG FAD FLAW MAZE MODE RAGE BREAK CRACK CRUSH FEVER FUROR MANIA VOGUE DEFECT IMPAIR MADDEN MADDLE WEAKEN WHIMSY DERANGE DESTROY FASHION SHATTER WHIMSEY DISTRACT
(NEWSPAPER —) STUNT
(PREF.) MANIC

CRAZED MAD REE AMOK LOCO WILD WOOD WOWF ZANY BALMY BATTY DAFFY DOTTY GIDDY MANIC NUTTY POTTY WACKY COOCOO DOTTLE INSANE LOONEY BERSERK FANATIC LUNATIC DATELESS DELEERIT DEMENTED DERANGED POSSESSED

CRAZINESS CRAZE LUNACY DEMENTIA

CRAZY (ALSO SEE CRAZED) APE OFF REE WET BATS BUGS GAGA GYTE HITE LOCO NUTS WILD ZANY BATTY BEANY BUGGY DAFFY DIPPY DOILT DOTTY FLAKY GOOFY KOOKY LOOLY LOONY POTTY WACKO WACKY WIGGY CRANKY CUCKOO DOTTLE FLAKEY FRUITY INSANE KOOKIE LOCKET MENTAL SCATTY SCREWY WHACKO WHACKY BANANAS BONKERS CRACKED LUNATIC PEEVISH SCRANNY BUGHOUSE COCKEYED CRACKERS DERANGED HALLICET HALUCKET MESHUGGA

CREAK CRY GIG GEIG GIRG JARG RASP YIRR CHARK CHEEP CHIRK CRAIK CRANK CROAK GRIND GROAN

CREAK FRATCH SCREAK SCRIKE SCROOP
SKRAIK SQUEAK COMPLAIN
(— OF TIN) CRY
CREAKING JARG SCREAK SCRIKE
CREAKY ARTHRITIC
CREAM DIP BEAT BEST FOOL HEAD
REAM CREME ELITE FROTH REAME
SAUCE WHOMP BONBON CHOICE
TRIFLE COLOGNE FATNESS
EMULSION OINTMENT
(ICE —) GELATA
CREAMING MANTLING
CREAM PUFF PUFF DUCHESSE
CREAMY RICH REAMY ACREAM
SMOOTH LUSCIOUS
CREASE GAW CLAM FOLD LINE LIRK
RUCK RUGA SEAM BLOCK CRESS
CRIMP PLAIT PLEAT PRESS SCARF
SCORE FURROW SCARPA SUTURE
WREATH CRUMPLE CRUNKLE
WRIMPLE WRINKLE
(SERIES OF —S) BREAK
(PL.) RASCETA
CREASED CRUMPLED ACCORDION
CREASELESS
(HAVING — LEGS) STOVEPIPE
CREATE COIN CREE FORM MAKE
PLAN BUILD CAUSE ERECT FORGE
IMPEL RAISE SETUP SHAPE WRITE
AUTHOR DESIGN IMPOSE INVENT
COMPACT COMPOSE CONJURE
FASHION IMAGINE PRODUCE
COMPOUND GENERATE CONSTRUCT
(— A DISTURBANCE) RIOT
(— CONFUSION) GARBOIL
(NEWLY -D) SUNRISE
CREATING CREANT
CREATION WORLD COSMOS EFFECT
NATURE POETRY EDITION FACTURE
FASHION POIESIS PRODUCT
SHAPING BERESHIT BUSINESS
CREATURE UNIVERSE
(MENTAL —) FANTASY PHANTASY
(VISIONARY —) DREAM
CREATIVE FERTILE FORMFUL
PLASTIC POIETIC FORGEFUL
GERMINAL NATURING POMATIVE
PROMETHEAN ORIGINATIVE
CREATOR MAKER AUTHOR FATHER
FORMER VARUNA WORKER KHEPERA
TAGALOA DESIGNER INVENTOR
OPERATOR PRODUCER TANGALOA
CREATURE MAN FOOD TOOL BEAST
BEING DABBA JOKER SLAVE THING
TRICK WIGHT ANIMAL FELLOW
MINION PERSON WRETCH CRITTER
GANGREL MINIKIN MINIMUS
SHAPING CRAYTHUR CREATION
HELLICAT
(— OF LITTLE VALUE) SHOT
(CANNIBALISTIC —) WENDIGO
WINDIGO
(CHARMING —) FAIRY

(DEFORMED —) MOONCALF
(DISORDERLY —) ROIT ROYT
(DWARF —) FAIRY GNOME
(ELFLIKE —) PERI
(EVIL —) HELLICAT
(FABLED —) LUNG SIREN MERMAN
WIVERN ALBORAK MERMAID
(FRIVOLOUS —) MOTH
(LITTLE —) MITING
(MANGY —) RONION RONYON
(MANLIKE —) HOMINID HOMONID
HOMINIAN
(MEAN —) LEFT
(MECHANICAL —) GOLEM
(MISERABLE —) SNAKE
(NONSENSE —) SNARK
(POOR —) EARTHWORM
(SILLY —) GOOSE
(SMALL —) ATOM GRIG BEASTIE
(SPRY —) WHIPPET
(STUNTED —) WIRL URLING WIRLING
(SUPERNATURAL —) MAN DRAGON
(TINY —) ELF ATOMY
(UNDERDEVELOPED —) SLINK
(UNDERSIZED —) DURGAN
(USELESS —) HUSHION
(VICIOUS —) DEVIL
(WICKED —) HELLICAT
(WORTHLESS —) SCULPIN SNIPJACK
(WRETCHED —) ARMINE
(3 —S OF A KIND) LEASH
(PL.) CREATION
CRECHE CRIB PUTZ MANGER
NURSERY
(— FIGURES) MAGI
CREDENCE FAITH TRUST BELIEF
BUFFET CREDIT CREANCE CREDENZA
CREDENTIAL VOUCHER CREDENCE
CREDENZA NICHE SHELF TABLE
BUFFET SERVER CREDENCE
CUPBOARD
CREDIBILITY FAITH CREDIT
CREDIBLE LIKELY CREDENT
FAITHFUL PROBABLE TROWABLE
PLAUSIBLE
CREDIT LOAN TICK ASSET CHALK
ENDOW FAITH HONOR IZZAT MENSK
MERIT STRAP TENET TRUST BELIEF
CHARGE ESTEEM IMPUTE RENOWN
REPUTE TICKET WEIGHT ACCOUNT
ASCRIBE BELIEVE CREANCE
JAWBONE OPINION WORSHIP
ACCREDIT CREDENCE HEADMARK
PRESTIGE
(HOCKEY —) ASSIST
CREDITABLE HONEST CREDIBLE
REPUTABLE
CREDITOR DEBTEE SHYLOCK
TRUSTER ADJUDGER APPRIZER
CRANSIER CREANCER
(TROUBLESOME —) DUN
CREDO FAITH
CREDULITY EASINESS

CREDULOUS FOND SIMPLE SPOONY
SPOONEY BOOBYISH CREDIBLE
GULLIBLE
CREED ISM LAY CULT SECT CREDO
DOGMA FAITH TENET BELIEF KELIMA
SYMBOL CREANCE KALIMAH
TROWING DOCTRINE SYMBOLUM
(KIND OF —) NICENE
CREEK BAY CUT GEO GIO GUT POW
RIA RIO RUN VLY VOE BECK BURN
COVE HOPE KILL PILL RILL SLEW
SLUE VLEI VLEY WASH WICK BACHE
BAYOU BIGHT BOGUE BROOK CRICK
DRAFT FLEET INLET ZANJA ARROYO
BRANCH BREACH CANADA ESTERO
SLOUGH STREAM DRAUGHT
ESTUARY RIVULET ZANJONA
MUSKOGEE
(AUSTRALIAN —) COWAL
(TIDE —) SLAKE
CREEK SEDGE THATCH
CREEL RIP CAUL CAWL HASK JACK
KELL RACK TRAP HARSK BASKET
JUNKET
(— FOR BOBBINS) BANK SKEWER
CREELER TUBER LIGGER
CREEP COON FAWN GEEK INCH NERD
RAMP CRAWL CROPE DRIFT GLIDE
PROWL SKULK SLINK SMOOT STEAL
TRAIL CRINGE GROVEL SCRIDE
SPRAWL TIPTOE WEIRDO CRAMBLE
CRAMMEL SNIGGLE WEIRDIE
TAURANGA
(— AS IVY) RIZZLE
(PL.) WILLIES
(PREF.) HERPETI HERPETO
CREEPER IVY JITI SHOE VINE
WORM CREEP CROPE SNAKE
COWAGE CRADLE IPECAC REPENT
ROMPER TECOMA CLAMPER
CLIMBER COWHAGE COWITCH
CRAWLER REPTANT REPTILE
RUNNING TRAILER FOXGLOVE
GUITGUIT PICUCULE WOODBINE
PERIWINKLE
CREEPING SLOW REPTANT REPTILE
SERVILE SARMENTOUS
SERPIGINOUS
(— OF FLESH) GREW GRUE
(PREF.) HERPET(I)(O)
(SUFF.) (— CREATURE) ERPETON
CREEPING CROWFOOT SITFAST
CRAWFOOT
CREEPING JENNY MONEYWORT
CREEPING SNOWBERRY MOXA
TEABERRY
CREESE KRIS STAB CRESS CRISE
SWORD DAGGER
CREMATE BURN
CREMATION SUTTEE
(PLACE OF —) GHAT GHAUT
CRENEL LOOP CORNEL KERNEL
CRENELET

CREOLE KRIO PATOIS CRIOLLO
DIALECT HAITIAN MESTIZO
(— STATE) LOUISIANA
(ENGLISH-BASED —) SRANAN
CREON (DAUGHTER OF —) GLAUCE
(FATHER OF —) MENOECEUS
(SISTER OF —) JOCASTA HIPPONOME
CREOSOTE BUSH LARREA
CREPE CRAPE FRIZZED NACARAT
PANCAKE CHIRIMEN CRINKLED
WRINKLED
CREPITATE SNAP GRATE RATTLE
CRACKLE
CRESCENT HORN LUNE MOON
ROOL CURVE LUNAR LUNOID
LUNULE MOONED SICKLE WAXAND
LUNETTE DEMILUNE MENISCUS
(END OF —) CUSP HORN
(PREF.) MENISCI MENISCO
CRESCENTLIKE BICORN
CRESCENT-SHAPED MOONY
LUNATE LUNATED
(PREF.) SELEN(O)
CRESCIVE WAXING GROWING
INCREASING
CRESOL FROTHER
CRESPHONTES (BROTHER OF —)
TEMENUS ARISTODEMUS
(FATHER OF —) ARISTOMACHUS
(SON OF —) AEPYTUS
CRESS EKER KERSE CUCKOO
MADWORT CRUCIFER WHITETOP
PEPPERGRASS
CRESSET TORCH BASKET BEACON
SIGNAL CRISSET FLAMBEAU
CREST COP TIP TOP ACME APEX
COMB EDGE HOOD KNAP PEAK RUFF
SEAL TUFT CHINE CROWN PLUME
RIDGE COPPLE CREASE CRISTA
CUMBRE FINIAL HEIGHT HELMET
SUMMIT TIMBER TIMBRE BEARING
FEATHER TOPKNOT CENTROID
CRESTING ECTOLOPH METALOPH
PINNACLE WHITECAP
(— OF BREAKER) SEEGE
(— OF HELMET) COMB CIMIER
(— OF HILL) KNAP
(— OF MINERAL VEIN) APEX
(— OF MOUNTAIN RANGE) ARETE
SAWBACK
(— OF PEACOCK) CHAPLET
(— OF RIDGE) EDGE
(— OF SNOW) CORNICE
(— ON BIRD) CROWN ECKLE COPPLE
(IMPERIAL —) KIKUMON
(WAVE —) FEATHER WHITECAP
(PREF.) CRISTI LOPH(I)(IO)(O)
(SUFF.) LOPH(US)
CRESTED COMBED MUFFED TAPPET
TAPPIT COPPLED CRISATE CROWNED
CRISTATE PILEATED CRISTATED
CRESTED GREBE CARGOOSE
CRESTED QUAIL COPPY

CRESTFALLEN COWED DEJECTED
CRESTING CHENEAU
CRETACEOUS CHALKY
CRETAN KEFTI MINOAN CANDIOT
CRETAN SPIKENARD PHU

CRETE
BAY: SUDA KANCA KISAMO MESARA
CAPE: BUZA LIANO SALOME SIDERO
   SPATHA STAVROS LITHINON
   SIDHEROS
CAPITAL: CANEA
GULF: KHANIA MERABELLO
MOUNTAIN: IDA DIKTE JUKTAS
   LASITHI THEODORE
NAME: CRETA KRETE CANDIA
TOWN: HAG LATO CANEA KHORA
   SITIA ZAKRO ANOYIA CANDIA
   KHANIA KISAMO RETIMO KISAMOS
   KASTELLI HERAKLION

CRETHEUS (FATHER OF —) AEOLUS
  (MOTHER OF —) ENARETE
  (SLAYER OF —) TURNUS
  (SON OF —) AESON PHERES
   AMYTHAON
  (WIFE OF —) TYRO
CRETIN IDIOT
CREUSA GLAUCE GLAUKE
  (FATHER OF —) CREON PRIAM
   ERECHTHEUS
  (HUSBAND OF —) AENEAS XUTHUS
  (MOTHER OF —) HECUBA PRAXITHEA
  (SLAYER OF —) MEDEA
  (SON OF —) ION DORUS ACHAEUS
   ASCANIUS
CREVALLE JACK JUREL
CREVASSE CHASM SPLIT MOULIN
  SCHRUND CLEAVAGE BERGSCHRUND
CREVICE KIN BORE LEAK NOOK
  PEEP SEAM VEIN BREAK CHINE
  CHINK CLEFT CRACK CREEK CUNNE
  GRIKE CRANNY STRAKE CRANNEL
  FISSURE GUNNIES KRAVERS
  OPENING SLIFTER CREVASSE
  PEEPHOLE
  (VOLCANIC —) SOLFATARA
CREW LOT MEN MOB SET BAND
  GANG GING HERD OARS SHIP TEAM
  UNIT COVIN EIGHT HANDS MEINY
  PARTY SQUAD STAFF COVINE MEINIE
  SEAMEN THRONG AIRCREW
  COMPANY FACULTY MANNING
  MEMBERS RETINUE EQUIPAGE
  (— OF SHEARERS) BOARD
CREWEL CRUEL CADDIS CADDICE
CRIB BED BIN BOX CAB COT CUB HUT
  KEY BOOM CRUB CURB DIVE JACK
  PONY RACK RAFT SKIN TROT BOOSE
  BOOSY CHEAT CRATE FRAME HOVEL
  STALL STEAL BUNKER CRATCH
  CRECHE CRITCH MANGER PIGSTY

PILFER CABBAGE ENGLISH PURLOIN
  BASSINET CORNCRIB CRIBBAGE
  CRIBBING CRIBWORK
CRIBBER SHORER STUMPSUCKER
CRICK KINK CREEK HITCH SPASM
  TWIST
CRICKET GRIG MOLE SNOB CHANGA
  SADDLE GRYLLID TWIDDLER
  ORTHOPTERAN
  (— HIT) SLOG
  (— SCORE OF 100 RUNS) TON
  (KIND OF —) MORMON
  (PREF.) GRYLLO
CRICKETER CUT COLT PLAYER
  RABBIT GENTLEMAN
CRICKET ON THE HEARTH
  (AUTHOR OF —) DICKENS
  (CHARACTER IN —) DOT MAY JOHN
  CALEB BERTHA EDWARD PLUMMER
  FIELDING TACKLETON PERRYBINGLE
CRIER HUER CRYER BEADLE HERALD
  WAILER BELLMAN MUEZZIN
  WRAWLER OUTCRIER
CRIME ACT SIN EVIL FACT LACK
  ABUSE ARSON BLAME CAPER FOLLY
  LIBEL WRONG FALSUM FELONY
  INCEST MURDER PIACLE FORFEIT
  FORGERY MISDEED OFFENCE
  OFFENSE INIQUITY SABOTAGE
  VILLAINY MALEFACTION
  MISDEMEANOR
  (— PHRASE) DOESNTPAY
  (ORGANIZED —) GANGLAND
CRIME AND PUNISHMENT
  (AUTHOR OF —) DOSTOEVSKI
  (CHARACTER IN —) SONIA DOUNIA
  LUZHIN PORFIRY PETROVICH
  RAZUMIHIN MARMELADOV
  RASKOLNIKOV SVIDRIGAILOV
CRIMINAL BAD SORE YEGG CROOK
  FELON TOUGH APACHE BASHER
  DACOIT GUILTY GUNMAN INMATE
  KILLER NOCENT SLAYER WARGUS
  WICKED CONVICT CULPRIT HEINOUS
  HOODLUM ILLEGAL ILLICIT MOBSTER
  NOXIOUS SEVENER VAUTRIN
  CRIMEFUL CULPABLE GANGSTER
  GAOLBIRD HABITUAL HARDCASE
  JAILBIRD PIACULAR SCELERAT
  (HABITUAL —) RECIDIVIST
  (PETTY —) ROUNDER
  (VIOLENT —) DESPERADO
  (PL.) AMALAITA
CRIMINATE IMPEACH
CRIMP BEND CURL FOLD FRIZ POKE
  POTE WAVE WEAK CLAMP CRISP
  FLUTE FRILL FRIZZ PINCH PLAIT
  BUCKLE GOFFER RUFFLE CRIMPER
  CRIMPLE CRINKLE FRIABLE GAUFFER
  WRINKLE OBSTACLE
CRIMSON LAC RED PINK GRAIN
  BLOODY JOCKEY MAROON MODENA

CARMINE SCARLET CRAMOISY
CREMOSIN
(— TIDE) BAMA
CRIMSON CLOVER NAPOLEON
CRIMSON LAKE SULTAN
CRINE HAIR
CRINED MANED
CRINGE BOW BEND CURB CURR
DUCK FAWN JOUK BINGE COWER
CRAWL CREEP QUAIL SNEAK SNOOL
STOOP WINCE YIELD BUCKLE
CROUCH GROVEL SHRINK SUBMIT
ADULATE CRINKLE DISTORT SCRINGE
TRUCKLE
CRINGER FLUNKEY
CRINGING ABJECT HANGDOG
SERVILE SPANIEL
CRINKLE BEND CURL KINK TURN
WIND CREPE CRISP PUCKER RIPPLE
RUMPLE RUSTLE CRACKLE CRANKLE
FRIZZLE WRINKLE
CRINKLED CRIMP CURLY BUCKLED
ENCOMIC CRISPATE
CRINKLY CREPY CREPEY
CRINOID POLYP CRINITE CAMERATE
COMATULA
(BODY OF —) CROWN
CRINOLINE CRIN HOOP
CRIPPLE MAR CRIP GIMP HARM HURT
LAME MAIM BACACH HOBBLE IMPAIR
INJURE SCOTCH WEAKEN CRAPPLE
CRUMPET DISABLE LAMETER
LAMIGER LAMITER HANDICAP
LAMESTER MUTILATE PARALYZE
(PL.) LAMZIEKTE
CRIPPLED GIMPY LAMED COUPLED
DISABLED
CRIPPLING MAIM MAYHEM
CRISIS FIT ACME CRUX FLAP HEAD
JUMP PASS TURN BRUNT CARDO
CRISE PANIC PERIL PINCH POINT
STATE STORM TRIAL STRAIT
DUNKIRK DECISION JUNCTURE
MOUNTAIN
(AUTHOR OF —) CHURCHILL
(CHARACTER IN —) BRICE GRANT
CARVEL COLFAX ABRAHAM LINCOLN
STEPHEN WHIPPLE CLARENCE
VIRGINIA
CRISP NEW COLD CURL FRIZ FROW
HARD BRISK CLEAR CRIPS CRUMP
CURLY FRESH FRIZZ NIPPY PITHY
SHARP SHORT SPALT STIFF TERSE
BITING BRIGHT CRISPY LIVELY
SNAPPY BRACING BRITTLE CONCISE
CRACKLY CRUNCHY CUTTING
FRIABLE FRIZZLE SMOPPLE INCISIVE
POTATOCHIP
CRISPED FUZZY FRIZZLY CRISPATE
CRISPINELLA
(SISTER OF —) BEATRICE
CRISPNESS SNAP

CRISSCROSS AWRY CROSS
NETWORK CONFUSED
CRITERION LAW NORM RULE TEST
TYPE AXIOM CANON CHECK GAUGE
MODEL PROOF TOUCH CRISIS
METRIC INDICIA MEASURE PLUMMET
STANDARD SHIBBOLETH
CRITIC MOME BOOER JUDGE MOMUS
RATER CARPER CENSOR CORNER
EXPERT PUNDIT SLATER SYNDIC
ZOILUS STYLIST ZOILIST COLLATOR
CRITIQUE DEBUNKER OVERSEER
REVIEWER THINGMAN ARISTARCH
AMERICAN CARY GILL KAEL KERR
LAHR MORE SOBY TATE AIKEN
BANGS BOGAN BREEN BROWN
CANBY CRIST CUPPY EBERT ELSON
FINCK FISKE GIBBS HEWES KALEM
KAZIN KOBBE LEVIN MABIE POUND
SIMON WHITE ALLSOP BECKER
BROOKS CHENEY DOWNES FULLER
GILMAN HUTTON KRASNA KRUTCH
LEDOUX LOWELL MANTLE MILLER
MUNSON NATHAN PARKER PHELPS
SHALIT SISKEL SONTAG TAYLOR
WILSON ALDRICH ANDREWS
AVAKIAN FIEDLER GRANICK
HUNEKER POIRIER SMAROFF
VENDLER WHIPPLE WIMSATT
ATKINSON BOOKSPAN CROWTHER
HAGEDORN SAARINEN ROSENFELD
WOOLLCOTT CHOTZINOFF
AUSTRALIAN HUGHES TURNER
AUSTRIAN KUH KRAUS
CANADIAN FRYE SMITH BIRNEY
CZECH HANSLICK
DANISH LANGE BRANDES
GERSTENBERG
DUTCH BRINK BILDERDIJK
JONCKBLOET VALCKENAER
ENGLISH BAX FRY BELL LAMB READ
SHAW WAIN WEST AGATE BOWRA
DILKE ELIOT ELWIN GAUNT GOULD
GREIN LAVES LEVIN MERES PAGET
PATER PATES RYMER SCOTT TYNAN
WAUGH ARNOLD BINYON COLLES
COLVIN DENNIS EMPSON HUXLEY
LEAVIS MORGAN PALMER RUSKIN
SYMONS THOMAS WALKER WARTON
AINSLIE BENTLEY BRADLEY COLLIER
COLLINS FREEMAN GIFFORD
GISSING JOHNSON KERMODE
LUBBOCK RALEIGH SHORTER
SITWELL STEPHEN TOYNBEE
WALKLEY WHIBLEY BEERBOHM
MARRIOTT SECCOMBE STEPHENS
MACCARTHY PARTRIDGE
SAINTSBURY SWINNERTON
FINNISH WALTARI
FRENCH GIDE BAYLE BAZIN BIDOU
BLAZE DENIS GILLE TAINE CASSOU
FAGUET FRANCE LANSON MENDES

OZANAM SARCEY VALERY BARTHES
BATTEUX BOURGET BREMOND
GAUTIER MERIMEE REGNIER
AUBIGNAC MEZIERES MONTEGUT
VALLETTE BRUNETIERE APOLLINAIRE
GERMAN BAB EYE KERR MERCK
MUNDT OPITZ MENZEL SCHOLL
WAAGEN LESSING NICOLAI RIBBECK
ZARNCKE ACIDALIUS
GREEK ELYTIS ZOILUS ARISTARCHUS
CALLIMACHUS
HUNGARIAN KOLCSEY
ICELANDIC BLONDAL
INDIAN ANAND
IRISH BOYD DEVERE MARTYN
ITALIAN PRAZ CECCHI OJETTI OVIDIO
BARETTI CAPUANA MONTALE
ZANELLA CARDUCCI CHIARINI
ALGAROTTI DESANCTUS
CASTELVETRO CAVALCASELLE
MEXICAN PAZ
NORWEGIAN WELHAVEN
POLISH LANGE
PORTUGUESE VASCONCELLOS
RUSSIAN PYPIN STASOV BELINSKI
SCOTTISH DENT MUIR ARCHER
WILSON JEFFREY
SPANISH CANETE
SWEDISH SIREN LEOPOLD KELLGREN
LEVERTIN
SWISS BODMER
WELSH SYMONS
CRITICAL EDGY HIGH NICE ACERB
ACUTE VITAL CHILLY CRITIC NASUTE
SEVERE URGENT ACERBIC ADVERSE
CARPING EXIGENT NERVOUS
PARLOUS CAPTIOUS CARDINAL
CAVILING DECISIVE EXACTING
JUDICIAL PRESSING SLASHING
TICKLISH CLIMACTERIC
CRITICISM DIG RAP FIRE FLAK GAFF
SLAM BLAME KNOCK SLATE ATTACK
CRITIC REVIEW STATIC CENSURE
COMMENT DESCANT LITCRIT
PANNING QUIBBLE SLASHER
SLATING ZOILISM BLUDGEON
CRITIQUE DIATRIBE JUDGMENT
STRICTURE
(PETTY —) NITPICKING
(POINTED —) JAB
(UNJUSTIFIED —) NITPICKING
CRITICIZE HIT PAN RAP RIP CARP
CRAB FLAY FLOG RIDE SKIN SLAM
SLUR TIDE YELP BLAME BLAST CAVIL
DECRY GRIPE JUDGE KNOCK ROAST
SCORE SLASH SLATE TRASH BERATE
CRITIC REBUKE REVIEW CENSURE
COMMENT CONDEMN CRITIZE
EXAMINE NITPICK SCARIFY
BADMOUTH CRITIQUE DENOUNCE
TOMAHAWK
(— MINUTELY) NITPICK

(— SEVERELY) FLAY JUMP
(— SLASHINGLY) SLASH SLATE
CRITIQUE CRITIC REVIEW CRITICISM
CRIUS (FATHER OF —) URANUS
(MOTHER OF —) GAEA
(SON OF —) PALLAS PERSES
ASTRAEUS
CRO CROY PAYMENT
CROAK CAW DIE GASP KILL PORK
ROUP CRAKE CREAK CRONK PLUNK
QUALM QUARK SPEAK CROAPE
GRUMBLE COMPLAIN FOREBODE
CROAKER SPOT RONCO CROCUS
RONCHO TOMCOD BUBBLER
CABEZON CORBINA CORVINA
CABEZONE HARDHEAD KINGFISH
SCIAENID
CROAKING CROAKY HOARSE
RANARIAN COAXATION
CROAT CHORWAT CHROBAT
SYRMIAN
(PL.) HRVATI HERVATI
CROATIA (ALSO SEE YUGOSLAVIA)
CAPITAL: ZAGREB
COIN: DINAR
GULF: KOTOR
LANGUAGE: CROATIAN
SERBOCROATIAN
MOUNTAIN: TROGLAV
MOUNTAIN RANGE: DINARIC ZAGORJE
PENINSULA: ISTRIAN
PLAIN: PANNONIAN PARAPANNONIAN
REGION: ISTRIA DALMATIA
RIVER: UNA KRKA KUPA SAVA DRAVA
CETINA
SEA: ADRIATIC
TOWN: SPLIT OSIJEK RIJEKA
WIND: BORA BURA JUGO MISTRAL
CROCARD BRABANT SCALDING
SLEEPING
CROCHET HOOK KNIT BRAID PLAIT
WEAVE CROTCHET
CROCK JAR PIG POT SMUT SOIL
SOOT STEAN STEEN STOOL CHATTY
CRITCH GOOLAH PANMUG SMUDGE
CRAGGAN TERRINE POTSHERD
CROCKERY CHINA CLOAM DISHES
PIGGERY POTWARE CLAYWARE
CROCODILE GOA CROC GATOR
MAGAR CAYMAN GAVIAL JACARE
LIZARD MUGGER YACARE CRAWLER
CREEPER DIAPSID REPTILE SAURIAN
SERPENT LORICATE
CROCODILE BIRD SICSAC TROCHIL
MESSMATE
CROCUS IRID LILY SAFFRON
COLCHICUM
CROFT FARM TORP CRAFT CRYPT
FIELD GARTH VAULT BLEACH CAVERN
PARROCK PIGHTLE
CROMLECH QUOIT CIRCLE DOLMEN
CROMMEL GORSEDD

CROMORNA CREMONA KRUMHORN

CRONE HAG AUNT TROT CRONY
WITCH BELDAM RIBIBE BELDAME

CRONOS
(DAUGHTER OF —) HERA

CRONY PAL CHUM BILLY GOSSY
NETOP GIMMER GOSSIP

CROOK BEND HOOK TURN WARP
CHEAT CHINK CLEEK CRANK CROMB
CROOM CRUMP CURVE GANEF
HUNCH NIBBY PEDUM STAFF THIEF
TRICK CRUMMY INDENT TWICER
CAMBUCA CROSIER CROZIER
CRUMMIE INCURVE POTHOOK
SLICKER ARTIFICE CHISELER
CRUMMOCK SWINDLER
(— A FINGER AT) BECKON
(— IN BRANCH) KNEE
(— OF HEAD) HEEL
(SHEPHERD'S   ) CROTCH KEBBIE

CROOKBACKED CROUCHIE

CROOKED CAM WRY AGEE ALOP
AWRY BENT GAME WOGH AGLEY
ASKEW BANDY BOWLY CRANK
CRUMP FALSE GLEED KINKY SNIDE
THRAW TIPSY WRONG ACROOK
AKIMBO ARTFUL ASLANT CAMMED
CAMSHO CRABBY CRAFTY CRANKY
CURVED DOGLEG HURLED THRAWN
TRICKY WEEWAW WEEWOW ZIGZAG
ASKANCE ASQUINT CORRUPT
CRABBED CURVOUS OBLIQUE
TURNING TWISTED WINDING
CAMSHACH THRAWART TORTUOUS
(PREF.) ANKYL(O) CROM

CROOKEDNESS PRAVITY RHEBOSIS

CROOKNECK CASHAW CUSHAW

CROON HUM LOW BOOM LULL SING
WAIL CHIRM CRONY WHINE LAMENT
MURMUR TEEDLE COMPLAIN

CROP BOB COW CUT LOP MAW SET
TOP CLIP CRAP CRAW KNAP MINE
REAP SETT SNIP STOW TRAP TRIM
WHIP FRUIT GRAZE PLANT QUIRT
SHAVE SHEAR SHIFT SWATH TILTH
TRASH BROWSE BURDEN DECERP
GATHER GEBBIE SILAGE BEARING
BURTHEN CRAPPIN CURTAIL
CUTTING HARVEST MAMMONI
MASHLUM TILLAGE GLEANING
PROFICHI TRASHIFY INGLUVIES
(— CANDLEWICK) SNUFF
(— OF A HAWK) GORGE
(— OF BIRDS) INGLUVIES
(— OF FRUIT) HANG
(— OF GRASS) LEA LEY SWATH
SWARTH SWATHE
(— OF OYSTERS) SET
(— OF POTATOES) GARDEN
(— OUT) BASSET
(— UP) EMERGE
(GREEN —S) SOILAGE

(INDIAN —) RABI KHARIF
(LARGE —) HIT
(RIDING —) ROP
(SECOND-GROWTH —) ROWEN
AFTERMATH
(PL.) FEED TILLAGE

CROPPED GOTCH SHAVED GOTCHED

CROPPER CARVER MUCKER PURLER
GRINDER PLUMPER

CROPPING EARMARK

CROQUET ROQUE BOMBARD

CROQUETTE CECIL OYSTER
KROMESKI KROMESKY

CROSIER BAGLE CROCE CROOK
PEDUM STAFF POTENT BACULUS
CAMBUCA CROZIER PASTORAL

CROSS GO CAM CUT MIX TAU ANKH
CRUX FORD FUNK MARK PASS ROOD
SIGN SOUR SPAN TREE WOOD
ANGRY CANGY CHUFF CORSE
GAMMY GURLY IRATE SURLY TEATY
TESTY THRAW TRAVE TRIAL YAPPY
BISECT CHUFFY CRABBY CRANKY
CROUCH DENIAL EMBLEM FRANZY
GIBBET GROUTY GRUMPY HIPPED
OUTWIT PATCHY SIGNUM SNAGGY
SNASTY SNUFFY SULLEN SYMBOL
TEETHY THWART TOUCHY WICKED
WOOLLY ATHWART BECROSS
CALVARY CRABBED CROSIER
CROZIER CRUSADE CRUSADO
FRABOUS FRETFUL FROWARD
OBLIQUE PASSAGE PATIBLE PEEVISH
PETTISH POTENCE SALTIER SALTIRE
CAMSHACH CRANTARA CROCIATE
CROISADE CROSSLET CROTCHED
CRUCIFIX DEBRUISE DEMISANG
FRAMPOLD FRATCHED FRUMPISH
OVERPASS PECTORAL PETULANT
PHRAMPEL SNAPPISH SWASTIKA
THUNDERY TRAVERSE VEXILLUM
WINDMILL
(— BETWEEN GRAPEFRUIT AND
TANGERINE) UGLI
(— BY PLANE) HOP
(— ONESELF) SAIN
(— OVER) SPAN TRAJECT
(DOUBLE —) BUSINESS
(KIND OF —) TAU
(MALTESE —) FIREBALL
(PREF.) CRUCI STAUR(O)

CROSSARM WISHBONE

CROSSBAR RUNG CROWN JUGUM
DRIVER TRANSOM
(— IN GATE) SWORD
(— IN SHAFT) STEMPEL STEMPLE
(— OF BALANCE) BEAM
(— OF DOOR) SLOAT
(— OF WINDOW) LOCKET

CROSSBEAM BAR BUNK SPUR
TRAVE GIRDER BOLSTER DORMANT
TRANSOM TRAVERSE

CROSSBEARER CRUCIFER
SPREADER
CROSSBILL FINCH
CROSSBOW PROD RODD BRAKE
LATCH PIECE PRODD TILLER
SLURBOW ARBALEST BALISTER
BALLISTA STEELBOW STOCKBOW
STONEBOW
(PART OF —) NUT IRON LOCK GUARD
SIGHT STOCK WEDGE GROOVE
STIRRUP TRIGGER BOWSTRING
CROSSBREED CUR HUSKY METIS
SANGA SANGU HYBRID
CROSS CARRIER CRUCIFER
CROSSCURRENT EDDY SURGING
CROSSCUT DRIFT OFFSET TUNNEL
COUPURE
CROSSCUT SAW BRIAR
CROSSCUTTER BUCKER
CROSSE STICK
CROSSED ACROSS SQUINT WOOFED
CRUCIAL THWARTING
(PREF.) CHIASTO
CROSSER STICKER
CROSSETTE EAR ANCON ELBOW
ANCONE CROSET
CROSS-EXAMINE GRILL TARGE
CROSSEXAMINE TARGE
CROSS-EYE ESOTROPIA
CROSS-EYED SQUINT
CROSS-FERTILIZATION
ALLOGAMY PHYTOGAMY
CROSS FORM URDE URDY
CROSS-GRAINED THWART UGLY
NURLY GNARLED HICKORY
CONTRARY FRAMPOLD
CROSSHEAD YOKE
CROSSING XG PASS CROSS LACED
MIXTURE PASSAGE TRAJECT
CRUCIATE OPPOSING OVERPASS
TRAVERSE CROSSOVER
(KIND OF —) ZEBRA
(NAVE —) TRANSEPT
CROSSLIKE CRUCIAL
CROSS-LINE
(— OF LETTER) SERIF
CROSSPATCH BEAR CRAB CRANK
GROUCH
CROSSPIECE BAR BAIL SPAR STEP
YOKE BEARD GLAND GRILL ROUND
STOCK PUTLOG THWART TOGGEL
TOGGLE BOLSTER TRANSOM
CROSSARM CROWFOOT FOOTRAIL
HEADRAIL TRAVERSE CHOPSTICK
(PL.) CROSSTREE
CROSS-QUESTION GRILL TARGE
TAIRGE
CROSSROAD LEET VENT WENT
WEENT CAREFOX CARFOUR
COMPITUM CROSSWAY
(PL.) TRIVIA
CROSSRUFF SAW SEESAW

CROSS-SHAPED CRUCIAL
CRUCIATE
CROSS-STAFF CROSS RADIUS
CROSIER CROZIER ARBALEST
CROSS STROKE BIND
CROSS-TEMPERED FRUMPISH
CROSSWALK ZEBRA
CROSSWISE CROSS ACROSS
ATHWART ACROSTIC DIAGONAL
OVERWART TRAVERSE WEFTWISE
CROSSWAYS
CROSSWORD (— PUZZLER)
CRUCIVERBALIST
CROSSWORT MAYWORT MUGWEED
MUGWORT
CROTALUM CROTAL CYMBAL
CROTCH FORK POLE POST CLEFT
NOTCH STAKE CRATCH CRUTCH
GRAINS CROTCHET
CROTCHET FAD TOY HOOK KINK
WHIM CRANK FANCY FREAK FIZGIG
MAGGOT VAGARY CORCHAT
CRANKUM
(HALF —) QUAVER
CROTCHETY KINKY CRANKY
SNARKY
CROUCH HUG BEND CLAP COOK
CURB DARE DROP FAWN FORM ROOK
RUCK COWER HOVER SQUAT STOOP
COORIE CRINGE CROOCH HUDDLE
HUNKER HURKLE HURTLE SCOOCH
SCOUCH CROODLE CROWDLE
SCROOCH SCRUNCH SQUATTER
CROUCHING SQUAT CROUCHANT
CROUD SCROUGE
CROUP CRUP HIVES CRUPPER
CROUPIER DEALER TOURNEUR
CROUTON DIABLOTIN
CROW AGA CAW CRY DAW BRAG
BRAN CRAW DOWP ROOK AYLET
BOAST CRAKE CROWD EXULT GLOAT
HOODY KELLY RAVEN VAUNT
CARNAL CHOUGH CORBIE CORVUS
HOODIE KOKAKO GORCROW
GRAPNEL JACKDAW SWAGGER
ABSAROKA BALDHEAD BLACKNEB
GAVELOCK GRAYBACK GREYBACK
(PREF.) CORACO CORVI
(SUFF.) CORAX
CROWBAR PRY SET CROW BETTY
JEMMY JIMMY LEVER SETUP SWAPE
FORCER GABLOCK PITCHER
GAVELOCK HANDSPEC
CROWBERRY HEATH HEATHER
CROWD FRY HUG JAM MOB SET TAG
TIP BIKE CRAM CRUT FARE GANG
HEAP HERD HOST JOSS MONG PACK
PAVE PILE PUSH RAFT ROCK ROTE
ROUT RUCK SERR SKIT SLUE SORT
STOW SWAD TURB WOOD BUNCH
CLOUD COHUE COVEY CRAMP
CRUSH CRWTH DROVE FLOCK

GROUP HORDE HURRY PLUMP POSSE PRESS ROTTA SERRY SHACK SHOAL STECH STIVE STUFF SWARM THREE VOLGE WEDGE BOODLE CHORUS CLIQUE HUBBLE HUDDLE HUSTLE IMPACT JOSTLE MITHER MOIDER OUTFIT PESTER RABBLE RESORT SCRUZE THRAVE THREAD THRIMP THRONG THRUST TOURBE TYMPAN VOLLEY BOUROCK CHROTTA CLUSTER COMPANY CONGEST IMPRESS JIMBANG SCROOGE SCROUGE SQUEEZE THICKEN THRUTCH CABOODLE ENTHRONG FREQUENT JINGBANG SANDWICH SATURATE VARLETRY CONCOURSE GATHERING MULTITUDE CLAMJAMFRY
(— ABOUT) FLOCK
(— AROUND) MOB BESIEGE
(— OUT) DISPLACE
(— TOGETHER) HUG HOTTER HOWDER HUDDLE CLUTTER CONTRUDE
(CONFUSED —) HURRY
(MOVING —) DROVE
(NOISY —) ROUT
(PREF.) OCHLO
CROWDED PANG CLOSE DENSE SPISS STIFF THICK FILLED SPISSY THRONG BUNCHED COMPACT OPPLETE POPULAR SERRIED STIPATE STUFFED TEEMING NUMEROUS POPULOUS JAMPACKED
CROWFOOT JOY PAGLE CREATE EXOGEN PAIGLE EELWARE GOLDCUP GOLLAND GOWLAND BANEWORT CRAWFOOT GOLDWEED HELLWEED
CROWING COCK
CROWN CAP TAJ TIP TOP BULL COIN GULL HELM PALE PATE PEAK POLL RIGO TIAR ADORN BASIL BEZEL BEZIL CREST MITER MITRE MURAL POLOS REGAL ROUND ROYAL TIARA ANADEM CANTLE CIRCLE CLIMAX CORONA DIADEM DOLLAR FILLET INVEST LAUREL POTONG REWARD SUMMIT TIMBER TROPHY UPWARD VALLAR VERTEX WREATH AUREOLE CHAPLET CORNICE CORONAL CORONET FORETOP GARLAND INSTALL PSCHENT STEPHEN TONSURE CORONALE CORONULE ENTHRONE PINNACLE SURMOUNT TURNPIKE
(— OF CHICORY) ENDIVE
(— OF EGYPT) ATEF PSCHENT
(— OF HEAD) NOLL PATE SKULL CANTLE POMMEL FORETOP
(— OF HILL) KNAP
(— OF LAUREL) BAY
(— OF ROCK) KRANTZ

(HALF —) GEORGE ALDERMAN
(PIECE OF —) BULL
(PLANT —) STOOL
(PREF.) CORONI CORONO STEPHAN(O)
CROWNED CORONATE LAURELED
(— WITH ROSES) ROSATED
CROW SHRIKE MAGPIE SQUEAKER
CROW'S NEST LOOKOUT
CROZER CHUCKER
CRUCIAL KEY ACUTE PIVOT NEEDLE SEVERE TRYING PIVOTAL SUPREME TELLING CRITICAL DECISIVE
CRUCIAN CARP GIBEL
CRUCIBLE POT DISH ETNA SHOE TEST CRUCE FOYER TRIAL CRUSET HEARTH MONKEY RETORT FURNACE CROSSLET
CRUCIFIX PAX ROOD CROSS
CRUCIFIXION RANSOM
CRUCIFY VEX HANG KILL HARRY MORTIFY TORMENT TORTURE CRUCIATE
CRUDE ILL RAW BALD BARE RUDE BRUTE CRASS GREEN GROSS HAIRY HARSH ROUGH TACKY CALLOW COARSE DOUGHY INCULT KUTCHA SAVAGE UNRIPE VULGAR ARTLESS GLARING SQUALID UNCOUTH AGRESTIC IGNORANT IMMATURE IMPOLITE INDIGEST PRIMITIVE
(NOT —) DELICATE
CRUDELY HARSHLY GAUCHELY
CRUDITY RUDENESS BARBARITY CRASSNESS GAUCHERIE ROUGHNESS
CRUEL ILL FELL GRIL GRIM HARD BLACK BREEM BREME BRUTE FELON HARSH RETHE SADIC STERN WROTH BITTER BLOODY BRUTAL DIVERS DREARY FIERCE IMMANE SAVAGE SEVERE UNJUST UNKIND UNMEEK UNMILD UNRIDE WANTON WICKED BESTIAL BOARISH BRUTISH GRIMFUL INHUMAN NERONIC SCADDLE SPITOUS WILROUN BARBARIC DIABOLIC FELONOUS FIENDISH INHUMANE PITILESS RUTHLESS SADISTIC TYRANNIC TRUCULENT
(THOUGHTLESSLY —) WANTON
CRUELLY FELL HARD CRUEL FELLY HARSHLY
CRUELTY RIGOR DURESS SADISM DEVILRY DEVILTRY FELLNESS SEVERITY
CRUET AMA JAR JUG VIAL BURET CRUSE BOTTLE CASTER CREVET CREWET GUTTUS AMPULLA BURETTE URCEOLE
CRUISE SAIL TRIP JUNKET STOOGE
(— AS A PIRATE) BUSK
CRUISER SHIP VALUER VESSEL WARSHIP ESTIMATOR

CRUISING ASEA
CRULLER WONDER OLYCOOK
OLYKOEK TWISTER DOUGHNUT
CRUMB BIT ORT MURL NIRL PIECE
LITTLE MORSEL CRIMBLE CRUMBLE
MEALOCK MURLACK REMNANT
FRAGMENT
(PL.) PANADA PANURE MOOLINGS
CRUMBLE ROT CRIM MULL MURL
MUSH BREAK BROCK CRUSH DECAY
RAVEL SLAKE SPALL SPOIL BUCKLE
MOLDER MYRTLE PERISH SLOUGH
CORRADE CRIMBLE MOULDER
COLLAPSE
(— DOWN) GRUSH
(— UNDER OVERWEIGHT) FLUSH
CRUMBLED UNDURE
(EASILY —) CRIMP BRUCKLE
CRUMBLY
CRUMBLING SAMEL SAMMEL
POWDERY
CRUMBLY NESH MURLY CRUMBY
CRUMMY FRIABLE PULVERULENT
CRUMPET CAKE MUFFIN PIKELET
CRUMPLE FOLD MOOL MUSS ROOL
WISP CRUSH SCREW BUCKLE
CREASE FURROW RAFFLE RUCKLE
RUMPLE CRIZZLE CRUNKLE FRUMPLE
SCRUNCH WRINKLE COLLAPSE
CONTRACT SCRUMPLE
CRUNCH BITE CHEW MUCH CHOMP
CRASH CRUMP CRUSH GNASH
GRIND PRESS RUNCH CRANCH
CRINCH GRANCH GROWSE CRAUNCH
SCRANCH SCRUNCH
CRUPPER CROUP CURPEL CURPIN
TAILBAND
CRUSADE WAR JEHAD JIHAD
CROISEE CAMPAIGN CROCIATE
CRUSADER PILGRIM TEMPLAR
EQUITIST REFORMER
(PL.) CROISES
CRUSADER IN EGYPT
(CHARACTER IN —) ADRIANO
ALADINO ARMANDO PALMIDE
DORVILLE ELMIRENO
(COMPOSER OF —) MEYERBEER
CRUSH BOW HUG JAM BEND BORE
BRAY CASE CHEW CRAM DASH
MASH MILL MULL PASH RAVE STUB
BRAKE BREAK BRIZZ CHAMP CHECK
CRASH CRAZE CREEM CROWD FORCE
FRUSH GRIND GRUSH PRESS QUASH
QUELL SMASH SMUSH SQUAB
SQUAT STAMP TREAD UNMAN
BRUISE BURDEN CRUNCH DEFOIL
DEFOUL KNATCH KNETCH SCOTCH
SCRUSH SCRUZE SQUASH SQUISS
SUBDUE THRING THRONG THWACK
ACCABLE BECRUSH CONQUER
CONTUSE CRACKLE CRUMPLE
DEPRESS DESTROY OPPRESS
OVERRUN REPRESS SCRUNCH

SCRUNGE SHATTER SQUEEZE
SQUELCH SUCCUMB TRAMPLE
COMPRESS FORBREAK OVERCOME
SQUABASH SUPPRESS OVERWHELM
(— BEANS) NIB
(— HAT) BONNET
(— IN) STAVE
(— ROCK) DOLLY DOLLEY DOLLIE
(— SPIRIT) BREAK
CRUSHABLE QUASHY
CRUSHED TAME BROKEN ECRASE
MUSHED CONTRITE CRUMPLED
CRUSHER NIBBER
CRUSHING FIERCE BRUISING
SMASHING SQUABASH
(SUFF.) TRIPSY
CRUST FUR PIP CAKE HULL RIND
SCAB SHELL SKULL COFFIN CRUSTA
ESCHAR GRATIN HARDEN RONDLE
SCRUFF ABAISSE CALICHE COATING
ENCRUST INCRUST CARAPACE
PELLICLE SCUTULUM WINEBALL
DURICRUST
(— IN BOILER) FUR
(— OF DIKE) SALBAND
(— OF DYKE) SALBAND
(— OF EARTH) SIAL SIMA
(— ON WINE) ARGAL ARGOL
(PIE —) HUFF COFFIN
(PL.) SORDES
CRUSTA PES
CRUSTACEAN BUG APUS CRAB
FLEA SCUD ZOEA ALIMA CARID KRILL
LOUSE PRAWN SCREW SCROW
CYPRID ENDITE ISOPOD SHRIMP
SLATER SQUILL ARTEMIA COPEPOD
CRAYLET DAPHNID DECAPOD
GRIBBLE HAYSEED LOBSTER
SQUAGGA SQUILLA AMPHIPOD
BARNACLE CIRRIPED CRAYFISH
GAMMARID LERNAEAN MONOCULE
OSTRACOD PAGURIAN SQUILLID
BRACHYURA PHYLLOPOD
SCHIZOPOD SHELLFISH
MALACOSTRACAN RHIZOCEPHALAN
(FEMALE —) HEN
CRUSTADE DARIOLE
CRUSTY CURT BLUFF BLUNT RUSTY
TESTY MOROSE SULLEN CRABBED
PEEVISH PETTISH STARCHY
SNAPPISH
CRUTCH FORK STILT CLUTCH
CRATCH CROTCH POTENT SADDLE
SCATCH STADDLE
CRUX NUB GIST HALF PITH CROSS
POINT PUZZLE RIDDLE PROBLEM
CRUX ANSATA ANKH
CRWTH ROTA ROTE CROWD CRUTH
ROTTA ROTTE CROUTH CHROTTA
CRY HO AHA BOO CAW CRI FAD HOA
HUE OLE PIP SOB YIP BAWL BELL
BUMP CALL COWL CROW EVOE FALL
GLAM GOWL HAIL HAWK HOOT

HOWL KEEN MEWL NOTE OYES OYEZ
PULE RAGE RAME RANE REEM RERD
ROOP SCRY SIKE TOOT WAIL WEEP
YELL YELP YOWL BARLA BLART
BLORE CHEVY CLEPE CRAKE CROUP
CRUNK GREDE GREET GROAN QUEAK
RUMOR SHOUT SOUND TROAT
UTTER VOGUE WHEWL WHINE
WHULE WRAWL BARLEY BELLOW
BOOHOO CHIVVY CLAMOR DEMAND
ENSIGN LAMENT OUTCRY QUETHE
SCREAM SHRIEK SLOGAN SNIVEL
SQUAIL SQUAWL SQUEAL TONGUE
WIMICK YAMMER EXCLAIM FASHION
HOSHANA SCREECH SPRAICH
GARDYLOO PROCLAIM SCRONACH
(— ALOUD) BLART GREDE
(— AT SIGHT OF WHALE) FALL
(— DOWN) DOWNCRY BERATTLE
(— FOR TRUCE) BARLA BARLY
BARLEY
(— HOARSELY) CROUP
(— LIKE ELEPHANT) BARR TRUMPET
(— LIKE PIG) WRINE
(— MOURNFULLY) YOWL
(— OF A BAT) CHIP
(— OF ABORIGINES) COOEE
(— OF BACCHANALS) EVOE
(— OF BIRD) CAW COO PEW BOOM
CAWK CLANG BIRDCALL
(— OF BITTERN) BILL
(— OF CAT) MEW MEWL MIAOU
MIAOW MIAUL MIAUW CALLING
(— OF CONTEMPT) BOO
(— OF DEER) BELL
(— OF DELIGHT) WHEF YIPES
(— OF DISCOVERY) EUREKA
(— OF DISGUST) PAH
(— OF ENTHUSIASM) BANZAI
(— OF GOOSE) HONK YANG
(— OF GUINEA HEN) POTRACK
(— OF HORROR) ACK
(— OF HOUND) MUTE MUSIC
(— OF JACKAL) PHEAL PHEALE
PHEEAL
(— OF MOURNING) KEEN TANGI
(— OF NEWBORN CHILD) VAGITUS
(— OF RAVEN) QUALM
(— OF SHEEP) BAA BLAT BLEAT
(— OF SNIPE) SCAPE
(— OF SORROW) ULLAGONE
(— OF SURPRISE) ACK
(— OF SURRENDER) KAMERAD
(— OF WATCHMAN) WATCH
(— OUT) BAY BAWL BRAY GALE GAPE
HOOT HOWL JERK SCRY BLORE
CHIRM CLAIM ESCRY SHOUT HALLOO
HOLLER SCREAM SHRIEK THREAP
THROPE BREATHE EXCLAIM RECLAIM
DISCLAIM PROCLAIM
(— TO CLEAR PASSAGE) HALL
(— TO COMBATANTS) BAILE
(— UP) CRACK

(BATTLE —) CRY ENSIGN MONTJOY
GERONIMO MONTJOYE
(DERISIVE —) BOO FIE POOF POOH
HUMBUG
(DISMAL —) HOWL WAIL YOWL
(DRINKING —) RIVO
(HOARSE —) CROAK
(HUNTING —) TIVY CHEVY CHIVY
CHEVVY STABOY YOICKS TALLYHO
TANTARA TANTIVY PILILLOO
(KIND OF —) FAR
(MAGICIAN'S —) PRESTO
(PROLONGED —) RANE
(RALLYING —) SLOGAN
(RAUCOUS —) CATCALL
(SHRILL) SKIRL SQUEAK SQUEAL
SCREECH YALLOCK
(WAR —) DIN ALALA HAVOC BANZAI
SLOGAN
(WORDLESS —) KEEN ULULU
CRY-BABY MARDY
CRYING PIPING URGING CLAMANT
HEINOUS VAGIENT PRESSING
REGNEANT
(— OF HOUND) BELLING
CRYPT PIT CRAFT CROFT CROWD
VAULT CAVERN GROTTO RECESS
SHROUD CHAMBER FOLLICLE
CRYPTIC DARK VAGUE HIDDEN
OCCULT SECRET OBSCURE ELLIPTIC
MYSTICAL SIBYLLIC
CRYPTOGAM ACROGEN
CRYPTOGAMOUS AGAMIC
AGAMOUS
CRYPTOGRAM CODE CRYPT CIPHER
CRYPTOGRAPH GEMATRIA
CRYPTOGRAPHER VIGENERE
CRYPTORCHID RIDGLING
CRYSTAL XL ICE DIAL DOME HARD
IRIS SEED XTAL CLEAR CRANK
GLASS GRAIN LUCID LUNET NICOL
TABLE GLASSY LIMPID MIRROR
NEEDLE PEBBLE QUARTZ TABLET
ACICULA DIAMOND DIPLOID GLASSIE
LUNETTE ORTHITE SPICULE
TWOLING ULEXITE YAJEINE ZOISITE
FIVELING FOURLING PELLUCID
TRICHITE TRILLING PERIMORPH
PHENOCRYST
(— FOREIGN TO ROCK) XENOCRYST
(— OF GREAT STRENGTH) WHISKER
(FINE —) BERYL
(ICE —S IN WATER) FRAZIL
(NEEDLE-SHAPED —S) RAPHIDES
(ROCK —) BRISTOL CITRINE
(TWIN —) TWIN MACLE TWINDLE
TWOLING FOURLING
(PL.) DRUSE GRAIN
(PREF.) CHRYSTO
(SUFF.) BLAST(IC)(Y) HEDRON
CRYSTAL GAZE SCRY
CRYSTAL GAZER SEER SCRYER
SKRYER

CRYSTALLINE PURE CRYSTAL PELLUCID
CRYSTALLITE BELONITE TRICHITE BACILLITE SCOPULITE
CRYSTALLIZE FIX FIRM JELL CANDY SUGAR NEEDLE CONGEAL SOLIDIFY
CRYSTALLOGRAPHY LEPTOLOGY
C-SHAPED SIGMATE
CTENIDIUM COMB
CTENOPHORE RIB NUDA CESTOID CYDIPPID JELLYFISH
CUADRA MANZANA
CUB FRY PEN BEAR CHIT COOP SHED TOTO STALL WHELP LIONET NOVICE CODLING REPORTER
(— SCOUT) WEBELOS

CUBA
BAY: NIPE PIGS
CAPE: CRUZ MAISI LUCRECIA
CAPITAL: HAVANA
CIGAR: HAVANA
COIN: PESO CENTAVO CUARENTA
DANCE: CONGA RUMBA DANZON RHUMBA GUARACHA PACHANGA
FALLS: TOA AGABAMA CABURNI
GULF: MEXICO ANAMARIA BATABANO
INDIAN: CARIB TAINO ARAWAK
ISLAND: PINES
ISLANDS: SABANA CAMAGUEY
MEASURE: VARA BOCOY TAREA CORDEL FANEGA
MOUNTAIN: TURQUINO
MOUNTAINS: CRISTAL MAESTRA ORGANOS TRINIDAD
PROVINCE: HAVANA ORIENTE CAMAGUEY MATANZAS
RIVER: ZAZA CAUTO
SWAMP: ZAPATA
TOWN: COLON MANES ALAMAR BAYAMO GUINES HAVANA BARACOA HOLGUIN PALMIRA ARTEMISA CAMAGUEY GUAYABAL MATANZAS SANTIAGO
TREE: JIQUE JIQUI
WEIGHT: LIBRA TERCIO

CUBAN LILY SCILLA
CUBBYHOLE CELL NOOK CUBBY
CUBE CUT DIE NOB KNOB BLOCK EIGHT SOLID TIMBO BABASCO CUBELET TESSERA BARBASCO QUADRATE TESSALLA
(— OF BREAD) CROUTON
(— OF COLORED GLASS) SMALTO
(— WITH 21 SPOTS) DIE
(MEAT —S) CABOB KABOB KEBOB
(PUZZLE —) RUBIC
(PL.) DICE
CUBIC SOLID CUBOID CUBICAL
CUBICALLY DIEWISE
CUBIC CENTIMETER FLUIGRAM

CUBICLE BAY CELL ROOM BOOTH CABIN NICHE STALL ALCOVE CARREL CARRELL
CUBIC METER STERE
CUBIT ELL CODO HATH COVID HASTA COUDEE
CUBITUS ULNA
CUB SHARK LAMIA GALEID REQUIEM
CUCKING STOOL THEW TUMBLER TUMBREL TUMBRIL
CUCKOLD TUP HORN BECCO VULCAN WITTOL ACTAEON CORNUTE CORNUTO HORNIFY RAMHEAD COKEWOLD
CUCKOLDED FORKED UNICORN
CUCKOLDISE GRAFT
CUCKOLD-MAKING HORNING
CUCKOLDRY HORNWORK
CUCKOO ANI GAG COWK CUCK FOOL GOUK GOWK KOEL KOIL CLOCK CRAZY KOKIL SILLY COUCAL DIDRIC HUNTER KOBIRD BOOBOOK CHATAKA DIEDRIC KOWBIRD SIRKEER CHOWCHOW PICARIAN RAINBIRD RAINFOWL
(PREF.) CUCULI
CUCKOOFLOWER HEAD PAGLE SPINK CUCKOO PAIGLE HEADACHE MILKMAID
CUCKOOPINT ARUM RAMP AARON AROID BOBBIN DRAGON BUCKRAM OXBERRY MANDRAKE
CUCKOO SPIT WOODSERE
CUCULLATE COWLED HOODED COVERED
CUCUMBER CUKE PEPO GOURD CONGER CUCURB PEPINO PICKLE GHERKIN PICKLER CUCURBIT PEPONIDA PEPONIUM
(BITTER —) COLOCYNTH
(SHRIVELED —) CRUMPLING
(WILD —) SICYOS CREEPER
(PREF.) CUCUMI
CUCURBIT BODY FLASK GOURD CUCURB ALEMBIC MATRASS
CUD CHEW QUID BOLUS QUEED RUMEN CUDGEL
CUDBEAR CORK PERSIO PERSIS CUDWEED
CUD-CHEWING RUMINANT
CUDDLE HUG LAP PET CARESS COSSET FONDLE HUGGLE KIDDLE KIUTLE NESTLE PETTLE CROODLE CRUDDLE EMBRACE SMUGGLE SNOOZLE SNUGGLE CANOODLE
CUDDLESOME HUGGABLE
CUDDY ASS LOUT BRIBE CABIN DONKEY GALLEY PANTRY CUDEIGH
(BELOVED OF —) BUXOMA
CUDGEL BAT CUD BEAT CANE CLUB CRAB DRUB KENT MACE RACK RUNG TREE BASTE BATON BILLY DRIVE

KEBBY KEVEL LINCH LINGE SHRUB
STAFF STAVE STICK THUMP TOWEL
ALPEEN BALLOW BASTON BILLET
GIBBET KEBBIE LIBBET THRASH
WASTER BELABOR BOURDON
DRUBBER SWADDLE SWINGLE
TROUNCE BLUDGEON SHILLALA
THWACKER SHILLALAGH

CUDWEED ENAENA CATFOOT

CUE QU NOD TAG TIP HINT MAST TAIL
WINK BRAID CLUFF PLAIT QUEUE
TWIST PROMPT SIGNAL PIGTAIL
(BILLIARD —) MACE MAST STICK
(MUSICAL —) PRESA
(PART OF —) TIP BUTT HILT JOINT
POINT SHAFT BUMPER FERRULE
(SHUFFLEBOARD —) SHOVEL
(TIP OF —) LEATHER

CUFF BOX BANK BLOW GOWF SLAM
SLAP SLUG SWAT TURF CLOUT
FIGHT GOWFF MISER SCUFF SCUFT
SMITE SOUSE BUFFET CODGER
FENDER MITTEN STRIKE TURNUP
COLPHEG SCUFFLE WHERRET
GAUNTLET HANDBLOW HANDCUFF
TURNBACK

CUIR DORADO

CUIRASS CURACE CURATE CURIET
LORICA THORAX

CUIRASSIER LOBSTER

CUISINE FOOD MENU TABLE
COOKERY KITCHEN
(KIND OF —) HAUTE
(SOUTHERN —) CAJUN CREOLE

CUITLATEC TECO

CUL-DE-SAC POCKET STRAIT
IMPASSE

CULL OPT CAST COIL DUPE GULL
PICK PIKE SIFT SORT ELECT GLEAN
PLUCK ASSORT CHOOSE GARBLE
GATHER REMOVE SELECT CULLING
SEPARATE

CULLET SCRAP

CULLODEN MOOR

CULM COOM HAULM SLACK COOMBE
REFUSE DEPOSIT
(PL.) SIRKI SIRKY

CULMINATE CLIMAX

CULMINATION END ACME APEX
AUGE CULM NOON ROOF BLOOM
CREST CROWN HIGHT POINT APOGEE
CLIMAX CULMEN CUMBLE HEIGHT
PAYOFF PERIOD SUMMIT VERTEX
ZENITH BLOWOFF

CULOTTE PANTDRESS

CULOTTES GAUCHOS

CULPABILITY BLAME FAULT GUILT
DEMERIT

CULPABLE FAULTY GUILTY LACHES
SINFUL IMMORAL TOBLAME
BLAMABLE CRIMINAL

CULPRIT FELON CONVICT CRIMINAL
OFFENDER

CULT CLAN DADA SECT CREED
KUKSU CHURCH CULTUS DOMNEI
MANISM NUDISM RITUAL SCHOOL
SHINTO AMIDISM DADAISM ICONISM
MYALISM MYSTERY WORSHIP
DEVILISM HUMANISM SATANISM
(— OF MALE VIRILITY) MACHISMO
(ADHERENT OF RELIGIOUS —) RASTA
RASTAMAN
(SUFF.) ISM

CULTCH CUTCH STOOL SCULCH

CULTIVATE EAR HOE CROP DISC
DISK FARM GROW PLOW REAR TEND
TILL WORK DRESS EARTH LABOR
NURSE RAISE STUDY TRAIN AFFECT
FOSTER FURROW HARROW MANAGE
MANURE PLOUGH RATOON SARCLE
SCHOOL ACQUIRE CHERISH
CONTOUR CULTURE EDUCATE
EMBRACE EXPLOIT HUSBAND
IMPROVE NOURISH PREPARE
SCRATCH CIVILIZE
(— FAVOR) BOOTLICK

CULTIVATED ABAD TAME CIVIL
GROWN POLITE SATIVE TOILED
POLITIC REFINED CULTURED
ARTIFICIAL
(ARTIFICIALLY —) HOTHOUSE

CULTIVATION CROP TILTH FINISH
GROWTH CULTURE TILLAGE TILTURE
LABORAGE MANURAGE REFINEMENT
(— IN MANNERS) FINISH
(MENTAL —) HUMANITY

CULTIVATOR JAT KMET RYOT ILAVA
SULKY FARMER GADABA HARROW
ILAVAN MAMOTY MILLER RIDGER
TILLER FLORIST GRUBBER HUSBAND
MEADOWER ROSARIAN SCUFFLER
(— GANG) RIG
(PL.) LAETI

CULTURAL HUMANIST

CULTURE ART AGAR STAB KULLI
NASCA NAZCA SHAKE SLANT SLOPE
TAJIN TASTE TILTH JHUKAR KULTUR
POLISH STREAK WILTON ABASHEV
ANANINO AZILIAN IRANISM
JHANGAR KAYENTA SOCIETY
STARTER TILLAGE HUMANISM
LEARNING
(ESKIMO —) DORSET
(MEXICAN —) MAZAPAN
(MIDDLEBROW —) MIDCULT
(PREF.) ETHEO

CULTURED CIVIL POLITE LETTERED

CULVERIN SLING CULVER LANTACA
PELICAN SPIROLE

CULVERT FOX GOUT DRAIN SLUIT
BRIDGE CONDUIT CULBERT PINNOCK
PONCEAU OVERPASS

CUMBER BURDEN CUMMER
SHACKLE

CUMBERSOME GOURD HEAVY
CLUMSY UNRIDE AWKWARD

LUGSOME ONEROUS WEIGHTY
CUMBROUS UNWIELDY
CUMMER GIRL LASS WOMAN
KIMMER
CUMMERBUND BAND BELT SASH
CUMMUTATIVE ABELIAN
CUMULATE HEAP GATHER COMBINE
CUMULATIVE CHAIN SUMMATIVE
CUNA CUEVA DARIEN
CUNEIFORM ULNARE WEDGED
CUNNER CANOE NIPPER WRASSE
BURGALL CHOGSET GOLDNEY
NIBBLER BERGGYLT BLUEFISH
CORKWING GILTHEAD
CUNNING ART OLD SHY SLY WIT
ARCH CUTE DEEP FAST FINE FOXY
KEEN SLIM SNOD TRAP WILY WISE
CANNY CRAFT DOWNY FAVEL GUILE
LOOPY PAUKY PAWKY POKEY SHARP
SMART ADROIT ARTFUL ASTUTE
CALLID CLEVER CRAFTY DAEDAL
DECEIT ENGINE FOXERY PRETTY
QUAINT SHREWD SUBTLE SUPPLE
TRICKY WISDOM COMPASS CRAFTLY
CURIOUS FINESSE KNOWING
PARLISH PARLOUS POLITIC PRACTIC
SLEIGHT SUBTILE VARMINT VULPINE
CONTOISE DEXTROUS MANAGERY
QUENTISE SKILLFUL SLEIGHTY
STEALTHY YEPELEIC
CUNNING LITTLE VIXEN
(CHARACTER IN —) LAPAK PRIEST
HARASTA TERYNKA FORESTER
SHARPEARS GOLDENMANE
SCHOOLMASTER
(COMPOSER OF —) JANACEK
CUNNINGLY YEPLY YEPELY
CUP AMA BOX CAN DOP MUG NOG
POT TOT TUN TYG CELL DOPP HORN
LOTA PECE SHOE SKEW TASS TOSS
BOUSE CALIX CHARK COGUE COPPE
CRUSE CYLIX DEPAS GLASS GODET
GRAIL KITTY PHIAL SCALE STEIN
STOOP STOUP TASSE TAZZA THECA
BEAKER BICKER BUCKET BUMPER
CAPPIE CHOANA COTYLA CRATER
CUPULA DOBBIN EGGCUP EYECUP
FALSIE FESSEL FINJAN GOBLET
JICARA KOTYLE MAZARD NAGGIN
NOGGIN OXHORN POTION RUMKIN
TASSIE VESSEL BRIMMER CAPSULE
CHALICE CHEERER CYATHUS
GODDARD KYATHOS QUONIAM
SCYPHUS SHERBET STIRRUP
THIMBLE TRINKET VENTOSE
BRIDECUP GRADUATE PANNIKIN
STANDARD TJANTING
(— FOR HOLDING DIAMOND) DOP
DOPP
(— FOR PERFUMES) CONCH
(— FOR YEAST) SKEP
(— IN SAUCER OF ALCOHOL) ETNA
(— OF FLOWER) BELL

(— OF TEA) DISH CUPPA SPEED
OYSTER
(— ON BULLET) GASCHECK
(— WITH COVER) HANAP
(ASSAYING —) CUPEL
(CAFE —) TASSE
(DRINKING —) CAN MUG NUT TIG
TUN TYG CANN HORN TASS TOSS
GODET BEAKER GOBLET HOLMOS
QUAICH RUMMER CHALICE
GODDARD TRINKET
(FAIRY —) COOLWORT
(FILLED —) BUMPER
(IRISH —) MADDER METHER
(IRON —) CULOT MUSHROOM
(LARGE —) FACER BLACKJACK
(LEATHER —) WELL GISPIN
(LONG-HANDLED —) CYATH DIPPER
CYATHUS KYATHOS
(MAPLE —) MAZER
(NAUTICAL —) THIEF
(ORNAMENTAL —) TAZZA
(PAPER —) DIXIE
(PASTRY —) DARIOLE
(PRIZE —) PEWTER
(SACRED —) GRAIL
(SHALLOW —) CYLIX TAZZA TASTER
CAPSULE
(SMALL —) DOP NOG TOT DOPP
TASS DOBBIN NAGGIN NOGGIN
TASSIE
(SQUARE —) MADDER METHER
(STIRRUP —) BONAILIE
(WINE-TASTING —) TASTEVIN
(WOODEN —) COG COGUE CAPPER
CAPPIE METHER QUAICH
(PL.) VALONIA
(PREF.) CALATHI CALICI COTYL(I)(O)
CUPULI CYATH(I)(O) POCILLI SCYPH(I)
(O)
(SUFF.) COTYL(LY)(OUS)
CUPBEARER HEBE SAKI CUPPER
GANYMEDE
CUPBOARD CUB KAS BOLE CASE
COIN SAFE AMBRY CHEST CUBBY
CUDDY HUTCH PRESS ABACUS
AUMBRY AWMRIE BUFFET CLOSET
LARDER LOCKER PANTRY SPENCE
ALMIRAH ARMOIRE CABINET
DRESSER PIESAFE SKIBBET
ALHACENA CREDENCE CREDENZA
TROSTERA
(ARCHERY —) ASCHAM
CUPEL TEST
CUPFUL CUP CAROUSE
CUP HOLDER ZARF
CUPID DAN AMOR EROS LOVE PUTTO
CHERUB AMORINO AMOURET
AMORETTO
(PL.) PUTTI
CUPIDITY LUST GREED DESIRE
AVARICE AVIDITY LONGING APPETITE
RAPACITY

CUPOLA DOME KILN TYPE VAULT BELFRY TURRET CALOTTE FURNACE LANTERN LOOKOUT CIMBORIO COCKLOFT
(ROUND —) THOLUS
CUPOLAMAN HEATER
CUPPED GLENOID
CUPPING GLASS VENTOSE
CUP-SHAPED PEZIZOID SCYPHATE
CUPULE CUP DOLSTER CYATHUS THUMBMARK
CUR DOG YAP FICE FIST FYCE MUTT TIKE TYKE FEIST KEOUT BRAKJE MESSAN MESSIN BOBTAIL MONGREL WHAPPET
CURABLE SANABLE
CURARE URARE URARI OORALI WOORALI
CURASSOW MITU COPPY HOCCO MITUA PAUXI
CURATE ABBE CURA AGENT VICAIRE MINISTER
CURATIVE HEALING IATRICAL PHYSICAL REMEDIAL SALUTARY SANATIVE
CURATOR KEEPER STEWARD GUARDIAN OVERSEER
CURB BIT LID CRUB FOIL KERB REIN SKID SNIP SNUB BRAKE CHECK CRIMP CURVE GUARD LEASH LIMIT MOUND ARREST BOTTLE BRIDLE COERCE COLLAR DECKLE GOVERN HAMPER STIFLE STRAIN SUBDUE THWART CONTROL CURBING INHIBIT REFRAIN REPRESS SHACKLE ATTEMPER COMPESCE MODERATE RESTRAIN RESTRICT WITHHOLD
(OFFICIAL —) LID
(WELL —) PUTEAL
CURCULIO TURK WEEVIL
CURCUMA ZEDOARY
CURD CRUD DAHI CHEESE CURDLE CASEINE CLABBER CONGEAL COAGULUM
(— IN MILK) ZIEGA
(—S AND WHEY) SLIP PINJANE
(BEAN —) TOFU
(PL.) SKYR FLEETINGS
(PREF.) THROMB(O)
CURDLE CAP LOP RUN SAM SET CRIM CURD EARN LEEP QUAR SAMM SOUR TURN WHIG YERN CARVE QUAIL QUARL SPOIL YEARN CAILLE LAPPER LOBBER LOPPER POSSET QUARLE CLABBER CONGEAL CRIDDLE CRUDDLE THICKEN CONDENSE
CURDLED CURDLY QUARRED SHOTTEN
(NOT —) UNCRUDDED
CURE DIP DRY DUN FIX BEEF BOOT CARE CORN HEAL HEED HELP JERK MEND SALT SANE SAVE AMEND BLOAT BOTEN LEECH REEST SMEEK SMOKE CHARGE CURATE KIPPER PHYSIC PRIEST RECURE REMEDY SEASON SUCCOR TEMPER WARISH BESMOKE RECOVER RESTORE THERAPY TREACLE ANTIDOTE BARBECUE CURATION GUERISON PRESERVE REVOCERY
(— A HABIT) BREAK
(— BY SMOKING) GAMMON SMUDGE
(— FISH) DUN ROUSE
(— GRASS) HAY
(— HAY) WIN
(— HERRINGS) BLOAT
(— IN SUN) RIZZAR
(— SKINS) DRESS
(COUGH —) SAPA SAPE
CURE-ALL BALM AVENS ELIXIR REMEDY PANACEA THERIAC
CURED SALT BLOATED
CURIO DOODAD
CURIOSITY CURIO ODDITY INTEREST
(— OF SMALL VALUE) GABION
(—S OF THE CITY) LIONS
(PL.) CURIOSA
CURIOUS ODD NOSY RARE SELI QUEER SELLE SELLY PRYING QUAINT SNOOPY CUNNING STRANGE UNUSUAL FREAKISH MEDDLING PECULIAR SINGULAR
(— ONE) PANDORA
CURL BOB BEND COIL FEAK FURL KINK LOCK PURL ROLL TUBE WAVE WIND ACKER CANON CRIMP CRISP DILDO FRILL FRIZZ QUIRL SPIRE TRESS TWIRE TWIST BERGER BUCKLE CANNON CRUCHE CURDLE FROWSE MULLET RIPPLE SPIRAL TUNNEL WRITHE CRIDDLE CRIMPLE CRINKLE CROCKET CRUDDLE EARLOCK FLEXURE FRIZZLE FROUNCE RINGLET SERPENT TENDRIL WHISKER FAVORITE LOVELOCK SQUIGGLE
(— HAIR) CROOK
(— OF SMOKE) WREATH
(— OF WIG) SNAKE
(— ON FOREHEAD) CRUCHE CROUCHE
(— OVER) BREAK
(— UP) CRUMP HUNCH SNIRL HUDDLE SHRINK SNUGGLE
(FRINGE OF —S) FRISETTE FRIZETTE
(METAL —) CHIP
(SMALL —) CROCK
(PREF.) CIRR(I)(O) CIRRH(I)(O)
CURLED CRISP FUZZY KINKY SPIRY CIRRATE COCKLED CRISPED FRIZZLY SAVOYED WREATHY CRISPATE CRUMPLED GAUFFRED GOFFFRED HELICINE SCROLLED
CURLER GOFFER TEASER CRIMPER FRIZZER MULLETS

CURLEW FUTE JACK SPOW KIOEA
SNIPE SPOWE WHAAP WHAUP
DIKKOP MARLIN SMOKER BANKERA
BUSTARD DOEBIRD BLUELEGS
WHIMBREL SICKLEBILL
CURLICUE ESS CAPER CURVE
CASSIS PARAPH SQUIRL FLOURISH
PURLICUE SCRIGGLE SQUIGGLE
CURLING CRISP
CURLING MARK TEE
CURLING MATCH SPIEL
CURLING STONE IRON STONE
LOOFIE GRANITE
(— SPIN) RAISE
CURL-PAPER CRACKER PAPILLOTE
CURLY WAVY CRISP CRULL OUNDY
CRIMPY RIPPLED CRINKLED
(— HAIR) VEDDOID
CURMUDGEON CRAB CHURL
HUNKS MISER GLEYDE GROUCH
NIGGARD
(LIKE A —) CRUSTY
CURMUDGEONLY STINGY
CURRANT PASA BERRY CASSIS
RAISIN RIZZAR RIZZLE CORINTH
(PL.) RIBES SPICE
CURRANT BUN WIG WIGG
CURRAWONG SQUEAKER
STREPERA
CURRENCY CASH COIN PASS BILLS
CATER MONEY SCRIP SERIES SPECIE
PASSAGE WILDCAT
(FRACTIONAL —) SPONDULIX
(SHELL —) UHLLO
CURRENT NOW WAY EDDY FLOW
FLUX FORD RACE RIFE TIDE VEIN
WAFT ALIVE DRIFT GOING RAPID
ROUST SCOUR SWIFT TENOR TESLA
TREND USUAL ABROAD ACTUAL
COEVAL COMMON COURSE DOUCHE
DURANT FLUENT LATEST LIVING
MOTION MOVING OFFSET OUTSET
RECENT RIZZER RULING SLUICE
STRAND STREAM TONGUE VOLANT
COUNTER DRAUGHT FLOWING
FRESHET GENERAL INDRAFT
INSTANT PASSANT PRESENT
RUNNING STICKLE THERMAL
TORRENT BACKWASH CURRANCE
DOWNCAST FREQUENT MILLRACE
OCCURRENT PASSABLE TIDERACE
TODAYISH UNDERTOW
(— IN SPEECH) WAIF
(— INSTRUMENT) AMMETER
(AIR —) DRAFT SHEET SPLIT
BREEZE DRAUGHT DOWNCAST
DOWNFLOW
(ELECTRIC —) STRAY
(HOT —) BACK
(JAPAN —) KUROSHIO KUROSIWO
(KIND OF —) RIP
(PREVAILING —) MAINSTREAM
(RAPID —) SWIFT TONGUE

(SOUND —) DISTORTION
(STRONG —) GALE ROOST ROUST
(PREF.) RHEO
CURRENTLY ANYMORE
CURRICULUM STREAM PROGRAM
PROGRAMME
CURRISH BASE CYNICAL DOGGISH
IGNOBLE SNARLING
CURRY COMB DRUB KARI CLEAN
DRESS GROOM BRUISE CAJOLE
CARREE POWDER PREPARE
TARKEEAN
(— FAVOR) HUG NUT QUILL COTTON
SMOOGE CUITTLE SMOODGE
CURSE BAN HEX POX BANE BLOW
CUSS DAMN JINX OATH PIZE WARY
BLAST BLESS CORSE SHREW SPELL
SWEAR WEARY WINZE DETEST
DEVOTE GOOFER GUFFER MAKUTU
MALIGN MAUGER MAUGRE
ACCURSE BESHREW MALISON
SWEARAT ANATHEMA EXECRATE
FORSPEAK MALEDICTION
CURSED DASH CUSSED DAMNED
DASHED ACCURSED
CURSER WARIER
CURSING BLESSING BLASPHEMY
CURSIVE RUNNING
CURSORILY OBITER
CURSORY FAST BRIEF HASTY QUICK
SHORT FITFUL ROVING SPEEDY
PASSANT PASSING SHALLOW
CARELESS RAMBLING
CURT BUFF RUDE TART BLUFF BLUNT
BRIEF BRUSK NIPPY SHORT SQUAB
TERSE ABRUPT CURTAL CUTTED
SNIPPY BRUSQUE CONCISE CRYPTIC
LACONIC CAVALIER SNAPPISH
SNIPPETY SUCCINCT
CURTAIL CUT LOP CLIP CROP DOCK
PARE STOP ABATE ELIDE SHORT
SLASH STUNT TRUNK DECURT
LESSEN REDUCE ABRIDGE BOBTAIL
CRACKLE SHORTEN DIMINISH
MINORATE RETRENCH
CURTAILED TAIL CUTTY SHORT
STUNT CURTAL BOBTAIL CONCISE
ABRIDGED
CURTAIN END BOOM DROP IRIS
MASK VEIL WALL BLIND DRAPE
SCENE SHADE SHEET VELUM
COSTER HANGER PURDAH SCREEN
SHROUD CEILING CONCEAL CORTINE
DRAPERY HANGING VITRAGE
ASBESTOS PORTIERE TRAVERSE
(CHURCH —) CLOTH RIDDEL
ENDOTYS ENDOTHYS
(THEATER —) IRON SCRIM TEASER
TRAVELER TORMENTER
(PL.) END DEATH
CURTAIN ROD TRINGLE
CURTAIN STRETCHER SCRAY
STRAINER

CURTAL CRAPE COURTAL CURTLAX
CURTSY BOB BOW DIP DOP BECK
DROP JOUK KNEE CONGE HONOR
CURCHY
CURUBA CASSA BANANA
CURVATED STUNT HOOKED
CURVATURE ARC PLY ARCH BENT
BOOL CURL CURVE SHEER SINUS
CAMBER CURVITY ADUNCITY
APOPHYGE CYRTOSIS GRYPOSIS
KYPHOSIS LORDOSIS
(— OF BONE) ARCUATION
(— OF DECK) SHEER
(— OF LEGS) RHEBOSIS
(— OF SHOE SOLE) SWING
(— OF SPINE) KYPHOSIS SCOLIOSIS
(— OF STOMACH) FUNDUS
(— OF STRAKE) SPILING
CURVE ARC BOW CUP ESS SAG ARCH
BEND BOUT COME CURB FADE HOOK
KNEE LINE OGEE TURN VEER WIND
AMBIT BIGHT BREAK CONIC CROOK
CRUMP CUBIC HELIX NONIC OGIVE
PEDAL POLAR QUIRK SLICE SWEEP
SWIRL TARVE TREND TWIST WITCH
BOUGHT CAMBER CIRCLE DEFLEX
JORDAN LITUUS SOLVUS SPIRAL
SPRING TOROID WIMPLE ADIABAT
BRACKET CAUSTIC CIRCUIT CISSOID
COMPASS CONCAVE CONTOUR
COSEISM CURVITY CYCLOID ELLIPSE
ENVELOP FESTOON FLEXURE
INCURVE INFLECT LIMACON
PHUGOID PROFILE QUARTIC
SCALLOP SINUATE SOLIDUS
CARDIOID CATENARY CONCHOID
DYGOGRAM ELASTICA EXTRADOS
FADEAWAY INTRADOS INVOLUTE
LIGATURE LIQUIDUS OPHIURID
PARABOLA SINUSOID TONOGRAM
TRACTRIX TROCHOID STROPHOID
CATACAUSTIC
(— DESCRIBED BY GRAPH) GRAM
(— IN HANDRAIL) KNEE
(— IN PLANKING) HANG
(— IN SAIL) ROACH
(— OF ARCH) INTRADOS
(— OF BALL) DROP
(— OF BIT) LIBERTY
(— OF COLUMN) APOPHYGE
(— OF FINGERNAIL) GRYPOSIS
(— OF HORSE'S NECK) CREST
(— OF PLANK) SNY
(— OF SHIP'S BOW) FLAIR FLARE
(— OF TIMBER) CUP
(— SATISFYING EQUATION) BRANCH
(— SPACE) KNOT
(— WHEN DRAWN) COME
(BASEBALL —) SNAKE
(CRICKET —) SWERVE
(DOUBLE —) CIMA CYMA
(KIND OF —) LAFFER LEARNING
PRACTICE

(PLANE —) ROSE STROPHOID
(PLANE CUBIC —) WITCH
(VERTICAL —) RAMP
CURVED BENT SOFT ADUNC CORBE
CURVE CURVY ROUND WOUND
CONVEX CURVEY GYRATE HAMATE
TURNED ARCUATE ARRONDI
CONCAVE CROOKED CURVANT
EMBOWED FALCATE SIGMOID
ADUNCOUS ANCHORAL AQUILINE
ARCIFORM CRUMPLED CYGNEOUS
DECURVED EXCURVED SCROLLED
ARCHIFORM
(PREF.) ANCYLO ANKYLO CAMPTO
CAMPYL(O) CURVI CURVO
CYRT(O)
(SUFF.) CLASTIC
CURVET HOP LEAP LOPE SKIP TURN
BOUND CAPER FRISK PRANK VAULT
CAVORT CROUPE FROLIC GAMBOL
PRANCE PANNADE CORVETTO
CROUPADE
CURVING SPIRY SIMOUS TWISTY
AQUILINE DRAWDOWN
(— IN) CONCAVE
(— OUTWARD) BOMBE
(DOWN —) EPINASTY
(SMOOTHLY —) FAIR
CUSH
(FATHER OF —) HAM
CUSH-CUSH CARA YAMPEE
CUSHION BAG COD MAT PAD PIG
BALL BANK BOSS PUFF SEAT SUNK
TRIM GADDI GADHI PANEL SQUAB
TRUSH BUFFER INSOLE JOCKEY
MUSNUD PILLOW SACHET BOLSTER
BRIOCHE COSSHEN HASSOCK
KNEELER MUFFLER PILLION REPOSAL
ROOTCAP CUTIDURE OREILLER
PULVINAR PINCUSHION
(KIND OF —) WHOOPEE
(LACE-MAKERS —) BOTT
(PIN —) PRINCOD
(SEAT —) BANKER
(TAILOR'S —) HAM
(PREF.) PULVILLI PULVINI
CUSHIONING DUNNAGE
CUSHIONLIKE PULVINAR
CUSHION PLANT POLSTER
CUSHIONY PADDY
CUSHITIC NUBIAN
CUSHY PLUM
CUSK COD TUSK TORSK BURBOT
CATFISH
CUSP APEX CONE HORN PEAK ANGLE
POINT STYLE TOOTH CORNER
SPINODE ENTOCONE HYPOCONE
METACONE PARACONE
CUSPID CANINE
CUSPIDOR GABOON CRACHOIR
SPITTOON
CUSSO KOSO KOUSSO BRAYERA
BRAZERA

CUSTARD FLAN FOOL CREME FLAWN
DOUCET DOWCET CHARLET PARFAIT
FLUMMERY DIABLOTIN ZABAGLIONE
(— PIE) QUICHE
CUSTARD APPLE ANONA ANNONA
PAWPAW CORAZON SWEETSOP
CUSTODIAN HACK GUARD BAILEE
CUSTOS KEEPER SEXTON WARDEN
WARDER CURATOR JANITOR
CERBERUS CLAVIGER GUARDIAN
CONCIERGE
CUSTODY LAP LAW MOS PAD TAX
URE USE WON ASAL DUTY FORM
GARB MODE MORE RITE ROTE RULE
THEW TOLL WONE WONT FUERO
GUISE HABIT HAUNT RITUS STYLE
SUNNA TRADE TREAD TRICK USAGE
VOGUE BYRLAW DASTUR DHARMA
GROOVE IMPOST MANNER MINHAG
MONTEM PRAXIS SUNNAH USANCE
COSTUME DUSTOOR DUSTOUR
FASHION FORMULA HALAKAH
TRIBUTE USAUNCE WARNOTH
BUSINESS ENDOGAMY HABITUDE
PRACTICE ASSUETUDE
CONSUETUDE PRESCRIPTION
(BINDING —) LAW
(BUSINESS —) TRADE GOODWILL
(CHILDBIRTH —) COUVADE
(CHURCH —) COMITY
(CORRUPT —) ABUSE
(FESTIVAL —) HOCKING
(OUTMODED —) ARCHAISM
(PRIMITIVE —) COUVADE
(RURAL —) HEAVING
(SECRET —) SANDE
(TEMPORARY —) FAD VOGUE
(PL.) MORES MOEUR HAIKWAN
FOLKLORE PROPRIETIES
CUSTOMARILY USUALLY
CUSTOMLY
CUSTOMARY PER RIFE TAME USED
NOMIC USUAL BEATEN COMMON
SOLEMN VULGAR WONTED CLASSIC
GENERAL REGULAR USITATE
EVERYDAY FAMILIAR HABITUAL
ORTHODOX
(NOT —) INSOLENT
CUSTOMER CHAP COVE BUYER
CLIENT PATRON SUCKER ACCOUNT
CALLANT CHAPMAN PATIENT
SHOPPER MERCHANT PROSPECT
(PRINTER'S —) AUTHOR
(PROBABLE —) PROSPECT
(TOUGH —) HARDCASE
(PL.) CUSTOM CLIENTELE

CUSTOMHOUSE ADUANA
DOGANA DOUANE
CUSTOM-MADE BESPOKE
BESPOKEN
CUSTOMS OFFICER SHARK
WAITER
CUT AX ADZ AXE BOB DAG DAP DIE
HAG HEW KIT LOP MOW NIP RIT SAW
SNY TAP ADZE BANG BITE BOLO
BOLT BUZZ CHIP CHOP CLIP CROP
DADO DOCK FACE FELL FILE GASH
GIRD HACK HASH HEWN JERK KNAP
LIMB MAKE MODE MUSH NICK OCHE
PARE RACE RASH RAZE REAP SIDE
SKIN SLIT SLOT SMIT SNEE SNEG
SNIP SNUB STOW SUMP SWAP
SWOP TAME TRIM VELL VIDE BEVEL
BLOCK BREAK CANAL CANCH CARVE
CHIVE CHYND CLEFT COPSE COUPE
CRIMP DRESS FLICK FRAZE FRITH
GOUGE GRAVE GRIDE GROOP
HOWEL KITTE KNIFE LANCE LATHE
MINCE NOTCH PLATE PRUNE RAZEE
SABER SABRE SCALP SCARP SCIND
SCORE SEVER SHAPE SHARE SHEAR
SHIVE SHRED SKICE SKISE SLASH
SLICE SLICK SLISH SLIVE SNICK SPLIT
STAMP SWEEP SWIPE SWISH TOUCH
TWITE VOGUE WHITE ABLATE
AJOURE BARBER BISECT BROACH
CAMBER CHISEL CLEAVE CORNER
CUTTED DIVIDE EXCISE FIGURE
FLETCH FLITCH FRENCH GROOVE
GULLET HACKLE HAGGLE IGNORE
INCIDE INCISE INDENT LESSEN
MANGLE OUTPUT RASURE REDUCE
RIPPLE SCORCH SCOTCH SCRIBE
SCYTHE SLIGHT SLIVER SNATHE
STRAIT STREAK SULLET SWINGE
TAILYE THWITE TRENCH AFFRONT
CONVERT CURTAIL CUTTING
DIACOPE DISCIDE DISSECT
DRAWCUT ENGRAVE FASHION
FRITTER HATCHET RAKEOFF SCALPEL
SCISSOR SCUTTLE SECTILE TAILZEE
WHITTLE DISSEVER FRACTION
INCISION INCISURE INTAGLIO
LACERATE MALAHACK RETRENCH
THWITTLE
(— AN OPENING) BREACH
(— ASLANT) RAKE
(— AT ANGLE) CANT BEVEL
(— A THREAD) CHASE
(— AT RANDOM) SLASH
(— AWAY) COPE SLIT UNDO ABATE
CONCISE
(— BACK) HEAD SPUR
(— BARK) CHIP
(— BEAM) KERF
(— CARS) LIFT
(— CHEESE) HARP
(— CLAY) SLING

(— CORNERS) SKIRT CHAMFER
CHAMPHER
(— CRUST) CHIP
(— DEEPER) DEENTER
(— DEEPLY) DIG SHANK
(— DIAGONALLY) CATER SLANT
(— DOWN) HEW MOW FELL STAG
STUB RAZEE SCANT SCARP ABRIDGE
SHORTEN RETRENCH
(— FANCY FIGURE) DASH
(— FINELY) DICE
(— FISH) SOLAY STEAK
(— FOR FODDER) CHAFF
(— GEAR TEETH) RATCH
(— GLASS) SPLIT
(— GRAIN) BAG FAG CRADLE SWINGE
(— HAIR) DOD
(— IN) INSECT INCISED
(— IN A TREE) FACE
(— IN BARK) RING
(— IN BARREL STAVE) HOWEL
(— IN CURVES) SCALLOP
(— IN EXCAVATIONS) GULLET
(— IN LARGE SLICES) WHANG
(— IN RELIEF) ENGRAVE
(— IN SOFT ROCK) CAVATE
(— IN SQUARES) CHECK
(— INTO LARGE SLICES) WHANG
(— INTO SLIPS) ZEST
(— INTO STRIPS) JERK FLETCH
FLITCH JULIENNE
(— INTO TREE) BOX
(— IN WHALE'S CARCASS) SCARF
(— JAGGEDLY) HACK SNAG
(— LEDGES) BENCH
(— LOGS) LUMBER
(— OFF) BOB LOP CLIP CROP DOCK
KILL PARE SHUT SLIT STAG BELEE
CROSS ELIDE PRUNE SCIND SEVER
SHAVE SHEAR SKIVE SLIPE SPIKE
COUPED DECIDE EXEMPT FORCUT
RESECT SHIELD STIFLE SWATCH
ABJOINT ABSCIND ABSCISE ABSCISS
CURTAIL EXSCIND ISOLATE PRECIDE
RESCIND AMPUTATE CLEIDOIC
DESECATE RESECATE RETRENCH
TRUNCATE LANDLOCKED
(— OFF BY BITS) DRIB
(— OFF END) BUTT
(— OF FISH) JOWL
(— OFF WOOL) DOD DODD
(— OF GEM) STAR BAGUET
BAGUETTE
(— OF GRAIN) MELL
(— OF MEAT) ARM SEY CROP HOCK
SHIN SIDE CHUCK SHANK STEAK
BRISKET FORESEY ICEBONE SIRLOIN
EDGEBONE FORERIBS
(— OF RIFLING) GROOVE
(— OPEN) SPLAY
(— OUT) AX DESS DINK CLICK
BROACH EXCIDE EXCISE EXSECT

(— PATH) FRAY
(— SALMON) CHINE
(— SHEEP) TOMAHAWK
(— SHORT) BOB COW HOG LOP BANG
CROP DOCK JIMP SNIB BOBBED
CURTAL HOGGED BOBTAIL CHAPPED
CONCISE SCANTLE PRESCIND
(— TENDONS) ENERVATE
(— THE THROAT) JUGULATE
(— THE WAVES) SNORE
(— THINLY) CURL
(— TO PIECES) CHOP DICE MINCE
BRITTLE FRITTER
(— TO SIZE) TAIL
(— TURF) VELL
(— UNDER) KIRVE
(— UNEVENLY) CHATTER
(— UP) TUSK CARVE CHINE JOINT
PRANK SPOIL TRAIN GOBBET
COLLOPED
(— UP SWAN) LIFT
(— WHALE BLUBBER) LEAN FLENSE
(— WITH BACKWARD SLOPE) COOT
(— WITH DIE) DRINK BLANK
(— WITH SHEARS) SHIRL
(— WITH SICKLE) BAG REAP
(COLD —S) ASSIETTE
(CREW —) BUTCH FLATTOP
(DEEP NARROW —) JAD
(FENCING —) STRAMAZON
(LARGE — OF FOOD) DODGE
(NOT —) UNCORVEN
(SHORT —) ATAJO
(SLIGHT —) SNICK SCOTCH
(THIN —) TARGET
(PREF.) SEC(O) TEMNO TOMO
(SUFF.) COPATE COPE SECT SECTED
TOMA TOME TOMIC TOMOUS TOMY
CUT-AND-DRIED CANNED
CUTANEOUS DERMAL
CUTCH GAMBIR CATECHU GAMBIER
CUTE COY KEEN TWEE COONY DINKY
DUCKY SHARP CLEVER PRETTY
SHREWD CUNNING DARLING
CUTICLE DERM HIDE SKIN SHUCK
THECA MEMBRANE PELLICLE
(— OF EGGSHELL) BLOOM
CUTLASS SWORD CURTAL DUSACK
HANGER TESACK CURTAXE
MACHETE SHABBLE CAMPILAN
CUTLASS FISH HIKU SAVOLA
KALKVIS MACHETE HAIRTAIL
CUTLERY SILVER FLATWARE
CUTLET SCHNITZEL
(KIND OF —) PORK VEAL
CUTOVER COUPE
CUTPURSE NIP BUNG THIEF
HORNTHUMB
CUTTER DIE REEF BOAT IRON MILL
PONE SLED BRAVO FACER FRAZE
SLOOP SMACK BAYMAN CHERRY
COLTER COTTER DOCKER EDITOR

FRAZER MINCER SLEIGH SLICER
CLIPPER COULTER DROMOND
INCISOR RUFFIAN KNIFEMAN
REVENUER SCHOKKER SHEPSTER
(— OF STONES) LAPIDARY
(BRICK —) RUBBER
(PEAT —) PINER
(WIRE —) SECATEUR
CUTTERHEAD WABBLER WOBBLER
CUTTHROAT THUG BRAVO CUTTER
RUFFIAN SWORDER
CUTTHROAT TROUT MYKISS
CUTTING CUT HAG RAW SET ACID
CARF CURT KEEN KERF SECT SETT
SLIP TART TWIG ACUTE BLEAK
CHECK CRISP EAGER EDGED GRIDE
SCION SCRAP SCROW SHARP SMART
BITING BITTER BORING ENTAIL
GODOWN GORING JAGGED PHYTON
PIPING SECANT SEVERE SNITHE
BURNING CAUSTIC GRIBBLE INCISAL
MORDANT NICKING OVERCUT
PAINFUL PIQUANT POLLING
SARMENT SATIRIC SECTION SLICING
CHILLING CLEARING INCISIVE
PIERCING POIGNANT QUICKSET
SCATHING SCISSION SNAPPISH
WOUNDING TRENCHANT
(— FOR DIRT-CAR TRACK) GULLET
(— FOR WATER) TAJO
(— FROM PLANT) SLIP SHROUD
SARMENT PROPAGULE TRUNCHEON
(— OF DEER) SAY
(— OFF) AVULSION
(— OF TREES) HAG
(— SHORT) ABORTIVE
(— TOOL) HOB
(DRILL —S) MUD
(OBLIQUE —) BARBING
(SECOND —) ROWEN
(WASTE —) SELVAGE SELVEDGE
(SUFF.) THEMA THESIS TOMA TOME
TOMIC TOMOUS TOMY
(— OUT) ECTOMY
CUTTLEBONE SEPIA SEPION
SEPIUM GLADIUS SEPIARY
CUTTLEFISH SEPIA SHELL SQUID
CUDDLE CUTTLE SCRIBE CATFISH
DECAPOD INKFISH MOLLUSK
OCTOPUS SCUTTLE
(PREF.) TEUTHIS
CUVETTE POT TUB TANK BASIN
BUCKET TRENCH CISTERN
CYANEE (DAUGHTER OF —) BYBLIS
(FATHER OF —) MAEANDER
(HUSBAND OF —) MILETUS
(SON OF —) CAUNUS
CYANIDE NITRILE CYANURET
PRUSSIATE
CYANIPPUS (FATHER OF —) PHARAX
(WIFE OF —) LEUCONE
CYANITE SAPPARE DISTHENE

CYANOGEN PRUSSIN PRUSSINE
CYANOTYPE BLUEPRINT
CYBELE RHEA KYBELE AGDISTIS
(DAUGHTER OF —) JUNO
(FATHER OF —) URANUS
(HUSBAND OF —) SATURN
(MOTHER OF —) GAEA
(SON OF —) JUPITER NEPTUNE
CYCAD BANGA CICAD ZAMIA
COONTIE CYCADITE
CYCHREUS (DAUGHTER OF —)
GLAUCE
(FATHER OF —) NEPTUNE POSEIDON
(MOTHER OF —) SALAMIS
CYCLADES (ISLAND OF —) IOS KEOS
DELOS MELOS NAXOS PAROS SYROS
TENOS ANDROS AMORGOS
KYTHNOS SANTORIN SERIPHOS
CYCLAMEN BACCHAR PRIMWORT
SOWBREAD
CYCLE AGE EON ERA AEON BIKE
EPOCH KALPA PEDAL PRIME
ROUND SAROS SECLE WHEEL
BAKTUN CIRCLE COURSE CYCLUS
PERIOD BICYCLE CIRCUIT DICYCLE
TRICYCLE
(— FURIOUSLY) SCORCH
(— OF TIME) ORB
(— OF WORK) ROTA JOURNEY
(— OF 3600 YEARS) SAROS
(—S CAUSED BY KARMA) SAMSARA
SANSARA
(BUSINESS —) JUGLAR KITCHIN
(GO THROUGH —S) ROTATE
(KIND OF —) CALVIN
(LUNAR —) SAROS
(ONE — PER SECOND) HERTZ
(SECONDARY —) EPICYCLE
CYCLIC CYCLAR ANNULAR CYCLICAL
PERIODIC
CYCLING (— TRACK) VELODROME
CYCLIST CYCLER WHEELER
WHEELMAN
CYCLOLITH CROMLECH
CYCLOMETER ODOGRAPH
VIAMETER
CYCLONE GALE GUST WIND BLAST
STORM BAGUIO TORNADO TWISTER
TYPHOON SECONDARY
NEUTERCANE
CYCLOPARAFFIN NAPHTHENE
CYCLOPEAN HUGE VAST STRONG
MASSIVE COLOSSAL GIGANTIC
CYCLOPS ARGES BRONTES
COPEPOD STEROPES
CYCLORAMA CYKE PANORAMA
CYCLOSIS STREAMING
CYCLOSTOME HAGFISH
CYCNUS (DAUGHTER OF —)
HEMITHEA
(FATHER OF —) ARES MARS
NEPTUNE POSEIDON

(MOTHER OF —) CALYCE PYRENE
PELOPIA
(SON OF —) TENES
(WIFE OF —) PROCLEA PHYLONOME
CYLINDER CAN EKE GIG TIN BEAM
BOMB BURR CAGE CANE DRUM LEAD
MUFF PIPE PRIM ROLL SLUG TUBE
WELL BLOCK CORER DRAIN FIBER
FIBRE FUDGE SCREW SHELL SPOOL
STELA STELE SWIFT BARREL BOBBIN
BUTTON COLUMN COPPER DECKER
DOFFER DUSTER FILTER GABION
PISTON PLATEN ROLLER SCREEN
TIPITI TUMBLE URCHIN WORKER
CUTCHER SLEEVER SLUDGER
SUCCULA FOLLOWER GRADUATE
NEURAXIS SPARKLET
(— AROUND MOLD) COTTLE
(— FOR DANCE RHYTHM) CLAVE
(— OF STEAM WHISTLE) BELL
(— OF TISSUE) CORTEX
(— OF YARN) CAKE
(— ON LOOM) BEAM
(—S PULLED THROUGH DUCT)
MANDREL
(— WITH PERFORATIONS) FLUSHER
(ARMORED —) BARBETTE
(GLASS —) MUFF
(HOLLOW —) PIPE TUBE
(MARKING —) LEAD
(NAPPING —) GIG
(RELAY —) BATON
(REVOLVING —) BEATER ROLLER
(TOOTHED —) SPROCKET
(WATERMARK —) DANDY
CYLINDRICAL ROUND TERETE
TOROSE CENTRIC TUBULAR
TERETIAL
(PREF.) TERETI
CYMA GOLA GULA OGEE DOUCINE
MOLDING CYMATIUM
CYMA REVERSA HEEL
CYMBA YET
CYMBAL ZEL ZILL CHIME TARGET
CROTALUM KYMBALON
(PAIR OF —S) HIGHHAT
(PL.) TAL BECKEN PIATTI
CYMBELINE
(AUTHOR OF —) SHAKESPEARE
(CHARACTER IN —) CAIUS HELEN
CLOTEN IMOGEN LUCIUS MORGAN
IACHIMO PISANIO BELARIUS
LEONATUS PHILARIO ARVIRAGUS
CORNELIUS CYMBELINE GUIDERIUS
POSTHUMUS
(SON OF —) ARVIRAGUS
GUIDERIUS
CYMBIUM MELO
CYME AXIS CYMULE BOSTRYX
CYMLING SIMNEL CYMBLIN
SCALLOP PATTYPAN
CYMOSE DEFINITE SYMPODIAL

CYMRY KYMRI WELSH
CYNIC SATYR TIMON DOUBTER
SNEERER APEMANTUS
CYNICAL CYNIC SULLEN CURRISH
DOGGISH DOGLIKE CAPTIOUS
SARDONIC SNARLING JAQUESIAN
MISOGYNIC PESSIMISTIC
MISANTHROPIC
CYNOCEPHALUS AANI
CYNORTES (BROTHER OF —)
HYACINTHUS
(FATHER OF —) AMYCLAS
(MOTHER OF —) DIOMEDE
(SON OF —) PERIERES
CYNOSURE SHOW LODESTAR
CYPRESS CULL SABINO SIPERS
FIREBALL AHUEHUETE BELVEDERE
CYPRESS SPURGE BALSAM
NAPOLEON
CYPRIPEDIUM CYP DUCK NERVINE

CYPRUS
CAPE: GATA GRECO ANDREAS
ARNAUTI ZEVGARI
CAPITAL: NICOSIA
COIN: PARA
MEASURE: OKA OKE PIK CASS DONUM
KOUZA GOMARI KARTOS MEDIMNO
MOUNTAIN: TROODOS
RIVER: PEDIAS PEDIEOS
TOWN: POLIS CITIUM PAPHOS
KYRENIA LARNACA MORPHOU
NICOSIA LIMASSOL FAMAGUSTA
WEIGHT: OKA OKE MOOSA KANTAR

CYRANO DE BERGERAC (AUTHOR
OF —) ROSTAND
(CHARACTER IN —) CYRANO ROXANE
VALVERT DEGUICHE CHRISTIAN
CYRENE (FATHER OF) HYPSEUS
(MOTHER OF —) CHLIDANOPE
(SON OF —) IDMON DIOMEDES
ARISTAEUS
CYRILLA TITI
CYRUS KORESH
CYST BAG SAC WEN POUCH CYSTUS
RANULA DERMOID HYDATID
HYGROMA SACCULE VESICLE
ATHEROMA DACRYOPS MUCOCELE
STEATOMA
CYSTOPTERIS FILIX
CYTOKININ ZEATIN
CYTOLYSIN AMBOCEPTOR
CYTOME SPHEROME
CYTOPLASM MASSULA OOPLASM
PLASMON DIASTEMA
(PREF.) PLASTO
CZAR CSAR IVAN TSAR TZAR PETER
AUTOCRAT NICHOLAS
CZARDAS CSARDAS
(SECTION OF —) FRISS LASSU
FRISZKA

CZECH CECH TSECH TSCEKH
BOHEMIAN

CZECH REPUBLIC
CAPITAL: PRAHA PRAGUE
COIN: CROWN DUCAT HALER HELLER
KORUNA
DANCE: POLKA REDOWA FURIANT
FOREST: BOHEMIAN
FORMER NAME: CZECHOSLAVAKIA
MEASURE: LAN SAH MIRA KOREC
LATRO STOPA MERICE STRYCH
MOUNTAIN: SNEZKA
MOUNTAIN RANGE: ORE GIANT
SUMAVA SUDETEN KRKONOSE
JAVORNIKY CARPATHIAN
KRUSNEHORY BILEKARPATY

PEOPLE: ROMA CZECH GYPSY
MORAVIAN
PLATEAU: BOHEMIAN
REGION: BOHEMIA MORAVIA
RIVER: MZE DYJE EGER ELBE ISER
LABE NISA ODER ODRA OHRE OLSE
OLZA OPPA BECVA OPAVA JIZERA
MOLDAU MORAVA SAZAVA VLTAVA
LUZNICE BEROUNKA
TOWN: AS ASCH BRNO CHEB EGER
MOST ZLIN BRUNN OPAVA PLZEN
PRAHA TABOR AUSSIG BILINA
KLADNO OSTROV PILSEN VSETIN
BUDWEIS HAVIROV JIHLAVA
OLOMOAC OSTRAVA TEPLICE
TEPLITZ KARLOVYVARY

D

D DE DEE DOG DELTA
DA DUCKTAIL
DAB DAP DOB DOT DUB HIT PAT
BLOW CHIT DAUD LICK LUMP PECK
SPOT CLOUT DHABB DIGHT LEMON
SMEAR BLOTCH EXPERT STRIKE
DABSTER PORTION SPLOTCH
FLATFISH FLOUNDER MARYSOLE
SANDLING
DABBER BALL PROD TAMPON
DABBING PICKING
DABBLE DAB DIB MESS DALLY
DIBBLE MEDDLE MUDDLE PADDLE
POTTER SOSSLE SPLASH TAMPER
TRIFLE DRABBLE MOISTEN PLOUTER
PLUTTER SMATTER SPATTER
DELIBATE SPRINKLE
(— WITH BLOOD) ENGORE
DABBLER AMATEUR DABSTER
DABBLING PLOUTER PLOWTER
DABCHICK GREBE DIPPER DOBBER
DOPPER PUFFER HENBILL DIDAPPER
DOPCHICK
DACE CHUB DARE DART CYPRINID
GRAYLING
DACHSHUND DACHS TECKEL
BADGERER
DACOIT DAKU DAKOO ROBBER
CRIMINAL
DACTYL TOE FOOT FINGER
(— AND IAMB) FEET
DACTYLOPODITE POLLEX
DACTYLOZOOID PALPON
DACTYLUS DACTYL DIGITUS
DAD BEAT BLOW DAUD HUNK LUMP
PAPA KNOCK THUMP FATHER STRIKE
DADA (FOUNDER OF —) ARP
DADAIST (— PAINTER) ARP
(— POET) TZARA
DADDY BABBO DEDDY
DADDY LONGLEGS SPINNER
LONGLEGS PHALANGID
DADO DIE GROOVE SOLIDUM
DAEDALUS (ANCESTOR OF —)
ERECHTHEUS
(NEPHEW OF —) TALUS
(SON OF —) ICARUS
DAEMON (ALSO SEE DEMON)
GHOST DAIMON PYTHON
EUDAEMON MISTRESS
(PL.) CURETES
DAFFODIL GLEN LILY DAFFY DILLY
JONQUIL ASPHODEL BELLWORT
CROWBELL
DAFT GAY MAD LOCO WILD ZANY
BALMY BATTY CRAZY DAFFY GIDDY
LOONY POTTY SILLY INSANE
FOOLISH IDIOTIC IMBECILE
DAG JAG DAGG STAB SLASH DAGGLE
PIERCE DAGGING DAGLOCK PRICKET
DAGAME SALAMO MADRONA
LEMONWOOD
DAGGER DAG SAX DIRK ITAC KRIS
SAEX SNEE SPUD STAB TANG CRISE
DAGUE KATAR KREES POINT PRICK
SKEAN STEEL ANLACE BODKIN
COUTEL CREESE DIESIS HANGER
KIRPAN KUTTAR PANADE PINKER
POPPER SKHIAN STYLET BALARAO
BAYONET COUTEAU DUDGEON
HANDJAR KANDJAR KHANJAR
OBELISK PONIARD SLASHER
STABBER BASELARD PUNCHEON
PUNTILLA STILETTO
(— AS CERAMICS COVER) HILLER
(— REFERENCE MARK) SPIT
(— WITH WAVY BLADE) KRIS CREESE
KREESE
(DOUBLE —) DIESIS
(PART OF —) HAFT BLADE
(SACRED —) KIRPAN
(PREF.) MACHAIRO
DAGOMBA DAGBANE DAGBANI
DAH DAO DOW DHAO
DAHLIA JICAMA POMPON
DAHOMEY (CAPITAL OF —)
PORTONOVO
(PEOPLE OF —) FON FONG BARIBA
(RIVER OF —) NIGER OUEME
(TOWN IN —) KANDI NIKKI ABOMEY
OUIDAH COTONOU
DAIL ASSEMBLY
DAILY ADAY ADAYS DIARY DIURNAL
QUOTIDIAN
DAINCHA NARDOO
DAINTIES EST ESTE SOCK CATES
DIABLOTIN
DAINTILY CHOICELY GINGERLY
MINIONLY
DAINTINESS FLUTTER DELICACY
DAINTY CATE FINE NICE RARE TEAR
TWEE ACATE DAINT DENTY FRILL
GENTY NAISH TREAT BONBON
CHOICE COSTLY FRIAND MIGNON
MINION PICKED REGALO SCARCE
SPICED SUNKET CURIOUS ELEGANT
FINICAL FINICKY MINIKIN REGALIA
TAFFETA TAFFETY DAINTITH
DAINTREL DELICACY DELICATE
ETHEREAL LIKEROUS MIGNIARD
TRYPHOSA
(PREF.) ABRO HABRO

DAIRY TAMBO LACTARY VACCARY
CREAMERY DEYHOUSE
(— PRODUCTS) MILCHIGS
DAIRYMAID DEE DEY DEYWOMAN
MILKMAID
DAIRYMAN AHIR MILKMAN
DAIS PACE SEAT BENCH LEWAN
STAGE TABLE CANOPY ESTATE
LISSOM PODIUM PULPIT SETTLE
ESTRADE TERRACE TRIBUNE
CHABUTRA FOOTPACE HALFPACE
HATHPACE HUSTINGS PLATFORM
DAISY BULL GOLD DANDY GOWAN
OXEYE BENNET MORGAN SHASTA
BONESET BOWWORT COMFREY
DOGBLOW BACKWORT BONEWORT
COMPOSIT HEXAFOIL KNITBACK
PISSABED MOONPENNY
BRUISEWORT MARGUERITE
DAISY CUTTER GRUB
DAISY FLEABANE ERIGERON
SCABIOUS
DAKOTA SIOUX LAKOTA
DALE HAW DELL DENE GLEN VALE
SPOUT BOTTOM DINGLE TROUGH
VALLEY
DALEA PAROSELA
DALIBOR (CHARACTER IN —) BENES
ZDENEK DALIBOR MAILADA
(COMPOSER OF —) SMETANA
DALLES DELLS RAPIDS
DALLIANCE TOY CHAT PLAY TALK
SPORT GOSSIP TOUSEL TOUSLE
TRIFLE COLLING
DALLIER PINGLER
DALLY TOY CHAT DAFF FOOL IDLE
JAKE JAUK PLAY SWAN WAIT DELAY
FLIRT SPORT TARRY COQUET DABBLE
DAWDLE LINGER LOITER PINGLE
TRIFLE WANTON DRINGLE SLIDDER
PHILANDER
DALLYING COQUETRY SISSETON
DALMATIAN COACHDOG
DALMATIC TUNICLE
DALPHON (FATHER OF —) HAMAN
DAM BAR BAY PEN REE BUND DAME
HEAD POND SADD SPUR STAY STEM
STOP SUDD WEIR BLOCK CAULD
CHECK CHOKE GARTH MOUND
POUND STANK ANICUT CAUSEY
HINDER MOTHER PARENT ANNICUT
BARRAGE BARRIER BURROCK
MILLDAM PENHEAD RAMPIRE
TAPPOON ABOIDEAU BLOCKADE
GRANDDAM OBSTACLE OBSTRUCT
RESTRAIN
(PART OF —) GATE PIER POOL SILL
WALL BASIN CREST OUTLET SLUICE
ROADWAY TAINTOR OVERFLOW
SPILLWAY POWERHOUSE
DAMAGE MAR BLOT BURN COST
HARM HURT JEEL LOSS RUIN SKIN
TEEN BLITZ BURST CLOUD CRACK
HAVOC PRANG SPOIL WOUND
WRONG BANJAX BATTER CHARGE
DANGER DEFACE DEFECT HINDER
IMPAIR INJURE INJURY INSULT
LESION SCATHE SORROW AFFLICT
DAMNIFY DEGRADE DISTURB
EXPENSE FOUNDER OFFENCE
OFFENSE PAYMENT SCRATCH
SCUTTLE SHATTER ACCIDENT
BUSINESS DISSERVE FRACTURE
FRETTING MISCHIEF SABOTAGE
(MINOR SURFACE —) DING
(PREF.) DAMNI
DAMAGED HURT CRAZY LESED
BROKEN CRACKED INJURED
DAMAGES INTEREST HAMESUCKEN
(EXCESSIVE —) SMART
SMARTMONEY
DAMAGING HARMFUL HURTFUL
SCATHING
DAMAN DAS CONY CONEY CUNNY
DASSY GANAM HYRAX DASSIE
WABBER ASHKOKO CHEROGRIL
DAMA PADEMELON TAMMAR
WALLABY
DAMASCENED WATERED
DAMASCENE WORK KOFTGARI
DAMASK LINEN DARNEX DORNIC
DORNICK VALANCE DAMASSIN
DRAWLOOM
DAMAYANTI (HUSBAND OF —) NALA
DAME DINT LADY DAMIE WOMAN
MATRON
DAME BLANCHE, LA (CHARACTER
IN —) ANNA BROWN JENNY GEORGE
DICKSON GAVESTON
(COMPOSER OF —) BOIELDIEU
DAME'S VIOLET EVEWEED
DAMKINA (HUSBAND OF —) EA
DAMMARA AGATHIS
DAMN DEE DEM DOG RAT BLOW
BURN DANG DARN DASH DING DRAT
DUMB DURN BLAME BLANK BLAST
BLESS CURSE FETCH TARAL WHOOP
BEDAMN BUGGER DEMPNE DEVOTE
GODDAM CONDEMN CONSARN
DOGGONE GODDAMN GOLDARN
GOLDURN CONFOUND EXECRATE
DAMNABLE RUDDY DAMNED
ODIOUS ACCURSED INFERNAL
DAMNABLY DEUCED CURSEDLY
DEUCEDLY
DAMNATION NATION PERDITION
DAMNATION DE FAUST
(CHARACTER IN —) FAUST
MARGUERITE MEPHISTOPHELES
(COMPOSER OF —) BERLIOZ
DAMNED DEE DAMN DARN DEED
DURN LOST BALLY DOOMS BLAMED
BLOODY DARNED DASHED DURNED
GODDAM GORMED TARNAL
BLASTED BLESSED CONSARN
DOGGONE ETERNAL GOLDARN

GOLDURN MUCKING ACCURSED
BLANKETY BLINKING DASHEDLY
FREAKING INFERNAL JIGGERED
DAMO (FATHER OF —) PYTHAGORAS
  (MOTHER OF —) THEANO
DAMP DEG FOG RAW WAK WET CLAM
DANK DEWY DULL MIST ROKY SOFT
WACK BLUNT DABBY HUMID JUICY
MALMY MOCHY MOIST MOOTH
MUGGY MUNGY MUSTY RAFTY
RAINY RAWKY SAPPY SEEPY SOBBY
SOGGY THONE WAUGH WEAKY
BLIGHT CLAMMY DAMPEN DEADEN
MUFFLE QUENCH RHEUMY STUPOR
BEDEWED DAMPISH DEPRESS
MOISTEN SQUIDGY DEJECTED
DISPIRIT HUMIDIFY HUMIDITY
MOISTURE
  (— OF EVENING) SERENE
  (CHOKE —) STYTHE
  (PREF.) HUMI(DI)
DAMPED SORDO
DAMPEN DEG DAMP MOIL CHILL
CRAMP FREEZE SPONGE MOISTURE
DAMPENER MULLER
DAMPER DAMP MUTE BREAD CHECK
CHECKER SORDINE REGISTER
DAMPNESS CLAM DAMP HUMIDITY
DAMSEL GIRL MISS WENCH MAIDEN
MOPPET DAMOSEL DAMOZEL
PUCELLE DONZELLA PRINCESS
DAMSELFISH PINTANO
DAMSELFLY NAIAD ODONATE
DAN GI DEN
  (MOTHER OF —) BILHAH
DANAKIL AFAR
DANAUS ANOSIA
  (BROTHER OF —) AEGYPTUS
  (DAUGHTER OF —) AMYMONE
  (FATHER OF —) BELUS
  (MOTHER OF —) ANCHINOE
DANCE BAL BOB HOP JIG MAI SON
BALL DRAG DUET DUMP FISH FOOT
FRUG HEEL HOOF HORA JAZZ JIVE
JUBA JUKE KOLO LEAP LOPE LOUP
MASK MILL MOVE PROM REEL SAIL
SHAG SKIT STEP BAILE BAMBA
BONGO BOOGY BRAWL CANON
CAPER CAROL CONGA DANZA DISCO
ENTRY FLING FLISK FRIKE FRISK
GOPAK HORAH LASYA LIMBO LINDY
MAMBO PAVAN POLKA RINKA
RUMBA SALLY SAMBA STOMP
SWING TANGO TRACE TREAD TWIST
VOLTA WALTZ ALTHEA AREITO
BALLET BALTER BOLERO BOOGIE
BOSTON BRANLE CANARY CANCAN
CEBELL CHACHA CORDAX DANZON
DIDDLE DREHER FADING FORMAL
FROLIC GERMAN HORMOS MASQUE
MINUET MOBBLE MONKEY MORRIS
NRITTA PASSAY RACKET RHUMBA
SHIMMY TODDLE TRESCA TUMBLE

VALETA VELETA ANTHEMA BEGUINE
CALINDA CANTICO COURANT
CZARDAS DANSANT FADDING
FARRUCA FOOTING FOXTROT
FURLANA GAVOTTE MEASURE
MORISCO PATTERN SALTATE
SARDANA SHUFFLE TEMPETE
TRESCHE TRIPPLE VOLTIZE ZIGANKA
ANGLAISE AURRESCU BAMBOULA
BUNNYHUG CACHUCHA CAKEWALK
CHACONNE COMPARSA COONJINE
COTILLON ENTRACTE ESTAMPIE
FANDANGO FANTASIA FLAMENCO
GALLIARD GALOPADE GUARACHA
HABANERA HEYDEGUY HORNPIPE
KOI ATTAM MATELOTE MERENGUE
SALTATION SHAKEDOWN
CARMAGNOLE SCHOTTISCHE
  (— ART) NATYA ORCHESIS
  (— ATTENDANCE) LACKEY LACQUEY
  (— CLUMSILY) BALTER
  (— DRAMA) NO NOH
  (— FACE TO FACE) SET
  (— FORM) PIVA
  (— IN CIRCLE) JIGGER
  (— METHOD) LABAN
  (— NIMBLY) CANARY
  (— RESEMBLING THE POLKA) BERLIN
  (— STEP) RIFF PICKUP
  (— STYLE) ABHINAYA
  (— SUGGESTIVELY) BUMP GRIND
  (— TYPE) TANDAVA
  (ACROBATIC —) ADAGIO
  (AFRICAN —) SHOUT
  (ARGENTINE —) CUANDO
  (AUSTRIAN —) LANDLER
  (BALINESE —) KEBYAR LEGONG
  (BALLROOM —) SON CONGO
TWOSTEP COTILLON
  (BOHEMIAN —) REDOWA FURIANT
  (BRAZILIAN —) SAMBA
  (CARNIVAL —) COOCH FOLIA
COOTCH
  (CEREMONIAL —) AREITO CANTICO
DUTUBURI
  (COQUETTISH —) PURPOSE
  (COUNTRY —) HAY CLOG RANT
CONFESS LANDLER MUSETTE
ZIGANKA ANGLAISE SARABAND
  (COURTSHIP —) CUECA BATUQUE
LEZGINKA
  (DANISH —) SEXTUR
  (FIESTA —S) AKRIEROS
  (FLAMENCO —) ALEGRIAS
  (FRENCH —) BAL BOREE BRAWL
GAVOT BRANLE BOURREE BOUTADE
BRANSLE GAVOTTE LAVOLTA
ALLEMANDE
  (GAY —) RANT GAILLARD GALLIARD
  (GESTURE —) SIVA
  (GREEK —) CORDAX KORDAX
KUMAIKA SIRTAKI SIKINNIS
  (GYPSY —) FARRUCA

(HAITIAN —) JUBA
(HAWAIIAN —) HULA
(HOBBYHORSE —) CALUSAR
(HOLIDAY —) PATTERN
(HUNGARIAN —) KOS
(IMPROMPTU —) BOUTADE
(INDIAN —) IRUSKA KATHAK
KANTIKOY
(IRISH —) FADING PLANXTY
(ITALIAN —) FORLANA FURLANA
BERGAMASK SALTARELLO
(JAPANESE —) BUGAKU KAGURA
(JAVANESE —) SERIMPI
(KIND OF —) TAP
(LIVELY —) JIG REEL GALOP GIGUE
POLKA RUMBA BOLERO CANARY
RHUMBA SPRING BOURREE
CORANTO FURLANA HOEDOWN
GALLIARD GALOPADE HORNPIPE
(MAORI —) HAKA
(MARTIAL —) PYRRHIC
(MEXICAN —) JARABE HUAPANGO
SANDUNGA
(MOURNFUL —) DUMP
(NORWEGIAN —) HALLING
(OLD-FASHIONED —) LOURE
PASSACAGLIA
(OLD ENGLISH —) CEBELL MORRIS
ARGEERS ANGLAISE
(PEASANT —) JOTA DANZON
BALITAO
(PERUVIAN —) CUECA KASWA
CACHUA
(POLISH —) POLACCA KUJAWIAK
POLONAISE VARSOVIENNE
(POLYNESIAN —) HULA
(PORTUGUESE —) FADO
(ROMAN —) TRIPUDIUM
(ROUND —) RAY BRAUL CAROL
WALTZ CAROLE MAXIXE
(RUSSIAN —) ZIGANKA
(RUSTIC —) HAY HEY HAYMAKER
(SPANISH —) JOTA POLO JALEO
BOLERO JARABE CHACONNE
FLAMENCO GUARACHA
MALAGUENA ZAPATEADO
SEGUIDILLA
(SPEAR —) BARIS
(SQUARE —) SQUARE ARGEERS
HOEDOWN LANCERS QUADRILLE
(STATELY —) PAVAN PAVANE
EMMELEIA SARABAND POLONAISE
(SWORD —) BACUBERT MATACHIN
(VENEZUELAN —) JOROPO
(WEDDING —) CANACUAS
(WEST INDIAN —) LIMBO
(WHIRLING —) TARANTELLA
(PREF.) CHORE(I)(O) CHORO ORCHESO
DANCE-DRAMA NOH
(JAPANESE —) NO
DANCER PONY CLOWN PONEY
ARTIST CORNER EXOTIC HOOFER
HOPPER MAENAD APSARAS

CLOGGER DANSEUR PASCOLA
PRANCER PRANKER SAILOUR
STEPPER TODDLER BALADINE
BAYADERE DANSEUSE DEVADASI
FIGURANT MORRICER
(BALLET —) ETOILE SOLISTE
CORYPHEE
(EGYPTIAN —S) GHAWAZI
GHAWAZEE
(JAVANESE —) SERIMPI
(JAVANESE —S) BEDOYO
(MASKED —) GAHE
(SQUARE —S) FLOOR
(SWORD —) MATACHIN
(ZUNI —) SHALAKO
DANCE-TUNE BRAWL BRANTLE
DANCING SWING ADANCE BALLET
CHANGE FROLIC MORRIS SALTANT
SURGING STEPPING TRIPSOME
(— MANIA) TARANTISM
DANCING-GIRL ALMA ALME ALMEH
ALAMAH BAYADERE
DANDELION BLOW BLOWER
CANKER DINDLE CHICORY HAWKBIT
BLOWBALL COMPOSIT PISSABED
(RUSSIAN —) KOKSAGYZ
DANDELION HEAD PUFF CLOCK
BUFFBALL BULLFICE BULLFIST
PUFFBALL
DANDER ANGER DUTCH SCURF
STROLL TEMPER WANDER HACKLES
PASSION SAUNTER DANDRUFF
DANDIFIED SPRUCE BUCKISH
ADONIZED
DANDIFY ADONIZE DANDYIZE
DANDLE DANCE DIDDLE DOODLE
FADDLE FONDLE PAMPER
DANDRUFF SCURF DANDER FURFUR
PORRIGO
DANDY FOP JAY ADON BEAU BUCK
DAND DUDE FINE JAKE MAJO PRIG
TOFF TRIG YAWL BLOOD DILDO
JEMMY SWELL ADONIS MIZZEN
BUCKEEN CAPSTAN COXCOMB
ELEGANT FOPPISH JESSAMY
MACARONI MUSCADIN SAILBOAT
DANDY HORSE HOBBY DRAISINE
DANDYISHNESS SPIFF
DANDYISM BUCKISM
DANE DANSKER LOCHLIN DUBHGALL
DANEWORT EBULUS LOCHLIN
DANEBALL DANEWEED DEADWORT
WALLWORT
DANGER FEAR RISK DOUBT PERIL
WATHE HAZARD PLIGHT EXTREME
PITFALL VENTURE DISTRESS
JEOPARDY
(— SIGNAL) RED
(MORAL —) SNARE
DANGEROUS BAD HOT ILL RUM
DEAR FOUL GRAVE NASTY RISKY
FICKLE KITTLE SCATHY SHREWD
UNSURE AWKWARD FEARFUL

PARLOUS UNCANNY DOUBTFUL
INSECURE PERILOUS UNCHANCY
BREAKNECK WANCHANCY
PRECARIOUS PESTIFEROUS
(MAKE LESS —) DEFUSE
(NOT —) CUSHY
(VERY —) TOXIC
DANGLE BOB LOP HANG LOLL
DROOP SWING DANDLE SHOGGLE
SHOOGLE SUSPEND SWINGLE
TROLLOP
DANGLER (— AFTER WOMEN)
PHILANDER
DANGLIN DANLI
DANGLING PENDANT VERSATILE
DANIEL (FATHER OF —) DAVID
(MOTHER OF —) ABIGAIL
DANK WET DAMP DONK HUMID
MADID MOIST CLAMMY COARSE
DAMPEN DANKISH DRIZZLE
WETNESS MOISTURE
DANSEUSE DANCER BALLERINA
DANUBE (— FEEDER) INN
DANZIG GDANSK
(— LIQUEUR) RATAFIA
DAPHNE (CHARACTER IN —) GAEA
APOLLO DAPHNE PENEIOS
LEUKIPPOS
(COMPOSER OF —) STRAUSS
DAPPER CHIC COOL NEAT TRIM
NATTY SNAZZY SPRUCE FINICAL
FOPPISH SPARKISH
DAPPLE COVER FLECK FRECK
DAPPLED BLOCKY DOTTED POMELY
FLECKED MOTTLED SPOTTED
FRECKLED
DAPPLE GREY LIARD
DARBHA KUSA KUSHA
DARDA (FATHER OF —) MAHOL
DARDANUS (CHARACTER IN —)
VENUS IPHISE TEUCER ANTENOR
ISMENOR DARDANUS
(COMPOSER OF —) RAMEAU
(DAUGHTER OF —) IDAEA
(FATHER OF —) ZEUS JUPITER
(MOTHER OF —) ELECTRA
(SON OF —) ILUS DEIMAS IDAEUS
ERICHTHONIUS
DARE OSS DAST DEFY FACE OSER
OSSE RISK BRAVE STUMP ASSUME
BANTER DACKER ATTEMPT BRAVADE
FASHION PRESUME VENTURE
(— NOT) DASSNT DAURNA DASSENT
DAREDEVIL MADCAP HARDYDARDY
DARING BOLD DARE DERF PERT
RACY RASH WILD BRAVE HARDY
MANLY NERVE PREST FELONY
HEROIC COURAGE DAIROUS
DAREFUL BOLDNESS DEVILISH
FEARLESS STALWART
DARIOLE MADELINE
DARK DIM DUN MUM DAD WAN BASE
BLAE DEEP DERK DERN DUSK EBON

HARD MALE MIRK MURK BLACK
BLIND BROWN CLOUD DINGY DUSKY
FAINT MIRKY MURKY ROOKY SHADY
SOOTY SWART UMBER UNLIT VAGUE
CLOSED CLOUDY CYPRUS DIMPSY
DISMAL DRUMLY GLOOMY OPAQUE
SOMBER SOMBRE SWARTH WICKED
APHOTIC DARKISH DUSKISH
MELANIC OBSCURE PITMIRK
RAYLESS STYGIAN SUNLESS
SWARTHY THESTER UNCLEAR
ABSTRUSE DARKLING DARKSOME
GLOOMFUL GLOOMING IGNORANT
LOWERING SINISTER CIMMERIAN
CALIGINOUS
(PREF.) AITHO MAVRO MEL(A)
MELAN(O)
(SUFF.) MELANE
DARK BEAVER PRALINE
DARK-COLORED SAD SWART
SOMBER SOMBRE SWARTH
SWARTHY
(PREF.) FUSCO
DARK-COMPLEXIONED BROWN
MELANOUS
DARKEN DIM DUN BLUR DULL DUSK
BEDIM BLIND CLOUD GLOAM GLOOM
POCHE SHADE SULLY SWART UMBER
DEEPEN ENDARK SHADOW BECLOUD
BENIGHT BLACKEN ECLIPSE
EMBROWN OBSCURE OPACATE
PERPLEX SLUBBER TARNISH
OVERCAST OBFUSCATE
OVERSHADOW
(— HAIR) BLEND
DARKENED SABLE CLOUDY
BLINDED LAMPLESS
DARKENING SCURF
DARK HORSE MOREL
DARKISH DIM
DARKLY DARK CLOSE SABLY MISTILY
DARKNESS DARK DERN DUSK MIRK
MURK BLACK GLOOM NIGHT SHADE
TAMAS SHADOW DIMNESS PITMIRK
PRIVACY SECRECY TENEBRA
GLOAMING INIQUITY MIDNIGHT
TENEBRES TWILIGHT NIGRITUDE
(PLACE OF —) EREBUS
(PREF.) SCOTO TENEBRI
DARKNESS AT NOON
(AUTHOR OF —) KOESTLER
(CHARACTER IN —) ARLOVA BOGRAV
IVANOV GLETKIN HARELIP KIEFFER
MICHAEL NICHOLAS RUBASHOV
DARLING JO JOE PET CHOU CONY
DEAR DUCK LIFE LOVE NOBS PEAT
ROON AROON ARUIN BULLY CHERI
DEARY DUCKS LIEVE SWEET WHITE
CHERIE DAUTIE DAWTIE MINION
MOPPET OCHREE POPPET ACUSHLA
ASTHORE BUNTING CUSHLAM
DILLING MINIKIN PIGSNEY PINKENY
QUERIDA STOREEN DEARLING

DUMPLING FAVORITE LIEBCHEN
LOVELING MACUSHLA PRECIOUS
SWEETING MAVOURNIN
MAVOURNEEN
DARLING PEA INDICO INDIGO
DARN DOG BLOW DERN DURN MEND
PATCH BUGGER RENTER REPAIR
DOGGONE
DARNED BLAME BLAMED DAGNAB
DAGNAG DANGED DEUCED DURNED
BLESSED BLINDING DOWNGONE
DARNEL RAY CRAP TARE WEED
CHEAT CHESS DRANK DRAWK
DRUNK EAVER GRASS IVRAY NEELE
COCKLE EGILOPS AEGILOPS
DART JET POP BOLT BUZZ CANE
CHOP COLP FLIT JOUK LEAP LICK
PILE PLAN PLAY ROUT ARROW
BOUND FLAME FLING FLIRT GLEAM
GLINT LANCE SCAMP SCOOT SHAFT
SHOOT SKITE SKIVE SPEAR SPEED
SPRIT START ANCHOR BULTEN
DARTLE ELANCE GLANCE LANCET
LAUNCH METHOD SCHEME SPRING
SQUIRT STRIKE SUMPIT THRUST
JAVELIN MISSILE STRALET VERUTUM
BRANDISH GAVELOCK JACULATE
SPICULUM BANDERILLA
 (— ABOUT) SPRINKLE
 (— OF LIGHTNING) STREAK
 (— OF MOLDING) ANCHOR
 (— REPEATEDLY) DARTLE
 (PART OF —) POINT SHAFT BARREL
FLIGHT
 (PREF.) JACULI TELI
DARTER SPECK
DARTING SALLY ARROWY
DARTLIKE SPICULAR
DASH DAD DAH PEP ZIP BANG BOLT
CAST DING DIVE ELAN GIFT HINT
HURL LASH LINE LUSH PASH PELT
POSS RACE RASH RUIN RULE RUSH
SHOW SLAM SOSH TICK VEIN WHAP
WHOP ABASH ARDOR BLANK BREAK
CHAFE CLASH CRASH CRUSH DRIVE
ECLAT FLASH FLING FRUSH KNOCK
PLASH PLOUT SKITE SLASH SLOSH
SMASH SPEED SPEND SPICE SPURN
START STYLE SWASH SWELL TASTE
THROW TOUCH TRICK BEDASH
DALLOP DASHEE DOLLOP ENERGY
HURTLE HYPHEN JABBLE RELISH
SHIVER SPIRIT SPLASH SPRINT
STRAIN STROKE THRUST ABANDON
BRAVURA BREENGE COLLIDE
DEPRESS DISPLAY HUNDRED
IMPINGE PANACHE SHATTER
SPATTER SPLOTCH TANTIVY VIRETOT
CONFOUND GRATUITY SPLINTER
 (— ABOUT WILDLY) GAD REEL
 (— AGAINST) BEAT
 (— DOWN) QUELL STRAM
STRAMASH

 (— IN PIECES) CRASH
 (— OF LIQUID) JAW
 (— OF SPIRITS) LACE LACING
 (— OUT) QUELL
 (— TOGETHER) COLLIDE
 (— UP) FLURR
 (— WITH WATER) JAW BLASH
SLASH
DASHARATHA (FATHER OF —) AJA
 (SON OF —) RAMA BHARATA
LAKSHMANA SHATRUGHNA
 (WIFE OF —) KAIKEYI SUMITRA
KAUSHALYA
DASHBOARD DASH FACIA DASHER
FASCIA
DASHED SWITCHED
DASHEEN TARO
DASHER DASH BEATER PLUNGER
DASHING BOLD BULLY DASHY
DOGGY SHOWY SMART SPICY
SWASH JABBLE SPANKY SWANKY
VELOCE DOGGISH GALLANT
GALLOWS LARKING STYLISH
SWAGGER VARMINT SLASHING
SPANKING SPIRITED
DASSIE HYRAX
DASTARD CAD SOT DAFF SNEAK
COWARD CRAVEN DULLARD HILDING
VILLAIN WITHING POLTROON
DASTARDLY BASE FOUL VILLAIN
COWARDLY POLTROON SNEAKING
DASYLIRION SOTOL
DASYPUS TATU
DASYURE TIGER YABBI DAPPLE
DATA DOPE FILE FACTS IMPUT INPUT
MATERIAL
 (— RETRIEVAL SYSTEM) VIDEOTEX
 (— STRUCTURE) ARRAY
 (COMPUTER —) FILE PUSHDOWN
 (ENTER —) READIN
 (INACCURATE —) GARBAGE
 (SHORT SECTION OF —) PACKET
 (STORE OF —) PUSHDOWN
 (USELESS —) GARBAGE
DATE DAY ERA SEE DRAG FARD FUSS
DATUM EPOCH FARDH FRUIT SAIDI
TRYST CUTOFF FARDH FRIEND HALAWI
JUJUBE RECKON GALLANT
ANTEDATE ASHARASI DEADLINE
 (— BACK) TRACE RELATE
 (— FIXED UPON) TERM
 (— OF DEATH) OBIT
 (— RIPENING) KIMRI RUTAB KHALAL
 (CHINESE —) BER
 (REGULAR —) STEADY
DATED GIVEN PASSE STALE
OUTMODED
DATELESS STAG
DATE PLUM LOTUS SAPOTE ZAPOTE
DATHAN (FATHER OF —) ELIAB
DATING (KIND OF —) OPEN
DATOLITE BAKERITE HUMBOLDTITE
DATUM FACT ITEM GIVEN DONNEE

DATURA DUTRA STRAMONY
TOGUACHA
DAUB DAB DOB MUD BALM BLOB
BLOT CLAG CLAM CLAT CLAY COAT
GAUM MOIL SOIL TEER CLAIK CLART
CLEAM COVER DITCH FLICK PAINT
SLAKE SLAUM SMEAR BEDAUB
CLATCH GREASE LABBER SMUDGE
SPLASH BESMEAR DRIBBLE PLASTER
SCLATCH SLUBBER SPLATCH
SPLOTCH SLAISTER
DAUBE LARD
DAUBED GAUMY
DAUBING DUBBING MOILING
DAUBY BLOTTY
DAUGHTER ANAC BINT DAME GIRL
CHILD FILLE FILLY KIBEI REGAN
ALUMNA CADETTE DOCHTER
GONERIL CORDELIA
(NISEI —) SANSEI
(PANTALOON'S —) COLUMBINE
(PRIEST'S —) NIECE
(PREF.) FILI
DAUGHTER OF THE REGIMENT
(CHARACTER IN —) MARIF TONZIO
SULPICE COUNTESS
(COMPOSER OF —) DONIZETTI
DAUNT AWE COW DAW ADAW DARE
DAZE FAZE MATE PALL STUN TAME
ABASH ACCOY AMATE BREAK CHECK
DETER DOMPT QUAIL APPALL
DANTON DISMAY SUBDUE CONQUER
CONTROL OVERAWE REPRESS
STUPEFY TERRIFY DISPIRIT
OVERCOME
DAUNTED MATE
DAUNTLESS BOLD GOOD BRAVE
AWELESS CHANTAN FEARLESS
INTREPID
DAUNUS (DAUGHTER OF —) FILIPPE
(FATHER OF —) PILUMNUS
(MOTHER OF —) DANAE
(SON OF —) TURNUS
(WIFE OF —) VENILIA
DAVENPORT DESK SOFA COUCH
DIVAN
DAVID TAFFY DAWKIN
(COMPANION OF —) JONATHAN
(DAUGHTER OF —) TAMAR
(FATHER OF —) JESSE
(SON OF —) AMNON ABSALOM
(WIFE OF —) ABIGAIL AHINOAM
DAVID COPPERFIELD (AUTHOR OF
—) DICKENS
(CHARACTER IN —) HAM DICK DORA
HEEP JANE MICK ROSA AGNES
BETSY CLARA DAVID EMILY JAMES
MEALY TOMMY URIAH BARKIS
DARTLE GRINBY STRONG WALKER
CREAKLE SPENLOW WILKINS
MICAWBER PEGGOTTY TRADDLES
TROTWOOD MURDSTONE WICKFIELD
STEERFORTH

DAVIDIST JORIST
DAVIT CRANE
DAW DA DAWN DRAB DAUNT MAGPIE
DAWPATE JACKDAW SLATTERN
SLUGGARD
DAWDLE LAG IDLE JAUK LOAF
MOON MUCK MULL POKE TOIT
DALLY DELAY DRILL KNOCK DADDLE
DAIDLE DIDDLE DOODLE DRETCH
FADDLE LINGER LOITER MUCKER
PICKLE PINGLE PINGLE POTTER
PUTTER TANTLE TRIFLE DRIDDLE
FINNICK QUIDDLE SAUNTER
LALLYGAG LOLLYGAG SHAMMOCK
SLUMMOCK
DAWDLER DAWDLE MUSARD
LOUTHER
DAWN DAW ROW EOAN MORN
BREAK CREEK LIGHT PRIME SHINE
SUNUP AURORA MORROW ORIENT
SPRING UPRISE DAWNING GREKING
MORNING SUNRISE COCKCROW
DAYBREAK
(PREF.) EO EOSINO
DAWN-HORSE EOHIPPUS
DAY DA DEI ERA SUN YOM DATE DIEM
DIES DIET JOUR TIME EPOCH LIGHT
FRIDAY MONDAY PERIOD SUNDAY
JOURNEY TUESDAY LIFETIME
SATURDAY THURSDAY WEDNESDAY
(— AND NIGHT) KALPA
(— BEFORE) EVE
(— OF BRAHMA) CAI PA KALPA
(— OF JOY)) FEAST
(— OF JUDGMENT) INQUEST
DOOMSDAY
(— OF ORIGIN) BIRTHDAY
(— OF REST) SABBATH
(— OF ROMAN MONTH) IDES NONES
CALENDS KALENDS
(DOG —S) CANICULE
(EVERY —) ALDAY
(EVIL —S) DISMAL
(FAST —) ASHURA FASTEN
(FIRST — OF AUGUST) LAMMAS
(FIRST — OF MAY) BELTANE
BEALTINE
(HOLY —) FEAST HOLIDAY
(HOT —) BROILER ROASTER
SCORCHER
(LAST — OF FESTIVAL) APODOSIS
(LAST — OF YEAR) HOGMANAY
(MARKET —) NUNDINE TIANGUE
(NO FLESH —) MAIGRE
(PATRON SAINT'S —) PATTERN
(QUARTER —) TERM
(SAINT'S —) FESTA FIESTA
(TWELFTH —) EPIPHANY
(UNLUCKY —S) DISMAL
(WEEK —) FERIA
(WORK —) WARDAY
(40 —S) QUARANTINE
(5 NAMELESS —S) UAYEB

(60TH OF —) GHURRY
(8TH — AFTER FEAST) UTAS
(PREF.) HEMER(O)
(LASTING BUT —) EPHEMERO
DAYAK DYAK IBAN BAHAU DUSUN KAYAN KENYA KENYAH KELABIT
DAYBOOK BOOK DIURNAL JOURNAL
DAYBREAK DAWN MORN SUNUP DAWNING DAYDAWN DAYLIGHT (PREF.) EO EOSINO
DAYDREAM DWAM MUSE DREAM DWALM FANCY VISION FANTASY REVERIE PHANTASY
DAYDREAMER MITTY REVEUR
DAYFLOWER COHITRE
DAYLIGHT DAY LIGHT DAYSHINE (BROAD —) FUIRDAYS
DAYWORKER DILKER
DAZE FOG DAMP DARE MAZE ROCK STUN DAUNT DAVER DIZZY DOZEN GALLY SWOON ASTONY BEDAZE BEMUSE BENUMB DAZZLE DEAFEN MUDDLE STUPOR TRANCE CONFUSE PETRIFY STUPEFY TORPIFY ASTONISH BEWILDER DUMFOUND PARALYZE
DAZED MAD ASEA DAMP ASSOT DIZZY DOYLT MUZZY SILLY TOTTY WOOZY CUCKOO DOILED GROGGY ROTTEN BEMUSED DONNERT SPOILED WITLESS ASTONIED BESOTTED DITHERED DONNERED WITHERED
DAZEDLY GROGGILY
DAZZLE DARE DAZE BLEND BLIND DROWN GLAIK SHINE FULGOR ECLIPSE BEWILDER OUTSHINE SURPRISE
DAZZLED BLINDED
DAZZLING FLARE FLASH GLAIK FLASHY GARISH ADAZZLE FLARING FULGENT GLARING RADIANT DIZZYING GORGEOUS
DDT TDE DICOPHANE
DEACON ADEPT CLERIC DOCTOR LAYMAN LEVITE MASTER PHILIP MINISTER
DEACONESS WIDOW
DEACTIVATE MOTHBALL
DEAD FEY LOW AWAY BONG BUNG COLD DEAF DOWD DULL FLAT GONE MORT NUMB POKY SURE TAME ADEAD AMORT BLIND DEEDS INERT NAPOO POKEY QUIET SLAIN STARK VAPID ASLEEP BYGONE FALLEN LAPSED NAPOOH PARTED REFUSE DEADISH DEFUNCT EXACTLY EXPIRED EXTINCT INSIPID SAINTED STERILE TEDIOUS ABSOLUTE COMPLETE DECEASED DEPARTED INACTIVE LIFELESS OBSOLETE SCUPPERED

(— AT TOP) RAMPICK
(BLESSED —) SAINT
(PREF.) NECR(O)
DEAD-ARM NECROSIS
DEAD-DRUNK BLIND
DEADEN DAMP DRUG DULL DUMB KILL MULL MUTE NUMB SEAR STUN BLUNT SLAKE BENUMB DAMPEN MUFFLE OBTUND OPIATE RETARD STIFLE WEAKEN MORTIFY PETRIFY REPRESS SLUMBER SMOTHER AMORTIZE ASTONISH ENFEEBLE (— A SCENT) FOIL
DEAD END PLACE
(AUTHOR OF —) KINGSLEY
(CHARACTER IN —) KAY JACK DRINA TOMMY GIMPTY HILTON MARTIN BABYFACE
DEADENED DEAD DEAF SEAR SERE
DEADENING PUGGING
DEADFALL SNARE
DEADHEAD SINK BOBBER SINKER
DEADHOUSE MORGUE MORTUARY
DEAD LETTER NIX
DEADLINE DATELINE
DEADLINESS LETHALITY
DEADLOCK TIE DRAW LOGJAM IMPASSE STANDOFF STOPPAGE
DEADLY WAN DIRE FELL MORT FATAL FERAL TUANT DEATHY FUNEST LETHAL MORTAL CAPITAL DEATHLY FATEFUL RUINOUS MORTIFIC VENOMOUS VIRULENT PESTILENT THANATOID PERNICIOUS
DEADLY CARROT DRIAS THAPSIA
DEADLY-NIGHTSHADE DWALE
DEAD NETTLE HENBIT
DEADS MULLOCK
DEAD SOULS
(AUTHOR OF —) GOGOL
(CHARACTER IN —) PAVEL ALEXEI PLATON KLOBUEFF KOPEYKIN MANILOFF NOZDREFF LYENITZEN PLATONOFF PLIUSHKIN SOBAKEVITCH KOSTANZHOGLO TCHITCHIKOFF TENTETNIKOFF BETRISHTCHEFF
DEAF SURD DUNCH DUNNY SORDA SORDO (PREF.) SURDI SURDO
DEAFEN DIN DORR DEAVE DEADEN
DEAFENING DEEVEY
DEAF-MUTE FENELLA SURDOMUTE
DEAFNESS ASONIA SURDITY ANACUSIA ANACUSIS COPHOSIS
DEAL GO END JOB DAIL DOLE LEND PART SALE TALE WHIZ ALLOT BOARD BROKE FETCH PLANK SERVE SEVER SHAKE SHARE SHIFT TRADE TREAT TROKE TRUCK WIELD YIELD BATTEN BESTOW DIVIDE HANDLE MEDDLE NUMBER PARCEL BARGAIN DELIVER INFLICT PIANOLA PORTION SCATTER

TRUCKLE WRESTLE DISPENSE
SEPARATE
(— CARDS) DRAW TALLY
(— CLANDESTINELY) TRINKET
(— DISHONESTLY) SHORTCHANGE
(— IN) SELL VEND
(— IN A TRIFLING WAY) PIDDLE
(— IN BRIDGE) BOARD
(— IN GRAIN) SWALE
(— OF CARDS) COUP SPOIL
GOULASH
(— OUT) HELP METE
(— SHREWDLY) JOCKEY
(— SPARINGLY) TAPE
(— WITH) HAND COVER DIGHT
TOUCH TREAT BUCKET CUSTOM
DEMEAN HANDLE ENTREAT
NEGOTIATE
(GOOD —) HANTLE
(GREAT —) MORT LOADS MIGHT
SIGHT JUGFUL OODLES SKINFUL
(POLITICAL —) DICKER
DEALER BANK CHAP AGENT
COPER BADGER DANKER BROKER
CADGER EGGLER GROCER JOBBER
JUNIOR MONGER SELLER TRADER
BUTCHER CHAPMAN KEELMAN
YOUNGER CHANDLER MERCHANT
OCCUPIER OPERATOR STICKMAN
TAILLEUR
(— IN CATTLE) COUPER COWPER
DROVER
(— IN CHEMICALS) SALTER
DRYSALTER
(— IN DRY GOODS) DRAPER
(— IN GRAIN) OWNER
(— IN OLD CLOTHES) FRIPPER
(— IN PAINTS) COLORMAN
(— IN TEXTILES) MERCER
(CARDS —) FARMER
(COAL —) COLLIER
(EXTORTIONATE —) SHAVER
(HORSE —) COPER COUPER COWPER
CHANTER SCORSER
(SCRAP —) TOTTER DIDAKAI
(SLAVE —) MANGO
(STOCK —) STAG JOBBER OUTSIDER
DEALFISH VAAGMAR VAAGMAER
RIBBONFISH
DEALING DOLE PRICE TRUCK TAFFIC
TRADING EXCHANGE
(BUSINESS —S) TROKE
(JUST —) DOOM
(TRICKY —) BROKING
(PL.) DEAL TRAFFIC BUSINESS
COMMERCE PRACTICE PRACTISE
(SUFF.) (— WITH) IC(AL)
DEAN DECAN DOYEN DEANER
SENIOR VERGER PREFECT PROVOST
SUBDEAN ARCHDEAN PRAEFECT
DEAR JO GRA HON JOE PET AGRA
CARA CHER CHOU CONY FAIR FOND
GOOD HIGH LAMB LIEF LOVE NEAR

NOBS SALT ANGEL BOSOM CHARY
CHERE CHERI CHUCK DEARY HONEY
LOVED PRICY SWEET TIGHT CHERIE
COSTLY DAUTIE DAWTIE DEARIE
DEARLY POPPET PRICEY SCARCE
SEVERE SQUALL TENDER WORTHY
BELOVED DARLING LOVABLE
PIGSNEY QUERIDA SPECIAL TOOTSIE
ESPECIAL ESTEEMED GLORIOUS
PRECIOUS VALUABLE
(SUFF.) (— ONE) EEN
DEARLY DEAR ALIFE DEEPLY KEENLY
RICHLY HEARTILY
DEARNESS CHERTE DEARTH
DEARTH LACK WANT CHERTE
FAMINE PAUCITY POVERTY
DEARNESS SCARCITY SOLITUDE
(SUFF.) PENIA
DEASPIRATION PSILOSIS
DEATH DEE END BALE BANE DEAD
DOOM EXIT FAIL FATE KILL MORS
MORT OBIT PASS REST WINK ANKOU
DECAY GRAVE GRUEL LETHE NIGHT
SLEEP CHARON CHARUS DEMISE
DEPART ENDING EXITUS EXPIRY
MURDER PERIOD REAPER WAGANG
ACHERON CURTAIN DECEASE
FUNERAL PARTING PASSAGE
QUIETUS SILENCE BIOLYSIS
CASUALTY CURTAINS FATALITY
NECROSIS RAWBONES THANATOS
MORTALITY NOTHINGNESS
(— ANGEL) AZRAEL
(— BY BURNING) STAKE
(— BY HANGING) HALTER
(— OF TISSUE) GANGRENE
(PREF.) LETHI THANAT(O)
(SUFF.) THANASIA
DEATH ADDER ELAPID ELAPOID
DEATH-AGONY
(— OF WHALE) FLURRY
DEATH CAMASS LOBELIA
DEATH INSTINCT THANATOS
DEATH IN VENICE
(CHARACTER IN —) TADZIO
ASCHENBACH
(COMPOSER OF —) BRITTEN
DEATHLESS ETERNAL UNDYING
IMMORTAL
DEATHLESSNESS ATHANASY
DEATHLIKE CHARNEL DEATHLY
GHASTLY MACABRE GHASTFUL
MORIBUND MORTUOUS
DEATHLY DEAD FATAL DEADLY
MORTAL GHASTLY STYGIAN
DEATHFUL MORTALLY
DEATH OF A SALESMAN
(AUTHOR OF —) MILLER
(CHARACTER IN —) BIFF HAPPY
LINDA LOMAN WILLY
DEATH'S-HEAD SKULL
DEBACLE ROUT COLLAPSE
STAMPEDE

DEBAR DENY TABU CROSS ESTOP REPEL TABOO DISBAR FORBID HINDER REFUSE BOYCOTT DEPRIVE EXCLUDE OUTSHUT PREVENT SECLUDE SUSPEND PRECLUDE PROHIBIT

DEBARK LAND GOASHORE

DEBARRED FROZEN OUTSHUT

DEBASE SINK ABASE ALLAY ALLOY AVILE DIRTY LOWER STOOP BEMEAN DEFILE DEMEAN DILUTE EMBASE IMPAIR NIDDER NITHER REDUCE REVILE VILIFY CORRUPT DEBAUCH DECLINE DEGRADE DEPRAVE PERVERT PROFANE TRADUCE VILLAIN VITIATE DEROGATE PROSTITUTE

DEBASED BASE VILE HEDGE BASTARD CORRUPT SQUALID CANKERED DEGRADED DEROGATE

DEBASEMENT TARNISH PROSTITUTION

DEBASING DOWNWARD

DEBATABLE MOOT DISPUTABLE

DEBATE AGON BEAT FRAY MOOT ARGUE FIGHT PLEAD STUDY ARGUFY COMBAT HASSEL HASSLE REASON STRIFE AGITATE CANVASS CONTEND CONTEST DISCEPT DISCUSS DISPUTE EXAMINE MOOTING PALAVER QUARREL WRANGLE ARGUMENT COLLOQUY CONSIDER CONTRARY MILITATE PARLANCE QUESTION CONTENTION (VIGOROUS —) SETTO

DEBATER PICADOR

DEBAUCH BUM BOUT FILE SPREE TAINT WHORE DEBASE DEBOSH DEFILE GUZZLE MISUSE SEDUCE SPLORE VILIFY CORRUPT DEBOISE DEPRAVE MISLEAD POLLUTE VIOLATE DISHONOR SQUANDER STRUMPET STUPRATE

DEBAUCHED LEWD RAKELY RAKISH DEBOIST DEBOSHED RAKEHELL

DEBAUCHEE RIP RAKE ROUE HOLOUR LECHER RAKEHELL

DEBAUCHERY RIOT RAKERY DEBAUCH PRIAPISM

DEBENTURE BOND SECURITY

DEBENZOLIZE STRIP

DEBILITATE SINK

DEBILITATED WEAK SEEDY FEEBLE INFIRM SAPPED ASTHENIC

DEBILITY ATONY ADYNAMY ASTHENY LANGUOR MALAISE ADYNAMIA ASTHENIA WEAKNESS MYASTHENIA (PREF.) ASTHEN(O) (SUFF.) ASTHENIA

DEBIR (SLAYER OF —) JOSHUA

DEBIT DEBT LOSS CHARGE

DEBONAIR AIRY JAUNTY POLITE CAVALIER GRACEFUL GRACIOUS

DEBORA E JAELE (CHARACTER IN —) JAELE DEBORA SISERA (COMPOSER OF —) PIZZETTI

DEBOUCH FALL MOUTH

DEBOUCHMENT EXIT INFLUX INFLUXION

DEBRIS GUCK SLAG DECAY FRUSH TRADE TRASH WASTE RAFFLE REFUSE RUBBLE RUDERA CRUMBLE ELUVIUM RUBBISH SLIDDER DETRITUS (— AT BASE OF CLIFF) SCREE (— IN WOOL) BUR BURR (— OF INSECTS) FRASS (— OF ROCKS) HEAD DRIFT SCREE TALUS ELUVIUM (FLOATING —) LAGAM JETSAM FLOTSAM (FLUFFY —) FLUE (FOREST —) SLASH

DEBT DUE SIN CHIT POST DEBIT FAULT STOCK ARREARS DEBITUM JUDGMENT TRESPASS (PL.) OBLATA WANIGAN ARREARAGE

DEBTOR OWER PEON SKIP DYVOUR DEBITOR YIELDER

DEBUT OPENING ENTRANCE

DEBUTANTE BUD DEB BELLE DEBBY INGENUE ROSEBUD

DECADENT EFFETE DECAYED HOTHOUSE OVERRIPE

DECAHYDRATE SODA

DECALOGUE WITNESS

DECAMP GUY PUT BOLT HIKE KITE ELOPE MOSEY SCOOT SCOUR SLOPE VAMOS DEPART ESCAPE LEVANT MIZZLE MORRIS POWDER VAMOSE ABSCOND DISCAMP VAMOOSE ABSQUATULATE

DECAMPING GUY

DECAN DECURION

DECANT EMIT POUR RACK UNLOAD TRANSFER

DECANTER CARAFE CARAFON URCEOLE GARDEVIN INGESTER

DECAPITATE BEHEAD DECOLLATE

DECAPITATION DECOLL HEADING

DECAPOD CRAB BUSTER

DECARBONIZE DECOKE

DECATING SPONGING

DECAY EBB ROT ROX BLET CONK DOAT DOTE DOZE FADE FAIL RUIN SEED WANE WEAR CROCK DEATH SHANK SLOOM SLOUM SPOIL WASTE BLIGHT CANKER CARIES FADING MARCOR MILDEW MOLDER MOSKER SICKEN WITHER CRUMBLE DECLINE FAILURE FORFAIR MORTIFY PUTREFY DECREASE FORDWINE (— IN WOOD) CONK DOZE

(— OF FRUIT) BLETTING
(INCIPIENT —) BLET
(TOOTH —) CARIES
(PREF.) SAPR(O)
(TOOTH —) CARIO
DECAYED BAD DEAF DOZY ROXY
FRUSH SEEDY DAISED MARCID
PUTRID ROTTEN SPAKED CARIOUS
RUINOUS SNAGGLED
DECAYING COLD DOTY SHABBY
CARIOUS
DECEASE DIE FAIL OBIT PASS DEATH
DEMISE PASSAGE
DECEASED DEAD LATE PARTED
DEFUNCT EXTINCT UMWHILE
DEPARTED UMQUHILE
DECEIT GAB DOLE FLUM GAFF GULL
RUSE SHAM TRAP TRAY WILE ABUSE
COVIN CRAFT DOLUS FRAUD GUILE
SARAB SWICK SWIKE CAUTEL
FELONY WOIDRE CUNNING DISSAIT
FAITERY FICTION ARTIFICE
COZENAGE FALSEDAD INTRIGUE
SPOOFERY SUBTLETY TRICKERY
TRUMPERY WILINESS
(— IN LOVE) COQUETRY
DECEITFUL JIVE RUSE BLIND BRAID
FALSE GAUDY JANUS LOOPY PUNIC
SLAPE SNAKY ARTFUL COVERT
CRAFTY DOUBLE FICKLE HOLLOW
ROTTEN TRICKY CUNNING EVASIVE
FICTIVE SIRENIC SLEEKIT SLIDDER
UNWREST WINDING COVINOUS
GUILEFUL ILLUSIVE INDIRECT
SHAMMISH TORTUOUS
MENDACIOUS
DECEITFULLY DOUBLE FALSELY
DECEITFULNESS SHAM DECEIT
FALSITY
DECEIVE BOB COG CON DOR FOB
FUB GAB GAS GUM KID LIE BILK
BRAG BUNK CRAP DUPE FAKE FLAM
FOOL GAFF GULL HAVE HOAX HYPE
JILT JOUK MOCK SCAM SELL SHAM
SILE SNOW TURN WILE ABUSE
AMUSE BLEAR BLEND BLENK BLIND
BLINK BLUFF CATCH CHEAT COZEN
CROSS CULLY DODGE DORRE FEINT
GLEEK GLOZE HOCUS LIETO LURCH
PATCH SHUCK SPOOF SWICK SWIKE
TRICK TROIL TRUFF TRUMP TRYST
BAFFLE BARRAT BEDOTE BEFLUM
BEFOOL BETRAY BLANCH BUBBLE
CAJOLE CLOINE CLOYNE DELUDE
DIVERT EUCHRE GAMMON HUMBUG
ILLUDE JUGGLE MISUSE NIGGLE
SUCKER TAKEIN WIMPLE BEGUILE
DEFRAUD MISLEAD OVERSEE
TRAITOR BEJUGGLE FLIMFLAM
HOODWINK OUTREACH
DECEIVER ANGLE CHEAT HOCUS
COGGER FAITOR FALSER GUILER
MOCKER TRAPAN TREPAN FALSARY

ILLUSOR JUGGLER SHARPER
SPOOFER TRUMPER WARLOCK
WERNARD IMPOSTOR LOSENGER
LOTHARIO MAGICIAN TREGETOUR
DECEIVING FALSE ILLUSIVE
DECELERATE SLOW
DECENCY GRACE DECORUM
HONESTY MODESTY CHASTITY
DECENNIUM DECADE
DECENT FAIR CHASTE COMELY
HONEST MODEST PRETTY PROPER
SEEMLY FITTING GRADELY JANNOCK
SHAPELY SIGHTLY DECOROUS
GRAITHLY WISELIKE
DECENTLY WHITE
DECEPTION BAM COG DOR GAG LIE
DOLE FLAM FLUM GAFF GULL HOAX
HYPE MAZE RIDE RUSE SELL SHAM
WILE ABUSE BLIND BLUFF CHEAT
COVIN CRAFT CURVE DOLUS DORRE
FAVEL FRAUD GLAIK GLEEK GUILE
MAGIC SHUCK SNARE SPOOF TRICK
BARRAT CAUTEL DECEIT DUPERY
HUMBUG JUGGLE ABUSION
BLAFLUM CHICANE CUNNING
EVASION FALLACY FALSERY FICTION
GULLAGE GULLERY KNAVERY
PRETEXT SLYNESS ARTIFICE
DISGUISE FALSEDAD FLIMFLAM
ILLUSION INTRIGUE PHANTASM
PRESTIGE SUBTLETY TRICKERY
TRUMPERY WILINESS
DECEPTIVE FLAM FALSE ARTFUL
BUBBLE SIRENIC TRICKSY DELUSIVE
DELUSORY FLIMFLAM ILLUSORY
IMPOSING SHAMMISH UNSICKER
DECEPTIVENESS FANTASTRY
DECIBEL
(10 —S) BEL
DECIDE FIX CAST DEEM HOLD RULE
TELL WILL AWARD JUDGE PATCH
PITCH DECERN DECISE DECREE
FIGURE REWARD SETTLE ADJUDGE
DERAIGN RESOLVE CONCLUDE
SENTENCE
(— UPON) SET ELECT CHOOSE
TERMINE
(RIGHT TO —) SAY
DECIDED FIRM FLAT MAIN FORMED
SETTLED DECISIVE RESOLUTE
DECIDEDLY DIRECTLY DISTINCTLY
DECIDUA CADUCA
DECIGRAM LI
DECIMA TENTH TITHE
DECIMAL DENARY REPEATER
(— PART) MANTISSA
DECIMATE TENTH DESTROY
DECIPHER READ SOLVE CIPHER
DECODE DETECT REVEAL DECRYPT
DISCOVER INDICATE UNPUZZLE
DECIPHERING EPIGRAPHY
DECISION ACT END CALL DOOM FIAT
GRIT ARRET AWARD CANON FAITH

ISSUE PARTY PLUCK POINT ACTION
CHOICE CRISIS DECREE DIKTAT
RULING ACUERDO CONSULT
INTERIM PRACTIC VERDICT FINALITY
JUDGMENT PLACITUM SENTENCE
SUFFRAGE UMPIRAGE
(— BY MAJORITY) VOTE
(— OF COURT) HOLDING
ABSOLVITOR
(— OF REFEREE) TKO
(— OF UMPIRE) OUT FOUL SAFE
(EXISTENTIAL —) LEAP
(FINAL —) ISSUE
(LEGAL —) FETWA
(MUSLIM LEGAL —) FETWA
DECISIVE FATAL FINAL CRISIC
PAYOFF VIRILE CRUCIAL DECIDED
CRITICAL CRUSHING DECRETAL
POSITIVE
DECISIVELY FINALLY
DECK FIG TOG BANK BUSK BUSS
DAUB DINK FLAT HEAP PINK POOP
PROW TIER TRIG ADORN ARRAY
COVER DIZEN DRESS EQUIP FLOOR
HATCH PRANK PRINK STORE
AWNING BEDECK BETRIM BLAZON
CLOTHE ENRICH FETTLE FOCSLE
LAUREL APPAREL BEDIGHT BEDIZEN
FEATHER FLOUNCE GEMMATE
TERRACE BEAUTIFY DECORATE
EMBLAZON PLATFORM FLYBRIDGE
(— OF CARDS) BOOK
(— OUT) BARB TIFF ARRAY DIZEN
SPICK BEDECK DAIKER FANGLE
FINIFY BEDIGHT
(HIGH —) POOP
(LOWEST —) ORLOP
DECKED CLAD BESEEN ARMORIED
LAURELED
(— OUT) CLAD SPIFFED
DECKHAND BOATMAN TRIMMER
BARGEMAN ROUSTABOUT
DECKHOUSE CABOOSE CAMBOOSE
PILOTHOUSE
DECKLE DECKEL FEATHEREDGE
DECKMAN TRIPPER LEVERMAN
DECLAIM GALE RANT RAVE ROLL
MOUTH ORATE SPEAK SPOUT
BLEEZE RECITE ELOCUTE INVEIGH
DENOUNCE DISCLAIM HARANGUE
PERORATE SINGSONG
DECLAIMER BARD SPEECHIFIER
DECLAMATION FROTHING
HARANGUE RHETORIC SPOUTING
PHILIPPIC
DECLARATION BILL CALL DICK
NARR TALE WORD COUNT FUERO
LIBEL PAROL AVOWAL DECEIT
MISERE ORACLE PAROLE PLACET
SAYING EXPRESS PROMISE RESOLVE
MANIFEST PLATFORM
(— IN BRIDGE) MAKE AUCTION
(— OF HOSTILITIES) DEFIANCE

(OFFICIAL —) AUTHORITY
(PUBLIC —) MANIFESTO
DECLARE BID KEN LAY SAY VOW
AVER AVOW DENY MAKE READ
SHOW SNUM SWAN TROW VOTE
AREAD AREED BRUIT KEETH KITHE
KYTHE POSIT SNORE SOUND SPEAK
STATE TRUTH VOUCH AFFIRM
ALLEGE ASSERT ASSURE AUTHOR
AVOUCH BLAZON COUTHE DEPONE
DESCRY EXPONE HERALD INDICT
NOTIFY PATEFY RELATE SPRING
UPGIVE ACCLAIM BEHIGHT DISCUSS
EXPRESS OUTTELL PROFESS
PROTEST PUBLISH SIGNIFY TERMINE
TESTIFY ANNOUNCE DENOUNCE
DESCRIBE INDICATE INTIMATE
MAINTAIN MANIFEST NUNCIATE
PROCLAIM RENOUNCE PREDICATE
(— ARBITRARILY) GAVEL
(— A SAINT) CANONIZE
(— INVALID) ANNUL
(— PUBLICLY) CRY
(— TRUE) SOOTHE
(— UNTRUE) DENY
(— WAR) DEFY
(SOLEMNLY —) AFFY SWEAR
DECLARED AVOWED STATED
DECLARER LAWMAN VIVANT
DECLINATION BIAS DECAY SLOPE
REGRET DECLINE DESCENT REFUSAL
SOUTHING SWERVING
DECLINE BEG DIP EBB SAG SET BALK
BEND BUST DENY DIVE DOWN DROP
FADE FAIL FALL FLAG FLOP HELD
SINK SLIP TURN VAIL WANE WELK
BAULK CHUTE DECAY DROLL DROOP
DWINE FAINT HEALD HIELD LAPSE
LOWER QUAIL REPEL SLACK SLOPE
SLUMP SPURN STOOP STRAY TABES
WAIVE DEBASE DEVALL FALTER
REFUSE REJECT RENEGE SICKEN
WEAKEN ATROPHY DESCEND
DESCENT DETRECT DEVIATE
DISAVOW DWINDLE ECLIPSE FAILURE
FALLOFF FORBEAR INFLECT
LETDOWN SINKAGE DECREASE
DOWNBEAT DOWNTURN FOREBEAR
LANGUISH MELTDOWN TOBOGGAN
WITHDRAW REPUDIATE
(— IN MARKET PRICE) SPILL
(— IN POPULATION) CRASH
(ECONOMIC —) SLUMPFLATION
(INTO A STATE OF —) SOUTH
(PREF.) CLIN
DECLINING DOWN AWANE BEARISH
FALLING WESTERN DECADENT
DECLIVITY BENT BREW FALL HANG
SIDE SKUG CLIFF COAST DEVEX
PITCH SCARP SLENT SLOPE CALADE
HANGER DECLINE DESCENT
HANGING DOWNHILL
DECLIVOUS PRONE SLOPING

DECOCT BOIL COOK SMELT EXCITE
KINDLE REFINE EXTRACT
DECOCTION BANG OOZE SAVE
BHANG APOZEM CREMOR PTISAN
TISANE APOZEMA DECOCTUM
DECODE CLEAR DECRYPT
DECOHERER TAPPER
DECOLLETE LOW
DECOMPOSE ROT FOUL FRIT DECAY
ATTACK DIGEST DEGRADE DISSOLVE
DECOMPOSED BAD PUTRID
DECOMPOSITION DECAY BREAKUP
BIOLYSIS EXCHANGE
(DOUBLE —) METATHESIS
(SUFF.) LYSE LYSIS LYST LYTE LYTIC
LYZE
DECORATE DO BIND BUSK CHIP CITE
DECK EDGE FRET GAUD PINK RAIL
RULE TIFF TIRE TRIM ADORN DRESS
FLOCK FRILL GRAIN INLAY MENSE
PANEL POKER TRAIL TRICK BEDECK
BUTTON DAIKER DAMASK DECORE
EMBOSS FLOWER FRESCO PARGET
POUNCE PURFLE SPONGE SUBORN
BECROSS CORONET ENCHASE
FESTOON FURNISH GADROON
GARNISH HISTORY IMPASTE
INWEAVE MINIATE PERFORM
BELETTER FLOURISH ORNAMENT
OVERWORK TITIVATE
DECORATED GIDDY LACED AJOURE
FLAMBE ORNATE ADORNED
DAMASSE FROGGED INCISED
WROUGHT COCKADED DISTINCT
FLORETED
(— WITH PENDANTS) SCARFED
(ELABORATELY —) RICH
DECORATING LIMNERY
DECORATION KEY BUHL FALL FUSS
IKAT BOULE DECOR DODAD HONOR
MEDAL PRIDE BOULLE DECKER
DECORE DESIGN DOODAB DOODAD
FINERY FLORET FRIEZE GOTHIC
NIELLO PLAQUE SETOFF TINSEL
ARTWORK BARBOLA DECKING
EPERGNE FLUTING GARNISH
TRACERY BAYADERE DENTELLE
DIAMANTE ESCALLOP FILIGREE
FLOURISH FOOFARAW FRETTING
FRETWORK FRIPPERY FURBELOW
INTARSIA ORNAMENT
(— IN GUEST CHAMBER) XENIUM
(— OF LEAVES) VIGNETTE
(— OF MONKEYS) SINGERIE
(— TECHNIQUE) PLANGI
(BOOK-COVER —) DENTELLE
(CURVED —) OGEE
(CUTOUT —) APPLIQUE
(ENAMEL —) WUTSAI
(FESTIVE) GALA
(INESSENTIAL —) SPINACH
(INLAID —) BUHL BOULE BOULLE
(MURAL —) TOPIA

(MUSICAL —) GRACE
(PAINTED —) ROSEMALING
(PORCELAIN —) KAKIEMON
(POTTERY —) BRODERIE
(RICH —) PARAMENT
(SCANDINAVIAN —) ROSEMALING
(TABLE —) DOILY
(WALL —) ARRAS
(WALL —S) TENTURE
(PL.) COLORS BUNTING GREENERY
DECORATIVE FANCY FIKIE
(OVERLY —) DITSY DITZY
DECORATOR PAINTER
DECOROUS CALM DONE GOOD NICE
PRIM DOUCE GRAVE QUIET SOBER
STAID CHASTE DECENT DEMURE
MODEST POLITE PROPER SEDATE
SEEMLY SERENE STEADY BECOMED
FITTING ORDERLY REGULAR SETTLED
BECOMING COMPOSED MANNERLY
DECOROUSLY FITLY
DECOROUSNESS CHASTITY
POLITESSE
DECORTICATE FLAY HULL HUSK
PARE PEEL PILL SKIN STRIP DENUDE
DECORUM DECENCY DIGNITY
FITNESS HONESTY MODESTY
PROPRIETY
DECOY COY BAIT CALL GOAD LURE
TOLE TOLL COACH CRIMP DRILL
PLANT ROPER SHILL STALE STALL
STOOL TEMPT TRAIN ALLURE
BUTTON CALLER CAPPER ENTICE
ENTRAP PIGEON SEDUCE TOLLER
TREPAN BARNARD BERNARD
DECOYER INVEIGLE SQUAWKER
(— FOR GAMBLERS) CAPPER
(— FOR SWINDLERS) BARNARD
BERNARD
(AUCTIONEER'S —) BONNET BUTTON
DECREASE EBB BATE DROP FALL
LOSS SINK WANE WELK WILK ABATE
CROCK DECAY LAPSE SWAGE TAPER
WANZE WASTE CHANGE DECESS
DECREW IMPAIR LESSEN NARROW
REDUCE SHRINK ATROPHY
CUTDOWN DECLINE DWINDLE
SHORTEN SLACKEN SUBSIDE
ABLATION DECIMATE DIMINISH
DOWNTURN MODERATE RETRENCH
(— IN FORCE) LAY
(— IN VOLUME) ABLATION
(— IN WIDTH) INTAKE
(— OF EFFICIENCY) FATIGUE
(— STITCHES) FASHION
DECREE ACT DIT LAW SAW SET
DOOM FIAT REDE RULE WILL WITE
AREAD AREED ARRET CANON EDICT
ENACT FIANT GRACE HATTI IRADE
JUDGE ORDER POINT SHAPE TENET
UKASE WRITE ARREST ASSIZE
DECERN DICTUM DIKTAT FIRMAN
INDICT MODIFY ORDAIN PLACIT

RECESS ADJUDGE APPOINT BESLUIT
COMMAND CONSULT DECREET
DICTATE DIVORCE ESCRIPT GEZERAH
MANDATE SETNESS STATUTE
WORKING DECISION DECRETUM
JUDGMENT PLACITUM PSEPHISM
RESCRIPT ROGATION SANCTION
SENTENCE ORDINANCE ABSOLVITOR
(— BEFOREHAND) DESTINE
(ECCLESIASTICAL —) CANON
SYNODICAL
(JUDICIAL —) AUTO
(MOHAMMEDAN —) IRADE
(OFFICIAL —) RESCRIPT
(PAPAL —) BULL DECRETAL
DECREPIT LAME WEAK UNORN
BEDRID CREAKY FEEBLE INFIRM
SENILE FAILING INVALID FORFAIRN
DECRY BOO CRAB SLUR LOWER
ROGUE DESCRY LESSEN ASPERSE
BARRACK CENSURE CONDEMN
DEBAUCH DEGRADE DETRACT
BELITTLE DEROGATE MINIMIZE
DECRYPT BREAK DECODE
DECURRENT DEFLUENT
DECUSSATION CHIASM CHIASMA
DEDAN (FATHER OF —) RAAMAH
JOKSHAN
(MOTHER OF —) KETURAH
DEDANS HAZARD
DEDICATE VOW VOTE DEVOW SACRE
SACRI DEVOTE DEVOVE DIRECT
HALLOW OBLATE ASCRIBE ENTITLE
CHRISTEN INSCRIBE INTITULE
SEPARATE NUNCUPATE
(— TO CHURCH) IMMOLATE
DEDICATED HOLY OBLATE SACRED
VOTIVE
DEDICATION CULT WAKF DEVOTION
DEDUCE PUT DRAW LEAD TAKE
BRING DRIVE FETCH GUESS INFER
TRACE DEDUCT DERIVE ELICIT
EVOLVE GATHER COLLECT EXPLAIN
EXTRACT SUBSUME CONCLUDE
DEDUCT BATE DOCK TAKE ABATE
ALLOW SHAVE DEFALK REBATE
RECOUP REDUCT REMOVE CURTAIL
SUBDUCT TAKEOUT TRADUCE
ABSTRACT DISCOUNT SEPARATE
SUBTRACT
DEDUCTION AGIO SALT CREDIT
DEDUCT REBATE BEAMAGE
DOCKAGE IMPRESS OFFTAKE
REPRISE DISCOUNT ERGOTISM
ILLATION STOPPAGE ABATEMENT
COROLLARY
(YEARLY —) REPRISE
DEDUCTIVE DOGMATIC
DEE DUANT
DEED DO ACT BILL BOOK CASE FACT
FAIT FEAT FIAT GEST HARD JEST
TURN WORK ACTUM ACTUS BROAD
CHART DOING GESTE ISSUE SANAD

THING TITLE ACTION CONVEY
ESCROW FACTUM POTTAH REMISE
SASINE SUNNUD TAILYE CHARTER
EXPLOIT FACTION TAILZIE CHIVALRY
HEIRLOOM PARERGON PRACTICE
PRACTISE TRANSFER HARDIMENT
PERFORMANCE
(BRUTAL —) ATROCITY
(CHARITABLE —S) ALMS
(DARING —) GESTE
(EVIL —) PRANK MALEFACTION
(GOOD —) BENEFIT MITZVAH
(HEBREW —) STARR
(KIND —) FAVOR
(PART OF —) HABENDUM
(VALIANT —) VALIANCE
(WICKED —) ILL
(PL.) DOINGS SERVICE MUNIMENTS
DEEM LET SAY SEE GIVE HOPE RECK
SEEM TELL JUDGE OPINE THINK
ESTEEM EXPECT ORDAIN RECKON
REGARD ACCOUNT ADJUDGE
BELIEVE RECOUNT RESPECT
SURMISE ANNOUNCE CONSIDER
JUDGMENT PROCLAIM
DE-EMPHASIZE DOWNPLAY
DEEMSTER DOOMSMAN
DE-ENERGIZE KILL CLEAR
DEEP LOW SAD SEA BASS BOLD
DUAT HOLL HOWE NEAL RAPT
ABYSS BROAD DEWAT GRAVE GREAT
GRUFF HEAVY OCEAN SOUND STIFF
STOOR STOUR HOLLOW INTENT
STRONG SULLEN ABYSMAL INTENSE
SERIOUS UNMIXED ABSORBED
ABSTRUSE COMPLETE POWERFUL
PROFOUND THOROUGH RECONDITE
(— IN COLOR) RICH
(— IN THE THROAT) GRUM
(PREF.) (— SEA) BATH(O)(Y)
DEEP-DYED ENGRAINED
DEEPEN CLOUD DARKEN DREDGE
ENHANCE THICKEN HEIGHTEN
DEEPEST INMOST DEEPMOST
DEEPLY DEEP INLY ADEEP DEARLY
SOUNDLY DEVOUTLY GROUNDLY
INWARDLY
DEEP-SEA DIPSY BATHYL DIPSEY
BATHYAL
DEEP-SEATED CHRONIC DEEP
INTIMATE PROFOUND INGRAINED
DEEP-TONED STOUR
DEER ELK RED REH ROE AXIS BUCK
DAIM HART HIND MILU MUSK OLEN
PARA PUDU RUSA SHOU SIKA STAG
WILD BROCK GEMUL MARAL MOOSE
SABIR SPADE STAIG CERVID CHITAL
CHITRA FALLOW GUEMAL HANGUL
HEARST HUEMUL PARRAH RASCAL
SAMBAR SAMBUR THAMIN VENADA
BROCKET BROWZER CARIBOU
CERVINE CERVOID CHEETAL DEERLET
FANTAIL GUAZUTI KASTURA

MUNTJAC PLANDOK SAMBHAR
THAMENG VENISON BOBOLINK
CARIACOU CARJACOU ELAPHURE
RUMINANT
(— IN 3RD YEAR) SPAY SOREL
SPAYAD SPAYARD
(— UNDER 1 YEAR) KID
(CASTRATED —) HAVIER
(FEMALE —) DOE ROE HIND
(FEMALE — IN 2ND YEAR) TEG
HEARST
(HINDQUARTERS OF —) FOUCH
FOURCHE
(MALE — IN 2ND YEAR) PRICKET
(MALE — IN 4TH YEAR) SORE
STAGGARD STAGGART
(MALE — OVER 5 YEARS) HART STAG
(RED —) OLEN SPAY MARAL
BROCKET
(RUSINE —) AXIS
(YOUNG —) KID FAWN SPITTER
(2-YEAR OLD —) KNOBBER
(PREF.) CERVI
DEER BUSH SOAPBUSH
DEER FERN HARDFERN
DEERFLY TABANID
DEERHAIR SEDGE BULRUSH
DEERHOUND DEERDOG
BUCKHOUND
DEERSKIN BUCK DEER
DEERSLAYER (AUTHOR OF —)
COOPER
(CHARACTER IN —) HARRY HETTY
NATTY UNCAS BUMPPO HUTTER
JUDITH THOMAS CHINGACHGOOK
DEFACE MAR FOUL RUIN SCAR
ERASE SHAME SPOIL CANCEL
DAMAGE DAMASK DEFAME DEFOIL
DEFORM DEFOUL EFFACE INJURE
INJURY DESTROY DETRACT
DISTORT SLANDER DISGRACE
DISHONOR MALAHACK MUTILATE
OUTSHINE
DEFACED FOUL
DEFACING DIMINUTION
DEFALCATE DRIB DEFALK
DEFAMATION LIBEL SMEAR
DEFAME DEFAMY DEPRAVE SCANDAL
SLANDER ASPERSION
DEFAMATORY SCANDALOUS
DEFAME FOUL ABASE BELIE CLOUD
LIBEL NOISE SMEAR ACCUSE
CHARGE DEFACE DEFOIL DEFOUL
FORGAB INFAME INJURE MALIGN
REVILE SUGGIL VILIFY ASPERSE
BLACKEN BLEMISH DEBAUCH
DETRACT DIFFAME PUBLISH
SCANDAL SLANDER SPATTER
TRADUCE DISHONOR INFAMIZE
VILIPEND
DEFAMER SYCOPHANT
DEFAULT FAIL FLAW LOSS MORA
ERROR FAULT OFFEND BLEMISH
FAILURE MISTAKE NEGLECT
OFFENSE OMISSION
(— ON DEBT) LEVANT
DEFAULTER DUCK
(PL.) JANKERS
DEFEASANCE DEFEAT UNDOING
DEFEASIBLE IMPERFECT
DEFEAT ACE EAT PIP WIN BALK BEAT
BEST BOWL CAST DING DOWN DRUB
FOIL HAVE JINK KILL LACE LICK LOSS
ROUT RUIN RUSH SINK SKIN STOP
TOLL TOSS TRAP TRIM UNDO WHAP
WHIP WHOP AVOID BREAK CHECK
FACER FALSE FLING FLOOR OUTDO
PASTE SHEND SKUNK SMITE SWAMP
THROW UPEND WASTE WHACK
WORSE WORST WRACK BAFFLE
CUMBER DEROUT EUCHRE HOSING
LARRUP MASTER MURDER OUTGUN
REBUFF STOUSH THWACK THWART
WAGGLE WEAKEN CLOBBER
CONQUER DEPRIVE DESTROY
LICKING OVERSET PEREMPT
REVERSE SCOMFIT SETBACK
SHELLAC SNOOKER SUBVERT
TROUNCE INFRINGE IRRITATE
OUTFIGHT OVERCOME SLOSHING
VANQUISH WATERLOO OVERPOWER
OVERTHROW
(— BY INGENUITY) OUTWIT
(— COMPLETELY) SKUNK
(— DECISIVELY) EAT DRUB SACK
BLAST CLEAN FLATTEN SHELLAC
(— IN BRIDGE) SET
(— IN LAWSUIT) CAST
(DECISIVE —) CLEANUP CLEANING
PLASTERING
(INTO —) DOWN
(UTTER —) MATE ROUT DEROUT
DEFEATED DOWN LOST KAPUT
BEATEN CRAVEN WHIPPED
DEFEATIST BOLO FATALIST
DEFECT BUG FLAW LACK MAIM
MOTE TWIT VICE WANE WANT WART
BOTCH CLOUD CRAZE ERROR FAULT
MINUS MULCT TOUCH DAMAGE
DESERT HIATUS INJURY LACUNA
MALADY MAYHEM PLIGHT VICETY
VITIUM ABSENCE BLEMISH DEMERIT
FAILING MISPICK PEELING PINHOLE
COLOBOMA CRESCENT DRAWBACK
WEAKNESS SHORTCOMING
(— IN ARTICULATION) PSELLISM
(— IN CRYSTAL) HOLE
(— IN ENAMEL) SCAB SAGGING
SCUMMING
(— IN FABRIC) GOUT SCOB BARRE
BRACK SMASH
(— IN GLASS) KNOT TEAR STONE
WREATH THREADS
(— IN IRON) SEAM
(— IN MARBLE) TERRAS TERRACE
TERRASSE

(— IN METAL) SNAKE BLOWHOLE
(— IN PRINTING PLATE) HICKY
HICKEY
(— IN STEEL) LAP
(— IN TIMBER) LAG SHAN COLLAPSE
(— IN YARN) SINGLING CORKSCREW
(— OF CHARACTER) HOLE SHADE
HAMARTIA
(LINT —) SPOT
(SPEECH —) BALBUTIES CLUTTERING
(TELEVISION —) FLOPOVER
DEFECTION LETDOWN APOSTASY
DESERTION
DEFECTIVE BAD ILL EVIL FOXY LACK
LAME MANK POOR SICK BAUCH
BAUGH BLIND FALSE FLAWY PASUL
COMMON FAULTY FLAWED MANGUE
MEAGER MEAGRE RAGGED HALTING
TOMFOOL VICIOUS DISGENIC
DYSGENIC MUTILOUS VITIATED
(— PRODUCT) LEMON
(MENTALLY —) WANTING
(PREF.) ATEL(O)
DEFECTOR APOSTATE DESERTER
FUGITIVE
DEFEND FEND HOLD KEEP SAVE
WARD WARN WEAR COVER GUARD
SHEND WATCH ASSERT FORBID
SCREEN SECURE SHIELD UPHOLD
WARISH BUCKLER BULWARK
CONTEST DERAIGN ESPOUSE
EXPOUND FLANKER JUSTIFY
PREVENT PROPUGN PROTECT
SHELTER SUPPORT WARRANT
ADVOCATE CHAMPION CONSERVE
GARRISON MAINTAIN PRESERVE
PROHIBIT SAFEGUARD
(— WITH SUCCESS) VINDICATE
DEFENDANT REA REUS ACCUSED
AVOWANT APPELLEE
DEFENDER FENDER PATRON
ADVOCATE ASSERTER ASSERTOR
CHAMPION GUARDIAN UPHOLDER
DEFENSE EGIS FORT PALE ROCK
WALL WARD WEAR AEGIS ALIBI
FENCE GRITH GUARD TOWER ABATIS
ANSWER BEHALF COVERT FRAISE
SCONCE BARRACE BARRIER
BASTION BULWARK CONTEST
COUNTER DEFENCE DILATOR
OUTWORK PARADOS RAMPART
SHELTER WARDING WARRANT
ADVOCACY APOLOGIA BOUNDARY
FRONTIER GALAPAGO GARRISON
MUNITION SECURITY SEPIMENT
DEFENSELESS BARE COLD NAKED
SILLY UNARMED HELPLESS
DEFENSIBLE TENABLE JUSTIFIABLE
DEFER BOW RISE STAY WAIT DELAY
DRIVE HONOR REFER REMIT STAVE
TARRY TRACK WAIVE YIELD ESTEEM
HUMBLE RETARD REVERE SUBMIT
ADJOURN SUSPEND CONSIDER

INTERMIT POSTPONE PROROGUE
PROTRACT SUSPENSE
DEFERENCE VAIL COURT HONOR
CRINGE ESTEEM HOMAGE REGARD
RESPECT WORSHIP CIVILITY
OBEISANCE
DEFERENT ECCENTRIC
DEFERENTIAL DUTIFUL OBEISANT
DEFERMENT STAY
DEFERVESCENCE LYSIS DECLINE
DEFIANCE DARE DEFI DEFY GAGE
BRAVE DEFIAL CHALLENGE
DEFIANT BOLD BARDY BRAVE STOUT
DARING STOCKY INSOLENT
STUBBORN OBSTREPEROUS
DEFIANTLY ACOCK
DEFICIENCY FAIL LACK WANT ANOIA
ERROR FAULT MINUS DEARTH
DEFECT INLAIK ULLAGE ABSENCE
ANOESIA BLEMISH DEFICIT FAILING
FAILURE POVERTY DELETION
SCARCITY SHORTAGE SHORTFALL
SHORTCOMING
(— OF BLOOD) ISCHEMIA
(— OF NERVOUS ENERGY) ANEURIA
(— OF OXYGEN) ASPHYXIA
(CARBON DIOXIDE —) ACAPNIA
(MENTAL —) IDIOCY AMENTIA
(PL.) SHORTS
(PREF.) ISCH
(SUFF.) PENIA
DEFICIENT BAD LEAN WANE BLUNT
MINUS SCANT BARREN FEEBLE
MEAGER MEAGRE SCARCE SCRIMP
SKIMPY BOBTAIL DISGENIC
DYSGENIC INDIGENT
(— IN BEAUTY) PLAIN
(— IN HEALTH) INVALID
(— IN TURGOR) FLACCID
(MENTALLY —) SOFT
(SUFF.) PRIVIC
DEFICIT SHORTAGE UNDERAGE
DEFILE GUT RAY ABRA BAWD BEDO
FILE FOIL FOUL GATE GOWL HALS
LIME MOIL MUCK PACE PASS SLIP
SLOT SLUT SMUT SOIL ABUSE
BERAY CLEFT CROCK DIRTY FILTH
GLACK GORGE HALSE NOTCH SLACK
SMEAR STAIN SULLY TAINT BEWRAY
DEBASE GULLET IMBRUE INFECT
RAVISH SMOUCH SMUTCH CORRUPT
DEBAUCH DEPRAVE DISTAIN
PASSAGE POLLUTE PROFANE
SLOTTER SMATTER TARNISH
VIOLATE DISHONOR MACULATE
DEFILED DIRTY IMPURE SPOTTY
UNCLEAN MACULATE
DEFILEMENT MOIL SOIL SULLAGE
TAINTURE
(PREF.) MEASMATO MIASMO MYS(O)
DEFILING PIKY PITCHY
DEFINE END FIX SET MERE TERM
BOUND LIMIT DECIDE CLARIFY

DELIMIT EXPLAIN EXPOUND DESCRIBE DISCOVER

DEFINED FORMED STRICT
(SHARPLY —) HARD

DEFINITE SET FIRM HARD SURE CLEAR FINAL FIXED SHARP FINITE FORMED LIQUID STRAIT CERTAIN EXPRESS LIMITED POINTED PRECISE DISTINCT EMPHATIC EXPLICIT LIMITING POSITIVE PUNCTUAL SPECIFIC

DEFINITELY BUT WELL FAIRLY EVERMORE

DEFINITION GLOSS CLARITY DIORISM
(— OF FORM) SFUMATO
(PREF.) ORISMO

DEFINITIVE LAST FINAL GRAND ORISTIC DEFINITE

DEFLATE EMPALE IMPALE CONTRACT

DEFLATED FLAT

DEFLATING SETDOWN

DEFLATION HANGOVER

DEFLECT GUT WRY BEND COCK SWAY WARP PARRY WREST WRING BAFFLE DETOUR DIVERT SWERVE DEVIATE DIVERGE INFLECT REFLECT REFRACT

DEFLECTION DROOP SWEEP WINDAGE
(— ON METER) KICK
(PREF.) SPHINGO

DEFLECTOR (AIR —) SPOILER

DEFLOWER FRAY DEFOIL DEFOUL FORLIE RAVAGE RAVISH DEFLORE DESPOIL VIOLATE UNMAIDEN UNVIRGIN

DEFORM MAR FLOW WARP GNARL DEFACE BLEMISH CONTORT DISFORM DISTORT DIFFORME DISGUISE DISHONOR MISSHAPE SHAUCHLE

DEFORMATION CREEP SPRING STRAIN FLEXURE FLOWAGE

DEFORMED GAMMY WRONG INFORM HALILE CROOKED HIDEOUS MISBORN FORMLESS UNMACKLY MISCREATE MISCREATED
(PREF.) CACH CAC(O)
(SUFF.) CACE

DEFORMITY GALL VICE BLEMISH HARELIP PRAVITY CLUBFOOT CLUBHAND FLATFOOT WANSHAPE

DEFRAUD ROB BEAT BILK FAKE GULL NICK ROOK SCAM TRIM WIPE CHEAT COZEN GOUGE LURCH MULCT SLICK STICK TRICK WRONG BOODLE CHOUSE CHOWSE RIPOFF DECEIVE SKELDER SWINDLE

DEFRAY PAY BEAR AVERT COVER ABSORB EXPEND PREPAY APPEASE REQUITE SATISFY DISBURSE

DEFT FEAT GAIN NEAT TALL TRIM AGILE HANDY NATTY QUICK SLICK ADROIT EXPERT HEPPEN NIMBLE SPRACK SPRUCE DELIVER DEXTROUS SKILLFUL

DEFTEST EFTEST

DEFTLY LIGHTLY SLICKLY DELIVERLY

DEFTNESS SLEIGHT

DEFUNCT DEAD EXTINCT DECEASED DEPARTED FINISHED

DEFY BRAG DARE DEFI FACE MOCK BEARD BRAVE FLOUT STUMP TEMPT CARTEL FORBID MAUGER MAUGRE REJECT AFFRONT BRAVADE DESPISE DISDAIN OUTDARE OUTFACE CHAMPION DEFIANCE OUTSCOUT RENOUNCE CHALLENGE

DEGENERATE ROT SINK DEBADE EFFETE UNKIND DEGENER DEGRADE DEPRAVE DESCEND DEGENDER DEROGATE
(— IN IDLENESS) RUST
(— TOWARD BARBARISM) WILDER

DEGENERATION WALLER ATROPHY ADIPOSIS PEJORATION

DEGRADATION FALL WOHL SHAME DEMISS DECLINE DESCENT ADULTERY COMEDOWN DEPOSURE IGNOMINY ABJECTION

DEGRADE BUST SINK ABASE BREAK DECRY LOWER SHAME SHEND STOOP STRIP UNMAN DEBASE DEMEAN DEMOTE DEPOSE EMBASE HUMBLE LESSEN REDUCE VILIFY CORRUPT DECLINE DEPRESS IMBRUTE REGRADE VILLAIN DIMINISH DISGRACE DISHONOR DISMOUNT DISPLUME SUPPLANT

DEGRADED BASE BROKE SEAMY ABJECT DEMISS FALLEN SORDID DEBASED DEGREED GRIECED OUTCAST

DEGRADING BASE VILE MENIAL SHAMEFUL
(PREF.) LY(O)

DEGRAS MOELLON

DEGREE PEG PIP POL BANK CAST DEAL FORM GREE HEAT PEEP POLL RANK RATE RUNG STEP TERM TIER CLASS GRADE GRADO GRECE GRICE HONOR LEVEL NOTCH ORDER PITCH PLACE POINT PRICK SHADE STAGE STAIR EXTENT GRIECE LENGTH MEDIUM SOEVER DESCENT DIGNITY MEASURE SAENGER STATION ACCURACY AEGROTAT QUANTITY STANDING STRENGTH
(— OF CLOSENESS) FIT
(— OF COLOR) SHADE
(— OF COMBINING POWER) VALENCE
(— OF CONTRAST) GAMMA
(— OF DEVIATION) LEEWAY
(— OF DISTINCTION) PHD

(— OF ELEVATION) ASCENT
(— OF ENGAGEMENT) DEPTH
(— OF EXCELLENCE) DIGNITY
(— OF FLAWLESSNESS) CLARITY
(— OF FORCE) KICK
(— OF HEIGHT) GRADE
(— OF IMPORTANCE) CALIBER
CALIBRE
(— OF INFESTATION) BURDEN
(— OF INTOXICATION) EDGE
(— OF KNOWLEDGE) SCIENTER
(— OF LIGHTNESS) VALUE
(— OF MIXTURE) ALLOY
(— OF OPACITY) DENSITY
(— OF PLENTIFULNESS) ABUNDANCE
(— OF PRESTIGE) PLACE
(— OF QUALITY) VALUE
(— OF SLOPE) PITCH SPLAY
(— OF STREAMLINING) FAIRNESS
(— OF THE SOUL) RUACH
(— OF WATER HARDNESS) GRAIN
(— OF WHITENESS) BLEACH
(CONFUSING —) WHIRL
(EXCESSIVE —) EXTREME
(GREATEST —) UTMOST OPTIMUM
(HIGHEST —) PINK SUMMIT
SUPREME SUBLIMITY
(INDEFINITE —) SEEM
(LEAST —) MINIMUM
(MINUTE —) DROP SHADE
(MUSICAL —) SPACE SUBTONIC
(RABBINICAL —) SEMICHA SEMIKAH
SEMICHAH
(SMALL —) ACE TAD HAIR INCH IOTA
SHADOW GLIMMER
(SOME —) BIT
(TO A GREAT —) INSPADES
(TO A MODERATE —) RATHER
SORTOF
(UTMOST —) MAX NTH SUM ACME
HEIGHT EXTREME EXTREMITY
(10 —S OF LONGITUDE) FACE
(15 —S) HOUR
(PREF.) (OF THE THIRD ALGEBRAIC —)
CUB(I)(O)
(SUFF.) ANCE ANT ENCE ITY NESS TY
DEGU OCTODONT
DEGUM STRIP
(— SILK) SOUPLE
DEHGAN SWAT SWATI
DEHORN SNUB DISBUD
DEHWAR DEHKAN
DEHYDRATE DRY DESICCATE
DEIANIRA (BROTHER OF —) TYDEUS
MELEAGER
(FATHER OF —) OENEUS
(HUSBAND OF —) HERCULES
(MOTHER OF —) ALTHAEA
DEIDAMIA HIPPODAMIA
(FATHER OF —) LYCOMEDES
(LOVER OF —) ACHILLES
(SON OF —) PYRRHUS
NEOPTOLEMUS

DEIFICATION APOTHEOSIS
DEIFY GOD BEGOD DIVINE GODDIZE
DIVINIFY DIVINIZE
DEIGN STOOP VOUCHSAFE
DEILEON (BROTHER OF —) PHLOGIUS
AUTOLYCUS
(FATHER OF —) DEIMACHUS
DEION (DAUGHTER OF —)
ASTERODIA
(FATHER OF —) AEOLUS
(MOTHER OF —) ENARETE
(SON OF —) ACTOR AENETUS
CEPHALUS PHYLACUS
(WIFE OF —) DIOMEDE
DEIPHOBUS (BROTHER OF —) PARIS
HECTOR
(FATHER OF —) PRIAM
(MOTHER OF —) HECUBA
(WIFE OF —) HELEN
DEIPYLE (FATHER OF —) ADRASTUS
(HUSBAND OF —) TYDEUS
(SISTER OF —) AEGIA ARGIA
(SON OF —) DIOMEDES
DEIPYLUS (FATHER OF —)
POLYMNESTOR
(MOTHER OF —) ILIONE
DEITY (ALSO SEE GOD AND
GODDESS) EA EL KA RA RE SU ABU
BEL GAD GOD RAN SHU SOL AKAL
AMEN AMON BAAL CAGN DEVA
FAUN FURY GWYN MIND MORS
RANA SIVA SOBK ALALA ALALU
AMIDA AMITA AMMON DAGAN
DAGON HAOMA HOBAL HORUS
HUBAL INUUS JANUS MIDER MITRA
MONAD SATYR SEBEK SHIVA SIRIS
SURYA ZOMBI ASHIMA ATHTAR
BATALA BUNENE CAISSA FATHER
FAUNUS IASION MARDUK MOLOCH
NIBHAZ OANNES ORISHA ORMAZD
ORMUZD RIMMON SOMNUS
SUCHOS SYLVAN VARUNA ZOMBIE
ALASTOR FORSETE FORSETI
GODDESS GODHEAD GODLING
GODSHIP HERSHEF IAPETUS
KHEPERA MANITOU NINURTA
NISROCH PHORCUS PHORKYS
RESHEPH SETEBOS SILENUS
TAGALOA TARANIS VIRBIUS
BAALPEOR BEELPEOR BELFAGOR
DEVARAJA DIVINITY ELAGABAL
GOVERNOR HACHIMAN MELKARTH
MERODACH PICUMNUS PILUMNUS
SEILENOS SILVANUS TANGALOA
TUTELARY ZEPHYRUS ZOOMORPH
(AVENGING —) ALASTOR
(BIBLE —) ELI ABBA ELOI
(HEATHEN —) IDOL
(INFERIOR —) GODKIN GODLING
DEMIURGE PETTYGOD
(PRESIDING —) NUMEN
(SHINTO —) KAMI
(SUPREME —) HANSA

(TUTELARY —) LAR NUMEN GENIUS
(ZOROASTRIAN —) HAOMA
(PL.) CABIRI PENATES
DEJECT ABASE LOWER HUMBLE
LESSEN FLATTEN DISPIRIT
DOWNCAST
DEJECTA EGESTA
DEJECTED BAD LOW SAD DAMP
DOWN GLUM POOR SUNK AMORT
MUDDY WAPED ABASED ABATTU
DEJECT DEMISS DROOPY GLOOMY
PINING SOMBER SOMBRE ALAMORT
DUMPISH HANGDOG HANGING
HUMBLED LUMPISH UNHAPPY
DOWNCAST DOWNWARD REPINING
WOBEGONE WRETCHED
MELANCHOLY
DEJECTEDLY HEAVILY
DEJECTION CRAB DAMP GLOOM
SLOTH DISMAY DISMALS HUMDRUM
SADNESS MELANCHOLY
DEJEUNER LUNCH BREAKFAST
COLAZIONE COLLATION
DEKASTERE
(ABBR.) DAS
DEL NABLA
DELAIAH
(FATHER OF —) MEHETABEEL
(SON OF —) SHEMAIAH

DELAWARE
CAPITAL: DOVER
COUNTY: KENT SUSSEX NEWCASTLE
INDIAN: LENAPE
STATE BIRD: BLUEHEN
STATE FLOWER: PEACH
STATE NICKNAME: FIRST BLUEHEN
DIAMOND
STATE TREE: HOLLY
TOWN: LEWES NEWARK SMYRNA
ELSMERE CLAYMONT WILMINGTON

DELAY LAG LET BLIN BODE HOLD
HONE LENG LING LITE MORA SIST
SLOW SLUG STAY STOP WAIT ABIDE
ABODE ALLAY BLINE CHECK DALLY
DEFER DEMUR DETER DRIFT DWELL
FRIST PAUSE REPRY SLOTH STALL
STENT STICK STINT TARDY TARRY
TRACT ARREST ATTEND BACKEN
BELATE DAWDLE DETAIN DILATE
DILUTE DRETCH ESSOIN FUTURE
HINDER HOLDUP IMPEDE LINGER
LOITER QUENCH REMORE RETARD
TAIGLE TARROW TEMPER WEAKEN
ADJOURN ASSUAGE BARRACE
CONFINE DRUTTLE FORSLOW
PROLONG RESPECT RESPITE
SLACKEN SOJOURN DEMURRAL
DILATION FORESLOW FOURCHER
HANGFIRE HESITATE MACERATE
MITIGATE MORATION OBSTRUCT
POSTPONE PROTRACT REPRIEVE

STOPPAGE DEMURRAGE
CUNCTATION OBSTRUCTION
(— IN COUNTDOWN) HOLD
(— IN EXECUTION) REPRIEVE
(— IN EXPLOSION) HANGFIRE
(— TRIAL) TRAVERSE
(LEGAL —) DILATOR INDUCIAE
(UNDUE —) LACHES
(WITHOUT —) PRONTO
(PL.) AMBAGES
DELAYED LATE TARDY LAGGED
BELATED OVERDUE
DELAYING TRAIN DILATORY
DELECTABLE TASTY DESIROUS
PLEASING BEAUTIFUL EXQUISITE
DELECTATE PLEASE
DELEGATE NAME SEND ASSIGN
COMMIT DELATE DEPUTE DEPUTY
LEGATE NUNCIO APPOINT CONSIGN
EMPOWER ENTRUST EMISSARY
RELEGATE TRANSFER
DELEGATION MISSION DELEGACY
(ATHENIAN —) DELIA
DELETE DELE EDIT OMIT BLACK
ERASE PURGE SLASH CANCEL
CENSOR DELATE REMOVE STRIKE
DESTROY EXPUNGE STONKER
CASTRATE
DELETERIOUS BAD PRAVE
HARMFUL HURTFUL NOXIOUS
PRAVOUS DAMAGING DELETERY
PERNICIOUS
DELI
(— ORDER) BLT
DELIBERATE COOL PORE RUNE
SLOW STUDY THINK VOULU ADVISE
CONFER DEBATE PONDER REGARD
ADVISED BALANCE BETHINK
CONSULT COUNCIL COUNSEL
DELIBER DELIVER REFLECT RESOLVE
STUDIED WILLING WITTING
CONSIDER DESIGNED MEASURED
MEDITATE PERPENSE PREPENSE
PROPENSE STUDIOUS
DELIBERATELY COOLY COOLLY
APURPOSE ADVISEDLY
DELIBERATENESS MATURITY
DELIBERATION ADVICE COUNCIL
COUNSEL LEISURE THOUGHT
VISEMENT
DELICACY BIT ROE CATE EASE NORI
TACT ACATE FRILL KNACK TASTE
CAVIAR DAINTY DELICE JUNKET
LUXURY NICETY REGALO TIDBIT
FINESSE RAREBIT REGALIA TENUITY
TRINKET AIRINESS DAINTITH
DAINTREL DELICATE KICKSHAW
LEGERETE NICENESS PLEASURE
SUBTLETY
(STUFFED —) DERMA
(PL.) CATES ACATES
DELICATE SLY AIRY FINE LACY NESH
NICE SOFT TEAR TWEE ZART DELIE

DORTY ELFIN FAIRY FRAIL LIGHT
SILKY TEWLY CASHIE CHOICE DAINTY
FLIMSY GENTLE GINGER INCONY
KITTLE MINION PASTEL PETITE
PULING QUEASY SILKEN SLIGHT
SUBTLE TENDER TICKLE TWIGGY
ELEGANT EPICENE FINICAL FRAGILE
MINIKIN REFINED SLIMMER SUBTILE
SUMMERY TAFFETA TAFFETY
TENUOUS TIFFANY WILLOWY
ARANEOUS CHARMING ETHEREAL
FEATHERY GOSSAMER GRACEFUL
HOTHOUSE LUSCIOUS MIGNIARD
PINDLING PLEASANT SENSIBLE
SUMMERLY TICKLISH UNLUSTIE
(— IN APPEARANCE) HUNGRY
(AFFECTEDLY —) ROSEWATER
(PREF.) ABRO HABRO
DELICATELY FINE SMALLY FAIRILY
MELTINGLY
DELICATESSEN DELI DELLY
GASTRONOME CHARCUTERIE
DELICIOUS TASTY YUMMY DAINTY
FRIAND DELICATE SCRUMPTIOUS
DELIGHT JOY GLEE GUST LITE
LOVE SEND TAKE BLESS BLISS
CHARM EXULT FEAST GRACE
GUSTO MIRTH REVEL SAVOR
SMACK ADMIRE ARRIDE DELICE
DIVERT LIKING PLEASE RAVISH
REGALE RELISH TICKLE DISPORT
ECSTASY ENCHANT GLADDEN
GRATIFY JOYANCE JOYANCY
LECHERY RAPTURE REJOICE
DELICATE ENTRANCE GLADNESS
PLEASURE SAVORING
(— IN) LOVE SAVOR
(PL.) DELICIAE
DELIGHTED GLAD
DELIGHTFUL NICE GREAT JAMMY
JOLLY MERRY SOOTH DREAMY
SAVORY ELYSIAN LEESOME
ADORABLE CHARMING DELICATE
DELITOUS GLORIOUS GORGEOUS
HEAVENLY LUSCIOUS SCRUMPTIOUS
DELIMER DRENCHER
DELIMIT FIX DEFINE SUBTEND
DELIMITATION
(PREF.) HORISMO
DELIMITED MERED MEERED
DELINEATE MAP DRAW ETCH LIMN
LINE CHALK CHART FENCE IMAGE
PAINT STELL TABLE TOUCH TRACE
TRICK BLAZON CIPHER DELINE
DEPICT DESIGN DEVISE SKETCH
SURVEY DEPAINT EXPRESS LINEATE
OUTLINE PICTURE PORTRAY
DECIPHER DEFIGURE DESCRIBE
TRAVERSE
DELINEATION DRAFT DESIGN
SKETCH SURVEY DRAUGHT
(CARELESS —) PERIGRAPH

DELINQUENCY FAULT GUILT
FAILURE MISDEED OFFENSE
OMISSION
DELINQUENT CRIMINAL
(JUVENILE —) HALBSTARKER
(PL.) KALANG
DELIQUESCE MELT LIQUEFY
DISSOLVE
DELIRIOUS FEY MAD OFF REE GYTE
LIGHT MANIC INSANE RAVING
FLIGHTY FRANTIC LUNATIC
MADDING BRAINISH DELEERIT
DELIERET DERANGED FRENETIC
FRENZIED
DELIRIUM FURY MAZE MANIA
FRENZY LUNACY RAVERY RAVING
MADNESS DELIRACY IDLENESS
INSANITY
DELIRIUM TREMENS JUMP
HORRORS JIMJAMS JIMMIES
POTOMANIA
DELITESCENT LATENT
DELIVER DO HIT LAY LET RID BAIL
BORN DEAL FREE GIVE LEND REDD
SAVE SELL SEND TAKE BEKEN BRING
COUGH LIVER SERVE SPEAK UTTER
ADDICT ASSIZE ASSOIL BETRAY
COMMIT CONVEY EXEMPT PREACH
RANSOM REDEEM RENDER RESCUE
RESIGN SUCCOR UNBIND BETEACH
BITECHE COMMEND CONSIGN
DECLAIM DICTATE OUTTAKE
PRESENT RECOVER RELEASE
RELIEVE DISPATCH EXORCISE
EXORCIZE LIBERATE
(— BALL) BOWL
(— BLOW) LEND POKE SEND
(— BLOWS ON HEAD) NOB
(— CHILD) LIGHT
(— FORCEFULLY) FASTEN
(— FORMALLY) SERVE
(— FROM EVIL SPIRIT) EXORCIZE
(— FROM SIN) SAVE
(— LECTURES) READ
(— LOGS) STOCK
(— MERCHANDISE) UTTER
(— OVER) BETAKE CONSIGN
(— RHETORICALLY) DECLAIM
(— SERMON) PREACH
(— SPEECH) ADDRESS
DELIVERANCE BOOT ESCAPE
RANSOM RESCUE SAVING DELIVERY
RIDDANCE SOLUTION VOIDANCE
SALVATION
(FESTIVAL OF —) PURIM
DELIVERED LANDED
(— FREE) FRANCO
(PRECISELY —) FLUSH
DELIVERER SOTER SAVIOR
DRAYMAN SAOSHYANT
DELIVERY FLY BAIL FLIER FLYER
ISSUE LIVERY RESCUE ADDRESS

AIRDROP BAILMENT SHIPMENT
ACCOUCHEMENT
(— IN SPEAKING) DICTION
(— OF BALL) BOWL
(— WAGON) FLY
(MAIL —) TAPPALL TAPPAUL
(PREF.) TOCO TOKO
(SUFF.) TOCIA TOCO(US) TOKIA
TOKO(US) TOKY

DELL DEN HOW DALE DEAN DENE
DILL DRAB GLEN VALE SLACK SLADE
TRULL WENCH DARGLE DIMBLE
DINGLE RAVINE VALLEY
(PL.) DALLES

DELPHINIUM DAUPHIN DOLPHIN
LARKSPUR

DELPHUS
(FATHER OF —) APOLLO NEPTUNE
POSEIDON
(MOTHER OF —) CELAENO MELANTHO

DELUDE BOB JIG BILK DUPE FOOL
HOAX MOCK AMUSE CHEAT COZEN
ELUDE EVADE GLAIK SPOOF TRICK
BAFFLE BANTER BEFOOL BUBBLE
CAJOLE DIDDLE ILLUDE BEGUILE
DECEIVE ENCHANT MISLEAD
OVERSEE BEJUGGLE HOODWINK
INVEIGLE OVERSILE

DELUGE SEA FLOW FLOOD SWAMP
DILUVY CATARACT INUNDATE
OVERFLOW SATURATE SUBMERGE
CATACLYSM

DELUNDUNG LINSANG ZINSANG
VIVERRINE

DELUSION MAZE MOHA ABUSE
DWALE FRAUD TRICK MIRAGE VISION
CHIMERA FALLACY FANTASM
PHANTOM WANHOPE ILLUSION
NIHILISM PHANTASM

DELUSTER DULL

DELUXE PALACE ELEGANT
ELABORATE SUMPTUOUS

DELVE DEN DIG DIP PIT CAVE DINT
MINE DITCH PLUMB BRUISE
BURROW EXHUME FATHOM INDENT
IMPRESS EXCAVATE INSCRIBE

DEMAGNETIZE DEPERM
DEPOLARIZE

DEMAGOGUE CLEON LEADER
ORATOR ROUSER DEMAGOG
JACOBIN SPEAKER TRIBUNE
JAWSMITH OCHLOCRAT

DEMAND ASK CRY TAX USE CALL
NEED RAME SALE CLAIM CRAVE
DRAFT EXACT GAVEL ORDER QUERY
SIGHT BEHEST CHARGE DESIRE
ELICIT EXPECT SNATCH SUMMON
ARRAIGN COMMAND CONSIST
DRAUGHT INQUIRE MANDATE
REQUEST REQUIRE SOLICIT
INSTANCE QUESTION POSTULATE
SCISCITATION

(— HIGHER PRICE) GAZUMP
(— PAYMENT) DUN CALL
(— RECOGNITION) CLAIM ASSERT
(STRONG —) PRESSURE
(PL.) EXIGENCE EXIGENCY

DEMANDABLE DUE EXIGIBLE
DEMANDED COMPULSORY
DEMANDING HEFTY EXIGENT
(— ATTENTION) ACUTE

DEMANTOID EMERALD OLIVINE
DEMARCATE DELIMIT SEPARATE
DEMARCATION CELL
DEMEAN ABASE CARRY LOWER
BEHAVE DEBASE DEPORT CONTAIN
DEGRADE DESCEND DEROGATE
MALTREAT

DEMEANOR AIR GARB MIEN PORT
FRONT HABIT ACTION HAVIOR
BEARING CONDUCT DISPOSE
FASHION CARRIAGE PORTANCE
(COLD —) MORGUE

DEMENTED MAD NUTS BUGGY
CRAZY LOONY NUTTY INSANE
SKEWED FATUOUS

DEMENTIA FATUITY INSANITY
DEMERIT MARK FAULT DESERT
BROWNIE
(PL.) GIG

DEMESNE MANOR PLACE REALM
DOMAIN ESTATE REGION DISTRICT

DEMETER CERES MISTRESS
DEMETRIUS
(BELOVED OF —) CELIA HERMIA
(MOTHER OF —) TAMORA

DEMIGOD AITU HERO KAMI YIMA
ADAPA SATYR GARUDA PAGODA
TRITON GODLING
(PL.) NEPHILIM

DEMIGODDESS URD NORN
HEROINE

DEMILUNE RAVELIN
DEMISE WILL DEATH CONVEY
DECEASE BEQUEATH

DEMISED LETTEN
DEMIT LOWER HUMBLE RESIGN
ABDICATE

DEMOCRACY POPULACY
COMMONALTY

DEMOCRAT DEMO DANITE HUNKER
SNAPPER DEMOCRAW LOCOFOCO
POPOCRAT
(CONSERVATIVE —) HARD

DEMOCRATIC LEFT POPULAR
DEMODULATE DETECT
DEMOISELLE KULM CRANE COOLEN
KAIKARA

DEMOLISH RASE RAZE RUIN ABATE
BREAK ELIDE LEVEL TOTAL WASTE
WRECK BATTER SLIGHT DESTROY
RUINATE SHATTER SUBVERT
UNBUILD DOWNCAST STRAMASH
PULVERIZE

DEMOLITION END FALL
DEMON ALP DEV HAG IMP NAT OKI AITU ATUA BADB BALI BHUT DEVA DOOK OGRE OKEE PUCK RAHU SURT WADE ASURA DEVIL DHOUL FIEND GENIE GHOST JUMBY LAMIA LESHY LESIY OTKON SATAN SATYR SHEDU SURTR TAIPO WITCH ABIGOR AFREET ARIOCH BILWIS DAEMON DAIMON DAITYA GENJIS JUMBIE MAMMON PILWIZ PISACA THURSE VRITRA YAKSHA YAKSHI ASMADAI ASMODAY DEMONIO HARPIER INCUBUS PISACHA VILLAIN WARLOCK ALICHINO ASHMODAI ASMODEUS BAALPEOR BEELPEOR CURUPIRA EUDAEMON OBIDICUT SUCCUBUS WATERMAN
(— OF WOODS) LESHY LESIY LESHEY
(ARABIC —) AFRIT AFREET AFRITE EFREET
(DESERT —) SATYR
(EVIL —) SHEDU
(FEMALE —) HAG LAMIA PISACHI SUCCUBUS
(NATURE —) GENIUS
(PETTY —) IMP
(WATER —) NICKER
(PL.) DASYUS
DEMONASSA (FATHER OF —) AMPHIARAUS
(HUSBAND OF —) THERSANDER
(MOTHER OF —) ERIPHYLE
(SON OF —) TISAMENUS
DEMONIAC DEMONIC LUNATIC SATANIC DEVILISH DIABOLIC FIENDISH INFERNAL
DEMONIACAL DEMONIAC INFERNAL
DEMONICE
(FATHER OF —) AGENOR
(MOTHER OF —) EPICASTE
(SON OF —) MOLUS EVENUS PHYLUS THESTIUS
DEMONSTRABLE ACTUAL
DEMONSTRATE GIVE SHOW CLEAR PROVE SPEAK EVINCE CONVICT DISPLAY PORTRAY CONVINCE INSTANCE MANIFEST
DEMONSTRATION SHOW SIGN TIME PROOF OVATION APODIXIS BALLYHOO DARSHANA MANIFEST
(— OF POWER) MANIFESTATION
(OSTENTATIOUS —) SPLURGE
DEMONSTRATIVE THAT THIS THESE THOSE EFFUSIVE EVINCIVE
DEMOPHON
(FATHER OF —) CELEUS THESEUS
(MOTHER OF —) PHAEDRA METANIRA
(NURSE OF —) DEMETER
DEMORALIZE UNMAN WEAKEN CONFUSE CORRUPT DEPRAVE PERVERT

DEMORALIZING INFECTIOUS SHATTERING
DEMOTE BUMP BUST REDUCE UNRANK DEGRADE DISRATE
DEMOTIC POPULAR ENCHORIAL
DEMOTION BUMP
DEMULCENT MANNA SALEB SALEP BORAGE GINSENG EMULSION SOOTHING
DEMUR COY GIB JIB SHY BALK STAY DELAY DOUBT PAUSE QUALM STICK BOGGLE LINGER OBJECT STRAIN DEMEORE SCRUPLE STICKLE STUMBLE SUSPEND DEMURRER HESITATE SUSPENSE
DEMURE COY MIM SHY MURE PRIM GRAVE SPAKE STAID SUANT SUENT MODEST SEDATE PRENZIE PRIMSIE COMPOSED DECOROUS
DEN MEW CAVE COVE DEAN DELL DIVE GLEN HELL HOLE HOLT HUNK LAIR LAKE NEST ROOM SHED SINK BIELD CABIN CAVEA COUCH DELVE HAUNT LODGE SLADE STUDY BURROW CAVERN COVERT GROTTO HOLLOW KENNEL RAVINE SHROUD LIBRARY RETREAT SPELUNK HIDEAWAY SNUGGERY WORKROOM
(— OF BEAR) WASH
(— OF INIQUITY) DOMDANIEL
(DRINKING —) BOTHAN
(FOUL —) SPITAL
(GAMBLING —) DEADFALL
DENARIUS DENAR PENNY DINDER
DENATURANT PYRIDINE
DENDRITE PROCESS
DENIAL NO NAY WARN DENAY DENIER NAYSAY DEFENSE DEMENTI REFUSAL REPULSE CONTRARY NEGATION TRAVERSE
(— OF AUTHORITY) ANARCHY
(— OF REALITY) NIHILISM
(— OF TRUTH) HERESY
DENIED LOST
DENIER DINERO NEGATOR DENARIUS DINHEIRO
(HALF —) MAIL MAILLE
DENIGRATE BEFOUL CRUCIFY DEROGATE
DENIM DUNGAREE
DENIZEN CITIZEN RESIDENT
(— BY BIRTH) NATIVE
(— OF HELL) HELLION

DENMARK
CAPITAL: COPENHAGEN
CHEESE: SAMSO
COIN: ORA ORE KRONE
COUNTY: AMT FYN RIBE SORO VEJLE AARHUS MARIBO ODENSE TONDER VIBORG AALBORG RANDERS AABENRAA BORNHOLM
INLET: ISE LIM FJORD VEJLE NISSUM

ODENSE HORSENS LOGSTOR
MARIAGER
ISLAND: OE ALS FYN MON AARO
AERO FANO FOHR MORS ROMO
BAAGO FAROE LAESO SAMSO
SANDO AMAGER FAEROE SEJERO
SUDERO FALSTER SEELAND
ZEALAND
MEASURE: ELL FOD MIL POT ALEN
FAVN RODE ALBUM KANDE LINJE
PAEGL TOMME ACHTEL PAEGEL
SKEPPE LANDMIL OLTONDE SKIFPPF
VIERTEL FJERDING
PARLIAMENT: RIGSRAAD FOLKETING
LANDSTING
PENINSULA: JUTLAND
POSSESSION: FAROE ICELAND
GREENLAND
RIVER: ASA HOLM OMME STOR
GUDEN SKIVE SUSAA VARDE
GELSAA STORAA VORGOD
GUDENAA LILLEAA LONBORG
SETTLERS: OSTMEN
STRAIT: KATTEGAT SKAGERRAK
TOWN: ARS HOV HALS KOGE NIBE
SORO VRAA FARUM HOBRO SKIVE
AARHUS DRAGOR KORSOR NYBORG
ODENSE SKAGEN STRUER VIBORG
AALBORG HERNING HORSENS
KOLDING RANDERS ALSINORE
BALLERUP GENTOFTE GLOSTRUP
ROSKILDE HELSINGOR
COPENHAGEN
TRIBE: DANES JUTES ANGLES CIMBRI
TEUTONS
TRIBUNAL: RIGSRAD RIGSRET
WEIGHT: ES LOD ORT VOG LAST MARK
PUND UNZE CARAT KVINT POUND
QUINT TONDE CENTNER LISPUND
QUINTIN LISPOUND SKIPPUND

DENOMINATE CALL NAME STYLE
TITLE DENOTE CHRISTEN INDICATE
NOMINATE
DENOMINATION CULT NAME SECT
CLASS FAITH TITLE VALUE CHURCH
SCHOOL SOCIETY CATEGORY
DENOMINATIONAL SECTARIAN
CONFESSIONAL
DENOTATION SIGN TOKEN EXTENT
NOTION SPHERE AMBITUS BREADTH
REFERENCE
DENOTE GIVE MARK MEAN NAME
NOTE SHOW SOUND IMPORT NOTIFY
BETOKEN CONNOTE EXPRESS
SIGNIFY DENOTATE DESCRIBE
INDICATE
DENOUEMENT END ENVOY ISSUE
PAYOFF OUTCOME SOLUTION
ANAGNOSIS
DENOUNCE DAN DAMN WRAY
ASCRY BASTE BLAST DECRY TAUNT
ACCUSE DELATE DESCRY DETEST
MENACE SCATHE ARRAIGN
CONDEMN DECLAIM DECLARE
UPBRAID EXECRATE PROCLAIM
THREATEN OBJURGATE
DENOUNCEMENT DELATION
DENSE SAD FAST FIRM CLOSE CRASS
DUNCH FOGGY GROSS HEAVY
MASSY MURKY SILLY SOLID SOUND
SPISS STIFF THEET THICK TIGHT
WOOFY OBTUSE OPAQUE SPISSY
STUPID THICKY THIGHT COMPACT
CROWDED INTENSE SERRIED
CONDENSE
(NOT —) TENUOUS
(PREF.) PACHY PYCN(O) PYKN(O)
DENSELY CLOSE
DENSITY FOG CANDY FASTNESS
GAUSSAGE SOLIDITY
(UNIT OF —) TESLA
(PREF.) DASY
DENT DASH DURT DING DINT DOKE
DUNT FAZE NICK CLOUR DELVE
DINGE NOTCH STOVE TOOTH BATTER
DUNTLE HALLOW INDENT BLEMISH
DEPRESS
(— OF REED) SPLIT
(PL.) BEER
DENTAL POINT
DENTATE TOOTHED
DENTICLE RASP
DENTICULATE SERRATE SERRATED
DENTICULATION JAG JAGG
DENTIFRICE WASH
DENTIL DENTEL DENTELLO DENTICLE
DENTINE IVORY DENTIN
DENTIST ODONTIST OPERATOR
DENTISTRY PROSTHODONTICS
DENTURE PLATE BRIDGE
(PL.) WALLIES
DENUDE BARE SCALP SHAVE STRIP
DIVEST NUDATE DESPOIL DENUDATE
DENUNCIATION BAN THREAT
THUNDER ANATHEMA DIATRIBE
DENY NAY NAIT NICK NITE WARN
BELIE DEBAR NITTE RENAY REPEL
WERNE ABJURE DISOWN FORBID
IMPUGN NAYSAY NEGATE OPPOSE
REFUSE REFUTE REJECT RENEGE
CONFUTE DEPRIVE DISAVOW
DISPUTE FORSAKE GAINSAY
PROTEST SUBLATE WITHSAY
ABNEGATE DENEGATE DISALLOW
DISCLAIM FORSWEAR NEGATIVE
RENOUNCE TRAVERSE WITHHOLD
REPUDIATE
(— ACCESS) CLOSE
(— RECOGNITION) BLINK
DEODORANT ROLLON
DEOXIDIZE REDUCE
DEOXIDIZED
(PREF.) DESOXY
DEPART GO DIE MUG OFF WAG
BLOW EXIT FLIT HOOK MOVE PACK

PART PASS PIKE QUIT SHED STEP
VADE VARY VOID WALK WEND WITE
AVOID BREAK FOUND LEAVE MOSEY
SEVER SHAKE SHIFT START TRUSS
AVAUNT BEGONE DECAMP DECEDE
DEMISE DESIST DIVIDE PERISH
RECEDE REMOVE RETIRE SKIDOO
SUNDER SWERVE WANDER
ABSCOND DEVIATE DISCEDE
FORSAKE RETREAT SKIDDOO
TAKEOFF VAMOOSE DISCOAST
FAREWELL SEPARATE TRESPASS
WITHDRAW
(— FROM HARBOR) SORTIE
(— FROM LIFE) DECEASE
(— IN HASTE) BREEZE
(— IN HURRY) SKIVE LAMMAS
(— SECRETLY) ABSCOND
ABSQUATULATE
(— SUDDENLY) FLEE DECAMP MIZZLE
(— WITH SPEED) VAMOOSE
DEPARTED DEAD BYGONE DEFUNCT
DECEASED DECEDENT
DEPARTMENT END PART OKRUG
REALM AGENCY BRANCH BUREAU
EXCISE MEMBER OKROOG SPHERE
FOUNDRY HANAPER PORTION
REVENUE SPICERY AGITPROP
CHANCERY DIVISION INDUSTRY
NOMARCHY PROVINCE SCULLERY
(— IN CHINA) FU
(— OF CHANCERY) HAMPER
HANAPER
(— OF KNOWLEDGE) STUDY
(ACADEMIC —) FACULTY
(NEWSPAPER —) COLUMN FEATURE
(TREASURY —) CAMERA
DEPARTURE BUNK EXIT BREAK
DEATH EXODE GOING LEAVE LUCKY
OUTGO CHANGE CONGEE DEPART
EGRESS EXODUS HEGIRA SETOFF
WAGANG WAYGANG DECEASE
EASTING OUTGANG PARTING
PARTURE RETREAT SAILING
TRUNDLE WAYGATE DEPARTER
FAREWELL OFFGOING REMOTION
(— FROM CORRECTNESS) ATROCITY
(— FROM SUBJECT) ASIDE
(— FROM THEME) CADENZA
(— OF SHIP) SORTIE
(CHARACTER IN —) LUISE TROTT
GILFEN
(COMPOSER OF —) D'ALBERT
(EMERGENCY —) BAILOUT
(GEOLOGICAL —) ANOMALY
(SECRET —) GUY SLIP
DEPEND BANK HANG LEAN PEND
RELY REST RIDE STAY TURN BUILD
COUNT FOUND HINGE TRUST LIPPEN
CONFIDE
DEPENDABILITY SECURITY
DEPENDABLE GOOD SURE TRIG
SIKER SOLID SOUND THERE SECURE

SICCAR SICKER STANCH STEADY
CERTAIN STAUNCH RELIABLE
SILVENDY SUREFIRE
DEPENDENCE MAINSTAY RELIANCE
SERVILITY
DEPENDENCY TALUK COLONY
APANAGE APPANAGE
DEPENDENT CHILD CLIENT HANGBY
MINION SPONGE VASSAL FEODARY
FEUDARY PRONEUR RELIANT
SERVILE SPONGER SUBJECT
WRAPPED BEHOLDEN CLINGING
CREATURE ENCLITIC EVENTUAL
FOLLOWER RETAINER
(— ON) ILLATIVE
(— ON DRUGS) HOOKED
(— PERSON) JUNKIE
(NOT —) ABSOLUTE
DEPENDING ATTENDANT
(— ON UNCERTAIN EVENTS)
ALEATORY
DEPICT HUE DRAW ETCH LIMN PICT
UNDO ENTER IMAGE PAINT SPEAK
WRITE BLAZON SHADOW DEPAINT
DISPLAY EXPRESS IMPAINT PICTURE
PORTRAY DESCRIBE EMBLAZON
RESEMBLE
(— IN MOSAIC) IMPAVE
(— WITH EXAGGERATION)
OVERPAINT
DEPICTED DEPAINT
(— AS BROKEN) ROMPU
DEPICTION SCAN SCHEMA
(PHOTOGRAPHIC —) RENOGRAM
DEPILATION PSILOSIS
DEPILATORY RUSMA EPILATOR
PELADORE PSILATRO
DEPILOUS BALD
DEPLETE DRAIN EMPTY PUNISH
REDUCE UNLOAD EXHAUST
BANKRUPT DIMINISH
DEPLETED WASTE BANKRUPT
DEPLETION DRAIN EROSION
DEPLORABLE SAD WOFUL WOEFUL
DOLOROUS GRIEVOUS WAILSOME
WRETCHED
DEPLORABLY SADLY
DEPLORE RUE MOAN SIGH WAIL
MOURN BEMOAN BEWAIL GRIEVE
LAMENT REGRET COMPLAIN
DEPLOY UNFOLD DISPLAY
DEPLOYMENT FORMATION
DEPOLYMERIZE DEGRADE
DEPONE SWEAR DEPOSE TESTIFY
DEPONENT AFFIANT DEPONER
EXAMINATE
DEPOPULATE RAVAGE DESOLATE
DISPEOPLE
DEPORT BEAR EXILE EXPEL BANISH
BEHAVE DEMEAN BEARING
CONDUCT DISPORT RELEGATE
DEPORTMENT AIR GEST MIEN PORT
GESTE HABIT TENUE ACTION

DEPORT HAVING MANNER ADDRESS
BEARING COMPORT CONDUCT
GESTURE HAVANCE BREEDING
CARRIAGE DEMEANOR MAINTAIN
PORTANCE
DEPOSE AVER ABASE PRIVE SWEAR
AFFIRM ASSERT BANISH DEPONE
DIVEST REDUCE REMOVE DEGRADE
DEPOSIT DESTOOL TESTIFY
DETHRONE DISCROWN DISPLACE
DEPOSIT FUR LAY PUT SET ADHI
BANK CAKE CAST CRUD DROP DUMP
FUND HIDE HOCK PAWN BLOOM
CHEST COUCH COVER DEPOT LODGE
PLACE SCURF STORE TOSCA
BESTOW DEPONE DEPOSE ENTOMB
ESCROW FLYSCH GARNER IMPOSE
INHUME PLEDGE REPOSE SALINE
SCORIA SCROLL SETTLE SINTER
TOPHUS ASHFALL CONSIGN
HORIZON DILUVIUM FOULNESS
SANDBANK PRECIPITATION
(— BALLOT) CAST
(— DRIFT-SAND) SUD
(— EGGS) BLOW SPAWN
(— FOR COPYRIGHT) ENTER
(— FROM HOT SPRINGS) SINTER
(— IN CHAMPAGNE) GRIFFE
(— IN EARTH) INTER INHUME
(— IN GUN BORE) FOULING
(— IN WINE CASK) CRUST TARTAR
(— OF DEBRIS) BRECCIA
(— OF LOAM) LOESS
(— OF ORE) BANK FLAT
(— OF PEBBLES AND SAND) BEACH
CASCALHO
(— OF SALT WATER) SOAK
(— ON LEATHER) BLOOM
(— ON LEAVES) HONEYDEW
(— STOLEN ANTIQUE) FENCE
(— USED AS FERTILIZER) FALUN
(ALLUVIAL —) APRON DELTA
(ARCHAEOLOGICAL —) LENS LENSE
(BANK —S) CASH
(BLACK —) STUPP
(BROKER'S —) MARGIN
(CORNEA —) ARCUS
(DEEP-SEA —) OOZE
(EARTHY —) GUHR MARL
(GEOLOGIC —) BLANKET HORIZON
(GLACIAL —) TILL DRIFT ESKAR
ESKER SHEET PLACER MORAINE
(GOUTY —) TOPHUS
(GRANULAR —) SABURRA
(GRAVEL —) LEAD
(KIDNEY —) GRAVEL
(MASS OF SEDIMENTARY —S) GOBI
(MINERAL —) FLAT LODE CARBONA
(MUDDY —) SLUDGE SLUMGULLION
(POWDERY —) BERGMEHL
(SEDIMENTARY —) SILT VARVE
TURBIDITE
(SHELLY —) CRAG

(SHOAL-WATER —) CULM
(SKELETAL —) CORAL
(STOMACH —) SABURRA
(TARRY —) GUM
(VALUABLE —) VEIN
(WELDING —) TACK
(PREF.) THESO
DEPOSITARY POSITOR SEQUESTER
DEPOSITION PAD BURIAL DEPOSIT
OPINION SILTING DEPOSURE
SEDIMENT
DEPOSITORY BANK DROP SAFE
AMBRY ATTIC VAULT DEPOSIT
OSSUARY SENTINE DEPOSITO
ESCROWEE OSSARIUM
DEPOT BANK BASE GARE AURANG
AURUNG STAPLE STATION
MAGAZINE TERMINAL TERMINUS
(MISSILE —) SILO
DEPRAVE TAINT DERASE DEFILE
INFECT MALIGN REVILE BESHREW
CORRUPT PERVERT VITIATE
DEPRAVED BAD EVIL UGLY VILE
PRAVE ROTTEN SHREWD WICKED
BESTIAL CORRUPT IMMORAL
PRAVOUS VICIOUS MISCREANT
DEPRAVITY VICE ABYSS ILLNESS
PRAVITY VILLAINY TURPITUDE
DEPRECATE PRAY INVOKE BESEECH
DEPRECATORY PEJORATIVE
DEPRECIATE FALL LACK SLUR
ABASE AVILE DECRY SLUMP DEBASE
EMBASE LESSEN MINISH REDUCE
SHRINK CHEAPEN DEBAUCH
DEGRADE DEPRAVE DEPRESS
DETRACT DISABLE SLANDER
OMALLEN DELITTLE DEROGATE
DISCOUNT DISPRIZE DISVALUE
MINIMIZE PEJORATE VILIPEND
WRITEOFF
DEPRECIATION AGIO DECRIAL
DISCOUNT
DEPREDATION PREY RAPINE
PILLAGE
DEPRESS BOW COW HIP LOW BATE
BEAR BORE DAMP DASH DENT FALL
FLAT SINK SUMP ABASE APPAL
BREAK CHILL COUCH CRUSH FAINT
LOWER SLUMP VAPOR WEIGH
APPALL DAMPEN DEBOSS DISMAY
HUMBLE INDENT LESSEN MURDER
SADDEN SETTLE SICKEN SLOUCH
STRIKE WEAKEN DECLINE DEGRADE
DESTROY FLATTEN OPPRESS
REPRESS BROWBEAT DIMINISH
DISPIRIT DOWNBEAR ENFEEBLE
(— STRINGS OF INSTRUMENT) FRET
DEPRESSANT HELLEBORE
DEPRESSED LOW SAD BLUE DAMP
DULL FLAT SICK SUNK COWED
WROTH BROODY BUMMED DISHED
GLOOMY HIPPED HOLLOW LONELY
OBLATE SOMBER TRISTE ACCABLE

DEPRESSED LETDOWN DEJECTED DOWNCAST DOWNSOME
(— AT THE POLES) OBLATE
(ECONOMICALLY —) HARD

DEPRESSING SAD BLUE COLD BLEAK CHILL DREAR DUSKY MUZZY OURIE DISMAL DREARY GLOOMY SOMBER SOMBRE TRISTE OPPRESSIVE

DEPRESSION COL DIP EYE GAT PAN PIT BUST CROP DAMP DELK DENT DOKE DOWN FALL FOSS FUNK GASH GLEN HOLL HOWE SLEW SLOT SLUE WELL ATRIO BASIN BLAHS BLUES BOSOM CANON COWAL CRYPT DELVE DINGE FOSSA FOSSE FOVEA GLOOM GROIN NADIR NAVEL ORBIT POLJE SALAR SCOOP SELLA SINUS SLUMP SWALE AMPHID BLIGHT BUCKLE CAFARD CANYON CAVITY CRATER CUPULE DIMPLE DISMAY FURROW GROOVE GULLEY GUTTER INDENT LACUNA RAVINE SAUCER SLOUGH SPLEEN VALLEY WALLOW ALVEOLA BLOWOUT BOGHOLE CHAGRIN CLAYPAN CONCAVE COUNTER FOSSULA FOSSULE FOVEOLA JIMMIES SADNESS SALTPAN SINKAGE SINKING VARIOLE BOTHRIUM DOLDRUMS DOWNBEND FAINTING FOLLICLE FOREDEEP FOSSETTE FOSSULET PUNCTURE SINKHOLE SOAKAWAY EPHIPPIUM MELANCHOLY OPPRESSION
(— BEHIND COW'S SHOULDERS) CROP
(— BETWEEN BREASTS) CLEAVAGE
(— BETWEEN HILLS) SWIRE
(— IN BOARD) SKIP
(— IN BOTTLE BOTTOM) KICK
(— IN DECK) COCKPIT
(— IN DOG'S FACE) STOP
(— IN FRUITS) EYE
(— IN GROUND) DALK DELK SOAK SWAG WELL SWALE CHARCO
(— IN MILLSTONE) BOSOM
(— IN NILE VALLEY) KORE
(— IN RANGE) PASS
(— IN RIDGE) COL
(— IN SNOW) SITZMARK
(— IN VELD) COMITJE KOMMETJE
(— OF EAR) SCAPHA
(— OF SPIRITS) JAWFALL
(— PRONE) VAPORISH
(ARTICULAR —) GLENE
(OBLONG —) CIRCUS
(SMALL —) DENT DIMPLE LACUNA FOLLICLE

DEPRIVATION COST LOSS MAIM WANT MAYHEM AMOTION MISTURE DEPRIVAL
(— OF SIGHT) DARKNESS
(SUFF.) STERESIS

DEPRIVE BAR ROB BATE DENY DOCK EASE GELD TWIN ABATE BENIM BREAK DEBAR EMPTY EXUTE PREVE SPOIL STRIP WRONG AMERCE DEFEAT DENUDE DEPOSE DEVEST DISMAY DIVEST FAMISH FORBAR HINDER HUSTLE REMOVE ABRIDGE BEGUILE BEREAVE CASHIER CURTAIL DECEIVE DEFORCE DEPRAVE DESPOIL DESTROY DISABLE EXHAUST FOREBAR GUDGEON PRIVATE UNDRESS BANKRUPT DENATURE DESOLATE DISANNUL EVACUATE
(— BY TRICKERY) NOSE MULCT
(— FRAUDULENTLY) GUDGEON
(— OF BRILLIANCE) DEADEN
(— OF COLOR) STAIN
(— OF COURAGE) UNNERVE
(— OF FOOD) STARVE
(— OF FREEDOM) FETTER
(— OF INDIVIDUALITY) FORDIZE
(— OF LIFE) DEADEN
(— OF OFFICE) DEPOSE
(— OF PAY) DOCK
(— OF POSSESSIONS) FLAY
(— OF REASON) DEMENT
(— OF SENSATION) BENUMB
(— OF SENSE) INEBRIATE
(— OF SIGHT) SEEL
(— OF STRENGTH) ENERVATE
(— OF VIRGINITY) DEFLOWER
(— WRONGFULLY) ROB
(PREF.) (— OF) DE DIS

DEPRIVED REFT SANS BANKRUPT DESOLATE

DEPTH DIP BURY DEEP DROP MOHO ABYSS MIDST SIDTH FATHOM HEIGHT ALTITUDE DEEPNESS PROFOUND SOUNDING STRENGTH PENETRATION
(— CHARGE) ASHCAN
(— OF NIGHT OR WINTER) HOLL HOWE
(— OF SAIL) HOIST
(— OF SHIP) GAGE GAUGE
(— OF SIN) SLOUGH
(— OF SPADE) SPIT GRAFT
(— OF WATER) DRAFT DRAUGHT
(—S OF SEA) PROFOUND
(LOWEST —) GROUND
(MORAL —) ABYSS
(PL.) MUD ABYSS HEART
(PREF.) BATH(O)(Y)

DEPUTATION MISSION THEORIA LEGATION

DEPUTE SEND ALLOT ASSIGN DEVOTE APPOINT DELEGATE

DEPUTY AIDE VICE AGENT ENVOY NABOB PROXY VICAR ANGELO COMMIS CURATE DEPUTE EXARCH FACTOR KEHAYA LEGATE MINION ADJOINT BAILIFF ESCALUS SUBDEAN CAIMACAM DELEGATE

ORDINARY PYLAGORE QAIMAQAM
TENIENTE VICARIAN
(— OF BISHOP) VICAR VIDAME
(BISHOP'S —) VIDAME
(PREF.) CO
DERACINATE UPROOT
DERAIL TOAD DERAILER THROWOFF
FRUSTRATE
DERANGE TURN CRAZE UNWIT
UPSET HAMPER RUFFLE CONFUSE
DERAIGN DISEASE DISTURB
PERTURB UNSHAPE DISORDER
DISPLACE UNSETTLE
DERANGED OUT GYTE CRAZY
CRAZED SKIVIE FRANTIC FURIOUS
BUGHOUSE DEMENTED DETRAQUE
INFORMAL
DERANGEMENT MANIA UPSET
FRENZY LUNACY DISEASE MADNESS
PHRENSY RUMMAGE DELIRIUM
DISORDER INSANITY
DERBY POT CADY KATY RACE BOXER
CADDY DICER KELLY SHIRE BOWLER
POTHAT BILLYCOCK
DERBY BLUE ELDERBERRY
DERELICT REMISS STREET FAILURE
BETRAYER CASTAWAY
DERELICTION FAILURE RELICTION
DERIDE BOO GECK GIBE HOOT JAPE
JEER JIBE LOUT MOCK RAZZ TWIT
DRAPE FLEER FLOUT KNACK LAUGH
RALLY SCOFF SCORN SCOUT TAUNT
EXPOSE ILLUDE IRRIDE CATCALL
LOWBELL RIDICULE
DERIDER IRRISOR
DERISION GECK JEER MOCK HOKER
SCORN SPORT MOWING ASTEISM
MOCKERY CONTEMPT IRRISION
RIDICULE
(EXPRESS —) SNELLH SNORT
DERISIVE JEERY SNIDE MOWING
SNEERY SNOOTY SATANIC
DERISORY IRRISORY SARDONIC
SCOFFING
DERIVATION ORIGIN DESCENT
PEDIGREE PARENTAGE
DERIVATIVE FURAN LININ SLOPE
ACOINE ACYLAL BORANE FURANE
INDOLE PHENOL RETENE ALKYLOL
ANALGEN DERIVED ENOLATE
FLAVONE FLUXION FULGIDE
FULVENE GERMANE SUCRATE
ALBUMOSE ANALGENE FLAVONOL
FORMAZAN HEMATINE INDAZOLE
STANNANE SECONDHAND
ADSCITITIOUS
DERIVE GET DRAW STEM TAKE
BRING CARRY DRIVE FETCH INFER
TRACE BORROW CONVEY DEDUCE
DESUME ELICIT EVOLVE GATHER
OBTAIN SPRING DESCEND EXTRACT
PROCEED RECEIVE TRADUCE
(IMPROPERLY —) WREST

DERIVED
(SUFF.) (— FROM) IC(AL)
DERMA LAYER CORIUM DERMIS
KISHKE
DERMATITIS ICH ICK CASCADO
CUTITIS
DERMATOGEN PROTODERM
DERMIS CUTIS DERMA CORIUM
DERNIER LAST FINAL DARREIN
DERNIER CRI CRY KICK LATEST
NEWEST FASHION
DEROGATE ANNUL DECRY LESSEN
REPEAL DETRACT SLANDER
RESTRICT WITHDRAW
DEROGATORY BAD
DERRICK JIB RIG LIFT SPAR CRANE
DAVIT HOIST STEEVE TACKLE
ERECTER ERECTOR GALLOWS
HANGING HANGMAN STIFFLEG
JINNYWINK
DERRIS TUBA DEGUELIA
DERVISH AGIB FAKIR FAKEER SADITE
SANTON DARWESH WHIRLER
CALENDER
DESALT DEIONIZE
DESATURATE SADDEN
DESCANT SING SONG COPULA
MELODY REMARK WARBLE
COMMENT QUINIBLE
DESCEND DIP SYE DIVE DROP DUCK
FALL SHED SINK SKIN VAIL AVALE
LIGHT LOWER SQUAT STOOP SWOOP
ALIGHT DERIVE DEVALL DEVAUL
SETTLE DECLINE DELAPSE DEVOLVE
SUBSIDE SUCCEED DISMOUNT
PREPONDERATE
(— BY ROPE) RAPPEL
(— INTO HELL) HARROW
DESCENDANT SON CION GHUZ
HEIR SEED SLIP CHILD GHUZZ SCION
BRANCH LINEAL DESCENT AARONITE
ASHERITE DAUGHTER EPIGONUS
(— OF IMMIGRANTS) BRAVA
(— OF JEW) CHUETA
(— OF MOHAMMED) EMIR
(— OF NOAH) AD
(—S OF MOHAMMED) ASHRAF
(INSIGNIFICANT —) TAG
(PL.) SEED DONMEH DUNMEH
STRAIN PROGENY OFFSPRING
POSTERITY
(SUFF.) ITE
DESCENDING FALL CADENT
DOWNWARD
(— FROM COMMON ANCESTOR)
AKIN
DESCENT JET KIN SET DIVE DOWN
DROP FALL KIND VAIL BIRTH BLOOD
CANCH CHUTE ISSUE PITCH SCARP
SHUTE SLOPE STOCK CLEUCH
CLEUGH ESCARP RAPPEL STRAIN
ASSAULT DECLINE DISSENT
EXTRACT FALLOUT INCLINE KINDRED

LINEAGE PROGENY ANCESTRY
BREEDING COMEDOWN DOWNCOME
DOWNFALL DOWNGATE DOWNHILL
GLISSADE INVASION PEDIGREE
PARENTAGE
(— IN MOUNTAINEERING) ABSEIL
(— OF AIRPLANE) LETDOWN
APPROACH
(— OF BIRD) STOOP
(— OF DEITY) AVATAR AVATARA
(— OF LIQUID) DRIBBLE
(— OF MASS) SLIDE
(— OF RIVER) LEAP
(FAMILIAR —) HAVAGE
(OVERWHELMING —) AVALANCHE
(PARACHUTE —) JUMP BAILOUT
(PLUNGING —) SPIN
DESCHAMPSIA AIRA
DESCRIBE DRAW GIVE LIMN READ
TELL BLAZE IMAGE LABEL PAINT
POINT STYLE WRITE DEFINE DENOTE
DEPICT DEVISE DILATE RELATE
REPORT SKETCH TITULE DECLARE
DEPAINT DISPLAY EXPLAIN EXPRESS
NARRATE OUTLINE PICTURE
PORTRAY PRESENT RECOUNT
STORIFY DESCRIVE INSCRIBE
REHEARSE
(— A LINE) CUT
(— AS) CALL
(— BRIEFLY) KODAK
(— GRAMMATICALLY) PARSE
(— VIVIDLY) PICTURE
DESCRIBER (VIVID —) PAINTER
DESCRIBING GRAPHIC
DESCRIPTION KIN IMAGE BLAZON
SKETCH SURVEY ACCOUNT DICTION
DISPLAY PICTURE LANDSKIP
RELATION TREATISE
(— OF A COUNTRY) FACE
(— OF VISION) AISLING
(BRIEF —) LEGEND
(RUSTIC —) IDYL IDYLL
(VIVID —) PICTURE PAINTING
DESCRY SEE SPY ESPY MAKE SCRY
ASCRY SIGHT BEHOLD BETRAY
DETECT REVEAL DISCERN DISPLAY
DENOUNCE DESCRIBE DISCLOSE
DISCOVER PERCEIVE
DESDEMONA (FATHER OF —)
BRABANTIO
(HUSBAND OF —) OTHELLO
DESECRATE ABUSE DEFILE POLLUTE
PROFANE VIOLATE TEMERATE
UNHALLOW
DESECRATION PROFANATION
DESENSITIZE DRUG DEADEN
DESERT DUE ERG RAT RUN AREG
ARID BOLT FAIL FLEE MEED SAND
SERT TURN VAST DITCH GUILT LEAVE
LURCH MERIT PLANT SERIR START
WAIVE WASTE WORTH BARREN
BETRAY DEFECT EXPOSE LONELY

RENEGE REWARD SHRINK THIRST
WESTEN ABANDON ABSCOND
CHICKEN DEMERIT FORSAKE
HORNADA OVERRUN WASTERN
WASTINE DESOLATE RENOUNCE
SOLITARY SOLITUDE WASTABLE
(PL.) GUILT
(PREF.) EREM(O)
DESERTED DEAD LONE WYSTY
LONELY FORLORN DESOLATE
FORSAKEN SOLITARY
(— WOMAN) AGUNAH
DESERTER RAT BOLTER BUGOUT
APOSTATE BUSHWACK FUGITIVE
RECREANT RENEGADE RUNAGATE
TURNTAIL
DESERTION BUGOUT RATTERY
APOSTASY
DESERT LEMON KUMQUAT
DESERVE EARN MEED RATE MERIT
REPAY SERVE ASSERVE BENEFIT
DEMERIT DISSERVE PROMERIT
DESERVED JUST COMING WORTHY
CONDIGN
DESERVING WORTHY CONDIGN
WORTHFUL ADMIRABLE
MERITORIOUS
DESICCATE DRY ARID SEAR SERE
DRAIN DEHYDRATE
DESICCATION XERANSIS
DESIDERATUM NEED DESIRE
DESIGN AIM END MAP CAST DRAW
GOAL IDEA MARK MEAN PLAN PLAT
PLOT TOOL TREE WORK ALLOT
CHECK DECAL DECOR DODAD DRAFT
DRIFT ETTLE FANCY MODEL MOTIF
NOTAN QUILT SHAPE STAMP STUDY
STYLE BOWPOT CACHET CORNER
CREATE DEVICE DEVISE DOODAD
DOODLE EMBLEM FIGURE FLORAL
FLOWER INCUSE INTEND INTENT
INVENT LAYOUT MODULE OBJECT
OBTENT PROJET SCHEME SKETCH
SYSTEM VERVER ALLOVER BOSCAGE
CARTOON CARVING CHASING
COMPOSE CONCERT COUNSEL
CROQUIS DESTINE DIAGRAM
DRAUGHT ETCHING FANTASY
FASHION OUTLINE PATTERN
PRETEND PROJECT PROPOSE
PURPORT PURPOSE REVERSE
SCALLOP SLEIGHT THOUGHT
APPLIQUE BAYADERE BOUGHPOT
CONTRIVE CYMATION CYMATIUM
ENGINEER FILIGREE FLOCKING
FORECAST GRAFFITO GROOVING
INTAGLIO PHANTASY PLATFORM
REMARQUE SINGERIE STRIPING
SUNBURST GOFFERING
SCHEMATISM
(— AS TITLE PAGE) VIGNETTE
(— ON BOOK) TOOL
(— ON CARPET) MEDALLION

(ON COIN) BEADING
(— ON FABRIC) BATIK BATTIK
(AIRCRAFT —) STEALTH
(ARTFUL —) MACHINATION
(BOOK —) FILET FILLET
(COMPUTER —) CAD
(CUP-SHAPED —) HUSK
(EMBLEMATIC —) IMPRESS
(ESSENTIAL —) BONES
(FASHION —) FORD
(OPENWORK —) POINTELLE
(OUTLINE —) KEYSTONE
(PERFORATED —) POUNCE
(SPOTTED —) SEME
(STRIPED —) STRIA STRIE
(TESSELLATED —) MOSAIC
(TEXTILE —) STRIPE HAIRLINE
DESIGNATE SET HAIL MARK MEAN
NAME SHOW ELECT LABEL SPEAK
STYLE TITLE ANOINT ASSIGN
DENOTE DESIGN FINGER INTEND
SETTLE TARGET APPOINT EARMARK
ENTITLE EXPRESS SPECIFY
SURNAME ALLOCATE DESCRIBE
IDENTIFY INDICATE NOMINATE
PRESCRIBE
DESIGNATION NAME TERM TYPE
LABEL STYLE TITLE CAPTION
HOMONYM ADDITION
(— OF PLACE) ADDRESS
DESIGNED PREPENSE SUPPOSED
(— FOR MALE AND FEMALE) UNISEX
DESIGNER ERTE STYLER FANCIER
PLANNER PLOTTER SCHEMER
STYLIST COLORIST ENGINEER
MEDALIST MOSAICIST
(FASHION —) DIOR FENLI RENTA
CASSINI
(PL.) COUTURE
DESIGNING ARTFUL CUNNING
JESUITIC PLANNING PLOTTING
SCHEMING
DESIRABLE FAIR GOOD KEEN
WORTH PLUMMY AMIABLE GRADELY
HEALTHY OPTABLE WELCOME
WISHFUL DESIROUS ELIGIBLE
ENVIABLE PLEASING SALUTARY
DESIRE HOT YEN ACHE CARE ENVY
EROS FAIN HAVE HOPE HOTS ITCH
KAMA KEEP LEST LIST LOAD LUST
MIND NEED PANT URGE WANT WILL
WISH WIST ARDOR BOSOM BRAME
COVET CRAVE FANCY GIMME GREED
GROAN HEART MANGE MANIA
NISUS QUEST STUDY TANHA TASTE
WILNE YEARN YISSE AFFECT APPETE
ASPIRE BEHEST BESOLN DEMAND
DEVICE HANKER HUNGER OREXIS
POTHOS PREFER TALENT THIRST
UTINAM YAMMER AVARICE AVIDITY
CONATUS COURAGE CRAVING
EROTISM FANTASY HIMEROS
HOPEFOR INKLING LONGING

PASSION STOMACH VOLUNTY
WILLING AMBITION APPETITE
COVETISE CUPIDITY PLEASING
NECESSITY
(— FOR LIFE) TANHA
(— WITH EAGERNESS) ASPIRE
(ARDENT —) THIRST
(IRRITATING —) ITCH
(SEXUAL —) HOTS PRIDE
(STRONG —) CUPIDITY SLAVERING
(UNCONTROLLABLE —) CACOETHES
(PREF.) (SEXUAL —) ERO EROTO
(SUFF.) OREXIA
DESIRE UNDER THE ELMS
(AUTHOR OF —) ONEILL
(CHARACTER IN —) EBEN ABBIE
CABOT PUTNAM EPHRAIM
DESIROUS AVID FAIN FOND LIEF
VAIN EAGER FRACK FRECK LUSTY
ARDENT WILFUL ANXIOUS THIRSTY
WILLFUL WILLING WISHING
APPETENT COVETOUS LIKEROUS
PRURIENT SPIRITED
DESIST HO LIN EASE HALT QUIT REST
SIST STOP WHOA CEASE LEAVE
SPARE STINT SWICK SWIKE WONDE
DEPART ABANDON FORBEAR
FORFEIT RESPITE SUBSIST
SURCEASE
(— FROM) CUT LEAVE REMIT
FORBEAR
DESK PEW AMBO SCOB BOARD
DESSE TABLE BUREAU CAISSE
PULPIT CONSOLE LECTERN PLUTEUS
COPYDESK STANDISH VARGUENO
(KIND OF —) ROLLTOP
DESMA CLON CLONE
DESMAN MOLE SQUASH MUSKRAT
ONDATRA
DESMANTHUS ACUAN
DESOLATE SAD BARE LORN RUIN
SACK SOLE VAST WILD ALONE
BLEAK DREAR GAUNT GUBAT OURIE
STARK UNKED UNKET UNKID WASTE
WASTY WYSTY BARREN DESERT
DISMAL DREARY GLOOMY GOUSTY
LONELY RAVAGE DESTROY FORLORN
GOUSTIE HOWLING LACKING
UNCOUTH WIDOWED WILSOME
DEPRIVED DESERTED FORSAKEN
SOLITARY WASTEFUL WOBEGONE
DESOLATION WOE RUIN GLOOM
GRIEF HAVOC WASTE RAVAGE
SADNESS
DESPAIR GLOOM UNHOPE WANHOPE
DESPAIRING HOPELESS
DESPERADO BRAVO BADMAN
BANDIT RUFFIAN CRIMINAL
RESOLUTE
DESPERATE MAD DIRE RASH
ACHARNE DESPERT EXTREME
FORLORN FRANTIC HEADLONG
HOPELESS PERILOUS RECKLESS

DESPERATELY BONE
DESPICABLE BUM BASE MEAN
ORRA VILE CHEAP DIRTY FOUTY
SCALY ABJECT PALTRY ROTTEN
SHABBY SORDID CAITIFF IGNOBLE
PITIFUL REPTILE PITIABLE
UNWORTHY WRETCHED
DESPICABLY DIRTILY
DESPISE DEFY HATE SCORN SCOUT
SPISE SPURN DETEST FORHOO
LOATHE SLIGHT VILIFY CONTEMN
DESPITE DISDAIN DISPRIZE MISPRIZE
VILIPEND
DESPITE BY VEX SPITE MALGRE
DESPISE
DESPOIL ROB PELF PILL POLL RAID
RAPE RUIN SKIN BOOTY HARRY
PLUME RAVEN REAVE RIFLE SPOIL
STRIP STRUB TRICE BEZZLE DIVEST
FLEECE HESPEL HUSPEL RAVAGE
RAVISH REMOVE BEREAVE DEPRIVE
DISROBE PILLAGE PLUNDER
UNSPOIL DEFLOWER DISARRAY
SPOLIATE SPUILZIE UNCLOTHE
DESPOINA KORE PERSEPHONE
DESPONDENCY DUMP HUMP
BLUES DUMPS GLOOM ATHYMY
MISERY ATHUMIA ATHYMIA DESPAIR
DESPOND
DESPONDENT SAD BLUE GLOOMY
FORLORN DEJECTED DOWNCAST
HOPELESS
DESPOT CZAR TSAR TZAR ANARCH
SATRAP TYRANT AUTARCH
MONARCH AUTOCRAT
DESPOTIC LORDLY ABSOLUTE
DOMINANT
DESPOTISM TYRANNY AUTARCHY
SULTANISM
DESQUAMATE PEEL
DESSERT EIS ICE PIE BABA CAKE
FOOL SKYR SNOW VOID BETTY
BOMBE COUPE DOLCE FRUIT GLACE
GRUNT JELLY LACTO SLUMP AFTERS
ECLAIR JUNKET MOUSSE PASTRY
POSTRE SPONGE SWEETS TRIFLE
BAKLAVA BANQUET PARFAIT
PAVLOVA PUDDING SHERBET
SOUFFLE SPUMONE STRUDEL
SUPREME DUMPLING FLUMMERY
FRUMENTY NAPOLEON PANDOWDY
SILLABUB DACQUOISE ENTREMETS
SOPAPILLA SOPAIPILLA
(BAKED —) CRISP
(CARAMEL) FLAN
DESTINATION END GOAL PORT
BOURN BILLET BOURNE
DESTINE DOOM EURE FATE MARK
ALLOT SHAPE SLATE WEIRD DEPUTE
DESIGN DEVOTE INTEND ORDAIN
APPOINT PURPOSE SENTENCE
DESTINY LOT DOLE DOOM EURE
FATE SORT KARMA MOIRA STARS

WEIRD KHARMA KISMET DESTINE
FORTUNE PORTION FOREDOOM
DESTITUTE BARE NACE POOR SANS
VOID CLEAN EMPTY NAKED NEEDY
WASTE BEREFT DEVOID VACANT
WASTED FORLORN LACKING
NAUGHTY VIDUATE WANTING
BANKRUPT BEGGARED DEFEATED
DEPRIVED DESOLATE FORSAKEN
HELPLESS INDIGENT INNOCENT
VIDUATED PENNILESS
(— OF) BUT
(— OF FEATHERS) DEPLUMATE
(— OF LEAVES) APHYLLOUS
(— OF LIGHT) DARK
(— OF TEETH) EDENTATE
(— OF WATER) ANHYDROUS
(SUFF.) (— OF) LESS
DESTITUTION NEED WANT FAMINE
PENURY BEGGARY DEFAULT
POVERTY
DESTROY BAG EAT END GUT MOW
RID ZAP BLOW CHEW FRAP FULL
KILL NUKE NULL RASE RAZE RUIN
RUSH SINK SLAY SMIT STRY TINE
UNDO VOID BREAK CRACK CRAZE
DECAY ELIDE ERASE ERODE FORDO
HAVOC MISDO PRANG QUADE QUAIL
QUELL SHEND SHOOT SMASH SMITE
SPEED SPEND SPILL SPLIT SPOIL
STROY SWAMP TOTAL TRASH
WASTY WRACK WRECK BLIGHT
CANCEL CUMBER DEFACE DEFEAT
DELETE DEVOID DEVOUR EFFACE
FAMISH FOREDO MURDER PERISH
QUENCH RANKLE RAVAGE STARVE
STIFLE UNMAKE UNPILE UNWORK
UPROOT UPTEAR ABOLISH
CONSUME CORRODE DEPRIVE
DISTURB ENECATE EXPUNGE
FLATTEN FORFARE FORLESE
MORTIFY NULLIFY OVERRUN
PEREMPT RUINATE SHAMASH
SHATTER SMOTHER SUBVERT
TERRIFY UNBUILD WHITTLE
AMORTIZE CONFOUND DECIMATE
DEMOLISH DESOLATE DESTRUCT
DISANNUL DISPLANT DISSOLVE
FRACTURE FRAGMENT IMMOLATE
INFRINGE MUTILATE OVERTURN
PARALYZE SABOTAGE STRAMASH
OBLITERATE
(— BARK) GIRDLE
(— BY FIRE) CONSUME
(— COMPLETELY) RUBOUT
(— FERTILITY) EXHAUST
(— FOR FUN) TRASH
(— SELF-POSSESSION) ABASH
(— TOTALLY) SMASH SWEEP
CUMBER SCUTTLE
(SUFF.) CLASE CLASIA CLAST(IC)
DESTROYED FLAT BLOWN KAPUT
KAPUTT

DESTROYER CAN HUN DEATH
TINCAN UNDOER VANDAL VICTOR
FLIVVER STROYER UNMAKER
WARSHIP APOLLYON DEVOURER
SABOTEUR
(— OF MACHINERY) LUDDITE
(SUFF.) CIDAL CIDE PHTHORA
DESTROYING FELL
(PREF.) ANTI
(SUFF.) CLASTIC
DESTRUCTIBLE FRAIL
DESTRUCTION BAR END HEW BANE
DOGS DOOM FIRE LOSS RACK RUIN
STRY TALA CRUSH DEATH DECAY
GRAVE HAVOC SMASH STRIP STROY
WASTE WRACK DEFEAT DISMAY
ENDING EXPIRY WONDER ABADDON
CARNAGE EROSION UNDOING
COLLAPSE DELETION DISPOSAL
DOWNFALL EVERSION EXCISION
SHAMBLES SMASHERY RUINATION
(— OF BONES) CARIES
(— OF ENVIRONMENT) ECOCIDE
(— OF SHIP'S PAPERS) SPOLIATION
(CELL —) LYSIS
(GOD OF —) SIVA
(GRADUAL —) CORROSION
(MALICIOUS —) SABOTAGE
(UTTER —) PERDITION
(SUFF.) LYSE LYSIS LYST LYTE LYTIC
LYZE
DESTRUCTIVE FELL FATAL DEADLY
MORTAL BALEFUL BANEFUL
DEATHLY EXITIAL FATEFUL HARMFUL
HUMLIKE HURTFUL NOISOME
NOXIOUS RUINOUS ANERETIC
DEATHFUL EXITIOUS WASTEFUL
WRACKFUL WREAKFUL ANAERETIC
PESTILENT
(— TO LIFE) BIOCIDAL
DESUETUDE BREACH DISUSE
DESULTORY IDLE HASTY LOOSE
ROVING AIMLESS CURSORY
RAMBLING UNSTEADY WAVERING
IRREGULAR
DETACH CUT DRAFT LOOSE SEVER
AVULSE LOOSEN UNBIND UNGLUE
UNWORK CRACKLE DISJOIN
DRAUGHT ISOLATE UNHINGE
UNRIVET UNSEIZE ABSTRACT
DISSOLVE DISUNITE PRESCIND
SEPARATE UNFASTEN WITHDRAW
DETACHABLE SLIP
DETACHED CUT COLD FREE ALONE
ALOOF LOOSE DEADPAN INSULAR
PORTATO SCIOLTO ABSTRACT
CLINICAL DISCRETE ISOLATED
OUTLYING SEPARATE SPICCATO
UNBIASED IMPERSONAL
(PREF.) APH APO
DETACHMENT POINT POSSE
ATARAXY OUTPOST ATARAXIA
AVULSION OUTGUARD

(SUFF.) LYSE LYSIS LYST LYTE LYTIC
LYZE
DETAIL CREW ITEM DODAD POINT
ACCENT ASSIGN DOODAB DOODAD
NICETY PARCEL RELATE RETAIL
ACCOUNT APPOINT ARTICLE ITEMIZE
MINUTIA NARRATE NULLING
RESPECT SEVERAL SPECIFY
INSTANCE REHEARSE SALIENCE
PARTICULAR PARTICULARITY
(—S OF MAP) CULTURE
(CLIMACTIC —) BEAUTY
(PETTY —) CHICKEN
(SPECIFIC —S) NITTYGRITTY
(UNIMPORTANT —S) TRIVIA
(PL.) DOPE FROUFROU FURNITURE
DETAILED NARROW PROLIX
CLOSEUP SPECIAL PUNCTUAL
TIRESOME
DETAIN BAIL HOLD KEEP STAY STOP
CHECK DELAY TARRY ARREST
ATHOLD COLLAR HINDER RETARD
TAIGLE IMPRISON RESTRAIN
WITHHOLD
DETECT SEE SPY ESPY FIND NOSE
SPOT CATCH SCENT SENSE SMOKE
SNIFF TRACE DESCRY DIVINE
EXPOSE REVEAL DEVELOP DISCERN
UNCOVER DECIPHER DISCOVER
OVERTAKE
DETECTIVE EYE TEC BULL BUSY
DICK JACK TRAP PLANT SNOOP
SPADE BEAGLE MOUSER RUNNER
SHADOW SHAMUS SLEUTH TAILER
TRACER GUMSHOE MAIGRET
SCENTER SNOOPER SPOTTER
TEMPLAR TRAILER BEAUMONT
DETECTOR FLATFOOT HAWKSHAW
HOUSEMAN OPERATOR SHERLOCK
OPERATIVE PINKERTON
PLAINCLOTHESMAN
(— FICTION AWARD) EDGAR
(— OF FICTION) LUPIN
(— STORY) WHODUNIT
(FICTIONAL —) CHAN LUPIN QUEEN
TRACY VANCE CARTER HOLMES
MARPLE POIROT CHARLES
DETECTOR ASDIC COHERER
REAGENT SFERICS SPHERICS
(ELECTRONIC —) SOLION
(KIND OF —) METAL
(LIE —) POLYGRAPH
DETENT DOG PALL PAWL CATCH
CLICK RATCH PALLET RATCHET
DETENTION DELAY ARREST
CAPTURE DETINUE JANKERS
DETAINER STOPPAGE
DETER BAR FEAR BLOCK BLUFF
CHECK DELAY DEHORT HINDER
RETARD PREVENT TERRIFY
DISSUADE PRECLUDE RESTRAIN
DETERGE PURGE CLEANSE
MUNDIFY

DETERGENT SOAP SYNDET ABLUENT PURGING RHYPTIC SMECTIC SOLVENT CLEANSER GARDINOL

DETERIORATE GO FAIL GIVE SLIP SOUR WEAR DECAY ERODE SPILL WORST APPAIR APPERE DEBASE IMPAIR SICKEN WORSEN DECLINE PERVERT FIREFANG

DETERIORATED MUSTY

DETERIORATING DECADENT

DETERIORATION DECAY IMPAIR MALADY DECLINE EROSION FAILURE DOLDRUMS PEJORATION

DETERMINABLE FIXED DEFINITE DEFINABLE GAUGEABLE

DETERMINANT CYTOGENE JACOBIAN CIRCULANT WRONSKIAN PLASTOGENE

DETERMINATE CERTAIN ORISTIC DEFINITE RESOLUTE RESOLVED SPECIFIC

DETERMINATION ACT HEST WILL ASSAY BLANK CAUSE ADVICE BEARING CONSULT PURPOSE RESOLVE ANALYSIS BACKBONE BIOASSAY DECISION DIVISION FIRMNESS FORECAST JUDGMENT JUDICIAL SENTENCE VOLITION

DETERMINATIVE FINAL FORMANT SHAPING LIMITING
(MOST —) DOMINANT

DETERMINE END FIT FIX GET RUN TEST WILL ASSAY AWARD JUDGE PITCH WIELD ADJUST ASSESS ASSIGN ASSOIL CHOOSE DECERN DECIDE DECREE DEFINE DESCRY DETECT DETERM DEVISE FIGURE GOVERN PERFIX SETTLE ACCOUNT ADJUDGE ANALYZE APPOINT ARRANGE COMPUTE DELIMIT DERAIGN DISPOSE RESOLVE TERMINE COGNOSCE CONCLUDE DISCOVER PINPOINT INFLUENCE
(— FINENESS) SET SETT
(— PATERNITY) AFFILIATE
(— RATE) ASSESS
(— ROOT) EXTRACT

DETERMINED SET BENT DERN FIRM GRIM BOUND GIVEN STOUT UPSET BITTER DOGGED GRITTY INTENT MULISH STURDY DECIDED SETTLED DECISIVE FOREGONE PERVERSE RESOLUTE RESOLVED STUBBORN

DETERMINER GENE CHANCE PLASMAGENE

DETERMINING CRUCIAL

DETERMINIST JABARITE

DETEST DAMN HATE ABHOR CURSE LOATHE CONDEMN DESPISE DISLIKE DENOUNCE EXECRATE ABOMINATE

DETESTABLE FOUL HORRID ODIOUS BLASTED HATABLE HATEFUL HELLISH HIDEOUS ACCURSED DAMNABLE HATEABLE INFAMOUS INFERNAL MALEDICT ABHORRENT ABOMINABLE

DETESTATION ODIUM HATRED HORROR LOATHING ANTIPATHY

DETHRONE DEPOSE DIVEST UNCROWN

DETONATE FIRE BELCH BLAST SHOOT EXPLODE DETONIZE

DETONATION BLAST KNOCK AMBITUS PINGING PINKING

DETONATOR CAP FUSE FUZE FUSEE FUZEE SQUIB TORPEDO INITIATOR

DETOUR BYPASS CIRCUIT REROUTE DIVERSION ROUNDABOUT

DETRACT TAKE DECRY DEDUCT DEFAME DETRAY DIVERT VILIFY ASPERSE TRADUCE BELITTLE DEROGATE DIMINISH DISTRACT MINIMIZE PROTRACT SUBTRACT WITHDRAW
(— FROM) IMPEDE

DETRACTION CALUMNY SCANDAL SLANDER ZOILISM

DETRIMENT COST HARM HURT LOSS SORE WOUND DAMAGE DAMNUM DENIAL INJURY BEATING EXPENSE JACTURE DISFAVOR MISCHIEF

DETRIMENTAL ADVERSE CAPITAL HARMFUL HURTFUL LOSSFUL DAMAGING INVIDIOUS PERNICIOUS PREJUDICIAL
(— TO HEALTH) HARD

DETRITUS OUTWASH SHINGLE SHEETWASH

DEUCALION (FATHER OF —) PROMETHEUS
(MOTHER OF —) CLYMENE
(SON OF —) HELLEN ORESTHEUS AMPHICTYON
(WIFE OF —) PYRRHA

DEUCE TWO DIANTRE DICKENS
(WILD —) FREAK

DEUCEDLY BLAME BLAMED

DEUEL (SON OF —) ELIASAPH

DEUTERIUM DIPLOGEN

DEUTEROGAMY DIGAMY

DEUTOMALA LABIUM

DEUX JOURNEES, LES
(CHARACTER IN —) ARMAND MIKELI MAZARIN
(COMPOSER OF —) CHERUBINI

DEVA DEV DEWA SURA ANGEL DEITY

DEVASTATE NUKE EXILE HARRY HAVOC WASTE DEVAST RAVAGE ATOMIZE DESTROY PILLAGE PLUNDER SCOURGE DEMOLISH

DEVASTATED WASTE

DEVASTATING DEADLY LETHAL SAVAGE CRUSHING FEROCIOUS MURDEROUS

DEVASTATION RUIN SACK EXILE
HAVOC WASTE WRACK HARASS
RAVAGE SACCAGE SACKAGE
SACCAGE
DEVASTATOR LOCUST
DEVELOP BUD RUN BOOM COOK
FORM GROW STEM TILL ARISE
BREAK BREED BUILD ERECT RIPEN
SHOOT APPEAR BRANCH DETECT
EVOLVE ENLARGE FLOWER FULFIL
MATURE REVEAL UNFOLD UNFURL
BLOSSOM BURGEON BURNISH
EDUCATE ENLARGE EVOLUTE
EXPOUND FULFILL UNCOVER
DEVELOPE DISCLOSE DISCOVER
DISVELOP ENGENDER GENERATE
INCUBATE MANIFEST
(— A HEAD) HEART
(— BULB) BOTTOM
(— COLOR) AGE
(— CRACKS) ALLIGATOR
(— FLAVOR) BREATHE
(— WELL) COTTON
DEVELOPABLE TORSE
DEVELOPED DEEP FORWARD
(— AFTER BIRTH) ACQUIRED
(FULLY —) BOLD ADULT FLORID
FORMED SUMMED
(GREATLY —) ADVANCED
(IMPERFECTLY —) ABORTIVE
(INCOMPLETELY —) SEED
DEVELOPER ELON SOUP METOL
ORTOL AMIDOL GLYCIN KACHIN
QUINOL BUILDER GLYCINE RODINAL
DEVELOPING
(SUFF.) PLASTIC
DEVELOPMENT WAX DRIFT EVENT
HATCH ESTATE GROWTH DESCENT
GENESIS PROCESS STATURE
BREEDING INCREASE ONTOGENY
PEDIGREE UPGROWTH UPSPRING
(— OF SEX) DIOECISM
(FULL —) BLOW MATURITY
(HIGHEST —) BLOOM
(NORMAL —) APHANISIA
(SUBSEQUENT —) SEQUEL
(THEMATIC —) CONTINUITY
(UNEXPECTED —) ACCIDENT
(PREF.) PLASTO
(SUFF.) PLASIA PLASIS PLASM(A)(IA)
(IC) PLAST(IC)(Y) PLASY
DEVI UMA KALI DURGA GAURI
CHANDI SHAKTI BHAVANI BHOWANI
HIMAVAT MAHADEVI HAIMAVATI
(FATHER OF —) HIMAVAT
(HUSBAND OF —) SHIVA
DEVIANT KINKY ABERRANT
DIVERGENT
DEVIATE ERR RUN WRY YAW LEAN
MISS VARY VEER BEVEL BREAK DRIFT
LAPSE SHEER SPORT START STRAY
WAIVE CHANGE DEPART DETOUR
DIVERT RECEDE SQUINT SWERVE

WANDER DECLINE DEFLECT DIGRESS
DIVERGE INCLINE REFLECT
ABERRANT ABERRATE DEROGATE
(— FROM VERTICAL) HADE
DEVIATING SKEW DEVIANT
DEVIOUS ERRATIC SINUOUS
ABERRANT INDIRECT
DEVIATION BOW YAW HELM JUMP
SKEW TURN DRIFT LAPSE QUIRK
SHEER TWIST ABRASH BATTER
CHANGE DETOUR FIGURE SPREAD
ANOMALY BRISURE LICENCE
LICENSE ACCURACY DRIFTAGE
LATITUDE SOLECISM VARIANCE
ABERRATION
(— OF COLOR) ABRASH
(STANDARD —) SIGMA
DEVICE (ALSO SEE INSTRUMENT)
ARM ART DIE DOG DOP EYE FAN FLY
FOB GAG GIN GUN HOG JIG KEY
MOP MOT PEN SET TIP TUP WAY WIT
ARCH BELL BOND BOOM BUFF COIN
COMB COUP DARE DOPP DRAG DRIP
FAKE FIRE FLAG FORK FROG FUSE
FUZE GAGE GATE GOBO GRAB GRIP
GYRO HASP HAUL HEAD HECK HORN
IRIS IRON JACK KEEP KITE LAMP
LENS LOCK MOVE MULE MUTE NAIL
PACE PAGE PAWK PLAN PLOW POKE
PUMP REEL SEAL SHOE SHUT SIGN
SLAY SLEY SLUR SNAP SPUD STOP
STUD SUMP TOOL TRAP TRIP VICE
WEIR WHIM WHIP WIND WING WOLF
ALARM APRON BADGE BALUN BITCH
BLOCK BREAK BRUSH CHECK CLAMP
CODER COVIN CRAMP CROSS DODGE
DRIER DRIFT DRIVE DRYER DUMMY
FADER FANCY FLAIL FLARE FLASH
FLIRT FLOAT GAUGE GLAND GORGE
GRIPE GUARD GUIDE GUILE HICKY
HINGE HOKUM IMAGE KAZOO KEYER
LADLE LASER LATCH LEVEL LIDAR
LINAC MATCH MODEM OTTER PARER
PLATE PROBE PUNKA SCREW SHADE
SHANK SHIFT SIEVE SIGHT SIGIL
SIREN SIZER SKATE SLAVE SLICK
SLIDE SLING SONDE SPOOL SPOUT
SQUIB STAMP STILL STOOL STOVE
SWEEP SWELL TABLE TABUT TAMER
THIEF TIMER TORCH TRUER TUNER
UNION VERGE AGRAFE AIRWAY
ALARUM ALINER ANCHOR ARREST
BAILER BASTER BEACON BEATER
BECKET BEDDER BEEPER BINDER
BLOWER BOBBIN BOOMER BRIDLE
BROOCH BUCKLE BUFFER BULLEN
BUMPER BUNGEE BUNTER BURNER
BUTTON CHARGE CIPHER COOKER
DASHER DECEIT DERAIL DESIGN
DIMMER DOFFER DOTTER DRIVER
DROGUE DUMPER EMBLEM ENGINE
EVENER FABRIC FALLER FEEDER
FENDER FILLER FILTER FINDAL

FINDER FORMER GADGET GLAZER
GOFFER GOGGLE GRADER GRATER
GRISLY GUIDER HANGER HEATER
HICKEY HOLDER HOOTER INVENT
JIGGER JOGGER KEEPER KICKER
LAYBOY LETOFF LIFTER LOOPER
MARKER MIRROR MODULE MORTAR
MOTHER NAVAID NIPPLE NONIUS
NOTION PACKER PEELER PICKUP
PLAYER PLOUGH PORTER POTEYE
PULLER PUNKAH REROLL RINGER
ROCKET ROLLER ROOTER ROTULA
ROUTER SACKER SADDLE SAFETY
SANDER SCALER SCHEME SCREEN
SEALER SEEKER SENSOR SETTER
SHAKER SHIELD SIFTER SIGNAL
SINKER SIPPER SLEIGH SLICER
SLIDER SLIMER SLOPER SLUICE
SOCKET SOLION SORTER SPACER
SPRING STONER STYLUS SUCKER
SWITCH TACTIC TAGGER TAPPER
TELLER TEMPLE TESTER TILLER
TRACER TUCKER TUNNEL TURNER
WARMER WASHER WEANER WEEDER
WHEEZE WINDER WINNOW WORKER
ADAPTER ADJUNCT AERATOR
AGRAFFE ALIGNER AUTOCUE
BALANCE BECKETT BIMETAL
BIMORPH BINDING BLEEDER
BLEEPER BLENDER BLINKER
BLOCKER BLOWOFF BLOWOUT
BOOKEND BOOSTER BREAKER
CALTROP CHIPPER CLAPPER
COMPASS DASHPOT DISHMOP
DIVISOR DRAWOFF DRESSER
DRINKER EARPICK EDUCTOR
EJECTOR EMPRESA EXCITER
FACEBOW FASHION FETLOCK
FICELLE FICTION FITMENT FIXTURE
FLASHER FLIPPER FLUSHER FLYFLAP
FRISKET GAUFFER GIMMICK
GLASSES GRAINER GRENADE
GRIDDLE GRILLER GRINDER GRIPPER
GRIZZLY GROMMET GROOVER
GROWLER GUDGEON GUZZLER
HATCHER HELIDON IGNITER IMAGINE
IMPRESA IMPRESS INFUSER
INHALER IRONMAN KICKOFF
KNOTTER LIGHTER MACHINE
MUFFLER OOGRAPH PIGTAIL
PLOTTER POINTER PRESSER
RATCHET RATTLER RECEDER
REDUCER RELEASE ROASTER
ROSETTE SAMPLER SCALPER
SCANNER SCOGGAN SCRAPER
SCUPPER SERVANT SETBACK
SETOVER SETWORK SHACKLE
SHEDDER SHIFTER SHIPPER
SHOOFLY SHUTTER SHUTTLE
SINKBOX SKIMMER SLAPPER
SLEEVER SLINGER SLITTER SLUDGER
SLUSHER SNAPPER SNIFFER
SNIGGLE SNORKEL SNUBBER

SNUFFER SNUGGER SONOVOX
SOUNDER SPARGER SPEEDER
SPLICER SPOTTER SPRAYER
SQUEEZE STACKER STAPLER
STARTER STEMMER STENTER
STIRRER STOPPER STRIKER STRIPER
SUCTION SWATTER SWEEPER
SYRINGE TAMBOUR TENDRIL
TENSION THEORIC THINNER TICKLER
TOKAMAK TREADLE TRINDLE
TRIPPER TRIPPET TUMBLER
TURNOUT TWISTER WASHOUT
WRINGER ABSORBER ADJUSTER
AQUASTAT BACKSTAY BAROSTAT
BIOMETER BLOCKING BOOTJACK
BRAILLER BREATHER BRONTEUM
BUSINESS BUSYBODY CATAPULT
CATHETER COLOPHON CONTOISE
COUPLING CROTCHET CRYOTRON
DAMPENER DEHORNER DERAILER
DIFFUSER DIRECTOR DISPOSER
DOORSTOP DROPHEAD DUPLEXER
EARPHONE EPISEMON ESPRESSO
EXPLODER FAIRLEAD FAKEMENT
FASTENER FLASHGUN FLYBRUSH
FUELIZER GASCHECK GATHERER
GIMCRACK GUNSTICK GYROSTAT
HALLMARK HANDTRAP HEADGEAR
HOLDBACK IMPROVER INKSTAND
IRENICON IRISCOPE ISOLATOR
KNOCKOUT LAUNCHER LEEBOARD
LOXOCOSM LUNARIUM MNEMONIC
MOLITION NEOSTYLE ODOGRAPH
OVERLIFT OVERRIDE PACIFIER
PARAVANE PENWIPER PINWHEEL
PULSATOR PYROSTAT QUADRANT
QUENTISE REFILTER REHEATER
REPEATER RETARDER REVERSER
SCORCHER SCOTCHER SCRAWLER
SCUTCHER SELECTOR SHRINKER
SILENCER SILVERER SINKBOAT
SMOOTHER SNOWPLOW
SNOWSHOE SPLITTER SPREADER
SPROUTER SQUEEGEE SQUEEZER
STOPWORK STRAINER STRINGER
STRIPPER STROPPER SURFACER
SWEATBOX TELETYPE TELLTALE
TERMINAL THROWOFF THROWOUT
TRAVELER TRAVERSE TRIANGLE
NEURISTOR PINSETTER PROJECTOR
STRATAGEM MARTINGALE
PERIPHERAL PINSPOTTER
ACCELERATOR
(— FOR BENDING PIPE) HICKEY
(— FOR BORING WELLS) TIGER
(— FOR CONCENTRATING ORE)
JIGGER
(— FOR PUTTING IN GEAR) STRIKER
(— IN LOOM) FEELER TEMPLE
(— ON FLAG) UNION
(— PLACED OVER CHIMNEY) JACK
(— PROTECTING DENTIST'S HAND)
THIMBLE

(— THAT CONVERTS SIGNALS) MODEM
(— TO LOCATE AN OBJECT) LIDAR
(— TO RETAIN COFFEE GROUNDS) GRECQUE
(ARTIFICIAL —) PROSTHESIS
(AUTOMATIC —) BRAIN
(BRAKE —) CALIPER
(CENTRIFUGAL —) CYCLONE
(CLEVER —) COUP KNACK
(COMPUTER —) WAND MOUSE TERMINAL ACCUMULATOR
(COMPUTER CONTROL —) PADDLE
(CONVERTING —) MODEM
(CUBICAL BULB —) FLASHCUBE
(DISTINGUISHING —) SPOT
(ELECTORNIC —) MASER
(ELECTRICAL —) OVONIC
(ELECTRONIC —) DME NEURISTOR
(FILM —) MOVIOLA
(FILM EDITING —) MOVIOLA
(GAMBLING —) HOLDOUT
(GLASSBLOWER'S —) DUMMY
(HAMPERING —) HOBBLES
(HEATING —) ETNA
(HERALDIC —S) ARMS
(LISTENING —) BUG
(LITERARY —) FRAME
(MAGICIAN'S —) FAKE FEKE CRAFT
(MIXING —) CRUTCHER
(MUSIC —) HOOK
(NAVIGATIONAL —) LORAN
(OPTICAL —) NIGHTSCOPE
(PAGING —) BEEPER
(POLISHING —) WAGWAG
(PYROTECHNIC —) FOUNTAIN
(RHETORICAL —) ANAPHORA
(ROTATION —) TACH
(SHIELDING —) GOBO
(SIGHTING —) ALIDADE
(SIGNALLING —) CRICKET
(SKILLFUL —) ART
(SOUND —) PINGER
(SPEECH —) ITALICS
(SWIMMING —) SNORKEL
(THEATRICAL —) SLOAT SLOTE
(TIMEKEEPING —) HOROLOGE
(TOROIDAL —) TOKAMAK
(WATER-RAISING —) JANTU SWEEP CHURRUS
(WEAVING —) BOAT ENGINERY
(SUFF.) STAT(IC)(ICS)
(MUSICAL —) INA INE
DEVIL DEL IMP BEN BHUT BOGY DEIL HAZE MAHU NICK PUCK QUED WOLF WOND ANNOY BOBBY BOGEY BOGIE CHORT CLOOT DEMON DEUCE EBLIS FIEND HARRY SATAN SCRAT SHEDU TAIPO TEASE AMAMON BELIAL DAEMON DIABLE DIABLO HORNIE NICKIE PESTER RAGMAN SORROW THURSE AMAIMON ANHANGA CLOOTIE DIANTRE

DICKENS GREMLIN LUCIFER MAHOUND RUFFIAN SERPENT SHAITAN TORMENT WARLOCK WENDIGO WINDIGO APOLLYON BAALPEOR BEELPEOR BELFAGOR CAGNAZZO CURUPIRA DEVILING DEVILKIN DIABOLUS MEPHISTO MISCHIEF OBIDICUT PLOTCOCK WIRRICOW WORRICOW WORRYCOW BEELZEBUB
(BLUE —S) MARE
(PREF.) DIABOL(O)
DEVILFISH RAY MANTA
DEVIL-IN-A-BUSH NIGELLA
DEVILISH DARING DEUCED DEVILY RAKISH WICKED DEMONIC EXTREME FIENDLY HELLISH INHUMAN SATANIC DEMONIAC DIABOLIC FIENDISH INFERNAL SATURNINE
DEVILISHLY DEUCED DEUCEDLY
DEVILKIN IMP
DEVIL'S CLUB FATSIA
DEVIL'S COACHHORSE DARDAOL
DEVIL'S DISCIPLE
(AUTHOR OF —) SHAW
(CHARACTER IN —) DICK ESSIE JUDITH DUDGEON ANDERSON BURGOYNE
DEVIL'S-MILK WARTWEED WARTWORT
DEVIL'S-TREE DITA
DEVIOUS DEEP ERRING LOUCHE ROVING SHIFTY SUBTLE TRICKY OBLIQUE PLAITED VAGRANT WINDING HAVERING INDIRECT RAMBLING SCHEMING TORTUOUS AMBAGIOUS MEALYMOUTHED
DEVISE AIM CAST COOK FIND GIVE PLAN PLOT WARP WILL ARRAY FANCY FRAME FUDGE IMAGE LEAVE SHAPE WEAVE ADVISE CONVEY DECOCT DESIGN DEVICE DIVIDE DIVINE INVENT SCHEME AGITATE APPOINT ARRANGE BETHINK COMMENT COMPASS CONCERT CONCOCT CONSULT IMAGINE PREPARE PROJECT BEQUEATH CONTRIVE
DEVISED INVENIT
DEVISER FINDER ARTIFICER
DEVISING DEVICE DEVISAL FORGERY
DEVITALIZE DULL DEADEN
DEVITALIZED DEGENERATE
DEVITRIFIED AMBITTY
DEVOID FREE VAIN VOID EMPTY BARREN EXPERT VACANT SINCERE WANTING DESOLATE
(— OF) BOUT EMPTY
(— OF HELP) AIDLESS
(— OF KINDNESS) CRUEL
(— OF MERCY) BRUTAL
(— OF MIND) AMENTAL
(— OF VALUE) HOLLOW

DEVOLUTION DESCENT
DEVOLVE FALL PASS VEST RESULT
BLOSSOM SUCCEED OVERTURN
TRANSFER TRANSMIT
DEVOTE VOW ALLY AVOW DOOM
GIVE LEND TAKE TURN APPLY
DEVOW ADDICT ATTACH BESTOW
DEPUTE DESIGN DEVOVE DIRECT
EMPLOY INTEND RESIGN ADDRESS
APPOINT CONSIGN DESTINE
DEDICATE VENERATE
(— TIME) BOTHER
(— TO MISERY) ACCURSE
DEVOTED MAD HIGH TRUE LIEGE
LOYAL PIOUS ARDENT DEVOUT
DOOMED ENTIRE FERVID LOVING
OBLATE VOTARY VOTIVE ADORING
ARDUOUS JEALOUS SERIOUS
ZEALOUS ADDICTED ATTACHED
CONSTANT FAITHFUL
(— TO COUNTRY) PATRIOTIC
(— TO ENJOYMENT) APOLAUSTIC
(OVERLY —) SUPERSTITIOUS
DEVOTEE CAT FAN NUN BUFF MONK
YATI ADEPT JNANI ADDICT BHAGAT
BHAKTA DEVOTO DEVOUT HEPCAT
VOTARY VOTEEN ZEALOT ADMIRER
AMATEUR BOPPIST BOPSTER
CINEAST FANATIC HEPSTER HIPSTER
SHAVIAN TARTUFE AMOURIST
BURNSIAN CABALIST DEVOTARY
FOLLOWER IBSENITE PARTISAN
PRIAPIAN SAVOYARD SIMPLIST
TARTUFFE VOTARESS VOTARIST
ALLIGATOR AFICIONADO
DEVOTION CULT ZEAL ARDOR PIETY
BHAKTI NOVENA ANGELUS ARABISM
CULTISM LOYALTY PIETISM FIDELITY
IDOLATRY JEALOUSY KAVVANAH
KAWWANAH RELIGION
NATIONALISM
(— OF ONESELF) VOW NARCISSISM
(— TO HUMAN WELFARE)
HUMANISM
(— TO LADIES) GALLANTRY
(FERVENT —) ADORATION
(PARENTAL —) PROGENITY
(PL.) HOLIES
(SUFF.) LATER LATRIA LATROUS
LATRY
DEVOTIONAL PIOUS SOLEMN
DEVOUR EAT JAW FRET GULP SWAP
SWOP VOUR GORGE RAVEN SCOFF
WASTE AFRETE ENGULF CONSUME
ENGORGE FRAUNCH SWALLOW
(— GREEDILY) SWILL
(RAVENOUSLY —) WOLF
(SUFF.) VORA VORE VOROUS
DEVOURER LOCUST
DEVOURING PREY EATING GREEDY
VORANT EDACIOUS
DEVOUT GOOD HOLY WARM FROOM
GODLY GRACY PIOUS HEARTY

INWARD SOLEMN CORDIAL DEVOTED
GODLIKE PITEOUS SAINTLY SINCERE
REVERENT PIETISTIC PRAYERFUL
RELIGIOUS PIETISTICAL
SANCTIMONIOUS
(NOT —) LINK
DEVOUTNESS PIETY DEVOTION
DEW DAG RIME BLOOM FROST TEARS
MOISTEN REFRESH MOISTURE
(— METER) PAGOSCOPE
(NIGHT —) SERENE
(PREF.) DROSO RORI
DEWBERRY MAYES
DEWDROP PEARL
DEWLAP JOWL GULLET JOLLOP
CHOLLER WATTLES
(— OF MALE MOOSE) BELL
DEWY DAMP RORY MOIST RORAL
RORIC RORID GENTLE ROSCID
DEXTERITY ART CHIC CRAFT KNACK
SKILL STROIL ABILITY ADDRESS
AGILITY APTNESS CUNNING FINESSE
SLEIGHT APTITUDE DEFTNESS
FACILITY
(— IN ARMS) CHIVALRY
DEXTEROUS APT FLY DEFT FEAT
HEND NEAT WISE ADEPT CANNY
CLEAN FEATY HANDY HAPPY HENDE
JIMMY QUICK READY SMART TIGHT
ADROIT ARTFUL CLEVER DRAFTY
CUNNING SLEIGHT DEXTROUS
HANDSOME SKILLFUL SLEIGHTY
DEXTEROUSLY YARELY HANDILY
DEXTRAN GLUCOSAN
DEXTROROTATORY POSITIVE
DEXTRORSE EUTROPIC
DEXTROSE AME CEROLOSE
DHAK DAK PALAS PULAS
DHAVA BAKLI
DHOLE KOLSUN
DHOW BUGALA LATEEN SAMBUK
SAMBOUK LATEENER
DHRITARASHTRA (BROTHER OF —)
PANDU
(FATHER OF —) VYASA
VICHITRAVIRYA
(SON OF —) DURYODHANA
(WIFE OF —) GANDHARI
DHYANA JHANA
DIABASE OPHITE DOLERITE
THOLEITE
DIABOLICAL CRUEL WICKED
DEMONIC HELLISH INHUMAN
SATANIC VIOLENT DEMONIAC
DEVILISH DIABOLIC FIENDISH
INFERNAL
DIABOLISM SATANISM
DIACETATE ACETIN
DIACONATE DEACONRY
DIACONICON PARABEMA
DIACRITIC HACEK TILDE UMLAUT
MODIFIER
DIAD DIGONAL TWOFOLD

DIADEM TAJ MIND CROWN TIARA
ANADEM CIRCLE EMBLEM FILLET
CIRCUIT CORONET HEADBAND
DIAERESIS TREMA CESURA
CAESURA DIALYSIS
DIAGNOSE ANALYZE IDENTIFY
KNOWLEDGE
DIAGONAL BIAS SLANT SLASH
COUNTER SOLIDUS VIRGULE
BENDWISE DIAGONIC
DIAGONALLY BIAS ASLOPE
BENDWAYS BENDWISE
DIAGRAM MAP PLAN PLOT TREE
CARTE CHART EPURE GRAPH PARSE
DESIGN FIGURE SCHEMA SCHEME
SYMBOL YANTRA ISOGRAM ISOTYPE
SECTION VIAGRAM PICTOGRAM
PICTOGRAPH
(KIND OF —) FEYNMAN
DIAGRAMMATIC GRAPHIC
DIAGRAPH OE
DIAL NOB CALL FACE KNOB WATCH
DIACLE JIGGER AZIMUTH CRYSTAL
DECLINER HOROLOGE INCLINER
RECLINER
DIAL BIRD DAYAL DHYAL
DIALECT (ALSO SEE LANGUAGE) HO
KA WU GEG GIZ KHA LAI SAC TWI
AMOY CANI CANT DRAA EFIK EGBA
EPIC GEEZ GHEG GONA GUEG IOWA
ITZA KORA MANX NAMA NORN
OGAM PALI SAUK SHOR SOGA TALK
TCHI TOSK TUBA ALTAI ARGOT
ASURI ATTIC CONOY DORIC FANTI
GHEEZ GHESE HAKKA IDIOM IONIC
IOWAY IRAQI KANSA KAREL KOINE
LADIN LINGO MAZUR MOTAN MUKRI
NGOKO OGHAM PARSI PUNIC SABIR
SAXON SCOTS SLANG TIGRE TSCHI
VALVE VOGUL ZMUDZ AEOLIC
AGNEAN ASANTE ATSINA AWADHI
BADAGA BRETON BROGUE CANTON
CREOLE DEBATE DUNGAN FAEROE
FANTEE FURLAN GASCON GULLAH
GUTNIC HARARI HARAYA IBANAG
ISINAI ITAVES JARGON KABYLE
KANSAS KHAMIR KORANA KVITSH
LADAKI LADINO LAHULI LALLAN
LEDDEN LIBYAN PARSEE PATOIS
PATTER PICARD SANTEE SCOTCH
SCOUSE SHARRA SKAGIT SPEECH
SUDANI SWATOW SYRIAC SZEKEL
TAVAST TONGUE TUSCAN YANKEE
ZENAGA ACADIAN AEOLIAN
AMOYESE ANGLIAN ASHANTI
BHOTANI BHUTANI BUNDELI
CATALAN CHILULA CHUVASH
CLATSOP COCKNEY CORNISH
CUZCENO CYPRIOT FAYUMIC
FOOCHOW GEECHEE GHEGISH
GUTNISH JAIPURI KARAITE KENTISH
KITKSAN KONKANI LADAKHI
LALLAND LEONESE LESBIAN

MALTESE MARSIAN MARWARI
MERCIAN MIDLAND MULTANI
MUNDARI OLONETS PANAYAN
PRAKRIT SAHIDIC SANPOIL SHORTZY
SOKOTRI SPOKANE SQUAXON
SWABIAN SZEKLER TIGRINA
VAUDOIS WALLOON ABANEEME
ACHIMIMIC AKHMIMIC ALGERINE
ARCADIAN ASSYRIAN BASILECT
BAVARIAN BHOJPURI BISCAYAN
BOEOTIAN BOHAIRIC CLAKAMAS
COLVILLE CORSICAN CYPRIOTE
FALERIAN FALISCAN FAROEISH
FRANCIEN FRIULIAN GARHWALI
HARARESE IZCATECO KANESIAN
KARELIAN KERMANJI KICKAPOO
KINGWANA LACANDON LANGUAGE
LAWLANTS MAGHREBI MAGHRIBI
MAITHILI MANDAEAN MANDARIN
MANISIAN MAZATECO MAZURIAN
MEMPHITE NABATEAN NEENGATU
PANAYANO PEKINESE RABBINIC
SALTEAUX SOULETIN SOUTHERN
TAUNGTHU TIORINTA TIRHUTIA
TUNISIAN VENERIAN VIENNESE
NORTHUMBRIAN
(ENGLISH — IN LIVERPOOL) SCOUSE
(ESKIMO —) INUIT INUKITTUT
(STRANGE —) GIBBERISH
(PL.) WU ANGLIAN
DIALECTIC PILPUL
DIALOGUE ION CRITO DIALOG
EPILOG PATTER PHAEDO TIMAEUS
COLLOQUY DUOLOGUE EPILOGUE
EXCHANGE PHAEDRUS
COLLOCUTION
(—S OF BUDDHA) SUTRA SUTTA
(COMIC —) LAZZO
DIAMETER BORE GAGE GEAR MOOT
GAUGE WIDTH MODULE
(— OF BULLET) CALIBER CALIBRE
(— OF PELVIS) CONJUGATA
(— OF PUPIL) APERTURE
(— OF WIRE) GAGE GAUGE
DIAMOND GEM ICE BORT LASK PICK
ROCK ROSE BAHIA BOORT BORTZ
DORJE FANCY FIELD JAGER JEWEL
LOZEN MACLE MELEE POINT RHOMB
RIVER SANCY SPARK STONE TABLE
VAJRA ADAMAS BOARTS CANARY
CARBON JAEGER LASQUE ORLOFF
PENCIL REGENT RONDEL SHINER
TABLET ADAMANT BRIOLET
CARREAU CRYSTAL FISHEYE INFIELD
LOZENGE PREMIER RHOMBUS
SPARKLE CORUNDUM KOHINOOR
RONDELLE SPARKLER BRIOLETTE
(— CUT TOO THIN) FISHEYE
(— MOLDER) DOP
(— STATE) DELAWARE
(— UNIT) INNING
(— USED FOR ENGRAVING) SHARP
(BLACK —) CARBONADO

(FLAT —) LASQUE
(GLAZIER'S —) QUARREL
(IMITATION —) SCHLENTER
(INFERIOR GRADE OF —) FLAT
(PASTE —) RHINESTONE
(PERFECT —) PARAGON
(PURE WHITE —) RIVER
(ROUGH —) BRAIT
(SINGLE —) SOLITAIRE
(TRANSPARENT —) CRYSTAL
(YELLOW —) CANARY
(PL.) MELANGE
DIAMOND BIRD PARDALOTE
DIAMORPHINE HEROIN
DIANA LUCINA TRIVIA ARTEMIS
(BROTHER OF —) APOLLO
(FATHER OF —) JUPITER
(MOTHER OF —) LATONA
DIANA MONKEY ROLOWAY
DIAPASON MONTRE DIAPASE
DIAPAUSE BLOCK
DIAPER FUR DIDY CLOUT DIDIE
NAPPY HIPPEN HIPPIN NAPKIN
NAPPIE DIAPERY
DIAPHANOUS CLEAR SHEER
FRAGILE DIAPHANE VAPOROUS
DIAPHONY ORGANUM TRIPHONY
DIAPHORETIC BUCCO BUCHU
BUCKU BORAGE DIAPNOIC HIDROTIC
SUDATORY SASSAFRAS
PILOCARPINE
DIAPHRAGM IRIS RIFF SLIT APRON
PHREN SKIRT WAFER DECKER
PLATEN MIDRIFF PHRAGMA
SKIRTING TRAVERSE TYMPANUM
(KIND OF —) IRIS
(PREF.) PHREN(O)
DIAPHRAGMATIC PHRENIC
DIARIST ENTERER
DIARRHEA LAX FLUX LASK GURRY
RELAX SCOUR SPRUE PURGING
SQUIRTS LIENTERY
DIARY LOG RECORD DAYBOOK
DIURNAL JOURNAL REGISTER
EPHEMERIS
DIASKEUAST EDITOR REVISER
DIASPORA GALUT GOLAH GALUTH
DIASPORE MIGRULE
DIASTASE MALT ENZYME AMYLASE
DIATOM BRITTLEWORT
ASTERIONELLA
DIATOMITE TRIPOLI
DIATONIC ACHROMATIC
DIATRIBE SATIRE SCREED
HARANGUE INVECTIVE
DIAZAPAM VALIUM
DIB DAP DIP DIBBLE DIBSTONE
DIBBLE DAP DIB DABBLE DIBBER
KIPPIN TRIFLE DIBBLER KIPPEEN
DIBRI
(SON OF —) SHELOMITH
DIBS COCKAL
DICAST HELIAST JURYMAN

DICE CHOP CUBE DEES BONES CRAPS
FLATS LOWMEN REJECT CHECKER
IVORIES
(— GAME) SET RAPHE MUMCHANCE
(— HAVING FOUR SPOTS) QUATRE
(FALSE —) GOAD TATS GOURD
GRAVIERS SQUARIER STOPDICE
(HIGHEST THROW AT —) APHRODITE
(LOADED —) TOPS DOCTOR
(LOWEST THROW AT —) AMBSACE
(PAIRED NUMBERS AT —) DUPLET
DOUBLETS
(2, 3, OR 12 ON 1ST —) MISSOUT
(PREF.) ASTRAGAL(O)
DICE-BOX RATTLE
DICE PLAYER THROWSTER
DICER HAT DERBY GAMBLER
GRAINER
DICERION DYKER
DICHASIAL BIPAROUS
DICHLORVOS DDVP
DICHONDRA LAWNLEAF
DICHOTOMY DUALITY
DICHROITE IOLITE
DICK TEC
DICKENS HECK DEUCE
(LITTLE —) IMP
DICKER ICRE SWAP DAKER BARTER
HAGGLE BARGAIN CHAFFER
EXCHANGE
DICKEY POOP WEAK DICKY FRONT
GILET SHAKY DONKEY RUMBLE
VESTEE HADDOCK PLASTRON
DICKIE SHAM DICKY FRONT SQUARE
TUCKER STARCHER
DICLINOUS IMPERFECT
DICTATE SAW SAY DITE TELL UTTER
WRITE DECREE DICTUM ENJOIN
IMPOSE INDITE OCTROY ORDAIN
SCHOOL COMMAND DELIVER
REQUIRE SUGGEST WARRANT
DICTAMEN PRESCRIBE
DICTATION DICTAMEN
DICTATOR CHAM CZAR DUCE TSAR
CAESAR PENDRAGON
DICTATORIAL BOSSY LORDLY
CZARIST POMPOUS TSARIST
ARROGANT DOGMATIC ORACULAR
POSITIVE ARBITRARY MAGISTERIAL
DICTION STYLE TERMS PHRASE
IMAGERY LANGUAGE PARLANCE
VERBIAGE
(BAD —) CACOLOGY
(SUFF.) ESE
DICTIONARY GRADUS ALVEARY
CALEPIN LEXICON GLOSSARY
WORDBOOK THESAURUS
(BRITISH —) OED
(PREF.) LEXICO
DICTUM SAY ADAGE AXIOM EDICT
DECREE SAYING DICTATE EFFATUM
OPINION APOTHEGM PRINCIPLE
STATEMENT

DID D CAN DED DEDE DYDE
(— NOT) DIDNA DIDNT
DIDACTIC DRY PREACHY SERMONIC
DIDO ANTIC CAPER PRANK TRICK
(BROTHER OF —) PYGMALION
(FATHER OF —) BELUS
(HUSBAND OF —) SICHAEUS
(LOVER OF —) AENEAS
DIDO AND AENEAS
(CHARACTER IN —) DIDO AENEAS
BELINDA MERCURY
(COMPOSER OF —) PURCELL
DIE GO BED DEE DOD END HOB HUB
PIP ROT SIX TAT BOSS COIN CONK
CUBE DADO DEAD DICE DROP EXIT
FADE FAIL FALL FINE FIVE FLIT KICK
MARK MOLD PART PASS PIKE PILE
SEAL TATT TINE WANE CROAK FORCE
FUDGE GHOST IVORY NAPOO PATAY
PRINT PUNCH QUAIL SHAPE SNUFF
SOUGH SPILL STALL STAMP STOCK
SWELT CHANCE DEMISE DEPART
DOCTOR EXPIRE FAMISH FINISH
FORCER FORMER FULLAM MATRIX
MULLAR PATRIX PERISH ROLLER
STARVE STRIKE TORFEL TORFLE
TRANCE VANISH WITHER BLOCKER
DECEASE STEPOUT SUCCUMB
TESSERA INTAGLIO LANGUISH
MISCARRY PUNCHEON TRESPASS
TRUSSELL
(— AWAY) FAIL SWOON
(— BEFORE) PREDECEASE
(— BY HANGING) SWING
(— DOWN) FLIT SINK ABATE
(— FOR DRAWING WIRE) WHIRTLE
WHORTLE
(— FOR MAKING DRAINPIPE) DOD
(— FOR MOLDING BRICK) KICK
(— FROM HUNGER) AFFAMISH
(— OF COLD) STARVE
(— OF HUNGER) STARVE
(— OF PEDESTAL) SOLIDUM
(— WITH 4 SPOTS) QUATRE
(— WITH 6 SPOTS) CISE SICE SISE
SIZE
(COINING —) SICCA
(FRAUDULENT —) FULHAM FULLAM
FULLOM
(HOLLOW —) GOURD
(IMPROPER —) FLAT
(LOADED —) TAT DOCTOR FULHAM
HIGHMAN LANGRET
(LOWER —) BED
(REVOLVING —) DREIDEL
DIEBACK STAGHEAD EXANTHEMA
DIED DYDE OBIIT WRATE
DIEHARD TORY BLIMP
DIESIS FEINT
DIET BANT FARE FAST FOOD SEIM
SEYM BOARD HOFTAG REDUCE
SEIMAS VIANDS VICTUS BANTING
DIETINE LANDTAG REGIMEN

RIKSDAG CONGRESS KREISTAG
VOLKSTAG
DIETARY LOCAL
(— LAWS) KASHRUTH
DIETER SLIMMER
DIETETICS SITOLOGY
DIETHER APIOL APIOLE DIOXANE
DIETING BANTING
DIFFER VARY RECEDE SQUARE
COMPARE DISCORD DISSENT
DIVERGE DISAGREE
DIFFERENCE SHED CHASM CLASH
FAVOR BREACH CHANGE DIFFER
ANOMALY DISCORD DISCORD
DISPUTE QUALITY VARIETY
DISTANCE DIVISION IMPARITY
VARIANCE
(— IN ELEVATION) HEAD
(— IN EXCHANGE) AGIO
(— IN LATITUDE) SOUTHING
(— IN LONGITUDE) EASTING
(— IN PITCH) COMMA INTERVAL
(— IN PRESSURE) DRAFT DRAUGHT
(— IN WIDTH) BILGE
(— OF OPINION) DISSENT
ARGUMENT
(— OF VESSEL'S DRAFT) DRAG
(ANGULAR —) EXPLEMENT
(GRADED —) GRADIENT
(MAKE A —) MATTER
(MINUTE —) SHADE
(POTENTIAL —) EMF
(PRICE —) BASIS
(SMALL —) NUANCE HAIRLINE
DIFFERENT FAR MANY SERE FRESH
OTHER PARTY DIVERS SCREWY
SUNDRY UNLIKE ANOTHER DISTANT
DIVERSE SEVERAL STRANGE
UNALIKE UNUSUAL VARIANT
VARIOUS CONTRARY DISTINCT
MANIFOLD SEPARATE OTHERWISE
OTHERGUESS NONIDENTICAL
(NOT —) IDENTIC INDENTICAL
(VERY —) WISE
(PREF.) DIVERSI HETER(O)
DIFFERENTIA MARK LIMIT
DIFFERENTIAL FLUXION
DIFFERENTIATE APLITE DIFFER
DISCERN HAPLITE CONTRAST
SPECIATE
DIFFERENTIATION ANABOLY
DEVIATION DICHOTOMY
(PREF.) ALL(O)
DIFFERING DIVERSE SINGULAR
DIVERGENT
DIFFICULT ILL HARD WICK CRAMP
CRANK GREAT HEAVY SPINY STEEP
STIFF AUGEAN CRABBY CRANKY
KNOTTY SEVERE STICKY STRAIT
STRONG TICKLE TRAPPY UNEASY
UNEATH UPHILL WENETH WICKED
ARDUOUS AWKWARD BRITTLE
COMPLEX CRABBED DIFFUSE

LABORED NERVOUS OBSCURE
PAINFUL PERPLEX PRACTIC SERIOUS
STICKLE UNNETHE ABSTRACT
CUMBROUS FIENDISH PUZZLING
SCABROUS STRUGGLE STUBBORN
TICKLISH
(— TO BEAR) BITTER
(— TO COMPREHEND) STRANGE
(— TO FOLLOW) DIRTY
(— TO GRASP) FUGITIVE
(— TO HANDLE) SPINOUS
(— TO MANAGE) SURLY STURDY
(— TO OBTAIN) CLOSE
(— TO OVERCOME) STRONG
(— TO PLEASE) CURIOUS
(— TO PRONOUNCE) BREAKJAW
(— TO RAISE) DORTY
(— TO SATISFY) CHOOSY CHOOSEY
(— TO UNDERSTAND) DEEP HIGH
SUBTLE CRABBED ABSTRACT
ABSTRUSE ESOTERIC
(PREF.) DYS MOGI

DIFFICULTY ADO BAR BOX ILL JAM
RUB BUMP CLOG COIL HEAT JAMB
KNOT LOCK NODE PAIN PINE SNAG
SORE WERE CHECK DOUBT GRIEF
NODUS PRESS RIGOR STAND STOUR
TRADE APORIA BOGGLE BUNKER
HABBLE HOBBLE PLIGHT PLUNGE
RUBBER SCRAPE STRAIT TIFTER
BARRIER DICKENS GORDIAN PITFALL
PROBLEM SQUEEZE ASPERITY
DISTRESS HARDNESS HARDSHIP
OBSTACLE SEVERITY STRUGGLE
(TEMPORARY —) HICCUP
(UNEXPECTED —) SNAG
(WITH —) SCARCELY
(PREF.) **(WITH —)** DYS MOGI

DIFFIDENCE DOUBT MODESTY
RESERVE SHYNESS DISTRUST
HUMILITY TIMIDITY

DIFFIDENT SHY BLATE CHARY
MODEST BASHFUL BACKWARD
RESERVED RETIRING SHEEPISH

DIFFUSE FULL SHED BLEED EXUDE
LARGE STREW WORDY DEFUSE
DERIVE DILATE DIVIDE EXPAND
EXTEND OSMOSE PROLIX SPREAD
SPRING COPIOUS DIALYSE DIALYZE
DIFFUND PERFUSE PERPLEX
PERVADE PUBLISH RADIATE SCATTER
SPARKLE SPRAWLY SPRENGE
SUFFUSE VERBOSE CONFUSED
DIFFUSED DIOSMOSE DISPERSE
PATULENT PATULOUS SPRANGLE
(NOT —) STRICT COMPACT

DIFFUSION SPREAD OSMOSIS
BLEEDING DEFUSION

DIG GET HOE JOB NIP CLAW DIKE
DYKE GIRD GORE GRUB HOWK LIKE
MINE MOOT PICK PION POKE PROD
ROOT SINK SLAM SMUG SPIT SPUD
SUMP SWOT DELVE DITCH DWELL

GAULT GRAFT GRAVE LODGE POACH
PROBE SNOUT SPADE START STOCK
BURROW DREDGE EXHUME GRAVEL
HOLLOW PLUNGE SHOVEL THRUST
TUNNEL BEDELVE COSTEAN
SPUDDLE UNEARTH EXCAVATE
UNDERSTAND
(— IN) EAT ENTRENCH
(— OUT) SCOOP STUMP EXHUME
(— OUT CREVICES) FOSSICK
(— PEAT) SHEUGH
(— POTATOES) LIFT
(— TRENCHES) GRIP LABOR
COSTEAN COSTEEN
(— UP) CAST GRUB STUB SPADE
STOCK EXHUME UPGRAVE DISINTER
(— WITH NAILS) SCRAPE
(— WITH SNOUT) GROUT
(— WITH STICK) CROW

DIGAMMA VAU

DIGEST COCT CODE DEFY ENDEW
ENDUE INDUE RIPEN CODIFY DECOCT
DOCKET MATURE SEETHE CONCOCT
EPITOME PANDECT SUMMARY
CONDENSE SYLLABUS
(— OF ROMAN LAWS) PANDECTS

DIGESTION PEPSIS COCTION
EUPEPSY EUPEPSIA
(SUFF.) PEPSIA PEPTIC

DIGESTIVE PEPSIN PEPTIC DIGERENT

DIGGER DIG PAL PLOW MINER
BANKER BILDAR DRUDGE PLOUGH
COMRADE PEATMAN PIONEER
PLODDER TRENCHER
(POST HOLE —) LOY

DIGGING DIG DIKAGE DYKAGE
STRIPPING

DIGHT DAB RUB DECK DINK DITE
WIPE ADORN DICHT DRESS EQUIP
ORDER RAISE TREAT MANAGE
REPAIR WINNOW APPOINT CONSIGN
PERFORM PREPARE

DIGIT TOE BYTE ONEK UNIT DOIGT
POINT THUMB DACTYL FIGURE
FINGER HALLUX MEDIUS NUMBER
DEWCLAW DIGITAL INTEGER
(BINARY —) BIT BINIT
(EXTRA —) PREPOLLEX
(GROUP OF EIGHT BINARY —S) BYTE
(PREF.) DACTYLIO DACTYL(O)
(SUFF.) DACTYLIA DACTYLOUS

DIGITAL KEY MANUAL

DIGITATE DIGITAL FINGERED

DIGNIFIED GRAND LOFTY MANLY
NOBLE REGAL STAID AUGUST
LORDLY SEDATE SOLEMN COURTLY
EXALTED STATELY TOGATED
ELEVATED ENNOBLED MAJESTIC

DIGNIFY DUB ADORN CROWN EXALT
GRACE HONOR RAISE ELEVATE
ENNOBLE PROMOTE

DIGNITARY DON WIG BABA RAJA
CANON RAJAH PRIEST SHERIF

DIGNITY HUTUKTU PRELATE
PROVOST SHEREEF ALDERMAN
HUTUKHTU VESTIARY
DIGNITY DOG CHIC FACE RANK BENCH
DINES HONOR IZZAT PRIDE STATE
AFFAIR BARONY LAUREL REPOSE
BARONRY BEARING DECORUM
DUKEDOM EARLDOM FITNESS
GRAVITY MAJESTY SHAHDOM
STATION WORSHIP CHIVALRY
EARLSHIP GRANDEUR NOBILITY
(— OF BISHOP) LAWN
(— OF CARDINAL) HAT
(— OF KING) PURPLE
(ACCIDENTAL —) JOY HAYZ
(EPISCOPAL —) MITER MITRE
CATHEDRA
(PAPAL —) TIARA
(SUFF.) DOM SHIP
DIGRAPH CH OE PH RH TH RRH
BIGRAM LIGATURE DIPHTHONG
DIGRESS VEER EXCUR DIVERT
SWERVE WANDER DEVIATE DIVERGE
EXCURSE DIGRESS DIVAGATE
DIGRESSION ASIDE VAGARY
DIGRESS ECRASIS EPISODE
EXCURSE PASSAGE TANGENT
DISGRESS EXCURSUS SIDESLIP
PARENTHESIS
(RHETORICAL —) ECBOLE
DIKE BAR RIB BANK BUND DICE DICK
DYKE GALL POND POOL DIGUE DITCH
GROIN LEVEE CAUSEY CRADGE
CHANNEL DIKELET POWDIKE
ABOIDEAU CAUSEWAY ESTACADE
SPREADER
DIKER COWAN COWEN
DIKETONE BENZIL BIACETYL
DIMEDONE
DIKI AH
(FATHER OF —) JOKTAN
DILACTONE LACTIDE ANEMONIN
DILAPIDATE DESTROY
DILAPIDATED BAD BEATEN CREAKY
RAGGED RUINED SHABBY WRECKY
CRAICHY CREACHY RUINOUS
DESOLATE TATTERED WOBEGONE
DILAPIDATION RUIN DECAY
DECREPITY DISREPAIR
DILATATION BULB SINUS VARIX
JARBOT SPREAD AMPULLA ECTASIA
ECTASIS ANEURISM DILATION
MYDRIASIS
(— OF ARTERY) ANEURYSM
(— OF TRACHEA) AIRSAC
(SUFF.) ECTASIA ECTASIS
DILATE TENT DELAY PLUMP SWELL
WIDEN DELATE EXPAND EXTEND
SPREAD AMPLIFY BROADEN
DESCANT DIFFUSE DISTEND
ENLARGE INFLATE PROLONG
STRETCH DISPERSE INCREASE
LENGTHEN PROTRACT DISCOURSE

DILATED TURGID VARICOSE
DILATING
(SUFF.) EURYSIS
DILATOR DIOPTER DIOPTRA DIOPTRY
DIVULSOR SPECULUM
DILATORY LATE SLOW SLACK SPARE
TARDY FABIAN REMISS DILATOR
LAGGARD LATREDE TEDIOUS
BACKWARD DELAYING INACTIVE
SLUGGISH
DILEMMA FIX FORK LOCK NODE
BRIKE POSER CHOICE PICKLE
PLUNGE CORNUTE SNIFTER
JEOPARDY QUANDARY
DILETTANTE LOVER SUNDAY
ADMIRER AMATEUR DABBLER
DABSTER ESTHETE AESTHETE
DILIGENCE HIE CARE HEED DILLY
EFFORT CAUTION HORNING
BUSINESS INDUSTRY SEDULITY
ASSIDUITY
DILIGENT BUSY HARD TIDY ACTIVE
EIDENT ITHAND STEADY CAREFUL
EARNEST HEEDFUL OPEROSE
PAINFUL PATIENT WORKFUL
CAUTIOUS CONSTANT LABOROUS
SEDULOUS STUDIOUS
DILL ANET CALM SOYA ANISE UMBEL
PICKLE SOOTHE DILLWEED
DILLIDALLY TARRY
DILLY ONER
DILLYDALLY LAG TOY LOAF DELAY
DILLY STALL LOITER TRIFLE
DILOGY ECHO
DILUENT CARRIER VEHICLE
DILUTE CUT BREW FUSE LEAN THIN
WEAK ALLAY BLUNT DELAY WATER
RAREFY REDUCE WEAKEN WHITISH
DIMINISH LENGTHEN WATERISH
(— LIQUOR) BREW SPLIT
(— WINE) GALLIZE
(VERY —) SMALL
DILUTED WASHY DILUTE REMISS
DILUTING ATTENUANT
DILUTION
(— OF A SERUM) TITER
DIM DIP WAN BLUR DARK DULL FADE
GRAY HAZY MIST PALE PALL VEIL
BEDIM BLEAK BLEAR BLIND DUSKY
DUSTY FAINT FOGGY MISTY STAIN
UNLIT BEMIST BLEARY CLOUDY
DARKEN DASWEN DIMPSY GLOOMY
OBTUSE SHADOW TWILIT BECLOUD
DARKISH DISLIMN ECLIPSE OBSCURE
OPACATE SHADOWY TARNISH
DARKLING OVERCAST CALIGINOUS
CREPUSCULAR
(NOT —) FRESH
DIME HOG HOGG DISME TENPENCE
TENPENNY
(HALF —) PICAYUNE
DIMEDON METHONE
DIMENHYDRINATE DRAMAMINE

DIMENSION BODY BULK SIZE SCOPE WIDTH ASSIZE DEGREE EXTENT HEIGHT LENGTH MOISON BREADTH PROPORTION MEASUREMENT
(COLOR —) CHROMA
(TYPE —) EM EN
(PL.) GAGE SIZE GAUGE GIRTH EXTENT SIDING MEASURE

DIMENSIONS
(PREF.) (THREE —) STERE(O)

DIMER (— IN EXCITED STATE) EXCIMER

DIMERCAPROL BAL

DIMIDIATE HALVED

DIMINISH GO CUT EBB SAP BATE BURN CHOP DAMP DROP EASE FADE FAIL FINE FRET MELT PARE PINK SINK WANE WEAR ABATE ALLAY BREAK CLOSE DRAFT DWARF ELIDE ERODE LOWER MINCE PETER SLACK SMALL TAPER DAMPEN DEBATE DECOCT DEDUCT DILUTE IMPAIR LESSEN MINISH REBATE REDUCE SLOUGH VANISH WITHER ABRIDGE ASSUAGE CORRODE CURTAIL DEGRADE DEPLETE DEPRESS DETRACT DIMINUE DRAUGHT DWINDLE FRITTER INHIBIT QUALIFY REFRACT RELIEVE TARNISH ADMINISH AMOINDER CONDENSE DECREASE DIMINUTE DISCOUNT MINORATE MITIGATE MODERATE RETRENCH
(— FRONT) PLOY

DIMINISHED SLACK ABATED GRAYED DIMINUTE

DIMINISHING TAPER CRITICAL FLAGGING
(— IN LOUDNESS) CALANDO

DIMINUTION FALL WASTE RABATE DECREASE PERDITION

DIMINUTIVE TOY WEE BABY TINY BANTY DWARF PETTY RUNTY SMALL YOUNG BANTAM LITTLE MIDGET PETITE POCKET MANIKIN MIDGETY MINIKIN SHRIMPY EXIGUOUS
(— OF BAR) SCARP CLOSET SCARPE
(SUFF.) CLE CULE CULUS EL ET ETTE KIN OCK SY ULA ULE

DIMLY DULLY DARKLY FEEBLY SHADOWY

DIMMED BLEARY CLOUDY GRAYED BLEARED

DIMMING GRAYOUT

DIMNESS DIM HAZE MIST SLUR GLOOM CALIGO DARKNESS

DIMPLE DOKE AHMADI AHMEDI RIPPLE GELASIN FOSSETTE

DIM-SIGHTED PURBLIND

DIMWIT DODO DOLT DUMMY AIRHEAD DINGDONG

DIN BUM DUN REEL RERD RIOT UTIS ALARM BABEL BRUIT CHIME CHIRM CLANG DEAVE DEEVE FRUSH NOISE RERDE ALARUM BELDER CLAMOR FRAGOR HUBBUB RACKET RANDAN RATTLE STEVEN TUMULT UPROAR CLANGOR CLATTER DISCORD TURMOIL DINGDONG TINTAMAR

DINAH (BROTHER OF —) LEVI SIMEON
(FATHER OF —) JACOB
(MOTHER OF —) LEAH

DINAR DENARE MARAVEDI

DINARZADE
(SISTER OF —) SCHEHERAZADE

DINDLE RING QUIVER THRILL TINGLE TINKLE TREMOR STAGGER VIBRATE

DINE EAT SUP FARE FEAST REGALE

DINER EPICURE GOURMAND

DING DIN BEAT DANG DASH KICK PUSH RING WHIP CLANG DRIVE EXCEL FLING KNOCK PITCH POUND PUNCH THUMP STROKE THRASH THRUST

DINGE DENT DINT BATTER BRUISE TARNISH

DINGHY PRAM SKIFF DINGEY ROWBOAT SHALLOP SNOWBIRD

DINGLE DEN DALE DELL GLEN VALE DIMBLE DUMBLE HOLLOW VALLEY

DINGMAN BUMPER

DINGO WARRAGAL WARRIGAL

DINGUS GADGET DOOHICKEY

DINGY DUN DARK BLACK DIRTY DUSKY GRIMY OURIE SMOKY DINGHY FUSCOUS SUBFUSC SMIRCHED

DINING CENATION
(— HALL) MESS
(PREF.) DEIPNO

DINING ROOM TRICLINIUM

DINKA JANGHEY

DINNER DINE HALL KALE MEAL MEAT NOON BEANO FEAST DINING REPAST BANQUET PUCHERO FUNCTION
(— AT HOME) EATIN
(CEREMONIAL —) SEDER
(PERTAINING TO —) PRANDIAL
(PREF.) DEIPNO

DINOSAUR DIAPSID SAURIAN DUCKBILL NODOSAUR SAUROPOD TROODONT ORNITHISCHIAN

DINT BEAT BLOW DENT DUNT NICK CLOUR DELVE DINGE FORCE NOTCH ONSET POWER PRESS SHOCK ATTACK CHANCE EFFORT STRIKE STROKE IMPRINT EFFICACY STRIKING

DIOCESAN EPISCOPAL

DIOCESE SEE EPARCHY DISTRICT BISHOPRIC

DIODE LED KENOTRON
(— THAT EMITS LIGHT) LED
(KIND OF —) ZENER
(LIGHT-EMITTING —) LED
(TYPE OF —) ZENER

DIOLEFIN DIENE ALLENE HEXADIENE

DIOMEDES (FATHER OF —) MARS TYDEUS
(MOTHER OF —) CYRENE DEIPYLE
(WIFE OF —) AEGIALE
DION (DAUGHTER OF —) EUPHRASIA
(FATHER OF —) HIPPARINUS
(SISTER OF —) ARISTOMACHE
(SLAYER OF —) CALLIPPUS
(TEACHER OF —) PLATO
(WIFE OF —) ARETE
DIONYSUS BACCHUS BROMIOS BROMIUS LENAEUS LIKNITES
DIONYZA
(HUSBAND OF —) CLEON
DIOPSIDE VIOLAN ALALITE PYROXENE
DIORITE CORSITE DIABASE ORNOITE APPINITE TONALITE
DIOSCURI ALCIS ANACES ANAKES CASTORES
DIOXIDE SILICA BINOXIDE
DIOXIN TCDD AGENTORANGE
DIP DAP DIB DOP SOP BAIL DROP DUCK DUNK LADE LAVE SINK SOAK BATHE DELVE LADLE LOWER MERSE PITCH SCOOP SLOPE SOUSE SWOOP TAINT CANDLE HOLLOW PLUNGE BAPTIZE DECLINE IMMERGE IMMERSE INCLINE MOISTEN DIPSTICK SUBMERGE GUACAMOLE
(— AND THROW) BAIL BALE
(— IN DANCING) CORTE
(— IN HOT WATER) PLOT
(— INTO) SAMPLE
(— OUT) KEACH
DIPENTENE CINENE CAJUPUTENE
DIPHOSPHATE UDP
DIPHTHONG BIVOCAL
DIPHTHONGIZED BROKEN
DIPLOIDIZE SPERMATIZE
DIPLOMA SANAD DEGREE SUNNUD CHARTER CODICIL PARCHMENT SHEEPSKIN
DIPLOMACY TACT POLICE TREATY
(KIND OF —) GUNBOAT SHUTTLE
DIPLOMAT DEAN ENVOY CONSUL ATTACHE MINISTER
(ISRAELI —) EBAN
DIPLOMATIC SUAVE FECIAL FETIAL
DIPLOPIA POLYOPA AMBIOPIA
DIPNOAN DIPNOID MUDFISH
DIPODY METER METRE DIIAMB SYZYGY
DIPPER BAIL GAWN PIET PLOW GOURD HANDY LADLE SCOOP SPOON BUCKET DUNKER PIGGIN PLOUGH TUNKER DUNKARD PICKLER CALABASH
(ASTRONOMICAL —) WAGON WAGGON
DIPPING DOOK MERSION
(SUFF.) CLINIC CLINOUS

DIPSOMANIA ENOMANIA POTOMANIA
DIPTERAN SYRPHID
DIPTEROCARP GURJUN
DIPTERON DIPTER
DIPTEROUS BIALATE
DIRDUM BLOW BLAME DURDUM OUTCRY REBUKE TUMULT UPROAR SCOLDING
DIRE DERN EVIL FELL AWFUL FATAL DEADLY DISMAL DREARY FUNEST TRAGIC WOFFUL DIREFUL DOLEFUL DRASTIC FEARFUL DREADFUL FUNESTAL HORRIBLE TERRIBLE ULTIMATE
DIRECT AIM BID CON KEN SAY SET WIS AGYE AIRT BAIN BEAM BEND BOSS CAST DEAD EDIT EVEN FLAT FULL GAIN HEAD HELM HOLD LEAD NEAR NIGH OPEN REIN SEND SOON SWAY TELL TURN WAFT WEND WILL WISE AIRTH APPLY AREAD AREED BLANK BOUND BURLY COACH DRESS ETTLE FLUSH FRAME FRANK GUIDA GUIDE NIGHT INDEX LEVEL ORDER PLUMP POINT REFER RIGHT SPEED STEER TEACH TRAIN UTTER WEISE WRITE ADVERT ARRECT CUSTOS DEVOTE ENJOIN ENSIGN FASTEN GOVERN GRAITH HANDLE HOMELY HONEST IMPART INDITE INFORM INTEND LINEAL MANAGE MASTER MOSTRA REFORM SQUARE STEADY STRECK TEMPER WITTER ADDRESS APPOINT COMMAND CONDUCT CONTROL CONVERT DEICTIC DESTINE EXECUTE EXPRESS FRONTAL GENERAL INSTANT MARSHAL OFFICER PRESIDE SPADISH ABSOLUTE ADMONISH CONVERSE DEDICATE DIRECTOR HOMESPUN IMMEDIAL INSTRUCT INTIMATE MANUDUCE MANUDUCT MINISTER OUTRIGHT REGULATE STRAIGHT
(— AGAINST) LAUNCH
(— ATTENTION) ATTEND
(— BLOW) MARK
(— DOCE) DLOW
(— FALL OF TREE) GUN
(— HELMSMAN) CON CONN
(— HORSE) HUP
(— ITSELF) TENT
(— ONE'S COURSE) HIT
(— PROCEEDINGS) PRESIDE
(— SECRETLY) STEAL
(— SIDEWAYS) SKLENT
(— TO GO) ADDRESS
(— UPWARD) MOUNT
DIRECTED FAST COMPULSORY
(— BACKWARD) RETROGRADE
(— FORWARD) ANTRORSE
(— TOWARD GOAL) HORMIC
(— UPWARD) ERECT

DIRECTING AIM LEADING PRINCIPAL
DIRECTION (ALSO SEE MUSICAL
DIRECTION) AIM RUN WAY AIRT BENT
CARE DUCT EAST EGIS GATE HAND
LEFT PART ROAD RULE WEST WORD
YARD AEGIS ANGLE COAST DRIFT
EAVER KIBLA NORTH ORDER PARTY
POINT QIBLA RANGE ROUTE SENSE
SOUTH TENOR TREND ASPECT
COURSE DESIGN ADDRESS BEARING
BIDDING CHANNEL COMMAND
CONDUCT CONTROL COUNSEL
DICTATE HEADING HELMAGE
MANDATE PRECEPT STRETCH
BEARINGS CALENDAR DELEATUR
DIAGONAL GUIDANCE STEERAGE
STEERING TENDENCY ORDINANCE
ORIENTATION PRESCRIPTION
(— IN WOOD) GRAIN
(— OF CURRENT) AXIS
(— OF FLOW) SET
(— OF ROCK CLEAVAGE) GRAIN
(— OF WIND) EYE CORNER
(— OUTWARD) BEAM
(—S FOR DELIVERY) ADDRESS
(DANCE —) CALL
(GENERAL —) RUN
(HORIZONTAL —) COURSE
AZIMUTH
(MUSICAL —) SEGUE
(NEW —) TURN
(OBLIQUE —) SKEW
(OPPOSITE —) EYE COUNTER
(SINGING —) GIMEL GYMEL
(PREF.) PHORO
(SUFF.) ERLY ERN
(— TO) WARD
DIRECTIVE MEMO GUIDE DICTATE
CIRCULAR
DIRECTLY DUE BANG BOLT DEAD
FLAT GAIN JUST MEAN PLAT PLUM
SLAP SOON PLAIN PLUMB PLUNK
POINT ROUND SHEER SMACK SOUSE
SPANG STANG ARIGHT CLEVER
SIMPLY SQUARE RIGHTLY SHEERLY
OUTRIGHT PROMPTLY SLAPDASH
STRAIGHT PRESENTLY
DIRECTNESS CLARITY IMMEDIACY
DIRECTOR BOSS HEAD COACH
GUIDE PILOT STAFF ARCHON
AUTEUR BISHOP LEADER MASTER
RECTOR WARDEN CURATOR
DESKMAN MANAGER PREFECT
STARETS STERNER TRAINER
ACCENTOR DISPOSER GOVERNOR
PRAEFECT PRODUCER TETRARCH
(BALLET —) REGISSEUR
(FILM —) AUTEUR
DIRECTORY PIE BOOK
DIRGE KEEN SONG ELEGY KINAH
LINOS LINUS QINAH TANGI HEARSE
LAMENT MONODY THRENE EPICEDE

REQUIEM CORONACH THRENODY
ULLAGONE
(PREF.) THREN(O)
DIRIGIBLE BLIMP AIRSHIP
DIRK SNEE SKEAN SWORD DAGGER
SKHIAN SKIVER WHINGER WHINIARD
DIRT FEN MUD PAY CRUD DUST GORE
GUCK MOOL MUCK NAST SOIL SUMP
CROCK EARTH FILTH GRIME GROUT
SEUCH SEUGH TRASH FULYIE FULZIE
GRAVEL GROUND GRUNGE REFUSE
MULLOCK SLOTTER MUCKMENT
(— ON PRINTING TYPE) PICK
DIRT-COLORED SORDID
DIRTINESS GRIME JAKES
DIRTY LOW RAY BASE CLAT DIRT
FOUL MOIL MUSS SOIL WORY
BAWDY BLACK CABBY DINGY FOGGY
GRIMY GUSTY HORRY MUDDY
NASTY POUSY SOILY SULLY BEMIRE
CLARTY CLATTY DEFILE DIRTEN
FILTHY FULYIE FULZIE GREASY
GRUBBY GRUNGY IMPURE MUSSED
POUCEY REECHY SCRIMY SLASHY
SLURRY SMIRCH SMUTTY SOILED
SORDID STORMY BEGRIME BROOKED
BROOKIE BRUCKLE CLOUDED
GRUFTED IMBROIN MUDDIED
PIGGISH RAUNCHY ROYNOUS
SCRUFFY SLOTTER SMUTCHY
SQUALID SULLIED TARNISH
UNCLEAN AMURCOUS SLOBBERY
SLOTTERY SOAPLESS
DIS BELITTLE
DISABLE OUT HOCK LAME MAIM
BREAK CHINK CROCK GRUEL UNFIT
WRECK BRUISE DISMAY UNABLE
WEAKEN CRIPPLE
(— CANNON) SPIKE
(— HORSE) NOBBLE
(— TANK) BELLY
DISABLED LAME INVALID
DISABLING BUM
DISACCHARIDE BIOSE LACTOSE
MALTOSE SUCROSE
DISACCUSTOM DISUSE
DISACKNOWLEDGE DISCLAIM
DISADVANTAGE HURT MISS RISK
LURCH WORRY DAMAGE DENIAL
INJURY STRIKE DICKENS PENALTY
UNSELTH UNSPEED DISAVAIL
DISFAVOR DRAWBACK HANDICAP
DISADVANTAGEOUS HURTFUL
INCONVENIENT
DISAFFECT DEBAUCH ALIENATE
ESTRANGE
DISAFFECTED FALSE UNTRUE
DISEASED DISLOYAL FORSWORN
PERJURED RECREANT
DISAFFECTION DECEIT MUTINY
DISEASE DISGUST DISLIKE
DISORDER HOSTILITY

DISAFFIRM DENY ANNUL REVERSE
DISCLAIM

DISAGREE VARY ARGUE CLASH
DIFFER DISCEPT DISCORD DISSENT
QUARREL CONFLICT

DISAGREEABLE BAD ILL ACID EVIL
FOUL PERT SOUR UGLY VILE AWFUL
CROSS HARSH NASTY STIFF GREASY
PUTRID ROTTEN SNUFFY STICKY
UNEASY UNGAIN BEASTLY CHRONIC
COMICAL GHASTLY HATEFUL
INGRATE IRKSOME NAUGHTY
UNLUSTY CHISELLY KINDLESS
TERRIBLE UNGENIAL UNLIKELY
UNLOVELY UNSAVORY

DISAGREEABLENESS ILLNESS
ASPERITY

DISAGREEABLY HARSHLY

DISAGREEING ODD DISSENTIVE

DISAGREEMENT BREE CLASH
CROSS FIGHT BREACH FRATCH
DISCORD DISGUST DISPUTE DISSENT
FISSURE MISLIKE QUARREL
WRANGLE ARGUMENT CLASHING
DISTANCY DIVISION FRICTION
SQUABBLE VARIANCE
MISUNDERSTANDING
(IN —) APART

DISALLOW FORBID REJECT
CENSURE DISCLAIM DISPROVE
PROHIBIT

DISAPPEAR DIE FLY DROP FADE FALL
FLEE LIFT PASS SINK WEND WHOP
BREAK CLEAR FAINT LAPSE SLIDE
SLOPE SNUFF REMOVE RETIRE
VANISH EVANISH IMMERGE
DISSOLVE EVANESCE
(— GRADUALLY) ELY FADE DRAIN
EVANESCE
(— SUDDENLY) COOK DUCK BURST
MIZZLE
(— UNEXPECTEDLY) LEVANT

DISAPPEARANCE ECLIPSE
FADEAWAY

DISAPPOINT BALK BILK FAIL FALL
MOCK SOUR UNDO CHEAT SNAPE
BAFFLE DEFEAT DELUDE OUTWIT
THWART BEGUILE DECEIVE DESTROY
FALSIFY NULLIFY DISPOINT

DISAPPOINTED OUTED BUMMED
THROWN SOREHEAD

DISAPPOINTING FIERCE
FALLACIOUS

DISAPPOINTMENT RUE BALK
DRAG SUCK BAULK LURCH DENIAL
DOWNER LETDOWN COMEDOWN

DISAPPROBATION ODIUM DISLIKE

DISAPPROVAL BAN BOOH HISS
VETO CATCALL CENSURE DISFAVOR
DISGRACE
(EXPRESSION OF —) TUT TUTTUT
(SHOW —) HISS

DISAPPROVE NIX GROAN REJECT
RESENT CENSURE CONDEMN
DISLIKE MISTAKE PROTEST
DISALLOW DISPROVE HARRUMPH

DISAPPROVED DISTASTED

DISAPPROVER WOWSER

DISARM SUBDUE UNSTEEL

DISARRANGE MESS MUSS DEFORM
GARBLE RUFFLE TIFFLE UNTIDY
UNTUNE CLUTTER CONFUSE
DERANGE DISTURB RUMMAGE
SLATTER TROUBLE COCKBILL
DISHEVEL DISORDER UNSETTLE
(— TYPE) SQUABBLE

DISARRANGEMENT DISARRAY

DISARRAY MESS TASH RIFLE STRIP
CADDLE DISRAY FUFFLE HUDDLE
DESPOIL UNDIGHT DISHEVEL
DISORDER

DISARRAYED UNKEMPT

DISASSEMBLE UNDO STRIP
DEMOUNT DISMOUNT
(— CASK) SHAKE

DISASSEMBLY TAKEDOWN
TEARDOWN

DISASSOCIATE SEVER SEPARATE

DISASTER ILL WOE BALE BLOW EVIL
FATE RUIN GRIEF MISHAP STROKE
REVERSE ACCIDENT CALAMITY
CASUALTY EXIGENCY FATALITY
(ONE WHO PREDICTS —)
CASSANDRA

DISASTROUS BAD ILL FATAL WEARY
SINISTER

DISAVOW DENY DEVOW ABJURE
DISOWN UNGANT REFUSE DECLINE
RETRACT ABNEGATE DISCLAIM
DISVOUCH RENOUNCE

DISAVOWAL DENIAL

DISBAND BREAK REDUCE REFORM
ADJOURN CASHIER DISMISS
RELEASE SCATTER DISSOLVE

DISBAR EXCLUDE

DISBELIEF ATHEISM SCRUPLE
ACOSMISM
(EXPRESSION OF —) TUT TUTTUT

DISBELIEVE DOUBT REJECT
SUSPECT DISCOUNT DISCREDIT

DISBELIEVER ATHEIST HERETIC
INFIDEL

DISBURDEN RID EASE CLEAR
UNLOAD DELIVER DISLOAD RELIEVE
(— BY CONFESSION) SHRIVE

DISBURSE SPEND DEFRAY EXPEND
OUTLAY DEBURSE

DISC (ALSO SEE DISK) DIAL DISK
GONG BLANK MEDAL PATEN PLATE
QUOIT COLTER RECORD RONDEL
SQUAIL COULTER DISCOID FRISBEE
PLATTER ROUNDEL TROCHUS
(— FOR PRESSING HERRINGS)
DAUNT

(— **ON BIT**) ROWEL
(— **ON SPINDLE**) WHORL
(— **ON TAMBOURINE**) JINGLE
(— **ON TARGET**) GONG FRISBEE
ROUNDEL
(**CILIATED** —) VELUM
(**COPPER** —) ROSETTE
(**FLESHY** —) SARCOMA
(**FLOPPY** —) DISKETTE
(**HOCKEY** —) PUCK
(**JELLYFISH** —) UMBRELLA
(**KIND OF** —) LASER SECCHI
(**POLISHING** —) LAP
(**TELEVISION** —) SCANNER
DISCANT HOCKET
DISCARD CAST DECK DEFY JILT
JUNK MOLT OMIT OUST SHED
CHUCK DITCH FLING SCRAP SHUCK
SLUFF THROW TRASH CHANGE
DECARD DISUSE DIVEST EXCUSS
REJECT SLOUGH ABANDON CASHIER
DISMISS EXPUNGE FORSAKE
ABDICATE JETTISON
(— **IN BRIDGE**) ECHO
DISCARDED DORMANT OFFCAST
DISCARDING DISPOSAL
DISCERN KEN SEE SPY WIT DEEM
ESPY KNOW READ SCAN JUDGE
SIGHT BEHOLD DESCRY DETECT
DEVISE NOTICE PIERCE SCERNE
DIGNOSCE DISCOVER PERCEIVE
(— **BY SMELL**) SCENT
DISCERNIBLE EVIDENT VISIBLE
APPARENT MANIFEST OBSERVABLE
DISCERNING SAGE WISE NASUTE
SHREWD SUBTLE SAPIENT
SAGACIOUS PERCEPTIVE PERCIPIENT
PENETRATING
DISCERNMENT EYE DOOM GOUT
TACT FLAIR SENSE SKILL TASTE
ACUMEN INSIGHT ELECTION
JUDGMENT SAGACITY SAPIENCE
PERCEPTION PENETRATION
DISCHARGE AX DO AXE CAN GUN
LET RUN BOLT BOOT CASS DUMP
EMIT FIRE FLOW FLUX FREE GIVE
KICK PASS POUR QUIT RIFF SACK
SEND SHOT VENT VOID BLAST BLEED
BRUSH CLEAR DRAIN EGEST EJECT
EMPTY EXPEL EXUDE FRUSH GLEET
GRASS ICHOR ISSUE LOOSE OZENA
PURGE RHEUM SHOOT SPEED START
VOMIT WHIFF YIELD ACQUIT ASSOIL
BOUNCE DEFRAY EFFECT EXCERN
EXEMPT EXHALE FEEDER LOCHIA
OZAENA TICKET UNLADE UNLOAD
ABSOLVE CASHIER DEBOUCH
DEFEASE DEHISCE DELIVER DERAIGN
DISBAND DISMISS EXCRETE
EXHAUST MISSION PAYMENT
PERFORM QUIETUS RELEASE
RELIEVE SATISFY SKITTER SOLUTIO
CATAPULT COMPOUND DEFECATE

DESPATCH DISGORGE DISPATCH
DISPLACE DISPLODE EMISSION
EVACUATE MITTIMUS OUTSHOOT
PERSOLVE SEPARATE SOLUTION
STREAMER
(— **ARROW**) TWANG
(— **AT RANDOM**) ROVE
(— **BULLET**) DRIVE
(— **CARGO**) STRIKE
(— **DEBT**) MEET CLEAR ACQUIT
LOOSING
(— **DUTY**) SERVE
(— **FROM HORSE'S FOOT**) FRUSH
(— **FROM NOSE**) RHEUM OZAENA
(— **FROM RESERVOIR**) HUSHING
(— **FROM WOUND**) SANIES
(— **MATTER**) WEEP
(— **OF DEBT**) SETOFF
(— **OF GAS**) FEEDER
(— **OF STREAM**) FALL SPOUT
(— **SUDDENLY**) HIKE
(**BLOODY** —) SHOW SANIES
(**CANNON** —) TIRE CANNON
(**CONCENTRATED** —) BARRAGE
(**CONTINUOUS — OF FIREARMS**)
FUSILLADE
(**DISHONORABLE** —) BOBTAIL
(**ELECTRIC** —) ARC SPARK LEADER
EFFLUVE STREAMER LIGHTNING
(**ELECTRIC** —S) STATIC
(**HEAVY** —) STORM
(**MENSTRUAL** —) PERIOD
(**SIMULTANEOUS** —) SALVO
BROADSIDE FUSILLADE
(**SUFF.**) CENOSIS RRHAGIA RRHEA
RRHOEA
DISCHARGED SPED SATISFIED
DISCHARGER EXCITATOR
DISCHARGING LABILE
DISCIPLE SON JOHN MARK CHELA
JUDAS MURID PETER PUPIL TEACH
TRAIN ANANDA DISPLE DORCAS
HEARER PUNISH APOSTLE AUDITOR
MATTHEW OVIDIAN SCHOLAR
SECTARY SRAVAKA STUDENT
ADHERENT FOLLOWER GALENIST
SECTATOR
DISCIPLINARIAN RAMROD TRAINER
MARTINET
DISCIPLINARY STRICT
DISCIPLINE THEW WHIP BREAK
DRILL INURE TEACH TRAIN TUTOR
CHURCH ETHICS FERULA FERULE
GOVERN INFORM PUNISH SEASON
TAIRGE VIRTUE CHASTEN CORRECT
CULTURE EDUCATE FURNACE
NURTURE SCOURGE DISCIPLE
DOCTRINE EXERCISE INSTRUCT
LEARNING MATHESIS PEDAGOGY
REGULATE RESTRAIN TEACHING
TRAINING TUTORING PHILOSOPHY
CASTIGATION
(**CHINESE** —) TAICHICHUAN

(MENTAL) YOGA
(RELIGIOUS —) CHURCH PENANCE SADHANA
DISCIPLINED INURED STEADY
DISCLAIM DENY DEVOW WAIVE ABJURE DISOWN REFUSE DISAVOW ABDICATE ABNEGATE DISALLOW RENOUNCE
DISCLOSE OPE RIP BARE BLOW CALL KNOW OPEN TELL BREAK COUGH UNRIP UNWRY UTTER BETRAY BEWRAY DESCRY DIVINE EVOLVE EXPOSE IMPART REVEAL SHRIVE UNBURY UNCASE UNHASP UNHIDE UNLOCK UNROLL UNSEAL UNSHUT UNVEIL UNWRAP CONFESS DEVELOP DISCUSS DISPLAY DIVULGE EXHIBIT EXPLAIN PROPALE UNCLOSE UNCOVER DISCOVER INDICATE MANIFEST UNBUNDLE UNKENNEL UNSECRET UNTHATCH
(— PARTIALLY) ADUMBRATE
DISCLOSED OUT
DISCLOSURE REVEAL SHRIFT COLORING DETGNIAL DISCLOSE OVERTURE APOCALYPSE
DISCOLOR FOX BURN FADE SPOT BLACK SMOKE STAIN TINGE SMIRCH STREAK DISTAIN TARNISH BESMIRCH
DISCOLORATION CORN BLEED SCALD SPECK STAIN TINGE FOXING LIVEDO MILDEW ARGYRIA BURNING MELASMA BRONZING BROWNING CHLOASMA CYANOSIS DYSCHROA SCALDING
(— IN FISH) PINKEYE
(— OF FRUIT) SUNBURN
(— OF TURKEYS) BLUEBACK
(— ON CHOCOLATE) BLOOM
(— ON CURED FISH) RUST
(SMALL —) FRECKLE
(SUFF.) CHROIA
DISCOLORED HAW FOUL DINGY FOXED RUSTY STAINED SCORCHED USTULATE
(— BY DECAY) DOTY FOXED
DISCOMFIT MATE ROIT ABASH ABAVE AFLEY SHEND SHENT UPSET WORST BAFFLE DEFEAT FEAGUE SQUASH CONFUSE CONQUER DISTURB
DISCOMFITURE LURCH
DISCOMFORT HELL PAIN UNEASE MALAISE PURGATORY
(FEELING OF —) BLAHS
DISCOMPOSE FEEZE PERTURB
DISCONCERT BASH BOWL FAZE FUSS HACK ABASH BLANK DAUNT FEEZE PHASE UPSET WORRY BAFFLE BLENCH MISPUT PUZZLE RATTLE SQUASH CONFUSE DISTURB FLUMMOX NONPLUS PERTURB SQUELCH BROWBEAT DISORDER

DISCONCERTED BLANK ASHAMED RATTLED CONFUSED
DISCONCERTING BAFFLING
DISCONNECT UNDO SEVER DIVIDE UNDOCK UNYOKE DISJOIN DISSOLVE DISUNITE SEPARATE UNCOUPLE
DISCONNECTED LOOSE ABRUPT BROKEN CHOPPY CURSORY DECOUSU SNATCHY RAMBLING STACCATO ASYNARTETE
DISCONSOLATE SAD GLOOMY WOEFUL DOLEFUL FORLORN UNCOUTH DEJECTED DESOLATE DOWNCAST HOPELESS
DISCONTENT ENVY ENNUI DISQUIET SOURNESS
DISCONTENTED DUMPY RESTLESS MALCONTENT
DISCONTINUANCE BREAK LAPSE DEMISE CUTBACK DISUNION SHUTDOWN CESSATION
DISCONTINUE END DROP HALT QUIT STOP BREAK CEASE CLOSE LETUP DECIDT DISUSE SUNDER DISRUPT SUSPEND INTERMIT SURCEASE
DISCONTINUITY JAR BREAK COMMA BREACH HIATUS
DISCONTINUOUS BROKEN DISJUNCT SALTATORY
DISCORD DIN JAR BROIL JANGLE SCHISM STRIFE DISLIKE FACTION FISSURE JARRING MISTONE CONFLICT DISTANCE DIVISION FRACTION MISCHIEF UNSAUGHT VARIANCE CACOPHONY
DISCORDANT AJAR RUDE CRONK HARSH FROWZY HOARSE JANGLY HIDEOUS JARRING SQUAWKY ABSONANT CONTRARY JANGLING SCORDATO
DISCOTHEQUE AGOGO DISCO
DISCOUNT AGIO BATTA SHAVE REBATE REDUCE DISCOMPT
DISCOURAGE CARP DAMP CHILL DAUNT DETER FROST DAMPEN DEJECT DISMAY FREEZE STIFLE DEPRESS FLATTEN INHIBIT DISPIRIT DISSUADE
DISCOURAGEMENT COLD DAMP CHILL DAUNT REBUFF LETDOWN PUTBACK
DISCOURAGING CHILL DREARY
DISCOURSE SAW CARP RANT READ TALE TALK TELL WORD DROOL FABLE ORATE PAPER SPEAK SPELL THEME TRACT TREAT COMMON DILATE EULOGY HOMILY PARLEY PREACH REASON SCREED SERMON THESIS TONGUE TREATY ACCOUNT ADDRESS COMMENT CONTEXT DECLAIM DELIVER DESCANT DIETARY DISCANT DISCUSS DISSERT ENTREAT

EXPOUND GRAMMAR LECTURE
NARRATE ORATION PARABLE
PRATING PRELECT PURPOSE RECITAL
TALKING ARGUMENT COLLOQUY
CONVERSE EXERCISE LOCUTION
LOQUENCE PARLANCE SPEAKING
SPELLING TRACTATE TREATISE
PHILIPPIC PROLUSION
(— OF LITTLE VALUE) STUFF
(— POLICY) GLASNOST
(LAUDATORY —) PANEGYRIC
(LONG —) SCREED
(OBSCENE —) SMUT
(PROLONGED —) DIATRIBE
(RAMBLING —) RHAPSODY
RIGMAROLE
(SERIOUS —) HOMILY
(SIMPLE —) PAP
(UNIMAGINATIVE —) PROSE
(PL.) EXOTERICS
(PREF.) LOG(O)
(SUFF.) LOG(ER)(IA)(IAN)(IC)(ICAL)
(IST)(UE)(Y)
DISCOURTEOUS RUDE SCURVY
UNCIVIL UNHENDE CAVALIER
IMPOLITE UNGENTLE
DISCOURTESY CUT SLIGHT
DISCOVER RIP SEE SPY WIT ESPY
FEEL FIND PICK TWIG CATCH LEARN
SPELL DEFINE DESCRY DETECT
DIVINE EXPOSE IMPART INVENT
LOCATE OVERGO REVEAL STRIKE
UNHIDE CONFESS DESCURE
DEVELOP DISCERN DISCURE DISPLAY
DIVULGE EXHIBIT EXPLORE
UNCOVER UNEARTH CONTRIVE
DECIPHER DESCRIBE DISCUREN
MANIFEST UNKENNEL
DISCOVERABLE VISIBLE
DISCOVERER SPY SCOUT
COLUMBUS EXPLORER INVENTOR
DISCOVERY FIND TROVE DESCRY
ESPIAL STRIKE DESCRIAL
DISCREDIT FOUL SLUT DECRY
DOUBT REFEL DEFACE DEFECT
ASPERSE BLEMISH DESTROY
IMPEACH SCANDAL SUSPECT
BELITTLE DISGRACE DISHONOR
DISTRUST REPROACH UNCREDIT
(SUFF.) ARD ART
DISCREDITABLE BLACK
UNHONEST
DISCREET SAGE WARY WISE CIVIL
WITTY HUSHED POLITE SILENT
CAREFUL GUARDED POLITIC
PRUDENT CAUTIOUS RESERVED
RETICENT
DISCREETLY SENSIBLY
DISCREPANCY VARIANCE
DISCREPANT VARIANT CONTRARY
DISSONANT
DISCRETE ETERNAL DISTINCT

DISCRETION TACT OPTION WISDOM
CONDUCT RETENUE COURTESY
JUDGMENT PRUDENCE
DISCRETIONARY ARBITRARY
DISCRIMINATE PART SEVER
SECERN DISCERN PERCEIVE
SEPARATE
DISCRIMINATED DISTINCT
DISCRIMINATING GOOD NICE
ACUTE SHARP ASTUTE CHOICE
NASUTE SELECT CHOOSEY CRITICAL
EXPLICIT
DISCRIMINATINGLY CHOICE
FINELY
DISCRIMINATION EYE BIAS DOOM
TACT TASTE ACUMEN AGEISM
CHOICE SEXISM FINESSE RESPECT
DELICACY SAPIENCE
(— AGAINST ANIMALS) SPECIESISM
(SYMBOL OF —) HANSA
DISCRIMINATIVE RESPECTIVE
DISCURSIVE ROVING CURSORY
RAMBLING DESULTORY
DISCURSIVELY WIDE
DISCUS DISC DISK QUOIT DISKOS
DISCOID
DISCUSS AIR MOOT RUNE TALK
ARGUE BANDY COVER DANDY
TRACT TREAT COMMON CONFER
DEBATE DICKER EMPARL EXCUSS
IMPARL PARLEY AGITATE BESPEAK
CANVASS COMMENT CONSULT
DESCANT DISCANT DISCEPT
DISCUTE DISPUTE DISSERT EXAMINE
NARRATE TRAVERSE CONJOBBLE
(— AT LENGTH) BAT
(— CASUALLY) MENTION
(— EXCITEDLY) AGITATE
(— LIGHTLY) BANDY
(— QUICKLY) SKIP
(— SECRETLY) ROUN
(— TERMS) CHAFFER
(— THOROUGHLY) EXHAUST
(— TO EXCESS) VEX
DISCUSSION MOOT DEBAT FORUM
COMMON CONFAB DEBATE HASSEL
HOMILY HUDDLE PARLEY TREATY
BARGAIN CANVASS COMMENT
COUNSEL DISCUSS DISPUTE
MOOTING PALAVER PRIBBLE
ARGUMENT CAUSERIE CHINFEST
COLLOQUY DIATRIBE ENTREATY
EXCURSUS QUESTION
(CONTROVERSIAL —) DISPUTE
(DIDACTIC —) HARANGUE
(HEATED —) FLAK
DISDAIN COY TUT DAIN DEFY PRIDE
SCORN SDAIN SPURN SDEIGN
SLIGHT CONTEMN DESPISE
CONTEMPT
DISDAINFUL COY DIGNE PROUD
SAUCY TOSSY SCORNY SLIGHT

SNIFFY SNUFFY DAINFUL HAUGHTY
ARROGANT DEIGNOUS PROUDFUL
SCORNFUL SNIFFISH TOPLOFTY
DISDAINFULLY SMALL SNIFFILY
DISEASE BUG FLU MAL ROT AIDS
BATS COTH CRUD EVIL FLAW GOUT
GRIP KURU NOMA PEST PHOS SORE
AGROM BATTS BEJEL BENDS CAUSE
COTHE CROUP DECAY DOLOR FEVER
GRIEF LUPUS PHOSS PINTA PINTO
SCALL SHAKE SPRUE SURRA
AINHUM ANGINA CANCER CARATE
CORYZA COURAP DENGUE GRAVEL
GRIPPE HERPES MALADY MORBUS
PALMUS PIEDRA POPEYE SCURVY
SICKEN SURRAH THRUSH UROSIS
ZOOSIS AILMENT CHOLERA
COXALGY DECLINE ENDEMIC
ENTASIA LANGUOR LEPROSY
MALEASE MISLIKE MYCOSIS MYIASIS
PATHEMA RAPHANY SCOURGE
SEQUELA SERPIGO SIBBENS
SORANCE SYCOSIS TETANUS
XERASIA ZYMOTIC ADENOSIS
ALASTRIM ATHEROMA BERIBERI
COXALGIA CRIPPLER CYNANCHE
DIAMONDS ENZOOTIC JAUNDICE
LEUKEMIA PALUDISM PANDEMIC
PELLAGRA RAPHANIA SCABBADO
SHINGLES SICKNESS SMALLPOX
SORRANCE STAGGERS SYPHILIS
UNHEALTH XANTHOMA ZOONOSIS
(— OF ANIMALS) SURRA
(— OF ANIMALS, GENERAL) ROT
CLAP CORE FIRE GOUT HUSK LICK
WEED APTHA CLEFT CLING CLOSH
COTHE CROOK DRUSE FARCY FLAPS
NENTA NGANA PAINS SPEED SWEAT
TAINT APHTHA AVIVES BROSOT
CANKER CARNEY CREEPS FARCIN
GARGET GRAPES LAMPAS NAGANA
ROUGET SPAVIN SURRAH WOBBLE
ANTHRAX BIGHEAD CALCINO
CALORIS CARCEAG DOURING
EARWORM EQUINIA FASHION
FISTULA FOUNDER FROUNCE
KETOSIS LAMPERS MURRAIN
MURRINA QUITTER QUITTOR
SLOBBER SOLDIER TAKOSIS
BULLNOSE CRATCHES CRIPPLES
FERNSICK FOOTHALT HORSEPOX
HYSTERIA MAWBOUND SLOBBERS
SNUFFLES THWARTER VACCINIA
EPIZOOTIC
(— OF APPLES) CORK BLOTCH
(— OF BANANAS) SIGATOKA
SQUIRTER
(— OF BARLEY) STRIPE
(— OF BEES) SACBROOD
(— OF BEETS) HEARTROT
(— OF BIRDS) GOUT
(— OF BLUEBERRY) BLUESTEM

(— OF CABBAGE) ANBURY
CLUBROOT
(— OF CATERPILLARS) WILT
FLACHERY
(— OF CATS) PANLEUCOPENIA
(— OF CATTLE) PUCK TURN BARBS
BLAIN CLOSH FARCY HOOVE HOOZE
SLOWS COWPOX GARGET GRAPES
HAMMER HEAVES ANTHRAX
BLACKLEG BLOATING
(— OF CEREALS) BRAND ERGOT
(— OF CHICKEN) PIP CORYZA
(— OF CHILDREN) PROGERIA
(— OF COTTON) HYBOSIS CYRTOSIS
STENOSIS
(— OF DUCKLING) KEEL
(— OF EYES) WALL GLAUCOMA
SYNECHIA TRACHOMA
(— OF FIGS) SMUT
(— OF FINGERNAILS) FLAW
(— OF FLAX) BROWNING
(— OF FOWLS) PIP CRAY ROUP
GAPES SOREHEAD
(— OF GRAIN) ILIAU ICTERUS
(— OF GRAPES) COLEUR ERINOSE
ROUGEAU ROUGEOT SHELLING
(— OF HAWKS) RYE CRAY CROAK
CROAKS FROUNCE FILANDER
(— OF HORSES) HAW CLAP CURB
MOSE MULE WEED FARCY LEUMA
VIVES APHTHA SCALMA THRUSH
BARBELS BROMINE QUITTOR
SARCOID AZOTURIA GLANDERS
HORSEPOX SCRATCHES STRANGLES
(— OF INSECTS) POLYHEDROSIS
(— OF LAMB) SWAYBACK
(— OF LETTUCE) STUNT
(— OF NARCISSUS) SMOLDER
SMOULDER
(— OF ONION) SMUDGE
(— OF ORANGE) LEPROSIS
(— OF PALMS) KOLEROGA
(— OF PLANTS) SCAB NECROSIS
(— OF PLANTS, GENERAL) POX ROT
BUNT CORK DROP FIRE GOUT KNOT
PULP SMUT BLAST DWARF EDEMA
ERGOT FLECK FLOCK GRUBS SCALD
SCALE SCURF SEREH SPIKE STUNT
TUKRA TWIST AUCUBA BLIGHT
BLOTCH BLUING BRAUNE CALICO
CANKER COLEUR GIRDLE OEDEMA
OIDIUM PETECA SMUDGE STREAK
STRIPE VIROSE BLISTER BLUEING
BRINDLE CRINKLE DIEBACK ERINOSE
EYESPOT FROGEYE HYBOSIS
MEASLES PRURIGO ROSETTE
SHATTER SMOLDER STIPPEN
TIPBURN TOMOSIS VIRUELA
WALLOON BLUESTEM BREAKING
BROWNING BUCKSKIN CLUBROOT
CYRTOSIS DARTROSE EXANTHEM
FLYSPECK GUMMOSIS KOLEROGA

LEPROSIS MELANOSE MELAXUMA
POLEBURN PSOROSIS RAPHANIA
SMOULDER STENOSIS VIROSITY
WHIPTAIL WILDFIRE CHLOROSIS
(— OF POTATO) CURL HAYWIRE
(— OF RABBITS) SNUFFLES
(— OF RICE) BLAST SPECK
(— OF RODENTS) TULAREMIA
(— OF SHEEP) CAW COE GID MAD
RAY ROT BANE BELT CORE HALT
SHAB WIND BLAST BLOOD BRAXY
GILLAR OVINIA PINING STURDY
ANTHRAX BRADSOT DAISING
RUBBERS SCRAPIE THWARTER
WILDFIRE BREAKSHARE
(— OF SILKWORM) UJI CALCINO
GATTINE PEBRINE FLACHERY
(— OF SUGARCANE) ILIAU SEREH
EYESPOT
(— OF SWINE) GARGET
(— OF TOBACCO) ETCH CALICO
BRINDLE FROGEYE
(— OF TOMATO) FERNLEAF
GRAYWALL
(— OF TONGUE) AGROM
(— OF TREES) KNOT CANKER
(— OF TULIPS) SHANKING
(— OF UNKNOWN ORIGIN) AINHUM
ACRODYNIA
(AGENT OF PLANT —) VIROID
(CAISSON —) CHOKES
(FATAL — OF NERVOUS SYSTEM)
KURU
(FOOT-AND-MOUTH —) AFTOSA
(FUNGUS —) PECK MYCOSIS
(KIDNEY —) RIPPLE
(KIND OF —) LYME KISSING
MINAMATA
(LUNG —) CON
(MUSHROOM —) FLOCK
(PINK —) ACRODYNIA
(PLANT —) ESCA YAWS
(SKIN —) ACNE SCAB FAVUS HIVES
LEPRA MANGE PSORA RUPIA SCALL
TINEA ECZEMA LICHEN TETTER
EXORMIA PORRIGO PRURIGO
PURPURA SERPIGO VERRUGA
CHLOASMA IMPETIGO MILIARIA
MYCETOMA SHINGLES VERRUGAS
VITILIGO PEMPHIGUS
(SWELLING —) EDEMA
(VENEREAL —) BURNING SYPHILIS
(WINE —) GRAISSE
(WOOLSORTER'S —) ANTHRAX
(PREF.) MORBI NOS(O) PATH(O)
(SUFF.) IASIS ITIS NOSUS OMATOSIS
OSIS SIS
(FUNGUS —) OSIS
DISEASED BAD EVIL SICKLY
MORBOSE PECCANT VICIOUS
MORBIFIC
(PREF.) CACH CAC(O) DYS
(SUFF.) CACE

DISEMBARK LAND ALIGHT ARRIVE
DEBARK UNBARK UNBOAT
DISBOARD
DISEMBARKATION LANDING
DISEMBARRASS EXTRICATE
DISEMBODIED SEPARATE
DISBODIED FLESHLESS
DISEMBODIMENT SOUL SPIRIT
DISEMBOGUE MOUTH
DISEMBOWEL GUT HULK PAUNCH
DEBOWEL EMBOWEL GARBAGE
UNTRIPE GRALLOCH
DISEMIC DIMORIC DICHRONOUS
DISENCHANT DISMAY
DISENCHANTED SOUR
DISENCUMBER RID FREE REDD
UNCUMBER
DISENCUMBERMENT RIDDANCE
DISENGAGE FREE CLEAR EDUCE
UNTIE DETACH EVOLVE LOOSEN
CUTOVER DISGAGE RELEASE
UNRAVEL LIBERATE UNCLUTCH
DISENGAGED OFF CLEAR
DISENTANGLE CARD COMB FREE
REED TOSE TOZE CLEAR LOOSE
RAVEL UNMAZE EVOLVE 3CUTCH
SLEAVE UNMAZE UNMESH RESOLVE
UNRAVEL UNREAVE UNTWINE
UNTWIST OUTTWINE UNTANGLE
DISENTANGLEMENT SOLUTION
DISESTEEM UMBRAGE DISVALUE
DISFAVOR DUTCH ODIUM DISLIKE
OFFENCE OFFENSE UMBRAGE
MALGRACE
DISFIGURE MAR BLUR FOUL MAIM
SCAR TASH AGRISE DEFACE DEFEAT
DEFORM INJURE MANGLE BLEMISH
DISGRACE DISGUISE MUTILATE
DISFIGURED FOUL DEFET DEFEIT
DEFORMED
DISFIGUREMENT SCAR BLEMISH
CATFACE DEFORMITY
DISGORGE SPEW VENT EGEST
EJECT EMPTY VOMIT
DISGRACE BLOT FOIL FOUL HISS
LACK SLUR SMIT SOIL SPOT TASH
ABASE CRIME ODIUM SCORN SHAME
SHEND SPITE STAIN TAINT BAFFLE
BEFOUL BISMER HUMBLE INFAMY
REBUKE STIGMA VILIFY AFFRONT
ATTAINT DEGRADE OBLOQUY
OFFENCE OFFENSE REPROOF
SCANDAL SLANDER UMBRAGE
CONTEMPT DISHONOR IGNOMINY
REPROACH SHENDING UNWORTHY
VILLAINY OPPROBRIUM
(PUBLIC —) ATIMY
DISGRACEFUL MEAN SOUR FILTHY
INDIGN IGNOBLE CRIMINAL
DEFAMOUS INHONEST SHAMEFUL
DISGRUNTLED SORE PEEVISH
DISGUISE DAUB FACE HIDE LAIN
LEAN MASK VEIL BELIE CLOAK

COLOR COUCH COVER FEIGN GLOZE
GUISE SHADE VISOR VIZOR COVERT
DEFORM IMMASK MANTLE MASQUE
VIZARD CONCEAL OBSCURE
PRETEND PURPORT COLORING
DISLIKEN MISGUISE PALLIATE
PRETENCE PRETENSE TRAVESTY
UMBRELLA SMOKEANDMIRRORS
(— INFORMATION) LAYNE

DISGUISED COVERT FUCATE
GILDED LATENT MYSTIC FEIGNED
PALLIATE TRAVESTY INCOGNITA
INCOGNITO

DISGUST IRK UGH CLOY PALL BLECH
LOATH REPEL SHOCK STALL DEGOUT
HORROR NAUSEA OFFEND REVOLT
SICKEN SCUNNER STOMACH
SURFEIT AVERSION DISTASTE
KREISTLE LOATHING NAUSEATE
SCOMFISH SICKNESS
(EXPRESSION OF —) BAH ICK ROT
RATS YECH YUCK PSHAW YECCH
PHOOEY
(INTERJECTION TO EXPRESS —) YUK
TUCK YECH YECCH
(SOUND OF —) RAZZ RASPBERRY
(WORD OF —) ICK

DISGUSTED IRK SICK IRKSOME

DISGUSTING FOUL PERT VILE
LOUSY MUCKY NASTY FILTHY
SCRIMY SICKLY BEASTLY CLOYING
FULSOME HATEFUL LOATHLY
MAWKISH NOISOME OBSCENE
SHITTEN FOULSOME LOATHFUL
NAUSEOUS SHOCKING VOMITOUS

DISH CAP CAUP CUSH DISC DISK
FOOL MEAT MOLD PLAT SOLE BASIN
BATEA COMAL DEVIL MOULD NAPPY
PATEN PINAX PLATE SHAPE BASQUE
BASSIE BICKER BLAZER BUTTER
CHAFER CRITCH CUSCUS ENTREE
FONDUE GOSSIP LUGGIE NAPPIE
OLIVES PADDLE PANADA PATERA
PATINA PHIALE RECIPE SAUCER
SUNDAE TAMALE TUREEN BALANCE
BOBOTEE BOBOTIE CAPSULE
CEVICHE CHARGER COCOTTE
COMPORT COMPOTE CRESSET
DORMANT DOUBLER EPERGNE
PAPBOAT PATELLA PLATEAU
PLATTER RAMEKIN SCUTTLE STIRFRY
SUPREME TERRINE TIMBALE
AMATORIO CIOPPINO CLAPDISH
COQUILLE COUSCOUS GALATINE
KEDGEREE MAZARINE POWSODDY
STANDARD ENTREMETS
(— IN PYRAMID STYLE) BUISSON
(— OF FISH) SUSHI
(— OF MEAT AND EGGPLANT)
MOUSSAKA
(— OF RAW FISH) SEVICHE
(— OF SLOPPY FOOD) SOSS
(— WITH TOAST) RAREBIT

(BAKING —) SCALLOP SCOLLOP
(BRAISED —) HASLET
(CASSEROLE —) POTAUFEU
(CHAFING —) CHAFER CHOFFER
SCALDINO
(CHEESE —) RACLETTE
(CHINESE —) LOMEIN SUBGUM
(CHOICE —) REGALE
(CONE-SHAPED —) BOMBE
(CURRIED MEAT —) VINDALOO
(EXQUISITE —) AMBROSIA
(FANCY —) SURPRISE
(FIRST —) STARTER
(FISH —) CIOPPINO
(FLAT —) ASHET COMAL CHARGER
(FRIED —) SKIRL
(HIGH-FLAVORED —) HOGO
(INDIAN —) BIRYANI BURIANI
(INDIAN — OF LEGUMES) DAL DAHL
DHAL
(IRISH —) COLCANNON
(JAPANESE —) SUSHI TEMPURA
TERIYAKI YAKITORI
(JEWISH —) CHOLENT
(LIGHT —) SOUFFLE
(MEAT —) SPIEDINO
(PASTA —) CARBONARA
(PHILIPPINE —) BURO
(PHILIPPINE FISH —) DOBO
(PIE —) COFFIN
(PILE OF —S) BUNG
(RICE —) PILAU
(ROMAN —) LANX PATERA PATINA
(SAILOR'S —) BURGOO SCOUSE
(SAUSAGE —) CHIPOLATA
(SCOTTISH —) BROSE
(SIDE —) OUTWORK
(SPANISH —) ADOBO
(SPANISH MEAT —) ADOBO
(SWEET —) JUNKET FLUMMERY
(TASTY —) MORSEL
(WARMED-UP —) RECHAUFFE
(WOODEN —) CUP CAUP BOWIE
GOGGAN LUGGIE KICKSHAW
(PL.) GARNISH BAKEWARE FLATWARE
ENTREMETS
(PREF.) LECO

DISHABILLE MOB DISARRAY
DISORDER NEGLIGEE

DISHAN (FATHER OF —) SEIR

DISHARMONY SCHISM ADHARMA
FRACTION

DISHCLOTH DISHRAG TORCHON

DISHCLOTH GOURD LOOFAH
PATOLA DISHRAG

DISHEARTEN AMATE DAUNT
FAINT DEJECT DEPRESS FLATTEN
UNHEART UNNERVE DISHEART
DISPIRIT

DISHEARTENED DULL GLUM
GLOOMY DOWNCAST DEPRESSED

DISHEARTENING GLOOMY
DESOLATE

DISHEVEL MUSS TOWSE RUFFLE TOUSEL TOUSLE TUMBLE TRACHLE DISARRAY DISORDER

DISHEVELED ROOKY BLOUSY BLOWZY FROWZY TUMBLED UNKEMPT FROWZLED SHEVELED SLIPSHOD TATTERED

DISHON (FATHER OF —) ANAH

DISHONEST BENT FOUL LEWD CRONK CROSS FALSE LYING QUEER SNIDE TWISTY UNFAIR UNJUST CORRUPT CROOKED JACKLEG KNAVISH INDECENT INDIRECT SHAMEFUL SINISTER UNCHASTE UNHONEST MENDACIOUS

DISHONESTLY DOUBLY FALSELY

DISHONESTY IMPROBITY

DISHONOR FILE FOUL ABASE ABUSE ATIMY ODIUM SHAME SPITE STAIN WRONG DEFAME DEFILE DEFORM INFAMY VILIFY DEGRADE DISTAIN OBLOQUY SLANDER VIOLATE DISGLORY DISGRACE DISPLUME IGNOMINY REPROACH VILLAINY ATTAINDER

DISHONORABLE BASE FOUL MEAN BLACK NASTY SHABBY YELLOW DISLEAL IGNOBLE SHAMEFUL UNHONEST UNWORTHY

DISHONORED DEFAMED

DISHPAN KEELER

DISH RACK FIDDLE

DISHWASHER SWILLER

DISILLUSION SOUR DISMAY

DISINCLINATION NILL UNLUST UNWILL DISLIKE QUARREL AVERSION DISTASTE

DISINCLINED LOTH LOATH AFRAID AVERSE HESITANT

(— TO) ABOVE

DISINFECT SCRUB SEASON CLEANSE SWEETEN

DISINFECTANT LYSOL IODINE PHENOL CREOLIN EUGENOL TACHIOL FUMIGANT HALAZONE PARAFORM ANTISEPTIC

DISINFECTION ANTISEPSIS

DISINGENUOUS FALSE UNFAIR OBLIQUE

DISINHERIT DEPRIVE DISHEIR ABDICATE DISHERIT

DISINTEGRATE BEAT DUST MELT BREAK DECAY ERODE GRUSH SLAKE SPLIT MOLDER CRUMBLE DISBAND RESOLVE SHATTER COLLAPSE DISSOLVE SEPARATE

DISINTEGRATING ROTTEN SCHIZOID

(SUFF.) CLASTIC

DISINTEGRATION DECAY BREAKUP EROSION BIOLYSIS COLLAPSE HEARTROT SOLUTION

(SUFF.) LYSE LYSIS LYST LYTE LYTIC LYZE

DISINTER EXHUME UNBURY UNTOMB UNGRAVE

DISINTERESTED FAIR CANDID APATHETIC IMPARTIAL

DISJOIN PART UNDO SEVER DETACH SUNDER UNTACK UNYOKE DISSOLVE DISUNITE SEPARATE

DISJOINED BITTY SEJOINED DIAZEUTIC

DISJOINTED BITTY

DISK (ALSO SEE DISC) EYE NOB ORB PAN SAW WAX WEB BURR CHAD DIAL DISC FLAN FLAT KNOB PALM PUCK STAR TUFT CAKRA DAUNT LAMIN MEDAL PATEN PLATE ROUND SABLE SABOT SPILL TOKEN TRUCK WAFER WHEEL WHORL BEZANT BOTTOM BUCKET BUMPER BUTTON CACHET CARTON CHAKRA CONCHA CONCHO CORONA DISCUS FLOPPY GHURRY HARROW PALLET PELLET RECORD RIFFLE RONDEL SEQUIN SHEAVE SQUAIL WASHER WEIGHT ZEQUIN ACETATE BLOTTER BOBECHE CHECKER CHIPPER CLIPEUS DIOPTER DISCOID FREEBEE FRISBEE GOGGLES KNICKER MEDALET PHALERA ROSETTE SLITTER SPINNER SPOTTER TONDINO DIFFUSER EYEPIECE HOLDFAST PLANCHET RONDELLE ROUNDLET ZECCHINO

(— FOR BARRELING HERRING) DAUNT

(— FOR CHEESE) FOLLOWER

(— FOR STRIKING HOURS) GHURRY

(— OF JELLYFISH) BELL

(— OF LAMELLAE) THYLAKOID

(— OF WAX) AGNUS

(— ON WOODEN ROD) SPILL

(— OPERATING SYSTEM) DOS

(BULL'S-EYE —) CARTON

(COIN-MAKING —) FLAN PLANCHET

(COMPUTER —) FLOPPY MINIFLOPPY

(CONTENTS OF —) DATA

(DOUBLE —) YOYO

(ECCENTRIC —) SHEAVE

(FLESHY —) SARCOMA

(FLOPPY —) DISKETTE

(HANDLED —) RIFFLE

(HOCKEY —) PUCK

(KIND OF —) FLOPPY

(MEDICATED —) LAMELLA

(METAL —) SLUG MEDAL

(ORNAMENTAL —) BANGLE SPANGLE

(PADDED IRON —) SPINNER

(PAPER —S) CONFETTI

(PLASTIC —) FRISBEE

(POTTER'S —) BAT

(REVOLVING —) WAFTER

(ROTATING —) SCANNER

(SOLAR —) ATEN AION
(SUN —) ATEN CAKRA CHAKRA
(TROCHAL —) CORONA
(WINGED —) FEROHER
(PREF.) DISC(I)(O)
DISLIKE DEFY DOWN HATE LOTH
LUMP MIND DERRY LOATH SPITE
DETEST PHOBIA REGRET RESENT
SPLEEN UNLIKE DESPISE MISLIKE
QUARREL SCUNDER SCUNNER
STOMACH AVERSION DESPISAL
DISFAVOR DISTASTE DYSPATHY
(— OF CHILDREN) MISOPEDIA
(FOOLISH —) TOY
DISLOCATE LUX SLIP BREAK SPLAY
UNSET LUXATE DISLOCK UNWREST
DISJOINT DISPLACE SEPARATE
DISLOCATED SHOTTEN DISLOCATE
DISLOCATION BREAK SHIFT SLIDE
THROW
(PL.) SETTLEMENTS
DISLODGE BEAT BOLT BUCK BUMP
EXPEL SHAKE SHIFT SWOOP
REMOVE DISROOT UNHORSE
UNHOUSE UNLODGE DISHABIT
(— BY BLASTING) BRUSH
(— FROM SADDLE) THROW
DISLODGING BUILDING
DISLOYAL FALSE FELON UNTRUE
DISLEAL
DISLOYALTY SWICK SWIKE
UNLEWTY UNTRUTH
DISMAL SAD WAN BLUE DARK DIRE
DOWF DREE DULL EERY GASH GLUM
GRAY GREY BLACK BLEAK DOWFF
DREAR EERIE LURID MORNE OORIE
OURIE SABLE SORRY SURLY SWART
WASTE WISHT DREARY DREICH
DREIGH GLOOMY GOUSTY LENTEN
SULLEN TRISTE DIREFUL DOLEFUL
FUNERAL GASHFUL GHASTLY
GOUSTIE JOYLESS OMINOUS
POCOSIN STYGIAN UNCOUTH
UNHAPPY DESOLATE DOLESOME
DOLOROUS FUNEREAL GROANFUL
LONESOME NOVEMBRY SOLITARY
WEARIFUL MELANCHOLY
DISMAL-LOOKING GASH
WOBEGONE
DISMALLY DERNLY DIRELY
DISMANTLE RASE RAZE STRIP
DIVEST STRIKE DEPRIVE DESTROY
UNCLOAK DISMOUNT
DISMAY BOWL FEAR RUIN ALARM
AMATE APPAL DAUNT DREAD FLUNK
APPALL ASTONY CHASSE FRIGHT
SUBDUE TERROR DEPRESS DEPRIVE
FOUNDER HORRIFY TERRIFY
AFFRIGHT CONFOUND
CONSTERNATION
(INTERJECTION EXPRESSING —)
OOPS WOOPS

DISMAYED ASTONIED
DISMAYING HIDEOUS
DISMEMBER LIMB MAIM PART REND
SEVER MANGLE UNLIMB DISCERP
DISLIMB DISSECT QUARTER
DISJOINT MUTILATE
DISMISS AX AXE CAN PUT BOOT
BUMP BUST CASH CAST DAFF DROP
DRUM FIRE KICK OUST QUIT SACK
SEND SHAB SWAP SWOP TURN VAIK
VOID AMAND AMOVE BREAK BRUSH
CHUCK DEMIT DIMIT DITCH EJECT
EXPEL FLIRT FLUNK LOOSE SCOUT
BANISH BOUNCE CHASSE CONGEE
DEHIRE DISMIT DISOWN REJECT
REMOVE SHELVE CASHIER DISBAND
DISCARD LICENCE LICENSE TURNOFF
DESELECT DISGRACE DISPATCH
DISPOINT RELEGATE SETASIDE
WITHDRAW
(— LIGHTLY) SNEEZEAT
DISMISSAL AX BOOT SACK BRUSH
CHUCK CONGE SHAKE AVAUNT
BOUNCE OUSTER KICKAXE REMOVAL
DISPATCH MITTIMUS REDUNDANCY
(LARGE-SCALE —) PURGE
(UNCEREMONIOUS —) CONGE
CONGEE
DISMISSED DEGOMME
(ONE WHO IS —) PUSHOUT
DISMOUNT AVALE AVOID LIGHT
ALIGHT DEVOID DESCEND FLYAWAY
UNHORSE UNMOUNT DISHORSE
UNSTRIDE
DISOBEDIENCE CONTEMPT
DISOBEDIENT BAD FORWARD
FROWARD NAUGHTY UNBUXOM
UNGODLY WAYWARD MUTINOUS
DISOBEY SIT REJECT
DISOBLIGE OFFEND REFUSE
AFFRONT NEGLECT
DISOBLIGING MEAN UNBAIN
UNBANE
DISORDER ILL MUX PIE CRUD FLAW
MESS MUSS RIOT RUFF STIR TOUT
CHAOS CRACK DERAY GRIME HAVOC
REVEL SNAFU SPLIT TOUSE TUKRA
UPSET BURBLE CHOREA DEFUSE
DESRAY HUDDLE JUMBLE LITTER
MALADY MASTIC MUCKER MUDDLE
RUFFLE TOUSLE TROPPO TUMULT
UNTIDY WALTER AILMENT CLUTTER
COBWEBS CONFUSE DERANGE
DISEASE DISTURB EMBROIL
FERMENT FLUTTER GARBOIL ILLNESS
MISDEED MISRULE OUTRAGE
PERTURB SHATTER TROUBLE
UNRAVEL UNSHAPE DISARRAY
DISHEVEL EPILEPSY MILIARIA
MISORDER NEUROSIS ROWDYISM
SICKNESS UNSETTLE COMMOTION
CONFUSION POLLINOSIS

(— OF BIRDS) PIP
(— OF EYES) HIPPUS
(— OF VISION) DIPLOPIA
(— OF WINES) CASSE
(COMPLETE —) CHAOS ANARCHY
(EATING —) BULIMIA
(MENTAL —) INSANITY PARANOIA
(NERVOUS —) VAPORS
(SPEECH —) LALOPATHY
(SUFF.) (SPEECH —) PHASIA PHEMIA
PHRASIA

DISORDERED ILL SICK WILD CRAZY
GAUMY LIGHT MESSY UNRID
BLOTTO FROUZY FROWSY FROWZY
INCULT INSANE MUSSED TURBID
CHAOTIC CLOUDED FORLORN
TUMBLED UNGLUED UNSIDED
CONFUSED DERANGED DISEASED
FEVERISH FLURRIED INCHOATE
SHAMBOLIC

DISORDERING CRIMP

DISORDERLY RAND RANDY ROWDY
RABBLE UNRULY BUNTING LAWLESS
ROARING CONFUSED FAROUCHE
LARRIKIN SLIPSHOD SLOVENLY
SLUTTISH SLATTERNLY

DISORGANIZE SHOCK UPSET
CONFUSE CONTUSE DERANGE
DISBAND DISRUPT DISORDER
DISSOLVE

DISOWN DENY RENAY UNOWN
REJECT DISAVOW RETRACT
ABDICATE DISALLOW DISCLAIM
RENOUNCE REPUDIATE

DISPARAGE LACK SLUR ABUSE
DECRY LOWER TRASH DEBASE
LESSEN SLIGHT BACKCAP DEBAUCH
DEGRADE DEMERIT DEPRESS
DETRACT DISABLE DOWNCRY
IMPEACH RUBBISH RUNDOWN
BELITTLE DEROGATE DIMINISH
DISCOUNT DISHONOR DISPRIZE
MINIMIZE MISLIKEN VILIPEND

DISPARAGEMENT DIASYRM
SNIDERY WASHWAY

DISPARAGING SNIDE SLIGHTING
PEJORATIVE

DISPARATE UNEQUAL SEPARATE

DISPARITY DISSENT DISTANCE
IMPARITY

DISPASSIONATE CALM COOL FAIR
STOIC SEDATE SERENE CLINICAL
COMPOSED MODERATE

DISPATCH RID FREE KILL MAIL NOTE
POST SEND SLAY WING BRIEF
ENVOY FLASH HASTE HURRY SHOOT
SPEED DIRECT EMPLOY HASTEN
ADDRESS COMMAND DELIVER
DISPEED EXPRESS HATCHET
BREVIATE CELERITY CONCLUDE
DESPATCH EXPEDITE TELEGRAM

DISPATCH BOAT AVISO PACKET

DISPATCHER STARTER

DISPEL FRAY SHOO CHASE ASSOIL
BANISH DISCUSS SATISFY SCATTER
DISPERSE

DISPENSATION LAW LILA GRACE
LIVERY ECONOMY FACULTY QUIENAL
TOTQUOT COVENANT DISPOSAL

DISPENSE DEAL DOLE HELP SHED
WEIGH EFFUSE EXCUSE EXEMPT
FOREGO MANAGE SPREAD ABSOLVE
ARRANGE DISPEND DRIBBLE
MINISTER
(— WITH) MISS WANT SPARE
SUSPENSE

DISPENSER BOMB MANAGER
STEWARD

DISPERSE DOT SOW FRAY MELT
PART ROUT SHED LOOSE SCALE
SEVER SKAIL STREW BAFFLE DEFEAT
DILATE DISPEL FANOUT SKIVER
SPARSE SPERSE SPREAD UNKNIT
VANISH WINNOW DIFFUSE DISBAND
DISJECT DISMISS DRIBBLE FRITTER
SCATTER SHATTER SPARKLE SPARPLE
SPERPLE DISSOLVE DISTRACT
SEPARATE SQUANDER STAMPEDE

DISPERSEDLY PASSIM

DISPERSING SCALE
(— SHADOWS) SCIALYTIC

DISPERSION CUT FOAM STAIN
SPREAD DEBACLE SCATTER
DIASPORA EMULSOID SOLUTION
STAMPEDE
(PREF.) LYO

DISPIRIT COW DAMP MATE MULL
CHILL DAUNT DEJECT DEPRESS
FLATTEN OPPRESS

DISPIRITED SAD BLUE DOWN DOWY
DOWIE ABATTU ABATTUE LETDOWN
SHOTTEN DOWNCAST DOWNSOME
SACKLESS UNHEARTY WOBEGONE

DISPIRITING COLD BLEAK CHILL
DISMAL

DISPLACE BUMP EDGE MOVE STIR
BANISH DEPOSE LUXATE MISLAY
REMOVE WINKLE DERANGE
SWALLOW UNHINGE UNPLACE
ANTEVERT DISLODGE DISPLANT
MISPLACE SUPPLACE SUPPLANT
UNSETTLE
(— LATERALLY) HEAVE

DISPLACED ATOPIC DEPAYSE

DISPLACEMENT JEE BUMP SLIP
HEAVE SCEND SHIFT START CUBAGE
OFFSET UPSLIP FALLING EVECTION
(— OF FAULT) THROW
(— OF STAR) ABERRATION
(DOWNWARD —) PTOSIS
(OPTICAL —) PARALLAX
(ROCK —) HITCH

DISPLAY ACT AIR BRAG DASH GAUD
OOZE ORGY POMP SHOW SIGN STAR
WEAR AGONY ARRAY BINGE BLAZE
BOAST DERAY ECLAT EMOTE FLASH

PRIDE SCENE SHINE SIGHT SPLAY
SPORT STAGE VAUNT BLAZON
DEPLOY DESCRY ESTATE EVINCE
EXPOSE EXTEND FLAUNT MUSTER
OSTENT OUTLAY PARADE REVEAL
RUFFLE SETOUT SPLASH SPRANK
SPREAD UNCASE APPROVE
BALLOON BRAVERY ETALAGE
EXHIBIT EXPRESS FANFARE FLUTTER
GAUDERY PAGEANT PRESENT
SHOWING SPLURGE TRADUCE
UNCOVER BEEFCAKE BLAZONRY
BOOKFAIR CEREMONY DISCLOSE
DISCOVER EMBLAZON EQUIPAGE
EVIDENCE EXERCISE EXPOSURE
FLOURISH INDICATE MANIFEST
PARAFFLE SPLENDOR TINSELRY
(— EXCITEMENT) FAUNCH
(— GLARINGLY) FLARE
(— OF COMPUTER TASKS) MENU
(— OF EMOTION) GUSH
(— OF GOODS) ETALAGE
(— OF SKILL) APPERTISE
(— OF STRONG COLORS) RIOT
(BOASTFUL —) JACTATION
(BOISTEROUS —) SPLURGE
(COMPUTER VIDEO — OF TASKS)
MENU
(DARING —) BRAVURA
(EMPTY —) GAUD EYEWASH
(EXCESSIVE —) OSTENTATION
(FLASHY —) CLAPTRAP
(FLORAL —) BLOW BLANKET
(IMPRESSIVE —) SWELL
(LAVISH —) PROFUSION
(LIGHT —) LED
(MOVE COMPUTER — UP OR DOWN)
SCROLL
(OSTENTATIOUS —) DOG GAUDERY
SWAGGER
(PRETENTIOUS —) PARAFLE
PARAFFLE
(RADAR —) SCAN
(SHOWY —) PYROTECHNICS
DISPLAYED SPLAY EXPANDED
DISPLEASE VEX MIFF ANGER
ANNOY PIQUE MISPAY MISSET
OFFEND DISLIKE DISSUIT MISLIKE
PROVOKE IRRITATE
DISPLEASED MAD GLUM UNEASY
UNFAIN
DISPLEASING BAD DRY PUTRID
IRKSOME TEDIOUS UNLOVELY
DISPLEASURE IRE ANGER MUMPS
PIQUE INJURY STRUNT UNLUST
UNWILL DISLIKE OFFENSE TROUBLE
UMBRAGE UNTHANK DISFAVOR
DISGRACE DISTASTE
DISPORT PLAY AMUSE FRISK SPORT
DIVERT FROLIC GAMBOL DISPLAY
DISPOSAL SALE BANDON CLEANUP
PROPINE BESTOWAL DEVOTION
DISPATCH

(— OF DEAD) FUNERAL
(ARBITRARY —) WILL
(QUICK —) WASHWAY
DISPOSE APT SET BEND CAST DUMP
GIVE MIND TRIM YARK ARRAY BRUSH
DIGHT ORDER PLACE POSIT ADJUST
ATTIRE BESTOW DIGEST SETTLE
TEMPER APPOINT ARRANGE
DISPONE GESTURE INCLINE PREPARE
RESOLVE DISPATCH REGULATE
(— OF) JOB SELL SCRAP FINISH
HANDLE WORKOFF
(— VARIOUSLY) STAGGER
DISPOSED APT FIT SET SIB LIEF
DIGHT GIVEN PRONE READY WRAST
MINDED MINDFUL SUBJECT WILLING
ADDICTED AFFECTED PREGNANT
PROCLIVE PROPENSE PROTENSE
TALENTED
(— AT INTERVALS) ALTERNATE
(— TO ACTION) ACTIVE
(— TO ASSOCIATE WITH ONE GROUP)
CLANNISH
(— TOWARD) AFFECTED
(FAIRLY —) CANDID
(FAVORABLY —) PROPITIOUS
(KINDLY —) FOND
(OPENLY —) LOOSE
(WELL —) FAIN INCLINED
DISPOSITION BENT BIAS MAKE
MIND MOOD RACE SORT TRIM TURN
DRIVE ETHOS FRAME GRAIN HABIT
HEART HUMOR SHAPE SPITE TACHE
AFFECT ANIMUS DESIGN GENIUS
HEALTH KIDNEY NATURE PTYXIS
SPIRIT SPRITE STRIND TALENT
TEMPER CONCEPT COURAGE
DISPOSE FACULTY STOMACH
APTITUDE ATTITUDE DISPOSAL
POSITURE PERSONALITY
(— OF DRAPERIES) CAST
(— OF PARTS) SYMMETRY
(— OF PAWNS) SKELETON
(— OF STRATA) OVERLAP
(— TO ANGER) CHOLER
(— TO RESIST) DEFIANCE
(BRIGHT —) OPTIMISM
(DEVILISH —) SATANISM
(GENEROUS —) HEART
(GENIAL —) BONHOMIE
(INHERITED —) RACE
(KINDLY —) CHARITY HUMANITY
(NATURAL —) KIND GRAIN TARAGE
INDOLES
(ORNAMENTAL —) DECOR
(ULTIMATE —) FATE
DISPOSITIONN
(FORGIVING —) MERCY
DISPOSSESS OUST EJECT EVICT
EXPEL STRIP WRONG DEPOSE
DIVEST BEREAVE CASHIER DEPRIVE
DISSEIZE SEPARATE
DISPOSSESSED LUMPEN

DISPOSSESSION OUSTER
DISPRAISE BLAME CENSURE
DISPROOF ELENCH REFUTE
  IMPROOF REPROOF
DISPROPORTIONATE UNEQUAL
DISPROVE BREAK REBUT REFEL
  NEGATE REFUTE CONFUTE EXPLODE
  IMPROVE REPROVE DISALLOW
  NEGATIVE REDARGUE
DISPUTABLE MOOT VAGUE UNSURE
  DUBIOUS FALLIBLE
DISPUTANT FENCER POLEMIC
  WRANGLER
DISPUTATION PARVIS PILPUL
  POLEMIC PROBLEM WRANGLE
  ARGUMENT COURSING DEBATING
  EXERCISE QUODLIBET
DISPUTATIOUS POLEMIC LITIGIOUS
  POLEMICAL
DISPUTE JAR ROW TAX CALL CHOP
  DENY FEUD FRAY FUSS HOLD MOOT
  ODDS RIOT SAKE SPAR SPAT TILT
  ARGUE BRAWL BROIL CABAL CHEST
  FLITE FLYTE HURRY PLEAD SPUTE
  SQUIB ARGUFY BARNEY BICKER
  CAMPLE CANGLE DABBER DACKER
  DAIKER DEBATE DIFFER FITTER
  FRATCH HAGGLE HASSLE IMPUGN
  MATTER NAGGLE SHARRY SQUALL
  SQUEAL THREAP BRABBLE CONTEND
  CONTEST DERAIGN DISCEPT
  DISCUSS DISSERT FACTION GAINSAY
  PRIBBLE QUARREL WRANGLE
  ARGUMENT CATFIGHT CONTRARY
  POLEMIZE QUESTION SKIRMISH
  SPARRING SPLUTTER SQUABBLE
  (POETICAL —) FLYTING PARTMEN
DISQUALIFY DEBAR UNFIT OUTLAW
  DISABLE
DISQUIET VEX FEAR FRET PAIN TOSS
  UNRO EXCITE UNCALM UNEASE
  UNREST AGITATE ANXIETY DISREST
  DISTURB INQUIET PERTURB SOLICIT
  TROUBLE TURMOIL UNPEACE
  UNQUIET
DISQUIETED UNEASY
DISQUIETING UGLY
DISQUIETINGLY UGLY
DISQUIETUDE CHAGRIN WANREST
  WANRUFE
DISRAELI DIZZY
DISREGARD BY SIT BLOW MOCK
  OMIT PASS WANE BELAY FLING
  WAIVE FORGET HUBRIS IGNORE
  SLIGHT UNHEED CASHIER DESPISE
  FORHEED LICENCE LICENSE NEGLECT
  OVERSEE DISCOUNT DISFAVOR
  DISPENSE DISVALUE EASINESS
  OVERHALE OVERLOOK OVERPASS
  UNREGARD
DISRELISH DISLIKE DISTASTE
DISREPUTABLE LOW BASE GAMY
  HARD WAFF GAMEY SEAMY SEEDY

SHADY TOUGH LOUCHE SHODDY
  RAFFISH SHAMEFUL UNHONEST
DISREPUTABLENESS BEGGARY
DISREPUTE DISFAME DISFAVOR
  DISHONOR REPROACH
DISRESPECT AFFRONT CONTEMPT
  RUDENESS
DISRESPECTFUL HARM SAUCY
  UNCIVIL IMPOLITE IMPUDENT
  INSOLENT
DISROBE STRIP CHANGE DIVEST
  DESPOIL UNDRESS
DISRUPT GASH REND TEAR BREAK
  CROSS HAMPER DISRUMP DISTRACT
  SONICATE
  (— WITH SOUND TREATMENT)
  SONICATE
DISRUPTED BROKEN DISRUPT
DISRUPTION BREACH BREAKUP
  DEBACLE RUPTURE SOLUTION
DISSATISFACTION PAIN DISTASTE
  VEXATION
  (FEELING OF —) BLAHS
DISSATISFIED UNEASY
  MALCONTENT
DISSATISFY MISPAY
DISSECT BAR ANALYZE DISJOIN
  SCALPEL UNPIECE
DISSECTED MATURE
DISSECTION ANATOMY ANALYSIS
DISSEMBLE ACT FOX LIE HIDE MASK
  CLOAK FEIGN BOGGLE SEMBLE
  CONCEAL DISGUISE SIMULATE
  SIMULIZE
DISSEMBLER SIMULAR
DISSEMBLING SLY BRAIDE IRONIC
  FICTION AESOPIAN IRONICAL
DISSEMINATE SOW BEAR BLAZE
  STREW EFFUSE SPREAD DIFFUSE
  PUBLISH SCATTER SPARPLE
  DISPERSE SEMINATE
DISSEMINATION PROPAGATION
DISSENSION JAR ODDS DEBATE
  STRIFE DISCORD DISLIKE DISSENT
  FACTION MISLIKE BROILERY
  DISPEACE DISTANCE DISUNION
  DISUNITY DIVISION FRACTION
  FRICTION SEDITION
DISSENT VARY DIFFER HERESY
  CONTEND PROTEST DISAGREE
DISSENTER HERETIC SECTARY
  RECUSANT SEPARATE RASKOLNIK
  (PL.) SEPARATION
DISSENTING PANTILE
DISSEPIMENT REPLUM SEPTUM
  PHRAGMA
DISSERTATION ESSAY THEME
  TRACT DEBATE MEMOIR SCREED
  THESIS DESCANT LECTURE
  MEMOIRS EXCURSUS EXERCISE
  TRACTATE TREATISE
  (— ON TEA) TSIOLOGY
DISSERVE HARM

DISSERVICE HARM DAMAGE
INJURY MISCHIEF
DISSIDENT FRONDEUR
DISSIMILAR UNLIKE DIFFORM
DIVERSE UNLIKEN
DISSIMILATE UNLIKEN
DISSIMULATION IRONY DECEIT
DISSIPATE BURN FRAY SPEND
WASTE BANISH DISPEL EXPEND
CONSUME DIFFUSE DISCUSS
FRITTER RESOLVE SCAMBLE
SCATTER SHATTER SWATTLE
TARNISH DISPERSE DISSOLVE
EMBEZZLE EVANESCE SQUANDER
DISSIPATED FAST HIGH LOST
SPORTY OUTWARD RACKETY
DISSIPATION RAKERY
DISSOLUTE LAX LEWD WILD LOOSE
SLACK RAKELY RAKISH SUBURB
UNTIED WANTON IMMORAL
LAWLESS VICIOUS DESOLATE
RAKEHELL RECKLESS RESOLUTE
SUBURBAN UNCURBED
DISSOLUTION END RUIN DECAY
BREAKUP DECEASE DIVORCE
DIALYSIS
(PREF.) LYS(I)
DISSOLVE CUT END DEFY FADE FUSE
MELT SOLV THAW BREAK FLEET
LOOSE SOLVE UNFIX DIGEST DISTIL
RELENT SOLUTE UNBIND UNGLUE
UNKNIT ADJOURN DESTROY
DISBAND DISJOIN DISTILL DIVORCE
LIQUEFY RESOLVE DISCANDY
DISUNITE SEPARATE
(— MEAT PARTICLES) DEGLAZE
(— OUT) LEACH
(PREF.) LY(O)
DISSOLVED SOLUT REMISS SOLUTE
RESOLUTE
DISSOLVING
(SUFF.) LYSE LYSIS LYST LYTE LYTIC
LYZE
DISSONANCE WOLF DISCORD
DIAPHONY
DISSONANT AJAR HARSH RAGGED
GRATING JARRING JANGLING
DISSUADE BLUFF DETER DEHORT
DIVERT RETIRE
DISTAFF ROCK FEMALE
DISTAFFINA (LOVER OF —)
BOMBASTES
DISTANCE DX HOP WAY BLUE GAIT
GATE LOOK PIPE SPAN STEP DEPTH
DRAFT RANGE SPACE GROUND
HEIGHT LENGTH SPREAD STANCE
STITCH BOWSHOT BREADTH
DRAUGHT FARNESS JOURNEY
MILEAGE MILEWAY RESERVE
STRETCH YARDAGE COLDNESS
COSECANT DIAMETER LATITUDE
HANDSPAN INTERVAL LATITUDE
OFFSCAPE OUTSTRIP

(— ALONG TRACK) LEAD
(— BETWEEN BATTENS) GAG
(— BETWEEN GEAR TEETH) PITCH
(— BETWEEN MASTS) INTERVAL
(— BETWEEN RAILS) GAGE GAUGE
(— BETWEEN RIVET-HEADS) GRIP
(— BETWEEN TACKS) REACH
(— FOR PUTTING COAL) RENK
(— FROM BELLY TO BACK) BODY
(— FROM CENTER) RADIUS
(— FROM EQUATOR) HEIGHT
(— FROM LOCK FACE) BACKSET
(— FROM THE EYE) DEPTH
(— IN ADVANCE) START
(— OF ARCHERY RANGE) BUTT
(— OF BOW SHOT) CAST
(— OF GOLF BALL) CARRY
(— OF HAUL) LEAD LEADAGE
(— OF TURNING SHIP) ADVANCE
(— OF VISION) KEN
(— ON FISHHOOK) BITE
(— ON GEAR WHEEL) ADDENDUM
(— OVER WHICH WIND BLOWS)
FETCH
(— UPWARDS) HEIGHT
(ANGULAR —) ANOMALY
(AT A —) LARGE
(GREAT —) INFINITY
(INTERVENING —) GAP
(PERPENDICULAR —) DROP CAMBER
ALTITUDE
(REMOVE TO A —) ELOIN
(SAFE —) BERTH
(SEA —) OUTING STEAMING
(SHOOTING —) SHOOT
(SHORT —) HAIR INCH SPIT STEP
SPELL BITTIE FOOTSTEP
(SHORT — AWAY) OUTBYE
(SMALL —) HAIR STEP
(UNIT OF —) LI YOJAN PARASANG
DISTANT DX COY FAR OFF AFAR
AWAY BACK COLD SIDE YOND ALOOF
CHILL FERNE HENCE FERREN
REMOTE YONDER FARAWAY
FOREIGN FROSTED REMOVED
STRANGE RESERVED
(— FROM COAST) MIDLAND
(— IN TIME) EARLY
(— PART) OFFSCAPE
(MORE —) YOND YONDER ULTERIOR
(MOST —) OUTMOST OUTERMOST
(PREF.) TEL(E)(EO)
DISTASTE HATE DEGOUT UNLUST
DISGUST DISLIKE MISLIKE AVERSION
MISTASTE
(— FOR FOOD) APOSITIA
DISTASTEFUL ICKY SOUR YUCKY
AUGEAN BITTER BEASTLY HATEFUL
BRACKISH NAUSEOUS SHOCKING
UNSAVORY REPUGNANT
DISTEMPER SOAK STEEP CHOLER
DILUTE GARGET GARGIL GARGLE
MALADY PANTAS AILMENT DISEASE

ILLNESS DISORDER DYSCRASE
SICKNESS UNSETTLE
(— OF COLT) STRANGLES
DISTEND BAG BLOW FILL GROW
HEFT BLOAT PLUMP STRUT SWELL
WIDEN DILATE EXPAND EXTEND
INTEND SPREAD BALLOON ENLARGE
INFLATE STRETCH
DISTENDED BIG FULL PENT TAUT
TRIG WIDE BLOWN POOCH TUMID
ASTRUT GRAVID BLOATED DISTENT
SWOLLEN INFLATED PATULENT
PATULOUS
DISTENDEDLY ASTRUT
DISTENTION BLOAT DISTENT
TYMPANY
DISTHENE CYANITE KYANITE
DISTICH SLOKA PROODE COUPLET
DISTILL DROP ELIX EMIT RATE STILL
DISTIL EXTILL INFUSE ALEMBIC
LIMBECK TRICKLE
DISTILLATE GUNDY ROSIN BENZIN
ALCOHOL BENZINE
DISTILLATION RUN DESCENT
DISTILLER ABKAR STILLER
DISTILLERY STILL JIGGER STILLERY
DISTINCT HOT FAIR FREE VIVE
BREME BRISK CLEAR PLAIN SHARP
VIVID PLUCKY PROPER SECRET
SUNDRY ANOTHER ASUNDER
DIVERSE EVIDENT LEGIBLE OBVIOUS
PRECISE SCIOLTO SEVERAL SPECIAL
APPARENT DISCRETE DIVIDUAL
PALPABLE PECULIAR SEPARATE
TRENCHANT
(— FROM) BESIDE
(NOT —) DIM OBSCURE
(PREF.) CHORI CHORIST(O) IDIO
DISTINCTION MARK NOTE RANK
SHED TEST CLASS GLORY HONOR
FIGURE LAUREL LUSTER LUSTRE
RENOWN DIORISM QUALITY QUILLET
ACCESSIT DIVISION GRANDEZA
SUBTLETY REFINEMENT
(ACADEMIC —) HONORS HONOURS
(LACKING —) VANILLA
(WITHOUT —) COMMON
DISTINCTIVE RARE JUICY DIRECT
PROPER SIGNAL PECULIAR
PHONEMIC SEPARATE SPANKING
TALENTED
DISTINCTIVENESS EMPHASIS
DISTINCTLY CLEAR REDLY FAIRLY
CLEARLY
DISTINCTNESS PLUCK CLARITY
SEVERALTY
(LACKING —) SMUDGY
DISTINGUISH DEEM KNOW MARK
SORT BADGE JUDGE LABEL SEVER
SKILL STAMP DECERN DEFINE
DESCRY DEVISE DIVIDE ENSIGN
SECERN SINGLE CONCERN DISCERN
DESCRIBE PERCEIVE SEPARATE

DISTINGUISHED CLEAR GREAT
NOTED SWELL BANNER FAMOUS
GENTLE MARKED SOLEMN EMINENT
INSIGNE NOTABLE SIGNATE SPECIAL
TOPPING DISTINCT ESPECIAL
LAUREATE RENOWNED SPLENDID
CONSPICUOUS
DISTINGUISHING BETWEEN
DISTORT WRY SKEW WARP CLOUD
COLOR FUDGE SCREW TWIST WREST
WRING CRINGE DEFACE DEFORM
DETORT GARBLE MANGLE SHEVEL
WRENCH WRITHE BLUBBER
CONTORT FALSIFY GRIMACE
PERVERT SHACHLE SHACKLE
SLANDER OUTIMAGE WIREDRAW
DISTORTED WRY AWRY BENT SKEW
ASKEW CRANK SKEWED WARPED
CROOKED DISTORT GNARLED
LOXOTIC WRITHEN CAMSHACH
DEFORMED DEGRADED STRAINED
TORTIOUS PERVERTED
DISTORTING CONVULSION
DISTORTION FIB HOG SAG WOW
WREST STRAIN FLUTTER GRIMACE
GARBLING SKEWNESS
(— IN WOOD) WARP DIAMONDING
(FACIAL —) GRIMACE
DISTRACT MAD AMUSE CRAZE
STROY BEMUSE DETRAY DIVERT
HARASS INSANE MADDEN MITHER
MOIDER PUZZLE TWITCH AGITATE
CONFUSE DETRACT DISTURB
EMBROIL PERPLEX SCATTER
BEWILDER CONFOUND FORHAILE
DISTRACTED GYTE WILD CRAZY
EPERDU STRACT FRANTIC MADDING
SCRANNY FRENETIC SCATTERED
DISTRACTION ALARM BLIND
ALARUM ESCAPE FRENZY TUMULT
ECSTASY
DISTRAIN NAM NAAM DRIVE POINT
STRAIN STRESS DISTRESS
POUNDAGE
DISTRAINT NAM NAAM POINT
DISTRAUGHT MAD CRAZED
FRANTIC DERANGED DISTRACT
DISTRAIT STRAUGHT
DISTRESS AIL ILL MAR VEX BITE
CARK GNAW HURT MOAN NEED PAIN
PORT PUSH TEAR TEEN AGONY
ANGER ANNOY DOLOR GRATE GRIEF
GRILL GRIPE LABOR PINCH PRESS
SMART TRYST TWEAK WORRY
WOUND WRING BARRAT DANGER
DURESS GRIEVE GRUDGE HARASS
HARROW LAMENT MISERY SORROW
STRESS TAKING THRONG WORRIT
AFFLICT ANGUISH ANXIETY
CHAGRIN DAYMARE DESTROY
DISEASE EXTREME HERSHIP
MISEASE OPPRESS PASSION
PENANCE PERPLEX STURBLE

TORMENT TORTURE TRAVAIL
TROUBLE UNQUERT AGGRIEVE
CALAMITY DARKNESS DISTASTE
DISTRAIN EXIGENCE FORHAILE
PRESSURE SORENESS STRAITEN
WANDRETH GRIEVANCE

DISTRESSED WRUNG DOWNGONE

DISTRESSFUL STRAIT

DISTRESSING BAD HOT SAD GRIM
HARD SORE BLEAK CHARY CRUEL
DIRTY SHARP BITTER SEVERE
SHREWD THORNY CARKING FEARFUL
GRIPING PAINFUL GRIEVOUS

DISTRIBUTE DOT SOW CAST DEAL
DOLE GRID METE SEED SORT TAME
ALLOT CLASS DIVVY ISSUE PLACE
SHARE SHIFT SPEND ASSIGN ASSORT
DEPART DEVISE DIGEST DIVIDE
EXPEND IMPART PARCEL REPART
SPARSE SPREAD ARRANGE DISPEND
DISPOSE EROGATE PRORATE
SCATTER ALLOCATE CLASSIFY
DESCRIBE DISBURSE DISPENSE
DISPERSE SEPARATE SPRINKLE
(— GUNFIRE) SEARCH
(— SEED) SOW SEED DRILL
(— TYPE) DISH THROW

DISTRIBUTED BALANCED DISPERSE

DISTRIBUTION DOLE SALE ARRAY
DIVVY DETAIL DIVIDE PARTING
DISPOSAL DIVIDEND

DISTRIBUTIVELY EACH APIECE

DISTRIBUTOR SOWER SHARER
CARRIER ZANJERO

DISTRICT DO AMT GAU LAN SOC
WAY WON AREA COIL FARM HUNT
LEET LIWA PALE PART SIDE SLUM
SOKE TEMA WARD WENE WICK
WOON AIMAK ANNEX COILA EXURB
HARSH JAGIR JEWRY MAHAL OKRUG
PAGUS PARTY SHIRE SOKEN TALUK
TEMAN TRACT VICUS AGENCY
BARRIO BOWERY CANTON CERCLE
CIRCLE COUNTY FOREST JAGHIR
MARKAZ MEMBER MERINA OKROOG
PARAMO PARISH POLLAM REGARD
REGION SIRCAR STAPLE STREET
SYSSEL VINTRY ZILLAH CALABAR
CIRCUIT CLASSIS COMARCA
COMMUNE COUNTRY CURRAGH
DEMESNE DIOCESE ENCLAVE
FREEDOM LIBERTY MAHALLA
MALACCA MAYFAIR MELIZKI
MISSION PIMLICO PURLIEU QUARTER
SEASIDE SLUMDOM THANAGE
THEBAID UPRIVER CHAPELRY
CIMARRON DISTRITO DIVISION
FAUBOURG GILDABLE LEGATION
MACASSAR MAGAZINE MONTANAS
PRECINCT PROVINCE REGIMENT
MAGISTRACY PREFECTURE
(— BORDERING RIVER) WATER
(— FOR GAME HUNTING) SHOOTING

(— OF COURT) LEET
(— OF JAPAN) DO KEN
(ADMINISTRATIVE —) ZILA ZILLAH
TOWNSHIP
(BROTHEL —) STEW
(BURNED —) QUEMADO
(CHINESE —) HIEN
(COASTAL —) RIVIERA
(ECCLESIASTICAL —) SYNOD
CLASSIS DIOCESE
(HUNTING —) WALK
(ICELANDIC —) SYSSEL
(ISLE OF MAN —) SHEADING
(JUDICIAL —) CIRCUIT
(MARKED-OFF —) PALE
(MOUNTAINOUS —) HIGHLAND
(OUTER —) END
(OUTWARD —) END
(OVERCROWDED —) WARREN
(POOR —) SLUM SLUMS
(POSTAL —) RAYON
(RURAL —) WAYBACK
(RURAL —S) STICKS
(RUSSIAN —) OBLAST STANITSA
STANITZA
(TENANT —) THIRL
(THEATER —) RIALTO
(TRIBAL —) GAU
(TURKISH —) ORDU SANJAK
(PL.) GAELTACHT

DISTRUST FEAR DOUBT DREAD
STRIFE DIFFIDE SUSPECT UNFAITH
UNTRUST DEFIANCE DISFAITH
MISFAITH MISTRUST QUESTION
WANTRUST

DISTRUSTFUL DIWLEERY JEALOUS

DISTURB JEE VEX BUSY FAZE FRET
FUSS JOLT RILE ROCK ROIL STIR
TOSS ALARM ANNOY BRASH DROVE
FEEZE KNOCK PHASE ROUSE SHAKE
STEER UPSET AFFRAY BOTHER
HARASS JOSTLE MOLEST RUFFLE
SQUEAK UNCALM UNEASE AGITATE
COMMOTE COMMOVE CONCUSS
DERANGE DISREST DRUMBLE
FRAZZLE GARBOIL INQUIET MISMAKE
PERTURB SCUFFLE SOLICIT STURBLE
TEMPEST TROUBLE CONVULSE
DISJOINT DISORDER DISQUIET
DISTRACT DISTRESS FRIGHTEN
(— BY HANDLING) TOUCH
(— SUDDENLY) START
(— THE PEACE) RIOT INQUIET

DISTURBANCE VEX BOIL BREE CAIN
COIL DUST RIOT ROUT STIR WIND
WORK ALARM BEANO BRAWL BROIL
DERAY FUGUE FUROR HURRY SHINE
SHOCK STEER STORM STROW STURT
TOUSE AFFRAY BOTHER BREEZE
CATHRO DESRAY FRACAS FRAISE
FURORE HUBBUB KICKUP POTHER
RUCKUS RUMBLE RUMPUS SHINDY
SQUALL STATIC TUMULT TURNUP

UPROAR BLUNDER BOBBERY
BRULYIE BRULZIE CHAGRIN CLATTER
CLUTTER DISTURB EMOTION
FERMENT GRINDER MADNESS
ROOKERY RUCTION TROUBLE
TURMOIL BROILERY BUSINESS
DISORDER FOOFARAW INCIDENT
REELRALL STRAMASH TRAVALLY
RABBLEMENT PERTURBATION
(— OF OCEAN) SEA
(ATMOSPHERIC —) STORM GRINDER
(DIGESTIVE —) BLOAT
(MENTAL —) FRENZY PHRENSY
DELIRIUM
(SEISMIC —) SEAQUAKE
DISTURBED CRACKED INQUIET
MAKADOO TROUBLE AGITATED
FLURRIED STREAKED
DISTURBING BREAK NASTY
HAUNTING
DISUNION DIVORCE
DISUNITE RIP PART SEVER UNTIE
DETACH DIVIDE SUNDER UNKNIT
UNLIME DISBAND DISJOIN DISLINK
DISSENT DIVORCE UNRAVEL
ALIENATE DISSEVER DISSOLVE
ESTRANGE SEPARATE UNSOLDER
DISUNITY DISCORD DISUNION
DIVISION
DISUSE MISUSE OUTAGE ABANDON
DISCARD DISUSAGE MISAPPLY
DISUSED DEAD WASTE DESUETE
EXOLETE OBSOLETE
DITCH GAW RUT SAP SOW DELF DICK
DIKE DYKE FOSS GOOL GOUT GRIP
GURT HOLL LEET LODE MOAT SEEK
SICK SIKE SINK TRIG CANAL CLAUD
DELFT DELVE FENCE FLEAM FOSSA
FOSSE GRAFF GRAFT GRAVE GRIPE
GROOP GULLY PUDGE RHEEN RHINE
RIGOL SEWER SHORE SLONK SLUIT
SOUGH STANK STELL ZANJA
GUTTER GUZZLE HOLLOW RELAIS
SHEUCH SHEUGH TRENCH ZANJON
ABANDON ACEQUIA CHANNEL
GRINDLE GRIPPLE LATERAL VANFOSS
ZANJONA WATERING
(— AROUND ARENA) EURIPUS
(MUDDY —) LETCH
(NARROW —) RELAIS
(OPEN —) STELL
(WIDE —) SLOT
(PREF.) FOSSI
DITCH GRASS ENALID
DITCH MILLET HUREEK PASPALUM
DITCH REED SPIRE BENNEL
DITHER FLAP STEW SHAKE TIZZY
BOTHER LATHER SHIVER TROUBLE
DITI (FATHER OF —) DAKSHA
(HUSBAND OF —) KASHYAPA
DITROCHEE DIPODY
DITSY CRAZY DIZZY GIDDY INANE
SILLY SPACY WIFTY SPACEY

DITTO SAME REPEAT LIKEWISE
DITTY DIT LAY DITE DYTE POEM SING
SONG THEME VERSE SAYING
DICTATE VINETTA
DIURETIC ZEA CAVA KAVA BUCCO
BUCHU CUBEB LAPPA PICHI SABAL
NASROL DROSERA EMICTORY
FUROSOMIDE PIPSISSEWA
DIVAGATE ROVE
DIVAN SOFA OTTOMAN SOCIABLE
DIVE BAR DEN DASH DUCK DUMP
JOINT SOUSE GAINER HEADER
PLUNGE SALOON BROTHEL
RATTRAP JACKNIFE SUBMERGE
JACKKNIFE
(— DEEP) SOUND
(KIND OF —) SWAN TWIST GAINER
JACKKNIFE
(MAKE A NOSE —) PEARL
DIVER AMA LOON DUCKER PEARLER
PLUNGER PLUNGEON
(SCUBA —) AQUANAUT
(SUFF.) DYTA DYTES
DIVERGE LEAVE BRANCH DIFFER
DIVIDE RAMIFY SPREAD SQUARE
SWERVE DEVIATE DIGRESS DIVERSE
DISAGREE DIVAGATE
DIVERGENCE DIP ERROR CHANGE
SPREAD SWERVE VAGARY
CONTRAST OBLIQUITY
(UNDUE —) OUTRAGE
DIVERGENT OFF APART REMOTE
TANGENT VARIANT
(MORE —) FARTHER
DIVERS EVIL MANY CRUEL SUNDRY
SEVERAL VARIOUS PERVERSE
DIFFERING
(PREF.) PARTI PARTY
DIVERSE EVIL SERE MOTLEY
SUNDRY UNLIKE VARIED ADVERSE
SEVERAL VARIOUS DISTINCT
PERVERSE SEPARATE VARIETAL
(PREF.) PARTI PARTY POLY VARI(O)
DIVERSIFIED MOTLEY EXTENDED
DIVERSIFY DOT FRET VARY CHECK
FRECK BEGARIE CHECKER VARIATE
SPRINKLE
DIVERSION JEU GAME MASK PLAY
ALARM FEINT FRISK HOBBY SPORT
ATTACK DEDUIT DIVERT LAUGHS
SCHEME SOLACE DISPORT PASTIME
ESCAPISM PLEASURE SIDESHOW
VARIORUM
(— OF STREAM) CAPTURE
DIVERSITY CHANGE DISCORD
DISSENT VARIETY CONTRAST
(PREF.) POLY
DIVERT SWAY AMUSE BLANK RELAX
SHUNT SPORT WRING DERAIL
DERIVE DETURN SIPHON SWITCH
SYPHON TICKLE BEGUILE CELIGHT
DECEIVE DEFLECT DETRACT DISPORT
PASTIME PERVERT REFLECT

ABSTRACT DISSUADE DISTRACT
ESTRANGE RECREATE
(— ATTENTION) COVER
(— HEADWATERS) BEHEAD
(— STREAM) CAPTURE
(— WATER) FLUME
DIVERTED MERRY AMUSED
DISTRACT
DIVERTICULUM UTERUS
OLEOCYST
DIVERTING DROLL AMUSING
FOOLISH PLEASANT SPORTFUL
LAUGHABLE
DIVEST BARE DOFF REFT TIRL EMPTY
EXUTE REAVE SHEAR SPOIL STRIP
DELAWN DENUDE DEPOSE DEVEST
DISMIT UNVEST BEREAVE DEPRIVE
DESPOIL DISROBE UNCOVER
UNDRESS DENATURE DETHRONE
UNCLOTHE
(— OF) ABDICATE
(— OF ARMOR) DEMAIL
(— OF VALUE) DEVALUE
DIVIDE CUT LOT CAST DEAL FORK
MERE PART RIFT SHED CLIP TEAR
ZONE BREAK CARVE CLASS CLEFT
DIVVY GAVEL JOINT SCALE SCIND
SEVER SHARE SHIFT SLICE SNACK
SPACE SPLIT SPRIT WHACK BEPART
BISECT BRANCH CANTLE CANTON
CLEAVE COTEAU DEPART DEVISE
DIFFER DOMIFY INDENT PARCEL
RAMIFY SECTOR SEJOIN SLEAVE
SUNDER ALIQUOT ANALYZE
ATOMIZE AVERAGE BRITTEN
COMPART DIFFUSE DIREMPT
DISCIDE DISPART DISSECT DIVERGE
FISSURE FRITTER PARTAKE
PRORATE ALLOCATE CLASSIFY
CROSSCUT DISCRETE DISSEVER
DISTRACT DISUNITE FRACTION
FRAGMENT GRADUATE HEMISECT
MEDISECT SEPARATE STRATIFY
UNSEEDER
(— BEEF) BLOCK
(— FILAMENTS) SLEAVE
(— INTO DISTRICTS) CANTON
(— INTO MEASURES) BAR
(— INTO PIECES) GOBBET
(— INTO 2 PARTS) HALVE BISECT
(— INTO 4 PARTS) QUARTER
(— LAND) STINT
(— NATURALLY) FALL
(— SMALL) SCANTLE
DIVIDED ENTE REFT SIDE CLEFT
FORKY SPLIT ATOMIC CLOVEN
PRONGY FISSATE FOURCHE
GYRONNY PARTITE SEPTATE
AEROLATE CAMERATE DIVIDUAL
FOURCHEE
(— BY VERTICAL LINES) PALY
(— INTO 4 PARTS) PALY QUARTERED
(— IN TWO) FOURCHE DIMIDIATE

(— TWICE) RETAILLE
(NOT —) GLORAL
(PREF.) CHORI(ST)(STO) FISSI PARTI
PARTY SCHIZ(O)
(SUFF.) FID FIDATE SECT SECTED
TOMOUS
DIVIDEND BONUS SHARE
DIVIDER BUNTON MERIST SEPTUM
SHARER BUNTING COMPASS
MULLION SEVERER DIVIDANT
DIVI-DIVI LIBIDIBI
DIVINATION OMEN SORS SORT
AUGURY MANTIC SORTES AUSPICE
SCRYING SORCERY GEOMANCY
TAGHAIRM
(— SCIENCE) MANTIC
(PREF.) MANTO
(SUFF.) MANCER MANCY MANTIC
DIVINE HOLY SORT SPAE TWIG
AREAD AREED ATMAN AUGUR DIVUS
GODLY GUESS PIOUS DEIFIC DETECT
DEVISE GODFUL HALSEN PRIEST
SACRED BLESSED FORESEE GODLIKE
PORTEND PREDICT PRESAGE
ARIOLATE CONTRIVE FOREBODE
FOREKNOW FORETELL HEAVENLY
IMMORTAL MINISTER PERCEIVE
UBIQUIST SPIRITUAL
DIVINER SEER AUGUR SIBYL
ARUSPEX AUGURER PROPHET
HARUSPEX
DIVING BELL NAUTILUS
DIVING BOARD RISE
DIVING SUIT GANGAVA
DIVINING ROD TWIG DOWSER
DIVINITY (ALSO SEE GOD AND
GODDESS) JOSS LLEU LLEW TIEN
AHURA DEITY HYBLA NUADA NUADU
NYMPH POWER ATHTAR VEDUIS
GLAUCUS GODDESS GODHEAD
GODSHIP HYBLAEA TARANIS VIRBIUS
TEUTATES VEDIOVIS
(— CIRCUIT BINDING) YAPP
(PL.) CABIRI ELOHIM
DIVISIBLE SECABLE DIVIDUAL
PARTIBLE
(— BY 2) AIM
DIVISION BAY BOX CUT DAG FIT JAG
LEG CHAP CLAN DOLE FARM FAUN
FORK GELD GELT GORE HOLD LITH
NEAT PACE PANE PART RANK RAPE
RIFT CAPUT CHASM CLASS CLEFT
CURIA DIGOR DIVVY DULAN DULAT
FIELD FIGHT GENOS GRANT GROUP
IJORE MURUT PERES REALM SHARD
SHARE SUBAH TAXIS THEME TOMAN
WHEEN BARONY CANTON COHORT
DECADE DECURY DEGREE DIVIDE
EOGAEA HAWIYA IMAHAL JHURIA
PORTIO SCHISM SEASON SECTOR
SUNDER VOLOST ZILLAH BREAKUP
COMARCA CUSTODY DIOCESE
DUALISM ENOMOTY FISSURE

FURLONG HASHIYA KINGDOM
KITKSAN NATUARY PARTAGE
PARTING ROULADE SECTION
SEGMENT SUBRACE ARPEGGIO
CATEGORY CLEAVAGE DECANATE
DIERESIS DISTRICT FASCICLE
MEROTOMY PARGANNA PRECINCT
SCISSION SCISSURE SHEDDING
SQUADRON SUBCLASS
(— BETWEEN PIERS) BAY
(— BETWEEN STALLS) BAIL
(— FOR TAXATION) GELD
(— IN DENMARK) AMT
(— IN HUNGARY) COMITAT
(— IN MINING BED) CLEAVE
(— OF ANGELS) CHOIR
(— OF ARMY) BATTLE LOCHUS
(— OF BEJA) BISHARIN
(— OF BOOK) CHAPTER FASCICLE
(— OF BUDDHIST CANON) PITAKA
(— OF BUILDING) STORY STOREY
(— OF CHAPTER) VERSE
(— OF CHARIOTEERS) FACTION
(— OF CHURCH) AISLE
(— OF COMPASS) POINT
(— OF CONTEST) HEAT INNING
(— OF COUNTY) RAPE BARONY
HUNDRED
(— OF CROPLAND) FLAT
(— OF DISCOURSE) HEADING
(— OF DRAMA) ACT SCENE
(— OF FAMILY) BRANCH
(— OF FIELD) RIG
(— OF FOOT) SEMEION
(— OF FOREST) WARD
(— OF GEOLOGICAL TIME) ERA
EPOCH PERIOD
(— OF GRASS) SPRIG
(— OF GREAT HORDE) DULAN DULAT
KANGLA KANGLI
(— OF HEADLINE) BANK DECK
(— OF HERALDIC SHIELD) POINT
(— OF ISLE OF MAN) SHEADING
(— OF KENT) LATHE
(— OF LAND) LAINE KONOHIKI
(— OF LEAF) LOBE
(— OF LEGION) COHORT HASTATI
MANIPLE TRIARII
(— OF LOG LINE) KNOT
(— OF MANCHU ARMY) BANNER
(— OF MANKIND) RACE
(— OF MEAL) COURSE
(— OF MUSICAL COMPOSITION)
MOVEMENT
(— OF NIGHT) WATCH
(— OF ORANGE) LITH
(— OF PARTED HAIR) LIST
(— OF PEOPLE) STREAM
(— OF PLAY) ACT SCENE
(— OF POEM) FIT DUAN CANTO
STANZA STROPHE
(— OF PROCESS) STAGING
(— OF ROAD) LANE

(— OF ROCKS) SYSTEM
(— OF ROSARY) DECADE CHAPLET
(— OF SCHOOL YEAR) TERM
SESSION
(— OF SOCIETY) CASTE ATOMISM
(— OF SONG) FIT
(— OF STOPE) FLOOR
(— OF STRUCTURE) STAGE
(— OF SUSSEX) RAPE
(— OF TREF) RANDIR
(— OF TRIBE) CURIA
(— OF UTTERANCE) COLON
(— OF WINDOW) DAY
(— OF YEAR) SEASON
(— OF YORKSHIRE) RIDING
(— OF ZILLAH) PARGANA
PERGUNNAH
(— OF ZODIAC) SIGN DECAN
(— OVER ISSUE) BREACH
(— SIGN) OBELUS
(ADMINISTRATIVE —) FU LATHE
CHARGE CIRCLE COUNTY EYALET
CUSTODY DIOCESE TOWNSHIP
(ANTHROPOLOGICAL —) STOCK
(ARMY —) MORA
(ASTROLOGICAL —) FACE
(CELL —) MITOSIS AMITOSIS
(ECCLESIASTICAL —) SCHISM
SOCIETY PRECINCT
(GEOLOGICAL —) ERA LIAS MALM
BUNTER KEUPER LUDIAN SERIES
LARAMIE ARNUSIAN RICHMOND
(HINGED —) LEAF
(ISLE OF MAN —) SHEADING
(MUSICAL —) ALLEGRO
(NUCLEAR —) FISSION
(PHILIPPINE —) ATO
(POLICE —) TANA THANA
(POLITICAL —) ATO CITY LATHE
STATE COUNTY PARISH BOROUGH
HUNDRED SURPLUS DISTRICT
PURCHASE WAPENTAKE
(POPULATION —) STRATUM
(SOCIAL —) HORDE
(TRIBAL —) CLAN
(SUFF.) KINESIS
DIVITIACUS (BROTHER OF —)
DUMNORIX
DIVORCE GET GETT AHSAN HASAN
KHULA SEVER TALAK SUNDER
ASUNDER DISBAND DISMISS
MUBARAT UNMARRY DISSOLVE
DISUNION DISUNITE SEPARATE
DIVOT CLOD TURF
DIVULGATION (UNAUTHORIZED —)
LEAK
DIVULGE BARE CALL SHOW TELL
BLURT BREAK SPILL UTTER VOICE
BABBLE BEWRAY EVULGE EXPOSE
IMPART REVEAL SPREAD UNFOLD
PROPALE PUBLISH UNCOVER
DISCLOSE DISCOVER EVULGATE
PROCLAIM

DIZZINESS HILO SWIM DINUS TIEGO
MEGRIM VANITY MERLIGO
SCOTOMY VERTIGO SWIMMING
WILLNESS
DIZZY DUNT ARIEL CRAZY DITSY
DITZY FAINT GIDDY LIGHT TOTTY
WESTY WOOZY FICKLE STUPID
FOOLISH SWIMMING UNSTEADY
DJIBOUTI (GULF OF —) TADJOURA
DNA (— SEGMENT) CISTRON
(— SEQUENCE) HOMEOBOX
DO D ACT DIV FAY TRY BILK BURN
CHAR COME DEAL DOST MAKE PASS
SUIT AVAIL BITCH CHEAT EXERT
GUISE SERVE SHIFT TRICK ANSWER
COMMIT NOBBLE RENDER ACHIEVE
EXECUTE PERFORM PRODUCE
SATISFY SUFFICE TRANSACT
(— AWAY WITH) BURK ABATE BURKE
FORDO BANISH FOREDO ABOLISH
AMOLISH CASHIER CONSUME
ABROGATE DEMOLISH DISSOLVE
IMBOLISH RETRENCH
(— BUSINESS) CHAFFER
(— CARELESSLY) SLIM
(— CASUAL WORK) GRASS
(— FOR) FIX GET JACK POOP SINK
FETCH NAPOO DIDDLE SCUPPER
(— IMPERFECTLY) HUDDLE
(— INJURY) BANE
(— IN SLOVENLY WAY) SLUBBER
(— NOT) DONT DINNA
(— OVER) REVAMP REMODEL
(— PENANCE) SATISFY
(— PIECEWORK) DACKER
(— SMARTLY) LINK
(— THOROUGHLY) FLOOR
(— WITHOUT) LACK SPARE FORBEAR
DISPENSE
(— WRONG) ERR SIN MISCARRY
(— YE) DEE
DOABLE AGIBLE
DOBLON ISABELLA
DOBRA JO JOE OCTAVE
DOCENT TUTOR TEACHER LECTURER
DOCILE CALM MEEK TALL TAME
TAWIE FACILE GENTLE DOCIOUS
DUCTILE DUTIFUL BIDDABLE
OBEDIENT TOWARDLY
DOCK BOB CUT PEN BANG CLIP
MOOR PIER QUAY RUMP SCUT BASIN
SHORE WHARF CAMBER COFFER
DOCKEN FIDDLE HAMBLE MARINA
SORREL STRUNT BOBTAIL CURTAIL
PARELLA PARELLE SHORTEN
CANAIGRE PATIENCE SHIPSIDE
(SPACE BETWEEN —S) SLIPWAY
DOCKAGE BERTHAGE
DOCKET LIST AGENDA
DOCKMACKIE VIBURNUM
DOCKWORKER (—S GROUP) ILA
DOCKYARD ARSENAL
(— WORKMAN) MATEY

DOCTOR (ALSO SEE PHYSICIAN)
DOC COOK DOPE DOSE FAKE PILL
BRUJO HAKIM LEECH SUGAR
TREAT CROCUS DEACON EXTERN
HAIKUN HEALER INTERN MAULVI
POWWOW CROAKER KORADJI
TEACHER MEDICATE PHYSICIAN
MANIPULATE
(— OF CANON LAW) JCD
(— OF LAWS) JD
(— UP) COOK FAKE EYEWASH
(— WINE) STUM
(IRISH —) OLLAV OLLAMH
(KIND OF —) SPIN
(PLAY —) FIXER
(QUACK —) CROCUS
(WITCH —) BOCOR BOKOR GOOFER
GUFFER WIZARD WITCHMAN
DOCTOR'S DILEMMA (AUTHOR OF
—) SHAW
(CHARACTER IN —) LOUIS RALPH
CULLEN COLENSO DUBEDAT PATRICK
RIDGEON WALPOLE JENNIFER
BONINGTON BLENKINSOP
DOCTRINAIRE ISMY
DOCTRINAL CREEDAL
DOCTRINE ISM DOXY LEAR LORE
RULE CREDO CREED DOGMA LIGHT
MAXIM TABLE TENET ZOISM AHIMSA
BABISM BELIEF DHARMA EGOISM
EROTIC GOSPEL HOLISM MALISM
MONISM NOETIC THEORY ACROAMA
AMIDISM ANIMISM ARTICLE ATAVISM
ATHEISM ATOMISM BAHAISM
DUALISM EGOTISM EVANGEL
KARAISM KRYPSIS MISHNAH
NEOLOGY NOETICS OPINION
PEELISM PRECEPT PROGRAM
REALISM SENSISM TRIKAYA
ACTIVISM AGATHISM ANALYTIC
ARIANISM ARYANISM BAJANISM
CHILIASM CYNICISM DARBYISM
DEVILISM DOCETISM DYNAMISM
ENERGISM FATALISM FINALISM
GOBINISM HEDONISM HYLOLOGY
IDENTISM IDEOLOGY ISLAMISM
MOLINISM NIHILISM PAJONISM
PAMNESIA PEJORISM POSITION
POSOLOGY PSYCHISM REGALISM
RHEMATIC SIDERISM SOLIDISM
SPHERICS TYPOLOGY UBIQUITY
VITALISM DITHEISM MECHANISM
MUTUALISM PANTHEISM PESSIMISM
PLURALISM NATURALISM
(BAD —) CACODOXY
(BUDDHIST —) ANATTA ANATMAN
(CONTRARY —) HERESY
(ESOTERIC —) CABALA QABBALA
CABALISM
(EVIL —) MOLOCH
(MUSLIM —) TAUHID TAWHID
(PL.) ESOTERY SCOTISM CREDENDA
DONATISM LABADISM SCRIBISM

(SUFF.) ISM LOGER LOGIA(N)
LOGIC(AL) LOGIST LOGUE LOGY
OLOGY

DOCUMENT DOC GET BILL BOND
BOOK CALL CHOP DEED FORM GETT
OLLA SEAL WRIT CHART DEMIT DIMIT
GRIEF LEASE PAPER PROOF SCRIP
SCRIT STIFF TARGE TEACH TITLE
BILLET BREVET CADJAN CAJANG
CEDULA COCKET DOCKET PATENT
RAGMAN SCHOOL SCRIPT SOURCE
SURVEY TICKET VOLUME ARCHIVE
CONDUCT DIPLOMA ELOHIST
ESCRIPT EXHIBIT INQUEST LICENSE
MISSIVE PLACARD PRECEPT
WARRANT WAYBILL WHEREAS
WRITING CITATION CONTRACT
COVENANT FURLOUGH INSTRUCT
MORTGAGE SCHEDULE SECURITY
TRANSIRE BORDEREAU
(CONDITIONAL —) SCRIP
(COPY OF —) VIDIMUS
(COURT —) WRIT PRODUCTION
(REGISTRATION —S) LOGBOOK
(PL.) BUMF ARCHIVE ARCHIVE
PALAPALA

DODAVAH (SON OF —) ELIEZER

DODDER SCAD SCALD SHAKE
DODDLE DOTHER FIDEOS TOTTER
TREMBLE FLAXDROP HAIRWEED
HALEWEED HELLWEED MULBERRY

DODDERING OLD ANILE INANE
INFIRM SENILE FOOLISH

DODDER LAUREL WOEVINE
MISTLETOE

DODDIE HUMLIE

DODECANESE (— ISLAND) KOS
SYME KASOS LEROS TELOS KHALKE
LIPSOS PATMOS NISYROS
KALYMNOS

DODGE RIG SHY BILK DUCK GAME
JINK JOUK LURK RUSE AVOID CHEAT
ELUDE EVADE FENCE FUDGE GLOSS
LURCH PARRY PLANT SHIFT SHIRK
SHUNT STALL TRICK ESCAPE FIDDLE
PALTER RACKET WHEEZE DECEIVE
EVASION PROFFER ARTIFICE
CROTCHET GILENYIE MALINGER
SIDESTEP

DODGER FLIER FLYER SOGER
HAGGLER HANDBILL
(DRAFT —) BUSHWACK

DODGING JINK

DODO (SON OF —) ELEAZAR
ELHANAN

DOE DA ROE TEG FAUN HIND NANNY
ALMOND BISCUIT
(— IN 1ST YEAR) FAWN
(BLUE —) FLIER FLYER

DOER ACTOR AGENT MAKER AUTHOR
FACTOR FEASOR WORKER FACIENT
MANAGER ATTORNEY EXECUTOR
(— OF ODD JOBS) JACK

(SUFF.) AST ATOR IST OR STER
STRESS

DOES S DOTH DUSE
(— NOT) DONT DISNA DOESNT

DOFF OFF DAFF VAIL AVALE DOUSE
DOWSE STRIP DIVEST REMOVE
UNDRESS

DOFFER DRUM DUFFER

DOFFING CAP

DOG CUR LAB MUT PUG PUP YAP
ALAN ALCO CHOW DANE FAUS GOER
HUND KIYI MONG MUTT PAWL STAG
TIKE TRAY TYKE ALAND ALANT
ARGOS BAWTY BEDOG BESET
BOUCH BOXER CALEB CANID CHIEN
CORGI DERBY DODGE HOUND
HUSKY LINER PELON POOCH PUPPY
RACHE RAKER RATCH SILKY SLING
SPITZ STALK WHELP AFGHAN
BANDOG BARBET BARKER BASSET
BAWTIE BEAGLE BELTON BORZOI
BOSTON BOWWOW BRIARD BUFFER
CANINE COCKER COLLIE COONER
DANCER DETENT DRIVER ESKIMO
FINDER GUNDOG HEADER HEELER
HUNTER JOWLER KELPIE KENNET
MISSET POODLE RANGER RATTER
SALUKI SEIZER SETTER SHADOW
SHOUGH SIRIUS SUSSEX TALBOT
TANUKI TOLLER TOWSER VIZSLA
YAPPER YAUPER YELPER BASENJI
BOARDER BULLDOG CARRIER
COURSER CRAMPON CREEPER
DOGGESS DROPPER GRIFFON
HARRIER LURCHER MALTESE
MASTIFF MONGREL OWTCHAH
POINTER SCOTTIE SHARPAI SKIRTER
SLEUGHI SPANIEL SPORTER STARTER
TERRIER TUMBLER WHIPPET
YAPSTER ABERDEEN AIREDALE
ALEUTANT ALSATIAN CERBERUS
COACHDOG COCKAPOO CYNHYENA
DEMIWOLF DOBERMAN ELKHOUND
FISSIPED FOXHOUND KEESHOND
LABRADOR LANDSEER LONGTAIL
MALEMUTE MALINOIS PAPILLON
PEKINESE SAMOYEDO SEALYHAM
SHEPHERD SIBERIAN SPRINGER
TURNSPIT VERMINER WATCHDOG
WATERRUG PEKINGESE
POMERANIAN AFFENPINSCHER
(— OF BUSTER BROWN) TIGE
(— OF INDIA) PARIAH
(— OF LATHE) DRIVER
(— OF ORPHAN ANNIE) SANDY
(— TRAINED AS DECOY) TOLLER
(BELGIAN —) SCHIPPERKE
(BIRD —) BOLTER
(CHAINED —) BANDOG
(CHINESE —) SHARPEI SHIHTZU
(COMICS —) OTTO
(COMMON NAME FOR —) ZEKE
(CORN —) FRANKFURTER

(DECOY —) PIPER
(ESKIMO —) HUSKY SIWASH
(FAMOUS —) ASTA FALA TIGE TOTO
(FARM —) KOMONDOR
(FEMALE —) GYP SLUT BITCH
DOGGESS
(FICTIONAL —) LAD TOBY SANDY
(FOXLIKE —) COLPEO
(GERMAN —) ROTTWEILER
(GUIDE —) SEEINGEYE
(HOUSE —) WAP WAPP
(HUNGARIAN —) PULI KUVASZ
(HUNTING —) ALAN BRACH RACHE
RATCH ALAUND BASSET HUNTER
KENNET LUCERN RACCHE SALUKI
SEIZER SETTER SLOUGH COURSER
DROPPER HARRIER POINTER STRIKER
(JAPANESE —) AKITA
(KIND OF —) FOO
(LAP —) MESSAN SHOUGH
(LARGE —) DANE TOWSER MASTIFF
KOMONDOR
(LIKE A —) CYNIC
(LONG-EARED —) BEAGLE
(LONG-HAIRED —) ALCO SHOCK
(MONGREL —) CUR BRAKJE
DEMIWOLF
(MOVIE —) ASTA LADY TOTO BENJI
TRAMP CHANCE LASSIE OLDYELLER
RINTINTIN
(NON-BARKING —) BASENJI
(PARTI-COLORED —) PIE PYE
(PART OF —) PAD PAW TOE ARCH
BACK DOME HOCK KNEE LOIN RUMP
STOP CHEEK CHEST CREST CROUP
ELBOW FLEWS THIGH CARPUS
DEWLAP MUZZLE STIFLE BRISKET
CUSHION KNUCKLE LEATHER
OCCIPUT PASTERN WITHERS
FOREHEAD HEELKNOB
(PET —) MINX LAPDOG MOPPET
(POPULAR — NAME) FIDO LADY SHEP
SPOT ROVER
(PRESIDENT'S —) FALA MINNIE
CHECKERS
(PUG —) MOPS
(PUNCH'S —) TOBY
(RACCOON —) TANUKI
(RUNNING —) LACKEY
(SHAGGY —) RUG OWTCHAH
(SHEEP —) CUR COLLIE KELPIE
BEARDIE MALINOIS SHEPHERD
(SHORT-BODIED —) PUG
(SMALL —) TOY FICE FIST DOGGY
FEIST LAIKA PIPER DOGGIE AMERTOY
SPANIEL PAPILLON PEKINESE
(VICIOUS —) TAEPO
(WATCH —) CUR GARM GARMR
(WELSH —) CORGI
(WILD —) ADJAG DHOLE DINGO
GUARA JACKAL AGOUARA
CIMARRON
(YELPING —) WAPPET

(PL.) DOGGERY
(PREF.) CYN(O)
DOGBANE KENDIR KENDYR ECHITES
FLYTRAP ALSTONIA MILKWEED
OLEANDER PERIWINKLE
DOGBOAT PIG
DOGCART GADDER TUMTUM
BOUNDER GADABOUT
DOG COLLAR TRASH
DOG DAYS CANICULE
DOG EAR LEATHER
DOG FENNEL HOGWEED
DOGFIGHT SCRAMBLE
DOGFISH DOG HOE HUSS TOPE
FLAKE HOUND HURSE MANGO
TOPER BOUNCE DAGGAR GALEID
MORGAY BONEDOG GABBACK
SPURDOG TRIAKID GRAYFISH
SEAHOUND
(PREF.) SCYLLIO SQUALI SQUALO
DOGGED DOUR SULLEN DOGGISH
DOGLIKE STUBBORN OBSTINATE
DOGGEREL NOMINY TRIVIA
DOGGREL SINGSONG
DOGGONE BLESSED DOWNGONE
DOGIE CALF LEPPY STRAY
DOG KEEPER FEWTERER
DOGLIKE CYNIC CYNOID DOGGED
DOGMA CREED TENET DICTUM
DOCTRINE DOCUMENT
DOGMATIC THETIC PONTIFIC
POSITIVE ARBITRARY CONFIDENT
PONTIFICAL
DOGMATISM BOWWOW
DOGMATIST BIGOT PHILODOX
DOG POUND GREENYARD
DOG ROSE BUCKY CANKER
BEDEGUAR DOGBERRY
DOG SALMON CHUM KETA
MORGAY DOGFISH
DOGSBODY DRUDGE
DOGSHORE DOG DAGGER
DOG'S MERCURY SAPWORT
DOG SNAPPER JOCU
DOGSTAIL BENT
DOGSTAR SIRIUS
DOGWOOD OSIER SUMAC CORNEL
CORNUS GAITER WIDBIN BARBASCO
FISHWOOD
DOILY MAT TIDE TIDY NAPKIN
DOING ACT DEED FACT STIR EVENT
ACTION FUNCTION PRACTIVE
(PL.) FARE GEAR
(SUFF.) ANT ENT PRACTIC PRAXIA
PRAXIS
DOIT DODKIN
DO-IT-YOURSELF DIY
DOLE LOT ALMS DEAL DOOL GIFT
GOAL METE PART VAIL ALLOT FRAUD
GRIEF GUILE MOURN POGEY SHARE
DECEIT GRIEVE RELIEF SORROW
CHARITY DEALING DESTINY
HANDOUT PAYMENT PORTION

BOUNDARY DIMENSUM DISPENSE
DIVISION GRATUITY LANDMARK
PITTANCE

DOLEFUL SAD DOWY DOWIE DREAR
HEAVY DISMAL DOOLFU DREARY
FUNEST RUEFUL FLEBILE DOLESOME
DOLOROUS FUNESTAL MOURNFUL
TRAGICAL

DOLERITE DIABASE

DOLICHOTIS MARA

DOLL GAL TOY BABE BABY MOLL
ARRAY DOLLY DOLLIE KEWPIE
MAIDEN MAUMET MOPPET MUNECA
POPPET POUPEE PUPPET KACHINA
KATCINA KATCHINA MISTRESS
(— UP) PRIMP SWANK
(PASTEBOARD —) PANTINE
(PREF.) PUPI

DOLLAR BALL BEAN BONE BUCK
CASE CLAM DURO FISH ROCK SCAD
SKIN SPOT ADOBE BERRY DALER
EAGLE PLONK PLUNK WHEEL
GOURDE PATACA DAALDER RINGGIT
SMACKER FROGSKIN PATACOON
SIMOLEON
(FIVE —S) NICKEL
(ONE MILLION —S) MEGABUCK
(SILVER —) SINKER
(SPANISH —) COB DURO COBBE
(TEN —S) DIME
(THOUSAND —S) GEE THOU GRAND

DOLLARFISH SHINER MOONFISH
STARFISH

DOLLOP GLOB

DOLL'S HOUSE
(AUTHOR OF —) IBSEN
(CHARACTER IN —) NORA RANK
HELMER LINDEN TORVALD
KROGSTAD CHRISTINA
(— CHARACTER) CHRISTINA

DOLLY DRAB HOBBY PEGGY PUNCH
SWAGE MAIDEN FOLLOWER
MISTRESS SLATTERN

DOLLYMAN BUCKER

DOLLYWAY DOCK

DOLMEN SENAM TOLMEN
CROMMEL CROMLECH MEGALITH

DOLOMITE ANKERITE PEARLSPAR

DOLOR CALOR GRIEF SORROW
ANGUISH SADNESS DISTRESS
MOURNING

DOLOROUS SAD DISMAL DOLEFUL
GRIEVOUS PATHETIC

DOLPHIN INIA SUSU BOUTO WHALE
DORADO KILLER PALACH TURSIO
BOLLARD COWFISH PELLOCK
PULLOCK SNUFFER CETACEAN
MAHIMAHI MUTILATE PORPOISE
(PREF.) DELPHIN DELPHO
(SUFF.) DELPHIS

DOLPHIN STRIKER MARTINGALE

DOLT ASS OAF PUT ASSE BOZO CALF
CHUB CLOD COOF DULT FOOL GOFF

MOKE PEAK POOP STUB BOOBY
CHUMP CLUNK DOBBY DUMMY
DUNCE FUNGE GOLEM IDIOT NUMPS
PATCH THICK BEFOOL CUDDEN
DIMWIT DOODLE DULTIE HOBBIL
NITWIT OXHEAD AIRHEAD BLUNTIE
DAWCOCK DULLARD JACKASS
SAPHEAD SCHNOOK BONEHEAD
BOSTHOON CLODPATE CLODPOLL
DUMBBELL IMBECILE LUNKHEAD
MACAROON MOONCALF NUMSKULL
LAMEBRAIN

DOLTISH DULL STUPID FOOLISH
PEAKISH SOTTISH TOMFOOL
BESOTTED BLOCKISH DOLTLIKE

DOMAIN LAND BOUND BOURN
REALM SCOPE STATE WORLD
BARONY BOURNE COUNTY DEMAIN
EMPERY EMPIRE ESTATE SPHERE
DEMESNE EARLDOM BIRTHDOM
DOMINION LORDSHIP PROVINCE
SEIGNORY STAROSTY
(— OF SULTAN) SOLDAN
(— OF THE UNCONSCIOUS)
SHADOWLAND
(MATHEMATICAL —) FIELD
(NETHER —) HELL
(TRANSCENDENT —) HEAVEN
(WOMAN'S —) DISTAFF

DOMBEYA ASSONIA

DOMBEY AND SON
(AUTHOR OF —) DICKENS
(CHARACTER IN —) GAY PAUL EDITH
CARKER CUTTLE DOMBEY WALTER
GRANGER FLORENCE

DOME CAP CIMA TYPE CROWN VAULT
COCKLE CUPOLA THOLOS CALOTTE
EDIFICE CIMBORIO HEMIDOME
(— OVER TOMB) WELI
(BUDDHIST —) TOPE
(KIND OF —) ONION
(OBSERVATION —) BLISTER
(POINTED —) IMPERIAL
(ROUND —) THOLUS
(SNOW-CAPPED —) CALOTTE

DOMER CLASPER

DOME-SHAPED BEEHIVE

DOMESTIC HIND HOME MAID MOZO
DOMAL TABBY FAMILY HAMEIL
HAMELT HEYDUC HOMELY HOMISH
HOUSAL INLAND INMATE INWARD
MENIAL NATIVE FAMELIC HEYDUCK
ONSHORE SCALDER SERVANT
FAMILIAR HOMEBRED HOMEMADE
INTIMATE
(PL.) FOLK

DOMESTICALLY ONSHORE

DOMESTICATE TAME ENTAME
AMENAGE RECLAIM CIVILIZE

DOMESTICATED CADE TAME
GENTLE INWARD DOMESTIC
FAMILIAR

DOMICILE CRIB HOME SHED ABODE
HOUSE MENAGE DWELLING
RESIDENCE
DOMINANCE SWAY INFLUENCE
DOMINANT BOSSY CHIEF FIFTH
TENOR MASTER RULING SOVRAN
CENTRAL REGNANT SUPREME
DOMINULE SUPERIOR PARAMOUNT
OVERBEARING PREPONDERANT
DOMINATE TOP BOSS HAVE RULE
CHARM REIGN COERCE DIRECT
GOVERN VASSAL BEWITCH
COMMAND CONTROL ENVELOP
POSSESS BESTRIDE DOMINEER
OVERRIDE OVERSWAY OVERTONE
(— THE MIND) POSSESS
(— THE WILL) MESMERIZE
DOMINATING SUPERIOR
BREATHLESS
DOMINATION EMPIRE CONTROL
STRINGS BOVARISM BOVARYSM
DOMINION POSSESSION
DOMINEER BOSS BRAG LORD RULE
BULLY FEAST REVEL TOWER COMPEL
COMMAND SWAGGER DOMINATE
OVERBEAR OVERLEAD OVERLORD
(— OVER) RIDE HECTOR
DOMINEERING SURLY LORDLY
HAUGHTY ARROGANT DESPOTIC
MASTERLY MASTERFUL
DOMINICA (CAPITAL OF —) ROSEAU
(MOUNTAIN PEAK IN —)
MORNEDIABLOTIN
DOMINICAN JACOBIN JACOBITE
PREACHER PREDICANT

DOMINIE MASTER PASTOR
DOMINION RULE SWAY CROWN
REALM REIGN DITION DOMAIN
EMPERY EMPIRE REGNUM CONTROL
DIOCESE DYNASTY KHANATE
MASTERY POUSTIE REGENCY
CALIFATE IMPERIUM LORDSHIP
SEIGNORY SIGNORIA SOVRANTY
OBEDIENCE
(PL.) DUCHY
DOMINO DIE BONE CARD FIVE MASK
TILE BLANK JETON STONE DOUBLE
JETTON MATADOR VENETIAN
(FIRST — PLAYED) SET
(PL.) MATATADOR MUGGINS
BONEYARD
DOMINO NOIR, LE (COMPOSER OF
—) AUBER
DOMITILLA (DAUGHTER OF —)
DOMITILLA
(HUSBAND OF —) VESPASIAN
(SON OF —) TITUS DOMITIAN
DOM PEDRO SNOOZER
DON CAPO WEAR ARRAY DRESS
ENDUE INDUE PUTON THROW
ASSUME CLOTHE INVEST ADDRESS
NOBLEMAN
DONALBAIN (FATHER OF —)
DUNCAN
DONATE GIE GIFT GIVE BESTOW
PRESENT
DONATION GIFT GRANT DONATIO
PRESENT DONATIVE BENEFACTION
(—S RECEIVED BY SINGERS) CARL
DON CARLOS (CHARACTER IN —)
EBOLI CARLOS PHILIP VALOIS
CHARLES RODRIGO ELISABETH
(COMPOSER OF —) VERDI
DONE GAR DEEN OVER BAKED
ENDED GIVEN COOKED THROUGH
FINISHED
(— AS DUTY) PERFUNCTORY
(— BY HAND) MANUAL
(— BY WORD OF MOUTH) PAROL
PAROLE
(— CARELESSLY) SCAMBLING
(— FOR) GONE SUNK KAPUT KAPUTT
FINISHED
(— IN FAITH) AF
(— IN PLAIN SIGHT) BRAZEN
(— POORLY) BOTCHY
(— THOROUGHLY) PERFECT
(— TOGETHER) CONCERTED
(— WITH) BY
(— WITHOUT DELIBERATION) SNAP
(— WRONG WAY) AWK
(TO BE —) PASS
DONEE DONATOR HERITOR RECEIVER
DON GIOVANNI
(CHARACTER IN —) ANNA ELVIRA
MASETTO OTTAVIO ZERLINA
GIOVANNI LEPORELLO
(COMPOSER OF —) MOZART
DONJON KEEP ROCCA DUNGEON
DON JUAN (MOTHER OF —) INEZ

DONKEY ASS BUSS DONK FUSS MOKE BURRO CHUMP CUDDY DICKY EQUID GENET GUDDA HINNY HORSE JENNY NEDDY BRAYER CUDDLE DICKEY JENNET ONAGER ASINEGO BUSSOCK FUSSOCK JACKASS LONGEAR CARDOPHAGUS
(MILNE —) EEYORE

DONKEY ENGINE DOCTOR DONKEY ROADER YARDER DOLLBEER

DONNA DEL LAGO (CHARACTER IN —) ELENA DOUGLAS GIACOMO MALCOLM RODERICK
(COMPOSER OF —) ROSSINI

DONNA DIANA (COMPOSER OF —) REZNICEK

DONNYBROOK MELEE

DONOR GIVER DONATOR

DO-NOTHING DONNOT DONOUGHT FAINEANT

DON PASQUALE (CHARACTER IN —) NORINA ERNESTO PASQUALE SOFRONIA MALATESTA
(COMPOSER OF —) DONIZETTI

DON QUIXOTE (AUTHOR OF —) CERVANTES
(CHARACTER IN —) PANZA PEDRO PEREZ ALONZO DAPPLE SAMSON SANCHO TOBOSO GUINART QUIXOTE CARRASCO DULCINEA NICHOLAS ROSINANTE

DONUM GIVER DEUNAM

DOODAD DODAD DOODAB DOFUNNY TRINKET GIMCRACK JIMCRACK

DOOHICKEY GISMO

DOOM KER LAW LOT DAMN FATE RUIN CURSE DEATH JUDGE ADDEEM DECREE DEVOTE STEVEN CONDEMN DESTINE DESTINY FORTUNE STATUTE DECISION FOREDOOM SENTENCE

DOOMED FEY DEAD DONE LORN FATAL DAMNED FORLORN ACCURSED FINISHED

DOOM PALM DOUM

DOOMSAYER DOOMSTER DOOMSDAYER

DOOMSMAN LAWMAN

DOOMSTER JUDGE

DOOR LID DROP EXIT FOLD GATE HECK SHUT TRAP ENTRY HATCH JANUA VALVE DAMPER JIGGER PORTAL RADDLE WICKET BARRIER DOORWAY INGRESS OPENING OUTDOOR PASSAGE POSTERN ANTEPORT ENTRANCE FOREDOOR POSTICUM SERVIDOR STOPPING TRAVERSE VOMITORY
(— IN MINE) STOPPING
(— OF ASH PIT) ARCH
(— OF MASONIC LODGE) TILE
(ADIT —) STULM

(AIRPLANE —) CLAMSHELL
(HALF —) HECK HATCH
(PART OF —) RAIL SILL STILE LINTEL MULLION
(ROMAN —S) FORES
(SLIDING —) SHUT SHOJI FUSUMA TRAVERSE
(STORM —) DINGLE
(STRONG —) OAK
(TRAP —) SLOT SCRUTO VAMPIRE VAMPYRE
(PREF.) THYRE(O) THYRO
(SUFF.) THYRIS

DOORFRAME BUCK

DOORHEAD DERNER

DOORKEEPER TILER TILIA USHER DURWAN PORTER WARDEN DOORMAN JANITOR OSTIARY DOORWARD HUISSIER JANITRIX PORTRESS WISKINKY

DOOR KNOCKER HAMMER RAPPER

DOOR LATCH SNECK HAGGADAY

DOORMAN FOOTMAN HALLMAN DOORWARD

DOORMAT COCOMAT

DOORPOST DURN JAMB PIER POST ALETTE POSTEL

DOORSILL SOIL

DOORSTOP BUMPER HOLDBACK

DOORWAY DOOR EXIT PORTAL OPENING

DOOZER PIP DARB LULU BEAUT DILLY CORKER SNORTER HUMDINGER

DOOZY LULU HUMDINGER

DOPATTA UPARNA DOOPUTTY

DOPE HOP LUG BOOB DRUG GOFF GOON GOOP INFO BOOBY OPIUM PASTE STUPE HEROIN INSIDE OPIATE SKINNY LOWDOWN PREDICT STUPEFY NARCOTIC
(— SMUGGLER) MULE

DOPED CRONK

DOPER GREASER

DOR BEE DORR JOKE MOCK BONGO CLOCK DORRE JOKER SCOFF TRICK BEETLE DRONER BUFFOON DECEIVE MOCKERY

DORADO CUIR XIPHIAS GOLDFISH

DORALICE (HUSBAND OF —) PHODOPHIL MANDRICARDO
(LOVER OF —) RODOMONT

DORBEETLE DOR CLOCK DRONER BUZZARD BUMCLOCK

DORIGEN (HUSBAND OF —) ARVIRAGUS
(LOVER OF —) AURELIUS

DORIMENE (HUSBAND OF —) SGANARELLE
(LOVER OF —) DORANTE

DORINDA (HUSBAND OF —) AIMWELL
(SISTER OF —) MIRANDA

DORIS (BROTHER AND HUSBAND OF
—) NEREUS
(FATHER OF —) OCEANUS
(MOTHER OF —) TETHYS
DORK JERK NERD DWEEB
DORMANCY TORPOR ABEYANCE
DORMANT FIXED INERT ASLEEP
LATENT TORPID RESTING SLEEPER
INACTIVE LATITANT SLEEPING
CONNIVENT
DORMER WINDOW LUCOMB
MEMBER DORMANT EYEBROW
LUCARNE LUTHERN
DORMITORY DORM HALL HOUSE
DORMER DORTER HOSTEL BULLPEN
COLLEGE DORTOUR CUBATORY
QUARTERS
DORMOUSE LOIR DRYAD LEROT
GLIRID SLEEPER
(PREF.) GLIRI
DORNICK DONEY LINEN DARNEX
DONACK DONNICK
DORPER DORSIAN
DORSAL NOTAL DORSER DOSSER
NEURAL TERGAL ABAXIAL HANGING
SUPERIOR POSTERIOR
(PREF.) OPISTH(O)
DORSUM BACK
DORUS (BROTHER OF —) LAODOCUS
POLYPOETES
(FATHER OF —) APOLLO HELLEN
XUTHUS
(MOTHER OF —) CREUSA ORSEIS
PHTHIA
(SLAYER OF —) AETOLUS
DOSAGE (RADIATION —) REM REP
REPP
(SCIENCE OF —) POSOLOGY
DOSE BOLE DOST SHOT BROMO
DATIO DOSIS DRAFT STORE TREAT
DATION DOCTOR DOSAGE DRENCH
POTION BOOSTER BROMIDE
CAPSULE DRAUGHT QUANTITY
(— OF SUBSTANCE) PULSE
(DRUG —) HIT
(NARCOTIC —) LOCUS BINDLE
LOCUST
DOSS BOW DOS KNOT TUFT
BUNCH
DOSSERET PULVINO
DOT SET CLOT DOTE LUMP MOTE
PECK SPOT STAR TICK COVER
DOWER DOWRY POINT PRICK PUNTO
SPECK BULLET CENTER CENTRE
DOTLET PERIOD STIGME TITTLE
TOCHER PUNCTUM PUNCTUS
SPECKLE SPOTTLE STIPPLE
FLYSPECK PARTICLE SPRINKLE
(— IN CODE) DIT
(— ON DICE) PIP
(— ON FOREHEAD) BOTTU
(— ON PATCH OF DIFFERENT COLOR)
ISLET

(BLACK —) DARTROSE
(PL.) LEADERS
DOTAGE DOTE FOLLY DRIVEL
SENILITY TWICHILD
DOTARD DOBBY DOTER SILLY DOBBIE
DOTANT SENILE DOTTREL DOTTEREL
IMBECILE LIRIPIPE LIRIPOOP
DOTCHIN STEELYARD
DOTE ROT DOVE DOZE FOND LIKE
LOVE TIRE ADORE DECAY ENDOW
BESTOW DOTAGE DOTARD DRIVEL
STUPOR IMBECILE
DOTING FON FOND GAGA DOTAGE
PAWING UXORIOUS
DOTTED SEME CRIBLE SEMEED
TICKED TOUCHY SPOTTED PUNCTATE
SPECKLED STIPPLED STELLATED
(— SWISS) LAPPET
DOTTER SPOTTER
DOTTEREL DUPE GULL WIND
PLOVER DOTTREL MORINEL
DOTTY TOTY CRAZY TOTTY FEEBLE
SPOTTY
DOUBLE KA BOW PLY DUAL FOLD
SORE TWIN CRACK DUPLE FETCH
ROUND SOSIE BIFOLD BINARY
BINATE DOPPIO DUPLEX MIDDLE
DIPLOID DOUBLET TWOFOLD
BIVALENT GEMINATE BIFARIOUS
SIMILITUDE
(— IMPRESSION) MACKLE
(— IN POKER) STRADDLE
(— MUSICAL NOTES) AUGMENT
(— UP) BUCK JACKKNIFE
(PHANTOM —) FETCH
(PREF.) BI BIN(I)(O) DI(S) DIPHY
DIPL(O) DISS(O) DITTO GEMINI
DOUBLE BASSOON FAGOTTONE
DOUBLE CHIN CHOLLER
DOUBLECROSS BITCH CHEAT
BETRAY DECEIVE SWINDLE
BUSINESS
DOUBLE-CROSSER RAT HEEL
DOUBLED GEMEL GEMINOUS
(PREF.) BIS
DOUBLE DAGGER DIESIS
DOUBLE-DEALING DECEIT
DUPLICITY
DOUBLE FLUTE DIAULOS
DOUBLEHEADER
(BASEBALL —) TWINIGHT
DOUBLENESS DUALITY PLENITUDE
(— OF ASPECT) POLARITY
DOUBLE-RIPPER BOBSLED
BOBSLEIGH
DOUBLE-RUNNER SKATE
DOUBLET SNIFF DOUBLE DUPLET
PALTOCK PLACCATE POURPOINT
DOUBLE-TALK NEWSPEAK
RAZZMATAZZ
DOUBLETREE EVENER SPREADER
DOUDLING LAP FOLD HEAD LOOP
(— OF THE BLIND) STRADDLE

DOUBLOON ONZA
DOUBLY
(PREF.) BI
DOUBT FEAR WEIR DEMUR DREAD
DWERE QUERY WAVER NIGGLE
BALANCE DIFFIDE DUBIETY SCRUPLE
SKEPSIS SUSPECT SWITHER
UMBRAGE DISTRUST DUBITATE
HESITATE MISTRUST QUESTION
STAGGERS MISLIPPEN
(EXTREME —) RACK
(PROFESSED —) APORIA
DOUBTER CYNIC SKEPTIC
DUBITANTE
DOUBTFUL JUBUS DOUBTY
UNSURE DUBIOUS FEARFUL
JEALOUS PERHAPS WILSOME
BOGGLISH DREADFUL JUBEROUS
PERILOUS WAVERING
QUESTIONABLE PROBLEMATICAL
DOUBTING DUBIOUS DUBITANT
DOUBTLESS WITTERLY
DOUCEUR TIP BONUS POURBOIRE
DOUCHE RINSE EYEWASH
DOUGH CASH DUFF FILO MASA
CRUST DAIGH MONEY MOOLA PASTE
PUPPY CHANGE DINERO HALLAH
NOODLE PHYLLO SPONGE WAMPUM
BRIOCHE CABBAGE MANDLEN
TEIGLACH
(BISCUIT —) CAKE
(BREAD —) SPONGE
(CASE OF —) PIROGI PIEROGI
(FERMENTING —) LEAVEN
(FRIED —) SPUD
(NOODLE —) FARFEL FERFEL
(PASTRY —) PHYLLO
(SWEET SQUARE OF —) SOPAPILLA
SOPAPILLA
DOUGHBOY YANK
DOUGHNUT NUT SINK DONUT
TORUS CYMBAL SINKER BEIGNET
CRULLER FATCAKE NUTCAKE
OLYCOOK OLYKOEK SIMBALL
TWISTER ZEPPOLE BISMARCK
FASNACHT
(SHAPED LIKE —) TOROIDAL
DOUGHTY FELL PREU TALL BRAVE
VALIANT INTREPID
DOUGHY SAD DUNCH SODDEN
DOUR DERN GLUM GRIM HARD SOUR
ROUGH STERN GLOOMY MOROSE
SEVERE STRONG SULLEN OMINOUS
TACITURN
DOUSE BEAT BLOW DOFF DUCK QUIT
STOW CEASE DOWSE RINSE SOUSE
DRENCH PLUNGE SLUICE STRIKE
STROKE IMMERSE DOWNPOUR
(— WITH LIQUOR AND IGNITE)
FLAMBE
DOUZEPER ANSEIS PALADIN
DOVE DOO DOW DOZE KUKU JONAH
CULVER CUSHAT JEMIMA PIGEON

COLUMBA DOVELET LAUGHER
NAMAQUA SLUMBER DOVELING
RINGDOVE
(— SOUND) CURR
(GROUND —) ROLA
(RING —) TOOZOO
(ROCK —) SOD
(SCALE —) INCA
DOVECOTE DOOCOT LOUVER
DOVECOT DOWCOTE PIGEONRY
COLUMBARY
DOVEKIE AUK ALLE BULL ROTCH
ROTGE DOVEKEY BULLBIRD
DOVELIKE
DOVETAIL COG JAG JAGG MESH
MERGE TENON
DOWDINESS FRUMPERY
DOWDY POKY FRUMP MOPSY POKEY
TACKY BLOWZY SHABBY STODGY
UNTIDY FRUMPISH SLOVENLY
DOWEL NOG PEG PIN COAK STUD
SPRIG JOGGLE PINTLE DULEDGE
DOWER DOS DOWRY ENDOW
TOCHER DOARIUM PORTION
HERITAGE MARITAGE
DOWITCHER SNIPE DRIVER SLEEPER
GRAYBACK GREYBACK LONGBEAK
DOWN BAS EAT HUP OFF BETE CAST
COOL DOON DOWL FELL FLIX FLUE
FUZZ HILL LINT MOXA PILE SOUR
ADOWN BELOW DOWLE EIDER
FLOOR FLUFF SOUTH BEDOWN
FRIEZE LANUGO PAPPUS CONSUME
HANDOUT HILLOCK PLUMAGE
DOWNLAND
(— AND OUT) QUISBY
(— AT THE HEEL) SLIPSHOD
(— THAT WAY) DOWNBY DOWNBYE
(— THE LINE) ALONG
(BE — WITH) HAVE
(BEAVER —) FLIX
(FAR —) DEEP DEEPLY
(FARTHEST —) BOTTOMMOST
(GO —) SET
(STRAIGHT —) DOWNRIGHT
(PREF.) CAT(A)(O) CATH DE HYPO
KAT(A) LACHN(O) OB PTIL(O) SUB
DOWN-AND-OUT DERELICT
DOWNBEAT THESIS
DOWNCAST BAD LOW SAD DOWN
ABJECT GLOOMY HANGING
DEJECTED HOPELESS
DOWNER DRAG
DOWNFALL PIT FALL FATE RUIN
TRAP ABYSS DECAY FINISH DESCENT
ECLIPSE UNDOING COLLAPSE
DOWNCOME FLAMEOUT TAILSPIN
(AUTHOR OF —) ZOLA
(CHARACTER IN —) JEAN WEISS
HONORE GOLIATH GUNTHER
MAURICE SILVINE FOUCHARD
MACQUART HENRIETTE LEVASSEUR
DELAHERCHE GARTLAUBEN

DOWNFEED OVERHEAD
DOWNFLOW VAIL DEFLUX
DOWNFOLD SADDLE DOWNWARP
DOWNGRADE DERATE
DOWNHILL DOWNDALE
  (SKI —) WEDEL
DOWN-HOME CORNPONE
DOWNPOUR POUR RAIN BRASH
  DOUSE DOWSE FLOOD PLASH SPILL
  SPOUT DELUGE TORRENT CATARACT
  AVALANCHE
DOWNRIGHT FAIR FLAT PURE RANK
  BLANK BLUNT PLAIN PLUMB PLUMP
  ROUND SHEER STARK ARRANT
  DIRECT FAIRLY STURDY REGULAR
  ABSOLUTE EVENDOWN POSITIVE
  THOROUGH
DOWNSPOUT SPOUT DOWNPIPE
  DOWNTAKE
DOWNSTAIRS BELOW
DOWNSTROKE DOWNBEAT
DOWNSWING DOLDRUMS
DOWNWARD ADOWN BELOW
  LOWER PRONE DEORSUM
  DOWNWITH
  (— ON ONE SIDE) SIDEWAYS
  (PREF.) BATH(O)(Y) CAT(A)(O) CATH
DOWNWIND LEEWARD
DOWNY SOFT FLUEY MOSSY NAPPY
  PILAR PLUMY QUIET CALLOW
  FLEDGY FLOSSY FLUFFY PILARY
  PLACID COTTONY CUNNING
  KNOWING SOOTHING
  (PREF.) HERE
DOWRY DOS DOT GIFT DOWER
  SULKA DOWAGE LOROLA LOBOLO
  TALENT PORTION
DOWSE WITCH
DOXOLOGIZE LAUD
DOXOLOGY GLORIA KADDISH
DOXY WENCH HARLOT
DOYEN DEAN DOYENNE
DOZE NAP NOD ROT DARE DORM
  DOTE DOVE DECAY DOVER SLEEP
  SLOOM CATNAP DROWSE MUDDLE
  SNOOZE DROPOFF MEMENTO
  PERPLEX SLUMBER SNOOZLE
  STUPEFY
DOZEN DIZZEN DOSAIN
  (FIVE —) TALLY
  (TWO —) THRAVE
DOZING DOGSLEEP
DRAB BOX DAW FOX SAD BLAH DELL
  DRUG DULL BESOM BLEAK DINGY
  DOLLY DREAR GRAVE GRAZE HEAVY
  MOUSY TRULL WENCH WHORE
  DREARY FRUMPY ISABEL MALKIN
  POISON PUSSEL STODGY PROSAIC
  PUCELLE SUBFUSC DOLLYMOP
  EVERYDAY POMPLESS
  (CHAETURA —) BEAR
DRABBLE DRAGGLE
DRACHM DRAM

DRACO ANGUIS DRAGON
DRAFT NIP SIP CHIT DOSE DRAG
  DRAM DRAW GLUT GULF GUST ITEM
  LEVY PLAN PLOT SUCK SWIG TOOT
  WORK BLAST CHECK DRINK EPURE
  SLOCK SWILL SWIPE TAPER WRITE
  DESIGN DRENCH GODOWN MINUTE
  POTION PROJET REDACT RETURN
  SCHEME SCROLL SKETCH WAUCHT
  WAUGHT ABBOZZO DRAUGHT
  DRAWING OUTLINE PATTERN
  PHILTER PROJECT BEVERAGE
  POTATION PROTOCOL
  (— OF AIR) COOKE
  (— OF A VESSEL) GAGE GAUGE
  (— OF COMPOSITION) SCORE
  (— OFF) SHED
  (— OF LAW) BILL
  (— OF PATTERN) STRIP
  (HEAVY —) WHITTER
  (LARGE —) SCOUR CAROUSE
  (MIDDAY —) NOONING
  (ORIGINAL —) PROTOCOL
  (ROUGH —) EBAUCHE BROUILLON
  SCANTLING
  (SECOND —) REDO REWRITE
  (SLEEPING —) DORTER
  (SMALL —) NIP SIP SUCK TIFF TIFT
DRAFTER HORSER
DRAFTSMAN DRAWER TRACER
  TIPPLER
DRAG DOG LAG TOW DRUG HALE
  HONE HOOK KITE RASH SHOE OKID
  SLUR TOLE TOLL TUMP CREEP
  DEVIL DRAWL DRIFT FLOAT GETUP
  LURRY NOWEL PLUCK RALLY GLIDE
  SNAKE SWEEP TEASE TRAIL TRAIN
  TRAWL TRICE DAGGLE DOWNER
  DROGUE LINGER OUTFIT REMORA
  SCHOOL TAIGLE TRAYNE DRAGBAR
  DRAGGLE GRAPNEL GRAPPLE
  SCHLEPP SKIDPAN ARRASTRA
  DRAGSHOE
  (— ALONG) LUG CRAWL SHOOL
  TRAYNE TRACHLE TRAUCHLE
  (— CARELESSLY) HIKE
  (— DOWN) DEGRADE
  (— FEET) SLODGE
  (— FORCIBLY) SNAKE
  (— HOME CARCASS OF GAME) TUMP
  (— IN DEEP WATER) CREEP
  (— JERKILY) SNIG
  (— LOGS) SKID
  (— OFF) HARRY
  (— OUT) DRAWL
  (PLANK —) RUBBER
DRAGGING LEADEN
  (— DEAD BULL FROM RING)
  ARRASTRE
DRAGGLE LAG DRAIL DAGGLE
  DRABBLE TRACHLE
DRAGNET FLUE TRAIN TRAWL
  DRAWNET TRAINEL

DRAGON AHI LUNG WORM DRAKE RAHAB NIDHOG VRITRA WYVERN BASILISK DRAGONET NIDHOGGR NITHHOGG
(— WITH 7 HEADS) HYDRA
(SEA —) QUAVIVER
(WINGLESS —) LINDWORM
(PREF.) DRACO(NT)(NTO)

DRAGONET FOX ILLECK FOXFISH GOWDNIE GURNARD JUGULAR SCULPIN LORICATE QUAVIVER

DRAGONFLY NAIAD ODONATE SKIMMER LIBELLULA

DRAGON TREE DRACAENA

DRAGROPE DRAG GUSS

DRAGSTER FUELER SLINGSHOT

DRAIN DRY FRY GAN GAW SEW TOP BUZZ COUP DAIL DALE DELF DIKE DRAG DRAW GOUT GRIP GURT LADE LODE MILK SIKE SINK SOAK SUFF SUMP TEEM TILE BLEED BUNNY CANAL DELFT DRAFT DREEN DRILL DROVE EMPTY FLEET GROOP GULLY LEECH RHINE SEUCH SEUGH SEWER SHORE SIVER STANK STELL EMULGE FILTER FURROW GUZZLE RIGGOT SHEUCH SHEUGH SIPHON SPONGE SWOUGH SYPHON TRENCH TROGUE TROUGH ZANJON ACEQUIA ALBERCA CAROUSE CARRIER CHANNEL CULVERT DEPLETE DRAUGHT EXHAUST GRINDLE GRIPPLE SCUPPER ZANJONA CANALIZE CARRIAGE SINKHOLE SUBDRAIN THURROCK
(— DRY) JIB
(— IN CHURCH) PISCINA
(— IN FEN) LEAM
(— IN MINE) SOUGH
(— IN STABLE) GROOP
(— SUGAR) POT
(COVERED —) THURROCK
(OPEN —) SIVER STELL KENNEL
(SMALL —) TRONE

DRAINAGE ADIT SAUR SOCK SULLAGE SUMPAGE

DRAINAGEWAY DRAW

DRAINER COLANDER

DRAINING SEEPAGE DRAINAGE EMULGENT

DRAINPIPE SINK SHELL WHELM LEADER QUELME

DRAKE STAG STAIG DRAKELET

DRAM GO NIP MITE SLUG TIFF TIFT DRAFT DRINK SOPIE CALKER CHASSE DRACHM JIGGER CAULKER SNIFTER MERIDIAN POTATION QUANTITY
(— OF LIQUOR) TOT SLUG SNIFTER
(— OF SPIRITS) NOBBLER

DRAMA RAS AUTO MIME PLAY LEGIT OPERA COMEDY NATAKA SCENES SOAPER TRAGIC ATELLAN COMEDIA HISTORY PROVERB THEATRE TRAGEDY DUODRAMA MONODRAM OPERETTA PASTORAL
(DANCE —) KATHAKALI
(JAPANESE —) NO NOH KABUKI
(MUSICAL —) OPERA SAYNETE OPERETTA

DRAMATIC WILD VIVID SCENIC THESPIAN
(— REPRESENTATION) WAYANG
(— WORK) PREQUEL
(HAVING LYRIC AND — QUALITIES) SPINTO

DRAMATIST (ALSO SEE PLAYWRIGHT) OG ACTOR IBSENITE

DRAMSHOP GROGSHOP

DRAPE HANG PALL VEST ADORN COVER CRAPE WEAVE CURTAIN FESTOON HANGING VALANCE

DRAPED BEHUNG

DRAPER TAILOR LINENMAN

DRAPERY SWAG BAIZE DRAPE SCENE CURTAIN REREDOS VALANCE MOURNING
(— ON BEDSTEAD) PAND
(PIECE OF —) HANGING

DRAPING BLOUSE DRAPERY

DRASTIC DIRE HARSH EXTREME RADICAL RIGOROUS
(NOT —) BLAND

DRAT DARN NUTS RATS PSHAW PHOOEY RABBIT SHUCKS DOGGONE

DRATTED BLESSED

DRAUGHT (ALSO SEE DRAFT) SLUG WAUGHT OENOMEL

DRAUPADI (FATHER OF —) DRUPADA

DRAVIDIAN GOND KOTA TODA TULU ARAVA COORG GONDI KHOND KLING MALTO ORAON TAMIL ANDHRA BADAGA BIRHOR BRAHUI KODAGU KURUKH TELEGU TELUGU COLLERY DRAVIDA TAMILIC KANARESE TAMILIAN

DRAW LUG TAG TEE TIE TOW TUG DRAG DUCT HALE HAUL LADE LIMN LINE LURE PUFF PULL RAKE SPAN TILL TIRE TOLL TREK VENT CATCH DRAFT DRILL EDUCE ENDUE EXACT HEAVE PAINT SKINK TRACE TRAIN TRECK ALLURE BUCKET DEDUCE DEPICT DERIVE DESIGN DEVISE ELICIT ENGAGE ENTICE INDUCE INHALE SELECT SKETCH STRIKE ATTRACT BEGUILE CONTOUR DETRACT DOGFALL DRAUGHT EXTRACT INSPIRE PORTRAY SCREEVE SCUMBLE INSCRIBE INVEIGLE OUTBRAID STANDOFF
(— A CARD) CUT
(— AIR) BREATHE
(— ALONG) TRACK TRAIN
(— APART) REAM DIVEL DIDUCE DIVERGE
(— ASIDE) SEDUCE

(— ASUNDER) TEAR
(— AT A PIPE) SHOOH SHAUGH
(— AWAY) ARACE DRAFT ABDUCT
ARACHE DRAUGHT ENTRAIN
ABSTRACT DISTRACT
(— AWKWARDLY) SCRAWL
(— BACK) FADE REVEL START WINCE
ARREAR RETIRE REVOKE SHRINK
CRINKLE RECLAIM RETRACT RETREAT
WITHTEE
(— BACK FROM) BLENCH FLINCH
RESILE TORFEL TORFLE DETRECT
(— BACK LIPS) GRIN
(— BOLT) SLOT
(— BY SUCTION) ASPIRATE
(— DEEP BREATH) SUSPIRE
(— DRINK) BIRL
(— EARTH AROUND) HILL
(— FIRST FURROW) FEER
(— FORTH) EDUCE EVOKE FETCH
ELICIT DEPROME EXHAUST
(— IN) PINK TRAP ENTRAP
(— IN DOTS) STIPPLLE
(— OFF) BROACH
(— ON) INDUE INDUCE SOLICIT
(— ON PAVEMENT) SCREEVE
(— ON UNCOLLECTED FUNDS) KITE
(— OUT) MILK SLUB EDUCE EVOKE
EXACT SKINK TRACT ELICIT EXHALE
EXTEND EXTORT EXTRACT
(— STITCHES TIGHT) YERK
(— TIGHT) FRAP THRAP STRAIN
(— TOGETHER) COWL LACE COART
GATHER CRIMPLE
(— UP) FORM MAKE HUCKLE INKNIT
UPWALE
(— WITH FORCE) STRAIN
DRAWBACK OUT LETDOWN
TAKEOFF DISCOUNT PULLBACK
DRAWBAR DRAGBAR BULLNOSE
DRAWLINK SLIPRAIL
DRAWBRIDGE PONTLEVIS
DRAWEE ACCEPTER
DRAWER TILL LIMNER LOCKER
TILLER ENTERER INTAKER SHUTTLE
(— OF WATER) GIBEONITE
(BOTTOM —) GLORYBOX
(CASH —) TILL
(COAL —) PUTTER
(TYPEWRITER —) BED
DRAWER-DOWN KNOBBLER
DRAWER-IN ENTERER HEALDER
HEDDLER
DRAWER-OFF RACKER
DRAWERS PANTS SHORTS LININGS
PANTIES SHALWAR CALSOUNS
CALZOONS SHINTYAN PANTALETS
PANTELETS SHULWAURS
PANTAI ETTES
DRAWGATE SLACKER
DRAWING DRAW CHALK DRAFT
ENVOI EPURE SEPIA TUSHE CRAYON
DESIGN DETAIL FIGURE FUSAIN

SKETCH CAMAIEU CARTOON
CROQUIS DIAGRAM DRAUGHT
HAULING ISOTYPE PULLING RETRAIT
TOUSCHE ADDUCENT CHARCOAL
CROSSING DOODLING FREEHAND
FROTTAGE HATCHING LINEWORK
SANGUINE SLUBBING SPECULUM
STICKMAN TRACTION TRANSFER
TRICKING
(— ASUNDER) DIVELLENT
(— BACK) ABDUCENT
(— IN) INDRAFT
(— IN RED CHALK) SANGUINE
(— LIQUOR) BIRLING
(— OFF) DERIVATION
(— OF LOTS) BALLOT
(— OUT) BATTUE
(— TOGETHER) STYPTIC
(CHARCOAL —) FUSAIN
(COMIC —) CARTOON DROLLERY
(MARGINAL —) REMARK
(PREHISTORIC —) PICTOGRAM
PICTOGRAPH
(PREPARATORY —) SINOPIA
(SIDEWALK —) SCREEVE
(PL.) GRAFFITI
(PREF.) GRAMO
(SUFF.) GRAM
DRAWING-IN DRAW ENTERING
DRAWING-ROOM SALON
DRAWING ROOM SALON PARLOR
DRAWKNIFE SHAVE JIGGER
DRAWL DRANT DRATE DRUNT TRAIN
LOITER PROLATE
DRAWN DRAFT STREIT DRAUGHT
GRAPHIC HAGGARD
(— APART) DISTRACT
(— AWAY) ABSTRACT
(— CLOSE) STRICT
(— OFF) DRAINED
(— OUT) DREE DREICH DREIGH
EXTENDED
DRAWPLATE AGATE FLATTER
DRAWSHEET TYMPAN
DRAWSTRING LATCH STRING
DRAY CART LORRY SCOOT SLOOP
WAGON CAMION JIGGER ROLLEY
RULLEY SLOVEN WHEERY
DREAD AWE DREE FEAR FRAY FUNK
WARD WERE ANGST AWFUL DOUBT
GRISE TIMOR ADREAD AGRISE
DISMAY ESCHEW HORROR TERROR
ANXIETY DISMISS DRIDDER
REDOUBT AFFRIGHT DREDDOUR
GASTNESS MISDREAD TERRIBLE
(SUFF.) PHOBE PHOBIA(C) PHOBIC
PHOBOUS
DREADED AWESOME BEDREAD
DREADFUL DERN DIRE AWFUL CRUEL
DISMAL GRISLY HORRID AWESOME
CARFFUL DIREFUL DRIDDER FEARFUL
GHASTLY GRIMFUL HIDEOUS
UNCOUTH DOUBTFUL DOUBTOUS

GHASTFUL HORRIBLE HORRIFIC
PERILOUS SCAREFUL SHOCKING
TERRIBLE TERRIFIC
DREADFULLY DIRELY GRISLY
ABYSMALLY
DREADNOUGHT TANK DAREALL
WARSHIP FEARLESS
DREAM METE MOON MUSE REVE
FANCY SWEVEN VISION AISLING
AVISION CHIMERA FANTASY
IMAGINE NIRVANA REVERIE
ROMANCE CHIMAERA DAYDREAM
PHANTASM SOMNIATE
(— UP) ENVISION
(FRIGHTENING —) NIGHTMARE
(PREF.) ONEIR(O) ONIR(O)
DREAMER POET METER MUSARD
FANTAST IDEALIST PHANTAST
DREAMINESS LANGUOR
DREAMING ADREAM TRAUMEREI
DREAMTIME ALCHERA
DREAMY KEF SOFT MOONY VAGUE
POETIC FARAWAY LANGUID
MUSEFUL ONEIRIC PENSIVE
DREAMFUL FANCIFUL SOOTHING
DREAR DERN BLEAK DISMAL
GLOOMY DOLEFUL
DREARY SAD DIRE DOWY DREE DULL
FLAT GLUM BLEAK CRUEL DOWIE
DRURY OURIE WASTE WISHT DISMAL
DREICH ELENGE GLOOMY GOUSTY
LONELY DOLEFUL GOUSTIE
HOWLING WILSOME GRIEVOUS
WEARIFUL
DREDGE MOP DRAG DREG SIFT
SCOOP TRAIN DEEPEN DRUDGE
SCRAPE SPONGE TANGLE GANGAVA
SCALLOP EXCAVATE SPRINKLE
(KIND OF —) EKMAN
(NATURALIST'S —) TANGLE
DREDGER DUSTER HEDGEHOG
DREDGING JILLING
DREGS LAG MUD CRAP FAEX LAGS
LEES SCUT SILT SUDS TAIL DRAFF
DREST DROSS DRUGS FECES FOOTS
GROUT JAUPS MAGMA BOTTOM
DRAINS DUNDER FECULA MOTHER
REFUSE SORDES SORDOR ULLAGE
DRIBBLE GROUNDS GRUMMEL
HEELTAP OUTWALE RESIDUE
RINSING GRUMMELS REMNANTS
SEDIMENT SETTLING
(— OF LIQUOR) TAPLASH
(— OF MOLTEN GLASS) DRIBBLE
(— OF SOCIETY) WASH LEGGE
CANAILLE
(— OF TALLOW) GREAVES
DREIBUND TRIPLICE
DREIDEL TRENDEL
DREI PINTOS, DIE (CHARACTER IN
—) GOMEZ PINTO GASTON
AMBROSIO CLARISSA PANTALEONE
(COMPOSER OF —) MAHLER

DRENCH SOP DOSE HOSE SIND SINK
SOAK TOSH BLASH DOUSE DOWSE
DRAFT DRINK DROKE DROUK
DROWN SLOCK SLUSH SOUSE STEEP
SWILL BUCKET DELUGE DOUCHE
IMBRUE INFUSE POTION SLUICE
DRUNKEN EMBATHE IMMERSE
INDRENCH PERMEATE SATURATE
SUBMERGE
DRENCHED DRUNKEN
DRENCHER INFUSER
DRENCHING DOUSE DOWSE
DOWNPOUR
DRESS AX AXE BED DON DUB FIG FIT
HOE KIT RAG RAY RIG TOG BARB
BEGO BOWN BUSK BUSS CLAY COAT
COMB DESK DILL DINK GALA GARB
GEAR GORE GOWN HONE HUKE
KNAP MIDI MILL MINI RAIL ROBE
SUIT TIFF TIRE TRIM TUBE TUCK
VEST WEAR ADORN ARRAY BIGAN
BRAWS CLEAN CLOTH CRUMB
CRUSH CURRY DIGHT DIZEN EQUIP
FLOAT FROCK GUISE HABIT IHRAM
MAGMA PREEN PRICK PRIMP PRINK
PRUNE SHAPE SHIFT TENUE THING
TRICK AGUISE ATTIRE ATTRAP
BARBER BETRIM BROACH CLOTHE
ENROBE FANGLE FETTLE FRAISE
GRAITH INVEST JELICK JUMPER
KIRTLE MAGPIE MULLET MUUMUU
OUTFIT PLIGHT REVEST SARONG
SHEATH SHROUD TOILET ADDRESS
AFFAITE APPAREL BANDAGE
BEDIZEN CHEMISE CLOTHES
COSTUME DALLACK DUBBING
GARMENT GARNISH HARNESS
HATCHEL RAIMENT TOGGERY
VESTURE ACCOUTER ACCOUTRE
CLEADING CLOTHING DECORATE
FEATHERS HANDMADE ORNAMENT
SUNDRESS TAILLEUR VESTMENT
EMBELLISH
(— A SKIN) WHEEL
(— DOWN) BRACE BERATE
(— ELEGANTLY) DINK
(— FISH) CALVER
(— FLAX) TED
(— FLINT) NAP KNAP
(— FOOD) SAUCE
(— FOR FELTING) CARROT
(— HAIR) TIRE TRUSS BARBER
(— HIDES) BEAM
(— HURRIEDLY) HUDDLE
(— IN FINE CLOTHES) DIKE BRANK
(— MEAT) LARD SHROUD
(— NEGLIGENTLY) MOB
(— OF OFFICE) ROBE
(— ORE) VAN
(— OVER) STOP
(— SHEEPSKINS) TAW
(— SHOWILY) PRANK
(— SMARTLY) DALLACK

(— STONE) DAB NIG DAUB DRAG
FACE GAGE HACK GAUGE NIDGE
POINT SCABBLE SCAPPLE
(— TAWDRILY) BEDIZEN
(— UNTIDILY) MAB
(— UP) BUSK DILL ADORN ARRAY
PRANK PRIMP PRINK SPICK WATER
FETTLE TOGGLE BECLOUT BEDRESS
TITIVATE
(— VULGARLY) DAUB
(— WITH CHISEL) DROVE
(— WITH SLIT SKIRT) CHEONGSAM
(— WITH TROWEL) STRIKE
(— WORN BY MAN) DRAG
(— WOUND) PANSE BANDAGE
(CIVILIAN —) MUFTI
(COAT —) SIMAR SYMAR SIMARRE
(EVENING —) FORMAL
(FESTIVE —) GALA
(HAWAIIAN —) MUUMUU
(HIGHLANDER —) FILABEG
(HOMESPUN —) RUSSET
(INCOMPLETE —) DISARRAY
(LONG —) MAXI
(LOOSE —) SACK SACQUE
(MORNING —) PEIGNOIR
(ONE-PIECE —) CAGE
(ORIENTAL —) CHEONGSAM
(PECULIAR —) LIVERY
(POPLIN —) TABINET TABBINET
(RUSSIAN NATIONAL —) SARAFAN
(SHOWY —) BRAVERY
(SLEEVELESS —) SKIMMER
(STYLE OF —) GETUP
(SUFF.) ESTHES
DRESSED CLAD DONE BOUND
RECLAD COATED COMBED HABITED
GOFFERED
(— GAILY) FRESH SPARKISH
(— IN WHITE) CANDIDATE
(LOOSELY —) DISCINCT
(NOT —) UNDIGHT
(RICHLY —) BROCADED
(ROUGHLY —) HEWN
(SHOWILY —) BEPRANKED
(STYLISHLY —) SMART
(WELL —) BRAW GASH
DRESSER AMBRY AWMRY ROBER
TAWER BUREAU FRAMER ENROBER
MODISTE CUPBOARD
(LEATHER —) LEVANTER
(WELSH —) TRIDARN
DRESSING CAST MAYO GRAVY
BANDAGE BEATING BLANKET
IODOFORM RAVIGOTE REMOLADE
SCOLDING STUFFING
MAYONNAISE
(— FOR WOUNDS) LINT SPONGE
(— OF STONE) SKIFFLING
(HAIR —) LACKER LACQUER
(KIND OF —) RANCH
DRESSING-GOWN KIMONO
PEIGNOIR

DRESSING ROOM SHIFT VESTRY
CAMARIN VESTUARY
DRESSING-TABLE LOWBOY
DRESSMAKER SEWER SEAMER
MODISTE STITCHER COUTURIER
TIREWOMAN
DRESSMAKING COUTURE
DRESS RACK FRIPPERY
DRESSY SHARP
DRIBBLE DRIB DRIP DROP CARRY
DRIVEL DRIBLET DRIPPLE DRIZZLE
SLABBER
DRIBLET CLOT PIECE
(PL.) SMALLS
DRIED SEAR SERE ADUST GIZZEN
TORRID WIZENED GIZZENED
DRIFT FAN JET SAG DENE DUNE
FORD HERD PLOT RACK SILT TIDE
TILL DRIVE DROVE FLEET FLOAT
FLOCK IOWAN SENSE SLIDE SLOOM
SLOUM TENOR TREND BROACH
COURSE DESIGN DEVICE DRIVER
OFFSET PODGER SCHEME STREAM
TUNNEL WINDLE CURRENT DIPHEAD
DRIBBLE GALLERY HEADING
IMPETUS IMPULSE LATERAL
OUTWASH PASTURE PROCESS
PURPORT SETBOLT DILUVIUM
DRIFTPIN TENDENCY
(— LANGUIDLY) SWOON
(— OF CLOUDS) CARRY
(— OF SAND OR SNOW) WREATH
(— SIDEWISE) CRAB
(— WITH ANCHOR DOWN) CLUB
(DOWNWARD —) DROOP
(GLACIAL —) CARY TILL IOWAN
(RUBBLE —) HEAD
DRIFTER HOBO TRAMP DROVER
SWAGMAN VAGRANT
DRIFTING ADRIFT DRIFTAGE
DRIFT PLUG DUMMY
DRIFTWAY DROVE
DRIFTWOOD WAFTURE
DRILL GAD JAR JIG RIG SOW TAP
BORE CORE SPUD AUGER BORER
CHARK CHURN DECOY DREEL PADDY
THIRL TRAIN TUTOR TWIRL WHIRL
ALLURE BROACH ENTICE FURROW
JUMPER PIERCE SCHOOL SEEDER
SINKER STOPER THRILL CHANNEL
DRIFTER JANKERS PLUGGER
STARTER EXERCISE INSTRUCT
PRACTICE
(— SYSTEM) MARTINET
(MASONRY —) AIGUILLE
(WEAPONS —) MANUAL
DRILLMAN STOPER
DRINK GO ADE ALE BIB BUM FIX GIN
HUM KIR LAP MOP NOG PEO POT
RUM RYE SIP SUP TEA TOT WET
BALL BEER BEND BENO BOLL BOGA
BOZA BREW BULL BUMP CHIA CHUG
COKE COLA DRAG DRAM FIZZ FLIP

GROG HAVE HORN JAKE LUSH MEAD
MIST NIPA NOGG PULL PURL SHOT
SIND SLUG SOAK SOMA SOPE SPOT
SWIG TIFF TOOT TOPE WHET AIRAH
ASSAI BEVER BINGE BLAND BOMBO
BOOZE BOUSE BOZAH BUBUD
BUMBO CIDER CRUSH DAISY DRAFT
FLOAT GLOGG HAOMA JULEP LAGER
MORAT NEGUS PAINT POSCA PUNCH
QUAFF ROUSE SETUP SKINK SLING
SLOCK SMACH SMASH SMILE
SMOKE SNIFF SNORT SOPIE SOUSE
SWATS SWILL THING TOAST TODDY
VODKA WHIFF ZOMBI ABSORB
BEZZLE BRACER BRANDY BUMPER
BURTON CALKER CASIRI CATLAP
CAUDLE CHASER COFFEE COOPER
DIBBLE DRENCH EGGHOT EGGNOG
FUDDLE GIMLET GODOWN GUGGLE
GUZZLE HOOKER IMBIBE MESCAL
POSSET POTION PTISAN RICKEY
ROBROY SHERBET SHANDY SIPPLE
SIRPLE SWANKY SWINGE TACKLE
TAMPOY TASTER TIPPLE VELVET
WAUCHT WAUGHT ZOMBIE
BRAGGET BRIMMER CAROUSE
CHEERER CHIRPER COBBLER
COLLINS CONSUME CORDIAL
DILUENT DRAUGHT EXHAUST
FLANNEL GUARANA GUARAPO
INHAUST MORNING NOONING
PROPOMA SHERBET SIDECAR
SNEEZER SNIFTER SUCTION
SUPPAGE SWALLOW TANKARD
TRILLIL AMARETTO APERITIF
BEVERAGE BRIDECUP BULLSHOT
CHUGALUG COCKTAIL HIGHBALL
LIBATION MAHOGANY NIGHTCAP
POTATION QUENCHER REFRESCO
RUMBARGE SANGAREE SPRITZER
SYLLABUB TEQUILLA PHOSPHATE
SUNDOWNER
(— AFTER A MEAL) DIGESTIF
(— AT DRAFT) TOP
(— EXCESSIVELY) TOPE BIBLE SOUSE
BEZZLE BIBBLE TIPPLE SWIZZLE
(— FROM FERMENTED MILK) AIRAN
KEFIR
(— GREEDILY) SLOP SWACK SWILL
GUTTLE GUZZLE
(— HEAVILY) TOOT SWINK
(— INTOXICATING LIQUOR) IRRIGATE
(— LIQUOR) TIP DRAM SOAK BOOZE
PAINT
(— NOISILY) SLURP
(— OF BEER) BUTCHER
(— OF BEER AND BUTTERMILK)
BONNY CLABBER
(— OF BEER AND GINGERALE)
SHANDYGAFF
(— OFF) COUP
**(— OF HONEY AND MULBERRY
JUICE)** MORAT

(— OF IMMORTALITY) SOMA
(— OF INDIA) SHRAB
(— OF LIQUEUR) FRAPPE
(— OF LIQUOR) WET DRAM JOLT
SHOT SPOT TASS WHET SETUP
WHIFF CALKER JIGGER TASTER
WETTING HIGHBALL NIGHTCAP
(— OF MOLASSES) SWITCHEL
(— OF THE GODS) AMRITA NECTAR
(— OF VINEGAR AND WATER)
POSCA
(— SOCIALLY) BIRL HOBNOB
(— SPARINGLY) BLEB
(— TOAST) PLEDGE
(— TO EXCESS) SOAK
(— TO EXCITE LOVE) PHILTER
(— TO LAST DROP) BUZZ
(— UP) CRUSH EPOTE CAROUSE
EXHAUST
(— WITHOUT PAUSE) CHUGALUG
(ACID —) SOUR
(ADDITIONAL —) EIK EKE
(ALCOHOLIC —) BENO BINO MIST
NIPA BOMBO BUDGE BUMBO DRAIN
JOUGH SHRAB SLING SNORT
SNIFTER
(AUSTRALIAN —) BEAL
(BRAZILIAN —) ASSAI ASSAHY
(BUTTERMILK AND WATER —) BLAND
(CURRANT —) CASSIS
(DIETETIC —) POSSET
(DRUGGED —) HOCUS
(FARINACEOUS —) PTISAN
(FERMENTED —) BOSA MEAD
BALCHE MUSHLA PULQUE CASSIRI
GUARAPO
(FREE —) SHOUT
(FRUIT —) SQUASH
(GREAT —) JORUM
(HALF-SIZED —) CHOTAPEG
(HEADY —) HUFFCAP
(HERBAL —) SNAPS
(HOT —) COPUS NEGUS SALOP
TODDY BISHOP EGGHOT PLOTTY
SALOOP CARDINAL
(INCLINED TO —) OUTWARD
(INSIPID —) SLUM
(INTOXICATING —) AVA GROG SUCK
BOOZE KUMISS SCOTCH DRAPPIE
PAIWARI SWIZZLE SKOKIAAN
(INTOXICATING —S) SAUCE BOTTLE
(LONG —) SWIPE HIGHBALL
(MAKE A — LAST) NURSE
(MEAN —) LAP
(MEDICINAL —) TISANE ADVOCAAT
(MIDDAY —) NOONING MERIDIAN
(MIXED —) TWIST
(NARCOTIC —) KAVA
(NON-ALCOHOLIC —) GAZOZ COOLER
(PALM —) ASSAI
(PARTING —) BONAILIE
(POISONOUS —) DRENCH
(RUSSIAN —) OBARNE OBARNI

(SACRED —) HOMA AMRIT HAOMA AMRITA
(SACRIFICIAL —) HOMA SOMA
(SMALL —) PEG DRAM SOPIE DALLOP WETTING
(SOFT —) SLUSH
(SOUR —) ALEGAR
(SPANISH —) SANGRIA
(STRONG —) BUB HUM BENO SICER FUDDLE SHICKER
(TASTELESS —) SLOP
(THIN —) SLOSH
(WEAK —) LAP BOOL BULL CATLAP
(WEST INDIES —) SANGAREE

DRINKER SOT LUSH TANK POTER TOAST TOPER BARFLY BENDER CUPMAN LUSHER SOAKER SPONGE IMBIBER INTAKER QUAFFER DRUNKARD
(EXCESSIVE — OF TEA) THEIC
(HEAVY —) JUICEHEAD
(WATER —) HYDROPOT

DRINKING BEVER DRAFT DRINKY GUZZLE DRAUGHT POTTING CAROUSAL POTATION
(CONTINUOUS —) BOUT

DRINKING-BOUT CAROUSE

DRIP LIP SIE SYE DROP LEAK SEGE SILE WEEP CANAL DRILL EAVES LABEL STILL DRIBBLE DRIPPLE LARMIER TRICKLE TRINKLE TRINTLE
(— WITH TINKLING SOUND) PINK
(PREF.) STALACTI(TI) STALAGMO

DRIPPING ADRIP ALEAK STAXIS WEEPING

DRIPSTONE BAT DING LABEL HOODMOLD

DRIVE CA CAW COT FOG HOY JOG AUTO BANG BEAR BEAT BUTT CALL CRAM DING DRUB DRUM FIRE FIRK FLOG GOAD HACK HERD HUNT HURL JASM JEHU KICK LASH MOVE PICK PILE POSS PUSH RACK RIDE SEND SERR SINK SLOG SPUR STAB STUB TOOL TOUR TURN URGE BRAWL CHASE CHECK COACT CROWD DRIFT DROVE FEEZE FLAIL FORCE HORSE HURRY IMPEL INFER LODGE MOTOR PEDAL POACH PRESS PULSE PUNCH REPEL ROUST SHOVE SLASH SMITE SPANK SWEEP TEASE ATTACK BATTER REETLE BENSEL CHARGE COMPEL CUDGEL DEDUCE DERIVE FERRET HAMMER HASTEN IMPACT JARVEY JOSTLE PLUNGE PROPEL BLUSTER ENFORCE IMPULSE OVERTAX SETDOWN TRAVAIL CATAPULT CONATION SHEPHERD TENDENCY MOTIVATION
(— A BALL) LACE SEND
(— A HORSE ONWARD) WHIG
(— AIR) BLOW
(— ANIMALS) HAZE

(— AT TOP SPEED) BARREL CAREER
(— AWAY) RID FIRK HUSH SHOO BANDY EXILE FEEZE FLEME HOOSH REPEL SMOKE SWEEP AROINT BANISH DEFEND DISPEL ENCHASE DISPLACE EXORCISE
(— BACK) RUSH REBUT REPEL CULBUT DEFEND REBATE REBUFF RETUND REPULSE REFRINGE
(— BACK AND FORTH) TENNIS
(— BEFORE STRONG WIND) SPOON
(— BRISKLY) JUNE
(— CLOSE BEHIND WHILE RACING) DRAFT
(— CRAZY) BUG
(— DISTRACTED) BEDEVIL
(— FORTH) ISH
(— FURIOUSLY) SCORCH
(— HARD) RAM SWEAT HACKNEY
(— HOME) CLINCH
(— HURRIEDLY) BUM BUCKET
(— IN) CRAM DINT PILE TAMP INJECT
(— IN A PARK) TOUR
(— INTO THE GROUND) STUB
(— INTO WATER) ENEW
(— LEISURELY) TOOTLE
(— LOGS) SPLASH
(— OFF) KEEP LIFT EXCOCT
(— OFF STAGE) EXPLODE
(— ON BACK ROADS) SHUNPIKE
(— OUT) BOLT FIRE DEPEL DROWN EJECT EXPEL KNOCK WREAK AROINT EXTURB ABANDON DISLODGE EXORCISE PROPULSE
(— RECKLESSLY) COWBOY
(— ROUGHLY) CHOUSE
(— RUDELY IN TRAFFIC) CUTIN
(— SLANTINGLY) TOE
(— SLOWLY) TAXI
(— TO BAY) EMBOSS
(— TO MADNESS) FRENZY
(— VIOLENTLY) THUD SMASH HURTLE
(— WITH BLOWS) SKELP COURSE
(— WITH SHOUTS) HOY HUE
(FREE GOLF —) MULLIGAN
(RECREATIONAL —) SPIN

DRIVEL GOO BLAH DOTE DRIP MUSH DROOL SLUSH DOTAGE DRUDGE FOOTLE HUMBUG MENIAL SLAVER DRIBBLE EYEWASH MAUNDER SLABBER TWADDLE NONSENSE SALIVATE CODSWALLOP

DRIVELING INANE SLAVERY FOOTLING IMBECILE SLOBBERY BLITHERING

DRIVEPIPE POINT

DRIVER MUG HACK JEHU MUSH WHIP DRABI URGER CABMAN CALLER COWBOY DROVER FLYMAN HAULER JARVEY JOCKEY MALLET MIZZEN MUSHER PONIER STAGER VANMAN WAINER CATCHER

COCHERO FLANKER HACKMAN
HOODLUM HURRIER JITNEUR
PHAETON SPANKER SPEEDER
SUMPTER TOPSMAN TRUCKER
WHIPMAN BANDYMAN BULLOCKY
CALESERO CAMELEER COACHMAN
DRAGSMAN ENGINEER GALLOWAY
GOADSMAN IMPULSOR JITNEUSE
MOTORMAN OVERSEER REINSMAN
TEAMSTER WHIPSTER
(— OF ANIMALS) DROVER SKINNER
(— OF ELEPHANT) MAHOUT
(— OF OMNIBUS) PIRATE
(CAMEL —) SARWAN CAMELEER
(FAST —) JEHU SPEEDER
(FIELD —) HAYWARD
(PACK-HORSE —) SUMPTER
(SKILLFUL —) REINSMAN
(TOWPATH —) HOGGY HOGGEE
(PREF.) ELATRO
DRIVEWAY DRIVE SWEEP AVENUE
DRIFTWAY
DRIVING PELTING COACHING
SLASHING
(— ALONG) SCUD
(— OF GAME) BATTUE
(— OF WIND) GUST
(— TOGETHER) DRIFT
(— TOWARD) APPULSE
DRIZZLE DEG MUG DANK DRIP DROW
HAZE LING RAIN SMUR STEW DRISK
MISLE SMURR MIZZLE DRISSEL
SCOUTHER SPRINKLE
(— OF RAIN) SKEW
DRIZZLY SOFT DRIPPY MIZZLY
DROGUE DRAG DRUG SLEEVE
DROLL ODD RUM WRY COMIC DROLE
FUNNY MERRY QUEER WITTY
JESTER JOCOSE AMUSING BUFFOON
COMICAL JOCULAR STRANGE
WAGGISH FARCICAL HUMOROUS
DROLLERY WIT JEST FARCE HUMOR
DROLERIE
DROMEDARY OONT CAMEL DELUL
DELOUL HAGEEN HAGEIN HYGEEN
MEHARI CAMAILE CAMELUS
DROMOND
DRONE BEE BUM HUM DRUM SLUG
SPIV DRANT DROLL IDLER SNAIL
THRUM BUMBLE BURDEN CHORUS
DRAUNT DRONEL DRONET LUBBER
BAGPIPE BUMBARD BUMBASS
HUMMING SHIRKER SLEEPER
SOLDIER SPEAKER LOITERER
SLUGGARD
DRONE BASS FOOT
DRONGO FORKTAIL
DRONING BOURDON HUMDRUM
HUMMING SINGSONG
DRONISH SLOW INDOLENT
SLUGGISH
DROOL FLAT DRIVEL SLAVER DRIBBLE
SLABBER SLOBBER SALIVATE

DROOP FAG LOB LOP SAG BEND
DROP FADE FLAG HANG LAVE LOLL
PEAK PINE SINK SWAG WEEP WILT
DAVER DREEP DROWK FLACK HEALD
HIELD MOURN BANGLE BLOUSE
DANGLE DEPEND NUTATE SLOUCH
CURTAIN DECLINE FLITTER
LANGUISH PENDENCY
DROOPING LOP DRAG FLAG LANK
LAZY LIMP GOTCH OURIE ADROOP
DROOPY FLAGGY NUTANT SLOUCH
SOPITE GOTCHED HANGING
LANGUID NODDING POPPIED
CERNUOUS TRAILING
(— OF EARS) LAVE
(— OF EYELID) PTOSIS
DROOPY DREEPY SLIMPSY
DROP DAP DIP SIE SYE BEAD BEDE
BLOB CAST DRIB DRIP DUMP FALL
GLOB GOUT OMIT SEGE SHED SILE
SINK SPOT STOP TEAR BREAK CLOTH
DROOP FLUMP GUTTA LAPSE LOWER
MINIM PEARL PLUMP PLUNK SLUMP
STILL SWOOP CANCEL DISTIL
DRAPPY EXTILL FUMBLE GOBBET
GOUTTE PLUNGE SINKER SLOUGH
SPRINK TUMBLE ABANDON CURTAIN
DESCENT DEWDROP DISCARD
DISMISS DISTILL DRAPPIE DRIBBLE
DRIBLET DROPLET EXPUNGE
FORSAKE GLOBULE GUTTULA
GUTTULE INCURVE LETDOWN
MELDROP PLUMMET RELEASE
SPATTER DECREASE DROPLING
(— ANCHOR) SLIP
(— ARGENT) LARME
(— AS SEEDS FROM A POD) ROSE
(— AWAY) DESERT
(— BAIT IN WATER) DAP
(— BY DROP) DROPWISE GUTTATIM
(— DOWN) VAIL
(— IN) STOP HAPPEN INSTIL INSTILL
(— INTO LIQUID) PLUMP
(— OFF) NAP NOD DOZE SNOOZE
(— OF GIN) DAFFY
(— OF SEALING-WAX) KISS
(— OUT) FLOUNCE
(ARCHITECTURAL —) GUTTA
(CHOCOLATE —) DRAGEE
(THEATRICAL —) TAB SCRIM
(UNEXPECTED —) DOYST
(PL.) GTT GUTT
(PREF.) GUTTI STAGMO STAGONO
STILLI
DROP-CURTAIN GREENY
DROP ELBOW PIERDROP
DROPLET GLOBULE
(PL.) DEW
DROPLIGHT PENDANT
DROPPER SINK BOBBER SINKER
PIPETTE
DROPPING FALL SCAT SKAT SHARD
COWSHARD

(— ABRUPTLY) BOLD
(— SHARPLY) ABRUPT
(PL.) SOIL SPOOR FLYINGS
DROPSICAL PUFFY EDEMIC
DROPSIED HYDROPIC
DROPSY EDEMA OEDEMA ASCITES
ANASARCA
DROPWORT HORSEBANE
DEADTONGUE
DROSS KISH LEES SCUM SLAG
CHAFF DREGS DRUSH SCOBS SLACK
SPRUE WASTE GARBLE REFUSE
SCORIA SCRUFF SHRUFF SINTER
CINDERS LEAVING OFFSCUM
DROSSEL SLUT HUSSY DRAZEL
DRAZIL
DROUGHT DRYTH DROUTH THIRST
ARIDITY DRYNESS ARIDNESS
DROVE MOB SENT ATAJO CROWD
DRIFT FLOCK MANADA BOASTER
DISTURB TROUBLE DRIFTWAY
DROVER DEALER DRIVER TOPMAN
TOPSMAN WHACKER HERDSMAN
DROWN DEAFEN DRENCH STIFLE
ADRENCH DRUNKEN INDRENCH
INUNDATE OVERTONE
DROWNED ADRENT
DROWNING NOYADE
DROWSE NOD SOG DOZE DOVER
DRONE SLEEP SNOOZE SLUMBER
DROWSINESS COMA DULLNESS
LETHARGY NARCOSIS
DROWSING DORMANT
DROWSY DOZY DULL LOGY HEAVY
NODDY SLEEPY SNOOZY SOPITE
STUPID SUPINE SWOONY DORMANT
LULLING NODDING POPPIED
COMATOSE CUMATOUS OSCITANT
SLUGGISH LETHARGIC
DRUB TAP WAP BANG BEAT BLOW
DRUM PAIK ARRAY CREAM CURRY
PASTE STAMP THUMP WHALE
ANOINT CUDGEL SCUTCH THRASH
BELABOR DRYBEAT SHELLAC
DRUBBING PAIK LICKING SACKING
DRUDGE DIG FAG TUG DROY DRUG
GRUB HACK MOIL PEON PLOD SERF
TOIL DROIL DRONE GRIND SCRAT
SCRUB SLAVE SWEAT DIGGER
DRIVEL ENDURE JACKAL MOILER
SCODGY SCOGIE SLAVEY SLUDGE
SUFFER GRUBBER HACKNEY
PLODDER SLAVERY SWEATER
TRACHLE DOGSBODY
DRUDGERY FAG MOIL SLOG TOIL
WORK GRIND LABOR SWEAT SWINK
FAGGERY SLAVERY TRACHLE
TURMOIL DRUDGISM
(ROUTINE —) TREADMILL
DRUG (ALSO SEE NARCOTIC) DEX
DOM HOP STP ACID ALOE ALUM
BUKU CURE DOPE DRAB DULL HEMP
LOAD MDMA NUMB SCAG SINA

BUCHU HOCUS JALAP LDOPA LOCUS
MECON NSAID OPIUM RUTIN SALOL
SENNA SPECE SPEED SULFA TONGA
TRUCK COOLER DEWTRY DOWNER
ELAVIL FINGER HEROIN IPECAC
JAMBUL LOCUST MYOTIC NOBRLE
OPIATE PEYOTE PEYOTL PITURI
POTION SIDDHI SIMPLE SULPHA
ANODYNE ASPIRIN ATEBRIN BOTANIC
CUSHION DAMIANA DAPSONE
DILATER ECBOLIC ECSTASY ETHICAL
HASHISH JAMBOOL LIBRIUM
METOPON PHILTER PHILTRE QUASSIA
STUPEFY STYPTIC SURAMIN
ZEDOARY ADJUVANT AROMATIC
ASPIDIUM ATARAXIC BANTHINE
HYPNOTIC KOROMIKO LAETRILE
LAXATIVE MEDICATE MEDICINE
MERSALYL NARCOTIC NEPENTHE
PEMOLINE QUAALUDE SALIVANT
SEDATIVE SPECIFIC THIAZIDE
TOXICANT ZERUMBET ATARACTIC
BARBITONE BEMEGRIDE BRETYLIUM
CAPTOPRIL CLONIDINE COLCHICUM
IBUPROFEN MELPHALAN NIALAMIDE
SALURETIC AMANTADINE
CLOFIBRATE CLOMIPHENE PAINKILLER
(— CAPSULE) QUAALUDE
(— CAPSULES) RED REDS
(— DOSE) HIT
(— IN TABLET OF VARIOUS COLORS)
RAINBOW
(— SMUGGLER) MULE
(— USER) DOPER FREAK DRUGGY
DRUGGIE ACIDHEAD JOYPOPPER
(BITUMINOUS —) MUMMY
(DEPRESSANT —) DOWNER
(FIVE DOLLAR — PACKET) NICKEL
(FREE FROM — ADDICTION) CLEAN
(INHALE A —) SNORT
(INJECT —) SKINPOP
(INJECT —S) SHOOT
(KIND OF —) SULFA ORPHAN
DESIGNER
(NONUSER OF —S) STRAIGHT
(NOT USING —S) STRAIGHT
(ONE WHO USES —S) DRUGGY
DRUGGIE
(ONE WHO USES A —) HEAD
(ONE WHO USES ILLICIT —S) FREAK
(ORAL DIURETIC —) THIAZIDE
(RENDER FREE FROM —S) DETOX
(STIMULANT —) UPPER
(STRENGTHENING —) ROBORANT
(TAKE —S ORALLY) POP
(TAKE —S THROUGH THE MOUTH)
DROP SWALLOW
(TAKE A — THROUGH THE MOUTH)
DROP
(TO INJECT —) SHOOT
(VEGETABLE —) FINGER
(PL.) DRUGGERY
(PREF.) PHARMACO

DRUGGED POPPIED
DRUGGET BAUGE BOCKING
DRUGGIST CHEMIST DRUGGER
GALLIPOT APOTHECARY
DRUGSTORE APOTHEC PHARMACY
DRUID SARONIDE
DRUM BAZ GIN GON GOO GYO BOWL
CAGE CHIH DRUB LALI MUYU POPO
QASA ROUT SKIN SPOT TOPH TRAP
ZUZU ADAPU BONGO CONGA
CRAWL DAVUL DRONE DUGGI ENNEN
EWTIE FOUCT FURIN GUMBE GUMBY
JAIRA KENON MBIRA NAKER QABIB
REBAB SARON SHAPE SNARE
SWASH TABOR THRUM TOMBE
TUPAN ZURLA AFUCHE AMBIRA
ATABAL BAMBUS BARREL CROCUS
GAMAKA GRELOT KANOON KEMPUL
KHANSI KURTAR LIVIKA RIGGER
TABRET TAMBOR TIMBRE TUMBLE
TUMMER TYMPAN UDAKKI ANACARA
BODHRAN BUBBLER CROAKER
DAULBAZ ENCLUME FRUSTUM
GHIRBAL GRUNTER RATTLER
REDFISH SLENTEM SNUBBER
TABORIN TAMBOUR TEMPEST
TIMBREL TUMBLER VOSHAGA
ZAMBONA BAMBOULA BARBUKKA
CANISTER CYLINDER DERBUKKA
DRUMFISH HUEHUETI HUEHUETL
MAQQAREH MOULINET MRIDANGA
TYMPANUM ABURUKUWA
BRONTERON DUMTAKTAK
MRIDANGAM PUTTIPUTI
ROMMELPOT TSANATSEL
CACCAVELLA
(— AS SHIP'S SIGNAL) SHAPE
(— FOR WINDING ROPE) CAGE
(— IN WINCH) GIPSY GYPSY
(— MADE FROM HOLLOW TREE)
GUMBE GUMBY
(— OF CAPSTAN) RUNDLE
MOULINE
(— OF INDIA) MRIDANGA
MRIDANGAM
(— ON WINDLASS) WILDCAT
(— UP BUSINESS) HUSTLE
(— UP INTEREST) BALLYHOO
(HEATED —) DRIER DRYER
(IGOROT —) GANGSA
(KIND OF —) STEEL
(NARROW —) RIGGER
(PAIR OF —S) TABLA
(PAIR OF HINDU —S) TABLA
(REVOLVING —) GURDY BARREL
RATTLER
(SUMERIAN —) ALA ALAL
DRUMBEAT DUB FLAM RUFF TUCK
MARCH RUFFLE SHUFFLE ASSEMBLY
BERLOQUE BRELOQUE
(— SOUND) TUCK
DRUM-BELLY HOOVE

DRUMFISH SPOT CROCUS BUBBLER
CROAKER DRUMMER DRUMSLER
SCIAENID
DRUMLIN DRUM SOWBACK
DRUMMER DRUM TABOR STICKS
TABRET ROADMAN SWASHER
TAMBOUR TUMBLER DRUMSLER
SALESMAN
DRUMMING TATTOO
DRUM ROLL DIAN DIANA
DRUMS ALONG THE MOHAWK
(AUTHOR OF —) EDMONDS
(CHARACTER IN —) HON JOHN LANA
MARK YOST BRANT JURRY NANCY
WOLFF ARNOLD GAHOTA JOSEPH
MARTIN DEMOOTH GILBERT
MCLONIS SCHUYLER MAGDELANA
MCKLENNAR
DRUMSTICK LEG STICK BAGUET
TAMPON BAGUETTE
DRUNK CUT FAP FOU REE WET GONE
HIGH LUSH NASE PAID RIPE SOSH
BLIND BOOZE BOSKY CLEAR DRINK
GONZO LITUP LUMPY LUSHY MALTY
MOPPY OILED QUEER SHICK STIFF
TIGHT TIPSY BAGGED BLOTTO
BOILED BOMBED BUZZED CANNED
FLUFFY GROGGY JAGGED LOADED
LOOPED MORTAL POTTED RIPPED
SLOPPY SODDEN SOSHED SOUSED
SOZZLY SPONGY SPRUNG STEWED
STINKO STONED TIDDLY UPPISH
UPPITY ZONKED BLOTTER BONKERS
BOTTLED CROCKED DRUNKEN
JINGLED MAUDLIN PICKLED
SCREWED SHICKER SLOPPED
SLOSHED SMASHED SOZZLED
SQUIFFY SWACKED UNSOBER
WRECKED COCKEYED GLORIOUS
MUCKIBUS PLEASANT SQUIFFED
STINKING WIPEDOUT BLITHERED
PIXILATED
DRUNKARD SOT LUSH SOAK WINO
BLOAT DIPSO DRUNK GULCH
RUMMY SOUSE TOPER BARFLY
LUSHER SOAKER SPONGE DRUNKER
FUDDLER POTSHOT SHICKER
STEWBUM TIPPLER TOSSPOT
BORACHIO HABITUAL SWILLTUB
DRUNKEN REE WAT GONE WINY
BLIND BOUSY DROWN DRUNK
BLOTTO FLUFFY SODDEN BACCHIC
DRUCKEN PICKLED SOTTISH
WHIPCAT DRENCHED SATURATE
SQUIFFED VINOLENT WOODSERE
DRUNKENNESS BUN IVRESSE
POTSHOT METHYSIS
DRUPE TRYMA DRUPEL DRUPELET
DRUPEOLE
DRUPELET GRAIN ACINUS
DRUPE STONE NUTLET
DRUSE GEODE

DRUSILLA (BROTHER OF —)
CALIGULA
(FATHER OF —) HEROD CALIGULA
GERMANICUS
(HUSBAND OF —) FELIX AZIZUS
AUGUSTUS
(MOTHER OF —) CYPROS CAESONIA
AGRIPPINA
(SON OF —) AGRIPPA TIBERIUS
DRY EBB KEX SEC TED WIN ADRY
ARID BAKE BLOT BRUT DULL EILD
GELD HASK KEXY KILN PINE SAVE
SERE SOUR WELT WIPE AREFY
CORKY DRAIN FROST GUESS HASKY
JUSKY MEALY PARCH PROSY SANDY
SECCO SMEEK SWEAT VAPID WIZEN
BARKEN BARREN BIRSLE BORING
CHIPPY ENSEAR GIZZEN HISTIE
JEJUNE SCORCH STARKY AREFACT
BRUSTLE INSIPID SAHARAN
SAPLESS SICCATE SQUALID STERILE
THIRSTY TORREFY XEROTIC
BARBECUE DROUGHTY INFUMATE
TIRESOME WOODSERE
(— HERRINGS) DEESE
(— IN SUN) RIZZAR
(— OFF) TOWEL
(— OF MILK) SEW EILD
(— PARTLY) SAMMY
(— UP) SERE WELK WITHER AREFACT
FORWELK SKELLER
(— WITH SMOKE) REAST REEST
(— WOOD) BEATH SWEAT SEASON
(KIND OF —) DRIP
(NOT —) SWEET
(PREF.) DEHYDR(O) JEJUN(O)
SCLER(O) SICCI TORTE XER(O)
DRYAD DRYAS NYMPH CAISSA
YAKSHA YAKSII II WOODMAID
DRYER DRIER STOVE SIROCCO
DRY GOODS DRAPERY
DRYING SICCANT
DRYING RACK CRIB
DRYNESS DROUTH ARIDITY
DROUGHT SICCITY XEROSIS
XEROTES HASKNESS AREFACTION
(— OF THE HAIR) XERASIA
DRYOPE (FATHER OF —) EURYTUS
(HUSBAND OF —) ANDRAEMON
(SISTER OF —) IOLE
(SON OF —) AMPHISSUS
DUAL TWIN BINARY DOUBLE
DUALIST TWOFOLD
DUALISM DVAITA
DUALITY DUAD TWINE TWONESS
DUANT DE DEE
DUB DIB RUB ADUB BLOW CALL
NAME POOL ADORN ARRAY DRESS
STYLE THUMP CLOTHE KNIGHT
PUDDLE SMOOTH STRIKE ENTITLE
BEGINNER DRUMBEAT ORNAMENT
DUBBIN DAUBING

DUBIOUS DICKY FISHY JUBUS
DOUBTY BEARISH DOUBTFUL
DOUBTING JUBEROUS PRECARIOUS
QUESTIONABLE
(NOT —) EXPRESS
DUCA D'ALBA, IL (CHARACTER IN
—) AMELIA EGMONT MARCELLO
(COMPOSER OF —) DONIZETTI
DUCHY SAVOY DUCATUS DUCHERY
DUKEDOM PARMESAN
DUCK AIX BOB BOW CAN DIG DIP
DOP MIG PET WIO CHAP COLK COOT
DIVE DOGS DOGY DOKE DUKW JOUK
LADY LORD PATO ROOK SMEE SMEW
TEAL TEUK BOOBY BUNTY CRICK
DILLY DODGE DOUSE DOWSE DUCKY
EIDER EVADE HOUND MOMMY
NODDY PADDY POKER RODGE
ROUEN SCAUP SHIRK SOUSE SPIKE
SPRIG STOOL BOBBER CALLOO
CALLOW CANARD CANNET DUCKIE
FELLOW GARROT HARELD PEKING
PERSON PLUNGE QUANDY RUNNER
SCOTER SMETHE ANATINE BARWING
BLACKIE BOWSSEN BUMMALO
CANETTE CRACKER DABBLER
DARLING DRABBET DUCKING
DUCKLET DUNBIRD FIDDLER
FLAPPER GADWALL GEELBEC
GREASER MALLARD OLDWIFE
PENTAIL PINKEYE PINTAIL POCHARD
REDHEAD REDLEGS REDWING
SCOOTER SLEEPER SPATTER
WADDLER WIDGEON YAGUAZA
BALDPATE BLUEBILL BLUEWING
BOATBILL BULLNECK DUCKLING
DUCKWING GARGANEY GRAYBACK
GREYBACK HARDHEAD IRONHEAD
MOONBILL MORILLON PIKETAIL
REDSHANK RINGBILL RINGNECK
SHOVELER SHUFFLER SQUEALER
WIRETAIL BERGANDER
(— AT CRICKET) BLOB
(— EGGS) PIDAN
(DEAD —) GONER
(KIND OF —) PEKING SITTING
(MALE —) DRAKE
(PART OF —) EAR EYE WEB BEAN BILL
CAPE HEAD NECK RUMP TAIL WING
FLUFF SHANK BREAST SADDLE
COVERTS NOSTRIL SHOULDER
PRIMARIES SECONDARIES
(STUFFED —) DUMPOKE
(YOUNG —) CANETON FLAPPER
FLOPPER
DUCKBILL OOTOCOID PLATYPUS
TAMBREET MONOTREME
DUCKING SOUSE
DUCKTAIL DA HAIRSTYLE
DUCKWEED GLIT GRAIN LEMNAD
LENTIL DIGMEAT DUCKMEAT
FROGFOOT

DUCT VAS MAIN PIPE TUBE VEIN
CANAL ALVEUS BUSWAY DUCTUS
MEATUS URETER CHANNEL CONDUIT
DUCTULE DUCTURE LACTEAL
LEADING PASSAGE TRACHEA
AQUEDUCT CALIDUCT DOWNTAKE
EFFERENT EMISSARY EXHALANT
GONADUCT GUIDANCE OLEODUCT
(PREF.) RHYN(O) VAS(I)(O)

DUCTILE SOFT DOCILE FACILE
PLIANT PLASTIC PLIABLE TENSILE
FLEXIBLE TRACTILE
(PREF.) ELAST(O)

DUD TOG FLOP LEMON STUMER
STUMOR FAILURE

DUDE FOP DANDY DUDINE JOHNNY
COXCOMB JACKEEN

DUDEGON PIQUE

DUDGEON IRE RAGE ANGER PIQUE
OFFENSE
(HIGH —) IRE

DUE HAK LOT OWE BACK CENS DEBT
FAIR FARM FLAT HAKH JUST MEED
OWED TOLL DROIT ENDOW ENDUE
FATED MERIT OWING COMING
CUSTOM DESERT EXTENT LAWFUL
MATURE PROPER UNPAID CONDIGN
EXACTLY FALDFEE FITTING JETTAGE
TALLAGE ADEQUATE DIRECTLY
HEREGELD HEREZELD RIGHTFUL
SUITABLE TRUNCAGE

DUEL TILT FENCE FIGHT AFFAIR
COMBAT DUELLO MENSUR CONTEST
MEETING CONFLICT DUELLIZE
HOLMGANG

DUELIST FIGHTER SPADASSIN

DUENNA DRAGON GRIFFIN GRIFFON
CHAPERON

DUES TOLLS DROITS CHIEFRY
INWARDS JETTAGE PAYMENT
PENSION QUAYAGE ALTARAGE
HAVENAGE SOUNDAGE THIRLAGE
WHARFAGE

DUET DUO TWO DUETTO TWOSOME
(BALLET —) ADAGIO

DUFF ALTER BRAND CHEAT FLOOR
PUDDING

DUFFER DUB MUFF SHAM CHEAT
BUFFER GEEZER HAWKER RABBIT
SHICER PEDDLER

DUG TEAT
(— UP) HOWKIT
(PREF.) ORYCTO

DUGONG SEACOW YUNGAN
COWFISH MANATEE HALICORE
MUTILATE SIRENIAN

DUGOUT ABRI BOAT BURY CAVE
BANCA BONGO BUNGO CANOE
DONGA DUNGA SHELL BAROTO
BUNKER CAYUCA CAYUCO CORIAL
TROUGH BANTING PIRAGUA
PIROGUE SHELTER BLINDAGE
LIPALIPA

DUHSHASANA (FATHER OF —)
DHRITARASHTRA

DUIKER IPITI DUYKER BLAUBOK

DUKE DUC DUX KNEZ PEER AYMON
CHIEF KNIAZ HERZOG LEADER
ORSINO AUMERLE GORLOIS
SOLINUS STEENIE HERETOGA
PROSPERO

DUKEDOM DUCHY ALBANY
DUCATUS

DULCET SWEET DULCID SIRUPY
SYRUPY SOOTHING

DULCIAN CURTAL

DULCIMER ROTA CANUN CITOLE
SANTIR CEMBALO MAGADIS
SANTOUR CYMBALOM PANTALON
SAUTERIE ZIMBALON

DULIA ADORATION

DULL DIM DOW DRY FAT LAX MAT
SAD ARID BLAH CLOD COLD DAMP
DEAD DILL DOWD DOWF DOWY
DRAB DREE DRUG DUMB FLAT GRAY
GREY LOGY MOPE MULL POKY
SLOW TAME THIN TURN BESOT
BLACK BLAND BLATE BLEAR BLIND
BLUNT BRUTE CRASS DENSE DINGY
DOWFF DOWIE DOWLY DREAR
DUBBY DUNCH DUNNY DUSTY
FISHY FOGGY GLAZY GRAVE GROSS
HEAVY HOHUM INERT LOURD
MATTE MORON MOSSY MUDDY
MUSTY MUZZY NOOSE PLUMP
POKEY PROSE PROSY SHADE SLACK
SOGGY STARY STILL SULKY TERNE
THICK UNAPT VAPID WASTE
BARREN BLEARY BOVINE CLOUDY
DAMPEN DARKEN DEADEN DISMAL
DRAGGY DREARY DRIECH DRIEGH
DROWSY EARTHY FRIGID FRUMPY
GLASSY HEBETE JEJUNE LEADEN
LOURDY MUFFLE OBTUND OBTUSE
OPAQUE PALLID REBATE RETUND
SLEEPY SLOOMY SODDEN SOMBER
SOMBRE STODGY STOLID STUFFY
STUPID SULLEN TIMBER TORPID
TRISTE TURBID URLUCH WOODEN
ADENOID BLUNTED CONFUSE
DEADISH DISEDGE DOLTISH
DOWFART DRAINED DULLISH
DUMPISH HUMDRUM INSIPID
IRKSOME LANGUID LUMPISH
MUMPISH PEAKISH PINHEAD
PROSAIC SHEATHE SOTTISH
STUPEFY TEDIOUS UNLUSTY
VACUOUS BACKWARD BANAUSIC
BEFUDDLE BLOCKISH BOEOTIAN
BROMIDIC COMATOSE COMATOUS
DIDACTIC DISCOLOR DULLSOME
EDGELESS FRUMPISH GAUMLESS
HEBETATE INFICETE LIFELESS
LISTLESS LOURDISH OVERCAST
PLODDING SLOTTERY SLUGGISH
SOULLESS STAGNANT TIRESOME

PINHEADED PONDEROUS
SATURNINE
(— EDGE OF) ABATE
(— IN MOTION) LOGY
(— IN SPEECH) PROSY
(— SCENT) FOIL
(— WITH LIQUOR) SEETHE
(BECOME —) PALL RUST
(MENTALLY —) DOPY DOPEY
BARREN
(PREF.) AMBLY(O) BRADY
DULLARD DOIT BOOBY DUNCE
IDIOT MORON DODUNK STUPID
BROMIDE DASTARD DOLDRUM
DULBERT POTHEAD BLINKARD
DULLHEAD
DULLED EMPTY HEAVY JADED
BROKEN CLOUDY GRAYED SODDEN
STUPID BLEARED
DULLISH DIRTY
DULL-LOOKING OWLISH
DULLNESS DRAB HAZE YAWN
CLOUD TAMAS FADEUR PHLEGM
TORPOR DIMNESS DOLDRUM
DULLITY DUNCERY FATUITY
LANGUOR OPACITY DUMBNESS
HEBETUDE SLOWNESS SOPITION
VAPIDITY SEGNITUDE STOLIDITY
(— OF SIGHT) AMBLYOPIA
DULL-SPIRITED MUZZY
DULL-WITTED FOZY WITLESS
BESOTTED DONNERED
(— PERSON) MOREPORK
DULLY FLATLY HEAVILY
DULSE DILLESK DILLISK SEAWEED
DULY DUE FITLY RIGHT RITELY
PROPERLY
DUMAH (FATHER OF —) ISHMAEL
DUMB DULL MUTE STONY SILENT
STONEY STUPID IDIOTIC
(— OX) BOZO
DUMBBELL DODO DUMMY
DUNCE IDIOT HALTER AIRHEAD
KNOTHEAD
DUMBFOUND DAZE STUN A
MAZE CONFUSE CONFOUND
SURPRISE
DUMBFOUNDED AWED STUPENT
DUMBNESS SILENCE APHRASIA
DUMBWAITER LIFT DUMMY
DUM-DUM AIRHEAD
KNUCKLEHEAD
DUMMY COPY DOLT MUTE SHAM
DUMBY FAGOT EFFIGY FAGGOT
PONTIC SHADOW SILENT PHANTOM
DUMBBELL
(SWORDSMAN'S —) PEL
DUMNORIX (BROTHER OF —)
DIVITIACUS
DUMP SUM TIP BEAT CASH COIN
COUP FALL HOLE JAIL MUSE NAIL
TOOM EMPTY HOUSE SHOOT
GRIEVE PLUNGE TIPPLE UNLOAD

BOGHOLE COUNTER DEPOSIT
REVERIE SADNESS STORAGE
(MINE —) BURROW
(PL.) SUDS MOPES SADNESS
DUMPCART DUMPER TUMBREL
TUMBRIL
DUMPER TIPMAN
DUMPLING COB CRUST KNODEL
PIROGI KNAIDEL NOCKERL PIEROGI
SPATZLE DOUGHBOY QUENELLE
SPAETZLE AGNOLOTTI
(POLISH —) PIEROGI
(RUSSIAN MEAT —S) PELMENI
PELMENY
(PL.) KLOSSE GNOCCHI
DUMPY DUNCH GROSS PUDGY
SQUAB SQUAT DUMPTY STOCKY
SQUATTY
DUN BUM TAN FORT KICK URGE
ANNOY BROWN CRAVE CROWD
DINGY FAVEL MOUND PRESS SEPIA
DUNNER LEADEN PESTER PLAGUE
DUNNISH SWARTHY
DUNCE ASS CLOD DODO DOLT DULT
GABY GONY BOBBY BOOBY DOBBY
IDIOT NINNY DULTIE HOBBIL
PEDANT DULLARD SOPHIST
NUMSKULL STUNPOLL TOMNODDY
WISEACRE
DUN-COLORED
(PREF.) PHAEO PHEO
(SUFF.) PHAEIN PHEIN
DUNDERHEAD OAF CLOD DOLT
SAPE DUNCE TURNIP GOMERIL
DUNE BAR DENE MEAL MOUND
TOWAN TWINE BARKAN BARCHAN
BARKHAN
(SAND —) DRAB SAIF SEIF
DUNG MIS CACK CHIP DOLL FIME
GORE MERD MUCK MUTE SOIL TATH
ARGAL ARGOL FECES FILTH FUMET
MIXEN SCARN SHARN BILLET
CASSON FIANTS LESSES MANURE
ORDURE SCUMBER SCUMMER
TREDDLE COWSHARD DROPPING
STALLAGE
(— AS FUEL) ARGOL CASSON
CASSONS
(— OF BEAST OF PREY) LESSES
(— OF DEER) FUMET FEWMET
(COW —) MIST UPLA COWSHARD
COWSHARN
(OTTER'S —) SPRAINTS
(SHEEP —) BUTTONS TREDDLE
TROTTERS
(PREF.) COPR(O) FIMI GUANI GUANO
MERDI SCAT(O) SCORI SPATILO
STERCO STERCOR(I)
DUNG BEETLE SCARAB
DUNGEON PIT CELL HELL HOLE
LAKE VAULT CACHOT DONJON
PRISON CONFINE OUBLIET REVOLVER
OUBLIETTE

DUNGHILL MIXEN MIDDEN MIXHILL
DUNGON DONGON SUNDARI
DUNK DIP SOP SOAK STEEP IMMERSE
MOISTEN
(— SHOT) JAM
DUNKER DIPPER TAUFER TUNKER
DUMPLER DUNKARD TUMBLER
DUNLIN STIB OXEYE PURRE STINT
DORBIE OXBIRD REDBACK LEADBACK
DUNNAGE FARDAGE
DUODECIMO TWELVEMO
DUPE APE BAM FOB FOP MUG BOOB
COAX CONY CULL DUST FOOL GECK
GULL HOAX LAMB ROOK SCAM
TOOL CHEAT CHUMP COKES CONEY
CULLY HEALD MOOTH MOUTH
PROOF REPRO SLANG STALE TRICK
BEFOOL BUBBLE CHOOSE CHOUSE
COUSIN DELUDE DERIDE MONKEY
PIGEON PLOVER SQUARE SUCKER
TAKEIN VICTIM BECASSE CATSPAW
CHICANE CULLION DECEIVE
GUDGEON MISLEAD SAPHEAD
SWINDLE YOUNKER DOTTEREL
HOODWINK RODERIGO DUPLICATE
DUPERY RAMP
DUPLE BINARY DOUBLE TWOFOLD
DUPLEX DOUBLE TWOFOLD
DUPLEXITY EQUIVOKE
DUPLICATE BIS COPY DUPE ALIKE
DITTO SPARE TALLY DOUBLE FLIMSY
REPEAT COUNTER ESTREAT
MISLEAD REPLICA TWOFOLD
LIKENESS
(PREF.) COUNTER
DUPLICATION DISOMATY
DUPLICATOR MIMEOGRAPH
DUPLICITY ART GUILE DECEIT
TRICKERY
DUPONDIUS BRONZE
DURABILITY WEAR FIBER FIBRE
STEEL DURANCE STAMINA
DURABLE FIRM HARD LASTY PAKKA
PUKKA STOUT STABLE STAPLE
LASTING SERVICE CONSTANT
ENDURING LIVELONG
DURABLENESS DURATION
DURAMEN HEARTWOOD
DURANCE DURANT DURESS
CUSTODY
DURANGO CARTOUCH
DURATION AGE DATE LAST LIFE
SPAN TERM TIME WHEN DUREE
KALPA SPACE LENGTH PERIOD
DURANCE LASTING INFINITE
LIFETIME STANDING
(— BREEZE) SLATCH
(— OF DWELLING) RESIDENCE
(BOUNDLESS —) INFINITE
(INFINITE —) ETERNITY
(RELATIVE —) VALUE
DURAZZO (WARD OF —) CALDORO
DURESS FORCE DANGER CRUELTY

DURANCE COERCION HARDNESS
PRESSURE
DURGA KALI CHAMUNDA
(HUSBAND OF —) SHIVA
DURIAN JAK JACK JAKFRUIT
DURING IN ON BIN AMID OVER TIME
AMONG INTRA WHILE AMIDST
WHILST WITHIN AMONGST DURANTE
PENDING ENDURING
(PREF.) DIA INTRA
DURRA DARI DURA MILO JOWAR
CHOLUM DHURRA JONDLA
SORGHUM FETERITA
DURUM WHEAT
DURYODHANA (BROTHER OF —)
PANDU
(FATHER OF —) DHRITARASHTRA
(SON OF —) LAKSHMANA
(WIFE OF —) DRAUPADI
DUSACK TESACK
DUSHYANTA (SON OF —) BHARATA
(WIFE OF —) SHAKUNTALA
DUSK DIM EVE DARK DIMPS GLOAM
GLOOM DIMMET DIMPSY DIMNESS
DUCKISH DARKNESS GLOAMING
OWLLIGHT TWILIGHT NIGHTFALL
DUSKINESS PHAEISM
DUSKY DIM DUN SAD WAN DARK
DUSK ADUSK BLACK BROWN DINGY
GRIMY MOORY TAWNY GLOOMY
PHAEIC SMUTTY SOMBER SOMBRE
SWARTH DARKISH DARLING
OBSCURE SUBFUSC SUBFUSK
SWARTHY BLACKISH
(PREF.) PERCNO PHAEO
DUST ROW COOM DIRT FOGO MUCK
MULL PILM SMUT BRISS CLEAN
COOMB FLOUR POUCE STIVE STOUR
DREDGE FILLER KITTEN POLLEN
POWDER SMEECH BEFLOUR EBURINE
REMAINS SAWDUST SMEDDUM
TURMOIL ANTELOPE BULLDUST
PUMICITE
(— IN FLOUR MILLS) STIVE
(— IN QUARTZ MILL) SLICKENS
(BLOOD —) HEMOCONIA
(CHOKING —) POTHER
(COAL —) COOM CULM DUFF COOMB
(COKE —) BREEZE
(COSMIC —) STARDUST
(DIAMOND —) SEASONING
(FIBER —) FLOCK
(FLAX —) POUCE POUSE
(THICK —) SMOTHER
(PREF.) CON(I)(ICO)(IDIO)(O)
(SUFF.) CONITE
DUST CLOUD STEW
DUST COVER WRAPPER
DUSTER COAT DEVIL WILLOW
ZEPHYR TORCHON DUSTCOAT
DUSTMAN GARBO
DUST-STORM DEVIL
DUST-UP TODO

DUSTY ADUST MOTTY MOTTLE POUCEY STOURY POWDERY UNDUSTED

DUTCH (SEE NETHERLANDS) HOGEN HOLLAND

DUTCH FOIL ORSEDE ORSEDUE

DUTCH GOLD CLINQUANT

DUTCHMAN HANS HOGEN BLANDA DUTCHY BELANDA DUTCHER MYNHEER BATAVIAN

DUTCHMAN'S BREECHES DICENTRA

DUTCHWOMAN FROW

DUTIFUL PIOUS DOCILE LAWFUL DEBTFUL DUTEOUS OBEDIENT OFFICIAL REVERENT OFFICIOUS

DUTIFULNESS PIETY

DUTY DO END JOB LOT TAX CALL CARE FYRD MUST ONUS PART PROW ROLE TAIL TASK TOLL WIKE CHORE DEVER ERMIN LADLE LIKIN OUGHT PREST RIGHT STINT WIKEN BLANCH BURDEN CHARGE COCKET DEVOIR DHARMA EXCISE EXITUS HERIOT IMPOSE IMPOST INGATE OFFICE RIVAGE TARIFF AVERAGE BAILAGE BOOMAGE FOSSAGE FURDUNG GRANAGE INDULTO KEELAGE LASTAGE PONTAGE PRIMAGE ROYALTY SCAVAGE SERVICE STATION TONNAGE TRIBUTE TRONAGE TUNNAGE BALLIAGE BUSINESS FUNCTION MALIKANA MALTOLTE REDDENDO WEIGHAGE OBLIGATION
(— FOR LEAD ORE) COPE
(— OF SPARING LIFE) AHIMSA
(CHINESE TRANSIT —) LIKIN
(CUSTOMS —) OCTROI
(FEUDAL —) HERIOT
(IMPORT —) ERMIN INDULTO
(MILITARY —) STABLES
(TIRING —) FATIGUE
(PL.) CUSTOMS INGATES ACTIVITY

DUX CHIEF LEADER SUBJECT HERETOGA

DWALE BELLADONNA

DWARF ELF PUG URF AETA CRUT GRIG GRUB NANA RUNT CRILE CROWL GALAR GNOME KNURL MIDGE PIGMY PYGMY SCRUB STUNT TROLL ABLACH ALVISS CONJON DROICH DURGAN DURGEN MIDGET SHRIMP ANDVARI ANDWARI BLASTIE CONGEON MANIKIN OVERTOP PACOLET WRATACK ALBERICH BELITTLE HOMUNCIO HOMUNCLE HUCKMUCK KNURLING MENEHUNE NANANDER
(PL.) CERCOPES NIBLUNGS NIBELUNGS
(PREF.) NAN(O) NANN(O)

DWARF DANDELION KRIGIA

DWARFED STUNTY STUNTED

DWARF ELDER WALLWORT

DWARFING BRACHYSM

DWARFISH ELFIN PIGMY PYGMY GRUBBY KNURLY NANOID RUNTISH STUNTED

DWARFISHNESS NANISM

DWARFISM NANISM ATELIOSIS

DWARF MALLOW CHEESE PELLAS

DWARF RASPBERRY PLUMBOG

DWEEB NERD

DWELL BIG COT DIG SIT WIN WON BIDE BIGG HAFT HARP LIVE STAY TELD WINE WONT ABIDE BIELD BOWER BROOD BUILD DELAY HOUSE LODGE PAUSE SHACK STALL TARRY LINGER REMAIN RESIDE TENANT CLIMATE COHABIT INHABIT CONVERSE
(— IN) BIG BIGG BEDWELL INHABIT
(— IRRITATINGLY) GRATE
(— ON) HARP BROOD GLOAT

DWELLER TENANT WONNER DENIZEN PALEMAN DOWNSMAN HABITANT OCCUPANT RESIDENT
(— BY SEA) PARALIAN
(BUSH —) HATTER
(CAVE —) CAVEMAN TROGLODYTE
(CITY —) SLICKER
(COAST —) BUFFALO ORARIAN
(LAKE —) LACUSTRIAN
(PL.) HUTHOLD
(SUFF.) ITE

DWELLING DAR HUT INN SEF WON CASA FARM FLAT FORT HAFT HALL HOME NEST ROOF SLUM TENT WIKE WONE ABODE BOWER CABIN DOMUS HOGAN HOOCH HOTEL HOUSE HOVEL JOINT MANSE MOTEL PLACE CASTLE DUGOUT DUPLEX HOMING HOOTCH MALOCA SHANTY TEEPEE WIGWAM WONING COTTAGE LODGING MANSION SALTBOX TRAILER TRIPLEX WONNING BUILDING BUNGALOW DOMICILE TENEMENT PENTHOUSE RESIDENCE
(— IN UNDERWORLD) CHTHONIC
(— PLACE) HOWF HOWFF
(— WITH ANOTHER) INMATE
(ATTRACTIVE —) BOWER
(CRUDE —) SHED SHEBANG
(ESKIMO —) IGLOO
(HERMIT'S —) CELL
(LAKE —) CRANNOG PALAFITTE
(MEAN —) SHANTY
(MISERABLE —) BURROW DOGHOLE
(NAVAJO —) HOGAN
(NEOLITHIC —) TERRAMARA
(ONE-ROOM —) CELL
(OVERCROWDED —) WARREN
(PORTABLE —) CAMPER
(RAMSHACKLE —) HUMPY
(RUDE —) BOTHY BOTHIE
(SMALL —) CRIB
(SUBTERRANEAN —) WEEM

(SWISS —) CHALET
(TEMPORARY —) BOTHY BOTHIE
(WRETCHED —) HOVEL
(PL.) HOUSING
DWINDLE FADE FAIL FINE MELT PINE
WANE DECAY DRAIN PETER TAPER
TRAIL WASTE MOLDER SHRINK
CONSUME DECLINE FRITTER
MOULDER DECREASE DIMINISH
FORDWINE
DWINDLING DOWN FLAGGING
DYAD PAIR
DYBBUK GILGUL
DYE (ALSO SEE DYESTUFF) AAL AZO
DIP LIT ANIL BLUE COLOR EMBUE
FUCUS IMBUE LOKAO STAIN SUDAN
TINCT VENOM ARCHIL IMBRUE
INFECT MADDER TINGER ENGRAIN
INTINCT LACMOID LOGWOOD
PUCCOON ZAMBESI AMARANTH
COLORANT DYESTUFF FUGITIVE
INDIGOID TINCTURE
(— FUR) FEATHER
(— NOT FAST) FUGITIVE
(BLACK —) GUAKO
(BLUE —) RUM ANIL ROOM SAXE
WOAD INDIGO METHYL ANILINE
CYANINE DICYANINE
(BROWN —) CACHOU
(GENERAL —S) NIL NILL AZINE
BROWN EOSIN GREEN DIANIL
EOSINE ISAMIN ORANGE PURPLE
VIOLET CYANINE FUCHSIN METANIL
PONCEAU PRIMULA ALIZARIN
AURANTIA CIBACRON DICYANIN
EURHODOL FUCHSINE HYPERNIC
INDULINE NIGROSIN TURNSOLE
VIRIDINE NIGROSINE SAFRANINE
(HAIR —) RASTIK
(KIND OF —) AZO SRA
(ORANGE —) KAMALA ROUCOU
(PURPLE —) CASSIUS GALLEIN
TURNSOLE
(RED —) AAL ANATO AURIN EOSIN
GRAIN HENNA RUBIN ANATTO
AURINE CERISE EOSINE RELBUN
RUBINE ALKANET ANNATTO
CORINTH CRIMSON MAGENTA
PONCEAU SAFFLOR ALIZARIN
AMARANTH BORDEAUX CORALLIN
CROCEINE
(SCARLET —) TULY GRAIN
(VIOLET —) MAUVE ARCHIL ORCHIL
LACMOID ARCHILLA
(VIOLET — SOURCE) MUREX
(YELLOW —) ARUSA FLAVIN CHRYSIN
FISETIN FLAVINE LAWSONE
WONGSHY AURAMINE

DYED INGRAIN
(PERMANENTLY —) FAST
DYED-IN-THE-WOOL INVETERATE
DYEING TINCTION
DYEPOT JIG VAT LEAD DYEBECK
DYER LISTER TINGER TINTER DYESTER
FIELDER SKEINER TAINTOR TINTIST
DYERMA ZARMA ZAREMA
DYERS' MULBERRY FUSTIC
DYERS'-WEED SOLIDAGO
DYESTUFF (ALSO SEE DYE) DYE LIT
WELD WOAD CHICA LOKAO WOULD
ANATTO BRAZIL KAMALA LITMUS
ORCEIN RELBUN ALKANET ARNATTO
CUDBEAR DYEWARE SAFFRON
INDULINE LUTEOLIN PITTACAL
PURPURIN
DYEWEED WOODWAX
DYEWOOD FUSTET FUSTIC
BARWOOD CAMWOOD HYPERNIC
DYING FEY DEATH MORENDO
PARTING MORIBUND
(— AWAY) CALANDO DILUENDO
MANCANDO PERDENDO
SMORZATO
DYNAMIC POTENT DRIVING KINETIC
FORCEFUL
DYNAMITE BLAST DUALIN
SAWDUST RENDROCK GELIGNITE
DYNAMO EXCITER TORNADO
(PART OF —) BRUSH FIELD FRAME
RIGGING ARMATURE COUPLING
COMMUTATOR
DYNASTY (OR MEMBER THEREOF)
HAN KIN SUI WEI YIN CHIN CHOU
HSIA RACE SUNG TANG YUAN
BUYID CHING PIAST REALM RULER
SHANG HAFSID PRINCE SAFAVI
SELJUK ABBASID ALMOHAD
ARSACID ATTALID AYUBITE AYYUBID
BOUIDES FATIMID HAFSITE IDRISID
JAGELLO LAKHMID MONARCH
OMAYYAD ROMANOV SAADIAN
SAFAWID SAMANID TULUNID
ABBASIDE AGHLABID AGLABITE
ASMONEAN BUWAIHID CAPETIAN
CHALUKYA DOMINION EDRISITE
GOVERNOR IDRISITE JAGIELLO
LORDSHIP SAFFARID SARGONID
SASANIAN SELEUCID SOFFARID
SASSANIDE
DYSENTERY FLUX SCOUR MENISON
TOXEMIA DIARRHEA
DYSPEPTIC CACOGASTRIC
DYSPHORIA FIDGET
DYSSODIA BOEBERA
DZIGGETAI HEMIONUS

E EASY ECHO
EA HEA ENKI
EACH A EA UP ALL ILK THE UCH ILKA
UCHE EVERY APIECE EITHER
EVERYONE
(OF —) ANA
EAGER HOT RAD YAN ACID AGOG
AVID EDGY FAIN FELL FOND FREE
GAIR HIGH KEEN RATH SOUR TARE
THRO VAIN WARM WAVE YARE YERN
AFIRE AGASP ANTSY BRIEF FIRST
FRACK FRECK HASTY HIGRE ITCHY
PRIME READY SHARP SNELL YIVER
ARDENT FIERCE GREEDY HETTER
INTENT STRONG TIPTOE ANXIOUS
ATHIRST BRITTLE BURNING
EMULOUS EXCITED FERVENT
FORWARD ITCHING PROVOKE
DESIROUS IRRITATE SPIRITED
VIGOROUS YEARNING SOLICITOUS
(— IN PURSUIT) SHARP
(— TO KNOW) INQUISITIVE
(VERY —) WILD
(WILDLY —) CRAZY
EAGERLY FAST FELL YERN HOTLY
BELIVE TIPTOE YARELY YEPELY
PRESTLY HUNGRILY INTENTLY
EAGERNESS GOG ELAN GARE ZEAL
ARDOR DESIRE FERVOR ARDENCY
AVIDITY ALACRITY CUPIDITY
DEVOTION FAINNESS FERVENCY
EAGLE AAR ERN CROW ERNE GIER
TERN HARPY AQUILA BERGUT
EAGLET FALCON FORMAL FORMEL
RAPTOR ALLERION BATALEUR
BATELEUR BEARCOOT BERGHAAN
RINGTAIL
(KIND OF —) LEGAL
(SEA —) ERN ERNE PYGARG
PYGARGUS
(PREF.) AET(O)
(SUFF.) AETUS
EAGLE OWL KATOGLE
EAGLESTONE AETITES
EAGLET BIRD LAIGLON
EAGLEWOOD AGAR ALOE AGILA
ALOES AGALLOCH AQUILARI
EAGRE BORE WAVE AEGIR HYGRE
EANFLED (FATHER OF —) EADWINE
(HUSBAND OF —) OSWIU
EAR LUG NEB CLIP HEAR HEED HOOK
LIST OBEY PLOW TILL AURIS BRACE
PINNA SENSE SOUSE SOWSE SPIKE
CANNON CONCHA CROSET EARLET
LISTEN AURICLE HEARING SENSORY
AUDIENCE PAVILION RECEPTOR
(— OF BELL) CANON CANNON

(— OF CORN) COB ICKER MEALIE
NUBBIN CORNCOB
(— OF GRAIN) RISOM SPIKE RIZZOM
(— OF WHEAT) SPICA WHEATEAR
(—S OF GRAIN) CAPES EARHEAD
(KIND OF —) TREE
(KIND OF —S) RABBIT
(OF THE —) AURICULAR
(PART OF —) LOBE TUBE CANAL
HELIX INCUS PINNA CONCHA
MEATUS SCAPHA STAPES TRAGUS
COCHLEA MALLEUS MEMBRANE
TYMPANUM ANTIHELIX ANTITRAGUS
(UNRIPE — OF CORN) TUCKET
(PREF.) AUR(I) AURICULO OT(ICO)(IO)
(O) SPICI SPICULI SPICULO
(— OF CORN) ATHERO STACHY(O)
(SUFF.) OTIC
EARACHE OTALGY OTALGIA
EAR-BONE OTOLITH
EARCOCKLE PURPLES
EARDRUM TABOR TABOUR TYMPAN
MYRINGA DRUMHEAD TYMPANUM
(PREF.) TRYPAN(O) TYMPAN(O)
EARED SEAL SEALION
EARFLAP LUG EARLAP EARTAB
EARMUFF
EARINE (LOVER OF —) AEGLAMOUR
EARL EORL GRAF JARL LORD PEER
COMES NOBLE CONSUL SIWARD
(— OF COVENTRY)
SNIPSNAPSNORUM
EARLDOM DERBY COUNTY
EARLIER ERE OLD ERST FORE ELDER
SUPRA UPPER BEFORE FORMER
HITHER RATHER SOONER FIRSTER
FURTHER PIONEER PREMIER
PREVIOUS
(PREF.) FORE PROTER(O)
(— THAN) PRE PRO
EARLIEST ERST FIRST ELDEST
MAIDEN PIONEER PREMIER RATHEST
FURTHEST PRIMROSE ABORIGINAL
(PREF.) EO
EAR LOBE LUG EARLAP
(— PEOPLE) OREJON
EARLY AIR ERE OLD GOOD HIGH RARE
RATH SOON FORME PRIMY RATHE
VERTY REARLY SUDDEN TIMELY
ANCIENT BETIMES ERLICHE
FORWARD YOUTHFUL MATUTINAL
(UNDULY —) PREMATURE
(PREF.) EO PALAE(O) PALE(O)
EARMARK BIT CROP SIGN SPLIT
LUGMARK OVERBIT SLEEPER
ALLOCATE OVERCROP UNDERBIT
EAR MUFF OREILET

EARN GET WIN FANG GAIN MAKE
TILL VANG ADDLE ETTLE GLEAR
MERIT GARNER HUSTLE OBTAIN
ACHIEVE ACQUIRE CHEVISE DEMERIT
DESERVE
(— BY LABOR) ADDLE SWINK
BESWINK

EARNEST ARRA DEAR DERN HARD
PAWN ARLES EAGER GRAVE SMART
SOBER STAID ARDENT ENTIRE
HANSEL HEARTY INTENT SEDATE
SOLEMN EMULOUS ENGAGED
FERVENT FORWARD HANDSEL
INTENSE SERIOUS SINCERE
ZEALOUS DILIGENT EMPHATIC
STUDIOUS
(IN —) AGOOD

EARNESTLY HARD DEARLY WISHLY
WISTLY EARNEST DEVOUTLY
DINGDONG ENTIRELY HEARTILY
INTENTLY INWARDLY

EARNESTNESS GLOW FERVOR
WARMTH GRAVITY DEVOTION
DILIGENCE

EARNINGS GET MAKING ADDLINS
PICKING ADDLINGS

EARPIECE BUTTON

EARPLUG STOPPLE TEMBETA
EARSPOOL

EARRING DROP GRIP EARBOB
EARLET PENDLE EARCLIP EARDROP
PENDANT EARSCREW
(— LOCALE) LOBE

EARS (KIND OF —) RABBIT

EAR SHELL ORMER ABALONE

EARSHOT SOUND HEARING
EARREACH

EARTH ERD ORB SET BALL BANK
BURY BYON CLAY CLOD DIRT DUST
FLAG FOLD GRIT LAND LOAM MARL
MASS MEAL MOLD MOOL MUCK
ROCK SOIL SORY STAR VALE YIRD
ADOBE CRUMB FLOSS GLEBE GLOBE
GROOT INTER LOESS MOULD REGUR
TERRA TRASS SWARD WIND WORLD
CENTER CENTRE COARSE GROUND
YACATA KOKOWAI MIDGARD
TERRENE TIERRAS TOPSOIL TRIPOLI
MAGNESIA MIDGARTH
(— FOR RAMPART) REMBLAI
(— INHABITANT) TERRAN
(— PROVIDING OCHER) KOKOWAI
(— SUITABLE FOR CULTIVATION)
LAYER
(BLACK —) MUCK SORY KILLOW
AMPELITE CHERNOZEM
(BLUE —) KIMBERLITE
(BROWN —) UMBER
(CLAYEY —) LAME LOAM
(DRY —) MOOL GROOT
(FULLER'S —) CRETA CIMOLITE
SMECTITE
(GEM-BEARING —) BYON

(HEAVY —) BARYTA
(LOOSE —) CRUMB GEEST
(MOIST —) SLAB SLIME
(POOR —) RAMMEL
(RAMMED —) PISE
(RED —) RUDDLE
(REFUSE —) MURGEON
(RIVER-BANK —) GREWT
(SMALL —) TERRELLA
(SOAP —) SOAPROCK
(STRAW-YELLOW —) BISMITE
(SUN-DRIED —) SWISH
(VITRIFIED —) FLOSS
(VOLCANIC —) TRASS TARRASS
(PREF.) AGRO GE(O) TELLUR(I)
TERR(A)(E)(I)
(SUFF.) GAEA GEA

EARTHEN FICT DIRTEN EARTHLY
YARTHEN

EARTHENWARE PIG POT DELF
CHINA CLOAM CROCK DELFT CLAYEN
JASPER ASTBURY BISCUIT FAIENCE
POTTERY TICKNEY BUFFWARE
CROCKERY MAJOLICA TALAVERA
(BROKEN PIECE OF —) CROCK

EARTHINESS SALT TERREITY

EARTHKIN TERRELLA

EARTHLY LAIRY CARNAL EARTHY
MORTAL EARTHEN GLEBOUS
MUNDANE SECULAR TERRAIN
TERRENE WORLDLY SUBLUNAR
TELLURIC TEMPORAL

EARTHMAN TERRAN

EARTHNUT ARNOT ARNUT CHUFA
HOGNUT JARNUT PEANUT PIGNUT
HARENUT HAWKNUT TRUFFLE

EARTH PIG ERDVARK AARDVARK

EARTHQUAKE QUAKE SEISM
SHAKE SHOCK TEMBLOR SEAQUAKE
(PREF.) SEISMO SISMO
(SUFF.) SEISM SEISMAL SEISMIC

EARTHSTAR GEASTER

EARTH STATION DISH

EARTHWALL TRINCHERA

EARTH WOLF AARDWOLF

EARTHWORK BANK RATH RING
AGGER CASTLE SCONCE PARADOS
RAMPART TERRACE
(PL.) PARADOS

EARTHWORM ESS MAD WORM
ANNELID DEWWORM IPOMOEA
MADDOCK ANGLEDOG BRANDLIN
EACEWORM FISHWORM RAINWORM
TWATCHEL BRANDLING LUMBRICID
OLIGOCHATE

EARTHY GROSS SALTY WORMY
CLODDY VULGAR EARTHLY TERRENE
BARNYARD TERREOUS VISCERAL

EAR TICK PINOLIA

EAR TRUMPET CORNET
AEROPHONE

EARWAX CERUMEN
(PREF.) CERUMINI

EARWIG GOLACH GOLOCH TOUCHBELL
EARWORM BOLLWORM
EASE CALM COSY COZY EASY REST ABATE ALLAY KNACK LETUP PEACE QUIET RELAX SLAKE LOOSEN PACIFY REDUCE RELIEF REPOSE SAUGHT SMOOTH SOFTEN SOOTHE APPEASE ASSUAGE COMFORT CONTENT FACULTY FLUENCY FREEDOM LEISURE LIBERTY LIGHTEN RELIEVE SLACKEN SUBSIDE DIMINISH FACILITY MITIGATE MODERATE PALLIATE PLEASURE SECURITY UNBURDEN
(— GENTLY) SLIDE
(— OF A BURDEN) LIGHT
(— OFF) FLOW CHECK START SLOUGH
(APATHETIC —) INDOLENCE
(AT —) OTIOSE
(CAREFREE —) ABANDON
EASEL FRAME SUPPORT SCAFFOLD
EASEMENT EASE EASING RELIEF HERBAGE TURBARY SERVITUS WAYLEAVE
EASE-TAKING PICKTOOTH
EASIEST EFTEST
EASILY EASY EATH WELL LIGHT EATHLY GENTLY GLIBLY HANDILY LIGHTLY READILY SLIGHTLY SMOOTHLY
(PREF.) EU
EASINESS GRACE FACILITY
EASING DETENTE
EAST OST ASIA MORN LEVANT ORIENT SUNRISE EASTWARD
(— OF) FOLLOWING
EAST AFRICA
(— TREE) PODO
EASTER PT PACE PASCH EOSTRE PASCHA PASQUE
EASTERN LEVANT ORTIVE AURORAL ORIENTAL
EASTERNER DUDE
EAST INDIAN
(— TREE) SAL AMLA DHAK TEAK KOKAN LANSA MAHUA MOHWA NIEPA PALAS PULAS ROHAN ROHUN SALAI SIMAL
EASTLAND ESTRICHE
EASTWARD EAST EASEL EASSEL
EASY CALM COZY CRIP EATH EITH GAIN GLIB MILD RIFE SNAP SOFT CUSHY JAMMY LARGE LIGHT PLAIN PRONE ROYAL SUAVE YEZZY CASUAL COMODO FACILE FLUENT FRUITY GENTLE GENTLY SECURE SIMPLE SMOOTH UNHARD ARTLESS GRADUAL LENIENT NATURAL CAREFREE CARELESS CAVALIER EXPEDITE FAMILIAR FRIENDLY

GRACEFUL HOMELIKE MODERATE TRANQUIL UNFORCED
(— IN MIND) SECURE
(— TO HANDLE) HANDSOME
(— TO SPEAK TO) AFFABLE
(— TO UNDERSTAND) PELLUCID
(— TO USE) CLEVER
(TAKE IT —) SIT LAZE
EASYGOING LAX QUIET DEGAGE
EAT FOG KAI SUP BITE CHOP CHOW DINE FARE FEED FRET GNAW GRUB HAVE HEYT MAKE PECK RUST TUCK DIGIN ERODE FEAST GRAZE MANGE MUNCH SCOFF STOKE TASTE WASTE ABSORB BEGNAW DEVOUR INGEST NIBBLE RAVAGE CONSUME CORRODE DESTROY SWALLOW VICTUAL
(— A MEAL) GRUB
(— AS HOGS) SLUICE
(— A SNACK) NOSH
(— AWAY) GNAW ERODE RANKLE CORRODE
(— BETWEEN MEALS) NOSH
(— BIG MEAL) STOKE
(— CRUNCHINGLY) GROUZE
(— GLUTTONOUSLY) GUDGE STUFF
(— GREEDILY) GAMP GAWP SLAB SLOP TUCK CHAUM MOOCH SCARF SCOFF GOBBLE GOFFLE GUTTLE GUZZLE PIGOUT RAUNGE GLUTTON GOURMAND
(— HEARTILY) THORN
(— IN GULPS) LAB
(— MINCINGLY) PICK PICKLE PIDDLE
(— NOISILY) SLOP GULCH SLURP GUTTLE SLOTTER
(— OUT) EXFDE
(— RUDELY) TROUGH
(— SLOVENLY) SLUP MUMMICK
(— SPARINGLY) DIET NIBBLE
(— TO EXCESS) COLF BEZZLE
(— UP) DEMOLISH
(— VORACIOUSLY) CRAM WORRY
(— WITH GUSTO) SMOUSE
(— WITHOUT CHEWING) BOLT
(SUFF.) ESTES PHAG(A)(E)(IA)(ISM) (IST)(O)(OUS)(US)(Y) VORA VORE VOROUS
EATABLE FOODY COOKER EDIBLE ESCULENT
EATEN CANKERED
(HALF —) SEMESE
(PREF.) BROTO
EATER PECKER DEVOURER
(GREEDY —) GOURMAND
EATING BIT FOOD ESURINE
(— BETWEEN MEALS) TIFFIN
(— COARSE FOOD) FOUL
(— DISORDER) BULIMIA
(— INTO) CANKEROUS
(— OUT) EXESION
(PREF.) PHAG(O)

EAVES EASE EASING
EAVESDROP DARK HARKEN LISTEN HEARKEN
EAVESDROPPER COWAN EARWIG SNOOPER DRAWLATCH
EAVES TROUGH CHENEAU
EBAL (FATHER OF —) SHOBAL
EBB FAIL FALL FLAG SINK WANE ABATE DECAY RECEDE REFLOW REFLUX RETIRE TIDING DECLINE REFLOAT SUBSIDE DECREASE DIMINISH
(— AND FLOW) ESTUS AESTUS FLUIDITY
EBBING AWANE REFLUENT REFLUOUS
(— AND FLOWING) TIDAL
EBED (FATHER OF —) JONATHAN
(SON OF —) GAAL
EBER (FATHER OF —) SALAH ELPAAL
EBLIS JANN IBLIS
EBONY EBON BLACK GABON GABOON WAMARA HEBENON IRONWOOD
EBULLIENCE OVERFLOW ELEVATION
EBULLIENT BRASH FERVID YEASTY BOILING
EBULLIOSCOPE ZEOSCOPE
EBULLITION SEETHE FERMENT OUTBURST
ECAD ECOPHENE
ECCENTRIC FEY NUT ODD OFF CARD DOER NUTS CRANK DOTTY KINKY OUTRE QUEER WEIRD WIPER CRANKY LOCOED OUTISH PSYCHO SCREWY SHAGGY WEIRDO WEIRDY BIZARRE CURIOUS DEVIOUS DINGBAT ERRATIC ODDBALL STRANGE TOUCHED ABNORMAL CRACKPOT FITIFIED PECULIAR SINGULAR
(— PERSON) KOOK
ECCENTRICITY KINK FERLY ODDITY ANOMALY CROTCHET QUIDDITY
(— OF CURVE) E
ECCLESIASTES KOHELETH QOHELETH
ECCLESIASTIC ABBE ABBOT CLERK VICAR ARCHON FATHER LECTOR LEGATE PRIEST KIRKMAN PRELATE SECULAR EPISTLER SUBDEACON
ECCLESIASTICAL CHURCH CANONIC CHURCHLY CHRISTIAN SPIRITUAL
ECHELES
(FATHER OF —) ACTOR
(FOSTER SON OF —) EUDORUS
(WIFE OF —) POLYMELA
ECHEVIN SCABINE SCABINUS
ECHIDNA NODIAK ANTEATER EDENTATE MONOTREME PORCUPINE
(CHILD OF —) HYDRA LADON ORTHUS SPHINX CERBERUS CHIMAERA
(FATHER OF —) PHORCYS CHRYSAOR

(MOTHER OF —) CETO CALLIRRHOE
(SLAYER OF —) ARGUS
ECHINODERM CYSTID CRINOID BLASTOID STARFISH
ECHINOPANAX FATSIA
ECHINO-SOREX GYMNURA
ECHION (FATHER OF —) MERCURY
(MOTHER OF —) ANTIANIRA
(SON OF —) PENTHEUS
(WIFE OF —) AGAVE
ECHO APE ECO BLIP RING SING CHORUS REPEAT REVERB SECOND IMITATE ITERATE RESOUND RESPEAK RESPOND REVOICE REDOUBLE RESPONSE
(— EFFECT) REVERB
(RADAR —) ANGEL
(RADIO —) ANGEL
ECLAT FAME GLORY RENOWN ACCLAIM SCANDAL APPLAUSE FACILITY PRESTIGE SPLENDOR
ECLECTIC BROAD LIBERAL
ECLIPSE DIM BIND BLOT HIDE BLIND CLOUD SHADE STAIN SULLY DARKEN DAZZLE DEFECT EXCEED OCCULT DEFAULT OBSCURE PRODIGY TRAVAIL OUTRIVAL OCCULTATION
ECLOGUE IDYL IDYLL BUCOLIC
ECOLOGIST BIONOMIST
ECOLOGY BIOLOGY BIONOMY MESOLOGY
ECONOMIC
(PREF.) EC(O) OEC(O) OIKO
ECONOMICAL WARY CHARY FENDY FRUGAL SAVING CAREFUL PRUDENT SPARING THRIFTY SCREWING
ECONOMICS PLUTONOMY
ECONOMIST HUSBAND MANAGER PHYSIOCRAT
AMERICAN DAY ELY GRAY OKUN POOR ADAMS ARROW ARROW BALCH BURNS CAREY CLARK DEWEY GRAMM HANEY HAUGE HICKS LUBIN MEYER SOLOW TOBIN WELLS WITTE YOUNG CARVER DEBREU DUNBAR DURAND ECCLES FISHER FOSTER GEORGE HADLEY HARVEY KATONA MILLIS RAGUET RIPLEY RIVLIN SPLAWN SUMNER TUCKER TURNER VEBLEN WALKER WEAVER WILLIS BULLOCK COMMONS CROWELL GARRETT JOHNSON KUZNETS TAUSSIG TUGWELL ANDERSON FRIEDMAN KEMMERER KOOPMANS LAUGHLIN LEONTIEF MITCHELL ROSOVSKY GALBRAITH HENDERSON HOLLANDER SAMUELSON MODIGLIANI WILLOUGHBY JANEWAY
AUSTRALIAN DONALD
AUSTRIAN BOHM HAYEK MISES SPANN MENGER

BELGIAN ZEELAND LEVELEYE
MOLINARI
CANADIAN HOWE MAVOR ERDMAN
LALONDE LEACOCK
DUTCH TINBERGEN
ENGLISH JAY COLE MILL WARD
WEBB WEST HAYEK HICKS HIRST
JAMES MEADE PAISH PETTY PRICE
STAMP ASHLEY BARBON BAXTER
COBDEN FARRER GIFFEN HOBSON
JEVONS KEYNES KIRKUP LAYTON
LESLIE REEVES ROGERS SALTER
SENIOR SHANKS TUCKER WILSON
BAGEHOT CHAPMAN CLAPHAM
FAWCETT GRESHAM MALTHUS
MALYNES RICARDO TOYNBEE
BELLERBY MARSHALL BEVERIDGE
EDGEWORTH HOLLOWOOD
MACMILLAN MARTINEAU
NICHOLSON OVERSTONE
CUNNINGHAM
FINNISH PROCOPE
FRENCH SAY LEVY RIST BODIN
GUYOT CAMBON HAUSER MONNET
ALIMAND BASTIAI BLANQUI
BLONDEL COURNOT FAUCHER
GARNIER GOURNAY MONTYON
QUESNAY SCHUMAN MIRABEAU
PECQUEUR ROEDERER WOLOWSKI
CHEVALIER LEVASSEUR SIEGFRIED
GERMAN RAU BONN HAHN ENGEL
FUCHS HARMS JUSTI KNIES LANGE
BRIEFS BUCHER CONRAD ECKERT
ENGARD GESELL GOSSEN HIRSCH
SERING ANDREAE DUHRING
EHEBERG GERLOFF HEIMANN
JASTROW LEDERER MICHELS
ROSCHER HUFELAND SCHAFFLE
BAMBERGER RODBERTUS
SCHMOLLER FLURSCHEIM
HAXTHAUSEN HELFFERICH
KESSELRING RAIFFEISEN
SCHUMPETER OPPENHEIMER
GREEK ANDREADES
IRISH SMIDDY CAIRNES BASTABLE
CANTILLON
ITALIAN BODIO CARLI GIOJA LORIA
NITTI PELLA ROSSI BOTERO PARETO
GALIANI BECCARIA GENOVESI
LUZZATTI SCIALOIA CERNUSCHI
PANTALEONI
NORWEGIAN FRISCH
POLISH GRABSKI WOJCIECHOWSKI
RUSSIAN BUNGE KANTOROVICH
VOZNESENSKI
SCOTTISH MILL SMITH MACLEOD
ANDERSON MCCULLOCH
SWEDISH OHLIN CASSEL MYRDAL
SWISS SISMONDI CHERBULIEZ
URUGUAYAN COSIO
ECONOMIZE HAIN SAVE SKIMP
STINT SCRAPE SCRIMP HUSBAND
UTILIZE RETRENCH

ECONOMY SPARE SAVING SYSTEM
THRIFT MANAGERY PARSIMONY
ECOTONE EDGE
ECSTASY JOY BLISS POWER SWOON
TRANCE DELIGHT EMOTION
MADNESS RAPTURE RHAPSODY
ECSTATIC HOT RAPT PYTHIAN
GLORIOUS
ECTENE IRENICON
ECTODERM EXODERM EPIBLAST
ECTOMORPHIC LINEAR ASTHENIC
LEPTOSOME
ECTROPION EVERSION
ECU CROWN SCUTE SHIELD

ECUADOR

ANCIENT NAME: QUITO
CAPE: ROSA PASADO PUNTILLA
CAPITAL: QUITO
COIN: SUCRE CONDOR CENTAVO
INDIAN: CARA INCA PALTA CANELO
JIVARO
ISLAND: PUNA WOLF MOCHA PINTA
RAITRA CHAVEZ DARWIN PINZON
WENMAN ISABELA
ISLANDS: COLON GALAPAGOS
LANGUAGE: JIBARO QUECHUA
SPANISH
MEASURE: CUADRA FANEGA
MOUNTAIN: ANDES SANGAY
CAYAMBE ANTISANA COTOPAXI
NATIVE: MONTUVIO
PROVINCE: LOJA AZUAY CANAR
COLON ELORO CARCHI GUAYAS
MANABI BOLIVAR LOSRIOS
COTOPAXI IMBABURA
RIVER: COCA MIRA NAPO DAULE
PINDO TIGRE GUAYAS TUMBES
ZAMORA CURARAY PASTAZA
AGUARICO BOBUNAZA CONONACO
NARANJAL PUTUMAYO
TOWN: JAMA LOJA MERA NAPO
PUYU TENA CANAR GUANO
MANTA PAJAN PINAS PIURA
QUITO YAUPI AMBATO CUENCA
IBARRA PUJILI TULCAN ZARUMA
AZOGUES CAYAMBE GUAMOTE
MACHALA PELILEO PILLARO
SALINAS BABAHOYO GUARANDA
RIOBAMBA
WATERFALL: AGOYAN
WEIGHT: LIBRA

ECUMENE HEARTH
ECUMENICAL LIBERAL CATHOLIC
ECZEMA TETTER EARWORM
MALANDERS
EDACITY GREED APPETITE VORACITY
EDDA SAGA
EDDISH ETCH ARRISH EEGRASS
EDDO TARO COCOYAM
EDDY CURL GULF PURL WASH WEEL
WELL ACKER GURGE SHIFT SWIRL

TWIRL WHIRL SWOOSH VORTEX
WIRBLE BACKSET WREATHE
(PREF.) DINO

EDDYING WALE

EDEMA BRAXY TUMOR DROPSY
BIGHEAD HYDROPS ANASARCA
SWELLING

EDEMATOUS BLOATED HYDROPIC

EDEN ADEN HEAVEN UTOPIA
ARCADIA ELYSIUM PARADISE
(FATHER OF —) JOAH

EDENTATA BRUTA

EDENTATE SLOTH AARDVARK
ANTEATER

EDGE AGE BIT HEM JAG LIP RIM
BANK BERM BRIM BROW CURB
DRAW FACE KANT LIMB LIST RAND
SIDE TRIM WELL WHET ARRIS BERME
BEVEL BLADE BOARD BRINK CHIMB
CHIME CREST EAVES FRILL KNIFE
LABEL LEDGE MARGE PEARL RULER
SHARP SIDLE SPLAY VERGE BORDER
CANTLE DECKLE FLANGE FORAGE
IMPALE LABRUM MARGIN NOSING
PLANGE MARGENT NOSEOUT
SELVAGE SHARPEN VANDYKE
BOUNDARY EMBORDER KEENNESS
MAJORITY OUTSKIRT SELVEDGE
STICKING UMSTROKE
(— FORWARD) CREEP
(— IN MINING DRIFT) ARRAGE
(— OF BASKET) FOOT
(— OF BED) STOCK
(— OF BIRD'S BILL) TOMIUM
(— OF BOOK) FERRULE BACKBONE
(— OF BOOK COVER) FLAP
(— OF BRILLIANT) GIRDLE
(— OF CASK) CHIME CHINE
(— OF COAL PILE) RUN
(— OF DAM) CREST
(— OF DUMP) TOE
(— OF FABRIC) SELVAGE SELVEDGE
(— OF FLAG) HOIST
(— OF MESA) CEJA
(— OF MINERAL VEIN) APEX
(— OF ROADWAY) SHOULDER
(— OF RUDDER) BEARDING
(— OF RUFFLE) HEADING
(— OF SAIL) FOOT HEAD LEACH
LEECH
(— OF SAW) SAFE
(— OF SHELL) HINGE
(— OF STRATUM) BASSET
(— OF STREAM) HAG
(— OF TOOL) BEZEL BEZIL
(— OF TOOTH) SCALPRUM
(— OF TROUSERS) CREASE
(— OF VAULT) GROIN
(— OF WOOD) WOODRIME
(—S OF COAT) LAP
(BEVELED —) CHAMFER
(CUTTING —) SHOE FRONTIER
VANGUARD

(DOUBLE —) FLAT
(EMBROIDERED —) SURFLE SURPHUL
(EXTERIOR —) AMBITUS
(FRONT — OF BOOK) FACE
(HAVING IRREGULAR —) EROSE
(ORNAMENTAL —) FRILL
(RAGGED —) RAG
(ROCKY —) ARETE
(ROUGH —S) FASH
(SHARP —) ARRIS BEARD
(UNPLOWED — OF FIELD) RAND
(UNTRIMMED —) DECKLE
(PREF.) AMBO

EDGED EDGY EROSE SHARP
CRENATE CUTTING
(— BY ARCS) INVECTED

EDGER WHETTER STRANDER

EDGEWISE (NOT —) FLATLONG

EDGING HEM CURB EDGE LACE LIST
FILET FRILL LEDGE PICOT BORDER
FILLET FRINGE LIMBUS BEADING
BINDING GIMPING HAMBURG
COQUILLE FRILLING PUNTILLA
RICKRACK SKIRTING SURROUND
PASSEMENTERIE
(— TO COLLAR) PIKADELL PICCADILL
PICCADILLO PICCADILLY
(GRASS —) VERGE

EDGY ANTSY EAGER FUSSY SHARP
TENSE ANGULAR NERVOUS CRITICAL
SNAPPISH

EDIBLE EDULE ALIBLE EATABLE
ESCULENT

EDICT ACT BAN LAW BULL FIAT TYPE
ARRET BANDO BULLA IRADE ORDER
SANAD UKASE ASSIZE DECREE
DICTUM NOTICE COMMAND
EMBARGO PLACARD PROCESS
PROGRAM STATUTE ECTHESIS
RESCRIPT

EDIFICE DOME CHURCH TURBEH
BUILDING ERECTION TETRAGON

EDIFY GROW BUILD FAVOR TEACH
BENEFIT IMPROVE PROSPER
CONVINCE INSTRUCT ORGANIZE

EDIFYING HIGH SAVORY ELEVATED

EDIT CUT EMEND DIRECT REDACT
REVIEW REVISE ARRANGE COMPILE
CORRECT PREPARE PUBLISH
REWRITE COPYREAD

EDITION KIND EXTRA FINAL FIRST
ISSUE PRINT STAMP ALDINE DIGLOT
SOURCE AUSGABE BULLDOG
HEXAPLA OCTAPLA VERSION
PRINCEPS VARIORUM
(FIRST —) PRINCEPS

EDITOR AUTHOR OVERSEER
REDACTOR
AMERICAN BOK DAY BOVA BOYD
BURR BYRD CARY DANA DELL DUNN
FARB FOSS FUNK HILL HOWE LUCE
REID ROSS SHAW WARE YUST ALLEN
BACON BYERS CANBY CLARK COLBY

DEBOW DUBAY ELSON FENNO
FODOR FOLEY GOULD GRADY KNOTT
LASCH LOCKE LYNES MABIE MOORE
NILES PAINE PRATT PUSEY RENSE
RIDER RUDER SHAWN SWOPE WHITE
ABBOTT AIKENS ANGELL ANGOFF
BALLOU BARRON BIRNIE BOWKER
BOWLES CAPPER CATTON CHURCH
CLARKE COWLEY DABNEY DANIEL
DENNIE DUBOIS FINLEY FLOWER
FORBES GILDER GIROUX HANSEN
HEARST HOOPER LARSEN LAWSON
LUMMIS MALONE MANTLE MARKEL
MARTIN MERWIN MONROE MUNSON
NATHAN PALLEN RASCOE WILLIS
ALDRICH BROWLES BURNETT
COUSINS DREISER EASTMAN
FADIMAN FERNALD FREEMAN
GANNETT HAPGOOD HAZLITT
HOFFMAN HOLLAND HUBBARD
JOHNSON LINCOLN LITTELL
LOVEJOY LOWNDES MENCKEN
NAVASKY ONASSIS STEDMAN
TAGGARD VIERECK WALLACE
ALLIBONE ANDERSON BARSOTTI
BENJAMIN CRAWFORD DOCTOROW
GINGRICH GRINNELL GRUENING
HUZTABLE LIPPMANN PETERSON
RUKEYSER SEDGWICK STRUNSKY
TAISHOFF THOMPSON VANDOREN
WHEELOCK ALTSHELER BARTHOLDT
BLACKWELL DUYCKINCK
KAEMPFFERT UNTERMEYER
CHAMBERLAIN CROWNINSHIELD
CANADIAN MCGEE NEWMAN
ENGLISH LEE MEE FELL FENN OPIE
PEEL READ RHYS RYLE TODD CRAIG
GIBBS HICKS WAUGH ALLOTT
BARNES BOOSEY DELANE GARVIN
HAWKES HUTTON HUXLEY KELTIE
SEAMAN BOWDLER BURNAND
CHAPMAN DUGDALE HYAMSON
KNOWLES VERRALL CHISHOLM
GOLDRING MUIRHEAD PROTHERO
QUENNELL RICKWORD SPEDDING
BOTTOMLEY CUSHENDUN
HOLINSHED HOLLOWOOD
PEMBERTON RAPPOPORT
MONTGOMERY
FINNISH WALTARI
FRENCH MIGNE MORTIER YRIARTE
CHAUMEIX HACHETTE
GERMAN BARTH HUBER MULLER
HUNGARIAN HARSANYI
IRISH RUSSELL ALLINGHAM
ITALIAN ASCOLI
MALTESE BUTTIGIEG
PANAMANIAN ARIAS
RUSSIAN CAHAN ARBATOV BLEEKER
SCOTTISH DYCE LAING CURRIE
DAVIES HERVEY SPENCE ANDERSON
HASTINGS LOCKHART FINDLATER
MOTHERWELL

EDITORIAL LEADER
EDO BENI BINI
EDRED (BROTHER OF —) EDMUND
  (FATHER OF —) EDWARD
  (MOTHER OF —) EADGIFU
EDUCATE REAR BREED TEACH
  TRADE TRAIN EXPAND INFORM
  SCHOOL DEVELOP NURTURE
  INSTRUCT
EDUCATED BRED CIVIL TAUGHT
  TRAINED INFORMED LETTERED
  LITERATE
EDUCATION CLERGY NURTURE
  BREEDING LEARNING NORTELRY
  PEDAGOGY TRAINING
  (— GROUP) NEA
  (LIBERAL —) HUMANITY
  (PHYSICAL —) GYM
EDUCATOR TEACHER
  AMERICAN BOK DAY FEW GAY HAM
  ILG AMES BATE BLOW BODE CASE
  CHEW COLN CONE FORD FRYE HALL
  HART HESS HILL HOLT HOPE HULL
  HYDE KOHL LEVI LIDZ LYND LYON
  MANN MAYR MOON ODUM PAGE
  RAND ROOS ROOT RUGG TARR TRUE
  WARD WARE WEST AARON ADAMS
  ADLER AIKEN AVERY AYRES BAKER
  BATES BAUGH BEARD BEERS BEGLE
  BERRY BOLEY BROWN BRYAN BYRNE
  CANBY CAPEN CAPPS CHASE CLAPP
  CLARK COONS CROSS CURRY
  DAMON DENNY DEWEY DOBIE ELIOT
  EWING FLORY FRANK FUESS GATES
  GAUSS GOULD HEDGE HUBEL
  JAMES JENKS JONES KNOTT KOZOL
  KRAPP KRAUS KUSCH LANGE LOCKE
  LOWES MANLY MEYER MEZES
  MINOT ORTON PATRI PERRY POUND
  PUSEY RILES ROLFE ROSSI SCOTT
  SHERA SMITH SMYTH SZASZ TAUBE
  TEMIN TYLER UNGER UPHAM WHITE
  WOLFF YOUNG ANGELL BAGLEY
  BAILEY BARNES BARZUN BASCOM
  BAXTER BOVARD BOWKER BOWMAN
  BRIGGS BUMPUS BUTLER CARMER
  CARTER CARVER CHIANG CONANT
  COOPER CORSON COUNTS CRONIN
  DABNEY DAVIES DOMAGK DONHAM
  DRAPER DUBOIS DURANT EURICH
  FERRIS FINLEY FINNEY FOWLER
  GAYLEY GEDDES GILMAN GOEBEL
  GRAVES GRIMKE HADLEY HARPER
  HARRIS HAWKES HAZARD HIBBEN
  HIGHET HOWARD JESSUP JEWETT
  JUDSON KELLER KEPPEL LANDIS
  LERNER LOVETT LOWELL MARTIN
  MATHER MCAFEE MEARNS MILLIS
  MONROE NORTON PALMER PARKER
  PEFFER PEIRCE PHELPS PORTER
  SARETT SCOPES SLOANE SPARKS
  SPROUL STRONG STROUP STUART
  THOMAS THWING WIGGIN WILDER

WRIGHT AGASSIZ ANAGNOS
ANDREWS BABBITT BARBOUR
BARNARD BARROWS BENEZET
BETHUNE BRADLEY BRAWLEY
CALKINS CARDOZO CLAXTON
COFFMAN COLBURN COMFORT
CONNELY DENNETT DOHERTY
DYKSTRA ERSKINE FARRAND
GARNETT GARRATY GARRETT
GILMORE GOODNOW GOODWIN
GOUCHER GUMMERE HASKINS
HERRICK HOPKINS HOUSTON
HUEBNER HULBERT HULBURT
JACKSON JARDINE JOHNSON
KHORANA KIMBALL KIMPTON
LEONARD LINCOLN LINDSAY
MATHEWS MCMURRY PADOVER
PATRICK PEABODY RAYMOND
RICKERT ROLLINS SCUDDER
SHUSTER TATLOCK TAUSSIG
THACHER VANDYKE VANHISE
VIERECK VOELKER WALLACE
WHEELER WILLARD WIMSATT
WOOLSEY ZEITLIN ALDERMAN
BANCROFT BASHFORD BLANDING
BREWSTER BRITTAIN CALLAHAN
CHANDLER COMMAGER COMSTOCK
COPELAND DJERASSI FLETCHER
FOERSTER GRISWOLD HARNWELL
HARRISON HOLLOWAY HUTCHINS
LANGSTON LAWRENCE MARQUAND
MATTHEWS MCGUFFEY MCKNIGHT
PENNIMAN PHILLIPS ROBINSON
SCHURMAN SEASHORE SILLIMAN
STODDARD SUZZALLO TUTWILER
WHEELOCK WILLIAMS WOODBURN
WOODWARD ARMSTRONG
AYDELOTTE CARPENTER
CHAUVENET FAIRBANKS FAIRCHILD
GOODSPEED GRANDGENT
GREENOUGH HENDERSON
KITTREDGE LOUNSBURY PARTRIDGE
PATTERSON PENDLETON SCHELLING
SHARPLESS SPAULDING THORNDIKE
WENTWORTH BLOOMFIELD
CHADBOURNE KILPATRICK
LONGSTREET PARRINGTON
STURTEVANT WASHINGTON
GILDERSLEEVE
ARGENTINIAN HOUSSAY
SAAVDEDRA AVELLANEDA
AUSTRALIAN GREER HOLME
CALDWELL
AUSTRIAN NEURATH
BELGIAN HEYMANS LAFONTAINE
CANADIAN ABEL GRANT OSLER
PRATT WIGLE CAPPON HUTTON
MACKAY MURRAY LEACOCK
MACLEAN MCLUHAN
CZECH KELSEN COMENIUS
DANISH LUND KROGH
DUTCH ASSER DEVRIES EIJKMAN
LORENTZ ZERNIKE COUPERIUS

ECUADORIAN ROCAFUERTE
EGYPTIAN HUSSEIN
ENGLISH DENT KING KLUG ALLEN
BEALE BOWRA CECIL CHAIN DYSON
ELTON FITCH GRANT KEBLE LUCAS
OGDEN PETTY ROUSE SMITH
SWANN ARNOLD BARNES CATLIN
COTTON FARMER HADDON HOGBEN
INGOLD KEYNES MORANT RAIKES
RIPMAN SADLER BAINTON BALFOUR
BALLARD COGHILL KENDREW
STARKIE WESTRUP CHAMBERS
CUNLIFFE SIDGWICK SPURGEON
MANSBRIDGE ABERCROMBIE
FRENCH EPEE ANDLER BOUTMY
CAMPAN DORIOT FONCIN WAILLY
ABELARD BELJAME BIDAULT
BUISSON CHINARD RENAULT
BOUTROUX COMPAYRE
GERMAN AHN ALER BAUR KERN
LAUE REIN CAMPE GRAFE LANGE
STURM CARNAP GEDIKE JENSEN
LIEBIG NATORP WITTIG ZIMMER
BECKMAN FISCHER FROEBEL
JASPERS SPEMANN DORPFELD
FOERSTER DIESTERWEG
TROTZENDORF
HUNGARIAN BEOTHY MANNHEIM
INDIAN HUSAIN GOKHALE
IRISH HUNTER WALTON STARKIE
ISRAELI SCHOLEM
ITALIAN PEI NATTA FEDELE DAPONTE
VILLARI BELTRAMI GALLENGA
LOMBROSO MALPIGHI MONTESSORI
JAPANESE NAGAI SUZUKI YUKAWA
ASAKAWA NEESIMA FUKUZAWA
MEXICAN CAMPOS
NORWEGIAN HASSEL ONSAGER
PORTUGUESE EGAS
RUSSIAN BAER RUBIN
SCOTTISH BELL BLAIR NEILL AYTOUN
DALGARNO
SWEDISH SIREN SIEGBAHN
SWISS HESS BLOCH PAULI GIRARD
KARRAR TOPFFER DUCOMMUN
FELLENBERG
EDUCE DRAW EVOKE ELICIT EVOLVE
EXTORT EXTRACT
EEL ELE APOD GRIG LING OPAH SNIG
TUNA APODE ELVER MORAY SIREN
APODAN CARAPO CONGER FAUSEN
MOREIA MURENE CONGRIO
KWATUMA LAMPREY MURAENA
SNIGGLE WRIGGLE CONGEREE
GYMNOTID KINGKLIP
(KIND OF —) MORAY
(YOUNG —) GRIG ELVER OLIVER
YELVER
(25 —S) STICK SWARM
EELGRASS DREW WRACK ENALID
EELPOUT BARD LING POUT QUAB
BURBOT CONGER GUFFER YOWLER
LYCODOID

EELSKIN (10 —S) TIMBER
EELSPEAR PILGER
EELWORM EEL NEMA
EERIE EERY SCARY TIMID WEIRD
WISHT CREEPY DISMAL GLOOMY
GOUSTY SPOOKY AWESOME
GHOSTLY GOUSTIE MACABRE
STRANGE UNCANNY ELDRITCH
GHOULISH POKERISH
EFFACE BLOT DASH DELE RASE RAZE
WEAR ERASE CANCEL DEFACE
SPONGE STRIKE DESTROY DISLIMN
EXPUNGE NULLIFY UNPAINT
WEAROUT
EFFECT DO SEE DENT DOES FECK
HAVE PRAY PREY TEEM WORK
CAUSE CLOSE ECLAT ENACT ETTLE
EVENT FORCE FRUIT ISSUE STAMP
ACTION ENERGY GROWTH INDUCE
INTENT OBTAIN RESULT SECURE
SEQUEL STEREO UPSHOT ACHIEVE
ACQUIRE ARRANGE COMPASS
CONDUCE EMOTION EXECUTE
FULFILL IMPRESS IMPRINT
OPERATE OUTCOME PERFORM
PROCURE PRODUCE PURPORT
REALIZE CAUSATUM COMPLETE
CONCLUDE CONTRIVE FRUITAGE
CONSEQUENT
(— OF PAST EXPERIENCE) MNEME
(BLURRED —) FUZZ
(COUNTERBALANCING —) STANDOFF
(DAZZLING —) ECLAT
(DECORATIVE —) CHIPPING
(ELECTRICAL —) STRAY
(ESTHETIC —) ATMOSPHERE
(FALSE —) FACADE
(FINAL —) AMOUNT
(GRANULAR —) SPECKLE
(ILL —) EVIL
(INTENSE —) STRESS
(KIND OF —) BOHR GUNN COANDA
DOMINO RIPPLE DOPPLER PLACEBO
HAWTHORNE MOSSBAUER
(MOTTLED —) SPRINKLE
(MUSICAL —) BEND SHADING
(OPTICAL —) PHANTASMAGORIA
(PAINFUL —) JAR
(PAINTING —) STIPPLE
(PENETRATING —) SEARCH
(PERNICIOUS —) BLAST
(PERSONAL —S) DUNNAGE
(SECONDARY —) OVERTONE
(SHATTERING —) BRISANCE
(THEATRICAL —) CURTAIN
(TO HAVE —) MILITATE
(TOTAL —) ENSEMBLE
(TOXIC —S) THEISM
(TREMOLO —) BEBUNG
(VISIBLE —) TOUCH
(SUFF.) ERGATE ERGY
EFFECTIVE ABLE HOME MEAN REAL
ALIVE GREAT HAPPY PITHY SIKER

SOUND VALID ACTIVE ACTUAL
CAUSAL COGENT DEADLY DIRECT
FRUITY POTENT SEVERE SICKER
SOVRAN CAPABLE FECKFUL
OPERANT TELLING VIRTUAL
ADEQUATE FORCEFUL POWERFUL
SMASHING STRIKING VIGOROUS
TRENCHANT
EFFECTIVELY NAITLY
EFFECTIVENESS AIM BANG CHIC
EDGE TEETH VOLTAGE EFFICACY
LEVERAGE
EFFECTUAL ACTUAL TOOTHY
ADEQUATE POWERFUL MAGISTRAL
EFFECTUATE FULFIL FULFILL
COMPLETE
EFFEMINATE NICE SOFT MILKY
MISSY NELLY SAPPY SISSY BITCHY
EFFETE FEMALE LYDIAN NELLIE
NIMINY PRISSY SILKEN TENDER
WANTON WEAKLY CITIZEN EPICENE
MEACOCK WOMANLY FEMINATE
FEMININE LADYLIKE OVERSOFT
WOMANISH
EFFERENT EXODIC
EFFERVESCE FIZZ HUFF KNIT
BUBBLE SPARKLE CARBONATE
EFFERVESCENCE FRET CRACKLE
SPARKLE
EFFERVESCENT UP BRISK FIZZY
QUICK BUBBLY ABUBBLE ELASTIC
BUBBLING
EFFERVESCING BRISK
EFFETE SERE WEAK JADED PASSE
SPENT BARREN DECADENT ETIOLATE
MORIBUND OUTMODED
EFFICACIOUS VALID MIGHTY
POTENT FORCIBLE POWERFUL
SINGULAR VIGOROUS VIRTUOUS
OPERATIVE
EFFICACY DINT FECK DEVIL FORCE
GRACE MIGHT POWER DEGREE
VIRTUE POTENCY VALIDITY
OPERATION
EFFICIENCY POWER SKILL AGENCY
ABILITY FACULTY DISPATCH
EFFICACY PERFORMANCE
EFFICIENT ABLE GOOD SMART VALID
POTENT CAPABLE FECKFUL
POWERFUL SPEEDFUL
EFFIGY GUY IDOL POPE SIGN DUMMY
IMAGE LIKENESS MONUMENT
EFFLORESCE GERMINATE
EFFLORESCENCE RASH BLOOM
BLOSSOM ROSEOLA ANTHESIS
ERUPTION WHITEWASH
EFFLUENCE ISSUE EFFLUX ELAPSE
EMANATE
EFFLUVIA SCENT
EFFLUVIUM AURA ODOR MIASMA
FLUXION SPECIES APORRHEA
EMISSION OUTGOING EMANATION
EFFLUX OUTGO OUTFLOW EFFUSION

EFFORT JOB TRY TUG DINT FIST HUMP JUMP MINT PASS SHOT TOIL ASSAY BRUNT BURST CRACK DRIVE ESSAY FLING LABOR NISUS PAINS POWER REACH STUDY THROE TRIAL ANIMUS DEVOIR FAVORS FIZZLE FUFFLE PINGLE STRAIN STROKE THRIFT ATTEMPT CONATUS MOLIMEN NITENCY SPLURGE STRETCH TENSURE TROUBLE WORKING ENDEAVOR EXERTION GOODWILL INDUSTRY MOLITION REACHING STRIVING STRUGGLE
(— FOR ONESELF) FEND
(ABORTIVE —) FIZZLE
(AGONIZED —) THROE
(ARTICULATIVE —) ACCENT
(EARNEST —) STUDY
(EFFECTIVE —) LICK
(FINAL —) CHARETTE
(INITIAL —) ASSAY
(MAXIMUM —) BEST
(SALVATIONIST —) ATTACK
(SINGLE —) HEAT TRICE
(STRENUOUS —) HASSEL HASSLE
(UNSUCCESSFUL —) ATTEMPT CLUNKER
(UTMOST —) DEVOIR BUSINESS
(VIOLENT —) BURST STRAIN OUTRAGE STRUGGLE
EFFORTLESS EASY
EFFORTLESSNESS EASE
EFFRONTERY BROW FACE GALL BRASS FRONT BRONZE AUDACITY BOLDNESS CHUTZPAH FOREHEAD TEMERITY
EFFULGENCE BLAZE GLORY RADIANT RADIANCE SPLENDOR
EFFULGENT BRIGHT FULGENT RADIANT SHINING
EFFUSE GUSH SHED FLING EFFUND EMANATE DISPENSE
EFFUSION EFFLUX FOISON SCREED SPILTH STREAM
EFFUSIVE GOOEY GUSHY LAVISH SLOPPY GUSHING BUBBLING
EFFUSIVENESS SLOP
EFT ASK EVET NEWT LIZARD TRITON
EGAD ADAD ECOD IGAD SGAD
EGEST VOID EXCRETE ELIMINATE
EGEUS (DAUGHTER OF —) HERMIA
EGG AI ABET GOAD GOOG OEUF OVUM PROD SEED SPUR URGE CHECK HUEVO OVULE SPORE DARNER INCITE OOCYTE PEEWEE ZYGOTE ACTUATE COCKNEY COKENEY OOPLAST OOSPERM PROTOVUM
(— CASE) POD
(— CLUTCH) LAUGHTER
(— OF FISH OR LOBSTER) BERRY
(— ON) HAG HAG EDGE GOAD URGE
(— ON ONE'S FACE) EMBARRASSMENT

(— PRODUCT) ZOON
(—S OF BEES) BROOD
(—S OF SILKWORM) GRAINE
(— WITH BACON) COLLOP
(ACID —) SLOWCASE
(CRACKED —) CHECK CRACK LEAKER
(DRIED —S) AHUATLE
(DUCK —S) PIDAN
(FLY'S —) BLOW FLYBLOW
(FOSSIL —) OVULITE
(GOLDEN —S) SUNCUP
(GOOSE —) BLOB
(HAVE AN —) LAY
(HUNT BIRDS' —S) OOLOGIZE
(INFERTILE —) CLEAR
(INSECT —) NIT BLOW
(PART OF —) YOLK SHELL WHITE ALBUMEN CHALAZA MEMBRANE BLASTODISC
(SHAPED LIKE AN —) OVOID
(SHAPE LIKE AN —) OVOID
(SMALL —) OVULE OVULUM
(PL.) OVA ROE SEED EYREN SPAWN CLUTCH ETTING AHUATLE
(PREF.) OARI(O) OIDIO OO OV(I)(O)
(— CASE) OOTHEC(O)
EGG AND DART ECHINUS
EGG CAPSULE OVISAC
EGG-CELL GAMETE
EGGFRUIT LUCUMA CANISTEL
EGGHEAD EINSTEIN HIGHBROW INTELLECTUAL
EGGNOG NOG CAUDLE ADVOCAAT
EGGPLANT BRINJAL SOLANUM BRINGELA EGGFRUIT
EGG-SHAPED OOID OVAL OVATE OVOID OOIDAL OBOVOID OVALOID OVIFORM
EGGSHELL SHARD CASCARON
EGG WHITE GLAIR ALBUMEN
EGG YOLK YELLOW VITELLUS
EGLAH (HUSBAND OF —) DAVID
EGLANTINE (FATHER OF —) PEPIN
(HUSBAND OF —) VALENTINE
EGO I ATTA SELF ATMAN EGOITY FYLGJA CONCEIT SUBJECT
EGOCENTRIC INSEEING
EGOISM PRIDE ONEISM VANITY CONCEIT EGOTISM OWNHOOD SELFNESS NARCISSISM
EGOIST (AUTHOR OF —) MEREDITH
(CHARACTER IN —) DALE LUCY CLARA HARRY OXFORD VERNON DECRAYE CROSSJAY DARLETON LAETITIA PATTERNE WHITFORD MIDDLETON CONSTANTIA WILLOUGHBY
EGOTISM EGO PRIDE EGOISM VANITY CONCEIT EGOMANIA SELFLOVE
EGREGIOUS FINE GROSS CAPITAL EMINENT FLAGRANT PRECIOUS SHOCKING

EGREGIOUSLY BEASTLY
EGRESS EXIT ISSUE OUTGO OUTLET
　EXITURE OUTCOME OUTGATE
　PASSAGE REGRESS OUTGOING
EGRET HERON PLUME GAULIN
　KOTUKU AIGRETTE GAULDING
EGYPT MIZRAIM

EGYPT

BAY: FOUL
CALENDAR: AHET APAP TYBI PAYNI
　SHEMU THOTH CHOIAK HATHOR
　MECHIR MESORE PAOPHI PACHONS
CAÑAL: SUEZ
CAPE: BANAS RASBANAS
CAPITAL: CAIRO ELQAHIRA
CHRISTIAN: COPT COPTIC
COIN: FILS DINAR GIRSH POUND
　DIRHAM GUINEA JUNAYH PIASTER
　MILLIEME
DAM: ASWAN
DESERT: LIBYAN
GOVERNORATE: SUEZ CAIRO CANAL
　SINAI BAHARIYA BAHRIYAH
　ALEXANDRIA
GULF: AQABA
ISTHMUS: SUEZ
KING: AY IB KA ITI ITY TUT DJER DJET
　HUNY PAMI PEPI SETI TEOS TETI
　UNIS ARSES BEBTI FOUAD ITETI
　KEBEH KHUFU KNIAN MENES
　NEBKA NECHO NEFER UDIMU ZEMTI
　ZOSER CHEOPS DARIUS FAROUK
　KHAFRE NARMER RANSES SENEDJ
　XERXES MENKURE PHARAOH
　PTOLEMY RAMESES SALADIN
　CHEPHREN THUTMOSE
LAKE: EDKU IDKU MARYUT MOERIS
　MANZALA BURULLUS MAREOTIS
LAKES: BITTER
MEASURE: APT DRA HEN PIK ROB
　DRAA KHET ROUB THEB ABDAT
　ARDAB CUBIT FARDE KELEH KILAH
　SAHME ARTABA AURURE FEDDAN
　KEDDAH ROBHAH SCHENE
　CHORYOS DARIBAH MALOUAH
　ROUBOUH TOUMNAH KASSABAH
　KHAROUBA
MOUNTAIN: SINAI GHARIB KATHERINA
NAME: UAR
NATIVE: ARAB COPT NILOT BERBER
　MUSLIM NUBIAN
OASIS: SIWA DAKHLA KHARGA
　FARAFRA BAHARIYA
OLD CAPITAL: SAITE
PENINSULA: SINAI
PORT: TOR SUEZ ATTUR DUMYAT
　QUSEIR RASHID SAFAGA SALLUM
　ROSETTA DAMIETTA HURGHADA
　PORTSAID ALEXANDRIA
PROVINCE: GIZA QENA QINA ASWAN
　ASYUT MINYA SOHAR DUMYAT
　FAIYUM SAWHAJ TAHRIR ALJIZAH

　BEHEIRA BENISUEF DAMIETTA
　GHARBIYA MINUFIYA SHARQIYA
RESERVOIR: ASWAN
RIVER: NILE
RUINS: ABYDOS THEBES MEMPHIS
　PYRAMIDS
SUN GOD: RA RE ATUM
TOWN: NO MUT DUSH GIZA IDFU ISNA
　QENA SAIS SIWA SUEZ ZOAN
　ASWAN ASYUT BENHA BULAQ
　CAIRO ELTUR FAYID GIRGA GIZEH
　LUXOR NAKHL SALUM SOHAG
　TAHTA TANIS TANTA ABYDOW
　AKHMIN DUMYAT ELQASR HELWAN
　RASHID THEBES BURSAID ROSETTA
　ZAGAZIG BENISUEF DAMIETTA
　ISMAILIA
WEIGHT: KAT KET OKA OKE HEML
　KHAR OKIA ROTL ARTAL ARTEL
　DEBEN KERAT MINAE MINAS OKIEH
　POUND RATEL UCKIA HAMLAH
　KANTAR DRACHMA QUINTAL
WELL: BIRTABA
WIND: KAMSIN SIROCCO KHAMSEEN

EGYPTIAN ARAB COPT GIPPY GYPPY
　TASIAN PHARIAN BADARIAN
　MEMPHIAN
EHUD (FATHER OF —) GERA BILHAN
EIDER COLK WAMP DIVER EDDER
　DUCKER SHOREYER
EIDOLON ICON GHOST IMAGE
　IDOLUM PHANTOM LIKENESS
EIGHT ETA ECHT AUGHT CHETH
　OCTAD OCTET OCTAVE OGDOAD
　OCTONARY
　(PREF.) OCT(A)(O)(U)
EIGHTEENMO OCTODECIMO
EIGHTEEN-WHEELER RIG
EIGHTFOLD OCTUPLE
EIGHTH AUGHT
　(— PART OF CIRCLE) OCTANT
EIGHTH NOTE UNCA CROMA
　CHROMA QUAVER
EIGHTY FOURSCORE
EIGHTY-SIX EJECT
EINSTEIN BRAIN
EIRE (SEE IRELAND)
EITHER ANY EDDER ITHER OTHER
　WHETHER
EJACULATE BELCH BLURT EJECT
　FLING EXCLAIM EMISSION
EJACULATION HOW COADS ZOWIE
　BEGORRA CRIMINE UTTERING
　(MYSTIC —) OM
EJACULATORY SPUTTERY
EJECT OUT BLOW BOOT CAST EMIT
　FIRE HOOF OUST SHED SPAT SPEW
　SPIT VOID WARP AVOID BELCH
　CHUCK ERUCT ERUPT EVICT EXPEL
　SHAKE SHOOT SPOUT SPURT VOMIT
　BANISH BOUNCE REJECT SQUIRT
　DEFORCE DISMISS EXCLUDE

EXTRUDE OBTRUDE DISGORGE
OUTBRAID
(— DROPS) SPUTTER
EJECTION BLOW OUSTER OUTING
EVICTION
EJECTOR LIFTER EDUCTOR
EKE IMP ALSO YEKE AUGMENT
ENLARGE HUSBAND STRETCH
APPENDIX INCREASE LENGTHEN
LIKEWISE UNDERLAY
ELABORATE LUSH FIKIE GREAT
LABOR DELUXE DRESSY ELABOR
ORNATE QUAINT REFINE CURIOUS
DEVELOP ENLARGE LABORED
PERFECT
(OVERLY —) NIGGLING
ELABORATED WROUGHT
ELABORATELY FANCILY
ELABORATENESS FINENESS
CURIOSITY
ELABORATION FINISH
(PETTY —) NIGGLING
ELAH (FATHER OF —) UZZI CALEB
BAASHA
(SLAYER OF —) ZIMRI
(SON OF —) HOSHEA
ELAINE (FATHER OF —) PELLES
BRANDEGORIS
(SON OF —) GALAHAD
ELAIS (FATHER OF —) ANIUS
(MOTHER OF —) DORIPPE
(SISTER OF —) OENE SPERMO
ELAMITE SUSIAN ANZANITE
ELAN DASH ZEST ARDOR DRIVE FLAIR
GUSTO VERVE SPIRIT WARMTH
PANACHE POTENCY
ELAND ORYX IMPOFO
ELAN VITAL ZOISM
ELAPS MICRURUS
ELAPSE GO RUN PASS ROLL SLIP
GLIDE SPEND EXPIRE RUNOUT
ELAPSED PAST
ELAPSING CURRENT
ELASAH
(FATHER OF —) SHAPHAN
ELASMOBRANCH PLACOID
ELASTIC QUICK GARTER RUBATO
SPONGY BUOYANT SPRINGY
STRETCH CHEVEREL CHEVERIL
FLEXIBLE STRETCHY VOLATILE
ELASTICITY GIVE LIFE ELATER
SPRING STRETCH
ELATE BYOU PUFF CHEER EXALT
EXULT FLUSH LOFTY RAISE SETUP
ELATED EXCITE PLEASE THRILL
ELEVATE GLADDEN INFLATE SUBLIME
SUCCESS ELEVATED HEIGHTEN
INSPIRIT JUBILATE
ELATED RAD HIGH RADE CHUFF
ELATE GIDDY HAPPY PROUD VAUDY
VOGIE WLONK CHUFFY JOVIAL
UPPISH UPPITY EXCITED EXULTED
JOCULAR SUBLIME EUPHORIC

EXULTANT GLORIOUS INFLATED
JUBILANT PRIDEFUL UPLIFTED
ELATER BEETLE CRINULA SKIPJACK
ELATION JOY GLEE RUFF RUFFE
BUOYANCY
ELATUS (FATHER OF —) ARCAS
(MOTHER OF —) ERATO
CHRYSOPELIA
(SON OF —) CYLLEN ISCHYS PEREUS
AEPYTUS STYMPHALUS
(WIFE OF —) LAODICE
ELBOW ELL BEND ANCON JOINT
NUDGE SHOVE CROSET ELBUCK
JOSTLE JUSTLE SPRING PIERDROP
(OUT AT THE —S) SEEDY
(PREF.) CUBITO ULNO
ELCAJA MAFURA
ELDER AIN IVA AINE WITE ELLER
OLDER PRIOR MAHANT PRIMUS
SENIOR ANCIENT NEGUNDO
STAROST TRAMMON ANCESTOR
BOUNTREE BOURTREE CARELESS
DANEWORT ELDERMAN PRESBYTER
ELDERLY AGED GRAY ALDER ANILE
ELDERN SENILE BADGERLY
GERIATRIC
ELDEST AYNE EIGNE OLDEST
PRIMUS
ELDRICH EERIE
ELEASAH (FATHER OF —) HELEZ
RAPHA
ELEAZAR (BROTHER OF —) ABIHU
NADAB ITHAMAR
(FATHER OF —) AARON ELIUD MAHLI
PAROSH ABINADAB PHINEHAS
(GRANDFATHER OF —) MERARI
ELECAMPANE INULA CANADA
ELFWORT SCABWORT
ELECT CALL PICK VOICE ASSUME
CHOOSE CHOSEN DECIDE ISRAEL
PREFER SELECT
ELECTION PROXY CHOICE LECTION
PRIMARY
ELECTIONEERING HUSTINGS
ELECTIVE OPTION OPTIONAL
ELECTOR VOTER ELISOR CHOOSER
ELIGENT INTRANT ELECTANT
ELECTORATE PEOPLE COUNTRY
ELECTRA LAODICE
(BROTHER OF —) ORESTES
(DAUGHTER OF —) IRIS AELLO
OCYPETE
(FATHER OF —) ATLAS OCEANUS
AGAMEMNON
(HUSBAND OF —) PYLADES
THAUMAS
(MOTHER OF —) ERATO TETHYS
PLEIONE CLYTEMNESTRA
(SON OF —) IASION DARDANUS
(UNCLE OF —) MENELAUS
ELECTRIC
(PREF.) POTAM(O)
(— RAY) NARC(O)

ELECTRICIAN WIRER GAFFER
JUICER BOARDMAN
ELECTRICITY JUICE POWER
PYROGEN ELECTRIC GALVANISM
(GENIUS OF —) TESLA
ELECTRIFY EXCITE THRILL STARTLE
ELECTROCARDIOGRAPHIC (—
EXAMINATION) STRESSTEST
ELECTROCUTE BURN EXECUTE
ELECTROCUTION CHAIR
ELECTRODE DE DEE GATE GRID
ANODE PLATE DYNODE CATHODE
IGNITER CROWFOOT REOPHORE
(PL.) ELEMENT
ELECTRODEPOSIT STRIKE
REGULINE
ELECTROLYTE STRIKE IONOGEN
ELECTROMAGNETIC (— UNIT)
OERSTED ABAMPERE
ELECTRON ION NEGATON POLARON
NEGATRON POSITRON CORPUSCLE
ELECTRONIC RADIONIC
(— DEVICE) WAWAPEDAL
ELECTRONICS (— WHIZ) TECHIE
(BRANCH OF —) OVONICS
ELECTRONOGRAPHY ONSET
ELECTRON TUBE TRIODE
ELECTROPHONE MARTENOT
ELECTROPLATE SILVER
ELECTROTYPE PATCH CLICHE
WORKER ELECTRO
ELECTRUM AMBER ELECTRE
ORICHALC
ELECTRYON (DAUGHTER OF —)
ALCMENE
(FATHER OF —) PERSEUS
(MOTHER OF —) ANDROMEDA
ELECTUARY DIASCORD LECTUARY
THERIACA MITHRIDATE
ELEGANCE CHIC GARB LUXE TONE
CLASP GRACE STYLE SWANK TASTE
FINERY GAIETY GAYETY LUXURY
NICETY POLISH COURTESY
EUPHUISM FINENESS FRIPPERY
GRANDEUR SPLENDOR
ELEGANT CHIC DINK FAIR FEAT FINE
FIXY GENT JIMP POSH CIVIL COMPT
FANCY GRAND NOBBY RITZY SHARP
SLEEK SWANK SWISH CHOICE
CLASSY DAINTY DELUXE DRESSY
FACETE MINION POLITE PRETTY
QUAINT SUPERB SWANKY URBANE
VENUST CAPITAL CLEANLY COURTLY
FEATISH FEATOUS GENTEEL MINIKIN
REFINED SMICKER DEBONAIR
DELICATE GINGERLY GRACEFUL
GRAZIOSO HANDSOME POLISHED
TASTEFUL CONCINNOUS
ELEGANTLY FINE TALLY FAIRLY
GENTLY GINGERLY
ELEGIAC MOURNFUL EPICEDIAL
ELEGY POEM SONG DIRGE KINAH
QINAH LAMENT MONODY EPICEDE

ELEKTRA (CHARACTER IN —) OREST
AEGISTH ELEKTRA CHRYSOTHEMIS
KLYTEMNESTRA
(COMPOSER OF —) STRAUSS
ELEMENT AIR ATOM DIAD DYAD
RECT WOOF BEARD ETHER FIBER
FIBRE IODIN METAL MONAD PUNCT
STUFF AETHER ARTIAD COSTAL
FACTOR HEPTAD LOSSER MATTER
MOMENT SIMPLE ACTINON ADAPTER
BUNCHER CARRIER CATCHER
ESSENCE FEATURE ACTINIDE
BACKBONE CEREBRAL EQUATION
PERISSAD RUDIMENT SELECTOR
THERBLIG
(— IN GRAPH) SPIKE
(— IN WAVE) DART
(— IN WORD GROUP) KOINON
(— OF ALCHEMIST) AIR FIRE EARTH
WATER
(— OF EXISTENCE) DHARMA
(— OF MACHINE) HORN SPIDER
(— OF WEALTH) COMMODITY
(— ON TV SCREEN) PIXEL
(ALIEN —) ALLOY
(ARCHITECTURAL —) SLAB
(BINDING —) CEMENT
(CHARACTER —) STRAIN
(CHARACTERISTIC —) PARAMETER
(CHEMICAL —) TIN GOLD IRON LEAD
NEON ZINC ARGON BORON RADON
XENON BARIUM CARBON CERIUM
CESIUM COBALT COPPER CURIUM
ERBIUM HELIUM INDIUM IODINE
MURIUM NICKEL OSMIUM OXYGEN
RADIUM SILVER SODIUM SULFUR
ARSENIC BISMUTH BROMINE
CADMIUM CALCIUM FERMIUM
GALLIUM HAFNIUM HOLMIUM
IRIDIUM KRYPTON LITHIUM
MERCURY NIOBIUM RHENIUM
RHODIUM SILICON TERBIUM
THORIUM THULIUM URANIUM
WOLFRAM YTTRIUM ACTINIDE
ACTINIUM ANTIMONY ASTATINE
CHLORINE CHROMIUM EUROPIUM
FLUORINE FRANCIUM HYDROGEN
LUTETIUM MASURIUM NITROGEN
NOBELIUM NONMETAL PLATINUM
POLONIUM RUBIDIUM SAMARIUM
SCANDIUM SELENIUM TANTALUM
THALLIUM TITANIUM TUNGSTEN
VANADIUM METALLOID PALLADIUM
PLUTONIUM
(COMMUNION —) GIFT
(CRIMINAL —) GANGLAND
(DECORATIVE —S) ART
(DOMINANT —) CAPSHEAF
(ELECTRIC —) IMPEDOR
(ESSENTIAL —) CORPUS
(EUCHARISTIC — S) HAGIA SPECIES
(FATAL —) BANE
(FIRST —) PRIMORDIAL

(FUNDAMENTAL —) STAMEN
KEYSTONE
(GLOOMY —) PALL
(HEATING —) CALANDRIA
(HYPOTHETICAL —) CORONIUM
(IMAGE —) PIXEL
(INTERFERING —) CRIMP
(LAMP —) GLOWER
(LEADING —) HEAD
(LINGUISTIC—) SERVILE INTENSIVE
(MILITARY —) SUPPORT
(MODIFYING —) LEAVENING
(MORAL —) DAENA
(MOST IMPORTANT —) CAPSTONE
(PRIMAL —) GUNA SALT ARCHE
(PRINCIPAL —) STAPLE
(SKELETAL —) SCLERE
(STRUCTURAL —) ARCUALE
(SUPPOSED —) PROTYLE WELSIUM
VICTORIUM
(SUSTAINING —) BREAD STAPLE
(TRACE —) MICRONUTRIENT
(TRANSITORY —S) SKANDHAS
(UNITING —) BOND
(UNSOUND —) ULCER
(PL.) DETAIL ALPHABET
(PREF.) (FIRST —TH) STOICHIO
(SUFF.) AD IUM
(CHEMICAL —) ID IDE INE IUM
ELEMENTAL PURE BASIC PRIMAL
SIMPLE PRIMARY ULTIMATE
PRIMITIVE
ELEMENTARY PRIMAL SIMPLE
INITIAL PRIMARY INCHOATE
ULTIMATE RUDIMENTARY
ELEMI ANEMI ANIME MATTI RESIN
CONIMA
ELEPHANT COW BULL CALF HINE
PUNK BABAR HATHI HATTY JUMBO
ROGUE MUCKNA TUSKER KOOMKIE
AIRAVATA LOXODONT MASTODON
OLIPHANT PACHYDERM
PROBOSCIDEAN
(— BOY) SABU
ELEPHANT BIRD AEPYORNIS
ELEPHANT FISH JOSEF JOSUP
JOSEPH
ELEPHANTIASIS TYRIASIS
ELEPHANTINE HUGE ENORMOUS
ELEPHANT'S-EAR TARO
ELEPHANT'S -EARS BEGONIA
ELEPHANT SHREW JUMPER
ELEUT KALMUK KALMYK KALMUCK
ELEVATE HAIN JUMP LIFT REAR RISE
EDIFY ELATE ENSKY ERECT EXALT
EXTOL GRIMP HEAVE HOIST MOUNT
RAISE TOWER REFINE UPLIFT
ADVANCE DIGNIFY ENHANCE
ENNOBLE GLORIFY PROMOTE
SUBLIME UPRAISE HEIGHTEN
INSPIRIT
ELEVATED EL FINE HIGH GREAT
LOFTY NOBLE RISEN STEEP AERIAL

AMOTUS ELATED RAISED RISING
WINGED BULLATE ELEVATO EXALTED
MOUNTED STILTED SUBLIME
MAJESTIC UPLIFTED
(— IN CHARACTER) HIGH
(NOT —) COMICAL
ELEVATION UP ARM BAND BANK
DOME DRUM GLEE HIGH HILL
HUMP LIFT RISE SPUR TOFT TOOT
UMBO AGGER BULLA GRADE
KNOLL MOUND PITCH RAISE RIDGE
SHOAL SWELL TOWER WHEAL
CONULE CRISTA HEIGHT PAPULE
UPLIFT DIGNITY FURCULA
MAJESTY UPRIGHT ALTITUDE
EMINENCE EVECTION HIGHNESS
LEVATION MOUNTAIN SWELLING
MONTICULE
(— OF CARTILAGE) ANTHELIX
(— OF CUTICLE) BLEB
(— OF SKIN) BLISTER
(— OF VOICE) ARSIS
(— ON TOOTH) STYLE
(— SEPARATING CREEKS) BUGOR
(ANGULAR —) STEEVE
(GUN —) RANDOM
(TURRET —) HOOD
(PREF.) ORO
ELEVATOR BIN CAGE LIFT SILO
HOIST BRIDGE LIFTER TEAGLE
HOISTER STACKER UPTAKER
UPLIFTER UPRAISER
(TAKE THE —) RIDEUP
ELEVEN
(PREF.) HENDEC(A) UNDEC(A)
ELEVENTH ELFT
ELF FAY HAG HOB IMP OAF PUG
DROW FANE OUPH PERI PIXY PUCK
DWARF ELFIN FAIRY GNOME OUPHE
PIGMY PIXIE ELFKIN GOBLIN SPIRIT
SPRITE URCHIN BLASTIE BROWNIE
INCUBUS SUCCUBUS
ELFIN ELF FEY CHILD ELFIC ELFISH
URCHIN
ELFISH ELFIN ELVAN ELVISH IMPISH
URCHIN ELFLIKE TRICKSY
ELFRIDA (HUSBAND OF —) EDGAR
(SON OF —) AETHELRED
ELIA LAMB
ELIAB (BROTHER OF —) DAVID
(DAUGHTER OF —) ABIHAIL
(FATHER OF —) HELON NAHATH
(SON OF —) ABIRAM DATHAN
ELIADA (FATHER OF —) DAVID
ELIADAH (SON OF —) REZON
ELIAKIM (FATHER OF —) ABIUD
MELEA HILKIAH
(SON OF —) AZOR JONAN
ELIAM (DAUGHTER OF —)
BATHSHEBA
ELIASAPH (FATHER OF —) LAEL
ELIASHIB (FATHER OF —) BANI
ZATTU

ELICIT CALL DRAW MILK PUMP CLAIM EDUCE EVOKE EXACT FETCH WREST WRING DEDUCE DEMAND ENTICE EXTORT INDUCE EXTRACT PROVOKE SOLICIT

ELIDE OMIT SKIP ANNUL IGNORE CURTAIL DESTROY NULLIFY DEMOLISH SUPPRESS

ELIEZER (FATHER OF —) JORIM MOSES BECHER ZICHRI DODAVAH

ELIGIBILITY FITNESS

ELIGIBLE FIT ACTIVE WORTHY SUITABLE
(— IN POKER) ACTIVE

ELIMELECH (SON OF —) MAHLON CHILION
(WIFE OF —) NAOMI

ELIMINATE FAN COMB EDIT KILL EDUCE EXPEL PURGE SCRUB DELETE EFFACE EXCEPT IGNORE REMOVE SCREEN WINNOW ABOLISH BLANKET BRACKET DIVULGE EXCLUDE EXCRETE RELEASE RULEOUT SCISSOR SILENCE SUBLATE TAKEOUT SEPARATE

ELIMINATION STRIP

ELIOENAI (FATHER OF —) NEARIAH

ELIPHAL (FATHER OF —) UR

ELIPHALET (FATHER OF —) DAVID

ELIPHAZ (FATHER OF —) ESAU
(MOTHER OF —) ADAH
(SON OF —) TEMAN

ELIPHELET (FATHER OF —) DAVID ESHEK

ELISABETH (HUSBAND OF —) ZACHARIAS
(SON OF —) JOHN

ELISHA (FATHER OF —) SHAPHAT

ELISHAH (FATHER OF —) JAVAN

ELISHAMA (FATHER OF —) DAVID
(SON OF —) NETHANIAH

ELISHAPHAT (FATHER OF —) ZICHRI

ELISHEBA (BROTHER OF —) NAHSHON
(FATHER OF —) AMMINADAB
(HUSBAND OF —) AARON

ELISHUA (FATHER OF —) DAVID

ELISION SYNCOPE

ELISIR D'AMORE (CHARACTER IN —) ADINA BELCORE NEMORINO DULCAMARA
(COMPOSER OF —) DONIZETTI

ELISSA (BROTHER OF —) PYGMALION
(FATHER OF —) BELUS METGEN
(HUSBAND OF —) ACERBAS SYCHAEUS SICHARBAAL
(SISTER OF —) ANNA

ELITE BEST LITE PINK CREAM CHOICE CIRCLE FLOWER GENTRY SELECT PERFECTI

ELIUD (FATHER OF —) ACHIM

ELIXIR DAFFY AMRITA SPIRIT AMREETA ARCANUM CORDIAL CUREALL ESSENCE PANACEA MEDICINE
(ALCHEMIST'S —) TINCT

ELIZAPHAN (FATHER OF —) UZZIEL

ELK ALCE DEER LAMA LOSH ALAND ALCES ELAND LOSHE MOOSE CERVID SAMBAR WAPITI SAMBHUR WAMPOOSE
(— HIDE) LOSH
(YOUNG —) DEACON

ELKANAH (FATHER OF —) KORAH
(SLAYER OF —) ZICHRI
(SON OF —) SAMUEL

ELK BARK BIGBLOOM

ELL ULNA WING ELBOW ALNAGE ADDITION

ELLIPSE OVAL

ELLIPSIS BRING ELLIPSE

ELLIPSOGRAPH TRAMMEL

ELLIPSOID CONOID ELLIPTIC SPHEROID

ELLIPSOIDAL OVAL

ELLIPTICAL OVAL OVATE OVOID OBLONG

ELLOBIUM AURICULA

ELM ULME ELVEN ULMUS WAHOO MEZCAL CHEWBARK ORHAMWOOD
(FRUIT OF —) SAMARA

ELMODAM (FATHER OF —) ER

ELMSEED
(PREF.) SAMARI

ELNAAM (SON OF —) JERIBAI JOSHAVIAH

ELOCUTION SPEECH DICTION ORATORY

ELOCUTIONIST READER RECITER

ELOIGN CONVEY REMOVE ABSCOND CONCEAL

ELON (FATHER OF —) ZEBULUN

ELONGATE EXTEND REMOVE STRETCH LENGTHEN PROTRACT
(— RAPIDLY) SHOOT

ELONGATED LANK LONG LINEAR OBLONG PROLATE SLENDER HAIRLIKE PRODUCED

ELOPE DECAMP ESCAPE ABSCOND

ELOQUENCE FACUND FLUENCY ORATORY

ELOQUENT VOCAL DISERT FACUND FERVID FLUENT SILVER RENABLE SPEAKING ORATORICAL

ELPAAL (BROTHER OF —) ABITUB
(FATHER OF —) SHAHARAIM
(MOTHER OF —) HUSHIM

ELPALET (FATHER OF —) DAVID

EL SALVADOR
CAPITAL: SANSALVADOR
COIN: PESO COLON CENTAVO
DANCE: PASILLO
DEPARTMENT: LAPAZ CABANAS MORAZAN SUNSONATE
GULF: FONSECA

INDIAN: PIPIL
LAKE: GUIJA ILOPANGO
MEASURE: VARA CAFIZ CAHIZ FANEGA
TERCIA BOTELLA CAJUELA
CANTARO MANZANA
POINT: REMEDIOS
PORT: CUTUCO ACAJUTLA
RIVER: JIBOA LAPAZ LEMPA
RUINS: TAZUMAL
TOWN: CUTUCO IZALCO CORINTO
METAPAN ACAJUTLA USULUTAN
SONSONATE AHUACHAPAN
VOLCANO: IZALCO
WEIGHT: BAG CAJA LIBRA

ELSE OR ENS ENSE OTHER BESIDES
INSTEAD
ELSEWHERE ALIBI EXCEPT THENCE
(FROM —) ALIUNDE
ELUCIDATE CLEAR LUCID EXPLAIN
SIMPLIFY
ELUDE BEAT FLEE FOIL JINK MISS
MOCK SLIP AVOID DODGE EVADE
BAFFLE BEFOOL DELUDE DOUBLE
ESCAPE BEGUILE DECEIVE
HEDGEHOP
ELUSIVE EELY LUBRIC SHIFTY
SUBTLE TRICKY TWISTY EVASIVE
BAFFLING FUGITIVE SLIPPERY
ELYSIUM EDEN ANNWFN PARADISE
ELYTRON HUSK SCUTE SHARD
SHERD SHEATH
ELYTRUM SHARD TEGMEN
ELZAPHAN (FATHER OF —) UZZIEL
EM EMMA
(HALF —) EN
EMACIATED LEAN POOR EMPTY
GAUNT MEAGER PEAKED SKINNY
WASTED TABETIC WASTREL
MARASMIC SKELETAL WANTHRIVEN
EMACIATING MARCID
EMACIATION NITON TABES MACIES
ATROPHY POVERTY ASTHENIA
MARASMUS
EMANATE FLOW ARISE EMANE
EXUDE ISSUE DERIVE EFFUSE
EXHALE OUTRAY SPRING BREATHE
OUTCOME PROCEED RADIATE
EMANATING EFFLUENT
EMANATION FUG AURA BEAM BLAS
AROMA GLORY NITON AZILUT
BREATH EFFLUX ELAPSE EIDOLON
MOFETTE OUTCOME PROCESS
SEPHIRA EMISSION PROCESSION
(— FROM A MEDIUM) ECTOPLASM
(SENSED —) KARMA
(PL.) SCENT
EMANCIPATE FREE MANUMIT
RELEASE LIBERATE UNFETTER
EMANCIPATION FREEDOM RELEASE
(FINAL —) NIRVANA
EMASCULATE GELD SOFTEN
EVIRATE CASTRATE ENERVATE

EMATHION (BROTHER OF —)
MEMNON
(FATHER OF —) TITHONUS
(MOTHER OF —) EOS
(SLAYER OF —) HERCULES
EMBALM BALM CERE MUMMY SPICE
BALSAM SEASON CONDITE
MUMMIFY
EMBANK BUND
EMBANKMENT BAY BAND BANK
BUND DIKE DYKE FILL QUAY ARGIN
DIGUE LEVEE MOUND REVET SCARP
BUNKER ESCARP STAITH BACKING
BANKING PARADOS PILAPIL
RAMPART RAMPIRE SEAWALL
APPROACH STRENGTH REVETMENT
EMBARGO EDICT ORDER IMBARGE
BLOCKADE STOPPAGE
EMBARK BANK SAIL SHIP ENGAGE
ENLIST INSHIP INVEST LAUNCH
IMBARGE
EMBARRASS SET CHAW CLOG FAZE
HACK LAND POSE ABASH ANNOY
SHAME UPSET BOGGLE CUMBER
GRAVEL HAMPER HINDER HOBBLE
IMPEDE PLUNGE PUZZLE RATTLE
CONFUSE ENTRIKE FLUMMOX
INVOLVE NONPLUS BEWILDER
CONFOUND DUMFOUND ENCUMBER
ENTANGLE HANDICAP IMPESTER
OBSTRUCT STRAITEN
EMBARRASSED AWKWARD
FLURRIED SHEEPISH
EMBARRASSING STICKY
AWKWARD HIDEOUS
EMBARRASSINGLY AWKWARDLY
EMBARRASSMENT FIX GENE
LURCH SHAME STAND CADDLE
CUMBER HOBBLE PUZZLE CHAGRIN
NONPLUS CONFUSION
EMBASSY SAND ERRAND AMBASSY
MESSAGE MISSION INBASSAT
LEGATION
EMBATTLED BATTLED CRENELE
BRETESSE CRENELEE
EMBAY BATHE DETAIN ENCLOSE
SHELTER SUFFUSE ENCIRCLE
SURROUND
EMBAYMENT FIORD FJORD
EMBDEN GOOSE
EMBED BED SET BOND IMBED LAYIN
STAMP CHARGE ENGAGE EMBOWEL
IMMERSE
(— IN SAND) DOCK
EMBEDDED INNATE ENGAGED
IMMERSED
EMBELLISH GEM DECK GILD LARD
TRIM ADORN DRESS FUDGE GRACE
BEDECK BETRIM BLAZON EMBOSS
ENRICH FIGURE FLOWER APPAREL
BEDRAPE EMBLAZE GARNISH
MYSTIFY VARNISH BEAUTIFY
DECORATE FLOURISH ORNAMENT

EMBELLISHED FLORID GESTED ORNATE COLORED FOCUSED BROCADED SPLENDID

EMBELLISHMENT FILIP GRACE FILLIP RELISH AGREMEN GARNISH GILDING WINDING AGREMENT FLOURISH MOUNTING ORNAMENT PARERGON TRAPPING TRICKING PASSAGGIO
(MUSICAL —) SERIF MELISMA ROULADE ARABESQUE
(PL.) FIXINGS

EMBER ASH COAL AIZLE GLEED IMBER CINDER
(RED-HOT —S) BAGA

EMBEZZLE STEAL PECULATE SQUANDER

EMBEZZLEMENT THEFT PLUNDERAGE

EMBITTER SOUR BITTER CURDLE ACIDIFY ENVENOM ACERBATE EMPOISON VERJUICE

EMBITTERED SOURED ACERBATE ENFESTED

EMBLAZON LAUD ADORN EXTOL BLAZON DISPLAY EMBLAZE EXHIBIT GLORIFY

EMBLAZONED CLOUE CLOUEE CRINED CRESTED BRISTLED
(— WITH ANTLERS) ATTIRED
(— WITH BEARD) BARBED

EMBLAZONMENT HERALDRY

EMBLEM BAR ANKH ATEN LOGO MACE ORLE SEAL SIGN STAR TYPE AWARD BADGE CREST CROSS EAGLE FAVOR IMAGE TIARA TOKEN DEVICE DIADEM ENSIGN FIGURE KAHILI SABCAT SHIELD SIGNAL SYMBOL TRISUL CHARACT IMPRESA IMPRESE SCEPTER SCEPTRE ALLEGORY CADUCEUS COLOPHON INSIGNIA
(— OF AUTHORITY) ROD SCEPTER
(— OF CUCKOLD) HORN
(— OF ENGLAND) ROSE
(— OF IMMORTALITY) AMARANTH
(— OF IRELAND) SHAMROCK
(— OF PIRACY) CROSSBONES
(— OF SCOTLAND) THISTLE
(— OF SOVEREIGNTY) GLOBE
(— OF VENGEANCE) SWORD
(— OF WALES) LEEK
(AUTOMOBILE —) MARQUE
(FLYER'S —) WINGS
(PRINTING —) COLOPHON
(SACRED —) HIEROGRAM

EMBLEMATIC TYPAL FIGURAL TYPICAL SYMBOLIC

EMBLIC AMLA AULA MYROBALAN

EMBODIMENT MAP SON SELF AVATAR GENIUS EPITOME IMAGERY BODIMENT
(— OF JUSTICE) ARISTIDES
(— OF PERFECTION) FLOWER
(VISIBLE —) PICTURE

EMBODY BODY UNITE INBODY CONTAIN EXPRESS COALESCE ORGANIZE
(— IN FLESH) INCARNATE

EMBOLDEN BOLD BIELD BRAVE ERECT NERVE ASSURE BOWDEN ENHARDY HEARTEN STOMACH

EMBOLUS CLOT STYLE

EMBOSOM BOSOM FOSTER CHERISH ENCLOSE IMBOSOM SHELTER SURROUND

EMBOSS BOSS HIDE KNOB KNOT ADORN BLOCK CHASE GOFFER INDENT POUNCE ANTIQUE CONCEAL ENCLOSE EXHAUST GAUFFER INFLATE ORNAMENT

EMBOSSED BOSSED RAISED ANTIQUE CHAMPED MATELASSE

EMBOSSING CELATURE

EMBOUCHURE LIP CHOPS LIPPING

EMBOWER BOWER

EMBOWERED ARBORED

EMBRACE ARM HUG CLIP COLL FOLD LOVE NECK PLAT SIDE ZONE ADOPT BOSOM BRACE CHAIN CLASP CLING CRUSH ENARM GRASP HALCH HALSE INARM OXTER PRESS TWINE ABRAZO ACCEPT ACCOLL AMPLEX BECLIP CARESS CLINCH COMPLY CUDDLE ENFOLD FATHOM HUDDLE INCLIP INFOLD PLIGHT SHRINE AMPLECT CHERISH CONTAIN ENCLOSE ESPOUSE INCLUDE INVOLVE ACCOLADE AMPLEXUS CANOODLE COMPLECT COMPRESS COMPRISE CONCLUDE ENCIRCLE

EMBRACING COLLING OSCULANT AMPLECTANT

EMBRASURE LOOP PORT VENT CRENEL CRENELLE PORTHOLE

EMBROCATION ARNICA EMBROCHE LINIMENT

EMBROIDER RUN TAT DARN FRET LACE BROUD COUCH FAGOT PANEL SMOCK BEWORK EMBOSS FAGGOT FRIEZE NEEDLE PURFLE STITCH SURFLE TISSUE BROIDER TAMBOUR ORNAMENT

EMBROIDERED BRODE BRODEE BROWDEN BROCADED

EMBROIDERER SPRIGGER

EMBROIDERY KANT LACE OPUS WORK BREDE ASSISI BONNAZ CREWEL EDGING HEDEBO APPAREL CHICKEN CUTWORK ORPHREY SETWORK TAMBOUR ARRASENE BRODERIE BROIDERY COUCHING FAGOTING LISTWORK PHULKARI SMOCKING TAPESTRY CREWELLERY NEEDLEPOINT

EMBROIL BROIL JUMBLE INVOLVE PERPLEX TROUBLE DISORDER DISTRACT ENTANGLE

EMBRYO GERM CADET FETUS OVULE FOETUS EMBRYON NEURULA PLANULA ACANTHOR BLASTULA GASTRULA PRINCIPE (PREF.) BLAST(O)

EMBRYONIC GERMINAL

EMCEE HOST

EME AUNT YEME UNCLE FRIEND NEIGHBOR

EMEND (ALSO SEE AMEND) EDIT MEND ALTER AMEND BETTER REFORM REPEAL REVISE CORRECT IMPROVE RECTIFY REDRESS EMENDATE

EMERALD BERYL GREEN EMRAUD EMERANT PRASINE SMARAGD

EMERALD FISH ESMERALDA

EMERGE BOB DIP BOLT LOOM PEER RISE BREAK ERUPT EXUDE ISSUE START APPEAR BECOME PLUNGE SPRING DEBOUCH EXTRUDE
(— FROM EGGSHELL) HATCH ECLOSE
(— FROM SLEEP) AWAKE
(— SLOWLY) PEEK

EMERGENCE NEED BIRTH PINCH EGRESS GROWTH PRICKLE BECOMING DEBOUCHE ECLOSION EMERSION ERUPTION EXIGENCE TENTACLE
(— FROM DARKNESS) BREAK
(SUDDEN —) OUTCROP

EMERGENCY NEED PEND PUSH PINCH CRISIS STRAIT SUDDEN EMERGENT EXIGENCY JUNCTURE

EMERGENT RISING ONCOMING

EMERGING EMANANT EMERGENT

EMERITA HIPPA

EMERY EMERIL SMIRIS ABRASIVE CORUNDUM

EMETIC ALUM PICK PUKE PUKER VOMIT IPECAC EVACUANT VOMITIVE VOMITORY

EMIGRANT EMIGRE EXODIST PATARIN SETTLER COLONIST PATERINE STRANGER
(— FROM MECCA) COMPANION

EMIGRATE MOVE REMOVE MIGRATE

EMIGRATION EXODUS HEGIRA HEJIRA SWARMING

EMILIA
(HUSBAND OF —) IAGO PALAMON

EMINENCE DUN NAB BALL BERG CRAG KNOT MONS MOTE NOTE POLE RANK RISE SCAR TOOT CHIEF HOYLE KNOLL PERCH STATE WHEAL WORTH ASCENT HEIGHT KRANTZ RENOWN RIDEAU STATURE ALTITUDE GRANDEUR TUBERCLE
(— OF HAND) SUBVOLA

EMINENT BIG ARCH HIGH CHIEF GRAND GREAT LOFTY NOBLE NOTED FAMOUS MARKED SIGNAL EXCELSE SUBLIME TOPPING GLORIOUS RENOWNED SINGULAR TOWERING PROMINENT CONSPICUOUS

EMIR AMIR AMEER NOBLE RULER LEADER PRINCE ADMIRAL GOVERNOR

EMISSARY SPY AGENT SCOUT LEGATE DELEGATE

EMISSION FUME GUST PUFF VENT ESCAPE

EMISSIVE EMITTENT EXHALANT

EMIT RUN BARK BEAM CAST DRIP GIVE GUSH HURL LASH MOVE OOZE PASS POUR REEK SEND SHED SPIT VENT VOID WARP AVOID BELCH EJECT ERUCT EXERT EXUDE FLASH FLING ISSUE UTTER YIELD DECANT DONATE EVOLVE EXHALE EXPIRE SPREAD BREATHE DISTILL EMANATE EXHAUST OUTSEND RADIATE REFLAIR ERUCTATE TRANSMIT
(— COHERENT LIGHT) LASE
(— FOAM) SPURGE
(— FORCEFULLY) FIRE
(— IN PUFFS) PLUFF
(— LIGHT) GLOW
(— ODOR) REEK STEAM
(— OUTCRIES) CHUNNER CHUNTER
(— PLAY OF COLORS) OPALESCE
(— RAYS) RADIATE IRRADIATE
(— SMOKE) SMEECH
(— SOUND) BUFF MOVE
(— SPARKS) SNAP
(— SPITTLE) SPAWL

EMITTING EMISSIVE SOUNDING
(SUFF.) (— LIGHT) ESCENT

EMMA (AUTHOR OF —) AUSTEN
(CHARACTER IN —) EMMA JANE BATES ELTON FRANK SMITH GEORGE MARTIN ROBERT WESTON FAIRFAX HARRIET CHURCHILL KNIGHTLEY WOODHOUSE

EMMENAGOGUE ALOE SAFFRON GROUNDSEL

EMMER SPELTZ AMELCORN

EMMET ANT ENEMY PISMIRE FORMICID

EMMOR (SON OF —) SHECHEM

EMOLLIATE SOFTEN

EMOLLIENT BALM LOTION LENIENT ICHTHYOL LENITIVE MALACTIC MOLLIENT SUPPLING

EMOLUMENT FEES WAGES INCOME PROFIT SALARY BENEFIT STIPEND (PL.) PERK

EMOTE HAM OVERACT

EMOTION IRE LOVE ONDE PANG STIR AGONY ANGER CHORD GRIEF HEART SHAME AFFECT EFFECT

MOTION RAPTUS SNIVEL SPLEEN
ECSTASY FEELING PASSION
VULTURE GRAMERCY MOVEMENT
SURPRISE SENTIMENT
(CONTROLLING —) LEITMOTIF
LEITMOTIV
(CONVULSIVE —) SPASM
(EVIL —) DEMON DAEMON
(PAINFUL —) PANG
(PERIOD OF —) CRISIS
(PREF.) THYM(O)
(SUFF.) THYMIA
EMOTIONAL MUSHY DRIPPY
EMOTIVE AFFECTIVE
(OPENLY —) TOUCHYFEELY
(UNDULY —) SPOONY SPOONEY
RHAPSODIC
EMOTIONLESS COLD
EMPATHY SYMPATHY
EMPEROR I IMP CZAR INCA KING
TSAR AKBAR RULER TENNO CAESAR
DESPOT KABAKA KAISER SULTAN
BAGINDA MONARCH VIKRAMA
AUGUSTUS IMPERIAL PADISHAH
(ROMAN —) GETA NERO OTHO OTTO
CARUS GALBA NEPOS NERVA TITUS
ADRIAN CAESAR JULIAN HADRIAN
CALIGULA
EMPERY DOMAIN EMPIRE EMPIRY
DOMINION
EMPHASIS ANGLE ACCENT STRESS
WEIGHT EMPIRISM SALIENCE
EMPHASIZE HIT CLICK PINCH PRESS
RUBIN ACCENT RETONE CHARGE
HARPON PLAYUP STRESS
FOREGROUND
EMPHATIC LOUD STRONG EARNEST
MARCATO SERIOUS ENFATICO
FORCIBLE MARCANDO POSITIVE
RESOUNDING
EMPHATICALLY FLATLY STRONGLY
POINTEDLY
EMPHYSEMA HEAVES
EMPIRE RULE SWAY POWER REALM
REIGN STATE DIADEM DOMAIN
EMPERY CONTROL KINGDOM
IMPERIUM
(— STATE) NEWYORK
(— STATE OF SOUTH) GEORGIA
(SELJUK —) RUM ROUM
EMPIRIC QUACK IMPOSTOR
EMPIRICAL POSITIVE
EMPIRICIST VIRTUOSO
EMPLACEMENT BATTERY GALLERY
PLATFORM
EMPLOY FEE PAY USE BUSK BUSY
HIRE PLOY TAKE WAGE WISE ADOPT
APPLY BESET IMPLY SPEND BESTOW
ENGAGE ENLIST INFOLD INVOKE
OCCUPY SUPPLY CONCERN
CONDUCT ENCLOSE IMPROVE
INVOLVE SERVICE UTILIZE PRACTICE

(— FLATTERY) COLLOGUE
(— ONESELF ABOUT) TOSS
(— SHIFTS) CHICANE
EMPLOYED APPLIED ENGAGED
EMPLOYEE HAND HELP BOOTS
CLERK FACTOR LEADER BELLBOY
BOOTBOY CALLBOY CARRIER
SERVANT CHASSEUR CIVILIAN
FLOORMAN IMPROVER
(— PROGRAM) ESOP
(— WHO RUNS ERRANDS) GOFER
GOPHER
EMPLOYER BOSS JOSS BLOKE
GAFFER ENGAGER MANAGER
PADRONE GOVERNOR
(SMALL —) CORK
EMPLOYMENT FEE JOB USE CALL
HIRE NOTE TASK TOIL USER WORK
CRAFT TRADE TREAD USAGE MISTER
THRIFT CALLING PURPOSE PURSUIT
SERVICE USAUNCE BUSINESS
EXERCISE POSITION RETAINER
VOCATION
(CASUAL —) GRASS
EMPORIUM MART SHOP BAZAR
STORE BAZAAR EMPORY MARKET
STAPLE MONOPOLE
EMPOWER POWER ENABLE ENTITLE
DELEGATE DEPUTIZE
EMPRESS IMPX EMPERESS IMPERIAL
KAISERIN
EMPTIED DRAINED
EMPTILY TOOMLY
EMPTINESS VAIN VOID INANE
ANEMIA VACUUM VANITY ANAEMIA
INANITY VACANCY VACUITY
LEERNESS
(— OF SPIRIT) ENNUI
EMPTY DRY FAT RID TIM AIRY BARE
BOSS BUZZ CANT DEAF DUMP EMPT
FALL FARM FREE GLIB HOWE IDLE
LEER NEAR POUR ROOM TEEM TOOM
VAIN VIDE VOID ADDLE AVOID BLANK
BLEED CLEAN CLEAR DRAIN EQUAL
EXPEL HUSKY INANE LEERY MOUTH
SCOOP SHOOT SKAIL STARK START
STRIP SWAMP TINNY WINDY BARREN
BUBBLE CHAFFY DEVOID GOUSTY
HOLLOW JEJUNE STRIKE SWASTY
UNEMPT UNLOAD VACANT VACATE
DELIVER DEPLETE EXHAUST EXPRESS
UNTAKEN VACUATE VACUOUS
VIDUOUS DISGORGE EVACUATE
EVANESCE NEGATION UNFILLED
(— AN EGG) BLOW
(PREF.) CEN(O) JEJUN(O) KEN(O)
EMPTY-HEADED VAIN DOLLISH
EMPTYING EVACUANT
(ACT OF —) KENOSIS
EMPTY-SOUNDING TOOM
EMPUSA MONSTER SPECTER
SPECTRE

EMPYREAN ETHER AETHER HEAVENS EMPYREUM

EMU EMEU RHEA RATITE

EMU APPLE COLANE

EMU BUSH BERRIGAN

EMULATE APE VIE COPY EMULE EQUAL EXCEL RIVAL COMPETE IMITATE

EMULATION STRIFE CONTEST PARAGON RIVALRY

EMULATOR RIVAL

EMULOUS EMULATE ENVIOUS CORRIVAL

EMULOUSLY AVIE

EMULSIFIABLE SOLUBLE

EMULSION PAP FLUID LATEX (SENSITIVE —) PHOTOGENE

EMU WREN STIPITURE

EN NUT

ENABLE ABLE EMPOWER ENTITLE QUALIFY INHABILE

ENACT LIVE MAKE PASS ADOPT STAGE DECREE EFFECT ORDAIN ACTUATE APPOINT PERFORM PORTRAY

ENACTMENT LAW DOOM ENACT NOVEL ASSIZE DECREE MEASURE PASSAGE STATUTE ENACTION ENACTURE

ENAMEL AMEL FLUX SLIP EMAIL GLAZE GLOSS PAINT SLUSH AUMAIL SHIPPO SMALTO DENTINE LIMOGES SCHMELZ (KIND OF —) CANTON

ENAMOR LOVE CHARM SMITE CAPTIVE

ENAMORED FOND EPRIS EPRISE MASHED AMOROUS CHARMED SMITTEN (VAINLY —) FOOLISH

ENARCHUS (NEPHEW OF —) MUSIDORUS (SON OF —) PYROCLES

ENCAMP TELD TENT LODGE PITCH INCAMP LAAGER BIVOUAC LEAGUER

ENCAMPMENT CAMP DOUAR ETAPE SIEGE LAAGER BIVOUAC CASTRUM HUTMENT TOLDERIA

ENCASE CASE WRAP HOUSE SHELL INCASE ENCHASE INCLOSE SURROUND ENCAPSULE

ENCELIA INCIENSO

ENCEPHALON CEREBRUM

ENCHAIN FETTER INCHAIN

ENCHANT CHARM DELUDE GLAMOR INCANT ATTRACT BECHARM BESPELL BEWITCH DELIGHT GLAMOUR BEDAZZLE ENSORCEL CAPTIVATE

ENCHANTED RAPT HAGGED CAPTIVE

ENCHANTER MAUGIS CHARMER MAGICIAN MALAGIGI ARCHIMAGE

ENCHANTING ORPHIC WIZARD HEAVENLY SPELLFUL

ENCHANTMENT HEX TAKE CHARM FAIRY MAGIC SPELL SPOKE CARACT CHANTRY DEVILRY GRAMARY SORCERY SORTIARY WITCHERY

ENCHANTRESS CIRCE FAIRY MEDEA ACRASIA URGANDA

ENCHARGE ENJOIN ENTRUST

ENCHASE INFIX ENRICH ENGRAVE

ENCHIRIDION MANUAL HANDBOOK TREATISE

ENCHORIAL NATIVE DEMOTIC DOMESTIC

ENCIPHER CODE CIPHER ENCRYPT

ENCIRCLE ORB BAND BELT BIND CLIP COIL GIRD GIRT HALO HOOP PALE RING RINK STEM WIRE ZONE BELAY BESET BRACE CLASP CROWN EMBAY EMBOW GIRTH HEDGE INORB ROUND TWINE TWIST BECLIP BEGIRD CIRCLE EMBALL ENGIRT ENLACE ENRING ENWIND FATHOM GIRDLE IMPALE SWATHE WRITHE BETREND COMPASS EMBRACE ENCLAVE ENCLOSE ENTWINE ENVIRON ENWHEEL SERPENT WREATHE CINCTURE CORSELET ENSPHERE IMMANTLE SURROUND

ENCIRCLED GIRT CINCT BELTED SUCCINCT

ENCIRCLEMENT EMBRACE

ENCIRCLING AROUND AMBIENT EMBRACE CORONARY ENCYCLIC (PREF.) AMPLEXI

ENCLAVE INLIER (— IN SOUTH AFRICA) BANTUSTAN

ENCLOAK MANTLE

ENCLOSE IN BAY BOX CAN HEM LAP MEW ORB PAR PEN PIN RIM BANK BUNG CAGE CASE COOP FORT GIRD HAIN HOOP PALE SPAR TINE WALL WARD WOMB YARD BOSOM BOUND BOWER BRICK CHEST CLOSE DITCH EMBAR EMBED EMBOX FENCE FRAME GARTH GRIPE HEDGE HOUSE IMBED INURN BOUGHT CARTON CASTLE CAVERN CIRCLE CORDON CORRAL EMBANK EMBOSS EMPALE EMPARK EMPLOY ENCASE ENCYST ENFOLD ENGULF ENLOCK FASTEN IMMURE IMPALE IMPARK INCASE INCLIP INHOOP INSACK INWALL JACKET PICKET POCKET SHUTIN TACKLE APPROVE CAPSULE COMPASS CONFIDE CONTAIN CURTAIN EMBOSOM EMBOWEL EMBOWER EMBRACE ENCHASE ENCLAVE ENGLOBE ENHEDGE ENVELOP HARNESS IMBOSOM IMMERSE IMPOUND INBOUND INCLUDE INFIELD PARROCK PINFOLD SHEATHE BULKHEAD COMPRISE

COMPRIZE CONCLUDE CONVOLVE
EMBORDER ENCIRCLE ENSHRINE
ENSPHERE IMPRISON LANDLOCK
PALISADE PARCLOSE SURROUND
(— IN ARMOR) EMPANOPLY
(— LOGS) CRIB
ENCLOSED BOUND CLOSED INDOOR
OBTECT SHUTIN INGROWN INTERNAL
ENCLOSING LIMITARY
(PREF.) PERI
ENCLOSURE HAG HAW HOK MEW
PAR PEN REE STY TYE BAWN BOMA
BYTH CAGE CAVE CELL COOP DOCK
FOLD HAIN HOCK HOPE KILN LIST
PALE PEEL SEPT SKIT SLOT TIGH
TOWN WALL WEIR YARD ALTIS
ATAJO BASIN BLIND BOOLY BOOTH
BOSOM CAROL CLOSE COURT
CRAWL CREEP CUBBY FENCE FRANK
GARTH GOTRA HUARD KENCH
KRAAL LOBBY MARAI PLECK POUND
REEVE STALL STELL AVIARY BOOLEY
BOXING CANCHA CARREL CORRAL
COWPEN CRUIVE DRYLOT GARDEN
HURDLE INTAKE KENNEL OUTSET
PALING PRISON SERAIL TAMBOR
TEOPAN TINING VIVARY WARREN
BELLOWS BOROUGH BULLPEN
CLOSURE COCKPIT EMBRACE
GALLERY GONDOLA HAINING
HENNERY HOUSING HUMIDOR
LANTERN PADDOCK PIGHTLE
PUDDOCK SEVERAL STUFFER
TAMBOUR AEDICULA CASEMATE
CHIPYARD CINCTURE CLAPNEST
CLAUSURE CLOISTER COMPOUND
DELUBRUM ENCEINTE ENCHASER
PARADISE POUNDAGE PRECINCT
PURPRISE SEPIMENT SERAGLIO
SKIRTING STOCKADE VIVARIUM
(— ABOUT ALTAR) BEMA
(— FOR BOWLING) ALLEY
(— FOR COCKPIT) CANOPY
(— FOR FISH) CROY YAIR YARE
KENCH SPILLER SPILLET
(— FOR JURY) BOX
(— FOR KNIGHTLY ENCOUNTERS)
BARRACE
(— FOR LIGHT) LANTERN
(— FOR ROASTING ORE) STALL
(— OF HOUSE) BAWN
(— ON AIRPLANE) NACELLE
(— SURROUNDED BY DITCH) COP
(ELEPHANT —) KEDDAH
(OBLONG —) CIRCUS
(PORTABLE —) PLAYPEN
(POULTRY —) HENNERY
(PRIVATE SEAT —) SKYBOX
(ROOFED —) SKYBOX
(SACRED —) SECOS SEKOS
(PREF.) CLAUSTRO SEPTATO
(SUFF.) SEPTATE
ENCOLPION PANAGIA

ENCOLURE MANE
ENCOMIAST EULOGIST
ENCOMIUM ELOGE ENCOMY
EULOGY PRAISE PLAUDIT TRIBUTE
PANEGYRIC
ENCOMPASS BEGO BELT CLIP GIRD
PALE RING SPAN WALL WRAP BELIE
BERUN BESET BIGAN BRACE CLOSE
CROWN ROUND BEGIRD BEGIRT
CIRCLE ENGIRD BESEIGE COMPASS
EMBOWEL EMBRACE ENCLOSE
ENVIRON INCLUDE SUBSUME
UMBESET CINCTURE ENCIRCLE
ENGIRDLE PURPRISE SURROUND
(— WITH ARMS) FATHOM
ENCOMPASSED AMID BAYED
AMIDST BEGIRT
ENCOMPASSING ROUND AMBIENT
CINCTURE PROFOUND INCLUSIVE
ENCORE BIS AGAIN RERUN ANCORA
RECALL REPEAT
ENCOUNTER BIDE BUMP COIL COPE
FACE FIND KEEP MEET MOOT RINK
BRUSH CLOSE FIGHT FORCE GREET
INCUR OCCUR ONSET SHOCK STOUR
VENUE ACCOST AFFRAY ANSWER
ASSAIL ATTACK BATTLE BREAST
CAREER COMBAT JOSTLE JUSTLE
OPPOSE RUFFLE ADDRESS AFFRONT
CONTEST COUNTER DISPUTE
HOSTING JOINING PASSAGE
CONFLICT CONFRONT CONGRESS
REANSWER RECONTER SKIRMISH
COLLISION
(— HOSTILELY) CROSS
(HOSTILE —) CLOSE
(MILITARY —) ACTION
(PUGILISTIC —) MILL
ENCOURAGE DAW EGG ABET BACK
FIRM URGE BOOST CHEER ERECT
FAVOR FLUSH HEART IMPEL NERVE
SERVE STEEL ADVISE ASSURE
EXHORT FOMENT FOSTER HALLOO
HARDEN INCITE INDUCE INVITE
NUZZLE REHETE SECOND SPIRIT
UPHOLD ADVANCE ANIMATE
CHERISH COMFORT CONFIRM
CONSOLE ENFORCE ENLIVEN
FLATTER FORTIFY FORWARD
HEARTEN INSPIRE PROMOTE
STOMACH UPCHEER UPRAISE
EMBOLDEN INSPIRIT REASSURE
ENCOURAGED BUCKED CONFIRMED
ENCOURAGEMENT BOOST FLUSH
HURRAH COMFORT FOMENTO
IMPETUS BLESSING SANCTION
ENCOURAGING HELPFUL FAVORING
ENCRATITE TATIAN AQUARIAN
ENCROACH JET PINCH POACH
IMPOSE INVADE TRENCH IMPINGE
INTRUDE SHINGLE ENTRENCH
INFRINGE INTRENCH TRESPASS
ENCROACHING INVASIVE

ENCROACHMENT BREACH INROAD
ENCROACH INVASION
ENCRUST CAKE CANDY BARKEN
BARKLE INCRUST
ENCRUSTATION SCALE
ENCRUSTED CAKED SCABROUS
ENCUMBER CLOG LOAD PACK
BESET CHECK CRAMP CROWD TRASH
ACCLOY BEMOIL BURDEN FELTER
HAMPER HINDER IMPEDE LUMBER
MITHER MOIDER RETARD SADDLE
WEIGHT BEPAPER INVOLVE OPPRESS
ACCUMBER ENTANGLE HANDICAP
OBSTRUCT OVERCOME OVERLOAD
ENCUMBERED HEAVY CONGESTED
ENCUMBRANCE CLOG LIEN LOAD
CLAIM BURDEN CHARGE CUMBER
TROUBLE MORTGAGE ALBATROSS
ENCYCLICAL PASCENDI
ENCYCLOPEDIA TOME
(GAME —) HOYLE
ENCYSTED CYSTIC SACCATE
SACCATED
END EN AIM DAG EAR FAG TIP BUTT
CUSP DATE DOUP FACE FATE FINE
FOOT GOAL HALT HEEL LAST MAIN
MARK SAKE STOP TAIL TERM VIEW
AMEND ANNUL ARTHA BLOCK
BREAK CAUSE CEASE CLOSE DEATH
ENSUE EVENT FINIS ISSUE LIMIT
LOOSE NAPOO OMEGA POINT PRICK
RAISE SCOPE SCRAP SHANK START
STASH THULE DECIDE DEFINE
DESIGN DOMINO EFFECT EFFLUX
ENDING EXITUS EXPIRE EXPIRY
FINALE FINISH INTENT NAPOOH
OBJECT PERIOD RESULT THIRTY
UPSHOT UTMOST WINDUP ABOLISH
ACHIEVE CLOSURE CURTAIN
DESTROY FANTAIL FINANCE
LINEMAN MEANING OUTGIVE
PURPOSE REMNANT BOUNDARY
COMPLETE CONCLUDE DESITION
DISSOLVE FINALITY SURCEASE
TERMINAL TERMINUS ULTIMATE
(— DEBATE) CLOTURE
(— OF ANTENNA) CLAVA
(— OF ANVIL) BICKIRON
(— OF ARCHERY PILE) STOPPING
(— OF ARROW) NOCK
(— OF BEEF LOIN) BUTT
(— OF BLANKET) DAGON
(— OF BONE) EPIPHYSIS
(— OF BOOM) JAW
(— OF BOW) EAR
(— OF BRICK) HEADING
(— OF BRISTLE) FLAG
(— OF BUILDING) GABLE
(— OF CAN) BREAST
(— OF CANE) FRAZE
(— OF CART) TIB
(— OF CRESCENT) HORN
(— OF EAR CANAL) AMPULLA

(— OF EGG) DOUP
(— OF EXISTENCE) DEMISE
(— OF FABRIC) FENT
(— OF FISHHOOK) SPEAR
(— OF FLAG) FLY
(— OF FROG) TOE
(— OF HALTER) CAPITULUM
(— OF HAMMER) CLAW POLL
(— OF HAMMERHEAD) PEEN
(— OF HORSE-COLLAR) GULLET
(— OF INGOT) CROP
(— OF KEEL) GRIPE
(— OF LEVER) FORK
(— OF LOAF) HEEL
(— OF MINERAL LODE) SLOVAN
(— OF MINE TUNNEL) FACE
(— OF MINING LEVEL) DEAN
(— OF MUZZLE) MUFFLE
(— OF NAIL) CLENCH
(— OF ONE'S LIFE) DOOM
(— OF PIER) CUTWATER
(— OF PIPE) TAFT SPIGOT
(— OF POCKETKNIFE HANDLE)
BOLSTER
(— OF RAILROAD CAR) BEND
(— OF ROAD) ROADHEAD
(— OF ROD) FORKHEAD
(— OF SHEEP SHEARING) CUTOUT
(— OF SHIP) STERN
(— OF SPINE) ACRUMION
(— OF TENON) HAUNCH
(— OF TOOL) BUTT
(— OF UTERUS) FUNDUS
(— OF WEAVER'S THREAD) THRUM
(— OF WORLD) PRALAYA
(— OF YARD) ARM YARDARM
(— ON) ABUT
(— ON POND) FOREBAY
(—S OF RIBBONS) FATTRELS
(—S OF SATURN'S RINGS) ANSA
(— UP WITH) NET
(CANDLE —) DOUP SNUFF
(DOMINO —) ACE
(FAG —) RUMP
(HANGING —) DAG DAGGE
(JAGGED —) SHRAG
(KIND OF —) TIGHT
(LOOSE —) TAG
(NARROWED —) NEB
(NORTH — OF COMPASS NEEDLE) LILY
(POINTED —) APEX
(POSTERIOR —) BOTTOM
(REEF —S) DEADMAN
(ROPE'S —) COLT FEAZE PIGTAIL
FEAZINGS
(SPECIAL —) SAKE
(TAPERING —) POINT
(TATTERED —) FRAZZLE
(ULTIMATE —) SUM TELOS
(UNPLEASANT —) GRIEF
(UPPER —) HEAD
(WARP —S) ACCIDENTAL
(PREF.) ACR(O) FINI TEL(IO)

ENDANGER DANGER HAZARD IMPERIL SCUPPER

ENDANGERED BESTED BESTEAD FRAUGHT

ENDANGERER MARPLOT

ENDEARMENT LOVE CARESS

ENDEAVOR DO AIM PUT TRY WIN BEST MINT SEEK WORK ASSAY ESSAY ETTLE EXERT OFFER STUDY TEMPT TRIAL AFFAIR ASSAIL DEVOIR EFFORT INTEND STRIFE STRIVE AFFORCE ATTEMPT CONATUS CONTEND CULTURE EMPRISE EMULATE IMITATE MOLIMEN NITENCY WORKING EXERTION PURCHASE STRUGGLE
(— TO CONCLUSION) STUDY
(BEST —) DEVOIR
(EARNESTLY —) FEND

ENDED DONE OVER PAST FINISHED
(— BY CONSONANT) CHECKED

ENDEMIC LOCAL ENDEMIAL

ENDING END CLOSE DEATH GRAVE FINALE BREAKUP FINANCE DESITION
(KIND OF —) NERVE
(MUSICAL —) CODA
(NERVE —) SPINDLE
(ROMAN —) CODA

ENDIVE CHICORY WITLOOF ESCAROLE SCARIOLE

ENDLESS ANANTA ETERNE ETERNAL FOREVER UNDYING UNENDED UNENDLY DATELESS FINELESS IMMORTAL INFINITE UNENDING

ENDMOST TIPMOST FARTHEST REMOTEST

ENDOCARP STONE PYRENA PUTAMEN

ENDOGENOUS INNATE AUTOGENIC

ENDOMORPHIC PYCNIC PYKNIC

ENDOPITE PETASMA

ENDOPLEURA TEGMEN

ENDORSE BACK SIGN ADOPT BOOST DOCKET ENDOSS SECOND APPROVE CERTIFY INDORSE SPONSOR SUPPORT ADVOCATE SANCTION RECOMMEND

ENDORSEE HOLDER

ENDORSEMENT FIAT FORM VISA RIDER BACKING APPROVAL HECHSHER SANCTION

ENDOSPERM FARINA ALBUMEN

ENDOSPORIUM INTINE

ENDOW DOW DUE DOTE GIFT RENT VEST BLESS CROWN DOWER ENDUE EQUIP FOUND INDUE SEIZE STATE STUFF ASSIGN CLOTHE DOTATE ENABLE ENRICH ENSOUL ESTATE IMPART INVEST CHARTER ENLARGE FURNISH INSTATE APPANAGE BENEFICE BEQUEATH ENTAILENT
(— WITH FORCE) DYNAMIZE

ENDOWED ABLE GIFTED FAVORED

ENDOWMENT CLAY FINE GIFT WAKF WAQF DOWER DOWRY GRACE GRANT CORPSE GENIUS TALENT APANAGE CHANTRY CHARISM FACULTY APPANAGE DOTATION PATRIMONY BENEFACTION
(NATURAL —S) BUMP DOTES TALENT
(PL.) ALTARAGE

ENDPAPER FLYLEAF

ENDPIECE BRACE CHUMP
(— OF STETHOSCOPE) BELL

ENDUE DUE ENDOW INDUE TEACH CLOTHE INVEST INSTRUCT

ENDURABLE LIVABLE BEARABLE LIVEABLE PORTABLE

ENDURANCE GAME LAST TACK PLUCK BOTTOM BEARING COMFORT DURANCE GRANITE LASTING STAMINA BEARANCE DURATION GAMENESS HARDSHIP PATIENCE STRENGTH

ENDURE GO ABY SIT VIE ABYE BEAR BIDE DREE DURE HOLD KEEP LAST TAKE TIDE WEAR ABEAR ABIDE ALLOW BROOK CARRY DRIVE POUCH SPARE STAND STICK STOUT THOLE TOUGH WIELD ABROOK ACCEPT DRUDGE HARDEN REMAIN SUFFER ABROOKE COMFORT FORBEAR PERSIST STOMACH SUPPORT SUSTAIN SWALLOW TOUGHEN UNDERGO WEARING CONTINUE FOREBEAR TOLERATE
(— LONGER) OUTLAST

ENDURING FAST SURE STOUT BIDING DURING STABLE STURDY ABIDING DURABLE ETERNAL LASTING PATIENT IMMORTAL REMANENT STUBBORN PERENNIAL

ENDWAYS ANEND ENDWISE

ENDYMION (DAUGHTER OF —) EURYDICE
(FATHER OF —) ZEUS JUPITER AETHELIUS
(MOTHER OF —) CALYCE
(SON OF —) EPEUS PAEON AETOLUS
(WIFE OF —) CROMIA ASTERODIA HYPARIPPE

ENEMA CLYSMA CLYSTER COLONIC LAVEMENT

ENEMY FOE AXIS BOYG FEID DEVIL FIEND SATAN FOEMAN HOSTILE CONTRARY OPPONENT
(— OF MANKIND) DEVIL FIEND SATAN
(PERSONAL —) HATER

ENEMY OF THE PEOPLE (AUTHOR OF —) IBSEN
(CHARACTER IN —) KIIL PETER MORTEN HORSTER HOVSTAD ASLAKSEN STOCKMANN

ENERGETIC BUSY FAST FELL HARD LIVE RASH SPRY BRISK DASHY LUSTY PITHY STOUT TIGHT VITAL

YAULD ZIPPY ACTIVE HEARTY
HUSTLE LIVELY SPROIL ACTIOUS
ANIMOSO ARDUOUS DASHING
DRIVING DYNAMIC ENERGIC
FURIOUS NERVOUS PUSHFUL
PUSHING VIBRANT EMPHATIC
ENERGICO FORCEFUL FORCIBLE
HUSTLING VIGOROUS
(— PERSON) TOWSER
ENERGETICALLY MANLY
FURIOUSLY
ENERGID PROTOPLAST
ENERGIZE LIVEN EXCITE ANIMATE
ENERGIZING KINETIC VIRTUAL
ENERGY U W GO GAS PEP VIM ZIP
BANG BENT BIRR DASH EDGE JASM
LIFE SAKT SNAP TUCK ZING ARDOR
ECLAT FORCE INPUT MOXIE NERVE
OOMPH POWER STEAM VIGOR
EFFORT FOISON INTAKE ORGONE
OUTPUT SPIRIT SPRAWL SPRING
SPROIL STARCH VIRTUE POTENCY
SPIRITS ACTIVITY AMBITION
DYNAMISM ENERGEIA MOTIVITY
PRAKRITI STRENGTH VIVACITY
(— PEAK) NUCLEUS
(EMOTIONAL —) LIBIDO
(LIBINAL —) CATHEXIS
(LIFE —) JIVA SAKTI SHAKTI
(LIGHT —) RAD
(LOW IN —) COLD
(MENTAL —) DOCITY PSYCHURGY
(POINT OF PHYSICAL —) CHAKRA
(POTENTIAL —) ERGAL
(QUANTUM OF —) PLASMON
(RADIANT —) SOUND ACTINISM
EINSTEIN
(VITAL —) HORME PANZOISM
(PREF.) (RADIANT —) PENETRO
(SOLAR —) HELI(O)
ENERVATE SAP COOK FLAG MELT
SOFTEN WEAKEN MOLLIFY UNNERVE
UNSINEW ENFEEBLE
ENERVATED LIMP BEDRID EFFETE
LANGUID LIFELESS BEDRIDDEN
ENERVATING MUGGY DREARY
ENERVATION COLLAPSE
ENFEEBLE SAP NUMB FAINT SHAKE
APPALL DEADEN FEEBLE IMPAIR
SOFTEN WEAKEN DEPRESS
UNSINEW AFFEEBLE ENERVATE
IMBECILE UNSTRONG
ENFEEBLED FEY NUMB
ENFILADE RAKE
ENFOLD (ALSO SEE INFOLD) LAP
FURL ROLL WRAP CLASP COVER
DRAPE ENROL IMPLY COMPLY
ENLACE ENROLL ENWIND ENWRAP
INCLIP INFOLD INWIND SHADOW
SWATHE WATTLE EMBRACE
ENCLOSE ENVELOP ENVIRON
INCLUDE INVOLVE UMBELAP
CONVOLVE

ENFORCE BULL LEVY EXACT
FORCE PRESS COERCE COMPEL
EFFECT FOLLOW INVOKE EXECUTE
IMPLANT
ENFORCED COMPULSORY
ENFORCER EXECUTOR MUSCLEMAN
ENFRAMEMENT CARTOUCH
ENG AGMA
ENGAGE DIP WED BOOK BUSY
GAGE HAVE HIRE JOIN LIST MESH
RENT SIGN TAKE WAGE AGREE
AMUSE CATCH ENTER LEASE PITCH
TRADE TRYST ABSORB ARREST
EMBARK EMPLOY ENLIST INDUCE
OBLIGE OCCUPY PLEDGE PLIGHT
TAKEON BESPEAK BETROTH
CONCERN CONDUCE CONSUME
ENGROSS IMMERSE INVOLVE
PROMISE THROWIN AFFIANCE
CONTRACT COVENANT ENTANGLE
INTEREST INTRIGUE PERSUADE
PREOCCUPY
(— ATTENTION) INTEREST
(— DEEPLY) DROWN
(— IN) GO CUT SUE HAVE JOIN LEAD
PROSECUTE
(— IN ARGUMENT) BALK BAULK
(— IN COMBAT) DEBATE STRIKE
(— IN DEBATE) STONEWALL
(— IN DISCUSSION) CONTEND
(— IN PRANKS) LARK
(— IN TILT) JUST JOUST
(— OVERMUCH) TROUBLE
(— WHOLLY) ABSORB CONSUME
IMMERSE
(SUFF.) (— IN) IZE
ENGAGED BENT BUSY FAST GONE
HIRED ACTIVE BONDED BOOKED
MESHED ASSURED BESPOKE
EARNEST ENTERED PLEDGED
TOKENED VERSANT ABSORBED
ATTACHED EMBEDDED EMPLOYED
INSERTED INTEREST INVOLVED
OCCUPIED PROMISED
(— IN) ABOUT
(— IN CONTROVERSY) DISPUTANT
(MENTALLY —) VERSANT
(WARMLY —) ZEALOUS
ENGAGEMENT AVAL DATE COWLE
SPURN ACTION AFFAIR BATTLE
COMBAT ESCROW PLIGHT STANZA
SURETY BARGAIN BOOKING
DUSTING SERVICE CONFLICT
RETAINER SKIRMISH WARRANTY
(— OF GEARS) MESH
(— TO MARRY) TRYST
(MILITARY —) DO SHOW
(SHORT —) RUN SNAP
(SINGLE —) GIG
(THEATRICAL —) SHOP
(WRITTEN —) COWLE
ENGAGING SOFT SAPID SWEET
TAKING

ENGENDER BEGET BREED CAUSE
EXCITE GENDER DEVELOP PRODUCE
GENERATE INGENDER OCCASION
ENGIDU EABANI
ENGINE GAS JET SIX FOUR GOAT
TANK EIGHT JINNY MOTOR OILER
STEAM BANKER DIESEL DOCTOR
DUDLER DUDLEY INGENE JORDAN
KICKER PUFFER RADIAL RAMJET
ROADER YARDER MACHINE POACHER
POTCHER SKIDDER STEAMER
TRACTOR TURBINE BULLGINE
COMPOUND DOLLBEER EXPANDER
GASOLINE IMPULSOR SCRAMJET
(— **FOR HAULING LOGS**) DUDLER
DUDLEY
(— **FOR THROWING MISSILES**) GIN
PETRARY SPRINGAL
(— **OF TORTURE**) GIN RACK
(— **OF WAR**) RAM SWEEP HELEPOLE
(— **PART**) STATOR
(**AIRPLANE** —) SCRAMJET
(**DONKEY** —) DOCTOR
(**FIRE** —) TUB
(**JET** —) ATHODYD
(**KIND OF** —) PLASMA WANKEL
(**MILITARY** —) BOAR TOWER BRICOL
FABRIC TREPAN BRICOLE DONDINE
PERRIER PETRARY TORMENT
WARWOLF BALLISTA DONDAINE
MANGONEL MARTINET SCORPION
(**RAILROAD** —) HOG GOAT YARDER
SWITCHER
(**REACTION** —) THRUSTER THRUSTOR
(**ROCKET** —) ARCJET VERNIER
(**SMOOTH RUNNING** —) HUMDINGER
(**TYPE OF ROTARY** —) WANKEL
ENGINEER PLAN GUIDE DRIVER
FANNER HOGGER MANAGE SAPPER
HOGHEAD PLANNER PLOTTER
CONTRIVE DESIGNER INGENIER
INVENTOR MANEUVER
AMERICAN AMY BURR BUSH DORR
DUNN EADS HERR HILL KRUG LAKE
LEAR PECK RICE ROUS WANG ALLEN
CARTY ELLET GANTT HAUPT HENCH
LAMME MILLS MOORE OWENS
PRATT STOUT TESLA AMDAHL
ARNOLD BEATTY BOGART COFFIN
CONRAD COOPER COWLES CRAVEN
FERRIS GARAND GREENE HAMMER
HOLLEY HOLLIS HOUDRY HUTTON
JACOBY JENNEY LAMONT LITTLE
MORGAN NEWELL PARKER PENDER
PINCUS PORTER RUMSEY STUMPF
WILSON WRIGHT BALDWIN BARRELL
BEHREND CLEMSON CROCKER
DEJONGH DRINKER EHRICKE
FANNING FREEMAN GODFREY
GRAYDON HASWELL KINEALY
KINTNER KNOWLES LATROBE
LEONARD PACKARD PARSONS
PATRICK GERRELL STRAUSS WHIPPLE

AMSTRUTZ DINKELOO EDGERTON
ELLSBERG ERICSSON GOETHALS
HARRISON HARTNESS HUNSAKER
KENNELLY MCALPINE MODJESKI
OVINGTON REYNOLDS RICHARDS
ROEBLING ZWORYKIN ARMSTRONG
CARPENTER GILLESPIE KETTERING
STEINMETZ TRAUTWINE ZACHARIAS
FARNSWORTH LETOURNEAU
LINDENTHAL RIESENBERG
STRICKLAND WORTHINGTON
ALEXANDERSON BRECKENRIDGE
AUSTRALIAN CLAPP
AUSTRIAN BIRAGO ENGERTH
MANNLICHER
CANADIAN DUMAS KLOTZ MARKLE
CHINESE KWOH
CUBAN MENOCAL
CZECH SKODA
DANISH POULSEN
DUTCH NORDEN STEVIN MUSSERT
ENGLISH FOX AIRD BAKER
BOYLE CLARK COOKE GABOR
GOOCH GROVE KEMPE MANCE
ROYCE AYRTON BRAMAH BRUNEL
CAYLEY CLARKE CUBITT DONKIN
FLOREY FOWLER HARRIS HEDGES
HINTON MCADAM WALLIS BERKLEY
BOULTON CAUTLEY CRAPPER
DUDDELL FLEMING HARTLEY
MURDOCK SIEMENS SMEATON
ANDERSON BRINDLEY BUCHANAN
CRAMPTON FERRANTI HAWKSHAW
REDMAYNE SYDENHAM GREATHEAD
GRIFFITHS HOPKINSON ISSIGONIO
WILLCOCKS WIMSHURST
HORNBLOWER TREVITHICK
BRAITHWAITE FITZMAURICE
FRENCH LAME ARCON MALUS
PRONY BERTIN CHAPPE COANDA
CUGNOT DEPREZ EIFFEL LEPLAY
MARTIN RATEAU RIQUET ALPHAND
BELIDOR BERLIER BERNARD BIERIOT
BLERIOT CLERGET GIFFARD LEBLANC
LENFANT LESSEPS TELLIER
BELGRAND PONCELET FOURNEYRON
HENNEBIQUE
GERMAN BACH BENZ KOCH OTTO
BOSCH KNORR AMMANN CRELLE
DIESEL GERBER LANGEN WANKEL
CARNALL CULMANN DAIMLER
SIEMENS FLETTNER EYTELWEIN
BAUERSFELD LILIENTHAL
BAUERNFEIND GOLDSCHMIDT
HASELWANDER
ITALIAN NERVI VINCI BUGATTI
CODAZZI FABRONI MARCONI
LATVIAN MOISSEIFF
POLISH NARUTOWICZ
RUSSIAN THEREMIN FEOKTISOV
SCOTTISH BARR BELL WATT BAIRD
CLERK ELDER EWING MCADAM
MURRAY NAPIER RANKINE TELFORD

BRUNLEES FAIRBAIRN STEVENSON
SYMINGTON
SPANISH CIERVA CANDELA
SWEDISH DALEN LAVAL POLHEM
BRINELL DAHLBERG
SWISS ILG FAVRE
ENGINEMAN HOISTER HOISTMAN
ENGINERY TIRE
ENGIRDLED CINCT
ENGLAND HOME ALBION LOGRIA
BLIGHTY BRITAIN LOEGRIA
HOMELAND

ENGLAND

AIRFORCE: RAF
BAY: TOR LYME WASH START MOUNTS
BIGBURY BIDEFORD CARDIGAN
FALMOUTH TREMADOC WEYMOUTH
CAPITAL: LONDON
CHANNEL: SOLENT BRISTOL ENGLISH
SPITHEAD
CHANNEL ISLAND: HERM SARK
JERSEY ALDERNEY GUERNSEY
COIN: ORA RIAL RYAL ACKEY ANGEL
CROWN GROAT NOBLE PENCE
PENNY POUND SPRAT UNITE
BAWBEE FLORIN GUINEA SESKIN
TESTON ANGELET CAROLUS
HAPENNY TUPPENY FARTHING
SHILLING SIXPENCE TUPPENCE
CONSERVATIVE: TORY
COUNTY: KENT DEVON ESSEX HANTS
NOTTS SALOP WIGHT DORSET
DURHAM LONDON SURREY SUSSEX
NORFOLK RUTLAND SUFFOLK
CHESHIRE CORNWALL SOMERSET
DANCE: MORRIS
FIRTH: SOLWAY
FOREST: ARDEN EPPING EXMOOR
DARTMOOR SHERWOOD
HEAD: SPURN BEACHY FORMBY
LIZARD CEMMAES TREVOSE
HILLS: MENDIP BRENDON CHEVIOT
MALVERN CHILTERN COTSWOLD
INVADER: DANE PICT ROMAN SAXON
NORMAN
ISLAND: HOLY LUNDY WIGHT COQUET
MERSEA THANET TRESCO WALNEY
BARDSEY HAYLING IRELAND
SHEPPEY ANGLESEA ANGLESEY
FOULNESS HOLYHEAD
ISLANDS: FARNE SCILLY CHANNEL
KING: HAL LUD BRAN BRUT CNUT
COLE KNUT LEAR HENRY JAMES
SWEYN ALFRED BLADUD BRUTUS
CANUTE EDWARD EGBERT GEORGE
ARTEGAL ELIDURE RICHARD
WILLIAM GORBODUC
LAKE: CONISTON
LIBERAL: WHIG
MEASURE: CUT ELL LEA MIL PIN ROD
RUN TON TUN VAT ACRE BIND BOLL
BUTT CADE COMB COOM CRAN

FOOT GILL GOAD HAND HANK HEER
HIDE INCH LAST LINE MILE NAIL
PACE PALM PECK PINT PIPE POLE
POOL ROOD ROPE SACK SEAM SPAN
TRUG TYPP WIST YARD YOKE
BODGE CABOT CHAIN COOMB CUBIT
DIGIT FLOAT FLOOR FLUID HUTCH
JUGUM MINIM OUNCE PERCH POINT
PRIME QUART SKEIN STACK TRUSS
BARREL BOVATE BUSHEL CRANNE
FATHOM FIRKIN GALLON HOBBET
HOBBIT LEAGUE MANENT OXGANG
POTTLE RUNLET SECOND SQUARE
STRIKE SULUNG THREAD TIERCE
AUCHLET FURLONG KENNING
QUARTER RUNDLET SEAMILE
SPINDLE TERTIAN VIRGATE
CARUCATE CHALDRON HOGSHEAD
LANDYARD PUNCHEON QUADRANT
QUARTERN STANDARD
MOUNTAIN: PEAK SCAFELL SKIDDAW
SNOWDON
MOUNTAINS: BLACK PENNINE
SNOWDON CAMBRIAN CUMBRIAN
NAME: ALBION BRITAIN BRITANNIA
PENINSULA: PORTLAND
POINT: NAZE LYNAS MORTE SALES
DODMAN LIZARD PRAWLE
HARTLAND LANDSEND GIBRALTAR
POLICEMAN: BOBBY COPPER PEELER
RACE TRACK: ASCOT
RESORT: BATH BRIGHTON BLACKPOOL
RIVER: CAM DEE DON ESK EXE LEA
NEN URE WYE AIRE AVON EDEN
LUNE NENE NIDD OUSE PENK TAME
TEES TILL TYNE WEAR YARE ANKER
COLNE DEBEN STOUR SWALE
TAMAR TAWAR TRENT TWEED
HUMBER KENNET MERSEY RIBBLE
ROTHER SEVERN THAMES WENSUM
WHARFE WITHAM DERWENT
PARRETT WAVENEY WELLAND
TORRIDGE
ROCKS: MANACLES
ROYAL HOUSE: YORK TUDOR STUART
HANOVER WINDSOR LANCASTER
PLANTAGENET
SCHOOL: ETON RUGBY HARROW
SEA: IRISH NORTH
SEAPORT: POOLE
SETTLER: JUTE PICT ANGLE SAXON
NORMAN
SOLDIER: TOMMY REDCOAT FUSILEER
STRAIT: DOVER
TOWN: ELY BATH DEAL ETON HULL
RYDE WARE YORK BLYTH BRENT
DERBY DOVER ERITH FLINT LEEDS
RIPON TRURO WIGAN BARNET
BOLTON BOOTLE CAMDEN DURHAM
EALING EXETER HANLEY JARROW
LEYTON LONDON OLDHAM OXFORD
YEOVIL BRISTOL BROMLEY
BURNLEY CHELSEA CROYDON

ENFIELD GRIMSBY HALIFAX
HORNSEY IPSWICH LAMBETH
NEWPORT NORWICH PRESTON
SALFORD SEAFORD WESTHAM
BRADFORD BRIGHTON CORNWALL
COVENTRY DEWSBURY HASTINGS
PLYMOUTH ROCHDALE WALLASEY
WALLSALL GREENWICH LIVERPOOL
SHEFFIELD BIRMINGHAM
MANCHESTER
TRIBE: ICENI
UNIVERSITY: LONDON OXFORD
CAMBRIDGE
VALLEY: COOM EDEN TEES TYNE
COMBE COOMB COQUET
WEIGHT: BAG KIP TOD TON KEEL LAST
MAST MAUN BARGE FAGOT GRAIN
MAUND POUND SCORE STAND
STONE TRUSS BUSHEL CENTAL
FANGOT FIRKIN FOTHER FOTMAL
POCKET QUARTER QUINTAL
SARPLER

ENGLISH SPIN SAXON AUSTRAL
BRITISH ENGLAND SAXONISH
SOUTHRON STANDARD
(— DIALECT IN LIVERPOOL) SCOUSE
(— MIXED WITH SPANISH) SPANGLISH
(IN —) ANGLICE
(TEACHING —) TEFL TESL TESOL
(PREF.) ANGLO
ENGLISHMAN PONGO SAXON
BRITON BRONCO GODDAM GRINGO
JOHNNY ROOINEK MACARONI
SOUTHRON ENGLISHER
(— IN INDIA) QUIHIQUIHYE
(— IN SOUTH AFRICA) ROOTNEK
(RICH —) MILOR MILORD
ENGLISHWOMAN INGLESA
ENGORGE GLUT GORGE DEVOUR
SWALLOW
ENGRAFT INSET
ENGRAM TRACE
(— PATTERN) MEANING
ENGRAVE CUT ETCH RIST CARVE
CHASE GRAVE HATCH PRINT SCULP
CHISEL INCISE SCULPT CRIBBLE
ENCHASE EXARATE IMPRESS
IMPRINT INSCULP STIPPLE INSCRIBE
ORNAMENT
ENGRAVED GRAVEN GRAPHIC
INCISED
(PREF.) GRAPTO
ENGRAVER POINT CHASER ETCHER
GRAVER ARTISAN INSCULP BURINIST
MEDALIST SCULLION WRIGGLER
(— OF STONES) LAPIDARY
ENGRAVING CUT PRINT SCULP
STAMP GRAVERY GRAVING GRAVURE
WOODCUT AQUATINT DRYPOINT
HATCHING INTAGLIO LINEWORK
MEZZOTINT
(PREF.) GLYPHO GLYPT(O)

ENGROSS BURY SINK SOAK AMASS
GROSS ABSORB ENGAGE ENROLL
ENWRAP OCCUPY SCROLL COLLECT
CONSUME IMMERSE INVOLVE
PREOCCUPY
ENGROSSED DEEP FULL RAPT
INTENT BEMUSED WRAPPED
ABSORBED IMMERSED PREOCCUPIED
ENGULF GULF ABYSM ABYSS SOUSE
SWAMP WHELM ABSORB DEVOUR
INVADE QUELME SLOUGH ENGORGE
SWALLOW SUBMERGE
ENHANCE FOIL LIFT BUILD ENARM
ENDOW EXALT RAISE DEEPEN
AUGMENT ELEVATE ENLARGE
EXHANCE GREATEN IMPROVE
SHARPEN HEIGHTEN INCREASE
ENHANCEMENT SAKE
ENHYDRA LATAX
ENID (HUSBAND OF —) GERAINT
ENIGMA WHY EGMA GRIPH REBUS
PUZZLE RIDDLE SPHINX GRIPHUS
MYSTERY PROBLEM PROVERB
ENIGMATIC HUMAN MYSTIC
CRYPTIC OBSCURE ELLIPTIC
MYSTICAL ORACULAR PUZZLING
RIDDLING MYSTIFYING
PERPLEXING
ENISLE MAROON
ENJAMBMENT OVERFLOW
ENJOIN BID JOIN WILL ENJUN ORDER
CHARGE DECREE DIRECT FORBID
COMMAND DICTATE REQUIRE
ADMONISH PROHIBIT
ENJOY GO JOY FAIN HAVE LIKE
BROOK FANCY PROVE SAVOR TASTE
WIELD ADMIRE DEVOUR GROOVE
RELISH DELIGHT
(— AT LEISURE) SIP
(— ONESELF) FEAST LAUGH
ENJOYABLE GOOD FRUITY AMIABLE
BLESSED CAPITAL GLORIOUS
SAVOROUS SPLENDID
ENJOYING FRUITIVE
ENJOYMENT FUN JOY USE BANG
BASK BOOT EASE GUST KAMA PLAY
ZEST FEAST GUSTO LIKING RELISH
COMFORT DELIGHT JOLLITY
JOYANCE JOYANCY FELICITY
FRUITION PLEASURE SKITTLES
(— FROM OTHERS' TROUBLES)
SCHADENFREUDE
ENKINDLE WARM STIRUP INCENSE
INFLAME
ENLARGE ADD EKE BORE GROW
HONE HUFF OPEN REAM ROOM
BUILD FARCE LARGE SWELL WIDEN
BIGGEN BRANCH BROACH DIDUCE
DILATE EXPAND EXTEND FRAISE
GATHER LARGEN OMNIFY SPREAD
AMPLIFY AUGMENT DISTEND
ENHANCE GREATEN IMPROVE
INGREAT MAGNIFY STRETCH

ENLARGE AMPLIATE CUMULATE FLOURISH
INCREASE
(— COAL MINE) SNUB
ENLARGED TUMID BLOATED
CLUBBED SWELLED SWOLLEN
AMPLIATE CAPITATE EXPANDED
EXTENDED VARICOSE
ACCRESCENT
ENLARGEMENT BULB DISC DISK
KNOP NODE CLAVA SWELL BLOWUP
BUNION GIBBER GROWTH SCYPHA
ENLARGE FOOTING SCYPHUS
STATION ANEURYSM INCREASE
SWELLING PROPAGATION
(— IN MINE SHAFT) STATION
(— IN MUSCLE) KNOT
(— OF BONE) EXOSTOSIS
(— OF GLAND) GOITER GOITRE
(— OF GULLET) CROP
(— OF MOLD) RAPPAGE
(— OF NERVE FIBER) BOUTON
(— OF ORGAN) STRUMA
(— ON HORSE'S LEG) SPLINT
(ABNORMAL —) ANEURYSM
(BONY —) SPAVIN SPAVINE
(MORBID —) TUMOR
(PREF.) MACR(O) MEG(A) MEGAL(O)
PLETHYSMO
(SUFF.) AUXE MEGALY
ENLARGING EVASE SWELLING
(PREF.) MICR(O)
ENLIGHTEN OPEN CLEAR EDIFY
TEACH ILLUME INFORM UNSEEL
EDUCATE LIGHTEN CIVILIZE
ENKINDLE INSTRUCT
ENLIGHTENED WISE LUMINOUS
ENLIGHTENMENT BODHI LIGHT
SATORI WISDOM CULTURE INSIGHT
SAMADHI AUFKLARUNG
ENLIST DRUM JOIN LEVY SOUD
ENROL ENTER HITCH PREST ENGAGE
ENROLL INDUCT JOINUP SIGNUP
IMPRESS RECRUIT REGISTER
(— AGAIN) REUP
ENLISTMENT LEVY HITCH PREST
LISTING
ENLIVEN DASH JAZZ WARM BRACE
BRISK CHEER PEPUP QUICK RAISE
ROUSE KITTLE REVIVE ANIMATE
COMFORT INSPIRE REFRESH
SMARTEN BRIGHTEN INSPIRIT
RECREATE
ENLIVENED MERRY
ENLIVENING GENIAL LIVELY VIVIFIC
CHIRPING
ENMESH TRAP CATCH SNARL
IMMESH ENSNARE ENTANGLE
ENMITY WAR FEUD SPITE WRAKE
ANIMUS HATRED MALICE RANCOR
STRIFE FOEHOOD AVERSION
ENNEAGON NONAGON
ENNOBLE LORD EXALT HONOR
NOBLE RAISE GENTLE UPLIFT
DIGNIFY ELEVATE GLORIFY GREATEN
NOBLIFY SUBLIME
ENNUI BORE TEDIUM ACCIDIE
BOREDOM DOLDRUM
ENOCH (FATHER OF —) CAIN JARED
(SON OF —) METHUSALEH
ENOCH ARDEN (AUTHOR OF —)
TENNYSON
(CHARACTER IN —) LEE RAY LANE
ANNIE ARDEN ENOCH MIRIAM PHILIP
ENORMITY GRAVITY
ENORMOUS BIG GOB HUGE REAM
VAST ENORM GREAT HEROIC MIGHTY
UNRIDE IMMENSE ABNORMAL
COLOSSAL FLAGRANT GIGANTIC
WHAPPING WHOPPING
ENOS (FATHER OF —) SETH
(GRANDFATHER OF —) ADAM
(SON OF —) CAINAN
ENOUGH BAS ENOW WELL WHEN
AMPLE ASSAI BASTA BELAY ANEUCH
PLENTY APLENTY SUFFICE ADEQUATE
(— SAID) VERBUMSAP
(HARDLY —) SKIMP
(MORE THAN —) PLENTY APLENTY
ENOUNCE STATE UTTER AFFIRM
DECLARE PROCLAIM
ENRAGE RAGE ANGER GRIEVE
MADDEN INCENSE INFLAME
STOMACH
ENRAGED MAD ASHY WODE WOOD
ANGRY IRATE LIVID SAVAGE
AGRAMED BERSERK CHOLERIC
INCENSED MADDENED
ENRAPTURE RAVISH TRANCE
ECSTASY ENCHANT ENRAVISH
ENTRANCE
ENRAPTURED RAPT ENRAPT
TRANCED ECSTATIC
ENRICH FAT BOOT FEED FRET LARD
RICH ADORN CROWN ENDOW
GUANO BATTEN FATTEN INVEST
FEATHER FORTIFY FURNISH GUANIZE
INCREASE ORNAMENT TREASURE
(— A GAS) CARBURET
(— A MINE) SALT
(— FUEL MIXTURE) CHOKE
ENRICHED FLORID
ENRICHMENT DITATION
ENROLL BEAR JOIN LIST POLL ENROL
ENTER WRITE ATTEST BILLET
ENFOLD ENLIST INDUCT MUSTER
RECORD ASCRIBE IMPANEL INITIATE
INSCRIBE REGISTER
ENROLLMENT LISTING REGISTRY
ENROOT ENRACE IMPLANT
ENSCONCE HIDE COVER SETTLE
CONCEAL SHELTER
ENSEMBLE CORPS DECOR WHOLE
COSTUME PANTSUIT
(— OF ARMS) ARMORY
(WOMAN'S —) PANTSUIT
ENSHEATHE EMBOSS

ENSHRINE SAINT SHRINE ENCHASE
ENTEMPLE
ENSHROUD WRAP
ENSIFORM ENSATE XIPHOID
GLADIATE
ENSIGN FLAG IAGO SIGN BADGE
COLOR SENYE AQUILA BANNER
BEACON PENNON PISTOL SIGNAL
SYMBOL ALFEREZ ANCIENT INSIGNE
DANEBROG GONFALON ORIFLAMB
PAVILION STANDARD
(—S ARMORIAL) ARMS
(IMPERIAL —) TUT
(JAPANESE —) SUNBURST
(PL.) ENSIGNRY HERALDRY
ENSILE SILO SILAGE
ENSLAVE THEW CHAIN SLAVE THIRL
ENTHRAL NESLAVE SLAVISH
ENTHRALL
ENSLAVED SLAVE THRALL
ENSLAVEMENT DULOSIS SLAVERY
ENSNARE NET WEB GIRN LACE LIME
MESH TOIL TRAP WRAP BENET
CATCH NOOSE SNARF SNARL
ALLURE ATTRAP ENGINE ENMESH
ENTOIL ENTRAP TANGLE TREPAN
BEGUILE DECEIVE ENGLEIM SNIGGLE
SPRINGE BIRDLIME INVEIGLE
OVERTAKE SURPRISE
ENSNARL ENTANGLE
ENSPHERE INORB SPHERE
ENSTATITE BRONZITE
ENSUE FOLLOW RESULT SUCCEED
(— UPON) SUE
ENSUING NEXT SUING SEQUENT
ENSURE ASSURE INSURE SECURE
BETROTH ESPOUSE WARRANT
AFFIANCE
ENTABLATURE
(PART OF —) CORONA FRIEZE TAENIA
CORNICE CYMATIUM ARCHITRAVE
ENTADA LENS
ENTAIL TAIL INCUR IMPOSE CONTAIN
INVOLVE REQUIRE TAILZIE
ENTAILED AYNE TAIL EIGNE
ENTAMOEBA LOSCHIA
ENTANGLE ELF LAP MAT TAT WEB
BALL CAST COLL FOUL HARL KNIT
KNOT LIME MESH MIRE TOIL WRAP
BROIL CATCH HALCH RAVEL SNAFU
SNARE SNARL BEFOUL
COMMIT COTTER ENGAGE ENLACE
ENMESH ENTRAP ENWRAP FANKLE
FELTER HAMPER HANKLE HATTER
INMAZE INMESH PESTER PUZZLE
RAFFLE RANGLE TACKLE TAIGLE
TANGLE WRAPLE CONFUSE
EMBRAKE EMBROIL ENSNARL
ENTRIKE IMBRIER INVOLVE PERPLEX
THAMMEL BEWILDER ENCUMBER
IMPESTER INTRIGUE STRAPPLE
ENTANGLED DEEP FOUL COTTY
TANGLY COMPLEX KNOTTED IMPLICIT

ENTANGLEMENT WEB FOUL KNOT
TWIT HITCH BUNKER COBWEB
ENTRAIL HEDGEHOG OBSTACLE
PERPLEXITY
ENTASIS SWELL
ENTELLUS HANUMAN
ENTENTE TREATY ALLIANCE
ENTER BOX DIP SET BEAR BOOK JOIN
POST ADMIT BEGIN BOARD BREVE
ENROL GETIN INCUR PROBE SHARE
START ACCEDE APPEAR BILLET
ENGAGE ENLIST ENROLL ENTHER
INCEPT INVADE PIERCE RECORD
SPREAD INGRESS INTRUDE
COMMENCE ENCROACH INITIATE
INSCRIBE NOMINATE REGISTER
PENETRATE
(— A COMPUTER PROGRAM) LOAD
(— BY FORCE) BREAK IRRUPT
INTRUDE
(— COMPUTER PROGRAM) BOOT
(— DATA) INPUT
(— HASTILY) BULGE
(IN ATTACK) FORCE
(— IN BOOK) ACCESS
(— IN BOOKS) ACCRUE
(— INFORMATION INTO COMPUTER)
WRITE
(— INTO) JOIN INTERN
(— NOISILY) STOMPIN TROMPIN
(— PROGRAM INTO COMPUTER)
LOAD
(— SLOWLY) SEEP
(— UNNOTICED) CREEP
(— UPON CAREER) INCEPT
(— UPON DUTIES) ASSUME
(— WITHOUT RIGHT) ABATE
ENTERING ENTRY INGOING INGRESS
INTRANT INCOMING
ENTEROTOXEMIA STRUCK
ENTERPRISE FIRM IRON PUSH TOGT
DRIVE ESSAY ACTION EMPIRE SPIRIT
VOYAGE ATTEMPT EMPRISE
HOLDING PROJECT VENTURE
BUSINESS CARNIVAL GUMPTION
VIRITOOT
(CRIMINAL —) JOB
(HARD —) DIFFICULTY
(REMEDIAL —) CRUSADE
(SPECULATIVE —) ADVENTURE
(UNPROFITABLE —) SINKHOLE
ENTERPRISING BOLD FORTHY
PUSHFUL PUSHING
ENTERTAIN INN BEAR BUSK EASE
FETE HAVE HOLD HOST AMUSE
ENJOY FEAST GUEST SPORT TREAT
DIVERT FROLIC GESTEN HARBOR
JUNKET RECULE REGALE RETAIN
SOLACE TICKLE ACCOUNT DEGUILE
CHERISH DISPORT KITCHEN
CONSIDER INTEREST RECREATE
(— IN THE MIND) HAVE
(— WITHOUT CHARGE) DEFRAY

ENTERTAINED OUGHT
ENTERTAINER BHAT HOST ACTOR
AMUSER ARTIST BUSKER DANCER
FIDDLE HARLOT SINGER ACTRESS
ARTISTE DISEUSE GLEEMAN
HETAERA HOSTESS REGALER
SPEAKER BEACHBOY COMEDIAN
HOSTELER MAGICIAN MINSTREL
(WEST AFRICA —) GRIOT
ENTERTAINING GOOD RICH TREAT
PRETTY AMUSING BEDSIDE
GUESTING SPORTFUL
ENTERTAINMENT BASH BILL FARE
FETE GALA GLEE PLAY SHOW BOARD
CHEER FEAST GAUDY OPERA REVUE
SPORT CIRCUS DIVERT DOMENT
GAIETY GAYETY HOSTEL INFARE
KERMIS NAUTCH SETOUT SHIVOO
WATTLE BANQUET BENEFIT
BUMMACK BUMMOCK BURLESK
CEILIDH CONCERT COSHERY FESTINE
FESTINO JOLLITY KERMESS PASTIME
RIDOTTO TAMASHA CAKEWALK
CARNIVAL COMMORTH DROLLERY
EASEMENT ENTREATY ENTREMES
FUNCTION GESTNING GESTONIE
GUESTING HOGMANAY JONGLERY
MUSICALE WAYZGOOSE
(BLUE —) NUDIE
(FAREWELL —) FOY
(OF INDIA —) TAMASHA
(TRIVIAL —) PAP
(VARIETY —) VODVIL VAUDEVILLE
ENTERTAINMNET
(CHEAP —) HONKYTONK
ENTHALPY H
ENTHRALL SEND CHARM THIRL
THRALL ENSLAVE ENTHRAL
CAPTIVATE
ENTHRALLED AGOG RAPT HOOKED
ENTHRONE CROWN EXALT STALL
ENSEAT THRONE THRONIZE
ENTHUSIASM BUG ELAN FIRE FURY
ZEAL ZEST ZING ARDOR ESTRO
FEVER FLAME FUROR HEART MANIA
OOMPH VERVE FERVOR HURRAH
SPIRIT WARMTH ABANDON
ARDENCY AVIDITY MADNESS
MUSTARD DEVOTION LYRICISM
(— IN BATTLE) EARNEST
(CONTAGIOUS —) FUROR FURORE
(EXCESSIVE —) MANIA
(LOSE —) COOL SOUR
(WILD —) DELIRIUM
ENTHUSIAST BUG FAN NUT BUFF
BIGOT DEMON FREAK ROOTER
VOTARY ZEALOT BOOSTER DEVOTEE
EUCHITE FANATIC FANCIER GROUPIE
FOLLOWER VOTARESS VOTARIST
(PHOTOGRAPHY —) SHUTTERBUG
(PL.) ARDITI
ENTHUSIASTIC GAGA KEEN NUTS
WARM HAPPY NUTTY RABID ARDENT

GUNGHO HEARTY STOKED CRACKED
FERVENT GLOWING CRACKERS
PASSIONATE
(BECOME —) FLIP
(EXCESSIVELY —) FANATIC
(VAINLY —) FOOLISH
ENTICE COG COY PUT WIN BAIT
COAX DRAW DRIB LEAD LOCK LURE
TICE TOLE TOLL WILE CHARM DECOY
DRILL LATHE SIREN SLOCK STEAL
TEMPT TRAIN TROLL TULLE ALLECT
ALLURE ATTICE CAJOLE ENLURE
INCITE INDUCE INVITE SEDUCE
ATTRACT BEWITCH SOLICIT
SUGGEST INVEIGLE PERSUADE
ENTICEMENT BAIT CORD LURE TICE
ENTICING SIREN ALLURING
ENTIRE ALL DEAD EVEN FULL HALE
MEAR MERE SOLE CLEAN EVERY
GROSS PLAIN QUITE ROUND SOUND
STARK TOTAL TUTTO UTTER WHOLE
VERSAL PERFECT PLENARY
ABSOLUTE COMPLETE ENDURING
GLOBULAR INTEGRAL LIVELONG
OUTRIGHT TEETOTAL UNBROKEN
(NOT —) PARTIAL
(PREF.) HOL(O) INTEGRI
ENTIRELY DEAD DEIN FAIR FULL
PURE CLEAN CLEAR FULLY PLAIN
QUITE STARK WHOLE BODILY
WHOLLY EXACTLY QUITELY
THROUGH CLEVERLY ABSOLUTELY
ENTIRETY WHOLE ENTIRE TOTALITY
(PREF.) PAM PAN
ENTITLE DUB CALL NAME TERM
AFFIX STYLE ENABLE CAPTION
EMPOWER QUALIFY INTITULE
NOMINATE
ENTITLED APPARENT ELIGIBLE
ENTITY ENS BODY FORM UNIT BEING
HABIT OUSIA SPACE THING ENERGY
ESSENCE INTEGER TOTALITY
ENTOMB BURY TOMB INTER INURN
ENCAVE HEARSE IMMURE INHUME
SHRINE
ENTOMBMENT BURIAL
ENTOMOLOGIST BUGHUNTER
AMERICAN SAY DYAR HORN BANKS
BRUES RILEY FORBES HARRIS
HOWARD MORGAN BURGESS
PACKARD POLLARD SCHWARZ
COMSTOCK COQUILLETT
DANISH FABRICIUS
DUTCH LYONNET
ENGLISH SCOTT LEFROY HAWORTH
ORMEROD WESTWOOD
FRENCH FABRE AUDOUIN LATREILLE
LACORDAIRE
GERMAN BRAUER
SWISS FOREL SAUSSURE
ENTOMOLOGY BUGOLOGY
ENTOMOPHTHORA EMPUSA
ENTOTROPHI DIPLURA

ENTOURAGE TRAIN COMITES
RETINUE
ENTRACTE INTERACT INTERVAL
INTERMEZZO
ENTRAIL BOWEL TRAIL INTRAIL
(PREF.) SPLANCHN(O)
ENTRAILS GUT GUTS DRAFT TRIPE
FIBERS GIBLET HALLOW HASLET
INWARD JAUDIE MUGGET PAUNCH
QUARRY QUERRE UMBLES INSIDES
NUMBLES CHAWDRON GRALLOCH
PUDDINGS PURTENANCE
(DEER'S —) QUARRY
ENTRANCE ADIT BOCA CUSP DOOR
GATE HALL PEND BOCCA CHARM
DEBUT ENTER ENTRY FOYER GORGE
INLET MOUTH PORCH STULM THIRL
TORAN ACCESS ATRIUM ENTREE
INFAIR INGANG INGATE INROAD
PORTAL RAVISH TORANA TRANCE
ZAGUAN DELIGHT GATEWAY
HALLWAY INGOING INGRESS INITIAL
INTRADO INTROIT PASSAGE
POSTERN ENTRESSE FOREGATE
VOMITORY PROPYLAEUM
(— TO SEWER) JAWHOLE
(— TO VALLEY) CHOPS
(ASTROLOGICAL —) CUSP
(CELLAR —) ROLLWAY
(FORCIBLE —) INROAD
(FORMAL —) DEBUT
(HARBOR —) BOCA
(HOSTILE —) INVASION
(HURRIED —) BOUT
(MINE —) EYE ADIT
(PRIVATE —) POSTERN
ENTRANCED RAPT CHARMED
TRANCED ECSTATIC
ENTRANCEMENT SPELL
ENTRANCING ORPHIC
ENTRANT INTRANT STARTER
BEGINNER
ENTRAP BAG EBB NET HOOK SNIB
TOIL TRAP CATCH CRIMP DECOY
NOOSE SNARE ALLURE AMBUSH
ATTRAP CAJOLE ENGAGE ENTOIL
TAIGLE TANGLE TREPAN BEGUILE
ENSNARE PITFALL ENTANGLE
INVEIGLE
ENTRAPMENT SETUP
ENTRAPPED
(— IN SEDIMENT) CONNATE
ENTREAT ASK BEG BID SUE WOO
PRAY PRIG SEEK URGE CRAVE HALSE
PLEAD PRESS TREAT ADJURE
APPEAL DESIRE INVOKE BESEECH
CONJURE EXORATE IMPLORE
PREVAIL PROCURE REQUEST SOLICIT
PERSUADE PETITION
ENTREATING TREAT CRAVING
ENTREATY DO CRY PLEA SUIT
APPEAL DEESIS PRAYER TREATY
BESEECH BIDDING ENTREAT

PURSUIT REQUEST URGENCY
PETITION PLEADING
ENTRECHAT
(PERFORM —S) LEAP
ENTREE ENTRY ACCESS BOUDIN
OSTIUM ENTRADA INTRADA
SOUFFLE ENTRANCE FRICANDO
MAZARINE
ENTREMES SAINETE SAYNETE
ENTRENCH DIGIN INVADE SCONCE
TRENCH ENCROACH TRESPASS
ENTRENCHED
(BECOME —) DIGIN
ENTRENCHMENT CLOSURE
COUPURE LODGMENT
ENTROPY S
ENTRUST ARET FIDE GIVE STOW
BEKEN TRUST CHARGE COMMIT
CREDIT LIPPEN ADDRESS BEHIGHT
COMMEND CONFIDE CONSIGN
DEPOSIT INTRUST BEQUEATH
DELEGATE ENCHARGE RECOMMEND
(— TO DEPUTY) DEVIL
ENTRY ADIT HALL ITEM STET BREAK
CLOSE DEBIT AUTHOR CREDIT
DOCKET ENTREE PORTAL POSTEA
RECORD RINGER TRANCE ENTRADA
INGRESS INTRADO PASSAGE
ENTRANCE ENTRESSE ENTRYWAY
NOTANDUM REGISTER VOCATION
(— IN CHRONICLE) ANNAL
(— WORD) HEADWORD
(LEDGER —) POSTING
ENTWINE FOLD LACE WIND BRAID
CLASP IMPLY PLASH TWINE TWIST
WEAVE ENLACE INWIND ENTWIST
INVOLVE SERPENT WREATHE
ENTWINED ACCOLLE BRAIDED
INWOVEN ACCOLLEE
ENUMERATE POLL TELL COUNT
SCORE DETAIL NUMBER RECITE
RECKON RELATE COMPILE COMPUTE
ITEMIZE RECOUNT ESTIMATE
REHEARSE
ENUMERATION LIST TALE COUNT
SCORE CENSUS ACCOUNT CATALOG
RECITAL CITATION
ENUNCIATE SAY UTTER DECLARE
DELIVER ENOUNCE ANNOUNCE
PROCLAIM
ENUNCIATION DICTION DELIVERY
(IMPERFECT —) LALLATION
ENVELOP BUR FOG LAP LOT POD
WEB BURR CASE COMA FOLD HUSK
MAIL ROLL BRACE CLOUD COVER
KNIFE ROUND BEGIRD BEGIRT
BEMIST BINDLE CLOTHE COCOON
CORONA CUPULE ENFOLD ENGIRT
ENTIRE ENWRAP FARDEL FOLDER
INFOLD INVEST JACKET MANTLE
MUFFLE POCKET SHEATH SHROUD
STIFLE SWATHE WRIXLE CALYMMA
CAPSULE CHORION ENCLOSE

ENVIRON INVOLVE SWADDLE
SWALLOW VESTURE WRAPPER
ENSPHERE ENVELOPE MANTLING
PERIANTH PERIDIUM POCHETTE
SURROUND WRAPPAGE
(— CLOSELY) SMOTHER
(— IN SMOKE) ENFUME
(GLASS —) BULB
(LUMINOUS —) CORONA
(NEBULOUS —) CHEVELURE
(OPEN —) JACKET
(PAY —) PACKET
(STAMPED —) ENTIRE
(VEGETABLE —) COD
ENVELOPE (— ENCLOSURE) SASE
(FRUIT —) CUPULE
(SUN'S —) CORONA
(PREF.) (OUTER —) PERIDI
(SUFF.) LEMMA
ENVELOPED WOMPLIT
ENVELOPING AMBIENT
ENVENOM VENOM CORRUPT
VITIATE EMBITTER EMPOISON
ENVIOUS YELLOW EMULOUS
JEALOUS ENVIABLE
ENVIRON HEM BEGO GIRD BIGAN
LIMIT VIRON ENVIRE GIRDLE SUBURB
COMPASS ENVELOP INCLOSE
INVOLVE PURLIEU DISTRICT
ENCIRCLE SURROUND
(PL.) SKIRT UMLAND BANLIEU
SUBURBS PRECINCT
ENVIRONMENT HOTBED MEDIUM
MILIEU AMBIENT CONTEXT ELEMENT
HABITAT SETTING TERRAIN
AMBIANCE CINCTURE PRECINCT
(— OF NURTURE) LAP
(ACADEMIC —) ACADEME
(DOMESTIC —) INTERIEUR
(NORMAL —) HOME
(PREF.) EC(O) OEC(O) OIK(O)
ENVISAGE FACE CONFRONT
ENVISION
ENVISION PICTURE
ENVOY AGENT ELCHI ENVOI DEPUTY
ELCHEE LEGATE LENVOY NUNCIO
EMBASSY TORNADA ABLEGATE
LEGATION METATRON
ENVY CHAW ONDE COVET GRUDGE
EMULATE BEGRUDGE GRUDGERY
JEALOUSY
ENWRAP FOLD ROLL CLASP IMPLY
ENFOLD INFOLD KIRTLE ENGROSS
ENVELOP OBVOLVE CONVOLVE
ENVELOPE INSWATHE
ENZOOTIC RABIES
ENZU SIN
ENZYME ASE ZYM ZYMO LYASE
RENIN CYTASE KINASE LIGASE
LIPASE LOTASE MUTASE OLEASE
PAPAIN PEPSIN RENNIN UREASE
ZYMASE ACYLASE ADENASE
AMIDASE AMINASE AMYLASE

APYRASE CASEASE CYCLASE
EMULSIN ENOLASE EREPSIN
FERMENT GUANASE HYDRASE
INULASE LACCASE LACTASE
MALTASE MYROSIN OXIDASE
PECTASE PEPSINE PHYTASE
PLASMIN PRUNASE TANNASE
TRYPSIN ALDOLASE ARGINASE
BROMELIN CATALASE CATALYST
CYTOLIST DIASTASE ELASTASE
EREPTASE ESTERASE FUMARASE
INVERTIN LYSOZYME NUCLEASE
PERMEASE PROTEASE RACEMASE
SEMINASE SYNTHASE THROMBIN
TRYPTASE UROKINASE
(PREF.) ZYM(O)
(SUFF.) ASE EIN EINE IN INE
EOANTHROPUS DAWNMAN
EOS MORNING
(SISTER OF —) SELENE
EPAPHUS (DAUGHTER OF —) LIBYA
(FATHER OF —) ZEUS JUPITER
(MOTHER OF —) IO
(WIFE OF —) MEMPHIS
EPAULET KNOT SWAB SWOB WING
SCALE SHELL
EPENDYTES HAPLOMA
EPENTHESIS ANAPTYXIS
EPEUS (BROTHER OF —) AETOLUS
(DAUGHTER OF —) HYRMINA
(FATHER OF —) ENDYMION
PANOPEUS
(WIFE OF —) ANAXIROE
EPHAH BATH
(FATHER OF —) JAHDAI MIDIAN
EPHELIS FRECKLE
EPHEMERAL BRIEF VAGUE HORARY
DIURNAL FUNGOUS PASSANT
PASSING EPISODAL EPISODIC
FUGITIVE MUSHROOM STAYLESS
MOMENTARY
EPHEMERIS DIARY TABLE RECORD
ALMANAC JOURNAL CALENDAR
EPHER (FATHER OF —) EZRA MIDIAN
EPHIPPIUM SADDLE
EPHOD VAKASS
(SON OF —) HANNIEL
EPHRAIM (FATHER OF —) JOSEPH
(MOTHER OF —) ASENATH
EPHRATAH (HUSBAND OF —) CALEB
(SON OF —) HUR
EPHRON (FATHER OF —) ZOAR
EPHTHALITE HAITHAL
EPI PEAK SPIRE FINIAL PINNACLE
EPIBLAST ECTODERM
EPIC EDDA EPOS SAGA GRAND ILIAD
NOBLE BYLINA EPOPEE HEROIC
LUSIAD BEOWULF EPYLLION
KALEVALA RAMAYANA
MAHABHARATA
(SUFF.) AD
EPICALYX CALYCLE
EPICARP HUSK RIND EXOCARP

EPICENE SEXLESS
EPICURE FRIAND FEASTER GLUTTON GOURMET GOURMAND PALATIST GASTRONOME GASTRONOMER
EPICUREAN APICIAN SENSUOUS
EPIDEMIC FLU PLAGUE POPULAR PANDEMIA PANDEMIC
EPIDERMIS SKIN CUTICLE ECDERON VELAMEN
EPIDOTE SCORZA
EPIGLOTTIS FLAP WEEZLE
EPIGRAM POEM ENGLYN EPITAPH
EPIGRAMMATIC LACONIC POINTED
EPIGRAPH EPIGRAM IMPRINT
EPILEPTIC FITIFIED
EPILOGUE CLOSE FINALE APPENDIX
EPIMANIKION CUFF
EPIMETHEUS (WIFE OF —) PANDORA
EPINAOS POSTICUM
EPINEPHRINE ADRENINE
EPINICION ODE
EPIPACTIS SERAPIAS
EPIPHANY TWELFTH
EPIPHARYNX PALATE EPIGLOTTIS
EPIPHRAGM TYMPANUM
EPIPHYTE KARO EPIPHYLL
EPIPHYTOTIC EPIDEMIC
EPIRUS (KING OF —) PYRRHUS
EPISCOPACY BISHOPRIC PRELATISM
EPISCOPAL PRELATIC
EPISODE GAG EPOCH EVENT SCENE STORY AFFAIR INCIDENT SEQUENCE OCCURRENCE
(COMIC —) BURLA SIGHTGAG
(MUSICAL —) COUPLET
EPISPASTIC VESICANT
EPISPERM TESTA
EPISTAXIS NOSEBLEED
EPISTERNUM MANUBRIUM
EPISTLE CANON JAMES LETTER PISTLE MISSIVE WRITING DECRETAL
EPISTLER SUBDEACON
EPISTOLOGRAPHIC DEMOTIC
EPISTROPHE EPODE ABGESANG
EPISTYLE PLATBAND
EPITHELIUM ENDODERM
EPITHET AKAL GOOD NAME TERM LABEL SMEAR TITLE BYWORD MONETA PHRASE AGNOMEN JAPHETIC MULCIBER
(PL.) LANGUAGE
EPITOME MAP SUM FLETA DIGEST PRECIS SCHEME COMPEND PITOMIE SUMMARY SUMMULA ABSTRACT BREVIARY LANDSKIP SYLLABUS SYNOPSIS ABRIDGMENT CONSPECTUS
EPITOMIZE RESUME ABRIDGE CURTAIL ABSTRACT COMPRESS CONDENSE CONTRACT DIMINISH
EPITONIUM SCALA
EPIZOA PARASITA

EPOCH AGE ERA DATE ECCA TIME DWYKA EVENT EOCENE PERIOD CLINTON OLIGOCENE
EPONYM LIMMU ANCIENT
EPOPEUS (BROTHERS OF —) ALOIDAE
(FATHER OF —) ALOEUS POSEIDON
(MOTHER OF —) CANACE IPHIMEDIA
(WIFE OF —) ANTIOPE
EQUABLE EVEN JUST EQUAL SUANT SMOOTH STEADY UNIFORM TRANQUIL
EQUAL AEQ PAR TIE COPE EGAL EVEN FERE JUST LIKE MAKE MATE MEET PEEL PEER SAME ALIKE LEVEL MATCH PARTY RIVAL TOUCH DOUBLE EQUATE EVENLY FELLOW MARROW PAREIL ABREAST BALANCE COMPEER EMULATE EQUABLE IDENTIC PARAGON PAREGAL UNIFORM ADEQUATE EQUALIZE EVENHAND PATCHING TRANQUIL
(— A BET) SEE
(— IN MEANING) BE
(— QUANTITY) ANA
(— TO) ANOTHER
(NOT —) UNMEET UNMETE
(PREF.) AEQUI EQUI IS(O) PARI
EQUALING TO
EQUALITY PAR TIE EQUITY OWELTY PARAGE PAREIL PARITY BALANCE EGALITE EGALITY ISOTELY EQUATION EVENHAND EVENNESS FAIRNESS
(— BEFORE THE LAW) ISONOMY
(— OF ELEVATION) ISOMETRY
(— OF MEASURE) ISOMETRY
(— OF POWER) ISOCRACY
(— OF RATIOS) ANALOGY
(— STATE) WYOMING
EQUALIZATION EQUATION DISCHARGE
EQUALIZE EVEN KNOT EQUAL LEVEL EQUATE SQUARE BALANCE ADEQUATE
EQUALIZER EVENER
EQUALLY AS BOTH LIKE ONCE SAME ALIKE EGALLY EVENLY JUSTLY EMFORTH
EQUANIMITY POISE PHLEGM TEMPER BALANCE EGALITY CALMNESS EVENNESS SERENITY SANGFROID
EQUATE EQUAL BALANCE EQUALIZE
EQUATING COMPARISON
EQUATION CUBIC IDENTITY
EQUATOR LINE GIRDLE EQUINOX
(— CROSSER) POLLIWOG
EQUATORIAL GUINEA (CAPITAL OF —) MALABO
(COIN OF —) EKUELE EKPWELE
(MONEY OF —) EKUELE EKPWELE
(MONEY OF —) CENTIME

(RIVER OF —) MUNI CAMPO BENITO
(TOWN OF —) BATA NSOK
SANTAISABEL
EQUES KNIGHT
EQUIDISTANT CENTRAL HALFWAY
EQUILIBRIUM POISE APLOMB
BALANCE STATION EQUATION
EVENHAND ISOSTASY
(— OF FLUID) LEVEL
(PREF.) STATO
EQUINE COLT FOAL MARE FILLY
HORSE ZEBRA EQUOID EQUINAL
HORSELY
EQUINIA MALLEUS
EQUIP ARM FIT IMP KIT RAY RIG ABLE
BEAM DECK FEAT FIND GEAR GIRD
GIRT HEEL REEK TRIM ARRAY DIGHT
DRESS ENARM ENDOW POINT SPEED
STUFF AGUISE ATTIRE BUCKLE
ORDAIN OUTFIT SUBORN APPAREL
APPOINT BEDIGHT FORTIFY
FRAUGHT FURNISH GARNISH
HARNESS PLENISH PREPARE
QUALIFY ACCOUTER ACCOUTRE
ACCOMPLISH
(— FOR ACTION) ARM
EQUIPAGE RIG CREW SAMAN SUITE
TRAIN SUPPLY RETINUE TURNOUT
UNICORN CARRIAGE
EQUIPMENT KIT FARE GEAR TIRE
STOCK STUFF ATTIRE CONREY
DUFFEL DUFFLE FITOUT GRAITH
OUTFIT SETOUT TACKLE APPAREL
BAGGAGE FITMENT HARNESS
PANOPLY ARMAMENT EQUIPAGE
MATERIAL MATERIEL MOUNTING
SUPELLEX
(— FOR CATCHING FISH) CRAFT
(— FOR JOURNEY) FARE
(CLASSROOM —) REGALIA
EQUIPOISE POISE BALANCE
EQUIPOTENTIAL LEVEL
EQUIPPED SEEN ARMED BODEN
THERE EQUIPT ARMORED INSTRUCT
WEAPONED
(FULLY —) SUMMED
(INADEQUATELY —) HAYWIRE
(LIGHTLY —) EXPEDITE
EQUISETUM CANDOCK
EQUITABLE EVEN FAIR JUST EQUAL
RIGHT EVENLY HONEST EQUABLE
UPRIGHT BONITARY RATIONAL
RIGHTFUL
EQUITY LAW EPIKY MARGIN EPIKEIA
HONESTY JUSTICE EQUALITY
EVENHAND FAIRNESS
EQUIVALENCE AMOUNT PARITY
EQUIVALENT KIND SAME EQUAL
NODEL COUSIN UNISON ANALOGUE
EVENHAND
(— IN MONEY) CHANGE
(— OF TWO BUSHELS) HUTCH
(FAIR —) VALUE

EQUIVOCAL FISHY SHADY DOUBLE
FORKED DUBIOUS EVASIVE HALFWAY
OBSCURE DOUBTFUL HAVERING
PUZZLING SIBYLLIC
EQUIVOCATE HAW HEM LIE DODGE
EVADE SHIFT BOGGLE ESCAPE
PALTER TRIFLE WAFFLE WEASEL
QUIBBLE SHUFFLE SCRAFFLE
PUSSYFOOT PREVARICATE
EQUIVOCATION QUIP QUIRK
EVASION QUIBBLE SHUFFLE
EQUIVOKE
EQUIVOQUE PUN
EQUULEUS FOAL
ER (FATHER OF —) JOSE
(SON OF —) ELMODAM
ERA AGE AEON DATE TIME EPOCH
STAGE PERIOD CENOZOIC
PALEOZOIC PROTEROZOIC
(EMPEROR'S —) KIMIGAYO
(GEOLOGICAL —) QUATENARY
(HINDU —) SAMVAT
(MUSLIM —) HEGIRA HEJIRA
ERADICATE DELE ROOT SLAY WEED
CROSS ERASE STAMP DELETE
EFFACE REMOVE UNROOT UPROOT
ABOLISH DESTROY EXPUNGE
OUTROOT SUPPLANT
(— HAIR) EPILATE
ERADICATOR ERASER
ERAL MOINE
ERAN (GRANDFATHER OF —)
EPHRAIM
ERASE BLOT DASH DELE RACE RASE
RASH RAZE ANNUL PLANE CANCEL
DEFACE DELETE EFFACE EXCISE
REMOVE SCRAPE SPONGE DESTROY
EXPUNGE OUTRAZE SCRATCH
UNWRITE WEAROUT OBLITERATE
ERASER RASER RUBBER
ERASTE (LOVER OF —) JULIE LUCILLE
ORPHISE
ERASURE RASURE ERASION
DELETION EXCISION
ERD SHREW RANNY
ERE OR AIR SOON EARLY PRIOR
BEFORE EREWHILE FORMERLY
EREBUS (FATHER OF —) CHAOS
(SISTER OF —) NOX
(SON OF —) CHARON
ERECHTHEUS (DAUGHTER OF —)
CREUSA PROCRIS CHTHONIA
ORITHYIA
(FATHER OF —) PANDION
(SLAYER OF —) JUPITER
(SON OF —) MERION CECROPS
PANDORUS
(WIFE OF —) PRAXITHEA
ERECT BIG SET BIGG LEVY REAR
RECT STEP STEY SWAY TELD AREAR
BRANT BUILD DRESS EXALT FRAME
MOUNT ONEND PUTUP RAISE SETUP
STAND ARRECT UPLIFT UPREAR

ADDRESS ATROPAL BRISTLE ELEVATE
STATELY UPRAISE UPRIGHT UPSTART
STANDING STRAIGHT VERTICAL
(— HASTILY) RUNUP
(— TENT) PITCH
(NOT —) LAZY COUCHED
ERECTED UPSET
ERECTION DOME HARD FABRIC
CHORDEE MACHINE
(— FOR SPECTATORS) STAND
(TEMPORARY —) SCAFFOLD
ERELONG ANON SOON
EREMITE LONER HERMIT ASCETIC
RECLUSE ANCHORET
EREWHILE ERE WHILOM
EREWHON (AUTHOR OF —) BUTLER
(CHARACTER IN —) HIGGS GEORGE
STRONG ZULORA CHOWBOK
AROWHENA NOSNIBOR
ERG REG EROGON
(PL.) AREG
ERGINUS (FATHER OF —) CLYMENUS
POSEIDON
(SON OF —) AGAMEDES TROPHONIUS
ERGO SO ARGO ARGAL HENCE
ERGOT SPUR CLAVUS ECBOLIC
(STAGE OF —) SPHACELIA
ERI (FATHER OF —) GAD
ERICHTHONIUS (FATHER OF —)
VULCAN DARDANUS
(MOTHER OF —) ATTHIS
(SON OF —) PANDION
ERIDANUS (FATHER OF —) OCEANUS
(MOTHER OF —) TETHYS
ERIE WENRO
ERIGONE (FATHER OF —) ICARIUS
AEGISTHUS
(MOTHER OF —) CLYTEMNESTRA
ERINYS FURY ALECTO MEGAERA
(PL.) DIRAE FURIAE SEMNAE
EUMENIDES
ERIOPHORUM DRAWLING
ERIPHYLE (FATHER OF —) TALAUS
(HUSBAND OF —) AMPHIARAUS
(SON & SLAYER OF —) ALCMAEON
ERISTIC DIALECTIC
ERITREA (CAPITAL OF —) ASMARA
ERMINE VAIR VARE STOAT WEASEL
ERMELIN FUTERET FUTTRAT MINIVER
CLUBSTER WHITRACK WHITTRET
ERNANI (CHARACTER IN —) CARLO
GOMEZ SILVA ELVIRA ERNANI
(COMPOSER OF —) VERDI
ERODE EAT ROT COMB ETCH GNAW
GULL WEAR CLIFF GULLY SCOUR
ABRADE DENUDE CORRODE DESTROY
ERODIUM HERONBILL
EROS AMOR KAMA CUPID AENGUS
POTHOS
EROSE ERODED UNEVEN
EROSION PIPING CHIMNEY NIVATION
SCOURING
(MECHANICAL —) PLANATION

ERO THE JOKER (COMPOSER OF —)
GOTOVAC
EROTIC SEXY LOVING STEAMY
AMATORY AMOROUS CURIOUS
LESBIAN THERMAL
EROTICA CURIOSA FACETIAE
ERR MAR SIN BOOT FAIL MISS SLIP
ABERR LAPSE MISGO STRAY
BUNGLE FORVAY SLIPUP WANDER
BLUNDER DEVIATE MISPLAY
MISTAKE SCRITHE STUMBLE
MISCARRY MISJUDGE
(— AT BRIDGE) RENEGE
ERRAND CHORE ENVOY JOURNEY
MISSION LEGATION
(— BOY) LOBBYGOW
(RUNNER OF —S) GOFER GOPHER
ERRANT STRAY ASTRAY ERRING
DEVIOUS PRICKANT
ERRATIC WILD CRAZY HUMAN
LOONY QUEER WACKY CRANKY
WHACKY STRANGE TANGENT
VAGRANT ACROSTIC ERRABUND
FITIFIED PLANETAL PLANETIC
TRAVELED VAGABOND PLANETARY
ERRATUM ERROR
ERRING ASTRAY ERRANT DEVIOUS
ERRINGLY FALSE
ERRONEOUS AMISS FALSE WRONG
UNTRUE ERRATIC MISTAKEN
STRAYING WRONGFUL
(PREF.) PSEUD(O)
ERRONEOUSLY AWRY
ERRONEOUSNESS FALLACY
ERROR X HOB SIN BALK BUBU BULL
FLUB HELL MUFF SLIP TRIP TYPO
BEARD BEVUE BONER DEVIL FAULT
FLUFF LAPSE SCAPE BOBBLE
BOOBOO FUMBLE GARBLE HOWLER
LAPSUS MISCUE NAUGHT SPHALM
BLOOMER BLUNDER DEFAULT
ERRATUM FALLACY FALSITY LITERAL
MISPLAY MISSTEP MISTAKE
OFFENSE RHUBARB SNAPPER
STUMBLE DELUSION HAMARTIA
MISPRINT MISSMENT SOLECISM
OVERSIGHT MISPRISION
(— IN PLEADINGS) JEOFAIL
ERS VETCH KERSANNE
ERSATZ FAUX
ERSE ERSCH IRISH CELTIC GAELIC
SCOTTISH
ERST ONCE FORMERLY RECENTLY
ERSTWHILE ONCE FORMER
FORMERLY
ERUCT RASP BELCH
ERUCTATION BRASH
ERUDITE LEARNED CLERGIAL
DIDACTIC
ERUDITION WIT LORE WISDOM
LETTERS LEARNING
ERUPT BOIL SPEW BELCH BURST
EJECT IRRUPT

ERUPTING ACTIVE
ERUPTION ITCH RASH REEF RUSH
AGRIA BLAIN BRASH BURST RUPIA
SALLY SALVO STORM BLOTCH
HYDROA NIRLES ACTERID BLOWOUT
ECTHYMA MORPHEA MORPHEW
PUSTULE SAWFLOM SUDAMEN
SYCOSIS EMPYESIS ENANTHEM
EXANTHEM MALANDER OUTBREAK
OUTBURST
(— ON CHIN) MENTAGRA
(CUTANEOUS —) HUMOR
(SKIN —) SPOT REDGUM TETTER
(SUFF.) ANTHEMA PHLYSIS
ERVUM LENS LENTILLA
ERYSICHTHON (FATHER OF —)
CECROPS TRIOPAS
(MOTHER OF —) AGRAULOS
(SISTER OF —) IPHIMEDIA
ERYSIPELAS POX ROSE BLAST
WILDFIRE
ERYTHROBLASTOSIS HYDROPSY
ERYX (FATHER OF —) BUTES
(MOTHER OF —) VENUS
(SLAYER OF —) HERCULES
ESAU EDOM
(BROTHER OF —) JACOB
(FATHER OF —) ISAAC
(LIKE —) HAIRY
(MOTHER OF —) REBEKAH
(SON OF —) JEUSH KORAH REUEL
JAALAM ELIPHAZ
(WIFE OF —) ADAH BASHEMATH
ESCALADE SCALE SCALADE
SCALADO ESCALADO
ESCAPADE LARK CAPER FLING
PRANK SALLY SCHEME SCRAPE
SPLORE RUNAWAY FREDAINE
ESCAPE FLY GUY LAM RUN BAIL
BALE BEAT BLOW BOLT FLEE GATE
HISS JINK JUMP LEAK MISS SHUN
SKEW SLIP VENT AVOID BREAK
CHAPE DODGE ELOPE ELUDE EVADE
FLANK ISSUE SCAPE SHIFT SKIRT
SMOKE SPILL ASTERT DECAMP
ESCHEW OUTLET POWDER SQUEAK
ABSCOND AVOLATE BLOWOUT
ELUSION EXHAUST GETAWAY
LEAKAGE MISTAKE OUTFLOW
SCRITHE SQUEEZE WILDING
BLOWBACK BREAKOUT ESCAPADE
ESCAPAGE EXSHEATH OUTSCAPE
OVERSLIP RIDDANCE OVERSLIP
(— FROM) FLY SHUN ILLUDE
(— FROM WORK) SNIB
(— LEGAL PROCESS) ABSCOND
(— NOTICE) ELUDE
(— OF FLUID) EFFUSION
(CUT OFF FROM —) HEMIN
(NARROW —) SHAVE
ESCAPEMENT SCAPE CRUTCH
ESCAPE FOLIOT VIRGULE KARRUSEL
ESCARGOT SNAIL

ESCAROLE ENDIVE SCAROLA
ESCARPMENT EDGE
ESCHAR SCAB CRUST ASCHER
ESCHAROTIC CAUSTIC
ESCHEAT FALL LAPSE REVERT
EXCHEAT FORFEIT
ESCHEW SHUN ABHOR AVOID
FORGO ESCAPE FOREGO ABSTAIN
ESCOLAR PALU ROVET OILFISH
ROVETTO MACKEREL
ESCORT MAN SEE SET TRY BEAR
BEAU COND LEAD SHOW TEND WAIT
BRING CARRY GUARD USHER
ATTEND CONVEY CONVOY FOLLOW
SQUIRE COLLECT CONDUCT
CONSORT ESQUIRE GALLANT
CAVALIER CHAPERON SHEPHERD
SAFEGUARD
(PAID —) GIGOLO
ESCRITOIRE DESK BUREAU LECTERN
ESCULENT EDIBLE EATABLE
ESCUTCHEON CREST SHIELD
(CENTER OF —) NOMBRIL
ESHBAN (FATHER OF —) DISHON
ESHCOL (BROTHER OF —) ANER
MAMRE
(COMPANION OF —) ABRAHAM
ESKER AS OS OSE KAME ESKAR
HOGBACK
ESKIMO ITA HUSKY INUIT INNUIT
AGOMIUT AMERIND ANGAKOK
KUNMIUT OKOMIUT ORARIAN
AGLEMIUT ESQUIMAU IKOGMIUT
KIDNELIK KINIPETU MAGEMIUT
MALEMIUT NUGUMIUT SINIMIUT
(— ASSEMBLY HOUSE) KASHIM
(— CULTURE) PUNUK
(— ISLAND) ALEUT
(— TENT) TUPEK TUPIK
ESLI (FATHER OF —) NAGGE
ESOPHAGUS GULLET SWALLOW
WEASAND
(PREF.) LAEMO LEMO
ESOTERIC DEEP INNER ARCANE
MYSTIC ORPHIC SECRET PRIVATE
ABSTRUSE RAREFIED RARIFIED
ESPADON ESPADA SPADON
SPADROON
ESPALIER CORDON LATTICE RAILING
TRELLIS PALISADE
ESPARTO ALFA HALFA SPART STIPA
ATOCHA
ESPAVE CARACOLI
ESPECIAL VERY CHIEF SPECIAL
PECULIAR UNCOMMON
ESPECIALLY SUCH EXTRA RATHER
CHIEFLY OVERALL SPECIAL
ESPIAL SPY ESPY EYING SCOUT
NOTICE
ESPINAL MONTE
ESPIONAGE SPYING
ESPLANADE BUND WALK DRIVE
MAIDAN MARINA

ESPOUSAL CEREMONY SPOUSAGE
BETROTHAL
ESPOUSE WED AFFY MATE ADOPT
MARRY DEFEND ENSURE SPOUSE
BETROTH EMBRACE HUSBAND
SUPPORT ADVOCATE MAINTAIN
ESPOUSED HANDFAST
ESPRESSO COFFEE
ESPUNDIA UTA
ESPY SEE ASPY SPOT ASCRY SIGHT
WATCH BEHOLD DESCRY DETECT
LOCATE NOTICE DISCERN OBSERVE
DESCRIBE DISCOVER
ESQUIRE RADMAN ARMIGER
ESCUDERO SERGEANT
ESSAY TRY SEEK ASSAY CHRIA
OFFER PAPER PROVE TASTE THEME
TRACT TRAIL CASUAL EFFORT
MEMOIR SAILYE SATIRE SCREED
THESIS ARTICLE ATTEMPT PROFFER
VENTURE WRITING CAUSERIE
ENDEAVOR EXERCISE EXERTION
TRACTATE TREATISE TURNOVER
(PRELIMINARY —) STUDY
ESSAYIST
AMERICAN DAY MORE VERY ADAMS
GRANT WHITE YOUNG BROOKS
COFFIN FISHER GUINEY HOLMES
HUTTON KILMER KRUTCH LOWELL
· EMERSON LAZARUS SISSMAN
WHIPPLE WHITMAN WHITTER
KOSINSKI REPPLIER STRUNSKY
TUCKERMAN SCHAUFFLER
AUSTRIAN BLEI
BELGIAN MAETERLINCK
CANADIAN MACMECHAN
CZECH CAPEK
ENGLISH HUNT LAMB BACON DRAKE
MUNRO MYERS PAGET PATER
POWYS SMITH GARROD MACHEN
MARTIN SEELEY STEELE TEMPLE
ADDISON BUDGELL CHAPONE
HAYWARD HAZLITT HEWLETT
MEYNELL RALEIGH SYMONDS
CHAMBERS CONGREVE DISRAELI
NEVINSON STERLING THOMPSON
DICKINSON STEVENSON
CHESTERTON DOBSONLEGALLIENNE
FRENCH ALAIN CAMUS ARAGON
MOUREY CHAMSON STAPFER
CHARTIER SCHOPFER MONTAIGNE
GERMAN ZWEIG FONTANE
GREEK XENOPHON
IRISH BOYD LECKY MAGEE
ITALIAN BRACCO CECCHI
MEXICAN REYES
POLISH BELCIKOWSKI MAKUSZYNSKI
SCOTTISH SMITH WILSON CARLYLE
THOMSON STEVENSON
SWEDISH EKELUND
ESSE BEING
ESSENCE ENS NET ALMA ATAR BASE
BONE CORE CRUX DRAW ESSE GIST

GUTS KIND ODOR OTTO PITH QUID
RASA SOUL YOLK ATTAR BASIC
BASIS BEING EIDOS FIBER FIBRE
FUMET HEART JUICE OTTAR OUSIA
STUFF BOTTOM EFFECT ENTITY
FLOWER INWARD MARROW NATURE
SPRITE ALCOHOL ELEMENT EXTRACT
FUMETTE GODHEAD INBEING
MEDULLA PERFUME RATAFIA
BERGAMOT CONCRETE ESSENTIA
(— OF BEING) SAT
(— OF FLOWERS) CONCRETE
(— OF GOD) SPIRIT DIVINITY
(— OF MEAT) BLOND
(— OF TEA) DRAW
(— OF VITAL MATTER) GLAME
(INNERMOST —) ATMAN
(UNIVERSAL —) FORM
(VITAL —) STAMINA
ESSENE ESSEE ASCETIC
ESSENTIAL KEY MUST REAL BASAL
BASIC VITAL ENTIRE FORMAL
INWARD CENTRAL CRUCIAL
NEEDFUL CARDINAL CRITICAL
INHERENT MATERIAL OBLIGATE
NECESSARY
(— TO LIFE) BIOGENOUS
(NOT —) ACCIDENTAL
(PL.) ABCS
ESSENTIALLY AUFOND
ESSONITE GARNET HYACINTH
ESTABLISH RED FIX PUT SET BASE
FAST FIRM FOOT MAKE REAR REST
ROOT SEAT BUILD DEFIX EDIFY
ENACT ERECT EVICT FOUND PLANT
PROVE RAISE SEIZE SETUP START
STATE STELL ATTEST AVOUCH
BOTTOM CEMENT CLINCH CREATE
ENROOT FASTEN FICCHE GROUND
INVENT INVEST LOCATE ORDAIN
RATIFY SETTLE STABLE VERIFY
ACCOUNT APPOINT APPROVE
CONFIRM ENSTATE INSTALL INSTATE
INSTORE POSSESS PREEMPT
SUSTAIN COLONIZE CONSTATE
CONTRACT ENSCONCE ENTRENCH
IDENTIFY INITIATE INSTRUCT
RADICATE REGULATE STABLISH
VALIDATE ASCERTAIN
(— FACT) APPROVE
(— FIRMLY) HAFT INDURATE
(— MORALS) ETHIZE
(— TRUMP) PITCH
ESTABLISHED SAD FAST FIRM SURE
LEGAL ROOTED SEATED SICCAR
STABLE STAPLE STATED STRONG
CERTAIN SETTLED STANDING
ESTABLISHMENT HONG MILL
SHOP STAB DAIRY FORGE JOINT
PLANT POWER SALON STORE
AGENCY CAISSE CENOBY ECESIS
LAYOUT MENAGE SALOON SCHOOL
ARSENAL ATELIER BROTHEL

COENOBY CONCERN DOWNSET
FACTORY FISHERY FOUNDRY
FUNDUCK SHEBANG AQUARIUM
AVERMENT BUSINESS CHEESERY
CREAMERY ERECTION HACIENDA
(— IN NEW HABITAT) ECESIS
(— OF COLONY) DEDUCTION
(BATHING —) THERM HAMMAM
HOTHOUSE
(DOMESTIC —) MENAGE
(DRINKING —) STUBE SALOON
BARROOM SHEBEEN
(GAMBLING —) HOUSE TRIPOT
(HORSE-BREEDING —) HARAS
(MONASTIC —) CLOISTER
(NAVAL —) DOCKYARD
(WHITE —) MAN

ESTAFETTE COURIER STAFETTE

ESTAMINET CAFE

ESTATE FEE ALOD COPY FEOD FIEF
HOME LAND POMP RANK UDAL
ACRES ALLOD DAIRA DOWER DOWRY
ESTER ESTRE ETHEL FINCA FUNDO
HABIT HOUSE MANOR STATE TALUK
VILLA ABBACY BARONY DEMISE
DOMAIN ENTAIL GROUND LIVING
MISTER QUINTA TALUKA ALODIUM
CHATEAU COMMONS DEMESNE
DIGNITY DISPLAY FORTUNE HAVINGS
MAJORAT ALLODIUM BENEFICE
COPYHOLD DOMINION EXECUTRY
FREEHOLD HACIENDA JOINTURE
LIFEHOLD LONGACRE MESNALTY
POSITION PROPERTY SENATORY
STANDING STAROSTY PATRIMONY
PERPETUITY
(— OF REBEL) FISC FISK
(— WITH SERFS) HAM
(CATTLE —) ESTANCIA
(HINDU —) CHAK
(PORTION OF —) LEGITIM
(REAL —) FUNDUS
(PL.) AMANI

ESTEEM AIM LET USE DEEM HOLD
RATE TALE ADORE COUNT FAVOR
HONOR PRICE PRIDE STEEM THINK
VALUE WEIGH WORTH ADMIRE
CREDIT EXTIME REGARD REPUTE
REVERE TENDER WONDER ACCOUNT
CONCEIT OPINION RESPECT
SUSPECT APPRAISE CONSIDER
ESTIMATE VENERATE

ESTEEMED DEAR PRECIOUS

ESTER ADP FMN BIXIN ETHER OLEIN
SARIN TABUN BORATE CAPRIN
ERUCIN FOLATE HUMATE LAURIN
MALATE OLEATE ACETATE ADIPATE
ANISATE AZELATE CINERIN ELAIDIN
FORMATE FUROATE GALLATE
HEPARIN INDICAN LACTATE LACTONE
LAURATE MALEATE MELLATE
NITRATE OCTOATE OXALATE
OXAMATE PECTATE PEPSIDE PICRATE

SORBATE STEARIN SULTONE
ABIETATE ACRYLATE ARSENATE
ARSENITE ARSONATE BEHENATE
BENZOATE CAFFEATE CONGENER
DIPHENAN ESTOLIDE FLUORIDE
FUCOIDIN KETIPATE LINOLATE
LINOLEIN MALONATE MARGARIN
MYRISTIN NUCLEATE PALMITIN
PIMELATE PIPERATE RACEMATE
SEBACATE SELENATE SILICATE
SINAPATE STEARATE SUBERATE
TARTRATE TOSYLATE PYRETHRIN
(SUFF.) OATE

ESTHER
(COUSIN OF —) MORDECAI
(FATHER OF —) ABIHAIL
(HUSBAND OF —) AHASUERUS

ESTHER WATERS
(AUTHOR OF —) MOORE
(CHARACTER IN —) FRED RICE LATCH
SARAH ESTHER JACKIE PEGGIE
TUCKER WATERS PARSONS WILLIAM
BARFIELD

ESTIMABLE GOOD SOLID WORTH
GENTLE HONEST WORTHY THRIFTY
VALUABLE

ESTIMATE AIM SET CALL CAST GAGE
RANK RATE READ RECK ASSAY AUDIT
CARAT CENSE COUNT GAUGE GUESS
JUDGE MOUNT PLACE PRIZE SCALE
STOCK TALLY VALUE WEIGH ASSESS
BUDGET ESTEEM RECKON REGARD
SURVEY ACCOUNT AVERAGE
BALANCE CENSURE COMPUTE
CONCEIT MEASURE APPRAISE
CONSIDER CRITIQUE CALCULATE
(— OF ONE'S SELF) OPINION
(— TOO HIGHLY) OVERRATE
(KIND OF —) POINT
(LOW COST —) LOWBALL

ESTIMATION AIM EYE CESS FAME
NAME ODOR PASS RATE COUNT
HONOR PRICE SIEGE VALUE CHOICE
ESTEEM REGARD REPUTE ACCOUNT
OPINION JUDGMENT PRESTIGE
(— OF STRAIGHTNESS) BONING
(HIGH —) CONCEIT
(LOW —) DISREPUTE

ESTIMATOR RATER CRUISER

ESTOC STOCK SWORD

ESTOILE STAR ETOILE

ESTONIA

CAPITAL: TALLINN
COIN: SENT KROON ESTMARK
DIALECT: TARTU
ISLAND: DAGO MUHU OESEL SAARE
    VORMSI HIIUMAA SAAREMAA
LAKE: PEIPUS
MEASURE: TUN ELLE LIIN PANG SUND
    TOLL TOOP FADEN VERST SAGENE
    VERSTA KULIMET VERCHOC
    TONNLAND

NATIVE: ESTH AESTI
PROVINCE: SAARE
RIVER: EMA NARVA PARNU KASARI
TOWN: NARVA PARNU REVAL TARTU
TALLINN
WEIGHT: LOOD NAEL PUUD

ESTONIAN ESTH
ESTOP BAR FILL PLUG STOP DEBAR
PREVENT
ESTRANGE PART WEAN ALIEN
AVERT DIVERT ALIENATE DISUNITE
STRANGER
ESTRANGED ALIEN FRAIM FREMIT
ESTRANGEMENT STANCE
DISTASTE
ESTRAY STRAY WANDER
ESTREAT COPY FINE EXACT RECORD
STREET EXTRACT EXTREAT
ESTREPEMENT STRIP
E STRING QUINT
ESTRIOL THEELOL
ESTROGEN MESTRANOL
TAMOXIFEN
ESTRONE THEELIN
ESTRUS HEAT SEASON
ESTUARY ARM RIA PARA WASH
CREEK FIRTH FLEET FRITH INLET
LIMAN ESTERO
ESURIENCE GREED HUNGER
ETCETERA ETC KTL
ETCH BITE FROST ENGRAVE
AQUATINT INSCRIBE
ETCHED FROSTED
ETCHER POINT
ETCHING ETCH AQUATINT
ETEOCLES (BROTHER OF —)
POLYNICES
(FATHER OF —) OEDIPUS
(MOTHER OF —) JOCASTA
ETERNAL ETERNE TARNAL AGELESS
ENDLESS LASTING UNAGING
ENDURING IMMORTAL TIMELESS
UNCAUSED
ETERNALLY AKE EER EVER ALWAYS
ETERNE FOREVER
ETERNITY AGE EON AEON OLAM
GLORY ETERNE ETERNAL EWIGKEIT
INFINITY PERPETUITY
ETESIAN ANNUAL PERIODIC
ETHAN (FATHER OF —) KISHI MAHOL
ETHANE DIMETHYL
ETHAN FROME
(AUTHOR OF —) WHARTON
(CHARACTER IN —) ETHAN FROME
ZEENA MATTIE PIERCE SILVER
ZENOBIA
ETHANOL ISOMER
ETHBAAL (DAUGHTER OF —)
JEZEBEL
ETHER AIR SKY APIOL ESTER PINOLE
ANISOLE ASARONE EPOXIDE
ETHYLIN HARMINE SAFROLE

SESAMIN SESAMOL SOLVENT
ACACETIN ELEMICIN EMPYREAN
GUAIACOL PHENETOLE
ETHEREAL AERY AIRY SKYEY AERIAL
SKYISH AIRLIKE ETHERIC FRAGILE
SLENDER DELICATE HEAVENLY
SUPERNAL VAPOROUS
ETHICAL ETHIC MORAL HONORABLE
ETHICS HEDONICO PHILOSOPHY

ETHIOPIA
ANCIENT CAPITAL: AXUM AKSUM
CAPITAL: ADDISABABA
COIN: BESA BIRR AMOLE GIRSH
DOLLAR TALARI ASHRAFI PIASTER
DEPRESSION: DANAKIL
FALLS: TISISAT BLUENILE
ISLANDS: DAHLAK
LAKE: ABE TANA ABAYA SHOLA
ZEWAY RUDOLF STEFANIE
LANGUAGE: GEEZ TIGRE SOMALI
AMHARIC GALLINYA TIGRINYA
MARRIAGE: DAMOZ QURRAN
SEMANYA
MEASURE: TAT KUBA SINJER SINZER
FARSAKH FARSANG
MOUNTAIN: RATU GUGE GUNA TALO
MOUNTAINS: AHMAR CHOKE
NAME: ABYSSINIA
NATIVE: AFAR GALLA ABIGAR
AMHARA ANNUAK HAMITE SEMITE
SOMALI TIGRAI CUSHITE DANAKIL
FALASHA
PORT: ASSAB MASSAWA
PRINCE: RAS
PROVINCE: BALE KEFA WELO ARUSI
GOJAM HARER SHEWA TIGRE
SIDAMO ERITREA
RIVER: OMO WEB BARO DAWA GILA
ABBAI AKOBO AWASH FAFAN
TAKKAZE
TOWN: EDD DESE GOBA GORE JIMA
THIO ADOLA ADUWA AKSUM ASSAB
AWASH DIMTU HARAR HARER
JIMMA MOJJO ASMARA DESSYE
DUNKUR GONDAR MAKALE MEKELE
GARDULA MASSAWA NAKAMTI
NEKEMTE DIREDAWA LALIBALA
MUSTAHIL
VALLEY: RIFT
WATERFALL: FINCHA DALVERME
TESISSAI
WEIGHT: KASM NATR OKET ALADA
NETER WAKEA WOGIET FARASULA

ETHIOPIAN SIDI HAMITE HARARI
AETHIOP AFRICAN CUSHITE
FALASHA
ETHIOPIC GIZ GEEZ GHEEZ
ETHNAN (FATHER OF —) ASHUR
(MOTHER OF —) HELAH
ETHNIC RACIAL
(— GROUP) ACHANG

ETHNOLOGIST AMERICAN GIBBS
HODGE LOWIE MASON SMITH
FEWKES MOONEY MORGAN
THOMAS BARROWS GODDARD
HENSHAW PILLING FLETCHER
GATSCHET GRINNELL CHURCHILL
SCHOOLCRAFT
AUSTRIAN MULLER LUSCHAN
WINTERNITZ
DANISH RASMUSSEN
DUTCH STEINMETZ NIEUWENHUIS
ENGLISH HADDON LATHAM
PRICHARD
FINNISH CASTREN
GERMAN BOEHM FINSCH GROSSE
KRAUSE BASTIAN GERLAND
STEINEN FROBENIUS FRIEDERICI
RUSSIAN KOPPEN
ETHOS MANNER
ETHYLENE ELAYL ETHENE ETHERIN
ETIOLATED DRAWN
ETIQUETTE FORM DECORUM
MANNERS
(— OF DRINKING TEA) CHANOYU
ETRUSCAN TUSCAN RASENNA
ETRURIAN TYRRHENE
(PL.) TURSENOI TYRRHENI
ETUDE STUDY
ETUI CASE ETWEE TWEEZE TWEEZER
EQUIPAGE RETICULE
ETYMOLOGY ORIGIN DERIVATION
ETYMON RADIX
EUAECHME (DAUGHTER OF —)
PERIBOEA
(FATHER OF —) MEGAREUS
(HUSBAND OF —) ALCATHOUS
EUBOEANS ABANTES
EUCALYPT GUM YATE APPLE BIMBIL
CARBUN JARRAH MALLEE MYRTAL
CARBEEN CUTTAIL MESSMAN
COOLABAH IRONBARK MESSMATE
WHITETOP YERTCHUK
EUCALYPTOLE CINEOL CINEOLE
EUCALYPTUS TUART MALLEE
TEWART BLUEGUM EUCALYPT
IRONBARK SUGARGUM WHIPSTICK
EUCHARIST HOUSEL MAUNDY
SUPPER MYSTERY VIATICUM
EUCHARISTIC (— ELEMENTS) HAGIA
EUCHITE SATANIST ADELPHIAN
MESSALIAN
EUCHRE LOVE
(— HAND) JAMBONE JAMBOREE
EUDAEMONIA HAPPINESS
EUDOCIMUS GUARA
EUDOXIA (FATHER OF —) BAUTO
(HUSBAND OF —) ARCADIUS
(SON OF —) THEODOSIUS
EUGENE ONEGIN
(CHARACTER IN —) OLGA GREMIN
LARINA ONEGIN OLENSKY TATYANA
TRIQUET
(COMPOSER OF —) TCHAIKOVSKY

EUGENIE GRANDET (AUTHOR OF
—) BALZAC
(CHARACTER IN —) NANON CHARLES
CRUCHOT EUGENIE GRANDET
DEGRASSINS
EULALIA NETI
EULENSPIEGEL OWLGLASS
EULOGIST PRAISER LAUREATE
PANEGYRIST
EULOGISTIC EULOGIC EPENETIC
MAGNIFIC LAUDATORY
EULOGY PRAISE TONGUE ADDRESS
ELOGIUM ORATION ENCOMIUM
PANEGYRE
EUMOLPUS (FATHER OF —)
NEPTUNE
(MOTHER OF —) CHIONE
(SON OF —) ISMARUS
EUNEUS (BROTHER OF —) THOAS
(FATHER OF —) JASON
(MOTHER OF —) HYPSIPYLE
EUNICE (SON OF —) TIMOTHEUS
EUNUCH CAPON SPORUS WETHER
GELDING HALFMAN CASTRATE
EUPHAUSID SHRIMP
EUPHEMISM DEE FIB GEE GOR
DASH GOSH GOLES GOLLY LAWKS
DIANTRE DICKENS CODEWORD
GRACIOUS
(— FOR DAMN) HANG
(— FOR MURDER) REMOVAL
EUPHEMUS (FATHER OF —)
NEPTUNE POSEIDON
(MOTHER OF —) EUROPA
(SON OF —) BATTUS
EUPHONIOUS TUNEFUL
EUPHORIA BLISS ELATION
EUPHORIC GIDDY
EUPHROSYNE JOY
EUPHUISM GONGORISM
EURASIAN BURGHER FERINGI
EUREKA RED PUCE
EURIPIDES (TRAGEDY OF —)
ELECTRA
EURO WALLAROO
EUROPA (BROTHER OF —) CILIX
CADMUS THASUS PHINEUS PHOENIX
(FATHER OF —) AGENOR
(HUSBAND OF —) ASTERIUS
(MOTHER OF —) TELEPHASSA
(SON OF —) MINOS SARPEDON
RHADAMANTHYS

EUROPE
(ALSO SEE SPECIFIC COUNTRIES)
LAKE: COMO GARDA ONEGA VANEM
GENEVA LADOGA LUGANO PEIPUS
VANERN ZURICH BALATON
MALAREN SCUTARI VATTERN
MAGGIORE CONSTANCE
NEUCHATEL
MOUNTAIN: DOM ETNA ELBRUS
KAZBEK LYSKAMM SHKHARA

JUNGFRAU NADELHORN
WEISSHORN ZUGSPITZE
MATTERHORN
NATION: ITALY SPAIN FRANCE GREECE
LATVIA MONACO NORWAY POLAND
RUSSIA SWEDEN ALBANIA
ANDORRA AUSTRIA BELGIUM
DENMARK ENGLAND ESTONIA
FINLAND GERMANY HOLLAND
HUNGARY ICELAND IRELAND
ROMANIA BULGARIA PORTUGAL
SCOTLAND SLOVAKIA SLOVENIA
SANMARINO LUXEMBOURG
YUGOSLAVIA NETHERLANDS
SOVIETUNION SWITZERLAND
VATICANCITY LIECHTENSTEIN
CZECHOSLOVAKIA
RANGE: ALPS URAL BALKAN KJOLEN
RHODOPE SUDETEN CAUCASUS
PYRENEES APENNINES CARPATHIAN
RIVER: PO AAR DON AARE EBRO ELBE
ODER DOURO DVINA LOIRE RHINE
RHONE SEINE TAGUS TIBER VOLGA
DANUBE THAMES DNIEPER VISTULA
DNIESTER

EUROPEAN FRANK SAHIB BOHUNK
EUROPE FRINGE INDIAN FERINGI
TOPIWALA
(— IN INDIES) BLIJVER
(WESTERN —) FRANK
EUROPEAN BARRACUDA SPET
EUROPEAN BASS BRASSE
EUROPEAN BISON AUROCHS
EUROPEAN CLOVER ALSIKE
EUROPEAN GULL MEW
EUROPEAN HERRING SPRAT
EUROPEAN JUNIPER CADE
EUROPEAN KITE GLEDE
EUROPEAN LAVENDER ASPIC
EUROPEAN LINDEN TEIL
EUROPEAN MINT HYSSOP
EUROPEAN OAK DURMAST
EUROPEAN PERCH RUFF RUFFE
EUROPEAN POLECAT FITCHEW
EUROPEAN PORGY BESUGO
EUROPEAN RABBIT CONY
EUROPEAN SHARK TOPE
EUROPEAN SPARROW WHITECAP
EUROPEAN STARLING STARNEL
EUROPEAN SWALLOW MARTIN
EUROPEAN THRUSH MAVIS OUZEL
EUROPEAN WIDGEON WHIM
WHEWER
EUROPEAN WREN STAG
EURYANTHE (CHARACTER IN —)
ADOLAR LYSIART EGLANTINE
EURYANTHE
(COMPOSER OF —) WEBER
EURYBIA (FATHER OF —) PONTUS
(MOTHER OF —) GAEA
(SON OF —) PALLAS PERSES
ASTRAEUS

EURYNOME (DAUGHTERS OF —)
GRACES CHARITES
(FATHER OF —) CHAOS OCEANUS
EURYPTERID SERAPHIM
EURYPYLUS (FATHER OF —)
NEPTUNE TELEPHUS
(MOTHER OF —) ASTYOCHE
(SLAYER OF —) PYRRHUS
HERCULES
EURYSACES (FATHER OF —) AJAX
(MOTHER OF —) TECMESSA
EURYSTHEUS (FATHER OF —)
STHENELUS
(MOTHER OF —) NICIPPE
(SLAYER OF —) HYLLUS
EURYTUS (DAUGHTER OF —) IOLE
(FATHER OF —) ACTOR AUGEAS
MELANEUS
(MOTHER OF —) GAEA
(SLAYER OF —) HERCULES
EUTECTIC STEADITE
EUTERPE (FATHER OF —) JUPITER
(MOTHER OF —) MNEMOSYNE
EUXANTHONE PURRONE
EUXOA AGROTIS
EVACUATE PASS VENT VOID AVOID
EMPTY EXPEL STOOL VACATE
DEPRIVE EXCRETE EXHAUST NULLIFY
VACUATE PERSPIRE
EVACUATION OFFICE DUNKIRK
MEDEVAC
EVADE BEG GEE BILK DUCK FLEE FOIL
JOUK JUMP SHUN SLIP VOID AVERT
AVOID BLINK DALLY DODGE ELUDE
FENCE FLANK PARRY SHIRK SKIRT
SKIVE BAFFLE BLENCH BYPASS
COROUT DELUDE ESCAPE ILLUDE
BEGUILE FINESSE OUTSLIP QUIBBLE
TURNOFF HEDGEHOP LEAPFROG
SIDESTEP
(— LEGAL PROCESS) ABSCOND
(— PAYMENT) BILK
(— QUESTIONS) QUIBBLE SHUFFLE
(— WORK) JOUK BLUDGE
EVADNE (FATHER OF —) PELIAS
NEPTUNE POSEIDON
(HUSBAND OF —) CAPANEUS
(MOTHER OF —) IPHIS PITANA
(SON OF —) IAMUS
EVALUATE RATE ASSESS PONDER
RECKON DISSECT APPRAISE
ESTIMATE
EVALUATION STOCK ESTIMATE
EVANDER (FATHER OF —) HERMES
(MOTHER OF —) CARMENTA
EVANESCE FADE VANISH
EVANESCENCE ANICCA
EVANESCENT FLEET EVANID
BRITTLE CURSORY EVASIVE FRAGILE
DELICATE FLEETING FLITTING
FUGITIVE STAYLESS
EVANGELICAL GOSPEL SIMEONITE
(— ACTIVITY) WARFARE

EVANGELIST LUKE MARK EVANGEL
GOSPELER SALVATIONIST
EVAPORATE DRY EXHALE AVOLATE
CONDENSE VAPORIZE
EVAPORATING
(— QUICKLY) VOLATILE
EVAPORATOR BOILER EFFECT
EVASION JINK SLIP DODGE QUIRK
SALVE SHIFT AMBAGE ESCAPE
SNATCH ELUSION OFFCOME
SHUFFLE TWISTER ARTIFICE
ESCAPISM VOIDANCE
(— OF DUTY) COMEOFF
(ARTFUL —) QUIRK
EVASIVE SLY EELY DODGY SHIFTY
SUBTLE TWISTY ELUSIVE ELUSORY
TRICKSY SLIPPERY SLIPSKIN
(TO BE —) STONEWALL
EVE DUSK EREB EREV EVEN VIGIL
SUNSET SUNDOWN
(NEW YEAR'S —) HAGMENA
HOGMANAY
EVELINA (AUTHOR OF —) BURNEY
(CHARACTER IN —) JOHN DUVAL
ARTHUR HOWARD ANVILLE
BELMONT CLEMENT EVELINA
ORVILLE VILLARS WILLOUGHBY
EVEN ALL DEN EEN TIE YET FAIR
HUNK JUST PAIR TIED TILL ALINE
CLEAN EQUAL EVERY EXACT FLUSH
GRADE HUNKY LEVEL MATCH PLAIN
RIVAL STILL SUANT SUENT SWEET
DIRECT ITSELF PLACID SILKEN
SMOOTH SQUARE STEADY ABREAST
BALANCE EQUABLE FLATTEN
REGULAR UNIFORM UPSIDES
EQUALIZE MODERATE PARALLEL
SOMUCHAS
(— NUMBERS) PAIR
(— OFF) LEVEL
(— THOUGH) IF ALTHO ALBEIT
ALTHOUGH
(MAKE —) WEIGH STEADY
(PREF.) ARTIO HOMAL(O) LEUR(O)
EVENING DEN EVE EREB EVEN SOIR
ABEND TARDE SUNSET VESPER
EVENTIDE VESPERAL
(— BEFORE PASSOVER) PARASCEVE
(— OF SONG) CEILIDH
(AT —) TEEN
(EARLY —) UNDERN
(YESTERDAY —) STREEN
EVENING PRIMROSE SUNCUP
SCABIOUS
EVENING STAR VENUS HESPER
VESPER EVESTAR HESPERUS
EVENLY FAIR PLAIN FLATLY EQUALLY
EVENNESS EQUALITY
EVENSONG VESPERS
EVENT HAP CASE FACT FATE FEAT
TILT CASUS DOING EPOCH FRAME
ISSUE THING ACTION EFFECT
FACTUM RESULT TIDING TIMING

EPISODE FIXTURE MIRACLE PORTENT
TRAGEDY INCIDENT OCCASION
OCCURRENCE PHENOMENON
(AMUSING —) COMEDY
(CHANCE —) ACCIDENT FORTUITY
(EXTRAORDINARY —) MIRACLE
(FORTUITOUS —) HAZARD
(GRAVE —) CALAMITY
(HAPPY —) GODSEND
(IMPORTANT —) ACE ERA
(INTRODUCTORY —) PROLOGUE
(KIND OF —) MEDIA
(PAST —S) HISTORY
(SEISMIC —) STARQUAKE
(SET OF —S) EPISODE
(SIGNIFICANT —) CRISIS
(SKI —) DOWNHILL
(SOCIAL —) BENEFIT
(SPORTING —) STAKE
(STAGED —) FRAMEUP
(SUPERNATURAL —) MIRACLE
(THEATRICAL —) DRAW
(TURNING-POINT —) LANDMARK
(UNEXPECTED —) STUNNER
ACCIDENT AFTERCLAP
(UNPLEASANT —) BUMMER
(YEARLY —) ANNUAL
EVENTFUL LIVELY NOTABLE
EVENTIDE VESPER EVENING
EVENTUAL LAST FINAL ULTIMATE
EVENTUALITY EVENT
EVENTUALLY YET FINALLY
EVENTUATE GO LEAD ISSUE
RESULT SUCCEED ULTIMATE
EVENUS (DAUGHTER OF —)
MARPESSA
(FATHER OF —) ARES MARS
EVER O AY SO AYE EER ONCE STILL
ALWAYS ETERNE FOREVER
EVERGLADE STATE FLORIDA
EVERGREEN BOX FIR IVY YEW ASIS
ATLE BAGO ILEX PINE TAWA ATLEE
BOLDO CAROB CEDAR HEATH HOLLY
LARCH SAVIN THUYA TOYON
BAUERA COIGUE DAHOON LAUREL
MASTIC SPRUCE BANKSIA BARETTA
BEBEERU BILIMBI GOWIDDE
HEMLOCK JASMINE TARATAH
BOXTHORN CALFKILL CARAUNDA
IRONWOOD TAMARISK TILESEED
(— SHRUB) GORSE
(PL.) CHRISTMAS
EVER-INCREASING ACCRESCENT
EVERLASTING ETERNE AEONIAL
AEONIAN AGELESS AGELONG
DURABLE ENDLESS ETERNAL
FOREVER LASTING TEDIOUS
ENDURING IMMORTAL INFINITE
TIMELESS PERPETUAL
EVERLASTINGLY ALWAYS FOREVER
EVERSION BLOWOUT BEARINGS
EVERT UPSET EVERSE SUBVERT
OVERTURN

EVERY ALL ANY ILK PER THE EACH
EVER ILKA ENTIRE EVERICH
COMPLETE
(— DAY) OD QUOTID
(— HOUR) QH
(— NIGHT) ON
(PREF.) PAM PAN
EVERYBODY ALL EACH EVERYMAN
EVERYONE
EVERYDAY USUAL HOMELY
PROSAIC ORDINARY WORKADAY
EVERY MAN IN HIS HUMOUR
(AUTHOR OF —) JONSON
(CHARACTER IN —) EDWARD KITELY
BOBADIL BRIDGET CLEMENT
KNOWELL MATTHEW WELLBRED
BRAINWORM
EVERYTHING ALL ATHING
(— TAKEN INTO ACCOUNT) ALLINALL
(COUNTING —) INALL
EVERYWHERE PASSIM UBIQUE
ALGATES AYWHERE OVERALL
ALLWHERE
EVICT OUST EJECT EXPEL
EVICTION OUSTER
EVIDENCE CLUE MARK SHOW SIGN
TEST PROOF SCRIP SMOKE TOKEN
TRACE TRIAL ATTEST AVOUCH
BETOKE RECORD REVEAL CHARTER
EXHIBIT HEARSAY SHOWING
SUPPORT ARGUMENT DISPROOF
DOCUMENT EVICTION INDICATE
MANIFEST MONUMENT MUNIMENT
WARRANTY ADMINICLE
(— OF DISEASE) SYMPTOM
(— OF FRESHNESS) BLOOM
(— OF RIGHT) TITLE
(— OF WRONGDOING) GOODS
(POSITIVE —) CONSTAT
(VERBAL —) PAROL
EVIDENT LOUD OPEN PERT APERT
BROAD CLEAR FRANK GROSS NAKED
PLAIN EXTANT LIQUID PATENT
WITTER EMINENT GLARING OBVIOUS
PROBATE VISIBLE APPARENT
DISTINCT FLAGRANT LUCULENT
MANIFEST PALPABLE
(PREF.) DELO
EVIL BAD DER ILL SIN BALE BASE DIRE
HARM LEWD PAPA POOR SORE VICE
VILE WICK YELL CRIME CURSE DEVIL
FELON FOLLY HYDRA MALUM OUEDE
SORRY WATHE WRONG CANCEL
DIVERS INJURY MALIGN MENACE
NAUGHT PLAGUE ROTTEN SHREWD
SINFUL UNFEEL UNFELE UNGOOD
UNWELL WICKED WONDER ADVERSE
BALEFUL CORRUPT DISEASE
DIVERSE HEINOUS HURTFUL
IMMORAL MISDEED NOXIOUS
SATANIC UNHAPPY UNSOUND
VICIOUS CALAMITY DEPRAVED
DEVILISH DISASTER GANGRENE

IMPROPER INIQUITY MISCHIEF
QUEDSHIP SINISTER NEFARIOUS
(— BEING) MARE
(— OF MANY PHASES) HYDRA
(— SPIRIT) JUMBIE
(IMAGINARY —) WINDMILL
(IMPENDING —) MENACE
IMMINENCE
(SOCIAL —) SCOURGE
(SPIRITUAL —) SCAB
(PREF.) MAL(E) PONERO
EVIL-DOER VILLAIN
EVILDOER BADMASH BUDMASH
SLASHER
EVIL EYE DROCHUIL MALOCCHIO
EVINCE SHOW ARGUE PROVE
SUBDUE BREATHE CONQUER
DISPLAY EXHIBIT EVIDENCE INDICATE
MANIFEST
EVISCERATE GUT DRAW BOWEL
PAUNCH GARBAGE
EVOCATION SADHANA
EVOCATIVE REDOLENT
EVOKE FIT MOVE STIR EDUCE
AROUSE ELICIT SUMMON EVOCATE
PROVOKE SUGGEST
EVOLUTION DRIFT GROWTH
BIOGENY DIOECISM HOROTELY
MANEUVER BRADYTELY
(PL.) AEROBATICS
EVOLUTIONISM DARWINISM
EVOLVE COOK EMIT EDUCE DERIVE
UNFOLD UNROLL BLOSSOM
DEVELOP EVOLUTE CONCEIVE
UNPLIGHT
EWE KEB TEG CROCK CRONE DRAPE
SHEEP GIMMER LAMBER RACHEL
THEAVE CHILVER
(— AND LAMB) COUPLE
(OLD —) BIDDY CROCK CRONE BIDDIE
(YOUNG —) THEAVE
EWER JUG CREW LAIR BASIN UDDER
PITCHER URCEOLE
EXACERBATE SOUR ENRAGE
FERMENT EMBITTER IRRITATE
EXACERBATION PAROXYSM
EXACT ASK DUE DEAD EVEN FINE
FLAT HAVE JUMP JUST LEVY NEAT
NICE TRUE VERY PRESS SCREW
WREAK WREST COMPEL DEMAND
ELICIT EVINCE EXTORT FORMAL
GRAITH MINUTE NARROW PROPER
SEVERE SQUARE STRAIT STRICT
CAREFUL CERTAIN COLLECT
COMMAND CORRECT ENFORCE
ESTREAT EXPRESS EXTRACT LITERAL
PARTILE PERFECT POINTED PRECISE
PRECISO REFINED REGULAR
REQUIRE ACCURATE CRITICAL
EXPLICIT FAITHFUL RIGOROUS
SPECIFIC
(— BY FINE) ESTREAT
(— SATISFACTION) AVENGE

(NOT —) PLATIC
(VERY —) RELIGIOUS
(PREF.) ORTH(O)
EXACTING NICE HARSH PICKY
STERN STIFF TIGHT SCREWY SEVERE
STRAIT STRICT ARDUOUS EXIGENT
FINICKY ONEROUS CRITICAL
IMPOSING IRONCLAD PRESSING
SCREWING PARTICULAR
PERSNICKETY
(— EXCLUSIVE DEVOTION) JEALOUS
EXACTION FEE TAX MART GOUGE
GRIPE
(— OF PROVISIONS) CESS COYNE
COIGNY
(ANCIENT IRISH —) SOREHON
(UNDUE —) EXTORTION
EXACTITUDE RIGOR
EXACTLY DUE AMEN BANG DEAD
EVEN FLAT FLOP FULL JUMP JUST
VERY PLUMB PLUNK QUITE RIGHT
SHARP SPANG TRULY ARIGHT
EVENLY ITSELF JUSTLY NICELY
PERFECT SLAPDAB DIRECTLY
MINUTELY SMACKDAB
EXACTNESS RIGOR TRUTH NICETY
ACCURACY DELICACY DISPATCH
FIDELITY IDENTITY JUSTNESS
SAPIENCE SEVERITY PRECISION
PARTICULARITY
(FUSSY —) FIKE
EXAGGERATE GAB MORE COLOR
BOUNCE CHARGE COLOUR EXTEND
OVERDO AMPLIFY ENHANCE
ENLARGE MAGNIFY OUTLASH
ROMANCE STRETCH INCREASE
OVERDRAW OVERLASH OVERPLAY
OVERTELL OVERSTATE OVERCHARGE
(— OPENING OF MOUTH) CHINK
EXAGGERATED CAMP SLAB TALL
COLORED FUSTIAN FABULOUS
INFLATED OVERDONE OVERSHOT
OVERWEENING
EXAGGERATING ARROGANT
EXAGGERATION BLAH REACHER
HYPERBOLE
EXALT HAUT LAUD REAR AREAR
BUILD DEIFY ELATE ENSKY ERECT
EXTOL HEAVE HEEZE HONOR MOUNT
RAISE TOWER ALTIFY ASCEND
EXHALE PREFER REFINE THRONE
UPREAR WORTHY ADVANCE
AUGMENT DIGNIFY ELEVATE
ENHANCE ENNOBLE FEATHER
GLORIFY GREATEN INSPIRE MAGNIFY
PROMOTE SUBLIME DIVINIZE
ENTHRONE GRADUATE HEIGHTEN
INHEAVEN PEDESTAL
EXALTATION LAUD AVATAR
ANAGOGE ANAGOGY ELATION
RAPTURE ERECTION
EXALTED HAUT HIGH ELATE GRAND
LOFTY NOBLE SHEEN SKYEY SOARY

ASTRAL TIPTOE TOPFUL HAUGHTY
SUBLIME ELEVATED EXALTATE
MAGNIFIC
EXALTING HUMAN
EXAM MUG
(— ANSWER) TRUE FALSE
(— TAKER) TESTEE
(HIGH SCHOOL —) PSAT
EXAMINATION EX MAY EXAM FACE
QUIZ TEST ASSAY AUDIT BOARD
CHECK FINAL GREAT POINT PROBE
STUDY TRIAL BIOPSY EXAMEN
NOTICE REVIEW SCHOOL SEARCH
SURVEY TRIPOS AUTOPSY BEARING
CANVASS CHECKUP DIVVERS
EXAMINE HEARING INQUEST
INQUIRY MIDYEAR OPPOSAL
TUGGERY ANALYSIS CRITIQUE
DOCIMASY EXERCISE NECROPSY
PHYSICAL RESEARCH SCANNING
SCRUTINY PRACTICAL PRELIMINARY
(BRITISH —) SLEVEL
(ELECTROCARDIOGRAPHIC —)
STRESSTEST
(PL.) HOURS
(SUFF.) SCOPE SCOPIC SCOPUS
SCOPY
EXAMINE ASK CON FAN SEE SPY
TRY BOLT CASE COMB FEEL LAIT
LINE LOOK OGLE QUIZ RIPE SCAN
SEEK SIFT TEST VIEW ASSAY AUDIT
CHECK ENTER GROPE PROBE QUEST
QUOTE SAMEN SENSE SOUND
STUDY VISIT APPOSE BEHOLD
CANDLE DEBATE PERUSE PONDER
REVIEW SCREEN SEARCH SURVEY
ANALYZE CANVASS COLLATE
DISCUSS EXPLORE INQUIRE INSPECT
OVERSEE PALPATE RUMMAGE
COGNOSCE CONSIDER OVERHAUL
TRAVERSE
(— BY TOUCH) PALPATE
(— CAREFULLY) SCAN SIFT PONDER
(— LAND) SOUM
EXAMINER POSER TRIER CENSOR
CONNER SABORA ANALYST
APPOSER AUDITOR CORONER
PROBATOR SEARCHER
EXAMPLE A CASE CAST COPY LEAD
NORM TYPE BEAUT BYSEN ESSAY
LIGHT MODEL PIECE EMBLEM PRAXIS
SAMPLE BOUNCER LEADING
LECTURE PATTERN PURPOSE
SAMPLER THEATER CALENDAR
ENSAMPLE EXEMPLAR EXEMPLUM
FORBYSEN FOREGOER INSTANCE
PARADIGM SPECIMEN
(CHOICE —) PEACH
(DISGRACEFUL —) BIZEN BYSEN
BYZEN MONSTROSITY
(EXTREME —) CAUTION
(FINEST —) PEARL
(INFERIOR —) EXCUSE

(INSTRUCTIVE —) LESSON
(NOTABLE —) MONUMENT
(OLDEST —) DOYEN
(PERFECT —) APOTHEOSIS
(STANDARD —) PROTOTYPE
(SUPERLATIVE —) BLINGER

EXANTHEMA DIEBACK ERUPTION

EXASPERATE IRE IRK MAD BAIT GALL HEAT URGE ANNOY BLOOD ENRAGE EXCITE NETTLE EXASPER INFLAME PROVOKE ROUGHEN ACERBATE IRRITATE

EXASPERATED SNAKY WROTH SNAKEY SNAKISH ACERBATE

EXASPERATION AGRO GALL HEAT AGGRO WRATH

EXCAVATE CUT DIG PIT HOLE HOWK MINE MOLE MUCK PION SINK DELVE DRILL DRIVE GRAVE NAVVY SCOOP STOPE BURROW DREDGE EXCAVE GULLET HOLLOW QUARRY

EXCAVATION CUT DIG PIT HOLE MINE REDD SINK SUMP BERRY DELFT DELPH DITCH GRAFT GRAVE HEUGH PILOT STOPE BURROW CAVITY DUGOUT GROOVE TRENCH BREAKUP CUTTING PADDOCK TUTWORK WORKING DENEHOLE SLUSHPIT
(TRIAL —) SONDAGE

EXCAVATOR DIG BILDAR CLEOID DIGGER DIPPER DRIFTER HATCHET PIONEER

EXCEED COW TOP BEST PASS EXCEL OUTDO OUTGO BETTER OUTRUN OUTVIE OVERDO OVERGO ECLIPSE OUTPASS OVERRUN OVERTAX PRECEDE SURPASS OUTRANGE OUTREACH OUTSTRIP OVERCOME OVERGANG OVERSTEP OVERWEND SURMOUNT PREPONDERATE
(— IN IMPORTANCE) OVERSHADOW
(— THE RESOURCES) BEGGAR

EXCEEDING VILE

EXCEEDINGLY ALL DONE PURE TRES VERY AMAIN BLAME BLAMED MASTER PROPER PURELY AWFULLY LICKING PARLOUS PASSING HEARTILY HEAVENLY HORRIBLE PROPERLY
(PREF.) PRE ULTRA

EXCEL CAP COB TOP BANG BEAT BEST DING FLOG MEND PASS STAR BLECK OUTDO OUTGO SHINE TRUMP BETTER EXCEED MASTER OUTRAY OVERDO OVERGO PRECEL ECLIPSE EMULATE OUTPEER SURPASS OUTCLASS OUTRANGE OUTRIVAL OUTSHINE OUTSTRIP OVERPEER SUPERATE SURMOUNT

EXCELLENCE ARETE MERIT PRICE VIRTU WORTH BEAUTY DESERT HEIGHT VIRTUE DIGNITY PROWESS GOODNESS SPLENDOR BRILLIANCE PREROGATIVE

(— OF QUALITY) STRIKE
(MORAL —) GRACE
(PL.) SANCTITIES

EXCELLENT FAB GAY RUM BEST BOSS BRAW COOL FINE GOOD HEND HIGH PURE RARE RIAL SLAP TALL TRIM ATHEL BEAUT BONNY BONZA BRAVE BULLY BURLY CRACK GREAT JAMMY JOLLY LUMMY PIOUS PRIME PRIMO SOLID SUPER SWELL TOUGH TRIED WALLY BONNIE BONZER BOSKER BUMPER CHEESY CHOICE CLASSY FAMOUS FREELY GENTLE GOODLY MELLOW PRETTY PROPER SELECT SPIFFY TIPTOP WICKED WIZARD WORTHY YANKEE BLIGHTY BOSHTER CAPITAL CORKING CURIOUS ELEGANT GALLANT IMMENSE QUALITY SNIFTER STAVING TOPPING CLIPPING COLOSSAL EXIMIOUS GENEROUS KNOCKOUT SPIFFING STUNNING SUPERIOR VALUABLE VIRTUOUS WAUREGAN YNGOODLY GANGBUSTERS
(— IN QUALITY) FRANK
(MOST —) BEST

EXCELLENTLY BRAWLY CLEVER FINELY FREELY PROUDLY DIVINELY FAMOUSLY

EXCELLING BEST PASSANT

EXCEPT BAR BUT CEP NOR NOT RATE BOUT OMIT ONLY SAVE ABATE FORBY SEVER EXEMPT FORBYE NOBBUT SAVING SCUSIN UNLESS BARRING BESIDES EXCLUDE OUTCEPT OUTSIDE OUTTAKE OUTWITH RESERVE WITHOUT FORPRISE OUTTAKEN RESERVED
(PREF.) PRETER

EXCEPTING BATING EXCEPT SAVING UNLESS BARRING

EXCEPTION DEMUR SALVO SAVING DISSENT OFFENSE DEMURRER FALLENCY FORPRISE INSTANCE
(— TO JUROR) CHALLENGE
(WITHOUT —) BARNONE

EXCEPTIONAL RARE EXEMPT ROUSING STRANGE UNUSUAL ABERRANT ABNORMAL ESPECIAL SINGULAR UNCOMMON

EXCEPTIONALLY AMAZING SPANKING

EXCERPT CITE PATCH QUOTE SCRAP EXTRACT OFFPRINT
(— FROM SONG) SNATCH

EXCESS OVER PLUS RIOT FLOOD INORD LUXUS PRIDE ACRASY SPILTH ACRASIA BALANCE DEBAUCH EXTREME MISRULE NIMIETY OUTRAGE OVERAGE OVERDET PROFUSE RIOTISE SURFEIT SURPLUS EXCEDENT GLUTTONY INTEREST

OVERLASH OVERMUCH OVERPLUS
PLEONASM PLETHORA PLEURISY
SATURNALIA OVERABUNDANCE
(— OF ACTION) OVERKILL
(— OF LOGS) BANK
(— OF METAL) FEEDHEAD
(— OF SOLAR MONTH) EPACT
(— OF VOTES) PLURALITY
(SUFF.) ARD ART

EXCESSIVE TOO OVER RANK ENORM
FANCY STEEP STIFF THICK UNDUE
DEADLY DEUCED WOUNDY BURNING
EXTREME FURIOUS NIMIOUS
OVERDUE SURFEIT ABNORMAL
CRIMINAL DEVILISH ENORMOUS
HORRIBLE INSOLENT OVERMUCH
TERRIBLE TERRIFIC PLETHORIC
(PREF.) POLY SUR

EXCESSIVELY TOO SUPER DEADLY
OVERLY STRONG UNDULY PARLISH
PARLOUS PASSING PLAGUEY
WOUNDLY DEVILISH PLAGUILY
(PREF.) HYPER

EXCHANGE RAP SET CASH CAUP
CHOP CODE COPE COUP KULA MART
SELL SWAP SWOP BANDY BOARD
BOLSA CORSE SHIFT STORE TRADE
TROKE TRUCK BARTER BOURSE
CAMBIO CHANGE DICKER EXCAMB
MARKET NIFFER RESALE RIALTO
SCORSE SHOPPE TOLSEL TOLZEY
VALUTA WISSEL WRIXLE BARROOM
CAMBIUM CHAFFER COMMUTE
CONVERT DEALING PERMUTE
TRAFFIC COMMERCE TRADEOFF
TRUCKAGE
(— COURTESIES) GAM
(— IN CHECKERS) CUT SHOT
(— OF BLOWS) HANDPLAY
(— OF PRISONERS) CARTEL
(— OF SYLLABLES) ANACLASIS
(— PREMIUM) AGIO
(— SMALL TALK) CHAFFER
(— THOUGHTS) CONVERSE
(— VISITS) GAM
(DANCE —) CROSSOVER
(FAIR —) GIFFGAFF
(FOREIGN —) DEVISE
(POETICAL —) FLYTING
(POST —) CANTEEN
(TELEPHONE —) CENTRAL
(PREF.) CAMBI(O)

EXCHEQUER FISC PURSE COFFER
KHALSA CHECKER FINANCE
TREASURY

EXCIPIENT OXYMEL

EXCISE CUT TAX CROP DUTY GELD
TOLL SLASH EXCIDE EXSECT IMPOST
RESECT EXSCIND ALCABALA
RETRENCH

EXCISEMAN GAGER GAUGER
EXCISOR

EXCISION CUT ERASURE ABLATION

EXCITABLE HYPER NAPPY NERVY
NERVOUS RACKETY

EXCITATION LASH
(CONVULSIVE —) SHOCK

EXCITE HOT CITE FIRE HEAT HYPO
SEND SPUR STIR URGE WAKE WHET
WORK YERK ALARM AMOVE ANGER
CHAFE ELATE ERECT FLAME FLUSH
IMPEL PIQUE RAISE ROUSE SCALD
SPOOK AROUSE AWAKEN BOTHER
DAZZLE DECOCT FLURRY FOMENT
GROOVE IGNITE INCEND INCITE
INVOKE JANGLE KINDLE LATHER
PROMPT SALUTE TICKLE TURNON
UPREAR WECCHE AGITATE ANIMATE
COMMOVE ENCHAFE FERMENT
INCENSE INFLAME PHILTER PROVOKE
QUICKEN STARTLE WHITTLE
DISQUIET ENGENDER EXCITATE
IRRITATE
(— MIRTH) DIVERT

EXCITED UP APE GAY HOT AGOG
GAGA GYTE PINK ABOIL AGLOW
CADGY EAGER MANIC PROUD RANTY
SKEER WIRED BLEEZY ELATED
HEATED STEAMY ATHRILL FEVERED
HAYWIRE SKEERED WAKENED
AGITATED ATWITTER ELEVATED
FEVERISH FLURRIED FRENETIC
STARTLED OVERWROUGHT
(EASILY —) KITTLE
(INTENSELY —) MAD AMOK

EXCITEMENT ADO GOG BUZZ FUME
FUSS GLOW HEAT HWYL KICK RUFF
STIR TOSS UNCO FEEZE FEVER
FUROR KICKS LARRY MANIA SETUP
SPARK STOUR UNCOW FRENZY
SPLASH WARMTH FERMENT
FRISSON NERVISM TAMASHA
WIDDRIM BROUHAHA DELIRIUM
INTEREST RACKETRY
(FILLED WITH —) HECTIC
(GREAT —) FEVER
(MENTAL —) WIDDRIM
(PLEASANT —) SUSPENSE
(SHOW —) ENTHUSE
(VIOLENT —) GARE

EXCITING HOT HIGH KICKY ZINGY
HECTIC AGACANT BURNING
PARLOUS RACKETY ROUSING
EXCITANT EXCITIVE PATHETIC
STIRRING TERRIFIC FASHIONABLE
(— HORROR) DIRE DIREFUL
(ENJOYABLY —) ZINGY

EXCLAIM CRY HOWL BLURT ESCRY
SNORT CLAMOR OUTCRY BESPEAK
(— IN AMAZEMENT) OOH
(— IN PROTEST) RECLAIM

EXCLAMATION (ALSO SEE
INTERJECTION) O AH AI AY BO EH EY
HA HI HO LA LO MY OH OW SO ST YO
AHA AIE BAH BAM BOO FEN FIE FOH
GEE GIP GRR GUP HAI HAW HAY HEM

HEP HEY HIC HOY HUH NOW OCH
OFF OHO OUF OUT PAH PEW POH
POX ROT SEE SUZ TCH TCK TUT UGH
VOW WEE WOW YAH YOW AHEM
ALAS AVOY BUFF DEAR DRAT EGAD
EVOE FAST GARN GOOD HAIL HECH
HECK HIST HOLA HUFF HUNH HUSH
HYKE OONS OUGH PHEW PHOO
PHUT PIFF PISH POOH PRUT PUGH
RATS RIVO SCAT SIRS SOFT SOHO
TCHU TUSH WALY WEEK WEET WELL
WHAM WHAT WHEE WHEW WHIR
WHIT WUGG YOOP YULE ALACK
BRAVO EWHOW FAINS FANCY FAUGH
FEIGH GLORY GOODY HEIGH HELLO
HOLLA HUFFA HULLO HUMPH HUZZA
JOSSA OHONE PSHAW RIGHT SALVE
SHISH SKOAL SORRY SUGAR TEREU
WAUGH WELOO WHING WHISK
WHIST WHOOP WIRRA WOONS
CARAJO CLAMOR ENCORE HALLOO
HEYDAY HOOTAY HURRAH INDEED
OUTCRY PERFAY QUOTHA RATHER
RIGHTO SHUCKS STEADY WALKER
WHOOSH ZOUNDS CARAMBA
DOGGONE GODSAKE HOSANNA
JEEPERS JIGGERS KERCHOO
KERWHAM NICHEVO PRITHEE
RUBBISH SALAMAT TANTIVY
THUNDER WELCOME WHOOPEE
FAREWELL WAESUCKS WELLAWAY
(— OF DISGUST) AUH FIE FOH PAH
UGH AUGH AVOY PHEW PISH POOT
PSHA PUGH FAUGH FEICH FEIGH
PSHAW WELOO
(— OF DISTRESS) AI AIE HARO
HARROW
(— OF DOUBT) HUM HUMPH
(— OF IMPATIENCE) GIP PHEW
(— OF INCREDULITY) AHEM INDEED
WALKER
(— OF REPUGNANCE) UGH
(— OF SURPRISE) HA OW GIP LAW
HEIN HUNH LACK LAND LAWK LORD
ODSO BABAI HEUGH LAWKS MARRY
CRIMINE CRIMINY HEAVENS JUCKIES
GORBLIMY GRAMERCY
(— OF TRIUMPH) AH IO GRIG HEUCH
HOOCH HURRAH
(BIBLICAL —) SELAH
(IRISH —) ARRA
(PROFANE —) BAN
EXCLAMATION POINT BANG
SHOUT SCREAMER
EXCLUDE BAR SHUT SINK CLOSE
DEBAR EJECT EXPEL FENCE BANISH
DISBAR EXCEPT EXEMPT FORBAR
FORBID REJECT BLANKET DEFAULT
EXPUNGE FOREBAR FOREIGN
OUTTAKE OUTWALL REPULSE
RULEOUT SECLUDE SHUTOUT
SUSPEND OSTRACIZE
(PREF.) DIS

EXCLUDED EXEMPT FOREIGN
EXCLUDING BAR BUT LESS BARRING
EXCLUSION TABU TABOO
OSTRACISM
EXCLUSIVE ALL ONLY RARE SOLE
VERY ALONE ELECT WHOLE NARROW
SELECT CLANNISH CLIQUISH
ENTIRELY RECHERCHE
(— OF) BEFORE
EXCLUSIVELY ALL ONLY ALONE
SINGLY ENTIRELY
EXCOGITATE CONSIDER
EXCOMMUNICATE CURSE
UNCHURCH
EXCOMMUNICATION BAN CURSE
HEREM EXCISION
EX-CONVICT LAG LAGGER
EXCORIATE FLAY GALL SCORE STRIP
ABRADE SCATHE SCORCH BLISTER
LAMBASTE
EXCREMENT LEE CRAP DIRT DREG
DUNG FRASS JAKES SIEGE HOCKEY
ORDURE REFUSE VOIDING CROTTELS
COLLUVIES
(— OF EARTHWORM) CAST
(— OF FOXES) SCUMBER
(— OF HARES) CROTTELS
(— OF INSECTS) FRASS
(PL.) DEJECTA
(PREF.) COPR(O) MERDI
EXCRESCENCE NOB PIN WEN BURL
BURR GALL HORN KNOB KNOT KNUR
LUMP SCAB WART FUSEE FUZEE
KNURL THORN EXCESS HURTLE
MORULA NUBBLE PIMPLE BOLSTER
PUSTULE RATTAIL SPINACH
CARUNCLE EPITHEMA TUBERCLE
(— ON BIRD'S THROAT) WATTLE
(— ON HORSE'S FOOT) FIG TWITTER
(— ON WHALE'S HEAD) BONNET
(FLESHY —) SARCOMA
(TUBERCULOUS —) WOLF
(PREF.) GANGLI GANGLO
EXCRETA EGESTA
EXCRETE EGEST SWEAT EXCERN
SECERN DEFECATE PERSPIRE
EXCRETION SORDES ECRISIS
PERISARC
EXCRUCIATE RACK GRIND AGONIZE
TORMENT TORTURE
EXCRUCIATING GRINDING
EXCULPATE FREE CLEAR REMIT
ACQUIT EXCUSE PARDON ABSOLVE
FORGIVE JUSTIFY RELEASE PALLIATE
EXCULPATION EXCUSE
EXCURSION DIP HOP ROW DIET
RIDE SAIL SPIN TOUR TRIP ESSAY
JAUNT RANGE SALLY START TRAMP
AIRING CANTER CRUISE FLIGHT
JUNKET OUTING PASEAR RAMBLE
SASHAY VAGARY VOYAGE JOURNEY
OUTLOPE OUTRIDE OUTROAD
CAMPAIGN ESCAPADE

EXCURSIONIST TRIPPER
EXCUSABLE VENIAL
EXCUSE OUT FAIK PLEA ALIBI COLOR
GLOSS PLANE REMIT SALVO SCUSE
STORY ACQUIT ESSOIN EXEMPT
PARDON REASON REFUGE SCONCE
SECURE SUNYIE ABSOLVE APARDON
APOLOGY CONDONE ESSOIGN
EVASION EXCUSAL FORGIVE
OFFCOME PRETEXT DISPENSE
OCCASION OVERLOOK PALLIATE
PRETENCE
(CONSCIENTIOUSLY —) SCRUPLE
EXCUSS SHAKE DISCARD DISCUSS
EXECRABLE BAD CURST CURSED
DAMNED HEINOUS ACCURSED
DAMNABLE WRETCHED
EXECRATE BAN DAMN ABHOR
CURSE DETEST DEVOTE
EXECRATION CURSE ANATHEMA
MALEDICTION
EXECUTE DO ACT CUT TOP BURN
DASH FILL GIVE HANG HAVE KILL
OBEY PASS PLAY SLAY FRAME
GANCH LYNCH SCRAG YIELD DESIGN
DIRECT EFFECT FINISH FULFIL
GARROT GIBBET MANAGE ACHIEVE
GAROTTE PERFORM STRETCH
COMPLETE DISPATCH EXPEDITE
PRACTICE PRACTISE
(— BOW) WREATHE
(— POORLY) DUB
(— SUCCESSFULLY) COMPLETE
EXECUTED GIVEN
(— EXQUISITELY) CURIOUS
(— WITH CARE) ACCURATE
(CRUDELY —) DAUBY
EXECUTION GANCH TOUCH EFFECT
FACTURE GARROTE HANGING
TECHNIC CARRÍAGE GARROTTE
PRACTICE PERFORMANCE
(— BY BURNING) STAKE
(— BY DROWNING) NOYADE
(— OF WILL) FACTUM
EXECUTIONER BURRIO HEADER
TORTOR BUTCHER HANGMAN
HEADMAN LOCKMAN CARNIFEX
EXECUTOR HEADSMAN CRUCIFIER
EXECUTIVE BOSS DEAN EXEC
MAYOR WARDEN CASHIER
MANAGER PODESTA PREMIER
GOVERNOR OFFICIAL
(— OFFICER) CEO
EXECUTOR DOER AGENT ALBACEA
SECUTOR ENFORCER MINISTER
EXEGESIS ANAGOGE ANAGOGY
MIDRASH HAGGADAH
EXEMPLAR COPY TYPE MODEL
FATHER MIRROR MODULE EIDOLON
EXAMPLE PARABLE PATTERN
PARADIGM
EXEMPLARY LAUDABLE

EXEMPLIFICATION SOUL SAMPLE
CONSTAT EXAMPLE
EXEMPLIFY SAMPLE SATISFY
ENSAMPLE MODELIZE
EXEMPT EXON FREE EXEEM EXEME
FRANK SEVER SPARE EXPERT FIDATE
IMMUNE EXCLUDE RELEASE
DISPENSE EXCEPTED PRIVILEGE
(— FROM DEATH) IMMORTAL
(PREF.) IMMUNO
EXEMPTION GRACE CHARTER
FREEDOM LIBERTY SWEATER
BLOODWIT IMMUNITY IMPUNITY
EXEQUATUR PLACET
EXERCISE ACT AIR DIP PLY URE USE
BEAR HAVE DRILL ETUDE EXERT
HALMA LATIN LONGE SWEAT AIRING
BREATH CAREER EMPLOY EXERCE
LESSON MANUAL PARADE PRAXIS
PUSHUP SCHOOL AUFGABE
BREATHE DISPLAY ENHAUNT
JOGGING PROBLEM ACTIVITY
EXERTION FORENSIC PALESTRA
PRACTICE PRACTISE
(— AUTHORITY) COMMAND
(— CONTROL) BOSS PRESIDE
(— HORSE) BREEZE
(— POWER) RULE
(—S TO REDUCE WEIGHT)
SLIMNASTICS
(ACADEMIC —) PRACTICUM
(BRIEF —) THEME
(CAVALRY —) MELEE
(DEVOTIONAL —) ANGELUS
(GYMNASTIC —) PRESSUP
(MARTIAL —) BARRIERS
(MUSICAL —) ETUDE SOLFEGE
VOCALISE
(PRACTICE —) DRYRUN
(PRELIMINARY —) WARMUP
PROLUSION
(PUNISHMENT —) PENSUM
(REDUCING —S) SLIMNASTICS
(RHYTHMICAL —) MEDAU
(STRONG —) INTENSION
(SYSTEM OF —) AEROBICS
(UNWARRANTED —) STRETCH
(PL.) ALLEGRO ATHLETICS
EXERT DO PLY PUT DRAW EMIT
HUMP STIR DRIVE SPEND SWING
BESTIR EXTEND PUTOUT REVEAL
STRAIN AFFORCE ENFORCE IMPRESS
CHARETTE ENDEAVOR EXERCISE
(— A SPELL) TAKE
(— POWER) ACT BEAR
(— PRESSURE) PRESS SQUEEZE
(— TRACTION) HAUL
EXERTING (— POWER) AGENT
EXERTION DINT HEFT BURST ESSAY
LABOR NISUS TRIAL WHILE ACTION
EFFORT MOTION PINGLE STRESS
STRIFE ATTEMPT TROUBLE
ENDEAVOR EXERCISE STRUGGLE

(EXCESSIVE —) STRAIN
(STRENUOUS —) HUMP
EXFOLIATE SCALE SPALL SPAWL
EXFOLIATION FURFUR
EXHALATION AURA FUME REEK
STEAM BREATH EXPIRY MIASMA
HALITUS MALARIA FUMOSITY
MEPHITIS
EXHALE CAST EMIT REEK EXUDE
STEAM WHIFF EXPIRE BREATHE
FURNACE REFLAIR RESPIRE
EXHALATE PERSPIRE
EXHALED SFOGATO
EXHAUST DO FAG SAP BEAT BURN
COOK COWL EMIT FAIL FLAG FLOG
JADE KILL MATE SOAK TIRE TUCK
BLAST BREAK CLEAN DRAFT DRAIN
EMPTY FORDO GRUEL LEECH PETER
SHOOT SPEND SWINK WASTE
WEARY ABRADE BETOIL BOTTOM
BUGGER EMBOSS FINISH FOREDO
HARASS HATTER OVERDO TAIGLE
TUCKER BREATHE CONSUME
DEPLETE DEPRIVE DRAUGHT
EXTRACT FATIGUE OUTWEAR
SCOURGE SURREIN TRACHLE
WEAROUT DISTRESS EDUCTION
EVACUATE FORSPEND FORSWINK
FORWEARY OVERWEAR OVERSPEND
EXHAUSTED TAM BEAT DEAD DONE
DUNG GONE WEAK WORN BLOWN
EMPTY JADED SPENT STANK TIRED
BARREN BEATEN BUSHED EFFETE
GROGGY MARCID PLAYED TOILED
TRAIKY ATTAINT DRAINED EMPTIED
FORDONE FORSUNG FORWORN
TEDIOUS WHACKED WORNOUT
BANKRUPT CONSUMED FOREDONE
FOREWORN FORFAIRN FORSPENT
FOUGHTEN HARASSED OUTSPENT
OVERWORN
(— OF AIR) HIGH
EXHAUSTING ARDUOUS IRKSOME
PREYING
EXHAUSTION EXHAUST FATIGUE
SELLOUT SOOREYN DISTRESS
GONENESS HEATSTROKE
PROSTRATION
EXHAUSTIVE FULL MINUTE
THOROUGH
EXHIBIT AIR PEN FAIR HAVE SHEW
SHOW TURN WEAR CARRY SPORT
STAGE BLAZON DEMEAN EVINCE
EXPOSE OPPOSE OSTEND PARADE
REVEAL APPROVE CONCENE
DIORAMA DISPLAY EXPRESS
MONSTER PERFORM PRESENT
PRODUCE PROJECT PROPOSE
TRADUCE BOOKFAIR BRANDISH
CONCEIVE DISCLOSE DISCOVER
EMBLAZON EVIDENCE FORTHSET
MANIFEST SHOWCASE
(— ALARM) GLOFF

(— DOGS) BENCH
(— IN SNARLING) GRIN
EXHIBITION EXPO FAIR SALE SHOW
DROLL ENTRY SALON SIGHT
ANNUAL PARADE SALARY ACADEMY
DISPLAY EXHIBIT PAGEANT PENSION
PRESENT SHOWING STAGERY
EXERCISE PERFORMANCE
(— OF DOGS) BENCH
(— ON STAGE) STAGERY
(ART —) SALON
(POETICAL —) FLYTE
(PUBLIC —) SPECIES
(RIDING —) CAROUSEL
EXHIBITIONER SERVITOR
EXHIBITIONIST HAM FLASHER
HAMFATTER
EXHIBITOR SHOWER
EXHILARANT GOOFBALL
EXHILARATE AMUSE CHEER ELATE
ANIMATE ELEVATE ENLIVEN
GLADDEN
EXHILARATED RAD GLAD HAPPY
HEADY STOKED ELEVATED
SPIRITED
EXHILARATING RACY SAPID
BREEZY LIVELY
EXHILARATION GAIETY JOLLITY
GLADNESS HILARITY
EXHORT URGE WARN CHARM
ADHORT ADVISE CHARGE DEHORT
ENGAGE INCITE PREACH CAUTION
ADMONISH DISSUADE
EXHORTATION ADVICE EXHORT
HOMILY COUNSEL PROPHECY
PREACHMENT
EXHORTER HORTATOR PREACHER
EXHUME DIG DELVE UNBURY
UNTOMB UNEARTH DISINTER
EXHUMATE
EXIGENCY NEED PUSH WANT
EXIGENT URGENCY JUNCTURE
OCCASION PRESSURE
EXIGENT DIRE VITAL URGENT
CRITICAL EXACTING PRESSING
EXIGUITY PAUCITY
EXIGUOUS MEAGER MEAGRE
EXILE EXUL POOR RUIN THIN EXPEL
GALUT WREAK BANISH DEPORT
GALUTH OUTLAW SCANTY WRETCH
EXULATE GERSHOM OUTCAST
PILGRIM REFUGEE SLENDER
DIASPORA FUGITIVE OUTLAWRY
RELEGATE OSTRACIZE
(PLACE OF —) ELBA
EXILED FOREIGN FUGITIVE
EXIST AM BE IS ARE LIE COME GROW
LIVE MOVE PASS DWELL CONSIST
SUBSIST
(— IN FULL SUPPLY) FLOW
EXISTENCE ENS ESSE LIFE SEIN
BEING DASEIN ENTITY IDEATE
INESSE ESSENCE IDEATUM REALITY

ENERGEIA IDENTITY STANDING
SURVIVAL PERSONALITY
(— **AFTER DEATH**) AFTERLIFE
(**DULL** —) DEATH
(**ETERNAL** —) SAT
(**EVER-CHANGING** —) SAMSARA
SANSARA
(**FIRST** —) ORIGIN
(**IN** —) GOING AROUND EXTANT
(**INDEPENDENT** —) ASEITY PERSEITY
(**PERMANENT** —) INHERENCE
(**WAKING** —) JAGRATA
(PREF.) ONTO
EXISTENT HARD REAL ALIVE BEING
ACTUAL EXTANT EXISTING
(— **IN DIFFERENT FORMS**)
ALLOTROPIC
(**CONTINUALLY** —) STUBBORN
EXISTING GOING ACTUAL EXTANT
PRESENT EXISTENT
(— **IN NAME ONLY**) DUMMY
(SUFF.) ANT ENT
EXIT ISH DOOR GATE VENT GOING
ISSUE LEAVE EGRESS EXITUS
OUTLET OUTWAY EXITION OUTGATE
OUTPORT PASSAGE DEBOUCHE
(**HURRIED** —) BOUT
EXITE BRACT
EX LIBRIS BOOKPLATE
EXOCYCLIC IRREGULAR
EXODUS EXODY EXITUS FLIGHT
HEGIRA HEJIRA EXODIUM
EXON EXEMPT
EXONERATE FREE ALIBI CLEAR
ACQUIT EXCUSE EXONER UNLOAD
ABSOLVE RELIEVE EXCULPATE
EXOPODITE EXOPOD SQUAMA
EXORABLE PRAYABLE
EXORBITANT STEEP UNDUE
ABNORMAL
EXORCISE LAY
EXORCIST BENET
EXORDIUM PREFACE PRELUDE
EXOSKELETON CORSLET
CORSELET
EXOSPORIUM EXINE EXTINE
EXOSPERM
EXOSTOSIS POROMA SPLINT
OSSELET RINGBONE
EXOTIC ALIEN FOREIGN STRANGE
ADVENTIVE RECHERCHE
EXOTOSPORE BLAST
EXOTROPIA WALLEYE
EXPAND OPE WAX BLOW BULK FLAN
FLUE FOAM GROW HUFF OPEN
FARCE FLASH RETCH SPLAY SWELL
WIDEN DIDUCE DILATE EXTEND
INTEND SPREAD SPROUT UNFOLD
UNFURL AMPLIFY BALLOON
BLOSSOM BOLSTER BROADEN
BURGEON DEVELOP DIFFUSE
DISPAND DISPLAY DISTEND EDUCATE
ENLARGE EXPANSE EXPLAIN

INFLATE STRETCH DISPREAD
INCREASE LENGTHEN OUTREACH
(— **AS A VESSEL**) FLAN
(— **FEATHERS**) PRIDE
(— **INTO PODS**) KID
EXPANDED NOWY OPEN OVERT
DILATE PATENT SPREAD DILATED
SWOLLEN INFLATED PATULENT
PATULOUS
EXPANDER EXTENDER
EXPANDING BOSOMY
EXPANSE AREA ROOM BOSOM
BURST FIELD REACH TRACT EXTENT
LENGTH SPREAD COUNTRY STRETCH
DISTANCE EXPANSUM SEPARATE
(— **OF ICE**) SHEET
(— **OF SEA ICE**) FIELD
(— **OF SPACE**) VOID
(— **OF WATER**) OCEAN
(**BROAD** —) ACRE MAIN
(**FLAT** —) LEVEL
(**GREAT** —) MAIN
(**IMMEASURABLE — OF TIME**)
ETERNITY
(**IMMENSE** —) OCEAN
(**INDEFINITE** —) VAGUE
(**UNBROKEN** —) MASS
(**VAST** —) SEA
(**WIDE** —) BREADTH
EXPANSIBILITY ELATER
EXPANSION ALA BULB WING FLUSH
SPLAY GROWTH SPREAD ECTASIA
ECTASIS EXPANSE HASTULA
ACROSYST COQUILLE DIASTOLE
DILATION INCREASE SWELLING
(— **IN SEEDS**) ALA WING
(— **OF COBRA'S NECK**) HOOD
(— **OF DECK**) SPONSON
(— **OF LEAF-BASE**) SPUR
(— **OF RIVER**) BROAD
(— **OF ROADWAY**) LAYBY
(**FOLIOSE** —) LAMINA
(**LITURGICAL** —) EMBOLISM
EXPANSIVE FREE WIDE BROAD
GENIAL ELASTIC LIBERAL GENEROUS
SPACIOUS SWELLING
EXPATIATE DWELL DILATE EXPAND
SPREAD AMPLIFY BROADEN
DESCANT DIFFUSE ENLARGE
SATISFY
EXPATRIATE EXILE EXPAT EXPEL
BANISH OUTLAW OUTCAST
EXPATRIATION EXILE
EXPECT ASK DEEM HOPE LITE LOOK
STAY TEND TROW WAIT WEEN ABIDE
AWAIT THINK ATTEND DEMAND
INTEND LIPPEN RECKON PRESUME
REQUIRE SUPPOSE SUSPECT
CALCULATE
(— **CONFIDENTLY**) TRUST
(— **TOO MUCH**) OVERWEEN
EXPECTANT ATIP ATIPTOE CHARGED
HOPEFUL INCHOATE

EXPECTANTLY AGOG TIPTOE
EXPECTATION HOPE VIEW WAIT
WEEN TRUST EXPECT FUTURE
ESPEIRE OPINION SUPPOSE
THOUGHT WEENING PROSPECT
(CONFIDENT —) TRUST
EXPECTED DUE NATURAL
SUPPOSED
EXPECTORANT CINEOL STORAX
CINEOLE EMETINE AMMONIAC
CREOSOTE GUAIACOL TEREBENE
EXPECTORATE SPIT
EXPECTORATION EMPTYSIS
EXPEDIENCE ARTIFICE
EXPEDIENT FIT WISE ATAJO CRAFT
DODGE JOKER KNACK SALVO SHIFT
DEVICE RESORT STRING DODGERY
POLITIC STOPGAP ARTIFICE
RESOURCE DESIRABLE MAKESHIFT
EXPEDITATE LAW
EXPEDITATION LAWING
EXPEDITE HIE EASY FREE HURRY
SPEED EXPEDE GREASE HASTEN
QUICKEN DISPATCH
EXPEDITION CAMP FARE PLOY
ROAD TREK DRAVE HASTE HURRY
RANGE SCOUT TRADE SAFARI
VOYAGE CARAVAN CRUSADE
ENTRADA JOURNEY OUTLOPE
SERVICE WARFARE WARPATH
COMMANDO HEADHUNT PROGRESS
(FISHING —) DRAVE
(HUNTING) SAFARI
(MILITARY —) HARKA CRUSADE
HOSTING JOURNEY WARPATH
EXPEDITIOUS FAST HASTY QUICK
RAPID READY SHORT PROMPT
SPEEDY
EXPEL CAN OUT USH BLOW BOLT
DRUM DUMP FIRE OUST VOID WARP
AVOID CHASE CHECK DEPEL EJECT
ERUPT EVICT EXILE KNOCK SPURT
BANISH BOUNCE DEBOUT DEPORT
DEVOID DISBAR DISOWN OUTPUT
OUTRAY REFUSE ABANDON
EXCLUDE EXPULSE EXTRUDE
OBTRUDE SCRATCH SECLUDE
SUSPEND DISLODGE DISPLACE
EVACUATE FORJUDGE
(— AIR) COUGH
(— FROM MEMBERSHIP) HAMMER
(— GAS) BELCH
(— SUDDENLY) SLIRT
(PREF.) DIS
EXPEND USE LEND SPEND SPORT
WASTE WREAK DEFRAY IMPEND
OCCUPY OUTLAY PONDER CONSUME
DISPEND EROGATE EXHAUST
OVERUSE DISBURSE SQUANDER
EXPENDITURE COST MISE OUTGO
PENSE CHARGE OUTLAY EXPENSE
OUTFLOW PENSION SPENDING
(— OF ENERGY) EFFORT

EXPENSE EX COST GAFF LOSS
BATTA PRICE SUMPT CHARGE
DAMAGE GERSUM ONCOST OUTLAY
OUTSET AVERAGE OVERHEAD
SUMPTURE
(— OF CARRYING) CARRIAGE
(— OF TREAT) SAM
(PL.) BATTA COSTS MISES
EXPENSIVE DEAR HIGH SALT PRICY
STEEP STIFF COSTLY LAVISH PRICEY
APICIAN LIBERAL THRIFTY
(— IN DIET) APICIAN
EXPERIENCE SEE TRY FEEL FIND
GUST HAVE HENT HOLD KNOW LIVE
TEST ASSAY EVENT PROOF PROVE
SKILL TASTE TRIAL USAGE BEHOLD
EXPERT FRAIST ORDEAL SAMPLE
SUFFER APPROVE CALVARY
CONTACT FEELING FURNACE
KNOWING REALIZE SUSTAIN
UNDERGO ESCAPADE
(— GOOD OR ILL FORTUNE) SPEED
(— OF INTENSE SUFFERING)
CALVARY
(— WITH BITTERNESS) BEAR
(CALAMITOUS —) ADVERSITY
(DRUG —) TRIP
(ENJOYABLE —) GROOVE
(EXCITING —) TRIP
(FIRST —) TIROCINIUM
(HALLUCINATORY —) TRIP FREAKOUT
(HORRIFYING —) NIGHTMARE
(HUMILIATING) PRATFALL
(IRRITATING —) RUB
(ORDINARY —) USE
(PAINFUL —) FIT
(PARTIAL —) GUST
(TASTE —) GUST
(TEDIOUS —) DRAG
(TRYING —) ORDEAL
(UNPLEASANT —) BUMMER MISERY
(VISIONARY —) PHANTOM
(WARNING —) LESSON
EXPERIENCED HAD MET OLD SEEN
USED SALTY EXPERT SALTED
TRADED ANCIENT PRACTIC THRIVEN
VETERAN WEIGHED SEASONED
(— INTENSIVELY) ACUTE
(ACTUALLY —) SPECIOUS
EXPERIENTIAL EMPIRIC
EXPERIMENT SHY TRY TEST ASSAY
ESSAY TRIAL ATTEMPT CONTROL
(PREF.) EMPIRICO EMPIRIO
EXPERIMENTAL SAMPLE
(NOT —) STANDARD
EXPERT ACE DAB PRO DEFT FULL
GOOD GURU PERT ADEPT CRACK
FLASH MAVEN MAVIN READY SHARP
SWELL ADROIT ARTIST CLEVER
FACILE HABILE KAHUNA MASTER
MAYVIN PANDIT PERTLY QUAINT
SUBTLE WIZARD ARTISTE ATTACHE
CAPABLE DABSTER MEISTER

PERFECT PERITUS SKILLED
DEXTROUS GAINSOME SKILLFUL
SPEEDFUL VIRTUOSO PROFESSED
PROFICIENT
(— IN JEWISH LAW) DAYAN
(— LEVEL IN JUDO) DAN
(— ON DRIVING LOGS) LAKER
(BANK —) SHROFF
(GREAT —) ONER
(SCIENTIFIC —) BOFFIN
(PL.) PERITI
(SUFF.) ICIAN
EXPERTISE MOXIE
EXPERTNESS SAVVY SKILL FACILITY
HABILITY
EXPIATE ABY SKUG ATONE AVERT
ASSOIL RANSOM
EXPIATORY PIACULAR
EXPIRATION END DEATH BREATH
EFFLUX ELAPSE EXPIRE EXPIRY
(SPASMODIC —) SNEEZE
EXPIRE DIE END EMIT FALL EXPEL
GHOST LAPSE ELAPSE EXHALE
INLAIK OUTRUN PERISH RUNOUT
EXPIRED UP DEAD EXPIATE
EXPIRING DYING
EXPIRY ISH CLOSE DEATH EFFLUX
EXPLAIN OPEN REDE SAVE SCAN
UNDO WISE AREAD AREED CLEAR
GLOSS GLOZE PLANE RECHE SOLVE
SPEED TOUCH DEFINE EXPAND
EXPLAT EXPONE REMENE RIDDLE
UNFOLD ABSOLVE ACCOUNT
AMPLIFY CLARIFY COMMENT
CONTRUE DECLARE DEVELOP
DISCUSS EXHIBIT EXPOUND JUSTIFY
RESOLVE CONSTRUE DESCRIBE
MANIFEST SIMPLIFY UNPLIGHT
UNWONDER
(— BY HYPOTHESIS) SALVE
EXPLAINER EXPONENT
EXPLAINING EXPONENT
EXPLANATION KEY NOTE FARSE
GLOSS SALVE SALVO ANSWER
CAVEAT ACCOUNT APOLOGY
ADDENDUM EXEGESIS INNUENDO
NOTATION SOLUTION
(PRELIMINARY —) PREFACE
EXPLETIVE ACH AND GEE BOSH
EGAD GOSH OATH BEGAD MODAL
BEHEAR GOSH SDEATH TUNKET DAMMISH
MORBLEU GOODYEAR GRACIOUS
EXPLICATE OPEN CLEAR EXPAND
UNFOLD ACCOUNT EXPLAIN
EXPLICATION CRIB ANALYSIS
EXPLICIT OPEN CLEAR EXACT FIXED
PLAIN EXPRESS PRECISE ABSOLUTE
DEFINITE IMPLICIT POSITIVE
PUNCTUAL SPECIFIC
EXPLICITLY BARELY DIRECT
FORMALLY
EXPLODE POP BLOW FIRE BELCH
BLAST BURST CRUMP ERUPT GOOFF

PLUFF SHOOT SQUIB SPRING
BACKFIRE DETONATE DISPLODE
EXPLOIT ACT USE DEED FEAT GEST
JEST MILK WORK GESTE GOUGE
STUNT PERFORM SUCCESS
CHIVALRY PARERGON PROPERTY
(— FINANCIALLY) RIPOFF
(— SUCCESSFULLY) PARLAY
EXPLOITATION RIPOFF
EXPLOITER KULAK
EXPLORATION SPY PROBE SEARCH
EXPLORE
(— OF CAVES) SPELEOLOGY
EXPLORATORY FRONTIER
PROBATIVE PROBATORY
EXPLORE DO DIP MAP SPY DIVE
DRAG FEEL VIEW CHART COAST
DELVE RANGE SCOUT SOUND
SEARCH EXAMINE PALPATE
BOTANIZE DISCOVER
(— CAVES) SPELUNK
(— FOR MINERALS) PROSPECT
EXPLORER CAVEMAN PIONEER
COLUMBUS
AMERICAN BOYD BYRD COOK GRAY
HALL KANE LONG PIKE BEEBE CLARK
FIALA GOULD HAYES JAMES LEWIS
MUSIL NILES PEARY RONNE AKELEY
ASHLEY BRYANT CARVER CATLIN
COLTER DELONG EKLUND GIMBEL
GREELY HENSON HERVEY LUMMIS
RAINEY WILKES AGASSIZ ANDREWS
BALCHEN BALDWIN BURNHAM
FREMONT POULTER STANLEY
VERRILL WELLMAN WORKMAN
BRAINARD BRIDGMAN LOCKWOOD
MELVILLE SCHWATKA ELLSWORTH
MACMILLAN DANENHOWER
HUNTINGTON HALLIBURTON
AUSTRALIAN WILLS MAWSON
STUART FORREST KENNEDY
LINDSAY WILKINS BERNACCHI
AUSTRIAN HUGEL PAYER GLASER
BAUMANN PAULITSCHKE
BELGIAN GERLACHE
CANADIAN MACKAY JOLLIET
SIMPSON BARTLETT PALLISER
IBERVILLE VINCENNES STEFANSSON
COLOMBIAN REYES
DANISH BOCK HOLM KOCH
FREUCHEN MIKKELSEN RAS
MUSSEN
DUTCH TASMAN NIEUWENHUIS
ENGLISH BACK BASS BENT BYNG
COOK EYRE BAKER BATES BRUCE
DAVYS EVANS FUCHS GRANT OATES
PARRY SCOTT SPEKE STURT YOUNG
BAILEY BURTON CONDER GROGAN
HEARNE HOWITT LANDER MAWSON
OSBORN PHILBY SABINE WILSON
CAMERON CHESNEY DAMPIER
DEWINDT GREGORY HOLDICH
JACKSON WEDDELL WHYMPER

WICKHAM FLINDERS FRANKLIN GRENFELL JOHNSTON SCORESBY ALEXANDER VANCOUVER WARBURTON INGLEFIELD MCCLINTOCK SCHOMBURGK SHACKLETON LIVINGSTONE YOUNGHUSBAND **FRENCH** BONIN MONTS BINGER BRAZZA CALLIE DULUTH GENTIL HAARDT ABBADIE CARTIER CRAMPEL CREVAUX FOUREAU GARNIER LASALLE NICOLET BONVALOT COUDREAU HENNEPIN MARCHAND RADISSON CAILLIAUD CHAMPLAIN IBERVILLE MARQUETTE VINCENNES **GERMAN** EMIN LENZ BARTH PFEIL POGGE REISS VOGEL DECKEN FLEGEL JUNKER PETERS ROHLFS FISCHER NEUWIED NIEBUHR OVERWEG WEGENER DENHARDT FILCHNER FRANCOIS HUMBOLDT KOLDEWEY KOTZEBUE WISSMANN FEDERMANN GUSSFELDT WEYPRECHT LEICHHARDT SCHLAGINTWEIT **ICELANDIC** ERICSON **IRISH** BURKE SHACKLETON **ITALIAN** ZENO CABOT CAGNI GESSI CASATI NOBILE ABRUZZI BELZONI CODAZZI FILIPPI PIAGGIA ALBERTIS ANTINORI BECCARIA COLUMBUS CADAMOSTO VERRAZANO SCHIAPARELLI **NEW ZEALAND** HAAST HILLARY **NORWEGIAN** ASTRUP NANSEN WISTING AMUNDSEN JOHANSEN SVERDRUP HEYERDAHL JOHANNESEN BORCHGREVINK **PORTUGUESE** CABRAL DAGAMA CABRILLO COVILHAO MAGELLAN FERNANDES **RUSSIAN** TOLL PAPANIN POTANIN WRANGEL PRZHEVALSKI BELLINGSHAUSEN **SCOTTISH** RAE PARK ROSS BRUCE LAING LAIRD BAIKIE CADELL FORBES THOMSON MITCHELL MACKENZIE CLAPPERTON LIVINGSTONE **SPANISH** ANZA OJEDA AYLLON BALBOA CABEZA CORTES DESOTO AGUIRRE ALARCON CORDOBA MENDOZA PIZARRO BASTIDAS CARDENAS CORONADO GRIJALVA ORELLANA VIZCAINO ESCALANTE ESTAVANICO **SWEDISH** HEDIN ANDREE NATHORST PALANDER ANDERSSON NORDENSKJOLD **SWISS** BODMER PICCARD MUNZINGER **EXPLOSION** POP BANG BLOW BLAST BURST CRUMP SALVO BLOWUP BOUNCE REPORT PLOSION INCIDENT OUTBURST (**FUEL** —) BACKFIRE (**SLIGHT** —) PLUFF **EXPLOSIVE** EGG TNT MINE AMVIS AMATOL JOVITE LIMPET POWDER TETRYL TONITE TORPEX TOUCHY TRITON ABELITE AMMONAL AZOTINE DUNNITE LIGNOSE LYDDITE PLOSIVE PRIMING PUDDING SHIMOSE THORITE AMMONITE CHEDDITE DYNAMITE ECRASITE ERUPTIVE GELATINE MAXIMITE MELINITE PYROLITE ROBURITE SABULITE SAXONITE SECURITE VOLATILE RACKAROCK SAMSONITE (— **COMPOUND**) TNT (**CHARGE OF** —) TULIP RESPONDER (**NOT** —) SOFT **EXPONENT** INDEX POWER (**SUFF.**) ICIAN **EXPORT** OUTCARRY (— **HERRING**) KLONDIKE **EXPORTATION** EXPORT OUTPORT **EXPOSE** AIR BARE GIVE OPEN RISK SHOW STRIP BEWRAY DEBUNK DETECT EXPONE GIBBET OBJECT OPPOSE REVEAL UNHUSK UNMASK DISPLAY EXHIBIT EXPOUND PILLORY PROPINE PUBLISH SUBJECT UNCOVER UNEARTH UNTRUSS BRANDISH DISCLOSE DISCOVER MUCKRAKE RIDICULE SATIRIZE UNCLOTHE UNSHROUD (— **FOR BLEACHING**) CROFT (— **INDECENTLY**) FLASH (— **ORE**) HUSH (— **PLAYING CARD**) BURN (— **SELF TO**) WAGE (— **SUDDENLY**) FLASH (— **TO AIR**) AERATE (— **TO ATTENTION**) PARADE (— **TO DANGER**) JUMP COMMIT SUBMIT (— **TO FUMES**) FUMIGATE (— **TO HAZARD**) RISK (— **TO HEAT**) AIR (— **TO INFAMY**) GIBBET (— **TO MOISTURE**) RET (— **TO RADIATION**) PUMP (— **TO SCORN**) PILLORY (— **TO SULFUR DIOXIDE**) STOVE (— **TO SUN**) INSOLATE SOLARIZE (— **TO SUN AND AIR**) FIELD **EXPOSED** AIRY BARE OPEN BLEAK LIABLE PUBLIC UNSAFE SUBJECT VEILLESS (— **TO**) AGAINST (— **TO DANGER**) INSECURE **EXPOSITION** EXPO FAIR GECK SHOW ZEND TRACT APERCU EXPOSE METHOD SURVEY ACCOUNT EXPOSAL MIDRASH ANALYSIS

EXEGESIS EXPOSURE EXTHESIS
HAGGADAH TREATISE
(— OF FEAST) SYNAXARY
EXPOSITORY EXEGETIC
EXPOSTULATE ARGUE OBJECT
DISCUSS EXAMINE PROTEST
EXPOSTULATION PROTEST
EXPOSURE ASPECT EXPOSE
EXPOSAL FLASHING FRONTAGE
PROSPECT
(— OF CARDS) SPREAD
(— OF KING) CHECK
(— TO AIR) AERATE AIRING
(BODY —) FLASH
(PHOTOGRAPHIC —) SHOT
(PUBLIC —) NOTORIETY
EXPOUND OPEN REDE UNDO GLOZE
SENSE TREAT DEFINE EXPONE
EXPOSE COMMENT DEVELOP
DISCUSS EXPLAIN EXPOSIT EXPRESS
CONSTRUE SIMPLIFY PHILOSOPHIZE
(— SCRIPTURES) PROPHESY
EXPOUNDER MUFTI MULLAH
SCRIBE EXPRESS EXPONENT
HERMETIC
(— OF THEORY) ALFAQUI
PHILOSOPHER
EXPRESS AIR BID PUT SAY CAST
EMIT FAST PASS POST VENT COUCH
EMOTE FRAME OPINE SPEAK STATE
UTTER VOICE WIELD BROACH
DEMEAN DENOTE DIRECT EVINCE
IMPORT PHRASE ABREACT BREATHE
DECLARE DICTATE EXPOUND
EXTREME TESTIFY DEFINITE
DESCRIBE DISPATCH EXPLICIT
INTIMATE MANIFEST
(— APPROVAL) AGREE ACCEDE
APPLAUD
(— AS LANGUAGE) LAY
(— AT LENGTH) EXPAND
(— A VIEW) OPINE
(— BY GESTURE) BECK
(— BY LAUGHTER) LAUGH
(— CONCERN) CLUCK
(— DISAPPROVAL) BOO CHIDE DECRY
GROAN CATCALL
(— DISDAIN) TUT
(— EFFERVESCENTLY) CHORTLE
(— FOLLY) EXPAND
(— GRATITUDE) THANK AGGRATE
(— GRIEF) DEPLORE
(— INDIRECTLY) IMPLY
(— IN OTHER WORDS) REDUCE
PARAPHRASE
(— IN WORDS) SAY DRAW SPEAK
PHRASE
(— NUMERICALLY) EVALUATE
(— ONE'S FEELINGS) FLOW
(— SORROW) LAMENT COMPLAIN
(— WILLINGNESS) CONSENT
(NOT AN —) LOCAL

EXPRESSION DIT HIT SAY CAST
EUGE FACE FORM MIEN POSE SHOW
SIGN TERM VULT WORD ADIEU GLIFF
IDIOM SNEER TOKEN VOICE BYWORD
DILOGY DIVERB EFFECT FACIES
ORACLE PHRASE SPEECH SYMBOL
COMMENT DESCANT EPITHET
EXPRESS GRIMACE ALLEGORY
AUSDRUCK DANICISM FELICITY
LACONISM MONOMIAL
(— IN FEW WORDS) BREVITY
(— OF ANNOYANCE) SOH
(— OF APPROVAL) EUGE PLACET
(— OF ASSENT) CONTENT
(— OF BEAUTY) ART
(— OF CHOICE) VOTE
(— OF CONTEMPT) COBLOAF
(— OF DELIGHT) WHEE
(— OF DISPLEASURE) FROWN
(— OF DISTASTE) FACE
(— OF HOMAGE) OVATION
(— OF JOY) GREETING
(— OF OPINION) EDITORIAL
(— OF RESPECT) DUTY
(— OF SADNESS) SHADE
(— OF SCORN) GECK
(— OF SINGLE IDEA) RHEME
(APT —) FELICITY
(CHEMICAL —) EQUATION
(COMMONPLACE —) BROMIDE
(CORRECT —) SUMPSIMUS
(CURT —) LACONIC
(FACIAL —) GRIN CHEER SCOWL
SMILE
(HACKNEYED —) CLICHE
(HIGH-FLOWN —) EUPHUISM
(INCONGRUOUS —) BULL
(LOUD —) CLAMOR
(MATHEMATICAL —) INDEX SERIES
BINOMIAL EQUATION FUNCTION
INTEGRAL
(MOCKING —) SCOFF
(MOMENTARY —) SHADE
(PECULIAR —) IDIOM
(PET —) CANT
(PUERILE —) BOYISM
(SARCASTIC —) GIBE JIBE
(SERIOUS —) EARNEST
(SINCERE —) CANDOR
(SYMBOLIC —) FORMULA
(TENDER —) LANGUISH
(TRITE —) CLICHE
(UNRESTRAINED —) EFFUSION
(VERBAL —) LETTER
(VOCAL —) TONE
(VULGAR —) SOLECISM
(WISE —) ORACLE
(SUFF.) LOG(ER)(IA)(IAN)(IC)(ICAL)
(IST)(UE)(Y)
EXPRESSIONLESS BLANK STONY
GLASSY LEADEN SODDEN VACANT
WOODEN TONELESS

EXPRESSIVE POETIC TONGUED
ELOQUENT EMPHATIC SPEAKING
EXPRESSIVENESS DICTION
DELICACY TOURNURE ELOQUENCE
EXPRESSLY NAMELY EXPRESS
PRESSLY FORMALLY
EXPRESSWAY FREEWAY SPEEDWAY
EXPROBATE CENSURE UPBRAID
EXPULSION EXILE BOUNCE
OUSTER BANNIMUS EJECTION
EXCISION
(— OF SPORES) ABJECTION
EXPUNGE BLOT DELE ERASE SLASH
CANCEL DELETE EFFACE EXCISE
SCRAPE DESTROY SCRATCH
DISPUNGE
EXPURGATE GELD PURGE
CASTRATE
EXPURGATION BOWDLERISM
EXQUISITE FOP DUDE FINE NICE
PERT PINK RARE DANDY EXACT
CHOICE DAINTY CAREFUL ELEGANT
GEMLIKE PERFECT REFINED
AFFECTED DELICATE ETHEREAL
MACARONI RECHERCHE
EXQUISITELY CHOICELY
EXSCIND CUT SEVER EXCISE
EXTANT ALIVE BEING LIVING VISIBLE
EXISTING MANIFEST
(PREF.) NEO
EXTEMPORE SUDDEN OFFHAND
IMPROVISO
EXTEMPORIZE ADLIB
EXTEND GO EKE LIE RUN BEAR BUSH
COME DATE DRAW GROW LAST
OPEN PASS PUSH RISE ROLL SPAN
SPIN BREDE BULGE CARRY COVER
FARCE REACH RENEW RETCH SEIZE
SHOOT STENT VERGE WIDEN
AMOUNT DEEPEN DEPLOY DILATE
EXPAND INTEND OUTLIE SPREAD
SPRING STRAIN STREAK THRUST
TRENCH AMPLIFY BROADEN DIFFUSE
DISPLAY DISTEND ENLARGE
OVERLAP OVERRUN PORRECT
PORTEND PRODUCE PROFFER
PROJECT PROLONG PROMOTE
PROTEND RADIATE STRETCH
CONTINUE ELONGATE INCREASE
LENGTHEN OUTREACH PROROGUE
PROTRACT PROTRUDE OUTSPREAD
PROPAGATE OUTSTRETCH
(— ACTIVITIES) BRANCH
(— AROUND) GIRTH
(— HAND) RAX
(— IN SPACE) DURE
(— IRREGULARLY) TRAIL
(— OVER) SPAN COVER CROSS
CONTAIN OVERLAP OVERRIDE
(— SAIL) SHEET
(— THE FRONT) DEPLOY
(— TO) LINE REACH

EXTENDED FAT LONG OPEN BROAD
EXTENT SPREAD EXTENSE LENGTHY
PROLATE SPLAYED EXPANDED
INTENDED
(PREF.) MEG(A) MEGAL(O)
EXTENDER INERT FILLER LIGNIN
EXTENDING BROAD
(— OVER) ASTRIDE
EXTENSION ARM EKE ELL AREA
CAPE LIMB SCOPE POCKET SATTVA
SPHERE SPREAD BREADTH STRETCH
ADDENDUM ADDITION DURATION
INCREASE PROTENSE
(— OF BUILDING MATERIAL) APRON
(— OF CREDIT) DATING
(— OF MINERAL VEIN) FLAT
(— OF RACE TRACK) CHUTE SHUTE
(— OF SHELL) LAPPET
(— OF TIME) RESPITE
(— OF WAGON FRAME) THRIPPLE
(BALLET —) BATTEMENT
EXTENSIVE HUGE VAST WIDE
AMPLE BROAD LARGE EXTENSE
IMMENSE EXPANDED FARFLUNG
INFINITE SPACIOUS SWEEPING
EXTENT DUE RUN TAX AREA BODY
BULK DEAL GAGE LEVY PASS SIZE
WRIT AMBIT DEPTH FIELD GAUGE
LIMIT RANGE REACH SCOPE SPACE
STENT SWEEP TRACK AMOUNT
ASSIZE ATTACK DEGREE LENGTH
SPREAD STREEK ACREAGE ASSAULT
BREADTH COMPASS CONTENT
EXPANSE PURVIEW SEIZURE
STRETCH VARIETY DISTANCE
INCREASE LATITUDE OUTREACH
QUANTITY STRAIGHT
(— OF FRONT) FRONTAGE
(— OF JURISDICTION) VERGE
(— OF LAND) HEIGHT CONTINENT
(— OF SPACE) ROOM
(— OF TIME) SPACE
(BROAD —) SWEEP MAGNITUDE
(GREATEST —) MAX MAXIMUM
(RELATIVE —) SCALE
(SOME —) BIT
(UNLIMITED —) INFINITY
(UTMOST —) FULL
(VAST —) DEEP
(VERTICAL —) ALTITUDE
EXTENTION
(— OF LETTER) TAIL
EXTENUATE THIN GLOZE MINCE
EXCUSE LESSEN SOOTHE WEAKEN
DIMINISH PALLIATE
EXTERIOR CRUST ECTAD ECTAL
OUTER SHELL EXTERN OUTSIDE
OUTWARD SURFACE EXOTERIC
EXTERNAL OUTLYING
(PREF.) OUT
EXTERMINATE WIPE EXPEL
UPROOT ABOLISH DESTROY

EXTERMINATION (RACIAL —)
GENOCIDE
EXTERNAL OUT OUTER EXTERN
OUTSIDE OUTWARD STRANGE
EXOTERIC EXTERIOR INCIDENT
PHYSICAL PERIPHERAL
(PREF.) ECT(O) OUT
EXTERNALITY OUTNESS
EXTERNALIZE OBJECTIFY
EXTERNALLY OUTWARD WITHOUT
EXTINCT DEAD BYGONE DEFUNCT
QUENCHED
(— MAN) KANJERA
(PREF.) NECR(O)
EXTINCTION DOOM FINE DEATH
EXPIRY DELETION
EXTINGUISH OUT DAMP DOUT
REDD DINCH ANNUL CHOKE CRUSH
DINCH DOUSE DOWSE DROWN
QUELL REPEL SLAKE SNUFF STAMP
ASLAKE QUENCH STANCH STIFLE
ABOLISH BLANKET DESTROY
ECLIPSE EXPIATE EXTINCT OBSCURE
OPPRESS SLOCKEN STAUNCH
SUPPRESS
(— BY CRUSHING) DINCH
(— CIGARETTE) SNUB
EXTINGUISHED OUT DEAD
EXTINCT
EXTINGUISHER DOUTER
STAUNCH BACKPACK QUENCHER
STANCHER
EXTIRPATE DELE ROOT STUB ERASE
EXPEL STAMP STOCK EXCISE EXTIRP
UPROOT DESTROY EXSCIND
OUTROOT SUPPLANT
EXTIRPATION ROOTAGE EXCISION
EXTOL CRY FETE HYMN LAUD BLESS
CRACK EXALT KUDOS ROOSE SPEAK
EXTOLL PRAISE ADVANCE APPLAUD
COLLAUD COMMEND ELEVATE
ENHANCE GLORIFY MAGNIFY
RESOUND UPRAISE EMBLAZON
EULOGIZE PROCLAIM
EXTOLMENT PRECONY
EXTORT MILK PEEL PILL RAMP BLEED
BRIBE EDUCE EXACT FORCE PINCH
WREST WRING COMPEL ELICIT
SPONGE STRAIN WRENCH WRITHE
EXTRACT OUTWREST
EXTORTION CHOUT GOUGE EXTORT
HOLDUP SCOTAL BRIBERY PILLAGE
CHANTAGE EXACTION RAPACITY
SHAKEDOWN
EXTORTIONATE HARD CRIMINAL
GRINDING
EXTORTIONER BRIBER POLLER
SHAVER BLEEDER VAMPIRE
EXTORTIONIST POLLER
EXTRA ODD GASH MORE ORRA OVER
PLUS ADDED SPARE SPECIAL
SURPLUS SUPERIOR LAGNIAPPE
(PREF.) HYPER SUPER

EXTRACT DIG PRY CITE COPY DRAW
KINO KOLA MILK PULL SOAK ANIMA
BLEED CUTCH DRAFT EDUCE ELUTE
EXACT KUTCH KYPOO QUOTE RENES
RUSOT SCRAP STEEP WRING CORTIN
CURARE DECOCT DEDUCE DERIVE
DEWTRY DISTIL ELICIT ELIXIR EVULSE
EXTORT GOBBET GUACIN MULIUM
OVARIN REMOVE RENDER RUSWUT
TRIPOS UZARON ABORTIN AMALTAS
ARCANUM CATECHU DESCENT
DISTILL DRAUGHT ERGOTIN
ESSENCE ESTREAT EXCERPT
EXHAUST FUMARIA INTRAIT
LIMBECK MONESIA PASSEWA
SUMMARY VANILLA ACETRACT
AMBRETTE GINGERIN HYPERNIC
INFUSION LICORICE PERICOPE
SEPARATE TIKITIKI TINCTURE
WITHDRAW
(— BY BOILING) DECOCT ELIXATE
(— BY DIGGING) GRUB
(— DATA FROM COMPUTER) READ
(— FORCIBLY) MULCT EVULSE
(— FROM ACACIA) KATH CASHOO
CATECHU
(— FROM BERBERIS) RUSOT RUSWUT
(— OF BARK) EUONYMIN
(— OF GINGER) JAKE JAKEY
(— ORE) STOPE
(— WITH LIQUID) LEACH
(ALOE —) ORCIN ORCINOL
(TANNING —) AMALTAS
EXTRACTION KIN BIRTH BROOD
STOCK ORIGIN DESCENT EDITION
ESSENCE EXTRACT EXTREAT
BREEDING TINCTURE
(— OF ROOTS) EVOLUTION
(— OF STEAM) BLEEDING
EXTRACTIVE AGAR BANG BHANG
AMAROID CARAGEEN
EXTRACTOR JUICER
EXTRADITE BANISH
EXTRANEOUS ALIEN OUTER EXOTIC
FOREIGN OUTLYING SPURIOUS
EXTRAORDINARILY BYOUS
EXTRAORDINARY ODD FREM
ONCO RARE BYOUS ENORM SMASH
DAMNED EXEMPT MIGHTY RAGING
SIGNAL AWESOME CORKING
CURIOUS HUMMING NOTABLE
SPECIAL STRANGE UNUSUAL
ABNORMAL ESPECIAL EXIMIOUS
FORINSEC FRABJOUS SINGULAR
SMASHING UNCOMMON
PHENOMINAL PRODIGIOUS
EXTRARETINAL PAROPTIC
EXTRATERRESTRIAL ALIEN
EXTRAVAGANCE CAMP FRILL
PRIDE WASTE LUXURY EXPENSE
RAMPANCY SQUANDER UNTHRIFT
WILDNESS PROFUSION SATURNALIA
(MENTAL —) MADNESS

EXTRAVAGANT MAD HIGH LUSH
WILD FANCY FISHY FOLLE LARGE
OUTRE COSTLY GOTHIC HEROIC
LAVISH SHRILL WANTON BAROQUE
BIZARRE COSTLEW FANATIC
FLAMING FURIOUS NIMIOUS
PROFUSE RAMPANT VAGRANT
INSOLENT PRODIGAL RECKLESS
ROMANTIC UNTHRIFT WANDERER
WASTEFUL BOMBASTIC PROFLIGATE
EXTRAVAGANTLY LARGE
EXTRAVAGANZA FEERIE
EXTRAVAGATION VIBEX
EXTRAVASATION EFFUSION
EXTREME NTH BLUE DEEP DIRE HIGH
LAST RANK SORE VILE ACUTE BLACK
CLOSE CRUEL DENSE DIZZY FINAL
GREAT LIMIT PITCH STEEP ULTRA
UNDUE UTTER ARDENT ARRANT
BRAZEN DEADLY FAROUT FIERCE
HEROIC LENGTH MORTAL SAVAGE
SEVERE STRONG UTMOST WOUNDY
ABYSMAL DRASTIC FEARFUL
FORWARD FRANTIC HOWLING
INTENSE OUTWARD PROFUSE
RADICAL SURFEIT VICIOUS VIOLENT
ALMIGHTY DEVILISH DREADFUL
EGYPTIAN ENORMOUS FABULOUS
FARTHEST GREATEST MERCIFUL
SPENDFUL TERRIBLE TERRIFIC
ULTIMATE EXQUISITE
(NOT —) SWEET
(TO THE —) INSPADES
(PL.) PASO
(PREF.) ACR(O) ARCH
EXTREMELY SO BIG DOG TOO WAY
BONE DEAD EVER FULL MAIN RANK
SELI THAT UNCO VERY AWFUL
BLACK BULLY BYOUS CRAZY CRUEL
EXTRA HEAPS RIGHT SELLE SOWAN
SUPER BITTER DAMNED DEADLY
DEUCED HIGHLY MIGHTY NATION
POISON SORELY SURELY UNCOLY
APLENTY AWFULLY BOILING
CRUELLY EXTREME GALLOWS
HOPPING INNERLY SOPPING STAVING
ALMIGHTY ENORMOUS MORTALLY
PRECIOUS PROPERLY
EXTREMISM JACOBINISM
EXTREMIST CRAZY ULTRA JACOBIN
RADICAL SANSCULOTTE
EXTREMITY END TIP HEAD NEED
PUSH TAIL CLOSE LIMIT SHIFT START
VERGE BORDER FINGER EXIGENT
EXTREME ACROSTIC ALTITUDE
DISASTER JUNCTURE OUTRANCE
TERMINAL
(— OF MOON) HORN
(— OF TENDRIL) HOLDFAST
(— OF TOOTH ROOT) APEX
(HORSE'S —) POINT
(REMOTEST —) CORNER
(PREF.) ACR(O)

EXTRICATE FREE HELP WIND CLEAR
LOOSE RESCUE SQUIRM OUTWIND
EXPEDITE LIBERATE UNTANGLE
(— ONESELF) WANGLE
EXTRINSIC ALIEN EVERY FOREIGN
OUTWARD EXTERNAL OUTLYING
EXTROVERT SYNTONIC
EXTRUDE BEAR SPEW EJECT EXPEL
SHOOT PROJECT PROTRUDE
EXUBERANCE BEANS PRICE
EXCESS LUXURY PLENTY ABANDON
LAUGHTER OVERFLOW RAMPANCY
EXUBERANT RANK BOUNCY FEISTY
LAVISH COPIOUS FERTILE GLOWING
PROFUSE RAMPANT EFFUSIVE
EXUDATE GUM SPEW SPUE MANNA
DIKAMALI GUAIACUM HONEYDEW
SARCOCOL
EXUDATION DIP GUM LAC SAP TAR
BALM KINO COPAL PITCH RESIN
ROSIN SUDOR ULMIN CHARAS
MASTIC SANIES CHURRUS GALIPOT
MOCHRAS SPEWING BLEEDING
EXUDENCE LAITANCE MOISTURE
EXUDE GUM DRIP EMIT OOZE REEK
SPEW BLEED STILL SWEAT EXTILL
STRAIN STREAM EXUDATE GUTTATE
SCREEVE SECRETE SWELTER
PERSPIRE
EXULT JOY CROW LEAP BOAST
GLOAT GLORY INSULT SPRING
MAFFICK REJOICE TRIUMPH
EXULTANT PROUD ELATED
PRIDEFUL
EXULTATION JOY GLEE PAEAN
OVATION RAPTURE
EXULTING EXULTANT JUBILANT
EXUVIATE MOLT
EYALET VILLAYET
EYAS NESTLING
EYE O EE HE ORB SPY DISC GAZE
GLIM LAMP LOOP MIEN OEIL OGLE
SCAN UVEA VIEW GLARE GLASS
GLENE NAVEL OPTIC SENSE SHANK
SIGHT TOISE WATCH BEHOLD
COLLAR EUCONE EYELET GOGGLE
OCULAR OCULUS OILLET PEEPER
POPEYE REGARD ROLLER SHINER
STEMMA VISION WINDOW WINKER
BLINKER EUCONIC EXOCONE
EYEBALL EYEHOLE OBSERVE
OCELLUS PIERCER PIGSNEY PINKANY
PINKENY SENSORY WITNESS
LATCHING NOISETTE OMMATEUM
RECEPTOR
(— AMOROUSLY) OGLE
(— DISEASE) STYE PINKEYE
(— FORMED BY ROPE) TONGUE
(— IN BIGHT) COLLAR
(— IN EGYPTIAN SYMBOLISM) UTA
(— MAKEUP) KOHL MASCARA
(— MOVEMENT) REM
(— OF BEAN) HILUM

(— OF CAMERA) LENS
(— OF FRUIT) NOSE
(— OF HINGE) GUDGEON
(— OF INSECT) STEMMA
(— OF POTATO) BUD
(— OF RA) SEKHET
(— SORENESS) LIPPITUDE
(BLACK —) KEEK MOUSE SHINER
(EVIL —) DROCHUIL MALOCCHIO
(JERKY — MOVEMENT) SACCADE
(KIND OF —) RIB LAZY
(METAL —) HONDA
(PART OF —) IRIS LENS FOVEA PUPIL
CORNEA MACULA SCLERA CHAMBER
CHOROID LIGAMENT CONJUNCTIVA
(PRIVATE —) GUMSHOE
(PL.) EEN EES NIE YEN YES EYNE
LAMPS LIGHTS SEEING GOGGLES
KEEKERS GLAZIERS GLIMMERS
(PREF.) OCELLI OCUL(I)(O) OMMA(TO)
OPHTHALM(O) OPTI(CO) OPTO
(SUFF.) OMMA OPHTHALMA
OPHTHALMUS OPIS OPS
(SUFF.) (DEFECT OR CONDITION OF —
) OPE OPIA OPIC OPIS OPS OPY
EYEBALL EYE BALL GLASS GLOBE
(— MOVEMENT) VERGENCE
(PREF.) OPHTHALM(O)
EYEBOLT SPRIG RINGBOLT
(INTERLOCKING —S) SNIBEL
EYEBRIGHT EYEWORT EUPHRASY
EYEBROW BREE BROW EEBREE
WINBROW WRIGGLE
EYE-CATCHING BOLD
EYE-CORNER
(PREF.) CANTH(O)
EYECUP EYEGLASS
EYED
(SUFF.) OPIS OPS
EYEGLASS QUIZ NIPPER MONOCLE

EYEGLASSES GLIMS SPECS LENSES
GLASSES LORGNON NIPPERS
BIFOCALS
EYEHOLE EYELET EYEPIT
EYELASH BREE LASH CILIUM
WINKER EYEBREE
(LOSS OF —S) MADAROSIS
(PL.) CILIA EAVES
(PREF.) CILI(I)(O)
EYELET MAIL PINK OELET AGRAFE
OILLET POUNCE AGRAFFE CRINGLE
GROMMET PEEPHOLE
EYELID HAW LID BREE WINDOW
EYEBREE PALPEBRA
(PL.) EAVES
(PREF.) BLEPHAR(O) CILI(I)(O)
(SUFF.) BLEPHARON CIL
EYEPIECE OCULAR EYEGLASS
(— OF TELESCOPE) POWER
EYESHADE VISOR OPAQUE
EYESHOT RANGE REACH EYESIGHT
EYESIGHT VIEW LIGHT SIGHT
EYE SOCKET ORBIT
EYESORE DESIGHT
EYESPOT EYEDOT STIGMA EYEHOLE
OCELLUS EYEPOINT
EYESTALK STIPES
EYETOOTH CUSPID DOGTOOTH
EYEWASH COLLYRIE EYEWATER
COLLYRIUM
EYING ESPIAL
EYOT AIT EIGHT ISLET
EYRE AIR ITER
EZBAI (SON OF —) NAARAI
EZBON (FATHER OF —) GAD BELA
EZEKIEL (FATHER OF —) BUZI
EZER (FATHER OF —) EPHRAIM
(SON OF —) HUSHAH
EZRA (SON OF —) EPHER
EZRI (FATHER OF —) CHELUB

F EF FF EFF FOX DIGAMMA FOXTROT
FABA VICIA
FABLE MYTH TALE FEIGN STORY
LEGEND TRIFLE FICTION PARABLE
POETIZE UNTRUTH ALLEGORY
APOLOGUE FABULATE FABULIZE
(— OF GOLD COAST) NANCY
(MORAL —) EMBLEM
(PREF.) MYTHO
FABRIC ABA BAN ACCA CORD DUCK
GOLD GROS HAIR HUCK IKAT SILK
SUSI TAPA TARS TUKE BATIK CHECK
CREPE DHOTI DOBBY DYNEL FANCY
GAZAR MOIRE NINON PRINT RUMAL
SCRIM SPLIT STUFF SUPER SURAH
SURAT TABBY TAMMY TARSE TERRY
TEWKE TULLE TWEED TWILL UNION
VICHY VOILE WEAVE WIGAN WOVEN
AGARIC ALACHA BENGAL BROCHE
BYSSUS CAFFOY CARPET COTTON
CREPON CYPRUS DACRON DAMASK
DIAPER DOBBIE EPONGE ESTRON
FLEECE HARDEN LAPPET LUSTER
LUSTRE MARBLE MASHRU MURREY
PLISSE POODLE SENNIT STRIPE
TAMINY TANJIB TARTAN TRICOT
TUSSAH VELURE VELVET WADMAL
WINCEY ZENANA ACETATE ALEPINE
ALLOVER BANDALA BANDING
BELTING BEWPERS BINDING
BUCKRAM CANILLE CHALLIS
CHEKMAK CHIFFON CYPRESS
DAMASSE DOESKIN DRABBET
EDIFICE ELASTIC EPINGLE FACONNE
FISHNET FUOTIAN MIXTURE
MORELLA ORGANZA PAISLEY
PLUMBET RASCHEL SAYETTE
SEGATHY SILESIA SUITING TABARET
TABINET TAFFETA TEXTILE TIFFANY
VESSETS AGARANEE BARRACAN
BOCASINE BOURETTE BROCATEL
CAMELINE CANNELLE CASEMENT
CHAMBRAY CRETONNE DIAMANTE
DUCHESSE FIBRANNE HAIRLINE
HANDMADE HARATEEN JACQUARD
KNITTING LUSTRINE MATERIAL
METALLIC MOLESKIN OSNABURG
SHANTUNG SHIRTING SICILIAN
SKIRTING SWANSKIN TAPESTRY
TARLATAN VALENCIA POINTELLE
VELVETEEN
(— CLOSURE) VELCRO
(— CONTAINING GOLD OR SILVER
THREAD) ACCA TASH TASS KINCOB
(— FOR STIFFENING) WIGAN
(— OF TWO OR MORE MATERIALS)
UNION
(— RESEMBLING TOWELING) AGARIC
(— WITH INWOVEN SCENES) ARRAS
(ABSORBENT —) HUCK
(BROCADED —) LAME LAMPAS
(CARPET —) DURRIE
(COARSE —) TAT BAFT CRASH HAIRE
DUFFEL RATINE STAMIN BAGGING
BOCKING DRABBET SACKING
STAMMEL DAGSWAIN FIBRANNE
(CORDED —) REP PIQUE DUCAPE
POPLIN OTTOMAN BENGALINE
(COTTON —) CREA DUCK JEAN LENO
LINO SUSI BAIZE BASIN DENIM DRILL
RUMAL SUPER SWISS VICHY WIGAN
BURRAH CALICO CANVAS CATGUT
CHILLO CHINTZ COUTIL COVERT
DIMITY MADRAS MUSLIN PENANG
SATEEN BLANKET DUOTIAN
CANTOON DAMASSE ETAMINE
FLANNEL GALATEA GINGHAM
HICKORY HOLLAND JACONET
ORGANDY ORLEANS PERCALE
TICKING BOCASINE BUCKSKIN
COTELINE COUTILLE CRETONNE
DRILLING DUNGAREE INDIENNE
SHEETING SILKALINE MARSEILLES
(CURTAIN —) NINON
(DECORATED —) DIAMANTE
(DELICATE —) HUSI JUSI
(DURABLE —) SCRIM SERGE
(ELASTIC —) GORING ELASTIC
(EMBOSSED —) CLOKY CLOQUE
(EMBROIDERED —) BALDAQUIN
(FIGURED —) BROCADE BROCATEL
(FINE —) PIMA SILK SUSI LINEN
DIMITY MERINO MOHAIR BATISTE
PERCALE
(GAUZELIKE —) BAREGE GOSSAMER
(GLAZED —) CIRE
(GLOSSY —) SATIN GLORIA SATEEN
PERCALINE
(GOAT'S-HAIR —) ABA TIBET
(HEAVY —) GROS CRASH DENIM
DRILL BURLAP CATGUT FRIEZE
LINENE TOBINE WHITNEY
(JUTE —) BALINE BURLAP
(KNITTED —) SUEDE BOUCLE JERSEY
TRICOT CHIFFON
(LIGHTWEIGHT —) GLORIA BUNTING
DELAINE FORTISAN PARAMATTA
SEERSUCKER
(LINEN —) HARN SINDON BEWPERS
BUCKRAM CAMBRIC DRABBET
HOLLAND NACARAT CRETONNE
(METALLIC —) LAME
(MOTTLED —) CHINE
(MOURNING —) ALMA

(MUSLIN —) TANJIB
(NYLON —) VELCRO
(OPEN-WEAVE —) LENO
(OPENWORK —) LACE SKIPDENT
(ORNAMENTAL —) GIMP LACE
LAMPAS GALLOON
(PEBBLY-SURFACED —) ARMURE
(PILED —) TERRY BOLIVIA KRIMMER
CHENILLE
(PRINTED —) BATIK CALICO ALLOVER
PERCALE TOURNAY
(RAFFIA —) RABANNA
(RIBBED —) CORD GROS PIQUE
COTELE FAILLE SOLEIL DROGUET
CORDUROY MAROCAIN MOGADORE
WHIPCORD
(RICH —) SAMITE SATEEN
(ROUGH —) TERRY HOPSACK
HOMESPUN
(SATIN —) CAMLET ETOILE
CHARMEUSE
(SHEER —) LAWN NINON SHEER
SWISS BAREGE DIMITY BATISTE
SOUFFLE VALENCE GOSSAMER
MOUSSELINE MARQUISETTE
(SHORT-NAPPED —) RAS
(SILK —) ACCA ALMA FUGI FUJI
GROS IKAT MOFF RASH ATLAS
CARDE NINON PEKIN RAJAH RUMAL
SATIN SHIKH SURAH TIRAZ ARMURE
BROCHE CAMACA CHAPPE CREPON
DIAPER DUCAPE FAILLE KHAIKI
MANTUA PONGEE SAMITE SENDAL
ALACHAH ALAMODE BROCADE
EPINGLE GROGRAM SARSNET
SCHAPPE YESTING BARATHEA
DUPPIONI EOLIENNE IMPERIAL
ORMUZINE SARCENET SARSENET
SHAGREEN SIAMOISE MARCELINE
MESSALINE BROCATELLE
(SOFT-NAPPED —) PANNE DUVETYN
(SOFT SILK —) KASHA BARATHEA
(STRIPED —) ABA STRIPE BAYADERE
MERALINE
(THIN —) CRISP GAUZE VOILE
PONGEE TAMISE HERNANI
MARABOU ORGANZA PERSIAN
(TWILLED —) REP SAY DENIM KASHA
SERGE SURAH COUTIL RUSSEL
BOLIVIA ESTAMIN FLANNEL ZANELLA
CAMELINE CASHMERE CORDUROY
DIAGONAL MARCELLA SHALLOON
VENETIAN
(UNBLEACHED —) DRABBET
(UNGLAZED —) CRETONNE
(UPHOLSTERY —) FRISE FRIEZE
BROCATEL MOQUETTE
(VELVETY —) TRIPE DUVETYN
(VINYL —) NAUGAHYDE
(VINYL-COATED —) NAUGAHYDE
(WATERPROOF —) MACINTOSH
MACKINTOSH
(WOOLEN —) REPP BAIZE DOILY

OSSET SERGE TAMIS TWEED BUFFIN
BURNET COTTON DJERSA DUFFEL
FRISCA MANTLE MOREEN MOTLEY
PERPET SAXONY SHAYAK SHODDY
STAMIN TAMISE VICUNA WADMAL
WITNEY BATISTE BOCKING BOLIVIA
CHEVIOT CHEYNEY CRYSTAL
DELAINE DRUGGET FRISADO
HEATHER RATTEEN STAMMEL
ALGERINE BATSWING BURBERRY
CASHMERE CATALOON CHIVERET
HARATEEN LAMBSKIN PRUNELLA
RATTINET SHALLOON SHETLAND
WOOLENET ZIBELINE
(WORSTED —) TABBY COBURG
ESTAMIN ETAMINE SAGATHY
BARATHEA
(WOVEN —) LENO TWEED TWILL
SOLBIL TISSUE GROGRAM TEXTURE
VALENCIA
FABRICATE COIN COOK FAKE FORM
MAKE MINT VAMP WARP BUILD
FORGE FRAME FRUMP WEAVE DEVISE
FANGLE INVENT CONCOCT FASHION
IMAGINE PRODUCE CONTRIVE
(— CLOTH) DRAPE
(— PAPER) CONVERT
FABRICATION LIE WEB TRIFLE
CHIMERA FICTION FINGURE
FORGERY UNTRUTH BASKETRY
PRETENSE
(PL.) INVENTORY
FABRICATOR LIAR COINER FORGER
FABULIST LIAR AESOP FABLER
FABULOUS FAB FEIGNED MYTHICAL
ROMANTIC
FACADE FACE FRONT FUCUS
FRONTAL FRONTLET
(— FEATURE) CEDILLA
FACE JIB MAP MUG NEB PAN BIDE
CHIV CLAD COPE DARE DEFY DIAL
GIZZ HEAD LEER LINE MASK MEET
MOUE MUNS PHIZ PUSS SIDE ABIDE
BEARD BRAVE BRICK BRUNT CASTE
CHECK CHEER COVER FACET FAVOR
FRONT GUARD INDEX REVET STAND
STONE VISOR VIZOR ASPECT
BRAZEN FACADE FACIES KISSER
MAZARD MUZZLE OPPOSE PHIZOG
VENEER VISAGE AFFRONT BAZOOKA
COMMAND DIGLYPH FASHION
FEATURE GRIMACE GRUNTLE
PROPOSE RESPECT REVERSE
SURFACE UPRIGHT CONFRONT
ENVISAGE EXTRADOS FEATURES
FROGFACE FRONTAGE FRONTIER
PROSPECT SEMBLANT
PERPENDICULAR
(— DOWN) DEFACE
(— IN DEFIANCE) AFFRONT
(— OF ANIMAL) MASK
(— OF CUBE) SQUARE
(— OF CUTTING TOOL) BEZEL BEZIL

(— OF GLACIER) SNOUT
(— OF PEDIMENT) TYMPANUM
(— OF STEAM HAMMER) TUP
(— OF STUMP) SCARF SCARPH
(— ON DOOR KNOCKER) MASCARON
(ONE'S DANCING PARTNER) SET
(— THE EAST) ORIENTATE
(— TO FACE) AFRONT BEFORE FACIAL DIRECTLY
(— WITH MARBLE) PIN
(— WITH MASONRY) REVET
(— WITH PLASTER) STUCCO
(— WITH STONE) BATCH
(CLOCK —) DIAL TABLE WATCH
(CRYSTAL —) PINAKOU
(CURVED —) EXTRADOS INTRADOS
(DIE —) ACE
(FANTASTIC —) ANTIC
(HALF DOMINO —) END
(HAVING SHORT BROAD —) LATERAL
(INNER —) CONCAVE
(MADE-UP —) MOP
(MINING —) BANK BREAST FOREHEAD LONGWALL
(MOCKING —) MOE MOWE
(QUARRY —) HEUGH
(ROCK —) CLIFF
(UPPER —) BROW
(WRY —) MOUTH GRIMACE
(PREF.) FACIO PROSOP(O)
FACE-ARBOR KNIFE
FACED
(SUFF.) PROSOPOUS
FACE GUARD FRONTAL
FACEMAN HAGGER WINNER
FACEPLATE FRONT DOGPLATE
FACER BUMPER DRIFTER TANKARD
FACET PANE STAR BEZEL CULET
PHASE COLLET STEMMA FACETTE
LOZENGE TEMPLET
FACETIAE CURIOSA
FACETIOUS FUNNY MERRY SMART
WITTY FACETE JOCOSE JOCULAR
HUMOROUS POLISHED
FACIAL
(PREF.) FACIO
FACIENT DOER
FACILE PAT ABLE EASY GLIB QUICK
READY EXPERT FLUENT GENTLE
AFFABLE DUCTILE LENIENT
FACILITATE AID EASE HELP FAVOR
SPEED ASSIST GREASE EXPEDITE
FACILITY ART EASE FEEL HELP ECLAT
KNACK SKILL ADDRESS COMMAND
FREEDOM PROWESS EASINESS
(PL.) ADDITIONS
FACING DADO HARL FRONT HARLE
LAPEL LINER PANEL SKIRT BEFORE
TOWARD VENEER AGAINST
FORNENT SURFACE BLACKING
CAMPSHOT CONFRONT COVERING
FACEWORK FORNENST OPPOSITE
PITCHING

(— AGAINST GLACIER) STOSS
(— AHEAD) FULL
(— APEX) ACROSCOPIC
(— AUDIENCE OBLIQUELY) EFFACE
(— EACH OTHER) AFFRONTE AFFRONTY
(— FOR WALLS) CASE
(— FROM GLACIER) STOSS
(— INWARD) INTRORSE
(— OF BODICE) VEST
(— OUTWARDS) EXTRORSE
(PREF.) OB
FACSIMILE FAX COPY IMAGE MODEL
REPLICA AUTOTYPE
FACT CASE DEED FAIT DATUM EVENT
SOOTH TRUTH DONNEE EFFECT
FACTUM VERITY COMPERT FORMULA
GENERAL INDICIA KEYNOTE
LOWDOWN REALITY PARTICULAR
(CONCLUSIVE —) CRUSHER
(DECISIVE —) CLINCHER
(FUNDAMENTAL —) KEYNOTE
(OBVIOUS —) TRUISM
(TRUE G) STRENGTH
(PL.) DATA FEAT
FACTION BLOC NERI PART SECT SIDE
WING CABAL JUNTO PARTY BRIGUE
CLIQUE SCHISM BIANCHI DISPUTE
PINFOLD QUARREL INTRIGUE
SPLINTER
(— OF SECEDERS) CAVE
(PARTY —) STASIS
FACTITIOUS SHAM WHIPPED
KRITRIMA
FACTOR GEN DOER GENE ITEM
AGENT ALLEL CAUSE MAKER ALLELE
AUTHOR CENTER DETAIL BAILIFF
CONTROL COUCHER CUSHION
ELEMENT ENTROPY FACTRIX
ISOLATE STEWARD ADHERENT
AUMILDAR COFACTOR DOMINANT
EQUATION GOMASHTA INCIDENT
INCITANT PARAMETER
(—S IN EVOLUTION) ANTICHANCE
(CYTOPLASMIC —) KAPPA
(DECISIVE —) CAPSTONE
(ECOLOGICAL —) INFLUENT
(ENVIRONMENTAL —) GEOGEN
(HEREDITY —) GENE INSTINCT
(HINDERING —) CRIMP
(INTELLIGENCE —) G
(MATHEMATICAL —) ROOT
(PERSONALITY —) SURGENCY
(RESTRICTIVE —) BARRIER
(UNFORSEEN —) JOKER
FACTORY HONG MILL SHOP PLANT
USINE AURANG AURUNG FABRIC
SUGARY CANNERY HATTERY
HOSIERY OFICINA SOAPERY
BUILDING COMPTOIR FABRIQUE
FILATURE HACIENDA OFFICINA
STAMPERY WORKSHOP
MANUFACTORY

FACTOTUM SIRCAR FAMULUS
COMPRADOR
(INDIAN —) SIRCAR SIRKAR
FACTUAL HARD REAL REAL TRUE ACTUAL
BEDROCK EARTHLY EMPIRIC LITERAL
PROSAIC
(INSUFFICIENTLY —) ABSTRACT
FACTUALLY INSOOTH
FACULTY ART WIT BOOM BUMP
EASE GIFT WILL FANCY POWER
SENSE TASTE BREATH BUDDHI
GIFTIE SEEING TALENT ABILITY
COLLEGE COUNSEL HABITUS
APTITUDE CAPACITY FELICITY
(— FOR DETECTING) NOSE
(— OF EXPRESSION) LANGUAGE
(CRITICAL —) JUDGMENT
(MENTAL —) HEADPIECE
(POETIC OR CREATIVE —) IDEALITY
PRINCIPLE
(REASONING —) DISCOURSE
(PL.) INDULTS
FAD BUG CULT FIKE RAGE WHIM
CRAZE FANCU HOBBY FOIBLE
MAGGOT CROCHET FASHION
WRINKLE
FADDISH TRENDY
FADDIST CRANK
FADE DIE DIM DOW FLY WAN BRIT
CAST FATE FLAT GIVE PALE PEAK
PINE PINK VADE WELK WILK WILT
BLANK DAVER DECAY FLEET PASSE
PETER QUAIL SWING SWOON
DARKLE PERISH VANISH WITHER
DECLINE INSIPID LIGHTEN DIMINISH
DISCOLOR DISSOLVE EVANESCE
LANGUISH
(— AWAY) DOW BREAK FLEET
WALLOW
FADED PASSE SHABBY EXOLETE
SHOPWORN
FADELESS AMARANTIN
FADGE FAY FIT SUIT
FADING FUGITIVE MANCANDO
SWINGING
FAERIE QUEENE (AUTHOR OF —)
SPENSER
(CHARACTER IN —) UNA GUYON
IRENE TALUS ACRASY AMORET
ARTHUR DUESSA TIMIAS ASTRAEA
MALEGER ARTEGALL CALIDORE
GLORIANA ORGOGLIO RADIGUND
ARCHIMAGO BELPHOEBE
BRITOMART FLORIMELL GRANTORTO
SCUDAMOUR
FAFNIR (FATHER OF —) HREIDMAR
(SLAYER OF —) SIGURD
FAG FLAG JADE TIRE TOIL DROOP
WEARY DRUDGE HARASS MENIAL
EXHAUST FATIGUE FRAZZLE
FAG-END LAG BUTT
FAGGED TASKIT
FAGGOT BROSNA CHUMPA FAGALD

FAGOT KID BUNT PILE PIMP BAVIN
FADGE NICKY NITCH FAGGOT KNITCH
GARBAGE
FAIL GO CUT EBB ERR PIP BANK BOMB
BUST CONK FALL FLAG FLOP FOLD
LACK LOSE MISS SINK SKEW SPIN
WANE APPAL BREAK BURST CRACK
FAULT FLUFF FLUKE FLUNK PETER
QUAIL SLAKE SMASH SPILL VAILE
APPALL BETRAY COPOUT DEFAIL
DEFECT DESERT FALTER FIZZLE
REPINE WINDER BACKOUT DECLINE
DEFAULT EXHAUST FALSIFY FINKOUT
FLICKER FLUMMOX FOUNDER
MISFARE MISGIVE SCANTLE
LANGUISH
(— AT) FLUB
(— IN DUTY) LAPSE
(— IN EARLY STAGES) ABORT
(— IN HEALTH) SINK BREAK
(— IN SPIRIT) QUAIL
(— IN STUDIES) BILGE
(— ON RIFLE RANGE) BOLO
(— TO ADVANCE) STICK
(— TO FOLLOW SUIT) RENIG
RENEGE
(— TO GAIN ALTITUDE) MUSH
(— TO GROW) MISS
(— TO NOTICE) OVERLOOK
(— TO PERFORM) CHOKE
FAILING BAD ILL BLOT FAULT FOIBLE
SENILE BLEMISH FAILURE FRAILTY
ABORTIVE WEAKNESS
(NEVER —) PERENNIAL
FAILURE DUD BALK BOMB BUST FAIL
FLOP FLUB FOIL LACK LOSS MISS
MUFF TRIP BAULK BILGE CRASH
DECAY ERROR FAULT FLUKE FLUNK
FROST GRIEF GUILT LAPSE LEMON
PLUCK SMASH BRODIE BUMMER
FIASCO FIZZLE OUTAGE STUMER
STUMOR TURKEY BLOOMER
CROPPER DEBACLE DECLINE
DEFAULT FLIVVER FLUMMOX
NEGLECT STUMBLE ABORTION
COLLAPSE DISASTER FAILANCE
FLOPEROO OMISSION
(— OF DAM) BLOW
(— OF FIREARM) STOPPAGE
(— OF MILK SECRETION) AGALAXY
AGALAXIA
(— OF MUSCLE) ACHALASIA
(— OF PAVEMENT) BLOWUP
(— OF PRIMER) HANGFIRE
(— OF VITALITY) DELIQUIUM
(— TO MEET) GAPE
(— TO NOTICE) OVERSIGHT
(— TO PLAY) GO
(— TO RAISE OAR) CRAB
(COMPUTER —) CRASH
(FLAT —) DUD
(POWER —) OUTAGE
(RIDICULOUS —) FIASCO

FAIN FOND GLAD LIEF EAGER PLEASED WILLING DESIROUS INCLINED

FAINEANT IDLE LAZY LOAFER

FAINT GO DIM LOW WAN WAW COLD CONK COOL DARK PALE PALL SOFT THIN WEAK LIGHT QUEAL QUEER SHADY SWELT SWOON TIMID WAUFF WAUGH WERSH EVANID FEEBLE REMISS REMOTE SICKLY WAMBLY FEIGNED FORGONE LANGUID OBSCURE SWITHER SYNCOPE WEARISH COWARDLY DELICATE LANGUISH LISTLESS SLUGGISH TIMOROUS
(— FROM HEAT) SWELTER
(— FROM HUNGER) LEERY
(— OF SCENT) COLD WAUGH

FAINTHEARTED TIMID COWARD CRAVEN COWARDLY UNHEARTY

FAINTHEARTEDNESS QUALM

FAINTING AFAINT SYNCOPE DELIQUIUM
(— SPELL) DROW DWAM DWALM

FAINTLY DIMLY FAINT SMALL

FAINTNESS TENUITY GONENESS WEAKNESS

FAINT-VOICED INWARD

FAIR GAY GEY MOP BEAU BELL CALM EVEN FINE GAFF GALA GOOD HEND JUST MART PLAY TIDE TIDY BAZAR BLOND CLEAN CLEAR EQUAL FERIA HENDE LARGE RIGHT ROUND SHEER TRYST WHITE AONACH BAZAAR BLONDE CANDID COMELY DECENT DINKUM HONEST KERMIS PRETTY SERENE SQUARE EXHIBIT JANNOCK KERMESS STATUTE BOOKFAIR DISTINCT FESTIVAL HORNFAIR MIDDLING RATIONAL STRAIGHT UNBIASED EQUITABLE OBJECTIVE REASONABLE
(— AND CALM) SETTLED
(— AND SQUARE) DINKUM
(HINDU —) MELA
(VILLAGE —) WALK

FAIR-DEALING HONEST

FAIRER SHIPWRIGHT

FAIRING SPAT SPINNER FAIRLING

FAIR-LEAD WAPP

FAIRLY WELL GAILY GAYLY GEYAN EVENLY JUSTLY MEANLY HANDILY PLAINLY RIGHTLY MIDDLING PROPERLY SUITABLY

FAIRNESS FAIR CANDOR EQUITY HONESTY JUSTICE EQUALITY EVENNESS FAIRHEAD FAIRHOOD

FAIRWAY HOLE WATERWAY
(ANGLED —) DOGLEG

FAIR-WEATHER SUNSHINE

FAIRY ELF FAY FEE HOB IMP FAIN PERI PIXY PUCK SHEE VILA OUPHE PECHT PIXIE SIDHE WIGHT COURIL FAERIE HATHOR KEWPIE SPIRIT SPRITE YAKSHA YAKSHI ARGANTE BANSHEE ORIANDA SHEOGUE SYLPHID URGANDA FOLLETTO MELUSINA
(— QUEEN) MAB
(IRISH —) SHEE SIDHE
(TRICKSY —) PUCK
(PL.) GENTRY

FAIRY BELL FOXGLOVE

FAIRYFOLK SHEE SIDHE

FAIRYLAND ANNWN ANNWFN FEERIE ELFLAND

FAITH DIN FAY FOY LAW LAY VAY FACK FAIX FEGS SLAM TROW CERTY CREED HAITH STOCK TOUCH TROTH TRUST TRUTH BELIEF CERTIE CREDIT GOSPEL CREANCE FACKINS AFFIANCE RELIANCE RELIGION
(BAD —) DUPLICITY
(MUSLIM —) CRESCENT
(RELIGIOUS —) SRADH SRADDHA SHRADDHA
(SHOW OF GOOD —) GESTURE
(PREF.) FIDE(I) PISTIO PISTO

FAITHFUL FAST FEAL FIRM GOOD JUST LEAL LIKE REAL TRIG TRUE FALSE HEMAN LIEGE LOYAL PIOUS SOOTH SWEER TIGHT TREST TRIED AEFALD ARDENT ENTIRE FIDELE HONEST LAWFUL PISTIC STANCH STEADY TRUSTY DEVOTED SINCERE STAUNCH ACCURATE CONSTANT RESOLUTE SPEAKING RELIGIOUS

FAITHFULNESS HSIN FEALTY VERITY LOYALTY FIDELITY TRUENESS

FAITHFUL SHEPHERDESS
(AUTHOR OF —) FLETCHER
(CHARACTER IN —) CHLOE ALEXIS AMORET CLORIN THENOT DAPHNIS PERIGOT AMARILLIS

FAITHLESS FALSE PUNIC FICKLE HOLLOW ROTTEN UNJUST UNTRUE ATHEIST APOSTATE DELUSIVE DISLOYAL SHIFTING UNSTABLE NIDDERING PERFIDIOUS

FAITHLESSNESS FALSITY PERFIDY UNTRUTH

FAKE DUD DUFF DUPE FEKE HOAX HOKE SHAM BOGUS CHEAT FALSE FEIGN FLAKE FRAUD FUDGE PHONY WANGLE DUFFING FALSIFY FURBISH GUNDECK PRETEND SWINDLE SIMULATE SPURIOUS ADULTERINE
(— OF STOWED ROPE) FLEET
(— OUT OF POSITION) JUKE
(FOOTBALL —) JUKE
(PREF.) PSEUD(O)

FAKER FAKIR QUACK HUMBUG CAMELOT PEDDLER
(— OF ART) TRUQUEUR

FAKIR FAKIH FAQUIR DERVISH

FALCHION FALX

FALCON EYAS HAWK SORE BESRA
HOBBY SAKER STOOP GENTLE
JAGGER JUGGER LANNER LUGGAR
LUGGER MERLIN MUSKET PREYER
RAPTOR SHAHIN TERCEL KESTREL
SAKERET BERIGORA BOCKEREL
FALCONET PEREGRIN SOREHAWK
(— **BOARD**) HACK
(— **IN FIRST YEAR**) SORE SOREHAWK
(**FEMALE** —) FORMAL FORMEL
LANNER
(**MALE** —) TASSEL TERCEL SAKERET
(**SMALL** —) HOBBY MERLIN KESTREL
(**WHITE** —) ICELANDER
FALCONER HAWKER OSTREGER
FALCONRY HAWKING
FALDSTOOL ORATORY
FALL GO EBB SAG SYE TIP BACK
BAND COME COUP DIVE DRIP DROP
DUNT FLOP HANG PICK PLOP RASH
RUIN RUSE SHED SILE SINK SLIP
SWAK SWAP SWAY SWOP TILT WHAP
WHOP ABATE CHUTE CLOIT CRASH
DROOP HANCE INCUR JABOT LAPSE
LIGHT LODGE PITCH PLUMB PLUMP
RAPID SAULT SHAKE SHOOT SKITE
SLIPE SLUMP SPILL SQUAB SQUAT
THROW TRACE TWINE ALIGHT
AUTUMN BRODIE DEVALL DOUNCE
DRYSNE FOOTER HAPPEN HEADER
JOUNCE PERISH PLUNGE RECEDE
SEASON SLOUGH STREEK STRIKE
TOPPLE TUMBLE CASCADE CROPPER
CROWNER DECLINE DEGRADE
DEPRESS DESCEND DEVOLVE
DRIBBLE ESCHEAT ILLAPSE
PLUMMET RELAPSE RETREAT
SQUELCH STUMBLE SUBSIDE
CATARACT COLLAPSE COMMENCE
DECREASE DOWNCOME PRECIPITATE
(— **ABRUPTLY**) DUMP
(— **APART**) BREAK SHIVER COLLAPSE
DISUNITE
(— **AWAY**) DEFECT
(— **BACK**) RECEDE RESORT
(— **BEHIND**) LAG
(— **DIZZILY**) SPIN
(— **DOWN**) CAVE FLOP SWAP SLUMP
REVERSE SWITHER
(— **DUE**) ACCRUE BEFALL
(— **FAST**) HOP
(— **FLAT**) PLAT FLIVVER
(— **FOR**) BITE
(— **FORWARD**) PECK PITCH
PROLAPSE
(— **FROM A HORSE**) PURL
VOLUNTARY
(— **FROM SURFBOARD**) WIPEOUT
(— **FROM UNDERMINING**) CALVE
(— **FROM VIRTUE**) LAPSE
(— **GRADUALLY**) EBB SAG
(— **GUY**) GOAT CHUMP SCAPEGOAT

(— **HEAVILY**) DING LUMP SOSS CLOIT
CLYTE GULCH PLOUT PLUMP SOUSE
SWACK THROW
(— **ILL**) TRAIK
(— **IN**) CAVE FOUNDER
(— **IN DROPS**) DRIP STILL DRIBBLE
(— **IN FLURRIES**) SPIT
(— **IN FOLDS**) BLOUSE
(— **IN RIVER**) SAULT
(— **INTO**) STRIKE
(— **INTO ERROR**) SLIP STUMBLE
(— **INTO FAINT**) DWAM DWALM
(— **INTO RUIN**) DECAY
(— **INTO SLUMBER**) DROWSE
(— **INTO TRAP**) DECOY
(— **INTO WATER**) DOP
(— **IN WITH**) INCUR
(— **OF DEW**) SEREIN SERENE
(— **OFF**) BATE SLIP SLACK
(— **OF RAIN**) SKIFF SKIFT ONDING
SHOWER
(— **OF SNOW**) SKIFF SKIFT ONCOME
SCOUTHER SNOWFALL
(— **OF WICKETS**) ROT
(— **ON BACK**) BACKER
(— **ON SUCCESSIVE DAYS**) CONCUR
(— **ON THE NOSE**) NOSER
(— **OUT**) BREAK LIGHT FORTUNE
QUARREL
(— **PRONE**) GRABBLE
(— **RAPIDLY**) SKID
(— **SHORT**) DROP FAIL FAULT
(— **SLOWLY**) SETTLE
(— **SUDDENLY**) BOLT PLOP SLUMP
(— **THROWING HORSE AND RIDER**)
CRUMPLER
(— **TO NOTHING**) DISSOLVE
(— **TO PIECES**) BUCKLE CRUMBLE
(— **UPON**) WARP
(— **VIOLENTLY**) BEAT
(**BAD** —) BUSTER
(**HEAVY** —) PASH POUR SWAG BLASH
CLOIT GULCH SKELP SOUSE SQUAT
MUCKER
(**INCOMPLETE WRESTLING** —) FOIL
(**SOFT** —) SCLAFF
(**SUDDEN** —) HANCE SQUAT SQUASH
TAILSPIN
FALLACIOUS SLY WILY ABSURD
CRAFTY UNTRUE DELUSIVE
GUILEFUL ILLUSORY
FALLACY IDOL ERROR FALLAX
IDOLUM SOPHISM EQUIVOKE
ILLUSION
(PL.) IDOLA
FALLEN DOWN FAUN FLAT SHED
LAPSED DECLASSE
(— **IN**) SUNKEN
FALLER GILL FLATHEAD
FALLFISH CHUB DACE CORPORAL
FALLGUY PATSY
FALL HERRING TAILOR

FALLIBLE HUMAN ERRANT ERRABLE
FALLING SIT CADENT CAVING
  PROLAPSE WINDFALL
  (— BACK) ESCHEAT
  (— BEHIND) LAG
  (— DOWN) RUIN
  (— IN FOLDS) FLOWING
  (— IN RUINS) DERELICT
  (— INTO) INFALL
  (— OFF) CADUCE LEEWAY CADUCOUS
  (— OF MINE ROOF) SIT
  (— OF RAIN) SPIT
  (— ON SOMETHING) INCIDENT
  (— OUT) DIFFICULTY
  (— SHORT) DEFICIT
  (PREF.) CADUCI
  (SUFF.) PTOMA PTOSIS
FALLOPIAN TUBE TUBAL
  (PREF.) FALL(O)
FALLOVER OSTREGER
FALLOW LEA PALE HOBBY BARREN
  VALEWE
  (PREF.) POLI(O)
FALLOW DEER DAMINE DAPPLE
FALLOWING ARDER
FALSE DEAD FAKE FLAM SHAM
  BOGUS FAUSE LYING PASTE PHONY
  WRONG FICKLE HOLLOW LUTHER
  PSEUDO UNTRUE ASSUMED
  BASTARD CROOKED FEIGNED
  APOSTATE DISLOYAL ILLUSIVE
  RECREANT RENEGADE SPECTRAL
  SPURIOUS MENDACIOUS
  (PREF.) PSEUD(O)
FALSE BEACHDROPS PINESAP
FALSE CRAWLEY PINEDROPS
FALSE FOXGLOVE FEVERWEED
FALSE HELLEBORE EARTHGALL
FALSEHOOD COG FIB LIE BUNG
  CRAM FLAM TALE CRACK LIETOR
  FABLE STORY FALSET UNFACT
  YANKER CRAMMER CRETISM
  FALSAGE FALSERY FALSITY FIBBERY
  FICTION LEASING PERFIDY PHANTOM
  ROMANCE UNTRUTH FALSHEDE
  ROORBACK STRAPPER
FALSE MERMAID FLOERKEA
  LIMNANTH
FALSENESS SHAM DECEIT
FALSE WINTERGREEN PYROLA
FALSEWORK CENTERING
FALSIES CHEATERS
FALSIFIER LIAR FALSER FORGER
  FALSARY
FALSIFY LIE COOK FAKE WARP
  ABUSE BELIE FEINT FORGE BETRAY
  DOCTOR FIDDLE WANGLE GUNDECK
  VIOLATE EMBEZZLE MISREPRESENT
FALSITY LIE ERROR VANITY
  UNTRUTH INVERITY
FALSTAFF (CHARACTER IN —) MEG
  FORD JOHN PAGE ALICE BROOK

CAIUS FENTON QUICKLY FALSTAFF
  NANNETTA
  (COMPOSER OF —) VERDI
FALTER FAIL HALT LIMP PAUSE
  WAVER BOGGLE FLINCH TOTTER
  FRIBBLE STAMMER STUMBLE
  TREMBLE HESITATE
FALTERING HINK HALTING·
FALX FALCULA
FAME BAY CRY LOSE NAME STAR
  WORD BRUIT ECLAT GLORY HONOR
  KUDOS PRICE RUMOR VOICE ESTEEM
  LAUREL RENOWN REPORT REPUTE
  TONGUE HEARSAY STARDOM
  WORSHIP
  (HALL OF —) OF (SEE HALL FAME)
  (ILL —) OPPROBRIUM
FAMED RIFE KNOWN NOTED
  EMINENT RENOMEE RENOWNED
FAMEUSE APPLE
FAMILIAR FLY BAKA BOKO BOLD
  COZY EASY FREE FULL HOMY TAME
  TOSH CLOSE CONNU GREAT HOMEY
  KNOWN PRIVY THICK USUAL
  ATHOME BEATEN CHUMMY
  COMMON ENTIRE FOLKSY GERMAN
  HOMELY INWARD KENNED STRAIT
  THRONG VERSED AFFABLE FAMULAR
  FOLKSEY POPULAR FREQUENT
  HABITUAL INTIMATE SOCIABLE
  STANDARD
  (— FEELING) DEJAVU
  (— WITH) KNOWING
  (MAKE —) POST
  (PRESUMPTUOUSLY —) INSOLENT
FAMILIARITY HABIT FREEDOM
  LIBERTY PRIVACY PRIVITY TRAFFIC
  HABITUDE INTIMACY CONSUETUDE
FAMILIARIZE HAFT VERSE
  ACCUSTOM ACQUAINT FREQUENT
FAMILIARLY HOMELY
FAMILY ILK KIN AIGA CLAN GING
  KIND LINE NAME RACE TEAM TRIP
  CINEL CLASS FLESH GOTRA GROUP
  HOUSE MEINY STIRP STOCK CLETCH
  FAIMLY PARAGE STEMMA STIRPS
  STRAIN ZEGRIS DYNASTY KINDRED
  LINEAGE ORLEANS PROGENY
  CATEGORY FIRESIDE
  (COSMOPOLITAN —) FELIDAE
  FABACEAE
  (FIRST —) FF
  (LANGUAGE —) CHON BANTU CLICK
  COCHE CUNAN KADAI STOCK
  AIMARA ATALAN AYMARA CHOLON
  GILIAK HUARPE LENCAN SERIAN
  URALIC BOTOYAN CADDOAN
  CARIBAN CATIBAN CHINOOK
  CHOLONA CHUMASH COPEHAN
  ESSELEN KARTHLI KARTVEL
  KERESAN SHASTAN ATAKAPAN
  CHANGOAN

(LARGE —) QUIVERFUL
(ONE-PARAMETER —) PENCIL
(RAISE A —) PARENT
(SUPER —) APINA APOIDEA
FAMINE LACK PINE WOLF DEARTH
HUNGER SCARCITY
FAMISH KILL STARVE DESTROY
ENFAMISH
FAMOUS MERE BREME FAMED
GRAND NOBLE NOTED FAMOSE
NAMELY EMINENT NAMABLE
NOTABLE RENOWNED
FAMULUS WAGNER SERVANT
FAN ONE RUN VAN BEAT BLOW BUFF
COOL WASH DELTA PUNKA WHIFF
BASKET BLOWER CHAMAR COLMAR
FANNER FLABEL FLIGHT PUNKAH
ROOTER SHOVEL SPREAD VENTOY
WINNOW ADMIRER DEVOTEE
FLABRUM FLYFLAP MPANGWE
PAHOUIN WHISKER EVENTAIL
FOLLOWER RHIPIDION
(— FOR BLOWER) WAFTER
(— OF ROCK GROUP) GROUPIE
(ALLUVIAL —) CONE APRON DELTA
(FEMALE — OF ROCK MUSICIAN)
GROUPIE
(FOOTBALL —) GRIDDER
(JAZZ —) CAT
(WINNOWING —) SAIL LIKNON
(PL.) FOLLOWING
(PREF.) FLABELLI RHIPI(D)(DO)
FANALOKA FOSSA FOUSSA
FANATIC MAD NUT BIGOT CRAZY
FIEND RABID ULTRA ZEALOT
DEVOTEE FURIOSO PHANTIC
PULAHAN PULIJAN BABAYLAN
FRENETIC
(TYPE OF —) PURIST
FANATICAL RABID ULTRA EXTREME
FURIOUS
FANCIED UNREAL DREAMED
AFFECTED
FANCIFUL ODD ANTIC FAIRY IDEAL
QUEER VIEWY DREAMY QUAINT
UNREAL BIZARRE CURIOUS FANCIED
LAPUTAN STRANGE WHIMSIC
CHIMERIC FANCICAL FILIGREE
NOTIONAL ROMANTIC VAPAROUS
WHIMSICAL
FANCY BEE FAD GIG IDEA ITEM LIKE
LOVE MAZE TROW WEEN WHIM
BRAID BRAIN DREAM FREAK GUESS
HUMOR SHINE AFFECT BEGUIN
FANGLE FIGURE FLOSSY IDEATE
LIKING MAGGOT MEGRIM NOTION
ORNATE SHINDY VAGARY VISION
WHIMSY CAPRICE CHIMERA CONCEIT
CONCEPT CROCHET FANCIED
FANCIFY FANTASY PROPOSE
ROMANCE SUSPECT THOUGHT
WRINKLE CHIMAERA CONCEIVE

CROTCHET DAYDREAM ILLUSION
PHANTASM PHANTASY
(FOOLISH —) CHIMERA CHIMAERA
(PASSING —) FIKE
(PERVERSE —) CROTCHET
(WILD —) TOY MAZE
(PL.) DREAMERY
FANDANGO MURCIANA
FANE FLAG BANNER FANACLE
FANFARE TUSCH HOOPLA HOORAY
HURRAH TUCKET TANTARA
FANFARON FLOURISH
FANFARONADE BLUSTER FANFARE
SWAGGER BOASTING
FANFLOWER TACCADA
FANG FAN EARN FALX TAKE TANG
TUSK VANG BEGIN PRONG SEIZE
SNARE TOOTH ASSUME OBTAIN
PANGWE CAPTURE PAHOUIN
PROCURE
FANON CAPE ORALE PHANO FANNEL
MANIPLE
FAN PALM YARAY ERYTHEA
FANTREE TALIPOT
FAN-SHAPED FLABELLATE ALARY
RHIPIDATE
FANTAIL COMET SHAKER WAGTAIL
FAN-TAN PARLIAMENT
FANTASIA FANTASY QUODLIBET
FANTASTIC ODD WILD ANTIC LUCIO
OUTRE QUEER ABSURD GOTHIC
ROCOCO TOYISH UNREAL ANTICAL
BAROQUE BIZARRE WHIMSIC
FANCIFUL FREAKISH ROMANTIC
SINGULAR
(— PERSON) KICKSHAW
FANTASY IDEA MYTH DREAM FANCY
DESIRE VISION CAPRICE CHIMERA
PHANTOM ROMANCE CHIMAERA
PHANTASM PHANTASY
(FUTURISTIC —) SPACEOPERA
FANTINE
(DAUGHTER OF —) COSETTE
FAR AWAY LONG MUCH ROOM SIDE
WELL WIDE CLEAN SIZES WIDEN
REMOTE DISTANT FARAWAY
ROOMWARD
(— AND AWAY) STREETS
(— OFF) OUTBYE
(— ON) ADVANCED
(— OUT) RAD WOW RADICAL
(— UP) HIGH
(SO —) ASYET UPTONOW
(PREF.) TEL(E) TELOTERO
FARAMONDO (COMPOSER OF —)
HANDEL
FARCE MIME DROLL EXODE FORCE
STUFF COMEDY GARLIC SOTTIE
EXODIUM MOCKERY TEMACHA
BURLETTA DROLLERY FARCETTA
(RELATING TO —) ATELLAN
FARCEUR WAG JOKER FORCER

FARCICAL BUFFO COMIC DROLL
ATELLAN
FARCTATE STUFFED
FARCY FARCIN EQUINIA FASHION
FARE DO GO EAT TRY COME DIET
FEND FOOD PATH RATE TIME TOLL
WEND CHEER CHEFE CHIVE FRAME
GOING LIGHT PRICE SPEED TABLE
TOKEN TRACK VIAND COMMON
FARING FETTLE HAPPEN TRAVEL
CARFARE JOURNEY MAKEOUT
PASSAGE PROCEED PROSPER
WAFTAGE WAYFARE FERRYAGE
PROGRESS
(— FOR FERRY) NAULUM FERRYAGE
(— WELL) SPEED
(COARSE —) HAWEBAKE
(USUAL —) ORDINARY
FAREWELL AVE BYE CIAO TATA VALE
ADIEU ADIOS ALOHA CONGE FINAL
LEAVE BYEBYE CHEERO SOLONG
BONALLY CHEERIO GOODBYE
LEAVING LULLABY PARTING
FAREWELL TO ARMS
(AUTHOR OF —) HEMINGWAY
(CHARACTER IN —) HENRY BARKLEY
RINALDI FREDERIC CATHERINE
FARFETCHED FARFET FORCED
DEVIOUS STRAINED EXQUISITE
FAR-FETCHED
(NOT —) NATURAL
FAR-FLUNG EXTENDED
**FAR FROM THE MADDING
CROWD**
(AUTHOR OF —) HARDY
(CHARACTER IN —) OAK TROY FANNY
ROBIN GABRIEL BOLDWOOD
EVERDENE BATHSHEBA
FARIDUN
(FATHER OF —) ABTIN
(MOTHER OF —) FIRANAK
(SON OF —) TUR IRAJ SALM
FARINA MEAL FLOUR FARINE POLLEN
STARCH
FARKLEBERRY BLUET
FARL PARLY FARREL
FARM FEU PEN CROP TACK TILL TORP
TOWN WALK CROFT DAIRY EMPTY
FIRMA HARAS MAINS MILPA PLACE
RANCH RANGE STEAD BARTON
BOWERY CHACRA ESTATE FURROW
GRANGE RANCHO TYDDEN TYDDYN
CLEANSE HENNERY KOLKHOZ
MAILING POTRERO POULTRY
SOVKHOS VACCARY ESTANCIA
HACIENDA HATCHERY LABORING
LOCATION STEADING TOWNSHIP
(— OUT) DIMIT ARRENT
(AUSTRALIAN —) STATION
(COLLECTIVE —) ARTEL KIBBUTZ
KOLKHOZ
(COMMUNAL —) KVUTZA KVUTZAH

(DAIRY —) WICK
(KIND OF — AS ASYLUM) FUNNY
(LARGE —) RANCH BARTON
(RENTED —) MAILING
(SMALL —) CHACRA
(STOCK —) ESTANCIA
(STUD —) STUD HARAS
(WEST INDIAN —) PEN
FARMER HOB MEO CARL FARM HOBB
KHOT KYLE RUBE RYOT TATE AILLT
AUMIL BOWER CARLE CEILE CLOWN
COLON HODGE KISAN COOKIE
GROWER HOGMAN JIBARO TILLER
YEOMAN BUCOLIC BUSHMAN
BYWONER COTTIER CROFTER
GRANGER HAYSEED HUSBAND
LANDMAN METAYER PLANTER
PLOWMAN RANCHER SCULLOG
TILLMAN TRUCKER AGRONOME
COCKATOO PRODUCER PUBLICAN
RURALIST SELECTOR AGRONOMIST
(AUSTRALIAN —) SELECTOR
(NORWEGIAN —) BONDER
(POOR —) PIKE
(PROSPEROUS —) KULAK
(SMALL —) BOOR COCKIE
(TENANT —) AILLT GEBUR SIRDAR
COLONUS SHAREMAN
SHARECROPPER
FARMHAND HAND HELP
FARMHOLD CROFT
FARMHOUSE FARM TOWN ONSET
GRANGE QUINTA CASERIO ONSTEAD
STEADING
FARMING SOIL FARMERY
HUSBANDRY
(— SYSTEM) NOTILL METAYAGE
FARMLAND ACREAGE
FARMSTEAD TOWN WICK STEAD
FARMERY ONSTEAD
FARMYARD WERF CLOSE BARTON
RICKYARD
FARO MONTE STUSS TIGER
PHARAOH
(— CARD) SODA
FARO BANK TIGER
FAR-OFF DISTANT
FAR-OUT RAD GONZO KINKY
FARRAGO OLIO
FAR-REACHING GREAT FARGOING
FARRIER SHOER SMITH MARSHAL
FARROW PIG ROW RAKE DRAPE
LITTER
FARSEEING ORACULAR
FARSIGHTED SHREWD SIGHTY
FARTHER YOND AHEAD STILL
LONGER FURTHER REMOTER
THITHER
FARTHEST ULTIMA ENDMOST
EXTREME FARMOST LONGEST
OUTMOST DOWNMOST FURTHEST
REMOTEST ULTIMATE

FARTHING RAG GRIG JACK QUAD
FADGE FERLING QUARTER
QUADRANS QUADRANT
(HALF —) CUE
(THREE —S) GILL
FARTHINGALE FERDEGEW
VERTUGAL
FASCIA BAND SASH FACIA FILLET
BANDAGE MOLDING LIGATURE
PLATBAND
FASCICLE BUNDLE PHALANGE
FASCICULUS HEFT BUNDLE
COLUMN TRACTUS
FASCINATE DARE CHARM RIVET
SEIZE WITCH ALLURE ENAMOR
ATTRACT BEWITCH ENCHANT
ENGROSS GLAMOUR PHILTER
PHILTRE ENSORCEL ENTRANCE
INTEREST INTRIGUE SIRENIZE
CAPTIVATE
FASCINATED HOOKED BESOTTED
FASCINATING NUTTY ORPHIC
TAKING SIRENIC CHARMING
FETCHING MESMERIC
FASCINATION CHARM SPELL
WITCHERY
FASCINE FAGOT FAGGOT SAUCISSE
FASCIOLA DISTOMA DISTOMUM
FASCIOLE SEMITA
FASCIST BLACK FASCISTA
FASHION GO CRY CUT FAD LAT TON
WAY CHIC FEAT FORM GARB GATE
KICK MAKE MODE MOLD RAGE RATE
SORT TURN TWIG WEAR WISE BUILD
CRAZE FEIGN FORGE FRAME GUISE
MODEL MOULD SHAPE STYLE TASTE
VOGUE WEAVE AGUISE ASSIZE
BUSTLE CAMBER CREATE CUSTOM
DESIGN FANGLE INVENT MANNER
METHOD TAILOR ALAMODE
COMPOSE IMAGERY PORTRAY
QUALITY CONTRIVE
(LATEST —) KICK
(OF PAST —) RETRO
(PREVAILING —) CRY
(SPECIAL —) TOUCH
FASHIONABLE HIP CHIC GOGO
LATE PINK POSH TONY DASHY
DOGGY DOSSY NOBBY RITZY SMART
SWELL SWISH VOGUE GIGOLO
JAUNTY MODISH TIMISH TONISH
TRENDY DASHING GALLANT
GENTEEL STYLISH SWAGGER
BELGRAVIAN
(NOT —) DEMODE
FASHIONABLY SMARTLY
FASHIONED HUED CARVED SHAPED
WROUGHT FEATURED
FASHIONING FINGENT
FASHION PLATE SWELL
FASSAITE PYRGOM
FAST HOT HUT COLD FIRM HARD
LENT SOON SURE WIDE AGILE APACE

BRISK CHEAP FIXED FLASH FLEET
HASTY QUICK RAPID ROUND SADLY
STUCK SWIFT TIGHT TOSTO CARENE
ESTHER FASTLY LIVELY SECURE
SPEEDY SPORTY STABLE STARVE
ABIDING EXPRESS HOTSHOT
HURRIED PROVISO RASPING
SETTLED SIKERLY STATION TAANITH
ENDURING FAITHFUL SPINNING
SPORTING WIKIWIKI
(— DAY) ASHURA
(DANGEROUSLY —) BREAKNECK
(MUSLIM —) MOHARRAM
(SUFF.) (MAKING —) PEXIA PEXIS
PEXY
FAST-DYED INGRAIN
FASTEN BAR DOG FAY FIX GAD GIB
KEY LAG PEN PIN SEW TAG TIE YOT
BELT BEND BIND BITT BOLT BRAD
CLIP FRET GIRD GIRT GLUE GRIP
HANG HANK HASP HOOK HOOP
HORN KILT KNIT KNOT LACE LASH
LINK LOCK MOOR NAIL ROPE SEAL
SNIB SOUD SPAN SPAR STAY WELD
WIRE AFFIX ANNEX BELAY BIGHT
BRACE CABLE CATCH CHAIN CHOCK
CINCH CLAMP CLASP CLING COPSE
CRAMP DEFIX GIRTH HALSH HITCH
INFIX LATCH PASTE RIVET SCREW
SEIZE SLOUR SNECK STEEK STICK
STRAP TRUSS WITHE ANCHOR
ATTACH BATTEN BUCKLE BUTTON
CEMENT CLINCH COTTER COUPLE
ENGAGE ENTAIL FATHER GARTER
HAMPER HANKLE INKNOT PICKET
SECURE SKEWER SOLDER STAPLE
STITCH STRAIN TETHER BRACKET
CONFINE CONNECT EMBRACE
GRAPPLE GROMMET PADLOCK
BARNACLE FORELOCK INTERTIE
OBLIGATE TRANSFIX
(— ABOUT) THRAP
(— ANCHOR) SCOW
(— A SAIL) CROSS
(— AS SPURS) SPEND
(— IN) EMBAR
(— PROMPTLY) CLAP
(— THE LEGS) HOBBLE
(— TO) TAG
(— TOGETHER) COAPT SEIZE SPLICE
CONNECT
(— WINGS ON) IMP
(— WITH A GIRTH) WARRICK
(— WITH NOTCHES) GAIN
(PREF.) HAPT(O)
FASTENED FAST SHUT BOUND
FIXED BOUNDEN
(PREF.) (— TOGETHER) SYNAPTO
FASTENER BAR GIB GIN NUT PIN
AGAL BOLT DOME FAST FROG HASP
LOCK NAIL SNAP STUD TACK CATCH
CLAMP CLASP LATCH RIVET SCREW
SPIKE STRAP TATCH THONG BUCKLE

BUTTON HATPIN STAPLE ZIPPER
FIXATOR LATCHET PADLOCK
SNAPPER TENDRIL FASTNESS
STAYLACE
FASTENING TEE TIE FROG HASP
SEAL SNAP SNIB STAY TACK TACHE
BUCKLE CLINCH LACING MUZZLE
STRIKE TINGLE BINDING CLOSURE
LATCHET MOUSING PINNING
SEIZING FORELOCK KNITTING
(— FOR HAWK'S WING) BRAIL
(— OF COPE) MORSE
(— ON HARPOON IRON) HITCH
(HOOK AND LOOP —) AGRAFE
AGRAFFE
(PL.) GRIPES
(PREF.) DESM(A)(IDI)(IDIO)(O)
(SUFF.) PEXIA PEXIS PEXY
FAST-GOING CLIPPING
FASTIDIOUS FINE NEAT NICE CHARY
DONCY FEEST FUSSY NAISH NATTY
PAWKY PICKY CHOICE CHOICY
CHOOSY DAINTY DONSIE MOROSE
FICKED QUAINT QUEASY SPRUCE
CHOOSEY CURIOUS ELEGANT
FINICAL FINICKY HAUGHTY PICKING
REFINED TAFFETA TAFFETY CRITICAL
DELICATE EXACTING GINGERLY
OVERNICE PICKSOME PRECIOUS
SCORNFUL SQUEAMISH PARTICULAR
PERSNICKETY SCRUMPTIOUS
(NOT —) GROSS
(OVERLY —) SAUCY
FASTIDIOUSNESS DAINTY NICETY
DELICACY
FASTIGIATE CONIC
FASTING RAMADAN
(PREF.) NEST(I)
FAST-MOVING SUDDEN
FASTNESS FORT CASTLE CITADEL
RETREAT FORTRESS
FAST-WORKING HOTSHOT
FAT GHI OIL TUB FOZY GHEE GRAS
LARD LIPA MORT RICH SAIM SUET
ADEPS BEEFY BROSY CETIN CHUFF
COCUM ESTER FLECK FLICK FOGGY
GROSS JUICY KEDGE KOKUM LARDY
LIPID LIPIN LUSTY OBESE PLUMP
PODGY PORKY PUDDY PUDGY
PURSY SAAME SPICK SQUAB STOUT
SUMEN THICK WASTY AXUNGE
BLOWSY CHOATY CHUBBY CHUFFY
DEGRAS FATTED FINISH FLESHY
GREASE LIPIDE LIPOID PLUFFY
PORTLY PUBBLE PUNCHY PYKNIC
ROTUND STOCKY STUFFY TALLOW
UCUUBA ADIPOSE BLOATED
BLUBBER CEROTIN FATNESS FERTILE
FLESHLY FULSOME LANOLIN
OPULENT PINGUID PURSIVE REPLETE
STEARIN EXTENDED FRUITFUL
MARROWED MURUMURU PALMITIN
UNCTUOUS

(— AROUND WHALE'S NECK) KENT
(— MEAT) SPECK
(— OF HIPPOPOTAMUS) SPECK
(— PERSON) SQUAB
(ANIMAL —) GLOR SAIM SUET ADEPS
GLORE GREASE TALLOW
(CHEW THE —) GAB JAW YAK
(FLOATING —) FLOT
(LARD —) FLARE FLECK FLICK
(LOW IN —S) SPA
(LUMP OF —) KEECH
(LUMPY —) CELLULITE
(NATURAL —) ESTER
(POULTRY —) SCHMALZ SCHMALTZ
(SOLID —) LARD KIKUEL STEARIN
(PREF.) ADIP(O) LIP(O) LIPAR(O) PI(O)
PIA(R)(RO) PINGUE PINGUI SEBI
STEAR(O) STEAT(O)
FATAL FEY DIRE MORT FERAL VITAL
DEADLY DISMAL DOOMED FUNEST
LETHAL MORTAL TRAGIC CAPITAL
DEATHLY EXITIAL FATEFUL KILLING
OMINOUS RUINOUS UNSONSY
BASILISK DESTINED EXITIOUS
FUNESTAL MORTIFIC
FATALITY DOOM ACCIDENT
CALAMITY DISASTER
FATA MORGANA MIRAGE
FAT-BELLIED GUTTY
FATE DIE END KER LOT CAST DOLE
DOOM EURE NORN RUIN SORT STAR
CAVEL EVENT GRACE KARMA MOIRA
MORTA WEIRD WHATE WRITE
ANANKE CHANCE KISMET DESTINY
FORTUNE OUTCOME PORTION
DOWNFALL FATALITY
(INEXORABLE —) HEAVEN
(PREF.) FATI
FATED DUE FEY FATAL DOOMED
DECREED DESTINED
FATEFUL FATAL FATED DEADLY
DOOMFUL OMINOUS DOOMLIKE
FATES CLOTHO MOERAE PARCAE
ATROPOS LACHESIS
(ONE OF —) URD NONA PARCA
SKULD CLOTHO DECUMA ATROPOS
LACHESIS VERDANDE
FATHEAD REDFISH
FATHEADED FOZY
FATHEADEDNESS FOZINESS
FATHER BU DA PA ABU AMA DAD POP
TAT ABBA ABOU AMBA ANBA ATEF
BABA BAPU DADA PAPA PERE SIRE
ADOPT BABBO BEGET DADDY FRIAR
PADRE PATER VADER PARENT PRIEST
SUBORN ELKANAH GENITOR TATINEK
BEAUPERE GENERATE GOVERNOR
PATRIARCH PATERFAMILIAS
(CHURCH —) APOLOGIST
(SEMIDIVINE —) PITRI
(SIDE OF —) AGNATE
(PL.) PP
(PREF.) PARRI PATR(I)(IO)(O)

FATHER GORIOT (AUTHOR OF —)
BALZAC
(CHARACTER IN —) EUGENE GORIOT
VAUTRIN DELPHINE ANASTASIE
DERESTAUD TAILLEFER VICTORINE
DENUCINGEN DEBEAUSEANT
DERASTIGNAC

FATHERLAND KITH HOMELAND

FATHER-LASHER GUNDIE COTTOID
SCULPIN BULLHEAD LORICATE

FATHERLESS ORBATE SIRELESS

FATHERS AND SONS (AUTHOR OF
—) TURGENEV
(CHARACTER IN —) KATYA PAVEL
ARKADY VASILY NIKOLAI BAZAROFF
FENICHKA KIRSANOFF ODINTZOFF
SITNIKOFF

FATHOM BRACE BRASS DELVE
FADME PLUMB SOLVE SOUND
TOUCH BOTTOM MEASURE
PLUMMET

FATIGUE FAG HAG TEU BEAT BORE
COOK JADE TASH TIRE TRAY SPEND
STALL TARRY THRIE TRAIK TRASH
WEARY HARASS OVERDO TAIGLE
TUCKER EXHAUST LANGUOR
TRACHLE FATIGATE VEXATION
(FLIGHT —) AERONEUROSIS

FATIGUED BEAT GONE JADED TIRED
WEARY TASKIT OUTWORN WEARIED
FATIGATE HARASSED OVERDONE
TUCKERED

FATIGUING HARD IRKSOME

FATLIKE LIPOID

FATNESS BLOOM GREASE

FATTEN FAT BEEF LARD SOIL BRAWN
FARCE FLESH FRANK PROVE SMEAR
STALL BATTEN BATTLE ENRICH
FINISH TALLOW THRIVE PINGUEFY
SAGINATE

FATTENING FRANK BATTEL
BATTABLE

FATTY SUETY BACONY GREASY
ADIPOSE ADIPOUS FATLIKE PINGUID
SEBIFIC STEARIC LIPAROID LIPAROUS
UNCTUOUS ALIPHATIC
(PREF.) LIPAR(O)

FATUITY INANITY

FATUOUS DOPY GAGA DOPEY INANE
SILLY SIMPLE STUPID UNREAL
FATUATE FOOLISH IDIOTIC WITLESS
DEMENTED ILLUSORY IMBECILE

FAUCES JAWS

FAUCET BIB TAP BIBB COCK QUILL
SPOUT VALVE CUTOFF DOSSIL
DOZZLE OFFLET SPIGOT BIBCOCK
HYDRANT PETCOCK TURNCOCK
(WOODEN —) HORSE

FAUGH BAH FOH VAH

FAUJDAR PHOUSDAR

FAULT BUG RUB SIN BEAM CLAG
COUP DEBT FAIL FLAW FLUB GALL
HOLE LACK LAST MOLE SAKE SLIP
SPOT VICE WANT WITE ABUSE
AMISS BLAME BREAK CULPA ERROR
FLUFF GUILT LAPSE SCAPE SHIFT
SLIDE SWICK TACHE BLOTCH DEFECT
FOIBLE RUNNER THRUST VICETY
VITIUM BLEMISH BLISTER BLUNDER
DEFAULT DEMERIT EYELAST FAILING
FAILURE FRAILTY MISTAKE NEGLECT
OFFENSE FAULTING PECCANCY
WEAKNESS
(— IN BADMINTON) SLING
(AT —) CULPABLE
(MINING —) COUP LEAP CHECK HITCH
(TRIFLING —) PECCADILLO
(PL.) FAULTAGE

FAULTFINDER MOMUS CARPER
CHIDER CRITIC MOMIST CAPTION
KNOCKER NAGSTER

FAULTFINDING CARPING CAPTIOUS
CRITICAL

FAULTILY BADLY

FAULTLESS PURE CLEAN RIGHT
CORRECT PERFECT PRECISE
FLAWLESS

FAULTY BAD ILL SICK AMISS UNFIT
WRONG FLAWED FAULTED PECCANT
VICIOUS BLAMABLE CULPABLE
SPURIOUS
(PREF.) DYS PARA

FAUN SATYR WOODMAN
WOODWOSE

FAUNA ANIMALS FAUNULA FAUNULE
ZOOLOGY
(FOSSIL —) BIOCHRON

FAUSSEBRAIE VAMURE VAUMURE

FAUST (AUTHOR OF —) GOETHE
(CHARACTER IN —) FAUST HELEN
SIEBEL WAGNER GRETCHEN
VALENTINE HOMUNCULUS
MARGUERITE MEPHISTOPHELES
(COMPOSER OF —) GOUNOD

FAUX PAS GAFF SLIP BONER ERROR
GAFFE BLOOMER FLOATER MISSTEP
MISTAKE SNAPPER

FAVOLA D'ORFEO (CHARACTER IN
—) PLUTO APOLLO CHARON
ORPHEUS MESSENGER PROSERPINA
(COMPOSER OF —) MONTEVERDI

FAVOR AID FOR ORE PRO BOON ESTE
FACE GREE HEAR HELP LIKE MAKE
BLESS BRIBE GRACE LEAVE MENSK
SERVE SPARE SPEED THANK TREAT
ASSIST ERRAND ESTEEM FAVOUR
LETTER NOTICE PENCEL UPHOLD
ADVANCE AGGRACE BENEFIT
ENFAVOR FEATURE FORWARD
GRATIFY INDULGE RESPECT
SUPPORT ADVOCACY BEFRIEND
COURTESY FAVORIZE GOODWILL
KINDNESS RESEMBLE SYMPATHY
ACCEPTANCE

FAVORABLE HOT BOON FAIR FREE
GOOD HIGH KIND ROSY TIDY CIVIL

CLEAR HAPPY LARGE MERRY TRINE
WHITE WILLY BENIGN DEXTER
GENIAL GOLDEN KINDLY TOWARD
BENEFIC EXALTED OPTIMAL
POPULAR PRESENT FAVONIAN
FRIENDLY GRACIOUS PLEASING
PROPENSE SPEEDFUL TOWARDLY
BENIGNANT PROPITIOUS
PROSPEROUS
(— TO PURCHASER) KEEN
(NOT —) INFAUST

FAVORABLY FAIR WELL HIGHLY

FAVORED WELL FAURD HAPPY
FAURED GIFTED BLESSED FAVOURED

FAVORER FAUTOR FRIEND FAVORITE

FAVORING FAVONIAN
(PREF.) PRO
(SUFF.) ABLE IBLE

FAVORITE BOY PET POT DEAR PEAT
CHALK GREAT INGLE WHITE MINION
DARLING FANCIED MINIKIN POPULAR
SPECIAL GRACIOSO WHITEBOY

FAVORITE, LA (CHARACTER IN —)
GUSMAN ALFONSO LEONORA
FERNANDO
(COMPOSER OF —) DONIZETTI

FAVORITISM BIAS FAVOR NEPOTISM

FAVUS TILE WHITECOMB

FAWN COG BUCK CLAW DEER FAON
JOUK ROOT COWER CRAWL CREEP
GLOZE HONEY SMARM TOADY
WHELP CRINGE CROUCH GROVEL
KOWTOW SHRINK SLAVER ADULATE
CROODLE CRUDDLE FLATTER
FLETHER HANGDOG SERVILE
SPANIEL TOADEAT TRUCKLE
WHEATEN BOOTLICK
(— UPON) SUCK SMOOGE ADULATE

FAWN-COLORED CERVINE

FAWNIA (LOVER OF —) DORASTUS

FAWNING SLEEK CRINGE GREASE
MENIAL SLEEKY SMARMY SUPPLE
FLETHER GLOZING HANGDOG
SERVILE SPANIEL FLATTERY

FAWNSKIN NEBRIS

FAY ELF FEY FAIRY FEIGH

FAZE DAUNT FEEZE PHASE WORRY

FEALTY FEE FEWTE HOMAGE
LOYALTY SERVICE TREWAGE FIDELITY

FEAR UG AWE DREE FLAY FUNK
WARD ALARM DOUBT DREAD JELLY
PANIC AFFRAY ALARUM DANGER
DISMAY FRIGHT HORROR PHOBIA
TERROR ANXIETY SUSPECT
AFFRIGHT DISQUIET DISTRUST
EERINESS MISDOUBT VENERATE
(— OF CROSSING STREETS)
DROMOPHOBIA
(— OF DRAFTS) AEROPHOBIA
(— OF FALLING) BATHOPHOBIA
HYPSOPHOBIA
(— OF HOME SURROUNDINGS)
ECOPHOBIA

(— OF OPEN PLACES) AGORAPHOBIA
(— OF THUNDER) ASTRAPHOBIA
(INTERJECTION TO EXPRESS —)
YIKES
(IRRATIONAL —) PARANOIA
(PREF.) PHOB(O)
(SUFF.) PHOBE PHOBIA(C) PHOBIC
PHOBOUS

FEARFUL ARGH DIRE AWFUL FERLY
PAVID TIMID WINDY WROTH AFRAID
COWISH FRIGHTY GHASTLY
NERVOUS PANICKY WORRIED
CAUTIOUS DOUBTFUL DREADFUL
GREWSOME GRUESOME HORRIBLE
HORRIFIC PARANOID SHOCKING
SKITTISH TERRIBLE TERRIFIC
TIMOROUS
(PREF.) DEIN(O) DIN(O)

FEARLESS BOLD BRAVE DARING
HEROIC AWELESS IMPAVID INTREPID

FEASIBLE FIT LIKELY POSSIBLE
PROBABLE SUITABLE

FEAST (ALSO SEE FESTIVAL) EAT FOY
PIG SUP DINE FARM FETE LUAU
MEAL TUCK UTAS AZYME CHEER
CHOES CITUA DIRGY FESTA FESTY
GAUDY REVEL TREAT ARTHEL AVERIL
BRIDAL DEVOUR DINNER DOUBLE
INFARE ISODIA JUNKET MAUNDY
REGALE REPAST SIMPLE SMOUSE
SPREAD AHAAINA BANQUET
BRIDALE DELIGHT FESTINO GRATIFY
GREGORY LAMBALE LEMURIA
SHEVUOS SYNAXIS ANALEPSY
CAROUSAL DOMINEER EPIPHANY
FESTIVAL GESTNING GESTONIE
HANUKKAH KOIMESIS PASSOVER
POTLATCH SHABUOTH VESTALIA
(— BEFORE JOURNEY) FOY
(— OF BOOTHS) SUCCOS SUKKOTH
(— OF LANTERNS) HON
(— OF LOTS) PURIM
(— OF WEEKS) SHEVUOS SHABUOTH
(— PLACE) IDGAH
(DRINKING —) BANQUET
(FUNERAL —) ARVAL ARVEL DIRGY
DIRGIE DREDGIE
(HARVEST —) BUSK
(JEWISH —) SENDAH
(LOVE —) AGAPE
(RELIGIOUS —) CANAO KANYAW
PENTECOST
(VILLAGE —) TANSY
(PREF.) DAPI FESTI FESTO HEORTO
(SUFF.) (— DAY) MAS

FEASTER CONVIVE

FEASTING FEAST CARNIVAL

FEAT ACT KIP DEED FATE GEST WORK
GESTE SPLIT STUNT TRICK CRADDY
CUTOFF EXPLOIT MASTERY MIRACLE
WORSHIP DEXTROUS PERFORMANCE
(— IN SURFING) SPINNER
QUASIMODO

(ACROBATIC —) SPLITS
(CRICKETER'S —) DOUBLE
(EASY —) PICNIC
(EFFECTIVE —) STROKE
(TUMBLING —) SCISSORS
(PL.) DAGS
FEATHER BOO PEN TAB DECK DOWN
FLAG HERL SETA STUB VANE ADORN
AXIAL PENNA PINNA PLUMA PLUME
QUILL REMEX CLOTHE COVERT
CRINET FLEDGE FLETCH FLIGHT
HACKLE MANUAL PINION SARCEL
SICKLE SQUAMA TIPPET TONGUE
AXILLAR BRISTLE FLEMISH IMPLUME
PRIMARY RECTRIX REMICLE STIPULE
TECTRIX TERTIAL TOPPING AXILLARY
SCAPULAR STREAMER TERTIARY
(BRISTLELIKE —) VIBRISSA
(HAWK'S —S) BRAIL BRAILS
(HORSE —) SPEAR
(NECK —) HACKLE
(NEW —) STIPULE
(OSTRICH TAIL —) BOO
(PINION —) SARCEL
(PRIMARY —) MANUAL
(TAIL —) SICKLE RECTRIX
(YELLOW —S) HULU
(PL.) GIG BOOT CAPE DOWN FLUE
MAIL BRAIL CRISSUM CUSHION
FLIGHTS PLUMAGE REMIGES SPURIAE
(PREF.) PENNAT(I)(O) PENNI PENNO
PINN(I)(O) PINNAT(I)(O) PLUMI
PTER(O) PTIL(O)
(SUFF.) PENNATE PENNINE PTILE
PTILUS
FEATHER BED TYE
FEATHER CLOAK AHUULA TEMIAK
FEATHERED FLEDGE FLEDGY
PLUMED PENNATE PINNATE FLIGHTED
(PREF.) PTENO
(SUFF.) PINNATE
FEATHERHEAD FOOL
FEATHERING STOCKING
FEATHER KEY FIN STOP SPLINE
FEATHER
FEATHER-LEGGED COOTY COOTIE
FEATHERLIKE PINNATE
FEATHERY LIGHT PLUMY FLEDGY
FLUFFY PLUMOSE PLUMEOUS
FEATLY NEATLY FOOTINGLY
FEATURE WAY FACE ITEM NOTE
STAR BREAK FAVOR GRACE MOTIF
TOKEN TRACT TRAIT TREAT ASPECT
CACHET FAVOUR SPLASH AMENITY
OUTLINE HALLMARK SALIENCE
(— OF WORD FORM) ASPECT
(ATTRACTIVE —) AMENITY
(DETERMINING —) LIMIT
(DISTINGUISHING —) TRAIT STROKE
HALLMARK
(ESSENTIAL —) CHARACTER
(FATAL —) BANE
(LINGUISTIC —) ISOGLOSS SURVIVAL

(MAIN —) CRUX
(MOST COGENT —) BEAUTY
(OBJECTIONABLE —) DISCOUNT
DRAWBACK
(SALIENT —) MOTIF
(TOPOGRAPHIC —) ARC
(TOPOGRAPHIC —S) LIE
(PL.) LAY FACE CONTOUR FASHION
GEOLOGY RETRAIT
FEAZE FRAY FAIZE ROUGHEN
FEBRIFUGE PEREIRA ANGOSTURA
FEBRILE PYRETIC FEVERISH
FECES DRAST HOCKEY ORDURE
(PREF.) COPR(O)
FECKLESS WEAK FEEBLE
FECULENCE DREG
FECULENT DREGGY
FECUND FERTILE FRUITFUL PROLIFIC
FED FAT MEATED
FEDERATION BUND CROM UNION
LEAGUE NATION COUNCIL ALLIANCE
FEDERACY TRIALISM
FEDORA (CHARACTER IN —) LORIS
FEDORA IPANOV ROMANOV
(COMPOSER OF —) GIORDANO
FEE FEU DUES DUTY FEAL FEUL FIEF
FIER HIRE RATE WAGE CAULP EXTRA
HANSE PRICE RIGHT ALNAGE
AMOBER BARONY CHARGE DASTUR
EMPLOY EXCISE REWARD SALARY
SHEKEL BUOYAGE DASTURI
DUMPAGE DUSTOOR FALDAGE
FIRNAGE FURNAGE GAOLAGE
GARNISH GRATIFY GUIDAGE
HALLAGE HOUSAGE JAILAGE
MULTURE PAYMENT PINLOCK
PREFINE STIPEND STORAGE
TALLAGE TRIBUTE VANTAGE
BOOTHAGE BOUNTITH CHUMMAGE
EXACTION FAREWELL GRATUITY
MALIKANA POUNDAGE REREFIEF
RETAINER SHIPPAGE WHARFAGE
(— TO LANDOWNER) TERRAGE
(— TO TEACHER) MINERVAL
(CUSTOMARY —) DASTUR
(CUSTOMS —) LOT
(ENTRANCE —) HANSA HANSE
INCOME
(GRINDING —) THIRLAGE
(INITIATION —) FOOTING
(INSTALLATION —) FOOTING
(PHYSICIAN'S —) SOSTRUM
(ROAD —) PIKE
(UNAUTHORIZED —) GARNISH
(PL.) EXHIBITS
FEEBLE LOW WAN FLUE LAME MEAN
PALE POOR PUNY SOFT WEAK
DONCY DOTTY FAINT SEELY SILLY
SOBER UNORN WANKY WASHY
WERSH WONKY CADUKE DEBILE
DONSIE DOTAGE FAINTY FLABBY
FLIMSY FOIBLE INFIRM PAULIE
PUISNE SCANTY SEMMIT SICKLY

SIMPLE TANGLE UNFIRM WANKLE
WEANLY DWAIBLY DWEEBLE
FRAGILE INVALID LANGUID QUEECHY
RICKETY SAPLESS SHILPIT SLENDER
SLIMPSY THREADY UNWIELD
UNWREST WEARISH DECREPIT
DROGHI IN FEATLESS IMBECILE
IMPOTENT INFERIOR LUSTLESS
MALADIVE RESOLUTE SACKLESS
THEWLESS THOWLESS UNSTRONG
UNWIELDY WATERISH YIELDING
NERVELESS

FEEBLE-MINDED ANILE DOTTY
DOTTLE FOOLISH MORONIC
WANTING IMBECILE

FEEBLENESS DOTAGE FEEBLE
POVERTY CADUCITY DEBILITY
WEAKNESS

FEED EAT HAY BAIT BEET BRAN CROP
DIET DINE FILL FOOD GLUT GRUB
MEAL MEAT OATS SATE AGIST FLESH
FLUSH GORGE GRASS GRAZE NURSE
SERVE STOKE TABLE BATTLE
BROWSE FODDER FOSTER INFEED
NOODLE REFETE REPAST SUCKLE
SUPPLY BLOWOUT FURNISH GRATIFY
HERBAGE INDULGE KEEPING
NOURISH NURTURE PASTURE
PROVENT SATIATE SATISFY SUBSIST
SURFEIT SUSTAIN VICTUAL
PROVENDER
(— ABUNDANTLY) STOKE
(— ANIMAL) SORT SERVE
(— AT NIGHT) SUP
(— CATTLE) SOIL
(— FOR CATTLE) FODDER STOVER
TACKLE
(— FORCIBLY) CRAM
(— GLUTTONOUSLY) BATTEN
(— GREEN FOOD TO CATTLE) SOIL
(— HIGH) FRANK
(— IN STUBBLE) SHACK
(— ON FLIES) SMUT
(— RAVENOUSLY) FRAUNCH
(— STOCK) FOG SOIL SOILING
(— TO REPLETION) ENGORGE
(— TO THE FULL) SATIATE
(— WELL) BATTLE
(GROUND —) CHOP
(HORSE'S —) OATS
(POULTRY —) SCRATCH
(RED —) HAYSEED
(STOCK —) BRAN
(WHALE —) GRIT
(PREF.) THREP(SO)

FEEDBOARD DECK

FEEDER HOGGER HOPPER PECKER
STOCKER
(YARN —) CARRIER

FEEDHEAD RISER FEEDER SINKHEAD

FEEDING RELIEF FOLDAGE PANNAGE
(— GROUND FOR FISH) MEADOW
(— THROUGH TUBE) GAVAGE

(FREE-CHOICE —) CAFETERIA
(IMPROPER —) MISDIET
(PREF.) PHAG(O)

FEEL FIND PALP GROPE SENSE THINK
TOUCH FIMBLE FINGER HANDLE
RESENT EXAMINE EXPLORE FEELING
SENSATE PERCEIVE
(— ACUTELY) SUFFER
(— AVERSION FOR) HATE LOATHE
(— CHILLY) CREEM
(— COMPASSION) PITY YEARN
(— DEJECTION) REPINE
(— FEAR) UG GRUE UGGE TREMBLE
(— GRIEF) GRIEVE DEPLORE
(— HAPPY OR BETTER) LIGHT
(— NAUSEA) WAMBLE
(— OF CLOTH) HAND
(— ONE'S WAY) GROPE FUMBLE
GRAMMEL
(— OUT) SOUND
(— PAIN) URN
(— REPUGNANCE) ABHOR
(— SHAME) BLUSH
(— WANT OF) MISS

FEELER DRAW KITE PALP SNIFF
PALPUS TACTOR ANTENNA SMELLER
PROPOSAL TENTACLE
(PREF.) ANTENNI

FEELING AURA FEEL PITY TACT VIBE
VIEW CHEER HEART HUMOR SENSE
SORGE TOUCH VIBES AFFECT
CEMENT MORALE CONSENT
EMOTION OPINION PASSION
VELUNGE ATTITUDE SENTIENT
SENSATION PRESENTIMENT
(— ILL) HOWISH
(— MIRTH) JOCUND
(— OF ACCORD) SYMPATHY
(— OF AMUSEMENT) CHARGE
(— OF ANTIPATHY) ALLERGY
(— OF ANXIETY) ANGST
(— OF CONTEMPT) DISDAIN
(— OF DISGUST) UG
(— OF DOUBT) SCRUPLE
(— OF HAVING SEEN BEFORE)
DEJAVU
(— OF HORROR) CREEP CREEPS
(— OF HOSTILITY) ANIMUS
(— OF JOY) GLOAT
(— OF LOSS) REGRET
(— OF NAUSEA) WAMBLE
(— OF OPPOSITION) KICK
(— OF PLEASURE) THRILL
(— OF RESENTMENT) GRUDGE
(— OF ROMANCE) STARDUST
(— OF UNEASINESS) MALAISE
(— OF WARMTH) GLOW
(— OF WEARINESS) ENNUI
(— OF WELL-BEING) EUPHORIA
(— PRODUCED BY DRUG) RUSH
(ACTIVE —) SWANKY
(ANGERED —) DUDGEON
(AWKWARD —) LUBBER

(BODILY —) TABET
(BRISTLING —) GOOSEFLESH
(COMPASSIONATE —) REMORSE
(CONCEITED —) SWELLING
(EXALTED —) ECSTASY
(FAMILIAR —) DEJAVU
(HUMILIATING —) SHAME
(ILL —) HARDNESS
(INMOST —S) HEART
(INTUITIVE —) HUNCH
(KINDLY —) GOODWILL
(LOW-BORN —) LOON
(MISCHIEVOUS —) SPALPEEN
(OFFENDED —) PET
(PALTRY —) SQUIB
(PLEASANT —) BUZZ
(RAGGED —) SNUDGE
(RAKISH —) RAFF
(REPRESSION OF —) STOICISM
(SCURVY —) SCALD
(SHOCKED —) SCANDAL
(SICKLY —) QUALM
(STRONG —) STAB
(STRONG, POSITIVE —) SOUL
(TENDEREST —S) QUICK
(TRIFLING —) TOMFOOL
(UNKIND —) ILLWILL
(PL.) HEART WITHERS
(PREF.) SENSI
(SUFF.) PATH(IA)(IC)(Y)
FEEN, DIE (CHARACTER IN —) ADA
GROMA ARINDAL
(COMPOSER OF —) WAGNER
FEET DOGS TONGS STAMPS
WALKERS GUNBOATS TRILBIES
PETTITOES
(— WASHING) MAUNDY
(BOARD —) FOOTAGE
(LARGE —) GUFFINS
(PREF.) PED(I)
(SUFF.) PEDE
(MEASURE OF —) METER
FEIGN ACT FAKE MINT MOCK SEEM
SHAM VEYN AVOID FABLE FALSE
FORGE PAINT PUTON SHAPE SHIRK
AFFECT ASSUME GAMMON INVENT
POSSUM CONCEAL FALSIFY FASHION
IMAGINE POETIZE PRETEND
ROMANCE DISGUISE SIMULATE
(— ASSENT) COLLOGUE
(— IGNORANCE) CONNIVE
(— ILLNESS) MALINGER
FEIGNED SHAM FALSE FEINT POETIC
PSEUDO SHADOW ASSUMED
COLORED FICTIVE PAINTED
FABULOUS FICTIOUS SIMULATE
SUPPOSED
(PREF.) PSEUD(O)
FEIGNING FICTION FORGERY
SIMULATION
FEIJOA ANDRE
FEINT FAKE MINT RUSE APPEL FAINT
SHIFT SPOOF TRICK FALSIFY FEIGNED

FEINTER FINCTURE PRETENSE
REVIRADO
FELDSPAR ALBITE AMBITE GNEISS
CELSIAN SYENITE ADULARIA
ANDESINE FELSPATH PERTHITE
PETUNTZE SANIDINE SUNSTONE
MOONSTONE
FELICIA AGATHAEA
FELICITATE HUG BLESS MACARIZE
FELICITOUS FIT HAPPY
FELICITOUSLY HAPPILY
FELICITY JOY BLISS SONSE
HEAVEN
FELINE CATTISH
FELL CUR FEN HEW COSH DOWN
DROP FALL HIDE HILL MOOR PELT
RUIN SKIN VERY CRUEL EAGER FIELD
GRASS GREAT SHARP DEADLY
FIERCE FLEECE INTENT MIGHTY
SAVAGE SHREWD TUMBLE BRUTISH
CRASHED DOUGHTY HIDEOUS
INHUMAN STRETCH TUMBLED
MOUNTAIN SPIRITED VIGOROUS
(— A TREE) HEW LODGE
FELLER GIDEON
FELLING FALL CUTTING
FELLOE BOD FELF FALLY
FELLOW S BO BOY BUB COD DON
EGG FOX GUY JOE LAD MAC MAN
MUN NUT WAG WAT YOB BALL BEAN
BEAU BIRD BOZO BUFF CARL CHAL
CHAP COOT COVE CUSS DEAN DICK
DUCK DUDE DULL GENT GILL GINK
HIND HUSK JACK JAKE JOHN LOON
MATE NABS PEER PRIG SNAP BILLY
BIMBO BLOKE BROCK BUDDY BULLY
CARLE CHIEL COVEY CULLY FRUIT
GROOM GUEST JOKER MATCH
PARTY SCOUT SKATE SLAVE SPORT
SPRIG SWIPE BEGGAR BILLIE BIRKIE
BOHUNK BUDDIE BUDDIE BUFFER
BUGGER BUSTER CALLAN CHIELD
CODGER CUFFIN CUTTER FELLER
FOOTER FOUTER FOUTRA GALOOT
GAZABO GEEZER HOMBRE JASPER
JOCKEY JOHNNY JOSSER KIPPER
PERSON SHAVER SINNER SIRRAH
SISTER SOCIUS TURNIP BASTARD
BROTHER CALLANT CHAPPIE
COMRADE CULLIES CULLION
CUSTRON KNOCKER PARTNER
SCROYLE SNOOZER BLIGHTER
CONFRERE DOTTEREL MERCHANT
NEIGHBOR SYNODITE
(AWKWARD —) JAY OAF CLUB
GAWK CLOWN LOOBY GALOOT
SLOUCH
(BASE —) CARL CARLE CULLION
(BASHFUL —) SHEEP
(BOLD —) HEARTY
(BRUTAL —) CLUBFIST
(CLOWNISH —) COOF BAYARD
LOBLOLLY

(CLUMSY —) BOOB FILE CAMEL FARMER LUBBER PALOOKA
(COMMON —) JACK LOUT
(CONCEITED —) JEMMY DALTEEN PRINCOX
(CONTEMPTIBLE —) DOG SCUT SMAIL SNAKE RABBIT SMATCH PEASANT
(CONTENTIOUS —) SQUARER
(CORPULENT —) POMPION
(COUNTRY —) JAKE JASPER
(CRUDE —) STIFF
(DASHING —) BUCK BLADE
(DASTARDLY —) HOUND
(DECEITFUL —) KNAVE
(DESPICABLE —) FOUTER FOUTRA HANGDOG SMATCHET
(DIRTY —) SCAB BROCK
(DISAGREEABLE —) GLEYDE
(DISSOLUTE —) RAKE ROUE RAKEHELL
(DROLL —) CARD
(DROWSY —) LUNGIS
(DRUNKEN —) BORACHIO
(DULL —) BURP DRIP FOGY CHUFF SUMPH LUNGIS HUMDRUM
(ENERGETIC —) HUSTLER
(FAT —) HIND GULCH GLUTTON
(FIERCE-LOOKING —) KILLBUCK
(FINE —) BAWCOCK
(FOOLISH —) SOP GABY GOFF ZANY GANDER JACKSON WIDGEON
(GAY —) GALLIARD
(GOOD —) BRICK BULLY TRUMP HEARTY TROJAN
(GOOD-FOR-NOTHING —) JACKEEN
(GREEDY —) SLOTE
(IDLE —) FANION FOOTER STOCAH LOLLARD SKULKER
(IGNORANT —) GOBBIN
(ILLBRED —) LARRIKIN
(IMPERTINENT —) JACK WHISK
(INSIGNIFICANT —) SQUIB
(JOLLY —) VAVASOR VAVASOUR
(LAZY —) BUM LUSK TOOL LENTO
(LOW —) RAG WAFF SWEEP LIMMER VARLET MECHANIC WHORESON
(LUBBERLY —) HULK
(MEAN —) CAD DOG BOOR BOUCH BUCKO CAVEL CHURL SCURF RASCAL CULLION BEZONIAN COISTREL COISTRIL SNEAKSBY SPALPEEN STINKARD
(NIGGARDLY —) SNUDGE
(NOISY —) MOUTH
(OLD —) GLYDE GAFFER GEEZER
(OLD-FASHIONED —) FOGY
(OVERBEARING —) GRIMSIR
(PROSAIC —) PRUNE
(PUNY —) SMAIK
(QUARRELSOME —) HECTOR
(QUEER OLD —) CODGER GEEZER
(RESIDENTIAL —) DON

(ROGUISH —) DOG
(RUDE —) BOOR JACK ROUGH
(SHABBY —) SHAB SQUEEF
(SHEEPISH —) SUMPH
(SHIFTLESS —) PROG SHACK PROGGER
(SHREWD —) COLT
(SILLY —) TOT GUMP ZANY SHEEP SMAIK BUFFER DOTTEREL MUSHHEAD
(SIMPLE —) DOODLE
(SLOVENLY —) SLUTE
(SLY —) FOX COON
(SNEAKING —) SNUDGE
(SORDID —) HUNKS
(SOUTH AFRICAN —) KEREL
(SPIRITED —) BRICK
(SPORTY —) PLAYBOY
(STRANGE —) CODGER
(STRAPPING —) SWANKY SWANKIE
(STUPID —) ASS BOOB CLOD COOF DAFF DOLT GUMP HASH MUFF SIMP BOOBY CUDDY DUNCE MORON STIRK BAYARD BUFFER FARMER FOOZLE GANDER ASINOCO DOWFART HUMDRUM CLODPATE CLODPOLE CLODPOLL CODSHEAD SOCKHEAD
(STURDY —) HUSKY
(SULLEN —) GLUMP
(SURLY —) CHUFF CHOUGH
(TEDIOUS —) FOOZLE
(TRICKISH —) HUMBUG
(TRICKY —) ROOK GREEK KNAVE SCAMP DODGER RASCAL
(UNCIVIL —) RUDESBY
(UNCOUTH —) JAKE KEMP TIKE
(VILE —) RAT SKUNK
(VULGAR —) TIGER
(WORTHLESS —) BUM CUR DOG HASH PROG RAFF WAFF JAVEL ROGUE SCAMP SHOAT SNAKE STUMER BROTHEL BUDMASH PROGGER VAURIEN TARTARET
(WRETCHED —) DEVIL DOGBOLT
(YOUNG —) BILLY BUCKO CADIE CADDIE
(PREF.) CO
(SUFF.) ENGRO
FELLOWMAN BROTHER NEIGHBOR
FELLOWSHIP GUILD HAUNT UNION FAMILY COMPANY ALLIANCE SODALITY
(CHRISTIAN —) KOINONIA
FELLY RIM FELF FELLOE KEENLY CRUELLY BITTERLY FIERCELY SAVAGELY TERRIBLY
FELO-DE-SE SUICIDE
FELON WILD CRUEL FETLOW FIERCE WICKED CONVICT CULPRIT PANARIS VILLAIN WHITLOW PHLEGMON RUNROUND MALEFACTOR
FELONY ARSON CRIME OFFENSE

FELT JIG PLAIT FILTER NUMNAH SENSED SOLEIL VELOUR DOUBLER FELTING PANNOSE
(— INTENSIVELY) ACUTE
(— THROUGH SENSES) SENSATE
(DEEPLY —) CORDIAL INTENSE
(PERSONALLY —) CONSCIOUS
(PL.) CLOTHING
(PREF.) PIL(O)

FELTWORK NEUROPIL

FEMALE DOE EWE HEN HER SHE SOW DAME GIRL GYNE LADY MORT ADULT JENNY SMOCK SQUAW WOMAN WAHINE WEAKLY DISTAFF FEMINAL WOMANLY DAUGHTER FEMININE GYNAECIC LADYLIKE WOMANISH PETTICOAT
(— ANCESTOR) TAPROOT
(IMPERFECT —) FREEMARTIN
(PARTHOGENETIC —) AMAZON
(PREF.) FEMINO GYN(AE)(AECO)(AEO) (ANDRO)(E)(ECO)(EO)(O) THELY
(SUFF.) ESS ETTE GYN(E)(IST)(OUS) INE TRIX

FEMININE FAIR SOFT WEAK WOMAN FEMALE TENDER WAHINE FEMINAL WOMANLY WOMANISH PETTICOAT
(SUFF.) ENNE INA INE

FEMININE WILES (CHARACTER IN —) BELLINA LEONORA FILANDRO GIAMPOLO ROMUALDO
(COMPOSER OF —) CIMAROSA

FEMININITY MUSLIN FEMINITY MULIEBRITY

FEMME FATALE VAMP SIREN

FEMORAL CRURAL
(PREF.) CRURO

FEMUR THIGH

FEN BOG CARR FAIN FELL FOWL MERE MOOR WASH BROAD FAINS MARSH SNIPE SWAMP VENTS MORASS MUSKEG QUAGMIRE

FENCE BAR HAW HAY BANK DIKE DUEL DYKE HAHA HAIN PALE PLAY RAIL STUB WALL WEIR WIRE BEARD DODGE FRITH GUARD HEDGE MOUND PALIS STICK STUMP DETENT FENDER FRAISE GLANCE HURDLE LEADER PALING PICKET RADDLE RASPER SCHERM SCRIME TIMBER BARRIER BULWARK CYCLONE DEFENSE ENCLOSE FENCING FENSURE IMPALER PASSAGE RAILING SWAGMAN BACKSTOP ENCHASER ENCLOSER GRAFFAGE HOARDING PALISADE PALISADO SEPIMENT SKIRMISH BRANDRETH BRANDRITH
(— AROUND BULLRING) BARRERA
(— AROUND MACHINERY) BRATTICE
(— CLOSING DITCH) WOLF
(— OF LOCK) STUB
(— OF LOGS) GLANCE

(CATTLE —) OXER WIPE SKERM SCHERM
(FISH —) WEIR KIDDLE LEADER
(METAL —) RAIL RAILING
(PREF.) HERCO PHRAGMO SEPTATO
(SUFF.) SEPTATE

FENCER DUELIST IMPALER PARRIER PROVOST SCRIMER SWORDER FOILSMAN BACKSWORD

FENCE RAIL DRAWBAR

FENCE SECTION PANE

FENCE-SITTER MUGWUMP

FENCING WIRE FENCE PALING ESCRIME PASSAGE SCIENCE SWORDING
(— THRUST) PASSADO
(JAPANESE —) KENDO

FEND WARD PARRY SHIRK DEFEND FORBID RESIST SUPPORT

FENDER SKID WING CAMEL GUARD SKATE BUFFER BUMPER SHIELD DOLPHIN PUDDING BOWGRACE MUDGUARD SPLASHER
(— FOR FIREPLACE) CURB KERB
(— NEAR HOLE) TELLTALE
(ROPE —) PUDDENING
(SHIP'S —) SKID

FENDER SKID GLANCER

FENESTRA FORAMEN

FENGHUANG FUM PHOENIX

FENKS FRITTERS

FENMAN WEBFOOT

FENNEC ZERDA

FENNEL ANIS DILL HEMP SOYA FERULE FINKEL COWBANE HOGWEED SPINGEL FINOCHIO FLORENCE CAROSELLA

FENNER ZERDA

FENRIS (FATHER OF —) LOKI
(MOTHER OF —) ANGURBODA
(SISTER OF —) HEL
(SLAYER OF —) VIDAR

FENSTER WINDOW

FENUGREEK BAUMIER MELLILOT
(SEEDS OF —) HELBEH

FERAL WILD BRUTAL DEADLY FERINE SAVAGE BESTIAL UNTAMED FUNEREAL UNBROKEN

FER-DE-LANCE BONETAIL JARARACA

FERMATA HOLD PAUSE TENOR CORONA

FERMENT FRY LOB ZYM BARM BREW FRET HEAT SOUR TURN WORK ZYME FEVER SWEAT YEAST DANDER ENZYME FLOWER FOMENT SEETHE SIMMER TUMULT UPROAR AGITATE QUICKEN TURMOIL DISORDER
(— IN SALIVA) PTYALIN
(DIGESTIVE —) TRYPSIN
(PREF.) ZYM(O)
(SUFF.) ZYME

FERMENTATION SWEAT CUVAGE
FERMENT MOWBURN WORKING
ZYMOSIS
FERMENTED SOD HARD
(IMPROPERLY —) FOXY
FERMENTING BARMY WORKING
FERN HEII NITO PULU TARA WEKI
BRAKE DUGAL EKAHA FROND
NARDO PITAU PONGA ULUHI WHEKI
AMAMAU DOODIA NARDOO
OSMUND PTERIS ACROGEN
ATERACH BOGFERN BRACKEN
OSMUNDA SYNANGE WOODSIA
ADIANTUM ASPIDIUM BAROMETZ
BUCKHORN BUNGWALL CETERACH
DAVALLIA DENDRITE FERNWORT
FILICITE GOLDBACK HARDFERN
KOLOKOLO MOONWORT MULEWORT
PARAREKA PILLWORT POLYPODY
SPOROGEN STAGHORN MAIDENHAIR
(KIND OF —) MALE
(PART OF —) AXIS CASE LEAF STEM
BLADE FROND PINNA STIPE TOOTH
MIDRIB RACHIS LEAFLET PETIOLE
PINNULE SUBLEAFLET
(PL.) FILICES
(PREF.) PTERID(O)
(SUFF.) PTERIS
FERN LEAF FROND CROSIER
FERNLIKE FERNY PTEROID
FEROCIOUS ILL FELL GRIM RUDE
WILD BRUTE CRUEL FERAL BLOODY
BRUTAL FEROCE FIERCE GOTHIC
RAGING SAVAGE ACHARNE
INHUMAN OMINOUS VIOLENT
WOLFISH PITILESS RAVENOUS
RUTHLESS TARTARLY
FEROCITY FERITY SAVAGERY
VIOLENCE ACHARNEMENT
FERRARA ANDREW
FERRET HOB MONK TAPE PADOU
MONACH WEASEL POLECAT
(— OUT) FOSSICK
(FEMALE —) GIL GILL JILL BITCH
(MALE —) HOB HOBB
FERRIAGE WAFTAGE
FERRIC OXIDE CROCUS
FERROCYANIDE PRUSSIATE
FERROTYPE GLAZE TINTYPE
FERROUS SIDEROUS
FERRULE CAP TIP CUFF RING SHOE
VIRL COLLET PULLEY RUNNER
VERREL VIROLE ARMGARN BUSHING
CRAMPET
FERRY FORD PASS PONT SCOW
PASSAGE TRAJECT TRANECT
TRANSFER
FERRYBOAT BAC PONT SCOW
FERRY
FERRYMAN CHARON FERRIER
WATERMAN
FERTILE FAT GOOD RANK RICH
GLEBY ARABLE BATFUL BATTLE

FECUND HEARTY STRONG TEEMING
ABUNDANT BATTABLE FRUITFUL
GENEROUS PREGNANT PROLIFIC
SPAWNING
FERTILITY HEART FATNESS
(PATRON OF —) YAKSHA
FERTILIZATION ENDOGAMY
POROGAMY
FERTILIZE FAT DUNG FISH LIME
MARL CHALK BATTEN ENRICH
FRUCTIFY
FERTILIZER FAT MARL GUANO
HUMUS ALINIT FLOATS MANURE
POLLEN POTASH CARRIER COMPOTE
HUMOGEN KAINITE NITRATE
TANKAGE AMMONITE CINEREAL
NITROGEN
FERULA NARTHEX
FERULE ROD RULER COLLET FENNEL
FERULA PALMER
FERVENCY WARMTH CANDENCY
FERVENT HOT KEEN WARM EAGER
FIERY ARDENT BITTER FERVID FIERCE
INWARD RAGING SAVAGE BOILING
BURNING GLOWING INTENSE
PECTORAL ROMANTIC VEHEMENT
RELIGIOUS
FERVID HOT ARDENT TROPIC
BOILING BURNING FERVENT
GLOWING ZEALOUS UNCTUOUS
VEHEMENT
FERVOR FIRE HEAT HWYL RAGE
SOUL ZEAL ARDOR SPIRIT WARMTH
PASSION CANDENCY DEVOTION
STRENGTH VIOLENCE
(— IN PRAYER) KAVVANAH
KAWWANAH
FESCUE VESTER
FESS BAR BAND PERT DANCE HUMET
(DIMINUTIVE —) TRANGLE
FEST GALA
FESTAL GAY GALA GAUDY FESTIVE
FESTUAL FEASTFUL
FESTER ROT BEAL RANK SCAR
RANKLE PUSTULE PUTREFY
FESTERING RANK FRETTY
FESTIVAL (ALSO SEE FEAST) ALE
BON PWE BUSK FAIR FEIS FETE GALA
HOLI MELA PUJA TIDE UTAS WAKE
DELIA FEAST FERIA FESTA GAUDY
HALOA PURIM REVEL ROUSE SEDAR
ADONIA BAIRAM BRIDAL CARNEA
DEWALI DIASIA DIPALA FIESTA
HOHLEE HUFFLE KERMIS KWANZA
LAMMAS LENAEA OPALIA PONGOL
POOJAH POSADA SUCCOS AGONIUM
AGRANIA BANQUET BELTANE
DASAHRA EQUIRIA FESTIAL HILARIA
KERMESS KWANZAN MATSURI
PALILIA SUKKOTH THIASOS TOXCATL
UPHELYA VINALIA AGHIONIA
AIANTEIA APATURIA ATHENAEA
BEALTINE BRUMALIA CARNIVAL

COTYTTIA DASAHARA DIIPOLIA
DIONYSIA DUSSERAH ENCAENIA
FASNACHT FLORALIA HANUKKAH
HIGHTIDE KALENDAE LUPERCAL
MARYMASS MATRALIA MITHRIAC
MUHARRAM MUNYCHIA NATIVITY
NEOMENIA POTLATCH STAMPEDE
TAARGELIA SATURNALIA
(FALL —) OCTOBERFEST
(HIGHLAND —) MOD
(MUSICAL —) EISTEDDFOD
(PL.) MOED VOTA
(SUFF.) MAS

FESTIVE GAY GALA JOLLY FESTAL
GENIAL JOYOUS FEASTLY HOLIDAY
JOCULAR CONVIAL FEASTFUL
MIRTHFUL SPORTIVE CONVIVIAL
(— TIME) TET

FESTIVITY GALA GAUD UTAS UTIS
BEANO FEAST MIRTH RANDY REVEL
GAIETY GAYETY SPLORE HOLIDAY
JOLLITY JOYANCE PATTERN
FESTIVAL FUNCTION MERRIMENT
MERRYMAKING
(RIOTOUS —) RAG

FESTOON SWAG TRIM WREATH
GARLAND DECORATE
(PL.) ENCARPUS

FETCH FET FESH GASP GIVE SHAG
TACK TAKE TEEM WAIN BRING
SWEEP TRICK DOUBLE STROKE
WRAITH ACHIEVE ATTRACT ARTIFICE
FETCHING INTEREST

FETCHED FOSH

FETCHING SWEET CRAFTY CUNNING
ALLURING PLEASING SCHEMING

FETE FAIR GALA FEAST HONOR
ROAST BAZAAR FIESTA HOLIDAY

FETID OLID RANK MUSTY PUTID
ROTTEN VIROSE NOISOME SANIOUS
MALODOROUS

FETIDLY FOULLY

FETISH OBI IDOL JUJU OBIA ZEME
ZEMI ZOGO ANITO ASCON CHARM
GUACA HUACA OBEAH OBIAH
TOTEM AMULET FETICH GRIGRI
NAGUAL VOODOO SHINTAI SORCERY
FETISHRY GREEGREE TALISMAN

FETLOCK COOT FOOTLOCK

FETTER BAND BEND BOLT BOND
FIND GYVE IRON SPAN BASIL BEWET
BILBO CHAIN SLANG SWATH ANKLET
GARTER HALTER HAMPER HOBBLE
HOPPLE IMPEDE LANGEL RACKAN
SWATHE CLINKER CONFINE ENCHAIN
ENSLAVE FETLOCK GARNISH
MANACLE SHACKLE SPANCEL
TRAMMEL RESTRAIN
(PL.) IRONS LINKS DARBIES GARNISH
GARTERS

FETTERBUSH PIPESTEM PIPEWOOD

FETTLE BEAT DECK FUSS MULL TIDY
TWIG VEIN DRESS GROOM WHACK

YARAK GIRDLE REPAIR SETTLE
STRIKE ARRANGE BANDAGE
FEATHER HARNESS

FETTLER BILLYER NOBBLER

FETTLING FIX FETTLE FIXING

FETUS BIRTH CHILD YOUNG AMELUS
BREECH EMBRYO FOETUS ABORTUS
CYCLOPS FEATURE AMORPHUS
(PREF.) EMBRY(O) FETI FETO FOETI
FOETO

FEUD FIEF FRAY BROIL AFFRAY
ENMITY FEODUM FEUDUM STRIFE
CONTEST DISPUTE QUARREL
VENDETTA

FEUDATORY FIEF VASSAL
ZAMINDAR ZEMINDAR

FEUILLE MORTE PHILAMOT

FEVER AGUE FIRE ARDOR CAUMA
DANDY LEUMA OCTAN CAUSUS
DENGUE FEBRIS HECTIC SEPTAN
SEXTAN SODOKU TYPHIA TYPHUS
VOMITO AMAKEBE FERMENT
FEVERET HELODES HOTNESS
MALARIA PINKEYE PYREXIA
QUARTAN TERTIAN TYPHOID
SYNOCHUS TERTIANA TYPHINIA
CALENTURE
(— OF HORSE) WEED SCALMA
(— OF PERU) VERRUGA
(— OF SHEEP) BRAXY
(BRAIN —) PHRENITIS
(HAY —) RHINITIS
(KIND OF —) LASSA
(MALARIAL —) TAP
(MARSH —) HELODES
(SPLENIC —) ANTHRAX
(TEXAS —) TRISTEZA
(WITHOUT —) APYRETIC
(YELLOW —) VOMITO
(PREF.) FEBRI PYR(ET)(ETO)
(SUFF.) PYRA

FEVERED DISEASED

FEVERFEW MAYWEED MUGWORT
PELLITORY

FEVERISH HOT FIERY FEVERY HECTIC
EXCITED FEBRILE FRANTIC RESTLESS

FEVERLESS APYREXIA

FEVERROOT GENSON

FEVER TREE BITTERBARK

FEVERWEED FITWEED

FEVERWORT BONESET

FEW LIT CURN LESS SOME SCANT
THREE WHEEN WHONE CURRAN
PICKLE SPOTTY LIMITED SEVERAL
EXIGUOUS
(PREF.) OLIG(O) PAUCI

FEWER LESS
(PREF.) MI(O)

FEWNESS PAUCITY

FEY DEAD CRAZY DYING ELFIN FATAL
DOOMED TOUCHED UNLUCKY
PIXILATED

FEZ TARBOOSH

FIADOR THEODORE
FIANCE TRUST SPOUSE FIANCEE
   PROMISE AFFIANCE INTENDED
FIASCO CRASH FLASK FROST FIZZLE
   FAILURE DISASTER
FIAT EDICT ORDER UKASE DECREE
   COMMAND DECISION SANCTION
FIB LIE YED FLAW WHID SLANT STORY
   FITTEN PUMMEL SILENT
   TARADIDDLE
FIBBER LIAR
FIBER TAL ADAD BASS BAST COIR
   ERUC FERU FLAX HARL HEMP IMBE
   JUTE LINE PITA SILK SUNN TULA
   ABACA AGUST AZLON CAJUN
   CAROA CHOEL ERIZO FIBRE GRAIN
   HARLE ISOTE ISTLE IXTLE IZOTE
   KAPOK KENAF KITUL LYCRA MESTA
   MURVA OAKUM MUCUNA NYTRIL RAMIE RAPHE SIMAL
   SISAL STRAW TERAP TOSSA TUCUM
   VIVER AMIRAY ARAMID ARGHAN
   BINDER BUNTAL BURITI CABUYA
   CATENA DACRON EMBIRA FIBRIL
   FIMBLE HINOKI KANAFF KENDIR
   KOHEMP MUCUNA NYTRIL RAFFIA
   SALAGO STAPLE STRAND STRING
   SUTURE THREAD TUCUMA TURURI
   VINYON YACHAN ZAPUPE ACETATE
   ACRYLIC ANONANG ARAMINA
   BASSINE CANTALA CASCARA
   CHANDUL CHINGMA COQUITA
   ESPARTO FILASSE FUNICLE
   GEBANGA GRAVATA GUAXIMA
   GUMIHAN HUARIZO KERATTO
   KITTOOL MOCMAIN PALMITE
   PANGANE PAUKPAN POCHOTE
   SABUTAN CANAPINA CURRATOW
   FILAMENT HARAKEKE HENEQUEN
   PIASSAVA TOQUILLA TRONADOR
   (— FROM PEACOCK FEATHERS) MARL
   (— OF PALM) DOH LIF ERUC COYOL
   COROZO GOMUTI KITTUL COQUITA
   GEBANGA
   (—S OF FLAX) HARE
   (CLUSTER OF —S) NEP
   (COARSE —) KEMP
   (COCONUT —) COIR KYAR
   (COTTON —) LINT STAPLE
   (FLAX —) TOW
   (KNOT OF —) NOIL
   (MANUFACTURED —) DYNEL ORLON
   ESTRON ACRILAN SPANDEX
   (MATTED —) SHAG
   (MINERAL —) ASBESTOS
   (MUSCLE —) RHABDIUM
   (NERVE —) EFFERENT DEPRESSOR
   (PULVERIZED —) FLOCK
   (SILKY —) PULU KAPOK KUMBI
   YACHAN CASTULI
   (TEXTILE —) SPANDEX
   (TWISTED —S) STRAND
   (WASTE —) FLY GOUT
   (WASTE —S) FLOSS

(WOODY —) BAST GRAIN SCUTCH
   (PL.) FUZZ KERATTO
   (PREF.) FIBRO IN(O)
FIBRIL AXONEME DESMOSE
   MYONEME MYOPHAN
FIBRILS
   (SUFF.)
   (NETWORK —) SPONGIA(E)(N)
   SPONGIUM
FIBRIN GLUTEN MYOSIN
FIBROCARTILAGE FABELLA
   MENISCUS
FIBROID DESMOID
FIBROMA INOMA FIBROID
FIBROUS FIBROSE STRINGY
   NEMALINE
FIBULA LACE CLASP BROOCH
   BUCKLE PERONE SPLINT
   (PREF.) PERONEO PERONO
FICHE FILMCARD
FICKLE GERY DIZZY FALSE GIDDY
   LIGHT UNSAD HARLOT KITTLE
   MOBILE PUZZLE SHIFTY VOLAGE
   WANKLE WANKLY CASALTY CASELTY
   FLATTER MOONISH MOVABLE
   MUTABLE VAINFUL VARIANT
   VOLUBLE GOSSAMER MOVEABLE
   SKITTISH STIRRING UNSTABLE
   UNSTEADY VARIABLE VOLATILE
   WAVERING
FICKLENESS CHANGE LEVITY
   EASINESS FICKLETY VARIANCE
FICO FIG FIGO TANTI
FICTILE FIGULINE
FICTION BAM TALE FABLE FALSE
   NOVEL ROMAN STORY DECEIT
   DEVICE FABULA FITTEN LEGEND
   COINAGE FANTASY FIGMENT
   FORGERY MARCHEN NOVELRY
   ROMANCE ROMANZA KAILYARD
   PHANTASY PRETENCE PRETENSE
   (CRIME —) NOIR
FICTITIOUS MADE BOGUS DUMMY
   FALSE PHONY FABLED POETIC
   ASSUMED FEIGNED PHANTOM
   FABULOUS FICTIOUS MYTHICAL
   ROMANTIC SIMULATE SPURIOUS
   LEGENDARY
   (PREF.) PSEUD(O)
FICUS PYRULA
FID PRICK NORMAN PRICKER
   SPLICER
FIDDLE BOW BOX GIG SAW VIOL
   CHEAT CROWD GEIGE GIGUE GUDOK
   CHORUS DIDDLE FITHEL POTTER
   TRIFLE URHEEN VIOLIN CHROTTA
   SARANGI SWINDLE HUMSTRUM
   (— STRING) THAIRM
   (— WITH) TWIDDLE
   (BASS —) GUTBUCKET
   (OLD —) REBEC
FIDDLER CRAB VIOLER VIOLIN
   CROWDER SCRAPER SIXPENCE

FIDDLER CRAB RACER FIDDLER OCYPODE SOLDIER
FIDDLESTICKS POOH PSHAW FIDDLE
FIDELIO (CHARACTER IN —) ROCCO FIDELIO LEONORE PIZARRO JAQUINO FLORESTAN MARZELLINE
(COMPOSER OF —) BEETHOVEN
FIDELITY TRUE ARDOR FAITH PIETY TROTH TRUTH FEALTY HONESTY LOYALTY ADHESION DEVOTION RELIGION VERACITY CONSTANCY
FIDGET MOP FIKE FIRK FUSS ROIL FIDGE FITCH HOTCH SHRUB SHRUG WORRY BREVIT FIGGLE FISSLE FISTLE FRIDGE FUSSER HIRSEL JIFFLE JIGGET NESTLE NIBBLE NIGGLE TIDDLE TRIFLE VIGGLE WORRIT NERVOUS RESTLESS TWITCHET
(— ABOUT TRIFLES) SPOFFLE
(STATE OF —) FANTAD FANTOD
(PL.) JUMPS
FIDGETY ANTSY FIKIE FUSSY ITEMY FEISTY FIGENT FLISKY KITTLE UNEASY RESTIVE TWITCHY RESTLESS
FIDUCIARY TRUSTEE TRUSTFUL
FIE SISS FAUGH
FIEF FEE HAN FEUD FEOFF TIMAR ZIAMET SATSUMA SUBFIEF BENEFICE
(— HOLDER) TIMARIOT
FIELD LEA LOT ACRE AGER AREA BENT CAMP FELL FLAT HADE INAM LAND LIST MEAD PALE PARK PLAY RAND TOWN WONG BRECK CAMPO CHAMP CLOUR CROFT EARTH GLEBE INNAM LAYER MILPA NILPA PADDY RANGE ROWEN SAWAH TILTH VELDE ARRISH CAMPUS CAREER CHAMPE DOMAIN FURROW GARDEN GROUND MACHAR MATTER MEADOW PADANG PINGLE SHIELD SPHERE CHARMEL COMPASS CULTURE DIAMOND FERRING GARSTON INFIELD MOWLAND NEWTAKE PADDOCK PARROCK PIGHTLE PURVIEW QUILLET TERRAIN THWAITE TILLAGE CLEARING PROVINCE
(— ADJOINING HOUSE) CROFT
(— AT CRICKET) SCOUT
(— OF ACTIVITY) GAME ARENA BARONY SPHERE TERRAIN
(— OF BATTLE) PLAIN
(— OF BLOODSHED) ACELDAMA AKELDAMA
(— OF CONTROL) DOMAIN
(— OF ENDEAVOR) BUSINESS
(— OF SNOW) NEVE SNOWPACK
(— OF STUDY) MAJOR GROUND
(— ON WHICH GRASS IS GROWN) MEAD MEADOW

(— SOWN FOR TWO SUCCESSIVE YEARS) HOOK
(ENCLOSED —) AGER TOWN CLOSE CROFT
(FOOTBALL —) GRIDIRON
(FRUITFUL —) CHARMEL
(GRASSY —) LEA PEN GARSTON
(HOP —) HOPYARD
(KIND OF —) SKEW
(LAVA —) PEDREGAL
(LITTLE-KNOWN —) BYWAY
(NEW GOLD —) RUSH
(PLOWED —) FURROW
(RICE —) SAWAH
(SMALL —) HAW CLOSE CROFT PADDOCK
(SPORTS —) ARENA PITCH
(STUBBLE —) HIRSH ROWEN ARRISH GRATTEN GRATTON
(TILTING —) LISTS
(TOBACCO —) VEGA
(UNEXPLOITED —) FRONTIER
(UNPLOWED EDGE OF —) RAND
(PL.) FIELDEN
(PREF.) AGRI AGRO ARVI CAMPI
FIELD BALM SHEEPMINT
FIELD CAMOMILE OXEYE
FIELDER GLOVEMAN
(CRICKET —) SLIP COVER FIELD GULLY POINT SCOUT GULLEY INFIELDER
FIELDFARE FELT JACK REDLEG FELLFARE HILLBIRD JACKBIRD REDSHANK SNOWBIRD VELTFARE
FIELDING (— ABILITY) GLOVE
FIELD MADDER SPURWORT
FIELD MOUSE VOLE MIGALE
FIELDPIECE GUN AMUSETTE GALLOPER
FIELD SCABIOUS BLUECAP
FIELDWORK LUNET REDAN LUNETTE REDOUBT
FIEND FEN FOE PUG FEND FYND DEMON DEVIL ENEMY SATAN TRULL WIZARD SHAITAN SUCCUBA TITIVIL BARBASON SUCCUBUS
FIENDISH CRUEL WICKED DEMONIC FIENDLY SATANIC DEMONIAC DEVILISH DIABOLIC INFERNAL
FIERCE ILL BOLD FELL GRIM KEEN RUDE THRO WILD WOOD ASPER BREME CRUEL EAGER FELON HATEL ORPED RETHE SHARP SMART STARK STERN STOUR STOUT WROTH ARDENT FEROCE GOTHIC HETTER IMMANE LUPINE RAGING RUGGED SAVAGE STURDY UNMEEK UNMILD WICKED BRUTISH FERVENT FURIOSO FURIOUS GRIMFUL INHUMAN MANKIND RABIOUS RAMPANT SCADDLE VICIOUS VIOLENT STERNFUL TIGERISH
(PREF.) LABRO

FIERCE-EYED WALLEYED
FIERCELY FELL HARD FELLY FIERCE
FIERCENESS FURY FEROCITY
FIERY HOT RED ADUST FIRED QUICK
SHARP ARDENT FLASHY IGNITE
BURNING FERVENT FLAMING
FURIOUS GLOWING HOTHEAD
IGNEOUS PARCHED PEPPERY VIOLENT
ADUSTIVE CHOLERIC FEVERISH
FRAMPOLD INFLAMED PHRAMPEL
SPIRITED SPITFIRE VEHEMENT
FIERY ANGEL (CHARACTER IN —)
RENATA AGRIPPA HEINRICH
RUPPRECHT MEPHISTOPHELES
(COMPOSER OF —) PROKOFIEV
FIERY RED SANDIX
FIERY-TEMPERED SPUNKY
FIESTA FETE FERIA PARTY HOLIDAY
(— COSTUME) POLLERA
FIFE STICK PIFERO PIFFERO
FIFTEEN FIVE
(PREF.) PENTADEC(A)
FIFTEENTH DOUBLETTE
FIFTH QUINT QUINTIN HEMIOLIA
(— ABOVE TONIC) DOMINANT
(PERFECT —) HEMIOLA HEMIOLIA
(PREF.) QUINT(I)
FIFTY (— YEAR ANNIVERSARY)
JUBILEE
FIFTY-FIFTY EVEN
FIG RIG FICO ARRAY BREBA DRESS
ELEME ELEMI PIPAL SABRA TANTI
BALETE BALITI FOUTER FOUTRA
GINGER LOBFIG PEEPUL TRIFLE
FURBISH GONDANG SICONUS
SYCONUS WARINGIN
(— CROP) MAMME
(PREF.) FICI SYCO
FIG BASKET CABAS
FIGHT BOX MIX WAP WAR WIN BEAT
REEF BLUE BOUT CAMP CLEM COCK
COPE COWP CRAB CUFF DUEL DUKE
FLOG FRAY LAKE MEET MELL MILL
SHOW SLUG SPAR TILT WAGE YOKE
BANDY BRAWL CLASH FIELD FLOIT
HURRY JOUST MATCH MELEE MIXUP
RAMMY SCRAP SETTO SHINE SPURN
STOUR TOUSE AFFAIR AFFRAY
BARNEY BATTLE BICKER BLOWUP
COMBAT DEBATE FEUCHT FRACAS
FRAISE HASSLE IMPUGN MEDDLE
OPPOSE RELUCT REPUGN RESIST
RIPPIT RUFFLE SHOWER STOUSH
STRIFE STRIKE STRIVE TOUSEL
TURNUP BARGAIN BRABBLE
CONTEND CONTEST COUNTER
JOURNEY QUARREL RUCTION
SIMULTY TUILYIE WARFARE
CONFLICT DOGFIGHT DUOMACHY
FINISHER GUNFIGHT MILITATE
SKIRMISH SLUGFEST SQUABBLE
STRUGGLE TIRRIVEE TIRRWIRR
TRAVERSE

(— AGAINST) BUCK OPPUGN
(— BETWEEN TWO) DUEL
DUOMACHY
(— FOR) SERVE CHAMPION
(— WITH CLUB) TIMBER
(FIST —) RIPPIT TURNUP
(GANG —) RUMBLE
(SEA —) NAUMACHY
(STREET —) HABBLE RUMBLE
(SUFF.) MACHIA MACHY
FIGHTER PUG VAMP BOXER COCKER
BATTLER DUELIST SLUGGER
SOLDIER WARRIOR ANDABATA
BARRATER BARRATOR CHAMPION
GUERILLA PUGILIST SCRAPPER
(FIRE —) EXEMPT HOTSHOT
(GUERILLA —) MAQUIS
BUSHWHACKER
(GUERILLA —S) MUJAMIDEEN
FIGHTING BLOW ACTION AFFRAY
DEBATE WARLIKE CONFLICT
MILITANT
(— WITH SHADOW) SCIAMACHY
FIGHTING FISH PLAKAT
**FIGLIA DI JORIO, LA (CHARACTER
IN —)** MILA ALIGI LAZARO
(COMPOSER OF —) PIZZETTI
FIG MARIGOLD SAMH MESEM
FICOID FOXCHOP FICOIDAL ICEPLANT
FIGMENT IDEA FICTION
FIGPECKER BECCAFICO
FIGURATE FLORID FIGURAL FIGURED
FIGURATO
FIGURATION FORM SHAPE DESIGN
OUTLINE
FIGURATIVE FLORID FIGURAL
FIGURED FLOWERY TYPICAL
ALLUSIVE TROPICAL
FIGURE FIG HUE VOL ROSH DOLL
FORM IDEA SIGN STAR ANGLE ANTIC
DATUM DIGIT FLIRT FRAME IMAGE
MAGOT MOTIF SHAPE SPADE SPRIG
AUMAIL BABOON CHANGE CIPHER
COCKUP CUTOUT DEVICE EFFIGY
EMBLEM ENTAIL FIGGER GOOGOL
INCUSE NUMBER PERSON SCHEME
SYMBOL TAILLE TATTOO CHASSIS
CHEVRON CHIFFER CHIFFRE
COMPUTE CONTOUR DRAWING
GESTALT IMPRESS NUMERAL
OUTLINE STATURE DIHEDRAL
FIGURATE GRAFFITO HEXAGRAM
LIKENESS SEMBLANT MARIONETTE
**(— FORMED BY INTERSECTING
LINES)** KNOT
(— IN PRAYER) ORANT
(— IN WOOD GRAIN) BURL FLAKE
(— MADE OF CORN) KNACK
(— MADE OF 3 LINES) TRIGRAM
TRIANGLE
(— OF SPEECH) IMAGE IRONY TROPE
APORIA CLIMAX FLOWER SCHEME
SIMILE VISION ZEUGMA ANALOGY

IMAGERY CHIASMUS DIALLAGE
METAPHOR METONYMY OXYMORON
SYLLEPSIS ABSCISSION
(— OUT) SUS DOPE SUSS BOTTOM
(—S OF SPEECH) COLORS
(— UP) ITEM
(— USED AS COLUMN) ATLAS
TELAMON CARYATID
(— USED AS MAGIC SYMBOL)
PENTACLE
(ANATOMICAL —) ECORCHE
(ARTIFICIAL —) GOLEM
(BIBLICAL —) ANGEL CHERUB
(BIZARRE —) GROTESQUE
(CARVED —) GLYPH FIGURINE
(CENTRAL —) HERO
(CIRCULAR —) HOOP
(CLAY —) HANIWA
(COMIC —) BILLIKEN
(CONSPICUOUS —) MARK
(CRESCENT-SHAPED —) LUNE
(DANCE —) SWING TRACE SQUARE
PURPOSE ASSEMBLE PROMENADE
(DOMINANT —) CAPTAIN
(DUMMY —) MANNEQUIN
(FEMALE —) ORANTE
(FOLDED PAPER —) FLEXAGON
(GEOMETRICAL —) BODY CONE CUBE
LUNE PRISM RHOMB SOLID CIRCLE
GNOMON ISAGON ISOGON OBLONG
SECTOR SPHERE SQUARE DIAGRAM
ELLIPSE LOZENGE PELCOID
POLYGON RHOMBUS SECTION
HEXAFOIL SPHEROID TRIANGLE
RECTANGLE POLYHEDRON
PARALLELOGRAM
(GREEK —) KOUROS
(GROTESQUE —) MAGOT BABOON
MAXIMON
(HAVING FULL ROUNDED —) ZAFTIG
ZOFTIG
(IDEAL —) EIDOLON
(IMAGINARY —) BOGEYMAN
(IMPORTANT —) PANJANDRUM
(INCISED —) INTAGLIO
(JAPANESE — ON GRAVE) HANIWA
(MATH —) SINE COSINE
(MUMMYLIKE —) USHABTI
(MUSICAL —) IDEA LICK OSTINATO
(ODD —) MAUMET
(OVAL —) SWASH ELLIPSE
(PAPER —) FLEXAGON
(PREHISTORIC —) CHACMOL
CHACMOOL
(QUADRILLE —) POULE
(QUEER —) GIG
(RHETORICAL —) COLOR COLOUR
(RHYTHMIC —) SNAP
(SCULPTURED —) CANEPHOR
(SHADOW —) SKIAGRAM
(SKATING —) SPIRAL BRACKET
COUNTER
(SPINDLE-SHAPED —) FUSEE FUZEE

(STUFFED —) DUMMY
(SYLLOGISTIC —) SCHEMA
(SYMBOLIC —) MORAL EMBLEM
(TAILOR'S —) MANNEQ MANNEQUIN
(TRIANGULAR —) TRIQUET
(UNDRAPED —) NUDE
(WINGED —) ANGEL EIDOLON
(WORSHIPPING —) ORANT
(PL.) DATA SPILING
(PREF.) EID(O)
(SUFF.) HEDRON
FIGURED FIGURY FACONNE
FIGUREHEAD DUMMY FRONT
SCROLL
FIGURINE TANAGRA CRIOPHORE
FIGWORT BARTSIA PILEWORT
PAULOWNIA PENSTEMON
BLUEHEARTS

FIJI

BAY: MBYA NATEWA NGALOA
SAVUSAVU
CAPITAL: SUVA
EASTERN GROUP: LAU
ISLAND: ELD KIA ONO AIWA KIOA
KORO MALI NGAU VIWA WAIA
AGATA MANGO MOALA NAIAU
RAMBI MAMOLO MATUKU MBENGA
MBULIA NAIRAI NAVITI NGAMEA
OVALAU TOTOYA YASAWA YENDUA
KAMBARA KANDAVU LAKEMBA
TAVEUNI VITILEVU
MOUNTAIN: NARARU MONAVATU
NIECE OR NEPHEW: VASU
POINT: VUYA
TOWN: BA MAU MBA MOMI NADI
REWA SUVA TUVU NANDI THUVU
ETUMBA LABASA NALOTO NAMOLI
NARATA NASALA NAVOLA SAGARA
LAUTOKA VATUKOULA

FIJIAN VITIAN
FILAGO GIFOLA
FILAMENT BRIN DOWL HAIR HARL
NEMA PILE SILK CHIVE CHORD FIBER
FIBRE FILUM TWIRE CIRRUS ELATER
HEATER MANTLE STRAND THREAD
CIRRHUS FIMBRIA FLIMMER RHIZOID
TEXTILE PARANEMA PHACELLA
STERIGMA PARAPHYSIS
(— MATERIAL) TUNGSTEN
(— OF FEATHER) BARB DOWL DOWLE
(— OF MINERAL) STRINGER
(— OF SILK) BRIN
(—S OF FLAX OR HEMP) HARL
(TWISTED —S) STRAND
(PL.) HACKLE
FILAMENTOUS BYSSOID STRINGY
HAIRLIKE
FILANDERS BACKWORM
FILARIASIS MUMU
FILBERT HAZEL COBNUT HAZELNUT
(SIEVE OF —S) PRICKLE

FILCH BOB FUD NIM ROB BEAT DRIB
FAKE PILK PRIG SMUG SNIP FETCH
LURCH PILCH SNAKE SNEAK STEAL
CLOYNE PILFER SMOUCH STRIKE
CABBAGE PURLOIN
FILE BOX ROW BARB DECK LINE LIST
RANK RASP RATE RISP ROLL SLIP
STUB EMERY ENTER FLOAT FOUND
GRAIL INDEX LABEL RIFLE TRACK
TRAIN ACCUSE ANSWER BEFOUL
CARLET DEFILE FILACE RASCAL
RUBBER STRING TOPPER ARCHIVE
ARRANGE CHOILER CONDEMN
DOSSIER EXHIBIT GRAILLE QUANNET
TICKLER DRAWFILE
(— DOWN SAW TEETH) JOINT
(— OFF) DEFILE
(— OF SIX SOLDIERS) ROT
(— USED BY COMBMAKERS) GRAIL
TOPPER GRAILER GRAILLE
(— WITH COURT OF LAW) BOX
(COARSE —) RAPE
(CURVED —) RIFFLER
(KIND OF —) INDIAN
FILE BOX SOLANDER
FILEFISH LIJA UNIE TURBOT
UNICORN BALISTID FOOLFISH
PLECTOGNATH
FILET DEBONE
FILIAL PIUS SONLY
FILIBUSTER FLIBUTOR
STONEWALL
FILIGREED LACED
FILING RASION LIMATION
(PL.) LEMEL SCOBS LIMAIL
FILIPENDULA ULMARIA
FILIPINO MORO KALINGA KANKANAI
FILL EKE HIT PAD BUNG CLOY CRAM
FEED GLUT HOLD LADE LINE MEET
PANG QUAR SATE STOP TEEM BELLY
BLOAT BULGE CHOKE ESTOP FLOCK
GORGE KEDGE PITCH PRIME STORE
STUFF CHARGE FULFIL INFUSE
OCCUPY QUERRE SUPPLY AGGRADE
DISTEND ENLARGE EXECUTE FILLING
FRAUGHT FULFILL IMPLETE INFLATE
INVOLVE PERFECT PERFORM
PERVADE PLENISH SATIATE SATISFY
SUFFUSE COMPLETE COMPOUND
FREQUENT PERMEATE
(— COMPLETELY) SATURATE
(— CUP TO BRIM) BRIM CROWN
BUMPER
(— FULL) FARCE STUFF
(— HORSES' TEETH) BISHOP
(— IN) NOG KILL STOP SLUSH INFILL
BALLAST
(— IN CHINKS) LIP
(— INTERSTICES) BLIND
(— IN WITH RUBBLE) HEART
(— LEATHER WITH OIL) FAT
(— OUT) DUNCH SWELL
(— THE BASES) LOAD

(— TO EXCESS) CROWD FLOOD
CONGEST SURFEIT
(— TO OVERFLOWING) FLOW
THWACK
(— UP) STOP BRICK CHOKE CLOSE
ESTOP STOAK FULFIL IMPACT
STODGE PLENISH
(— UP HOLE) STIFLE
(— WITH) SWILL
(— WITH ALE) RACK
(— WITH ANXIETY) ALARM ALARUM
(— WITH CARGO) STOW
(— WITH CLAY) CAT PUG
(— WITH FEAR) APPAL APPALL
(— WITH HORROR) ABHOR
(— WITH LIGHT) GLUT
(— WITH LIQUOR) TUN SKINK
(— WITH METAL) BACK
(— WITH MORTAR) GROUT
(— WITH ODORS) EMBALM
(— WITH RUBBISH) BASH
(— WITH TERROR) AMAZE
(ONE'S —) SLITHERS
FILLED BIG ALIVE FLUSH QUICK
SATED SOLID GRAVID LOADED
CROWDED HAUNTED IMPLETE
OPPLETE REPLETE SWOLLEN
FREQUENT INSTINCT POPULOUS
(— OUT) BOLD FULL
(— TO EXCESS) FLOWN
(— WITH AIR) INFLATED
(— WITH EXCITEMENT) ABUZZ
(— WITH FEAR) AFRAID
(— WITH INTERSTICES) AREOLAR
(— WITH MOISTURE) FAT
(— WITH PRIDE) YNPRIDID
FILLER GARA BOGUS SILEX SILKA
SQUIB BALAAM LIGNIN FILLING
LOADING WRAPPER
(— FOR CRACKS) SPACKLE
(QUILT —) BATT BATTING
FILLET BAND BONE GIRT LIST ORLE
ORLO SOLE TAPE AMPYX CROWN
FACET FILET GORGE LABEL LEDGE
MITER MITRE QUIRK SCROD SNOOD
STRAP STRIA TIARA VITTA ANADEM
BENDEL BINDER CIMBIA COMBLE
CORONA DIADEM FASCIA INFULA
LISTEL NORSEL POTONG QUADRA
REGLET REGULA RIBBON ROLLER
TAENIA TURBAN TURBOT ANNULET
BANDAGE BANDEAU CLOISON
CORONET EYEBROW FACETTE
FRONTAL GARLAND LAMBEAU
MOLDING TRESSON TRINGLE
BANDELET CINCTURE FRONTLET
HAIRLACE HEADBAND PLATBAND
TRESSOUR TRESSURE UNDERCUT
(— OF HERRING) ROLLMOP
(BEEF —) TOURNEDOS
(PREF.) TAENI(A)(O)
FILLIFORM CATENOID
FILL-IN MODESTY

FILLING GOB FILL MODE PLUG WEFT
WOOF INLAY STUFF FILLER
STOPPING STUFFING FIBERFILL
(— OF COLUMN FLUTES) CABLING
(— OF GAPS) CONFAB
(— UP) CLOSURE RIPIENO
(BASKET —) SLEW
(DENTAL —) INLAY
(SILK —) SHIKII
FILLIP BLOW FLIP SNAP SPUR TOSS
URGE FILIP FLASH FLIRT FLISK IMPEL
BUFFET INCITE MOMENT PROJECT
STIMULATE
(— ON THE NOSE) SNITCH
FILLY COLT FOAL GIRL
FILM H BRAT HAZE HULL KELL MIST
SCUM SKIM SKIN VEIL WEFT
BLEAR COVER FLAKE FLICK GLAZE
LAYER MYLAR PEARL PLATE SCALE
SHOOT SHORT BUBBLE MOTHER
PATINA SCRUFF CUTICLE FEATURE
PHILOME TAFFETA TOPICAL
TRAILER BEESWING FIRECOAT
NEGATIVE PELLICLE MICROFILM
MONOLAYER
(— OF AIR) PLASTRON
(— OF ICE) VERGLAS
(— OF OIL) SLICK
(— OF OXIDE) TARNISH
(— OF TARTAR) SCALE PLAQUE
(— ON COPPER) PATINA
(— ON PORRIDGE) BRAT
(— ON TEETH) PLAQUE
(— ON WINE) BEESWING
(— OVER EYE) WEB
(— OVER THE EYES) WEB
(DISCARDED —) OUTTAKE
(ORIGINAL —) MASTER
(POLYESTER —) MYLAR
(X-RAY —) BITEWING
FILMING
(REALISTIC —) VIDEOVERITE
FILMY FINE HAZY GAUZY MISTY
SHEER WISPY CLOUDY CLOUDED
TIFFANY FILMLIKE GOSSAMER
FILOSOFO DI CAMPAGNA, IL
(CHARACTER IN —) NARDO EUGENIA
LESBINA RINALDO TRITEMIO
(COMPOSER OF —) GALUPPI
FILTER CLAY RAPE SEEP SIFT SILE
DRAIN SEITZ SIEVE BOUGIE CANDLE
COLATE CONTEX LAUTER MEDIUM
PURIFY REFINE STRAIN BAGHOUSE
COLATURE FILTRATE INFILTER
STRAINER
FILTERER CLARIFIER
FILTH FEN KET DIRT DUNG GORE
MUCK NAST SLUT SOIL SUDS
ADDLE BILGE DRECK GLEAM GLEET
JAKES POUCE SWILL DEFILE FULYIE
FULZIE IMMUND ORDURE SORDES
SORDOR VERMIN SLOTTER

SQUALOR SULLAGE FOULNESS
MUCKMENT SNOTTERY WORTHING
COLLUVIES
(PREF.) COPR(O)
FILTHINESS MUCOR SQUALOR
SULLAGE CENOSITY
FILTHY LOW FOUL MIRY VILE BAWDY
DIRTY DROVY DUNGY GROSS LAIRY
MUCKY NASTY AUGEAN BAWDRY
CRUMBY CRUMMY CRUSTY PINNA
IMMUND IMPURE SORDID BEASTLY
BESTIAL HOGGISH OBSCENE
PIGGISH SQUALID UNCLEAN
ORDUROUS SLUTTISH
FILTRATE MALLEIN
FILTRATION BAGGING COLATURE
(KIND OF —) GEL
FIN ARM RAG RIB ANAL BURR FANG
HAND KEEL SAIL FLASH PINNA
CAUDAL FINLET ACANTHA FEATHER
FLIPPER PINNULE VENTRAL
FORELIMB PECTORAL
(BOMB —) VANE
(PREF.) PTER(O) PTERYG(O)
FINAGLE CHEAT TRICK REVOKE
DECEIVE FENAGLE
FINAL LAST UTTER FINIAL LATTER
RUNOFF ULTIMA UTMOST DARREIN
DERNIER EXTREME FINALIS
OUTMOST PARTING SUPREME
ABSOLUTE DECISIVE DECRETAL
DEFINITE EVENTUAL FAREWELL
ULTIMATE
(— STANZA) ENVOI
(NOT —) NISI
FINALE END CODA FINIS ENDING
WRAPUP CLOSING
FINALITY END ERGO
FINALLY YET LAST AFINE ATLAST
LASTLY
FINANCE TAX BACK BANK FUND
GOODS REVENUE TAXATION
TREASURE
FINANCIAL FISCAL MONETARY
PECUNIARY
FINANCIER BANIAN BANYAN
MONEYMAN
(AUTHOR OF —) DREISER
(CHARACTER IN —) FRANK HENRY
AILEEN BUTLER EDWARD SEMPLE
STENER LILLIAN WINGATE
COWPERWOOD
FINBACK WHALE FINNER GIBBAR
FINFISH RORQUAL JUBARTAS
FINCH FINK MORO PAPE JUNCO
SERIN TERIN BURION CANARY CITRIL
LINNET PALILA SISKIN TOWHEE
BUNTING CHEWINK PEEWEEP
REDHEAD REDPOLL SENEGAL
SPARROW TANAGER WAXBILL
AMADAVAT COMBASOU FIRETAIL
GOULDIAN GROSBEAK HAWFINCH

LONGSPUR SNOWBIRD BRAMBLING
SEEDEATER
(— FLOCK) CHARM
(SOUTH AMERICAN —) REDSISKIN

FIND GET RUG MEET VAIL CATCH
INVENT LOCATE STRIKE ADJUDGE
FINDING DISCOVER SCROUNGE
(— FAULT) CARP BARGE BLAME
CAVIL GRONT KNOCK PINCH SCOLD
NATTER ARRAIGN
(— GUILTY) ATTAINT CONVICT
(— OUT) AFIND CHECK ESSAY LEARN
SPELL TROVE DETECT CONTRIVE
DECIPHER DISCOVER
(— REFUGE) BIEL BIELD
(— SOLUTION) SOLVE
(— THE SUM) SUMMATE
(— TIME) EEM

FINDER SIGHT SEEKER FOUNDER

FINDING TROVER INQUEST VERDICT
(POLICE —) MO

FINE AOK CRO GAY RUM TAX BEIN
BIEN BOTE BRAW CAIN CROP DIRE
ERIC FAIR GENT GOOD HUNK JAKE
LEVY MOOI NEAT NICE PURE RARE
SEPT SLAP TALL TEAR TINE TRIM
ABWAB BONNY BRAVE BULLY CHECK
DAISY DANDY DELIE DUCKY FRAIL
GAUDY GRAND GREAT HUNKY
ISSUE KELTY MULCT NIFTY NOBLE
RORTY SHARP SHEER SMALL SPALE
SWANK SWEET SWELL UNLAW
WALLY WHITE AMENDE AMERCE
BONNIE BUNZER BRAWLY BRIGHT
CHEESY CHOICE CLEVER COSTLY
CRAFTY DAINTY FACETE FINISH
FLUTED GERSUM HERIOT HUNGRY
INCONY MELLOW ORNATE PEACHY
PRETTY PROPER QUAINT RANSOM
SARAAD SCONCE SERENE SILKEN
SLIGHT SPIFFY TENDER CLARIFY
CONDEMN CORKING CREANCE
CUNNING ELEGANT ESTREAT
FERDWIT FINICAL FORFEIT FRAGILE
GALANAS GALLANT GALLOWS
GRADELY GRASSUM IMMENSE
MARCHET MERCHET MURDRUM
ORFGILD PENALTY PERFECT
REFINED SCUTAGE STAVING
TENUOUS TOPPING VALIANT
WERGILD ABSOLUTE BLOODWIT
BUDGEREE CAVALIER CLINKING
DELICATE DUSTLIKE FLITWITE
FOOTGELD HANDSOME LASHLITE
MARITAGE PENALIZE PESHKASH
PINPOINT PLEASANT SKILLFUL
SPLENDID SUPERIOR WARDWITE
WIRESPUN COPACETIC
MAGNIFICENT
(— AGAINST SERVANTS) CHECK
(— FOR KILLING) BOTE
(— IN LIEU OF FLOGGING) HIDE

(BLOOD —) ERIC WITE
(FEUDAL —) RELIEF
(OSTENTATIOUSLY —) GAUDY
(PRINTING OFFICE —) SOLACE
(VERY —) BUNKUM SPLENDID
(PL.) SILT FLOUR
(PREF.) LEPT(O)

FINE-DRAW RANTER

FINE-LOOKING SPICY WALLY SPIFFY

FINELY FINE GAILY GAYLY WALLY
BRAGLY RARELY SMALLY BRAVELY
SMICKLY SWEETLY

FINENESS ALLOY GRAIN TRICK
DENIER FINERY PURITY THREAD
EXILITY FINESSE DELICACY
(— AS RECKONED BY CARATS) TITLE
(— OF FABRIC) CUT GAGE GAUGE
(— OF METAL) STANDARD
(— OF PITCH) COUNTS

FINERY GAUD WALY ARRAY BRAWS
WALLY BAUBLE BAWDRY BEAUTY
FEGARY GAIETY GAYETY TAWDRY
BRAVERY GAUDERY REGALIA
BEAUTERY ELEGANCE FINENESS
FOFARRAW FOLDEROL FOOFARAW
FRIPPERY ORNAMENT RIBANDRY
(TAWDRY —) FRIPPERY

FINESPUN HAIR THIN TWITTERY

FINESSE ART TACT CHEAT SKILL
TRICK PURITY SERENE CUNNING
ARTIFICE DELICACY SUBTLETY
THINNESS

FINF-TUNE TWEAK

FINFOOT SUNBIRD

FINGER TOY PAUT PLAY DIGIT INDEX
PINKY DACTYL HANDLE MEDDLE
MEDIUS PADDLE PILFER PINKIE
POLLEX ANNULAR DIGITAL MINIMUM
MINIMUS PURLOIN DIGITIZE
THRIMBLE
(— IDLY) TWIDDLE
(— INFECTION) FELON
(CROOK A — AT) BECKON
(FORE —) INDEX
(LITTLE —) PINKY PINKIE PIRLIE
MINIMUS AURICULAR
(RING —) ANNULAR RINGMAN
ANNULARY
(THIRD —) RINGMAN
(PL.) HOOKS
(PREF.) DACTYL(IO)(O) DIGITI DIGITO
(SUFF.) DACTYLIA DACTYLOUS

FINGERFLOWER FOXGLOVE

FINGERING DOIGTE

FINGERLING PARR TROUTLET

FINGERNAIL DIGGER
(RELATING TO —) ONYCHOID
(SUFF.) ONYCHA ONYCHES ONYCHIA
ONYCHIUM ONYCHUS ONYX

FINGERPRINT DAB ARCH LOOP
WHORL LATENT

FINGERPRINTING (KIND OF —) DNA

FINGERROOT FOXGLOVE
FINGERSTALL COT
FINIAL EPI NOB TEE TOP CROP KNOB
KNOP KNOT BUNCH CREST CROWN
FINAL POPPY PRICKET ORNAMENT
PINNACLE
FINICAL NICE FUSSY CHOOSY
DAINTY DAPPER JAUNTY PRETTY
PRISSY SPRUCE CHOOSEY FINICKY
FINIKIN FOPPISH MINCING PERJINK
PICKING SMICKER DELICATE
FINICALLY SMICKLY GINGERLY
FINICKY NICE DINKY FIKEY FIKIE
PRISSY FINICAL FINIKIN PRECISE
FINISH DO DIE END CHAR EDGE FACE
FINE MILL OVER PASS SINK SNUG
STOP BLOOM BOUND CEASE CHARE
CHEVE CLOSE CROWN ENDUP FEEZE
GLACE GLAZE LIMIT SPEED UPPER
BOTTOM BUSHEL FULFIL FULLDO
PLISSE POLISH SETTLE WINDUP
ABSOLVE ACHIEVE DEPETER
EXECUTE FLUTING FULFILL PERFECT
SURFACE COMPLETE CONCLUDE
DEPRETER DRESSING FINALIZE
FROSTING TERMINAL
(— CAREFULLY) NEATEN
(— CLOTH) BURL CONVERT
(— FILMING) WRAP
(— METAL) PLANISH
(— OFF) DASH CRUSH ABSOLVE
ACCOMPLISH
(— OF FABRIC) CIRE HOLLAND
(— OF PAPER) STIPPLE
(— STONE) COMB BOAST DROVE
(— WITH A SEAM) FELL
(— WORK) FLOOR
(CALENDERED —) CHASING
(DULL —) MAT MATTE
(GLAZED —) GLACE LACKER
LACQUER
(PHOTO —) MAT MATT MATTE
(STUCCO —) SPATTER
(SUPERFICIAL —) BLAZONRY
FINISHED BY DID OER PAU ARCH
DONE DOWN FINE GONE OVER
PAST PURE RIPE SHOT ENDED
EXACT KAPUT NAPOO ROUND
CLOSED NAPOOH ORNATE
PERFECT REFINED ROUNDED
STOPPED THROUGH BANKRUPT
CLIMAXED GOFFERED LUSTERED
POLISHED
(— IN NATURAL COLOR) FAIR
(— WITH NAP) BRUSHED
(ABSOLUTELY —) SUNK
(HIGHLY —) SUAVE
(IMPERFECTLY —) RUDE
FINISHER EYER ENDER CORKER
GAFFER BEETLER CEMENTER
ENAMELER SOCKDOLOGER
FINISHING CRUSHING

FINITE LIMITED
FINK (PLAY THE —) RATON

FINLAND
CAPITAL: HELSINKI HELSINGFORS
COIN: PENNI MARKKA
DIVISION: IJORE VILLIPURI
GOD: TAPIO JUMALA
ISLAND: ALAND KARLO AALAND
  HAILUTO VALLGRUND
ISTHMUS: KARELIA
LAKE: JUO MUJO KEMI KIVI NASI OULO
  PURU PYHA SIMO ENARE HAUKI
  INARI KALLA LAPPA LESTI PUULA
  LENTUA SAIMAA SOUNNE SYVARI
  KOITERE NILAKKA PIELINEN
LANGUAGE: AVAR LAPP UGRIC
  MAGYAR OSTYAK TAVAST SAMOYED
  ESTONIAN
MEASURE: KANNU TUNNA VERST
  FATHOM SJOMIL OTTINGER
  SKALPUND TUNNLAND
MOUNTAIN: HALTIA
NAME: SUOMI
PARLIAMENT: EDUSKUNTA
PROVINCE: HAME KYMI OULU LAPPI
  VAASA KUOPIO MIKKELI UUSIMAA
RIVER: II KALA OULU SIMO TENO
  IVALO LOTTA OUNAS SIIKA IIJOKI
  LAPUAN MUONIO PASVIK TORNIO
  KITINEN KOKEMAKI
TOWN: ABA ABO KEM KEMI OULU
  PORI VASA ENARE ESPOO KOTKA
  LAHTI TURKU VAASA IMATRA
  KUOPIO MIKKELI TAMPERE HELSINKI
TRIBE: HAME VEPS VEPSE UGRIAN
  KARJALAISET SUOMALAISET

FINLET PINNULE
FINN FIOUN INGER OSTIAK OSTYAK
TAVAST INGRIAN CHEREMIS
INGERMAN SWEKOMAN
(PL.) SUOMI
FINNISH
(PREF.) FENNO
FINNOCK HERLING
FINTA GIARDINIERA, LA
(CHARACTER IN —) ONESTI ANCHISE
ARMINDA BELFIORE SANDRINA
SERPETTA VIOLANTE
(COMPOSER OF —) MOZART
FIORD FJORD INLET
FIORIN KNOTGRASS
FIORITURA ORNAMENT
FIPPLE FLUTE RECORDER
FIR VER LARCH SAPIN BAUMIER
LASHORN PINABETE
FIR CLUB MOSS FOXFEET
FIRE CAN FEU LOW AGNI APOY BALE
BRIO BURN HEAT KILN LOWE POOP
SACK SWAP SWOP ZEAL ARDOR
ARSON BLAST BLAZE BREAK BURST

EMPTY FEVER GLEED INGLE LIGHT
LOGHE LOOSE LOUGH PLUFF SERVE
SHOOT SQUIB STOKE AROUSE
ENGHLE EXCITE FERVOR IGNITE
INCITE KINDLE SMUDGE SPIRIT
SPLEEN VULCAN ANIMATE BONFIRE
BURNING BURNOUT CHIMNEY
DISMISS EMITTER EXPLODE
FURNACE GLIMMER INFLAME
INSPIRE SMOLDER BACKFIRE
BALEFIRE CAMPFIRE DETONATE
HELLFIRE ILLUMINE IRRITATE
NEEDFIRE SMOULDER VIVACITY
PORCELAINIZE
(— A REVOLVER) FAN
(— ON) AFIRE
(— THE CHARGE) HIT
(— TWO ROUNDS) DOUBLE
(— UPON) GUN SPRAY
(BALL OF —) DYNAMO
(CROSS —) GANTLET GAUNTLET
(DAMPENED —) SMOTHER
(FOREST —) BREAK
(LITTLE —) SPONK SPUNK
(MASSED —) ARTILLERY
(PEAT —) GREESAGH
(RUNNING-OUT —) DANDY
(SIGNAL —) BALE BEACON BALEFIRE
(PREF.) EMPYRO IGNEO IGNI PHLOGO
PYR(ET)(ETO)(ITI)(O)
(SUFF.) PYRA
FIRE ALARM FIREBOX
FIREARM ARM GUN IRON SHOT
TUBE FIRER ORGAN PIECE RIFLE
JEZAIL MAGNUM MAUSER MUSKET
PISTOL POPPER BOMBARD CARBINE
CURRIER DEMIHAG HANDGUN
PINFIRE SHOOTER SPANNER
ARQUEBUS BROWNING CULVERIN
EXPELLER EXPLODER PETRONEL
REVOLVER
(PL.) HARDWARE ARTILLERY
FIRE ARROW MALLEOLUS
FIREBACK REREDOS MACARTNEY
FIREBALL BOLIDE
FIRE BEETLE COCUYO CUCUYO
ELATER ELATERID
FIREBOAT PALANDER
FIREBRAND BLAZE BRAND BLEERY
BOUTEFEU RABBLEROUSER
FIREBRICK QUARLE
(PL.) GROG
FIREBUG BUG ARSONIST
FIRE CARRIER PORTFIRE
FIRECLAY THILL
FIRE COVER CURFEW CURPHEW
FIRECRACKER DEVIL SQUIB
BANGER PETARD SALUTE CRACKER
SNAPPER FIREWORK WHIZBANG
FIRE-CURED DARK
FIREDAMP GAS FOULNESS
WILDFIRE

FIREDART PHALARICA
FIREDOG DOG IRON ANDIRON
FIRE ENGINE RIG TUB MANUAL
FIRE EXTINGUISHER SQUIRT
EXTINCTOR
FIRE FIGHTER EXEMPT HOTSHOT
FIREFLY CUCUYO FIREBUG GLOWFLY
LAMPFLY FIREWORM GLOWWORM
LAMPYRID
FIREGUARD FENDER
FIRELINE GUTTER
FIRELOCK FUSEE FUZEE SPANNER
FIREMAN VAMP FIRER FUELER
STOKER TEASER TIZEUR FIREBOY
HOSEMAN BAKEHEAD FURNACER
FIREPLACE FOCUS FOGON FORGE
FOYER GRATE INGLE TISAR HEARTH
CHIMNEY CHEMINEE
(— AND CHIMNEY) STACK
(— STONE) MANTEL
(PORTABLE —) BARBECUE
BARBEQUE
FIREPLUG PLUG HYDRANT
FIRER STOKER BLASTER
FIRESIDE SMOKE HEARTH
FIRESTAND HASTER HASTENER
FIRE THORN PYRACANTH
FIREWEED FIRETOP ROSEBAY
PILEWEED PILEWORT
FIREWOOD FIRE LENA SLAB WOOD
CHUNK FAGOT BILLET BILLOT
ELDING FIRING TALWOOD FIREBOTE
TALLWOOD TALSHIDE
FIREWORK JET SUN GERB DEVIL
GERBE PEEOY SAXON SHELL SQUIB
WHEEL FIZGIG MAROON PETARD
ROCKET SALUTE SHOWER TRACER
CASCADE SERPENT SPARKER
TORPEDO VOLCANO FOUNTAIN
SPARKLER GIRANDOLE
(PL.) FUN FIRE
FIRE WORSHIPPER PARSI GHEBER
GHEBRE PARSEE
FIRING FIRE FUEL COUGH SALVO
BURNING DRUMFIRE
FIRKIN VESSEL
FIRM HUI PAT BUFF FAST HARD IRON
NASH SURE TAUT TRIG TRIM CHAMP
CORKY CRISP DENSE FIRMA FIXED
HARDY HOUSE LOYAL RIGID SOLID
SOUND STARK STIFF STITH STOUT
SWITH TIGHT TOUGH CEMENT
HARDEN HEARTY SECURE SETTLE
SICCAR SICKER SINEWY STABLE
STANCH STEADY STEEVE STOLID
STRONG STURDY TRUSTY ADAMANT
CERTAIN COMPACT COMPANY
CONCERN CONFIRM CONTEXT
DECIDED DURABLE STAUNCH
UNMOVED CONSTANT FAITHFUL
FIDUCIAL ODDURATE RESOLUTE
SUBSTANT UNSHAKEN

(— BUT EASILY CUT) SEMISOFT
(NOT —) FUZZY
(PREF.) PAGIO
FIRMAMENT SKY DEEP POLE CARRY
ETHER CANOPY HEAVEN EXPANSE
EMPYREAN EMPYREUM EXPANSUM
FIRMLY BUFF FAST FIRM HARD
SADLY STARK TIGHT HARDLY
SQUARE SURELY SOLIDLY SECURELY
STRONGLY
FIRMNESS BODY GRIT IRON ETHAN
PROOF FIXURE COURAGE FIRMITY
GRANITE BACKBONE DECISION
FASTNESS SECURITY SOLIDITY
STRENGTH TENACITY
(— OF CHARACTER) SAND
(— OF PURPOSE) RESOLVE
FIRN NEVE
FIRST ERST FUST GULE HEAD HIGH
MAIN AHEAD ALPHA CHIEF FORME
NIEVE PRIMA PRIME PRIMO MAIDEN
PRIMAL PRIMUS VIRGIN FIRSTLY
HIGHEST INITIAL LEADING PREMIER
PRIMARY EARLIEST FOREHAND
FOREMOST FORMERLY ORIGINAL
PARAVANT PREMIERE PRINCEPS
(— PRIZE) BLUE
(— SERGEANT) TOP
(— STATE) DELAWARE
(PREF.) PRIMI PRIMO PROT(O)
(— IN TIME) ARCH
FIRSTBORN AYNE EIGNE ELDEST
FIRST-CLASS PUCKA GAY TOP BOSS
POSH FLASH PRIME PUKKA BUNKUM
STUNNING
FIRST-FRUITS ANNATES
FIRSTHAND DIRECT PRIMARY
ORIGINAL
FIRST-RATE AOK SLAPUP TIPTOP
BOSS BRAG GOOD JAKE MAIN SLAP
BULLY DANDY LUMMY PRIME SLEEK
SLICK SUPER SWELL BONSER
BONZER BOSKER CHEESY FAMOUS
TIPTOP BLIGHTY BOSHTER CAPITAL
SKOOKUM STELLAR TOPPING
CHAMPION CLINKING CLIPPING
TOPNOTCH
FIRTH ARM KYLE FRITH INLET
COPPICE ESTUARY
FISCAL BURSAL MONETARY
FISH AU ID AKU AWA AYU BIB CAT
COD DAB DAP DIB EEL FIN GAR GIG
GOO HEN IDE IHI JIG JUG ORF RAY
SAR TAI UKU BANK BARB BASS BLAY
BOCE BOGA CARP CAST CERO CHUB
CHUG CHUM CLOD CRAB CUSK DACE
DORY DRAG DRAW DRUM ERSE
FUGU GADE GHOL GOBY GRIG HAKE
HIND HUCH HUSO JACK JUNK LINE
LING LOTE MADO MERO MOLA OPAH
PEAL PEGA PIKE POOR POUT PRIM
QUAB RAIL RUDD RUFF SCAD SCUP
SEER SHAD SOLE SPET SPIN SPOT

TILE TORO TUNA ULUA ACARA
AHOLE AKULE ANGLE ATULE BEGTI
BETTA BINNY BLAIN BLEAK BOLTI
BOLTY BREAM BULLY BULTI CABIO
CATLA CHIRO CISCO COBIA CONEY
DANIO DORAB DOREE DRAIL DRIFT
DRIVE ELOPS ERIZO FLOAT FLUKE
FOGAS FRIAR GADID GRUNT GUPPY
HILSA HUCHO JUREL KILLY LAKER
LANCE MANTA MIDGE MINIM MORAY
OTTER PERCH PIABA PLATY PORGY
POWAN POWER REINA ROACH SAIDE
SARGO SAURY SEINE SHARK SKATE
SMELT SNOEK SNOOK SPRAT SQUID
SULEA SWEEP TENCH TETRA TRABU
TRAWL TROLL TROUT TUNNY
UMBRA VIUVA VORAZ WAHOO WHIFF
AIMARA ALEVIN ANABAS ANGLER
BARBEL BARBER BENNET BICHIR
BISKOP BLENNY BONITO BOWFIN
BUMPER BURBOT CALLOP CANDIL
CAPLIN CARANX CARIBE COFI HO
COTTID CREOLE CUCHIA CUNNER
DARTER DASSIE DENTEX FISHET
GANOID GINNEL GULPER GUNNEL
HAMLET HAPUKU HILSAH HUSSAR
INANGA KOKOPU LAUNCE LEDGER
LIGGER LOUVAR MAIGRE MARLIN
MEDAKA MENISE MILTER MINNOW
MOLLIE MOULD MULLET NONNAT
PHOEBE PLAICE POMPON PUFFER
PUNECA REDFIN REMORA ROBALO
ROUGHY RUNNER SABALO SALELE
SALEMA SALMON SAPSAP SARDEL
SAUGER SAUREL SERRAN SHINER
SIERRA SIMARA SPARID SUCKER
TAILER TAIMEN TANDAN TARPON
TAUTOG TESTAR TETARD TINOSA
TOMCOD TURBOT VENDIS WALLER
WEAVER WIRRAH WRASSE ZINGEL
ALEWIFE ALFIONA ANCHOVY
BACALAO BARBUDO BATFISH
BEARDIE BERGYLT BERYCID BOXFISH
BRAGGLE BUFFALO BUMMALO
CABEZON CANDIRU CAPELIN
CAPLING CATFISH CAVALLA CAVALLY
CHIMERA CHROMID CICHLID CLUPEID
CONVICT CORVINA COWFISH
CRAPPIE CROAKER CTENOID CUTLIPS
CYCLOID DRABBLE DREPANE
DRUMMER EELPOUT ESCOLAR
FATHEAD FINFISH GALJOEN GEELBEC
GEELBEK GOBIOID GOGGLER
GOLDEYE GOURAMI GRAYSBY
GROUPER GRUNION GRUNTER
GUAPENA GUAVINA GUDGEON
GULARIS GURNARD GWYNIAD
HADDOCK HAGFISH HALIBUT
HARMOOT HERRING HINALEA
HOGFISH HOUTING ICEFISH ICHTHUS
INCONNU JAWFISH JEWFISH
JUGULAR LABROID LAGARTO
LONGFIN MACHETE MAHSEER

MAYFISH MOJARRA MOONEYE
MORWONG OARFISH OLDWIFE
OQUASSA PEGASUS PIGFOOT
PINTADO PIRANHA POISSON
POLLACK POMFRET POMPANO
PUPFISH RASBORA RONQUIL
SANCORD SARDINE SAUROID
SAVELHA SAWFISH SCALARE
SCAROID SCHELLY SCULPIN
SENNETT SEVRUGA SILURUS
SLEEPER SMUTTER SNAPPER
SOLDIER SPAWNER STERLET
SUNFISH TELEOST TOMTATE
TOPKNOT TORPEDO TUBFISH
UMBRANA UNICORN VENDACE
VIAJACA WAREHOU WAUBEEN
WHAPUKA WHAPUKU WHITING
ALBACORE ALFONSIN APOGONID
ARAPAIMA ATHERINE BAITFISH
BALISTID BIGMOUTH BILLFISH
BLENNOID BLUEBACK BLUEFISH
BOARFISH BONEFISH BRISLING
BROTULID BULLHEAD CACKEREL
CANCHITO CARANGID CARANGIN
CARDINAL CATALINA CATALUFA
CHANCITO CHIMAERA CHOANATE
CHROMIDE CORACINE CREVALLE
CREVALLY CROSSOPT CYPRINID
DEALFISH DIPNEUST DITREMID
DONCELLA DRAGONET DRUMFISH
DUMBFISH ECHENEID ELEOTRID
EPISCATE FALLFISH FILEFISH
FLAGFISH FLATFISH FLATHEAD
FLOUNDER FOOLFISH FROGFISH
FUNDULUS GAMBUSIA GEELBECK
GILTHEAD GOATFISH GOLDFISH
GRAINING GRAYFISH GRAYLING
GREYSKIN HAIRFISH HALFBEAK
HANDFISH HANDLINE HAPLOMID
HARDHEAD HARDTAIL HOMOCERC
HORNFISH HORSEMAN JACKFISH
JUMPROCK KABELJOU KARMOUTH
KELPFISH KINGFISH LADYFISH
LUMPFISH MACKEREL MENHADEN
MILKFISH MOONFISH PICKEREL
PILCHARD PIRARUCU PORKFISH
QUERIMAN ROBALITO ROCKFISH
ROCKLING ROSEFISH SAILFISH
SALANGID SANDFISH SANDGOBY
SCIAENID SCOMBRID SCOTSMAN
SEERFISH SKILFISH SKIPJACK
SOAPFISH STUDFISH STURGEON
TALLYWAG TARWHINE TERAGLIN
TILEFISH TOADFISH TREEFISH
TREVALLY WARMOUTH WEAKFISH
WHISTLER WRYMOUTH QUILLBACK
SCORPAENO NEEDLEFISH
SHEEPSHEAD SHOVELHEAD
SHOVELNOSE SILVERSIDES
MOUTHBREEDER
(— BROTH) DASHI
(— BY TROLLING) DRAIL
(— FOR EELS) GRIG SNIGGLE
(— FOR SALMON) SNIGGER
(— LIGHTLY) DAP
(— NETTED) LIFT
(— NOT UNDERSIZED) COUNT
KEEPER
(— PRODUCT) SURIMI
(— TAPE) SNAKE
(— THROUGH ICE) CHUG
(— UNDERWATER) GUGGLE
(— WITH HANDS) GUMP GUDDLE
(AQUARIUM —) GUPPY RASBORA
(BAKED —) COULIBIAC
(BLIND —) PINKFISH
(CURED —) DUNFISH
(DISH OF RAW —) SEVICHE
(FABLED —) MAH
(FEMALE —) RAUN SPAWNER
(FIGHTING —) PLAKAT
(FRIED —) ESCABECHE
(HAWAIIAN —) AU
(HERALDIC —) CHABOT
(INDIAN —) ROHU
(NUMBER OF —) SCHOOL
(OLD —) MOSSBACK
(PART OF —) EYE FIN JAW ANUS
CHEEK NARIS SCALE MAXILLA
MANDIBLE OPERCULUM
PREMAXILLA
(PULPED —) POMACE
(PUREE OF —) BRANDADE
(QUANTITY OF —) MAZE
(RAW —) SASHIMI
(REFUSE —) CHUM SHACK
(SALTED —) COR
(SMALL —) TIDDLER
(SMOKED —) FUMADO
(SPLIT —) KLIPFISH
(STEWED —) MATELOTE
(THIN —) RACER
(YOUNG —) FRY ALEVIN
(25 LBS. OF —) STICK
(PREF.) ICHTHY(O) ISCI
(SUFF.) CHROMIS ICHTHYS
FISH BASKET POT CAUL CREEL
SLATH
FISH BOX TRUNK
FISH BRINER COBBERER
FISH CLEANER GILLER
FISH DRESSER IDLER
FISHER MART EELER PEKAN SABLE
SOBOL TAIRA TAYRA MARTEN
SEINER WEJACK MARTRIX TRAWLER
TROLLER
(SPONGE —) HOOKER
FISHERMAN (ALSO SEE ANGLER)
TOTY EELER ANGLER GIGMAN
GILLER KEDGER MAIMUL SEINER
WORMER ADMIRAL DORYMAN
DRAGMAN DRIFTER PRAWNER
RODSTER SHANKER SMELTER
STRIKER TRAWLER TROTTER
TROWMAN PETERMAN PISCATOR
SEASONER SHRIMPER

FISHERY FISHING PISCARY SEALERY
FISHGARTH WEIR
FISHHOOK FLY GIG HOOK LARI
ANGLE DRAIL KIRBY LARIN SLEEK
ANGULE SPROAT KENDALL
ABERDEEN BARBLESS CARLISLE
LIMERICK
(PART OF —) EYE GAP BARB BEND
POINT SHANK
(PL.) PULLDEVIL
FISHING PIKING ANGLING BANKING
BASSING GRAINING SNOEKING
(— TOOL) OVERSHOT
FISHING GROUNDS HAAF
FISHING ROD GAD
FISHING TACKLE TEW LEDGER
FISHLINE GIMP TROT SNELL TRAWL
DIPSEY LIGGER BOULTER GANGION
OUTLINE SETLINE TRIMMER
HAIRLINE TROTLINE
FISH LOUSE GISLER
FISHMONGER PESSONER
FISH NEST REDD
FISHNET FLUE SEINE SETNET
FISHPOND STEW VIVER PISCINA
VIVARIUM
FISHPOUND MADRAGUE
FISH SPEAR GRANES WASTER
LEISTER
FISHTAIL SKID UROSOME
FISHWAY PASS RACEWAY
FISHY DULL FUNNY GLASSY VACANT
FISSION BREAKING CLEAVAGE
CLEAVING GAMOGENY SCISSION
FISSURE GAP CHAP CONE FLAW
GOOL GULL LEAK LOCH LODE REFT
RENT RIFT RIMA RIME SEAM SLIT
TEAR VEIN VENT CHASM CHINE
CHINK CLEFT CRACK FLAKE GRIKE
PIPER PORTA SHAKE SPLIT ZYGON
CLEAVE CRANNY DIVIDE LESION
RICTUS RIMULA SPRING SULCUS
BLEMISH CREVICE FISSURA
MOFETTE OPENING SWALLET
APERTURE BLOWHOLE CLEAVAGE
COLOBOMA CREVASSE INCISURE
QUEBRADA SCISSURA TRAVERSE
(— IN BUILDING STONE) DRY
(— IN HEEL) GAUG
(— IN LIMESTONE) GRIKE
(— IN MAST) SPRING
(— IN PLATEAU) ABRA
(— OF LIVER) PORTA
(UNDERGROUND —) SWALLET
SWALLOW
(PL.) RHAGADES
(PREF.) RHAGADI
(SUFF.) SCHISIS SCHIST
FISSURED RIMATE CHAPPED
CLEFTED FISSATE
FIST JOB PUD DUKE NAVE NEIF NIEF
FOIST GRASP INDEX NIEVE CLENCH
CLUTCH DADDLE EFFORT MAULER

MAULEY PINKER STRIKE ATTEMPT
CLUBFIST FISTNOTE PUFFBALL
TIGHTWAD
FISTFIGHT SETTO TURNUP
FISTICUFF BOX NEVEL FISTIFY
FISTULA EGILOPS
(PREF.) SYRING(O)
FISTULOUS TUBULAR
FIT GO APT FAY GEE JAG PAN RIG SET
SIT ABLE AGUE BOUT FEAT FURY
GOOD HARD KINK MEET MESH PANG
RIPE SORT SUIT TRIM TURN WELL
WHIM ADAPT ADEPT APPLY BESIT
CHINK CLICK DIGNE EXIES FADGE
FANCY FITLY FRAME FRISK FUROR
HAPPY ICTUS MATCH PITCH QUEME
QUIRK READY RIGHT SERVE SPASM
SPELL START STOUR SWOON TALLY
ACCESS ADJUST ANSWER ATTACK
BECOME BEHOVE BESORT DUEFUL
FINISH FITTEN HABILE HEPPEN
LIABLE PROPER SEASON SEEMLY
SPLEEN SQUARE STREAK STROKE
STRONG SUITED WORTHY ADAPTED
BEHOOVE CAPABLE CONCENT
CONDIGN CONFORM CORRECT
DESPAIR FASHION FITTING HEALTHY
PREPARE QUALIFY SEIZURE
TANTRUM WIDDRIM ADEQUATE
BECOMING DOVETAIL ELIGIBLE
GLOOMING IDONEOUS OUTBREAK
PAROXYSM PASSABLE SUITABLE
SYNCOPES
(— CLOSELY) FAY CHOCK
(— CORNER TO CORNER) BUTT
(— FOR THE GALLOWS) WIDDIFOW
(— IN) GO NESTLE
(— INTO SOCKET) FANG
(— LOOSELY) SLOP
(— NAUTICALLY) RIG
(— OF ANGER) WAX FRAP FUME
HUFF RAGE SNIT TIFF FLING RAVERY
SPLEEN
(— OF DEPRESSION) HUMP
(— OF ILL HUMOR) DOD PET TIG
FUNK POUT TOUT GRUMPS
(— OF ILLNESS) DROW TOUT FLING
(— OF ILL TEMPER) MAD TANTRUM
(— OF LAUGHTER) GIRD KINK
(— OF NERVOUSNESS) TWITCHET
(— OF RESENTMENT) PIQUE SNUFF
(— OF SHIVERING) AGUE GROOSE
(— OF STUBBORNNESS) REEST
(— OF SULKS) GEE STRUM
(— OF SULLENNESS) DOD
(— OF TEMPER) WAX BAIT BIRSE
HISSY PADDY TETCH GROUCH
SPLEEN SQUALL BRAINGE
(— OF WEEPING) CRY
(— OF YAWNING) GAPE
(— ONE WITHIN ANOTHER) NEST
(— OUT) ARM RIG BUSK BEFIT EQUIP
ASTORE CLOTHE OUTFIT APPAREL

APPOINT FURNISH HABILLE
ACCOUTER
(— RIFLE BARREL) BED
(— TIGHTLY) STUFF
(— TO BE DRUNK) SORBILE
(— TOGETHER) MESH NEST COAPT
JOINT COHERE ASSEMBLE
(— UP) RIG
(— WITH COMPACTNESS) BOX
(— WITH FETTERS) GARNISH
(FAINTING —) SWOON SYNCOPE
(RITUALLY —) KOSHER
(PL.) LUNES
(SUFF.) ABLE IBLE

FITCH LINER

FITFUL GERY CATCHY GERFUL
GLEAMY CURSORY FLIGHTY
RESTLESS UNSTABLE VARIABLE
SPASMODIC

FITLY FIT PAT DULY FEATLY GLADLY
MEETLY TIDELY APROPOS HAPPILY
PROPERLY SUITABLY

FITNESS FORM APTNESS DECENCY
DECORUM DIGNITY APTITUDE
CAPACITY IDONEITY JUSTNESS
PROPERTY CONGRUITY

FITTED APT ADLE ADAPT KEYED
SUITED ADAPTED ENGAGED
ADJUSTED ASSORTED ELIGIBLE

FITTER TUBER GASMAN

FITTING TO APT CAP DUE LUG
PAT BUTT FAIR FEAT FORK HARP
JUMP JUST KIND MEET CLEAT
HAPPY QUEME WORTH BECOME
CLENCH CLEVIS LEADER PROPER
SADDLE SEEMLY WASHER
ADAPTER CONGRUE PENDANT
SERVING SHACKLE SUCTION
TACTFUL CONDULET DECOROUS
GRACEFUL RIGHTFUL SUITABLE
RECEPTACLE
(— FOR MILL-STONE) RIND RYND
(— TIGHTLY) CLOSE
(GREASE —) ZERK
(LIGHT —) PLUG LUMINAIRE
(PIPE —) CROSS ELBOW
(PL.) BRASS COVER REPAREL
FITMENTS

FITZGERALD ELLA

FIVE CINQ FUNF CINQUE EPSILON
QUINQUE
(— CENTS) JITNEY NICKEL
(— HUNDRED DOLLARS, POUNDS)
MONKEY
(— IN CRAPS) PHOEBE
(— OF TRUMPS) PEDRO
(— YEARS) LUSTRUM
(GAME CALLED —S) HANDBALL
(TWO —S) QUINAS
(PREF.) CINQUE LEPT(O) PEN(T)(TA)
(TH) QUINQU(E)

FIVES BALL SNACK

FIVESTONES SNOBS

FIX DOX JAM PEG PIN SET CLEW CLUE
FAST FIRM GAFF GLUE HOLD HOLE
JAMB LOCK MEND MOOR NAIL PICK
RELY SEAL SPOT STAY AFFIX ALLOT
DEFIX FOUND GRAFT GRAVE IMBED
INFIX LIMIT PLACE PLANT POINT
POSIT SEIZE STATE STEEK STELL
STICK TRYST ADJUST ANCHOR
ARREST ASSIGN ASSIZE ATTACH
CEMENT CLINCH DEFINE ENROOT
ENTAIL FASTEN FICCHE FIXATE
FREEZE GROUND IMPALE REPAIR
REVAMP SETTLE SQUARE TEMPER
APPOINT ARRANGE CALCIFY
CONFIRM DELIMIT DESTINE
DILEMMA GRAPPLE IMPLANT
IMPRESS IMPRINT PREPARE STATION
PINPOINT RENOVATE TRANSFIX
(— A FIGHT) RIG
(— A MAST) STEP
(— AMOUNT) AFFEER
(— ATTENTION) NAIL
(— DEEPLY) GRAVE
(— FIRMLY) SEAL FREEZE IMPACT
INCUBE RAMPIRE
(— IMMOVABLY) RIVET
(— IN AMAZEMENT) PETRIFY
(— IN MUD) MIRF
(— IN POSITION) SHIP
(— PRICE) ASSIZE CHARGE SETTLE
(— THE MIND) INTEND
(— UP) CLEW CLUE
(— UPON) CHAP AFFIX
(— WORK OF ART) REDO
(GAMBLING —) RIG STCK

FIXATION TIC FETICH FETISH
(SUFF.) PAGUS PEXIA PEXIS PEXY

FIXATIVE FIXER SKATOLE AMBRETTE
EUDESMOL HYRACEUM LABDANUM

FIXED PAT PUT SAD SET GOT FAST
FIRM FLAT HARD GIVEN SIKER STAID
UPSET FINITE FROZEN INTENT
MENDED SICKER STABLE STATED
STEADY STRONG CERTAIN DORMANT
EMPIGHT HABITED LIMITED SETTLED
SITFAST STATARY STATIVE STELLED
ACCURATE ARRANGED ATTACHED
CONSTANT DEFINITE EXPLICIT
FASTENED IMMOBILE IRONCLAD
MOVELESS RESIDENT RESOLUTE
STANDING STUBBORN
(NOT —) FLUID SHIFTY MOVABLE
FUGITIVE INSECURE MOVEABLE
(PREF.) APLANO

FIXEDLY SAD FAST FIRM FIXLY
INTENTLY

FIXEDNESS FASTNESS

FIXER HYPO PATCH

FIXTURE ANNEX EVENT GUARD
FAUCET SHIELD BRACKET CREEPER
KNOCKER THIMBLE
(LIGHTING —) SCONCE
(STORE —) GONDOLA

FIZZING FIZZY GASSING
FIZZLE FLOP FUSS BARNEY FAILURE
FLIVVER
(— OUT) DIE
FLABBINESS MYATONIA
FLABBY LAX FOZY LASH LIMP WEAK
BAGGY FLASH FOGGY FRUSH SAPPY
WOOZY CASHIE DOUGHY FEEBLE
FLAGGY FLAPPY LIMBER QUAGGY
WATERY FLACCID YIELDING
FLABELLUM RHIPIDION
FLACCID LIMP WOOZY FLABBY
FLAGGY EMARCID FLACKED
YIELDING
FLAG FAG LAG SAG SOD FAIL FANE
FLAT HOOK IRIS JACK JADE LECK
PINE TIRE TURF WAFT WAIF WILT
CREST DROOP FAINT FLAKE SEDGE
SLAKE UNION VEXIL WHEFT WHIFF
BANNER BOUGEE BURGEE COLORS
CORNET EMBLEM ENSIGN FANION
GUIDON LEVERS PENCEL PENNON
SIGNAL TABARD WIMPLE ANCIENT
BEEWORT CALAMUS CATTAIL
CURTAIN DECLINE DRAPEAU
FANACLE LABARUM PENDANT
PENNANT SCOURGE BANDEROL
BRATTACH GONFALON HANDFLAG
LANGUISH PAVILION STANDARD
STREAMER TRICOLOR VEXILLUM
WATCHMAN
(— CORNER) UNION
(— OF DENMARK) DANEBROG
(— OF TRANSVAAL) VIERKLEUR
(— OF TRUCE) KARTEL
(— OF U.S.) GRIDIRON
(— ON LANCE) PAVON
(BLUE — WITH WHITE SQUARE)
PETER
(CAVALRY —) STANDARD
(KNOTTED —) WAFT
(PIRATE —) ROGER BLACKJACK
(SERPENT-LIKE —) DRACO ANGUIS
(SHIP'S —) DUSTER
(TURKISH —) ALEM
(WATER —) SAG
(PL.) BUNTING
FLAG BEARER GUIDON ANCIENT
FLAGELLANT WHIPPER SCOURGER
(PL.) ALBI
FLAGELLATE MONAS NOCTILUCA
FLAGELLUM WHIP CILIUM RUNNER
KONSEAL WHIPLASH
(PREF.) BLEPHAR(O) MASTIG(O)
(SUFF.) KONT
FLAGEOLET PIPE ZUFOLO BASAREE
LARIGOT SIBILUS ZUFFOLO
MONAULOS
FLAGGING WEAK LANGUID
FLAGITIOUS WICKED CORRUPT
HEINOUS CRIMINAL FLAGRANT
GRIEVOUS

FLAGON GUN STOUP BOTTLE
VESSEL FLACKET FLAGONET
REHOBOAM
FLAGRANT BAD RED RANK GROSS
ODIOUS STRONG WANTON WICKED
BLATANT GLARING HATEFUL
HEINOUS SCARLET VIOLENT
SHAMEFUL
FLAGSHIP FLAG ADMIRAL
FLAGSTONE FLAG LECK SLAB
FAVUS
FLAIL BEAT FLOG WHIP DRASH FRAIL
THRAIL THRASH THRESH SWINGLE
SWIPPLE STRICKLE THRESHEL
FLAIR RAY BENT ELAN NOSE ODOR
SMELL VERVE GENIUS TALENT
LEANING PANACHE
FLAKE CHIP FILM FLAG FLAW RACK
SNOW FLANK FLECK FLOCK LAMIN
SCALE SLATE SPALL SPAWL STRIP
APHTHA HURDLE LAMINA PALING
FLAUGHT SHAVING FLOCCULE
FRAGMENT
(— OF DIRT) SMUT
(— OF METAL) FLITTER
(— OF SNOW) FLAG
(— OF SOOT) STRANGER
(PREF.) LEPID(O)
(SUFF.) LEPIS
FLAKY SCALY WACKY OFFBEAT
SHIVERY
FLAMBE JUBILEE
FLAMBEAU TORCH
FLAMBOYANCE BLARE PANACHE
FLAMBOYANT BAROCK FLORID
GARISH ORNATE BAROQUE BUCKEYE
FLAMING GORGEOUS
FLAME LOW FIRE GLOW LOWE LUNT
ARDOR BLAZE FLARE FLASH GLARE
GLEED INGLE LIGHT RESEPH
TONGUE BURNING FLAMELET
INKINDLE
(ACETYLENE —) CALCIUM
(SMALL —) SPUNK FLAMELET
FLAMMULE
(PL.) GLEED
FLAME SCARLET FLORENTINE
FLAME TREE KURRAJONG
FLAMING LIVE AFIRE FIERY FLAMY
VIVID AFLARE ARDENT BLAZING
BURNING FLARING FLAGRANT
FLAMMA, LA
(CHARACTER IN —) AGNES CERVIA
BASILIO DONELLO SILVANA
(COMPOSER OF —) RESPIGHI
FLAN PLANCHET
FLANGE BEAD BOSS BEZEL COLLAR
COLLET FLANCH SHROUD FEATHER
DUCKBILL FOLLOWER
(— OF GIRDER) BOOM
(WITHOUT —) BALD
FLANGER FLAYER GOUGER

FLANK LEEK LISK SIDE WING CHEEK
  SKIRT THIGH BORDER FLITCH
  (— OF ARCH) HANCH HAUNCH
  (PL.) ILIA
  (PREF.) LAPAR(O)
FLANNEL LANA DOMETT SAXONY
  STAMIN RUBBISH WHITTLE
  MOLLETON NONSENSE SWANSKIN
FLAP ADO FAN LUG ROB TAB TAG TAP
  WAP BATE BEAT BLOW CLAP FLIP
  FLOG FLOP GILL LOBE LOMA SLAM
  SLAT WAFF WELT ALARM APRON
  FLACK FLAFF FLICK BALLUP BANGLE
  LAPPET LIBBET STRIKE TONGUE
  WAFFLE WALLOP WINNOW AILERON
  BLINDER CLICKET FLACKER FLAPPET
  FLICKER FLOUNCE FLUTTER
  SWINDLE VALANCE AVENTAIL
  BACKFLAP COATTAIL CODPIECE
  TURNOVER AGITATION COMMOTION
  CONFUSION
  (— OF BOOTEE) FLY
  (— OF GARMENT) LAP
  (— OF HAT OR CAP) VALANCE
  (— OF HINGE) LEAF
  (— ON HOLSTER) FLOUNCE
  (— ON SADDLE) SKIRT JOCKEY
  (— VIOLENTLY) FLOG SLAT
  (CARDIAC —) CUSP
  (FLESHY —) GILL
  (MUD —) BOOT
  (TROUSERS' —) FALL
FLAPPER FLAP WING FLOPPER
  SNICKER
FLAPPING WAFF WHUTTER
FLARE BELL FLUE BLAZE FLAME
  FLASH FLECK FUSEE LIGHT SPIRT
  TORCH FLANCH SIGNAL SPREAD
  FLICKER TRUMPET OUTBURST
  (— ON SHIPBOARD) DUCK
  (— UP) ERUPT KINDLE
  (RAILROAD —) FUSEE
  (PL.) TROUSERS
FLARING BELL FLUE EVASE GAUDY
  AFLARE FLIPPY FLAMING GLARING
  SWAGGER BOUFFANT DAZZLING
FLASH DOT BEAT DASH LAIT LAMP
  LASH LEAM POOL RUSH SHOT STAB
  WINK BLASH BLAZE BURST FLAME
  FLARE FLOSH FLUFF GLADE GLAIK
  GLEAM GLENT GLINT GLITZ LEVIN
  MARSH SPARK STEAM BOTTLE FILLIP
  GLANCE QUIVER REPORT BLUETTE
  FLAUGHT FOULDRE GLIMMER
  GLIMPSE GLISTEN GLITTER INSTANT
  LIGHTEN QUICKEN SHIMMER
  SPARKLE TWINKLE BULLETIN
  SPLINTER SUNBURST CORUSCATE
  SCINTILLATION
  (— FORTH) OUTRAY
  (HOT —) FLUSHING
  (NEWS —) FUDGE

FLASHBACK THROWBACK
FLASHING CURB FLASH STEEP
  ARDENT BRIGHT FLASHY
  FORWARD LAMPING SHINING
  CREASING METEORIC SLASHING
  SNAPPING
FLASHLIGHT BUG GLIM FLASH
  TORCH PENLITE PENLIGHT
FLASHY GAY FLAT GAUD LOUD
  BAVIN FIERY GAUDY NOBBY SHOWY
  SLEEK ZOOTY FLOSSY FROTHY
  GARISH SLANGY SPORTY STUNTY
  INSIPID RAFFISH TINHORN DAZZLING
  FLASHING SPORTING TIGERISH
  VEHEMENT
FLASK BOX PIG BODY HEAD HELM
  JACK OLPE SNAP BETTY BULGE
  DEWAR FRAME GIRBA GOURD
  BOTTLE FIASCO FLACON GUTTUS
  HELMET LAGENA AMPULLA
  BOMBOLA CANTEEN FLASKET
  MATRASS TICKLER WARBURG
  CHRISMAL CUCURBIT
  (POCKET —) TICKLER
  (PREF.) OLPIDI
FLAT DEAD DOWD DULL EVEN FADE
  FLUE PLAT SLOB TAME ABODE AFLAT
  RANAL BLAND BLUNT DUSTY
  HAUGH LEVEL MOLLE MUSTY PLAIN
  PLANE PRONE ROOMS SEBKA SLAKE
  VAPID WALSH AGRUFE BORING
  CALLOW DREARY FLASHY JEJUNE
  LEADEN PLANAR QUATCH SEBKHA
  SILENT SIMOUS DECIDED FLIPPER
  INSIPID INSULSE PLATOID PROSAIC
  SHILPIT TABULAR UNIFORM
  DIRECTLY LIFELESS TENEMENT
  UNBROKEN WATERISH CHAMPAIGN
  POINTLESS PROSTRATE
  (— AND CIRCULAR) DISCOID
  (— AND SHORT) CAMUS CAMUSE
  (— IN MUSIC) BEMOL MOLLE
  (— OF SWORD) PLAT
  (MUD —) SLOB SLAKE CORCASS
  (NOT —) BRISK
  (SALT —) SALINA
  (THEATRICAL —) JOG
  (PREF.) PLAN(I) PLAT(Y)
FLATBOAT ARK SCOW PULLBOAT
FLATCAR FLAT IDLER LORRY
  (ON A —) PIGGYBACK
FLATFISH DAB RAY BUTT DACE KITE
  SLIP SOLE TONG BREAM BRILL
  FLUKE QUIFF RHINA WHIFF ACEDIA
  CARTER PLAICE TURBOT HALIBUT
  SUNFISH TORPEDO FLOUNDER
  MARYSOLE
FLATHEAD SALISH
FLATIRON IRON GOOSE STEEL
  SADIRON
FLATLY
  (PREF.) PLANO

FLATNESS BATHOS SILENCE
EVENNESS KURTOSIS
(— OF NOSE) SIMITY
FLAT-NOSED CAMUS
FLATTEN BEAT COMB DECK EVEN
PLAT CRUSH GRADE LEVEL PLUSH
SPLAT BEETLE CLINCH DEJECT
SMOOTH SPREAD SQUASH DEPRESS
EXPLAIN PANCAKE PLANISH SUBSIDE
SURBASE COMPRESS DISPIRIT
FLATTENED ECRASE OBLATE
DILATED PLANATE TABULAR
FLATTER BULL CLAW COAX DAUB
FAGE FUME PALP SOAP WORD
CHARM FLOAT GLOZE HONEY PAINT
ROOSE SLEEK SMALM BECOME
BUTTER CAJOLE CRINGE FICKLE
FLEECH FRAISE GLAVER KITTLE
PEPPER PHRASE SAWDER SLAVER
SMOOGE SOOTHE STROKE ADULATE
BEGUILE BEHONEY BLARNEY
FLETHER FLUTTER INCENSE PALAVER
SOOTHER SWEETEN WHEEDLE
BESLAVER BLANDISH BOOTLICK
COLLOGUE
FLATTERER FLOIT COGGER DAUBER
EARWIG GLOZER JENKINS PRONEUR
SOOTHER BOOTLICK CLAWBACK
COURTIER DAMOCLES INCENSER
LOSENGER SLAVERER SMOOTHER
FLATTERING SOAPY SMARMY
SMOOTH BUTTERY CANDIED
COURTLY GLAVERING
FLATTERY BULL BUNK DAUB FLUM
MUSH SOAP FRAIK GLOZE SALVE
TAFFY BUTTER CARNEY FLEECH
GREASE PHRASE SAWDER SLAVER
BLARNEY DAUBING EYEWASH
FAWNING FLETHER INCENSE
PALAVER CAJOLERY ADULATION
FLATULENCE WIND VAPOR
FLATULENT GASSY WINDY TURGID
POMPOUS VENTOSE FLATUOUS
INFLATED
FLATWARE SILVER
FLATWORM ACOEL FLUKE PLATODE
RADIATE POLYCLAD
FLAUNT BOSH SHOW WAVE BOAST
SKYRE STOUT VAUNT PARADE
DISPLAY FLUTTER TRAIPSE
BRANDISH FLOURISH
FLAUNTING GAUDY PURPLE SKYRIN
FLAGGERY
FLAVONE CHROMONE
FLAVOR GAMY GOUT MASK ODOR
RASA SALT TANG ZEST AROMA
ASSAI CURRY DEVIL SAPID SAPOR
SAUCE SAVOR SCENT SMACK SPICE
TASTE TINGE ASARUM ASSAHY
INFUSE RANCIO RELISH SEASON
TARAGE FLAVOUR PERFUME
SUPTION VARIETY HAUTGOUT
PIQUANCY

(DEVELOP —) BREATHE
(DISTINCTIVE —) TACK SMACK
(HIGH —) HOGO
(SHARP —) TWANG
(SPECIAL —) GUST
(UNPLEASANT —) TACK
FLAVORED SPICY TINCT SPICED
FLAVORFUL SAPID SAVOROUS
FLAVORING DIP MOCHA ALMOND
CASSIS VANILLA MIREPOIS
FLAVORLESS BLAND STALE SILENT
WATERISH
FLAW BUG FIB GAP LIE MAR RUB
WEM BANE BLOT CHIP FLEE GALL
HOLE RASE RIFT SPOT WIND
BOTCH BRACK BURST CHICK CLEFT
CRACK CRAZE FAULT FLAKE PLUME
SPECK BLOTCH BREACH DEFECT
FOIBLE LACUNA LESION BLEMISH
BLISTER DEFAULT EYELAST
FEATHER FISSURE NULLIFY
SUNSPOT VIOLATE WHITLOW
FRACTURE FRAGMENT GENDARME
WINDFLAW
(— IN CASTING) BUCKLE
(— IN CLOTH) BRACK
(— IN DIAMOND) GENDARME
(— IN MARBLE) TERRACE
(— IN METAL) SNAKE
(— IN PRECIOUS STONE) FEATHER
(— IN STEEL) STAR
(— IN STONE) DRY
(— IN WICK) THIEF
(MORAL —) SMIRCH
FLAWED CRACKED
FLAWLESS CLEAN SOUND PERFECT
FLAX LIN POB TOW CARD FLIX HARL
LINE LINT ROCK GRAIN HURDS
BREADS BYSSUS KORARI PEANUT
PEBBLE SCUTCH LINSEED FLAXWORT
HARAKEKE
(— DISEASE) PASMO
(PREPARE —) RET
(PREF.) BYSSI BYSSO LINO
FLAXEN FLAXY BLONDE
FLAXWEED TOADFLAX
FLAY SKIN SCULP STRIP FLEECE
UNCASE CENSURE PILLAGE
REPROVE SCARIFY
FLEA LOP SCUD FLECH FLECK PULEX
TUNGA CHEGRE CHIGOE VERMIN
PULICID SANDBOY
(— INFESTED) PULICOSE
(PREF.) PULI
FLEABANE SKEVISH SCABIOUS
WHITETOP
FLEA BEETLE THRIPS
FLEAM BEVEL
FLEAWORT CAMMOCK FLEASEED
PSYLLIUM
FLECHE SPIRE SPIRELET
FLECK FLAKE FREAK DAPPLE FLEECE
POUNCE STREAK STIPPLE

FLEDERMAUS, DIE (CHARACTER IN —) ADELE FALKE FRANK ALFRED ORLOFSKY ROSALINDE EISENSTEIN (COMPOSER OF —) STRAUSS

FLEDGED FLUSH FLIGGED

FLEDGLING SQUAB NESTER FLIGGER BIRDLING

FLEE FLY LAM RUN BOLT FLEG LOUP SCUR SHUN TURN ELOPE ELUDE SKIRR SPEED DECAMP ESCAPE RUNOFF VANISH ABANDON ABSCOND FORSAKE SCAMPER LIBERATE SKEDADDLE (SUFF.) FUGAL FUGE

FLEECE JIB KET TEG BUCK CAST FELL GAFF MORT PLOT ROOK SKIN TEGG TEGS CHEAT FLICK PASHM PLOAT SHAVE SHEAR SHEEP SWEAT PASHM PIGEON PUSHUM TOISON SHEARING (— OF MEDIUM GRADE) SUPER (POOREST PART OF —) ABB

FLEEING FUGIENT HOTFOOT RUNNING FUGITIVE

FLEER GIBE JIBE LEER FLIRE FLOUT SCOFF SNEER

FLEET BAY FAST FLIT NAVY SAIL SKIM SWIM CREEK DRAIN DRIFT EVAND FLOAT FLOTA HASTY INLET POWER QUICK RAPID SWIFT ARGOSY ARMADA FLIGHT HASTEN NIMBLE SPEEDY CARAVAN COMPANY FLOTILLA NAVARCHY WARCRAFT

FLEETING BRIEF BUBBLE CADUCE FLYING VOLAGE CURSIVE FLIGHTY PASSING POSTING SHADOWY VOLATIC CADUCOUS FUGITIVE VOLATILE

FLESH KIN BEEF BODY FELL GAME LAMB LINE MEAT RACE WEED SLATE STOCK FAMILY MUSCLE SEASON CARNAGE KINDRED MANKIND NATURAL HUMANITY MOONLIGHT (— ABOUT CHIN AND JAWS) GILL (— OF CALF) SLINK (— OF GOAT) CHEVON (— OF KID) CABRITO (— OF SHEEP) TRAIK (— ON LOWER JAW) CHOLLER (— OUT) CLOTHE (— UNDER SKIN) FELL (ANIMAL —) BRAWN (DEAD —) MURRAIN (HORSE —) JACK (LIFELESS —) MUMMY (PUTREFYING —) CARRION (SUN-DRIED —) TAPA (SUPERFLUOUS —) LUMBER (PREF.) CARNI CRE(O) CREATO KRE(O) SARC(O) (SUFF.) SARC

FLESHBRUSH STRIGIL

FLESH-COLORED SARCOLINE

FLESH-EATING CARNAL CARNIVOROUS

FLESHER LINING

FLESHINESS FULLNESS CORPULENCE

FLESHLESS LENTEN

FLESHLY CARNAL FLESHY SENSUAL SARKICAL

FLESHY FAT BEEFY LUSTY OBESE PLUMP PULPY STOUT ANIMAL BODILY BRAWNY CARNAL BUNTING CARNOSE SARCOUS CARNEOUS

FLETCH WING FLIGHT

FLEUR-DE-LIS LIS LYS LILY LUCY FLEUR

FLEX BEND

FLEXED PENCHE

FLEXIBILITY WHIP FLUIDITY

FLEXIBLE ACDC LIMP LUSH SOFT BUXOM LIMSY LITHE WANDY WITHY FLOPPY LIMBER LITHER PLIANT SUPPLE DUCTILE ELASTIC FINGENT FLEXILE FLEXIVE LISSOME PLIABLE SPRINGY WILLOWY WINDING WRIGGLE BENDSOME YIELDING (PREF.) CAMPTO

FLEXURE ARCH BEND BENT CURL FOLD CURVE TWIST SIGMOID WINDING

FLICK PIC FILM FLIP CLICK FLACK FLANK FLECK FLIRT FLISK MOVIE CINEMA (SKIN —) NUDIE (PL.) CINEMA

FLICKER FAIL FLIT LICK WINK BLINK FLAME FLARE FLICK FLUNK WAVER BICKER FITTER SHIVER YUCKER BLINTER FLIMMER FLITTER FLUTTER SKIMMER TREMBLE TWINKLE WHIFFLE FLICHTER HIGHHOLE

FLICKERING FLICKY FLUTTER LAMBENT FLEXUOUS UNSTEADY

FLICKERTAIL STATE NORTHDAKOTA

FLIER ACE BIRD KIWI FLYER PILOT AIRMAN AVIATOR LEAFLET CIRCULAR PAMPHLET

FLIGHT FLY GUY HOP LAM BOLT BUNK LAKE PAIR ROUT WING CHEVY FLOCK GLIDE GRICE SCRAP VOLEE CHIVVY EXODUS FUGACY HEGIRA HEJIRA JOYHOP SPIRAL BOUQUET EVASION FLAUGHT FLYOVER MIGRATE MISSION SCAMPER STEPWAY REGIFUGE STAMPEDE SWARMING (— APPROVAL) AOK (— OF BALL) HOOK DRIVE SLICE (— OF BIRDS) VOLARY VOLERY VOLLEY (— OF FANCY) SALLY (— OF GEESE) SKEIN (— OF SNIPE) WISP

(— OF STEPS) RISE TRAP GRECE
PITCH SCALE STOOP PERRON STAIRS
STEPWAY STAIRWAY
(— OF WILD FOWL) SKEIN
(— OF WOODCOCK) RODING
(ABORTIVE —) ABORT
(HASTY —) TIFT
(HAWK'S —) CAREER
(HIGH —) TOWER
(IN —) ALOFT
(LATE NIGHT —) REDEYE
(SUDDEN —) START STAMPEDE
(UNAUTHORIZED —) BUGOUT
(UPWARD —) SOAR
(PREF.) AERO
(SUFF.) FUGAL FUGE PHOBE PHOBI(A)
(AC)(C) PHOBUS
FLIGHTY ANILE BARMY GIDDY LIGHT
SWIFT FITFUL GARISH UNFIRM
VOLAGE WHISKY FLYAWAY FOOLISH
GIGGISH MOONISH ROCKETY
FLEETING FREAKISH HELLICAT
SKIPPING VOLATILE
(— PERSON) TRIVVET
FLIMFLAM CON
FLIMSINESS INANITY
FLIMSY LIMP THIN VAIN WEAK FRAIL
GAUDY JERRY FEEBLE PALTRY
SLEAZY SLIGHT SLIMSY HAYWIRE
SHALLOW TENUOUS TIFFANY
GIMCRACK GOSSAMER JIMCRACK
TWITTERY
FLINCH SHY FUNK GAME JARG
BLUNK BUDGE FEIGN QUAIL SHUNT
START WINCE WONDE BLANCH
BLENCH FALTER FLENSE RECOIL
SHRINK SCRINGE SCUNNER
SQUINCH
FLINCHER VELLINCH
FLINDER FLITTER SMITHERS
FLINDERSIA SILKWOOD
FLINDOSA CUDGERIE
FLING SHY BUZZ CAST DART
DASH DING EMIT FLAP FLEG GIBE
HURL KICK LASH PECK PICK SLAT
TOSS WARP BRAID CHEAT DANCE
FLIRT LANCE PITCH SHOOT SLING
SNEER SWING THROW WHANG
BAFFLE EFFUSE HURTLE LAUNCH
PLUNGE REBUFF SPIRIT ENFORCE
FLOUNCE REPULSE SARCASM
SCATTER SWINDLE SHYLANCE
SPANGHEW
(— HEADLONG) RUINATE
(— MISSILES) CHUNK
(— UPWARD) HAUNCH
(HIGHLAND —) WALLOCH
FLINT CORE BLANK CHERT MISER
SILEX EOLITH QUARTZ REJECT
ESLABON FURISON SCRAPER
GRATTOIR GUNFLINT
(PREF.) SILICEO SILICI SILICO
FLINTINESS HEART

FLINTLOCK FUSEE FUSIL FUZEE
MUSKET SPANNER FIRELOCK
MIQUELET SNAPHAAN
FLINTWOOD WHITETOP
FLIP SKY TAP FLAP SNAP TOSS TRIP
FLANK FLICK FLIRT GOAPE SLIRT
SMART FILLIP FLITCH GOGAGA
LIMBER NIMBLE PLIANT PROPEL
(— OUT) GOAPE
FLIP-FLOP SANDAL REVERSAL
FLIPPANT AIRY FLIP GLIB FLUENT
LIMBER NIMBLE
FLIPPER ARM FIN PAW HAND SWELL
PADDLE FLAPPER SPRINGER
FLIRT TOY FIKE FLIP MASH TICK VAMP
FLICK ROVER SLIRT JILLET MASHER
TRIFLE GALLANT PICKEER TWINKLE
COQUETTE PHILANDER
FLIRTATION FIKE PASSADE
COQUETRY PHILANDER
FLIT DART FLOW SCUD FLECK FLEET
FLICK FLIRT FLOAT FLURR HOVER
QUICK SCOOT SKIFF SWIFT NIMBLE
FLICKER FLUTTER
FLITCH FLICK GAMMON LONGWOOD
MIDDLING
FLOAT BOB FLY KIT SEA BOOM BUOY
CORK DRAG FLOW FLUX HAWK
HONE HOVE LIVE PONT RAFT RIDE
SAIL SCOW SOAR SWIM TILT WAFT
WAVE BALSA BLADE CAMEL DERBY
DRIFT DRIVE FLEET FLOOD FLUSH
GRAIL HOVER LADLE QUILL SHOAD
SWOON BILLOW BOBBER BUCKET
BUNGEY CANNEL DOBBER PADDLE
PONTON RADEAU STREEL TOPPER
CAISSON DRINGLE FLATTER FLOTTER
FRESHEN OROPESA PAGEANT
PLANKER PLUMMET PONTOON
SLICKER LEVITATE PICKOVER
(— AIMLESSLY) DRIFT
(— DELIGHTFULLY) COWD
(— FOR HERRING NET) BOWL
(— FOR RING BUOY) LEMON
(— LOGS) DRIVE
(— OF REEDS) KELEK LIGGER
(— PAST) GLACE
(— PROPERLY) WATCH
(CANOE —) AMA
(FISHLINE —) BOB CORK BOBBER
DOBBER TRIMMER
(PLASTERER'S —) DARBY
FLOATBOARD BLADE FLOAT LADLE
FLOATER STIFF
FLOATING FREE WAFT AWASH
LOOSE ADRIFT AFLOAT FLYING
NATANT BUOYANT FLYAWAY
PENDENT DRIFTING FLUITANT
SHIFTING UNFUNDED
FLOCCILATION TILMUS
FLOCK MOB POD BAND BANK BEVY
FOLD GAME GANG HERD MANY
PACK ROUT SAIL SORT TEAM TRIP

WISP BROOD BUNCH CHARM COVEY
CROWD DRIFT DROVE FLAKE FLECK
GROUP PLUMP SEDGE SHOAL
SWARM TRIBE TROOP COVERT
FLIGHT GAGGLE HIRSEL MANADA
MEINIE RAFTER SCHOOL SCURRY
VOLERY COMPANY GOOSERY
THICKEN PADDLING
(— OF BIRDS) POD BANK HERD TEAM
WISP BROWN COVEY SEDGE SIEGE
TRIBE FLIGHT VOLERY
(— OF BITTERNS) SEDGE SIEGE
(— OF DUCKS) PADDLING
(— OF FINCHES) CHARM CHIRM
(— OF GEESE) SKEIN GAGGLE
(— OF HERONS) SEDGE SIEGE
(— OF LARKS) EXALTATION
(— OF LIONS) PRIDE
(— OF MALLARDS) SORD SUTE
(— OF NIGHTINGALES) WATCH
(— OF PARTRIDGE) COVEY
(— OF PEACOCKS) MUSTER
(— OF PIGEONS) KIT LOFT
(— OF PLOVER) WING
(— OF ROOKS) ROOKERY
(— OF SANDPIPERS) FLING
(— OF SHEEP) FOLD HIRSEL
(— OF SHELDRAKE) DOPPING
(— OF SNIPE) WISP
(— OF SWANS) BANK GAME MARK
(— OF TURTLE-DOVES) DOLE
(— OF WIDGEONS) COMPANY
(— OF WILDFOWL) SCRY SKEIN
(— TOGETHER) RAFT
(SMALL —) SPRING
(PREF.)
(— OF WOOL) FLOCCI
FLOCKING REPAIR
FLOE PAN
FLOG CAT TAN TAW BEAT CANE
CHOP HIDE LASH LICK LUMP TOCO
WALE WARM WELK WHIP YANK
BIRCH EXCEL FIGHT FLAIL HORSE
KNOUT LINGE QUILT SAUCE SKEEG
SWISH WHANG BREECH COTTON
LARRUP LATHER STRIKE SWITCH
THRASH WALLOP WATTLE BALEISE
BELABOR COWHIDE SCOURGE
SJAMBOK TROUNCE CARTWHIP
CHAWBUCK SLAISTER URTICATE
VAPULATE
(— WATER) SCRINGE
FLOGGER HORSING SWISHER
FLOGGING TOCO TOKO TANNING
BIRCHING WHIPPING
FLOOD SEA BORE BUOY FLOW FLUX
POUR TIDE EAGRE FLOAT FLUSH
SPATE SWAMP SWILL WATER
DELUGE EXCESS RAVINE SLUICE
SPLASH DEBACLE FLOTTER FRESHET
NIAGARA TORRENT ALLUVION
CATARACT INUNDATE OVERFLOW
SURROUND

FLOODED AWASH AFLOAT
FLOODGATE CLOW DRAG GOLE
HATCH SLUICE STAUNCH CATARACT
PENSTOCK
FLOODING UP PROUD FLOWAGE
DILUVIAL FLOATING
FLOODLIGHT OLIVET
FLOODPLAIN BENCH DAMBO
FLOOR BECK DECK DROP FLAT LAND
LOFT PAVE SEAT BOARD FLOAT
GRASS PIANO PIECE SOLAR STAGE
STORY BELFRY FLIGHT GROUND
SOLLAR PLANCHE BARBECUE
FLOORING HALFPACE PAVEMENT
SUBFLOOR
(— OF COAL MINE) SOLE THILL
(— OF COAL SEAM) SILL
(— OF FORGE) HEARTH
(— OF GLASS FURNACE) SIEGE
(— OF OCEAN) SEABED
(— OF SPORTS RING) CANVAS
(— OF WOOLSHED) BOARD
(FOREST —) SEEDBED
(GROUND —) TERRENO BASEMENT
(OPENWORK —S) GRATINGS
(RAISED —) LEEWAN HALFPACE
(THEATRE —) GALLERY
(THRESHING —) MOWSTEAD
(UPPER —) LOFT
FLOORBOARD FOOTLING
(BOAT'S —) BURDEN
(BOAT'S —S) BURDEN
FLOORING STAGE PARQUET
TERRAZZO
(— FOR STACK) RICKSTAND
FLOORMAN CALLBOY
FLOP DOG BOMB SWOP WHOP
SQUAB BUMMER TURKEY FAILURE
TRAGEDY
FLORA CYBELE FLORULA
(— AND FAUNA) BIOTA
FLORAL TREE LEAF
FLORENCE FLASK BEITY
FLORENCE IRIS ORRIS TREOS
FLORESTAN
(WIFE OF —) LEONORA
FLORID FINE HIGH BUXOM FRESH
RUDDY ORNATE ROCOCO RUBIED
ASIATIC FLOWERY TAFFETA
BLOOMING FIGURATE RUBICUND
SANGUINE SPLENDID VIGOROUS

FLORIDA
BAY: BISCAYNE APALACHEE
  WACCASASSA
CAPITAL: TALLAHASSEE
COLLEGE: ROLLINS
COUNTY: BAY LEE DADE GULF LEON
  POLK BAKER DIXIE HARDEE HENDRY
  NASSAU ORANGE ALACHUA
  BREVARD BROWARD MANATEE
  OSCEOLA VOLUSIA PINELLAS
  SARASOTA

INDIAN: AIS OCALE UTINA CALUSA
CHATOT POTANO TIMUCUA
SEMINOLE
ISLANDS: KEYS
KEY: WEST LARGO BISCAYNE
LAKE: DORA APOPKA HARNEY JESSUP
NEWNAN LEDWITH ARBUCKLE
KISSIMMEE OKEECHOBEE
NATIVE: CONCH CRACKER
RIVER: BANANA INDIAN AUCILLA
MANATEE SCAMBIA SUWANEE
OCHLAWAHA
STATE BIRD: MOCKINGBIRD
STATE NICKNAME: SUNSHINE
STATE TREE: PALMETTO
TOWN: TICE COCOA MIAMI OCALA
TAMPA ORLANDO PALATKA
SEBRING TAMARAC SARASOTA
PENSACOLA
UNIVERSITY: STETSON
WETLANDS: GLADES

FLORIDIAN CRACKER
FLORIMEL (HUSBAND OF —)
MARINEL
FLORIN GULDEN
FLORIPES (BROTHER OF —)
FIERABRAS
(HUSBAND OF —) GUY
FLOSS FLUFF SKEIN WASTE CADDIS
SLEAVE CADDICE
FLOSSER FANNER
FLOSS-SILK TREE SAMOHU
FLOTSAM JETSAM WILSAM
WAFTURE WAVESON DRIFTAGE
FLOATAGE
FLOUNCE FLAP HUFF SKIT SLAM
FLING FRILL RUCHE PEPLUM RIPPLE
ROBING ROUNCE RUFFLE VOLANT
FALBALA FALBELO FROUNCE
RUCHING FLOUNDER FURBELOW
STRUGGLE
FLOUNDER DAB GAD BUTT KEEL
POLE ROLL TOSS BREAM FLUKE
SLOSH WITCH WRELE GADOID
GROVEL MEGRIM MUDDLE PLAICE
TOLTER TURBOT WALLOP WALLOW
WARSLE BLUNDER FLASKER
FLOUNCE PLOUNCE STUMBLE
SUNFISH TOPKNOT VAAGMAR
ANACANTH FLATFISH FOOLFISH
PLUNTHER SANDLING
FLOUR AMYL ATTA DUST CONES
HOVIS BINDER CLEARS FARINA
FLOWER PATENT POLLEN SICKEN
TSAMBA WHITES BOXINGS
BRAVURA CRIBBLE CANAILLE
(— OF MALT) SMEDDUM
(COARSE —) THIRD CHISEL BOXINGS
CRIBBLE
(COVER WITH —) DREDGE
(FINE —) CONES SUJEE
(LOW-GRADE —) TAIL

(PARTICLE OF —) CHOP
(POTATO —) FROW
(UNSORTED —) ATTA
(PREF.) ALEURO
FLOURISH TAG WAG BOOM BRAG
FUSS GROW LICK RIOT RISE SHOW
TUCK WAVE ADORN BLOOM BOAST
CHEVE GLOSS QUIRK REIGN SHAKE
SWASH SWING SWISH TUSCH VAUNT
CATTER PARADE PARAPH QUAVER
SQUIRL THRIVE BLOSSOM BURGEON
CADENZA DISPLAY ENLARGE
FANFARE GAMBADE GAMBADO
PASSAGE PROSPER ROULADE
SUCCEED TRIUMPH WAMPISH
ARPEGGIO BRANDISH CURLICUE
INCREASE ORNAMENT SKIRMISH
(— OF BAGPIPE) WARBLER
(— OF TRUMPET) MORT SENNET
TUCKET
FLOURISHING FAR FRIM FRUM PERT
GREEN PALMY PEART VITAL BLOOMY
FLORID GOLDEN FLORENT HEALTHY
VERNANT THRIVING VEGETOUS
PROSPEROUS
FLOURY MEALY
FLOUT BOB GIBE JEER JERK JIBE
LOUT MOCK FLEER FLITE FRUMP
SCOFF SCOMM SCORN SCOUT
SNEER TAUNT DERIDE INSULT
BETONGUE
FLOW GO EBB ERN JET PUT RUN SET
SUE BORE COMB FLIT FLUX FUSE
GUSH HALE LAVA LAVE MELT PASS
POUR RAIL ROLL SEND SHED SILE
SLIP SOAK SWIG TAIL TEEM TIDE
WELL AVALE DRAIN DRIFT EAGRE
EXUDE FLEAM FLEET FLOAT FLOOD
FLUSH FRESH GLIDE ISSUE QUELL
RIVER SCOOT SLIDE SPEND SPILL
SPURT SWILL TRILL ABOUND AFFLUX
COURSE CURSUS DELUGE GUGGLE
GUTTER POPPLE RECEDE RINDLE
SPRING STREAM CURRENT DEVOLVE
DISTILL DRIBBLE EMANATE
FLOWAGE FLUTTER FLUXION
ILLAPSE INDRAFT MEANDER
SPURTLE TRINKLE TRINTLE
ALLUVION BACKWASH CURRANCE
CURRENCY DOWNFLOW EMISSION
FOUNTAIN GOWITHIT INUNDATE
(— AGAINST) LAP LAVE BATHE
(— BACK) EBB
(— BEYOND BANKS) DEBORD
SURROUND
(— DOWN) AVALE
(— IN) INFLOW INFLOOD
(— IN RILLS) DRILL
(— IN RIVULETS) GUTTER
(— IN SPURTS) SALTATION
(— INTERMITTENTLY) HEAD
(— NOISILY) BICKER
(— OF AIR) SIDEWASH

(— OF ELECTRICITY) BOLT
OSCILLATION
(— OF LANGUAGE) STRAIN
(— OF METAL) CREEP
(— OF RADIO SIGNAL) BEAM
(— OF SOUNDS) CADENCE
(— OUT) EMIT ISSUE EFFUSE SPREAD
EXHAUST RESOLVE
(— OVER) BERUN
(— SLOWLY) SEEP EXUDE GLEET
(—TOGETHER) CONCUR CONFLOW
(— WITH) FLEET
(CONTINUOUS —) LAPSE
(COPIOUS —) HALE RIVER
(LAVA-) COULE COULEE
(RHYTHMICAL—) LILT
(STRONG —) TORRENT
(TIDAL—) BORE AEGIR EAGER EAGRE
(PREF.) RHEO RHYSI
(SUFF.) FLUENCE FLUENT FLUOUS
FLUX RRHAGIA RRHEA RRHOEA
FLOWER (ALSO SEE PLANT AND
HERB) BUD GAY BEST BLOW FLAG
IRIS IXIA PINK POLE POSY ROSE
ARROW ASTER BLOOM BLUET
BREAK DAISY ELITE FANCY FLOUR
GOWAN LILAC PANSY PHLOX TRUSS
TULIP TUTTY AZALEA CHOICE
CORYMB CROCUS CYMULE DAHLIA
DATURA FLORET MAYPOP ORCHID
SCILLA SEASON SHOWER SINGLE
STEVIA UNFOLD AMELLUS
ANEMONE ARBUTUS BLETHIA
BLOSSOM BOSTRYX CAMPANA
DEVELOP ESSENCE FLEURET
FLOSCLE GAZANIA GENTIAN
GERBERA IPOMOEA PETUNIA
PICOTEE TORENIA BELAMOUR
CAMELLIA CYCLAMEN DAFFODIL
DIANTHUS GARDENIA GERANIUM
HEPATICA HIBISCUS HYACINTH
PRIMROSE SNOWDROP SPARAXIS
(— FOR BUTTONHOLE).
BOUTONNIERE
(— STATE) FLORIDA
(— WITH 6 SEGMENTS) SEXFOIL
(ART OF —ARRANGING) IKEBANA
(AXIS OF —) CYME SPIKE UMBEL
CORYMB MIASMA RACEME
(COTTON —) SQUARE
(DEFORMED —) BULLHEAD
(DOUBLE —) BURSTER
(DRIED —S) BRAYERA
(GLOWING —) TORCH
(IMAGINARY —) AMARANTH
(PART OF —) OVARY PETAL SEPAL
STALK STYLE ANTHER CARDEL PISTIL
STAMEN STIGMA PEDICEL FILAMENT
PEDUNCLE PERIANTH RECEPTACLE
(SHOWY —) ORCHIS
(STRIPED —) BIZARRE
(UNFADING —) AMARANTH
(PL.) SPRAY BOUQUET

(PREF.) ANTH(O) FLORI
(SUFF.) ANTHEMA ANTHEMUM
ANTHERA ANTHEROUS ANTHERY
ANTHES ANTHOUS ANTHUS FLORAL
FLOROUS
FLOWER-BED KNOT BORDER
FLOWER-BUD CAPER CLOVE
FLOWERFLY SYRPHID
FLOWERHEAD CALATHUS
FLOWERING AFLOWER FLOWERY
ANTHESIS BLOOMING
FLOWERING GLUME LEMMA
FLOWERLESS ANANTHOUS
FLOWER-LIKE ANTHOID
FLOWER-OF-AN-HOUR SHOOFLY
FLOWER-PECKER KAKAWAHIE
FLOWERPOT POT CACHEPOT
FLOWERY BLOWN BLOOMY FLORID
POSIED FLORENT PRIMROSE
FLOWING FAIR FLUX LAVE SIDE
AFLOW FLOAT FLUID FLUOR QUICK
TIDAL AFFLUX DEFLUX FLUENT
FUSILE LIVING COPIOUS CURRENT
CURSIVE EMANANT FLUXING
FLUXION FLUXIVE RUNNING SLIDING
STREAMY DEFLUENT DILUENDO
FLUVIOSE
(— AT LOW SPEED) SLACK
(— BACK) EBB
(— IN) INFLUX INFLUENT INFLUXION
(— OF GLAZE) STREAMING
(— OF TIDE) FLOOD
(— OUT) ELAPSE EFFLUENT
(— SMOOTHLY) VOLUBLE
PROFLUENT
(— TOGETHER) CONFLUX
(PREF.) (— OUT) EFFLUVIO
FLOWOFF RUNOFF
FLU (TYPE OF —) ASIAN
FLUR BOOT ERRATUM
FLUCAN SELVAGE SELVEDGE
FLUCTUATE SWAY VARY VEER YOYO
FLEET SWING WAVER BALANCE
VIBRATE WAMPISH UNDULATE
UNSTEADY VACILLATE
FLUCTUATING WAVY HECTIC
LABILE RUBATO ERRATIC FLUXIVE
WAYWARD UNSTABLE UNSTEADY
FLUCTUATION CYCLE FADING
JIGGLE FLICKER FLUTTER VIBRATO
OSCILLATION
(— IN LAKES) SEICHE
(— OF LAKE SURFACE) SEICHE
FLUE NET BARB DOWN OPEN PIPE
THIN VENT FLARE FLUFF FLUKE
TEWEL FUNNEL TUNNEL UPTAKE
CHIMNEY OUTTAKE PASSAGE
DOWNTAKE
FLUE-CURED BRIGHT
FLUENCY SKILL
FLUENT GASH GLIB FLUID READY
FACILE LIQUID SMOOTH STREAM
COPIOUS CURRENT FLOWING

FLUIDIC RENABLE VERBOSE
VOLUBLE ELOQUENT FLIPPANT

FLUFF FUG FLUE FUZZ LINT OOZE
PUFF BEARD ERROR FLOSH FLOSS
WHEEL MISTAKE

FLUFFING WHEELING

FLUFFY SOFT DOWNY DRUNK FILMY
FLUEY FUZZY LIGHT LINTEN PLUFFY
FEATHERY UNSTEADY
(NOT —) CLOSE

FLUID INK SAP MASS RASA BLOOD
FLUOR HUMOR JUICE LATEX SERUM
SPERM SWEAT WATER FLUENT
LIQUID WATERY COOLANT FLOWING
FLUIBLE FLUXILE GASEOUS SYNOVIA
EMULSION FLOATING FLUXIBLE
FORESHOT PERSPERATION
(ANIMAL —) SERUM
(BODY —) CHYLE
(EAR —) PERILYMPH
(EGYPTIAN PRIMEVAL —) NU NUN
(ELECTRIC —) VRIL
(ETHEREAL —) ICHOR
(LIVER —) BILE
(LUBRICATING —) SYNOVIA
(MAMMARY —) MILK
(PLANT —) SERO
(SLIMY —) MUCUS
(SOLDERING —) FAKE
(SUPPURATION —) PUS
(THICK VISCOUS —) GRUME
(WATERY —) LYE SANIES SEROSITY
(WORKING —) AIR
(PREF.) SERO

FLUIDITY LENGTH
(— UNIT) RHE

FLUKE FLUE PALM BLADE GRASP
SCALE PLAICE DISTOME PLATODE
SCRATCH FLATWORM FLOUNDER
BILHARZIA
(— OF ANCHOR) HOOK KILLICK
(— OF WHALE'S TAIL) BLADE

FLUME CHUTE DITCH SHUTE
SLUICE

FLUMMERY SOWENS WASHBREW

FLUMMOX ABASH ADDLE
CONFOUND EMBARRASS
DISCONCERT

FLUNK BUST FAIL SKEW SPIN
FLICKER

FLUNKY SNOB TOADY COOKEE
JEAMES LACKEY FOOTMAN
SERVANT STEWARD

FLUORESCENCE BLOOM

FLUORESCENT PSYCHEDELIC

FLUORINE PHTOR PHTHOR

FLUORITE CAND FLUX FLUOR

FLURRY ADO FIT FACT FRET GUST
PIRR SPIT STIR TEAR HASTE SKIFF
SKIRL BOTHER BUSTLE SCURRY
SQUALL CONFUSE FLUSKER
FLUSTER FLUTTER FOOSTER
SWITHER WHITHER SPITTING

FLUSH JET EVEN GLOW HUSH JUMP
POOL ROSE BLOOM BLUSH COLOR
ELATE FLASH FLUSK FRESH KNOCK
LEVEL RAISE ROUGE SCOUR START
VIGOR AFLUSH EXCITE HECTIC
LAVISH MANTLE MORASS REDDEN
RUDDLE SLUICE SPRING THRILL
ANIMATE BOBTAIL CRIMSON
SUFFUSE ABUNDANT AFFLUENT
PRODIGAL ROSINESS
(— GAME) SERVE
(— IN SKY) SUNGLOW
(NOT —) FLAT

FLUSHED RED ROSY BEAMY FIERY
FLOWN FLORID FLUSHY HECTIC
CRIMSON RUBICUND

FLUSTER PAVIE SHAKE BOTHER
FLURRY FUDDLE MUDDLE POTHER
RATTLE CONFUSE FLUSKER
FOOSTER SWITHER BEFUDDLE
FLOWSTER FLUSTRUM

FLUTE NAY FIFE FUYE PIPE AULOS
CRIMP CUENA PUNGI QUENA STICK
STYKE TIBIA TWILL CANNEL
DOUCET FLAUTO GEWGAW GOFFER
POOGYE ZUFOLO CHAMFER
DIAULOS FLAMFEW FLUTING
GAUFFER HEMIOPE MAGADIS
MATALAN PICCOLO SIBILUS SIFFLOT
TONETTE TRANGAM WHISTLE
ZUFFOLO FLAUTINO MONAULOS
RECORDER
(— OF A COLUMN) STRIGA CHANNEL
(— STOP) VENTAGE
(CHINESE —) TCHE
(EAST INDIAN —) MATALAN
(EUNUCH —) KAZOO
(JAPANESE —) FUYE SHAKUHACHI
(LYDIAN —) MAGADIS
(MOSLEM —) NAY
(PHOENICIAN —) GINGRAS
(PL.) NEHILOTH
(PREF.) AUL(O)

FLUTED QUILLED

FLUTEMOUTH CORNETFISH

FLUTE PLAYER AULETE FLUTER
FLUTIST TIBICEN TOOTLER AULETRIS
FLAUTIST

FLUTING STRIX FULLER GADROON
STRIGIL COULISSE QUILLING

FLUTTER BAT FAN FUG BATE BLOW
BUZZ FLAP FLIT FLOW FLUE OOZE
PLAY WAFF WAVE FLACK FLAFF
FLARE FLECK FLICK FLOSS FLURR
HOVER PULSE SHAKE WAVER
BANGLE FLAUNT FLURRY RUFFLE
SWIVET TREMOR WAFFLE WALLOP
WINNOW FLACKER FLAFFER
FLASKER FLATTER FLAUGHT FLICKER
FLITTER FLUSKER SKIMMER
WAGTAIL WHIFFLE FLICHTER
SQUATTER VOLITATE
(IN A —) PITAPAT

FLUTTERING AWING FLITTY
  WHUTTER AFLUTTER FLICKERY
FLUTTERINGLY PITAPAT
FLUTTER-TONGUING GROWL
FLUX FLOW FUSE LASK MELT BORAX
  FLOAT FLOOD ISSUE RESIN ROSIN
  SMEAR SMELT FUSION CURRENT
  EURIPUS FLOWING LEAKAGE
  OUTFLOW
  (— UNIT) WEBER MAXWELL
FLY BEE FAG FAN GAD HOP RUN FIRK
  FLEA FLEE FLEG FLIT FRIT GNAT KITE
  KIVU LASH LEAP MELT RACK RAKE
  SAIL SCUD SMUT SOAR SOLO WHEW
  WHIR WHIZ WIND WING ZIMB AGILE
  ALERT EMPID FLEET FLIER FLOAT
  FLURR FLUSH FLYER GLIDE LATCH
  MIDGE MUSCA OXFLY PERLA PHORA
  PILOT POPUP QUICK SEDGE SHARP
  SKIRL SKIRR STOUR WHAMF WHIRR
  ZEBUB ASILID AVIATE BANGLE
  BLOWER BOTFLY BREEZE DAYFLY
  ESCAPE FLIGHT FLYBOY GADFLY
  GORFLY JARFLY LEPTID MEDFLY
  MOTUCA NIMBLE PALMER PHORID
  PUNKIE RANDON ROBBER SEPSID
  SEROOT SPRING TIPULA TSETSE
  VANISH VERMIN WINNOW AVIGATE
  AVOLATE BROMMER CANOPID
  CHALCID CONOPID FORMATE
  GRANNOM KNOWING LOVEBUG
  ORTALID PYRALIS SCIARID TYRPHID
  AIRPLANE BIBIONID BRACONID
  COACHMAN DIPTERAN DROPPING
  EPHYDRID EULOPHID GLOSSINA
  HORSEFLY HOUSEFLY RUBYTAIL
  SIMULIID TACHINID TATUKIRA
  VOLITATE
  (— AFTER GAME) RAKE
  (— AIMLESSLY) BANGLE
  (— ALOFT) SOAR TOWER
  (— AWAY) CARRY
  (— CLUMSILY) FLIGHTER
  (— ERRATICALLY) GAD
  (— INTO RAGE) FUFF RARE
  (— LOW) DICE DRAG HEDGEHOP
  (— NEAR THE GROUND) ACCOST
  (— OUT) EXPIRE
  (— RAPIDLY) SCUR SKIRR
  (— TOO HIGH) SCUD
  (— WIDE) MISS
  (BITING —) PIUM
  (FISHING —) BEE DUN OAK BUZZ
  GNAT HARL HERL SMUT WASP ZULU
  ABBEY ALDER BAKER FAIRY NYMPH
  SEDGE BADGER BOBFLY CADDIS
  CAHILL CANARY CLARET DOCTOR
  HACKLE MILLER ORIOLE WILLOW
  BABCOCK BUTCHER CADDICE
  COLONEL DROPPER DUBBING
  GRANNOM HUZZARD SPINNER
  WATCHED WATCHET BUCKTAIL
  CATSKILL COACHMAN FERGUSON

GOVERNOR STREAMER WOODRUFF
  WRENTAIL
  (KIND OF —) FACE
  (MAY —) DUN DRAKE
  (POP —) BLOOP BLOOPER
  (SHEEP —) FAG KED
  (STONE —) SALLY
  (PREF.) MUSCI MYI(O)
  (SUFF.) MYI(A)(O)
FLYBLOWN BLOWN STRUCK
FLYBOAT FLUTE FLIGHT
FLYCATCHER TODY PEWEE PEWIT
  CHEBEC COBWEB MILLER PEEWEE
  PHOEBE PIPIRI RAFTER TYRANT
  YETAPA ELEPAIO FANTAIL GRIGNET
  GRINDER PITIRRI TOMFOOL TYRANNI
  BEAMBIRD FIREBALL FIREBIRD
  FLYEATER FORKTAIL GERYGONE
  KINGBIRD KISKADEE PITANGUA
  WALLBIRD SCISSORTAIL
FLYER (FLEXIBLE —) SLED
FLY, FISHING (PART OF —) EYE TAG
  BODY BUTT HEAD HORN TAIL WING
  CHEEK JOINT HACKLE RIBBING
  TOPPING
FLYING AWING FLIGHT VOLANT
  WAVING FLOTANT VOLATIC AVIATION
  FLOATING
  (— MANEUVER) LUFBERY
  (— TAIL DOWN) CABRE
  (STUDY OF — OBJECTS) UFOLOGY
FLYING DUTCHMAN, THE
  (CHARACTER IN —) ERIK SENTA
  DALAND
  (COMPOSER OF —) WAGNER
FLYING FISH SKIPPER VOLADOR
FLYING FOX KALONG PTEROPID
FLYING GURNARD ANGLER
  BATFISH LATCHET LOPHIID
  VOLADOR
FLYING LEMUR COBEGO COLUGO
  KUBONG
FLYING MACHINE AVIATOR
  AEROSTAT
FLYING PHALANGER CUSCUS
  SQUIRREL
FLYING SAUCER UFO
FLYING SQUIRREL TAGUAN
  ASSAPAN
FLYMAN LOFTMAN
FLYSCH MACIGNO
FLYWHEEL FLY FLIER FLYER WHORL
  WHARVE
FOAL CADE COLT FILLY PODDY
  SLEEPER
FOAM FOB SUD BARM BEES BOIL
  FUME HEAD KNIT REAM SCUD SCUM
  SUDS WORK CREAM FROST FROTH
  SPUME YEAST RUBBLE FLOWER
  FLURRY FREATH IMBOST LATHER
  SEETHE BLUBBER DESPUME
  MELDROP
  (PREF.) APHR(O) SPUMI

FOAMING AFOAM NAPPY YEASTY SPUMOUS MANTLING SPUMANTE
FOAMY BARMY BEADY SPUMY SUDSY FROTHY SPUMOSE
FOB FUB SPUNG POCKET
FOCAL POINT OMPHALOS
FOCUS AIM FIX PUT POINT PURSE TRAIN CENTER CLIMAX DIRECT FASTEN FIXATE HEARTH TEMPLE NUCLEUS CONVERGE FOCALIZE GANGLION
FODDER HAY FEED FOOD SOIL VERT GOOMA MANGE VETCH EATAGE FORAGE FOTHER PODDER SILAGE STOVER FARRAGE PODWARE PROVAND BROWSING ENSILAGE ROUGHAGE
FODDERCAGE TUMBREL
FODDERER FOGGER
FOE ENEMY FIEND RIVAL FOEMAN HOSTILE OPPOSER OPPONENT WRANGLER
(STUBBORN —) WRANGLER
FOG FF DAG RAG DAMP DAZE HAAR HAZE MIST MOKE MOSS MURK PRIG RACK ROKE SMOG SMUR SOUP BEDIM BRUME CLOUD GRASS HUMOR MUDDY SMIRR SPRAY STOUR VAPOR MUDDLE NEBULA SALMON STUPOR FOGGAGE OBSCURE POGONIP SMOTHER BEWILDER MOISTURE
(— OF THE NILE) QOBAR
(FROZEN —) BARBER
(LIGHT —) GAUZE
(SEA —) HAAR HARR
FOGBOW DOG FOGDOG SEADOG MISTBOW FOGEATER
FOGDOG DOG STUBB FOGBOW SEADOG FOGEATER
FOGGINESS CLOUDING
FOGGY DIM DULL HAZY MIRK MOKY MURK ROKY DENSE DIRTY GROSS MISKY MISTY MURKY ROOKY ROUKY SPEWY CLOUDY GREASY GROGGY MARSHY MILKEN SMURRY BRUMOUS MUDDLED OBSCURE CONFUSED NUBILOUS VAPOROUS
FOGHORN SIREN TYFON RIPPER MEGAFOG
FOG-SIGNAL DIAPHONE
FOGY DODO FOGEY DUFFER FOGRAM FOOZLE STODGER MOSSBACK
FOGYISH MUSTY
FOIBLE VICE FAULT FERLY FEEBLE FAILING FRAILTY WEAKNESS
FOIL BACK BALK EPEE FILE FOIN SOIL TAIN BLADE BLANK BLUNT CHEAT ELUDE EVADE FALSE STAIN STUMP SWORD TRACK TRAIL BAFFLE BLENCH BOGGLE CHATON DEFEAT DEFILE FLORET OFFSET OUTWIT STIGMA STOOGE THWART BEGUILE

FAILURE FOILING FOLIATE LAMETTA PAILLON POLLUTE REPULSE STONKER TRAMPLE DISGRACE
(— STRIPS) WINDOW
(FENCING —) EPEE BLUNT FLORET FLEURET
(PART OF —) END TIP BELL GRIP HILT BLADE FORTE GUARD POINT BUTTON FOIBLE HANDLE POMMEL MOUNTING
(POINTED —) TANG
(TIN —) TAIN
FOIST WISH FUDGE FATHER SUBORN FOISTER SHOEHORN
FOLD BOW FLY LAP PEN PLY SET WAP BEND COTE CREW CRUE DART FAIL FALX FAUN FELD FLAP FURL HANK HOOD LIRK LOOP RUCK RUGA SWAG TUCK WRAP BREAK CLASP CRIMP CRISP CROZE DRAPE FAULD FLIPE FLOCK FLYPE FRILL GROIN LAYER PARMA PINCH PLAIT PLEAT PLICA PRANK QUILL SINUS YIELD BOUGHT BUCKLE COLLOP CREASE CRISTA CUTTLE DEWLAP DIAPIR DOUBLE ENFOLD FORNIX FRENUM FURDLE GATHER GUSSET HURDLE INFOLD LABIUM LAPPET MANTLE PIPING PLIGHT PUCKER RIMPLE RUMPLE WIMPLE CAPSIZE CRINKLE CRUMPLE EMBRACE ENVELOP FLEXION FLEXURE PINFOLD PLACATE PLICATE REVERSE ROLLING ROULEAU TURNING VALVULA CRIMPING FLECTION FLITFOLD QUILLING SCAPULET SPLENIUM SURROUND PLICATION REPLICATE REFLECTION
(— CLOTH) RAG
(— DOWN) COLLAPSE
(— FOR CATTLE) BAWN
(— IN HOOD) SHOVE
(— INWARD) CRIMP
(— OF MEMBRANE) CRISTA
(— OF SKIN) APRON DEWLAP SHEATH OMENTUM FORESKIN MESENTERY
(— ROCKS) DEFORM
(—S OF TOGA) SINUS
(CARDIAC —) CUSP
(GEOLOGICAL —) DIAPIR CLOSURE EXOCLINE SYNCLINE MONOCLINE
(LOOSE —) LAPPET
(RESTRAINING —) FRENUM FRAENUM
(SCOTTISH —) CAT
(SHEEP —) REEVE
(PREF.) PLEXI PLICATO PLICI PTYCH(O) SINU(ATO) VALVI VALVO
(SUFF.) FARIOUS PLEX PLICATE PLOID
(COVERING —) STEGE STEGITE
FOLDAGE SOC SOKE
FOLDED SHUT DOUBLE FANLIKE PLICATE PLICATED REFLEXED WREATHED

(**— AND WAVED**) GYROSE
(PREF.) PLICATO
FOLDER KIT BOOK FILE FOLD ATLAS
COVER FOLIO BINDER CLEANER
HANDOUT LEAFLET STROKER
PAMPHLET
FOLDING KNOT
(**— OF LEAF**) PTYXIS
(**— PAPER**) ORIGAMI
FOLDOUT GATEFOLD
FOLIACEOUS LEAFY PHYLLOID
FOLIAGE HERB SHADE GREENS
LEAVES SHROUD BOSCAGE GILLERY
LEAFAGE LEAFERY UMBRAGE
FRONDAGE GREENERY
(**CARVED —**) KNOT
FOLIATED SPATHIC
FOLIATION SEXFOIL TREFOIL
CINQFOIL SEPTFOIL
FOLIC ACID PGA
FOLIO CASE ATLAS FOLIUM
FOLK SOULS DAIONE PEOPLE
(**— TALES**) LORE
(**FAIRY —**) SHEE SIDHE
(**STRANGE —**) FRAIM FREMD
(PL.) GENTRY
FOLKLORE (**IMITATION —**) FAKELORE
FOLKSONG SON TONADA
VOLKSLIED
FOLKSY HOMY HOMEY HOMESPUN
FOLKTALE DROLL FABULA MARCHEN
FOLLETTO DUSIO
FOLLICLE CRYPT LACUNA OVISAC
CONCEPTACLE
FOLLOW GO PAD SUE TAG COME
COPY HUNT NEXT OBEY SEEK SHAG
TAIL TAKE TOUT ADOPT AFTER
CHASE DODGE ENSUE SNAKE SPOOR
TRACE TRACK TRAIL TREAD ADHERE
ATTEND DANGLE FOLLER OCCUPY
PURSUE RESULT SECOND SHADOW
SUIVEZ TAGGLE HOTFOOT IMITATE
OBSERVE PROFESS REPLACE
SUCCEED VALOUWE PRACTICE
SUPPLANT
(**— A COURSE**) RUN
(**— A POINTER'S LEAD**) BACK
(**— CLOSELY**) TAILGATE
(**— HOSTILELY**) DOG
(**— INSIDIOUSLY**) DOG
(**— IN SUCCESSION**) VARY
(**— SCENT**) ROAD CARRY
(**— SLAVISHLY**) ECHO
(**— SLOWLY**) DRAGGLE
(**— THROUGH**) PRESS
(**— TRACK**) SLEUTH
(**— UP**) SUE ATTEND
(**— UPON**) WAIT
FOLLOWER FAN IST SON APER BEAU
ZANY ADEPT CHELA GILLY BILDAR
COHORT DRIVEN ENSUER GILLIE
GUDGET KNIGHT LACKEY SEQUEL
SUITOR SULTER VOTARY ACACIAN

ACOLYTE CARRIER DEVOTEE
EPIGONE FLATTER GRIFTER POLIGAR
PURSUER RETINUE SECTARY
SEQUENT SPANIEL SUPPOST
TRAILER ADHERENT DISCIPLE
FAITHFUL FAVORITE HENCHMAN
MYRMIDON OBSERVER OFFSIDER
PARTISAN RETAINER SECTATOR
SERVITOR SATELLITE PURSUIVANT
(**— OF ART**) BOHEMIAN
(**— OF CELEBRITY**) GROUPIE
(**CAMP —**) BUMMER GUDGET
LASCAR
(**CRANE —**) SPOTTER
(**SERVILE —**) SLAVE LACKEY
ANTHONY
(PL.) FOLK SECTA SEQUACES
(SUFF.) ITE
FOLLOWING LAST NEXT SECT SUIT
AFTER FIRST INTOW SUANT TRACE
TRAIN BEHIND SEQUEL ENSUANT
ENSUING SEQUENT AUDIENCE
BUSINESS SECUNDUM SEGUENDO
TRAILING VOCATION
FOLLOW UP FOLO
FOLLY ATE SIN RAGE LAPSE MORIA
SOTIE BETISE DOTAGE LUNACY
NICETY WANWIT DAFFERY DAFFING
FOOLERY FOPPERY IDIOTCY
MADNESS MISTAKE SOTTAGE
UNSKILL FONDNESS FOOLHEAD
IDLENESS LEWDNESS MOROLOGY
NONSENSE RASHNESS SURQUIDY
UNTHRIFT UNWISDOM WILLNESS
WOODNESS SIMPLICITY
FOMALHAUT DIFDA DIPHDA
FOMENT SOW ABET BREW SPUR
ROUSE STUPE AROUSE EXCITE
INCITE AGITATE FERMENT INSPIRE
FOND TID DAFT DEAR DOTE FAIN
FOOL FUND KIND VAIN WEAK CRAZY
SILLY STOCK STORE ARDENT
BEFOOL CARESS CHOICE DEARLY
DOTING FONDLE FONDLY LOVING
SIMPLE TENDER AMATORY
AMOROUS BEGUILE BROWDEN
FONDISH FOOLISH INSIPID PARTIAL
DESIROUS ENAMORED SANGUINE
TRIFLING UXORIOUS
(**FOOLISHLY —**) SPOON SPOONY
(PREF.) (**— OF**) PHIL(O)
(SUFF.) (**— OF**) PHIL(A)(AE)(E)(OUS)
(US)
FONDLE PET BABY BILL CLAP COAX
DAUT DAWT FOND NECK TICK WALY
DAUNT INGLE NURSE WALLY
CARESS COCKER CODDLE COSSET
CUDDLE CUTTER DANDLE GENTLE
KIUTLE MUZZLE PAMPER SLAVER
STROKE TANTLE TIDDLE CHERISH
FLATTER SMUGGLE TWATTLE
BLANDISH CANOODLE
FONDLING NINNY NURSLING

FONDLY DEAR FOND DEARLY
FOOLISH
FONDNESS GRA LOVE FANCY FOLLY
TASTE DOTAGE NOTION FEELING
DEARNESS WEAKNESS
(— FOR WOMEN) PHILOGYNY
(SUFF.) (— FOR) ITIS
FONS (FATHER OF —) JANUS
(MOTHER OF —) JUTURNA
FONT BILL FUND PILA BASIN FOUNT
SOURCE SPRING LAVACRE PISCINA
BENITIER DELUBRUM
FONTANEL MOLD MOULD
FENESTRA
FOOD BIT KAI PAP SAP BAIT BITE
BUNK CARB CATE CHIH CHOP CHOW
CRAM DIET DISH EATS FARE FARM
FUEL GEAR GRUB HASH JOCK KAIL
KALE MEAT NOSH PECK PLAT PROG
SALT SOCK STEW TACK TOKE TUCK
BREAD BROMA CARBO CHEER
CHUCK FLUFF FORAY GRILL SCAFF
SCOFF SCRAN TABLE THING TOMMY
TREAT TRIPE APPAST BUTTER
DODGER DOINGS EATING FODDER
FOSTER LIVING MAIGRE MORSEL
MUKTUK PABLUM PANADA PANADE
REFETE STOVER SUNKET TACKLE
TUCKER VIANDS VIVERS WRAITH
ALIMENT FAUSTER HANDOUT
INGESTA KEEPING KITCHEN
NURTURE PABULUM PASTURE
PECKAGE PROVANT PULTURE
EATABLES FLUMMERY GRUBBERY
NUTRIENT PEMMICAN PROVIANT
TRENCHER VICTUALS PROVENDER
NOURISHMENT
(— AND DRINK) BOUGE CHEER
LOWANCE
(— AND LIQUOR) GEAR
(— AND LODGING) FOUND
EASEMENT
(— BANNED DURING PASSOVER)
HAMETZ CHAMETZ
(— EATEN AS RELISH) KITCHEN
(— EATEN BETWEEN MEALS)
BAGGING
(— FOR ANIMALS) FODDER FORAGE
(— FOR CATTLE) BROWSE TACKLE
(— FROM KELP) KOMBU
(— IN SLICES) LEACH
(— IN STOCK) LARDER
(— NOT RITUALLY CLEAN) TEREPHAH
(— OF DUCK EGGS) BALUT
(— OF RUMINANTS) CUD
(— OF THE GODS) AMRITA AMREETA
AMBROSIA
(— OF WHALE) KRILL
(— OF WORKMEN) TOMMY
(— ON TABLE AT ONE TIME) MESS
(— PRESERVATIVE) TINFOIL
(— TO BE CONSUMED ELSEWHERE)
TAKEOUT CARRYOUT

(ASIAN —) TEMPEH
(ASIATIC —) TEMPEH
(BABY —) PAP
(BEE —) CANDY
(BREAKFAST —) GRANOLA
(CHINESE —) DIMSUM
(COOKED —) CURY BAKEMEAT
(DAILY —) TUCKER
(EXTRA —) GASH
(FILLING —) STODGE
(FLAVORLESS —) HOGWASH
(GROUND —) DUST
(HAWAIIAN —) POI
(HEAVENLY —) MANNA
(INDIGESTIBLE —) STODGE
(JAPANESE —) TERIYAKI
(KIND OF —) JUNK FINGER
(LIQUID —) LAP SLOP SOUP GRUEL
LEBAN LEBEN SUPPING
(LUXURIOUS —) CATE CATES
JUNKET
(MADE OF SEVERAL —S) PANACHE
(MIRACULOUS —) MANNA
(RICH —) CHEER
(SEMILIQUID —) SWILL
(SLICED —) PIZZA
(SNACK —) MUNCHIES
(SOFT —) PAP
(STARCHY —) AMYLOID
(TAPIOCA-LIKE —) SALEP
(WATERY —) SLIPSLOP
(WRAPPED —) TAMALE
(PREF.) SITIO SITO TROPH(O)
(SUFF.) PHAGA PHAGE PHAGIA
PHAGOUS PHAGUS PHAGY TROPHIA
TROPHIC TROPHY
(WANT OF —) ATROPHIA
FOODLESS JEJUNE VICTLESS
FOODSTUFF TRADE CEREAL
COOKABLE
FOOFARAW ADO FUSS TODO FRILL
BOTHER
FOOL APE ASS BAM BOB COD CON
DAW DOR FON FOP FOX FUN GIG KID
MUG NIT NUP POT RIG SAP SOT TOY
BULL BUTT CAKE CHUB CLOT COLT
DINK DOLT DUPE FOND FUTZ GECK
GOER GOFF GOOP GOWK GYPE HARE
HAVE HOIT JAPE JEST JOKE JOSH
MOME MUCK NIZY POOP RACA RACH
SIMP TONY TOOT TWIT YOYO ZANY
ASINO BLIND BLUFF BUFFO CHUMP
CLOWN DALLY FUNGE GALAH GLAIK
GOOSE GREEN HORSE IDIOT KNAVE
MORON NINNY NIZEY NODDY PATCH
PATSY SAMMY SCREW SILLY SNIPE
SPOOF STICK STIFF STIRK TOMMY
TRICK BUFFLE COUSIN CUCKOO
CUDDEN DELUDE DIMWIT DISARD
DOTARD DOTTLE FOLEYE FOOTER
GAMMON JESTER MOTLEY MUCKER
MUSARD NIDGET NIMSHI NINCOM
NUPSON SAWNEY SHMUCK STRING

TAMPER WITTOL ASINEGO BECASSE
BUFFOON CHARLEY CHARLIE
COXCOMB DAGONET DECEIVE
DIZZARD FATHEAD FOOLISH FRIBBLE
GOMERAL GOMERIL HAVERAL
JACKASS LACKWIT MADLING
MISLEAD NATURAL OMADAWN
PINHEAD PLAYBOY SCHMUCK
STOOKIE TOMFOOL WANTWIT
WITLING ABDERITE BADINAGE
DRIVELER FONDLING HOODWINK
IMBECILE MONUMENT OMADHAUN
TOMNODDY BAMBOOZLE
NINCOMPOOP LIGHTWEIGHT
(— **AROUND**) FUTZ JIVE SKYLARK
LALLYGAG
(— **AWAY**) FRIBBLE
(**BORN** —) MOONCALF
(**LEARNED** —) MOROSOPH
(**NATURAL** —) INNOCENT
(PL.) FOOLERY
FOOLERY GAME FOLLY BARNEY
MOTLEY BAUBLERY
FOOLHARDY RASH BRASH
FOOLATUM
FOOLISH FAT SOT BETE DAFT DUMB
FOND FOOL GAGA GYPE IDLE MADE
NICE RASH SOFT VAIN VOID WEAK
ZANY BALMY BARMY BATTY BOGGY
BUGGY DILLY DIPPY DIZZY DOILT
EMPTY FONNE GAWKY GOOFY
GOOSY INANE INEPT JERKY LOONY
NODDY POTTY SAPPY SAWNY
SCREW SEELY SILLY YAPPY ABSURD
CUDDEN DOTISH DOTTLE FONDLY
GLAKED GOTHAM GOWKIT HARISH
INSANE MOMISH MOPISH SHANNY
SIMPLE SLIGHT SOFTLY SPOONY
STOLID STULTY STUPID TAWPIE
UNWISE VACANT ASININE DAMFOOL
DOLTISH ETOURDI FANGLED
FATUOUS FLIGHTY FOLLIAL FOPPISH
GLAIKIT GOOSISH GULLISH IDIOTIC
PEEVISH PUERILE SOTTISH TOMFOOL
UNWITTY WANTWIT WITLESS
ABDERIAN FOOTLING FOPPERLY
HEADLESS HEEDLESS HIGHLAND
IMBECILE SENSELESS
(PREF.) STULT(I)
FOOLISHLY IDLY FONDLY SIMPLE
SIMPLY
FOOLISHNESS JAZZ PUNK FOLLY
BARNEY BUNKUM FADDLE LEVITY
LUNACY RUBBLE VANITY FATUITY
PORANGI BUNCOMBE FONDNESS
INSANITY TOMMYROT ABSURDITY
SAPPINESS
FOOT FIT PAT PAW PEG PES BASE
COOT FUSS GOER HEEL HOOF PIED
SOLE TAIL BASIS PIECE BOTTOM
CLUTCH GAMMON PATTEN PODIUM
RHYTHM TOOTSY TRILBY WALKER
FOOTING GAMBONE MEASURE

METREME PEDICEL TOOTSIE
FOREFOOT
(— **OF ANIMAL**) PAD PAW HOOF
TROTTER
(— **OF APE**) HAND
(— **OF INSECT**) TARSUS
(— **OF WINE GLASS**) MULE
(**CHINESE** —) CHEK CHIH
(**DOUBLE** —) DIPODY
(**HALF** —) SEMIPED
(**HOLLOW OF** —) VOLA
(**LARGE AWKWARD** —) CAVE
(**METRIC** —) IAMB BASIS DIAMB
IONIC PAEAN CHOREE DACTYL
DIIAMB IAMBUS SYZYGY ANAPEST
BACCHIC PYRRHIC SPONDEE
TROCHEE ANAPAEST BACCHIUS
CHORIAMB DOCHMIUS EPITRITE
MOLOSSUS TRIBRACH TRIMACER
(**STEWED OX** —) COWHEEL
(**TUBE** —) SUCKER
(**WEB** —) FOURCHETTE
(PREF.) PED(I)(O) PEDATI PEDICULO
PEZO POD(O)
(SUFF.) PED(E) POD(A)(AL)(E)(IA)(IUM)
(OUS) PUS
FOOTAGE SETUP
FOOTBALL GRID HURLY ROUGE
FOOTER HURLING LEATHER PIGSKIN
KICKBALL
(— **FORMATION**) SHOTGUN
WISHBONE
(— **LINEMAN**) NOSEGUARD
(— **LINE SHIFTING**) STUNT
(— **PASS PATTERN**) FLY
(— **PATTERN**) FLY
(— **PLAY**) DRAW DELAY SWING
KEEPER AUDIBLE REVERSE ROLLOUT
SCRAMBLE
(— **PLAYER**) HUFF LANE RICE BROWN
DITKA ELWAY FOUTS SMITH STARR
YOUNG AIKMAN BLOUNT BUTKUS
CSONKA DEACON DUDLEY GRANGE
GREENE MARINO NAMATH NEVERS
PAYTON SAYERS SHARPE TAYLOR
THOMAS THORPE TITTLE UNITAS
DONOVAN DORSETT FLANKER
GIFFORD HORNUNG MONSTER
MONTANA RIGGINS SIMPSON
BRADSHAW SLOTBACK STAUBACH
JURGENSEN NOSEGUARD
TARKENTON HIRSCHSHELL
(— **RECEIVER**) WIDEOUT
(— **TEAM**) JETS RAMS BEARS BILLS
COLTS LIONS BROWNS CHIEFS
EAGLES GIANTS OILERS SAINTS
BENGALS BRONCOS COWBOYS
FALCONS PACKERS RAIDERS VIKINGS
CHARGERS DOLPHINS PATRIOTS
REDSKINS SEAHAWKS STEELERS
CARDINALS BUCCANEERS
FORTYNINERS
(**AUSTRALIAN** —) RULES

(KIND OF —) CAMP
(KIND OF — PASS) SPOT SCREEN
(RUSH ON — PLAYER) BLITZ
(SHORT PASS IN —) FLARE
FOOTBOARD CRAMPET CRAMPIT
FOOTBOY PAGE PEDES
FOOTBRIDGE PLANK LIGGER
FOOTLOG
FOOTED FITTIT PEDATE
(SUFF.) PEDE PODOUS
FOOTFALL PAD STEP TREAD
FOOTSTEP
FOOTGEAR PATTEN FOOTWEAR
FOOTHILL SLOPE
FOOTHOLD TIP HACK STEP FOOTING
TOEHOLD BEACHHEAD
FOOTING PAR FOOT TROD BASIS
EARTH TRACK HEADING PIECING
TOEHOLD FOOTHOLD
FOOTLESS APODAL
FOOTLIGHTS FOOTS FLOATS LIGHTS
FOOTLIKE PEDATE
FOOTMAN SKIP FLUNKY JEAMES
LACKEY VARLET DOORMAN
FOOTPAD BOTTOMER CHASSEUR
HIRCARRA WAGONMAN
FOOTNOTE IBID IBIDEM
FOOTPACE MAT DAIS CARPET
HALFPACE PREDELLA
FOOTPAD PAD WHYO PADDER
ROBBER FOOTMAN PADFOOT
SCOURER LANDRAKER
FOOTPATH LANE TROD JETTY SENDA
TRAIL FOOTWAY HIGHWAY PARAPET
RAMPIRE SIDEWALK TROTTOIR
(— TO A PASTURE) DRUNG
(RAISED —) CLAPPER
FOOTPICK CASCROM
FOOTPIECE STEP
FOOTPRINT PAD PUG STEP TROD
PRICK SPOOR TRACE TRACK TRADE
TREAD FOOTING ICHNITE PUGMARK
VESTIGE FOOTMARK
(DEER'S —S) SLOT
(HARE'S —) PRICK
(OTTER'S —) SEAL
(PREF.) ICHN(O)
FOOTREST COASTER HASSOCK
STIRRUP
(— OF SPADE) TRAMP
FOOTROPE HORSE
FOOTROT HALT
FOOTS SEDIMENT
FOOTSCRAPING SAND
FOOT-SOLDIER KERN PEON KERNE
(PL.) INFANTRY
FOOTSORENESS SURBATE
FOOTSTALK STRIG PODIUM PEDICEL
PETIOLE PEDUNCLE
(PREF.) PEDICULO
FOOTSTEP PAD STEP TROD CLAMP
VESTIGE FOOTBEAT FORESTEP
(PREF.) ICHN(O)

FOOTSTOOL TUT LOVE MORA
STOOL BUFFET SAMBLE CRICKET
HASSOCK OTTOMAN FOOTREST
FOOT-WASHING NIPTER
FOOTWAY PATH CATWALK
FOOTPATH
(— ALONGSIDE BRIDGE) BANQUETTE
FOOTWEAR CLOG FEET
FOOTYBALL (— PLAYER) SCATBACK
FOP TO ADON BEAU BUCK DUDE
DUPE FOOL KNUT PRIG TOFF DANDY
FLASH PUPPY MASHER MOPPET
VANITY COXCOMB JESSAMY
GIMCRACK MACARONI MACAROON
MUSCADIN POPINJAY SKIPJACK
FOPPISH APISH DANDY FOPPY
SAPPY SILLY DAPPER PRETTY
SPRUCE STUPID BEAUISH BUCKISH
FANGLED FINICAL FOOLISH
DANDYISH SKIPJACK
FOR P IN TO PRO TIL VER TILL SINCE
FORWHY BECAUSE FORNENT
FAVORING
(— A LONG TIME) YORE
(— CASH) SPOT
(— EXAMPLE) EG VG
(— FEAR THAT) LEST
(— INSTANCE) AS SAY
(— THE EMERGENCY) PRN
(— THE MOST PART) FECKLY
GENERALLY
(— TIME BEING) ACTUALLY
(PREF.) PRO
FORAGE ERS OAT RYE CORN GUAR
MAST PROG RAID ETAPE FORAY
BREVIT RUSSUD ZACATE GOITCHO
HAYLAGE PICKEER BOOTHALE
SCROUNGE
(— PLANT) ERS
FORAGE-CAP KEPI
FORAGER OUTRIDER
FORAMEN PORE EXOSTOME
METAPORE TROCHLEA
FORAMINIFER NUMMULITE
FORAY RAID MELEE CREAGH
FURROW INROAD MARAUD RAVAGE
RAZZIA SORTIE CHAPPOW HERSHIP
PILLAGE SPREAGH SPREATH
FORBEAR LET BEAR HELP HOLD
SHUN SIRE AVOID FORGO SPARE
WAIVE DEPORT DESIST ENDURE
PARENT RETAIN ABSTAIN DECLINE
REFRAIN RESPITE ANCESTOR
FOREBEAR WITHDRAW
(— PROSECUTION) COMPOUND
(— TO SPEAK) OVERGO
FORBEARANCE MERCY LENITY
NONACT PARDON QUARTER
MILDNESS PATIENCE
FORBEARING CLEMENT LENIENT
PATIENT MERCIFUL TOLERANT
FORBID BAN BAR NIX DEFY DENY
FEND TABU VETO WARN DEBAR

TABOO DANISH DEFEND ENJOIN
IMPEDE OPPOSE REFUSE SHIELD
FORFEND FORWARN GAINSAY
INHIBIT WITHSAY DISALLOW
FORSPEAK PRECLUDE PROHIBIT
PROSCRIBE
(— ENTRANCE) SHUT
FORBIDDANCE BAN VETO FORBODE
FORBIDDEN TABU TABOO BANNED
DENIED VERBOTEN
(— AS FOOD) TREF TREFA
(SOMETHING —) NONO
FORBIDDING DOUR GRIM HARD
BLACK GAUNT STERN FIERCE
GLASSY GLOOMY GRISLY ODIOUS
STRICT FORBODE GRIZZLY
REPULSIVE
(— CLOSED MEETINGS) SUNSHINE
FORCE GAR GAS GUT HAP JAM LID
VIM VIS ZIP BANG BEAR BEAT BEND
BIRR BODY CLIP CRAM DINT DOOM
DRAG EDGE FECK FOSS GRIP GUTS
HEAD JAMB JINX MAIN MAKE MANA
SNAP SOCK ABATE AGENT ARDOR
BRAWL BRING BRUSH CLAMP COACT
CRAFT CROWD CRUSH DEMON
DRAFT DRIVE EXACT EXERT FOHAT
GAVEL IMPEL KARMA MIGHT PAINT
PEISE POACH POINT POWER PRESS
PRIZE PUNCH REPEL SHEAR SHOVE
SINEW STEAM STUFF THROW
WAKAN WREST CHARGE COERCE
COMPEL CUDGEL DURESS EFFECT
EFFORT ENERGY EXTORT HIJACK
HOTBED IMPACT IMPOSE JOSTLE
MUSCLE OBLIGE POWDER RAVISH
SHAKTI STRAIN STRESS WRENCH
ABILITY AFFORCE BLUSTER
CASCADE COGENCE COGENCY
CONCUSS DRAUGHT DYNAMIC
IMPETUS IMPRESS IMPULSE
LASHKAR OPPRESS REQUIRE
SQUEEZE TORMENT VIOLATE
WAKANDA ACTIVITY ADHESION
AFFINITY BULLDOZE COACTION
COERCION DYNAMISM EFFICACY
HOTHOUSE MOMENTUM PRESSURE
STRENGTH VALIDITY VIOLENCE
VIRILITY NECESSITATE
(— AIR UPON) BLOW
(— AN ENTRANCE) RANDOM THRUST
(— APART) SUNDER DISPART
(— BACK) REPEL RAMBARRE
(— BY THREAT) SWAGGER
(— DOWN) CLEW CLUE DETRUDE
DISMOUNT
(— IN) INJECT INTRUDE
(— OPEN) BURST JIMMY SPORT
RANFORCE
(— OUT) SPEW EJECT ERUPT EVICT
EXPEL KNOCK WRING EXTUND
EXPRESS
(— PASSAGE) SQUEEZE

(— TO MOVE) STICTION
(— WAY) CROWD WREST WRING
(— WITH LEGAL AUTHORITY) POSSE
(AIR —) LUFTWAFFE
(ALLEGED —) OD
(ARMED —) CREW HEAD POWER
CONREY ARMAMENT BATTALIA
(CONCENTRATED —) PITH
(CONFINING —) LID
(CONSTRAINING —) STRESS
(COSMIC —) EVIL
(CREATIVE —) NATURE
(DRIVING —) STEAM SWINGE
(EVOLUTIONARY —) BATHMISM
(EXPLOSIVE —) MEGATON
(HYPOTHETICAL —) FORTUNE
(KIND OF —) LORENTZ
(LACK OF — TO DEFEAT) UNDERKILL
(LIFE —) SHAKTI
(MAIN —) BRUNT
(MILITANT —) SWORD
(MILITARY —) FYRD LEGION WERING
BAYONET OCCUPATION
ESTABLISHMENT
(MOVING —) SOLICITATION
(NAVAL —) FLEET
(PHYSICAL —) NERVE
(PREPONDERATING —) SWAY
(PROTECTIVE —) CONVOY
(RELIGIOUS —) SANCTITY
(SACRED —) KAMI
(SPIRITUAL —) SQUI
(UNRESTRAINED —) FURY
(UPWARD —) BUOYANCY
(PL.) ARMY WILL COLORS
(SUFF.) (UNIT OF —) DYNE
FORCED LABORED ENFORCED
FALSETTO SARDONIC SPURIOUS
STRAINED SFORZANDO
FORCEFUL RUDE GREAT GUTSY
PITHY STIFF STOUT MIGHTY PUNCHY
STRONG VIRILE DYNAMIC STHENIC
VIOLENT BRUISING ELOQUENT
EMPHATIC ENFATICO FORCIBLE
VIGOROUS TRENCHANT
FORCEFULNESS PUNCH
EMPHASIS
FORCEMEAT FARCE BOUDIN
GODIVEAU QUENELLE STUFFING
FORCEPS DOG FURCA TONGS
TENAIL BULLDOG CLAMMER
PINCERS PINSONS RONGEUR
CROWBILL DENTAGRA PINCETTE
VULSELLA TENACULUM
(PREF.) FORCI LABID(O)
FORCIBLE VIVE STOUT VALID
COGENT MIGHTY POTENT STRONG
FORCIVE NERVOUS VIOLENT
WEIGHTY EMPHATIC FORCEFUL
POWERFUL PREGNANT PUISSANT
VEHEMENT VIGOROUS
FORCIBLY AMAIN SADLY HARDLY
MAINLY HEAVILY STRONGLY

FORD PASS RACK RIFT WADE WATH DRIFT STREAM CURRENT FORDING PASSAGE PASSING CROSSING (PAVED —) STEAN STEENING

FORE VAN WAY AFORE AHEAD FRONT PRIOR FORMER FURTHER

FOREARM CUBIT CUBITAL CUBITUS

FOREBEAR ANCESTOR

FOREBODE BODE GIVE OMEN ABODE AUGUR CROAK BETIDE DIVINE BETOKEN MISBODE OMINATE PORTEND PREDICT PRESAGE FORETELL
(— EVIL) CROAK

FOREBODING OMEN BLACK FATAL AUGURY BODING DISMAL GLOOMY ANXIETY BALEFUL BANEFUL DRUTHER OMINOUS PRESAGE BODEMENT SINISTER ABODEMENT PROGNOSTICATION

FOREBODINGLY DIRELY

FOREBRAIN CEREBRUM PROENCEPHALON

FORECAST BODE CAST SCHEME CAUTION FORESEE FORESET PREDICT FOREDEEM FOREDOOM FORETELL PROPHESY ADUMBRATE PREVISION PROGNOSIS PREDICTION PROGNOSTICATION

FORECASTER SEER ORACLE PROPHET

FORECASTLE FOCSLE ISLAND

FORECOURT VESTIBULE

FOREDOOM JINX DESTINY

FOREFACE CUSHION

FOREFATHER AYEL SIRE ELDER PITRI PARENT ANCESTOR FOREBEAR PROGENITOR PRIMOGENITOR

FOREFINGER INDEX

FOREFOOT PAW PUD GRIPE

FOREFOOTING MANGANA

FOREFRONT VAN FRONT VAWARD

FOREGO FORGO WAIVE ESCHEW ABSTAIN NEGLECT PRECEDE REFRAIN ABNEGATE DISPENSE RENOUNCE

FOREGOING PAST ABOVE ANTERIOR PREVIOUS PRECEDING

FOREGROUND PROSCENIUM

FOREHEAD BROW FRONS FRONT FRONTLET SINCIPUT
(— INDENTATION) STOP
(— MARK) KUMKUM
(HIGH —) LEPTENE
(PREF.) FRONTI FRONTO METOPO

FOREHEARTH SETTLER

FOREIGN UNCO ALIEN FREMD WELSH ALANGE EXILED EXOTIC FRENCH REMOTE UNKIND DISTANT ECDEMIC EPIGENE EXCLUDE FRAMMIT HEATHEN OUTBORN OUTLAND OUTWARD STRANGE BARBARIC EPIGENIC EXTERIOR EXTERNAL FORINSEC OVERSEAS PEREGRIN STRANGER BARBAROUS OUTLANDISH TRAMONTANE
(— TO) DEHORS
(ONE ATTRACTED TO — THINGS) XENOPHILE
(PREF.) ALIENI EXOTO

FOREIGNER ALIEN HAOLE ALLTUD GRINGO PAKEHA GREENER OUTBORN OUTLAND PARDESI ETRANGER OUTSIDER PEREGRIN PORTUGEE STRANGER MLECHCHHA OUTLANDER
(— IN JAPAN) GAIJIN
(— LIVING IN CHINA) TAIPAN
(PREF.) XEN(O)
(SUFF.) XENE XENOUS XENY

FOREIGN-LOOKING EXOTIC

FOREKNOW DIVINE FORESEE FOREWIT

FOREKNOWLEDGE PRESAGE

FORELEG GAMB

FORELOCK TOP BANG QUIFF COTTER TOUPET FORETOP TOPPING FOREBUSH

FOREMAN BOSS BULL CORK JOSS LUNA PUSH CHIEF DOGGY BUNTER GAFFER GANGER LEADER RAMROD SIRDAR TENTER CAPATAZ CAPORAL CAPTAIN FOUNDER HEADMAN MANAGER MANDOER OVERMAN SHOOFLY SKIDDER STEWARD FOREHAND GANGSMAN OVERSEER
(— OF JURY) CHANCELLOR

FOREMOST TOP HEAD HIGH MAIN CHIEF FIRST FORME FRONT GRAND BANNER FORMER LEADING RANKING SUPREME VANMOST CHAMPION
(— PART) VAWARD

FOREORDAIN FATE SLATE DESTINE FORESAY PREDOOM FORECAST

FOREORDINATION FATE

FOREPART FRONT FOREHEAD
(— OF FACE) CHAP
(— OF HEAD) SINCIPUT
(— OF HORSE'S HEAD) CHANFRIN
(— OF SHIP) STEM FORWARD CUTWATER ENTRANCE

FOREPOLE LATH SPILE SPILING

FORERUN HERALD OUTRUN PRECEDE PRELUDE ANNOUNCE FORESHOT

FORERUNNER OMEN SIGN USHER AUGURY HERALD ANCESTOR FOREGOER FOURRIER OUTRIDER PRODROME MESSENGER PRECURSOR

FORERUNNING PRECURSE

FORESADDLE RACK

FORESEE SEE READ DIVINE PURVEY PREVISE PROVIDE ENVISAGE ENVISION FORECAST FOREKNOW PROSPECT PREFIGURE

FORESHADOW HINT FIGURE
HERALD BESPEAK FORERUN
PATTERN PRELUDE PRESAGE
UMBRATE FORETYPE ADUMBRATE
FORESHORE HARD SHORE
HARDWAY SEASHORE
FORESHOW BODE ABODE AUGUR
BETOKEN PORTEND SIGNIFY
FORETELL PROPHESY
FORESIGHT FEAR VISION FOREWIT
PRESAGE FORECAST FORELOOK
PROSPECT PRUDENCE
(LACKING —) MYOPIC
FORESIGHTED CAGY CAGEY
CANNY
FOREST BUSH GAPO MATA RUKH
WOLD WOOD FIRTH GLADE GUBAT
MATTA MATTO MONTE SYLVA TAIGA
WASTE WEALD JUNGLE TIMBER
BOSCAGE CALYDON COPPICE
CAATINGA WOODLAND
(— CITY) PORTLAND SAVANNAH
CLEVELAND
(— FOR DEER) FIRTH
(DENSE —) JUNGLE
(IMMENSE —) MONTANA
(RAIN —) SELVA
(RIVERSIDE —) GAPO
(SHAKESPEAREAN —) ARDEN
(SIBERIAN —) URMAN
(STUNTED —) CAATINGA
KRUMMHOLZ
(PREF.) HYL(O) SILVI SYLVI
FORESTAGE APRON
FORESTALL BEAT HELP AVERT
DETER LURCH STALL DEVANCE
FORERUN OBVIATE PREVENE
PREVENT FORSTEAL STAVEOFF
ANTICIPATE
FORESTALLER KIDDER GROSSER
FORESTAYSAIL JUMBO
FORESTER FOSTER WALKER
MONTERO TINEMAN TREEMAN
WOODMAN WOODSMAN
FORETASTE GUST HANSEL TEASER
EARNEST HANDSEL ANTEPAST
PROSPECT PRELIBATION
FORETELL BODE ERST READ SPAE
AUGUR INSEE WEIRD WRITE DIVINE
HALSEN HERALD BESPEAK FORESAY
PORTEND PREDICT PRESAGE
ANNOUNCE FOREBODE FORECAST
FORESHOW PROPHESY SOOTHSAY
FORETELLING PROPHECY
FORETHOUGHT CAUTION
FORECAST PREPENSE PRUDENCE
FORETOKEN OMEN AUGUR
PORTEND PROMISE FORECAST
FORESHOW FORESIGN
FOREVER AY AKE AYE EVER ETERN
ALWAYS ETERNE ENDLESS ETERNITY
EVERMORE
FOREWARN WEIRD PREMONISH

FOREWARNING HINT PORTENT
PREMONITION
FOREWING PRIMARY
FOREWORD PROEM PREFACE
PREAMBLE
FORFEIT WED FINE LOSE TINE WITE
CHEAT CRIME DEDIT FORGO LAPSE
FOREGO SCONCE DEFAULT ESCHEAT
FORWORK PENALTY FORFAULT
FORFEITURE FINE BLIND MULCT
TINSEL ESCHEAT FORFEIT PENALTY
FORGE FOGE MINT TILI WELL CLICK
FALSE FEIGN SMITH STOVE HAMMER
SMITHY STEADY STITCH STITHY
SWINGE CHAFERY FALSIFY FASHION
BLOOMERY
FORGED BOGUS SPURIOUS
FORGER SMITH FALSER FALSARY
LEVERMAN
FORGERY SHAM FALSUM FICTION
BLOOMERY
FORGET LOSE OMIT WANT FLUFF
BILEVE UNKNOW UNMIND NEGLECT
OVERLOOK
FORGETFUL FLAKY SPACY
OBLIVIOUS
FORGETFULNESS SWIM FLUFF
LETHE AMNESIA AMNESTY OBLIVION
(PREF.) LETHO
FORGET-ME-NOT MYOSOTE
FORGETTING
(PREF.) LETHO
FORGING HOOP CLICK JACKET
FORGIVE REMIT SPARE ASSOIL
EXCUSE PARDON ABSOLVE
CONDONE OVERLOOK
FORGIVENESS GRACE PARDON
FORGIFT
FORGIVING GRACE HUMANE
CLEMENT MERCIFUL
MAGNANIMOUS
FORGOTTEN DERELICT UNMINDED
FORINT FLORIN
FORK CROC EVIL HOOK TANG TINE
CLEFT CLOFF FURCA GLACK GRAIN
GRAIP PRONG TWIST BISECT
BRANCH CLITCH CROTCH DIVIDE
FEEDER GAFFLE HACKER OFFSET
TWISEL BIPRONG FOURCHE
FRUGGIN HAYFORK TOASTER
CROTCHET EQUULEUS GRAINING
PITCHFORK
(— OF BODY) SHARE
(— OF PENNON) FANON
(— OF WINDPIPE) BRONCHUS
(— OVER) PAYOUT
(FISHING —) SPEAR
(MEAT —) TORMENTOR
(THATCHER'S —) GROM
(TUNING —) DIAPASON
(PREF.) FURCI
FORKED BIFID FORKY FURCAL
PRONGY DIVIDED FURCATE LITUATE

BIFORKED BIRAMOUS BRANCHED
FOURCHEE SUBBIFID

FORKING STAR

FORLORN LORN LOST REFT ALONE
ABJECT FORFAIRN FORSAKEN
HELPLESS HOPELESS PITIABLE
WITLOSEN

FORM AME DIG FIG HEW HUE SET
BLEE BODY CASE CAST CAUL DOME
FLOW GARB IDEA KERN KITE MAKE
MODE MOLD PLAN RITE SEAT THEW
TURN BENCH BLANK BLOCK BOARD
BUILD BUNCH CHART CHECK CRUSH
DUMMY EIDOS ERECT FORGE FORMA
FORME FRAME GALBE GUISE IMAGE
MATCH MEUSE MODEL SHAPE SPELL
STAMP THROW USAGE ADJUST
CHALAN COUPON CREATE CUSTOM
DEVISE DOCKET FIGURE FILLER
HANGER INVENT MANNER REMOVE
RITUAL SCHEMA SCHOOL SPONGE
STRIKE SYSTEM TAILLE AGENDUM
ARRANGE COMPOSE CONFECT
CONTOUR DEVELOP FASHION
FEATURE FORMULA GESTALT
IMPANEL INVOICE LITURGY
MAKEDOM OUTLINE PATTERN
PORTRAY PORTURE PRODUCE
PROFILE SPECIES STATURE BILLHEAD
CEREMONY COMPOUND CONCEIVE
CONTRIVE FORMWORK INSTRUCT
LIKENESS MODALITY ORGANIZE
SEMBLANCE
(— A HEAD) POME
(— A NETWORK) PLEX
(— A RING) ENVIRON
(— ASSUMED AFTER DEATH)
KAMARUPA
(— BRANCHES) BREAK
(— BY CUTTING OFF) ABJOINT
(— CONNECTION) ALLY
(— FOR BELL FOUNDING) SWEEP
(— FOR CONCRETE) BOXING
(— FOR HOLDING BARREL) SQUAW
(— FOR MOLD) JACKET
(— FOR PRESSING VENEERS) CAUL
(— FRUIT) KNIT
(— INTO A CHAIN) CATENATE
(— INTO BALL) CONGLOBE
(— INTO RINGLETS) CRISP
(— LEATHER) CRIMP
(— MOUND) TUMP
(— OF GOVERNMENT) ESTATE
KINGSHIP
(— OF PREDICATION) CATEGORY
(— POLITICAL SUCCESSION) CAVE
(— WITH PLASTER) RUN
(— YARN INTO THREAD) CABLE
(ANCESTRAL —) BLASTAEA
STEMFORM
(CEREMONIAL —) RITE
(CONVENTIONAL —) AMENITY
(DEXTROROTATORY —) CAMPHOR

(DISPLAY —) MANNEQUIN
(IMPERFECT —) SEMIFORM
(IRREGULAR —) PSEUDOMORPH
(ISOMETRIC —) DIPLOID
(LINGUISTIC —) FOSSIL GERUND
(LITERARY —) KNACK
(LITURGICAL —) SERVICE
(LYRICAL —) SESTINA
(MUSICAL —) RAGA SUITE
(POETIC —) CINQUAIN
(POINTED —) ANGLE
(SCHOOL —) SHELL
(SHOE —) LAST FILLER
(SHORTENED —) ABBREVIATION
(SONG —) BAR
(SPECTRAL —) SHADOW
(SPEECH —) LEXEME IDIOLECT
(SPIRAL OR CIRCULAR —) GYRE
(STRUCTURE —) MORPHOLOGY
(TOP —) GROOVE
(VERB —) FUTURE CONATIVE
DEFINITE DURATIVE
(VERSE —) EPODE BALLAD PANTUM
SONNET KYRIELLE LIMERICK
(VISIBLE —) RUPA
(WILD —) AGRIOTYPE
(WORD —) ETYMON ANOMALY
(PREF.) IDO MORPH(O) PLASMATO
(SUFF.) FY GEN(E)(ESIA)(ESIS)(ETIC)
(IC)(IN)(OUS)(Y) IFY MORPH(A)(AE)(IC)
(ISM)(OSIS)(OTIC)(OUS)(Y) PLASIA
PLASIS PLASM(A)(IA)(IC) PLAST(IC)(Y)
PLASY
(HAVING — OF) IC(AL)
(IN THE — OF) OID(AL)

FORMAL DRY SET BOOK PRIM
BUDGE CHILL COURT EXACT STIFF
SOCIAL SOLEMN STOCKY ANGULAR
BOOKISH LOGICAL NOMINAL
ORDERLY OUTWARD PRECISE
REGULAR SOLWARD STARCHY
STATELY STILTED ABSTRACT
ACADEMIC AFFECTED ELEVATED
FORMULAR OFFICIAL PUNCTUAL
STARCHED WHITETIE

FORMALDEHYDE FORMAL
MONOSE HARDENER METHANAL

FORMALISM ACADEMISM

FORMALIST PEDANT SCHOLASTIC

FORMALISTIC COURT ACADEMIC

FORMALITY FORM POMP SASINE
STARCH BUCKRAM DECENCY
WIGGERY CEREMONY PHARISAISM

FORMALIZE STIFFEN

FORMALLY FORMLY STARCHLY

FORMAT SIZE GETUP SHAPE STYLE

FORMATION FORM RANK SPUR
BIOME FLIGHT GROWTH HARROW
MASSIF SPREAD POTENCE BOTRYOID
(— ENCLOSING MINE WORKING)
GROUND
(— ENCOUNTERED IN DRILLING)
STRAY

(— OF BRAIN) FORNIX
(— OF BRANCHES) CANOPY
(— OF CRYSTAL) SHOOT
(— OF JOINT) ANKYLOSIS
(— OF PLANES) JAVELIN
(— OF SCAR) ULOSIS
(— OF WILDFOWL) WEDGE
(— ON TOAD) SPADE
(— RESEMBLING ICICLE) STIRIA
(BATTLE —) HERSE
(BRAIN —) FORNIX
(CLOUD —) NUBECULA
(DANCE —) SET
(DIAGONAL —) HARROW
(DRIPSTONE —) COLUMN
(ECOLOGICAL —) BIOME
(FLIGHT —) SQUADRON
(FOOTBALL —) SHOTGUN
WISHBONE
(GEOLOGIC —) BOEL CULM CHICO
STRAY MARKER MEDINA CURTAIN
MANLIUS MATAWAN POTOMAC
TERRAIN AQUIFUGE FERNANDO
KOOTANIE KOOTENAI LOCKPORT
TOPATOPA YORKTOWN
(GLAUIAL —) ARETE
(HABIT —) FIXATION
(INDENTED —) CLEFT
(INFANTRY —) TERTIA ECHELON
(LAND —) BOOTHEEL
(MILITARY —) SNAIL FLIGHT
(MORBID —) GROWTH
(NAVAL —) SCREEN
(POINTED —) BEAK
(THICKET —) MAQUIS
(PREF.) PLASTO
(TAIL —) CERC(O)
(SUFF.) GENESIA GENESIS OSIS
POEIA POESIS POIEIS POIETIC
FORMATIVE CREANT PLASTIC
DEMIURGIC
(SUFF.) POEIA POESIS POIEIS
POIETIC
FORMED BUILT BOOKIT DECIDED
MATURED SETTLED WROUGHT
TIMBERED
(— AT BASE OF MOUNTAIN)
PIEDMONT
(— INTO STEPS) GRADY
(— ON SURFACE OF EARTH)
EPIGENE
(IMPERFECTLY —) ABORTIVE
(STURDILY —) BUXOM
(PREF.) APO PLASTO
FORMEE PATE PATTEE
FORMER DIE OLD ERER ERST FERN
FORE LATE ONCE PAST ELDER
FORME GAUGE GUIDE MAKER OTHER
PRIOR BYGONE RATHER WHILOM
ANCIENT ANOTHER CREATOR
EARLIER FIRSTER FURTHER ONETIME
PRIDIAN QUONDAM TEMPLET
UMWHILE PRETERIT PREVIOUS

PRISTINE SOMETIME STRICKLE
UMQUHILE PRECEDING
(PREF.) PROTER(O)
FORMERLY ERE NEE OLD ERST FORE
ONCE THEN YORE GRAVE WHILOM
WHILST ONETIME QUONDAM
SOMETIME UMQUHILE
FORMIDABLE MEAN STOUR
FEARFUL ALARMING DREADFUL
MENACING TERRIBLE FEROCIOUS
REDOUBTABLE
(— PERSON) TARTAR
FORMING
(SUFF.) GENIC GEROUS
FORMLESS ARUPA DOUGHY
ANIDIAN CHAOTIC DEFORMED
INDIGEST
FORMOSA (SEE TAIWAN)
FORMULA LAW MIX DATE FIAT
FORM RULE CANON CREED DHIKR
GRAPH INDEX LURRY KEKULE
MANTRA METHOD RECIPE THEORY
RECEIPT APOLYSIS CLAUSULE
DOXOLOGY EXORCISM
(— OF FAITH) KELIMA
(MAGICAL —) CARACT
(OFFICIAL —) PROTOCOL
(WORD —) PATERNOSTER
(PL.) RAKA RAKAH
FORMULARY SYMBOL
FORMULATE PUT CAST DRAW
FRAME DEVISE CAPSULE COMPOSE
FORMULE PLATFORM
FORMULATED STATED WRITTEN
FORMULATION (— OF A TRUTH)
COUNT CREED DOGMA APHORISM
APOTHEGM DOCTRINE
(SUFF.) (SYSTEMATIC —) ICS
FORMWORK SHUTTERING
FORNIX VAULT PSALIS
FORSAKE DENY DROP FLEE QUIT
SHUN ABAND AVOID FORGO LEAVE
WAIVE DEFECT DEPART DESERT
FORGO FORHOO FORLET REFUSE
REJECT ABANDON DISCARD
FORLESE DESOLATE FORHOOIE
RENOUNCE WITHDRAW
FORSAKEN LORN FORLORN
DESERTED DESOLATE LASSLORN
FORSETE (FATHER OF —) BALDER
FORSOOTH EVEN MARRY QUOTH
FORSWEAR DENY ABJURE REJECT
ABANDON PERJURE ABNEGATE
MANSWEAR RENOUNCE
FORSYTE SAGA (AUTHOR OF —)
GALSWORTHY
(CHARACTER IN —) JON VAL JUNE
MONT FLEUR HOLLY IRENE JULIA
MONTY DARTIE JOLYON PHILIP
SOAMES ANNETTE FORSYTE
LAMOTTE MICHAEL PROFOND
PROSPER SWITHIN TIMOTHY
BOSINNEY WINIFRED

FORT PA DUN LIS PAH LISS PEEL SHEE
SPUR WORK COTTA REDAN SIDHE
CASTLE SANGAR SCHERM SCONCE
STRONG BASTION BULWARK
CITADEL CLOSURE REDOUBT
BASTILLE CASTILLO FASTHOLD
FASTNESS FORTRESS MARTELLO
PRESIDIO
(FAIRY —) LIS LIOS LISS SHEE SIDHE
(HILL —) RATH
(MAORI —) PA PAH
(RUINS OF —) ZIMBABWE
(SMALL —) GURRY FORTIN BASTIDE
FORTLET FORCELET
FORTE FORT LOUD STARK METIER
STRONG EMINENCY STRENGTH
FORTESCUE COBBLER SCORPION
FORTH OUT AWAY FURTH
(PREF.) E OUT
FORTHCOMING PROXIMATE
FORTHRIGHT BALD BURLY GUTTY
CANDID
FORTHRIGHTLY FRANKLY
FORTHRIGHTNESS CANDOR
PLUMPNESS
FORTHWITH EFT NOW ANON AWAY
BEDENE DIRECT BETIMES FORTHON
DIRECTLY
FORTIFICATION BAWN BOMA FORT
MOAT WALL REDAN TOWER ABATIS
CASHEL CASTLE GLACIS LAAGER
BASTION BULWARK CITADEL
DEFENCE DEFENSE PARAPET
PILLBOX RAMPART RAVELIN
REDOUBT FORTRESS MUNITION
RONDELLE STRENGTH
(LINE OF —S) TROCHA
(PART OF —) BERM MOAT ANGLE
DITCH FLANK GORGE SCARP SLOPE
COVERT ESCARP GLACIS PARADE
BASTION CURTAIN PARAPET
RAMPART SALIENT TENAILLE
BANQUETTE TERREPLEIN
COUNTERSCARP
FORTIFIED ARMED CONFIRMED
FORTIFY ARM MAN BANK FORT LINE
WALL WARD FENCE SPIKE STANK
BATTLE IMMURE MUNIFY MUNITE
BULWARK COMFORT DEFENSE
GARNISH RAMPIRE BASTILLE
EMBATTLE FORTRESS RAMFORCE
STOCKADE
FORTITUDE GRIT GUTS SAND FIBER
FIBRE HEART NERVE PLUCK METTLE
BRAVERY COURAGE HEROISM
STAMINA BACKBONE PATIENCE
STRENGTH
(AUTHOR OF —) WALPOLE
(CHARACTER IN —) TAN HANZ NORA
BOBBY BRANT CLARE JERRY PETER
ZANTI EMILIO LAUNCE GALLEON
JERRARD MONOGUE STEPHEN
ZACHARY BROCKETT ROSSITER

WESTCOTT CARDILLAC GOTTFRIED
AITCHINSON
FORTNIGHT (HALF A —) WEEK
FORTNIGHTLY BIWEEKLY
FORTRESS (ALSO SEE FORT) BURG
KEEP KASBA PIECE PLACE ROCCA
CASBAH CASTLE ALCAZAR BARRIER
BOROUGH CASTRUM CHATEAU
CITADEL KREMLIN ZWINGER
ALCAZAVA BASTILLE FASTNESS
STRENGTH
(AUTHOR OF —) WALPOLE
(CHARACTER IN —) ADAM JOHN
KRAFT PARIS ROGUE BENJIE CAESAR
JUDITH REUBEN TEMPLE UHLAND
WALTER HERRIES SUNWOOD
JENNIFER MARGARET ELIZABETH
GOLIGHTLY CHRISTABEL
(NORTH AFRICAN —) KABBAH
FORTUITOUS CASUAL CHANCE
RANDOM FORTUIT FORTUNEL
FORTUITY LUCK CHANCE
FORTUNATE EDI FAT HAP SRI GOOD
SHRI WELL CANNY FAUST HAPPY
LUCKY RIGHT WHITE DEXTER
EUROUS BLESSED FAVORED
WEIRDLY GRACIOUS
FORTUNATELY FAIR HAPPILY
FORTUNE DIE HAP LOT URE BAHI
DOOM FALL FARE FATE HAIL LUCK
PILE SEEL STAR EVENT GRACE ISSUE
LINES SONSE SPEED WEIRD WHATE
CHANCE ESTATE MISHAP RICHES
WEALTH DESTINY SUCCESS
THEEDOM VENTURE ACCIDENT
CASUALTY FELICITY STOCKING
(GOOD —) SELE SONSE SPEED
THRIFT FURTHER GOODHAP
BONCHIEF FELICITY
(ILL —) DOOM THRAW
(PREF.) TYCH(O)
**FORTUNES OF RICHARD
MAHONY** (AUTHOR OF —)
RICHARDSON
(CHARACTER IN —) TOM JOHN LUCY
MARY ZARA CUFFY OCOCK POLLY
SARAH LALLIE MAHONY RICHARD
TURNHAM CUTHBERT
FORTUNE-TELLER SEER SIBYL
SYBIL SPAEMAN SORTIARY
SPAEWIFE
(PL.) CHALDAEI
FORTY DAYS OF MUSA DAGH
(AUTHOR OF —) WERFEL
(CHARACTER IN —) TER HAIK MARIS
SARKIS BEREKET GABRIEL STEPHAN
GONZAGUE HAIGASUN HULIETTE
KILIKIAN BAGRADIAN NOKHUDIAN
FORUM COURT PLATFORM TRIBUNAL
FORWARD ON TO AID BOG BUG GAY
ABET BAIN BOLD FORE FREE HELP
PERT SEND SHIP STEP AHEAD
ALONG AVANT BARDY BRASH CAGER

EAGER FAVOR FORTH TRACK FRECK
FRONT HASTY PAWKY PUSHY RANDY
READY RELAY REMIT SAUCY SERVE
SPACK ULTRA AFFORD ARDENT
AVAUNT BEFORE BRIGHT COMING
DEVANT FORRIT FORTHY HASTEN
NUZZLE ONWARD PROMPT REMAIL
ROUDAS SECOND TOWARD
ADVANCE BETIMES EARNEST
EXTREME FURTHER PROMOTE
PUSHING RADICAL SOLICIT
ADPLANTE ARROGANT FROMWARD
IMMODEST IMPUDENT MALAPERT
ONCOMING PERVERSE PETULANT
TELLSOME TOWARDLY TRANSMIT
OBTRUSIVE
(MOST —) HEADMOST
(PREF.) ANTE
(LEANING —) PRONO

FORWARDNESS IMMODESTY
FOR WHOM THE BELL TOLLS
(AUTHOR OF —) HEMINGWAY
(CHARACTER IN —) MARIA PABLO
PILAR JORDAN ROBERT ANSELMO
FORZA DEL DESTINO, LA
(CHARACTER IN —) CARLO ALVARO
LEONORA CALATRAVA
(COMPOSER OF —) VERDI
FOSSA FOSS FOVEA GALET TRENCH
VALLIS FOSSULA FOSSETTE
FOSSE DITCH GRAFF
FOSSIL CYCAD CYSTID DOLITE
EOZOON FUCOID ICHITE PINITE
AMBRITE BLASTID CHAMITE CRINITE
ICHNITE JUNCITE LITUITE NEREITE
OVULITE REMANIE TYLOPOD
ZOOLITE ZOOLITH AISTOPOD
AMMONITE ANCODONT ASTROITE
BACULITE BALANITE BIOCHRON
BLASTOID BUFONITE CALAMITE
CERATITE CONCHITE CONODONT
ECHINITE EOHIPPUS FAVOSITE
FILICITE FUSULINA GEDANITE
GYROLITH MIMOSITE PEUCITES
POLYPITE SALIGRAM SCAPHITE
SERAPHIM SPONGOID SYNAPSID
TARSIOID CARPOLITE TRILOBITE
OSTRACODERM
(PREF.) NECR(O) ORYCT(O)
(SUFF.) LITE LITH(IC) LITIC
FOSSILIZE PETRIFY
FOSTER REAR NURSE COCKER
HARBOR NUZZLE SUCKLE CHERISH
DEPOSIT EMBOSOM GRATIFY
INDULGE NOURISH NOURSLE
NURTURE BEFRIEND CULTIVATE
FOSTERAGE NURSERY
FOSTER-CHILD DALT DAULT
FOSTERED (ARTIFICALLY —)
SPOONFED
FOSTERER NORRY
FOUL BAD BASE EVIL HORY RANK
ROIL VILE BAWDY BLACK DIRTY

DITCH FUNKY GRIMY GURRY HORRY
KETTY LOUSY MUDDY MUSTY
NASTY RUSTY SULLY WEEDY
CLARTY DEFAME DIRTEN DREGGY
FILTHY GREASY IMPURE MALIGN
ODIOUS PUTRID ROTTEN SOILED
SORDID UNFAIR VIROSE ABUSIVE
BEASTLY DEFACED FULSOME
HATEFUL ILLEGAL IMBROIN
NOISOME OBSCENE PROFANE
SLOTTER SMEARED SQUALID
TETROUS UNCLEAN VICIOUS
AMURCOUS ENTANGLE FECULENT
INDECENT MEPHITIC SLOTTERY
STAGNANT STINKING TRAUCHLE
WRETCHED
(— UP) ERR BOTCH
(BASKETBALL —) HACK
FOULMOUTHED RIBALD ROUDAS
ABUSIVE OBSCENE PROFANE
FOULNESS FEDITY PRAVITY
(— OF MOUTH) SABURRA
FOUL-SMELLING FUNKY
FOUL-UP SNAFU
FOUMART POLECAT
FOUND FIX TRY YET BASE CAST
REST STAY BEGIN BOARD BUILD
ENDOW ERECT PLANT SETUP START
ATTACH BOTTOM DEPART GROUND
INVENT EQUIPPED PRACTICE
PROVIDED SUPPLIED
FOUNDATION BED BASE BODY
FIRM FOND FUND GIST ROOT SILL
SOLE BASIS FOUND STOCK STOOL
ANLAGE BOTTOM CRADLE GROUND
LEGACY MATRIX PODIUM RIPRAP
BEDDING BEDROCK CHANTRY
COLLEGE MORTISE PINNING
RADICAL ROADBED SUBBASE
WARRANT BACKBONE DONATION
MATTRESS MIREPOIX PEDESTAL
PLATFORM STANDARD UNDERLAY
(— FOR WIG) CAUL
(— OF BASKET) SLATH SLARTH
(FLOATING —) CRIB
(LACE —) RESEAU
(PRECARIOUS —) STILT
FOUNDATIONER GOWNBOY
COLLEGER
FOUNDATION-STOP DIAPASON
FOUNDED FUSILE
FOUNDER FAIL IMAM SINK AUTHOR
CASTER DYNAST EPONYM HELLEN
YETTER AFOUNDE STUMBLE
BELLETER MISCARRY LAMINITIS
PATRIARCH
(— OF COLONY) OECIST OIKIST
FOUNDLING WAIF ORPHAN
FOUNT FONS FONT SOURCE
FOUNTAIN URN AQUA FOND HEAD
KELD PANT PILA SYKE WELL DIRCE
FOUNT GURGE QUELL SURGE
ORIGIN PHIALE PIRENE SOURCE

SPRING BUBBLER CONDUIT SPRUDEL
AGANIPPE SALMACIS UPSPRING
WELLHEAD
(— ON SHIP) SCUTTLEBUTT
(INK —) DUCT
(SODA —) SPA
(PREF.) PEGO
(SUFF.) CRENE
FOUNTAINHEAD ORIGIN
SOURCE
FOUNTAIN PEN STICK STYLO
FOUR MESS CATER DELTA DALETH
FEOWER TETRAD QUARTET
QUATRAL MURNIVAL QUADRATE
(— OF ANYTHING) GUNDA
(— OF TRUMPS) TIDDY
(— TIMES A DAY) QID
(— YEAR PERIOD) PYTHIAD
(GROUP OF —) TETRAD
(PREF.) QUADR(I)(U) QUADRATO
QUATER TESSARA TETR(A)
(— ATOMS OF HYDROGEN)
TETRAZ(O)
(— TIMES) QUATER TETRAKIS
(HAVING — PARTS) TETR(A)
FOURCHETTE FORGET SIDEWALL
WISHBONE
FOURFOLD FOURBLE QUATERN
**FOUR HORSEMEN OF
APOCALYPSE**
(AUTHOR OF —) IBANEZ
(CHARACTER IN —) JULIO CHICHI
MARCELO DESNOYER HARTROTT
FOURIERISM SOCIALISM
FOUR-O'CLOCK FRIARBIRD
FOURPENNY BIT JOE FLAG JOEY
GROAT
FOURSQUARE FRANK
FOURTEENER SEPTENAR
FOURTH DELTA QUART FARDEL
FORPIT FERLING QUARTER
QUADRANT
(— HOUR) SEXT
(— OF BAHMANI EMPIRE) TARAF
(— OF CAKE) FARL FARLE
(— OF YEAR) RAITH
(AUGMENTED —) TRITONE
(PREF.) QUART(I) TETART(O)
FOUSSA CIVET GALET
FOVEOLA VARIOLE
FOWL HEN RED COCK GAME GRIG
JAVA ROCK SLIP BIDDY CHUCK
CLUCK COPPY DUMPY MALAY
MANOC MARAN SILKY ANCONA
ASHURA BANTAM BRAHMA CAMBAR
COCHIN HOUDAN LAMONA LEGBAR
POLISH REDCAP SULTAN SUSSEX
BUFFBAR CAMPINE CHICKEN
CORNISH DORKING FRIZZLE
HAMBURG LEGHORN MINORCA
OKLABAR POULTRY ROOSTER
SPANISH SUMATRA COCKEREL
CUBALAYA DELAWARE DUCKWING

DUNGHILL GAMECOCK LANGSHAN
SHANGHAI SHOWBIRD VOLAILLE
(AGGREGATION OF —) RAFT
(CASTRATED —) CAPETTE
(CRESTED —) TOPKNOT
(GUINEA —) KEET COMEBACK
(MALE —) STAG
(STUFFED —) FARCI
(TAILLESS —) RUMKIN
(5-TOED —) SILKY SILKIE
FOWLER BIRDMAN
FOWLING-PIECE SHOTGUN
FOX DOG KIT PUG TOD ASSE FOOL
STAG WILD ADIVE BRANT CAAMA
SWIFT TRICK VIXEN ZORRO ARCTIC
BAGMAN CANDUC COLFOX CORSAC
FENNEC LOWRIE OUTWIT RENARD
RUSSEL BEGUILE CHARLEY CHARLIE
KARAGAN REYNARD STUPEFY
VULPINE CUSTOMER MUSKWAKI
OUTAGAMI PLATINUM
(KIND OF —) KIT
FOX-AND-GEESE MERELS
FOXGLOVE POPPY POPDOCK
THIMBLE FLAPDOCK POPGLOVE
FOX GRAPE ISABELLA LABRUSCA
FOXHOUND WALKER
FOX HUNTER PINK
FOX-LIKE ALOPECOID
FOXTAIL CAUDA CHAPE COUGH
KNEED TWITCH SETARIA GAMELOTE
FOXY SLY WILY COONY SHREWD
CUNNING VULPINE DEXTROUS
FOYER HALL LOBBY ANTEROOM
FRACAS BOUT BRAWL MELEE MUSIC
BICKER RUMPUS SHINDY UPROAR
QUARREL SHINDIG FRACTION
INCIDENT
FRACTION BIT CUT PYO FLUX PART
BREAK PIECE SCRAP BREACH LITTLE
MOIETY DECIMAL GLUTOSE WETNESS
(— OF RADIATION) ALBEDO
(NAPHTHA —) LIGROIN
(PREF.) MER(I)(O)
(SUFF.) MER(E)(IC)(OUS)(Y)
FRACTIONAL ALIQUOT FRACTED
PARTIAL
FRACTIOUS MEAN UGLY CROSS
UNRULY CRABBED PEEVISH WASPISH
PERVERSE SNAPPISH
FRACTURE BUST FLAW REND BILGE
BREAK CLEFT CRACK FAULT JOINT
BREACH DEFORM HACKLE DIACOPE
FISSURE RUPTURE DIACLASE
FRACTION
(PREF.) RHEGMA RHEGNO
(SUFF.) CLASE RHEXIS RRHEXIS
FRACTURED SPLIT BROKEN
FRACTURING SLIP STRAIN FAILURE
FRA DIAVOLO (CHARACTER IN —)
PAMELA DIAVOLO LORENZO ZERLINA
COCKBURN
(COMPOSER OF —) AUBER

FRAGILE FINE FROW WEAK FRAIL
FROWY LIGHT SWACK FEEBLE
FROUGH INFIRM SLIGHT TENDER
BRICKLE BRITTLE FROUGHY
SLENDER TIFFANY DELICATE
EGGSHELL ETHEREAL FRACTILE
SLATTERY BREAKABLE
FRAGILITY DELICACY
FRAGMENT BIT END ORT ATOM
BLAD CHIP DRIB FLAW GROT MOIT
MOTE PART RUMP SHED SNIP WISP
ANGLE BLAUD BRACK BREAK BROKE
CATCH CHUNK CLOUT CRUMB FRUST
GIGOT PIECE RELIC SCRAP SHARD
SHERD SHIVE SHRED SPALL SPELL
SPLIT CANTLE FARDEL FILING
GOBBET MORSEL REMAIN SCREED
SHIVER SIPPET SLIVER CANTLET
EXCERPT FLINDER FLITTER FRITTER
FRUSTUM MACERAL MAMMOCK
REMANIE REMNANT SEGMENT
SHATTER SHAVING SNIPPET
AVULSION CHIPPING DETRITUS
FRACTION OARTICLE POTSHERD
SCANTLET SKERRICK SPLINTER
(— CUT OFF) CANTLE
(— OF BONE) SEQUESTER
SEQUESTRUM
(— OF BRICK) BRICKBAT
(— OF DIAMOND) CLEAVAGE
(— OF ICE) CALF
(— OF LAVA) FAVILLA LAPILLUS
(— OF MELODY) LAY
(— OF ROCK) CRAG CLAST AUTOLITH
LAPILLUS
(— OF SAIL) HULLOCK
(OF OOD) TAG
(— OF STONE) SCABBLING
(— OF UNFINISHED WORK) TORSO
(— OF VEIN MATERIAL) SHOAD
SHODE
(—S OF CLOUD) SCUD
(—S OF DIAMOND) BORT
(—S OF SAND) FINES
(CAST IRON —) POTLEG
(ICE —S) BRASH
(JAGGED —) BROCK
(LITERARY —) ANALECTA
(LITERARY —S) ANALECTA
(MASS OF —S) BRASH
(PLANT —) SHIVE
(SHELL —S) SHRAPNEL
(WOODY —S FOUND IN FOOD)
CHAD
(PL.) BRASH FRUSH SCRAPS CINDERS
FITTERS GUBBINS SMATTER
FLINDERS LEFTOVER SMITHERS
SMITHEREENS
FRAGMENTAL CLASTIC
FRAGMENTARY HASHY SNIPPY
SCRAPPY DIVIDUAL
FRAGRANCE BALM ODOR AROMA
SCENT SMELL SWEET BREATH

FLAVOR FRAGOR BOUQUET INCENSE
PERFUME SUAVITY
FRAGRANT NOSY RICH BALMY
OLENT SPICY SWEET SAVORY SPICED
ODORANT ODOROUS PERFUMY
SCENTED AROMATIC FLAGRANT
NECTARED ODORIFIC REDOLENT
FRAIL FINE POOR PUNY WEAK CRAZY
REEDY SEELY SILLY BASKET BROTEL
CROCKY FLIMSY INFIRM SICKLY
SINGLE SLIGHT SLIMSY SQUEAL
TICKLE TOPNET BRITTLE BRUCKLE
FRAGILE SLENDER SLIMSY
UNHARDY DELICATE PINDLING
FRAILTY FAULT FOIBLE INVENT
FAILING DELICACY WEAKNESS
(HUMAN —) ADAM
FRAMBESIA PIAN YAWS BUBAS
MORULA
FRAME BED BIN BOW BOX FLY GYM
MAT SET BAIL BEAM BIER BULK
BULK BUNK CANT CASE CAUM CELL
CLAM CRIB CURB DESK DRAG FORM
FROG GATE GILL HACK HARP HECK
JACK MOLD PORT RACK SASH SLEY
SOLE STEP AIRER ANGLE BANJO
BLADE BLIND BLOCK BUILD CADRE
CHASE CLEAT CRATE CROOK DRAFT
EASEL FLAKE FLASK FLEAK FLOAT
GRATE HERSE HORSE MOUNT
OXBOW PERCH PRESS SCRAY SETUP
SHAPE STAND STATE STEAD STOCK
STOOL TRAIL TRAMG BARROW BATTEN
BINDER BUCCAN BUCKET CASING
CHEVAL COFFIN CRADLE CRATCH
CRUTCH DECKLE DIRNDL FABRIC
FENDER GANTRY GRILLE HANGER
HARROW HOTBED HURDLE PERSON
PILLAR QUADRA REDACT REEDER
SCREEN SETTLE SLEDGE SPIDER
SQUARE STAPLE TANGLE TENTER
TESTER ARMRACK BREAKER
CABINET CARRIER CASEBOX
CHASSIS COAMING COASTER
CRAMPON CRIMPER DRAUGHT
DROSSER FASHION FRAMING
FRISKET GALLOWS GARLAND
GATEWAY GIGTREE GRATING
HAYRACK HOUSING ICEBOAT
MACHINE MONTURE OXBRAKE
PORTRAY SETTING STADDLE
TRANSOM TRESTLE TRIBBLE
BARBECUE BOWGRACE CARRIAGE
CASEMENT CONCEIVE CONTRIVE
DOORCASE GRAFFAGE GRIDIRON
GRILLAGE HALBERDS HOGFRAME
PLOWHEAD RAILROAD RECEIVER
RETAINER SKELETON THRIPPLE
TRIANGLE TURNPIKE BRANDRITH
OUTRIGGER
(— FOR ARCH) COOM COOMB
(— FOR BEEHIVE) SECTION
(— FOR CANDLES) HEARSE

(— FOR CARRYING STRAW) KNAPE
(— FOR CASK) GANTRY STALDER
(— FOR CATCHING FISH) HATCH
(— FOR CLOTHES DRYING) AIRER
(— FOR CONFINING HORSE) TRAVE TRAVAIL
(— FOR COW'S HEAD) BAIL
(— FOR DRYING FISH) HACK HAIK
(— FOR DRYING SKINS) HERSE
(— FOR FISHING LINE) CADAR CADER
(— FOR GLAZING LEATHER) BUCK
(— FOR HAWKS) CADGE
(— FOR HONEYCOMB) SECTION
(— FOR KILLING PIGS) CREEL
(— FOR LENS) BOW
(— FOR ROLLER BEARINGS) CAGE
(— FOR SMOKING MEAT) BOUCAN BUCCAN
(— FOR STACK) HAYRACK STADDLE
(— FOR WASHING ORE) BUDDLE
(— OF A VESSEL) HULL
(— OF MIND) HAZE SPITE SPIRIT TEMPER FEELING POSTURE
(— OF PIER) JETTY
(— OF SAW) HUSK
(— OF SPINNING MULE) SQUARE
(— OF STRAW) SIME
(— OF TINWORK) MARQUITO
(— ON STAGE) CEILING
(— TO CATCH STARFISH) TANGLE
(— TO CLEAN SHIP'S BOTTOM) HOG
(— TO DRY CLOTHES) AIRER
(— WHICH JOINS) YOKE
(BELL —) SWEEP
(BOBBIN —) BANK
(CARRIAGE —) BRAKE BREAK
(CLOTHES —) AIRER
(COUNTING —) ABACUS
(DIVING —) LUNET LUNETTE
(EMBROIDERY —) TENT TABORET TAMBOUR
(FISHING —) DREDGE
(GLAZIER'S —) FRAIL
(HARNESS —) HEALD
(LOOM —) SLAY SLEY LATHE BATTEN SLEIGH
(MINING —) APRON
(PHOTOGRAPHY —) BUTTERFLY
(PORTABLE —) BIER CACAXTE
(PRINTING —) CHASE PRESS
(SHIP'S —) CANT
(SLUBBING —) BILLY
(STRETCHING —) TENT SLEDGE TENTER
(TANNING —) BEAM
(WINDOW —) CHESS
(2-WHEELED —) GILL
(PL.) PROFILE
FRAMED NATE NATED ENGAGED
FRAMEWORK BED BENT BIER BONE BUCK BULK CAGE CRIB DURN GRID RACK SASH BONES CADRE CHUTE COPSE CREEL FLAKE SHELL STOCK BELFRY BRIDGE BUSTLE CABANE CASING CRADLE DESIGN FABRIC GOCART GUARDS HARROW HEARSE REBATO SHIELD STROMA WATTLE CABINET CARCASS CLIMBER COMMODE DERRICK FRAMING FULCRUM JACKBOX LATTICE PANNIER REBATER RETABLE STADDLE TRESTLE BARBECUE BEDSTEAD BULKHEAD CARRIAGE CRADLING CRIBWORK GRIDIRON GRILLAGE OSSATURE SCAFFOLD SHELVING SHOWCASE SKELETON TEMPLATE
(— AROUND HATCHWAY) FIDDLEY
(— FOR BUILDING SHIP) STOCKS
(— FOR CORNSTACK) HOVEL
(— FOR PEAL OF BELLS) CAGE
(— OF REFERENCE) SCHEMA
(— TO EXPAND SKIRTS) BUSTLE PANNIER
(EMPTY —) HUSK
(FOLDING —) SCREEN
(SCULPTOR'S —) ARMATURE
FRAMING CURB LEAD BELFRY ARMATURE BEDPLATE
FRAMLEY PARSONAGE
(AUTHOR OF —) TROLLOPE
(CHARACTER IN —) LUCY MARK FANNY SMITH LUFTON THORNE CRAWLEY ROBARTS SOWERBY DUNSTABLE
FRANC LEU LEY
FRANCE
(PREF.) GALLO

FRANCE

BAY: BISCAY ARACHON
CAPE: HAGUE
CAPITAL: PARIS
CHEESE: BLEU BRIE BONBEL BOURSIN MUNSTER CAMEMBERT MARCILLAT ROQUEFORT
COIN: ECU SOL SOU GROS AGNEL BLANC BLANK FRANC LIARD LIVRE LOUIS OBOLE SAIGA SCUTE BLANCA DENIER DIZAIN TESTON AGNEAUX CENTIME TESTOON CAVALIER NAPOLEON
DANCE: GAVOT BRANLE CANARY CANCAN BOUTADE GAVOTTE
DEPARTMENT: AIN LOT VAR AUBE AUDE CHER EURE GARD GERS JURA NORD OISE ORNE TARN AISNE INDRE ISERE LOIRE RHONE YONNE ARIEGE CANTAL CREUSE LOZERE NIEVRE CORREZE GIRONDE MOSELLE
DIVISION, ANCIENT: ARLES PERCHE NEUSTRIA AQUITAINE AQUITANIA
DYNASTY: CAPET VALOIS BOURBON ORLEANS CAPETIAN MEROVINGIAN

FOOD: PATE CREPE CANAPE MOUSSE QUICHE BRIOCHE SOUFFLE ESCARGOT PIPERADE POTAUFEU TOURNEDO

ISLAND: RE YEU CITE CORSE GROIX HYERE OLERON USHANT CORSICA

KING: ODO EUDES PEPIN CLOVIS LOTHAIR

LAKE: ANNECY CAZAUX

MEASURE: POT SAC AUNE LINE MINE MUID PIED VELT ARPEN CARAT LIEUE LIGNE MINOT PERCH PINTE POINT POUCE TOISE VELTE ARPENT HEMINE LEAGUE QUARTE SETIER CHOPINE HEMINEE POISSON SEPTIER BOISSEAU QUARTAUT ROQUILLE QUARTERON

MILITARY ACADEMY: STCYR SAINTCYR

MOUNTAIN: PUY DORE BLANC CINTO FOREZ PELAT COTEDOR MOUNIER VENTOUX VIGNEMALE CHAMBEYRON

MOUNTAIN RANGE: ALPS ECRINS VOSGES CEVENNES PYRENEES MARITIMES

NAME: GAUL GAULE GALLIA

NATIONAL ANTHEM: MARSEILLAISE

NATIVE: CELT GAUL FRANK BASQUE BRETON GASCON NORMAN PICARD CATALAN GALLOIS LORRAIN FRANCIEN LIGURIAN PROVENCAL BURGUNDIAN

PORT: CAEN BREST CALAIS TOULON LEHAVRE BORDEAUX CHERBOURG DUNKERQUE MARSEILLE

PROTESTANT: HUGUENOT

PROVINCE: FOIX ANJOU AUNIS BEARN ALSACE ARTOIS COMTAT POITOU AUVERGNE BRETAGNE BRITTANY LIMOUSIN LORRAINE PROVENCE TOURAINE

RACE TRACK: AUTEUIL LONGCHAMPS

REPUBLIC CALENDAR: NIVOSE FLOREAL VENTOSE BRUMAIRE FERVIDOR FRIMAIRE GERMINAL MESSIDOR PLUVIOSE PRAIRIAL FRUCTIDOR THERMIDOR VENDEMIAIRE

RESORT: PAU NICE CANNES MENTON RIVIERA

RIVER: AIN ILL LOT LUY LYS VAR AIRE AUBE AUDE CHER DRAC EURE GARD GERS LOIR OISE ORNE TARN VIRE ADOUR AISNE AULNE DROME INDRE ISERE LOIRE MARNE MEUSE RHONE RISLE SAONE SEINE SELLE SOMME VIAUR YONNE ALLIER ARIEGE ESCAUT SAMBRE SCARPE VEZERE VIENNE DURANCE GARONNE GIRONDE MAYENNE MOSELLE CHARENTE DORDOGNE

STOCK EXCHANGE: BOURSE

STRAIT: BONIFACIO

TOWN: AY EU AIX DAX GEX PAU AGDE AGEN ALBI ALES AUBY AUCH BRON CAEN LAON LOOS METZ NICE OPPY ORLY RIOM SENS SETE STLO TOUL UZES VAUX VIMY VIRE ARLES ARRAS BLOIS BREST DIJON DINAN DOUAI ERNEE LAVAL LILLE LISLE LYONS NANCY NERAC NESLE NIMES ORNES PARIS REIMS ROUEN SEDAN TOURS TULLE VICHY AMIENS ANGERS CALAIS LEMANS LONGWY NANTES PANTIN RENNES RHEIMS SAHLAT SENLIS SEVRES TARARE TARBES TOULON TROYES TULLUM VALOIS VERDUN BAREGES CASTRES LIMOGES ORLEANS ROUBAIX VALENCE BORDEAUX CLERMONT GRENOBLE MULHOUSE ROCHELLE TOULOUSE MARSEILLE STRASBOURG

TRIBE: REMI AEDUI ARVERNI SALUVII ALLOBROGES

VERSE FORM: LAI ALBA AUBADE RONDEL BALLADE DESCORT RONDEAU VIRELAI VIRELAY

WATERFALL: GAVARNIE

WEIGHT: GROS MARC ONCE CARAT LIVRE POUND TONNE TONNEAU ESTERLIN

WIND: MISTRAL

WINE: MACON MEDOC GRAVES CHABLIS POMEROL BORDEAUX BURGUNDY MUSCADET SAUTERNE CHAMPAGNE

WINE DISTRICT: MEDOC ALSACE BORDEAUX BURGUNDY CHAMPAGNE

FRANCESCA DA RIMINI
   (CHARACTER IN —) PAOLO FRANCESCA GIANCIOTTO MALATESTINO
   (COMPOSER OF —) ZANDONAI

FRANCHISE SOC SOKE VOTE CHASE FERRY HONOR INFANG CHARTER FREEDOM LIBERTY CONTRACT FREELAGE SUFFRAGE TENEMENT

FRANCISCAN MINOR MINORITE

FRANCOLIN COQUI TETUR TITAR REDWING PHEASANT

FRANCOPHILE GALLOMAN

FRANGIBLE BRITTLE

FRANGIPANI SHAKEWOOD

FRANK FREE OPEN RANK BLUFF BLUNT BURLY LUSTY NAIVE PLAIN BRAZEN CANDID DIRECT FORTHY HONEST SALIAN ARTLESS GENUINE LIBERAL PROFUSE SINCERE CAREFREE CAVALIER GENEROUS OUTFRONT STRAIGHT VIGOROUS OUTSPOKEN FOURSQUARE OPENHEARTED PLAINSPOKEN

FRANKENSTEIN (AUTHOR OF —)
SHELLEY
(CHARACTER IN —) HENRY ROBERT
VICTOR WALTON CLERVAL JUSTINE
WILLIAM ELIZABETH
FRANKENSTEIN
FRANKFURTER DOG HOTDOG
REDHOT CORNDOG
FRANKINCENSE THUS OLIBAN
OLIBANUM
FRANKLY FREELY OPENLY PLAINLY
CANDIDLY
FRANKNESS CANDOR FREEDOM
OPENNESS
FRANKPLEDGE BORROW FRIBORG
FRANSERIA RAGWEED
FRANTIC MAD WOOD RABID INSANE
MANIAC FURIOUS LUNATIC VIOLENT
DERANGED FEVERISH FRENETIC
FRENZIED MANIACAL
FRAPPE ICE GRANITE
FRATERCULA MORMON
FRATERNAL BROTHERLY DIZYGOTIC
NONIDENTICAL
FRATERNITY FRAT FRARY HOUSE
ORDER FRATRY QUALITY SOCIETY
SODALITY
FRATERNIZE FRAT COTTON
FRAUD GYP DOLE FAKE GAFF GAUD
GULL JAPE JUNT LURK RUSE SHAM
SKIN WILE CHEAT COVIN CRAFT
DOLUS FAKER FAVEL GLAIK GUILE
HOCUS LURCH SHARK SHIFT SHUCK
SWICK SWIKE TRICK BROGUE
DECEIT FIDDLE FULLAM HUMBUG
INTAKE STUMER WRENCH FLIVVER
KNAVERY ROGUERY STUMOUR
SWINDLE BOODLING COZENAGE
IMPOSTER OPERATOR SUBTLETY
TRUMPERY
FRAUDULENT SKIN WILY CRONK
COGGED CRAFTY QUACKY ABUSIVE
CROOKED CUNNING KNAVISH
CHEATING COVINOUS FRAUDFUL
GUILEFUL QUACKISH SINISTER
SPURIOUS
FRAXINELLA DITTANY RUEWORT
FRAY FRET BROIL BROOM FEAZE
MELEE RAVEL AFFRAY BUSTLE
CHAUVE FRIDGE TIFFLE CONTEST
FRAZZLE
FRAYED WORN FLAGGY RAVELED
RAVELLY
FRAZER FINNER
FREAK FIRK FLAM WHIM FANCY
HUMOR LUSUS MAVEN MOODS
SCAPE SPORT HIPPIE MEGRIM
SPLEEN WHIMSY CAPRICE CROTCHET
ESCAPADE FLIMFLAM WHIMWHAM
MONSTROSITY
(CRAZY —S) LUNES
FREAKISH FREAKY BIZARRE FLIGHTY
MAGGOTY WHIMSIC CRANKISH

FRECKLE CHIT EPHELIS FRECKEN
LENTIGO SUNSPOT HEATSPOT
FERNTICLE FERNTICKLE
FRECKLED FRECKLY FLECKLED
FREE LAX LET MOD RID BOLD EASE
LISS OPEN PERT REDD SHED SHUT
CLEAN CLEAR FLUID FRANK LARGE
LISSE LOOSE READY SCOUR SLAKE
SPARE UNTIE ACQUIT DEGAGE
DEVOID EXEMPT FACILE FLUENT
FREELY GRATIS IMMUNE LOOSEN
SOLUTE UNSLIP VACANT VAGILE
CLEANSE DELIVER GRIVOIS INEXACT
LASKING LIBERAL MANUMIT
RELEASE SCIOLTO UNBOUND
UNBOWED UNSLAVE UNTWIST
WELCOME WILLING ABSOLUTE
AUTARKIC BUCKSHEE EASINESS
EXPEDITE FACILITY FREEHAND
GRIVOISE INDIGENT LAXATIVE
LIBERATE UNBRIDLE FOOTLOOSE
(— AND EASY) GLIB CAVALIER
FAMILIAR
(— BROOK OF WEEDS) RODE
(— FROM) EX REDD DEVOID DISPATCH
(— FROM ACCUSATION) SACKLESS
(— FROM ACIDITY) DULCIFY
(— FROM AMBIGUITY) HOMELY
DECIDED
(— FROM ANXIETY) CONTENT
(— FROM ARTIFICIAL) ARTLESS
(— FROM BIAS) CANDID
(— FROM CARE) EASY CARELESS
(— FROM CHARGE) FDD PURGE
FRANCO
(— FROM CONSTRAINT) CASUAL
(— FROM DEDUCTIONS) NET
(— FROM DEFECT) HAIL HALE SOUND
(— FROM DIRT) BRIGHT
(— FROM DOUBT) RESOLVE
(— FROM DRUG ADDICTION) CLEAN
(— FROM ELECTRICAL CHARGE) DEAD
(— FROM ERROR) LEAL SOUND
CORRECT ACCURATE
(— FROM EVIL) RESCUE
(— FROM EXTREMES) EQUABLE
(— FROM FLAWS) GOOD
(— FROM FROST) FRESH
(— FROM IMPURITIES) FINE DRESS
DEFECATE DEPURATE
(— FROM KNOTS) ENODE ENODATE
(— FROM MARKS) BLANK
(— FROM MICROORGANISMS)
ASEPTIC STERILE
(— FROM OBLIGATION) ACQUIT
EXCUSE
(— FROM PENALTY) ABSOLVE
(— FROM RESTRAINT) ABANDONED
(— FROM STONES) CHESSOM
(— FROM WHITE) SATURATE
(— OF DIFFICULTIES) AFLOAT
(— OF FAT) ENSEAM
(— OF OVERTONES) PURE

(— OF TAR) WRECK
(— ONE'S SELF) SOLVE
(— PLUNGER) ARM
(— THROW AREA) KEYHOLE
(PREF.) ELEUTHER(O) IMMUNO LIBRO
(— FROM) DE
FREEBASE COCAINE
FREEBOARD QUICKSIDE
FREEBOOTER TORY RIDER ROVER
THIEF PIRATE RAIDER BRIGAND
CATERAN CORSAIR PINDARI
PILLAGER RAPPAREE SNAPHANCE
FREEBORN INGENUOUS
FREEDMAN LEYSING TITYRUS
(PL.) LAET
FREEDOM RUN EASE FRITH LARGE
UHURU ACCESS STREET APATHIA
BREADTH LEISURE LIBERTY LICENCE
LICENSE RELEASE AUTONOMY
FREELAGE FREENESS IMMUNITY
IMPUNITY LARGESSE WITHGATE
(— FROM BIAS) CANDOR
(— FROM CALAMITY) WELFARE
(— FROM CONSTRAINT) ABANDON
(— FROM DANGER) SECURITY
(— FROM ERROR) ACCURACY
(— FROM GUILT) SHRIVE
(— FROM MIXTURE) PURITY
(— FROM NOISE) QUIET
(— OF ACCESS) ENTREE
(— OF ACTION) SWINGE LATITUDE
(— OF MOVEMENT) RANGE
(— OF SPEECH) PARISIA
(— TO PROCEED) HEAD
(— TO RETURN) RECOURSE
(CARELESS —) ABANDON
(LIMITED —) PLAY
(PREF.) ELEUTHER(O)
FREEHOLD BARONY REALTY
FREEHOLDER SWAIN BONDER
YEOMAN FRANKLIN
FREEING LIVERY ACQUITAL
FREE LANCE ROUTIER
FREELY FREE LIEF LARGE LARGELY
READILY HEARTILY
FREEMAN BUR AIRE BARON CEORL
HAULD BONDER CITIZEN FRANKLIN
ROTURIER
(POOR —) THETE
FREEMASON FRATER MORGAN
NOACHITE
(ONE NOT A —) COWAN
FREESTONE HAZEL
(— STATE) CONNECTICUT
FREETHINKER INFIDEL SKEPTIC
AGNOSTIC
FREEZE ICE RIME CATCH CHILL FROST
CURDLE FRAPPE HARDEN STARVE
STEEVE CONGEAL GLACIATE
FREEZING COLD FREEZY FRIGID
FROSTY GLACIAL ICECOLD CRYONICS
GELATION
(PREF.) CRY(O) KRY(O)

FREIGHT COST LOAD CARGO GOODS
ASTRAY BURDEN LADING FRAUGHT
HOTSHOT PLUNDER PORTAGE
TRUCKAGE
(— CAR) TRUCK
FREISCHUTZ, DER (CHARACTER IN
—) MAX CUNO AGATHE HERMIT
KASPAR SAMIEL AENNCHEN
(COMPOSER OF —) WEBER
FREMD FRAIM FRAMMIT
FRENCH CREOLE FRANCO GALLIC
GALLIAN GALLICAN
(— MIXED WITH ENGLISH) FRANGLAIS
(CANADIAN —) JOUAL
(PREF.) FRANCO GALLO
FRENCH GUIANA (CAPE OF —)
ORANGE
(CAPITAL OF —) CAYENNE
(RIVER OF —) MARONI
(TOWN OF —) MANA KOUROU
FRENCH HONEYSUCKLE SULLA
FRENCH LAVENDER STECHADOS
FRENCHMAN GAUL PICARD
FRENCHY MONSIEUR PARLEYVOO
FRENCH MULBERRY SOURBUSH
FRENCH NUDE ALESAN
FRENCH REPUBLIC MARIANNA
MARIANNE
FRENCH SUDAN (SEE MALI)
FRENCHWOMAN GRISETTE
FRENULUM TENDON
FRENUM BRIDLE FRAENUM
FRENULUM VINCULUM
FRENZIED MAD AMOK MUST RABID
RAMAGE BERSERK FANATIC FRANTIC
MADDING FRENETIC FURIBUND
POSSESSED
FRENZY AMOK FURY GERE MOON
MUST RAGE AMUCK FUROR MANIA
MUSTH FURORE RAVING MADNESS
OESTRUS SWIVVET DELIRIUM
INSANITY
FREQUENCY HERTZ PITCH CREBRITY
FREQUENT USE BANG KEEP HAUNT
HOWFF OFTEN THICK AFFECT
COMMON HOURLY INFEST RESORT
ENHAUNT OFTTIME CREBROUS
FAMILIAR PRACTICE ACCUSTOMED
(PREF.) SYCHNO
FREQUENTLY OFT OFTEN HOURLY
UNSELDOM
FRESH GAY HOT NEW WET FLIP GOOD
RACY SMUG WARM BRISK CRISP
GREEN MOIST QUICK RUDDY SASSY
SMART SOUND SWEET VIVID CALLER
CALVER FLORID LIVELY MAIDEN
REDHOT STRONG UNUSED VERNAL
VIRENT VIRGIN ANOTHER NOUVEAU
UNFADED VERDANT NOUVELLE
ORIGINAL SPANKING YOUTHFUL
(NOT —) PALE STALE
(PREF.) CENO
(SUFF.) CENE

FRESHEN PERK BRACE FRESH
RENEW BREEZE CALLER REVIVE
CHOUNCE PEARTEN REFRESH
SWEETEN FRENCHEN
FRESHENER BRACER
FRESHET TIDE FLOOD FRESH SPATE
TORNADO
FRESHMAN FOX BEJAN FROSH
BÉJANT GREENY PENNAL FRESHER
(GERMAN —) PENNAL
FRESHNESS DEW SASS VERD
NOVELTY VERDURE VIRIDITY
ORIGINALITY
FRET DIK NAG ORP RUB RUX VEX CARK
FASH FRAY FUSS GALL GNAW RAGE
STEW YIRM CHAFE CRAKE CRISP
FLISK GRATE PIQUE WORRY WREAK
ABRADE CORSIE CRYSAL HARASS
MUCKLE NETTLE PLAGUE REPINE
RIPPLE RUFFLE CHRYSAL GRECQUE
GRIZZLE MEANDER SCRUPLE
SQUINNY ALIGREEK IRRITATE
FRETFUL CROSS GIRNY ORPIT TEATY
TEENY TESTY FRETTY PENCEY
SULLEN TATCHY TWISTY FRECKET
PEEVISH PETTISH SPLEENY
CAPTIOUS CRANKOUS FRETSOME
FROPPISH PETULANT PINDLING
QUERULOUS
FRETTED FRETTY MAGGED
FRETTING FRET EATING
FREY FREYR YNGVI
(FATHER OF —) NJORD
(SISTER OF —) FREYA
FREYA
(BROTHER OF —) FREY
(FATHER OF —) NJORD
(HUSBAND OF —) ODIN
FRIABLE CRIMP CRISP CRUMP FLAKY
FRUSH MEALY SHORT CRUMBY
CRUMMY FLUFFY PUTRID CHESSOM
CRUMBLY POWDERY POWDERY
RESOLUTE ROTTENLY SHATTERY
(NOT —) SAD
FRIAR FRATE FREER MINIM MINOR
BHIKKU FRATER GELONG GOSAIN
LISTER BHIKSHU JACOBIN LIMITER
SERVITE BREVIGER CAPUCHIN
JACOBITE MINORIST MINORITE
PREACHER AUGUSTINE CARMELITE
CORDELIER MENDICANT
BENEDICTINE
FRIARBIRD COLDONG PIMLICO
MONKBIRD
FRIAR SKATE DOCTOR
FRICANDEAU GRENADINE
FRICASSEE POTPIE
FRICATIVE BUZZ HISS OPEN YOGH
DURATIVE
FRICTION BUZZ DRAG HISS CHAFE
WINDAGE
(PREF.) TRIBO
(SUFF.) TRIPSIS

FRICTIONLESS SMOOTH
FRIED FRIT SAUTE
FRIEDCAKE WONDER CRULLER
FATCAKE DOUGHNUT
FRIEND AME AMI AMY BOR CAD EME
PAX AMIE BHAI CHUM NABS OPPO
PARD WINE AMIGA AMIGO BRICK
BUDDY INGLE NETOP TROUT AIKANE
BELAMY COBBER COUSIN CUMMER
GOSSIP INWARD KIMMER PRINCE
QUAKER ACHATES COMRADE
SOCIETY COCKMATE COMPADRE
DEMOPHIL FEDERATE HICKSITE
INTIMADO INTIMATE TILLICUM
CATERCOUSIN
(— OF BRIDEGROOM) PARANYMPH
(—S NOT SPEAKING) CUTS
(BOSOM —) CONFIDANT
(CLOSE —) PRIVY COBBER
COMPADRE
(DIVINE —) SOCIUS
(FAMILIAR —) CRONY GREMIAL
SPECIAL
(GIRL —) DOXY DRAG DONEY DOXIE
STEADY
(INTIMATE FEMALE —) CUMMER
(PRIVATE —) PRIVADO
(WOMAN —) GIMMER
(PL.) FOLK KITH SOCE FOLKS
SOCIETY
FRIENDLESS FORLORN
FRIENDLINESS AMITY AFFINITY
BONHOMIE GOODWILL
FRIENDLY COSH EASY GOOD HOLD
HOMY KIND TOSH CADGY CHIEF
COUTH GREAT HOMEY MATEY THICK
AMICAL CHATTY CHUMMY FOLKSY
FORTHY HOMELY KINDLY SMOOTH
AFFABLE AMIABLE AMICOUS
COUTHIE AMICABLE HOMELIKE
INTIMATE SOCIABLE NEIGHBORLY
FRIENDSHIP PAX AMITY AMOUR
FRIEZE KELT FRISE CUSHION FALDING
FRISADO FRIEZING
FRIGATE ZABRA
FRIGATE BIRD IOA IWA ALCATRAS
FRIGATE MACKEREL BONITO
TASSARD
FRIGG FREA FRIJA
FRIGGA (HUSBAND OF —) ODIN
(SON OF —) BALDER
FRIGHT COW BOOF FEAR FLEG FRAY
ALARM GHAST GLIFF GLOFF PANIC
SCARE AFFRAY GASTER GLIFFY
SCHRIK TERROR STARTLE SWITHER
FRIGHTEN GASTNESS GLIFFING
FRIGHTEN AWE COW FLY SHY SOB
BAZE BREE DARE DOSS FEAR FLEG
FLEY FRAY FUNK HARE HAZE SHOO
AFEAR AFLEY ALARM APPAL BLUFF
GALLY GHOST GLIFF HAZEN SCARE
SHORE SPOOK AFFRAY ALARUM
APPALL BOGGLE BOOGER COWARD

FLAITE FLIGHT FRIGHT GALLEY
GALLOW AFFREUX FRECKEN
SCARIFY STARTLE TERRIFY AFFRIGHT
MISTRYST
(— BIRDS) KEEP
(PREF.) TERRI TERRORI

FRIGHTENED RAD EERY FRIT GAST
EERIE GHAST WINDY AFEARD AFRAID
AGHAST SCARED SCAREY STURTIN
GHASTFUL
(EASILY —) TIMID SKITTISH

FRIGHTENING EERY DREAD EERIE
GOURY HAIRY FRIGHTY GHASTLY
SHIVERY DREADFUL FEARSOME
FLEYSOME

FRIGHTFUL WAN DIRE GRIM UGLY
AWFUL FERLY HORRID UGSOME
AFFREUX DIREFUL FEARFUL
GASHFUL GHASTLY HIDEOUS
ALARMING DREADFUL ELDRITCH
FEARSOME GHASTFUL HORRIBLE
HORRIFIC TERRIBLE TERRIFIC

FRIGID DRY ICY COLD BLEAK FISHY
ARCTIC FROSTY FROZEN WINTRY
GLACIAL FREEZING SIBERIAN

FRIGIDITY GLARE

FRILL DIDO PURL JABOT RUCHE
RUFFLE ARMILLA FLOUNCE SPINACH
SPINAGE CHITLING CRIMPING
FRILLERY FURBELOW
(— OF HAIR) APRON
(PL.) PUFFERY FOOFARAW FRILLERY

FRILLINESS CHICHI

FRILLING RUCHE ROUCHE SWEEPER

FRILLY CHICHI

FRINGE WLO EDGE GILL LOMA RUFF
WELT BEARD THRUM BORDER
EDGING MARGIN PELMET TASSEL
BULLION CREPINE EYELASH FEATHER
FIMBRIA MACRAME SELVAGE
TRAILER VALANCE WHISKER CILIELLA
FRISETTE INDUSIUM PENUMBRA
SELVEDGE TRIMMING
(— OF TEETH) PERISTOME
(SOFT —S) THRUM
(PL.) ZIZITH TZITZIS TZITZIT
(PREF.) CROSS(O) FIMBRI(O) LACINI
THYSAN(O)

FRINGED JUBATE CILIATE LACINIATE

FRINGEFOOT UMA

FRINGEPOD LACEPOD

FRINGETAIL VEILTAIL

FRINGE TREE SHAVINGS

FRIPPERY FLIPPERY TRINKUMS
(PL.) GAUDERY

FRISK COLT FISK PLAY ROLL SKIP
WHID BOUND CAPER SKICE CAREER
CAVORT CURVET FRISCO FROLIC
TITTUP WANTON FRISCAL FRISKLE

FRISKY GAY PERT FRISK CROUSE
FEISTY KIPPER LIVELY WANTON
BUCKISH COLTISH JIGGISH PLAYFUL
SKITTISH SPORTIVE

FRISON KNUB

FRIT FRETT CALCINE

FRITTER FOOL FRIT TEAR BOLLO
DRILL WASTE BANGLE DRIVEL
LOUNGE BEIGNET DRIBBLE FLITTER
SLATTERN

FRIVOLITY LEVITY FRIBBLE INANITY
ITEMING FUTILITY NONSENSE
NUGACITY

FRIVOLOUS GAY DAFT VAIN GIDDY
INANE LIGHT PETTY SILLY WASHY
FLIMSY FRILLY FRIVOL FROTHY
FUTILE TOYISH YEASTY FATUOUS
FRIBBLE LIGHTLY NIDGETY SHALLOW
TRIVIAL GIMCRACK JIMCRACK
SKITTISH TRIFLING

FRIVOLOUSNESS FUTILITY

FRIZZ FRIZ CREPE FRIZE FRIZZLE
FROUNCE

FRIZZED CRISPY

FRIZZLE CRAPE CREPE

FRIZZLY FUZZY CRIMPY FRIZZY

FRIZZY FUZZY CRIMPY FRIZZLY

FROCK DUD JAM GOWN JUMP SLIP
OLOF WRAP LAMMY SMOCK TRUSS
TUNIC CLERIC JERSEY LAMMIE
MANTLE ROCHET SUKKENYE

FROCK COAT CRISPIN

FROG PAD POD KICK FROSH FROSK
FROUD PADDO PADDY RANID RONCO
ANURAN PEEPER TOGGLE CHARLIE
CRAWLER CREEPER CROAKER
CUSHION FRESHER FROGLET
PADDOCK PODDOCK QUILKIN
BULLFROG FERREIRO FROGGING
PLATANNA REPLACER
(— IN LOOM) HEATER
(— OF HORSE'S HOOF) FRUSH
CUSHION
(TREE —) HYLA NOTOTREMA
(PREF.) BATRACH(O) RANI

FROG CRAB RANININAN

FROGFISH ANGLER SLIMER
TOADFISH

FROGGER CHASER TRAILER
ZOOGLER

FROGGY RANARIAN

FROGHOPPER HOPPER CERCOPID

FROGMOUTH MOPOKE MOREPORK
PODARGUE

FROGS (AUTHOR OF —)
ARISTOPHANES
(CHARACTER IN —) AEACUS CHARON
BACCHUS DIONYSUS HERCULES
XANTHIAS AESCHYLUS EURIPIDES
(SUFF.) BATRACH(O)(US)

FROLIC BUM GAY RIG BLOW COLT
GAME GELL HAZE JINK LAKE LARK
ORGY PLAY PLOY RANT REEK ROMP
TEAR CAPER FREAK FRISK MERRY
PRANK RANDY ROUSE SALLY SPORT
SPREE BUSTER CAVORT CURVET
FRATCH GAMBOL PLISKY POWWOW

PRANCE ROLLIX SHINDY SPLORE
VAGARY WANTON DISPORT
GAMMOCK MARLOCK PLISKIE
ROLLICK SCAMPER SKYLARK
SPANIEL STASHIE WASSAIL
CAROUSAL JAMBOREE

FROLICSOME GAY DAFT ROID
ANTIC BUXOM CADGY FRISK GILPY
LARKY FRISKY LIVELY WANTON
ANTICAL JOCULAR LARKING
LARKISH PLAYFUL WAGGISH
ESPIEGLE FRISKFUL FROLICKY
GAMESOME LARKSOME PRANKISH
SPORTFUL SPORTIVE

FROLICSOMENESS HEYDAY

FROM A AB DE EX OF FAE FRA FRO
VAN VON ASOF THROM AGAINST
(— A DISTANCE) ALOOF
(— BEGINNING TO END) THROUGH
(— ELSEWHERE) ALIUNDE
(— OFF) AFFA
(— SIDE TO SIDE) OVER CROSS
ATHWART
(— THIS PLACE) HENCE
(— THIS TIME) HENCE
(PREF.) AP APH APO

FROND FERN TRESS CROSIER
FRONDLET

FRONT BOW VAN BROW FACE FORE
HEAD PROW THIN AFORE VAUNT
BEFORE DEVANT FACADE FACING
FORMER OPPOSE SECTOR VAWARD
ADVANCE FORWARD FRONTAL
FURTHER OBVERSE PALATAL
PREFACE RESPECT SLENDER
FOREHEAD FOREMOST FOREPART
FORESIDE FRONTAGE
(— OF ASTROLABE) WOMBSIDE
(— OF BARN) FOREBAY
(— OF BIRD'S NECK) GUTTUR
(— OF BODY) GROUF
(— OF HEAD) VISAGE FORETOP
(— OF HELMET) VENTAIL
(— OF SHIRT) BOSOM
(— OF WATERWHEEL BUCKET) START
(— UPON) AFFRONT
(PREF.) ANTER(O) PRO
(IN —) FORE PRO(S)(SO)
(IN — OF) ANTE ANTER(O) PRAE
PRE

FRONTAL PALL FRONT SINDON
TABULA FRONTON METOPIC
FRONTLET SUFFRONT
(ALTAR —) TABULA

FRONTIER BOUND COAST FRONT
MARCH BORDER BARRIER FRONTURE
OUTLYING
(FORTIFIED —) LIMES

FRONTING OBVIOUS

FRONTISPIECE FRONT UNWAN
FRONTIS

FRONTLET TIARA FRONTAL
CHAMFRON

FRONT PAGE (AUTHOR OF —)
HECHT MACARTHUR
(CHARACTER IN —) EARL BURNS
GRANT HILDY PEGGY WALTER
HARTMAN JOHNSON WILLIAMS

FRONTPIECE GORE

FROST ICE COLD HOAR RIME RIND
(GROUND —) PERMA
(PREF.) CRYMO PAGO RHIGO
(HOAR —) PACHNO

FROSTED GLACE PRUINOSE

FROSTING ICING DIVINITY

FROSTWEED ROCKROSE

FROSTY ICY COLD RIMY CHILL CRISP
FRORE GELID GLARY HUNCH BOREAL
FRIGID FROREN CHILLING INIMICAL
PRUINOUS
(NOT —) OPEN

FROTH FOB BARM FOAM HEAD REAM
SCUM SUDS WORK CREAM SPUME
YEAST FLOWER FREATH LATHER
SPURGE

FROTHER CREOSOTE

FROTHING HUMMING MANTLING

FROTHY BARMY FOAMY LIGHT
REAMY SPEWY SPUMY SUDSY
FLASHY YEASTY SPUMOSE
SPUMOUS WHIPPED SPUMANTE

FROWARD RANK CROSS AWKWARD
PEEVISH WAYWARD CONTRARY
FROPPISH PERVERSE PETULANT
PROTERVE SHREWISH UNTOWARD

FROWN GLUM LOUR GLOOM GLOUT
GLUMP LOWER SCOWL GLOWER
GLUNCH FROUNCE FRONTLET

FROWNING GLUM GLUNCH

FROWZY BLOUSY BLOWSY BLOWZY
RAFFISH FROWZLED SCABROUS
SLOVENLY

FROZEN FAST FIXED FRORE FRORY
GELID GLARY FRAPPE FROREN
GLACIAL

FRUCTIFICATION CONK AECIDIUM
BASIDIUM APOTHECIUM

FRUCTOSE ACROSE

FRUGAL EASY MILD CANNY CHARY
ROMAN SCANT SPARE MEAGER
SAVING SCANTY SCARCE SCOTCH
SKIMPY CAREFUL PRUDENT
SCRIMPY SLENDER SPARING THRIFTY
PROVIDENT PARSIMONIOUS

FRUGALITY SPARE THRIFT
ECONOMY PARCITY MANAGERY

FRUGALLY HARD CHARILY SAVINGLY

FRUIT BEL FIG HAW UVA AKEE ATTA
BAEL BITO COYO DATE DIKA DROP
GEAN JACK LIME NOOP PEAR PLUM
POMF SEED SLOE SNAP SORB AKENE
ANISE APPLE BERRY CLING COUMA
DRUPE GENIP GOURD GRAPE GUAVA
HAZEL ILAMA LEMON LIMON
MANGO MELON OLIVE PAPAW PEACH
RIPER SORVA TRYMA ACHENE

ACINUS ALMOND BANANA BUTTON
CEDRON CEREZA CHERRY CITRON
CITRUS COBNUT COCHAL COCONA
DAMSON DURIAN EMBLIC EMBOLO
GUARRI JUJUBE KEEPER LEGUME
LONGAN LOQUAT MAMMEE
MARANG MAYPOP MUYUSA
NARRAS ORANGE PAPAYA PAWPAW
PELLAS POMATO RESULT SAPOTA
SQUASH UVALHA WAMPEE WESTME
ZAPOTE APRICOT ATEMOYA
AVOCADO AZAROLE BILIMBI
BLOATER CARAWAY CHAYOTE
CHECKER CIRUELA COCONUT
CURRANT DESSERT GEEBUNG
GENIPAP GHERKIN KUMQUAT
MURCOTT PIGFACE PRODUCT
RIPENER SERVICE SHALLON SOROSIS
SOURSOP TANGELO ACHENIUM
BAYBERRY BELLERIC BILBERRY
CALABASH CANISTEL CAPSICUM
CARDAMUM CITRANGE COCOPLUM
CUCUMBER DEWBERRY DOGBERRY
EGGFRUIT FOLLICLE FRUITAGE
FRUITERY FRUITLET GOLKAKRA
INKBERRY LIMEQUAT OSOBERRY
PIEPRINT PODOCARP RAMBUTAN
SEBESTEN SEEDBALL SHADDOCK
SWEETSOP SYCONIUM CARYOPSIS
CHERIMOYA NECTARINE PINEAPPLE
SAPODILLA TAMARILLO
CHERIMOYER CLEMENTINE
MANGOSTEEN
(— LIKE APPLE) MEDLAR
(— OF CACTUS) OABRA
(— OF CAPER) CAPOT
(— OF CITRON) ETROG ETHROG
(— OF HEMLOCK) CONIUM
(— OF OAK) ACORN
(— OF PALM) SALAK PUPUNHA
(— OF ROSE) HEP HIP BUTTON
(— ON TREES) HANG
(—S COOKED IN SYRUP) COMPOTE
(AGGREGATE —) ETAERIO
DRUPETUM HETAERIO
(ASTRINGENT —) GAB GAUB
CHEBULE
(AVOCADO-LIKE —) ANAY
(CANDIED —) CONSERVE
(CARMINATIVE —) BADIAN
(COILED —) STROMBUS
(COLLECTIVE —) SYNCARP
(COMPOUND —) SYNCARP
(DRIED —) PASA CUREB MUMMY
SABAL OREJON CAPSULE EMBELIA
(EARLY —) PRIMEUR HASTINGS
(FALLEN —) SHEDDER WINDFALL
(FIRST —S) ANNATES BIKKURIM
PRIMICES
(FLESHY —) SYCONIUM SARCOCARP
(FUZZY —) KIWI
(GOURD —) PEPO
(GRAPEFRUIT-LIKE —) SUHA

(GRAPELIKE —) WAMPEE
(HAWTHORN —) PEGGLE
(IMPERFECT —) SPECH NUBBIN
(MASHED —) FOOL
(MEDICINAL —) DRUPE AIWAIN
AJOWAN EMBELIA
(ONE-SEEDED —) AKENE ACHENE
(PALMYRA —) PUNATOO
(PLUMLIKE —) CARISSA CIRUELA
(PRESERVED —) SUCCADE
CONFITURE
(PRICKLY —) HEDGEHOG
(SELF-FERTILIZED —) AUTOCARP
(SLICED DRIED —) SNITS SNITZ
SCHNITZ
(SPURGE —) TAMPOE
(SUPERIOR —) TOPPER
(UNRIPE OAK —) CAMATA
(WINGED —) SAMARA
(WOODY —) XYLOCARP
(PREF.) CARP(O) FRUCTI FRUGI
(BEAK-LIKE —) RYNCO
(SUFF.) CARP(OUS)(US)(Y)
FRUIT BAT KALONG
FRUIT-BEARING FERTILE
FRUIT DOVE KUKU
FRUITFUL FAT FOODY BATTEL
FECUND FRUITY GRAVID FERTILE
TEEMFUL UBEROUS ABUNDANT
CHILDING FRUITIVE PREGNANT
PROLIFIC PLENTEOUS
FRUITFULNESS UBERTY FATNESS
FRUITGROWER FRUITIST
FRUITLESS DRY GELD VAIN ADDLE
BARREN FUTILE STERILE USELESS
ABORTIVE BOOTLESS
FRUIT PIGEON KUKU LUPE KUKUPA
MANUMA MANUTAGI
FRUIT ROT BLET
FRUIT STONE COB PYRENE
PUTAMEN
(PREF.) PYREN(O)
FRUMP JUDY
FRUSTRATE BALK BEAT BILK CRAB
DASH DISH FOIL LAME BAULK BLANK
BLOCK CHECK CROSS ELUDE SMEAR
THRAW WRECK BAFFLE BLIGHT
BUGGER DEFEAT DELUDE DERAIL
KIBOSH OUTWIT SCOTCH THWART
ANIENTE DECEIVE FALSIFY PREVENT
CONFOUND INFRINGE STULTIFY
FRUSTRATED DISHED MANQUE
FRUSTRATER MARPLOT
FRUSTRATING BOOTLESS
FRUSTRATION FOIL SUCK DEFEAT
FIASCO
FRUSTRUM GUTTA
FRUSTULE TESTULE HYPOTHECA
FRY SILE BROOD FRIZZ KRILL SAUTE
FRIZZLE GREYFISH
(HANGTOWN —) OMELET
(KIND OF —) HANGTOWN
FRYER FRIER FRIZZER SPRINGER

FRYING PAN FRYPAN SPIDER CREEPER SKILLET

FUCHSIA CORREA KONINI FUCHSIN EARDROPS

FUCHSIN ROSEINE SOLFERINO

FUCHSINE RUBIN RUBINE MAGENTA ROSANILINE

FUDDLE FUZZLE FLUSTER

FUDDLED FAP REE DOPY BOSKY DOPEY SWASH TIPSY WOOZY MAUDLIN TOSTICATED

(**— WITH MALT LIQUOR)** SWIPEY

FUDGE HUNCH SNUDGE PENUCHE DIVINITY

FUEL GAS OIL POB COAL COKE FIRE PEAT UPLA ARGOL AVGAS ACETOL BUNKER ELDING FIRING NAPALM SHRUFF TIMBER COALITE GASOHOL PABULUM SYNTHOL FIREBOOT FIREBOTE GASOGENE GAZOGENE TRIPTANE

(**GAS —)** ETHANE

(**JELLED —)** NAPALM

(**ROCKET —)** BORANE HYDYNE

FUGITIVE HOT FLEME FLYER FUGIE SCAMP OUTLAW FLEEING LAMSTER REFUGEE RUNAWAY FLEETING RUNAGATE UNSTABLE

(**PL.)** MANZAS

FUGUE FUGA RICERCAR

(**— THEME)** DUX

(**PART OF —)** STRETTA

FULA PEUL PEUHL FELLANI FELLATA

FULANI PEUL PEUHL

FULCRUM BAIT GLUT

(**— FOR OAR)** ROWLOCK

FULFILL FILL FULL KEEP MEET HONOR ANSWER COMPLY FULFIL REDEEM ACHIEVE PERFORM SATISFY COMPLETE COMPLISH ACCOMPLISH

(**— A TERM)** EXPIRE

FULFILLMENT PASS EFFECT FUNCTION PERFORMANCE

(**— OF GOD'S WILL)** KINGDOM

(**IMAGINARY —)** FANTASY

FULGURATION BLICK

FULL BAD BIG FAT FOW COOL DEEP FAIR GOOD JUST PANG RANK TRIG TUCK AMPLE AWASH BROAD CLEAR FLUSH LARGE LUCKY PIENO PLAIN PLENY ROUND SATED SOLID TIGHT TOTAL WHOLE ENTIRE GOGGLE HONEST STRONG BAPTIZE BRIMFUL COPIOUS DESTROY DIFFUSE FULFILL FULSOME LIBERAL OROTUND PERFORM PLENARY REPLETE TEEMING TRAMPLE WEALTHY ABSOLUTE ADEQUATE BOUFFANT BRIMMING CHOCKFUL COMPLETE EXTENDED FREQUENT PREGNANT RESONANT THOROUGH

(**— CLOTH OR YARN)** WALK

(**— OF AIR)** LIGHT

(**— OF BLANKS)** LACUNOSE

(**— OF CHINKS)** RIMOSE

(**— OF DELAY)** MOROSE

(**— OF DEVILTRY)** HEMPY HEMPIE

(**— OF DIRT)** FOUL

(**— OF EGGS)** GRAVID

(**— OF ENERGY)** STOUT SWANK

(**— OF ENTHUSIASM)** RARING

(**— OF ERRORS)** FOUL

(**— OF FLAWS)** CRAZY

(**— OF FUN)** FROLIC

(**— OF HAPPINESS)** SUNSHINY

(**— OF INTEREST)** AGOG

(**— OF IRON)** SIDEROSE

(**— OF LIFE)** SPUNKY ANIMATE

(**— OF LOOPS)** KINKY

(**— OF MATTER FOR THOUGHT)** MEATY

(**— OF PROMISE)** PREGNANT

(**— OF RUSHES)** SPRITTY

(**— OF SAND)** ARENOSE

(**— OF SLEEP)** SOPOROSE

(**— OF SMALL OPENINGS)** POROUS

(**— OF SPIRIT)** GENEROUS

(**— OF VIGOR)** FLUSH GREEN LUSTY ANIMATED SPIRITED

(**— OF ZEST)** RACY

(**NOT —)** SCANT

(**VERY —)** SKELPING

(**PREF.)** PLENI PLERO

(**SUFF.) (— OF)** IOUS OSE OUS

FULL-BLOODED PLETHORIC

FULL-BLOWN JUICY

FULLBODIED FAT LOFTY HEARTY ROBUST

FULL-BOSOMED BUXOM

FULLER GAG HARDY HARDIE ROLLER TUCKER WALKER BLOCKER CREASER THICKER CLOTHIER

FULL-FACED AFFRONTE AFFRONTY

FULL-FLAVORED BOLD RACY

FULL-FLEDGED ALLOUT ENTIRE SUMMED

FULL-GROWN ADULT RIPE GROWN MATURE SEEDED

FULL-LENGTH UNCUT

FULLLNESS (**— OF TONE)** VOLUME

FULLNESS BODY FLAIR FLARE FULTH PLENUM FULNESS PLEROMA SATIETY

FULL-SOUNDING ROUND SONOROUS

FULLY ALL DOWN EVEN INLY WELL AMPLY LARGE ENOUGH FAIRLY THRICE WHOLLY CLEARLY LARGELY UTTERLY CLEVERLY ENTIRELY INWARDLY MATURELY

FULMAR HAG NELLY NODDY HAGDON NELLIE MALDUCK MALMOCK STINKER MALLEMUCK

FULMINATE BLOW RAIL FULMINE

FULSOME FAT SUAVE FOULSOME

FUMARIC BOLETIC LICHENIC

FUMAROLE HORNITO

FUMBLE BOOT DROP MUFF MULL PIRL BOBBLE BOGGLE FAFFLE MUMBLE PRODDLE MISFIELD THRUMBLE

FUMBLER STUMER BUNGLER STUMOUR

FUMBLING HALTING

FUME FUFF RAGE REEK STEW EWDER SMOKE STIFE STORM VAPOR SEETHE SNUFFLE FUMIGATE
(— A CASK) STUM

FUMID SMOKY SMOKEY

FUMIGATE SMEEK SMOKE PASTIL CYANIDE PASTILLE

FUMIGATION GASSING

FUMIGATOR AERATOR

FUMITORY FUMARIA FUMEROOT FUMEWORT

FUN GIG GAME GELL JEST JOKE LAKE PLAY BORAK BOUND HUMOR KICKS MIRTH MUSIC SPORT FROLIC GAIETY GAYETY DAFFERY DAFFING GAMMOCK WHOOPEE
(MAKE — OF) JAPE RIDE
(UNRESTRAINED —) HELL

FUNCTION ACT JOB MAP RUN USE DUTY FORM ROLE WORK POWER ACTION AGENCY MATRIX MISTER OFFICE SQUASH CONCEPT FACULTY ISOLATE MAPPING OPERATE PERFORM SERVICE WORKING ACTIVITY BUSINESS MINISTRY PROVINCE
(— EFFECTIVELY) AVAIL
(—S OF JUDGES) ERMINE
(APPARENT —) STUDY
(CHEMICAL —) PARACHOR
(CLERICAL —) DIET
(ECCLESIASTICAL —) DIET
(ESSENTIAL —) DHARMA
(LAVISH —) WINGDING
(MATHEMATICAL —) DEL FORM METRIC INVERSE QUARTIC
(SPECIAL —) CEREMONY
(USEFUL —) PURPOSE
(WORD —) DEIXIS
(SUFF.) CY URE

FUNCTIONAL DYNAMIC

FUNCTIONARY BEADLE FLUNKY CAPTAIN FLUNKEY CHAPRASI

FUNCTIONING ALIVE AFLOAT

FUNCTIONLESS OTIOSE

FUND BOX BANK FOND MASS CHEST KITTY MOUNT SLUSH STOCK STORE ESCROW CHALUKA JACKPOT RESERVE HALUKKAH PECULIUM
(COMMON —) POT POOL
(POLITICAL —S) BARREL
(RESERVE —) REST
(PL.) CAJA PURSE COFFER

FUNDAMENT NOCK TAIL BOTTOM FUNDUS

FUNDAMENTAL NET BASE BASAL BASIC KLANG PRIME VITAL BOTTOM PRIMAL SIMPLE BASILAR BEDROCK ORGANIC PRIMARY RADICAL ABSOLUTE CARDINAL ORIGINAL RUDIMENT SUBSTRAT ULTIMATE PRIMORDIAL RUDIMENTARY
(PL.) ABCS NITTYGRITTY

FUNDAMENTALLY AUFOND

FUNDUS FORNIX

FUNERAL TANGI BURIAL EXEQUY BURYING CORTEGE FUNFRRE FUNERARY MORTUARY

FUNERAL DIRECTOR BLACKMAN

FUNEREAL BLACK FERAL DISMAL SOLEMN FUNEBRE FUNERAL DIRGEFUL EXEQUIAL MOURNFUL SEPULCHRAL

FUNGI MYCOFLORA

FUNGICIDE MANEB NABAM ZINEB CAPTAN FERBAM CALOMEL BORDEAUX DICHLONE

FUNGOID MYCOID FUNGOUS

FUNGOSO (FATHER OF) SORDIDO

FUNGUS BUNT MOLD SMUT BLACK BRAND ERGOT FUNGE HYPHO MOREL MOULD PHOMA SPUNK SWARD TRUFF VALSA VERPI AGARIC BOLETE FUNGAL MILDEW OIDIUM AMANITA BOLETUS CHYTRID FUNGOID GEASTER LEPIOTA TRUFFLE AECIDIUM CLATHRUS CORNBELL EUMYCETE FUSARIUM HELVELLA MUCEDINE MUSHROOM OOMYCETE OTOMYCES PHALLOID POLYPORE PUFFBALL RHIZOPUS SAPROGEN SPOROGEN TREMELLA TUCKAHOE STINKHORN NEUROSPORA PENICILLIUM
(KIND OF —) PORE
(PLANT —) UREDO
(UNICELLULAR —) BEES EAST YEAST
(PREF.) AGARICI BASIDIO HYDNO MYC(ET)(ETO)(O)
(SUFF.) MYCES MYCET(O) MYCETE(S) MYCOSIS
(— DISEASE) OSIS

FUNK FUNG NESH

FUNKY HIP FOUL PANICKY

FUNNEL CAST STACK TEWEL TRUNK FILLER FUMMEL HOPPER SIPHON SYPHON TUNNEL TUNNER TRUMPET TUNDISH HYPONOME WINDSAIL
(UNDERGROUND —) SWALLET SWALLOW
(PREF.) CHOAN(O)
(SUFF.) CHOANITE CHOANITIC

FUNNY ODD GOOD COMIC DROLL MERRY QUEER COMICAL JOCULAR RISIBLE STRANGE HUMOROUS
(VERY —) SPLITTING SIDESPLITTING

FUR FOX BEAR CALF COON FLIX FLUE FOIN GRAY GREY GRIS MINK PEAN

PELF PELL PILE SEAL VAIR BUDGE
COYPU CROSS FITCH FLICK GENET
GRISE OTTER PAHMI SABLE SCARF
SHUBA BADGER BEAVER COUGAR
DESMAN ERMINE FISHER GALYAC
JACKET MARTIN NUTRIA PELAGE
POTENT RABBIT SPRING SUSLIK
TANUKI CALABER CARACAL FITCHET
FITCHEW FURRURE MINIVER
TOPCOAT CACOMIXL ERMINOIS
KOLINSKI
(— OF LAMBSKIN AND WOOL)
BUDGE
(— OF SABLE) ZIBELINE
(— RESEMBLING PERSIAN LAMB)
KRIMMER
(BEAVER —) WOOM CASTOR
(GRAY —) GRAY GREY GRIS GRISE
CRIMMER LETTICE
(HERALDIC —) PEAN
(LAMB —) CARACUL KARAKUL
(NUMBER OF — SKINS) TIMBER
TIMMER
(RABBIT —) CONY SCUT CONEY
FLICK LAPIN HATTER SUSLIK SEALINE
SOUSLIK ERMILINE
(SQUIRREL —) SISEL CALABAR
(SQUIRREL OR MARTIN —) AMICE
POPEL
(STONE MARTEN'S —) FOIN
(PL.) PELTRY FURRIERY
(PREF.) DORA
FURBEARER PLATINUM
FURBELOW DIDO FRILL FALBALA
FURBISH DO FIG RUB FAKE FINE
VAMP CLEAN SCOUR FINIFY POLISH
BURNISH VARNISH RENOVATE
FURCATE FORKY BRANCH FURCAL
FURCULA SPRING FURCULUM
FURCULUM WISHBONE
FURFOOZ GRENELLE
FURIES DIRAE ALECTO ERINYS
ERINYES MEGAERA ERINNYES
TISIPHONE
FURIOUS MAD GRIM WOOD YOND
ANGRY BRAIN GIDDY IRATE LIVID
RABID SHARP FIERCE FURIAL FURIED
INSANE RENISH STORMY ACHARNE
FRANTIC HOPPING MADDING
MANKIND PELTING RAGEOUS
REDWOOD RUSHING TEARING
VIOLENT FRENZIED MAENADIC
TOWERING VEHEMENT VESUVIAN
WRATHFUL
FURIOUSLY CRAZY ANGERLY
TEARING
FURL FOLD HAND ROLL STOW WRAP
FRESE TRUSS FARDEL FURDLE
TAKEIN
FURLED IN
FURLONG SHOT STADE
FURLOUGH LEAVE BLIGHTY

FURNACE ARC KILN OVEN TANK
BENCH CUPEL DRIER DRYER FORGE
MOUTH TISAR BURNER CALCAR
COCKLE CUPOLA HEATER ATHANOR
CHAFERY CRESSET FIREPOT
PUDDLER ROASTER BESSEMER
BLOOMERY CALCINER CHAUFFER
FIREWORK IRONCLAD LIMEKILN
PRODUCER REFINERY TRYWORKS
(— DOOR) TWEEL
(ALMOND —) ALMAN
(ARC —) HEROULT
(GLASS-HEATING —) TISAR
(PLUMBER'S —) DEVIL
(PORTABLE —) DANDY CRESSET
FURNACEMAN BUSTLER DROSSER
SMELTER IMPROVER REHEATER
FURNISH ARM SOW DECK FEAT FEED
FILL FRET FRUB GIVE LEND TRIM
VEST ARRAY BESEE ENDOW EQUIP
FRAME INDUE PITCH POINT SERVE
SPEED STOCK STORE STUFF AFFORD
GRAITH INSURE INVEST OUTFIT
RENDER SUPPLY ADVANCE APPAREL
APPOINT BRACKET GARNISH
INSTORE PERFORM PLENISH
PRESENT PRODUCE PROVIDE
SUFFICE ACCOUTER DECORATE
FRUBBISH MINISTER ACCOMMODATE
(— ABUNDANTLY) FREQUENT
(— ANALYSIS) ACCOUNT
(— FULLY) CHARGE
(— REFRESHMENT) EASE
(— WITH) BESEE
(— WITH DRINK) BIRL BYRL
(— WITH MEALS) BOARD
(— WITH NEW PARTS) RETROFIT
(— WITH POWER) QUALIFY
(— WITH STEEP SLOPE) ESCARP
(— WITH STRENGTH) MAN
(— WITH TROOPS) GARRISON
(— WITH WINGS) IMP
FURNISHED ARMED BODEN GARNI
(COMFORTABLY —) BEIN
FURNISHING ADVANCE FITMENT
(PL.) STUFF BAGGAGE PENATES
FURNITURE ADAM BUHL TIRE
SAMAN STOOL STUFF GRAITH
FITMENT INSIGHT MEUBLES
MOVABLE EQUIPAGE ORNAMENT
SUPELLEX TACKLING
(— PIECE) ETAGERE
(CHEAP —) BORAX
(SHIP'S —) HARNESS
(STORED —) LUMBER
(STYLE OF —) SHERATON
FURORE FUROR BROUHAHA
FURRED PURED LOADED
FURRING PACKING
FURROW FUR GAP GAW RIB RUT
FURR GRIP HINT LINE PLOW RAIN
RILL ROUT RUCK SEAM SULK CHASE

DRAIN DRILL EARTH FIELD RIGOL
SCORE SEUGH STRIA GROOVE
GUTTER INDENT SULCUS SUTURE
TRENCH BREAKER CHAMFER
CHANNEL CRUMPLE FEERING
PLOWING QUILLET SCRATCH
WINDROW WRINKLE CARRIAGE
NOTAULIX THOROUGH VALLECULA
(PREF.) AULAC(O) HOLC(O) LIRELLI
SULCI SULCO

FURROWED SEAMED EXARATE
FURROWY SULCATE TRENCHED

FURROWING KNOT DRESS

FURRY SHAGGY

FUR SEAL URSAL

FURTHER MO AID YET ALSO HELP
YOND ADDED AGAIN FRESH SPEED
SUPRA BEYOND EXTEND SECOND
ADVANCE DEVELOP FARTHER
FORWARD PROMOTE MOREOVER
REMANENT ULTERIOR

FURTHERMORE BESIDES FURTHER
OVERMORE

FURTIVE SLY PRIVY CLAMMY SECRET
SHIFTY SNEAKY HANGDOG
MEACHING MYSTICAL SNEAKING
STEALTHY THIEVISH CLANDESTINE

FURTIVELY SLILY SLYLY SIDELINS

FURTIVENESS STEALTH

FURUNCLE BOIL

FURY HAG IRE MAD WAX BURN RAGE
ANGER BRETH DREAD FUROR IRISH
RIGOR WRATH ALECTO BELDAM
CHOLER FRENZY FURORE MADNESS
MEGAERA WIDDRIM DELIRIUM
FEROCITY VIOLENCE WOODNESS
TISIPHONE

FURZE FUN FUZZ LING ULEX WHIN
GORSE WHINCOW

FUSE RUN CAKE FLOW FLUX FRIT
FUZE MELT WELD BLEND FOUND
FUSEE FUZEE QUILL SMELT SQUIB
SWAGE TRAIN UNITE MINGLE
SPITTER COALESCE CONCRETE
CONFLATE COPULATE PORTFIRE
SAUCISSE COLLIQUATE

FUSED CONNATE

FUSEE FUZEE SPINDLE VESUVIAN
VESUVIUS

FUSELAGE BODY
(— MEMBER) LONGERON

FUSIFORM FUSATE SPINDLE

FUSIL (DIVIDED INTO —S) PLUMETE

FUSION ZYG FLUX UNION FUSURE
CHIASMA FLUXION CYTOGAMY
MITAPSIS PLASMOGAMY
(PREF.) ZYG(O)(OTO)
(SUFF.) APSIS

FUSS DO ADO ROW TEW COIL FAFF
FIKE FIRK FIZZ FRET ROUT SONG
STIR TIME TODO TOUSE TOWSE
TRADE WHAUP BOTHER CADDLE
DIRDUM FANTAD FETTLE FISSLE
FISTLE FIZZLE FRAISE FUFFLE
FUSTLE HOORAY HURRAH PHRASE
POTHER RACKET SETOUT STROTH
TURNUP FOOSTER FRIGGLE FUSSIFY
NAUNTLE POOTHER SPUFFLE
SPUTTER TAMASHA BUSINESS
FOOFARAW SCRONACH

FUSSBUDGET PRIG

FUSSBUDGETY SPOFFISH

FUSSINESS DAINTY FADDLE FIKERY
FOOSTER

FUSSING BOTHER

FUSSY BUSY FIKY FIXY DITSY DITZY
FUDGY PICKY CHICHI FIDDLY FIDFAD
PROSSY SPOFFY SPRUCE STICKY
FIDGETY NIGGLING NOTIONAL
SPOFFISH SQUEAMISH PERSNICKETY

FUSTET ZANTE FUSTIC

FUSTIAN RANT HOLMES PILLOW
BOMBAST TWADDLE CORDUROY
MOLESKIN

FUSTIC LIME MORA FUSTET
DYEWOOD AMARILLO

FUSTINESS FOIST FROWST

FUSTY FOIST MOLDY MUSTY FOISTY
RANCID FROWSTY MALODOROUS

FUTILE IDLE TOOM VAIN OTIOSE
USELESS BOOTLESS FECKLESS
FOOTLESS FUTILOUS HELPLESS
NUGATORY

FUTILITY VANITY NUGACITY
VAINESSE

FUTTAH WHATA

FUTURE TOBE LATER SKULD AVENIR
COMING ONWARD OPTION TOCOME
TOWARD LAVENIR FUTURITY
ONCOMING
(— TIME) MANANA

FUZZ LINTERS

FUZZY LINTY LOUSY MUZZY WOOLY
WOOLLY

FYTTE PASSUS

G

G GEE GOLF GEORGE
GA AKRA ACCRA INKRA
GAAL (FATHER OF —) EBED
GAB GOB YAP BLAB CHIN CHINFEST
GABBLE WAB CANK CHAT CONK
  JAVER BABBLE GAGGLE HABBLE
  PATTER RABBLE TATTER YABBLE
  CLATTER JAUNDER TWADDLE
  TWITTER SLIPSLOP SLUMMOCK
GABBRO BOJITE NORITE EUCRITE
GABION KISH KEESH BASKET
  WALING CORBEIL
GABLE GAVEL GOFOL DETAIL
  DORMER GABLET KENNEL MEMBER
  PINION AILERON PEDIMENT
GABON (CAPITAL OF —) LIBREVILLE
  (LAKE OF —) ANENGUE AZINGUO
  (MOUNTAIN OF —) MPELE IBOUNDJI
  (NATIVE OF —) FANG ADOUMA
  ECHIRA OKANDE
  (RIVER OF —) ABANGA IVINDA
  OGOOUE NGOUNIE
  (TOWN OF —) OYEM BONGO KANGO
  MITZIC OMVANE MAKOKOU
GABOON OKOUME
GABRIELINO TOBIKHAR
GAD GAR RUN FISK GAUD JAZZ RAKE
  JINKET GADLING TRAIPSE VIRETOT
  (— ABOUT) HAIK ROLL STRAM
  GALLANT TROLLOP
  (BROTHER OF —) ASHER
  (FATHER OF —) JACOB
  (MOTHER OF —) ZILPAH
GADABOUT GAD GOER GADDER
  TRAIPSE
GADDI (FATHER OF —) SUSI
GADFLY GAD CLEG GLEG BRIZE
  CLEGG STOUT WHAME BOTFLY
  BREEZE GADBEE OESTRID TABANID
  HORSEFLY
  (PREF.) ESTRA ESTRI ESTRO OESTR(I)
GADGET DODAD GISMO GIZMO
  HICKY DINGUS DOODAD GILGUY
  HICKEY JIGGER JIMJAM WIDGET
  CONCERN DOFUNNY GIMMICK
  WHATNOT BUSINESS DOHICKEY
  GIMCRACK JIMCRACK HOOTNANNY
  CONTRAPTION THINGAMAJIG
  WHANGDOODLE
  (PL.) GIBBLES GUBBINS GADGETRY
GADI (SON OF —) MENAHEM
GADUS MORRHUA
GADWALL RODGE VOLANT
  GADWELL REDWING SHUTTLE
GAEL CELT KELT SCOT GOIDEL
  GAEDHEAL
GAELIC ERSE IRISH

GAFF CLIP SPAR SPUR YARD GAFFLE
  GABLOCK GAFFLET SLASHER
  GAVELOCK
  (— MACKEREL) GAMBEER
GAFFE SLIP
GAFFER STAGEHAND
GAG YAK YUK BOFF GEGG JOKE
  PONG SCOB YOCK YUCK HEAVE
  KEVEL SCOBE AGUAJI MUZZLE
  WHEEZE
  (KIND OF —) SIGHT
GAGA (GO —) FLIP
GAGARIN YURI
GAGE (ALSO SEE GAUGE) LAY PAWN
  WAGE GAUGE JEDGE NORMA
  WAGER FEELER PLEDGE SPIDER
  SCANTLE STANDARD UDOMETER
GAHAM (FATHER OF —) NAHOR
  (MOTHER OF —) REUMAH
GAHERIS (MOTHER OF —)
  MORGANSE
GAIETY JOY GALA JEST RANT CHEER
  MIRTH BAWDRY FROLIC GAYETY
  LEVITY BAUDERY BEGONIA DAFFERY
  DAFFING GAYNESS JOLLITY
  JOYANCE ROLLICK BUOYANCY
  FESTIVAL HILARITY VIVACITY
  (NOISY —) RACKET
GAILY GAY GAYLY BRAVELY LIGHTLY
GAIN BAG DAP GET NET POT WIN
  BEAR BOOT DRAW GROW HAVE
  LAND MAKE PELF SACK TILL ADDLE
  BOOTY CATCH LATCH LUCRE REACH
  SCORE ARRIVE ATTAIN CHIEVE
  DERIVE GATHER INCOME OBTAIN
  PROFIT RACKUP STRAIN CAPTURE
  CONQUER EMBRACE GAYMENT
  GETTING HARVEST POSSESS
  PROCURE REALIZE VANTAGE
  WINNING CLEANING CONQUEST
  PURCHASE PERQUISITE
  (— ADMISSION) ENTER
  (— ADVANTAGE) GLEEK
  (— ASCENDANCY) PREVAIL
  (— BY EXTORTION) SQUEEZE
  (— BY FORTUNE) DRAW HAZARD
  (— COMMAND OF) MASTER
  (— IN FAVOR) PROPITIATE
  (— KNOWLEDGE) EDIFY LEARN
  (— OVER) ENGAGE
  (— UNDERSTANDING) SMOKE
  (— WITHOUT DEDUCTION) CLEAR
  (DISHONEST —) MEED
  (ESTIMATED —) ESTEEM
  (ILL-GOTTEN —) PELF BOODLE
  (ILLICIT —) SPLOSH
  (MATERIAL —) PUDDING

(UNEXPECTED —) DUNCE
(PL.) PICKING PLUNDER GANANCIAS
GAINFUL LUCROUS GAINSOME
GAINSAY DENY FORRID IMPUGN
OPPOSE REFUTE RESIST DISPUTE
RECLAIM WITHSAY AGAINSAY
CONTRAVENE
GAIT BAT JOG GANG LOPE PACE
RACK SKIP STEP TROT VOLT WALK
AMBLE AUBIN GOING STALK TRAIN
ALLURE CANTER GALLOP LOUNGE
SLOUCH SWINGE TODDLE WADDLE
WALLOW WAMBLE WOBBLE
DOGTROT HICKORY PIAFFER
SAUNTER SCUTTLE SHAMBLE
SHUFFLE WALKING WAUCHLE
(— OF ILL-BROKEN HORSE) CHACK
(DEFECTIVE —) WINDING
(LIMPING —) HIRPLE
(UNGAINLY —) SLOUCH
(UNSTEADY —) STAGGER
(4-BEAT —) AMBLE
GAITER SPAT VAMP STRAD BONNET
BRAGAS COCKER GASKIN GUETRE
HOGGER HUGGER LEGGIN PUTTEE
GAMBADE GAMBADO LEGGING
STARTUP BOOTIKIN CUTTIKIN
SPATTERDASH
(PL.) UPPERS GASKINS GAMASHES
GRAMOCHES
GAIZE MALMSTONE
GAJO GORGIO
GALABIA ROBE
GALACTITE MILKSTONE
GALACTOSIDE IDEIN IDAEIN
GALAGO LEMUR LEMUROID
GALAHAD (MOTHER OF —) ELAINE
GALAL (FATHER OF —) ASAPH
JEDUTHUN
GALANAS GAINES
GALAOR (BROTHER OF —) AMADIS
GALATEA (DAUGHTER OF —)
LEUCIPPUS
(FATHER OF —) NEREUS
(HUSBAND OF —) PYGMALION
(LOVER OF —) ACIS
(MOTHER OF —) DORIS
(SON OF —) PAPHUS METHARME
GALAX COLTSFOOT
GALAXY NEBULA SPIRAL
(KIND OF —) SEYFERT
(PREF.) GALACT(O)
GALBANUM FERULA GALBAN
ALBETAD
GALCHA PAMIR
GALE BLOW GELL HELM WIND GAGEL
PERRY STOUR BUSTER EASTER
BAYBUSH BURSTER GALEAGE
TEMPEST FLEAWOOD GALEWORT
NORWESTER
(KIND OF —) NEAR
GALEA MITRA HELMET
GALGA INGUSH

GALIBI CARIBI KALINA
GALINGALE CYPRESS WANHORN
CHINAROOT
GALIPOT BARRAS GALLIPOT
TACAMAHAC
GALJOEN BLACKFISH
GALL GA GAW BAIT FELL FRET NERVE
WRING ANBURY COCKLE HARASS
HUTZPA ANBERRY BEDEGAR
CHUTZPA GALLNUT HUTZPAH
KNOPPER NUTGALL BEDEGUAR
CECIDIUM CHUTZPAH FLEASEED
IRRITATE OAKBERRY SEEDGALL
SPURGALL TACAHOUT
(SAND —) SALT NATRON SANDIVER
(PL.) PURPLES
(PREF.) CHOL(E)(O)
(SUFF.) CHOLIA CHOLY
GALLANT GAY BEAU PROW BLADE
BRAVE BULLY CIVIL JOLLY LOVER
NOBLE PREUX SHOWY SPARK SWAIN
DONZEL ESCORT HEROIC POLITE
RUTTER SPARKY SQUIRE SUITOR
AMATORY AMORIST AMOROSO
AMOROUS CONDUCT GALANTE
GREGORY SPARKER STATELY
TOPPING YOUNKER BELAMOUR
CAVALIER CICISBEO FEMALIST
GALLIARD HANDSOME POLISHED
GALLANTRY GAME DRURY DRUERY
BRAVERY COURAGE PROWESS
CHIVALRY PARAMOUR
GALLBERRY INKBERRY
GALLED RAW
GALLEON CARAC CARRACK
GALLOON
GALLERY POY SAP COOP GODS
JUBE LOFT PAWN ALURE BOYAU
ORIEL PRADO ARCADE BURROW
DEDANS NARROW PIAZZA SCHOOL
SOLLAR SUBWAY TUNNEL BALCONY
GALERIE HEADWAY MIRADOR
TERRACE VERANDA BARTISAN
BRATTICE CANTORIA CORRIDOR
HOARDING PARADISE PREAMBLE
SCAFFOLD TRAVERSE VERANDAH
BLINDSTORY
(— IN BAZAAR) PAWN
(— IN HOUSE OF COMMONS)
VENTILATOR
(— MADE BY INSECT) MINE
(— OF FORT) CASEMATE
(CHURCH —) JUBE LAFT LOFT
(MINE —) BORD BROW SLOVAN
(MINSTREL'S —) ORIEL
(OPEN —) LOGGIA
(UNDERGROUND —) HYPOGEE
HYPOGEUM
GALLEY FUST CUDDY DRAKE FOIST
STICK BIREME GALIOT HEARTH
ZYGITE BASTARD CABOOSE
DRUMOND GALLIOT HEXERIS
KITCHEN LYMPHAD TRIREME

UNIREME CAMBOOSE COOKROOM
CROMSTER GALLEASS RAMBERGE
(— BOTTOM) SLICE
(CHIEFTAIN'S —) BIRLING BIRLINN
(PHILIPPINE —) CALAN
(VIKING —) AESC DRAKE
GALLEY SLAVE FORSADO
SFORZATO
GALLFLY CYNIPID
GALLIMAUFRY HASH OLIO
GALLINACEOUS RASORIAL
GALLINAE RASORES
GALLINAZO VIRU VULTURE
GALLING BITTER
GALLINULE COOT KORA MOHO RAIL
GORHEN PUKEKO SKITTY MOORHEN
STANKIE SULTANA DABCHICK
HYACINTH MANUALII RAILBIRD
RICEBIRD SWAMPHEN
GALLIVANT KITE ROAM ROVE
GALLANT
GALLNUT
(PREF.) CECIDIO CEDIDO
GALLON GAWN CONGIUS
(— OF ORE) DISH
(EIGHTH —) OCTARIUS
(HALF —) POTTLE
(128 —S) LEAGUER
GALLOON ORRIS
GALLOP FOG RUN AUBIN PRICK
CANTER CAREER COURSE TITTUP
WALLOP TANTIVY
GALLOWS NUB CRAP DROP FORK
TREE BOUGH CHEAT FURCA WIDDY
GIBBET WOODIE DERRICK FORCHES
JUSTICE POTENCE STIFLER
WARYTREE
GALLOWS BIRD HEMPY WIDDY
HEMPIE HEMPSEED WIDDIFOW
CRACKROPE
GALOOT OAF
GALOSH ARCTIC ZIPPER EXCLUDER
OVERSHOE
GALUTH GOLUS GOLAHI
GALVANIC VOLTAIC
GALVANIZE ZINC ZINCIFY
SHERADISE
GALVANOMETER DETECTOR
REOMETER
GAMBADO BOOT ANTIC CAPER
GAITER LEGGING
GAMBESON WAMBAIS
GAMBIA (CAPITAL OF —) BANJUL
(COIN OF —) BUTUT DALASI
(LANGUAGE OF —) JOLA WOLOF
FULANI MALINKE
(MONEY OF —) DALASI
(NATIVE OF —) JOLA PEUL WOLOF
DIOLAS FULANI MANDINGO
SERAHULI
(TOWN OF —) KAUUR MANSA
FATOTO BINTANG BRIKAMA
KUNTAUR

GAMBIA POD BABLOH
GAMBIER CATECHU
GAMBIT PLOY MANEUVER
GAMBLE BET DICE GAFF GAME NICK
PLAY PUNT RISK SPORT STAKE
WAGER CHANCE GAMMON HAZARD
PLUNGE FLUTTER
(— AGAINST) BUCK
GAMBLER PIKER SPORT CARROW
DEALER PLAYER PUNTER HUSTLER
PLAYMAN PLUNGER SLICKER
THROWER BLACKLEG GAMESTER
HAZARDER
GAMBLER, THE (CHARACTER IN —)
ALEXEY BLANCHE PAULINE
(COMPOSER OF —) PROKOFIEV
GAMBLING GAMING HAZARDRY
(— CHARGE) VIG VIGORISH
(— DEVICE) PACHINKO
GAMBLING HOUSE HELL TRIPOT
GAMBO GOOSE SPURWING
GAMBOL HOP PLAY ROMP CAPER
FRISK KEVEL PRANK CAREER CAVORT
FROLIC PRANCE GAMBADO
CAPRIOLE
GAMBREL ROOF CAMMOCK
SPREADER
GAME COB FUN JEU JIG GAMY LAKE
MAIL PLAY DANCE DOZEN GAMEY
PARTY SPIEL SPORT WATHE BATTUE
DOZENS MORRIS QUARRY RAMSCH
VENERY JENKINS KNICKER
BREATHER FIGHTING FOREGAME
FRONTENIS
(— CALLED FIVES) HANDBALL
(— EASILY WON) LAUGHER
(— FOR FISHERMEN) SKISH
(— LIKE HANDBALL) FIVES
(— LIKE HOCKEY) DODDART
(— NARROWLY WON) SQUEAKER
(— OF CAT) BILLET
(— OF FIVE HUNDRED) EUCHRE
(— OF FOOTBALL) BOWL CAMP
(— OF FORFEITS) KEN
(— OF HOCKEY) BANDY SHINNY
(— OF INSULTS) DOZENS
(— OF MARBLES) TAW BOWL BONCE
GULLY KEEPS KNUCKS MIGGLES
(— OF MENTAL SKILL) GO CHESS
CHECKERS
(— OF NINEPINS) KAILS KAYLES
(— OF PRISONER'S BASE) CHEVY
CHIVVY
(— WITH BOOMERANG) BRIST
(— WITH COUNTERS) DUMPS GOOSE
(— WITH SHUTTLECOCK) TAHYING
(BACKGAMMON —) HIT IRISH
(BALL —) CAT TUT SNOB CATCH
RUGBY SOCCER SQUASH TENNIS
CRICKET KNAPPAN ONEOCAT
BASEBALL FOOTBALL HANDBALL
SLUGFEST SOFTBALL BROOMBALL
(BASQUE —) JAI

(CALL THE —) LIMIT
(CARD —) AS HUC LOO MAW NAP
OMBRE PIT PUT SET BRAG CENT FARO
FISH FROG GRAB JASS LANT PINK
POOL POPE POST RUFF SANT SKAT
SLAM SNAP SOLO STUD VINT BEAST
BUNCO BUNKO CARDS CARIE CHICO
CINCH COMET CRIMP DECOY GILET
GLEEK GRAND LEAST MONTE
NODDY OMBER OMBRE PEDRO PITCH
POKER PRIME RUMMY SCOPA
SLAMM STOPS STUSS TRUMP
WHIST BANKER BASSET BIRKIE
BOODLE BOSTON BRIDGE CASINO
CHEMMY COMMIT ECARTE EIGHTS
EUCHRE FARMER FLINCH HEARTS
HOWELL LOADUM PANFIL PIQUET
QUINZE RAMSCH ROUNCE SLOUGH
SMUDGE SPIDER TOURNE AUCTION
AUTHORS BELOTTE BEZIQUE
CANASTA CASSINO CAYENNE
CHICAGO COONCAN GARBAGE
HUNDRED JACKPOT PLAFOND
PONTOON PRIMERO REVERSI
SCOPONE SETBACK TRIUMPH
VINGTUN VITESSE BACCARAT
BASEBALL BRISCOLA COMMERCE
CONQUIAN CONTRACT CRIBBAGE
FREAKPOT HANDICAP IMPERIAL
NAPOLEON PATIENCE PENCHANT
PENNEECH PINOCHLE SHOWDOWN
SKINBALL SKINNING SLAPJACK
TREDILLE TRESILLO VERQUERE
VIDERUFF
(CARNIVAL —) HOOPLA
(CHILDREN'S —) TAG DIBS JACKS
KICKBALL PEEKABOO
(CONFIDENCE —) RAMP SCAM STING
MURPHY BIGMITT
(COURSE —) GOLF
(COURT —) PELOTA SQUASH TENNIS
HANDBALL
(DICE —) FARE TRAY BINGO CRAPS
NOVUM RAPHE HAZARD BARBUDI
ADDITION BARBOTTE CAMEROON
HOOLIGAN
(DRAWN —) SPOIL REFAIT
(DRINKING —) HIJINKS
(EGYPTIAN —) SENT SENIT
(FOLLOW THE —) HUNT
(GAMBLING —) EO TAN FARO HAND
KENO PICO BOULE CRAPS MACAO
MONTE POKER PROPS RONDO
STUSS BRELAN HAZARD RONDEAU
ROULETTE
(GENERAL —) HEI HIT HOB NIM TAG
TAW TIG BALL BASE BULL BUNT
BUZZ CENT DIBS DUCK FARE GOLF
HOLE JOWL KENO MALL PALM POLO
POOL SLAM SNOB TICK BANDY
BINGO BONCE BOULE CHESS CHUBA
CHUNK CLOSH DARTS DOLOS FIVES
GOOSE HALMA HOUSE IRISH JACKS

LOTTO LURCH NOVUM NULLO PITCH
PUSSY RUGBY SALTA SALVO SCRUB
TOUCH TROCO WHOOP BEAVER
BEETLE CAROMS CHIVVY CHUNKY
CLUMPS COBNUT COCKAL COOTIE
CRAMBO FEEDER GOBANG GRACES
HAZARD HOOPLA HUBBUB JEREED
KAYLES MERELE PACHIS PELOTA
PLUMPS RAGMAN RINGER SEESAW
SHINNY SIPPIO SKILLO STICKS
TENNIS TIGTAG TIPCAT TIVOLI
TRIGON TRUCKS BALLOON
BEANBAG BEEBALL BOWLING
COBBLER CONKERS CROQUET
CURLING DIABOLO DODDART
DOUBLES DREIDEL ENDBALL
GOGGANS HANGMAN HURLBAT
LOGGATS MAHJONG MATADOR
MUGGINS NETBALL PALLONE
PASSAGE PEEVERS PUSHPIN
QUINTET RINGTAW SARDINE
SQUAILS STATUES TENPINS
TOMBOLA ANAGRAMS BALKLINE
BASEBALL CHARADES CHECKERS
CHOUETTE DOMINOES DOUBLETS
DRAUGHTS DUCKPINS FIVEPINS
FOOTBALL FORFEITS GIVEAWAY
HARDHEAD KICKBALL KORFBALL
LEAPFROG NINEPINS PARCHESI
PEEKABOO PETANQUE PURPOSES
PUSHBALL PYRAMIDS RINGTOSS
ROULETTE ROUNDERS SCRABBLE
SKITTLES STOBBALL STOWBALL
TRAPBALL VERQUERE PARCHEESI
PHILOPENA SHUFFLEBOARD
(GUESSING —) LOVE MORA CANUTE
(INDIAN —) CHUNKY HUBBUB
(INFERIOR —) CHECK
(JAPANESE —) GO
(KIND OF —) VIDEO
(MEXICAN —) FRONTENIS
(NUMBERS —) BUG
(OUTDOOR —) GOLF POLO HURLY
ROQUE RUGBY SOCCER CROQUET
HURLING BASEBALL FOOTBALL
LACROSSE
(PROGRESSIVE —) DRIVE
(PUZZLE —) GLAIK
(QUIZZING —) TRIVIA
(REHEATED —) SALMI SALMIS
(SWINDLING —) BUNCO BUNKO
(SWISS —) JASS
(THREE BOWLING —S) SERIES
(TRAPSHOOTING —) SCOOT
(VIDEO —) ATARI
(WAR —) BARRIERS
(WORD —) GHOST HANGMAN
ANAGRAMS
(PL.) LUDI

GAMECOCK STAG STAIG
GAMEKEEPER GAMIE KEEPER
WALKER WARNER VENERER
WARRENER

GAMESTER DICER PLAYER
GAMBLER PLAYMAN SHARPER
HAZARDER TABLEMAN
GAMETE OVUM SPERM OOCYTE
ZYGOTE GAMETOID OOGAMETE
OOSPHERE
GAMETOCYTE GAMONT CRESCENT
GONOCYTE
GAMETOPHYTE GERMLING
GAMIN TAD ARAB URCHIN
GAVROCHE
GAMMA AGMA
GAMMON BAM
GAMP ORRIS UMBRELLA
GAMUT GAMME RANGE SCALE
SERIES COMPASS DIAGRAM
GANDAREWA (SLAYER OF —)
KERESASPA
GANDER STEG STAIG GANNER
(— AND GEESE) SET
GANDHARI (HUSBAND OF —)
DHRITARASHTRA
GANEF RASCAL
GANESA GUNPUT GANAPATI
GANG MOB SET BAND CORE
CREW GING PACK PAIR PUSH TEAM
BATCH BUNCH GROUP HORDE SPELL
SQUAD CHIURM COFFLE GAGGLE
LAYOUT MOHOCK SCHOOL
COMPANY
(— MEMBER) WHYO
(— MEMBER) SKINHEAD
(— OF CONVICTS) PUSH
(— OF FISHHOOKS) PULLDEVIL
(— OF MINERS) CORE
(— OF WITCHES) COVEN
(GROUP OF —S) MAFIA
(ROWDY —) TRIBULATION
GANGBUSTERS SOCKO
GANGLING GAWKY RANGY GANGLY
GANGLION TUMOR CEREBRUM
GANGPLANK BROW GANGWAY
GANGRENE NOMA CANKER
GANGER SPHACEL NECROSIS
MORTIFICATION
(PREF.) NECR(O) SPHACELO
GANGSTER HOOD PUNK WHYO
APACHE BANDIT COWBOY GUNMAN
GUNSEL CHOPPER
GANGUE MATRIX LODESTUFF
VEINSTONE
GANGWAY BROW ROAD SLIP
LOGWAY TUNNEL CATWALK
COULOIR GATEWAY
GANJA GUNJAH CANNABIS
GANNET BOOBY GAUNT SOLAN
PIQUERO SEAFOWL ALCATRAS
GANTRYMAN DROPMAN
GANYMEDE (BROTHER OF —) ILUS
ASSARACUS
(FATHER OF —) TROS
(MOTHER OF —) CALLIRRHOE

GAOLER (ALSO SEE JAILER) ADAM
ALCAIDE
GAP SAG FLAW GAPE GOWL GULF
MUSE NICK SLAP SLOP WANT BREAK
BRECK CHASM CHAUM CHAWN
CLOVE FRITH MEUSE MUSET NOTCH
SHARD SHERD VUIDE BREACH
GULLET HIATUS LACUNA SPREAD
THROAT VACUUM CLOSING OPENING
VACANCY VACUITY APERTURE
DIASTEMA ENTREFER INTERVAL
MULTIGAP QUEBRADA
(— IN BANK OF STREAM) GAT
(— IN FENCE) SLAP
(— IN FOOTBALL LINE) SLOT
(— IN MEMORY) AMNESIA
(— IN TURF) BUNKER
(— SERVING AS PASS) COL
(VOCAL CORD —) RIMA
(PREF.) CHASMO
GAPE GAN GAP GANT GAUP GAWK
GAWP GAZE GOVE GRIN YAWN
CHAUN GERNE HIATE STARE RICTUS
DEHISCE INHIATE
(PREF.) CHAEN(O)
GAPER COMBER
GAPING GALP AGAPE HIANT CHAPPY
CHASMA GAWISH MOUTHED
RINGENT ADENOIDAL
GAR HOUND SNOOK AGUJON
CHERNA GARFISH GARPIKE BILLFISH
GOREFISH GURDFISH HORNBEAK
HORNFISH HORNKECK LONGJAWS
LONGNOSE
GARAGE HANGAR LOCKUP SIDING
GARRIDGE
(ROW OF —S) MEWS
GARAM MASALA SPICES
GARAVANCE CARAUNA GARBANZO
GARB (ALSO SEE APPEAL AND
DRESS) COWL GEAR TOGA VEST
DRESS GUISE HABIT STOLA APPAREL
CLOTHES COSTUME RAIMENT
GLADRAGS
(LIGHT —) STRIP
(MUSLIM —) IHRAM
(PARTICOLORED —) MOTLEY
(PLAY —) ROMPERS
(RED —) SCARLET
(SPECIAL —) REGALIA
(UNIVERSITY —) ACADEMICALS
GARBAGE GASH SLOP OFFAL TRASH
WASTE GIBLET REFUSE SCRAPS
(— IN — OUT) GIGO
(— IN, — OUT) GIGO
GARBAGEMAN DUSTMAN
GARBLE GELD JUMBLE MANGLE
DISTORT GARBLING MUTILATE
MISREPRESENT
GARDANT AFFRONTE
GARDEN HAW EDEN KNOT TILL YARD
ARBOR GARTH CIRCLE POMACY

POMARY QUINTA ROSARY SHAMBRA
VERGER VIHARA ACADEMY HERBARY
OLITORY ORCHARD ROCKERY
TOPIARY CHINAMPA FLORETUM
HORTYARD KALEYARD LEIGHTON
PARADISE PARTERRE POTAGERE
ROSARIUM CULTIVATE
(— CITY) CHICAGO
(— PLOT) ERF
(— STATE) NEWJERSEY
(BEER —) BRASSERIE
(SECLUDED —) PLEASANCE
(PREF.) HORT(I) TOPI
(SUFF.) ETUM

GARDENER MALI PONICA TILLER
CROPPER PLANNER BOSTANGI

GARDEN HELIOTROPE VALERIAN

GARDENIA TIARA

GARDENING TOPIARY

GARDEN ROCKET RUGOLA
ARUGULA EVEWEED

GARDEN-VARIETY AVERAGE

GARDEN WARBLER JACK HAYBIRD
BECAFICO FAUVETTE FIGEATER

GARFISH (SEE GAR)

GARGAMELLE (SON OF —)
GARGANTUA

GARGANEY TEAL CRICK

GARGANTUA AND PANTAGRUEL
(AUTHOR OF —) RABELAIS
(CHARACTER IN —) JOHN BRIDE
BACBUC TRIPPE BADEBEC PANURGE
ANARCHUS JOBERLIN GARGANTUA
TRIBOULET GARGAMELLE
GRANGOSIER HOLOFERNES
PANTAGRUEL PICROCHOLE
PONOCRATES ENTOMMEURES
TROUILLOGAN RAMINAGROBIS

GARGANTUAN HUGE VAST GIANT
HOMERIC TITANIC ENORMOUS
GIGANTIC HOMERIAN

GARGET MASTITIS

GARGLE GURGLE COLLUTORY

GARGOYLE BOSS

GARIBALDI GOLDFISH

GARISH GAUDY GIDDY SHOWY
CRIANT GLARING

GARISHNESS GLARE

GARLAND BAY LEI CROWN TORAN
VITTA ANADEM CORONA CRANTS
ROSARY WREATH CHAPLET
CORANCE CORONAL FESTOON
(PREF.) STEMMATI STEPHAN(O)

GARLIC AJO MOLY RAMP CHIVE
PORET ALLIUM PORRET RAMSON

GARMENT GI DUD TOG BACK BRAT
COAT GOWN PELL PELT RAIL ROBE
SARI SARK SHAG SILK SLIP SLOP
SULU VEST WEED ABAYA BUREL
BURKA CENTO CLOAK CLOTH COTTE
CYMAR DRESS FROCK HABIT HAORI
JOSEY JUPON KHAKI MANGA

NABOB SHAWL SHIFT SHIRT SIMAR
SKIRT STOLE WRIEL ALPACA ATTIRE
BARROW BLOUSE BOUBOU BURKHA
CAFTAN CAMLET CAPOTE CHAMMA
COTTON CYCLAS ERMINE EXOMIS
FECKET HUIPIL JACKET JERSEY
JUMPER KERSEY KIRTLE MOHAIR
MOTLEY SARONG SHORTY SHROUD
STROUD TAMEIN ZIZITH AMICTUS
BLOUSON BROIGNE BUNTING
CAMBLET CASSOCK CHIRIPA
CRAWLER CUCULLA CULOTTE
DOUBLET FALDING FLOCKET
GROGRAM PALETOT PELISSE
RAIMENT SHORTIE SURCOAT
SWEATER VESTURE WRAPPER
BATHROBE BODYSUIT CAMELINE
CAPUCHIN CHAUSSES COLOBIUM
CORSELET COVERALL DEERSKIN
EPIBLEMA GAMBESON GUERNSEY
HIMATION INDUMENT PADUASOY
PULLOVER SCAPULAR SEALSKIN
SLIPOVER SNOWSUIT VESTMENT
WEARABLE PETTICOAT REDINGOTE
STROUDING
(— OF DERVISH) KHIRKAH
(— OF HERALD) TABARD
(— OF HIGH PRIEST) EPHOD
(— OF PATCHES) CENTO
(ARAB —) ABA
(ARABIAN —) ABA
(BABY'S —) BARROW CRAWLER
CREEPER
(BADLY-MADE —) DRECK
(BLUE —) MAZARINE
(BURIAL —) SHROUD
(COARSE —) BRAT STROUD
(DEFENSIVE —) JACK BROIGNE
GAMBESON
(ECCLESIASTICAL —) STOLE RHASON
ROCHET CASSOCK
(ECCLIASTICAL —) FANON ORALE
CHASUBLE
(ETHIOPIAN —) CHAMMA
(HINDU —) SARI SAREE
(INFANT'S —) BARRY BARROW DIAPER
BUNTING SLEEPER PANTYWAIST
(INQUISITION —) SANBENITO
(JAPANESE —) HAORI
(LEATHER —) BUFF
(LINEN —) LINE
(LONG —) JIBBA KANZU STOLE
JIBBEH MANDYAS PELISSE HIMATION
(MALAY —) SARONG
(MEDIEVAL —) ROCHET CHAUSSES
DALMATIC GAMBESON
(MONK'S —) SCAPULAR
(MOURNING —) SABLE
(ONE-PIECE —) BODYSUIT JUMPSUIT
(ONE-PIECE WOMAN'S —) CATSUIT
(OUTER —) BRAT COAT GOWN HAIK
HYKE SLOP WRAP FROCK HAORI

NABOB PALLA PILCH SMOCK
DOLMAN ROCHET CHEMISE GALABIA
PALETOT SURCOAT SWEATER
HIMATION OVERSLOP
(PADDED —) TRUSS
(PENITENTIAL —) CILICE
(PULLOVER —) DASHIKI
(RED —) SCARLET
(ROMAN —) TOGA
(SLEEVELESS —) ABA CAPE COWL
VEST MANTLE CUCULLA GANDURAH
(SQUARE —) KAROSS
(SYRIAN —) ABAYA
(THIN —) GOSSAMER
(TIGHT-FITTING —) HOSE COTTE
TRICOT LEOTARD
(WOMAN'S —) IZAR BURKA CYMAR
NABOB SIMAR BURKHA CHITON
JOSEPH PEPLOS PEPLUM VISITE
BLOUSON BURNOUS
(PL.) GEAR COSTUME GARNISH
FLANNELS
(PREF.) RHACO
GARNER REAP MOPUP STORE
GATHER IMBARN COLLECT
GARNET YAG YIG GRENAT PYROPE
ANTHRAX GRANATE OLIVINE
VERMEIL ESSONITE MELANITE
ROSOLITE YANOLITE CARBUNCLE
RHODOLITE UVAROVITE
(SYNTHETIC —) YAG
(YTTRIUM IRON —) YIG
GARNISH LARD TRIM ADORN DRESS
EQUIP MENSE STICK FURNISH
PARSLEY TOPPING CHUMMAGE
DECORATE DUXELLES ORNAMENT
GARNISHED GARNI
(— WITH GRAPES) VERONIQUE
(— WITH VEGETABLES)
BOUQUETIERE
GARNISHEE CHECK FACTOR
GARNISH
GARRET ATTIC SOLAR SOLLAR
MANSARD COCKLOFT
GARRISON WARD STUFF PRESIDY
WARNISON
GARROTE STRANGLE
GARRULITY POLYLOGY
GARRULOUS GABBY TALKY WORDY
BABBLY TONGUY VOLUBLE
GARTER GARTEN LEGLET ELASTIC
STRAPPLE
GARTH CORTILE OUTGARTH
GARUM LIQUAMEN
GAS DAMP XENON FLATUS GENAPP
LEAVEN OXYGEN PETROL EXHAUST
KRYPTON PROPANE YPERITE
AFTERGAS ETHERION FIREDAMP
HYDROGEN STANNANE VESICANT
(— CONSTANT) R
(— FUEL) ETHANE
(COLORLESS —) OXAN OXANE
KETENE GERMANE STIBINE SILICANE

(EXPLOSIVE —) METHYLAMINE
(KIND OF —) NERVE
(MARSH —) METHANE
(NERVE —) SARIN
(NONCOMBUSTIBLE —) INERT
(POISONOUS —) ARSINE ADAMSITE
AQUINITE CYANOGEN PHOSGENE
BRETONITE PHOSPHINE
(RADIOACTIVE —) THORON
(TEAR —) ACROLEIN
(VOLCANIC —) MOFETTE
(PREF.) MANO PNEUM(O)(ON)(ONO)
PNEUMA PNEUMAT(O)
(CONTAINING —) PYOPNEUMO
(PRESENCE OF —) PHYS(O)
(SUFF.) (INERT —) ON
GAS-BURNER BUNSEN
GASCONADE BRAG CROW BOAST
BLUSTER
GASEOUS AERIFORM GASIFORM
VOLATILE
GASH CUT CHOP LASH BLASH CRIMP
GANCH GRIDE SCORE SLASH SLISH
SCOTCH SLUICE TRENCH INCISION
INCISURE
(— A FISH) RIM
GASKET LUTE CASKET GASKIN
GROMMET SCISSIL
GASKIN BRAGAS
GASOLINE AVGAS JUICE PETROL
BENZINE NATURAL
GASP FOB BLOW GAPE KINK PANK
PANT CHINK CROAK FETCH THRATCH
GASPING CHINK
GASTEROPOD WHELK STROMB
UNICORN PTEROPOD
GASTRONOME EPICURE
GASTROPOD SLUG DRILL HARPA
OLIVA SNAIL BUCKIE NERITE
ABALONE MOLLUSK TOXIFER
UNIVALVE VELUTINA PULMONATE
PROSOBRANCH
GAT HEATER
GATAM (FATHER OF —) ELIPHAZ
GATE BAB BAR JET HEAD LIFT PORT
SASH SLAP TAKE YATE YETT ENTRY
HATCH JANUA PURSE SALLY SPRAY
STICK TORAN ENAJIM ESCAPE
FENDER FUNNEL HARROW INGATE
LIGGAT PADDLE PORTAL RUNNER
TIMBER TORANA WICKET ZAGUAN
BARRIER CLICKET FIVEBAR
GATEWAY LIDGATE POSTERN
SHUTTER ABOIDEAU ANTEPORT
DECUMANA ENTRANCE FOREGATE
GURDWARA PENSTOCK TOLLGATE
TOWNGATE TRIMTRAM TURNPIKE
ELECTRODE
(— OF CASTLE) BAR
(— OF DRYDOCK) CAISSON
(BACK —) POSTERN
(COMPUTER —) AND
(CUSTOMS —) BARRIER

(IRRIGATION —) CHECK TAPON TAPPOON
(LICH —) SCALLAGE TRIMTRAM
(RUNNING —) FUNNEL
(SAW —) FRAME
(SAWMILL —) SASH
(SLALOM —S) HAIRPIN
(SLUICE —) HATCH VALVE
(TEMPLE —) VIMANA
(TIDE —) ABOIDEAU ABOITEAU
(WATER —) SLUICE
(PREF.) PYL(E)
GATEADO DIOMATE
GATEHOUSE BAR LODGE
GATEKEEPER WARDEN CERBERUS GATEWARD PORTITOR STILEMAN
GATEMAN GUARD
GATEPOST DURN HARR HEEL PIER POST SHAFT POSTEL
GATEWAY DAR DOOR GATE LOKE PORT TORU PYLON TORAN TORII BARWAY GOPURA TORANA PROPYLON
(COMPUTER —) PORT
GATHER GET LEK POD WIN BAND BREW CLAN CLOT CHOP CULL FURL HERD HIVE HOST PICK REAP RELY TUCK AMASS BANGE BROOM BUNCH FLOCK GI FAN GUESS INFER LEASE PLUCK RAISE SWEEP ACCRUE COMPEL CORRAL DECERP DERIVE GARNER HUDDLE HUSTLE IMBARN MUSTER RAMASS SCRAPE CLUSTER COLLATE COLLECT COMPILE CONGEST CONVENE CONVOKE HARVEST RAMMASS RECRUIT ASSEMBLE CUMULATE SHEPHERD
(— AS ARMY) HOST
(— BY SCRAPING) SCRATCH
(— GRAPES) VINDEMIATE
(— GRASS SEED) STRIP
(— HEADWAY) SET
(— HERBS) SIMPLE
(— IN A HEAP) HATTER
(— IN RAGS) TAT
(— SEWING) GAGE GAUGE
(— UP) KILT
(SUFF.) LEGE
GATHERED KILTED CUMULATE
GATHERER GEDDER TUCKER RUFFLER CHICLERO PLICATOR PUCKERER
GATHERING BEE HUI LED LEK SUM FAIR FEST KNOT SING SIVA LEVEE SHINE TRYST AFFLUX INDABA MUDDLE PLISSE POWWOW RUELLE SMOKER COLLECT COMMERS COMPANY FUNFEST HARVEST HOSTING HUSKING JOLLITY KLATSCH MEETING MOOTING NYMPHAL ROCKING TURNOUT ASSEMBLY CONCLAVE FUNCTION JAMBOREE PANIONIA POTATION

RECOURSE SINGSONG SOCIABLE STAMPEDE
(— FOR DANCING) FANDANGO
(— OF ANIMALS) DRIVE
(— OF ARMED MEN) HOSTING
(— OF CLOTH) SHIRR SHIRRING
(— OF FILM) CISSING
(— OF SCOUTS) CAMPOREE JAMBOREE
(— OF TEAM) HUDDLE
(— OF WITCHES) COVEN
(— OF WOMEN) HENPARTY
(— PLACE) LESCHE
(BASUTO —) PITSO
(FORMAL —) HALL
(RELIGIOUS —) SHOUT
(SOCIAL —) BEE FRY BAKE BALL CLUB DRUM STAG WINE BAILE BINGE BINGO DANCE MIXER SHIVOO SMOKER CANTICO COTERIE KLATSCH SHINDIG SQUEEZE BARBECUE CAMPFIRE CLAMBAKE TALKFEST RECEPTION SYMPOSIUM
(STUDENTS' —) KOMMERS
(THREE DAY —) CURSILLO
(SUFF.) (FESTIVE —) FEST
GAU BANT
GAUCHE CLUMSY AWKWARD
GAUD GAY GAUDY FANGLE VANITY TRINKET
GAUDINESS GLARE GLITTER
GAUDY GAY LOUD CHEAP FLARY SHOWY VAUDY BRAZEN FLASHY FLIMSY FLORID GARISH GAWISH SKYRIN TAWDRY TINSEL BRANKIE CHINTZY FLARING GAUDISH GLARING BRUMMAGEM MERETRICIOUS
GAUGE (ALSO SEE GAGE) BORE GAGE MOOT PLUG SIZE TRAM GADGE NORMA RANGE DENTIN FEELER FORMER GABARI DEPTHEN TEMPLET TRAMMEL ESTIMATE INDICANT MEASURER STANDARD SURFACER TEMPLATE MANOMETER
(— FOR SLATES) SCANTLE
(RAIN —) UDOMETER
GAUGER SURVEYOR
GAUL GALLIA
(PL.) PICTONES
GAULISH
(PREF.) GALLO
GAUNT BONY GRIM LANK LEAN SLIM THIN PINED SPARE THIRL BARREN HAGGED HOLLOW MEAGER MEAGRE SHELLY SKINNY HAGGARD SCRAWNY SLENDER DESOLATE RAWBONED CADAVEROUS
GAUNTLET TOP CUFF GLOVE GANTLET GAINPAIN GANTLOPE
GAUR BISON SELADANG
GAUZE LISSE MARLI MARLY UMPLE CYPRUS CYPRESS TIFFANY CARBASUS

GAUZY FILMY
GAVE GIN GUV YAF YAFE
GAVEL HAMMER GAVELAGE
GAVIAL NAKOO LIZARD GHARIAL
LORICATE
GAVOTTE MUSETTE
GAWK GAWKY GAWNEY LUMPKIN
RAMMACK
GAWKY GOWKIT ANGULAR
AWKWARD GAWKISH
GAY MAD AIRY BOON DAFT GLAD
GLEG HIGH RORY TRIM WILD BONNY
BUXOM GAUDY JOLLY LIGHT MERRY
NITID RIANT RORTY SUNNY VAUDY
WLONK ALEGER BLITHE CHEERY
FLASHY FRISKY FROLIC GARISH
JOCUND JOVIAL JOYFUL JOYOUS
KIPPER LIVELY SOCIAL SPORTY
WANTON BOBBISH CHIPPER FESTIVE
GALLANT GIOJOSO GLEEFUL
LARKING RACKETY SMICKER
SMILING TITTUPY WINSOME
CAVALIER DEBONAIR FROHLICH
GAMESOME PLEASANT PRIMROSE
SPARKISH SPLENDID SPORTIVE
GAY-FEATHER LIATRIS
GAYUMART (SLAYER OF —)
ANGROMAINYUS
(SON OF —) SIYAMAK
GAYWINGS MAYWINGS
GAZE EYE PRY CAPE GAPE GOUK
GOWK LEER LOOK MOON OGLE PEER
PORE SCAN TOOT GLAIK GLARE
GLOAT GLORE SIGHT STARE TWIRE
VISIE WLITE ASPECT GLOWER
REGARD AFTEREYE
GAZELLE AHU GOA ADMI AOUL
CORA DAMA MOHR ADDRA ARIEL
KORIN MHORR DZEREN GROUSE
ALGAZEL CHIKARA CORINNE
DIBATAG TABITHA CHINKARA
GAZELLE HOUND SALUKI
GAZETTE COURANT JOURNAL
(— OF CRIMES) HUE
GAZEZ (FATHER OF —) CALEB HARAN
(MOTHER OF —) EPHAH
GE TAPUYAN
GEAN MERRY MURIE MURRY GUIGNE
GASKINS
GEAR KIT SPUR TACK TRIM IDLER
TOOTH FOURTH GRAITH HYPOID
PINION TACKLE CLOBBER GEARING
HARNESS REVERSE RIGGING
SEGMENT TRILOBE BACKPACK
HEADGEAR OVERDRIVE
(— OF DIVER) ARMOR
(CAR —) LOW HIGH FIRST SECOND
REVERSE
(CHAFING —) SCOTCHMAN
(DEFENSIVE —) ARMORY
(RUNNING —) CARRIAGE
(TRANSMISSION —) HIGH FIRST
SPEED FOURTH SECOND REVERSE

GEARED GIRT
GEARWHEEL UNILOBE WABBLER
WOBBLER
GEB KEB SEB
GEBER (FATHER OF —) URI
GECKO FANFOOT TARENTE
GEKKONID LACERTID
GEDALIAH (FATHER OF —) AHIKAM
(SLAYER OF —) ISHMAEL
GEE WOW GOSH GOLLY JEEPERS
GEELBEC SALMON TERAGLIN
GEEPOUND SLUG
GEESE SET
GEEZER COOT
GEIGER TREE ALOEWOOD
SEBESTEN
GEL JELL JELLY LIVER GELATE
ALCOGEL
GELATIN AGAR GLUE COLLIN
GLUTIN GLUTOID HAITSAI NORGINE
ISINGLASS
GELATINOUS COLLOID MUCULENT
COLLOIDAL JELLYLIKE
GELD LIB GELT ALTER CASTRATE
GELDING HORSE SPADE SPADO
GEM GIM JADE ONYX OPAL RUBY
SARD AGATE BERYL BIJOU CAMEO
JAZEL JEWEL PEARL SPARK STONE
TOPAZ ZIMME AMULET BAGUET
CRUSTA GARNET IOLITE JASPER
PEBBLE PYROPE RONDEL ZIRCON
ASTERIA CITRINE DIAMOND
DOUBLET EMERALD JACINTH
KUNZITE ONEGITE PERIDOT SPARKLE
ACHROITE AMATRICE AMETHYST
BAGUETTE HYACINTH INTAGLIO
MARQUISE ORIENTAL RONDELLE
SAPPHIRE SARDONYX HIDDENITE
MOONSTONE RUBICELLE
(— CARVED IN RELIEF) CAMEO
INTAGLIO
(— ENGRAVED WITH CHARM)
ABRAXAS
(— OF IMPERFECT BRILLIANCY)
LOUPE
(— REFLECTING LIGHT IN 6 RAYS)
ASTERIA
(— STATE) IDAHO
(— SURFACE) BEZEL FACET
(IMITATION —) PASTE
(MYTHICAL —) CARBUNCLE
(TRANSPARENT —) IOLITE
(UNCUT —) ROUGH CABOCHON
GEMALLI (SON OF —) AMMIEL
GEMARIAH (FATHER OF —) HILKIAH
SHAPHAN
(SON OF —) MICHAIAH
GEMMA BUD GEMMULE
SOREDIUM
GEMMULE SPORE BROODSAC
GEMMY EMERALD
GEMSBOK ORYX KOKAMA
GEMSBUCK

GEMSTONE JADE STAR CHEVEE
PYROPE SPINEL EMERALD FISHEYE
CROSSCUT HYALITHE MORGANITE
TANZANITE
(PART OF —) BEZEL CROWN CULET
FACET TABLE GIRDLE PAVILION
(SYNTHETIC —) YAG

GENA CHEEK

GENDER SEX KIND CLASS FEMININE

GENE GEN ALLEL ALLELE AMORPH
FACTOR LETHAL PRIMER CYTOGENE
MODIFIER POLYGENE RECESSIVE
(— MATERIAL) DNA
(GROUP OF 8) OPERON
(SET OF —S) HAPLOTYPE

GENEALOGY PEDIGREE

GENERAL (ALSO SEE SOLDIER) MAIN
MOST BROAD GROSS ATAMAN
COMMON HETMAN PUBLIC VULGAR
CURRENT GENERIC MARSHAL
SUMMARY AUFIDIUS CANIDIUS
CATHOLIC ECUMENIC ENCYCLIC
OVERHEAD PANDEMIC PUFIDIUS
STRATEGE BRIGADIER
(PL.) DIADOCHI
(PREF.) CAEN(O) CEN(O) COEN(O) PAN

GENERALITY CREDO GENERALE

GENERALIZATION LAW AXIOM
BROMIDE

GENERALIZE WIDEN EXTEND
SPREAD BROADEN

GENERALIZED GROSS GLOBAL

GENERALLY ASARULE BROADLY
LARGELY OVERALL ROUNDLY
MOSTWHAT

GENERALSHIP STRATEGY

GENERATE MAKE SIRE TEEM BEGET
BREED IMPEL SPAWN STEAM CREATE
FATHER GENDER IMPOSE KITTLE
DEVELOP INBREED PRODUCE
ENGENDER
(— PUS) DIGEST

GENERATION AGE KIND TIME
WORLD STRAIN STRIND DESCENT
DIPLOID GETTING KINDRED
GAMOBIUM GENITURE SAECULUM
THEOGONY TRIPLOID UPSPRING
OFFSPRING
(FUTURE —S) POSTERITY
(SPONTANEOUS —) ABIOGENESIS
(SUFF.) GON(E)(IDIUM)(IMO)(IUM)(Y)

GENERATIVE GENIAL GAMETIC
GENESIC GENETIC SEEDFUL
SEMINAL PROLIFIC

GENERATOR KIPP BUZZER DYNAMO
RULING ELEMENT DIPHASER
GENERANT OSCILLATOR

GENEROSITY GRACE LARGE
BOUNTY GENTRY BREADTH
FREEDOM HONESTY COURTESY
GOODNESS KINDNESS LARGESSE

GENEROUS BIG FREE OPEN SOFT
FRANK HEFTY LARGE NOBLE LIBERAL
GRACIOUS HANDSOME INSORDID
LARGEOUS MAGNIFIC OPENHANDED

GENEROUSLY LUCKY MANLY
KINDLY FRANKLY

GENESIS BIRTH ORIGIN BERESHIT
GENETICS

GENET BERBE CIVET DAPPLE
VIVERRINE

GENEVA GIN

GENIAL BEIN BIEN WARM DOUCE
SONSY DOULCE FORTHY FURTHY
HEARTY KINDLY MELLOW MENTAL
CHEERFUL GRACIOUS PLEASANT

GENIALITY BONHOMIE

GENICULATE KNEED ELBOWED

GENIE GENIUS HATHOR SANDMAN

GENII XIN JANN

GENIN BUFAGIN

GENIP GINEP JAGUA IRONWOOD

GENIPAP LANA GENIP JAGUA
GUENEPE

GENISTA FURZE RETAMA

GENITAL SECRET
(PL.) HARNESS PRIVITY GENITURE

GENITALS
(PREF.) FDE(O)

GENIUS KA FIRE GIFT HAPI KALI
TURN ANGEL BRAIN DEMON GENIO
KNACK NUMEN DAEMON INGENY
INGINE TALENT WIZARD DUSTMAN
DUAMUTEF EINSTEIN FRAVASHI
PENCHANT SILVANUS
(— OF LANGUAGE) IDIOM

GENOA GEANE

GENOTYPE BIOTYPE LOGOTYPE

GENOUILLERE KNEELET

GENRE EPIC KIND SORT TYPE CLASS
STYLE FABLIAU SPECIES CATEGORY

GENS CLAN HOUSE

GENSERIC (BROTHER OF —)
GONDERIC GONTHARIS
(FATHER OF —) GODIGISDUS

GENTEEL NICE GENTY GENTIL
JAUNTY POLITE STYLISH GRACEFUL

GENTIAN BIT FELWORT AGUEWEED
GALLWEED BALDMONEY
PENNYWORT

GENTILE ARIAN ARYAN HEATHEN

GENTILITY COUTH POLISH CIVILITY
GENTRICE NICENESS

GENTLE MOY CALM DEFT DEWY FAIR
HEND KIND MEEK MILD MURE NESH
SLOW SOFT SOOT TAME BLAND
CANNY LIGHT LITHE MILKY QUIET
SMALL SOBER SWEET BENIGN
BONAIR CADISH DOCILE FACILE
LYDIAN MODEST PLACID REMISS
SILKEN SILVER SOFTLY TENDER
AFFABLE AMABILE CLEMENT
GRADUAL SOAKING SUBDUED
DEBONAIR DELICATE DOVELIKE
EGGSHELL LAMBLIKE LENITIVE
MAIDENLY MANSUETE MODERATE

PEACEFUL SARCENET TOWARDLY
TRANQUIL
(— AS OF THE WIND) LOOM
GENTLEFOLK GENTRY GENTILITY
GENTLEMAN NIB SIR BABU GENT
TOFF BABOO CURIO DORAY SAHIB
SENOR GEMMAN MILORD SENHOR
SIGNOR YONKER BRAVERY GALLANT
GENTMAN MYNHEER CAVALIER
MIRABELL SEIGNEUR SEIGNIOR
SQUIREEN
(— COMMONER) HAT
(— TRAINING FOR KNIGHTHOOD)
DONZEL
(— WITHOUT FORTUNE) STALKO
(COUNTRY —) SQUIRE
(GIPSY —) RYE
(MALAY —) TUAN
(MILITARY —) CADET
(POOR —) BUCKEEN
(WOULD-BE —) SHONEEN
(PL.) HERREN CHIVALRY
GENTLEMAN-AT-ARMS
PENSIONER
GENTLEMANLY JAUNTY
GENTLENESS FLESH LENITY
AMENITY DOUCEUR CLEMENCY
KINDNESS MANSUETUDE
GENTLY SOFT CANNY SOAVE EASILY
FAIRLY LIGHTLY EASYLIKE PRETTILY
TENDERLY
GENTRY COUNTY GENTRICE
SQUIRAGE SZLACHTA
GENUBATH (FATHER OF —)
HADAD
GENUFLECTION VENIE KNEELING
GENUINE ECHT GOOD LEAL PURE
REAL TRUE VRAI PLAIN PUKKA SOLID
ACTUAL ARRANT DINKUM DIRECT
HONEST KOSHER PISTIC CURRENT
GERMANE GRADELY SINCERE
VERIDIC GRAITHLY STERLING
RIGHTEOUS
(NOT —) TIN SHAM BOGUS PLASTIC
PRETENDED
(SEEMINGLY —) COLORABLE
(SUFF.) (NOT —) ASTER
GENUINENESS VERIDITY
GENUS KIND CLASS ANALOG
GENDER GENERAL
(— OF ALGAE) DASYA FUCUS
BANGIA CHORDA CODIUM HYPNEA
NOSTOC PADINA DIATOMA
LEMANEA LIAGORA PTILOTA
VALONIA ZYGNEMA ANABAENA
BRYOPSIS CAULERPA CERAMIUM
CHONDRUS CONFERVA CUTLERIA
DICTYOTA DUMONTIA GELIDIUM
GOMONTIA HALIMEDA LERAMIUM
LESSONIA NEMALION OOCYSTIS
PALMELLA PORPHYRA STRIARIA
TAONURUS ULOTHRIX
(— OF AMOEBA) CHAOS

(— OF AMPHIBIAN) HYLA RANA
SIREN PROTEUS AMPHIUMA
NECTURUS
(— OF ANT) ATTA ECITON LASIUS
PONERA TERMES FORMICA
PHEIDOLE TAPINOMA
(— OF ANTELOPE) ORYX KOBUS
BUBALIS GAZELLA MADOQUA
REDUNCA ANTILOPE EGOCERUS
(— OF APE) PAN PONGO SIMIA
(— OF APHID) ADELGES CHERMES
(— OF ARACHNID) ACARUS
GALEODES
(— OF ARMADILLO) DASYPUS
XENURUS
(— OF ASCIDIAN) CIONA MOLGULA
BOLTENIA PYROSOMA
(— OF ASCLEPIAD) STAPELIA
(— OF AUK) ALCA ALLE
(— OF BABOON) PAPIO
(— OF BACTERIA) VIBRIO EIMERIA
ERWINIA GAFFKYA PROTEUS
SARCINA BACILLUS BRUCELLA
SERRATIA SHIGELLA YERSINIA
BORDETELLA
(— OF BADGER) MELES ARCTONYX
HELICTIS
(— OF BAMBOO) DENDROCALAMUS
(— OF BARNACLE) LEPAS BALANUS
ELMINIUS
(— OF BASIDIOMYCETE) BOVISTA
(— OF BAT) EUDERMA PETALIA
DESMODUS DIPHYLLA MOLOSSUS
MORMOOPS NOCTILIO NYCTERIS
PLECOTUS PTEROPUS VAMPYRUM
(— OF BEAN) ABRUS
(— OF BEAR) URSUS EUARCTOS
MELURSUS
(— OF BEAVER) CASTOR
(— OF BEE) APIA APIS BOMBUS
ANDRENA TRIGONA COLLETES
HALICTUS MELIPONA
(— OF BEETLE) AMARA FIDIA HISPA
LAMIA LARIA LYTTA MELOE SAGRA
ALTICA ASILUS CLERUS ELATER
LYCTUS PTINUS SILPHA ACILIUS
ADELOPS AGRILUS ANOBIUM
ANOMALA BRUCHUS CARABUS
CASSIDA EPITRIX PRIONUS SAPERDA
SITARIS ADORETUS AGRIOTES
APHODIUS CALOSOMA CATORAMA
CYBISTER DYNASTES DYTISCUS
EPICAUTA EUMOLPUS HARPALUS
LAMPYRIS MEGASOMA PASSALUS
POPILLIA SCOLYTUS SPHINDUS
TENEBRIO DERMESTES
(— OF BIRD) ARA ALCA APUS CRAX
CREX GYPS JYNX MIRO MITU MOHO
OTIS PICA RHEA SULA TYTO XEMA
AJAJA ANOUS ANSER ARDEA
ARGUS ASTUR BUCCO FALCO GAVIA
GOURA GUARA GYGIS IRENA JUNCO
LARUS LERWA LOXIA MIMUS MITUA

MUNIA PIPRA PITTA SITTA TODUS
UPUPA VIDUA VIREO ALAUDA
ALCEDO ANHIMA ANTHUS AQUILA
BONASA BRANTA CAPITO CIRCUS
COLIUS CORVUS DACELO ELANUS
FULICA GALLUS JACANA LANIUS
LEIPOA LIMOSA MARECA MENURA
MEROPS MILVUS MONASA NESTOR
NUMIDA PASSER PASTOR PERDIX
PERNIS PROGNE QUELEA RALLUS
SAPPHO SCOPUS SIALIA SPINUS
STERNA SYLVIA TETRAO TRERON
TRINGA TROGON TURDUS TURNIX
VULTUR ANHINGA APTERYX
ARTAMUS BUCEROS CACICUS
CAPELLA CARIAMA CERTHIA CHIONIS
CICONIA CINCLUS COLINUS
COLUMBA COTINGA CUCULUS
ELAENIA GALBULA GARRUPA
HALCYON HIRUNDO IBYCTER
ICTERUS KAKATOE LAGOPUS
LOPHURA LYRURUS MALURUS
MANACUS MESITES MILVAGO
MOMOTUS ORIOLUS PANDION
PAROTIA PIRANGA PITYLUS
PLAUTUS PLOCEUS PORZANA
REGULUS SEIURUS SERINUS
STURNUS TANAGRA TIMALIA
TOTANUS XENICUS ZENAIDA
ACCENTOR ACCIPTER ACREDULA
AFROPAVO AGELAIUS AMIZILIA
BOTAURUS BUCORVUS BURHINUS
CHAETURA COLYMBUS CORACIAS
COTURNIX DELICHON DIATRYMA
DINORNIS DIOMEDEA DREPANIS
EMBERIZA EUPHONIA EURYPYGA
FULMARUS GARRULUS GEOSPIZA
GERYGONE GLAREOLA GRALLINA
GYPAETUS IONORNIS LUSCINIA
MACHETES MYCTERIA NEOPHRON
NOTORNIS NUMENIUS OREORTYX
PENELOPE PHAETHON PITANGUS
PLATALEA PLEGADIS PODARGUS
PRIONOPS PRUNELLA PUFFINUS
RUPICOLA SALTATOR SAXICOLA
SCOLOPAX SPEOTYTO SPIZELLA
STRUTHIO TRAGOPAN TYRANNUS
(— OF BIVALVES) MYA PINNA
ANOMIA MACTRA NUCULA ETHERIA
MYTILUS PANDORA COLYMBUS
HINNITES PISIDIUM SAXICAVA
TRIDACNA XYLOTRYA SPHAERIUM
(— OF BOWFIN) AMIA
(— OF BRACHIOPOD) ATRYPA CRANIA
ATHYRIS DISCINA SPIRIFER
(— OF BRYOPHYTE) RICCIA
(— OF BRYOZOAN) BUGULA
ESCHARA FLUSTRA RETEPORA
(— OF BUG) ANASA CIMEX EMESA
CORIXA TINGIS
(— OF BUTTERFLY) CALIGO COLIAS
DANAUS MORPHO PIERIS THECLA
EURYMUS JUNONIA KALLIMA

LYCAENA PAPILIO STRYMON
VANESSA ARGYNNIS HESPERIA
LEMONIAS MELITAEA SPEYERIA
(— OF CABBAGE) COS
(— OF CACTUS) CEREUS NOPALEA
OPUNTIA HARRISIA
(— OF CANTELOUPE) CUCUMIS
(— OF CAT) FELIS ACINONYX
HEMIGALE
(— OF CATTLE) BOS NEAT TAURUS
(— OF CEPHALOPOD) SEPIA SPIRULA
(— OF CETACEAN) INIA
(— OF CHINK) LACUNA
(— OF CHIPMUNK) EUTAMIAS
(— OF CILIATE) COLPODA CHILODON
EUPLOTES
(— OF CIVET) FOSSA PAGUMA
(— OF CLAM) ENSIS GEMMA SOLEN
SPISULA
(— OF COCKLE) CHIONE
(— OF COCKROACH) BLATTA
(— OF CODFISH) GADUS
(— OF CORAL) ASTREA FUNGIA
MAENDRA OCULINA PORITES
ACROPORA TUBIPORA
(— OF CRAB) UCA MAIA BIRGUS
CANCER GRAPSUS OCYPODE
PAGURUS LITHODES PORTUNUS
(— OF CRANE) GRUS
(— OF CRAYFISH) CAMBARUS
(— OF CRICKET) ACHETA GRYLLUS
(— OF CRUSTACEAN) APUS HIPPA
JAOUS LIGIA MYSIS CYPRIS LIGYDA
SELLUS TRIOPS ARGULUS ARTEMIA
ASTACUS BOPYRUS CALAPPA
CHELURA DAPHNIA EMERITA
HOMARUS IDOTHEA LERNAEA
NEBALIA SQUILLA CAPRELLA
ESTHERIA GAMMARUS LEUCIFER
LIMNETIS LIMNORIA NEPHROPS
PHRONIMA
(— OF CTENOPHORE) BEROE
CESTUM
(— OF CUCUMBER) CUCUMIS
(— OF CURASSOW) CRAX
(— OF DEER) AXIS DAMA PUDU RUSA
CERVUS MAZAMA MOSCHUS
RUCERVUS
(— OF DIATOM) DIATOMA SYNEDRA
MERIDION NAVICULA
(— OF DODO) DIDUS
(— OF DOG) CUON CANIS LYCAON
(— OF DORMOUSE) GLIS
(— OF DRAGONFLY) AESCHNA
(— OF DUCK) AIX ANAS AYTHYA
MERGUS NYROCA NETTION
SPATULA CLANGULA FULIGULA
(— OF EAGLE) AQUILA
(— OF ECHINODERM) ASTERIAS
(— OF EDENTATE) MANIS
(— OF EEL) CONGER ECHIDNA
MURAENA ANGUILLA GYMNOTUS
MORINGUA

(— OF FERN) FILIX TODEA ANEMIA
AZOLLA DOODIA CYATHEA ISOETES
ONOCLEA OSMUNDA PELLAEA
WOODSIA ADIANTUM ASPIDIUM
ATHYRIUM BLECHNUM CETERACH
CIBOTIUM CLEMATIS DAVALLIA
LYGODIUM MARATTIA SALVINIA
SCHIZAEA VITTARIA
(— OF FIREFLY) LAMPYRIS
(— OF FISH) AMIA ESOX HURO LOTA
MOLA RAJA ZEUS ALOSA BADIS
BERYX BETTA DORAS ELOPS GADUS
GOBIO HUCHO LATES MANTA MUGIL
PERCA SALMO SARDA SOLEA
UMBRA ALBULA ANABAS APOGON
BAIGRE BARBUS BELONE CARANX
CLUPEA COTTUS DIODON GERRES
GOBIUS HIODON KUHLIA LABRUS
LATRIS MOBULA MYXINE NOMEUS
PAGRUS PSETTA REMORA SCARUS
SPARUS TRIGLA TRUTTA TURSIO
WEEVER ABRAMIS ALOPHAS
ALOPIAS ARACANA ASPREDO
BROTULA CARAPUS CLARIAS
DREPANE ECHIDNA GARRUPA
GIRELLA GYMNORA LEPOMIS
LIMANDA LUCANIA LYCODES
OSMERUS PEGASUS PRISTIS
SCIAENA SCOMBER SEPIOLA
SERIOLA SIGANUS SILLAGO
SILURUS SPHYRNA SQUALUS
SYNODUS THUNNUS TORPEDO
TOXOTES TRIODON XIPHIAS
ZOARCES AMEIURUS ANABLEPS
ANGUILLA ARAPAIMA ASTYANAX
ATHERINA BALISTES BODIANUS
CARANGUS CHIMAERA CLADODUS
CTENODUS CYPRINUS DAPEDIUS
DIPLODUS DIPTERUS DOROSOMA
ECHENEIS ETRUMEUS FUNDULUS
GADOPSIS GALAXIAS GAMBUSIA
GOBIESOX HAEMULON ICOSTEUS
KYPHOSUS LEBISTES LUTIANUS
MEGALOPS MORMYRUS MUSTELUS
NOTROPIS OPHIDION PALOMETA
PANTODON PHOCAENA POLYODON
PYGIDIUM SERRANUS SQUATINA
COREGONUS MYCTOPHUM
(— OF FLAGELLATE) COCOS GONIUM
OPHION SYNURA VOLVOX ATTALEA
CARYOTA EUGLENA GIARDIA
BORASSUS CERATIUM EUDORINA
HEXAMITA HYDRURUS
(— OF FLEA) PULEX BOSMINA
(— OF FLY) DACUS MUSCA MYMAR
PERLA PHORA ASILUS CEPHUS
FANNIA PIMPLA RHYSSA SCIARA
TIPULA CALIROA CHALCIS DIOPSIS
EPHYDRA HYLEMYA MIASTOR
ORTALIS OSCINIS PANORPA TACHINA
THEREVA ACROCERA AGROMYZA
ANOMALON APHIDIUS BORBORUS
CHELONUS CHRYSOPA CHRYSOPS

GLOSSINA PSYCHODA SCHEDIUS
SIMULIUM STOMOXYS
(— OF FLYING SQUIRREL) BELOMYS
(— OF FOSSIL) AMPYX ERYON
ADAPIS ATRYPA BAIERA ERYOPS
GEIKIA HYENIA KLUKIA MAMMUT
OLENUS ORTHIS RHYNIA ANDRIAS
ANTEDON APTIANA ASAPHUS
DICERAS EXOGYRA GANODUS
HAMITES HYBODUS KNORRIA
LESKEYA LESLEYA LOXOMMA
MESONYX MOROPUS MYLODON
OTOZOUM PHACOPS PHIOMIA
PROAVIS PROETUS WALCHIA
AGLASPIS AGNOSTUS AMYNODON
APHELOPS ARCHELON BIRKENIA
BRONTOPS CALIPPUS CALYMENE
CAYTONIA CERATOPS CLYMENIA
CTENODUS DAPEDIUS DEINODON
DIATRYMA DINOHYUS DIPLODUS
DIPTERUS ENCHODUS ENCRINUS
EODISCUS EOHIPPUS EOSAURUS
EUSMILUS GORDONIA GRYPHAEA
HALLOPUS HELIGMUS ILLAENUS
LANARKIA LEBACHIA LECROSIA
LEGUATIA LESTODON LITUITES
MACLUREA MARRELLA METOPIAS
OLDHAMIA PLACODUS PORTHEUS
RUTIODON SMILODON SPIRIFER
STEGODON STEGOMUS TAONURUS
THELODUS XIPHODON ZAMICRUS
CONULARIA
(— OF FOX) ALOPEX VULPES
UROCYON
(— OF FROG) RANA ANURA HYLODES
(— OF FUNGUS) FOMES IRPEX
PHOMA TUBER VALSA VERPA
ALBUGO BREMIA CAEOMA EMPUSA
FUMAGO HYDNUM ISARIA OIDIUM
PEZIZA TORULA ZYTHIA ACRASIA
ACRASIN AMANITA BOLETUS
CANDIDA CHALARA CYATHUS
ELSINOE ERYSIBE FABRAEA
GEASTER LEPIOTA MONILIA NECTRIA
OZONIUM PACHYMA PYTHIUM
RHIZINA RUSSULA SIMBLUM
STEREUM STICTIS STILBUM
TYPHULA XYLARIA ACHORION
AECIDIUM AGARICUS BOTRYTIS
CALVATIA CLATHRUS CLAVARIA
COLLYBIA COPRINUS CORYNEUM
CYPHELLA CYTTARIA DAEDALEA
DIPLODIA ENDOTHIA ENTOLOMA
ENTYLOMA ERYSIPHE EXOASCUS
FUSARIUM GEASTRUM GNOMONIA
GRAPHIUM HELOTIUM HELVELLA
LENZITES MERULIUS MYCOGONE
PAXILLUS PHOLIOTA PUCCINIA
RHIZOPUS RHYTISMA SEPTORIA
SORDARIA SPICARIA TAPHRINA
TERFEZIA TRAMETES TREMELLA
TROCHILA USTILAGO USTULINA
VENTURIA CORDICEPS

(— OF GALLFLY) CYNIPS
(— OF GASTROPOD) FICUS HARPA
LIMAX OLIVA EBURNA PATELLA
TENEBRA SCYLLAEA STROMBUS
(— OF GEESE) CHEN ANSER
NETTAPUS
(— OF GNAT) SCIARA
(— OF GOAT) IBEX CAPRA
OREAMNOS
(— OF GRASS) POA ZEA AIRA COIX
AVENA BRIZA ORYZA STIPA APLUDA
ARUNDO BROMUS ELYMUS HOLCUS
LOLIUM LYGEUM MELICA MILIUM
NARDUS PHLEUM SECALE UNIOLA
ZOYSIA BAMBUSA BUCHLOE
CHLORIS CYNODON FESTUCA
HILARIA HORDEUM LAGURUS
LEERSIA MELINIS MOLINIA PANICUM
SETARIA SORGHUM ZIZANIA
AEGILOPS AGROSTIS ARISTIDA
AXONOPUS BULBILIS CENCHRUS
DACTYLIS ELEUSINE GLYCERIA
GYNERIUM IMPERATA PASPALUM
PHALARIS SPARTINA SPINIFEX
TRISETUM TRITICUM
(— OF GRASSHOPPER) LOCUSTA
(— OF GUAN) CRAX
(— OF GULL) XEMA LARUS
(— OF HAWK) BUTEO CIRCUS
(— OF HERB) GYP IVA AMMI ARUM
BETA GEUM GLAX HERE LENS MEUM
MUSA OLAX RUTA SIDA SIUM
ADOXA AJUGA APIOS APIUM CALLA
CANNA CAREX CARUM CICER DALEA
DRABA ERUCA ERVUM FEDIA GALAX
GAURA GILIA GLAUX HOSTA INULA
LAPPA LAVIA LAYIA LEMNA LINUM
LOASA LOTUS LUFFA MADIA MALVA
NAPEA PANAX PARIS PHACA PHLOX
PILEA RHEUM RHOEO RUBIA SEDUM
TACCA URENA VICIA VIGNA VINCA
VIOLA ZIZIA ACAENA ACNIDA
ACORUS ACTAEA ADONIS ALISMA
ALLIUM ALSINE AMOMUM ANOGRA
ARABIS ARALIA ARNICA ASARUM
ATROPA BACOPA BAERIA BASSIA
BELLIS BIDENS BLITUM BLUMEA
BORAGO CAKILE CALTHA CASSIA
CELSIA CICUTA CISTUS CLEOME
CNICUS COLEUS CONIUM COPTIS
COSMOS CRAMBE CREPIS CRINUM
CROCUS CROTON CUNILA CYNARA
DAHLIA DATURA DAUCUS DIODIA
DONDIA ECHIUM ELODEA ELODES
EMILIA EUCLEA FILAGO GALEGA
GALIUM GIFOLA GYNURA ISATIS
ISMENE KOCHIA KUHNIA KUHNIA
LAMIUM LECHEA LUZULA MALOPE
MENTHA MIMOSA MONTIA MUCUNA
MUILLA NERINE NERIUM NESLIA
ONONIS OTHAKE OXALIS PICRIS
PISTIA PYROLA RESEDA RESTIO
RHEXIA RIVINA RUPPIA SAGINA

SALVIA SCILLA SESBAN SESELI
STEVIA SUAEDA THALIA TULIPA
VIORNA ZINNIA ABRONIA ADLUMIA
AETHUSA ALEGRIA ALETRIS
ALKANNA ALPINIA ALTHAEA
ALYSSUM AMORPHA AMSONIA
ANCHUSA ANEMONE ANETHUM
ANYCHIA APHANES ARACHIS
ARCTIUM ARNEBIA ARUNCUS
BABIANA BARTSIA BEGONIA
BOEBERA BUTOMUS CACALIA
CAJANUS CALYPSO CARLINA
CELOSIA CHELONE CIRCAEA CIRSIUM
CLARKIA COMARUM CROOMIA
CURCUMA CUSCUTA CYTINUS
DATISCA DECODON DERINGA
DIASCIA DROSERA ELATINE
EOMECON EPISCIA ERODIUM FELICIA
FICARIA FRASERA FREESIA FUMARIA
GAZANIA GERBERA GLECOMA
GLYCINE GUNNERA HALENIA
HECHTIA HEDEOMA HOMERIA
HUGELIA HYPOXIS IRESINE JASIONE
KICKXIA KNAUTIA KOELLIA LACTUCA
LAPPULA LAPSANA LEWISIA LIATRIS
LINARIA LINNAEA LOGANIA LOPEZIA
LUNARIA LUPINUS LYCHNIS
LYTHRUM MARANTA MEDEOLA
MIMULUS MITELLA MOLLUGO
MONESES MUSCARI NEMESIA
NIGELLA OTHONNA PAEONIA
PAPAVER PAVONIA PEGANUM
PETUNIA PLUCHEA PRIMULA
RORIPPA ROTALIA RUELLIA SALSOLA
SAMOLUS SCANDIX SENECIO
SEDAMUM SHORTIA SILYBUM
SINAPIS SOLANUM SONCHUS
STACHYS STATICE SUCCISA SWERTIA
TAGETES TALINUM TELLIMA
THAPSIA THESIUM THLASPI THURNIA
TORENIA TORILIS TOVARIA TRILISA
URGINEA VALLOTA VERBENA
ZEBRINA ACALYPHA ACANTHUS
ACHILLEA ACONITUM AGALINIS
AGERATUM ALLIARIA ALLIONIA
ALOCASIA AMBROSIA AMMOBIUM
ANDRYALA ANGELICA ANTHEMIS
ANTICLEA APOCYNUM ARCTOTIS
ARENARIA ARGEMONE ARISAEMA
ASPERULA ATRIPLEX BAPTISIA
BARBAREA BARTONIA BERGENIA
BERTEROA BETONICA BISTORTA
BOLTONIA BORRERIA BRASSICA
BRUNONIA BUCHNERA CALATHEA
CAMASSIA CAMELINA CANNABIS
CAPSICUM CERINTHE CLEMATIS
COCHARUS COLLOMIA COLUMNEA
COMANDRA COOPERIA CRASSULA
CUBELIUM DENTARIA DIANTHUS
DICENTRA DIPSACUS DISPORUM
DYSSODIA ECHINOPS EPIFAGUS
ERANTHIS EREMURUS ERIGENIA
ERIGERON ERYNGIUM ERYSIMUM

EUCHARIS EUTHAMIA FITTONIA
FLAVERIA FLOERKEA FRAGARIA
GALACTIA GENTIANA GERARDIA
GESNERIA GILLENIA GLAUCIUM
GLECHOMA GLORIOSA GLOXINIA
GOODENIA GRATIOLA GUZMANIA
HELENIUM HELONIAS HEPATICA
HESPERIS HEUCHERA HIBISCUS
HIPPURIS HOSACKIA HOTTONIA
HUDSONIA HYDROLES HYSSOPUS
IONIDIUM ISNARDIA JATROPHA
JUSSIAEA JUSTICIA KNEIFFIA
KOHLERIA LAPORTEA LAVATERA
LEONOTIS LEONURUS LEPIDIUM
LEPTILON LIMONIUM LOPHIOLA
LYCOPSIS MACLEAYA MANFREDA
MANTISIA MEDICAGO MEIBOMIA
MYOSOTIS MYOSURUS OBOLARIA
OENANTHE OPOPANAX ORONTIUM
PAROSELA PHACELIA PHORMIUM
PHYMOSIA PHYSALIS PHYSARIA
PLANTAGO PLUMBAGO POLYGALA
POLYMNIA POTERIUM PRUNELLA
PSORALEA RAPHANUS RHAGODIA
SABBATIA SAMBUCUS SANICULA
SARCODES SAROTHRA SATUREIA
SCABIOSA SCOLYMUS SESBANIA
SESUVIUM SEYMERIA SIDALCEA
SILPHIUM SOLIDAGO SPERGULA
SPIGELIA SPINACIA STOKESIA
TAENIDIA THASPIUM TIARELLA
TRIBULUS TRILLIUM TROLLIUS
TUECRIUM UVULARIA VACCARIA
VALERIAN VANELLUS VERATRUM
VERNONIA VERONICA VISCARIA
WATSONIA XANTHIUM RUDBECKIA
(— OF HERON) ARDEA EGRETTA
(— OF HORSE) EQUUS CALIPPUS
EOHIPPUS
(— OF HYDROZOAN) DIPHYES
PHYSALIA
(— OF HYENA) HYAENA CROCUTA
(— OF INSECT) NEPA APHIS EMESA
JAPYX SIREX BOREUS CICADA
COCCUS CORIXA EMPUSA ICERYA
KERMES MANTIS PHASMA PODURA
SIALIS THRIPS CHALCIS FORMICA
FULGORA LEPISMA ORYSSUS
RANATRA STYLOPS VEDALIA
BACILLUS CAMPODEA EPHEMERA
LABIDURA LACCIFER LECANIUM
LYONETIA MACHILIS MANTISPA
NERTHRUS REDUVIUS
(— OF ISOPOD) IDOTEA IDOTHEA
CIROLANA
(— OF JAY) GARRULUS
(— OF JELLYFISH) CYANEA AURELIA
AEQUOREA
(— OF JERBOA) DIPUS
(— OF KELP) AGARUM
(— OF LANGUR) SIMIAS
(— OF LEAFHOPPER) AGALLIA
EMPOASCA

(— OF LEECH) HIRUDO HAEMOPIS
(— OF LEMUR) INDRI GALAGO
(— OF LIANA) BAUHINIA
(— OF LICE) APHIS PSYLLA ARGULUS
ONISCUS BOVICOLA ERIOSOMA
GONIODES LIPEURUS
(— OF LICHEN) CORA USNEA STICTA
EVERNIA GRAPHIS LECIDEA LOBARIA
PHYSCIA CETRARIA CLADONIA
LECANORA PARMELIA ROCCELLA
STRIGULA
(— OF LILY) CAMAS CAMASS
QUAMASH
(— OF LIMPET) ACMAEA
(— OF LIZARD) UTA AGAMA DRACO
GEKKO AMEIVA ANGUIS ANOLIS
IGUANA EUMECES LACERTA
PYGOPUS SCINCUS ACONTIAS
CHIROTES COLEONYX LYGOSOMA
RHINEURA
(— OF LOCUST) TETRIX TETTIX
(— OF MACAW) ARA
(— OF MAMMAL) BOS SUS HOMO
LAMA ALCES BISON CAPRA TAYRA
DUGONG FRISON AELURUS AILURUS
BUBALUS GALIDIA GYMNURA
LINSANG OTOCYON AUCHENIA
CYCLOPES CYNOGALE SURICATA
TRAGULUS
(— OF MAPLE) ACER
(— OF MARSUPIAL) DASYURUS
MACROPUS POTOROUS TARSIPES
(— OF MARTEN) MARTES
MUSTELA
(— OF MEDUSA) SARSIA
GERYONIA
(— OF MICROSPORIDIAN) GLUGEA
(— OF MILDEW) ERYSIPHE UNCINULA
(— OF MILLIPEDE) JULUS
(— OF MINT) ICIMUM NEPETA
MELISSA PERILLA PHLOMIS
ORIGANUM
(— OF MITE) ACARUS ACERIA
LEPTUS DEMODEX ACARAPIS
(— OF MOLD) MUCOR FULIGO
MELIOLA
(— OF MOLE) TALPA SCALOPS
SCALOPUS
(— OF MOLLUSK) ARCA DOTO LEDA
LIMA CHAMA DONAX EOLIS FICUS
HARPA LIMAX MUREX OLIVA VENUS
AEOLIS ANOMIA BANKIA CASSIS
CHITON LEPTON LUCINA OSTREA
PECTEN PHOLAS PYRULA SEMELE
TEREDO TETHYS ACTAEON ASTARTE
ATLANTA CARDITA CARDIUM
CYPRAEA CYPRINA DOSINIA ETHERIA
EXOGYRA LINGULA TELLINA
BUCCINUM GRYPHAEA HALIOTIS
LIMACINA LUTRARIA MODIOLUS
NAUTILUS PINCTADA SCYLLAEA
STROMBUS
(— OF MONGOOSE) GALIDIA

(— OF MONKEY) AOTES AOTUS
CEBUS ATELES MACACA CACAJAO
COLOBUS NASALIS SAIMIRI PITHECIA
(— OF MOOSE) ALCES
(— OF MOSQUITO) AEDES CULEX
STEGOMYIA
(— OF MOSS) BRYUM CHILO
EUXOA MNIUM SAMIA SESIA TINEA
ACTIAS ALYPIA ARCTIA BOMBYX
COSSUS DATANA HYPNUM LESKEA
PLUSIA PSYCHE SPHINX THYRIS
URANIA AGROTIS ALABAMA
APATELA ARCHIPS ATTACUS
BARBULA CHAMBUS FUNARIA
GRIMMIA PHASCUM PRONUBA
PYRALIS SESAMIA TORTRIX
ZEUZERA ZYGAENA ANDREAEA
CATOCALA DAWSONIA DIATRAEA
DICRANUM ENDROMIS EPHESTIA
EUPREPIA GALLERIA GELECHIA
HEPIALUS PLUTELLA PRODENIA
PYRAUSTA SATURNIA SPHAGNUM
THUIDIUM
(— OF MOTH) CHILO ABRAXAS
(— OF MOUSE) MUS APODEMUS
(— OF MUSKMELON) CUCUMIS
(— OF MUSKRAT) FIBER ONDATRA
(— OF NARWHAL) MONODON
(— OF NEMATODE) ACUARIA
ALAIMUS ANGUINA NECATOR
(— OF NUDIBRANCH) GLAUCUS
(— OF OATS) AVENA
(— OF OPOSSUM) MARMOSA
(— OF ORCHID) DISA VANDA BLETIA
LAELIA PHAJUS ACINETA AERIDES
ANGULOA BRASSIA CORDULA
EUCOSIA IBIDIUM ISOTRIA LIPARIS
LISTERA MALAXIS POGONIA VANILLA
ANGRECUM ARETHUSA BLETILLA
CALANTHE CATTLEYA CYTHEREA
FISSIPES GOODYERA MILTONIA
ONCIDIUM PERAMIUM SERAPIAS
SOBRALIA TRIPHORA
(— OF OSTRICH) STRUTHIO
(— OF OTTER) LUTRA
(— OF OWL) BUBO NINOX STRIX
KETUPA NYCTEA AEGOLIUS
SPEOTYTO
(— OF OXEN) BIBOS
(— OF OYSTER) OSTREA AVICULA
(— OF PALM) NIPA ARECA ASSAI
COCOS HOWEA SABAL ARENGA
ELAEIS INODES KENTIA RAPHIA
RHAPIS ATTALEA BACTRIS CALAMUS
CARYOTA CORYPHA ERYTHEA
EUTERPE GEONOMA LATANIA
LICUALA PHOENIX SERENOA
THRINAX BORASSUS HYPHAENE
IRIARTEA LODOICEA MAURITIA
(— OF PARASITE) STRIGA CUSCOTA
CUSCUTA HYDNORA OLPIDIUM
CASSYTHIA
(— OF PARRAKEET) ARATINGA

(— OF PARROT) NESTER AMAZONA
KAKATOE
(— OF PEACOCK) PAVO
(— OF PENGUIN) EUDYPTES
(— OF PHALANGER) DROMICIA
(— OF PIGEON) GOURA DUCULA
COLUMBA
(— OF PLANT) ALOE ARUM COLA
DION FABA IRIS IXIA PUYA SOJA
ADOXA AGAVE ASTER BATIS CANNA
CHARA DIOON DRYAS INULA NAIAS
PIPER RUMEX TRAPA TYPHA XYRIS
YUCCA ZILLA ABROMA ACACIA
AIZOON ALBUCA ANANAS CACTUS
CUPHEA DATURA EXACUM FERULA
IBERIS JAMBOS JUNCUS LICHEN
LILIUM MAYACA MORAEA NUPHAR
PHRYMA RICCIA SILENE SMILAX
STRIGA URTICA VISCUM ALONSOA
ASTILBE BALLOTA CABOMBA
CUCUMIS CYPERUS DIONAEA
DROSERA ENCELIA EPACRIS EPIGAEA
EURYALE FAGELIA GLYCINE GODETIA
HELXINE HOOKERA ISOETES
ISOLOMA KARATAS LYCOPUS
MANIHOT MONARDA NELUMBO
NITELLA RAOULIA RICINUS
STEMONA SYRINGA TRIURUS
TURNERA WOLFFIA WYETHIA
ZOSTERA ABUTILON ACANTHUS
ADIANTUM ANABASIS ANTHYLIS
BRASENIA BRODIAEA BROMELIA
CALADIUM CAPSICUM CYCLAMEN
FURCRAEA FURCRAEA GALTONIA
GASTERIA GERANIUM LATHRAEA
LATHYRUS MARSILEA MONGTERA
NYMPHAEA PANDANUS PEDALIUM
PELVETIA PERESKIA SAURURUS
SPARAXIS THEVETIA TIGRIDIA
TRITONIA VELLOZIA VICTORIA
ZINGIBER
(— OF POLYZOAN) LEPRALIA
LOXOSOMA
(— OF POPLAR) ALAMO
(— OF PORCUPINE) COENDOU
HYSTRIX
(— OF PORPOISE) INIA PHOCAENA
(— OF PRAWN) PALAEMON
(— OF PROTOZOAN) BODO HYDRA
MONAS ADELEA AMOEBA ACINETA
ARCELLA EIMERIA STENTOR
DIDINIUM EUGLYPHA ISOSPORA
UROGLENA
(— OF RABBIT) LEPUS
(— OF RACCOON) OLINGO
(— OF RAT) ANISOMYS
(— OF REPTILE) SPHENOGON
(— OF RHIZOPOD) AMOEBA GROMIA
LAGENA HATTERIA PELOMYXA
(— OF RODENT) MUS CAVIA DIPUS
LEPUS ZAPUS GEOMYS LEMMUS
SPALAX CYNOMYS DINOMYS
ECHIMYS LEGGADA MERINES

NESOKIA ZYZOMYS ALACTAGA
ARVICOLA CAPROMYS CITELLUS
CRICETUS HAPLODON HYDROMYS
LAGIDIUM MICROTUS MYOTALPA
ORYZOMYS
(— OF ROTIFER) HYDATINA PEDALION
(— OF RUST) UREDO HEMILEIA
UROMYCES
(— OF SALAMANDER) ANDRIAS
EURYCEA SIREDON TRITURUS
(— OF SCALE) KERMES LECANIUM
(— OF SCALLOP) HINNITES
(— OF SCORPION) BUTHUS SCORPIO
CHELIFER
(— OF SEA ANEMONE) MINYAS
ACTINIA
(— OF SEACOW) RHYTINA
(— OF SEA FAN) GORGONIA
(— OF SEAL) PHOCA HYDRURGA
MIROUNGA ZALOPHUS
(— OF SEA OTTER) ENHYDRA
(— OF SEA SLUG) ELYSIA
(— OF SEA URCHIN) ARBACIA
CIDARIS DIADEMA ECHINUS
(— OF SEAWEED) ULVA FUCUS
ALARIA LAMINARIA RHODYMENIA
(— OF SEDGE) FUIRENA SCIRPUS
SCLERIA SCHOENUS
(— OF SHARK) LAMNA GALEUS
ISURUS ACRODUS ALOPIAS
SPHYRNA SQUALUS CLADODUS
MENASPIS SQUATINA
(— OF SHEEP) OVIS
(— OF SHELL) PUPA LAMBIS
EXOGYRA LATIRUS MALLEUS
TROCHUS HAMINOEA MACLUREA
OLIVELLA TRIGONIA UMBRELLA
(— OF SHREW) SOREX BLARINA
(— OF SHRIMP) CRAGO CRANGON
(— OF SHRUB) IVA ACER BIXA BRYA
HOYA ILEX INGA ITEA MABA OLEA
RHUS ROSA SIDA THEA ULEX ALNUS
ANONA BIOTA BUTEA BUXUS CATHA
DALEA DIRCA ERICA EURYA FICUS
HAKEA IXORA LEDUM MALUS
OCHNA PADUS RIBES RUBUS SABIA
SALIX TAXUS THUJA TREMA UNONA
URENA VITEX ABELIA ACAENA
ADELIA ALHAGI AMYRIS ANNONA
ARALIA ARONIA AUCUBA AZALEA
BAPHIA BAUERA BETULA BLUMEA
BYBLIS CANTUA CASSIA CELTIS
CERCIS CISTUS CITRUS CLEOME
CLUSIA COFFEA CORDIA COREMA
CORNUS CORREA CROTON DAPHNE
DATURA DERRIS DIOSMA DONDIA
DRIMYS ECHIUM EVODIA FATSIA
FEIJOA GARRYA GNETUM GREWIA
GUAREA KALMIA KERRIA LARREA
LIPPIA LITSEA LUCUMA LYCIUM
MIMOSA MYRICA MYRICA MYRTUS
OCOTEA OLINIA OPILIA PENAEA
PERSEA PIERIS PROTEA PTELEA

PUNICA QUIINA RAMONA RANDIA
ROCHEA ROYENA RUSCUS SALVIA
SAPIUM SCHIMA SELAGO SESBAN
SORBUS STEVIA STYRAX SUAEDA
TECOMA AECULUS AMORPHA
ARBUTUS ARDISIA ARMERIA
ASIMINA ASSONIA BANKSIA
BAROSMA BENZOIN BORONIA
BUMELIA BURSERA CALLUNA
CARISSA CASASIA CERASUS
CESTRUM CLETHRA CNEORUM
COLUTEA CORYLUS COTINUS
CUNONIA CYRILLA CYTISUS DEUTZIA
DOMBEYA DURANTA EHRETIA
ENCELIA EPACRIS EPHEDRA
EUCHLEA EUGENIA EURSERA
FABIANA FUCHSIA GENISTA
GMELINA GYMINDA HAMELIA
HOVENIA KARATAS LAGETTA
LANTANA MAHONIA MERATIA
MONIMIA MORINDA MUTISIA
MYRRHIS NANDINA NEMESIA
OLEARIA OTHONNA PAVETTA
PAVONIA PENTZIA PIMELEA PISONIA
PURSHIA QUASSIA QUERCUS
RAPANEA REMIJIA RHAMNUS
RHODORA ROBINIA ROMNEYA
RUELLIA SALSOLA SENECIO
SKIMMIA SOLANUM SOPHORA
SPIRAEA SURIANA SYRINGA
TAMARIX TELOPEA XIMENIA
XYLOPIA XYLOSMA ZELKOVA
ACALYPHA ALANGIUM ALSTONIA
ANAGYRIS ATRIPLEX BALOGHIA
BAUHINIA BERBERIS BORRERIA
BUCKLEYA BUDDLEIA CAMELLIA
CAPPARIS CAPSICUM CARAGANA
CASSIOPE CASTANEA CODIAEUM
COLLETIA CONDALIA CONNARUS
COPROSMA CORIARIA CRATAEVA
DAVIESIA DENDRIUM DILLENIA
DODONAEA DOVYALIS DRACAENA
DUBOISIA EMPETRUM EUONYMUS
EUPTELEA EXOSTEMA FRAXINUS
GALACTIA GOODENIA GORDONIA
GUAIACUM HIBISCUS HIRTELLA
IONIDIUM JASMINUM JATROPHA
JUSTICIA KNIGHTIA KRAMERIA
LABURNUM LAVATERA LAWSONIA
LEONOTIS MAGNOLIA MAYTENUS
MICHELIA MYOPORUM NOTELAEA
PALIURUS PAROSELA PHILESIA
PHOTINIA PHYMOSIA PLUMIERA
POLYGALA POTERIUM PROSOPIS
PSORALEA RHAGODIA ROLLINIA
RORIDULA RUSSELIA SAMBUCUS
SATUREIA SAURAUIA SESBANIA
SOLANDRA SORBARIA SPARTIUM
TABEBUIA TORRUBIA TRECULIA
VARRONIA VERNONIA VERONICA
VIBURNUM VOCHYSIA WITHANIA
ZIZYPHUS MENZIESIA
(— OF SILKWORM) BOMBYX

(— OF SKUNK) MEPHITIS
(— OF SLOTH) BRADYPUS
(— OF SLUG) DOTO ARION DORIS
LIMAX ELYSIA GLAUCUS
(— OF SNAIL) HUA PILA CONUS
FUSUS GALBA HELIX MITRA OVULA
PHYSA THAIS TURBO CERION
EULIMA NATICA NERITA RISSOA
TRITON ANCYLUS BITTIUM BULINUS
BUSYCON CYMBIUM LATIRUS
LITIOPA LYMNARA MELANIA
MODULUS PURPURA RANELLA
VALVATA VERTIGO VITRINA ZONITES
ACHATINA ALOCINMA ELLOBIUM
FOSSARIA GYRAULUS HELICINA
HELISOMA JANTHINA KATAYAMA
LITORINA NERITINA OLEACINA
SUCCINEA
(— OF SNAKE) BOA ERYX NAIA NAJA
ASPIS BITIS BOIGA ECHIS ELAPS
CAUSUS DABOIA ELAPHE HURRIA
ILYSIA LIGUUS NATRIX PYTHON
VIPERA ATHERIS BOAEDON COLUBER
ECHIDNA MEHELYA OPHIDIA
ZAMENIS BOTHROPS BUNGARUS
CERBERUS CROTALUS DEMANSIA
EUNECTES FARANCIA LACHESIS
MICRURUS STORERIA TYPHLOPS
(— OF SPIDER) ARANEA LYCOSA
MYGALE AGALENA ARGIOPE
ATTIDAE NEPHILA PHOLCUS
LINYPHIA ULOBORUS
(— OF SPIROCHETE) BORRELIA
(— OF SPONGE) SYCON GEODIA
SCYPHA ASCETTA CHALINA GRANTIA
SPONGIA SYCETTA LEUCETTA
(— OF SPOROZOAN) NOSEMA
(— OF SQUID) LOLIGO SEPIOLA
(— OF SQUIRREL) SCIURUS
(— OF SUBSHRUB) LECHEA ARMERIA
ASCYRUM BEGONIA FELICIA
ATRIPLEX COLUMNEA
(— OF SWAN) OLOR CYGNUS
(— OF TAKIN) BUDORCAS
(— OF TAPEWORM) BERTIA LIGULA
DAVAINEA HARRISIA
(— OF TAYRA) GALERA GALICTIS
(— OF TELEDU) MYDAUS
(— OF TERN) GYGIS STERNA
(— OF THISTLE) CNICUS CARDUUS
(— OF TICK) ARGAS ARGUS IXODES
HYALOMMA
(— OF TOAD) BUFO HYLA PIPA
ALYTES XENOPUS ASCAPHUS
(— OF TREE) ACER BIXA BRYA COLA
HURA ILEX INGA MABA OLAX OLEA
RHUS THEA ABIES AEGLE ALNUS
ANIBA BIOTA BUTEA BUXUS CARYA
CEIBA CYCAS DURIO EURYA FAGUS
FICUS HAKEA HEVEA HOPEA IXORA
KHAYA LARIX MALUS MELIA MESUA
MORUS NYSSA OCHNA PADUS PICEA
PINUS PYRUS SALIX TAXUS THUJA

TILIA TOONA TREMA TSUGA ULMUS
UNONA VITEX XYLIA ABROMA
ACHRAS AKANIA AMOMIS AMYRIS
ANDIRA ANNONA ARALIA AUCUBA
AZALEA BAPHIA BETULA BOMBAX
CANTUA CARAPA CARICA CASSIA
CEDRUS CELTIS CERCIS CITRUS
CLUSIA COFFEA CORDIA CORNUS
DATURA DRIMYS EPERUA EPERVA
EUCLEA EVODIA FEIJOA GARRYA
GENIPA GINKGO GNETUM GREWIA
GUAREA IDESIA ILLIPE LAURUS
LITCHI LITSEA LUCUMA LYCIUM
MAMMEA MIMOSA MYRCIA MYRICA
OCOTEA OLNEYA OSTRYA OWENIA
PAPPEA PARITI PERSEA PRUNUS
PTELEA QUIINA RANDIA ROYENA
SAPIUM SAPOTA SCHIMA SENCIO
SESBAN SHOREA SIMABA SORBUS
STYRAX TECOMA AGATHIS
ARBUTUS ARDISIA ASIMINA
ASSONIA BANKSIA BUMELIA
BURSERA CANANGA CANELLA
CASASIA CATALPA CEDRELA
CERASUS CLETHRA COPAIVA
CORYLUS COTINUS CUNONIA
CUPANIA CYDONIA CYRILLA
DOMBEYA ECHINUS EHRETIA
EPACRIS EUGENIA FERONIA
GMELINA GUAZUMA GYMINDA
HAGENIA HALESIA HICORIA HOVENIA
HUMIRIA JUGLANS KADELIA
KOKOONA LAGETTA LICANIA
LINGOUM MACLURA MICONIA
MORINDA MORINGA MURRAYA
OCHROMA OLEARIA PANGIUM
PIMENTA PISONIA PLANERA
POPULUS PROTIUM PSIDIUM
QUASSIA QUERCUS RAPANEA
REMIJIA RHAMNUS ROBINIA
 UCHINUS SENECIO SEQUOIA
SLOANEA SOLANUM SOPHORA
SURIANA SYRINGA TAMARIX
TECTONA TELOPEA TORREYA
TROPHIS VATERIA XIMENIA XYLOPIA
XYLOSMA ZELKOVA AESCULUS
ALANGIUM ALBIZZIA ALSTONIA
ANTIARIS AVERRHOA BALANOPS
BALOGHIA BAUHINIA BRABEJUM
BROSIMUM BUDDLEIA CABRALEA
CAMELLIA CANARIUM CAPPARIS
CARAGANA CARPINUS CARYOCAR
CASEARIA CASTANEA CASTILLA
CECROPIA CINCHONA CODIAEUM
CONDALIA CYBISTAX DII LENIA
DIPTERYX DODONAEA DOVYALIS
DRACAENA DUBOISIA EUCOMMIA
EUONYMUS EUPTELEA EXOSTEMA
FITZROYA FRAXINUS FUNTUMIA
GARCINIA GARDENIA GORDONIA
GUAIACUM HIBISCUS HIRTELLA
HOMALIUM HYMENAEA ILLICIUM
JATROPHA KANDELIA KNIGHTIA

LABURNUM LAPORTEA LAVATERA
LECYTHIS LEUCAENA LYSILOMA
MAGNOLIA MALLOTUS MAYTENUS
MESPILUS MICHELIA MIMUSOPS
MYOPORUM NOTELAEA PHOTINIA
PISCIDIA PISTACIA PLATANUS
PLUMIERA PONCIRUS PROSOPIS
QUILLAJA RAVENALA ROLLINIA
SAMADERA SAMBUCUS SANTALUM
SAPINDUS SAURAUIA SESBANIA
SIMARUBA SPONDIAS SWARTZIA
TABEBUIA TAXODIUM TORRUBIA
TRECULIA VARRONIA VERONICA
VIBURNUM VIRGILIA VOCHYSIA
(— OF TUNICATE) SALPA ASCIDIA
DOLIOLUM
(— OF TURTLE) EMYS AMYDA
CHELUS CHELYS CARETTA CHELONE
CLEMMYS TESTUDO TRIONYX
ARCHELON CHELONIA CHELYDRA
PELUSIOS
(— OF TWINER) STEMONA
(— OF UNIVALVE) DOLIUM
(— OF VINE) ROSA ABRUS ABUTA
PISUM TAMUS UNONA VIGNA VITIS
AKEBIA CISSUS COBAEA DERRIS
ENTADA HEDERA MUCUNA PETREA
POTHOS SICANA SICYOS SOLLYA
VIORNA ARAUJIA BASELLA
BOMAREA BRYONIA ECHITES
EMBELIA EPACRIS FALCATA
HUMULUS IPOMOEA MIKANIA
PISONIA SECHIUM UNCARIA
ZANONIA ANAMIRTA ATRAGENE
BIGNONIA CLEMATIS COCCULUS
DEGUELIA DOLICHOS EUONYMUS
JASMINUM KENNEDYA PANDOREA
PUERARIA SECAMONE SERJANIA
TACSONIA WISTARIA
(— OF WALRUS) ODOBENUS
(— OF WASP) SPHEX VESPA BEMBEX
CYNIPS SCOLIA TIPHIA CHRYSIS
EUMENES MASARIS MUTILLA
ANDRICUS CHLORION ODYNERUS
POLISTES POMPILUS SPHECIUS
(— OF WEASEL) MUSTELA
(— OF WEED) CAPSELLA
(— OF WEEVIL) APION HYPERA
SITONA CLEONUS CALANDRA
CALENDRA CURCULIO
(— OF WHALE) CETE ARETA KOGIA
BALAENA ORCINUS ZIPHIUS
PHYSETER
(— OF WOLVERINE) GULO
(— OF WORM) DERO SPIO ALARIA
EUNICE KERRIA MERMIS NEREIS
SYLLIS ACHAETA ACHOLOE ASCARIS
DUGESIA EISENIA FILARIA GLYCERA
GORDIUS HESIONE LEODICE
POLYNOE SABELLA SAGITTA
SERPULA SETARIA SPIRURA TUBIFEX
ARABELLA ASCAROPS BIPALIUM
BONELLIA COOPERIA DOCHMIUS

ECHIURUS FASCIOLA GEOPLANA
PHORONIS SPADELLA SUBULURA
SYNGAMUS SYPHACIA
(— OF ZORIL) ICTONYX
(PREF.) GEN(O)
(SUFF.) IA
GEODE DRUSE
GEOGRAPHER AMERICAN BAKER
DAVIS GUYOT RONNE ATWOOD
BOWMAN BRYANT SEMPLE
DAVIDSON HUTCHINS MITCHELL
ROBINSON GROSVENOR
HUNTINGTON
ARAB BAKRI
AUSTRIAN KORISTKA PAULITSCHKE
CANADIAN PALLISER
DUTCH BLAEU
EGYPTIAN PTOLEMY
ENGLISH BEKE PEEL KEANE BEAZLEY
EVEREST HAKLUYT MARKHAM
RENNELL THOMPSON GREENOUGH
MACKINDER FRESHFIELD
FRENCH JOMARD RECLUS VALLOT
ANVILLE DELISLE DEMANGEON
GERMAN BEHM KOHL BANSE PENCK
VOGEL ANDREE BEHAIM CLUVER
RATZEL RITTER APIANUS EBELING
GERLAND HETTNER KIEPERT
KRUMMEL PESCHEL SCHONER
BERGHAUS BRUCKNER BUSCHING
DRYGALSKI PETERMANN
RICHTHOFEN CHRISTALLER
GREEK SCYLAX STRABO MARINUS
PYTHEAS DIONYSIUS PAUSANIAS
ERATOSTHENES
HUNGARIAN TELEKI
ICELANDIC THORODDSEN
ITALIAN BALBI CODAZZI AMORETTI
MARSIGLI
POLISH LELEWEL
PORTUGUESE CORDEIRO
RUSSIAN SEMENOV GERASIMOV
KROPOTKIN SHOKALSKI
PRZHEVALSKY
SCOTTISH MILL BROWN JOHNSTON
SPANISH COSA
SWEDISH HEDIN
GEOLOGIST AMERICAN DALY DANA
HALL KEMP KING REID TARR CROSS
GUYOT HAGUE HOBBS LEITH MCGEE
ORTON SCOTT SMITH SPURR WHITE
ARNOLD ATWOOD BAYLEY DUTTON
EMMONS FOSTER HAYDEN HOLMES
IRVING JAGGAR LAWSON LESLEY
MARCOU MATHER MENARD POWELL
SHALER UPJOHN WRIGHT BALLARD
BARRELL BRANNER GILBERT
HOLLICK IDDINGS JOHNSON
MACLURE MERRILL PIRSSON
RANSOME RUSSELL TALMAGE
VANHISE WHITNEY WRATHER
LEVERETT MASURSKY MITCHELL
NEWBERRY PUMPELLY SILLIMAN

WINCHELL HITCHCOCK JOHANNSEN
SALISBURY TWENHOFEL
CHAMBERLIN LOUDERBACK
WASHINGTON
AUSTRALIAN DAVID MAWSON
AUSTRIAN BECKE HAUER SUESS
HAIDINGER HOCHSTETTER
MOJSISOVICS
BELGIAN RENARD
CANADIAN BELL ADAMS LOGAN
DAWSON TYRRELL WALLACE
DANISH KOCH
DUTCH TROMP
ENGLISH BELT TATE FUCHS JUKES
LYELL SMITH SORBY ANSTED
BONNEY CLARKE FORBES HOLMES
MAWSON SCROPE DAWKINS
GREGORY HOLLAND MANTELL
BUCKLAND LYDEKKER PHILLIPS
SEDGWICK GREENOUGH
MURCHISON PRESTWICH
STRICKLAND
FRENCH FOUQUE ARCHIAC DAURREE
DELESSE BARRANDE BEAUMONT
BERTRAND DOLOMIEU DUFRENOY
LAPPARENT
GERMAN BUCH ABICH COHEN
DECHEN ROEMER WERNER ZITTEL
ALBERTI BISCHOF CREDNER GEINITZ
LEONHARD QUENSTEDT
KEYSERLING ROSENBUSCH
ICELANDIC THORODDSEN
IRISH OLDHAM
ITALIAN MERCALLI
NEW ZEALAND HAAST
NORWEGIAN BROGGER KJERULF
RUSSIAN ORRUCHEV
SCOTTISH HALL CROLL LYELL GEIKIE
HUTTON MILLER RAMSAY OGLIVIE
PLAYFAIR MACCULLOCH
SWEDISH ANTEVS TORELL HISINGER
NATHORST NORDENSKJOLD
SWISS HEIM DELUC
GEOMETRIC CUBIST CUBISTIC
(— TERM) SECANT
GEOMETRY EUCLID SPHERICS
(KIND OF —) SOLID
GEOPHAGY PICA

GEORGIA

CAPITAL: ATLANTA
COLLEGE: SPELMAN MOREHOUSE
COUNTY: BIBB CLAY COBB COOK HALL
TIFT WARE BANKS BRYAN BUTTS
DOOLY EARLY FLOYD GRADY PEACH
RABUN TROUP WORTH COFFEE
COWETA DEKALB ECHOLS ELBERT
FANNIN FULTON JASPER LANIER
OCONEE TWIGGS WILKES CATOOSA
LAURENS LUMPKIN GWINNETT
MUSCOGEE
INDIAN: GUALE YUCHI CHIAHA
OCONEE YAMASEE

LAKE: LANIER MARTIN HARDING
NOTTELY BANKHEAD HARTWELL
SINCLAIR
MOUNTAIN: STONE KENNESAW
NATIVE: CRACKER
PRESIDENT: CARTER
RIVER: PEA FLINT ETOWAH OCONEE
PIGEON CONECUH SATILLA
ALTAMAHA OCMULGEE
STATE BIRD: THRASHER
STATE NICKNAME: PEACH
STATE TREE: LIVEOAK
TOWN: JESUP MACON JASPER OCILLA
AUGUSTA CONYERS DECATUR
ELLIJAY GRIFFIN VIDALIA MARIETTA
MOULTRIE SAVANNAH VALDOSTA
WAYCROSS
UNIVERSITY: EMORY GATECH MERCER

GEORGIA (ALSO SEE RUSSIA)

CAPITAL: TIFLIS TBILISI
COIN: RUBLE
LANGUAGE: KARTVELIAN
MOUNTAIN: USHBA SHKHARA
TETNULD DIDIABULI RUSTAVELI
MOUNTAIN RANGE: LIKHI KARTLI
LOMISI LIKHSKY MESKHET
CAUCASUS LOMISSKY MESKHETI
KARTLIYSKY KARTALINIAN
PEOPLE: GORJ OSSET GEORGIAN
KARTVELI SAKARTVELO
PLAIN: KARTLI COLCHIS KOLKHIDA
KARTALINIAN
RIVER: KURA RIONI INGURI KODORI
MTKVARI
TOWN: GORI POTI BATUMI KUTAISI
RUSTAVI SUKHUMI KHASHURI
MTSKHETA
VOLCANO: KAZBEK MKINVARI

GEORGIAN ADZHAR CRACKER
GEORGIA PINE LONGLEAF
GEPHYREAN STARWORM
GER STRANGER
GERAINT (WIFE OF —) ENID
GERANIUM DOVEFOOT FLUXWEED
SHAMEFACE
GERANIUM LAKE SPARK NACARAT
GERANIUM PINK BERMUDA
GERBIL JIRD
GERIANOL ISOLATE
GERM BUG CHIT SEED SPARK SPAWN
SPERM GERMEN GERMULE MICROBE
SEMINAL RUDIMENT SEEDLING
SEMINARY SEMINIUM
(— CELL) GONE
(PREF.) BLAST(O) SPERM(A)(ATI)
(ATIO)(ATO)(I)(IO)(O)
(SUFF.) BLAST(IC)(Y) SPERM(A)(AE)
(AL)(IA)(IC)(OUS)(UM)(Y)
GERMAN BALT HANS ALMAN HEINE
JERRY ALMAIN DUTCHY HEINIE

TEUTON TEDESCO COTILLON
GERMANIC TUDESQUE
(PREF.) TEUTO
GERMANDER POLY BETONY
FOXTAIL SOVENEZ SCORDIUM
GERMANE GERMAN APROPOS
RELEVANT PERTINENT
GERMANIC GOTHIC GOTHONIC
TEUTONIC
GERMAN MEASLES ROSEOLA
RUBELLA
GERMAN SHEPHERD ALSATIAN
GERMAN SILVER ALBATA

GERMANY
ANCIENT: ALMAIN ALMAINE
ANCIENT TRIBESMAN: JUTE TEUTON
VISIGOTH OSTROGOTH
CANAL: KIEL WESER LUDWIG
CAPITAL: BERLIN
CHEESE: MUENSTER TILSITER
LIMBURGER
COAL REGION: RUHR SAAR SARRE
COIN: MARK KRONE TALER GULDEN
KRONEN THALER PFENNIG
GROSCHEN
DIALECT: KOLSCH KOELSCH BALTISCH
HESSISCH
DYNASTY: HOHENSTAUFEN
HOHENZOLLERN
FOOD: WURST KNODEL SPATZLE
STRUDEL MARZIPAN ROULADEN
HANSEATIC CITY: KOLN LUBECK
COLOGNE HAMBURG LUEBECK
ISLAND: USEDOM WOLLIN FEHMARN
FRISIAN
LAKE: DUMMER WURMSEE
AMMERSEE BODENSEE CHIEMSEE
MURITZEE CONSTANCE
LANGUAGE: DEUTSCH
MEASURE: AAM IMI OHM FASS FUSS
LAST RUTE SACK STAB CARAT
EIMER KANNE KETTE LINIE MAASS
METZE RUTHE SIMRI MASSEL
MORGEN OXHOFT SEIDEL STRICH
JUCHART KLAFTER TAGWERK
SCHEFFEL SCHOPPEN STUBCHEN
VIERLING
MONEY: NOTGELD OSTMARK
MOUNTAIN: FELDBERG WATZMANN
MOUNTAIN RANGE: ORE ALPS HARZ
RHON HARDT HUNSRUCK
NAME: REICH ASHKENAZ GERMANIA
DEUTSCHLAND
NATIVE: GOTH SAXON TEUTON
PORT: EMDEN BREMEN HAMBURG
ROSTOCK STETTIN
RESORT: EMS BADEN AACHEN
RIVER: ALZ EMS INN EDER EGER ELBE
ISAR LAHN LECH MAIN NAAB NAHE
ODER OKER REMS RUHR SAAR SIEG
ALLER DONAU EIDER FULDA HAVEL
HUNTE ILLER LEINE LIPPE MOSEL

MULDE PEENE REGEN RHEIN RHINE
SAALE SAUER SPREE UCKER VECHT
WERRA WESER DANUBE ELSTER
KOCHER NECKAR NEISSE RANDOW
TAUBER WARNOW ALTMUHL
JEETZEL PEGNITZ SALZACH
UNSTRUT
STATE: BADEN HESSE LIPPE BAYERN
BREMEN HESSEN SAXONY BAVARIA
HAMBURG PRUSSIA SAARLAND
BRUNSWICK
TOWN: AUE EMS HOF ULM BONN
GERA GOCH HAAR HAMM JENA KIEL
KOLN LAHR SUHL AALEN AHLEN
EMDEN ESSEN FURTH GOTHA
HAGEN HALLE HERNE MAINZ
MOLLN NEUSS PIRNA TRIER
AACHEN ALTENA ALTONA BARMEN
BERLIN BREMEN CASSEL DACHAU
DESSAU ERFURT KASSEL LINDEN
LUBECK MUNICH PLAUEN TREVES
BAMBERG BRESLAU COBLENZ
COLOGNE COTTBUS CREFELD
DRESDEN GORLITZ HAMBURG
HANOVER LEIPZIG MAYENCE
MUNCHEN MUNSTER POTSDAM
ROSTOCK SPANDAU ZWICKAU
AUGSBURG CHEMNITZ DORTMUND
DUISBURG FREIBURG LIEGNITZ
MANNHEIM NURNBERG SCHWERIN
WURSELEN WURZBURG
DARMSTADT KARLSRUHE
MAGDEBURG NUREMBERG
OSNABRUCK STUTTGART
WUPPERTAL DUSSELDORF
HEIDELBERG OBERHAUSEN
UNIVERSITY TOWN: FREIBURG
HEIDELBERG
WEIGHT: LOT GRAN LOTE LOTH UNZE
LOTHE PFUND STEIN PRUNDE
DRACHMA ZENTNER VIERLING
WINE: MOSELLE RIESLING

GERMFREE AXENIC
GERMICIDE KRELOS MERBROMIN
GERMINABLE PREGNANT
GERMINATE BUD HIT CHIP CHIT
GERM SHOOT SPIRE SPRIT BRAIRD
SPROUT STRIKE PULLULATE
GERMINATION CATCH
GERSHOM (FATHER OF —) LEVI
MOSES
(MOTHER OF —) ZIPPORAH
GERSHWIN IRA GEORGE
GERYON (DOG OF —) ORTHUS
(FATHER OF —) CHRYSAOR
(MOTHER OF —) CALLIRRHOE
(SLAYER OF —) HERCULES
GESAN TAPUYAN CHAVANTE
GESHAM (FATHER OF —) JAHDAI
GESTATION GOING BREEDING
PREGNANCY
GESTE DEED

GESTICULATE GESTURE
GESTURE CUT FIG BECK BERE GEST
SIGN FILIP GESTE HONOR SANNA
ACTION BECKON BREATH CUTOFF
FILLIP MOTION SALUTE SIGNAL
CURTSEY FASHION FLICKER
MURGEON ACCOLADE CEREMONY
(— OF DERISION) SNOOK
(— OF DOUBT) SHRUG
(— OF SALUTATION) SALAAM
(AFFECTED —) GAATCH
(HAND —) MUDRA
(HINDU —) NAMASTE
(OBSCENE —) BIRD
(OSTENTATIOUS —) POMP
(THREATENING —) MINT
(USELESS —) FUTILITY
GET COP DIG GIT WIN EARN FALL
GAIN GRAB HAVE HENT TAKE TILL
AFONG ANNEX CATCH COVER FETCH
LATCH DERIVE OBTAIN PUZZLE
SECURE ACQUIRE CAPTURE
COMPARE CONQUER PROCURE
PRODUCE RECEIVE PERCEIVE
* (— ABOARD) FLIP
(— ABOUT) BEGO NAVIGATE
(— ALONG) DO GEE FARE FEND
AGREE FADGE FODGE SPEED FETTLE
(— AROUND) BYPASS COMPASS
FINESSE FLUMMER OUTFLANK
(— AT) ACCESS ATTAIN
(— AWAY) LAM RYNT SLIP EVADE
CHEESE ESCAPE
(— BACK) REDEEM RETIRE RECOVER
(— BETTER OF) WAX BEST DING
DOWN DAUNT FLING SHEND SHENT
STICK STING JOCKEY OVERGO
RECOVER OVERCOME SURMOUNT
(— BY ARTIFICE) WIND
(— BY ASKING) KICK
(— BY CUNNING) WHIZZLE
(— BY EXTORTION) GRATE
(— BY FLATTERY) COG
(— CLEAR OF) STRIP
(— DISHONESTLY) FIRK
(— DOWN) ALIGHT
(— DRUNK) SOUSE
(— IN RETURN) REAP
(— LOST) STRAY TRAIK
(— ON) AGE FARE BOARD CHEFE
CHEVE FRAME MOUNT SHIFT
EXPLOIT
(— ON WELL) LIKE
(— OUT) LEAK SCRAM CHEESE
OUTWIN VOETSAK
(— PAST) BEAT HURDLE
(— POSSESSION) CARRY
(— READY) GET BOUN PARE RANK
BOWNE BRACE FRAME FETTLE
ORDAIN APPAREL
(— RID) CAST DISH DUMP FREE JUNK
SHAD TOSS ERASE SHAKE SHIFT
SHOOT SLOUGH UNLOAD DELIVER

DISCARD EXTRUDE DISPATCH
DISSOLVE
(— SURREPTITIOUSLY) SNEAK
(— THE POINT) SAVVY
(— TO BOTTOM OF) FATHOM
(— UNDER CONTROL) RAIM
(— UNDER WAY) ROLL
(— UP) ARISE HUDDUP UPRISE
HAIRPIN
(PREF.) (— OFF) DE
GETA SABOT
GETHER (FATHER OF —) ARAM
GETHSEMANE (LOCALE OF —)
OLIVET
GETTING (— ON) TOWARD
(— OUT OF BED) LEVEE
GET-TOGETHER DO DRINK HOBNOB
BAMBOCHE POTLATCH
GET-UP ATTIRE
GETUP SETOUT
GEWGAW DIE TOY WALY KNACK
WALLY BAUBLE FANGLE FEGARY
JIGGER FLAMFEW TRANGAM
TRINKET FOLDEROL GIMCRACK
JIMCRACK TRIMTRAM
GEYSER BORE JETTER

GHANA

CAPITAL: ACCRA
COIN: PESEWA
DAM: AKOSOMBO
LAKE: VOLTA BOSUMTWI
LANGUAGE: GA EWE TWI FANTI
   HAUSA DAGBANI DAGOMBA
MONEY: CEDI NEWCEDI
MOUNTAIN: AFADJATO
NATIVE: GA EWE AHAFO BRONG FANTI
   ASHANTI DAGOMBA MAMPRUSI
REGION: VOLTA ASHANTI
   BRONGAHAFO
RIVER: OTI PRA DAKA TANO AFRAM
   VOLTA ANKOBRA KULPAWN
TOWN: HO WA ODA AXIM FIAN KETA
   TALA TEMA ACCRA BAWKU ENCHI
   LAWRA LEGON SAMPA YAPEI
   DUNKWA KARAGA KPANDU KUMASI
   NSAWAM OBUASI SWEDRU TAMALE
   TARKWA WASIPE ANTUBIA
   DAMONGO MAMPONG PRESTEA
   SEKONDI SUNYANI WINNEBA
   AKOSOMBO KINTAMPO TAKORADI
WIND: HARMATTAN

GHARRY SHIGRAM
GHASTLY WAN GASH GRIM PALE
BLATE GHAST LURID UNKET UNKID
DISMAL GOUSTY GRISLY PALLID
CHARNEL DEATHLY FEARFUL
GASTFUL GRIZZLY GRUGOUS
HIDEOUS MACABRE DREADFUL
GRUESOME HORRIBLE SHOCKING
TERRIBLE
GHAWAZI BARAMIKA

GHAZEL ODE POEM
GHERKIN CUCUMBER CORNICHON
GHETTO JEWRY JUDAISM
GHIBELLINE WAIBLING
GHOST HAG KER BHUT HANT JUBA
WAFF BUGAN CADDY DUFFY DUPPY
FETCH GAIST GUEST HAUNT JUMBY
LARVA PRETA SHADE SPOOK UMBRA
CHUREL IDOLON SOWLTH SPIRIT
SPRITE TAISCH ANTAEUS ANTAIOS
BOGGART BUGGANE GYTRASH
PHANTOM SPECTER SPECTRE
VAMPIRE BARGHEST GUYTRASH
PHANTASM REVENANT
(PREF.) SPECTRO SPOOKO
GHOSTFISH WRYMOUTH
GHOSTLY EERY EERIE GOUSTY
SHADOWY UNCANNY WEIRDLY
CHTHONIC GHASTFUL SPECTRAL
GHOST MOTH SWIFT HEPIALID
GHOSTS (AUTHOR OF —) IBSEN
(CHARACTER IN —) HELEN JACOB
ALVING OSWALD REGINA MANDERS
ENGSTRAND
GHOST-WRITER SPOOK
GHOULISH SATANIC
GHUZ OGHUZ
GI DOGFACE SOLDIER
GIAI NHANG
**GIANNI SCHICCHI (CHARACTER IN
—)** BUOSO DONATI LAURETTA
RINUCCIO SCHICCHI
(COMPOSER OF —) PUCCINI
GIANT ORC ANAK ETEN HUGE OGRE
OTUS WATE YMER YMIR AFRIT
BALOR CACUS HYMIR JOTUN MIMAS
MIMER THRYM TITAN TROLL AFREET
ALBION FAFNIR GIGANT GOEMOT
PALLAS THJAZI THURSE TITYUS
WARLOW ANTAEUS CYCLOPS
GOLIATH WARLOCK ASCOPART
BELLERUS COLBRAND GIGANTIC
GOEMAGOT GOGMAGOG
MASTODON MORGANTE ORGOGLIO
TYPHOEUS PROCRUSTES
(1-EYED —) CYCLOPS
(100-EYED —) ARGUS
(100-HANDED —) GYGES COTTUS
BRIAREUS
(1000-ARMED —) BANA
(PL.) ANAK ANAKIM COTTUS
ALOADAE REPHAIM NEPHILIM
ZAMZUMMIM
(PREF.) GIGANT(I)(O)
GIANTESS NORN ARGANTE
GIANT FULMAR NELLY STINKER
STINKPOT
GIANT GRASS OTATE
GIANT HERON GOLIATH
GIANTISM ACROMEGALY
GIANTLIKE CYCLOPIC CYCLOPEAN
CYCLOPIAN

GIANT LILY FIGUE MAGUEY
GIANT PUFFBALL FUZZ FUZZBALL
**GIANTS IN THE EARTH (AUTHOR
OF —)** ROLVAAG
(CHARACTER IN —) OLE PER ANNA
HANS OLSA BERET HANSA PEDER
GIARDIA LAMBLIA
GIB JIB SHOE DEMUR SLIPPER
GIBBAR GIBBERT JUBARTAS
GIBBER CHAT CHATTER
GIBBERISH GREEK JABBER JARGON
CHOCTAW ABRACADABRA
GIBBET STOB TREE CROOK JEBAT
GALLOWS POTENCE EQUULEUS
GIBBON LAR WAWA UNGKA WUYEN
CAMPER HULOCK HOOLOCK
SIAMANG HYLOBATE
GIBBOUS CONVEX HULCHY HUMPED
SACCATE
GIBE (ALSO SEE JIBE) BOB RUB GIRD
JAPE JEST JIBE PROG QUIB QUIP
SKIT WIPE FLEER FLING FLIRT FRUMP
GLEEK KNACK SCOFF SCOMM
SCORN SLANT SNEER DERIDE
GLANCE HECKLE BROCARD
SARCASM RIDICULE
GIBING SNASH
GID DUNT GIDDY STURDY GOGGLES
POTHERY VERTIGO
GIDDALTI (FATHER OF —) HEMAN
GIDDINESS LUNACY SOORAWN
GIDDY GAGA AREEL BARMY DITSY
DITZY GLAKY INANE LIGHT SILLY
SPACY WESTY GIGLET GLAKED
GOWKED GOWKIT SHANNY STURDY
VOLAGE GLAIKET LARKING
HALUCKET HELLICAT SKIPPING
GIDDY-HEADED HELLICAT
GIDEON (FATHER OF —) JOASH
GIDEONI (SON OF —) ABIDAN
GIFT BOX FOY QUO SOP BENT BOON
DASH ENAM MEED SAND BONUS
BRIBE CAULP CUDDY DONUM FLAIR
GRANT KNACK TOKEN BEFANA
CADEAU DASHEE DONARY GENIUS
GERSUM GIFTIE GIVING HANSEL
LEGACY RECADO REGALO TALENT
XENIUM APTNESS BEFFANA BENEFIT
CHARISM CHARITY DEODATE
DONATIO DOUCEUR ETRENNE
FACULTY FAIRING GIFTURE HANDSEL
PRESENT PROPINE REGALIO
SUBSIDY TASHRIF TRIBUTE
AMATORIO APTITUDE BENEFICE
BESTOWAL BLESSING COURTESY
DONATION DONATIVE GARRISON
GIVEAWAY GRATUITY MORTUARY
OBLATION OFFERING POTLATCH
SPORTULA BENEFACTION
REMEMBRANCE PHILANTHROPY
PRESENTATION
(— FROM HUSBAND TO WIFE) ARRAS

(— OF GOD) GRACE
(— OF MONEY) POUCH GARNISH
BAKSHISH BAKSHEESH
(— OF NATURE) DOWER DOWRY
(— RECEIVER) DONEE
(— TO GOD) DEODATE
(— TO ROMAN PEOPLE) CONGIARY
(CHARITABLE —) ALMS ENAM
PITTANCE
(COMPULSORY —) SIXENIA
(LIBERAL —) LARGESSE
(NATURAL —) TALENT
(NEW YEAR'S EVE —) ETRENNE
HAGMENA HOGMANAY
(SPIRITUAL —) CHARISM CHARISMA
(PL.) OBLATA MISSILES
GIFTBOOK ANNUAL KEEPSAKE
GIG RUN TUB MOZE BANDY BUGGY
CHAIR GIGGE CHAISE CLATCH
DENNET WHISKY CALESIN TILBURY
STANHOPE ENGAGEMENT
GIGANTIC HUGE GIANT MAMMOTH
TITANIC COLOSSAL ENORMOUS
GIGANTAL ATLANTEAN MONSTROUS
BROBDINGNAGIAN
GIGGER TEASELER
GIGGLE TEHEE KECKLE NICKER
TEEHEE TITTER SNICKER TWITTER
GIGLET JIG
GIL BLAS
GIL BLAS (AUTHOR OF —) LESAGE
(CHARACTER IN —) GIL BLAS LEWIS
PEREZ AURORA MENCIA SCIPIO
ANTONIA ARSENIA ROLANDO
ALPHONSO DOROTHEA FABRICIO
MATTHIAS OLIVAREZ SANGRADO
GILD GILT BEGILD ENGILD ORFGILD
GILDED GILT AURATE INAURATE
GILDER TRACER
GILEAD (FATHER OF —) MACHIR
(SON OF —) JEPHTHAH
GILGAMESH IZDUBAR
GILL JILL QUAD GHYLL PLICA GILLIE
LAMELLA BRANCHIA QUADRANT
(—S OF BIVALVE) BEARD
(PL.) GINNERS CHOLLERS
BRANCHIAE
(SUFF.) BRANCH(IA)(IATE)
GILLAR PITTO
GILLIE GILLY HENCHMAN
GILLS
(PREF.) BRANCHI(O)
GILLYFLOWER STOCK GILVER
GELOFRE GILLIVER
GILT SOW
GILTHEAD CONNER MELANURE
GIMBAL GEMEL JEMBLE
GIMCRACK QUIP BAUBLE FIZGIG
GEWGAW JIMJAM TRIFLE TRANGAM
TRINKET JIMCRACK WHIMWHAM
GIMLET SCREW WIMBLE PIERCEL
PIERCER

GIMMICK GAFF SHTIK SHTICK
SCHTICK
GIMP TAR ORRIS GUIMPE GIMPING
GIN MAX CRAB GRIN LACE RUIN TAPE
TRAP CLEAN JACKY SNARE SNARL
DIDDLE GENEVA JAMBER JAMMER
SPRINGE TITTERY TWANKAY
EYEWATER HOLLANDS SCHIEDAM
SCHNAPPS
(— AND TREACLE) MAHOGANY
(BAD —) RUIN
(DROP OF —) DAFFY
GINATH (SON OF —) TIBNI
GINGER PEPPER RATOON AROMATIC
ZINZIBER COLTSFOOT
GINGERBREAD SPICE PARKIN
PEPPERCAKE
GINGERLY GINGER WARILY CHARILY
EDGINGLY
GINGERROOT HAND RACE
(PL.) ASARUM
GINGHAM CHAMBRAY
GINKGO ICHO
GINSENG SANG FATIL PANAX
ARALIA IVYWORT REDBERRY
GIOCONDA, LA (CHARACTER IN —)
ENZO CIECA LAURA ALVISE
BARNABA GIOCONDA GRIMALDO
(COMPOSER OF —) PONCHIELLI
GIRAFFE OONT CAMEL DAPPLE
KAMEEL SERAPH CAMAILE
RUMINANT
GIRASOL OPAL
GIRD BELT BIND GIRR GIRT HASP
YERK CLOSE SCOFF ENGIRD ENRING
FASTEN GIRDLE BEGIRD ACCINGE
ENVIRON CINCTURE SURROUND
GIRDER BEAM GIRD GIRT GIRTH
TABLE TRUSS BINDER SUMMER
WARREN GIRDING TWISTER
BUCKSTAY STRINGER
GIRDING CINCTURE
GIRDLE OBI ZON BARK BELT CEST
GIRD HOOP SASH ZONA ZONE
CEINT GIRTH MITER PATTE SARPE
WAIST BODICE CESTUS CINGLE
CIRCLE MOOCHA TISSUE ZODIAC
ZONULA ZOSTER BALDRIC
BALTEUS CENTRUM CENTURE
COMPASS GIRDING SHINGLE
CEINTURE CINCTURE CINGULUM
SURROUND
(— FOR HELMET) TISSUE
(— OF CASSOCK) SURCINGLE
(— OF DIATOM) HOOP
(BRIDE'S —) CEST CESTUS
(LITTLE —) ZONULE ZONLET
(ROYAL —) MALO
(SACRED —) KUSTI
(PREF.) ZON(I)(O) ZOSTERI ZOSTERO
(SUFF.) PLEURA
GIRDLED KUNG

GIRL BIT GAL HER KIT POP SHE SIS TIB
TID TIT BABE BABY BINT BIRD CHIT
DAME DEEM DELL GILL JANE JILL
JUDY LASS MARY MOPS MORT PERI
PUSS SLUT WREN BEAST BUNNY
FILLY FLUFF GUIDE KITTY LUBRA
QUEAN SISSY SKIRT TIDDY TITTY
TOOTS TRULL BURDIE CALICO
CLINER CUMMER DALAGA DAMSEL
DEEMIE FEMALE FIZGIG GEISHA
GIRLIE LASSIE LOVELY MAGGIE
NUMBER PIGEON SHEILA SISTER
SUBDEB TOMATO CAMILLA COLLEEN
CRUMPET DAMOSEL MADCHEN
MAUTHER TENDREL BONNIBEL
FARMETTE FEMININE GRISETTE
MUCHACHA
(— NOT YET 13) PRETEEN
(— OF MEXICAN DESCENT) CHICANA
(AGILE —) YANKER
(AWKWARD —) HOIT
(BEATIFIED —) BEATA
(BEAUTIFUL —) PERI BELLE
(BOISTEROUS —) GILPY GILPEY
(BOLD —) HOIDEN HOYDEN
(CAMP FIRE —) ARTISAN
(CHORUS —) CHORINE CORYPHEE
(CLUMSY —) TAUPIE TAWPIE
(COUNTRY —) MEG JOAN
(DANCING —) ALMA DASI ALMAH
KISANG KISAENG BAYADERE
DEVADASI
(DANCING —S) GHAWAZI
(DEAR —) PEAT
(DUMPY —) CUTTY
(FLIGHTY —) GOOSECAP
(FLIRTATIOUS —) JADE JILLET
(FLOWER —) NYDIA
(FORWARD —) STRAP
(FROLICSOME —) GILPY
(GANGSTER'S —) MOLL
(GIDDY —) GIG GIGLET GIGLOT
JILLET
(GREEK —) HAIDEE
(GYPSY —) GITANA
(HIRED —) BIDDY BIDDIE
(IMPUDENT —) STRAP
(JAPANESE —) GEISHA
(LITTLE —) SIS COOKY SISSY COOKIE
LASSOCK
(MISCHIEVOUS —) CUTTY HUSSY
(MODEST —) BLUSHET
(NAIVE —) INGENUE
(NON-JEWISH —) SHIKSE SHICKSA
(PERT —) MINX HUSSY
(PRETTY —) PRIM BUNNY
(PRETTY—) BUNNY
(PRETTY —) CUTEY CUTIE
(ROMPING —) STAG TOMBOY
(SAUCY —) SNIP
(SEDUCTIVE —) LOLITA
(SERVANT —) SLUT
(SHIFTLESS —) MYSTERY

(SILLY —) SKIT
(SINGING —) ALMA ALMEH
(SLENDER —) SYLPH
(SMALL —) PINAFORE
(SPIRITED —) FILLY
(UNATTRACTIVE —) FRUMP
(UNMARRIED —) MOUSME TOWDIE
MUSUMEE MADEMOISELLE
(WANTON —) GIG FILLOCK
(WILD —) BLOWZE
(WORKING —) ORISETTE
(WORTHLESS —) HUSSY
(YOUNG —) BUD MODER TITTY
MAIDEN MOTHER BAGGAGE
COLLEEN FLAPPER GIRLEEN
ROSEBUD
(PL.) GIRLERY GIRLHOOD
(PREF.) PUPI
GIRLFRIEND LADY STEADY
(GANGSTER'S —) MOLL
GIRL OF THE GOLDEN WEST
(CHARACTER IN —) DICK JACK
RANCE MINNIE JOHNSON RAMERREZ
(COMPOSER OF —) PUCCINI
GIRT CINCT
GIRTH GIRD GIRT TAPE CINCH GARTH
GIRSE GRETH WANTY CINGLE
WARROK COMPASS GIRDING
SHINGLE WEBBING
GIST JET NET NUB SUM CHAT CORE
GITE KNOT MEAT PITH GREAT HEART
JOIST POINT SENSE BURDEN
KERNEL ESSENCE PURPORT
SUMMARY STRENGTH
GITH MELANTHY
GIVE ADD GIE HOB TIP BEAR DEAL
DOLE HAND METE SELL TAKE WEVE
WHIP YEVE ALLOW AWARD COUGH
GRANT REFER YIELD ACCORD
AFFORD BESTOW CONFER DEMISE
DOTATE FASTEN IMPART IMPOSE
IMPUTE RENDER SUPPLY CONSIGN
DELIVER FORGIVE FURNISH PRESENT
PROPINE BEQUEATH DISPENSE
(— A BOOST) BOLSTER
(— ADHERENCE) ASSENT
(— ADMITTANCE) ACCEPT
(— ADVICE) READ ADVISE
(— AN ACCOUNT) TELL RELATE
REPORT
(— ANYTHING NAUSEOUS TO) DOSE
(— A PLACE TO) SITUATE
(— APPROVAL) CONSENT
(— A REASON) ACCOUNT
(— A REMEDY) MINISTER
(— AS CONCESSION) YETTE
(— AS EXPLANATION) ASSIGN
(— ASSURANCE) EFFRONT
(— ATTENTION TO) HEED
(— AUTHORITY) ENABLE EMPOWER
ACCREDIT
(— AWAY) PART

(— BACK) REFUND RETURN RESTORE
(— BIRTH) KIT BEAR BORN DROP FIND
MAKE BEGET BREED ISSUE WORLD
FARROW KINDLE LITTER DELIVER
FRESHEN
(— BY WILL) DEVISE
(— CARE) NURSE
(— CLAIM TO) REMISE
(— COUNSEL) AREAD AREED
(— CREDIT FOR) FRIST
(— CURRENCY TO) PASS
(— EAR) HARK HARKEN LISTEN
HEARKEN
(— EXPRESSION TO) EMOTE FRAME
VOICE
(— FORM) CUT
(— FORTH) WARP YIELD AFFORD
CONCEIVE
(— GROUND) RETIRE
(— HEED) LOOK ATTEND
(— IN) BOW RELENT CONCEDE
COLLAPSE
(— IN EXCHANGE) SWAP SWOP
(— INFORMATION) WARN
(— IN MARRIAGE) BESTOW SPOUSE
(— INSTRUCTION) LEAR
(— NAME TO) BAPTIZE
(— NOTICE) WARN HERALD APPRISE
PUBLISH ANNOUNCE INTIMATE
(— NOTICE TO APPEAR) GARNISH
(— OBLIQUE EDGE) CANT
(— OFF) EMIT SEND SHED EXUDE
FLING DIVIDE EXPIRE EFFUSE EVOLVE
EXHALE EXCRETE SEPARATE
(— ONE'S SELF OVER TO) ADDICT
(— ONE'S WORD) PROMISE
(— OUT) BOOM LEAK EXUDE ISSUE
PETAL EVOLVE EMANATE OUTGIVE
(— OVER) LIN
(— PAIN) AGGRIEVE
(— PLACE) VAIL BACCARE
(— PLEDGE) GAGE
(— PROMINENCE TO) FEATURE
(— RELUCTANTLY) BEGRUDGE
(— SATISFACTION) ABY ABYE
ABEGGE
(— SPARINGLY) INCH
(— STRENGTH TO) NERVE
(— SUPPORT) ASSIST ANIMATE
(— TEMPORARILY) LEND
(— TIP) TOUT
(— TONGUE) CRY YEARN
(— UP) PUT BURY DROP PART CHUCK
DEMIT DEVOW FORGO LEAVE RAISE
REMIT SHOOT SPARE SPEND WAIVE
ABJURE ADDICT BETRAY DESERT
DEVOTE FOREGO MIZZLE REFUSE
RELENT RENDER RESIGN VACATE
ABANDON DEPOSIT DESPAIR
FLUMMOX FORBEAR FORGIVE
REFRAIN RELEASE ABDICATE
RENOUNCE
(— VENT TO) EMIT ISSUE DISCHARGE

(— VOICE) BOLT ACCENT
(— WARNING) ALERT
(— WAY) GO FAIL FOLD KEEL MOVE
SINK VAIL BREAK BUDGE BURST
FAINT SLAKE YIELD BUCKLE FALTER
RELENT SWERVE FOUNDER RECLAIM
SUCCUMB
(— WITNESS) DEPOSE
GIVE AND-TAKE SWAP
GIVEN APT DONEE NATHAN PROMPT
(— TO) ALL AFTER
(SUFF.) (— TO) ABLE IBLE LEW
GIVER DONOR
(— OF ALMS) ALMONER
(— OF LIFE) APHETA
(NAME—) EPONYM
GIVING DOLE BOUNTY DATION
REMISE
(— BY WILL) TESTATION
(— HELP) ADJUTANT
(— MILK) FRESH
(— NO MILK) YELD YELL
(— TROUBLE) CUMBROUS
GIZMO DOODAD GADGET
GIZZARD CROP GIGERIUM
GIZZARD SHAD SKIPJACK
GLABROUS BALD SMOOTH
GLABRATE LEVIGATE
GLACIAL (— FORMATION) ARETE
GLACIARIUM RINK
GLACIATE ICE
GLACIATION MINDEL
(— STAGE) RISS WURM
GLACIER BRAE ICECAP STREAM
CALOTTE ICEBERG PIEDMONT
(FACING A —) STOSS
(FACING AGAINST —) STOSS
(PREF.) GLACIO
GLACIOLOGY CRYOLOGY
GLACIS ESPLANADE
GLAD GAY FAIN LIEF VAIN CANTY
HAPPY PROUD BLITHE FESTUS
GLADLY JOCUND JOYFUL JOYOUS
GLADFUL GLEEFUL JOCULAR
ANIMATED CHEERFUL CHEERING
FESTIVAL GLADSOME PLEASING
GLADDEN JOY GLAD BLESS BLISS
CHEER EXULT MIRTH BLITHE
COMFORT GLADIFY LIGHTEN
REJOICE
(PREF.) TERP(I)(SI)
GLADE LAWN LAUND SLADE SHRADD
SUNGLADE SUNSCALD
(PREF.) NEMO
GLADIATOR THRAX RETIARY
SAMNITE SECUTOR ANDABATA
GLADIOLUS GLAD IRID LILY LEVERS
LILIUM GLADIOLA
GLADLY GLAD LIEF FAINLY LIEFLY
LOVELY HAPPILY
GLADNESS JOY GLAD GLEE BLISS
MIRTH BLITHE FAINNESS GLADSHIP
PLEASURE

GLADSOME BLITHE
GLAGA KASA KUSA TALTHIB
GLAMOR SCRY UTIS OOMPH PIZAZZ
BRABBLE PIZZAZZ BALLYHOO
GLAMORIZE POT GLORIFY
GLAMOROUS GLAM EXOTIC
ALLURING CHARMING
GLAMOUR HALO PAZAZZ PIZAZZ
PIZZAZZ PRESTIGE
GLANCE EYE RAY SEE BEAM CAST
GLIM LEER PEEK SCRY SKEG VIEW
WINK BLENK BLINK BLUSH CAROM
FLASH GLEEK GLENT GLIDE GLIFF
GLINT GLISK GRAZE PRINK SCREW
SIGHT SKIME SLANT SQUIZ TWIRE
APERCU ASPECT CARROM GANDER
REGARD SCANCE STRIKE VISION
EYEBEAM EYESHOT EYEWINK
GLIMPSE BELAMOUR GLIFFING
OEILLADE
(— OFF) GLACE
(— THROUGH) SAMPLE
(LOVE —) AMORET
(MELANCHOLY —) DOWNCAST
(SHARP —) DART
(SIDELONG —) SHEW SLENT SKLENT
(SLY —) GLEG GLIME GLOAT
GLAND MILT NOIX SETA CLYER
CRYPT GONAD LIVER MAMMA
ACINUS BREAST KERNEL THYMUS
TONSIL ADRENAL CRUMENA
NECTARY PAROTID PAROTIS TEARPIT
THYROID CONARIUM ENDOCRIN
FOLLICLE FOLLOWER GANGLION
GLANDULA GLANDULE HOOFWORM
PROSTATE SCIRRHUS SPERMARY
TESTICLE
(PREF.) ADEN(O) SCIRRH(O)
(SUFF.) ADEN SCIRRHUS
GLANDERS FARCY MALLEUS
GLANDULAR EARTHY INNATE
SEXUAL ADENOID PHYSICAL
ADENOIDAL
GLANS NUT GLAND
GLARE BEAT GAZE BLARE BLAZE
BLOOM FLAME GLAZE STARE
GLITTER ICEBLINK RADIANCE
GLARING HARD RANK GLARY
AGLARE GARISH BURNING FLARING
STARING FLAGRANT
GLASGOW (NATIVE OF —)
GLASWEGIAN
GLASS CUP VER CALX FLAT FLUX
FRIT JENA MOIL PONY VITA CHARK
FACER FLINT GLAZE STOOP STOUP
VERRE VITRE CALGON CEMENT
CULLET RUMMER SPECKS VITRUM
ALEYARD BIFOCAL BRIMMER
CHIRPER CRYSTAL PERLITE SCHMELZ
TALLBOY VITRITE FROSTING
OBSIDIAN SCHOPPEN PERSPECTIVE
(— IN STATE OF FUSION) METAL
(— OF A MIRROR) STONE

(— OF BEER) BREW
(— OF BRANDY) SNEAKER
(— OF SPIRITS) CHASSE
(— OF WHISKY) KELTY RUBDOWN
(— OF WINE) APERITIF
(— STICKING TO PUNTY) COLLET
(BEER —) SHELL SEIDEL PILSNER
PILSENER
(BELL-SHAPED —) CUP CLOCHE
(BURNING —) SUNGLASS
(CHEVAL —) PSYCHE
(COLORED —) SMALT SMALTO
TINTER SCHMELZ
(COLORED —S) GOGGLES
(CUPPING —) VENTOSE
(CURVED —) LENS
(DESSERT —) COUPE
(DRINKING —) GOBLET RUMKIN
PILSNER PIMLICO SCUTTLE TUMBLER
SCHOONER
(EUROPEAN ORNAMENTAL —)
PELOTON
(EXAMINATION —) SLIDE
(FULL —) BUMPER
(FUSIBLE —) FLUX
(HALF —) SPLIT
(ICE CREAM —) SLIDER
(KIND OF —) CUSTARD CRANBERRY
(LEAD —) STRASS
(LIQUEUR —) PONY PONEY
(LIQUOR —) GUN
(MAGNIFYING —) LOUPE
(MASS OF MOLTEN —) PARISON
(METEORITIC —) TEKTITE
MOLDAVITE
(OPALESCENT —) OPALINE
(OPAQUE —) HYALITHE
(ORNAMENTAL —) PELOTON
(PIECE OF —) PANE
(PIECE OF HOT —) BIT
(PULVERIZED —) FROSTING
(REFUSE —) CALX CULLET
(RUBY —) SCHMELZE
(RUSSIAN —) CHARK
(SHERBET —) SUPREME
(SHERRY —) COPITA
(SMOKED —) SHADE
(STAINED —) VITRAIL
(TALL —) RUMMER
(THIN —) MOUSSELINE
(VOLCANIC —) PUMICE PERLITE
(WINDOW —) PANE
(WINE —) FLUTE
(PL.) SHELLS
(PREF.) HYAL(O) VITR(EO)(I)(O)
GLASSBLOWER MUMBLER
GLASS CRAB SPECTER SPECTRE
GLASSES EYEWEAR
(TINTED —) SHADES
GLASSHOUSE STOVE HOTHOUSE
GLASS-LIKE VITRIC
GLASS MENAGERIE (AUTHOR OF
—) WILLIAMS

(CHARACTER IN —) TOM JAMES LAURA AMANDA OCONNOR

GLASSWARE AGATA AURENE BURMESE FAVRILE OPALINE STEUBEN VITRICS AMBERINA CORALENE

GLASSWORK GLAZING GLAZIERY

GLASSWORKER GANGMAN GLAZIER SNAPPER GLASSMAN SERVITOR

GLASSWORT KALI KELPWORT SALTWORT SAMPHIRE

GLASSY GLIB FILMY GLAZY GLAZEN GLASSEN HYALINE HYALOID VITREAL VITREOUS

(PREF.) HYAL(O)

GLAUCE (FATHER OF —) CREON

(HUSBAND OF —) JASON

GLAUCUS (FATHER OF —) MINOS ANTHEDON SISYPHUS HIPPOLOCHUS

(MOTHER OF —) MEROPE PASIPHAE

GLAZE DIP LEAD SIZE SLIP GLASS SLEET SMEAR ENAMEL QUARRY CELADON COPERTA EELSKIN GLASSEN GLAZING GLIDDEN COUVERTE TIGEREYE

(— OF ICE) GLARE

(POTTERY —) SMEAR

GLAZED FILMY GLACE GLASSEN GLOSSED

GLAZED WARE GLOST

GLAZIER PUTTIER

(TOOL OF —) SPRIG LADKIN

GLEAM RAY BEAM GLOW LEAM WAFT WINK BLENK BLINK BLUSH FLASH GLAIK GLEEN GLENT GLINT GLISK GLIST GLOSE SHINE SKIME SPUNK STARE STEEM TWIRE GLANCE SCANCE FOULDRE GLIMMER GLITTER SHIMMER CORUSCATE SCINTILLA

(— FAINTLY) SHIMMER

(— OF LIGHT) LEAM PINK GLAIK SCANCE

(FAINT —) SCAD

GLEAMING FAW GLOW CLEAR GLINT STEEP ABLAZE BRIGHT GLEAMY ADAZZLE SHINING GLOOMING

GLEAN CULL EARN REAP LEASE DEDUCE GATHER COLLECT SCRINGE

GLEANER STIBBLER

GLEANING CROP GATHERING

(LITERARY —S) ANALECTA ANALECTS

GLEBE SOD CLOD LAND SOIL TERMON KIRKTOWN

GLEE GLY JOY SONG MIRTH SPORT GAIETY DELIGHT ELATION WASSAIL HILARITY MADRIGAL

GLEEFUL GAY MERRY JOYOUS JOCULAR GLEESOME

GLEEMAN GONGMAN MINSTREL

GLEN DEN GILL GLYN GRIFF HEUCH HEUGH KLOOF SLACK SLADE TEMPE CANADA DINGLE POCKET

GLIADIN GLUTIN PROLAMIN

GLIB PAT FLIP SLICK CASUAL GLOSSY OFFHAND RENABLE SHALLOW VOLUBLE FLIPPANT

GLIBLY SLICK

GLIBNESS UNCTION

GLIDE GO SKI FLOW SAIL SILE SKIM SLIP SLUR SOAR SWIM COAST CREEP DANCE FLEET GLACE GRAZE LAPSE MERGE PLANE SCOOP SHIRL SKATE SKIFF SKIRR SKITE SLADE SLEEK SLICK SLIDE SLIPE STEAL GLANCE GLIDER SASHAY SNOOVE ILLAPSE SCRIEVE SCRITHE SKITTER SLITHER AIRPLANE GLISSADE VOLPLANE SEMIVOWEL

(— AWAY) ELAPSE

(— BY) PASS FLEET

(— IN) ILLAPSE

(— OFF) EXIT

(MUSICAL —) PORTAMENTO

GLIDER BIPLANE SCOOTER PARAWING SAILPLANE

(KIND OF —) HANG

GLIDING LAPSE TRAIL SLIDING

(— OF THE VOICE) DRAG

(— OVER) LAMBENT

GLIMMER FIRE GLIM GLOW IDEA LEAM STIM BLINK FLASH GLEAM GLOOM STIME SIMPER BLINTER FLIMMER GLIMPSE GLITTER SHIMMER SPARKLE TWINKLE SUNBLINK

GLIMMERING GHOST AGLIMMER GLOOMING

GLIMPSE ESPY IDEA WAFF WAFT BLINK BLUSH FLASH GLIFF GLINT GLISK SIGHT STIME TINGE TRACE WHIFF GLANCE GLEDGE LUSTER SCANCE GLIMMER INKLING

(BRIEF —) APERCU

(FLEETING —) SHIM SNATCH

GLINT PEEP FLASH GLEAM GLENT GLANCE SPARKLE

GLIS MYOXUS

GLISSANDO GLISS SMEAR GLISSADE

GLISTEN FLASH GLISK GLISS GLIST SHINE GLISTER GLITTER SHIMMER SPANGLE SPARKLE RUTILATE

GLISTENING SHINY AGLISTEN

GLITCH FLAW SNAG

GLITTER FLASH GLARE GLEAM GLEIT GLINT GLITZ GLORE SHEEN SHINE SKYRE STARE BICKER LUSTER SCANCE GLIMMER GLISTEN GLISTER SKINKLE SPANGLE SPARKLE TWINKLE BRANDISH RADIANCE RUTILATE CORUSCATE

(FALSE —) GILT

GLITTERING GEMMY SHEEN SHINY
STEEP FULGID SPANGLY AGLITTER
GLITTERY RUTILANT BRILLIANT
CLINQUANT

GLOAMING EVE DUSK GLOAM
GLOOMING TWILIGHT

GLOAT GAZE GLUT TIRE EXULT
PREEN

GLOBAL PLANETARY

GLOBE ORB BALL BOWL CLEW CLUE
POME AGGER GEOID MONDE
MOUND ROUND SPHERE COMPASS
GEORAMA GLOBULE GRENADE
AQUARIUM ROUNDURE

GLOBEFISH FUGU TOBY TOADO
ATINGA BOTETE PUFFER BLAASOP
BURFISH OOPUHUE BLOWFISH

GLOBEFLOWER BOLT GOLLAND
GOWLAND CORCHORUS

GLOBE THISTLE ECHINOPS

GLOBOSE COCCOID COCCOUS
CAPITATE GLOBULAR

GLOBULAR GLOBED ROTUND
GLOBATE GLOBOSE GLOBICAL

GLOBULE BEAD BLOB DROP GLOB
PEARL BUBBLE BUTTON REGULUS
GLOBULET SPHERULE
(— OF TAPIOCA) FISHEYE

GLOBULIN MAYSIN MYOSIN VIGNIN
ARACHIN CORYLIN EDESTIN
LEGUMIN TUBERIN VICILIN
ANTIBODY BIOLOGIC EXCELSIN
GLYCININ MUSCULIN ORYZENIN

GLOCKENSPIEL BELL LYRA
CARILLON

GLOMERULE GLOME FASCICLE

GLOOM DAMP DUSK MURK CLOUD
DREAR FROWN SOMBER DESPAIR
DIMNESS GLOOMTH SADNESS
DARKNESS MIDNIGHT

GLOOMINESS DUMPS

GLOOMY DUN SAD WAN BLUE COLD
DARK DOUR DREE DULL EERY GLUM
MIRK MURK ADUSK ADUST BLACK
BROWN DOWFF DREAR DUSKY EERIE
FERAL GUMLY HEAVY LURID MOODY
MORNE MUDDY MUNGY MUSTY
MUZZY ROOKY SABLE SORRY STERN
SULKY SURLY SWART TRIST CLOUDY
DISMAL DREARY DREICH DROOPY
DRUMLY GLUMMY MOROSE
SOLEMN SOMBER SULLEN TETRIC
THRAWN OBSCURE STYGIAN
THESTER DARKSOME DESOLATE
DOLESOME DOWNBEAT DOWNCAST
FUNEREAL GLOOMING LOWERING
OVERCAST TRISTFUL PESSIMISTIC

GLORIA HALO GLORY AUREOLE

GLORIFICATION AVATAR

GLORIFY HERY LAUD BLESS DEIFY
EXALT EXTOL HERSE HONOR PRIDE
WURTH ENHALO KUDIZE PRAISE
CLARIFY ELEVATE MAGNIFY DIVINIZE
EMBLAZON EULOGIZE PROCLAIM
STELLIFY

GLORIOLE HALO AUREOLE

GLORIOUS SRI DEAR DERE MERE
SHRI GRAND PROUD BRIGHT
EMINENT RENOWNED

GLORY JOY ORE SUN FACE FAME
GLOR HALO HORN BLAZE BOAST
EXULT HONOR KUDOS PRIDE
WULDER AUREOLA CLARITY
GARLAND GLORIFY RADIANCE
SPLENDOR WORTHING

GLORY-PEA KOWHAI KAKABEAK
KAKABILL KOWHAI

GLOSS GILL COLOR DUNCE GLASS
GLAZE GLOZE JAPAN SHEEN SHINE
BLANCH LUSTER LUSTRE POSTIL
REMARK VENEER BURNISH
EXPOUND VARNISH FLOURISH
PALLIATE POLITURE WHITEWASH
(— OVER) FARD HUSH SALVE SLEEK
SOOTHE

GLOSSA LINGUA

GLOSSARY GLOSS CLAVIS

GLOSSIPHONIA CLEPSINE

GLOSSY GLOZE NITID SHINY SILKY
SLEEK SLICK SATINY SMOOTH

GLOVE KID CUFF GAGE MITT COFFE
BERLIN MITTEN CHEVRON DANNOCK
GANTLET GOMUKHI GAUNTLET
(— FOR RUBBING SKIN) STRIGIL
(BISHOP'S —) GWANTUS
(BODY OF —) TRANK
(BOXING —) MUFFLE
(HEDGER'S —) DANNOCK
(HUSKING —) HUSKER
(PART OF —) THUMB TRANK GUSSET
BINDING FOURCHETTE

GLOVEMAKER DOMER GLOVER
CLASPER FINGERER

GLOVER TRANKER

GLOW ARC LOW AURA BURN FIRE
LEAM LOOM LOWE BLAZE BLOOM
BLUSH FLAME FLASH FLUSH GLAZE
GLEAM GLEED GLORY GLOSS GLOZE
SHINE STEAM CORONA KINDLE
WARMTH FLUSTER LIGHTEN
(— OF PASSION) ESTUS AESTUS
(— WITH INTENSE HEAT) IGNITE

GLOWER GAZE GLOW GLARE
GLOOM GLORE SCOWL

GLOWING HOT RED LIVE ROSY
WARM AGLOW FIERY LIGHT QUICK
RUDDY VIVID ABLAZE ARDENT
ORIENT BURNING CANDENT
FERVENT RADIANT SHINING
FLAGRANT RUTILANT

GLOWWORM FIREFLY FIREWORM
GLOWBIRD LAMPYRID

GLOZE FAWN PAINT SMOOTH
FLATTERY

GLUCINUM BERYLLIUM

GLUCOSE AME GLYCOSE DEXTROSE

GLUCOSIDE GEIN APIIN RUTIN TUTIN
ADONIN BINDER CORNIN DURRIN
FRAXIN FUSTIN IRIDIN PICEIN UZARIN
ACACIIN ARBUTIN DAPHNIN DIOSMIN
ESCULIN ESTEVIN GITALIN GITONIN
GITOXIN HEDERIN HELECIN INDICAN
LOGANIN LOTUSIN LUPININ OUABAIN
POPULIN ROBININ SALICIN TABACIN
TEUCRIN ADONIDIN CARTHAME
ERICOLIN GENISTIN GOSSYPIN
MORINDIN NARINGIN PARIGLIN
PARILLIN PRUNASIN QUINOVIN
SAPONINE SCILLAIN SINIGRIN
SYRINGIN THEVETIN VERNONIN
VIBURNIN VICIANIN
GLUE PAD EPOXY MOUNT STICK
BEGLEW CEMENT FUNORI FUNORIN
STICKER STICKUM TAUROCOL
(BEE —) PROPOLIS
(WEAK —) SIZE
(PREF.) COLL(A)(O)(OIDIO)(OIDO)
GLOEO
(SUFF.) COLL GLIA GLOEA
GLUE-LIKE
(PREF.)
(— SUBSTANCE) GLI
GLUEY GLUISH STICKY STRINGY
VISCOUS ADHESIVE
GLUM CLUM DOUR GRUM SURLY
GLOOMY GLUMPY MOROSE SULLEN
DEJECTED
GLUMALES POALES
GLUME PILE FLIGHT
(FLOWERING —) LEMMA
(PL.) CHAFF
GLUSIDE SACCHARIN
GLUT CLOY FILL GULP QUAT SATE
CHOKE DRAFT GORGE BATTEN
ENGLUT EXCESS MARROW PAMPER
PAUNCH ENGORGE GLUTTON
SATIATE SURFEIT SWALLOW
OVERFEED SAGINATE SATURATE
GLUTEAL NATAL
GLUTELIN AVENINE ORYZENIN
GLUTENIN AVENIN ZYMOME
ZYMOMIN
GLUTINOUS ROPY SIZY ROPEY
SLIMY TOUGH STICKY VISCID
(PREF.) GLOEO GLOIO
GLUTTED QUAT GORGED SATIATED
GLUTTER VEER
GLUTTON HOG PIG GLUT GORB
GUTS GULCH MIKER GLOTUM
HELLUO MACCUS EPICURE GUTLING
LURCHER MOOCHER RAVENER
SWILLER CARCAJOU DRAFFMAN
GOURMAND GULLYGUT
(STUPID —) GRUB
GLUTTONIZE BIZLE BEZZLE
GLUTTONOUS GREEDY GLUTTON
HOGGISH GOURMAND
GLUTTONY GULE EDACITY SURFEIT
GLYCERIDE BUTYRIN

GLYCINE SOJA
GLYCOL CARBOWAX
GLYCOPROTEIN MUCIN MUCOID
GLYCOSIDE APIIN CROCIN ACACIIN
CYMARIN DIGOXIN GITALIN GITOXIN
HEDERIN HYPERIN LOGANIN
LOTUSIN SAPONIN ALDESIDE
ANDROSIN ANTIARIN HOLOSIDE
KETOSIDE
GLYPTOLOGIST JEWELLER
GNARL NOB KNOB KNUR KNARL
KNURR SNIRL WARRE DEFORM
GNARLED GNARLY KNARRY KNOTTY
CRABBED KNOTTED KNURLED
GNASH TUSK CHAMP CRASH GANCH
GRASH GRATE KNASH
GNAT KNAW SMUT MIDGE PUNKY
STOUT KNATTE SCIARA SCIARID
SCINIPH BLACKFLY DIPTERAN
GNATLING
(PREF.) CULIC(I)
GNATCATCHER SYLVIID
GNATHION MENTON
GNAW EAT NAB BITE FRET TIRE
CHELE GNARL MOUSE SHEAR
ARRODE BEFRET BEGNAW CANKER
CHAVEL NATTLE NIGGLE ROUNGE
CHIMBLE CHUMBLE CORRODE
GNAWED
(PREF.) BROTO
GNAWING EATING RODENT FRETFUL
ARROSION ROSORIAL
GNOME NIS ADAGE NISSE PECHT
PYGMY KOBOLD VAKSHA YAKSHI
GNOMIDE GREMLIN HODEKEN
ERDGEIST
GNOMON COCK INDEX STILE STYLE
FESCUE STYLUS
GNOSTIC CLEVER SHREWD
KNOWING PERATES EBIONITE
MANDAEAN SEVERIAN SIMONIAN
SIMONITE
GNU KOKOON BRINDLE
GO BE DE ACT GAE HOP ISH LAY NIM
PEP TEE WAG BANG BEAR BING
BOWN BUSK DRAW FAND FARE FOND
GANG HARK HAUL HUMP MOVE QUIT
RAIK ROAM ROLL SEEK SHOT SILE
SLAP SNAP STAB STEP TAKE TEEM
TOUR WADE WANE WEAR WEND
WEVE WIND WISE WORK YEAD YEDE
AMBLE BOUND CARRY CHEVE
DEMON DRESS FETCH FRAME
HAUNT KNOCK LEAVE MOSEY PLUCK
REACH SCRAM SHAKE SLOPE SPEED
TOUCH TRACE TRACK TRENE TRINE
TRUSS WHIZZ YONGE BECOME
BETAKE CHIEVE CRUISE DEPART
EXTEND QUATCH QUETCH REPAIR
RESORT RESULT RETIRE SASHAY
STRAKE STRIKE TODDLE TRAVEL
WEAKEN JOURNEY SCRITHE
DIMINISH WITHDRAW

(— **ABOUT**) JET BEGO BIGAN
(— **ABOUT DEJECTEDLY**) PEAK
(— **ABOUT GOSSIPING**) COURANT
(— **AHEAD**) HOLD
(— **AIMLESSLY**) ERR BUMMLE
(— **ALONG**) PATH
(— **ALONG WITH**) ACCOMPANY
(— **AROUND**) SKIRT BYPASS CIRCUE
COMPASS ENCOMPASS
(— **ASHORE**) LAND
(— **ASTRAY**) ERR MAR WRY MANG
WILL MISGO DELIRE FORVAY
MISWEND DEROGATE MISCARRY
(— **AWAY**) AGO HOP OFF BEAT BUNK
HIKE NASH PART SHOO VADE CLEAR
HENCE IMSHI LEAVE SCRAM SHIFT
BEGONE BUGGER DEPART REMOVE
VACATE SKIDDOO ELONGATE
(— **AWAY AT ONCE**) SCRAM
(— **BACK**) RECEDE RETURN REGRESS
RETRACE
(— **BACK IN TIME**) MOUNT
(— **BAD**) SOUR
(— **BEFORE**) LEAD FOREGO PRECEDE
ANTECEDE PREAMBLE
(— **BEYOND**) SURPASS FOREPASS
(— **BRISKLY**) JUNE
(— **BROKE**) BUST
(— **BY**) PASS
(— **BY WATER**) SAIL
(— **COURTING**) WENCH
(— **DOGGEDLY**) PLUG
(— **DOWN**) SET SINK VAIL DROOP
SOUND DESCEND
(— **EASILY**) AMBLE
(— **ERRATICALLY**) KICK
(— **FAST**) HURRY SPLIT BARREL
BEELINE
(— **FOR**) ATTEMPT
(— **FORTH**) AGO DEPART FORTHGO
(— **FORWARD**) HUP HUPP ADVANCE
AGGRESS PROCEED
(— **FOWLING**) AUCUPATE
(— **FURTIVELY**) SLINK SNEAK STEAL
(— **HANG**) SNICK
(— **HEAVILY**) LOB LAMPER
(— **IN**) ENTER INGRESS
(— **IN A HURRY**) SCUFFLE
(— **IN CROWDS**) PILE
(— **IN HASTE**) LEN LAMMAS
(— **IN PURSUIT**) SUE
(— **IN SEARCH**) QUEST
(— **INTO BUSINESS**) EMBARK
(— **IT ALONE**) SOLO
(— **LAME**) FOUNDER
(— **LEISURELY**) BUMMEL JIGGET
JIGGIT
(— **LIGHTLY**) TIPTOE
(— **MAD**) CRAZE MADDLE
(— **NEAR**) APPROACH
(— **NOISILY**) LARUM
(— **OFF**) MOG DISCHARGE

(— **ON**) DO GARN LAST PASS PERGE
FURTHER PROCEED
(— **ON BOARD**) BOARD EMBARK
ENTRAIN
(— **ON FOOT**) SHANK
(— **ON TO SAY**) ADD
(— **OUT**) EXIT ISSUE SLOCK EGRESS
EXEUNT QUENCH SORTIE
(— **OVER**) KNEE REVOLT SURPASS
OVERGANG
(— **OVER AGAIN**) RENEW REVISE
RETRACE
(— **PROSPEROUSLY**) COTTON
(— **QUICKLY**) BOP GET HIE BUZZ
LAMP PIKE SCAT SPEED
(— **RAPIDLY**) LAMP SPLIT
(— **SHARES**) SNACK
(— **SIDEWAYS**) SIDLE
(— **SLOWLY**) CRAWL CREEP
(— **SLUGGISHLY**) SHACK
(— **SMOOTHLY**) SLIP SKATE
(— **STEALTHILY**) SHIRK SLINK SNEAK
GUMSHOE
(— **SUDDENLY**) CLAP SCOOT
(— **SWIFTLY**) SKISE STRIP HIGHBALL
(— **THE ROUNDS**) PATROL
(— **THROUGH**) SUFFER
(— **THROUGHOUT**) COAST
(— **THROUGH WATER**) SQUATTER
(— **TO BED**) KIP DOSS FLOP SNUG
(— **TO EXCESS**) DEBORD
(— **TO HARBOR**) VERT
(— **TOO FAR**) OUTREACH
(— **TO PIECES**) SNURP
(— **TO SCHOOL**) SCOLEY
(— **TO SLEEP**) HUSHABY
(— **TO WAR**) RISE
(— **UP**) CLIMB AMOUNT ASCEND
(— **WEARILY**) HAGGLE
(— **WELL**) COOK
(— **WITH**) ASSENTTO
(— **WITH EFFORT**) HIKE
(— **WITH IT**) FLOW
(— **WRONG**) MISS FAULT CURDLE
MISFARE BACKFIRE
GOAD EGG GAD GIG HAG BAIT BROD
BROG DARE EDGE GAUD LASH MOVE
PROD SPUR URGE WHIP YERK
ANKUS HARRY IMPEL PIQUE PRICK
PROGG PUNGE STING VALET INCITE
NEEDLE OXGOAD ANKUSHA
HOTFOOT INFLAME PROVOKE
IRRITATE SLAPJACK STIMULUS
GOADMAN GADMAN GAUDSMAN
GOADSTER
GOAL BYE DEN END BASE BUTT DOLE
DOOL HAIL HALE MARK METE PORT
BOURN FINIS IDEAL SCOOP SCOPE
SCORE DESIGN DESTINY HORIZON
SIGHTS DESTINY HORIZON
TERMINUS OBJECTIVE
(— **IN GAMES**) HUNK

(FIELD —) BASKET
(REMOTE —) THULE
(UNATTAINABLE —) STAR
GO-ASHORE KOHUA
GOAT BOK TUR IBEX TAHR BEDEN
BILLY BOVID EVECK SEROW ALPINE
ANGORA AOUDAD CAPRID CHAMAL
JEMLAH MAZAME NUBIAN PASANG
SAANEN WETHER CHAMOIS
AEGAGRUS CAPRIPED MARKHOOR
BOUQUETIN
(DOMESTIC —) HIRCUS
(FEMALE —) DOE NANNY DOELING
(MALE —) BUCK BUCKLING
(YOUNG —) KID KIDDY TICCHEN
GOATLING
(PREF.) AEG(I)(O) CAPRI EGO
GOAT ANTELOPE GORAL SEROW
GOORAL
GOAT CHEESE CHEVRE
GOATEE TUFT
GOATFISH MOANO
GOATHERD DAMON
GOAT-LIKE CAPRINE GOATISH
HIRCINE
GOAT MOTH COSSID
GOATSBEARD ROSACEAN
GOATSKIN CRUST CASTOR
CHEVRETTE
GOATSUCKER PUCK PEWKE POTOO
EVEJAR BULLBAT DORHAWK
GRINDER SPINNER DOORHAWK
EVECHURR NIGHTJAR PAURAQUE
GOB TAR CLOT GOAF SALT SWAB
SWOB WASTE GOBBET SWABBY
GOBBET BIT CHUNK MORSEL
GOBBLE MOP BOLT SLOP EATUP
GOFFLE GORBLE
GOBBLEDYGOOK PEDAGESE
BAFFLEGAB
GO-BETWEEN AGENT BAWD FIXER
MEANS BROKER DEALER PANDAR
CONTACT MEDIATOR
GOBLET TASS DINOS GLASS HANAP
POKAL SKULL STOOP STOUP
BEAKER BUMPER HOLMOS RUMKIN
CHALICE SCYPHUS SNIFTER TALLBOY
JEROBOAM STANDARD STEMWARE
(PREF.) CALICI
GOBLIN (ALSO SEE HOBGOBLIN)
COW HAG NIS PUG BHUT BOGY
MARE PUCK BOGEY NISSE OUPHE
POOKA BODACH BOGGLE BOOGER
CHUREL EMPUSA FOLIOT SPRITE
BOGGARD BOGGART BROWNIE
BUGBEAR KNOCKER PADFOOT
BARGHEST BOGEYMAN FOLLETTO
GOBY MAPO BULLY BIGHEAD
CHALACO GOBIOID GUAVINA
GUDGEON MUDFISH BULLHEAD
PINKFISH SANDGOBY
GOCART SULKY WALKER STROLLER

GOD (ALSO SEE DEITY) AS EA EL ER
RA VE ANU BEL BES COG DAD DES
DEV DIS DOD EAR GAR GAW GEB
GOG GOL GOM GUM ING KEB LAR
LOK MEN MIN ODD ORO SEB SUN
TEM TYR ULL UTU VAN AITU AMEN
AMON ARES ASUR ATEO ATUA ATYS
BAAL BEER BRAN BURE CHAC COCK
DEUS DEVA DIEU ESUS FONS FREY
GAWD GOSH HAPI HOLY HOTH INTI
JOVE KANE KING LIFE LLEU LOKE
LOKI LOVE LUGH MARS MIND NABU
NEBO NUDD ODIN PTAH SHEN SHIN
SOMA SOUL TANE THOR TIKI ULLR
UTUG VAYU XIPE YAMA ZEUS
ARAWN ASHUR ASURA ATTES ATTIS
COMUS DAGDA DEITY DEOTA DUVEL
DYAUS DYLAN EBISU ELOAH FREYR
GHOST GOLES GOLLY GRAVE GUACA
HESUS HIEMS HORUS HOTHR HUACA
HYMEN INDRA JUDGE KINGU LADON
LIBER LLUDD MAKER MENTU MIDER
MOMUS NJORD NUMEN PALES
PICUS SILEN TAMUZ THOTH TINIA
TRUTH TYCHE URASH WAKEA
WODIN WOTAN ZOMBI ADITYA
ADONAI ADONAY ANSHAR ANUBIS
APOLLO ASEITY AUTHOR CHAMOS
CONSUS DEVATA DHARMA ELATHA
ELOHIM FATHER FAUNUS GANESA
HEAVEN HERMES HOENIR MEZTLI
MILCOM MITHRA NEREUS NERGAL
OSIRIS PATRON PENEUS PLUTUS
PUSHAN SESHAT SOCIUS SOURCE
SPIRIT SUTEKH SYLENE TAAROA
TAMMUZ TARTAK TERAPH TRITON
TRIVIA VARUNA VEDUIS VERITY
VISHNU VULCAN WISDOM YAKSHA
YAKSHI ZOMBIE ARRAXAS ADRANUS
ALPHEUS ANTEROS BELENUS
CHEMOSH DAIKOKU DELLING
ETERNAL GODHEAD HANUMAN
IAPETUS JEHOVAH JUPITER
KANALOA MERCURY MITHRAS
MUTINUS NEPTUNE NJORTHR
PROTEUS PRYDERI REMPHAN
ROBIGUS SAVITAR SERAPIS TRIGLAV
VATICAN VEJOVIS ZAGREUS
ALMIGHTY ASTRAEUS BISHAMON
CAMAXTLI DEMIURGE DEVOTION
DIVINITY GUCUMATZ INFINITE
JIUROJIN KUKULKAN MIXCOATL
MORPHEUS POSEIDON SABAZIOS
SUMMANUS TANGAROA TERMINUS
TUTELARY VEDIOVIS ZEPHYRUS
OMNIPOTENT
(— OF AGRICULTURE) PICUS URASH
FAUNUS AMAETHON NINGIRSU
(— OF ARTS) SIVA
(— OF ATMOSPHERE) HADAD
(— OF BOUNDARIES) TERMINUS
(— OF COMMERCE) MERCURY

(— OF CORN) CAT
(— OF DAY) HORUS
(— OF DESTRUCTION) SIVA
(— OF EARTH) BEL GEB KEB SEB DAGAN
(— OF EVIL) SET FOMOR FOMORIAN ZERNEBOCK
(— OF FERTILITY) SHANGO
(— OF FIRE) AGNI GIRRU NUSKU RUDRA VULCAN
(— OF FLOCKS) PAN
(— OF HAPPINESS) HOTEI JUROJIN
(— OF HEAVENS) ANU JUMALA
(— OF HOUSEHOLD) LARES PENATES
(— OF JUSTICE) FORSETE FORSETI
(— OF LEARNING) IMHOTEP
(— OF LOVE) AMOR ARES EROS KAMA BHAGA CUPID AENGUS
(— OF MOCKERY) MOMUS
(— OF MOON) SIN ENZU NANNAR
(— OF NATURE) MARSYAS
(— OF POETRY) BRAGE BRAGI
(— OF RAIN) PARJANYA
(— OF REGENERATION) SIVA
(— OF RIDICULE) MOMUS
(— OF SEA) LER VAN AEGIR DYAUS NEPTUNE PROTEUS PALAEMON POSEIDON
(— OF SKY) ANU GWYDION
(— OF SLEEP) HYPNOS HYPNUS MORPHEUS
(— OF SOUTHEAST WIND) EURUS
(— OF STORM) ZU ADAD ADDA ADDU MARUT RUDRA TESHUP
(— OF SUN) RA RE SHU SOL TEM TUM UTU AMON ATEN ATMU ATUM BAAL LLEU UTUG SAMAS SEKER SURYA APOLLO HELIOS SOKARI KHEPERA PHOEBUS SHAMASH PHAETHON TONATIUH
(— OF THUNDER) THOR DONAR PERUN PERKUN PEROUN SHANGO TLALOC HURAKAN TARANIS
(— OF UNDERWORLD) DIS BRAN GWYN YAMA HADES ORCUS PLUTO
(— OF VEGETATION) ATYS ATTIS
(— OF WAR) ER IRA ORO TIU TYR ARES COEL IRRA MARS MENT ODIN THOR MONTU NINIB MEXITL SKANDA CAMULUS MEXITLI NINURTA ENYALIUS NINGIRSU QUIRINUS
(— OF WEALTH) BHAGA KUBERA KUVERA PLUTUS
(— OF WIND) ADAD ADDA ADDU VAYU MARUT AEOLUS BOREAS EECATL
(— OF WISDOM) TAT THOTH
(— WILLING) DV
(ANCIENT GREEK —) CHAOS
(BLIND —) HOTH HOTHR
(EGYPTIAN — OF MUSIC) BES
(FALSE —) BAAL IDOL MAUMET

(FEMALE —) GODDESS
(HAWAIIAN —) AUMAKUA
(HOUSEHOLD —) PENATE
(IMMORTAL —) AKAL
(INFERIOR —) PANISK
(NORSE —) AESIR
(PAGAN —) DEMON
(RAM-HEADED —) AMON KHNUM KHNEMU
(TIMELESS —) AKAL
(TUTELARY —) LAR
(UNKNOWN —) KA
(WOOD —) SILEN SILENUS
(PL.) DI DII KAMI AESIR IGIGI SUPERI PANTHEON TRIMURTI
(PREF.) DEI DEO THE(O)
GODDESS (ALSO SEE DEITY) AI NU ANA ANU ATE AYA DEA DON NUT OPS UNI VAC ANTA BADB BODB CACA DANA DANU ERIS ERUA FRIA HELA HERA JORD JUNO MAIA MEDB NIKE NINA NONA NORN PELE SAGA SATI TARA UPIS ALLAT AMENT ANATH ANTUM ARURU BAUBO CERES CHLOE DEESS DIANA DIANE DIRGA DOLMA DOMNU EPONA FREYA FRIGG HYBLA IAMBE ISTAR KOTYS MAEVE NANAI NINTU PAKHT PALES PARCA SALUS SEDNA SKADI TANIT TYCHE USHAS VENUS VESTA ADEONA AESTAS ANATUM ANUKIT APHAIA ATHENA BELILI BENDIS BOOPIS BRIGIT CYBELE CYRENE EOSTRE FRIGGA GEFJON HELENA HESTIA HYGEIA INNINA KISHAR LIBERA MOTHER NINGAL PEITHO PHOBOS POMONA PRORSA RUMINA SEKHET SELENE SEMELE SKATHI SOTHIS TANITH TEFNUT TRIVIA URANIA VACUNA YDGRUN ANAHITA ANAITIS ARTEMIS ASHERAH DEMETER DERCETO FERONIA FJORGYN GALATER GODHEAD KOTYTTO LARENTA LARUNDA MAJAGGA MAJESTA MINERVA MORNING MORRIGU MYLITTA NEKHEBT NEMESIS PALATUA PARBATI PARVATI SALACIA ADRASTEA AGLAUROS ANGERONA BELISAMA CARMENTA CENTEOTL COCAMAMA DESPOINA DICTYNNA GULLVEIG MORRIGAN NEPHTHYS PARBUTTY PRAKRITI RHIANNON SEFEKHET THOUERIS VICTORIA
(— IN CHARIOT) SELENE
(— OF AGRICULTURE) BAU OPS DEMETER CENTEOTL
(— OF AIR) AURA
(— OF BEAUTY) VENUS LAKSHMI
(— OF BURIAL) LIBITINA
(— OF CHILDBIRTH) LEVANA LUCINA
(— OF DAWN) EOS USAS USHAS AURORA MATUTA

(— OF DEW) HERSE
(— OF DISCORD) ATE ERIS
(— OF EARTH) GE LUA SEB ERDA GAEA GAIA TARI ARURU DIONE JORTH TERRA SEMELE TELLUS THEMIS DAMKINA PERCHTA
(— OF FATE) NONA NORN MOIRA
(— OF FERTILITY) MA ISIS MAMA NERTHUS
(— OF FLOWERS) FLORA CHLORIS
(— OF FORTUNE) TYCHE FORTUNA
(— OF GRAIN) CERES
(— OF HEALING) EIR GULA
(— OF HEALTH) DAMIA HYGEIA VALETUDO
(— OF HEARTH) VESTA HESTIA
(— OF HISTORY) SAGA
(— OF HOPE) SPES
(— OF INFATUATION) ATE
(— OF JUSTICE) DIKE MAAT THEMIS ASTRAEA NEMESIS JUSTITIA
(— OF LEGISLATION) EUNOMIA
(— OF LOVE) ATHOR FREYA VENUS FREYJA HATHOR
(— OF LUCK) FORTUNA
(— OF MAGIC) HECATE
(— OF MARRIAGE) HERA
(— OF MATERNITY) APET
(— OF MERCY) KWANNON
(— OF MOON) SELENE
(— OF MOTHERHOOD) ISIS
(— OF NIGHT) NOX NYX
(— OF OCEAN) NINA
(— OF OVENS) FORNAX
(— OF PEACE) PAX IRENE NERTHUS
(— OF PLEASURE) BES
(— OF PLENTY) OPS
(— OF RAINBOW) IRIS
(— OF SEASONS) DIKE HORA
(— OF THE DEAD) HEL HELA
(— OF THE HUNT) DIANA VACUNA ARTEMIS
(— OF THE MOON) LUNA MOON DIANA SELENA SELENE TANITH ARTEMIS
(— OF THE SEA) INO RAN DORIS BRANWEN EURYNOME
(— OF TRUTH) MAAT
(— OF VEGETATION) OPS CERES COTYS COTYTTO
(— OF VENGEANCE) ARA NEMESIS
(— OF VICTORY) NIKE
(— OF WAR) ENYO ANATH ANATU ANUNIT BELLONA
(— OF WATER) ANAHITA
(— OF WEALTH) LAKSHMI
(— OF WISDOM) ATHENA MINERVA
(— OF YOUTH) HEBE JUVENTAS
(COW-HEADED —) ISIS
(ESKIMO —) SEDNA
(FERTILITY —) ASTARTE
(MARRIAGE —) VOR
(PRESIDING —) QUEEN
(SUBORDINATE —) DEMIURGE
(THUNDER-SMITTEN —) SEMELE KERAUNIA
(3-HEADED —) HECATE
(PL.) HORAE MATRIS POINAE ASYNJUR

GO-DEVIL SLED WEIGHT HANDCAR SCRAPER CULTIVATOR TRAVOIS ALLIGATOR
GODFATHER GOSSIP GODPAPA PADRINO SPONSOR GODPHERE
GODHEAD DEITY GODHOOD DIVINITY
GODLESS WICKED ATHEIST IMPIOUS PROFANE UNGODLY
GODLESSNESS ATHEISM
GODLIKE DEIFIC DIVINE IMMORTAL OLYMPIAN
GODLINESS PIETISM SANCTITY
GODLING DEVATA GENIUS GODKIN GODLET PANISC DEMIGOD PANISCUS
GODLY HOLY WISE PIOUS DEVOUT GRACIOUS
GODMOTHER CUMMER GOSSIP SPONSOR GODMAMMA MARRAINE
GODOWN WAREHOUSE
GODPARENT SPONSOR
GOD'S S
GODSON FILLEUL GODCHILD
GOD TREE CEIBA
GODWIT PICK PRINE BARKER MARLIN SCAMMEL YARWHIP RINGTAIL SHRIEKER SPOTRUMP YARDKEEP YARWHELP
GOFFER QUILL FULLER GAUFFER
GOG (FATHER OF —) SHEMAIAH
GO-GETTER HUSTLER
GOGGLER SCAD
GOGLET COOJA SERAI MONKEY SURAHI GURGLET SURAHEE
GOING FARE GAIT BOUND AGOING WAYING PASSADO SLEDDING
(— ABOUT) AROUND
(— BEYOND OTHERS) ULTRA
(— IN) INEUNT INFARE INGOING
(— ON) FARE AGATE TOWARD
(— OUT) EGRESS
(— UP) ANABASIS
(GET —) BEGIN
(SUFF.) GRESS
GOITER WEN GLANS GOITRE STRUMA BRONCHOCELE
GOITERED ANTELOPE ZENU
GOITROUS STRUMOUS
GOLD OR ORO RED SOL DORE GILT GULL ALTUN AURUM GUILD METAL OCHER OCHRE RIDGE SHINY GOLDEN OBRIZE ORMOLU YEI LOW BULLION SPANKER
(— PIECE) TALI
(GREENISH —) AENEUS AENEOUS
(IMITATION —) PINCHBECK
(PREF.) AUR(I) AUREO CHRYS(O) ORI

GOLDBEATER (TOOL OF —) WAGON
GOLDBRICK LOAF SHIRK SLACKER
GOLDCREST MOON TIDLEY
MUDDLER TROCHIL
GOLD DUST (PENNY'S WORTH
OF —) PESEWA
GOLDEN RED DORE GOLD BLEST
DURRY GOLDY SUNNY AUREAL
BLONDE GILDEN GILTEN AUREATE
AUREOUS HALCYON AURULENT
DEAURATE
(— STATE) CALIFORNIA
GOLDEN-AGER RETIREE
GOLDEN ASS (AUTHOR OF —)
APULEIUS
(CHARACTER IN —) ISIS MILO FOTIS
LUCIUS CHARITES PAMPHILE
SOCRATES BYRRHAENA LEPOLEMUS
THRASILLUS ARISTOMENES
GOLDEN BOWL (AUTHOR OF —)
JAMES
(CHARACTER IN —) ADAM STANT
MAGGIE VERVER AMERIGO
CHARLOTTE
GOLDEN CHAIN LABURNUM
GOLDEN CLUB TAWKEE TAWKIN
TUCKAHOE
GOLDEN EAGLE RINGTAIL
GOLDENEYE CUR GARROT
COBHEAD GOWDNIE BULLHEAD
IRONHEAD MORILLON WHIFFLER
WHISTLER
GOLDEN LION TAMARIN
MARMOSET
GOLDEN ORIOLE PIROL WITWALL
GOLDEN PLOVER KOLEA
FROGSKIN SQUEALER WHISTLER
GOLDEN RAGWORT LIFEROOT
GOLDENROD BONEWORT
SOLIDAGO JIMMYWEED
GOLDENSEAL EYEBALM EYEROOT
ICEROOT PUCCOON
GOLDEN SHINER CHUB DACE
WINDFISH
GOLDFINCH JACK FINCH GOLDY
GOWDY CANARY REDCAP FLAXBIRD
GRAYPATE
GOLDFINNY CONNER GOLDNEY
CORKWING
GOLDFISH FUNA MOOR COMET
CALICO FANTAIL CYPRINID VEILTAIL
GOLD-LEAF ORMOLU
GOLD-OF-PLEASURE FLAX
MADWORT OILSEED
GOLDSINNY CONNER CORKWING
GOLDSMITH SONAR AURIFEX
ENGLISH HILLIARD
FRENCH MEISSONIER
GERMAN JAMNITZER
ITALIAN LEONI ROBBIA
WELSH MYDDELTON
GOLF (— CLUB) IRON WOOD BAFFY
CLEEK MASHY SPOON WEDGE

BULGER DRIVER MASHIE PUTTER
BRASSIE MIDIRON NIBLICK
(— COURSE) GREEN LINKS
(— PLAYER) BALL BERG KING KITE
VARE BRAID FALDO FLOYD HAGEN
HOGAN IRWIN JONES LOCKE LOPEZ
MILLS PRICE RAWLS SMITH SNEAD
STACY SUGGS ALCOTT CAPONI
CARNER GEDDES HAYNIE HILTON
LANGER MALLON MILLER MORRIS
NELSON PALMER PLAYER VARDON
WATSON WRIGHT BERNING BRADLEY
COUPLES DEMARET INKSTER
SARAZEN SHEEHAN THOMSON
TREVINO ZOELLER ANDERSON
NICKLAUS ZAHARIAS WHITWORTH
BALLESTEROS
(— SCORE) ACE PAR BOGEY EAGLE
BIRDIE
(— STROKE) BAFF CHIP HOOK PUTT
DRIVE PITCH SLICE
(FREE SHOT IN —) MULLIGAN
(PUTTING TENSION IN —) YIPS
(SHORT — PUTT) GIMME TAPIN
GOLFER TEER
GOLLY GEE WOW GOSH JEEPERS
GOMER (FATHER OF —) JAPHETH
(HUSBAND OF —) HOSEA
GOMUTI EJOO IROK ARENG KITTUL
SAGWIRE SAGOWEER
GONAD OVARY GERMEN
GONCALO ALVES KINGWOOD
GONDOLA GON BARGE GUNDALOW
(— GUIDE) POLER
GONE AWAY LOST NAPOO USEDUP
(— BY) AGO DONE PAST AGONE
PASSE BEHIND BYGONE
(— OUT OF USE) EXTINCT
(— TO PIECES) HAYWIRE
GONERIL (SISTER OF —) REGAN
GONE WITH THE WIND (AUTHOR
OF —) MITCHELL
(CHARACTER IN —) FRANK OHARA
RHETT ASHLEY BUTLER WILKES
CHARLES KENNEDY MELANIE
HAMILTON SCARLETT
GONG BELL CLOCK GANGSA
DOORBELL
(SERIES OF —S) BONANG
GONGORISM CULTISM
GONOPHORE MEDUSOID
SPOROSAC
GOO GUCK GUNK TRIPE
GOOD BAD BON GAY TOP TRY ABLE
BEAU BEIN BIEN BOON BRAW FINE
GAIN HEND NICE NOTE PROW SAKE
BONNE BONNY BONUM BRAVE
BULLY CANNY FRESH GWEED JELLY
KAPAI PAKKA PUKKA SEELY SOUND
VALID BENIGN BRAWLY BUCKRA
DIVINE EXPERT FACTOR FORBYE
HONEST MABUTI PRETTY PROFIT
PROPER WEALTH BENEFIT COPIOUS

CORKING FAIRISH FORTHBY GODLIKE
GRADELY HELPFUL LIBERAL SNIFTER
STAVING TRAINED UPRIGHT
BUDGEREE GRAITHLY INTEREST
LAUDABLE PLEASING SALUTARY
SKILLFUL SUITABLE
(— FOR NOTHING) NAPOO NAUGHT
(ESPECIALLY —) RARE
(EXCEPTIONALLY —) SLAMBANG
(EXTREMELY —) SLICK
(FAIRLY —) TIDY MIDDLING
(HOLD —) BEAR
(INFINITELY —) HOLY
(MARVELOUSLY —) FANTABULOUS
(MIGHTY —) SKOOKUM
(NO —) DUFF VOID NAPOO NAPOOH
VOIDED
(PRETTY —) FAIR TIDY
(RELATIVELY —) SMOOTH
(STRIKINGLY —) RATTLING
(SUPERLATIVELY —) BRAG BEAUTIFUL
(SUPREMELY —) IMMENSE
GORGEOUS
(SURPASSINGLY —) SUPERIOR
(VERY —) HOT TOP DANDY DICTY
GRAND NIFTY BONZER BOSHTA
BOSKER BOSHTER NAILING
SPLENDID SWINGING
(PREF.) AGATH(O) BENI EU
GOOD-BYE CIAO LATER BY BYE TATA
GOODBYE TATA
GOOD-BYE ADDIO ADIEU
GOODBYE ADIEU
GOOD-BYE ADIOS
GOODBYE ADIOS
GOOD-BYE LULLABY FAREWELL
SAYONARA
GOODBYE (IMPOLITE —) SCRAM
GOOD COMPANIONS (AUTHOR OF
—) PRIESTLEY
(CHARACTER IN —) DEAN HUGH
NUNN ELSIE INIGO JERRY JIMMY
SUSIE TRANT JESIAH OAKROYD
ELIZABETH JOLLIFANT LONGSTAFF
MCFARLANE JERNINGHAM
GOOD EARTH (AUTHOR OF —)
BUCK
(CHARACTER IN —) LIU LUNG NUNG
OLAN PEAR WANG CHING HWANG
LOTUS
GOOD-FOR-NAUGHT LOSEL
GOOD-FOR-NOTHING STIFF
VAURIEN BUM ORRA SLIM SLINK
DONNOT KEFFEL RIBALD STUMER
BRETHEL FUSTIAN SCROYLE
SHOTTEN SKEEZIX SKELLUM
SKYBALD VAURIEN WOSBIRD
VAGABOND
GOOD FRIDAY PARASCEVE
GOOD-HUMORED SONSY
GOOD-KING-HENRY BLITE
ALLGOOD MARKERY MERCURY
CHENOPOD

GOOD-LOOKING BRAW FAIR FOXY
MOOI BONNY GAWSY COMELY
PRETTY SEEMLY EYESOME GRADELY
WINSOME GOODLIKE HANDSOME
STUNNING
GOODLY BOON PROPER GOODLIKE
GOOD-NATURED SONSY CLEVER
AMIABLE
GOODNESS BONTE BONUM MENSK
PROOF BONITY BOUNTY SATTVA
VIRTUE KINDNESS
GOODS FEE BONA GEAR KIND PELF
CARGO STUFF TRADE WORLD
WRACK ADVANCE CAPITAL CHATTEL
EFFECTS FINANCE HAVINGS INSIGHT
TRAFFIC CHAFFERY HIGGLERY
PROPERTY
(— BARTERED) DICKER
(— CAST OVERBOARD) JETSAM
(— SUNK IN SEA) LAGAN LIGAN
LAGEND
(DRY —) DRAPERY
(HOUSEHOLD —) INSIGHT
(IMPERFECT —) FENT
(INFERIOR —) BRACK
(PIECE —) CUTTANEE
(SECONDHAND —) BROKERY
(SLOW-SELLING —) JOBS
(STOLEN — THROWN AWAY) WAIF
(SURPLUS —) OVERAGE
(VALUABLE —) SWAG
GOOD-SIZED TIDY HEFTY GAWSIE
GOOD-TASTING DAINTY
GOODWIFE GOODY VROUW
GOODWILL GREE PHILANTHROPY
GOODY-GOODY PI MOLLYCODDLE
GOOEY CLARTY
GOOF SAP BOOB FLUB BONER GOOFER
GOOFBALL DOOFUS
GOOGLY BOSEY WRONGUN
GOOK SLIME
GOON HOOD THUG GORILLA
MUSCLEMAN
GOOSANDER JACKSAW RANTOCK
GOOSE ELK OIE LAMA NENE ROUT
ANSER BRANT BRENT EMDEN
HANSA HOBBY ROMAN SOLAN
WAVEY CAGMAG CANADA EMBDEN
GALOOT GANDER GOSLET HISSER
HONKER SOLAND AFRICAN BLACKIE
BUSTARD GAGGLER GOSLING
GRAYLAG GREASER GREYLAG
OUTARDE WIDGEON BALDHEAD
BARGOOSE BARNACLE BERNICLE
SPURWING TOULOUSE
(— GENUS) ANSER
(MYTHICAL —) GANZA
(PART OF —) BOW EAR EYE TOE WEB
BEAN BILL CAPE FOOT KEEL RUMP
WING FLUFF SHANK BREAST COVERT
DEWLAP SADDLE FEATHER NOSTRIL
SHOULDER SECONDARY
(PREF.) CHEN(O)

GOOSEBERRY BLOB FABE FAPE POHA BRAGAS GOBLIN GOZILL GROZER DOWNING GASKINS GROZART CARBERRY CATBERRY DOGBERRY EATBERRY FEABERRY GOOSEGOG HOUGHTON INDUSTRY KIWIFRUIT
(PL.) THAPES
GOOSE EGG DUCK
GOOSEFOOT BLITE ORACH BASSIA KOCHIA ORACHE QUINOA ALLSEED PIGWEED
GOOSEGIRL GOSSARD
GOOSE GRASS HERIF HARIFFE CLEAVERS
GOOSEHERD GOZZARD GOOSEBOY
GOOSENECK LAMP ROOSTER
GOPHER TUZA GAUFFRE GEOMYID MUNGOFA QUACHIL SALAMICH TUCOTUCO
(— STATE) MINNESOTA
GOPHER BALL HOMER
GOPHERMAN SWAMPER
GOPHERWOOD FUSTIC
GORBODUC (SON OF —) FERREX PORREX
GORDIUS (SON OF —) MIDAS
GORE CLY CLOY GARE HIKE HIPE HOOK HORN PICK PIKE SHOT CRUOR GODET STICK GORING GUSSET
GOREVAN AUBURN
GORGE GAP JAM FILL GASH GAUM GLUT JAMB KHOR RENT SATE BREAK CAJON CANON CHASM CHINE CLUSE DRAFT FARCE FLUME GULLY GURGE KLOOF PONGO POUCH STECH STRID STUFF TANGI CANYON DEFILE NULLAH PIGOUT RAVINE STODGE STRAIT THROAT COULOIR DATIATE DRAUGHT ENGORGE SATIATE SLABBER BARRANCA QUEBRADA
GORGED ACCOLLE
GORGEOUS VAIN GRAND SHOWY COSTLY DAZZLING GLORIOUS SPLENDID
GORGERIN NECK NECKING
GORGIBUS (DAUGHTER OF —) CELIE
GORGING STODGE
GORGON HAG MEDUSA STHENO EURYALE
(MOTHER OF —S) CETO
GORGOPHONE (FATHER OF —) PERSEUS
(HUSBAND OF —) OEBALUS PERIERES
(MOTHER OF —) ANDROMEDA
(SON OF —) ICARIUS APHAREUS LEUCIPPUS TYNDAREUS
GORILLA APE GOON THUG PIGMY PYGMY
GORING CORNUPETE
GORMANDIZE STECH STEGH GUTTLE
GORMANDIZER HELLUO GLUTTON

GORSE ULEX WHIN FURZE GORST
GORY BLOODY
GOSHAWK GOS ASTUR TERCEL
GOSLING GULL
GOSPEL SPELL DHARMA EVANGEL KERUGMA KERYGMA SYNOPTIC
(PL.) TEXT
GOSSAMER MOUSEWEB STARDUST
GOSSIP EME GAB GUP PIE WAG AUNT BLAB BUZZ CANT CLAT CONK COZE DIRT DISH NEWS TALK CAUSE CLACK CLASH CLYPE COOSE CRACK FERLY FRUMP GOSSY SIEVE YENTA BABBLE CACKLE CADDLE CALLET CAMPER CLAVER CUMMER FERLIE JANGLE KIMMER NORATE TATTLE TITTLE CLATTER COMPERE GOSTHER HASHGOB NASHGAB SCANDAL TATTLER TRATTLE CAUSERIE CHITCHAT GOSSIPRY QUIDNUNC SCHMOOZE NEWSMONGER SCUTTLEBUTT
(MALICIOUS —) SCANDAL
(OUTPOURING OF —) EARFUL
GOSSIPY BUZZY NEWSY CHATTY
GOTH GOTHIAN SUIOGOTH VISIGOTH
GOTHAM ABDERA
GOTHAMITE ABDERITE
GOTHIC OGIVAL
GOTTERDAMMERUNG
(CHARACTER IN —) HAGEN GUNTHER GUTRUNE SIEGFRIED WALTRAUTE BRUNNHILDE
(COMPOSER OF —) WAGNER
GOUGE DIG PUG BENT SCUFF CHISEL EXTORT FLUKAN GOUGER HOLLOW SCRIBE FLOOKAN SCORPER SELVAGE SELVEDGE STICKING
(— OUT) BULLDOZE
(V-TYPE —) VEINER
GOUGER CHISELLER
GOURD MATE PEPO LUFFA ABOBRA JICARA PATOLA ANGURIA DISHRAG HECHIMA CALABASH CUCURBIT PEPONIDA PEPONIUM
GOURMAND EATER EPICURE GLUTTON GORMAND
GOURMET PALATE EPICURE GOURMAND
GOUT GUT CLOT DROP SPLASH PODAGRA PODAGRY CHIRAGRA ARTHRITIS
(— IN HAND) CHIRAGRA
(SUFF.) AGRA
GOUTTE DROP ICICLE
GOUTWEED AXWEED ASHWEED ACHEWEED AISEWEED BOLEWORT GOATWEED GOUTWORT
GOUTY PODAGRAL PODAGRIC
GOVERN RUN WIN CURB KING LEAD REDE REIN RULE SWAY WALD WARD WIND YEME GUIDE JUDGE REGLE

STEER TREAT WIELD BRIDLE DIRECT
MANAGE ORDAIN POLICE POLICY
TEMPER COMMAND CONDUCT
CONTROL PRESIDE REFRAIN
DISPENSE DOMINATE IMPERATE
MODERATE OVERRULE OVERSWAY
POLICIZE REGULATE RESTRAIN

GOVERNED BENT

GOVERNESS ABBESS DUENNA
FRAULEIN MISTRESS MADEMOISELLE

GOVERNING REGENT REGITIVE

GOVERNMENT GATE LAND RULE
KREIS METRO POWER STATE STEER
DURBAR HAVANA POLICY RULING
CABINET CZARISM DIARCHY
DYARCHY RECTION REGENCY
REGIMEN TSARISM CIVILITY
ENDARCHY GOBIERNO HEGEMONY
ISOCRACY ISOCRYME KINGSHIP
STEERING ABSOLUTISM
(— BY FEW) OLIGARCHY
(— BY GOD) THEONOMY
(— BY MANY) POLYARCHY
(— BY MOB) OCHLOCRACY
(— BY SMALL CLASS) OLIGARCHY
(— BY THREE) TRIARCHY
(— BY WEALTHY) PLUTOCRACY
(— BY WOMEN) GYNARCHY
GYNOCRACY
(— BY 10) DECARCHY
(— BY 2) DIARCHY DUARCHY
(— NOTE) TBOND
(— OF CEYLON) DISSAVA
(— OF TURKEY) GATE PORTE
(ARBITRARY —) ABSOLUTISM
(BAD —) MISRULE
(CHURCH —) FREEOCY
(INDIAN —) CIRCAR SIRCAR
(ITALIAN —) QUIRINAL
(MALAYSIAN —) KOMPENI
(MOROCCAN —) MAGHZEN MAKHZAN
(REGIONAL —) METRO
(RUSSIAN —) KREMLIN
(SWAHILI —) SERKALI
(TURKISH —) PORTE
(PREF.) CRATO
(WITHOUT —) ANARCH(O)
(SUFF) ARCH ARCHIG ARCHY CRACY
CRATIC)

GOVERNMENTAL ARCHICAL

GOVERNOR BAN BEY DEY EARL
KAID LORD NAIK TUTU VALI BANUS
CLEON DEWAN DIWAN HAKIM
NABOB NAZIM PACHA PASHA SHEIK
SUBAH TUPAN AUTHOR DYNAST
GRIEVE LEGATE MOODIR MYOWUN
NAIGUE NAIQUE PATESI PENLOP
RECTOR REGENT SACHEM SATRAP
SHEIKH SHERIF TUCHUN WARDEN
CATAPAN DAROGHA LEONATO
PODESTA RECTRIX SERKALI SHEREEF
TOPARCH TSUNGTU VICEROY
WIELDER AUTOCRAT BURGRAVE

ETHNARCH HOSPODAR LANDVOGT
MISTRESS PENTARCH RESIDENT
SUBAHDAR TETRARCH CASTELLAN
PRESIDENT PROCONSUL
(— OF ALGIERS) DEY DISAWA
(— OF BURMA) WUN WOON
(— OF EGYPT) MUDIR
(— OF FORTRESS) ALCAIDE ALCAYDE
(— OF SHIRE) ALDERMAN
(— OF TAMMANY) SACHEM
(BYZANTINE —) EXARCH CATAPAN
(CEYLON —) DISAWA
(GERMAN —) LANDVOGT
(GREEK —) ETHNARCH
(JAPANESE —) SHOGUN TYCOON
(PAPAL —) LEGATE
(ROMAN —) TETRARCH
(SELJUK —) ATABEG ATABEK
(SPARTAN —) HARMOST
(TURKISH —) BEY WALI MUDIR KEHAYA

GOVERNOR-GENERAL VALI

GOWDIE SCULPIN

GOWK CUCKOO

GOWN OOB SAC GITE GORE HUKE
JAMA RAIL SACK SILK TOGA BANIA
DRESS FROCK GOUND HABIT JAMAH
MANTO TABBY TOOSH BANIAN
DANIYA CAFTAN CAMISE CANDYS
CHITON JESUIT JOHNNY KIMONO
KIRTLE KITTEL LEVITE MANTUA
ARISARD CASSOCK GARMENT
JOHNNIE SLAMKIN SULTANA
SULTANE WRAPPER CAMISOLE
GANDOURA MAZARINE PEIGNOIR
(HAWAIIAN —) MOLOKU MUUMUU

GOYA CURRANT

GOYIM GENTES

GRAB NAB NAP RAP GLAM GOPE
GLAUM SCRAB CLUTCH COLLAR
GRATCH DIMPLII NIPPER NOBBLE
SNATCH CRAPPLE GRABBLE
GRAPNEL GRAPPLE NIPPERS

GRAB BAG LUCKYDIP

GRABBY ARID

GRABEN TROUGH

GRABWEED BISHOPWEED

GRACE EST ORF BEAT ESTE GARB
HELD SWAY ADORN COULE FAVOR
HONOR MENSE MENSK MERCY
POISE SLIDE THANK VENUS BEAUTY
BECOME BEDECK CHARIS POLISH
RELIGH THALIA AGGRACE CHARISM
COMMEND DIGNITY FINESSE
GRATIFY MELISMA MORDENT
BACKFALL BEAUTIFY BLESSING
DECORATE EASINESS ELEGANCE
FELICITY GRATUITY LEVATION
ORNAMENT
(— OF FORM) FLOW SWAY
TOURNURE

GRACEFUL AIRY FEAT GENT BONNY
GENTY GRATE COMELY FEATLY
FELINE FLUENT GAINLY QUAINT

SEEMLY SILKEN VENUST ELEGANT
FITTING GENTEEL GRACILE SYLPHID
WILLOWY CHARMING DELICATE
GRACIOUS LEGGIERO MACEVOLE
SWANLIKE SYLPHISH
(PREF.) ABRO HABRO
GRACEFULLY FAIR FEATLY HAPPILY
LEGGIERO
GRACEFULNESS JOLLITY ELEGANCE
GRACELESS AWKWARD
GRACES CHARITES
GRACIOUS GOOD HEND HOLD KIND
MILD CIVIL GODLY HAPPY LUCKY
SUAVE WINLY BENIGN GENIAL
GENTLE GOODLY KINDLY AFFABLE
CORDIAL WINSOME BENEDICT
DEBONAIR GENEROUS HANDSOME
MERCIFUL PLEASING SOCIABLE
BENIGNANT
GRACIOUSLY FAIR SWEETLY
GRACIOUSNESS GRACE MENSK
FACILITY GRATUITY
GRACKLE BEO DAW JACKDAW
BOATTAIL TINKLING TROOPIAL
GRADATION HUE CLINE ABLAUT
CLIMAX NUANCE GEOCLINE
STRENGTH
GRADE CUT BANK CHOP EVEN FORM
MARK RANK SIZE STEP GLIDE LEVEL
ORDER PLANE SCORE SIEGE STAGE
ASCENT DEGREE RATING STAPLE
TRIAGE FAILURE INCLINE INSPECT
DEMISANG GRADIENT GRADUATE
MERIDIAN STANDARD
(— DOWN) FAULT
(— LUMBER) SURVEY
(— OF BEEF) GOOD CUTTER
(— OF LIFE) PLANE
(— OF LUMBER) CULL
(— OF OAK) WAINSCOT
(— OF OFFICER) CORNET
(— ROAD) IMPROVE
(—S ONE THROUGH TWELVE) ELHI
(—S 1 THROUGH 12) ELHI
(ABLAUT —) GUNA
(DESIGNED FOR USE IN —S 1-12) ELHI
(POOR —) DEE
(SUPERIOR —) SUPER
(THIRD —) FAIR
GRADER PLANER CLASSER SCRAPER
GRADIENT GRADE LAPSE SLOPE
ASCENT INCLINE DOWNHILL
(SUFF.) CLINAL CLINE
GRADIN GRADINO PREDELLA
GRADUAL EASY FLAT SLOW GRAIL
GENTLE LENTOUS STEPWISE
PIECEMEAL
GRADUALLY GENTLY EDGINGLY
GRADATIM INCHMEAL PIECEMEAL
GRADUATE ALUM GRAD GRADE
ALUMNA DIVIDE FELLOW ALUMNUS
GRADATE BACHELOR
(EISTEDDFOD —) OVATE

GRADUATED SCALAR MEASURED
GRADUATION CLICK
GRAFT BUD IMP PIE CION WORK
GRAFF GRAVY INEYE SCION BOODLE
INARCH PAYOLA SPLICE ENGRAFT
IMPLANT JOBBERY SQUEEZE
TOPWORK APPROACH BOODLING
GRAFTING INSITION
GRAFTED ENTE
GRAFTER BOODLER
GRAFTING GRAFTAGE INSITION
(PREF.) GREFFO
GRAIL CUP GRAAL CHALICE SANGRAAL
GRAIN JOT RUN RYE WAY CORN
CURN DANA KERN PILE RICE SAND
SEED WALE WOOD EMMER FIBER
FIBRE FUNDI GAVEL GLEBE GRIST
PANIC SCRAP SPARK STUFF TRACE
WHEAT ANNONA BARLEY BRAINS
CEREAL CURRAN GROATS KERNEL
FRUMENT GRANULE PANICLE
VICTUAL GRAINING PARTICLE
STRAIGHT SWEEPAGE
(— FOR MUSH) KASHA
(— FROM MASH TUN) DRAINS
(— LEFT AFTER HARVEST) GAVEL
SHACK
(— MEASURE) THRAVE
(— OF BOARD) BEAT
(— OF CORN) BEAT
(— OF GOLD) PIPPIN
(— OF WOOD) BATE
(—S OF PARADISE) MALAGUETTA
(CHAFF OF —) BRAN
(COARSE —) THIRD
(COARSELY GROUND —) MEAL GRITS
KIBBLE
(DAMAGED —) SALVAGE
(EAR OF —) SPIKE RISSOM RIZZON
(GERMINATED —) MALT
(GROUND —) GRIST
(HANDFUL OF —) REAP
(HULLED —) GRITS GROUT GROATS
SHELLING
(HUSKED —) SHEALING SHILLING
(MILLET —) CUSCUS
(MIXED —) MASLIN
(MIXED —S) DREDGE
(PARCHED —) GRADDAN
(REFUSE —) SHAG DRAFF
(SACRIFICIAL —) ADOR
(SHOCK OF —) COP
(STACK OF —) HOVEL
(STORED —) MOW
(STREAKED —) ROEY
(PL.) PICKLES RAGGING
(PREF.) CHONDR(I)(IO)(O) COCC(O)
GRANI GRANUL(I)(O) SITIO SITO
(SUFF.) COCCAL COCCIC
GRAIN BEETLE CADELLE
GRAINER DICER BOARDER
GRAINSMAN THROWER DRAFFMAN
GRAIN SORGHUM DURRA SHALLU

GRAM KHESARI
(MILLIONTH —) GAMMA
GRAMMAR DONAT SYNTAX
GRAMARY PRISCIAN
(TYPE OF —) TAGMEMIC
GRAMMARIAN PRISCIAN
GRAMPUS ORC ORCA COWFISH
DOLPHIN SPRINGER
GRANARY GOLA GUNJ SILO GOLAH
GUNGE LATHE GARNER GIRNEL
GRANGE HORREUM RESERVE
CORNLOFT GRAINERY
GRAND OLD AIRY BRAW EPIC MAIN
TALL CHIEF GREAT LOFTY NOBLE
PIANO PROUD SHOWY SWELL
WLONK ANDEAN AUGUST COSMIC
EPICAL FAMOUS GLOBAL KINGLY
LORDLY SIGHTY SUPERB SWANKY
EXALTER IMMENSE STATELY
SUBLIME COSMICAL FOREMOST
GLORIOUS GORGEOUS IMPOSING
MAJESTIC SPLENDID MAGNIFICENT
(PREF.) BEL
GRAND CANYON STATE
ARIZONA
GRANDCHILD OE OY OYE
(GREAT —) IEROE
GRANDDAUGHTER NIECE
GRANDEE DON GRAND OMRAH
BASHAW GRANDO MAGNATE
GRANDEUR POMP STATE ESTATE
FIGURE PARADE MAJESTY
ELEGANCE GRANDEZA HAUTESSE
NOBILITY SPLENDOR VASTNESS
GRANDFATHER AIEL NONO BOBBY
GRAMP ATAVUS GRAMPS BELSIRE
GRANDAD GRANDPA GRANDFER
GUIDSIRE
(GREAT —) NONO
(GREAT-GREAT-GREAT —)
QUATRAYLE
GRAND HOTEL (AUTHOR OF —)
BAUM
(CHARACTER IN —) ANNA OTTO
FLAMM GAIGERN PREYSING
ELISAVETA FLAEMMCHEN
KRINGELEIN GRUSINSKAYA
OTTERNSCHLAG
GRANDILOQUENT TALL HEROIC
TURGID BOMBAST MAGNIFIC
RHETORICAL
GRANDIOSE GRAND COSMIC
TURGID SUBLIME COSMICAL
IMPERIAL
GRANDISSIMUS (AUTHOR OF —)
CABLE
(CHARACTER IN —) KEENE AURORA
HONORE JOSEPH PALMYRE
AGRICOLA CLOTILDE FUSILIER
NANCANOU FROWENFIELD
GRANDISSIMUS
GRANDMOTHER GRAM GRAN
NANA LUCKY NANNY GRANNY

GUDAME LUCKIE BELDAME
NOKOMIS BABUSHKA GRANDAME
GRANDMOTHERS (AUTHOR OF —)
WESTCOTT
(CHARACTER IN —) JIM EVAN ROSE
ALWYN FLORA HENRY NANCY RALPH
TOWER CANNON SERENA LEANDER
MARIANNE
GRANDPARENT TUTU TUPUNA
(OF —S) AVAI
GRAND SLAM VOLE
GRANDSON NEPHEW NEPOTE
GRANITE MOYITE RUNITE GREISEN
SYENITE ALASKITE RAPAKIVI
PEGMATITE
(— STATE) NEWHAMPSHIRE
(DECOMPOSED —) GROWAN
(PREF.) PEGMATO SYENO
GRANITEWARE GRAYWARE
GRANNY TUTU BABUSHKA
GRANT AID FEU BOOK BOON CEDE
ENAM GALE GIFT GIVE HEAR LEND
LOAN MISE SEND STOW YARK ADMIT
ALLOT ALLOW AWARD BONUS
CHART COWLE FLOAT FUERO LEASE
SEIZE SPARE TITHE YETTE YIELD
ACCEDE ACCORD AFFORD ASSENT
BESTOW DETAKE BETEEM BOUNTY
CONFER DESIGN EXTEND FIRMAN
IMPART JAGEER NOVATE OCTROI
PATENT PERMIT REMISE ADJUDGE
APPOINT COLLATE CONCEDE
CONSENT DISPONE INDULGE
LICENSE PRESENT PROMISE
SUBSIDY TRIBUTE APPANAGE
BESTOWAL CONTRACT DONATION
EXCHANGE MONOPOLY PITTANCE
TRANSFER CONCESSION
ACKNOWLEDGE
(— AS PROPER) ACCORD
(— FOR EXPENSES) SUPPLY
(— IN REMISSION) PARDON
(— OF LAND) FEU ENAM GALE PATA
SASAN CASATE
(— PERMISSION) ALLOW DISPENSE
(— RELIEF) FORGIVE
(— TIME) FRIST
(INDIAN —) ENAM COWLE SASAN
JAGEER JAGHIR
(PL.) PORK
GRANTING IF ALTHO REMISE
ALTHOUGH ACCORDANCE
GRANTOR LESSOR
GRANULAR CORN OPEN GRAINY
GRANULATE CORN KERN GRAIN
SUGAR
GRANULATED CORN GRANULAR
GRANULATION SUGARING
GRANULE GRIT GRANUM LUCULE
NODULE BIOBLAST GONIDIUM
GRANULET
(— IN PROTOPLASM) PLASTID
(ALTMANN'S —S) BIOPLAST

(ICE —S) FRAZIL
(SUFF.) PLAST
GRAPE UVA EDEN VINE BERRY GRAIN
PINOT TOKAY ACINUS AGAWAM
ISABEL MALAGA MONICA MUSCAT
RAISIN VERDEA WORDEN CATAWBA
CONCORD HAMBURG MALMSEY
MISSION NIAGARA SULTANA
CABERNET DELAWARE GRAPELET
HANEPOOT ISABELLA LABRUSCA
MALVASIA MORILLON MOUNTAIN
MUSCATEL NUCULANE RIESLING
SLIPSKIN SYLVANER THOMPSON
VINIFERA MUSCADINE
(GARNISHED WITH —S) VERONIQUE
(PREPARED WITH —S) VERONIQUE
(PL.) RAPE UVAE
(PREF.) ACINI UVI UVULO
GRAPEFRUIT POMELO POMOLO
POMMELO TORONJA SHADDOCK
POMPELMOUS POMPELMOOSE
GRAPE HYACINTH MUSK
GRAPE JUICE MUST SAPA STUM
GRAPENUTS TERRAPIN
GRAPEROOT BERBERIS
GRAPES
(PREF.)
(BUNCH OF —) BOTRY(O) STAPHYL(O)
**GRAPES OF WRATH (AUTHOR OF
—)** STEINBECK
(CHARACTER IN —) AL JIM TOM
JOAD NOAH ROSE CASEY MULEY
CONNIE GRAVES RUTHIE WINFIELD
GRAPESTONE
(PREF.) ACINI
GRAPEVINE
(PREF.) AMPEL(O)
GRAPH CHART CURVE OGIVE TRACE
CONTOUR DIAGRAM PROFILE
ISOPLETH
(BOTTOMS OF —S) XAXES
(KIND OF —) FEYNMAN
GRAPHIC PICTORIAL PICTURESQUE
GRAPHITE WAD KISH LEAD WADD
KEESH PENCIL PLUMBAGO
MODERATOR
GRAPNEL CROW DRAG GRAB CREEP
CREEPER GRABBLE GRAPPLE
SNIGGER GRABHOOK
GRAPPLE DOG CLOSE GRASP GRIPE
LATCH BUCKLE CLINCH GRABBLE
GRAPNEL GRIPPLE SNIGGER
SNIGGLE WRESTLE
(— QUARRY) BIND
GRAPPLING IRON CLIP DRAG
CLASP CRAMP CORVUS CRAMPER
CRAMPON CREEPER GRAPNEL
GRAPPLE HARPAGO
GRAPTOLITHA XYLINA
GRASP HUG NAP SEE CLAM CLAW
CLUM FAKE FANG FIST GLAM GRAB
GRIP HAND HENT HOLD SNAP SPAN
TAKE VICE CATCH CINCH CLAMP

CLASP CLAUT CLEUK GRIPE GROPE
LATCH SAVVY SEIZE SENSE SHAKE
SPEND CLENCH CLINCH CLUTCH
COLLAR FATHOM GOUPEN RUMBLE
SNATCH CLAUGHT COMPASS
ENCLOSE GRAPPLE GRIPPLE SMITTLE
CONCEIVE HANDFAST HOLDFAST
(— FULLY) SWALLOW
(— MENTALLY) ENVISAGE
(— OF REALITY) EPIPHANY
(PREF.) CHADA
GRASPING HARD NIPPY SNACK
GRABBY GREEDY GRIPPY HAVING
TAKING BROKING MISERLY PUGGING
COVETOUS HANDGRIP AVARICIOUS
GRASS BON FAG FOG POA RAY BENT
COIX DISS DOOB GAMA HERB ICHU
KANS KUSA MUNJ MUSK RAGI TARE
TORE USAR ANKEE BARIT BROME
COGON COUCH CROFT DRAWK
DRINN FLAWN FUNDI GARSE GIRSE
GLAGA GRAMA HARIF HAVER HICHU
ILLUK KOGON KIJSHA KWEEK MELIC
MUHLY PANIC QUILA REESK ROOSA
SEREH SPIRE STIPA SUDAN ZORRA
BARLEY BHABAR BHARTI DARNEL
EMOLOA FESCUE FIORIN GLUMAL
KIKUYU QUITCH RAGGEE REDTOP
RIPGUT SCUTCH TOETOE TWITCH
ZACATE AMOURET CANNACH
DOGFOOT ESPARTO EULALIA
FESTUCA FINETOP FOXTAIL GALLETA
GOLDEYE HERBAGE HORDEUM
JARAGUA MATWEED MUSCOVY
PANICLE PASTURE PIGROOT SETARIA
SORGHUM TIMOTHY TOCUSSO
TUSSOCK VETIVER ZACATON
AEGILOPS BLUESTEM BROWNTOP
CALFKILL CAMALOTE CELERITY
COCKSPUR DOGSTAIL DRAWLING
DROPSEED EELGRASS ELEUSINE
FINEBENT GAMELOTE MANGRASS
MATGRASS PASPALUM SANDBURR
SANDSPUR SANDSTAY SPANIARD
SPARTINA SPINIFEX SWEEPAGE
TEOSINTE WHITETOP MARIJUANA
(— AMONG GRAIN) DRAWK
(— FOR STOCK) EATAGE
(— FOR THATCHING) BANGO
(— ON BORDER OF FIELD) RAND
(— READY FOR REAPING) SWATH
SWATHE
(— USED FOR MAKING PAPER)
ESPARTO
(AROMATIC —) KHUS CUSCUS
KHUSKHUS
(BEACH —) STAR
(BERMUDA —) DOOB SCUTCH
(CEREAL —) SORGO SORGHUM
(COARSE —) FAG RISP TATH COGON
REESK LALANG SNIDDLE
(COUCH —) CUTCH KWEEK QUITCH
SCUTCH STROIL SQUITCH

(CURED —) HAY
(DEAD —) FOG FOGGAGE
(DITCH —) ENALID
(GOOSE —) CLIVERS CLEAVERS
(KIND OF —) COUCH QUACK
(MEADOW —) POA
(NUT —) COCO COCOA
(ORCHARD —) DOGFOOT
(PART OF —) AWN TIP APEX CULM
LEAF NODE ROOT STEM BLADE
BRACT GLUME SHOOT FLORET
FLOWER LIGULE SHEATH TILLER
PEDICEL RHIZOME SPIKELET
(PASTURE —) TORE GRAMMA
(POVERTY —) HEATH
(QUAKING —) SHAKER
(REED —) CARRIZO
(REEDLIKE —) BENT DISS
(STORED FORAGE —) HAYLAGE
(SUDAN —) GARAWI
(SWEET —) SORGO
(PREF.) CHORTO GRAMIN(I)(O) HERBI
GRASS-EATING
(PREF.) POE
GRASSERIE JAUNDICE
GRASSHOPPER GRIG CICADA
HOPPER QUAKER SAWYER TETTIX
ACRIDID CRICKET KATYDID SKIPPER
ACRIDIAN LANGOSTA
GRASSLAND HAM LEA RAKH VELD
VELDT BOTTOM MEADOW PATANA
LEYLAND PASTURE SAVANNA
(ARGENTINE —) CAMPO
(RUSSIAN —) STEPPES
(SWAMPY —) EVERGLADE
(TRACT OF —) PRAIRIE
(PL.) SCHIH
GRASS PEA LANG KHESARI
GRASSQUIT QUAT QUIT CIVITE
GRASS TREE BLACKBOY
GRASSY HERBY
GRATE JAR FRET GRIT RASP CHARK
CHIRK DANDY DEVIL GRIDE GRIND
RANGE STOVE ABRADE CHAFER
SCRAPE SCREAK SCREEK SCROOP
GRATING MANGRATE
(FALSE —) DANDY
GRATEFUL KIND SAPID WELCOME
THANKFUL
GRATEFULNESS GRATUITY
GRATER RISP
GRATIANO (BROTHER OF —)
BRABANTIO
(WIFE OF —) NERISSA
GRATIFICATION GLUT GUST
LUXURY RELISH REWARD SATIETY
DELICACY GRATUITY PLEASURE
TICKLING SATISFACTION
GRATIFIED GLAD PROUD CHARMED
CONTENT PLEASED
GRATIFY PAY BABY FEED LUST SATE
AMUSE FEAST FLESH GRACE HUMOR
MIRTH QUEME SAVOR SERVE SETUP

STILL WREAK ARRIDE FOSTER
OBLIGE PAMPER PLEASE REGALE
SALUTE TICKLE AGGRATE CONTENT
DELIGHT FLATTER GLADDEN
INDULGE SATISFY PLEASURE
(— THE PALATE) SEASON
GRATIFYING GOOD COMELY
DELICATE GRATEFUL
GRATING GRID HACK HARP HECK
JACK RACK CRATE CRUDE GRILL
HARSH RANGE RASPY TRAIL BAFFLE
CRATCH GITTER GRILLE HOARSE
RUGGED WICKET BAFFLER ECHELLE
ECHELON BABRACOT CATAPULT
GRIDIRON METALLIC SCRANNEL
STRIDENT PORTCULLIS
(— OVER DRAIN) SIVER SYVER
GRATIS FREE FREELY BUCKSHEE
GRATITUDE THANK THANKS
GRATUITY
GRATUITOUS FREE WANTON
BASELESS NEEDLESS
GRATUITY FEE TIP BOON DASH VAIL
PILON SPIFF SPILL BOUNTY
CUMSHAW DASTURI DOUCEUR
PRESENT PRIMAGE BAKSHISH
BONAMANO BUCKSHEE COURTESY
DUSTOORI GRATUITO REAPDOLE
BAKHSHISH BAKSHEESH PERQUISITE
(CHRISTMAS —) BOX
(GAMBLER'S —) TOKE
(PL.) LARGESSE
GRAVE BED DRY LOW PIT SAD URN
BALK BASS BIER CELL CIST DEEP
DELF FOSS GRIT HIGH HOME KIST
LAIR LAKE MOLD MOOL RUDE SADE
SAGE TOMB URNA DELFT FOSSE
GRAFF GROVE HEAVY MOULD SHEOL
SOBER STAID STIFF SUANT VAULT
BURIAL DEMURE GRIEVE HEARGE
SEDATE SEVERE SOLEMN SOMBER
SOMBRE STEADY AUSTERE EARNEST
FUNERAL PITHOLE SERIOSO SERIOUS
SOBERLY CATONIAN DECOROUS
MATRONAL SERMONIC SATURNINE
GRAVECLOTHES LINEN
CEREMENTS
GRAVEDIGGER RATEL BEDRAL
BURIER FOSSOR PITMAN BEDERAL
GRAVEL GRIT ARENA GEEST GRAIL
CHESIL RANGLE SAMMEL SHILLA
BALLAST CALICHE CHANNEL RATCHEL
SHINGLE STANNER BLINDING
(— AND SAND) DOBBIN
(— DEPOSIT) LEAD
(— IN KIDNEYS) ARENA
(LOOSE —) SLITHER
(SCREENED —) HOGGINS
(PREF.) CROCO
GRAVELLY HASKY CHISELLY
GLAREOUS
GRAVELY SADLY DEEPLY
GRAVE MOUND TUMULUS

GRAVER BURIN STYLE PLASTIC SCORPER
GRAVESTONE BAUTA PLANK STELA STELE STONE TABLE CIPPUS JUMPER THROUGH
GRAVEYARD CEMETERY
GRAVID HEAVY WOMBED PREGNANT
GRAVIMETER DOODLEBUG
GRAVITATIONAL UNIT SLUG
GRAVITY WEIGHT DIGNITY EARNEST SOBRIETY
(KIND OF —) ZERO
GRAVY JUS SOP BREE FOND LEAR BLANC BUNCE JIPPER
GRAY ASH BAT FOG ASHY BEAR BLAE BLUE DOVE DUSK GREY GRİS GULL HOAR IRON LEAD SALT ACIER CAMEL CRANE HOARY LYART MOUSE STEEL WHITE CASTOR CINDER DENVER FROSTY FRUSTY GREIGE GRISLY ISABEL LEADEN NICKEL NUTRIA PEWTER QUAKER STRING BLUNKET CRUISER GRANITE GRIZARD GRIZZLE GRIZZLY HUELESS MURINUS NEUTRAL PELICAN PILGRIM SARKARA SPARROW ALUMINUM BLONCKET CHARCOAL CINEREAL CINEROUS EVENGLOW FELDGRAU PLATINUM PLYMOUTH
(BROWNISH —) TAUPE
(DARKEST —) BLACK
(GOOSE —) LAMA
(MOLE —) TAUPE
(MOTH —) SHEEPSKIN
(STREAKED WITH —) LYARD
(VIOLET —) GRIDELIN
(PREF.) GLAUC(O) POLI(O)
GRAYBACK DOWITCH GRAYCOAT GREYBACK
GRAYBEARD OLDSTER
GRAY CRANE COOLEN COOLUNG
GRAY DRAB ACIER
GRAYISH NEUTRAL
GRAYLING PINK OMBRE UMBER HERRING UMBRANA BLUEFISH SALMONID
GRAYNESS CANITIES
GRAY PARROT JAKO
GRAYSBY CONY CONEY
GRAY WHALE RIPSACK GRAYBACK HARDHEAD
GRAZE BITE CROP FEED SCUR SKIM AGIST BRUSH GRASS GRIDE RANGE SCAMP SCUFF SHAVE SKIFF SKIRR STOCK BROWSE CHASE FODDER GLANCE RIPPLE SCRAPE SCRAZE PASTURE
GRAZIER PASTURER SQUATTER TREKBOER
GRAZING BIT FEED GRASS COLLOP RASANT FOLDING PASCUAGE
GREASE COOM SAIM SEAM ADEPS BLECK COOMB SMEAR SPICK ARMING

AXUNGE CREESH ENSEAM LIQUOR POMATE ALEMITE SAINDOUX
(— IN HARD CAKES) SEAK
(— UP) LARD
(PIG'S —) MORT
(WOOL —) YOK DEGRAS LANOLIN
(PREF.) SEBI
GREASE-HEELS GRAPES
GREASER DOPER
GREASEWOOD CHICO CHEMIZO
GREASY FAT GLET OILY RICH FATTY PORKY YOLKY SMEARY TRAINY CREESHY PINGUID TALLOWY UNCTUOUS
GREAT BAD BIG FAR FAT FIT OLD RAD BARO COOL DEEP DREE FELL FINE GONE GURT HUGE KEEN MAIN MUCH RIAL SOME TALL UNCO VAST VILE AMPLE BURRA CHIEF DANDY FELON GRAND LARGE MEKIL STOUR SUPER SWEET SWELL TOUGH YEDER FIERCE GAPING HEROIC MICKLE NATION STRONG SUPERB CAPITAL EMINENT EXTREME GALLOWS HOWLING IMMENSE INTENSE STAVING TITANIC VIOLENT VOLUMED ALMIGHTY CRACKING ELEVATED ENORMOUS FAVORITE GALACTIC GALAXIAN GIGANTIC HORRIBLE INFINITE PRECIOUS TERRIFIC MONSTROUS MAGNIFICENT
(— LAND) ALASKA
(IMMEASURABLY —) ABYSMAL
(TOO —) OVERDUE
(VERY —) MAIN SORE AWFUL STEEP ARDENT DEADLY IMMANE INGENT MORTAL EXTREME FRANTIC GHASTLY HOWLING SUBLIME DREADFUL MOUNTAIN MONUMENTAL
(PREF.) ARCH MAGN(I) MAHA MEG(A) MEGAL(O)
(HOW —) QUANTI
(SUFF.) MEGALY
GREAT AUK PENGUIN PINWING GAREFOWL
GREAT BARRIER (— ISLAND) OTEA
GREAT BRITAIN (SEE ENGLAND)
GREATCOAT GREGO JEMMY JOSEPH POSTEEN OVERCOAT
GREAT DANE BEARHOUND
GREATER SUPERIOR
(PREF.) MEIZO
GREATER STITCHWORT HEAD SNAPPER HEADACHE SNAPJACK SNAPWORT
GREATER YELLOWLEGS YELPER
GREATEST UTMOST EXTREME MAXIMAL
(— EXTENT) MAX MAXIMUM
(— POSSIBLE) ALL SUPREME
GREAT EXPECTATIONS (AUTHOR OF —) DICKENS

(CHARACTER IN —) JOE PIP ABEL BIDDY DOLGE SARAH ORLICK PHILIP PIRRIP POCKET PROVIS BENTLEY DRUMMLE ESTELLA GARGERY HERBERT JAGGERS MATTHEW HAVISHAM MAGWITCH COMPEYSON PUMBLECHOOK

GREAT GATSBY (AUTHOR OF —) FITZGERALD
(CHARACTER IN —) JAY TOM NICK BAKER DAISY MCKEE GATSBY GEORGE JORDAN MYRTLE WILSON BUCHANAN CARRAWAY CATHERINE WOLFSHIEM

GREAT-GRANDCHILD IEROE
GREAT GRANDFATHER NONO BESAIEL GRANDSIR
GREAT LAKE ERIE HURON ONTARIO MICHIGAN SUPERIOR
GREATLY FAR MUY FELL MUCH AMAIN SWITH FINELY MAINLY STRONG SWYTHE SWEETLY WOUNDLY MIGHTILY
GREAT MOLE RAT ZEMMI ZEMNI
GREATNESS FORCE GRANDEUR GRANDEZA MUCHNESS
GREAT RAGWEED KINGHEAD
GREAT TITMOUSE SHARPSAW
GREAVE JAMB JAMBE JAMBEAU (PL.) CRAP HOSE GRAVES
GREBE LEAD LOON DIVER GAUNT WITCH DIPPER DOBBER DUCKER FINFOOT HENRILL PYGOPOD ARSEFOOT CARGOOSE DABCHICK DIDAPPER GRUIFORM
GRECE GRICE DEGREE GRIDOLN

GREECE

ANCIENT LOCATIONS: ELIS DORIS PYLOS ACHAEA ACTIUM ATTICA DELPHI EPIRUS HELLAS LOCRIS PHOCIS SPARTA THEBES TIRYNS BOEOTIA CORINTH EPEIROS LACONIA MACEDON MEGARIS MYCENAE PAESTUM
ARMY UNIT: TAXIS
BAY: ELEUSIS SALAMIS PHALERON
CAPE: KRIOS MALEA SPADA AKRITAS MATAPAN SIDEROS DREPANON GRAMBYSA TAINARON
CAPITAL: ATHENS ATHENAI
COIN: OBOL HECTE DIOBOL LEPTON STATER DRACHMA DIOBOLON
COLUMN: DORIC IONIC CORINTHIAN
DANCE: PYRRHIC ROMAIKA
DIALECT: COAN ATTIC DORIC ELEAN EOLIC IONIC AEOLIC MELIAN THERAN ACHAEAN ARCADIAN
DISTRICT: ARTA ELIS CANEA CHIOS CORFU CRETE DRAMA EVROS KHIOS PELLA SAMOS ZANTE ACHAEA ACHAIA ATTICA EPIRUS EUBOEA KILKIS KNANIA KOZANE LARISA

LESBOS LEUKAS PHOCIS PIERIA SERRAI THRACE XANTHE AETOLIA ARCADIA ARGOLIS BOEOTIA CORINTH KAVALLA LACONIA LARISSA LASITHI MTATHOS PREVEZA RHODOPE CYCLADES IOANNINA KARDITSA KASTORIA MAGNESIA MESSENIA PHLORINA RETHYMNE SALONIKA THESSALY TRIKKALA MACEDONIA
GULF: VOLOS ATHENS MESARA PATRAI PATRAS ARGOLIS CORINTH KAVALLA KNANION LACONIA LEPANTO MESSINI RENDINA SARONIC STRIMON MESSENIA SALONIKA SINGITIC THERMAIC TORONAIC
HOME OF GODS: OLYMPUS
ISLAND: DIA IOS KEA KOS NIO CEOS KEOS MILO SYME SYRA CHIOS CORFU CRETE DELOS KASOS KHIOS LEROS MELOS MILOS NAXOS PAROS PAXOI PAXOS PSARA RODOS SAMOS SARIA SYROS TELOS TENOS THERA THIRA TINOS ZANTE ANAPHE ANDROS CANDIA CERIGO CHALKE EUBOEA EVVOIA GAVDOS IKARIA ITHACA ITHAKI LEMNOS LESBOS LEUKAS LEVKAS PATMOS RHENEA RHODES SIFNOS SKYROS THASOS AMORGOS CIMOLUS CYTHERA KERKYRA KIMOLOS KYTHERA KYTHNOS LEVITHA MYKONOS NISYROS SALAMIS SIPHNOS KALYMNOS MYTILENE SANTORIN SERIPHOS
ISLANDS: IONIAN CYCLADES SPORADES DODECANESE STROPHADES
LAKE: KARLA VOLVE COPAIS KOPAIS PRESPA TOPOLIA KASTORIA TACHINOS VISTONIS
LETTER: MU NU PI XI CHI ETA PHI PSI RHO TAU BETA IOTA ZETA ALPHA DELTA GAMMA KAPPA OMEGA SIGMA THETA LAMBDA EPSILON OMICRON UPSILON
MARKET PLACE: AGORA
MEASURE: PIK BEMA PIKI POUS BARIL CADOS CHOUS CUBIT DIGIT MARIS PEKHE PODOS PYGON XYLON ACAENA BACHEL BACILF RARILE COTULA DICHAS GRAMME HEMINA KOILON ORGYIA PALAME PECHYS SCHENE AMPHORA CHENICA CHOENIX CYATHOS DIAULOS HEKTEUS METRETA STADION STADIUM STREMMA CONDYLOS DAKTYLOS DEKAPODE DOLICHOS MEDIMNOS METRETES PALAISTE PLETHRON PLETHRUM SPITHAME STATHMOS
MOUNTAIN: IDA IDHI OSSA ATHOS PAROS ELIKON PARNON PELION

PILION WITSCH HELICON OLYMPUS
VURANON KRAGNOVO SMOLIKAS
TAYGETOS PARNASSUS
MOUNTAINS: OETA OTHRYS PINDUS
RODOPI RHODOPE HYMETTOS
TAYGETUS
NAME: ELLAS HELLAS
PENINSULA: ACTE AKTE AKTI MOREA
SITHONIA PELOPONNESE
PORT: SYRA CORFU PYLOS SYROS
VOLOS MEGARA PATRAI PATRAS
KAVALLA KERKYRA PIRAEUS
SALONIKA
RIVER: IRI ARDA ARTA AURO AXIOS
DOONA EVROS LERNA ALFIOS
NESTOS PENEUS PINIOS STRUMA
VARDAR ALPHEUS EUROTAS
EVROTAS ILISSOS PENEIOS ROUFIAS
SARANTA STRIMON ACHELOUS
AKHELOOS ALIAKMON KEPHISOS
RHOUPHIA
RUINS: DELOS PELLA SAMOS CORINTH
ELEUSIS ELEVSIS ACROPOLIS
SEA: CRETE AEGEAN IONIAN
MIRTOON
STATE: PHOCIS
TOWN: IOS KEA KOS ARTA ELIS KYME
PETA SYME YDRA ADREA AGYIA
ARGOS CANEA CHIOS CORFU
DRAMA KARYA MELOS NAXOS
NEMEA PELLA POROS PSARI PYLOS
PYRGI SAMOS SYROS TENOS
VAMOS VATHY VOLOS VYRON
ZANTE ACTIUM ATHENS CANDIA
DAPHNI DELPHI EDESSA ITHACA
JANINA KOZANE LARISA MEGARA
NIKHIA PATRAS RHODES SERRAI
SERRES SPARTA THEBES TIRYNS
XANTHE ATHENAI CORINTH ELEUSIS
KERKYRA LARISSA MYCENAE
PIRAEUS IOANNINA KOMOTINE
MARATHON PHARSALA SALONIKA
TRIKKALA PERISTERI
VALLEY: NEMEA
VERNACULAR: DEMOTIC
WEIGHT: MNA OKA OKE MINA OBOL
LITRA LIVRE MANEH POUND DIOBOL
DRAMME KANTAR OBOLOS OBOLUS
STATER TALENT CHALCON CHALQUE
DRACHMA DIOBOLON TALANTON
WOMEN: THYIAD

GREED AVARICE AVIDITY HOGGERY
CUPIDITY RAPACITY
GREEDINESS AVARICE AVIDITY
GULOSITY
GREEDY AVID GAIR GORB YELP
AVIDE EAGER GUTTY YIVER GRABBY
GUNDIE KITISH STINGY GLUTTON
GRIPPLE HOODOCK MISERLY PIGGISH
COVETOUS ESURIENT GRASPING
RAVENOUS LICKERISH
(PREF.) LICHNO

GREEK GREW ATTIC HADJI KOINE
METIC ARGIVE IONIAN KLEPHT
ACHAEAN ACHAIAN AEOLIAN
GRECIAN GRIFFON HELLENE
GRECANIC HELLADIC HELLENIC
ITALIOTE SICELIOT
(— RESISTANCE GROUP) EDES ELAS
(MODERN —) ROMAIC
(PREF.) GRAECO GRECO HELLENO
GREEN (ALSO SEE COLOR) NEW RAW
LEEK NILE VERD VERT CRUDE FRESH
LODEN NAIVE CALLOW VIRENT
NOUVEAU SINOPLE UNFIRED
VERDANT BAYBERRY IMMATURE
NOUVELLE VAGABOND VIRIDIAN
WEDGWOOD WOODLAND
UNTRAINED
(— MOUNTAIN STATE) VERMONT
(COOKED —S) SALAD
(GRAYISH —) RESEDA
(KIND OF —) MOSS KELLY PARIS
(NILE —) BOA
(PALE —) ALOE ALOES
(YELLOWISH —) GLAUZY ABSINTHE
GLAUCOUS
(PREF.) CHLOR(O) PRASEO PRASO
VERD(O) VIRID(I)
GREEN AMARANTH REDROOT
GREENBACK NOTE FROGSKIN
(PL.) GREEN LETTUCE
GREEN BAY TREE
(AUTHOR OF —) BROMFIELD
(CHARACTER IN —) CYON LILY ELLEN
GIGON IRENE JULIA SHANE HATTIE
WILLIE HARRISON KRYLENKO
TOLLIVER
GREENBRIER SMILAX
SARSAPARILLA
GREEN CORMORANT SHAG
GREENERY VERDURE
GREENFISH BLUEFISH
GREENHEART BIBIRU BEBEERU
GREEN HERON KIALEE
GREENHORN JAY MUG YAP JAKE
PUTT TYRO IKONA GREENY ROOKIE
SUCKER INNOCENT SOFTHORN
(— ON WHALER) WAISTER
GREENHOUSE STOVE GREENERY
HOTHOUSE ORANGERY COOLHOUSE
GREENISH BERYL SANIOUS
GREENISH-YELLOW RESEDA

GREENLAND

AIR BASE: THULE
BAY: DISKO BAFFIN MELVILLE
CAPE: JAAL GRIVEL WALKER
BISMARCK BREWSTER FAREWELL
LOWENORN
CAPITAL: GODTHAAB
DISCOVERER: ERIC
MOUNTAIN: FOREL PAYER KHARDYU
GUNNBJORN
STRAIT: DAVIS DENMARK

TOWN: ETAH NORD THUI E IIMANAK GODHAVN IVIGTUT GODTHAAB JULIANEHAB EGEDESMINDE SUKKERTOPPEN HOLSTEINSBORG

GREENLING TROUT BOREGAT BOD-IERON LORICATE ROCKFISH
GREEN MANSIONS (AUTHOR OF —) HUDSON
(CHARACTER IN —) ABEL RIMA NUFLO
GREEN MONKEY GUENON
GREENNESS VERD VERT VERDURE VERDANCY VIRIDITY
GREEN ONION RARERIPE
GREEN PIKE JACK
GREENROOM FOYER
GREENSHANK TATTLER
GREENSTONE POUNAMU
GREEN SUNFISH REDEYE
GREENWEED WOODWAX
GREEN WOODPECKER ECCLE SPRITE YAFFLE YOCKEL YUKKEL HEWHALL HEWHOLE SNAPPER SPEIGHT YAFFLER POPINJAY WOODHACK WOODWALL
GREET CRY JOY CROW HAIL HALSE ACCOST HERALD SALAAM SALUTE ADDRESS RECEIVE WELCOME
GREETING HOW CIAO HIYA ALOHA GREET HELLO HOWDY KOMBO ACCOST CHEERO SALAAM SALUTE SHALOM ADDRESS CHEERIO COMMEND SI AINTE WELCOME REMEMBRANCE
GREGARIOUS GREGAL SOCIAL
GREGE NUTRIA
GRENADA (CAPITAL OF —) STGEORGES
(ISLAND OF —) CARRIACON
GRENADE EGG TROMBE GRENADO FIREBALL PINEAPPLE
GRENADIER RATTAIL WHIPTAIL
GRENADINE FLORENCE
GRENDEL (SLAYER OF —) BEOWULF
GREREN (— LIGHT) GOAHEAD
GRETCHEN (BELOVED OF —) FAUST
GRETTIR THE STRONG (AUTHOR OF —) UNKNOWN
(CHARACTER IN —) ATLI GEST GLAM GRIM JARL ANGLE BJORN EINAR ASMUND ILLUGI OGMUND OXMAIN SKEGGI STEINN THORIR DROMUND GRETTIR MAKSSON HALLMUND LONGHAIR REDBEARD SNAEKOLL STEINVOR THORFINN THORGILS SLOWCOACH THORBJORN THORSTEINN
GREY (SEE GRAY)
GREYHOUND GREW SALUKI BANJARA SAPLING TUMBLER WHIPPET
GREYISH BEIGE

GRID BOUCAN BUCCAN GRIDDLE GRIDIRON
(CIRCULAR —) DISC DISK
GRIDDLE COMAL GRILL GIRDLE GRILLE BRANDER
GRIDDLE CAKE AREPA LATKE CHAPATTY CORNCAKE FLAPJACK SLAPJACK
GRIDIRON GRID GRILL TRAIL BRANDER BROILER GRIDDLE
GRIEF VEX WOE CARE DILL DOLE DOOL DREE HARM HURT MOAN MOOD PAIN RUTH SORE TEEN TINE AGONY DOLOR GRAME RUING TRIAL WRONG BARRAT DESIRE MISHAP REGRET SORROW STOUND WONDER ANGUISH CHAGRIN EMOTION FAILURE OFFENSE SADNESS THOUGHT TROUBLE WAESUCK WAYMENT DISASTER DISTRESS HARDSHIP
(— STEM) KELLY
(SECRET —) CANKER
(PREF.) DOLORI LYPO
GRIESEN ZWITTER
GRIEVANCE BEEF GRIEF PEEVE BURDEN BYGONE GRAVAMEN HARDSHIP
GRIEVE VEX CARE DOLE DUMP EARN ERME HONE HURT PAIN PINE SIGH WAIL GRAME GRIPE MOURN SORRY WOUND YEARN ATHINK CORSIE LAMENT REPINE SORROW AFFLICT CHAGRIN CONDOLE GRIZZLE TROUBLE WAYMENT COMPLAIN DISTRESS
GRIEVED WOE GRAME SORRY
GRIEVING SORRY
GRIEVOUS SAD DEAR DEEP DERF HARD SORE CHARY DIRTY GRIEF HEAVY SORRY WEARY BITTER DREARY SEVERE SHREWD CAREFUL HEINOUS WEIGHTY DOLOROUS ATROCIOUS
GRIEVOUSLY DERNLY FOULLY SORELY HEAVILY
GRIFFE SPUR
GRIFFIN GRIPE GRYPHON EPIMACUS
GRILL ASK REJA BRACE BROIL DEVIL TRAIL AFFLICT BROILER GRILLADE
GRILLE FACE REJA HAZARD
GRILLROOM GROOM
GRILSE PEAL SEWIN FINNAC GRAWLS BOTCHER FORKTAIL
GRIM DOUR GASH SOUR BLEAK CRUEL GAUNT STERN GRIMLY GRISLY HORRID SEVERE SULLEN TORVID GHASTLY GRIZZLY HIDEOUS MACABRE TORVOUS PITILESS RUTHLESS
GRIMACE MOP MOW MUG POT FACE GIRN IRPE MOUE MUMP YIRN FLEER

MOUTH SNEER SNOOT GIMBLE
SHEYLE STITCH MURGEON SIMAGRE
GRIMALKIN CAT HAG MOLL CRONE
WITCH BELDAM HARRIDAN
GRIME DIRT SMUT COLLY SMOUCH
SMUTCH
GRIMME COQUETOON
GRIMNESS TORVITY
GRIMP CLIMB
GRIMY DINGY GRUBBY STAINED
SCABROUS
GRIN DRAD GIRN MUMP FLEER RISUS
SNEER SIMPER GRIZZLE
GRIND DIG SAP BONE BRAY CHEW
FILE GRUN MILL MULL MUZZ SMUG
SWOT CRUSH FLOAT FLOUR GRATE
GRIDE GRIST QUERN CRUNCH
DRUDGE POWDER EMERIZE GRISTLE
SWOTTER LEVIGATE
(— COARSELY) KIBBLE
(— DIAMONDS) SKIVE
(— SMALL) BRAY
(— TEETH) GNASH GRATE GRINT
GRISBET
(— TO POWDER) TRITURATE
(— WITH WATER) PUG
GRINDER SUB HERO CRASH HOAGY
MOLAR HOAGIE MULLER BRUISER
TORPEDO PEPPERMILL
GRINDING BREAK MOLAR
ABRASION
(— OF CORN) MULTURE
(— OF MEAL) BREAK GRIST
(— OF TEETH) BRUXISM
(PL.) SWARF
GRINDSTONE MANO PAVER STONE
GRIP BITE BURR CLIP FANG FIST HOLD
HOLT TAKE VICE CHOKE CINCH
CLAMP CLASP GRASP GRIPE PINCH
SALLY SEIZE BARREL CLINCH
CLUTCH CRADLE FREEZE EMBRACE
HANDBAG HOLDING SEIZURE
ADHESION FOOTLOCK HANDFAST
HANDGRIP HANDHOLD STAGEHAND
(— OF A SWORD) FUSEAU
(— OF BELL ROPE) SALLY
(— TO A SPAR) DOG
GRIPE BEEF CARP CRAB FRIB BITCH
CREATE GROUSE HOLLER KVETCH
NATTER SNATCH GRIZZLE COMPLAIN
GRIPER GRIZZLER
GRIPES TORMINA
GRIPING GRIPPLE PINCHING
GRIPPER TALON KEEPER NIPPER
GRIPPING STONY STONEY
GRIQUA BASTARD BASTAARD
GRIS-GRIS AMULETS
GRISKINISSA (HUSBAND OF —)
ARTAXAMINOUS
GRISLY GRIM GHASTLY GRIZZLY
HIDEOUS GRUESOME
GRISON HURON GALICTIS
GRIST PABULUM

GRISTLE CARTILAGE
GRIT SAND GRIND PLUCK SPUNK
BOTTOM BRAVERY DECISION
GRITROCK RUBSTONE
(— FROM AXLE) SWARF
(PL.) CUTLINGS
GRITH MUND GYRTH
GRITTY SANDY SHARP GRISTY
CHISELLY SABULINE SABULOUS
GRIVET TOTA WAAG GEUNON
NISNAS
GRIZZLE ROAN
GRIZZLED GRISLY STREAKED
GRIZZLY BEAR (— STATE)
CALIFORNIA
GROAN MOAN ROME GRANK GRUNT
STECH COMPLAIN
GROANER PUN JOKE
GROAT BIT FLAG GILL HARP
GROATS
(PREF.) ATHERO
GROCER SPICER EPICIER PEPPERER
GROCERY BODEGA PULPERIA
GROG RUMBO TEMPER CHAMOTTE
GROGGERY SHANTY GROGSHOP
GROGGY SHAKY UNSTEADY
WAVERING
GROGSHOP SHANTY DOGGERY
GROGGERY
GROIN LISK PIER SHARE CLITCH
INGUEN GRUNZIE
(PREF.) INGUIN(O)
GROMMET RING BECKET COLLAR
EYELET CRINGLE GARLAND
GROMWELL PUCCOON REDROOT
SALFERN GRAYMILL
GROOM LAD MAFU NEAT SYCE
CURRY DRESS MAFOO PREEN PRIMP
STRAP SWIPE TIGER BARBER
BATMAN FETTLE FOGGER GUINEA
MEHTAR OSTLER HOSTLER
MARSHAL COISTREL COISTRIL
GROOMLET STRAPPER
GROOMING TOILETTE
GROOVE RUT BEAD DADO GAIN
KERF LUCE NOCK PORT RAKE SLOT
CANAL CHASE CROZE FLUTE FOSSA
GLYPH GORGE GOUGE GUIDE JOINT
QUIRK REGAL RIFLE RIGOL SCARF
SCORE STRIA SWAGE CREASE
CULLIS FULLER FURROW GUTTER
KEYWAY RABBET RAGGLE RAGLET
REBATE RIFFLE RUNNER SCROBE
SULCUS THROAT TRENCH CHAMFER
CHANNEL GARLAND KEYHOLE
PLOWING SULCATE BOTHRIUM
GROOVING PHILTRUM CANNELURE
VALLECULA
(— FOR SLIDING DOOR) REGLE
(— IN AUGER) POD
(— IN COLUMN) FLUTE
(— IN HORSE'S TOOTH) MARK
(— IN MASONRY) RAGGLE

(— IN SLUICE) RIFFLE
(— IN STAVES) CROZE
(— IN STONE) JAD
(— IN TIRE) SIPE
(— OF RECORD) TRACK
(— ON UPPER LIP) PHILTRUM
(— ON WEEVIL) SCROBE
(— ON WHALE) SCARF
(—S ON ROCK) LAPIES
(— UNDER COPING) GORGE
(JOINER'S —) SEAM
(RECTANGULAR —) REGLET
GROOVED FLUTED MILLED EXARATE
SULCATE
GROOVER FLUTER
GROOVY IN HIP RAD COOL FAROUT
SMOOTH STRIATE
GROPE CLAM CLAW FEEL POKE RIPE
GLAUM GRAIP FUMBLE GUDDLE
GRABBLE GRAPPLE GROPPLE
GRUBBLE SCRABBLE
(— AWKWARDLY) FUMBLE
GROSBEAK FINCH HAWFINCH
GROSGRAIN ROYALE
GROSS FAT DULL FOUL LUMP RANK
BROAD CRASS FOGGY GREAT GUTTY
LARGE MACRO SLUMP THICK WHOLE
ANIMAL COARSE EARTHY FILTHY
GREASY SORDID STRONG BLOATED
FULSOME CLODDISH FLAGRANT
INDECENT SLUTTISH
GROSSO MATAPAN
GROTESQUE ANTIC WOOZY
ROCOCO BAROQUE BIZARRE
GROTESCO FANCIFUL
GROTTO CAVE GROT ANTRE SPEOS
CAVERN LUPERCAL
GROUCH BEAR CRAB SULK CRANK
GROUSE SOURBALL SOURPUSS
GROUND SEW SOD SUE BASE CLOD
DIRT FOLD FOND GIST LAND MOLD
REST ROOT SOIL STAY WOLD EARTH
FIELD FIRTH FOUND MOULD PLACE
SCORE SOLUM STAIN TRAIN TUTOR VENUE
CREASE MATTER REASON SMACKED
FORELAND INITIATE
(— AT TOP OF SHAFT) BANK
(— COVERED WITH RUBBLE) TITI
(— FOR COMPLAINT) BEEF
(— OF FLAG) FIELD
(— OF LACE) FOND
(— OVERLYING TIN DEPOSIT)
BURDEN
(BOGGY —) SOG CARR SNAPE
(BROKEN —) HAG
(BURYING —) CEMETERY
(CAMPING —) AUTOCAMP
(COLLEGE —S) CAMPUS
(DUMPING —) TIP TOOM
(FALLOW —) BRISE
(FEEDING —) HAUNT
(FIRM-HOLDING —) LANDFANG
(FIGHTING —) HAAF

(FROZEN —) TJAELE
(GRASSY —) LAWN CLOWRE
(GRAZING —) HERDWICK
(HARD —) HARDPAN
(HUNTING —) CHASE
(LOW —) INCH SWALE TALAO
(MIDDLE —) LIMBO
(MUDDY —) SLOB
(NEW ENCLOSED —) TINING
(ORIGINAL —) URGRUND
(PARADE —) MAIDAN
(PASTURE —) HIRSEL
(RECREATION —) PARK
(RISING —) HURST HYRST
(SLOPING —) CLEVE
(SOLID —) HILL
(SPONGY —) BOG
(SWAMPY —) PUXY CRIPPLE
(UNCULTIVATED —) JUNGLE
(UNUSED —) AREA
(WET WASTE —) MOOR REESK
(PL.) GROUT STOCK
(PREF.) CHAMAE CHAME GE(O) PEDO
SOLI
(ON THE —) HUMI
GROUND BEETLE CARABID
GROUND COVER AJUGA VETCH
MYRTLE
GROUNDER COMEBACKER
GROUND HEMLOCK SHINWOOD
GROUND HOG MARMOT
GROUND IVY GILL HEWE HOVE JILL
YARROW ALEHOOF CATFOOT
GAGROOT MILFOIL TUNHOOF
FOALFOOT
GROUNDLESS IDLE FALSE
BASELESS
GROUNDLINE SETLINE
GROUNDMAN GRUNT
GROUNDMASS PASTE CEMENT
MATRIX
GROUNDNUT GOBBE PEANUT
PIGNUT
GROUND PINE FOXTAIL STAGHORN
GROUNDS RATIONALE
GROUNDSEL SIMSON DOGBUSH
SENCION SENECIO BINDWEED
BIRDSEED
GROUNDSMAN CURATOR
GROUND SQUIRREL GOPHER
GRINNY SUSLIK MEERKAT SCIURID
SOUSLIK SCIURINE
GROUND THRUSH PITTA
GROUNDWORK BASE FOND FUND
BASIS BOTTOM FUNDUS
GROUP MOB SET BAND BEVY BODY
CREW DECK FOLD GANG KNOT PAIR
RING SECT SORT STEW TEAM TREF
ARRAY BATCH BREED BUNCH CASTE
CLASS CLUMP COVEY FIRCA FLOCK
GENUS GLOBE PLUMP SABHA SKULK
SQUAD STACK TALLY WHEEN CIRCLE
CLUTCH COHORT FAMILY GRUPPO

PARCEL RUBRIC AGGROUP BATTERY
BOILING BOUROCK BRACKET
CLASSIS CLUSTER COLLEGE
COMMUNE COMPANY CONSORT
FELLOWS FLUTTER QUOTITY
SECTION SEVERAL SOCIETY
ALLIANCE CATEGORY CLASSIFY
DIVISION FAISCEAU FLOTILLA
GROUPING
(— HIRED TO APPLAUD) CLAQUE
(— OF ANGELS) FLIGHT
(— OF ARTIFACTS) CACHE
(— OF ATOMS) CLUSTER RADICAL
(— OF BADGERS) CETE
(— OF BLOOD CELLS) NEME
(— OF BUILDINGS) BLOCK CLUSTER
(— OF CASTINGS) SPRAY
(— OF CATS) CLOWDER
(— OF CELLS) GLAND ISLET LAURA
CENTER CORONA EPITHEM
SEMILUNE
(— OF CHIMNEYS) STACK
(— OF COMMUTERS) VANPOOL
(— OF COMPUTER JOBS) BATCH
(— OF CRAFTSMEN) ARTEL
(— OF DECOYS) STOOL
(— OF DEITIES) CABEIRI
(— OF DIALECTS) AEOLIC
(— OF EELS) SWARM
(— OF EIGHT) OCTAD OCTET
OCTETTE
(— OF EIGHT BINARY DIGITS) BYTE
(— OF FAMILIES) FINE
(— OF FIVE) PENTAD CINQUAIN
(— OF FOUR) MESS QUARTET
(— OF FRIENDS) BUNCH
(— OF FURNISHINGS) ENSEMBLE
(— OF HAITIANS) COMBITE
COUMBITE
(— OF HORSEMEN) QUADRILLE
(— OF HOUSES) BOROUGH
(— OF HUTS) BUSTI KRAAL BUSTEE
(— OF ILLUSTRIOUS PERSONS)
PANTHEON
(— OF INDIAN STATES) AGENCY
(— OF ISOGLOSSES) BUNDLE
(— OF KINDRED) SIOL
(— OF KINSMEN) AHL
(— OF KITTENS) KENDLE KINDLE
(— OF LAYMEN) COFRADIA
(— OF LIONS) PRIDE
(— OF LISTENERS) AUDIENCE
(— OF MARTENS) RICHESSE
(— OF MILITARY VEHICLES)
DEADLINE
(— OF MOLDINGS) DANCETTE
(— OF NERVE CELLS) GANGLIA
(— OF NINE) ENNEAD NONARY
(— OF NUCLEONS) SHELL
(— OF OFFSPRING) CLUTCH
(— OF ORGANISMS) FORM STRAIN
(— OF PARACHUTISTS) STICK
(— OF PERSONS) BAG CLUB KNOT

SWAD CROWD DROVE CIRCLE
GAGGLE KENNEL
(— OF RETORTS) BENCH SETTING
(— OF RUFFIANS) PUSH
(— OF SCHOLARS) ULAMA
(— OF SCULPTURE) MORTORIO
(— OF SEVEN) HEPTAD SEPTET
HEBDOMAD
(— OF SIX) HEXAD SENARY
(— OF SLAVES) COFFLE
(— OF SOILS) LATERITE
(— OF SOLDIERS) DRAFT COHORT
(— OF STARS) ASTERISM
(— OF STRATIFIED BEDS) FACIES
(— OF STUDENTS) SEMINAR
(— OF SYLLABLES) FOOT
(— OF SYMBOLS) FORMULA
(— OF SYMPTOMS) SYNDROME
(— OF TAXA) CLADE
(— OF TEN) DECADE DENARY
(— OF TENTS) CAMP CANVAS
(— OF THEATERS) CIRCUIT
(— OF THREE) TRIO GLEEK TRIAD
TRINE TROIKA
(— OF TRAITS) COMPLEX
(— OF TROUT) HOVER
(— OF VERSES) SYSTEM
(— OF WEAPONS) NEST
(— OF WINGS) RUFFLE
(— OF WIRES) DROP
(— OF WORDS) ACCENT GENITIVE
(— OF 10 NOTES) DECUPLET
(— OF 100) SENATE
(— OF 1000) CHILIAD
(— OF 12) DOZEN
(— OF 2 VOWELS) DIGRAM
DIGRAPH
(— OF 40 THREADS) BEER BIER
(— OF 60 PIECES) SHOCK
(— TO RAISE CAMPAIGN MONEY)
PAC
(ASSISTANCE —) AINI
(ATHLETIC —) TEAM
(ATOMIC —) LIGAND
(AUTHORITATIVE —) CONCLAVE
(AVANT-GARDE —) UNDERGROUND
(CONFUSED —) SNARL
(CORE —) CADRE
(CRIME SYNDICATE —) FAMILY
(ECOLOGICAL —) GUILD
(ETHNIC —) LI ACHANG BALAHI
BATTAK ETHNOS CHINGPAW
(ETHNOLOGICAL —) ISLAND
(EXCLUSIVE —) ELECT
(EXPERT —) PANEL
(FAMILY —) GWELY
(GREEK RESISTANCE —) EDES ELAS
(HARMONIOUS —) DOVECOTE
(INTIMATE —) COTERIE
(KINSHIP —) SUSU
(LANGUAGE —) ATALAN
(LARGE —) PASSEL
(LINKED —) NEXUS

(LIVELY —) GALA
(MEMBER OF COMMANDO —) FEDAYEE
(NON-MOSLEM —) MILLET
(PAGAN —) BATAK BATANGAN
(PERFORMING —) COMBO TROUPE ENSEMBLE
(PHILOSOPHICAL —) CENACLE
(POLITICAL —) BLOC PARTY FASCIO COMMONS MACHINE
(SEGREGATED —) GHETTO
(SMALL —) PLUMP
(SOCIAL —) KITH SEPT TRIBE FAMILY INGROUP
(WEALTHY SOCIAL —) JETSET
(PREF.) (CULTURAL —) ETHNO
(SUFF.) AD ET OME SOME
GROUPED AGMINATE
GROUPER GAG HIND MERO GUASA HAMEL SCAMP AGUAJI BONACI CHERNA GROPER HAMLET WARSAW BACALAO GARLOPA GARRUPA GOURAMI JEWFISH REDFISH LAPULAPU REDBELLY ROCKFISH SCIRENGA SERRANID
(KIND OF —) WARSAW
(YOUNG —) SNAPPER
GROUPING KIND ARRAY BATTERY KINDRED DIVISION GROUPAGE SODALITY SYNTAGMA
(— OF POTTERY) SERIES
GROUSE CRAB BITCH GANGA GRIPE PEEVE GORHEN GROUCH HOOTER ATTAGEN CHEEPER GAZELLE GORCOCK PINTAIL COMPLAIN MOORBIRD MOORFOWL PARTRIDGE PTARMIGAN
(YOUNG —) POULT SQUEALER
GROUT GROOT LARRY SLUSH GROUTING
GROUTER GUNITER
GROVE CAMP HEWT HOLT MOTT SHAW TOFT TOPE WONG ALTIS BLUFF COPSE GLADE HURST HYRST GARDEN GREAVE GROVET ISLAND OLIVET SCROBE SPRING ACADEMY ARBORET BOSCAGE COPPICE SPINNEY THICKET WOODING SERINGAL WODELEIE
(— OF ALDERS) CARR
(— OF MANGO TREES) TOPE
(— OF OAKS) ENCINAL
(— OF OSIERS) HOLT
(— OF SUGAR MAPLES) CAMP
(SACRED —) ALTIS SARNA
(SMALL —) SHAW
(PREF.) NAEMOR
(SUFF.) ETUM
GROVEL FAWN ROLL CREEP CRINGE TUMBLE WALLOW WELTER GRABBLE FLOUNDER
GROVELING PRONE WORMY ABJECT HANGDOG REPTILE

GROW AGE BUD GET HIT ICH WAX BOLL COME CROP ECHE ITCH MAKE RISE SEED THEE THRO WEAR EDIFY ISSUE PLANT PROVE RAISE SHOOT SWELL ACCRUE BATTEN BECOME DOUBLE EXPAND EXTEND GATHER SPRING SPROUT THRIVE AUGMENT BROADEN BURGEON DEVELOP DISTEND ENLARGE IMPROVE NOURISH ADOLESCE FLOURISH HEIGHTEN INCREASE MUSHROOM THRODDEN PROLIFERATE
(— ANGRY) STIVER
(— BETTER) IMPROVE
(— COLD) QUENCH
(— DARK) GLOAM GLOOM NIGHT DARKEN DARKLE
(— FAINT) DIE APPAL APPALL
(— FAT) FEED BATTEN
(— IN LENGTH) ELONGATE
(— IRREGULARLY) SCRAMBLE
(— LESS) ABATE SLAKE ASSUAGE DECREASE
(— LIGHT) DAWN
(— LOUDER) SWELL
(— LUXURIANTLY) THRIVE
(— MAD) WOOD
(— MILD) GIVE
(— OLD) AGE OLD SENESCE
(— OVER) INVADE
(— PLUMP) PLIM
(— RAPIDLY) SNOWBALL
(— RICH) FATTEN
(— SOUND) HEAL
(— SPIRITLESS) FLAG
(— STILL) HUSH
(— STRONG) FORTIFY STORKEN
(— THIN) PEAK
(— TOGETHER) JOIN KNIT ACCRETE CONCREW COOSIFY COALESCE
(— TO HEAD) CABBAGE
(— TO STALK) SPINDLE
(— UNDER GLASS) GLASS
(— UNTIDILY) STRAGGLE
(— UP) STEM ACCRUE
(— WEAK) FAINT
(PREF.) (— TOGETHER) SYMPHY(O)
GROWING GROWY ONGOING CRESCENT CRESCIVE ACCRESCENT
(— ANGRY) IRASCENT
(— IN AIR) AERIAL
(— IN CLUSTERS) RACEMOSE
(— IN GRAIN FIELDS) SEGETAL
(— IN HEAPS) ACERVATE
(— IN MEADOW) PRATAL
(— IN PAIRS) BINATE
(— IN RUBBISH) RUDERAL
(— IN WATER) AQUATIC
(— ON A STEM) CAULINE
(— OUT) ENATE
(— RAPIDLY) BOOMING
(— THICKLY) HOUSY
(— VIGOROUSLY) THRIFTY

(— **WILD**) SAVAGE AGRARIAN
AGRESTAL
(**GOOD FOR** —) ARABLE
(**SUFF.**) PLASIA PLASIS PLASM(A)(IA)
(IC) PLAST(IC)(Y) PLASY
(— **IN OR ON**) COLE COLINE COLOUS
GROWL YAR GNAR GURL GURR
NARR RASE ROIN ROME WIRR YARR
YIRR GARRE GNARL GNARR GROIN
SNARL GOLLAR HABBLE GRUMBLE
MAUNDER
GROWLER CLARENCE
GROWLING GROIN SURLY
GROWN THRIVEN
(— **COLD**) DEAD
(— **FROM SEED**) MAIDEN
(— **HIGH**) LOGGY
(— **TOGETHER**) ADNATE ACCRETE
(**FULL** —) GREAT MATURE
(**WELL** —) THRODDY
GROWN-UP ADULT GROWN MATURE
GROWTH FUR WAX BUSH COAT
CORN FILM GROW JUBA RISE SPUR
SUIT DUVET FLUSH GUMMA MAQUI
STAND STOCK STOOL SWELL
BUTTON CALLUS CANCER CLAVUS
EATAGE EPULIS FRINGE FUNGUS
LANUGO SCREEN SPROUT TYLOSE
UPCOME WASTME AUXESIS
BRACKEN COPPICE ERINEUM
FUNGOID MACCHIE SARCOID
STATURE TYLOSIS BEARDING
CARUNCLE ENDOGENY INCREASE
SETATION SWELLING UPSPRING
ACCRETION
(— **IN EYE**) FILM
(— **OF BEARD**) DOWN
(— **OF HAIR**) SUIT
(— **OF HORN**) BUTTON SPIDER
(— **OF PLANKTON**) BLOOM
(— **OF SHOOTS**) STOOL
(— **OF TREES**) MOTTE BOSQUE
BOSCAGE COPPICE SHINNERY
(— **ON HORSE'S LEG**) FUSEE FUZEE
(— **ON VESSEL'S BOTTOM**) GARR
(**ABUNDANT** —) FLUSH
(**CANCEROUS** —) WOLF
(**DENSE** —) BRUSH FOREST
SHINNERY
(**DOWNY** —) LANUGO
(**GREEN** —) GREENTH
(**HARD** —) STONE
(**LUXURIANT** —) FLOURISH
(**ROUGH** —) STUBBLE
(**RUDIMENTARY** —) STUB STUMP
(**SIDE** —) SPRIG
(**SPARSE** —) SCRAGGLE
(**SUPERFICIAL** —) MILDEW
(**TRANSPARENT** —) DRUSE
(**VIGOROUS** —) THRIFT
(**WOODY** —) STUBBLE
(**2ND** — **OF GRASS**) FOG
(**PREF.**) AUXANO AUXO

(**SUFF.**) PHYTA PHYTE(S) PHYTIC
PHYTUM PLASTY TROPHIA TROPHIC
TROPHY
(**INHIBITION OF** —) STASIA STASIS
GROWTH OF THE SOIL (**AUTHOR
OF** —) HAMSUN
(**CHARACTER IN** —) AXEL ISAK BREDE
INGER OLINE OLSEN STROM BARBRO
SIVERT ARONSEN ELESEUS REBECCA
GEISSLER LEOPOLDINE
GRROVE (— **ALONGSIDE MOLDING**)
QUIRK
GRUB BOB DIG CHOW EATS HUHU
MOIL MOOT ROOT ROUT STUB
WORM CHUCK GROUT MATHE
SCRAN SNOUT WROTE ASSART
ESSART GRUGRU MAGGOT MUZZLE
ROOTLE NEASCUS PIGROOT
FLAGWORM GRUBWORM
MUCKWORM SKINWORM
GRUBBY TIRED
GRUBROOT STARWORT
GRUDGE DOWN ENVY DERRY PEEVE
SCORE SPITE ANIMUS GROUCH
GRUNCH GRUTCH MALICE MALIGN
SPLEEN DESPITE EYELAST SIMULTY
GRUDGING JEALOUSY
GRUEL SLOP BLEERY BURGOO
CAUDLE CONGEE CROWDY SKILLY
SOFKEE BROCHAN CROWDIE
LOBLOLLY WANGRACE
GRUESOME UGLY GRISLY GROOLY
HORRID SORDID FEARFUL GHASTLY
HIDEOUS MACABRE
GRUFF BLUFF ROUGH SURLY
CLUMSE SULLEN AUSTERE BEARING
BRUSQUE CLUMPST
(**PL.**) TAILINGS
GRUIFORMES GRALLAE
GRUMBLE CARP GIRN GREX HONE
KREX ROIN BLEAT BROCK CROAK
DRUNT GROIN GROWL GRUMP
GRUNT MUNGE GROUCH GROUSE
GRUDGE GRUNCH MUMBLE
MUNGER MURMUR MUTTER NOLLER
PEENGE REPINE RUMBLE SQUEAL
TARROW YAMMER CHANNER
CHUNNER CHUNTER GNATTER
GRIZZLE GRUNTLE MAUNDER
MURGEON QUADDLE SWAGGER
COMPLAIN
GRUMBLER GROUCH QUADDLE
GROGNARD
GRUMBLING BITCH DRUNT GRIPE
GROIN GRUDGE MURMUR
MURGEON
GRUMP SULK GRUMBLE COMPLAIN
GRUMPY ILL CROSS DUMPY SURLY
GLUMPY GLUMPISH GRUMPISH
GRUNGY DUMPY
GRUNION SMELT
GRUNT OINK BURRO GROIN HUMPH
RONCO SARGO GRUMPH RONCHO

BURRITO CROAKER GRUNTER GRUNTLE PIGFISH PINFISH TOMTATE KNORHAAN KOORHAAN PORKFISH REDMOUTH RONCADOR

GUACHARO FATBIRD OILBIRD

GUAICURU CADUVEO

GUAM (BAY OF —) AGAT YLIG CETTI AJAYAN UMATAC
(CAPITAL OF —) AGANA
(HARBOR OF —) APRA
(ISLAND OF —) CABRAS
(MOUNTAIN OF —) TENJO LAMLAM
(PENINSULA OF —) OROTE
(TOWN OF —) UPI ARRA ASAN TOTO YONA AGANA LUPOG MAGUA MERIZO UMATAC MALOLOS

GUAMA INGA PACAY

GUAN JACU ORTALIS PHEASANT

GUANA CHANE

GUANABANA SOURSOP

GUANACO LLAMA

GUANCHE CANARIAN

GUANO OSITE

GUAPENA SERRAN SERRANA AGUAVINA

GUARANTEE (ALSO SEE GUARANTY) BAIL BAND SEAL CINCH COVER ASSURE AVOUCH ENGAGE ENSURE INSURE RATIFY SECURE SURETY CAUTION CERTIFY HOSTAGE WARRANT AWARRANT GUARANTY PRESTATE SECURITY WARRANTY

GUARANTEED ASSURED CERTIFIED FOOLPROOF

GUARANTOR ENGAGER GRANTOR GUARAND SPONSOR GUARANTY

GUARANTY (ALSO SEE GUARANTEE) ANDI AVAL PAWN SEAL CAUTIO PLEDGE WARRANT SECURITY WARRANTY

GUARD BOW LEG NIT PAD SEE CARE CURB HERD HOLD KEEP KNOW LOOK REDE SAVE STOP STUB TENT TILE WAIT WEAR WERE WITE YEME ASKAR AWARD BLESS BLOCK CHECK COVER FENCE FORAY HEDGE HINGE PILOT SCREW SKIRT TUTOR WAKEN WATCH ASKARI BANTAY BASKET BRACER BRIDLE BUMPER BUTTON CONVOY DEFEND DRAGON ESCORT FENDER GHAFIR GUNMAN JAILER KAVASS KEEPER MIDDLE POLICE SCREEN SECURE SENTRY SHIELD SHROUD WAITER WARDER YEMING BULWARK CHERISH ESGUARD FRONTAL GHAFFIR GHATWAL GUARDER KEEPING PANDOUR PRESIDY PROTECT SOULACK TRABANT WARDAGE WARRANT CHAPERON DEFENDER GARRISON MUDGUARD OUTGUARD PEDESTAL PILOTMAN PRESERVE SECURITY

SENTINEL SHEPHERD SPLASHER WARDSMAN WATCHMAN
(— ON FOIL) BUTTON
(— WHILE IN TRANSIT) RIDE
(AXLE —) HOUSING
(COACH —) SHOOTER
(CONSULAR —) KAVASS
(IMPERIAL —) BOSTANGI BOSTANJI
(KEYHOLE —) LAPPET
(LET DOWN —) NAP
(MOUNTED —) SHOMER
(NECK —) CAMAIL
(ON —) AWARE EXCUBANT
(PRISON —) HACK SCREW CHASER JAILER
(STIRRUP —) TAPADERA
(SWORD —) BOW TSUBA
(WRIST —) BRACER
(PL.) HEAVIES

GUARDED WARY IMMUNE MANNED

GUARDEDLY GINGERLY

GUARDHOUSE BRIG CLINK BULLPEN HOOSEGOW

GUARDIAN HERD ANGEL ARGUS TUTOR YEMER CUSTOS KEEPER MIMING PASTOR PATRON SHOMER WARDEN CORONER CURATOR GARDANT GARDEEN GRIFFIN BARTHOLO BELLERUS CERBERUS CREANCER DEFENDER ECKEHART FRAVASHI GOVERNOR GUARDANT PROTUTOR TUTELARY
(— OF GARDENS) PRIAPUS
(— OF HOME) SIF
(WORLD —) LOKAPALA MAHARAJA
(PL.) SELLI SELLOI

GUARDIANSHIP WARD TUTELA CUSTODY KEEPING TUITION WARDAGE WARDING CUSTODIA GUARDAGE TUTELAGE WARDENRY WARDSHIP

GUARDROOM WARDROOM

GUARDSMAN GUARDEE

GUASA MERO

GUATEMALA
CAPITAL: GUATEMALA
COIN: PESO CENTAVO QUETZAL
DANCE: ELSON GUARIMBA
DEPARTMENT: PETEN IZABAL JALAPA QUICHE SOLOLA ZACAPA JUTIAPA ESCUINTLA
GULF: HONDURAS
INDIAN: MAM CHOL ITZA IXIL MAYA XINCA CARIBE QUICHE POKOMAM
LAKE: DULCE GUIJA PETEN IZABAL ATITLAN
MEASURE: VARA CUARTA FANEGA TERCIA CAJUELA MANZANA
MOUNTAIN: AGUA FUEGO PACAYA TAJANA ATITLAN TELIMAN TAJAMULCO
PORT: OCOS BARRIOS LIVINGSTON

RIVER: AZUL BRAVO DULCE LAPAZ
BELIZE CHIXOY NEGINO PASION
SAMALA CHIAPAS MOTAGUA
SARSTUN POLOCHIC
RUINS: TIKAL
TOWN: OCOS COBAN VIEJA CHAHAL
CHISEC CUILCO FLORES IZTAPA
JALAPA SALAMA SOLOLA TACANA
TECPAN YALOCH ZACAPA ANTIGUA
CUILAPA JUTIAPA SANJOSE
PROGRESO
VOLCANO: AGUA FUEGO PACAYA
TACANA ATITLAN TAJUMULCO
WEIGHT: CAJA LIBRA

GUAVA ARACA MYRTAL GUAYABA
GUAYABO GOIABADA
GUAYCURU MBAYA
GUDDLE GUMP NOODLE HANDFISH
GUDGEON PIN QUAB CHALDER
TRUNNION
GUDRUN (FATHER OF —) HETEL
(HUSBAND OF —) ATLI
GUELDER-ROSE GAITER OPULUS
DOGWOOD WHITTEN DOGBERRY
SNOWBALL VIBURNUM
GUENDOLEN (HUSBAND OF —)
LOCRINE
GUENON GRIVET NISNAS VERVET
TALAPOIN TALLAPOI MOUSTACHE
GUEREZA COLOBIN COLOBUS
GUERILLA (VIETNAMESE —)
VIETCONG
GUERRILLA COWBOY GORILLA
JAYHAWK SKINNER BUSHWACK
FELLAGHA KOMITAJI
GUERRILLERO KOMITAJI
GUESS AIM CALL HARP REDE SHOT
WEEN AREAD COUNT ETTLE FANCY
INFER TWANG DEVISE DIVINE
RECKON IMAGINE SURMISE SUSPECT
(— CORRECTLY) TOUCH
(WILD —) STAB
GUEST COME GOER HOST DINER
INVITEE VISITOR SYMPHILE VISITANT
(— AT RANCH) DUDE
(UNINVITED —) SHADOW
(PL.) LEVEE COMPANY
(PREF.) XEN(O)
(SUFF.) XENE XENOUS XENY
GUEST-HOUSE GASTHOF
GUESTHOUSE BANDB
GUFA KUFA GOOFAH KUPHAR
GUFFAW GAFF ROAR HEEHAW
GUIDANCE AIM DUCT EGIS AEGIS
STEER CONDUCT GUIDAGE
HELMAGE LEADING WISSING
AUSPICES ENGINERY REGIMENT
STEERAGE
GUIDE GUY LAY PIR TIP AIRT BEAD
CURB GAGE GATE LEAD PASS REIN
RULE SWAY WISE CARRY CHARM
DRESS FRAME GAUGE LIGHT MAHDI

MOROC PILOT STEER TEACH WEISE
ADALID BARKER BEACON BEDWAY
CONVOY DIRECT ESCORT FORMER
GILLIE GOVERN INFORM LEADER
MANAGE MENTOR POPPET
CONDUCE CONDUCT COURIER
GHILLIE INSPIRE MARSHAL MERCURY
PIONEER SHIKARI STERNER TRACKER
CALENDAR CICERONE DIRECTOR
DRAGOMAN ENGINEER FAIRLEAD
LODESMAN PEDESTAL POLESTAR
PRACTICO REPEATER SHIKAREE
SIGNPOST
(— ON GUN) SIGHT
(MORAL —) LABARUM
(RAILWAY —) ABC BRADSHAW
(SPIRITUAL —) PIR GURU BISHOP
DIVINE
(TRAFFIC —) MUSHROOM
(SUFF.) AGOGUE AGOGY
GUIDEBOOK ABC GUIDE WAYBOOK
BAEDEKER HANDBOOK ROADBOOK
GUIDELINE SLUG DIRECTIVE
PARAMETER
GUIDEPOST GUIDE PARSON
WAYMARK WAYPOST SIGNPOST
GUIDERIUS (FATHER OF —)
CYMBELINE
GUIDEWAY SLAY SLEY SLEIGH
SLIDEWAY SWANNECK
GUIDING POLAR BEHIND HOMING
LEADING
GUIDO (WIFE OF —) ALERIA
GUILD HUI GILD HOEY HONG YELD
CRAFT HANSA HANSE GREMIO
GUIDRY SCHOLA BASOCHE COLLEGE
COMPANY MYSTERY
(CHINESE —) TONG
GUILE DOLE WILE CHEAT CRAFT
FRAUD TRAIN CAUTEL DECEIT
HUMBUG CUNNING FALLACY
ARTIFICE
GUILELESS PLAIN CANDID HONEST
ARTLESS ONEFOLD IGNORANT
INNOCENT SACKLESS UNNOOKED
GUILLEMOT AUK COOT LARY LAVY
LOOM QUET TURR URIA ARRIE
CUTTY FROWL MURRE SCOUT TOIST
TYSTE GRYLLE LUNGIE MAGGIE
MARROT SCRABE TINKER DOVEKEY
DOVEKIE SEACOOT SKIDDAW
TARROCK WILLOCK PUFFINET
ROCKBIRD SCUTTOCK SPRATTER
GUILT SIN SAKE WITE BLAME CULPA
FAULT PIACLE PLIGHT NOCENCE
OFFENSE HAMARTIA INIQUITY
GUILTLESS FREE PURE CLEAN
UNSAKED INNOCENT SACKLESS
GUILTY FAULTY NOCENT WICKED
CORREAL HANGDOG NOXIOUS
PECCANT BLAMEFUL CRIMINAL
CULPABLE GUILTFUL
(— OF ERROR) LAPSED

GUINEA MEG BEAN QUID QUEED
  GEORGE SHINER GEORDIE
  (HALF —) SMELT

GUINEA

CAPE: VERGA
CAPITAL: CONAKRY
COIN: FRANC
ISLAND: TOMBO TRISTAO
ISLAND GROUP: LOS
MEASURE: JACKTAN
MONEY: SYLI CAURI
MOUNTAIN: TAMGUE
MOUNTAINS: LOMA NIMBA
NATIVE: SUSU TOMA KISSI FULANI
  GUERZI MALINKE KOURANKE
  LANDUMAN
RIVER: NIGER BAFING FALEME
  SENEGAL KONKOURE TINKISSO
TOWN: BOKE FRIA KADE LABE BENTY
  BEYLA COYAH KOULE MAMOU
  DABOLA DALABA DOUAKO FABALA
  KANKAN KINDIA BOFOSSO
  CONAKRY DUBREKA FARANAH
  KONFARA KOUMBIA OUASSOU
  SIGUIRI KEROUANE
WEIGHT: AKEY PISO UZAN BENDA
  SERON QUINTO AGUIRAGE

GUINEA-BISSAU (ARCHIPELAGO OF
  —) BIJAGOS
  (CAPITAL OF —) BISSAU
  (RIVER OF —) GEBA CACHEU
  MANSOA CORUBAL
GUINEA FOWL KEEL KEET PEARL
  MEBACK GALEENY PINTADO
  COMEBACK GALLINEY
  (SOUND OF —) POTRACK
GUINEA GRASS PANIC PANICLE
  SACATON ZACATON GAMELOTE
GUINEA PEPPER PIMENTO
GUINEA PIG CAVY
  (MALE —) BOAR BUCK
GUINEA RUSH ADRUE
GUISE HUE FORM GARB COLOR
  COVER SHAPE MANNER PERSON
  APPAREL CLOTHES GUISARD
  LIKENESS
GUISER MUMMER
GUITAR AX AXE BOX KIT PIPA DOBRO
  JAMON KITAR SITAR TIPLE CUATRO
  GIMBRI KITTAR SANCHO SATTAR
  CITHERN CITTERN MACHETE
  UKULELE CHARANGO CHITARRA
  BOTTLENECK
  (ACOUSTIC —) DOBRO
  (JAPANESE —) SAMISEN SHAMISEN
  (KIND OF —) FOLK PEDALSTEEL
  (PART OF —) KEY NUT PEG BASE
  BODY BONE FRET HEAD HEEL HOLE
  NECK BRACE GUARD WAIST BRIDGE
  SADDLE STRING ROSETTE
  FINGERBOARD

GUITARFISH RAY BATOID PURAQUE
GUITGUIT PITPIT
GULANCHA GILO GILOE
GULCH COULE GULLY SLUIT CANYON
  COULEE RAVINE
GULDEN FLORIN GUILDER
  (100,000 —) TUN
GULÉS MARS RUBY TORTEAU
GULF SINE CHAOS GULPH VORAGE
  VORAGO
  (BOTTOMLESS —) ABYSM ABYSS
GULFWEED SARGASSO
GULL COB COX MEW COBB CONY
  COOT CULL DUPE FOOL GOLL LARI
  MALL PINT PIRR SELL SKUA XEME
  ALLAN ALLEN ANNET BOSUN CHEAT
  CHUMP COBBE COKES CROCK CULLY
  HOODY JAGER LARID LARUS PEWIT
  SCULL SMELT YAGER BONXIE
  BUBBLE CHOUSE COUSIN JOCKEY
  PEEWIT PIGEON SIMPLE TEASER
  TULIAC VICTIM WAGGEL WHILLY
  CROCKER DECEIVE MEDRICK
  PICKMAW POPELER SCAURIE
  SEABIRD SEAFOWL SWARBIE
  TARROCK TRUMPIE BLACKCAP
  DIRTBIRD DOTTEREL DUNGBIRD
  SEEDBIRD
  (LIKE A —) LAROID
  (YOUNG —) SCAURY SCAURIE
GULLET MAW GULE LANE GORGE
  GARGLE PECHAN THROAT KEACORN
  STOMACH SWALLOW WEASAND
  GURGULIO
  (PREF.) ESOPHAG(O) LAEMO LEMO
  RUMENO
GULLIBLE GOOFY GREEN SIMPLE
  CULLIBLE
GULLIVER GRILDRIG
GULLY BOX GEO GUT DRAW GULL
  RAIK RAKE SICK SIKE DONGA DRAFT
  GOYLE GULCH SLAKE SLUIT ZANJA
  ARROYO GULLET GULLEY GUTTER
  NULLAH RAVINE SHEUCH SHEUGH
  CHIMNEY COULOIR DRAUGHT
  BARRANCA
GULLYWASHER TORRENT
  CLOUDBURST
GULP BOLT GAUP GLUT GULL POOP
  SOPE SWIG GULCH QUILT SLOSH
  SWIPE ENGLUT GLUTCH GOBBLE
  GOLLOP PAUNCH SLABBER
  SWALLOW SWATTLE SLUMMOCK
  (— NOISILY) SLORP
GUM ASA AMRA BLOB FILL GOOM
  LOAD TUNO ALGIN AMAPA BABUL
  CUMAY DHAVA ACAJOU ANGICO
  BALATA BARRAS CHICLE KARAYA
  TOUART TUPELO CARANNA
  CARAUNA CHICLET GINGIVA
  GUMWOOD PERRIER BORRACHA
  CARABEEN DEXTRINE DRESSING
  FEVERGUM CALENDULIN

(ACACIA —) GEDDA
(AROMATIC —) MYRRH
(ASTRINGENT —) KINO
(CHEWING —) WAX CHICLE
(FRAGRANT —) BUMBO
(KIND OF —) ESTER XANTHAN
(PERSIAN —) SARCOCOLLA
(RED —) JARRAH
(UNGRADED —) SORTS
(WOOD —) XYLAN
(PL.) ULA
(PREF.) COMMI GUMMI GUTTI
GUM ARABIC KIKAR ACACIA ACACIN
GUMBO MUD OKRA
GUMBOIL PARULIS
GUMBO-LIMBO JOBO BIRCH
GOMART MASTIC NEGRITO
ALMACIGO ARCHIPIN
GUMDROP GUM JUJUBE
GUMMER BIDDY BIDDIE SCRAPER
SCUFFER SCUFFLER SCUPPLER
GUMMY GLUEY CLAGGY MASTIC
GUMMOUS
GUMPTION GRIT NOUS NERVE
PLUCK SENSE SPUNK SPRAWL
GUMS
(PREF.) GINGIV(O) ULEMO ULO
GUMSHOE TEC
GUM SUCCORY HOGBITE
GUM TREE KARI KARRI TOOART
TOUART TUPELO EUCALYPT
GUMWEED GRINDELIA SUNFLOWER
GUN GAT POP BREN HAKE PIAT ROER
STEN TUBE BARIL FIFTY FIRER FUSEE
FUZEE RAKER REWET RIFLE ARCHIE
BERTHA CANNON CHASER CULVER
DUCKER HEATER INCHER JEZAIL
MINNIE QUAKER RANDOM ROSCOE
SPIGOT SWIVEL TUPARA CALIVER
FIREARM HACKBUT HANDGUN
JINGALL LANTACA MUZZLER
AMUSETTE ARQUEBUS CHAUCHAT
CULVERIN FIRELOCK GALLOPER
OERLIKON PEDERERO REVOLVER
SHAGBUSH STERLING TROMBONE
(—FOR DISCHARGING STONES)
PERRIER
(AFGHAN —) JEZAIL
(BOAT —) BASE
(KIND OF —) ZIP BURP RIOT STUN
HIRED
(LOWER-DECK —) BARKER
(MACHINE —) CHOPPER GATLING
(SPRING —) STEL
(TOP —) ACE
(TOY —) SPARKLER
(TYPE OF —) BURP BOFORS
(PL.) FLAK CHASE ARTILLERY
GUNA RAJAS TAMAS SATTVA
GUNBOAT SKIP BARCA GONDOLA
TINCLAD
GUN CARRIAGE PANEL MADRIER
GALLOPER

GUNCREWMAN PLUGMAN
GUNDOBAD (BROTHER OF —)
GODOMAR CHILPERIC GODEGISEL
(FATHER OF —) GUNDIOCH
GUNDOG POINTER
GUNFLINT STONE
GUNI (FATHER OF —) NAPHTALI
GUNITE SHOTCRETE
GUNK GOO
GUNLOCK ROWET FIRELOCK
GUNMAN HOOD GUNSEL GUNSMAN
TORPEDO ENFORCER GANGSTER
GUNNEL BLENNY SWORDICK
GUNNER GUN POPPER FIREMAN
SHOOTER ENGINEER
GUNNY TAT BURLAP BAGGING
SACKING
GUNNYSACK CORNSACK
GUNPOWDER SULFUR SULPHUR
(— SIZE) PEBBLE
GUNSHOT REPORT
GUNSIGHT VISIE HAUSSE
GUNSTOCK BLANK TIPSTOCK
GUNSTONE OGRESS PELLET
GUNTHER (SISTER OF —) KRIEMHILD
(WIFE OF —) BRUNEHILDE
GUNTRAM (BROTHER OF —)
SIGEBERT CHARIBERT CHILPERIC
(CHARACTER IN —) ROBERT
GUNTRAM FREIHILD FRIEHOLD
(COMPOSER OF —) STRAUSS
(FATHER OF —) CLOTAIRE
GUNWALE GUNNEL PORTOISE
GUNZ SCANIAN
GUPPY MILLIONS BELLYFISH
GUR GOOR KHAUR JAGGERY VOLTAIC
GURGE EDDY SWIRL
GURGLE GLOX GLUG BRAWL CLUNK
QUARK SLOSH BICKER BUBBLE
BULLER BURBLE GOLLER GUGGLE
RUCKLE
GURGLINGLY TRILLIL
GURJUN YANG
GURNARD CUR TUB PIPER ELLECK
ROCHET BATFISH CAPTAIN GRUNTER
LATCHET SOLDIER TRIGLID TUBFISH
VOLADOR HARDHEAD KNORHAAN
LORICATE
GURO KWENI
GURU MENTOR
GUSH JET BOIL FLOW FOAM HUSH
RAIL SLOP WALM BELCH SLUSH
SMALM SMARM SPATE SPIRT SPURT
STOUR SWOSH BURBLE PHRASE
SWOOSH WALLOW WHOOSH
SLOBBER
(SENTIMENTAL —) SLOSH
GUSHING SLOPPY SMARMY
EFFUSIVE
GUSSET GORE INSET MITER MITRE
QUIRK PIECETTE
GUST BUB FLAN GALE GUSH WAFF
WAFT WIND BLAST FRESH SLANT

FLURRY HUFFLE SQUALL FLAUGHT
WILLIWAW WINDFLAW WINDBLAST
(— OF RAIN) SKIT
(— OF WIND) FLAM FLAN FUFF GALE
GUSH PIRR SCUD TIFT BERRY BLAST
BLORE FLAFF THODE SQUALL
WINDFLAW
GUSTATION TASTE
GUSTO GUST ZEST VERVE RELISH
UNCTION
GUSTY DIRTY PUFFY BLASHY
BLASTY FRETFUL GUSTFUL SQUALLY
GUT GIB BOWEL CECUM CLEAN
CAECUM CATGUT HOLLOW STRING
ELISION GRALLOCH VISCERAL
(FISH —) GIP GILL
(TWISTED —) THARM THERM
(PL.) MOXIE BOWELS COJONES
PUDDING ENTRAILS
GUTHRIE ARLO
GUTSY BALLSY PLUCKY SPUNKY
GUTTA SOH DROP PUAN SIAK SUSU
DUJAN GERIP SANGE SUNDIK
CAMPANA JANGKAR SEMARUM
TRENAIL TRUNNEL HANGKANG
KETAPANG
GUTTER GRIP REAN SIKE GRIPE
GULLY RIGOL SIVER SPOUT SWEAL
BOTTOM CANNEL CULLIS GROOVE
GUZZLE KENNEL RIGGOT RUNNEL
STRAND TROUGH VENNEL CHANNEL
CHENEAU GRIZZLE
(— OF STREET) KENNEL
(MINING —) BOTTOM HASSING
(ROOF —) RONE
(PL.) LIMBERS
GUTTERMAN SWAMPER
GUTTURAL GRUM BURRY HARSH
THICK
GUY BOD CAT EGG JOE NUT BIRD
BOZO DUDE GENT GINK HUSK JACK
JOHN STUD BLOKE CABLE COOKY
JOKER SCOUT SPOOF STIFF BUFFER
COOKIE FELLOW GAZABO GAZEBO
GAZOOK GILGUY HOMBRE JASPER
JIGGER MALKIN MAUMET MAWKIN
KNOCKER BLIGHTER
(FALL —) GOAT CHUMP SCAPEGOAT
GUYANA (CAPITAL OF —)
GEORGETOWN
(RIVER OF —) CUYUNI BERBICE
DEMERARA MAZARUNI ESSEQUIBO

(TOWN OF —) ITUNI BILOKU ISSANO
MACKENZIE
(WATERFALL IN —) MARINA KAIETEUR
GUY MANNERING (AUTHOR OF —)
SCOTT
(CHARACTER IN —) GUY MEG LUCY
BROWN DANDY HARRY JULIA
BERTRAM DINMONT GLOSSIN
SAMPSON MANNERING MERRILIES
ELLANGOWAN HATTERAICK
GUY ROPE STAY VANG
GUZ GAZ GEZ ZAR ZER GUDGE
GUZERAT KANKREJ
GUZZLE BUM GUM SOT TUN BEND
GULL SLOSH SWILL GOOZLE
GUDDLE SWATTLE SWIZZLE
CHUGALUG
GUZZLER BENDER
GWYNIAD SCHELLY
GYASCUTUS PROCK
GYLE BEER GAIL BREWING
GYMKHANA AUTOCROSS
GYMNASIUM GYM PALESTRA
TURNHALL PALAESTRA
GYMNAST SOKOL BENDER TURNER
ACROBAT TUMBLER
(FAMOUS —) KORBUT
GYMNASTIC (— SOCIETY) SOKOL
GYNOECIUM BRUSH APOCARP
GYNOPHORE PODOGYN
GYPSUM GYP GYPS YESO GESSO
LUDIAN PARGET GYPSITE SATINITE
SELENITE ALABASTER
GYPSY FAW ROM CALO APTAL CAIRD
GIPSY ROMNI BOSHAS GITANO
ROMANY TINKER AZUCENA CZIGANY
MOONMAN TINKLER TZIGANE
ZINCALO ZINGARO BOHEMIAN
EGYPTIAN FLAMENCO ZIGEUNER
(MALE —) ROM
(NON —) GORGIO
(SEA —) BAJAU
(PL.) ROMANESE
GYRATE GYRE SPIN TURN TWIRL
WHIRL CURVET INGYRE ROTATE
REVOLVE SQUIRREL
GYRATION PRECESSION
GYRATORY GIDDY GYRAL
GYRFALCON JERKIN
GYRON GIRON ESQUIRE
GYROSE SINUATE
GYVE FETTER

H ETA HOW AITCH HOTEL ASPIRATE
HABERDASHER OUTFITTER
HABERDASHERY TOGGERY
HABERGEON HAUBERK
HABILIMENT GARB HABIT APPAREL
  RAIMENT CLOTHING
  (PL.) CLOTHES EQUIPAGE
HABILITATE ENABLE
HABIT LAW PAD SET USE WON COAT
  GARB GATE SUIT THEW WONT
  FROCK HAUNT JONES TACHE TRADE
  TRICK USAGE CUSTOM GROOVE
  MANNER PRAXIS TALENT CLOTHES
  FOLKWAY HABITUS WONTING
  CROTCHET HABITUDE PHYSIQUE
  PRACTICE PRACTISE ASSUETUDE
  CONSUETUDE
  (— OF GRINDING TEETH) BRUXISM
  (BAD —) HANK VICE MISTETCH
  CACOETHES
  (CHARACTERISTIC —) TRICK
  (DEPRAVED —) CACHEXY CACHEXIA
  (MONASTIC —) SCHEMA
  (SPEECH —S) ACCENT
  (PL.) DAPS
  (PREF.) HEXICO
HABITABLE BIGLY LIVABLE
HABITAT ECE HOME RANGE PATRIA
  STATION LOCALITY
  (NATURAL —) ELEMENT
  (PREF.) EC(O) OEC(O) OIKO
HABITATION HOLD TELD TENT
  ABODE BIELD HABIT HOUSE BIDING
  WONING DOMICILE DWELLING
  PANTHEON TENEMENT RESIDENCE
  (— SITE) YACATA
  (COMMUNAL —) PUEBLO
  (QUIET —) SHADE
  (UNDERGROUND —) HOLE
HABITUAL USUAL COMMON HECTIC
  CHRONIC REGULAR FREQUENT
  ORDINARY
HABITUATE USE HOWF ENURE
  FLESH HABIT INURE ADDICT SEASON
  HACKNEY ACCUSTOM ACQUAINT
  OCCASION
HABITUATED WONT SEASONED
  ACCUSTOMED
HABITUDE HABIT SCHESIS
HABITUE DENIZEN COURTIER
HABRONEMIASIS BURSATI
  BURSATTEE
HACEK WEDGE
HACHALIAH (SON OF —) NEHEMIAH
HACK CAB HAG HEW BOLO CHIP
  HAKE DEVIL HATCH CABBIE DRUDGE
  FIACRE HACKLE HAGGLE HODMAN

JOBBER MANGLE SCOTCH HACKNEY
  MATTOCK VETTURA MUTILATE
  (LITERARY —) GRUB DEVIL
HACKBERRY EGGBERRY HACKTREE
  HAGBERRY ONEBERRY
HACKBUT HAGBUT DEMIHAG
  HACKBUSH
HACK GHARRI SHIGRAM
HACKLE COMB RUFF HECKLE
  NAPPER RUFFER HATCHEL
  ROUGHER
HACKNEY HACK MIDGE NODDY
HACKNEY CARRIAGE MIDGE
  FIACRE JARVEY VETTURA
HACKNEYED HACK WORN BANAL
  HOARY STALE TRITE CANNED CLICHE
  COMMON FOREWORN TIMEWORN
HAD D HED HEDDE
  (— NOT) HADNA HADNT
HADAD (FATHER OF —) ISHMAEL
HADADEZER (FATHER OF —)
  REHOB
HADDOCK GADE GADID SCROD
  DICKEY HADDIE
  (DRIED —) CRAIL RIZZAR SPELDING
  SPELDRIN
HADE UNDERLIE
HADES DIS PIT ADES HELL AIDES
  ORCUS PLUTO SHEOL SHADES
  TARTAR ACHERON AIDONEUS
  TARTARUS
  (FATHER OF —) SATURN
  (GODDESS OF —) HEKATE
  (RIVER IN —) STYX LETHE
  (RIVER OF —) STYX
  (WIFE OF —) PROSERPINA
HADORAM (FATHER OF —) TOU
  JOKTAN
HAECCEITY THISNESS
HAEMON (FATHER OF —) CREON
  PELASGUS
  (SON OF —) THESSALUS
HAEMUS (FATHER OF —) BOREAS
  (MOTHER OF —) ORITHYIA
  (SON OF —) HEBRUS
  (WIFE OF —) RHODOPE
HAFF LAGOON
HAFNIUM CELTIUM
HAFT HEFT HOVE HELVE DUDGEON
HAFTER HANDLER
HAG ATE MARE CRONE REBEC RUDAS
  SHREW SIBYL VECKE WITCH BELDAM
  HECATE ROUDAS BELDAME
  HAGGARD HELLCAT HARRIDAN
HAGAR (MISTRESS OF —) SARAH
  (SON OF —) ISHMAEL
HAGBOAT HOGGET HOGGIE

HAGFISH HAG BORER VECKE MYZONT SUCKER PLACOID MYXINOID
HAGGARD PALE THIN GAUNT WISHT HAGGED
HAGGI (FATHER OF —) GAD
HAGGITH (HUSBAND OF —) DAVID (SON OF —) ADONIJAH
HAGGLE CHOP PRIG DODGE BADGER BANTER BOGGLE DICKER HACKER HIGGLE HUCKLE NAGGLE NIFFER PALTER SCOTCH THREEP BARGAIN CHAFFER HUCKSTER
HAGGLER DODGER
HAGGLING BARGAIN CHAFFER
HAGIOGRAPHA KETUBIM
HAGIOSCOPE SQUINT SQUINCH
HAIDA SKITTAGET
HAIL AVE HOY HALE GREET SALVE SPEAK STORM ACCOST BAYETE HAGGLE HALLOO HERALD SALUTE ACCLAIM
(SOFT —) GRESIL GRAUPEL
(PREF.) CHALAZI CHALAZO
HAILSTONE STONE
HAINAI IONI
HAIR FAX JAG RIB WIG BARB CROP FLUE GLIB HEAD KEMP PELF PILE SETA WIRE BEARD CRIMP CRINE FRIZZ FRONT PILUS QUIFF ANGORA BRILLS BRUTUS CRINET FIBRIL FROWZE MERKIN SETULA THATCH TRAGUS CULOTTE FLI FLOCK GLOCHIS TOPKNOT WHISKER CAPILLUS COLLETER PALPOCIL TENTACLE TRICHODE TRICHOME VIBRISSA
(— BROWN) ARGALI
(— OF ANIMALS) FUR PELF
(— OF HORSES OR COWS) CERDA
(— OF TERRIER) FALL
(— ON HORSE'S HOOF) CRONET
(— ON LEAF) GLAND
(— ON TEMPLES) HAFFET HAFFIT
(— ON THIGHS) CULOTTE
(— OVER EYES) BROW GLIB EYELASH
(BARBED —) GLOCHIS
(BRAID OF —) QUEUE PIGTAIL
(BUNDLE OF —) LEECH
(CAMEL'S —) DEER
(COARSE —) KEMP BRISTLE
(CURLED —) FRIZZ
(CUTDOWN —) STUMPS
(FALSE —) WIG JANE FRONT PERUKE
(FRIZZED —) FROWZE
(GRAY —) GRIZZLE
(LOCK OF —) TUZ FEAK TATE FLOCK TRESS
(LONG HEAVY —) MANE
(LOOSE —) COMBINGS
(MATTED —) SHAG ELFLOCK
(MOP OF —) MANE SHOCK TOUSLE
(NOSE —) VIBRISSA

(PERSON WITH SHORT —) SKINHEAD
(PLANT —) COLLETER
(ROOT —) FIBRIL
(SNARL OF —) TANGLE
(SOFT —) DOWN LANUGO
(STINGING —) STING STIMULUS
(STINGING —S) COWHAGE
(STRAIGHTEN —) CONK
(STRAY LOCK OF —) TAG
(STYLE —) CORNROW
(TREAT —) CONK
(TUFT OF —) PLUME KROBYLOS
(WAVING LOCK OF —) WIMPLER
(WHITE —) SNOW SNOWS
(PL.) SETAE COWAGE COWHAGE HACKLES
(PREF.) CAPILLI CHAET(I)(O) CHETO COME COMI CRINI HIRSUTO LACHN(O) PIL(I)(O) TRICH(O) TRICHINO VILLI
(SUFF.) CHAETA CHAETES CHAETUS COMA THRICHOUS THRIX TRICHA TRICHI(A) TRICHY
HAIRBREADTH HERMELE WHISKER
HAIR BROWN QUAIL
HAIRBRUSH TOILETRY
HAIRCLOTH HAIR CILICE
HAIRCUT BOB CUT CROP BUTCH SHINGLE DUCKTAIL
HAIRDO AFRO COIF BEEHIVE FRISURE PAGEBOY
HAIRDRESSER WAVER FRICEUR COIFFEUR
HAIRDRESSING FRISURE BANDOLINE
HAITI FRAME PALISADE
HAIRINESS PILOSISM PILOSITY
HAIRLESS BALD PELON CALLOW ATRICHIC DEPILOUS GLABROUS
(— PERSON) PILGARLIC
HAIRLIKE PILIFORM TRICHOID
HAIRLINE WHISKER
HAIRNET KELL SNOOD
HAIRPIECE MERKIN POSTICHE
HAIRPIN ACUS BODKIN SKEWER
HAIRSPLITTING FINE PILPUL
HAIRSTYLE DA AFRO CONK SHAG UPDO BINGLE MOHAWK CORNROW PAGEBOY DUCKTAIL PONYTAIL DREADLOCKS
HAIRWORM GORDIID GORDIOID
HAIRY FAXED MOSEY PILAR ROUGH COMATE COMOUS PILARY PILINE PILOSE CRINITE CRINOSE HIRSUTE PILEOUS VILLOUS UNSHAVEN
(PREF.) DASI DASY HEBE

GULF: GONAVE
INDIAN: TAINO
ISLAND: VACHE GONAVE TORTUE
    NAVASSA TORTUGA
ISLAND GROUP: CAYMITES
LAKE: SAUMATRE
MAGIC: OBI OBEAH
MOUNTAIN: NORD CAHOS NOIRES
    LAHOTTE LASELLE TROUDEAU
NATIONAL HERO: OGE
PLAIN: NORD CAYES JACMEL
    LEOGANE ARCAHAIE CULDESAC
    GONAIVES
PRIEST: BOCOR HOUNGAN
RELIGION: OBEAH
RIVER: GUAYAMOUC ARTIBONITE
SPIRIT: LOA BAKA BOKO
TOWN: AQUIN CAYES FURCY LIMBE
    HINCHE JACMEL JEREMIE LEOGANE
    SALTROU GONAIVES KENSCOFF

HAKAM CACAM HAHAM CHOCHEM
    KHAKHAM
HAKE GADE HAIK LING GADOID
    CODLING HADDOCK WHITING
    ANACANTH QUODLING
HAKENKREUZLER SWASTIKA
HALBERD BILL PIKE GLAIVE GLEAVE
    POLEARM PARTISAN
    (PART OF —) BEAK BUTT BLADE
    SPIKE
HALBERDIER DRABANT
HALCYON CALM ALCYON GOLDEN
HALE FIT YELL FRACK FRECK TRAIL
    ROBUST STRONG HEALTHY
    VIGOROUS
HALER HELLER
HALF M ARF ELF DEMI HAUF HOVE
    SEMI SIDE MEDIO HALFEN HALFLY
    MOIETY MEDIETY
    (— AND —) ONE
    (— GALLON) POTTLE
    (— OF BLADE) FORTE
    (— OF DRAW) BRACKET
    (— OF EM) EN
    (— OF INNING) BOTTOM
    (— OF MOLD) VALVE
    (FRUIT —S) SLABS
    (PREF.) DEMI HEMI SAM SEMI
    (ONE AND A —) SESQUI
HALFBACK (OFFENSIVE —)
    SLOTBACK
HALFBEAK GAR IHI BALAO PIPER
    BALLYHOO
HALF-BLOOD DEMISANG
HALF BOOT PAC BUSKIN BOTTINE
HALF-BREED BREED METIF METIS
    SAMBO MUSTEE RAMONA CABOCLO
    MESTIZO METISSE DEMISANG
    HARRATIN MIXBLOOD
HALF-CASTE TOPAZ TOPASS
HALF-CONSCIOUSNESS DOVER
HALF-CRAZY FIFISH

HALF CROWN GEORGE ALDERMAN
HALF-DEAD ALAMORT
HALF DENIER MAILE MAILLE
HALF DOBRA PECA
HALF-DRUNK MAUDLIN
HALF-EATEN SEMESE
HALF-FARTHING CUE MITE MINUTE
HALF-GABLE AILERON
HALF GAINER ISANDER
HALF-GROWN HALFLIN
HALF-GUINEA SMELT
HALF-HEARTED LUKEWARM
HALFHEARTED TEPID
HALF HITCH ROLLING
HALF MASK LOUP DOMINO
HALF-MOON LUNETTE DEMILUNE
HALF NOTE MINIM
HALFPENCE GROCERY
HALFPENNY OB MAG MEG DUMP
    GRAY GREY MAIK MAIL MAKE MEKE
    OBOL SOUSE STAMP BAUBEE
    BAWBEE MAILLE HAPENNY PATRICK
    STUIVER
    (COUNTERFEIT —) RAP GRAY
    (IRISH —) PATRICK
    (THICK —) DUMP
HALF-PIKE SPONTON DEMIPIKE
    SPONTOON
HALF-PINT CUP JACK CUPFUL
HALF REST SOSPIRO
HALF SOLE TAP
HALF STEP CHROMA
HALFTONE DROPOUT
HALF TURN DEMIVOLT
HALF-WIT ASS DOLT DUNCE
    HAVEREL TOMFOOL STAUMREL
    UNDERWIT
HALF-WITTED SOFT DOTTY SIMPLE
    HALUCKET IMBECILE STAUMREL
HALF-YEARLY BIANNUAL
HALIBUT BUT BUTT FLITCH TURBOT
    FLATFISH
HALIFAX BALLYHACK
HALIOTIS ABALONE
HALIRRHOTHIUS (FATHER OF —)
    NEPTUNE
    (MOTHER OF —) EURYTE
    (SLAYER OF —) MARS
HALL HA AULA HELL IWAN SALA
    AIWAN ATRIO BALAI BURSA CURIA
    DIVAN ENTRY FOYER HOUSE
    OECUS SALLE SALON ATRIUM
    CAMERA DURBAR EXEDRA GARDEN
    LESCHE SALOON SCHOOL SENATE
    TOLSEY TRANCE APADANA
    CHAMBER DANCERY GALLERY
    HALLWAY KURHAUS KURSAAL
    MEGARON PASSAGE VINGOLF
    ANTEROOM ARCHEION ASSEMBLY
    BASILICA CHOULTRY COLISEUM
    CORRIDOR FOREHALL HASTROND
    HOSPITAL RAADZAAL TOLBOOTH
    VALHALLA

(— FOR PERFORMANCES) ODEON ODEUM

(— OF JUSTICE) COURT

(— WITH STATUES) VALHALLA

(DINING —) MESS COMMON REFECTORY

(LECTURE —) SCHOLA

(MISSION —) CITADEL

(MUSIC —) GAFF

(TOWN —) CABILDO RATHAUS TRIBUNAL

(UNIVERSITY —) BURSA

HALLMARK CROWN TRAIT SHOPMARK

HALL OF FAME (AVIATION —) ELY SIX BYRD LAHM LEAR LINK LUKE MOSS POST RYAN WADE EAKER GLENN LEMAY PIPER REEVE ARNOLD BOEING CESSNA FOKKER HUGHES LEVIER MARTIN ROGERS SPAATZ SPERRY TOWERS TRIPPE TURNER WALDEN WRIGHT YAEGER CHANUTE EARHART GRUMMAN LANGLEY LOENING SHEPARD TWINING MITCHELL NORTHROP SIKORSKY ARMSTRONG LINDBERGH MCDONNELL RICKENBACKER

(BASEBALL —) OTT COBB DEAN FORD FOXX HOYT KELL KLEM MACK MAYS MIZE RUTH WYNN AARON BANKS BERRA COMBS EVERS FRICK GOMEZ GROVE HAFEY KINER LEMON LOPEZ LYONS PAIGE PLANK RUSIE SPAHN TERRY VANCE WALSH WANER WHEAT YOUNG ALSTON CHANCE CRONIN CUYLER FELLER FRISCH GEHRIG GOSLIN KALINE KOUFAX LAJOIE LANDIS MANTLE MANUSH MCGRAW MUSIAL RICKEY SISLER TINKER WAGNER WILSON WRIGHT YAWKEY APPLING AVERILL BURKETT HORNSBY HUBBARD HUGGINS JOHNSON PENNOCK RUFFING SIMMONS SPEAKER STENGEL TRAYNOR BOUDREAU COMISKEY DIMAGGIO GRIFFITH MACPHAIL MARICHAL MCCARTHY ROBINSON WILLIAMS COVELESKI BRICKHOUSE MARANVILLE

(BASKETBALL —) GALE GOLA PAGE REED WEST COUSY FULKS GREER HAGAN HYATT LUCAS MIKAN ARIZIN BARLOW BAYLOR COOPER FOSTER HANSON HOLMAN KRAUSE MURPHY PETTIT PHILIP RAMSEY ROOSMA SEDRAN TWYMAN WOODEN BECKMAN BRADLEY BRENNAN DEHNERT GRUENIG KURLAND POLLARD SCHAYES SCHMIDT SHARMAN WACHTER BORGMANN ENDACOTT LAPCHICK LUISETTI MACAULEY SCHOMMER

MCCRACKEN STEINMETZ VANDIVIER DEBERNARDI DEBUSSCHERE

(BUSINESS —) FORD HAAS LUCE OCHS VAIL GARST HEINZ ROUSE SLOAN BATTEN DISNEY DORIOT DUPONT HILTON KAISER LASKER MELLON MORGAN OGILVY PENNEY SCHIFF SCHWAB EASTMAN SARNOFF WHITNEY CARNEGIE FRANKLIN MCCORMICK VANDERBILT ROCKEFELLER WESTINGHOUSE WEYERHAEUSER

(FOOTBALL —) MIX KAY BELL HEIN HUFF LARY MARA OTTO FEARS GROZA GUYON HALAS HAYES LAYNE LILLY LYMAN MUSSO NEALE RINGO ROYAL BADGRO BLANDA BUTKUS GRANGE HINKLE KINARD MATSON MCAFEE ROONEY THORPE TITTLE TRIPPI UNITAS ALWORTH GILLMAN LUCKMAN MILLNER LOMBARDI MITCHELL WARFIELD JURGENSEN PARSEGHIAN

(GOLF —) BERG FORD HOPE BOROS BURKE DUTRA EVANS HAGEN HOGAN JONES SHUTE SMITH SNEAD ARMOUR COOPER DIEGEL GHEZZI LITTLE NELSON OUIMET PALMER PICARD RUNYAN TRAVIS DEMARET GULDAHL HARBERT MANGRUM REVOLTA SARAZEN ZAHARIAS DEVICENZO

(THEATER —) DREW KERR BROOK HECHT KELLY SIMON PRINCE DUNNOCK CHAMPION KINGSLEY LANSBURY MCARTHUR MEREDITH SONDHEIM STRASBERG YOUNGMANS BLOOMGARDEN

HALLOO HO HOO LOO ALEW BAWL LURE WHOOP ACCOST TALLYHO

HALLOW BLESS HALWE DEDICATE SANCTIFY

HALLOWED HOLY SACRED BLESSED

HALLSTAND HATRACK

HALLUCINATION DWALE ACOASMA ACOUASM ACOUSMA FANTASY PHONEME DELUSION ILLUSION PHANTASY ZOOSCOPY

HALLUCINOGEN ACID

HALLUX TALON

HALLWAY ENTRY FOYER TRANCE

HALMA HOPPITY

HALMALILLE PETWOOD

HALO DOG BURR GLOR NIMB GLORY SHINE AREOLA CIRCLE CORONA GLORIA NIMBUS SUNDOG AREOLET AUREOLE BOROUGH CINCTURE

HALOHESH (SON OF —) SHALLUM

HALT HO HOP ALTO BAIT BALK HOLD LIMP SKID STAY STOP TRIP WAIT BAULK BLOCK BREAK CEASE CHECK HILCH HITCH STAND STICK ARREST BARLEY FREEZE PULLUP SCOTCH

STANCE CONTAIN CRIPPLE STATION STOPPAGE
(— GAME) CALL
(— TO DOGS) TOHO
(REFRESHMENT —) DRIVEIN
HALTER EVIL SOLE BRANK NOOSE TRASH WANTY WIDDY WITHE POISER CAUSSON CAVESON JAQUIMA POINTEL BALANCER NECKLACE HACKAMORE
HALTING BODE LAME ZOPPA CRIPPLE LIMPING
HALVE BISECT DIVIDE DIMIDIATE
(PL.) HALVERS
HALVING HAPLOSIS
HAM PIG EMOTE GAMMON JAMBON JARRET PESTLE GAMBONE PROSCIUTTO
(— IT UP) EMOTE
(BROTHER OF —) SHEM JAPHET
(FATHER OF —) NOAH
(PICNIC —) CALA CALI
(SON OF —) CUSH PHUT CANAAN MIZRAIM
(PL.) HUNKERS
HAMATUM UNCIFORM
HAMBURGER WIMPY
HAMESUCKEN HAMFARE
HAMITE BORAN BORANA DANAKIL DANKALI
HAMLET KOM BURG DORP TOON TOWN TREF VILL ALDEA CASAL HAMEL SITIO STEAD THORP VICUS ALDEIA BUSTEE THORPE CLACHAN KAMPONG KIRKTON KIRKTOWN
(AUTHOR OF —) SHAKESPEARE
(CHARACTER IN —) OSRIC HAMLET HORATIO LAERTES OPHELIA BERNARDO CLAUDIUS GERTRUDE POLONIUS REYNALDO CORNELIUS FRANCISCO MARCELLUS VOLTIMAND FORTINBRAS ROSENCRANTZ GUILDENSTERN
HAMMEDATHA (SON OF —) HAMAN
HAMMER AX AXE BIT DOG PEG SET CALL COCK DROP HORN MALL MASH MAUL MELL SETT TILT CAVIL KEVEL KNOCK MADGE POUND SMITE THUMP BEETLE BUCKER CLOYER DRIVER FALLER FULLER MALLET MARTEL NOPPER OLIVER PLEXOR SCUTCH SLEDGE TACKER TILTER KNAPPER KNOCKER MALLEUS PLESSOR STRIKER CRANDALL MALLEATE MJOLLNIR SCUTCHER TREMBLER
(— FOR DRESSING STONE) KEVEL
(— OF GUNLOCK) DOG COCK DOGHEAD
(— OUT) ANVIL
(BRICKLAYER'S —) SCOTCH SCUTCH SCUTCHER
(FLATTEN BY —) PEEN

(LEADEN —) MADGE
(MINER'S —) BULLY
(PART OF —) BELL CLAW FACE GRIP HEAD NECK PEEN POLL CHEEK HANDLE
(PAVING —) REEL
(PERCUSSION —) PLEXOR PLESSOR
(PNEUMATIC —) GUN BUSTER
(POINTED —) PICK
(SLATE-CUTTER'S —) SAX
(STEAM —) IMPACTER IMPACTOR
(THOR'S —) MJOLNIR MJOLLNIR
(TUNING —) KEY
(WAR —) MARTEL
HAMMERED BEATEN WROUGHT
HAMMERHEAD PEEN UMBRE CORNUDA UMBRETTE
HAMMERKOP UMBER UMBRETTE
HAMMERLOCK BAR ARMLOCK
HAMMERMAN STRIKER
HAMMOCK SACK HUMMOCK
(— CARRIED BY BEARERS) DANDY
(— SLUNG ON POLE) MACHILA
(WOODEN —) KATEL KARTEL
HAMMOLEKETH (BROTHER OF —) GILEAD
(FATHER OF —) MACHIR
HAMPER BIN COT MAR PED TUB BEAT BIND CLOG CURB FLAT HURT LOAD SLOW TUCK BLOCK CABIN CRAMP CRATE MAUND RUSKY SERON BASKET BURDEN FETTER HALTER HINDER HOBBLE HOPPLE IMPEDE TANGLE BUFFALO CONFINE HANAPER MANACLE PANNIER PERPLEX SHACKLE TRAMMEL ENCUMBER ENTANGLE OBSTRUCT RESTRAIN RESTRICT STRAITEN
HAMPERING STIFLING DIFFICULT
HAMSTER CRICETID
HAMSTRING HOX HOCK LAME HOUGH IMPEDE ENERVATE
HAMUL (FATHER OF —) PHAREZ
HAMUTAL (FATHER OF —) JEREMIAH
(HUSBAND OF —) JOSIAH
(SON OF —) JEHOAHAZ ZEDEKIAH
HANAMEEL (COUSIN OF —) JEREMIAH
(FATHER OF —) SHALLUM
HANAN (FATHER OF —) AZEL ZACCUR MAACHAH IGDALIAH
HANANI (FATHER OF —) HEMAN
(SON OF —) JEHU
HANANIAH (FATHER OF —) AZUR BEBAI HEMAN ZERUBBABEL
(GRANDSON OF —) IRIJAH
(SON OF —) ZEDEKIAH
HANAPER HAMPER
HAND M CAT DAB FAM FIN HAN PAW PUD CLAW DEAL DUKE GIVE GOLL HALF JACK LOOF MAIN MANO MITT PART PASS SPAN CAMAY CLAUT CLEUK FLUSH GLAUM GRASP GRIPE

INDEX MANUS NIEVE POWER SHARE
STIFF STOCK BRIDGE CLUNCH
CLUTCH DADDLE DOUBLE FAMBLE
GOWPEN HANDLE MAULEY MINNIE
STAGER WORKER CLAWKER
FAMELEN FLAPPER FLIPPER POINTER
WORKMAN GRAPPLER MORTMAIN
(— COUNTING ZERO) BACCARA
BACCARAT
(— DOWN) DEVOLVE TRADUCE
BEQUEATH TRANSMIT
(— GESTURES) MUDRA
(— IN POKER) FULL SKIP BLAZE FLUSH
SKEET TIGER BICYCLE JACKPOT
SKIPPER IMMORTAL STRAIGHT
(— IN WHIST) MORT TENACE
(— ON) BUCK SPREAD
(— ON HIP) AKIMBO
(— OVER) GIVE REACH BETEACH
BITECHE DELIVER
(— UP STRAW) SERVE
(— WITH 5 HIGHEST TRUMPS)
JAMBOREE
(AT —) NEAR CLOSE
(BABY'S —) SPUD
(BIG AND UNGAINLY —) MAIG
(BRIDGE —) BID DUMMY DOUBLE
CHICANE LAYDOWN
(CLENCHED —) FIST
(COLD —S) SHOWDOWN
(CURSIVE —) CIVILITE
(DECK —) HAWSEMAN
(DUMMY —) BOARD
(ELDEST —) EDGE SENIOR
(EUCHRE —) JAMBONE
(EXTRA — IN LOO) MISS
(FRENCH —) COULEE
(GRASPING —) CLAUT
(GREEN —) FARMER JACKEROO
(LEFT —) SINISTRA
(LONE —) JAMBONE
(PART OF —) PAD BALL HEEL PALM
DIGIT INDEX THUMB WRIST CARPUS
CREASE FINGER PINKIE THENAR
MINIMUS BRACELET LIFELINE
FINGERTIP FOREFINGER
HYPOTHENAR TRANSVERSE
(PERSIAN —) SHIKASTA
(POKER —S) BOARD
(RANCH —) COWBOY
(REEL —) SPINDLER
(RIGHT —) DEXTER
(ROUND —) RONDE
(SECTION —) SNIPE
(SKILLFUL —) DAB
(SLAPPING OF RIGHT —) HIGHFIVE
(SPARE — IN CARDS) CAT JAMBOREE
(UNSKILLED —) DABSTER
(UPPER —) BULGE EMINENCE
(WEAK CARD —) BUST
(PREF.) CHEIR(O) CHIR(O) MANI MANU
PALMATI PAI MI
(SUFF.) CHEIRIA CHIRIA

HANDBAG BAG CABA NEIF CABAS
PURSE SATCHEL ENVELOPE
GRIPSACK POCHETTE RETICULE
POCKETBOOK
HANDBALL PALM
HANDBARROW DIER HANDY TRUCK
BARROW
HANDBELL SKELLAT TANTONY
HANDBILL BILL FLIER FLYER LIBEL
DODGER
HANDBOOK VADY GRADUS
MANUAL BAEDEKER
HANDBOW STONEBOW
HANDCAR DRAG
HANDCART PRAM DANDY HURLY
TRUCK GOCART TROLLY TROLLEY
HANDCUFF CUFF STAY LINKER
NIPPER STAYER MANACLE TRAMMEL
WRISTER BRACELET HANDBOLT
HANDLOCK LIGAMENT SNITCHER
WRISTLET
(PL.) IRONS SNAPS DARBIES NIPPERS
HANDEDNESS
(SUFF.) CHEIRIA CHIRIA
HANDER-IN INGIVER
HANDFUL M MAN GRIP LOCK WISP
YELM CLAUT GRIPE LITCH GOUPIN
GOWPEN HANTLE YAFFLE FISTFUL
MANIPLE
(— OF GRAIN) RIP REAP SINGLE
SONGLE
(— OF LEAVES) PATRIN
(DOUBLE —) GOWPEN
(LAST — OF HARVEST) KIRN
(SMALL —) PUGIL
**HANDFUL OF DUST (AUTHOR OF
—)** WAUGH
(CHARACTER IN —) JOCK JOHN LAST
TODD TONY BEAVER BRENDA
MENZIES MESSINGER
HANDGRIP TUFFING
HANDGUN GAT HAKE ROSCOE
CALIVER HANDARM ARQUEBUS
REVOLVER ARQUEBUSE
HANDICAP START BURDEN DENIAL
HAMPER HINDER IMPEDE STRIKE
PENALTY ENCUMBER PENALIZE
(SPORTS —) BISQUE
HANDICAPPED CRIMP CRIMPED
HANDICRAFT MYSTERY ARTIFICE
MECHANIC HANDCRAFT
HANDICRAFTSMAN ARTISAN
HANDILY HANDY GAINLY
HANDINESS YARAGE
HANDING (— OVER) TRADITION
HANDIWORK MACHINE
(SAILOR'S —) SCRIMSHAW
HANDKERCHIEF WIPE CLOUT
FOGLE HANKY ROMAL STOOK WIPER
HANKIE MADRAS NAPKIN SUDARY
TIGNON BANDANA BELCHER
FOULARD KERCHER MANIPLE
ORARIUM SNEEZER BANDANNA

KERCHIEF MOCKETER MONTEITH
MOUCHOIR SUDARIUM VERNACLE
VERONICA

HANDLE BOW EAR FAN LUG NIB NOB
PAD PIN PLY USE ANSA BAIL BALE
BOOL BUTT CROP FEEL FIST GAUM
GRIP HAFT HALE HAND HANK HILT
KILP KNOB LIFT RAPE RUNG STOP
GRASP GRIPE GROPE HELVE MOUNT
SHAFT SPOKE STAIL STALE START
STEAL STELE STOCK SWING TREAT
WIELD BECKET FETTLE FINGER
FUSEAU HANGER LIFTER MANAGE
MANURE POMMEL ROUNCE TILLER
CONDUCT DUDGEON WOOLDER
BEERPULL BELLPULL BITSTALK
BITSTOCK DISPENSE HANDGRIP
HANDHOLD HANDLING MOPSTICK
STAGHORN PENHOLDER
MANIPULATE
(— AWKWARDLY) FUMBLE THUMBLE
(— BADLY) ILLGUIDE
(— CLUMSILY) PAW FUMBLE
(— IMPROPERLY) GAUM
(— MODISHLY) GALLANT
(— OF AXE) HELVE
(— OF BENCH PLANE) TOAT TOTE
(— OF CANNON) MANIGLION
(— OF DAGGER) DUDGEON
(— OF KETTLE) BAIL
(— OF LADLE) SHANK
(— OF OAR) GRASP
(— OF PLOW) HALE STAFF START
STILT PLOWTAIL
(— OF PRINTING PRESS) ROUNCE
(— OF RAKE) STALE
(— OF SCYTHE) TACK SNATH SNEAD
THOLE SNATHE SNEATH
(— OF SPOON) STEM
(— OF SWORD) HAFT HILT
(— OF WHIP) CROP
(— RECKLESSLY) FOOL
(— ROUGHLY) MALL MAUL TOWSE
MUZZLE GRABBLE MANHANDLE
(— VIOLENTLY) BOUNCE
(CRANK —) WINK
(CROSSBOW —) TILLER
(CURVED —) BOOL BOUL
(DETACHABLE —) KILP
(LIFTING — OF GUN) DOLPHIN
(PUMP —) BRAKE SWIPE
(ROPE —) SHACKLE
(WOODEN —) TREE
(PL.) HALES

HANDLED (EASILY —) BANTAM

HANDLER DOCKHAND
(AIRPLANE —) AIREDALE
(SUFF.) STER STRESS

HANDLEY CROSS (AUTHOR OF —)
SURTEES
(CHARACTER IN —) JOHN PIGG
HARDY MELLO BELINDA BRAMBER

DOLEFUL MICHAEL SWIZZLE
JORROCKS FLEECEALL BARNINGTON

HANDLING USE CONTROL
(SEVERE —) KILLING
(SKILLFUL —) CONDUCT
(UNSKILLFUL —) BUNGLING

HANDMAID ANCILLA

HAND-MILL QUERN PEPPERMILL

HANDOUT DOWN

HANDRAIL BAR RAIL MANROPE
BANISTER EASEMENT MOPSTICK
TOADBACK

HANDSAW STADDA

HANDSHAKE SHAKE SHRUG

HAND-SHAPED PALMATE

HANDSOME BRAW FAIR FINE MOOI *
NICE PERT TALL BONNY FETIS FITTY
FUSOM LUSTY ADONIC BRAWLY
CLEVER COMELY FARAND GOODLY
HEPPEN LIKELY PROPER SEEMLY
ADONIAN AVENANT ELEGANT
FEATISH FEATOUS FEWSOME
GALLANT LIBERAL SMICKER
GOODLIKE STUNNING VENEREAN
WEELFARD

HANDSOMELY FAIRLY HANDSOME

HANDSTONE MANO

HAND STRAP TOGGEL TOGGLE

HANDSTROKE TALLY

HANDWORK MACRAME TOOLING

HANDWRITING PAW FIST HAND
WRITE DUCTUS NESHKI NIGGLE
SCRIPT SCRIVE BATARDE WRITING
BACKHAND HANDWRIT
(ARABIC —) NESKI NASKHI NESKHI
(BAD —) CACOGRAPHY
(CRAMPED —) NIGGLE

HANDY DAB DEFT GAIN NEAT WEME
JEMMY LUSTY QUEME READY TIGHT
ADROIT CLEVER HEPPEN KNACKY
DEXTROUS EXPEDITE HANDSOME
SKILLFUL

HANDYMAN MOZO JUMPER
GREASER SWAMPER

HANG NUB TOP CRAP DRAG FALL
HANK KILT PEND TREE TUCK DRAPE
DROOP HOVER KETCH NOOSE
SCRAG STRAP SWING TRINE TRUSS
TWIST ANHANG APPEND DANGLE
DEPEND GIBBET HALTER IMPEND
SLOUCH STRING TALTER DOGGONE
HANGING LANTERN STRETCH
SUSPEND
(— ABOUT) DRING HOVER
(— AROUND) KNOCK HANKER LOITER
SLINGE
(— BACK) LAG BOGGLE
(— BEHIND) PLOD
(— CRIMINAL) STRAP TOTTER
(— DOWN) DIP LOP LAVE DROOP
DEPEND FESTOON PROPEND
(— HEAVILY) SWAG

(— IN POSITION) SET
(— IN SUSPENSE) POISE
(— LOOSELY) BAG SAG FLAG FLOW
LOLL BANGLE DANGLE PAGGLE
(— OF GARMENT) SET
(— ONE'S HEAD) SLINK
(— ON THE LINE) DRIPDRY
(— OUT) LILL
(— OVER) HOVER WAUVE IMPEND
WHAUVE
(— PICTURE NEAR CEILING) SKY
(— SOGGILY) TROLLOP
(— VERTICALLY) PLUMB
(— WITH TAPESTRY) TAPIS
(PREF.) CREMO
HANGAR DOCK GARAGE AIRDOCK
HANGER PASSIVE SHABBLE
BASELARD WHINYARD
(— FOR CARCASSES) STANG
(COAT —) SHOULDER
(CRANK —) BRACKET
(LACE-MAKING —) WORKER
(SWORD —) CARRIAGE
HANGER-ON BUR CAD BURR SPIV
LEECH TOADY CLIENT HANGBY
HEELER LACKEY SPONGE LACQUEY
PENDING PARASITE
(— OF CELEBRITY) GROUPIE
HANGING FLAG HEMP TURN ARRAS
BAGGY DRAPE SWING CELURE
DORSEL DOSSER DERRICK DRAPERY
PENDENT PENSILE ANTEPORT
HANGMENT PARAMENT
(— LOOSE) LUPPY BAGGED
(— LOW) SIDE
(— THREATENINGLY) IMMINENT
(ALTAR —) FRONTAL
(LIMPLY —) FLAGGY SLIMPSY
(WALL —) CEILING DRAPERY
TENTURE KAKEMONO
(PL.) TAPIT TAPPET DRAPERY
PARAMENT
HANGMAN KETCH HANGER HANGIE
TOPMAN DERRICK GREGORY
TOPSMAN VERDUGO CARNIFEX
SCRAGGER
(HALTER OF —) TOW
HANGMAN'S DAY FRIDAY
HANGNAIL AGNAIL
HANGOUT NEST HAUNT JOINT
SCATTER
HANGOVER HOLDOVER RESIDUUM
KATZENJAMMER
HANG-UP BAG
HANIEL (FATHER OF —) ULLA
HANK HASP SKEIN BOBBIN SELVAGEE
(— OF FLAX) HEAD
(— OF TWINE) RAN
(— OF YARN) SLIP
HANKER HANK ITCH LONG YEARN
LINGER
HANKERING ITCH HANKER

HANKUL ENMUN ONMUN
HANNAH (HUSBAND OF —)
ELKANAH
(SON OF —) SAMUEL
HANNIEL (FATHER OF —) EPHOD
HANOCH (FATHER OF —) REUBEN
HANS BRINKER (AUTHOR OF —)
DODGE
(CHARACTER IN —) HANS RAFF
GLECK HILDA GRETEL BOEKMAN-
BRINKER MEVROUW
HANSOM CAB SHOFUL SHOWFUL
HANUMAN ENTELLUS
HANUN (FATHER OF —) NAHASH
ZALAPH
HAP REDE CHANCE FORTUNE
HAPPING
HAPHAZARD CASUAL CHANCE
CHANCY RANDOM BUCKEYE
SCRATCH CARELESS SCRAMBLY
SLAPDASH TUMULTUARY
HAPHAZARDLY ANYHOW
SLAPDASH
HAPLESS POOR UNLUCKY
HAPLY HAPS HAPPILY
HAPPEN BE DO GO HAP COME
COOK FALL FARE GIVE LUCK PASS
RISE TIDE TIME BREAK EVENE
EVENT LIGHT OCCUR SHAPE
ARRIVE BECOME BEFALL BETIDE
CHANCE TUMBLE FORTUNE
STUMBLE SUCCEED BECHANCE
OVERCOME
(— AGAIN) RECUR
(— TOGETHER) CONCUR
HAPPENING HAP FACT EVENT
THING CHANCE TIDING TIMING
INCIDENT OCCASION OCCURRENCE
(ACTUAL —) FACT
(UNCANNY —) WEIRD
(UNEXPECTED —) ACCIDENT
HAPPILY FAIN FITLY GLADLY
JOYOUSLY
HAPPINESS JOY WIN GLEE SELE
SONS WEAL BLISS GLORY MIRTH
SOOTH FELICE WEALTH DELIGHT
ECSTASY FELICIA RAPTURE UTILITY
FELICITY GLADNESS HILARITY
(PLACE OF —) CAMELOT
HAPPY FIT COSH FAIN GLAD GLEG
SELI WELY BONNY FAUST FELIX
LIGHT LUCKY MERRY PROUD SEELY
SONSY SUNNY WHITE BLITHE
BONNIE BRIGHT JOYFUL COMICAL
GLEEFUL HALCYON JOCULAR
PERFECT SEELFUL WEALFUL
WEIRDLY BLISSFUL CAREFREE
DISPOSED FROHLICH GRACIOUS
SUNSHINE
(PREF.) FELICI
HARA-KIRI SEPPUKU
HARALD (FATHER OF KING —) OLAF

HARAN (BROTHER OF —) ABRAHAM
(DAUGHTER OF —) ISCAH MILCAH
(FATHER OF —) CALEB TERAH
(MOTHER OF —) EPHAH
(SON OF —) LOT
HARANGUE RANT ORATE SPOUT
CONCIO PATTER SCREED SERMON
SPEECH SPRITZ TIRADE ADDRESS
DECLAIM EARBASH DIATRIBE
PERORATE
HARASS FAG GIG HAG HOX MAG
NAG RAG TAW VEX BAIT CARK FRAB
FRET GALL GNAW HAKE HALE HARE
HAZE HOCK JADE PAIL PUSH RIDE
SEEK TIRE TOIL TOSS WORK ANNOY
BESET BULLY CHAFE CHASE CHEVY
CHIVY CURSE FLISK GRIND GRIPE
HARRY HOUND HURRY PRESS
TARGE TEASE TRASH WEARY
WORRY BADGER BOTHER CHIVVY
CHOUSE CUMBER FERRET HASSLE
HATTER HECKLE HECTOR HESPEL
HOORAY HURRAH INFEST MOLEST
MURDER OBSESS PESTER PINGLE
PLAGUE POTHER PURSUE AFFLICT
AGITATE BEDEVIL DRAGOON
HAGRIDE HARRAGE OPPRESS
PERPLEX PROVOKE TERRIFY
TORMENT TRAVAIL TROUBLE
TURMOIL BULLYRAG DISTRACT
DISTRESS EXERCISE FORHAILE
IRRITATE SPURGALL SUPPRESS
PERSECUTE
(— MENTALLY) GRUDGE
HARASSED BESTEAD HARRIED
HAUNTED
(— BY) BEFORE
HARASSING WARM
HARBINGER OMEN ANGEL USHER
HERALD FORAGER FORAYER FURRIER
OUTRIDER PRODROME
(— OF SUMMER) SWALLOW
HARBOR REE BEAR DOCK HOLD PIER
PORT BASIN BAYOU CHUCK CREEK
HAVEN HITHE SLADE BREACH
BUNDER COTHON FOSTER REFUGE
OUTPORT PORTLET SEAPORT
SHELTER CARENAGE ENHARBOR
SHIPRADE
(— A CRIMINAL) RESET
(SUBMARINE —) PEN
HARBOR SEAL DOTANT DOTARD
RANGER SEALCH TANGFISH
HARD DRY FIT ILL COLD DEAR DOUR
DURE FAST FIRM IRON MEAN NASH
OPEN CHAMP CLOSE CORKY HARSH
HORNY ROCKY SMART SNELL SOLID
SOUND STEEL STERN STIFF STONY
STOOR STOUT TIGHT BOARDY
BRAWNY COARSE FLINTY GLASSY
KITTLE KNOBBY KNOTTY ROBUST
RUGGED SEVERE STARKY STINGY

STRICT STRONG STURDY UNEATH
UNNETH WOODEN ADAMANT
ARDUOUS AUSTERE CALLOUS
HARDWAY HORNISH ONEROUS
SUBDURE CORNEOUS DILIGENT
HARDBACK HARDENED IRONHARD
OBDURATE PETROSAL RIGOROUS
SCLEROID SCLEROSE TOILSOME
(— BY) FORBY FORTHBY
(— TO BEAR) FIERCE
(— TO MANAGE) SALTY
(— TO PLEASE) FINICKY CONCEITY
(— TO REACH) CUMBROUS
(— TO READ) BLIND
(— TO SATISFY) EXIGENT EXIGEANT
(— TO SELL) STICKY
(— TO UNDERSTAND) DIFFUSE
(PREF.) DURO SCLER(O) STERE(O)
HARD-BILL SEEDEATER
HARD-BITTEN GNARLED
HARDEN SET TAW BAKE BEEK CAKE
FIRM HARN KERN SEAR BRAZE
ENURE FLESH INURE SETUP STEEL
STONE BRONZE ENDURE FREEZE
OBDURE OSSIFY POTASH SEASON
TEMPER CALCIFY EMBRAWN PETRIFY
STIFFEN THICKEN CONCRETE
ENHARDEN INDURATE SOLIDIFY
(— QUILL) DUTCH
(CASE —) STEEL
HARDENED DRAW HARD LOST
SALTED CALLOUS COCTILE
CRUSTED FIBROUS INDURATE
OBDURATE
HARDENING SET POROMA
SCLEROMA OSSIFICATION
(— OF TISSUES) SCLEREMA
SCLERIASIS
HARDHACK SPIREA IRONBUSH
WHITECAP
HARDHEAD LION BOCHE
HARDHEARTED STERN STONY
OBDURATE
HARDICANUTE (FATHER OF —)
CANUTE
(HALF-BROTHER OF —) HAROLD
(MOTHER OF —) EMMA
HARDIHOOD PLUCK COURAGE
AUDACITY
HARDLY ILL SCANT BARELY RARELY
SCARCE UNEATH SCARCELY
HARDNESS SEG GRAIN PROOF
RIGOR STEEL DURESS DURITY
ADAMANT HARDSHIP SEVERITY
SOLIDITY
(— OF CHARACTER) HEART
(— SCALE) MOHS
HARD-OF-HEARING DULL DUNCH
DEAFISH
HARDPAN PAN CLAYPAN MOORPAN
MOORBAND ORTSTEIN
HARDSCRABBLE ARID

HARDSHIP HARD GRIEF PINCH RIGOR STOUR THRONG UNWEAL SQUEEZE ASPERITY HARDNESS
(PL.) EXTREMES
HARDTACK PANTILE
(— AND MOLASSES) BURGOO
HARD TIMES (AUTHOR OF —) DICKENS
(CHARACTER IN —) JUPE JAMES SISSY JOSIAH LOUISA SLEARY THOMAS SPARSIT STEPHEN GRAGRIND BLACKPOOL BOUNDERBY HARTHOUSE MCCHOAKUMCHILD
HARDWARE TRIM IRONWARE
(COMPUTER —) MONITOR
HARDWOOD ASH HARD BREAKAX LEAFWOOD
HARDWORKING EIDENT
HARDY DOUR HARD WIRY LUSTY MANLY STOUR STOUT TOUGH GARDEN INURED RUGGED STURDY SPARTAN STUBBED GAILLARD GALLIARD STUBBORN
HARE PUG WAT BAWD CONY PUSS SCUT BAWTY CUTTY LEPUS PUSSY MALKIN MAUKIN BELGIAN LEPORID POUSSIE VENISON BAUDRONS KLIPHAAS LEPORINE
(— IN FIRST YEAR) LEVERET
(— TRACK) PRICK
(FEMALE —) DOE
(GREAT —) MANABOZHO
(KIND OF —) VARYING SNOWSHOE
(LITTLE CHIEF —) CONY PIKA
(MALE —) BUCK
(PATAGONIAN —) MARA
(SIBERIAN —) TOLAI
(PL.) FLICK
(PREF.) LAG(O) LEPORI
HAREBELL BLAWORT THIMBLE BLAEWORT BLUEBELL
HAREBRAINED GIDDY WINDY
HARELIP LAGOSTOMA
HAREM SERAI ZENANA ANDERUN HAREMLIK SERAGLIO
(ROOM IN —) ODA ODAH
HAREPH (FATHER OF —) CALEB
(SON OF —) BETHGADER
HARE'S-EAR MODESTY BUPLEVER
HARHAIAH (SON OF —) UZZIEL
HARIJAN PANCHAMA
HARK (— BACK) HOICKS
HARL WHIRL
HARLEQUIN DUCK SQUEALER
(FEMALE —) LADY
(MALE —) LORD
HARLOT PUG DRAB LOON SLUT HIREN PAGAN QUEAN RAHAB STRAP TWEAK WHORE RIBALD TOMBOY DELILAH MERMAID WAGTAIL MERETRIX MISWOMAN STRUMPET
(PREF.) PORN(O)

HARLOTRY PUTAGE BITCHERY
HARM NEY NOY NYE WEM ARME BALE DANE DERE HURT SCAT SORE TEEN WERD ABUSE ANNOY GRAME HERME LOATH QUALM SHEND SPOIL TOUCH WATHE WEMMY WOUGH WOUND WRAKE WREAK WRONG DAMAGE DAMNUM DANGER GRIEVE INJURE INJURY SCATHE SORROW WONDER DESPITE DISEASE FORFEIT IMPEACH TROUBLE UNQUERT BUSINESS DISAVAIL DISSERVE ENDAMAGE MISCHIEF NOCUMENT NUISANCE
(— REPUTATION) DEFAME
(DO —) ENVY
(PREF.) NOCI
HARMFUL BAD EVIL HARM NASTY NOXAL NOCENT NOCIVE NOYFUL UNSELY BANEFUL HURTFUL NOISOME NOXIOUS DAMAGING INIMICAL SINISTER PERNICIOUS
HARMFULNESS VICE MALICE
HARMINE BANISTERINE
HARMLESS SAFE SELI TAME CANNY SEELY SILLY WHITE DOVISH FEARLESS HURTLESS INNOCENT SACKLESS UNHARMED
(MAKE —) DEFANG
HARMONIA (DAUGHTER OF —) INO AGAVE SEMELE AUTONOE
(FATHER OF —) MARS
(HUSBAND OF —) CADMUS
(MOTHER OF —) VENUS
(SON OF —) POLYDORUS
HARMONIC OVERTONE
HARMONICA HARP EUPHON SYRINX AEOLINE PANPIPE ARMONICA ZAMPOGNA MOUTHORGAN
HARMONIOUS HAPPY SWEET COSMIC SILKEN UNITED MUSICAL SPHERAL TUNEFUL BALANCED CHARMING HARMONIC PEACEFUL ACCORDING CONCINNOUS CONCORDANT
(— RELATIONSHIP) SYNC
(PREF.) SYMPHO
HARMONITE RAPPIST RAPPITE
HARMONIUM ORGAN VOCALION
HARMONIZE GO FIT GEE KEY JIBE SORT TUNE AGREE ATONE BLEND CHORD GROUP HITCH RHYME ACCORD ASSORT ATTUNE COTTON COMPORT CONCENT CONCORD CONSORT ORDINATE ACCOMMODATE
HARMONIZING HENOTIC
HARMONY SUIT TUNE CHIME CHORD UNITY ACCORD ATTUNE COSMOS HEAVEN MELODY UNISON BALANCE CONCENT CONCERT

HARMONY CONCORD CONSENT CONSORT KEEPING RAPPORT DIAPASON FABURDEN SYMPATHY SYMPHONY CONGRUITY
(— OF COLORS) TONE

HARNEPHER (FATHER OF —) ZOPHAH

HARNESS TUG GEAR HAME LEAF REIN YOKE BRACE CROWN DRAFT FRONT GEARS SLING TRACE COLLAR FETTLE GULLET INSPAN TACKLE DRAUGHT GEARING GIGTREE LORMERY SIMBLOT TOGGERY DRAWGEAR ENCLOSER HEADGEAR TACKLING TURNBACK
(— FOR LOOM) LEAF HEALD MOUNTING
(— FOR PULLING GUNS) BRICOLE
(DECORATIVE —) CAPARISON
(PART OF —) BIT REIN GIRTH TRACE COLLAR BLINDER BREECHING CRUPPER BELLYBAND BREECHING CHECKREIN
(WEAVING —) HEADLE HEDDLE

HARNESSED ANTELOPE GUIB GUIBA BOSCHBOK BUSHBUCK

HARNESS MAKER KNACKER WHITTAW

HAROLD I HAREFOOT

HARP ARPA FORK LYRE VINA NABLA NANGA HARPER SABECA CHROTTA DECHORD SAMBUKE AUTOHARP CLARSACH
(— ON) RUBIN
(CELTIC —) TELYN CLARSACH
(FINNISH —) KANTELA KANTELE
(ICELANDIC —) LANGSPIL
(JAPANESE —) KOTO
(JEW'S —) TRUMP
(PART OF —) BASE BODY FOOT NECK BOARD PEDAL PILLAR STRING
(PERSIAN —) SANG
(TRIANGULAR —) TRIGON TRIGONON

HARPER MINSTREL

HARPOON IRON FIZGIG GRAINS FISHGIG HARPAGO STRIKER HARPAGON

HARPOONED FAST

HARPOONER STRIKER

HARP SEAL HARP BEATER SADDLER

HARPSICHORD SPINET CEMBALO CLAVIER CLAVECIN HASPICOL

HARPY HAG AELLO CELAENO OCYPETE PODARGE

HARQUEBUS HAGBUT CALIVER HACKBUT ARQUEBUS

HARQUEBUSIER CARABIN

HARRIDAN HAG

HARRIER HAWK KAHU BEAGLE FALLER MILLER PUTTOCK HARROWER

HARROW COG CHIP DISC DISK DRAG HARO TINE BRAKE BREAK HERSE DREDGE DRUDGE FALLOW LADDER SPADER CUTAWAY LACERATE OXHARROW

HARROWED HAGGARD

HARROWING TINE TINING TEARING
(— OF HELL) ANASTASIS

HARRY DUN HAG BRACE CHIVEY CHIVVY FERRET HARASS CRUCIFY

HARSH ILL ACID BULL DOUR FOUL HARD HASH HASK IRON RUDE SOUR ACERB ACRID ASPER BRUTE CRONK CRUDE GRILL GRUFF HEAVY HUSKY RASPY ROUGH ROUND RUVID SHARP SNELL STARK STERN STIFF STOUR STOUT BRUTAL COARSE FLINTY GRAVEL GRISLY HOARSE RAGGED RASPED RUGGED SEVERE SHREWD STURDY SULLEN TETRIC UNKIND UNRIDE AUSTERE CRABBED RASPING RAUCOUS SQUAWKY VIOLENT ABRASIVE ACERBATE ASPERATE ASPEROUS CATONIAN CLASHING DRACONIC GRAVELLY GRINDING GUTTURAL JANGLING OBDURATE RIGOROUS SCABROUS SCRANNEL STRIDENT STROUNGE STUBBORN TETRICAL UNGENTLE UNKINDLY
(— OF VOICE) STEER

HARSHLY HARD HARSH SHORTLY

HARSHNESS WOLF RIGOR DURESS CATOISM CRUDITY CRUELTY DUREZZA RAUCITY ACERBITY ACRIMONY ASPERITY FELLNESS HARDNESS HASKNESS MORDANCY SEVERITY

HART SPADE VENISON

HARTEBEEST ASSE TORA TORI BUBAL CAAMA KAAMA KONZE LECAMA BUBALIS CONGONI KONGONI SASSABY

HART'S-TONGUE LONGLEAF

HARUM (SON OF —) AHARHEL

HARUMAPH (SON OF —) JEDAIAH

HARUSPEX SEER ARUSPEX ARUSPICE EXTISPEX

HARUZ (DAUGHTER OF —) MESHULLEMETH

HARVEST IN WIN CROP HEAP PICK RABI REAP SLED SNAP FOISON GATHER HAIRST RUBBEE UPROOT COMBINE GRABBLE INGATHER SHEARING
(— OF GRAPES) VENDAGE

HARVESTER COMBINE

HARVEST FISH WHITING MOONFISH STARFISH

HARVEST HOME KIRN MELL HOCKEY HORKEY

HARVESTING SLEDDING

HARVESTMAN CARTER CARTARE

HARY JANOS (COMPOSER OF —) KODALY

HAS S AS HATH
(— NOT) NAS AINT
HASADIAH (FATHER OF —)
ZERUBBABEL
HAS-BEEN WUZZER
HASH RAPE MINCE HACHIS MUDDLE
RAGOUT
HASHABIAH (COMPANION OF —)
EZRA
(FATHER OF —) BUNNI KEMUEL
JEDUTHUN MATTANIAH
HASHABNIAH (SON OF —)
HATTUSH
HASHISH HEMP ASSIS CHARAS
HASHUBAH (FATHER OF —)
ZERUBBABEL
HASID ASSIDEAN
HASKALAH (FOLLOWER OF —)
MASKIL
HASP COP HAPS COPSE SPRENT
HASSAR DORAD
HASSOCK TUT BOSS PESS POUF
TOIT TRUSH BUFFET TUFFET
HASTE HIE POST RACE RAGE RAPE
CHASE FEVER HASTY HURRY SPEED
BUSTLE FLURRY SWIVET DISPATCH
RAPIDITY STROTHER PRECIPITATION
(HEADLONG —) SPURN
(IN —) HOTFOOT
(IN GREAT —) AMAIN
(WITH —) EXPRESS
HASTEN HIE RAP RUN BUSK DUST
FIRK PELL PLAT POST RACE RAPE
RUSH SPUR URGE CATCH CHASE
DRIVE FLEET HASTE HURRY PRESS
PREST SLATE SPEED STEER EXPEDE
SCURRY STREAK SWITHE ADVANCE
FORWARD HACKNEY HOTFOOT
PREVENT QUICKEN SLITHER
SWIFTEN WITHHIE DISPATCH
EXPEDITE ACCELERATE
(— AWAY) FLEE SHERRY SQUIRR
HASTILY HOTLY RAPELY RASHLY
FOOTHOT HOTFOOT HYINGLY
HEADLONG
HASTY FAST RAPE RASH BRASH
FLEET QUICK FLYING RAPELY
CURSORY HOTHEAD HURRIED
PEPPERY TEARING HASTEFUL
HEADLONG SUBITANE
(TACTLESSLY —) BRASH
HAT DIP FEZ LID NAB ATTE BAKU
CADY COIF DISC DISK FELT FLAT HIVE
HOOD KNAB MOAB SLOP TILE TOPI
BEANY BENJY BENNY BERET BOXER
CADDI CORDY DERBY DICER GIBUS
JERRY KELLY MILAN MITER MITRE
SHAKO SHELL TARAI TERAI TOPEE
TOQUE TRUSH ABACOT BEANIE
BEAVER BOATER BOWLER BRETON
BUMPER CADDIE CASQUE CLAQUE
CLOCHE COCKUP COIFFE FEDORA

GALERO HELMET PANAMA PILEUS
RAFFIA SAILOR SHOVEL SLOUCH
TITFER TOPPER TURBAN VIGONE
BANDEAU BANGKOK BLOOMER
BRIMMER BYCOKET CATSKIN
CAUBEEN CHAPEAU FANTAIL
HATTING HATTOCK HOMBURG
LEGHORN PETASOS PILLBOX
PLATEAU PLATTER SALACOT
SCRAPER SHALLOW SKIMMER
SMASHER STETSON TARBUSH
TRICORN BONGRACE CAPELINE
GOSSAMER HEADGEAR JIPIJAPA
MONTABYN MUSHROOM NABCHEAT
RAMILIES REHOBOAM ROUNDLET
SOMBRERO TARBOOSH TARBOUCH
BORSALINO
(— BLOCKER) ROPER
(— MAKER) MODISTE MILLINER
(— OF MERCURY) PETASUS
(BEAVER —) CASTOR
(CARDINAL'S —) GALERO
(CLERGYMAN'S —) SHOVEL
(COCKED —) BICORNE RAMILIE
SCRAPER
(COWBOY —) STETSON
(FABRIC —) TOQUE
(FELT —) DERBY JERRY TARAI TERAI
ALPINE BOWLER TRILBY BILLYCOCK
(FLAT-TOP —) TAM
(HARD —) LABORER
(HIGH —) KYL PLUG TILE TOPPER
(IRON —) GOSSAN GOZZAN
(KIND OF —) COSSACK PORKPIE
(MILITARY —) BUSBY BEARSKIN
(OILSKIN —) SQUAM
(OPERA —) GIBUS CLAQUE
(PART OF —) BOW BRIM CROWN
PINCH LINING BINDING HATBAND
SWEATBAND
(PITH —) TOPI TOPEE
(RED —) GALERO
(SILK —) KYL BEAVER SHINER
CATSKIN
(STIFF —) TILE DERBY KELLY BOATER
BOWLER SAILOR
(STOVEPIPE —) CAROLINE
(STRAW —) BAKU FLAT HOOD KADY
KATY TOYO BENJY BENNY CADDY
STRAW BASHER BOATER PANAMA
LEGHORN
(TOP —) PLUG TOPPER
(UNBLOCKED —) CONE
(WATERPROOF —) TARPAULIN
(WIDE-BRIMMED —) FLAT BENJY
TARAI SMASHER SUNDOWN
(3-CORNERED —) TRICORN
HATBAND BAND WEED WEEPER
HAT BRIM LEAF TARFE TURNUP
HATCH HECK BREED BROOD CLECK
CLOCK COVEY GUICHET UNSHELL
DISCLOSE INCUBATE

HATCHED (NEWLY —) SQUAB
HATCHERY CHICKERY
HATCHET MOGO HACHE GWEEON THIXLE CLEAVER FRANCISC TOMAHAWK
(PREF.) SECURI
HATCHING CLETCH BREEDING ECLISION
HATCHWAY HATCH SCUTTLE
HATE FIRE TEEN ABHOR SPITE DETEST HATRED LOATHE UNLOVE DESPITE
HATEFUL FOUL LOTH BLACK CURST DIRTY HATEL LOATH CURSED ODIOUS HEINOUS HIDEOUS ACCURSED FLAGRANT ABOMINABLE
HATER ULYSSES
HATH MOOLUM
HATHATH (FATHER OF —) OTHNIEL
HATING
(PREF.) MIS(O)
HAT MONEY TAMPANG
HAT-PLANT SOLA
HATRED DOSA ENVY HATE HELL ONDE HAINE ODIUM SPITE ENMITY RANCOR AVERSION ABHORRENCE
(— OF CHILDREN) MISOPEDIA
(— OF MARRIAGE) MISOGAMY
(— OF MEN) MISANDRY MISANTHROPY
(— OF NEW IDEAS) MISCAINEA
(— OF REASONING) MISOLOGY
(— OF WOMEN) MISOGYNY
(PREF.) MIS(O)
HATTER GADGER HURRER
HATTUSH (FATHER OF —) HASHABNIAH
HAUBERK BYRNIE
HAUGHTILY BIGLY
HAUGHTINESS AIR PRIDE HEIGHT MORGUE ORGUIL DISDAIN HAUTEUR STOMACH HAUTESSE
HAUGHTY DAIN HIGH RANK STAY DIGNE DORTY HUFFY LOFTY LUSTY POTTY PROUD STOUT SURLY TAUNT FEISTY FIERCE HAUGHT QUAINT SNOOTY UPPISH DISTANT HAUTAIN HONTISH PAUGHTY STATELY SUBLIME ARROGANT CAVALIER DEIGNOUS FASTUOUS GLORIOUS IMPERIAL INSOLENT ORGULOUS PRIDEFUL SCORNFUL SNIFFISH SUPERIOR TOPLOFTY PEREMPTORY
HAUL KEP LUG RUG TEW TOW TUG CART DRAG DRAW DRAY HALE HURL JUNK PULL SKID TAKE TOTE TRAM BOUSE DRAVE HEAVE LIGHT ROUSE SNAKE TOUSE TOWSE TRACT TRICE TRAVOY DRAUGHT SCHLEPP CORDELLE HANDBANK
(— AFT) TALLY
(— DOWN) STRIKE

(— IN) GATHER
(— LOGS) TODE SLOOP SWAMP SIWASH HANDBANK
(— OF FISH) TACK DRAVE
(— OF NET) LIFT
(— SAIL) BUNT CLEW CLUE
(— SHIP) SPRING
(— TO DECK) BOARD
(— UP AND FASTEN) TRICE
(— WITH TACKLE) BOUSE
HAULAGE DOOK
HAULAGEWAY GANGWAY
HAULING HALE CARTAGE
HAUNCH HIP HOOK HUCK HANCE HUCKLE
(PL.) GRUG HUNKERS
HAUNT DEN HANT HOME HOWF KEEP NEST WALK GHOST HOWFF SPOOK STALK INFEST KENNEL OBSESS OUTLAY PURSUE REPAIR PURLIEU FREQUENT PRACTICE
(— OF ANIMALS) LIE HOME
(FAMILIAR —) SLAIT
HAUNTED SPOOKY
HAUNTING BESETTING
HAUSTELLATE GLOSSATE
HAUSTORIUM SINK SINKER SUCKER
HAUTBOY OBOE WAIT
HAUTEUR PRIDE HEIGHT MORGUE
HAVE A AN OF OWN HOLD BOAST ENJOY OUGHT WIELD POSSESS
(— ON) WEAR
HAVEN ARK HOPE PIER PORT HITHE HARBOR HAVENET
HAVILAH (FATHER OF —) CUSH JOKTAN
HAVING
(SUFF.) IOUS OSE OUS
HAVOC HOB HELL RUIN WASTE RAVAGE
HAW HOI HECK SLOE WIND WYND BOOTS PEGGLE ALISIER

HAWAII

BAY: POHUE HALAWA KIHOLO MAMALA KAMOHIO KANEOHE WAIAGUA KAWAIHAE MAUNALUA
BEACH: WAIKIKI
CAPITAL: HONOLULU
CHANNEL: AUA KAIWI KALOHI PAILOLO
COUNTY: MAUI KAUAI HAWAII HONOLULU
CRATER: KILAUEA
DESERT: KAU
DISTRICT: KONA PUNA
FISH: ULUA AKULE MOANO
FORMER NAME: SANDWICH
HARBOR: PEARL
HEAD: DIAMOND
ISLAND: MAUI OAHU KAUAI KAULA LANAI NIIHAU MOLOKAI

MOUNTAIN: KAALA KOHALA
   KAMAKOU MAUNAKEA LANAIHALE
MOUNTAIN RANGE: KOHALA KOOLAU
   WAIANAE
NATIVE: KANAKA
STATE BIRD: NENE GOOSE
STATE FLOWER: HIBISCUS
STATE NICKNAME: ALOHA
STATE TREE: CANDLENUT
TOWN: EWA AIEA HANA HILO LAIE
   PAIA KAPAA KEAAU LIHUE MAILI
   KAILUA KEKAHA PAHALA HONOKAA
   KAHULUI KANEOHE WAHIAWA
   WAIANAE WAILUKU HONOLULU
   PAPAIKOU
TREE: KOA NAIO WILIWILI
VALLEY: MANOA
VOLCANO: KILAUEA HUALALAI
   MAUNAKEA MAUNALOA

HAWAIIAN KANAKA KAMAAINA
HAWFINCH KATE GROSBEAK
HAWK IO EYAS KITE SELL ALLAN
   BATER BUTEO CADGE EYESS HOICK
   HOUGH REACH RIVER STOOP
   BAWREL FALCON FOOTER HIGGLE
   KEELIE MERLIN MUSKET OSPREY
   PALLET PEDDLE RAMAGE RAPTOR
   RIFLER SHIKRA VERMIN BUZZARD
   GOSHAWK HAGGARD HARRIER
   HERONER KESTREL LENTNER
   STANIEL SWOOPER BRANCHER
   CARACARA HARROWER LENTINER
   PASSAGER ROUGHLEG SPARHAWK
   TALENTER TARTARET
   MORTARBOARD
   (— FIGHT) CRAB
   (CAGE FOR —S) MEW
   (COUPLE OF —S) CAST
   (CROP OF —) GORGE
   (FEMALE —) FORMAL FORMEL
   (MALE —) JACK TASSEL TERCEL
   (SMALL —) ELANET
   (UNTAMED —) HAGGARD
   (YOUNG —) EYAS NIAS BOWET
   BOWESS BRANCHER
   (PREF.) HIERACO
HAWKER CRIER CRYER BADGER
   CADGER COSTER DUFFER JOWTER
   PEDDER PETHER CAMELOT
   CHAPMAN HIGGLER MERCURY
   PEDDLER CRATEMAN GLASSMAN
   HUCKSTER
HAWKEYE STATE IOWA
HAWKING FALCONRY
HAWKMOTH SPHINX
HAWK PARROT HIA
HAWKWEED DINDLE BUGLOSS
   FIREWEED OXTONGUE
HAWSE BAG JACKASS
HAWSER FAST WARP HEADLINE
HAWTHORN HAW MAY QUICK
   THORN AIGLET MAYBUSH

COCKSPUR MAYBLOOM MAYTHORN
   QUICKSET
   (FRUIT OF —) HAZEL PEGGLE
HAY HEI RIP MATH RAKH RISP FETTLE
   STOVER WINDLIN SWEEPAGE
   (— CUT FINE) CHAFF
   (— PUT IN BARN) END
   (— SPREADER) TEDDER
   (BUNDLE OF —) TRUSS
   (PILE OF —) TUMBLE
   (ROW OF —) WINDROW
   (SECOND-GROWTH —) EDDISH
   (SMALL LOAD OF —) HURRY
   (SMALL PIECE OF —) TATE
HAYCOCK MOW COIL HOVEL QUILE
   SHOCK DOODLE HIPPLE LAPCOCK
   HAYSHOCK
HAYFIELD PARK RAKH MOWING
HAYFORK PIKE PICKEL
HAYLOFT LOFT TALLET SCAFFOLD
HAYMAKER PICKMAN
HAYMOW GOAF HAYLOFT OVERDEN
   OVERHEAD
HAYRACK HECK HAYRIG THRIPPLE
HAYSTACK COB PIKE RICK HOVEL
   HAYRICK STACKAGE
HAYSUCK EYSOGE
HAY SWEEP BUCK
HAYWARD MEADSMAN
HAZAN CANTOR CHAZZAN
HAZARD DIE LAY LOT JUMP PAWN
   RISK WAGE JENNY LOSER PERIL
   CHANCE DANGER NIFFER BALANCE
   IMPERIL VENTURE ENDANGER
   JEOPARDY SANDTRAP
   (BILLIARDS —) INOFF
   (GOLF —) TRAP BUNKER
   (ROAD —) ESS
HAZARDOUS NICE NACTY
   RISKY CHANCY QUEASY RISQUE
   UNSAFE UNSURE PARLOUS
   PERILOUS
HAZARDOUSLY CHANCILY
HAZE FOG URE FILM GLIN MIST REEK
   SMOG TRUB DEVIL GAUZE HAZLE
   SMEETH
   (— AND SMOKE) SMAZE
HAZEL AGLET AIGLET COBNUT
   MUFFIN FILBERT HAZELNUT
   NOISETTE
   (— FOR THATCHING) SPRAYS
HAZEL HOE PULASKI
HAZELNUT NIT HAZEL FILBERT
HAZEL TREE AVELLANO
HAZILY DIMLY
HAZINESS HAZE GRAYOUT
HAZO (FATHER OF —) NAHOR
   (MOTHER OF —) MILCAH
HAZY DIM ABLUR FOGGY MISTY
   MUZZY SMOKY THICK VAGUE
   BLURRY CLOUDY DREAMY OBSCURE
   SMUISTY NEBULOUS
   (NOT —) OPEN

HE A E HI HO HEH HEY HIM HYE SHE
ESSO ILLE THON CESTUI
(— DIED) OB
(— GAVE AND DEDICATED) DDD
(— MADE) F FEC
(— PAINTED IT) PNXT
(— READS) LEG
(— WAS NOT FOUND) NEI
HEAD BIT BUT COP DON FAT MIR NAB
NOB PEN POW TOP BEAN BOSS CAPE
COCO CONK COSP CROP DATU DEAN
DOME HELM JOLE JOWL KAID KNOB
LEAD LOAF MAKE MASK NOLL PASH
PATE POLL RAIS TETE TURN YEAD
ALDER ATTIC BLADE BLOCK BONCE
CHIEF CHUMP CROWN DATTO MAZER
ONION RISER SCALP SHODE SKULL
START TIBBY TROPE BELFRY BLANCH
CABEZA CENTER CHAULE COBBRA
COCKER DAROGA EXARCH GARRET
GATHER HEADER KAISER MAHANT
MAZARD NAPPER NODDLE PALLET
RUBRIC SCONCE CAPITAL CAPTAIN
COCONUT COSTARD COSTREL
COXCOMB CRUMPET CUPHEAD
GENARCH HEADING HEGUMEN
NUCLEUS PRELATE TOPKNOT
CALABASH CEPHALON DECURION
DIRECTOR DUFFADAR FOUNTAIN
HEADLINE INITIATE PHYLARCH
POINTING TOPPIECE CAPERNOITIE
(— IN PARTICULAR DIRECTION) STEM
(— OF ABBEY) ABBOT
(— OF ALEMBIC) MITER MITRE
(— OF BEAR, WOLF OR BOAR) HURE
(— OF CABBAGE) LOAF
(— OF CEREAL) EAR
(— OF CHAIR) MAKER
(— OF CLOVER) COB SUCKER
(— OF COLUMN) CHAPITER
(— OF COMET) COMA
(— OF CONVENT) ABBESS SUPERIOR
(— OF CRIME SYNDICATE) CAPO
(— OF DANDELION) BLOWBALL
(— OF DRILL BRACE) CUSHION
(— OFF AGAIN) RESUME
(— OF FAMILY) ALDER COARB
COMARB GOODMAN
(— OF FISH) JOWL
(— OF GANG) TINDAL
(— OF GOVERNMENT) MUKHTAR
(— OF GRAIN) ICKER
(— OF GUILD) ALDERMAN
(— OF HAIR) SUIT CRINE FLEECE
CHEVELURE
(— OF HARPOON) BOMB
(— OF HERRING) COB
(— OF INSTITUTION) WARDEN
(— OF JEWISH ACADEMY) GAON
(— OF LANCE) MORNE MOURNE
(— OF LOOM) JACQUARD
(— OF MONASTERY) HEGUMEN
(— OF MUSHROOM) BUTTON

(— OF MUSICAL INSTRUMENT)
SCROLL
(— OF NUNNERY) DAME
(— OF ORDER) MURSHID
(— OF PROJECTILE) OGIVE
(— OF RING) CHATON
(— OF RIVET) BULLHEAD FLATHEAD
SNAPHEAD
(— OF SEPT) COARB COMARB
(— OF STATE) CAUDILLO PRINCEPS
(— OF TAPEWORM) SCOLEX
(— OF TREE) COMA
(— OF 10 MONKS) DEAN
(— ON) SQUARE
(— PREMATURELY) BUTTON
(— USED AS TARGET) SARACEN
(— WRAP) SNOOD
(ACADEMIC) DEAN
(BAKED SHEEP'S —) JAMES JEMMY
(BALD —) PILGARLIC
(BARBED —) FLUKE
(DRAGON'S —) RAHU
(EMPTY —) MONAD
(FLOWER —) DAISY ARNICA BUTTON
PINBALL
(FLOWER —S) CURD ANTHEMIS
(FROM — TO FOOT) CANAPE
(LATHE —) POPPET
(NAIL —) ROSEHEAD
(POPPY —) POST
(PRINTED —) BOXHEAD
(SEED — OF FLAX) HOPPE
(SHRUNKEN —) TSANTSA
(PL.) GEONIM
(PREF.) CEPHAL(O) CORY(PH)(PHO)
CRANIO
(SUFF.) CEPHALIC CEPHALOUS
CEPHALUS CEPHALY PATE
HEADACHE HEAD SODA BUSTHEAD
HEADWARK MIGRAINE CEPHALALGY
HEADBAND MITER MITRE VITTA
CARCAN DIADEM TAENIA CIRCLET
GARLAND CARCANET FOOTBAND
STEPHANE
HEADBOROUGH VERGES
HEADCAP SETHEAD CAPELINE
HEADCLOTH ROMAL RUMAL
HEADDRESS FLY TOP TOY APEX
COIF FRET HEAD HORN KELL PARE
POUF TETE TIRE TOUR AEGIS AMPYX
CROWN GABLE LAUTU PASTE POLOS
PSHEM SHAKO TIARA TOWER VITTA
ALMUCE ATTIRE ATTOUR BONNET
CASQUE CORNET FAILLE HENNIN
KENNEL KULLAH MOBCAP PINNER
TIRING TUINGA BANDORE
COMMODE FLANDAN MORTIER
PSCHENT STEEPLE TABLITA THERESE
TRESSON TUTULUS BILIMENT
BINNOGUE BYCOCKET CAPRIOLE
COIFFURE HEADGEAR HEADTIRE
KAFFIYEH MASKETTE STEPHANE
TRESSURE

(— OF DOGES) TOQUE
(— OF GODS) MODIUS
(— OF POPE) REGNUM
(— WITH LONG LAPPET) PINNER
(HIGH —) TOWER STEEPLE FONTANGE
(MEDIEVAL —) BARB
(WIDOW'S —) BANDORE
HEADED KNOTTED
(— OUT) RIZZOMED
(SUFF.) PATED
HEADER BINDER BONDER NOBBER
SADDLE KNOBBER HEADSMAN
STRETMAN
HEADFAST HEADROPE
HEADFIRST HEADLONG
HEADFOREMOST TOPSAIL
HEADFRAME POPPET GALLOWS
HEADGEAR (ALSO SEE HEADDRESS)
HIVE PASTE BONNET BRIDLE
HEADWEAR
HEADHUNTER LAKHER TAIYAL
ATAIYAL QUIANGAN
HEADING END HEAD STOW LEMMA
PILOT TROPE WICKET CAPTION
DIPHEAD HEADILY STENTON
WITCHET FOREHAND STENTING
(MASTHEAD —) EDITOR
HEADLAND KOP PEN RAS BILL CAPE
HEAD MULL NASE NAZE NESS NOOK
NOUP PEAK SCAW THRUM
FORELAND PROMONTORY
HEADLESS ACEPHALOUS
(PREF.) ACEPHALO
HEADLINE HEAD STAR LABEL BANNER
CAPTION DROPLINE SCREAMER
STREAMER SCAREMONGER
HEADLONG FULL BANK AHEAD
HASTY PRONE STEEP SUDDEN
RAMSTAM TANTIVY GADARENE
HEADLING RECKLESS PRECIPITATE
HEADMAN BAAS JARL CHIEF DATTO
MALIK PATEL POMBO VIDAN
ATAMAN CABEZA HETMAN INDUNA
LOWDAH LULUAI POTAIL TOPMAN
KOMARCH ALDERMAN CABOCEER
CAPITANO HEADSMAN KONOHIKI
MALGUZAR MOKADDAM PENGHULU
PRINCEPS STAROSTA TENIENTE
HEADMASTER HEAD RECTOR
REGENT PRECEPTOR
HEADMOST FOREMOST
HEADNOTE SYLLABUS
HEADPHONE
(PL.) CANS
HEADPIECE CAP POT BASKET
CASQUE HELMET PALLET TESTER
TREMOR BASINET BRASSET
CASQUET CHAMFRON TESTIERE
HEADPIN KINGPIN
HEADQUARTERS BASE DEPOT
YAMEN AGENCY FONDACO
EXCHANGE BATTALION
(MILITARY —) SHAKO PENTAGON

HEADROPE BALK BAULK HEADLINE
HEADSET PHONES
HEADSHIP CHIEFTY
(SPIRITUAL —) KHALIFAT
HEADSPACE OUTAGE
HEADSTALL HALTER BRADOON
BRIDOON JAQUIMA
HEADSTOCK POPPET
HEADSTONE STELE
HEADSTRONG RASH COBBY
RACKLE STOCKY UNRULY HOTSPUR
RAMSTAM VIOLENT WAYWARD
PERVERSE STUBBORN
HEADWAITER CAPTAIN
HEADWAY WAY DENT SEAWAY
WAYGATE HEADROOM
HEADWORD ENTRY
HEADY BOLD WINY NAPPY HUFFCAP
HEAL CURE HALE KNIT MEND SAIN
AMEND COVER LEECH SALVE SOUND
WHOLE PHYSIC RECURE SUPPLE
TEMPER WARISH CLEANSE GUARISH
RECOVER REDRESS RESTORE
MEDICATE
(— OVER) INCARN
HEALD CAMB DUPE HAVEL
HEALED WHOLE
HEALER CURER ALTHEA SHAMAN
POWWOWER PRACTITIONER
(SUFF.) IATRIST
HEALING IATRIC POWWOW
BALSAMIC CURATION IATRICAL
SANATION
(PREF.) IATR(O)
(SUFF.) IATRIA IATRIC(S) IATRIST
IATRY
HEALTH SAP HAIL HEAL SONS
QUART SALEW LIKING PLEDGE
SALUTE SANITY EUCRASY SLAINTE
EUCRASIA TONICITY VALETUDE
VALIDITY GESUNDHEIT
(— ORGANIZATION) HMO
(GOOD —) PROST PLIGHT PROSIT
VERDURE GESUNDHEIT
(ILL —) SICKNESS
(NORMAL —) USUAL
(RESTORE CONDITION OF —) REHAB
(PREF.) HYGE(I) HYGI SALUTI
HEALTHFUL HEALTHY HYGIENIC
SALUTARY SANATORY SANITARY
HEALTHY FIT FIER FIRM HALE IRON
SAFE SANE SANO TIDY WELL BONNY
HODDY QUART SOUND STOUT VALID
ENTIRE HEARTY ROBUST BOUNCING
LAUDABLE SALUTARY SANITARY
VEGETOUS VIGOROUS
(PREF.) SANI
HEALTHY-LOOKING BONNY
BONNIE
HEAP COP CUB HOT MOW PIE SOW
TON BALF RING BULK DECK DESS
HILL HOTT LEET PILE POKE POOK
RAFF REEK RUCK SESS TASS TUMP

AMASS CLAMP CLUMP COUCH
CROWD SHOCK SORUS STACK
WOPSE BURROW HIPPLE HOTTER
ISLAND JALOPY MEILER OODLES
QUARRY RICKLE RUCKLE SCRAPE
SORITE TOORIE BOUROCK CUMULUS
ENDORSE HAYCOCK HAYRICK
HURROCK TOOROCK TUMMELS
WINDROW BASURALE CONGERIES
ACCUMULATE ACCUMULATION
(— HAY) UNCOCK
(— OF DEAD BODIES) CARNAGE
(— OF GAME) QUARRY
(— OF GRAIN) BING
(— OF MORTAR) BINK
(— OF ORE) PANEL MONTON
(— OF PRODUCE) BURY CLAMP
(— OF REFUSE) BURROW BASURAL
(— OF RUBBISH) GAGING
(— OF SILVER ORE) TORTA
(— OF SLAIN) CARNAGE
(— OF STONES) AHU MAN CAIRN
SCRAE SCREE HURROCK MONTJOY
(— OF VEGETABLES) HOG
(— REPROACHES) KICK
(— TOGETHER) AGGEST HOWDER
LUMBER CUMULATE
(— UP) HILL SACK AGGEST
ACERVATE AGGERATE OVERHEAP
(COMBUSTIBLE —) PYRE
(MANURE —) HOTT MIXEN
(PROMISCUOUS —) RAFF
(STONE —) CAIRN
(PREF.) CUMULI CUMULO SOREDI
SORI SORO THOMO
HEAPED COCKED ACERVATE
CUMULATE
HEAR EAR LIST OYES OYEZ LEARN
LITHE HARKEN LISTEN HEARKEN
(— CONFESSION) SHRIVE
(— DIRECTLY) IMPINGE
(PREF.) ACOU(O) AUDIO
HEARD AUDIBLE
(EASILY —) CLEAR
(VAGUELY —) RUMOROUS
HEARER AUDIENT AUDITOR
HEARING EAR LIST OYER AUDIT
SOUND ASSIZE AUDIENCE
AUDITION
(DISORDERED —) PARACUSIS
(PREF.) ACOU(O)
(SUFF.) ACOUSIA ACOUSIS ACUSIA
ACUSIS
HEARKEN HARK HEAR HEED LIST
TEND LITHE ATTEND HARKEN
INTEND
HEARSAY REPORT ACCOUNT
HEARSE HACK CATAFALCO
HEART AB COR ANGI CORE GIST HATI
PUMP RAAN SOUL YOLK ANGIO
BOSOM BOWEL CHEER JARTA QUICK
BREAST CENTER CENTRE DEPTHS
HASLET MIDDLE NATURE TICKER

VISCUS COURAGE EMOTION
ESSENCE FEELING
(— OF DIXIE) ALABAMA
(— OF ROTTEN TREE) DADDOCK
(DEAR —) DILIS
(PREF.) ANGI ANGIO CARDI(A)(O)
CORDI PHREN(O)
(AROUND THE —) PERICARDI(O)
(SUFF.) CARDIA CARDIUM
HEARTACHE SORROW
HEARTBEAT STROKE
(SUFF.) CROTIC
HEARTBREAK HOUSE (AUTHOR
OF —) SHAW
(CHARACTER IN —) DUNN ELLIE
MANGAN HESIONE MAZZINI
HUSHABYE SHOTOVER
UTTERWORD
HEARTBURN PYROSIS
HEART CHERRY GASKINS
HEARTEN BIELD CHEER HEART
SPIRIT EMBOLDEN INSPIRIT
HEARTFELT DEAR DEEP REAL TRUE
INFELT INWARD CORDIAL GENUINE
SINCERE
HEARTH EARD SOLE TEST ASTRE
CUPEL EARTH FOCUS FOGON FOYER
INGLE SMOKE CHIMNEY
(— GODDESS) VESTA
HEARTH-MONEY FUMAGE
HEARTILY INLY AGOOD DEARLY
FREELY WARMLY SHEERLY
DINGDONG INWARDLY STRONGLY
HEARTINESS GOODWILL
HEARTLESS SARDONIC
HEARTLESSNESS CYNICISM
HEART OF MIDLOTHIAN (AUTHOR
OF —) SCOTT
(CHARACTER IN —) MEG JOHN DAVID
DEANS EFFIE MADGE BUTLER
GEORGE JEANIE REUBEN GEORDIE
PORTEUS STAUNTON ROBERTSON
MURDOCKSON
HEARTSEASE PANSY
HEARTSICK (BE —) ACHE
HEARTSORE ACHING
HEARTTHROB DUNT FLAME
HEARTWOOD ALOES HEART SAPAN
SPINE GUAYAB BUBINGA DURAMEN
TRUEWOOD
HEARTY REAL WARM BUXOM COBBY
FRECK HEAVY STOUT DEVOUT
ENTIRE ROBUST STANCH BOBBISH
CORDIAL EARNEST HEALTHY
RAFFING SINCERE HEARTFUL
VIGOROUS BOISTEROUS
HEAT HET HOT RUT SUN TAP BOIL
FIRE GLOW SALT WARM ARDOR
BEATH BROIL CALOR CAUMA CHAFE
FEVER PRIDE PROUD STECH TEPOR
TRIAL ACHAFE ANNEAL DEGREE
DIGEST FERVOR HEATEN IGNITE
SCORCH SEASON SIZZLE SPARGE

WARMTH CALCINE CALORIC
ENCHAFE FERMENT FLUSTER
INCENSE INFERNO PASSION
SWELTER UPERIZE CALIDITY
PRESSURE MICROWAVE
(— GENTLY) SOAK
(— OF BATTLE) PRESS
(— SCRAP IRON) BUSHEL
(— SWEETEN, AND SPICE) MULL
(— TOBACCO) SAP
(ROWING —) REPECHAGE
(SCORCHING —) EWDER
(TRIAL —) REPECHAGE
(PREF.) CALORI PYR(O) THERM(ATO)
(O)
(BURNING —) KAUMO
(MODIFIED BY —) COCTO
(SUFF.) THERM(Y)
HEATED WARM FIERCE STEAMY
HEATER GAT GUN FIRE COCKLE
PISTOL SMOKER CHAFFER CHOFFER
LATROBE
(WATER —) BOILER
HEATH BENT YETH BESOM BRIAR
BRIER ERICA ERICAD COMMONS
HEATHER RHODORA CRAKEBERRY
(PREF.) ERICO
HEATHCOCK GROUSE
HEATHEN AKKUM PAGAN ETHNIC
PAYNIM GENTILE PROFANE SARACEN
GENTILIC
HEATHENISM ODINISM OTHINISM
PAGANISM
HEATHER BENT GRIG LING DROOM
ERICA HEATH HADDER
HEATHERY LINGY
HEATH PEA CARMELE
HEATING BAKEOUT BURNING
HEATLESS ATHERMIC
HEAVE GAG BUNG HEFT HOVE KECK
LIFE QUAP FETCH HOIST SCEND
SURGE BUCKLE KECKLE POPPLE
ESTUATE
HEAVEN SKY HIGH ABOVE BLISS
DYAUS ETHER GLORY ASGARD
CANAAN HIMMEL SVARGA SWARGA
URANUS WELKIN KINGDOM
OLYMPUS DEVALOKA EMPYREAL
EMPYREAN PARADISE SVARLOKA
VALHALLA
(12TH PART OF —) HOUSE
(PL.) ARCH LIFT LANGI HEIGHT
REGION SPHERE ELEMENT TENGERE
EMPYREAN KAMALOKA
(PREF.) URAN(I)(O) URANOSO
HEAVENLY ABOVE DIVINE ANGELIC
BLESSED URANIAN ETHEREAL
OLYMPIAN AMBROSIAL
HEAVEN'S MY DESTINATION
(AUTHOR OF —) WILDER
(CHARACTER IN —) BAT HERB BRUSH
COREY EFRIM LOUIE MCCOY BURKIN
CROFUT GEORGE JESSIE MARGIE

MORRIE DOREMUS QUEENIE
ROBERTA BLODGETT ELIZABETH
HEAVENWARD ZIONWARD
HEAVER COALY DANNER HEFTER
HEAVILY SOSS CLOIT CLYTE HEAVY
PLUMP SADLY SOUSE SWACK
HEAVINESS DOLE HEFT GLOOM
POISE WEIGHT GRAVITY
(— OF MIND) GLOOM
HEAVING HEFT SWELL
HEAVY FAT HOT SAD CLIT DEEP
DOWF DULL HARD BEEFY BURLY
DENSE DOWFF DUNCH GRAVE GREAT
GROSS HEFTY HOGGY STIFF THARF
THERF THICK WROTH CHARGE
CLUMPY CLUMSY COSMIC DOUGHY
DRAGGY HEARTY LEADEN LIVERY
LOGGER SODDEN STODGY STRONG
STUPID WOODEN INSIPID LABORED
LIVERED LUMPING MASSIVE
ONEROUS OUTSIZE PESANTE
WEIGHTY CUMBROUS GRIEVOUS
PERSANTE PREGNANT THUMPING
PONDEROUS SATURNINE
(— LOOKING) HORSY
(PREF.) BARY GRAVI HADR(O)
HEAVY-FOOTED SOGGY LEADEN
INFICETE
HEBDOMAD WEEK
HEBDOMADARY WEEKLY
HEBE (FATHER OF —) JUPITER
(HUSBAND OF —) HERCULES
(MOTHER OF —) JUNO
HEBER (GRANDFATHER OF —) ASHER
(SON OF —) SOCHO
(WIFE OF —) JAEL
HEBILW RABBINIC
HEBRIDES (ISLAND OF —) IONA
HARRIS
(ISLAND OF —) MULL SKYE ULST
BARRA ISLAY LEWIS
HEBRON (FATHER OF —) KOHATH
HECATE TRIVIA
(FATHER OF —) PERSES
(MOTHER OF —) ASTERIA
HECKELPHONE OBOE HAUTBOY
HECKLE BAIT GIBE HACK RAZZ
HARRY BADGER DERIDE HARASS
HECTOR NEEDLE HATCHEL
HECTIC ETIK SEPTIC HECTIVE
FEVERISH FRENETIC FRENZIED
HECTOLITER VAT
(5.82 —S) LEAGUER
HECTOR BAIT HUFF BULLY HARRY
TEASE WORRY HARASS HECKLE
BLUSTER BRAVADO BROWBEAT
(FATHER OF —) PRIAM
(MOTHER OF —) HECUBA
(SLAYER OF —) ACHILLES
(WIFE OF —) ANDROMACHE
HECUBA (DAUGHTER OF —)
POLYXENA
(FATHER OF —) DYMAS CISSEUS

(HUSBAND OF —) PRIAM
(SON OF —) PARIS HECTOR HELENUS
POLYDORUS
HEDDA GABLER (AUTHOR OF —)
IBSEN
(CHARACTER IN —) THEA BRACK
DIANA HEDDA EILERT GABLER
GEORGE TESMAN ELVSTED JULIANA
LOVBERG
HEDDLE CAMB DOUP HAVEL HEALD
(PL.) CAAM
HEDGE BAR HAW HAY HYE OXER
SAVE BEARD EDDER FENCE FRITH
FUDGE HOVER MOUND QUICK
COPPER FRIGHT RADDLE ENCLOSE
QUICKSET RUFFMANS SEPIMENT
SURROUND THICKSET
(PREF.) SEPI SEPTATO
(SUFF.) SEPTATE
HEDGE BINDWEED CREEPER
HELLWEED WOODBINE
HEDGEHOG ORCHEN TENREC
URCHIN ECHINUS ERICIUS YLESPIL
HEDGEPIG HERISSON
HEDGE LAUREL TARATA
HEDGE MUSTARD BANKWEED
FLUXWEED
HEDGE NETTLE STACHYS
HEDGE PARSLEY HOGWEED
HEDGE-PRIEST PATRICO
HEDGE SPARROW DICKY DONEY
DICKEY EYSOGE PHILIP CHANTER
DUNNOCK HAYSUCK PINNOCK
TITLING ACCENTOR
HEDGEWOOD LAYER
HEED EAR CARK COME CURE GAUM
HEAR KEEP LOOK MIND NOTE OBEY
RECK TEND TENT VISE WARE YEME
AWAIT TASTE VALUE ATTEND INTENT
NOTICE REGARD REMARK REWARD
CAUTION OBSERVE RESPECT
SUSPECT THOUGHT OBSERVATION
HEEDFUL WARE ATTENT DILIGENT
VIGILANT REGARDFUL
(ANXIOUSLY —) JEALOUS
HEEDFULNESS CARE CAUTION
HEEDLESS DEAF RASH BLIND DIZZY
GIDDY BLITHE REMISS UNWARY
LANGUID UNHEEDY CARELESS
LISTLESS MINDLESS RECKLESS
WISTLESS NEGLECTFUL
HEEDLESSLY BLIND HEADLONG
HEEL CAD TIP BUTT CALX FROG JERK
HIELD LOUSE SPIKE TALON DOTTLE
BUDMASH INCLINE BOOTHEEL
(— IN) SHOUGH
(— OF GATE) HARR
(— OF HORSESHOE) SPONGE
(— OF SWORD BLADE) TALON
RICASSO
(— OVER) SEEL TILT CAREEN
(PREF.) CALCANEO TAL(I)(O)
HEEL BEVEL RAND

HEELING ALIST
HEEL PLATE SHOD CLEAT
HEELTAPS LEES DREGS
HEFT WEIGHT
HEFTY HEAVY
HE-GOAT
(PREF.) HIRCO
HEIFER IO QUI QUEE QUEY QUOY
BULLER STOCKER
(— IN 2ND YEAR) STIRK
(YEARLING —) BURLING
HEIGH-HO HECH
HEIGHT SUM ACME ALTO APEX FELL
HIGH LOFT MOTE PINK TUNE CREST
HICHT STATE ALTURE INCHES
SUMMIT CEILING COMMAND
HEIGHTH STATURE SUPREME
ALTITUDE EMINENCE HAUTESSE
SIDENESS VERTICAL ACROPOLIS
(— OF AMBITION) EVEREST
(— OF EXALTATION) RUFF RUFFE
(— OF EXCELLENCE) TIPTOP
(— OF FASHION) GO
(— OF INSPIRATION) ESTRO
(— OF PERFECTION) PRIME
(— OF PROSPERITY) GLORY
(— OF ROOM) STUD STUDDING
(— OF SAIL) HOIST
(GREATEST —) NOON SUMMIT
ZENITH
(ROCKY —) KNOT
(PREF.) ACR(O) BATHO BATHY BATO
HYPS(I)(O)
HEIGHTEN ENDOW EXALT FORCE
RAISE ACCENT BOLSTER ELEVATE
ENHANCE SUBLIME ESCALATE
(— FLAVOR) PETUNE
HEINOUS SWART CRYING WICKED
SCARLET FLAGRANT GRIEVOUS
ATROCIOUS
HEIR SCION SPRIG COHEIR HERITOR
LEGATEE APPARENT PARCENER
(— APPARENT) ATHELING ETHELING
(CELTIC —) TANIST
(CELTIC CHIEF'S —) TANIST
(FEMALE —) DISTAFF
(PREF.) HEREDI HEREDO
HEIRESS BEGUM PORTIA FORTUNE
HERITRIX
HEIRLOOM
(PL.) CIMELIA
HEL (FATHER OF —) LOKI
(MOTHER OF —) ANGURBODA
HELAH (HUSBAND OF —) ASHUR
(SON OF —) TEKOA
HELEB (FATHER OF —) BAANAH
HELEK (FATHER OF —) GILEAD
HELEN (PURSUER OF —) PARIS
HELENUS (FATHER OF —) PRIAM
(MOTHER OF —) HECUBA
(SON OF —) CESTRINUS
(WIFE OF —) ANDROMACHE
HELEZ (FATHER OF —) AZARIAH

HELI (SON OF —) JOSEPH
HELIANTHEMUM SUNROSE
HELICAL SPIRAL
HELICAON (FATHER OF —) ANTENOR
(MOTHER OF —) THEANO
(WIFE OF —) LAODICE
HELICOPTER HOVER COPTER
CHOPPER MEDEVAC WINDMILL
WHIRLYBIRD
(— TO REMOVE CASUALTIES)
DUSTOFF
(ARMED —) GUNSHIP
(MOVE LIKE A —) HOVER
HELIOGRAPH (USE A —) SIGNAL
HELIOPOLIS ON
HELIOS HYPERION PHAETHON
(DAUGHTER OF —) CIRCE PASIPHAE
(FATHER OF —) HYPERION
(MOTHER OF —) THEIA
(SISTER OF —) EOS SELENE
(SON OF —) AEETES PHAETHON
HELIOSIS SUNBURN
HELIOTROPE HELIO BENNET.
SETWALL GIRASOLE TURNSOLE
VALERIAN
HELIPORT SKYPORT
HELIX COIL SPIRAL
HELIXIN HEDERIN
HELL PIT POT HECK PAIN ABYSS AVICI
BLAZE DEUCE HADES SHEOL BLAZES
NARAKA TARTAR TOPHET TUNKET
ABADDON GEHENNA HELLBOX
INFERNO TORMENT TARTARUS
BARATHRUM PERDITION
PANDEMONIUM
(RIVER IN —) STYX LETHE
(PREF.) TARTARO
HELLBENDER TWEEG MENOPOME
HELLE (BROTHER OF —) PHRIXUS
(FATHER OF —) ATHAMAS
(MOTHER OF —) NEPHELE
HELLEBORE POKE BUGBANE
ITCHWEED LINGWORT LUNGWORT
NOSEWORT POKEROOT VERATRUM
EARTHGALL
HELLEN (FATHER OF —) DEUCALION
(MOTHER OF —) PYRRHA
(SON OF —) DORUS AEOLUS XUTHUS
(WIFE OF —) ORSEIS
HELLER HALER HALERZ
HELLERI SWORDTAIL
HELL-FIRE BRIMSTONE
HELLGRAMMITE DOBSON SIALID
CLIPPER CRAWLER SPRAWLER
HELLION TERROR
HELLISH HELLY AVERNAL SATANIC
STYGIAN DEVILISH INFERNAL
TOPHETIC
HELLKITE FIEND
HELLO CIAO HALLO HILLO HULLO
HILLOA CHINCHIN
HELM KEY STEER STERN TIMON
HELMET TIMBER STEERAGE

HELMET CAP POT CASK HELM HOOD
ARMET CREST GALEA MAZER
MOUND BARBEL BEAVER CASQUE
CASTLE GALERA HEAUME MORION
PALLET SALADE SALLET TESTER
BASINET CASQUET GALERUM
GALERUS AVENTAIL BURGANET
BURGONET HEADGEAR KNAPSCAP
SCHAPSKA SKULLCAP TARNHELM
TESTIERE KNAPSKULL
(— PART) VENTAIL
(CRASH —) SKIDLID
(PITH —) TOPI TOPEE
(PREF.) GALEI
HELMET-SHAPED GALEATE
HELMSMAN PILOT STEER GLAUCUS
TIMONEER
HELON (SON OF —) ELIAB
HELP AID BOT ABET AMOI BACK
BOOT CAST LIFT STOP AVAIL BOOST
FAVOR FRITH HEEZE RESET SPEED
START STEAD YELDE ASSIST HELPER
RELIEF REMEDY SECOND SUCCOR
UPTAKE BENEFIT BESPEED BESTEAD
CHEVISE COMFORT FORWARD
FURTHER HELPING IMPROVE
PRESIDY PROMOTE REDRESS
RELIEVE SUPPORT SUSTAIN
ADJUMENT BEFRIEND SUFFRAGE
(— FORWARD) FRANK FURTHER
(— IN GROWTH) NOURISH
(— ON) ADVANCE
(— ONWARD) FORWARD
(— OUT) FIRK
(HIRED —) LABOR
HELPER AID CAD FOAL HELP MATE
PAGE ANSAR AIDANT BARBOY
COOKEE DIENER FLUNKY JUMPER
NIPPER TENTER WAITER ADJOINT
ADJUNCT ADJUTOR ANCILLA
CASHBOY GALOPIN SUMPMAN
SWAMPER HELPMATE OFFSIDER
SCULLION TROUNCER
(— IN GLASSWORKS) SNAPPER
(BLACKSMITH'S —) STRIKER
(CHIMNEY SWEEP'S —) CHUMMY
(COOK'S —) SLUSHY
(COOPER'S —) TUBBIE
(HORSESHOER'S —) FLOORMAN
(LEGAL —) PARACLETE
(PICKPOCKET'S —) BULKER
(YOUNG —) FOAL
HELPFUL GOOD AIDANT AIDFUL
HELPLY SECOND SPEEDY USEFUL
ADJUVANT HELPSOME OBLIGING
SINGULAR SERVICEABLE
HELPING HELP ORDER AIDANT
PORTION SERVING ADJUTORY
ADJUVANT
(SECOND —) FOLLOW
HELPLESS NUMB SILLY ABJECT
UNABLE AIDLESS FORLORN
FECKLESS HAVELESS REDELESS

HELPLESSNESS ADYNAMIA
HELTER-SKELTER TAGRAG
PELLMELL
HELVE HELM SHAFT
HELVE HAMMER OLIVER
HEM HUM WLO FELL SLIP WELT
HEDGE SPLAY PURFLE TURNUP
HEMMING TURNING SURROUND
(— AND HAW) HAVER
(— GLOVE) WRIST
(— IN) BOX LAP GIRD BEBAY BESET
IMPALE BESIEGE COMPASS ENCLOSE
ENVIRON STRAITEN SURROUND
(— IN FISH) EBB
(— OF SAIL) TABLING
(— OF TROUSERS) CUFF
(PREF.) LIMBI
HEMAM (BROTHER OF —) HORI
(FATHER OF —) LOTAN
HEMAN (FATHER OF —) JOEL ZERAH
(GRANDFATHER OF —) SAMUEL
HEMATITE ORE OLIGIST SANGUINE
HEMDAN (FATHER OF —) DISHON
HEMICRANIA MIGRAINE
HEMIEPES ENOPLION
HEMIMORPHITE CALAMINE
HEMIOLIC SESCUPLE
HEMISTICH SECTION
HEMITHEA (BROTHER OF —) TENES
(FATHER OF —) CYCNUS
(MOTHER OF —) PROCLEA
HEMLOCK BUNK CASH KELK
BENNET CICUTA COWBANE DEATHIN
SHINWOOD
HEMOPHILIAC BLEEDER
HEMORRHAGE STAXIS APOPLEXY
BLEEDING HEMOPTOE PETECHIA
HEMOSTATIC RHATANY ERIGERON
HEMP IFE KEF KIF TOW BANG CARL
POOA RINE SANA SUNN ABACA
BHANG DACHA DAGGA FIQUE
GANJA HURDS MURVA RAMIE SABZI
SISAL AMBARY CABUYA FIMBLE
LIAMBA NALITA SINAWA AMYROOT
CABULLA GAGROOT NIYANDA
PANGANE PITEIRA SOSQUIL
BIRDSEED CANNABIS CHUCKING
LOCOWEED NECKWEED NEPENTHE
MARIJUANA
(KIND OF —) ALOE
(REFUSE —) HARDS HURDS
(PREF.) CANNABI
HEMP AGRIMONY EUPATORY
HEMPWEED
HEMPEN NOGGEN
HEMP NETTLE IRONWORT
HEMPWEED BONESET DUCKBLIND
HEN FOWL BIDDY CHUCK LAYER
BROODY MABYER PULLET SULTAN
CLOCKER HOVERER PARTLET
LANGSHAN
(— THAT HAS NOT LAID) TOWDIE
(— WITH CHICKENS) CLUCK

(— WITH SHORT LEGS) GRIG
(BROODY —) SITTER
(FATHER OF —) ZEPHANIAH
(FATTENED —) POULARD
(MUD —) COOT
(1-YEAR-OLD —) YEAROCK
HENBANE HEBENON CHENILLE
HENCE AWAY ERGO HYNE THUS
AVAUNT HETHEN HEREOUT
HENCEFORTH YET ERGO HENCE
HENCHMAN FELLOW SATRAP
SERVANT FOLLOWER RETAINER
UNDERLING
HEN COOP CAVY CAVIE
HENGEST (BROTHER OF —) HORSA
(KINGDOM FOUNDED BY —) KENT
(SON OF —) AESC
HEN HARRIER FALLER KATABELLA
(IMMATURE —) RINGTAIL
(MALE —) MILLER
HENHOUSE ROOST
HENNA MENDY ALCANNA ALHENNA
CAMPHIRE
HENNIN STEEPLE
HENPECK NAG
HENRY QUAD HAWKIN SECOHM
HEINRICH QUADRANT
HENRY ESMOND (AUTHOR OF —)
THACKERAY
(CHARACTER IN —) HOLT FRANK
HENRY JAMES MOHUN ESMOND
RACHEL STUART BEATRIX FRANCIS
HENRY IV-PART I (AUTHOR OF —)
SHAKESPEARE
(CHARACTER IN —) JOHN OWEN
PETO BLUNT HENRY PERCY POINS
EDMUND SCROOP THOMAS VERNON
WALTER DOUGLAS HOTSPUR
MICHAEL QUICKLY RICHARD
BARDOLPH FALSTAFF GADSHILL
MORTIMER ARCHIBALD GLENDOWER
LANCASTER WESTMORELAND
HENRY IV-PART II (AUTHOR OF —)
SHAKESPEARE
(CHARACTER IN —) DAVY DOLL FANG
JOHN PETO WART BLUNT GOWER
HENRY POINS RUMOR SNARE
FEEBLE MORTON MOULDY PISTOL
SCROOP SHADOW SURREY THOMAS
MOWBRAY QUICKLY SHALLOW
SILENCE TRAVERS WARWICK
BARDOLPH BULLCALF CLARENCE
FALSTAFF HARCOURT HASTINGS
HUMPHREY COLEVILLE LANCASTER
TEARSHEET WESTMORELAND
NORTHUMBERLAND
HENRY V (AUTHOR OF —)
SHAKESPEARE
(CHARACTER IN —) NYM GREY JAMY
YORK ALICE BATES COURT GOWER
HENRY LEWIS EXETER ISABEL PISTOL
SCROOP THOMAS BEDFORD
BOURBON CHARLES MONTJOY

ORLEANS WARWICK BARDOLPH
BURGUNDY FLUELLEN GRANDPRE
RAMBURES WILLIAMS ERPINGHAM
KATHARINE MACMORRIS SALISBURY
GLOUCESTER WESTMORELAND
HENRY VIII (AUTHOR OF —)
SHAKESPEARE
(CHARACTER IN —) ANNE VAUX
BUTTS DENNY HENRY SANDS
BULLEN LOVELL SURREY THOMAS
WOLSEY ANTHONY BRANDON
CRANMER NORFOLK SUFFOLK
CAMPEIUS CAPUCIUS CROMWELL
GARDINER GRIFFITH NICHOLAS
PATIENCE GUILDFORD KATHARINE
BUCKINGHAM ABERGAVENNY
HENRY VI-PART I (AUTHOR OF —)
SHAKESPEARE
(CHARACTER IN —) JOAN JOHN
LUCY HENRY BASSET EDMUND
TALBOT THOMAS VERNON ALENCON
BEDFORD CHARLES RICHARD
SUFFOLK WARWICK WILLIAM
BEAUFORT BURGUNDY FASTOLFE
GARGRAVE MARGARET MORTIMER
REIGNIER GLANSDAI F LAPUCELLE
SALISBURY WOODVILLE
GLOUCESTER PLANTAGENET
HENRY VI-PART II (AUTHOR OF —)
SHAKESPEARE
(CHARACTER IN —) SAY CADE
DICK HUME IDEN JACK JOHN
VAUX BEVIS GOFFE HENRY PETER
SMITH EDWARD GEORGE HORNER
SCALES ELEANOR HOLLAND
MATTHEW MICHAEL RICHARD
SIMPCOX STANLEY SUFFOLK
WARWICK BEAUFORT CLIFFORD
HUMPHREY JOURDAIN MARGARET
SOMERSET STAFFORD ALEXANDER
SALISBURY SOUTHWELL
BUCKINGHAM BOLINGBROKE
PLANTAGENET
HENRY VI-PART III (AUTHOR OF —)
SHAKESPEARE
(CHARACTER IN —) BONA HUGH
JOHN HENRY LEWIS MARCH
EDMUND EDWARD EXETER GEORGE
OXFORD RIVERS BOURBON
NORFOLK RICHARD RUTLAND
STANLEY WARWICK CLIFFORD
HASTINGS MARGARET MONTAGUE
MORTIMER TEMBROKE SUMERSET
STAFFORD MONTGOMERY
PLANTAGENET WESTMORELAND
NORTHUMBERLAND
HEP (NOT —) ICKY
HEPATICA AI TRINITY
HEPATITIS FAVISM JAUNDICE
HEPHAESTUS LEMNIAN
(FATHER OF —) ZEUS
(MOTHER OF —) HERA
(WIFE OF —) CHARIS

HEPHZIBAH (HUSBAND OF —)
HEZEKIAH
(SON OF —) MANASSEH
HER A ARE SHE HARE HERS HURE
HERA JUNO
(FATHER OF —) CHONOS KRONOS
(HUSBAND OF —) ZEUS
HERALD BODE LYON USHER BEADLE
DECLARE FORERUN PREFACE
STENTOR USHFRIN BLAZONER
PRECURSE PROCLAIM ROTHESAY
MESSENGER
HERALDIC FECIAL FETIAL
HERALDRY ARMORY
HERB ANU APE PIA RUE UDO WAD
ALOE ANET ANYU ARUM COUS DILL
HEMP IRID LEEK MINT MOLY POLY
RAPE RUTA SAGE SOLA WOAD WORT
YAMP YARB AVENS AWIWI BLITE
BRUSH CANNA CHIVE CREAT CROUT
DAGGA DAISY DRABA GALAX
GAURA GILIA GRASS HOSTA LOASA
LUFFA MEDIC MUNGO NANCY
ORACH SEDGE SEDUM SENNA
SOLAH STOCK SULLA TANSY THYME
ZIZIA ALLIUM ARALIA ARNICA
AXSEED BAGPOD BAMBAN BANANA
BLINKS BORAGE CANCER CATGUT
CATNIP CENIZO CICELY CISTUS
CLOVER COCASH COLEUS CONIUM
COWISH COWPEA CRAMBE ELODEA
ENDIVE ERYNGO FENNEL GALAXY
GINGER HARMEL HYSSOP KOCHIA
KRIGIA KRIGLA LOOFAH LOVAGE
RAMTIL RATTLE ROBERT SESAME
SESELI SHEVRI WASABI ABRONIA
ALPINIA ALTHAEA ALYSSUM
AMORPHA AMSONIA ANCHUSA
ANEMONE ANGELON ARACHIS
BABIANA BABROOT BARTSIA
BIRDEYE BLINKER BONESET
BUGSEED BUGWEED CHICORY
CUDWEED CULVERS DEWDROP
DYEWEED EPISCIA ERODIUM FREESIA
FROGBIT FUMMORY GERBERA
GINSENG GOITCHO GOSMORE
GOUAREE GUAYULE GUNNERA
HARMALA HEDEOMA HENBANE
HERBLET IRESINE ISOLOMA JONQUIL
LABIATE LEWISIA LINNAEA
MARANTA MIMULUS MUDWEED
MUDWORT MULLEIN MUSTARD
NAILROD NEMESIA NIEVETA
PAVONIA PETUNIA PINESAP
PINWEED PUCHERA ROSELLE
SAFFLOR SALSIFY SEEDBOX SKIRRET
SOWBANE SPIGNEL STACHYS
ABELMOSK ABELMUSK ACANTHUS
ACONITUM AGERATUM ALOCASIA
ALUMROOT AMBROSIA AMMOBIUM
ANGELICA ARGEMONE ASPHODEL
BEDSTRAW CALATHEA CAPEWEED
CARELESS CENTAURY CHENILLE

COLLOMIA COSTMARY COWWHEAT
CRASSULA CROMWELL DANEWEED
DEERWEED DROPWORT ECHINOPS
EGGPLANT EREMURUS ERIGERON
EUCHARIS FEVERFEW FLEABANE
FOWLFOOT GAYWINGS GERARDIA
GESNERAD GESNERIA GHETCHOO
GLOXINIA GOATROOT GUZMANIA
HAREBELL HEPATICA HEUCHERA
HIBISCUS HOLEWORT HONEWORT
HOROKAKA HUDSONIA IRONWEED
LICORICE LOCOWEED MANDRAKE
MANFREDA MANYROOT MARDOWRT
MARJORAM MARTYNIA MURRNONG
PHACELIA PINKROOT PLUMBAGO
POKEWEED SACALINE SAINFOIN
SALICORN SAMPHIRE SANDBURR
SCABIOUS SHINLEAF SMALLAGE
SNOWDROP SOAPROOT SOAPWORT
STAPELIA SUNDROPS TETRIFOL
TOCALOTE WOODRUFF
MONEYWORT PUSSYTOES
RUDBECKIA SAXIFRAGE SPIKENARD
NASTURTIUM PENNYCRESS
PERIWINKLE SARRACENIA
(— COUNTERACTING POISON)
CANCER
(— OTHER THAN GRASS) FORB
(AROMATIC —) MINT ANISE CLARY
CATNIP CAAPEBA CHERVIL DITTANY
(BIENNIAL —) LEEK PARSLEY
ANGELICA
(BULBOUS —) LILY CANNA ALLIUM
CRINUM GARLIC NERINE SQUILL
BABIANA SHALLOT DOGTOOTH
SLANGKOP
(FABULOUS —) MOLY PANAX PANACE
(FLOATING —) FROGBIT
(FORAGE —) FITCHES GOITCHO
(MEDITERRANEAN —) CRAMBE
(MYTHICAL —) MOLY
(POISONOUS —) CONIUM HEMLOCK
MONKSHOOD
(PL.) POTAGERIE
HERBAGE HAY BITE GRASS GRAZE
PICHI ADONIS SACATE ZACATE
GRAZING
HERB EVE IVA IVY
HERB GRACE RUE
HERBICIDE IPE DIQUAT DIURON
SILVEX DALAPEN DALAPON LINURON
MONURON ATRAZINE PARAQUAT
PICLORAM PROPANIL SIMAZINE
HERB IMPIOUS DOWNWEED
HOARWORT
HERB PARIS TRUE ONEBERRY
TRUELOVE
HERB ROBERT JENNY ROBIN
ROBERT
HERCULEAN HUGE
HERCULES ERCLES ALCIDES
HERSHEF OETAEUS OVILLUS
HERAKLES

(BROTHER OF —) IPHICLES
(CAPTIVE OF —) IOLE
(FATHER OF —) JUPITER
(MOTHER OF —) ALCMENA
(WIFE OF —) HEBE MEGARA
DEIANIRA
HERCULES ALLHEAL OPOPANAX
HERCULES-CLUB ARALIA IVYWORT
RUEWORT SHOTBUSH
HERD BOW GAM MOB BAND CREW
GAME GANG HEAD RACE ROUT
RUCK TAIL TEAM TRIP DROVE FLOCK
HEARD TROOP CAVIYA CHOUSE
HIRSEL HUDDLE MANADA MEINIE
REMUDA SPREAD THRAVE CREAGHT
RANGALE SHEPHERD
(— CATTLE) TAIL WRANGLE
(— OF CATTLE) FLOTE
(— OF COLTS) RAG
(— OF HORSES) RACE HARAS
HARRAS REMUDA
(— OF SEALS) PATCH
(— OF WHALES) GAM
(— OF WILD SWINE) SOUNDER
HERDBOY BOUCHAL
HERDER DROVER FEEDER HERDBOY
HERDSMAN AMOS SENN GAUCHO
HERDER LOOKER PASTOR HERDBOY
LLANERO THYRSIS VAQUERO
BEASTMAN DAMOETAS GARTHMAN
NEATHERD PASTORAL PASTURER
RANCHERO SWANHERD WRANGLER
HERE ICI ADSUM READY WHERE
HEREAT HITHER PRESENT
(— AND THERE) ABOUT ABROAD
AROUND PASSIM SPARSIM
HEREAFTER BEYOND
HEREDITAMENT LAND
HEREDITARY INBORN INNATE
KINDLY LINEAL PATERNAL
HEREDITY
(— UNIT) RNA
HEREIN WITHIN
HERESY DOCETISM KETZEREI
MISBELIEF
HERETIC BUGGER KETZER ZINDIQ
LOLLARD PATARIN PROFANE
SECTARY JUDAIZER MISCREANT
SABELLIUS MISBELIEVER
(PL.) ACEPHALI
HERETICAL HERETIC HETERODOX
MISCREANT
HERETO HITHER
HERETOFORE ERST BEFORE
ERENOW EREWHILE FORMERLY
HEREWARD THE WAKE (AUTHOR
OF —) KINGSLEY
(CHARACTER IN —) BRAND GODIVA
MARTIN WILLIAM ALFTRUDA
HEREWARD TORFRIDA LIGHTFOOT
HERITAGE DESCENT HEIRDOM
HEIRSHIP PATRIMONY
HERMA MERCURY

HERMAPHRODITE MOPH SCRAT ANDROGYNOUS
HERMAPHRODITIC BISEXED BISEXUAL MONOECIOUS
HERMAPHRODITISM GYNANDRY
HERMAPHRODITUS (FATHER OF —) MERCURY
(MOTHER OF —) VENUS
HERMENEGILD (FATHER OF —) LEOVIGILD
HERMES MERCURY AGORAIOS CYLLENIUS
(FATHER OF —) ZEUS
(MOTHER OF —) MAIA
HERMIA (BELOVED OF —) LYSANDER
(FATHER OF —) EGEUS
HERMIONE (FATHER OF —) MENELAUS
(HUSBAND OF —) PYRRHUS
(MOTHER OF —) HELEN
HERMIT ARME MUNI HANIF MINIM ANCHOR SANTON SULLEN ASCETIC EREMITE RECLUSE TAPASVI ANCHORET MARABOUT SOLITARY
HERMITAGE ASHRAM ASHRAMA RECLUSE
HERNIA BURST RAMEX BREACH RUPTURE MEROCELE
(SUFF.) CELE COELE COELUS
HERO CID KIM RAB AJAX EGIL IDAS KAMI MAUI NALA NATA OFFA RINK YIMA ADAPA BERNE DEBON ETANA FAUST GHAZI HODER HOTHR IRAYA KIPPS MARKO ORSON TASSO TIMON VOTAN EGMONT FIGARO GIDEON GOLIAS HEROIC IASION IOLAUS MAUGIS MINYAS OSSIAN PELHAM PENROD RIENZI ROLAND RUSTAM SIGURD TARZAN USHEEN VATHEK ALCESTE DOGATYR DEMIGOD FAUSTUS GLUSKAP GRINDER INGOMAR JAMSHID MACBETH MANRICO MARMION MAZEPPA ORLANDO OTHELLO PALADIN RAFFLES TANCRED THALABA THESEUS TROILUS ULYSSES VOLPONE WERTHER WIDSITH WIELAND ACADEMUS ARGONAUT CHAMPION FANSHAWE FERUMBAS FRITHJOF GAEDHEAL GILGAMES LAMMIKIN MALAGIGI MORGANTE OROONOKO PALMERIN PARSIFAL PERICLES RASSELAS RODOMONT SUPERMAN TRISTRAM WAVERLEY
(LOVER OF —) LEANDER
(TRIBAL —) JUDGE
HERODIAS (BROTHER OF —) AGRIPPA
(FATHER OF —) ARISTOBULUS
(HUSBAND OF —) HEROD
HEROIC EPIC FELL GREAT NOBLE EPICAL FEATLY EXTREME GALLANT VALIANT FEARLESS HEROICAL HOMERIAN INTREPID SPLENDID

HEROIN JUNK SCAG SKAG SNOW HORSE JONES SMACK STUFF
HEROINE AIDA EMMA MIMI RUTH JULIE MEDEA NORMA SEDNA THAIS ESTHER FEDORA GUDRUN HELENA JUDITH JULIET MARTHA MIGNON PAMELA PHEDRE RAMONA ROMOLA SALOME SILVIA TRILBY UNDINE ERMINIA EVELINA GALATEA GINEVRA GRAINNE HEROESS MONIMIA SHIRLEY ZENOBIA ZULEIKA ATAI ANTA ISABELLA MARGARET PATIENCE POMPILIA ROSMUNDA SOFRONIA
HEROISM VALOR BRAVERY COURAGE PROWESS
HERON QUA POKE SOCO CRAIG CRANE EGRET FRANK HERNE PADDY QUAWK YAROA AIGRET GAULIN KIALEE KOTUKU QUAKER SQUAWK BITTERN CRABIER GOLIATH HANDSAW QUABIRD SQUACCO BOATBILL GAULDING HERONSEW UMBRETTE
(— FLOCK) SIEGE
HERON'S-BILL ERODIUM
HERPES DARTRE TETTER
HERPES ZOSTER ZONA SHINGLES
HERRING ALEC BRIT CHUB SHAD SILD BLOAT CAPON CISCO DORAB HILSA MARAY MATIE SPRAT KIPPER POLLAN TAILOR ANCHOVY BLOATER CLUPEID NAILROD ROLLMOP SHADINE BLUEBACK BRISLING BUCKLING CROPSHIN GRAYBACK QUODDIES SCUDDAWN STRADINE
(— SEASON) DRAVE
(— UNIT) LAST MAZE
(FEMALE —) RAUN
(LAKE —) KIYI CISCO
(RED —) CAPON SOLDIER
(SMOKED —) BLOATER
(YOUNG —) COB BRIT SILD SILE SILL SOIL WILE BRITT COBBE MATIE SPRAT SARDINE SPERLING
(2, 3 OR 4 —S) WARP
HERS HERN SHISN
HERSE (FATHER OF —) CECROPS
(SISTER OF —) AGRAULOS
(SON OF —) CEPHALUS
HERSELF HI HER SELF ITSELF
HERSEY (— LOCALE) ADANO
HERSHEF ARSAPHES
HESHVAN BUL CHESHVAN
HESIONE (FATHER OF —) LAOMEDON
(HUSBAND OF —) TELAMON
(RESCUER OF —) HERCULES
HESITANCY HANG
(— IN SPEECH) BALBUTIES
HESITANT SHY CAGY CHARY GROPING HALTING RETICENT SUSPENSE
(NOT —) FACILE

HESITATE COY HEM BALK STAY STOP CHECK CRANE DEMUR DOUBT FORCE PAUSE STALL STAND STICK SUSSY WAVER BOGGLE FALTER HANKER LINGER MAMMER RELUCT SCOTCH TARROW TARTLE BALANCE PROFFER SCRUPLE STAGGER STAMMER SWITHER THRIMBLE
(— IN SPEAKING) HACKER
HESITATING JUBUS HALTING BACKWARD DOUBTFUL JUBEROUS TIMOROSO
HESITATION HANG HINK WAND PAUSE STAND STICK SUSSY SWITHER (SPEECH —) STAMMER
HESPERUS VESPER
HESRON (FATHER OF —) REUBEN
HESSIAN BURLAP
HESTIA (FATHER OF —) KRONOS (MOTHER OF —) RHEA
HETAERA LAIS THAIS PHRYNE MISTRESS
HETER-
(PREF.) XEN(O)
HETERODOX HERETIC SINISTRAL
HETERODOXY HERESY CACODOXY
HETEROGENEOUS MIXED MOTLEY UNLIKE DIVERSE PIEBALD ASSORTED
HETEROMYS SACCOMYS
HETEROSEXUAL STRAIGHT
HETEROTROPHIC HOLOZOIC
HETEROXENOUS INDIRECT
HETEROZYGOUS CROSS SPLIT IMPURE
HETMAN ATAMAN
HEW CUT HAG CHIP SNAG STUB SHRED SLICE
(— OUT) CARVE
(— STONE) CHAR
HEWER JOEY GETTER GIDEON FACEMAN
HE WHO GETS SLAPPED
(AUTHOR OF —) ANDREYEV
(CHARACTER IN —) ALFRED ZINIDA BENZANO BRIQUET JACKSON MANCINI REGNARD CONSUELO
HEX WITCH VOODOO WHAMMY
HEXAGON SEXANGLE
HEXAGONAL HEX DIMETRIC
HEXAGRAM PENTACLE
HEXAMETER MIURUS RHOPALIC (DACTYLIC —) EPOS HEROIC
HEXOBARBITAL EVIPAL
HEXOSAN MANNAN GLUCOSAN MANNOSAN
HEYDAY MAY HIGHDAY
HEY PRESTO SUDDENLY
HEZEKIAH (FATHER OF —) AHAZ NEARIAH (MOTHER OF —) ABI
HEZION (SON OF —) TABRIMON
HEZRON (FATHER OF —) PHAREZ REUBEN

HIATUS GAP BREAK CHASM BREACH HIATAL LACUNA
HIBERNATE SHACK WINTER SLUMBER
HIBERNATING LATITANT
HIBERNIA EIRE ERIN IRELAND JUVERNA
HIBERNIAN IRISHMAN IVERNIAN
HIBISCUS ROSELLE
HICCUP YEX YOX HICK HOCKET HOQUET SINGULTUS
HICK BOOR HIND JAKE BACON BUSHMAN CORNBALL CHAWBACON
HICKORY NOGAL PIGNUT BULLNUT SHAGBARK
HICKORY NUT TRYMA PIGNUT BULLNUT KISKITOM
HICKWALL ECCLE HECKLE HICKWAY
HID LATENT
HIDDEN HID SHY DEEP DERN LOST TECT BLIND CLOSE DOGGO DUSKY PERDU PRIVY ARCANE BURIED COVERT INNATE LATENT MASKED MYSTIC OCCULT SECRET VEILED BOSOMED CLOUDED COVERED CRYPTIC OBSCURE RECLUSE SUBTILE ABDITIVE ABSTRUSE CRYPTOUS HIDEAWAY PALLIATE SCREENED SECLUDED SNEAKING CRYPTICAL RECONDITE
(PREF.) CRYPT(O) KRYPT(O)
HIDE HOD WRY BUFF BURY CASE CROP DARK DERN FELL FELT HILL HOOD JOUK LEAN MASK PELL PELT SCAB SKIN SKUG SNUG STOW VEIL WELL BELIE BELLY BLIND CACHE CLOAK CLOUD COUCH COVER DITCH EARTH FLANK GLOSS LAYNE LOSHE MANSE PLANT SHADE SPOIL STASH STEER TAPIS BURROW BUSHEL CASATE EMBOSS ENCASE ENCAVE ENWOMB FOREST HUDDLE IMBOSK LIELOW MANENT PELAGE SCREEN SHADOW SHIELD SHROUD ABSCOND CONCEAL COWHIDE EMBOWEL FLAUGHT OBCLUDE OVERLAY SECLUDE SECRETE SPREADY TAPPICE CARUCATE DISGUISE ENSCONCE HIDELAND HOODWINK PALLIATE PLOWLAND SQUIRREL SUPPRESS CLANDESTINE
(— AS AN EEL) MUD
(— IN WOODS) WOOD BUSHWACK
(— UNDER) BUSHEL
(CALF'S —) DEACON
(DRESSED —S) LEATHER
(HALF OF —) BEND
(HAVING SOFT —) MELLOW
(SHEEP'S —) SLAT
(TANNED —) CROP
(THICKEST —S) BACKS
(UNDRESSED —) KIP
(PL.) JUFTI JUFTS

(PREF.) DERM(AT)(ATO)(O) DORA
(SUFF.) DERM(A)(ATOUS)(IA)(IS)(Y)

HIDE-AND-GO-SEEK BOGLE
WHOOP BOGGLE

HIDEAWAY MEW LAIR SHANGRILA

HIDEBOUND BORNE NARROW
BIGOTED

HIDEOUS FELL GASH GRIM UGLY
AWFUL TOADY DEFORM GRIMLY
GRISLY HORRID ODIOUS OGRISH
GHASTLY DEFORMED DREADFUL
FIENDISH GRUESOME HORRIBLE
SHOCKING TERRIBLE MONSTROUS

HIDEOUSLY FOULLY

HIDING DERN MICHING SECRECY
ADDITIVE HIDEAWAY

HIDING-PLACE CACHE

HIEMAL WINTRY

HIERACIUM DINALE HAWKWEED

HIERARCHY SATRAPY

HIEROGLYPH CIPHER
(PL.) SIGNARY

HIEROPHANT PRIEST

HIGGLE HUCK HAGGLE

HIGH UP AIT AIRY DEAR HAUT MAIN
MUCH RANK TALL ACUTE ALOFT
BRENT CHIEF CLOSE DRUNK FIRST
GREAT HAUTE LOFTY MERRY NOBLE
SHARP SPACY STEEP BOMBED
COSTLY RIPPED SHRILL SPACEY
STONED ZONKED EMINENT EXALTED
HAUGHTY STICKLE SUBLIME
TOPPING VIOLENT ELEVATED
FOREMOST PIERCING TOWERING
WIPEDOUT SPACEDOUT
(— AND MIGHTY) HOGEN
(— IN CHROMA) STRONG
(— IN PITCH) ALT ACUTE
(— IN RANK) MUCH
(— ON DRUGS) STONED
(— PITCH) ORTHIAN
(BE —) FLY
(MOST —) SERENE
(PRETTY —) STIFFISH
(VERY —) TAUNT RAREFIED RARIFIED
(PREF.) ALTI HYPS(I)(O)
(ON —) HYPS(I)(O)

HIGHBORN NOBLE GENEROUS

HIGHBOY TALLBOY

HIGHBRED SOFT REFINED

HIGHBROW EGGHEAD

HIGH-CLASS CLASSY UPSTAGE

HIGH-CLIMBER TOPPER

HIGH-COLORED BLOWSY BLOWZY

HIGH-CROWNED COPATAIN

HIGHER OVER ABOVE SENIOR
SUPERIOR
(PREF.) SUPER(O) SUPRA

HIGHEST ACE TOP HEXT FIRST
EXTREME MAXIMAL SUPREME
BUNEMOST HIGHMOST OVERMOST
(— IN DEGREE) LAST

HIGHFALUTIN PAUGITY

HIGH-FED BEANY

HIGH-FLAVORED GAMY

HIGH FLOWN TALL TUMID

HIGH-HANDED BOSSY CAVALIER

HIGH-HAT SNOOT

HIGHLAND RAND CERRO

HIGHLANDER GAEL TARTAN
NAINSEL PLAIDMAN REDSHANK
TREWSMAN UPLANDER
(PL.) TREWS TARTAN

HIGHLIGHT ADORN HEIGHTEN
PINPOINT SALIENCE

HIGHLY THRICE

HIGH-MINDED HAUGHT

HIGHNESS ALTESSE ALTEZZA
ALTITUDE
(— OF PRICE) DEARTH

HIGH-PITCHED ACUTE PROUD
PIPING TREBLE ORTHIAN SHRIEKY

HIGH-POWERED INTENSE
MAGNUM

HIGH-PRICED DEAR

HIGH-RIGGER TOPPER

HIGH-SOUNDING BIG BOMBAST
MAGNIFIC SONORANT SONOROUS
SOUNDING

HIGH-SPIRITED METTLED CRANK
FIERY FIERCE LIVELY GALLANT
GINGERY RAMPANT CAVALIER
VASCULAR

HIGH-SPIRITEDNESS SPLEEN

HIGH-STRUNG HYPER TENSE
NERVOUS

HIGHTAIL (— IT) LEAVE SCRAM

HIGH-TONED TONY DICTY DICKTY

HIGHWAY VIA WAY DELT ITER PATH
PIKE ROAD TOBY BOLOS ARTERY
CAUSEY COURSE RUMPAD SKYWAY
STREET BELTWAY CALZADA
FREEWAY RAMPIRE THRUWAY
ARTERIAL AUTOBAHN BROADWAY
CAUSEWAY CHAUSSEE HIGHROAD
MOTORWAY SPEEDWAY
(— ROBBERY) TOBY
(LOCATED OFF THE —) DEVIOUS
(PART OF —) EXIT GORE LANE LOOP
RAMP ACCESS BRIDGE ISLAND
MEDIAN DIVIDER ROADWAY
JUNCTION OVERPASS SHOULDER
UNDERPASS INTERSECTION

HIGHWAYMAN PAD RIDER SCAMP
BANDIT CUTTER PADDER RODMAN
BRIGAND FOOTPAD LADRONE
PRANCER RODSMAN TOBYMAN
BIDSTAND DAMASTES HIGHTOBY
HIJACKER LANCEMAN OUTRIDER
BANDOLERO

HIGH-WROUGHT INTENSE

HIKE UP MUSH WALK MARCH RAISE
TRAMP RAMBLE ADVANCE INCREASE

HILARIOUS MAD RORTY JOVIAL
JOCULAR NAUGHTY CHIRPING
GLORIOUS

HILARITY GIG JOY GLEE LAUGH MIRTH GAIETY GAYETY DEVILRY JOLLITY WHOOPEE MERRIMENT

HILKIAH (FATHER OF —) AMZI HOSAH (SON OF —) ELIAKIM GEMARIAH JEREMIAH

HILL BEN DEN DUN HOE HOW KOP LOW PUY TOR VAN ALTO BANK BERG BRAE BULT BUMP COTE DAGH DENE DOWN DRUM FELL HIGH HONE KNAP LOMA LUMP MESA MOOR MOTE NOUP PAHA TOFT ZION BARGH BUTTE CERRO CLIFF COAST HEUGH KNOCK KNOLL KOPJE MORRO MOUND MOUNT STILL SWELL TELLE WATCH ASCENT BARROW BEACON COBBLE COLLIS COPPLE CUESTA HEIGHT HEUVEL LOMITA SPRUNT STRONE CAELIAN CAPITOL COLLINE DRUMLIN HILLOCK NUNATAK PICACHO SOWBACK VIMINAL AREOPAGY CATOCTIN DRUMLOID FOOTHILL MONTICLE QUIRINAL MONADNOCK
(— OF SAND) DENE DUNE
(— OF STRATIFIED DRIFT) KAME
(— UP) MOLD
(ARABIAN —) TEL
(BROAD-TOPPED —) LOMA
(CONICAL —) LAW PAP PINGO
(CRAGGY —) TOR
(FORTIFIED —) RATH
(HIGH —) BEN
(ISOLATED —) HUM TOFT BARGH BUTTE
(LAST —) STRONE
(LOW —) HOW BAND DENE WOLD KOPPIE SOWBACK
(NIPPLELIKE —) PAP
(NORTH AFRICAN —) JEBEL DJEBEL
(RESIDUAL —) CATOCTIN
(ROUNDED —) DODD HONE MAMELON
(SAND —) DENE
(SHARP-POINTED —) KIP KIPP PIKE
(SMALL —) KNAP KNOLL KOPJE KOPPIE HILLOCK MOLEHILL
(STEEP —) BREW BROW STILL
(STONY —) ROACH
(SUGAR-LOAF —) SPITZKOP
(WOODED —) HOLT HURST
(PREF.) BUNO

HILLARY (CONQUEST OF —) EVEREST

HILLBILLY HOEDOWN

HILL-FORT RATH

HILLOCK HOW LOW NOB BOSS BULT DOWN KAME KNAP KNOB TERP TOFT TUMP BERRY HEAVE HURST KNOCK KNOLL KOPJE MOUND TOMAN BARROW BURROW COPPET HILLET HUMMOCK MAMELON TUMMOCK TUMULUS MOLEHILL

HILLSIDE BENT BRAE COTE EDGE CLEVE FALDA SLADE SLOPE FELLSIDE SIDEHILL

HILLTOP DOD NAB PIKE RISE KNOLL

HILLY KNOBBY

HILT HAFT BASKET POIGNET HANDGRIP
(— OF DAGGER) DUDGEON
(PART OF —) BOW CUT GRIP RING GUARD BUTTON POMMEL CAPSTAN LANGUET QUILLON RICASSO CROSSPIECE COUNTERGUARD

HILUM EYE SCAR HILUS PORTA NUCLEUS CICATRIX

HIM A EN HE HEM HIN LUI MUN

HIMATION PALLION PALLIUM

HIMERUS (FATHER OF —) LACEDAEMON
(MOTHER OF —) TAYGETE
(SISTER OF —) CLEODICE

HIMSELF HIM IPSE SELF HISSEL ITSELF HERSELF HISSELF

HIND ROE CONY HINE HINT CONEY HEARST HINDER VENISON CABRILLA

HIND-BODY ABDOMEN

HINDBRAIN RHOMBENCEPHALON

HINDER BAR DAM KEP LET MAR ROB CLOG HELP SLOW SLUG STAY STOP TENT WARN AFTER BLOCK CHEAT CHECK CHOKE CRAMP DEBAR DELAY DETER EMBAR ESTOP HEDGE SLOTH STYMY THROW TRASH ARREST CUMBER DETAIN FORBID FORLET HAMPER HARASS HINNER IMPEDE IMPEND INJURE RETARD RETRAL SCOTCH TAIGLE UNHELP ABSTAIN DEPRIVE FORELAY IMPEACH INHIBIT OCCLUDE PREVENT TRACHLE ENCUMBER HANDICAP IMPEDITE OBSTRUCT PRECLUDE PROHIBIT POSTICOUS
(PREF.) POSTERO

HINDERED FOUL

HINDERER LETTER

HINDERMOST LAG ACHTER

HINDQUARTER HIND HAUNCH
(HALF —) LEG
(PL.) FOUCH CRUPPER HAUNCHES

HINDRANCE BAR LET RUB BALK CURB REIN SLUG SNAG STAY STOP BLOCK CHECK DELAY HITCH TRASH ARREST CUMBER DENIAL HINDER OBJECT REMORA UNHELP SHACKLE UNSPEED DISCOUNT DRAWBACK HOLDBACK OBSTACLE PULLBACK

HINDU BABU BABOO SUDRA BABHAN BANIAN BANYAN GENTOO JAJMAN BANIAN KHATRI NAYADI SHUDRA THAKUR VAISYA MUSAHAR VAIRAGI
(— ASCETIC) SADHU
(— ASSOCIATION) SANGH

(— **CASTE**) TELI VARNA
(— **CUSTOM**) SATI SUTTEE
(— **ENERGY**) SAKTI SHAKTI
(— **IDOL**) SWAMI
(— **INTERJECTION**) OM AUM
(— **PHILOSOPHY**) YOGA VEDANTA
(— **PRACTICE**) PURDAH
(— **RITE**) PUJA POOJA
(— **SAGE**) RSI RISHI
(— **SCRIPTURE**) VEDA
(— **SECT**) SIKH
(— **VARNA MEMBER**) SUDRA
(— **WORSHIPER**) SAKTA
(— **WRITING**) VEDA
(— **WRITINGS**) SMRTI TANTRA
(**TWICE-BORN** —) KSATRIYA
HINDUSTANI URDU HINDI OORDOO
   DAKHINI
HINDWING BALANCER
HINGE RUN BAND BUTT FLAP HARR
   TRIM TURN CARDO CROOK GEMEL
   JOINT MOUNT NODUS SKELL SKEWL
   TWIST DEPEND GARNET GEMMEL
   GIMMER HANGLE JIMMER SNIBEL
   CHARNEL COXCOMB FULCRUM
   HOLDBACK
(— **OF BIVALVE SHELL**) CARDO
(— **OF HELMET**) CHARNEL
(— **TOGETHER**) SCISSOR
(**HALF OF** —) FLAP
(**PHILATELIC** —) STICKER
(**PREF.**) GINGLYMO
HINGED SWING
(**SUFF.**) POMATOUS
HINNY BURDON FUNNEL JENNET
HINT CUE TIP AGTE ITEM MINT TANG
   WIND WINK CHEEP IMPLY INFER
   POINT SPELL STEER TOUCH TRACE
   WHIFF ALLUDE BREATH GLANCE
   OFFICE SMATCH TIPOFF WHEEZE
   INKLING LEADING MEMENTO
   POINTER SUGGEST UMBRAGE
   WHISPER WRINKLE ALLUSION
   INDICATE INNUENDO INTIMATE
   TELLTALE
(**HUNT** —) CLUE
HINTERLAND BLED BACKLAND
HIP HEP MOD COXA HUCK FUNKY
   PITCH SHOOP HAUNCH HUCKLE
   TRENDY TUNEDIN HIPBERRY
   TURNEDON
(— **JOINT**) COXA THURL
(— **OF ROSE**) BERRY CHOOP SHOOP
(— **OF TARGET**) SPOT
(**PREF.**) COX(O) ISCHI(O) OSPHY(O)
HIPBONE FINBONE PINBONE
   EDGEBONE SIDEBONE
HIPPARCHUS (**BROTHER OF** —)
   HIPPIAS
(**FATHER OF** —) PISISTRATUS
HIPPARETE (**BROTHER OF** —)
   CALLIAS

(**FATHER OF** —) HIPPONICUS
(**HUSBAND OF** —) ALCINIADES
HIPPEUS KNIGHT
HIPPIE FREAK
HIPPOCAMPUS ERGOT HIPPO
   SEAHORSE
HIPPOCOON (**BROTHER OF** —)
   TYNDAREUS
(**FATHER OF** —) OEBALUS
(**MOTHER OF** —) GORGOPHONE
(**SLAYER OF** —) HERCULES
HIPPODAMIA (**FATHER OF** —)
   ADRASTUS OENOMAUS
(**HUSBAND OF** —) PELOPS
   PEIRITHOUS
(**SON OF** —) ATREUS TROEZEN
   PITTHEUS THYESTES
HIPPOLYTUS (**FATHER OF** —)
   THESEUS
(**MOTHER OF** —) HIPPOLYTE
(**STEPMOTHER OF** —) PHAEDRA
HIPPOMENES (**FATHER OF** —)
   MEGAREUS
(**MOTHER OF** —) MEROPE
(**WIFE OF** —) ATALANTA
HIPPONACTEAN SCAZON
HIPPOPOTAMUS HIPPO ZEEKOE
   BEHEMOTH BUNODONT
HIPPOTHOE (**FATHER OF** —) MESTOR
(**MOTHER OF** —) LYSIDICE
(**SON OF** —) TAPHIUS
HIPPOTRAGUS OZANNA
   EGOCERUS
HIPSTER HEPCAT
HIRAH (**COMPANION OF** —) JUDAH
HIRE FEE JOB HAVE MEED RENT SIGN
   WAGE LEASE PREST WAGES EMPLOY
   ENGAGE RETAIN SALARY TAKEON
   BESPEAK CHARTER CONDUCE
   CONDUCT FREIGHT STIPEND
(— **CATTLE**) TACK
HIRED PAID TEEKA TICCA WAGED
HIRELING HACK VENAL HACKNEY
   MYRMIDON WAGELING MERCENARY
   PENSIONER PENSIONARY
HIRSUTE HAIRY PILOSE SHAGGY
   TRESSY
HIS S AS ES IS HISN
HISPID STRIGOSE STRIGOUS
HISS BLOW FUFF HISH HIZZ QUIZ SISS
   SIZZ GOOSE WHISS FISSLE FIZZLE
   SIFFLE WHOOSH WHISTLE SIBILATE
(— **OF SWORD**) SOUGH
HISSING BIRD AFFLATUS SIBILANT
HIST PEACE
HISTONE GLOBIN
HISTORIAN MORONI STORIER
   ANNALIST
   AMERICAN FAY FOX GAY NYE BEER
   BOYD DODD FEIS FISH GARR HART
   KANE MAYS SHEA ZINN ADAMS
   AMORY BEARD BEMIS CURTI ELSON

BRANDENBURG FALLMERAYER
GARDTHAUSEN GREGOROVIUS
SECKENDORFF
GREEK DURIS GREEN ARRIAN
STRABO BIKELAS EPHORUS
LAMBROS SOZOMEN TIMEAUS
DEXIPPUS EUSEBIUS HERODIAN
POLYBIUS XENOPHON CRATIPPUS
DIONYSIUS HERODOTUS HESYCHIUS
PHILISTUS TIMAGENES
ANAXIMENES CLITARCHUS
HELLANICUS HIERONYMUS
PHYLARCHUS THEOPOMPUS
THUCYDIDES ARISTOBULUS
MEGASTHENES OLYMPIODORUS
AGATHARCHIDES
HEBREW JOSEPHUS
HUNGARIAN FEJER TOLDY PAULER
TELEKI FESSLER FRAKNOI MAILATH
MANNHEIM MARCZALI SZILAGYI
ICELANDIC SNORRI
IRISH BURY LECKY CHESNEY
GILBERT WADDING
ITALIAN AMARI CANTU VOLPE
CANALE CIAMPI DENINA EMILIO
FEDELE GIOVIO NOVATI VASARI
ACCOLTI FERRERO VILLANI VILLARI
AMMIRATO CIBRARIO GIANNONE
MOLMENTI MURATORI BERTOLINI
LIUTPRAND SALVEMINI
GUICCIARDINI
MEXICAN ALAMAN PEREYRA
CLAVIJERO BUSTAMANTE
NORWEGIAN KOHT LANGE MUNCH
DIETRICHSON
PERUVIAN ULLOA
POLISH KUBALA BIELSKI CHODZKO
DLUGOSZ LELEWEL SZUJSKI
ASKENAZY JABLONSKI BOBRZYNSKI
KUCHARZEWSKI
PORTUGUESE GOES MELO LOPES
BARROS CASTANHEDA
ROMAN CATO LIVY NEPOS CORDUS
FLORUS TROGUS SALLUST TACITUS
APPIANUS VALERIUS EUTROPIUS
SUETONIUS FENESTELLA
RUMANIAN IORGA KOGALNICEANU
RUSSIAN KAVELIN POGODIN
BRUCKNER KARAMZIN MILYUKOV
SOLOVIEV TURGENEV VENGEROV
DRUZHININ POKROVSKI
HRUSHEVSKY KOSTOMAROV
SCOTTISH MILL BOECE BROWN
LAING BURTON TYTLER CARLYLE
GILLIES NEILSON SPALDING
ROBERTSON MACKINTOSH
MACPHERSON
SPANISH AVILA LOPEZ XEREZ PINELO
PULGAR TORENO DESCLOT
GOMARRA HERRERA MARIANA
MONCADA FERRERAS LAFUENTE
MENENDEZ SEPULVEDA
MONTESINOS

SWEDISH DALIN BESKOW GEIJER
CARLSON FRYXELL FORSSELL
MESSENIUS
SWISS KOPP BLUMER GELZER
MULLER STUMPF TSCHUDI
SISMONDI GAGLIARDI BURCKHARDT
HISTORICAL GENETIC
HISTORIOGRAPHER SCALD SKALD
HISTORY STORY ANNALS LEGEND
RECORD SURVEY ACCOUNT
ANCESTRY PROPHECY RELATION
(— OF EXPERIENCES) MEMOIRS
(— OF JAPAN) KOJIKI
(LIFE —) COURSE
(MUSE OF —) CLIO
(PAST —) RECORD
(PERIOD OF JAPANESE —) HEIAN
(PREVIOUS —) BACKGROUND
(TRIBAL —) PHYLOGENY
HISTRION ACTOR
HISTRIONIC ACTORY ACTORISH
ACTRESSY
HIT BAT BOP BOX DOT GET HAT JOB
PEG PIP WOW BASH BEAN BEAT BELT
BIFF BLOW BOFF BONK BUST CHOP
CONK DING FOUR GOLD NAIL PINK
POKE PUCK PUNT RUFF SLAM SLAP
SLUG SOCK SWAT SWIP TAKE TANK
TUNK WART WIPE ANGLE BOFFO
CHECK CLOUT CLUNK CROWN FIVER
FLICK GOUFF KNOCK PASTE POTCH
PRANG PUNTA PUNTO SCORE SLASH
SLOSH SMASH SMITE SNICK SOCKO
SWIPE TAINT TOUCH VENUE ATTAIN
DOUBLE FOURER HURTLE SCLAFF
STRIKE VOLLEY ATTAINT BOFFOLA
CONNECT MUZZLER SANDBAG
SHELLAC WHERRET BLUDGEON
BOUNDARY LENGTHER STRICKEN
(— A KEY) STRIKE
(— BALL) CUR FLY DINK DRIVE
SHOOL SKITE SNICK
(— BUNT) DRAG
(— GAME) STOP
(— GENTLY) BABY
(— GLANCINGLY) TIP
(— GOLF BALL) CAN BLAST EXPLODE
(— HARD) DUMP SLOG SLUG PASTE
SKELP SOUSE DEVVEL STOUSH
STONKER
(— IN BOXING) LEADOFF
(— IN FACE) CLOCK
(— IN FIELD HOCKEY) CORNER
(— IN TILTING) TAINT
(— IT OFF) CLICK
(— LIGHTLY) KISS
(— ON BULL'S-EYE) GOLD
(— POORLY) DUB
(— SHARPLY) CLIP
(— SUDDENLY) ZAP
(— TOGETHER) CLASH
(— UPON) FIND
(— WITH FOOT) KICK SPURN

(BASE —) BINGLE DOUBLE SAFETY SINGLE TRIPLE SCRATCH SMOTHER
(BOXING —) SLUG PUNCH
(CRICKET —) SLOG BOUNDARY
(EASILY —) SITTING
(FENCING —) HAI HAY VENUE
(SHARP —) LICK
(SMASH —) SOCKEROO
(SOLID —) LINEDRIVE
HITCH JET TUG WED HALT HIKE ITCH KNOT LIFT PULL CATCH HOTCH SPELL TRACE FASTEN HIRSLE INSPAN MAGNUS SHUFFLE CONTRETEMPS
(— IN ROPE) CATSPAW
(NOSE —) BOZAL
HITCHHIKE HOP THUMB
HITCHHIKER PICKUP
HITCHING KNOT SHRUG
HITHER HERE
HITHERTO YET BEFORE
HITLERITE NAZI
HIT-OR-MISS CASUAL CHANCE HOBNOB CARELESS
HITTER SWATTER
HITTING BATTING SLOGGING
HITTITE HATTI KHATTI TABALIAN
HIVE GUM BIKE SKEP PYCHE STAND STATE STOCK SWARM APIARY ALVEARY BEEHIVE SWARMER
(— PLACED OVER ANOTHER) SUPER
HIVES CROUP UREDO
HLORRITHI THOR THORR
HOAGIE TORPEDO
HOAR GRAY RIME HOARY
HOARD HEAM KEEP POSE SAVE AMASS HUTCH MISER STASH STOCK COFFER MAGPIE MUCKER STOUTH GENIZAH HUSBAND SQUIRREL TREASURE
(— OF SAVINGS) STOCKING
(SECRET —) POSE
(THIEF'S —) PLANT
HOARDER MUCKER STORER HUSBAND
HOARFROST RAG HOAR RIME RIND
HOARINESS HOAR ROOP MUCOR
HOARSE RAW FOGGY GRUFF HEAZY HUSKY RAWKY ROKEY ROUGH ROUPY STOUR CROAKY CROUPY RASPED ROUPIT GRATING RAUCOUS
HOARSENESS FROG ROUP QUACK RAUCITY HASKNESS BARYPHONIA
HOARY AGED GRAY GREY HOAR WHITE FROSTY ANCIENT HOARISH INCANOUS
HOATZIN ANNA HANA HOACTZIN
HOAX BAM COD FUN GAG HUM KID RAG RIG BILK DUPE FAKE GAFF GEGG GUNK JOSH QUIZ RAMP RUSE SELL SHAM SKIT CHEAT FRAUD GREEN

SHAVE SPOOF TRICK WINDY CANARD DIDDLE HUMBUG STRING BLAFLUM DECEIVE FLIVVER ARTIFICE
HOB HUB PUNCH MATRIX
HOBAB (BROTHER-IN-LAW OF —) MOSES
HOBBER LEANER
HOBBLE GIMP LOCK SPAN BUNCH HILCH HITCH STILT STUMP HABBLE HIRPLE HOPPLE LANGLE LANKET TOLTER CRAMBLE CRAMMEL CRIPPLE SHACKLE SHAFFLE SPANCEL STAGGER TRAMMEL SIDELINE
HOBBLEBUSH DOGWOOD
HOBBLING LAME
HOBBY BUG FAD HOBBLER PASTIME AVOCATION
HOBBYHORSE HOBBY PLAYMARE
HOBBYIST BUG
HOBGOBLIN (ALSO SEE GOBLIN) COW HAG HOB PUG BOGY PUCK BOGEY BUCCA BUGAN POKER SCRAT SPOOK BOODIE BOWSIE EMPUSA SPOORN BUGABOO RAWHEAD BOGGLEBO COLTPIXY POPLEMAN PUCKEREL WORRICOW
HOBNAIL HOB HUB PUNCH TACKET
HOBNAILED TACKETY
HOBO BO BOE BUM STIFF TRAMP VAGRANT VAGABOND SUNDOWNER
HOCK HAM HOX HEEL ANKLE HOUGH HUXEN SINEW SKINK IMPAWN JARRET CAMBREL GAMBREL HOCKSHIN SUFFRAGO
HOCKEY HURLY HORKEY HURLEY SHINNY CAMMOCK HURLBAT
(— DISK) PUCK
(— PLAYER) DYE ORR ROY HALL HOWE HULL BUCYK DIONE MOORE SHORE CLARKE COWLEY DRYDEN DURNAN GOULET HARVEY MALONE MIKITO MORENZ PILATE PLANTE POLVIN ULLMAN VACHON BOURQUE GRETZKY LAFLEUR LEMIEUX MESSIER RATELLE SAWCHUK WORSLEY CHEEVERS CONACHER ESPOSITO SCHRINER THOMPSON TROTTIER LAROCOQUE MAHOVLICH PERREAULT DELVECCHIO
(— STAR) ORR
(— TEAM) JETS BLUES KINGS BRUINS DEVILS FLAMES FLYERS OILERS SABRES SHARKS CANUCKS RANGERS WHALERS CAPITALS PENGUINS REDWINGS SENATORS CANADIENS ISLANDERS LIGHTNING NORDIQUES BLACKHAWKS MAPLELEAFS NORTHSTARS
(AREA IN FRONT OF — GOAL) CREASE
(ILLEGAL CHECK IN —) SPEARING
(INFRACTION IN —) SPEARING

HOCKEY STICK HOOKY HURLY
STICK BULGER SHINNY CAMBUCA
CAMMOCK DODDART HURLBAT
HOCUS-POCUS CANTRIP
JUGGLERY FAKERY HUMBUG
FLIMFLAM QUACKERY
HOD TRAY
(**FATHER OF —**) ZOPHAH
HODAVIAH (**FATHER OF —**)
HASSENUAH
HOD CARRIER PADDY
HODESH (**HUSBAND OF —**)
SHAHARAIM
HODGEPODGE CHOW HASH MESS
OLIO RAFF SALAD BOLLIX JUSSEL
MAGPIE MEDLEY MELANGE
CHIVAREE CHOWCHOW HOTCHPOT
KEDGEREE MISHMASH PASTICHE
PORRIDGE SCRAMPUM PATCHWORK
HODOMETER VIAMETER
HOE BROD CHIP CLAT HACK HOWE
SHIM CLAUT LARRY THIRD CHONTA
HACKER PAIDLE PECKER SARCLE
GRUBBER PULASKI SCRAPER
SCUFFLE GRIFFAUN STRADDLER
(**— HANDLE**) STAIL
(**HORSE —**) NIDGET NIGGET
(**PART OF —**) BLADE SHANK HANDLE
FERRULE
HOECAKE CORNCAKE
HOG BEN SOW BOAR GALT GILT
PORK DUROC GRUNT SHOAT
BARROW HOGGET HOGGIE OINKER
PORKER PORKET YORKER BACONER
BUTCHER GRUNTER HOGLING
MONTANA DADIRUOA DUNODONT
HEREFORD LANDRACE VICTORIA
RAZORBACK
(**KIND OF —**) ROAD
(**PREF.**) SUI
HOGAN ABODE LODGE TEPEE
DWELLING
HOGBACK RIDGE FLATIRON
HOGFRAME
HOGCHOKER SOLE
HOGFISH CAPITAN LADYFISH
LORICATE SCORPION
HOGGER HUGGER HOGHEAD
HOGGISHNESS GRILL GRYLL
HOGLAH (**FATHER OF —**)
ZELOPHEHAD
HOGNOSE SNAKE ADDER
FLATHEAD
HOG PLUM AMRA JOBO
HOGSHEAD CASK CARDEL
HOG'S-MEAT TOSTON HOGWEED
HOG-TIE HAMPER
HOGWASH SLOP DRAFF SWASH
SWILL PIGWASH
HOIST FID HEFT KILT LIFT SWAY SWIG
WHIM WHIP CRANE ERECT HEAVE
HEEZE HEIST HOICK HOOSH HORSE

RAISE WEIGH JAMMER LAUNCH
LIFTER TUGGER WHIMSY DERRICK
(**— A LOG**) CANNON
(**— ANCHOR**) CAT
(**— FISH**) BRAIL
(**— FLUKES**) FISH FANCIER
HOISTED (**— TIGHT**) ATRIP
HOISTMAN CAGEMAN
HOKUM BLAA BLAH HOKE JUNK
HOLD HOD OWN BULK DEEM FEEL
FILL GAOL GAUM GIVE GRIT HANK
HAVE HELD HEND HILT HOLE HOLT
HOOK JAIL KEEP LOCK NAIL RELY
SOFT STOW AFONG AHOLD AHOLT
BELAY CARRY CINCH CLAMP CLING
GRASP GRIPE LATCH LEASE PAUSE
POISE ROCCA STORE WOULD
ADHERE ADSORB ARREST CLUTCH
DETAIN HANDLE INTERN MANURE
OCCUPY REGARD REPUTE RETAIN
ADJUDGE CAPTURE CLAUGHT
CONFINE CONTAIN ENCLOSE
FERMATA GRAPPLE HOLDING
RECEIVE SEIZURE SUBSIST SUSPEND
COMPRISE FOOTHOLD FOREHOLD
HANDFAST HANDHOLD HEADLOCK
HOLDFAST PURCHASE THURROCK
(**— A BELIEF**) SUPPOSE
(**— AS PRECIOUS**) TREASURE
(**— AS TRUE**) ACCEPT
(**— AT BAY**) DOMPT
(**— BACK**) STAY STOP WELL BELAY
LAYNE STINT BOGGLE DETAIN
FLINCH HINDER RETIRE SHRINK
CONTAIN DETRACT FORBEAR INHIBIT
RECLAIM REFRAIN REPRESS
SLACKEN HESITATE RESTRAIN
SUPPRESS WITHDRAW
(**— BACK ON LEASH**) TRASH
(**— CLOSELY**) CRADLE CUDDLE
(**— CONSULTATION**) ADVISE
(**— CORONER'S INQUEST**) CROWN
(**— DEAR**) CHERISH
(**— DOWN**) PINION CONTAIN
(**— FAST**) FIX BAIL BITE CLING SNARL
CLENCH CLINCH SECURE STABLE
(**— FIRMLY**) CLIP INSIST
(**— FORTH**) ORATE SPIEL
(**— FROM**) ABSTAIN
(**— GOOD**) APPLY SERVE
(**— IN CHECK**) REIN GOVERN
REPRESS COMPESCE
(**— IN CONTEMPT**) SMILE DISPRIZE
(**— IN PLACE**) ANCHOR
(**— OF PLASTER**) KEY
(**— ON COURSE**) STEM FETCH STAND
(**— ON FINAL NOTE**) TENOR
(**— ON SHORE**) LANDFAST
(**— OUT**) DREE LAST STAY OFFER
EXTEND PROTEND STRETCH
SUSTAIN
(**— PROTECTIVELY**) LAP

(— TIGHTLY) CLIP STICK
(— TOGETHER) BOND COHERE
CONSIST
(— UP) ROB BEAR HALT STAY ERECT
HEIST IMPEDE UPHOLD RUMPADE
SUPPORT SUSTAIN TRADUCE
(— UP BY LEADING STRINGS) DADE
(— UP TO CONTEMPT) FLEER
(— UP TO PUBLIC NOTICE) GIBBET
(SHIP'S —) HOLE HOLL FISHHOLD
(WRESTLING —) CROTCH NELSON
KEYLOCK CHANCERY HEADLOCK
SCISSORS SIDEHOLD
(PREF.) CHADA
HOLDBACK DAM
HOLDER WYE HAVER STOCK DIPPER
SOCKET CRACKER CASSETTE
JAGIRDAR
(— FOR CARRYING GLASS) FRAIL
(— FOR COIL) SPOOL
(— FOR CUP) ZARF
(— FOR FLOWERS) FROG JARDINIERE
(— FOR FOOD) COZY COSEY
(— FOR TOOLS) TURRET
(— FOR WHIP) BUCKET
(— OF BENEFICE) ABBE
(— OF GRANT) ENAMDAR
(ALLOTMENT —) CLERUCH
(CANDLE —) SPIDER GIRANDOLE
(FLOWER —) FROG
(LAMP —) BODY
(TAPE —) CASSETTE
(PL.) GRIPPERS
(PREF.) PORTE
HOLDFAST CLINCH HAPTERON
HOLDIKEN HADDIN
HOLDING HAL COPY COTE HOLD
TAKE GRASP HONOR HADDIN POFFLE
TENANT TENURE TENANCY
COMMENDA
(— DIFFERENT OPINIONS) APART
(— FAST) IRON
(— OF LAND) ROOM
(— OF OFFICE) OCCUPATION
(— OF SECURITIES) CARRY
(PL.) FLOCKS PROPERTY
HOLDUP HEIST STICKUP
HOLE CAN CUP EYE GAP PIT TAP
BORE BURY LEAK MAIL MUSE PECK
PINK POCK PUKA WANT CHINK DITCH
FLOSS FOSSE MEUSE SINUS SLACK
SPRUE SQUAT TEWEL THIRL THURL
BURROW CAVITY CENTER CENTRE
CRANNY CRATER EYELET HOLLOW
LACUNA OBTAIN OILLET PIERCE
POCKET POUNCE WEEPER BLOWOUT
BOGHOLE BOTHROS DIBHOLE
EYEHOLE KEYHOLE MORTICE
MORTISE OILHOLE OPENING
PINHOLE POTHOLE SCUTTLE
SWALLET VENTAGE ACCEPTER
APERTURE BLOWHOLE BOREHOLE

COALHOLE CRABHOLE FUMAROLE
HANDHOLE KNOCKOUT KNOTHOLE
OVERTURE PEEPHOLE POSTHOLE
PUNCTURE WELLHOLE WINDHOLE
PERTUSION PERFORATION
(— CAUSED BY LEAK) GIME
(— FOR MOLTEN METAL) SUMP
(— FOR WIRE) HUB HUBB
(— IN BANK OF STREAM) GAT
(— IN GARMENT) FRACK
(— IN GUILLOTINE) LUNET LUNETTE
(— IN HEDGE) SMEUSE
(— IN HIDE) BOTHOLE
(— IN KEEL) LIMBER RUFFLE
(— IN KIVA) SIPAPU
(— IN ONE STROKE) ACE
(— IN STREAM BED) DUMP
(— INTO MOLD) GEAT SPRUE
(— IN WIND INSTRUMENT) LILL
(— THREE BELOW PAR) ALBATROSS
(AIR —) SPIRACLE
(BREATHING —) SUSPIRAL
(DEEP —) POT GOURD
(FOX —) KENNEL
(FULL OF —S) POROSE
(GOLF —) CUP DOGLEG
(KIND OF —) OZONE
(MELON —) GILGAI
(RABBIT —) CLAPPER
(SAND —) BUNKER
(SINK —) SOAKAWAY
(SPY —) JUDAS
(TO —) GOBBLE HAZARD
(VOLCANIC —) FUMAROLE
(VOLCANIC STEAM —S) SOFFIONI
(WATER —) DUB CHARCO
(WELL-LIKE —) CASCAN
(PREF.) TREMATO TROGLO
HOLIDAY HOL PLAY TIDE WAKE FERIE
FESTA MERRY FIESTA JOVIAL
FESTIVE HALEDAY PLAYDAY
YEARDAY PASSOVER SHABUOTH
WAYGOOSE
(EASTERN —) TET
(HALF —) REMEDY
(PL.) FERIA
HOLINESS PIETY HALIDOM
SANCTITY SANCTIMONY
HOLLA SOLA
HOLLAND (ALSO SEE
NETHERLANDS) FROGLAND
HOLLANDAISE GULASH GOULASH
HOLLAND BLUE ORION
HOLLANDER DUTCHMAN
HOLLANDS GIN GENEVA
HOLLER HALLO HOLLO HALLOO
KYOODLE
HOLLO SOLA
HOLLOW DEN DIP KEX BOSS BOWL
CAVE COMB COOM COVE DALK DELL
DENT DINT DISH DOCK DOKE FOLD
GORE HOLE HOLL HOWE IDLE KEXY

KHUD SINK SLOT THIN VAIN VOID
WAME BASIN BIGHT CAVUM CHASE
CLEFT CUPPY DELVE DOWFF EMPTY
FALSE FOSSA GAUNT GOYLE GULCH
GULLY HEUCH LAIGH NOTCH SCOOP
SINUS SLOCK SWAMP WOMBY
ARMPIT BULLAN CAVITY CORRIE
DIMPLE HOLLER INDENT KETTLE
MATRIX POCKET RECESS SOCKET
SUNKEN VACANT WALLOW BOXLIKE
CONCAVE UNSOUND VACUITY
CAVITARY CHELIDON CORELESS
CRUCIBLE FISTULAR FOSSETTE
NOTCHING SPECIOUS
(— AMONG HILLS) SWAG SLOCK
(— BETWEEN BREASTS) SLOT
CLEAVAGE
(— BETWEEN WAVES) TROUGH
(— IN COIL OF CABLE) TIER
(— IN HILL) COOM CLASH COMBE
COOMB CORRIE
(— IN SNOW) IGLOO
(— IN TILE) KEY
(— OF ARM) LEAD ARMPIT
(— OF EAR) ALVEARY
(— OF EYEBALL) ORBIT ORBITA
(— OF FOOT) VOLA
(— OF HANDS) GOUPEN GOWPEN
(— OF HORSE'S TOOTH) MARK
(— OF KNEE) HAM
(— OF ROOF) VALLEY
(— OUT) CUT DIG BORE HOWK KERF
CAVERN EXCISE
(LONG —) GROOVE
(NOT —) SOLID FARCTATE
(PASSING —) CRESCENT
(ROUND —) CIRQUE
(SECLUDED —) GLEN
(SPRINGY —) GAW
(WOODED —) GULLY
(PREF.) CAEL(I)(O) CAVI CAVO CEL(O)
COEL(I)(O)
(SUFF.) COELOUS COELUS
HOLLOWED HOWKIT CONCAVE
SPOUTED
HOLLOW-EYED HAGGARD
HOLLOWNESS VANITY INANITY
VACUITY CONCAVITY
HOLLY HOLM HULL ILEX MATE
DAHOON HOLLIN HULVER TOLLON
YAUPON CATBERRY INKBERRY
MILKMAID
HOLLYHOCK HOCK ALTHEA
MALLOW
HOLM AIT ISLET ISLAND BOTTOMS
HOLM-OAK ILEX
HOLOFERNES (SLAYER OF —)
JUDITH
HOLOTHURIAN TREPANG
HOLY SRI SHRI HUACA SAINT SANTO
DEVOUT DIVINE SACRAL SACRED
BLESSED PERFECT SAINTLY SINLESS
BLISSFUL INNOCENT REVEREND
SPIRITUAL SANCTIMONIOUS
(— MAN) SADHU
(— OF HOLIES) ADYT ADYTUM
(ALL —) PANAGIA
(PREF.) HAGI(O) HIERATICO HIER(O)
HOSIO SANCTI SANCTO SEMNO
(SUFF.) HIERIC
HOLY BASIL TULCE TOOLSY
HOLY SPIRIT PARACLETE
HOLY STONE REAR BIBLE
HOLY WOOD LIGNUM
HOMAGE FEE COURT HONOR
YMAGE FEALTY MANRED INCENSE
LOYALTY MANRENT MANSHIP
OVATION SERVICE TREWAGE
EMINENCE OBEISANCE
(PAY —) GENUFLECT
(PAY — TO) KNEEL
(SUPREME —) LATRIA
HOME BYE DEN HAM BASE CASA
HAME HUNK WIKE ABODE ASTRE
BEING DOMUS FOYER HAUNT
SMOKE HEARTH HEIMAT BLIGHTY
SHELTER DOMICILE FIRESIDE
ROOFTREE
(— FOR THE POOR) HOSPICE
(— OF REFUGE) HOSPICE
(— OF THE BLESSED) GIMLE
(AT THE — OF) CHEZ
(FUNERAL —) CHAPEL
(HARVEST —) KERN KIRN MELL
HOCKEY
(IN THE — OF) CHEZ
(KIND OF —) MOTOR
(NURSING —) CLINIC
(REST —) FARM HOSTEL
(PREF.)
(RETURN —) NOST(O)
HOMELAND HAVAIKI BANTUSTAN
HOMELESS ROOFLESS VAGABOND
HOMELIKE HOMEY HAMEIL HAMILT
HOMISH HOMESOME
HOMELINESS YEOMANRY
HOMELY FOUL UGLY PLAIN DUDGEN
RUGGED PLAINLY EVERYDAY_
FAMILIAR HOMELIKE
HOME PLATE RUBBER
HOMER KOR CHOMER
HOME RUN SWAT SWOT BLAST
DINGER
HOMESICKNESS HEIMWEH
NOSTALGIA
HOMESPUN KERSEY RUSSET
RAPLOCH
HOMESTEAD TOFT TREF ONSET
PLACE WORTH GRANGE TYDDYN
FARMERY ONSTEAD STEADING
HOMESTEADER NESTER
HOMETHRUST HAI HAY
HOMEWORK PREP
HOMICIDE DEATH MORTH KILLING

HOMILETIC KERYSTIC
HOMILY PRONE OMELIE POSTIL
SERMON
HOMINY SAMP NASAUMP
HOMOEOMERY GERM SEED
(PL.) SPERMATA
HOMOGENEITY SAMENESS
HOMOGENEOUS LIKE SOLID
GLOBAL SIMPLE COMPACT MASSIVE
SIMILAR
(PREF.) HOL(O) IS(O)
HOMOGENOUS ENTIRE
HOMOLOGUE CYANINE HOMOTYPE
(PREF.) NOR
HOMOPHONY MONODY
HOMORGANIC COGNATE
HOMOSEXUAL GAY FLIT
(— WOMAN) LESBIAN
(FEMALE —) DIKE DYKE
HOMOZYGOUS PURE ISOGENIC

HONDURAS

CAPITAL: TEGUCIGALPA
COIN: PESO CENTAVO LEMPIRA
DEPARTMENT: YORO COLON COPAN
VALLE OLANCHO
GULF: FONSECA
INDIAN: MAYA PAYA SUMO ULVA
CARIB LENCA PIPIL TAURA JICAQUE
MISKITO MOSQUITO
ISLAND: ROATAN
ISLANDS: BAY BAHIA
LAKE: CRIBA YOJOA BREWER
MEASURE: VARA MILLA MECATE
TERCIA CAJUELA MANZANA
MOUNTAINS: PIJA AGALTA CELAQUE
PORT: LACEIBA TRUJILLO
RIVER: COCO SICO ULUA AGUAN
LEMPA NEGRO TINTO WANKS
PATUCA SULACO GUAYAPE
OLANCHO SEGOVIA SANTIAGO
RUINS: TENAMPUA
TOWN: TELA YORO COPAN LAPAZ
ROATAN GRACIAS LACEIBA
TRUJILLO YUSCARAN JUTICALPA
WEIGHT: CAJA LIBRA

HONE HO STROP STROKE STRICKLE
HONEST FAIR GOOD JAKE TRUE
AFALD FRANK LEGIT ROUND SOUND
WHITE CANDID DEXTER DINKUM
ENTIRE PROPER RUSTIC SINGLE
SQUARE SINCERE UPRIGHT
RIGHTFUL STRAIGHT
(BARELY —) SHARP
HONESTLY TRULY DINKUM
HONEST INDEED SINGLY SQUARE
SQUARELY
HONESTY FAITH HONOR SATIN
CANDOR EQUITY LUNARY REALTY
VERITY JUSTICE LUNARIA PROBITY
BOLBONAC FAIRNESS FIDELITY
MOONWORT SATINPOD YEOMANRY

HONEY MEL MELL HINNY HONEYBUN
(— BEVERAGE) MULSE
(COLOR OF —) AMBER
(ROSE-FLAVORED —) RODOMEL
(PREF.) MELI(TTO) MELL(I)
HONEYBEE (ALSO SEE BEE) BEE
GYNE KING DRANE DRONE QUEEN
DINGAR DRONER EGATES CYPRIAN
DEBORAH DESERET KOOTCHA
MELISSA STINGER ACULEATE
ANGELITO
HONEY BUZZARD PERN
HONEYCOMB COMB FRAME
WAXCOMB
(PREF.) CERIO FAVI
HONEYCOMBED FAVOSE
FAVEOLATE
HONEYCREEPER IIWI MAMO PALILA
DREPANID GUITGUIT
HONEYDEW MANNA MILDEW
HONEY EATER OO IAO TUI MOHO
MINER TENUI MANUAO MAOMAO
ROSTER BELLBIRD WURRALUH
HONEYED SWEET HYBLAN SUGARY
SUGARED HYBLAEAN LUSCIOUS
HONEY GUIDE MOROC
HONEY MESQUITE ALGAROBA
HONEYPOD
HONEY PLANT HOYA HUAJILLO
HONEY-STONE MELLITE
HONEYSUCKLE VINE SUCKLE
WEIGELA BINDWEED SUCKLING
WOODBINE

HONG KONG

BAY: SHEKO REPULSE
CAPITAL: VICTORIA
COIN: CENT DOLLAR
DISTRICT: WANCHAI
GARDENS: TIGERBALM
ISLAND: LANTAO
MOUNTAIN: CASTLE VICTORIA
PENINSULA: KOWLOON
TOWN: KOWLOON

HONING (— DEVICE) OILSTONE
HONK KONK YANG CRONK
HONKER GOOSE
HONOR BAY ORE CLIO FAME FETE
HORN KUDO LAUD ADORE CROWN
GLORY GRACE HERRY IZZAT MENSE
MENSK SPEAK TREAT CREDIT
DECORE ENHALO ESTEEM HOMAGE
HONOUR LAUREL PRAISE REVERE
SALUTE WORTHY DIGNITY EMBLAZE
GLORIFY HONESTY MANSHIP
RESPECT WORSHIP ACCOLADE
DECORATE GRANDEZA TASHREEF
(PL.) ACES
(PREF.) TIMO
HONORABLE DEAR FREE GOOD
DIGNE NOBLE OPIME WHITE GENTLE
HONEST HONORA LORDLY SQUARE

UPRIGHT GENEROUS HANDSOME
HONORARY
HONORABLENESS HONESTY
HONORABLY GENTLY
HONORARIUM SALARY DOUCEUR
ALTARAGE HONORARY
HONORED GOOD FAMOUS LAUREL
LAURELED PRESTIGIOUS
HONORIFIC MAGNIFIC
HOOD HOW COIF COWL GOON HEAD
HUDE JACK AMICE ALMUCE BIGGIN
BONNET BURLET CALASH CAMAIL
CANOPY CAPOTE CUTOFF DOMINO
FUNNEL MANTLE RAFFIA BANGKOK
BASHLYK CALOTTE CAPUCHE
MOBSTER BLINDAGE CALYPTRA
CAPUCCIO CAPUTIUM CHAPERON
CUCULLUS FOOLSCAP GANGSTER
LIRIPIPE LIRIPOOP MAZARINE
TROTCOZY NITHSDALE
(— AND CAPE COMBINED) FALDETTA
(— FOR EVENING WEAR) CAPELINE
(— OF BOILER) VOMIT
(— OF CARRIAGE) HEAD
(— OF MAIL) COIF CAMAIL COIFFE
(— OF REFRACTORY MATERIAL)
MANTLE
(— OF VEHICLE) TOP CAPOTE
(— ON CUPBOARD) TREMOR
(— ON HORSES) BLINKER
(— OVER DOOR) MARQUISE
(— OVER SIGNAL LIGHT) VISOR
(LENS —) SUNSHADE
(MONK'S) COWL
(STIRRUP —) TAPADERO
(STRAW —) JAVA
(WOMAN'S) CURTOUT VOLUPER
HOODED COWLED GALEATE
CUCULLATE
HOODED CROW HOODIE
GRAYBACK GREYBACK
HOODED MERGANSER SMEW
SNOWL SPIKE TADPOLE TOWHEAD
MOSSHEAD
HOODED SEAL WIG HOOD
HOODCAP
HOODLUM YOB HOOD LOUT PUNK
BADDY YOBBO YOKEL BADDIE
SKOLLY LURCHER HOOLIGAN
LARRIKIN
HOODOO JINX
HOODWINK MOP DUPE FOOL SEEL
BLEAR BLIND BLUFF CHEAT BAFFLE
CLOYNE DELUDE GAMMON WIMPLE
AVEUGLE BEGUILE BLINKER DECEIVE
MISLEAD INVEIGLE
HOOEY BUSHWAH
HOOF CLOOF CLOOT COFFIN UNGUIS
UNGULA CLOOTIE HOOFLET
FOREHOOF
(PREF.) UNGULI
HOOFED UNGULATE
HOO-HA ADO

HOOK DOG GAB JIG PEW TUG CLIP
DRAG FLAG GAFF HAKE HUCK KILP
MEAK NOCK PEVY PRIN PUGH SETT
SKID STAY TACK CATCH CHAPE
CLEEK CLICK CRAMP CROME CROOK
DRAIL HAMUS ONCIN PEAVY PREEN
SARPE SPOON TACHE UNCUS
BECKET DETENT HANGLE HINGLE
PINTLE TENTER AGRAFFE GAMBREL
GRUNTER HAMULUS HITCHER
HOOKLET KNUCKLE NUTHOOK
PELICAN PENNANT PINHOOK
POTHOOK RAMHEAD SNIGGLE
SPERKET UNCINUS BOATHOOK
CROTCHET GRABHOOK PORTHOOK
PULLBACK VULSELLA WEEDHOOK
(— FISH) FOUL HANG SNAG DRAIL
HITCH STRIKE SNIGGLE FISHHOOK
(— FOR BACON) COMB
(— FOR KETTLE) KILP HANGLE
TRAMMEL
(— FOR POT) DRACKEN POTHOOK
SLOWRIE
(— FOR TWISTING HEMP) WHIRL
WHIRLER
(BENCH —) JACK
(BOAT —) HITCHER
(BOXING —) CROSS
(BUTCHER'S —) GAFF
(COUPLING —) JIGGER
(KIND OF —) MOUTH
(LONG-HANDLED —) HOCK MEAK
(MUSICAL —) FLAG PENNANT
(PRUNING —) SARPE CALABOZO
(REAPING —) HINK TWIBILL
(SAFETY —) CLEVIS
(SKIDDING —S) GRAB
(2 —S FASTENED AT SHANKS)
DOUBLES
HOOKAH KALIAN CHILLUM
NARGHILE
HOOKED ADUNC UNCATE UNCOUS
ADUNCAL FALCATE HAMATED
HAMULAR ADUNCATE ADUNCOUS
AQUILINE HAMIFORM UNCINATE
HOOKEDNESS ADUNCITY
HOOKER-OUT STICKMAN
HOOK-SHAPED ANKYROID
HOOKUP CIRCUIT
HOOKWORM STRONGYL
HOOLIGAN ROUGH ROWDY TOUGH
APACHE GOONDA LARRIKIN
(SOUTH AFRICAN —) TSOTSI
(PL.) AMALAITA
HOOP RIB BAIL BAND BOND BOOL
CLIP GIRD GIRR PASS RING TIRE
GARTH GIRTH FRETTE HOOPLE
LAGGIN WICKET CIRCLET GARLAND
TROCHUS TRUNDLE
(— FOR A SPAR) BANGLE
(— FOR BARREL) BAND GIRD GIRTH
(— FOR LAMPSHADE) HARP
(— FOR ORE BUCKET) CLEVIS

(— FOR WINNOWING GRAIN) WEIGHT
(— NET) TRUNK
(— OF WHEEL) STRAKE
(— TO STRENGTHEN GUN) FRETTE
(HALF —) BAIL BALE
HOOPED RUNG
HOOPLA FANFARE
HOOPOE HOOP UPUPA WHOOP
IRRISOR DUNGBIRD PICARIAN
HOOPSKIRT TUBTAIL
HOOP SNAKE WAMPUM
HOOPSTER CAGER
HOOSE HUSK
HOOSEGOW JUG JAIL POKY POKEY
HOOSIER SCHOOLMASTER
(AUTHOR OF —) EGGLESTON
(CHARACTER IN —) BUD PETE JONES
MEANS RALPH SMALL WHITE
HANNAH MARTHA SANDER SHOCKY
WALTER HAWKINS JOHNSON
MATILDA PEARSON THOMSON
HOOSIER STATE INDIANA
HOOT CURR WHOO WHOOP WHOOT
EXPLODE ULULATE
(— OF REPROACH) FIE
HOOVE BLOAT
HOOVER VACUUM
HOP HIP NIP FLIP JUMP LEAP BOUND
HITCH SWINE FLIERS GAMBOL
SPRING TITTUP CROWHOP HOPBIND
HOPVINE LUPULUS SKIPPER
HOPBUSH AKE AKEAKE
HOP CLOVER SHAMROCK
SUCKLING
HOPE WON DEEM SPES TROW
COMBE THINK TRUST DESIRE
EXPECT PERDUE ESPEIRE THOUGHT
SPERANZA VELLEITY
(VAIN —) PIPE WANHOPE
HOPEFUL FOND BUOYANT
SANGUINE WENLICHE
HOPEFULNESS OPTIMISM
HOPELESS DULL ALLUP ABJECT
FORLORN DOWNCAST
HOPELESSNESS ANOMIE DESPAIR
HOPHNI (BROTHER OF —) PHINEHAS
(FATHER OF —) ELI
HOP HORNBEAM DEERWOOD
HARDHACK IRONWOOD
HOPI MOKI MOQUI
HOP-LIKE LUPULINE
HOPPER CURB JACK BUNKER
CLOSET HOPPLE MACARONI
HOPPLE HOBBLE PASTERN SIDELANG
HOPS SHATTER
(— BETWEEN 2 AND 4 YEARS) OLDS
HOPSCOTCH POTSY HOPPERS
PALLALL PEEVERS
HOP TREE RUEWORT WINGSEED
HORDE ARMY CAMP CLAN PACK
CROWD GROUP SWARM LEGION
THRONG
(INNER —) BUKEYEF

HOREHOUND HENBIT MARVEL
WONDER MARRUBE
HORI (FATHER OF —) LOTAN
(SON OF —) SHAPHAT
HORIZON LAYER VERGE COMPASS
FINITOR ORTERDE SKYLINE
HORIZONTAL LEVEL LINEAR NAIANT
ACLINAL STRAIGHT
HORIZONTALLY FLATLY BARWAYS
BARWISE ENDLONG FESSWAYS
FESSWISE
HORMIGO QUIRA
HORMONE HGH ACTH KININ
CORTIN LUTEIN EQUILIN ESTRIOL
ESTRONE GASTRIN INSULIN
RELAXIN STEROID THEELIN THEELOL
ANDROGEN ECDYSONE ENDOCRIN
ESTROGEN FLORIGEN GALACTIN
LACTOGEN OESTRIOL SECRETIN
CORTISONE
(PITUITARY —) ACTH
HORN BEAK BATON BUGLE CONCH
CORNO CORNU SHOOT ANTLER
CLAXON KLAXON OXHORN TOOTER
ALPHORN ALTHORN ANTENNA
BUFFALO CLARONE FOGHORN
HELICON HUTCHET OUTHORN
PRICKET SHOPHAR UNICORN
BEAKIRON BUCKHORN CLAVICOR
CORNICLE OLIPHANT SLUGHORN
STAGHORN WALDHORN
NOISEMAKER
(— NOTE) MORT
(— OF COW) SCUR
(— OF CRESCENT MOON) CUSP
(— OF DILEMMA) PIKE
(— OF DRINK) SLOSH
(— OF YOUNG STAG) BUNCH
(BUDDING —) SHOOT
(DRINKING —) RHYTON
(ENGLISH —) CA
(FRENCH —) CORNO
(GREY —) COLUMN
(HUNTER'S —) HUTCHET WALDHORN
(INSECT'S —) ANTENNA
(IVORY —) OLIFANT
(RAM'S —) SHOPHAR SHOFAR
(RUDIMENTARY —) SLUG
(STUNTED —) SCUR
(PREF.) CORNEO CORNI CORNU
(SUFF.) CERA(S) CEROS CEROUS
CERUS CORN
HORNBEAM HARDBEAM HARDHACK
HORNWOOD IRONWOOD
HORNBILL TOCK CALAO TOUCAN
BUCEROS HOMURAI BROMVOEL
PICARIAN YEARBIRD
HORNBLENDE SIDERITE
HORNED FORKED CORNUTE
(PREF.) CERA CERVI CORNEO CORNI
CORNU
HORNED DACE CHUB
HORNED POUT CATFISH

HORNED SCREAMER ANHIMA
KAMACHI KAMICHI UNICORN
HORNED VIPER WAMPUM
CERASTES
HORNET VESPA VESPID STINGER
HORNGELD CORNAGE
HORNLESS NAT NOT MOIL POLL
DODDY MULEY POLEY DODDED
HUMBLE HUMMEL MAILIE MULLEY
POLLED ACEROUS
HORNPIPE MATELOTE
HORN POPPY SQUATMORE
HORNSTONE CHERT KERALITE
HORNSWOGGLE DUPE
HORNTAIL SIREX ORYSSID
UROCERID WOODWORM
HORNWORT COONTAIL HORNWEED
HORNWRACK SEAMAT
HORNY WAUKIT CALLOUS CERATOID
CORNEOUS KERASINE KERATOID
HORNYHEAD CHUB
HOROSCOPE SCOPE THEME FIGURE
GENESIS NATIVITY
HORRIBLE DIRE GRIM UGLY AWFUL
BLACK GREAT GRISLY HORRID
GEARFUL GHASTLY HIDEOUS
HORRENT UNSLOGH DREADFUL
GRUESOME HORRIFIC SHOCKING
TERRIBLE MONSTROUS
HORRID GRIM UGLY AWFUL ROUGH
RUGGED SNUFFY UGSOME WICKED
HIDEOUS DREADFUL GRUESOME
HORRIBLE SHOCKING
HORRIFIC FEARFUL
HORRIFIED AGHAST GHASTLY
HORRENT
HORRIFY APPAL AGRISE DISMAY
ENHORROR
HORROR FEAR DREAD TERROR
CONSTERNATION
(PL.) JIMJAMS
HORRORS CREEPS
HORSA (BROTHER OF —) HENGIST
HORS D'OEUVRE CANAPE RELISH
OUTWORK ZAKUSKA
(PL.) ASSIETTE
HORS D'OEUVRE) TAPA
HORSE BAY COB CUT DUN GEE GRI
NAG PAD POT RIP TIT ARAB AVER
BARB DOON GOER GROG HACK
HAND HOSS JADE MARE MOKE PRAD
PROD QUAD RACK RIDE ROAN ROIL
SKIN STUD TEAM TURK WEED YAWD
ZAIN AIVER ARION ARVAK BEAST
BIDET BLACK BROCK CAPLE CAPUL
CHUNK CLYDE CREAM CROCK
DUMMY EQUID FAVEL GLYDE GRANI
HAIRY HOBBY MILER MOREL PACER
PINTO PIPER POLER PUNCH RACER
ROGUE RUNSY SCREW SHIER SHIRE
SKATE SOMER STEED STIFF TACKY
WALER WIDGE ALEZAN AMBLER
BANKER BOLTER BRONCO BRUMBY

BUCKER BUSSER CABBER CALICO
CASTER CHASER CHEVAL COLLOP
CURTAL CUSSER DAPPLE DOBBIN
DRIVER ENTIRE EQUINE FENCER
FILLER GANGER GARRON GLEYDE
GRULLA HUNTER JUMPER KEFFEL
LEADER MAIDEN MORGAN NUBIAN
ORLOFF OUTLAW PELTER PLATER
POSTER PULLER RACKER ROARER
ROUNCY RUNNER SAVAGE SORREL
STAGER TARPAN TRACER TURKEY
VANNER WARPER WEAVER ALSVINN
ALSVITH ARABIAN BARBARY
BELGIAN BOARDER CABALLO
CHARGER CLICKER CLIPPER
COACHER COCOTTE COURSER
CRIBBER CRIOLLA CRITTER DRAFTER
FLEMISH GALATHE GELDING
GIGSTER GRUNTER HACKNEY
KNACKER LEEFANG MONTURE
MUSTANG NEIGHER PACOLET
PALFREY PIEBALD PRANCER
PRANKER RATTLER REESTER
REFUSER REMOUNT RUNAWAY
SADDLER SLEDDER SLEEPER
SPANKER STAGGIE STEPPER
SUFFOLK SUMPTER TRAPPER
TRESTLE TROOPER TROTTER
WHEELER ARDENNES BATHORSE
BUCKSKIN CHESTNUT CHEVALET
COCKTAIL COLICKER CREATURE
CYLLAROS DEMISANG DESTRIER
EOHIPPUS FOOTROPE FRIPPERY
GALLOPER GALLOWAY HRIMFAXI
KADISCHI MACHINER OUTSIDER
PALOMINO RIDGLING ROADSTER
SKEWBALD STALLION STIBBLER
TRIPPLER WHISTLER YARRAMAN
CLYDESDALE
(— ACT) MANAGE
(— ANCESTOR) EOHIPPUS
(— CERTAIN NOT TO WIN) STIFF
(— ESTABLISHMENT) HARAS
(— LOSING FIXED RACE) STUMER
STUMOUR
(— OF ACHILLES) XANTHUS
(— OF ALEXANDER THE GREAT)
BUCEPHALUS
(— OF CALIGULA) INCITATUS
(— OF DALE EVANS) BUTTERMILK
(— OF DICK TURPIN) BLACKBESS
(— OF DON QUIXOTE) ROSINANTE
(— OF DUKE OF WELLINGTON)
COPENHAGEN
(— OF GENERAL CUSTER)
COMANCHE
(— OF GENERAL SHERMAN) RIENZI
(— OF LONE RANGER) SILVER
(— OF MOHAMMED) ALBORAK
(— OF NAPOLEON) MORENGO
(— OF ORLANDO) VEGLIANTINO
(— OF RINALDO) BAYARD
(— OF ROBERT E. LEE) TRAVELLER

(— **OF ROY ROGERS**) TRIGGER
(— **OF SIGURD**) GRANI
(— **OF STONEWALL JACKSON**)
LITTLESORREL
(— **OF TEX RITTER**) WHITEFLASH
(— **OF TOM MIX**) TONY
(— **OF ULYSSES GRANT**) CINCINNATI
(— **OF UNIFORM DARK COLOR**) ZAIN
(— **OF WILL ROGERS**) SOAPSUDS
BOOTLEGGER
(— **RACE**) WALKOVER
(—**S RUNNING BEHIND**) RUCK
(— **THAT WON'T START**) STICK
(**ARABIAN** —) ARAB KOHL ARABIAN
(**BALKY** —) JIB JIBBER
(**BREED OF** —) SHETLAND
APPALOOSA PERCHERON
CLYDESDALE LIPPIZANER
(**BROKEN-DOWN** —) JADE CROCK
SCREW DURGAN GARRAN
(**CALICO** —) PINTO
(**CASTRATED** —) GELDING
(**CLUMSY** —) STAMMEL
(**DECREPIT** —) SKATE GLEYDE
(**DRAFT** —) HAIRY PUNCH SHIRE
BEETEWK BELGIAN SUFFOLK
PERCHERON
(**DROVE OF** —S) ATAJO
(**EASY-PACED** —) PAD
(**FALLOW** —) FAVEL
(**FAMILY** —) DOBBIN
(**FAMOUS** —) SILVER TRIGGER
(**FAST** —) GANGER
(**FEMALE** —) MARE FILLY
(**FLEMISH** —) ROIL
(**GOLD** —) PALOMINO
(**GRAY** —) SCHIMMEL
(**HIGH-SPIRITED** —) STEPPER
(**IMAGINARY** —) AULLAY
(**IMMUNIZED** —) BLEEDER
(**INFERIOR** —) PLUG CAYUSE PLATER
(**JUMPING** —) LEPPER
(**MALE** —) STALLION
(**NEAR** —) HAND
(**OLD** —) JADE PLUG PROD YAUD
AIVER CROCK
(**PACK** —) BIDET SUMPTER
(**PART OF** —) EAR EYE JAW RIB FACE
HOCK HOOF KNEE LOIN MANE NECK
NOSE POLL TAIL BELLY CHEEK
CROUP ELBOW FLANK MOUTH THIGH
BREAST CANNON GASKIN HAUNCH
STIFLE BUTTOCK CORONET FETLOCK
FOREARM NOSTRIL PASTERN
WITHERS FOREHEAD FORELOCK
SHOULDER THROATLATCH
(**PIEBALD** —) CALICO
(**RANGE** —) FANTAIL
(**ROAN** —) SCHIMMEL
(**SADDLE** —) MOUNT
(**SHAFT** —) SHAFTER THILLER
(**SHAGGY** —) ALTAI
(**SLUGGISH** —) HOG

(**SMALL** —) NAG TIT BIDET GENET
HOBBY CANUCK JENNET GALLOWAY
(**STOCKY** —) COB
(**TEAM OF** —S) CARTWARE
(**TEAM OF 3** —S **WITH LEADER**)
UNICORN
(**TRICK** —) SIMON
(**TV** —) MRED
(**UNBROKEN** —) BRONCO
(**VICIOUS** —) LADINO
(**WILD** —) BRONC FUZZY BRUMBY
KUMRAH OUTLAW TARPAN
JUGHEAD BANGTAIL FUZZTAIL
WARRIGAL
(**WINGED** —) PEGASUS
(**WORN-OUT** —) HACK GARRAN
KNACKER CROWBAIT
(**WORTHLESS** —) JADE SHACK
KEFFEL
(**YOUNG** —) TIT COLT FOAL STAG
STOT STAGGIE
(**2-YEAR OLD** —) TWINTER
(**3** —S **ABREAST**) TROIKA
(**3** —S **ONE BEHIND ANOTHER**)
RANDEM
(**4** —S **ABREAST**) QUADRIGA
(**PL.**) MANADA STABLE UNICORN
(**PREF.**) HIPP(O)
(**SUFF.**) HIPPUS
HORSE BALM KNOBWEED
KNOTROOT RICHWEED
HORSE BLANKET RUG MANTA
HORSE BOY TRACER
HORSE CHESTNUT CONKER
HORSE-CLOTH MANTA
HORSECLOTH HOUSE HOUSING
HORSE DEALER COPER CHANTER
COURSER
HORSE-EYE JACK XUREL
HORSE FENNEL SESELI
HORSEFLESH JACK
HORSEFLY BOT GAD CLEG CLEGG
STOUT BOTFLY BREEZE GADBEE
GADFLY BULLDOG DEERFLY TABANID
HORSEHAIR SETON
HORSELAUGH GUFFAW
HORSELEECH ALUKAH
HORSELOAD SEAM
HORSE MACKEREL TUNNY
SAUREL
HORSEMAN RIDER CHARRO
COWBOY HUSSAR KNIGHT RUTTER
COURIER PICADOR PRICKER
CAVALIER GALLOPER
(**PL.**) HORSE CAVALRY
HORSEMANSHIP CAVALRY
HORSEMINT RIGNUM
HORSE MUSHROOM WHITECAP
HORSE NETTLE SOLANUM
HORSEPLAY HIJINKS
(**PANTOMIME** —) RALLY
HORSEPOWER SOUP
HORSEPOX GREASE

HORSE-RACE DERBY
HORSE-RADISH MAROR MOROR
REDCOLL
HORSE-RADISH TREE BEN BEHN
BEHEN
HORSESHOE TIP SHOE PLATE
HOBBER LUNETTE
HORSETAIL TAIL PRELE TOADPIPE
HORSETAIL LICHEN TREEHAIR
HORSETAIL TREE AGOHO AGOJO
HORSEWEED COCASH COWTAIL
HOGWEED FIREWEED SCABIOUS
HORSEWHIP BEAT CHABOUK
HORTATORY EMOTIVE
HORTICULTURIST
          (ALSO SEE BOTANIST)
HORUS SEPT SOPT SEPTI HORMAKHU
(FATHER OF —) OSIRIS
(MOTHER OF —) ISIS
HOSACKIA ACMISPON
HOSE LINE VAMP HOSEN GASKIN
BROGUES BULLION HOSIERY
CHAUSSES HANDLINE HOSEPIPE
HOSEA OSEE
(FATHER OF —) BEERI
HOSHAIAH (SON OF —) AZARIAH
JEZANIAH
HOSHEA (FATHER OF —) NUN
AZAZIAH
HOSIERY HOSE KNEESOCK
KNITWEAR
(— WORKER) LOOPER
HOSPICE IMARET DIACONIA
HOSPITAL
HOSPITABLE DOUCE CLEVER
DOULCE SOCIAL CORDIAL FRIENDLY
HOSPITAL BEDLAM CRECHE SPITAL
COLLEGE LAZARET PESTHOUSE
POLYCLINIC
(— AREA) ICU
(— WARD) ICU
(MENTAL —) SNAKEPIT
(MOVABLE —) AMBULANCE
(PRIVATE —) HOME
HOSPITALITY SALT MENSE
XENODOCHY
HOSPODAR VOIVOD GOSPODAR
HOST SUM ARMY FYRD WARE
CROWD EMCEE HORDE JASON
MAKER POWER SWARM WERED
LEGION LODGER NATION THRONG
BALEBOS COMPANY FYRDUNG
SACRING VIANDER LANDLORD
PARTICLE MULTITUDE
(— OF INVADERS) HERE
(EUCHARISTIC —) LAMB SACRING
(PL.) SABAOTH
(SUFF.) XENOUS XENY
HOSTA NIOBE FUNKIA
HOSTAGE BORROW PLEDGE SURETY
RANSOMER
HOSTEL INN ENTRY HOSTAGE
KINGDOM HOSPITAL

HOSTELRY AUBERGE PARADOR
HOSTESS TAUPO LANDLADY
CHATELAINE
HOSTILE FOE HARD UGLY ALIEN
BLACK ENEMY FREMT HATEI STOUT
DEADLY FRIGID INFEST ADVERSE
ASOCIAL FIENDLY OPPOSED
UNQUERT WARLIKE CONTRARY
INIMICAL OPPOSITE
HOSTILITY WAR FEID FEUD HATE
ANIMUS ENMITY HATRED RANCOR
SCHISM DAGGERS RUPTURE
(PL.) WAR ARMS ARMOR WARFARE
HOSTLER NAGMAN OSTLER
HORSEBOY
HOT WARM ADUST CALID EAGER
FIERY ARDENT CALIDO ESTIVE
FERVID IGNITE STOLEN SULTRY
TORRID ANIMOSE ANIMOUS BOILING
BURNING CANDENT FERVENT
PEPPERY THERMAL CALIENTE
CAYENNED FEVERISH SEETHING
SIZZLING GANGBUSTERS
(— WATER) GOUP
HOTBED BED NEST HOTHOUSE
HOT-BLOODED VASCULAR
HOTBOX SMOKER STINKER
HOTDOG DOG FRANK WEENIE
WEINER WIENER WIENIE
FRANKFURTER
(— KIND OF PERSON) FIREBRAND
HOTEL INN SPA DIGS FLOP FONDA
HOUSE HYDRO HOSTEL HOTTLE
POSADA FLEABAG FONDACO
FUNDUCK GASTHOF HOSTELRY
(— AT AIRPORT) AIRTEL
(— NEAR AIRPORT) AIRTEL
(WATERSIDE —) BOATEL
HOTELKEEPER HOTELIER
HOTHAM (FATHER OF —) HEBER
HOTHAN (SON OF —) SHAMA JEHIEL
HOT-HEADED BRAINISH MADBRAIN
HOTHIR (FATHER OF —) HEMAN
HOTHOUSE STEW STOVE PINERY
FRUITERY
HOT ROD DRAGSTER
HOTSHOT HONCHO
HOT-TEMPERED PEPPERY
CHOLERIC SPITFIRE
HOTTENTOT NAMA TOTTY HOTNOT
KOKANA WITBOOI QUAEQUAE
(PL.) BALAO BALAWU
HOUND DOG PIE BAIT HARL HUNT
MUTE BESET BRACE BRACH ENTRY
HARRY LEASH LIMER SLATE AFGHAN
BASSET BEAGLE CANINE HARASS
HUNTER JOWLER LEAMER LUCERN
SLEUTH TUFTER CURTISE ENTRADA
GELLERT REDBONE SKIRTER
BARUKHZY BLUETICK BRATCHET
COURSING FOXHOUND
(BITCH —) BRACH
(CRY OF —) MUSIC

(EXTINCT —) TALBOT
(KIND OF —) BIZAN IBIZAN
(RELAY OF —S) VANLAY
(SLEUTH —) TALBOT
(SPECTRAL —) SHUCK
(PL.) RACHES
HOUND'S-TONGUE TORYWEED
HOUR URE TIDE TIME CURFEW
GHURRY
(CANONICAL —) NONE SEXT PRIME
TERCE MATINS TIERCE ORTHROS
VESPERS COMPLINE EVENSONG
(HALF —) BELL
(KILOWATT —) KELVIN
(KIND OF —) HAPPY
(LAST —S) DEATHBED
(STUDY —) PREP
(6 —S) QUADRANT
(PREF.) HORO
HOURGLASS (PART OF —) BULB
SAND FRAME WAIST
HOURLY HORAL HORARY
HOUSE BOX KEN CASA CRIB DOME
DUMP FIRM FLET HALL HELL HOLE
HOME RACE ROOF STOW ABODE
ADOBE AERIE BAHAY BANDA COVER
DACHA DOMUS HOOCH HOOSE
JACAL LODGE MEESE PLACE STAGE
WHARE BESTOW BIGGIN BOTTLE
CAMARA CASITA CASTLE CHEMIS
CLOTHE DUPLEX FAMILY HEARTH
HOOTCH MAISON PALACE PARISH
SINGLE STABLE WIGWAM BASTIDE
BIGGING CABOOSE CASSINE
EUDEMON FAZENDA HOGGERY
HOUSING MESUAGE QUARTER
SHELTER AEDICULA BARADARI
BUNGALOW DOMICILE DOVECOTE
DWELLING HACIENDA MEDSTEAD
MESSUAGE TENEMENT NOVITIATE
(— AND LAND) DEMESNE
(— AND 5 ACRES) COTE
(— FOR DOGS) KENNEL
(— FOR WOMEN) HAREM
(— IN BOROUGH) HAW
(— OF A MARABOUT) KOUBA
(— OF CORRECTION) BRIDEWELL
(— OF ILL-FAME) KIP
(— OF KNIGHTS TEMPLARS)
PRECEPTORY
(— OF LEGISLATURE) SEANAD
CHAMBER ASSEMBLY
(— OF PARLIAMENT) COMMONS
LAGTING REICHSTAG
(— OF PROSTITUTION) CRIB BAGNIO
BORDEL
(— OF REFUGE) MAGDALEN
MAGDALENE
(— OF THIEVES) KEN
(— OF WORSHIP) BETHEL CHURCH
(— WITH TRIANGULAR FRONT)
AFRAME
(APARTMENT —) INSULA

(ASTROLOGICAL —) ANGLE
(AUSTRALIAN —) HUMPY
(CHANGE —) DRY
(CHAPTER —) CABILDO
(CHEAP EATING —) SLAPBANG
(CLAY —) ADOBE TEMBE
(COACH —) REMISE
(COMMUNAL —) MORONG
(COUNTRY —) PEN DACHA CASINO
GRANGE QUINTA BASTIDE CHATEAU
(COW —) VACCARY
(DAIRY —) WICK
(DISREPUTABLE —) KEN
(EATING —) COOKSHOP
(EMPTY —) SQUAT
(ESKIMO —) IGLU IGLOO TOPEK
KASHGA KASHIMA
(FIJI —) BURE
(FORTIFIED —) GARRISON
(FULL —) SRO
(GAMBLING —) BANK HELL RIDOTTO
(GOVERNMENT —) KONAK
(GREEK —) FRAT SORORITY
FRATERNITY
(GRINDING —) HULL
(GROUP OF —S) CLUSTER
(HAWAIIAN —) HALE
(LODGING —) INN KIP HOST ENTRY
HOTEL HOSTEL
(LOG —) TILT
(MANOR —) HAM HALL COURT
PLACE SCHLOSS SEIGNEURY
(MERCANTILE —) HONG
(PLANETARY —) TOWER
(POULTRY —) ARK HENNERY
(PUBLIC —) INN PUB HOWF HOWFF
JOINT HOSTEL SHANTY CANTEEN
POTSHOP SNUGGERY
(RANCH —) HUT
(RELIGIOUS —) CELL CONVENT
KELLION MONASTERY PRESBYTERY
(RENTED —) LET
(REST —) DAK KHAN SERAI
(RETREAT —) CENACLE
(ROOMING —) DOSS FLOP FLEABAG
(ROYAL —) AERIE
(SENATE —) CURIA
(SMALL —) COT HUT BACH CELL
CABIN HOVEL SHACK CASITA
COTTAGE MAISONETTE
(SOD —) SODDY
(STILT —) CHIKEE CHICKEE
(SUMMER —) TRELLIS
(TENEMENT —) LAND CHAWL
(THATCHED —) BANDA
(TOY —) COBHOUSE
(TURKISH —) KONAK
(TYPE OF —) PREFAB
(PREF.) DOMI ECO OECO OIKO
STEG(O)
(SUFF.) OECA OECIA STEGE STEGITE
HOUSEBOAT BARGE HOUSER
WANGAN WANIGAN DAHABEAH

HOUSEBREAKER MILL JACOB
  MILLKEN
HOUSEBREAKING CRACK
HOUSECARL THINGMAN
HOUSECOAT DUSTER
HOUSED (— IN) PUTUPAT
  (NOT —) OUTLER
HOUSEFINCH BURION LINNET
  REDHEAD
HOUSEHOLD HIRED HOUSE FAMILY
  HOUSAL MEINIE MENAGE FIRESIDE
  MAINPAST
  (— GOD) LAR
  (PREF.) EC(O) OEC(O) OIKO
HOUSEHOLDER ASTRER
  GOODMAN GUIDMAN NAUKRAR
  FRANKLIN
HOUSEKEEPER HUSSY MATRON
HOUSELEEK JUBARB AYEGREEN
  HOMEWORT SENGREEN SILGREEN
HOUSEMATE DOMESTIC
HOUSE OF MIRTH (AUTHOR OF —)
  WHARTON
  (CHARACTER IN —) GUS BART JUDY
  LILY GRYCE PERCY SIMON BERTHA
  DORSET GEORGE SELDEN TRENOR
  LAURENCE PENISTON ROSEDALE
HOUSE OF SEVEN GABLES
  (AUTHOR OF —) HAWTHORNE
  (CHARACTER IN —) MAULE PHOEBE
  VENNER JAFFREY CLIFFORD
  HEPZIBAH HOLGRAVE PYNCHEON
HOUSEWARMING INFARE
HOUSEWIFE DAME FRAU FROW
  WIFE HUSSY VROUW BUSHWIFE
  HAUSFRAU
  (MEAN —) NIP
HOUSEY-HOUSEY BINGO
HOUSING BOX BAGE CASE DRUM
  TRAP BANJO BLIMP GLOBE HOUSE
  KIOSK BARREL RADOME SHIELD
  HOUSAGE SHELTER DOGHOUSE
  PADCLOTH PECTORAL PEDESTAL
  SHABRACK
  (HORSE'S —) BASE
  (PLASTIC —) RADOME
  (RADAR —) BLISTER
  (PL.) HOLSTERS
HOVA IMERINA
HOVEL HUT COSH CREW CRIB CRUE
  HELM HULK HULL BOTHY CHOZA
  HUTCH LODGE BOTHIE BURROW
  CRUIVE PONDOK
HOVELER HOBBLER HUFFLER
HOVEN BLOATING
HOVER BAIT FLIT HANG HOVE LOOM
  BROOD POISE FLUTTER HOVERER
HOW AS FOO HOO HOWE HOWEER
  HOWEVER QUOMODO WHEREBY
HOWDAH TOWER AMBARI
  AMBAREE
HOWEVER BUT THO YET ONLY
  HOWSO STILL THOUGH

HOW GREEN WAS MY VALLEY
  (AUTHOR OF —) LLEWELLYN
  (CHARACTER IN —) HUW BETA DAVY
  IVOR OWEN EVANS IANTO GWILYM
  IESTYN MARGED MORGAN
  BRONWEN ANGHARAD GRUFFYDD
HOWITZER HOWITZ LICORN UNICORN
HOWITZER SHELL OBUS
HOWL BAY WAP WOW BAWL GOWL
  GURL HURL RAVE WAUL WAWL YAWL
  YOLL YOUT YOWL TIGER WHEWL
  WRAWL BEHOWL STEVEN ULULATE
  (— VOCIFEROUSLY) TONGUE
HOWLER BONER ERROR ARAGUATO
HOWLER MONKEY MONO ARABA
  HOWLER GUARIBA GUEREBA
  STENTOR ALOUATTE
HOWLING ULULANT
HOY TJALK BILANDER CRUMSTER
HOYDEN MEG BLOWZE RIGSBY
  TOMBOY
HREIDMAR (SON OF —) REGIN
  FAFNER FAFNIR
H-SHAPED ZYGAL
HUAMUCHIL INGA
HUAVE WABI HUABI
HUB HOB BOSS NAVE STOCK CENTER
  CENTRE FAUCET HUBBLE SOCKET
  SPIDER OMPHALOS
  (— AND SPOKES) SPEECH
HUBBLE UPROAR TELESCOPE
HUBBLE-BUBBLE CALEAN KALIAN
  CALAHAN
HUBBUB ADO DIN COIL FLAP STIR
  CLAMOR FRAISE HUBBLE RABBLE
  RACKET TUMULT BOBBERY CLUTTER
  BROUHAHA HUBBABOO ROWDYDOW
  SPLATTER
HUCHEN HUSO
HUCHNOM TATU
HUCKLEBERRY HURT ERICAD
  CRACKERS
HUCKLEBERRY FINN (AUTHOR OF
  —) TWAIN CLEMENS
  (CHARACTER IN —) JIM TOM DUKE
  FINN HUCK JANE KING POLLY SALLY
  SUSAN WILKS JOANNA PHELPS
  SAWYER WATSON DOUGLAS
  GRANGERFORD SHEPHERDSON
HUCKSTER BADGER CADGER
  KIDDER HAGGLER KIDDIER TRUCKER
  OUTCRIER
HUDDLE RUCK HUNCH CRINGE
  CROUCH FUMBLE HOWDER HURTLE
  SCRUMP SHRIMP SHRINK CROODLE
  SCRINCH SCROOCH SCRUNCH
  SHUFFLE
HUDIBRAS (AUTHOR OF —) BUTLER
  (CHARACTER IN —) RALPHO
  CROWDERO HUDIBRAS SIDROPHEL
HUE RUD BLEE BLUE COND CYAN
  CHLOR COLOR GREEN LEMON
  SHOUT TAINT TINCT CHROMA

(DULL —) DRAB
(SOMBER —) DARK
HUELESS GRAY GREY
HUFF DOD PET BLOW RUFF TIFF
DRUNT SNUFF OFFENSE
(— AND PUFF) PANT
HUFFY FUFFY SHIRTY
HUG CLIP COLL COUL MOLD CREEM
CRUSH HALSE PRESS CUDDLE
HUDDLE HUGGLE STRAIN CHERISH
EMBRACE SQUEEZE
HUGE BIG FELL MAIN VAST ENORM
GIANT GREAT JUMBO LARGE STOUR
HEROIC IMMANE BANGING BUMPING
DECUMAN HIDEOUS IMMENSE
MASSIVE MONSTER TITANIC
COLOSSAL ENORMOUS GALACTIC
GIGANTIC MOUNTAIN PYTHONIC
SLASHING SWAPPING THUMPING
HUMONGOUS THWACKING
MOUNTAINOUS
HUGENESS ENORMITY
HUGUENOT CAMISARD
HUGUENOTS, LES (COMPOSER OF
—) MEYERBEER
HUISACHE WABI AROMO CASSIE
POPINAC OPOPANAX
HUL (FATHER OF —) ARAM
(GRANDFATHER OF —) SHEM
HULDAH (HUSBAND OF —) SHALLUM
HULK CHOP HULL CORSE
HULL HUD POD BODY BULK HULK
HUSK PILL BURSE CASCO SWELL
(— OF COTTON BOLL) BUR BURR
(— OF SHIP) BODY HULK BOTTOM
(PART OF —) BEAM DECK KEEL RAIL
BATTEN RABBET CEILING FUTTOCK
KEELSON GARBOARD PLANKING
STRINGER WATERWAY STANCHION
SHELFPIECE SPIRKETING
HULLABALOO DIN FLAP FUROR
MANIA CLAMOR HUBBUB RACKET
BROUHAHA
HUM BUM BLUR BRUM BUZZ HUSS
TUNE CHIRM CROON DRONE FEIGN
SOUGH SOWFF THRUM HUMBLE
TEEDLE FREDDON TRUMPET
BOMBINATE
(— OF VOICES) CHIRM
HUMAN BEING BIPED MANLY FINITE
FLESHY HUMANE MORTAL MANNISH
HOMININE HUMANIST
(— BEING) CYBORG
(— LINKED TO SPACE
ENVIRONMENT) CYBORG
(BIONIC — BEING) CYBORG
(PREF.) HOMI HOMIN(I)
HUMAN BEING MAN WIGHT
MORTAL PERSON ADAMITE
CREATURE RATIONAL
(PREF.) ANTHROP(O)
HUMAN COMEDY (AUTHOR OF —)
SAROYAN

(CHARACTER IN —) BESS MARY
ARENA HOMER KATEY TOBEY
ACKLEY GEORGE GROGAN HUBERT
LIONEL MARCUS THOMAS BYFIELD
ULYSSES MACAULEY SPANGLER
HUMANE CIVIL KINDLY TENDER
MERCIFUL
HUMANELY MANLY
HUMANITARIAN (ALSO SEE
PHILANTHROPIST) PUBLIC
PHILANTHROPIC
HUMANITY FLESH MENSK WORLD
MANHEAD MANHOOD MANSHIP
SPECIES ADAMHOOD HUMANISM
KINDNESS LENITUDE
HUMBLE LOW BASE HOWE MEAN
MEEK MILD MURE POOR TAME VAIL
ABASE ABATE BUXOM DEMIT DIMIT
LOWER LOWLY PLAIN SILLY SMALL
SOBER WORMY ATTERR DEJECT
DEMEAN DEMISS EMBASE HONEST
MASTER MODEST REDUCE SIMPLE
SLIGHT UNPUFF AFFLICT DEGRADE
DEPRESS FOOLISH IGNOBLE
MORTIFY OBSCURE CONTRITE
DISGRACE
(— ONESELF) STOOP GROVEL
HUMBLED SMALL ABASED
DEJECTED
HUMBLENESS HUMILITY
HUMBLER INFERIOR
HUMBLING SETDOWN ABJECTION
HUMBLY SIMPLE
HUMBUG BOO FIE GAS GUM HUM
KID BOSH BUNK FLAM GAFF GAME
GUFF JAZZ SHAM CHEAT FRAUD
FUDGE GUILE JOLLY SPOOF SPOOK
TRICK BARNEY BLAGUE BUNKUM
GAMMON BLARNEY EYEWASH
FLUMMER HOGWASH VERNEUK
BUNCOMBE FLIMFLAM FLUMMERY
HUCKMUCK IMPOSTER NONSENSE
(SORT OF —) BEE
HUMDINGER ACE PIP DARB LULU
ONER BEAUT DILLY DOOZY CORKER
DINGER HUMMER SNORTER
RIPSNORTER
HUMDRUM IRKSOME PROSAIC
BOURGEOIS
HUMERAL VEIL
HUMERUS ARM
HUMID WET DAMP DANK MOIST
SOGGY STICKY SULTRY WETTISH
HUMOROUS
HUMIDITY
(PREF.) HYGR(O)
HUMILIATE ABASE ABASH SCALP
SHAME NIDDER NITHER DEGRADE
MORTIFY PUTDOWN UNPLUME
DISGRACE
HUMILIATED SMALL ASHAMED
HUMILIATION DUST COMEDOWN
DISGRACE

HUMILITY MODESTY MEEKNESS
MILDNESS
HUMIN MELANIN
HUMMEL FALTER
HUMMING AHUM BROOL SINGING
HUMMINGBIRD RUBY STAR
MANGO SYLPH TENUI TOPAZ
AMAZON COQUET HERMIT HUMMER
ROSTER SAPPHO COLIBRI EMERALD
HUMBIRD JACOBIN RAINBOW
SNOWCAP TROCHIL WARRIOR
CALLIOPE COQUETTE FIRETAIL
FROUFROU MIMOTYPE PICARIAN
SAPPHIRE WHITETIP
HUMMOCK HUMP KNOLL CHENIER
HAMMOCK TUSSOCK
HUMOR CUE PIN TID WIT BABY BILE
CANT COAX MOOD TIFF VEIN WHIM
FRAME IRONY TUTOR MEGRIM
PAMPER PHLEGM SANIES SOOTHE
SPLEEN SPRITE TEMPER FOOLING
GRATIFY INDULGE VITREUM VITRINA
ARCHNESS DISHUMOR DROLLERY
EYEWATER FUMOSITY SANGUINE
VITREOUS
(BAD —) BATS THROW
(ILL —) BILE DUDGEON
(KIND OF —) WRY
(QUIET —) DRYNESS
(SLIMY —) HIPPOMANES
(WATERY —) ICHOR
HUMORIST JOKER FUNSTER
FUNMAKER FUNNYMAN
AMERICAN NYE LEAF SHAW WARD
LEWIS SHUTE SMITH LELAND
LOOMIS MASSON ROGERS MARQUIS
THOMSON PERELMAN STREETER
SULLIVAN SHILLABER
AUSTRIAN SAPHIR
CANADIAN LEACOCK
ENGLISH PAIN WARD SEAMAN
FRENCH RABELAIS
GERMAN RICHTER
IRISH MAHONY
HUMOROUS DROLL FUNNY PAWKY
QUEER JOCOSE COMICAL GIOCOSO
PLAYFUL WAGGISH PLEASANT
SARDONIC
HUMP BOSS HUNK BULGE
BUNCH CROUP CRUMP HULCH
HUNCH GIBBER GIBBUS HUMMIE
GIBBOUS
(— ACROSS ROAD) RAMP
(PREF.) HYB(O)
HUMPBACK LORD CRUMP PUNCH
WHALE KYPHOSIS
HUMPBACKED HUMPED HUMPTY
GIBBOSE GIBBOUS
(PREF.) CYPH(O) HYB(O)
HUMPBACKED SALMON HADDO
HOLIA
HUMPED HULCH HUMPY HUTCH
HUMPTY HUNCHY BUNCHED

HUMPHRY CLINKER (AUTHOR OF
—) SMOLLETT
(CHARACTER IN —) JERRY LYDIA
GEORGE WILSON BRAMBLE CLINKER
HUMPHRY JENKINS MATTHEW
MELFORD OBADIAH TABITHA
DENNISON WINIFRED LISMAHAGO
HUMUS MOR MOLD MULL HUMIN
MOULD
HUN AVAR BOCHE BULGAR MAGYAR
VANDAL
(KING OF —S) ATLI ETZEL ATTILA
(KING OF THE —S) ATLI ETZEL ATTILA
HUNCH HUMP HUNK HULCH
HUNCHET SCRUNCH
HUNCHBACK URCHIN HUMPBACK
HUNCHBACK OF NOTRE DAME
(AUTHOR OF —) HUGO
(CHARACTER IN —) CLAUDE FROLLO
PHOEBUS ESMERALDA GRINGOIRE
QUASIMODO CHATEAUPERS
HUNDRED RHO CENT CENTUM
HUNDER HUNNER CANTRED
CANTREF CENTARY
(— THOUSAND) LAC LAKH
(NINE —) SAN SAMPI
(ONE — DOLLARS) BILL
(5 —) D
(PREF.) CENT(I) HECATO HECATOM
HECATON HECT(O)
HUNDREDFOLD CENTUPLE
HUNDRED-HANDED BRIAREAN
HUNDREDTH CENTESIMAL
(— OF INCH) POINT
(— OF RIGHT ANGLE) GRAD GRADE
HUNDREDWEIGHT CENT CENTAL
CENTENA CENTNER HUNDRED
QUINTAL
HUNGARIAN HUN KUMAN MAGYAR
(PREF.) UGRO

HUNGARY		
CANAL: SIÓ SARVIZ		
CAPITAL: BUDAPEST		
COIN: GARA BALAS FILLER FORINT		
KORONA		
COUNTY: VAS PEST ZALA BEKES FEJER		
HEVES TOLNA NOGRAD SOMOGY		
BARANYA		
DANCE: CZARDAS		
DYNASTY: ARPAD ANGEVIN		
FOREST: BAKONY		
GYPSY: SZIGANE TZIGANE		
KING: BELA GEZA IMRE ARPAD ISTVAN		
KALMAN MATTHIAS		
LAKE: FERTO BALATON VELENCE		
BLATENSEE		
MEASURE: AKO HOLD JOCH YOKE		
ANTAL ITCZE MAROK METZE		
HUVELYK MERFOLD		
MONEY: PENGO		
MOUNTAIN: KEKES BAKONY MECSEK		
BORZSONY KORISHEGY		

MOUNTAIN RANGE: BUKK MATRA
MECSEK CARPATHIAN
MUSICAL INSTRUMENT: TAROGATO
NATIVE: HUN SERB CROAT GYPSY
MAGYAR SLOVAK UGRIAN
PLAIN: PUSZTA
REGIME: KADAR
RIVER: DUNA MURA RAAB RABA SAJO
ZALA BODVA DRAVA DRAVE IPOLY
KAPOS KOROS MAROS RABCA
TARNA TISZA DANUBE HENRAD
POPRAD SZAMOS THEISS ZAGYVA
VISTULA BERRETYO
TOWN: ABA ACS OZD VAC BUDA EGER
GYOR MAKO PAPA PECS PEST TATA
ZIRC KOMLO CEGLED MOHACS
SOPRON SZEGED DBRECEN
MISKOLC SZENTES DEBRECEN
SZEGEDIN
WEIGHT: VAMFONT VAMMAZSA
WINE: EGER TOKAJ TOKAY
SZEKSZARD

HUNGER BELL CLEM WANT ACO-
RIA DESIRE FAMINE CRAVING
APPETITE
(— PANGS) MUNCHIES
HUNGRY YAP HOWE KEEN LEER
YAUP EAGER EMPTY THIRL UNFED
HOLLOW JEJUNE PECKISH YAPPISH
ANHUNGRY ESURIENT
HUNK DAD DAUD JUNK STUD
ADONIS MOUNTAIN
(— OF BREAD) TOMMY
HUNKY STUDLY MUSCULAR
ATTRACTIVE
HUNKY-DORY JIMDANDY
HUNT DOG GUN JAG MOB RUN
GREW JACK LARK PUMP SEAL SEEK
SHOP CHASE CHEVY DRIVE HOUND
REVAY STALK TRACK TRAIL BATTUE
BEAGLE BREVIT CHEVVY COURSE
FALCON FERRET SEARCH SHIKAR
VANLAY ENCHASE AUCUPATE
PIGSTICK SCROUNGE VENATION
(— BIG GAME) GHOOM
(— DEER) FLOAT
(— DOWN) QUARRY
(— DUCKS) TOLL
(— FOX) CUB
(— HINT) CLUE
(— WITH HAWK) FLY
(— WITH SPEAR) STICK
HUNTER GUN HUNT PINK JAGER
BIRDER CHASER GUNNER JAEGER
NIMROD THERON ACTAEON
BUSHMAN CATCHER COURSER
MONTERO SHIKARI SHOOTER
SKIRTER STALKER TRAILER VENERER
CEPHALUS CHASSEUR FIELDMAN
HUNTSMAN TRAILMAN
(— ON SNOW) CRUSTER
(BUFFALO —) CIBOLERO

(MYTHOLOGICAL —) GWYN ORION
(RING OF —S) TINCHEL TINCHILL
HUNTING DRAG HANK AHUNT
WATHE SHIKAR VENERY CUBBING
GUNNING BEAGLING PURCHASE
SHOOTING SURROUND VENATION
(— SIGNAL) SEEK
HUNTRESS DIANA
HUNTSMAN WHIP HUNTER JAEGER
ACTAEON CATCHER COURSER
MONTERO SCARLET VENATOR
VENERER CHASSEUR
HUPHAM (FATHER OF —) BENJAMIN
HUR (GRANDSON OF —) BEZALEEL
(SON OF —) REPHAIAH
HURAM (FATHER OF —) BELA
HURDLE TRAY FLAKE FRITH PANEL
STALE STICK DOUBLE RADDLE
SLEDGE WATTLE
HURDS TOW
HURDY-GURDY LIRA ROTA LANTUM
VIELLE SAMBUKE HUMSTRUM
SYMPHONY
HURI (SON OF —) ABIHAIL
HURL BUM BUN CAST CLOD DASH
DUST FIRE PASH PELT PICK SLAT
SOAK SOCK DRIVE FLING HEAVE
LANCE PITCH SLING SMITE SPANG
SWING THIRL THROW WHIRL
LAUNCH THRILL HURLBAT SWITHER
WHITHER JACULATE PRECIPITATE
HURLY-BURLY HURL RACKET
UPROAR
HURRAH HAIL HUZZA HOORAY
HURRAY BRAVISSIMO
HURRICANE BAGUIO PRESTER
FURACANA FURICANE WILDWIND
HURRIED HASTY RAPID THRONG
HASTEFUL SNATCHED
HURRY ADO FOG HIE NIP RAP RUB
RUN BUSK DASH DUST HUMP PELT
PLAT POST RAPE RESE RUSH STIR
TEAR TIFT TROT URGE WHIR CHASE
CROWD HASTE HYPER LURRY
MOSEY PRESS SESSA SKIRT SPEED
STAVE STOUR WHIRL BUCKET
BUNDLE BUSTLE HASTEN HUSTLE
POWDER STROTH TATTER WHORRY
HOTFOOT QUICKEN SCUDDLE
SKELTER SLITHER WHITHER
DISPATCH EXPEDITE SPLUTTER
ACCELERATE
(— ABOUT) SCOUR
(— A HORSE) SPUR
(— AWAY) FLEE BUNCH SCREW SKIRT
(— CLUMSILY) TAVE TEAVE
(— NOISILY) SPLUTTER
(— OFF) DUST
(— UP) BUSK
(GO IN A —) ZOOM
HURRYING FLUSTER
HURT CUT HOT NOY DERE FIKE GALL
HARM PAIN SCAT ABUSE BLAME

GRIEF GRIPE PINCH SORRY SPITE
THORN WATHE WOUND BRUISE
DAMAGE GRIEVE IMPAIR INJURE
INJURY LESION MIFFED MITTLE
PAINED PUNISH SCATHE STRAIN
STROKE WINGED AFFLICT HURTING
OFFENCE OFFENSE SCADDLE
MISCHIEF NUISANCE
(— EASILY) FROISSE
(— FEELINGS) CUT TOUCH
(— REPUTATION) LIBEL
(— SEVERELY) KILL
(EASILY —) GINGER
(PREF.) NOCI
HURTFUL BAD ILL EVIL MALIGN
NOCENT NOCIVE NOUGHT SHREWD
TAKING BALEFUL BANEFUL
HARMFUL MALEFIC NOCUOUS
NOXIOUS SCADDLE UNQUERT
GRIEVOUS HURTSOME SCATHFUL
HURTLE HURL FLING THIRL
HUSBAND EKE MAN WER BOND
CHAP FERE KEEP LORD MAKE MATE
SAVE SIRE BARON CHURL HOARD
HUBBY MATCH STORE MANAGE
MASTER MISTER SPOUSE CONSORT
GOODMAN GUIDMAN HENPECK
PARTNER CONSERVE
(— OF ADULTRESS) CUCKOLD
(— OF SQUAW) SANNUP
(AFFIANCED —) FUTURE
(SUPPLEMENTARY —) PIRRAURU
(PL.) PUNALUA
(PREF.) MARITI
HUSBANDMAN BOND BOOR CARL
CLOWN COLON RUSTIC TILLER
ACREMAN HUSBAND PLOWMAN
TILLMAN AGRICOLE
HUSBANDRY GAINER GAINOR
THRIFT ECONOMY MANAGERY
HUSH SH HSH MUM PAX HESH HOOT
LULL BURKE SHUSH STILL WHISH
WHIST WHUSH HUDDLE BESTILL
HUSHABY SILENCE
HUSHED QUIET STILL GENTLE
WHISHT
HUSHIM (HUSBAND OF —)
SHAHARAIM
HUSK BUR COD HUD KEX SID ARIL
BARK BURR COAT COSH HOSE
HUCK HULK PILL SEED SHIV SKIN
HOOSE SCALE SHACK SHALE
SHAUP SHELL SHILL SHOOD SHUCK
SHUDE COLDER DEHUSK FLIGHT
SLOUGH BOLSTER CARCASS
CASCARA
(— OF NUT) SHACK BOLSTER
(— OF OATS) SHUD SHOOD FLIGHT
(CORN —) HOJA
(PL.) BHUSA CHAFF BHOOSA
HULKAGE SHELLING
(PREF.) LEMMO LEPO LOPO SILIQUI
(SUFF.) LEMMA

HUSKY HUSK CODDY FOGGY THICK
FURRED BUIRDLY HULKING
BOUNCING SIBERIAN
HUSSITE TABORITE
HUSSY MINX SLUT BESOM CUTTY
GIPSY GYPSY MADAM STRAP HIZZIE
LIMMER DROSSEL
HUSTINGS BEMA
HUSTLE FAN PEG HUMP JUMP BLITZ
SKELP BUCKET BUNDLE BUSTLE
JOSTLE RABBLE RUSTLE SCUFTER
HUSTLECAP PINCH
HUSTLER HUSTLE PEELER BUSTLER
FIREBALL
HUT COE COT BARI BUTT COSH COTE
CREW CRIB HALE HULK HULL ISBA
IZBA SHED SKEO TENT TILT BASHA
BENAB BOHIO BOOTH BOTHY CABIN
CHAWI CHOZA HOOCH HOVEL
HUMPY HUTCH JACAL KRAAL LODGE
SCALE SETER SHACK SHIEL TOLDO
TOPEK WHARE WURLY BOHAWN
BOTHAN CANABA CHALET GUNYAH
GUNYEH HOOTCH MIAMIA PONDOK
RANCHO REFUGE SAETER SCONCE
SHANTY SHELTY WIGWAM WIKIUP
BALAGAN BARRACK BOUROCK
CAMALIG COTTAGE GOONDIE
HUDDOCK HUTMENT SHEBANG
YAKUTAT BARABARA CHANTIER
RONDAWEL SHIELING THOLTHAN
TUGURIUM
(— FOR TEMPORARY USE) CORF
(— IN VIETNAM) HOOCH HOOTCH
(— OVER MINING SHAFT) COE
(ABORIGINAL —) MIMI WURLY
GUNYAH MIAMIA WURLEY GOONDIE
(FISHERMAN'S —) SKEO SKIO
(HEATED —) HOTHOUSE
(HERMIT'S —) CELL
(KIND OF —) NISSEN
(NAVAJO —) HOGAN
(POULTRY —) IGLOO
(RITUAL —) SUCCAH SUKKAH
(SAMOYED —) CHUM
(SENTRY —) BOX
(SIBERIAN —) JURT
(SOUTH AFRICAN —) STRUIS
(PREF.) CALIO
HUTCH ARK BUDDLE RABBITRY
HUTIA UTIA JUTIA PILORI
HUZ (FATHER OF —) NAHOR
HUZZAH SHOUT
HWYL FERVOR EXCITEMENT
HYACINTH LILY MUSK LILIUM
CROWTOE FLOATER GREGGLE
JACINTH BLUEBELL CROWFOOT
HAREBELL JACOUNCE
HYACINTH BEAN LABLAB
BONAVIST BONNYVIS DOLICHOS
HYACINTHUS (FATHER OF —)
AMYCLAS
(MOTHER OF —) DIOMEDE

HYALITE OPAL
HYALOGEN NEOSSIN
HYBRID DZO ZHO MULE ZOBO
CROSS GRADE HINNY LIGER
COYDOG GALYAK MOSAIC MULISH
SPLAKE TURKEN BASTARD BIGENER
CATTALO JERSIAN MONGREL
PLUMCOT ZEBRASS ZEBRULA
ZEBURRO CARIDEER CITRANGE
KAFERITA LIMEQUAT ZEBRINNY
(PREF.) NOTH(O)
HYBRIDIZE CROSS
HYDRA POLYP
HYDRANT CHUCK FIREPLUG
(PART OF —) NUT CHAIN BARREL
BONNET STANDPIPE CONNECTION
HYDRANTH SIPHON SYPHON
HYDRATE SLAKE
HYDRAULIC
(PREF.) HYDR(I)(O)
HYDRAZINE DIAMIDE
HYDRAZOATE AZIDE
HYDRIA KALPIS
HYDROCARBON ARENE CUMOL
FREON GUTTA IDRYL INDAN IRENE
TOLAN XYLOL ALKANE ALKYNE
ALLENE BUTANE BUTYNE CARANE
CETANE CETENE CYMENE DECANE
ETHANE ETHENE HEXINE INDANE
INDENE MELENE NONENE OCTANE
OCTENE OCTINE PICENE PINENE
PYRENE RETENE TOLANE TOLUOL
XYLENE AMYLENE AZULENE
BENZENE CHOLANE CYCLENE
DECALIN ETHERIN FULVENE
HEPTANE HEPTENE HEPTYNE
LYCOPIN MUCKITE MYRCENE
OLEFINE PENTINE PENTYNE
PHYTANE PROPANE STYRENE
TETROLE TOLUENE BIPHENYL
CADALENE CADINENE CAMPHANE
CARBURAN CEROTENE CETYLENE
CHRYSENE CORONENE CUMULENE
DECYLENE DIOLEFIN DIPHENYL
DOCOSANE DYSODILE EICOSANE
ETHYLENE EUDALENE FLUORENE
HEXYLENE ILLIPENE ISOPRENE
LYCOPENE MENTHENE NONYLENE
OCTYLENE PARAFFIN PRISTANE
PYRACENE RUTYLENE SABINENE
SQUALENE STILBENE
(SUFF.) YLENE
HYDROCHLORIC ACID
(SUFF.) CHLORHYDRIA
HYDROCYANIC PRUSSIC
HYDRODAMALIS RHYTINA
HYDROEXTRACTOR BUZZER
WHIZZER
HYDROFLUORIC PHTHORIC
HYDROFOIL FOIL
HYDROGEN HYDRO PROTIUM
(HEAVY —) DIPLOGEN

HYDROGRAPHER AMERICAN
MAURY MITCHELL
ENGLISH SMYTH MURRAY
GERMAN NEUMAYER
NORWEGIAN SVERDRUP
HYDROHEMATITE TURGITE
HYDROID POLYP OBELIA ACALEPH
ZOOPHYTE
HYDROLEA NAMA
HYDROMEL ALOJA
HYDROMETER SPINDLE
HYDROPERITONEUM ASCITES
HYDROPHOBIA LYSSA RABIES
HYDROPHOBIC LYSSIC
HYDROPHYLLIUM BRACT
HYDROPLANE SKIM GLIDER
HYDROXIDE ALKALI HYDRATE
HYDRIDE
HYDROXYL
(SUFF.)
(CONTAINING —) OLIC
HYDROZINCITE CALAMINE
HYENA HINE DABUH SIMIR HYAENID
HYGIENIC SANITARY
HYGRODEIK PAGOSCOPE
HYLAS (FATHER OF —) THIODAMAS
(LOVER OF —) DRYOPE
(MOTHER OF —) MENODICE
HYLLUS (FATHER OF —) HERCULES
(MOTHER OF —) DEIANIRA
(SLAYER OF —) ECHEMUS
(WIFE OF —) IOLE
HYLOZOIST PHYSICIST
HYMEN CHERRY BRIDEGOD
MAIDENHEAD
HYMENIUM THECIUM
HYMENOCALLIS ISMENE
HYMN ODE FUGE LAUD SING DIRGE
GATHA PAEAN PSALM YASHT YMPNE
ANTHEM CARVAL CHORAL HIMENE
HIRMOS MORPHA ORPHIC THEODY
VESPER CHORALE EXULTET HEIRMOS
INTROIT CANTICLE CATHISMA
DOXOLOGY ENCOMIUM PSALMODY
SEQUENCE TRISAGION TROPARION
(— COLLECTION) MENAION
(MEXICAN —) ALABADO
(VEDIC —) MANTRA
(PL.) HYMNODY
HYMNAL HYMNARY HYMNBOOK
HYPATIA (AUTHOR OF —) KINGSLEY
(CHARACTER IN —) AMAL MIRIAM
AUFUGUS HYPATIA ORESTES
PELAGIA RAPHAEL VICTORIA
HERACLIAN PHILAMMON
HYPE EXCITE PROMOTE PUFFERY
INCREASE
HYPER EXCITABLE
HYPERACTIVE MANIC
HYPERBOLE AUXESIS
HYPERCORACOID RADIAL
SCAPULA

HYPERCRITICAL NICE CAPTIOUS CRITICAL
HYPERDULIA ADORATION
HYPEREMIA RUBOR
HYPEREMIC CONGESTED
HYPERENOR (BROTHER OF —) EUPHORBUS POLYDAMAS
(FATHER OF —) PANTHOUS
(MOTHER OF —) PHRONTIS
(SLAYER OF —) MENELAUS
HYPERICUM TUTSAN
HYPERION (DAUGHTER OF —) AURORA
(FATHER OF —) URANUS
(MOTHER OF —) GAEA
(WIFE OF —) THEA
HYPERON BARYON
HYPEROPIC FARSIGHTED
HYPERSENSITIVITY ATOPY ALLERGY
HYPHA STOLON
HYPHEN BAND
(PL.) LEADERS
HYPNOTIC AMYTAL BROMAL CHLORAL SECONAL BARBITAL NARCEINE SOPORIFIC
HYPNOTISM DEVIL BRAIDISM HYPNOSIS MESMERISM
HYPNOTIST OPERATOR SVENGALI
HYPO FIXER
HYPOBLAST ENDODERM HYPODERM
HYPOCHONDRIA HIP HYP HYPO MEGRIM
HYPOCHONDRIAC ARGAN HIPPY HIPPIST ATRABILIAR
HYPOCOTYL RADICLE TIGELLA TIGELLUS
HYPOCRISY SHAM POPEHOLY PHARISAISM
HYPOCRITE CANT BIGOT CHEAT FACER FRAUD BLIFIL CAFARD

HUMBUG MUCKER MAWWORM SIMULAR CHADBAND DECEIVER TARTUFFE
HYPOCRITICAL FALSE SLAPE DOUBLE CANTING PLASTER POPEHOLY SPECIOUS
HYPOCYCLOID ASTROID
HYPODERMIS SKIN
HYPOPHARYNX LINGUA LABIELLA
HYPOSTASIS PERSON
HYPOSTATIZE ENTIFY
HYPOSTOME MANUBRIUM
HYPOTENUSE SUBTENSE
HYPOTHESIS SYSTEM THEORY PREMISE WEGENER SUPPOSAL POSTULATE
HYPOTHETICAL IDEAL
HYPOTRACHELIUM GORGERIN
HYPSEUS (DAUGHTER OF —) CYRENE
(FATHER OF —) PENEUS
(MOTHER OF —) CREUSA
(WIFE OF —) CHLIDANOPE
HYPTIS OREGANO
HYRAX DAS CONY CONEY DAMAN WABUR DASSIE WABBER ASHKOKO KLIPDAS HYRACOID
HYRMINA (FATHER OF —) EPEUS
(HUSBAND OF —) PHORBAS
(SON OF —) ACTOR
HYRNETHO (BROTHER OF —) AGELAUS CALLIAS EURYPYLUS
(FATHER OF —) TEMENUS
(HUSBAND OF —) DEIPHONTES
HYSTERIA MOTHER NERVES PIBLOKTO TARASSIS
(PRONE TO —) VAPORISH
(RELIGIOUS —) LATA
HYSTERICAL FRANTIC NERVOUS SHRIEKY

I A Y HI HY CHE ICH ISS SHE ITEM UTCH
INDIA UTCHY
  (— AM) ISE CHAM ICHAM
  (— HAD) CHAD
  (— WILL) CHILL ICHULLE
  (— WOULD) CHUD
IALEMUS (FATHER OF —) APOLLO
  (MOTHER OF —) CALLIOPE
IALMENUS (BROTHER OF —)
  ASCALAPHUS
  (FATHER OF —) ARES APOLLO
  (MOTHER OF —) ASTYOCHE
  CALLIOPE
IAMB IAMBIC IAMBUS
  (— AND DACTYL) FEET
  (DOUBLE —) DIIAMB
IAMUS (FATHER OF —) APOLLO
  (MOTHER OF —) EVADNE
IAPETUS (FATHER OF —) URANUS
  (MOTHER OF —) GAEA
  (SON OF —) ATLAS MENOETIUS
  (WIFE OF —) ASIA CLYMENE
IAPYGIANS MESSAPII
IAPYX (BROTHER OF —) DAUNIUS
  PEUCETIUS
  (FATHER OF —) LYCAON DAEDALUS
IASION (BROTHER OF —) DARDANUS
  (FATHER OF —) ZEUS JUPITER
  (LOVER OF —) CERES DEMETER
  (MOTHER OF —) ELECTRA
  (SON OF —) PLUTUS
IATROCHEMICAL SPAGYRIC
IATROCHEMISTRY SPAGYRIC
IBANAG CAGAYAN
IBEX KYL TEK TUR ZAC GOAT KAIL
  BEDEN EVECK IZARD JAELA EVICKE
  SAKEEN
IBHAR (FATHER OF —) DAVID
IBIS GUARA GANNET HADADA JABIRU
  TURKEY CICONIID IRONHEAD
IBNEIAH (FATHER OF —) JEROHAM
ICARIUS (BROTHER OF —)
  TYNDAREUS
  (DAUGHTER OF —) ERIGONE
  PENELOPE
  (FAITHFUL DOG OF —) MOERA
  (FATHER OF —) OEBALUS
  (MOTHER OF —) GORGOPHONE
ICARUS (FATHER OF —) DAEDALUS
  (MOTHER OF —) NAUCRATE
ICE YS GEAL FROST GLACE CRYSTAL
  VERGLAS
  (— IN ROUGH BLOCKS) RUBBLE
  (ANCHOR —) FRAZIL
  (DRIFTING FRAGMENT OF —) PAN
  CALF

  (GROUND —) FRAZIL
  (PATCH OF —) RONE
  (PINNACLE OF —) SERAC
  (RIDGE OF —) HAMMOCK HUMMOCK
  (SEA —) GLACON SLUDGE
  (SHORE —) FAST
  (SLUSHY —) SISH
  (SOFT —) SLOB LOLLY
  (THIN NEW —) DISH PANCAKE
  (THIN OR FLOATING —) FLOE GRUE
  BRASH
  (WATER —) SHERBET
  (PREF.) CRYSTALL(I)(O) GLACI(O)
  (SUFF.) CRYST
ICE AX PIOLET
ICEBERG BERG GROWLER FLOEBERG
  (OFFSHOOT OF —) CALF
ICEBOAT SKEETER
ICE CREAM BISK CREAM GLACE
  AUFAIT BISQUE NOUGAT TASTER
  SPUMONI TORTONI
  (— BETWEEN WAFERS) SLIDER
  (— MOLD) BOMBE
  (— TREAT) MALT
ICE CREAM CONE CORNET
ICED COLD GLACE FRAPPE
ICEFISH SALANGID
ICE FLOE PAN
ICEHOUSE IGLU IGLOO
  (— WORKER) AIRMAN

ICELAND

BALLAD: RIMUR
BAY: FAXA HUNA
CAPITAL: REJKJAVIK REYKJAVIK
COIN: AURAR EYRIR KRONA
DISH: SKYR SVIO BLOOMOR HAROFISK
EPIC: EDDA SAGA
FIRST SETTLER: ARNARSON
FJORD: BREIDHA
GEYSER: GRYLA
GIANT: ATLI
GLACIER: HOFSJOKULL LANGJOKULL
  VATNAJOKULL
HERO: BELE ERIC LEIF SIGUROSSON
LAKE: MYVATN THORISVATN
MEASURE: SET ALIN LINA ALMUD
  TURMA ALMENN ALMUDE FERFET
  POTTUR FATHMUR FERALIN
  FERMILA OLTUNNA SJOMILA
MOUNTAIN: JOKUL
PARLIAMENT: ALTHING
REPUBLIC: LYOVELDIO
RIVER: HVITA JOKULSA THJORSA
TOWN: AKRANES AKUREYRI KEFLAVIK
  KOPAVOGUR

VOLCANIC ISLAND: SURTSEY
VOLCANO: LAKI ASKJA HEKLA
 ELDFELL
WATERFALL: GULL DETTI GULLFOSS
 DETTIFOSS
WEIGHT: PUND POUND

ICE-STONE CRYOLITE
ICHABOD (FATHER OF —)
 PHINEHAS
 (GRANDFATHER OF —) ELI
ICHNEUMON URVA NYMSS
 MEERKAT VANSIRE
ICHOROUS GLEFTY
ICHTHYOSIS FISHSKIN
ICHU HICHU STIPA
ICICLE ICARY ICKLE YOKEL TANGLE
 SHOGGLE SHOOGLE COCKBELL
ICINESS GLARE
ICING ICE PIPING ALCORZA FROSTING
 MERINGUE
ICON IKON EIKON IMAGE DEESIS
ICONOCLAST DEBUNKER
ICONOSTASIS DIASTYLE
ICTEROHEMATURIA CARCEAG
ICTONYX ZORILLA
ICTUS ACCENT STRESS DOWNBEAT
ICY GELID BOREAL FRIGID WINTRY
 GLACIAL
ID ES ORF GARDON SYPHILID

IDAHO
CAPITAL: BOISE
COUNTY: ADA GEM BUTTE CAMAS
 LATAH LEMHI POWER TETON BLAINE
 BONNER CARNAS CASSIA JEROME
 OWYHEE BENEWAH KOOTENAI
DAM: OXBOW BROWNLEE
INDIAN: BANNOCK KALISPEL
 NEZPERCE SHOSHONI
LAKE: BEAR GRAYS PRIEST
MOUNTAIN: RYAN BORAH RHODES
 TAYLOR BIGBALDY BLUENOSE
MOUNTAIN RANGE: CABINET SELKIRK
NICKNAME: GEM
RIVER: SNAKE LOCHSA SALMON
 PAYETTE
SPRINGS: SODA HOOPER LAVAHOT
STATE BIRD: BLUEBIRD
STATE FLOWER: SYRINGA
TOWN: ARCO BUHL MALAD NAMPA
 BURLEY DRIGGS DUBOIS MOSCOW
 WEISER CASCADE CHALLIS ORIFINO
 REXBURG POCATELLO

IDAS (BROTHER OF —) LYNCEUS
 (FATHER OF —) APHAREUS
 (MOTHER OF —) ARENE
 (WIFE OF —) MARPESSA
IDDO (FATHER OF —) ZECHARIAH
 (SON OF —) AHINADAB
IDE ORFE

IDEA EGG GIG KINK EIDOS IMAGE
 THING ANONYM DHARMA ECTYPE
 FIGURE INTENT NOTICE NOTION
 RECEPT THREAP THROPE BEGRIFF
 CONCEIT CONCEPT GIMMICK
 GLIMPSE MAROTTE OPINION
 PROJECT SPECIES SURMISE
 THOUGHT GIMCRACK NOTIONAL
 BRAINCHILD PRECONCEPTION
 (—S OF LITTLE VALUE) STUFF
 (CENTRAL —) ARGUMENT
 (COMMONPLACE —) SHIBBOLETH
 (CONSERVATIVE —S) FOGYISM
 (DOMINANT —) CLOU
 (DULL STUPID —S) STODGE
 (FAINT —) GLIMMER
 (FALSE —) FALLACY
 (FANTASTIC —) VAPOR MAGGOT
 (FAVORITE —) HORSE
 (FIXED —) TICK
 (FUNDAMENTAL —) KEYNOTE
 (GENERAL —) HANG
 (IRRATIONAL —) FOLLY
 (MAIN —) POINT
 (MUSICAL —) SENTENCE
 (ODD —) FREAK
 (OVERWORKED —) CLICHE
 (PLATONIC —) ESSENCE
 (RECURRING —) BURDEN
 (STALE —S) BILGE
 (SUPERSTITIOUS —) FREIT
 (TRANSCENDENT —) FORM
 (TRITE —) PABLUM PABULUM
 (PL.) EIDE THOUGHT
 (PREF.) IDEO
IDEAL ISM IDEA DREAM AERIAL
 BEAUTY DOMNEI DREAMY EDENIC
 MENTAL UNREAL PATTERN PERFECT
 UTOPIAN ABSTRACT FANCIFUL
 IDEALITY NOTIONAL QUADRATE
 ORIFLAMME
 (— OF BEAUTY) KALON
IDEALISM IDEOLOGY
IDEALIST IDEIST UTOPIAN FICHTEAN
 UTOPIAST
IDEALIZE PLATONIZE
IDEALIZED POETICAL
IDENTICAL LIKE SAME SELF VERY
 ALIKE EQUAL METOO EVENLY
 PROPER CORRECT IDENTIC NUMERIC
 SELFSAME
IDENTIFIABLE NAMEABLE
IDENTIFICATION IDENT DOCUMENT
 EQUATION RECOGNITION
 (— METHOD) DNA
IDENTIFIED SIGNATE
IDENTIFIER LINK BIRDER
IDENTIFY PEG TAB MARK NAME
 RANK SPOT IDENT PLACE TALLY
 FINGER DISCERN DIAGNOSE
 PINPOINT
 (— WITH) ENTER

IDENTITY SEITY UNITY IPSEITY ONENESS EQUALITY SAMENESS
(— OF PITCH) UNISON
(PERSONAL —) SEITY

IDEOGRAPH CHARACTER
(PL.) KANJI

IDEOGRAPHIC REAL

IDEOLOGICAL MENTAL

IDEOLOGY ISM

IDIOBLAST SPHERE IDIOSOME

IDIOCY ANOIA ANOESIA FATUITY IDIOTRY MOROSIS IDIOTISM

IDIOM CANT ARGOT JUANG DORISM IFUGAO JARGON MEDISM SPEECH AEOLISM ANOMALY GRECISM PAHLAVI PEHLEVI TURKISM DANICISM DORICISM IDIOTISM IONICISM LANGUAGE LOCALISM PARLANCE RURALISM

IDIOMORPHIC EUHEDRAL

IDIOPHONE RATTLE

IDIOSOME SPHERE

IDIOSYNCRASY TIC WAY QUIRK IDIASM RUMNESS

IDIOT FON OAF SOT DAFF DOLT FOOL AMENT BOOBY DUNCE FONNE CRETIN HOBBIL NIDGET NIDIOT DINGBAT DULLARD NATURAL OMADAWN PINHEAD IMBECILE INNOCENT SLAVERER
(AUTHOR OF —) DOSTOEVSKI
(CHARACTER IN —) LEF GANYA AGLAYA PARFEN MYSHKIN NATASYA EPANCHIN ROGOZHIN FILIPOVNA ARDALIONOVITCH

IDIOTIC DAFT DOPY ZANY IDIOT FATUOUS FOOLISH WANTWIT IMBECILE

IDLE COLD DEAD HACK HAKE HANG HULL JAUK LAKE LAZE LAZY LUSK MUZZ ORRA SOFT SORN TICK VAIN VOID DALLY EMPTY ORROW SHOOL SLIVE THOKE WASTE COOTER DAIDLE DANDER DREAMY FOOTER GAMMER LOUNGY O'RANT OTIOSE SLIMSY TEETER TIDDIE TIFFLE TRIFLE TRUANT UNUSED VACANT DRONISH IDLEFUL IDLESET LOAFING SAUNTER SHACKLE SLUMBER SLUTHER UNLUSTY VACUOUS WHIFFLE BASELESS BOOTLESS FAINEANT INACTIVE INDOLENT SHAMMOCK SLAISTER SLOTHFUL TRIFLING WORKLESS
(TO BE —) SLOTH

IDLENESS LAZE RUST SLOTH IDLETY IDLESET IDLESSE IGNAVIA VACANCY VACUITY FLANERIE IDLEHOOD INACTION
(— PERSONIFED) LAURENCE LAWRENCE
(LIVE IN —) MAROON

IDLER BUM GAUM HAKE JAUK KERN LOON DRONE BADAUD BUMBLE DONNOT IDLEBY LUBBER PLAYER QUISBY RODNEY STALKO TRUANT BLELLUM BUCKEEN DAWDLER FAITOUR FRANION IDLESBY LOLLARD LOUNGER LOUTHER LURDANE SLOUNGE TRIFLER DOLITTLE FAINEANT IDLESHIP LAYABOUT LAZARONE UNWORKER WHIFFLER

IDLE WHEEL IDLER RUNNER

IDLY TOOMLY VAGUELY

IDMON (DAUGHTER OF —) ARACHNE
(FATHER OF —) APOLLO
(MOTHER OF —) CYRENE ASTERIA

IDOCRASE EGERAN CYPRINE VESUVIAN

IDOL GOD BAAL ICON JOSS LION TIKI WOOD ZEMI ANITO BESAN EIKON GUACA HOBAL HUACA IMAGE STOCK SWAMI IDOLET IDOLUM MAMMET MAUMET MINION PAGODA POPPET PUPPET TERAPH EIDOLON MAHOMET BAPHOMET MAUMETRY PANTHEUM
(HEATHEN —) DEVIL
(PREF.) EIDOLO IDOLO

IDOLATER AKKUM PAGAN BAALIST BAALITE HEATHEN IDOLIST

IDOLATROUS PAGAN IDOLISH

IDOLATRY BAALISM IMAGERY ADULTERY MAUMETRY

IDOLIZE GOD IDOL ADORE ADMIRE WORSHIP

IDUMAEAN EDOMITE

IDUN (HUSBAND OF —) BRAGI

IDYIA (DAUGHTER OF —) MEDEA
(FATHER OF —) OCEANUS
(HUSBAND OF —) AEETES
(MOTHER OF —) TETHYS
(SON OF —) APSYRTUS

IDYL IDYLL BUCOLIC ECLOGUE

IDYLLIC HALCYON PASTORAL THEOCRITEAN

IDYLLS OF THE KING (AUTHOR OF —) TENNYSON
(CHARACTER IN —) BORS ENID BALAN BALIN ISOLT ARTHUR ELAINE GARETH GAWAIN MERLIN MODRED VIVIEN ETTARRE GALAHAD GERAINT LYNETTE PELLEAS BEDIVERE LANCELOT TRISTRAM GUINEVERE PERCIVALE

IF AN AND GIF GIN THO GEVE IFFEN INCASE SOBEIT THOUGH PROVIDED
(— EVER) ONCE
(— NOT) BUT ELSE NISI
(PREF.) (AS —) QUASI

IF WINTER COMES (AUTHOR OF —) HUTCHINSON
(CHARACTER IN —) MARK NONA EFFIE MABEL PERCH SABRE TYBAR BRIGHT FARGUS HAROLD FORTUNE TWYNING

IGAL (FATHER OF —) JOSEPH NATHAN

IGDALIAH (SON OF —) HANAN
IGEAL (FATHER OF —) SHEMAIAH
IGERNA (HUSBAND OF —) UTHER
　GORLOIS
　(SON OF —) ARTHUR
IGNEOUS PLUTONIC
　(SOURCE OF — ROCK) MAGMA
　(PREF.) PLUTONO
IGNIS FATUUS WISP SPUNKIE
　WILDFIRE
IGNITE TIND FLASH LIGHT SHOOT
　SPARK ILLUME KINDLE CALCINE
　LIGHTEN
IGNITED LIVING BURNING
　(CAUSE TO BECOME —) RETROFIRE
IGNITER PUNK SPARKER
IGNITION FIRE LIGHTING
IGNOBLE LOW BASE MEAN VILE
　ABJECT GRUBBY SORDID CURRISH
　SERVILE UNNOBLE BASEBORN
　SHAMEFUL
IGNOBLY BASELY
IGNOMINIOUS BASE VILE
　INFAMOUS SHAMEFUL
IGNOMINY SHAME REBUKE
　SCANDAL DISGRACE DISHONOR
IGNORAMUS IDIOT IGNARO SIMPLE
　AMHAAREZ
IGNORANCE IRONY TAMAS
　AGNOSY AVIDYA AVIJJA BETISE
　NICETY RUDITY UNSKILL DARKNESS
　IDIOTISM NESCIENCE
　(BOLD —) BAYARD
　(FEIGNED —) IRONY
　(PREF.) AGNOIO
IGNORANT LAY DARK NICE RUDE
　VAIN GREEN GROSS SILLY INGRAM
　SIMPLE ARTLESS REDNECK SECULAR
　UNAWARE UNCOUTH UNKNOWN
　IMPERITE INNOCENT INSCIENT
　INSCIOUS NESCIENT UNTAUGHT
　BENIGHTED
　(— OF EVIL) INNOCENT
IGNORANTLY SIMPLY
IGNORE BALK BLOW OMIT SINK
　SNUB VAIN BAULK BLINK ELIDE
　BYPASS MISKEN SLIGHT DESPISE
　MISKNOW NEGLECT TUNEOUT
　CONFOUND OVERJUMP OVERLEAP
　OVERLOOK OVERPASS
IGOROT BONTOK NABALOI
　KANKANAI
IGUANA GUANA GUANO LEGUAN
IGUVINE UMBRIAN
IJO DJO BONI BONNY
IKKESH (SON OF —) IRA
ILAIRA (FATHER OF —) LEUCIPPUS
　(HUSBAND OF —) CASTOR
　(MOTHER OF —) PHILODICE
　(SISTER OF —) PHOEBE
ILEUM
　(PREF.) ILEO
ILEUS MISERERE

ILIA RHEA
　(FATHER OF —) NUMITOR
　(SON OF —) REMUS ROMULUS
ILIAD (AUTHOR OF —) HOMER
　(CHARACTER IN —) AIAS HELEN
　PARIS PRIAM ATHENA HECTOR
　NESTOR ACHILLES DIOMEDES
　MENELAUS ODYSSEUS PANDARUS
　AGAMEMNON APHRODITE
　PATROCLUS ANDROMACHE
ILIONE (BROTHER OF —) POLYDORUS
　(FATHER OF —) PRIAM
　(HUSBAND OF —) POLYMNESTOR
　(MOTHER OF —) HECUBA
　(SON OF —) DEIPYLUS
ILIUM TROY
ILK KIN KIDNEY
ILL BAD EVIL ILLY SICK AEGER CRONK
　CROOK DONCY FUNNY WISHT
　GROGGY INJURY POORLY SICKLY
　UNWELL SICKISH VICIOUS MISCHIEF
　PHYSICAL
　(— AT EASE) ASHAMED AWKWARD
　FAROUCHE
　(PREF.) MAL(E) MIS
ILL-ADVISED FOOLISH
ILL-BALANCED LOPSIDED
ILL-BEHAVED UNTHEWED
ILL-BEING ILLTH
ILL-BODING DIRE DISMAL
ILL-BRED HOYDEN CADDISH
　CHURLISH PLEBEIAN MISLEARED
ILL-CHOSEN UNSORTED
ILL-CONSIDERED HASTY
ILL-DEFINED BLIND VAGUE
　MONGREL
ILL-DRESSED FRUMPY FRUMPISH
ILLEGAL BLACK LAWLESS
　UNLAWFUL WRONGOUS
　ADULTERINE
　(NOT —) COLD
ILLEGALITY NONO UNLAW
ILLEGIBLE BLIND
ILLEGITIMACY BASTARDY
ILLEGITIMATE BASE BASTARD
　BOOTLEG NATURAL NOTHOUS
　MISBEGOT NAMELESS UNLAWFUL
　WRONGFUL MISBEGOTTEN
　(PREF.) NOTH(O)
ILL-FATED UNHAPPY UNSONCY
　UNCHANCY
ILL-FAVORED UGLY UNSONCY
ILL-FEELING PIQUE
ILL-FORMED SCRAWLY INFORMED
ILL HUMOR TID BILE DRUNT GRUMP
　THRAW FANTEE SPLEEN DUDGEON
　FANTIGUE
ILL-HUMORED FOUL GLUM CROOK
　DUDDY GRUMPY MOROSE STUFFY
　SULLEN CROOKED FRETFUL
　PEEVISH
ILLIBERAL LITTLE NARROW INSULAR
　BANAUSIC GRUDGING

ILLICIT SLY BLACK ILLEGAL
  UNLAWFUL
ILLIMITABLE INFINITE

ILLINOIS

CAPITAL: SPRINGFIELD
COLLEGE: AURORA EUREKA OLIVET
  QUINCY SHIMER
COUNTY: BOND CASS COOK KANE
  OGLE COLES MACON BUREAU
  DUPAGE GRUNDY HARDIN MASSAC
  PEORIA IROQUOIS MACOUPIN
  SANGAMON
FRENCH SETTLEMENT: CAHOKIA
HILLS: SHAWNEE
INDIAN: FOX SAUK
LAKE: MICHIGAN
NICKNAME: SUCKER PRAIRIE
PRESIDENT: REAGAN
RIVER: OHIO ROCK WABASH ELKHORN
  MACKINAW SANGAMON
STATE BIRD: CARDINAL
STATE FLOWER: VIOLET
STATE TREE: OAK
TOWN: PANA ALEDO ALTON CAIRO
  CARMI DIXON FLORA LACON OLNEY
  PARIS PEKIN ALBION CANTON
  EUREKA GALENA HARDIN HAVANA
  HERRIN JOLIET NORMAL OTTAWA
  PEORIA QUINCY SKOKIE URBANA
  VIENNA CHICAGO DECATUR
  GENESEO MENDOTA NOKOMIS
  TAMPICO KANKAKEE ROCKFORD

ILLINOISIAN SUCKER
ILLIPE BASSIA VIDORICUM
ILLITERATE UNREAD IGNORANT
  MUSELESS UNTAUGHT
ILL-MADE AWKWARD
ILL-NATURED SHREWD CRABBED
  SHREWISH ACID UGLY NASTY SURLY
  CRABBY SNARLY SULLEN THWART
  CANKERY PEEVISH
ILLNESS DROW TOUT BRASH CHILL
  TRAIK MORBUS PLUNGE DISEASE
  SICKNESS
  (IMAGINARY —) HYPOCHONDRIA
  (MENTAL —) MANIA MONOMANIA
  (MINOR —) HURRY
  (MOMENTARY —) DROW
  (SUDDEN —) WEED SWEAM
ILL-NOURISHED SHELLY
ILLOGICAL MAD SPURIOUS
ILL-OMENED OBSCENE DISMAL
  UNLUCKY
ILL-SHAPED WEEDY
ILL-SMELLING FUSTY STINKING
ILL-TEMPERED SURLY ILL FESS
  MEAN PUXY ACRID CHUFF NURLY
  RATTY CAMMED CHUFFY CURSED
  GIRNIE SHRILL SNAGGY RAMPANT
  ROPABLE VICIOUS CAMSHACH

  LUNGEOUS SHREWISH VIXENISH
  MALODOROUS
ILL-TREAT FOB HOIN MISDO
  AFFRONT
ILLUMINATE FIRE LIMN CLEAR
  LIGHT ENLIMN ILLUME KINDLE
  BESHINE CLARIFY EMBLAZE LIGHTEN
  MINIATE RADIATE EMBRIGHT
  FLOURISH ILLUMINE LUMINATE
  (— FAINTLY) TWILIGHT
ILLUMINATED FIRELIT
ILLUMINATION E GLIM GLORY
  LIGHT SHINE LIGHTING LUMINARY
  (— INCREASE) WOMP
  (— UNIT) PHOT
  (MANUSCRIPT —) MINIATURE
ILLUMINE SUN FIRE LAMP CLEAR
  LUMINE ENLIGHT
ILL-USAGE ABUSE
ILLUSION MAYA DEATH DREAM
  ERROR FAIRY FANCY FLESH TRICK
  MATTER CHIMERA ELUSION FALLACY
  FICTION MOCKERY PHANTOM
  RAINBOW ZOLLNER DELUSION
  PHANTASM PRESTIGE
ILLUSIVE PHANTOM
ILLUSORY FALSE EVANID FATUOUS
  PHANTOM TRICKSY APPARENT
  ILLUSIVE SPECTRAL
ILLUSTRATE INSTANCE
ILLUSTRATION CUT GAY ICON IKON
  SHOW SPOT INSET FIGURE COMPARE
  DISIMILE EXEMPLUM INSTANCE
  VIGNETTE
ILLUSTRATIVE CLASSIC
ILLUSTRATOR ERTE
ILLUSTRIOUS GRAND NOBLE
  NOTED SHEEN BRIGHT CANDID
  HEROIC EMINENT EXALTED GLORIED
  SHINING GLORIOUS HEROICAL
  LUCULENT MAGNIFIC PRECLARE
  RENOWNED SPLENDID STARLIKE
  BRILLIANT REDOUBTABLE
  (MOST —) ILMO ILLMO
ILL WILL SPITE ENMITY GRUDGE
  MALICE MAUGER MAUGRE RANCOR
  DESPITE AMBITION
ILL-WISHER FOE
ILUS (FATHER OF —) TROS
  (MOTHER OF —) CALLIRRHOE
  (SON OF —) LAOMEDON
ILVAITE YENITE LIEVRITE
ILYSIA TORTRIX
IMAGE DAP GOD MAP FORM ICON
  IDOL IKON JOSS MAKE SEAL SIGN
  SPIT TIKI AGNUS DITTO EPHOD
  FANCY HERMA IMAGO MEDAL
  MORAL PAINT PRINT SAMMY SANTO
  SHAPE SIGIL SWAMI SWAMY TOTEM
  AGALMA ALRAUN EFFIGY EMBLEM
  FIGURE MAUMET MODULE POPPET
  RECEPT REFLEX SHRINE SPHINX

STATUE SVAMIN TERAPH VISAGE
WEEPER EIDOLON EXPRESS
FANTASY GODLING IMAGERY
KATCINA PICTURE PROPOSE
CONCEIVE DAIBUTSU OPTOGRAM
PORTRAIT SURPRINT ZOOMORPH
SEMBLANCE SIMILITUDE
SIMULACRUM RESEMBLANCE
(— IN CHINESE COSTUME)
MANDARIN
(— OF CHRIST) SUDARIUM
(— OF DEITY) SWAMI GODKIN
SVAMIN GODLING
(— OF SAINT) BULTO SAINT SANTO
GEORGE SANTON
(— OF WOOD) XOANON
(— RECALLED BY MEMORY) IDEA
(CULT —) JOSS
(FALSE —) GHOST GHOSTING
(GOOD-LUCK —) ALRAUN ALRUNA
(HEAVENLY —) FRAVASHI
(LINGERING —) SHADE
(MENTAL —) FANCY IMAGO RECEPT
CONCEPT FANTASY SPECIES
PHANTASM
(RADAR —) BLIP
(REFLECTED —) SHADOW SPECIES
(SEQUENCE OF —S) REVERIF
(VAGUE —S) FRINGE
(PL.) IMAGERY TERAPHIM
(PREF.) EID(O)(OLO) EIKON(O) ICON(O)
IDOLO IKON(O) TYP(I)(O)
IMAGERY ICONISM
IMAGINARY IDEAL AERIAL FEIGNED
FICTIVE SHADOWY CHIMERAL
CHIMERIC FANCIFUL FICTIOUS
MYTHICAL NOTIONAL QUIXOTIC
ROMANTIC SCENICAL VISIONAL
BARMECIDE
IMAGINATION CHIC BRAIN FANCY
FLAME NOTION FANTASY PROJECT
THOUGHT
(DROLL —) HUMOR
IMAGINATIVE FORMFUL CREATIVE
FANCIFUL POETICAL
IMAGINE SEE WIS REDE WEEN
DREAM FANCY FEIGN FRAME GUESS
IMAGE THINK DEVISE FIGURE IDEATE
INVENT RECKON COMPASS CONCEIT
CONJURE FANCIFY FANTASY
FEATURE PICTURE PORTRAY
PROJECT PROPOSE SUPPOSE
SURMISE SUSPECT CONCEIVE
DAYDREAM JEALOUSE
IMAGINED FANCIED SUPPOSED
IMAGINER FANCIER
IMAGINING FICTION PHANTOM
IMAGO MOTH
IMAM IMAUM MAHDI
IMBALANCE DRIVE DYSCRASIA
IMBECILE MAD DOTE FOOL AMENT
ANILE DAFFY IDIOT CRANKY DOTARD

DOTING DOTISH CONGEON
FATUOUS
IMBECILITY AMENTIA FATUITY
IMBIBE DRINK SMACK ABSORB
SPONGE INHAUST SWALLOW
IRRIGATE
(— NOISILY) SLURP
IMBIBING SUCTION
IMBIBITORY SPONGY
IMBRIUS (FATHER OF —) MENTOR
(SLAYER OF —) AJAX
(WIFE OF —) MEDESICASTE
IMBRUE EMBREW INSTEEP
IMBUE SOAK STEW COLOR CROWN
EMBUE ENDUE INDUE SCENT STEEP
TINCT ENSOUL IMBIBE INFUSE
LEAVEN SEASON ANIMATE INGRAIN
INSENSE INSTILL SATURATE
TINCTURE INOCULATE
IMBUED INSTINCT REDOLENT
IMHOTEP (FATHER OF —) PTAH
(MOTHER OF —) SEKHMET
IMIDE LACTIM SACCHARIN
IMITATE APE COPY ECHO MIME
MOCK ZANY ENSUE FORGE IMAGE
MIMIC AFFECT ANSWER FOLLOW
PARROT SEMBLE COPYCAT EMULATE
PAGEANT PATTERN PASTICHE
RESEMBLE SIMULATE
(— WITH RECORDED SOUND)
LIPSYNC LIPSYNCH
(PREF.) MIMO
IMITATION COPY FAKE FAUX SHAM
DUMMY IMAGE MIMIC ALPACA
ANSWER BUMPER ECTYPE SHADOW
CAMBLET FOULARD IMITANT
MIMESIS MOCKAGE MOCKERY
CHENILLE PARROTRY PASTICHE
POSTIQUE
(— OF COIN) COUNTER
(BURLESQUE —) TRAVESTY
(COTTON —) CAMBRIC
(EXAGGERATED —) BURLESQUE
(UNSUBSTANTIAL —) GHOST
(PREF.) NE
(SUFF.) EEN ETTE
IMITATIVE ARTY MIMIC ARTFUL
ECHOIC SHODDY MIMETIC SIMULAR
SLAVISH APATETIC EPIGONAL
IMITATOR APE MIME ZANY MIMIC
COPIER COPYIST EPIGONE
EMULATOR EPIGONUS HOMERIST
(SUFF.) MIMUS
IMMACULATE CLEAN CANDID
CHASTE BLOTLESS PRISTINE
SPOTLESS UNSOILED
IMMANENCE INBEING
IMMATERIAL MENTAL SLIGHT
ETHEREAL FORMLESS SEPARATE
TRIFLING
IMMATURE RAW CRUDE GREEN
SAPPY SMALL VEALY YOUNG

BOYISH CALLOW JEJUNE LARVAL
NEANIC TENDER GIRLISH HALFLIN
IMPUBIC LADDISH NOUVEAU
PUERILE UNBAKED JUVENILE
NEPIONIC UNWEANED SHIRTTAIL
IMMATURITY NONAGE
IMMEASURABLE UNTOLD
ABYSMAL INFINITE
IMMEDIACY HERE
IMMEDIATE CLOSE DIRECT MODERN
PARATE SUDDEN INSTANT PRESENT
PROXIMAL SYNECTIC POSTHASTE
IMMEDIATELY PDQ TIT ANON ASAP
AWAY FAST JUST ONCE SOON
PLUMB RIGHT ASTITE DIRECT
PRESTO PRONTO SUBITO DIRECTLY
HEREUPON OUTRIGHT STRAIGHT
IMMEDIATENESS INSTANCY
IMMEMORIAL DATELESS
IMMENSE HUGE VAST GIANT
GRAND GREAT LARGE UNMEET
UNRIDE TITANIC ENORMOUS
GIGANTIC INFINITE SLASHING
WHOOPING PLANETARY
IMMENSELY ALOT EVER
IMMENSITY VAST IMMANE
IMMENSE ENORMITY GRANDEUR
HUGENESS
IMMERSE DIP SINK SOAK COVER
DOUSE MERGE MERSE SOUSE STEEP
DRENCH PLUNGE BAPTIZE BOWSSEN
DEMERGE EMBATHE ENSTEEP
IMMERGE DISSOLVE
IMMERSED DEEP INNATE
IMMERSION DIP DUNKING MERSION
IMMERSIONIST DIPPER
IMMIGRANT LAG BALT ISSEI JIMMY
METIC POMMY GUINEA HALUTZ
CHALUTZ INCOMER PILGRIM
COMELING
IMMINENCE INSTANCY
IMMINENT TOWARD PENDING
PROXIMATE
IMMIX BLEND
IMMOBILE FIXED INERT STILL
FROZEN DORMANT GLACIAL
TRANCED MOVELESS
(PREF.) ANKYL(O)
IMMOBILIZATION FUSION
FIXATION
IMMOBILIZE PIN FREEZE SPLINT
STIFFEN
IMMOBILIZED STIFF
IMMODERATE FREE DIZZY UNDUE
LAVISH UNMETH EXTREME
OVERWEENING
IMMODERATENESS EXCESS
IMMODEST FREE BRAZEN OBSCENE
INDECENT PETULANT UNCHASTE
SHAMELESS
(NOT —) DELICATE
IMMORAL BAD ILL EVIL IDLE LOOSE
WRONG WANTON CORRUPT VICIOUS

CULPABLE DEPRAVED INDECENT
SLIPPERY
IMMORTAL DIVINE ENDLESS
ETERNAL GODLIKE UNDYING
ENDURING UNDEADLY
IMMORTALITY AMRITA ATHANASY
ETERNITY
IMMOVABLE PAT SET FAST FIRM
FIXED RIGID ADAMANT SITFAST
CONSTANT IMMOBILE IMMOTIVE
OBDURATE
IMMUNE FREE SALTED REFRACTORY
IMMUNITY SOC CHARTER
FREEDOM LIBERTY WOODGELD
PROTECTION
IMMUNOGLOBULIN IGA IGE IGM
UGG
IMMURE MURE WALL CONFINE
CLOISTER IMPRISON
IMMUTABILITY ONENESS
IMMUTABLE ETERNAL
IMNAH (FATHER OF —) ASHER
IMOGEN (FATHER OF —) CYMBELINE
(HUSBAND OF —) POSTHUMUS
IMP PUG BRAT LIMB DEMON TERROR
URCHIN DEVILET DEVILING DEVILKIN
FOLLETTO
(PRINTING-HOUSE —) RALPH
IMPACT HIT JAR BEAT BITE BLOW
BUMP DASH DUSH JOLT SLAM
BRUNT CLASH FEEZE PEISE POISE
PULSE SHOCK SKITE GLANCE
STROKE CONTACT IMPULSE
COLLISION
(— OF VALUES ON YOUTH)
YOUTHQUAKE
(HAVING STRONG —) GUT
IMPAIR MAR BLOT HARM HURT MAIM
MANK SOUR WEAR ALLOY CLOUD
CRACK CRAZE DECAY ERODE QUAIL
SPOIL TAINT ACRAZE DAMAGE
DEADEN DEFACE HINDER INJURE
LABEFY LESSEN REDUCE SICKEN
WEAKEN WORSEN BLEMISH CRIPPLE
DISABLE IMPEACH REFRACT
SHATTER STRETCH VITIATE
DECREASE ENFEEBLE IMBECILE
IMPERISH INFRINGE LABEFACT
(— BY INACTIVITY) RUST
(— ESSENTIALLY) RUIN
(— GRADUALLY) WASTE
IMPAIRED HURT STALE CROCKY
FLYBLOWN
(— BY AGE) FUSTY
(— IN TONE) BREATHY
(HEARING —) DEAF
(SPEECH —) APHASIC
(PREF.) DYS
IMPAIRMENT ALLAY FAULT SPOIL
DOTAGE IMPAIR INJURY LESION
BEATING DEFICIT DISEASE EROSION
WEARING AKINESIA PAIRMENT
(— OF CONSCIOUSNESS) ABSENCE

IMPALA PALLA PALLAH REDBUCK
ROOIBOK ROODEBOK ROOYEBOK
IMPALE BAIT SPIT GANCH GANSH
SPEAR SPIKE STAKE STICK STING
SKIVER TRANSFIX
IMPALPABLE ELUSIVE
IMPART GIVE SEND SHED TELL
BREAK DRILL SHARE YIELD
BESTOW COMMON CONFER
CONVEY DIRECT IMPUTE INSTIL
PARTEN REVEAL DELIVER DIVULGE
PURPORT DISCOVER INSTRUCT
INTIMATE
(— **KNOWLEDGE**) TEACH INFORM
(— **SECRETS**) CONFIDE
(— **TONE**) TONE
(— **ZEST**) ANIMATE
IMPARTIAL EVEN FAIR JUST EQUAL
LEVEL CANDID NEUTER UNBIASED
IMPARTIALITY CANDOR EQUITY
EQUACITY EVENNESS
IMPARTIALLY FAIRLY EQUALLY
IMPASSABLE WICKED INVIOUS
PASSLESS ROADLESS TRACKLESS
IMPASSE LOGJAM DEADLOCK
IMPASSION COMMOVE
IMPASSIONED ARDENT FERVID
FERVENT FEVERISH PERFERVID
IMPASSIVE STOIC FROZEN STOLID
PASSIVE STOICAL APATHETIC
PHLEGMATIC
IMPASSIVENESS APATHY MORGUE
STOICISM
IMPATIENT HOT ANTSY EAGER
HASTY SHARP TESTY FRETFUL
PEEVISH RESTIVE TIDIOSE CHOLERIC
PETULANT
IMPATIENTLY HASTILY
IMPEACH CALL ACCUSE CHARGE
INDICT ARRAIGN CENSURE IMPLEAD
TRAVERSE
IMPEACHMENT APPEAL
IMPECCABLE SINLESS
IMPECUNIOUS POOR
IMPEDE BOG DAM GUM JAM LET
MAR CLOG GRAB JAMB KILL SLUG
SNAG ANNOY BLOCK CHECK CHOKE
DELAY EMBAR ESTOP HITCH SLOTH
SPOKE BAFFLE FETTER FORBID
FORSET HAMPER HARASS HINDER
HOBBLE PESTER RETARD STYMIE
IMPEACH PREVENT SHACKLE
ENCUMBER HANDICAP OBSTRUCT
PRECLUDE
IMPEDED FOGBOUND
IMPEDIMENT BAR RUB CLOG SNAG
STOP BLEAR BLOCK HITCH SPOKE
STICK BURDEN RUBBER SCOTCH
BLINDER EMBARGO OBSTACLE
OBSTANCY
(— **IN SPEECH**) HAAR HALT
IMPEDIMENTA STUFF
IMPEDING CATCH HEAVY FOULING

IMPEL PAT PUT BEAR BEAT CALL
CAST GOAD HURL MOVE SEND URGE
WHIP CARRY DRIVE FEEZE FORCE
KNOCK PRESS PRICK PULSE COMPEL
EXCITE INCITE INDUCE PROPEL
ACTUATE DESTINE INSPIRE INSTINCT
MOTIVATE
(— **TO GREATER SPEED**) GATHER
IMPELLER RUNNER
IMPEND BREW HANG DEPEND
OVERHANG
IMPENDING TOWARD PENDENT
PENDING IMMINENT MENACING
IMPENETRABLE HARD DENSE
MURKY PROOF THICK AIRTIGHT
HARDENED
IMPENITENT OBDURATE
IMPERATIVE AMUST VITAL
PRESSING MASTERFUL
IMPERCEPTIBLE OCCULT SUBTLE
IMPERFECT ILL HALF POOR AMISS
BLIND FUZZY ROUGH BOTCHY
FAULTY PLATIC ATELENE STICKIT
UNWHOLE VICIOUS INPARFIT
MUTILOUS
(**PREF.**) ATEL(O)
IMPERFECTED INCHOATE
IMPERFECTION BUG RUB WEN
FLAW KINK MOLE SLUR VICE WART
ERROR FAULT BLOTCH DEFECT
FOIBLE BLEMISH CRUDITY DEFAULT
DEMERIT FAILING FRAILTY
WEAKNESS
(— **IN BOTTLE**) HEELTAP
(— **IN GLASS**) STRIA STREAK
(— **IN LEATHER**) FRIEZE
(— **IN SILK**) CORKSCREW
(— **IN WICK**) THIEF WASTER
IMPERFECTIVE ATELIC
IMPERFECTLY ILL HALF AMISS
ROUGHLY
IMPERFORATION ATRESIA
IMPERIAL TUFT ROYAL KINGLY
PURPLE MAJESTIC
IMPERIALIST KHAKI CAESAR
CAESAREAN
IMPERIL RISK EXPONE EMPERIL
ENDANGER JEOPARDY
IMPERIOUS BOSSY SURLY
LORDLY HAUGHTY DESPOTIC
IMPERIAL MASTERLY PRESSING
MASTERFUL
IMPERISHABLE ETERNAL UNDYING
ENDURING IMMORTAL
IMPERMANENCE ANICCA
IMPERMANENT FLEETING
IMPERMEABLE AIRTIGHT
IMPERSONAL COLD DEADPAN
INHUMAN ABSTRACT
IMPERSONALITY UNSELF
IMPERSONATE POSE TYPIFY
PERSONIFY
IMPERSONATION GENIUS

IMPERSONATOR APER ACTOR
MIMIC CACHINA KACHINA KATCINA
IMPERTINENCE PAWK SNASH
AUDACITY
IMPERTINENT GAY FREE PERT RUDE
FRESH SASSY SAUCY PUSHING
IMPERENT IMPUDENT OBTRUSIVE
OFFICIOUS MEDDLESOME
IMPERTURBABILITY ATARAXY
ATARAXIA SANGFROID
IMPERTURBABLE COOL PLACID
GLACIAL TRANQUIL UNFLAPPABLE
IMPERVIOUS DEAD GASTIGHT
HARDENED HERMETIC MOTHPROOF
(— TO HEAT) ADIATHERMIC
(— TO LIGHT) OPAQUE
(SUFF.) PROOF
IMPETUOSITY BIRR ELAN FURY
HASTE WRATH FOUGUE POWDER
RANDOM SPLEEN
IMPETUOUS HOT RAMP RASH RUDE
BRASH EAGER FIERY FRECK HASTY
HEADY SHARP ARDENT BROTHE
FIERCE FLASHY LAVISH RACKLE
STRONG BUCKISH FURIOUS
HOTHEAD HOTSPUR RAMSTAM
VIOLENT BRAINISH EMPRESSE
HEADLONG SLAPDASH VEHEMENT
PRECIPITATE
IMPETUS BIRR FARD SEND DRIFT
GRACE SWING YMPET BENSEL
IMPACT POWDER RAVINE SWINGE
SWOUGH IMPULSE MOMENTUM
IMPIGNORATE PAWN
IMPINGE FALL IMPACT ASSAULT
CROSSCUT ENCROACH
IMPINGEMENT IMPACT
IMPIOUS UNHOLY ATHEIST ATHEOUS
GODLESS UNGODLY DOWNWEED
HOARWORT NEFANDOUS NEFARIOUS
IMPISH IMPY ELFISH PUCKISH
WARLOCK
IMPLACABLE STOUT DEADLY
MORTAL
IMPLACABLY FATALLY
IMPLANT FIX IMP SET SOW HAFT
ROOT GRAFT INFIX INLAY ENRACE
ENROOT FASTEN INFUSE INSTIL
ENFORCE ENGRAFT IMPRESS
INSPIRE ENTRENCH INSTINCT
IMPLANTED INBORN INSITE
IMPLEMENT (ALSO SEE TOOL) AX
AXE BAT CARD DISC DISK FORK
GRAB HACK HONE HOOK LOOM
PLOW SPUD SPUR TOOL CROOK
DRILL FLINT LANCE SCRUB SHEAR
SLICK SPADE SPOON STEEL STICK
TRIER AMGARN BEAMER BLADER
BROACH CALOR COOLER DIBBLE
DREDGE DRIVER DUSTER EOLITH
FLAKER FLUTER HACKER HARROW
INVOKE LADDER LIPPER LUNATE
MARKER MEALER PACKER PADDLE
PALLET PESTLE PLOUGH RIMMER
SCREEN SCYTHE SEATER SEEDER
SERVER SHEARS SHOVEL SICKLE
SLICER SMOOTH BREAKER CHOPPER
CLEANER CLEAVER ENFORCE
FLESHER FLYFLAP GAROTTE
GRUBBER HARPOON HUSTLER
KNAPPER MATTOCK NUTPICK
SKIMMER SLABBER SLASHER
SLEEKER SLICKER SPATTLE SPATULA
SPITTLE SPURTLE STAMPER STICKER
SWATHER UTENSIL AGITATOR
BUSHWACK MEASURER SCUTCHER
SEARCHER SHREDDER SKETCHER
SPLITTER SPREADER STRIPPER
TERRACER THWACKER TOLLIKER
TRANCHET TWEEZERS WARKLOOM
WORKLOOM NUTCRACKER
(— FOR CUTTING CHEESE) HARP
(— FOR HANGING POT) HALE
(—S OF HUSBANDRY) WAINAGE
**(— TO PREVENT MALT FROM
OVERFLOWING)** STROM
(ANCIENT —) POINT SLICE AMGARN
EOLITH NEOLITH RACLOIR PALEOLITH
(BAKER'S —) PEEL
(CLIMBING —) CREEPER
(ESKIMO —) ULU
(GARDENING —) HOE RAKE SEEDER
SICKLE
(HEDGING —) TRAMP
(IRRIGATION —) CROWDER
(LOGGING —) TODE
(POTTER'S —) PALLET SPATTLE
(PREHISTORIC —) CELT FLAKER
(SHOVEL-LIKE —) SCOOP
(SOLDERING —) DOCTOR
(TORTURE —) ENGINE
(UPROOTING —) MAKE
(WINNOWING —) FAN
(PL.) GEAR CUTLERY GAINAGE
FLAUGHTS
(SUFF.) LABE
IMPLEMENTATION PERFORMANCE
IMPLICATE DIP ENWRAP CONCERN
EMBROIL INCLUDE INVOLVE
IMPLICATION CLAIM IMPLIAL
INNUENDO
IMPLICIT COVERT
IMPLIED TACIT IMPLICIT
IMPLORATION PETITION
IMPLORE ASK BEG CRY PRAY CHARM
CRAVE PLEAD INVOKE OBTEST
BESEECH CONJURE ENTREAT
SOLICIT PETITION
IMPLOSION INRUSH
IMPLY HINT ARGUE CARRY COUCH
INFER EMPLOY ENTAIL IMPORT
INDUCE CONNOTE CONTAIN
INCLUDE INVOLVE PRESUME SIGNIFY
SUGGEST SUPPOSE PREDICATE
IMPOLITE RUDE UNCIVIL
IMPOLITENESS CRUDITY

IMPONDERABLE FRIGORIC
IMPORT SAY WIT BEAR BODY GIST
TOUR DRIFT FORCE IMPLY MORAL
SCOPE SENSE SOUND SPELL TENOR
VALOR AMOUNT CHARGE DENOTE
INGATE INTENT MATTER SPIRIT
BETOKEN MEANING PRETEND
SIGNIFY CARRIAGE INDICATE
(PL.) INWARDS
IMPORTANCE BORE MARK PITH
FORCE POISE WORTH CHARGE
IMPORT MATTER MOMENT REMARK
STRESS STROKE WEIGHT ACCOUNT
ESSENCE GRAVITY VALENCY
EMPHASIS MAGNITUDE
SIGNIFICANCE
**IMPORTANCE OF BEING
EARNEST (AUTHOR OF —)** WILDE
(CHARACTER IN —) JACK ALGIE
PRISM CECILY EARNEST ALGERNON
WORTHING BRACKNELL
GWENDOLEN MONCRIEFF
IMPORTANT BIG KEY DEAR DREE
HIGH MAIN REAL GRAVE GREAT
HEAVY MAJOR GAPING MIGHTY
NEEDLE STRONG URGENT VALOUR
CAPITAL CENTRAL CRUCIAL EMINENT
MATTERY PIVOTAL SERIOUS
WEIGHTY EVENTFUL MATERIAL
PRESSING MOMENTOUS
OVERBEARING SIGNIFICANT
(— PERSON) LION
(HIGHLY —) VITAL
(MOST —) TOP ULTIMATE
(MOST — ONE OF GROUP) FLAGSHIP
IMPORTER MILLINER
IMPORTUNATE URGENT INSTANT
DEVILING EXIGEANT PRESSING
IMPORTUNE BEG WOO BEAT BONE
PREY PRIG TOUT URGE PRESS TEASE
BESEECH RESOLICIT INSTANT SOLICIT
TERRIFY INSTANCE
IMPORTUNITY BRASS URGENCY
IMPOSE LAY SET TOP CLAP GIVE
LEVY MUMP POLE SORN ABUSE
APPLY CLAMP INPUT STAMP TRUMP
BURDEN CHARGE ENJOIN ENTAIL
FASTEN FATHER IMPONE IMPUTE
BLAFLUM DICTATE INFLICT IRROGATE
(— UPON) FOB GAG HUM LAY DUPE
SELL CULLY TRAIL BLUDGE DELUDE
EXCISE HUMBUG NUZZLE CULLION
DECEIVE HOODWINK
IMPOSED BOUNDEN
IMPOSING BIG EPIC BUDGE BURLY
GRAND HEFTY NOBLE PROUD
AUGUST EPICAL FEUDAL PORTLY
HAUGHTY POMPOUS STATELY
HANDSOME MAGNIFIC SONORANT
SONOROUS
(— UPON) PRACTICE PRACTISE
IMPOSITION BAM COD HUM LEVY
SELL TAIL GOUGE IMPOT CHOUSE

GAMMON INTAKE TAILLE IMPOSAL
ARTIFICE IMPOSURE
(MILITARY —) CESS
(SCHOOL —) PENSUM
IMPOSSIBLE OUT HOPELESS
IMPOST LAY TAX CAST LEVY TAIL
TASK TOLL ABWAB ANNALE AVANIA
EXCISE GABELLE POUNAMU
TALLAGE TONNAGE TRIBUTE
CHAPTREL SPRINGER
(PL.) CUSTOMS
IMPOSTOR FOB FAKE GULL IDOL
CHEAT FAKER FRAUD GOUGE QUACK
BUNYIP FOURBE HUMBUG MUMPER
EMPIRIC FAITOUR PROCTOR
SHAMMER PHANTASM
IMPOSTURE BAM GAG FAKE HOAX
SHAM CHEAT FRAUD TRICK DECEIT
HUMBUG JUGGLE ARTIFICE
DELUSION JUGGLERY
IMPOTENCE ACRATIA UNMIGHT
WEAKNESS
(— THROUGH MAGIC) LIGATURE
IMPOTENCY UNWELTH
IMPOTENT WEAK FRIGID PAULIE
UNABLE STERILE UNMIGHTY
IMPOUND FIND POIND POUND
INTERN PINFOLD
IMPOVERISH PILL CLOUD BEGGAR
IMPOOR SICKEN DEPLETE DEPRESS
EMPOVER BANKRUPT POVERISH
PAUPERISE
IMPOVERISHED POOR OBOLARY
BANKRUPT INDIGENT
IMPRACTICAL CRAZY FECKLESS
IMPRECATE WISH SWEAR
IMPRECATION DASH OATH PIZE
WISH BLAME CURSE DAMME
DAMMIT CONSARN ANATHEMA
IMPREGNABILITY STRENGTH
IMPREGNABLE FAST PROOF
IMPREGNATE BIG HOP DOPE FILL
LIME MILT BREED IMBUE STOCK
STUFF TINCT AERATE CHARGE
INFORM INFUSE LEAVEN SEASON
SETTLE ASPHALT ENVENOM
IMPREGN CHROMATE CONCEIVE
CREOSOTE FRICTION FRUCTIFY
GRAPHITE MEDICATE PERMEATE
SATURATE SILICATE TINCTURE
(SUFF.) (— WITH) URET(UM)
IMPREGNATED BRED COATED
IMPRESS FIX BITE CORN DING DINT
ETCH GRAB MARK AFFIX BRAND
CLAMP CRIMP DRIVE GRAVE GRILL
INFIX PRESS PRINT REACH SEIZE
STAMP STEAD WRITE AFFECT
ENSEAL FASTEN INCUSE INDENT
SALUTE STRIKE ANTIQUE ENGRAVE
ENSTAMP IMPLANT IMPREST
IMPRINT INSENSE AUTOTYPE
INSCRIBE NEGATIVE
(— CONSIDERABLY) WOW

(— **DEEPLY**) DELVE ENGRAVE
(— **SUDDENLY**) SMITE
(— **VERY MUCH**) SLAY
(— **WITH FEAR**) AFFRIGHT
(**FAIL TO** —) UNDERWHELM
IMPRESSED AGOG BLIND ANTIQUE INDENTED
IMPRESSIBLE WAXY
IMPRESSION CUT HIT AURA CAST CHOP DENT DINT IDEA MARK MOLD SEAL STEP STIR FANCY GOUGE IMAGE MOULD PRINT STAMP STATE ECTYPE EFFECT ENGRAM FIGURE INCUSE OFFSET SIGNET SPLASH STRIKE EOPHYTE ETCHING FANTASY IMPRESS MOULAGE OPINION SEALING SQUEEZE STENCIL TOOLING BLANKING ENGRAMMA NEGATIVE PRESSION PRESSURE STAMPAGE TOOLMARK PHOTOGENE
(— **OF DIE**) CLICHE
(— **ON COIN**) CROSS
(— **WITHOUT INK**) ALBINO
(**AUDITORY** —) SOUND
(**DOUBLE** —) MACKLE MACULE
(**GENERAL** —) REPUTE
(**IMMEDIATE** —) APERCU
(**LATER** —) REPRINT
(**LUMINOUS** —) PHOSPHENE
(**MAKE AN** → **ON**) GRAB
(**MENTAL** —) GRAVING
(**STRONG** —) HUNCH
(**TRANSITORY** —) SNAPSHOT
(**VIVID** —) SPLASH
(**PREF.**) TYP(I)(O)
(**SUFF.**) TYPAL TYPE TYPIC TYPY
IMPRESSIONABLE SOFT WAXY WAXEN TENDER PLASTIC PASSIBLE
IMPRESSIONIST LUMINIST
IMPRESSIVE BIG FAT EPIC AWFUL GRAND NOBLE PROUD SOCKO EPICAL SOLEMN PESANTE STATELY TEARING TELLING WEIGHTY FORCIBLE IMPOSING SMASHING SONORANT SONOROUS STUNNING MAGNIFICENT
IMPRESSIVENESS WEIGHT
IMPREST LOAN
IMPRIMATUR SEAL LICENSE APPROVAL SANCTION
IMPRINT DINT ETCH MARK SIGN STEP PRESS STAMP CUTOFF FASTEN STRIKE ENGRAVE ENSTAMP IMPRESS APREYNTE COLOPHON EPIGRAPH PRESSION PRESSURE STAMPAGE
(— **ON CHEEK**) FASTEN
(**PUBLISHER'S** —) COLOPHON
IMPRISON JUG LAG NUN BOND GAOL HULK JAIL QUOD SEAL SHOP WARD CROWD EMBAR GRATE COMMIT IMMURE JIGGER PRISON SLOUGH CONFINE INTOWER BASTILLE

IMPRISONED FAST
IMPRISONMENT BAND BOND ARREST CHAINS DURESS PRISON CUSTODY DURANCE
IMPROBABLE FISHY UNLIKE UNLIKELY
IMPROMPTU GLIB MAGGOT SUDDEN OFFHAND
IMPROPER BAD PAH PAW AMISS LARGE SPICY UNDUE UNFELE UNJUST ILLICIT INDECENT PERVERSE TORTIOUS UNSEEMLY WRONGOUS MALODOROUS
IMPROPERLY AMISS
IMPROPRIETY SOLECISM
IMPROVE FIX BEET GAIN GOOD GROW HELP MEND AMEND EDIFY EMEND GRADE MOISE SMART TOUCH BETTER ENRICH PROFIT ADVANCE BENEFIT CORRECT CULTURE ELEVATE PERFECT PROMOTE RECTIFY UPGRADE UPSWING
(— **APPEARANCE OF HORSE**) BISHOP
(— **APPEARANCE OF TEA**) FACE
(— **CONDUCTIVITY**) AGE
IMPROVED BETTER
IMPROVEMENT AMENDS PICKUP POLICY PROFIT REFORM REDRESS UPSWING
IMPROVIDENT PRODIGAL WASTEFUL
(— **PERSON**) MICAWBER
IMPROVISATION THEME CALYPSO
IMPROVISE JAM COOK FAKE PONG VAMP WING ADLIB FANTASY
(— **MUSICALLY**) JAM FAKE NOODLE
(— **NONSENSE SYLLABLES**) SCAT
IMPRUDENCE FOLLY
IMPRUDENT FESS RASH FALSE UNWARY FOOLISH RECKLESS
IMPUDENCE GALL BRASS CHEEK MOUTH NERVE SLACK BRONZE PUPPYISM
IMPUDENT BOLD COXY FACY RUDE BANTY BARDY BRASH FRESH GALLY LIPPY SASSY SAUCY BRASSY BRAZEN CHEEKY STOCKY BIGGETY CHUNKED FORWARD GALLOWS PERKING INSOLENT MALAPERT AUDACIOUS BAREFACED
IMPUDENTLY COOLY COOLLY FRESHLY
IMPUGN DENY FALSE DISPUTE IMPEACH
IMPULSE FIT BIAS RESE SEND URGE DRIVE NISUS SPEND START DESIRE MOTIVE SIGNAL SPLEEN YETZER CALLING CONATUS IMPETUS INSTINCT MOVEMENT STIRRING
(— **CARRIER**) AXON
(**BLIND** —) ATE
(**ELECTRICAL** —) KICK

(SPONTANEOUS —) ACCORD
(SUDDEN —) SPLEEN
(SUPERNATURAL —) AFFLATUS
(PREF.) OSMO
IMPULSION SWING IMPULSE
IMPULSIVE QUICK FITFUL
HEADLONG IMPETUOUS
IMPURE DRY FOUL LEWD GROSS
HORRY MUDDY FILTHY TURBID
UNPURE MONGREL SCABBED
UNCLEAN VICIOUS INDECENT
MACULATE PRURIENT MACULATED
IMPURITY CRUD DONOR DROSS
DOPANT FEDITY ACCEPTER
ACCEPTOR FOULNESS
(— IN LINT) SHALE
(— IN MINERAL) GANG GANGUE
(PL.) SCUM GARBLE SLUMMAGE
IMPUTABLE OWING
IMPUTATION SCANDAL
IMPUTE LAY PUT RET ARET EVEN
WITE COUNT REFER ARRECT CHARGE
FASTEN IMPOSE OBJECT RECKON
REPUTE ASCRIBE ENTITLE IMPEACH
IN A I N Y AT TO BAJO INBY INTO
UPON ALONG INTIL ATHOME
(— ACCORDANCE) AFTER
(— ADDITION) EKE TOO ALSO ABOVE
AGAIN ALONG FORBY STILL BEYOND
BESIDES FARTHER FURTHER
MOREOVER OVERPLUS THERETIL
(— ADVANCE) AHEAD FORTH BEFORE
(— A FAINT) AWAY
(— ANY CASE) EVER HOWEVER
(— A SERIES) SERIATIM
(— A STATE OF ACTION) ENERGIC
(— BEHALF OF) PRO
(— CASE THAT) AUNTERS
(— CIRCULATION) ABROAD
(— CONNECTION WITH) FORNENT
FERNINST
(— EARNEST) AGOOD
(— EXCESS OF) OVER
(— FACT) SOOTH TRULY INDEED
ITSELF MERELY VERILY ACTUALLY
VERAMENT
(— FAITH) IVADS EFECKS YFACKS
(— FRONT) FORE AFACE FORNE
AGAINST PARAVANT
(— FULL) ALONG
(— GOOD SEASON) BETIMES
(— GOOD SPIRITS) BOBBISH
(— GRACEFUL MANNER) ADAGIO
(— JEST) AGAME
(— NO MANNER) NOWISE NAEGATES
(— ONE DIRECTION) ANON
(— ORDER) FOR ATAUNT ATAUNTO
(— PLACE OF) FOR WITH INSTEAD
(— POSSESSION) WITHIN
(— PROGRESS) AFOOT TOWARD
(— PROPER MANNER) DULY
(— RESPECT TO) ANENT
(— RETURN FOR) AGAINST

(— ROTATION) ABOUT
(— SO FAR AS) AS QUA
(— SOLE CONTROL) ABSOLUTE
(— SOOTH) PARFEY PERFAY
(— SPITE OF) FOR ALTHO MALGRE
AGAINST DESPITE MALGRADO
(— SUSPENSE) PENDING
(— THE DOING OF) WITH
(— THE FIELD) ABROAD
(— THE FIRST PLACE) IMP IMPRIMIS
(— THE FUTURE) HENCE
(— THE MORNING) MANE
(— THE REAR) AREAR ASTERN
(— THE REGIONS OF UNBELIEVERS)
IPI
(— THE SAME PLACE) IBID IBIDEM
(— THE SAME WAY) AS
(— TOWARD) INOWER
(— TRUTH) MARRY SOOTH CERTES
INDEED VERILY SOOTHLY FORSOOTH
(— VAIN) WASTELY
(— VIEW OF THE FACT THAT)
SEEING
(— WHAT MANNER) HOW QUOMODO
(NOT —) OUT
(PREF.) A IL IM IN INTRO IR
INABILITY (— TO FEED) APHAGIA
(— TO MASTICATE) AMASESIS
(— TO SPEAK) ALOGIA ANEPIA
DUMBNESS
(— TO WALK) ABASIA
(— TO WRITE) AGRAPHIA
INACCESSIBILITY FASTNESS
INACCESSIBLE COY REMOTE
UNGAIN WICKED SHADOWY
INACCURATE SOUR FALSE LOOSE
FAULTY UNJUST INEXACT IMPROPER
SLIPSHOD
INACHUS (DAUGHTER OF —) IO
(FATHER OF —) OCEANUS
(MOTHER OF —) TETHYS
(SON OF —) PHORONEUS
INACTION RUST
INACTIVATE MOTHBALL
INACTIVE LAX DEAD DRUG FLAT
IDLE LAZY MESO SLOW HEAVY INERT
NOBLE SLACK SULKY ASLEEP
SEDENT STATIC SUPINE TORPID
CESSANT DORMANT PASSIVE
RESTIVE COMATOSE COMATOUS
DEEDLESS DILATORY FAINEANT
SLOTHFUL SLUGGISH THEWLESS
THOWLESS QUIESCENT
INACTIVITY SLOTH ANERGY
TORPOR ANERGIA ABEYANCE
IDLENESS CESSATION SEGNITUDE
INADEQUACY DEFECT FRAILTY
SCARCITY
INADEQUATE BAD BARE POOR THIN
INEPT SCANT SHORT SLACK FEEBLE
STRAIT FOOLISH INVALID SLENDER
HIGHLAND INFERIOR MISERABLE
(PREF.) MAL

INADEQUATELY BADLY SLACK
SLACKLY
INADVERTENCE LAPSUS
INADVERTENT CARELESS
INAJA JAGUA
INALIENABLE INHERENT
INAMORATA AMORADO AMORETTO
INANE DITSY DITZY DIZZY EMPTY
GIDDY JERKY SILLY VAPID JEJUNE
VACANT FATUOUS FOOLISH INSIPID
PUERILE VACUOUS IMBECILE
SLIPSLOP TRIFLING SENSELESS
INANGA MINNOW
INANIMATE DEAD DULL BRUTE
INERT DEADLY STOLID STUPID
LIFELESS
INANIMITY CONSENSUS
INANITY FATUITY VACUITY
INAPPLICABLE SPURIOUS
INAPPROPRIATE INEPT UNAPT
UNDUE FOREIGN UNHAPPY
(SOMETHING —) CAMP
INAPT UNHAPPY BACKWARD
FOOTLESS MALAPROPOS
INARTICULATA LYOPOMA
INARTICULATE DUMB LAME THICK
INARTISTIC CRUDE ARTLESS
INATTENTION ABSENCE NEGLECT
APROSEXIA
INATTENTIVE DEAF SLACK ABSENT
REMISS SUPINE DREAMSY UNTENTY
CARELESS DISTRAIT HEEDLESS
MINDLESS
INAUDIBLE SECRET
INAUDIBLY INWARDLY SECRETLY
INAUGURATE AUGUR BEGIN SETUP
HANDSEL INITIATE
INAUGURATION HANDSEL
INAUSPICIOUS BAD ILL EVIL FOUL
ADVERSE OBSCENE OMINOUS
UNHAPPY UNLUCKY SINISTER
INAUTHENTIC SPURIOUS
INBORN GENIAL INBRED INNATE
NATIVE CONNATE NATURAL
HABITUAL INHERENT
INBRED INBORN INNATE
INBREED SELF
INBREEDING ENDOGAMY
INCA INGUA OREJON
INCALCULABLE UNTOLD SUMLESS
UNKNOWN
INCA MAGIC FLOWER CANTUT
CANTUTA
INCANDESCENCE GLOW
INCANDESCENT BRIGHT
INCANTATION CHARM DAWUT
SPELL CARMEN FETISH MANTRA
SHAZAM CANTION CHANTRY
GREEGREE
INCAPABLE DEAD NUMB UNABLE
HANDLESS
INCAPACITATE NAPOO UNFIT
NOBBLE UNABLE DISABLE

INCAPACITATED FLAT DISABLED
STRICKEN
INCARCERATE JAIL IMMURE
CONFINE IMPRISON
INCARNATE BODIED EMBODY
CARNATE ENFLESH HUMANIFY
PERSONIFY
INCARNATION RAMA IMAGE
ADVENT AVATAR GENIUS MNEVIS
TERTON HUTUKTU EPIPHANY
PERSONIFICATION
INCAUTIOUS RASH UNWARY
UNCHARY UNTENTY CAREFREE
RECKLESS
INCENDIARY FIREBUG ARSONIST
BOUTEFEU
INCENSE CENSE INFLAME KETURAH
PROVOKE IRRITATE THYMIAMA
(— INGREDIENT) ONYCHA
(— VESSEL) SHIP
(PREF.) THURI
INCENSE-BOAT NAVICULA
INCENSED RAW HETUP IRATE RILED
WROTH WRATHFUL
INCENTIVE BROD GOAD SPUR PRICK
MOTIVE IMPETUS IMPULSE INCITIVE
STIMULUS MOTIVATION
INCEPTION ORIGIN ANCESTRY
INCESSANT STEADY ENDLESS
CONSTANT
INCESSANTLY FOREVER
INCH UNCH PRIME UNCIA
(ABOUT 7 —S) FISTMELE
(100TH OF —) POINT
(4 —S) HANDFUL
(48TH OF —) IRON
(9 —S) SPAN
INCHOATE FORMLESS
INCIDENT GO EVENT LIABLE
CAUTION EPISODE PASSAGE
SUBJECT ACCIDENT CASUALTY
OCCASION OCCURRENCE
(AMUSING —) BAR BREAK
(LITERARY —) BIT
INCIDENTAL BY BYE SIDE STRAY
CASUAL EPISODIC GLANCING
INCIDENT OCCURRENT
INCIDENTALLY BYHAND OBITER
APROPOS BYTHEWAY
INCINERATE COMBUST CREMATE
INCINERATOR BURNER
SALAMANDER
INCIPIENCE BUD
INCIPIENT INITIAL GERMINAL
INCHOATE
INCISE CHOP RASE LANCE INCIDE
CHANNEL ENGRAVE
INCISION CUT GASH SLIT SNIP ISSUE
SCORE BROACH SCOTCH STREAK
CUTDOWN DIACOPE APLOTOMY
CECOTOMY COLOTOMY
CULDOTOMY
(SUFF.) TOMY

INCISIVE ACID KEEN CRISP SHARP BITING BRUTAL CUTTING ACULEATE PIERCING TRENCHANT

INCISIVENESS MORDANCY

INCISOR CUTTER NIPPER GATHERER

INCITE EGG HIE HOY PUT SIC TAR ABET BEET BUZZ EDGE FIRE GOAD LASH MOVE PROD SICK SNIP SPUR STIR URGE WHET AWAKE CHIRK EGGON IMPEL PRICK PROKE SPARK SPURN STING TEMPT AROUSE BESTIR ENTICE EXCITE EXHORT FILLIP FOMENT HALLOO INDUCE KINDLE NETTLE PROMPT UPSTIR URGEON ACTUATE ANIMATE COMMOVE INCENSE INSPIRE PROMOVE PROVOKE QUICKEN SOLICIT INCITATE MOTIVATE
(— SECRETLY) SUBORN
(— TO ATTACK) SET HIRR SOOL

INCITEMENT GOAD PROD SPUR STING MOTIVE EGGMENT STIRRING
(— OF LITIGATION) BARRATRY

INCITER FEEDER MONITOR INCENSOR INCENTOR

INCLEMENCY RIGOR CRUELTY TYRANNY ASPERITY HARDNESS SEVERITY

INCLEMENT RAW HARD RUDE SOUR GURLY STARK COARSE RUGGED SEVERE UNFINE UNKINDLY
(NOT —) OPEN CIVIL

INCLINATION DIP GEE MAW PLY SET BENT DIAS BROO CANT CARE DRAG DRAW EDGE FALL GUST HANG LEAN LIKE LIST LOVE LUST MIND SLEW TURN VEIN WILL BEVEL BOSOM DRAFT DRIFT FANCY GRAIN HABIT HIELD HUMOR KNACK LURCH PITCH POISE SLANT SLOPE STUDY SWING TASTE THEAT TREND AFFECT ANIMUS ANLAGE ASCENT DESIRE DEVICE GATHER GENIUS INTENT LIKING MOTION NOTION PONDUS RELISH SQUINT TALENT YETZER APTNESS CONATUS COURAGE CURRENT DESCENT DRAUGHT FANTASY INKLING LEANING STOMACH VERSANT WILLING APPETITE APTITUDE CLINAMEN DEVOTION GRADIENT PENCHANT TENDENCY VELLEITY VERGENCY WOULDING PROCLIVITY PROPENSITY
(— DOWNWARD) DIP DESCENT HANGING
(— FROM VERTICAL) RAKE
(— OF OARSMAN'S BODY) LAYBACK
(INWARD —) BATTER
(PLEASUREFUL —) RELISH
(PREDOMINATE —) STRENGTH

INCLINE APT BOW DIP KIP TIP WRY BEAR BEND BIAS BREW CANT CAST DUCK DOOK DOOR DROP GIVE HANG HEEL HELD HILL LEAN LIKE LIST PECK PEND RAKE SEEL STAY SWAY TILT TURN BEVEL CLIMB CLINE DROOP FLECT HIELD JINNY OFFER PITCH SHAPE SLANT SLOPE SOUND VERGE AFFECT GLACIS INTEND SHELVE STEEVE UPBROW DECLINE DESCEND GANGWAY PROPEND PROCLINE PROCLIVE
(— SKI) EDGE
(PREF.) CLIN(O)

INCLINED APT FIT SIB BENT CANT FAIN LIEF RIFE VAIN ALIST ARAKE ATILT GIVEN LEANT PRONE READY ASLOPE COUCHE MINDED PROMPT SLOPED SUPINE FORWARD HANGING OBLIQUE PRONATE STUDIED AFFECTED DISPOSED ENCLITIC PREGNANT PROPENSE SIDELING TALENTED
(— TO DRINK) BIBULOUS
(— TO LEARN) WALTY
(READILY —) PROMPT

INCLINING HILLY SHELVY SLOPING CERNUOUS PROPENSE SIDELING
(SUFF.) CLINIC CLINOUS

INCLUDE ADD LAP HAVE TAKE ANNEX COUCH COVER IMPLY EMPLOY ENSEAM RECKON BELOUKE COLLECT CONNOTE CONTAIN EMBRACE IMMERSE INVOLVE RECOUNT SUBSUME COMPRISE CONCLUDE
(— IN LIST) ENGROSS

INCLUDING TO CUM
(— EVERYTHING) OVERALL

INCLUSIVE GRAND CAPABLE CATHOLIC

INCLUSIVELY BROADLY

INCLUSUS RECLUSE

INCOHERENT FUZZY BROKEN RAVING INCHOATE

INCOHERENTLY IDLY

INCOMBUSTIBLE APYROUS ASBESTIC

INCOME GAIN PORT RENT RENTE LIVING PEWAGE PEWING PROFIT SALARY FACULTY INTRADO INTRATE PRODUCE REVENUE STIPEND INTEREST PROCEEDS POCKETBOOK
(— OF BENEFICE) ANNAT
(ANNUAL —) RENTE
(FRENCH —) RENTE
(UNFORESEEN —) GRAVY

INCOMMENSURATE UNEQUAL

INCOMMODE VEX ANNOY MOLEST PLAGUE TROUBLE DISQUIET

INCOMPARABLE ALONE

INCOMPATIBILITY SOLECISM ANTIPATHY

INCOMPATIBLE ALIEN REPUGNANT

INCOMPETENT INEPT UNFIT SLOUCH UNABLE UNMEET FECKLESS HANDLESS HELPLESS SPLITTER

INCOMPLETE WANE BLIND ROUGH BROKEN UNDONE DIVIDED LACKING PARTIAL SKETCHY IMMATURE INCHOATE SEGMENTAL (GRAMMATICALLY —) PENDANT (PREF.) ATEL(O) DEMI SEMI
INCOMPLETELY BADLY HALVES
INCOMPOSITE PRIME
INCOMPREHENSIBILITY ACATALEPSY
INCOMPREHENSIBLE PARTIAL COCKEYED
INCONCLUSIVE FUZZY
INCONGRUITY JAR ANOMALY SOLECISM
INCONGRUOUS ALIEN ABSURD ANOMALOUS
INCONNU CONY NELMA CONNIE SHEEFISH
INCONSEQUENTIAL NUGATORY
INCONSIDERABLE WEAK LIGHT PETTY LITTLE
INCONSIDERATE RASH UNKIND ASOCIAL RECKLESS
INCONSISTENCY HOLE
INCONSISTENT ALIEN REPUGNANT
INCONSPICUOUS OBSCURE
INCONSTANCY CHANGE LEVITY
INCONSTANT FICKLE BRUCKLE FLUXILE MOONISH MUTABLE PROTEAN SLIDING VARIOUS FLUXIBLE METEORIC MOVEABLE STRUMPET VARIABLE CHAMELEON MERCURIAL VERSATILE
INCONTESTABLE SURE CLEAN CERTAIN POSITIVE
INCONTINENCE ENURESIS
INCONTINENT LOOSE LAXATIVE
INCONTROVERTIBLE GRAND
INCONVENIENCE FASH BOTHER CUMBER STRESS SQUEEZE DISQUIET
INCONVENIENT UNKED CLUMSY UNBANE UNGAIN AWKWARD UNHANDY ANNOYING UNCHANCY UNTOWARD
INCOORDINATION ASTASIA
INCORPORATE MIX FOLD FUSE JOIN ANNEX KNEAD MERGE UNITE ABSORB EMBODY ENGRAIN ENTRAIN INWEAVE INCORPSE (— IN WALL) ENGAGE
INCORPOREAL AERY BODILESS ASOMATOUS
INCORRECT BAD ILL OFF FALSE WRONG PECCANT UNRIGHT UNSOUND VICIOUS PERVERSE (PREF.) CAC(O)
INCORRIGIBLE HARD
INCORRUPTIBLE IMMORTAL
INCREASE UP ADD EIK EKE IMP WAX BUMP ECHE GAIN GROW HELP HIKE HYPE ITCH JACK JUMP MEND MORE MUCH PLUS PUSH RISE SOAR THEE THRO BOOST BUILD BULGE CLIMB CROWD FLUSH FRESH GOOSE HEAVE LARGE RAISE SPURT SWELL ACCENT ACCESS ACCRUE BETTER BIGGEN CHANGE CREASE DEEPEN DOUBLE EXPAND EXTEND EXTENT GATHER GROWTH PUMPUP SPREAD SPRING UPTICK ADVANCE AMPLIFY AUCTION AUGMENT AUXESIS BALLOON DISTEND ELEVATE ENGROSS ENHANCE ENLARGE GREATEN IMPROVE INFLATE MAGNIFY STEEPEN SURCRUE ACCRESCE ADDITION COMPOUND ESCALATE FLOURISH HEIGHTEN LENGTHEN MAJORATE MAXIMATE MAXIMIZE MULTIPLY THRODDEN PROPAGATE PROLIFERATE
(— ACCORDING TO RATIO) SCALEUP
(— AT USURY) OCKER
(— GREATLY) ACCUMULATE
(— HEAT OF KILN) RUSTLE GLISTER
(— IN BUSINESS) UPBEAT
(— IN PAY) FOGY FOGIE
(— IN SIZE) AUXESIS
(— IN STRENGTH) FRESHEN
(— KNOWLEDGE) ENRICH
(— OF DEPTH) OVERFALL
(— OF LOUDNESS) CRESCENDO
(— OF POWER) SURGE
(— OF WEALTH) THRIFT
(— POWER) SOUP
(— PRICE BY BIDDING) CANT
(— RAPIDLY) SOAR MUSHROOM
(— SPEED) JAZZ GOOSE ACCELERATE
(— STITCHES) FASHION
(— SUDDENLY) LEAP
(PRICE —) RIST
(SALARY —) FLOWON
(SHORT-TERM —) BOOMLET
(TEMPORARY —) BULGE
(PREF.) AUXO
(SUFF.) AUXE OSIS
INCREASING GROWING CRESCENT CRESCIVE DILATANT SWELLING CUMULATIVE
(— RAPIDLY) BOOMING
INCREDIBLE TALL STEEP DAMNED FABULOUS COCKAMAMY COCKAMAMIE
INCREDULITY UNBELIEF
INCREDULOUS INFIDEL
INCREMENT DOSE DELTA INCREASE
INCRIMINATE ACCUSE
INCRUST FOUL
INCRUSTATION CRUD MOSS CRUST SCALE TARTAR FOULING FURRING
INCUBATE SIT BROOD CLOCK COVER HATCH
INCUBATION PASSAGE
INCUBATOR FURNACE HATCHER COUVEUSE ISOLETTE

INCUBUS DUSE MARE DUSIO NIGHTMARE

INCULCATE BREED INFIX INCULK INFUSE IMPLANT IMPRESS INSTILL

INCULCATED BRED

INCUMBENT COARB BEARER

INCUR RUN BEAR GAIN WAGE CONTRACT

INCURABLE BOOTLESS HOPELESS

INCURRENT INHALANT

INCURSION RAID ROAD FORAY INFALL INROAD RAZZIA DESCENT HOSTING INBREAK INCURSE ANABASIS INVASION

INCUS AMBOS ANVIL

INDEBTED LIABLE DEBTFUL BEHOLDEN

INDEBTEDNESS DEBT SCORE

INDECENCY IMPURITY PRIAPISM RIBALDRY

INDECENT PAW BLUE FOUL LEWD RANK BAWDY GROSS NASTY SAUCY GREASY IMPURE PAWPAW SMUTTY CURIOUS GRIVOIS IMMORAL OBSCENE IMMODEST IMPROPER SHAMEFUL UNCOMELY

INDECENTLY DIRTY

INDECISION DEMUR DOUBT MAYBE POISE SWITHER
(PSYCHOTIC —) ABULIA

INDECISIVE DRAWN HALTING
(BE —) TEETER

INDECISIVENESS SUSPENSE

INDECOROUS RUDE COARSE FORWARD UNCIVIL IMMODEST IMPOLITE IMPROPER INDECENT UNSEEMLY UNTOWARD GRACELESS TASTELESS

INDEED SO ARU NAY TOO WIS YEA AWAT DEED EVEN IWIS JUST SURE MARRY QUOTH TIENS ATWEEL ITSELF PARDIE SURELY FAITHLY FRANKLY SOOTHLY FORSOOTH VERAMENT

INDEFATIGABLE TIRELESS

INDEFENSIBLE INVALID

INDEFINABLE NAMELESS

INDEFINITE HAZY FUZZY GROSS LOOSE VAGUE DIVERS INEXACT AORISTIC NUBILOUS

INDEFINITELY IN

INDELIBLE FAST FIXED

INDELICATE RAW FREE WARM BROAD GROSS ROUGH COARSE GREASY IMPOLITE IMPROPER UNSEEMLY

INDEMNIFICATION RELIEF

INDEMNIFY PAY REPAY RECOUP SATISFY WARRANT

INDENT JAG BRIT DENT GIMP MUSH NICK CHASE DELVE NOTCH STAMP TOOTH WHEEL BRUISE CRENEL ENGRAIL GAUFFER

INDENTATION CHOP DENT DINT DOKE FOIL KINK SCAR BOSOM BULGE CLEFT CRENA DINGE NOTCH SINUS DIMPLE FURROW GROOVE INDENT RECESS IMPRESS CRENELLE TOOTHING
(— IN BOTTLE) KICK
(— IN DOG'S FACE) STOP
(— IN SHELL) EYE

INDENTED WAVED CRENATE NOTCHED SINUATE

INDENTURE BIND INDENT ESCALLOP SYNGRAPH

INDEPENDENCE AUTARKY FREEDOM AUTARCHY
(— OF GOD) ASEITY ASEITAS
(POLITICAL —) SWARAJ

INDEPENDENT FREE PROUD SEEKER BIGGITY DIVIDED MUGWUMP SECTARY ABSOLUTE PECULIAR POSITIVE SEPARATE
(STATISTICALLY —) ORTHOGONAL
(PREF.) SELF

INDEPENDENTLY APART

INDESCRIBABLE TERMLESS INEFFABLE

INDETERMINATE AORISTIC FORMLESS INFINITE

INDEX PIE FIST HAND ARNETH ELENCH PIGNET TONGUE POINTER ALPHABET EXPONENT REGISTER
(COMPUTER —) KWIC KWOC

INDIA

ANCIENT NAME: BHARAT

CAPE: COMORIN

CAPITAL: NEWDELHI

CASTE: JAT MAL AHIR GOLA JATI MALI DHORI SANSI SUDRA VARNA DACOIT DHANUK LOHANA VAISYA AGARWAL BRAHMAN DHANGAR

COAST: MALABAR

COIN: LAC PIE ANNA FELS LAKH PICE TARA ABIDI CRORE PAISA RUPEE

COLLEGE: TOL

DESERT: THAR

DISTRICT: SIRI NASIK PATNA SIMLA ZILLAH MALABAR NELLORE MOFUSSIL

GULF: KUTCH CAMBAY MANNAR

ISLAND: CHILKA

LAKE: WULAR CHILKA COLAIR DHEBAR SAMBHAR

LANGUAGE: URDU HINDI TAMIL TELUGU SANSKRIT

MEASURE: ADY DHA GAZ GUZ JOW KOS LAN SER BYEE COSS DAIN DHAN HATH JAOB KUNK MOOT PARA RAIK RATI SEIT TAUN TENG TOLA AMUNA BIGHA CAHAR COVID CROSA DANDA DRONA GARCE GIREH HASTA PALLY PARAH RATTI SALAY YOJAN ADHAKA ANGULA

COVIDO CUDAVA CUMBHA GEERAH
LAMANY MOOLUM MUSHTI PALGAT
PARRAH ROPANI TIPREE UNGLEE
YOJANA ADOULIE DHANUSH
GAVYUTI KHAHOON NIRANGA
PRASTHA VITASTI OKTHABAH
MOUNTAIN: MERU GHATS KAMET
MASTUJ TANKSE KALAHOI SIWALIK
VINDHYA SULEIMAN
MOUNTAIN RANGE: SATPURA
VINDHYA ARAVALLI HIMALAYA
NATIVE: TODA HINDU TAMIL
PROVINCE: HAR ASSAM BIHAR
ANDHRA BENGAL KERALA MADRAS
MYSORE ORISSA PUNJAB GUJARAT
HARYANA KASHMIR MANIPUR
REGION: MALABAR
RIVER: AI DOR SON TEL KOSI KUSI
NIRA REHR SIND BETWA BHIMA
DAMOH GOGRA INDUS JAWAI RAPTI
SANKH SONAR TAPTI TUNGA
CHENAB GANGES KISTNA PENNER
SUTLEJ WARDHA CAUVERY
CHAMBAL IRAWADI KRISHNA
NARMADA NARMEDA HEMAVATI
HYDASPES MAHANADI NERBUDDA
VINDHYAS
SEAPORT: DAMAN BOMBAY COCHIN
MADRAS CALCUTTA
STATE: ASSAM BIHAR KERALA
MYSORE ORISSA PUNJAB GUJARAT
MANIPUR
STRAIT: PALK
TERRITORY: DIU GOA DAMAN
MINICOY AMINDIVI
TOWN: DIU AGRA DAMA GAYA PUNA
REWA ADONI AKOLA ALWAR ARCOT
BHERA DACCA DATIA DELHI GIROT
KALPI PATAN PATNA POONA SALEM
SIMLA SURAT TEHRI AJMERE
AMBALA BARELI BARODA BHOPAL
BOMBAY CHAMBA COCHIN
DUMDUM HOWRAH INDORE JAIPUR
KANPUR LAHORE MADIRA MADRAS
MADURA MEERUT MULTAN
MUTTRA MYSORE NAGPUR
RAMPUR UJJAIN ALIGARH BENARES
BIKANER CALICUT CAWNPUR
DINAPUR GWALIOR JODHPUR
KARACHI KURNOOL LASWARI
LUCKNOW RANGOON RANGPUR
AMRITSAR BHATINDA BHATPARA
CALCUTTA DINAPORE JABALPUR
KOLHAPUR MANDALAY MIRZAPUR
PESHAWAR SHOLAPUR SRINAGAR
VARANASI
TRIBE: AO GOR BHIL BADAGA
SHERANI
WATERFALL: JOG GOKAK CAUVERY
WEIGHT: MOD PAI SER VIS DHAN
DRUM KONA MYAT PALA PANK PICE
RAIK RATI RUAY SEER TANK TOLA
YAVA ADPAD BAHAR CANDY CATTY

HUBBA MASHA MAUND PALLY
POUAH RATTI RETTI RUTEE TICAL
TICUL TIKAL ABUCCO DHURRA
KARSHA CHITTAK PEIKTHA

INDIAN LO RED ROJO INJUN TAWNY
ABNAKI INDISH REDMAN BHARATI
HOSTILE NAIKPOD REDSKIN LONG-
HAIR MUSKOGEE PENOBSCOT SHA-
HAPTIAN NARRAGANSET
(— LEADER) NEHRU
(AMERICAN —) AIS AUK FOX HOH
KAW OTO REE SAC SIA UTE WEA ZIA
ADAI COOS CREE CROW DOEG ERIE
EYAK HANO HOPI HUPA IOWA KATO
KOSO MOKI MONO OTOE OTTO PIMA
PIRO SAUK TANO TAOS TEWA TIOU
TOAG UTAH WACO YUMA ZUNI
ACOMA ALSEA BANAK BIDAI CADDO
CHAUI COMOX CONOY COREE CREEK
HANIS HOOPA HUECO HURON JEMEZ
KANIA KANSA KAROK KERES KIOWA
KOROA KUSAN LENCA LIPAN MAKAH
MANSO MIAMI MINGO MODOC
MOQUI NAMBE OMAHA OSAGE
OSTIC OZARK PECOS PINAL PIUTE
PONCA SAMBO SARSI SEWEE SIOUX
SITKA SKIDI SLAVE SNAKE SOOKE
TETON TEXAS TIGUA TONTO TWANA
TYIGH UINTA UNAMI WAPPO WASCO
WASHO WIYOT YAMEL YAZOO YUCHI
YUROK AGAWAM AHTENA APACHE
ATSINA ATUAMI AVOYEL BILOXI
CALUSA CAYUGA CAYUSE CHATOT
CHERAW CHETCO COOSUC CUPENO
DAKOTA DIGGER EYEISH FARAON
GILENO HAINAI HAISLA ISLETA
KAIBAB KAINAH KANSAS KICHAI
KOSIMO KUITSH LAGUNA LENAPE
MANDAN MAUMEE MAYEYE
METOAC MICMAC MIKMAK MOHAVE
MOHAWK MUNSEE NASHUA NATICK
NAUSET NAVAHO NAVAJO NEUTER
NOOTKA OGLALA ONEIDA OREJON
OTTAWA PAIUTE PAPAJO PATWIN
PAWNEE PEORIA PEQUOD PEQUOT
PIEGAN PODUNK PUEBLO QUAPAW
QUERES RIKARI SALISH SAMISH
SANTEE SAPONI SATSOP SENECA
SHASTA SILETZ SIOUAN SIWASH
SKAGIT SOKOKI SUMASS SUMDUM
SUTAIO SYLVID TAPOSA TENINO
TOHOME TOLOWA TONGAS TUNICA
TUTELO UMPQUA WALAPI WAPATO
WATALA WAXHAW WEANOC WIKENO
WINTUN YAKIMA YAMASI ZUNIAN
ABENAKI ALABAMA ALIBAMU
AMERIND ANDARKO ANDASTE
ARIKARA ATAKAPA AYAHUCA
BANNOCK CAHOKIA CALOOSA
CATAWBA CHILCAT CHILULA
CHINOOK CHOCTAW CHUMASH
CHUMAWI CIBECUE CLALLAM

CLATSOP COCHITI COLCINE COWLITZ
DEADOSE DHEGIHA DWAMISH
ESSELEN GOSHUTE HELLELT
HIDATSA HUCHNOM HUICHOL
INGALIK JUANENO KANAWHA
KLAMATH KOASATI KOHUANA
KOPRINO KUNESTE KUTCHIN
KUTENAI LUISENO MASHPEE
MASKOKI MOHEGAN MOHICAN
MONACAN MONSONI MONTAUK
MOUSONI NANAIMO NASCAPI
NATCHEZ NIANTIC NIMKISH
NIPMUCK OJIBWAY PACIFID
PADUCAH PAMLICO PICURUS
QUAITSO SALINAN SANETCH
SANPOIL SERRANO SHAPTAN
SHAWANO SHAWNEE SIKSIKA
SIUSLAW SONGISH SPOKANE
SQUAXON STIKINE TAMAROA
TESUQUF TIMUCUA TLINGIT
TONKAWA TUALATI TULALIP
TUTUTNI UGARONO WAILAKI
WALPAPI WAMESIT WANAPUM
WASHAKI WEWENOC WHILKUT
WICHITA WISHOSK WITUMKI
WYANDOT YANKTON YAQUINA
YAVAPAI YOJUANE YONKALA
ABSAROKA ACHOMAWI ACHUMAWI
ALGONKIN AMERICAN AMOSKEAG
APALACHI ARIVAIPA ARKANSAS
ASTAKIWI ATFALATI ATSUGEWI
CAHINNIO CAHUILLA CANARSIE
CHAWASHA CHEHALIS CHEMAKUM
CHEROKEE CHEYENNE CHIMAKUM
CHOPTANK CHOWANOC CLACKAMA
COLUMBIA COLVILLE COMANCHE
COQUILLE COYOTERO DELAWARE
DIEGUENO ETCHIMIN FLATHEAD
HITCHITI HUNKPAPA ILLINOIS
IROQUOIS KALISPEL KAWAIISU
KICKAPOO KIKATSIK KLASKINO
KLIKITAT KONOMIHU LAMANITE
MALECITE MASCOTIN MENOMINI
MIKASUKI MINITARI MISSOURI
MOGOLLON MUSCOGEE MUSKWAKI
NEHANTIC NESPELIM NOTTOWAY
OKINAGAN ONONDAGA PAMUNKEY
PANAMINT PATUXENT PAVIOTSO
PENACOOK PISHQUOW POWHATAN
PUYALLUP QUATSINO QUERECHO
QUILEUTE QUINAULT ROCKAWAY
SAHAPTIN SAULTEUR SAVANNAH
SEMINOLE SHIVWITS SHOSHONE
SIHASAPA SINGSING SINKIUSE
SINKYONE SINTSINK SISSETON
SOUHEGAN SQUAMISH SQUEDUNK
TLAKLUIT TOBIKHAR TOPINISH
TSIHALIS TUSHEPAW TUSKEGEE
UMATILLA WABANAKI WACHUSET
WAHPETON WETUMPKA YAHUSKIN
YAMACRAW DOUSTIONI ·
SQUAWTITS
(BRAZILIAN —) BUGRE

(CANADIAN —) DENE COMOX HAIDA
SLAVE TINNE DOGRIB HAISLA LASSIK
MICMAC SARSEE BEOTHUK GOASILA
KHOTANA KOYUKON CHISEDEC
COWICHAN HEILTSUK KIMSQUIT
KWAKIUTL LILLOOET SALTEAUX
SHUSHWAP
(FEMALE —) SQUAW KLOOCH
(MALE —) BUCK SANNUP SIWASH
(MEXICAN —) MAM OVA CHOL CORA
JOVA MAYA MAYO ROTO SERI TECA
TECO XOVA AZTEC CHIZO CHORA
HUABI HUAVE KAMIA NAHUA OPATA
OTOMI YAQUI ZOQUE CAHITA
CHOCHO CONCHO FUDEVE KILIWI
NEVOME OTONIA PAKAWA TARASC
TOLTEC ZOTZIL ACOLHUA AKWAALA
AMISHGO CHATINO CHINCHA
CHINIPA CHONTAL COTONAM
COUHIMI GUASAVE HUASTEC
HUAXTEC MAZATEC MISTECA
MIXTECA NAYARIT SINALOA
TEGUIMA TEHUECO TEPANEC
TEPEHUA TZENTAL TZOTZIL
ZACATEC ZAPOTEC CHANABAL
CHAPANEC CHUCHONA COLOTLAN
COMANITO CONICARI GUASAPAR
HUASTECO IRRITILA JACALTEC
JANAMBRE LACANDON LAGUNERO
TARUMARI TECPANEC TEXCOCAN
TEZCUCAN TOTONACO TZAPOTEC
YUCATECO
(OTHER —) GE ITE ONA URO URU
YAO AGAZ ANDE ANTA ANTI AUCA
BABU CAME CANA CARA CHUJ COTO
CUNA DENE DIAU DUIT INCA ITEN
ITZA IXIL MOJO MOXO MURA MUSO
MUZO PEBA PIRO RAMA TAMA TAPE
TATU TOBA TRIO TUPI TUPY ULUA
ULVA ACROA ARARA ARAUA ARUAC
AUETO BAURE BETOI BRAVO BUGRE
CAITE CAMPA CANCA CARIB CHANE
CHIMU CHITA CHOCO CHOKO CHOLA
CHOLO CHONO COCTO COLAN
CUEVA DIRIA GUANA GUATO HUARI
JAVAH KASKA LENCA MOCOA
MOZCA OPATA OYANA PALTA PAMPA
PASSE PETEN PINTO PIOJE PIOXE
PIPIL POKAN POKOM QUITU SENCI
SIUSI SMOOS TAINO UAUPE UMAUA
VEJOZ WAURA XINCA YAGUA
YAMEO YUNCA YUNGA AGUANO
AIMARA AKAVAI AKAWAI AMORUA
ANDOKE ANTISI APANTO APARAI
APIACA ARAWAK AROACO ATORAI
AYMARA BABINE BANIVA BETOYA
BORORO BRIBRI BRUNKA CAHETE
CAIGUA CANCHI CANELO CARAHO
CARAJA CARAYA CARIRI CAUQUI
CAVINA CAYAPA CHAIMA CHARCA
CHAYMA CHICHA CHISCA CHOCOI
CHORTI COCAMA COCOMA COCORA
COFANE COLIMA COTOXO CUCAMA

CULINO CUMANA DOGRIB DORASK
GALIBI GOYANA GUAIMI GUAQUE
GUAYMI HUARPE HUBABO IGNERI
INCERI IXIAMA JIVARO JUCUNA
JUMANA JURUNA KARAYA KEKCHI
KUCHIN LENGUA LUCAYO MACUSI
MAKUSI MANGUE MANIVA MIRANA
MUYSCA NAHANE NASCAN
OMAGUA OTOMAC PAPAGO
PKOMAM PURUHA QUICHE SABUJA
SACCHA SALIBA SALIVA SAMUCU
SEKANE SETIBO SIPIBO SUERRE
TACANA TAGISH TAHAMI TAMOYO
TAPAJO TAPUYA TARUMA TECUNA
TICUNA TIMOTE TOTORO TUCANO
TUNEBO UIRINA UITOTO VILELA
WAIWAI WITOTO WOOLWA YAHGAN
YAHUNA YARURO YURUNA ZAPARA
ACHAGUA ACKAWOI AKAMNIK
ANDAQUI ANGAITE APALAII APINAGE
ARECUNA ARHUACO BEOTHUK
BILQULA CACHIBO CAINGUA
CALIANA CAMACAN CARANGA
CARIBAN CARIBEE CARRIER CASHIBO
CHARRUA CHIBCHA CHIMANE
CHIMILA CHIRINO CHONCHO
CHOROTE CHUMULU CHUNCHO
CHURAPA CHUROYA CIBONEY
CJACOGO COROADO FRENTON
FUEGIAN GITKSAN GOAHIVO
GOAJIRA GUAHIVO GUARANI
GUARANY GUARAYO GUARRAU
GUARUAN GUATUSO GUETARE
HUANUCO HUATUSO ITONAMA
JACUNDA JICAQUE KALIANA
KOPRINO KULIANA LUCAYAN
MAIPURE MISKITO MONGOYO
MORCOTE NICARAO PAMPERO
PAYAGUA PEDRAZA PIARROA
POKOMAM PUELCHE PUQUINA
QUECHUA QUEKCHI RANQUEL
SARIGUE SATIENO SHUSWAP
SINSIGA SIRIONE TAHLTAN TALUCHE
TALUHET TAMANAC TARIANA
TARRABA TAYRONA TELEMBI
TIMBIRA TIRRIBI TSONECA UARAYCU
UCAYALE VOYAVAI WOYAWAY
YUSTAGA ZUTUHIL AGUARUNA
AHOUSAHT AKIYENIK ALACALUF
AMAHUACA APOLISTA ARAQUAJU
AWISHIRA BOTOCUDO CAINGANG
CALINAGO CANAMARY CANOEIRO
CAQUETIO CARIBISI CARIJONA
CARIPUNA CAYUBABA CHAMBOIA
CHANDALA CHAVANTE CHIQUITO
CHIRIANA COLORADO COMIAKIN
CONCHUCU CORABECA CUSTENAU
GUAYAQUI GUAYCURU JAVITERO
KANHOBAL KLASKINO LOROKOTO
MACARANA MAYORUNA MISSKITO
MOSQUITO NIQUIRAN OCHOZOMA
OROTINAN PACAVARA PALENQUE
PARUKUTU PINALENO POIGUARA

POKONCHI POPOLOCO POTYUARA
PUPULUCA QUATSINO QUERENDY
QUIMBAYA SHIRIANA SNONOWAS
SUBTIABA TADOUSAC TAPACURA
TENAKTAK TOCOBAGA TOROMONA
TSATTINE TUMUPASA UAREKENA
URUKUENA USPANTEC YURUCARE
(SOUTH AFRICAN —) COOLY COOLIE
(SPANISH-AMERICAN —) CHOLO

INDIANA
CAPITAL: INDIANAPOLIS
COLLEGE: BALL BETHEL DEPAUW
  GOSHEN MARIAN PURDUE WABASH
COUNTY: JAY CASS CLAY KNOX OWEN
  PIKE RUSH VIGO BOONE FLOYD
  WELLS JASPER TIPTON DAVIESS
  PULASKI
INDIAN: MIAMI HAWNEE
LAKE: MONROE MANITOU WAWASEE
  MICHIGAN
NATIVE: HOOSIER
RIVER: OHIO WHITE WABASH
STATE BIRD: CARDINAL
STATE FLOWER: PEONY
STATE TREE: TULIP
TOWN: GARY PERU PAOLI VEVAY
  ALBION ANGOLA BRAZIL GOSHEN
  JASPER KOKOMO MUNCIE SHOALS
  WABASH

INDIAN BEECH KURUNJ
INDIAN BREAD TUCKAHOE
INDIAN CORN KANGA MAIZE
  CHOLUM JAGONG MEALIES
INDIAN FIG SABRA
INDIAN FISH FLATFISH
INDIAN GOOSEBERRY EMBLIC
INDIAN HEMP KEF KIF SANA
  DAGGA SABZI AMYROOT DOGBANE
INDIANIAN HOOSIER
INDIAN JALAP TURPETH
INDIAN LICORICE JEQUIRITY
INDIAN MADDER MUNJEET
INDIAN MALLOW SIDA DAGGA
  PIEPRINT
INDIAN MILLET JONDLA
INDIAN MULBERRY AL AAL ACH
  ALROOT
INDIAN PIPE FITROOT EYEBRIGHT
  WAXFLOWER
INDIAN POKE ITCHWEED
  HELLEBORE
INDIAN RED BOLE
INDIAN SHOT ALIIPOE
INDIAN TOBACCO GAGROOT
  LOBELIA PUKEWEED SOURBUSH
INDIAN YELLOW PIOURY PURREE
INDIA-RUBBER BUNGEE BUNGIE
INDIC (— LANGUAGE) URDU VEDIC
INDICATE RUN SAY BODY CITE HINT
  LOOK MAKE MARK READ SHOW
  ARGUE INDEX INFER POINT PROVE

SPEAK ALLUDE ATTEST BETRAY
DENOTE DESIGN EVINCE FINGER
IMPORT NOTIFY REVEAL BESPEAK
BETOKEN CONNOTE DECLARE
DISPLAY POINTTO PORTEND SIGNIFY
SPECIFY ADMONISH ANNOUNCE
DECIPHER DISCLOSE EVIDENCE
MANIFEST OUTPOINT REGISTER
SIGNALIZE
(— BY SOUNDING) STRIKE
(— WILLINGNESS) AGREE

INDICATION BECK CLEW CLUE HINT
LEAD MARK NOTE SHOW SIGN
CURVE INDEX PROOF SCENT TOKEN
AUGURY BEACON INDICE REMARK
SAMPLE SIGNAL AUSPICE MENTION
PROFFER SYMPTOM ALLUSION
ARGUMENT EVIDENCE MONITION
MONUMENT NOTATION SIGNANCE
TELLTALE
(— OF APPROVAL) CACHET
(— OF CONTROL) COLLAR
(— OF LIGHT) AUREOLE
(— OF OFFICE) SEAL
(— OF SOMETHING TO COME)
PROGNOSTIC PROGNOSTICATION
(INFALLIBLE —) ORACLE
(OBSCURE —) SHADOW
(VAGUE —) GLIMMER
(PL.) INDICIA

INDICATOR PIN HAND OMEN SIGN
FLOAT INDEX LITMUS SHOWER
STYLUS TARGET LACMOID POINTER
DETECTOR TELLTALE
(— LIGHT ON COMPUTER) CURSOR
(— OF BALANCE) COCK
(— OF HOUR) GNOMON
(DIRECTION —) FLASHER
(ECONOMIC —) LAGGER LEADER
(ELECTRONIC — TUBE) NIXIE

INDICIA POSTAGE

INDICT DITE CRIME PANEL ACCUSE
ATTACH CHARGE INDITE ARRAIGN
ARTICLE IMPEACH TROUNCE
WARRANT

INDICTMENT CHARGE DITTAY

INDIFFERENCE APATHY PHLEGM
ATARAXY DISDAIN ATARAXIA
COLDNESS EASINESS FROIDEUR
STOICISM

INDIFFERENT COLD COOL DEAD
DRAM EASY SOSO ALOOF BLASE
EQUAL HOHUM SOBER STOIC
CASUAL DEGAGE FRIGID SUPINE
CALLOUS LANGUID NEUTRAL
DETACHED LISTLESS LUKEWARM
MEDIOCRE RECKLESS SUPERIOR
UPSITTEN APATHETIC

INDIFFERENTIST POLITIC

INDIFFERENTLY DRYLY
HUMDRUM

INDIGENCE NEED WANT PENURY
BEGGARY POVERTY TENUITY

INDIGENE ENDEMIC

INDIGENOUS DESI NATIVE
DOMESTIC HOMEBORN ABORIGINAL

INDIGENT POOR NEEDY BEGGARLY
HAVELESS

INDIGESTIBLE STUDGY

INDIGESTION APEPSY APEPSIA
DYSPEPSY

INDIGNANT ANGRY WROTH
ANNOYED UPTIGHT INCENSED

INDIGNATION IRE RAGE ANGER
WRATH DESPITE DISDAIN DUDGEON
JEALOUSY

INDIGNITY CUT SLUR SCORN
INSULT SLIGHT AFFRONT OFFENCE
CONTUMELY

INDIGO ANIL NILL SHOOFLY
(PREF.) INDI(CO)

INDIRECT SLY SIDE DEVIOUS
OBLIQUE CIRCULAR GLANCING
OVERHEAD OVERWART SIDELONG
SIDEWAYS SIDEWISE ROUNDABOUT
(— WAY) AMBAGE

INDIRECTION CIRCUITY

INDIRECTLY ROUND SECOND
HAND

INDIRECTNESS OBLIQUITY

INDISCREET RASH HASTY SILLY
WITLESS CARELESS HEEDLESS

INDISCRETION FOLLY LAPSE
FREDAINE

INDISCRIMINATE MIXED MINGLED
SWEEPING PROMISCUOUS

INDISCRIMINATELY PELLMELL

INDISPENSABLE CENTRAL
NEEDFUL CRITICAL

INDISPOSED ILL MEAN SICK ILLISH
UNWELL

INDISPOSITION AIL BRASH
MALADY AILMENT SICKNESS
(— TO MOTION) INERTIA

INDISPUTABLE SURE CERTAIN
EVIDENT MANIFEST POSITIVE
APODICTIC

INDISTINCT DIM DARK DULL HAZY
FAINT FUZZY INNER LIGHT MISTY
MUDDY SHADY THICK VAGUE
BLEARY CLOUDY DREAMY INWARD
SLURRY WOOLLY BLEARED BLURRED
OBSCURE SHADOWY UNCLEAR
NEBULOUS
(— IN SOUND) NEUTRAL
(— IN UTTERANCE) CHOKING

INDISTINCTNESS BLUR
CONFUSION

INDITE PEN DITE DRAW

INDIVIDUAL GEE MAN ONE HEAD
SORT UNIT BEING MONAD THING
PROPER SINGLE SPIRIT VERSAL
APOMICT ATAVISM AZYGOTE
BIONTIC DIPLOID FINETIC ISOLATE
MONADIC NUMERIC SEVERAL
SPECIAL EVERYONE IDENTITY

SEPARATE SINGULAR SOLITARY
SPECIMEN PERSONAGE
(COLOR-BLIND —) MONOCHROMAT
(COUNTRIFIED —) HOBNAIL
(DESPICABLE —) HEEL
(DULL —) BOEOTIAN
(FOOLISH —) SOP
(HAUGHTY —) POT
(IDENTICAL —) CLONE
(IMMATURE —) ADULTOID
(IMPUDENT —) BOLDFACE
(INDEPENDENT —) MAVERICK
(IRRITABLE —) SNAPPER
(LEADING —) KEY
(MOSAIC —) GYNANDER
(MUTANT —) SALTANT
(PHYSIOLOGICAL —) BION
(PROSAIC —) PHILISTINE
(ROUGH-LOOKING —) BOHUNK
(SKILLED —) ADEPT
(SLOVENLY —) GROBIAN
(STUPID —) HOBBIL
(TRICKY —) BILK
(UNDERSIZED —) KIT KITT
(WINGED —) ALATE
(YOUNG —) KID
(PL.) FRY
INDIVIDUALITY KA SEITY QUALITY
SELFDOM HECCEITY IDENTITY
SELFHOOD
INDIVIDUALIZE ATOMIZE
INDIVIDUALLY APART APIECE
SINGLY PROPERLY
INDIVIDUATION AHANKARA
INDIVISIBLE PUNCTUAL
INDO-CHINESE SERIFORM
INDOCTRINATE BRIEF INSTRUCT
INDO-EUROPEAN ARIAN ARYAN
JAPHETIC
INDOLE KETOLE
INDOLENCE SLOTH LANGUOR
IDLESHIP MUSARDRY SLUGGING
(— PERSONIFIED) LAURENCE
LAWRENCE
INDOLENT IDLE LAZY FAINT INERT
SWEER DROWSY OTIOSE SUPINE
DRONISH LANGUID WILSOME
FAINEANT INACTIVE LISTLESS
LOUNGING SLOTHFUL SLUGGISH
PICKTOOTH
INDO-MALAYAN (— TREE) SUPA

INDONESIA
CAPITAL: DJAKARTA
COIN: RUPIAH
GULF: BONE TOLO TOMINI
ISLAND: ALOR BALI BURU JAVA
CERAM IRIAN SUMBA WETAR
BAWEAN BORNEO BUTUNG
FLORES KOMODO LOMBOK
MADURA PELENG CELEBES
SALAJAR SUMATRA SUMBAWA
SULAWESI

ISLAND GROUP: ARRU EWAB SUNDA
BANJAK NATUNA ANAMBAS
MOLUCCA TABELAN SABALANA
LAKE: RANAU TOWUTI
LANGUAGE: BAHASA MALAYAN
MOUNTAIN: BULU NIUT RAJA DEMPO
MURJO NIAPA LEUSER SLAMET
MENJAPA OGOAMAS SAMOSIR
KATOPASA KERINTJI MAHAMERU
RINDJANI TALAKMAU
MOUNTAINS: MULLER BARISAN
QUARLES SCHWANER
NATIVE: BUGI
PROVINCE: RIAU ATJEH DJAMBI
MALUKU LAMPUNG BENGKULU
RIVER: HARI MUSI DIGUL KAJAN
PAWAN BARITO KAMPAR KAPUAS
MAHAKAM
SEA: JAVA BANDA CERAM TIMOR
FLORES ARAFURA CELEBES
STRAIT: SUNDA LOMBOK MAKASSAR
TOWN: PALU MEDAN MALANG
MANADO BANDUNG KENDARI
MAKASAR SEMARANG SURABAJA
PALEMBANG SURAKARTA
VOLCANO: GEDE AGUNG DEMPO
RAUNG MARAPI MERAPI SINILA
SLAMET SUNDORO TAMBORA
KERINTJE RINDJANI
WEIGHT: CATTY OUNCE THAIL

INDONESIAN NESIOT SADANG
INDOORS WITHIN
INDRA SAKKA SAKRA
INDRI BABACOOTE
INDUBITABLE SURE EVIDENT
APPARENT MANIFEST UNIVOCAL
INDUCE GET DRAW LEAD MOVE
URGE WORK ARGUE BRIBE BRING
CAUSE IMPEL INFER TEMPT WEIGH
ADDICT ADJURE ALLURE ENGAGE
ENTICE IMPORT INCITE INVITE
OBTAIN REDUCE SEDUCE SUBORN
ACTUATE PREVAIL PROCURE
PROVOKE SOLICIT MOTIVATE
PERSUADE WIREDRAW
(— BY BRIBERY) FIX
INDUCEMENT BAIT MOTIVE
REASON FEATURE PERSUASION
INDUCT STALL INSTAL KNIGHT
INITIATE
INDUCTANCE HENRY
INDUCTION EPAGOGE
INDULGE PET BABY CADE CANT
FEED GLUT ALLOW HUMOR JOLLY
SPOIL TUTOR WALLY WREAK
COCKER FOSTER PAMPER PETTLE
DEBAUCH GRATIFY
(— IN PRIDE) PRIDE
(— ONESELF) WALLOW WANTON
(— TO EXCESS) PAMPER DEBAUCH
SURFEIT
INDULGED CADE

INDULGENCE LAW BINGE FAVOR
FOLLY MERCY SPREE EXCESS INDULT
PARDON PATENT JUBILEE QUIENAL
SURFEIT COURTESY DELICACY
EASINESS GLUTTONY POCULARY
(FREE —) SWING
(SEXUAL —) LECHERY
INDULGENT FOND GOOD MEEK
MILD SPOONY LENIENT TOLERANT
INDURATE HARDEN INDURE
INDURATED SCLEROID SCLEROUS
INDURATION SCLEROMA
INDUSTRIOUS BUSY DEEDY EIDENT
STEADY OPEROSE PAINFUL DILIGENT
SEDULOUS VIRTUOUS WORKSOME
INDUSTRY TOIL LABOR SCREEN
VIRTUE CERAMICS SEDULITY
INDWELLING IMMANENT INHERENT
INE (WIFE OF —) AETHELBURH
INEBRIATE SOUSE FERRIATED
INEBRIATED DRUNK DRINKY
INEFFACEABLE INBURNT
INDELIBLE
INEFFECTIVE DUD WEAK CLUMSY
DREEPY FLABBY FUTILE FLACCID
HALTING STERILE BUMBLING
INEFFECTIVELY ILL BADLY FEEBLY
INEFFECTUAL WAN DEAD IDLE
TAME VAIN VOID JERKY FUTILE
SPINDLY USELESS BOOTLESS
FAINEANT FIDDLING NUGATORY
INEFFICIENT ILL LAME POOR
CLUMSY DOLESS ROTTEN UNABLE
SLOUCHY USELESS FECKLESS
HANDLESS
INELASTIC DEAD
INELEGANT RUDE HOYDEN
AWKWARD
INELOQUENT WANMOL
INEPT DORKY INAPT ABSURD
AWKWARD FOOTLESS MALADROIT
INEPTITUDE PIFFLE
INEQUAL ROUGH
INEQUALITY ODDS CAHOT WHELK
ANOMALY EVECTION IMPARITY
NUTATION
(— OF SURFACE) WAVE
INEQUITABLE HARD
INERADICABLE LASTING INDELIBLE
PERMANENT
INERT DEAD DULL LAZY SLOW HEAVY
NOBLE SULKY LEADEN SODDEN
STUPID SUPINE TORPID PASSIVE
INACTIVE INDOLENT LIFELESS
SLOTHFUL SLUGGISH STAGNANT
THEWLESS THOWLESS
INERTIA TAMAS
INESCAPABLE DEAD NECESSARY
INESTIMABLE SUMLESS PRICELESS
INEVITABILITY FINALITY
INEVITABLE DUE SURE DIRECT
CERTAIN FATEFUL FOREGONE
INEXACT FREE ROUGH CLOUDY

INEXHAUSTIBLE INFINITE
INEXORABLE STERN STONY STRICT
RIGOROUS
INEXPEDIENCY IMPOLICY
INEXPEDIENT UNWISE
INEXPENSIVE LOW CHEAP
DIMESTORE REASONABLE
INEXPERIENCED RAW PUNY CRUDE
FRESH YOUNG UNSEEN KITLING
STRANGE INEXPERT INSOLENT
PRENTICE UNTRADED
INEXPERT ILL RUDE CRUDE GREEN
SIMPLE
INEXPLICABLE FELL
INFALLIBLE FAILSAFE SUREFIRE
UNERRING FOOLPROOF
INFAMOUS BASE RUDDY BLOODY
NOTOUR ODIOUS BLEEDING
FLAGRANT NIDERING SHAMEFUL
NEFARIOUS OPPROBRIOUS
INFAMY STAIN BAFFLE DEFAME
SHONDE DISHONOR IGNOMINY
OPPROBRIM OPPROBRIUM
INFANCY CRADLE BABYHOOD
INFANT BABE BABY TINY WEAN
CHILD MINOR PREMIE CHRISOM
MILKSOP PREEMIE BALDLING
BANTLING
(NAKED —) SCUDDY
(NEWLY-BORN —) NEONATUS
(VORACIOUS —) KILLCROP
INFANTILE BABYISH
INFANTRY FOOT PANTERIE
FOOTFOLK
INFANTRYMAN GI ASKAR
ZOUAVE DOGFACE DRAGOON
DOUGHBOY PIOUPIOU SOREFOOT
VOETGANGER
INFATUATE FOOL ASSOT BESOT
INFATUATED MAD FOND GAGA
GONE ASSOT CRAZY DOTTY ENTETE
ENGOUEE FOOLISH BESOTTED
INFATUATION ATE PASH RAVE
CRUSH FOLLY BEGUIN
(TRANSIENT —) CRAZE
(SUFF.) (— FOR) MANE MANIA(C)
(— WITH) ITIS
INFECT EMIT TAINT CANKER DEFILE
EMPEST ENTACH INFEST POISON
CORRUPT DISEASE POLLUTE
SMITTLE CONTAMINATE
INFECTED SEPTIC FUNGUSED
(NOT —) BLAND
INFECTION COLD DOSE SMIT FELON
TAINT FUNGUS
INFECTIOUS TAKING SMITTLE
CATCHING SMITABLE SMITTING
VIRULENT
INFEFTMENT SASINE
INFER DRAW PICK READ TAKE EDUCE
GUESS JUDGE ALLEGE DECIDE
DEDUCE DEDUCT DERIVE DIVINE
GATHER INDUCE REASON COLLECT

INCLUDE PRESUME SURMISE
CONCLUDE CONSTRUE

INFERENCE EDUCT SEQUEL
ANALOGY SEQUELA ILLATION
SEQUENCE SEQUITUR OBSERVATION
PRESUMPTION

INFERIOR BAD BUM DOG ILL JAY
LOW OFF SAD EVIL LESS MEAN
POOR PUNK SLIM SOUR WAFF
BASER BAUCH BELOW CHEAP
DOGGY GROSS LOUSY LOWER
PETTY PLAIN SCALY SCRUB TACKY
TATTY WORRY BEHIND CAGMAG
COARSE COMMON CRAPPY FEEBLE
FEMALE IMPURE LESSER MEASLY
PALTRY PEDARY PUISNE PUISNY
ROTTEN SECOND SHABBY SHODDY
WOODEN BADDISH CRIPPLE
HUMBLER NAGGISH POPULAR
SCRUBBY SUBJECT ABNORMAL
ANTERIOR DEROGATE ORDINARY
PARAVAIL TERRIBLE
(PREF.) DEMI INFRA SUB
(SUFF.) ASTER EEN
(— ONE) LING

INFERIORITY LESSNESS MEANNESS

INFERNAL BLACK AVERNAL
BLASTED ETERNAL HELLISH SATANIC
SHEOLIC STYGIAN CHTHONIC
DAMNABLE DEVILISH PLUTONIC
PLUTONIAN

INFERTILE DEAD DEAF DOUR LEAN
POOR THIN CLEAR EFFETE STERILE

INFEST COE VEX BESET INFECT
PESTER PLAGUE OVERRUN
TORMENT

INFESTATION SCALE PLAGUE
STRIKE MYIASIS LOAIASIS
PEDICULOSIS

INFESTED MITY BLOWN BROOD
BUGGY FLUKY FLUKED GRUBBY
HAUNTED FLYBLOWN

INFIDEL DEIST KAFIR GIAOUR
PAYNIM ATHEIST SARACEN SKEPTIC
AGNOSTIC MISCREANT
MISBELIEVER

INFIDELITY PERFIDY ADULTERY
TRAHISON

INFIELD CARPET INTOWN DIAMOND

INFILTRATE FILTER CRETIFY
COLONIZE

INFILTRATION SEEPAGE ADIPOSIS
SATURATION

INFINITE CHAOS COSMIC ENDLESS
ETERNAL IMMENSE

INFINITENESS ETERNITY

INFINITESIMAL PUNCTUAL

INFINITIVE SUPINE VERBID
(FRENCH —) ETRE

INFINITY OLAM ANANTA ETERNITY

INFIRM LAME WEAK ANILE CRAZY
CRONK SHAKY CRANKY FEEBLE
SICKLY UNFIRM UNSURE CASALTY

CRAICHY DOWLESS DWAIBLE
FRAGILE INVALID SAPLESS UNFEARY
DODDERED FIRMLESS INSECURE
RESOLUTE UNSTRONG

INFIRMARY SICKBAY

INFIRMITY WOE CRAZE DOTAGE
FOIBLE UNHEAL DISEASE FAILING
FRAILTY UNMIGHT DEBILITY
SICKNESS WEAKNESS

INFIX INLAY INSET ENGRAVE
IMPLANT INGRAIN

INFIXED INHERENT

INFLAME RAW BURN FIRE GOAD
HEAT STIR ANGER BLAIN FLAME
SCALD SHAME AROUSE ENAMOR
EXCITE FESTER IGNITE INCEND
KINDLE MADDEN RANKLE EMBRASE
FLUSTER INCENSE ESCHAUFE
(— WITH LOVE) ENAMOR

INFLAMED RED ANGRY FIERY
ABLAZE FRETTY HEATED TORRID
FLAGRANT

INFLAMMABLE FIERY ARDENT
TOUCHY PICEOUS TINDERY

INFLAMMATION ACNE FIRE ANGER
FELON GLEET SCALD SEBEL AGNAIL
ANCOME BLIGHT CANKER DEFLUX
GREASE IRITIS CATARRH CECITIS
CHAFING COLITIS COXITIS FISTULA
GONITIS ILEITIS QUITTOR SUNBURN
ADENITIS ANGIITIS AORTITIS
BURSITIS CHILITIS CYCLITIS CYSTITIS
SHINGLES
(SUFF.) ITIS

INFLATE HOVE HUFF KITE PLIM PUFF
BLOAT BOLNE HEAVE SWELL DILATE
EMBOSS EXPAND HUFFLE INBLOW
PUMPUP TUMEFY BLADDER
BOMBAST DISTEND FORBLOW
OUTSWELL SUFFLATE

INFLATED TRIG BLOWN FLOWN
GASSY PUFFY TUMID TURGID
BOMBAST BULLATE FUSTIAN
OROTUND STILTED SWOLLEN
TURGENT BLADDERY OUTBLOWN
TOPLOFTY TUMOROUS VANITOUS
BOMBASTIC OVERBLOWN
PLETHORIC

INFLATION FLATUS CADENCE
TYMPANY

INFLECT COMPARE DECLINE

INFLECTION SIGN TONE ARSIS
ACCENT FLEXION LATINISM
MODULATION

INFLECTIONAL FORMAL

INFLEXIBILITY ACAMPSIA

INFLEXIBLE ACID DOUR FIRM HARD
IRON EAGER SOLID STERN STIFF
STONY STOUR SEVERE STRICT
STUFFY ADAMANT RESTIVE
GRANITIC IRONCLAD OBDURATE
PREFRACT RESOLUTE RIGOROUS
STIFFISH STUBBORN ADAMANTINE

INFLICT DO ADD PUT SET GIVE SEND
INFER YIELD IMPOSE RAMROD
STRIKE
(— CHASTISEMENT) WREAK
(— HURT) BRUISE
(— INJURY) AGGRIEVE
(— PAIN) LAY CHASTISE
INFLICTION (— OF PUNISHMENT)
AUTODAFE
INFLORESCENCE CHAT CYME
AMENT ARROW BRUSH SPIKE UMBEL
CORYMB FLOWER RACEME SPADIX
TASSEL BOSTRYX PANICLE THYRSIS
CYATHIUM FASCICLE NUCAMENT
INFLOW INSET AFFLUX INCOME
INFLUX INCOURSE
INFLOWING AFFLUENT
INFLUENCE IN WIN BEND BIAS
COAX DRAG DRAW HAND HANK
HEFT LEAD MOVE PULL PUSH RULE
SUCK SWAY BRIBE CHARM CLOUT
COLOR ENACT FORCE GRACE IMPEL
JUICE MOYEN POWER REACH SPELL
VAPOR VOGUE WEIGH AFFECT
ALLURE CREDIT EFFECT COVERN
IMPORT INDUCE INFLOW INFLUX
MOTIVE OBSESS PONDUS SALUTE
SHADOW STROKE WEIGHT ACTUATE
ATTINGE ATTRACT BEARING
BEWITCH BLARNEY BOSSDOM
CAPTURE CONCUSS CONTROL
DISPUTE ENCHANT GRAVITY IMPRINT
INCLINE INSPIRE MASTERY SUASION
TENDRIL DOMINION HEGEMONY
INTEREST LEVERAGE MEDICINE
PRESTIGE SANCTION STRENGTH
CAPTIVATE
(— BY GIFTS) GREASE
(— BY THREATS) INTIMIDATE
(— CORRUPTLY) BRIBE
(— FOR DESTRUCTION) MAELSTROM
(— OF GODS) MANA
(— OF PERSONALITY) MAGNETISM
(— OF THE STARS) BLAS
(— UNREASONABLY) OBSESS
(ATTEMPT TO —) JAWBONE
(BENIGN —) UNCTION
(CONSTRAINING —) STRESS
PRESSURE
(CONTROLLING —) SWAY
(CORRUPTING —) SMOUCH SMUTCH
(DEPRESSING —) CHILL
(DIABOLICAL —) DEVILDOM
(DISRUPTIVE —) GREMLIN
(DOMINANT —) GENIUS STREAM
(DULLING —) DAMPER
(ELEVATING —) LIFT
(HARMFUL —) UPAS GRUDGE
(INJURIOUS —) RUST
(MALEVOLENT —) DISASTER
(MALIGN —) TAKING
(PERNICIOUS —) BALE BLAST
(SINISTER —) MALICE

(SOOTHING —) SALVE
(SPIRITUAL —) NUMEN
(SURROUNDING —) AIR AMBIENCE
(UNDER — OF ALCOHOL OR DRUGS)
ZONKED
INFLUENCING INFUSIVE
INFLUENTIAL BIG GRAVE
POWERFUL
INFLUENZA FLU LEUMA GRIPPE
PINKEYE
INFLUX STORM INCOME INFLOW
INRUSH ILLAPSE
(— IN A MINE) COURSE
(— OF TIDE) INSET
INFOLD WRAP IMPLY TWINE EMPLOY
INWRAP ENVELOP INVOLVE
CONVOLVE
INFORM KEN BEEF BLOW FINK NOSE
POST SHOP SHOW TELL WARN WISE
LEARN PEACH ADVISE ASSURE
DELATE DETECT NOTIFY PREACH
SNITCH WITTER APPRISE EDUCATE
IMPEACH INSENSE PARTAKE
POSSESS RESOLVE SIGNIFY
SUGGEST ACQUAINT DENOUNCE
INFORMED INSTRUCT SPARSILE
(— AGAINST) SHOP RUMBLE
DENOUNCE
INFORMAL BREEZY CASUAL CHATTY
COMMON FOLKSY TWEEDY
INTIMATE SLIPSHOD SOCIABLE
NEGLIGENT OFFICIOUS
INFORMANT AUTHOR INFORMER
SQUEALER SYCOPHANT
INFORMATION AIR GEN OIL WIT
CLEW CLUE DOPE INFO LORE NEWS
NOTE TALE WIRE WORD DATUM
GRIFF SCOOP SKILL ADVICE INSIDE
LIGHTS NOTICE APPRISE PEMICAN
READOUT TIDINGS WITTING
BRIEFING NOTITION PEMMICAN
(— ON VIDEO SCREEN) DISPLAY
(BODY OF —) DIGEST
(CONDENSED —) PEMICAN
PEMMICAN
(INCIDENTAL —) SIDELIGHT
(SECRET —) ARCANUM
(SUFF.) ANA IANA
INFORMED UP HEP WISE AWARE
WITTY KNOWING LEARNED
(WELL —) UPON
INFORMER FINK NARK NOSE PIMP
SPIV STAG RUSTY SNEAK SPLIT
BEAGLE CANARY FINGER SETTER
SNITCH TELLER DELATOR STOOLIE
TANQUAM APPROVER PROMOTER
SQUAWKER SQUEAKER SQUEALER
TELLTALE SYCOPHANT
WHISTLEBLOWER
INFORTUNE MARS SATURN
INFRACTION BREACH OFFENCE
TRESPASS
(— IN HOCKEY) SPEARING

INFRARED ULTRARED
INFREQUENCY SELDOMCY
INFREQUENT RARE SELDOM
FUGITIVE SPORADIC UNCOMMON
INFRINGE IMPOSE INVADE TRENCH
IMPINGE INFRACT INTRUDE
ENCROACH REFRINGE TRESPASS
INFRINGEMENT FOUL BREACH
TRESPASS VIOLENCE
INFRINGER PIRATE
INFULA FANON LABEL LAPPET
HEADBAND
INFUNDIBULUM FUNNEL PAVILION
INFURIATE ENRAGE ENFELON
INFUSE DRAW MASK IMBUE IMMIT
SPOIL STEEP AERATE AERIFY IMMISS
INFLOW INFORM INFUND INVEST
LEAVEN BREATHE DISTILL ENGRAIN
IMPLANT INFOUND INSPIRE INSTILL
SUFFUSE SATURATE
(— TEA) TRACK
(— WITH HATRED) TURN
INFUSED SHOT
INFUSION SHADE CARDIN INCOME
TISANE HORDEATE
(— OF MALT) WORT GROUT
(BITTER —) RUE
INFUSORIAN LEPOCYTE
INGA GUAVA
INGATE GATE LEDGE TEDGE
INGATHERING HARVEST
INGENIOUS SLY CUTE FAST FEAT
FINE ACUTE SHARP SMART WITTY
ADROIT BRAINY CLEVER CRAFTY
DAEDAL GIFTED KNACKY PRETTY
QUAINT SUBTLE CUNNING POLITIC
SKILLFUL
INGENUITY ART WIT ENGINE
ADDRESS COMPASS ARTIFICE
CONTOISE INDUSTRY QUENTISE
INGENUOSITY NAIVETE
INGENUOUS FREE FRANK NAIVE
PLAIN CANDID HONEST SUBTLE
ARTLESS NATURAL SINCERE
INNOCENT
INGENUOUSNESS NAIVETE
INGEST EAT INCEPT ENGLOBE
SWALLOW
INGESTION SLURP
INGOT GAD SOW WEDGE LINGOT
NIGGOT CROPHEAD
(— OF BRASS) STRIP
(— OF SILVER) SHOE TING SCHUYT
(SILVER —) SYCEE
(SILVER —S) SYCEE
(SOAKING —S) HEAT
INGRAIN GRAIN INFUSE ENFLESH
INGRAINED INWORN
INGRATE SNAKE
INGRATIATE FLATTER
INGRATIATING BLAND SILKY SLEEK
SLICK SOAPY SILKEN SMOOTH
INGRATITUDE UNTHANK

INGREDIENT FACTOR AMALGAM
BINDING ELEMENT ADJUVANT
(ACTIVE —) ANIMA
(FUNDAMENTAL —) BASIS
(FUSIBLE —) BOND
(MAIN —) BASE
(SALVE —) ALOE
INGRESS ENTRY ENTRANCE
INGROWTH APODEMA
INGUEN GROIN
INHABIT BIG WIN WON COVER
DWELL HABIT OCCUPY BEDWELL
INDWELL POSSESS POPULATE
INHABITANT INMATE BURGHER
CITIZEN DENIZEN DWELLER PEOPLER
BORDERER CONFINER DEMESMAN
HABITANT INCOLANT INHOLDER
(— OF ALASKA) SOURDOUGH
(— OF BORDER REGION) MARCHER
(— OF CITY) CIT CITIZEN
(— OF EXTREME NORTH)
HYPERBOREAN
(— OF INDIA) BHARATA
(— OF JUNGLE) JUNGLI
(— OF MAINE) DOWNEASTER
(— OF MOON) LUNARIAN
(— OF SWISS ALPS) GRISON
(— OF TORRID ZONE) ASCIAN
(— OF VIRGINIA) COOHEE
(— OF WISCONSIN) BADGER
(EARTH —) TERRAN
(OLDEST —) PATRIARCH
(PL.) SIDE WARE
(SUFF.) COLA ITE OT OTE
INHABITING
(SUFF.) COLE COLINE COLOUS
INHALATION SNUFF BREATH
(PREF.) ANEM(O)
INHALE DRAW TAKE SMOKE SNIFF
SNUFF ATTRACT BREATHE INHAUST
INSPIRE RESPIRE ASPIRATE
(— A DRUG) SNORT
(PREF.) INSPIRO
INHALER SNIFTER
INHARMONIOUS ABSURD RUGGED
ABSONANT
INHERE CONSIST INEXIST
INHERENCE INBEING
INHERENT KIND INBORN INNATE
INWARD NATIVE PROPER INGENIT
NATURAL HABITUAL IMMANENT
INTEGRAL INTERNAL RESIDENT
INHERIT HEIR SUCCEED
INHERITANCE KIND ENTAIL
HEIRDOM HEIRSHIP HEREDITY
HERITAGE LANDFALL VACANTIA
(— OF CATTLE) ERF
(PARTICULATE —) MENDELISM
INHERITED INBORN INNATE
CONGENITAL
(SUFF.) CLINOUS CLINY
INHIBIT COOP CURB SNUB CRIMP
DETER FORBID STIFLE SUPPRESS

INHIBITED COLD
INHIBITION AKINESIS
INHIBITOR PARGYLINE PHENELZINE
INHIBITORY COLYTIC
INHOSPITABLE STERN DESERT
INHUMAN FELL CRUEL BRUTAL
FIERCE IMMANE SAVAGE BESTIAL
MANLESS DEVILISH KINDLESS
INHUMANE WANTON
INHUMANITY CRUELTY
INHUME BURY INTER ENTOMB
INIMICAL BAD FROSTY HOSTILE
(— TO LIFE) ANTIBIOTIC
INIQUITOUS ILL DARK WRONG
SINFUL WICKED NEFARIOUS
INIQUITY SIN EVIL VICE CRIME GUILT
DARKNESS MISCHIEF
INITIAL LETTER VIRGIN ASPIREE
PRINCIPAL
(INTERWOVEN —S) CIPHER
(PL.) PERFINS
INITIALLY ATFIRST
INITIATE HEAD MYST OPEN ADEPT
ADMIT BEGIN BREAK ENTER EPOPT
FOUND START GROUND INDUCE
INDUCT INVENT LAUNCH MYSTES
ORPHIC BAPTIZE INSTALL INSTATE
OPERATE ORPHEAN SYMMIST
YTIGGER COMMENCE ESOTERIC
INCHOATE ORIGINATE
INITIATION DIKSHA OPENING
ENTRANCE
(— OF GROWTH) BUDBREAK
INITIATIVE PEP LEAD GETUP ACTION
AMBITION GUMPTION OVERTURE
INJECT DRIVE IMMIT
(— DRUG) SKINPOP
(— DRUGS) SHOOT MAINLINE
INJECTION JAG HYPO SHOT
BOOSTER CLYSTER INSERTION
INJUDICIOUS UNWISE
INJUDICIOUSNESS ACRISY
INJUNCTION HEST BEHEST CHARGE
IMPOSE RUBRIC BIDDING DICTATE
EXPRESS MANDATE PRECEPT
INJURE DO GAS ILL MAR BURN
CHEW DERE ENVY GALL HARM HURT
MAUL TEAR TEEN WERD ABUSE
BLAST CRAZE DIRTY MISDO RIFLE
SCALD SHEND SMITE SPOIL STEER
WOUND WRONG BRUISE DAMAGE
DEFACE DEFECT DEPAIR GRIEVE
HINDER IMPAIR INJURY MANGLE
NOBBLE PUNISH RANKLE SCATHE
SCOTCH STRAIN AFFLICT AFFRONT
CONTUSE DAMNIFY DESPITE
FORWORK MISBEDE TERRIFY
AGGRIEVE DISASTER DISSERVE
FORSLACK IMPERISH INTERESS
MISCHIEF MISGUIDE MUTILATE
PREJUDGE SPURGALL
(— BY ASPERSION) SPATTER
(— BY FALSE REPORT) SLANDER

(— BY GLANCE OF BASILISK) STRIKE
(— BY TREADING UPON) FITTER
(— SCENT) STAIN
(— SERIOUSLY) DO KILL SPOIL
(— SLIGHTLY) ANNOY
(— THE BACK) CHINK
(— WITH GRENADE) FRAG
(DELIBERATELY —) FRAG
(SEVERELY —) WASTE
INJURED HURT LESED BLASTED
(EASILY —) NICE
INJURIOUS BAD ILL EVIL NOCENT
NOYANT NOYFUL SHREWD ABUSIVE
HARMFUL HURTFUL NOXIOUS
SCADDLE DAMAGING GRIEVOUS
SINISTER TORTIOUS TORTUOUS
WRACKFUL WRONGFUL PERNICIOUS
INJURIOUSLY HEAVILY
INJURY ILL JAM MAR BALE BANE
BURN EVIL HARM HURT JEEL LOSS
RUIN SCAT TEEN TORT WITE ABUSE
BLAME CHAFE CRUSH GRIFF SCALD
SCORE SPITE SPOIL TOUCH WATHE
WRACK WRONG BREACH BRUISE
DAMAGE DANGER IMPAIR LESION
SCATHE STRAIN STROKE TRAUMA
BEATING DESPITE EXPENSE OFFENSE
OUTRAGE PAYMENT SCADDLE
SCRATCH SORANCE BUSINESS
CASUALTY CREPANCE INTEREST
MISCHIEF NUISANCE
(— OF HORSES) TREAD CREPANCE
(— OF PLANTS) SUNSCALD
(— TO REPUTATION) SCANDAL
(CHIEF —) FOCUS
(MALICIOUS —) REVENGE
(SERIOUS —) MAYHEM
INJUSTICE WRONG INJURY INJURIA
UNRIGHT HARDSHIP INEQUITY
(GROSS —) INIQUITY
INK BEAT SIGN COLOR ARNEMENT
ATRAMENT
(DISPENSER OF —) SQUID
(KIND OF —) RED INDIA
(PRINTER'S —) CYAN
INK-BALL DABBER PUMPET
INKER SLOSHER
INKING PAD TOMPION
INKLE SPINEL
INKLING HOE HINT ITEM SCENT
GLIMMER GLIMPSE UMBRAGE
INKSTAND STANDISH
INKWELL FOUNT INKSTAND
INKY BLACK ATRAMENTOUS
INLAID PIQUE CONTISE
(— DECORATION) BUHL BOULE
BOULLE
(— WORK) KOFTGARI
INLAND MAUKA INMORE INWARD
MIDLAND INTERIOR
INLAY PICK PIKE COUCH HATCH INLET
PIQUE SPELL CRUSTA ENAMEL
IMPAVE INDENT NIELLO TARSIA

ENCHASE ENCRUST INCRUST
COMMESSO
INLAYING TARKASHI
INLET ARM BAY CUT GEO RIA VOE
COVE DOCK HOPE MERE SLEW WICK
BAYOU BRACE CHUCK CREEK FIORD
FJORD FLEET HAVEN LOGAN LOUGH
STOMA ESTERO HARBOR INFALL
SLOUGH TONGUE DOGHOLE
INDRAFT SUCTION CALANQUE
SEAPOOSE
(— OF THE SEA) EA
(MUDDY —) SUMP
(REGULATED —) SLUICE
(TIDAL —) GAP
INLIER WINDOW
INLYING INNERLY
INMATE FISH LODGER TENANT
BEADSMAN DOMESTIC PRISONER
(BEDLAM —) ABRAMMAN
ABRAHAMMAN
(RELIGIOUS —) NOVICE
INMOST SECRET RETIRED
INN PUB KHAN STOP VENT ANGEL
BANDB FONDA HOTEL MESON
SERAI TAMBO VENTA CABACK
HARBOR HOSTEL HOSTRY IMARET
POSADA PUBLIC SHANTY TABARD
ALBERGE AUBERGE BOLICHE
CAFENEH CAFENET FONDACO
FONDOUK HOSTAGE LOCANDA
OSTERIA SOJOURN SURAHEE
CHOULTRY GASTHAUS HOSTELRY
ORDINARY SERAGLIO WAYHOUSE
ROADHOUSE
(KIND OF —) MOTOR
INNARDS GIZZARD INWARDS
STUFFING
INNATE BORN KIND INBORN INBRED
CONNATE INGRAIN NATURAL
INHERENT INSTINCT
(— QUALITY) LARGESS
INNER BEN END INSIDE INWARD
INWITH MENTAL INTERIOR INTERNAL
PECTORAL
(— LIGHT) SEED
(PREF.) ENT(O) ESO
(— PARTS OF BODY) BATHY
INNER MONGOLIA
(CAPITAL OF —) HOHHOT HUHEHOT
INNERMOST UPPER INMOST
MIDMOST INTIMATE
INNERVATE AROUSE
INNINA ISHTAR
INNING END HAND HEAD FRAME
(PL.) KNOCK WICKET
INNKEEPER HOST DUENA TAPPER
VENTER GOODMAN HOSTESS
HOSTLER PADRONE BONIFACE
HOSTELER
(PL.) CAUPONES
INNOCENCE BLUET WHITE CANDOR
PURITY SIMPLICITY

INNOCENT SOT DEWY FREE NAIF
PURE CANNY CLEAR NAIVE SEELY
SILLY WHITE CHASTE DOVISH
HONEST SIMPLE CHRISOM LAMBKIN
UPRIGHT ARCADIAN HARMLESS
IGNORANT PASTORAL PRIMROSE
SACKLESS UNGUILTY ZACCHEUS
INNOCUOUS HARMLESS INNOCENT
INNOVATE NOVELIZE
INNOVATION NOVEL NOVELTY
INNOVATOR HERETIC
INNUENDO HINT SLUR SLIPE
INNUMERABLE MYRIAD
NUMBERLESS
INO (BROTHER OF —) POLYDORUS
(FATHER OF —) CADMUS
(HUSBAND OF —) ATHAMAS
(MOTHER OF —) HARMONIA
(SISTER OF —) AGAVE SEMELE
AUTONOE
(SON OF —) LEARCHUS PALAEMON
MELICERTES
INOCULATE SEED PLANT INFUSE
ENGRAFT EQUINATE
INOCULATION JAG
INOCULUM STAB STREAK
IN-OFF JENNY
INOFFENSIVE HARMLESS
INOPERATIVE OFF DEAD RESTY
SILENT NUGATORY
INOPPORTUNE UNTIMELY
INORDINATE WILD UNDUE
ENORMOUS
INORGANIC MINERAL
INOSITOL DAMBOSE
INPOURING INFLUX
INQUEST CROWN QUEST ASSIZE
OFFICE INQUIRY
INQUIET UNEASY
INQUILINE GUEST
INQUIRE ASK AXE SEEK QUERY
SPERE DEMAND FRAYNE SEARCH
EXAMINE HEARKEN QUESTION
INQUIRER ASKER QUERENT
INQUIRY PROBE QUERY THANK
TRIAL DEMAND EXAMEN TRACER
DOCIMASY QUESTION RESEARCH
SCRUTINY SPEERING
INQUISITION CUSTOM INQUIRY
QUAESTIO
INQUISITIVE NOSY PEERY PRYING
CURIOUS MEDDLING QUIZZICAL
INROAD RAID BREACH INBREAK
INVASION
INSALUBRIOUS NOXIOUS
INSANE MAD WUD DAFT NUTS WILD
WOOD BALMY BATTY BUGGY CRAZY
DIPPY MANIC QUEER WRONG
CRANKY LOCOED SCREWY FLIGHTY
FRANTIC FURIOUS LUNATIC WITLESS
BUGHOUSE DEMENTED DERANGED
DISTRACT
(— ONE) MANIAC

INSANITY RAGE CRACK CRAZE FOLIE
MANIA FRENZY LUNACY MADNESS
VESANIA DELIRIUM DEMENTIA
WOODNESS ACROMANIA
PSYCHOSIS

INSATIABLE GREEDY VORACIOUS

INSCRIBE DELVE ENTER WRITE
BLAZON DOCKET ENDOSS INDITE
LEGEND LETTER SCRIBE SCRIVE
SCROLL ASCRIBE ENDORSE
ENGROSS DEDICATE DESCRIBE
EMBLAZON ENSCROLL INTITULE

INSCRIBED INWRIT WRITTEN
DESCRIPT

INSCRIPTION HEAD ELOGY CACHET
LEGEND LETTER ELOGIUM EPIGRAM
EPITAPH MENTION TITULUS WRITING
COLOPHON EPIGRAPH GRAFFITO
INSCRIPT SCRIBING
(— ON ROCK) PETROGLYPH
(— ON TOMBSTONE) ELOGE
ELOGIUM
(3-LETTER —) TRIGRAM

INSCRUTABLE EQUIVOCAL
MYSTERIOUS

INSECT ANT BEE BUG DOR DUN ELF
FLY NIT ANER FLEA GNAT GOGO
GYNE MOTH PELA PEST PUPA SPIT
WASP WETA ZIMB APHID APHIS
BICHO BORER FLYER GOGGA GUEST
IMAGO LOUSE MINER ROACH SCALE
BEETLE BLIGHT CALLOW CICADA
CIXIID EARWIG EMBIID HAWKER
HOPPER INSTAR MANTIS NITTER
PODURA PSOCID SAPPER SAWFLY
THRIPS VERMIN WALKER WEEVIL
ATTACUS BLATTID BOATMAN
BRUMMER BUZZARD CRAWLER
CREEPER CRICKET CYNIPID DEALATE
DRUMMER FARWORM FIREBUG
FIREFLY GALLFLY GIRDLER GRAYFLY
HEXAPOD JAPYGID KATYDID
PHASMID SANDBOY SCINIPH
SKIPPER SPECTRE STAINER STYLOPS
TERMITE VAGRANT WEBWORM
ALDERFLY ALKERMES BLACKFLY
BRACONID DIPTERAN FIREBRAT
FULGORID GLOWWORM HOMOPTER
HORNTAIL LACEWING LECANIUM
MEALYBUG PRONYMPH SEMIPUPA
SEXUPARA SPHECOID STINKBUG
STYLOPID SYMPHILE
(— STAGE) PUPA IMAGO LARVA
(IMMATURE —) NYMPH
(LOWEST —S) AMETABOLA
(PART OF —) EYE CLAW COXA WING
FEMUR TIBIA CERCUS LABRUM
PALPUS TARSUS THORAX ABDOMEN
ANTENNA OCELLUS MANDIBLE
SPIRACLE OVIPOSTOR PROTHORAX
TYMPANIUM MESOTHORAX
METATHORAX OVIPOSITER
TROCHANTER

(PL.) HEXAPODA
(PREF.) ENTOM(O)
(SUFF.) CORIS

INSECTICIDE DDD DDT DIP EPN
CUBE FLIT MINEX MIREX NALED
SEVIN TIMBO ALDRIN DERRIS
ENDRIN RONNEL CALOMEL ISODRIN
LINDANE MENAZON OVICIDE
PHORATE CARBARYL CHLORDAN
CULICIDE DIELDRIN FENTHION
NICOTINE ROTENONE SCHRADAN
ANTRYCIDE MALATHION PARATHION
PYRETHRUM

INSECTIVORE MOLE SHREW
AGOUTA DESMAN TENREC
MOONRAT ALAMIQUI

INSECURE DICKY EEMIS LOOSE
SHAKY INFIRM TICKLE UNFAST
UNSAFE UNSURE CASALTY

INSECURITY DANGER

INSEMINATE BREED

INSENSATE SURD FATUOUS

INSENSIBILITY DAMP APATHY
STUPOR TORPON

INSENSIBLE DEAD DULL LOST
NUMB BRUTE DENSE MARBLE
OBTUSE SEARED STUPID WOODEN
DATELESS APATHETIC

INSENSITIVE DEAD BLUNT CRASS
STONY OBTUSE STUPID BOORISH

INSEPARABLE WRAPPED

INSERT SLIP SPUD STOP BOTCH
DICKY ENROL ENTER FUDGE IMMIT
INFER INFIX INLET INSET SETIN
STUFF COLLET GUSSET INWORK
INWEAVE GATEFOLD INTROMIT
SANDWICH SLASHING SUBTRUDE
THROWOUT
(— IN SHOE) CUSHION
(— STONE CHIPS) PIN
(— SURREPTITIOUSLY) FOIST
(SKIRT —) GORE

INSERTION FLOWER BEADING
(TAPERED —) MITER MITRE

INSET GODET INSERT
(DRESS —) MOTIF

INSHEATHE EMBOSS

INSIDE IN BEN ATHIN INBYE INNER
INWITH KEYHOLE INTERIOR
(— OF ANGLE BAR) BOSOM
(— OF OUTER EAR) BUR BURR
(PREF.) END(O)

INSIDIOUS SLY SNARY COVERT
SUBTLE GUILEFUL

INSIGHT KEN SIGHT APERCU
THEORY NOSTRIL

INSIGNIA TYPE BADGE ORDER SIGNS
COLLAR GEORGE CADUCEUS
COMMENDA HERALDRY OPINICUS
PONTIFICALS
(HERALDIC —) ARMOR
(MILITARY —) EAGLE

INSIGNIFICANCE NOTHINGNESS

INSIGNIFICANT NULL POOR PUNY DINKY FOOTY PETIT PETTY POTTY SCRUB SMALL HUMBLE NAUGHT PALTRY PUISNE SIMPLE SLIGHT FOOLISH NAUGHTY NIFLING NOMINAL PELTING PIMPING SCRUBBY TENUOUS TRIVIAL BAUBLING INFERIOR PEDDLING PITIABLE SNIPPING TRIFLING TRIPENNY

INSINCERE FALSE DOUBLE HOLLOW FEIGNED LIPDEEP ARTIFICIAL

INSINCERITY ARTIFICE DISGUISE

INSINUATE HINT MINT WIND CRAWL SCREW TWIST ALLUDE GLANCE INFUSE INSTIL WRITHE IMPLANT INNUATE

INSINUATING SNIDE SILKEN SMARMY

INSINUATION HINT INKLING

INSIPID DRY WAW BLAH DEAD FADE FLAT FOND FOZY LASH TAME BANAL BAUCH BLAND FLASH INANE PROSY STALE VAPID WALSH WAUGH FLASHY FRIGID JEJUNE SWASHY THREEP WAIRSH WALLOW EXOLETE FATUOUS INSULSE MAWKISH PROSAIC SAPLESS SHILPIT WEARISH WEERISH LIFELESS UNSAVORY WATERISH

INSIST AVER PRESS ASSERT THREAP CONSIST
(— PEEVISHLY) CRAIK
(— UPON) SOLICIT

INSISTENCE URGENCY INSTANCY

INSISTENT LOUD ADAMANT INSTANT EMPHATIC FRENZIED IMPOSING

INSISTER STICKLER

INSOLE CUSHION SLIPSOLE

INSOLENCE GUM LIP SASS CHEEK MOUTH PRIDE SNASH HUBRIS DISDAIN AUDACITY SURQUIDY CONTUMELY PETULANCE

INSOLENT FACY PERT RUDE WISE BARDY BRASH LUSTY PROUD CHEEKY LORDLY WANTON ABUSIVE DEFIANT PAUGHTY ARROGANT IMPUDENT PETULANT SCORNFUL AUDACIOUS

INSOLUBLE HOPELESS

INSOLVENT BANKRUPT

INSOMNIA AHYPNIA AGRYPNIA

INSOUCIANT CAVALIER

INSPECT SEE SUS VET CASE ESPY LOOK SUSS BRACK CHECK SIGHT VISIT INLOOK PERUSE SURVEY EXAMINE OVERSEE CONSIDER OVERLOOK OVERVIEW
(— CASUALLY) BROWSE
(— COINS) SHROFF
(— MERCHANDISE IN BALTIC) BRACK
(— TROOPS) REVIEW

INSPECTION EYE PRY VIEW CHECK SIGHT REVIEW SURVEY BEDIKAH CHECKUP INSIGHT INSPECT PERUSAL VIDIMUS OVERHAUL OVERVIEW SCRUTINY
(— OF CLOTH) ALNAGE
(— OF TROOPS) REVIEW
(KIT —) RAGFAIR

INSPECTOR SAYER SNOOP BISHOP CENSOR CONNER JUMPER LOOKER VIEWER GRAINER MOOCHER PERCHER SAMPLER SNOOPER VEADORE EXAMINER SEARCHER
(— OF COAL) KEEKER
(— OF COTTON LOOMS) TACKLER
(— OF ELECTRIC LAMPS) AGER
(ECCLESIASTICAL —) EXARCH

INSPIRATION FIRE SIGH POESY ANIMUS SPIRIT SPRITE IMPULSE MADNESS PEGASUS AFFLATUS AGANIPPE INFLATUS
(— IN ORATORY) HWYL
(ORATORICAL —) HWYL

INSPIRE FIRE MOVE CHEER ELATE EXALT SPARK BEACON INBLOW INCUSS INDUCE INFORM INFUSE KINDLE PROMPT ACTUATE ANIMATE EMBRAVE ENFORCE ENLIVEN HEARTEN IMPLANT PREMOVE QUICKEN SUGGEST CATALYZE ENTALENT INSPIRIT MOTIVATE SUFFLATE

INSPIRED AWED VATIC AFFLATED DAEMONIC ENTHEATE VISIONED

INSPIRER SOUL

INSPIRING INFUSIVE SPLENDID STIRRING
(— AWE) FORMIDABLE

INSPIRIT CHEER ELATE HEART ROUSE SPIRIT ANIMATE CHERISH COMFORT ENLIVEN HEARTEN INSPIRE QUICKEN ALACRIFY

INSPISSATE STIFFEN THICKEN

INSPISSATED STIFF THICK

INSTABILITY ANOMY ANOMIE SLIDDER FLUIDITY

INSTALL SEAT CHAIR STALL INDUCT INVEST ENSTOOL POSSESS ENTHRONE INITIATE

INSTALLATION INDUCTION
(— OF MINISTER) INFARE
(FLOATING —) PLATFORM
(MILITARY —) GARRISON

INSTALLMENT KIST SERIAL EARNEST CONTRACT
(— OF SERIAL) HEFT
(— OF WAGES) COMPO
(— SELLER) TALLYMAN
(FIRST —) HANDSEL
(NEXT —) SEQUEL

INSTALMENT (— OF EPIC) RHAPSODY
(— OF SERIAL) HEFT

INSTANCE SEC CASE PINK SAMPLE EXAMPLE PURPOSE ENSAMPLE EXEMPLAR
(EXTREME —) CAPSHEAF
INSTANT POP SEC HINT WHIP WINK BLICK CLINK CRACK FLASH GLENT GLIFF GLISK JIFFY POINT SHAKE SOUND START TRICE WHIFF WIGHT BREATH FLIFFY MINUTE MOMENT SECOND PRESENT CLIFFING
(PRECISE —) TIME
INSTANTANEOUS PRESTO DIRECTLY
INSTANTANEOUSLY OUTRIGHT
INSTANTLY SLAP SWITH PRONTO SWITHE DIRECTLY MOMENTLY
INSTAR STAGE
INSTEAD EITHER
(PREF.) ANTI PRO
INSTEP WRIST TARSUS
(PREF.) PEDI(O)
INSTIGATE EGG ABET GOAD MOVE SPUR URGE IMPEL SETON ATTICE ENTICE EXCITE FOMENT INCITE INDUCE INVOKE PROMPT SPIRIT SUBORN ACTUATE INCENSE INSTINCT
INSTIGATION MOTION MOTIVE EGGMENT INSTANCE INSTINCT
INSTIGATOR AUTHOR MOTIVE SOURCE MONITOR
INSTILL GRAFT INFIX IMPART INFUSE INSTIL BREATHE IMPLANT
INSTINCT KIND FILLED NATURE CHARGED IMPULSE CAPACITY TENDENCY
INSTINCTIVE INNATE NATURAL INHERENT ORIGINAL
INSTITUTE BEGIN BRING ERECT FOUND RAISE START STUDY FOMENT INVENT KINDLE ORDAIN ACTIVATE
(— MEMBER) PIARIST
INSTITUTION BANK CAMP FOLD CLINIC FRIARY SCHOOL ACADEMY CHARITY COLLEGE GALLERY JUBILEE LIBRARY SHELTER STATION VERITAS SEMINARY ORPHANAGE OBSERVATORY PENITENTIARY
(— FOR HOMELESS CHILDREN) PROTECTORY
(— FOR INSANE) ASYLUM
(CHARITABLE —) SPITTLE DEACONRY HOSPITAL
(DRUIDICAL —) GORSEDD
INSTRUCT KEN REAR SHOW WISE BREED COACH DRILL EDIFY ENDUE GUIDE TEACH TRAIN CHARGE DIRECT GROUND INFORM INFORM LESSON PREACH REFORM SCHOOL COMMAND EDUCATE INSENSE POSSESS ADMONISH DOCUMENT
(— BEFOREHAND) PRIME

INSTRUCTED SCIENCED
INSTRUCTION LORE ADVICE ASSIZE CHARGE LESSON COUNSEL PRECEPT TUITION WISSING COACHING DOCTRINE DOCUMENT MONITION PEDAGOGY PROPHECY TEACHING TUTELAGE
(COMPUTER —) MACRO
(DIVINE —) LAW
(SACRED —) TORAH
(SERIES OF COMPUTER —S) LOOP
(PL.) BRIEF BRIEFING
INSTRUCTIVE DOCENT DIDACTIC
INSTRUCTOR DON SOAK SCREW TUTOR MENTOR REGENT ACHARYA CRAMMER MONITOR TEACHER BEACHBOY CHAIRMAN ELDERMAN
(RELIGIOUS —) SWAMI
INSTRUMENT (ALSO SEE MUSICAL INSTRUMENT) DEED TOOL WRIT AGENT SLANG THEME FACTUM OCTANT TEREBRA UTENSIL SYNGRAPH
(— FOR ACQUIRING KNOWLEDGE) ORGANON
(— NOT UNDER SEAL) PAROL
(— OF DESTRUCTION) SWORD
(— OF DIVINATION) EPHOD
(— OF TORTURE) BOOT RACK BRAKE BRANK FURCA GADGE WHEEL TUMBREL BARNACLE SQUEEZER SCARPINES PILLIWINKS
(—S OF WAR) ENGINERY
(CALCULATING —) ABACUS
(DETECTING —) SQUID
(FINANCIAL —) ITEM
(KEYBOARD —) MELLOTRON
(LEGAL —) DEED GRANT FACTUM SASINE SCRIPT CHARTER CODICIL DUPLICATE
(METEOROLOGICAL —) LIDAR
(NAUTICAL —) OCTANT
(NAVIGATIONAL —) LORAN TELERAN
(NEGOTIABLE —) HUNDI HOONDEE
(OFFICIAL —) SLANG
(PREHISTORIC —) CELT
(SCIENTIFIC —) HELIOSTAT
(SCIENTIFIC OR OTHER —) AWL FAN HOE KEY MET RAX SAX BROG CLAM COMB DIAL DRAG FILE FORK GAGE HOOK PALM PLOW RACK RING SPAR ARMIL BEVEL BLADE BRACE BRAKE CHAIN CLAMP CORER DATER DOLLY DRILL FLAIL FLOAT FLUKE GAUGE GLASS INDEX KNIFE LADLE LEVER METER MISER PILOT RAZOR SCALE SCOPE SLATE SLICE SLING SPADE SPEAR SPRAY STAMP STEEL SWIFT THROW TONGS TUNER WHISK ABACUS BEATER BEETLE BODKIN BRIDGE CHOWRY CIRCLE DOUCHE ENGINE ERASER FERULE FOLDER GRATER LEAPER MORTAR NEEDLE

PALLET PESTLE PICKER PLOUGH
PULLER PUMPER RAMMER RASPER
RATTLE RUBBER SCALER SCORER
SCRIBE SCUTCH SCYTHE SHEARS
SQUARE SQUIRT STADIA STRAIK
STROBE STYLET STYLUS TACKLE
TICKER WIMBLE ALIDADE BELLOWS
BREAKER CADRANS CLEAVER
COMPASS DIOPTER DOLABRA
DOUBLER FISTUCA GRAFTER
GRAINER GRAPPLE HATCHEL
LAYOVER MASSEUR MEASURE
OOMETER OOSCOPE PAVIOUR
PELORUS PIERCER PINCERS PRICKER
PRINTER PYROPEN QUADRAT
SCRAPER SEXTANT SHOCKER
SHUTTLE SLITTER SOUNDER
SPLAYER SPRAYER STRIGIL SUNDIAL
SWINGLE TRAMMEL TRIMMER
WHISTLE ANALEMMA ATOMIZER
BARNACLE BIRDCALL BLOWPIPE
BUTTERIS CALLIPER COALRAKE
DECAPPER DETECTOR DIAGRAPH
DIPMETER DIVIDERS EQUULEUS
ERGMETER EXPLORER FATHOMER
GEOPHONE HOROLOGE IMPINGER
IRISCOPE ISOGRAPH ISOSCOPE
JOVILABE MESOLABE MHOMETER
ODOMETER OHMMETER PHOTOMER
QUADRANT RECORDER RINGHEAD
RUMMAGER SCISSORS SEARCHER
SQUEEGEE STILETTO STRICKLE
TJANTING TRIANGLE VELLINCH
VIAGRAPH YAWMETER
(SURGICAL OR MEDICAL —) GAG
HOOK SPUD FLEAM PROBE SCALA
SCOOP SNARE SOUND STAFF STYLE
BILABE BOUGIE BROACH GORGET
LANCET SEEKER TREPAN TROCAR
UNGULA VECTIS XYSTER AGRAFFE
AIRDENT DILATER FORCEPS
HARPOON LEVATOR LIGATOR
MYOTOME PELICAN PLUGGER
RONGEUR SCALPEL SOUNDER
SYRINGE TRACTOR TRILABE
TURNKEY ANOSCOPE AURILAVE
AXOMETER BISTOURY DIRECTOR
DIVULSOR ECRASEUR ELEVATOR
EXSECTOR HEMOSTAT KERATOME
MYOGRAPH SPECULUM TREPHINE
(VOID —) NULLITY
(PREF.) (POINTED —) SCOLO
(WIND —) AEOLO
(SUFF.) LABE METER METR(E)(O)(Y)
STAT(IC)
(MUSICAL —) INA
(SURGICAL REMOVAL —) ECTOME
INSTRUMENTAL MEDIATE
ORGANIC SERVILE SERVIENT
MINISTERIAL
INSTRUMENTALIST KLEZMER
SIDEMAN

(SUPPLEMENTARY —) RIPIENO
RIPIENIST
INSTRUMENTALITY HAND MEANS
AGENCY MEDIUM CHANNEL
COUNCIL MINISTRY
**(— FOR ACQUISITION OF
KNOWLEDGE)** ORGANON
(NAVAL —S) BEACH
INSUBORDINATE FACTIOUS
MUTINOUS UNWIELDY
INSUBORDINATION MUTINY
INSUBSTANTIAL AIRY PUNY
INANE WISPY FROTHY POROUS
SLENDER SPECTRAL VAPOROUS
INTANGIGLE
INSUBSTANTIALITY FRAILTY
INSUFFICIENCY PAUCITY
(PREF.) OLIG(O)
INSUFFICIENT POOR WANE SHORT
SCANTY
INSUFFICIENTLY BARELY FEEBLY
THINLY
INSULATE ISLE DEADEN ISLAND
ISOLATE
INSULATION LAGGING ISOLATION
INSULATOR NOB KNOB CLEAT
TAPLET VITRITE MEGOHMIT
STANDOFF
(PL.) STRING
INSULT CAG FIG JOEY RUMP SLAM
SLAP SLUR ABUSE CHECK FLOUT
FRUMP SLANG INJURE INJURY
OFFEND OUTRAY RUFFLE SCRAPE
ABUSION AFFRONT OFFENCE
OUTRAGE BRICKBAT DISHONOR
CONTUMELY
INSULTING RUDE ABUSIVE
ARROGANT INSOLENT
INSULTINGLY FOULLY
INSURANCE LINE CHOMAGE
COVERAGE INDEMNITY
(— AGENT) TWISTER
(UNEMPLOYMENT —) DOLE POGEY
INSURE COVER ASSURE ENSURE
FURNISH
INSURER ABANDONEE
INSURGENT REBEL RISER CHOUAN
OAKBOY TAIPING BARRABAS
CAMISARD STEELBOY
INSURRECTION RIST MUTINY
REVOLT UPROAR OUTBREAK
SEDITION UPRISING REBELLION
INSURRECTO GUGU
INTACT SOUND WHOLE ENTIRE
MAIDEN
(PREF.) INTEGRI
INTAGLIO ENTAIL DIAGLYPH
(PART OF —) INCAVO
INTAKE
(AIRCRAFT ENGINE —) AIRSCOOP
INTANGIBLE VAGUE SUBTLE
AERIFORM SLIPPERY

INTEGER SUM NORM TOTITIVE

INTEGRAL FLUX NEEDFUL

INTEGRANT ELEMENT

INTEGRATE FUSE PIECE COMBINE
FULFILL ORGANIZE

INTEGRATED FUSED INTEGRAL

INTEGRATION BALANCE HARMONY

INTEGRITY HONOR TRUTH HONESTY
JUSTICE PROBITY CHASTITY
STRENGTH SINCERITY

INTEGUMENT KEX ARIL PILL SKIN
TESTA TUNIC SWATHE CUTICLE
ENVELOP EPIDERM EXODERM
PRIMINE TUNICLE VELAMEN
EPISPERM PERISARC SCABBARD
SECUNDINE
(PREF.) SCYT(O)
(SUFF.) DERM(A)(ATOUS)(IA)(IS)(Y)

INTELLECT MIND NOUS HEART
INWIT MAHAT SKILL BRAINS NOTICE
REASON SPIRITS THINKING
(HIGHEST —) NOUS

INTELLECTUAL BLUE GAON IDEAL
BOOKSY MENTAL NOETIC SOPHIC
BRAHMIN EGGHEAD GNOSTIC
CEREBRAL HIGHBROW LONGHAIR
SOPHICAL DIANOETIC SPIRITUAL
(PL.) EGGMASS

INTELLIGENCE AIR CIT SAT CHIT
KNOW MIND NEWS NOTE NOUS
WORD AGIEL SAVVY SENSE SMART
ADVICE BRAINS ESPRIT INGENY
NOTICE PSYCHE SMARTS WITTING
MENTALITY
(— IN EGYPTIAN LORE) CHU
(— OF PLANET JUPITER) JOPHIEL
(LACKING —) VACUOUS
(LIVELY —) WIT

INTELLIGENT APT GASH PERT
ACUTE ALERT SHARP SMART SPACK
AKAMAI BRAINY BRIGHT CLEVER
MENTAL SHREWD SPRACK WITFUL
KNOWING INFORMED LUMINOUS
RATIONAL SKILLFUL
(— GROUP) MENTA

INTELLIGENTSIA CLERISY

INTELLIGIBLE CLEAR PLAIN
LUMINOUS PELLUCID PERVIOUS
REVELANT PERCEIVABLE

INTELLIGIBLY SIMPLY

INTEMPERANCE ACRASY EXCESS
ACRASIA OUTRAGE

INTEMPERATE SHRILL SURFEIT
(NOT —) SWEET

INTEND GO AIM FIX CAST MEAN
MIND MINT PLAN PLOT TEND ALLOT
ALLOW ETTLE TIGHT ATTEND
DESIGN RECKON SETOUT BEHIGHT
DESTINE FORELAY PRETEND
PROPOSE PURPORT PURPOSE
FOREMIND MEDITATE PRETENSE

INTENDED ON FIANCEE SUPPOSED

INTENSE HOT ACID COLD DEEP HARD
HIGH KEEN BLANK DENSE GREAT
HEAVY QUICK SHARP TENSE VIVID
ARDENT BRAZEN FIERCE INTENT
PITCHY SEVERE STRONG BURNING
CHARGED CHRONIC CUTTING
EXTREME FERVENT FRANTIC
FURIOUS VICIOUS VIOLENT
EGYPTIAN GRIEVOUS POWERFUL
PROFOUND SEETHING TERRIFIC
VEHEMENT
(VIOLENTLY —) RABID

INTENSELY VERY STIFF HIGHLY
ACUTELY CURSEDLY FERVIDLY
MORTALLY SHREWDLY

INTENSIFICATION
(PREF.) DE

INTENSIFIED ACUTE

INTENSIFY RISE URGE EXALT RAISE
ACCENT DEEPEN HEATUP BOLSTER
ENFORCE ENHANCE IMPROVE
INFLAME MAGNIFY SHARPEN
THICKEN CONDENSE HEIGHTEN
INCREASE REDOUBLE

INTENSION INTENT MEANING

INTENSITY EDGE HEAT ARDOR
DEPTH DRIVE FEVER FIELD VIGOR
ACCENT DEGREE DOSAGE FERVOR
FRENZY STRESS CURRENT FEROCITY
STRENGTH VIOLENCE
(— OF DISEASE) ACUITY
(— OF EMOTION) ARDENCY

INTENSIVE HARD HIGH EXTENDED

INTENSIVELY HARD SOLIDLY

INTENT SET DEEP DOLE FELL HENT
MIND RAPT TENT READY GAUGE
DRIFT ETTLE FIXED HEART PRICK
SCOPE TENOR TENSE EFFECT SPIRIT
COUNSEL INTENSE PRESENT
PURPOSE STUDIED WISTFUL
(CRIMINAL —) DOLE
(EVIL —) DOLUS

INTENTION AIM END GOAL HENT
MIND VIEW WILL HEART SCOPE
ANIMUS ATTENT DESIGN DEVICE
EFFECT INTENT OBJECT REGARD
COUNSEL COURAGE EARNEST
FORESET MEANING PROPOSE
PURPORT PURPOSE SUPPOSE
THOUGHT PRETENSE OBJECTIVE
(CRIMINAL —) DOLE

INTENTIONAL SET WILLFUL
WILLING WITTING INTENDED

INTENTLY BUSILY WISHLY EAGERLY
FIXEDLY

INTER BURY EARTH ENTER GRAVE
PLANT ENTOMB INHUME INEARTH

INTERACTION COUPLING

INTERAGENT MEDIUM MIDDLER

INTERBREED CROSS

INTERBREEDING APOGAMY
MIXTURE PANMIXY CROSSING

INTERCALATE INSERT
INTERCALATION EMBOLISM
INTERCEPT KEP HEAD KEEP STOP
CATCH NORMAL ABSCISS TRAMMEL
GAINCOPE INTERPEL RETRENCH
INTERCEPTION CUTOFF
INTERCESSION MOYEN DIPTYCH
PLEADING
INTERCESSOR MEANS PLEADER
ADVOCATE MEDIATOR
INTERCHANGE CHANGE ANAGRAM
COMMUTE PASSAGE PERMUTE
COMMERCE EXCHANGE
(— OF OPINION) COUNSEL
(— OF WORDS) SPEECH
(PREF.) TRANS
INTERCHANGEABLE FUNGIBLE
INTERCHANGED CROSS
INTERCOLUMNIATION EUSTYLE
SYSTYLE DIASTYLE
INTERCOMMUNICATION
LIAISON
INTERCONNECTED SYNDETIC
INTERCONNECTION BONDING
INTERCOURSE GAM DEAL MANG
MONG TRADE TRUCK TURGY
BAWDRY HOBNOB NEGOCE COITION
DEALING MIXTURE QUARTER
SOCIETY TRAFFIC BUSINESS
COMMERCE CONVERSE RECOURSE
RELATIONS
INTERDICT BAN TABU DEBAR TABOO
FORBID UTRUBI INHIBIT PROHIBIT
SUPPRESS
INTERDICTION VETO
INTEREST BUG DIP FAD USE BENT
GOOD HAND HOLD PART CLOSE
COLOR DRIVE FAVOR FETCH GAVEL
HOBBY RENTE RIGHT STAKE STUDY
USAGE USURA USURY BEHALF
ENGAGE EQUITY ESTATE FAENUS
FERVOR FINGER INCOME USANCE
ATTRACT CONCERN RESPECT
USAUNCE CONTANGO INCREASE
VIGORISH
(— OF HUSBAND) CURTESY
(— ON LAND) CLOSE
(— PAID TO MONEYLENDER) VIG
VIGORISH
(ACTIVE —) SYMPATHY
(EXORBITANT —) JUICE
(LEGAL —) EASEMENT
(POLITICAL —) FENCE
(SECURITY —) LIEN
(SPECIAL —) MEAT ANGLE
INTERESTED HIPPED ENGAGED
SERIOUS CONCERNED
(— IN) INTO
(UNEASILY —) PRURIENT
INTERESTING FRUITY CURIOUS
PIQUANT STORIED ABSORBING
INTERFACE PORT
(COMPUTER —) PORT

INTERFERE CUT MAKE ANNOY
BLOCK CHECK HITCH POACH BAFFLE
HAMPER HINDER HOBBLE IMPEDE
MEDDLE STRIKE TAMPER INTRUDE
INTROMIT
(— SLIGHTLY) BRUSH
(— WITH) AIL JOLT MESS CROSS
HECKLE BLANKET DISTURB
INTERFERENCE BALK CHOKE
THUMP HINDER JOSTLE MEDDLE
CONFLICT FREINAGE
INTERFERING CUT
INTERFEROMETER ETALON
INTERFLUVE DOAB
INTERGROWTH PERTHITE
INTERIM BREAK VACANCY
INTERIOR BEN BELLY BOSOM INNER
ENTIRE INLAND INWARD INWITH
MIDDLE GIZZARD ENTRAILS
INTERNAL
(— OF CUPOLA) CALOTTE
(— OF TEMPLE) CELLA
(— OF VESSEL) HOLD
(— PART) MANTLE
INTERJECT POKE ENTER SQUIB
INJECT THRUST
INTERJECTION
(ALSO SEE OATH) AW ER HA LO BAH
BOO COO FIE GAD GEE GIP GUP HAH
HAY HEH HEY HOY HUH LAW OOH POW
WOW AHEM AHOY ALAS ANAN BOOH
CHUT CIAO DAMN DEAR EGAD EVOE
FORE GOSH HAHA HAIL HECH HECK
HEHE HEIL HELL HOLA JOVE ODSO
OOPS OUCH OYEZ PISH POOH POSH
RATS SHOO WELL WHEW ADIOS ALACK
ARRAH BASTA BEDAD BRAVO BULLY
FAITH FANCY FAUGH GOLLY GOODY
HALLO HEIGH HOLLA HUZZA MAFEY
MARRY MERCY MUSHA OHONE PROST
PSHAW RIGHT SUGAR TENEZ ZOWIE
ATWEEL BARLEY CRIKEY CRIPES
EUREKA HARROW JIMINY OUTCRY
PHOOEY PROSIT RIGHTO SHUCKS
YIPPEE BEGORRA CARAMBA CRIMINE
HEAVENS BEGORRAH GADZOOKS
LACKADAY
(— EXPRESSING APOLOGY) OOPS
WOOPS
(— INDICATING DISMAY) UHOH
(— OF AGREEMENT) UHHUH
(— OF NEGATION) UHUH
(— TO EXPRESS DISGUST) YUK YECH
YUCK YECCH
(— TO EXPRESS FEAR) YIKES
(— TO EXPRESS PLEASURE)
YUMYUM
(BIBLICAL —) SELAH
INTERLACE LACE WARP BRAID
WEAVE ENLACE PLEACH WATTLE
ENTRAIL INWEAVE WREATHE
INTERLACED BRACED FRETTED
PLEACHED

INTERLACEMENT KNOT
INTERLACING RETE TWINY
INTERLINING DOUBLER
INTERLOCK KNIT LOCK MESH PITCH
ENGAGE FINGER TANGLE DOVETAIL
INTERLOPE INTRUDE
INTERLUDE JIG JEST LETUP
COMEDY VERSET TEMACHA
TRIUMPH ANTIMASK ENTRACTE
ENTREMES RITORNEL VERSETTE
PARENTHESIS
(OPERATIC —) RITORNELLO
(QUIET —) LACUNA
(ROMANTIC —) IDYL IDYLL
INTERMEDDLER STRANGER
INTERMEDDLING GESTION
INTERMEDIARY MEAN AGENT
MOYENER MEDIATOR TRAMPLER
MIDDLEMAN
INTERMEDIATE MEAN MESNE
FILLER ISATIN MEDIAL MEDIUM
MIDDLE NEUTRAL MIDDLING
(PREF.) MEDI MES(O)
INTERMEDIATOR BROKER
INTERMENT BURIAL BURYING
DEPOSIT HUMATION
INTERMINABLE ETERNAL INFINITE
TIMELESS UNENDING
INTERMINGLE MIX BRAID
COALESCE IMMINGLE INTERMIT
INTERMIX
INTERMINGLED AMONG AMONGST
INTERMINGLING
(SUFF.) MIXIS
INTERMISSION REST WAIT BREAK
DWELL PAUSE DEVALL RECESS
NOONING DELACHE RESPITE
INTERVAL SURCEASE VACATION
(— OF FEVER) APYREXIA
(— OF PAIN) SABBATH
INTERMISSIVE CESSANT
INTERMIT CEASE DEFER DEVAUL
SUSPEND
INTERMITTENT BROKEN FITFUL
PERIODIC
INTERMIX BLEND MEDLEY MINGLE
INTERMIXTURE CROSS INTIMACY
INTERNAL INLY INNER ENTIRE
INLAND INNATE INSIDE INWARD
DOMESTIC
(PREF.) INTRA
INTERNALLY INLY INSIDE INWARD
INWARDLY
INTERNET (CONNECTED TO —)
ONLINE
INTERNODE ROSETTE
INTERPELLATION FLOWER
INTERPENETRATED SHOT
INTERPLAY AUSPICE
INTERPOLATE FARCE FARSE FOIST
FUDGE INSERT THRUST
INTERPOLATION GAG FARSE
(ACTOR'S —) GAG

INTERPOLATOR DIASKEUAST
INTERPOSE BAR CHOP POKE DEMUR
OBJECT STRIKE THRUST THWART
MEDIATE STICKLE
INTERPRET MAKE OPEN READ SCAN
TAKE AREAD AREED FANCY GLOSS
GLOZE RECHE DEFINE DIVINE INTEND
CLARIFY COMMENT DECLARE
ENGLISH EXPLAIN EXPOUND
CONSTRUE DECIPHER SIMPLIFY
INTERPRETATION REDE GLOSS
SENSE GOSPEL STRAIN ANAGOGE
BARAITA COMMENT DOBHASH
EPIKEIA MEANING READING
CABALISM EXEGESIS INNUENDO
MOONSHEE SOLARISM SOLUTION
INTERPRETER BROKER DUBASH
MUNSHI UNDOER EXEGETE
LATINER MUNCHEE CADALIST
DRAGOMAN EXPONENT LINKSTER
TRUCHMAN
(— OF DREAMS) ONEIROCRITIC
(— OF SCRIPTURE) TROPIST
(PL.) HAHAM SELLI SELLOI CHOCHEM
HAKAMIM
INTERRELATED INTIMATE
INTERRELATIONSHIP ACCORD
LIAISON COMMERCE
INTERROGATE ASK GRILL TARGE
DEBRIEF EXAMINE INQUIRE
INTERROGATION EROTESIS
QUESTION
INTERROGATORY EROTETIC
INTERRUPT CUT MAR NIP CHOP
STOP TAKE BREAK CHECK CHACK
EMBAR ARREST DERAIL DERANGE
DISRUPT FORBREAK INTERMIT
INTERPEL OBSTRUCT
INTERRUPTED BROKEN CHOPPY
SNATCHY
INTERRUPTER BUZZER
INTERRUPTION BLIP CESS JUMP
STOP BLOCK BREAK CHECK DWELL
LAPSE PAUSE BREACH HIATUS
HOCKET HOQUET ISLAND OUTAGE
CAESURA CUTBACK DIASTEM
BLOCKING BREAKAGE SOLUTION
STOPOVER
(— OF SOUND) BLIP BLEEP
(WITHOUT —) FLUSH
INTERRUPTOR TIKKER BREAKER
CHOPPER RHEOTOME
INTERSECT CUT CROSS BISECT
INCISE CROSSCUT
INTERSECTING SECANT CRUCIAL
COMPITAL
INTERSECTION LEET CHINE CROSS
CURVE CHIASMA CROSSING
CROSSWAY JUNCTION
INTERSESSION WINTERIM
INTERSEXUAL EPICENE
INTERSEXUALITY GYNANDRY
INTERSPACE SPACE POCKET

INTERSPERSE DOT SALT SHED
MEDDLE THREAD CHECKER
INTERSOW SPRINKLE
INTERSTICE GAP PORE SEAM CHINK
GRATE SPACE AREOLA AREOLE
RIFFLE CELLULE VACUITY
(PL.) CANCELLI
INTERSTRATIFY INTERBED
INTERTWINE KNIT LACE WARP
PLAIT TWINE FELTER TANGLE
WAMPLE WARPLE WRITHE ENSNARL
COMPLECT IMPLEACH INTERTEX
INTERTWINED INWOUND
INTERTWIST RADDLE
INTERVAL GAP LAG CENT GULF
REST SAND SEXT SPOT STEP BLANK
BREAK COMMA CYCLE FIFTH LAPSE
PRIME QUINT SIXTH SPACE SWING
TENTH THIRD BREACH DECIMA
DEGREE DIESIS DITONE FOURTH
MERLON SECOND SLATCH SYSTEM
ADVANCE DIASTEM DISCORD
HEADWAY HEMIOLA INTERIM
PASTIME RESPITE SCHISMA SETTIMO
STADIUM TRITONE DIAPASON
DIAPENTE DISTANCE ELEVENTH
ENTRACTE FONTANEL INTERACT
MICROTONE PARENTHESIS
(— BETWEEN FINGERS) SUBVOLA
(— BETWEEN ROPE STRANDS)
CONTLINE
(— OF BRIGHTNESS) FLICKER
(— OF CALM) LULL
(— OF EASE) REPRIEVE
(— OF FAIR WEATHER) SLATCH
(— OF HARSH WEATHER) SNAP
(— OF ROPE STRANDS) CONTLINE
(— OF SEMITONE) APOTOME
(— OF TIME) WINDOW
(AT REGULAR —S) SPACED
(MUSICAL —) TONE FIFTH NINTH
SIXTH TENTH THIRD FOURTH OCTAVE
SECOND UNISON SEVENTH TRITONE
MEANTONE
(REST —) SOB
(SHORT —) STREAK
(TIME —) HEADWAY
INTERVALE BOTTOM
INTERVENE CHOP STEP STRIKE
MEDIATE OBVIATE STICKLE INTERCUR
INTERVENING MESNE MIDDLE
MEDIAN
(PREF.) INTER
INTERVIEW BUZZ CONTACT
AUDIENCE CONGRESS
INTERWEAVE MAT PLAT CRISP
PLAIT PLASH PLEACH RADDLE
TANGLE WATTLE ENTWINE TEXTURE
TRELLIS COMPLECT ENTANGLE
IMPLEACH INTERTEX
INTERWEAVING BREDE CROWN
INTIMATE
(— OF INITIALS) CIPHER

INTERWOVEN INWOVEN IMPLICIT
INTIMATE
(— WITH COLORS) PIRNIT
INTESTINAL INNER ENTERAL
ENTERIC SPLANCHNIC
INTESTINE GUT ROPE BOWEL INNER
THARM INWARD MIDDLE THAIRM
(PORTION OF —) JEJUNUM
(PL.) VISCUS INGANGS CHITLINS
(PREF.) COL(O) ENTER(O)
INTHROW RIDGE
INTIMACY LIAISON PRIVACY
AFFINITY CHUMMERY GOSSIPRY
INTRIGUE MUTUALITY
(UNDUE —) LIBERTY
INTIMATE PAL SIB BOON GRIT HINT
HOME HOMY KIND NEAR NEXT PACK
TOSH BOSOM CHIEF CLOSE GREAT
HOMEY PALLY PRIVY THICK ALLUDE
ENTIRE FRIEND HOMELY INTIME
INWARD NOTICE SECRET STRAIT
STRICT THRANG THRONG CHAMBER
CLOSEUP GREMIAL INNERLY
INNUATE KEYHOLE PRIVADO PRIVATE
SIGNIFY SPECIAL SUGGEST
UPCLOSE COCKMATE ESPECIAL
FAMILIAR FREQUENT FRIENDLY
INDICATE INTIMADO
(INGRATIATINGLY —) PALSY
(MOST —) MIDMOST
(PL.) FOLKS
INTIMATELY INLY NEAR TOSH WELL
COZILY CLOSELY INWARDLY
INTIMATION CUE HINT ITEM WARN
WIND SCENT NOTICE OFFICE
GLIMMER INKLING CIRCULAR
INNUENDO MONITION
INTIMIDATE COW HAZE ABASH
BULLY COWER DAUNT DETER PSYCH
HECTOR PSYCHE TERRIFY
BROWBEAT BULLDOZE BULLYRAG
FRIGHTEN
INTO IN INTIL WITHIN
(PREF.) IL IM IN INTRO IR
INTOLERABLY PLAGUY
INTOLERANCE BIGOTRY
INTOLERANT CLOSED BIGOTED
INTONATION FALL CHANT ITALICS
(LOCAL —) TWANG
(MONOTONOUS —) SINGSONG
INTONE CANT SING TONE CHANT
CHAUNT ENTUNE MODULATE
CANTILLATE
INTOXICANT BOZA HASH BHANG
CHARAS MESCAL PEYOTE COCAINE
HASHISH HASHEESH MARIJUANA
INTOXICATE FOX TIP TOX CORN
FLAW GOOF SOAK TODDY FUDDLE
MUDDLE SOZZLE SPRING TIPSIFY
DISGUISE OVERTAKE SPRINKLE
INTOXICATED CUT FAP LIT WET
HIGH LUSH RIPE SHOT SOSH TOFT
TOSY BOSKY BUFFY DRUNK FRESH

FRIED FUNNY HEADY LACED NAPPY
PIPED TIGHT BLOTTO BOILED
GROGGY LOADED LOOPED MELLOW
PIPPED QUAINT SCREWY SKEWED
SLEWED SLOPPY SODDEN SOSHED
SOZZLE STEWED TANKED UPPISH
UPPITY WASTED ZONKED EBRIATE
EXALTED FLECKED JINGLED
POTSHOT SCREWED SLOPPED
SMASHED SPIFFED SQUIFFY
UNSOBER WRECKED BESOTTED
COCKEYED DELCERIT ELEVATED
OVERSEEN OVERSHOT PLEASANT
SQUIFFED TEMULENT TOXICATE
WIPEDOUT

INTOXICATING HARD HEADY STARK
HUFFCAP

INTOXICATION WINE FUDDLE
IVRESSE LOCOISM DISGUISE
EBRIOSITY TEMULENCE
(— OF ANIMALS) DUNZIEKTE

INTRACTABLE BAD HARD SALTY
STACK SURLY FIERCE KITTLE SULLEN
THWART UNRULY CRABBED
HAGGARD RESTIVE ROPABLE
WAYWARD CHURLISH INDOCILE
MUTINOUS OBDURATE PERVERSE
SHREWISH

INTRADA ENTREE

INTRADOS SOFFIT

INTRANSITIVE NEUTER

INTREPID BOLD BRAVE HARDY
HEROIC PRETTY SAVAGE DOUGHTY
VALIANT RESOLUTE

INTREPIDITY GAME VALOR
COURAGE

INTRICACY KNOT INTRIGUE

INTRICATE HARD MAZY BLIND
DAEDAL IMPLEX KNUBBY KNOTTY
SUBTLE TANGLY TRICKY COMPLEX
CRABBED CURIOUS GORDIAN
PERPLEX PUZZLED SINUOUS
INVOLUTE INVOLVED
ANFRACTUOUS
(ARTIFICIALLY —) CONTRIVED

INTRIGUE PLOT ANGLE CABAL
CLOAK STORY AFFAIR AMOUNT
BRIGUE DECEIT SCHEME CONNIVE
FACTION FINAGLE JOBBERY TRINKET
TRINKLE ARTIFICE CHEATING
COLLOGUE PRACTICE PRACTISE
STRATEGY TRIPOTER

INTRIGUER JESUIT SCHEMER
DESIGNER TRINKETER

INTRIGUING EXCITING SCHEMING

INTRINSIC REAL TRUE INBORN
INBRED INNATE INWARD NATIVE
GENUINE NATURAL ABSOLUTE
IMMANENT INHERENT INTERNAL
INTIMATE

INTRINSICALLY PERSE PROPERLY

INTRODUCE READ DEBUT ENTER
FRONT IMMIT INFER PLANT START

USHER BROACH HERALD INDUCE
INDUCT INFUSE INJECT INSERT
INVECT INVOKE LAUNCH PREFER
FORERUN IMPLANT INSTILL INVEIGH
PRECLDE PREFACE PRELUDE
PRESENT SHUFFLE SPONSOR
TROTOUT ACQUAINT INNOVATE
INTROMIT WIREDRAW
(— AIR INTO) AERATE
(— AS FIRST ACT) INITIATE
(— FROM WITHOUT) IMPORT
(— SURREPTITIOUSLY) FOIST

INTRODUCTION LASSU PROEM
PRONE INTRADA INTROIT ISAGOGE
MENTION PREFACE ENTRANCE
EXORDIUM PREAMBLE PROLOGUE
PRELUSION
(— INTO STOMACH) GAVAGE
(— OF DRAMA) PROTASIS
(— OF NEW PRODUCT) ROLLOUT
(— OF NOVELTY) CHANGE
(MUSICAL —) INTRO INTRADA
OVERTURE
(SUFF.) PHORESIS

INTRODUCTORY EXORDIAL
ISAGOGIC LIMINARY PROTATIC
SYSTATIC PRELUSIVE PRELIMINARY

INTROIT REQUIEM

INTRORSE ANTICAL

INTROSPECTION INLOOK
REFLEX

INTRUDE JET ADATE BARGE CRASH
POACH BOTHER CHISEL INGYRE
INJECT INVADE IRRUPT THRUST
AGGRESS OBTRUDE ENCROACH
INFRINGE TRESPASS

INTRUDER INTRUS INCOMER
INVADER STRANGER

INTRUSION INVASION

INTRUSIVE NOSY FRESH NOSEY
SPURIOUS
(PREF.) XEN(O)

INTUITION HUNCH PRESAGE
INSTINCT

INTUITIONIST EIDETIC

INULIN ALANTIN

INUNDATE FLOW DROWN FLOOD
INUND SWAMP DELUGE OVERFLOW
SUBMERGE SURROUND

INUNDATED AWASH

INUNDATION FLOW FLOOD SPATE
WATER DELUGE ALLUVIO FRESHET
ALLUVION FLOODAGE OVERFLOW

INURE URE BREAK ENURE STEEL
HARDEN SCHOOL SEASON
ACCUSTOM INDURATE ACCLIMATIZE

INVADE ASSAIL INTRUDE ENCROACH
INTRENCH TRESPASS

INVADER HUN PICT

INVADING INGRUENT

INVAGINATION GULLET

INVALID BAD BUM NULL CHRONIC
NUGATORY

INVALIDATE UNDO AVOID BREAK CANCEL INFIRM IMPROVE INVALID VITIATE
INVALUABLE COSTLY PRECIOUS PRICELESS
INVARIABLE STEADY UNIFORM CONSTANT
INVARIABLENESS ONENESS
INVARIABLY EVER ALWAYS
INVASION RAID INROAD DESCENT INBREAK INJURIA
(— BY BACTERIA) SEPSIS
INVECTIVE ABUSE HOKER SATIRE RAILING DIATRIBE REPROACH
INVEIGH RANT INVECT DECLAIM DENOUNCE
INVEIGLE COAX ROPE WILE CHARM DECOY SNARE ALLURE ENTICE SEDUCE
INVENT COIN FIND FORM MINT VAMP FEIGN FRAME FRUMP CREATE DESIGN DEVISE IDEATE CONCOCT CONJURE CONTRIVE DISCOVER
INVENTED MADE
INVENTION FANCY DEVICE FINDAL NOTION FANTASY FICTION FIGMENT FORGERY WITCRAFT
(DRAMATIC —) IBSENISM
INVENTIVE ADROIT FERTILE CREATIVE MECHANIC ORIGINAL PREGNANT
INVENTIVENESS WIT ARTIFICE
INVENTOR TALOS COINER FINDER FRAMER MINTER CREATOR MINTMAN ENGINEER ARTIFICER
AMERICAN HOE LEE BELL COLT EADS FELT GRAY HALL HOWE HUNT IVES LAND LINK LOWE MOOG OLDS OTIS PAGE READ VAIL WOOD ADAMS ALLEN BLAKE BOWIE BROWN COWEN DAVIS DOLBY EARLE ELLIS EVANS FIELD FITCH GIBBS HYATT LEWYT LIBBY LOCKE MCKAY MOODY MOREY MORSE NOYES PERKY PRATT PUPIN RUBIC TESLA WHITE BENDIX BISELL BITTER BORDEN BORTON BOYDEN BOYKIN CAHILL CHURCH CLYMER CURTIS DURYEA EDISON FARBER FOLMER FRENCH FULTON GARAND GAYLEY GORDON GORRIE HAMLIN HAYNES HORGAN HOUDRY HUGHES HUSSEY JANNEY JATVIK JUDSON KALMUS LOOMIS PITNEY PORTER SAXTON SHOLES SINGER SPANEL SPERRY TIMKEN TUPPER WARING WESSON WILCOX WILSON WRIGHT ACHESON APPLEBY BABBITT BETHELL BIGELOW BRADLEY CARRIER CORLISS CURTISS EASTMAN GATLING GODFREY HAMMOND HOLLAND JACUZZI JENKINS KNOWLES LANSTON PERKINS PULLMAN SCHICCK

SELLERS STEVENS TAINTER THURBER WHITNEY ZAMBONI BACHRACH BERLINER BIRDSEYE BOGARDUS BUSHNELL DAHLGREN DEFOREST ELLSBERG ERICSSON EVINRUDE GILLETTE GOODYEAR HALSTEAD WATERMAN ABPLANALP BURROUGHS BUTTERICK DRAWBAUGH HONEYWELL HOTCHKISS INGERSOLL MCCORMICK HERRESHOFF WESTINGHOUSE
AUSTRIAN PORSCHE KEMPELEN WELSBACH
BELGIAN SAX BAEKELAND
CANADIAN ABBOTT FESSENDEN
CHINESE TSAI
DUTCH BORDEN COSTER DREBBEL
ENGLISH KAY MOON WATT DUNNE MAXIM MILLS SMITH AYRTON BRAMAH BRUNEL DONKIN GURNEY HOLDEN LISTER PITMAN WALLIS BABBAGE BESEMER BUDDING BURGESS DELARUE GAUDENS MORLAND MURDOCK SIEMANS STARLEY CROMPTON OUGHTRED STURGEON ACKERMANN APPLEGATH ARKWRIGHT ARMSTRONG HEATHCOAT WHITWORTH CARTWRIGHT HARGREAVES STEPHENSON TREVITHICK WHEATSTONE
FRENCH LYOT COANDA FOUCHE GIRARD LENOIR MONIER PROGIN LAENNEC LUMIERE CHRETIEN DAGUERRE DELSARTE JACQUARD CHASSEPOT CHARDONNET MONTGOLFIER
GERMAN FOCKE BUNSEN DIESEL DREYSE MAUSER WANKEL DAIMLER SIEMENS FLETTNER BAUERSFELD
GREEK CTESIBIUS ARCHIMEDES
IRISH BRENNAN
ITALIAN MARCONI
NORWEGIAN KRAG
SCOTTISH GED BARR WATT BAIRD DUNLOP MILLER GREGORY NEILSON TWADDELL MACINTOSH SYMINGTON
SWEDISH DALEN NOBEL POLHEM
SWISS ZWICKY PICCARD SCHWEPPE VETTERLI
INVENTORY BILL LIST STOCK ACCOUNT INVOICE TERRIER ANAGRAPH DATABASE REGISTER SCHEDULE
INVERSE
(PREF.) OB
INVERSION WALDEN CHIASMUS ENTROPION
(— OF STITCHES) PURL
INVERT CANT TURN REVERT REVERSE
INVERTASE SUCRASE

INVERTEBRATE INSECT MOLLUSC
MOLLUSK
INVERTED AWKWARD
INVEST DON DUB PUT BELT FUND
GARB GIFT GIRD GIRT GOWN LOCK
SINK VEST WRAP BELAY BLOCK
ENDOW ENDUE FEOFF INDUE
CLOTHE EMBODY ENROBE FORSET
OCCUPY ORDAIN BESIEGE COMPASS
ENFEOFF ENVELOP INSTATE
OBSERVE BENEFICE BLOCKADE
SURROUND
(— IN ARMOR) EMPANOPLY
(— ONESELF) COVER ASSUME
(— WITH) INFEFT
(— WITH AUTHORITY) SCEPTER
ACCREDIT
(— WITH ENERGY) CATHECT
(— WITH HONOR) DIGNIFY
(— WITH SOVEREIGN DIGNITY)
ENTHRONE
(SUFF.) (— WITH ATTRIBUTES OF) FY
IFY
INVESTED GARTERED
(— WITH AUTHORITY) REGENT
INVESTIGATE SPY SUS SIFT SUSS
CHECK PROBE SOUND STUDY
EXCUSS FATHOM SEARCH DISCUSS
EXAMINE EXPLORE INQUIRE
INDAGATE SCRUTATE
(— QUICKLY) SKIP
INVESTIGATION CHECK PROBE
TRIAL EXAMEN PILPUL SEARCH
DELVING INQUEST INQUIRY
LEGWORK ZETETIC ANALYSIS
QUESTION RESEARCH SCRUTINY
SOUNDING
INVESTIGATOR SNOOP TRIER
SLEUTH GUMSHOE SPOTTER
FIELDMAN
(NARCOTICS —) NARC NARK
(PRIVATE —) SHAMUS
INVESTING AMBIENT
INVESTITURE VESTURE INDUMENT
INVESTMENT DOG FLIER CUTICLE
CATHEXIS PANNICLE
(— OF TOWN) SIEGE
(RISKY —) SPECULATION
INVETERATE BLACK SWORN
ROOTED CHRONIC HARDENED
INVIDIOUS ENVIOUS HATEFUL
INVIGORATE PEP BRACE CHEER
RAISE RENEW VIGOR VIVIFY
COMFORT ENFORCE ENLIVEN
FORTIFY INNERVE INSINEW REFRESH
INSPIRIT
INVIGORATING BRISK CRISP FRESH
TONIC VITAL HEARTY LIVELY
BRACING CORDIAL VEGETANT
INVIOLABILITY SANCTITY
INVIOLABLE SACRED SECURE
STYGIAN
INVIOLATE SACRED

INVISIBLE HID BLIND SECRET
UNSEEN VIEWLESS SIGHTLESS
(PREF.) APHAN(O) CRYPT(O) KRYPT(O)
INVITATION BID CALL CARD INVITE
BIDDING CALLING
(— TO CONTEND) DARE
(— TO RIDE) GETIN GETON HOPIN
HOPON CLIMBON
INVITE ASK BID WOO BEAR CALL
LURE PRAY TOLL CLEPE COURT
LATHE TEMPT TRYST ALLURE DESIRE
ENTICE INDITE ATTRACT CONVITE
PROVOKE REQUEST SOLICIT
INVITING ADORABLE HOMELIKE
INVOCATION WISH DAWUT NANDI
BISMILLAH
INVOICE BILL BRIEF CHALAN
FACTURE MANIFEST BORDEREAU
INVOKE WISH CLEPE EVOKE APPEAL
ATTEST ODTEST CONJURE ENTREAT
PROVOKE SOLICIT INVOCATE
(— EVIL) BESHREW IMPRECATE
INVOLUCRE HULL HUSK CUPULE
CALYCLE CALYCULE EPICALYX
INVOLUNTARY FORCED REFLEX
HELPLESS
INVOLUTE INVOLVED
INVOLUTED SCREWY
INVOLUTION ATRESIA
INVOLVE DIP LAP MOS MIRE WRAP
BROIL CARRY COUCH IMPLY RAVEL
DIRECT EMPLOY ENGAGE ENTAIL
HANKLE INWRAP TANGLE COMPORT
CONCERN CONNOTE EMBRACE
EMBROIL ENSNARE ENTWINE
ENVIRON IMMERSE INCLUDE
ENCUMBER ENTANGLE INTEREST
(— IN DIFFICULTY) STEAD
INVOLVED IN DEEP GONE INTO
BLIND KNOTTY COMPLEX ENGAGED
PLAITED IMPLICIT INVOLUTE
CONCERNED ANFRACTUOUS
INWARD ENTAD INNER INWITH
BENWARD INNERLY HOMEFELT
INTRINSIC
(PREF.) IL IM IN INTRO IR OB
INWICK INRING
IO (BROTHER OF —) PHORONEUS
(FATHER OF —) INACHUS
(SON OF —) EPAPHUS
IODINE (SOURCE OF —) KELP
(PREF.)
(REMOVAL OF —) DESIODO
IOLAUS (COMPANION OF —)
HERCULES
(FATHER OF —) IPHICLES
(MOTHER OF —) AUTOMEDUSA
(WIFE OF —) MEGARA
IOLE (FATHER OF —) EURYTUS
(HUSBAND OF —) HYLLUS
IOLITE IBERITE PELIOMA
ION ACID ADION ANION CATION
ISOMER KATION LIGAND AMPHION

HYDRION OXONIUM SPECIES
ZWITTERION
(— DURATION) LIFETIME
(FATHER OF —) XUTHUS
(MOTHER OF —) CREUSA
(SON OF —) GELEON ARGADES
HOPLETES AEGICORES
(PREF.) IONTO
(SUFF.) (CHARGED —) ONIUM
IONIA (GULF OF —) ARTA
IONIAN (— ISLAND) CORFU
IONIZATION BURST
IOPHON (FATHER OF —) SOCRATES
(MOTHER OF —) NICOSTRATE
IOTA JOT TAD WHIT GHOST TITTLE
SCRUPLE SCINTILLA
IOU SCRIP MARKER

IOWA

CAPITAL: DESMOINES
COLLEGE: COE DORDT LORAS
CORNELL PARSONS GRINNELL
WARTBURG
COUNTY: IDA LEE SAC CASS LINN
PAGE POLK TAMA ADAIR BOONE
CEDAR EMMET FLOYD LUCAS SIOUX
BREMER KEOKUK OBRIEN DUBUQUE
KOSSUTH MAHASKA OSCEOLA
LAKE: CLEAR STORM SPIRIT
NICKNAME: HAWKEYE
PRESIDENT: HOOVER
RIVER: CEDAR SKUNK BIGSIOUX
MISSOURI
STATE BIRD: GOLDFINCH
STATE FLOWER: WILDROSE
STATE TREE: OAK
TOWN: ADEL AMES LEON ALBIA
MASON ONAWA OSAGE PERRY
SIOUX ALGONA ELDORA KEOKUK
LEMARS MARION SIBLEY VINTON
ANAMOSA OTTUMWA WATERLOO
DAVENPORT

IOWAN HAWKEYE
IPECAC ITOUBOU
IPHIANASSA (FATHER OF —)
PROETIUS
(HUSBAND OF —) BIAS
(MOTHER OF —) ANTIA
IPHICLUS (BROTHER OF —) HERCULES
(FATHER OF —) PHYLACUS
AMPHITRYON
(MOTHER OF —) ALCMENA
(SON OF —) PODARCES PROTESILAUS
(WIFE OF —) CLYMENE
IPHIDAMAS (FATHER OF —)
ANTENOR
(MOTHER OF —) THEANO
(SLAYER OF —) AGAMEMNON
IPHIGENIA (BROTHER OF —) ORESTES
(FATHER OF —) AGAMEMNON
(MOTHER OF —) CLYTEMNESTRA
(SISTER OF —) ELECTRA

IPHIMEDIA (HUSBAND OF —) ALOEUS
(SON OF —) OTUS EPHIALTES
IPHINOE (FATHER OF —) PROETUS
(MOTHER OF —) ANTIA
(SISTER OF —) LYSIPPE IPHIANASSA
IPHIS (FATHER OF —) LIGDUS
(MOTHER OF —) TELETHUSA
(WIFE OF —) IANTHE
IPHITUS (BROTHER OF —) CLYTIUS
(FATHER OF —) EURYTUS
(SISTER OF —) IOLE
(SLAYER OF —) HERCULES
IPIL VESI
IPOMOEA NIL NILL BATATAS
MANROOT TURBITH TURPETH
SCAMMONY
IPSEITY SELFHOOD
IRA (FATHER OF —) IKKESH
IRACUND IREFUL
IRAD (FATHER OF —) ENOCH
(GRANDFATHER OF —) CAIN
(SON OF —) MEHUJAEL

IRAN

CAPE: HALILEH
CAPITAL: TEHRAN TEHERAN
COIN: PUL ASAR CRAN LARI RIAL BISTI
DARIC DINAR LARIN SHAHI TOMAN
STATER ASHRAFI KASBEKE PAHLAVI
DESERT: KERMAN
FORMER NAME: PERSIA
GOVERNORSHIP: ILAM YAZD SEMNAN
ZANJAN HAMADAN LORESTAN
LAKE: NIRIS NIRIZ TASHT TUZLU
URMIA SAHWEH SISTAN MAHARLU
NEMEKSER URUMIYEH
LANGUAGE: ZEND PAHLAVI
MEASURE: GAZ GUZ MOV ZAR ZER
CANE FOOT GAREH JERIB KAFIZ
MAKUK QASAB ARTABA CHARAC
CHEBEL GARIBA GHALVA OUROUB
CAPICHA CHENICA FARSAKH
FARSANG MANSION MISHARA
PAIMANEH PARASANG SABBITHA
STATHMOS
MOUNTAIN: CUSH KUSH HINDU
KHOSF ARARAT HAMUNT BINALUD
KHORMUJ SABALAN DEMAVEND
MOUNTAIN RANGE: ELBURZ SIAHAN
ZAGROS JAGATAL
PEOPLE: LUR KURD MEDE SART KAJAR
MUKRI PERSE TAJIK HADJEMI
PERSIAN
PORT: JASK BUSHIRE PAHLEVI
PROVINCE: FARS GILAN KERMAN
TEHRAN ESFAHAN KHORASAN
KORDESTAN
RIVER: MAND MUND SHUR ARAKS
JAGIN KARUN RABCH SEFID
BAMPUR GORGAN HALIRI TIGRIS
KARKHEH MASHKEL SAFIDRUD
ZAYENDEH EUPHRATES
STRAIT: HORMUZ

TOWN: FAO KOM QUM AMOL ARAK SARI YAZD AHWAZ KHVOY NIRIZ RASHT RESHT ABADAN DEZFUL GORGAN KASVIN KERMAN MASHAD MESHED SHIRAZ TABRIZ TAURIS HAMADAN ISFAHAN SANANDAJ
WEIGHT: SER DRAM DUNG ROTL SANG SEER ABBAS ARTEL MAUND PINAR RATEL BATMAN DIRHEM GANDUM KARWAR MISCAL NAKHOD NIMMAN ABBASSI TCHEIREK

IRANIAN TAT SART GALCHA SHUGNI BACTRIAN BARTANGI
(— SOVEREIGN) SHAH

IRAQ

CAPITAL: BAGDAD BAGHDAD
COIN: DINAR DIRHAM
DISTRICT: BASRA KURDISTAN
FORMER NAME: MESOPOTAMIA
MOUNTAINS: ZARGOS KURDISTAN
OASIS: MANIYA
PEOPLE: ARAB KURD
PORT: FAO BASRA
RIVER: ZAB TIGRIS EUPHRATES
TOWN: ANA HIT AFAQ AMARA BAIJI BASRA ERBIL HILLA MOSUL NAJAF HILLAH KIRKUK TIKRIT KARBALA

IRASCIBILITY BILE CHOLER
IRASCIBLE WARM ANGRY CROSS FIERY GASSY HASTY IRATE SHARP TECHY TESTY CRANKY CRUSTY IREFUL ORNERY SPUNKY TETCHY TOUCHY ANGULAR BILIOUS FRETFUL IRACUND PEEVISH TINDERY TOUSTIE WASPISH CAPTIOUS CHOLERIC PETULANT SNAPPISH STOMACHY
IRATE MAD SORE ANGRY HEATED CHOLERIC WRATHFUL
IRE FURY ANGER STEAM WRATH
IREFUL ANGRY HETUP JEALOUS

IRELAND

BAY: MAL CLEW SLIGO BANTRY DINGLE GALWAY TRALEE DONEGAL DUNDALK KILLALA BLACKSOD DROGHEDA
CAPE: CLEAR
CAPITAL: TARA DUBLIN BELFAST
COIN: RAP REAL
COUNTY: CORK DOWN LEIX MAYO CAVAN CLARE KERRY LOUTH MEATH SLIGO ANTRIM ARMAGH CARLOW GALWAY OFFALY TYRONE ULSTER DONEGAL KILDARE LEITRIM WEXFORD WICKLOW KILKENNY LIMERICK MONAGHAN FERMANAGH LONDONDERRY
ISLAND: ARAN TORY SALTEE RATHLIN
LAKE: DOO KEY REE TAY CONN DERG ERNE MASK CARRA GOWNA LEANE RAMOR BODERG COOTER ENNELL DROMORE OUGHTER SHEELIN
MEASURE: MILE BANDLE
MONEY: PUNT
MOUNTAIN: OX CAHA ANTRIM GALTEE KEEPER MOURNE MULREA DONEGAL ERRIGAL KENNEDY KIPPURE WICKLOW LEINSTER
MOUNTAIN RANGE: GALTY STACKS COMERAGH
OTHER NAME: EIRE ERIN BANBA IERNE IRENA ULSTER BOGLAND HIBERNIA INISFAIL
PEOPLE: CELT ERSE GAEL CELTIC HIBERNIAN
PERTAINING TO: CELTIC GAELIC
POINT: CAHORE CARNSORE
PORT: CORK
PROVINCE: ULSTER MUNSTER CONNACHT LEINSTER CONNAUGHT
RIVER: LEE BANN DEEL ERNE NORE SUIR BOYNE CLARE FEALE FLESK FOYLE LAUNE BANDON BARROW LIFFEY KENMARE MUNSTER SHANNON
TOWN: CORK NAAS TRIM ADARE CAVAN ENNIS OMAGH SLIGO ARMAGH CARLOW DUBLIN GALWAY LURGAN TRALEE LIMERICK TIPPERARY

IRENE (FATHER OF —) JUPITER
(MOTHER OF —) THEMIS
IRENIC CALM HENOTIC PEACEFUL
IRENICA AITESIS
IRI (FATHER OF —) BELA
IRIDESCENCE LUSTER LUSTRE REFLET
(— ON METAL) TARNISH
IRIDESCENT SHOT IRISED IRIDINE IRISATE OPALINE PAVONINE
IRIS EYE SET FLAG LILY LUCE LUCY SEGG AZURE IREOS ORRIS SEDGE FLAGON LEVERS LILIAL LILIUM SHADOW SUNBOW ALCAZAR BABIANA FLAGGER GLADDON FLAGLEAF
(FATHER OF —) THAUMAS
(MOTHER OF —) ELECTRA
(PREF.) IRIDICO IRIDIO IRID(O)
IRISH ERSE EIRANN IRISHRY MILESIAN HIBERNIAN
(— KING) RIG
(ILLITERATE —) KEELMAN
(MEMBER OF — REPUBLICAN ARMY) PROVO
(PREF.) HIBERNO
IRISHMAN MAC PAT CELT GAEL KELT SCOT GREEK IRISH PADDY YREIS TEAGUE GRECIAN IRISHER MILESIAN ORANGEMAN
(LEARNED —) OLLAMH

IRISH MOSS SLOKE CHONDRUS
IRISHWOMAN HARP
IRK BORE ITCH ANNOY WEARY
BOTHER
IRKSOME DULL WARM WEARY
HUMDRUM OPEROSE PAINFUL
TEDIOUS ANNOYING TIRESOME
IRKSOMENESS TEDIUM
IROKO ODUM ODOOM MUVULE
KAMBALA
IRON BIT DOG IRE AIRN MARS WIRE
ANGLE ANVIL BASIL BRAND DRAIL
DRIFT FLOSS HORSE NEGRO PRESS
SPIKE STEEL WAVER ANCONY
BEATER CALKER CAUTER FERRUM
GAGGER GOFFER JAGGER OSMUND
CAUTERY COBIRON CRAMPER
FERRITE FURISON GAMBREL
GAUFFER PRICKER SADIRON
FLATIRON TRICOUNI
(— FOR CLOSING STAVES) HORSE
(— FOR STRIKING COINS) PILE
(— OF MILLSTONE) RIND RYND
(— ORE) LIMNITE
(— PIECES) POTLEG
(— PLATE) TRAMP
(— SHORTAGE) ANEMIA
(— SUPPORTING SPIT) COBIRON
(— TO SUPPORT BEAM) TORSEL
(ANGLE —) LATH STIFFENER
(BASKETWORK —) BEATER
(BOOM —) WITHE WYTHE
(BRANDING —) BURN
(CAST —) METAL YETLIN SPIEGEL
YETLING PROMETAL SEMISTEEL
(CLIMBING —) GAFF SPUR CREEPER
(CRUDE CASTING OF —) PIG
(DRIVING —) CLEEK
(GLASSBLOWING —) BAIT
(GOLF —) WEDGE JIGGER MASHIE
MIDIRON NIBLICK
(GRAPPLING —) CRAMPON
CRAMPOON
(HATTER'S —) SLUG
(LEG —S) SLANGS
(MASS OF WROUGHT —) BLOOM
(METEORIC —) SIDERITE
(PASTY —) SPONGE
(PIG —) SPIEGEL KENTLEDGE
(PRIMING —) DRIFT
(PUDDLING —) RABBLE
(RUSSIAN —) SABLE
(SHEET —) TERNE
(SOLDERING —) COPPER
(SPECULAR —) HEMATITE
(TAILOR'S —) GOOSE
(TAMPING —) DRIVER
(8 PIGS OF CAST —) FODDER
(PL.) GARTERS
(PREF.) FERRI FERRO SIDER(O)
(SUFF.) SIDERITE
IRONBARK MUGGA
IRON BROWN NEGRO

IRONCLAD ARMORED IRONSIDE
IRON, GOLF (PART OF —) TOE FACE
GRIP HEAD HEEL NECK NOSE SOLE
HOSEL SHAFT
IRON GRAY BAT
IRON HAT GOSSAN
IRONIC DRY WRY ACERB ACERBIC
SATIRIC SARCASTIC
IRONICAL BLAND CRUEL PAWKY
IRON-LIKE MARTIAL
IRON MAN TALUS
IRONMONGERY HARDWARE
IRON-OXIDE RED TARRAGONA
IRONSMITH FERRER
IRONSTONE DOGGER SIDERITE
IRONWEED FLATTOP VERNONIA
WINGSTEM
IRONWOOD TITI COLIMA MOPANE
MOPANI PURIRI WAMARA CYRILLA
JOEWOOD AXMASTER BURNWOOD
FIREWOOD
IRONWORKER LOHAR MOSCHI
IRONWORT SIDERITE
IRONY SATIRE ASTEISM SARCASM
RIDICULE
IROQUOIS HURON MINGO CAYUGA
MENGWE
IRRADIATE XRAY EMBEAM
IRRATIONAL MAD REE SURD WILD
BRUTE SILLY ABSURD RAVING
STUPID BESTIAL FOOLISH
IRRECONCILABLE HOSTILE
FRONDEUR
IRREDUCIBLE BASIC
IRREGULAR ODD DUMB WILD
BUMPY EROSE FANCY MIXED WOPSY
ATYPIC CATCHY FITFUL PATCHY
RAGGED RUGGED SPOTTY UNEVEN
UNLIKE WEEWAW ANAXIAL ATACTIC
BAROQUE CATERAN CRABBED
CROOKED CURSORY DEVIOUS
DIFFORM ERRATIC FRECKET
MUTABLE SCRAWLY SNATCHY
UNEQUAL WAYWARD ABNORMAL
ATYPICAL DOGGEREL INFORMAL
PINDARIC SCRAGGLY SCRAMBLY
UNLAWFUL UNSTABLE UNSTEADY
VARIABLE AMORPHOUS
SCRAMBLING PROMISCUOUS
(— IN SHAPE) BAROQUE
(HAVING — EDGE) EROSE
(PREF.) AMETR(O) ANOM ANOMAL(O)
IRREGULARITY SNAG DEFECT
RUFFLE ANOMALY ACCIDENT
(— IN YARN) SLUB SNICK
IRREGULARLY UNDULY
IRRELEVANT INEPT
IRRELIGIOUS PAGAN WICKED
HEATHEN IMPIOUS PROFANE
SENSUAL
IRREMEDIABLE HELPLESS
HOPELESS
IRREPROACHABLE SPOTLESS

IRRESISTIBLE KILLING MESMERIC
OPPOSELESS
IRRESISTIBLY FATALLY
IRRESOLUTE FICKLE INFIRM
UNSURE WANKLE DOUBTFUL
UNSTABLE
IRRESPONSIBLE WILDCAT
CAREFREE FECKLESS SKITTISH
IRRESPONSIVE LEADEN
IRRETRIEVABLE HOPELESS
IRREVERENCE IMPIETY
IRREVERENT ATHEIST AWELESS
IMPIOUS PROFANE
IRREVOCABLE DEAD
IRREVOCABLY FATALLY FINALLY
IRRIGATE FLOAT WATER SYRINGE
IRRIGATION KAREZ
IRRIGATOR FLOATER
IRRITABILITY BATE NERVES SPLEEN
ERETHISM SORENESS VAGOTONY
SENSITIVITY
IRRITABLE BAD EDGY BIRSY CROOK
FIERY FUSSY HASTY HUFFY JUMPY
MUSTY NAGGY RASPY TESTY TETTY
TILTY TOITY CRANKY GROWLY
NETTLY PATCHY SNUFFY SPUNKY
STOCKY TEETHY TETCHY TOUCHY
BILIOUS CRABBED FRATCHY FRETFUL
HORNETY HUFFISH KICKISH PECKISH
PEEVISH SPLEENY TEDIOUS TWITCHY
WASPISH CHOLERIC LIVERISH
PETULANT SNAPPING SNAPPISH
STOMACHY SPLENETIC
IRRITANT PHOSGENE
IRRITATE BUG EAT GET IRE IRK NAG
RUB TAR TEW TRY VEX BURN CRAB
FIRE FRET GALL GOAD GRIG GRIT
ITCH NARK RASP RILE ROIL SOUR
TEEN ANGER ANNOY CHAFE EAGER
FRUMP GRATE GRILL GRIPE PEEVE
PIQUE STING TARRY ABRADE
BOTHER FRIDGE GRAVEL HARASS
HECTOR NETTLE PUTOUT RUFFLE
AFFRONT INCENSE INFLAME
NERVOUS PROVOKE STOMACH
ACERBATE
IRRITATED RILY SORE HUFFY RAGGY
MUFFED SHIRTY EMPORTE
FRATCHED SOREHEAD
(EASILY —) TESTY
IRRITATING ACRID HARSH PESTY
CORSIE ELVISH GRAVEL FRETFUL
GALLING IRKSOME PUNGENT
RASPING ANNOYING FRETSOME
GRAVELLY NETTLING SCRATCHY
SPITEFUL STINGING TIRESOME
MADDENING NETTLESOME
IRRITATION AGRO FRET TEEN
AGGRO BIRSE PIQUE STEAM NEEDLE
RUFFLE TEMPER WARMTH ANTPRICK
FLEABITE PINPRICK VEXATION
IRRUPTION BREAK INROAD INBREAK
INBURST ERUPTION INVASION

IRU (FATHER OF —) CALEB
IS S YS BEES
(— NOT) NIS AINT ISNT
ISAAC (FATHER OF —) ABRAHAM
(MOTHER OF —) SARAH
(SON OF —) ESAU JACOB
(WIFE OF —) REBEKAH
ISABELLA (BROTHER OF —) CLAUDIO
(HUSBAND OF —) BIRON VILLEROY
VINCENTIO
(LOVER OF —) ZERBINO
(SLAYER OF —) RODOMONT
ISABELLE (GUARDIAN OF —)
SGANARELLE
(HUSBAND OF —) VALERE
ISAIAH ESAY ESAIAS
(FATHER OF —) AMOZ
ISANDER (BROTHER OF —)
HIPPOLOCHUS
(FATHER OF —) BELLEROPHON
(SISTER OF —) LAODAMIA
ISCAH (BROTHER OF —) LOT
(FATHER OF —) HARAN
(SISTER OF —) MILCAH
ISCHEMIA ANEMIA
ISCHIAL SCIATIC
ISEULT (FATHER OF —) HOEL
ANGUISH
(HUSBAND OF —) MARK
(LOVER OF —) TRISTAN
ISFENDIYAR (BROTHER OF —)
BISHUTAN
(FATHER OF —) GUSHTASP
(SLAYER OF —) RUSTAM
(SON OF —) BAHMAN
ISHBAK (FATHER OF —) ABRAHAM
(MOTHER OF —) KETURAH
ISHBOSHETH (FATHER OF —) SAUL
ISHI (SON OF —) ZOHETH
ISHIAH (FATHER OF —) IZRAHIAH
ISHMAEL (FATHER OF —) AZEL
ABRAHAM JEHOHANAN NETHANIAH
(MOTHER OF —) HAGAR
(SON OF —) ZEBADIAH
ISHMAIAH (FATHER OF —)
OBADIAH
ISHPINGO CINNAMON
ISHSHAKKU PATESI
ISHTAR NINNI
ISHUAH (FATHER OF —) ASHER
ISHUI (FATHER OF —) SAUL
(MOTHER OF —) AHINOAM
ISINGLASS AGAR LEAF MICA PIPE
KANTEN CARLOCK
ISIS (BROTHER OF —) OSIRIS
(FATHER OF —) SATURN
(MOTHER OF —) RHEA
ISLAM ABBASID
(— CALL TO PRAYER) AZAN
ISLAMIC (— CUSTOM) SUNNA
ISLAND CAY ILE CALF CAYO HOLM
INCH ISLE JAVA POLO ENNIS MALTA
MAYDA AVALON ITHACA OGYGIA

REFUGE RIALTO CIPANGO JAMAICA
MADEIRA TOWHEAD BLEFUSCU
CALAURIA DOMINICA GUERNSEY
LILLIPUT LUGGNAGG
(— IN EVERGLADES) HAMMOCK
(— OF REIL) INSULA
(ARTIFICIAL —) CRANNOG
(CORAL —) ATOLL
(FABLED —) MERU UTOPIA
(FLOATING —) HOVER
(FLYING —) LAPUTA
(FORTIFIED —) CRANNOG
(LEGENDARY —) BRAZIL OBRAZIL
(LITTLE —) AIT KAY KEY ISLET
(LOW —) KEY
(ROCKY —) SKERRY
(SANDY —) BEACH BARRIER
(SMALL —) CAY EYET EYOT ISLE
ISLET NUBBLE SANDKEY
(PREF.) NESO
ISLANDER KANAKA ISLEMAN
INSULARY
ISLE CAY IZLE ISLET SKERRY
ISLET OE AIT CAY KEY EYOT HAFT
HOLM ILOT MOTU ROCK ISLOT
STACK NUBBLE
ISMENE (FATHER OF —) OEDIPUS
(MOTHER OF —) JOCASTA
(SISTER OF —) ANTIGONE
ISOBAR MEIOBAR MESOBAR
PLEIOBAR
ISOGRAM ISOPLETH
ISOLATE SPORE ENSILE ISLAND
DISSECT SECLUDE COLONIZE
INSULATE PRESCIND SEPARATE
SEQUESTER
ISOLATED LONE POCKET UNIQUE
OUTLYING SOLITARY STRANDED
SECESSIVE
ISOLATION HERMITRY LONENESS
SOLITUDE SEQUESTER
ISOMER PYRAN TOSYL XYLENE
ETHANOL CUMIDINE DECOSANE
DODECANE CARBOLINE
ISOMERIC ISO ALLO
ISOMETRIC ALLO CUBIC REGULAR
TESSULAR
ISOPLETH GEOTHERM
ISOPOD SLATER ASELLUS BOPYRID
GRIBBLE EPICARID
ISOTOPE MUON IONIUM THORON
ACTINON CARRIER PROTIUM
TRITIUM
ISOTYPE COTYPE SYNTYPE
ISPAGHUL SPOGEL
ISPAHAN HERAT HERATI

ISRAEL
CAPITAL: JERUSALEM
COIN: AGORA AGURA POUND PRUTA
PRUTAH SHEKEL
COLLECTIVE FARM: KIBBUTZ
DESERT: NEGEV

FORMER NAME: CANAAN PALESTINE
GULF: AQABA
LAKE: HULEH TIBERIAS
MEASURE: CAB HIN KOR LOG BATH
EPHA EZBA OMER REED SEAH CUBIT
EPHAH HOMER KANEH QANEH
MOUNT: TABOR
MOUNTAIN: NAFH SAGI HARIF MERON
RAMON ATZMON CARMEL
PLAIN: ESDRAELON
RIVER: FARIA MALIK SOREQ JORDAN
QISHON SARIDA YARKON LAKHISH
SEA: DEAD GALILEE
SEAPORT: EILAT ELATH ASHDOD
TELAVIV
TOWN: ACRE RAMA EILAT HAIFA
HOLON JAFFA JENIN JOPPA RAMLE
SAFAD BATYAM HEBRON NABLUS
JERICHO NATANYA TELAVIV
TULKARM NAZARETH

ISRAELI SABRA
(— AIRPORT) LOD
(— STUDY CENTER) ULPAN
ISRAELITE JEW SAINT HEBREW
JACOBITE
(PL.) ZION
ISSUE END ISH COME EMIT FALL
FLOW GIVE GUSH HEAD MISE REEK
TERM VENT ARISE COUNT EVENT
FRUIT LOOSE OUTGO SETON SOURD
UTTER EFFECT EFFUSE EGRESS
EMERGE ESCAPE EXITUS MUTTON
RESULT SEQUEL SETTER SPRING
UPPING BALLOON DEBOUCH
DESCENT DRIZZLE EMANATE
ESSENCE EXSURGE OUTCOME
PROCEED PROGENY REDOUND
REFLAIR SUCCESS EXPEDITE
FONTANEL INCREASE ISSUANCE
KINDLING OUTGOING
(— AND ORDER) BID
(— SLOWLY) EXUDE
(— SPASMODICALLY) BELCH
(— SUDDENLY) SALLY
(— WITH FORCE) SPOUT
(BOND —) CONSOL
(FAVORABLE —) SPEED FORTUNE
(FINAL —) FATE UPSHOT UTMOST
(NEW —) REMAKE
(NUMEROUS —) SPAWN
(REAL —) CRUX
ISSUED OUT
ISSUING EMANANT JESSANT
MANATION
ISTHMUS BALK STRAIT TARBET
ISTLE PITA IXTLE JUAMAVE
GUAPILLA
IT HE HIT MUN ESSO TAGGER
(— FOLLOWS) SEQ SEQU
(— HAS BEEN SWORN) JURAT
ITALIAN ITALIC AUSONIAN
MACARONI

ITALIANA IN ALGIERI, L'
   (CHARACTER IN —) ELVIRA TADDEO
   LINDPRO ISABELLA MUSTAPHA
   (COMPOSER OF —) ROSSINI
ITALITE VESRITE
ITALY AUSONIA HESPERIA SATURNIA

ITALY

CAPE: TESTA CIRCEO LICOSA LINARO
   COLONNE FALCONE PASSERO
   RIZZUTO SANVITO TEULADA
   VATICANO
CAPITAL: ROMA ROME
CHEESE: ROMANO FONTINA RICOTTA
   BELPAESE PARMESAN TALEGGIO
COIN: LIRA LIRE TARI GRANO PAOLI
   PAOLO SCUDO SOLDO DANARO
   DENARO DUCATO SEQUIN TESTONE
   ZECCHINO
FAMILY: ASTI ESTE AMATI CENCE
   DORIA BORGIA MEDICI SFORZA
FOOD: PASTA PIZZA SCAMPI GNOCCHI
   LASAGNE POLENTA RAVIOLI
   RISOTTO SPUMONI TORTONI
   CAPONATA LINGUINE MACARONI
   PEPERONI
GULF: GAETA GENOA OROSEI
   SALERNO TARANTO CAGLIARI
   ORISTANO
ISLAND: ELBA LERO CAPRI LEROS
   PONZA GIGLIO ISCHIA LINOSA
   SALINA SICILY USTICA ALICUDI
   ASINARA CAPHAIA GORGONA
   LEVANZO PANAREA PIANOSA SICILIA
   VULCANO FILICUDI SARDINIA
ISLANDS: EGADI LIPARI TUSCAN
   PELAGIE PONTINE TREMITI
LAKE: COMO ISEO NEMI GARDA
   ALBANO LESINA LUGANO VARANO
   BOLSENA PERUGIA MAGGIORE
   BRACCIANO
MEASURE: PIE ORNA CANNA PALMA
   PALMO PIEDE PUNTO SALMA STAIO
   STERO BARILE MIGLIE MIGLIO
   MOGGIO RUBBIO TAVOLA TOMOLO
   BOCCALE BRACCIO SECCHIO
   GIORNATA POLONICK QUADRATO
MOUNTAIN: ETNA ROSA VISO AMARO
   BLANC CORNO SOMMA CIMONE
   BERNINA VESUVIUS
MOUNTAIN RANGE: ALPS ORTLES
   APENNINES MARITIMES
NATIVE: ITALO LATIN OSCAN ROMAN
   SABINE TIRANO TUSCAN LOMBARD
   SIENESE LIGURIAN VENETIAN
NATIVE:) PISAN PISANO
PASS: FREJUS BERNINA BRENNER
   SPLUGEN
PORT: BARI POLA ZARA GENOA TRANI
   ZADAR RIMINI SALERNO TRIESTE
PROVINCE: ASTI COMO ENNA PISA
   AOSTA CUNEO FORLI LECCE NUORO
   PARMA PAVIA RIETI SIENA UDINE

   FOGGIA MATERA MODENA PADOVA
   RAGUSA TRENTO VERONA BRESCIA
   PISTOIA SASSARI VITERBO
REGION: CARSO APULIA LATIUM
   MARCHE MOLISE PUGLIA SICILY
   UMBRIA ABRUZZI LIGURIA
   TUSCANY VENETIA CALABRIA
   CAMPANIA LOMBARDY PIEMONTE
   SARDINIA
RESORT: LIDO SANREMO TAORMINA
RIVER: PO ADDA AGRI ANIO ARNO LIRI
   NERA RENO SELE TARO ADIGE CRATI
   MANNU OGLIO PARMA PIAVE SALSO
   STURA TIBER TIRSO ANIENE BELICE
   MINCIO OFANTO PANARO RAPIDO
   SANGRO SIMETO TANARO TEVERE
   TICINO BIFERNO BRADANO CHIENTI
   METAURO MONTONE OMBRONE
   PESCARA RUBICON SECCHIA
   TREBBIA VOLTURNO
SEA: IONIAN ADRIATIC LIGURIAN
STRAIT: MESSINA OTRANTO
   BONIFACIO
TOWN: BRA RHO ACRI ALBA ASTI BARI
   COMO DEGO ELEA ENNA ESTE FANO
   GELA IESI LODI NARO NOLA PISA
   POLA ROMA ROME ACQUI ANZIO
   AOSTA ASOLA AVOLA CAPUA
   CUNEO EBOLI FIUME FORLI GENOA
   IMOLA LECCE LUCCA MASSA MILAN
   MONZA OSTIA PADUA PARMA PAVIA
   RIETI SIENA TEANO TRENT TURIN
   UDINE VELIA ALCAMO AMALFI
   ANCONA ANDRIA AREZZO CEFALU
   FAENZA FOGGIA GENOVA MANTUA
   MESTRE MILANO MODENA NAPLES
   NAPOLI NOVARA RIVOLI SPEZIA
   TRENTO VARESE VENICE VERONA
   BERGAMO BOLOGNA BOLZANO
   BRESCIA CARRARA CASERTA
   CATANIA COSENZA CREMONA
   FERRARA FIRENZE GORIZIA IMPERIA
   LEGHORN LIVORNO MARSALA
   MESSINA PALERMO PERUGIA
   PISTOIA POMPEII RAVENNA
   TARANTO TRIESTE BRINDISI
   CAGLIARI FLORENCE PIACENZA
   SORRENTO SYRACUSE
VOLCANO: ETNA SOMMA VULCANO
   VESUVIUS STROMBOLI
WATERFALL: FRUA TOCE
WEIGHT: CARAT LIBRA ONCIA POUND
   CARATO DENARO LIBBRA OTTAVA
WINE: SOAVE CHIANTI MARSALA
   ORVIETO

ITCH EWK EACH REEF RIFF YEUK
   YEWK YUKE PSORA TICKLE ITCHING
   SCABIES PRURITUS CACOETHES
   VANILLISM
   (PREF.) ACARI ACARO PSOR(O)
ITCHING ITCHY YEUKY PRURIENT
   PRURITUS URTICANT

ITCHY SCRATCHY
ITEM ANA JOB TOT ENTRY PIECE
  POINT THING DETAIL PARCEL
  ARTICLE SEVERAL PARTICULAR
  (— IN SERIES) COURSE
  (— OF PROPERTY) CHATTEL
  (— OF VALUE) ASSET
  (APPENDED —) ADDENDUM
  (CHOICE —) PLUM
  (COLLECTOR'S —) SPOIL
  (DECORATIVE —) CONCEIT
  (DESIRED —S) WISHLIST
  (LUXURY —) BOUTIQUE
  (NEWS —) FACTOID DISPATCH
  (OFF-BRAND —) GENERIC
  (UNPUBLISHED —S) ANECDOTE
  (VALUELESS —) BEAN
  (PL.) CHECKAGE
ITEMIZE DETAIL
ITERATE ECHO REPEAT REITERATE
ITERATION PLEONASM
ITHIEL (FATHER OF —) JESAIAH
ITHRA (SON OF —) AMASA
  (WIFE OF —) ABIGAIL
ITHRAN (FATHER OF —) DISHON
ITHREAM (FATHER OF —) DAVID
  (MOTHER OF —) EGLAH
ITHURIEL'S-SPEAR GRASSNUT
ITINERANT ERRANT ROADMAN
  RUNNING AMBULANT STROLLER
  STROLLING PERIPATETIC
ITINERARY DIET JOURNAL WAYBILL
  (— OF ROYAL PROGRESS) GEST
ITINERATION EYRE
ITS HIS
ITSELF IT HERSELF
ITSY-BITSY WEE
ITTAI (FATHER OF —) RIBAI
ITYS (FATHER OF —) TEREUS
  (MOTHER OF —) PROCNE
ITZA PETEN
IULUS ASCANIUS
IVANHOE (AUTHOR OF —) SCOTT
  (CHARACTER IN —) JOHN BRIAN

  GIRTH ISAAC LUCAS ROBIN WAMBA
  CEDRIC ROWENA ULRICA MAURICE
  REBECCA RICHARD WILFRED
  REGINALD BEAUMANOIR
IVATAN BATAN
IVORY EBURE DENTINE ELEPHANT
  (DUST OF —) EBURINE
  (WALRUS —) RIBZUBA RIBAZUBA
IVORY BLACK ABAISER

IVORY COAST		
CAPE: PALMAS		
CAPITAL: ABIDJAN		
DAM: BANDAMA		
LANGUAGE: DIOULA		
MOUNTAIN: NIMBA		
PEOPLE: ABE AKAN ATLE KOUA		
KROU MANDE ABOURE LAGOON		
MALINKE VOLTAIC		
RIVER: KOMOE BANDAMA CAVALLY		
SASSANDRA		
TOWN: MAN DALOA TABOU		
BOUAKE GAGNOA KORHOGO		
SASSANDRA		

IVORY GULL SNOWBIRD
IVORY NUT ANTA TAGUA JARINA
IVORY PALM TAGUA COROJO
  COROZO
IVORY TREE PALAY
IVY TOD GILL HOVE IVIN JILL PICRY
  ARALIA HEDERA HIBBIN ALEHOOF
  ARALIAD IVYWORT BINDWEED
  FOALFOOT
  (— LEAGUER) ELI
  (PREF.) HEDERI
IWW WOBBLY
IXION (FATHER OF —) PHLEGYAS
  (SISTER OF —) CORONIS
  (WIFE OF —) DIA
IYNX (FATHER OF —) PAN
  (MOTHER OF —) ECHO
IZHAR (FATHER OF —) KOHATH
IZMIR SMYRNA

J

J JAY JIG JULIETT
JAALAM
  (FATHER OF —) ESAU
JAAL GOAT BEDEN JAELA
JAASIEL (FATHER OF —) ABNER
JAAZANIAH (FATHER OF —) AZUR
  SHAPHAN JEREMIAH
JAB GAG GIG JAG JOB POKE STAB
  STICK
JABAL (BROTHER OF —) JUBAL
  (FATHER OF —) LAMECH
  (MOTHER OF —) ADAH
JABBER YAP CHAT YACK JAVER
  BURBLE GABBER GABBLE JOBBER
  NATTER YABBER YATTER CHATTER
JABESH (SON OF —) SHALLUM
JABIRU STORK CICONIID
JABOT RUFFLE
JACANA PARRA
JACARANDA BROWN DATE
  TALLYHO
JACARE CAIMAN CAYMAN
JACHIN (FATHER OF —) SIMEON
JACINTH LIGURE
JACK DIB FLAG JACA CRICK DICKY
  KNAVE NANCA COLORS KATHAL
  SCALET SETTER WENZEL MATADOR
  BLOCKING JACKFISH POLIGNAL
  SOURJACK TURNSPIT UPLIFTER
  (— IN BOWLS) BABY MARK KITTY
  MASTER MISTRESS
  (— IN CARDS) PAM PUR TOM BOWER
  CNAFE KITTY KNAPE KNAVE MAKER
  KNIGHT VARLET WENZEL VARLETTO
  (— OF CLUBS) PAM NODDY BRAGGER
  MATADOR
  (— OF SAME SUIT) NOB
  (— OF TRUMPS) TOM JASS JASZ
  BOWER HONOR PLAYBOY
  (PIANO —) HOPPER STICKER
  SAUTEREAU
  (ROASTING —) TURNSPIT
  (SPINNING —) BEAT
JACKAL DIEB JACK KOLA THOS
  CANID CANINE DRAGON SILVER
  THOOID SIACALLE
JACKAROO RINGNECK
JACKASS JACK
JACKASS FISH MORWONG
  TERAKIHI
JACK BEAN OVERLOOK
JACK CREVALLE TORO
JACKDAW DAW KAE JACK SHELL
  CADDOW CARDER CHOUGH KADDER
  CADESSE DAWCOCK DAWPATE
  GRACKLE
JACKER SLIPMAN TORCHER

JACKET SAC COAT ETON JACK JUMP
  JUPE SACK VEST ACTON COVER
  DICKY JUPON PARKA POLKA SHRUG
  WAMUS BANIAN BASQUE BIETLE
  BLAZER BOLERO CARACO CORSET
  DOLMAN FECKET GANSEY JERKIN
  JERSEY JUMPER RAILLY REEFER
  SACQUE SADDLE SLEEVE SLIVER
  SONTAG TABARD TEMIAK WAMPUS
  WARMUS ZOUAVE BEDGOWN
  CANEZOU LOUNGER NORFOLK
  PALETOT PALTOCK PEACOAT RISTORI
  SPENCER SURCOAT SWEATER
  CAMISOLE CARDIGAN CHAQUETA
  HANSELIN JIRKINET MACKINAW
  OVERSLOP PENELOPE SEALSKIN
  CARMAGNOLE ROUNDABOUT
  WINDBREAKER WINDCHEATER
  (— FOR TURKEY) APRON
  (— LINED WITH STEEL) PLACCATE
  (— OF BOOK) DUSTCOVER
  (— OF INDIA) BANIAN BANIYA
  (— UNDER ARMOR) ACTON TRUSS
  HAQUETON
  (CROCHETED —) SONTAG
  (DINNER —) TUXEDO
  (ETON —) DUMFREEZER
  (HOODED —) GREGO ANORAK
  GRIEKO
  (HUSSAR'O —) PELISSE
  (KIND OF —) MAO NEHRU SAFARI
  (LADY'S —) BRUNSWICK
  (LIFE —) MAEWEST
  (LOOSE —) VAREUSE
  (MALAY —) BAJU BADJU KABAYA
  (MILITARY —) TUNIC
  (PART OF —) FOB HEM DART FLAP
  SEAM VENT GORGE LAPEL BUTTON
  COLLAR INSEAM PIPING POCKET
  REVERS SLEEVE ARMHOLE
  OUTSEAM BUTTONHOLE
  (PEASANT'S —) SAYON
  (UNDRESS MILITARY —) SHELL
  (WORK —) BAWNEEN
JACKFRUIT JACA KATHAL
  SOURJACK
JACKHAMMER SINKER PLUGGER
JACKKNIFE DIVE JACK PIKE
  BARLOW
JACKMAN SHELLMAN
JACK-OF-ALL-TRADES DOCTOR
  TINKER GIMCRACK
JACK-PUDDING ZANY CLOWN
  BUFFOON
JACKS DIBS
JACKSCREW CRICK
JACKSMELT PEIXEREY

JACKSNIPE GID JED JACK PEERT SCAPE SNIPE SNIGHT CHOROOK CREAKER JUDCOCK SQUATTER
JACKSTAY JACK HORSE PARREL JACKROD RAILWAY
JACKSTRAW SPILIKIN
JACK TREE NANGKA
JACOB ISRAEL
  (BROTHER OF —) ESAU
  (DAUGHTER OF —) RACHEL DEBORAH
  (FATHER OF —) ISAAC
  (MOTHER OF —) REBEKAH
  (SON OF —) ACER LEVI ASHOR JOSEPH
JACOB'S LADDER POLEMONIUM
JACQUARD FACONNE
JADA (BROTHER OF —) SHAMMAI
  (FATHER OF —) ONAM
JADE YU DUN TIT HACK JAUD MINX PLUG SLUT TIRE HUSSY QUEAN TRASH BEJADE HARASS RANNEL AXSTONE HILDING POUNAMU
  (DIRTY —) SLAISTER
JADED BLASE FORGONE SHOPWORN DISJASKIT
JADEITE YU
JAEGER LARI SKUA ALLAN BOSUN LARID SHOOL BONXIE TEASER TULIAC TRUMPIE DIRTBIRD DUNGBIRD
JAEL (HUSBAND OF —) HEBER
  (VICTIM OF —) SISERA
JAFFIER (WIFE OF —) BELVIDERA
JAG BUN JOG BARB GIMP JAUG LOAD SOSH TOOT SKATE TOOTH INDENT
JAGELLO (WIFE OF —) HEDWIG
JAGGED JAGGY HACKLY RAGGED RUGGED SCRAGGY SHAGGED SNAGGED INDENTED SCRAGGLY TATTERED
JAGGERY GUR GOOR GOUR KHAUR KHAJUR KITTUL
JAGUAR CAT OUNCE TIGER PANTHER UTURUNCU
JAHANGIR (FATHER OF —) AKBAR
JAHATH (FATHER OF —) LIBNI SHIMEI SHELOMOTH
JAHAZIAH (FATHER OF —) TIKVAH
JAHAZIEL (FATHER OF —) HEBRON ZECHARIAH
JAHDO (FATHER OF —) BUZ
  (SON OF —) JESHISHAI
JAHLEEL (FATHER OF —) ZEBULUN
JAHZEEL (FATHER OF —) NAPHTALI
JAI ALAI PELOTA
  (— BASKET) CESTA
  (— COURT) FRONTON
JAIL CAN GIB JUG PEN BOOB CAGE COOP CRIB DUMP GAOL HELL HOLD HOLE KEEP LAKE LOCK NICK SLAM STIR WARD CHOKY CLINK GRATE KITTY LIMBO LODGE POKEY TENCH TRONK BUCKET CARCEL COOLER ENJAIL JIGGER LIMBUS LOCKUP TOLZEY FREEZER FURNACE GEHENNA KIDCOTE PINFOLD SLAMMER TOLLERY BASTILLE CALABOZO HOOSEGOW IMPRISON MILLDOLL TOLLHALL BRIDEWELL CALABOOSE
  (— TERM) JOLT
JAILBIRD CON LAG TERMER PRISONER
JAILER ADAM GAOLER KEEPER WARDEN ALCAIDE TURNKEY INCLUDER
JAIR (FATHER OF —) KISH
  (SON OF —) ELHANAN MORDECAI
JAKAN (FATHER OF —) EZER
JAKE FINE HICK FELLOW
JAKES AJAX GONG
JALAP MECHOACAN
JALON (FATHER OF —) EZRA
JALOPY HEAP BUGGY CRATE CLUNKER
JAM DIP CRAM JAMB BLOCK CHOKE CROWD CRUSH JEELY STICK JEELIE KONFYT THRONG JACKPOT PRESERVE MARMALADE
  (— FOR LACK OF LUBRICATION) SEIZE
  (TRAFFIC —) GRIDLOCK
JAMAICA (CAPITAL OF —) KINGSTON
  (RELIGIOUS ADHERENT OF —) RASTA RASTAMAN
  (RIVER OF —) BLACK COBRE MINHO
  (TOWN OF —) MAYPEN PORTANTONIO SPANISHTOWN
JAMAICA COBNUT OUABE PIGNUT
JAMAICA DOGWOOD BABASCO BARBASCO FISHWOOD
JAMAICAN (— MUSIC) SKA
JAMAICA RAINBIRD TOMFOOL
JAMAICA VERVAIN GERVAO
JAMAICIN BERBERINE
JAMB DURN ALETTE HAUNCH REVEAL DOORPOST
  (PL.) COVING
JAMBOREE BASH
JAMES JEM JIM JIMMY SEAMAS SHAMUS
  (BROTHER OF —) JOHN JESUS JOSES
  (COUSIN OF —) JESUS
  (FATHER OF —) CLOPAS
  (MOTHER OF —) MARY SALOME
JAMIN (FATHER OF —) RAM SIMEON
JAMMAICA PEPPER ALLSPICE
JANAKA (DAUGHTER OF —) SITA
JANAMEJAYA (FATHER OF —) PARIKSHIT
JANE EYRE (AUTHOR OF —) BRONTE
  (CHARACTER IN —) EYRE JANE JOHN MARY REED ADELE DIANA ELIZA GRACE POOLE BERTHA BESSIE

EDWARD ELLIOT INGRAM LEAVEN RIVERS TEMPLE VARENS BLANCHE FAIRFAX GEORGIANA ROCHESTER
JANGLE CLAM SQUABBLE
JANGLING HARSH JANGLY AJANGLE
JANISSARY CREOLE RABINUBIA
JANITOR DURWAN PORTER SERVITOR
JANIZARY SOLAK SOLACH
JANNA (FATHER OF —) JOSEPH
  (SON OF —) MELCHI
JANSENIST RIGORIST
JANUARY ENERU
  (— IN SPANISH) ENERO
JANUS IANUS BIFRONT
JAOB JOW
JAPAN NIPPON YAMATO CIPANGO

JAPAN

ABORIGINE: AINU
BAY: ISE MUTSU OTARU ARIAKE ATSUMI SENDAI SURUGA TOYAMA WAKASA UCHIURA
CAPE: TOI ESAN MINO NOMA SHIO TOYA OUZU ERIMO KYOGA RURUI MUROTO NOJIMA TODOGA SHIRIYA ASHIZURI SHAKOTAN
CAPITAL: TOKIO TOKYO
COIN: BU RIN SEN YEN OBAN KOBAN OBANG TEMPO ICHEBU ITZEBU KOBANG
FORMER CAPITAL: EDO
ISLAND: IKI SADO AWAJI RONIN HONDO KURIL REBUN HONSHU KIUSHU KURILE KYUSHU RYUKYU CIPANGO LOOCHOO RISHIRI SKIKOKU HOKKAIDO IKISHIMA OKIGUNTO OKUSHIRI TSUSHIMA YAKUJIMA
ISLAND GROUP: OKI GOTO BONIN VOLCANO
LAKE: OMI BIWA TOYA TOWADA CHUZENJI KUTCHAWA SHIKOTSU INAWASHIRO
MEASURE: BU JO SE BOO CHO KEN TAN HIRO SHAKU TSUBO
MOUNTAIN: ZAO FUJI ASAHI ASAMA YESSO ASOSAN ENASAN HIUCHI KIUSIU YARIGA FUJISAN HAKUSAN KUJUSAN TOKACHI FUJIYAMA
PORT: UBE OTARU YAHATA YAWATA
PREFECTURE: MIE GIFU NARA OITA SAGA AICHI AKITA CHIBA EHIME FUKUI GUMMA HYOGO IWATE KOCHI KYOTO SHIGA AOMORI KAGAWA MIYAGI NAGANO TOYAMA NIIGATA OKINAWA SAITAMA TOTTORI NAGASAKI WAKAYAMA YAMAGATA TOKUSHIMA
SEA: SUO AMAKUSA
STRAIT: SUO BUNGO OSUMI NEMURO TANEGA TOKARA TSUGARU TSUSHIMA

STREET: GINZA
TOWN: OME TSU GIFU KOBE KURA MITO NAHA NARA OITA OTSU SAGA UEDA AKITA ATAMI CHIBA FUKUI KIOTO KOCHI NIKKO OSAKA OTARU SAKAI UJINA URAWA CHOSHI MATSUE NAGOYA SASEBO SENDAI TAKADA TOYAMA FUKUOKA NIIGATA OKAYAMA OKAZAKI SAPPORO HAKODATE KAMAKURA KANAZAWA KAWASAKI KUMAMOTO NAGASAKI YOKOHAMA YOKOSUKA HIROSHIMA
VOLCANO: ASO USU FUJI ASAMA ASOSAN HAKUSAN FUJIYAMA
WATERFALL: KEGON
WEIGHT: MO FUN KIN KON RIN SHI KATI KWAN NIYO CARAT CATTY MOMME PICUL KWAMME HIYAKKIN

JAPAN CEDAR SUGI
JAPANESE JAP JAPONIC
  (— ART OF SELF-DEFENSE) AIKADO
  (— CONGLOMERATE) ZAIBATSU
  (— STYLE OF PAINTING) YAMATO
  (ABORIGINAL —) AINU
  (OF — CULTURAL PERIOD) YAYOI
  (PERIOD OF — HISTORY) HEIAN
JAPANESE APRICOT UME
JAPANESE CHERRY SAKURA
JAPANESE DEER SIKA
JAPANESE GELATIN AGAR
JAPANESE IRIS SHADOW
JAPANESE PERSIMMON KAKI
JAPANESE PLUM KELSEY
JAPANESE PORGIE TAI
JAPANESE QUINCE JAPONICA
JAPANESE VELVET RIRODO
JAPE GAUD JOKE BEGUNK
JAPHETH (BROTHER OF —) HAM SHEM
  (FATHER OF —) NOAH
  (SON OF —) JAVAN
JAPHIA (FATHER OF —) DAVID
JAPONICA ASTILBE
JAQUENETTA
  (LOVER OF —) ARMADO
JAR TUN CELL JANG JARG JOLT JURR OLLA BANGA BOCAL CADUS CRUSE KADOS SHOCK DOLIUM HUSTLE HYDRIA IMPACT JUDDER KALPIS PANKIN PINATA PITHOS TINAJA CANOPUS CONCUSS POTICHE PSYKTER STAMNOS TERRINE MARTABAN STINKPOT
  (— FOR LIQUOR) GREYBEARD
  (— VIOLENTLY) STAVE
  (BELL —) CLOCHE
  (BULGING —) OLLA
  (EARTHENWARE —) CAN NAN CROCK GAMI A PIPKIN PITHOS TERRINE
  (PHYSICIST'S —) LEYDEN
  (POROUS —) GURGLET

(SQUAT —) KORO
(STONE —) STEEN STONE CROPPA
(STRAWBERRY —) PLANTER
(WATER —) KANG BANGA CHATTI
CHATTY GUMLAH HYDRIA
(2-HANDLED —) AMPHORA
(PREF.) DOLIO URCEI
JARASANDHA (FATHER OF —)
BRIHADRATHA
(SLAYER OF —) BHIMA
JARDINIERE POT
JARED (SON OF —) ENOCH
JARGON CANT JIVE RANE SLUM
ARGOT IDIOM LINGO SLANG LINGUA
LINSEY PATOIS PATTER PIDGIN
SHELTA SIWASH CHINOOK CHOCTAW
DIALECT JARGOON PALAVER
BARRIKIN KEDGEREE PARLANCE
POLYGLOT SCHMOOZE SHOPTALK
GOBBLEDEGOOK GOBBLEDYGOOK
GOGGLEDEGOOK
(— OF TINKERS) KENNICK
(THIEVES' —) FLASH
(TINKER'S —) KENNICK
(UNINTELLIGIBLE —) BARAGOUIN
JARHA (MASTER OF —) SHESHAN
JARIB (FATHER OF —) SIMEON
JARRING JARG RUDE SOUR HARSH
ROUGH DARING STRIDENT
JASHUB (FATHER OF —) BANI
ISSACHAR
JASMINE BELA MALATI PIKAKE
JESSAMY WOODBINE
JASON (VESSEL OF —) ARGO
(WIFE OF —) MEDEA
JASPER JASPIS MORLOP DIASPER
BASANITE CREOLITE WEDGWOOD
JATAYU (FATHER OF —) GARUDA
(SLAYER OF —) RAVANA
JAUNDICE AURIGO GULSACH
ICTERUS JANDERS YELLOWS
JAUNDERS GRASSERIE
(PREF.) ICTER(O)
JAUNDICED ICTERODE
JAUNT TRIP SALLY JAUNCE VAGARY
JOURNEY
JAUNTILY AIRILY BOUNCILY
JAUNTING CAR SIDECAR
OUTSIDER
JAUNTY PERK PERT TRIM COCKY
PERKY SASSY DAPPER JANTEE
SHANTY FINICAL PERKING
DEBONAIR

JAVA
INDONESIAN NAME: DJAWA
ISLAND: BALI LOMBOK MADURA
MEASURE: PAAL
MOUNTAIN: GEDE MURJO RAOENG
SEMERU SLAMET SEMEROE
SOEMBING
PORT: BATAVIA SURABAJA TJILATJAP
RIVER: SOLO LIWUNG BRANTAS

TOWN: BOGOR DESSA KEDIRI
MALANG BANDUNG BATAVIA
JAKARTA SEMARANG SURABAJA
WEIGHT: POND TALI

JAVA ALMOND PILI CANARI KA-
NARI TALISAY
JAVA COTTON KAPOK
JAVA HEAD (AUTHOR OF —)
HERGESHEIMER
(CHARACTER IN —) TAOU YUEN
RHODA EDWARD GERRIT JEREMY
NETTIE VOLLAR AMMIDON DUNSACK
WILLIAM
JAVAN (FATHER OF —) JAPHETH
JAVANESE KRAMA KROMO
JAVANESE SKUNK TELEDU
JAVA PLUM DUHAT JAMBUL
LOMBOY JAMBOOL
JAVA SPARROW MUNIA PADDY
RICEBIRD
JAVELIN COLP DART PILE ACLYS
PILUM SPEAR JAREED LANCET
ASSAGAI HARPOON HURLBAT
JAVELOT ACONTIUM GAVELOCK
JAW JIB BEAK CHAP CHAW CHOP
JOWL WANG ANVIL CHAFT CHEEK
CHOKE SCOLD CHAWLE FEELER
JAWBONE MAXILLA MANDIBLE
(— OF FORCEPS) BEAK
(— OF SPIDER) FANG
(— OF VISE) CHAP
(—S OF BIRD) BILL
(FALSE —) CLAMP
(RECEDING NOSE AND UNDERSHOT
—) LAYBACK
(PL.) MAW BITS THROAT
(PREF.) (UNDER —) GENYO
(SUFF.) GNATHA(E) GNATHI(A)(C)(SM)
GNATHOUS GNATHUS
JAWBONE JOWL WANG MAXILLA
CHAWBONE
(PREF.) MAXILLI MAXILLO
JAWBREAKING CRACKJAW
JAY JAYPIET SIRGANG BLUECOAT
MEATBIRD
JAYHAWK RAID
JAYHAWKER KANSAN
JAZERANT GESSERON
JAZZ BOP HYPE JIVE BEBOP HOTCHA
RICKYTICK
(— DATE) GIG
JEALOUS YELLOW EMULOUS
ENVIOUS
JEALOUSY ENVY YELLOWS
EMULATION ZELOTYPIA
JEAN FROCKING
**JEAN-CHRISTOPHE (AUTHOR OF
—)** ROLLAND
(CHARACTER IN —) ADA JEAN
GRAZIA KRAFFT LOUISA MICHEL
COLETTE LORCHEN OLIVIER
STEVENS MELCHIOR GRUNEBAUM

JEANPAULIA BAIERA
JEATERAI (FATHER OF —) ZERAH
JECHOLIAH (HUSBAND OF —) AMAZIAH
  (SON OF —) UZZIAH AZARIAH
JEDAIAH (FATHER OF —) HARUMAPH
JEDIAEL (FATHER OF —) SHIMRI MESHELEMIAH
JEDIDAH (HUSBAND OF —) AMON
  (SON OF —) JOSIAH
JEEP PEEP SEEP BANTAM
JEER BOB BOO MOB GECK GIBE GIRD JAPE JEST JIBE MOCK SKIT WIPE FLIRT FLOUT FLUTE FLYTE FRUMP GLAIK LAUGH SCOFF SCOMM SNEER TAUNT CHIACK DERIDE BARRACK RIDICULE
JEERING BIRD FLOUT DERISIVE
JEEVES VALET
JEHALELEL (SON OF —) AZARIAH
JEHIEL (BROTHER OF —) JEHORAM
  (FATHER OF —) HOTHAN HACHMONI JEHOSHAPHAT
  (SON OF —) GIBEON OBADIAH SHECHANIAH
JEHIZKIAH (FATHER OF —) SHALLUM
JEHOADDAN (HUSBAND OF —) JOASH
  (SON OF —) AMAZIAH
JEHOAHAZ (FATHER OF —) JEHU JOSIAH JEHORAM
  (SON OF —) JEHOASH
JEHOASH (FATHER OF —) AHAZIAH JEHOAHAZ
JEHOHANAN (SON OF —) ISHMAEL
JEHOIACHIN (FATHER OF —) JEHOIAKIM
JEHOIADA (FATHER OF —) PASEACH
  (SON OF —) BENAIAH
  (WIFE OF —) JEHOSHEBA
JEHOIAKIM (FATHER OF —) JOSIAH
  (SON OF —) JEHOIACHIN
JEHONADAB (FATHER OF —) RECHAB
JEHONATHAN (FATHER OF —) UZZIAH
JEHORAM (BROTHER OF —) AHAZIAH
  (FATHER OF —) AHAB JEHOSHAPHAT
  (SLAYER OF —) JEHU
  (WIFE OF —) ATHALIAH
JEHOSHAPHAT (FATHER OF —) ASA AHILUD NIMSHI PARUAH
  (SON OF —) JEHU JEHORAM
JEHOSHEBA (FATHER OF —) JORAM
  (HUSBAND OF —) JEHOIADA
  (SON OF —) JOASH
JEHOVAH JAH LORD JAHVE YAHWEH
  (— WITNESS) PIONEER
JEHOZABAD (FATHER OF —) OBEDEDOM
  (MOTHER OF —) SHOMER SHIMRITH

JEHOZADAK (FATHER OF —) SERAIAH
  (SON OF —) JESHUA
JEHU (FATHER OF —) HANANI JOSIBIAH JEHOSHAPHAT
  (SON OF —) JEHOAHAZ
  (VICTIM OF —) JEHORAM
JEHUDI (FATHER OF —) NETHANIAH
JEHUSH (FATHER OF —) ESHEK
JEJUNE DRY ARID MEAGER INSIPID
JEKAMIAH (FATHER OF —) SHALLUM
JELL COME FIRM
  (INCENDIARY —) NAPALM
JELLY GEAL JEEL JELL GELEE CULLIS JUJUBE ALCOGEL FISNOGA GELATIN JELLIFY FLUMMERY HYDROGEL QUIDDANY MARMALADE
  (AGAR-AGAR —) KANTEN
  (CALF'S-FOOT —) SULZE
  (FRUIT —) ROB
  (INFLAMMABLE —) NAPALM
  (MEAT —) ASPIC
  (PREF.) GELATI
JELLYFISH JELLY QUARL CARVEL MEDUSA ACALEPH AURELIA BLUBBER MEDUSAN SLOBBER SUNFISH SCYPHULA SEACROSS STROBILA SEANETTLE
  (PART OF —) ARM BELL MOUTH MARGIN STOMACH TENTACLE UMBRELLA MANUBRIUM
  (PREF.) MEDUSI
JELLYLIKE SLABBY
JEMIMA (FATHER OF —) JOB
JEMMY BETTY JIMMY
JEMUEL (FATHER OF —) SIMEON
JENNET ASS
JENNY ASS MULE BETTY JINNY
JEOPARDIZE STAKE EXPOSE HAZARD IMPERIL ENDANGER
JEOPARDY RISK PERIL DANGER HAZARD
JEPHTHAH (FATHER OF —) GILEAD
JEPHUNNEH (SON OF —) CALEB
JEQUIRITY BEAN EYEN RUTTEE
JERAH (FATHER OF —) JOKTAN
JERAHMEEL (FATHER OF —) MAHLI HEZRON HAMMELECH
JERBOA GERBIL JUMPER
JERED (FATHER OF —) MAHALALEEL
  (SON OF —) ENOCH
JEREED TZIRID
JEREMIAD LAMENT TRAGEDY
JEREMIAH (DAUGHTER OF —) HAMUTAL
  (FATHER OF —) HILKIAH
  (SON OF —) JAZANIAH
JEREMOTH (SON OF —) ELAM HEMAN MUSHI ZATTU
JERIMOTH (DAUGHTER OF —) MAHALATH
  (FATHER OF —) BELA DAVID HEMAN MUSHI AZRIEL BECHER

JERIOTH (HUSBAND OF —) CALEB
JERK BOB GAG JET NUD TIT BOUT
CANT DINK DORK FIRK GIRD HIKE
JERT JIRT JOLT JOUK KICK NERD
PECK PUTZ SNAP SNIG YANK YERK
BRAID CHUCK DWEEB FLIRT HITCH
HOICK SCHMO SLIRT SNAKE SPANG
SPASM SURGE TWEAK TWICK FILLIP
JIGGER SCHMOE SHMUCK SWITCH
TWITCH WRENCH FLOUNCE
SACCADE SADSACK SCHMUCK
SPANGHEW SCHLEMIEL
JERKED MEAT TASAJO
JERKILY HITCHILY
JERKIN SAYON JACKET
JERKY NERVY SHARP CHOPPY
ELBOIC FLICKY FLINGY HITCHY
JIGGETY CHOPPING PALMODIC
RATCHETY SACCADIC
JEROBOAM REHOBOAM
(FATHER OF —) JOASH NEBAT
(WIFE OF —) ANO
JEROHAM (FATHER OF —) PASHUR
(SON OF —) ADAIAH AZAREEL
AZARIAH ELKANAH IBNEIAH
JERSEY FROCK SHIRT GANSEY
TRICOT ZEPHYR MAILLOT SINGLET
CAMISOLE GUERNSEY
JERUSALEM ZION ARIEL SOLYMA
AHOLIBAH
JERUSALEM ARTICHOKE TUBER
CANADA GIRASOL
JERUSALEM CHERRY SOLANUM
JERUSALEM DELIVERED
(AUTHOR OF —) TASSO
(CHARACTER IN —) HUGH OTHO
SWENO ARMIDA OLINDO ALADINE
ERMINIA GODFREY RINALDO
TANCRED ARGANTES BOUILLON
CLORINDA SOLIMANO SOPHRONIA
JERUSALEM OAK AMBROSIA
JERUSALEM SAGE PHLOMIS
SAGELEAF
JERUSALEM THORN CASCOL
RETAMA
JERUSHA (FATHER OF —) ZADOK
(HUSBAND OF —) UZZIAH
JESAIAH (BROTHER OF —)
PELATIAH
(FATHER OF —) HANANIAH
JESHAIAH (FATHER OF —)
JEDUTHUN REHABIAH
(MOTHER OF —) ATHALIAH
JESHARELAH (FATHER OF —)
ASAPH
JESHER (FATHER OF —) CALEB
(MOTHER OF —) AZUBAH
JESIAH (FATHER OF —) UZZIEL
JESSAMINE JASMINE WOODBINE
JESSE (FATHER OF —) OBED
(SON OF —) DAVID
JESSICA (FATHER OF —) SHYLOCK
(HUSBAND OF —) LORENZO

JEST BAR BOG COD COG FUN GAB
JOE TAX BULL GAME GAUD GIRD
JAPE JOKE JOSH PLAY QUIP QUIZ
RAIL SKIT BOURD BREAK CHAFF
CLOWN DROLL FLIRT GESTE GLEEK
SPORT THING BANTER GLANCE
JAPERY RAILLY TRIFLE DICTERY
GAMMOCK JOLLITY WAGGERY
DROLLERY RAILLERY
(— SPITEFULLY) SLENT
JESTER FOOL MIME BUFFO CLOWN
DROLL IDIOT JAPER JOKER PATCH
WAMBA DISOUR MOTLEY YORICK
BADCHAN BOURDER BUFFOON
DIZZARD DROLLER JOCULAR
JUGGLER PICADOR SCOFFER
SCOGGIN TOMTRAM MERRYMAN
OWLGLASS PLEASANT RAILLEUR
TRINCULO
JESTING DROLL JAPERY SCOPTIC
WAGGISH
(COARSE —) RIBALDRY
(RUDELY —) INFICETE
JESUI (FATHER OF —) ASHER
JESUIT PAULIST TERTIAN IGNATIAN
LOYOLITE
JESUS GEE GIS IHC IHS JHS YHS
JESU WISDOM
(SAYINGS OF —) AGRAPHA
JET SST BOLT NOIR TAIL TANG BREAK
DUMBY DUMMY JETTO SALLY
SCOOT SPOUT SPRAY SPURT AIRBUS
CANDLE DELUGE DOUCHE GAGATE
SQUIRT FANTAIL JETTEAU SPATTER
SPURTER FOUNTAIN SOFFIONE
UPSPRING
(— OF FLAME) TONGUE
(— OF METAL) BREAK
(— OF VOLCANIC STEAM) STUFA
(KIND OF —) JUMP LEAR PLASMA
(SMALL —) SQUIB
(SUBSONIC —) AIRBUS
JET-BLACK BUGLE
JETHER (FATHER OF —) EZRA JADA
GIDEON
(SON-IN-LAW OF —) MOSES
(SON OF —) AMASA
JETHRO (DAUGHTER OF —)
ZIPPORAH
(SON-IN-LAW OF —) MOSES
JETTING SALIENT
JETTISON DUMP DITCH JETSAM
JETTY JET PEN DIKE PIER GROIN
JUTTY BRIDGE OVERHANG
JEUSH (FATHER OF —) ESAU BILHAN
REHOBOAM
(MOTHER OF —) AHOLIBAMAH
JEW SAINT ESSENE JUDEAN LITVAK
SEMITE SMOUCH SMOUSE TOBIAD
BARABAS GRECIAN KARAITE
MARRANO APIKOROS CONVERSO
GALICIAN JUDAHITE LANDSMAN
SEPHARDI

(—6 OUT OF ISRAEL) DIASPORA
(BALKAN —) LADINO
JEWEL GEM JOY DROP OUCH BIJOU
REGAL STONE BROOCH GEORGE
TRIFLE CRAPAUD GARI AND
POUNDER
(MATCHING SET OF —S) PARURE
(PL.) BULSE PERRIE
JEWELER GEMMARY LAPIDARY
JEWELRY ICE JUNK OUCH PARURE
COLLARET LAPIDARY
(CHEAP — MATERIAL) OROIDE
(MOCK —) LOGIE
(PIECE OF —) GAUD
JEWELS OF THE MADONNA
(CHARACTER IN —) GENNARO
MALIELLA RAFFAELE
(COMPOSER OF —) WOLFFERRARI
JEWELWEED CEROLINE EARJEWEL
SNAPWEED
JEWFISH MERO GUASA WARSAW
PERCOID JUNEFISH MULLOWAY
SERRANID
JEWISH JUDAIC SEMITIC
(— BODY) VAAD
(— COMMUNITY) KEHILLAH
(— QUARTER) MELLAH
(— SCHOOL) ALJAMA
(PREF.) JUDAEO JUDEO
JEW OF MALTA (AUTHOR OF —)
MARLOWE
(CHARACTER IN —) JACOMO MARTIN
ABIGAIL BARABAS MATHIAS
CALYMATH ITHAMORE LODOWICK
BELLAMIRA BERNARDINE
JEWRY GHETTO JUDAISM
JEW'S-HARP HARP TROMP TRUMP
GEWGAW FLAMFEW TRANGAM
GUIMBARD
JEW'S MALLOW DESI
JEZANIAH (FATHER OF —)
HOSHAIAH
JEZEBEL GILLIVER
(FATHER OF —) ETHBAAL
(HUSBAND OF —) AHAB
(SLAYER OF —) JEHU
JEZER (FATHER OF —) NAPHTALI
JEZOAR (FATHER OF —) ASHER
(MOTHER OF —) HELAH
JEZREEL (FATHER OF —) HOSEA
JIB GIB BALK BAULK DEMUR GIGUE
STICK GIBBET SPITFIRE
JIBE (ALSO SEE GIBE) FIT GEE KAY
GAFF GIBE JAPE JERK MOCK SKIT
AGREE FLIRD MARCH SNACK
SQUARE THRUST
JIBSAM (FATHER OF —) TOLA
JIDLAPH (FATHER OF —) NAHOR
JIFFY SEC JIFF BRAID FLISK WHIFF
GLIFFY GLIFFING
JIG BUCK FRISK GIGUE SQUID
GARLIC JIGGER JIGGET JITTER
LOCATOR

(— FOR WASHING ORE) HUTCH
(FISHING —) PILK
JIGGER SHOT DANDY PIQUE
DOODAD GADGET JIGMAN VATMAN
CHIGGER
JIGGLE DIDDLE JUGGLE TEETER
JIHAD WAR JEHAD STRIFE CRUSADE
JILT GUNK KICK SACK BEGOWK
BEGUNK MITTEN
JIMMY PRY OPEN BETTY JAMES
JEMMY ·
JIMNA (FATHER OF —) ASHER
JIMSONWEED DATURA DEWTRY
JIMSON FIREWEED STRAMONY
JINGLE TUNE CHIME CHINK CLINK
DINGLE RICKLE TINKLE CHINKLE
CLERIHEW DINGDONG JINGLING
(MEANINGLESS —) SPORT
JINGLING SMIT JANGLE RIGADIG
TINKLING
JINGO WARRIOR WARMONGER
JINGOISM CHAUVINISM
JINKER WHIM
JINN DJIN JANN AFRIT EBLIS GENIE
AFREET DJINNI SHAITAN
(PL.) JINNI
JINNI MARID AFREET ALUKAH
GENIUS YAKSHA YAKSHI JINNIYEH
JINRIKIMAN KURUMAYA
JINRIKISHA GOCART KURUMA
RICKSHAW
JINX HEX JONAH HOODOO WHAMMY
JIPIJAPA CHIDRA PANAMA PALMILLA
TOQUILLA
JITTERBUG TRUCKING
JITTERY EDGY JUMPY TENSE
SPOOKY AJITTER ILLATEASE
JIVARO JIBARO SHUARA XIBARO
JIVE BOP ROCK
JIVER HEPCAT
JOAB (BROTHER OF —) ASAHEL
ABISHAI
(MOTHER OF —) ZERUIAH
(SLAYER OF —) BENAIAH
(UNCLE OF —) DAVID
(VICTIM OF —) ABNER
JOAH (FATHER OF —) ASAPH JOAHAZ
ZIMMAH OBEDEDOM
(SON OF —) EDEN
JOAHAZ (SON OF —) JOAH ·
JOAN JUG JONE
(— OF ARC) PUCELLE
JOANNA (FATHER OF —) RHESA
(HUSBAND OF —) CHUZA
JOASH (FATHER OF —) AHAB BECHER
AHAZIAH SHEMAAH JEHOAHAZ
(SON OF —) GIDEON
(VICTIM OF —) ZECHARIAH
JOB LAY TUT CHAR CRIB FIST SHOP
TURN BERTH CHORE FIRST PLACE
BILLET HOBJOB HUSTLE JOBSITE
SWEATER BUSINESS POSITION
(EASY —) BLUDGE

(FATHER OF —) ISSACHAR
(HIGH-PAYING EASY —) PLUM
(KIND OF —) NOSE
(SMALL —) CHORE JOBBLE
JOBAB (FATHER OF —) JOKTAN
JOBBER BRAGER DEALER FLUNKY
BROGGER COURSER
JOB'S TEARS COIX ADLAI ADLAY
JOCHEBED (HUSBAND OF —)
AMRAM
(SON OF —) AARON MOSES
JOCKEY JOCK RIDER ROPER WASTER
CHANTER EQUISON TURFITE
SKIPJACK
(— FOR POSITION) DICE
(DISC —) DEEJAY
JOCOSE JOCO LEPID JOCULAR
PLAYFUL
JOCOTE MOMBIN
JOCOTE DE MICO BARBAS
JOCULAR GAY AIRY GLAD JOKY
DROLL FUNNY HAPPY JOLLY MERRY
WITTY BLITHE ELATED JAPISH
JOCOSE JOCUND JOKISH JOVIAL
JOYFUL JOYOUS LIVELY BUOYANT
COMICAL FESTIVE GLEEFUL PLAYFUL
WAGGISH ANIMATED CHEERFUL
DEBONAIR GLADSOME HUMOROUS
JOCATORY JOKESOME LAUGHING
MIRTHFUL BURLESQUE
JOCULARITY FUN WAGGERY
JOCUND BUDGE MERRY JOCANT
JOCULAR
JOE JO
(HALF —) JOANNES JOHANNES
JOED (FATHER OF —) PEDAIAH
JOEL (BROTHER OF —) NATHAN
(FATHER OF —) NEBO SAMUEL ZICHRI
PEDAIAH PETHUEL IZRAHIAH
(SON OF —) HEMAN
JOELAH (FATHER OF —) JEROHAM
JOE-PYE WEED EUPATORY
JOEWOOD JOEBUSH BARBASCO
IRONWOOD
JOG BOB HOD JAG JIG JOT MOG KICK
LOPE POKE SHOG SPUD STIR TROT
WHIG DUNCH HOTCH MOSEY NUDGE
TWEAK DIDDLE JITTER JOGGLE
JUNDIE
(— ALONG) FADGE FODGE
(— AWKWARDLY) DODGE
(— WITH ELBOW) DUNCH
JOGGER LOPER LAYBOY RUNNER
JOGGLE HOTCH JUGGLE SHOGGLE
SHOOGLE
JOGLI (SON OF —) BUKKI
JOHA (FATHER OF —) BERIAH
JOHANAN (FATHER OF —) JOSIAH
KAREAH TOBIAH AZARIAH ELIOENAI
HAKKATAN
(SON OF —) AZARIAH
JOHANNES JOE PECA

JOHN IAN JEAN JOCK JONE JUAN
SEAN JOHANN SEAGHAN GIOVANNI
(BROTHER OF —) JAMES
(FATHER OF —) ZEBEDEE ZACHARIAS
(MOTHER OF —) SALOME ELISABETH
JOHN BROWN'S BODY (AUTHOR
OF —) BENET
(CHARACTER IN —) CLAY JACK LUCY
LUKE DUPRE SALLY SOPHY SPADE
VILAS ELLYAT MELORA SHIPPY
WINGATE WEATHERBY
BRECKINRIDGE
JOHNNYCAKE CORNCAKE
JOIADA (FATHER OF —) ELIASHIB
JOIAKIM (FATHER OF —) JESHUA
JOIN ADD COP FAY MIX OUP PAN TAG
TIE UNY ALLY COPE FUSE GAIN
GLUE KNIT LINK MEET MELL SEAM
SOUD TAIL TEAM YOKE ANNEX
BLEND ENTER FRANK FUSE JOINT
MERGE TENON UNITE WRING
ACCEDE ADJECT ADJOIN ASSIST
ATTACH CEMENT COCKET COMMIT
CONCUR ENGAGE INDENT JOGGLE
MARROW MINGLE PIECEN RELATE
RELIDE SPLICE STITCH STRIKE
COMBINE CONJOIN CONNECT
CONTACT INJOINT JOINING MORTISE
SHACKLE ACCOUPLE COALESCE
COMPOUND COPULATE DOVETAIL
JUNCTION ACCOMPANY
COMPAGINATE
(— BATTLE) JOUST ENGAGE
(— BY SEWING) STITCH SUTURE
(— CLOSELY) FAY AFFY WELD GRAFT
(— IN COMBAT) BUCKLE
(— IN MARRIAGE) WED TACK HITCH
COUPLE
(— MECHANICALLY) DOCK
(— THE PARTS OF) PIECE
(— TOGETHER) CLOSE COAPT FRANK
HITCH COUPLE ENGLUE ENJOIN
ASSEMBLE COAGMENT COALESCE
(— UP) ACCEDE
(PREF.) ARTIO
JOINED JOINT ALLIED DIRECT
SEAMED ACCOLLE ADJUNCT
APPINED EMBOITE ADJUGATE
COMBINED CONJUNCT COPULATE
INTEGRAL
(PREF.) GAM(ETO)(O) ZEUCTO
ZEUGLO
JOINER SNUG WRIGHT JOINTER
JOINING BAR JOIN SEAM BRIDE
CLOSE SPLICE BETWEEN JOINDER
ADDITION JUNCTION JUNCTIVE
JUNCTURE SYNECTIC
JOINT BED HAR HIP JAY BUTT COXA
FISH HEAD HELL HOCK JOIN KNEE
LITH LOCK SEAL SEAM TUCK ANKLE
BRAZE BUILD CARDO CHASE ELBOW
MITER MITRE PLACE SCAPE SCARF

SPALD UNION UNITE WRIST BOXING
COMMON HAUNCH MUTUAL
SCARPH SPLICE STIFLE SUTURE
TOGGLE UNITER ARTHRON ARTICLE
COGGING DIGITAL FETLOCK
FLEXURE ISCHIUM JOINING
KNUCKLE SCATTER SHIPLAP
SIAMESE CONJOINT CONJUNCT
COUPLING DIACLASE DOVETAIL
FLASHING JOINTURE JUNCTURE
SUBJOINT SUFFRAGO TROCHOID
VARIATOR
(— ABOVE HOCK) STIFLE
(— OF APPENDAGE) SEGMENT
(— OF BIRD'S WING) FLEXURE
(— OF FLAIL) CAPEL
(—OF INSECT LEG) PHALANX
(— OF MEAT) BARON SADDLE
(— OF SHIP) CHASE
(— OF STEM) NODE
(ANKLE —) COOT
(ELBOW —) NOOP
(FLEXIBLE —) HINGE
(GROOVED —) RABBET
(HIP —) COXA THURL
(MASONRY —) JOGGLE
(MINING —) CLEAT SLINE
(QUARRYING —) CUTTER
(SCARF —) BOXING
(THE —) STIR PRISON
(UNIVERSAL —) CARDAN
(VERTICAL —) BUILD
(WHEEL-LIKE —) TROCHITE
(PREF.) ARTHR(O) ARTI CO CONDYL(O)
HARMO HOM(O)
JOINTED ARTHROUS
JOINTED CHARLOCK KRAUT
RUNCH
JOINTER JOINER SKIMMER
JOINT FIR EPHEDRA
JOINT GRASS PASPALUM
JOINTLY
(PREF.) CO COL COM CON COR
JOINTURE DOWER
JOIST GEEST LEDGE BRIDGE RAGLIN
DORMANT SLEEPER CARRIAGE
(PL.) PIGGIN JOISTING
JOJOBA PIGNUT SHEEPNUT
JOKE BAR DOR FUN GAB GAG GIG
JOE KID ROT WIT YAK YUK FOOL
GAFF GAME GAUD GEGG JAPE JEST
JOSH LICE NOTE QUIP QUIZ TYPE
YUCK YUCK BREAK CRACK FLIRT
GLEEK GRIND LAUGH PRANK RALLY
SPORT TRICK BANTER JAPERY
PLISKY WHEEZE JOKELET WAGGERY
CHESTNUT
(— COLLECTION) ANA
(PRACTICAL —) BAR FUN GAG RIG
HOAX REAK SHAVIE HOTFOOT
(STALE —) GROANER CHESTNUT
(PL.) JAPERY

JOKER BUG DOR WAG CARD CLOWN
GRIND SLAVE FARCER FOOLER
GAGGER JOKIST FARCEUR GIMMICK
FUNNYMAN HUMORIST JOKESTER
JOKESTER WAG WIT
JOKIM (FATHER OF —) SHELAH
JOKING JOSH BANTER JOCOSE
(PRACTICAL —) GAME
JOKSHAN (FATHER OF —) ABRAHAM
(MOTHER OF —) KETURAH
(SON OF —) DEDAN SHEBA
JOKTAN (FATHER OF —) EBER
JOLLIFICATION RAG RANT BEANO
JOLLY SINDIG
JOLLITY MIRTH GAIETY HILARITY
JOLLITRY
JOLLY GAY KID BOON BUXOM
GAWSY MERRY RORTY SONSY
WALLY BLITHE CROUSE JOVIAL
STRING JOCULAR RAUGHTY
DISPOSED
JOLLY BOAT YAWL DANDY
JOLT JAR JET JIG JOG JOT JUT BELT
BUMP DIRD DIRL HIKE JOWL JUMP
KICK SHOG JAUNT HOTTER IMPACT
JOGGLE JOSTLE JOUNCE JUMBLE
JOLTING JERKY BUMPITY HOTTERY
JONA (SON OF —) PETER
JONADAB (COUSIN OF —) AMNON
(FATHER OF —) SHIMEAH
(UNCLE OF —) DAVID
JONAH JINX JONAS HOODOO
(FATHER OF —) AMITTAI
JONAN (FATHER OF —) ELIAKIM
JONATHAN (BROTHER OF —)
JOHANAN
(COMPANION OF —) DAVID
(FATHER OF —) SAUL ASAHEL
JOIADA KAREAH ABIATHAR
(SON OF —) MEPHIBOSHETH
JONES HABIT HEROIN ADDICTION
(ARCHITECT —) INIGO
JONQUIL JONK LILY DAFFODIL
JORAM (FATHER OF —) TOI AHAB
JEHOSHAPHAT

JORDAN
CAPITAL: AMMAN
COIN: DINAR
GULF: AQABA
MOUNTAIN: BUKKA DABAB ATAIDA
MUBRAK
REGION: PEREA BASHAN PERAEA
RIVER: HOR JORDAN YARMUK
TOWN: AQABA ARIHA IRBID KARAK
ZARQA ZERKE NABLUS JERICHO

JORIM (FATHER OF —) MATTHAT
JOSE (FATHER OF —) ELIEZER
JOSEPH JOSEY GIUSEPPE
(FATHER OF —) HELI JACOB JUDAH
MATTATHIAS

(MOTHER OF —) RACHEL
(SON OF —) IGAL JESUS
(WIFE OF —) MARY ASENATH
JOSEPH ANDREWS
(AUTHOR OF —) FIELDING
(CHARACTER IN —) ADAMS BOOBY
FANNY PETER JOSEPH PAMELA
POUNCE THOMAS WILSON
ANDREWS GOODWILL SLIPSLOP
JOSEPHINE BLUSH PHENY
JOSEPH VANCE
(AUTHOR OF —) DEMORGAN
(CHARACTER IN —) JOE BONY JANEY
NOLLY SIBYL VANCE JOSEPH LOSSIE
THORPE VIOLET BEPPINO DESPREZ
PHEENER RANDALL SPENCER
PERCEVAL CHRISTOPHER
MACALLISTER
JOSES (BROTHER OF —) JESUS
(FATHER OF —) ELIEZER
JOSH GUY KID RIB JEST JOKE CHAFF
STRING
JOSHAVIAH (FATHER OF —)
ELNAAM
JOSHBEKASHAH (FATHER OF —)
HEMAN
JOSHI JOTI JOTISARU
JOSHUA JESUS
(FATHER OF —) NUN JOZADAK
JOSIAH (FATHER OF —) AMON
ZEPHANIAH
(MOTHER OF —) JEDIDAH
JOSIBIAH (SON OF —) JEHU
JOSTLE JOG JOLT JOSS PUSH SHOG
CROWD ELBOW HUNCH JUNDY
SHOVE HURTLE HUSTLE JOGGLE
JUNDIE JUSTLE SHOULDER
JOSTLING SCRAMBLE
JOT ACE DOT ATOM IOTA MARK MITE
TARE WHIT GRAIN MINIM POINT
TWINT WIGHT TITTLE SCRUPLE
SMIDGEN SYLLABLE
(— DOWN) NICK
JOTHAM (FATHER OF —) GIDEON
UZZIAH
(MOTHER OF —) JERUSHAH
JOTTING TOT
JOTUNN GEIRROTH
JOUNCE HIKE JOLT JAUNT
JOURNAL TOE BOOK DIARY PAPER
BLAZER SERIAL DAYBOOK DIURNAL
GAZETTE GUDGEON JOURNEY
CASHBOOK NOCTUARY TRUNNION
(SEA —) LOGBOOK
JOURNAL BEARING RHODING
JOURNALISM NEWSWRITING
JOURNALIST SCRIBE WRITER
BYLINER DIARIAN
AMERICAN BLY DIX NEW BAER BAUM
CAIN CAPA CERF CHEW COBB CONY
CROW DALY DANA DREW EDEL EDGE
GELB HOWE HUIE HUNT IDOE KENT
LOEB MOTT OTIS OWEN PAGE PAUL

PECK POST PRAY PYLE RAAB REED
REID ROSS SANN SNOW WALN
WEBB WEED WIND ADAMS ALSOP
BACHE BAKER BEACH BEALS BEEBE
BENET BRANN BROUN CANBY CREEL
DUANE EARLY ELSER FISKE FLYNN
GREEN GUILD HABER HARTE HOPPE
HOUSE IRWIN JAMES KEOGH KROCK
LAHEY LASKY LEWIS LOCKE MCCOY
MEANS MOLEY MOORE MORSE
NOVAK NOYES OGDEN OHARA
OMARR PAINE PIATT POORE PRIME
QUINN RALPH REEDY ROWAN
ROYKO SAXON SCALI SIDEY SOBOL
STONE STOWE SWING SWOPE TIEDE
TOWLE TWAIN UPTON UTLEY WALSH
WHITE WILLE YOUNG ZEVIN ALLSOP
ASBURY BAILEY BIERCE BIRNIE
BISHOP BLIVEN BONSAL BOWERS
BOWLES BUGBEE BURMAN CAPUTO
CHILDS CROUSE DECTER FOWLER
GILDER GILMER GODWIN GRAHAM
GRAVES GREENE HAMILL HARSCH
HARVEY HASKIN HATTON HERSEY
HICKOK HOWARD HOWELL KEIRAN
KENNAN KNEBEL LAFFAN LAWSON
LELAND LUBELL MANNES MANTLE
MARDEN MEDILL MILLER MILLIS
MOLLOY MORRIS MORTON MOWRER
NELSON NEWELL PEGLER REDMAN
RESTON RIDDER RUNYON SAFIRE
SAVAGE SEAMAN SEATON SELDES
SHIRER STREIT TAYLOR TERKEL
TILTON TOLAND TUCKER TURNER
WALKER WALTER WARMAN WIESEL
WILCOX WILSON YARMON ANTHONY
AXTHELM BARRETT BIGELOW
BOMBECK BRENNAN BULLARD
CARROLL CONNIFF DANIELS DREIFUS
EASTMAN EDWARDS FARRELL
FEARING FISCHER FREEMAN
FRENEAU GALLICO GARRETT
GERVASI GIBBONS GREELEY
GUNTHER HALLOCK HASSARD
HELOISE KENDALL LOSSING
MANNING MARQUIS MELONEY
OCONNOR OURSLER OVERTON
POLLARD PRINGLE RANDALL
RAYMOND REDPATH RITCHIE
RUSSELL SANBORN SERVISS
SMALLEY STANTON VANLOON
VEILLER VILLARD WELLMAN
WHEELER WOLFERT YARDLEY
BROWNELL BUCHWALD CREELMAN
JOHNSTON LAWRENCE LIPPMANN
MCINTYRE MCKELWAY MEREDITH
PULITZER ROBINSON STARRETT
STEFFENS STILLMAN STODDARD
SULLIVAN THOMPSON TOWNSEND
WESTCOTT WHITLOCK WILLIAMS
BENEFIELD BERNSTEIN MACDONALD
MARCOSSON MCCORMICK
MOREHOUSE PATTERSON

WATTERSON WOOLLCOTT
CHAMBERLIN WEITZENKORN
ARGENTINIAN AVELLANEDA
AUSTRALIAN DONALD WARNER
FAWKNER PATERSON MOOREHEAD
AUSTRIAN BAHR SEIDL HEVESI
SAPHIR CASTELLI
BRAZILIAN BANDEIRA
CANADIAN LAUT RYAN BROWN
DAFOE BOWELL BRIAND DUNTON
HEWITT RASKIN PAASSEN WHITMAN
DECELLES SINCLAIR FRECHETTE
CZECH CAPEK NERUDA HAVLICEK
DANISH PALUDAN JORGENSEN
GOLDSCHMIDT
DUTCH SCHIMMEL
ENGLISH LOW MEE BELL FOOT FYFE
GORE HARE LANE LUCY MAIS SALA
SIMS TOYE ARRAN BANKS BLAKE
COTES CROWE DICEY DORAN GIBBS
LEMON LEVIN LEWIS LOCKE MIALL
MOULT SCOTT SHIEL STEAD STEED
WERTH ARKELL ARNOLD BAINES
BANGOR BARKER BEGBIE BENHAM
BOADEN BROOKS BUCKLE CANTON
CASTLE CHIROL DARWIN DILLON
DIVINE FORBES GARVIN GIBBON
HANNAY MACKAY MANNIN MAYHEW
MORLEY MURRAY NORMAN REEVES
SQUIRE TRAILL WATSON BENTLEY
BOLITHO BURGESS BYWATER
CARLILE CHORLEY COBBETT
DURANTY ENNEVER GILLOTT
HAMMOND HASKELL HERBERT
HORABIN LEHMANN MEYNELL
MITFORD ROBERTS SHORTER
SPENDER STANLEY WALLACE
BAERLEIN CARSWELL CHISHOLM
COCKBURN COURTNEY FLETCHER
HOBHOUSE LAWRENCE LOCKHART
MONTAGUE MORRISON ROBINSON
SLOCOMBE STEEVENS STRACHEY
TOWNSEND WOODFALL BLANCHARD
COLERIDGE COLQUHOUN
CRANKSHAW GREENWOOD
LESTRANGE MACDONELL
MONYPENNY THORNBURY
BALLANTYNE BRAILSFORD
CHATTERTON CHESTERTON
FONBLANQUE HUDDLESTON
MASSINGHAM THURSFIELD
HOLLINGSHEAD
FRENCH BLUM KARR MACE PUJO
BULOZ CAPUS CLAIR DUPUY GOSSE
GRIMM HAMEL HAVES HERVE MEYER
MILLE SOREL STEEG VERON BABEUF
BERTIN BODARD CARNOT CARREL
DAUDET DELORD DUCAMP FONTAN
FRERON GOZLAN HEBERT LEROUX
MAZADE NISARD PICHON ROMIER
SARCEY SCHWOB UZANNE BRISSOT
CARRERE CHARMES GENOUDE
HAUREAU LARBAUD LINGUET

MATHIEU MICHAUD MIRBEAU
NALECHE RECOULY REINACH
REYBAUD SCHERER SIMONDS
TABOUIS TILLIER VIARDOT
CALMETTE CLARETIE DUJARDIN
GIRARDIN GUEROULT JOUVENEL
MAZELINE NEFFTZER PELLETAN
PERTINAX PROUDHON QUILLARD
RENAUDOT RIVAROLI VEUILLOT
BAINVILLE CAILLAVET CAVAIGNAC
DESCHAMPS MIRECOURT
ROCHEFORT SAUERWEIN VACQUERIE
BARTHELEMY DESMOULINS
LACRETELLE MONTLOSIER
TASCHEREAU TAILLANDIER
MONTALEMBERT
GERMAN LONS BUSCH GIDAL
THOMA BECKER DREYER EISNER
GEROLD GORRES GROSSE GUBITZ
HARDEN ZENGER BARTELS FRANZOS
GUTZKOW HAMMANN KALISCH
MARTENS BERNHARD FRAENKEL
ROHRBACH LIEBNECHT SCHUCKING
STREICHER BEUMELBURG
POSCHINGER
HUNGARIAN BAJZA HERZL BALAZS
HUSZAR MORICZ RAKOSI
INDIAN ABBAS MEHTA
IRISH BELL LYND WEST CONNOR
LESLIE OBRIEN OKELLY PIGOTT
DESMOND OCONNOR ROLLESTON
ITALIAN NENNI ANCONA MONETA
FALLACI MORAVIA BALTISTI
ALBERTINI FEDERZONI
JAPANESE HEARN INUKAI
FUKUZAWA KAWAKAMI
NEW ZEALAND BALLANCE
NORWEGIAN FINNE VINJE
BRATTELI
PARAGUAYAN BENITEZ
PERUVIAN CANDAMO
RUSSIAN KATKOV SHUKOV
CHERNOV NOVIKOV DOBROLYUBOV
SCOTTISH BELL DENT REID BLACK
CALER MUNRO FORBES CHALMERS
CARRUTHERS
SOUTH AFRICAN WOODS
SWEDISH MYRDAL THORILD
STRANDBERG
SWISS DROZ FAZY MEYER MURET
GIROUD DUCOMMUN
WELSH EVANS CUDLIPP
JOURNEY BE GO JOG RUN WAY DIET
EYRE FARE FORE GAIT GANG GATE
HIKE JUMP RACE RAIK RIDE ROAD
STEP TOUR TREK TRIP TURN WENT
BROAD COVER DRIVE JAUNT REISE
SITHE THAIK TRAIL TURUS WEENT
COMINO ERRAND FLIGHT HEGIRA
JUNKET TRAVEL VAGARY EMBASSY
ENTRADA EXCURSE JORNADA
JOURNAL MEANDER PASSAGE
STRETCH TRAVAIL TROUNCE

WALKING WAYFARE GODSPEED
PROGRESS PILGRIMAGE
(— BY SEA) VOYAGE
(— DOWNSTREAM) DESCEND
(DAY'S —) DIET
(DESERT —) JORNADA
(FATIGUING —) TRAIK
(LONG —) TREK
(PART OF —) LEG
(TEDIOUS —) TRANCE
(PL.) PERIPATETICS
JOURNEYING CRUISE
JOURNEYMAN YEOMAN
JOUST PLAY TILT JOSTLE JUSTLE
TOURNEY
JOUSTER TILTER
JOVIAL GAY BOON JOVY BULLY
JOLLY MERRY GENIAL HEARTY
MELLOW WANTON BACCHIC
HOLIDAY JOCULAR CONVIVIAL
RANTIPOLE
JOVIALITY JOLLITY ROLLICK
HILARITY
JOWL CHOW CHAULE
(PL.) CHOPS
JOY JO WIN GLEE LIST PLAY BLISS
CHEER DREAM EXULT MIRTH REVEL
GAIETY HEYDAY DELIGHT ECSTASY
ELATION JOYANCE RAPTURE
REVELRY FELICITY GLADNESS
HILARITY PLEASURE
JOYFUL GAY GLAD BEAMY JOLLY
BLITHE FESTUS JOCUND JOVIAL
JOYANT JOYOUS GAUDFUL
GLADFUL GLEEFUL JOCULAR
GLADSOME
JOYFULLY FAIN FAINLY GLADLY
JOYOUSLY
JOYLESS DESOLATE LUSTLESS
UNBLITHE
JOYOUS GAY GLAD JOLLY MERRY
YOUSE BLITHE JOVIAL FESTIVE
GIOJOSO GLEEFUL JOCULAR
SMILING FRABJOUS FROHLICH
SUNSHINY
JOYOUSNESS HILARITY
JOYRIDE SPIN
JOY STICK CONTROL
JOZABAD (FATHER OF —) JESHUA
JOZACHAR (VICTIM OF —) JOASH
JUBAL (FATHER OF —) LAMECH
(MOTHER OF —) ADAH
JUBILANT ELATED JOYFUL
EXULTANT
JUBILATION JOY JOYANCE JUBILEE
JUDA (FATHER OF —) JOSEPH
HANANIAH
(MOTHER OF —) JOANNA
JUDAH (FATHER OF —) JACOB
(MOTHER OF —) LEAH
(SON OF —) ONAN
JUDAHITE JEW

JUDAISM JEWISM HEBRAISM
JUDAS TREE CERCIS
JUDEA JEWRY
JUDEO-SPANISH JUDESMO
JUDEZMO LADINO
**JUDE THE OBSCURE (AUTHOR OF
—)** HARDY
(CHARACTER IN —) SUE DONN JUDE
FAWLEY RICHARD ARABELLA
DRUSILLA BRIDEHEAD PHILLOTSON
JUDGE (ALSO SEE JURIST) DAN JUS
SEE WIG CADI CAID CAZY DEEM
DOOM HOLD IMAM JUEZ JURY KAZI
QADI RATE RULE SCAN AWARD
COUNT COURT DAYAN GAUGE
HAKIM INFER JUDEX MINOS OPINE
PUNEE TRIER WEIGH BREHON
CENSOR CRITIC DANIEL DECERN
DEEMER DICAST DOOMER INTEND
JUDGER JURIST OPINER PUISNE
SAMSON SAMUEL SETTLE SQUIRE
ACCOUNT ADJUDGE ALCALDE
ARBITER BENCHER BRIDOYE
CENSURE DISCERN FLAGMAN
FOUJDAR HELIAST JURYMAN
JUSTICE MUNSIFF PODESTA
REFEREE SCABINE SHAMGAR
SUPPOSE APPRAISE CENTENAR
CONCLUDE CONSIDER DEEMSTER
DEMPSTER DIRECTOR DOOMSMAN
DOOMSTER ESTIMATE FOREDEEM
JEPHTHAH JUDGMENT JUDICATE
LINESMAN MINISTER MITTIMUS
ORDINARY QUAESTOR RECORDER
REGICIDE SCABINUS STRADICO
(— OF UNDERWORLD) AEACUS
(PREF.) KRIT(O)
JUDGMENT ACT EYE BOOK DEEM
DOME DOOM REDE VIEW ARRET
AWARD FANCY JUISE SENSE SIGHT
SKILL TASTE ADVICE ASSIZE DECREE
ESTEEM JUWISE OUSTER STEVEN
ACCOUNT CENSURE CONCEIT
HOLDING OPINION THOUGHT
VERDICT WITTING DECISION
ESTIMATE JUDICIAL JUDICIUM
SAGACITY SAPIENCE SENTENCE
THINKING PREJUDICE OBSERVATION
(PREF.) GNOMO
JUDICATORY SYNOD
JUDICIOUS SAGE WISE POLITIC
PRUDENT CRITICAL JUDICIAL
MODERATE SENSEFUL SENSIBLE
WISELIKE
JUDITH (FATHER OF —) BEERI
(HUSBAND OF —) ESAU
JUDITH PARIS (AUTHOR OF —)
WALPOLE
(CHARACTER IN —) ADAM EMMA
JOHN CARDS DAVID PARIS STANE
JUDITH REUBEN WALTER WARREN
DOROTHY FRANCIS GAUNTRY

GEORGES HERRIES SUNWOOD
WILLIAM FORESTER JENNIFER
CHRISTABEL FERNYHIRST
JUDO (— EXERCISES) KATA
(— LEVEL) DAN
(— PRACTICE) RANDORI
(— SCHOOL) DOJO
(EXPERT LEVEL IN —) DAN
(EXPERT LEVEL OF —) DAN
JUG CAN EWER JACK JUST OLLA
ASCUS ASKOS BUIRE GAMLA GOTCH
JORUM JUBBE STEAN BOGGLE
CROUKE GOGLET GOMLAH HYDRIA
CREAMER PITCHER CRUISKEN
LECYTHUS LEKYTHOS OENOCHOE
PROCHOOS
(— FOR BEER) GROWLER
(— WITH SPOUT) BUIRE DOLLIN
(ALE —) TOBY
(BEER —) BOCK
(BULGING —) GOTCH
(CREAM —) POURER POURIE
(LEATHER —) JACK BOMBARD
(ONE-HANDLED —) URCEUS
(SPOUTLESS —) OLPE
JUGATED BAJOIRE
JUGGERNAUT IDOL
JUGGLE TRICK BAFFLE FUMBLE
CONJURE SHUFFLE
JUGGLER HARLOT CONJURER
JONGLEUR TREGETOUR
JUGGLERY GUILE HANKYPANKY
HOCUSPOCUS LEGERDEMAIN
JUGHEAD SAP
JUGLONE NUCIN
JUGULARES DERIPIA
JUGUM FIBULA JUGULUM
JUICE JUS SEW BREF BROO FOND
OOZE PULL SUCK ANIMA BLOND
BLOOD CLOUT GRAVY HUMOR
LASER MOBBY PERRY CASIRI
CREMOR JIPPER LIQUOR SUCCUS
CAMBIUM AGUAMIEL HYPOCIST
VERJUICE INFLUENCE
(— OF COCONUT) MILK
(— OF TREE) SAP LYCIUM JELUTONG
(— OF UNRIPE FRUIT) OMPHACY
(APPLE —) CIDER
(CANE —) SLING
(CASSAVA —) CASSAREEP
CASSARIPE
(CONCENTRATED —) SIRUP SYRUP
(DRIED —) ALOE KINO
(ETHEREAL —) ICHOR
(FERMENTED —) SURA GRAPE
(FRUIT —) ROB ROHOB
(GRAPE —) MUST SAPA STUM
(INSPISSATED —) HYPOCIST
(INTOXICATING —) SOMA
(LETTUCE —) THRIDACE
(MEAT —) BLOND
(POPPY —) CHICK MECONIUM

(TOBACCO —) AMBEER AMBIER
(VITAL —) SAP
(PL.) ESSENCE HUMIDITY
(PREF.) CHYL(I)(O) MYRO OPO
(SUFF.) CIDAL CIDE
JUICY FAT FRIM FRUM NAISH SAPPY
FRUITY SUCCOSE WATERISH
JUJUBE BER ELB TSAO LOTUS
LOTEBUSH LOTEWOOD ZIZYPHUS
JUKEBOX PICCOLO NICKELODEON
JULIUS CAESAR (AUTHOR OF —)
SHAKESPEARE
(CHARACTER IN —) CATO CASCA
CINNA CLITO PORTA VARRO BRUTUS
CAESAR CICERO CIMBER DECIUS
JULIUS LUCIUS MARCUS STRATO
CASSIUS FLAVIUS LEPIDUS
MESSALA PUBLIUS ANTONIUS
CLAUDIUS LIGARIUS LUCILIUS
MARULLUS METELLUS OCTAVIUS
PINDARUS POPILIUS TITINIUS
CALPURNIA DARDANIUS TREBONIUS
VOLUMNIUS ARTEMIDORUS
JUMBLE PI PIE ROG HASH MESS
MUSS RAFF BOTCH BOLLIX BUMBLE
FUDDLE GARBLE HUDDLE JABBLE
JUMPER JUNGLE MEDLEY MOMBLE
MUDDLE PALTER RAFFLE WELTER
WUZZLE CLUTTER CONFUSE
EMBROIL GOULASH SHUFFLE
DISORDER MISHMASH PASTICHE
RHAPSODY SMACHRIE
(— OF SOUNDS) LURRY
JUMBLED CRAZY HASHY JUMBLY
MEDLEY HUDDLING MACARONIC
JUMP HOP LEP NIP DART JETE LEAP
LUTZ SKIP SKIT STEN STOT TUMB
BOUND CAPER HALMA SALTO
SAULT SPANG SPEND START STOIT
VAULT DOUBLE FOOTER HURDLE
INSULT LAUNCH SPRING SPRUNT
STARRE WALLOP CISEAUX
CROWHOP SALTATE SKYLARK
BALLONNE
(— ABOUT) SKIT CAPER
(— FROM AIRCRAFT) BAIL BALE
(— IN FENCING) BALESTRA
(— ON HORSEBACK) LARK
(— ON SKATES) AXEL SALCHOW
(— TO CONCLUSION) SALTUS
(ELECTRICAL —) ARC
(PL.) ALLEGRO
JUMPER LAMMY SWAGE BARKER
LEPPER HANDYMAN
JUMPING SALIENT SALTANT
JUMPING-JACK PANTINE
JUMPING JACK PANTINE
JUMPY ITCHY NERVOUS
JUNCO SNOWBIRD
JUNCTION HIP FROG JOIN NODE
SEAM CLOSE CROWN RAPHE UNION
FILLET INFALL CONTACT JOINING

MEETING UNITION ABUTMENT
JUNCTURE CONSERTION
(— OF EARTH AND SKY) HORIZON
(— OF STREAMS) GRAINS
(— OF THREADS) FELL STOP
(— ON TOOTH) CERVIX
(ROAD —) TOLL
JUNCTURE PASS SEAM PINCH
CRISIS STRAIT ARTICLE BRACKET
JOINING OPHRYON EXIGENCY
JOINTAGE JOINTURE OCCASION
QUANDARY
JUNEBERRY SHADBLOW
SHADBUSH SERVICEBERRY
JUNE BUG DOR BUZZARD
DUMCLOCK
JUNGLE BUSH RUKH SHOLA
BOONDOCK
(AUTHOR OF —) SINCLAIR
(CHARACTER IN —) ONA JACK
DUANE JONAS CONNOR JURGIS
MARIJA RUDKUS ANTANAS
ELZBIETA STANISLOVAS
JUNGLE BENDY WEENONG
JUNGLE BOOK (AUTHOR OF —)
KIPLING
(CHARACTER IN —) KAA KHAN AKELA
BALOO HATHI SHERE BULDEO
MESSUA MOWGLI TABAQUI
BAGHEERA BANDARLOG
JUNIOR PUNY CADET YOUNG
PUISNE YOUNGER
JUNIPER CADE EZEL GORSE GORST
RETEM SAVIN SABINE
JUNK CRAM GEAR GOOK TOPE
DRECK REFUSE SCULCH DISCARD
PLUNDER TONGKANG
(WORTHLESS —) SLUM
JUNKET TRIP KNACK JINKET SAFARI
JUNKMAN TATTER SCRAPMAN
SCAVENGER
JUNO MONETA PRONUBA
JUNO AND THE PAYCOCK
(AUTHOR OF —) OCASEY
(CHARACTER IN —) JACK JUNO
MARY BOYLE JERRY JOXER DEVINE
JOHNNY BENTHAM CHARLIE
TANCRED
JUNTO CABAL
JUPITER JOVE STATOR FORTUNE
MUSHTARI TERMINUS
(SATELLITE OF —) LEDA
(PREF.) JOVI ZENO
JUPITER'S BEARD JOUBARB
SENGREEN
JUR LWO LUOH
JUREL RUNNER CREVALLE HARDTAIL
JURGEN (AUTHOR OF —) CABELL
(CHARACTER IN —) LISA HELEN
JURGEN MERLIN SEREDA ANAITIS
CHLORIS DESIREE DOLORES
DOROTHY KOSHCHEI GUENEVERE
JURIDIC LEGAL

JURISDICTION SOC BAIL SOKE
FUERO HONOR REALM VERGE
ABBACY BANDON BEYLIK DANGER
DIWANI RIDING SPHERE DEANERY
DEWANEE DROSTDY EMIRATE
FOUDRIE KHANATE BAILIERY
CHAPELRY FOUJDARY LIGEANCE
PASHALIC PROVINCE
(— OF BISHOP) SEE
(COERCIVE —) SWORD
(MORMON —) KEYS
(REMOVE FROM —) ELOIN
(SUFF.) DOM
JURISPRUDENCE LAW BYRLAW
REPORTS
JURIST JUDGE MUFTI BREHON
LAWYER DOTTORE
AMERICAN DAY JAY LEE BEAN BOND
BORK DANA DANE DYER GOFF GRAY
HALL HAND HUNT KENT NOTT POPE
REED RUSK SHAW TAFT TAIT WARE
ZANE ADAMS BETTS BLACK BLAIR
BROWN CASEY CHASE DAVIS DAWES
DUANE EATON FIELD FREAR GRIER
LAMAR LIMAN LOGAN MIKVA
MOODY MOORE PAINE RANDA
SMITH STONE STORY TANEY TYLER
WAITE WAYNE WEARE WHITE WYTHE
YATES BAYLOR BREWER BURGER
BURTON BUTLER BYRNES CATRON
CLARKE COOLEY CRATER CURTIS
DANIEL DARROW DONLON DULLES
FOLGER FORTAS FULLER GASTON
GIBSON HARLAN HOLMES HUDSON
HUGHES JEROME KENYON LANDIS
LOWELL LURTON MARTIN MEDINA
MILLER MINTON MORRIS MURPHY
NELSON PARKER PECORA PETERS
PITNEY POWELL SCALIA SEWALL
SHIRAS SIRICA STRONG SUMNER
SWAYNE UPSHUR VINSON WARREN
WILBUR BALDWIN BRADLEY
CARDOZO CLAYTON CUSHING
DOUGLAS DRAYTON GRIFFIN
JACKSON JOHNSON JUSTICE
LINDSEY MCKENNA PARSONS
ROBERTS SANBORN SANFORD
SHERMAN STEVENS STOWELL
TRIMBLE VOELKER WHARTON
WHEATON ANDERSON BLACKMUN
BRANDEIS CLIFFORD GOLDBERG
GRISWOLD GROSSCUP KIRCHWAY
LAWRENCE MACVEAGH MARSHALL
MATTHEWS MCKINLEY MITCHELL
PENFIELD ROSENMAN RUTLEDGE
SEDGWICK STAFFORD WALWORTH
WOODBURY ELLSWORTH
GREENLEAF GROESBECK
HOPKINSON PENDLETON
REHNQUIST SHARSWOOD
UNDERWOOD WHITTAKER
YOUNGDAHL BLATCHFORD
CELEBREZZE MCREYNOLDS

POINDEXTER TROWBRIDGE
WASHINGTON FRANKFURTER
VANDEVANTER
ARGENTINIAN CALVO DRAGO
ALBERDI QUESADA CASTILLO
AUSTRIAN GROSS UNGER GLASER
ZELLER REDLICH LAMMASCH
RINTELEN SCHMERLING
BELGIAN NYS PICARD LAURENT
DESCAMPS GERLACHE
BOLIVIAN SILES SAAVEDRA
BRAZILIAN PESSOA BARBOSA
BARROSO PECANHA
CANADIAN CARON JETTE ARMOUR
DAVIES MULOCK STUART DOHERTY
LACOSTE FOURNIER HAULTAIN
NEWCOMBE RICHARDS ROBINSON
THOMPSON HALIBURTON
FITZPATRICK
CHILEAN EGANA DONOSO
COSTA RICAN CARRILLO
CUBAN URRUTIA
CZECH HACHA
DUTCH GEER ASSER LODER
GROTIUS OPZOOMER BYNKERSHOEK
ENGLISH MAY AMOS CAVE COKE
HALE HOLT KING REID ANSON
BOWEN BRYCE GROVE HURST IMPEY
JAMES MAINE PRATT SCOTT TWISS
VINER ABBOTT ATKYNS AUSTIN
BARNES CARSON DAVIES FINLAY
GATLEY HENLEY HEWART HUGHES
MERSEY NORTON PALMER SANKEY
SELDEN AMULREE BRACTON
DARLING DENNING GODFREY
HOLLAND JENKINS MOULTON
PLOWDEN RUSSELL WIDGERY
CAMPBELL CHALMERS HAILSHAM
JEFFREYS CALDECOTE FORTESCUE
HERSCHELL LITTLETON OPPENHEIM
BLACKSTONE FITZHERBERT
FRENCH ADAM GIDE MOLE DOMAT
FLACH WEISS CASSIN COCHIN
DEMETZ DONEAU DUGUIT GOHIER
HOTMAN MERLIN PITHOU DECAZES
HENAULT LECONTE NOGARET
RENAULT CUJACIUS DUMOULIN
GODEFROY PASQUIER PORTALIS
AGUESSEAU BEAUMANOIR
EPREMESNIL LAFERRIERE
GERMAN UZ BAR FALK GANS HUGO
KAHL POST WACH ZORN CROME
FRANK HANEL KRAUS MOSER SPAHN
TEMME WITTE AEGIDI AHRENS
FICKER GERBER GNEIST HITZIG
KELSEN LABAND MEZGER PREUSS
BOCKING COCCEJI GOLDAST
GOSCHEL HEFFTER KOSTLIN
RICHTER THIBAUT WICHERT
ANCILLON DERNBURG EICHRODT
FISCHART GEFFCKEN HABERLIN
HEDEMANN HUFELAND ALTHUSIUS
EBERMAYER FEUERBACH HINSCHIUS

KIRCHMANN PUFENDORF
HEINECCIUS KOHLRAUSCH
GOLDSCHMIDT KANTOROWICZ
MITTERMAIER HOLTZENDORFF
GREEK POLITES
INDIAN SAPRU
IRISH BALL MORRIS OHAGAN
MACNEILL ODALAIGH FITZGIBBON
ITALIAN AZO FIORE ROCCO
ACCORSO ALCIATI CARRARA
GRAVINA MANCINI ORLANDO
TANUCCI BARTOLUS BULGARUS
GAROFALO IRNERIUS ANZILOTTI
ROMAGNOSI FILANGIERI
PIERANTONI
JAPANESE ADACHI
MEXICAN IGLESIAS
NEW ZEALAND STOUT BULLER
MANING
NORWEGIAN FALSEN HAGERUP
PANAMANIAN PORRAS
PARAGUAYAN BAEZ
PERUVIAN CORNEJO
ROMAN GAIUS LABEO CELSUS
FRONTO PAULUS ULPIAN SABINUS
SALVIUS PAPINIAN PROCULUS
SCAEVOLA SULPICIUS TRIBONIAN
MODESTINUS GREGORIANUS
RUSSIAN KAVELIN MARTENS
MUROMTSEV MEYENDORFF
VINOGRADOFF POBEDONOSTSEV
SCOTTISH HOME CRAIG FORBES
ERSKINE GIFFORD JEFFREY LORIMER
BROUGHAM
SPANISH GALVEZ PINELO AGUSTIN
SWEDISH UNDEN
SWISS DUBS MUSY HILTY HUBER
LARDY MEILI BLUMER DELOLME
URUGUAYAN BRUM
JUROR JURAT ASSIZER JURYMAN
CENTUMVIR
JURY ARRAY PANEL QUEST ASSIZE
JURATA COUNTRY EMPANEL
INQUEST
(**— COUNTY**) VISNE
JURYMAN DICAST JURIST ASSIZER
JURY-RIGGED HAYWIRE
JUST ALL DUE EVEN FAIR FLOP LEAL
MERE ONLY TRUE EQUAL FIRST
LEVEL NOBUT ROUND VALID ZADOC
CANDID GIUSTO HONEST JUSTIN
JUSTUS MERELY SQUARE EQUABLE
LEESOME MERITED UPRIGHT
ACCURATE LIEFSOME RATIONAL
RIGHTFUL SKILLFUL UNBIASED
(**— AS**) AFTER
(**— HOVE CLEAR**) ATRIP
(**— IN TIME**) SONICA
(**ONLY —**) HARDLY SCARCELY
JUSTAUCORPS JUSTICO
JUSTICE LAW DOOM RIGHT SKILL
DHARMA EQUITY REASON HONESTY
SHALLOW SILENCE DEEMSTER

JUDGMENT JUSTITIA JUSTNESS
RECORDER
(— OF PEACE) BEAK SQUIRE
(AUTHOR OF —) GALSWORTHY
(CHARACTER IN —) HOW RUTH DAVIS
FROME JAMES FALDER WALTER
CLEAVER COKESON WILLIAM
HONEYWILL
(RETRIBUTIVE —) NEMESIS
(PREF.) DICAEO
JUSTIFIABLY FAIRLY
JUSTIFICATION CALL COLOR
EXCUSE APOLOGY DEFENCE
WARRANT APOLOGIA
JUSTIFIED FAIR JUST
JUSTIFY AVOW CLEAR PROVE SALVE
DEFEND EXCUSE HONEST DERAIGN
EXPLAIN RECTIFY SUPPORT

WARRANT DARRAIGN MAINTAIN
SANCTION UNDERPIN VINDICATE
JUST-IN-TIME KANBAN
JUSTLY WELL TRULY EVENLY FAIRLY
EQUALLY HANDILY SQUARELY
JUSTNESS SQUARE FITNESS
JUSTICE ACCURACY
JUSTUS JESUS
JUT HANG BULGE JETTY JUTTY
BEETLE EXTEND IMPEND EXTRUDE
JUTE PAT DESI PAUT DAISEE
ARAMINA CHINGMA
JUTTING HANGING
JUVENILE TEEN YOUNG JEJUNE
PUERILE YOUTHFUL
JUXTAPOSED ADJACENT
JUXTAPOSITION BALANCE
CONTACT CONTRAST NEARNESS

K

K KA KAY KILO KING
KAABA CAABA ALCAABA
KABAYA BADJU CABIE
KABELJOU KOB
KABISTAN KUBA
KABOB KEBOB SHASLIK
KABUKALLI CUPIUBA
KACHA (FATHER OF —) BRIHASPATI
   CHITRARATHA
   (MOTHER OF —) MADIRA
KACHARI BODO
KACHIN SINGFO SINGPO CHINGPAW
KADAGA COORG
KADAMBARI (FATHER OF —)
   CHITRARATHA
   (MOTHER OF —) MADIRA
KAFFIR KATI XOSA FINGO TEMBU
   CAFFRE INFIDEL TAMBUKI WAIGULI
   (— BOY) UMFAAN
KAGU GRUIFORM
KAHODA (SON OF —) ASHTAVAKRA
KAIKAWAKA CEDAR
KAIKAWUS (FATHER OF —)
   KAIQUBAD
   (WIFE OF —) SAUDABAH
KAIKEYI (HUSBAND OF —)
   DASHARATHA
   (SON OF —) BHARATA
KAIKHUSRAU (FATHER OF —)
   SYAWAUSH
   (MOTHER OF —) FARANGIS
KAINGIN SWIDDEN
KAKI TRIUMPH
KAKU (GRANDFATHER OF —)
   ZOHAK
   (SLAYER OF —) MINUCHIHR
KALAPOOIAN LAKMIUT
KALE COLE KAIL COLLARD SPROUTS
   BORECOLE
KALEVALA (AUTHOR OF —)
   UNKNOWN
   (CHARACTER IN —) KULLERVO
   ILMARINEN VAINAMOINEN
   LEMMINKAINEN
KALI (HUSBAND OF —) SIVA SHIVA
KALMASHAPADA (FATHER OF —)
   SUDASA
KALMUCK ELEUT UIRAD KHOSHOT
KALPA EON AEON
KALUMPIT ANAGEP
KAMA (DAUGHTER OF —) TRISHA
   (FATHER OF —) DHARMA
   (MOTHER OF —) LAKSHMI
   SHRADDHA
   (SON OF —) ANIRUDDHA
   (WIFE OF —) RATI PRITI
KAMAHI BIRCH TOWAI
KAMALA WURRUS ROTTLERA

KAME AS ESKAR ESKER
KAMICHI SCREAMER
KAMPUCHEA (SEE CAMBODIA)
KANA IROFA IROHA
KANGAROO ROO EURO BILBI FLIER
   FLYER TUNGO BOOMER FOSTER
   WOILIE DIDELPH POTOROO WALLABY
   BETTONGA BOONGARY FILANDER
   FORESTER WALLAROO
   (FEMALE —) DOE GIN
   (YOUNG —) JOEY
KANGAROO APPLE GUNYANG
   POROPORO
KANGAROO RAT JERBOA
   BETTONG POTOROO
KANHOBAL CONOB
KANKANAI IGOROT
KANS KUSA GLAGA KUSHA
   GLAGAH
KANSA (FATHER OF —) UGRASENA
   (SLAYER OF —) KRISHNA
KANSAN JAYHAWK

KANSAS		
CAPITAL: TOPEKA		
COLLEGE: BAKER TABOR BETHANY		
STERLING WASHBURN		
COUNTY: ELK GOVE LINN LYON NESS		
RENO GEARY PRATT ROOKS TREGO		
BARTON COFFEY NEMAHA NEOSHO		
BOURBON LABETTE ATCHISON		
FORT: RILEY SCOTT		
INDIAN: KANSA KIOWA PAWNEE		
WICHITA COMANCHE		
LAKE: CHENEY KIRWIN NEOSHO		
MILFORD		
MOUNTAIN: SUNFLOWER		
NATIVE: JAYHAWK		
NICKNAME: JAYHAWKER SUNFLOWER		
PRESIDENT: EISENHOWER		
RIVER: SALINE SOLOMON ARKANSAS		
MISSOURI		
STATE BIRD: MEADOWLARK		
STATE FLOWER: SUNFLOWER		
STATE TREE: COTTONWOOD		
TOWN: ALMA GOVE HAYS IOLA		
COLBY DODGE HOXIE LAKIN LEOTI		
SEDAN LARNED SALINA ABILENE		
CHANUTE LIBERAL ULYSSES		
WICHITA		

KAOLIANG SORGHUM
KAOLIN PIPECLAY
KAPOK CEIBO FLOSS
KARAISM ANANISM
KARAKA KOPI

KARA KIRGHIZ BURUT BOUROUT
KARATAS PITA
KARATE (— SCHOOL) DOJO
  (EXPERT LEVEL IN —) DAN
  (EXPERT LEVEL OF —) DAN
  (KOREAN —) TAEQUONDU
KAREN SGAU SGAW
KARENNI PADAUNG
KARMA FATE
  (BAD —) DEMERIT
KARNA (FATHER OF —) SURYA
  (MOTHER OF —) KUNTI PRITHA
  (SLAYER OF —) ARJUNA
KARTTIKEYA (FATHER OF —) RUDRA
  SHIVA
KASKA NAHANE
KAT KHAT QUAT CAFTA
KATE KAI
KATHERINE (HUSBAND OF —)
  PETRUCHIO
KAUNAS KOVNO
KAURI COWRIE BERAIROU
KAUSHALYA (HUSBAND OF —)
  DASHARATHA
  (SON OF —) RAMA
KAVA AVA AWA YAQONA KAVAKAVA
  YANGGONA
KAW AKHA
KAYANUSH (BROTHER OF —)
  FARIDUN PURMAYAH

KAZAKHSTAN
(ALSO SEE RUSSIA)
CAPITAL: ALMATY ALMAATA
COIN: RUBLE
DESERT: BARSUKI KARAKUM
  KYZYLKUM
LAKE: ALAKOL TENGIZ ZAYSAN
  BALKHASH SILETITENIZ
  SELETYTENGIZ
LANGUAGE: KAZAKH KIPCHAK
  QIPCHAQ
MOUNTAIN: KHANTENGRI
MOUNTAIN RANGE: ALTAI ULUTAU
  TIENSHAN CHINGIZTAU
  DZUNGARIAN TARBAGATAY
NAME: KAZAK KAZAKH
PENINSULA: MANGYSHLAK
PLATEAU: USTYURT
RIVER: URAL YAIK ISHIM TOBOL
  IRTYSH SYRDARYA
SEA: ARAL CASPIAN
TOWN: OMSK YAIK RUDNY URALSK
  ALMAATA TROITSK CHIMKENT
  ORENBURG KARAGANDA
  QARAGHANDY PETROPAVLOVSK
  SEMIPALATINSK
VALLEY: FERGANA

KAZOO BAZOO GAZOO ZARAH HEW-
  GAG MIRLITON
KEEL FIN BACK SEEL BARGE CARINA
  CRISTA RADDLE SERRULA

(— OF BIRD'S MANDIBLE) GONYS
(AFTERPART OF —) SKAG SKEG
(PREF.) CARINI
KEELBILL ANI
KEELBIRD ANI
KEEN DRY FLY GAY SHY YAP ACID
  DEAR FINE GAIR GLEG HIGH HOWL
  NUTS PERT TART TEEN WAIL WARM
  WILD ACUTE ALERT BREME BRIEF
  BRISK EAGER QUICK SHARP SMART
  SNELL SPICY VIVID ARGUTE ASTUTE
  BITTER CAOINE GREEDY LIVELY
  SEVERE SHREWD SHRILL CUNNING
  HAWKING MORDANT PARLISH
  PARLOUS PUNGENT SERIOUS
  THIRSTY OBSERVANT SAGACIOUS
  TRENCHANT PERSPICACIOUS
  (PREF.) OXY
KEENER HOWLER
KEENLY KEEN FELLY DEARLY
  ACUTELY
KEENNESS EDGE ACUITY ACUMEN
  PUNGENCY
  (— OF SIGHT) ACIES
KEEN-SCENTED NASUTE
  NOSEWISE
KEEN-SIGHTED EAGLE
KEEP HUG HAVE HOLD SALT SAVE
  STOW WAIT WITE BLESS ROCCA
  WITIE COFFER DETAIN REDUIT
  CONFINE CONTAIN DEFORCE
  HUSBAND KEEPING OBSERVE
  RESERVE WARRANT CONSERVE
  MAINTAIN PRESERVE RESTRAIN
  WITHHOLD
(— ABREAST) FOLLOW
(— A COURSE) CAPE
(— AFLOAT) BUOY
(— AN EYE ON) STAG
(— APART) DOTTLE ISOLATE
  SEPARATE
(— A SMALL SHOP) CRAME
(— ASUNDER) PART
(— AT A DISTANCE) ESTRANGE
(— AWAY) ABSENT
(— AWAY FROM) ABHOR AVOID
(— A WOUND OPEN) TENT
(— BACK) DAM HAP ROB STAY
  ARREAR DETAIN RETARD RESERVE
(— COMPANY WITH) GANG MOOP
  CONSORT
(— FOR SALE) STOCK
(— FREE) ESCHEW
(— FROM BOILING OVER) KEEL
(— FROM BURNING) REDD
(— GUARD) SENTINEL
(— HIDDEN) HOARD SECRETE
(— IN) CAGE
(— IN CIRCULATION) WIND
(— IN EXCITEMENT) ALARM ALARUM
(— IN MIND) RETAIN
(— IN ORDER) TARGE
(— IN STOCK) CARRY

(— IN THE TRACK) GATHER
(— OFF) FEND WEAR EXPEL FENCE SHIELD
(— OUT) BAR EXPEL
(— POSSESSION) HARBOR
(— SCORELESS) BLANK
(— SECRET) HUSH WHIST
(— STRAIGHT) DIRECT
(— TABS ON) FINGER
(— TIME) GO
(— TOGETHER) WHIP
(— TO ONESELF) BOSOM
(— UNTIL YEAR OLD) HOG
(— UP) SUBSIST SUSTAIN CONTINUE
(— WAITING) DELAY
(— WARM) STIVE STOVE FOSTER
(— WATCH) BARK TOUT WAIT BEWAKE
(PREF.) SOZ(O)
(— OFF) ALEXI
KEEPER NAB KEEP SCREW TUTOR YEMER CUSTOS GAOLER JAILER LIFTER LOOKER PARKER PASTOR RAHDAR RANGER WARDEN BAILIFF CURATOR GEARMAN PIKEMAN PROVOST BEARWARD DEERHERD DOLLYMAN ELDERMAN FEWTERER GUARDANT GUARDIAN HOUNDMAN TRAITEUR WARRENER
(— OF CATTLE) HAYWARD
(— OF DOGS) FEWTERER
(— OF ELEPHANT) MAHOUT
(— OF INN) PUBLICAN
(— OF LOCK) NAB
(— OF PRISON) GAOLER JAILER WARDEN ALCAIDE PROVOST
(DOOR —) DURWAN
KEEPING CARE WARD TRUST CHARGE CUSTODY STORAGE DETAINER
KEEPSAKE DRURY TOKEN GIFTBOOK SOUVENIR
KEEVE TUB VAT KIEVE
KEG CAG PIN TUB CADE CASK KNAG WOOD ANKER BARRICO COSTREL
KELOID SCAR
KELP KILP LEAG VAREC WRACK GIRDLE SEAWEED BELLWARE
KELPIE NIX BARB
KELT SLAT LIGGER
KENAF DA GOMBO MESTA AMBARI KANAFF PAPOULA STOKROOS
KENILWORTH (AUTHOR OF —) SCOTT
(CHARACTER IN —) AMY HUGH TONY GILES JANET SMITH ALASCO DICKIE DUDLEY EDMUND FOSTER SLUDGE SUSSEX VARNEY WALTER GOSLING MICHAEL RALEIGH RICHARD ROBSART WAYLAND DOBOOBIE ELIZABETH LAMBOURNE LEICESTER TRESSILIAN FLIBBERTIGIBBET
KENNEL DTALL VENERY VENISON DOGHOUSE

KENO HOUSE
KENTISH (— UNIT) YOKE

KENTUCKY

CAPITAL: FRANKFORT
COLLEGE: BEREA ASBURY CENTRE BRESCIA URSULINE
COUNTY: BATH BELL BOYD HART TODD ADAIR BOYLE TRIGG WOLFE ESTILL MENIFEE MAGOFFIN
INDIAN: SHAWNEE CHEROKEE IROQUOIS
LAKE: CUMBERLAND
RIVER: DIX OHIO SALT BARREN
STATE BIRD: CARDINAL
STATE FLOWER: GOLDENROD
STATE NICKNAME: BLUEGRASS
STATE TREE: TULIP
TOWN: INEZ BEREA CADIZ DIXON HYDEN MCKEE PARIS CORBIN HARLAN HAZARD GLASGOW GREENUP PADUCAH DANVILLE COVINGTON LEXINGTON OWENSBORO

KENYA

BAY: FORMOSA
CAPITAL: NAIROBI
COIN: SHILLING
LAKE: MAGADI RUDOLF NAIVASHA VICTORIA
LANGUAGE: LUO KIKUYU SWAHILI
MEASURE: WARI
MOUNTAIN: ELGON KENYA KULAL NYIRU MATIAN LOGONOT
PEOPLE: LUO MERU BANTU KAMBA KISII LUHYA MASAI NANDI KIKUYU OGADEN BALUHYA HAMITIC HILOTIC TURKANA KIPSIGIS
RIVER: LAK ATHI TANA KEIRO TURKWELL
TOWN: MERU KITUI NAROK KIPINI KISUMU MOYALE NAKURU NAYUKI ELDORET MALINDI MOMBASA

KERATIN HORN
KERCHIEF CURCH DORAG ROMAL RUMAL ANALAV CYPRUS MADRAS NAPKIN PEPLUM CYPRESS KERCHER PANUELO THERESE BABUSHKA BANDANNA HEADRAIL KAFFIYEH KINGSMAN
KERESAPA (BROTHER OF —) URVAKHSHAYA
(FATHER OF —) THRITA
KERF CARF SKAFF GROOVE UNDERCUT
KERI QRI KERE
KERMANSHAH COCONUT
KERMES GRAIN
KERNEL NUT BUNT CORE KERN MEAT PITH BERRY GOODY GROAT

ACINUS ALMOND CARNEL PICKLE
NUCLEUS PICHURIM
(CORN —S) HOMINY
(UNHUSKED —S) CAPES
(PL.) NIXTAMAL
(PREF.) CARY(O) KARY(O)
KEROGEN SAPROPEL
KEROSINE PARAFFIN
KERSENNEH ERS ERVIL
KERSEY WASHER ORDINARY
KESTREL FANNER KEELIE STANIEL
STANNEL STANYEL STANCHEL
WINDHOVER
KETA CHUM
KETCH SAIC
KETONE IRONE ACETOL ARMONE
CARONE CARVOL COTOIN HEXONE
IONONE QUINOL ACETOIN ACETONE
ACYLOIN BENZOIN CAMPHOR
CARVONE DYPNONE FLAVONE
JASMONE MUSCONE PHORONE
SHOGAOL THUJONE ACRIDONE
ANTHRONE BAECKEOL BUTANONE
BUTYRONE CHALCONE CHALKONE
CHROMONE DEGUELIN EXALIONE
FENCHONE MENTHONE PROPIONE
PULEGONE ROTENONE STEARONE
TAGETONE THIENONE VALERONE
XANTHONE
KETTLE LEAD STEW DIXIE BOILER
CANNER FESSEL MARMIT MASLIN
TRIPOD VESSEL CALDRON SKILLET
STEWPOT CALABASH FLAMBEAU
KETTLEDRUM NAKER ATABAL
KETTLE TIMBAL TYMBAL TIMBALE
TYMPANY
KEVEL CAVEL HAMMER KNAPPER
KEWPIE DOLL
KEX KECKSY
KEY CAY KAY CLEW CLUE CRIB FLAT
ISLE JACK KING NOTE PLUG PONY
BASAL DITAL INDEX SCREW TASTO
WREST BUTTON CHIAVE CIPHER
CLAVIS COTTER OPENER SAMARA
SPLINE WINDER DIGITAL LANGUET
PASSKEY SPEAKER LATCHKEY
TONALITY
(— FOR TUNING HARP) WREST
(— OF KEYBOARD INSTRUMENT)
CHIP MANUAL
(— OF LIFE) ANKH
(— OF ORGAN) TASTO DIGITAL
(— OF PIANO) IVORY NATURAL
(— OF SPINET) CHIP
(— ON WOODWIND INSTRUMENT)
LANGUET SPEAKER
(—S OF CARILLON) CLAVECIN
(— UP) STRING
(ARITHMETICAL —) ADDITIVE
(ASH —) PIGEON
(FALSE —) GLUT
(FEATHER —) FIN STOP SPLINE
FEATHER

(KIND OF —) CHURCH
(PART OF —) BOW BLADE WARDING
SHOULDER SERRATION
(SKELETON —) GILT TWIRLER
(TELEGRAPH —) BUG TAPPER
(WHITE —) NATURAL
(PREF.) CLAVI CLEID(O) CLEIST(O)
(SUFF.) CLEISIS CLISIS
KEYBOARD MANUAL CELESTA
CELESTE CLAVIER PEDALIER
(PRACTICE —) DUMBPIANO
(TYPEWRITER —) QWERTY
(PREF.) CLAVI
KEY-DESK CONSOLE
KEYHOLE KEY SLOT LOCKHOLE
KEYNOTE A B D E KEY MESE TONIC
FINALIS
KEYSTONE KEY QUOIN VERTEX
SAGITTA VOUSSOIR
(— STATE) PENNSYLVANIA
KEYWAY SPLINE KEYSLOT
KEZIA (FATHER OF —) JOB
KHA KA KHMU KACHE LAMET
KHALAT SEERPAW
KHAN CAN CHAM HAWN SERAI
TACON CHAGAN KHAKAN
KHAS-KURA NEPALI PAHARI
PARBATI GORKHALI
KHATTISH HATTIC
KHEDIVE QUITEVE
KHELLIN VISAMMIN
KHOTANA KOYUKON
KHUSKHUS CUSCUS VETIVER
KIANG ONAGER CHIGETAI HEMIONUS
KIBBLE GIG KETTLE
KIBBLER CRACKER
KICK BOOT FICK FLEG FLIG FOOT
FUNK HEEL HOOF LASH PORR POTE
PUNT RUSH SHIN TRIP TURF YERK
ANGLE BUNCH FLING KEVEL PAUSE
PUNCH SCENE SKELP SPANG SPURN
CHARGE CORNER FITTER KICKER
KICKUP OBJECT SPIRAL VOLLEY
DROPOUT FOUETTE KICKOFF
DROPKICK PLACEKICK
(— ABOUT) SPARTLE
(— AS A HORSE) FLING WINCE
(— AT GOAL) SHOOT
(— HEELS UP) SPURN
(— IN) ANTEUP
(— ON SHINS) HACK SHINNER
(— OUT) SPUR
(— OVER) CATCH
(BALLET —) BRUSH
(KIND OF —) SQUIB
(SOCCER —) CORNER
(SWIMMING —) THRASH
KICKBACK RECOIL
KICKER TEDDER WINCER
KICKOFF (BEFORE —) PREGAME
KICKSHAW TIDBIT TITBIT
KID COD FUN POD RIB TUB FAWN
FOOL GOAT JIVE JOKE JOSH CHAFF

KID CHILD FAGOT HORSE JOLLY KIDDY SPOOF TEASE KIDLET SQUIRT DECEIVE EANLING FATLING TICCHEN YOUNGER CHEVEREL YEANLING
(UNDRESSED —) SUEDE
(WHIZ —) BRAIN GENIUS EINSTEIN

KIDDING JOKE SPOOFERY

KIDNAP STEAL ABDUCT HIJACK PANYAR SPIRIT

KIDNAPER PLAGIARY SNATCHER SPIRITER

KIDNAPING SNATCH PLAGIUM PLAGIARY

KIDNAPPED (AUTHOR OF —) STEVENSON
(CHARACTER IN —) ALAN BRECK COLIN DAVID RIACH SHUAN BALFOUR RANSOME CAMPBELL EBENEZER HOSEASON RANKEILLOR

KIDNEY NEAR NEER REIN TYPE CLASS NEPHRON
(PL.) REINS ROGNONS
(PREF.) NEPHR(O) RENI RENO
(SUFF.) NEPHRITIS NEPHROSIS

KIDNEY BEAN FRIJOLE
(PL.) FASELS

KIER KEEVE PUFFER

KIESELGUHR DOPE GUHR

KILL DO BAG END GET ICE MOW OFF OUT PIP ZAP BANE BOLO COOK COOL DOIN DOWN FELL MORT NECK SLAY TAME WING BLAST BRAIN CROAK CULLE FETCH FORDO GANCH MISDO NAPOO QUELL SABER SCRAG SHOOT SMITE SNUFF SPEED SPEND SPILL SPOIL STALL STICK SWELT SWORD WASTE CORPSE DEADEN DIDDLE FAMISH FINISH HANDLE IMPALE MARTYR MURDER POISON RUBOUT STARVE UNLIVE ACHIEVE BUTCHER DESTROY EXECUTE FLATTEN HATCHET KILLING MORTIFY SMOTHER STONKER SUICIDE DEATHIFY DISPATCH DISSOLVE IMMOLATE JUGULATE STILETTO
(— ANIMALS) CONTROL
(— BY STONING) LAPIDATE
(— BY SUBMERSION) STIFLE
(— CALF AFTER BIRTH) DEACON
(— CATTLE) PITH
(— EVERY TENTH) DECIMATE
(— GAME) SATCHEL
(— OFF) ENECATE
(— SMALL GAME) BARK
(— TIME) GOOF
(— WITH GRENADE) FRAG
(DELIBERATELY —) FRAG

KILLDEER PLOVER KILLDEE DEERKILL

KILLED KILT WINGED SKITTLED
(FRESHLY —) GREEN

KILLER GUN BRAVO GUNMAN SLAYER TORPEDO MURDERER THRESHER
(SUFF.) CIDAL CIDE

KILLER WHALE ORCA DOLPHIN GRAMPUS

KILLIFISH KELLY KILLY MINNOW COBBLER GUDGEON MAYFISH MUDFISH PANCHAX FUNDULUS ROCKFISH SACALAIT STUDFISH SWAMPINE MUMMICHOG

KILLING FELL KILL MORT QUELL TUANT MURDER CLEANUP HANGING CLEANING DISPATCH FELICIDE HOMICIDE MANSLAUGHTER
(MERCY —) EUTHANASIA

KILLJOY NARK GLOOM LEMON GRINCH SOURPUSS

KILN BING KEEL LEHR OAST CULLE DRIER GLAZE STOVE TILER COCKLE CUPOLA TILERY FURNACE CALCINER LIMEKILN

KILOGRAM (— OF MARIJUANA) KEY
(— OF MARIJUANA OR HEROIN) KEY
(— OF NARCOTIC) KEY
(907 —S) NETTON

KILOMETER LI CLICK KLICK

KILORAD KRAD

KILOWATT-HOUR KELVIN

KILT QUELT PIUPIU FILIBEG PHILIBEG PETTICOAT

KILTER SKEET

KIM (AUTHOR OF —) KIPLING
(CHARACTER IN —) ALI KIM OHARA ARTHUR HURREE LURGAN MAHBUB BENNETT KIMBALL CREIGHTON MOOKERJEE

KIN SIB KATI KITH CATTY CUNNE FLESH FAMILY AFFINITY RELATION

KIND ILK KIN LOT BOON CAST FAIR FORM GOOD HAIR HEND LIKE MAKE MEEK MILD MODE MOLD NICE RATE SELY SOFT SORT SUIT TRIM TYPE WING BREED BROOD CLASS GENRE GENUS GESTE ORDER SPICE STAMP BENIGN BLITHE FACILE GENDER GENTLE GOODLY HUMANE KIDNEY KINDLY MANNER MISTER NATURE SPEECE STRAIN STRIPE TENDER CLEMENT EDITION FASHION FEATHER FLESHLY LENIENT QUALITY REGIMEN SPECIAL SPECIES SPECKLE FRIENDLY GENEROUS MANSUETE OBLIGING BENIGNANT INDULGENT OFFICIOUS PERSUASION
(— OF) A
(— OF PEOPLE) FOLK
(DIFFERENT IN —) DIVERS
(DISTINCTIVE —) BRAND
(OF EVERY —) ALKIN
(PREF.) GEN(O)

KINDLE BEET BLOW FIRE LUNT MOVE TAKE TEND TIND FLAME LIGHT QUICK SPARK SPUNK ACCEND ALIGHT DECOCT ENFIRE EXCITE IGNITE ILLUME EMBLAZE ESPRISE INCENSE INFLAME SOLICIT KINDLING

KINDLINESS CANDOR
KINDLING FIRE BAVIN FAGOT TWIGS
TINDER IGNITION
KINDLY FAIR GAIN KIND NESH AGREE
COUTH HENDE NAISH BENIGN
BLITHE COUTHY GENIAL HOMELY
AMIABLE BENEFIC INNERLY
FAVOROUS GENEROUS GRACIOUS
QUEMEFUL TOWARDLY
KINDNESS LOVE ALOHA FAVOR
BOUNTY CANDOR LENITY BENEFIT
SERVICE CLEMENCY EASINESS
GOODNESS HUMANITY LENITUDE
MILDNESS
KIND OF
(SUFF.) EE
KINDRED KIN SIB KIND KITH BLOOD
FLESH HOUSE FAMILY KOBONG
NATION STRIND COGNATE KINFOLK
KINSMEN RELATED SIBSHIP AFFINITY
COGNATION CONGENIAL
CONGENEROUS
KINE KYE COWS CATTLE
KINETIC ACTUAL
(— POTENTIAL) L
KING RI SO ASA BAN DAM LOT LUD
PUL REX REY RIG ROY AGAG AMON
ATLI BALI BELI BIJA BORS BRAN
BRES CRAL CZAR JEHU KRAL LEIR
MARK NUDD NUMA OMRI OTTO
PHUL RAJA RIAL SIRE TSAR TZAR
WANG YIMA ARDRI BALOR BELUS
CONOR CREON DAGDA DAHAK
EGLON ETZEL GYGES HEROD HIRAM
HOGNI HOSEA IPHIS IXION JOASH
LAIUS LLUDD LYCUS MESHA MIDAS
MINOS NADAB NEGUS NORSE
NUADA PEKAH PRIAM RAJAH
SAMMY SWAMI ZIMRI ZOHAK
AEOLUS AGENOR AILILL ALARIC
ALBOIN ALONSO ALOROS AR1OCH
BLADUD CODRUS DIOMED DUNCAN
ELATHA FINGAL FRODHI FROTHI
GOEMOT INKOSI KABAKA LEMUEL
LYCAON MEMNON MINYAS NESTOR
NODONS OENEUS OGYGES PELEUS
PELIAS SAUGHT SHESHA SVAMIN
TEUCER URIENS UZZIAH VASUKI
ADMETUS AHAZIAH AMAIMON
AMYCLAS ANGEVIN ARDRIGH
ARTEGAL ATHAMAS BAGINDA
BELINUS BUSIRIS CACIQUE CEPHEUS
CROESUS ELIDURE EPAPHUS
EPOPEUS ETHBAAL EURYTUS
GUNTHER HYGELAC INACHUS
JAMSHID JEHOASH JEHORAM
KINGLET LAERTES LATINUS LEONTES
MENAHEM MONARCH PANDION
PHINEUS POLYBUS REGULUS
ROMULUS ROYALET SMERDIS
SOLOMON VOLSUNG ACRISIUS
ADRASTUS AEGYPTUS ALBERICH
AMRAPHEL ASNAPPER BAHMANID

BRENNIUS CLAUDIUS COPHETUA
ELDORADO ETEOCLES ETHELRED
GILGAMES GOEMAGOT GOGMAGOG
GORBODUC HEZEKIAH HROTHGAR
JEHOAHAZ JEROBOAM KINGLING
LAOMEDON LISUARTE MANASSEH
MELIADUS MENELAUS ODYSSEUS
ORCHAMUS OSNAPPAR OVERKING
PADISHAH PEKAHIAH PENTHEUS
RAMESSID REHOBOAM RODERICK
RODOMONT ROITELET SARPEDON
SHEPHERD SISYPHUS TANTALUS
GILGAMESH
(— AND QUEEN OF TRUMPS) BELLA
(— CHANGED TO WOLF) LYCAON
(— OF ARMS) GARTER NORROY
(— OF BEASTS) LION
(— OF DWARFS) ALBERICH
(— OF FAIRIES) OBERON
(— OF JUDAH) ASA
(— OF TRUMPS) HONOR
(— WITH 10 WIVES) HEROD
(IRISH —) RI RIG ARDRI ARDRIGH
(NEIGHBOR OF —) QUEEN BISHOP
(POLYNESIAN —) ALII ARII ARIKI
(PREF.) REGI
KING ARTHUR (MOTHER OF —)
IGRAINE
KINGBIRD PIPIRI PETCHARY
KINGBOLT KING KINGPIN MAINPIN
KING CRAB LIMULID LIMULUS
PANFISH
KINGDOM WEI ELAM REALM REIGN
WORLD ESTATE MONERA MORVEN
REGION REGNUM SAXONY MITANNI
(ANCIENT IONIAN —) EPIRUS
KINGFISH BARB CERO HAKE HAKU
MINK OPAH TOMCOD CHENFISH
SCIAENID TOMMYCOD
KINGFISHER HALCYON PODITTI
TOROTORO
KING JOHN (AUTHOR OF —)
SHAKESPEARE
(CHARACTER IN —) JOHN BIGOT
ESSEX HENRY JAMES LEWIS MELUN
PETER ARTHUR BLANCH ELINOR
GURNEY HUBERT PHILIP ROBERT
DEBURGH LYMOGES BRETAGNE
PANDULPH PEMBROKE CHATILLON
CONSTANCE SALISBURY
FAULCONBRIDGE
KING LEAR (AUTHOR OF —)
SHAKESPEARE
(CHARACTER IN —) KENT LEAR
CURAN EDGAR REGAN ALBANY
EDMUND OSWALD GONERIL
BURGUNDY CORDELIA CORNWALL
GLOUCESTER
KINGLET REGULI
KINGLY REGAL ROYAL REGNAL
BASILIC IMPERIAL MAJESTIC
PRINCELY
KING-OF-ARMS NORROY

KING PARAKEET WELLAT
KINGPIN TOPBANANA
KING'S EVIL CRUELS CREWELS
  CRUELLS
KING'S HENCHMAN, THE
  (CHARACTER IN —) EADGAR
  AELFRIDA AETHELWOLD
  (COMPOSER OF —) TAYLOR
KINGSHIP STOOL THRONE KINGDOM
  ROYALTY DEVARAJA KINGHOOD
KING SOLOMON'S MINES
  (AUTHOR OF —) HAGGARD
  (CHARACTER IN —) GOOD JOHN
  JOSE ALLAN HENRY KHIVA TWALA
  CURTIS GAGOOL GEORGE IGNOSI
  UMBOPA FOULATA SCRAGGA
  INFADOOS SILVESTRE VENTVOGEL
  QUATERMAIN
KING'S PEACE GRITH
KING'S ROW (AUTHOR OF —)
  BELLAMANN
  (CHARACTER IN —) DRAKE ELISE
  JAMIE NOLAN RANDY RENEE TOWER
  CASSIE GORDON LOUISE MCHUGH
  PARRIS SANDOR PERDOFF
  MONAGHAN CASSANDRA
  WAKEFIELD
KING'S SCHOLAR TUG
KING VULTURE PAP PAPA
KININ KALLIDIN
KINK NIB SNICK BUCKLE DOGLEG
  KINKLE
  (— IN ROPE) GRIND
KINKAJOU POTTO HEYRAT APOROSO
KINKING FLUTING
KINKY NAPPY ENCOMIC KINKLED
KINO BIJA BIJAOAL
KINSHIP SIB BLOOD NASAB STOOL
  ENATION KINDRED SIBNESS SIBSHIP
  AFFINITY AGNATION RELATION
  PROPINQUITY
KINSMAN KIN SIB ALLY BLOOD
  AFFINE AGNATE COUSIN FRIEND
  BROTHER GOTRAJA KINDRED
  WINEMAY BANDHAVA RELATION
  RELATIVE COLLATERAL
KINSWOMAN SISTER KINDRED
  RELATIVE
KIOSK STALL STAND
KIP SKIP GRASSER KIPSKIN UPSTART
KIRGHIZ QYRGHYZ
KIRGIZ (MOUNTAIN RANGE IN —) ALAI
KIRIBATI (CAPITAL OF —) TARAWA
  BAIRIKI
  (FORMER NAME OF —)
  GILBERTISLANDS
  (ISLAND OF —) BERU MAKIN
  ABAIANG ABEMAMA NONOUTI
  TABITEUEA
KIRN MELL
KISH (FATHER OF —) JEHIEL
  (SON OF —) SAUL
KISMET FATE

KISS BA LIP NEB BASS BUSS PECK
  PREE MOUTH POGUE SLAKE SMACK
  BEKISS CARESS SALUTE SLAVER
  SMOOCH SMOUCH OSCULATE
  (— OF PEACE) PAX
  (— WETLY) SLOBBER
  (STOLEN —) SMOORICH
KISSING LIPWORK
KIT CHIT DUFFEL KITTEN OUTFIT
  POCHETTE
  (LUMBERMAN'S —) TURKEY
  (MESS —) CANTEEN
KITCHEN BUT GALLEY CABOOSE
  CUISINE KITCHIE COOKROOM
  (— CONTAINER) CANISTER
  (SHIP'S —) CABOOSE
KITCHEN-GARDEN OLITORY
KITE LAP CHIL CYTE HAWK GLEDE
  CHILLA DRACHE DRAGON ELANET
  FALCON PREYER SENTRY MILVINE
  PUDDOCK PUTTOCK FORKTAIL
  HELLKITE
KITH COUSINRY
KITTEN KIT KITTY KITTLE CATLING
  KITLING
KITTIWAKE GULL WAEG ANNET
  KITTY PICKUP HACKLET TARROCK
  TIRRLIE
KITTY CAT POT BADRANS BAUDRONS
KIVA ESTUFA
KIWI APTERYX
  (BROWN —) ROA
KLAMATH WEED AMBER
  GOATWEED
KLANG PHONE
KLIPSPRINGER KAINSI KLIPBOK
KLONDIKE CANFIELD SOLITAIRE
KLUTZ BOOB
KNACK ART FEAT FEEL GATE GIFT
  HANG CATCH QUIRK SKILL TRICK
  TALENT SLEIGHT WRINKLE INSTINCT
  (— FOR DISCOVERY) NOSE
KNACKER CLAPPER
  (PL.) BONES
KNAPSACK WALLET MOCHILA
  MUSETTE SNAPBAG SNAPSACK
KNAPWEED SWEEP BLUETOP
  FLATTOP BALLWEED BELLWEED
  BOLEWEED BULLWEED BUNDWEED
  CENTAURY CLUBWEED CROPWEED
  HARDHEAD IRONHEAD IRONWEED
  KNOTWEED MATFELON
KNAVE BOY ELF LAD NOB PAM PUR
  TOM JACK BOWER CHEAT DROLE
  MAKER NODDY ROGUE TIGER VIPER
  COQUIN FRIPON HARLOT KNIGHT
  PICARO RASCAL VARLET WENZEL
  CAMOOCH CUSTREL PEASANT
  VILLAIN BEZONIAN COISTREL
  SWINDLER VARLETTO
  (— OF CLUBS) PAM
KNAVERY ROPERY CATZERIE
  PATCHERY RASCALITY

KNAVISH ROGUISH SCAMPISH
KNAWEL KNOTWEED KNOTWORT
KNEAD ELT TEW MOLD POST BRAKE
STOCK PETRIE MASSAGE
(— HIDES) STOCK
KNEADING
(— MACHINE) BRAKE
KNEADING-TROUGH HUTCH
KNEE GENU HOCK CROOK KNAPPER
SLEEPER SUFFRAGO
(— HOLLOW) HAM
(— OF COMPOSING STICK) SLIDE
(PREF.) GENU GONY
KNEECAP CAP ROTULA PATELLA
(PL.) MARROWBONES
KNEE-JERK AUTOMATIC
KNEEL SIT KNEE COUCH SHIKO
KOWTOW
KNEELER SPRINGER
KNEELING SHIKO BENDED
KNEEPAN ROTULA PATELLA
KNELL BELL RING TOLL KNOLL
STROKE
KNICKERBOCKERS PLUSFOURS
KNICKKNACK TOY CURIO KNACK
TRICK GEWGAW NOTION PRETTY
BIBELOT GIMCRACK TCHOTCHKE
KNICKNACK CURIO
KNIFE DAH DIE PIN SAX ULU BOLO
BUCK MOON SAEX SHIM SHIV SNEE
SPUD TANG BOWIE BURIN CHIVE
CUTTO FACON GULLY KNIVE KUKRI
PANGA SHANK SHAVE SKEAN SLICE
BARLOW BARONG CAMPIT CARVER
COLTER COUTEL CUTTLE CUTTOE
DAGGER DOCTOR JIGGER PANADE
PARANG PAVADE PORKER PULLER
RIMMER SICKLE SLICER TREVET
TRIVAT WORKER BREAKER CATLING
CHOPPER COUTEAU FIPENNY
KIOTOME MACHETE PALETTE
SCALPEL SEVERER SKINNER
SLASHER SNICKER STICKER
SUNDANG TICKLER WHITTLE
BELDUQUE BILLHOOK CALABOZO
JOCTELEG SERPETTE THWITTLE
YATAGHAN SNICKERSNEE
(— FOR BREAKING FLAX) BEATER
(— FOR LEATHER) PIN
(— FOR RUBBER DOUGH) DOCTOR
(BLACKSMITH'S —) BUTTERIS
(BOWIE —) TOOTHPICK
(BURMESE —) DAH DAO DOW
(CURRIER'S —) CLEANER
(ENGRAVER'S —) CRADLE
(ESKIMO —) ULU
(MORO —) BARONG
(PART OF —) NEB TIP WEB BACK
EDGE HEEL HILT BLADE CHOIL
GUARD POINT RIVET FULLER
HANDLE POMMEL BOLSTER QUILLON
ROCASSO
(SHOEMAKER'S —) BUTT

(SURGICAL —) LANCET CATLING
SCALPEL BISTOURY EXSECTOR
(TANNER'S —) GRAINER
(WHALER'S —) SPADE
KNIFE-PLEATED KILTED
KNIGHT N DUB ELF SIR ADUB GANO
TULK EQUES EQUIS HORSE LANCE
RIDER THANE TOLKE CABALL
ERRANT KEMPER PENCEL RITTER
ROGERO GENILON PALADIN
YOUNKER ALMANZOR BACHELOR
BANNERET CAVALIER COLVILLE
GANELONE IRONCLAD ISENBRAS
PALMERIN RUGGIERO
(— IN CHESS) HORSE
(— OF ROUND TABLE) GAN KAY
BORS OWEN GARETH GAWAIN
MODRED CARADOC CRADOCK
GALAHAD GANELON EGLAMORE
LANCELOT PALMERIN PERCIVAL
TRISTRAM
(BOASTFUL —) KAY
(CARPET —) DAMMARET
(MERCENARY —) FREELANCE
(NEIGHBOR OF —) ROOK BISHOP
(ROMAN —) MAECENAS
KNIGHT-ERRANT KEMPER
PALADIN
KNIGHTHOOD CAVALRY
KNIGHTS (AUTHOR OF —)
ARISTOPHANES
(CHARACTER IN —) CLEON DEMUS
NICIAS AGORACRITUS
DEMOSTHENES
KNIPHOFIA TRITOMA
KNIT SET BIND KNOT PLAIT PURSE
UNITE WEAVE COMPACT CONNECT
WRINKLE CONTRACT
(— STOCKINGS) SHANK
(KIND OF —) WEFT
KNITTED FLAT WOVEN
KNITTING PURL
(— OF BONES) POROSIS
KNITTING LOOP STEEK
KNITTING NEEDLE WIRE
KNOB BOB BUR NOB NUB BEAD BOLL
BOSS BURR CLUB DENT HEAD HEEL
KNOP KNOT KNUB LIFT NODE NOOP
PULL SNUG STUD TORE BERRY
BULLA BUNCH FORTE GEMMA
KNURL NATCH ONION PLOOK PLUKE
BUTTON CROCHE EMBOSS NOBBLE
NUBBLE PIMPLE PISTON POMMEL
FERRULE HORNTIP KNOBBLE
BELLPULL DOORKNOB DRAWSTOP
OMPHALOS
(— OF HAIR) TOORIE
(— OF ROCK) BUHR BURR KNUCKLE
(— ON BILL OF SWAN) BERRY
(— ON BUTT OF CANNON) GRAPE
(— ON CHAIR) POMMEL
(— ON DEER'S ANTLER) OFFER
CROCHE

(— **ON ROPE**) MOUSE
(**TY** —) VOL
(**PREF.**) CONDYL(O) TYL(O)
KNOBBED NODOSE TOROSE
BULLATE TUBEROUS TYLOTATE
KNOBBY GOUTY NODAL KNOTTY
TOROSE WHELKY GOUTISH KNOBBLY
SCRAGGED
KNOCK CON DAD HIT JOW JUT POP
PUN RAP WAP BANG BASH BEAT
BUMP CALL CHAP CHOP DASH DAUD
DING DUMP DUNT HACK JOLT JOWL
KNAP NOCK NOIT PINK PLUG POLT
POSS PUSH ROUT SLAM SLAY SNOP
TANK TIRL WHAP WHOP CLOUR
CLUMP KNOIT POUND SMITE SNOCK
STAVE STRAM THUMP BOUNCE
DUNTLE KNATCH KNETCH STOTER
CANVASS PINKING
(— **ABOUT**) RUMBLE
(— **DOWN**) MOW DROP DUMP FELL
FLOOR GRASS LEVEL SMITE SOUSE
HURTLE RAFFLE UNPILE CLOTHESLINE
(— **FOR A LOOP**) FLOOR
(— **OFF**) SECURE
(— **ON HEAD**) MAZER MAZARD
(— **OUT**) OUT SAP CONK COOL KAYO
FLATTEN STIFFEN
(— **UNCONSCIOUS**) COLDCOCK
(— **WITH THE HORNS**) DISH
(**IGNITION** —) PING
KNOCKER CROW RISP HAMMER
WHACKER
(**DOOR** —) CROW HAMMER RAPPER
KNOCK-KNEED VARUS VALGUS
KNOCKOFF COPY
KNOCKOUT KO KAYO CRUSHER
NOBBLER
(**PRETENDED**) DIVE
KNOLL NOB HIGH KNAP KNOB KNOW
TOFT HEAVE HURST HYRST MOUND
SHOAL COPPLE BOUROCK
HUMMOCK
KNOP NOB KNOB KNOSP KNAPPE
KNOT BOB BOW RUN FAG NIB NOB
NUB PIN TIE BEND BURL BURR CHOU
CLOD CLOT CLUB HARL KILL KNAG
KNAR KNOB NODE NOIL NURL SLUG
SNUB TRUE WAFT WALL BUNCH
CLOVE CROWN DUNNE GNARL
GNARR HALCH HALSH HATCH HITCH
KNURL MOUSE NODUS NOEUD
SNARL SNICK SWIRL TWIST WARRE
BOUGHT BUTTON CLINCH CROCHE
FINIAL GRANNY MASCLE SORTIE
TANGLE BOWKNOT BOWLINE
CHIGNON COCKADE GORDIAN
MAYBIRD CICISBEO DRAWKNOT
GRAYBACK KNITTING SLIPKNOT
TRUELOVE CLOVEHITCH
SHEEPSHANK
(— **IN CLOTH**) FAG NEP BURL
(— **IN COTTON FIBERS**) NEP

(— **IN SIGNAL FLAG**) WAFT WEFT
WHEFT
(— **IN WOOD**) NUR PIN BURL BURR
KNAG KNAR KNUR NURR SNUB
GNARL KNAUR KNURL KNURR
(— **IN YARN**) SLUG SNICK
(— **OF HAIR**) BOB BUN COB PUG
CLUB KNURL CHIGNON
(**EMBROIDERY** —) PICOT
(**KIND OF** —) LOVER LOVERS
(**LOVE** —) AMORET
(**ORNAMENTAL** —) BOW
(**SHOULDER** —) WING
(**WALL** —) WALE
(**PREF.**) NODI
KNOTGRASS LIGNUM HOGWEED
PIGWEED BINDWEED BIRDWEED
DOORWEED KNOTWEED
KNOTWORT PINKWEED POLYGONY
WIREWEED
KNOTTED KNIT NOUE TIED NOWED
NODOSE SWIRLY CRABBED
NODATED SCRAGGY
KNOTTY HARD CRAMP GOUTY
NODAL COMMON CRAGGY GNARLY
KNAGGY KNAPPY KNURRY NODOSE
NODOUS COMPLEX GNARLED
GOUTISH JOINTED KNARRED
KNOTTED SCABROUS
KNOTWEED LIGNUM ALLSEED
HOGWEED JUMPSEED POLYGONY
POLYGONUM
KNOW CAN CON KEN WIS WIT WOT
CITE HAVE SABE WEET WIST WOTH
SAVVY SKILL COGNIZE
(— **NOT**) NOOT
(—**S NOT**) NOTE
(**DID NOT** —) KENDNA
(**DO NOT** —) KENNA
KNOWABLE SENSABLE
KNOW-HOW CRAFT MOXIE SMART
SMARTS SAVVY SKILL
KNOWING FLY HEP HIP SLY FOXY
GASH INON ONTO SPRY WISE
AWARE CANNY DOWNY JERRY
LEERY SPACK WITTY EXPERT SCIENT
SCIOUS SHREWD WITFUL WITTER
GNOSTIC SAPIENT WISEDUP
(— **SUPERFICIALLY**) SCIOLOUS
(**SUFF.**) GNOSIA GNOSIS GNOSTIC
GNOSY
KNOWINGLY CANNILY SCIENTER
SHREWDLY WITTERLY
KNOW-IT-ALL MAVIN SAVANT
KNOWLEDGE CAN WIT BOOK KITH
KNOW LAIR LEAR LORE NOTE INWIT
JNANA SAVVY SKILL VIDYA ADVICE
AVIDYA CLERGY GNOSIS NOESIS
NOTICE WISDOM CUNNING DIANOIA
HEARING KNOWING MEANING
SCIENCE WITTING DAYLIGHT
DOCTRINE EPISTEME LEARNING

LETTRURE NOTITION PRUDENCE
SAPIENCE SCIENTIA COGNIZANCE
(— OF ALL THINGS) OMNISCIENCE
(— OF SPIRITUAL TRUTH) GNOSIS
(ABSOLUTE —) PANSOPHY
(EXPERT —) SKILL
(FAMILIAR —) HANG
(GENERAL —) GROUNDING
(INWARD —) INWIT
(LATER —) AFTERWIT
(MYSTERIOUS —) ARCANUM
(PIECEMEAL —) SMATTER
(PRACTICAL —) INSIGHT
(PRIVATE —) PRIVITY
(PUBLIC —) LIGHT
(SLICK —) ANGLE
(SLIGHT —) INKLING SMATTER
(SPIRITUAL —) GNOSIS
(SUPERFICIAL —) SCIOLISM
(SUPERIOR —) MASTERY
(SUPREME —) PRAJNA
(SYSTEMATIZED —) SCIENCE
(UNIVERSAL —) PANSOPHY
(PREF.) EPISTEMO GNOSIO
(SUFF.) GNOSIA GNOSIS GNOSTIC
GNOSY ICS SOPH(ER)(IC)(IST)(Y)
KNOWLEDGEABLE KNOWING
SKILLED STUDIED
KNOWN EVER COUTH COMMON
(ACTUALLY —) SPECIOUS
(ALSO — AS) AKA
(GENERALLY —) PUBLIC
(LITTLE —) FAMELESS
(NOT —) DARK SILENT
(OTHERWISE — AS) ALIAS
(PUBLICLY —) EXOTERIC
(UNMISTAKABLY —) STATED
(WIDELY —) COMMON
KNOW-NOTHING SAM
KNUCKLE KNUCK JARRET
(PREF.) CONDYL(O)
KNUCKLEBONE DIB DOLOS TALUS
COCKAL SHACKLE
KNUCKLEHEAD SAP DUMDUM
KNURL MILL NULL DWARF SNARL
KNURLING NULLING REEDING
KNULLING
KOALA BEAR BAALU BALOO SLOTH
KOOLAH WOMBAT CARBORA
PHALANGER
KOANGA (CHARACTER IN —) JOSE
PEREZ SIMON KOANGA PALMYRA
MARTINEZ
(COMPOSER OF —) DELIUS
KOBOLD NIS GNOME NISSE
HODEKEN HUTCHEN
KOEL KOIL KOKIL RAINBIRD
KOHATH (FATHER OF —) LEVI
(SISTER OF —) JOCHEBED
KOHL COHOL ALCOHOL
KOHLRABI BROMATIUM
KOKAN LAMPATIA
KOKO LEBBEK

KOKOON GNU
KOKUM GARCINIA
KOKUMIN BAN
KOLA COLA BICHY GOORANUT
KOLAIAH (SON OF —) AHAB
KOMATIC SLED
KOMATIK SLED
KOMBU KOBU KAMBOU CHAKOBU
KOMMETJE WALLOW COMITJE
KONAK YALI
KOOK NITWIT DINGBAT DINGALING
KOOKABURRA KOOKA JACKASS
KOOKY CRAZY OFFBEAT
KOPECK KAPEIKA
KORAH (FATHER OF —) ESAU IZHAR
ELIPHAZ
(MOTHER OF —) AHOLIBAMAH
KORAKAN RAGI RAGGI RAGGY
KORAN KITAB QURAN ALCORAN
(SECTION OF —) SURA SURAH
KORE DESPOINA
(FATHER OF —) IMNAH
KOREA (SEE NORTH KOREA OR
SOUTH KOREA)
KOREC MIRA
KORINA LIMBA
KOS COAN
KOSHER (NOT —) TREF
KOSIN KOUSSIN TAENNIN BRAYERIN
KOSO PANAMINT
KOULAN GOUR
**KOVANSHCHINA (CHARACTER IN
—)** ENNA IVAN MARFA ANDREY
DOSIFEY GOLITSYN KHOVANSKY
(COMPOSER OF —) MUSSORGSKY
KOWHAI GOAI PELU LOCUST
SOPHORA
KOWTOW KNEEL SHIKO
KOYUKON TENA KHOTANA
KRAAL CRAW MANYATTA ZIMBABWE
KRAIT ADDER KORAIT BUNGARUM
KRATER KELEBE
KRAUNHIA WISTARIA
KREIS CIRCLE
**KREUTZER SONATA (AUTHOR OF
—)** TOLSTOY
(CHARACTER IN —) LIZA VASYLA
POZDNISHEF TRUKHASHEVSKY
KRIEMHILD (BROTHER OF —)
GERNOT GUNTHER GISELHER
(FATHER OF —) GIBICH
(HUSBAND OF —) ATTILA SIEGFRIED
KRIS CREASE CREESE DAGGER
KRISHNA VASUDEVA
(BROTHER OF —) BALARAMA
(FATHER OF —) VASUDEVA
(FOSTER FATHER OF —) NANDA
(FOSTER MOTHER OF —) YASHODA
(MOTHER OF —) DEVAKI
(UNCLE OF —) KANSA
KRISTIN LAVRANSDATTER
(AUTHOR OF —) UNDSET
(CHARACTER IN —) ULF IVAR GAUTE

MUNAN SIMON SKULE ERLEND JOFRID NAAKVE AASHILD HALVARD KRISTIN LAVRANS RAMBORG ULVHILD BJORGULF JARDTRUD NIKULAUS RAGNRID ANDRESSON BJORGULFSON IVARSDATTER LAVRANSDATTER
KRONE CROWN CORONA
KRU KROOBOY KROOMAN
KRUMMHORN CREMONA CROMORNE
KSHATRIYA THAKUR
KUA MAKUA MAKWA
KUBA BUSHONGO KABISTAN
KUDZU VINE KOHEMP
KUI KHONDI
KU KLUXER KLUXER KLUCKER KLANSMAN
KUKURUKU IKPERE
KULANAPAN POMO
KUMAN POLOVTZY
KUMBUK ARJAN ARJUN
KUMMEL ALLASCH
KUMQUAT NAGAMI
KUNTI (FATHER OF —) PANDU SHURA (SON OF —) BHIMA KARNA ARJUNA YUDHISHTHIRA
KURRAJONG CALOOL LACEBARK
KURUKH ORAON
KUSA DARBHA
KUSHAIAH (SON OF —) ETHAN
KUSIMANSEL MANGUE
KUTCHIN LOUCHEUX

KUWAIT (— NATIVE) ARAB (CAPITAL OF —) ALKUWAIT (OIL FIELD OF —) WAFRA BAHRAH BURGAN SABRIYA MINAGISH RAUDHATAIN (OTHER NAME OF —) KOWEIT KUWEIT (TOWN OF —) MAGWA AHMADI HAWALLI ABDULLAH FAHAHEEL
KVASS ALE BEER QUASH
KWENI GURO
KYANITE DISTHENE
KYOODLE YAP
KYPHOSIS HUMPBACK

KYRGYZSTAN
(ALSO SEE RUSSIA)
CAPITAL: FRUNZE BISHKEK PISHPEK
COIN: SOM
LAKE: ISSYKKUL
MOUNTAIN: VICTORY KHANTENGRI
MOUNTAIN RANGE: ALAY KIRGIZ ZAALAY CHATKAL FERGANA TIENSHAN TRANSALAY KOKSHAALTAU KUNGEYALATAU TERSKEYALATAU
NAME: KYRGYZ KIRGHIZIA KIRGIZIYA
RIVER: CHU NARYN SYRDARYA
TOWN: OSH TOKMAK BISHKEK KYZYLKIYA PREZHEVALSK
VALLEY: CHU TALAS FERGANA

KYURINISH LESGHIN LEZGHIAN

L

L EL LIMA FIFTY
LAADAH (FATHER OF —) SHELAH
  (GRANDFATHER OF —) JUDAH
LAADAN (FATHER OF —) GERSHOM
LAAGER LEEGTE LEAGUER
LABAN (DAUGHTER OF —) LEAH
  RACHEL
  (FATHER OF —) BETHUEL
  (SISTER OF —) REBEKAH
LABDACUS (FATHER OF —)
  POLYDORUS
  (MOTHER OF —) NYCTEIS
  (SON OF —) LAIUS
LABDANUM MYRRH
LABEL TAG BILL FILE MARK FICHE
  STAMP TALLY TITLE DIRECT DOCKET
  TICKET ENDSEAL LAMBEAU STICKER
  (— ON SUIT OF CLOTHES) ETIQUET
LABELLUM LIP LABEL PETAL
  (PART OF —) HYPOCHIL
LABIAL ROUND
LABIATE HOREHOUND
LABIUM LIP LABRUM
LABOR ADO FAG TUG WIN CARK
  MOIL TASK TAVE TILL TOIL WORK
  BEGAR DELVE GRAFT GRIND HEAVE
  PAINS SWEAT SWINK TEAVE TREAD
  WHILE YAKKA CORVEE DRUDGE
  EFFORT HAMMER STRIVE BULLOCK
  FATIGUE MANUARY OPIFICE
  PROCURE SERVICE SLAVERY TRAVAIL
  TROUBLE TURMOIL BUSINESS
  DRUDGERY EXERTION GROANING
  INDUSTRY LABORAGE STRUGGLE
  (— ARDUOUSLY) BILDER
  (— HARD) THRASH THRIPPLE
  (— LEADER) DEBS
  (— UNDER) SUFFER
  (DAY'S —) DARG JOURNEY
  (DIFFICULT —) DYSTOCIA
  (EXCESSIVE —) STRAIN
  (FORCED —) BEGAR CORVEE
  (HARD —) HARD BULLWORK
  (HIRED —) TOGT
  (IMPOSED —) TASKAGE
  (MENTAL —) HEADWORK
  (ROUTINE —) SCUTWORK
  (SEVERE —) AGON
  (UNPAID —) CORVEE
LABORATORY LAB SHOP KITCHEN
  OFFICINA WORKSHOP PHYTOTRON
LABOR CAMP GULAG
LABORED HEAVY FORCED SWEATY
  STRAINED
LABORER (ALSO SEE WORKER AND
  WORKMAN) BOY BHAR ESNE HIND

JACK JOEY MOZO PEON TOTY BAGDI
CHURL GUASO HUNKY NAVVY PALLI
PINER STIFF BALAHI BEGARI
BOHUNK COALER COOLIE DAYMAN
DILKER DOCKER FELLAH FLUNKY
FOGGER HEAVER HODMAN HOLEYA
JIBARO LUMPER RAFTER TASKER
WAYMAN WORKER BRACERO
BYWONER CREWMAN DAYSMAN
DIGGORY DIRGLER DRAINER
DVORNIK GRECIAN HARDHAT
HOBBLER MANUARY MAZDOOR
PICKMAN PIONEER PIPEMAN
PLOWMAN SANDHOG SCOURER
SHIPPER SMASHER SOUGHER
SPALLER STOCKER SWINKER
TOTYMAN WORKMAN BIJWONER
CHAINMAN COTTAGER DOLLYMAN
FARMHAND FLOORMAN GANGSMAN
HOLDSMAN SPADEMAN SPALPEEN
STRAPPER TIDESMAN ROUSTABOUT
  (DOCK —) SEAGULL
  (INEXPERIENCED —) GREENER
  (LOWLY —) GRUNT
LABORIOUS HARD HEAVY STIFF
  TOUGH SWEATY UPHILL ARDUOUS
  OPEROSE SLAVISH TOILFUL DILIGENT
  LABOROUS TOILSOME
LABRADOR TEA LEDUM GOWIDDIE
LABRYS AX AXE
LABURNUM AWBER
LABYRINTH MAZE CIRCUIT
  MEANDER
LABYRINTHINE TORTUOUS
  BYZANTINE
LAC LACCA LACQUER
LACE VAL BEAT BEST FOND GOTA
  LASH PEAK FILET LACIS LIVEN ORRIS
  POINT SCREW SPRIG WEAVE BLONDE
  CADDIS CORDON DEFEAT EDGING
  GRILLE LACING LASHER THRASH
  TUCKER VENISE ALENCON ALLOVER
  BULLION CURRAGH CUTWORK
  FOOTING GALLOON GUIPURE
  HONITON LATCHET MACRAME
  MALINES MECHLIN MELANGE
  NANDUTI TAMBOUR TATTING
  TORCHON TROLLEY ARGENTAN
  BOBBINET BONEWORK BOOTLACE
  BRUSSELS DENTELLE ILLUSION
  LACEWORK LIMERICK PEARLING
  STAYLACE COLBERTINE
  NEEDLEPOINT
  (— EDGING) PUNTILLA
  (— IN PLACE OF COLLAR) RUCHE
  (— MAKER) TWISTHAND

(— PATTERN) TOILE
(KIND OF —) CLUNY
(KNOTTED —) TATTING
LACEBARK LAGETTO DAGUILLA
　LACEWOOD
LACE BUG TINGITID
LACEDAEMON (DAUGHTER OF —)
　CLEODICE
　(FATHER OF —) ZEUS JUPITER
　(MOTHER OF —) TAYGETE
　(SON OF —) HIMERUS
　(WIFE OF —) SPARTA
LACERATE REND TEAR GANCH
　ENGORE HARROW MANGLE SCARIFY
　FRACTURE
LACERATION RIP TEAR WOUND
LACERTA LIZARD
LACEWING NEUROPTERAN
LACEWOOD SYCAMORE
LACEWORK DENTELLE
LACHRYMOSE SAD TEARY WEEPY
　MAUDLIN
LACINARIA LIATRIS
LACING LACET LINGEL ECHELLE
　LANGUET
　(RAWHIDE —S) BABICHE
LACINIATION DAG
LACK FAIL LANK LIKE LOSS MAIM
　MISS NEED VOID WANE WANT FAULT
　MINUS DEARTH DEFECT INLAIK
　ABSENCE BLEMISH DEFAULT
　FAILURE PAUCITY REQUIRE VACANCY
　SCARCITY SOLITUDE WANTROKE
　(— CONFIDENCE) DOUBT
　(— FAITH) DIFFIDE
　(— HARMONY) DISAGREE
　(— OF APPETITE) ANOREXIA
　(— OF CLARITY) DARKNESS
　(— OF CONFIDENCE) MISTRUST
　(— OF COORDINATION) ASYNERGY
　DYSERGIA
　(— OF DEVELOPMENT) AGENESIS
　(— OF EARNESTNESS) ITEMING
　(— OF EFFUSIVENESS) RESERVE
　(— OF EMOTION) APATHY
　(— OF ENERGY) ATONY ANERGY
　ATONIA
　(— OF FLAVOR) SILENCE
　(— OF FORESIGHT) MYOPIA
　(— OF HARMONY) DISCORD
　DISUNITY
　(— OF INTENTION) ACCIDENT
　(— OF INVOLVEMENT) DISTANCE
　(— OF ORDER) ATAXY ATAXIA
　DISARRAY
　(— OF PATRIOTISM) INCIVISM
　(— OF REFINEMENT) CRUDITY
　(— OF SENSE) FOLLY
　(— OF SENSE OF SMELL) ANOSMIA
　(— OF STEADINESS) LEVITY
　(— OF SYMPATHY) DYSPATHY
　(— OF VIGOR) LANGUOR

(— OF VITALITY) ANEMIA ADYNAMIA
(— OF WIND) CALM
(— OF WORTH) IMMERIT
(— STRENGTH) DROOP
LACKADAISICAL LANGUID
　LISTLESS
LACKEY SKIP SLAVE LAPDOG
　LACQUEY STAFFIER
LACKING BUT SHY BARE FREE SANS
　WANT ALACK GNEDE MINUS SHORT
　ABSENT BARREN DEVOID WITHIN
　WANTING DESOLATE INDIGENT
　(PREF.) LONCH(O)
LACKLUSTER DULL FISHY CLOUDY
　GLASSY
LACONIA (CAPITAL OF —) SPARTA
LACONIAN SPARTAN
LACONIC CURT SHORT CONCISE
　POINTED SPARTAN SUCCINCT
LA CORUNA GROIN
LACQUER LAC DOPE DUCO JAPAN
　CHATON LACKER URUSHI VARNISH
LACRIMAL
　(PREF.) DACRY(O)
LACTATION (— PERIOD) NOTE
LACTONE CUMARIN LIMONIN
　MECONIN DIKETENE
LACTOSCOPE PIOSCOPE
LACUNA GAP BREAK HIATUS
LACUSTRINE LAKISH
LAD BOY BUB MAN BOYO CARL CHAP
　DICK HIND JOCK LOON LOUN SNAP
　BILLY BUCKO CADDY CHIEL GROOM
　YOUTH BURSCH CADDIE CALLAN
　FELLOW LADDIE LADKIN MANNIE
　NIPPER SHAVER CALLANT
　MUCHACHO SPRINGER STRIPLING
　(AWKWARD —) GROMET GRUMMET
　(MISCHIEVOUS —) GAMIN
　(MY —) AVICK
　(SERVING —) GILLIE GOSSOON
LADDER STY STEE JACOB SCALE
　AERIAL BANGOR ESCAPE PULEYN
　GANGWAY POLEYNE POMPIER
　(— IN HOSE) RUN
　(— TO LOFT) TRAP
　(FIREMAN'S —) STICK
　(FISH —) FISHWAY
　(JACOB'S —) CHARITY
　(REVOLVING —) POTENCE
　(ROPE —) ETRIER
LADDER-LIKE SCALAR
LADDIE JOCKEY LATHIE LADDOCK
　LADDIKIE
LADE BAIL LAVE LADEN TRUSS
　BURDEN ONLOAD FRAUGHT
　(— INTO COOLER) STRIKE
LADEN HEAVY BELAST LOADED
　FRAUGHT FREIGHT GESTANT
LA-DI-DA TOOTOO EXTREME
LADING LOAD CARGO BURDEN
　FREIGHT

LADINO SPANIOL
LADLE DIP JET GAWN SKEP CLATH
CYATH KEACH STOOP DIPPER LADING
CUVETTE CYATHUS KYATHOS
POTSTICK
(— FOR MOLTEN METAL) SHANK
(— OUT SOUP) SLEECH
(— WITH HANDLES) CYATH SHANK
CYATHUS KYATHOS SKIPPET
(BRINE —) LOOT
(LARGE —) SCOOP
(PREF.) ARYTENO
LADRONE TULISAN LATHERIN
LADY BIBI BURD DAMA DAME RANI
DONNA HANUM BEEBEE DOMINO
FEMALE KADINE KHANUM RAWNIE
SAHIBA SENORA LADYKIN
MADONNA SENHORA BELAMOUR
SINEBADA
(— OF HIGH RANK) BEGUM
(— OF HOUSE) GOODWIFE
(BEAUTIFUL —) CLEAR
(LEADING —) PREMIERE
(TURKISH —) KHANUM
(YOUNG —) DEB MISS DAMSEL
MAIDEN DAMOZEL DEBUTANTE
(PL.) LADYHOOD
LADYBUG VEDALIA
LADYFISH WRASSE PUDIANO
BONEFISH BONYFISH DONCELLA
LADYISH TENPOUNDER
LADYLIKE FEMALE
LADYLOVE LADY DELIA MINION
MISTRESS
LADY'S-COMB NEEDLES
LADY'S-MANTLE DEWCUP
PADELION
LADY'S-SLIPPER DUCK YELLOW
NERVINE YELLOWS UMBILROOT
(PREF.) CYPRI CYPRO
LADY'S-SMOCK SPINK
LADY WINDERMERE'S FAN
(AUTHOR OF —) WILDE
(CHARACTER IN —) LORTON
ERLYNNE AUGUSTUS MARGARET
DARLINGTON WINDERMERE
LAEL (SON OF —) ELIASAPH
LAERTES (FATHER OF —) ARCESIUS
(MOTHER OF —) CHALCOMEDUSA
(SON OF —) ULYSSES
(WIFE OF —) ANTICLEA
LAG DRAG DRAW SLOG DELAY TRAIL
HOCKER LAGGER LINGER LOITER
STRING DRIDDLE LAGGING
(— IN PRODUCTION) SLIPPAGE
(KIND OF —) JET
LAGGARD SLOW TARDY LAGGER
TORTOISE
LAGGING TARDY JACKET DEADING
LAGGARD CLEADING DRAWLING
FOREPOLE
LAGNIAPPE TIP GIFT BONUS EXTRA
PILON PRESENT

LAGOMORPH HARE PIKA RABBIT
LAGOON HAFF POOL BAYOU LIMAN
LAGUNA SALINA
LAHAD (FATHER OF —) JAHATH
LAHMI (BROTHER OF —) GOLIATH
LAID (— ACROSS WALL) INBOND
(— DOWN) THETIC THETICAL
(— WASTE) BARE
LAIR DEN LAY FORM HOLD SHED
COUCH EARTH HAUNT LODGE
MEUSE SQUAT HARBOR KENNEL
SPELUNK
(— OF FOX) KENNEL
(— OF OTTER) HOLT HOVER
(— OF WILD BOAR) SOUNDER
LAISH (SON OF —) PHALTIEL
LAISSE TIRADE
LAITY FOLK LAYMEN PEOPLE
LAIUS (FATHER OF —) LABDACUS
(SON OF —) OEDIPUS
(WIFE OF —) JOCASTA
LAKE LAY SEA VLY BAHR JAIL JHIL
LAGO LLYN LOCH MERE MOAT SHOR
TANK TARN VLEI VLEY BAYOU CHOTT
JHEEL LERNA LIMAN LOUGH SPARK
TUBIG LAGOON NYANZA STROND
ANCYLUS CARMINE LAKELET
TURLOUGH
(CASHEW —) AUBURN
(DRY —) PLAYA
(FENNY —) BROAD
(MOUNTAIN —) TARN
(RELATING TO —S) LIMNAL
(SALT —) SHOT CHOTT SHOTT
SALINA SALINE
(SHALLOW —) PLAYA
(SMALL —) GURGES MARIGOT
(TEMPORARY —) PINAG
(YELLOW —) PINK
(PREF.) LIMN(I)(O)
(SUFF.) LIMNION
LAKE CARP DRUM LAKER
LAKE-DWELLING CRANNOG
LAKE HERRING KIYI CISCO
GRAYBACK
LAKE TROUT POGY TOGUE
LAKE WHITEFISH POLLAN
LAKME (CHARACTER IN —) LAKME
GERALD NILAKANTHA
(COMPOSER OF —) DELIBES
LAKSHMANA (FATHER OF —)
DURYODHANA
(SLAYER OF —) ABHIMANYU
LAKSHMI SRI SHREE
(HUSBAND OF —) VISHNU
LALAPALOOZA ONER
LAMA ELK AUCHENIA
LAMB BUM PET PUR CADE DEAR
DUPE ELIA LOME SOCK YEAN AGNUS
PESAH PODDY AGNEAU COSSET
HIEDER LAMBIE LAMKIN PESACH
SUCKER WASTER WEANER CHILVER
EANLING FATLING HOGLING

PASCHAL PERSIAN RUFFIAN
TWAGGER BAAHLING LAMBLING
PASSOVER YEANLING
(— AND WHEAT) KIBBE
(SCYTHIAN —) BAROMETZ
(SHOULDER OF —) BANJO
(SIDE OF —) CONCERTINA
LAMBASTE BEAT WHIP CREAM
SCOLD SCORE CENSURE SQUABASH
LAMBENT BRIGHT RADIANT
LAMBREQUIN MANTLING
LAMBSKIN LAMB BAGDAD
BAGHDAD SALZFELLE
LAMB'S QUARTERS MUCKWEED
LAMB'S WOOL WASSAIL
LAME BUM GAME HALT LAHN
GAMMY GIMPY GRAVEL TINSEL
CRIPPLE CRIPPLY HALTING HIPHALT
GORGERIN SPAVINED
(— A HORSE) STUB NOBBLE
(— WITH HORSESHOE NAIL) ACCLOY
LAMEBRAIN CLOD KNUCKLEHEAD
LAMECH (DAUGHTER OF —) NAAMAH
(SON OF —) NOAH JABAL JUBAL
TUBALCAIN
(WIFE OF —) ADAH ZILLAH
LAMELLA PLICA FOLIUM FORNIX
LAMELLAR SPATHIC
LAMELLIBRANCH PELECYPOD
LAMENESS HALT
LAMENT CRY WEY CARE DOLE HONE
HOWL KEEN MEAN MOAN PINE SIGH
TEAR WAIL WALY WEEP CROON
DUMKA GREET KINAH MOURN PLAIN
QINAH BEHOWL BEMOAN BEWAIL
BEWEEP KOMMOS KOMMOS PLAINT
REGRET REPINE SORROW SQUAWK
THREAP YAMMER BEMOURN
CONDOLE DEPLORE EJULATE
ELEGIZE GRIZZLE BEGRAIL THRENOS
WAYMENT COMPLAIN CORONACH
MOURNING THRENODY ULLAGONE
WELLAWAY
LAMENTABLE YEMER FUNEST
RUEFUL DOLEFUL PITIFUL PITIABLE
PLAINFUL YAMMERLY
LAMENTATION KEEN MOAN WAIL
DOLOR LINOS RUING TANGI LAMENT
PLAINT REGRET SORROW THRENE
PLANGOR TRAGEDY WAYMENT
WILLAWA CORONACH MOURNING
PATHETIC WAILMENT WELLAWAY
LAMENTING
LAMINA FILM LAME LAMP LEAF
OBEX BLADE FLAKE LAMIN PLATE
SCALE SHELL TABLE FOLIUM
CAPSULE
LAMINATE LEAFY FLAGGY
LAMINATED BUILT FOLIATE
TABULAR
LAMINATION SLABBING
LAMINITIS FOUNDER
LAMMAS DAY GULE TERM

LAMMERGEIER AREND OSSIFRAGE
LAMP ARC EYE SEE DAVY GLIM INKY
JACK SLUT ALDIS ARGAND ASTRAL
BULLET HELION LAMPAD TARGET
ILLUMER LAMPION LAMPLET
LANTERN LUCERNE LUCIGEN
SUNLAMP SUNSPOT AEOLIGHT
CIRCLINE GASLIGHT SIDELAMP
TORCHERE PHOTOFLASH
PHOTOFLOOD
(— FOR FIREPLACE) KYLE
(CHIMNEYLESS —) TORCH
(DARKROOM —) SAFELIGHT
(IRON —) CRUSIE
(KIND OF —) POLE
(MAKESHIFT —) BITCH
(NIGHT —) VEILLEUSE
(PART OF —) CAP CORD HARP SHELL
FINIAL NIPPLE SOCKET SWITCH
WASHER NECKWING
(SAFETY —) DAVY GEORDIE
(STAGE —S) BATTEN
(TYPE OF —) GOOSENECK
(4-CORNERED —) CHILL
(PL.) CLUSTER
(PREF.) LYCHNO
LAMPBLACK LINK SOOT
LAMPETIA (FATHER OF —) APOLLO
HELIOS
(MOTHER OF —) NEAERA
(SISTER OF —) PHAETHUSA
LAMP HOLDER HUSK
LAMPLIGHTER LEERIE
LAMPOON PIPE SKIT GESTE LIBEL
SQUIB IAMBIC SATIRE BERHYME
PASQUIN COCKALAN RIDICULE
SATIRIZE PASQUINADE
LAMPOONER PASQUIL PASQUIN
LAMPREY EEL PRIDE LAMPER
MYZONT RAMPER SAYNAY SUCKER
LAMPERN
LAMP RING CRIC
LAMPSHADE GLOBE
(PART OF —) RIB RING SHADE SPIDER
LAMPSTAND TORCHERE
LAMPWARE (— STYLE) TOLE
LAMPWICK MATCH
LANATE WOOLY LANOSE WOOLLY
LANCE PIC CANE DART SHAFT SPEAR
STAFF BROACH ELANCE GLAIVE
GLEAVE LANCET ROCKET LANCELET
SPICULUM
(KING ARTHUR'S —) RON
LANCE GUARD VAMPLATE
LANCE HEAD MORNE SOCKET
LANCELET AMPHIOXUS
LANCER LANCE SOWAR UHLAN
LANCE REST QUEUE FEWTER
LANCET FLEAM FLEEM LANCELET
LANCEWOOD YAYA CIGUA CANFLA
YARIYARI
LAND ERD ERF NOD RIB AGER DIRT
FOLD GALE GISH GORE JODO MARK

SITE SOIL EARTH EJIDO ETHEL FIELD
GLEBE JUGER PLANT SHORE SOLUM
ALIGHT ASSART FUNDUS GROUND
COMMONS COUNTRY DEMESNE
ELLASAR HOLDING LANDING
LIBRATE QUILLET TERRENE ALLODIAL
BOOKLAND COMMONTY FARMLAND
FLEYLAND FOLKLAND POMERIUM
PRAEDIUM
(— A PLANE) GREASE
(— BETWEEN FURROWS) SELION
(— BETWEEN RIVERS) DOAB
(— BORDERING SEA) SHORE
(— CLEARING) KAINGIN
(— CONVERTED TO TILLAGE) TWAITE
THWAITE
(— HAVING VALUE OF POUND PER
YEAR) LIBRATE
(— IN CONACRE) MOCK
(— IN GRASS) LAYER
(— LEFT FALLOW) ARDER
(— MEASURE) RIG
(— OF BLISS) GOKURAKU
(— OF GIANTS) UTGARTHAR
(— OF MANSION) DEMESNE
(— OF OPPORTUNITY) ARKANSAS
(— OF PLENTY) GOSHEN
(— OF REGION) MOLD MOULD
(— PLOWED IN A DAY) JORNADA
(— RECOVERED FROM SEA) INTAKE
INNINGS
(— REGULARLY FLOODED) SALTING
(— SURROUNDED BY WASTE) HOPE
(— UNIT) URE KIPUKA MECATE
MORGEN MANZANA VIRGATE
(ALLUVIAL —) BATTURE
(ANCESTRAL —) ETHEL
(ARABLE —) LEA LEY LAINE
(ARID —) DESERT STEPPE
(BOTTOM —) SLASH CALLOW
STRATH
(CHURCH —) GLEBE TERMON
(CHURCH —S) CROSS
(CLEAR —) BUSHHOG
(CLEARED —) ASSART
(COMMON —) EJIDO EXIDO STRAY
(CONTINENTAL —) MAIN
(CULTIVATED —) FARM ARADA TILTH
CULTURE FEERING WAINAGE
LABORAGE METAIRIE
(ENCLOSED —) CLOSE INTAKE
(FREEHOLD —) MULK
(GRAVELLY —) GEEST GRAVES
(GRAZING —) GRASS HIRSEL HIRSLE
FEEDING
(HEATHY —) ROSLAND
(HERITABLE —) ODAL UDAL
(IMAGINARY —) FAERIE COCKAYNE
LILLIPUT
(LEASED —) TACK
(LONG STRIP OF —) SLANG SPONG
(LOW —) BOG FEN GALL INKS CARSE
BOTTOM

(LOW RICH —) CARSE
(NATIVE —) SOD KITH BLIGHTY
BIRTHDOM HOMELAND
(OBDURATE —) TILL
(ON —) ASHORE
(PARCEL OF —) FEU LOT MOCK
(PASTURE —) HA ALP FEED HOGA
WALK GRASS VELDT LEASON
SCATHOLD SCATLAND
(PLATEAU —) HIGHVELD
(PLOWED —) ARADA FALLOW
FURROW BREAKING
(PRIVATE —) SEVERAL
(PROMISED —) CANAAN
(PURE —) JODO SUKHAVATI
(RECLAIMED —) POLDER THWAITE
(RESOWN —) HOOKLAND
(ROUGH —) BRAKE
(SAVANNAH —S) LALANG
(SCRUBBY —) SCROG SCROGS
(SMALL PARCEL OF —) SUERTE
(SWAMPY —) WOODSERE
(TIMBER —S) STICKS
(WASTE —) HEATH
(WESTERN —) HESPERIA
(WET —) SOAK SWAMP SWANG
(WOODED —S) STICKS
(PL.) ACRES SUCKEN LAENDER
NOVALIA
(PREF.) CHERSO CHOR(O)
(SUFF.) GAEA GEA

LANDBOOK TERRIER
LAND-CRAB HORSEMAN
LANDED PRAEDIAL
LANDFORM CUSP CUESTA
LANDHOLDER LAIRD COSCET
TALUKDAR
LANDHOLDING BARONY
LANDING BANK VTOL YARD STAITH
LANDAGE ARRIVAGE FOOTPACE
HALFPACE LANDFALL
(— IN WATER) SPLASHDOWN
(ABRUPT —) PANCAKE
(BOAT —) SLIP
(CRASH —) PRANG
(SMOOTH —) GREASER
LANDING PLACE GHAT HARD
SCALE PALACE ARRIVAGE
LANDING STAGE MEAR STAGE
STAIR STAITH STELLING
LANDLADY WIFE DUENA PADRONA
GOODWIFE
LAND-LOCK EMBAY
LANDLOCK EMBAY
LAND-LOCKED MEDITERRANEAN
LANDLORD HOST LEASER
LESSOR GOODMAN PADRONE
ZAMINDAR
LANDMARK COPA DOLE DOOL
MARK MERE BAKEN BOUND CAIRN
MARCH MEITH SENAL CIPPUS
SEAMARK
LANDMASS BULGE

LANDOWNER THANE BONDER
SQUIRE CACIQUE EFFENDI FREEMAN
BHUMIDAR FRANKLIN ZAMINDAR
(PL.) GAMORI GEOMOROI
LANDSCAPE VIEW BOCAGE
PAYSAGE SCENERY LANDSKIP
LANDSLIDE SLUMP LANDFALL
LANDSLIP
LANDSLIP SLIDE
LANDSMAL MAL NYNORSK
LAND SPRING LAVANT
LANDVOGT BAILIFF
LANE GUT WAY GANG LOAN LOKE
PASS RACE VEIN WIND WYND ALLEY
CHASE DRANG DRONG ENTRY
BOREEN VENNEL LANEWAY
LOANING TWITTEN DRIFTWAY
(AIR TRAFFIC —) CORRIDOR
(FREE-THROW —) PAINT
(NARROW —) CHAR CHARE TEWER
BOREEN RUELLE
(OCEAN —) SEAWAY
LANGOUSTINE PRAWN
LANGUAGE (ALSO SEE DIALECT)
BAT KWA LIP CHIB CODE LEED RUNE
TALE TESO LEDEN LINGO SLANG
VEDIC LANGUS LINGUA SPEECH
TONGUE YABBER ACCENTS CABLESE
DIALECT IDIOLECT LEGALESE
PARLANCE PILIPINO
(— AKIN TO SHAN) THAI
(— COMBINATION) SPANGLISH
(— ENDING) ESE
(— FAMILY) URALIC
(— IN SURINAME) SRANAN
(— THAT CONDEMNS) ABUSE
(— VARIETY) BASILECT
(ARTIFICIAL —) RO IDO NEO ARULO
NOVIAL VOI APUK ESPERANTO
(BANTU —) TSWANA KIRUNDI
UMBUNDU TSHILUBA
(BIBLICAL —) ARAMAIC
(COMPUTER —) ADA BAL RPG ALGOL
BASIC COBOL PROLOG SNOBOL
FORTRAN
(ENGLISH WITH YIDDISH —)
YINGLISH
(FIGURATIVE —) IMAGERY
(FLORID —) SILLABUB
(FOOLISH —) STUFF FLUMMERY
(FOUL —) SMUT ORDURE
(GYPSY —) CALO
(IMPUDENT —) SNASH
(INCOMPREHENSIBLE —) CHOCTAW
(INDO-ARYAN —) SINHALA
(INTERNATIONAL —) ANGLIC
(KIND OF —) MACHINE
(LATIN —) GRAMMAR HUMANITY
(NONSENSICAL —) BANTER
(OBSCENE —) BAWDY BAWDRY
(OF — OR BEHAVIOR) ETIC
(OF — STRUCTURE) EMIC
(OF A —) EMIC

(ORDINARY —) PROSE
(OVERPRETENTIOUS —) BOMBAST
(PERT —) SAUCE
(PIDGIN —) SABIR CAVITENO
FANAKALO
(PLAIN —) CLEAR
(PROPAGANDISTIC —) NEWSPEAK
(SECRET —) ARGOT
(SHOWY —) FLUBDUB
(SIGN —) ASL AMESIAN
(SLEAZY —) SMARM
(SPECIFIC —) GA GE HO MO VU AIS
AKA ATA EDO EFE EPE EVE EWE FAN
FON FOX FUL GEG HET ICA IJO ILA
KAI KAU KOL KOT KRU KUI LAB LAI
LAZ MON MRU SIA TWI UDI YAO ZIA
AFAR AGAO AGAU AGNI AHOM AINU
AKAN AKIM ALUR AMBO ANDI ANTA
ARUA AVAR BARI BEJA BIAK BODO
BONI BORA BUBE BUGI BULU CARA
CHAM CHIN CHOL CHUJ COOS CORA
COTO CREE CROW CUNA DENE
DOBU DYAK EFIK EKOI ERIE EYAK
FANG FIJI FULA FUNG GARO GEEZ
GHEG GOLA GOLD HARE HEHE HOPI
HOVA HULA HUPA IBAN IDJO IJAW
IXIL KADU KAFA KAMI KAVI KAWI
KELE KOCH KOMI KONO KOTA KUKI
KURI LAHU LAKH LAPP LASI LATI LAZI
LESU LETT LUBA MANX MAYA MOLE
MORO NAGA NAMA NIAS NIUE
NUBA NUPE OGOR PAIA PALI PECU
PEUL PUME RAMA SAHO SERB SERI
SGAW SHAN SIUS SORB SULU
SUMO SUMU SUSU TAAL TIAM TIBU
TINO TODA TSHI TUPI TUPY VEPS
VOTE XOSA ZULU ALEUT ALSEA
ARAUA AUETO AZTEC BAJAU BALTI
BANTU BASSA BATAK BATTA BAURE
BEMBA BHILI BICOL BILIN BONNY
CAMPA CARIB CAYUA CHANE CHIMU
CHOCO CHOPE COFAN COIBA
COMAN CUEVA CUMAN CUNZA
CZECH DAFLA DAYAK DIERI DINKA
DUALA DUTCH DYULA EMPEO FANTI
FINGO FUNJI GAFAT GALLA GANDA
GETAN GETIC GOLDI GONDI GREBO
GREEK GUAMO GUATO GURMA
GYPSY HABAB HAIDA HAIKH HATSA
HAUSA HINDI HUABI HUARI HURON
HUSKY HYLAM IGALA ILOKO IRAYA
IRISH JAKUN JATKI JUANG JUTIC
KABYL KAMBA KAMIA KANDH KAREN
KAROK KHASI KHMER KHOND KHUZI
KIOWA KISSI KIWAI KOINE KOLIS
KONDE KONGO KORKU KORWA
KOTAR KUMUK KUMYK KUSAN
KWOMA LAMBA LAMUT LANGO
LATIN LENCA LENDU LHOKE LHOTA
LIMBA LIMBU LUIAN LUNDA MAGHI
MAHRA MAHRI MALAY MALTO
MAORI MAZUR MBUBA MEDIC
MENDI MIKIR MODOC MOSSI

MUONG MURMI MURUT NAHUA
NOGAI NORSE NYORO ORAON ORIYA
OROMO OSAGE OSCAN PALAU
PAMIR PELEW PEUHL PLATT PUNIC
RONGA SAKAI SAMAL SANTO
SAXON SCOTS SERER SHILH SHINA
SHONA SICEL SIKEL SLAVE SOTHO
SOYOT SUOMI SWAZI TAINO TAMIL
TELEI TONGA TURKI UDISH UIGUR
URIYA UZBEK VOGUL WAYAO WELSH
WOLOF YAKUT YUNCA ZERMA
ABIPON ABKHAS ACAWAI ACHOLI
ADIGHE ADZHAR AFGHAN AHTENA
ALTAIC ANDAKI ANDHRA ANDOKE
ANGAMI APACHE APANTO APIACA
ARABIC ARANA ARAONA ARAWAK
ARUNTA ATAROI AVANTI AYMARA
BAGOBO BAHASA BAITSI BAKELE
BANIVA BASQUE BASUTO BEAVER
BHOTIA BHUMIJ BIHARI BILAAN
BILOXI BOHUNK BONTOC BORORO
BRAHUI BRETON BRIBRI BUKAUA
BULGAR BURIAT CAGABA CANITA
CARAJA CARIAN CARIRI CAUQUI
CAVINA CAYAPA CAYUGA CAYUSE
CEBUAN CHAGGA CHAIMA CHANGO
CHOCHO CHOKWE COCAMA CONIBO
COPTIC CREOLE DAKOTA DANISH
DOGRIB DYERMA ESKIMO EUDEVE
FRENCH FULANI FULNIO FUTUNA
GADDAN GALCHA GALIBI GATHIC
GENTOO GERMAN GILAKI GILIAK
GILYAK GOTHIC GUAIMI GUETAR
GUINAU GULLAH GURIAN HAINAN
HANTIK HARARI HATTIC HEBREW
HERERO HIBITO IBANAG IBIBIO
IFUGAO IGNERI IGOROT INDIAN
INDOIS INNUIT INUPIK ISINAI ISLETA
IVATAN KABARD KACHIN KAFFIR
KAIBAL KALMUK KAMASS KANAKA
KANURI KATIRI KEKCHI KHALKA
KHAMTI KHARIA KHOWAR KIKUYU
KILIWA KODAGU KODAGU KOIARI
KOIBAL KOLAMI KOREAN KORYAK
KOTIAK KPELLE KUNAMA KURNAI
KURUKH KYURIN LADINO LAGUNA
LAHNDA LAHULI LENAPE LEPCHA
LIBYAN LIUKIU LIVIAN LUSHAI
LUVIAN LUWIAN LYCIAN LYDIAN
MAGAHI MAGYAR MANCHU
MANOBO MBONDO MBUNDA
MEDIAN MEGREL MICMAC MINOAN
MISHMI MISIMA MOHAWK MONTES
MUYSCA MYSIAN NEPALI NEWARI
NINGPO NOOTKA NUBIAN NYANJA
OJIBWA ONEIDA OORIVA OSTIAK
OTOMAC OVAMPO PAHARI PAIUTE
PALAIC PAPAGO PAPUAN PASHTO
PAZAND POLISH PUSHTO PUSHTU
RASHTI REJANG ROMANY SAFINE
SAKIAN SALISH SAMOAN SANGIL
SANGIR SARCEE SASSAK SAVARA

SEDANG SEKANI SELKUP SELUNG
SEMANG SENECA SENUFO SESUTO
SHARRA SHASTA SILETZ SINDHI
SLOVAK SOMALI SONRAI SUBIYA
SURHAI SUSIAN TARTAR TAVGHI
TELEGU TELEUT TETTUM THONGA
TIPURA TUNGUS VANNIC VOTYAK
YANKEE YARURA YORUBA ZAREMA
ABENAKI ACHAGUA AEQUIAN
AKWAALA AKWAPIM ALABAMA
ALTAIAN AMANAYE AMHARIC
AMORITE AMUESHA APINAYE
ARAMAIC ARAPAHO ARAUCAN
ARECUNA ARGOBBA ARICARA
ARMORIC ASHANTI ASURINI
ATACAMA ATAKAPA AUSTRAL
AVESTAN AXUMITE BAGHELI
BAGIRMI BAINING BAKONGO
BALANTE BALUCHI BAMBARA
BANGALA BANNACK BASHKIR
BENGALI BEOTHUK BERBERI
BHOTIYA BHUTANI BOSNIAN BRITISH
BULANDA BUNDELI BUNYORO
BURMESE BUSHMAN CALIANA
CALINGA CARRIER CASHIBO
CATALAN CATAWBA CAWAHIB
CHACOBO CHARRUA CHATINO
CHEBERO CHECHEN CHIBCHA
CHIMILA CHINOOK CHIRINO CHIWERE
CHONTAL CHOROTI CHUKCHI
CHUMASH CHUROYA CHUVASH
CIBONEY CIMBRIC CLALLAM
COCHIMI CORNISH COTONAM
COWLITZ CYMRAEG DAGBANE
DAGOMBA DANAKIL DANKALI
DARGHIN DEUTSCH DHEGIHA
DRAVIDA ENGLISH ESCUARA
ESSELEN EUSKERA FINNISH FLEMISH
FOOCHOW FRIESIC FRISIAN GAULISH
GOAJIRO GUAHIBO GUARANI
GUAYAKI GURUNSI GYARUNG
HAITIAN HANUNOC HIDATSA HITTITE
HUASTEC HUCHNOM HUICHOL
HURRIAN IBERIAN ILOKANO
ILONGOT INGALIK IPURINA ITALIAN
ITELMES ITONAMA JACUNDA
JAGATAI KAKHYEN KALINGA
KALMUCK KAMASIN KANAUJI
KANNADA KASHUBE KASSITE
KIKONGO KIPCHAK KIRANTI KIRGHIZ
KIRUNDI KLAMATH KOASATI
KONKANI KOYUKON KUBACHI
KULAMAN KURDISH KUTCHIN
KUTENAI LAMPONG LATVIAN
LESGHIN LINGALA LOATUKO
LUGANDA MAGADHI MAHICAN
MALINKE MALTESE MAPUCHE
MARATHI MASKOKI MERCIAN
MEXICAN MINAEAN MINGREL
MISKITO MITANNI MOABITE
MOCHICA MONUMBO MORATTY
MORISCO NAHUATL NICOBAR

OJIBWAY OSMANLI OSSETIC
PAHLAVI PALAUNG PANJABI
PARBATE PERMIAK PERMIAN
PERSIAN PICTISH PRAKRIT PUNJABI
PUQUINA QUECHUA QUERCHI
SABAEAN SALINAN SAMBALI
SAMNANI SAMNITE SAMOYED
SANDAWE SANTALI SANTANA
SEMITIC SERBIAN SHAWANO
SHAWNEE SHILLUH SHIPIBO
SHUSWAP SIAMESE SIRIONO
SIUSLAW SOGDIAN SONGHAI
SONGISH SORBIAN SPANIOL
SPANISH STIKINE SUBANUN
SVANISH SWAHILI SWEDISH
TAGALOG TIBETAN TUAMOTU
TURKISH UMBRIAN UMBUNDU
VISAYAN WALLOON WENDISH
YENISEI YIDDISH ZABERMA
ZONGORA ABANEEMF ACHINESE
ACHUMAWI AKKADIAN AKSUMITE
ALACALUF ALBANIAN ALFURESE
AMAHUACA AMERICAN AMMONITE
ANGOLESE ANNAMESE ANZANIAN
APALACHI ARMENIAN ASSAMESE
ASSYRIAN ATJINESE AWISHIRA
BACTRIAN BALINESE BARBACOA
BECHUANA BHOJPURI BISCAYAN
BOSNISCH BOTOCUDO CAHUILLA
CAINGANG CANARESE CANOEIRO
CAQUETIO CARELIAN CARIJONA
CAYUBABA CHALDEAN CHAMORRO
CHEHALIS CHEMAKUM CHEYENNE
CHINGRAW OHIQUITO CHITRALI
COCONUCO COLUMBIA COMANCHE
CORAVECA CROATIAN CUSTENAU
DELAWARE DIEGUENO EGYPTIAN
ELAMITIC ETHIOPIC ETRUSCAN
FALISBAN FORMOSAN FRANKISH
FUI FULDE GALICIAN GALLEGAN
GEORGIAN GERMANIC GORKHALI
GUAICURU GUJARATI HADENDOA
HAWAIIAN HITCHITI ILLINOIS
ILLYRIAN IROQUOIS JAPANESE
JAVANESE KANARESE KANAWARI
KANKANAI KASHMIRI KASUBIAN
KERMANJI KIMBUNDU KOLARIAN
LANDSMAL LANUVIAN LIGURIAN
LIHYANIC LILLOOET LIVONIAN
LUSATIAN MADURESE MAHRATTI
MAKASSAR MALAGASY MANDINGO
MARSHALL MASOVIAN MAYATHAN
MAZOVIAN MONGOLIC MUSKOGEE
NUMIDIAN NYAMWEZI ONONDAGA
OSSETIAN PAMPANGO PHRYGIAN
PILIPINO POLABIAN PORTUGAL
PRUSSIAN RABBINIC ROMANIAN
SABELLIC SANSKRIT SAWAIORI
SCOTTISH SCYTHIAN SEBUNDOY
SEECHELT SHAMBALA SHIRIANA
SHOSHONE SICILIAN SKIPETAR
SLAVONIC SOUTHRON SQUAMISH

SUBARIAN SUBTIABA SUMATRAN
SUMERIAN TAHITIAN TALMUDIC
TAMASHEK THRACIAN TURCOMAN
VENETIAN VOLSCIAN WOGULIAN
YUGOSLAV YUKAGHIR CANAANITE
MONGOLIAN
(STRONG —) FRENCH
(SWAHILI —) KISWAHILI
(UNCLEAN —) SEWERAGE
(UNIVERSAL —) PASILALY
(WELSH —) CYMRAEG
(PL.) BALTIC FINNIC MAHORI SEMITIC
SUDANIC ILLYRIAN
(PREF.) GLOSS(O) GLOTT(I)(O) KI
(SUFF.) ESE GLOT

LANGUE D'OC LEMOSI LIMOSI
LANGUET LANGUID LANGUAGE
LANGUID WAN LANK DOWIE FAINT
DREAMY FEEBLE SICKLY SUPINE
TORPID CARELESS FLAGGING
HEEDLESS INDOLENT LISTLESS
SLUGGISH
LANGUISH DIE FADE FALL FLAG PINE
WILT DROOP DWINE FAINT QUAIL
SWOON SICKEN WITHER DECLINE
LANGUISHING FADE SICK LANGUID
LOVESICK
LANGUOR KEF KIF BLAHS ENNUI
MALAISE DEBILITY LASSITUDE
LANGUR DOUC MAHA LOTONG
LUTONG SIMPAI WANDEROO
LANK LEAN THIN GAUNT LANKY
SLANK MEAGER MEAGRE SCRANKY
SLUNKEN
LANKY LEAN RENKY SLINK GANGLY
GANGLING
LANOLIN LANUM DEGRAS
LANSEH DUKU LANSA LANZON
LANTANA OREGANO
LANTERN (ALSO SEE LAMP) BUAT
BOUET BOWET CROWN DARKY
LIGHT CUPOLA LOUVER PHAROS
SCONCE THOLUS CIMBORIO
LANTHORN LUMINARIA
(— ON ROOF) FEMEREIL
(DARK —) DARKY ABSCONCE
ABSCONSA
(ELEVATED —) PHAROS
(OPTICAL —) EPISCOPE
LANTERN FISH INIOME
LANTERN FLOUNDER MEGRIM
LANTERN FLY FULGORID
LANTERN PINION RUNDLE
TRUNDLE
LANYARD CORD WAPP GILGUY
LANIARD BACKROPE
LAODAMIA (BROTHER OF —)
ISANDER HIPPOLOCHUS
(FATHER OF —) ACASTUS
BELLEROPHON
(HUSBAND OF —) PROTESILAUS
(MOTHER OF —) HIPPOLYTE

(SLAYER OF —) ARTEMIS
(SON OF —) SARPEDON
LAODICE (FATHER OF —) PRIAM
(HUSBAND OF —) HELICAON
(MOTHER OF —) HECUBA
LAOIGHIS LEIX
LAOMEDON (DAUGHTER OF —)
HESIONE
(FATHER OF —) ILUS
(MOTHER OF —) EURYDICE
(SON OF —) PRIAM CLYTIUS

```
                LAOS
CAPITAL: VIENTIANE
COIN: KIP
MEASURE: BAK
MOUNTAIN: BIA LAI LOI SAN COPI
   KHAT ATWAT KHOUNG TIUBIA
PEOPLE: LU KHA LAO MEO YAO THAI
RIVER: NOI DONE KHONG MEKONG
   NAMHOU SEBANG
TOWN: NAPE PAKSE XIENG PAKLAY
   THAKHEK SAVANNAKHET
   LUANGPRABANG
WATERFALL: MEKONG
```

LAP LEP LIP BARM FOLD GORE LICK
SLAP SLOD SOSS SUCK WASH WELT
SKIVE LAPPER LAPPET LICKUP
SHOVEL INTERLAP
(— IN STEEL) SPILL
(— OF STRAKES) LAND
(KIND OF —) PACE
(LOSE A —) RISE ARISE STAND
LAPACHOL TECOMIN
LAPBOARD PANEL
LAPDOG MESSAN MESSET SHOUGH
LAPEL LAPPET REVERE REVERS
LAPIDARY STONER GEMMARY
LAPIDIST
LAPIDOTH (WIFE OF —) DEBORAH
LAPILLUS RAPILLO
(PL.) CINDER
LAPIS LAZULI AZURE
LAP-JOINTED CLINCH
LAPP LAPPISH LAPPONIC
LAPPED FOLIATED
LAPPET LAP PAN BARBE FANON
LABEL CORNET INFULA PINNER
(PREF.) LACINI
LAPSE DROP FADE FALL HALT SLIP
ERROR FAULT FOLLY SPACE TRACT
EFFLUX HIATUS LAPSUS DELAPSE
ESCHEAT FAILURE PASSAGE
PROCESS RELAPSE RESOLVE SLIDING
ABEYANCE CADUCITY
(— INTO WRONGDOING) STUMBLE
(— OF MEMORY) BLACKOUT
(MENTAL —) ABERRATION
(PL.) LACHES
LAPSED CADUCOUS
LAPSING CADUCOUS

LAPSTRAKE CLINCH
LAPTOP PORTABLE
LAPWING WEEP WYPE PEWIT
PEEWEE PEEWIT PLOVER TIRWIT
HORNPIE PEEWEEP PIEWIPE TEUCHIT
FLOPWING PEESWEEP TEEWHAAP
TERUTERU
LARBOARD PORT BABURD
LARCENY THEFT FELONY ROBBERY
BURGLARY STEALAGE
LARCH ALERCE LARICK SPRUCE
JUNIPER EPINETTE TAMARACK
LARD MORT SAIM ADEPS DAUBE
ENARM FLARE FLECK FLICK AXUNGE
ENLARD INLARD NEUTRAL
SAINDOUX
LARDED PIQUE CADUCE CADUCOUS
LARDER CAVE PANTRY SPENCE
BUTTERY LARDINER
LARGE BIG BULL DEEP FEAT GOOD
LONG MAIN ROOM TALL AMPLE
BULKY BURLY GRAND GREAT GROSS
HUSKY JOLLY LARGY MACRO MAXIM
RENKY ROUND SMART SPACY WALLY
GAWSIE GOODLY HEROIC MAXIMA
STRONG TRABAL BOWERLY CAPITAL
COPIOUS FAIRISH FEARFUL HEALTHY
HULKING LASKING LIBERAL MASSIVE
OUTSIZE SIZABLE BOUNCING
CHOPPING OUTSIZED PLUMPING
SENSIBLE SWACKING
(— AND HOLLOW) CAVAL
(— AND ROUND) SIDE
(— IN DIAMETER) STOUT
(APPALLINGLY —) HIDEOUS
(EXTRA —) MAXI
(EXTREMELY —) GIANT DECUMAN
GIGANTIC
(FAIRLY —) SMART
(INDEFINITELY —) NTH INFINITE
(MODERATELY —) FAIR TIDY PRETTY
(UNUSUALLY —) HEAVY SKELPIN
SKELPING
(VERY —) HUGE JUMBO ROYAL
BOXCAR BUMPER INGENT NATION
GOLIATH INTENSE BEHEMOTH
SLAPPING SPANKING SWINGING
WHACKING HUMONGOUS
(PREF.) MACR(O) MEGA MEGAL(O)
(HOW —) QUANTI
LARGE-FOOTED MEGAPOD
LARGE-FRAMED ROOMY
LARGE-LETTERED UNCIAL
LARGELY BIG HARD BIGLY
LARGENESS BULK MICKLE
BREADTH FREEDOM GIANTISM
LARGEOUR
LARGE-SCALE EPIC
LARGEST BEST MAXIMUS
LARIA BRUCHUS
LARIAT ROPE LASSO NOOSE RIATA
CABESTRO

LARK GAME ROMP ANTIC PRANK
FROLIC PEEWEE SCHEME GAMMOCK
LAVROCK LAYROCK SKYLARK
CALANDER LAVEROCK
LARKA KOLS HO
LARKSPUR LOCOWEED
LARNITE BELITE
LARRIGAN PAC
LARRIKIN NUT ROWDY HOODLUM
LARVA BOT BLOW BOTT CRAB GRUB
HUHU SLUG TURK WOLF WORM
ALIMA ASCON BARDY BRUKE ERUCA
LEECH OTTER REDIA SYCON CORBIE
COSSID DRAGON EPHYRA GRUGRU
HOPPER LEPTUS LEUCON LOOPER
MAGGOT MEASLE PEDLAR TORCEL
WABBLE WORMIL WOUBIT ATROCHA
BUDWORM CADELLE CREEPER
DIPORPA FIGWORM FLYBLOW
GORDIAN HYDATID HYPOPUS
PEDDLER PLANULA PLUTEUS
PREPUPA VELIGER WIGGLER
ACTINULA ANTIZOEA ARMYWORM
BOLLWORM BOMBYCID BOOKWORM
CASEWORM CERCARIA COENURUS
CYRTOPIA DEUTOVUM DROPWORM
EPHYRULA FIREWORM FURCILIA
GEOMETER GILTTAIL GLOWWORM
GNATWORM LEAFTIER LEAFWORM
MEALWORM MUCKWORM NAUPLIUS
PILIDIUM ROOTWORM SCYPHULA
SEMIPUPA SILKWORM SKINWORM
SPANWORM SPRAWLER STAGWORM
SURIMAGO TORNARIA VERMICLE
WASPLING WIREWORM WOODGRUB
WOODWORM
LARVACEA ATREMATA COPELATA
LARVAL NEPIONIC
LARYNGITIS CROUP
LARYNX
(PREF.) LARYNG(O)
LASCIVIOUS LEWD NICE SALT
HORNY RANDY LUBRIC WANTON
BLISSOM FLESHLY GOATISH PAPHIAN
PRURIENT SALACIOUS
LASCIVIOUSNESS LECHERY
ASELGEIA LUXURITY LUBRICITY
LASERWORT SILPHIUM
LASH CUT BEAT FIRK FLOG JERK LACE
WELT WHIP WIRE YERK LEASE LEASH
SCORE SKEEG SLASH THONG TRICE
WHALE CANVAS CILIUM LAINER
LAUNCH STRIPE SWINGE SWITCH
FLYFLAP KURBASH SCOURGE
(— BOWSPRIT) GAMMON
(— OUT) THRASH
(— TOGETHER) RACK
LASHER THONGMAN
LASHING YARK YERK GAMMON
LISTING MOUSING SEIZING SLATING
FRAPPING
(PL.) OODLES OODLINS SLITHERS

LASS TIB GILL PRIM TRULL DAMSEL
KUMMER LASSIE DAMOZEL LASSIKY
TENDREL MUCHACHA
(COUNTRY —) JENNY
LASSITUDE BLAHS COPOS STUPOR
LANGUOR MALAISE LETHARGY
LASSO LASH LAZO ROPE RIATA
LARIAT CABESTRO
LAST ABY LAG DURE GOON HOLD
KEEP RIDE SAVE ABIDE FINAL SERVE
ABEGGE ENDURE LATEST LATTER
REMAIN ULTIMA UTMOST DARREIN
DERNIER EXTREME PERDURE
SUPREME CONTINUE EVENTUAL
HINDMOST LATEMOST REARMOST
TERMINAL ULTIMATE AFTERMOST
(— BUT ONE) PENULT
(— OUT) SPIN STAY
(AT —) FINALLY
(THE —) OMEGA
(PREF.) ESCHATO POSTREMO ULTIMO
LAST DAYS OF POMPEII (AUTHOR
OF —) BULWER LYTTON
(CHARACTER IN —) IONE BURBO
JULIA NYDIA DIOMED ARBACES
CLODIUS GLAUCUS SALLUST
APAECIDES
LASTING FIXED LASTY DURANT
DURING STABLE ABIDING DURABLE
DUREFUL CONSTANT ENDURING
LIVELONG REMANENT STANDING
(— FOR LONG PERIOD) AEONIC
AEONIAL
(— FOR ONE DAY) DIARY DIURNAL
LASTINGNESS STAY DURATION
LAST OF THE MOHICANS
(AUTHOR OF —) COOPER
(CHARACTER IN —) CORA WEBB
ALICE DAVID GAMUT MAGUA
MUNRO NATTY UNCAS BUMPPO
DUNCAN HAWKEYE HEYWARD
MONTCALM CHINGACHGOOK
LAST PURITAN (AUTHOR OF —)
SANTAYANA
(CHARACTER IN —) JIM IRMA ROSE
ALDEN BOBBY EDITH MARIO PETER
WEYER BOWLER OLIVER DARNLEY
HARRIET SCHLOTE BUMSTEAD
LAST SUPPER CENA COENA
MAUNDY
LAT STAMBHA
LATCH FLY PIN HASP RISP SHUT
CATCH CHAIR CLICK CLINK SNECK
SNICK KEEPER CLICKET
LATCHET DAG TAB SANDAL
LANGUET
LATCHING LASKET
LATCHKEY CLICKET PASSKEY
LATE LAG NEW DEEP RIPE SLOW
TARDY RECENT TARDIVE UMWHILE
ADVANCED LATEWARD SOMETIME
UMQUHILE

(— COMER) CUNCTATOR
(— IN DEVELOPING) SEROTINOUS
LATE GEORGE APLEY
(AUTHOR OF —) MARQUAND
(CHARACTER IN —) JOHN MARY APLEY AMELIA GEORGE ELEANOR HORATIO MONAHAN OREILLY WILLIAM WILLING BOSWORTH PRENTISS CATHARINE
LATELY LATE ALATE NEWLY
LA TENE MARNEAN
LATENT HIDDEN MASKED ABEYANT DORMANT PASSIVE LATITANT QUIESCENT
(PREF.) CRYPT(O) KRYPT(O)
LATER POI SIN ANON POST SYNE AFTER ELDER NEWER BEHIND FUTURE LATTER PUISNE ANOTHER INFERIOR UMUHILE
(PREF.) HYSTERO INFRA META POST
LATERAL SIDE
(PREF.) PLEUR(O)
LATERALLY SIDELONG
LATERITE CABOOK KUNKUR
LATEST LAST LATTER FARTHEST FURTHEST
LATEX GUTTA SORVA ANTIAR SENAMBY
LATH BAT LAG SLAT SPAIL SPALE SPELL SWALE REEPER SPLENT SPLINT STOOTH LATHING FOREPOLE LATHWORK
LATHE LAY SLEY TURN LAITH THROW BEATER WISKET
(— FOR CYLINDERS) BROAD
(— OF LOOM) LAY
(TURNING —) THROW
(WATCHMAKER'S —) TURN TURNS MANDREL
LATHER FOAM SUDS FROTH FREATH SAPPLES
LATHERED SOAPY
LATIGO STRAP
LATIN ROMAN HISPERIC LATINITY SCATTERMOUCH
(— COMPOSITION) VULGUS
LATIN-AMERICAN LATIN LADINO LATINO HISPANIC
LATINUS (DAUGHTER OF —) LAVINIA
(FATHER OF —) FAUNUS
(SON-IN-LAW OF —) AENEAS
(WIFE OF —) AMATA
LATITUDE SCOPE SPACE WIDTH EXTENT HEIGHT
(HELIOCENTRIC —) LIMIT
LATONA (DAUGHTER OF —) DIANA
(FATHER OF —) COEUS
(MOTHER OF —) PHOEBE
(SON OF —) APOLLO
LATRIA ADORATION
LATRINE BOG REAR PRIVY TOILET BOGGARD

LATTER LAST FINAL RECENT SECOND PRESENT
(— PORTION) AUTUMN
LATTICE MESA GRATE HERSE TWINE GRILLE PINJRA UMBREL GRATING CANCELLI
(— OF POINTS) SATIN
(MOVING —) APRON
(PREF.) CLATHR
LATTICED CLATHRATE
LATTICE PLANT LACELEAF
LATTICEWORK ARBOR GRATE GRATING ESPALIER TUKUTUKU

LATVIA	
CAPITAL: RIGA	
COIN: LAT RUBLIS KAPEIKA SANTIMS	
MEASURE: STOF KANNE STOFF STOOF VERST ARSHIN KULMET SAGENE VERCHOC KROUCHKA POURVETE	
NAME: LATVIJA LETTLAND LETTONIE	
NATIVE: LETT	
PEOPLE: LETT	
RIVER: AA OGRE DVINA GAUJA VENTA SALACA LIELUPE	
TOWN: CESIS LIBAU DVINSK LIBAVA TUKUMS JELGAVA LIEPAJA REZEKNE DUNABURG VALMIERA DAUGAVPILS	
WEIGHT: LIESPFUND	

LAUAN KALUNTI
LAUD EXTOL PRAISE ADVANCE APPLAUD COMMEND GLORIFY MAGNIFY EMBLAZON EULOGIZE MACARIZE
LAUDATION PUFF EULOGY PRAISE PANEGYRIC
LAUDATORY SNEER EPENETIC PRAISING
LAUDER ESTEE
LAUGH YAK YUK GAFF YOCK YUCK CHUCK FLEER LEUGH RISUS ARRIDE NICKER TITTER CHORTLE GRIZZLE SNICKER SNIGGER SNIRTLE TWITTER LAUGHTER
(— CONTEMPTUOUSLY) SNORT DERIDE
(— GLEEFULLY) CHECKLE
(— HYSTERICALLY) CHECKLE
(— IN AFFECTED MANNER) GIGGLE
(— IN COARSE MANNER) FLEER GUFFAW
(— LIKE HEN) CACKLE
(— LOUDLY) GAFF GUFFAW
(— MOCKINGLY) FLEER
(— OUT LOUD) CRACKUP
(— QUIETLY) GULE SMUDGE CHUCKLE SNIRTLE
(BELLY —) BOFF BOFFOLA
(LOUD —) GAUSTER
LAUGHABLE ODD RICH COMIC DROLL FUNNY MERRY QUEER WITTY

AMUSING COMICAL RISIBLE
STRANGE WAGGISH FARCICAL
HUMOROUS LAUGHING PLEASANT
SPORTIVE RIDICULOUS
LAUGHING RIANT RIDENT IRRISION
MIRTHFUL
(— MATTER) MOWS
LAUGHING GULL PEWIT
LAUGHING JACKASS
KOOKABURRA
LAUGHING OWL WEKAU WHEKAU
LAUGHINGSTOCK GUY BUTT JEST
JOKE SONG SPORT DERISION
RIDICULE
LAUGHTER JOKE MIRTH RISUS
SNIRT CACKLE LAWTER SPLEEN
HILARITY RISIBILITY
(HYSTERICAL —) CACHINNATION
(VULGAR —) HAWHAW
(PREF.) GELOTO
LAUNCE LANT LANCE SMELT
AMMODYTE SANDLING
LAUNCH PUT BURST DRIVE LANCE
ELANCE STRIKE BAPTIZE PINNACE
PROMOTE STEAMER TELSTAR
VIBRATE CATAPULT
(— HOSTILELY) DIRECT
LAUNCHER
(ROCKET —) BAZOOKA
LAUNCHING BLASTOFF
LAUNDER TYE WASH TRUNK SLUICE
STRAKE LAUNDRY
LAUNDRESS TRII BY LAVENDER
LAUNDRY WASH BAGWASH
LAVATORY WASHATERIA WASHETERIA
(PUBLIC —) STEAMIE
LAUREL BAY IVY LAURY UNITE
WICKY DAPHNE KALMIA MALLET
MYRTLE CAJEPUT IVYWOOD
WOEVINE BREWSTER CALFKILL
(GROUND —) ARBUTUS
LAUREL OAK ACAJOU
LAURIC PICHURIC
LAURUSTINE VIBURNUM
LAUSUS (FATHER OF —) NUMITOR
MEZENTIUS
(SISTER OF —) ILIA
(SLAYER OF —) AMULIUS
LAUTVERSCHIEBUNG SHIFT
LAVA AA ASHES SPINE COULEE
LATITE SCORIA VERITE FAVILLA
LAPILLO MALPAIS ASPERITE
ORENDITE PAHOEHOE
(MUD —) MOYA LAHAR
(SCORIACEOUS —) AA SLAG
(SLAGGY —) SCORIA
LAVABO LAVATORY
LAVAGE LAVATION LAVEMENT
LAVALAVA SULU
LAVAN KALUNTI
LAVATORY LOO BASIN CHALET
CLOSET LAVABO OFFICE LATRINE
LAVETTE WASHROOM CLOAKROOM

LAVE LIP WASH BATHE SPLASH
LAVENDER BEHN ASPIC BEHEN
SPICK SPIKE INKROOT LAVANDIN
STICHADO
LAVENGRO (AUTHOR OF —)
BORROW
(CHARACTER IN —) JOHN MOLL
ARDRY HERNE PETER ISOPEL JASPER
BERNERS FRANCIS LEONORA
TAGGART LAVENGRO SAPENGRO
SLINGSBY WILLIAMS WINIFRED
PETULENGRO
LAVER SION SLAKE SLOKE LOUTER
PHIALE AMANORI CISTERN
CANTHARUS
LAVINIA (FATHER OF —) LATINUS
(HUSBAND OF —) AENEAS
(MOTHER OF —) AMATA
LAVISH FREE LASH LUSH FLUSH
LARGE SPEND SPORT WASTE COSTLY
WANTON COPIOUS OPULENT
PROFUSE GENEROUS LUCULLAN
PRODIGAL SQUANDER WASTEFUL
REDUNDANT MUNIFICENT
LAVISHNESS WASTE FINERY LAVISH
LAW ACT FAS IUS JUS LAY LEX ADAT
DOOM JURE RULE CANON DROIT
NOMOS TORAH BYELAW BYRLAW
DECREE DHARMA EQUITY BROCARD
DANELAW DERECHO HALACHA
HALAKAH JUSTICE PRECEPT
SETNESS STATUTE JUDGMENT
JUDICIAL ROGATION STATEWAY
TANISTRY ORDINANCE
(—S OF MANU) SUTRA SUTTA
(— VIOLATOR) SCOFFLAW
(BEDOUIN —) THAR
(DIETARY —S) KASHRUTH
(ELEMENTARY —) BROCARD
(EQUAL —) ISONOMY
(ISLAMIC —) ADA BAI ADAT SHERI
SHARIA SHERIAT
(JEWISH —) MISHNA MISHNAH
(KIND OF —) LEASH
(MARRIAGE —) LEVIRATE
(MOSAIC —) TORAH
(OPPOSING —) ANTINOMY
(PROPOSED —) BILL
(UNIVERSAL —) HEAVEN
(PL.) LORS
(PREF.) JURIS LEGI LEGO NOM(O)
THESMO
(SUFF.) LEGE NOMY
LAW-ABIDING LAWFUL
LAWBREAKER FELON HOUGHER
LAWFUL DUE JUST LEAL TRUE VERY
LEGAL LEGIT LICIT LOYAL VALID
KINDLY LEEFUL ENNOMIC LEESOME
INNOCENT LIEFSOME RIGHTFUL
LAWGIVER MINOS MOSES SOLON
LAWYER LAWMAKER
LAWLESS LEWD UNRULY ILLEGAL
MOBBISH ANARCHIC

LAWLESSNESS ANOMY ANOMIE
ANARCHY
LAWMAKER LEGIFER
LAWN ARBOR GRASS LINON SWARD
UMPLE CYPRUS BATISTE QUINTIN
TIFFANY
LAWSUIT LIS CASE SAKE SECTA
ACTION BRABBLE
LAWYER (ALSO SEE JURIST) JET
PEAT AVOUE PATCH SHARK BREHON
JURIST LAWMAN LEGIST SQUIRE
WRITER COUNSEL MUKHTAR
TEMPLAR DEFENDER LEGISTER
TRAMPLER BARRISTER MOUTHPIECE
PETTIFOGGER
(PALTRY —) PETTIFOGGER
(UNSCRUPULOUS —) SHYSTER
LAX DULL FREE LASH LAZY LINK
SLOW SWAG WIDE LARGE LOOSE
RELAX SLACK TARDY REMISS
BACKWARD INACTIVE DISSOLUTE
NEGLIGENT
LAXATIVE LAX LASK CASCARA
APERIENT HYDROMEL LAPACTIC
RELAXANT SOLUTIVE TARAXACUM
LAXITY LASCHETY LATITUDE
LAY LIE SET CLAP LAIC LEWD SLEY
SONG WAGE BIGHT CIVIL COUCH
DITTY LATHE LEDGE QUIET STAKE
STILL COMMON HAZARD IMPOSE
IMPUTE MELODY APPEASE ASCRIBE
LAYDOWN POPULAR SECULAR
SIRVENTE TEMPORAL
(— ASIDE) DOFF DOWN DUMP SHUCK
DEPOSE DIVEST DEPOSIT
PIGEONHOLE
(— AWAY) STORE
(— BARE) BARE NAKE TIRL TIRVE
DENUDE DETECT OPPOSE UNCOVER
DENUDATE
(— CLAIM) ASSERT BESPEAK
ARROGATE
(— CROSSWISE) COB
(— DOWN) ABDICATE PRESCRIBE
(— EGGS) BLOW WARP LEDGE
OVIPOSIT
(— FLAT) SQUAT ADPRESS
(— HOLD OF) FANG GRIP HENT TAKE
GRIPE LATCH ATHOLD ATTACH
COLLAR COMPRISE
(— IN) EMBED
(— IN BIGHTS) JAG
(— IN COIL) FLEMISH
(— IN PLEATS) FOLD
(— IT ON) COAT
(— LOW) STREW STRIKE
(— OFF) FORE IDLE STOP
(— OF LOOM) BEATER
(— ON) APPLY INFLICT
(— OPEN) BREAK CHINE EXPOSE
UNMASK
(— OUT) FRAY PLAT ARRAY RANGE
SPELD SPEND BEWARE DESIGN
EXTEND SPREAD STREAK STREEK
CHECKER DEVELOP STRETCH
CONTRIVE
(— PRONE) LEVEL
(— RUBBLEWORK) SNECK
(— SIEGE) INVEST
(— SMOOTH) EVEN
(— SNARE FOR RABBITS) HAY
(— STONE) PAVE
(— STRAIGHT) COMB
(— TYPE) CASE
(— UP) HEAP HIVE ADDLE HOARD
HUTCH STOCK TREASURE
(— WASTE) PEEL WEST HARRY
HAVOC HARASS RAVAGE DESTROY
DESOLATE FORWASTE
LAYABOUT IDLER
LAYBOY JOGGER
LAYDOWN LAYOUT SPREAD
LAYER BED FLY HEN LAY BARK CAKE
COAT DASS FACE FILM FLAP FOLD
LAIR LOFT RIND SEAM SKIN WEFT
ZONA CHESS COUCH COVER CRUST
CUTIS FLAKE FLASH LEDGE SCALE
CARPET COURSE FASCIA FILLER
FOLIUM INTINE LAMINA LISSOM
STREAK BLANKET COATING CUTICLE
EPICARP FEATHER FLAVEDO
GANGMAN INLAYER LAMELLA
PACKING PHELLEM PROPAGO
PROVINE STRATUM SUBCOAT
SUPPORT ECTOCYST ECTOSARC
ENDOCYST ENDODERM EPIBLAST
EPIBLEMA EPISPORE EPITHECA
INTERBED MOLLISOL PERIOPLE
PERISARC SUBCRUST PERIPLAST
PHELLODERM
(— IN FUNGI) HYMENIUM
(— OF ATMOSPHERE) MESOSPHERE
OZONOSPHERE
(— OF BLOOD VESSEL) EXTIMA
EXTERNA
(— OF CELLS) EXINE CORTEX EXTINE
CAMBIUM PHELLEM TAPETUM
PERICYCLE
(— OF CLAY) GLEY VARVE SELVAGE
SELVEDGE
(— OF CONCRETE) RAFT
(— OF EARTH) SPIT
(— OF EYE) RETINA
(— OF FAT) LEAF FINISH
(— OF FELT) BAT BATT
(— OF FIBER) LAP
(— OF FINE MATERIAL) CUSHION
(— OF FOREST GROWTH) SUBSTORY
OVERSTORY
(— OF FUEL) FIREBED
(— OF GLASS) CASING
(— OF IRIS) UVEA
(— OF MEAT) SPINE
(— OF MORTAR) SCREED
(— OF NERVE FIBERS) ALVEUS
(— OF ORGANIC MATTER) FLOOR

(— OF PLASMA) BUFFCOAT
(— OF ROCK) CAP SHELF SHELL
SLATE FOLIUM SEPTUM BLISTER
SKULLCAP
(— OF ROOTS) SOLE
(— OF SEDIMENT) WARP
(— OF SHALE) BONE
(— OF SHEEPSKIN) FLESHER
(— OF SHOE HEEL) LIFT
(— OF SILT) VARVE
(— OF SKIN) DERM DERMA EPIDERM
(— OF SOIL) SOLUM CALLOW
CASING HARDPAN HORIZON
(— OF STONES) DASS DESS
(— OF TANBARK) HAT
(— OF TISSUE) BED DARTOS FASCIA
SEROSA ELASTICA EPIBLEMA
PERIDERM
(— OF TOBACCO LEAVES) HANGER
(— OF TURF) FLAW KERF
(— OF WHITE MATTER) CAPSULE
(— OF WOOD) CORE
(BONY —) LAMELLA CEMENTUM
(BOTTOM —) BEDDING
(FLAT —) BED FLAP FLAKE
(FROZEN —) PERMAFROST
(GERM —) MESODERM
(IMPERVIOUS —) LINING
(OUTER —) HUSK
(THIN —) SCRAPE
(UNDERLYING —) SUBSTRATUM
(UPPER —) SURFACE
(PREF.) LAMELLI LAMIN(I) PTYCH(O)
STRATI
(SUFF.) CLINAL CLINE LAMIN
(— OF SKIN) DERMIS
(GERM —) BLAST(IC)(Y)
LAYERING LAP GOOTEE STOOLING
LAYMAN LAIC CLERK IDIOT DEACON
SECULAR DEFENSOR EXHORTER
EXOTERIC FAMILIAR STRANGER
WORLDMAN
LAYOFF FURLOUGH
LAYOUT MISE DUMMY SETOUT
(— OF CARDS) TABLEAU
LAZARETTO SPITAL SPITTLE
LAZARUS (SISTER OF —) MARY
MARTHA
(SISTER OF —) MARTHA
LAZINESS LAZE SLOTH SLOUCH
OISIVITY
LAZULITE SIDERITE
LAZY ARGH IDLE LASS DOXIE DRONY
FAINT INERT LINGY LUSKY RESTY
SLOAN SLOTH CLUMSY LIMPSY
LURDAN LUTHER ORNERY SWEERT
TRAILY CLUMPST DRONISH LUSKISH
PEAKISH SLIVING DROGHLIN
FAINEANT FECKLESS INDOLENT
LITHERLY OSCITANT SLOTHFUL
SLUGGARD THOWLESS TRIFLING
SHIFTLESS
LAZY EYE AMBLYOPIA

LEA LAY GRASS LAYER LAYLAND
LEALAND
LEACH TAP LETCH SOFTEN
LEAD GO TEE VAN WIN BEAR DADE
GIVE GROW HAVE HEAD HERD LEED
SLIP TAKE TEEM WORK BLAZE
BOUND BRING CARRY GREBE GUIDE
MAYNE PILOT PRESA SOUND START
TRAIN TREAT CONVEY DEDUCE
DIRECT ESCORT INDUCE INDUCT
LEADER SATURN BEGUILE CAPTAIN
CONDUCE CONDUCT LEADING
MARSHAL PIGTAIL PIONEER
PLUMBUM PLUMMET LEADSMAN
MANUDUCE MANUDUCT SQUIRREL
(— A BAND) BATON
(— AND SUPPORT) DADE
(— ASIDE) CHAR SINGLE
(— ASTRAY) ERR MANG TURN WARP
BEFOOL BETRAY ENTICE WANDER
WILDER DEBAUCH MISLEAD
MISWEND PERVERT SOLICIT TRADUCE
BEWILDER INVEIGLE MISGUIDE
(— AWAY) CHAR ABDUCT DIVERGE
(— BACK) REDUCT
(— FORCIBLY) ESCORT
(— IN CARD GAME) SNEAK
WHITECHAPEL
(— IN RACE) LAP
(— IN SINGING) PRECENT
(— INTO ERROR) ABUSE DELUDE
(— MONOXIDE) MASSICOT
(— ON) TRAIL
(— PASSIVE EXISTENCE) VEGETATE
(— POISONING) PLUMBISM
(BLACK —) WAD WADD GRAPHITE
(COLOR —) PLOMB
(DEEP-SEA —) DIPSY DIPSEY
(MOCK —) DLENDE
(OVERLAPPING —) DRIP
(PLUMBING —) BLUEY
(SYMBOL FOR —) PB
(WHITE —) KREMS CERUSE
(PREF.) GALENO MOLYBD(O)
PLUMB(I)(O)
(SUFF.) AGOGUE AGOGY
LEAD-COLORED WAN BLAE
LEADEN HEAVY INERT PLUMBEAN
LEADER BO BOH COB DUX HOB MIR
CAST COCK DUCE DUKE HEAD HOBB
JEFE NAIG NAIK OMDA SOUL TYEE
CHIFF DOYEN ELDER FIRST MAHDI
MOSES OMDEH PILOT SEYID TRACE
ARCHON CALIPH DESPOT HEADER
HONCHO RECTOR SAYYID TYCOON
ACREMAN ADVISER CAPTAIN
CONDUCT DEMAGOG DRUNGAR
FOREMAN FUEHRER INDUCER
PRIMATE ACCENTOR CAUDILLO
DIRECTOR FUGLEMAN HEADSMAN
HERETOGA LODESMAN PANDARUS
STRATEGE AYATOLLAH PENDRAGON
PROTAGONIST

(— OF ARMY) VAIVODE VOIVODE
(— OF DACOITS) BOH
(— OF FLOCK) PATRIARCH
(—,OF GUISERS) SKUDLER
(— OF MINING GANG) CORPORAL
(— OF MUTINEERS) ELECTO
(— OF REVOLT) ANARCH
(BAND —) BATONEER
(CHOIR —) CANTOR PRECENTOR
(CHORUS —) CHORAGUS
(COSSACK —) ATAMAN HETMAN
(FASCIST —) RAS
(HOLY —) MAHATMA
(INTELLECTUAL —) BRAIN
(MINING —) CORPORAL
(MOB —) MOBOCRAT
(MUSLIM —) MAHDI
(POLITICAL —) SACHEM
(PRAYER —) IMAM
(RELIGIOUS —) AGA AGHA LAMA
SHEIKH
(SCOUT —) AKELA SIXER
(SPIRITUAL —) GURU SADDIK
GUARDIAN
(TAMMANY —) SACHEM
(SUFF.) ARCH ARCHIC ARCHY
LEADERSHIP LEAD AEGIS MANRED
CONDUCT IMAMATE LEADING
MANRENT CHIEFDOM GUIDANCE
HEADSHIP HEGEMONY
(— BY TALENTED) MERITOCRACY
LEADING BIG BEST COCK DUCT
HEAD LEAD MAIN AHEAD CHIEF
FIRST BANNER PREMIER STELLAR
GUIDANCE PROMINENT
(— OUTWARD) EMISSARY
(— TO NOTHING) IDLE
LEAD MONOXIDE MASSICOT
LEADSMAN SOUNDER
LEADWORK PLUMBAGE PLUMBING
LEADWORT CROWTOE PLUMBAGO
LEAF PAD BACK BARB BUYO FLAG
FLAP FOIL FOLD GEAR PAGE PALM
STUB BLADE BLANK FLIER FLYER
FOLIO FROND GRASS GUARD LEAVE
SCALE SEPAL SIGHT SPILL TEPAL
BONNET CADJAN CARPEL COUPON
FOLIUM FRAISE FULZIE NEEDLE
PEPPER DAMIANA FOLDOUT
HARNESS LEAFLET TREFOIL
WITNESS PHYLLADE PHYLLOME
MICROPHYLL
(— FAT) FLICK
(— FROM AXIL) BRACT
(— OF BOOK) PAGE FOLIO INSET
PLATE FLYLEAF
(— OF CALYX) BARB
(— OF CORN) HUSK
(— OF COROLLA) PETAL
(— OF DOOR) VALVE
(— OF HEDDLES) GEAR
(— OF PALM) FAN OLA PAN CHIP
OLLA FROND LATANIER

(— OF SPRING) BACK
(—S OF CORIANDER) CILANTRO
(BETEL —) PAN SIRIH
(BIBLE —) COSTMARY
(DEAD —) FLAG
(EXTRA —) INSERT
(HOLLOW —) PHYLLODE
(PART OF —) RIB TIP APEX BASE
LOBE STEM VEIN BLADE SINUS
LAMINA MARGIN MIDRIB PETIOLE
LEAFSTALK
(RUDIMENTARY —) CATAPHYLL
(SPRING —) WRAPPER
(STRAWBERRY —) FRAISE
(THIN —) LAMELLA
(TOBACCO —) LUGS STRIP CUTTER
WRAPPER
(WASTE GOLD —) SKEWING
(PREF.) FOLI(O) PETAL(I)(O) PHYLL(I)
(O)
(SUFF.) FOLIATE FOLIOUS PETALOUS
PHYLL(A)(OUS)(UM)(Y)
LEAFAGE FOLIAGE
LEAFHOPPER HOPPER JASSID
THRIPS HOMOPTER
LEAFLET FLIER PINNA TRACT MAILER
FOLIOLE STUFFER
(—S DROPPED FROM AIR) BUMF
(PAIR OF —S) JUGUM
(PL.) SENNA CAROBA
LEAFLIKE PHYLLINE
LEAFMOLD KOLINSKY
LEAFSTALK HAFT CHARD PETIOLE
LEAFY GREEN LEAVY FOLIATE
FOLIOSE FRONDOSE
LEAGUE BOND BUND BANDY BOARD
GUEUX HANSA PARTY UNION WHEEL
CIRCUIT COMPACT ALLIANCE
SYSTASIS COALITION
(— OF NATIONS) GENEVA
(BUSH —S) STICKS
(MINOR —S) BUSHES
LEAGUED FEDERATE
LEAH (DAUGHTER OF —) DINAH
(FATHER OF —) LABAN
(HUSBAND OF —) JACOB
(SISTER OF —) RACHEL
(SON OF —) LEVI JUDAH REUBEN
SIMEON ZEBULUN ISSACHAR
LEAK BLAB BLOW WEEP GEYZE
SPUNK INLEAK SIGGER SPRING
ZIGGER LEAKAGE MELTERS SCREEVE
(— IN ELECTRIC CIRCUIT) FAULT
LEAKAGE ESCAPE SEEPAGE
(— OF ELECTRICITY) CREEPAGE
(— OF GAS) SLIP
(— OF WIND) RUNNING
LEAKING ALEAK DRIBBLE NAILSICK
LEAKY LEAK UNTIGHT GIZZENED
LEAL FAITHFUL
LEAN BEAR BEND BONY HANG HEEL
LANK PEND POOR PRIN RACY RELY
REST SEEL STAY SWAY THIN TOOM

EMPTY GAUNT HIELD LANKY LEANY
SLANK SOUND SPARE STOOP
HOLLOW MEAGER RECUMB SKINNY
SPRING UPLEAN ANGULAR FATLESS
HAGGARD INCLINE SCRAGGY
SCRAWNY SLUNKEN STRINGY
MACILENT SCRAGGED SCRANNEL
(— FOR SUPPORT) ABUT
(— FORWARD) PROCLINE
(— OVER) WHAUVE
(PREF.) CLIN(O)

LEANDER (LOVE OF —) HERO

LEANDRE (FATHER OF —) GERONTE
(LOVER OF —) LUCINDE

LEANER HOBBER

LEANING AGEE BIAS DRIFT FLAIR
TREND PENCHE HANGING ACCLINAL
ENCLITIC FROMWARD PROPENSE
PROCLIVITY PROPENSITY
(— BACKWARD) SUPINE
(STRONG —) GENIUS PENCHANT

LEANNESS LANK POVERTY
SPARENESS

LEAN-TO SHED LINTER OUTSHOT
SKILLION

LEAP +LY HOP POP BEND DART DIVE
FALL GIVE JUMP LOPE LOUP RAMP
RISE SKIT WIND BOUND BREAK
CAPER DANCE EXULT FLIER FLYER
FRISK LUNGE PRIME SALTO SAULT
SCOPE SCOUP SPANG STEND VAULT
BOUNCE BREACH CURVET INSULT
LAUNCH SPRENT SPRING SPRUNT
WALLOP REBOUND SALTARY
SALTATE SUBSULT BUCKJUMP
LEAPFROG SPANGHEW UPSPRING
(— BACK) RESULT SPRUNT
(— FOR JOY) EXULT
(— IN DANCING) STOT
(— LIGHTLY) SKIP
(— OF HORSE) CURVET BALOTADE
CAPRIOLE CROUPADE
(— OF WHALE) BREACH
(— OUT) SALLY
(— OVER) FREE OVER SKIP CLEAR
HURDLE
(— UPON) ASSAIL POUNCE
(BALLET —) FISH JETE ASSEMBLE
CABRIOLE FISHDIVE ELEVATION
ENTRECHAT
(FENCING —) VOLT VOLTE
(FROLICSOME —) CAPER
(SKATING —) AXEL
(SUICIDAL —) BRODIE
(PL.) ALLEGRO
(PREF.) SCIRTO

LEAPING GAMBOL SPRING
RAMPANT SALIENT SALTANT

LEAR (DAUGHTER OF —) REGAN

LEARCHUS (BROTHER OF —)
MELICERTA
(FATHER OF —) ATHAMAS
(MOTHER OF —) INO

LEARN DO CON GET SEE WIT ARAL
FIND HAVE HEAR LEAR LERE EDIFY
GLEAN STUDY RECORD REALIZE
RECEIVE DISCOVER ASCERTAIN
(— FROM EXPERIENCE) ASSAY

LEARNED BLUE SEEN LERED LORED
DUCTUS BOOKISH CLERKLY
CUNNING ERUDITE STUDIED TUITIVE
ACADEMIC CLERGIAL LETTERED
OVERSEEN POLYMATH PROFOUND
SCIENCED
(— GROUP) LITERATI
(— MAN) OLLAV
(AFFECTEDLY —) INKHORN
(SOMETHING TO BE —) LIRIPIPE

LEARNEDLY CLERKLY

LEARNER PUPIL NOVICE SCHOLAR
TRAINEE PRENTICE ABECEDARIAN
(LATE —) OPSIMATH

LEARNING ART WIT BOOK LEIR LERE
LORE CLERGY WISDOM APPRISE
CUNNING GRAMMAR INSIGHT
LETTERS WISTING BOOKLEAR
BOOKLORE DOCTRINE HUMANISM
LETTRURE MATHESIS PEDANTRY
(— LATE IN LIFE) OPSIMATHY
(SUFF.) MATHY

LEASE FEU FEW LET SET FARM HIRE
RENT TACK COWLE DIMIT FIRMA
LISSE DEMISE POTTAH RENTAL
ASSEDAT CHARTER SETTING
BACKTACK SUBLEASE
(— AGAIN) SUBLET

LEASEHOLDER LIVIER

LEASH LEAD LYME SLIP LEASE
TRASH COUPLE STRING OWINGE
(— OF HOUNDS) HARL
(DOG —) SLIP TRASH TIRRET
(HAWK'S —) LOYN LUNE TIRRET
CREANCE

LEASING LOCATIO

LEAST LEST MINIMAL MINIMUM
MINIMUS
(AT —) HURE

LEAST FLYCATCHER CHEBEC

LEAST SANDPIPER PEEP OXEYE
STINT

LEATHER ELK KID BEND BOCK BUFF
CALF CAPE HIDE NAPA ROAN SEAL
ADUST ALUTA BAT AT FLANK NIGER
RETAN SUEDE BULGAR CASTOR
CHAMMY CHROME LIZARD ORIOLE
OXHIDE PEBBLE RUSSET SHAMMY
SKIVER TURKEY BELTING BUFFING
CANEPIN CHAMOIS COWHIDE
COWSKIN DEGRAIN DOGSKIN
DONGOLA HEADCAP HOGSKIN
KIDSKIN MURRAIN PANCAKE
PECCARY PERSIAN SAFFIAN
ANTELOPE BUCKSKIN BULLNECK
CABRETTA CALFSKIN CAPESKIN
CHEVEREL COLTSKIN CORDOBAN
CORDWAIN DEERSKIN GOATSKIN

KANGAROO LAMBSKIN SHAGREEN
SHEEPSKIN
(— FOR DRESSING FLAX) RIBSKIN
(— FROM SHEEPSKIN) ROAN
(— SHREDS) MOSLINGS
(— STRIP) RAND
(ARABIAN —) MOCHA
(ARTIFICIAL —) KERATOL PEGAMOID
(BOARDED —) BOX
(BOOKBINDING —) ROAN
(CORDOVAN —) CORDOBAN
CORDWAIN
(GOAT —) MOROCCO MAROQUIN
(GRAINED —) ROAN
(KIND OF —) NAPA
(MOROCCO —) LEVANT MAROQUIN
(PATCH OF —) CLOUT
(PRUSSIAN —) SPRUCE
(RUSSIAN —) YUFT BULGAR RUSSIA
JUCHTEN
(SHEEPSKIN —) BOCK BUCK NAPA
MOCHA
(SOFT —) OOZE ALUTA
(SUPERIOR —) BUFF
(THICK —) BUTT
(UNTANNED —) RAWHIDE
(WASH —) LOSH LOSHE
(PREF.) SCYT(O)
LEATHERBACK LUTH
LEATHERFISH LIJA FOOLFISH
LEATHERJACKET FILEFISH
ZAPATERO
LEATHERLEAF CASSANDRA
LEATHERNECK GYRENE MARINE
LEATHERWOOD DIRCA WICOPY
BURNWOOD FIREWOOD IRONWOOD
LEADWOOD ROPEBARK
LEATHERWORKER TAWER BEDDER
CHAMAR MADIGA FLUFFER CHUCKLER
LEAVE GO GET LET BUNK DROP FADE
FLEE HOOK LEAF PART QUIT VADE
VOID WALK AVOID CONGE FAVOR
FORGO GOOUT GRACE SHOVE SPLIT
WAIVE BUGGER BUGOFF DEPART
DESERT DEVOID FORLET PERMIT
RETIRE SECEDE STRAND VACATE
FORLEIT FORLESE FORSAKE
LARGESS LIBERTY LICENSE
FAREWELL PATIENCE UNTENANT
PERMISSION SABBATICAL
(— ALONE) FORBEAR DESOLATE
(— BEHIND) LET PLANT DISTANCE
OUTSTRIP
(— BRIGHT TRAIL) STREAM
(— BY WILL) BEQUEATH
(— COVER) BREAK
(— HASTILY) SCUR SKIP SKIRR
(— HURRIEDLY) CUT BLOW BOLT
FLEE JUMP SCAT SKIP
(— IN ISOLATION) MAROON
(— IN SAFEKEEPING) CHECK
(— NOTHING TO BE DESIRED)
SATISFY

(— OF ABSENCE) ABSIT EXEAT
LIBERTY FURLOUGH
(— OFF) CEASE DEVAL PETER BILEVE
CHEESE DESIST SURCEASE
(— OUT) BATE OMIT SKIP SLIP ELIDE
(— PORT) SAIL CLEAR
(— QUICKLY) SCREW
(— SECRETLY) STEAL
(— SUDDENLY) KITE
(— UNDONE) PRETERMIT
LEAVED
(SUFF.) PHYLLOUS
LEAVEN ZYM ZYMO RAISE YEAST
INFUSE RAISING SOURING
(PREF.) ZYM(O)
LEAVENING EMPTINGS
LEAVES PATRIN FOLIAGE LEAFAGE
LEAFERY
(— OF BAOBAB TREE) LALO
(— OF ORCHID) FAHAM
(— OF TOBACCO) LEAF FLYINGS
SECONDS
(— ON STEM AFTER WITHERING)
INDUVIAE
(— USED AS STYPTIC) MATICO
(— USED FOR TEA) MANUKA
(BOILED — OF POTHERB) CHARD
(DRIED —) LAUHALA
(FALLEN —) DUFF
(MEDICINAL —) COCA FILE BUCCO
BUCKU FARFARA FUMARIA
(PALM —) ATAP ATTAP CADJAN
CAJANG
(TEA —) SOUCHONG
(WITHERED —) PININGS
(SUFF.) (HAVING —) CLEMA
PHYLLOUS
(NUMBER OF —) MO
LEAVE-TAKING VALE ADIEU
CONGEE PARTING WAYGANG
FAREWELL WAYGOING
LEAVING BIT ORT TAG
(PL.) RAFF SNUFF REFUSE RESIDUE
RESIDUUM
(PREF.) LIPO

LEBANON
CAPITAL: BEIRUT BEYROUTH
COIN: LIVRE PIASTRE
MOUNTAIN: ARUBA HERMON
SANNINE KENISSEH
PLAIN: ELBIKA
RIVER: JOZ LYCOS DAMOUR LITANI
HASBANI LEONTES ORONTES
KASEMIEH
SEAPORT: TYRE SAIDA SIDON BEIRUT
TOWN: SUR TYRE ALEIH HALBA SAIDA
SIDON ZAHLE JUNIYE ZAHLAH
QARTABA TRIPOLI MERJUYUN
VALLEY: BEQAA

LEBBEK KOKO KOKKO SIRIS
LEBKUCHEN LEKACH

LECHER GOAT LECH LETCH LUXUR GATYR PALLIARD
LECHEROUS LEWD SALT PRIME RANDY WANTON BOARISH CODDING GOATISH LUSTFUL SATYRIC LIKEROUS SCABROUS SPORTIVE STUPROUS SALACIOUS (PREF.) LUBRI
LECHERY LUXURY
LECTERN DESK EAGLE LUTRIN LATERAN LATTERIN
LECTION GOSPEL EPISTLE READING PERICOPE PROPHECY
LECTIONARY LEGEND
LECTOR LISTER READER
LECTURE JOBE CREED FORUM HOMILY LECTOR LESSON SERMON ADDRESS EARBASH HEARING PRELECT READING JOBATION ORDINARY
LECTURER DOCENT LECTOR READER DRYASDUST
LED (EASILY —) DUCTILE
LEDA (DAUGHTER OF —) HELEN CLYTEMNESTRA
(FATHER OF —) THESTIUS
(HUSBAND OF —) TYNDAREUS
(SON OF —) CASTOR POLLUX
LEDGE BEAD BERM DESS LINE STEP ALTAR BENCH CLINT LINCH SHELF SNOUT BEARER OFFSET SETTLE STANCE CHANNEL LEDGING RETABLE
(— BEHIND ALTAR) GRADIN GRADINE
(FIRESIDE —) STOCK
LEDGEMAN BREAKER
LEDGER BOOK SLAB LIEGER JOURNAL OVERLIER
LEDGER BOARD RIBBON
LEE LEW LEEWARD
LEECH GILL HARPY LEACH APODAN SANGSUE BDELLOID HELMINTH
(PREF.) BDELL(A) HIRUDINI
(SUFF.) BDELLA
LEEK FOUAT ALLIUM PORRET SCALLION SENGREEN ROCAMBOLE
(— COLORED) PRASINE
(PREF.) PRASEO PRASO
LEEK GREEN RESEDA
LEER LEAR LOOK OGLE FLEER LEERY SKIME SMIRK TWIRE
LEERFISH GARRICK
LEES LAGS ADDLE DRAFF DREGS DROSS GROUT AMURCA BOTTOM DUNDER MOTHER SORDOR ULLAGE GROUNDS EMPTINGS SEDIMENT WINEDRAF
LEEWAN SOFA DIVAN
LEEWARD DOWNWIND
LEEWARD ISLANDS (ISLAND OF —) KURE ARUBA NEVIS NIHOA LAYSON MIDWAY NECKER ANTIGUA MONTSERRAT

LEEWAY ROOM ROPE DRIFT
LEFT G CAR KAY KAY GAWK NEAR PORT OTHER TOWARD DESERTED SINISTER
(— BEHIND) RELICT
(— EYE) OL OS
(— HELPLESS) STRANDED
(— OVER) ODD ORRA REMAINDER
(BE — ON BASE) DIE
(TURN —) HAW
(PREF.) LAEV(O) LEV(O) SINISTR(O)
LEFT HAND MG MS SM SIN GAUCHE
(— PAGE) VERSO
LEFTHANDED CAR GAUCHE AWKWARD DUBIOUS OBLIQUE KITHOGUE SOUTHPAW
LEFT-HANDER SOUTHPAW
LEFTIST RAD RADICAL
LEFTOVER END ORT REMNANT SURPLUS REMAINDER
(— YARN) THRUMS
(TOBACCO —) TOPPER
(PL.) SCRAN ANALECTS
LEG ARM GAM PEG PIN CRUS GAMB JAMB LIMB TRAM BOUGH GAMBE JAMBE REACH SHANK STICK STUMP BENDER GAMBON GAMMON LEGLET MOGGAN OVIGER PESTLE PLANTA PROLEG WALKER FORELEG TRESTLE FORELIMB
(— OF CRUSTACEAN) PODITE
(— OF HAWK) ARM
(— OF LAMB) GIGOT WADDLER WOBBLER
(— OF TABLE) BALUSTER
(— OF WHEELBARROW) STILT
(—S OF ARTIFICIAL FLY) HACKLE
(— USED FOR FOOD) PESTLE
(ARTIFICIAL —) PYLON
(FURNITURE —) CABRIOLE
(HAVING CREASELESS —S) STOVEPIPE
(LAST —) HOMESTRETCH
(MILK —) WEED
(TROUSER —) SLOP
(WIRE —S) SLING
(WOODEN —) PEG STUMP TIMBER
(PL.) PROPS TONGS STAMPS STICKS
(PREF.) SCEL(O)
(SUFF.) SCELES
(LOWER —) CNEMA CNEMIA CNEMIC CNEMUS
LEGACY ENTAIL LEGATE BEQUEST HERITAGE WINDFALL
LEGAL LEAL LICIT SOUND VALID LAWFUL SQUARE JURIDIC RIGHTFUL
(DOING — WORK) PROBONO
LEGALISM NOMISM SCRIBISM
LEGALISTIC COURT
LEGATE ENVOY DEPUTY EXARCH LEGATUS CONSULAR LEGATARY PANDULPH
LEGATION MISSION
LEGATO SMOOTH

LEGEND EDDA MYTH POSY SAGA TALE FABLE STORY TITLE THREAP CAPTION CUTLINE HAGGADA
(MAP —) KEY
(PREF.) MYTHO
LEGENDARY FABLED FICTIOUS
LEGERDEMAIN JUGGLERY PRESTIDIGITATION
LEGERDEMAINIST JUGGLER
LEGGING SPAT COCKER BOTTINE GAMBADO JAMBEAU BALATONG BOOTIKIN CHIVARRA
(LEATHER —) STRAD
(PL.) CHAPS SHANKS BROGUES COGGERS GAMASHES LEATHERS OVERALLS
LEGIBLE FAIR READABLE
(NOT —) OBSCURE
LEGION HOST TERZO TERZIO
LEGIONARY ANT DRIVER FORAGER
LEGISLATION DYSNOMY LAWMAKING
LEGISLATOR SOLON LAWGIVER LAWMAKER
LEGISLATURE DIET COURT THING LAGTING RIKSDAG LANDRATH RIGSRAAD
LEGITIMATE JUST TRUE VERY LEGAL LEGIT LOYAL HONEST KINDLY KOSHER LAWFUL REABLE SQUARE NATURAL LEGITIME
LEGITIMATELY FAIRLY MULIERLY
LEGPIECE JAMBEAU
LEGUME DAL POD URD DAHL DHAL GUAR PULSE LENTIL LOMENT PEANUT PODDER COCHLEA LEGUMEN PODWARE SOYBEAN STROMBUS
LEHUA OHIA
LEIPOA LOWAN MEGAPOD PHEASANT
LEISHMANIASIS UTA ESPUNDIA
LEISTER SPEAR WASTER
LEISURE TIME TOOM VOID OTIUM RESPITE VACANCY VACATION
LEISURELY SLOW SOODLY TIMELY TOOMLY GRADUAL PICKTOOTH
LELEX (FATHER OF —) NEPTUNE POSEIDON
(MOTHER OF —) LIBYA
(SON OF —) MYLES
LEMAN UNDERPUT
LEMMING CRICETID
LEMMUS MYODES
LEMNISCUS FILET FILLET LAQUEUS
LEMON DOG DUD CEDRA CHLOR LEMONY CEDRATE FAILURE KUMQUAT
LEMONADE COOLER
LEMON GRASS TANGLAD
LEMON SOLE MARYSOLE
LEMON VERBENA ALOYSIA

LEMUR LORI MAKI VARI AVAHI INDRI KOKAM LORIS POTTO SIFAC ADAPID AYEAYE COBEGO COLUGO GALAGO KUBONG MACACO MAHOLI MONKEY SIFAKA APOSORO MEERKAT NATTOCK PRIMATE SEMIAPE TARSIER AMPONGUE BABAKOTO MONGOOSE PRIMATAL TARSIOID
LEND OCKER PREST SECOND ADVANCE IMPREST
(— AT INTEREST) GAVEL
(— ITSELF) ALLOY
LENDING (— AGENCY) MOUNT
LENGTH LUG DREE TOWT PITCH SCOPE SIDTH COURSE EXTENT TOWGHT FOOTAGE DISTANCE LEGITUDE SIDENESS
(— ATHWARTSHIP) ABURTON
(— OF BRIDGE) BAY
(— OF CABLE) SCOPE SHACKLE
(— OF CHAIN) SHOT
(— OF CLOTH) CUT BOLT YARD
(— OF FIBER) STAPLE
(— OF FISHING LINE) CAST
(— OF GEAR TOOTH) FACE
(— OF HAIR) KNOT
(— OF HAIR IN FISHING LINE) IMP
(— OF LIFE) LONGEVITY
(— OF LINE) LOYN
(— OF METAL) SHAPE
(— OF MOUTH) GAPE
(— OF NET) LEAD
(— OF PISTON STROKE) TRAVEL
(— OF ROPE) DRIFT SPOKE BRIDLE COURSE STOPPER
(— OF SERVICE) STANDING
(— OF SHOEMAKER'S THREAD) END
(— OF SOUND) QUANTITY
(— OF THREAD) STITCH
(— OF TILE) GAUGE
(— OF TIMBER) BALK FLITCH
(— OF TIME) DURATION
(— OF TRIP) GATE
(— OF WALL) PANE
(— OF WINDMILL ARM) WHIP
(— OF YARN) KNOT TAPE CHASE SKEIN
(— UNIT) FERMI
(— OF ORGAN PIPE) FOOTAGE
(AT FULL —) ALONG
(CONTINUOUS —) STRETCH
(FOCAL —) FOCUS
(PROJECTING —) SPONSON
(UNIT OF —) PIC PIK ROD FOOT INCH KILO PIKE REED VARA WRAP YARD FERMI METER SHAKU POLLEX FURLONG PLETHRON
(UTMOST —) EXTREME
(PREF.) MEC(O)
LENGTHEN EKE LONG DILATE EXPAND EXTEND LENGTH AMPLIFY DISTEND PRODUCE PROLONG

STRETCH ELONGATE INCREASE
PROTRACT
(— BY INTERPOLATION) FARSE
LENGTHENING HOLD ECTASIS
DIASTOLE
LENGTHWISE ALONG ALENGTH
ENDLONG ENDWAYS ENDWISE
VERTICAL
LENGTHY LONG LARGE PROLIX
LONGFUL EXTENDED
LENIENCY FAVOR MERCY LENITY
CHARITY CLEMENCY LENIENCE
LENIENT LAX EASY KIND MILD SOFT
FACILE GENTLE HUMANE LENITIVE
LENITIVE MILD MITIGANT SEDATIVE
LENITY MERCY HUMANITY
KINDNESS LENITUDE
LENO GAUZE
LENS EYE CROWN GLASS OPTIC
FLASER PEBBLE READER APLANAT
BIFOCAL CONCAVE CONTACT
DOUBLET ACHROMAT EYEGLASS
EYEPIECE HYPERGON LENTICLE
LUNETTES MENISCUS MAGNIFIER
PANTOSCOPE
(JEWELER'S —) LOUPE
(KIND OF —) FRESNEL
(WITHOUT —) APHAKIA
(PREF.) PHAC(O)
LENT CAREME IMPREST
LENTICULAR PHACOID
LENTIGO FRECKLE
LENTIL LENS LINT TILL LENTILE
LENTICLE
(PREF.) PHAC(O)
LEOFRIC (FATHER OF —) LEOFWINE
(WIFE OF —) GODIVA
LEONORE (GUARDIAN OF —) ARISTE
(SISTER OF —) ISABELLE
LEONTOCEBUS MIDAS
LEOPARD PARD TIGER PARDAL
WAGATI LIBBARD PAINTER PANTHER
PARDALE CATAMOUNT
(SNOW —) IRBIS OUNCE
LEOVIGILD (SON OF —)
ERMENEGILD
(WIFE OF —) GOISWINTHA
LEPCHA RONG RONGPA
LEPER LAZAR MESEL LAZARUS
LEPIDOMELANE ANNITE
LEPIDOPTERA GLOSSATA
LEPIDOPTERIST AURELIAN
LEPIDOSIS SCALING
LEPRECHAUN ELF SPRITE LURACAN
LEPROSY LEPRA MESEL SCALL
ALPHOS LAZARY MESELRY
LEPROUS MESELY MESELED
LEPTON MITE MUON
LEPTOSPIROSIS JAUNDICE
LERP LAAP
LESBIAN FEM DIKE DYKE FEMME
EROTIC SAPPHIC TRIBADE SAPPHIST
LESBIANISM SAPPHISM

LESION PIT GALL HIVE SORE CRATER
ESCHAR LEPRID ANTHRAX CHANCRE
FISSURE LEPROMA BEESTING
ERUPTION LEUKEMID TERTIARY
LESOTHO
(MONEY OF —) LOTI MALOTI

LESOTHO
CAPITAL: MASERU
COIN: RAND
FORMER NAME: BASUTOLAND
LANGUAGE: SOTHO SESOTHO
MONEY: LOTI SENTE MALOTI LICENTE LISENTE
MOUNTAINS: MALUTI
PEOPLE: BASOTHO
RIVER: ORANGE CALEDON
TOWN: LERIBE MASHAI MORIJA PITSENG QUTHING SEKAKES MAFETENG
WATERFALL: MALETSUNYANE

LESPEDEZA SERICEA
LESS FEW MIN MENO FEWER MINOR
LESSER SMALLER WANTING
(— BY A COMMA) MINOR
(PREF.) HYPO MEIO MIMIO MIO
(— THAN NORMAL) HYPO
LESSEE FARMER TERMOR HUURDER
TACKSMAN
LESSEN CUT EBB BATE DOCK EASE
FAIK FRET KILL LESS SINK WANE
ABATE BREAK LOWER MINCE SMALL
TAPER BUFFER DEADEN DEJECT
IMPAIR INLESS MINIFY MINISH
NARROW REMAIT HEDUCE WEAKEN
AMENUSE ASSUAGE CURTAIL
DEPLETE DEPRESS ELEVATE LIGHTEN
RELIEVE SHORTEN CONTRACT
DECREASE DEROGATE DIMINISH
DISCOUNT EMBEZZLE MITIGATE
MODERATE PALLIATE
(— FORCE) GELD
(— IN VALUE) SHRINK CHEAPEN
(— SENSITIVITY) DULL
(— STRENGTH) WEAR
(— TENSION) RELAX
(— VELOCITY) DEADEN
LESSENING LETUP PERDITION
(— OF PRISON TERM) REMISSION
(— PAIN) PAREGORIC
LESSER PETIT MINUTE SMALLER
INFERIOR
(PREF.) MINI MI(O)
(SUFF.) (— ONE) ET ETTE
LESSER CELANDINE PILEWORT
LESSON TAX LEAR TASK STUDY
EXAMPLE LECTURE PRECEPT
READING DOCUMENT LIRIPOOP
RECITATION
(DIFFICULT —) SOAK
(TORAH —) PARASHAH
LESSOR SETTER

LEST UNLESS ANANTER ANAUNTERS
LET LAT SET HIRE ALLOW LEASE
LEAVE LETTEN PERMIT SUFFER
TENANT
(**— BAIT BOB**) DIB
(**— BECOME KNOWN**) SPILL
(**— BURN**) BISHOP
(**— CONTINUE**) DRILL
(**— DOWN**) VAIL DEMIT DIMIT LOWER
STOOP STRIKE SUBMIT
(**— DOWN ROCK FACE**) ABSEIL
(**— FALL**) DROP VAIL AVALE AWALE
DEPOSE
(**— FLY**) PEG BOLT FIRE WING
(**— GO**) DROP FAIK QUIT DEMIT
BILEVE DEMISE DISMIT UNHAND
DISCARD UNSEIZE
(**— HIM TAKE**) SUM
(**— IN**) IMMIT INLET IMMISS ADHIBIT
(**— IT BE REPEATED**) REPET
(**— IT STAND**) STET
(**— KNOW**) ACQUAINT
(**— LAND**) GAVEL
(**— LOOSE**) FREE SLIP LIBERATE
(**— OUT**) BLAB TEAM WAGE ALTER
BREAK SPILL ARRENT BROACH
(**— SLIP**) BALK BAULK CHECK
FOREGO
(**— UP**) EBB EASE ABATE
LETDOWN DRAG DOWNER
HANGOVER
LETHAL FATAL DEADLY MORTAL
LETHARGIC LOGY INERT DROWSY
SLEEPY TORPID DORMANT PASSIVE
COMATOSE COMATOUS SLUGGISH
SLUMBROUS
LETHARGY COMA LOGY SLOTH
STUPOR TORPOR SLUMBER
HEBETUDE INACTION SOPITION
(**FEELING OF —**) BLAHS
LETO LATONA
LETT BALT
LETTER EF EL EM EN EX HE MU NU
PE PI XI AIN AYN BEE CEE CHI DAK
DEE EDH ESS ETA ETH GEE HET JAY
KAY LIL MEM NUN PEE PHI PSI RHO
SIN TAU TAV TEE VEE WAW YOD
YOK ZED ZEE ALEF ALIF AYIN BETA
BETH BILL BULL CHIT DEAD HETH
IOTA KAPH RESH SHIN SORT TETH
YODH YOGH ZETA AITCH ALEPH
ALPHA BLIND BREVE CAPON DELTA
DEMIT FAVOR GAMMA GIMEL GRAPH
KAPPA KNOWN KOPPA OMEGA
SADHE SIGMA STAVE STIFF THETA
ZAYIN ACCENT ADVICE ANSWER
BILLET CADJAN CARTEL CHARTA
COCKUP DALETH FAVVER ITALIC
LAMBDA LAMEDH MEDIAL SAMEKH
SCRIPT SIGLUM SUNNUD SYMBOL
VERSAL CODICIL COLLINS CONTROL
DIGAMMA DIPLOMA EPISTLE
EPSILON KAREETA MISSIVE

OMICRON SPECIAL UPSILON
AEROGRAM ASCENDER ENCYCLIC
MONITORY NUNDINAL PASTORAL
(**— OF DEFIANCE**) CARTEL
(**— OF PERMISSION**) EXEAT
(**—S DIMISSORY**) APOSTOLI
(**—S OF MARQUE**) MART
(**ANGLO-SAXON —**) EDH ETH THORN
(**AUTHORIZING —**) BREVE
(**BEGGING —**) SCREEVE
(**BLACK —**) GOTHIC
(**BREAD AND BUTTER —**) COLLINS
(**CAPITAL —**) CAP UNCIAL CAPITAL
FACTOTUM MAJUSCULE
(**FRIENDLY —**) SCREED
(**INITIAL —**) BLOOMER
(**LOVE —**) POULET
(**LOWERCASE —**) MINISCULE
(**OBSOLETE —**) EPISEMON
(**OFFICIAL —**) BRIEF
(**PAPAL —**) BULL TOME BREVE
ENCYCLIC
(**PRIVATE —**) BOOK
(**SHORT —**) CHIT LINE NOTE BILLET
LETTERET
(**SILENT —**) MUTE
(**SMUGGLED —**) KITE
(**SUBSCRIPT —**) SUBFIX
(**WORD —**) LOGOGRAM
(**PL.**) MAIL APOSTOLI
(**PREF.**) EPISTOLO
LETTER BOX APARTADO
LETTER CARRIER CORREO
MAILMAN POSTMAN
LETTERER SKETCHER
LETTERING FAC WRITE INCUSE
CALLIGRAPHY
(**— ON TV SCREEN**) CRAWL
(**TV —**) CRAWL
LETTERPRESS TEXT CAPTION
LETTING FIRMA LOCATIO
LETTING-OUT DROPPING
LETTISH LATVIAN
LETTUCE COS BIBB GRASS SALAD
KARPAS SALLET ICEBERG ROMAINE
FIREWEED MILKWEED
LETUP (**WITH NO —**) ONEND
LETUSHIM (**FATHER OF —**) DEDAN
LEUCIPPE (**BROTHER OF —**)
CALCHAS
(**FATHER OF —**) MINYAS THESTOR
(**SISTER OF —**) THEONOE
(**SON OF —**) TEUTHRAS
LEUCIPPUS (**BROTHER OF —**)
APHAREUS
(**DAUGHTER OF —**) PHOEBE HILAIRA
(**FATHER OF —**) OENOMAUS
PERIERES
(**MOTHER OF —**) GORGOPHONE
(**WIFE OF —**) PHILODICE
LEUCITE LENAD
LEUCITITE ITALITE SPERONE
ALBANITE CECILITE

LEUCOCYTE POLY NEOCYTE
HEMAMEBA MONOCYTE OXYPHILE
LEUCOMA ALBUGO WALLEYE
LEUCORRHEA WHITES
LEUCOTHEA (FATHER OF —)
ORCHAMUS
(MOTHER OF —) EURYNOME
LEUKEMIA CHLOROMA LEUKOSIS
LEVANT EASTERN WORMSEED
LEVANTINE SCATTERMOUCH
LEVEE DIKE DYKE WALL WEIR
DURBAR STOPBANK
LEVEL DONE EVEN FAIR FLAT GLAD
LUTE PLAT RAZE SHIM VIAL COUCH
EQUAL FLUSH GRADE PLAIN PLANE
POINT SLICK SOLID CHARGE DOUBLE
EVENLY FIELDY NIVEAU SLIGHT
SMOOTH STRIKE TUNNEL FLATTEN
GALLERY GANGWAY REGULAR
DEMOLISH LEVELLER SUBGRADE
(— AFTER PLOWING) BUSH
(— AND SCATTER) GELD
(— A RAFTER) EDGE
(— OFF) HAMMER BULLDOZE
(— OF SOCIETY) STRATUM
(— OF STAGE) STUDY
(— PLACE) PLANILLA
(COMMON —) PAR
(ENERGY —) SINGLET
(EXPERT — OF KARATE) DAN
(EYE —) EYELINE
(HIGHER —S) BRASS
(HIGHEST —) SUMMIT
(LOWEST —) FLOOR BOTTOM
HARDPAN
(MINING —) KIP HEAD GALLERY
GANGWAY
(NOT ON THE —) ALOP
(ON THE —) TRUE
(STRATIGRAPHIC —) HORIZON
(TOP —) HIGH CEILING
(PREF.) PLAN(I)
LEVELED BENT
LEVELER DIGGER
(PL.) ACEPHALI
LEVELING EGALITE EGALITY
LEVER KEY PRY BEAM GAUL HOOK
HORN JACK SWAY TREE BRAKE FLAIL
FLIRT HELVE PEDAL PINCH PLUTO
PRIZE SPOON STANG STANK SWIPE
THROW BINDER CLUTCH COUPER
DETENT FEELER GAFFLE HAMMER
HEAVER HOPPER LOWDER PORTER
ROCKER TAPPET TILLER BALANCE
BOOTLEG CROWBAR POINTER
RAMHEAD SHIPPER SWINGLE
TREADLE TRIGGER TUMBLER
BACKFALL GAVELOCK SELECTOR
THROTTLE
(— ARM) NIGGER
(— FOR CROSSBOW) GAFFLE GARROT
(— FOR TURNING RUDDER) HELM
TILLER

(— IN KNITTING MACHINE) JACK
(— IN TIMEPIECE) PALLET
(— LIKE CANTHOOK) PEAVY PEAVIE
(— OF GIN) START
(CONTROL —) JOYSTICK
(GEARSHIFT —) STICK
(LUMBERMAN 'S —) PEAVY PEAVEY
(ORGAN —) BACKFALL KNEESTOP
KNEESWELL
(SPINNING —) BOOTLEG
(SPOKELIKE —) SWINGLE
(THROTTLE —) GUN
(WEAVING —) LAM LAMM SWELL
BINDER TIPPLER
LEVERAGE PRY PRIZE
LEVI (FATHER OF —) JACOB
ALPHAEUS
(MOTHER OF —) LEAH
(SON OF —) KOHATH MERARI
GERSHON
LEVIGATE DUST
LEVITATE RISE FLOAT
LEVITY FOLLY HUMOR GAIETY
FLIPPANCY WHIFFLERY
LEVOROTATORY LAEVO LEVOGYRE
NEGATIVE
LEVY CUT TAX CESS MISE REAR
LEVEL RAISE ASSESS EXTEND
EXTENT IMPOSE IMPOST UPTAKE
IMPRESS TRIBUTE DISTRAIN
DISTRESS SHIPPAGE
(— A TAX) GELD GELT TAIL STENT
(— DISTRESS) DRIVE
(IRISH —) MART
LEVYING EXACTION
LEWD NICE BAWDY FOLLY PRIME
RANDY HARLOT IMPURE LACHES
LUBRIC RAKISH WANTON HIRCINE
LEERING LUSTFUL OBSCENE
RAMMISH RIGGISH SCARLET
SENSUAL WHORISH PRURIENT
SLUTTISH UNCHASTE SALACIOUS
LEWDNESS FOLLY RAKERY LECHERY
HARLOTRY PUTANISM LUBRICITY
SCULDUDDERY
LEXICOGRAPHER AMERICAN GOVE
ALLEN EVANS GOULD CARHART
MATHEWS WEBSTER WHEELER
BARNHART BARTLETT WORCESTER
BRAZILIAN MORAES
ENGLISH WYLD COLES DYCHE
ROGET SCOTT SMITH BAILEY
BLOUNT CRAGIE FARMER FLORIO
FOWLER MURRAY ONIONS WALKER
BRADLEY CAWDREY JOHNSON
MINSHEU WITHALS BULLOKAR
COCKERAM COTGRAVE AINSWORTH
COCKERELL PARTRIDGE STORMONTH
RICHARDSON
FRENCH LITTRE ROBERT BEAUJAN
GODEFROY LAROUSSE FURETIERE
GERMAN ERMAN MURET SACHS
FLUGEL SCHNEIDER

GREEK POLLUX SUIDAS PAMPHILUS
ICELANDIC BLONDAL
ITALIAN CESARI CALENUS FANFANI
FACCIOLATI FORCELLINI
NEW ZEALAND PARTRIDGE
POLISH LINDE
SCOTTISH GRANT MURRAY OGILVY
LEXICON CALEPIN WORDBOOK
LIABILITY DEBT DEBIT CHARGE
TRIBUTE OBLIGATION
LIABLE APT ABLE OPEN GUILTY
EXPOSED OBVIOUS ONEROUS
SUBJECT AMENABLE INCIDENT
(— TO MISCHANCE) RISKY
(— TO SIN) PECCABLE
(NOT —) EXEMPT IMMUNE
(SUFF.) ABLE IBLE
LIAISON BOND AFFAIR AFFAIRE
LINKING INTIMACY INTRIGUE
LIANA CIPO BEJUCO GUARANA
BUSHROPE
LIANG TAEL
LIAR LEAR ANANIAS BOUNCER
CRACKER CRAMMER PROCTOR
WARLOCK WERNARD FABULIST
LIBATION AMBROSIA
LIBEL DEFAME MALIGN VILIFY
SLANDER
LIBELOUS FAMOUS SCANDALOUS
LIBER PHLOEM
LIBERAL WET FAIR FREE GOOD OPEN
WHIG BROAD FRANK LARGE NOBLE
SOLUTE JANNOCK PROFUSE
ADVANCED CATHOLIC GENEROUS
HANDSOME LARGEOUS PRODIGAL
SEPARATE MUNIFICENT
(CANADIAN —) GRIT
(NOT —) CHARY SPARE
LIBERAL ARTS MUSES
LIBERALITY LARGE BOUNTY
BREADTH CHARITY FREEDOM
HONESTY LARGESS
LIBERALLY LARGE BROADLY
LIBERATE FREE QUIT FRITH REMIT
UNGYVE UNWRAP DELIVER
MANUMIT RELEASE UNSLAVE
UNFETTER UNTHRALL
LIBERATION LIB FREEDOM RELEASE
DELIVERY KAIVALYA DISCHARGE
(— OF SPORE) ABSCISSION

LIBERIA

CAPITAL: MONROVIA
CUSTOM: SANDE
HILLS: BOMI
MEASURE: KUBA
MOUNTAIN: UNI NIETE NIMBA WUTIVI
MOUNTAINS: BONG SATRO
PEOPLE: GI KRU KWA VAI VEI GOLA
KROO KROU TOMA BASSA GIBBI
GISSI GREBO KPELLE KROOBY
KRUMAN KROOBOY MANDINGO
RIVER: CESS LOFA MANO LOFFA

MANNA MORRO CESTOS DOUOBE
STJOHN STPAUL CAVALLY
SANPEDRO
TOWN: GANTA GRIBO REBBO HARPER
ZORZOR NANAKRU TAPPITA
BUCHANAN MARSHALL SASSTOWN

LIBERTINE ROUE PUNKER PANURGE
STRIKER LOTHARIO LOVELACE
STRINGER
LIBERTY MAY SOC EASE LARGE
LEAVE SCOPE ACCESS LEEWAY
SCOUTH STREET FREEDOM LARGESS
LICENSE WITHGANG
(— OF ACTION) PLAY SWING
(— OF CHOICE) FREEWILL
(— OF ENTRANCE) INGRESS
(— OF GOING OUT) ISH
(— OF TURNING PIGS INTO FIELDS)
SHACK
(— TO BUY AND SELL) TOLL
(— TO HUNT) CHASE
(AT —) FREE IDLE
(PARTIAL — OF HAWK) HACK
(SEXUAL —) INTIMACY
(UNDUE —) HEAD
LIBERTY CAP PILLEUS
LIBIDINIZATION EGOISM
LIBIDINOUS FLESHY FLESHLY
LIBNI (FATHER OF —) MAHLI
GERSHON
LIBRA AS PONDUS
LIBRARIAN
AMERICAN COLE DANA HILL HUNT
KOCH LANE DEWEY EAMES EVANS
GREEN MUDGE POOLE SHERA SMITH
WROTH CUTTER FOLSOM HUMMEL
JEWETT MEARNS PUTNAM WINSOR
CARLSON EDMANDS MUMFORD
SONNECK VANNAME WELLMAN
BARTLETT BOSTWICK COGSWELL
HAVILAND MACLEISH SAUNDERS
SPOFFORD HENDERSON
YARMOLINSKY
CANADIAN READY
ENGLISH BOND COXE DIBDIN LARKIN
PANIZZI PATMORE THOMPSON
FRENCH DUPUY OMONT
BONNECHOSE TASCHEREAU
GERMAN EBERT BURGER
PERUVIAN ULLOA
SPANISH MACHADO
LIBRARY DEN AMBRY BIBLE
MUSEUM BHANDAR BOOKERY
ATHENEUM
LIBRETTO BOOK WORD TESTO
TEXTBOOK

LIBYA

ALPHABET: TIFINAGH
CAPITAL: BENGASI BENGAZI TRIPOLI
COIN: DIRHAM
DESERT: FEZZAN MURZUK MURZUCH

GULF: SIDRA GIRTE
MEASURE: SAA BOZZE DONUM JABIA
   TEMAN BARILE MISURA MATTARO
MOUNTAIN: BETTE
OASIS: JALO KUFRA SEBHA FEZZAN
   GIOFRA TAZERRO GIARABUB
SEAPORT: HOMS DERNA SIDRI
   TOBRUK BENGAZI
TOWN: BRAK DERJ HOMS BARKA
   DERNA SEBHA SIDRI UBARI ZAWIA
   ELMARJ GARIAN MURZUQ REMADA
   TOBRUK MISURATA
WEIGHT: KELE UCKIA GORRAF
   TERMINO KHAROUBA

LICE CREEPERS
  (FISH —) EPIZOA
LICENSE TAG CHOP GALE HEAD
  EXEAT LEAVE SLANG SWING
  BANDON CAROON FIRMAN INDULT
  PATENT PERMIT READER TICKET
  CAROOME CERTIFY CROTTLE
  FACULTY FREEDOM INDULTO
  LIBERTY LICENCE PLACARD
  WARRANT ESCAMBIO IMMUNITY
  MORTMAIN PASSPORT TEZKIRAH
  (— FOR CART) CAROOME
  (— PLATE) NUMBER
  (PEDDLER'S —) SLANG
LICENTIOUS GAY LAX FREE LEWD
  WILD FRANK LARGE LOOSE FILTHY
  RIBALD UNRULY WANTON CYPRIAN
  FLESHLY IMMORAL LAWLESS
  LIBERAL UNYOKED
LICENTIOUSNESS DIRT LICENSE
LICHEN RAG MOSS MANNA USNEA
  ARCHIL CORKIR KORKIR ORCHIL
  CROTTAL CROTTLE CUDBEAR
  EVERNIA OAKMOSS PARELLA
  ARCHILLA CAPEWEED LECANORA
  LUNGWORT PARMELIA ROCKHAIR
  TREEHAIR WARTWORT
LICIT LEGAL LAWFUL LEEFUL
LICK LAP LIKE SUCK MOUTH SLAKE
  CONQUER
LICKER-IN TUMBLE
LICKING LAMBENT GRUELING
LICKSPITTLE LACKEY
LICORICE POMFRET SWEETROOT
LICORICE PILL CACHOU
LICYMNIUS (FATHER OF —)
  ELECTRYON
  (MOTHER OF —) MIDEA
  (SISTER OF —) ALCMENA
  (SLAYER OF —) TLEPOLEMUS
  (WIFE OF —) PERIMEDE
LID DIP BRED DECK TYMP COVER
  BRIDLE EYELID POTLID CLAPPER
  CLICKET CLOSURE SCUTTLE
  SHUTTER COVERCLE OPERCULUM
  (SUFF.) POMATOUS
LIE FIB GAB KIP LAY LIG LIN SIT YED
  CRAM FALL FLAW LIGG REST RIDE

WHID DEVIL DWELL FABLE FEIGN
LEASE STAND STORY BOUNCE
FITTEN PALTER RAPPER RESIDE
SPRAWL VANITY YANKER BOUNCER
CONSIST CRACKER CRAMMER
CRUMPER FALSITY GRABBLE
LEASING PLUMPER TWISTER
UNTRUTH WHACKER WHISKER
WHOPPER MENDACITY TARADIDDLE
PREVARICATE
(— AHEAD) AWAIT
(— ALONGSIDE) ACCOST
(— AROUND) COMPASS
(— AT ANCHOR) HOVE
(— AT FULL LENGTH) STRETCH
(— CONCEALED) DARKLE
(— CONTIGUOUS) CONFINE
(— DETECTOR) POLYGRAPH
(— DORMANT) SLEEP
(— DOWN) LEAN COUCH CHARGE
(— FLAT ON BELLY) GROVEL
(— HEAD TO WIND) TRY
(— HIDDEN) LURK MICHE TAPPISH
(— IN AMBUSH) HUGGER
(— IN BED) KIP THOKE
(— IN WAIT) AWAIT LOWER AMBUSH
  FORELAY
(— IN WATER) DOUSE DROWN
(— LOW) TAPPICE
(— NEXT TO) ADJOIN
(— OPPOSITE TO) SUBTEND
(— OVER) COVER
(— PRONE) GROVEL GRABBLE
(— PROSTRATE) STREEK
(— QUIET) SNUDGE
(— SNUG) CUDDLE
(— UNEVENLY) SAG
(— WITH SAILS FURLED) HULL
(RIG —) CAULKER
(IMPUDENT —) BOUNCE
(MONSTROUS —) STRAMMER
(PREF.) (— HID) LANTHAN(O) LANTHO

LIECHTENSTEIN

CAPITAL: VADUZ
CASTLE: GUTEMBURG
MOUNTAIN: RHATIKON
RIVER: RHINE SAMINA
ROMAN NAME: RHAETIA
TOWN: HAAG BALZER SCHAAN
  NENDELN
TRIBE: ALAMANNI

LIED BALLAD
LIEF DEAR LEAVE LEEVE LIEVE FREELY
  GLADLY BELOVED
LIEN MORTGAGE
LIEU STEAD
LIEUTENANT LUFF ZANY LOUEY
  JAYGEE KEHAYA CAIMAKAM
  QAIMAQAM TENIENTE WOODVILE
  SHAVETAIL
  (— JUNIOR GRADE) JAYGEE

LIFE IT VIE ZOE HIDE JIVA PUFF SNAP
TUCK VALE ANIMA BEING BLOOD
DEMON HEART LIFER QUICK SWEAT
BIOSIS BREATH CANDLE COURSE
ENERGY SPIRIT SPRITE LIFELET
LIFEWAY VITALITY VIVACITY
(— AFTER DEATH) FUTURITY
(— IN HEAVEN) GLORY
(— IN SOCIETY) SAMSARA SANSARA
(— OF FURNACE LINING) CAMPAIGN
(— OF THE SEA) HALIBIOS
(ACADEMIC —) ACADEMIA
(ANIMAL —) FLESH
(ANIMAL AND PLANT —) BIOS BIOTA
BIOLOGY EDAPHON
(CLOISTERED —) VEIL
(EARLY —) YOUTH
(ETERNAL —) GRACE
(HOME —) DOMESTICITY
(INTELLECTUAL —) JIVATMA
(LOCAL —) BIOTA
(MONASTIC —) CLOISTER
(MORAL —) DAENA
(MOSS —) BRYOLOGY
(PLANT —) BIOS BIOTA FLORA
BOTANY
(PUBLIC —) WORLD
(ROBUST —) JUICE
(SIGN OF —) PULSE
(SINGLE —) CELIBACY
(TERRESTRIAL —) GEOBIOS
(WAY OF —) BAG SCENE FASTLANE
(WITHOUT —) AZOIC
(PREF.) BI(O) EMBIO PSYCH(O) VIT(A)
(O)
(NOT —) ABIO
(SUFF.) BIA BIONT BIOSIS BIOTIC
BIOUS BIUM BIUS BY PSYCHE
LIFE BELT SAFETY
LIFEBLOOD BLOOD SWEAT
LIFE-FORCE KUNDALINI
(YOGI —) KUNDALINI
LIFE FOR THE TSAR, A
(CHARACTER IN —) SOBININ
SUSANIN ANTONIDA
(COMPOSER OF —) GLINKA
LIFELESS ARID BLAH DEAD DULL
FLAT AMORT HEAVY INERT VAPID
ANEMIC TORPID SAPLESS DESOLATE
GRIPLESS INACTIVE
(PREF.) ABIO
LIFELESSLY DEADLY INERTLY
LIFELESSNESS ANEMIA
LIFELIKE VIVE QUICK EIDETIC
NATURAL ANIMATED SPEAKING
LIFE PRESERVER FLOAT NEDDY
LIFESAVER HERO
LIFETIME AGE DAY WORLD LIVING
LIFEDAY DURATION LIFELONG
(— OF FLOWER) ANTHESIS
LIFE WITH FATHER (AUTHOR OF —)
DAY

(CHARACTER IN —) DELIA GULICK
CLARENCE MARGARET
LIFEWORK (ARTIST'S —) OEUVRE
LIFT WIN BOOM BUOY CAST COCK
HEFT JACK REAR TOSS WEVE ARSIS
BOOST BREAK ELATE HEAVE HITCH
HOICK HOIST HOOSH MOUNT PRESS
RAISE SPOUT STEAL WEIGH BUCKET
CLEECH SNATCH TAKEUP ELEVATE
ENHANCE HEELTAP NAUNTLE
BOOKLIFT CHAIRWAY ELEVATOR
LEVITATE
(— HAT) DOFF
(— IN PAWNSHOP) SPOUT
(— IN VEHICLE) SETDOWN
(— IN WEIGHT LIFTING) SQUAT
(— OF WAVE) SCEND
(— OF WEIGHTS) SNATCH
(— ONESELF) SOAR
(— QUICKLY) PERK
(— UP) HOVE CRANE ERECT EXALT
EXTOL HORSE WEIGH ADVANCE
ELEVATE NAUNTLE
(— WITH BLOCK AND TACKLE) BOUSE
(KIND OF —) SKI
(SKI —) GONDOLA
LIFTED ARRECT SUBLIME
LIFTER GAGGER SERVER HOISTER
HOISTMAN
LIFTING HIKE UPTAKE
LIFT VALVE POPPET
LIGAMENT BAND BOND ARTERY
FRENUM PAXWAX STRING ZONULE
ARMILLA LIGATURE
(PREF.) DESM(A)(IDI)(IDIO)(O)
SYNDESM(O)
LIGAMENTOUS DESMOID
LIGATE BAR
LIGATURE ASH CLAM PLICA DIGRAM
PNEUMA STIGMA BANDAGE
DIGRAPH FUNICLE LIGAMENT
LIGATION
(— OE) ASH
LIGGER TRIMMER
LIGHT BUG DAY GAY HAP LAW SHY
SUN AIRY EASY FAIR FALL FINE FIRE
FLIT FLUX GLIM LAMP LEET LUNT
MILD SLUT SOFT BAVIN BLAZE
CORKY FANAL FILMY FLAME FLEET
FUFFY LEGER LOUGH MERRY PITCH
QUICK SHEER SPILL WHITE BEACON
BRIGHT CHAFFY FLOATY FLOSSY
FLUFFY FROTHY GENTLE HAPPEN
ILLUME KINDLE LANCET LUSTER
LUSTRE MARKER PASTEL PHAROS
SIGNAL SLUSHY STINGY STRIKE
STROBE SUTTLE VOLAGE BENGOLA
BUOYANT CRESSET FRAGILE
GLITTER LAMBENT SFOGATO
SMITHER SUMMERY TORTAYS
TRIVIAL UNGRAVE BACKFIRE
DAYLIGHT DELICATE DIAPHANE

ELECTRIC EXPEDITE FEATHERY
GASLIGHT GOSSAMER LEGGIERO
LUMINARY PALOUSER SUNLIGHT
SUNSHINE
(— AND BRILLIANT) LAMBENT
(— AND FIRE ON HORSE'S MANE)
HAG
(— AND FREE) FLYAWAY
(— AND QUICK) VOLANT
(— CANDLES) TOLLY
(— DISPLAY) LED
(— FROM NIGHT SKY) AIRGLOW
(— IN WINDOW) LANCET
(— OF MORNING) AURORA
(— ON TV SCREEN) SNOW
(— UP) FLASH GLOZE ILLUME
RELUME GLORIFY
(— UPON) STRIKE
(BRIGHT —) GLARE GLEAM
(BURST OF —) FLASH
(CIRCLE OF —) HALO NIMBUS
(EMIT —) LASE
(EMIT COHERENT —) LASE
(FAINT —) GLIMMER SCARROW
(FEEBLE —) TAPER GLIMMER
(FITFUL —) SHIMMER
(GREEN —) GOAHEAD
(HARBOR —) BUG
(INDICATOR —) BEZEL
(INDICATOR — ON SCREEN) CURSOR
(INNER —) SEED
(KIND OF —) KLEIG KLIEG
(LASER — EMITTER) LIDAR
(NEBULOUS —) CHEVELURE
(NEW —) SEPARATE
(NIGHT —) MORTAR
(PARKING —S) DIMMERS
(PATCH OF —) CURSOR
(PERSIAN GOD OF —) MITHRAS
(REFLECTED —) SKYME
(SHIP'S —) FANAL
(SMALL —) TAPER
(STUDIO —) KLIEG
(TRAFFIC —) BLINKER
(WAVERING —) FLICKER
(PL.) BUFF
(PREF.) LUCI LUMIN(I)(O) PHOS
PHOT(O)
LIGHT-COLORED BLONDE
LIGHTED LUMINOUS
LIGHTEN ALAY CLEAR LEVIN LIGHT
RAISE ALLEGE BLEACH ENCLEAR
FOULDRE MOLLIFY SWEETEN
THUNDER LEVIGATE
LIGHTENING BREAK
(— OF HAIR) FROSTING
LIGHTER KEEL SCOW ACCON BARGE
CASCO PRAAM WHERRY DROGHER
GABBARD GONDOLA PONTOON
CHOPBOAT
LIGHTERMAN KEELER KEELMAN
LIGHT-FOOTED SPRY

LIGHT-GREEN
(PREF.) CHLOR(O)
LIGHT-HEADED IDLE BARMY LIGHT
LIVELY CARRIED GLAIKET SKITTISH
LIGHT-HEARTED GAY GLAD GIDDY
BUOYANT WINSOME CAREFREE
DEBONAIR VOLATILE
LIGHTHEARTEDNESS BUOYANCY
LIGHTHOUSE FANAL LIGHT MINAR
BEACON PHAROS LANTERN
(PREF.) PHARO
LIGHT IN AUGUST (AUTHOR OF —)
FAULKNER
(CHARACTER IN —) DOC JOE GAIL
LENA ALLEN BROWN BYRON
GROVE HINES LUCAS BOBBIE
BURDEN JOANNA EUPHEUS
CHRISTMAS HIGHTOWER
LIGHTLESS APHOTIC
(PREF.) APHOTO
LIGHTLY LIGHT AIRILY FAIRILY
HOVERLY LEGGIERO SLIGHTLY
LIGHT-MINDED BLITHE ETOURDI
LIGHTNESS CHEER VALUE GAIETY
LEVITY AIRINESS BUOYANCY
LEGERETE LEGERITY
(— OF MOVEMENT) BALLON
LIGHTNING BOLT FIRE LAIT LEVIN
FULMEN METEOR FOULDRE
SULPHUR THUNDER FIREBALL
FIREBOLT WILDFIRE
LIGHT-O'-LOVE COCOTTE LEVERET
LIGHT-TEXTURED FOZY
LIGHTWOOD FATWOOD
LIGIA LIGYDA
LIGNEOUS WOODY XYLOID
LIGNIN LIGNOSE XYLOGEN
LIGNITE JET
LIGNUM VITAE GUAYACAN
POCKWOOD
LIGROIN BENZINE CANADOL
LIGULA LANGUET
LIGULE STRAP LIGULA
LIKE AS ALA DIG DOTE LIST LOVE
ALIKE ENJOY EQUAL FANCY SAVOR
TASTE ADMIRE AFFECT BELIKE
LIKELY MATTER PLEASE SEMBLE
SIMILE THEWAY CONCEIT SIMILAR
SEMBLANT SUITABLE SEMBLABLE
(— A GLAND) ADEMOSE ADENOUS
(— BETTER) PREFER
(— HAIR) CRINITE
(VERY —) SIAMESE
(PREF.) HOME(O) HOMOE HOMOI SYM
(SUFF.) AR EOUS ESQUE IC(AL) INE IS
ISH ISTIC LY ODE OID(AL) SOME
LIKELIHOOD APTNESS
LIKELY APT FAIR LIKE READY LIABLE
PROOFY SEEMLY GRADELY SMITTLE
APPARENT FEASIBLE POSSIBLE
PROBABLE PROSPECTIVE
(MOST —) BELIKE

LIKEN EVEN LIKE REMENE SEMBLE COMPARE ASSEMBLE CREDIBLE RESEMBLE SIMILIZE

LIKENESS DAP BLEE ICON IDOL MAKE SECT BLUSH DUMMY GLIFF IMAGE MORAL SHAPE EFFIGY FIGURE STATUE ANALOGY KINSHIP PATTERN PICTURE RETRAIT EQUALITY HOMOLOGY PARALLEL PORTRAIT SEMBLANCE SIMILARITY
(**— OF ORIGIN**) ISOGENY
(**DISTORTED —**) CARICATURE
(**PERFECT —**) SPIT

LIKENING SIMILE

LIKEWISE EKE TOO ALSO ITEM EITHER EQUALLY LIKEWAYS
(**— NOT**) NOR

LIKHI (**FATHER OF —**) SHEMIDAH

LIKING GOO GRA PAY GOUT GUST LIKE LIST LUST FANCY FLAIR GUSTO HEART SHINE SKILL SMACK TASTE THEAT SWALLOW AFFINITY APPETITE FONDNESS PENCHANT
(**ECCENTRIC —**) FOIBLE
(**MENTAL —**) PALATE
(**SUFF.**) (**— FOR**) PHIL(A)(AE)(E)(IA) (ISM)(IST)(OUS)(US)

LIKUTA
(**PL.**) MAKUTA

LILAC LILAS MAUVE LAYLOCK

LILACIN SYRINGIN

LILIOM (**AUTHOR OF —**) MOLNAR
(**CHARACTER IN —**) WOLF JULIE MARIE FICSUR LILIOM LOUISE MUSKAT LINZMAN HOLLUNDER

LILLIPUTIAN TINY

LILY ALOE IXIA KELP SEGO AZTEC CALLA CLOTE AUGUST LILIUM VALLEY COCUISA MONOCOT ASPHODEL LILYWORT MARTAGON NENUPHAR
(**AFRICAN —**) AGAPANTHUS
(**CLIMBING —**) GLORIOSA
(**PALM —**) TI
(**SEA —**) CRINOID
(**WATER —**) CANDOCK CAMALOTE
(**PREF.**) LIRIO
(**SUFF.**) CRINUS

LILY OF THE VALLEY LILIUM MUGGET MUGUET MUGWET LILYWORT SHINLEAF

LIMA BEAN HABA LIMA

LIMB ARM LEG CLAW FOOT KNOT LITH TRAM WING ARTUS BOUGH SPALD SPAUL SWAMP BRANCH MEMBER PODITE FEATURE FLIPPER FORCEPS PLEOPOD NECTOPOD
(**PREF.**) MEL
(**SUFF.**) (**CONDITION OF —**) MELIA

LIMBA AFARA FRAKE

LIMBER BAIN FLIP LIMP LUSH AGILE LINGY LITHE LISSOM SEMMIT SUPPLE SWANKY BRUSHER BRUTTER KNOTTER LIMMOCK PLIABLE FLEXIBLE FLIPPANT

LIME CALX LIMA CEDRA CEDRAT CHUNAM CITRON FUSTIC
(**— IN BRICK**) BOND
(**KIND OF —**) KEY
(**WILD —**) COLIMA
(**PREF.**) CAL(AREO)(I)(IO)(O)

LIMEN THRESHOLD

LIMESTONE CAM HUM CALP CAUK CAUM LIAS LYAS MALM CHALK POROS ROACH CLUNCH KUNKUR MARBLE OOLITE CIPOLIN SCAGLIA DOLOMITE PISOLITE TRAVERTINE
(**— REGION**) KARST
(**DECOMPOSED —**) ROTTENSTONE

LIME TREE LIME TEIL LINDEN

LIMEY TAR

LIMIT CAP END FIX BIND BUTT FINE HOLD LINE LIST MARK MERE PALE TAIL BLOCK BOUND COAST GAUGE HEDGE SCANT STENT STINT VERGE BORDER BOURNE DEFINE EFFLUX EXTENT FINISH FINITE HAMPER LENGTH MODIFY NARROW PALING SCRIMP TROPIC UPSHOT ASTRICT CLOSURE COMPASS CONFINE CONTENT HORIZON MAXIMUM MEASURE OUTSIDE BOUNDARY CONTRACT DEADLINE IMPRISON LIMITARY LIMITATE OUTGOING OUTREACH RESTRAIN RESTRICT SOLSTICE TERMINUS PARAMETER
(**— EFFECT**) ALLAY
(**— IN A FOREST**) BAIL
(**— MOTION**) HOLD
(**— OF STATUTE**) PURVIEW
(**— OF VISION AT SEA**) KENNING
(**EXTREME —**) HEIGHT
(**LOWER —**) FLOOR
(**TAKE TO THE —**) TAX
(**UPPER —**) CEILING
(**UTTER —**) EXTREME
(**PL.**) AMBIT CANCELS ENVIRONS PERIMETER
(**PREF.**) ORI

LIMITATION TAIL FRAME STINT DENIAL CLOTURE RESERVE
(**— OF DEBATE**) CLOTURE
(**— OF INHERITANCE**) TAIL
(**— OF WANTS**) STOICISM
(**PL.**) SWADDLE

LIMITED MILD TAIL BORNE BRIEF SHORT SMALL FINITE NARROW STINTY STRAIT BOUNDED SPECIAL CONFINED DEFINITE LIMITARY PAROCHIAL SECTARIAN MEASURABLE PROVINCIAL RESTRICTED
(**— IN APPEAL**) CHICHI
(**— IN SCOPE**) MODERATE

LIMITING DEFINITE ADJECTIVE EXCLUSIVE
(**— LINE**) RUBICON

LIMITS (NEAR OUTER — OF PLAY)
DEEP
LIMMA DIESIS
LIMMU EPONYM
LIMO (KIND OF —) STRETCH
LIMON (BROTHER OF —) SCEPHRUS
(FATHER OF —) TEGEATES
(MOTHER OF —) MAERA
LIMONENE CINENE CARVENE
CITRENE
LIMONITE BOGORE BOGIRON
PEAIRON
LIMONIUM STATICE
LIMOUSINE LIMO BERLIN SALOON
SUBURBAN
LIMP HIP HOP CLOP GIMP HALT HIMP
HOIT SOFT THIN HENCH HILCH HITCH
LINGY LOOSE LOPPY SLAMP STILT
FLABBY FLIMSY HAMBLE HIMPLE
HIRPLE HOBBLE LENNOW LIMBER
LIMPSY FLACCID LIMMOCK SHAFFLE
UNSMART DRAGGLED DROOPING
CLAUDICATION
LIMPET CHINK OPIHI SHELL ACMAEA
LIMPIN FLIDDER
LIMPID PURE CLEAR LUCID BRIGHT
CRYSTAL PELLUCID
LIMPING HALT LAME GIMPY LIMPY
ZOPPA HALTING
LIMPLY LANKLY
LINAGE SPACE
LINALOOL LICAREOL
LINCHPIN FORELOCK
LINCOLN (IN-LAW OF —) TODD
LINCTUS LOOCH LOHOCH LOHOCK
LINDEN LIN LIME LYNE TEIL TILIA
TILLET LINWOOD BASSWOOD
DADDYNUT WOODLIND
LINE BAR BOX FIX RAY ROW TAW
BOFF CASE CEIL COLA CRIB DASH
FACE FILE GAME GAPE LACE LARD
LATH LEAD LING MAIN MARK RACE
RANK RULE STOP TAUM WHIP
AGONE FAINT FEINT FLEET HATCH
LIGNE LINEA METER RANGE SCORE
SPIEL STRIA TOUCH TRACE TRAIL
TRAIN TWIST BINDER CABURN
CEVIAN CREASE DEGREE DOUBLE
EARING GASKET ISOBAR ISOHEL
ISOPAG ISOTAC METIER NETTLE
SECANT SECOND SPRING STREAK
STRING STRIPE AZIMUTH BABBITT
CATLINE CONTOUR CREANCE
ENVELOP GUNLINE HIPLINE ISOCHOR
ISOGRAM ISOHYET ISONEPH ISORITH
ISOSTER ISOTOME KNITTLE MARLINE
NACARAT SCRATCH WINDROW
BALKLINE BISECTOR BOUNDARY
BUSINESS CHAMPAIN DATELINE
DEADLINE DIAGONAL DIAMETER
DRAGLINE DRUMLINE FISHBACK
GANTLINE GEODESIC GIRTLINE
HAIRLINE HANDLINE HEXAPODY

ISOGLOSS ISOGONIC ISOPHANE
ISOPHENE ISOPLERE ISOTHERE
ISOTHERM LANDWIRE LIFELINE
MARTINET SLIPBAND STRINGER
SUBCLONE SUBSTILE SUBSTYLE
UPSTROKE PERPENDICULAR
(— AROUND STAMP) FRAME
(— AS CENTER FOR REVOLVING)
AXIS
(— HEARTH) FIX FETTLE
(— IN GLASS) STRING
(— IN HAT) HEADLINE
(— MINESHAFT) TUB
(— OF ACTION) LAY
(— OF BATTLE) FRONT
(— OF BUSINESS) WAY
(— OF CELLS) ANNULUS
(— OF CLIFFS) SCARP BREAKS
(— OF COLOR) SLASH STREAK
(— OF DANCERS) CHAIN
(— OF DESCENT) SIDE STEM STIRP
STOCK PHYLUM STRAIN ANCESTRY
BREEDING
(— OF DETERMINANT) COLUMN
(— OF DEVELOPMENT) STREET
(— OF DEVOLUTION) ENTAIL
(— OF FAMILY) STEM
(— OF FIBERS) CHRYSAL
(— OF FIRE HOSE) LEAD
(— OF FLOTATION) BEARINGS
(— OF FORTIFICATION) LIMES
ENCEINTE
(— OF HAY) WAKE WALLOW
(— OF HEALTH) HEPATICA
(— OF HIGH TIDE) LANDWASH
(— OF HOUSES) BLOCK
(— OF INTERSECTION) GROIN
BUTTOCK
(— OF JUNCTION) MEET SEAM
(— OF LIGHTNING) STREAK
(— OF MERCHANDISE) NAMEPLATE
(— OF MERCURY) HEPATICA
(— OF PERSONS) QUEUE CORDON
STICKLE
(— OF PORES) HATCHING
(— OF SOLDIERS) RAY FILE RANK
WAVE CORDON
(— OF STITCHING) BASTING
(— OF TACK) PITCH
(— OF TALK) SPIEL
(— OF TIMBERS) BOOM STOCKADE
(— OF TREES) STRIP
(— OF TYPE) SLUG KICKER
(— OF UNION) SUTURE
(— ON A LETTER) SERIF
(— ON BOOK COVER) BAND
(— ON COAT) GORGE
(— ON DOLPHIN) STOP
(— ON HIGHWAY) BARRIER
(— ON WEATHER MAP) ISOBAR
(— THAT CUTS ANOTHER) SECANT
(— TO BIND CABLES) CABURN
(— TO FASTEN SAIL) EARING GASKET

(— TO RAISE FLAG) LANIARD LANYARD
(— TO START RACE) TRIG
(— TOUCHING ARC) TANGENT
(— UP) LAY QUEUE
(— WITH BRICKS) GINGE
(— WITH PANELLING) WAINSCOT
(— WITH STONES) STEEN STEYN
(— WITH TIMBER) CRIB
(ANCHOR —) RODING
(BEARING —) CUT
(BOTTOM —) NET
(BOUNDARY —) MERE FENCE BORDER ISOGLOSS
(BOUNDING —) SIDE BOUNDARY PERIMETER
(BRIEF —) ITEM
(COASTAL —) SEAMARK
(CONNECTING —) LIGATURE
(CONTINUOUS —) STRETCH
(CONTOUR —) ISOBASE ISOCHASM ISOTHERM
(CURVED —) ARC SLUR SWEEP
(CUTTING —) SECANT
(DEMARCATION —) BOMBLINE
(DIAGONAL —) BIAS
(DIVIDING —) EDGE MIDRIB DIVISION FRONTIER
(ELECTRIC —) HIGHLINE
(ENCIRCLING —) RIM
(FACIAL —) TRAIT
(FINISHING —) TAPE WIRE
(FISHING —) TOME TROT FLEET SNELL SNOOD LEADER LEDGER NORSEL BACKING BOULTER OUTLINE SPILLER SPILLET TRIMMER BLOWLINE CORKLINE FISHLINE SNAGLINE TROTLINE
(HORIZONTAL —) LEVEL
(IMAGINARY —) AGONE HINGE GROOVE ISOBAR ISOGAM ISOHEL ISOPAG HORIZON ISOBASE ISOBATH ISOGRIV ISOHYET ISOLINE ISOTACH ISOBRONT ISOCHASM ISOCHEIM ISOCHLOR ISOCHORE ISOCRYME ISOGLOSS ISOPHOTE ISOPLETH ISOSTERE ISOTHERM
(INCISED —) SCORE
(INCLINED —) CANT
(LIMITING —) RUBICON
(LONGITUDINAL —) MERIDIAN
(MEDIAN —) RAPHE
(METRICAL —) EIGHT STAFF STICH DIMETER SAPPHIC STICHOS MONOMETER OCTAMETER PENTAMETER
(MINESHAFT —) BRATTICE
(MUSICAL —) ACCOLADE
(NAUTICAL —) EARING LACING GESWARP MARLINE PAINTER RATLINE DOWNHAUL MESSENGER
(ONE-TENTH OF —) GRY
(PERPENDICULAR —) CATHETUS

(PLOTTED —) ADIABAT
(RADIATING —) BEAM
(RAILROAD —) STEM STUB
(RAISED —) RIDGE
(SPECTRUM —) GHOST DOUBLET SINGLET TRIPLET MULTIPLET
(STARTING —) SCRATCH
(STRAIGHT —) CHORD BEELINE STRAIGHT
(SUPPLY —) AIRLIFT UMBILICAL
(SURVEYING —) WAD BASE CHAIN
(THEATRICAL —S) FAT
(THIN —) THREAD
(TOW —) CORDELLE
(TRANSPORTATION —) FEEDER CARRIER
(WAVY —) SQUIGGLE
(ZIGZAG —) DANCETTE
(42 —S) LENGTH
(PREF.) LINEO STICHO
(SUFF.) STICH(OUS)
(STRAIGHT —) TRIX
LINEAGE GET KIN KIND RACE TEAM BIRTH BLOOD SPACE STIRP STOCK FAMILY HAVAGE NATION PARAGE SOURCE SPRING STRAIN DESCENT KINDRED PROGENY SUCCESS ANCESTRY PEDIGREE PARENTAGE
LINEAL DIRECT
LINEAMENT LINE TRACT TRAIT FEATURE
LINEAR RUNNING
LINECUT ZINCO
LINED MASONED
LINEMAN END GUARD CENTER TACKLE FORWARD WIREMAN CHAINMAN
LINEN LIN BUCK LAWN CRASH IRISH TOILE BARRAS DAMASK DIAPER NAPERY RAINES SENDAL BATISTE DORNICK HOLLAND LOCKRAM TABLING BARANDOS OSNABURG PLATILLA
(— CLOSET) LOCKER
(— FOR SHIRTS) SARKING
(— TO COVER CHALICE) PALL
(CHINESE —) KOMPOW
(COARSE —) HARN BARRAS
(FINE —) LAKE LAWN BYSSUS DAMASK DIAPER RAINES
(HOUSEHOLD —) NAPERY TABLING
(SCRAPED —) LINT
(SHADE OF —) ECRU
(SPANISH —) CREA
(TWILLED —) SILESIA
(PREF.) BYSSI BYSSO LINO
LINER SHIP BASKET SCRIBER STEAMER
LINES
(PREF.)
(TWO CROSSED —) CHIASMO CHIASTO

LINET (BROTHER OF —) LIONES
(HUSBAND OF —) GARETH
LINEUP SHOWUP
LING BURBOT DRIZZLE STOKVIS
LINGA DILDO
LINGCOD CULTUS
LINGER LAG HANG HOVE LING STAY
CLING DALLY DELAY DEMUR DWELL
HAUNT HOVER PAUSE TARRY
DRETCH HANKER LOITER TAIGLE
TARROW DRINGLE
LINGERER LUNGIS LAGGARD
LINGERIE FRILLIES PRETTIES
LINGERING SLOW DELAY MOROSE
TARDANT DRAGGING
LINGO BAT CANT JARGON LINGUA
PATTER DIALECT
LINGUA GLOSSA TONGUE
LINGUAL GLOSSAL
LINGUIST (ALSO SEE PHILOLOGIST)
LINGUISTIC GLOTTIC
LINGUISTICS GRAMMAR
PHILOLOGY
LINIMENT EIK EMBROCHE
OPODELDOC
LININ PLASTIN
LINING FUR BACK COAT BAIZE BRASS
FACING PANNEL BABBITT BUSHING
CEILING FURRING FURRURE THIMBLE
TINNING TUBBING CLEADING
DOUBLING DOUBLURE FIREBACK
SHEETING UNDERLAY WAINSCOT
PERCALINE
(— FOR ROOF) SARKING
(— FOR WALL) FIRRING FURRING
(— FOR WELL) STEENING STEYNING
(— OF BEARING) JEWEL
(— OF CYLINDER) BUSH
(— OF FURNACE) BASQUE FIREBACK
(— OF HAT) TIP CAUL
(— OF SMELTING LADLE) SCULL
(MINESHAFT —) CRIB
(WOODEN —) LAG BRATTICE
(SUFF.) PLEURA
LINK JAR TIE TOW JOIN KNIT LUNT
SHUT YOKE CLEEK COMMA NEXUS
COPULA COUPLE FASTEN FETTER
TOUGHT CODETTA CONNECT
COUPLER ENCHAIN INVOLVE LIAISON
SHACKLE CATENATE IDENTIFY
VINCULUM COLLIGATE
(— ARMS) CLEEK
**(— FOR TWO COMPUTERS BY
PHONE)** MODEM
(— IN NETWORK) LEG
(COMPOUND —) SWIVEL
(WOODEN —) LAG
LINKAGE BOND CELL COUPLING
LINKWORK
LINKED CONNEX CATENATE
INTEGRAL
LINKING HOOKUP ANNECTANT
(— DEVICE) LINCHPIN

LINKMAN LINKBOY LIGHTMAN
LINKS MACHAIR
(BOGGY —) MACHAIR
LINNET FINCH TWITE LENARD LINTIE
REDPOLL REDFINCH
LINSANG CIVET ZINSANG
LINSEED LINGET
LINSEY-WOOLSEY WINCEY
LINT FLY FLUE FLICK CADDIS CADDICE
CHARPIE CARBASUS
(SCRAPED —) XYSTUS
LINTEL CAP CLAVY HANCE CLAVEL
DARNER SUMMER SQUINCH
TRANSOM BRESSUMMER
(— OF FIREPLACE) MANTEL
LINUS (BROTHER OF —) ORPHEUS
(FATHER OF —) APOLLO OEAGRUS
ISMENIUS
(MOTHER OF —) CALLIOPE
PSAMATHE
LION CAT LLEW MORNE SHEDU
SIMBA LIONEL LIONET LEOPARD
(MOUNTAIN —) PUMA COUGAR
(PREF.) LEON LEONT(O)
LION MONKEY LEONCITO
LION-TAILED MONKEY MACACO
MACAQUE WANDEROO
LIP BLOB BRIM EDGE MASK PUSS
SASS APRON CHOPS GROIN MOUTH
SPOUT TUTEL LABIUM LABRUM
ROUTER CHILOMA LABELLUM
UNDERLIP
(— DISEASE) PERLECHE
(— OF BELL) SKIRT
(— OF COROLLA) GALEA
(— OF FLOWER) HELM
(— OF ORCHID) SLIPPER
(— OF PITCHER) BEAK
(— OF VESSEL) SPOUT
(—S OF MOOSE) MUFFLE
**(CHAD WOMAN WITH DISTENDED —
S)** UBANGI
(FLAT —) APRON
(LOWER —) JIB FIPPLE
(PL.) LABRAS CUSHION
(PREF.) CHEIL(O) CHIL(O)
(SUFF.) CHIL(IA)(O)(US)
LIPARITE RHYOLITE
LIPASE PIALYN
LIPIDE FAT CERIDE ADIPOID STERIDE
TETHELIN
LIPLIKE LABIAL
LIPOCHROME LUTEIN
LIPOID FAT ADIPOSE
LIPOMA STEATOMA
LIPOPROTEIN HDL LPL
(PLASMA —) VLDL
LIPPED LABIATE
LIPPIA WRIGHT ALOYSIA
LIP PLUG LABRET TEMETA
LIPPY STIMPART
LIPS
(PREF.) LABIO

LIQUEFACTION (— OF GEL)
SOLATION
LIQUEFIED FUSILE POTATE REMISS
RESOLVED
LIQUEFY RUN FUSE MELT RELENT
LIQUATE DISSOLVE ELIQUATE
LIQUEUR EAU OUZO RAKI AURUM
CREME NOYAU CHASSE GENEPI
KUMMEL PASTIS PERNOD RACKEE
STREGA ANESONE CORDIAL
CURACAO PERSICO RATAFIA RATIFIA
ABSINTHE ADVOCAAT ALKERMES
AMARETTO ANGELICA ANISETTE
CALVADOS MANDARIN PRUNELLE
VESPETRO MARASCHINO
BENEDICTINE
(PL.) EAUX
LIQUID AQUA BREE BLASH DRINK
FLUID LEACH MOIST ACETAL FLUENT
FURANE AEROSOL BUCKING
CINEOLE EYEWASH FLOWAGE
VINASSE BLACKING EFFLUENT
EFFUSION EXCITANT FURFURAN
LEACHATE LIBATION SOLUTION
(— AFTER SALT CRYSTALLIZATION)
BITTERN
(— IN CELL) EXCITANT
(— UNIT) TUN CHENG SHENG SHING
POTTLE MUTCHKIN PUNCHEON
(ACID-RESISTANT —) GROUND
(COLORING —) HENNA
(COOKING —) BREE BROO BROTH
STOCK
(DISABLING —) MACE
(DISTILLED —) SPIRIT
(FILTHY —) ADDLE
(INSULATING —) ASKAREL
(MAY BE —) ASSETS
(OILY —) ANILINE CHLORAL PICAMAR
CARDANOL CREOSOTE
(PERFUMED —) COLLEN COLOGNE
(REFUSE —) SCOURAGE
(REFUSE —S) SEWAGE
(SIZING —) GLAIK
(STERILIZED —) JOHNIN
(STINKING —) CACODYL
(SYRUPY —) HONEY
(TANNING —) LIME
(THICK —) DOPE GLOP SIRUP SYRUP
(THICK, STICKY —) GLOP
(VISCOUS —) TAR SCHRADAN
(VOLATILE —) ETHER ALCOHOL
DILUENT LIGROIN
(WEAK —) BLASH SLIPSLOP
(PREF.) LATICI
LIQUIDATE SINK SLAY SETTLE
LIQUIDATION CLEANUP
LIQUOR ALE BUB DEW GAS LAP OKE
PAD POT RUM SUP TAP WET BEER
BREE FIRE FIZZ GEAR GROG LUSH
PURL SUCK SWIG TAPE TIFF BOGUS
BUDGE CEBUR DRINK GLASS HOOCH
JUICE KEFIR MOBBY NAPPY PERRY

PISCO SAUCE SHRAB SHRUB SICER
SKINK STICK BOTTLE CASSIS CHICHA
DIDDLE DOCTOR FOGRAM FUDDLE
GATTER GENEVA GUZZLE HYDROL
KIRSCH MAOTAI MASTIC MESCAL
POTTLE ROTGUT SAMSHU STRUNT
TIPPLE WHISKY BITTERN BRACKET
BRAGGET GROCERY PHLEGMA
SPUNKIE SUCTION TAPLASH
TEQUILA WAIPIRO WHISKEY
ABSINTHE BRAGWORT EYEWATER
HYDROMEL MEDICINE OKOLEHAO
POTATION RUMBOOZE FIREWATER
(— CABINET) TANTALUS
(— CASE) GARDEVIN
(— FROM MUST) ARROPE
(— FROM PEARS) PERRY PERRIE
(— FROM WOOL-SCOURING) SUD
SUDS
(— MIXED WITH WINE) DOCTOR
(— SALE) ABKARI
(— TAKEN IN SODA WATER) CINDER
(ACID —) VERJUICE
(ALCOHOLIC —) GIN ARAK HOOCH
ARRACK BRANDY SAMSHU AQUAVIT
BITTERS SNOOTFUL
(ALCOHOLIC —S) ARDENT
(BITTER —) TIRE
(CHEAP —) SMOKE
(COLORLESS —) GLYCID.GLYCOL
GLYCIDOL GUAIACOL
(CRAB APPLE —) WHERRY
(DISTILLED —) DEW SOTOL GRAPPA
PHLEGM SCHNAPPS
(DRUGGED —) HOCUS
(HARD —) BOOZE
(INTOXICATING —) GROG LOAD LUSH
TAPE BUDGE GUZZLE KUMISS
HASHISH MOONSHINE
(MALT —) ALE BUB BEER STOUT
ENTIRE PORTER STINGO
(MOTHER —) HYDROL BITTERN
(POT —) BREWIS
(RICE —) SAMSHU
(SPIRITUOUS —) DEW GROG MOBBY
STRUNT WAIPIRO KAOLIANG
(STRAIGHT —) SHORT
(STRONG —) RUG TUBA VINO
HOGAN RUMBO STINGO
(TAN —) OOZE
(TANNING —) LAYAWAY TAILING
(WATERED —) BLASH
(WEAK —) BULL SLIPSLOP
LIRA LIRE ZWANZIGER
(ONE-TWENTIETH —) SOLDO
LIRIPIPE TIPPET
LISSOME LITHE LIMBER NIMBLE
SUPPLE SVELTE FLEXIBLE
LIST TIP BILL FILE HEEL LEET NOTE
POLL ROLL ROON ROTA SWAG BRIEF
CANON GISTS INDEX PANEL SCORE
SCRIP SCROW SLATE AGENDA
CENSUS COLUMN DETAIL DOCKET

ERRATA HUDDLE LEGEND PURREL RAGGER RAGMAN RECORD ROSTER SCREED SCROLL SERIES CATALOG CITATOR COMPILE DIPTYCH ITEMIZE LISTING NOTITIA WAYBILL CALENDAR CINCTURE HANDLIST PLATBAND REGISTER SCHEDULE SYNONYMY TITULARY
(— OF BOOKS) CANON
(— OF CANDIDATES) LEET SLATE TERNA
(— OF CAPABILITIES) REPERTOIRE
(— OF CHURCH DATES) ORDO
(— OF CONTESTANTS) DRAW SEEDING
(— OF CRIMINAL CONVICTIONS) RECORD
(— OF DISEASES) NOSOLOGY
(— OF INGREDIENTS) FORMULA
(— OF JURORS) TALES
(— OF MAP SYMBOLS) LEGEND
(— OF PASSERS WITHOUT HONORS) GULF
(— OF RATES) TARIFF
(— OF SAINTS) CANON
(— OF SECURITIES) PORTFOLIO
(— OF THEATRICAL PARTS) CAST
(COMPUTER —) MENU
(GENEALOGICAL —) BEGATS
(IMPRESSIVE —) ARRAY
(LEGAL —) TABLEAU
(LONG —) LITANY
(MAKE A —) CATALOG
(OBITUARY —) NECROLOGY
(PRAYER —) BEADROLL
(WINE —) CARD
(PL.) CAREER BARRAGE
LISTEL QUADRA
LISTEN HARK HEAR LIST TEND TENEZ ATTEND HARKEN INTEND WHISPER
(— TO) DIG EAR HARK HEAR CATCH ATTEND
LISTENER AUDITOR OTACUST
LISTENING PRICK AUDIENT HEARING
(— DEVICE) BUG
(PREF.) ACOU
LISTER SULKY RIDGER
LISTERA OPHRYS
LISTING AGEE ITEM FRAME PARADE LASHING
(— OF JURORS) ARRAY
LISTLESS DOPY DULL WOFF DOWFF FAINT MOONY DONSIE SUPINE LANGUID UNLISTY UNLUSTY CARELESS INDOLENT THOWLESS TONELESS UNHEARTY
LISTLESSLY DAVIELY
LISTLESSNESS ACEDIA APATHY UNLUST VACUITY
LISUARTE (DAUGHTER OF —) ORIANA
(FATHER OF —) ESPLANDIAN

LITANY AITESIS ROGATION
LITE LOCAL LOWCAL
LITERAL VERBAL TEXTUAL
LITERALLY SIMPLY
LITERARY BLUE BOOKISH LITERATE
(— MATERIAL) KITSCH
(— WORK) PREQUEL
(SUFF.) (— STYLE) ESE
LITERATE LETTERED
LITERATI CLERISY
LITERATURE FICTION LETTERS CLAPTRAP
(— CLANDESTINELY DISTRIBUTED) SAMIZDAT
(CLANDESTINE —) SAMIZDAT
(EROTIC —) EROTOLOGY
(OBSCENE —) SCATOLOGY
(RUSSIAN SUPPRESSED —) SAMIZDAT
(SACRED —) VEDA SRUTI
(WISDOM —) CHOKMAH HOKHMAH
LITHE BAIN SPRY WIRY SWACK CLEVER LIMBER LISSOM SILKEN SUPPLE SVELTE WANDLE LISSOME FLEXIBLE

LITHUANIA

CAPITAL: VILNA WILNA VILNIUS
COIN: LIT LITAS MARKA CENTAS FENNIG OSTMARK AUKSINAS SKATIKAS
FORMER CAPITAL: KOVNO KAUNAS
NAME: LITVA LIETUVA
PEOPLE: BALT LETT ZHMUD LITVAK YAI VYAG
RIVER: NEMAN NERIS RUSNE VENTA DUBYSA LIELUPE NEMUNAS PREGOLYA
TOWN: MEMEL VILNA JELGAVA VILNIUS KAPSUKAS KLAIPEDA SIAULIAI

LITHUANIAN BALT ZHMUD
LITIGANT SUER SUITOR
LITIGATE LAW PLEAD CONTEST
LITIGATION LAW LIS MOOT SUIT LAWING PLEADING PLEASHIP
LITMUS LAKMUS TURNSOLE
LITOTES MEIOSIS
LITTER DIG PIG BIER RAFF REDD BREED CABIN CLECK DOOLY DRECK HAULM MULCH SEDAN TRASH DOOLIE FARROW GOCART KINDLE KITTEN MAHMAL REFUSE CLUTTER LETTIGA LOUSTER MAMMOCK NORIMON RUBBISH RUMMAGE SCAMBLE BRANCARD CARRIAGE KINDLING MUNCHEEL PAVILION STRETCHER
(— FOR LIVESTOCK) BEDDING
(— OF PIGS) FAR FARE FARROW
(— ON PACK ANIMAL) CACOLET
(CAMEL —) KAJAWAH

(FOREST —) DUFF
(MOLE —) CACOLET
(SENT TO MECCA) MAHMAL
LITTERBUG SLOB
LITTERED FOUL
LITTLE FEW LIL PEU WEE CURN LITE
POCO TINY VEEN CHOTA CRUMB
SMALL TASTE WHONE BITTIE
DAPPER LEETLE MINUTE PETITE
PICKLE PUSILL KENNING MODICUM
THOUGHT FRACTION SNIPPING
(— BY LITTLE) EDGINGLY INCHMEAL
(— LESS THAN) ABOUT
(— MUSICALLY) POCO
(— ONE) RUNT BUTCHA POPPET
(A —) SOMEWHAT
(INDEFINITELY —) NTH
(PREF.) OLIG(O) PARVI PAUCI PUSILL(I)
STEN(O)
(SUFF.) ISK KIN STENOSIS ULE
(— ONE) CLE ELLA ETTE IE ILLA
LITTLE DEMON (AUTHOR OF —)
SOLOGUB
(CHARACTER IN —) SASHA LIUDMILA
PYLNIKOV PEREDONOV RUSTILOVA
NEDOTYKOMKA
LITTLE DORRIT (AUTHOR OF —)
DICKENS
(CHARACTER IN —) AMY JOHN
CASBY FANNY FLORA ARTHUR
DORRIT EDWARD PANCKS CHIVERY
CLENNAM MEAGLES WILLIAM
BLANDOIS PLORNISH BARNACLES
LITTLE MINISTER (AUTHOR OF —)
BARRIE
(CHARACTER IN —) DOW ROB ADAM
GAVIN MICAH NANNY BABBIE
OGILVY DISHART MCQUEEN RINTOUL
WEBSTER MARGARET
LITTLENESS ATOMITY
LITTLE WOMEN (AUTHOR OF —)
ALCOTT
(CHARACTER IN —) JO AMY MEG
BETH DEMI JOHN BHAER DAISY
FRITZ KIRKE MARCH BROOKE
CARROL LAURIE MARMEE LAURENCE
THEODORE
LITTORAL COAST
LITURGY FORM RITE ABODAH
MAARIB MINHAG NEILAH MINCHAH
MYSTERY HIERURGY SHAHARIT
LIVE BE USE WIN KEEP LEAD STAY
ALERT ALIVE DWELL EXIST GREEN
HABIT LEEVE QUICK SHACK VITAL
HARBOR LIVELY LIVING REMAIN
RESIDE BREATHE INHABIT SUBSIST
CONTINUE CONVERSE VIGOROUS
(— AT ANOTHER'S EXPENSE)
COSHER
(— BY BEGGING) CADGE SKELDER
(— BY STRATAGEMS) SHARK
(— FROM DAY TO DAY) EKE
(— IN CONTINENCE) CONTAIN

(— IN LUXURY) STATE
(— IN PEACE) COEXIST
(— IN SAME PLACE) STALL
(— ON) SURVIVE
(— RIOTOUSLY) JET
(— TEMPORARILY) CAMP
(— THROUGH) PASS TIDE
(— TOGETHER) AGREE COHABIT
(— WELL) BATTEN
LIVE-BOX CAR
LIVE-FOREVER LULANG ORPINE
LIVELIHOOD BEING BREAD LIVING
LIFEHOOD
LIVELINESS PEP BRIO FIRE FIZZ LIFE
PUNCH SPUNK BOUNCE ESPRIT
GAIETY SPIRIT ENTRAIN SPARKLE
ACTIVITY VITALITY VIVACITY
LIVELONG LEELANG ENDURING
LIVELY GAY TID AIRY BRAG CANT
FAST FESS GLEG KECK LIVE PERT
RACY SPRY TAIT TRIG VITE VIVE
WARM YARE AGILE ALERT ALIVE
BONNY BRISK BUXOM CANTY CHIRK
COBBY CORKY CRISP DESTO FRESH
FRISK JAZZY KEDGE KINKY MERRY
PAWKY PEART PEPPY POKEY RUDDY
SASSY SMART VIVID WHICK ACTIVE
BLITHE BOUNCY BRIGHT CHEERY
CHIRPY COCKET CROOSE CROUSE
DAPPER FIERCE FRISCH GINGER
JOCUND KIPPER LIVING NIMBLE
QUIVER SEMMIT SPARKY SPRACK
TROTTY VEGETE WHISKY WIMBLE
ALLEGRO ANIMATE ANIMOSE
BOBBISH BUCKISH BUOYANT
GIGGISH GIOCOSO JOCULAR KINETIC
LEBHAFT POINTED ROUSING SPIRITY
SPRINGY TITTUMY TITTUPY WINCING
ANIMATED BOUNCING CHIRRUPY
FRISKFUL FRISKING GALLIARD
SANGUINE SKITTISH SMACKING
SPANKING SPIRITED SPORTIVE
STEERING STIRRING TRIPSOME
VEGETOUS VOLATILE SPARKLING
(— PERSON) SWINGER
(BE —) SWING
(TO BE —) SWING
LIVEN LACE CHEER ANIMATE
LIVE OAK ENCINA
LIVER MAW FOIE HEPAR VISCUS
PUDDING
(— ATROPHY) LUPINOSIS
(— OF LOBSTER) TOMALLEY
(PREF.) HEPATICO HEPAT(O)
LIVER-COLORED HEPATIC
LIVERPOOL (NATIVE OF —) SCOUSE
SCOUSER LIVERPUDLIAN
LIVERWORT HEPATICA MOSSWORT
LIVERY SUIT CLOTH LIVRE UNIFORM
CLOTHING
LIVESTOCK FEE WARE STOCK
STORE STUFF CHATTEL BESTIALS
FATSTOCK

LIVE WIRE HUSTLER
LIVID HAW WAN BLAE BLUE
LIVING KEEP ALIVE BEING BREAD
GOING QUICK VITAL WHICK AROUND
LIVELY VIABLE ZOETIC ANIMATE
SUPPORT ANIMATED BENEFICE
(— IN THE WORLD) SECULAR
(— IN WAVES) LOTIC
(— NEAR THE GROUND) EPIGEAN
(— ON BANKS OF STREAMS) RIPAL
RIPARIAN
(— THING) QUICK
(DARE —) CRUST
(ECCLESIASTICAL —) BENEFICE
(PREF.) ONT(O) VIVI
(— ORGANISMS) BIO
(SUFF.) (— IN OR ON) COLE COLINE
COLOUS
LIVING-ROOM PARLOR
LIVRE FRANC
LIXIVIATE LEACH
LIXIVIUM LYE
LIZARD DAB EFT GOH UMA UTA
DABB GILA IBIT SEPS TEGU TEJU
URAN AGAMA ANOLE BLUEY DRACO
GECKO GUANO SKINK SNAKE SWIFT
TEIID TOKAY TWEEG VARAN AMEIVA
ANGUID ARBALO DRAGON GOANNA
HARDIM IGUANA LACERT LEGUAN
MOLOCH TEIOID WORRAL ZONURE
BUMMAJO CAUDATE CHEECHA
DIAPSID MONITOR REPTILE SAURIAN
SCINCID SCINCUS TUATARA
TUCKTOO BASILISK KAKARIKI
MOKAMOKA SCINCOID SCORPION
SLOWWORM TEGUEXIN WHIPTAIL
ZONUROID CHAMELEON
CHUCKWALLA PLEURODONT
(PREF.) LACERTI SAUR(O)
(SUFF.) SAUR(A)(IA)(IAN)(US)
LIZARD FISH ULAE INIOME
SOAPFISH SPEARING
LLAMA ALPACA VICUNA GUANACO
LLUDD NUDD
LO SEE ECCE
LOACH DOJO BEARDIE MUDFISH
LOAD BUN JAG LUG TON BUCK CARK
CRAM DECK DRAW FILL HAUL LADE
LAST LUMP PACK RAKE SEAM STEM
STOW TOTE TURN BARTH CARGO
DRAFT PITCH PRIME STACK TRUSS
TURSE BURDEN CHARGE COMBLE
DEMAND FODDER FOTHER HAMPER
LADING LOADEN THRACK WEIGHT
BALLAST CARLOAD DERRICK
DRAUGHT ENDORSE FRAUGHT
FREIGHT ONERATE OPPRESS
BACKPACK CARRIAGE ENCUMBER
HEADLOAD SHIPLOAD PLANELOAD
(— A DIE FOR CHEATING) COG
(— FABRICS) WEIGHT
(— OF COAL) KEEL
(— OF HAY OR CORN) HURRY

(— OF LAMBS) DECK
(— OF LOGS) PEAKER BUNKLOAD
(— OF WOOL) TOD
(— ON BACK) ENDORSE INDORSE
(— SHIP) STEM
(— TO CAPACITY) SATURATE
(— TO EXCESS) ENCUMBER
(ELECTRIC —) DEMAND
(EXCESSIVE —) SURCHARGE
(HORSE —) SEAM SUMAGE
(LAST — OF GRAIN) WINTER
(SMALL —) JAG JAGG JOBBLE
(PL.) BUSHEL
LOADER CHARGER
LOADING LADING MARGIN
ARRASTRE
(— PLACE) PIER
LOADSTONE MAGNET SIDERITE
LODESTONE
LOAF BAP BUM COB AZYM HACK
HAKE HULL LAKE MIKE SLIM SORN
BANGE BREAD BRICK DRING MOUCH
SHOOL SLIVE SLOSH BLUDGE
BROGUE CADDLE DIDDLE GEORGE
HALLAH RODNEY SLINGE WASTEL
HOOSIER MANCHET SHACKLE
SLOUNGE SOLDIER OBLATION
PANHAGIA QUARTERN SHAMMOCK
(— AROUND) HULL HOWFF SLOSH
RODNEY GOLDBRICK
(— OF BREAD) COB BATON FADGE
MICHE TOMMY HALLAH TAMMIE
(BROWN —) GEORGE
(KIND OF —) DELI
(ROUND —) BUN COBURG
(SMALL —) BAP COB NACKET
(SUGAR —) TITLER
LOAFER BUM CAD YOR BEAT CRUB
STIFF BUMBLE BUMMER CADGER
KEELIE SLOUCH SLOVEN BLUDGER
COASTER FAITOUR HOODLUM
SLINKER SOLDIER COBERGER
HOOLIGAN LARRIKIN LAYABOUT
SEASONER
LOAFING IDLE MIKE
LOAM RAB LAME MALM MARL SLIP
LOESS REGUR CLEDGE
LOAMY MELLOW
LOAN DHAN LEND LENT PREST
CREDIT DONATE MUTUUM ADVANCE
FIXTURE IMPREST
LOANBLEND HYBRID
LOATH LOTH LAITH LEATH SWEER
DAINTY BACKWARD
LOATHE UG HATE SHUN ABHOR
LAITH WLATE AGRISE DETEST
DESPISE SCUNDER SCUNNER
NAUSEATE
LOATHING NAUSEA REVOLT
DISGUST SCUNNER
LOATHLY LAIDLY
LOATHSOME FOUL UGLY VILE
POCKY LAIDLY UNLIEF HATEFUL

LOATHLY MAWKISH OBSCENE
TETROUS WLATFUL DEFORMED
NAUSEOUS WLATSOME NEFANDOUS
ABOMINABLE
LOB ARC
LOBBY HALL FOYER NARTHEX
PASSAGE TAMBOUR ANTEROOM
COULISSE
LOBBYIST PROMOTER
LOBE ALA FIN LAP AXIS LIST MALA
ALULA EXITE FIBER FIBRE FLUKE
GALEA LOBUS THECA TOOTH UVULA
EARLAP FILLET FOLIUM GLOSSA
INSULA LAPPET LIGULE LOBING
MANTLE VANNUS VERMIS AROLIUM
AURICLE HEMAPOD LACINIA
LOBULUS AMYGDALA EPICHILE
GLABELLA LABELLUM PALPIFER
PHYLLOID SQUAMULE
(— OF ANTHER) THECA
(— OF LEAF) LACINIA PINNULA
PINNULE SEGMENT
(— OF WHALE'S TAIL) FLUKE
(PREF.)
(— OF BRAIN) LEUC(O)
LOBED CUT LOMATINE
(SUFF.) FID FIDATE
LOBLOLLY LOUT MIRE PINE GRUEL.
LOBSTER CRAY HOMARD DECAPOD
SHEDDER CRAWFISH CRAYFISH
LANGOSTA MACRURAN
(— ENCLOSURE) CRAWL
(— LESS THAN 10 INCHES LONG) JOE
(FEMALE —) HEN
(NORWAY —) SCAMPO
(SMALL —) PAWK NANCY
(UNDERSIZED —) SHORT
LOBSTER POT COY CRAIL CREEL
TRUNK FISHPOT
LOBULARIA KONIGA
LO-CAL LITE
LOCAL HOME NATIVE LIMITED TOPICAL
VICINAL REGIONAL EPICHORIC
(NOT —) AZONIC
(PREF.) TOP(O)
LOCALE AREA SITE LOCAL PLACE
SCENE
LOCALITY SPA HAND PLAT SPOT
LOCUS PLACE POINT SITIO SITUS
STEAD HABITAT LATITUDE POSITURE
SITUATION
(BARREN —) GALL
(BEAUTIFUL —) XANADU
(GUARDED —) POST
LOCALIZE SITUATE POSITION
LOCATE SITE SPOT PITCH PLACE
BESTOW BILLET SETTLE SITUATE
PINPOINT
(— AT INTERVALS) SPOT
(— WATER) DIVINE
LOCATED SET FIXED SEATED
SITUATED
(— OFF THE HIGHWAY) DEVIOUS

LOCATING SYSTEM SOFAR
LOCATION FALL HOME PLOT SEAT
PLACE SITUS WHERE UBIETY
AMENITY STATION HOMESITE
STANDING
(ESSENTIAL —) EYE
(FOREST —) CHANCE
(GEOGRAPHIC —) SEAT
(MINING —) MYNPACHT
(NATURAL —) HABITAT
(SUFF.) TOPE TOPY
LOCH LOUGH LOCHAN
LOCK COT KEY FEAK FRIB HOLD TRIM
YALE CHUBB CLASP SASSE TRESS
DUBBEH ENLOCK LUCKEN DAGLOCK
EARLOCK KEYLOCK PINLOCK
SPANNER DEADLOCK FORELOCK
(— IMPROPERLY) BIND
(— IN RIVER) SASSE
(— OF HAIR) COT TAG TUZ COTT
CURL FEAK TATE FLAKE FLOCK
FLUKE QUIFF TRESS TANGLE
COWLICK EARLOCK FRIZZLE
SERPENT WIMPLER FORELOCK
SIDELOCK
(— OF WOOL) TAG COTT FRIB FLOCK
STAPLE HASLOCK
(— UP) JAIL STOW ENCAGE CABINET
(CANAL —) COFFER CHAMBER
(DIRTY —) FRIB
(MATTED —) COT COTT DAGLOCK
(MUSKET —) ROWET
(PART OF —) REWET STRIKE
(WHEEL —) REWET
LOCKED FAST LUCKEN
LOCKER HUTCH ASCHAM
LOCKERMAN NIBBLER SCOTCHER
SNIBBLER
LOCKET BRELOQUE
LOCKJAW TETANUS TRISMUS
LOCKNUT JAMNUT KEEPER
LOCKOUT SHUTOUT
LOCKS MOP
LOCKSMITH LOCKYER
LOCKUP JUG BRIG GAOL JAIL LOCK
LOGS STIR CHOKY CLINK TRONK
COOLER HOOSEGOW ROUNDHOUSE
LOCOMOTION FLYING LATION
LOCOMOTIVE HOG PIG PUG BOGY
GOAT HOGG MULE SHAG TANK
BOGIE DINKY DUMMY MOGUL PILOT
DIESEL DOCTOR DOLLIE DONKEY
ENGINE LOADER PUSHER SMOKER
YARDER BOBTAIL BOOSTER
SHUNTER STEAMER CALLIOPE
CHOOCHOO COMPOUND DOLLBEER
(— WITHOUT CARS) WILDCAT
(EXTRA —) HELPER
(PART OF —) CAB ROD BELL DOME
HOSE LAMP STEP BRACE HINGE
PILOT TRUCK BOILER JACKET
TENDER COUPLER SANDBOX
WHISTLE CYLINDER HANDRAIL

INJECTOR SANDPIPE HEADLIGHT
RESERVOIR DRIVEWHEEL
SMOKESTACK
LOCOMOTOR ATAXIA TABES
LOCOWEED LOCO LEGUME PEAVINE
CRAZYWEED
LOCRINE (DAUGHTER OF —)
SABRINA
(FATHER OF —) BRUTE BRUTUS
LOCULUS THECA
LOCUS PLACE EVOLUTE SURFACE
SYNAPSE CONCHOID ENVELOPE
HOROPTER
LOCUST WETA BRUKE CICAD HONEY
ACACIA CICADA QUAKER SKIPPER
TETRIGID VOETGANGER
LOCUST TREE CAROB ACACIA
LOCUST ROBINIA ALGAROBA
LODE LEAD REEF VEIN LEDGE
COURSE FEEDER QUARRY SCOVAN
COUNTER
LODOLETTA (CHARACTER IN —)
ANTONIO FLAMMEN LODOLETTA
(COMPOSER OF —) MASCAGNI
LODESTONE MAGNET SIDERITE
TERRELLA
LODGE DIG HUT INN LIE BEAT CAMP
HOST KEEP ROOM STAY STOW TENT
BOWER CABIN COUCH COURT
GROVE GUEST HOGAN HOTEL
HOUSE HOWFF LAYER LOGIS STICK
TARRY ALIGHT BESTOW BILLET
BURROW COSHER GESTEN GRANGE
HOSTEL RESIDE SETTLE BARRACK
LODGING QUARTER SOJOURN
EMBOLIZE HARBINGE
(— AND EAT) COSHER
(— FOR SAFEKEEPING) DEPOSIT
(— IN COURT) BOX
(DRUID —) GROVE
(LOCAL —) COURT
(SPORTSMAN'S —) SHEAL
LODGEPOLE PINE TAMARACK
LODGER INMATE ROOMER TENANT
LODGING BED CRIB FERM GIST HAFT
HOST NEST GEAST LOGIS HARBOR
HOSTEL LIVERY HOSPICE HOUSING
COUCHANT GUESTING
(— FOR SOLDIERS) CASERN
(— OF MARABOUT) KOUBA
(CHEAP —) DOSS
(TEMPORARY —) SHELTER
(VILE —) KENNEL
(PL.) PAD DIGS DIGGINGS
LODGINGHOUSE INN KIP GITE
STOP HOTEL LOGIA LOCANDA
PENSION HOSTELRY
LODICULE SQUAMULA SQUAMULE
LOESS LIMON
LOFT BALK FLAT GOLF JUBE LAFT
ATTIC SOLAR GARRET SOLLAR
HAYLOFT COCKLOFT SCAFFOLD
TRAVERSE

(— GOLF BALL) PITCH
(HAY —) TALLET TALLIT
LOFTIEST SUPREME
LOFTINESS PRIDE HEIGHT DIGNITY
MAJESTY EMINENCE GRANDEUR
HIGHNESS CELSITUDE
(— OF SPIRIT) MAGNANIMITY
LOFTSMAN LINESMAN
LOFTY AIRY HIGH LOFT TALL BRENT
ELATE GRAND GREAT NOBLE PROUD
SKYEY STEEP WINGY AERIAL
ANDEAN HAUGHT TOPFUL TOWERY
UPWARD WINGED ANDESIC
ARDUOUS EMINENT EXCELSE
HAUGHTY SUBLIME ARROGANT
ELEVATED GENEROUS MAJESTIC
OLYMPIAN TOWERING
LOG NOG BUNK CLOG DRAG SKID
CHOCK CHUCK CHUNK PIECE STICK
STOCK BATTEN BILLET PEAKER
PEELER SAWLOG SAWLOG BACKLOG
DAYBOOK DEADMAN DEGRADE
JOURNAL LOGBOOK DEADHEAD
(— AS ANCHOR) DEADMAN
(— AS RAFTER) VIGA
(— BINDING A RAFT) SWIFTER
(— CAR) BUNK
(— FASTENED TO TRAP) DRAG
(— SUPPORTING MINE ROOF) NOG
(— WITHOUT BARK) BUCKSKIN
(— WITH SPIKES IN END) DEADENER
(ENCLOSED —S) BOOM
(FLOATING —S) DRIVE
(LOAD OF —S) PEAKER
(PILE OF —S) DECK ROLLWAY
(SAWED —) BOULE
(SLABBED —) CANT
(SMALL —) LOGGET
(SPLIT —) PUNCHEON
(STRIPPED —) BATTEN
(SUNKEN —) DEADHEAD
LOGANIN MELIATIN
LOGARITHM DENSITY
(— SYMBOL) PF PH PK RH
(NEGATIVE —) PH
LOGBOOK LOG JOURNAL
LOGE BOX BOOTH LODGE STALL
LOGGER RIDER BOWMAN DECKER
FALLER GOPHER HOOKER LIMBER
MARKER SCORER CHOPPER
FROGGER GRABBER SPOTTER
CATTYMAN
LOGGIA LODGE BALCONY
MIRADOR
LOGIC NYAYA LOGICS CANONIC
WITCRAFT
(— OF DISCOVERY) HEURETIC
LOGICAL SANE RAISONNE RATIONAL
LOGISTILLA
(SISTER OF —) ALCINA MORGANA
LOGMAN CHASER CHOPPER
LOGO LABEL EMBLEM
LOGOGRAM IDEOGRAM

LOGOMACHY (ONE ENGAGED IN —)
DEBATER
LOGOS WORD
LOGOTYPE SIG
LOG PERCH DARTER HOGFISH
ROCKFISH
LOGROLLING BIRLING
(— TOURNAMENT) ROLEO
LOGWOOD BRAZIL ADMIRAL
DYEWOOD BLUEWOOD HYPERNIC
CAMPEACHY
LOGY DROWSY GROGGY
LOHAN RAKAN
LOHENGRIN (CHARACTER IN —)
ELSA HENRY ORTRUD FREDERICK
GOTTFRIED LOHENGRIN TELRAMUND
(COMPOSER OF —) WAGNER
(FATHER OF —) PARSIFAL
(WIFE OF —) ELSA
LOIN LEER LISK ALOYAU LUNYIE
(— STEAK) FILET FILLET TOURNEDOS
(PORK —) GRISKIN
(2 UNCUT —S) BARON
(PL.) REINS FILLET SADDLE
(PREF.) LUMB(O) OSPHY(O)
LOINCLOTH IZAR MALO MARO
DHOTI LUNGI PAGNE PAREU
MOOCHA PANUNG DHOOTIE
LOIS (DAUGHTER OF —) EUNICE
(GRANDSON OF —) TIMOTHY
LOITER LAG CLUG FOOL HAKE HANG
HAWM HAZE HOVE LOUT MIKE MUCK
SLUG COOSE DELAY DRAWL KNOCK
MOUCH SHOOL SIDLE TARRY
COOTER DAWDLE LAGGER LINGER
MUCKER STRAKE TAIGLE PROJECT
SHAFFLE LALLYGAG LOLLYGAG
SCOWBANK SLAMMOCK SLUMMOCK
HANGAROUND
LOITERER DRONE IDLER LAGGER
LAGGARD LURCHER
LOITERING SLIMSY LAGGARD
LOKAPALA MAHARAJA
LOKI (DAUGHTER OF —) HEL
(FATHER OF —) FARBAUTI
(MOTHER OF —) NAL LAUFEY
ANGRBODHA
(SLAYER OF —) HEIMDALL
(WIFE OF —) SIGYN ANGURBODA
LOLITA NYMPHET
LOLL FUG IDLE LAZE LOUT FROWST
LOLLUP LOUNGE SOZZLE SPRAWL
RECLINE SCAMBLE SCOWBANK
LOLLAPALOOZA LULU ONER
LOLLIPOP LOLLY SUCKER SUCKABOB
LOLO NOSU
LONDON SMOKE COCKAGNE
(— DISTRICT) SOHO CHEAPSIDE
(BRIDGE IN —) TOWER ALBERT
PUTNEY CHELSEA WATERLOO
(DISTRICT OF —) SOHO ACTON
ADELPHI ALSATIA BRIXTON CHELSEA
MAYFAIR

(MONUMENT IN —) GOG MAGOG
NELSON CENOTAPH VICTORIA
(RIVER OF —) THAMES
(STREET OF —) BOND FLEET
CANNON SAVILE DOWNING
WARDOUR HAYMARKET
(SUBURB OF —) KEW FINCHLEY
LONDONER FLATCAP
LONE LANE SOLE ALONE APART
SINGLE SOLITARY
(— STAR STATE) TEXAS
LONELINESS ONENESS VACANCY
SOLITUDE
LONELY LORN ONLY SOLE VAST
ALONE UNKET UNKID WISHT
ALANGE DEAFLY SULLEN DEAVELY
FORLORN LONEFUL SOLEYNE
DESOLATE SECLUDED SOLITARY
(PREF.) EREM(O)
LONESOME ALONE DOLEY LONELY
LANESOME SOLITARY
LONG HO DIE FAR FIT YEN ACHE DREE
HANK HONE ITCH LANG SIDE TALL
WILN WISH YAWN CRAVE DREAM
GREEN LATHY LONGA MOURN
STARK WEARY YEARN ARIGUE
ASPIRE DESIRE DREICH HANKER
HUNGER LINGER LONGUS PROLIX
STOUND THIRST LENGTHY TEDIOUS
WEILANG GEMINATE INFINITE
(— AGO) FERN LANGSYNE
(— AND SLENDER) REEDY SQUINNY
(— AND UNIFORM IN WIDTH)
LINEAR
(— FOR) CARE HONE COVET CRAVE
TASTE ASPIRE DESIRE SUSPIRE
(— RESTLESSLY) ITCH
(— SINCE) YORE
(EXTRA —) MAXI
(TEDIOUSLY —) MORTAL
(PREF.) DOLICH(O) LONGI LONGO
MACR(O) MEC(O)
LONG-BILLED CURLEW
SMOKER
LONGBOAT SLOOP
LONG-BODIED RACY RANGY
LONGERON SPAR
LONGEVITY VIVACITY
(— CHARACTER) SHOU
LONGING YEN ENVY ITCH LUST PINE
WISH BRAME YEARN DESIRE
HANKER TALENT THIRST ATHIRST
CRAVING THIRSTY WILLING WISHFUL
WISTFUL APPETENT APPETITE
CUPIDITY HOMESICK PRURIENT
LONGINGLY WISTLY
LONGITUDE (PLANET'S —) EPOCH
LONGITUDINALLY ENDLONG
LONG-LASTING CHRONIC
LONG-LEGGED RANGY
LONGLEGS STILT
LONGLINE BULTOW
LONG-LIVED LONGEVE MACROBIAN

LONGSHOREMAN DOCKER
HOBBLER WHARFIE DOCKHAND
STEVEDORE ROUSTABOUT
LONG-STANDING OLD
LONG-SUFFERING MEEK PATIENT
ENDURING PATIENCE
LONG-TAILED MACRURAL
LONG-TAILED WHIDAH REDBILL
LONG TOM SKIPPER
LONG-WINDED PROLIX PROSAIC
LOOK LA LO AIR EYE KEN SEE SPY
CAST GAWK GAZE GIVE GLOM HEED
KEEK LATE LUCK MARK MIEN POKE
SEEM SWAP VIEW WAIT ACIES
BLUSH DEKKO FAVOR FLASH GLEAM
GLEER GLIFF GLINT SCREW SIGHT
SQUIZ VIZZY WLITE APPEAR ASPECT
EYEFUL GANDER GLANCE REGARD
REWARD VISION EYESHOT EYEWINK
INSIGHT SEEMING DISCOVER
LANGUISH OEILLADE
(**— ABOUT**) BELOOK SPECTATE
(**— AFTER**) TENT ATTEND FATHER
FETTLE PROCURE
(**— AMOROUSLY**) SMICKER
(**— ASKANCE**) GLIM LEER SKEW
BAGGE GLENT GLEDGE SKLENT
(**— AT**) DIG SEE GLOM LAMP VIEW
VISE GLISK ADVISE BEHOLD REGARD
REWARD CONSIDER SPECTATE
(**— BACK**) RETROSPECT
(**— CLOSELY**) PRY ESPY SCAN
(**— CROSS-EYED**) SHEYLE
(**— DOWN UPON**) SNOB DESPISE
(**— DULLY**) BLEAR
(**— EVERYWHERE**) COMB
(**— FIXEDLY**) GAZE KYKE GLORE
STARE
(**— FOR**) SPY FOND SEEK AWAIT
GROPE EXPECT PROPOSE RESPECT
(**— FORWARD**) EXPECT FORESEE
ENVISAGE ENVISION
(**— GLANCINGLY**) BLINK
(**— GLOOMY**) SCOWL
(**— IN SNEAKING MANNER**) SNOOP
(**— INTENTLY**) GLOSE VISIE GLOWER
EYEBALL
(**— INTO**) SOUND SEARCH
(**— JOYOUS**) SMILE
(**— LIKE**) IMITATE
(**— OBLIQUELY**) GLIME GOGGLE
SQUINT·
(**— OF DERISION**) FLEER
(**— OF PLANETS**) ASPECTS
(**— ON**) SPECTATE
(**— OUT**) FEND MIND CHEESE
JIGGERS OUTLOOK
(**— OVER**) SCAN TOISE BROWSE
SURVEY EXAMINE
(**— SEARCHINGLY**) COMB PEER PORE
TOOT
(**— SLYLY**) PEEP GLINK
(**— SOUR**) GLUNCH

(**— STEADFASTLY**) GLOAT
(**— SULKY**) LUMP
(**— SULLEN**) LOUR LOWER
(**— TO**) RESPECT
(**— UPON AS**) ACCOUNT
(**— WILDLY**) GLOP WAUL WHAWL
(**— WITH FAVOR**) SMILE
(**AMOROUS —**) SMICKER
(**ANGRY —**) SCOWL
(**BRIEF —**) GLIM GLINT GLIMPSE
(**CLOSE —**) VISIE
(**LOVING —**) BELGARD
(**OBLIQUE —**) SQUINT
(**QUICK —**) SCRY GLENT
(**SEARCHING —**) SCRUTINY
(**SEVERE —**) FROWN
(**SIDELONG —**) GLEE GLIME
(**SLY —**) GLEG GLIME TWIRE
(**SULLEN —**) GLOOM GLOUT GLUNCH
(**TENDER —**) LANGUISH
(**WANTON —**) LEER
(**PL.**) DAPS
(**PREF.**) (**— THROUGH**) PERSPECTO
LOOKER BEAUTY HERDSMAN
SEARCHER
LOOKER-ON BEHOLDER
LOOK HOMEWARD ANGEL
(**AUTHOR OF —**) WOLFE
(**CHARACTER IN —**) BEN GANT LUKE
DAISY ELIZA HELEN JAMES LAURA
EUGENE GROVER OLIVER LEONARD
MARGARET
LOOKING (**— ASKANCE**) SQUINT
(**— BACKWARD**) REVIEW
RETROSPECT
(**— OBLIQUELY**) SQUINT
(**— UP**) ROSY
LOOKING BACKWARD (**AUTHOR
OF —**) BELLAMY
(**CHARACTER IN —**) WEST EDITH
LEETE JULIAN BARTLETT PILLSBURY
LOOKOUT HUER TOUT SCOUT
WATCH BANTAY CONNER TOOTER
FUNERAL OUTLOOK ATALAYAN
BANTAYAN BARTIZAN COCKATOO
PROSPECT TOWERMAN WATCHOUT
OBSERVATORY
LOOM BEAM BULK HULK LEEM
DOBBY FRAME GLOOM BEETLE
DOBBIE DRAWLOOM HANDLOOM
JACQUARD OVERPICK
(**— ATTACHMENT**) LAPPET
(**PREF.**) HIST(O)
LOOM AXLE ROCKTREE
LOOM BAR EASER DAGGER
LOOMFIXER TACKLER
LOOM HARNESS LEAF HEADLE
SIMBLOT MOUNTING
LOON DIVER IMBER WABBY COBBLE
DUCKER GUNNER WHABBY
PYGOPOD
LOONY MAD DAFT CRAZY INSANE
WEIRDO FOOLISH

LOOP BOW EYE LUG NOB TAB TAG
ANSA BEND COIL FAKE HANK KINK
KNOB KNOP LEAF LINK LOUP PURL
BIGHT BRIDE CHAPE COQUE GUIDE
KINCH LACET LATCH NOOSE PEARL
PICOT SHANK STRAP TERRY WITHY
BECKET BILLET BUCKLE FOLIUM
HANGER HOLDER KEEPER KINKLE
PARRAL SPIRAL STAPLE STITCH
TWITCH COCKEYE COUPURE
CRINGLE CRUPPER GROMMET
KNUCKLE LATCHET SEGMENT
ANTINODE COURONNE
(— AND THIMBLES) CLEW CLUE
(— BY ICESKATER) SPOON
(— FOR HOISTING) SLING
(— FOR REINS) TERRET TERRIT
(— FOR REMOVING TUMORS)
SNARE
(— IN KNITTING) STEEK
(— IN MINER'S ROPE) SLUG
(— IN NEEDLEWORK) BRIDE
(— OF INTESTINES) KNUCKLE
(— OF IRON) OOLLY
(— OF ROPE) FAKE BIGHT FLAKE
KINCH NOOSE ANCHOR BECKET
PARRAL SNORTER SNOTTER
(— OF SCABBARD) FROG
(— OF TUBING) SCROLL
(— ON ARMOR) VERVELLE
(— ON SAIL) LASKET
(— ON SPINNING FRAME) BAND
(— ON SWORD BELT) HANGER
(HANGING —) FESTOON
(HARNESS —) COCKEYE
(HEDDLE —) DOUP
(KIND OF —) LIPPES
(ORNAMENTAL —) PICOT
(SHOULDER —) EPAULET
(SURGICAL —) CURET CURETTE
(TIGHT —) KINK KINKLE
(TWISTED —) KINK
(PREF.) FUNDI
LOOPER INCHWORM SPANWORM
LOOPHOLE LOOP CATCH CHINK
MEUSE EYELET OILLET WICKET
BARBICAN PORTHOLE
LOOSE GAY LAX EASY EMIT FREE
GLAD LASH LIMP OPEN SOFT UNDO
WIDE WILD BAGGY CRANK FRANK
LARGE LIGHT RELAX SLACK UNTIE
VAGUE WASHY ADRIFT FLUFFY
LIMBER SLOPPY SOLUTE SPORTY
SUBURB UNBIND UNGIRT UNLASH
UNTIED WOBBLY ABSOLVE
CHESSOM FLYAWAY IMMORAL
MOVABLE RELAXED SETFREE
SHOGGLY STRINGY UNBOUND
UNHITCH UNTIGHT DIFFUSED
DISCINCT FLOATING INSECURE
LAXATIVE SHATTERY UNSTABLE
(— AN ANCHOR) TRIP

(— ARROW) BOLT
(MORALLY —) FRANK
(PREF.) LAXI
LOOSE-JOINTED LANKY SHACKLY
LOOSELY SLACK LARGELY SLACKLY
LOOSEN LAX BREAK SLACK UNTIE
LAXATE LIMBER UNBEND RESOLVE
SLACKEN UNGRIPE UNLOOSE
UNSCREW DISHEVEL UNSTRING
(— ANCHOR) TRIP
(— ROCK) GAD
LOOSENESS SLACK LAXITY
LATITUDE
(PREF.) LYO
LOOSENING START SOLUTIVE
SOLUTORY
(PREF.) LYS(I)
LOOSESTRIFE KILLWEED PEATWEED
PEATWOOD PRIMWORT
LOOSING
(SUFF.) LYSE LYSIS LYST LYTE LYTIC
LYZE
LOOT SACK SWAG BOOTY HARRY
SPOIL STEAL THEFT BOODLE
MARAUD HERSHIP PILLAGE PLUNDER
SNAFFLE
LOOTING SACK
LOP DOD LAP CLIP DODD OCHE SNED
SNIG SNIP TRIM SHRAG SHRED SHRUB
STUMP TRASH TWINE SHROUD
SNATHE TRASHIFY TRUNCATE
(— OFF) COW DOD CROP DODD HEAD
SNAG SNED PRUNE SHRED TRUNK
DEFALK AMPUTATE
LOPE SHAG
LOPPED
(PREF.)
(— OFF) TRUNCATO
LOPPER CLABBER
LOPPINGS SHROUD
LOQUACIOUS GABBY FUTILE
SPEECHFUL
LOQUACITY PRATE PRATTLE
FUTILITY
LOQUAT BIWA NISPERO
LORAL FRENAL
LORD BEL DAM DEN DON GOD HER
LOR MAR SID SIR DION DOMN EROS
HERR LAUK LOSH NAIK SIRE TUAN
ANGUS ARAWN BARON LAFEU LIEGE
LUDDY NIGEL OMRAH RABBI SAHIB
SWAMI THANE DOMINE DUMAIN
KYRIOS PRABHU SAYYID SIGNOR
TANIST THAKUR CAMILLO CERIMON
JACQUES JEHOVAH MARCHER
OGTIERN VAVASOR BHAGAVAT
DESPOTES DRIGHTEN GRANDPRE
LORDLING MARGRAVE OVERLORD
PALATINE SEIGNEUR SEIGNIOR
SUPERIOR SUZERAIN THALIARD
(— OF DARKNESS) HYLE
(— OF UNIVERSE) ORMAZD ORMUZD

(— OF WORLD) LOKINDRA
(FEUDAL —) DAUPHIN VAVASOR
SUZERAIN
(JAPANESE —) KAMI
(JUDAIC —) ADONAI
(MUSLIM —) OMRAH
LORD CHANCELLOR WOOLPACK
LORD JIM (AUTHOR OF —) CONRAD
(CHARACTER IN —) JIM DAIN BROWN
STEIN WARIS MARLOW DORAMIN
LORDLINESS PRIDE
LORDLY PROUD SUPERB ARROGANT
DESPOTIC
LORDOSIS SWAYBACK
LORDSHIP NAVY DYNASTY
ERECTION SEIGNORY SIGNORIA
LORE LEAR LORUM MASTAX
LEARNING
LORGNETTE STARER
LORICA LORIC SHEATH SHIELD
LORIKEET PARROT WARRIN CORELLA
WEROOLE
LORIS KOKAM LEMUR SLOTH
LEMUROID
LORN ALONE
LORNA DOONE (AUTHOR OF —)
BLACKMORE
(CHARACTER IN —) FRY TOM ALAN
JOHN RIDD ANNIE DOONE DUGAL
ENSOR LORNA CARVER FAGGUS
JEREMY REUBEN BRANDIR STICKLES
HUCKABACK
LORRY RIG DRAG RULLY TRUCK
CAMION ROLLEY TIPPER
JAGANNATH JUGGERNAUT
LORY LOORY CORELLA LORIKEET
LOSE LET TIN AMIT DROP TINE WANT
FORGO LAPSE LEASE TRAIL GAMBLE
MISLAY FORBEAR FORFEIT FORLESE
SLATTER
(— AT CARDS) BUST
(— BET) WRONG
(— BRILLIANCE) FAINT
(— BY DEATH) BURY
(— BY GAMING) GAME
(— BY STUPIDITY) BLUNDER
(— CONTROL) BLOW CRACK
(— COURAGE) DREEP TAINT
(— DELIBERATELY) THROW
(— FLAVOR) FOZE APPAL APPALL
(— FORCE) COLLAPSE
(— FRESHNESS) FADE WILT WITHER
(— HEART) JADE FAINT QUAIL
COLLAPSE
(— HOPE) DESPAIR DESPOND
(— IT) SNAP
(— LUSTER) TARNISH
(— MOISTURE) GUTTATE
(— NERVE) CHICKEN
(— OFFICE) FALL
(— ONE'S BREATH) CHINK
(— ONE'S WAY) STRAY

(— ONE'S SKILL) SLIP
(— POWER) FAIL DISSOLVE
(— SELF-POSSESSION) ABASH
(— SPIRIT) JADE
(— STRENGTH) GO FADE FAIL PALL
WEAKEN LANGUISH
(— SUPPORT) ERODE
(— UNDER HORIZON) SINK
(— VISION) DAZZLE
(— WARMTH) COOL CONGEAL
(— WEIGHT) ENSEAM
(— ZEAL) QUENCH
LOSER ALSORAN
LOSING (BEGIN — STREAK) GOCOLD
LOSS ACE BATH COST HARM LEAK
LOST MISS LAPSE QUALM WASTE
BURIAL DAMAGE DAMNUM DEFEAT
INJURY TINSEL AVERAGE DEBACLE
DEFICIT EXPENSE JACTURE
LEAKAGE LEESING MISTURE
REPRISE AMISSION BREAKAGE
CLEANING MISSMENT PERDITION
SACRIFICE
(— BY EVAPORATION) ULLAGE
(— BY SIFTING) ULLAGE
(— IN WORKING) SLIPPAGE
(— OF ABILITIES) COLLAPSE
(— OF ABILITY TO WRITE) AGRAPHIA
(— OF ACTIVITY) AKINESIA
(— OF APPETITE) ASITIA ANOREXIA
(— OF BRILLIANCY) ECLIPSE
(— OF CARGO) AVERAGE
(— OF CONSCIOUSNESS) SWOON
ABSENCE APOPLEXY BLACKOUT
FAINTING
(— OF ELASTICITY) SET
(— OF ELECTRICITY) EFFLUVE
(— OF EXPRESSION) AMIMIA
(— OF FEELING) APOPLEXY
ANESTHESIA ANAESTHESIA
(— OF FORTUNE) RUIN DECAY
(— OF GOOD NAME) IGNOMINY
(— OF GOODS) SHRINKAGE
(— OF HAIR) DEFLUX ALOPECIA
PTILOSIS
(— OF HONOR) ATIMY
(— OF HOPE) DESPAIR
(— OF MEMORY) AMNESIA
BLACKOUT
(— OF PRESTIGE) DISHONOR
(— OF SCENT) CHECK
(— OF SENSE OF SMELL) ANOSMIA
(— OF SIGHT) ANOPSY ANOPSIA
(— OF SIZE) WANE
(— OF SOUND) APOCOPE SYNCOPE
APHERESIS
(— OF SPEECH) ALALIA APHASIA
APHONIA
(— OF VOICE) ANAUDIA APHONIA
(— OF VOWEL) APHESIS
(— OF WILL POWER) ABULIA
(AT A —) ASEA

(CONTRACT —) LESION
(TAKE A — ON) EAT
(SUFF.) ZEMIA
LOST ASEA GONE LORN TINT ATSEA
STRAY WASTE ASTRAY BUSHED
HIDDEN NAUGHT FORFEIT FORLORN
MISSING CONFUSED OBSCURED
BENIGHTED
(— IN THOUGHT) PREOCCUPIED
LOST HORIZON (AUTHOR OF —)
HILTON
(CHARACTER IN —) HUGH BRIAC
CHANG HENRY CONWAY LOTSEN
BARNARD CHARLES ROBERTA
BRINKLOW MALLISON PERRAULT
RUTHERFORD
LOST LADY (AUTHOR OF —) CATHER
(CHARACTER IN —) IVY BLUM NIEL
FRANK OGDEN PETERS HERBERT
ELLINGER POMMEROY CONSTANCE
FORRESTER
LOT BAG CUT HAP PEW CHOP CROP
DEAL DOLE DOOM DRAW FALL FATE
HEAP PACK PART PILE REDE SKIT
SLEW SLUE SORS SORT BATCH
BLOCK BREAK BUNCH CAVEL FIELD
GRACE GRIST GROSS LINES SHARE
SHOOT SIGHT SITHE STAND TEEMS
TROOP WEIRD AMOUNT BARREL
BOODLE BUNDLE CHANCE DICKER
FARDEL HANGUP OODLES PARCEL
TICHEL BOILING DESTINY FEEDLOT
FORTUNE OODLINS PORTION
SANDLOT BACKYARD CABOODLE
JINGBANG MOUTHFUL RIMPTION
WOODLAND
(— OF PERSONS) BOODLE
(— OF TEA) BREAK
(— OF 60 PIECES) SHOCK
(BUILDING —) ERF
(BURIAL —) LAIR
(FATHER OF —) HARAN
(GREAT —) SWAG
(MISCELLANEOUS —) RAFT
(SISTER OF —) ISCAH MILCAH
(UNCLE OF —) ABRAHAM
(VACANT —) COMMON COMMONS
(PREF.) CLERO SORTI
LOTAN (FATHER OF —) SEIR
LOTION WASH EYEWASH EYEWATER
LAVATORY
(HAND — INGREDIENT) ALOE
LOTOPHAGUS EATER
LOTS MANY HEAPS TEEMS BUSHEL
HODFUL
LOTTERY AMBO LOTTO SWEEP
TERNO RAFFLE TOMBOLA
LOTTO KENO BINGO TOMBOLA
(— GAME) HOUSE
LOTUS LOTE LOTOS PADMA
NELUMBO WANKAPIN
(SACRED —) PADMA
LOTUS TREE SADR ZIZYPHUS

LOUCHEUX KUTCHIN
LOUD HARD HIGH MAIN CRUDE
FORTE GAUDY GREAT HEAVY SHOWY
STARK STOUR WIGHT BRASSY
BRAZEN COARSE CRIANT FLASHY
GARISH HOARSE VULGAR BLATANT
CLAMANT HAUTAIN VIOLENT
BIGMOUTH FRENZIED PIERCING
SLAMBANG STREPENT STRIDENT
VEHEMENT STREPITANT
(NOT —) LOW SOFT
(RATHER —) MEZZOFORTE
LOUDHAILER BULLHORN
LOUDLY BOST ALOUD FORTE
STARK
LOUDNESS STRESS SONORITY
MAGNITUDE
(— UNIT) PHON SONE
(UNIT OF —) PHON
LOUDSPEAKER WOOFER SPEAKER
TWEETER BULLHORN SQUAWKER
LOUD-SPOKEN RANDY
LOUIS LUIGI LODOWIC

LOUISIANA
CAPITAL: BATONROUGE
COLLEGE: LSU TULANE DILLARD
GRAMBLING
COUNTY: CADDO ACADIA PARISH
TENSAS LAFOURCHE
CULTURE: TCHEFUNCTE
DIALECT: CREOLE
FESTIVAL: MARDIGRAS
INDIAN: ADAI WASHA ATAKAPA
LAKE: IATT CLEAR LARTO BORGNE
SALINE DARBONNE MAUREPAS
MOUNTAIN: DRISKILL
NATIVE: CAJUN CREOLE ACADIAN
NICKNAME: CREOLE PELICAN
PARISH: WINN CADDO ACADIA IBERIA
SABINE TENSAS ORLEANS RAPIDES
OUACHITA CALCASIEU
RIVER: RED AMITE BOEUF SABINE
TENSAS OUACHITA
STATE BIRD: PELICAN
STATE FLOWER: MAGNOLIA
STATE TREE: CYPRESS
STREAM: BAYOU
TOWN: JENA MANY HOMER HOUMA
EDGARD GRETNA MINDEN MONROE
RUSTON BASTROP VIDALIA
BOGALUSA TALLULAH
NEWORLEANS

LOUISIANIAN CAJUN ACADIAN
LOUNGE HAWM LOAF LOLL SORN
SOSS BANGE TRAIK DACKER
FROUST FROWST GLIDER LOLLUP
LOPPET RIZZLE SLINGE SOZZLE
LAMMOCK SAUNTER SLOUNGE
LOUNGER IDLER SLOUNGER
LOUPE LENS
LOUR FROWN

LOUSE BOB DUG SOW CRAB CRUMB
BOOGER BRAULA COOTIE GISLER
PALMER SISTEN VERMIN MORPION
PUCERON GRAYBACK
(FISH —) GISLER ARGULUS
(PLANT —) APHID APHIS
(WOOD —) SOW ISOPOD SLATER
(YOUNG —) NIT
(PREF.) ONISCI PEDICUL(I)(O)
LOUSEWORT RATTLE SNAFFLES
LOUSINESS PEDICULOSIS
LOUSY SEEDY CRAPPY CRUMMY
PEDICULOUS
LOUT HOB LOB LUG YOB BOOR CHUB
COOF GAUM GAWK HOOD JAKE
LOON NOWT SWAB SWAD BOOBY
CHUMP CUDDY GNOFF LOOBY
LOURD ROBIN THRUM WHAUP
YAHOO YOBBO YOKEL BOHUNK
CLUNCH GORRIN HOBLOB LOUNDY
LUBBER LUNGIS SLOUCH TRIPAL
BUMPKIN GROBIAN HALLION
HAWBUCK HOODLUM LOBCOCK
PALOOKA LOBLOLLY
(COUNTRY —) KERN BUMPKIN
LOUTISH SWAB HULKY SLOOMY
BOORISH HULKING VILLAIN
BOEOTIAN CLOWNISH
LOUVER SLAT LOUVRE LUFFER
DIFFUSER FEMERELL
(PL.) SHUTTER
LOVABLE AMABEL CUDDLY AMIABLE
ADORABLE DOVELIKE LOVESOME
ENDEARING
LOVABLENESS DEARNESS
LOVAGE SMELLAGE
LOVE GRA LOU AMOUR EROS KAMA
LIKE ALOHA AMOUR CUPID DRURY
FANCY HEART MINNE AFFECT
TENDRE CHARITY EMBRACE FEELING
PASSION DEVOTION KINDNESS
LOVEHOOD PARAMOUR
(— IN RETURN) REDAME
(— OF COUNTRY) PATRIOTISM
(— OF CRUELTY) SADISM
(— OF MANKIND) PHILANTHROPY
(— OF MARVELOUS) TERATISM
(— OF THE ARTS) VIRTU
(— OF WOMEN) PHILOGYNY
(— TO EXCESS) IDOLIZE
(— TOWARD DEITY) BHAKTI
(ARDENT —) PASSION
(CHRISTIAN —) CHARITY
(EXCESSIVE —) IDOLATRY
(INTENSE —) FIRE
(MY —) MACHREE
(NATURAL —) STORGE
(SELF-GIVING —) AGAPE
(SENTIMENTALLY IN —) SPOONY
(UNLAWFUL —) LEMANRY
(PREF.) ERO(TO)
(SUFF.) PHIL(A)(AE)(E)(IA)(ISM)(IST)
(OUS)(US)

LOVED DEAR BELOVED
(MUCH —) SWEET
LOVE-DRUG DAGGA
LOVE FEAST AGAPE
LOVE KNOT AMORET
LOVELINESS BEAUTY
LOVELOCK EARLOCK
LOVELY DREAMY LOVING TENDER
AMIABLE AMOROUS ADORABLE
LOVESOME
LOVEMAKING AMOUR
LOVER GRA LAD MAN BEAU CHAP
AMANT AMOUR DRURY LEMAN
ROMEO SPARK SWAIN AMADIS
AMANTE MARROW MINION SQUIRE
ADMIRER AMORIST AMOROSO
CELADON GALLANT PATRIOT
SPARKER SPECIAL SPRUNNY
AMORETTO BELAMOUR CASANOVA
CICISBEO PARAMOUR STREPHON
INAMORATO
(— BOY) ROMEO
(MODEL —) LEILAH
(SILLY —) SPOON
LOVE SEAT CAUSEUSE
LOVE'S LABOR'S LOST
(AUTHOR OF —) SHAKESPEARE
(CHARACTER IN —) DULL MOTH
BOYET MARIA ARMADO DUMAIN
ADRIANO BEROWNE COSTARD
MERCADE ROSALINE FERDINAND
KATHERINE NATHANIEL
HOLOFERNES JAQUENETTA
LONGAVILLE
LOVING DEAR FOND TENDER
AMATORY AMOROUO
(PREF.) PHIL(O)
(SUFF.) PHIL(A)(AE)(E)(OUS)(US)
LOW BAS BOO LAW MOO BASE BASS
KEEN MEAN NEAP OPEN ORRA ROUT
SLOW VILE WEAK BLORE DIRTY
GROSS HEDGE LAICH PUTID SHORT
SMALL SNIDE THIRD CALLOW
EARTHY FILTHY GENTLE GRUBBY
HARLOT HUMBLE LIMMER MENIAL
ORNERY RASCAL RIBALD SECRET
SHABBY SILKEN TURPID VULGAR
BESTIAL IGNOBLE RAFFISH REPTILE
SLAVISH SUBMISS HOLSTEIN
SOUTERLY
(— AS OF A VOWEL) OPEN
(— DOWN) SIDE
(— IN LIGHTNESS) DULL
(— IN PERCEPTION) CRUDE
(— IN PITCH) GRAVE
(— IN PRICE) MODERATE
(— IN QUALITY) HEDGE
(— IN SATURATION) GRAYISH
(— IN SPIRITS) BLUE DOWN GLOOMY
DOWNCAST
(— IN TONE) SOFT SUBMISS
(— IN WATER) RACE
(— NUMBERS) MANQUE

(— POINT) TROUGH
(IMMEASURABLY —) ABYSMAL
(PREF.) CHAMAE CHAME TAPIN(O)
LOW-BORN PLEBEAN VILLAIN
PLEBEIAN
LOWBORN WAFF
LOWBRED BASTARD PLEBEIAN
LOWCAL LITE
LOW-DOWN BUCKASS
LOWER CUT DIP LOW BASE BATE
DOWN DROP DUCK FELL SINK VAIL
ABASE ABATE ALLOY AVALE BELOW
BLAME COUCH COWER DECRY DEMIT
DOUSE FROWN GLOOM LEVEL
SCOWL STOOP BEMEAN DEBASE
DEJECT DEMEAN EMBASE GLOWER
HUMBLE JUNIOR LESSEN MODIFY
NETHER REDUCE SETTLE STRIKE
SUBDUE SUBMIT BENEATH DECLASS
DEGRADE DEPRESS SHORTEN
DIMINISH DOWNWARD INFERIOR
MODERATE
(— BANNER) VAIL
(— BY HALF STEP) FLAT
(— IN ESTEEM) CHEAPEN
DEROGATE
(— IN PITCH) FLAT SHADE
(— ONESELF) SINK BEMEAN
DESCEND
(— PRICES) BEAR
(— SAIL) AMAIN
(— SLIGHTLY) SHADE
(— THE HEAD) STOOP
(PREF.) BATH(O)(Y) CATO INFERO
INFRA NERTERO
(— IN STATUS) INFRA
(MAKE —) DE
LOWERING DIP DUCK DOWLY
HEAVY LAPSE BEETLE SULLEN
PEJORATION
(— OF BODY) FONDU
(— OF LAND) ABLATION
LOWEST LAST LEAST EXTREME
LOWMOST PRIMARY PARAVAIL
NETHERMOST
(— CLASS) LAG
(— POSSIBLE) KNOWDOWN
LOWING MUGIENT
LOWLAND LAICH POLDER LALLAND
DOWNLAND
(— BESIDE RIVER) INKS
(BARREN —) LANDES
LOWLANDER SAXON ZHMUD
SASSENACH
LOWLIER LESS
LOWLIFE SCUM AMEBA
LOWLINESS
(— OF MIND) HUMILITY
LOWLY LOW BASE SILLY HUMBLE
BASEBORN
LOW-LYING CALLOW LALLAN
INFERIAL SUBJECTED

LOW-MINDED BASE MEAN
LOWNESS LOWTH
(— OF PITCH) GRAVITY
(— OF SPIRITS) GLOOM SPLEEN
MEGRIMS
LOW-PITCHED GRUFF
LOW-SPIRITED HIPPED DEJECTED
LOW SUNDAY QUASIMODO
LOX (PARTNER OF —) BAGEL
LOY SLICK
LOYAL FAST FEAL FIRM HOLD LEAL
REAL TRUE LIEGE PIOUS SOUND
ARDENT HEARTY LAWFUL SECRET
STANCH CONSTANT FAITHFUL
STALWART YEOMANLY
(BE — TO) OBEY
(REMAIN —) STANDBY
LOYALIST TORY
LOYALLY SURELY
LOYALTY ARDOR FAITH FEALTY
HOMAGE LEALTY REALTY SPIRIT
REALITY DEVOTION FIDELITY
CONSTANCY NATIONALISM
LOZENGE TAB JUBE COIGN QUOIN
CACHOU JUJUBE MASCLE PASTIL
QUARRY ROTULA RUSTRE TABLET
TABULE TROCHE CREMULE
DIAMOND TABELLA PASTILLE
ROSEDROP
(— OF CEMENT) WAFER
LOZI ROZI BAROTSE
LSD ACID
LUBBER LOUT SWAB LOOBY SLOUCH
LOBCOCK LILBURNE
LUBBERLY AWKWARD
LUBRICANT DOPE GREASE
AQUADAG UNGUENT
LUBRICATE OIL DOPE GLIB GREASE
LUBRIFY
LUBRICATOR OILER OILCAN
LUCARNE LUCOMBE
LUCE GED
LUCENT BRIGHT LUCIBLE
LUCERNE LEGUME ALFALFA
LUCIA DI LAMMERMOOR
(CHARACTER IN —) LUCY EDGAR
HENRY ARTHUR ASHTON BUCKLOW
RAVENSWOOD
(COMPOSER OF —) DONIZETTI
LUCIANA (SISTER OF —) ADRIANA
LUCID SANE CLEAR AERIAL BRIGHT
LIMPID CRYSTAL DILUCID LITERATE
LUCULENT LUMINOUS
LUCIDITY SANITY CLARITY
LUCIFER DEVIL MATCH PHOSPHOR
LUCK HAP CESS EURE SONS SPIN
GRACE ISSUE CHANCE THRIFT
FORTUNE HANDSEL SUCCESS
VENTURE HAMINGJA
(BAD —) ACE DOLE DEUCE HOODOO
UNLUCK AMBSACE MISCHANCE
(BAD — TO YOU) YLAHAYLL

(GOOD —) HAP SONCE SONSE
FORTUNE THEEDOM
(ILL —) UNHAP DIRDUM DISGRACE
MISHANTER
(RELATING TO —) ALEATORY
(STROKE OF —) MANNA
(UNEXPECTED —) BUNCE
LUCKILY HAPPILY
LUCKY HOT CANNY HAPPY JAMMY
SEELY SONSY CHANCY LUCKLY
LUCKFUL ONAROLL GRACIOUS
PROVIDENTIAL
LUCRATIVE FAT GOOD GAINFUL
LUCRE GELT SWAG DROSS MOOLA
LUCREZIA BORGIA
(CHARACTER IN —) ALFONSO
GENNARO LUCREZIA
(COMPOSER OF —) DONIZETTI
LUD (FATHER OF —) SHEM
LUDICROUS AWFUL COMIC DROLL
ABSURD COMICAL FOOLISH
HIDEOUS RISIBLE FARCICAL
BURLESQUE
LUDO UCKERS
LUFF DERRICK
LUFFA LOOFAH SPONGE
LUG EAR HUG TUG WAG SNUG SPUD
TOTE ZULU PATCH WALTZ SCHLEP
LUGE SLED
LUGGAGE BAGS SWAG TRAPS
HATBOX BAGGAGE CARRYON
TRUSSERY
(AIRPLANE —) CARRYON
LUGGAGE-CARRIER GRID
LUGGAGE CASE IMPERIAL
LUGGAR JAGGAR JINGER LAGGAR
LUGGER CAT TOUP CUCH FIFIE
LUGUBRIOUS BLACK TEARY
BALEFUL DOLEFUL DOLOROUS
LACHRYMOSE
LUGWORM LOB LUG LOBWORM
SANDWORM
LUIGINO TEMIN
LUISA MILLER (CHARACTER IN —)
WURM LUISA MILLER WALTER
RODOLFO FREDERICA
(COMPOSER OF —) VERDI
LUKEWARM LEW LUKE TEPID WLACH
LULL CALM DRUG FODE HUSH ROCK
CROON HUSHO LETUP SLACK STILL
LACUNA SOPITE HUSHABY HUSHEEN
LULLABY LULL BALOO BALOW
LULLAY HUSHABY HUSHEEN
ROCKABY
LULLING DROWSY CIRCEAN
LULU PIP DARB ONER BEAUT DOOZY
CORKER DOOZER SNORTER
HUMDINGER
LUMBER BURR DEAL RAFF NANMU
STOCK STRIP CUMBER FINISH FLITCH
RAFFLE REFUSE SAMCHU SHORTS
TIMBER DEGRADE DUNNAGE

GUMWOOD RUMMAGE TRUNDLE
STEPPING
(INFERIOR —) SAPS SCOOT
LUMBERING AWKWARD LUMBERLY
LUMBROUS
LUMBERJACK JACK AXMAN
LOGGER TOPPER TIMBERER
(COMPETITION FOR —S) ROLEO
LUMBERMAN PINER DOGGER
SCORER CHOPPER GIRDLER
TIMBERER
LUMINAIRE LAMP
LUMINANCE HELIOS
LUMINARY STAR LIGHT CANDLE
PLANET
LUMINESCENCE FLAME
LUMINOSITY FIRE GLOW LIGHT
VALUE
LUMINOUS LIGHT LUCID SHINY
BRIGHT LUMINANT
LUMMOX BOZO GALOOT LOBSTER
PALOOKA
LUMP BAT BUB COB CUB DAB DAD
FID GOB JOB LOB NIB NOB NUB WAD
BLOB BURL CLAG CLAM CLOT COOL
COWL DUNT GLOB JUNK KNOB
KNOT NIRL PONE SWAD TOKE
BLOOM BUNCH CHUCK CHUNK
CLAUT CLUMP CLUNK GLEBE HUNCH
KNOLL KNURL MOUSE SLUMP
STONE WEDGE WODGE CLUNCH
DOLLOP GOBBET HUBBLE HUDDLE
LUMPET NUBBLE NUGGET CLUMPER
CLUNTER PUMPKNOT
(— IN CLOTH) BURL
(— IN GLASS) YOLK
(— OF BLACK LEAD) SOP
(— OF BLOOD) CLOD
(— OF CLAY) BAT
(— OF COAL) NUBBLING
(— OF DOUGH) DIP
(— OF FAT) KEECH
(— OF GLASS) BLOOM
(— OF IRON) OOLLY
(— OF LAVA) BOMB
(— OF LINT) SLUG
(— OF MEAT) OLIVE
(— OF METAL) MASS SLUG
(— OF ORE) ROCK HARDHEAD
(— OF RUBBER) THIMBLE
(— OF SALT) SALTCAT
(— OF WOOD) CHUMP
(— OF YEAST) BEE
(— ON HORSE'S BACK) SITFAST
(— ON SKIN) MILIUM
(LARGE —) BLAD DOLL HUNK
(LITTLE —) NODULE KNOBBLE
(ROUNDED —) CLOT
(PREF.) THROMB(O)
LUMPFISH GROSS PADDLE
SUCKER
LUMPISH STODGY CHUCKLE

LUMPSUCKER PADLE PADDLE
SEAOWL
LUMPY GOBBY CHUNKY CLOGGY
CLUNCH COBBLY STODGY BUNCHED
NODULAR NODULOSE
LUNACY MOON FOLLY MADNESS
DELIRIUM INSANITY
LUNARIA SATINPOD
LUNARY VOLVELLE
LUNATIC NUT GELT LOONY
WACKO BEDLAM MADMAN
MANIAC WEIRDO CRAZOID FANATIC
FRANTIC CRACKPOT MOONLING
MOONSICK MOONSTRUCK
MOONSTRICKEN
LUNCH CUT BAIT CRIB TIFF BEVER
PIECE SNACK BRUNCH NACKET
TIFFIN UNDERN BAGGING
ELEVENS DEJEUNER DRINKING
ELEVENER LUNCHEON NUNCHEON
COLLATION
(— ORDER) BLT
(DAIRY —) CREMERIE
(MINER'S —) SNAP
LUNCHEON CRIB LUNCH STULL
TIFFIN DEJEUNE DINETTE
NOONMEAT
LUNCHROOM EATERY
LUNETTE OUTWORK
LUNG PULMO DRAGON LONGUE
(PREF.) PNEO PNEUM(A)(ATO)(O)(ON)
(ONO) PULMO PULMON(I)
LUNGE FOIN PASS SPAR POINT
VENUE CHARGE ALLONGE
LUNGFISH CYCLOID DIPNOAN
MUDFISH SIRENOID
LUNGS LIGHTS VISCUS BELLOWS
(PERTAINING TO —) PULMONIC
LUNKHEAD DOLT DOPE JUGHEAD
LUNULE ALBEDO
LUO DHOLUO
LUPIN ARSINE
LUPINE SUNDIAL
LURCH JOLL STOT SWAG PITCH
STOIT CAREEN STOITER STUMBLE
SWAGGER
(LEAVE IN THE —) DITCH
LURCHING DRUNKEN ROLLING
LURE CON JAY BAIT HOOK ROPE
TOLL WISE DECOY DRILL FEINT
SLOCK SNARE SNOOK SPOON SQUID
STALE TEMPT TROLL ALLURE
CAPPER CLARET ENTICE ENTRAP
RABATE SEDUCE TREPAN VELURE
ATTRACT GUDGEON INVEIGH
PHANTOM PITFALL WOBBLER
BUCKTAIL INVEIGLE LUREMENT
(— INTO GAMBLING) HUSTLE
(— OF CARRION) TRAIN
(— WILDFOWL) STOOL
LURI ALUR
LURID RED PURPLE SULTRY CRIMSON
GHASTLY

LURK DARE LOUT COUCH LOWER
SKULK SLINK SNEAK AMBUSH
DARKLE
LURKING LURKY GRASSANT
LATITANT
LUSCIOUS FOND RICH SWEET
CREAMY DULCET DELICATE
LUSH SOT RICH DRUNK GREEN
LUSTY MOIST TOPER SAVORY
FERTILE OPULENT PROFUSE
THRIVING
LUST HELL ITCH KAMA BLOOD PRIDE
DESIRE LIBIDO LIKING LUXURY
NICETY PASSION COVETISE CUPIDITY
CARNALITY
(SUFF.) LAGNIA
LUSTER NAIF GLASS GLINT GLOSS
SHEEN SHINE WATER LUSTRE
POLISH REFLET BURNISH GLIMPSE
GLISTER LUSTRUM NITENCY
FULGENCE LUSTRATE RADIANCY
SPLENDOR
(— OF FIBER) BLOOM
(BRONZE-LIKE —) SCHILLER
LUSTERLESS MAT WAN DEAD DULL
FISHY STARY
LUSTFUL HOT GAMY GOLE LEWD
RANK SALT CADGY LUSTY PRIME
RANDY RUTTY WANTON BEASTLY
CODDING FLESHLY FULSOME
GOATISH JEALOUS RAMMISH
RUTTISH LIKEROUS SALACIOUS
LUSTFULNESS SATYRISM
LUSTILY CRANK HOTLY
LUSTING ITCHY
LUSTRATION ABHISEKA
LUSTROUS CLEAR DOGGY NITID
BRIGHT GLOSSY ORIENT SHEENY
SILKEN SILVER SHINING SPLENDID
LUSTY BRAG CANT BURLY CRANK
FLUSH FRACK FRANK FRECK GUTSY
HARDY JUICY RANDY STIFF STOUT
GAWSIE ROBUST STURDY LUSTFUL
LUSTICK BOUNCING PHYSICAL
SKELPING SPORTIVE VIGOROUS
LUTE TAR BIWA LAUD DOMRA NABIA
NABLE REBAB REBEC SAROD CITOLE
ENLUTE LORICA LUTING SCREED
VIELLE ANGELOT BANDORE DICHORD
DYPHONE MANDOLA MANDORE
MINIKIN PANDORE THEORBO
VIHUELA ANGELICA ARCHLUTE
PENORCON TAMBOURA TEMPLATE
TRICHORD
LUTER DAUBER PASTER
LUTJANID JEWFISH

LUXEMBOURG
CAPITAL: LUXEMBOURG
HIGHEST POINT: BURGPLATZ
LOWLAND: BONPAYS GUTLAND
MEASURE: FUDER
MOUNTAIN RANGE: ARDENNES

PLATEAU: ARDENNES
RIVER: OUR SURE SAUER ALZETTE
  MOSELLE
TOWN: BOUS FICH ROODT WILTZ
  PETANGE VIANDEN DIEKIRCH
  DUDELANGE ETTELBRUCK
  DIFFERDANGE

LUXURIANT GOLE LUSH RANK RICH
FRANK PROUD LAVISH WANTON OP-
ULENT PROFUSE RAMPANT TEEMING
PAMPERED PRODIGAL
LUXURIANTLY FATLY
LUXURIATE BASK REVEL FROWST
WALLOW WANTON
LUXURIOUS HIGH LUSH NICE POSH
RANK SOFT GAUDY PLUSH SWANK
CAPUAN DELUXE GILDED PALACE
SILKEN SWANKY WANTON APICIAN
ELEGANT DELICATE LUCULLAN
PRODIGAL REGALADO SENSUOUS
TRYPHENA TRYPHOSA SUMPTUOUS
LUXURIOUSLY HIGH DELUXE
LUXURY FRILL FINERY OUTRAGE
DELICACY ELEGANCE PLEASURE
RICHNESS PRINCELINESS
LUXURY-LOVING DELICATE
LUZON (— VOLCANO) TAAL
LYCANTHROPE WEREWOLF
LYCAON (DAUGHTER OF —)
CALLISTO
(FATHER OF —) PELASGUS
LYCEUM PLATFORM
LYCHNIS FIREBALL NONESUCH
LYCIUM RUSOT
LYCOPODIUM MOSS FOXTAIL
CROWFOOT STAGHORN
LYCURGUS (BROTHER OF —)
POLYDECTES
(FATHER OF —) DRYAS EUNOMUS
(SON OF —) OPHELTES
LYCUS (BROTHER OF —) AEGEUS
PALLAS IPHINOE
(FATHER OF —) PANDION
(MOTHER OF —) PYLIA
(WIFE OF —) DIRCE
LYDIA MAEONIA
LYE LEY BOUK BUCK STRAKE LESSIVE
LIXIVIUM SOAPLEES
LYING FLAT FALSE LEASE CRETISM
LEASING MENTERY ACCUBATION

MENDACIOUS
(— APART) DISSITE
(— AT BASE OF MOUNTAINS)
PIEDMONT
(— CLOSE) QUAT
(— DOWN) DOWN LODGED
CUMBENT DORMANT COUCHANT
(— HID) LATITANT
(— IDLE) INACTIVE
(— ON BACK) SUPINE
(— ON FACE) PRONE PROCUMBENT
(— ON GROUND) REPENT REPTANT
(— OPEN) PATENT
(— OVER) JACENT
(— UNDER GRASS) LEA
LYING-IN INLYING CHILDBED
GROANING
LYMPH CHYLE VIRUS
(PREF.) CHYL(O)
(SUFF.) CHYLIA
LYMPHAD GALLEY
LYMPHANGITIS WEED FILLING
LYMPHATIC LACTEAL
LYMPHOGRANULOMA BUBO
LYMPHOMATOSIS FISHEYE
LYNCEUS (BROTHER OF —) IDAS
(FATHER OF —) AEGYPTUS
APHAREUS
(WIFE OF —) HYPERMNESTRA
LYNCH HANG DEWITT
LYNX LOSSE OUNCE PISHU BOBCAT
GORKUN LUCERN CARACAL LUCIVEE
WILDCAT CARCAJOU
LYRE ASOR HARP LYRA SHELL CHELYS
KINNOR KISSAR TRIGON CITHARA
TESTUDO BARBITON PHORMINX
TRICHORD TRIGONON
LYREBIRD LYRETAIL PHEASANT
LYRIC LAY LIED HOKKU LALAN MELIC
GHAZEL TENSON CANCION
CHANSON DESCORT MADRIGAL
(HAVING — AND DRAMATIC
QUALITIES) SPINTO
(LOVE —) ALBA
(PL.) SONG
LYRICAL ODIC MELIC
LYSIPPE (FATHER OF —) PROETUS
(HUSBAND OF —) MELAMPUS
(MOTHER OF —) ANTIA
(SISTER OF —) IPHINOE IPHINASSA
LYTTA WORM

M

M EM EMMA MIKE METRO
 (WRONG USE OF —) MYTACISM
M-1 GARAND
MAACAH (HUSBAND OF —) DAVID
 (SON OF —) ABSALOM
MAACHAH (FATHER OF —) NAHOR
 URIEL TALMAI
 (HUSBAND OF —) JEHIEL MACHIR
 REHOBOAM
 (MOTHER OF —) REUMAH
 (SON OF —) HANAN ABIJAH ACHISH
 ABSALOM SHEPHATIAH
MAADAI (FATHER OF —) BANI
MA'AM MARM MISTRESS
MAARIB ARBIT ARBITH
MAASEIAH (FATHER OF —) ADAIAH
 BARUCH SHALLUM
 (SON OF —) AZARIAH ZEDEKIAH
 ZEPHANIAH
MAATH (FATHER OF —) MATTATHIAS
MAAZ (FATHER OF —) RAM
MACA ENIMAGA
MACABRE SICK SCARY HORRIBLE
MACACA PITHECUS
MACADAMIZE METAL
MACAO (CHINESE NAME OF —)
 AOMEN
 (ISLAND OF —) TAIPA COLOANE
MACAQUE KRA BROH BRUH MACAC
 TOQUE MACHIN MONKEY RHESUS
 RILAWA WANDEROO
MACARIA (FATHER OF —) HERCULES
 (MOTHER OF —) DEIANIRA
MACARIZE LAUD
MACARONI FOP DANDY DITALI
MACARONIC SKEW
MACAROON AMARETTO
MACAW ARA ARARA PARROT
 MARACAN ARACANGA COCKATOO
MACAW-TREE MACOYA
 MACAHUBA
MACBETH (AUTHOR OF —)
 SHAKESPEARE
 (CHARACTER IN —) ROSS ANGUS
 BANQUO DUNCAN HECATE LENNOX
 SEYTON SIWARD FLEANCE MACBETH
 MACDUFF MALCOLM MENTEITH
 CAITHNESS DONALBAIN
MACE CROC MALL MAUL POKER
 VERGE MALLET SPARTH CATTAIL
 (PART OF —) HEAD HILT SPIKE
 FLANGE HANDLE
 (REED —) DOD DODD
 (ROYAL —) SCEPTER SCEPTRE
MACE-BEARER BEADLE VERGER
 MACEMAN

MACERATE RET SOUR STEEP
MACHAON (BROTHER OF —)
 PODALIRIUS
 (FATHER OF —) AESCULAPIUS
 (MOTHER OF —) CORONIS
MACHETE BOLO GULOC PANGA
 PARANG CURTAXE CUTLASS
 CUTLASS
MACHI (COMPANION OF —) CALEB
 JOSHUA
 (SON OF —) GEUEL
MACHIAVELLIAN CRAFTY
 CUNNING GUILEFUL
MACHINATE TAMPER
MACHINATION ARTIFICE INTRIGUE
 SCHEMERY
**MACHINE (ALSO SEE DEVICE AND
 ENGINE)** GIN HOG JIG SAW AGER
 BABY COMB GEAR JACK LIFT MULE
 PUMP RASP TRAY WHIM WINK
 ADDER AWNER BALER BENCH BILLY
 BOARD BRAKE BREAK COPER CRANE
 DEVIL EDGER ERNIE FRAME FUDGE
 FUGAL JENNY JERRY JOLLY LATHE
 LAYER METER MIXER MOWER NAVVY
 RAKER RESAW ROVER SCREW SETUP
 SHEEN SIZER STAMP SULKY TRONE
 VINER WILLY BARKER BEADER
 BEAMER BEATER BEETLE BENDER
 BILLER BINDER BOLTER BUCKLE
 BUMPER BUTTER CANTER CAPPER
 CARDER CONCHE COOLER CREWER
 DECKER DOFFER DONKEY DRAPER
 DREDGE DUSTER ENGINE FLAKER
 FOLDER FOOTER FORMER GADDER
 GAPPER GLAZER GRADER GRATER
 GUMMER HEADER HEMMER HOBBER
 HOGGER HOOPER HULLER HUSKER
 IRONER JIGGER JORDAN KICKER
 LEGGER LIFTER LINTER LOGGER
 MAILER MANGLE MILLER MITRER
 NAPPER NETTER NIBBER NIPPER
 PACKER PEGGER PINNER PLATER
 PUMPER RIPPER ROSSER ROTARY
 ROUTER SANDER SCUTCH SEALER
 SEAMER SHAKER SHAPER SHAVER
 SINGER SKIVER SLICER SORTER
 SPACER STOCKS STOKER TEDDER
 TENTER TWINER VANNER WASHER
 WELDER WILLOW ABRADER
 AUTOMAT AVIATOR BACKHOE
 BATCHER BELLOWS BLENDER
 BLUNGER BOTTLER BRANNER
 BREAKER CANDROY CAPSTAN
 CHIPPER COMBINE CRUSHER
 DIBBLER DRESSER EMULSOR

ENCODER ENROBER ERECTOR
EXOSTRA FLANGER FLOSSER
FREEZER GARNETT GLASSER
GRAINER GRINDER GROOVER
GROUTER HUMIDOR IRONMAN
JOINTER KNITTER KNOTTER
MACHINA MANGLER MATCHER
MITERER PERRIER PLODDER
PLUCKER POTCHER PRINTER
QUILLER REPRESS RIVETER ROASTER
SAMMIER SCALPER SHEARER
SHEETER SIROCCO SLABBER
SLASHER SLITTER SLOTTER
SLUBBER SLUGGER SMASHER
SPALLER SPEEDER SPINNER
SPONGER SPOOLER SPRAYER
STACKER STAMPER STAPLER
STEAMER STEMMER STICKER
TENONER TEREBRA TOOTHER
TRAMPER TREATER TRIMMER
TRUSSER TWILLER TWISTER
TYPOBAR WHIPPER WHIZZER
AERIFIER AIRCRAFT BROACHER
CALENDER CANCELER CARTONER
CLINCHER COLLATOR COMPRESS
DUNGBECK ELEPHANT EXPLODER
EXTRUDER FILATORY FINISHER
FLYWINCH FORKLIFT GATHERER
HARDENER HAYMAKER HERCULES
HUMMELER IMPACTER KILLIFER
MORTISER MOULINET ODOGRAPH
OROGRAPH PROFILER PULSATOR
SCHIFFLI SCUTCHER SHREDDER
SOFTENER SPLITTER SPREADER
SPRIGGER SQUEEZER STITCHER
STRANDER STRIPPER SURFACER
TEMPERER THREADER THRESHER
THROSTLE TRAVELER TRISPAST
TUNNELER UPSETTER WINNOWER
ADDRESSER
(ANCIENT MILITARY —) BALISTA
BALLISTA
(BETTING —) PARIMUTUEL
(POLITICAL —) APPARAT
(STAGE —) PAGEANT
MACHINE-GUN POMPOM
MITRAILLEUSE
MACHINE GUN STINGER
CHAUCHAT
MACHINERY MINT TOPCAP
SUCCULA APPARATUS
MACHINE SHOP TURNERY
MACHINIST FRILLER THINNER
MACHINER
MACHIR (FATHER OF —) AMMIEL
MANASSEH
MACHISMO MACHO
MACHNADEBAI (FATHER OF —)
BANI
MACKEREL CERO CHAD PETO SCAD
TINK BLINK OPELU SNOEK TUNNY
BONITO SAUREL TINKER BLINKER

BLOATER SCOMBER TASSARD
ALBACORE HARDHEAD SCOMBRID
SEERFISH
(— ABOUT 8 OR 9 INCHES) TINK
TINKLIT
(KING —) CERO
(PICKLED —) SCALPEEN
(POOR BONY —) SLINK SLINKER
(SNAKE —) ESCOLAR
(YOUNG —) SPIKE
(PREF.) SCOMBRI
MACKLE SLUR SHAKE MACULA
MACROGAMETE OVUM
MACROSCOPIC GROSS
MACROSPECIES LINNEON
MAD FEY AWAY GITE GYTE HYTE
WOOD YOND ANGRY BATTY BRAIN
CRAZY DIPPY FOLLE MANIC RABID
WACKO WACKY BEDLAM FRENZY
INSANE MANIAC WOODEN BERSERK
BONKERS FANATIC FRANTIC
FURIOUS LUNATIC MADDING
MADDOCK MANKIND REDWOOD
WITLESS DELIRANT DEMENTED
DISTRACT INFORMAL MANIACAL
MINDLESS RAVENING POSSESSED
(GET —) SEERED

MADAGASCAR

CAPITAL: ANTANANARIVO
FORMER NAME: MALAGASYREPUBLIC
ISLAND GROUP: ALDABRA
LAKE: ITASY ALAOTRA
MEASURE: GANTANG
NATIVE: HOVA SAKALAVA
PEOPLE: HOVA COTIER MARINA
RIVER: IKOPA MANIA SOFIA MANGOKY
MANGORO ONYLAHY
TOWN: IHOSY MANJA TULEAR
MAJANGA NOSSIBE TSIVORY
TAMATAVE ANTISIRABE

MADAI (FATHER OF —) JAPHET
MADAM MEM MUM BAWD MAAM
PANI DONNA MADAME SENORA
SENHORA SIGNORA GOODWIFE
MISTRESS SINEBADA
MADAMA BUTTERFLY
(CHARACTER IN —) SUZUKI
CIOCIOSAN PINKERTON SHARPLESS
(COMPOSER OF —) PUCCINI
MADAME BOVARY (AUTHOR OF —
) FLAUBERT
(CHARACTER IN —) EMMA LEON
BOVARY DUPUIS HOMAIS CHARLES
HELOISE ROUAULT LHEUREUX
RODOLPHE BOULANGER
MADAR YERCUM
MADCAP RASH
MADDEN ENRAGE INCENSE
INFLAME DISTRACT
MADDENED ENRAGED FRENZIED

MADDER GAMENE LIZARY ALIZARI
GARANCE MUNJEET TANAGRA
GARANCIN SPURWORT WOODRUFF
MAD-DOG SKULLCAP MADWEED
HOODWORT
MADE SET BUILT COMPACT
PREPARED TIMBERED
(— FLUID BY HEAT) FUSILE
(— LATELY) NEW
(— OF DISSIMILAR PARTS) MIXED
(— OF FLAX) LINEN
(— OF GRAIN) OATEN CEREAL
(— OF IVORY) EBURNEAN
(— OF SILVER) ARGENT
(— OF STONE) STONEN
(— OF TWIGS) VIRGAL
(— SHORT) CURTAL
(— TART) EUCHRED
(— TO ORDER) BESPOKEN
(— TRANSLUCENT) AJOURE
(— UP) ACCRETE
(— WITH CEDAR) CEDARN
(CUNNINGLY —) SLY
(PREF.) (— OF) DIA
(SUFF.) (— OF) INE
MADE-BEAVER SKIN CASTOR
MADEIRA ISLANDS (ISLAND OF —)
GRANDE DEZERTE
(TOWN OF —) FUNCHAL
(WINE OF —) BUAL TINTA MALMSEY
SERCIAL VERDELHO
MADELON POLIXENE
MADHGOUSE SCRUM
MADHOUSE ASYLUM BEDLAM
MADHUCA BASSIA ILLIPE
MADLY WOOD CRAZY
MADMAN GELT WACKO BEDLAM
MANIAC CRAZOID FURIOSO LUNATIC
WOODMAN
MADNESS MAD FURY MOON WOOD
FOLIE FOLLY FUROR MANIA BEDLAM
FRENZY LUNACY DEWANEE ECSTASY
MOONERY WIDDRIM DELIRIUM
DEMENTIA PIBLOKTO WILLNESS
WOODNESS WOODSHIP
(PREF.) LYSSO MANIC
(SUFF.) MANE MANIA(C)
MADONNA LADY VIRGIN
MADREPORE FUNGID
MADRIGAL ENSALADA
MADRONA LAUREL MANZANITA
MADTOM TADPOLE
MADWORT ALYSSUM BUGLOSS
MAENAD FROW BASSARID
BACCHANTE
(PL.) BACCHAE
MAFIA MOB GANG CLIQUE
MAFIC FEMIC
MAFURA ROKA ELCAJA
MAGANI BAGANI
MAGAZINE MAG BOOK DRUM FLAT
IGLOO SLICK STORE RETORT
ALMACEN JOURNAL CASSETTE

(BLACKWOOD'S —) MAGA
(FASHION —) ELLE
(OLD MUSIC —) ETUDE
(SCIENCE FICTION —) FANZINE
MAGDALEN MAUDLIN
MAGGOT MAD GRUB MAWK WORM
METHE GENTLE WARBLE WORMIL
MADDOCK SKIPPER MUCKWORM
MAGGOTY MAWKISH
MAGIC JUJU MAYA RUNE CRAFT
FAIRY GOETY SPELL TURGY GOETIC
TREGET VOODOO ALCHEMY CANTRIP
CONJURY DEVILRY GLAMOUR
GRAMARY MAGICAL SORCERY
BRUJERIA HECATEAN WIZARDRY
NECROMANCY
(BLACK —) GOETY GOETIC MALEFICE
(PERSONAL —) CHARISM CHARISMA
(WHITE —) TURGY
MAGICAL WIZARD WONDER
HERMETIC NUMINOUS THEURGIC
**MAGIC FLUTE, THE (CHARACTER
IN —)** PAMINA TAMINO PAPAGENA
PAPAGENO SARASTRO
MONOSTATOS
(COMPOSER OF —) MOZART
MAGICIAN MAGE BOKOR MAGUS
UTHER CUNJAH GOETIC GOOFER
GUFFER MAGIAN MERLIN WABENO
WIZARD CHARMER GWYDION
KOSCHEI WARLOCK WIELARE
WISEMAN CONJURER FETISHER
SORCERER THEURGIC TROLLMAN
ARCHIMAGE
**MAGIC MOUNTAIN (AUTHOR OF
—)** MANN
(CHARACTER IN —) HANS NAPHTA
BEHRENS CASTORP CAUCHAT
CLAVDIA JOACHIM ZIEMSSEN
KROKOWSKI PEEPERKORN
SETTEMBRINI
MAGISTERIAL LOFTY PROUD
AUGUST CURULE LORDLY HAUGHTY
STATELY ARROGANT DOGMATIC
MAGISTERY MASTERY
MAGISTRACY AMT PRYTANY
MAGISTRATE BEAK FOUD EPHOR
JUDGE JURAT MAYOR PRIOR REEVE
AMTMAN ARCHON AVOYER BAILIE
BAILLI CENSOR CONSUL FISCAL
KOTWAL SYNDIC ALCALDE BAILIFF
BURGESS DUUMVIR ECHEVIN
EPHORUS JUSTICE NOMARCH
PODESTA PRAETOR PREFECT
PROVOST STEWARD SUFFETE
TRIBUNE ALABARCH ALDERMAN
CAPITOUL DEFENSOR DEMIURGE
DICTATOR GOVERNOR MITTIMUS
PHYLARCH PRYTANIS RECORDER
STRADICO STRATEGE HUNDREDER
CORREGIDOR
(— IN CHANNEL ISLANDS) JURAT
(— OF ANCIENT ROME) EDILE AEDILE

(— OF INDIA) COTWAL KOTWAL
(— OF MECCA) SHERIF SHEREEF
(— OF VENICE AND GENOA) DOGE
(MOHAMMEDAN —) CADI CADY SHERIF
(SCOTCH —) PROVOST STEWARD

MAGMA ICHOR
MAGMATIC JUVENILE
MAGNANIMITY HEIGHT FREEDOM
MAGNANIMOUS BIG FREE GREAT LARGE LOFTY NOBLE HEROIC EXALTED GENEROUS
MAGNATE BARON MOGUL TITAN BASHAW TYCOON
MAGNESIA PULVIL
MAGNET FIELD ADAMAS MAGNES ADAMANT SOLENOID TERRELLA LODESTONE
MAGNETIC (— FIELD MEASURER) SQUID
MAGNETISM IT DEVIL OOMPH
MAGNETITE LOADSTONE LODESTONE
MAGNETIZE TOUCH SATURATE
MAGNETOMETER DOODLEBUG
MAGNIFICATION POWER
MAGNIFICENCE GITE POMP FLARE GLORY STATE PARADE JOLLITY ROYALTY GRANDEUR SPLENDOR
MAGNIFICENT RIAL GRAND NOBLE PROUD ROYAL AUGUST LAVISH IMMENSE POMPOUS STATELY SUBLIME GLORIOUS GORGEOUS MAGNIFIC PALATIAL PRINCELY SPLENDID
MAGNIFICENT OBSESSION (AUTHOR OF —) DOUGLAS (CHARACTER IN —) BRENT HELEN JOYCE NANCY WAYNE DAWSON HUDSON ROBERT ASHFORD MERRICK
MAGNIFY LAUD BLESS ERECT EXALT PRAISE ADVANCE DISTEND ENLARGE GLORIFY GREATEN INCREASE MAXIMIZE MULTIPLY
MAGNIFYING (PREF.) MICR(O)
MAGNIFYING GLASS LOUPE READER
MAGNILOQUENT TURGID BOMBAST
MAGNITUDE BULK MASS SIZE DATUM LEVEL SOLID EXTENT FIGURE PERIOD EXTREME CONSTANT FUNCTION INFINITE
MAGNOLIA YULAN BIGBLOOM CUCUMBER MAURICIO (— STATE) MISSISSIPPI
MAGOG (FATHER OF —) JAPHETH
MAGPIE MAG PIE PIET PYAT CISSA KOTRI MADGE NINUT MARGET NANPIE PIANET PIEMAG SIRGANG

HAGISTER MARGARET PHEASANT PIENANNY CHATTERBOX
MAGPIE LARK PEEWEE GRALLINA
MAGPIE ROBIN DAYAL DHYAL
MAGUEY AGAVE MESCAL CANTALA
MAGYAR SZEKEL SZEKLER
MAHALAH (MOTHER OF —) HAMMOLEKETH (UNCLE OF —) GILEAD
MAHALATH (FATHER OF —) ISHMAEL JERIMOTH (HUSBAND OF —) ESAU REHOBOAM
MAHALI (FATHER OF —) MERARI
MAHATMA SAGE ARHAT
MAHAZIOTH (FATHER OF —) HEMAN
MAH-JONGG WOO
MAHLAH (FATHER OF —) ZELOPHEHAD
MAHLI (FATHER OF —) MUSHI MERARI
MAHLON (DAUGHTER OF —) NAOMI (SON OF —) ELIMELECH (WIFE OF —) RUTH
MAHOE EMAJAGUA
MAHOGANY SIPO ALMON CAOBA CEDAR ROHAN ACAJOU AGUANO SAPELE THITKA ALBARCO AVODIRE BAYWOOD GUNNUNG MADEIRA RATTEEN TABASCO BANGALAY HARDTACK TANGUILE (INDIAN —) TOON (PHILIPPINE —) BAGTIKAN
MAHONIA ASHBERRY ODOSTEMON
MAHOUND MACON
MAHUA FULWA MOWHA MOWRA MADHUCA PHULWARA
MAHUANG EPHEDRA
MAHWA ILLIPE ILLUPI
MAIA (FATHER OF —) ATLAS (MOTHER OF —) PLEIONE (SON OF —) MERCURY
MAID MAY AYAH GIRL LASS MEDE SLUT CHINA WENCH WOMAN MAIDEN SLAVEY TWEENY VIRGIN ANCILLA GENERAL MAIDKIN PHYLLIS PUCELLE WENCHEL BONIBELL BRANGANE HANDMAID SUIVANTE TIREMAID (— IN WAITING) DAMSEL DAMOZEL (— OF-ALL-WORK) SLAVEY GENERAL (— OF HONOR) MARIE (KIND OF —) METER (KITCHEN —) SCOGIE (LADY'S —) AYAH ABIGAIL TIREMAID (NURSE —) BONNE (OLD —) TABBY SPINSTER (WAITING —) ABIGAIL SUIVANTE
MAIDEN MAY BIRD BURD DAME GIRL MAID DALAGA DAMSEL FROKIN MEISJE COLLEEN CYDIPPE DAMOZEL MADCHEN DAUGHTER (— WITH BASKET ON HEAD) CANEPHOR (MOUNT IDA —) OREAD

(MUSLIM —) HURI HOURI
(WEAVING —) ARACHNE
(PREF.) PARTHENO
MAIDENHAIR GINGKO ADIANTUM
MAIDENLY VIRGIN GIRLISH
VIRGINAL
MAIDEN PINK SPINK DIANTHUS
MAIDSERVANT LASS BIDDY BONNE
SKIVVY ANCILLA LISETTE
MAIEUTIC HEBAMIC
MAIGRE BAR SCIAENID WEAKFISH
MAIL BAG DAK HOOD POST ARMOR
MATTER AIRMAIL JACKPOT MAILBAG
ORDINAR POSTAGE POSTBAG
SEAPOST TAPPALL ORDINARY
(IMPROPERLY ADDRESSED —) NIX
NIXY NIXIE
(JUNK —) CATALOG
(KIND OF —) HATE VOICE
MAILBAG BAG POUCH POSTBAG
MAILBOX POST PILLAR POSTBOX
MAILLECHORT ARGENTON
MAILLOT SWIMSUIT
MAILMAN POSTMAN BREVIGER
MAIM LAME BREAK TRUNK HAMBLE
MANGLE MAYHEM SCOTCH CRIPPLE
MUTILATE TRUNCATE
(— AN ANIMAL) LAW MANK
MAIMED GAMMY SPAVINED
(PREF.) PERO
MAIMING MAYHEM
MAIN HIGH LINE MOST CHIEF GRAND
GREAT OCEAN PRIME SHEER MIGHTY
CAPITAL LEADING CARDINAL
FOREMOST

MAINE
CAPITAL: AUGUSTA
COLLEGE: BATES COLBY BOWDOIN
COUNTY: KNOX WALDO KENNEBEC
AROOSTOOK PENOBSCOT
SAGADAHOC PISCATAQUIS
INDIAN: ABNAKI
LAKE: GRAND SEBEC SEBAGO
RANGELEY SCHOODIC MOOSEHEAD
CHESUNCOOK
MOUNTAIN: BIGELOW CADILLAC
KATAHDIN
NATIVE: MANIAC
RIVER: SACO KENNEBEC AROOSTOOK
KENNEBAGO PENOBSCOT
STATE BIRD: CHICKADEE
STATE FLOWER: PINECONE
STATE NICKNAME: LUMBER PINETREE
STATE TREE: PINE
TOWN: BATH ORONO AUBURN
BANGOR BELFAST HOULTON
KITTERY MACHIAS BOOTHBAY
LEWISTON OGUNQUIT PORTLAND
SKOWHEGAN

MAINLAND
(PREF.) EPEIRO

MAINLY BROADLY CHIEFLY LARGELY
MAINSTAY KEY ATLAS SINEW
STOOP PILLAR BACKBONE RELIANCE
MAIN STREET (AUTHOR OF —)
LEWIS
(CHARACTER IN —) ERIK HUGH WILL
CAROL MILFORD VALBORG
KENNICOTT
MAINTAIN AVER AVOW BEAR FEND
FIND HOLD KEEP LAST SAVE ADOPT
ARGUE CARRY CLAIM ESCOT SALVE
ADHERE ALLEGE ASSERT AVOUCH
DEFEND INTEND RETAIN THREAP
UPHOLD UPKEEP CONFIRM CONTEND
DECLARE DISPUTE JUSTIFY NOURISH
SUBSIST SUPPORT SUSTAIN
CONTINUE PRESERVE
(— AS TRUE) AVOUCH SOOTHE
(— POSITION) STALL
(— SOLEMNLY) VOW
(— WITHOUT REASON) ARROGATE
MAINTAINER FOUNDER RETAINER
MAINTENANCE KEEP LIVING
UPKEEP ALIMONY CUSTODY
FINDING KEEPING PREBEND SERVICE
(— OF POPULATION) BALANCE
MAITHILI TIRHUTIA
MAIZE CORN GRAIN CEREAL INDIAN
JAGONG STAPLE MEALIES
DJAGOONG
(— CRUSHED WITH PESTLE) STAMP
MAJAGUA HAU BARU BOLA MAHO
MOJO BURAO GUANA MAHOE
PURAU BALIBAGO CORKWOOD
EMAJAGUA
MAJESTIC HIGH AWFUL GRAND
LOFTY REGAL ROYAL AUGUST
KINGLY SUPERB STATELY SUBLIME
ELEVATED IMPERIAL MAESTOSO
SPLENDID
MAJESTY DIGNITY AUGUSTUS
GRANDEUR KINGSHIP
MAJOON BANG BHANG
MAJOR BEY DUR DURUM SHARP
CAPITAL GREATER MAGGIORE
MAJOR BARBARA (AUTHOR OF —)
SHAW
(CHARACTER IN —) LOMAX SARAH
CUSINS BARBARA CHARLES
STEPHEN ADOLPHUS BRITOMART
UNDERSHAFT
MAJORCA (SEAPORT IN —) PALMA
MAJORITY BODY BULK FECK MOST
CORPSE SUBSTANCE
(ABSOLUTE —) QUORUM
MAJOR LEAGUE BIGS
MAKARAKA IDDIO
MAKARI KOTOKO
MAKE DO CUT GAR LET MAY FORM
GIVE LEVY BRAND BUILD CAUSE
COVER FETCH FORGE FRAME SEIZE
SHAPE STAMP AUTHOR COBBLE
CREATE GRAITH INDUCE RENDER

CONFECT FASHION IMAGERY IWURCHE PERFORM PRODUCE CONTRIVE GENERATE
(— A BLUNDER) GOOF
(— ACKNOWLEDGMENT) CONFESS
(— ACTIVE) ENERGIZE
(— A DIFFERENCE) SKILL
(— A DRINK LAST) NURSE
(— ADVANCES) SOLICIT IMPORTUNE
(— AGAIN) RENEW
(— AMENDS) ABYE ATONE ABEGGE ANSWER REDEEM EXPIATE REDRESS
(— A MESS OF) PIE
(— ANGRY) GRAMY WRATH
(— A RUG) HOOK
(— AS PROFIT) GROSS
(— ATTRACTIVE) GILD
(— A VISIT) COSHER
(— AWAY WITH) ABOLISH EMBEZZLE
(— BARE) STRIP DENUDE
(— BELIEVE) LET PRETEND
(— BETTER) AMEND HEIGHTEN
(— BLUE) HIP
(— BRIGHT) ENGILD ILLUME CLARIFY
(— BRISK) PERK
(— BROWN) TAN
(— BY STAMPING) MINT
(— CANDLE) DIP DRAW
(— CERTAIN) ASSURE ENSURE
(— CHANNEL IN) THROAT
(— CHEERFUL) SOLACE
(— CHOICE) OPT CHOOSE SELECT
(— CLAMMY) ENGLEIM
(— CLEAR) DECLARE DEVELOP DISCUSS EXHIBIT EXPOUND LIGHTEN DESCRIBE
(— COLD) REFREID
(— COMPLETE) SPHERE
(— CONSPICUOUS) ENNOBLE
(— CONTENT) SATISFY
(— CULTIVABLE) EMPOLDER
(— CUT PRIOR TO LAYERING) TONGUE
(— DEMANDS) POSTULATE
(— DESTITUTE) BEREAVE
(— DIFFERENT) ALTER CHANGE
(— DIRTY) MOIL GRIME
(— DISPLAY OF) AFFECT DISCOVER
(— DRUNK) FOX SOUSE FUDDLE SOZZLE
(— DRY) HAZLE HAZZLE
(— EARLIER) ADVANCE
(— EFFERVESCENT) AERATE
(— EFFIGY) GUY
(— EFFORT) PUSH
(— END OF) SNIB FETCH
(— ENDURING) ANNEAL
(— EQUAL) WEIGH EQUATE
(— EVEN) GLAZE LEVEL WEIGH SQUARE
(— FACES) GIMBLE MURGEON
(— FALSE PRETENSES) SHAM
(— FAST) FIX BAIL FAST GIRD KNIT

MAKE STOP BELAY HITCH BUCKLE FASTEN SECURE
(— FAT) BATTEN
(— FIRM) FIX BRACE FASTEN
(— FIT) APTATE STRIKE
(— FOOLISH) DAFF GREEN NUGIFY STULTIFY
(— FOOL OF) DOR BORE DOLT DORRE BEGOWK DOODLE
(— FOOTSORE) SURBATE
(— FOR) HEAD
(— FROTHY) MILL
(— FULL) FARCE FULFILL
(— FUN OF) GUY KID GAFF JAPE JEST JOSH RIDE DROLL GLAIK SCOUT SMOKE
(— FUSS OVER NOTHING) FAFF
(— GLAD) FAIN
(— GLASS) FOUND
(— GLOSSY) SLEEK
(— GLOW) FURNACE
(— GOLDEN) ENDORE
(— GOOD) ABET SUPPLY RESTORE SUPPORT RETRIEVE
(— GRINDING NOISE) GRINCH
(— GURGLING SOUND) CROOL
(— HAPPY) BLESS ENJOY REFORM BEATIFY SATISFY FELICIFY
(— HARD) TAW STEEL ENDURE HORNIFY
(— HARDY) FASTEN
(— HEADWAY) STEM WALK ENFORCE
(— HEALTHY) SANIFY
(— HELPLESS) STAGGER
(— HOLY) BLESS SACRE HALLOW SANCTIFY
(— HORSE SEEM YOUNGER) BISHOP
(— ILL) MORBIFY
(— IMMOBILE) FREEZE
(— IMPACT) ASSAIL
(— INCURSION) HARRY
(— INSIGNIFICANT) MICRIFY
(— INTO BUNDLE) FARDEL
(— INTO LAW) ENACT
(— INVALID) DAMASK
(— JOINT) SYPHER
(— KNOWN) BID OUT GIVE WISE AREAD BEKEN BREAK KITHE SOUND SPEAK BEWRAY BROACH COUTHE DENOTE DESCRY EXPOSE INFORM REVEAL SPREAD CONFESS DECLARE DELIVER DIVULGE PUBLISH SIGNIFY UNCOVER ANNOUNCE DECIPHER DISCLOSE DISCOVER INDICATE PROCLAIM PROMULGE
(— LESS) MINISH
(— LESS DENSE) THIN RAREFY
(— LESS SEVERE) MITIGATE
(— LIABLE) DANGER
(— LOVE) WOO COURT SPOON GALLANT
(— LUKEWARM) WLECCHE
(— LUSTERLESS) FLATTEN

(— MANIFEST) EVINCE EXPLAIN
(— MELANCHOLY) HYP
(— MELODIOUS) ATTUNE
(— MELODY) DREAM
(— MENTION) SPEAK
(— MERRY) JET GAUD CHEER SPORT
FROLIC SHROVE DISPORT REHAYTE
(— METALLIC SOUND) CHINK
(— MISTAKE) ERR BOOB GOOF
(— MONOTONOUS NOISE) DRONE
(— MORAL) ETHICIZE
(— MUCH OF) DAWT DANDLE
(— MURMURING NOISE) BUM
(— NEAT) FEAT SMUG TIDY GROOM
(— NEST) TIMBER
(— NEW AGAIN) RENOVATE
(— NONMAGNETIC) DEGAUSS
(— NUMB) DAZE ETHERIZE
(— OFF) BAG BOLT HOOK ANNEX
HEIST MOSEY SLOPE SPIRIT
SCARPER
(— ONE) UNE
(— ONE'S WAY) AIRT BORE TRADE
PLY FRAME
(— OPEN) AIR PATEFY
(— OUT) FARE FILL GLEAN SKILL
DISCERN DECIPHER
(— OVER) TURN ALIEN CHANGE
RECOCT DELIVER REFORGE
(— PALE) CHALK
(— PLEASANT) SWEETEN
(— POIGNANT) SAUCE
(— PREGNANT) ENWOMB
(— PROGRESS) GAIN STEM GATHER
(— PROUD) WLENCH
(— PUBLIC) BLOW BLAZE BREAK
BLAZON DELATE DIVULGE FANFARE
PUBLISH BULLETIN
(— QUIET) ALLAY QUIET APPEASE
(— RATTLING NOISE) TIRL
(— READY) DO BUN GET BOUN
BOWN BUSK YARK BELAY BOWNE
DRESS PREST PRIME FETTLE GRAITH
ADDRESS APPAREL DISPOSE
PREPARE
(— RECORD OF) REFER
(— REFERENCE) MENTION
(— RESISTANCE) REBEL
(— RESOLUTE) STEEL
(— RETURN FOR) REQUITE
(— RICH) FREIGHT IMBURSE
(— ROSY) FLUSH
(— RUSTLING SOUND) FISSLE FISTLE
(— RUTTING CRY) FREAM
(— SCANTY LIVING) EKE
(— SERIES OF NOTES) TINKLE
(— SHIFT) SCAMBLE
(— SIGN OF CROSS) BLESS
(— SMALL) MICRIFY BELITTLE
(— SMALLER) MINIFY COMPRESS
(— SMOOTH) SLAB GLAZE SLEEK
GENTLE HAMMER SCRAPE LEVIGATE
(— SOFT) NESH GENTLE

(— SOGGY) SOP
(— SOUR) FOX WIND
(— SPIRITLESS) MOPE
(— SPORT OF) LARK
(— SPRUCE) PERK SMARTEN
(— STRAIGHT) ADDRESS
(— STRONG) STEEL FASTEN FORTIFY
(— STUPID) MOIDER STULTIFY
(— SUITABLE) ADAPT
(— SURE) SEE INSURE
(— THIN) EMACIATE
(— TIDY) RED REDD
(— TIPSY) FLUSTER
(— TRANSITION TO) MODULATE
(— TRIM) SMUG
(— UNEVEN) RUFFLE RUMPLE
(— UP) UP COOK FORM SPELL INDITE
SETTLE ANALYZE COMPACT
COMPOSE COMPUTE CONCOCT
CONFECT FASHION COMPOUND
COMPRISE DISPENSE
(— UP ACCOUNTS) BREVE
(— USELESS) SPIKE SPOIL
(— USE OF) FEE BUSK APPLY AVAIL
BROOK SERVE SPEND EMPLOY
EXECUTE IMPROVE UTILIZE
(— VIBRANT SOUND) CHIRR
(— VOID) ABATE ANNUL
(— WAR) WARRAY
(— WET) DRAGGLE
(— WHISTLING NOISE) WHEW
(— WHITE) BLANCH BLEACH
CANDIFY
(— WORSE) IMPAIR PEJORATE
(PREF.) POETICO POETO
(SUFF.) EN FECT FEIT FIC(AL)(ATE)
(ATION)(ATIVE)(ATOR)(ATORY)(E)
(ENCE)(ENT)(IAL)(IARY)(IENT) FIER
FIQUE FY IFY POEIA POESIS POIESIS
POIETIC
MAKE-BELIEVE BORAK DUMMY
ASSUMED PRETENCE
MAKER DOER JACK KNAVE SMITH
FACTOR FORGER FORMER WORKER
WRIGHT CREATOR DECLARER
OPERATOR
(— OF ARROWS) FLETCHER
(— OF BARRELS) COOPER
(— OF POTS) POTTER
(— OF SADDLETREES) FUSTER
(— OF SONGS) BULBUL
(— OF TALLOW) CHANDLER
(DRIP-COFFEE —) MACCHINETTA
(SUFF.) STER STRESS
MAKESHIFT JURY RUDE JERRY
TOUSY BEWITH CUTCHA KUTCHA
APOLOGY JACKLEG STOPGAP
RESOURCE TIMENOGUY
MAKEUP FACE BUILD GETUP HABIT
PAINT ROUGE SETUP SHAPE FACIES
FORMAT ANATOMY CONSIST
FEATURE EYELINER PHYSIQUE
TRAVESTY MAQUILLAGE

MAKING FACT
　(SUFF.) FACIENT FACT(ION)(IVE)(ORY)
　FIC FICATION
MALABAR BAY
MALABAR ALMOND KAMANI
　ALMENDRO
MALACCA CANE
MALACEAE POMACEAE PYRACEAE
MALADJUSTMENT SCAR
MALADROIT ILL INEPT AWKWARD
　UNHANDY BUNGLING
MALADY AMOK EVIL MORB CAUSE
　GRIEF ONCOME AILMENT DISEASE
　ILLNESS DISORDER MISCHIEF
　SICKNESS
　(SUFF. — ARISING FROM) ITIS
MALAGASY LEMURIAN
MALAGASY REPUBLIC (SEE
　MADAGASCAR)
MALAGIGI (COUSIN OF —) RINALDO
MALAISE UNEASE
MALAPROPISM SLIPSLOP
MALAR JUGAL
MALARIA AGUE MIASMA SHAKES
　QUARTAN PALUDISM
　(— PARASITE) VIVAX
MALARIAL PALUDAL PALUDOSE
　PALUDOUS

```
              MALAWI
CAPITAL: LILONGWE
COIN: KWACHA TAMBALA
FORMER CAPITAL: ZOMBA
FORMER NAME: NYASALAND
HIGHLANDS: SHIRE
LAKE: NYASA
LANGUAGE: YAO CEWA BANTU NGONI
  TONGA NYANJA TUMBUKA
MOUNTAIN: MLANJE
PEOPLE: YAO BANTU CHEWA NGURU
  NYANJA
RIVER: SHIRE
TOWN: DOWA CHOLO MZUZU NCHEU
  ZOMBA KARONGA BLANTYRE
  LILONGWE
VALLEY: RIFT
```

MALAY AMOK ASIL AMUCK BAJAU
　ILOCO JAKUN MANOBO ILOKANO
MALAYAN (— TREE) TERAP
MALAY APPLE OHIA JAMBO KAVIKA

```
            MALAYSIA
CAPITAL: KUALA LUMPUR
COIN: SEN TRA TRAH RINGGIT
ISLAND: ARU GOA KAI OBI OMA ALOR
  BALI GAGA JAVA MUNA MURU
  SULU AMBON BANDA BOHOL
  BUTON CERAM LUZON MISOL
  PANAY SANGI SUMBA TIMOR
  WETAR BANGKA BOETON DOEROE
  BORNEO BUTUNG FLORES LOMBOK
  MADURA PELENG SANGIR TALAUR
  WAIGEU AMBOINA CELEBES
  JAMDENA MINDORO MOROTAI
  PALAWAN SALAJAR SALWATI
  SUMATRA SUMBAWA BELITONG
  DJAILOLO TANIMBAR
ISTHMUS: KRA
LANGUAGE: TAGALOG
MONEY: DOLLAR RINGGIT
MOUNTAIN: BULU NIUT RAJA MURJO
  NIAPA LEUSER SLAMET BINAIJA
  RINDJANI
PEOPLE: ATA BAJAU SEMANG
  BISAYAN TAGALOG VISAYAN
RIVER: KUTAI PERAK BARITO PAHANG
STATE: KEDAH PERAK SABAH JOHORE
  PAHANG PENANG PERLIS MALACCA
  SARAWAK
TOWN: IPOH DAVAO ILOILO KANGAR
  KUPANG MANADO KUANTAN
  KUCHING MALACCA SANDAKAN
  SEREMBAN
WEIGHT: TAEL WANG TAMPANG
```

MALCHAM (FATHER OF —)
　SHAHARAHIM
　(MOTHER OF —) HODESH
MALCHIAH (FATHER OF —) HARIM
　PAROSH RECHAB
MALCHIEL (FATHER OF —) BERIAH
MALCHIRAM (FATHER OF —)
　JEHOIACHIN
MALCHISHUA (FATHER OF —)
　SAUL
MALCONTENT FRONDEUR
MALDIVES (CAPITAL OF —) MALE
　(MONEY OF —) LAARI RUFIYAA
　RUFIYAN
MALE HE DOG HIM MAN TOM BUCK
　BULL COCK JACK ADULT MANLY
　SPEAR JOHNNY MANFUL MASCLE
　VIRILE LALAQUI MANKIND MANLIKE
　MANNISH PURUSHA
　(— OF ANIMALS) TOM BUCK BULL
　JACK STUD STALLION
　(EFFEMINATE —) NANCE
　(GELDED —) GALT
　(SWAGGERING —) GREASER
　(YOUNG —) GROOM
　(PREF.) ANDR(O)
　(SUFF.) ANDRIA ANDROUS ANDRY
MALECITE ETCHEMIN
MALEDICTION BAN WISH CURSE
　MALISON ANATHEMA
MALEFACTOR BADDY FELON
　BADDIE CULPRIT CRIMINAL
　EVILDOER
MALEFIC TAKING
MALEFICENT BALEFUL
MALELEEL (FATHER OF —) CAINAN
MALEO MEGAPOD
MALE ORCHIS CUCKOO CROWTOE
　CULLION PURPLES RAGWORT
　CROWFOOT

MALEVOLENCE SPITE ENMITY
GRUDGE HATRED MALICE RANCOR
SPLEEN MALIGNITY
MALEVOLENT ILL EVIL FELL
MALIGN HATEFUL HOSTILE SPITEFUL
RANCOROUS
MALFEASANCE MISCONDUCT
MALPRACTICE
MALFORMATION CURL ERROR
HEMITERY MONSTROSITY
(— OF CARNATION) TWITTER
(— OF FRUIT) CATFACE
MALFORMED SHAMBLE
MALFUNCTION GLITCH

MALI
ANCIENT CITY: TIMBUKTU
CAPITAL: BAMAKO
FORMER NAME: FRENCHSUDAN
LAKE: DO DEBO GAROU KORAROU
LANGUAGE: DOGON DYULA MANDE
MARKA PEULH BAMBARA MALINKE
SENOUFO SONGHAI
MOUNTAIN: MINA MANDING
PEOPLE: MOOR PEUL TUAREG
BAMBARA MALINKE SONGHAI
SENOUFO
RIVER: BANI BAGOE BAKOY NIGER
BAOULE AZAOUAK SENEGAL
TOWN: GAO SAN KATI KITA NARA
BAMBA KAYES MOPTI NIONO NIORO
SEGOU SIKASSO

MALICE DOLE ENVY HAIN PIQUE
SPITE VENOM VIRUS ENMITY
GRUDGE RANCOR SPLEEN DESPITE
AMBITION MALIGNITY
MALEVOLENCE
MALICIOUS SHREW SNIDE TEENY
BITTER DOGGED MALIGN WANTON
HATEFUL HEINOUS LEERING
SPITOUS VICIOUS CANKERED
NARQUOIS SINISTER SPITEFUL
VENOMOUS VIPEROUS
MALIGN ILL FOUL ABUSE LIBEL
WRONG BEWRAY DEFAME REVILE
VILIFY ASPERSE DEPRAVE HURTFUL
SLANDER TRADUCE BLASPHEME
MALIGNANCY FEROCITY
MALIGNANT EVIL ATTRY BLACK
FELON FERAL SWART ATTERY
MALIGN BALEFUL ENVIOUS HATEFUL
HELLISH PEEVISH REPTILE VICIOUS
WARLOCK CANKERED SHREWISH
SPITEFUL VENOMOUS VIPEROUS
VIRULENT WRATHFUL RANCOROUS
(NOT —) BENIGN INNOCENT
MALIGNITY GALL LIVER VENOM
VIRUS HATRED MALICE RANCOR
DESPITE
MALINGER MIKE DODGE SHIRK
SKULK
MALINGERER SCONCER

MALL MART WALK ALLEE
(SHOPPING —) GALLERIA
MALLARD TWISTER
(FLOCK OF —S) SORD SUTE
PADDLING
MALLEABLE MILD SOFT DUCTILE
PLASTIC BATTABLE
MALLEIN MORVIN
MALLEMUCK MOLLIE MALMARSH
MALLET MALL MAUL MELL GAVEL
BEATER BEETLE DRIVER HAMMER
DRESSER FLOGGER STRIKER
PLOWMELL
(— FOR BREAKING CLODS) BILDER
(CURRIER'S —) MACE
(HATTER'S —) BEATER
(PAVER'S —) TUP
(PREF.) MALLEI MALLEO SPHYRA
MALLEUS HAMMER OSSICLE
PLECTRUM
MALLOTHI (FATHER OF —) HEMAN
MALLOW MAW DOCK HOCK ALTEA
KOKIO MALVA MAUVE TAUPE
CHEESE ESCOBA GEMAUVE
ABUTILON PIEPRINT
MALLUCH (FATHER OF —) BANI
MALMSEY MALVASIA MALVOISIE
MALNUTRITION CACHEXY
CACHEXIA CACOTROPHY
MALODOROUS GAMY HIGH NOSY
OLID RANK FETID SMELLY VIROSE
VIROUS NOISOME
MALPRACTICE (UNDERHAND —S)
SKULDUGGERY
MALT WORT
(GROUND —) GRIST
(REMAINS OF —) DRAFF
MALTA (ANCIENT NAME OF —)
MELITA
(CAPITAL OF —) VALLETTA
(ISLAND OF —) GOZO COMINO
(MONEY OF —) LIRA
(TOWN OF —) QORMI RABAT
HAMRUN SLIEMA XAGHRA ZABBAR
BIRKIRKARA
MALTASE GLUCASE
MALTESE CROSS (LIKE A —) PATE
PATEE PATTEE
MALTHA BREA
MALTHOUSE MALTING
MALTOSE AMYLON
MALTREAT MAUL ABUSE DIGHT
DEFOUL DEMEAN HESPIL HUSPEL
MISUSE THREAT BEDEVIL MISGUIDE
MANHANDLE
MALTREATMENT ABUSE
MALVA DOCK MALLOW
MAMAMU MU
MAMBA COBRA ELAPOID
MAMMA MA MOM MAMA WIFE
MOMMA WOMAN MOTHER
MAMMAL OX ASS BAT CAT COW
DOG FOX PIG YAK BEAR BOAR COON

DEER GOAT HARE LION LYNX MINK
MOLE PUMA SEAL ZEBU BEAST
BISON CAMEL COATI COYPU GENET
HORSE HYENA LEMUR LLAMA
MOOSE OKAPI OTTER PANDA RATEL
SABLE SHEEP SHREW SKUNK SLOTH
SWINE TAPIR TIGER WHALE ZORIL
ALPACA ANIMAL BADGER COUGAR
CULPEO DESMAN DUGONG FISHER
FOUSSA GOPHER GRISON JAGUAR
MARTEN MONKEY OCELOT OLINGO
TENREC VICUNA WALRUS WOMBAT
BUFFALO CARIBOU DOLPHIN
ECHIDNA GIRAFFE GLUTTON
GUANACO HIPPOID HUANACO
MANATEE OPOSSUM PECCARY
POLECAT PRIMATE RACCOON
SUCKLER SURICAT TARSIER
TYLOPOD WILDCAT AARDVARK
AARDWOLF ANTELOPE BANXRING
CACOMIXL CREODONT ELEPHANT
FALANAKA HEDGEHOG KINKAJOU
MAMMIFER PANGOLIN PINNIPED
REINDEER SQUIRREL PRONGHORN
RHINOCEROS
(— EXTINCT) STEGODONT
MAMMALIA MASTOZOA
MAMMEE ABRICO ABRICOT
MAMMILLA PAP TEAT NIPPLE
MAMMOTH HUGE LARGE GIGANTIC
MAMRE (BROTHER OF —) ANER
ECHCOL
MAN BO HE BOY GEE GUY HIM LAD
TAO WAT WER BUCK CHAL CHAP
COVE DICK EARL GENT GOME HOMO
JACK JONG MALE RINK TULK BERNE
BIMBO BIPED BLOKE CHURL COVEY
CULLY FORCE FREKE GROOM GUEST
HEART HOMME HORSE JOKER
SEGGE SWAIN WIGHT BIMANE
CHIELD CUFFIN FELLOW HOMBRE
MANTZU WEPMAN BIMANUS
HOMONID KINSMAN MANKIND
(— AFFECTING FOREIGN WAYS)
MACARONI
(— DRESSED AS WOMAN) BESSY
MALINCHE
(— IN DEBT) DYVOUR
(— IN GAMES) PIECE
(— IN PRIVATE STATION) IDIOT
(— IN TUG-OF-WAR) ANCHOR
(— LEADING 12TH NIGHT) BEAN
(— OF ALL WORK) MOZO
(— OF AUTHORITY) AGHA SEIGNIOR
(— OF BEAUTY) APOLLO
(— OF BRASS) TALOS
(— OF COURAGE) LION
(— OF GREAT WEALTH) NABOB
(— OF HIGH RANK) CHAM KHAN
THAKUR GRANDEE
(— OF POWER) MAGNATE
(— OF SUBSTANCE) IDLEMAN
(— OF THE COMMON PEOPLE) JACK

(— OF VIGOR) WYE
(— OF VIOLENCE) RABIATOR
(— OF WAR) ANDREW CARAVEL
CRUISER
(— TO MAN) SINGLE
(ARTIFICIAL —) GOLEM
(ATTRACTIVE —) FOX HUNK
(BACKGAMMON —) BLOT BUILDER
(BALD —) PILGARLIC
(BEST —) BRIDEMAN PARANYMPH
(BIG —) COB BRUISER MUGWUMP
(BLESSED —) BEATUS
(BRISK —) SPARK
(CASTRATED —) SPADO EUNUCH
(CHIEF —) FOREMAN OPTIMATE
(CHURLISH —) NABAL BODACH
(CLEANING —) BUSBOY
(COMMON —) CARL STREET
YEOMAN
(COVETOUS —) HUNKS
(CRAFTY —) FOX
(CRUEL —) OGRE BRUTE
(DISAGREEABLE —) GLEYDE
(DISCREET —) PRUDHOMME
(DISLIKED —) CUT
(DISSOLUTE —) RAKE
(ECCENTRIC —) GEEZER
(EDUCATED —) EFFENDI
(EFFEMINATE —) DILDO FAIRY NANCE
PUNCE SISSY JESSIE COCKNEY
MEACOCK MIDWIFE MILKSOP
ANDROGYN MOLLYCODDLE
(END —) BONES BRAKE
(ENLISTED —) GI SNIPE AIDMAN
AIRMAN KEEPER STORES ARMORER
STRIKER SONARMAN
(ENTIRE —) EGO
(EXTINCT —) TEPEXPAN
(FAITHFUL —) TRUEMAN
(FANCY —) PONCE
(FASHIONABLE —) TOUPET ELEGANT
FOPLING GALLANT
(FIRST —) ASK ADAM ASKR TIKI
FOREMAN
(FLASHILY-DRESSED —) LAIR
(FOPPISH —) BLOOD
(FREE —) LIBER
(GRAY-HAIRED —) GRIZZLE
(GREAT —) VAVASOR
(HARDHEARTED —) KNARK
(HAUGHTY —) BASHAW
(HOLDUP —) FOOTPAD
(HOLY —) SADHU SAINT SANNYASI
(HONORS —) WRANGLER
(IDEAL —) SUPERMAN
(IMMORAL —) REP
(INEFFECTUAL —) DUFFER
(INSANE —) FURIOSO
(LADY'S —) FOPLING DAMMARET
(LAME —) BACACH
(LEARNED) ULEMA LAMDAN
OLLAMH PUNDIT SAVANT SOPHIST
(LECHEROUS —) SATYR

(LEWD —) BROTHEL
(LIAISON —) COURIER
(LITERARY —) GIGADIBS
(LITTLE —) MANNET SHRIMP
MANNIKIN
(LUSTFUL —) GOAT
(MAINTENANCE —) CAMPMAN
(MARRIED —) HUSBAND BENEDICT
(MECHANICAL —) ROBOT
(MEDICINE —) PEAI DOCTOR
SHAMAN ANGAKOK
(MEEK —) MOSES
(MIGHTY —) SAMSON
(ODD-JOB —) JOEY
(OLD —) HAG OLD BOOL CUFF GAFF
CRONE DOBBY UNCLE BODACH
DUFFER FATHER GAFFER NESTOR
GERONTE STARETS ECKEHART
VELYARDE PATRIARCH
(OLD-CLOTHES —) POCO
(ONE-ARMED —) WINGY
(ONE-EYED —) ARIMASP
(ONE-FOOTED —) MONOPODE
(OVERFASTIDIOUS —) DUDE
(PARTY —) SIDESMAN
(POOR —) PAUPER
(PRIMITIVE —) URMENSCH
(PRINCIPAL —) HERO TOPARCH
(RASH —) HOTSPUR
(RICH —) DIVES NABOB CROESUS
(RIGHT-HAND —) HENCHMAN
(RIGHTEOUS —) SADDIK
(SERVING —) GARCON
(SOUND-EFFECTS —) CRAWK
(STERN —) GRIMSIRE
(STRAIGHT —) STOOGE
(STRONG —) KWASIND
(STRONG-ARM —) HOOD GORILLA
(STUPID —) SUBMAN
(SWAGGERING YOUNG —) GREASER
(THICKSET —) GRUB KNAR SPUD
(TOUGH —) KNAR
(UNEMPLOYED —) BATLAN
(UNKNOWN —) INCOGNITO
(UTILITY —) JUMPER
(VICIOUS —) YAHOO
(WEAK —) WIMP
(WELL-BUILT —) HUNK
(WHITE —) BOSTON BUCKRA PAKEHA
CACHILA
(WHITE — LIVING WITH ABORIGINE)
COMBO
(WILD —) WOODMAN WOODWOSE
(WISE —) NAB HAKAM MAGUS
SABIO SOLON SOPHY NESTOR
WIZARD SOLOMON TOHUNGA
(WIZENED —) GNOME
(WOMANISH —) JENNY
(WRETCHED —) CAITIFF
(YOUNG —) BOY LAD JONG PUNK
YOUTH BOCHUR DAMSEL EPHEBE
KNIGHT BOUCHAL BUCKEEN

YOUNKER BOYCHICK COCKEREL
SPRINGAL
(PREF.) ANDR(O) ANTHROP(O)
HOMI(NI)
(SUFF.) ANDRIA ANDROUS ANDRY
ENGRO VIR(ATE)
MAN-ABOUT-TOWN JOHNNY
CLUBMAN FLANEUR
MANABOZHO MICHABOU
WINABOJO
MANACLE BAND BOND DARBY
HAMPER TIRRET SHACKLE
HANDCUFF HANDLOCK
(PL.) IRONS CHAINS
MANAGE DO GET MAN RUN BEAR
BOSS COPE CURB FEND HACK HOLD
KEEP LEAD MAKE RULE TEND TOOL
WIND WORK BROOK CARRY DIGHT
FORTH FRAME GUIDE MAYNE ORDER
SHIFT SPEND STEER SWING WIELD
CONVEY DEMEAN DEVISE DIRECT
FETTLE GOVERN HANDLE INTEND
MANURE TEMPER AGITATE
CONDUCT DISPOSE EXECUTE
FINAGLE HUSBAND MINSTER
OFFICER OPERATE SOLICIT STEWARD
CONTRIVE ENGINEER NEGOTIATE
(— AWKWARDLY) FOOZLE
(— CLUMSILY) KEVEL
(— SKILLFULLY) MANIPULATE
(— SUCCESSFULLY) HACK
(— TO BEAR) AFFORD
(— WITH CARE) NURSE
MANAGEABLE EASY YARE BANTAM
DOCILE WIELDY DUCTILE FLEXIBLE
YIELDING
MANAGEMENT CARE HEEL WORK
CHARGE CONDUCT CONTROL
ECONOMY GESTION RUNNING
CARRIAGE DEMEANOR ENGINERY
MANAGERY MANEUVER REGIMENT
STEERAGE
(DELICATE —) NICETY
(DOMESTIC —) MENAGE
HUSBANDRY
(GOOD —) EUTAXY
(SKILLFUL —) PRACTICE PRACTISE
MANAGER BOSS DOER EXEC AGENT
DAROGA DEPUTY PURSER SYNDIC
AMILDAR CURATOR ERENACH
HUSBAND STEWARD WIELDER
AUMILDAR DIRECTOR DISPOSER
ENGINEER HERENACH INSTITOR
(— OF ENTERTAINERS) ROADIE
(— OF FARM) HIND GRIEVE
(ASSISTANT —) CAPORAL
(MINE —) CAPTAIN
(POLITICAL —) FUGLEMAN
(STAGE —) REGISSEUR
(SUFF.) EER
MANAHATH (FATHER OF —) SHOBAL
MANAKIN PIPRA

MAN-AT-ARMS KNIGHT
MANATEE DUGONG SEACOW
  COWFISH HOGFISH MERMAID
  LAMANTIN MUTILATE SIRENIAN
MANBARKLAK JARANA KAKARAL
MANCALA WARI
MANCHE (— CAPITAL) STLO
MANCHU SHERRY
MANCHURIA (CHINESE NAME FOR
  —) MANCHOW
  (PENINSULA OF —) LIAOTUNG
  (PROVINCE OF —) JILIN LIAONING
  HEILONGJIANG
  (RIVER OF —) AMUR LIAO YALU
  ARGUN USSURI SUNGARI
MANDAEAN SABAEAN
MANDANE (FATHER OF —)
  ASTYAGES
  (HUSBAND OF —) CAMBYSES
  (SON OF —) CYRUS
MANDARIN TOWKAY CHINESE
MANDARIN ORANGE SATSUMA
MANDATE BREVE ORDER BEHEST
  CHARGE DECREE FIRMAN BIDDING
  COMMAND PRECEPT PROCESS
  MANDAMUS MANDATUM
  WARRANTY
  (— OF GOD) JUDGMENT
MANDATORY OBLIGATORY
MANDIBLE BEAK JOWL SETA
  RAMUS JAWBONE GNATHITE
  (— PART) MALA
MANDINGO MANDE MALINKE
  WANGARA
MANDOLIN OUD MANDORA
MANDRAKE ALRAUN DUDAIM
MANDREL ROD BALL STUD SLEEVE
  CHEMISE SPINDLE TRIBLET
MANDRICARDO
  (BELOVED OF —) ANGELICA
  (FATHER OF —) AGRICAN
  (SLAYER OF —) ORLANDO
MANDRILL MAIMON MORMON
MANE JUBA MONE CREST PITRI
  ENCOLURE
MAN-EATER
  (PL.) ANTHROPOPHAGI REQUIN
  REQUIEM
MANEGE TRAIN
MANEUVER PLAY TURN WISE
  GAMBIT JOCKEY MANURE PESADE
  VRILLE FINAGLE FINESSE ARTIFICE
  DEMARCHE ENGINEER EXERCISE
  STRATEGY WINDLASS
  (— GENTLY) EASE
  (— IN AUTO RACING) SLINGSHOT
  (— IN SPACE) DOCK
  (— IN SURFING) CUTBACK
  (— OF MOTORCYCLE OR BICYCLE)
  WHEELIE
  (AERIAL —) BUNT LOOP SPIN
  FISHTAIL WINGOVER

  (BICYCLE —) WHEELIE
  (BULLFIGHTING —) VERONICA
  (ILLEGAL —) GAME
  (KIND OF —) HEIMLICH VALSALVA
  (ROADWAY —) UTURN
  (ROCK-CLIMBING —) LAYBACK
  (SKIING —) SNOWPLOW
  (VEHICLE —) WHEELIE
  (WRESTLING —) ESCAPE BUTTOCK
MANEUVERABLE YAR YARE
MANEUVERING FINESSE FLANKING
  FOOTWORK
MANEUVRE (DRESSAGE —) PESADE
MANGE ITCH REEF SCAB CANKER
  DARTARS SCABIES
MANGER BIN BUNK CRIB HECK
  STALL CRATCH
MANGLE MAR HACK IRON MOUTH
  BRUISE GARBLE HACKLE IRONER
  MAGGLE MURDER MAMMOCK
  LACERATE MUTILATE
MANGO DIKA AMHAR AMINI BAUNO
  AMCHOOR CARABAO PAHUTAN
  (POINT OF —) NAK
MANGOSTEEN SANTOL GARCINIA
MANGROVE BACAO GORAN
  MANGLE MYRTAL BACAUAN
  CERIOPS COURIDA HANGALAI
  LANGARAI
MANGUE CHOLUTECA CHOROTEGA
MANGY SCABBY ROINISH SCABETIC
MANHANDLE MAUL MESS ROUGH
  SCRAG WORKOVER
MANHATTAN ROBROY
MANHATTAN TRANSFER
  (AUTHOR OF —) DOSPASSOS
  (CHARACTER IN —) BUD GUS JOE
  HERE JOHN RUTH STAN CONGO
  ELLEN EMERY EMILE HARRY JIMMY
  SUSIE GEORGE MCNIEL NELLIE
  OKEEFE PRYNNE BALDWIN HARLAND
  MERIVALE PEARLINE THATCHER
  GOLDWEISER OGLETHORPE
MANHOOD ADAMHOOD
MANIA RAGE CRAZE FUROR FRENZY
  DELIRIUM HYSTERIA INSANITY
  CACOETHES
MANIAC KILLER MADMAN FANATIC
  LUNATIC
  (KIND OF —) EGO
MANIFEST HAVE NUDE OPEN RIFE
  SENE SHOW APERT CLEAR FRANK
  GROSS KITHE NAKED OVERT PLAIN
  PROVE SPEAK SUTEL ARRANT
  ATTEST COUTHE EVINCE EXTANT
  GRAITH LIQUID OSTEND PATENT
  PHANIC APPROVE BETOKEN
  CONFESS DECLARE EVIDENT EXHIBIT
  EXPRESS OBVIOUS SIGNIFY VISIBLE
  APPARENT DISCLOSE DISCOVER
  INDICATE PALPABLE PROCLAIM
  (NOT —) LATENT

(PREF.) PHANER(O) PHANTA(SMO) PHANTO

MANIFESTATION ACT SON BEAM COMA SIGN GLINT AVATAR COMING EFFECT OSTENT ADVANCE DISPLAY EXPRESS OUTSIDE SHOWING EPIPHANY MANIFEST
(BARELY PERCEPTIBLE —) SCINTIL
(BRIEF —) GLEAM
(DIVINE —) SPIRIT SHEKINAH
(HORRIBLE —) CHIMAERA
(MORAL —) SOUL
(VAGUE —) GLIMMER
(SUFF.) PHANE PHANOUS PHANT PHANY

MANIFESTLY WITTERLY
MANIFESTO PLACARD
MANIFOLD MANY TURRET VARIOUS FELEFOLD MANYFOLD MULTIPLE MULTIPLEX REPLICATE
(SUFF.) PLOID

MANIKIN ECORCHE PANTINE PHANTOM HOMUNCIO HOMUNCLE MANNIKIN

MANILA HEMP ABACA
MANIOC CASSAVA CATELLA MANDIOCA

MANIPLE BAND FANON ORALE FANNEL COMPANY HANDFUL SUDARIUM

MANIPULATE COG RIG COAX COOK DIAL FAKE HAND STIR TOOL CROOK HUMOR KNEAD SHAPE TREAT WIELD CHIVVY GOVERN HANDLE JOCKEY MANAGE WANGLE MASSAGE SHUFFLE
(— BY DECEPTIVE MEANS) RIG
(— DISHONESTLY) RIG SHUFFLE
(— FRAUDULENTLY) FIDDLE

MANIPULATION PASS JUGGLERY MANAGERY

MANITO ORENDA POKUNT MANITOU TAMANOAS

MANITOBA (CAPITAL OF —) WINNIPEG
(RIVER OF —) RED SEAL SWAN NELSON ROSEAU SOURIS PEMBINA CHURCHILL SASKACHEWAN
(TOWN OF —) CARMAN BRANDON DAUPHIN KILLARNEY SWANRIVER

MANKIND MAN FLESH SHEEP WORLD BIMANA SPECIES HUMANITY UNIVERSE MORTALITY

MANLIKE MALE MANLY MANNISH HOMINOID

MANLINESS ARETE VIRTUS MANSHIP

MANLY BOLD MALE HARDY MANNY DARING VIRILE MANLIKE

MAN-MADE SYNTHETIC UNNATURAL CULTURAL SYNTHETIC

MANNA TREHALA WINDFALL

MANNER AIR BAT JET LAT WAY FORM GAET GARB GATE KIND MAKE MIEN MODE RATE SORT THEW TOUR WISE WONE GUISE LATES SHAPE STYLE TENUE TRICK COURSE CUSTOM METHOD MISTER STRAIN ADDRESS AMENITY FASHION QUALITY QUOMODO CARAPACE DEMEANOR LANGUAGE
(— OF APPROACH) ABORD
(— OF DOING) ACTION
(— OF HANDLING) HAND
(— OF MAKING ANYTHING) FACTURE
(— OF PERFORMING) HAND
(— OF SITTING) ASANA
(— OF SPEAKING) SLUR SOUGH ACCENT GRAMMAR PARLANCE
(— OF SWIMMING) STROKE
(— OF WALKING) STEP
(AFFECTED —) AIR
(AMUSING —) DROLLERY
(ARROGANT —) BRAG HAUTEUR
(CHARACTERISTIC —) TOUCH
(EMOTIONAL —) STRAIN
(FORBIDDING —) SHELL
(FORMAL —) STARCH
(GRAND —) PANACHE
(HABITUAL —) SONG
(LIVELY —) JAZZ
(OUTWARD —) TOUR FRONT
(RESTRAINED —) RESERVE
(SECRET —) STEALTH
(SMOOTH —) JAPAN
(SWAGGERING —) SIDE PANACHE
(UNUSUAL —) SINGULARITY
(USUAL —) HABIT
(PL.) ADDRESS CORNERS HAVINGS BREEDING
(SUFF.) WISE
(AFTER THE — OF) FASHION
(IN A —) LY
(IN THE — OF) IC(AL)

MANNERED CUTE CUTESY MORATE THEWED

MANNERISM TIC POSE TRICK IDIASM
(EXAGGERATED —) CAMP
(PL.) DAPS

MANNERLY CIVIL POLITE
MANNERS MORES HAVANCE HAVINGS PSANDOS BEAUETRY BREEDING

MANNITOL MANNITE PUNICIN
MANOAH (SON OF —) SAMSON
MAN-OF-WAR CARAVEL
MAN-OF-WAR FISH PASTOR
MANON (CHARACTER IN —) MANON GRIEUX LESCAUT BRETIGNY
(COMPOSER OF —) MASSENET

MANON LESCAUT (CHARACTER IN —) MANON GRIEUX GERONTE
(COMPOSER OF —) PUCCINI

MANOR HAM HOF BURY HALL TOWN VILL BARONY ESTATE COMMOTE MANSION LORDSHIP TOWNSHIP
MANPOWER BRAWN LABOR
MANROOT IPOMOEA
MANROPE LIMMER
MANSERVANT
(ALSO SEE SERVANT) LAD MOZO GROOM VALET ANDREW BUTLER TEABOY
MANSFIELD PARK (AUTHOR OF —) AUSTEN
(CHARACTER IN —) TOM MARY WARD FANNY HENRY JULIA MARIA PRICE YATES EDMUND NORRIS THOMAS BERTRAM CRAWFORD RUSHWORTH
MANSION DOME SEAT HOTEL HOUSE MANSE SIEGE TOWER CASTLE HARBOR HOSTEL CHATEAU
(— OF THE MOON) ALNATH
MANSLAUGHTER BLOOD FELONY HOMICIDE
MANTEL CLAVY CLAVEL
MANTELET MANTA MANTLE MANTLET GALAPAGO
MANTELPIECE BRACE PAREL CLAVEL MANTEL MANTLING
MANTICORE MONTEGRE
MANTIS CAGN RACER REARER MANTOID PROPHET
MANTIS CRAB SQUILLA
MANTIS SHRIMP SQUILL
MANTLE CAPA HOSE PALL REAM ROBE CLOAK CREAM FROCK JABUL LAMDA PALLA TUNIC CAMAIL CAPOTE KHIRKA KIRTLE ROCHET SLAVIN SOLMAN TABARD CHLAMYS CHRISOM CHUDDAR FERIDJI MANTEAU PAENULA PALLIUM SLEEVES WHITTLE WRAPPER BARRACAN CHRYSOME MANTELET REGOLITH RICINIUM STOCKING
(PREF.) CHLAMYD(O) PHARO
MANTLEROCK REGOLITH
MANTO (DAUGHTER OF —) TISIPHONE
(FATHER OF —) HERCULES TIRESIAS
(HUSBAND OF —) RHACIUS
(SON OF —) OCNUS MOPSUS AMPHILOCHUS
MANTRA OM DHARANI GAYATRI MANTRAM SAVITRI
MANTUA MANTY SEMAR
MANTZU MIAOTZE
MANUAL VADY COACH GREAT TUTOR PORTAS CAMBIST CEMBALO DIDACHE MANUARY BOMBARDE HANDBOOK KEYBOARD ORDINARY PORTHORS SYNOPSIS
(MAGICIAN'S —) GRIMOIRE
(NAVIGATION —) BOWDITCH

MANUAO IAO
MANUBRIUM HYPOSTOME
MANUFACTORY ARSENAL
MANUFACTURE COIN FAKE MAKE FORGE PERFORM PRODUCE WORKING BOOKWORK
(— OF LIQUOR OR DRUGS) ABKARI
(ILLEGAL —) COINING
MANUFACTURED STORE
MANUFACTURER BRAND MAKER WRIGHT DISKERY SPINNER SUPPLIER
(ORIGINAL EQUIPMENT —) OEM
MANUMIT FREE DELIVER RELEASE LIBERATE
MANURE HOT MIG DUNG LIME MUCK SAUR SOIL TATH FECES GUANO MIXEN FULZIE SEASON SLEECH COMPOST FOLDING GOODING POUDRET DRESSING WORTHING
MANURED BONED
MANUS HAND
MANUSCRIPT CODEX FLIMSY MATTER SCRIPT UNCIAL CURSIVE PANDECT PAPYRUS PINTURA WITNESS EXEMPLAR PARCHMENT
MANX CAT RUMPY
MANX SHEARWATER CREW PUFFIN SCRABE SCRABER
MANY TEN ALOT FELE LOTS MUCH SERE SLEW FORTY GREAT MAINT MOULT SCADS OODLES TWENTY ENDLESS JILLION SEVERAL VARIOUS BEAUCOUP MANIFOLD COUNTLESS
(BEING —) NUMEROUS
(GOOD —) HANTLE
(GREAT —) MORT RAFF SWITH
(PREF.) MULT(I) PLURI POLY
(HOW —) POSO QUOT
MANYATTA KRAAL
MANY-COLORED POLYCHROME BONT
MANY-HANDED BRIAREAN
MANYPLIES FARDEL OMASUM MANIFOLD PSATERIUM
MANYROOT RUELLIA
MANY-SIDED VERSATILE VARIOUS
MAO NEHRU
MAOCH (SON OF —) ACHISH
MAORI
(— IMAGE) TIKI
(— LAW) UTU
(— VILLAGE) PA PAH KAINGA
(NOT —) PAKEMA
MAP KEY CARD DICE PLAT PLOT CARTE CENTO CHART DRAFT INSET QUART STILL DRAUGHT GRAPHIC CARTGRAM GATEFOLD PLATFORM CARTOGRAM
(— OF HEAVENS) HOROSCOPE
(CELESTIAL —) PLANISPHERE
(PREF.) CARTO CHARTO

MAPAU MAPLE MATIPO TARATA
PIRIPIRI
MAPLE MAZER DOGWOOD
SYCAMORE WINGSEED
(FLOWERING —) ABUTILON
(GROVE OF —) SAPBUSH
MAQUILLAGE MAKEUP
MAR BLOT SCAR SMIT SNIP BLOOM
BOTCH SHEND SPILL SPOIL BLOTCH
DEFACE DEFEAT DEFORM EFFACE
IMPAIR INJURE MANGLE BLEMISH
DISGRACE
MARABOU STORK ARGALA
MORABIT ADJUTANT
MARANAO LANAO
MARASMUS MARCOR ATHREPSIA
MARAUD RAID DACOIT PICKEER
PILLAGE
MARAUDER TORY BANDIT BUMMER
LOOTIE PIRATE CATERAN LADRONE
(PL.) BLACKS
MARAUDING BANDITRY OUTRIDING
MARBLE MIB MIG PEA TAW ALLY
BOOL BOWL DUCK DUMP MARL
AGATE AGGIE ALLEY BONCE COMMY
IMMIE IVORY LINER PUREY RANCE
DOGGLE MARMOR MARVEL MIGGLE
PARIAN PEEWEE STEELY CARRARA
CIPOLIN GLASSIE GRIOTTE KNICKER
PARAGON PITCHER SHOOTER
BROCATEL DOLOMITE KNUCKLER
(— WORKER'S TOOL) BURIN
(BLACK —) JET
(IMITATION —) SCAGLIOLA
(SIENA —) BROCATELLO
(PL.) TAW BOWLS PLUMPS HUNDRED
MARBLED MIRLY
MARCH FILE HIKE LIDE MARK MUSH
SLOG ROUTE TRACE TRINE TROOP
WALTZ DEFILE DOUBLE PARADE
REVIEW DEBOUCH STRETCH
FOOTSLOG PROGRESS
(— BEHIND) COVER
(— IN FRONT OF) LEAD
(— OBLIQUELY) INCLINE
(DAY'S —) ETAPE
(START OF —) HUP
(PL.) FRONTIER
MARCHING (— UP) ANABASIS
MARCHIONESS MARCHESA
MARQUISE
MARCOT GOOTE
MARCOTTAGE GOOTEE
MARE SEA YAD YADE YAUD GILLIE
GILLOT GRASNI HUNTRESS
MARE'S-TAIL HIPPURID
MARGARET MEG META MARGET
MARGOT GRETCHEN
MARGARINE BUTTERINE
MARGATE PORGY
MARGAY TIGER
MARGIN HEM RIM VAT BANK BRIM
BROW CURB EDGE FOLD HAIR INCH

LIMB LIST RAND BRINK EAVES
MARGE VERGE BORDER FRINGE
LABRUM LACING CUSHION
DRAUGHT MARGENT SELVAGE
HAIRLINE
(— OF CARAPACE) DOUBLURE
(— OF CIRCLE) LIMB
(— OF LIP) PROLABIUM
(— OF PAGE) BACK
(— OF SAFETY) LEEWAY
(— OF SEA) STRAND
(— OF SHELL) LABRUM LIMBUS
(— OF SUPERIORITY) LEAD
(— OF WING) TERMEN
(—S OF HERD) SWING
(NARROW —) ACE NECK WHISKER
(SEA —) COAST
MARGOSA NIM NEEM NEEMBA
MARGRAVE RUDIGER MARKGRAF
MARIA (FATHER OF —) OCTAVIO
PETROBIUS
(HUSBAND OF —) PETRUCHIO
MARIANA SILYBUM
MARIGOLD GOLD GULL SAMH
AZTEC BOOTS GOLDE GOOLS HELIO
BACLIN BUDDLE GOLDCUP GOLDING
GOLLAND KINGCUP MARYBUD
TAGETES
MARIJUANA BOO POT HERB WEED
DAGGA GANJA GRASS GANJAH
MOOCAH CANNABIS CARNABIS
LOCOWEED MARYJANE PANAMARED
SINSEMILLA
(BUTT OF — CIGARETTE) ROACH
(CHEMICAL IN —) THC
(KILOGRAM OF —) KEY
(ONE OUNCE OF —) LID
(ONE WHO SMOKES —) POTHEAD
(ONE WHO TAKES —) POTHEAD
(OUNCE OF —) CAN LID
(PUFF ON — CIGARETTE) TOKE
MARINA DOCK BASIN BOATEL
MARINADE SOUSE
MARINE JOLLY GALOOT GULPIN
GYRENE TOPMAN MARINAL
HALIMOUS MARITIME NAUTICAL
AEQUOREAL THALASSIC THALASSIAN
(PREF.) ENALI(O) THALASS(O)
THALASSI(O) THALATTO
MARINER MARINE SAILOR SEALER
SEAMAN BUSCARLE SEAFARER
WARRENER
(PL.) SEAFOLK
MARINHEIRO ACAJOU
MARIONETTE PUPPY POPPET
PUPPET
MARITAL INTIMATE HUSBANDLY
MARITIME MARINE HALIMOUS
NAUTICAL
MARJORAM ORIGAN ORIGANE
AMARACUS
MARK AIM END HOB HUB MOT POP
BELT BLOT BUOY BUTT CHOP CLIP

DELE DINT FAZE FIST GOAL KEEL
LINE MIND NOTE RIST SCAR SEAR
SIGN SMOT SMUT SPOT TEND TEXT
TICK VIRE WAND WIND BADGE
BOTTU BRAND BREVE CHANT CHECK
CLOUD DATUM DITTO DRAFT FLECK
FRANK GHOST GRADE HACEK HILUM
KNIFE LABEL MARCH MARCO MEITH
NOKTA POINT PRINT PROOF ROVER
SCART SCOPE SCORE SCUFF SPOOR
STAMP SWIRL TOKEN TOUCH TRACE
TRACK TRACT WATCH WHITE
ACCENT ALPIEU BEACON BESPOT
BLOTCH BUTTON CARACT DAGGER
DAPPLE DENOTE DIRECT INDICE
LETTER MARKER NOTICE OBJECT
SMUTCH STREAK STRIKE STROKE
SUCKER SYMBOL TARGET UPSHOT
WICKER WITTER BETOKEN CEDILLA
CHARBON COCKSHY DEMERIT
DIAMOND DRAUGHT EROTEME
EXCUDIT FINMARK IMPRESS IMPRINT
INSIGNE KENMARK SCARIFY
SERRATE SIGNARY SPECKLE STRIATE
SYMPTOM VESTIGE WAYMARK
BRACELET CROWFOOT DATEMARK
DIASTOLE DISPUNCT EVIDENCE
FOOTMARK FOOTSTEP IDENTIFY
IDEOGRAM MONUMENT NOTATION
(— A BIRD) BAND
(— AFTER ASSAY) TOUCH
(— AO PAID) RECEIPT
(— AS SPURIOUS) ATHETIZE
(— BOUNDS) STAKE
(— BY BURNING) CHAR
(— BY CUTTING) SCRIBE
(— BY PLOWING) STRIKE
(— CROSSWISE) CRANK
(— DENOTING CORRUPT PASSAGE)
OBELUS
(— DIRECTIONS) ADDRESS
(— IN ARCHERY) CLOUT HOYLE
ROVER WHITE
(— IN BOOK) PRESSMARK
(— IN CANON) LEAD
(— IN CURLING) TEE COCK
(— INDICATING CONTRACTION)
CORONIS
(— INDICATING DIRECTION) ARROW
(— IN QUOITS) MOT
(— OF ACKNOWLEDGEMENT)
ACCOLADE
(— OF CADENCY) MARTLET
(— OF CONDEMNATION) THETA
(— OF DISGRACE) STAIN STIGMA
(— OF DISHONOR) ABATEMENT
(— OF DISTINCTION) BELT
(— OF ESTEEM) LAUREL GARLAND
(— OFF) DIVIDE STRIKE SUBTEND
(— OFF LAND) FEER PHEER
(— OF OFFICE) SEAL
(— OF OWNERSHIP) SWANMARK
(— OF PURITY) HALLMARK

(— OF RANK) PIP
(— OF REFERENCE) OBELISK
(— OF SERVITUDE) YOKE
(— OF SIGNATURE) CROSS
(— OF SUPERIORITY) BELL
(— OF WEAVER) KEEL
(— ON ANIMAL'S FACE) BLAZE
STRIPE
(— ON CHART) VIGIA
(— ON DICE) PIP
(— ON EXAM) PASS
(— ON FEATHER) BAR SPANGLE
(— ON FOREHEAD) KUMKUM
(— ON PENNSYLVANIA BARNS)
HEXAFOOS
(— ON SHEEP) SMIT BUIST
(— ON SHIP) SURMARK
(— ON SKIN) PLOT CREASE
(— ON STAMP) CONTROL
(— OUT) BLIN CANCEL DELINE
AIRMARK APPOINT COMPART
DESCRIBE
(— OVER GERMAN VOWEL) UMLAUT
(— OVER LETTER N) TILDE
(— OVER LONG VOWELS) MACRON
(— RIGS) FEER
(— SHEEP OR CATTLE) BASTE BUIST
DEWLAP
(— TIME) BEAT COUNT
(— TO BE ATTAINED) BOGEY BOGIE
(— TO GUIDE VESSELS) MYTH
(— TO SCARE DEER) SHEWEL
(— TRANSVERSELY) LADDER
(— UNDER LETTER C) CEDILLA
(— UNDER SIGNATURE) PARAPH
(— WITH LINES) HATCH CAMLET
(WITH POINTED ROLLER) GRILL
(— WITH RED) RUBRICATE
(— WITH RIDGES) RIB
(— WITH STRIPES) WALE STREAM
(— WITH TAR) BASTE
(ACCENT —) VERGE
(ANGULAR —) HOOK
(AVERAGE —) CEE
(BALLOT —) SCRATCH
(BOUNDARY —) DOOL MEAR MERE
TERM WIKE MEITH STAKE
LANDMARK
(CADENCY —) BRISURE
(CANCELLATION —) BUMPER KILLER
(CIRCULAR —) SEAL
(CON MAN'S —) DUPE
(CURLY —) TWIDDLE
(DIACRITICAL —) TIL BREVE GRAVE
HACEK TILDE MACRON TITTLE
(DIRTY —) SMIRCH
(DISTINCTIVE —) BADGE INDICIA
(DISTINGUISHING —) ITEM COCARDE
EARMARK INSIGNE
(DOUBLE-DAGGER —) DIESIS
(EAGY —) YAP SMELT PIGEON
(EIGHTH —) URE
(EXACT —) NICK

(EXCLAMATION —) SCREAMER
(IDENTIFICATION —) MOLE CREST
SPLIT SIGNET WATTLE EARMARK
KENMARK LUGMARK COLOPHON
(LOW-WATER —) DATUM
(MAGICAL —) SIGIL
(MERIDIAN —) MIRE
(MUSICAL —) PRESA CORONA
(NAVIGATION —) PERCH
(PARAGRAPH —) PILCROW
(POOR —) DEE
(PRINTER'S —) PARALLEL
(PROOFREADER'S —) STET CARET
DELE
(PUNCTUATION —) DASH STOP
BRACE BREVE COLON COMMA
HYPHEN PERIOD BRACKET DIERESIS
ELLIPSIS DIACRITIC SEMICOLON
PARENTHESIS
(RANDOM —) ROVER
(RED —) HICKEY
(SCORING —) TALLY
(SECTARIAN —) BOTTU TILAKA
(SERVICE —) COMSAT
(SKATE —) CUSP
(SMALL ROUND —) DOT
(SURVEYOR'S —) PICKET
(TRAMP'S —) MONICA MONNIKER
(WHITE —) RACHE
(PL.) POINTING
(PREF.) STIGONO
MARKED FAR GREAT SCORED
SEVERE SPOTTY COLORED EMINENT
MARCATO POINTED SCARRED
SPECKED SPOTTED
(— BY COLORED RINGS) AREOLATE
(— BY FURROWS) RIVOSE
(— BY INTELLIGENCE) ABLE
(— BY PROSTRATION) ALGID
(— BY REFINEMENT) ELEGANT
(— BY RIDGES) SERRIED
(— BY SHREWDNESS) ADROIT
(— BY SIMILARITY) AKIN
(— BY SIMPLICITY) ATTIC
(— BY WAVY LINES) GYROSE
(— OUT) DISTINCT
(— SPOTS OR LINES) MACULATE
(— UP) FOUL
(— WITH BANDS) ZONATE
(— WITH SMALLPOX) FRETTEN
(— WITH SPOTS OR LINES) NOTATE
(— WITH WHITE) BAUSOND
(EXTREMELY —) INTENSE
MARKEDLY BYOUS
MARKER HOB HUB IOU DOLE FLAG
MARK SPAD STUMP TYPER BUTTON
GUIDON HOBBLE HUBBLE TABBER
DAYMARK SCRIBER
(BRIDGE —) PYLON
(STONE —) STELE
MARKET CURB GUNJ MART PORT
SALE SOOK SOUK VEND VENT
CHEAP CROSS GUNGE HALLE PASAR

PRICE TRONE TRYST BAZAAR
BOURSE MERCAT OUTLET PARIAN
RIALTO STAPLE POULTRY CHEAPING
DEBOUCHE EMPORIUM EXCHANGE
MACELLUM
(CATTLE —) TRISTE
(KIND OF —) BEAR BULL FLEA
OPENAIR
(MEAT —) SHAMBLES
(OLD CLOTHES —) RAGFAIR
MARKETABLE SUK SUQ SOUK
STAPLE SALABLE VENDIBLE
MARKET-DAY NUNDINE
MARKETING (SYSTEM OF —)
ADMASS
MARKETPLACE SUK SUQ SAUK
SOOK SOUK TRON AGORA CHAWK
CHOWK HALLE PLAZA BAZAAR
RIALTO EMPORIUM
MARKET-TOWN BORGO
MARKING EYE HOOD COLLAR
CLOUDING SCARRING SCRIBING
(— OF WOOD) CURL GRAIN
(— ON FEATHER) SPANGLE
(— ON MARS) CANAL
(—S ON STEEL) DAMASK
(ANIMAL —) SADDLE SHIELD
(CATTLE —) JINGLEBOB
(CRESCENT-SHAPED —) LUNULA
LUNULE
(DROP-SHAPED —) GUTTA
(POSTAL —) INDICIA OVERPRINT
(RINGLIKE —) ANNULUS
(STRIPED —) STRAKE
MARKKA FINMARK
MARKSMAN SHOT MARKER
PLUFFER SHOOTER SHOTMAN
SHOOTIST
MARL MALM MARLITE
MARLI MARIE
MARLIN AU AGUJA
MARLINESPIKE FID JAEGER
PRICKER STABBER
MARMALADE CHEESE SQUISH
CODINIAC
MARMALADE TREE CHICO MAMEY
MAMMIE SAPOTE ZAPOTE
MARMOSET MICO TITI SAGOIN
JACCHUS OUITITI QUIRCAL SAIMIRI
TAMARIN WISTITI ORABASSU
MARMOT BOBAC PAHMI GOPHER
SUSLIK SCIURID SIFFLEUR
WHISTLER
MARMOTA ARCTOMYS
MAROON AZTEC ENISLE PICNIC
STRAND CIMARRON
MARQUEE TENT CANOPY
MARQUISE
MARQUETRY INLAY
MARQUISE NAVETTE
MARQUISETTE LENO
MARRAM SEAREED MATGRASS
MATWEED

MARRANOS ANUSIM
MARRED CUPPY SCABBY SLURRED
  SPECKED
MARRIAGE MUTA DAIVA HYMEN
  KARAO UNION BEENAH BRIDAL
  BUCKLE SPLICE SPOUSE EXOGAMY
  NUPTIAL PUNALUA SPOUSAL
  WEDDING WEDLOCK CONUBIUM
  LEVIRATE OPSIGAMY
  (— AFTER DEATH OF FIRST SPOUSE)
  DIGAMY
  (— AT ADVANCED AGE) OPSIGAMY
  (— BELOW POSITION) HYPOGAMY
  (— CONTRACT) KETUBAH
  (— OUTSIDE FAMILY) EXOGAMY
  (— PORTION) TOCHER
  (— VOW) IDO
  (— WITH AN INFERIOR)
  MESALLIANCE
  (— WITHIN GROUP) ENDOGAMY
  (COMMUNAL —) HETAIRISM
  (SECOND —) BIGAMY
  (PREF.) GAMO
  (SUFF.) GAM(AE)(IST)(OUS)(Y)
  GAMETE
MARRIAGEABLE NUBILE
MARRIED COVERT WEDDED
  ESPOUSED
  (NOT —) SOLE
MARROW KEEST MARIE MERCH
  MERGH MEDULLA
  (PREF.) MEDULLI MYELINO MYEL(O)
  MYELO
  (SUFF.) MYELIA MYELITIS
MARRY TIE WED FAST WIFF WIVE
  CLEEK HITCH MATCH BUCKLE
  CROTCH ENSURE MARROW SPLICE
  HUSBAND NUPTIAL WEDLOCK
  DESPOUSE
  (— OFF) BESTOW
  (— UNSUITABLY) MISYOKE
  (PREF.) GAMETO GAMO
  (SUFF.) GAM(AE)(IST)(OUS)(Y)
  GAMETE
MARS ARES MAMERS MARMAR
  MAVORS MASPITER TEUTATES
  (FATHER OF —) JUPITER
  (MOTHER OF —) JUNO
  (SON OF —) REMUS ROMULUS
  (PREF.) AREO
MARSH BOG FEN HAG CARR DANK
  FELL FLAM FLAT HOPE JHIL MASH
  MIRE OOZE QUAG ROSS SOIL SUDS
  TARN VLEI VLEY WASH WHAM FLASH
  GLADE JHEEL LIMAN SLACK SLASH
  SLUMP SWAMP MORASS PALUDE
  PUDDLE CIENAGA CORCASS
  POCOSIN PONTINE QUAGMIRE
  STROTHER TURLOUGH
  (SALT —) SALT SEBKA SALINA
  SALINE
  (PREF.) ELO HELO LIMN(I)(O)
  PALUDI

MARSHAL ARRAY ORDER MUSTER
  PARADE JERONIMO MARECHAL
  MOBILIZE
  (— FACTS) HASH
MARSHALL ISLANDS (CAPITAL:)
  MAJURO
  (COIN:) DOLLAR
  (ISLAND:) JALUIT MAJURO
  ENIWETOK KWAJALEIN
  (LANGUAGE:) ENGLISH JAPANESE
  MARSHALLESE
  (PEOPLE:) MARSHALLESE
MARSH BOG QUAG
MARSHBUCK SITUTUNGA
MARSH ELDER JACKO
MARSH FEVER HELODES
MARSH GAS METHANE
MARSH HARRIER PUDDOCK
  PUTTOCK
MARSHLAND MAREMMA
MARSHMALLOW MALLOW
  WYMOTE
MARSH MARIGOLD BOOTS CAPER
  CRAZY GOOLS DRAGON GAMOND
  GOWLAN COWSLIP ELKSLIP
  GOLDCUP KINGCOB KINGCUP
  MARYBUD DRUNKARD
MARSH PENNYWORT PENNYROT
  WATERCUP
MARSH PINK SABBATIA
MARSH TEA LEDUM
MARSH TREFOIL BUCKBEAN
MARSH WREN LONGBILL
MARSHY BOGGY FOGGY MOORY
  MOSSY PONDY SNAPY SPEWY
  CALLOW MARISH PLASHY QUAGGY
  QUASHY SLUMPY HELODES
  MOORISH PALUDAL QUEACHY
  PALUDINE WATERISH
MARSILEA NARDOO
MARSUPIAL KOALA QUOLL CUSCUS
  POSSUM QUOKKA WOMBAT
  BETTONG DASYURE OPOSSUM
  POTOROO KANGAROO BANDICOOT
  PETAURIST
MARSUPIUM POUCH
MART STAPLE EMPORIUM
MARTEN FOIN PEKAN SABLE SOBOL
  FISHER MARTRIX MUSTELID
  MUSTELIN
  (GROUP OF —S) RICHESSE
  (SUFF.) ICTIS
MARTENSITE SORBITE
MARTHA (BROTHER OF —) LAZARUS
  (CHARACTER IN —) JULIA NANCY
  LIONEL MARTHA HARRIET PLONKETT
  (COMPOSER OF —) FLOTOW
  (SISTER OF —) MARY
MARTIAL BELLIC WARLIKE WARRIOR
  BELLICAL MILITARY
  (— ART) TAEKWONDO
MARTIAL ARTS BUDO JUDO KENDO
  AIKIDO KARATE JUJITSU

(— SCHOOL) DOJO
(— TRAINEE) NINJA
(PERSON TRAINED IN —) NINJA
  KARATE KUNGFU
MARTIN MARTLET SWALLOW
  MARTINET
MARTIN CHUZZLEWIT
(AUTHOR OF —) DICKENS
(CHARACTER IN —) GAMP MARK
  MARY SETH JONAS MERCY SARAH
  GRAHAM MARTIN TAPLEY ANTHONY
  CHARITY PECKSNIFF CHUZZLEWIT
MARTINI GIBSON
(KIND OF —) VODKA
MARTINMAS TERM
MARTYR STEPHEN WITNESS
  SUFFERER
MARTYRDOM MARTYRY PASSION
MARVEL MARL MUSE FERLY
  SELLY ADMIRE WONDER
  MAGNALE MIRACLE MONSTER
  PORTENT PRODIGY SELCOUTH
  ADMIRATION
MARVELOUS FAB SUPER SUPERB
  EPATANT MIRIFIC STRANGE
  FABULOUS WONDROUS
  MIRACULOUS
MARVY RAD COOL
MARX BROTHERS (ONE OF —)
  CHICO HARPO ZEPPO GROUCHO
MARY MOLL POLL MAMIE MAURA
  MOLLY MIRIAM MARILLA
MARY JANE MARIJUANA

MARYLAND
BATTLESITE: ANTIETAM
CAPITAL: ANNAPOLIS
COLLEGE: HOOD GOUCHER STJOHNS
COUNTY: KENT CECIL TALBOT
  CALVERT HARFORD ALLEGANY
  SOMERSET
INDIAN: CONOY NANTICOKE
LAKE: PRETTYBOY
MOUNTAIN: BACKBONE
NATIVE: WESORT TERRAPIN
NICKNAME: COCKADE OLDLINE
RIVER: CHESTER POTOMAC
  CHOPTANK PATUXENT
STATE BIRD: ORIOLE
STATE TREE: OAK
TOWN: BELAIR DENTON EASTON
  ELKTON TOWSON LAPLATA
  ABERDEEN BETHESDA POCOMOKE
  BALTIMORE

MARYSOLE CARTER LEADER
  CARTARE
MARZIPAN MARCHPANE
(— BASE) ALMOND
MASAI WAKWAFI WAKWAVI
MASCEZEL (BROTHER OF —)
  GILDO
MASCOT BILLIKEN

MASCULINE MALE BUTCH DOGGY
  MACHO RUDAS VIRILE LALAQUI
  MANLIKE
(EXAGGERATEDLY —) MACHO
(PREF.) ANDR(O) MASCULO
(SUFF.) ANDRIA ANDROUS ANDRY
MASCULINITY (EXAGGERATED —)
  MACHISMO
(EXAGGERATED AWARENESS OF —)
  MACHISMO
MASH PAP BEER CHAP MASA MASK
  MESH SLOP CHAMP CREEM SMASH
  SMUSH MUDDLE STILLAGE
(FATHER OF —) ARAM
MASHED CHAPPED DAUPHINE
MASHER FLIRT BEETLE
MASJID MOSQUE
MASK FACE HIDE JEST LOUP SLUR
  VEIL BLOCK BLOOP CLOAK COVER
  GRILL GUISE LARVE POINT VIZOR
  DOMINO GRILLE MUZZLE SCREEN
  VEILER VIZARD BECLOUD CONCEAL
  CURTAIN MASKOID ANTEMASK
  DEFILADE DISGUISE MASCARON
  PRETENSE
(— OUT) CROP
(GAS —) CANARY
(HALF —) LOO LOUP DOMINO
(KIND OF —) SKI
(PHOTOGRAPHIC —) MATTE
(PL.) AREITO
MASKED LARVATED VIZARDED
MASKED BALL (CHARACTER IN —)
  HORN ANGRI AMELIA RENATO
  TOMASI ULRICA ARMANDO RIBBING
  SAMUELE ARVIDSON GUSTAVUS
  RICCARDO ANCKERSTROEM
(COMPOSER OF —) VERDI
MASKER GUISARD MASQUER
MASKING MUMMERY MUMMING
  COLORING
MASKLIKE PERSONATE
MASLIN MESTLEN MASHLOCH
  MUNGCORN MASSELGEM
MASNADIERI, I
(CHARACTER IN —) CARLO AMALIA
  FRANCESCO MASSIMILIAN
(COMPOSER OF —) VERDI
MASON LAYER BUILDER MASONER
  COMACINE KNOBBLER LAMMIKIN
  SCUTCHER
MASONRY ASHLAR MANTLE RUSTIC
  BACKING BLOCAGE MOELLON
  NOGGING ISODOMUM QUOINING
  ROCKWORK EMPLECTON
  RUBBLEWORK
(UNDRESSED —) RAGWORK
MASQUE MASK COMUS DEVICE
  ANTIMASK DISGUISE
MASQUER REX
MASQUERADE BALL MASK GUISE
  DOMINO MASQUE PARADE
  MASKERY DISGUISE

MASQUERADER RAGSHAG
MASQUERADING CARNIVAL
MASS BAT BED GOB SOP TOD WAD
BODY BULK CLOD GOUT HEAP HEFT
KNOT LEAD LUMP MOLE OBIT STOW
SWAD AMASS BATCH BLOOM CLAMP
CLASH CLUMP CROWD CRUST DIRGE
GLOBE GORGE GROSS MATTE MISSA
PRESS SLUMP SOLID SPIRE STORE
WODGE COMMON GOBBET NUGGET
PROPER VOLUME WEIGHT BOUROCK
CONGEST DENSITY MASKINS
MESKINS MYSTERY REQUIEM
SALOMON CALAPITE CONGERIE
ENDOSOME FLOCCULE MOUNTAIN
MYCETOMA SOULMASS
ACCUMULATION
(— IN THE WHITE NILE) SUDD
(— OF BACTERIA) SLIME BAREGINE
SYMPLASM
(— OF BLOSSOMS) BLOW
(— OF BLUBBER) MELON
(— OF BRANCHES) SPRAY
(— OF BUBBLES) FOAM
(— OF BUSHES) SHAG
(— OF CARPELS) SOREMA
(— OF CELLS) COMB CANCER
MORULA CUMULUS STALACE
PULVINUS
(— OF CLOUDS) BANK
(— OF COAL) JUD
(— OF COLORS) BLOB
(— OF COTTON) FUSSOCK
(— OF CURED RUBBER) LOAF
(— OF DEBRIS) SLIDE
(— OF DOUGH) DUMPLING
(— OF FIBERS) KAPOK
(— OF FILAMENTS) FLOCCUS
MYCELIUM
(— OF FILTH) GORE
(— OF FRAGMENTS) BRASH
(— OF GAS) PROMINENCE
(— OF GOLD) BONANZA
(— OF HAIR) GLIB TOUPET
(— OF HYPHAE) MEDULLA
(— OF ICE) BERG CALF FLOE FLAKE
PATCH ICICLE STURIS GROWLER
ICEBERG FLOEBERG
(— OF INSECTS) CACHE
(— OF IRON) BALL BLOB CORE
BLOOM INDUCTOR
(— OF LAVA) BOMB SPINE
(— OF LEAVES) FOLIAGE
(— OF LIMESTONE) HUM
(— OF LOOSE BOULDERS) CLATTER
(— OF METAL) SOW INGOT BUTTON
(— OF MOLTEN GLASS) GOB BLOOM
GATHER PARISON
(— OF MUD) CLASH
(— OF ORE) BACK SLUG BUNNY
SQUAT REGULUS
(— OF PEOPLE) CROWD HORDE
(— OF POMACE) CHEESE

(— OF ROCK) DOME NECK HORSE
LEDGE NAPPE SCALP SNOUT INLIER
SARSEN BOULDER FOOTWALL
(— OF SAND) PAAR
(— OF SOAP) CURD
(— OF SPORES) SORUS
(— OF SUGAR) FONDANT
(— OF SUGAR CRYSTALS) STRIKE
(— OF TISSUE) COLLAR GANGLION
NUCELLUS
(— OF TREES) THICKET
(— OF WATER) HEAD
(— OF YARN) COP BALLOON
(— OF YOLK) LATEBRA
(— OVERHANGING) CORNICE
(—S OF DRIFTWOOD) EMBARRAS
(— TOGETHER) HUDDLE
(ALPINE —) FLYSCH
(AMORPHOUS —) JUMBLE
SYMPLASM .
(BILLOWY —) CLOUD
(BUSHY —) SHOCK
(COMPACT —) BRIQUET
(CONCENTRATION OF MOON —)
MASCON
(CONFUSED —) COT JUMBLE
JUNGLE PILEUP CLUTTER RUMMAGE
SHUFFLE
(DISORDERLY —) SCRAMBLE
(EGG —) BUNION CULTCH SPONGE
(FATTY —) BEAN HEADSKIN
(FECAL —) SCYBALUM
(FLATTISH —) DAB
(FLUFFY —) PUFF
(FLUID —) FLUOR
(GLASSY —) SLAG
(GLOBULAR —) MOORBALL
(INDISTINCT —) SMUDGE
(IRREGULAR —) CUB
(LIVING —) BLASTEMA
(MOIST —) PULP
(MOUNTAIN —) OROGEN
(NUCLEAR —) SHIELD
(OVERSPREADING —) PALL
(PART OF —) INTROIT
(PEAR-SHAPED —) BOULE
(POROUS —) FILTER
(PROJECTING —) BOSS
(PULPY —) SQUELCH
(RECTANGULAR —) BRICK
(ROOT —) SOLE
(ROUNDED —) COB NOB KNOB
BOLUS KUGEL BULLET RONDLE
(SEDIMENTARY —) GOBI
(SHAPED —) PAT LOAF
(SHAPELESS —) JELLY
(SLIPPERY —) SIND SLUD SLUDDER
(SLUSHY —) POSH
(SOFT —) MASH MOXA MUMMY
(STICKY —) CLAG
(SWOLLEN —) CERE
(TANGLED — OF HAIR) MOP KNURL
(TUFTY —) FLOC

(UNCTUOUS —) LANOLIN
(UNIT OF —) DALTON
(UPRIGHT —) COLUMN
(PL.) MEINY MEINIE TRENTAL
POPULACE
(PREF.) ONCO
(SUFF.) IUM OME
MASSA (FATHER OF —) ISHMAEL

MASSACHUSETTS
CAPE: ANN COD
CAPITAL: BOSTON
COLLEGE: SMITH AMHERST SIMMONS
WHEATON WILLIAMS RADCLIFFE
WELLESLEY
COUNTY: DUKES ESSEX BRISTOL
NORFOLK SUFFOLK BERKSHIRE
NANTUCKET BARNSTABLE
INDIAN: NAUSET POCOMTUC
ISLAND: DUKES NANTUCKET
LAKE: ONOTA QUABBIN ROHUNTA
WEBSTER
MOUNTAIN: BRODIE POTTER ALANDER
EVERETT GREYLOCK
MOUNTAIN RANGE: BERKSHIRE
POND: WALDEN
PRESIDENT: BUSH KENNEDY
RIVER: NASHUA CHARLES CONCORD
QUABOAG TAUNTON CHICOPEE
DEERFIELD MERRIMACK
STATE BIRD: CHICKADEE
STATE FLOWER: MAYFLOWER
STATE NICKNAME: BAY OLDBAY
OLDCOLONY
STATE TREE: ELM
TOWN: AYER LYNN OTIS ATHOL BARRE
LENOX AGAWAM DEDHAM GROTON
LOWELL NAHANT NATICK REVERE
SAUGUS WOBURN HOLYOKE
IPSWICH PEABODY TAUNTON
BROCKTON CHICOPEE COHASSET
SCITUATE UXBRIDGE YARMOUTH
CAMBRIDGE NANTUCKET
WORCESTER PITTSFIELD
SPRINGFIELD
UNIVERSITY: CLARK TUFTS HARVARD
BRANDEIS

MASSACRE SLAY POGROM
CARNAGE SCUPPER WIPEOUT
BUTCHERY SLAUGHTER
MASSAGE ROLF WISP KNEAD
FACIAL MODIFY PETRIE SHAMPOO
SHIATSU TRIPSIS BLANDISH
LOMILOMI ANATRIPSIS MANIPULATE
(— OF DEEP MUSCLES) ROLFING
(— WITH FINGERS) SHIATSU SHIHTZU
(MUSCLE —) ROLF ROLFING
(ONE WHO —S) ROLFER
MASSAGER MASSEUR VIBRATOR
MASSECUITE GUR FILLMASS
MASSED DENSE
MASSENA QUAIL COPPY

MASSIVE BIG BEAMY BULKY GROSS
HEAVY LUSTY MASSY SOUND STERN
STRONG HEALTHY HULKING
VOLUMED TIMBERED MONUMENTAL
MAST BUCK MAIN POLE SPAR OVEST
STICK STING DRIVER JIGGER MIZZEN
ARTEMON ASHERAH MASTAGE
PANNAGE SPANKER FOREMAST
JURYMAST MAINMAST SHIPMAST
MIZZENMAST
(FALLEN —) SHACK
(SIXTH —) DRIVER
MASTAX TROPHI
MASTER DON HER JOE MAS RAB
SAB SIR ARCH BAAS BEAK BEST
BOSS COCK FACE HERR JOSS KING
LORD MIAN SIRE TUAN BWANA
LEARN MARSE MASSA RABBI SAHIB
SWAMI SWAMY SWELL BRIDLE
BUCKRA CASTER DEACON DOMINE
HUMBLE MAITRE PATRON RECTOR
RHETOR SIRCAR WAFTER CAPTAIN
CONQUER DOMINIE DOMINUS
EFFENDI MAESTRO NAKHODA
OGTIERN PADRONE RABBONI
AMAISTER BARGEMAN BEMASTER
KINGFISH LANDLORD MAGISTER
OVERCOME SLOOPMAN SURMOUNT
VANQUISH
(— OF CEREMONIES) EMCEE VERGER
COMPERE CHAIRMAN
(— OF CRAFT) KAHUNA
(— OF HOUSEHOLD) BALABOS
GOODMAN
(— OF REVELS) ALYTARCH
(— OF WHALER) SPOUTER
(FENCING —) LANISTA
(INFERIOR —) KNIFER
(PREF.) ARCH
MASTER-AT-ARMS JAUNTY
JAUNTIE
MASTER BUILDER (AUTHOR OF —)
IBSEN
(CHARACTER IN —) ALINE HILDA
BROVIK RAGNAR SOLNESS
MASTERFUL BOSSY LORDLY VIRILE
HAUGHTY ARROGANT MAGERFUL
PEREMPTORY
MASTER OF BALLANTRAE
(AUTHOR OF —) STEVENSON
(CHARACTER IN —) CHEW DASS
BALLY BURKE HENRY JAMES TEACH
ALISON DURRIE GRAEME FRANCIS
SECUNDRA MACKELLAR
DURRISDEER
MASTERPIECE GEM TOPPIECE
MASTERSTROKE COUP
MASTERY GREE GRIP GRIPE
COMMAND MAISTRY OVERHAND
MASTHEAD FLAG HIGHTOP
MASTICATE GUM CHAW CHEW
MASTICATORY PAN BUYO
MASTIC BULLY JOCUM JOCUMA

MASTIC TREE ACOMA AUSUBO COCUYO COCULLO LENTISK
MASTIFF ALAN MASTY BANDOG TIEDOG
MASTIGONEME FLIMMER
MASTITIS CLAP WEED GARGET
MAST TREE ASAK
MASTURBATE ABUSE
MASTURBATION ONANISM FROTTAGE
MASTWOOD POON KAMANI
MAT COT RUG TOD BASS FLAT FLET FOOT HAIR MOSS NIPA PACE RAFT SHAG TAUT DOILY KILIM TATTY COTTER FELTER FOOTER PAUNCH PETATE TARGET TATAMI THATCH COASTER CUSHION DOORMAT KAITAKA MATTING FOOTPACE FROSTING MATTRESS SPANDREL
 (— BORDER) TANIKO
 (BOWLING —) FOOTER
 (FIBER —) IE BASS
 (PALM-LEAF —) YAPA
 (PICTURE-FRAME —) FLAT
 (POLYNESIAN —) LAUHALA
 (SCOURING —) BEAR
 (TABLECLOTH —) GARDNAP
 (PL.) DUNNAGE
MATACHIN BOUFFON
MATACO CORONADO
MATADOR MAT ESPADA CAPEADOR
 (— MOVEMENT) PASE
MATCH GO CAP VIE BOUT COPE EVEN FERE LUNT MAKE MATE MEET MILL MOTE PAIR PEEL PEER SIDE SUIT AGREE AMATE EQUAL FINCH FUSEE FUZEE MOUSE PARTY RIVAL SPUNK TALLY VENUE VESTA ASSORT BESORT CANCEL COMMIT FELLOW KIPPIN MARROW QUADER RUBBER SAMPLE SWATCH COMPEER EXAMPLE IGNITER ILLUMER KINDLER KIPPEEN LIGHTER LUCIFER PARAGON PAREGAL PATTERN PENDANT SINGLES APPROACH BONSPIEL BREATHER CONGREVE EUPYRION FOURSOME INFLAMER LOCOFOCO PARALLEL PORTFIRE REANSWER VESUVIAN VESUVIUS SEMIFINAL PREMINARY QUARTERFINAL
 (— AT DICE) MAIN
 (— FOR FIRING CANNON) MOUSE
 (— IN POKER) SEE CALL
 (BOXING —) SPAR FIGHT PRELIM SLUGFEST
 (CURLING —) SPIEL BONSPIEL
 (DANCING —) KANTIKEY
 (DISHONEST —) CROSS
 (GOLF —) NASSAU FOURSOME
 (LARGE-HEADED —) FUZEE
 (SCOLDING —) FLYTE FLYTING
 (SHOOTING —) TIR SHOOT
 (SLOW —) LUNT SMIFT SQUIB

 (TILTING —) CAROUSEL CARROUSEL
 (UNEQUAL —) DISPARAGE
 (WORTHY —) ROLAND
 (PL.) LIGHTS
MATCHED INSYNC ASSORTED
MATCHING MARROW SUITABLE
 (NOT —) ODD
MATCHLESS ALONE UNIQUE NONESUCH PEERLESS
MATCHMAKER SHADCHAN
MATE CAWK FERE METE PAIR PEER BILLY BREED BUDDY BULLY CHINA CLASP CULLY DICKY MATCH PARTY TALLY YERBA BUNKIE COBBER FELLOW FUTURE MARROW PAREIL SPOUSE BROTHER COMPEER COMRADE CONSORT HUSBAND PARAGON NEIGHBOR PIRRAURA
 (— WELL) NICK
 (BOATSWAIN'S —) BUFFER
 (GUNNER'S —) LADY
 (SECOND —) DICKY
MATERIAL FINE MOLD COMPO GAUZE GOUGE HYLIC METAL MOULD PASTE PLASS STUFF THING TRADE BORROW CARNAL CYANUS FABRIC GRAITH HOGGIN MATTER PAPREG PUBLIC THINGY APPAREL FOOTING SUBJECT TEXTILE UNIDEAL WEIGHTY ADDITIVE CORPORAL ECONOMIC EQUIPAGE RELEVANT SENSIBLE SNOODING TANGIBLE THINGISH OBJECTIVE PHENOMENAL
 (— ELIMINATED) CULLAGE
 (— FOR FERMENTING) GUILE
 (— FOR OYSTER BEDS) CULCH CULTCH
 (— IN GRAIN) DOCKAGE
 (— IN MAKING CEMENT) ADDITION
 (— IN NEEDLEWORK) INKLE
 (— OF CORDED SILK) CRYSTAL
 (— OF SCREENINGS) HOGGIN HOGGING
 (— REMOVED BY SAW CUT) KERF
 (—S FOR MAKING GLASS) FRIT
 (— USED IN WAXING) BALL
 (— WEIGHED) DRAFT DRAUGHT
 (ABSORBENT —) DOPE
 (ALLUVIAL —) SHINGLE
 (ANCIENT —) MURRA MURRHA
 (ARTISTIC —) KITSCH
 (BAGGING —) HOPSACK
 (BITUMINOUS —) KEROGEN
 (BONY —) COSMINE
 (BUILDING —) LATH ADOBE BRICK STAFF SWISH TABBY TAPIA SILLAR CONCRETE
 (BUILDING —S) TIGNUM
 (CLAY —) TAPIA
 (CLAYEY —) GOUGE
 (COLORING —) TINCTION
 (COMBUSTIBLE —) KINDLING
 (CONSTRUCTION —) BREEZE

(CORE —) NIFE
(CUSHIONING —) AIRFOAM
(DEPOSITED —) FOOTS
(DIAMOND —) BORT
(DOWNY —) FLUE
(DRESS —) FOULE VOILE PEELING
COTILLON EOLIENNE
(DYEING —) SUMAC SUMACH
(EMBOSSED —) CLOQUE
(EMROIDERY —) ARRASENE
(EXCAVATED —) SPOIL
(FACING —) ENAMEL
(FILLING —) FIBERFILL
(FISSIONABLE —) STUFF
(FOUNDATION —) UNDERLAY
(GLUTINOUS —) GELATIN
(GRANULAR —) BASIS
(HARD —) CARBIDE
(HEAT-RESISTANT —) ALSIFILM
(ILLUSTRATIVE —) ART
(INSECTICIDAL —) SCABRIN
(INSULATING —) KERITE PECITE
BLANKET LAGGING OKONITE
MEGOTALC
(LEFTOVER —S) ARISINGS
(LOOSE —) SAND GRAVEL DETRITUS
(MINING REFUSE —) ATTLE
(MINUTE —) SESTON
(MOLDING —) PREPREG
(NUTRITIVE —) FUEL
(OPAQUE —) MASK
(ORGANIC —) EXINITE
(PAPER-THIN —) FOIL
(PATCHING —) BOTCH
(PETRIFIED —) GEMSTONE
(POLISHING —) RABAT
(POWDERED —) FINES
(PRIMORDIAL —) BLASTEMA
(RAW —) STOCK STAPLE
(REFRACTORY —) GROG BULLDOG
CASTABLE
(RESIDUAL —) CEMENT
(RESOURCE —) SWIPE
(REVERSIBLE —) DAMASK
(SEDIMENTARY —) SILT
(SILK —) HONAN PEKIN FOULARD
SARCENET
(SLIMY —) GLIT SWARF
(SMOKING —) KEF KIF
(STIFF —) CANVAS
(STIFFENING —) BOXING
(TANNING —) BADAN SYNTAN
(THIN SLICE OF —) WAFER
(TILE-STRENGTHENING —) WEB
(TRASHY —) SLUSH
(TWEEDY —) HOMESPUN
(TYPE-HIGH —) BEARER
(UNPUBLISHED —) INEDITA
(UNSOLICITED —) SLUSH
(UPHOLSTERY —) LAMPAS
(VOLCANIC —) EJECTA TEPHRA
(WATERPROOF —) KERATOL

(WORTHLESS —) GARBLE
(WOVEN —) LAPPET
(PL.) STOCK STUFF
(PREF.) HYL(O)
(SUFF.) (PLASTIC —) PLASM(A)
MATERIALISM HYLISM SOMATISM
(DIALECTICAL —) DIAMAT
MATERIALISTIC SENSATE SENSUAL
BANAUSIC
MATERIALIZE REIFY DESCEND
MATER LECTIONIS GRAPHY
MATERNITY WARD NATUARY
MATGRASS NARD MATWEED
MATH MUTH MONASTERY
(KIND OF —) NEW
MATHEMATICIAN ALGORIST
GEOMETER
AMERICAN SEE FINE WEST WEYL
AIKEN BEGLE BROWN FISKE GIBBS
GODEL HARDY MASON MOORE
MUSES POLYA SMITH YOUNG
CAJORI HOPPER KASNER KEYSER
LEHMER LOOMIS MILLER NEWTON
OSGOOD PEIRCE RUNKLE VEBLEN
WIENER DICKSON GODFREY
METZLER NEUMANN SAFFORD
BANNEKER BIRKHOFF BOWDITCH
COOLIDGE FRANKLIN WELCHMAN
MURNAGHAN HUNTINGTON
VONNEUMANN WILCZYNSKI
RITTENHOUSE
AUSTRIAN HAGEN DOPPLER
PURBACH
BELGIAN LEMAITRE
BRAZILIAN GUSMAO
DUTCH BLAEU VLACQ CEULEN
STEVIN HUYGENS SNELLIUS
GRAVESANDE MUSSCHENBROEK
EGYPTIAN HYPATIA PTOLEMY
ENGLISH DEE LAMB MUIR PELL
ALLEN BONDI BOOLE COTES DIRAC
ELLIS HARDY JEANS MURIS ROUTH
SHARP SMITH WALES ATWOOD
BARLOW BARNES BARROW BRIGGS
CAYLEY COCKLE DARWIN DIGGES
GUNTER HADLEY HUTTON KELVIN
LARMOR NEWTON ROBINS STOKES
TAYLOR WALLIS WEDDLE BABBAGE
DODGSON HARRIOT LUBBOCK
MAKEHAM MASERES PEACOCK
RECORDE RUSSELL WHEWELL
WHISTON CLIFFORD GLAISHER
GOMPERTZ LEYBOURN MACMAHON
OUGHTRED RAYLEIGH BRONOWSKI
DUNSTABLE GREENHILL NICHOLSON
TODHUNTER WHITEHEAD
WHITTAKER WOODHOUSE
CODDINGTON GELLIBRAND
SACROBOSCO SAUNDERSON
FRENCH BIOT FINE LAME LEVY
BORDA BOREL CHEZY COMTE LEROY
MONGE PRONY RAMUS STURM

VIETE BEAUNE BEZOUT BOSSUT
CAUCHY FERMAT FERNEL GALOIS
JORDAN MOIGNO PASCAL PICARD
BOUGUER BROCARD CHARLES
CHASLES CHUQUET COURNOT
DARBOUX FOURIER GERMAIN
GOURSAT HERMITE KOENIGS
LACROIX LAPLACE POINSOT
POISSON PUISEUX VERNIER
ALEMBERT BERTRAND CLAIRAUT
CORIOLIS DEMOIVRE GERGONNE
HACHETTE HADAMARD LAGRANGE
LAGUERRE LEBESGUE LEGENDRE
MERSENNE MONTUCIA PAINLEVE
POINCARE PONCELET ROBERVAL
BRIANCHON CONDORCET
DESARGUES DESCARTES LIOUVILLE
BURCKHARDT DEPARCIEUX
MAUPERTUIS
GERMAN GAUSS HESSE KLEIN
MAYER MISES PASCH PFAFF RUNGE
WOLFF BALMER CANTOR JACOBI
KUMMER MOBIUS MULLER STIFEL
APIANUS CLEBSCH FRIESEN HILBERT
KASTNER LAMBERT LEIBNIZ
PLUCKER RIEMANN WIDMANN
ARONHOLD BLASCHKE CLAUSIUS
DEDEKIND DROBISCH LEIBNITZ
MERCATOR RHATICUS SCHOTTKY
SCHUBERT DIRICHLET GRASSMANN
KRONECKER LINDEMANN
BIEBERBACH EISENSTEIN
HINDENBURG PRINGSHEIM
TSCHIRNHAUS WEIERSTRASS
KONIGSBERGER
GREEK CONON EUCLID PAPPUS
DIOCLES PTOLEMY ANTIPHON
AUTOLYCUS OENOPIDES SOSIGENES
APOLLONIUS ARCHIMEDES
DIOPHANTUS PYTHAGORAS
DINOSTRATUS
HUNGARIAN BOLYAI
INDIAN ARYABHATA RAMANUJAN
IRISH BALL KELVIN SALMON
HAMILTON BROUNCKER
ITALIAN CEVA BALDI FRISI PEANO
AGNESI GRANDI CARDANO
CREMONA GALILEO PACIOLI RICCATI
BELTRAMI BRIOSCHI CAMPANUS
MALFATTI BOSCOVICH CAVALIERI
FIBONACCI TARTAGLIA BELLAVITIS
MASCHERONI TORRICELLI
JAPANESE SEKI
NORWEGIAN LIE ABEL STORMER
GULDBERG
POLISH BARTEL CIOLEK WRONSKI
PORTUGUESE NUNES
RUSSIAN KRYLOV LIAPUNOV
CHEBYSHEV KOLMOGOROV
KOVALEVSKI LOBACHEVSKI
SCOTTISH TAIT IVORY KEILL LESLIE
NAPIER BURGESS FORSYTH

GREGORY MAXWELL PLAYFAIR
STIRLING
SWISS EULER AMSLER CRAMER
GULDIN BYRGIUS STEINER
BERNOULLI CHRISTOFFEL
MATHEMATICS MATHESIS
MATING NICK COUPLE DIALLEL
BREEDING HOMOGAMY PANMIXIA
(RANDOM —) PANGAMY
MATRASS BOLTHEAD CUCURBIT
MATRED (DAUGHTER OF —)
MEHETABEL
(FATHER OF —) MEZAHAB
MATRIMONIAL MARITAL NUPTIAL
SPOUSAL CONJUGAL
MATRIMONIO SEGRETO, IL
(CHARACTER IN —) FIDALMA
PAOLINO CAROLINA ELISETTA
GERONIMO ROBINSON
(COMPOSER OF —) CIMAROSA
MATRIMONY WEDLOCK MARRIAGE
MATRIMONY VINE JASMINE
JESSAMY ROXTHORN
MATRIX PI BED MAT SORT PLASM
SHELL SLIDE DYADIC MASTER
MOTHER STRIKE STROMA CALYMMA
FORMULA MATRICE PATTERN
PROPLASM
MATRON DAME
MATTAN (SON OF —) SHEPHATIAH
MATTANIAH (FATHER OF —) BANI
ELAM HEMAN ZATTU
(SON OF —) ZACCUR
MATTE SLURRY REGULUS
MATTED COTTY FELTY PINNY FELTED
TAGGED TAUTED WAUKIT STRINGY
FELTLIKE CESPITOSE
MATTENAI (FATHER OF —) JOIARIB
MATTER BIT RES BONE CASE GEAR
HYLE ITEM RECK WHAT AMPER
FORCE PARTY SKILL STUFF THEME
TOPIC AFFAIR ARGUFY BEHALF
DITTAY IMPORT ARTICLE CONCERN
MATERIA SHEBANG SIGNIFY
SUBJECT BUSINESS COMETHER
MATERIAL
(— ADDED TO BOOK) APPENDIX
(— AROUND THE TEETH) TOPHUS
(— CONSTITUTING PERFUME)
ESSENCE
(— DISCHARGED) FLUX
(— EJECTED) CAST
(— FOR PRINTING) COPY
(— IN DISPUTE) ISSUE
(— OF BUSINESS) SHAURI
(— OF CHANCE) LOTTERY
(— OF CONCERN) FUNERAL
(— OF CONSCIENCE) REMORSE
(— OF DISCOURSE) SUBJECT
(— OF FACT) SENSE
(— OF INTEREST) GRIST
(— OF NO IMPORTANCE) TOY

(— TO) CONCERN
(ALLUVIAL —) GEEST
(BRAIN —) ALBA
(CARTILAGINOUS —) GRISTLE
(COLORING —) DYE COLOR CROCK
EOSIN MORIN PIURI ALNEIN ANATTO
BUTEIN FUSTIC INDIGO ORCEIN
PIOURY ANNATTO CARMINE
CASTORY CUDBEAR LIGULIN
OENOLIN PIGMENT PUNICIN
TURACIN XANTHIN ALGOCYAN
ALIZARIN BRAZILIN FUSTERIC
LAPACHOL SCOPARIN TINCTION
TINCTURE
(CORRUPT —) PUS ATTER
(DECAYED ORGANIC —) DUFF
(DECAYING —) DUFF
(DIFFICULT —) PROBLEM
(DISCHARGED —) EXUDATE
(ESSENTIAL —) POINT
(EXPLANATORY —) HAGGADA
(FATTY —) SEBUM
(FECAL —) SIEGE
(FILTHY —) GUNK
(FOREIGN —) SOIL DROSS
(FOUL —) FILTH SORDES
(FRONT —) FOREWORD
(GELATINOUS —) BREAK SPAWN
(GRAY —) GLIOSA CINEREA
(HYPOTHETICAL —) PROTYLE
(INANIMATE —) AJIVA
(INDECENT —) STUFF
(INFECTIOUS —) MIASMA
(INFLAMMABLE —) TINDER
(MINERAL —) FLOAT FLOATS
(NERVE —) CINEREA
(POTENTIAL —) PRAKRITI
(PRIMARY —) PRADHANA
(PRINTED —) BOX DISPLAY
(PRIVATE —) SECLUSION
(PULVERIZED —) ATTRITUS
(READING —) BODY
(SLIMY —) GLAIR
(SMALL —) MINUTIA
(SOFT —) PASH
(SUBJECT —) SCOPE CONTENT
(SUPPURATIVE —) PUS
(TRIVIAL —) JOKE
(TYPESET —) CHASE
(WASTE —) DIRT DRAFF DROSS
RAMMEL SEWAGE EXCRETA
(WORTHLESS —) SLAG CHAFF
GANGUE GARBAGE
(WRITTEN —) SCRIVE
(PL.) HARNESS SQUARES
(PREF.) HYL(O)
(SUFF.) (COLORING —) PHYLL
MATTER-OF-FACT THINGY
PROSAIC PROSAICAL DRY PROSE
LITERAL PROSAIC
MATTER-OF-FACTNESS PROSE
MATTHAN (GRANDSON OF —)
JOSEPH

MATTHEW (FATHER OF —)
ALPHAEUS
MATTING MAT TAT BAST BEAR
BUMP SIRKI TATTY SAWALI TATAMI
COCOMAT RABANNA
MATTOCK MAT BILL HACK MATAX
PICKAX TUBBAL TWIBIL GRUBBER
MATTRESS BED MAT TICK DIVAN
FUTON QUILT RESAI REZAI PALLET
BISCUIT MATRACE PAILLASSE
PALLIASSE
(INFLATABLE —) LILO
MATURATE MATTER
MATURE AGE OLD BOLD FULL GRAY
RIPE ADULT MANLY RIPEN SHOOT
ACCRUE AUTUMN DECOCT DIGEST
MELLOW SEASON SEEDED CONCOCT
DEVELOP FURNISH PERFECT
PROVECT MATURATE
(PREF.) TEL(E)(O)
MATURED ADULT GROWN FORMED
HEADED MELLOW SEEDED
HOMOGAMY
(SEXUALLY —) HIGH
MATURING (— EARLY) RATHRIPE
MATURITY AGE RIPENESS
MATWEED NARD NARDUS
MATZOTH MATZOS AFJKOMEN
MAUDLIN BEERY MOIST FUDDLED
MAUDLINISM BATHOS
MAUL FAN PAW TUG MALL MELL
GAVEL GLAUM BEATER BEETLE
BEMAUL MUZZLE SCAMBLE
MAUND MAO MEIN MAHAN
MAUNDER HAVER
MAUNDY NIPTER MANDATE
MAURITANIA (CAPITAL OF —)
NOUAKCHOTT
(COIN OF —) KHOUM
(MONEY OF —) OUGUIYA
(RIVER OF —) SENEGAL
(TOWN OF —) ATAR NEMA AGMAR
KAEDI OUJAF
MAURITANIAN MOOR
MAURITIUS (CAPITAL OF —)
PORTLOUIS
(CHANNEL OF —) QUOIN
(ISLAND OF —) AGALEGA GABRIEL
RODRIGUEZ
(RIVER OF —) GRAND POSTE
REMPART
(TOWN OF —) VACOAS TRIOLET
CUREPIPE SOUILLAC
MAUSOLEUM MOLE TOMB SHRINE
TURBEH BARADARI
MAUVE MALLOW PURPLE MAUVINE
MAVEN ADEPT EXPERT
MAVERICK STRAY
MAW MAA CRAW CROP GORGE
CROPPY THROAT
MAWKISH CUTE SAPPY SOPPY
SOUPY WALSH DRIPPY SICKLY
VANILLA

MAXILLA SETA GNATHITE
CULTELLUS
MAXILLIPED JAWFOOT GNATHITE
MAXIM SAW SAY DICT ITEM NORM
RULE TEXT WORD ADAGE AXIOM
GNOME LARGE MOTTO DICTUM
SAYING SYMBOL BROCARD DICTATE
IMPRESA PRECEPT PROVERB
APHORISM APOTHEGM DOCTRINE
MORALISM PROTASIS SENTENCE
(PL.) LOGIA
MAXIMUM FULL MOST PEAK CREST
EXTREME OUTSIDE SUMMARY
ULTIMATE
MAXIXE CARIOCA
MAXWELL LINE WEBER
MAY CAN MUN MOTE MOWE MUST
PRIME SHALL HEYDAY HAWTHORN
SYCAMORE
(3D OF —) RUDMASDAY
MAYA PRAKRITI
MAYAN COCOM
(— CALENDAR PERIOD) UAYEB UINAL
(— GOD) CHAC CHAAC
MAYAPPLE MANDRAKE
MAYBE MEBBE HAPPEN PERHAPS
POSSIBLY
MAY DAY BELTANE
MAYFISH ROCKFISH
MAYFLOWER ARBUTUS
MAYFLY DUN DOON DRAKE NAIAD
DAYFLY SPINNER EPHEMERA
MAYHEM FELONY
MAYONNAISE MAYO GOULASH
DRESSING
(GARLIC —) AIOLI
MAYOR MAIRE BAILIFF DEMARCH
PODESTA PROVOST HIZZONER
PALATINE
(BULGARIAN —) KMET
(IRISH —) SOVRAN SOVEREIGN
(SPANISH —) ALCALDE
MAYOR OF CASTERBRIDGE
(AUTHOR OF —) HARDY
(CHARACTER IN —) JOPP SUSAN
DONALD NEWSON FARFRAE
LESUEUR LUCETTA MICHAEL
RICHARD HENCHARD ELIZABETH
TEMPLEMAN
MAYORSHIP CHAIR
MAYPOLE SHAFT
MAYPOP MAYCOCK MARACOCK
MAYWEED BALDER COTULA
MATHER HOGWEED COMPOSIT
DILLWEED
MAZE JUNGLE WARREN CONFUSE
BEWILDER LABYRINTH
MAZEPPA (CHARACTER IN —) MARIA
ANDREY MAZEPPA KOCHUBEY
(COMPOSER OF —) TCHAIKOVSKY
MAZUMA
(ALSO SEE MONEY) LUCRE
MCCOY QUILL

ME I MA US MOI
MEAD MEATHE BRAGGET HYDROMEL
METHEGLIN
MEADOW LEA ABEL MEAD VEGA
WISH WONG FIELD GRASS LEASE
MARSH SWALE WARTH CALLOW
PARAMO SAETER SMOOTH POTRERO
THWAITE CHINAMPA
(ARTIFICIAL —) CHINAMPA
(FLOODED —) SALTING
(IRISH —) BAAN
(LOW —) ING INCH INGE HAUGH
-CALLOW
(NORWEGIAN —) SAETER
(PREF.) PRATI
(SUFF.) ING
MEADOW CROWFOOT
FROGWORT
MEADOW GRASS POA
MEADOWLAND ALP MOWING
MOWLAND
MEADOWLARK ACORN MEDLAR
MEADOW MOUSE VOLE
MEADOW PEA COWPEA
MEADOW PIPIT WEKEEN CHEEPER
TIETICK TITLING LINGBIRD TWITLARK
MEADOW SAFFRON UPSTART
COLCHICUM
MEADOW SAXIFRAGE SESELI
MEADOWSWEET SPIREA
MEADWORT
MEAGER RAID BARE LANK LEAN
NICE POOR THIN GAUNT NAKED
SCANT SILLY SKIMP SOBER SPARE
JEJUNE LEFPIT LENTEN MEAGRE
NARROW PILLED SCANTY SLIGHT
SPARSE STINGY SCRAGGY SCRANNY
SCRIMPY SCRUBBY SLENDER
SPARING STARVED STERILE
MARGINAL SCRANNEL SCRATCHY
MISERABLE
MEAGERLY BARELY SPARELY
SPARINGLY
MEAGERNESS ECONOMY EXILITY
TENUITY SPARENESS
MEAL AMYL ATTA BAKE CENA CHOW
FARM FEED HASH KAIL MEAT MONG
NOSH TUCK COENA FLOUR MANGE
SCOFF BUFFET COMIDA DINNER
FARINA MANGER POLLEN REPAST
SPREAD SQUARE SUPPER UNDERN
BLOWOUT COOKOUT CRIBBLE
MELTITH NAGMAAL NOONING
SETDOWN ALMUERZO CORNMEAL
EVENMETE MEALTIDE ORDINARY
TRENCHER
(— AND WATER) DRAMMOCK
(— FROM CASSAVA ROOT) FARINE
FARINHA
(— FROM ORCHID ROOT) SALEP
(— GROUND BY HAND) GRADDAN
(— OF FELLOWSHIP) AGAPE
(— STIRRED WITH MILK) STUROCH

(ACORN —) RACAHOUT
(AFTERNOON —) TEA
(CEREMONIAL —) SEDER
(COARSE —) GRIT GROUT KIBBLE
CRIBBLE GURGEONS
(COLLEGE —) HALL
(CORN —) MASA ATOLE NOCAKE
(ELABORATE —) FEAST BANQUET
(EXCESSIVE —) SURFEIT
(FIRST —) ALMUERZO
(FULL —) GORGE
(HASTY —) SNAP CHACK
(HEARTY —) AIT
(HEAVY —) TIGHTENER
(IMPROMPTU —) BITE CHECK
(LIGHT —) BAIT BEVER CHACK CHECK
FOURS NUNCHEON
(MIDDAY —) NOON
(MORNING —) BRUNCH
(PERTAINING TO —) PRANDIAL
(PURIM —) SEUDAH
(SCANTY —) PICK
(SMALL —) SNAP MORSEL
(SOLITARY —) SULLEN
(UNSORTED —) ATTA
(PL.) TUCKER
(PREF.) ATHERO
MEALTIDE MELTITH
MEALTIME CHOW MELTETH
MEALY FLOURY FARINOSE PERONATE
MEALYBUG COCCID
MEAN LOW BASE CLAM HARD LEAN
MIDS NICE POKY POOR SLIM VILE
AGENT ARGUE DINGY DIRTY DUSTY
FOOTY GRIMY KETTY LOUSY MANGY
MESNE MEZZO MIDST MINGY
MOYEN MUCKY NASTY PETIT PETTY
RATTY RUNTY SCALD SCALL SCALY
SCRUB SEEDY SILLY SMALL SNIDE
SNIVY SORRY SOUND SPELL ABJECT
BADASS BEMEAN COMMON DENOTE
DESIGN DIRTEN FEEBLE FROWZY
FRUGAL GRUBBY HUMBLE HUNGRY
IMPORT INSECT INTEND LEADEN
LITTLE MEASLY MEDIAL MEDIUM
MENIAL MIDDLE NARROW ORNERY
PALTRY PEANUT PILLED POKING
RASCAL SCABBY SCREWY SCUMMY
SCURVY SHABBY SLIGHT SNIFTY
SNIPPY SORDID SQUALL STRAIT
TEMPER YELLOW AVERAGE CAITIFF
CHANNEL CHETIVE COMICAL
CONNOTE HACKNEY HATEFUL
HILDING IGNOBLE MESQUIN
MISERLY MOTETUS OBSCURE
PEAKING PELTING PIGGISH PIMPING
PITIFUL PORTEND REPTILE ROINISH
SCABBED SHABBED SIGNIFY VICIOUS
BEGGARLY CHURLISH DOGGEREL
MEDIOCRE MIDDLING NIGGLING
PICAYUNE PITIABLE RASCALLY
RIFFRAFF SHAMEFUL SNEAKING
TWOPENNY WRETCHED

MEANDER ROVE WIND STRAY
TWINE CIRCLE WIMPLE WINDLE
SERPENT WINDING STRAGGLE
MEANING WIT HANG DRIFT SENSE
SOUND IMPORT INTENT SEMEME
PURPORT PURPOSE CARRIAGE
INNUENDO SENTENCE STRENGTH
REFERENCE SIGNIFICANCE
(BASIC —) EFFECT
(DOUBLE —) WHIM EQUIVOKE
(ESSENTIAL —) CORE CONTENT
(IMPLIED —) EMPHASIS
(LITERAL —) LETTER
(MANIFEST —) FACE
(PRECISE —) VALUE
(REAL —) SPIRIT
(SECONDARY —) OVERTONE
(SECRET —) HEART
(SENSE THE — OF) READ
(SIGNIFICANT —) PITH
(SUBTLE —) OVERTONE
MEANINGFUL RICH PREGNANT
MEANINGFULNESS BODY
MEANINGLESS BANAL EMPTY
ABSURD FECKLESS SENSELESS
(— LETTER OR CODE) NULL
MEANLY POORLY SLIGHT
COMMONLY
MEANNESS BEGGARY
MEANS MIDS AGENT DRIVE
MESNE MOYEN PURSE THEME
AGENCY AVENUE ENGINE MATTER
MIDDES POCKET STRING WRENCH
BALANCE BENEFIT DEMESNE
FACULTY FASHION QUOMODO
COURTESY
(— OF ACCESS) DOOR AVENUE
(— OF COMMUNICATION) CANAL
COMMERCE
(— OF DEFENSE) HORN HEDGE
SHIELD BULWARK
(— OF ENTRANCE) INGRESS
(— OF ESCAPE) CHINK SCAPE
FLIGHT
(— OF ESTIMATE) GAGE GAUGE
(— OF INFLUENCING) HOLD
(— OF LIVING) ALIMONY
(— OF OFFENSE) ARM
(— OF PROTECTION) SAFETY
(— OF SECURITY) WALL
(— OF SUPPORT) HOLD ALIMENT
SUPPORT
(— OF TESTING) CHECK
(— TO END) FULCRUM
(ARTIFICIAL —) MACHINE
(BY THIS —) HEREBY
MEANSPIRITED POOR SUPINE
CURRISH BANAUSIC RECREANT
MEANTIME MEAN WHILE WHILES
INTERIM
MEANTONE TERTIAN
MEANWHILE WHILST INTERIM
MEANTIME

MEANY BRUTE
MEASLES RUBEOLA MORBILLI
(BLACK —) ESCA APOPLEXY
MEASURE (ALSO SEE UNIT AND
WEIGHT) AB BU EM EN HO KO LI MO
RI SE TU AAM ARE AUM BAG CAB
CHO DRA ELL FAT FEN FIT FOU FUN
GAD GAZ GUZ HIN HOB IMI KAB KAN
KIP KOR KOS LEA LOG LUG MAU MIL
MOY PIK RIG RIN ROD SAA SHO TON
TUN VAT VOG WEY ACRE ALMA AUNE
BARN BATH BEKA BOLL BOUW DUTT
CADE CENT CHIH COOM COSS DEPA
DOSE DRAA DRAM DYNE EPHA EPHI
FALL FANG FOOT FULL GAGE GERA
GILL GIRT GOAD GRAM GREX HAND
HATT HIDE HOOP HOUR IMMI INCH
KNOT KOKU LAST MEAL METE MILE
MUID NAIL NOOK OMER PACE PINT
PIPE POLL RATE REAM RIME ROOD
ROPE ROTL SAAH SACK SALM SEAH
SEAM SIZE SKEP SPAN STEP TAKT
TAPE TIME TRAM TRUG TSUN VARA
WIST YARD ALMUD AMBER ANKER
ARDAB ARDEB ARURA BEKAH BIGHA
BLANK BODGE BRASS CABAN CABLE
CABOT CANDY CARAT CARGA CATTY
CAVAN CHAIN CHANG CHING CLOVE
COOMB CRANS CUBIT CUMAL CUNIT
DENUM DEPOH DIGIT DRAFT DUNAM
DUNUM EPHAH GAUGE GERAH GIRTH
HOMER HUTCH JUGER LABOR LAGEN
LIANG LIBRA LIGNE LIPPY LITER LITRE
MEITH METER METRE MINIM MODEL
OUNCE PEISE PERCH PLANK POUND
QUIRE RASER RHYME SALMA SCALE
SCORE SHAKU SHENG SHING SIEVE
SLEEP STACK STERE STONE STOOP
STOUP THERM TOISE TOVET TRACE
VERST YOJAN APATAN ARCHIN
ARPENT ARSHIN ASSIZE BARREL
BATMAN BEMETE BOVATE BUNDLE
BUSHEL CANADA CANTAR CHOMER
CHOPIN COLLOP COUDEE COVIDO
CUERDA DAVACH DAVOCH DECARE
DEGREE DENIER DIPODY DIRHAM
DRACHM ENGLER EXTENT FANEGA
FATHOM FEDDAN FINGER FIRKIN
FIRLOT FLAGON FODDER FORPET
FOTHER GALLON GRAMME HALEBI
HIDAGE KISHEN LEAGUE MICRON
MODIUS MODULE MOGGIO MORGEN
NUMBER OITAVA OUROUB OXHIDE
QANTAR REASON SAZHEN SETIER
SQUARE STERAD STRIKE SULUNG
TERMIN THRAVE WINDLE YOJANA
ADOULIE AMPHORA ANAPEST
ARSHINE BATTUTA BRACCIO
BREADTH CADENCE CALIPER
CALORIE CENTARE CENTNER
CENTRAD CHITTAK COMPASS
CONGIUS CONTAIN DECIARE DIOPTER
DRACHMA DRAUGHT ENTROPY

FARSAKH FARSANG FRUNDEL
FURLONG HECTARE HEMINEE KILIARE
NOCKTAT QUARTAN QUARTER
SCHEPEL SCRUPLE SECCHIO
SKEPFUL SKIPPLE SPANGLE SPINDLE
STADION STADIUM TERTIAN VIRGATE
ALQUEIRE CAPACITY CARUCATE
CENTIARE CHETVERT CRANNOCK
DACTYLIC DECAGRAM DECIGRAM
DESIATIN DIAPASON HOGSHEAD
INNOCENT LANDYARD METEWAND
MUTCHKIN PARASANG PLOWGANG
PLOWGATE SCHOONER SCHOPPEN
STANDARD PRECAUTION
(— DEPTH) SOUND
(— FOR DRINKS) JIGGER
(— FOR FISH) COT VOG CRAN LAST
DRAFT HAMPER DRAUGHT
(— FOR SHELLFISH) WASH
(— OF BEER) HANDLE
(— OF BUTTER) SPAN
(— OF CHAFF) FAN
(— OF COAL) TEN CORF KEEL
CHALDER CHALDRON
(— OF DEVELOPMENT) AGE
(— OF DIAMONDS) BULSE
(— OF DISCREPANCY) LEEWAY
(— OF EELS) BIND STICK
(— OF EFFICIENCY) DUTY
(— OF FURS) MANTLE
(— OF GRAIN) MOY COOP
(— OF HERRINGS) MEASE
(— OF HONCE) HAND
(— OF LIQUOR) FIFTH
(— OF MEDICINE) DOSE DROP
(— OF MERCURY) FLASK
(— OF MINING CLAIMS) MERE
(— OF OUTER SPACE) PARSEC
(— OF PEAS) COP
(— OF RAISINS) FRAIL
(— OF ROTATION) ANGLE
(— OF SILK) DRAMMAGE
(— OF STRAW) KEMPLE
(— OF SUPERIORITY) LEAD
(— OF TIMBER) TON STANDARD
(— OF WAR) BLOCKADE
(— OF WATCHES) LIGNE
(— OF WATERCRESS) HAND
(— OF WEIGHT FOR ARROWS)
SHILLING
(— OF WHISKY) CRUISKEN CRUISKEEN
(— OF WOOD) CORD STACK STERE
(— OF WOOL FINENESS) BLOOD
(— OF WORK) POOL
(— OF YARN) LEA RAP CLEW HEER
THREAD SPANGLE SPINDLE
(— OUT) BATCH
(ANGULAR —) ARC
(COERCIVE —) SANCTION
(COUNTERFEIT —) SLANG
(DANCE —) TRACE
(DUE —) MANNER
(FULL —) SATIETY COMPLEMENT

(LIQUID —) CUP GILL PINT MINIM
QUART GALLON
(OLD LIQUID —) TIERCE
(PHARMACISTS'S —) MINIM
(QUANTITATIVE —) MAGNITUDE
(ROAD —) SCHENE
(RUSSIAN —) VERST SAGENE
(SANCTIONED —) STANDARD
(SIAMESE —) NIOU
(TAKE —S) ACT
(PREF.) METR(O)
(SUFF.) METER METR(E)(O)(Y)
(BY A SPECIFIED —) MEAL
MEASURED NUMEROUS
MEASURE FOR MEASURE
(AUTHOR OF —) SHAKESPEARE
(CHARACTER IN —) ELBOW FROTH
LUCIO PETER ANGELO JULIET
POMPEY THOMAS CLAUDIO
ESCALUS MARIANA VARRIUS
ABHORSON ISABELLA OVERDONE
FRANCISCA VINCENTIO BARNARDINE
MEASURELESS ENDLESS INFINITE
MEASUREMENT GAGE DEPTH
GAUGE LEVEL MEITH METAGE
DIALING MEASURE SOUNDING
(— BY LINES) STICHOMETRY
(— FOR TAXATION) HIDE HIDAGE
(— OF CLOTH) ALNAGE
(— OF FINENESS) SET SETT
(CIRCULAR —) RADIAN
(EARTH —) GEODESY
(LUMBER —) LAST
(TIME —) HOROMETRY
MEASURER METER
(— OF LAND) SURVEYOR
MEASURING
(SUFF.) METRY
MEASURING-ROD METEWAND
METEYARD METESTICK
MEAT BEEF FISH FOOD LAMB LEAN
LIFT PORK FLESH STEAK VIFDA
VIVDA BUCCAN CAGMAG CONFIT
FLEECE MATTER NUTTON TARGET
PECKAGE
(— AND FISH) LAULAU
(— COOKED ON SKEWERS) SATE
HASLET HASSLET
(— COOKED WITH SKEWERS)
SASSATIE
(— DRIED IN SUN) JERKY CHARQUI
PEMMICAN
(— OF CONCH) SCUNGILI
(— OF KID) CAPRETTO
(— ON SKEWERS) YAKITORI
(— WITH VEGETABLES) STEW
MULLIGAN
(BOILED —) SOD SODDEN BOUILLI
(BROILED —) GRISKIN GRILLADE
(BUFFALO —) FLEECE
(CANNED —) SPAM
(CHOPPED —) BURGER
(COCONUT —) COPRA

(CURED —) HAM
(CUT OF —) ARM
(DRIED —) MUMMY
(FAT —) SPECK
(FROZEN —) FRIGO
(INFERIOR —) CAGMAG STICKING
(JERKED —) BILTONG CHARQUI
(KIND OF —) MINCE
(LEAN —) MUSCLE
(MINCED —) CHUET JIGOTE RISSOLE
SANDERS
(POTTED —) RILLETT
(RABBIT —) LAPAN
(RAGOUT OF —) HARICOT
(ROAST —) BREDE CABOB
(ROLLED —) BIRD
(SALTED —) JUNK MART
(SIDE —) SOWBELLY
(SLICED —) CARPACCIO
(SLICE OF —) BRACIOLA BRACIOLE
(SMALL PIECES OF —) SATAY
(SMOKED —) BUCCAN
(THIN SLICES OF —) PICCATA
MEAT CURER BATHMAN
MEATHEADED DENSE
MEAT HOOK GAMBREL
MEAT JELLY ASPIC
MEATLESS PARVE LENTEN PAREVE
MEAT PIE PASTY
MEATUS BUR BURR ALVEARY
MEATY PITHY
MECATE MCCARTY
MECHANIC JOINER WRIGHT
ARTISAN FELTMAN SHOPMAN
WORKMAN BANAUSIC OPERATIVE
MECHANICAL FROZEN INHUMAN
METALLIC AUTOMATIC
(NOT —) HORMIC
MECHANICALLY BLINDLY
MECHANISM FAN BOND FEED GEAR
KITE LIFT MOTE APRON CATCH
CROWD FORCE ORGAN SHAKE SLIDE
SPARK STEER ACTION BOTTOM
CUTOFF INFEED MOTION SICKLE
STRIKE AUTOVAC BUILDER CHANNEL
CONTROL EJECTOR GIGBACK
GRIPPER GUNLOCK HOLDOUT
SETTING TRIPPER ACTUATOR
ELEVATOR KINETICS RACKWORK
ROLAMITE SELECTOR SETWORKS
SIGNALER STEERING STOPWORK
THROWOUT
(— OF HEREDITY) PANGENESIS
MECHANIZE DESKILL AUTOMATE
MECHLIN MALINES
MECONIN OPIANYL
MEDAL GOLD GONG STAR AWARD
MODEL STAMP PLAQUE SILVER
MEDALET OSCELLA VERNICLE
MEDALLION
(PL.) EXONUMIA
MEDALLION CAMEO TONDO
PADUAN PATERA PANHAGIA

MEDAN (FATHER OF —) ABRAHAM
(MOTHER OF —) KETURAH
MEDDLE TIG FOOL MELL MESS MIRD
NOSE POKE TOUCH DABBLE FIDDLE
FINGER HECKLE POTTER PUTTER
TAMPER TANGLE TINKER
(— IRRESPONSIBLY) TRIFLE
MEDDLER SNOOP YENTA SNOOPER
BUSYBODY KIBITZER STICKLER
STIFFLER BUTTINSKY
MEDDLESOME NOSY FRESH NEBBY
MEDDLING BUSY
MEDEA (AUNT OF —) CIRCE
(BROTHER OF —) ABSYRTUS
APSYRTUS
(FATHER OF —) AEETES
(HUSBAND OF —) JASON AEGEUS
(MOTHER OF —) IDYIA
(SISTER OF —) CHALCOPE
CHALCIOPE
MEDIA ELASTICA
(ONE OF THE —) PRESS RADIO
TELEVISION
MEDIAL MEDIAN MEDIUM MIDDLE
AVERAGE
MEDIAN MEDIAL MESIAL AVERAGE
MIDLINE
(— STRIP) MALL TERRACE
MEDIANT THIRD
MEDIATE MEAN REFEREE INTERCEDE
MEDIATING MIDWAY MIDWAY
MEDIATOR MEANS MEDIUM
DAYSMAN MIDDLER PLACATER
STICKLER MODERATOR
MEDIC DOC HOP DOCTOR NONESUCH
SHAMROCK
MEDICAL IATRIC PHYSIC IATRICAL
PAEONIAN
(— WORK) ALMONING
(PREF.) (— TREATMENT) IATR(O)
MEDICAMENT REMEDY SMEGMA
FRONTAL EPULOTIC
MEDICINAL IATRIC PHYSIC MEDICAL
THERIAL PHYSICAL SALUTARY
THERICAL OFFICINAL
MEDICINE DRUG MUTI PEAI DROPS
GRUEL STEEL STUFF TONIC TRADE
AMULET ECLEGM ELIXIR MAGUAL
PHYSIC POWDER REMEDY SIMPLE
ALOETIC ANODYNE ANTACID
CORDIAL HEPATIC LUCHDOM
MIXTURE NERVINE OPORICE
PLACEBO POROTIC PYROTIC SPLENIC
AROMATIC DIAPENTE DIGESTER
DRUGGERY EARDROPS ECCRITIC
EMULGENT LAXATIVE LEECHDOM
LENITIVE LOBLOLLY PECTORAL
PHARMACY PULMONIC RELAXANT
SEDATIVE SPECIFIC STOMATIC
CATHARTIC PURGATIVE
PRESCRIPTION
(— BOTTLE) VIAL PHIAL
(AMOUNT OF —) DOSAGE

(CHINESE —) SENSO
(COLD —) CONTAC
(QUACK —) NOSTRUM
(SHIP'S —) LOBLOLLY
(SYSTEM OF —) AYURVEDA
(UNIVERSAL —) PANACEA
(PL.) GALIANES
(PREF.) IAMATO IATRO PHARMACO
MEDICINE MAN PEAI DOCTOR
KAHUNA PIACHE POWWOW
SHAMAN SINGER ANGEKOK
TOHUNGA CONTRARY POWWOWER
MEDICK SNAIL
MEDIEVAL OLD GOTHIC
MEDIOCRE BUSH HACK MEAN SUCH
MEDIUM AVERAGE INFERIOR
MIDDLING MODERATE PASSABLE
MEDITATE CAST CHEW MUSE
BROOD GLOAT STUDY THINK WEIGH
PONDER RECORD BETHINK
COMMENT IMAGINE PREPEND
REFLECT REVOLVE COGITATE
CONSIDER PURPENSE RUMINATE
MEDITATION MOYEN STUDY THINK
ZAZEN DHYANA MUSING REVERIE
THOUGHT HIGGAION
(PLACE OF —) ZENDO
MEDITATIVE MUSING MUSEFUL
PENSIVE RUMINANT
MEDITERRANEAN MIDLAND
MEDIUM BATH EVEN LENS MEAN
ETHER JUICE MIDST MOYEN
ORGAN BALIAN BISTER BISTRE
DIGEST MIDDLE MIDWAY ORACLE
SLUDGE TEMPER PSYCHIC VEHICLE
MEDIOCRE SHOWCASE
CONTINUUM
(— FOR DISCUSSION) PLATFORM
(— OF DIVINE REVELATION) ORACLE
(— OF EXCHANGE) CURRENCY
(— OF EXPRESSION) VOICE
(— OF TRANSMISSION) AIR AIRWAVE
(CULTURE —) AGAR STAB BROTH
HYRAX SLANT CULTURE BOUILLON
(ENVELOPING —) SWATH
(PAINTING —) TEMPERA
(PLANT GROWTH —) PERLITE
(REFINING —) ALEMBIC
MEDIUM, THE (CHARACTER IN —)
FLORA MONICA
(COMPOSER OF —) MENOTTI
MEDLAR MESPIL LAZAROLE
MEDLEY OLIO BABEL REVUE JUMBLE
CHIVARI CLANGOR FARRAGO
GOULASH MELANGE MIXTURE
BROUHAHA KEDGEREE MACARONI
MISHMASH RHAPSODY SLAMPAMP
VARIORUM CHARIVARI MACEDOINE
(— OF TUNES) QUODLIBET
MEDOC WINE LAFITTE
MEDREGAL BONITO
MEDULLA PITH MARROW
MEDULLA OBLONGATA BULB

MEDUSA JELLY QUARL GORGON
BLUBBER GERYONID
(FATHER OF —) PHORCYS
(MOTHER OF —) CETO
(SLAYER OF —) PERSEUS
(PL.) BRACT
MEEK LOW DAFT MURE LOWLY
GENTLE HUMBLE NEBBISH PACIFIC
LAMBLIKE YIELDING
MEEKNESS MANSUETUDE
MEERSCHAUM PIPE GRAVEL
KIEFEKIL SEPIOLITE
MEET FIT KEP SEE COPE FACE FILL
HENT NOSE ABIDE CLOSE CROSS
FRONT GREET INCUR OCCUR PIECE
TOUCH ANSWER BATTLE BEMEET
COMBAT CONCUR FULFIL INVENT
SEMBLE CONTACT CONTEST
CONVENE CONVENT COUNCIL
FULFILL RUNINTO SATISFY
ASSEMBLE CONFRONT CONVERGE
GAINCOPE
(— A BET) SEE
(— A NEED) SUFFICE
(— AT END) BUTT
(— FACE TO FACE) AFFRONT
(— FORCIBLY) SMITE
(— SQUARELY) ENVISAGE
(— VIOLENTLY) CHECK HURTLE
(— WITH) GET SEE BUMP FIND
STRIKE
(ATHLETIC —) GALA GYMKHANA
MEETING MOD FEIS MOOT CLOSE
FORUM SABHA SHINE STOUR
SYNOD TRYST ACCESS AUMAGA
CAUCUS CHAPEL CLINIC HUDDLE
POWWOW SEANCE CABINET
CHAPTER COLLEGE CONTACT
CONVENT COUNCIL JOLLITY
MOOTING OCCURSE REVIVAL
SEMINAR SITTING SYNAXIS
ASSEMBLY CONGRESS CONSULTA
DELEGACY ECCLESIA EXERCISE
JUNCTION OSCULANT TERTULIA
WARDMOTE CONCOURSE
COLLOQUIUM
(— FULLY ATTENDED) PLENUM
(— OF BARDS) GORSEDD
(— OF NEIGHBORS) HUSKING
(— OF SCHOLARS) LEVY
(— OF WITCHES) ESBAT SABBAT
SABBATH
(— OF WORSHIPERS) SERVICE
(— STANDARDS) FIT
(ANGLO-SAXON —) GEMOTE
(APPOINTED —) RENDEVOUS
(ENDWISE —) ABUTMENT
(EVENING —) SOIREE
(FORBIDDING CLOSED —S)
SUNSHINE
(GENERAL —) PRIME
(NOT —) PARALLEL

(POLITICAL —) CAUCUS
(PRIVATE —) CONCLAVE
(RACE —) REGATTA
(SECRET —) CABAL CONSULT
CONCLAVE
(SOCIAL —) CLUB JOLLY HOBNOB
(SPORTS —) GYMKHANA
(TOWN —) TUNMOOT
MEETINGHOUSE MORADA
MEETING PLACE AMBALAM
CENACLE TINWALD
MEGALOMANIAC MONARCHO
MEGAPHONE VAMPHORN
MEGAPODE MALEO LEIPOA
MEGARA (FATHER OF —) CREON
(HUSBAND OF —) HERCULES
MEGAREUS (FATHER OF —)
HIPPOMENES
(MOTHER OF —) OENOPE
(SON OF —) EUIPPUS
(WIFE OF —) IPHINOE
MEGILP GUMPTION
MEGINNING
(— OF ACTIVITY) DAYONE
MEHETABEL
(HUSBAND OF —) HADAD
(MOTHER OF —) MATRED
MEHIR (FATHER OF —) CHELUB
MEHTAR BUNGY BHUNGI
MEHUJAEL (FATHER OF —) IRAD
MEIOSIS LITOTES REDUCTION
**MEISTERSINGER VON
NURNBERG, DI** (CHARACTER IN —
) EVA HANS VEIT DAVID FRITZ SACHS
POGNER KOTHNER WALTHER
STOLZING MAGDALENE
BECKMESSER
(COMPOSER OF —) WAGNER
MELAMPUS SEER
(BROTHER OF —) BIAS
(FATHER OF —) AMYTHAON
(MOTHER OF —) IDOMENE
(SON OF —) MANTIUS
ANTIPHATES
(WIFE OF —) LYSIPPE
MELANCHOLIA ATHYMY ATHYMIA
SADNESS
MELANCHOLIC HYPPISH
MELANCHOLY WO LOW SAD WOE
BLUE DRAM DULL DUMP MARE
ADUST BLUES DEARN DOWIE DREAR
DUSKY GLOOM SORRY WISHT
GLOOMY SOMBER SOMBRE
SORROW SPLEEN SULLEN YELLOW
CHAGRIN DOLEFUL DUMPISH
ELEGIAC SADNESS SPLEENY
THOUGHT ATRABILE LIVERISH
TRISTFUL
MELANESIAN DOBUAN KANAGA
KANAKA EFATESE
MELANGE OLIO GOMBO GUMBO
SMORGASBORD

MELANIPPUS (FATHER OF —)
THESEUS HICETAON
(LOVER OF —) COMAETHO
(MOTHER OF —) PERIGUNE
(SON OF —) IOXUS
MELANISM PHAEISM
MELANTERITE INKSTONE
MELANTIUS (SISTER OF —) EVADNE
MELATOPE EYE
MELCHI (FATHER OF —) ADDI JANNA
MELCHIAH (SON OF —) PASHUR
MELD SET SAMBA SPREAD BOLIVIA
DECLARE
MELEA (FATHER OF —) MENAN
MELEAGER (FATHER OF —) OENEUS
(MOTHER OF —) ALTHAEA
MELECH (FATHER OF —) MICAH
MELEF BRAWL MEDLEY RUMBLE
DOGFIGHT PELLMELL WINGDING
MELIA (FATHER OF —) OCEANUS
(SON OF —) ISMENUS TENERUS
AEGIALEUS PHORONEUS
MELIBOEA (FATHER OF —) AMPHION
(HUSBAND OF —) NELEUS
(MOTHER OF —) NIOBE
MELIORATE MITIGATE
MELISMA JUBILUS
MELL KIRN
MELLIFLUOUS SUGARED
HYBLAEAN
MELLOW AGE OMY HAZE LUSH
MALM PLUM RICH RIPE SOFT FRUSH
RIPEN FLUTED GOLDEN MATURE
MELLOWED BEERY
MELODIOUS SOFT SOOT TUNY
SWEET TUNED ARIOSO DULCET
MELODIC MUSICAL SIRENIC
SONGFUL TUNADLE TUNEFUL
CANOROUS CHARMING NUMEROUS
SOUNDFUL
(EXCESSIVELY —) SIRUPY SYRUPY
MELODRAMA HAM SOAP TANK
MELODY AIR HUM LAY ARIA LILT
NOTE TUNE CANTO CHANT CHARM
DREAD MELOS MIRTH NIGUN
CANTUS CHORAL GHAZEL MONODY
NIGGUN STROKE CANZONA
CANZONE CHORALE DESCANT
HARMONY MEASURE MELISMA
PLANXTY ROSALIA CARILLON
CAVATINA DIAPASON VOCALISE
(— COMPASS) AMBITUS
(MOURNFUL —) DUMP
(PASTORAL —) MUSETTE
(SIMPLE —) PLAINSONG
(SYNAGOGAL —S) CHAZANUT
HAZANUTH
MELON PEPO GOURD MANGO
CASABA CITRON DUDAIM MAYCOCK
CUCURBIT HONEYDEW PEPONIDA
PEPONIUM
(KIND OF —) CRANSHAW CRENSHAW

MELT FLY RIN RUN BLOW FADE FLOW
FLUX FUSE THAW DEICE FOUND
LEACH SMELT SWEAL SWELT TOUCH
GUTTER RELENT SOFTEN DISTILL
FORMELT RESOLVE DISCANDY
DISSOLVE ELIQUATE COLLIQUATE
(— AWAY) SWEAL
(— DOWN) RENDER
(— IRREGULARLY) DROZE
MELTED RUN FONDU FUSED FUSILE
MELTING SOFT FUSILE FUSION
MELTWATER OUTWASH
MELVILLE (BOOK BY —) OMOO
MEMBER LIMB LITH PART BRANCH
FELLOW FILLET GIRDER SOCIUS
AMANIST COMPART ERANIST
FAIRING ALBRIGHT AULARIAN
BRIDLING
(— OF ANSAR) HELPER
(— OF BALLET) FIGURANT
(— OF BAND) SIDEMAN
(— OF BODYGUARD) HUSCARL
(— OF BROTHERHOOD) ESSENE
SENUSSI
(— OF CHURCH) BROTHER
PARISHIONER
(— OF CLAN) CHILD CALEBITE
(— OF CLERGY) DEFENSOR
(— OF COAST GUARD) SPAR
(— OF COUNCIL) CONSUL
HEEMRAAD
(— OF COURT) DICAST EPHETE
(— OF CREW) HAND IDLER LAYER
DRIVER STROKE BOWSMAN
FORETOP BRAKEMAN SHAREMAN
(— OF CULT) ANGEL AMIDIST
(— OF FACULTY) COUNSEL
LECTURER
(— OF FAMILY) FETII
(— OF FRATERNAL ORDER) ELK
SHRINER FORESTER KIWANIAN
(— OF FRATERNITY) GREEK
(— OF FRENCH ACADEMY)
IMMORTAL
(— OF GANG) HENCHMAN
(— OF GENTRY) SEIGNEUR
(— OF GIRL SCOUTS) BROWNIE
(— OF GREEK ARMY) EVZONE
(— OF GUILD) COMACINE
HOASTMAN
(— OF HOUSEHOLD) FAMILIAR
(— OF HUNTING PARTY) STANDER
(— OF INN OF COURT) ANCIENT
BENCHER
(— OF IRISH REPUBLICAN ARMY)
PROVO
(— OF ITALIAN ARMY) ALPINO
(— OF KNOW-NOTHING PARTY) SAM
(— OF LEGISLATURE) SOLON DEPUTY
DELEGATE
(— OF LITERARY GROUP) FELIBRE
(— OF LOWEST CLASS) LUMPEN

(— OF MIDDLE CLASS) BURGHER
(— OF PARLIAMENT) CONTENT
THINGMAN
(— OF PRIMROSE LEAGUE) KNIGHT
(— OF RELIGIOUS ORDER) DAME
FRIAR EUDIST FRAILE FRATER
HERMIT JESUIT SISTER ALEXIAN
BEGUINE BRINSER DERVISH HUSSITE
SEPARTE SERVANT SERVITE
CENOBITE EXORCIST HUMANIST
PENITENT SALESIAN THEATINE
(— OF RETINUE) SEQUEL SEQUENT
(— OF RUSSIAN ARISTOCRACY)
BOIAR BOYAR BOYARD
(— OF SAME GENUS) CONGENER
(— OF SECRET ORGANIZATION)
DEMOLAY
(— OF SECRET SOCIETY) BOXER
DANITE
(— OF SECT) BABI SHIA BABEE
DRUSE HASID KHOJA SHIAH AUDIAN
BEREAN BRAHMO CATHAR DIPPER
DOPPER IBADHI JUMPER KHLYST
SHIITE SMARTA WAHABI AISSAWA
AJIVIKA AUDAEAN CAÏNITE CHASSID
DREAMER EMPIRIC EUCHITE IBADITE
ISAWIYA ISMAILI RAPPIST SENUSSI
SEVENER AQUARIAN CALIXTIN
DARBYITE DUKHOBOR EBIONITE
FAMILIST GLASSITE LABADIST
MANDAEAN SADDUCEE SEVERIAN
SHAFIITE SIMONIAN STUNDIST
(— OF STAFF) ATTACHE
(— OF STATE) CITIZEN
(— OF STOCK EXCHANGE)
BOARDMAN
(— OF TEAM) SPARE BOBBER KICKER
(— OF TRIBE) LEVITE JUDAHITE
LAMANITE
(— OF UPPER CLASS) EFFENDI
(— OF VARNA) SUDRA SHUDRA
(— OF WHITE RACE) HAOLE
(— OF WINDOW) APRON
(— OF YOUTH GANG) HOMEBOY
(—S OF CLASS) FRY
(—S OF PROFESSION) FACULTY
(—S OF SECT) SKOPTSY
(—S OF TRIBUNAL) ACUERDO
(ARCHITECTURAL —) FAN ARCH FLAT
SILL SPAN GABLE SOCLE STILE STILT
CORBEL FASCIA CONSOLE CORNICE
(CHURCH —) GREEK LATIN DANITE
DUNKER KIRKER TUNKER AZYMITE
BAPTIST BEGHARD BROTHER
DUNKARD KIRKMAN SECEDER
ARMENIAN BRYANITE CATHOLIC
DISCIPLE DOWIEITE JACOBITE
(CHURCH —S) FAITHFUL
(EVERY —) ALL
(FEEBLEST —) WRIG
(FULL —) GREMIAL
(OLDEST —) FATHER

(OVERHANGING —) BRACKET
(POLITICAL —) CADET ENDEK SHIRT
GUELPH HUNKER LEADER APRISTA
LEFTIST LIBERAL ABHORRER
BUCKTAIL DEMOCRAT HERODIAN
LABORITE
(PROJECTING —) TENON
(SECRET —) CRYPTO
(SENIOR —) DOYEN
(TENSION —) HANGER
(TERMINAL —) TOE
(SUFF.) AD CRAT
(— OF A CLASS) ANDER MER(E)(IC)
(IS)(OUS)(Y)
MEMBERS
(SUFF.)
(— OF THE FAMILY) IDAE
(— OF THE SUBFAMILY OF) INAE
MEMBERSHIP SEAT GARTER
GUILDRY
MEMBRANE RIM WEB CAUL COAT
DURA FELL HEAD TELA GALEA
HYMEN VELUM AMNION AMNIOS
EXTINE INTINE MENINX MOTHER
MUCOSA PLEURA RETINA SEPTUM
SEROSA TIMBAL TUNICA TYMPAN
BLANKET CAPSULE CHORION
CHOROID CUTICLE DECIDUA EPICYTE
HYALOID OOLEMMA PERIOST
PUTAMEN STRATUM VELAMEN
ECTODERM ENDOCYST ENVELOPE
EPENDYMA EPISPORE EXOLEMMA
INDUSIUM INTEXINE LABELLUM
PATAGIUM PELLICLE STRIFFEN
ALLANTOIS PERIPLAST PERIOSTEUM
PERITONEUM
(— OF BRAIN) MATER
(— OF EGG) POTAMEN
(— OF EYE) SCLERA SCLEROTIC
(— OF GRAIN) INTINE
(— OF ORANGE) ZEST
(NICTITATING —) HAW
(TYMPANIC —) TYMPAN MYRINGA
DRUMHEAD DRUMSKIN
(PL.) ADNEXA ANNEXA MENINGES
(PREF.) CHORI(O) HYMEN(O)
MENING(O) MYRINGO VEL(I)
(SUFF.) YMENITIS
MEMBRANOUS HUSKY SKINNY
HYMENOID SCARIOSE SCARIOUS
MEMENTO RELIC TOKEN MEMORY
TROPHY KEEPSAKE REMINDER
SOUVENIR
MEMINNA PEESOREH
MEMNON (FATHER OF —) TITHONUS
(MOTHER OF —) AURORA
(SLAYER OF —) ACHILLES
MEMOIR ELOGE RECORD HISTORY
MEMORIAL
MEMORABLE GRAND SIGNAL
CLASSIC NOTABLE MEMORIAL
NAMEABLE NOTEWORTHY

MEMORANDA (SET OF —) TICKLER
MEMORANDUM BILL CHIT CHIT MEMO
NOTE SLIP BRIEF JURAT CAHIER
CIPHER DOCKET MEMOIR MINUTE
TICKET JOTTING MEMORIAL
NOTANDUM PROTOCOL BORDEREAU
DIRECTIVE
MEMORIAL AHU AGALMA CAHIER
FACTUM MEMOIR MEMORY RECORD
TROPHY DENKMAL MEMENTO
MENTION EBENEZER MONUMENT
REMEMBRANCE
MEMORIZE LEARN MANDATE
REMEMBER
MEMORY MIND EPROM HEART
IMAGE STORE RECALL RECORD
MEMENTO STORAGE MEMORIAL
SOUVENIR
(— CHIP) DRAM
(— ON COMPUTER CHIP) RAM ROM
(— SUBDIVISION) PAGE
(BAD —) FORGETTERY
(COMPUTER —) RAM ROM PAGE
CACHE STACK SCRATCHPAD
(MECHANICAL —) ROTE
(OF POOR —) FLUFFY
(PAINFUL —) SCAR
(PROGRAMMABLE —) EPROM
(SMALL COMPUTER —) SCRATCHPAD
(STORED COMPUTER —) FIRMWARE
(PREF.) MNEM(I)(O)
(SUFF.) MNESIA(C) MNESIS MNETIC
MEN THEY ORANG INNUIT MANHEAD
MANHOOD MANKIND MENFOLK
HUMANITY
(BLESSED —) BEATI
MENACE BOAST IMPEND THREAT
BOGEYMAN MINATORY THREATEN
MENACING STOUT SURLY FIERCE
TOWARD MINATORY MINACIOUS
MENAHEM (FATHER OF —) GADI
(VICTIM OF —) SHALLUM
MEN-AT-ARMS CHIVALRY
MEND DO FIX BEET DARN HEAL HELP
KNIT STOP TINK AMEND CLOUT
EMEND GRAFT MOISE PATCH
COBBLE DOCTOR FETTLE RANTER
REFORM REPAIR SOLDER SPETCH
TINKLE IMPROVE INWEAVE REDRESS
RIGHTLE
(— BY ADDING FEATHERS) IMP
(— CLUMSILY) BOTCH
(— MEN'S CLOTHES) BUSHEL
MENDACIOUS FALSE DISHONEST
MENDACITY LYING DECEIT FALSITY
UNTRUTH
MENDER TINKER KETTLER
BEATSTER
MENDICANCY BEGGARY
MENDICANT NAGA DANDI FAKIR
FRIAR UDASI BEGGAR BHIKKU
FAKEER FRATER GOSAIN AJIVIKA

BAIRAGI EUCHITE VAIRAGI
PANDARAM SANNYASI PASSIONIST
MENDING COBBLE
MENEL NELL
MENELAUS (BROTHER OF —)
AGAMEMNON
(FATHER OF —) ATREUS PLISTHENES
(MOTHER OF —) AEROPE
(SISTER OF —) ANAXIBIA
(WIFE OF —) HELEN
MENHADEN POGY PORGY BUNKER
CHEBOG SHINER ALEWIFE BUGFISH
BUGHEAD CLUPEID ELLFISH
FATBACK OLDWIFE SAVELHA
SHADINE WHITING BONYFISH
HARDHEAD
MENHIR BOUTA GORSEDD PEULVAN
CATSTONE HAGIOLITH
MENIAL FAG BASE LOON PAGE
KNAVE DRIVEL HARLOT POTBOY
VARLET SERVILE SLAVISH BANAUSIC
SCULLION SERVITOR
MENILITE OPAL
MENISCOID CRESCENT
MENNONITE HOOKER AMISHMAN
AMMANITE HUTERITE
MENOETIUS (BROTHER OF —)
ATLAS PROMETHEUS
(FATHER OF —) ACTOR
(MOTHER OF —) AEGINA
(SON OF —) PATROCLUS
MENOPAUSE CLIMAX
MENSTRUATE FLOW
MENSTRUATING SICK
MENSTRUATION FLOW CURSE
FLUOR CRAMPS PERIOD COURSES
(FIRST —) MENARCHE
(PREF.) MENO
(SUFF.) (— CONDITION) MENIA
MENSTRUUM SOLVENT
MENTAL IDEAL GENIAL INWARD
MINDLY PHRENIC PSYCHIC CEREBRAL
MENTALITY MIND SENSE ACUMEN
REASON SPIRIT PSYCHISM
MENTHA LABIATE
MENTHANE TERPANE
MENTHOL CAMPHOR
MENTION CALL CITE HINT MIND
MING MINT NAME CHEEP CLEPE
SPEAK TOUCH MEMBER NOTICE
SPEECH MEANING SPECIFY
SUGGEST CITATION INSTANCE
MEMORATE REHEARSE REMEMBER
REFERENCE REPETITION
(— BY NAME) NEMN NEMME
NEMPNE
(— CASUALLY) DROP
(— FIRST) PROMISE
(— PUBLICLY) PLUG
(HONORABLE —) ACCESSIT
MENTOR GURU TEACHER CICERONE
MENTUM PERULA

MENU CARD CARTE
  (COMPUTER —) DISPLAY
MEONOTHAI (FATHER OF —)
  OTHNIEL
MEPACRINE ATABRIN ATABRINE
MEPERIDINE DEMEROL
MEPHIBOSHETH (BROTHER OF —)
  ARMONI
  (FATHER OF —) SAUL JONATHAN
  (MOTHER OF —) RIZPAH
  (SON OF —) MICHA
MEPHISTOPHELIAN SATANIC
MEPROBAMATE MILTOWN
MERAB (FATHER OF —) SAUL
  (HUSBAND OF —) ADRIEL
MERARI (FATHER OF —) LEVI
MERCAPTAN THIOL
MERCEDARIAN NOLASCAN
  RANSOMER
MERCENARY HACK VENAL JACKAL
  HESSIAN PINDARI HIRELING
  WAGELING
MERCER SILKMAN
MERCERIZE SCHREINER
MERCHANDISE LINE CARGO CHEAP
  GOODS STUFF WARES ARTWARE
  CHAFFER SHIPPER TRAFFIC
  CHAFFERY SALEWARE
  (CHEAP SHODDY —) BORAX
  (RETURNED —) COMEBACK
MERCHANT ARAB SETH SETT TELI
  WALLA BADGER BANIAN DEALER
  FACTOR KITELY NEPMAN RETAIL
  SELLER TAIPAN TRADER ANTONIO
  CHAPMAN GOLADAR HANSARD
  HOWADJI CHANDLER HUCKSTER
  MARCHAND POVINDAH SOUDAGUR
  STOREMAN
  (COAL —) HOASTMAN
  (GRAIN —) LAMBADI
  (GREAT —) TAIPAN
  (HINDU —) BUNIA BUNNIA
  (WINE —) VINTNER
MERCHANT OF VENICE (AUTHOR
  OF —) SHAKESPEARE
  (CHARACTER IN —) GOBBO TUBAL
  PORTIA ANTONIO JESSICA LORENZO
  NERISSA SALANIO SALERIO
  SHYLOCK BASSANIO GRATIANO
  LEONARDO SALARINO STEPHANO
  BALTHASAR LAUNCELOT
MERCIFUL KIND MILD HUMANE
  RUEFUL TENDER CLEMENT LENIENT
  MILDFUL PITIFUL SPARING
  GRACIOUS QUEMEFUL
MERCILESS GRIM CRUEL SHARP
  BLOODY FIERCE SAVAGE WANTON
  PITILESS
MERCURY HG AZOCH AZOTH
  DRAGON HERMES SPIRIT CHIBRIT
  MARKERY TEUTATES QUICKSILVER
  (FATHER OF —) JUPITER
  (MOTHER OF —) MAIA

MERCY LAW ORE HORE PITY RUTH
  GRACE GRITH BLITHE LENITY
  CHARITY QUARTER CLEMENCY
  LENIENCY COMPASSION
  (— TO ANTAGONIST) QUARTER
  (PREF.) MISERI
MERE BARE NUDE ONLY PURE PUTE
  SOLE VERY NAKED SHEER SINGLE
  (PREF.) PSIL(O)
MEREL PIN
MERELY BUT JUST ONLY BARELY
  PURELY SIMPLY SINGLY SOLELY
  ALONELY UTTERLY ENTIRELY
  SCARCELY
MEREMOTH (FATHER OF —) BANI
  URIAH
MERETRICIOUS CHEAP GAUDY
  GILDED TAWDRY PUNKISH
MERGANSER SMEE SMEW HARLE
  SNOWL SPIKE HERALD SAWNEB
  WEASER BRACKET GARBILL
  JACKSAW RANTOCK SAWBILL
  TADPOLE TOWHEAD TWEEZER
  WHEEZER EARLDUCK MOSSHEAD
  SHELDRAKE
MERGE FUSE JOIN MELD SINK
  BLEND ENTER GLIDE UNIFY UNITE
  VERGE MINGLE COALESCE
  COMMERGE CONFLATE LIQUESCE
MERGING BLEND FUSION
MERICARP COCCUS
MERIDIAN (THOSE LIVING UNDER
  SAME —) ANTOECI
MERIDIONAL NOON NOONTIDE
MERINGUE KISS
MERINO DELAINE
MERISTEM PERIBLEM
MERIT DUE EARN MEED PUNY
  BROOK FOUND THANK WORTH
  DESERT PRAISE VIRTUE WRIHTE
  DEMERIT DESERVE PUDDING
  (— CONSIDERATION) COUNT
  (POSSESSING —) WORTHY
MERITED JUST
  (NOT —) INDIGN
MERITOCRACY ELITE
MERITORIOUS CAPITAL MERITORY
  THANKFUL VALOROUS
MERL BLACKIE
MERLIN (MISTRESS OF —) VIVIAN
  VIVIEN
MERLON COP
MERMAID ARIEL NIXIE SIREN
  MERROW MERWOMAN
MERMAN SEAMAN MANFISH
MERODACH (FATHER OF —) EA
  (WIFE OF —) ZARPAINT
MEROPE (BROTHER OF —)
  PHAETHON
  (FATHER OF —) ATLAS OENOPION
  PANDAREUS CRESPHONTES
  (HUSBAND OF —) POLYBUS
  SISYPHUS POLYPHONTES

(MOTHER OF —) PLEIONE CYPSELUS
HARMOTHOE
(SISTER OF —) AEDON CLEOTHERA
(SON OF —) AEPYTUS
MEROPODITE FEMUR MEROS
MEROZOITE AGAMETE
MERRILY GAILY GAMELY LIGHTLY
LUSTICK JOYOUSLY
MERRIMENT FUN JOY GALE GLEE
JEST UTAS DERAY MIRTH FROLIC
SPLEEN DAFFERY DAFFING FESTIVE
JOLLITY WAGGERY HILARITY
MERRY GAY BOON CANT GLAD GOLE
BONNY BUXOM CADGY CRANK
DROLL JOLLY LIGHT LUSTY MURRY
SUNNY VOGIE VOKIE BLITHE COCKET
FROLIC JOCANT JOCOSE JOCUND
JOVIAL JOYOUS LIVELY FEASTLY
GLEEFUL HOLIDAY JOCULAR
LUSTICK RAFFING WINSOME
CHIRPING DISPOSED FESTIVAL
GAMESOME GLEESOME LAUGHING
PLEASANT SPANKING SPORTFUL
SPORTIVE CONVIVIAL
(RIOTOUSLY —) SATURNALIAN
(UNREASONABLY —) DAFT
MERRY-ANDREW AIRY ZANY ANTIC
DROLL JESTER BUFFOON
MERRY-GO-ROUND CAROUSEL
TURNABOUT ROUNDABOUT
MERRYMAKING ALE MAY RAG
KIRN PLOY REVEL GAIETY JUNKET
RACKET SPLORE WHOOPEE
CARNIVAL FESTIVITY
MERRYTHOUGHT WISHBONE
MERRY WIDOW (CHARACTER IN —)
ZETA HANNA MIRKO DANILO GLAWARI
(COMPOSER OF —) LEHAR
MERRY WIVES OF WINDSOR
(AUTHOR OF —) SHAKESPEARE
(CHARACTER IN —) NYM ANNE FORD
HUGH JOHN PAGE CAIUS EVANS
ROBIN RUGBY FENTON PISTOL
SIMPLE QUICKLY SHALLOW SLENDER
WILLIAM BARDOLPH FALSTAFF
MERUS PALM
MESA HILL LOMA BENCH MESILLA
PLATEAU TERRACE CARTOUCH
MESADENIA CACALIA
MESCAL PEYOTE PEYOTL WOKOWI
MEXICAL CHALLOTE
MESCALERO FARAON
MESECH (FATHER OF —) JAPHET
MESENTERY CROW RUFFLE
MESH NET MASK MOKE CHAIN PITCH
SHALE ACCRUE ENGAGE MASCLE
SCREEN INTERLOCK SCREENING
(— IMPROPERLY) BUTT
(IN —) DIRECT
MESHA (FATHER OF —) CALEB
SHAHARAIM
(MOTHER OF —) HODESH
MESHED ENGAGED

MESHEZABEEL (FATHER OF —)
ZERAH
(SON OF —) PETHAHIAH
MESHILLEMOTH (FATHER OF —)
IMMER
MESHULLAM (FATHER OF —)
BERECHIAH BESODEIAH
ZERUBBABEL
(SON OF —) SALLU
MESHULLEMETH (FATHER OF —)
HARUZ
(HUSBAND OF —) MANASSEH
(SON OF —) AMON
MESOCARP FLESH
MESOMORPHIC SOMAL SOMATIC
ATHLETIC
MESON RHO KAON MUON PION
OMEGA BARYTRON MESOTRON
MESOPODIUM PETIOLE
MESOPOTAMIA (— REGION)
SUMER
(TREE OF —) HOMA
· **MESOTONIC** TERTIAN MEANTONE
MESQUITE HONEY KEAWE PACAY
CASHAW ALGAROBA HONEYPOD
IRONWOOD MOSQUITO
MESS JAG JAM MIX MUX PIE SOP
CLAT FIST HASH JAMB MUCK MULL
MUSS SLUB SOSS STEW SUSS
BOTCH CAUCH JAKES STREW SWILL
BOLLIX BUNGLE CADDLE CLATCH
JUMBLE MUCKER PICKLE PUDDLE
SOZZLE TUMBLE EYESORE
MAMMOCK MULLOCK SCAMBLE
SLOTTER COUSCOUS DISORDER
LOBLOLLY SHAMBLES SLAISTER
(— AROUND) JUKE
(— OF FOOD) SAND
(— OVER) ABUSE
(GREASY —) GAUM
(SLOPPY —) SLOBBER SLAISTER
(WATERY —) SLOSH
MESSAGE CHIT MODE SAND SEND
WIRE WORD RUMOR TELEX BREVET
CIPHER ERRAND GOSPEL LETTER
SCROLL BLINKER BODWORD
DEPECHE EMBASSY MISSION
SENDING TIDINGS AEROGRAM
CREDENCE DISPATCH GRAFFITO
MAILGRAM VOICEMAIL
(— BY FLAGS) HOIST
(— FROM GOD) ANGEL
(CHRISTIAN —) EVANGEL
(CIPHER —) SCYTALE
(COMPLIMENTARY —) RECADO
(INDICATING — IS RECEIVED)
WILCO
(SECRET —) PRIVATE
(SEND —) TELEX
(SEQUENCE OF —S) QUEUE
MESSALIAN EUCHITE
MESSENE (FATHER OF —) TRIOPAS
(HUSBAND OF —) POLYCAON

MESSENGER BODE PEON POST
SAND SEND TOTY VAUX ANGEL
ENVOY MUMMU VISOR BEADLE
BROKER BUNENE CHIAUS HERALD
LEGATE NUNCIO PIGEON RUNNER
APOSTLE CARRIER CASHBOY
CONTACT COURANT COURIER
EXPRESS FORAGER FORAYER
MALACHI MERCURY MESSAGE
MISSIVE NAMTARU PATAMAR
TOTYMAN TROTTER TRUMPET
EMISSARY FOREGOER HIRCARRA
LOBBYGOW NUNCIATE ORDINARY
PORTATOR APPARITOR
(— OF APSU AND TIAMAT) MUMMU
(— OF GOD) ANGEL
(— OF SHAMASH) BUNENE
(— OF THE GODS) HERMES MERCURY
(MOUNTED —) COSSID ESTAFET
(RELIGIOUS —) APOSTLE
(UNDERWORLD —) NAMTARU
MESSIAH CHRIST WOVOKA
(MUSLIM —) MAHDI
MESSINESS YUCK
MESSMATE YUBA
MESSUAGE HAW TOFT MEESE
MIDSTEAD
MESSY GOOEY SLOPPY SOZZLY
STICKY
MESTIZO CHOLO LADINO CURIBOCA
MAMELUCO
MESTOR (DAUGHTER OF —)
HIPPOTHOE
(FATHER OF —) PERSEUS
(MOTHER OF —) ANDROMEDA
(WIFE OF —) LYSIDICE
METAL ORE TIN BODY DIET GOLD
IRON LEAD ZINC BARIUM CESIUM
CHROME COBALT COPPER INDIUM
LATTIN NICKEL ORMOLU OSMIUM
RADIUM SILVER SODIUM BISMUTH
CADMIUM CALCIUM HAFNIUM
IRIDIUM LITHIUM MERCURY
RHENIUM RHODIUM THORIUM
TUTANIA URANIUM YTTRIUM
ALUMINUM ANTIMONY CHROMIUM
DEADHEAD PLATINUM RUBIDIUM
SCANDIUM TANTALUM TINCTURE
TITANIUM TUNGSTEN VANADIUM
(— IN MASS) BULLION
(— IN PLATES) LATTEN
(— IN SHEETS) LEAF PLATE
(— STRIP) SPLINE
(BABBITT —) LINING
(BASE —) BILLON
(COARSE —) MATTE
(DECORATED —) TOLE
(GROUND —) BRONZING
(HEAVIEST —) OSMIUM
(IMPURE MASS OF —) REGULUS
(LIGHTEST —) LITHIUM
(LIQUID —) MERCURY
(MASS OF —) INGOT

(MOLTEN —) TAP SQUIRT
(OLD POT —) POTIN
(ORNAMENTED —) NIELLO
(PERFORATED —) STENCIL
(PIECE OF CRUDE —) SLUG
(POINTED —) NAIL
(POROUS —) SPONGE
(PRECIOUS —) ORE GOLD PLATE
SILVER PLATINUM
(SEMIFINISHED —) SEMIS
(SHEET —) LATTEN DOUBLES
KALAMEIN
(TYPE —) QUAD QUADRAT
(UNREFINED —) PIGIRON
(WASTE —) GATE SPRUE
METALLIC HARD THIN TINNY
METALLOPHONE SARON
(BALINESE —) GANGSA
METALLURGIST AMERICAN HUNT
HOLLEY PETERS SHIMER
ENGLISH PERCY MUSHET THOMAS
HADFIELD
FRENCH HEROULT
METALOPHONE (BALINESE —)
GANGSA
METALWARE TOLE LORMERY
GRAYWARE PONTYPOOL
METALWORK ZOGAN
METALWORKER BARMAN FOONER
FORKMAN FOUNDER SUDSMAN
METAMERE SOMITE SEGMENT
MEROSOME
METAMERIC SEGMENTAL
METAMORPHIC
(PREF.) BLAST(O)
METAMORPHOSE TURN SHAPE
INDENIZE TRANSMEW
METAMORPHOSIS METABOLE
PETALODY PHYLLODY SEPALODY
(SUFF.) ODY
METANIRA (HUSBAND OF —)
CELEUS
(SON OF —) DEMOPHON
TRIPTOLEMUS
METAPHOR IMAGE TROPE FIGURE
KENNING
METAPHORICAL FIGURAL
FIGURATE TROPICAL
METASTOMA LABIUM
METATE QUERL
METE DEAL DOLE GIVE ALLOT AWARD
MATCH SERVE MEASURE APPORTION
METEMPSYCHOSIS SAMSARA
METEOR STAR ARGID CETID COMID
DRAKE LUPID LYRID URSID ANTLID
AUGUST BOLIDE BOOTID CORVID
CYGNID DRAGON HYDRID LEONID
LIBRID LYNCID LYRAID PHASMA
PISCID TAURID AQUARID AQUILID
ARIETID AURIGID CAMELID CANCRID
CEPHEID CORONID GEMINID
MEATURE ORIONID PEGASID
PERSEID POLARID PRODIGY

COLUMBID CRATERID DRACONID
ERIDANID FIREBALL FORNAXID
HERCULID LACERTID SAGITTID
SCORPIID SHOTSTAR TOUCANID
VIRGINID
(SUFF.) ID
METEORITE BAETYL BOLIDE
ANDRITE ATAXITE EUCRITE AEROLITE
AEROLITH BAETULUS BAETYLUS
IREOLITE SIDERITE SKYSTONE
METEOROLOGIST AMERICAN
EDDY ESPY WARD ROTCH FERREL
MARVIN CLAYTON REDFIELD
CARPENTER
AUSTRIAN FALR HANN PERNTER
ENGLISH REID SHAW DINES GALTON
GLAISHER
FRENCH MOREUX PELTIER
GERMAN DOVE FICKER WEGENER
BRUCKNER NEUMAYER
NORWEGIAN MOHN SVERDRUP
RUSSIAN TILLO
SCOTTISH MILL BUCHAN
SWEDISH MALMGREN
SWISS WILD DELUC
METEOROLOGY AEROLOGY
METER IONIC METRE SEVEN ALCAIC
RHYTHM CADENCE GAYATRI
MEASURE SUBMETER VIAMETER
YAWMETER
(CUBIC —) STERE
(MILLIONTH OF —) MICRON
(NETHERLANDS —) ELL
(SQUARE —) ARE CENTIARE
(VEDIC —) GAYATRI
(10,000 —S) GREX
(10 CUBIC —S) DEKASTERE
METHADONE AMIDONE
METHANE FORMENE
METHANOL WOODINE CARBINOL
METHAQUALINE QUAALUDE
METHEGLIN MEAD
METHOD ART WAY DART FORM
GARB GATE KINK LINE MIDS MODE
REDE RULE SORT ORDER STYLE
TRACK USAGE COURSE ENGINE
MANNER STEREO SYSTEM FASHION
PROCESS TACTICS WRINKLE
ADJUVANT STANDARD
(— OF ANGLING) HARLING
(— OF APPEALING) DHARNA DHURNA
(— OF COLORING TEA) FACING
(— OF CONSTRUCTION) JACAL
(— OF CULTIVATION) JUM JOOM
STUMPING
(— OF DIETING) BANTING
(— OF DISTILLATION) DESCENT
(— OF ELECTION) SCRUTINY
(— OF FATTENING POULTRY) GAVAGE
(— OF INDUCTION) CANON
(— OF INSTRUCTION) SCHOOL
(— OF INVESTIGATION) ORGANON
ORGANUM

(— OF MILKING) NIEVLING
(— OF MURAL DECORATION) KHASI
(— OF PROCEDURE) GAME
(— OF SELECTING POPE) SCRUTINY
(— OF TRACKING) DOVAP
(— OF TREATMENT) SCOPE
(CLEVER —) KINK KINKLE
(FIXED —) FORMULA
(MEDICAL —) CUSHION
(OUTMODED —) ARCHAISM
(PAINTING —) GOUACHE
(PRINTING —) AQUATONE
(SCIENTIFIC —) BACONISM
(SURVEYING —) STADIA
(USUAL —) COURSE PRACTICE
METHODICAL TRIG EXACT FORMAL
SEVERE ORDERLY REGULAR
ORDINARY ORDINATE
METHODIST JUMPER WESLEYAN
SWADDLING
METHODIZE ORDER REGULATE
METHODOLOGY TECHNIC
METHUSAEL (FATHER OF —)
MEHUJAEL
(SON OF —) LAMECH
METHUSELAH (FATHER OF —)
ENOCH
METHYLAL FORMAL
METICULOUS FUSSY NARROW
STICKY CAREFUL FINICAL FINICKY
PARTICULAR
METION (BROTHER OF —) CECROPS
(FATHER OF —) ERECHTHEUS
(MOTHER OF —) PRAXITHEA
METONYM SYNONYM
METRICAL MEASURED
(— QUANTITY) MATRA
METRICS PROSODY
METRONOME (PART OF —) BOX KEY
CASE PIVOT SCALE SHAFT WEIGHT
PENDULUM
METROPOLIS CITY SEAT CAPITAL
METROPOLITAN EPARCH EXARCH
METTLE PITH SAUL PRIDE SPUNK
GINGER SPIRIT COURAGE SMEDDUM
METTLESOME FIERY PROUD
SKEIGH SPUNKY STUFFY FLIGHTY
GINGERY SPIRITED
MEUSE
(PREF.)
(RIVER —) MOSA
MEW PEN WOW CAGE CAST COOP
GULL MEWL MOLT SHED MEUTE
MIAOU MIAOW SEAGULL HIDEAWAY
INTERMEW SEEDBIRD
CONFINEMENT
MEWER WRAWLER
MEWL WRAWL
MEWS ALLEY COURT STREET
STABLES
MEXICAN AZTEC
(AMERICAN OF — DESCENT)
CHICANO

MEXICAN-AMERICAN PACHUCO
MEXICAN ELM MEZCAL
MEXICAN ONYX TECALI
MEXICAN PERSIMMON
  CHAPOTE
MEXICAN POPPY ARGEMONE
MEXICAN TEA BASOTE APASOTE
  FISHWEED WORMSEED

MEXICO
CAPITAL: MEXICOCITY
COIN: PESO TLAC ADOBE CLACO
  TLACO AZTECA CENTAVO PIASTER
LAKE: CHAPALA
MEASURE: PIE VARA ALMUD BARIL
  JARRA LABOR LEGUA LINEA SITIO
  FANEGA PULGADA
MOUNTAIN: BUFA BLANCO CUPULA
  PEROTE ORIZABA
PENINSULA: BAJA YUCATAN
PEOPLE: MAM CHOL CORA MAYA MIXE
  PIMA SERI TECO XOVA AZTEC
  NAHUA OPATA OTOMI ZOQUE
  EUDEVE MIXTEC TOLTEC NAYARIT
  TEPANEC TOTONAC ZACATEC
  ZAPOTEC TEZCUCAN TOTONACO
  ZACATECO
RIVER: BRAVO LERMA BALSAS
  GRANDE PANUCO TABASCO
  GRIJALVA SANTIAGO
STATE: LEON NUEVO COLIMA OAXACA
  SONORA CHIAPAS DURANGO
  HIDALGO NAYARIT SINALOA
  TABASCO YUCATAN CAMPECHE
  QUINTANA VERACRUZ
TOWN: LEON LAPAZ TEPIC ARIZPE
  COLIMA JALAPA JUAREZ MERIDA
  OAXACA PARRAL POTOSI PUEBLA
  CANANEA DURANGO GUAYMAS
  MORELIA ORIZABA PACHUCA
  TAMPICO TORREON CULIACAN
  ENSENADA MAZATLAN MONCLOVA
  SALTILLO TLAXCALA VERACRUZ
VOLCANO: COLIMA TOLUCA JORULLO
  PARICUTIN POPOCATEPETL
WEIGHT: BAG ONZA CARGA LIBRA
  MARCO ADARME ARROBA OCHAVA
  TERCIO QUINTAL

MEZAHAB (DAUGHTER OF —)
  MATRED
MEZEREON DAPHNE
MEZZANINE ENTRESOL
MIAO HMONG
MIAROLITIC DRUSY
MIASMA REEK MALARIA MAREMMA
MIB MIGGLE
MIBSAM (FATHER OF —) SIMEON
  ISHMAEL
MICA DAZE TALC GLIST SLUDE
  BIOTITE GLIMMER ALURGITE
  FUCHSITE PHENGITE MUSCOVITE
  PHLOGOPITE

MICAH (FATHER OF —) UZZIEL
  MERIBBAAL
  (SON OF —) ABDON
MICAH CLARKE (AUTHOR OF —)
  DOYLE
  (CHARACTER IN —) JACOB MICAH
  SAXON CLANCY CLARKE GERVAS
  JOSEPH REUBEN DECIMUS STEPHEN
  LOCKARBY MONMOUTH TIMEWELL
MICAIAH (FATHER OF —) IMLAH
MICE (BREEDING PLACE FOR —)
  MURARIUM
➤**MICHA** (FATHER OF —)
  MEPHIBOSHETH
  (SON OF —) MATTANIAH
MICHAEL MIKE MICKY MICHEL
  MIGUEL
  (FATHER OF —) IZRAHIAH
  JEHOSHAPHAT
  (SLAYER OF —) JEHORAM
  (SON OF —) OMRI SETHUR
MICHAH (FATHER OF —) UZZIEL
MICHAIAH (FATHER OF —) URIEL
  GEMARIAH
  (HUSBAND OF —) REHOBOAM
  (SON OF —) ABIJAH
MICHAL (FATHER OF —) SAUL
  (HUSBAND OF —) DAVID PHALTI

MICHIGAN
BAY: SAGINAW THUNDER KEWEENAW
  STURGEON
CAPITAL: LANSING
COLLEGE: ALMA WAYNE ADRIAN
  ALBION CALVIN OLIVET OWOSSO
  OAKLAND
COUNTY: BAY CASS IRON LUCE CLARE
  DELTA IONIA IOSCO ALCONA
  OCEANA OGEMAW OSCODA
  OTSEGO GOGEBIC OSCEOLA
  TUSCOLA KALKASKA
INDIAN: OTTAWA
LAKE: BURT TORCH HOUGHTON
MOUNTAIN: CURWOOD
NATIVE: WOLVERINE
NICKNAME: LAKE WOLVERINE
RIVER: CASS BRULE HURON DETROIT
  SAGINAW STCLAIR ESCANABA
  MONTREAL MENOMINEE
STATE BIRD: ROBIN
STATE FLOWER: APPLEBLOSSOM
STRAIT: MACKINAC
TOWN: MIO ALMA CARO HART FLINT
  IONIA LANSE ADRIAN ALPENA
  BADAXE OWOSSO PAWPAW
  WARREN DETROIT LANSING LIVONIA
  PONTIAC SAGINAW ANNARBOR
  CADILLAC ESCANABA KALKASKA
  MANISTEE MUNISING MUSKEGON
  CHEBOYGAN KALAMAZOO

MICIPSA (FATHER OF —) MASINISSA
MICONIA TAMONEA

MICOPLASMA PPLO
MICROBAR BARYE
MICROBE GERM
MICROBIOLOGIST AMERICAN
  NATHAN
  FRENCH LWOFF
  SWISS ARBER
MICROCEPHALIC PINHEAD
MICROFICHE FICHE FILMCARD
MICROFILM COM.
  (SHEET OF —) FICHE
MICROMETER MU BIFILAR
  (— CALIPER) MIKE
MICRON MU
MICRONESIA (CAPITAL:) PALIKIR
  (COIN:) DOLLAR
  (ISLAND:) KOSRAE ULITHI WOLEAI
  POHNPEI MORTLOCK
  (PEOPLE:) TRUKESE POHNPEIAN
  (STATE:) YAP CHUNK KOSRAE
  POHNPEI
  (TOWN:) TOL WENU
MICRONESIAN KANAGA NAURUAN
  (— ISLAND) NUI GUAM ROTA TRUK
  MAKIN NAURU WOTHO MAJURO
MICROORGANISM BUG GERM
  AZOFIER BUTYRIC MICROBE
  BACILLUS MYCOPLASMA
MICROPHONE BUG MIKE
  PARABOLA
  (KIND OF —) LAVALIERE
  (REMOVE CONCEALED —) DEBUG
  (SHIELD FOR —) GOBO
MICROPYLE FORAMEN
MICROSCOPE GLASS SCOPE
  (PART OF —) ARM BASE CLIP KNOB
  LENS LIMB TUBE STAGE FILTER
  HOLDER APERTURE EYEPIECE
  CONDENSER DIAPHRAGM
  NOSEPIECE OBJECTIVE
  ADJUSTMENT
MICROSCOPIC SMALL MINUTE
MICROSECOND
  (HUNDREDTH OF —) SHAKE
MICROSPECIES JORDANON
MICROSPOROPHYLL STAMEN
MICROTONE SRUTI SHRUTI
MICROTUS ARVICOLA
MICROWAVE ZAP NUKE
MIDBRAIN MESENCEPHALON
MIDDAY NOON UNDERN MIDNOON
  NOONDAY MERIDIAN NOONTIME
MIDDEN BASURAL SAMBAQUI
MIDDLE MEDIO MESNE NAVEL
  CENTER MEDIAL MEDIAN MESIAL
  CENTRAL MEDIATE MEDILLE
  (— OF SAIL) BUNT
  (— OF SHIP) WAIST
  (— OF WINTER) HOLL HOWE
  (— WAY) VIAMEDIA
  (PREF.) MEDI(O) MES(O) MESIO
  MEZZO
MIDDLE-AGED MIDDLING

MIDDLE EAST
  (— NATIVE) WOG
MIDDLEMAN BUTTY BROKER
  DEALER FOGGER JOBBER LUMPER
  BUMAREE BUMMAREE BUTTYMAN
  HUCKSTER REGRATER
MIDDLEMARCH (AUTHOR OF —)
  ELIOT
  (CHARACTER IN —) FRED TYKE WILL
  CALEB CELIA GARTH JAMES RIGGS
  VINCY BROOKE EDWARD JOSHUA
  CHETTAM LYDGATE RAFFLES
  TERTIUS CASAUBON DOROTHEA
  LADISLAW NICHOLAS ROSAMOND
  BULSTRODE FEATHERSTONE
MIDDLER PLATEMAN
MIDDLETONE HALFTONE
MIDDLING FAIR MEAN SOSO
  NEUTRAL MEDIOCRE MEETERLY
  (PL.) DUNST FARINA SHARPS
  SIZINGS SEMOLINA WEATINGS
MIDGE GNAT SMUT PUNKY MIDGET
  MINGIE PUNKIE WEEVIL
MIDIAN (FATHER OF —) ABRAHAM
  (MOTHER OF —) KETURAH
MIDMOST
  (PREF.) MESATI
MIDNIGHT NOON NOONTIDE
MIDPOINT BASION PORION
  STOMION GNATHION
MIDRIB COSTA SHAFT MIDVEIN
  (— OF LEAF) PEN
MIDRIFF APRON SKIRT
  (PREF.) PHREN(O)
MIDSHIPMAN WART MIDDY PLEBE
  REEFER SNOTTY OLDSTER
MIDST DEPTH CENTER MIDDLE
  MIDWARD
  (PREF.)
  (IN THE —) INTER
MIDSUMMER DAY JOHNSMAS
MIDSUMMER NIGHT'S DREAM
  (AUTHOR OF —) SHAKESPEARE
  (CHARACTER IN —) MOTH PUCK
  SNUG EGEUS FLUTE SNOUT
  BOTTOM COBWEB HELENA HERMIA
  OBERON QUINCE THESEUS TITANIA
  LYSANDER DEMETRIUS HIPPOLYTA
  STARVELING MUSTARDSEED
  PHILOSTRATE PEASEBLOSSOM
MIDWAY MEDIO GAYWAY
  HALFWAY
MIDWIFE BABA DHAI GAMP HOWDY
  LUCKY COMMER CUMMER GRANNY
  HOWDIE KIMMER LUCINA LUCKIE
  GRANNIE HEBAMME
MIEN AIR BROW PORT VULT
  ALLURE ASPECT DEMEAN MANNER
  OSTENT BEARING DEMEANOR
  PORTANCE
MIFF TICKOFF
MIFFED IRKED
MIG MIB DUCK

MIGHT ARM BULK MOTE FORCE MOUND POWER SHOULD STRENGTH
(PREF.) CRATO
MIGHTILY HEFTILY
MIGHTINESS
(HIGH —) HOGEN
MIGHTY FELL HIGH KEEN MAIN MUCH RANK RICH VAST FELON GREAT HEFTY STERN STOOR POTENT STRONG VIOLENT ENORMOUS FORCEFUL POWERFUL PUISSANT SAMSONIC
(PREF.) DEIN(O) DIN(O) MEG(A)(AL) (ALO)
MIGNON (CHARACTER IN —) MIGNON MEISTER SPERATA WILHELM LOTHARIO
(COMPOSER OF —) THOMAS
MIGNONETTE WELD WOLD RESEDA LUTEOLA
MIGRAINE MEGRIM
MIGRANT MOVER
MIGRATE RUN FLIT TREK DRIFT FLIGHT COLONIZE
MIGRATION TREK EXODUS FLIGHT EELFARE EMOTION PASSAGE DIASPORA
MIGRATORY PEREGRINE
(NOT —) RESIDENT SEDENTARY
MIKADO DAIRI
MIKIR ARLENG
MIKLOTH (FATHER OF —) JEHIEL
(MOTHER OF —) MAACHAH
MILCAH (FATHER OF —) HARAN ZELOPHEHAD
(HUSBAND OF —) NAHOR
MILD LEW MOY CALM COLD EASY FAIR LENT MEEK NESH PLUM SOFT TAME WARM BALMY BLAND BUXOM GREEN LIGHT LITHE MELCH MELSH MILKY NAISH QUIET BENIGN FACILE GENIAL GENTLE HUMBLE KINDLY REMISS SMOOTH AFFABLE AMIABLE CLEMENT LENIENT SARSNET VELVETY BENEDICT DOVELIKE FAVONIAN LENITIVE MERCIFUL SARCENET SARSENET SOOTHING TRANQUIL
(— CLOSELY) JIB
(PREF.) LENI
MILDEW OIDIUM
MILDLY FEEBLY GENTLY
MILDNESS MILD LENITY SUAVITY CLEMENCY HUMILITY KINDNESS
MILE (GO —S) DEGREE
(NAUTICAL —) KNOT KAIRI
(ONE-EIGHTH —) FURLONG
(SEA —) NAUT
(SIXTY —S) DEGREE
(THIRD —) LI
(3 —S) HOUR LEAGUE
MILESTONE MILLIARY

MILETUS (FATHER OF —) APOLLO
(MOTHER OF —) ARIA DEIONE
(SON OF —) BYBLIS CAUNUS
(WIFE OF —) CYANEE
MILFOIL AHARTALAV
MILIEU CLIMATE TERRAIN AMBIENCE
MILITANT WARRISH FIGHTING
(ONE WITH — ATTITUDE) HAWK
MILITARISTIC PRUSSIAN
MILITARY MARTIAL WARLIKE MILITANT SOLDIERY
(— OBJECTS) MILITARIA
(— POST) THANA
(— SCIENCE) LOGISTICS
MILITIA FYRD ARRAY MILICE
MILITIAMAN CHOCO UHLAN LUMPER TRAINER FENCIBLE SHIRTMAN
(TURKISH —) TIMARIOT
MILK COW LAC FUZZ LAIT PAIL SKIM BLEED JUICE MILCH MULCT BOTTLE ELICIT RAMMEL STROKE SUCKLE EXPLOIT
(— CLOSELY) JIB
(— DRY) STRIP
(— OUT) EMULGE
(— PAN) LEAD
(— PRODUCT) KHOA
(— SICKNESS) TIRES
(BREAST —) SUCK DIDDY
(COW'S —) MESS
(CURDLED —) SKYR TYRE TAYER LOPPER CLABBER TATMJOLK
(FERMENTED —) KUMISS MATZOON
(NEW —) RAMMEL
(PINT OF —) PINTA
(SOUR —) SKYR WHIG BONNY BLEEZE BLINKY CLABBER JOCOQUE
(WATERY —) BLASH
(PREF.) GALACT(O) LACT(I)(O)
(SUFF.) GALACTIA
MILK CART KIT PRAM BUNGEY
MILKFISH AWA BANGOS SABALO SAVOLA BANDENG SABALOTE
MILKING (— PARLOR) BAIL
(— TIME) MEAL
MILKLESS PARVE PAREVE
MILKMAN KITTER CHALKER
MILK PAIL TRUG LEGLEN
MILK SHAKE FRAPPE
MILK SNAKE ADDER
MILKSOP SOP MOLLY SISSY COCKNEY MEACOCK
MILK-SUGAR LACTOSE
MILKWEED ANGLEPOD
MILKWOOD MELKHOUT
MILKWORT SENECA SENEGA CENTAURY GAYWINGS POLYGALA
MILKY MILCHY LACTARY LACTEAL OPALOID LACTEOUS
MILKY WAY GALAXY
(PREF.) GALACT(O)

MILL FULL MILN REED STAR BREAK
FLOUR KNURL QUERN CHERRY
FANNER STAMPS BLOOMER
MOLINET PUGMILL SMUTTER
ARRASTRA ARRASTRE BUHRMILL
SPINNERY TRAPICHE WALKMILL
(CHOCOLATE —) MOLINET
(FULLING —) STOCKS
(SHINGLING —) FORGE
(SUGAR —) CENTRAL TRAPICHE
(PREF.) MOLARI MYL(O)
MILLBOARD TARBOARD
MILLDAM WEIR WARREN WARRANT
MILLED GRAINED
MILLENARIAN CHILIAST
MILLENIUM CHILIAD
MILLER MILLMAN STOCKER
MULTURER NILLWARD
MILLER'S-THUMB BLOB CULL
CABOT CHABOT COTTOID MUDDLER
BULLHEAD
MILLET BUDA KODA KOUS MOHA
ARZUN BAJRA CHENA CUMBU
DUKHN DURRA GRAIN HIRSE KODRA
MILLY PANIC PROSO TENAI WHISK
BAJREE DHURRA HUREEK JONDLA
JOWARI MILIUM RAGGEE DAGASSA
PANICLE ZABURRO BIRDSEED
KADIKANE
(PREF.) MILIO
MILLHAND CROPMAN
MILLIGRAM
(200 —S) CARAT
MILLILITER MIL
MILLIMETER LI
(THOUSANDTH OF —) MICRON
MILLINER ARTISTE MODISTE
MILLING GRAINING
MILLION CONTO QUENT
(THOUSAND —S) GILLION MILLIARD
(10 —) CRORE
(1000 —) MILLIARD
(PL.) GUPPY
(PREF.) MEGA
MILLIONTH
(PREF.)
(ONE —) MICR(O)
MILLIPEDE JULID POLYPOD
DIPLOPOD PILLWORM RINGWORM
WIREWORM
MILLISECOND SIGMA
**MILL ON THE FLOSS (AUTHOR OF
—)** ELIOT
(CHARACTER IN —) BOB TOM KENN
LUCY DEANE GLEGG GUEST JAKIN
WAKEM MAGGIE PHILIP PULLET
STEPHEN STELLING TULLIVER
MILLPOND DAM MILLDAM
BINNACLE MILLPOOL
MILLRACE LADE LEAD LEAT
FOREBAY TAILRACE MILLSTREAM
MILLRYND INK

MILLSTONE RYND STONE BEDDER
LEDGER LIGGER RUNNER
(LOWER —) METATE
(UPPER —) MANO
(PL.) RUN
MILLSTREAM DAM LADE FLEAM
MILLWORKER DOGGER
MILO SORGHUM
MILPA LADANG
MILQUETOAST CASPAR
MILT MILK SEED SPLEEN
MILTONIST DIVORCER
MIMAS (FATHER OF —) THEANO
(MOTHER OF —) AMYCUS
(SLAYER OF —) MEZENTIUS
MIME ACTOR MIMER MIMIC
(PL.) MIMIAMBI
MIMEOGRAPH RONEO
MIMIC APE HIT COPY ECHO MIME
MINT MOCK ECHOER MOCKER
MONKEY BUFFOON COPYCAT
IMITATE PAGEANT
(PREF.) MIM(EO)(O)
MIMICKING TAKEOFF SIMULANT
IMITATIVE
MIMICRY APERY MIMESIS MOCKAGE
MOCKERY
MIMOSA AROMA ACACIA CASSIE
ALBIZZIA HUISACHE TURMERIC
MINCE CHOP SHEAR FINICK
MINCED HACHE
MINCEMEAT GIGOT MINCE
MINCING NIMINY FINICAL MINIKIN
MIGNIARD SKIPJACK
MINCINGLY FINE GINGERLY
MIND CIT CHIT HEAD HEED LOAF
MOOD NOTE NOUS OBEY RECK
SOUL RESEE BRAIN PHREN SENSE
SKULL WATCH ANIMUS MATTER
NOTICE PSYCHE REGARD COURAGE
SENSORY SUBJECT THINKER
THOUGHT
(CONSCIOUS —) SENTIENT
(INFINITE —) GOD
(RIGHT FRAME OF —) TUNE
(STATE OF —) BAG
(YEAR'S —) MINNING
(PREF.) MENTI NOO PHREN(O)
PSYCH(O)
(SUFF.) (CONDITION OF —) THYMIA
MINDFUL HEEDY MINDLY HEEDFUL
OBSERVANT
MIND READER MENTALIST
MINE BAL DIG PIT DELF HOLE HUEL
MEUM BARGH DELFT DELPH METAL
STOPE WHEAL COYOTE GOPHER
GROOVE RESCUE BONANZA
BORASCA COALPIT MINERAL
OPENCUT TORPEDO GOLCONDA
MYNPACHT PROSPECT
(— BY BLASTING) SHOOT
(— IRREGULARLY) GOPHER

(— PASSAGE) SLUM
(COAL —) ROB COALPIT COLLIERY
(KIND OF —) CLAYMORE
(MILITARY —) FOUGADE FOUGASSE
CAMOUFLET
(OLD —) GWAG
(RICH —) GOLCONDA
(TIN —) STANNARY
(UNPRODUCTIVE —) DUFFER SHICER
BORASCA
MINER PECK PICK PYKE BARER
DOGGY ARTIST BUCKER CUTTER
DAMMER DELVER DIGGER GANGER
GETTER HAGGER JUMPER MATTER
PELTER REEFER SNIPER STOPER
TINNER TOPMAN VANNER COLLIER
CRUTTER DIRGLER FEIGHER GEORDIE
GROOVER HITCHER HUTCHER
LEADMAN PICKMAN PIKEMAN
PIONEER PLUGMAN ROCKMAN
SNUBBER ENTRYMAN HEADSMAN
STRIPPER WINZEMAN
(— WHO WORKS ALONE) HATTER
MINERAL JET GEET HOST MINE
SPAR TALC BERYL BLOOM EARTH
EMERY FLUOR GLEBE GUEST LENAD
SQUAT TRONA ACMITE ALAITE
AUGITE BARITE BARYTE BLENDE
CASTOR CERITE COCKLE CURITE
DAVYNE EGERAN EHLITE ERRITE
GALENA GARNET GLANCE GYPSUM
HALITE HAUYNE HELVIN HUMITE
ILLITE IOLITE LABITE MIXITE NATRON
NOSEAN NOSITE PINITE RUTILE
SALITE SILICA SPHENE SPINEL
ADAMINE ADAMITE ADELITE ALTAITE
ALUMITE ALUNITE AMOSITE
ANATASE APATITE ATOPITE AXINITE
AZORITE AZULITE AZURITE BAUXITE
BAZZITE BELLITE BIOTITE BISMITE
BITYITE BOHMITE BOLEITE BORNITE
BRUCITE CALCITE CELSIAN CYANITE
DIAMOND DICKITE DUFTITE EDENITE
EPIDOTE ERIKITE ERINITE EUCLASE
FLOKITE GAGEITE GAHNITE GEDRITE
GLADITE GOTHITE GUMMITE HELVITE
HESSITE HOPEITE HOWLITE HULSITE
IHLEITE ILVAITE INESITE INYOITE
ISERITE JADEITE JARLITE JOSEITE
KEMPITE KERNITE KOPPITE KOTOITE
KYANITE LANGITE LARNITE LAURITE
LAUTITE LEHIITE LEIFITE LEONITE
LEPTITE LEUCITE LOWEITE MARTITE
MELLITE MULLITE OKENITE OLIVINE
PALAITE PENNINE PETZITE PYRITES
RATHITE REALGAR RETZIAN RHAGITE
RINKITE ROMEITE ROSSITE SENAITE
SODDITE SVABITE SYLVITE THORITE
TURGITE ULEXITE UTAHITE UVANITE
VAUXITE VOGLITE VRBAITE WARBITE
WIIKITE ZEOLITE ZINCITE ZOISITE
ZORGITE ZUNYITE AIKINITE
ALLANITE ALLUVIAL ALUNOGEN

AMBONITE ANAUXITE ANCYLITE
ANDORITE ANKERITE ARIEGITE
ARMENITE ARTINITE ASBOLITE
AUGELITE AUTUNITE AWARUITE
BADENITE BAKERITE BARARITE
BARYLITE BAVENITE BETAFITE
BEYERITE BILINITE BIXBYITE
BLAKEITE BLOEDITE BOOTHITE
BORACITE BOWENITE BRAGGITE
BRAUNITE BRAVOITE BROMLITE
BRONZITE BROOKITE BRUSHITE
CALCSPAR CARBOCER CEROLITE
CHIOLITE CHLORITE CHROMITE
CIMOLITE CINNABAR CLEVEITE
COHENITE COLUSITE COOKEITE
COSALITE CREEDITE CROCOITE
CRYOLITE DANALITE DAPHNITE
DATOLITE DELTAITE DENDRITE
DIALLAGE DIASPORE DIGENITE
DIOPSIDE DIOPTASE DIXENITE
DOLOMITE DYSODILE EGUEIITE
ELIASITE ELPIDITE EMBOLITE
ENARGITE EPSOMITE ERIONITE
EUCOLITE EULYTINE EULYTITE
EUXENITE EVANSITE FASSAITE
FAYALITE FELDSPAR FERSMITE
FIBROLITE FLINKITE FLUORITE
FOOTEITE FUCHSITE FUSINITE
GEMSTONE GENTHITE GIBBSITE
GINORITE GOETHITE GOYAZITE
GRIPHITE GROTHINE GROUTITE
GYROLITE HANKSITE HANUSITE
HARTTITE HATCHITE HAUERITE
HAUYNITE HEMATITE HOMILITE
HUGELITE IDOCRASE INDERITE
IODYRITE JALPAITE JAROSITE
JEZEKITE KALINITE KAMACITE
KASOLITE KEHOEITE KLEINITE
KOKTAITE KOLSKITE KRAUSITE
LAGONITE LAVENITE LAZULITE
LAZURITE LEVYNITE LEWISITE
LIMONITE LINARITE LOMONITE
LOWIGITE MARSHITE MEIONITE
MELILITE MELONITE MESITITE
MESOLITE MIERSITE MIMETITE
MISENITE MOLYSITE MONAZITE
MONETITE MORAVITE MOSESITE
NADORITE NASONITE NEPOUITE
NOCERITE NOSELITE OXAMMITE
PEGANITE PETALITE PIMELITE
PINNOITE PISANITE PODOLITE
PORODINE PRICEITE PRIORITE
RINNEITE ROSELITE SAGENITE
SALEEITE SALESITE SAPONITE
SASSOLIN SCAWTITE SHANDITE
SHARPITE SHORTITE SIDERITE
SMALTITE SMITHITE SODALITE
SPADAITE SPURRITE STANNITE
STIBNITE STILBITE STOLZITE
STRUVITE STURTITE SZMIKITE
TAGILITE TANGEITE TEALLITE
TENORITE TILASITE TITANITE
TRIPLITE TROILITE TYROLITE

TYSONITE URANOTIL VEGASITE
VOLTAITE VOLTZITE WEHRLITE
WEISSITE WELLSITE WILKEITE
WURTZITE XENOLITE XENOTIME
YENTNITE ZARATITE MILLERITE
MUSCOVITE NEPHELINE NICCOLITE
PHENACITE TANZANITE WILLEMITE
STISHOVITE
(BLACK —) JET GEET CERINE YENITE
KNOPITE NIOBITE ALLANITE
GRAPHITE HIELMITE ILMENITE
ONOFRITE MAGNETITE SAMARSKITE
(BLUE —) MOLYBDENITE
(BRIGHT —) BLENDE
(BROWN —) CERINE EGERAN
GUILDITE JAROSITE
(FIBROUS —) ASBESTOS
(GRAY-WHITE —) TRONA HOPEITE
(GREEN —) AMESITE GAHNITE
ILESITE PRASINE PREHNITE
SMECTITE
(MOTTLED —) SERPENTINE
(ORANGE —) SANDIX
(RADIATED —) ASTROITE
(RADIOACTIVE —) CURITE
(RARE —) CYMRITE EUCLASE
TYCHITE BARYLITE
(RED —) GARNET RHODOCHROSITE
(SOFT —) TALC KERMES
(TRANSPARENT —) MICA POLLUX
ABRAZITE SODALITE
(WHITE —) BARITE HOWLITE STILBITE
(YELLOW —) TOPAZ PYRITES
PENTLANDITE
(YELLOWISH-GREEN —) EPIDOTE
ECDEMITE
(PREF.) ORYCT(O)
(SUFF.) CLASE INF ITE LITE LITH(IC)
LITIC XENE
MINERALOGIST AMERICAN HUNT
KUNZ BRUSH KRAUS EGLESTON
WHITLOCK CLEAVELAND
AUSTRIAN BORN BECKE WULFEN
HAIDINGER TSCHERMAK
ENGLISH BROOKE CLARKE GREGOR
MILLER PHILLIPS
FRENCH HAUY ROME DAUBREE
FRIEDEL LACROIX LAUMONT
DOLOMIEU DUFRENOY
BRONGNIART
GERMAN MOHS COHEN RASPE
DECHEN KOBELL WERNER ZIRKEL
KARSTEN NEUMANN AGRICOLA
LEONHARD QUENSTEDT
ITALIAN SELLA BRUGNATELLI
RUSSIAN FERSMAN
SWEDISH GAHN HISINGER
SEFSTROM CRONSTEDT
BLOMSTRAND
MINERAL TAR MALTHA
MINERAL WATER SELTZER
MINERVA MENFRA
MINESWEEPER ALGERINE

MINGLE MIX FUSE JOIN MELL MOLD
MONG MOOL ADMIX BLEND MERGE
TWINE COMMIX FELTER HUDDLE
JUMBLE MEDDLE MEDLEY COMBINE
COALESCE CONFOUND
(PREF.) MISCE
MINGLED FUSED MIXED MEDLEY
CONFUSED PELLMELL
(PREF.) MYXTI
MINGLING MIX PELLMELL
(— OF VOWELS) CRASIS
(PREF.) MIXO
(SUFF.) MIXIS
MINIATURE BABY SMALL LITTLE
POCKET MINIKIN
MINIM HALFNOTE
MINIMAL BASAL LIMINAL MARGINAL
MINIMIZE DECRY MINCE LESSEN
MINIFY SMOOTH SCISSOR BELITTLE
DISCOUNT
MINIMUM BARE BEDROCK
(— OF CAPITAL) SHOESTRING
(— OF VISION) STIME STYME
MINING WORK MINERY SPATTER
GROOVING
(KIND OF —) PLACER
MINION PEAT SATAN MIGNON
DARLING MINIKIN CREATURE
SATELLITE
MINIONETTE EMERALD
MINISTER PRIG AGENT CLERK
DEWAN ELDER ENVOY HAMAN
PADRE VIZIR ATABEG DEACON DIVINE
GALLAH HELPER PANDER PARSON
PASTOR PESHWA PRIEST VIZIER
BROTHER DOMINIE OFFICER
PESHKAR PREFECT PALATINE
PREACHER SECRETARY
(— OF FINANCE) DEWAN
(— TO) TEND SERVE INTEND
(— TO PASSIONS) PANDER
(— WITHOUT SETTLEMENT)
STIBBLER
(PRIME —) PADRONE
(WAR —) SERASKIER
MINISTRANT
(PL.) SELLI SELLOI
MINISTRATION SERVICE TENDANCE
MINISTRY SERVICE
MINIUM SANDIX
MINIVER LASSET
MINK FAG HURON NORSE VISON
JACKASH KOLINSKY MUSTELIN
PLATINUM

MINNESOTA

CAPITAL: STPAUL
COLLEGE: BETHEL STOLAF WINONA
  BEMIDJI HAMLINE AUGSBURG
  CARLETON
COUNTY: LYON PINE TODD ANOKA
  MOWER AITKIN DAKOTA ISANTI
  ITASCA MCLEOD NOBLES ROSEAU

WASECA WILKIN CHISAGO
WABASHA CROWWING HENNEPIN
OTTERTAIL
INDIAN: SIOUX OJIBWA CHIPPEWA
LAKE: LEECH ITASCA BEMIDJI
SUPERIOR
MOUNTAIN: EAGLE MISQUAH
MOUNTAIN RANGE: CUYUNA MESABI
MISQUAH
NICKNAME: NORTHSTAR
RIVER: SAUK RAINY STCROIX
STATE BIRD: LOON
STATE TREE: REDPINE
TOWN: ADA ELY MORA ANOKA EDINA
FOLEY AUSTIN CHASKA DULUTH
MILACA NEWULM WADENA
WASECA WINONA BEMIDJI
FOSSTON HIBBING IVANHOE
MANKATO BRAINERD PIPESTONE

MINNESOTAN GOPHER
MINNOW PINK BANNY GUPPY HITCH
MINIM MINNY BAGGIE MENNON
DOGFISH FATHEAD GULARIS
PHANTOM PINHEAD PINKEEN
BONYTAIL CYPRINID FLATHEAD
GAMBUSIA MOONFISH SATINFIN
(PL.) MENISE
MINOR FLAT LESS MOLL WARD PETIT
PETTY INFANT LESSER SLIGHT
(PERIOD OF BEING A —) NONAGE
MINORESS CLARE CLARISSE
MINORITY FEW NONAGE INFANCY
MINOS (DAUGHTER OF —) ARIADNE
PHAEDRA
(FATHER OF —) JUPITER LYCASTUS
(MOTHER OF —) EUROPA
(SLAYER OF —) COCALUS
(SON OF —) ANDROGEOS
DEUCALION
(WIFE OF —) PASIPHAE
MINSTER CHADBAND
MINSTREL BARD LUTER BADHAN
HARPER JOCKEY BADCHAN
GLEEMAN JOCULAR PARDHAN
PIERROT SONGMAN JONGLEUR
MINSTRELSY GLEE DREAM
MINT NEW COIN NANA SAGE AJUGA
BASIL ORGAN THYME HYSSOP
SAVORY STRIKE ALLHEAL BALLOTA
CAPMINT LABIATE MONARDA
OLITORY OREGANO PERILLA
PHLOMIS POTHERB STACHYS
BERGAMOT CALAMINT IRONWORT
LAMPWICK LAVENDER MARJORAM
SAGELEAF SELFHEAL SKULLCAP
PATCHOULI PATCHOULY
PENNYROYAL PEPPERMINT
MINTER MONEYER
MINTING COINING
MINUCHIHR (DAUGHTER OF —)
NAUDAR
(FATHER OF —) IRAJ

MINUET MINAWAY
MINUS LESS WANTING
MINUTE FINE NICE TINY CLOSE
MINIM PRIME SMALL ATOMIC
MOMENT NARROW INSTANT
SCRUPLE DETAILED
(LAST —) DEADLINE
(ORIGINAL —) PROTOCOL
(24 —S) GHURRY
(PL.) ACTA
MINX JADE PEAT SLUT SNIP HUSSY
HUZZY LIMMER SNICKET
MIRACLE SIGN ANOMY MARVEL
WONDER PRODIGY THEURGY
(SITE OF —) CANA
(PREF.) THAUMA(TO)
MIRACLE PLAY GUARY
MIRACULOUS MARVELOUS
(NOT —) NATURAL
MIRAGE SERAB CHIMERA FLYAWAY
LOOMING ILLUSION TOWERING
MIRANDA (FATHER OF —) PROSPERO
(LOVER OF —) FERDINAND
MIRE BOG DUB CLAY GLAR LAIR MOIL
SLOB SLUB SLUE SLUR ADDLE
CLART EMBOG FANGO GLAUR LATCH
SEUGH SLAKE SLOSH SLUSH SQUAD
STALL SLOUGH SLUDGE SLUTCH
CLABBER GUTTERS SLUBBER
LOBLOLLY WORTHING
MIREILLE (CHARACTER IN —) RAMON
OURRIAS VINCENT MIREILLE
(COMPOSER OF —) GOUNOD
MIRIAM (BROTHER OF —) MOSES
MIRITI PALM ITA BURITI MORICHE
MIRLITON KAZOO
MIRO TOMTIT
MIRROR APE FLAT BERYL GLASS
IMAGE STEEL STONE PEEPER
PSYCHE REFLEX SHINER SHOWER
CONCAVE HORIZON REFLECT
DIAGONAL SPECULUM
(— BETWEEN WINDOWS) PIER
GLASS
(PREF.) CATOPTRO
MIRTH GLEE CHEER DREAM SPORT
GAIETY BAUDERY DISPORT JOLLITY
HILARITY
(CONTEMPTUOUS —) SPORT
(VIOLENT —) SPLEEN
MIRTHFUL CADGY MERRY RIANT
FESTIVE GLEEFUL JOCULAR
DISPOSED LAUGHFUL CONVIVIAL
MIRY OOZY PUXY LAIRY MUCKY
SLAKY CLAGGY CLASHY LUTOSE
MIRISH POACHY SLABBY GUTTERY
SLOUGHY
MISADVENTURE GRIEF ACCIDENT
CALAMITY CASUALTY DISASTER
MISHANTER
MISANTHROPE CYNIC HATER
TIMON
(AUTHOR OF —) MOLIERE

(CHARACTER IN —) ORONTE
ALCESTE ARSINOE ELIANTE
CELIMENE PHILINTE
MISANTHROPIC CYNICAL
MISANTHROPY CYNICISM
TIMONISM
MISAPPLIED ABUSIVE
MISAPPLY ABUSE CROOK WREST
DISUSE MISUSE
MISAPPREHEND MISTAKE
MISAPPREHENSION ILLUSION
MISBECOME MISSIT MISSEEM
MISBEHAVE MISUSE MISBEAR
MISFARE MISHAVE MISLEAD
MISGUIDE
MISBEHAVIOR MALVERSATION
MISBELIEF MISCREED
MISCALCULATE DUTCH MISCAST
MISCOUNT
MISCALL BECALL MISNAME
MISCARRIAGE FAIL MISHAP
FAILURE ABORTION
(PREF.) ECTRO
MISCARRY FAIL WARP ABORT
MISGO FOUNDER MISFARE MISGIVE
BACKFIRE
MISCARRYING ABORTIVE
MISCELLANEOUS CHOW ORRA
SUNDRY ASSORTED CHOWCHOW
MISCELLANY ANA VARIA MEDLEY
WHATNOT CHOWCHOW GIFTBOOK
MISCHANCE CALAMITY CASUALTY
DISASTER
MISCHIEF HOB ILL BALE BANE EVIL
HARM HURT JEEL WRACK INJURY
MURCHY SORROW WONDER
DEVILRY KNAVERY MALICHO
SCADDLE DEVILTRY MALLECHO
MISCHIEF-MAKING URCHIN
MISCHIEVOUS BAD SLY ARCH IDLE
PIXY ROYT ELFIN HEMPY PIXIE
ROYET ELFISH ELVISH GALLUS
HEMPIE IMPISH NOCENT NOYANT
SHREWD SULLEN WICKED GALLOWS
HARMFUL KNAVISH LARKISH
MOCKING NAUGHTY PARLISH
PLISKIE PUCKISH ROGUISH SCADDLE
UNHAPPY UNLUCKY WAGGISH
LITHERLY LUNGEOUS SPORTIVE
SPRITISH VENOMOUS WANSONSY
MISCHIEVOUSNESS ROGUERY
MISCONCEPTION DELUSION
ILLUSION
MISCONDUCT CULPA DOLUS
OFFENCE OFFENSE DISORDER
MALFEASANCE
MISCONSTRUCTION STRAIN
MISCONSTRUE MISJUDGE
MISCREANT KNAVE
MISDEED ILL MISS SLIP AMISS
UNWORK DEFAULT FORFEIT
OFFENCE OFFENSE DISORDER
(CATCH A —) DETECT

MISDEMEANOR SIN CRIME FAULT
DELICT OFFENCE OFFENSE DISORDER
MISDIRECT PERVERT MISGUIDE
MISER CUFF SKIN CHUFF CHURL
FLINT GRIPE HAYNE HUNKS NABAL
PIKER SCRAT SCRIB CODGER HUDDLE
NIPPER PELTER SCRIMP SNUDGE
WRETCH DRYFIST GOBSECK
NIGGARD SCRAPER SCROOGE
CHINCHER GATHERER HAPTERON
HARPAGON HOLDFAST MUCKERER
MUCKWORM PINCHGUT
CURMUDGEON
MISERABLE WOE EVIL GRAY PUNK
SOUR DAWNY DEENY DUSTY MISER
WOFUL YEMER ABJECT CHETIF
CRUMBY CRUMMY ELENGE FEEBLE
PRETTY UNSELY WOEFUL BALEFUL
FORLORN PITIFUL SCRUFFY
UNHAPPY WANSOME FORSAKEN
PITIABLE SCRANNEL UNTHENDE
WRETCHED
MISERABLES, LES (AUTHOR OF —)
HUGO
(CHARACTER IN —) JEAN JAVERT
MARIUS COSETTE EPONINE FANTINE
VALJEAN JONDRETTE MADELEINE
PONTMERCY THENARDIER
FAUCHELEVANT
MISERERE SUBSELLA
MISERLINESS AVARICE MISERISM
SNUDGERY TENACITY
MISERLY WOE GARE MEAN NEAR
GRIPPY KNIVEY STINGY CHINCHE
PELTING WANSITH SCRAPING
SNUDGERY
MISERY WO WOE BALE RUTH GNEDE
GRAME WREAK THREAT ANGUISH
MISEASE TRAGEDY CALAMITY
DISTRESS WANDRETH WOWENING
MISFIRE SKIP SNAP
MISFORTUNE ILL BLOW DOLE DREE
EVIL HARM RUTH TEEN CROSS
CURSE HYDRA SCATH TRAIK
DAMAGE DIRDUM MISERY MISHAP
RUBBER SCATHE SORROW UNHEAL
UNLUCK WANHAP WROATH
AMBSACE MALHEUR MISCARE
MISFALL MISFATE MISLUCK REVERSE
TRAGEDY TROUBLE UNSELTH
UNSPEED CALAMITY DISASTER
DISGRACE DISTRESS MISCHIEF
ADVERSITY MISCHANCE
MISGIVING DOUBT QUALM
MISGOVERN MISRULE
MISGUIDED WET
MISHAEL (BROTHER OF —)
ELIZAPHAN
(FATHER OF —) UZZIEL
MISHAM (FATHER OF —) ELPAAL
MISHANDLE BUNGLE
MISHAP SLIP GRIEF SHUNT SITHE
UNHAP WANHAP FORTUNE MISTIDE

ACCIDENT CASUALTY MISCHIEF
PRATFALL
(MINOR —) GLITCH
MISHEARING OTOSIS
MISHIT DUFF
MISHMA (BROTHER OF —) MIBSAM
(FATHER OF —) ISHMAEL
MISHMASH OLIO BOTCH GOULASH
MISINFORM MIZZLE
MISINTERPRET WARP WREST
WRITHE MISREAD PERVERT
MISCOUNT
MISJUDGE MISDEEM MISWERN
MISLAY LOSE DISPLACE MISPLACE
MISLEAD COG ERR BUNK DUPE
GULL HOAX HYPE JIVE BLUFF CHEAT
FALSE SHUCK BETRAY DELUDE
SEDUCE WILDER CONFUSE DEBAUCH
DECEIVE MISLEAR INVEIGLE
MISGUIDE BAMBOOZLE
MISLEADING JIVE BLIND FALSE
CIRCEAN TORTIOUS
MISMANAGE MULL BLUNK
BLUNDER MISLEAD MISRULE
ILLGUIDE MISGUIDE
MISOGYNIC CYNICAL
MISPLACE MISLAY MISPUT MISSET
DISPLACE
MISPLACED LOST MALPOSED
MISPLAY BLOW DUFF ERROR FLUFF
FUMBLE
MISPRINT LITERAL
MISPRONOUNCE MISCALL
STUMBLE
MISQUOTE GIVE
MISREPRESENT SKEW ABUSE
BELIE COLOR MISUSE DISTORT
FALSIFY SLANDER MISCOLOR
MISREPRESENTATION FRAUD
CALUMNY DAUBERY GARBLING
MISS ERR HIP SHE FAIL LACK LOSE
SKIP SLIP SNAB FORGO HANUM
MISSY PANNA SKIRT DESIRE KUMARI
FRAULEIN MISTRESS OVERLOOK
OVERSLIP SEÑORITA
(CLOSE —) SHAVE
(NARROW —) SHAVE
MISSEL BIRD MAVIS SHIRL DRAINE
JAYPIE MISTLE SHRITE SYCOCK
CHERCOCK
MISSHAPE DEFORM
MISSHAPEN UGLY BLOWN DEFORM
THRAWN DEFORMED UNSHAPED
MALFORMED
(PREF.) DYSMORPHO
MISSILE ABM GUN SAM BALL BIRD
BOLT DART MIRV NIKE SHOT PLUMB
SHAFT STONE BULLET EXOCET
ROCKET SEEKER BOMBARD FIREPOT
GRENADE MISSIVE OUTCAST
PROJECT AERODART BRICKBAT
MINUTEMAN PROJECTILE
SIDEWINDER

(— DEPOT) SILO
(ANTIBALLISTIC —) ABM
(BALLISTIC —) ICBM ATLAS
(DEFECTIVE —) DUD
(SURFACE-TO-AIR —) SAM
(PL.) MITRAILLE
(PREF.) TELI
MISSING LACK WANT ABSENT
WANTING
(— OF CUE) FLUFF
(PREF.) E
MISSION SAND TASK CHARGE
ERRAND SORTIE VISITA MESSAGE
BUSINESS DEVOTION LEGATION
NUNCIATURE
(— OF MERCY) RESCUE
MISSIONARY APOSTLE COLPORTER

MISSISSIPPI
CAPITAL: JACKSON
COLLEGE: RUST ALCORN BELHAVEN
MILLSAPS TOUGALOO
COUNTY: TATE HINDS JONES LAMAR
LEAKE PERRY YAZOO ALCORN
ATTALA COPIAH JASPER PANOLA
TIPPAH TUNICA CHOCTAW NESHOBA
NOXUBEE ITAWAMBA YALOBUSHA
INDIAN: TIOU BILOXI TUNICA
CHOCTAW NATCHEZ CHICKASAW
LAKE: ENID SARDIS BARNETT
GRENADA OKATIBBEE
MOUNTAIN: WOODALL
NATIVE: MUDCAT TADPOLE
NICKNAME: BAYOU MAGNOLIA
RIVER: LEAF PEARL YAZOO BIGBLACK
STATE BIRD: MOCKINGBIRD
STATE FLOWER: MAGNOLIA
STATE TREE: MAGNOLIA
TOWN: IUKA MARKS BILOXI LAUREL
PURVIS TUNICA TUPELO WINONA
BELZONI CORINTH GRENADA
NATCHEZ WIGGINS GULFPORT
MERIDIAN KOSCIUSKO

MISSIVE NOTE BILLET LETTER
EPISTLE MESSAGE MISSILE
MISSLE BUS

MISSOURI
CAPITAL: JEFFERSONCITY
COLLEGE: AVILA DRURY TARKIO
LINCOLN WEBSTER STEPHENS
COUNTY: RAY COLE DENT IRON LINN
ADAIR BARRY HENRY MACON RALLS
TANEY GRUNDY PETTIS PLATTE
DAVIESS NODAWAY
INDIAN: OSAGE
LAKE: OZARKS TABLEROCK
MOUNTAIN: TAUMSAUK
NATIVE: PUKE PIKER
NICKNAME: SHOWME BULLION
PLATEAU: OZARK
PRESIDENT: TRUMAN

RIVER: OSAGE
STATE BIRD: BLUEBIRD
STATE FLOWER: HAWTHORN
STATE TREE: DOGWOOD
TOWN: AVA EDINA ELDON HAYTI
   LAMAR MACON MILAN ROLLA
   BUTLER GALENA KAHOKA NEOSHO
   POTOSI BETHANY BOLIVAR
   CAMERON LEBANON MOBERLY
   PALMYRA SEDALIA STLOUIS
   HANNIBAL SIKESTON

MISSPEAK ERR
MISSTATEMENT ERRATUM
MISSTEP TRIP
MIST DAG FOG MUG URE DAMP DRIP
  DROW FILM HAAR HAZE MOKE RACK
  ROKE SCUD SMUR BRUME CLOUD
  DRISK GAUZE STEAM MIZZLE
  NEBULE SEREIN SERENE SMEETH
  (COLD —) DROW BERBER
  (DRIZZLING —) SMUR DRISK SMIRR
  SMURR
  (SMOKY —) SMOG
  (WHITE —) HAG
  (PL.) SMOKES
  (PREF.) NEBULI NIMBI
MISTAKE ERR BALK GAFF GOOF
  MISS SLIP TRIP ERROR FAULT FLUFF
  GAFFE LAPSE BARNEY BOBBLE
  ESCAPE MISCUE SLIPUP STUMER
  BLOOMER BLOOPER BLUNDER
  CONFUSE DEFAULT JEOFAIL
  STUMOUR WRONGER CONFOUND
  MISPRINT MISPRISE
  (CLERICAL —) TYPO
  (STUPID —) BUBU BONER CLANGER
  (PL.) ERRATA
MISTAKEN WET WRONG ASTRAY
  VICIOUS OVERSEEN OVERSHOT
  TORTIOUS
  (NOT —) RIGHT
MISTER DON REB HERR SENOR
  SENHOR SIGNOR GOODMAN
  SIGNIOR GOVERNOR MONSIEUR
MISTFLOWER EUPATORY
MISTILY FOGGILY
MISTINESS FILM HAZE
MISTLETOE MISSEL ALLHEAL
  GADBUSH
MISTREAT BANG ABUSE SHAFT
  BATTER SAVAGE VIOLATE
MISTRESS MRS PUG TOY AMIE BIBI
  DAME DOLL DOXY LADY MISS PURE
  AMIGA AMOUR DOLLY DONNA
  DUENA FANCY LEMAN LUCKY
  MADAM NANCY WOMAN BEEBEE
  MINION MISSIS MISSUS NEAERA
  PARNEL SAHIBA SENORA TACKLE
  WAHINE BEDMATE DELILAH HERSELF
  HETAERA KITTOCK LEVRET
  METREZA PADRONA SENHORA
  SIGNORA SULTANA CAMPASPE

DESPOINA DULCINEA FARMWIFE
GOODWIFE GUDEWIFE HAUSFRAU
LADYLOVE LANDLADY MIGNIARD
PARAMOUR PECULIAR SINEBADA
TIMANDRA COURTESAN INAMORATA
(— OF CEREMONIES) FEMCEE
MISTRUST MISTROW SURMISE
  DISTRUST JEALOUSE JEALOUSY
  MISDOUBT
MISTY HAZY MOKY BLEAR DAGGY
  FILMY FOGGY MISKY MOCHY
  MOOTH MURKY RAWKY ROKEY
  ROUKY BLURRY CLOUDY GREASY
  MIZZLY SMURRY STEAMY BRUMOUS
  OBSCURE NEBULOUS NUBILOUS
  VAPOROUS
MISUNDERSTAND MISKNOW
  MISTAKE
MISUNDERSTANDING
  MALENTENDU
MISUSE ABUSE ABUSION PERVERT
  MALTREAT
MITE BIT ATOM CENT DITE DRAM
  ATOMY BICHO SPECK ACARID
  ACARUS CHIGOE LEPTUS MINUTE
  SMIDGE ACARIAN BDELLID CHIGGER
  DEMODEX SMIDGEN ARACHNID
  DIBRANCH FARTHING HANDWORM
  ORIBATID SANDMITE
  (TEXAS —) SPIDER
  (PREF.) ACAR(I)(O)
MITER MITRE TIMBER TIMBRE
MITERWORT COOLWORT
MITICIDE ACARICIDE
  PHOSPHAMIDON
MITIGATE BALM COOL EASE HELP
  ABATE ALLAY DELAY MEASE RELAX
  REMIT SLAKE ASLAKE LENIFY
  LESSEN MODIFY PACIFY SOFTEN
  SOOTHE SUCCOR TEMPER ASSUAGE
  COMMUTE CUSHION ELEVATE
  MOLLIFY QUALIFY RELEASE RELIEVE
  SWEETEN PALLIATE ALLEVIATE
  (— PAIN) PLASTER
MITIGATING LENITIVE
MITIGATION REMORSE
MITOCHONDRION SARCOSOME
MITT MUFF
MITTEN BOOT CUFF MITT MUFF
  LOOFIE MUFFLE NIPPER MUFFLER
MIX BOX BEAT CARD DASH FUSE JOIN
  KNIT MELL MENG MESS STIR ADMIX
  ALLOY BLEND BRAID IMMIX KNEAD
  MISCE TWINE BLUNGE CAUDLE
  COMMIX CRUTCH GARBLE JUMBLE
  MEDDLE MEDLEY MINGLE MUDDLE
  PERMIX STODGE TEMPER WUZZLE
  BLUNDER SHUFFLE SWIZZLE
  CONFOUND LEVIGATE SCRAMBLE
  (— AND STIR WHEN WET) PUG
  (— AT RANDOM) SHUFFLE
  (— CONFUSEDLY) BROIL
  (— FLOCKS) BOX

(— LIQUORS) BREW
(— PLASTER) GAGE GAUGE
(— TEA) BULK
(— WINE) PART
(— WITH WHITE) LOAD
(— WITH YEAST) BARM
(— WOOL OF DIFFERENT COLORS)
TUM
(CONCRETE —) SOUP
(LIQUOR —) SODA QUININE SELTZER
MIXABLE MISCIBLE
MIXED CHOW IMPURE MEDLEY
MOTLEY PIEBALD STREAKY
CHOWCHOW
(— BLOOD) MESTIZO
(— CHALICE) KRASIS
(— UP) HAYWIRE
(NOT —) SINCERE
(PREF.) MIXO
MIXER HOG BANBURY MUDDLER
PICKLER
(CEMENT —) BOXMAN
(CONCRETE —) PAVER
(FOOD —) BEATER
MIXTURE AIR MIX BODY BREW DASH
FEED HASH MANG MELD MONG
MULL OLIO PUER SOUP STEW ALGIN
ALLOY BLEND BLENT BROMO
DOUGH GUMBO SALAD STUFF
FOURRE GARBLE GUNITE LIGNIN
MASLIN MEDLEY MELLAY MINGLE
MOTLEY TEMPER AMALGAM
COMPOST CUSTARD FARRAGO
FILICIN FORMULA GOULASH
HEADING KOGASIN MELANGE
MISTION MISTURA MIXTION
MONGREL OLLAPOD RECEIPT
TIMBALE ALKYLATE BLENDURE
DRAMMOCK EMULSION POSSODIE
POWSOWDY SOLUTION MACEDOINE
MENAGERIE MISCELLANY
SALMAGUNDI SMORGASBORD
(— ADDED TO WINE) DOSAGE
(— ATTRACTIVE TO PIGEONS)
SALTCAT
(— FOR CAKE) BATTER
(— FOR DRESSING LEATHER) DUBBIN
DUBBING
(— OF ALE AND OATMEAL) STOORY
(— OF ALKALOIDS) ADONIDIN
JABORINE
(— OF BARKS) TONGA
(— OF CEMENT AND STONE)
BUMICKY
(— OF CLAY AND CHALK) MALM
(— OF CLAY AND ROCK) BODY
(— OF CLAY AND SAND) LOAM
(— OF DRUGS) SPECIES
(— OF ELEMENTS) DIDYMIUM
(— OF FEEDS) MASH
(— OF IMPURE ARSENIDES) SPEISS
(— OF OATS AND BARLEY) DREDGE
(— OF PRINCIPLES) EUONYMIN

(— OF PROTEINS) CROTIN
(— OF SALTS) SOYATE
(— OF SAND AND STONES) CHAD
(— OF SAWDUST AND GLUE)
BADIGEON
(— OF SHALE AND SANDSTONE)
HAZLE
(— OF SLAG AND ORE) BROWSE
(— OF VINEGAR AND HONEY)
OXYMEL
(— OF VITAMINS) BIOS
(— OF WHITE AND BLACK) GRIZZLE
(— OF WINE, HONEY AND SPICES)
CLARY
(— TO ADULTERATE LIQUORS) FLASH
(— TO DOCTOR WINE) GEROPIGA
(— TO WHITEN BREAD) HARDS
(— USED AS A FERMENT) BUB
(— USED AT SEDER) HAROSET
CHAROSES
(ACUTE —) ACUTA
(AERIFORM —) GAS
(CARVER'S —) COMPO
(CAULKING —) BLARE
(CHEMICAL —) SYNGAS
(CLAY —) COB SLIP
(COATING —) COLOR
(CONFUSED —) MESS CHAOS
FUDDLE SOZZLE
(CRUMBLY —) STREUSEL
(EXPLOSIVE —) DUALIN FIREDAMP
(FOOD —) FILLING
(FREEZING —) CRYOGEN
(GILDING —) ASSIETTE
(HYDROCARBON —) ABIETENE
(ITALIAN CONDIMENT —) TAMARA
(JUMBLED —) BOTCH PASTICHE
(MECHANICS' —) PUTTY
(PLASTIC CEMENT —) CLOY
(PRESERVATIVE —) STUFF
(SEASONED —) STUFFING
(SMOKING —) CHARAS CHURRUS
(TANNING —) PURE
(THICKENING —) ROUX
(UNPALATABLE —) DRAMMOCK
(WATERY —) SLURRY
(WELDING —) THERMIT
(SUFF.) CRASE CRASIS CRASY
MIZZAH (FATHER OF —) REUEL
(GRANDFATHER OF —) ESAU
MIZZEN DANDY
MIZZONITE DIPYRE
MKS UNIT JOULE
MNEMONIC MEMORIAL
MOAN HONE MOON REEM WAIL
CROON GROAN MOURN MUNGE
QUIRK SOUGH MUNGER
MOANING SOUGH DIRGEFUL
MOAT FOSS DITCH FOSSE GRAFF
RUNDEL
MOB CREW GANG HERD RAFF ROUT
COHUE CROWD HURRY MAFIA PLEBE
PLEBS MOBILE RABBLE TUMULT

VUULGE DOGGERY CANAILLE
RIFFRAFF VARLETRY CLAMJAFRY
(PREF.) OCHLO
MOBCAP MOB
MOBILE THIN FLUID ROVING
MOVEABLE
(— ARTIST) CALDER
(FREELY —) THIN
MOBSTER HOODLUM
MOBY DICK (AUTHOR OF —)
MELVILLE
(CHARACTER IN —) AHAB STURR
ISHMAEL FEDALLAH QUEEQUEG
STARBUCK
MOCCASIN PAC CONGO TEGUA
SHOEPACK
(— WITH LEGS) LARRIGAN
(PL.) SHANKS
MOCCASIN FLOWER NERVINE
MOCHA BARK
MOCHICA YUNCA
MOCHILA MACHEER KNAPSACK
MOCK DO BOB DOR GAB MOW COPY
DEFY GECK GIBE GIRD JAPE JEER
JEST JIBE PLAY QUIZ BOURD DORRE
ELUDE FLEER FLIRT FLOUT FRUMP
HOKER KNACK MIMIC RALLY SCOFF
SCORN SCOUT SLEER SPORT TAUNT
BEMOCK DELUDE DERIDE ILLUDE
NIGGLE IMITATE MURGEON RIDICULE
MOCKER MOWER GIRDER BOURDER
FLOUTER SCORNER RAILLEUR
MOCKERNUT BULLNUT
MOCKERY DOR GAB MOW GLEE
JEER BOURD DORRE FARCE FLOUT
GLAIK SCOFF SPORT BISMER
HETHING LUDIBRY MOCKADO
MOCKAGE DERISION ILLUSION
RIDICULE SCOFFERY
(GOD OF —) MOMUS
MOCKING GAB ACID SPORT SCOPTIC
IRRISORY NARQUOIS SARDONIC
TRUMPERY
MOCKINGBIRD MIMUS MOWER
MOCKER
MOCK ORANGE SYRINGA
PHILADELPHUS
MOCOA COCHE
MOD HEP HIP YEYE TRENDY
MODE CUT JET TON WAY FORM GATE
MOOD RAGA TONE TWIG WISE FERIO
FINAL GENUS MODUS STATE STYLE
VOGUE ACTING BAROCO CESARE
COURSE DATISI FAKOFO FANGLE
FESAPO MANNER METHOD BAMALIP
CALEMES CAMENES DABITIS
DARAPTI DIBATIS DIMARIS DIMATIS
DISAMIS FAPESMO FASHION
FERISON FESTINO CELARENT
DOKMAROK FELAPTON FRESISON
TONALITY
(— OF BEHAVIOR) THEW HABITUDE
(— OF BEING) CATEGORY

(— OF CONDUCT) LAW
(— OF DRESS) HABIT TENUE
(— OF DRESSING HAIR) MADONNA
(— OF EXPRESSION) IRONY
(— OF MORAL ACTION) CONDUCT
(— OF PARTITIONING) CANT
(— OF PROCEDURE) ORDER SYSTEM
(— OF RULE) REGIME
(— OF SPEECH) ACCENT LATINISM
PARLANCE
(— OF STANDING) STANCE
(— OF STRUCTURE) BUILD
(PREVAILING —) GARB
(TEMPORARY —) VOGUE
MODEL WAX COPY FORM MOLD
NORM CANON DUMMY IDEAL LIGHT
MOULD NORMA SHAPE DESIGN
FUGLER GABARI MODULE PRAXIS
SOURCE BOZZETO DIORAMA
EXAMPLE GABARIT MODULET
PARAGON PATTERN PICTURE
SAMPLER CALENDAR ENSAMPLE
EXEMPLAR EXEMPLUM FORMULAR
FUGLEMAN MAQUETTE MODELLER
MODULIZE PARADIGM PROPLASM
SPECIMEN TYPORAMA MANNEQUIN
PLANETARIUM
(— MATERIAL) BALSA
(— OF EARTH) TERRELLA
(— OF FOOT) CAST
(— OF HUMAN BODY) FORM
MANIKIN
(— OF PERFECTION) PARAGON
(— OF SOLAR SYSTEM) ORRERY
(— OF STATUE) ESQUISSE
(INFERIOR —) JALOPPY
(MATHEMATICAL —) SPACE
(PRELIMINARY —) MAQUETTE
PROPLASM
(PREF.) TYP(I)(O)
MODERATE BATE COOL CURB EASE
EASY EVEN MEEK SOFT ABATE
ALLAY ALLOY LIGHT LOWER MEZZO
MODER REMIT SLACK SLAKE SOBER
SWEET ARREST BRIDLE DECENT
GENTLE LESSEN MEANLY MIDWAY
MODEST MODIFY REMISS SEASON
SOFTEN SUBMIT TEMPER CENTRAL
CHASTEN CONTROL SLACKEN
ATTEMPER CENTRIST MEETERLY
MIDDLING MITIGATE MODERATO
ORDINATE PALLIATE PASSABLE
CONTINENT ABSTEMIOUS
MEASURABLE REASONABLE
(— IN BURNING) SOFT
(— OF THE WIND) LOOM
MODERATELY GEY FAIR MEAN
MEANLY MEETLY PRETTY MIDWISE
MEETERLY MIDDLING
MODERATENESS CLEMENCY
MODICITY
MODERATION MEAN STAY MINCE
SPARE MANNER MEDIUM REASON

COMPASS MEDIETY MODESTY
SOBRIETY ABATEMENT IMMODESTY
MODERATO MASSIG
MODERATOR ANCHOR
ANCHORMAN
MODERN NEW LATE RECENT
NEOTERIC SPACEAGE
MODERNE ARTDECO
MODEST COY MIM SHY DEFT MURE
NICE PURE SNUG BLATE DOUCE
LOWLY QUIET SMALL CHASTE
DEMURE HUMBLE PUDENT SIMPLE
VIRGIN CLERKLY PUDICAL DISCREET
MAIDENLY PUDIBUND RESERVED
RETIRING SHAMEFUL VERECUND
VIRTUOUS
MODESTY AIDOS PUDOR NICETY
DECENCY PUDENCY SHYNESS
CHASTITY FOREHEAD HUMILITY
PUDICITY
MODICUM DROP BREAK SPICE
PENNORTH SCANTLING SEMBLANCE
PENNYWORTH
MODIFICATION BOB ECAD FORM
SALT CHANGE ENGRAM FACIES
SANDHI SINGLE UMLAUT
ENGRAMMA
(— **OF A REMEDY**) TINCTION
(**GLOTTAL** —) STOP
MODIFIED VARIANT
MODIFY EDIT VARY ALTER AMEND
HEDGE TOUCH BUFFER CHANGE
DOCTOR MASTER TEMPER ARABIZE
COMPARE FASHION MASSAGE
QUALIFY ATTEMPER DENATURE
GRADUATE MODERATE FAUCALIZE
(— **ARTICULATION**) COLOR
(— **COLOR**) TONE
MODILLION ANCON MODEL TRUSS
CARTOUCH
MODISH CHIC MODY SOIGNE TIMISH
TONISH STYLISH
MODISHNESS CHIC
MODRED (**FATHER OF** —) ARTHUR
(**MOTHER OF** —) MARGAWSE
MODULATE SINK INFLECT QUALIFY
MODULATION ACCENT CHANGE
CADENCE BUNCHING PASSAGIO
MODULE LEM UNIT COMPONENT
(**KIND OF** —) LUNAR
(**LUNAR EXCURSION** —) BUG LED
MOGUL NABOB NAWAB RULER
VICEROY PADISHAH
MOHAIR MOIRE
MOHAMMED MAHOMET MAHOUND
MUDEJAR PROPHET
(**SITE OF** — **TOMB**) MEDINA
(**UNCLE OF** —) ABBAS
MOHAMMEDAN MOSLEM PAYNIM
MAHOMET
MOHAMMEDANISM TURBAN
TURKERY MAUMETRY
MOHAWK NICKER

MOHR MHORR GAZELLE
MOHUR MOOR AHMEDI
MOIETY MEDIETY
MOIST WET DAMP DANK DEWY NESH
UVID DABBY GIVEY GREEN HUMID
JUICY MADID MOCHY SAMMY SAPPY
SLACK SOAKY SOCKY SPEWY
SWACK WASHY WEEPY CLAMMY
MOISTY STICKY WETTISH
HUMOROUS MUCULENT
(**PREF.**) HUMI(DI) HYGR(O) UDO
MOISTEN DIP WET DAMP MOIL
BASTE BATHE BEDEW JUICE LATCH
LEACH STEEP WOKIE DABBLE
DAMPEN HUMECT HUMIFY IMBRUE
MADEFY SPARGE TEMPER HUMIDIFY
IRRIGATE IRRORATE
(— **LEATHER**) SAM SAMMY
MOISTURE DEW WET BREE DAMP
DANK ROKE HUMOR MOIST WATER
PHLEGM AQUOSITY HUMIDITY
(— **DEFICIENT**) XERIC
(— **FROM SKIN**) SWEAT
(— **IN STONE**) SAP
(— **ON BEARD**) BARBER
(**CONDENSED** —) BREATH
(**REMOVE CONDENSED** —) DEFOG
(**PREF.**) HUMI(DI) HYGR(O) UDO
MOJARRA SHAD PATAO
MOKI MOGUEY MOKIHI
MOKSHA MUKTI
MOLAR WANG FORMAL MOLARY
GRINDER
(**PREF.**) MYL(O)
MOLASSES DIP LICK CLAGGUM
THERIAC TREACLE LONGLICK
(**PREF.**) MELASSI
MOLD DIE FEN PIG PLY SOW CALM
CAST CURB FORM MULL MUST SOIL
TRAP BLOCK CHAPE CHILL FRAME
INGOT MODEL MOULD MUCOR
PLASM PRINT SHAPE SNARE STENT
STINT VALVE COFFIN GABARI
INFORM LINGET MATRIX SQUARE
BASTARD FASHION FESTOON
MATRICE RILLETT SANDBOX SKILLET
TEMPLET COQUILLE FUMAGINE
HOODMOLD PROPLASM TEMPLATE
WHISKERS PENICILLIUM
(— **FOR METAL**) SOW SKILLET
(— **OF ASPIC**) DARIOLE
(— **OF SHIP**) SWEEP
(— **THAT ATTACKS HOPS**) FEN
(**CHEESE** —) CHESSEL
(**SLIME** —) MYCETOZOAN
MYXOMYCETE
(**PREF.**) PLASM(ATO)(O)
(**SUFF.**) PLASIA PLASIS PLASM(A)(IA)
(IC) PLAST(IC)(Y) PLASY
MOLDAVITE TEKTITE
MOLDBOARD REEST
(— **SURFACE**) WREST
MOLDED FICTILE

MOLDER ROT MURL DECAY ERODE CAPPER MANGLE MOSKER FIGURER PLASTER PLASTIC

MOLDINESS MUST FINEW MUCOR VINEW

MOLDING BEAD COVE CYMA DADO GULA KEEL LIST OGEE OVAL CABLE FILET GORGE LABEL LEDGE ROVER STAFF BANDLE BASTON BILLET CASING COLLAR CONGEE COVING FILLET LISTEL MULLER REGLET SQUARE ZIGZAG ANNULET BEADING CARLING CHAPLET CORNICE DOUCINE ECHINUS EYEBROW FINGENT HIPMOLD LOZENGE MOULAGE NECKING SURBASE TONDINO TRINGLE ASTRAGAL BAGUETTE BANDELET CASEMATE CASEMENT CINCTURE CYMATION CYMATIUM DANCETTE DOGTOOTH FUSAROLE HOODMOLD KNURLING MOULDING NAILHEAD NECKMOLD ARCHIVOLT BOLECTION
(CONCAVE —) GORGE CONGEE SCOTIA CAVETTO
(CONVEX —) REED CABLE OVOLO THUMB TORUS BASTON REEDING ASTRAGAL FUSAROLE
(OGEE —) TALON
(OUTSIDE —) BACKBAND
(PL.) TORI LEDGMENT

MOLDY FUSTY HOARY MUCID MUGGY MUSTY VINNY FOISTY MOULDY FOUGHTY

MOLE COB UNT COBB MAII OONT PIER PILE TAPE WANT JUTTY MOODY NEVUS TALPA TAUPE ANICUT MOUDIE HYDATID SLEEPER TALPOID MOLDWARP MOONCALF SORICOID STARNOSE UROPSILE ZANDMOLE
(PREF.) TALPI

MOLE CRICKET CHANGA

MOLECULE ACID ATOM BASE AMMINE CHIRAL DIPOLE HEXANE HYDROL LIGAND PRIMER HYDRONE SPECIES TEMPLATE OCTAPEPTIDE
(CLUSTER OF —) CAP
(PROTEIN —) BIOGEN

MOLEHILL TUMP HOYLE WANTHILL

MOLE RAT SEMNI ZEMMI ZOKOR SLEPEZ SPALACID ZANDMOLE

MOLEST GALL HAUNT TEASE BOTHER HARASS HECKLE INFEST PESTER MISLEST TROUBLE

MOLID (FATHER OF —) ABISHUR
(MOTHER OF —) ABIHAIL

MOLL FLANDERS (AUTHOR OF —) DEFOE
(CHARACTER IN —) MOLL JEMMY ROBIN FLANDERS

MOLLIFIER SLAVE

MOLLIFY HUSH ALLAY RELAX ADULCE GENTLE PACIFY RELENT SOFTEN SOOTHE TEMPER ASSUAGE DULCIFY SWEETEN ATTEMPER MITIGATE UNRUFFLE

MOLLIFYING MILD SUPPLING

MOLLUSK ARK CLAM CONE PIPI SPAT BORER CHAMA CHANK CHINK CLAMP CONCH COWRY DORIS DRILL MUREX PINNA SNAIL VENUS AEOLID BAILER BUBBLE CERION CHITON COCKLE COURIE DOLIUM JINGLE LEPTON LIMPET MUSSEL NERITA OYSTER PECTEN PHOLAD PURPLE SEMELE STROMB ABALONE ADMIRAL ASTARTE BIVALVE CARDITA DECAPOD JUNONIA MOLLUSC PIDDOCK SALPIAN SCALLOP TOHEROA TREPANG TROPHON DUCKFOOT FIGSHELL HALIOTIS NAUTILUS PTEROPOD SAXICAVA STROMBUS UNIVALVE VERMETUS SHELLFISH NUDIBRANCH PERIWINKLE
(— TRIBE) NAIADES
(LARVAL —) VELIGER
(YOUNG —) SPAT

MOLLYCODDLE BABY MOLLY WANTON INDULGE MILKSOP

MOLOSSUS (FATHER OF —) PYRRHUS
(MOTHER OF —) ANDROMACHE

MOLT MEW CAST MUTE SHED MOULT DISCARD EXUVIATE INTERMEW

MOLTEN FUSED

MOLTING BROKEN ECDYSIS

MOLUCCAS (ISLAND OF —) ARU KAI OBI BURU LETI SULA AMBON BABAR BANDA CERAM WETAR BATJAN TIDORE MOROTAI TERNATE TANIMBAR HALMAHERA

MOLUS (BROTHER OF —) EVENUS
(DAUGHTER OF —) MOLIONE
(FATHER OF —) ARES MARS
(MOTHER OF —) DEMONICE

MOLYBDENUM (EXCESS OF —) TEART

MOMBIN JOCOTE

MOMENT MO GIRD HINT SAND TICK AVAIL BLINK BRAID CLINK CRACK GLIFF GLISK JIFFY SHAKE SNIFT

SPURT STOUN TRICE VALUE FILLIP
GLIFFY MINUTE PERIOD SECOND
STOUND WEIGHT YAWING ARTICLE
INSTANT INSTANCE MOMENTUM
TWINKLING
(— FOR LEGERDEMAIN ACTION)
TEMPS
(— OF STRESS) CRISE
(APPROPRIATE —) PLACE
(CRITICAL —) BIT INCH CORNER
(DECISIVE —) CRISIS
(EXACT —) BIT POINT
(OPPORTUNE —) KAIROS
(PRECISE —) NICK
(SCHEDULED —) TIME
MOMENTARY MOMENTAL
TRANSIENT
MOMENTOUS FELL GRAVE
EPOCHAL FATEFUL WEIGHTY
EVENTFUL PREGNANT
MOMENTOUSNESS GRAVITY
MOMENTUM WAY FORCE SPEED
IMPETUS
MON PEGUAN TALAING
MONACO (NATIVE OF —)
MONEGASQUE

MONACO

ANCIENT NAME: MONOECUS
CAPITAL: MONACO MONACOVILLE
DYNASTY: GRIMALDI
LANGUAGE: FRENCH
PEOPLE: MONEGASQUES
PRINCE: LOUIS ALBERT HONORE
ANTOINE CHARLES RAINIER
FLORESTAN
RIVER: VESUBIE
SECTION: MONTECARLO
LACONDAMINE MONACOVILLE

MONAD ATOM JIVA AMEBA HENAD
MONAS
MONADIC UNARY
MONADNOCK BARABOO
MONARCH KING QUEEN DANAID
DIADEM PRINCE DANAINE EMPEROR
AUTOCRAT
MONARCHIAN PRAXEAN
MONARCHICAL KINGLY
MONARCHY KINGDOM
MONASTERY WAT ABBEY BADIA
LAURA RIBAT TEKKE TEKYA FRIARY
MANDRA VIHARA BONZERY CERTOSA
CONVENT KHANKAH MINSTER
MONKERY CLOISTER LAMASERY
(ALGERIAN —) RIBAT
(BUDDHIST —) TERA KYAUNG
BONZERY LAMASERY
(CARTHUSIAN —) CERTOSA
(HINDU —) MATH
(MOSLEM —) TEKKE TEKYA KHANKAH
(PREF.) MANDRI
(SUFF.) MINSTER

MONASTIC MONKLY MONKISH
ABBATIAL CENOBIAN MONACHAL
MONASTICISM MONKERY
MONKISM
MONDAY LUNDI
MONETARY EXPLICIT PECUNIARY
NUMISMATIC
MONEY (ALSO SEE COIN) AES BOX
DIB FAT FEE FEI GET OOF ORO SAP
TIN WAD BUCK CASH COAT COIN
COLE CRAP CUSH DUBS DUST FUND
GATE GELT GILT GOLD HOOT JACK
JAKE KALE LOOT LOUR MALI MINT
MOSS MUCK PELF ROLL SALT SAND
SHAG SOAP SWAG BEANS BLUNT
BRASH BRASS BREAD BUNCE BUNTS
CHINK CHIPS CLINK DARBY DIMES
DOUGH DUMPS FUNDS GREEN
GRIGS IMPUT LOLLY LUCRE MEANS
MOOLA MOPUS OCHER PURSE
RHINO ROCKS ROWDY SCADS SHINY
SMASH SPUDS STIFF STUFF SUGAR
ARGENT BARATO BARREL BOODLE
CHANGE CUNYIE DANARO DINERO
DOREMI FARLEU FARLEY FEUAGE
FLIMSY FUMAGE GRAITH HANSEL
KELTER MAZUMA POCKET SHEKEL
SILLER SILVER SPENSE SPLOSH
STAMPS STEVEN STUMPY TALENT
WAMPUM WISSEL ADVANCE
CABBAGE CHATTEL CHINKER
COUNTER CRACKER CRUSADE
DEPOSIT FALDAGE GUNNAGE
OOFTISH SCRATCH SPANKER
SPECIES STOCKER CRIMPAGE
CURRENCY DEMIMARK INCOMING
INTEREST SPENDING STERLING
STOCKING XERAPHIN SPONDULIX
WAMPUMPEAG SPONDULICKS
WHEREWITHAL
(— BET) COMEBACK
(— DUE) DEVOIRS
(— FOR LIQUOR) WHIP
(— HOLDER) TILL
(— LENT) LUMBER
(— MANAGER) GUNSLINGER
(— OF ACCOUNT) ECU ORA
(— PAID TO BIND BARGAIN) ARLES
(— TAKEN IN) DRAWING
(ADDITIONAL —) BONUS
(AVAILABLE —) CAPITAL
(BAD —) SMASH
(BAR —) BONK TANG
(BASE —) SHICE
(BRIBE —) SOAP BOODLE
(COINED —) SPECIE
(COUNTERFEIT —) BOGUS QUEER
BOODLE DUFFER SHOWFUL SLITHER
(EARNEST —) ARLES ARRHA DEPOSIT
HANSEL HANDGELD HANDSALE
(EXPENSE —) DIET
(EXTORTED —) PROTECTION
(FERRY —) NAULUM

(HARD —) SPECIE
(HAT —) TAMPANG
(HAVING NO —) FLYBLOWN
(INVESTED —) STOCK
(KIND OF —) NEAR
(LARGE SUM OF —) NUT
(NEAR —) ASSETS
(ON THE —) EXACTLY
(PAPER —) BUCK GREEN SCRIP
CABBAGE CURRENCY FROGSKIN
(PASSAGE —) SHIPHIRE
(PLEDGE —) EARNEST
(PRIZE —) PEWTER
(PROTECTION —) ICE
(PUSH —) SPIFF
(READY —) CASH DARBY PREST
READY STUFF STUMPY
(REFUNDED —) DRAWBACK
(SHELL —) PEAG HAWOK WAKIKI
WAMPUM
(SILVER —) SYCEE
(SMALL SUM OF —) SPILL
(STANDARD BANK —) BANCO
(SUBSISTENCE —) BATTA
(SYSTEM OF — TRANSFER) GIRO
(TRAVELLING —) VIATICUM
(WIRE —) LARI LARIN LARREE
(10 DOLLARS IN —) SAWBUCK
MONEYBAG FOLLIS
MONEY BELT ZONE
MONEY BOX TILL CHEST PIRLIE
MONEY-CHANGER SARAF SHROFF
CAMBIST ARGENTER
MONEY-CHANGING AGIO
AGIOTAGE AGIO
MONEY DRAWER TILL SHUTTLE
MONEYED RICH WEALTHY
MONEYLENDER BANYA CHETTY
USURER LOMBARD MAHAJAN
MARWARI SHYLOCK BUMMAREE
MONEYMAKING BANAUSIC
MONEYWORT MANG MYRTLE
PRIMWORT
MONGER DEALER
MONGOL HUN KALKA BALKAR
BURIAT DAGHUR SHARRA BERBERI
KALMUCK KHALKHA SILINGAL
(PL.) IIU
MONGOLIA (CAPITAL OF —)
ULANBATOR ULAANBAATAR
(DESERT IN —) GOBI
(MONEY OF —) MONGO TUGHRIK
(RIVER OF —) ORHON DZAVHAN
KERULEN SELENGE
(TOWN OF —) ONON MUREN
DARHAN BULAGAN CHOIREN
TAMTSAK ULANBATOR
CHOYBALSAN
MONGOOSE MUNG URVA CIVET
MUNGO MONGOE MEERKAT
VANSIRE
MONGREL CUR DOG FICE FIST MUTT
CROSS FEIST LIMER POOCH SCRUB
HYBRID PYEDOG BASTARD CURRISH
PIEBALD DOGGEREL
MONIKER NAME ALIAS
MONILIALES HYPHO
MONIMIA (GUARDIAN OF —) ACASTO
(HUSBAND OF —) CASTALIO
(LOVER OF —) POLYDORE
MONISM HENISM ONEISM
MONITION TUITION
MONITOR CRT MARKER MENTOR
LANTERN PREFECT
MONITOR LIZARD IBID IBIT URAN
VARAN WARAL GOANNA WORRAL
MONITOR KABARAGOYA
MONK BO FRA CUM LAMA MARO
ARHAT BONZE CLERK FRATE FRIAR
PADRE YAHAN ARAHAT BHIKKU
CULDEE GALLAH GETSUL GOSAIN
MONACH SANTON VOTARY CALOYER
CLUNIAC GALLACH JACOBIN
STARETS STUDITE ATHONITE
BACHELOR BASILIAN MARABOUT
MONASTIC OLIVETAN SANNYASI
TALAPOIN TRAPPIST BALDICOOT
CELESTINE THELEMITE BERNARDINE
CISTERCIAN
(CHIEF —) ABBOT
(PL.) AGAPETI ACOEMETI
MONKEY APE CAY KRA PUG SAI TUP
BEGA BROH BRUH DOUC KAHA
MONA MONK MONO SAKI SIME TITI
TOTA WAAG ZATI ARABA CEBID
DIANA JACKO JOCKO KAHAU
MUNGA OATAS PATAS PONGO
PUGGY SAJOU TOQUE UNGKA
BANDAR COAITA COUXIA GRISON
GRIVET GUENON HOWLER LANGUR
MACACO MARTEN MIRIKI MONACH
NISNAS OLINGO OUDARI PINCHE
RILAWA SAMIRI SIMIAN SIMPAI
TEETEE VERVET WARINE WEEPER
WISTIT BHUNDER COLOBIN GUARIBA
GUEREZA HANUMAN KALASIE
LUNGOOR MACAQUE MEERKAT
MOUSTOC OUAKARI PRIMATE
ROLOWAY SAIMIRI SAPAJOU
STENTOR TAMARIN ARAGUATO
CAIARARA CAPUCHIN DURUKULI
ENTELLUS LEONCITO MANGABEY
MARMOSET MARTINET MUSTACHE
ORABASSU PRIMATAL TALAPOIN
TCHINCOU WANDEROO BRACHYURA
MALBROUCK
(HOWLER —) ALOUATTA
(KIND OF —) GREASE VERVET
COLOBUS
(LIKE A —) PUGGISH
(PREF.) PITHEC(O)
MONKEY BREAD BAOBAB
ADANSONIA
MONKEY FLOWER MIMULUS
MONKEYPOT LECYTH KAKARALI
LECYTHIS SAPUCAIA

MONKEY PUZZLE BUNYA PINON PINION
MONKEYSHINE DIDO SINGERIE (PL.) HORSE
MONKFISH MONK LOTTE RHINA SQUATINA
MONKISH CENOBIAN MONASTIC
MONK PARROT LORO
MONKSHOOD ATIS ACONITE ACONITUM NAPELLUS MOUSEBANE
MONO MONACHI
MONOACETATE ACETIN
MONOCARPELLARY SIMPLE
MONOCHORD MAGAS MAGADIS UNICHORD
MONOCHROME CAMAIEU MONOTINT
MONOCLE QUIZ LORGNON EYEGLASS
MONOCLINOUS PERFECT
MONOECISM SYNOECY SYNOEKY
MONOGRAM IHS JHS YHS CIPHER HERALD CHRISMON
(LITERARY —) GBS RLS TSE
MONOGRAPH STUDY MEMOIR BULLETIN DISCOURSE
MONOLITH MENHIR PILLAR (CIRCLE OF —S) CROMLECH
MONOLITHIC GLOBAL
MONOLOGIST DISEUSE
MONOLOGUE MONOLOGY SOLILOQUY
MONONUCLEOTIDE AMP
MONOPHTHONGAL PURE
MONOPHTHONGIZE SMOOTH
MONOPHYSITE AGNOETE AGNOITE JACOBITE (PL.) ACEPHALI
MONOPLANE TAUBE PARASOL
MONOPODE SKIAPOD
MONOPOLIZE LURCH ABSORB CONSUME ENGROSS
MONOPOLY REGIE TRUST CARTEL APPALTO (GOVERNMENT —) REGIE
MONOSACCHARIDE OSE DIOSE HEXOSE KETOSE MONOSE GLYCOSE HEPTOSE PENTOSE PYRANOSE
MONOTONOUS ARID DEAD DULL FLAT WASTE DREARY SAMELY SODDEN ADENOID HUMDRUM INSIPID IRKSOME ONENOTE TEDIOUS BORESOME DRUDGING SAMESOME SINGSONG UNVARIED VEGETABLE
MONOTONY DRAB DRYNESS HUMDRUM DULLNESS SAMENESS
MONOTREME ECHIDNA DUCKBILL
MONOXENOUS DIRECT
MONSIEUR BEAUCAIRE (AUTHOR OF —) TARKINGTON (CHARACTER IN —) BEAU MARY NASH VALOIS CARLISLE MIREPOIX PHILLIPE MOLYNEAUX WINTERSET CHATEAURIEN
MONSOON VARSHA
MONSTER OGRE BILCH LARVA MORMO RAHAB TERAS UNMAN ELLOPS GERYON MAKARA SHRIMP TYPHON BICORNE CHIMERA CYCLOPS DIDYMUS DIPYGUS ECHIDNA GRENDEL GRIFFIN GRIFFON PRODIGY SLAPPER UNBEAST WARLOCK JANICEPS LINDWORM MOONCALF TARASQUE TYPHOEUS UROMELUS LEVIATHAN
(— WITH 100 EYES) ARGUS
(— WITH 100 HANDS) BRIAREUS
(FABULOUS —) OGRE KRAKEN WIVERN TANIWHA
(FEMALE —) HARPY LAMIA SCYLLA
(HALF-BULL HALF-MAN —) MINOTAUR
(HERALDIC —) SATYRAL
(IMAGINARY —) CHIMERA
(INVISIBLE —) BUNYIP
(LOCH —) NESS NESSIE
(MAN-DEVOURING —) OGRE LAMIA
(MYTHICAL —) HARPY SCYLLA SPHINX CHIMERA WARLOCK MINOTAUR
(SEA —) ORC BELUE PHOCA KRAKEN PISTRIX ZIFFIUS WASSERMAN
(SUPERNATURAL —) LARVA
(TWO-BODIED —) DISOMUS
(WATER —) NICKER
(9-HEADED —) HYDRA
(PREF.) TERAT(O)
(SUFF.) PAGUS
MONSTRANCE SUN
MONSTROSITY FREAK DIPYGUS MONSTER ABORTION IMMANITY MOONCALF TERATISM (SUFF.) DYMUS
MONSTROUS VAST ENORM GIANT FIENDLY FLAMING HIDEOUS TITANIC BEHEMOTH COLOSSAL DEFORMED ENORMOUS FLAGRANT GIGANTIC PYTHONIC SLAPPING NEFARIOUS PRODIGIOUS
MONTAGNARD SEKANI

MONTANA
CAPITAL: HELENA
COLLEGE: CARROLL
COUNTY: HILL TETON TOOLE CARBON CUSTER FERGUS MCCONE WIBAUX BIGHORN PONDERA RAVALLI CHOUTEAU FLATHEAD MISSOULA
INDIAN: CROW ATSINA SALISH ARAPAHO KUTENAI SIKSIKA SHOSHONE
LAKE: HEBGEN FLATHEAD FORTPECK MEDICINE
MOUNTAIN: AJAX BALDY COWAN SPHINX TORREY GRANITE HILGARD

TRAPPER GALLATIN PENTAGON
SNOWSHOE
MOUNTAIN RANGE: CRAZY LEWIS
ROCKY BIGBELT
NICKNAME: BIGSKY MOUNTAIN
TREASURE
RIVER: MILK TONGUE KOOTENAI
MISSOURI
STATE BIRD: MEADOWLARK
STATE FLOWER: BITTERROOT
TOWN: BUTTE HAVRE MALTA TERRY
CIRCLE CONRAD HARDIN HELENA
HYSHAM SCOBEY BOZEMAN
CHINOOK CHOTEAU EKALAKA
FORSYTH GLASGOW ROUNDUP
BILLINGS MISSOULA

MONTANIST PHRYGIAN

MONTENEGRO
CAPITAL: CETINJE
COIN: PARA FLORIN PERPERA
LAKE: SCUTARI SHKODER
MOUNTAIN: DURMITOR
NAME: ZETA ILLYRIA CRNAGORA
TSERNAGORA
PORT: BAR ULCINJ ANTIVARI
DULCIGNO
RIVER: IBAR ZETA DRINA MORACA
TOWN: NIKSIC CETINJE TITOGRAD
PODGORICA

MONTEZUMA AZTEC
MONTH AB AV BUL MAY PUS SOL ZIF
ZIW ABIB ADAR AHET AOUT APAP
ASIN ELUL IYAR JETH JULY JUNE
KUAR MAGH MOON TYBI AGHAN
APRIL ASARH CHAIT ENERO IYYAR
MAIUS MARCH NISAN PAYNI RABIA
RAJAB SAFAR SAWAN SEBAT SHVAT
SIVAN SIWAN TEBET THOTH TIZRI
UINAL AUGUST BHADON CHOIAK
JUMADA JUNIUS KARTIK KISLEV
KISLEW KISLEY MECHIR MESORE
NISSAN NIVOSE PAOPHI PHAGUN
SAPHAR SHABAN SHABAT SHEVAT
TAMMUZ TEBETH TISHRI VEADAR
ABAGHAN APRILIS BAISAKH
BYSACKI CHAITRA CHISLEV ETHANIM
FLOREAL HESHVAN JANUARY
MARTIUS OCTOBER PACHONS
PHALGUN RAMADAN SARAWAN
SHAABAN SHAWWAL THAMMUZ
VENTOSE BRUMAIRE DECEMBER
DULKAADA FEBRUARY FERVIDOR
FRIMAIRE GAMELION GERMINAL
MESSIDOR MUHARRAM NOVEMBER
PLUVIOSE POSEIDON PRAIRIAL
SEXTILIS ZULKADAH SEPTEMBER
(— OF ISLAMIC YEAR) RABI SAFAR
(IN NEXT —) PROXIMO
(IN PRECEDING —) ULTIMO
(PRESENT —) INSTANT

(SIX —S) SEMESTER
(SYNODIC —) LUNATION
(PREF.) MENO
(SUFF.) MESTER
MONTHLY MENSAL
MONTMORILLONITE SMECTITE
MONUMENT VAT WAT LECH TOMB
CROSS STONE TABUT TITLE BILITH
DOLMEN HEARSE HEROON MEMORY
RECORD TROPHY ARCHIVE CHAITYA
CHHATRI CHORTEN DENKMAI
FUNERAL TRILITH BILITHON
CENOTAPH MEMORIAL MONOLITH
TROPAION
(— IN CHURCH) SACELLUM
(— OF BALEARIC ISLANDS) TALAYOT
(— OF BALEARIC ISLES) TALAYOT
(— OF HEAPED STONES) CAIRN
(— WITHIN CHURCH) SACELLUM
(PILLARLIKE —) SHAFT STELA STELE
MONUMENTAL EPIC
MOO LOW
MOOCH BUM CADGE SPONGE
MOOCHER MIKER CADGER GRAFTER
SKELDER SPONGER FREELOADER
MOOD CUE FIT TID MIND TIFF TIFT
TONE TUNE VEIN WHIM DEVIL
FRAME FREAK HEART HUMOR SPITE
PLIGHT SPIRIT SPLEEN SPRITE
STRAIN TALENT TEMPER CAPRICE
FANTASY FEATHER JUSSIVE
ATTITUDE OPTATIVE
(— IN LOGIC) BARBARA
(— OF BAD TEMPER) MAD DORTS
(— OF DEPRESSION) FUNK LETDOWN
(CROSS —) FRUMPS
(FRIVOLOUS —) JEST
(GROUCHY —) DODS
(IRRITABLE —) GRIZZLE
(PENSIVE —) MELANCHOLY
(SULKY —) PET
(SULLEN —) STRUNT SULLENS
MOODY SAD GLUM SULKY BROODY
GLOOMY MOROSE SULLEN
MOODISH PENSIVE
MOOLA DOUGH
MOOLAH GELT MONEY
MOON BUAT LAMP LUNA MAHI
DIANA LUNET LUCINA PHOEBE
CHANDRA CYNTHIA LEWANNA
LUNETTE MOONLET FOGEATER
MENISCUS SATELLES
(AREA ON —) MARE TERRA
(FULL —) PLENILUNE
(LARGE MASS ON —) MASCON
(NEW —) PRIME
(PART OF COURSE OF —) MANSION
(SING TO THE —) BAY
(WANING —) WANIAND
(PREF.) LUNI MENI SELEN(I)(O)
MOON AND SIXPENCE (AUTHOR
OF —) MAUGHAM
(CHARACTER IN —) AMY ATA DIRK

TIARE BLANCHE CHARLES COUTRAS
STROEVE STRICKLAND
MOONBLIND LUNATIC
MOONEYE HIODONT
MOONEYE CISCO BLOATER
MOON-EYED LUNATIC
MOONFISH OPAH SUNFISH
JOROBADO
MOONFLOWER ACHETE
MOONLIGHT FLESH MOONGLOW
MOONRAT GYMNURE
MOONSET MOONDOWN MOONFALL
MOONSHINE BREW MOON SHINE
SHINNY BOOTLEG BLOCKADE
MOONSTONE (AUTHOR OF —)
COLLINS
(CHARACTER IN —) CUFF EZRA JOHN
BLAKE BRUFF CANDY LUKER RACHEL
GABRIEL GODFREY ROSANNA
FRANKLIN JENNINGS SPEARMAN
VERINDER ABLEWHITE BETTEREDGE
HERNCASTLE MURTHWAITE
MOONSTRUCK MAD LOONY
LUNATIC
MOONWORT LUNARY HONESTY
MOOR FEN BENT FELL MOSS POST
BEACH BERTH HOVEL TURCO
COMONTE MARRANO MOGRABI
MOORMAN MORESCO MORISCO
COMMONTY
(INFERTILE —) LANDE
MOOR COCK GORCOCK MUIRCOCK
MOORED GIRT
MOORING DOCK MOORAGE
MOORLAND ROSLAND OUTFIELD
MOOSE BELL ELAND CERVID
ORIGNAL
(YOUNG —) CALF
MOOSEWOOD DIRCA
MOOT MUTE STIR PORTMOOT
MOP BOB SOP SWAB MALKIN MERKIN
MOPPET SCOVEL
(— FOR CLEANING CANNON) MERKIN
(— OF HAIR) TOUSLE
(BAKER'S —) MALKIN MAWKIN
MOPANE IRONWOOD
MOPE MOON MUMP PEAK POUT
SULK BOODY BROOD GLOOM
MOPING FUSTY DUMPISH
MOPOKE FROGMOUTH
MOPSUS SEER
(FATHER OF —) AMPYCUS RHACIUS
(MOTHER OF —) MANTO CHLORIS
MORA LOVE TIME LIMMA SEMEION
MORAL TAG PURE CIVIL ETHIC
EPIMYTH ETHICAL UPRIGHT
HONORARY
(MAN OF —S) AESOP
(PL.) THEW
MORALIST ETHICIAN
MORALISTIC DIDACTIC
MORALITY MORALS VIRTUE
MORALIZING PI

MORASS BOG FEN FLOW MOSS
ROSS SUMP FLUSH MARSH SLACK
POLDER SLOUGH QUAGMIRE
MORAY PUSI ELGIN HAMLET
MURAENA
MORBID SICK MORBOSE PECCANT
MORDANT HANDLE SPIRIT CAUSTIC
STRIKER SCATHING
MORDECAI (FATHER OF —) JAIR
(WARD OF —) ESTHER
MORE MO MAE PIU OTHER HELDER
(— OR LESS) HALFWAY
(— THAN) BUT OVER ABOVE RISING
PLUSQUAM
(— THAN ADEQUATE) AMPLE
(— THAN ENOUGH) TOO
(— THAN HALF) BETTER
(— THAN ONE) SEVERAL
(— THAN ONE OR TWO) SUNDRY
(— THAN SUFFICIENT) ABUNDANT
(— THAN THIS) YEA
(LITTLE —) ADVANTAGE
(ONE —) ANOTHER
(PREF.) MALLO PLEIO PLEO PLIO
(— THAN) PLU SUPER
MOREEN TABBY
MOREL HELVELLA MORIGLIO
MORELLO MOREL GRIOTTE
MULBERRY
MOREOVER EFT EKE TOO ALSO
MORE AGAIN EITHER BESIDES
FARTHER FURTHER THERETO
LIKEWISE OVERMORE
MOREPORK OWL PEHO RURU
MOPOKE MOPEHAWK
MORGUE LIBRARY MORTUARY
MORION CABASSET
MORMON COHAB SAINT DANITE
PATRIARCH
(— STATE) UTAH
MORMONE CALCITONIN
MORNING GAY MORN MATIN
MORROW UNDERN COCKCROW
MORNTIME
(IN THE —) MANE
MORNING GLORY NIL KOALI
TWINER GAYBINE IPOMOEA
MANROOT PILIKAI BINDWEED
SCAMMONY MOONFLOWER
(— GROWING AMONG GRAIN) BEAR
MORNING-GOWN PEIGNOIR
MORNING STAR VENUS DAYSTAR
LUCIFER MERCURY BARTONIA
MORO LUTAO SAMAL YAKAN ILLANO
JOLOANO MARANAO
MOROCCO MAROQUIN

MOROCCO		
CAPE: NUN NOUN		
CAPITAL: RABAT		
COIN: OKIA RIAL OKIEH DIRHAM MOUZOUNA		
DISTRICT: ERRIF		

FRENCH NAME: MAROC
MEASURE: KALA SAAH FANEGA
   IZENBI TOMINI
MOUNTAIN: TOUBKAL
MOUNTAIN RANGE: RIF ATLAS
PEOPLE: MOOR BERBER KABYLE
   MOSLEM MUSLIM
PORT: SAFI CEUTA RABAT SAFFI
   AGADIR TETUAN LARACHE
   MAZAGAN MELILLA MOGADOR
   TANGIER
PROVINCE: CEUTA MELILLA
RIVER: DRA SOUS WADI SEBOU
   TENSIFT MOULOUYA
TOWN: FES FEZ SAFI OUJDA RABAT
   AGADIR MEKNES KENITRA TANGIER
   TETOUAN MARRAKECH
   CASABLANCA
WEIGHT: ROTL ARTAL ARTEL GERBE
   RATEL KINTAR QUINTAL

MORON FOOL AMENT IMBECILE
MORONITY MOROSIS
MOROSE SAD ACID GLUM GRUM
  SOUR MOODY RUSTY SURLY
  CRUSTY GLOOMY SEVERE STINGY
  SULLEN CRABBED CROOKED
  PEEVISH STROUNGE SATURNINE
  SPLENETIC
MOROSELY CRUSTILY
MOROSENESS ASPERITY
MORPHEME BASE ETYMON
  COGNATE
MORPHINE SNOW
MORPHOLOGICAL FORMAL
MORRIS MILL MERELS
MORSE WALRUS
MORSEL BIT NIG ORT TIT BITE GNAP
  SNAP SCRAN TIDBIT BUCKONE
  MORCEAU NOISETTE PARTICLE
  SKERRICK
  (— OF CHEESE) TRIP
  (— OF CHOCOLATE) BUD
  (— OF SEASONED MEAT) GOBBET
  (CHOICE —) TIDBIT TITBIT
  (PREF.) PSOMO
MORTAL BEING DYING FATAL
  HUMAN VITAL DEADLY FINITE
  LETHAL BRITTLE DEATHLY DEATHFUL
  (FIRST —) YAMA
MORTALITY FLESH MURRAIN
MORTALLY DEADLY FATALLY
MORTAR DAB COMPO DAGGA
  GROUT LARRY ROYAL SORKI SWISH
  CANNON CEMENT HOLMOS MINNIE
  POTGUN BEDDING COEHORN
  DAUBING PERRIER POUNDER
  PUGGING SOORKEE
  (— AND PESTLE) DOLLY DOLLIE
  (— EXTRUDED BETWEEN LATHS) KEY
  (— FOR ROCKETS) TROMBE
  (— FOR SALUTES) CHAMBER
  (— MADE WITH STRAW) BAUGE

  (ANTISUBMARINE —) SQUID
  (INFERIOR —) SLIME
  (SMALL —) HOBIT ROYAL TINKER
  (THIN —) LARRY
MORTARBOARD CATERCAP
  TRENCHER
MORTAR BOAT PALANDER
MORTGAGE DIP LAY BOND LIEN
  ENGAGE MONKEY OBLIGE WADSET
  WEDDEED THIRLAGE
  (KIND OF —) ARM
MORTGAGOR REVERSER
MORTIFICATION ENVY SHAME
  SPITE CHAGRIN GANGRENE
  NECROSIS VEXATION
MORTIFIED ASHAMED
MORTIFY ABASE ABASH SHAME
  SPITE DEMEAN HUMBLE CHAGRIN
  CRUCIFY MACERATE
MORTISE GAIN COCKET
  (SIDE OF —) CHEEK
MORTUARY MORGUE FUNERARY
  SAWLSHOT SEPULCHRAL
MORWONG TARAKIHI
MOSAIC BUHL BOULE INLAY AUCUBA
  BOULLE EMBLEM MUSIVE SCREEN
  FRISOLEE INTARSIA TERRAZZO
  (— PIECE) SMALTO TESSARA
  (POTATO —) CRINKLE
  (WOOD —) TARSIA INTARSIA
MOSCOW (NATIVE OF —)
  MOSCOVITE
MOSEL (— FEEDER) SAAR
MOSES (BROTHER OF —) AARON
MOSEY ROAM ANKLE DAUNTER
MOSLEM MOOR HADJI HAFIZ HANIF
  ISLAM MALAY SALAR PAYNIM SHIITE
  TURBAN ISLAMIC MOORMAN
  SANGGIL SARACEN ISLAMITE
  SANGUILE
  (— SCHOLAR) ALIM ULAMA ULEMA
  (— SECT) SUNNI
MOSQUE JAMI MOSCH DURGAH
  MASJID MESKED
MOSQUITO GNAT AEDES CULICID
  GAMBIAE SKEETER ANOPHELE
  DIPTERAN
  (PREF.) CULIC(I) EMPID(O)
MOSS FOG MNIUM USNEA HYPNUM
  MUSKEG AEROGEN FOXFEET
  GULAMAN HAIRCAP PILIGAN
  TORTULA CROWFOOT MOSSWORT
  SPHAGNUM STAGHORN
  (— HANGING FROM TREE) WEEPER
  (PL.) MUSCI
  (PREF.) BRY(O) MUSC(I)(O) SPHAGNI
  SPHAGNO
MOSSBUNKER MENHADEN
MOSSHORN STEER
MOSSI MOLE MORE
MOSSI-GURUNSI GUR
MOSS PINK PHLOX
MOSSTROOPER RIDER

MOSSY OLD FOGGY HOARY
MUSCOSE
MOST BEST MOSTLY FARTHEST
(PREF.) PLEISTO
MOSTLY MOST FECKLY CHIEFLY
MOSTDEAL
MOT JEST ZINGER
MOTE ATOM ATOMY FESCUE
MOATHILL
(PL.) DUST
MOTEL COURT
MOTH IO GEM NUN PUG DART HAWK
LUNA MOTE PAGE ACREA APPLE
ATLAS EGGAR EGGER FLAME
GAMMA IMAGO MORMO PISKY
PLUME SAMIA SWIFT THORN USHER
WITCH ANTLER BAGONG BUGONG
BURNET COSSID DAGGER DATANA
HERALD HUMMER JUGATE LACKEY
LAPPET MILLER MOODER MUSLIN
PLUSIA PRALID QUAKER RUSTIC
SPHINX THISBE TINEID TISSUE
TUSSUR VENEER ARCTIAN ARCTIID
BAGWORM BUDWORM CRAMBID
CRININE DELTOID DRINKER EMERALD
EMPEROR EUCLEID FESTOON
FIGWORM FOOTMAN FRENATE
HOOKTIP NOCTUID PEGASUS
PSYCHID PYRALIS SLICKER STINGER
SYLINID TINEOLA TORTRIX TUSSOCK
URANIID VAPORER ZYGENID
AEGERIID ARMYWORM BOMBYCID
CATOCALA CECROPIA CINNABAR
COCHYLIS FISHTAIL FORESTER
GEOMETER GOLDTAIL GRISETTE
HAWKMOTH HEPIALID KNOTHORN
MOTHWORM PHYCITID PLUTELLA
SPHINGID SPRAWLER WAINSCOT
SATURNIID PALMERWORM
(— BREEDER) AURELIAN
(VERY SMALL —) MICRO
(PREF.) PHALAENO SETO
MOTH BALL REPELLER
MOTHER INA MOM DAME MAMA
MERE MADRE MAMMA MAMMY
MATER MINNY MODUR MITHER
MULIER MUTTER VENTER GENETRIX
(— OF GOD) THEOTOKOS
(— OF THE GODS) RHEA
(DIVINE —) MATRIGAN
(GREAT —) AGDISTIS
(NOURISHING — OF MAN) CYBELE
(OF THE SAME —) UTERINE
(SEVEN —S) MATRIS
(SIDE OF —) ENATE
(PREF.) MADRE MATR(I)(O) METRO
MOTHERLAND COUNTRY
MOTHERLY MATERNAL MATRONAL
MOTHER-OF-PEARL NACRE PEARL
ABALONE
MOTIF SPRIG DESIGN DEVICE MOTIVE
SCALLOP APPLIQUE MORESQUE
MOTILE ZO ZOO

MOTION WAY FARD FEED GIRD MOVE
SIGN WHID HURRY PAVIE APPORT
MOMENT MOTIVE TRAVEL UNREST
IMPULSE ACTIVITY MOVEMENT
OVERTURE
(— ASEA) SCEND
(— OF AIR) AIRFLOW
(— OF CONTEMPT) FICO
(— OF HORSE) AIR
(— TO) ALLATIVE
(ABRUPT —) CHOP
(BACKWARD —) STERNWAY
(CAM —) COULIER
(CIRCULAR —) GYRE COMPASS
(CONFUSED —) GURGE
(DANCE —) CAPER
(DIZZY —) SWIMBEL
(EXPRESSIVE —) GESTURE
(FORWARD —) HEADWAY
(GLIDING —) SWIM SKITTER
(HASTY —) WAFF
(HEAVING —) ESTUS AESTUS
(HURRIED —) HUSTLE
(ILLEGAL —) BALK BAULK
(IRREGULAR —) SWAG
(JERKING —) BOB LIPE JIGGLE
(LATERAL —) DRIFT
(QUIVERING —) TREMOR
(RAPID —) SCOUR BRATTLE
(REARING —) PESADE
(RECIPROCATING —) SEESAW
(ROCKING —) SHOOGLE
(ROTARY —) SWAY BACKSPIN
SIDESPIN
(SHOWY —) FANFARE
(SIDEWAYS —) CRAB
(SLOW —) CRAWL
(SPINNING —) ENGLISH
(SUNWISE —) DEASIL
(SWEEPING —) WHISK
(SWIMMING —) FLUTTER
(TREMULOUS —) SHAKE
(UNDULATING —) WAVE
(UNSTEADY —) WABBLE WOBBLE
(UPWARD —) HEAVE
(VIGOROUS —) SKELP
(VIOLENT —) JERK RAPT BENSEL
(WAVERING —) SHAKE
(WAVING —) WAFF
(WHIRLING —) SWIRL
(PREF.) CIN(E)(EMATO)(EMO)(ET)(ETO)
KIN(E)(EMATO)(EMO)(ET)(ETO) KINESI
MOTI MOTO PHORO
(SUFF.) CINESIA KINESIA KINESIS
KINETIC
MOTIONLESS DEAD ASLEEP STATIC
IMMOBILE STAGNANT STIRLESS
MOTION PICTURE PIC CINE FILM
FLICK MOVIE BIOPIC CINEMA TALKIE
CHEAPIE SMELLIE FLICKERS
TELEFILM PHOTODRAMA
(PL.) SILENTS
(PREF.) CINE(MATO)(MO)(T)(TO)

MOTIVATE PROPEL ACTUATE
ANIMATE INSPIRE
MOTIVATED COVERT
MOTIVATION DRIVE
MOTIVE GOAD SAKE SPUR CAUSE
MOTIF SCORE ACTUAL DESIRE
OBJECT REASON REGARD SPRING
ATTACCO IMPULSE PATTERN
RESPECT RINCEAU SUBJECT
INSTANCE STIMULUS
(— FOR OBEDIENCE) SANCTION
(ALLEGED —) PRETEXT
(CHIEF —) MAINSPRING
(PRINCIPAL —) MAINSPRING
MOTLEY MIXED MEDLEY RAGTAG
MOTTLED PIEBALD UNKEMPT
(PREF.) PARTI PARTY
MOTMOT HOUTOU SAWBILL
PICARIAN
MOTOR AUTO TOOT TOUR MOVER
ENGINE BOOSTER ROTATOR
TURBINE EFFERENT OUTBOARD
MOTORBIKE MOPED
MOTORBOAT KICKER LAUNCH
AUTOBOAT RUNABOUT HYDROFOIL
MOTORCAR LIMO COUPE MOTOR
SEDAN JALOPY FLIVVER JALOPPY
STEAMER CABRIOLET DOODLEBUG
LIMOUSINE KNOCKABOUT
(MINIATURE —) KART
(MINIATURE — FOR RACING) KART
(RACING —) KART
MOTORCYCLE BIKE CYCLE MOPED
MOTOR STEED TRICAR CHOPPER
AUTOETTE DIRT BIKE MINIBIKE
TRICYCLE PIPSQUEAK
(PART OF —) HORN SEAT TANK TIRE
BRAKE GUARD LEVER LIGHT VALVE
WHEEL CLUTCH FENDER SADDLE
SIGNAL CALIPER EXHAUST MUFFLER
TOOLBOX HANDGRIP THROTTLE
GEARSHIFT TAILLIGHT TENSIONER
CARBURETOR TACHOMETER
SPEEDOMETER
(SMALL —) MINIBIKE
MOTORIST AUTOIST
(SELFISH —) ROADHOG
MOTORMAN CARMAN WATTMAN
TROLLYMAN
MOTORTRUCK DRAY LORRY
CAMION BOBTAIL FLATBED
MOTTLE CHECK TABBY SPONGE
MOTTLED JAZZ PIED CHINE PINTO
TABBY CALICO MARLED MOTLEY
RUMINATE SPLASHED
MOTTO MOT LOGO WORD ADAGE
AXIOM POESY CACHET DEVICE
EUREKA LEGEND REASON IMPRESA
EPIGRAPH
(— IN A RING) POSY
(— OF CALIFORNIA) EUREKA
(— OF MAINE) DIRIGO
MOUE FACE

MOUFLON MUSIMON
MOULDER CRUMBLE
MOULDING (HOLLOW —) SCOTIA
(ZIGZAG —) DANCETTE
MOULIN CHIMNEY
MOUND AHU COP HOW LAW LOW
BALK BANK BOSS BUND BUTT GOAL
HILL HUMP KNOW MOLE POME TELL
TEPE TERP TUFT TUMP AGGER
BERRY DHERI ESKAR ESKER KNOLL
MONDE MOTTE MOUNT PINGO
RAISE STUPA TOMAN BARROW
CAUSEY MEILER RIDEAU ANTHILL
BOUROCK HILLOCK MAMELON
BACKSTOP BARBETTE SNOWBANK
TEOCALLI
(— ABOUT A PLANT) TUMP
(— FOR MEMORIAL) CAIRN
(— IN BUILDING MATERIAL) DIMPLE
(— OF DETRITUS) WASH
(— OF ICE) DOME
(— OF WOOD TO BE CHARRED)
MEILER
(ANCIENT —) TEL TELL
(BURIAL —) LAW LOW TOR TOLA
BERRY GUACA HUACA BARROW
KURGAN TUMULUS
(FORTIFIED —) DUN
(GLACIAL —) KAME
(KING'S —) POME
(MILITARY —) BARBETTE
(PALISADED —) MOTTE
(VOLCANIC —) HORNITO
(PREF.) BUNO
MOUND BIRD MEGAPODE
MOUNT BEN STY BACK HEAD HIDE
RISE SCAN ARISE BIPOD BOARD
CLIMB GETON HEAVE HINGE SCALE
SPEEL SPIRE SWARM ASCEND
ASPIRE BREAST MORIAH CHARGER
COLLINE HAIRPIN HARNESS
BESTRIDE MOUNTAIN MOUNTING
MOUNTURE SURMOUNT
(— A HORSE) FORK LIGHT WORTH
(— BY STEPS) SCAN
(— HIGH) SOAR
(— NEAR TROY) IDA
(— ON PIN) STICK
(— ON WINGS) SOAR
(— UP) ACCRUE
(— UP TO) RUNTO
(STEREOTYPE —) CORE
MOUNTAIN BEN KOP BERG CIMA
DAGH FELL KLIP KNOB MONS MONT
NEBO PICO PIKE JEBEL MOUNT
RANGE BARROW BUNDOC GILEAD
GUNONG HEIGHT PISGAH HELICON
MONTURE NUNATAK MONADNOCK
(— INHABITED BY SPIRIT) GUACA
HUACA
(— MASS) OROGEN
(— PASS) GHAT GHAUT
(— STATE) MONTANA

(— TRACT) DUAR
(AT BASE OF —) PIEDMONT
(BUDDHIST SACRED —) OMEI
(FABLED —) KAF MERU
(GREEK —) OSSA PELION HELICON
OLYMPUS MAENALUS
(HIGH —) ALP
(ROUND —) REEK
(SMALL —) NOB KNOB BUTTE
(SNOW —) JOKUL
(SUBMARINE —) GUYOT SEAMOUNT
(PREF.) MONTI ORE(O) ORI ORO
MOUNTAIN ASH SORB SORBUS
DOGBERRY MOZEMIZE ROUNTREE
WINETREE
MOUNTAIN BEAVER SEWELLEL
MOUNTAIN BINDWEED
SOLDANEL
MOUNTAIN CAP SCALP
MOUNTAIN CLIMBER CRAGSMAN
MOUNTAIN CRANBERRY
FOXBERRY
MOUNTAINEER WASIR WAZIR
HEIDUC HAYDUCK HILLMAN
ORESTES MONTESCO TIERSMAN
(PL.) GUTI GUTIANS
MOUNTAIN GOAT IBEX MAZAME
MOUNTAIN LAUREL IVY HEATH
ERICAD KALMIS LAUREL IVYWOOD
CALFKILL
(THICKET OF —) SLICK
MOUNTAIN LINNET TWITE
MOUNTAIN LION PUMA COUGAR
MOUNTAIN MAHOE EMAJAGUA
MOUNTAIN MISERY TARWEED
MOUNTAINOUS RANGY ALPINE
VICIOUS
MOUNTAIN PARSLEY FLUELLEN
MOUNTAIN RANGE KAF QAF TIER
SIERRA SAWBACK DINDYMUS
MOUNTAIN SICKNESS VETA
MOUNTAINSIDE FELLSIDE
MOUNTAINTOP MAN DOME
MOUNTAIN WOOD ROCKWOOD
MOUNTEBANK ANTIC BALADIN
BALADINE IMPOSTOR OPERATOR
MOUNTED CARDED SADDLE
ASTRIDE EASELED EQUITANT
MOUNT ETNA MONGIBEL
MOUNTING MOUNT SCAPE ASCENT
FLIGHT MONTANT SOAKING
ASPIRANT INCABLOC MOUNTURE
(— OF GEM) CHASE
(STYLE OF —) SETTING
MOURN DOLE KEEN SIGH WAIL
PLAIN BEWAIL GRIEVE LAMENT
SORROW GRIZZLE
MOURNER WAILER WEEPER
(HIRED —) SALLIE SAULIE
(PROFESSIONAL —) MUTE BLACK
KEENER
MOURNFUL SAD BLACK MINOR
SORRY WEEPY RUEFUL TRISTE

DERNFUL FUNEBRE SIGHFUL
WAILFUL DEJECTED DIRGEFUL
ELEGIOUS FUNEREAL MAESTIVE
MESTFULL PLANTFUL YEARNFUL
PLAINTIVE
MOURNING DOLOR SHIVA DISMAL
SORROW WIDOWED
(— CLOTH) RADZIMIR
MOURNING BECOMES ELECTRA
(AUTHOR OF —) ONEILL
(CHARACTER IN —) ADAM EZRA ORIN
BRANT DAVID HAZEL NILES PETER
MANNON LAVINIA CHRISTINE
MOUSE MURINE MYGALE RODENT
SHINER VERMIN ARVICOLE CRICETID
MYOMORPH
(COMPUTER —) TRACKBALL
(LIKE A —) MURIFORM
(MEADOW —) VOLE
(STRIPED —) KUSU
(PREF.) MURI MY(O) SMINTHO
(SUFF.) MYS
MOUSEBIRD COLY
MOUSE-COLORED DUN
MOUSE DEER PLANDOK
MOUSE GRAY SAKKARA SPARROW
MOUSELIKE MURINE
MOUSETRAP TIPE
MOUSING KEEPER
MOUSY DRAB
MOUTH OS GAB GAM GOB JIB MUG
MUN NEB ORF ROW YAP BEAK BEAL
BOCA HEAD MUSS PUSS SHOP TRAP
YAWN BAZOO BOCCA BRACE CHOPS
CODON STOMA TUTEL GEBBIE
KISSER MUZZLE RABBLE RICTUS
SUCKER THROAT CLAPPER FLUMMER
ORIFICE OSTIOLE STOMACH
LORRIKER PAVILLON
(— AND THROAT) COPPER WHISTLE
(— OF CANYON) ABRA
(— OF GLASS FURNACE) BOCCA
(— OF HARBOR) BOCA
(— OF PERITHECIUM) OSTIOLE
(— OF RIVER) BEAL BOCA LADE
ENTRY FIRTH INFLUX OSTIUM
ESTUARY OSTIARY OUTFALL
(— OF SHAFT) BRACE
(— OF TRUMPET) BELL CODON
PAVILLON
(— PARTS OF ARTHROPOD) TROPHI
(AWAY FROM —) ABORAL
(KILN —) KILNEYE KILNHOLE
(SORE — OF SHEEP) ECTHYMA
(TOWARD —) ORAD
(TOWARD THE —) ORAD
(WRY —) MURGEON
(PL.) ORA
(PREF.) BUCCO ORI ORO OSCULI
STOM(A)(AT)(ATO)(O)
(SUFF.) STOMA(TA)(TE)(TOUS)
STOME STOMI(A) STOMOUS
STOMUM STOMY

MOUTHFUL GAG GOB SUP GNAP
SWIG GOLEE GOBBET
MOUTH-ORGAN HARP HARMONICA
MOUTHPART BILL
MOUTHPIECE BAR BEAK BOCAL
MOUTH FIPPLE SYRINX PROPHET
(— OF BAGPIPE) MUSE
(— OF OTHERS) FUGUEMAN
(— OF PIPE) STEM
MOUTHWASH GARGLE
COLLUTORIUM
MOUTH-WATERING SALIVANT
MOVABLE FREE LOOSE MOBILE
PORTABLE REMUABLE
(PL.) MEUBLES
MOVE GO ACT AWE FIG GEE GET
WAG BOOM BORE BUCK BUMP CALL
DRAW FIRK FLIT GOAD HEAT KNEE
MAKE PIRL ROLL SILE SPUR STEP
STIR SWAY WORK ANKLE BLITZ
BUDGE CARRY CAUSE CROWD
DRAFT HEAVE IMPEL LIGHT MARCH
MUDGE QUECH REMUE ROUSE
SHAKE SHIFT TOUCH GAMBIT
HANDLE HUSTLE INCITE INDUCE
KINDLE MOTION PROMPT QUITCH
REMBLE SASHAY STRAKE ACTUATE
AGITATE ANIMATE DISTURB
DRAUGHT FLUTTER INSPIRE
MIGRATE PROVOKE AMBULATE
BULLDOZE CATAPULT DEMARCHE
DISLODGE DISPLACE MOTIVATE
(— ABOUT) ROLL WEND DISPACE
SHUFFLE CONVERSE LOCOMOTE
(— ACROSS) THWART
(— ACROSS SCREEN) CRAWL SCROLL
(— ACTIVELY) YANK
(— AIMLESSLY) GAD POKE BOGUE
(— ALONG) SHOG
(— APART) ABDUCT SPREAD
(— A RESOLUTION) FIRST
(— ASIDE) SKEW
(— AS IN STUPOR) DAVER
(— ASUNDER) SINGLE
(— AT TOP SPEED) LICK
(— AWAY) CUT MOG DECAMP
RECEDE
(— AWKWARDLY) HODGE HIRSEL
LARRUP SHAMBLE SLUMMOCK
(— BACK) FADE ARSLE RECUR
RECEDE RETIRE RETREAT
(— BACKWARD AND FORWARD) GIG
SWAY DARTLE DIDDLE SHUFFLE
SHUTTLE
(— BOOM OR SAIL) JIB
(— BRISKLY) FAN HALE STIR FRICK
FRIKE FRISK KNOCK SQUIRT TRANCE
TRAVEL WHIPPET
(— BY FITS AND STARTS) JIFFLE
(— BY JERKS) HITCH JIGGET JIGGLE
JINKLE
(— BY SMALL SHOCKS) JOG
(— BY WHEELS) ROLL TRUNDLE

(— CHESS PIECE) DEVELOP
(— CLUMSILY) HOIT JOLL PAUT
BARGE KEVEL HIRSEL LUMBER
TOLTER GALUMPH STUMBLE
(— COMPUTER VIDEO DISPLAY)
SCROLL
(— DIAGONALLY) CATER
(— DOWN) SILE STOOP DECLINE
DESCEND
(— FORCIBLY) SHOVE
(— FORWARD) BREAK ADVANCE
PROGREDE
(— FROM SIDE TO SIDE) WAG
(— FURTIVELY) LEER GLIDE SLINK
SLIVE SNEAK STEAL
(— GRADUALLY) EDGE
(— GRATINGLY) SCRAPE
(— HAPHAZARDLY) BUCKET
(— HASTILY) DOUN SKIRR
(— HAUGHTILY) SWOOP
(— HEAVILY) LUG LUMP FLUMP
LUMBER
(— IN AGITATION) SEETHE
(— IN AWKWARD MANNER) GANGLE
(— IN CIRCLES) MILL PURL
(— IN MARBLES) FULK
(— IN ON) NEAR
(— IN RIPPLES) CURL
(— IN SHAMBLE) SHUFFLE
(— IN SHUFFLING MANNER) MOSEY
(— IN SMALL DEGREES) INCH
(— INWARDLY) ENMOVE
(— IN WATER) SQUELCH
(— IN WAVES) LAP CRINKLE
(— JERKILY) JAG BUCK FLIT KICK
FLIRT BUCKET TWITCH
(— LANGUIDLY) MAUNDER
(— LAZILY) HULK
(— LEISURELY) AMBLE
(— LIGHTLY) BRUSH FLUFF
(— LOOSELY) SLOP
(— NERVOUSLY) DITHER
(— NIMBLY) KILT LINK WHIP DANCE
(— OFF) FIRK RYNT MOSEY MORRIS
(— ON) MOG VAMP AVAUNT
SUCCEED WHIGFARE
(OUT) BLOW
(— OUT OF SIGHT) SINK
(— QUICKLY) BOB FIG CLIP DUCK FIRK
FLAX FLIT GIRD JINK KITE SCUR
WHAP WHEW WHID WHOP YANK
FLASH GLENT SKEET SKIRR SKITE
SPANK SQUIB STAVE STOUR THROW
NIDDLE STRIKE WALLOP SKIMMER
(— QUIETLY) SLIP
(— RAPIDLY) BANG BOLT BUZZ HEEL
HURL SKIR THUD CHASE GLINT
SCOUR CAREER GIGGIT HURTLE
WHIRRY AGITATE CLATTER HIGHTAIL
(— RESTLESSLY) FIG GAD FIKE ITCH
CHURN SQUIB JIFFLE KELTER
(— SHAKILY) HOTTER
(— SIDEWAYS) SKID SLEW SLUE

(— SIDEWISE) CRAB EDGE SIDLE SLENT
(— SINUOUSLY) WRIGGLE
(— SLOWLY) LAG MOG INCH PANT PAUT SLUG BOGUE CRAWL CREEP DRAWL FUDGE SHLEP SLOOM SNAIL HAGGLE LINGER SCHLEP SCHLEPP TRINTLE
(— SMOOTHLY) SLIP DRIFT FLOAT GLIDE SLEEK GLISSADE
(— SPIRALLY) GYRATE
(— STEADILY) FORGE
(— STEALTHILY) GLIDE SLINK SMOOT SNAKE
(— STIFFLY) CRAMBLE CRAMMEL
(— SUDDENLY) BOLT LASH YERK GLENT START FLOUNCE STARTLE
(— SWIFTLY) CUT FLY BOOM HARE LEAP RAKE SCUD SPIN BREEZE COURSE WUTHER SWIFTEN
(— THROUGH AIR) FLY
(— TO AND FRO) FAN FLOP DODGE SHAKE WIGWAG AGITATE
(— TO ANOTHER PLACE) ADJOURN
(— TO LEEWARD) DRIVE
(— TREMULOUSLY) WAPPER
(— TRIPPINGLY) WALTZ WAPPER
(— UNEASILY) FIDGET
(— UNSTEADILY) BICKER BUMBLE FALTER HOBBLE WABBLE WAMBLE WELTER WOBBLE BLUNDER STAGGER STUMBLE
(— UP AND DOWN) BOB HOWD SEESAW TEETER
(— UPWARD) ARISE ASCEND GRADUATE
(— VESSEL) KEDGE
(— VIGOROUSLY) FLOG STRAY
(— VIOLENTLY) DASH FLOG HURL LASH LEAP SWASH AGITATE COMMOVE
(— WAVERINGLY) FLEET
(— WEAKLY) FLAG
(— WITH BEATING MOTION) FLAP
(— WITH EFFORT) ACHE WADE
(— WITH LEAPS) SKIP SPRING
(— WITH NOISY ACTIVITY) BUSTLE
(— WITH POMP) SWEEP
(— WITH SHORT TURNS) ZIGZAG
(CHESS —) KEY COOK NECK PLOY GAMBIT KEYMOVE
(STRATEGIC —) TACK
(SUCCESSFUL —) SCORE
(SUDDEN —) GAMBADE
MOVED MOSSO ANIMATE FRANTIC INSTINCT
(— BY LOVE) AMOROUS
(EASILY —) FLESHLY SKINLESS
MOVEMENT EDDY MOTO PLAY STIR CARRY CAUSE FLICK FLISK FLOAT FRONT GESTE MUDGE TREND UKIYO ACTION CURSUS ENTREE MOMENT MOTION PIAFFE SPRAWL STROKE

CURRENT FURIANT GAMBADO
GESTURE KINESIS PIAFFER UKIYOYE
BUSINESS CHARTISM FEMINISM
FUTURISM HASKALAH STIRRING
PERIPATETICS
(— BY ORGANISMS) TAXIS
(— FOR POLITICAL UNION) ENOSIS
(— FROM POINT TO POINT) PASSAGE
(— IN BULLFIGHT) SUERTE
(— OF AIR) SPIRIT
(— OF CHORUS) STROPHE
(— OF CLOUDS) CARRY
(— OF COMPUTER BITS) SHIFT
(— OF EYES) NYSTAGMUS
(— OF HAND) PASS
(— OF HORSE) LEVADE PIAFFE
(— OF LEG) STEP
(— OF LOOM) MOUSING
(— OF NEEDLE) STITCH
(— OF PLANTS) NUTATION
(— OF PROTOPLASM) CYCLOSIS
(— OF QUADRILLE) TRENISE
(— OF ROPE) SURGE
(— OF SHIP) STERNWAY
(— OF SHUTTLE) SHOOT
(— OF TIDE) LAKIE
(— OF TROOPS) LIFT
(— OF WATER) BOBBLE
(— TO AND FRO) SHUTTLE
(— TOWARD GOAL) STRIDE
(AGITATED —) WORKING
(ART —) CUBISM
(AVANT-GARDE —) UNDERGROUND
(BACKWARD —) BACKUP BACKLASH BACKWASH
(BALLET —) PLIE BATTU FRAPPE FOUETTE FLICFLAC
(BOBBING —) BOBBLE
(BODILY —) ACTION
(BOWEL —) LAXATION
(BOWING —) LEG
(BOXING —) SPAR
(BRISK —) SNAP
(BROWNIAN —) PEDESIS
(CAVALRY —) CARACOLE
(CIRCULAR —) CYCLING
(CLEVER —) PAW
(CONFUSED —) MILLING
(CONVULSIVE —) SPASM
(DANCE —) FRIS BRISE CLOSE GIGUE GLIDE LASSU SPIRAL BATTERIE
(DARTING —) FLIRT
(DECISIVE —) UPCOME
(DOWNWARD —) DECLINE
(DROLL —) GAMBADE GAMBADO
(ENLIGHTENMENT —) HASKALAH
(EXPANSION —) BOOM
(EYE —) REM SACCADE
(FANTASTIC —) GAMBADO
(FENCING —) VOLT
(FLAPPING —) FLAFF
(FLUCTUATING —) PLAY

(FORWARD —) SWEEP ADVANCE PROGRESS INCESSION PROCESSION
(FROLICKING —) FRISK GAMBOL
(GRADUAL —) CREEPISM
(GRAZING —) SKIFF
(GREEK UNDERGROUND —) EAM
(GYMNASTIC —) KIP SWING DISMOUNT
(HUMOROUS —) BURLA
(IMPATIENT —) FLOUNCE
(INCIPIENT —) MINT
(INDEPENDENCE —) SWADESHI
(INVOLUNTARY —) REFLEX
(JAPANESE ART —) YAMATO YAMATOE
(JERKING —S) BALLISM
(JERKY —) SNATCH
(JERKY EYE —) SACCADE
(LATERAL —) LEEWAY
(MASS —) STAMPEDE
(MASSAGE —) SCIAGE
(MILITARY —) BOUND MANEUVRE
(MUSICAL —) AIR DUET BURLA DUMKA LARGO ADAGIO ENTREE FINALE PRESTO ANDANTE PRELUDE SCHERZO POSTLUDE SARABAND SYMPHONY ALLEMANDE INTERMEZZO
(NOISELESS —) WHID
(OBLIQUE —) GLANCE
(OSCILLATING —) HUNT
(PAINTING —) FAUVISM TACHISM TACHISME VORTICISM
(POETRY —) IMAGISM
(POLITICAL —) LEFTISM GAULLISM
(QUADRILLE —) POULE
(QUICK —) PAW DART WHID WHIP YERK GLENT SHAKE GLANCE
(RATIONALISTIC —) DEISM
(REELING —) STAGGER
(RELIGIOUS —) JOCISM BABIISM PIETISM STUNDISM
(RETROGRADE —) SLIP CREEP
(RETURN —) BACKHAUL
(RHYTHMIC —) DANCE
(ROCKING —) HOWD
(ROWING —) HOICK
(SKATING —) MOHAWK CHOCTAW
(SKILLED —) SUERTE
(SNATCHING —) CLUTCH
(SPASMODIC —) JUMP HICCUP SPRUNT HICCOUGH
(SPRINGY —) LILT
(STAGGERING —) WAMBLE
(STEALTHY —) SLINK
(SUDDEN —) HITCH SPANG START FLICKER
(SWAYING —) SWAG
(SWEEPING —) SWINGE
(SWIFT —) SWOOSH
(TERRORIST —) NIHILISM
(THEOLOGICAL —) ARIANISM
(TUMULTUOUS —) HORROR EMOTION

(TURNING —) CARACOLE
(UNEXPECTED —) LUNGE
(UNSTEADY —) WABBLE WOBBLE
(UP AND DOWN —) SEESAW
(UPWARD —) BULGE SCEND
(UPWARD — OF VESSEL) SCEND
(WALKING —) AMBLE
(WATCH —) EBAUCHE BAGUETTE
(WAVING —) WAFT
(ZIGZAG —) TACK MEANDER
(PREF.) KINESI KINETO KIN(O)
(SUFF.) CINESIA KINESIA KINESIS KINETIC

MOVEMENTS
(SUFF.)
(PERFORMANCE OF —) PRACTIC PRAXIA PRAXIS

MOVER MOTIVE CLIPPER
(KIND OF —) PEOPLE

MOVIE (ALSO SEE MOTION PICTURE) PIC FILM FLICK BIOPIC FLICKS SLEEPER MELODRAMA
(— WITH BLOODSHED) SHOOTEMUP
(ANIMATED —) TOON CARTOON
(BIOGRAPHICAL —) BIOPIC
(CRIME —) FILMNOIR
(SUCCESSFUL —) MEGAHIT
(PL.) PICTURES

MOVIES (DEVOTEE OF —) CINEPHILE

MOVING WAY HIGH ASTIR GOING QUICK AFLOAT MOVENT ANIMATE CURRENT AMBULANT FLITTING PATHETIC POIGNANT TOUCHING AFFECTING
(— ABOUT) AROUND AMBULANT
(— AIMLESSLY) ERRANT
(— BACKWARDS) CRAB
(— DOWN LINE) ACTIVE
(— FORWARD) ADVANCE
(— HAPHAZARDLY) AFLOAT
(— IN MANY DIRECTIONS) DIFFUSE
(— JERKILY) ATWITCH
(— RAPIDLY) STICKLE SKELPING
(— SLOWLY) SOFT GLACIAL TEDIOUS
(— TO AND FRO) AGITATED
(NOT —) STICKY STABILE

MOVINGLY PATETICO

MOW CUT BARB GOAF SKIM TASS CRADLE SCYTHE SICKLE DESECATE
(— BEANS) THROAT
(— FOR STORING GRAIN) TOSS
(— OF CORN) CANSH
(HAY —) TASS

MOWER MEADER
(FOREMOST —) LORD

MOWING MATH MOWTH SHEAR
(SECOND —) AFTERMATH

MOXIE GALL SPIRIT

MOZA (FATHER OF —) CALEB ZIMRI

MOZAMBIQUE (CAPE OF —) DELGADO
(CAPITAL OF —) MAPUTO
(LAKE OF —) CHUALI NHAVARRE

(MONEY OF —) METICAL
(RIVER OF —) SAVE MSALU RUVUMA
LIMPOPO LUGENDA ZAMBEZI
(TOWN OF —) MAUA TETE BEIRA
MAPAI ZUMBO CHEMBA MANICA
NAMAPA PAFURI CHIMOIO NAMPULA
MOZZETTA CAMAIL
MR HERR SIGNOR SIGNIOR SIGNORE
MR MIDSHIPMAN EASY
(AUTHOR OF —) MARRYAT
(CHARACTER IN —) EASY JACK
AGNES MESTY WILSON REBIERA
GASCOIGNE MIDDLETON
MRS MME FRAU MISS PANI HANOUM
SENORA SENHORA SIGNORA
GOODWIFE
MRS DALLOWAY (AUTHOR OF —)
WOOLF
(CHARACTER IN —) PETER SALLY
SETON SMITH WALSH HOLMES
KALMAN WILLIAM BRADSHAW
CLARISSA DALLOWAY SEPTIMUS
MRS WARREN'S PROFESSION
(AUTHOR OF —) SHAW
(CHARACTER IN —) FRANK PRAED
VIVIE CROFTS GEORGE SAMUEL
WARREN GARDNER
MUCH FAR FELE MICH REAL WELL
GREAT HEAPS MOLTO MOULT SIZES
MICKLE MUCHLY ABUNDANT
BEAUCOUP MUCHWHAT
(— CALLED FOR) LEEFTAIL
(PRETTY —) GAILY GAYLY
(SO —) ALL SUCH TANTO INSOMUCH
(TOO —) TROP TROPPO
(VERY —) ALL BADLY GREAT HEAPS
LOADS SWITHE SWYTHE APLENTY
GEYLIES GREATLY
(PREF.) ERI MULT(I) POLY SYCHNO
(HOW —) POSO QUANTI
MUCH ADO ABOUT NOTHING
(AUTHOR OF —) SHAKESPEARE
(CHARACTER IN —) HERO JOHN
PEDRO URSULA VERGES ANTONIO
CLAUDIO CONRADE FRANCIS
LEONATO BEATRICE BENEDICK
BORACHIO DOGBERRY MARGARET
BALTHASAR
MUCILAGE GUM MUCUS MUCAGO
MUCILAGINOUS MALACOID
MUCK CACK SOIL
MUCOID BLENNOID
MUCUS SNOT MUCOR BUBBLE
MUCAGO PHLEGM SNIVEL PITUITE
(PREF.) BLENN(I)(O) MUC(I)(O)(OSO)
MYX(O)
(SUFF.) MYXA
MUD DAB FEN CLAY DIRT DUBS FANC
GLAR LAIR MIRE MOIL SAUR SIND
SLAB SLEW SLOB SLOP SLUB SLUD
SLUE SLUR SUMP CLART FANGO
GLAUR GUMBO SLAKE SLIME SLOSH
SLUSH SPOSH SQUAD WAISE PELOID

SLOUGH SLUDGE CLABBER
GUTTERS MURGEON SLOBBER
SLODDER SLUDDER SLUTHER
SULLAGE
(LACUSTRINE —) GYTTJA
(LIQUID —) SLUSH
(OF DRIED —) CUTCHA
(THIN —) SLUR
(PREF.) LIMI LIMO PEL(O) TELMAT(O)
MUDAR AK AKUND ASHUR MADOR
YERCUM AKMUDDAR
MUDCAP ADOBE
MUD CAT FLATHEAD
MUDCAT STATE MISSISSIPPI
MUDDLE MIX BALL DOZE HASH
MASH MESS MULL MUZZ SOSS
ADDLE SNAFU BEMUSE BURBLE
FANKLE FOITER FUDDLE HUDDLE
JUMBLE MAFFLE MIZZLE MOFFLE
MUCKER POTHER PUDDLE TANGLE
BECLOUD BEDEVIL BLUNDER
CONFUSE EMBROIL FLUSTER
POOTHER STUPEFY BEFUDDLE
BEWILDER CONFOUND DISORDER
FLIUNDER
MUDDLED ADDLE BEERY FOGGY
FUZZY MUSED MUZZY DRUMLY
GROGGY BESOTTED CONFUSED
MUDDY DEEP FOUL GLET OOZY ROIL
SICK DIRTY DROVY DUBBY GUMLY
ROILY SLAKY CLAGGY CLARTY
CLASHY DREGGY DROUMY DRUMLY
GROUTY LIMOUS PUDDLY SALLOW
SLABBY SLOBBY SLOPPY SLUBBY
SLUDGY TURBID CLATCHY GUTTERY
MUDDIFY MUDDISH SLOUGHY
CLABBERY LUTULENT SLOBBERY
(— BY STIRRING) STUDDLE
MUDFISH BOWFIN KOMTOK
MUDFLAT PLAYA
MUDFLOW LAHAR MUDSPATE
MUDGUARD WING CUTTOO
SPLASHER
MUDHOLE PULK SLOUGH LOBLOLLY
MUD MINNOW DOGFISH MUDFISH
MUD PUPPY DOGFISH
MUERMO ULMO
MUEZZIN CRIER
MUFF ERR BLOW BOBBLE MUFFLE
SNUFFKIN
MUFFIN COB GEM SINK COBBE
HAZEL SINKER MANCHET PIKELET
POPOVER
MUFFLE MOB MOP PAD DAMP DULL
MUTE NOSE WRAP BUMBLE DEADEN
MUZZLE SHROUD STIFLE ENVELOP
(— A BELL) CLAM
(— THE HEAD) MOBLE
MUFFLED DEAD DEAF DULL CLOSE
THICK HOLLOW INWARD MOBBED
WRAPPED
MUFFLER SCARF MUFFLE SILENCER
MUFTI JURIST CIVVIES

MUG TOT BOCK CANN FACE PUNK
THUG STEIN KISSER NOGGIN
PEWTER SCONCE SEIDEL CANETTE
GODDARD TANKARD BLACKPOT
PANNIKIN SCHOPPEN
(ALE —) TOBY
(LIQUOR —) CAN GUN
(TWO-HANDLED —) SCONCE
MUGGER GOA HAM
MUGGING YOKING
MUGGINS SNIFF
MUGGY ROZY MUNGY PUGGY
STICKY MUGGISH FOTHERY
MUGWORT BULWAND MUGWEED
MUISCA CHIBCHA
MUISHOND ZORIL ZORILLE
MULATTO PARDO GRIFFE GRIQUA
GRIFFIN TERCERON
MULBERRY AL AAL ACH AUTE KOZO
MORE WAUKE ALROOT MURREY
MORELLO SOURBUSH SYCAMINE
(PREF.) MOR(I)
MULBERRY FIG SYCAMORE
MULCT ROB FINE CHECK AMERCE
SCONCE FORFEIT PENALTY
MULE BUCKER HYBRID ACEMILA
IRONMAN JARHEAD JUGHEAD
RATTAIL SUMPTER CENCERRO
HARDTAIL QUADROON QUATERON
(DROVE OF —S) ATAJO MULADA
(MOHAMMED'S —) ALBORAK
MULE ARMADILLO MULITA
MULE DRIVER SKINNER
MULE SHOE PLANCHE
MULETEER ASSMAN ARRIERO
MULE TRAIN
(— DRIVER) WAGONER
MULISH BALKY STUPID STUBBORN
OBSTINATE
MULL CHAW BOSOM STUDY FETTLE
MULMUL PONDER STEATIN
COGITATE MEDITATE
MULLAH ULAMA ULEMA
MULLEIN TORCH AGLEAF ICELEAF
DOVEWEED FELTWORT FOXGLOVE
HAGTAPER LUNGWORT VERBASCO
MULLER DAMPENER
MULLET BOBO LISA LIZA BOURI
GARAU KANAE MOLET HARDER
MULLOID GOATFISH MUGILOID
SPRINGER
(UNPIERCED —) STAR
MULLIGRUBS COLIC
MULLION MONIAL
MULLOWAY JEWFISH KINGFISH
SCIAENID
MULTICOLORED PIED CALICO
MULTIFARIOUS MANIFOLD
MULTIFARIOUSNESS VARIETY
MULTIFORM DIVERSE
MULTILINGUAL POLYGLOT
MULTIPLE DECUPLE PARALLEL
SEPTUPLE MULTIPLEX

MULTIPLICAND FACIEND
MULTIPLICATION INCREASE
DUPLATION
MULTIPLICITY MULTEITY
MULTIPLIER FACIENT COFACTOR
MULTIPLY VIE BREED LAYER DOUBLE
INVOLVE ENGENDER INCREASE
MANIFOLD PROPAGATE PROLIFERATE
(— BY ITSELF) SQUARE
MULTIPLYING
(PREF.) POLY
MULTITUDE SEA ARMY CRAM HEAP
HIVE HOST ROUT RUCK CLOUD
CROWD FLOTE MEINY POWER SHOAL
SWARM HIRSEL HOTTER LEGION
MAMPUS MEINIE NATION THRONG
SMOTHER PLURALITY
(PL.) FLOCKS
MULTITUDINOUS LEGION MYRIAD
MANIFOLD NUMEROUS
MULTIVALENT POLYAD
MULTURE THIRL THIRLAGE
MUM CLUM DARK MUMMER
MUMBLE CHEW MOUP MUMP
BROCK CHELE MOUTH CHAVEL
FAFFLE FUMBLE HOTTER HUMMER
MAFFLE MOFFLE PALTER DRUMBLE
FLUMMER GRUMBLE
(— PEEVISHLY) WITTER
MUMBLER MAFFLER
MUMBLETY-PEG KNIFE
MUMMER ACTOR GUISER GUISARD
MUMMERY MORRIS HODENING
PUPPETRY
MUMMICHOG MUDFISH
MUMMY CONGO MUMMIA SKELET
(PREF.) MOMIO
MUMMY BROWN BAY SNUFF
TAMARACK
MUMMY CASE SLEDGE
MUMPS BRANKS PAROTITIS
MUNCH CHEW NOSH CHUMP
MANGE MUNGE
MUND GRITH
MUNDA KOLARIAN
MUNDANE WORLD EARTHLY
FLESHLY SECULAR TERRENE
SUBSOLAR
MUNG BEAN MUG GRAM MONGOE
BALATONG
MUNIA MAYA PADDA
MUNICIPAL TOWN CIVIL
MUNICIPALITY CITY TOWN
CABILDO
MUNIFICENCE BOUNTY ROYALTY
LARGESSE
MUNIFICENT ROYAL LIBERAL
MUNIFIC PROFUSE MAGNIFIC
PRINCELY OPENHANDED
MUNITION
(PL.) ARMAMENT ORDNANCE
MUNJ MOONJA MANJEET
(CULMS OF —) SIRKI SIRKY

MUNTIACUS CERVULUS
MUNTJAC KAKAR RATWA KIDANG
MURAL TOPIA FRESCO
MURCIA (RIVER OF —) SEGURA
(TOWN OF —) MULA LORCA TOTANA
MURDER HIT OFF BANE KILL SLAY
BLOOD BURKE DEATH SCRAG
FELONY RUBOUT KILLING MURDRUM
MURTHER THUGGEE HOMICIDE
MASSACRE THUGGERY THUGGISM
PATRICIDE
(FEATURING —) SNUFF
(PREMEDITATED —) HIT
MURDERER BANE CAIN KILLER
ASSASSIN
MURDER IN THE CATHEDRAL
(COMPOSER OF —) PIZZETTI
MURDEROUS FELL GORY CRUEL
FELON BLOODY CARNAL SAVAGE
DEATHFUL SANGUINARY
MURKINESS HAZE GLOOM
MURKY DARK BLACK DIRTY MIRKY
MUDDY CLOUDY PUDDLY
MURMUR COO HUM BRUM BURR
CLUM CURR HUZZ MUSE BRAWL
BROOL GRANK INKLE MOURN
RUMOR SOUCH SOUGH BABBLE
BURBLE GRUDGE GRUTCH HUMMER
MUTTER PIPPLE REPINE RUMBLE
CROODLE MURGEON WHIMPER
WHISPER WHITTER COMPLAIN
(— AGREEABLY) CHIRM
(— AMOROUSLY) COO
(— OF PAIN) MOAN
(— OF STREAM) PURL
(CONFUSED —) BABBLE
(DEEP —) BROOL
MURMURING BUZZ BRABBLE
MURGEON RUMOROUS
MURRAH SURTI
MURRAIN PLAGUE
MURRAL DALAG
MURRE TINK ARRIE LUNGIE STRANY
TINKER ROCKBIRD
MURREY SANGUINE
MUSA SABA
MUSANG POWCAT POLECAT
MUSCA FLY
MUSCADINE BULLACE
SCUPPERNONG
MUSCAT (SEE OMAN)
MUSCLE EYE PEC BOWR LIRE THEW
FLESH MOUSE PSOAS SINEW
BENDER BICEPS CORACO FLEXOR
LACERT PENNON RECTUS SOLEUS
TENSOR AGONIST AMBIENS
CANINUS DELTOID DILATOR
ERECTOR EVERTOR FLECTOR
GLUTEUS ILIACUS LEVATOR
MUSCULE NASALIS OBLIQUE
ROTATOR SCALENE SCALLOP
TRICEPS VAGINAL ABDUCTOR
ADDUCTOR ADJUSTER ANCONEUS

ARRECTOR ATOLLENT BIVENTER
DIDUCTOR EXTENSOR GEMELLUS
GRACILIS INVERTOR MASSETER
MENTALIS OBLIQUUS OMOHYOID
OPPONENS PALMARIS PATHETIC
PECTORAL PERONEUS PROCERUS
PRONATOR RETENTOR SCALENUS
SERRATUS SPINALIS SPLENIUS
TEMPORAL TIBIALIS HAMSTRING
OBTURATOR SARTORIUS
(— MASSAGE) ROLF ROLFING
(HAVING LUMPY —S) LOADED
(THIGH —) HAMSTRING
(PL.) BRAWN THEWS
(PREF.) INO MUSCUL(O) NERVI NERVO
(SUFF.) EUS MYA MYARIA
MUSCLE-BOUND (NOT —) SPRY
MUSCLE SUGAR INOSITE INOSITOL
MUSCOVITE MICA
MUSCOVY DUCK PATO SCOVY
MUSCULAR ROPY HEFTY HUSKY
THEWY BRAWNY ROBUST SINEWY
STRONG TOROSE NERVOUS
ATHLETIC
MUSCULATURE DETRUSOR
(SUFF.) (HAVING —) MYA MYARIA
MUSE CLIO DUMP MESE MULL NETE
REVE AMUSE AOIDE DREAM ERATO
MNEME STUDY THINK HYPATE
MELETE PONDER THALIA URANIA
EUTERPE REFLECT CALLIOPE
COGITATE CONSIDER MEDITATE
POLYMNIA RUMINATE MELPOMENE
POLYHYMNIA TERPSICHORE
(— OF ASTRONOMY) URANIA
(— OF COMEDY) THALIA
(— OF EPIC POETRY AND
ELOQUENCE) CALLIOPE
(— OF HISTORY) CLIO
(— OF LOVE POETRY) ERATO
(— OF MIMIC ART) POLYHYMNIA
(— OF POETRY AND DANCE)
TERPSICHORE
(— OF THE FLUTE) EUTERPE
(— OF TRAGEDY) MELPOMENE
(PL.) PIERIDES
MUSETTE OBOE
MUSEUM MOMA MUSEE PRADO
LOUVRE
(— IN NEW YORK CITY) MET MOMA
FRICK CLOISTERS GUGGENHEIM
(— PIECE) RELIC
(PREF.) MUSEO
MUSH SAMP KASHA SLUSH MUSHER
SEPAWN SOFKEE POLENTA
SAGAMITE SCRAPPLE
(LIKE —) SOGGY
MUSHI (FATHER OF —) MERARI
MUSHROOM FAT CEPE FLAT GROW
DEATH ENOKI MITRA MOREL AGARIC
BEAVER BUTTON FUNGUS AMANITA
BLEWITS BOLETUS BROILER LEPIOTA
SHITAKE MUSHRUMP SHIITAKE

WHITECAP ENOKIDAKE
CHAMPIGNON SHAGGYMANE
CHANTERELLE TEONANACATL
(— HUNTER) MYCOPHILE
(PART OF) CAP GILL RING STEM
STALK STIPE VOLVA PILEUS
ANNULUS MYCELIUM
(PREF.) MYC(O) MYCET(O)
MUSHY SOFT SOPPY
MUSIC RAG DRAG FUNK GLEE JAZZ
NOME NOSH BEBOP CANOR CHIME
DREAM GIMEL GYMEL MURKY NOISE
SWING DREHER FUSION MUSICA
DESCANT FORLANA LANCERS
LANDLER MUSICAL MUSICRY
FALSETTO FANDANGO GUARACHA
(— FOR ENTRANCE) ENTREE
(— OF LOUISIANA) ZYDECO
(— OF SOUTHERN LOUISIANA)
ZODICO ZYDECO
(— OF WEST INDIES) REGGAE
(— SUNG IN UNISON) PLAINSONG
(BACKGROUND —) MUZAK
(BAGPIPE —) PIBROCH
(CALYPSO —) GOOMBAY
(CHURCH —) ANTIPHON ANTIPHONY
(CONCERTED —) ENSEMBLE
(COUNTRY —) BLUEGRASS
(DANCE —) DISCO
(EVENING —) DREAM SERENA
(IDENTIFYING —) SIG
(INDIAN —) RAGA
(JAMAICAN —) SKA REGGAE
(JAPANESE COURT —) GAGAKU
(JAZZ —) SKIFFLE
(JAZZ OR FOLK —) SKIFFLE
(KIND OF —) POP RAP SOUL TEXMEX
COUNTRY JAZZROCK SOFTROCK
TECHNOPOP
(LATIN AMERICAN —) SALSA
(LIVELY —) GALOP FURLANA
(MOD —) RAP
(MORNING —) AUBADE
(NEGRO —) SOUL
(NIGHT —) TAPS
(OLD — MAGAZINE) ETUDE
(PASSAGE OF —) MORCEAU
(PATTERN OF HINDU —) RAGA TALA
(PIECE OF —) ARIA HYMN MASS TRIO
ALBUM ETUDE FUGUE MOTET
OPERA RONDO SONATA ARIETTA
CANTATA CHORALE PRELUDE
QUARTET CONCERTO ENSEMBLE
MADRIGAL NOCTURNE OPERETTA
ORATORIO RHAPSODY SONATINA
SYMPHONY SIMPHONIA
(PIPED —) MUZAK
(PLAY — WELL) COOK
(RECORDED BACKGROUND —)
MUZAK
(RESOUNDING —) HIGGAION
(ROCK —) PUNK BIGBEAT
BUBBLEGUM

(ROUGH —) CHARIVARI
(SAD —) MESTO
(SENTIMENTAL —) SCHMALZ
SCHMALTZ
(STACCATO —) SECCO
(SYNCOPATED —) RAGTIME
(TYPE OF —) SERIAL SERIALISM
MINIMALISM
(UNSOPHISTICATED —) FUNK
(VOCAL STYLE OF —) DOWOP
DOOWOP
(WEST INDIAN —) REGGAE
(WRITE —) NOTATE COMPOSE
(ZULU —) KWELA
MUSICAL LYRIC SWEET LIQUID
LYRICAL TUNABLE TUNEFUL
CANOROUS HARMONIC NUMEROUS
(— CLOSING) CODA
(— DIRECTION) BIS PIU ADUE ARCO
BRIO FINE MENO MUTA POCO ANIME
ASSAI DOLCE GRAVE GUSTO LARGO
LENTO MEZZO MOLTO MOSSO
OSSIA PRIMO SECCO SEGNO SEGUE
SOPRA TACET TEMPO TUTTI ADAGIO
ARIOSO DOPPIO FREDDO MARCIA
PRESTO RUBATO SEMPRE SIMILE
SUBITO TENUTO TROPPO VELOCE
VIVACE AGITATO ALLEGRO AMABILE
ANIMATO ATTACCA FURIOSO
GIOCOSO MARCATO MORENDO
PIETOSO SORDINO TREMOLO
DOLOROSO MAESTOSO MODERATO
SALTANDO SEMPLICE SPICCATO
CRESCENDO GLISSANDO OBBLIGATO
SOSTENUTO SPIRITOSO
(SUFF.) (— DEVICE) INA INE
(— INSTRUMENT) INA
MUSICAL INSTRUMENT AX AXE
GLY GUE KIN OUD OIN TAR UKE ZEL
ALTO ASOR BELL CRUT DRUM GLEE
GLEW GORA HARP HORN KORA
KOTO LIRA LUTE LYRE OBOE ROTE
SANG SAWM TAAR TUBA VINA VIOL
ANVIL AULOS BANJO BLOCK BUGLE
CELLO CHENG CRWTH CUICA DOMRA
FLUTE GORAH GOURA GUDOK
GUIRO GUSLA GUSLE KAZOO MBIRA
NABLA ORGAN RAMKI REBAB REBEC
ROCTA RUANA SAROD SHAWM
SHELL SHENG TARAU TELYN TRUMP
VEENA VIOLA ZANZE ZINKE BALAFO
BONANG CARASA CITOLE CORNET
CROUTH CYMBAL DOUCET FIDDLE
GENDER GLARIN GUITAR GUSLEE
JARANA RAPPEL REBECK RIBIBE
SABECA SANCHO SANTIR SPINET
TABRET TREBLE TYMPAN URHEEN
VIOLET VIOLIN ZITHER ALTHORN
ANGELOT ANKLONG ARGHOOL
BAGPIPE BANDORE BANDURA
BASSOON BAZOOKA CELESTA
CHEKKER CHIKARA CITHARA
CLARINA CLAVIER CLAVIOL DICHORD

DOLCIAN DOLCINO DULCIAN
FISTULA FLUTINA GAMELIN GITTERN
HELICON KANTELE MAGADIS
MARIMBA OCARINA PANDURA
PIBCORN RACKETT SAMISEN
SARANGI SARINDA SAXHORN
SERPENT SISTRUM SORDONO
THEORBO TRUMPET UKULELE
URANION VIHUELA ADIAPHON
AKALIMBA AUTOHARP AUTOPHON
BARBITON BERIMBAU BOUSOUKI
BOUZOUKI CALLIOPE CASTANET
CLARINET CORNPIPE CRESCENT
DULCIMER DYOPHONE EUPHONON
FIDICULA FLAUTINO HORNPIPE
HUMSTRUM KRUMHORN LAPIDEON
MARTENOT MELODION NEGINOTH
NEHILOTH PENORCON PHONIKON
PSALTERY SCHWEGEL SERINGHI
SOURDINE SYMPHONY TAMBOURA
TAROGATO TRIANGLE TRICHORD
TROMBONE VIRGINAL ZAMBOMBA
ACCORDION BOMBARDON
SAXOPHONE DIDGERIDOO
DIDJERIDOO MELLOPHONE
PEDALSTEEL TETRACHORD
VIBRAPHONE
(AFRICAN —) KORA MBIRA
(ANCIENT —) ASOR LUTE LYRE
CRWTH REBEC
(BALINESE —) GANGSA
(STRINGED — OF INDIA) SARANGI
(PL.) BRASS FAMILY STRINGS
PERCUSSION
MUSICALITY HARMONY
MUSIC HALL GAFF MELODEON
MUSICIAN BARD WAIT ASAPH
LINOS VIOLA BOPPER BUSKER
MUSICO PLAYER VIOLER VIOLIN
BANDMAN BOPSTER CELLIST
GAMBIST ORPHEUS TWANGER
VIOLIST KORAHITE MARIACHI
MINSTREL MUSICKER THRUMMER
TWANGLER CITYBILLY
MINNESINGER
(FOLK —) FOLKY FOLKIE
(JOB OF —) GIG
(NOISY —) RANTER
(WEST AFRICA —) GRIOT
(WEST AFRICAN —) GRIOT
(WORK AS —) GIG
(PL.) ENSEMBLE WAITSMEN
MUSING PENSIVE MUSARDRY
MUSK MOOST CATTAIL MIMULUS
AMBRETTE FIXATIVE
(PREF.) MOSCHI
MUSK DEER CERVID KASTURA
MUSKEG BOG FEN
MUSKELLUNGE LONGE MUSKIE
MUSKET FUSIL FUZIL MATCH
DRAGON JINGAL BUNDOOK CALIVER
ENFIELD GINGALL BANDHOOK
BISCAYAN BISCAYEN CULVERIN

ESCOPETA SNAPHAAN TOPHAIKE
MATCHLOCK
MUSKET BALL GOLI
MUSKETEER FUSILEER STRELITZ
(THREE —S) ATHOS ARAMIS
PORTHOS
MUSKET FORK GAFFLE
MUSK MALLOW ABELMOSK
MUSKMELON MANGO ATAMON
WUNGEE SPANSPEK CANTALOUPE
MUSKOGEE CREEK SEMINOLE
MUSK OX OVIBOS
(WOOL OF UNDERCOAT OF —) QIVIUT
MUSKRAT SQUASH ONDATRA
MUSQUASH
MUSK SHREW SONDELI
MUSK TURTLE STINKER STINKPOT
MUSKWOOD CAOBA
MUSKY MOSCHATE
MUSLIM LAZ ALIM SIDI SWAT TURK
ARAIN HAFIZ IBADHI KAZAKH
TURBAN ABBADID AYYUBID BAGIRMI
BASHKIR IBADITE KHAKSAR
MUDEJAR SUNNITE ALAOUITE
ISLAMIST ISLAMITE QADARITE
SIFATITE
(— BEADS) TASBIH
(— BROTHERHOOD) TARIQA
(— CALL TO PRAYER) AZAN
(— CHIEF) RAIS REIS
(— DOCTRINE) TAWHID
(— FOUNDATION) WAKF WAQF
(— JUDGE) CAID QAID
(— LEADER) MAM
(— MYSTIC) SUFI
(— OFFICIAL) OMRAH
(— PLAY) TAZIA
(— PRACTICE) PURDAH
(— PRINCIPLE) TAQIYA
(— SCHOLARS) ULAMA ULEMA
(— SECT) SUNNI WAHHABI MURJIITE
(— TOMB) TABUT
(— TREE) TUBA
(— WOMAN OF RANK) BEGUM
(EDUCATED —) MULLAH
(PL.) SHIA SHIAH SUNNI
MUSLIN BAN MULL DORIA SWISS
GURRAH MULMUL SHALEE SHILLA
TANJIB BETEELA FACTORY JAMDANI
ORGANDY STENTER COTELINE
SEERHAND TARLATAN
(PL.) COSSAS
MUSQUASH MUSKRAT ONDATRA
MUSS FUFFLE RUMPLE GLOMMOX
UNDRESS
MUSSEL CLAM UNIO NAIAD
ANODON JINGLE LACERT MUCKET
PALOUR BIVALVE GLOCHID
MYTILID UNIONID BULLHEAD
DEERHORN
(PREF.) CONCH(O) MYTILI MYTILO
MUSSELCRACKER BISKOP
MUSSULMAN MOSLEM

MUST BIT BUD BUT MAN MAY MUN BOOD MAUN MOTE SAPA STUM DULCE GOTTA OUGHT SHALL
(— BE TAKEN) SUM
(— NOT) MAUNNA
MUSTACHE WALRUS VALANCE WHISKER
MUSTACHE MONKEY MOUSTOC
MUSTANG PONY BRONCO SPHINX
MUSTARD ZEST CRESS SENVY SINEWY AWLWORT CADLOCK KEDLOCK SINAPIS CHADLOCK CHARLOCK FLIXWEED AUBRIETIA
(— PLANT) WASABI
(PREF.) SIN
MUSTARD GAS YPERITE
MUSTARD PLASTER SINAPISM
MUSTELUS GALEUS
MUSTER LEVY ENROL RAISE SPUNK GATHER HOSTING MARSHAL RECRUIT
(— OUT) DEMOB
MUSTINESS FUST MUST
MUSTY HOAR FUNKY FUSTY HOARY MOLDY MUCID RAFTY VINNY FOISTY FROWZY RANCID FOUGHTY FROWSTY COBWEBBY
MUTABLE FICKLE MUTATORY VARIABLE
MUTATE SPORT
MUTATION SHIFT SPORT CHANGE MUANCE SILKIE ANAGRAM VARIANT SALTATION
(VOWEL —) UMLAUT
MUTE PAD DUMB ECHO LENE SURD BLACK MEDIA WHIST DAMPER MUFFLE SILENT STIFLE TENUIS SORDINE SOURDINE
(— AT FUNERAL) SALLIE
(— FOR TRUMPET) DERBY
MUTED DULL SORDO STILL DISCREET SOURDINE
MUTENESS SILENCE DUMBNESS
MUTILATE MAR HACK MAIM BREAK GARBLE HAMBLE INJURE MANGLE MARTYR MITTLE CONCISE CASTRATE EMBEZZLE
(— AN ANIMAL) LAW
MUTILATION STRIP CONCISION
MUTINEER PANDY MUTINADO
MUTINOUS UNRULY
MUTINY REVOLT STRIFE REBELLION
MUTINY ON THE BOUNTY
(AUTHOR OF —) HALL NORDHOFF
(CHARACTER IN —) BYAM BLIGH PEGGY ROGER GEORGE ROBERT TEHANI BURKITT ELLISON MAIMITI STEWART TINKLER WILLIAM FLETCHER MILLWARD MORRISON MUSPRATT CHRISTIAN
MUTISM ALALIA
MUTTER CROOL MOTRE HOTTER HUMMER MUMBLE MURMUR PATTER THROAT CHANNER CHUNNER CHUNTER GRUMBLE MAUNDER TOOTMOOT MUSSITATE
MUTTERING GROWL
MUTTON BRAXY VIFDA VIVDA MOUTON BRAXIES
(LEG OF —) CABOB WABBLER WOBBLER
MUTTONBIRD OII
MUTTONFISH SAMA ABALONE EELPOUT MOJARRA
MUTTONHEAD DOLT
MUTUAL COMMON RECIPROCAL
(PREF.) CO INTER
MUZZLE GAG NOSE MOUTH SNOUT FOREFACE GUNPOINT
(— FOR FERRET) COPE
(— OF CANNON) CHOPS
MUZZLE-LOADER CAPLOCK MUZZLER
MYALGIA COURBATURE
MYALL YARRAN WARRIGAL

MYANMAR

BAY: BENGAL HUNTER HEANZAY
CAPITAL: RANGOON
DIVISION: PEGU MAGWE ARAKAN KARENNI SAGAING MANDALAY IRRAWADDY TENASSERIM
FORMER CAPITAL: AVA
GULF: MARTABAN
MEASURE: LY DHA CON LAN MAU NGU SAO TAO TAT BYEE DAIN PHAN SEIT TAUN TENG THAT SALAY SHITA THUOC LAMANY PAI GAT TRUONG CHAIVAI OKTHABAH
MONEY: KYAT
MOUNTAIN: POPA NATTAUNG SARAMATI VICTORIA
MOUNTAINS: CHIN NAGA DAWNA KACHIN KARENNI PEGUYOMA
NATIVE: AO VU WA AOR LAI LAO MON PYU TAI CHIN KADU KUKI LOLO MIAO NAGA SEMA SGAU SGAW SHAN THAI KAREN KHMER LHOTA BIRMAN BURMAN KACHIN RENGMA PALAUNG ARAKANESE
PLATEAU: SHAN
PORT: AKYAB BASSEIN HENZADA MOULMEIN
RIVER: HKA NMAI PEGU MEKONG SALWIN SHWELI KALADAN MALIKHA MYITNGE SALWEEN SITTANG CHINDWIN INDAWGYI IRRAWADDY
SEA: ANDAMAN
TOWN: YE AVA PEGU AKYAB BHAMO KARBE KATHA MINBU PAPUN PROME TAVOY HSENWI HSIPAW LASHIO MAYMYO MONYWA SHWEBU BASSEIN HENZADA PAKOKKU RANGOON MANDALAY MOULMEIN

WEIGHT: TA CAN MAT MOO PAI VIS BINH DONG KYAT RUAY VISS BAHAR BEHAR CANDY TICAL TICUL ABUCCO PEIKTHA

MY ANTONIA (AUTHOR OF —) CATHER
(CHARACTER IN —) JIM JAKE LENA OTTO WICK ANTON CUZAK FUCHS LARRY BURDEN CUTTER ANTONIA DONOVAN HARLING LINGARD MARPOLE AMBROSCH SHIMERDA
MYCELIUM SPAWN MYCELE TAPESIUM
MYCTERIA TANTALUS
MY DEAR MACHREE
MYDRIATIC PHENYLEPHRINE
MYIASIS STRIKE
MYNA APER MINA MYNAH GRACKLE
MYNES (BROTHER OF —) EPISTROPHUS
(FATHER OF —) EVENUS
(WIFE OF —) BRISEIS
MYOCOMMA FLAKE
MYRIAD HOST TOMAN COUNTLESS
MYRIAPOD JULID POLYPOD PAUROPOD MILLIPEDE
MYRRH STACTE
MYRRHA (SON OF —) ADONIS
MYRTLE MYRT LILAC BALTIC JAROOL ARRAYAN JAPONICA RAMARAMA
MYSELF SELF MYSEN HERSELF
MYSID SHRIMP
MYSOST PRIMOST
MYSTERIES OF PARIS (AUTHOR OF —) SUE
(CHARACTER IN —) FLEUR SARAH CICELY MURPHY WALTER FERRAND GEORGES JACQUES RODOLPH CHOUETTE CLEMENCE HARVILLE POLIDORI MACGREGOR RIGOLETTE
MYSTERIES OF UDOLPHO (AUTHOR OF —) RADCLIFFE
(CHARACTER IN —) EMILY DUPONT MORANO MONTONI LUDOVICO STAUBERT VILLEFORT LAURENTINI VALANCOURT
MYSTERIOUS DIM DARK DEEP EERY SELI EERIE SABLE WAKON ARCANE EXOTIC MYSTIC OCCULT SECRET CRYPTIC PUCKISH UNCANNY UNCOUTH ABSTRUSE ESOTERIC NUMINOUS SIBYLLIC CRYPTICAL
MYSTERIOUSLY DARKLY EERILY HEIMLICH
MYSTERY MIST RUNE CABALA ENIGMA SECRET ARCANUM PROBLEM SECRECY
(— STORY) WHODUNIT
(— WRITER FIRST NAME) ERLE ELLERY
(RELIGIOUS —) SACRAMENT
(PREF.) MYST(ERI)(ERIO)(ICO)
MYSTIC SUFI OCCULT ORPHIC SECRET EPOPTIC ESOTERIC
MYSTICAL MISTY MYSTIC ANAGOGIC TELESTIC
MYSTICALLY GHOSTLY
MYSTICISM CABALA SUFIISM
MYSTIFY BEAT BEFOG BOTHER MUDDLE PUZZLE BECLOUD CONFUSE BEWILDER
MYSTIQUE AIR AURA
MYTH SAGA FABLE LEGEND MYTHOS ALLEGORY
MYTHICAL FABLED FABULOUS FICTIOUS
MYTHOMANIAC LIAR

N

N EN NU NAN NOVEMBER
NAAM (FATHER OF —) CALEB
NAAMAH (BROTHER OF —)
 TUBALCAIN
 (FATHER OF —) LAMECH
 (MOTHER OF —) ZILLAH
 (SON OF —) REHOBOAM
NAARAH (HUSBAND OF —) ASHUR
NAASSENE OPHITE
NAB HAT NIB GRAB HEAD KNAB NAIL
 CATCH SEIZE ARREST CLUTCH
 COLLAR NIBBLE NOBBLE SNATCH
 CAPTURE APPREHEND
NABAL (WIFE OF —) ABIGAIL
NABALOI IBALOI IGOROT
NABK NUBK NABAK NEBUK NABBUK
 NEBACK NEBBUK NEBBUCK
NABOB DIVES NAWAB NOBOB
 DEPUTY VICEROY GOVERNOR
 PLUTOCRAT
 (— DEPUTY) NAWAB
 (PL.) NABOBRY
NACELLE CAR BOAT BASKET
 CHASSIS COCKPIT SHELTER
NACHSCHLAG SPRINGER
 AFTERNOTE
NACKET BOY CAKE LUNCH NOCKET
NACRE PEARL SHELLFISH
NADAB (FATHER OF —) AARON
 SHAMMAI
 (MOTHER OF —) ELISHEBA
NADIR BATHOS BEDROCK
 (OPPOSED TO —) ZENITH
NAG CUT RAG TIT BAIT CARP FRAB
 FRET FUSS GNAW JADE MOKE PLUG
 PONY PROD RIDE SNAG TWIT YAFF
 ANNOY COBRA HOBBY HORSE
 SCOLD SKATE SNAKE STEED TEASE
 BADGER BERATE BOTHER DOBBIN
 GARRAN GLEYDE HAGGLE HARASS
 HECKLE HECTOR KEFFEL PADNAG
 PESTER PLAGUE ROUNCY WANTON
 HACKNEY HENPECK TORMENT
 DINGDONG HARANGUE IRRITATE
 PARAMOUR CATAMARAN
 (AMBLING —) HOBBY
NAGA SEMA COBRA KABUI LHOTA
 SNAKE
NAGGING NIGGLING
NAGKASSAR SURIGA
NAGOR TOHI ANTELOPE REEDBUCK
NAHANE KASKA
NAHATH (FATHER OF —) ZOPHAI
NAHBI (FATHER OF —) VOPHSI
NAHOOR SHA SNA SHEEP URIAL
 BHARAL OORIAL

NAHOR (BROTHER OF —) HARAN
 ABRAHAM
 (FATHER OF —) SERUG
 (SON OF —) TERAH
 (WIFE OF —) MILCAH
NAHSON (FATHER OF —)
 AMMINADAB
 (SISTER OF —) ELISHEBA
 (SON OF —) SALMON
NAHUATL AZTEC CAZCAN MEXICA
NAHUM ELKOSHITE
NAIAD NAIS NYMPH MUSSEL
 HYDRIAD
NAIF BABE
NAIL CUT FIX HOB NAB PIN TEN
 BOSS BRAD BRAG BROD CLAW CLOY
 DUMP HOOF PILE SLUG SPAD STUB
 STUD TACK TRAP AFFIX CATCH
 CLOUT DRIVE GROPE PLATE SCALE
 SEIZE SPEED SPICK SPIKE SPRIG
 TALON BULLEN CLENCH CLINCH
 COOLER CORKER DETAIN FASTEN
 GARRON HAMMER SECURE SINKER
 TACKET TENTER TINGLE UNGUIS
 UNGULA CAPTURE CLINKER
 FASTENER HOLDFAST ROSEHEAD
 SPARABLE SPIKELET TENPENNY
 TRICOUNI
 (— BITING) ONYCHOPHAGIA
 (— GROWTH) ONYCHAUXIS
 (— OBLIQUELY) TOE
 (HEADLESS —) SPRIG
 (HOOKED —) TENTER TENTERHOOK
 (INGROWN —) ONYXIS ACRONYX
 (MARKING —) SPAD SPEED
 (OLD HORSESHOE —) STUB
 (SHOEMAKER'S —) CLOUT SPARABLE
 (TOED —) TOSHNAIL
 (PREF.) GOMPHO HELO ONYCH(O)
 UNGUI
 (SUFF.) ONYCHA ONYCHES ONYCHIA
 ONYCHIUM ONYCHUS ONYX
NAILROD STICKWEED
NAIVE OPEN RACY FRANK GREEN
 CANDID JEJUNE SIMPLE ARTLESS
 NATURAL CHILDISH INNOCENT
 UNTAUGHT WIDEEYED CHILDLIKE
 GUILELESS INGENUOUS PRIMITIVE
 UNTUTORED UNWORLDLY
 (— GIRL) INGENUE
NAIVETE GREENNESS SIMPLICITY
NAKED BALD BARE MERE NUDE
 OPEN CLEAR EXACT PLAIN STARK
 ADAMIC BARREN CUERPO SCUDDY
 SIMPLE EXPOSED LITERAL OBVIOUS
 MANIFEST STARKERS STRIPPED

SMOCKLESS UNADORNED
UNCLOTHED UNCOVERED
(PREF.) GYMN(O) NUDI
NAKED OAT PILLAS PILCORN
PILKINS
NAKEDWOOD MABI SNAKEWOOD
NAKHI MOSO MOSSO
NAKONG SITUTUNGA
NAMAYCUSH CREE FISH LAKER
LONGE LUNGE TOGUE TROUT
LONGUE SISCOWET
NAMBY-PAMBY WET INANE SILLY
VAPID CODDLE INSIPID KEEPSAKE
NAME DUB FIX NOM SET CALL CITE
FAME NAIL NOMB NOUN READ TERM
ALIAS CLAIM CLEPE COUNT ETHIC
NEVEN NOMEN POINT QUOTE STYLE
TITLE ACCUSE ADDUCE APPEAL
GOSSIP MONICA REPUTE SELECT
ALLONYM APPOINT BEHIGHT
DECLARE ENTITLE EPITHET MENTION
MONIKER SPECIFY VOCABLE
CATEGORY CHRISTEN COGNOMEN
IDENTIFY IDENTITY INDICATE
MONICKER NOMINATE ENUMERATE
PATRONYMIC NOMENCLATURE
(— OF NEWSPAPER) MASTHEAD
(— OF PLACE) TOPONYM
(— TABLET) FACIA
(— WRITTEN BACKWARDS) ANANYM
(ADDED —) AGNAME AGNOMEN
(ALTERNATIVE —) BUNCH
(ANCESTOR'S —) EPONYM
(ANOTHER —) ALIAS
(ASSUMED —) PEN ALIAS
ONOMASTIC PSEUDONYM
SOBRIQUET
(BAD —) CACONYM
(DAY —) AHAU
(DERIVATION OF —) EPONYMY
(FAMILIAR —) NICKNAME
(FAMILY —) SURNAME
(FIRST —) FORENAME PRAENOMEN
(GENERIC —) PRAENOMEN
(GOOD —) HONOR CREDIT
(PEN —) PSEUDONYM
(POPULAR DOG —) FIDO LADY SHEP
SPOT ROVER
(REGISTERED —) AFFIX
(TECHNICAL —) ONYM
(UNSUITABLE —) MISNOMER
(WELL-SUITED —) EUONYM
(PREF.) NOMEN ONOMATO
(SUFF.) NOMEN NYM ONYM
NAMED DIT CITED HIGHT NEMPT
DUBBED YCLEPT ONYMOUS
YCLEPED
NAMELESS BAS
(— ONE) WHO
NAMELY FOR VIZ SCIL NOTED TOWIT
FAMOUS SCILICET
NAMEPLATE MASTHEAD
(AUTOMOBILE —) MARQUE

NAMESAKE EPONYM JUNIOR
HOMONYM
NAMIBIA (BAY OF —) WALVIS
(CAPITAL OF —) WINDHOEK
(DESERT OF —) KALAHARI
(PEOPLE OF —) NAMAS BANTUS
BUSHMEN HEREROS OVAMBOS
NANA (AUTHOR OF —) ZOLA
(CHARACTER IN —) NANA ROSE
HUGON LOUIS SATIN FONTAN
GEORGE HECTOR MIGNON MUFFAT
SABINE XAVIER ESTELLE STEINER
BEUVILLE DAGUENET FAUCHERY
PHILIPPE DECHOUARD
NANDI BANANDE MUNANDI KIPSIKIS
NANDU RHEA
NANISM DWARFISM
NANNAR SIN
NANNY GOAT NURSE
(ORIENTAL —) AMAH
NANTICOKE TOAG
NAOMI MARA
(DAUGHTER-IN-LAW OF —) RUTH
NAOS CELLA SHRINE TEMPLE
NAP GIG KIP NOD RAS CALK CAMP
DOWN DOZE FUZZ LINT OOZE PICK
PILE RUFF SHAG WINK COVER DOVER
FLUFF GRASP SEIZE SLEEK SLEEP
STEAL CATNAP DROWSE SIESTA
SNOOZE DROPOFF EMERIZE RECLINE
SLUMBER
(TO RAISE —) TEASE
NAPE NOD CUFF NECK NUKE POLL
NUCHA NUQUE SCRAG SCUFT
SCURF NODDLE SCRUFF TURNIP
NIDDICK
(PREF.) NUCH(I)
NAPERY LINEN DAMASK DOILIES
NAPKINS
NAPHTALITE ENAN AHIRA
NAPHTHA NEFTE PETROLEUM
NAPKIN CLOTH DOILY TOWEL DIAPER
NAPERY KERCHIEF SUDATORY
HANDCLOTH SERVIETTE
NAPLES BISCUIT LADYFINGER
NAPLESS BARE HARD
NAPOLELEON (AIDE TO —) NEY
NAPOLEON (— III) LOUIS
BOUSTRAPA
(BATTLE OF —) ULM ACRE JENA
WATERLOO
(BIRTHPLACE OF —) CORSICA
(BROTHER-IN-LAW OF —) MURAT
(GAME LIKE —) PAM
(ISLAND OF —) ELBA HELENA
CORSICA
(MARSHALL OF —) NEY
(MOTHER OF —) HORTENSE
(PLACE OF VICTORY FOR —) LODI
LIGNY
NAPPE DECKE
NAPPY ALE DISH DOWNY HEADY
KINKY WOOLY LIQUOR SHAGGY

STRONG WOOLLY COTTONY
FOAMING VILLOUS
NARC TMAN
NARCISSUS LILY PLANT CRINUM
EGOIST FLOWER LILIUM JONQUIL
POLYANTHUS
(FATHER OF —) CEPHISSUS
(LOVED BY —) ECHO
(MOTHER OF —) LIRIOPE
(TRUMPET —) DAFFODIL
NARCOTIC (ALSO SEE DRUG) KAT
KEF BANG DOPE DRUG HEMP JUNK
BHANG DAGGA ETHER OPIUM
HEROIN OPIATE ANODYNE COCAINE
CODEINE HASHISH METOPON
NARCEIN HYPNOTIC MORPHINE
TAKROURI DIACODION MARIJUANA
SOPORIFIC CHLORODYNE
(— AGENT) GAZER
(— DOSE) LOCUS
(— ORGANIZATION) DEA
(— OVERDOSE) OD
(— PLANT) DUTRA MANDRAKE
(INJECT —) SHOOTUP
(SALE OF —S) SCORE
(SMALL AMOUNT OF —) SNIFTER
(PL.) JUNK STUFF
NARCOTICS JUNK HEROIN
NARCOTINE OPIANE
NARD SPICE ANOINT RHIZOME
MUSKROOT SPIKENARD
NARDOO ARDOO NARDU CLOVER
NARGIL COCONUT
NARGILEH PIPE HOOKA HOOKAH
NARGHILE
NARK SPY VEX NOTE ANNOY TEASE
OBSERVE INFORMER IRRITATE
NARRA NAGA ASANA APALIT
NARRATE SPIN TELL BRUIT STATE
STORY DEPICT DETAIL DEVISE RECITE
RELATE REPORT DISCUSS RECOUNT
STORIFY DESCRIBE REHEARSE
NARRATION TALE FABLE STORY
DETAIL ACCOUNT HAGGADA RECITAL
SYNAXAR ALLEGORY DELIVERY
DIEGESIS HAGGADAH
NARRATIVE EPIC JOKE MYTH SAGA
TALE CHORE DRAMA FABLE PROSE
STORY COMEDY JATAKA LEGEND
ACCOUNT EPISODE HISTORY
MEMOIRS MIDRASH NOVELLA
PARABLE RECITAL ALLEGORY
ANECDOTE APOLOGUE ARETALOGY
HAGIOLOGY
(— OF VOYAGE) PERIPLUS
(— POEM) EPIC EPOS SAGA
(BRIEF —) ANECDOTE
(PL.) ACTA EXEMPLA
NARRATOR TESTO TELLER RELATOR
SAGAMAN TALESMAN RACONTEUR
NARROW JERK LEAN MEAN NEAR
POKY SLIT TRUE BORNE CLOSE
CRAMP PINCH RIGID SCANT SHARP

SMALL SOUND TAPER ANGUST
BIASED LINEAR LITTLE MEAGER
STRAIT STRICT TWITCH BIGOTED
ERICOID LIMITED PRIMARY SLENDER
THRIFTY CONDENSE CONTRACT
PAROCHIAL PROVINCIAL
(— DOWN) CONFINE
(— DOWN STAVES) BUCK
(— INLET) RIA
(— IN OUTLOOK) SUBURBAN
(— IN PRINCIPLE) STRAITLACED
(NOT —) CATHOLIC
(VERY —) HAIRBREADTH
(PREF.) AUGUSTI DOLICH(O) STEN(O)
(SUFF.) STENOSIS
NARROWED LISTED INSWEPT
CONTRACT ANGUSTATE
NARROWING CAP CHOKE INTAKE
STENOSIS
NARROWLY WIDE STRAITLY
NARROW-MINDED REDNECK
BORNE PETTY
NARROWNESS BIAS BIGOTRY
LOCALISM PAROCHIALISM
NARSINGA TRUMPET
NARTHECIUM ABAMA
NARTHEX HALL STOA ENTRY FOYER
LOBBY PORCH PORTICO PRONAOS
VESTIBULE
NARWHAL MONODON
NASAB NUSUB KINSHIP
NASAL NOSY NARINE RHINAL
TWANGY ADENOID STRINGY
(PREF.) NASIO RHIN(O)
NASCENCY BIRTH ORIGIN GENESIS
BEGINNING
NASEBERRY SAPODILLA
NASHGAB OAF GOSSIP
NASI OFFICER PATRIARCH
NASICORN RHINOCEROS
NASTIKA ATHEIST
NASTURTIUM CAPUCINE
NOSEWORT RADICULA STURSHUM
STURTION
NASTY BAD PAH FOUL MEAN UGLY
DIRTY SNIDE FILTHY HORRID ODIOUS
RIBALD SCUZZY BAGGAGE BEASTLY
DEFILED HARMFUL OBSCENE
SQUALID UNCLEAN INDECENT
NAUSEOUS SPITEFUL STITEFUL
DANGEROUS MALICIOUS OFFENSIVE
NAT NOT DEMON SPIRIT
NATA (WIFE OF —) NANA
NATAL INBORN INNATE NATIVE
GLUTEAL CONGENIAL
NATAL BROWN MAHAL
NATAL PLUM AMATUNGULA
NATANT AFLOAT FLOATING
SWIMMING
NATATORIUM BATH POOL
NATCHEZ STINKER STINKARD
NATION BENI FOLK GEAT HOST LAND
LEDE RACE VOLK AEDUI CASTE

CLASS FANTE FANTI REALM STATE
TRIBE FANTEE GEATAS PEOPLE
WAGOGO ARVERNI COUNTRY
SOCIETY LANGUAGE COMMUNITY
MANDATORY MINISTATE MULTITUDE
(— SYMBOL) FLAG CREST
(HEBREW —) JACOB
(LARGE —) COLOSSUS
(PREF.) ETHN(O)
NATIONAL CITIZEN FEDERAL
GENTILE GENTILIC
(— DEMOCRACY) ENDEX
NATIONALISM JINGOISM
PHYLETISM
NATIONALIST CHINA (SEE
TAIWAN)
NATIONALITY FLAG
NATIVE (ALSO SEE PEOPLE AND
TRIBE) ABO ITE RAW SON TAO BORN
FREE GOOK HOME KIND LIVE NEIF
WILD INNER NATAL PUNTI EPIROT
GENIAL INBORN INNATE KINDLY
MOTHER NORMAL SIMPLE VIRGIN
CITIZEN DENIZEN DZUNGAR
ENDEMIC GENUINE NATURAL
PAISANO POLISTA DOMESTIC
GRASSCUT HABITUAL HOMEBORN
HOMEMADE INHERENT LANDSMAN
ORIGINAL PRIMEVAL PRISTINE
RESIDENT YAMMADJI ABORIGINE
CONGENIAL INGRAINED INHERITED
INTRINSIC ORIGINARY TAWNYMOOR
ABORIGINAL
(— BEAR) KOALA
(— BEECH) FLINDOSA
(— MINERAL) LIVE
(— OF ALBANIA) SKIPETAR
(— OF ANJOU) ANGEVIN
(— OF BENGAL) KOL
(— OF CANADA) HABITANT
(— OF CHINA) CELESTIAL
(— OF FENS) SLODGER
(— OF FLORIDA KEYS) CONK CONCH
(— OF GALLOWAY) GALWEGIAN
GALLOVIDIAN
(— OF GLASGOW) GLASWEGIAN
(— OF ILLINOIS) SUCKER
(— OF IRELAND) BOGTROTTER
(— OF LIVERPOOL) SCOUSE
(— OF LONDON) COCKNEY
(— OF LOW CLASS) TAO
(— OF MADAGASCAR) HOVA
(— OF MALAYA) INFIEL
(— OF MANCHESTER) MANCUNIAN
(— OF MARITIME PROVINCES)
BLUENOSE
(— OF N. CAROLINA) TARHEEL
(— OF NEW GUINEA) BOONG
(— OF NEW SOUTH WALES)
CORNSTALK
(— OF PHILIPPINES) GUGU
(— OF SCOTLAND) GEORDIE

(— OF SOUTHERN ILLINOIS)
EGYPTIAN
(— OF TYNESIDE) GEORDIE
(— OF W. AUSTRALIA) GROPER
(— PLANT) INDIGINE
(— WHO TEACHES) CATECHIST
(BORN AND BRED AS A —) CREOLE
(FREE —) TIMAWA
(UNCIVILIZED —) MYALL
(SUFF.) ESE ITE OT OTE
(— OF) ER IER YER
NATIVE SON (AUTHOR OF —)
WRIGHT
(CHARACTER IN —) JAN MAX MARY
BORIS MEARS BESSIE BIGGER
DALTON ERLONE THOMAS BRITTEN
BUCKLEY
NATIVITY BIRTH JATAKA GENESIS
GENITURE HOROSCOPE
NATTERJACK NEWT TOAD
NATTY CHIC NEAT POSH TIDY TRIG
TRIM NIFTY SMART SPICY DAPPER
JAUNTY SPIFFY SPRUCE FOPPISH
VARMINT
NATURAL RAW AFRO BORN EASY
FOOL HOME KIND OPEN RACY REAL
WILD NAIVE USUAL CANCEL CASUAL
COMMON CONJON CRETIN DIRECT
EARTHY HOMELY INBORN INBRED
INNATE KINDLY MOTHER NATIVE
NORMAL PHYSIC ARTLESS GENUINE
QUADRUM REGULAR INHERENT
LIFELIKE ORDINARY PHYSICAL
UNCOINED PRIMITIVE REALISTIC
UNASSUMED UNFEIGNED
(— LOGARITHM) LN
(— TALENT) DOWER FLAIR
(NOT —) DYED AFFECTED
(PREF.) PHYSICO PHYSI(O)
NATURALIST AMERICAN LEA COPE
DALL LONG MUIR SNOW WARD
FLAGG HYATT LEIDY LUCAS MASON
ORTON PEALE SETON TEALE ABBOTT
AKELEY BARTON DELONG FOSSEY
GODMAN HOLDER MORTON NELSON
PORTER SAVAGE STORER WALKER
WILKES WILSON AGASSIZ ANDREWS
BACHMAN BUCKLEY DITMARS
FUERTES GIBBONS HOLLAND
HOLLING MERRIAM PEATTIE
SCUDDER WALCOTT COOLIDGE
HALDEMAN HOLBROOK JENNINGS
SCHWATKA BURROUGHS INGERSOLL
SUBLETETE RAFINESQUE
SCHOOLCRAFT
AUSTRALIAN BANFIELD
DANISH BERGSOE WINSLOW
DUTCH CAMPER HOEVEN HOMBERG
SWAMMERDAM LEEUWENHOEK
ENGLISH RAY BELL BAKER BANKS
BATES BRADY FORBE GOSSE LEACH
NORTH BAILEY DARWIN HUDSON

SLOANE BORLASE CATESBY
DUGMORE EDWARDS NEEDHAM
PENNANT WALLACE BRODERIP
BURCHELL LYDEKKER STEBBING
SWAINSON BOWERBANK JEFFERIES
CARRUTHERS TEGETMEIER
WILLIAMSON ATTENBOROUGH
FRENCH BELON CHENU BUFFON
CUVIER BAILLON DAUBENY DUMERIL
GERVAIS LAMARCK LESUEUR
ORBIGNY PEIRESC POUCHET
POUPART REAUMUR ADDANSON
AUDEBERT BONPLAND DESHAYES
LACEPEDE RONDELET CASTELNAU
DAUBENTON BROUSSONETT
GERMAN OKEN WIED JAGER LIBAU
SEITZ MULLER PALLAS MARTIUS
NEUWIED SCHWANN SIEBOLD
STELLER CHAMISSO ERXLEBEN
HUMBOLDT JUNGHUHN SCHUBERT
EHRENBERG KIELMEYER
BURMEISTER KEYSERLING
TREVIRANUS ESCHSCHOLTZ
SOEMMERRING SCHLAGINTWEIT
ITALIAN REDI RISSO BONELLI
BROCCHI FABRONI FONTANA
SCOPOLI AMORETTI MARSIGLI
ALDROVANDI SPALLANZANI
VALLISNIERI
NORWEGIAN ASBJORNSEN
RUSSIAN EICHWALD FEDCHENKO
CHIKHACHEV
SCOTTISH BROWN BAIKIE-FORBES
HERDMAN JARDINE THOMSON
RICHARDSON MACGILLIVRAY
SPANISH OOBO AZARA MUTIS
SWEDISH ARTEDI FORSKAL
ZETTERSTEDT
SWISS HEER HUBER BONNET
GESNER AGASSIZ TSCHUDI
SAUSSURE TREMBLEY CLAPAREDE
POURTALES RUTIMEYER
NATURALIZE ADAPT ADOPT
ACCUSTOM ACCLIMATE ENDENIZEN
HABITUATE
NATURALLY SN NATCH KINDLY
GENIALLY
NATURALNESS EASE NAIVETE
NATURE ILK BENT BIOS CAST CLAY
FORM HAIR KIND MAKE MOOD RACE
SORT TRIM TYPE COLOR OUSIA
SHAPE STATE TENOR ANIMAL
DHARMA FIGURE HEAVEN KIDNEY
PHYSIS STRIPE ESSENCE FEATHER
INBEING QUALITY SPECIES PRAKRITI
UNIVERSE CHARACTER
QUALIFICATION
(— DIVINITY) NYMPH
(— GOD) PAN
(— GODDESS) CYBELE ARTEMIS
(— OF GOD) DIVINITY
(— PRINT) PHYTOGRAPH

(— SPIRIT) NAT
(— WORSHIP) PHYSIOLATRY
(APPARENT —) STUDY
(BY ITS VERY —) IPSOFACTO
(CONCEALED —) LATENCY
(COURSE OF —) TAO
(DIVINE —) DEITY
(EMOTIONAL —) HEART
(ESSENTIAL —) ESSE FORM
GENIUS
(GOOD —) BONHOMIE
(HUMAN —) FLESH MANHEAD
MANKIND
(INHERENT —) GENIUS
(INNER —) SOUL
(INTRINSIC —) BOTTOM
(MORAL —) ETHNOS
(OF THE SAME —) HOMOGENEOUS
(ORGANIC —) BIOS
(PERT. TO —) COSMO
(ROUGH —) SPINOSITY
(SENSUAL —) BLOOD
(SPECIAL —) IDIOM
(SPIRITUAL —) INTERNAL
(TRIFLING —) FRIVOLITY
(TRUE —) ESSE PROPRIETY
(TRUE — OF THINGS) WHERE
(ULTIMATE —) ESSENCE
(UNREGENERATE —) ADAM
(PREF.) PHYSI(O)
(SUFF.) (HAVING — OF) IC ICAL
(OF — OF) COUS
NATURIST NUDIST
NAUGHT NIL EVIL ZERO AUGHT
NAGHT OUGHT CIPHER NOUGHT
WICKED NOTHING USELESS
WORTHLESS
NAUGHTY BAD PAW SAD EVIL
WRONG PAWPAW SHREWD WICKED
OBSCENE WAYWARD IMPROPER
NAUPATHIA SEASICKNESS
NAURU (CAPITAL OF —) YAREN
(DISTRICT OF —) BOE EWA AIWO
IJUW BAITI BUADA NIBOK UABOE
YAREN ANABAR ANETAN MENENG
ANIBARE
(FORMER NAME OF —)
PLEASANTISLAND
(TOWN OF —) ANNA ORRO ANABAR
RONAWI YANGOR
NAUSEA PALL QUALM DISGUST
NAUSITY LOATHING SICKNESS
ANTIPATHY DIZZINESS
NAUSEATE TURN TWIST WLATE
REVOLT SICKEN DISGUST SCUNNER
STOMACH DISTASTE SCOMFISH
NAUSEATED ILL SICKISH QUALMISH
SQUFAMISH
NAUSEATING NASTY WAUGH
QUEASY BILIOUS FULSOME
BRACKISH STAWSOME LOATHSOME
REVOLTING SICKENING

NAUSEOUS NASTY FULSOME
OFFENSIVE
NAUSICAA (FATHER OF —) ALCINOUS
(MOTHER OF —) ARETE
NAUSITHOUS (FATHER OF —)
NEPTUNE POSEIDON
(MOTHER OF —) PERIBOEA
(SON OF —) ALCINOUS
NAUTICAL (ALSO SEE NAVIGATION)
NAVAL MARINE NAUTIC MARINAL
OCEANIC TARRISH MARITIME
NAVIGABLE
(— FLAG) CORNET PENNON
NAUTILUS MOLLUSK ARGONAUT
ARGONAUTA
(— COMMANDER) NEMO
NAVAHO DINE NAVAJO LONGHAIR
(— GROUP) OUTFIT
(— RITE) WAY
NAVAL SEA MARINE NAUTICAL
NAVIGABLE
(— DEPOT) BASE
(— FORCE) NAVY FLEET ARMADA
SQUADRON
(— JAIL) BRIG
NAVAL OFFICER AMERICAN ROE
CONE DALE DYER HART HULL HUSE
KING LAND LEVY LUCE MAYO SIMS
ALLEN AMMEN BARRY BEALE CAPPS
CLARK DAVIS DEWEY DUERK EVANS
FISKE FITCH FOOTE GRANT JONES
LEAHY LEARY MAHAN MAURY PERRY
PRATT ROWAN STARK WALKE
BARNEY BENSON BIDDLE BREESE
CARNEY CONNER EBERLE GREENE
HALSEY HEWITT HOWELL KEARNY
KIMMEL KNIGHT MCCAIN MOORER
MORRIS NIMITZ PALMER PORTER
RODMAN SCHLEY SEMMES TALBOT
TOWERS TUCKER WILKES WORDEN
BRISTOL BULLOCH CHESTER
CUSHING DALGREN DECATUR
ELLIOTT GLEAVES GRAVELY GRIDLEY
HOLLINS HOPKINS KIMBALL KINKAID
MOFFETT NIBLACK SCHENCK
SIGSBEE STEWART TRUXTUN
WHIPPLE WILLSON WINSLOW
YARNELL ZUMWALT BUCHANAN
CAPERTON CHADWICK CHAUNCEY
FARRAGUT GHORMLEY INGRAHAM
LAWRENCE PAULDING PERCIVAL
RICKOVER ROBINSON ROUSSEAU
SHUBRICK SPRUANCE STANDLEY
STIRLING THATCHER GLASSFORD
PILLSBURY SCHROEDER SELFRIDGE
BAINBRIDGE GREENSLADE
MACDONOUGH WAINWRIGHT
GOLDSBOROUGH
BELGIAN GERLACHE
BRAZILIAN MELLO
CANADIAN GARNEAU
DANISH HOLM JUEL AMDRUP
ADELAER

DUTCH TROMP RUYTER ALMONDE
DEWINTER HELFRICH
ENGLISH BALL BYNG HOOD HOPE
HOWE LUCE MEUX ALLIN ANSON
BAYLY BLAKE BLIGH BOYLE BROKE
DRAKE EVANS FOLEY HARDY HAWKE
KEYES LEAKE LYONS NOBLE PARRY
TRYON AYLMER AYSCUE BEATTY
BENBOW BOWERS BURNEY CARDEN
COFFIN COLOMB FENNER FISHER
FRASER GORDON HALSEY HERVEY
HORNBY JERRAM LAWSON LAYTON
LITTLE MADDEN MONSON NELSON
OSBORN PARKER RODNEY SYFRET
VERNON WILSON ADDISON BARCLAY
BEDFORD BELCHER CRADOCK
DOUGLAS GAMBIER HARWOOD
HAWKINS JACKSON MCCLURE
MORESBY NASMITH SEYMOUR
ANDERSON BEAUFORT BOSCAWEN
BROTHERS COCHRANE JELLICOE
TRELAWNY TYRWHITT BACKHOUSE
BERESFORD CALLAGHAN CHATFIELD
COLLINSON FREMANTLE GRENVILLE
NARBROUGH NICHOLSON
CODRINGTON CUNNINGHAM
SOMERVILLE TROUBRIDGE
FITZMAURICE MOUNTBATTEN
FRENCH BART LOTI BELLOT DARLAN
FORBIN GRASSE COURBET DUPERRE
ESTAING FARRERE GUICHEN
MOUCHEZ CORBIERE FLEURIAS
FLEURIEU MUSELIER NOAILLES
CASABIANCA
GERMAN SPEE KONIG HIPPER
MULLER RAEDER BEHNCKE CANARIS
CAPELLE DOENITZ LUCKNER TIRPITZ
JACHMANN LANGSDORFF
GREEK KANARES MIAOULES
HUNGARIAN HORTHY
ITALIAN DORIA LAURIA JACCHINO
RICCARDI
JAPANESE ITO KATO TOGO URIU
KONDO OKADA SAITO YONAI
NAGANO NOMURA FUCHIDA
SHIMADA YOSHIDA KAMIMURA
SUETSUGU
NORWEGIAN TORDENSKJOLD
PERUVIAN GRAU
PORTUGUESE CASTRO
RUSSIAN GREIG KOLCHAK MAKAROV
ALEKSEEV APRAKSIN GORSHKOV
KUZNETSOV BELLINGHAUSEN
SCOTTISH BARTON
SPANISH ULLOA GRAVINA
MENENDEZ
SWEDISH LINDMAN EHRENSVARD
**NAVARRAISE, LA (CHARACTER IN
—)** ANITA ARAQUIL GARRIDO
ZUCCARAGA
(COMPOSER OF —) MASSENET
NAVE HOB HUB NEF APSE BODY FIST
PACE AISLE NATHE NIEVE CENTER

NAVEL NOMBRIL OMPHALOS
UMBILICUS
(PREF.) OMPHAL(O) UMBILI(CI)
(SUFF.) OMPHALUS
NAVIGABLE BOATABLE PORTABLE
NAVIGATE KEEL SAIL DRIVE GUIDE
SKIFF STEER AVIATE COURSE CRUISE
DIRECT MANAGE TRAVEL CONDUCT
CONTROL JOURNEY OPERATE
TRAVERSE ASTROGATE
NAVIGATION HOMING VOYAGE
NAUTICS PASSAGE SAILING TRAFFIC
CABOTAGE SHIPPING
(— MEASURE) TON KNOT SEAM
FATHOM
(— SYSTEM) LORAN TACAN
SHORAN
(SYSTEM OF —) DACCA DECCA
NAVIGATOR FLYER NAVVY PILOT
AIRMAN AVIATOR COPILOT LABORER
AERONAUT SEAFARER SPACEMAN
NEPTUNIAN NEPTUNIST
DANISH BERING
DUTCH BERING HARTOG BARENTS
HOUTMAN LEMAIRE HEEMSKERK
ENGLISH FOX COOK ADAMS BYRON
DIXON DRAKE BAFFIN BARLOW
BUTTON CLERKE HUDSON SOMERS
WALLIS BARLOWE GILBERT
GOSNOLD RALEIGH WEDDELL
CAVENDISH FROBISHER LANCASTER
VANCOUVER CHANCELLOR
WILLOUGHBY
FRENCH CARTIER BETHENCOURT
BOUGAINVILLE
GERMAN BEHAIM KOTZEBUE
GREEK EUDOXUS PYTHEAS
ICELANDIC ERICSON
ITALIAN ZENO CABOT VESPUCCI
NORWEGIAN ERIC
PORTUGUESE CAM DIAS DIAZ GAMA
CUNHA ZARCO CABRAL DAGAMA
GARCIA QUEIROS GILIANES
MAGELLAN FERNANDES
RUSSIAN LUTKE GOLOVNIN
KRUSENSTERN
SPANISH CANO GALI NINO SOLIS
PINZON TORRES BERMUDEZ
FERNANDEZ
NAVITE BASALT
NAVVY HAND WORKER LABORER
NAVIGATOR
NAVY FLEET SHIPFERD
(— BOARD) ADMIRALTY
(— OFFICER) CPO AIDE MATE BOSUN
CHIEF ENSIGN ADMIRAL ARMORER
CAPTAIN COMMANDER
COMMODORE
(— RADIO OPERATOR) SPARKS
(— VESSEL) PT SUB CARRIER
CRUISER FLATTOP DESTROYER
SUBMARINE TRANSPORT
NAWAB NABOB RULER VICEROY

NAY NO NAI NEI NOT DENY EVEN
NYET FLUTE NEVER DENIAL REFUSE
REFUSAL NEGATIVE
NAZARD STOP NASAT
NAZE NASE HEADLAND
NAZI BROWN HITLERITE
(— SYMBOL) FYLFOT SWASTIKA
NAZIM VICEROY GOVERNOR
NEAERA (DAUGHTER OF —) AUGE
EVADNE LAMPETIS PHAETHUSA
(FATHER OF —) PEREUS
(HUSBAND OF —) ALEUS STRYMON
(SON OF —) CEPHEUS LYCURGUS
AMPHIDAMAS
NEANDERTHAL CAVEMAN
NEANIC IMMATURE YOUTHFUL
NEAR AD AT BY IN GIN KIN NAR AKIN
BAIN DEAR FAST GAIN HARD HEND
INBY MEAN NEXT NIGH ABOUT
ANEAR ANENT ASIDE CLOSE EWEST
FORBY HANDY HENDE JUXTA MATCH
NUDGE ROUND SHORT TOUCH
ALMOST AROUND BESIDE CLIMAX
HEREBY NARROW STINGY TOWARD
WITHIN ADVANCE AGAINST FORTHBY
SIMILAR THRIFTY VICINAL ADJACENT
APPROACH IMMINENT INTIMATE
CONTIGUOUS
(— AKIN) GERMANE
(— POINT) PP
(— THE BEGINNING) EARLY FORMER
(— THE EQUATOR) LOW
(— THE MOUTH) ADORAL
(— THE SURFACE) EBB FLEET
(— THE WIND) HIGH AHOLD
(CONVENIENTLY —) HANDSOME
(PREF.) AC AD AF AG AL AP AS AT BY
ENGY EPH EPI JUXTA PERI PLESI(O)
PROS
NEARBY AROUND GAINLY LOCALLY
ADJACENT
(ONES —) THESE
NEARER HITHER
(— FRANCE) CISALPINE
(— ROME) CISALPINE
(— THE REAR) AFTER
(PREF.) (— IN TIME) CIS CITRA
NEAREST NEXT EWEST CLOSEST
NEARMOST PROCHAIN PROXIMAL
IMMEDIATE PROXIMATE
(— THE STERN) AFTERMOST
(PREF.) PROXIMO
NEARIAH (FATHER OF —) ISHI
SHEMAIAH
NEARLY GAIN JUST LIKE MOST
MUCH ABOUT CLOSE ALMOST
FECKLY WELLNIGH VIRTUALLY
PRACTICALLY
NEARNESS AFFINITY VICINITY
PROPINQUITY
NEARSIGHTED MYOPIC PURDLIND
NEAT GIM NET COGH COWS DEFT
DINK FEAT FEEL FEIL GENT JIMP

MACK NICE OXEN PRIM PURE SMUG
SNOD SNUG TIDY TOSH TRIG TRIM
BULLS CLEAN CLEAR COMPT CRISP
DINKY DONCY DONSY DOUCE EXACT
FEATY FETIS GENTY JEMMY NATTY
NIFTY PREST QUEME SMART SMIRK
SPICK TERSE TIGHT ADROIT BOVINE
CATTLE CLEVER DAINTY DAPPER
DIMBER DONSIE HEPPEN MINION
POLITE QUAINT SPANDY SPRUCE
BANDBOX CONCISE FEATOUS
ORDERLY PERJINK PRECISE REFINED
SHAPELY TRICKSY UNMIXED
MENSEFUL SKILLFUL STRAIGHT
TASTEFUL DEXTEROUS SHIPSHAPE
UNDILUTED WHOLESOME
NEATLY SNUG DEFTLY FAIRLY FEATLY
SMARTLY SPRUCELY
NEATNESS MENSE DEFTNESS
ELEGANCE SPRUCERY
NEATNIK (NOT A —) SLOB
NEB EAR NIB TIP BEAK BILL NOSE
POINT SNOUT
NEBAIOTH (FATHER OF —) ISHMAEL
NEBAT (SON OF —) JEROBOAM
NEBO (FATHER OF —) MARDUK
MERODACH
(WIFE OF —) TASHMET

NEBRASKA
CAPITAL: LINCOLN
COLLEGE: DANA DOANE DUCHESNE
HASTINGS
COUNTY: GAGE LOUP OTOE DEUEL
DUNDY KEITH SARPY CHERRY
COLFAX FURNAS HOOKER NEMAHA
VALLEY BUFFALO ANTELOPE
BOXBUTTE KEYAPAHA
INDIAN: OTO OMAHA PONCA PAWNEE
PRESIDENT: FORD
RIVER: LOGAN DISMAL PLATTE
ELKHORN NIOBRARA
STATE BIRD: MEADOWLARK
STATE FLOWER: GOLDENROD
STATE NICKNAME: BLACKWATER
CORNHUSKER TREEPLANTERS
STATE TREE: ELM
TOWN: ORD ALMA COZAD OMAHA
PONCA TRYON WAHOO GERING
MULLEN NELIGH PENDER TEKAMAH
OGALLALA REDCLOUD THEDFORD
UNIVERSITY: CREIGHTON

NEBRIS FAWNSKIN
NEBULA SKY CRAB SPOT VAPOR
BALAXY GALAXY SPIRAL PLANETARY
NEBULIZE ATOMIZE
NEBULOUS DIM DARK HAZY FOGGY
MISTY MUDDY VAGUE WISPY
CLOUDY MYSTIC TURBID CLOUDED
EVASIVE SHADOWY UNCLEAR
DREAMLIKE

NECESSARILY NEEDS NEEDLY
PERFORCE
NECESSARY NEEDY PRIVY VITAL
FRIEND TOILET KINSMAN NEEDFUL
FORCIBLE INTEGRAL OBLIGATE
BEHOVEFUL ESSENTIAL INTRINSIC
(PL.) ALIMENT MISTERS
NECESSITATE FORCE IMPEL
COMPEL DEMAND ENTAIL OBLIGE
REQUIRE CONSTRAIN
NECESSITY USE CALL DUTY FATE
FOOD LACK MUST NEED TASK WANT
DRINK ANANKE BEHOOF BESOIN
MISTER MUSCLE NEEDBE URGENCY
PERFORCE REQUIREMENT
(— OF MOVING) ZUGZWANG
(BY —) PRESENTLY
(OF —) PERFORCE
(PL.) BREAD
(PREF.) DEONTO
NECK COL NUB PET CAPE CRAG CROP
HALS KISS WAKE BEARD CHOKE
CRAIG HALSE SCRAG SPOON SWIRE
TRAIL BEHEAD CARESS CERVIX
COLLET COLLUM FONDLE STRAIT
CHANNEL EMBRACE ISTHMUS
SQUEEZE TUBULUS LALLYGAG
(— ARTERY) CAROTID
(— MUSCLE) SCALENUS
(— OF BOTTLE) THROTTLE
(— OF LAMB) TARGET
(— OF VOLCANO) CORE
(BACK OF —) NOD NAPE NUCH
NUQUE SCRUFF NIDDICK
(BOW —) HAWSE
(PERT. TO —) JUGULAR CERVICAL
(RED —) ROOINEK
(PREF.) CERVIC(I)(O) COLLI DER(O)
TRACHEL(O)
(SUFF.) DERUS
NECK AND NECK TIE EVEN CLOSE
NECKBAND BAND COLLAR COLLET
SHIRTBAND
NECKCLOTH BOA TIE RUFF AMICE
CHOKE SCARF STOLE CHOKER
CRAVAT BURDASH NECKTIE
PANUELO STARCHER BARCELONA
SOLITAIRE STEINKIRK
NECKERCHIEF GIMP RAIL FOGLE
BELCHER FOULARD NECKLET
KERCHIEF NECKATEE NECKCLOTH
NECKENGER
NECKING COLLAR GORGERIN
NECKLACE BEE LEI TORC BEADS
CHAIN NOOSE CARCAN CHOKER
COLLAR GORGET SANKHA TAWDRY
TORQUE BALDRIC CHAPLET RIVIERE
SAUTOIR LAVALIER NEGLIGEE
ESCLAVAGE
(PREF.) MONILI
NECKLET (FEATHER —) MARABOU
MARABOUT

NECKLINE COWL SCOOP
NECK RUFF FRAISE QUELLIO
NECKTIE BOW TIE ASCOT SCARF
CHOKER CRAVAT GRAVAT OVERLAY
(— PARTY) HANGING LYNCHING
(PART OF —) EDGE SEAM TACK
APRON SHELL FACING MARGIN
POCKET HEMMING TIPPING
NECKBAND INTERLINING
(STRING —) BOLO
(WOMAN'S —) TAWDRY
NECKWEAR ASCOT
NECROMANCER GOETIC MAGICIAN
NECROMANCY GOETY MAGIC
GRAMARY SORCERY WIZARDRY
EGROMANCY
NECROPOLIS CEMETERY
NECROPSY AUTOPSY
NECROSIS MORTIFICATION
NECTAR HONEY AMRITA AMBROSIA
NECTAR BIRD EATER HONEY
SUNBIRD
NECTARINE PEACH BRUNION
NECTRON NECTARIN
NECTARY SPUR GLAND NECTARIUM
NEDABIAH
(FATHER OF —) JECONIAH
NEDDER ADDER
NEDDY HORSE DONKEY
NEE BORN
NEED ASK NUD LACK TAKE THAR
WANT CRAVE DRIVE THARF BEHOOF
BEHOVE BESUIN DEMAND DESIRE
EGENCE MISTER STRAIT BEHOOVE
NEEDHAM POVERTY REQUIRE
URGENCY DISTRESS EXIGENCY
MISCHIEF EMERGENCE EXTREMITY
NECESSITY
NEEDED NECESSARY
NEEDFIRE WILDFIRE
NEEDFUL VITAL INTEGRAL
ESSENTIAL NECESSARY REQUISITE
NEEDLE RIB SEW VEX YEN ACUS
DARN GOAD TIER WIRE ANNOY
BLUNT POINT SHARP SPIKE STRAW
STYLE BODKIN DARNER HECKLE
STYLUS OBELISK PRICKER PROVOKE
SPICULE TUMBLER
(— HOLE) EYE
(— SORTER) HANDER
(COMB. FORM) ACU
(PART OF —) EYE HOLE CROWN
POINT SHANK
(PINE —) SPILL
(PINE —S) PININGS
(SHAPED LIKE A —) ACEROSE
(PL.) ACUS
(PREF.) ACU RAPHI RAPHIDI
NEEDLE BUG NEPID RANATRA
NEEDLEBUSH URY PINBUSH
NEEDLEFISH GAR SNOOK AGUJON
BELONID LONGJAW

NEEDLE GUN RIFLE DREYSE
NEEDLELIKE ACUATE ACERATE
ACEROSE ACEROUS ACIFORM
ACICULAR BELONOID SPLINTERY
NEEDLEMAN TAILOR
NEEDLE-POINTED ACEROSE
NEEDLESHAPED ACIFORM
ACETIOUS
NEEDLESS AMOK
NEEDLESTONE NATROLITE
NEEDLEWORK SEWING SAMPLER
SEAMING TATTING KNITTING
WOOLWORK HEMSTITCH INSERTION
STITCHERY EMBROIDERY
STITCHCRAFT
NEEDY BARE POOR INDIGENT
NEEDSOME HUNGARIAN PENNILESS
PENURIOUS NECESSITOUS
NEEP NEPE TURNIP
NE'ER-DO-WELL LOSER BUM PELF
SKELLUM SCHLEMIEL SHIFTLESS
WORTHLESS RAPSCALLION
NEFANDOUS IMPIOUS
EXECRABLE
NEFARIOUS BAD WICKED HEINOUS
IMPIOUS FLAGRANT HORRIBLE
INFAMOUS ATROCIOUS
NEFERT (HUSBAND OF —)
AMENEMHAT
NEGATE DENY SUBLATE
NEGATION NAY NOT EMPTY
DENIAL REFUCAL ANNULMENT
NONENTITY
(PREF.) DIS
NEGATIVE NA NE NO CON NAE NAY
NIT NIX NON NOR NOT NUL DENY
FILM VETO MINUS NEVER NAYWARD
STAMPER APOPHATIC PRIVATIVE
(— PREFIX) IL IM IN IR UN DIS NON
(— PRINCIPLE) YIN
(PHOTOGRAPHIC —) CLICHE
(PREF.) INEQUI
NEGATOR NAYSAYER OPPONENT
NEGLECT DEBT FAIL HANG OMIT
SHUN SLIP FAULT FORGO SHIRK
SLOTH WAIVE BYPASS CESSER
FOREGO FORGET IGNORE LACHES
LOITER PERMIT SLIGHT DEFAULT
DISOBEY FAILURE OVERSEE RESPECT
FORSLACK OMISSION OVERLOOK
OVERSLIP RECKLESS DISREGARD
MISLIPPEN OVERSIGHT PRETERMIT
MISPRISION
(— OF DUTY) INCIVISM
NEGLECTED TACKY SHABBY
UNDONE DORMANT OBSOLETE
NEGLECTFUL LAX REMISS
CARELESS DERELICT HEEDLESS
RECKLESS DISSOLUTE NEGLIGENT
NEGLIGEE ROBE MANTEAU
MATINEE UNDRESS PEIGNOIR
NIGHTGOWN DISHABILLE

NEGLIGENCE CULPA LACHES DEFAULT LASCHETY DISREGARD OVERSIGHT

NEGLIGENT LAX LASH SOFT SLACK CASUAL OVERLY REMISS CARELESS DERELICT DISCINCT RECKLESS SLOVENLY YEMELESS DISSOLUTE NEGLECTFUL

NEGLIGIBLE FAT

NEGOTIATE DEAL SELL BROKE FLOAT TREAT TROKE TRUCK TRYST ADVISE ASSIGN CONFER DICKER DIRECT MANAGE PARLEY SETTLE ARRANGE BARGAIN CHAFFER CONDUCT CONSULT DISCUSS ENTREAT CONCLUDE ENTREATY TRANSACT TRANSFER TEMPORIZE

NEGOTIATION DEAL DICKER PARLEY TREATY PASSAGE ENTREATY PRACTICE

NEGRITO ATA ATI ITA AETA AKKA BATWA BLACK KARON SEMANG TAPIRO ABENLEN BAMBUTE

NEGRITUDE SOUL

NEGRO FON JUR LUO LWO SUK AKIM ALUR BENI BINI BONI EGBA FONG IRON MADI MOKE NUBA NUPE SIDI BENIN BLACK BONGO CUFFY DINKA DJUKA FULUP FUZZY HATSA MUNGO SEPIA SEREC SMOKE TEMNE GULLAH HUBSHI AKWAPIM DAHOMAN GEECHEE QUASHIE SANDAWE SHELLUH SHILLUK BECHUANA ETHIOPIAN MANGBATTU
(— BLOOD) TARBRUSH
(GOLD COAST —) GA FANTI
(LIBERIAN —) KRU VAI VEI GREBO ICROO KRUMAN KROOBOY
(MALE —) BUCK
(OLD —) UNCLE

NEHEMIAH (ADVERSARY OF —) TOBIAH
(FATHER OF —) AZBUK HACHALIAH

NEHUSHTA (FATHER OF —) ELNATHAN
(HUSBAND OF —) JEHOIAKIM
(SON OF —) JEHOIACHIN

NEIGH NIE NVE WHI HINNY NICKER WHINNY WIGHER WHICKER

NEIGHBOR BOR ADJOIN BORDER FELLOW NEIPER ACCOLENT BORDERER CONFINER UCALEGON
(PL.) KITH CONFINES
(SUFF.) GETON

NEIGHBORHOOD WAY AREA HAND ZONE VENUE BARRIO LOCALE REGION PURLIEU SECTION DISTRICT ENVIRONS PRESENCE PROCINCT VICINAGE VICINITY BAILIWICK COMMUNITY PROXIMITY TERRITORY VOISINAGE
(SQUALID —) SLUM

NEIGHBORING NIGH NEARBY CONFINE VICINAL ACCOLENT ADJACENT

NEIGHBORLY FOLKSY FOLKSEY AMICABLE

NEITHER NOT NATHER NITHER NOWDER
(— RIGHT NOR WRONG) ADIAPHOROUS

NELEUS (BROTHER OF —) PELIAS
(DAUGHTER OF —) PERO
(FATHER OF —) NEPTUNE
(MOTHER OF —) TYRO
(SON OF —) NESTOR
(WIFE OF —) CHLORIS

NELLORE ONGOLE

NEMA EELWORM FILAMENT NEMATODE ROUNDWORM

NEMATOCYST CNIDA DESMONEME PENETRANT

NEMATODE EELWORM ROUNDWORM

NEMESIS BANE FATE UPIS AGENT AVENGER PENALTY

NEMUEL (BROTHER OF —) ABIRAM DATHAN
(FATHER OF —) ELIAB SIMEON

NENTSI SAMOYED SAMOYEDE

NEOPHYTE TYRO EPOPT NOVICE ROOKIE AMATEUR CONVERT BEGINNER PROSELYTE YOUNGLING

NEOPLASM TUMOR GROWTH TUMOUR SARCOMA NEWGROWTH

NEOTERIC NEW LATE FRESH NOVEL MODERN RECENT

NEP KNOT CATNIP CATMINT CLUSTER

NEPAL
CAPITAL: KATMANDU KATHMANDU
COIN: MOHAR RUPEE
MOUNTAIN: EVEREST
MOUNTAIN RANGE: HIMALAYA
NATIVE: KHA AOUL LIMBU MURMI NEWAR GURKHA GORKHALI
RIVER: KALI KOSI MUGU SETI BABAI BHERI RAPTI SARDA GANDAK KARNALI NARAYANI
TOWN: ILAM MUGU GALWA JUMLA PATAN BIRGANJ POKHARA BHADGAON LALITPUR BHAKTAPUR BIRATNAGAR

NEPENTHE DRUG PLANT POTION ANODYNE

NEPHEG (FATHER OF —) DAVID IZHAR

NEPHELE (DAUGHTER OF —) HELLE
(HUSBAND OF —) ATHAMAS
(SON OF —) LEUCON PHRIXUS

NEPHELINE LENAD MINERAL
SOMMITE ELEOLITE
NEPHEW OY OYE NEVE VASU NEFFY
NEVOY NIECE NEPOTE BENVOLIO
NEPHRIC RENAL
NEPHRITE YU JADE AXSTONE
POUNAMU TREMOLITE
NEPTUNE LER PAN SEA GREEN
OCEAN PLATE SEAGOD
(BROTHER OF —) PLUTO JUPITER
(CONSORT. OF —) SALACIA
(DISCOVERER OF —) GALLE
(EMBLEM OF —) TRIDENT
(FATHER OF —) SATURN
(MOTHER OF —) RHEA
(SISTER OF —) JUNO
NER (NEPHEW OF —) SAUL
(SON OF —) ABNER
NERD CLOD DINK DORK DRIP JERK
WONK DWEEB TWERP
(COMPUTER —) WEENIE
NEREID NYMPH NEREIS THALIA
THETIS CYMODOCE
NEREIDES (FATHER OF —) NEREUS
(MOTHER OF —) DORIS
NERGAL (BROTHER OF —) NINAZU
(FATHER OF —) ENLIL
(MOTHER OF —) NINLIL
NERI (FATHER OF —) MELCHI
(SON OF —) SALATHIEL
NERIAH (FATHER OF —) MAASEIAH
(SON OF —) BARUCH SERAIAH
NERISSA (HUSBAND OF —)
GRATIANO
NERO TYRANT FIDDLER
(MOTHER OF —) AGRIPPINA
(SUCCESSOR TO —) GALBA
(VICTIM OF —) LUCAN SENECA
(WIFE OF —) OCTAVIA
NERONE (CHARACTER IN —) MAGO
NERO SIMON FANUEL RUBRIA
ASTERIA
(COMPOSER OF —) BOITO
NERVE RIB BEND CORD GALL GRIT
GUTS LINE SAND VEIN BALLS BRASS
CHEEK CHORD CRUST PLUCK PUDIC
SINEW SPUNK STEEL TENON VAGUS
VIGOR APLOMB COSTAL DARING
DENTAL ENERGY FACIAL HUTZPA
LUMBAR RADIAL SACRAL STRING
AXILLAR CHUTZPA COELIAC
COURAGE HUTZPAH SAPHENA
SCIATIC SPINDLE ABDUCENS
AUDACITY BOLDNESS CERVICAL
CHUTZPAH COOLNESS EFFERENT
EMBOLDEN GUMPTION STRENGTH
TEMERITY AUTONOMIC ENCOURAGE
EYESTRING ACCELERATOR
(— CELL) ANAXON NEURON
DIAXONE DENDRAXON
(— CENTER) BRAIN CORTEX PLEXUS
(— CONNECTOR) SYNAPSE

(— FIBERS) PONS
(— NETWORK) RETIA PLEXUS
(— SLEEP) NEURO HYPNOTISM
(TYPE OF AFFERENT —) EXCITOR
(PL.) HORRORS JITTERS
(PREF.) NEUR(I)(O)
(SUFF.) NEURA(L) NEURE NEURIA
NEURIC
NERVE CELL DIAXON
NERVELESS DEAD WEAK BRAVE
INERT UNNERVED FOOLHARDY
POWERLESS
NERVOUS EDGY TOEY ANTSY
FUSSY GOOSY HYPER JUMPY
TENSE TIMID WINDY WIRED FIDGET
SINEWY SPOOKY TOUCHY UNEASY
FEARFUL FRETFUL JITTERY RESTIVE
SCADDLE NEUROTIC TIMOROUS
EXCITABLE SENSITIVE TREMULOUS
TWITTERLY
(— MALADY) APHASIA NEURITIS
(— SEIZURE) TIC ANEURIA
NERVURE RIB COSTA NERVE
NEURON CUBITAL
NERVY BOLD RASH JERKY PUSHY
BRAZEN SINEWY STRONG FORWARD
JITTERY IMPUDENT INTREPID
VIGOROUS EXCITABLE
NESS RAS CAPE SKAW SUFFIX
HEADLAND
NEST BED DEN EST JUG WEB AERY
BIKE BINK DRAY DREY EYRY HOME
LAIR NIDE REDD SHED TRAP ABODE
AERIE BROOD EYRIE HAUNT HOUSE
NIDUS SWARM CLUTCH COLONY
CUDDLE HOTBED NIDIFY RESORT
WURLEY CABINET LODGING
RETREAT VESPIARY WITHYPOT
LARVARIUM PENDULINE RESIDENCE
TERMITARY
(— OF ANIMALS) BED
(— OF ANT) FORMICARY
(— OF BOXES) INRO
(— OF EGGS) CLUTCH
(SQUIRREL'S —) CAGE DRAY DREY
(PREF.) CALIO NIDI OECO
(SUFF.) OECA OECIA
NESTER FLEDGLING
NESTLE JUG LAP LIE PET NEST SNUG
FITIN NICHE SPOON BURROW
CUDDLE FIDGET NUZZLE PETTLE
SETTLE SNUDGE CHERISH SHELTER
SNUGGLE SNUZZLE
NESTLING BABY BIRD EYAS
NEST POULT SQUAB CUDDLE
RETREAT BIRDLING NIDULATE
FLEDGLING
NEST OF GENTLEFOLK (AUTHOR
OF —) TURGENEV
(CHARACTER IN —) LIZA FYODOR
PANSHIN VARVARA KALITINE
PAVLOVNA LAVRETSKY

NESTOR SAGE SOLON LEADER
ADVISER ADVISOR COUNSELOR
PATRIARCH
(FATHER OF —) NELEUS
(MOTHER OF —) CHLORIS
(SON OF —) ANTILOCHUS
(WIFE OF —) ANAXIBIA EURYDICE
NESTORIAN WISE
NET BAG GIN HAY LAM POT WEB
CAUL FIKE FLAN FLEW FLUE FYKE
GAIN HAAF KELL LACE LAUN LAWN
LEAD LEAP MESH MOKE NEAT PURE
RETE SALE SEAN TOIL TRAP TRIM
WEIR BRAIL CATCH CLEAN CLEAR
DRIFT GAUZE LACIS PITCH POUND
SCOOP SEINE SEIZE SNARE SNOOD
TRAWL TRINK TULLE YIELD BAGNET
BASKET BRIGHT COBWEB ENMESH
ENTRAP FABRIC GROUND LEADER
MALINE MASILE PANTER PROFIT
RAFFLE SAGENE SAPIAO TOWNET
TUNNEL DRAGNET ENSNARE FLYTAIL
LAMPARA MALINES NETWORK
PROTECT RETICLE RINSING SCRINGE
SHELTER SPILLER STALKER TRAINEL
TRAMMEL MESHWORK SALAMBAO
BUCKSTALL RETICULUM
(PREF.) DICTY(O) DIKTYO(N) RETI
RETINO
NETHANEEL (BROTHER OF —)
DAVID
(FATHER OF —) ZUAR JESSE
OBEDEDOM
(SON OF —) SHEMAIAH
NETHANIAH (FATHER OF —) ASAPH
ELISHAMA
(SON OF —) JEHUDI ISHMAEL
NETHER DOWN BELOW LOWER
UNDER NEDDER DOWNWARD
INFERIOR INFERNAL

NETHERLANDS

CANAL: ORANJE JULIANA DRENTSCH
CAPITAL: AMSTERDAM
CHEESE: EDAM GOUDA LEYDEN
COIN: CENT DOIT RYDER FLORIN
GULDEN STIVER DUCATON ESCALIN
GUILDER STOOTER
ISLAND: TEXEL MARKEN AMELAND
VLIELAND
MEASURE: EL AAM AHM AUM ELL
KAN MUD VAT ZAK DUIM LOOD MIJL
ROOD ROPE VOET ANKER CARAT
ROEDE STOOP WISSE BUNDER
KOPPEN LEGGER MAATJE MUDDLE
MUTSJE STREEP SCHEPEL
MINGELEN OKSHOOFD STEEKKAN
NAME: HOLLAND
NATIVE: DUTCH DUTCHMAN
PROVINCE: DRENTHE LIMBURG
UTRECHT ZEELAND FRIESLAND
GRONINGEN GELDERLAND
OVERIJSSEL
RIVER: EEMS LECK MAAS WAAL YSEL
DONGE HUNSE YSSEL DINTEL
DOMMEL KROMME MEAUSE
SCHELDT
TOWN: EDE ASSEN BREDA HAGUE
AALTEN ARNHEM LEIDEN ZWOLLE
HAARLEM TILBURG UTRECHT
AALSMEER ENSCHEDE NIJMEGEN
AMSTERDAM EINDHOVEN
GRONINGEN ROTTERDAM
WEIGHT: ONS LAST LOOD POND
BAHAR GREIN KORREL WICHTJE
ESTERLIN

NETHERWORLD HADES SHADES
NETLIKE MESHY NETTY RETIARY
RETICULAR
NETTING BAR CAUL LING MESH
TULLE SCREEN DEEPING FISHNET
FOOTING BOBBINET WIREWORK
NETTLE VEX FRET LINE ANNOY
CNIDA ETTLE PEEVF PIQUE STING
HENBIT ORTIGA RUFFLE SPLICE
URTICA AFFRONT BLUBBER BLUETOP
KNITTLE PROVOKE STINGER IRRITATE
CLOWNHEAL GLIDEWORT PELLITORY
SMARTWEED
(— RASH) HIVES UREDO URTICARIA
(— TREE) LOTUS GYMPIE
(WHITE DEAD —) ARCHANGEL
(PREF.) CNID(O)
NETTLERASH HIVES
NETWORK WEB CAUL FRET GRID
KELL MAZE MESH MOKE RETE CHAIN
LACIS BRIDGE COBWEB CRADLE
PLEXUS RESEAU SAGENE SYSTEM
DRAGNET DIPLEXER GRIDIRON
KNITTING WATTLING RETICULUM
(— OF BLOOD VESSELS) RETE
TOMENTUM
(— OF CRACKS) CRACKLE
(— OF LINES) RETICLE
(— OF REFRACTORY MATERIALS)
MANTLE
(— ON MAP) GRATICULE
(COMPUTER —) LAN
(NUCLEAR —) SKEIN
(PL.) RETIA
NEUME PES VIRGA CLIVIS PNEUMA
PODATUS PUNCTUM VIRGULA
CLIMACUS QUILISMA SEQUENCE
TORCULUS SCANDICUS
NEURAL DORSAL NERVAL NEURIC
NEURALGIA SCIATICA COSTALGIA
NEURILEMMA
(PREF.) LEMMO
NEURITE AXON AXONE
NEURITIS SCIATICA
NEUROGLIAL
(PREF.) GLI(O)
NEUROLOGIST AMERICAN BEARD
DERCUM PRINCE COLLINS CORNING
MERRITT MITCHELL

AUSTRIAN FREUD
ENGLISH ASH GOWERS JACKSON
FRENCH RAYMOND DEJERINE
GERMAN NISSL GUDDEN MOBIUS
ALZHEIMER
ITALIAN GOLGI
PORTUGUESE MONIZ
SCOTTISH FERRIER
NEUROTIC DRUG NERVOUS
(— CONDITION) LATAH
NEUTRAL GRAY INERT SWEET
AMORAL MIDDLING NEGATIVE
UNBIASED COLORLESS IMPARTIAL
(— IN COLOR) SOBER
(OPTICALLY —) INACTIVE
NEUTRALIZE KILL ANNUL BLUNT
ERASE CANCEL ABOLISH BALANCE
CORRECT DESTROY NULLIFY VITIATE
NEGATIVE OVERRIDE SATURATE
FRUSTRATE
NEUTRINO LEPTON

NEVADA
CAPITAL: CARSONCITY
COUNTY: NYE ELKO LANDER STOREY
WASHOE MINERAL PERSHING
INDIAN: WASHO PAIUTE
LAKE: MUD MEAD RUBY TAHOE
WALKER PYRAMID WINNEMUCCA
PEAK: BOUNDARY
RIVER: REESE TRUCKEE HUMBOLDT
STATE BIRD: BLUEBIRD
STATE FLOWER: SAGEBRUSH
STATE NICKNAME: SILVER
SAGEBRUSH
STATE TREE: ASPEN
TOWN: ELY ELKO RENO EUREKA
FALLON NELLIS PIOCHE SPARKS
TONOPAH LASVEGAS LOVELOCK

NEVE ICE FIRN SNOW NEPHEW
GLACIER
NEVER NAY NIE NOT NARY NARRA
NIVER NOWHEN
NEVER-NEVER DREAMLAND
NEVERTHELESS BUT YET STILL
ALWISE THOUGH ALGATES HOWBEIT
HOWEVER WHETHER NATHELESS
NONETHELESS
NEVUS MOLE SPOT TUMOR NAEVUS
SPIDER SPILUS FRECKLE LENTIGO
SPILOMA BIRTHMARK
NEW HOT NEO NEU RAW LATE MINT
NOVA FRESH GREEN MOIST NOVEL
YOUNG MODERN RECENT REDHOT
UNUSED VIRGIN ANOTHER FOREIGN
STRANGE UNTRIED UPSTART
INITIATE NEOTERIC ORIGINAL
YOUTHFUL BEGINNING
(— BUT YET OLD) NOVANTIQUE
(BRAND —) SPICK
(COMB. FORM) NEO
(LOVE OF WHAT IS —) NEOPHILIA

(PREF.) CAEN(O) CEN(O) NE(O) NOV(I)
(O)
(SUFF.) CENE
NEWBORN YEANLING
NEW BRUNSWICK
(CAPITAL OF —) FREDERICTON
(COUNTY OF —) KINGS QUEENS
SUNBURY MADAWASKA
(MOUNTAIN OF —) CARLETON
(TOWN OF —) BURTON MONCTON
BATHURST GAGETOWN
NEW CALEDONIA (— BIRD) KAGU
(CAPITAL OF —) NOUMEA
(ISLAND OF —) HUON BELEP DEPINS
LOYALTY WALPOLE
(SEAPORT OF —) NOUMEA
NEWCASTLE GOTHAM
NEWCOMER CADET SETTLER
COMELING FRESHMAN JACKEROO
MALIHINI RINGNECK GREENHORN
IMMIGRANT KIMBERLIN
(— IN EAST) GRIFFIN GRIFFON
NEWCOMES (AUTHOR OF —)
THACKERAY
(CHARACTER IN —) ANN KEW JOHN
BRIAN CLARA CLIVE ETHEL JAMES
ROSEY ALFRED BARNES BINNIE
HOBSON RIDLEY THOMAS
NEWCOME PULLEYN FARINTOSH
MACKENZIE
NEW DEAL (— AGENCY) CCC NRA
NYA TVA WPA
NEWEL POST VICE SPINDLE
NEW ENGLAND (— INHABITANT)
YANK YANKEE JONATHAN
(— SETTLER) PILGRIM PURITAN
NEW-FANGLED UPSTART
NEWFANGLED MODERN
NEWFOUNDLAND (— CAPE) RAY
RACE BAULD
(— HOUSE) TILT
(— INHABITANT) OUTPORTER
(CAPITAL OF —) STJOHNS
(ISLAND OF —) BELL FOGO GROAIS
MIQUELON
(RIVER OF —) GANDER HUMBER
EXPLOITS
(TOWN OF —) GANDER HOWLEY
WABANA CORNERBROOK

NEW GUINEA
BAY: ORO MILNE HOLNICOTE
GOODENOUGH COLLINGWOOD
CAPITAL: PORTMORESBY
COIN: KINA
GULF: HUON PAPUA
ISLAND: BUKA MANUS MUSSAU
ISLAND GROUP: CRETIN NINIGO
SAINSON SOLOMON
MONEY: KINA TOEA
MOUNTAIN: ALBERT VICTORIA
NATIVE: ARAU BOONG KARON
PAPUAN

PORT: LAE DARU WEWAK MADANG
RIVER: FLY HAMU SEPIK KIKORI
  PURARI AMBERNO
TOWN: LAE WAU DARU SORON
  AITAPE KIKORI RABAUL SAMARAI

NEW HAMPSHIRE
CAPITAL: CONCORD
COLLEGE: DARTMOUTH
COUNTY: COOS BELKNAP GRAFTON
  MERRIMACK
LAKE: SQUAM OSSIPEE SUNAPEE
  UMBAGOG WINNIPESAUKEE
MOUNTAIN: MORIAH PAUGUS
  WAUMBEK CHOCORUA
  MONADNOCK
MOUNTAIN RANGE: WHITE
NOTCH: CRAWFORD FRANCONIA
PRESIDENT: PIERCE
RIVER: SACO ISRAEL BELLAMY
  SOUHEGAN MERRIMACK
  PISCATAQUA
STATE NICKNAME: GRANITE
TOWN: DOVER KEENE EXETER
  NASHUA HANOVER LACONIA
  OSSIPEE

NEW HEBRIDES (CAPITAL OF —)
  VILA
  (ISLAND OF —) EPI TANA EFATE
  MAEWO MABRIM MALEKULA

NEW JERSEY
CAPITAL: TRENTON
COLLEGE: UPSALA
COUNTY: ESSEX OCEAN SALEM
  UNION BERGEN CAMDEN MERCER
  MORRIS SUSSEX WARREN PASSAIC
  MONMOUTH
INDIAN: DELAWARE
PRESIDENT: CLEVELAND
RIVER: DENNIS HAYNES MANTUA
  RAMAPO MULLICA PASSAIC
  RARITAN COHANSEY TUCKAHOE
STATE BIRD: GOLDFINCH
STATE FLOWER: VIOLET
STATE NICKNAME: GARDEN
STATE TREE: REDOAK
TOWN: LODI SALEM CAMDEN
  NEWARK NEWTON NUTLEY
  RAHWAY TOTOWA BAYONNE
  CLIFTON HOBOKEN HOHOKUS
  MATAWAN NETCONG ORADELL
  PARAMUS PASSAIC TEANECK
  TENAFLY TRENTON WYCKOFF
  CARTERET FREEHOLD METUCHEN
  PATERSON SECAUCUS WATCHUNG
  HACKENSACK
UNIVERSITY: RUTGERS PRINCETON

NEWLY ANEW AGAIN AFRESH LATELY
  FRESHLY NEWLINS RECENTLY

NEWMARKET MICHIGAN
  SARATOGA GRABOUCHE

NEW MEXICO
CAPITAL: SANTAFE
COUNTY: LEA EDDY LUNA MORA
  QUAY TAOS OTERO CATRON
  CHAVES DEBACA HIDALGO
  SOCORRO VALENCIA
CULTURE: MIMBRES
INDIAN: SIA TANO TEWA TIWA ZUNI
  JEMEZ PECOS APACHE NAVAHO
  NAVAJO PUEBLO
MOUNTAIN: WHEELER
RIVER: UTE GILA PECOS SAN
  JOSE
STATE BIRD: ROADRUNNER
STATE FLOWER: YUCCA
STATE NICKNAME: SUNSHINE
  LANDOFENCHANTMENT
STATE TREE: PINON PINYON
TOWN: JAL MORA AZTEC BELEN
  RATON CLOVIS DEMING GALLUP
  GRANTS ARTESIA SANTAFE
  SOCORRO CARLSBAD LASVEGAS
  TUCUMCARI ALAMOGORDO

NEWNESS NOVITY
NEWS BUZZ DOPE UNCA UNKO
  WORD CLASH FERLY ADVICE BUDGET
  CRACKS FERLIE GOSPEL NOTICE
  REPORT EVANGEL KHUBBER TIDINGS
  WITTING NOUVELLE KNOWLEDGE
  SPEERINGS
  (— AGENCY) AP UP DNB INS UPI
  TASS ANETA DOMEI REUTERS
  (— BEAT) SCOOP
  (— INTERRUPTION) UPDATE
  (— ITEM) FACTOID
NEWSBOY NEWSY CAMELOT
  CARRIER PAPERBOY
NEWSCASTER ANCHORMAN
NEWSMONGER GOSSIP TATTLER
  NOVELANT NOVELIST QUIDNUNC
  REPORTER
NEWSPAPER RAG NEWS DAILY
  ORGAN PAPER PRESS SHEET TIMES
  ARRIBA HERALD SERIAL SUNDAY
  COURANT DIURNAL GAZETTE
  JOURNAL MERCURY TABLOID
  TRIBUNE NEWSPRINT
  (— EDITION) EXTRA FINAL
  (— SECTION) ROTO METRO
  (— USED BY PICKPOCKET) STIFF
  (FEEBLE —) SQUEAK
  (SECTION OF —) ROTO
  (PL.) PRESS
NEWSPAPERMAN HEARST
  PRESSMAN
NEWSPERSON REPORTER
NEWSSTAND BOOTH KIOSK STALL
  STAND BOOKSTALL

NEWSWORTHY NEWSY
NEWT ASK EFT ESK EVET EBBET
EFFET LIZARD TRITON AXOLOTL
CRAWLER CREEPER REPTILE
MANKEEPER
NEW YEAR'S DAY NAURUZ
NOROOSE NOWROZE
NEW YEAR'S EVE HAGMENA
HOGMANAY

NEW YORK

AVENUE: PARK FIFTH MADISON
FLATBUSH
BAY: JAMAICA PECONIC MORICHES
BOROUGH: BRONX KINGS QUEENS
BROOKLYN MANHATTAN
BUILDING: RCA PANAM CHRYSLER
FLATIRON
CANAL: ERIE GOWANUS
CAPITAL: ALBANY
COLLEGE: RARD CCNY IONA PACE
FINCH UNION HUNTER VASSAR
WAGNER ADEI PHI BARNARD
CANISIUS HAMILTON SKIDMORE
COUNTY: ERIE BRONX ESSEX KINGS
TIOGA WAYNE YATES BROOME
CAYUGA NASSAU ONEIDA OSWEGO
OTSEGO PUTNAM QUEENS SENECA
ULSTER CHEMUNG GENESEE
NIAGARA STEUBEN SUFFOLK
CHENANGO DUTCHESS HERKIMER
ONONDAGA RICHMOND ROCKLAND
SARATOGA SCHUYLER
INDIAN: CAYUGA MOHAWK ONEIDA
SENECA MOHICAN MONTAUK
IROQUOIS ONONDAGA
ISLAND: FIRE LONG ELLIS STATEN
FISHERS LIBERTY SHELTER
GOVERNORS MANHATTAN
LAKE: ERIE CAYUGA GEORGE ONEIDA
OTISCO OTSEGO OWASCO PLACID
SENECA CONESUS HONEOYE
ONTARIO SARANAC SCHROON
SUCCESS SARATOGA
MOUNTAIN: BEAR MARCY
MOUNTAINS: TACONIC CATSKILL
ADIRONDACK
NICKNAME: EMPIRE GOTHAM
PRESIDENT: FILLMORE VANBUREN
ROOSEVELT
PRISON: TOMBS ATTICA SINGSING
RIVER: TIOGA HARLEM HOOSIC
HUDSON MOHAWK OSWEGO
GENESEE NIAGARA
SQUARE: TIMES UNION HERALD
MADISON
STATE BIRD: BLUEBIRD
STATE FLOWER: ROSE
STATE NICKNAME: EMPIRE
EXCELSIOR
STATE TREE: SUGARMAPLE
STREET: WALL BOWERY BROADWAY

SUBWAY: BMT IND IRT LEX
TOWN: RYE OVID ROME DELHI ILION
ISLIP NYACK OLEAN OWEGO UTICA
ATTICA AUBURN CARMEL COHOES
ELMIRA GOSHEN ITHACA MALONE
ONEIDA OSWEGO TAPPAN WARSAW
ARDSLEY BABYLON BATAVIA
BUFFALO CONGERS ENDWELL
GENESEO HEWLETT MAHOPAC
MASSENA MERRICK MINEOLA
MONTAUK ONEONTA PENNYAN
POTSDAM SUFFERN SYOSSET
WANTAGH YAPHANK YONKERS
BETHPAGE CATSKILL HERKIMER
KINGSTON OSSINING SYRACUSE
TUCKAHOE ROCHESTER
UNIVERSITY: LIU NYU ADELPHI
COLGATE CORNELL FORDHAM
HOFSTRA YESHIVA COLUMBIA
WATERFALL: NIAGARA

NEW YORK CITY (BOROUGH OF —)
BRONX QUEENS BROOKLYN
MANHATTAN STATENISLAND
(COUNTY OF —) BRONX KINGS
QUEENS RICHMOND
(ISLAND OF —) WARD ELLIS
RANDALL WELFARE
(PARK OF —) GRANT BRYANT
BATTERY CENTRAL
(SUBWAY OF —) BMT IND IRT

NEW ZEALAND

BAY: OHUA HAWKE LYALL AWARUA
CLOUDY GOLDEN FITZROY
PEGASUS POVERTY DANGAUNU
CAPE: EGMONT FAREWELL PALLISER
CAPITAL: WELLINGTON
GULF: HAURAKI
ISLAND: OTEA STEWART PUKETUTU
LAKE: OHAU HAWEA TAUPO PUKAKI
PUPUKE TEANAU TEKAPO WANAKA
BRUNNER ROTORUA WAKATIPU
MOUNTAIN: COOK FLAT OWEN CHOPE
LYALL MITRE OTARI EGMONT
STOKES AORANGI PIHANGA
TUTAMOE TYNDALL ASPIRING
EARNSLAW
NATIVE: ATI ARAWA MAORI RINGATU
PENINSULA: MAHIA OTAGO
RIVER: MOKAU ORETI WAIPA CLUTHA
TAIERI TAMAKI WAIHOU WAIROA
MATAURA WAIKATO WAITAKI
CLARENCE MANAWATU WANGANUI
RANGITIKEI
STRAIT: COOK FOVEAUX
TOWN: LEVIN ORETI OTAKI TAUPO
CLUTHA FOXTON NAPIER NELSON
OAMARU PICTON TIMARU DUNEDIN
MANUKAU RAETIHI ROTORUA
AUCKLAND HAMILTON KAWAKAWA
CHRISTCHURCH

VOLCANO: RUAPEHU NGAURUHOE
TONGARIRO
WATERFALL: BOWEN HELENA
STIRLING SUTHERLAND

NEW ZEALANDER KIWI ENZED
DIGGER
NEXT POI NEAR SYNE THEN UNTO
WISE AFTER EWEST FIRST LATER
NEIST RIGHT BESIDE COMING
SECOND TIDDER TOTHER CLOSEST
NEAREST DIRECTLY PROCHAIN
PROCHEIN UPCOMING ADJOINING
IMMEDIATE
(— AFTER) THEN FOLLOWING
(— IN ORDER) EKA
(— MONTH) PROXIMO
(— OF KIN) GOEL
(— TO LAST) PENULT
(PREF.) (— IN ORDER) EKA
NEXUS TIE BOND LINK CHAIN
NGAIO KIO KAIO NAIO TREE
NHANG GIAI
NIAM-NIAM ZANDE AZANDE
AZANDI ZANDEH AZANDEH
BABUNGERA
NIB NEB PEN BEAK BILL KINK TEAT
POINT PRONG SCORER
NIBBLE EAT NAB NIB NIP BITE GNAW
KNAB KNAP MOOP MOUP NOSH
PECK PICK CHAMP GNARL MOUSE
PIECE SHEAR ARRODE BROWSE
CHAVEL NATTLE PICKLE PILFER
CHIMBLE GNABBLE GNATTER
KNABBLE SNAGGLE
NIBELUNGENLIED (AUTHOR OF —)
UNKNOWN
(CHARACTER IN —) UTA ETZEL
HAGEN IRING GERNOT HUNOLD
LUDGER BLOEDEL GUNTHER
ORTLIEB BRUNHILD DANKWART
DIETRICH GISELHER KRIEMHILD
SIEGFRIED HILDEBRAND
NIBLICK BLASTER
NICANOR (WIFE OF —)
CLEOPATRA

NICARAGUA
CAPITAL: MANAGUA
COIN: PESO CENTAVO CORDOBA
DEPARTMENT: LEON BOACO RIVAS
CARAZO ESTELI MADRIZ MASAYA
ZELAYA MANAGUA
ISLAND: OMETEPE
LAKE: MANAGUA
MEASURE: VARA CAHIZ MILLA SUERTE
TERCIA CAJUELA ESTADAL
MANZANA
MOUNTAIN: MADERA MOGOTON
PORT: CORINTO
RIVER: COCO TUMA WANKS GRANDE
ESCONDIDO

TOWN: LEON BOACO RIVAS MASAYA
OCOTAL SOMOTO GRANADA
MANAGUA JINOTEGA MATAGALPA
CHINANDEGA
WEIGHT: BAG CAJA TONELADA

NICCOLITE ARITE KUPFERNICKEL
NICE APT FIT FEAT FINE GOOD JUMP
KIND NEAT NYCE PURE TRIM CANNY
EXACT FUSSY NIECE SWEET BONITA
BONITO DAINTY GENTIL MINUTE
PEACHY QUAINT QUEASY SPICED
STRICT SUBTLE TICKLE CORRECT
ELEGANT FINICAL GENTEEL MINCING
PERJINK PICKING PRECISE PRUDISH
REFINED DECOROUS DELICATE
EXACTING PLEASANT PLEASING
TICKLISH PARTICULAR
SCRUMPTIOUS
(TOO —) SUPERFINE
(PREF.) (PERTAINING TO —) NICENO
NICELY JUMP
NICETY HAIR QUIDDIT DELICACY
JUSTNESS QUIDDITY CRITICISM
CURIOSITY PRECISION
(PL.) PERJINKITIES
NICHE BAY WRO APSE CANT COVE
NOOK SLOT AMBRY HERNE HOVEL
NIECE NITCH PLACE ALCOVE
ANCONA BOXING COVERT CRANNY
EXEDRA GROOVE MIHRAB RECESS
RINCON EDICULE HOUSING RETREAT
ROUNDEL AEDICULA CREDENCE
TOKONOMA HABITACLE
PIGEONHOLE TABERNACLE
NICHOLAS NICKLEBY (AUTHOR OF
—) DICKENS
(CHARACTER IN —) BRAY HAWK KATE
FRANK GRIDE NOGGS RALPH SMIKE
NEWMAN SQUEERS VINCENT
CRUMMLES MADELINE MULBERRY
NICHOLAS NICKLEBY WACKFORD
CHEERYBLE MANTALINI
NICIPPE (FATHER OF —) PELOPS
(HUSBAND OF —) STHENELUS
(MOTHER OF —) HIPPODAMIA
(SON OF —) EURYSTHEUS
NICK CUT JAG MAR NAG NOB CHIP
DENT DINT HACK NACK SLAP SLIT
CHEAT CHICK GOUGE NITCH NOTCH
PRICK SCORE SLACK SNICK TALLY
TRICK ARREST RECORD DEFRAUD
(— OF TIME) GODSPEED
NICKEL JIT COIN JITNEY NIMBUS
(ALLOY OF —) INVAR KONEL MONEL
(CONTAINING —) NICCOLIC
(SYMBOL OF —) NI
(WOODEN —) SLUG
NICKELODEON JUKEBOX
NICKEL-SILVER PAKFONG PAKTONG
PACKFONG
NICKER NEIGHER

NICKNAME DUB TAG DOEG NICK ALIAS AGNAME BYNAME BYWORD HANDLE MONICA TONAME AGNOMEN CRACKER EKENAME MISNAME MONIKER NICKERY COGNOMEN MONARCHO MONICKER TARTUFFE SOBRIQUET
NICKNAMING PROSONOMASIA
NICOMEDE (HALF-BROTHER OF —) ATTALE
(STEPMOTHER OF —) ARSINOE
NICOSTRATA (FATHER OF —) LADON
(HUSBAND OF —) ECHENUS
(SON OF —) EVANDER
NICOSTRATUS (BROTHER OF —) MEGAPENTHES
(FATHER OF —) MENELAUS
(MOTHER OF —) HELEN
NICOTINIC ACID NIACIN
NICTATE WINK BLINK CLOSE TWINK TWINKLE NICTITATE
NIDDICK NAPE
NIDE NID NEST BROOD LITTER
NIDGE NIG SHAKE QUIVER
NIDGET HOE FOOL IDIOT
NIDIFY NEST
NIDOR ODOR AROMA SAVOR SCENT SMELL
NIDUS NEST
NIECE OY OYE NEPHEW
NIELLO TULA
NIEPA NIOTA KARINGHOTA
NIEVE FIST HAND NEIF SERF NATIVE
NIFTY FINE GOOD KEEN SMART STYLISH
NIGER JOLIBA KWORRA RAMTIL
(CAPITAL OF —) NIAMEY
(MOUTH OF —) NUN
(NATIVE OF —) PEUL HAUSA DJERMA FULANI SONGHA TOUBOU TUAREG
(OASIS IN —) KAOUAR
(REGION OF —) AIR
(RIVER OF —) DILLIA
(TOWN OF —) SAY GAYA TERA BAGAM FACHI GOURE MADAMA MARADI TAHOUA ZINDER

NIGERIA
CAPITAL: LAGOS
COIN: KOBO NAIRA
NATIVE: ARO EBO EDO IBO IJO VAI BENI EBOE EFIK EJAM EKOI NUPE BENIN HAUSA FULANI YORUBA
PLATEAU: JOS
PORT: LAGOS CALABAR
PROVINCE: ISA OYO KANO NUPE ONDO IJEBU OGOJA WARRI OWERRI ADAMAWA
RIVER: OLI GANA YOBE BENUE NIGER KADUNA SOKOTO GONGOLA HADEJIA KOMADUGU
STATE: IMO OYO KANO OGUN ONDO BENUE BORNO KWARA LAGOS BAUCHI SOKOTO ANAMBRA GONGOLA
TOWN: ABA ADO EDE IFE ISA IWO JOS BIDI BUEA KANO OFFA YOLA AKURE ENUGU IKEJA LAGOS MINNA ZARIA BAUCHI IBADAN ILESHA ILORIN KADUNA MUSHIN OWERRI TAKOBA CALABAR ONITSHA OSHOGBO ABEOKUTA
TREE: AFARA

NIGGARD CARL CHURL CLOSE MISER NIGON PIKER SCART TIGHT NIGGER SCRIMP SCRUNT STINGY CHINCHE DRYFIST NITHING SCROOGE PINCHGUT PUCKFIST SCRIMPER EARTHWORM PINCHBECK PINCHFIST PUCKFOIST SKINFLINT PINCHPENNY
NIGGARDLY MEAN CLOSE NIRLY STINT NARROW NIDING NIGHLY NIRLED SCANTY SCREWY SKIMPY SORDID STINGY STRAIT CHINCHE COSTIVE MISERLY NITHING PENURIOUS PARSIMONIOUS
NIGGERFISH CONY HIND CONEY GROUPER GUATIVERE
NIGGLE DOUBT
NIGGLER NITPICKER
NIGGLING PETTY PICAYUNE
NIGH AT NEAR ANEAR ANIGH CLOSE ALMOST NEARLY ADJACENT
NIGHT PM EVE DARK NUIT SOIR DARKY DEATH NACHT NOCHE SLEEP DARKMANS DARKNESS
(— AND DAY) NYCHTHEMERON
(CHILDREN OF —) ERINYS FURIES ERINNYES
(COMB. FORM) NYCTI
(DEPTH OF —) HOLL
(GODDESS OF —) NOX NYX
(LAST —) YESTREEN
(NORSE —) NATT NOTT
(PERT. TO —) NOCTURNAL
(STAY OUT ALL —) PERNOCTATE
(PREF.) NOCT(I)(O) NYCT(I)(O)
NIGHT APE DURUKULI
NIGHT BELL (CHARACTER IN —) ENRICO SERAFINA PISTACCHIO
(COMPOSER OF —) DONIZETTI
NIGHT BLINDNESS NYCTALOPIA
NIGHTCAP HOW COWL DOWD HOUVE PIRNY BIGGIN PIRNIE DORMEUSE SUNDOWNER
NIGHTCLUB CAFE CLUB SPOT AGOGO BOITE DISCO BISTRO NITERY CABARET DANCERY NIGHTERY
NIGHTDRESS SLOP WILYCOAT WYLIECOAT

NIGHTFALL EEN EVE DARK DUSK
EVEN SHUTTING TWILIGHT
(OCCURRING AT —) ACRONICAL
NIGHTGOWN SLOP TOOSH NIGHTY
BEDGOWN NIGHTIE WYLIECOAT
NIGHTHAWK PISK CUIEJO BULLBAT
NIGHTINGALE JUG BULBUL
FLORENCE PHILOMEL ROSSIGNOL
(— SOUND) JUG
(SWEDISH —) LIND JENNY
(PL.) WATCH
NIGHTJAR PUCK POTOO EVEJAR
DERHAWK SPINNER WHEELER
MOREPORK POORWILL NIGHTHAWK
NIGHT LAMP VEILLEUSE
NIGHTMARE ALP HAG MARA MESS
DREAM FANCY FIEND VISION
INCUBUS CACODEMON CAUCHEMAR
EPHIALTES
(— CAUSER) MARE
NIGHTMARE ABBEY (AUTHOR OF
—) PEACOCK
(CHARACTER IN —) EMILY FATOUT
FLOSKY GLOWRY STELLA TOOBAD
CELINDA CYPRESS ASTERIAS
LISTLESS SCYTHROP GIROUETTE
MARIONETTA CHRISTOPHER
NIGHTSHADE HERB DWALE MOREL
TOMATO HENBANE MORELLE
PETUNIA SANDBUR SOLANUM
MANDRAKE TROMPILLO
NIGHT'S LODGING (AUTHOR OF —)
GORKY
(CHARACTER IN —) LUKA BARON
PEPEL SAHTIN BUBNOFF NATASHA
ALYOSCHKA KVASCHNYA KOSTILIOFF
WASSILISSA
NIGHT WATCHMAN CHARLEY
CHARLIE
NIGHTWEAR PJS JAMMIES
PAJAMAS
NIHIL NIL NICHIL NOTHING
NIHILIST ANARCHIST SOCIALIST
NIKE VICTORY
(BROTHER OF —) BIA ZELUS CRATOS
(FATHER OF —) PALLAS
(MOTHER OF —) STYX
NIL ZERO NILGAI IPOMOEA NOTHING

NILE
ARABIC NAME: ALBAHR
AS GOD: HAPI
BIRD: IBIS WRYNECK
BOAT: BARIS CANGIA NUGGAR
DAHABEAH
CAPTAIN: RAIS REIS
DAM: ASWAN
FALLS: RIPON
FISH: BAGRE SAIDE BICHIB DOCMAC
MORMYRID MORMYROID
ISLAND: RODA PHILAE
LATIN NAME: NILUS
NATIVE: MADI NILOT
NEGRO: JUR LUO LWO SUK
PLANT: SUDD LOTUS
REGION: NUBIA
SOURCE: TANA TSANA
TOWN: QUS ABRI ARGO IDFU ISNA
QINA ASYUT CAIRO REJAF SAITE
ROSETTA
TRIBUTARY: ATBARA KAGERA
VALLEY DEPRESSION: KORE

NILE GREEN BOA
NILGAI NIL NYLGAU ANTELOPE
NEELGHAU
NIMBLE FLY DEFT FLIP FLIT GLEG
LISH SPRY SWAK YALD YARE AGILE
BRISK FLEET LIGHT NIPPY QUICK
SWACK TRICK WIGHT YAULD ACTIVE
ADROIT CLEVER FEIRIE LIMBER
LISSOM LIVELY PROMPT QUIVER
SPRACK SUPPLE VOLANT WANDLE
DELIVER LISSOME SWIPPER
FLIPPANT TRIPPING CITIGRADE
SENSITIVE SPRIGHTLY
(PREF.) PRESTI
NIMBLENESS HASTE AGILITY
SLEIGHT LEGERITY DEXTERITY
LIGHTNESS
NIMBLE-WITTED VOLABLE
NIMBUS AURA HALO NIMB CLOUD
GLORY SHINE VAPOR GLORIA
AUREOLA AUREOLE
NIMIETY EXCESS
NINAZU (BROTHER OF —) NERGAL
(FATHER OF —) ENLIL
(MOTHER OF —) NINLIL
NINCOMPOOP ASS BOOB DOLT
FOOL POOP NINNY NINCOM WITLING
BLOCKHEAD SIMPLETON
NINE IX NIE NYE TEAM COMET
POTHOOK
(— A.M.) UNDERN MIDMORN
(— ANGLED FIGURE) NONAGON
(— DAYS DEVOTION) NOVENA
(— FOLD) NONUPLE
(— HEADED MONSTER) HYDRA
(— HUNDRED) SAN
(— INCHES) SPAN
(— OF CLUBS OR DIAMONDS) COMET
(— OF DIAMONDS) BRAGGER
(— OF TRUMPS) DIX MENEL SANCHO
(— YEAR CYCLE) JUGLAR
(GROUP OF —) ENNEAD
(MUSIC FOR —) NONET
(PREF.) ENNE(A) NON(A) NOVEM
NOVEN
NINEBARK ROSACEAN SEVENBARK
NINEHOLES BUMBLEPUPPY
NINEPIN KAIL SQUAIL SKITTLE
SKITTLES
(PL.) BOWLS KEELS KAYLES
NINEPEGS
NINETEENTH LARIGOT
NINETIETH NONAGESIMAL

NINETY KOPPA
NINEVEH (FOUNDER OF —) NINUS
NINE WORLDS HEL ASGARD
AI FHEIM MIDGARD NIFLHEIM
VANAHEIM JOTUNNHEIM
MUSPELLSHEIM SVARTALFAHEIM
NINLIL (HUSBAND OF —) ENLIL
(SON OF —) NERGAL NINAZU
NINNI ISHTAR
NINNY DOLT FOOL LOUT DUNCE
GOOSE IDIOT NONNY PATCH SAMMY
SPOON FONDLE NOODLE SAPHEAD
FONDLING BLOCKHEAD NIDDICOCK
PEAKGOOSE SIMPLETON
NINON SHEER
NINSUN (SON OF —) GILGAMESH
NINTH (EVERY —) NONAN ENNEATIC
(PREF.) NON(A)
NINTU (DAUGHTER OF —) UTTU
(HUSBAND OF —) ENKI
(SON OF —) NINSAR
NINURTA (FATHER OF —) ENLIL
NINUS (FATHER OF —) DCLUO
(SON OF —) NINYAS
(WIFE OF —) SEMIRAMIS
NIOBATE TODDITE SIPYLITE
COLUMBATE
NIOBE HERB,HOSTA FUNKIA
(BROTHER OF —) PELOPS
(FATHER OF —) TANTALUS
(HUSBAND OF —) AMPHION
(SISTER-IN-LAW OF —) AEDON
NIOBIC COLUMBIC
NIOBIUM COLUMBIUM
NIP CUT SIP VEX BITE BUMP CLIP
DRAM GIVE KNIP NIPE PECK SNUB
TANG TAUT TUCK BLAST CHEAT
CHECK CHILL CLAMP DRAFT FROST
PINCH SEIZE SEVER SNAPE SNEAP
THIEF BENUMB BLIGHT CATNIP
TIPPLE TWITCH WITHER SARCASM
SQUEEZE WETTING COMPRESS
FROSTBITE VELLICATE
NIPA PALM ATAP ATTAP DRINK
NIPPER BOY LAD CLAW CRAB GRAB
HAND BITER CHELA MISER THIEF
CUNNER URCHIN GRIPPER INCISOR
BRAKEMAN
NIPPERS DOG NIP BITS NIPS TONGS
GRATER PLIERS TURKIS FORCEPS
PINCERS OSTEOTOME
NIPPLE BUD DUG PAP TIT BEAN TEAT
DIDDY DUMMY SPEAN NIBBLE
PILLAR MAMILLA PAPILLA THELIUM
(— POINT) THELION
(PREF.) EPITHELI(O) MAMM(I)(ILLI)
MAST(O) PAPILLI PAPILLO THEL(O)
NIPPLEWORT BALLOGAN
WARTWEED WARTWORT
NIPPY BOLD SHARP
NIREUS (FATHER OF —) CHAROPUS
(MOTHER OF —) AGLAIA
(SLAYER OF —) EURYPYLUS

NIRVANA EDEN EMPTINESS
NIS NIX NISSE GOBLIN KOBOLD
BROWNIE
NISAN ARIB
NISEI (— SON OR DAUGHTER) SANSEI
NISUS POWER EFFORT IMPULSE
ENDEAVOR
(DAUGHTER OF —) SCYLLA
(FATHER OF —) PANDION HYRTACUS
(MOTHER OF —) IDA
NITER NITRE PETER PETRE POTASH
SALTPETER
NITHER BLAST DEBASE SHIVER
TREMBLE
NITID GAY BRIGHT GLOSSY SPRUCE
SHINING LUSTROUS NITIDOUS
NITO AGSAM
NITON RADON
NITRATE SALT ESTER COTTON
AZOTATE
(PREF.) NITR(O)
NITRIC AZOTIC
NITRIDE BORAZON
NITRITE AZOTITE
NITROGEN GAS AZOTE ALKALIGEN
(PREF.) AZ(O)
NITROGLYCERIN TNT SOUP NITRO
SIRUP SYRUP GLONOIN GLONOINE
NITWIT DAW NIT BOOB DINK DOLT
DOPE KOOK DRONGO DINGBAT
DIZZARD DINGALING SIMPLETON
NIX NO HARD NECK NICKER NOBODY
SPIRIT SPRITE UNDINE NOTHING
NJAVE ADJAB DIAVE
NJORD (DAUGHTER OF —) FREYA
(SON OF —) FREY
(WIFE OF —) SKADHI
NO NA NE NAE NAH NAW NAY NIT NIX
NUL BAAL BAIL BALE NEIN NONE
NYET NAPOO AIKONA NAPOOH
NOGAKU
(— MORE) NAPOO
(— ONE) NIX NEMO
(— POINTS IN TENNIS) LOVE
(PREF.) NULLI
NOADIAH (FATHER OF —) BINNUI
NOAH NOE
(DOVE OF —) COLUMBA
(FATHER OF —) LAMECH
ZELOPHEHAD
(GRANDFATHER OF —) METHUSALEH
(GRANDSON OF —) ARAM MAGOG
(GREAT-GRANDSON OF —) HUL
(MEXICAN —) COXCOX
(RAVEN OF —) CORVUS
(SON OF —) HAM SEM SHEM
JAPHETH
(WINE CUP OF —) CRATER
NOB NAB BLOW HEAD NAVE KNAVE
SWELL HANDLE TIPTOPPER
NOBEL PRIZE
(— IN CHEMISTRY) LEE BERG BERG
CECH CRAM HAHN HOFF KLUG KUHN

LEHN OLAH TODD UREY ALDER
ASTON BOSCH BROWN COREY CURIE
DEBYE DIELS EIGEN ERNST FLORY
FUKUI HABER HUBER KARLE LIBBY
NATTA PREGL SMITH SODDY SYNGE
TAUBE TAUBE ALTMAN CALVIN
HARDEN HASSEL KARRER LELOIR
MARCUS MICHEL MULLIS NERNST
PERUTZ PRELOG RAMSAY SANGER
SANGER SUMNER WERNER WITTIG
BERGIUS BUCHNER GIAUQUE
GILBERT GILBERT HOFFMAN
KENDREW KENICHI MOISSAN
NORRISH ONSAGER OSTWALD
POLANYI RUZICKA SEABORG
SEMENOV WALLACH WIELAND
WINDAUS HAUPTMAN LANGMUIR
MITCHELL MULLIKEN PEDERSON
TISELIUS HERSCHBACH MERRIFIELD
DEISENHOFER
(— IN **ECONOMICS** FOGEL MILLER
DOUGLASS
(— IN **ECONOMICS**) ARROW KLEIN
KLEIN LEWIS OHLIN SIMON SIMON
SOLOW STONE TOBIN TOBIN ALLAIS
DEBREU DEBREU FRISCH MYRDAL
SHARPE KUZNETS SCHULTZ
SCHULTZ STIGLER STIGLER
BUCHANAN FRIEDMAN HAAVELMO
LEONTIEF MARKOWITZ MODIGLIANI
(— IN **LITERATURE**) PAZ BOLL BUCK
COLA GIDE MANN SHAW AGNON
BUNIN CAMUS ELIOT HESSE HEYSE
LEWIS PERSE SACHS SIMON YEATS
ANDRIC BELLOW ELYTIS ELYTIS
EUCKEN FRANCE MAFOUZ MILOSZ
MILOSZ NERUDA ONEILL SARTRE
SINGER SINGER TAGORE BECKETT
BRODSKY CANETTI CENETTI
GOLDING GOLDING KIPLING
LAXNESS MARQUEZ MAURIAC
MISTRAL MONTALE ROLLAND
RUSSELL SEIFERT SOYINKA
WALCOTT BJORNSON CARDUCCI
FAULKNER GORDIMER ŁAGERLOF
MORRISON CHURCHILL HEMINGWAY
PASTERNAK STEINBECK LAGERKVIST
MAETERLINCK
(— IN **MEDICINE**) DAM CORI DALE
HESS KATZ KOCH ROSS ROUS VANE
WALD ARBER BLACK BLOCH BOVET
BROWN BUMET CHAIN COHEN CRICK
CURIE DOISY ELION EULER GOLGI
HENCH HUBEL HUBEL JERNE KREBS
KREBS KROGH LOEWI LURIA LYNEN
MINOT MONIZ MONOD NEHER
OCHOA SHARP SNELL SNELL TATUM
YALOW BARANY BEADLE BEKESY
BISHOP BORDET CARREL CLAUDE
DOMAGK ECCLES ENDERS FISHER
FLOREY GASSER GILMAN GRANIT
HOLLEY HUXLEY KOCHER KOHLER
KOSSEL LORENZ MURRAY PALADE

PAVLOV RICHET SPERRY SPERRY
THOMAS VARMUS WIESEL WIESEL
AXELROD BEHRING DAUSETT
FIBIGER HERSHEY HODGKIN
KHORANA LAVERAN NATHANS
NICOLLE ROBERTS RODBELL
SAKMANN SCHALLY THELLER
DELBRUCK MILSTEIN TONEGAWA
BERGSTROM GOLDSTEIN HITCHINGS
BENACERRAF MCCLINTOCK
MCCLINTOCK MONTALCINI
SAMUELSSON
(— IN **PEACE**) ORR THO HULL KING
MOTT PIRE ROOT SATO TUTU ASSER
BAJER BALCH BEGIN DAWES FRIED
GOBAT LANGE PASSY SADAT
ADDAMS ANGELL BRANDT BRIAND
BUNCHE BUTLER CASSIN CREMER
DUNANT MENCHU MONETA MYRDAL
NANSEN QUIDDE ROBLES WALESA
WALESA WIESEL WILSON BORLAUG
BUISSON DEKLERK JOUHAUX
KELLOGG LUTHULI MANDELA
PAULING RENAULT SANCHEZ
THERESA BRANTING CORRIGAN
ESQUIVEL ESQUIVEL SAKHAROV
GORBACHEV KISSINGER ROOSEVELT
SODERBLOM SCHWEITZER
HAMMARSKJOLD AUMGSANSUUKYI
(— IN **PHYSICS**) LEE BOHR BORN
HESS LAMB LAUE MOTT NEEL
RABI RYLE TAMM TING WIEN YANG
BASOV BETHE BLOCH BOTHE BRAGG
BRAUN CURIE DALEN DIRAC ESAKI
FERMI FITCH GABOR HERTZ HULSE
KUSCH PAULI RUSKA SEGRE SHULL
ALFVEN BARKLA BINNIG CRONIN
CRONIN FOWLER FOWLER GENNES
GLASER HEWISH LANDAU MULLER
PERRIN PLANCK RAMSEY ROHRER
RUBBIA STRUTT TAYLOR TAYLOR
TOWNES WIGNER WILSON YUKAWA
BARDEEN BEDNORZ CHARPAK
DEHMELT GELLMAN GLAEVER
GLASHOW KAPITSA KENDALL
LORENTZ MARCONI RICHTER
SHAWLOW EINSTEIN FRIEDMAN
KLITZING LEDERMAN ROENTGEN
SCHWARTZ SIEGBAHN BROCKHOUSE
BLOEMBERGEN STEINBERGER
CHANDRASEKHAR CHANDRASEKHAR
NOBILITY RANK ELITE GRACE
GENTRY STATUS DIGNITY KWAZOKU
PEERAGE QUALITY STATION
BARONAGE SZLACHTA ELEVATION
(**MEMBER OF TATAR —**) MURZA
(**ROMAN —**) RAMNES
NOBLE DON ALII DOGE DUKE EARL
EDEL EPIC FAME FREE GENT GOOD
GRAF HIGH JARL JUST KAMI KUGE
LORD PEER PURE RIAL ARIKI ATHEL
BARON BROAD BURLY COUNT
DUCAL ERECT ETHEL FURST GRAND

GREAT HIRAM KHASS LOFTY MANLY
MORAL MURZA PROUD ROYAL STATE
AUGUST COUSIN DAIMIO EPICAL
FLAITH GENTLE GESITH HAUGHT
HEROIC JUNKER KINGLY LORDLY
LUCUMO MANFUL SIRDAR SUPERB
THAKUR WORTHY YONKER ACERBAS
CACIQUE GALLANT GLAUCUS
GLORIED GRANDEE HIDALGO
LIBERAL MAGNATE MARQUIS
PATRICK STAROST STATELY
STEWARD SUBLIME TOISECH
VOLPONE PANGLIMA PRINCELY
(MINOR —) VIDAME

NOBLEMAN DUKE EARL EMIR LORD
PEER SOUL BARON COUNT ORLOV
PARIS THANE COUSIN MILORD
ORLOFF THAKUR YONKER GRANDEE
HIDALGO MAGNATE MARQUIS
STAROST VOLPONE YOUNKER
ADELIGER ALDERMAN ALMAVIVA
BELARIUS MARCHESE MARQUESS
LANDGRAVE MAGNIFICO

NOBLE-MINDED MANFUL LIBERAL

NOBLENESS HONOR DIGNITY
(— OF BIRTH) EUGENY

NOBLEWOMAN LADY MILADY
DUCHESS PEERESS BARONESS
COUNTESS

NOBODY NIX NEMO NONE NADIE
NOMAN SCRUB SCARAB NOTHING
JACKSTRAW

NOCENT GUILTY HARMFUL HURTFUL
NOXIOUS CRIMINAL

NOCTURNAL NIGHT NOXIAL
NIGHTLY NIGHTISH MOONSHINE
(— ANIMAL) COON POSSUM
OPOSSUM
(— BIRD) OWL
(— CARNIVORE) RATEL
(— MAMMAL) BAT LEMUR
(— SIGNS) ZODIAC

NOCTURNE LULLABY UHTSONG
PAINTING SERENADE

NOD OK BOB BOW ERR NAP NID NIP
BECK BEND DOZE NAPE SIGN SLIP
SWAY WINK DROOP LAPSE ASSENT
BECKON DODDLE DROWSE NODDLE
NUTATE SALUTE SIGNIFY
(— OFF) DOZE

NODDING DROWSY NUTANT
ANNUENT CERNUOUS DROOPING
NUTATION

NODDLE HEAD PATE BRAIN SKULL

NODDY AUK FOOL JACK NOIO TERN
KNAVE NINNY DROWSY FULMAR
NOODLE SLEEPY HACKNEY
TOMNODDY SIMPLETON

NODE BOW BUMP KNOB KNOT LUMP
PLOT JOINT NODUS POINT TUMOR
BULBIL NODULE DILEMMA GRANULE
KNUCKLE FOLLICLE PHYTOMER
SWELLING TUBERCLE

(— OF GRASS) KNOT
(— OF POEM) PLOT
(— OF STEM) JOINT

NODULE BOB AUGE BUMP KNOT
LUMP MASS NODE YOLK FLINT
GEODE PHYMA MILIUM BLISTER
CATHEAD GRANULE LEPROMA
NABLOCK SARCOID AMYGDALE
AMYGDULE COALBALL TUBERCLE
WHITEHEAD
(— OF FLINT) CORE
(CHALCEDONY —) ENHYDROS
(PL.) BEADING

NOEL XMAS CAROL NOWEL NATALIS
CHRISTMAS

NOGAH (FATHER OF —) DAVID

NOGGIN ALE CUP MUG NOG PEG PIN
BEAN GILL HEAD PAIL PATE DRINK
GOGGAN NAGGIN NOODLE

NO-GOODNIK SCALAWAG

NOHAH (FATHER OF —) BENJAMIN

NOIL FIBER PINION

NOISE (ALSO SEE SOUND) ADO AIR
BUM DIN GIG HUM POP ROW BANG
BOOM BRAY BUMP BURR CLAM COIL
HOOT KLOP MUSH PEAL RALE RASH
REEL RERD ROTE ROUT SLAM ZING
ALARM BABEL BLARE BLAST BLOOP
BRAWL BRUIT BURLE CHANG CHIRM
CLICK DREAM GRASS JERRY KNOCK
LARRY LARUM LEDEN PLASH QUONK
REERE RERDE RUMOR SLORP SNORE
SOUND STEER SWISH WHANG
BICKER CACKLE CLAMOR DUNDER
GOBBLE GOSSIP HUBBUB NORATE
OUTCRY PUDDER RACKET RANTAN
RATTLE REPORT SPLASH SQUAWK
STEVEN STRIFE TUMULT UPROAR
BLUSTER BRATTLE CLITTER CLUTTER
CRACKLE ORATION SCANDAL
SPATTER STREPOR STRIDOR
FLICFLAC QUONKING TINTAMAR
CONFUSION
(— OF DISAPPROVAL) RASPBERRY
(EARTHQUAKE —) BRONTIDES
(ELECTRIC —) GRASS
(EXPLOSIVE —) REPORT
(LOUD —) THUNDER
(RESOUNDING —) WHAM WHANG
(SCRAPING —) SCROOP
(PREF.) (— OF FALLING OBJECT) KER

NOISELESS QUIET STILL SWEET
TACIT SILENT APHONIC CATLIKE

NOISEMAKER BELL HORN GRAGER
RATTLE CLAPPER SQUEAKER

NOISETTE HAZEL HAZELNUT

NOISING
(— ABROAD) AIR

NOISOME FOUL OLID RANK FETID
NASTY PUTRID RANCID HARMFUL
HURTFUL NOXIOUS NUISOME
ODOROUS STINKING OFFENSIVE
MALODOROUS

NOISY LOUD CLASHY CREAKY BLATANT DINSOME FRANTIC MOILING RACKETY RIOTOUS ROUTOUS BRAWLING CLATTERY SONOROUS STREPENT HILARIOUS RATTLEBAG SCAMBLING BOISTEROUS

NOLL HEAD NODDLE NOODLE

NOMA CANKER

NOMAD ARAB BEJA LURI MOOR SAKA SHUA ALANI GYPSY IGDYR JAREG ROVER SHUWA NOMADE ROAMER ROVING SEMITE SLUBBI TUAREG BAZIGAR BEDOUIN SARACEN SCENITE SHORTZY SHUKRIA SOLUBBI TOUAREG KABABISH SCYTHIAN SHINWARI AMALEKITE MIGRATORY PEREGRINE
(— PEOPLE) ALANI
(ETHIOPIAN —) GALLA
(PL.) AKHLAME

NOMADIC ERRATIC VAGRANT VAGABOND FOOTLOOSE ITINERANT

NOMBRIL NAVEL

NOM DE PLUME PENNAME TELONISM PSEUDONYM

NOME ELIS NOMOS MELODY NOMARCHY PROVINCE

NOMENCLATURE LIST NAME TERM ONYMY NAMING GLOSSARY REGISTER CATALOGUE

NOMINAL PAR BASIC PAPER FORMAL SLIGHT UNREAL TITULAR TRIVIAL PLATONIC TRIFLING
(— RECOGNIZANCE) DOE

NOMINATE CALL LEET NAME ELECT NEVEN SLATE SELECT APPOINT ENTITLE PRESENT PROPOSE SPECIFY DESIGNATE POSTULATE

NOMINY SPEECH RIGMAROLE

NONAGE NEANT INFANCY MINORITY PUPILAGE

NONAGENARIAN OLDSTER

NONAGREEMENT DISSENT

NON-ALCOHOLIC SMALL

NO NAME (AUTHOR OF —) COLLINS
(CHARACTER IN —) NOEL CLARE FRANK GARTH KIRKE NORAH ANDREW GEORGE WRAGGE BARTRAM BYGRAVE LECOUNT MAGDALEN VANSTONE

NON-ARAB SHANGALLA

NONASPIRATE LENE

NONBELIEVER PAGAN ATHEIST AGNOSTIC

NONCE NANES NONES NOANCE PRESENT PURPOSE OCCASION

NONCHALANT COOL GLIB ALOOF CASUAL JAUNTY CARELESS DEBONAIR NEGLIGENT

NON-CHRISTIAN PAYNIM INFIDEL

NONCITIZEN TENSOR PEREGRINUS

NONCLERICAL LAY LAIC

NONCOMBUSTIBLE APYROUS

NONCOMMITTAL NEUTRAL

NONCONFORMIST REBEL NONCON BEATNIK DEVIANT FANATIC HERETIC SECTARY BOHEMIAN RECUSANT DISSENTER
(— IN ART) FAUVE

NONCONFORMITY HERESY ADHARMA DISSENT NEGLECT REFUSAL RECUSANCE RECUSANCY

NONCONTINUOUS DISCRETE

NON-CONVERGENCE ABERRATION

NONDESCRIPT BLAH DRAB DULL

NONDISCLOSURE FRAUD

NONDO LOVAGE ANGELICO

NONDUALISM ADVAITA

NONE NO UN NAE NIN ZIP NANE NARY NEEN NONES
(PREF.) NULLI

NONEGO NOTSELF

NONELASTIC BROAD

NONENTITY ZERO AUGHT CIPHER NOBODY NOUGHT NOTHING NULLITY NEGATION

NONESSENTIAL CASUAL FRILLY UNNEEDED EXTRINSIC
(— IN RELIGION) ADIAPHORON

NONESUCH APPLE MODEL PARAGON PATTERN PARADIGM MATCHLESS NONPAREIL UNRIVALED

NON-EXISTENCE ABSENCE NOTHING

NONEXISTENT NULL NAPOOH NOUGHT NONBEING BARMECIDE
(PRACTICALLY —) FAT
(PREF.) NULLI

NONFEASANCE BREACH

NON GRATA UNWELCOME

NONGYPSY GAJO

NONINJURY AHIMSA

NON-JEW GOI GOY

NONJUROR USAGER

NON-LATIN SAXON

NONLEGATO DETACHE DETACHED

NON-MOSLEM GENTILE

NONMOTILE
(PREF.) APLANO

NONNASAL ORAL

NO-NO TABU TABOO

NONPAREIL BEST ONER POPE TYPE PARAGON PERFECT SUPREME UNEQUAL NONESUCH PEERLESS UNRIVALED

NONPAYMENT DISHONOR

NONPLUS SET FAZE POSE STOP BLANK FLOOR POSER STICK STUMP TRUMP BAFFLE GRAVEL PUZZLE RATTLE CONFUSE MYSTIFY PERPLEX STAGGER QUANDARY DULCARNON EMBARRASS

NONPLUSSED BLANK FOOLISH
NONPOISONOUS SAFE EDIBLE
NON-POLYNESIAN PAKEHA
NONPROFESSIONAL BUM LAY
LAIC AMATEUR
NONSENSE BAH GAS GUP PAH ROT
BILK BLAA BLAH BOSH BUFF BULL
BUNK COCK CRAP FLAM FLUM GAFF
GOOK GUFF JIVE JUNK PISH POOH
PUNK TOSH BALLS BEANS BILGE
BLASH DROOL FOLLY FUDGE HAVER
HOOEY NERTS SPOOF STITE STUFF
TRASH TRIPE WAHOO BABBLE
BETISE BLAGUE BUNKUM DRIVEL
FADDLE FOLDER FOOTLE IDIOCY
KIBOSH LINSEY MALARK NAVERS
PIFFLE RUBBLE SQUISH TRIVIA
BLARNEY BLATHER EYEWASH
FARRAGO FLANNEL INANITY
LOCKRAM MALARKY RHUBARB
RUBBISH TOSHERY TRIFLES
TWADDLE BUNCOMBE CLAPTRAP
COBBLERS DISHWASH FALDEROL
FLIMFLAM FLUMMERY GALBANUM
MACARONI MOROLOGY PISHPOSH
PISHTOSH SKITTLES SPLUTTER
TOMMYROT TRUMPERY ABSURDITY
FRIVOLITY MOONSHINE POPPYCOCK
SILLINESS BALDERDASH
CODSWALLOP JABBERWOCK
TARADIDDLE JABBERWOCKY
GOBBLEDYGOOK
(— CREATURE) GOOP SHOO SNARK
SHIMOO
(SENTIMENTAL —) SLAWER
NONSENSICAL ABSURD
NONSURFER HODAD
NONUSER (— OF DRUGS) STRAIGHT
NON-VIOLENCE AHIMSA
NOODLE BEAN FOOL HEAD NIZY
NOLL PATE MOONY NINNY NIZEY
NODDY PASTA PASTE SAMMY
BOODLE GUDDLE NODDLE NOGGIN
DAWCOCK LOKSHEN NOGHEAD
NOUILLE BLOCKHEAD SIMPLETON
CAPERNOITIE
(— DISH) PANSIT RAVIOLI KREPLACH
(JAPANESE — SOUP) RAMEN
(STUPID —) BOODLE
(PL.) MEIN FARFEL FERFEL LASAGNA
LASAGNE LOKSHEN FETTUCINI
NOOK IN BAY OUT WRO CANT COVE
GLEN HERN HOLE NALK NUCK NUIK
ANGLE HALKE HERNE NEUCK NICHE
ALCOVE CANTLE CORNER CRANNY
RECESS CREVICE NOOKERY RETREAT
(FIREPLACE —) INGLE
NOON M APEX DINE NOWN SEXT
DINNER MIDDAY UNDERN MIDNOON
MERIDIAN
NOONDAY (— REST) NAP SIESTA
MERIDIAN

NOOSE TIE TOW BOND DULL FANK
GIRN HEMP LACE LOOP ROPE TRAP
BIGHT CATCH GRANE HITCH HONDA
KINCH LASSO LATCH LEASH SNARE
SNARL WIDDY CAUDLE CHOKER
CLINCH ENTRAP HALTER LARIAT
SPRING TETHER TIPPET TWITCH
CHOCKER ENSNARE EXECUTE
LANIARD LANYARD SPRINGE
NECKLACE SQUEEZER TWITCHEL
(— FOR HAULING LOG) CHOKER
CHOCKER
(— FOR SNARING FISH) DULL
(— IN A CORD) KINCH
(HANGMAN'S —) SQUEEZER
NOOTKA AHT AHOUSAHT
MOATCAHT MOOACHAHT
NORATE NOISE RUMOR GOSSIP
NORAX (FATHER OF —) HERMES
MERCURY
(MOTHER OF —) ERYTHEA
NORDIC ARIAN ARYAN
NORI AMANORI
NORITE GABBRO OLIGOSITE
NORM PAR MODE RULE TYPE CANON
GAUGE MODEL NORMA DHARMA
MEDIAN AVERAGE MODULUS
PATTERN STANDARD TEMPLATE
NORMA MOLD RULE GAUGE MODEL
SQUARE PATTERN TEMPLET
STANDARD TEMPLATE
(CHARACTER IN —) NORMA
ADALGISA POLLIONE
(COMPOSER OF —) BELLINI
NORMAL PAR FULL HOME JUST
MEAN SANE WISE CLEAR ERECT
USUAL FORMAL NATIVE SCHOOL
AVERAGE NATURAL NEUTRAL
REGULAR TYPICAL ORDINARY
STANDARD CUSTOMARY
NORMANDY (BEACH IN —) OMAHA
(CAPITAL OF —) ROUEN
(RIVER IN —) EURE ORNE SEINE
NORN FATE URTH WURD WYRD
NORNA SKULD URDHR URTHR
VERDHANDI VERTHANDI
NORSE ICELANDIC
NORSEL BAND LINE ORSEL FILLET
NOSSEL ORSELLER
NORTH SEPTENTRION
(PREF.) ARCT(O)

MOUNTAIN: WOOD LOGAN WALSH ROBSON STEELE TOLUCA LUCANIA PARICUTIN TAJUMULCO POPOCATEPETL
NATION: CANADA MEXICO UNITEDSTATES
RIVER: GILA MILK JAMES LIARD OSAGE PEACE PEARL PECOS SNAKE YUKON BALSAS BRAZOS FRASER HUDSON MOBILE NEOSHO PANUCO PLATTE POWDER SABINE TANANA KLAMATH KOYUKUK POTOMAC SUSITNA CIMARRON COLUMBIA DELAWARE MISSOURI NIOBRARA PENOBSCOT PORCUPINE RIOGRANDE STLAWRENCE MISSISSIPPI

NORTH CAROLINA
CAPE: FEAR LOOKOUT HATTERAS
CAPITAL: RALEIGH
COLLEGE: ELON CATAWBA DAVIDSON
COUNTY: ASHE DARE HOKE HYDE NASH PITT WAKE AVERY DAVIE GATES ROWAN SURRY BERTIE BLADEN CRAVEN ONSLOW YADKIN YANCEY CATAWBA PAMLICO CURRITUCK
INDIAN: ENO COREE CHERAW MORATOK PAMLICO CHOWANOC HATTERAS
MOUNTAIN: HARRIS MITCHELL
PRESIDENT: POLK JOHNSON
RIVER: HAW TAR NEUSE CHOWAN LUMBER PEEDEE YADKIN ROANOKE
SOUND: BOGUE CROATAN PAMLICO
STATE BIRD: CARDINAL
STATE FLOWER: DOGWOOD
STATE NICKNAME: TARHEEL OLDNORTH TURPENTINE
STATE TREE: PINE
TOWN: BOONE SYLVA BURGAW DOBSON DURHAM LENOIR SHELBY SPARTA EDENTON HICKORY ROXBORO TARBORO GASTONIA CHARLOTTE
UNIVERSITY: DUKE

NORTH DAKOTA
CAPITAL: BISMARCK
COLLEGE: JAMESTOWN
COUNTY: DUNN EDDY SLOPE STARK WELLS DICKEY DIVIDE GRIGGS KIDDER OLIVER TRAILL PEMBINA ROLETTE
INDIAN: MANDAN ARIKARA HIDATSA
MOUNTAIN: WHITEBUTTE
RIVER: RUSH CEDAR HEART JAMES SOURIS DESLACS SHEYENNE WILDRICE

STATE BIRD: MEADOWLARK
STATE FLOWER: PRAIRIEROSE
STATE NICKNAME: SIOUX FLICKERTAIL
STATE TREE: ELM
TOWN: MOTT CANDO FARGO MINOT ROLLA AMIDON LAKOTA LINTON MOHALL BOWBELLS NAPOLEON

NORTHERN PIKE ARCTIC BOREAL NORLAND NORTHEN
(— BEAR) POLAR RUSSIA
(— CONSTELLATION) URSA ANDROMEDA

NORTH KOREA
CAPITAL: PYONGYANG
COIN: JUN WON CHUN HWAN
PROVINCE: CHAGANG KANGWON TANGGANG
RIVER: NAM YALU IMJIN TUMEN TAEDONG
TOWN: HAEJU HEIJO KEIJO ANDONG ANTUNG HYESAN JUSHIN POCHON SAINNI WONSAN HAMHUNG HUICHON HUNGNAM KAESONG KANGGYE SARIWON SINUIJU CHONGJIN

NORTHMAN DANE
NORTH STAR STATE MINNESOTA
NORTHWEST TERRITORY
(CAPITAL OF —) YELLOWKNIFE
(DISTRICT OF —) FRANKLIN KEEWATIN MACKENZIE
(RIVER OF —) BACK KAZAN DUBAWNT COPPERMINE
(TOWN OF —) RAE INUVIK DISCOVERY SNOWDRIFT

NORWAY LEVANGER
CAPE: NORDKYN NORDKAPP
CAPITAL: OSLO
COIN: ORE KRONE
COUNTY: AMT OSLO FYLKE TROMS BERGEN TROMSO FINMARK HEDMARK OPPLAND OSTFOLD NORDLAND ROGALAND TELEMARK VESTFOLD
DANCE: GANGAR HALLING SPRINGAR SPRINGLEIK
FJORD: OSLO SOGNE HARDANGER TRONDHEIM
INLET: IS KOB RAN ALST ANDS BOKN NORD OFOT SALT SUNN TYRI VEST FIORD FJORD FOLDA LAKSE SOGNE BJORNA HADSEL HORTENS TRONDHEIM
ISLAND: VEGA BOMLO DONNA FROYA HITRA HOPEN SENJA SMOLA ALSTEN AVEROY BOUVET HINNOY KARMOY KVALOY SOLUND SOROYA VANNOY GURSKOY LOFOTEN

MAGEROY SEILAND JANMAYEN
SVALBARD RINGVASSOY
LAKE: ALTE ISTER MJOSA SNASA
FEMUND ROSTAVN TUNNSJO
ROSTVATN
MEASURE: FOT MAL POT ALEN MAAL
KANDE FATHOM SKIEPPE
MOUNTAIN: SOGNE KJOLEN
NUMEDAL BLODFJEL SNOHETTA
TELEMARK USTETIND JOTUNHEIM
PARLIAMENT: LAGTING STORTING
ODELSTING
PLATEAU: DOVRE FJELD HARDANGER
RIVER: OI ENA ALTA OTRA RANA TANA
BARDU BEGNA GLAMA LAGEN
ORKLA OTTER RAUMA REISA
GLOMMA LOUGEN NAMSEN PASVIK
DRAMSELVA
TOWN: GOL NES BODO MOSS ODDA
OSLO VOSS BJORT FLORO HAMAR
MOLDE SKIEN SKJAK BERGEN
HORTEN LARVIK NARVIK ALESUND
ARENDAL DRAMMEN SANDNES
STAVANGER
WATERFALL: VETTI SKYKJE VORING
WEIGHT: LOD MARK PUND
SKAALPUND BISMERPUND

NORWEGIAN (FORM OF —) BOKMAL
(LITERARY FORM OF —) NYNORSK
NOSE CAP NEB NIZ PRY PUG SPY
BEAK BOKO CONK NACE CROIN
LORUM NASUS SCENT SMELL SNIFF
SNOOP SNOOT SNOUT TRUNK
BEEZER CYRANO DETECT GNOMON
MUFFLE MUZZLE NOZZLE PECKER
ROOKIE SEARCH SNITCH SOCKET
ADVANCE PERFUME SMELLER
DISCOVER INFORMER OLFACTOR
PERCEIVE PROBOSCIS SCHNOZZLE
(— A LOG) SNIPE
(— BAG) MORRAL
(— CARTILAGE) SEPTUM
(— DISEASE) OZENA OZOENA
(— DIVE) VRILLE
(— FLUTE) PUNGI POOGYE
(— INFLAMMATION) CORYZA RHINITIS
(— MEDICINE) ERRHINE
(— OF AIRPLANE) PROW
(— OF ANIMAL) GROIN
(— OPENING) NARE
(— OUT) EDGE
(— PARTITION) VOMER
(— PIECE) NASAL
(— RING) PIRN
(BLUNT —) SNUB
(FLAT —) PUG SNUB
(PREF.) NAS(I)(O) NASUTI RHIN(O)
(SUFF.) RHINA RHINE RHINIA
RHINOUS RHINUS RRHINE RRHINIA
NOSEBAND BOSAL MUSROL
CAVESSON

NOSEBLEED EPISTAXIS
RHINORRHAGIA
NOSEGAY BOB ODOR POSY POESY
SCENT TUTTY BOUQUET CORSAGE
PERFUME
NOSH SNACK
NOSINESS CURIOSITY
NOSING CURB
NOSTALGIA LONGING YEARNING
NOSTALGIC RETRO ELEGIAC
OLDTIMEY ELEGIACAL
(FASHIONABLY —) RETRO
NOSTOLOGY GERIATRICS
NOSTRADAMUS SEER PROPHET
PHYSICIAN
NOSTRIL ALA NARE NARIS THIRL
THRILL BLOWHOLE
(PERT. TO —) NARIAL NARINE
(PL.) NARES NARIS SNUFFERS
(PREF.) NARI
NOSTRUM ELIXIR SECRET
NOSU LOLO
NOSY BEAKY PRYING CURIOUS
FRAGRANT INTRUSIVE
NOT NA NE NAE NAY NOR PAS BAAL
BAIL BALE NICHT SHORN SORRA
NOUGHT POLLED SHAVEN NEITHER
HORNLESS NEGATIVE
(— ANY) NO NUL NANE NARY NONE
NAIRY NOKIN STEAD
(— AT ALL) NEVER LITTLE NOWAYS
NOWHIT NOWICE
(— FINAL) NISI
(— THE SAME) OTHER ANOTHER
DIFFERENT
(— TO BE REPEATED) NR
(— WANTED) DETROP SUPERFLUOUS
(ALMOST —) SCARCELY
(COULD —) NOTE
(PREFIX MEANING —) IL IM IN IR UN
NON
(PREF.) A ANTI DIS E IL IM IN IR NON
UM UN
NOTABLE VIP FINE FABLED FAMOUS
GIFTED NOTARY SIGNAL UNIQUE
EMINENT STORIED SUBLIME
DISTINCT ESPECIAL EVENTFUL
HISTORIC MEMORABLE NOTORIOUS
NOTEWORTHY
NOTARY NOTAR GRAFFER GREFFIER
NOTEBOOK OBSERVER OFFICIAL
SCRIVENER
NOTARY PUBLIC TABELLION
NOTATION HOLD MEMO NOTE
ENTRY SYSTEM MARKING
(— OF DANCING) ORCHESOGRAPHY
(MUSICAL —) TABLATURE
(PHONETIC —) ROMIC
NOTATOR NOTER RECORDER
NOTCH CUT DAG DAP GAP HAG JAG
JOG PEG COPE DENT DINT GAIN
GIMP KERF MUSH NICK NOCK SLAP

SLOT SNIP STEP WARD CRENA
GABEL GRADE HILUM SCORE SHARD
SHERD SWICK TALLY CRENEL
CROTCH DEFILE DEGREE HOLLOW
INDENT JOGGLE RAFFLE RECORD
SCOTCH CRENATE GUDGEON
SERRATE INCISION UNDERCUT
(— **BETWEEN HILLS**) SLAP
(— **ON VERTEBRAE**) HYPANTRUM
(— **TO FELL TREE**) UNDERCUT
NOTCHED EROSE JAGGY RAGULE
RAGULY SERRATE CRENATED
SERRATED
NOTE BON DOG IOU JOT KEY SEE
TEN UNE BILL CARD CENT CHIT ESPY
FAME FLAT GOOD HEED MARK
MEMO NAME NOIT SIGN SOLE SONG
TENT TONE TUNE VIEW CHECK FIVER
GLOZE LABEL PRICK SHORT SIXTH
SOUND STIFF TENTH TOKEN TRAIT
TWANG ATTEND BILLET DEGREE
EXCUSE FIGURA FLIMSY LETTER
MELODY MINUTE NOTICE POLICY
RECORD REGARD REMARK RENOWN
REPORT SECOND STRAIN TENNER
BETOKEN COMMENT DISCORD
MESSAGE MISSIVE NATURAL
OBSERVE PUNCTUS REDBACK
ANNOTATE BLUEBACK BRADBURY
BREVIATE DISPATCH EMINENCE
MARGINAL PERCEIVE POSTFACE
TREASURY GREENBACK POSTSCRIPT
(— **FROM TRAIN**) BUTTERFLY
(— **OF ASSAULT**) WARISON
(— **OF HUMOR**) TRAIT
(— **OF SCALE**) DO FA LA MI RE SI SO
TI UT ARE SOL
(— **OF SNIPE**) SCAPE
(— **OF WARNING**) WATCHWORD
(— **ON SHOPHAR**) TEKIAH
(—**S ON HUNTING HORN**) SEEK
(— **TO RECALL DOG**) FORLOIN
(**ALTERED** —) ACCIDENTAL
(**BANK** —**S**) CABBAGE
(**BASS** —) DRONE
(**BIRD'S** —) JUG CHIRP
(**BUGLE** —) MOT
(**EDITOR'S** —) STET
(**EIGHTH** —) UNCA QUAVER
(**EMBELLISHING** —) ORNAMENT
(**ESCAPE** —) ECHAPPEE
(**EXPLANATORY** —) ANAGRAPH
SCHOLIUM ANNOTATION
(**FUNDAMENTAL** —) ROOT
(**GRACE** —) NACHSCHLAG
(**HALF** —) MINIM
(**HARSH** —) BLOB
(**HIGH-PITCHED** —) BEEP
(**HIGHEST** —) ELA
(**LEADING** —) SUBTONIC
(**LONG** —) LARGE
(**LOVE** —) POULET
(**LOWEST** —) KEY GAMUT

(**MARGINAL** —) TOT QUOTE POSTIL
APOSTIL
(**MUSICAL** —) ALT RAY HALF MESE
MIND BREVE GAMUT SHARP TONIC
WHOLE EIGHTH ALAMIRE MEDIANT
PUNCTUS QUARTER CROTCHET
DOMINANT LICHANOS PARAMESE
SUBTONIC PIZZICATO
SUBDOMINANT APPOGGIATURA
(**NONHARMONIC** —) CAMBIATA
(**POUND** —) BRADBURY
(**PROMISSORY** —) DOG GOOD HUNDI
CEDULA ASSIGNAT
(**QUARTER** —) CROTCHET SEMIMINIM
(**SIXTEENTH** —) DEMIQUAVER
SEMIQUAVER
(**SIXTY-FOURTH** —)
HEMIDEMISEMIQUAVER
(**THIRTY-SECOND** —) SUBSEMIFUSA
DEMISEMIQUAVER
(**TREASURY** —) TBILL
(**TWO** —**S**) DUPLET
(**WARBLING** —) CHIRL
(**WHOLE** —) SEMIBREVE
(**WRONG** —) CLINKER
(**100-POUND** —) CENTURY
(**PL.**) ANA GAMUT STRAIN NUMBERS
TIRALEE MARGINALIA
NOTEBOOK LOG DIARY NOTARY
RECORD STREET JOURNAL
NOTECASE WALLET POCKETBOOK
NOTED COUTH FAMED GREAT
NAMELY EMINENT INSIGNE
RENOWNED DISTINGUE
NOTEPAPER BOUDOIR
NOTEWORTHY BIG SOLEMN
EMINENT NOTABLE SALIENT SPECIAL
BODACIOUS MEMORABLE
OBSERVABLE
NOTHING NIL NIX ZIP FREE LUKE
NADA NILL RIEN WIND ZERO AUGHT
BLANK NIHIL SQUAT ZILCH CIPHER
NAUGHT NOBODY NOUGHT TRIFLE
NULLITY SCRATCH USELESS
BAGATELLE DIDDLYSQUAT
(— **BUT**) ALL
(— **DOING**) NAPOO NAPOOH
(— **MORE THAN**) MERE
(— **OTHER THAN**) ONLY
NOTHINGNESS NOT NADA ZERO
NOUGHT VACUITY NIHILITY
NOTICE AD BAN SEE SPY CALL ESPY
GAUM GOME HEED IDEA KEEP MARK
MIND NEWS NOTE PIPE RIDE SIGN
SPOT TWIG ALARM AWAIT COUNT
EDICT FLOAT NOTAM ORDER QUOTE
ADVICE ALLUDE BILLET ESPIAL
NOTION PERMIT READER REGARD
REMARK REWARD AFFICHE ARTICLE
DISCERN MENTION OBSERVE
PLACARD PROGRAM WARNING
BULLETIN MONITION PERCEIVE
WITTERING

(— UNEXPECTEDLY) CATCH
(ADVANCE —) HERALDRY
PREMONITION
(COMMENDATORY —) PUFF BLURB
(DEATH —) OBIT OBITUARY
(FAVORABLE —) RAVE
(FINAL —) OBIT OBITUARY
(LEGAL —) CAVEAT
(MARRIAGE —) BANS BANNS
(OFFICIAL —) EDICT SUMMONS
BULLETIN CITATION
(PUBLIC —) BAN EDICT BULLETIN
SPOTLIGHT
NOTICEABLE CRUDE GROSS
FLASHY MARKED SIGNAL EVIDENT
NOTABLE POINTED SALIENT
HANDSOME PALPABLE STRIKING
OBTRUSIVE PROMINENT
CONSPICUOUS OUTSTANDING
(UNDESIRABLY —) CONSPICUOUS
NOTIFICATION DRUM NOTE AVISO
NOTICE SUMMONS
(PUBLIC —) SIGN
NOTIFY ALL BID CRY JOG CITE PAGE
TELL WARN ADVISE INFORM NOTICE
SIGNAL APPRISE DECLARE FRUTIFY
PUBLISH ACQUAINT INTIMATE
NOTION BEE GEE BUZZ IDEA IDEE
KINK MAZE OMEN VIEW WHIM
FANCY FREIT IMAGE SENSE THING
WARES BELIEF CEMENT DESIRE
DONNEE GADGET MAGGOT NOTICE
THEORY VAGARY WHIMSY BROMIDE
CONCEIT CONCEPT FANTASY
INKLING MAROTTE OPINION
THOUGHT WHIMSEY WRINKLE
CATEGORY FOLKLORE PHANTASY
SUPPOSAL WHIMWHAM INTENTION
SENTIMENT WHIRLIGIG
(FALSE —) IDOL
(FANCIFUL —) VAPOR REVERY REVERIE
(FIXED —) TICK
(FOOLISH —) VAPOR VAPOUR
(PUERILE —) BOYISM
(SUPERSTITIOUS —) FREET FREIT
(VISIONARY —) ABSTRACTION
(WRONG —) FALLACY
(PL.) SMALLS SMALLWARE
NOTORIETY FAME ECLAT GLORY
HONOR RUMOR RENOWN REPUTE
PUBLICITY
NOTORIOUS BIG KNOWN ARRANT
COMMON CRYING FAMOUS NOTARY
STRONG EVIDENT NOTABLE
NOTOIRE APPARENT FLAGRANT
INFAMOUS MANIFEST EGREGIOUS
NOTORNIS TAKAHE
NOTUS (BROTHER OF —) EURUS
BOREAS ZEPHYRUS
(FATHER OF —) AEOLUS ASTRAEUS
(MOTHER OF —) EOS
NOTWITHSTANDING BUT FOR
THO YET EVEN WITH ASIDE ALGATE

MAUGER MAUGRE THOUGH
AGAINST ALGATES DESPITE
HOWBEIT HOWEVER ALTHOUGH
NATHLESS WHATRECK
NOUGAT NUT CANDY NUTSHELL
NOUGHT BAD NIL NOT NOWT ZERO
NOCHT WRONG NOTHING USELESS
WORTHLESS
NOUMENAL ONTAL ONTIC
NOUN MANE WORD THING SUPINE
NOMINAL CONSTRUCT INCREASER
(INDECLINABLE —) APTOTE
(KIND OF —) COMMON PROPER
DIPTOTE REGULAR TRIPTOTE
MONOPTOTE
(QUOTATION —) HYPOSTASIS
(VERBAL —) GERUND
NOURISH AID FEED FOOD GROW
BREED NORSH NURSE TRAIN BATTLE
BREAST FOISON FOSTER NORICE
REFETE SUCCOR SUCKLE SUPPLY
CHERISH DEVELOP EDUCATE
NURTURE NUTRIFY PROVIDE
SUPPORT SUSTAIN MAINTAIN
CULTIVATE REPLENISH STIMULATE
(PREF.) NUTRI
NOURISHING ALMA RICH ALIBLE
BATTLE HEARTY STRONG NUTRIENT
ALIMENTAL HEALTHFUL NUTRITIVE
WHOLESOME NUTRITIOUS
NOURISHMENT DIET FARE FETE
FOOD KEEP MEAT MANNA FOISON
FOSTER ALIMENT PABULUM
PASTURE NUTRIMENT REFECTION
(— FOR MIND) PABULUM
(PREF.) THREPSO
NOURONIHAR (FATHER OF —)
FAKREDDIN
(LOVER OF —) VATHEK
NOUS MIND REASON ALERTNESS
INTELLECT
NOUVEAU RICHE PARVENU
UPSTART
NOVA SCOTIA (CAPITAL OF —)
HALIFAX
(COUNTY OF —) DIGBY HANTS
PICTOU
(STRAIT OF —) CANSO
(TOWN OF —) TRURO PICTOU
SYDNEY ARICHAT BADDECK
DARTMOUTH
NOVA SCOTIAN ACADIAN
BLUENOSE
NOVEL HOT NEW BOOK EPIC RARE
FRESH PROSE RECIT ROMAN STORY
DARING RECENT SERIAL THRILL
FICTION ROMANCE STRANGE
UNUSUAL NEOTERIC ORIGINAL
THRILLER UNCOMMON NARRATIVE
PAPERBACK
(BRIEF —) CONTE
(PREF.) CAEN(O) CEN(O)
NOVELIST (ALSO SEE AUTHOR)

NOVELTY FAD NEWEL RENEW CHANGE NEWNESS PRIMEUR WRINKLE CURIOSITY FRESHNESS
NOVEMBER 1 SAMUIN SAMHAIN
NOVEMBER 11 MARTINMAS
NOVICE DUB HAM BOOT COLT PUNK PUNY TIRO TYRO CHELA GOYIN PUPIL ROOKY YOUTH DRONGO RABBIT ROOKIE TYRONE ACOLYTE AMATEUR CONVERT GRIFFIN LEARNER STARTER STUDENT YOUNKER BACHELOR BEGINNER FRESHMAN INEXPERT NEOPHYTE ARCHARIOS GREENHORN NOVITIATE TENDERFOOT ABECEDARIAN (MILITARY —) CADET
NOVITIATE FUCHS NOVICERY PROBATION
NOW NOO YET ARAH HERE AHORA ARRAH NONCE SINCE TODAY EVENOO EXTANT ANYMORE CURRENT INSTANT PRESENT FORTHWITH PRESENTLY (— AND THEN) SOMETIMES STOUNDMEAL (BUT —) ERSTWHILE (FROM — ON) EVERMORE (JUST —) ENOW FRESH
NOWADAYS ANYMORE
NOWEL DRAG
NOX NYX (BROTHER OF —) EREBUS (FATHER OF —) CHAOS
NOXIOUS BAD ILL EVIL FETID DEADLY NOCENT NOYOUS PUTRID BALEFUL BANEFUL DAMPISH HARMFUL HURTFUL NOCUOUS NOISOME SCADDLE TEDIOUS VICIOUS INFAMOUS VIRULENT INJURIOUS MIASMATIC OFFENSIVE PESTILENT POISONOUS PERNICIOUS (— AIR) MALARIA (MORALLY —) UNWHOLESOME
NOZZE DI FIGARO, LE (CHARACTER IN —) FIGARO BARTOLO BASILIO SUSANNA BARBARINA CHERUBINO MARCELLINA (COMPOSER OF —) MOZART
NOZZLE BIB JET TIP BEAK BIBB NOSE ROSE VENT GIANT SNOUT SPOUT TWEER GROVEL OUTLET MONITOR NIAGARA ORIFICE SHUTOFF ADJUTAGE ROSEHEAD VERMOREL NOSEPIECE (BLAST FURNACE —) TUYERE (MINING —) GIANT
NUANCE SHADE NICETY FINESSE GRADATION VARIATION
NUB EAR HUB JAB JAG KEY NOB CORE CRUX GIST HANG KNOB KNOT KNUB LUMP NECK PITH SNAG HEART NUDGE POINT KERNEL NUBBIN EXECUTE

NUBBIN EAR STUB STUMP
NUBIA WRAP CLOUD SCARF
NUBIAN NUBA BARABRA HADENDOA (— MUSICAL INST.) SISTRUM
NUBILOUS FOGGY MISTY VAGUE CLOUDY OBSCURE
NUCHA NAPE NECK NUKE NUCHE
NUCLEAR ELEMENTARY
NUCLEATE SEED
NUCLEOLUS (PREF.) PYREN(O)
NUCLEON MESON BARYON MESOTRON
NUCLEOSIDE VICINE INOSINE CYTIDINE ADENOSINE
NUCLEOTIDE GTP (SEQUENCE OF —S) EXON
NUCLEUS HUB CELL CORE GERM KERN PITH ROOT SEED CADRE FOCUS HEART MIDST SPERM UMBRA CENTER COLONY DEUTON KARYON KERNEL MIDDLE ISOTOPE NIDULUS HABENULA MEROCYTE MESOPLAST (— OF ATOM) DEUTERON (— OF CELL) KARYON (— OF STARCH GRAIN) HILUM (— OF SUNSPOT) UMBRA (ATOMIC —) SPECIES (CELL —) SYNCARYON HEMIKARYON (PREF.) (— OF CELL) CARY(O) KARY(O)
NUCLIDE ISOTONE
NUDE BARE LOOSE MODEL NAKED SEASAN STATUE UNCLAD DENUDED EXPOSED PICTURE PAINTING STARKERS STRIPPED UNDRESSED (FRENCH —) ALESAN (NOT —) DECENT (RUN —) STREAK
NUDGE JOG NOG NUB WAG GOAD JOLT KNUB LUMP PEST POKE POTE PROD PUSH BLOCK CHUCK DUNCH ELBOW
NUDIBRANCH SEASLUG
NUDISM NATURISM GYMNOSOPHY
NUDIST ADAMITE NUDIFIER GYMNOSOPH
NUDITY SCUD
NUDNICK PEST
NUDNIK PEST
NUGATORY IDLE NULL VAIN EMPTY PETTY FUTILE HOLLOW INVALID TRIVIAL USELESS TRIFLING FRUSTRATE WORTHLESS
NUGGET EYE LOB GOLD HUNK LUMP MASS SLUG PRILL YELLOW
NUISANCE BANE BORE EVIL HARM HURT PAIN PEST STING INJURY PLAGUE TERROR VEXATION ANNOYANCE
NUKE ZAP DESTROY DEVASTATE
NULL NIL VOID EMPTY INEPT IRRITE INVALID NULLIFY USELESS VACUOUS NUGATORY FRUSTRATE

NULLAH GORGE GULLY NULLA NALLAH RAVINE
NULLIFY BEAT FLAW LAME NULL UNDO VETO VOID ABATE ANNUL ELIDE ERASE LAPSE CANCEL DEFEAT NEGATE OFFSET REPEAL REVOKE ABOLISH COUNTER DESTROY ABROGATE EVACUATE STULTIFY FRUSTRATE
NULLIFYING DIRIMENT
NULLITY NIHILITY
NUMB DEAD DRUG DULL STUN DAZED FUNNY STONY ASLEEP BENUMB CLUMSY DEADEN STUPID TORPID STUNNED STUPEFY ENFEEBLE HEBETATE HELPLESS RIGESCENT TABETLESS
NUMBED ASLEEP
NUMBER SUM BAND BODY COPY CURN DRAW FECK HERD HOST LOTS MAIN MANY MESS MORT SLEW SURD TALE TELL COUNT DATUM DIGIT FOLIE GRIST GROUP INDEX ISSUE SCADS SCORE STAND TOTAL WHOLE ADDEND AMOUNT BUNDLE CIPHER ENCORE FACTOR FIGURE FILLER HIRSEL MYRIAD POLICY RECKON SCALAR TICHEL CHIFFER COMPUTE DECIMAL DIVISOR FOLIATE INTEGER NUMERIC SEVERAL CARDINAL FRACTION NUMERATE QUANTITY CALCULATE MAGNITUDE MULTITUDE MULTIPLIER MULTIPLICAND
(— BETWEEN 4 AND 10) MAIN
(— OF ARROWS) END
(— OF ATOMS) CHAIN
(— OF BEASTS) HERD
(— OF BOMBS) STICK
(— OF BRICKS) CLAMP
(— OF CATTLE) SOUM
(— OF FUR SKINS) TIMBER
(— OF HANKS OF YARN TO POUND) COUNT
(— OF HAWKS) CAST
(— OF HONEYBEES) CLUSTER
(— OF LINKED MINES) GIRANDOLA GIRANDOLE
(— OF NEEDLES) GAGE GAUGE
(— OF PERSONS) STABLE
(— OF POEMS) EPOS
(— OF SHEARERS) BOARD
(— OF TEA CHESTS) BREAK
(— OF THREADS PER INCH) PITCH
(— OF TRICKS) BOOK
(— OF WORDS) FOLIO
(—S GAME) BUG
(— THROWN IN CRAPS) POINT
(BALLET —) ENTREE
(CARDINAL —) ONE TWO ALEF ALEPH THREE
(CHOSEN —) FEW
(COMPLEX —) IMAGINARY

(CONSIDERABLE —) WHEEN HATFUL FISTFUL
(DESCRIBABLE —) SCALAR
(EXCESS —) ADVANTAGE
(EXCESSIVE —) SPATE
(EXTRA —) ENCORE
(GOLDEN —) PRIME
(GOOD —) THRAVE THREAVE
(GREAT —) LAC HEAP HOST LAKH MORT BREAK HIRST MEINY POWER SHOAL SIGHT SWARM LEGION MYRIAD INFINITE INFINITY THOUSAND MULTITUDE MULTIPLICITY
(GREAT —S) FLOCKS
(GREATER —) MO
(INDEFINITE —) LAC STEEN SUNDRY THRAVE JILLION SEVERAL THREAVE UMPTEEN
(IRRATIONAL —) SURD
(LARGE —) ARMY FECK HERD HOST LUMP PECK SLEW ARRAY CROWD FORCE POWER SCADS SHEAF SPATE STACK STORE WORLD GALLON GOOGOL HIRSEL HIRSLE LEGION MELDER BILLION JILLION PLURALITY
(LARGE —S) STRENGTH
(LEAF —) FOLIO
(LEAST WHOLE —) UNIT
(ODD —S) IMPAIR
(OF ANIMALS) PACK
(OPPOSITE —) COUSIN
(ORDINAL —) FIRST THIRD SECOND
(PUT ON SERIAL —) FOLIO
(SMALL —) FEW CURN CURRAN HANDFUL PAUCITY SPATTER
(SUNSCREEN —) SPF
(TOTAL —) AMOUNT
(VAST —) HORDE
(WHOLE —) ALL DIGIT INTEGER
(ZERO —) NOTHING
(PL.) STRENGTH
(PREF.) ARITHMETICO ARITHM(O) LOGARITHMO NUMERO
(SUFF.) ARITHM PLY
(— TERMINATION) TEEN
(— THAT FILLS) FUL FULL
(ORDINAL —) ETH
NUMBERED MENE
NUMBERING TALE COUNT FOLIATION
NUMBERLESS MYRIAD
NUMBERS
(PREF.)
(ODD —) PERISSO
NUMBFISH TORPEDO
NUMBING WARELESS
NUMBLES UMBLES INNARDS NOMBLES VISCERA ENTRAILS
NUMBNESS STUPOR TORPOR STUPIDITY
(PREF.) NARC(O)
NUMBSKULL OAF

NUMEN DEITY GENIUS SPIRIT
VESTAL DIVINITY
NUMERAL (ALSO SEE NUMBER)
SUM WORD DIGIT CIPHER FIGURE
LETTER CHAPTER NUMERIC
(**— STYLE**) ROMAN ARABIC
(**CLOCK —**) CHAPTER
NUMERATIVE PEN SEGREGATIVE
NUMERICAL SCALAR
NUMEROUS BIG LOTS MAIN MANY
RANK RIFE GREAT LARGE STOUR
DIVERS GALORE LEGION MYRIAD
SUNDRY UNRIDE COPIOUS
CROWDED ENDLESS FEARFUL
FERTILE PROFUSE SEVERAL TEEMING
UMPTEEN ABUNDANT FREQUENT
MANIFOLD MULTIPLE POPULOUS
THRONGED EXTENSIVE MULTIFOLD
NUMBERFUL PLENTIFUL
(**— AND POWERFUL**) MAIN
(**MODERATELY —**) FAIR
(**VERY —**) EXCESSIVE
(**PREF.**) MYRI
NUMIDIA (**BIRD OF —**) DEMOISELLE
(**CITY OF —**) HIPPO
(**KING OF —**) JUGURTHA
NUMITOR (**GRANDSON OF —**)
REMUS ROMULUS
NUMSKULL NUM DAFF DOLT FLAT
BOOBY DUNCE LACKWIT BONEHEAD
BLOCKHEAD LAMEBRAIN NUMBSKULL
NUN BIRD SMEW CLARE CLERK
MONIAL PIGEON SISTER TERESA
VESTAL VOWESS CLUNIAC CONFINE
DEANESS DEVOTEE EXTERNE
MINCHEN MONKESS RECLUSE
TEATINE THEATIN BASILIAN
CHAPLAIN CLARISSE PRIORESS
TITMOUSE URBANIST URSULINE
VISITANT VOTARESS ANGELICAL
CARMELITE LORETTINE PRIESTESS
RELIGEUSE TRAPPISTINE
(**— BIRD**) MONASE TITMOUSE
(**— HEADDRESS**) WIMPLE
(**— HOOD**) FAILLE
(**— MOTH**) TUSSOCK
(**— ORDER**) MARIST TRAPPIST
DOMINICAN LORETTINE
(**CHIEF —**) ABBA ABBESS MOTHER
(**LATIN —**) VESTA
(**SON OF —**) JOSHUA
NUNCIATE NUNCIO ANNOUNCER
MESSENGER
NUNCIO ENVOY NUNCE LEGATE
NUNTIUS DELEGATE MESSENGER
NUNCUPATE DECLARE DEDICATE
INSCRIBE PROCLAIM DESIGNATE
PRONOUNCE
NUNCUPATIVE ORAL SPOKEN
UNWRITTEN
NUNNERY ABBEY NUNRY CONVENT
CLOISTER MINCHERY
(**HEAD OF —**) ABBESS

NUPSON FOOL SIMPLETON
NUPTIAL BRIDAL GENIAL THORAL
MARITAL WEDDING ESPOUSAL
HYMENEAL MARRIAGE
(**PL.**) SPOUSAL WEDDING ESPOUSAL
HYMENEALS WIFETHING
NUQUE NAPE NECK
NURISTANI KAFIRI
NURSE LPN SIP AMAH AYAH BABA
CARE DHAI FEED NANA NUSS REAR
SUCK TEND BONNE MAMMY NANNY
NORSH ATTEND BAYMAN CRADLE
FOMENT FOSTER GRANNY KEEPER
NANNIE NORICE NUZZLE SISTER
SITTER SUCKLE UMFAAN CHERISH
FURTHER NOURISH NURTURE
PROMOTE CULTIVATE ENCOURAGE
NURSEMAID
(**— A GRIEVANCE**) SULK
(**— OF HIAWATHA**) NOKOMIS
(**— OF ULYSSES**) EURYCLEA
(**— OF ZEUS**) AMALTHEA CYNOSURA
(**— SHARK**) GATA
(**GULLIVER'S —**) GLUMDALCLITCH
(**WET —**) DHAI DHOLL
NURSEMAID AYAH BONNE
NURSERY RACE CRECHE HOTBED
BROODER FOSTERAGE
NURSLING BABY NORRY NURRY
FOSTER FOUNDLING
(**PREF.**) THREMMATO
NURTURE CARE DIET FEED FOOD
REAR TEND BREED NURSE TRAIN
COCKER CRADLE FOSTER NUZZLE
CHERISH EDUCATE SUPPORT
BREEDING NORTELRY TRAINING
EDUCATION ESTABLISH NUTRIMENT
(**PREF.**) TROPH(O)
NUSAIRI ANSARIE
NUT ACA BEN BUR COB GUY JOU NIT
TAP ANTA BURR COLA CORE DOLT
FOOL FROG HEAD KOLA LORE MAST
NITE PILI PITH SEED TASK ACORN
BETEL BONGA BUNGA CRANK FLAKE
FRUIT GLANS HAZEL HICAN JUVIA
PECAN TRYMA ALMOND BONDUC
BRAZIL CASHEW FELLOW HICCAN
ILLIPE KERNEL PEANUT PIGNON
PINION PYRENE CASTANA FILBERT
HICKORY PROBLEM APPLENUT
BEECHNUT BREADNUT CHESTNUT
GOORANUT LARRIKIN CAPOTASTO
CHINKAPIN ECCENTRIC MACADAMIA
PHILOPENA
(**— COAL**) ANTHRACITE
(**— GRASS**) SEDGE
(**— OF VIOLIN BOW**) FROG
(**— PINE**) PIGNON PINOON PIGNOLIA
(**CASHEW —**) SEDGE ANACARD
(**CONSORT OF —**) GEB KEB SET
(**DAUGHTER OF —**) ISIS NEPHTHYS
(**FALLEN —S**) SHACK
(**KIND OF —**) PEA

(PALM —) BETEL LICHI BABASSU
COCOANUT COQUILLA
(PERT. TO —) NUCAL
(RIPE —) LEAMER
(RUSH —) CHUFA
(SON OF —) RA OSIRIS
(PL.) MASTAGE
(PREF.) CARY(O) KARY(O) NUCI

NUT-BEARING NUCIFEROUS

NUTCRACKER XENOPS CRACKER
PILLORY MEATBIRD NUTCRACK
NUTHATCH NUCIFRAGA NUTPECKER

NUTHATCH SITTA TOMTIT XENOPS
JARBIRD SITTINE TITMOUSE
NUTJOBBER

NUTHOOK BEADLE CONSTABLE

NUTLET NUCULE PYRENA PYRENE
GYROLITH

NUTMEG SEED TREE SPICE BEAVER
CALABASH NOTEMIGGE
NOTEMUGGE
(— COVERING) MACE
(— STATE) CONNECTICUT
(PREF.) MYRISTICI

NUTRIA FUR COYPU GREGE NEUTRIA
RAGONDIN

NUTRIENT STARTER
(PLANT —S) SIDEDRESS
(PL.) FOOD HEMOTROPHE

NUTRIMENT DIET FOOD KEEP
VIANDS ALIMENT PABULUM
SUPPORT NOURISHMENT

NUTRITION EUTROPHY TROPHISM
(IMPERFECT —) DYSTROPHY
DYSTROPHIA
(PREF.) TROPH(O)
(SUFF.) TROPHIA TROPHIC TROPHY

NUTRITIOUS BATTLE BAITTLE
TROPHIC

NUTRITIVE ALIBLE

NUTS KEEN BALMY BUGGY CRAZY
INSANE ENTHUSIASTIC

NUT-SHAPED NUCIFORM

NUTSHELL SHELL INCLUDER

NUTTY BATS GAGA LOCO NUTS
RACY ZANY BATTY BUGGY CRAZY
QUEER SPICY FRUITY LOVING
SPRUCE AMOROUS FOOLISH
PIQUANT ZESTFUL DEMENTED
PLEASANT ECCENTRIC FLAVORFUL

NUX VOMICA SNAKEWOOD

NUZZLE DIG PET ROOT NURSE
SNUFF BURROW CARESS FONDLE
FOSTER NESTLE NUDDLE NURTURE
SNOOZLE SNUGGLE SNUZZLE

NYCTEUS (BROTHER OF —) LYCUS
(DAUGHTER OF —) ANTIOPE
(FATHER OF —) HYRIEUS
(MOTHER OF —) CLONIA

NYE EYAS NEST NIDE BROOD FLOCK

NYLON
(PL.) HOSIERY

NYMPH FLY GIRL MAIA MITE MUSE
PINK PIXY PUPA TICK AEGLE DRYAD
HOURI LARVA NAIAD NIXIE OREAD
SIREN SYLPH DYBLIS CYRENE
DAMSEL DAPHNE HELICE HESTIA
KELPIE MAIDEN NEREID SPRITE
SYRINX UNDINE CORYCIA ERYTHEA
HESPERA LIRIOPE OCEANID
CALLISTO CYNOSURA EURYDICE
MARPESSA PROSOPON BUTTERFLY
HAMADRYAD
(— BELOVED BY PAN) SYRINX
(— BELOVED OF NARCISSUS) ECHO
(— CHANGED TO BEAR) CALLISTO
(— OF FOUNTAIN) EGERIA SALMACIS
(— OF HILLS) OREAD
(— OF MEADOWS) LIMONIAD
(— OF MESSINA STRAIT) SCYLLA
(— OF MT. IDA) OENONE
(CITY —) POLIAD
(LAKE —) NAIAD LIMNIAD
(OCEAN —) SIREN GALATEA
OCEANID SEAMAID
(QUEEN OF —S) MAB
(RIVER —) NAIAS NAIAD
(SEA —) MERROW NEREID CALYPSO
GALATEA MERMAID
(WATER —) NAIS EGERIA LOTELI
UNDINE APSARAS HYDRIAD
JUTURNA RUSALKA EPHYDRIAD
(WOOD —) DRYAD NAPEA ARETHUSA
(PL.) HYADS THRIAI CAMENAE
(PREF.) NYMPHO

NYMPHAEA CASTALY CASTALIA

NYMPHET LOLITA

NYMPHOMANIAC (BOVINE —)
BULLER

NYNORSK LANDSMAL LANDSMAAL

NYROCA AYTHYA

NYSSA TUPELO

NYSTAGMUS TIC WINK

NYX NOX NIGHT
(— PERSONIFIED) NIGHT
(BROTHER OF —) EREBUS
(DAUGHTER OF —) DAY ERIS LIGHT
(HUSBAND OF —) CHAOS
(SON OF —) CHARON

O HO OH OCH ZERO CIPHER OMICRON
OAF AUF BOOR CLOD DOLT FOOL
LOUT CLOWN DUNCE IDIOT KLUTZ
OUPHE YOKEL MUCKER NASHGAB
PALOOKA POMPION BLOCKHEAD
FOUNDLING SCHLEMIEL SIMPLETON
OAHU (— BAY) KAHANA
(— BIRD) JIBI
OAK CLUB CORK HOLM ILEX BRAVE
BRIAR EMORY HOLLY ROBLE ROBUR
ACAJOU BAREEN CERRIS ENCINA
KERMES STRONG TOUMEY VALOMA
AMBROSE BELLOTA BELLOTE
DURMAST EGILOPS KELLOGG
PALAYAN TURTOSA BEEFWOOD
BLUEJACK CHAMPION CHAPARRO
FLITTERN WAINSCOT BLACKJACK
CHINKAPIN QUERCITRON
(— BARK) CRUT
(— FRUIT) MAST ACORN CAMATA
BELLOTE
(JERUSALEM —) AMBROSE
(WHITE —) ROBLE
(YOUNG —) FLITTERN
(PREF.) DRY(O) QUERCI
OAKUM OCCAM
OAKWOOD MESA
OAR AIR BOW PLY ROW PALM PEEL
POLE ALOOF BLADE ROWER SCULL
SPOON SWAPE SWEEP YULOH
PADDLE PALLET PROPEL OARSMAN
PROPELLER
(— BLADE) PALM PEEL WASH
(— FULCRUM) LOCK THOLE
OARLOCK ROWLOCK
(BOW —) GOUGER
(HANDLE OF —) GRASP
(INBOARD PORTION OF —) LOOM
(PART OF —) GRIP LOOM BLADE
SHAFT
(STERN —) SCULL SKULL
(PREF.) COPE(O) REMI
OARLOCK LOCK THOLE ROWLOCK
OARS CREW
OARSMAN OAR REMEX ROWER
BOWMAN STROKE BENCHER
SCULLER WATERMAN
OASIS BAR OJO SPA MERV SIWA
WADI WADY SPRING
OAST HOST KILN OVEN COCKLE
OASTHOUSE
OAT AIT WOT FEED FOOD PIPE POEM
SKEG SONG AUCHT CHEAT GRAIN
HAVER PEARL ANGORA EGILOPS
(— HUSK) SHOOD FLIGHT
(— RENT) AVENAGE
(EDIBLE PORTION OF —) GROATS

(FALSE WILD —S) FATUOID
(HUSKED —) SHEALING
(NAKED —) PILLAS PILCORN
(UNTHRASHED —) OATHAY
(WILD —S) HAVERGRASS
(PL.) CORN GRAIN HAVER GROUTS
PROVENDER WHITECORN
OATCAKE CAPER HAVERCAKE
SOURBREAD
OATEN AITEN
OATH OD ADS BAN DAD DOD GAD
GAR GOL GOR GUM ODD SAM VOW
BOND CRUM CUSS DARN DRAT ECOD
EGAD GEEZ GOSH HECK JEEZ JING
NIGS OONS SANG SLID SLUD WORD
BEDAD BEGAD BEGOB BLIMY CURSE
DAMME DEUCE GOLLY HOKEY
MORDU PARDY SACRE SFOOT SLIFE
SNIGS SWEAR YERRA ADSBUD
APPEAL CRACKY CRIKEY CRIPES
CRUMBS FEALTY JABERS JERNIE
NEAKES PARDIE PLEDGE RAPPER
SBLOOD SLIGHT STRUTH ZOUNDS
BEGORRA BEGORRY BEJESUS
BYRLADY CORBLEU GADSLID
GEEWHIZ GEEWIZZ JEEPERS
JIMMINY MORBLEU ODSFISH
ODZOOKS PROMISE THUNDER
ANATHEMA BEJABERS BODYKINS
CRICKETY GADZOOKS JURAMENT
PITIKINS SANCTION SEREMENT
SNIGGERS SPLUTTER AFFIDAVIT
BEJABBERS BLASPHEMY
DODGASTED EXPLETIVE PROFANITY
SACRAMENT SLIDIKINS
SWEARWORD
OATMEAL OATS STODGE YELLOW
POTTAGE DRAMMOCK PORRIDGE
(— BREAD) ANACK JANNACK
(— CAKE) PONE SCONE
OATS (MIXED ROLLED —) GRANOLA
(PREF.) AVENO
OBADIAH ABDIAS
(FATHER OF —) AZEL JEHIEL
SHEMAIAH
(SON OF —) ISHMAIAH
OBAL (FATHER OF —) JOKTAN
OBCLUDE HIDE OCCLUDE
OBDURATE FIRM HARD BALKY
HARSH INERT ROCKY ROUGH STARK
STONY DOGGED INURED MULISH
RUGGED SEVERE STURDY SULLEN
ADAMANT CALLOUS HARDENED
PERVERSE STUBBORN IMPASSIVE
UNBENDING
OBEAH OBI OBIA CHARM FETISH
VOODOO

OBECHE ARERE AYOUS SAMBA
OBED (FATHER OF —) BOAZ JARHA
　SHEMAIAH
　(MOTHER OF —) RUTH
　(SON OF —) JESSE AZARIAH
OBEDEDOM (FATHER OF —)
　JEDUTHUN
OBEDIENCE ORDER FEALTY
　CONTROL SERVICE DOCILITY
　OBEISANCE
OBEDIENT BENT RULY TALL TAME
　BUXOM DOCILE PLIANT DEVOTED
　DUTEOUS DUTIFUL HEEDFUL
　MINDFUL ORDERLY SUBJECT
　AMENABLE BIDDABLE YIELDING
　ATTENTIVE OBSERVING SERVIABLE
　TRACTABLE
　(— TO THE HELM) HANDY
OBEDIENTIARY PRIOR
OBEDIENT PLANT DRAGONHEAD
OBEISANCE BOW LEG JOUK BINGE
　CONGE HONOR SALAM CONGEE
　CRINGE CURTSY FEALTY HOMAGE
　SALAAM CURTSEY DEFERENCE
　HUMBLESSO REFERENCE
OBELISK MARK PYLON SHAFT
　DAGGER GUGLIA GUGLIO NEEDLE
　OBELUS PILLAR AGUGLIA
　MONUMENT HAGIOLITH
OBELUS DAGGER OBELISK
OBERON KING POEM FAIRY OPERA
　SATELLITE
　(CHARACTER IN —) HUON PUCK
　FATIMA OBERON TITANIA
　SHERASMIN
　(COMPOSER OF —) WEBER
　(WIFE OF —) TITANIA
OBESE FAT FOZY BEEFY PLUMP
　PUDGY PUFFY PURSY STOUT FLESHY
　PORTLY PYKNIC ROTUND TURGID
　ADIPOSE PORCINE PURSIVE
　BLUBBERY LIPAROUS CORPULENT
OBESITY FAT FATNESS LIPOSIS
　ADIPOSIS FOZINESS ADIPOSITY
OBEY EAR HEAR HEED MIND DEFER
　YIELD COMPLY FOLLOW OBFISH
　SUBMIT CONFORM EXECUTE
　OBSERVE OBTEMPER
　(— HELM) STEER
OBFUSCATE DIM BEFOG CLOUD
　DARKEN MUDDLE OBFUSK CONFUSE
　MYSTIFY OBSCURE PERPLEX
　STUPEFY BEWILDER
OBI OBE SASH CHARM OBEAH FETICH
　FETISH GIRDLE
OBIT MASS REST DEATH NOTICE
　OBITAL DECEASE RELEASE SERVICE
　OBITUARY NECROLOGY OBSEQUIES
OBITUARY NECROLOGY
OBJECT AIM END TAP BALK BEEF
　CARE CARP FINE GOAL IDEA ITEM
　KICK MAIN MIND PASS SAKE WHAT
　ARGUE CAVIL DEMUR GRIPE PINCH

POINT SCOPE SIGHT TELOS THING
AFFAIR DESIGN EMBLEM ENTITY
FIGURE GADGET INTENT MATTER
MOTIVE OPPOSE TARGET ARTICLE
DINGBAT DISLIKE DISSENT MEANING
PROTEST PURPOSE QUARREL
REALITY RECLAIM NOUMENON
TENDENCY CHALLENGE INTENTION
SPECTACLE
(— HAVING FLAWS) SPOIL
(— OF ABHORRENCE) ANATHEMA
(— OF AMBITION) MAIN
(— OF ART) VASE CURIO VIRTU
ANTIQUE BIBELOT FIGURINE
(— OF CONTEMPT) SCORN
(— OF CRITICISM) BUTT
(— OF DERISION) SCOFF
(— OF DEVOTION) IDOL TOTEM
FETISH
(— OF DISGUST) UG
(— OF DREAD) BOGY BOGEY BOGIE
BOGGIE BUGBEAR
(— OF INTEREST) SIGHT
(— OF KNOWLEDGE) SCIBILE
(— OF LAUGHTER) JEST
(— OF LOATHING) SCUNNER
(— OF LOVE) FLAME
(— OF PILGRIMAGE) CAABA KAABAH
(— OF PRIDE) GLORY
(— OF PURSUIT) SHADOW
(— OF RELIANCE) STAY
(— OF REVERENCE) MANITO
(— OF RIDICULE) FUN GAME
(— OF SCORN) GECK SCOFF BYWORD
HISSING DERISION
(— OF TERROR) BUG BUGABOO
BUGBEAR
(— OF THOUGHT) CONSTRUCT
(— OF WONDER) ADMIRATION
(— OF WORSHIP) GOD IDOL JUJU
MUMBOJUMBO
(— TO BE TILTED AT) QUINTAIN
(ALLURING —) DELILAH
(BELOVED —) MINION DARLING
MISTRESS
(BIZARRE —) GROTESQUE
(BULKY —) WODGE
(CELESTIAL —) QUASAR
(CONICAL —) ACORN
(CONSPICUOUS —) LANDMARK
(CONTAMINATED —S) FOMITES
(CURVED —) BELLY
(CYLINDRICAL —) BOLE
(DECORATIVE —) BIBELOT
(DESIRABLE —) GRAIL
(FACTORY-MADE —S) ARTWORK
(FLAT —) DISCUS
(HEAVY —) WEIGHT
(MINUTE —) ATOM MITE
(PALTRY —) TRINKET
(POINTED —) SPIKE
(ROUND —) COB RONDEL TRINDLE
TRUNDLE

(SACRED —) URIM ZOGO GUACA HUACA SHRINE CHURINGA
(SILLY —) INANITY
(SMALL —) PIRLIE
(STRANGE —S) CURIOSA
(STUDY OF FLYING —S) UFOLOGY
(TEACHING —S) REALIA
(TRANSCENDENTAL —) ENTITY
(TRIVIAL —) GUBBINS
(ULTIMATE —) TELOS
(UNIDENTIFIED FLYING —) BOGEY
(VILE —S) SCUM
(WORTHLESS —) SPLINTER
(PREF.) (FILTHY OR DIRTY —) RHYPARO RHYPO

OBJECTION OB BAR BUT BEEF CRAB FUSS KICK CAVIL DEMUR DOUBT BOGGLE CHESON NIGGLE QUARREL QUIBBLE SCRUPLE DEMURRAL QUESTION CHALLENGE CRITICISM EXCEPTION

OBJECTIONABLE VILE AWFUL HORRID GHASTLY UNLUSTY UNLIKELY FRIGHTFUL OBNOXIOUS OFFENSIVE
(BE —) SUCK

OBJECTIVE AIM END FAIR GAME GOAL HOME REAL SAKE OUTER ACTUAL AMORAL ANIMUS DESIGN MOTIVE TARGET THRUST PURPOSE DETACHED TANGIBLE UNBIASED DIRECTION INTENTION POSITIVAL QUAESITUM ULTIMATUM

OBJECTOR (CONSCIENTIOUS —) CONCHY CONCHIE

OBJETS D'ART VIRTU

OBJURGATE BAN JAW DAMN RAIL ABUSE CHIDE CURSE DECRY BERATE REBUKE REPROVE UPBRAID VITUPER EXECRATE CASTIGATE

OBLATE MONK OFFER DEDICATE MONASTIC

OBLATION CORBAN OFLETE SACRED CHARITY ANAPHORA DEVOTION OFFERING SACRIFICE

OBLIGATE COMMIT STRICT

OBLIGATED BOUND LIABLE BEHOLDEN

OBLIGATION DUE IOU TIE VOW BAIL BAND BOND CALL DEBT DUTY KNOT LOAD LOAN MUST NOTE OATH ONUS SEAL CHECK OUGHT SCORE ARREAR BURDEN CHARGE CONSOL CORVEE CUSTOM FEALTY PLEDGE ANNUITY BONDAGE PROMISE TRIBUTE CONTRACT HYPOTHEC SECURITY WARRANTY AGREEMENT LIABILITY
(— NOT TO MARRY) CELIBACY
(— TO RENDER RENT) CUSTOM
(— TO SECRECY) SEAL
(LABOR —) CORVEE

(MORAL —) BOND DUTY
(PL.) STRINGS

OBLIGATORY BINDING BOUNDEN FORCIBLE IMPOSING LIGATORY INCUMBENT MANDATORY

OBLIGE PUT HOLD PAWN DRIVE FAVOR FORCE COMPEL ENGAGE PLEASE GRATIFY REQUIRE CONCLUDE MORTGAGE OBLIGATE CONSTRAIN ACCOMMODATE

OBLIGED FAIN BOUND DEBTED BOUNDEN DEBTFUL FAVORED PLEASED PLEDGED BEHOLDEN GRATEFUL OBSTRICT BEHOLDING OBLIGATED

OBLIGING KIND BUXOM CIVIL CLEVER TOWARD AMIABLE FAVOROUS AGREEABLE COURTEOUS FAVORABLE OFFICIOUS

OBLIQUE AWRY BIAS SIDE SKEW ASKEW BEVEL CROSS SLANT ASLANT ASWASH LOUCHE SQUINT THWART ASKANCE AWKWARD CROOKED EMBELIF EVASIVE SCALENE SIDLING SLOPING DIAGONAL INCLINED INDIRECT SIDELONG SIDEWAYS SIDEWISE SLANTING TORTUOUS INDICULAR UNDERHAND
(— IN MINING) CLINIC
(— STROKE) SLASH SOLIDUS
(— WORK) SWASHWORK
(PREF.) LECHRI(O) LOX(O) PLAGI(O)

OBLIQUELY AGEE AWRY BIAS AGLEE ASIDE ASKEW AWASH SLANT SLOPE ASLANT ASWASH ASKANCE ASQUINT EMBELIF BIASWISE SIDELONG SIDEWAYS SIDEWISE

OBLIQUITY BIAS DIRT SWEEP DIRTINESS

OBLITERATE INK BLOT DELE RASE RAZE WIPE ANNUL BLACK COVER ERASE SMEAR CANCEL DELETE EFFACE SPONGE ABOLISH DESTROY EXPUNGE OUTRAZE SCRATCH OVERSCORE

OBLITERATION BLOT RASURE ERASURE NEGATION SYNIZESIS

OBLIVION LETHE LIMBO PARDON AMNESTY NIRVANA SILENCE OUBLIANCE

OBLIVIOUS AMORT BLISSFUL HEEDLESS OBLIVIAL FORGETFUL

OBLONG CHITON EVELONG AVELONGE EVENLONG ELONGATED
(ROUNDED —) ELLIPSE

OBLOQUY ABUSE BLAME ODIUM INFAMY CALUMNY CENSURE REPROOF CONTEMPT DISGRACE DISHONOR OBLIRCUE

OBNOXIOUS FOUL PERT VILE CURST CURSED FAULTY HORRID

LIABLE ODIOUS RANCID SEPTIC
HATEFUL INVIDIOUS OFFENSIVE
REPUGNANT VERMINOUS
(— PERSON) CREEP
OBOE PIPE REED WAIT AULOS
SHAWM SURNAI SURNAY HAUTBOY
MUSETTE PIFFERO CHIRIMIA
HAUTBOIS SCHALMEY SZOPELKA
CHALUMEAU HECKELPHONE
(— DI CACCIA) TENOROON
FAGOTTINO
(BASS —) RACKETT
(PREF.) AUL(O)
OBOLE MAIL MAILLE
OBSCENE PAW FOUL LEWD NAST
BAWDY GROSS NASTY ROCKY
COARSE FILTHY IMPURE RIBALD
SMUTTY VULGAR XRATED KNAVISH
PROFANE RAUNCHY IMMODEST
INDECENT LOATHSOME OFFENSIVE
REPULSIVE SALACIOUS
(— CULT) AISCHROLATREIA
OBSCENITY DIRT FILTH RIBALDRY
SCULDUDDERY
(PREF.) COPR(O)
OBSCURATION COVER ECLIPSE
OBSCURE DIM FOG BLOT BLUR
DARK DEEP HARD HART HAZY HIDE
PALE SLUR VEIL BEDIM BEFOG
BLACK BLANK BLEND BLIND CLOUD
COVER DUSKY FAINT FOGGY GLOOM
INNER LOWLY MIRKY MISTY MUDDY
MURKY SHADE SMEAR STAIN
VAGUE BEMIST CLOUDY DARKEN
DARKLE DEADEN DELUDE GLOOMY
HUMBLE MYSTIC OCCULT OPAQUE
REMOTE SHADOW SOMBER SUBTLE
BECLOUD BENIGHT CLOUDED
CONCEAL CONFUSE CRABBED
CRYPTIC ECLIPSE ENCRUST
ENVELOP OBLIQUE OVERLAY
OVERTOP SHADOWY SLUBBER
TARNISH UNCLEAR UNKNOWN
UNNOTED ABSTRUSE DARKLING
DISGUISE DOUBTFUL FAMELESS
MYSTICAL NAMELESS NUBILOUS
OBSTRUSE ORACULAR OVERSILE
CALIGINOUS
(MAKE —) BECLOUD
(PREF.) APHAN(O)
OBSCURED HAZY HIDDEN BLINDED
CLOUDED DUSKISH DARKSOME
DISGUISED INFUSCATE
OBSCURITY FOG MIST CLOUD
GLOOM SHADE CALIGO SHADOW
DIMNESS OPACITY PRIVACY SILENCE
DARKNESS TENEBRES BLINDNESS
SECLUSION
(DELIBERATE —) OBLIQUITY
(PL.) MURLEMEWES
OBSECRATE BEG PRAY BESEECH
ENTREAT PETITION

OBSEQUIES MASS OBIT PYRE WAKE
RITES SERVICE FUNERALS
OBSEQUIOUS SLICK MENIAL
SUPPLE COURTLY DEVOTED
DUTEOUS DUTIFUL FAWNING
SERVILE SLAVISH VERNILE
CRINGING OBEDIENT OBEISANT
TOADYING ASSIDUOUS ATTENTIVE
COMPLIANT
(— PERSON) LIMBERHAM
OBSEQUY RITE EXEQUY RITUAL
FUNERAL CEREMONY
OBSERVANCE ACT FORM RITE RULE
FREET HONOR CUSTOM REGARD
KEEPING CEREMONY PRACTICE
ADHERENCE ATTENTION DEFERENCE
INDICTION SOLEMNITY
(— OF PROPRIETIES) DECORUM
BREEDING ETIQUETTE
(RELIGIOUS —) NOVENA
SACRAMENT
(REVERENTIAL —) PUJA
(SUPERSTITIOUS —) FREET FREIT
(PL.) FUNERAL CEREMONY
OBSERVANT ALERT EYEFUL
CAREFUL HEEDFUL MINDFUL
DILIGENT VIGILANT WATCHFUL
REGARDFUL PERCEPTIVE
OBSERVATION EYE SPY HEED IDEA
NOTE RAOB VIEW SIGHT WATCH
ESPIAL LOGION NOTICE REGARD
REMARK AUSPICE AUTOPSY
COMMENT CONTACT DESCANT
OPINION EYESIGHT GAZEMENT
SCHOLION SCHOLIUM ASSERTION
ATTENTION ESPIONAGE
COGNIZANCE PERCEPTION
(— BY BALLOON) PIBAL
(BASED ON —) EYEBALL
(ECOLOGICAL —S) ANNUATION
(PRELIMINARY —) PROEM
(STALE —) GROANER
OBSERVATIONISM SCHAULUST
OBSERVATORY LICK TOWER
LOOKOUT PALOMAR
OBSERVE LO EYE SEE SPY ESPY
HEED HOLD KEEP LOOK MAKE MARK
MIND NARK NOTA NOTE OBEY SPOT
TENT TOUT TWIG VIEW WAIT YEME
ABIDE QUOTE SMOKE STUDY UTTER
WATCH ADHERE ADVERT ATHOLD
BEHOLD DETECT DEVISE FOLLOW
NOTICE NOTIFY REGARD REMARK
SURVEY COMMENT DISCERN
EXPRESS MENTION PROFESS
RESPECT WITNESS PERCEIVE
PRESERVE SPECTATE ADVERTISE
CELEBRATE SOLEMNIZE
(— CLOSELY) SMOKE
(— DULLY) BLEAR
(— FOOTBALL POSITION) KEY
(— OPPOSING POSITION) KEY

OBSERVER O BIRDER CORNER WATCHER AUDIENCE INFORMER ONLOOKER BYSTANDER SCRUTATOR SPECTATOR

OBSESS RIDE BESET HAUNT HARASS INVEST OBSEDE BESIEGE HAGRIDE POSSESS PREOCCUPY

OBSESSED CRAZY DOTTY HAPPY HIPPED BESOTTED

OBSESSION TIC CRAZE MANIA SIEGE MAGGOT ECSTASY FIXATION IDEEFIXE
(SUFF.) (— WITH) ITIS

OBSIDIAN CORE LAVA IZTLE IZTLI LAPIS

OBSOLETE OLD DEAD PAST DATED PASSE BYGONE EFFETE ABOLETE ANCIENT ARCHAIC CLASSIC DISUSED EFFACED EXTINCT OUTWORN OUTDATED OUTMODED OVERWORN DISCARDED

OBSTACLE BAR DAM LET BOYG BUMP DRAG HUMP JUMP OBEX SNAG STAY STOP BLOCK CHECK CLAMP CRIMP FENCE HITCH HYDRA SPOKE STICK STILE ABATIS BUNKER FRAISE HOCKET HURDLE LOGJAM OBJECT RETARD ANSTOSS BARRIER CHICANE FIVEBAR STOPPER BLOCKADE MOLEHILL BARRICADE CONDITION HINDRANCE ROADBLOCK TURNAGAIN
(— TO VIRTUE) SLANDER
(GOLF —) HAZARD
(INSURMOUNTABLE —) IMPASSE

OBSTETRICIAN ACCOUCHEUR

OBSTETRICS TOCOLOGY TOKOLOGY MAIEUTICS MIDWIFERY

OBSTINACY BRASS CONTUMACY

OBSTINATE SET SOT DOUR FIRM SULY BALKY FIXED ROWDY RUSTY STIFF STOUT TOUGH ASSISH CUSSED DOGGED KNOBBY MULISH STEEVE STUFFY STUPID STURDY SULLEN THRAWN UNRULY ASININE BULLISH CRABBED FROWARD PEEVISH RESTIVE WILLFUL CROTCHED OBDURATE PERVERSE PREFRACT RECUSANT RENITENT STOMACHY STUBBORN FOREIGHT PIGHEADED STONEWALL TENACIOUS
(— IN THE WRONG) PERVERSE
(— ONE) MULE
(NOT —) SUPPLE

OBSTREPEROUS LOUD WILD NOISY RORTY UNRULY RAUGHTY CLAMOROUS

OBSTRUCT BAR DAM DIT GAG JAM CLOG COOP CRAB DITT FILL FOUL JAMB STOP TRIG TRIP BESET BLANK BLOCK CHAIN CHECK CHOKE CROSS DELAY HEDGE THROW ARREST CUMBER FORBAR HAMPER HOBBLE IMPEDE OPPOSE PESTER RETARD STIFLE THWART WAYLAY WINDER BARRIER FORELAY OCCLUDE BLOCKADE EMBOLIZE ENCUMBER FLOUNDER OBTURATE OPPILATE BARRICADE EMBARRASS INCOMMODE

OBSTRUCTION BAR DAM GAG LET RUB BOOM BUMP CLOG SLUG SNAG STAY STOP BLOCK CHOKE GORCE HITCH SPOKE HAMPER TAPPEN THWART BARRACE BARRAGE BARRIER BLINDER CHOKAGE EMBOLISM OBSTACLE STOPPAGE AMBUSCADE EMPHRAXIS OCCLUSION
(— IN OILWELL) BRIDGE
(— IN RIVER) GORGE
(— IN TEAT) SPIDER
(— IN VALVE) GAG
(— OF BLOOD VESSEL) EMBOLISM
(— OF PINE LEAVES) TAPPEN
(— OF TONE) VEIL
(INNER —) LOAD
(LEGISLATIVE —) STONEWALL FILIBUSTER

OBTAIN BEG BUM BUY EKE GET PAN WIN EARN FANG FIND GAIN HENT REAP ANNEX CADGE CATCH ETTLE REACH AREACH ARECHE ARRIVE ATTAIN BORROW DERIVE EXPEDE SECURE SPONGE ACHIEVE ACQUIRE CAPTURE CHEVISE COMPASS DEMERIT EXTRACT POSSESS PREVAIL PROCURE RECEIVE SUCCEED PURCHASE SCROUNGE
(— BY CHANCE) DRAW
(— BY HEAT) EXCOCT
(— BY REQUEST) IMPETRATE
(— BY THREAT) EXTORT
(— CONTROL) ENGROSS
(— DISHONESTLY) CROOK SHARP FLEECE NOBBLE SKELDER
(— MONEY FROM) BLEED
(— PERMISSION) CLEAR

OBTAINABLE GOING GETTABLE AVAILABLE DERIVABLE SECURABLE

OBTAINED (— AT SCENE OF CRIME) LATENT
(— DIRECTLY) FIRSTHAND
(WRONGFULLY —) HOT EXTORTED

OBTEST PLEAD

OBTRUDE DIN JET SORN EJECT EXPEL GLARE FLAUNT IMPOSE MEDDLE THRUST INTRUDE INTERFERE

OBTRUSIVE FRESH PUSHY GARISH BLATANT FORWARD PUSHING BUMPTIOUS INTRUSIVE

OBTUND DULL BLUNT QUELL DEADEN

OBTURATOR MUSHROOM
OBTUSE DIM DULL BLINK BLUNT
CRASS DENSE THICK BOVINE
OPAQUE STUPID STUBBED
BOEOTIAN HEBETATE PURBLIND
(NOT —) ACUTE
OBVERSE FACE FRONT CONVERSE
(— OF COIN) MAN HEAD
OBVIATE PREVENT PRECLUDE
FORESTALL
OBVIOUS LOUD OPEN BROAD CLEAR
CRUDE FRANK GROSS NAKED OVERT
PLAIN SLICK STARK LIABLE PATENT
BLATANT EVIDENT EXPOSED
GLARING SHALLOW SUBJECT
VISIBLE APPARENT DISTINCT
MANIFEST PALPABLE BAREFACED
PROMINENT
(NOT —) DEEP INNER ARCANE
HIDDEN MASKED OCCULT SECRET
SUBTLE DELICATE DOUBTFUL
PROFOUND INEVIDENT
OBVIOUSNESS PATENCY
OBVOLUTE CONTORTED
OVERLAPPING
OCA OKA TUBER OXALIS SORREL
SOURSOP
OCARINA CAMOTE
OCCASION SEL BOUT CALL GIVE
HINT NEED SELE SITH TIDE TIME
TURN BREAK BREED CASUS CAUSE
CHARE EVENT INTER NONCE RAISE
SITHE SLANT STOUR WHILE YIELD
AFFAIR AUTHOR CHANCE COURSE
EXCUSE PERIOD REASON STOUND
CHESOUN INSPIRE OPENING
PRETEXT QUARREL CEREMONY
ENGENDER EXIGENCY FUNCTION
INCIDENT INSTANCE CONDITION
ENCHEASON HAPPENING
(— GRIEF) GRIEVE
(— OF EXCITEMENT) ALARM
ALARUM
(DEFINITE —) TIDE
(EXCITING —) BLAST
(FAVORABLE —) ADVANTAGE
(FESTIVE —) UTAS BEANO HOLIDAY
SHINDIG BEANFEAST MERRYMAKING
(HAPPY —) SIMHAH SIMCHAH
(SOCIAL —) COFFEE
(SPECIAL —) CEREMONY
OCCASIONAL ODD ORRA STRAY
ANTRIN CASUAL DAIMEN SCARCE
POPPING EPISODIC FUGITIVE
SPORADIC IRREGULAR
OCCASIONALLY EVERY ATTIMES
BETIMES SOMETIME SOMETIMES
OCCASIVE SETTING WESTWARD
OCCIDENTAL WEST PONENT
WESTERN HESPERIAN WESTERNER
OCCLUDE SHUT SORB CLOSE
ABSORB OBSTRUCT

OCCLUSAL MORSAL
OCCLUSION CORONARY
ARTICULATION
(SUFF.) CLEISIS CLISIS
OCCULT MAGIC ARCANE HIDDEN
LATENT MYSTIC SECRET VOODOO
ALCHEMY CRYPTIC ECLIPSE
UNKNOWN ESOTERIC MYSTICAL
SIBYLLIC CONCEALED RECONDITE
SIBYLLINE
(— SCIENCE) ESOTERICS
(PREF.) CRYPT(O) KRYPT(O)
OCCULTATION ECLIPSE
OCCULTISM MAGIC CABALA
MYSTERY
OCCUPANCY POSSESSION
OCCUPANT HOLDER INMATE
RENTER TENANT CITIZEN DWELLER
RESIDENT INCUMBENT
(— OF THEATER GALLERY) GOD
(SUFF.) ITE
OCCUPATION ART JOB LAY USE
CALL GAME LINE NOTE PLOY TOIL
WORK BERTH CRAFT GRAFT TRADE
BILLET CAREER EMPLOY METIER
RACKET SPHERE TENURE THRIFT
CALLING CONCERN CONTROL
MYSTERY PURSUIT QUALITY
SERVICE ACTIVITY BUSINESS
FUNCTION INDUSTRY INVASION
PLUMBING VOCATION
(— OF MIND) ABSORPTION
(PLEASURABLE —) RECREATIO
(PROFITABLE —) THRIFT
(SUBORDINATE —) HOBBY
AVOCATION
(TEDIOUS —) DRAG
OCCUPIED BUSY FULL HELD KEPT
RAPT TOOK INUSE ACTIVE INTENT
ENGAGED ABSORBED CAPTURED
(— WITH) INTO
(FULLY —) ENGROSSED
(NOT —) IDLE
OCCUPY LIE SIT USE BUSY FILL HAVE
HOLD KEEP TAKE WARM AMUSE
BELAY BESET DWELL ABSORB
BETAKE EMPLOY ENGAGE EXPEND
FULFIL OBTAIN TENANT COHABIT
CONCERN CONTAIN ENGROSS
ENTREAT IMPROVE INHABIT INVOLVE
OVERSIT PERVADE POSSESS
SWALLOW DISSOLVE GARRISON
INTEREST POPULATE POURPRISE
(— AS SUBSTITUTE) SUPPLY
(— ILLEGALLY) JUMP
(— ONESELF) TIRE TRADE ENTREAT
(— QUARTERS) CAMP
(— THOUGHTS) OBSESS
OCCUR BE GO COME COOK FALL
GIVE MAKE MEET PASS RISE SORT
ARISE BREAK CLASH EXIST INCUR
LIGHT APPEAR ARRIVE BEFALL

BETIDE CHANCE HAPPEN PROCEED
TRANSPIRE
(— AGAIN) RECUR REPEAT
(— BY CHANCE) LIGHT
(— TO) CROSS ENTER STRIKE
OCCURRENCE GO HAP CASE FACT
ITEM NOTE REDE EVENT WEIRD
EPISODE PASSAGE INCIDENT
JUNCTURE OCCASION ENCOUNTER
FREQUENCE HAPPENING
(CHANCE —) ADVENTURE
CONTINGENT
(COMMON —) USE FREQUENCY
(FREQUENT —) COMMUNITY
(HALLUCINATORY —) FREAKOUT
(SIMULTANEOUS —) SYNCHRONY
COINCIDENCE
(SUDDEN —) ZAP STROKE OUTCROP
(SUPERNATURAL —) MIRACLE
(UNEXPECTED —) SUDDEN BLIZZARD
BOMBSHELL
(UNFORTUNATE —) CASUALTY
(UNUSUAL —) ODDITY
OCCURRING (— AT NIGHTFALL)
ACRONICAL
(— AT REGULAR INTERVALS) HORAL
(— AT TWILIGHT) CREPUSCULAR
(— BY TURN) ALTERNATE
(— CASUALLY) SPORADIC
(— EVERY EIGHT DAYS) OCTAN
(— EVERY FOURTH YEAR)
PENTETERIC
(— FREQUENTLY) COMMON
(— INFREQUENTLY) OCCASIONAL
(— IN USUAL PLACE) ENTOPIC
(SELDOM —) RARE INFREQUENT
OCEAN SEA BLUE BRIM DEEP MAIN
POND BRINE DRINK ARCTIC INDIAN
EXPANSE NEPTUNE PACIFIC
ATLANTIC ANTARCTIC
(— FLOATING MATTER) ALGAE
LAGAN FLOTSAM
(— ROUTE) LANE
(— SPRAY) IRONWOOD CREAMCUPS
(— SWELL) SEA
(DEEP PART OF —) HADAL
(OF THE DEEP —) HADAL
(ON THE —) ASEA
(PERTAINING TO — DEPTHS) HADAL
(RELATING TO — BELOW 6000
METERS) HADAL
(PL.) ALOT
OCEANIA MALAYA AUSTRALIA
MELANESIA POLYNESIA
(REPUBLIC IN —) FIJI
(SACRED OBJECT OF —) ZOGO
OCEANIC NAVAL MARINE PELAGIC
NAUTICAL AEQUOREAL
OCEANOGRAPHER
(ALSO SEE HYDROGRAPHER)
OCEANUS TITAN
(DAUGHTER OF —) DORIS OCEANID
EURYNOME

(FATHER OF —) URANUS OURANOS
(MOTHER OF —) GAEA GAIA
(SISTER OF —) TETHYS
(SON OF —) NEREUS
(WIFE OF —) TETHYS
OCELLUS EYE EYELET STEMMA
EYESPOT
OCELOT CAT TOGER LEOPARD
WILDCAT
OCHER RUD SIL KEEL OAKER OCHRE
TIVER ABRAUM RADDLE ALMAGRA
TANGIER
(BLACK —) WAD WADD
(RED —) RUD KEEL TIVER ABRAUM
REDDLE RUBRIC RUDDLE KOKOWAI
(YELLOW —) SIL SPRUCE
OCOTILLO COACHWHIP
CANDLEWOOD
OCRAN (SON OF —) PAGIEL
OCREA OCHREA SHEATH
OCTAHEDROID HYPERCUBE
TESSERACT
OCTAVE UTAS UTIS EIGHT EIGHTH
OTTAVA EIGHTVO HUITAIN DIAPASON
SHEMINITH
(— FLUTE) FLAUTINO
(— OF THE SEVENTH) FOURTEENTH
(— SINGING) MAGADIZE
(DIMINISHED —) SEMIDIAPASON
(FATHER OF —) ARGANTE
(TRIPLE —) TRIDIAPASON
OCTAVIA (BROTHER OF —)
AUGUSTUS
(HUSBAND OF —) ANTONY
OCTAVO EIGHTS
OCTET OCTAVE OCTUOR HUITAIN
OTTETTO
OCTOPUS HEE POLYP POULP PREKE
SQUID CUTTLE CATFISH POLYPOD
POLYPUS SCUTTLE DIBRANCH
OCTOPEAN DEVILFISH
(— ARM) TENTACLE
(AUTHOR OF —) NORRIS
(CHARACTER IN —) DYKE TREE
HILMA LYMAN HOOVEN MAGNUS
SARRIA BEHRMAN CARAHER
DELANEY DERRICK PRESLEY
RUGGLES VANAMEE ANNIXTER
SHELGRIM CEDARQUIST
GENSLINGER
(SECRETION OF —) INK
OCTOROON METIS MESTEE
MUSTEE MESTIZO METISSE
OCTAROON
OCTROI TAX GRANT PRIVILEGE
OCTUPLE EIGHTFOLD
OCUBY RUM
OCULAR OPTIC VISUAL OCULARY
OPTICAL ORBITAL EYEPIECE
OCULUS MUNDI OPAL
OCYRRHOE (FATHER OF —)
CHIRON
(MOTHER OF —) CHARICLO

ODD AUK AWK OUT RUM FELL LEFT LONE ORRA RARE ANTIC CRAZY DIPPY DITSY DROLL EERIE EXTRA FLAKY FUNKY FUNNY IMPAR KINKY OUTRE QUEER SPACY UNKET UNKID WEIRD FLAKEY FREAKY IMPAIR QUAINT SINGLE SPACEY UNEVEN UNIQUE AZYGOUS BAROQUE BIZARRE COMICAL CURIOUS ERRATIC STRANGE UNEQUAL UNUSUAL FANCIFUL FREAKISH PECULIAR SINGULAR UNPAIRED BURLESQUE ECCENTRIC FANTASTIC GROTESQUE LAUGHABLE SQUIRRELY UNMATCHED WHIMSICAL
(— JOBMAN) JOEY
(PREF.) AZYGO IMPARI

ODDBALL GEEK KOOK SPOOK WEIRDO DINGBAT CRACKPOT

ODDITY GIG QUIP JIMJAM ANOMALY RUMNESS QUIZZITY PECULIARITY
(PL.) PURLICUES

ODDMAN UMPIRE ARBITER FLOATER REFEREE

ODDS BISK EDGE CHALK PRICE BISQUE DISCORD DISPUTE QUARREL HANDICAP VARIANCE ADVANTAGE DISPARITY
(— AND ENDS) ORTS STEW BROTT REFUSE SCRAPS GIBLETS SECONDS FEWTRILS REMNANTS SHAKINGS ETCETERAS FRAGMENTS
(AT —) ACROSS
(EXTRAVAGANT —) POUNDAGE
(FAVORABLE —) PERCENTAGE

ODE HYMN POEM SONG LYRIC PAEAN PSALM GHAZEL MONODY ODELET CANZONA CANZONE EPICEDE CANTICLE PALINODE PINDARIC SERENATA STASIMON EPICEDIUM EPINICION PARABASIS
(— OF LAMENTATION) THRENE THRENODY

ODED (SON OF —) AZARIAH

ODENATHUS (WIFE OF —) ZENOBIA

ODEON HALL ODEUM GALLERY THEATER

ODIN OTHIN WODAN WODEN WOTAN
(BROTHER OF —) VE VILI
(CREATED BY —) ASK EMBLA
(DAUGHTER-IN-LAW OF —) NANNA
(DESCENDANT OF —) DOYLD
(FATHER OF —) BOR BORR
(HALL OF —) VALHALLA
(HORSE OF —) SLEIPNER SLEIPNIR
(MANSION OF —) GLADSHEIM
(MOTHER OF —) BESTLA
(PALACE OF —) SYN
(RAVEN OF —) HUGIN MUNIN
(RING OF —) DRAUPNIR
(SHIP OF —) NAGLFAR SKIDBLADNIR
(SON OF —) TYR THOR VALI BALDR BALDER
(SPEAR OF —) GUNGNIR
(SWORD OF —) GRAM
(THRONE OF —) HLIDSKJALF
(WIFE OF —) FRIA RIND FRIGG RINDR FRIGGA
(WOLF OF —) GERI FREKI

ODIOUS FOUL LOTH UGLY VILE LOATH INFAND ODIBLE HATABLE HATEFUL HEINOUS HIDEOUS DAMNABLE FLAGRANT INFAMOUS ABHORRENT INVIDIOUS OBNOXIOUS OFFENSIVE REPUGNANT

ODIUM HATRED STIGMA DISLIKE AVERSION DISFAVOR DISGRACE DISHONOR ANTIPATHY
(PUBLIC —) ENVY

ODOACER (FATHER OF —) EDECON

ODOMETER ODOGRAPH VIAMETER WAYWISER HODOMETER PEDOMETER

ODONTALGIA TOOTHACHE

ODOR AIR FUME FUNK NOSE OLID TANG WAFF WAFT AROMA EWDER FETOR FLAIR FUMET NIDOR SCENT SMACK SMELL SNUFF SPICE STINK BREATH FLAVOR FOETOR HODURE REPUTE STENCH BOUQUET ESSENCE FUMETTE NOSEGAY PERFUME VERDURE PUNGENCE EFFLUVIUM EMPYREUMA FRAGRANCE REDOLENCE
(— FROM FLOWERS) FUME
(— OF GAME) FUMET
(— OF HAY) NOSE
(BAD —) EWDER FROWST STENCH
(DISGUSTING —) STINK
(FOUL —) FIST MEPHITIS
(FRESH —) YMUR
(PUNGENT —) SPICE
(SPICY —) BALM
(STUDY OF —S) OSMICS
(UNPLEASANT —) PONG
(PREF.) OSM(O)
(SUFF.) OSMA OSPHRESIA

ODORIFEROUS BALMY OLENT ODOROUS FRAGRANT

ODOROUS FOUL BALMY OLENT SMELLY NOISOME ODORANT AROMATIC FRAGRANT NIDOROSE NIDOROUS PERFUMED REDOLENT SCENTFUL SMELLFUL

ODYSSEUS ULYSSES
(ADVISER OF —) ATHENA
(DOG OF —) ARGOS
(FATHER OF —) LAERTES SISYPHUS
(FRIEND OF —) MENTOR
(ISLAND OF —) ITHACA
(SON OF —) TELEGONUS TELEMACHUS
(WIFE OF —) PENELOPE

ODYSSEY (AUTHOR OF —) HOMER
(CHARACTER IN —) ARETE CIRCE HELEN AEOLUS NESTOR EUMAEUS

ALCINOUS MENELAUS NAUSICAA
ODYSSEUS PENELOPE DEMODOCUS
EURYCLEIA TEIRESIAS POLYPHEMUS
TELEMACHUS

OEAX (BROTHER OF —) PALAMEDES
(FATHER OF —) NAUPLIUS
(MOTHER OF —) CLYMENE

OEBALUS (FATHER OF —) TELON
(SON OF —) ICARIUS HIPPOCOON
TYNDAREUS
(WIFE OF —) GORGOPHONE

OECIST OEKIST COLONIZER

OEDIPUS OEDIPAL
(BROTHER-IN-LAW OF —) CREON
(DAUGHTER OF —) ISMENE
ANTIGONE
(FATHER OF —) LAIUS
(FOSTER MOTHER OF —) PERIBOEA
(MOTHER OF —) JOCASTA
(SON OF —) ETEOCLES POLYNICES
(WIFE OF —) JOCASTA

OEIL-DE-BOEUF OCULUS

OEILLADE OGLE ELIAD EYLIAD
GLANCE ILLIAD

OENEUS (DAUGHTER OF —) GORGE
DEIANIRA
(FATHER OF —) PORTHEUS
(SON OF —) TOXEUS TYDEUS
MELEAGER
(WIFE OF —) ALTHAEA

OENOCHOE JUG EWER OLPE
PROCHOOS

OENOMAUS (DAUGHTER OF —)
HIPPODAMIA
(FATHER OF —) ARES MARS
(MOTHER OF —) STEROPE
(SON OF —) LEUCIPPUS
DYSPONTEUS HIPPODAMUS

OENOMETER VINOMETER

OENONE (FATHER OF —) CEBREN
(LOVER OF —) PARIS
(SON OF —) CORYTHUS

OENOPION (DAUGHTER OF —)
MEROPE
(FATHER OF —) DIONYSUS
(WIFE OF —) HELICE

OESTRID FLY
(— LARVA) BOT

OESTRUS RUT FURY HEAT STING
DESIRE ESTRUS FRENZY IMPULSE
STIMULUS

OEUVRE OPUS WORK

OF A O BY DE OFF VAN VON FROM
HAVE TILL WITH ABOUT
(— AGE) AE
(— ALL) AVA ALDER ALLER
(— COURSE) NATCH
(— DEATH) M
(— EACH) ANA PER SING
(— THIS DAY) HODIERNAL
(— THIS MONTH) HM
(SUFF.) AL AR ILE INE ISH ISTIC ITIC
ITIOUS ORIOUS ORY

OFF BY AFF FAR ODD WET AFAR AGEE
AWAY DOFF DOWN GONE LESS
ALONG ASIDE RIGHT WONKY
WRONG ABSENT CUCKOO DEPART
REMOTE DISTANT FURTHER
REMOVED SEAWARD TAINTED
ABNORMAL OPPOSITE
(— GUARD) TARDY
(— THE PATH) ASTRAY
(— THE SUBJECT) AFIELD
(— THE WIND) ROOM ROOMWARD
(FAR —) DISTANT
(PREF.) AP APH APO DE

OFFAL GURRY WASTE REFUSE
CARRION DOGMEAT GARBAGE
LEAVING RUBBISH GRALLOCH
(— OF FISH) GURRY STOSH
(MILLING —S) GRIT

OFFBEAT ODD FLAKY

OFF-BEAT KOOKY

OFFBEAT KOOKY SPACY WACKY
WEIRD KOOKIE SPACEY

OFFBREAK GOOGLY

OFF-CENTER ECCENTRIC
EXCENTRIC

OFF-COLOR BLUE RISQUE
SUGGESTIVE

OFFENCE (— AGAINST STATE)
SEDITION

OFFEND CAG ERR PET SIN VEX GALL
HARM HUFF HURT MIFF RASP RASS
ABUSE ANGER ANNOY GRATE GRILL
PIQUE SHOCK SPITE TOUCH WRONG
AGUILT ATTACK GRIEVE INJURE
INSULT NETTLE REVOLT AFFRONT
DEFAULT DISDAIN MORTIFY
OUTRAGE PROVOKE REGRATE
STOMACH UMBRAGE VIOLATE
CONFRONT DISTASTE IRRITATE
TRESPASS DISOBLIGE DISPLEASE

OFFENDED HUFF MIFF SORE
AVERTED FROISSE INJURED
INSULTED

OFFENDER SINNER CULPRIT
MISDOER PECCANT HABITUAL
OFFENDANT
(FIRST —) STAR

OFFENDING PECCANT

OFFENSE PET SIN HUFF LACK SLIP
WITE ABUSE CRIME ERROR FAULT
GRIEF GUILT MALUM PIQUE SNUFF
ATTACK BIGAMY DELICT FELONY
PIACLE PRITCH REATUS STRUNT
AFFRONT DEFAULT DEMERIT
DUDGEON LARCENY MISDEED
OUTRAGE SCANDAL UMBRAGE
PECCANCY TRESPASS EXTORTION
INDECORUM INDIGNITY
THEFTBOTE
(— AGAINST LAW) MALUM DELICT
DELICTUM
(— AGAINST MORALITY) EVIL CRIME
(SLIGHT —) PECCADILLO

OFFENSIVE BAD ACID EVIL FOUL
HARD UGLY BILGY CRUDE DIRTY
FETID GROSS NASTY SLIMY YUCKY
COARSE FROWZY GARISH HORRID
RANCID RIBALD ROTTEN ABUSIVE
BEASTLY FULSOME HATEFUL
HIDEOUS NOISOME PECCANT
RASPING SCARLET DREADFUL
INVADING MEPHITIC SHOCKING
STINKING UNSAVORY LOATHSOME
OBNOXIOUS REPUGNANT
REVOLTING SCANDALOUS
(— SIGHT) EYESORE
OFFENSIVENESS ODIUM
OFFER GO BID PUT BODE GIVE HAND
LEND PLEA POSE SHOW TAKE TEND
DEFER HEAVE PARTY SHORE START
ADDUCE AFFORD ALLEGE DELATE
INJECT OBLATE OPPOSE PREFER
SUBMIT SUPPLY TENDER ADVANCE
BIDDING COMMEND EXHIBIT
PRESENT PROFFER PROPINE
PROPOSE SUGGEST OVERTURE
PROPOSAL VOLUNTEER
(— A STAKE) SET
(— EXCUSE) ALIBI
(— FOR SALE) HAWK EXPOSE
(— INDUCEMENT) INVITE
(— IN EXCUSE) PLEAD
(— IN OPPOSITION) OBJECT
(— IN SACRIFICE) IMMOLATE
(— OF MARRIAGE) PROPOSAL
(— PROOF) APPROVE
(— PUBLICLY) JACTITATE
(— RESISTANCE) FEND
(— TO VERIFY) AVER
(— UP) APPEAL
(LAST —) ULTIMATUM
(PUBLIC —) SALE
(SOLEMN —) PLEDGE
(UNACCEPTED —) POLLICITATION
OFFERING BID ALMS BALI DALI DEAL
GIFT HOST SOMA DOLLY ENTRY
CORBAN NUZZER OFLETE PIACLE
PRESENT RETABLO TRIBUTE
ANATHEMA DEVOTION DONATION
LIBATION OBLATION PESHKASH
PIACULUM SACRIFICE
(— TO GOD) CORBAN DEODATE
(— TO HOUSEHOLD DEITIES) BALI
(EUCHARISTIC —) ANAPHORA
(PEACE —S) PACIFICS
(RELIGIOUS —) OBLATION
(SACRIFICIAL —) HOLOCAUST
(THEATRICAL —) FLUFF
(PL.) HIERA ALTARAGE INFERIAE
OFF-GLIDE EXIT VOCULE DETENTE
OFFHAND AIRY CURT GLIB SOON
ADLIB BLUSH HASTY ABRUPT
BREEZY CASUAL BRUSQUE READILY
CARELESS CAVALIER GLANCING
INFORMAL EXTEMPORE IMPROMPTU
UNSTUDIED

OFFICE HAT JOB SEE BOMA DUTY
NONE PART POST ROLE ROOM SHOP
TASK TOGA WIKE WORK PLACE
STINT TRUST WIKEN YAMEN ABBACY
AGENCY BUREAU CHARGE DAFTAR
DIWANI DUFTER METIER MISTER
BULLPEN CAMARIN CENTRAL
DEWANEE DROSTDY EDILITY
MYSTERY SERVICE STATION
SURGERY AEDILITY CAPACITY
CUTCHERY ENSIGNCY FUNCTION
KINGSHIP MINISTRY POSITION
PROVINCE WOOLPACK BAILIWICK
BANKSHALL SITUATION
(— BOY) CHOKRA
(— CHIEF) BOSS MANAGER
(— OF BISHOP) LAWN
(— OF JUDGE) BENCH ERMINE
(— OF PROFESSOR) CHAIR
(— OF ROMAN CURIA) DATARY
DATARIA
(— OF RULER) REGENCY
(— OF THE DEAD) DIRGE
(— WORKER) CLERK STENO TYPIST
SECRETARY
(BRANCH —) WING
(CASHIER'S —) CAISSE
(CLERICAL —) CASSOCK
(DIVINE —) AKOLUTHIA
(ECCLESIASTICAL —) FROCK
BENEFICE EXORCIST
(HIGH —) DIGNITY
(LITURGICAL —) SEXT SERVICE
(MAGISTRATE'S —) KACHAHRI
(MORNING —) ORTHRON ORTHROS
(NAVAL —S) BEACH
(PAY —) WANIGAN
(POLICE —) NICK
(PRIESTLY —) DACHIDOCY
(PRINTING —) CHAPEL IMPRIMERY
(RECORD —) CHANCERY
(RESIGN AN —) DEMIT
(TIMEKEEPER'S —) PENNYHOLE
(SUFF.) ATE CY DOM SHIP URE
OFFICEHOLDER IN WINNER
OFFICIAL PLACEMAN
OFFICER (ALSO SEE OFFICIAL) COP
TAB AIDE EXEC EXON FLAG HOLD
NASI SWAB VOGT AGENT CHIEF
CRIER DEWAN DIWAN GRAND GRAVE
GROOM JURAT SEWER TAXOR
USHER ALCADE BEADLE BEAGLE
BEDRAL BUTLER CENSOR DEPUTY
DIRECT ENSIGN GAILLI GEREFA
HERALD KOTWAL LAWMAN LICTOR
MANAGE ORATOR PARNAS REDTAB
SYNDIC TINDAL ADJOINT AGISTOR
ALNAGER ASSIZER BAILIFF
COMMAND CONDUCT CORONER
DUUMVIR EPAULET FEDERAL
FEODARY GAVELER GENERAL
JEMADAR KLEAGLE LOBSTER
MUSTANG NAPERER PANTLER

PATROON REGIDOR SANCTUM SCHEPEN SHERIFF SPEAKER STEWARD WHIPPER WOODMAN ADJUTANT ALDERMAN ALGUACIL ANDREEVE BANNERET CHAFFWAX COFFERER CURSITOR DOORWARD FORESTER GOVERNOR GRASSMAN MERESMAN MINISTER PALATINE PURVEYOR QUESTEUR REPORTER TIPSTAFF VISCOUNT WOODWARD CONSTABLE DIKEGRAVE FINANCIER INTENDANT MODERATOR PAYMASTER SCHOOLMAN TAHSILDAR

(— OF CHURCH) ABBOT ELDER DEACON SEXTON ANTISTES DEFENSOR LAMPADARY SACRISTAN
(— OF COURT) MACER MASTER BAILIFF FEODARY FILACER CURSITOR DEMPSTER EXAMINER SERGEANT ASSOCIATE BYRLAWMAN SURROGATE
(— OF FORESTS) AGISTER AGISTOR
(— OF KING'S STABLES) AVENER
(— OF TABLE) SEWER
(BARDIC —) DRUID
(CAVALRY —) CORNET
(CHIEF —) NASI DEWAN DAROGA PARNAS PRESIDENT
(CHIEF EXECUTIVE —) CEO
(CHURCH —) SEXTON
(COLLEGE —) RECTOR
(COURT —) REEVE SUMMONER
(CUSTOMS —) GAGER SHARK GAUGER JERQUER DOUANIER SEARCHER SURVEYOR TIDESMAN
(FOREST —) RANGER
(GREEK —) STRATEGOS STRATEGUS
(JAPANESE —) SHIKKEN
(KIND OF —) PETTY
(LAW —) GANGBUSTER
(MASONIC —) EAST KING DEACON STEWARD
(MILITARY —) NAIG NAIK COMES MAJOR SUBAH SIRDAR NAIQUE RANKER SARDAR SIRDAR CAPTAIN COLONEL GENERAL JEMADAR MARSHAL SUBADAR WARRANT COMMANDER RABSHAKEH SHAVETAIL
(MINOR —) CHINOVNIK
(MONASTERY —) CELLARER
(MUNICIPAL —) SCHOUT VARLET
(NAVAL —) CPO EXON MATE SWAB BOSUN ENSIGN PURSER YEOMAN ADMIRAL CAPTAIN MUSTANG SPOTTER YOUNKER COXSWAIN SUNDOWNER MIDSHIPMAN
(PAPAL —) DATARY
(POLICE —) COP PIG PEON RURAL COPPER EXEMPT JAVERT KOTWAL ROZZER RUNNER SBIRRO ALYTARCH

SEARCHER THANADAR DETECTIVE ROUNDSMAN
(PRESIDING —) CHAIRONE CHAIRPERSON
(PRISON —) SCREW WARDER
(PUBLIC —) JUDGE FISCAL NOTARY PODESTA
(ROMAN —) LICTOR
(SHERIFF'S —) FANG BEAGLE BAILIFF BULLDOG HUISSIER
(SHIP'S —) MATE FANTOD
(STAFF —) TAB AIDE REDTAB ADJUTANT
(TOLL —) SCAVAGER
(TURKISH —) AGA AGHA MUTE VIZIR VIZIER BIMBASHI BINBASHI
(UNIVERSITY —) DEAN REGENT PROVOST
(WARRANT —) MACHINIST
(PL.) BRAID BRASS STAFF
OFFICIAL (ALSO SEE OFFICER) AGA BEG DEY VIP AMIN BOSS KUAN KWAN TRUE AGENT AHONG AMALA AMBAN AMEEN AMLAH CLERK EDILE EPHOR GYANI HAJIB HOMER JURAT LIMMU LINER MAYOR NAZIR OMRAH REEVE SAHIB AEDILE ARCHON ATABEG BASHAW CENSOR CONSUL EPARCH EPONYM FISCAL FORMAL GABBAI GRIEVE HAZZAN HERALD LAWMAN MASTER NOTARY PANDIT PREVOT RABMAG SATRAP SCRIBE SEALER SINGER TAOTAI TAOYIN TRONER VERGER WARDEN WEDANA ALMONER APOSTLE ASIARCH BURGESS CERTAIN JEMADAR LANDRAT MARSHAL MOORMAN PRISTAW REFEREE STALLAR STARTER SUBASHI VAIVODE ALDERMAN APPROVED CARDINAL CELLARER CUSTOMER DOGBERRY GOVERNOR LINESMAN MANDARIN PROVIDER PRYTANIS VESTIARY VISCOUNT WHIFFLER EXECUTIVE MAJORDOMO OMBUDSMAN SELECTMAN MAGISTRATE
(— APPROVAL) VISA VISE
(— DECREE) WRIT UKASE
(— OF CARTHAGE) SUFFETE
(BLUNDERING —) DOGBERRY
(EISTEDDFOD —) DRUID
(GAME —) REF UMP SCORER UMPIRE REFEREE
(MUSLIM —) OMRAH
(PALACE —) PALADIN
(POMPOUS —) BUMBLE
(PRETENTIOUS —) PANJANDRUM
(UNIVERSITY —) PROCTOR
(PL.) KEYS PHAR OMLAH
OFFICIATE ACT FILL SERVE SUPPLY PERFORM CELEBRATE
OFFICIATOR DEICIDE

OFFICIOUS BUSY COOL PERT SAUCY
FORMAL FORTHY PUSHING
ARROGANT IMPUDENT INFORMAL
MEDDLING OFFICIAL INBEARING
PRAGMATIC
OFFING OFF FUTURE PICTURE
OFFISH CLAMMY UPSTAGE
OFFSCOURINGS MUD SCURF
OFF-SEASON LAYOFF
OFFSET SLAB STEP ALTAR CRIMP
ERASE POISE CANCEL CONTRA
JOGGLE REDEEM SETOFF BALANCE
COUNTER LATERAL RETREAT
SETBACK PROPAGULE
(— ON BULB) SPLIT
OFFSHOOT GET PUP ROD SON LIMB
SPUR BOUGH ISSUE SCION SHOOT
SPRIG BRANCH FILIAL GROWTH
MEMBER OFFSET SPROUT ADJUNCT
APOPHYSIS FILIATION OUTGROWTH
RAMIFICATION
(— OF LAKE) BAYOU
(— OF RELIGIOUS ORDER) REFORM
OFFSHORE DEEPWATER
OFFSPRING BOY FRY IMP KID KIN
SON BRAT BURD CHIT HEIR SEED
SLIP BIRTH BREED BROOD CHILD
FRUIT ISSUE SCION SPAWN BEGATS
DUSTEE EMBRYO FOSTER GRIQUA
JUMART PROLES RESULT STRAIN
STRIND MORISCO NISHADA
OUTCOME PRODUCE PRODUCT
PROGENY PRODUCE CHILDREN
DAUGHTER DEMISANG GENITURE
INCREASE KINDLING BAIRNTEAM
MUSTAFINA
(— OF EUROPEAN-INDIAN)
MAMELUCO
(— OF FAIRIES) CHANGELING
(— OF NEGRO AND MULATTO)
GRIFFE
(— OF STALLION AND ASS) HINNY
FUNNEL
(— OF WITCH) HAGSEED
HOLDIKEN
(MYTHICAL —) JUMART
(PREMATURE —) CASTLING
(WITHOUT —) ATOKAL ATOKOUS
(PREF.) GEN(O) GON(O) PAEDO PEDO
PROLI
(SUFF.) ITE TOKOUS
OFF-THE-RACK READYMADE
OF HUMAN BONDAGE (AUTHOR
OF —) MAUGHAM
(CHARACTER IN —) CAREY EMILY
ERLIN FANNY NORAH PRICE SALLY
WEEKS LAWSON LOUISA NESBIT
PHILIP ROGERS THORPE ATHELNY
CLUTTON HAYWARD MILDRED
WILLIAM CRONSHAW WILKINSON
OFICINA WORKS OFFICE FACTORY
OFLETE WAFER OBLATION OFFERING

OF MICE AND MEN (AUTHOR OF —
) STEINBECK
(CHARACTER IN —) SLIM CANDY
SMALL CROOKS CURLEY GEORGE
LENNIE MILTON
OFTEN OFT AFTEN OFTLY COMMON
EFTSOONS FREQUENT REPEATED
(VERY —) CONTINUALLY
OF TIME AND THE RIVER
(AUTHOR OF —) WOLFE
(CHARACTER IN —) ANN GANT JOEL
WANG BASCOM ELINOR EUGENE
PIERCE ROBERT WEAVER COULSON
FRANCIS HATCHER MORNAYE
PENTLAND
OGDOAD EIGHT OCTOAD OGDOAS
OCTONARY
OGEE (ALSO SEE MOLDING) CYMA
GULA TALON MOLDING
OGIVAL HEATER
OGLE EYE GAZE LEER LOOK MASH
STARE GLANCE EXAMINE MARLOCK
SMICKER OEILLADE
OGRE ORC BOYG BRUTE DEMON
FIEND GHOUL GIANT HUGON
TYRANT YAKSHA BUGABOO
BUGBEAR MONSTER WINDIGO
OGRESS PELLET GUNSTONE
OGTIERN LORD MASTER
OGYGIAN ANCIENT PRIMEVAL
OH OU OW ACH OUCH

OHIO	
CAPITAL: COLUMBUS	
COLLEGE: KENT HIRAM KENYON XAVIER ANTIOCH OBERLIN DEFIANCE	
COUNTY: ERIE PIKE ROSS DARKE MIAMI STARK GALLIA HARDIN SUMMIT LICKING CUYAHOGA HAMILTON	
INDIAN TRIBE: ERIE WYANDOT	
NATIVE: BUCKEYE	
NICKNAME: BUCKEYE	
PRESIDENT: TAFT GRANT HAYES HARDING GARFIELD HARRISON MCKINLEY	
RIVER: MIAMI MAUMEE SCIOTO CUYAHOGA MUSKINGUM	
STATE BIRD: CARDINAL	
STATE FLOWER: CARNATION	
STATE TREE: BUCKEYE	
TOWN: ADA ENON LIMA TROY ADENA AKRON BEREA CADIZ NILES XENIA CANTON DAYTON ELYRIA LORAIN MENTOR TOLEDO CHARDON COLUMBUS SANDUSKY CLEVELAND	

OIL BEN FAT ILE ULE BALM CHIA DIKA
FUEL ZEST BRIBE CRUDE JUICE
OLEUM SMEAR STOCK TRAIN ULYIE
ULZIE ACEITE ANOINT BINDER

BUTTER CARDOL CHRISM CREESH
EUPION GREASE LIQUOR SAFROL
SMOOTH ZACHUN CEDRIUM
ESSENCE LANOLIN MYRRHOL
PHLOROL RETINOL VETIVER
BERGAMOT COUMARAN ERIGERON
GINGEROL PHTHALAN SDRAVETS
TETRALIN CARVACROL LUBRICATE
PETROLEUM
(— BEETLE) MELOE MELOID
(— CAKE) SEEDCAKE
(— CAN) OILER
(— CASK) RIER
(— FROM ORANGE FLOWERS)
NEROLI
(— FROM RESIN) RETINOL
(— IN PAINTS) TUNG
(— LAMP) LUCIGEN
(— OF TURPENTINE) CAMPHENE
CAMPHINE
(— PALM) OILBERRY
(— PAN) SUMP
(— PLANT) SESAME
(— ROCK) SHALE LIMESTONE
(— TREE) EBOE POON TUNG MAHWA
(— VESSEL) DRUM OLPE CRUET
CRUSE TANKER CRESSET
(— WELL) DUSTER GASSER GUSHER
WILDCAT
(AROMATIC —) SPIKENARD
(BUTTER —) GHEE
(COAL —) PHOTOGEN
(CONSECRATED —) CHRISM
(FISH —) GURRY
(FIXED —) COCUM KOKAM KOKUM
(FLOWER —) ATAR NARD OTTO
ATTAR OTTAR CAFFEOL BERGAMOT
CAFFEONE GERANIOL
(FUEL —) DERV
(INFERIOR —) MIDDLING
(KIND OF —) CASTOR
(KIND OF COOKING —) CORN COPRA
OLIVE
(LINSEED —) CARRON LINOLEUM
(MINERAL —) NAPHTHA KEROSENE
(ORANGE —) NEROLI
(ORANGE-FLOWER —) NEROLI
(PINE —) FROTHER
(PUNGENT —) CAJUPUT
(REMAINING FUEL —) RESID
(RESIDUAL —) RESID
(SESAME —) GINGILI SIRITCH
(SOLID —) KIKUEL
(VEGETABLE —) MACASSAR
(VULCANIZED —) FACTICE
(WHALE —) SPERM TRAIN
(WOOL —) YOLK
(PREF.) ELAEO ELAIO ELEO OLEI OLEO
OILBIRD FATBIRD GUACHARO
OIL CAKE POONAC RESIDUE
OILFISH ESCOLAR
OILILY SLEEK

OILSEED TIL TEEL SESAME LINSEED
RAPESEED
OILSKIN OIL OILER SQUAM OILCASE
OILCOAT SLICKER
OILSTONE HONE SHALE
WHETSTONE
OIL WELL GUSHER
OILY FAT GLIB LIMY BLAND FATTY
LOEIC OLEIC SLEEK SOAPY SUAVE
GREASY OILISH OLEOSE OLEOUS
SMARMY SMOOTH SUPPLE PINGUID
SERVILE SLIPPERY UNCTUOUS
COMPLIANT PLAUSIBLE
(PREF.) LIPAR(O)
OINTMENT UNG BALM MULL NARD
PASTE SALVE SMEAR BALSAM
CERATE CEROMA CHARGE CHRISM
GREASE POMADE REMEDY
UNGUENT EYESALVE POPULEON
REMOLADE SPIKENARD WHITFIELD
(— OF GODS) AMBROSIA
OJIBWAY CHIPPEWA SAULTEUR
CHIPPEWAY
OKA OCHA OQUE OQUI OCQUE
OKAPI GIRAFFINE
OKAY OK YES HUNK OKEH HUNKY
APPROVE CORRECT SANCTION
AUTHORIZE SAYTHEWORD
(JAPANESE —) HAI
OKIA OKET OUNCE
OKINAWA (CAPITAL OF —) NAHA

OKLAHOMA

CAPITAL: OKLAHOMACITY
COLLEGE: CAMERON LANGSTON
PHILLIPS
COUNTY: KAY COAL LOVE ADAIR
ATOKA CADDO GREER OSAGE
ALFALFA OKFUSKEE OKMULGEE
INDIAN TRIBE: WACO WICHITA
TAWAKONI
LAKE: EUFAULA OOLOGAH
MOUNTAINS: OUACHITA
NATIVE: OKIE SOONER
NICKNAME: SOONER
RIVER: RED GRAND WASHITA
ARKANSAS CANADIAN CIMARRON
STATE FLOWER: MISTLETOE
STATE TREE: REDBUD
TOWN: ADA JAY ALVA ENID HUGO
ALTUS MIAMI PONCA TULSA
ELRENO GUYMON IDABEL LAWTON
MADILL TALOGA VINITA ANTLERS
SAPULPA SHAWNEE ANADARKO
FORTSILL MUSKOGEE

OKRA GOBO OKRO BAMIA BENDY
GOBBO GOMBO GUBBO GUMBO
OCHRA BENDEE MALLOW BANDAKA
BANDICOY BANDIKAI
OLD AGY ELD AGED AULD COLD
WOLD YALD ANILE HOARY MOSSY
STALE WOULD EFFETE FORMER

FOROLD INFIRM MATURE SENILE
SHABBY VETUST AGEABLE ANCIENT
ANTIQUE ARCHAIC ELDERLY
FORWORN OGYGIAN UMWHILE
DECREPIT MEDIEVAL OBSOLETE
DODDERING GERIATRIC HACKNEYED
SENESCENT VENERABLE
(— AND MELLOW) CRUSTY
(— BAILEY) GAOL JAIL PRISON
(— CLOTHESMAN) POCO
(— FAITHFUL) GEYSER
(— HAND) LONGTIMER
(— MAID) SPINSTER THORNBACK
(— MAN) ANTIQUITY WHITEBEARD
(— SOD) EIRE ERIN IRELAND
(— SQUAW) DIVER HOUND MOMMY
CALLOO CALLOW COWEEN DUCKER
QUANDY OLDWIFE SCOLDER
COCKAWEE LONGTAIL SHARPTAIL
SOUTHERLY
(— WOMAN) HAG CRONE GAMMER
(BEING LESS THAN 13 YEARS —)
PRETEEN
(GROWING —) SENESCENT
(OF —) WHILOM ERSTWHILE
(PREF.) PALAE(O) PALAI(O) PALE(O)
SENI
(— AGE) GER(I)(O) GERATO
GERONT(O) PRESBY(O)
(PREF.) (— MAN) GER(I)(O)
GERONT(O) PRESBY(O)
OLD AND THE YOUNG (AUTHOR
OF —) PIRANDELLO
(CHARACTER IN —) COSTA MAURO
SALVO SELMI AURITI GIULIO
AURELIO CORRADO MORTARA
ROBERTO CAPOLINO DIANELLA
FLAMINIO GERLANDO IPPOLITO
NICOLETTA LAURENTANO
OLD BAY STATE MASSACHUSETTS
OLD CURIOSITY SHOP (AUTHOR
OF —) DICKENS
(CHARACTER IN —) KIT DICK FRED
NELL BRASS QUILP SARAH CODLIN
JARLEY MARTON THOMAS BARBARA
NUBBLES SAMPSON SWIVELLER
CHRISTOPHER
OLD DOMINION STATE VIRGINIA
OLDEN ANTIQUE
OLDER MORE ALDER ELDER SENIOR
ANCESTOR
OLDEST
(PREF.) EO
OLD-FASHIONED MOSSY RETRO
CORNBALL SCHMALTZY
NEANDERTHAL CORNY DOWDY
FUSTY PASSE FOGRAM FOGRUM
QUAINT STODGY ANCIENT ANTIQUE
ARCHAIC ARRIERE ELDERLY
VINTAGE FRUMPISH OBSOLETE
CRINOLINE PRIMITIVE RINKYDINK
OLDFANGLED
(FASHIONABLY —) RETRO

OLD FRANKLIN STATE
TENNESSEE
OLD LINE STATE MARYLAND
OLD MAID (AUTHOR OF —)
WHARTON
(CHARACTER IN —) JOE TINA DELIA
JAMES LOVELL CLEMENT RALSTON
SPENDER CHARLOTTE
OLD MORTALITY (AUTHOR OF —)
SCOTT
(CHARACTER IN —) JOHN BASIL
EDITH HENRY JENNY MAUSE CUDDIE
MORTON BALFOUR FRANCIS
GRAHAME OLIFANT BOTHWELL
DENNISON EVANDALE HEADRIGG
MARGARET BELLENDEN
CLAVERHOUSE
OLD-TIMER SOURDOUGH
OLD WIVES' TALE (AUTHOR OF —)
BENNETT
(CHARACTER IN —) JOHN CYRIL
POVEY BAINES CHIRAC GERALD
SAMUEL SCALES SOPHIA HARRIET
FAUCAULT CONSTANCE CRITCHLOW
OLD-WOMANISH ANILE
OLEANDER LAUREL NERIUM
DOGBANE ROSEBAY
OLEFIN ALKENE
OLEIC RAPIC RAPINIC
OLEORESIN GUM ANIME APIOL
ELEMI TOLUS BALSAM GURJUN
IRIDIN COPAIBA GALIPOT LABDANUM
TACAMAHAC
OLFACTION NOSE SMELL OSMESIS
SMELLING ESPHRESIS
OLIGARCHIC FEUDAL
OLIGARCHY KREMLIN
OLIGOCLASE SUNSTONE
OLIMPIA (HUSBAND OF —) BIRENO
OBERTO
OLINDO (HUSBAND OF —) SOFRONIA
(SAVIOR OF —) CLORINDA
OLIO STEW MEDLEY FARRAGO
MELANGE MIXTURE MISHMASH
MACEDOINE PASTICCIO
POTPOURRI
OLIPHANT HORN ELEPHANT
OLIPRANCE ROMP SHOW FROLIC
JOLLITY
OLIVE OLEA MORON BRUNET LIERRE
OLIVER OXHORN PIMOLA RESEDA
BAROUNI CITRINE MISSION
MORILLON OLEASTER
(— FLY) DACUS
(AMERICAN —) DEVILWOOD
(OVERRIPE —) DRUPE
(PREF.) DRUPI
(—OIL) ELAEO ELAIO ELEO
OLIVER NOLL HAMMER HOLLIPER
(BROTHER OF —) ORLANDO
(WIFE OF —) CELIA
OLIVER TWIST (AUTHOR OF —)
DICKENS

(CHARACTER IN —) BILL JACK NOAH
ROSE TOBY BATES FAGIN HARRY
MONKS NANCY SALLY SIKES TWIST
BEDWIN BUMBLE CORNEY EDWARD
MAYLIE OLIVER CHARLEY CRACKIT
DAWKINS GRIMWIG LEEFORD
BROWNLOW CLAYPOLE LOSBERNE
SOWERBERRY
OLIVET PEARL
OLIVIA (HUSBAND OF —) SEBASTIAN
OLIVINE PERIDOT
OLLA JAR JUG OLE POT OLAY
PUCHERA PUCHERO
OLLA PODRIDA HASH OLIO MEDLEY
POTPOURRI
OLM PROTEUS SALAMANDER
OLOGY ISM SCIENCE
OLYMPIAN CELESTIAL
OLYMPIAS (FATHER OF —)
NEOPTOLEMUS
(HUSBAND OF —) PHILIP
(SLAYER OF —) CASSANDER
(SON OF —) ALEXANDER
OLYNTHUS ASCULA
OMAGUA CAMBEVA
OMAH SASQUATCH
OMAN (CAPITAL OF —) MASQAT
MUSCAT
(LANGUAGE OF —) ARABIC BALUCHI
(MOUNTAIN OF —) SHAM HAFIT
HARIM NAKHL TAYIN AKHDAR
(NATIVE OF —) ADNAN QAHTAN
BALUCHI
(TOWN IN —) SUR NIGWA MASQAT
MATRAH SALALAH
OMAR (FATHER OF —) ELIPHAZ
OMASUM BOOK BOUK BIBLE
FARDEL MANYPLIES
OMBER SOLO UMBRE HOMBRE
MEDIATOR QUADRILLE
OMEGA END LAST
OMELET AMLET AMELET FOOYUNG
FOOYOUNG FRITTATA
OMEN BODE LUCK SIGN ABODE
AUGUR BODER FREET FREIT GUEST
TOKEN WEIRD WHATE AUGURY
HANDEL HANSEL AUSPICE PORTENT
PRESAGE PRODIGY WARNING
CEREMONY FOREBODE SOOTHSAY
HARBINGER
OMENTUM WEB CAUL ZIRBUS
EPIPLOON
OMINOUS DIRE DOUR GRIM BLACK
DOOMY FATAL BODING DISMAL
SHREWD AUGURAL BALEFUL
BANEFUL BODEFUL DIREFUL
DOOMFUL FATEFUL MENACING
SINISTER THUNDERY PROPHETIC
PORTENTOUS
OMISSION OUT BALK BAULK
CHASM SALTUS DEFAULT ELISION
FAILURE MISPICK NEGLECT SILENCE
PASSOVER OVERSIGHT

(— OF A LETTER) APOCOPE
(— OF SYLLABLES) SYNCOPE
(TACIT —) SILENCE
OMIT CUT LET BALK BATE DROP EDIT
KILL MISS PASS SKIP SLIP ABATE
ELIDE OBMIT SPARE BELEVE CANCEL
DELETE EXCEPT FORGET IGNORE
DISCARD EXPUNGE NEGLECT
DISCOUNT OVERLEAP OVERLOOK
OVERSKIP OVERSLIP DISREGARD
PRETERMIT
OMITTED VIDE
OMMATIDIUM FACET FACETTE
OMNIBUS BUS BUSS BARGE HERDIC
JOGGER PIRATE AUTOBUS
MOTORBUS KITTEREEN
OMNIPOTENT GOD ABLE DEITY
GREAT ARRANT MIGHTY ALMIGHTY
POWERFUL UNEQUALED UNLIMITED
OMNIPRESENCE UBIQUITY
OMNISCIENT WISE LEARNED
POWERFUL PANSOPHIC
OMOPLATE SCAPULA
OMPHALE
(FATHER OF —) IARDANUS
(HUSBAND OF —) TMOLUS
(SON OF —) TANTALUS
OMPHALOS HUB BOSS KNOB NAVEL
CENTER UMBILICUS
OMRI (FATHER OF —) BECHER
MICHAEL
(SON OF —) AHAB
ON O AN IN TO LIT ONE SUR ATOP
AWAY OVER UPON ABOUT ABOVE
AHEAD ALONG ANENT ABOARD
WITHIN FORWARD
(— ACCOUNT OF) IN FOR
(— A HATCH) ABROOD
(— ALL SIDES) ABOUT AROUND
(— AND ON) EVER FOREVER TEDIOUS
(— EARTH) BELOW
(— END) TOGETHER
(— FOOT) UP AFOOT TOWARD
FOOTBACK
(— HAND) ALONG
(— HIGH) ALOFT
(— THE CONTRARY) BUT RATHER
(— THE MOVE) AFOOT
(— THE OTHER HAND) BUT AGAIN
HOWEVER ALTHOUGH
(— THE OTHER SIDE) OVER ACROSS
(— THE WAY) AWAY AGATE
(— TIME) PROMPT
(— TOP OF) ATOP ABOVE ALOFT
(— WHAT ACCOUNT) WHY
(FATHER OF —) PELETH
(PREF.) IL IM IN IR SUPER
ONAGER ASS GOUR KULAN KOULAN
ONAGRA ALACRAN CATAPULT
SCORPION
ONAM (FATHER OF —) SHOBAL
JERAHMEEL
(MOTHER OF —) ATARAH

ONAN (FATHER OF —) JUDAH
ONCE ANE EEN ERST AINCE ONCET
WHILE YANCE FORMER WHILOM
QUONDAM UMWHILE FORMERLY
SOMETIME UMQUHILE WHENEVER
ERSTWHILE
(— MORE) YET ANEW AGAIN ENCORE
ITERUM
(AT —) PRESTO
ONDATRA FIBER
ONE J AE AN HE UN ACE AIN ANE
ANY EIN MAN OON TAE UNA UNE
WON YAE YAN YEN YIN YOU SAME
SOLE SOME TANE TEAN THIS TONE
TOON UNAL UNIT WHON WONE
ALONE ALPHA UNITY WOONE
ABOARD FELLOW PERSON SINGLE
UNIQUE UNITED CERTAIN NUMERAL
PRONOUN SIMPLUM UNBROKEN
SINGLETON UNDIVIDED UNMARRIED
(— AFTER ANOTHER) ABOUT
TANDEM SERIALLY SERIATIM
(— BORN A SERF) NEIF NEIFE
(— BY ONE) APIECE SINGLY
OVERHEAD
(— CONDEMNED WRONGFULLY)
CALAS
(— CURIOUS TO KNOW ALL)
QUIDNUNC
(— DETESTED) WARLING
(— DEVOTED TO PARTICULAR ART)
IST
(— EASILY TRICKED) CULLY
(— ENGAGED IN MARAUDING)
LOOTIE
(— ENROLLED IN ARMY) DRAFTEE
(— FOLLOWED BY 100 ZEROES)
GOOGOL
(— GIVEN TO DEVILTRY) HELLION
(— HELD IN CONTEMPT) FINK
(— HIGHEST IN RANK) SUPREME
(— INSTRUCTED IN SECRET SYSTEM)
EPOPT
(— LATE) SERO
(— MANAGING ENTERTAINERS ON
ROAD) ROADIE
(— NOT A REGULAR MASON)
COWAN
(— OF PAIR) FELLOW DOUBLET
(— OF TRIPLETS) TRILLING
(— OVERZEALOUS) HYPER
(— SENT FORTH) APOSTLE
(—S NEARBY) THESE
(— TENTH) TITHE
(— THAT IRKS OR ANNOYS) PAIN
(— THAT UNDERGOES CHANGE)
MUTANT
(— THOUSAND) MIL
(— TWENTY-FOURTH) CARAT
(— UNKNOWN) QUIDAM
(— VERSED IN LITERATURE) SAVANT
(— WHO BRINGS MEAT TO TABLE)
DAPIFER

(— WHO DISPLAYS
FASTIDIOUSNESS) EPICURE
(— WHO DOCTORS SOMETHING)
COOK
(— WHO EXCELS) ACE
(— WHO FABRICATES) SMITH
(— WHO FOLLOWS ARMY) SUTLER
(— WHO FORSAKES FAITH)
APOSTATE
(— WHO FRUSTRATES PLAN)
MARPLOT
(— WHO HAS ATTAINED PERFECTION)
SIDDHA
(— WHO IS AWAY) ABSENTEE
(— WHO IS DISMISSED) PUSHOUT
(— WHO IS STRANGE OR ECCENTRIC)
WEIRDO
(— WHO LOADS SHIP) BUNKER
(— WHO MAKES LIVING BY
TRICKERY) CADGER
(— WHO MANAGES) GERENT
(— WHO REGULATES GUN) TRAINER
(— WHO REMOVES NUISANCE)
ABATOR
(— WHO REPRESENTS NEWEST) NEO
(— WHOSE MIND IS IMPAIRED BY
AGE) DOTARD
(— WHO TESTS) CONNER
(— WHO USES DRUGS) DRUGGY
DRUGGIE
(— WHO WANTS TO BE SOMEONE
ELSE) WANNABE
(— WITH FIRST-HAND INFORMATION)
INSIDER
(APPEALING —) GAS
(BLESSED —) BHAGAVAT
(CONSPICUOUS —) STANDOUT
(EVIL —) WOND SHAITAN SHEITAN
(EXTRAORDINARY —) DOOZY
DOOZER
(LITTLE —) BUTCHA PICKANINNY
(LOVED —) MINION
(MOST IMPORTANT —) FLAGSHIP
(NOT —) NARY
(SUPERIOR —) LAMA
(SWEET —) HONEYCOMB
(TIMELESS —) AKAL
(TIRESOME —) DRIP
(PREF.) HENO MON(O) UNI
(— AND A HALF TIMES) SESQUI
(— AND THE SAME) HOM(O)
(— ANOTHER) ALLELO
(— BILLIONTH) NANO
(— MILLIONTH) MICR(O)
(— TRILLIONTH) PICO
(SAME —) AUT(O) AUTH(I)
(SUFF.) (— BELONGING) AN EAN IAN
(— BELONGING TO) IE ING
(— BELONGING TO A GROUP) ID
(— BELONGING TO A LINE) ID
(— HAVING) ANDER
(— HAVING TO DO WITH) IE
(— OCCUPATIONALLY CONNECTED

WITH) ER IER YER
(— OF A KIND) ING
(— OF A QUALITY) IE
(— SKILLED) AN EAN IAN
(— THAT ADVOCATES A DOCTRINE)
IST
(— THAT DABBLES) IST
(— THAT DOES) ER IER YER
(— THAT HAS) ER IER YER
(— THAT MAKES) IST
(— THAT OPERATES) IST
(— THAT PERFORMS) ER IER IST YER
(— THAT PRACTICES) IST
(— THAT PRODUCES) ER IER IST YER
(— THAT SPECIALIZES) IST
(— THAT STUDIES) IST
(— THAT YIELDS) ER IER YER
(LESSER —) IDIUM
(LITTLE —) IE
(SMALL —) IDIUM IUM
ONEGITE AMETHYST GEMSTONE
ONE-LINER JEST JOKE
ONENESS UNION UNITY CONCORD
ONEHOOD UNICITY UNITUDE
IDENTITY SAMENESS AGREEMENT
ONE-NIGHT STAND GIG
ONE-NOTE MONOTONOUS
ONE-RAYED MONACT
ONEROUS HARD HEAVY ARDUOUS
ONEROSE WEIGHTY EXACTING
GRIEVOUS LABORIOUS
ONESELF
(PREF.) SUI
(BY, FOR, PERT. TO —) AUT(O) AUTH(I)
ONE-SIDED ECCENTRIC UNILATERAL
ONETIME FORMER FORMERLY
ERSTWHILE
ONFALL ONSET ATTACK ASSAULT
ON-GLIDE TENSION ENTRANCE
ONION BOLL CEPA LEEK LILY SYBO
CIBOL INGAN PEARL ALLIUM LILIUM
PORRET BERMUDA CEBOLLA
HOLLEKE PICKLER SHALLOT
AYEGREEN RARERIPE SCALLION
VALENCIA
(ROPE OF —S) REEVE
(SEASONED WITH —S) LYONNAISE
(SPRING —) SYBO CIBOL SYBOE
SYBOW
(STRING OF —S) TRACE
ONKOS TOPKNOT
ONLOOKER BOOK EYER GAZER
WITNESS AUDIENCE BEHOLDER
OVERSEER BYSTANDER SPECTATOR
ONLY ALL BUT JUST LONE MERE
ONCE SAVE SOLE AFALD ALONE
ARRAH FIRST MERED NOBUT OLEPY
ANERLY BARELY MERELY NOBBUT
SIMPLE SINGLE SINGLY SOLELY
ALLENALY EXCEPTING
(— THIS) MERE
(BEING —) SIMPLE
ONMUN HANGUL HANKUL

ONOMATOPOEIA
(PREF.) KE(R)
ONOMATOPOEIC ECHOIC IMSONIC
MIMETIC IMITATIVE
ONRUSH BIRR SHAKE ATTACK
TIDEWAY
ONSET DASH DINT FALL FARD RESE
RUSH BRAID BREAK BRUNT FAIRD
FRUSH START STORM STOUR VENUE
ACCESS AFFRET ATTACK CHARGE
COURGE IMPACT INSULT ONDING
ONFALL POWDER THRUST ASSAULT
BRATTLE BEGINNING ENCOUNTER
ONSLAUGHT
ONSETTER CAGER HITCHER
ONSLAUGHT LASH BLAST ONSET
ATTACK ASSAULT DESCENT
SISERARA SALIAUNCE
ONSTEAD ONSET FARMHOUSE
HOMESTEAD
ONTARIO (CANAL IN —) TRENT
RIDEAU
(CAPITAL OF —) TORONTO
(LAKE IN —) SIMCOE
(TOWN IN —) EMO GALT LONDON
OTTAWA WINDSOR HAMILTON
KINGSTON KITCHENER
ONTO ATOP ABOARD
ONTOGENY DEVELOPMENT
ONTOLOGY METAPHYSICS
ONUS DUTY LOAD BLAME BURDEN
CHARGE WEIGHT INCUBUS
ONWARD AWAY AHEAD ALONG
FORTH UPWARD FORTHON FORWARD
TOWARDS FORERIGHT
ONYX ONIX NICOLO TECALI ONYCHIN
JASPONYX SARDONYX
(MEXICAN —) ALABASTER
OOCYTE PROGAMETE GAMETOCYTE
OODLES HEAP LOTS MANY TONS
RAFTS SCADS SLEWS LASHINGS
SLITHERS ABUNDANCE
OOGONIUM NUCULE OOCYST
OOGONE
OOLAK WOLLOCK
OOLITE PISOLITE ROESTONE
OOLONG TEA
OOMPH PEP VIGOR ENERGY
OOPAK TEA
OORALI CURARE
OORIAL SHA SHEEP URIAL
OOTHECA OVISAC
OOZE OZ BOG MUD SEW SOP DRIP
EMIT LEAK MIRE SEEP SLEW SLOB
SLUE WEEP EXUDE GLEET MARSH
SLIME SWEAT WEEZE EXHALE
SICKER SLEECH SLOUGH SLUDGE
SQUASH SQUDGE STRAIN SCREEVE
TEICHER TRANSUDE PERCOLATE
(— OUT) SEW SPEW SPUE
(PREF.) STACTO
OOZING WEEPY SQUDGY SEEPAGE
SPEWING WEEPING

OOZY OASY SEEPY WASHY SLEECHY ULIGINOUS

OPACATE DIM DARKEN

OPACITY BODY
(— OF CORNEA) ONYX NEBULA LEUCOMA

OPAH CRAVO SUNFISH KINGFISH MARIPOSA MOONFISH

OPAL GEM NOBLE RESIN FIORITE GIRASOL HYALITE ISOPYRE GIRASOLE JASPOPAL MENILITE SEMIOPAL CACHOLONG GEYSERITE

OPALESCENT OPALED OPALINE IRISATED

OPALEYE GREENFISH

OPAQUE DIM DARK DULL DENSE MUDDY SHADY THICK VAGUE OBTUSE STUPID CLOUDED OBSCURE ABSTRUSE EYESHADE

OPEN GO CAP DUP LAX OPE AIRY AJAR BARE FAIR FLUE FREE GIVE NEAR PERT UNDO VIDE AGAPE APERT BEGIN BLOWN BREAK BROAD BURST CHINK CLEAR CRACK FLARE FRANK FRESH JIMMY LANCE LOOSE MUSHY NAKED OVERT PLAIN RELAX SPALD SPLAT SPLAY START UNBAR UNPEG UNTIE UNZIP APPERT CANDID DIRECT ENTAME EXPAND EXPOSE FACIAL FORTHY GAPING HONEST HARLE OUVERT PATENT PUBLIC SINGLE SPREAD UNBOLT UNDRAW UNFOLD UNFURL UNGLUE UNLOCK UNROLL UNSEAL UNSHUT UNSPAR UNSTOP UNTINE UNWINK UNWRAP VACANT ARTLESS BLOSSOM DISPART FIELDEN OBVIOUS OUTLINE SINCERE THROUGH UNCLOSE UNHINGE APPARENT COMMENCE DISCLOSE EXPLICIT EXTENDED INITIATE MANIFEST OUTFRONT PERVIOUS RESERATE UNFASTEN CHAMPAIGN OSTENSIBLE
(— AIR) ALFRESCO
(— AND CLEANSE) WILLOW
(— A VEIN) BROACH
(— CLOTH) SCUTCH
(— COUNTRY) VELDT WEALD
(— EYES OR LIPS) SEVER
(— THE WAY) INVITE PIONEER
(— TO PURSUIT) FAIR
(— UP) START DEVELOP DISPART DISCLOSE
(— VIOLENTLY) SPORT
(— WIDE) YAWN EXPAND STRETCH
(— WIDELY) GAPE
(BARELY —) AJAR
(FULLY —) WIDE AGAPE YAWNING
(HALF —) MID AJAR
(SLIGHTLY —) AJAR
(TOO —) OVERBARISH

OPENBILL OPENBEAK

OPENED APPAUME ECHAPPE

OPENER KEY KNOB LATCH SESAME APERIENT
(— IN POKER) PAIR JACKS
(FURROW —) SHOE STUBRUNNER
(OYSTER —) HUSKER

OPENHANDED FREE LIBERAL GENEROUS RECEPTIVE

OPENING OS CUT EYE GAP YAT ANUS BOLE BORE DAWN DOOR DROP FENT FLUE GATE HOLE LOOP PASS PORE PORT PYLA RIFT RIMA SLAP SLIT SLOT SPAN VENT VOID YAWN YEAT BLEED BRACK BREAK CHASM CHINK CLEFT CROSS DEBUT GRILL HILUM INLET LIGHT MOUTH SCOOT SINUS START THIRL WIDTH ADITUS AVENUE BREACH CASING CHANCE GRILLE HIATUS INTAKE LACUNA MEATUS OILLET OUTLET PORTAL SLUICE SPREAD AIRPORT CREVASS CREVICE DISPLAY FISSURE ORIFICE OUTCAST SWALLET APERIENT APERTURE BUNGHOLE CREVASSE ENTRANCE OVERTURE PLUGHOLE SCISSURE TEASEHOLE
(— BELOW PENTHOUSE) GALLERY
(— FOR ESCAPE) MUSE MEUSE
(— FOR SLEEVE) SCYE
(— FROM SEA) INDRAFT
(— IN ANTHER) STOMIUM
(— IN DECK) SCUTTLE
(— IN EARTH) GROTTO CHIMNEY
(— IN EARTH) MOFETTE
(— IN EARTH) SWALLOW
(— IN FLOOR OR ROOF) HATCH SKYLIGHT
(— IN GARMENT) FENT ARMHOLE
(— IN LOCK TUMBLER) GATING
(— IN MINE) EYE ADIT RAISE SHAFT WINZE WINNING
(— IN MOLD) POUR
(— IN PICTURE FRAME) SIGHT
(— IN PILLAR OF COAL) JENKIN
(— IN ROCK) GRIKE
(— IN SALMON TRAP) SLAP
(— IN SEA CAVE) GLOUP
(— IN SKIRT) PLACKET
(— IN SPONGE) APOPYLE
(— IN STAGE) DIP
(— IN TENNIS COURTS) GRILLE HAZARD GALLERY
(— IN TROUSERS) SPARE
(— IN VAULT) LUNET LUNETTE
(— IN WALL) BOLE DREAMHOLE
(— OF BALL) PROMENADE
(— OF BUD) ANTHESIS
(— OF EAR) BUR BURR
(— OF ESOPHAGUS) CARDIA
(— OF EYE) PUPIL
(— OF GEYSER) CRATER
(— OF HOCKEY GAME) BULLY
(— OF PRAIRIE) BAY

(— OF SHELL) GAPE
(— OF SKIRT) SPARE
(— OF STOMACH) PYLORUS
(— THROUGH BULWARKS)
GANGWAY GUNPORT SCUPPER
(— TO ASH PIT) GLUT
(— WIDE) DEHISCENT
(— WITH LID) SCUTTLE
(— WITHOUT TREES) BLANK
(ARCHED —) ALCOVE ARCADE
(CHECKERS —) ALMA DYKE FIFE
CROSS CENTER SOUTER BRISTOL
GLASGOW PAISLEY WHILTER
DEFIANCE SWITCHER
(CHESS —) DEBUT GAMBIT DEFENCE
DEFENSE
(EROSIONAL —) FENSTER
(FISTULOUS —) SYRINX
(FUNNELLIKE —) CHOANA
(GRILL —) GUICHET
(JAR —) PITHOIGIA
(MOUTHLIKE —) STOMA OSTIUM
(NARROW —) VISTA
(SMALL —) PORE SLOT CHINK
STOMA CRANNY EYELET LACUNA
CATHOLE CREVICE DOGHOLE
FORAMEN GUICHET PINHOLE
QUARREL FENESTRA
(WINDOWLIKE —) SPLITE FENESTRA
(PREF.) APERTO CHASMO TREMATO
(SUFF.) PORA PORE PYL(E)
STOMA(TA)(TE)(TOUS) STOME
STOMI(A) STOMOUS STOMUM
STOMY TREMA(TA)
OPENLY BARELY FREELY BROADLY
FRANKLY PUBLICE ROUNDLY
STRAIGHT
OPEN-MINDED LIBERAL
OPENMOUTHED GAPING GREEDY
RAVENOUS CLAMOROUS
OPENNESS CANDOR FREEDOM
PATENCY DAYLIGHT FRANKNESS
ROUNDNESS
OPENWORK LATTICE TRACERY
CAGEWORK FILIGREE FRETTING
FRETWORK
OPEN-WORKED AJOURISE
OPERA AIDA FAUST LAKME MANON
NORMA THAIS TOSCA BOHEME
CARMEN DAPHNE ERNANI LOUISE
MIGNON OTELLO RIENZI SALOME
ELEKTRA FIDELIO BURLETTA
FALSTAFF IOLANTHE LOKACOLO
PARSIFAL TRAVIATA WALKYRIE
LOHENGRIN PAGLIACCI RHEINGOLD
RIGOLETTO SIEGFRIED TROVATORE
(— DIVISION) SCENA
(— GLASS) GLASS JUMELLE
LORGNET LORGNETTE
(— HAT) GIBUS CLAQUE
(— SONG) ARIA
(— STAR) DIVA
(COMIC —) BUFFA BURLETTA
(HORSE —) WESTERN
(KIND OF —) SOAP
(SOAP —) SUDSER
(SPANISH —) ZARZUELA
(TV OR RADIO —) SOAP
(16TH CENTURY —) PASTORALE
OPERA GLASSES JUMELLE
LORGNETTE
OPERANT EFFICIENT OPERATIVE
OPERATE GO ACT CUT MAN RUN
PUSH TAKE WORK DRIVE MULES
STEER AFFECT EFFECT MANAGE
CONDUCT PROCEED FUNCTION
(— BY HAND) MANIPULATE
(— GUNS) SERVE
(— MINE) FLUSH
(— MOTOR VEHICLE) VROOM
(— RADIO) BLOOP
(CAUSE TO —) POWERUP
OPERATIC LYRIC
OPERATING GOING ATWORK
(FULLY —) AFLOAT
OPERATION DEED PLAY BLAST
ACTION AGENCY EFFECT OSTOMY
VIRTUE PROCESS CREATION
EXERCISE FACELIFT FUNCTION
PRACTICE EXECUTION INFLUENCE
PROCESSUS
(ARITHMETIC —) PROOF
(FRAUDULENT —) SCAM
(MILITARY —S) CAMPAIGN
(REGULAR —S) ECONOMY
(SURGICAL —) CECOPEXY
(UNDERCOVER —) STING
(SUFF.) (— FOR OPENING) STOMY
OPERATIONAL LIVE
OPERATIONS
(SUFF.) ICS
OPERATIVE EYE HAND ARTIST
LIVING ARTISAN OUVRIER MECHANIC
DETECTIVE EFFECTIVE
OPERATOR DEL DOER AGENT BAKER
DEWER NABLA PILOT QUACK
BEAMER BILLER BOLTER BUMPER
BUSMAN CAPPER DEALER DEGGER
DRIVER DUNGER DYADIC GAGGER
JOCKEY KICKER RAGGER TRADER
AVIATOR BREAKER CENTRAL
CHEESER DENTIST FACIENT GLASSER
JOGGLER MANAGER OPERANT
SURGEON IDENTITY MOTORMAN
CONDUCTOR
(INFERIOR —) PLUG
(LOGICAL —) NOT
(RADIO —) HAM CBER SPARKS
SPARKER
(TRUCK —) GIPSY GYPSY
(SUFF.) STER STRESS
OPERCULUM LID FLAP ONYCHA
OPERCLE APTYCHUS COVERING
EYESTONE MANDIBLE

OPERETTA ZARZUELA
OPEROSE BUSY IRKSOME DILIGENT
LABORIOUS
OPHELIA (BROTHER OF —) LAERTES
(FATHER OF —) POLONIUS
OPHELTES (FATHER OF —) LYCURGUS
(NURSE OF —) HYPSIPYLE
OPHIDIAN ASP EEL SNAKE CONGER
REPTILE SERPENT
OPHIR (FATHER OF —) JOKTAN
OPHITE CAINIAN CAINITE
OPHIUROID ARGUS SANDSTAR
OPHRAH (FATHER OF —) MEONOTHAI
OPHTHALMOLOGIST OCULIST
OPIATE DOPE DRUG HEMP DWALE
OPIUM DEADEN ANODINE HYPNOTIC
NARCOTIC SEDATIVE DORMITARY
PAREGORIC SOPORIFIC
OPIFICER OPIFEX WORKMAN
ARTIFICER
OPINE DEEM JUDGE THINK PONDER
BELIEVE SUPPOSE OPINIATE
OPINION CRY EYE MOT BOOK DOXY
FAME IDEA MIND VIEW WEEN
DOGMA FANCY FUTWA GUESS
HEART INPUT SENSE SIGHT TENET
THINK VARDI VARDY VOICE ADVICE
ASSENT BELIEF DEVICE DICTUM
ESTEEM GROUND NOTION REPUTE
SCHISM CENSURE CONCEIT
CONCEPT CONSENT COUNSEL
DIANOIA FEELING HOLDING
MEASURE SEEMING THINKSO
THOUGHT TROWING VERDICT
DECISION DOCTRINE JUDGMENT
SUFFRAGE PREJUDICE SENTIMENT
PERSUASION
(COLLECTION OF —S) SYMPOSIUM
(EXAGGERATED —) BIGHEAD
(EXPRESSION OF —) VOTE
(FAVORABLE —) BROO ESTEEM
(MOHAMMEDAN —) FUTWA
(SET OF PROFESSED —S) CREDO
(UNORTHODOX —) HERESY
(WRONG —) CACODOXY
(PREF.) DOXO
(SUFF.) DOX(Y)
OPINIONATED DOGMATIC
CONCEITED OBSTINATE PRAGMATIC
OPINIONATIVE ENTETE
O PIONEERS (AUTHOR OF —)
CATHER
(CHARACTER IN —) LOU CARL EMIL
IVAR FRANK MARIE OSCAR AMEDEE
BERGSON SHABATA TOVESKY
ALEXANDRA LINDSTRUM
OPIUM HOP MUD DOPE DRUG OPIE
POST CHANDU CHANDOO
MECONIUM TOXICANT
(— ALKALOID) CODEIN CODEINE
MORPHINE NARCOTIN NARCOTINE
PAPAVERIN

(— POPPY) NEPENTHE
(OF —) THEBAIC
(RESIDUE IN — PIPE) YENSHEE
(TINCTURE OF —) LAUDANUM
(PREF.) MECON(O) OPIO
OPIUMISM THEBAISM
OPOSSUM QUICA YAPOK POSSUM
YAPOCK MARMOSE OYAPOCK
SARIGUE VULPINE MARSUPIAL
PHILANDER TACUACINE
(— SHRIMP) MYSID MYSOID
(FAMOUS —) POGO
OPPONENT FOE ANTI ENEMY PARTY
RIVAL ALOGIAN NEMESIS OPPOSER
ADVERSARY ASSAILANT
(— OF GOV CLINTON) BUCKTAIL
(— OF WAR) PEACENIK
(BOORISH —) BOEOTIAN
(FORMIDABLE —) TIGER
(IMAGINARY —) WINDMILL
OPPORTUNE FIT PAT HAPPY LUCKY
READY TIMELY APROPOS FITTING
TIMEFUL SUITABLE FAVORABLE
OPPORTUNELY TIMELY APROPOS
HAPPILY
OPPORTUNIST CREEPER
OPPORTUNISTIC SHUFFLING
OPPORTUNITY GO MAY OPE SEL
EASE HENT MEAN MINT ROOM SELE
SHOT TIDE TIME SIGHT SLANT SPACE
ACCESS CHANCE SEASON SQUEAK
LEISURE OPENING RESPITE VANTAGE
APPROACH FACILITY OCCASION
ADVANTAGE
(— FOR ACTION) OPENING
(— OF ACTIVITY) SCOPE
(— TO PROCEED) WAY
(FAVORABLE —) SHOW TIME
OPPOSE PIT VIE WAR BUCK COPE
DEFY FACE HEAD MEET NOSE STEM
WARN WEAR ARGUE BLOCK CHECK
CLASH CROSS FIGHT FRONT OCCUR
REBEL REBUT REPEL BATTLE BREAST
COMBAT DEFEND NAYSAY OBJECT
OBTEND OPPUGN REPUGN RESIST
THWART WITHER CONTEST COUNTER
GAINSAY OBVIATE REVERSE WITHSET
CONFLICT CONFRONT CONTRARY
CONTRAST FRONTIER OBSTRUCT
TRAVERSE ENCOUNTER WITHSTAND
ANTAGONIZE
(— BY ARGUMENT) REBUT
(— ONE IN AUTHORITY) REBEL
DEFORCE
OPPOSED ANTI ALIEN AVERSE
ADVERSE AGAINST COUNTER
HOSTILE CONTRARY ABHORRENT
ANTARCTIC REPUGNANT
(PERSISTENTLY —) RENITENT
OPPOSER GAINSAYER
OPPOSING RENITENT RELUCTANT
(PREF.) COUNTER

OPPOSITE TO ANENT POLAR
ACROSS ANENST AVERSE FACING
WITHER ADVERSE COUNTER
FORNENT INVERSE OBVIOUS
REVERSE ANTIPODE CONTRARY
CONTRAST CONVERSE ANTIPODAL
REPUGNANT RECIPROCAL
(— MIDDLE OF SHIP'S SIDE) ABEAM
(— OF TRUTH) DEVIL
(— THE ALTAR) WEST
(— THE SUN) ANTISOLAR
(PREF.) ANTI ENANTIO
(DO THE —) DIS
OPPOSITION CON FLAK ATILT
CLASH FLACK STOUR STATIC
SYZYGY THWART DISCORD TENSION
CLASHING CONTRAST DISTANCE
OBSTACLE POLARITY ANIMOSITY
COLLISION HOSTILITY RENITENCY
(— TO GOD) ANTITHEISM
(ELECTRICAL —) IMPEDANCE
(PREF.) (IN —) CONTRA
OPPRESS SIT HOLD LADE LOAD PEIS
RACK RAPE RIDE SWAY THEW
CROWD CRUSH GRIND GRIPE HEAVY
PEISE POISE PRESS WEIGH WRONG
BETOIL BURDEN DEFOIL DEFOUL
EXTORT HARASS HARROW NIDDER
NITHER RAVISH SUBDUE THREAT
AFFLICT DEPRESS INGRATE OVERLAY
REPRESS SQUEEZE TRAMPLE
CONFRONT DISTRESS ENCUMBER
PRESSURE SUPPRESS OVERPOWER
OVERTHROW OVERWEIGH
OVERWHELM
(— WITH DREAD) HAGRIDE
(— WITH HEAT) SWELTER
OPPRESSED SERVILE
OPPRESSION ROD GRIPE PRESS
BURDEN THRALL MIZRAIM
DULLNESS PRESSURE EXTORTION
GRIEVANCE LASSITUDE
OPPRESSIVE HOT DIRE DOWY HARD
CLOSE DOWIE FAINT HARSH HEAVY
BITTER LEADEN SCREWY SEVERE
SMUDGY SULTRY TORRID URGENT
WEIGHT ONEROUS SLAVISH
GRIEVOUS GRINDING RIGOROUS
OPPRESSIVELY STRAIT
OPPRESSIVENESS LANGUOR
OPPRESSOR CSAR CZAR NERO
TSAR TZAR EGLON TYRANT
INCUBUS
OPPROBRIUM ENVY ABUSE ODIUM
SCORN SHAME INFAMY INSULT
CALUMNY DISDAIN OFFENSE
SCANDAL DISGRACE DISHONOR
REPROACH CONTUMELY
OPS (ASSOCIATE OF —) CONSUS
(CONSORT OF —) SATURN
(DAUGHTER OF —) CERES
(FESTIVAL OF —) OPALIA

(PERSONIFICATION OF —) FAUNA
TERRA TELLUS
OPT CULL PICK WISH ELECT CHOOSE
DECIDE OPTATE SELECT
(— ABRUPTLY) PLUMP
OPTIC EYE OCULAR VISUAL
OPTICAL VISIBLE
(— APPARATUS) LENS GLASS ALIDAD
ALIDADE OPTOMETER PERISCOPE
TELESCOPE
(— DEVICE ON RIFLE) SNIPERSCOPE
OPTIMIST POLLYANNA UTOPIANIST
OPTIMISTIC GLAD ROSY SUNNY
JOYOUS UPBEAT BULLISH HOPEFUL
ROSEATE EUPEPTIC SANGUINE
EXPECTANT
OPTION UP CALL DOWN CHOICE
SPREAD REFUSAL STRADDLE
PRIVILEGE
OPTIONAL ELECTIVE VOLUNTARY
PERMISSIVE
OPULENCE LUXE
OPULENT FAT LUSH RICH WELI
AMPLE FLUSH PLUSH SHOWY
LAVISH MONEYED PROFUSE
WEALTHY ABUNDANT AFFLUENT
LUXURIANT PLENTIFUL SUMPTUOUS
OPUS WORK ETUDE STUDY
(OVERLABORED —) LUCUBRATION
OQUASSA QUASKY
OR NE ARE AUT ERE ORE GOLD OSSIA
OTHER TOPAZ EITHER YELLOW
ORACHE SALTBUSH GREASEWOOD
ORACLE SEER TRIP SIBYL TRIPOD
TRIPOS DIVINER AUTOPHONE
ORACULAR OTIC VATIC ORPHIC
DELPHIC VATICAL DELPHIAN
PYTHONIC PROPHETIC
ORAL ALOUD PAROL VOCAL BUCCAL
PAROLE SONANT SPOKEN VERBAL
UTTERED UNWRITTEN NONCUPATIVE
ORALE FANON
ORANGE KING MOCK CERES CHILE
CHILI CHINO FLAME GENIP HEDGE
JAFFA NAVEL OSAGE TENNE
AURORA BODOCK BRAZIL COPPER
MIKADO NAVAHO SUNTAN TEMPLE
TITIAN UVALHA COWSLIP FLORIDA
LEATHER MACLURA NARTJIE
PAPRIKA PONCEAU PUMPKIN
RANGPUR SEVILLE TANGELO
TANGIER BERGAMOT BIGARADE
CHINOTTI CLAYBANK FLAMINGO
HONEYDEW JACINTHE MANDARIN
MARATHON MOROCCAN POMANDER
SUNBURST VALENCIA BUCCANEER
CARNELIAN PERSIMMON TANGERINE
(— BLOSSOM INGREDIENT) GIN
(— GRASS) KNITWEED PINEWEED
(— HAWKWEED) FIREWEED
HIERACIUM
(— MEMBRANE) ZEST

(— MILKWORT) CANDYWEED
(— PIECE) LITH SEGMENT
(— ROCKFISH) FLIOMA
(— SEED) PIP
(— TREE) SATSUMA
(BROWNISH —) SPICE
(LARGE —) KING
(MOCK —) SERINGA
(OSAGE —) HEDGE BODOCK
(SOUR —) CURACAO BIGARADE
CHINOTTO
(SWEET —) CHINA CHINO
(YELLOW —) SAFFRON
ORANGEBIRD TANAGER
ORANGE HAWKWEED
PAINTBRUSH
ORANGELEAF KARAMU
ORANGEMAN MARKSMAN
ORANGEWOOD OSAGE
ORANG LAUT BAJAU
ORANGUTAN APE MIAS ORANG
PONGO SATYR SATIRE SATURY
PRIMATE SALTIER SATYRUS
WOODMAN WOODSMAN
ORAON KURUKH
ORARION STOLE
ORATE PLEAD SPEAK SPIEL SPOUT
ADDRESS DECLAIM LECTURE
BLOVIATE HARANGUE DISCOURSE
SPEECHIFY
ORATION EULOGY HESPED SERMON
ADDRESS CONCION HARANGUE
SUASORIA OLYNTHIAC PANEGYRIC
PHILIPPIC
(— OF CICERO) PHILIPPIC
(FUNERAL —) ELOGE ELOGY
MONODY ELOGIUM ENCOMIUM
ORATOR RHETOR DEMAGOG
SPEAKER STUMPER CICERONE
BOANERGES DEMAGOGUE PLAINTIFF
SPOKESMAN
ORATORICAL ELOQUENT
RHETORICAL
ORATORIO ELIJAH RORATORIO
ORATORY CHAPEL SACRARY
ORACULUM SPEAKING ELOCUTION
ELOQUENCE PROSEUCHE
(EXAGGERATED —) RHETORIC
ORB EYE SUN BALL MOON STAR
EARTH GLOBE MOUND ORBIT
CIRCLE PLANET SPHERE CIRCUIT
ENCLOSE ENCIRCLE SURROUND
FIRMAMENT
ORBED LUNAR ROUND GLOBATE
ORBIT AUGE PATH APSIS CYCLE
TRACK CIRCLE SOCKET SPHERE
CIRCUIT ELLIPSE EYEHOLE
ECCENTRIC
(POINT IN —) APSIS APOGEE EPIGEE
SYZYGY PERIGEE
ORC OGRE ORCA GIANT WHALE
GRAMPUS

ORCHARD HOLT TOPE ARBOR
GROVE ARBOUR GARDEN HUERTA
OLIVET VERGER ARBUSTUM
FRUITERY PEACHERY POMARIUM
SUGARBUSH
(— GRASS) DOGFOOT COCKSFOOT
ORCHESTRA BAND GROUP CHAPEL
CAPELLE CONSORT GAMELAN
KAPELLE ENSEMBLE GAMELANG
SYMPHONY SINFONIETTA
PHILHARMONIC
(— BELLS) GLOCKENSPIEL
(— CIRCLE) PARQUET PARTERRE
(SECTION OF —) BRASS WINDS
WOODS STRINGS WOODWINDS
PERCUSSION
ORCHESTRATE SCORE ARRANGE
COMPOSE
ORCHESTRION HARMONICON
APOLLONICON
ORCHID FAAM FAHAM PETAL VANDA
CYMBID DUFOIL LAELIA PURPLE
AERIDES ANGULOA BOATLIP
CALYPSO CULLION FLYWORT
LYCASTE POGONIA VANILLA
ARETHUSA CALANTHE DENDROBE
GYNANDER LABELLUM ONCIDIUM
RAMSHEAD SATYRION CORALROOT
HABENARIA PUTTYROOT
TWAYBLADE SNAKEMOUTH
(KIND OF —) VANDA
ORCHIS CROWTOE CROWFOOT
CRAKEFEET
ORDAIN LAW PUT DEEM DOOM
LOOK MAKE SEND WILL WITE ALLOT
ENACT JAPAN ORDER SHAPE WIELD
WRITE DECREE PRIEST ADJUDGE
APPOINT ARRANGE BEHIGHT
COMMAND DESTINE DICTATE
FORTUNE INSTALL PREPARE
PRESCRIBE
ORDEAL FIRE GAFF TEST AGONY
TRIAL CALVARY GAUNTLET
(— TREE) AKAZGA TANGHIN
TANGUIN
ORDEAL OF RICHARD FEVEREL
(AUTHOR OF —) MEREDITH
(CHARACTER IN —) TOM LUCY BERRY
CLARE MOUNT ADRIAN AUSTIN
BLAIZE CAROLA HARLEY RIPTON
FEVEREL RICHARD BAKEWELL
THOMPSON GRANDISON
DESBOROUGH MONTFALCON
ORDER BAN BID ILK RAY SAY TAX
BOON CALL CASE CHIT FIAT FORM
ORDO RANK RULE SAND SECT STOP
SUIT TELL TIFF TRIM WILL WORD
ALIGN ARRAY CHIME CLASS DIGHT
EDICT GENUS GRADE GUIDE HAVOC
PRESS QUIET RANGE SHIFT STATE
TAXIS WHACK ASSIGN AVAUNT
BEHEST BILLET CEDULA CHARGE

COSMOS CURFEW DECREE DEGREE
DEMAND DIKTAT DIRECT ENJOIN
FIRMAN FOLLOW GRAITH HOOKUM
INDENT KILTER MANAGE METHOD
NATURE ORDAIN POLICE POTENT
SERIES SETTLE SYNTAX SYSTEM
ADJUDGE ARRANGE BESPEAK
BIDDING BOOKING COMMAND
COMPOSE DISPOSE EMBARGO
FLOATER MANDATE PRECEPT
PROCESS SOCIETY CATEGORY
KODASHIM METHODIZE ORDINANCE
PRESCRIBE
(— BACK) REMAND
(— OF ANGELS) CHOIR QUIRE
MIGHTS THRONES DOMINIONS
PRINCIPALITIES
(— OF BATTLE) BATTALIA
(— OF BELLS) CHANGE
(— OF COURT) SIST VACATUR
(— OF CRUSTACEANS) ISOPODA
(— OFF) TURN
(— OF HOLY BEINGS) HIERARCHY
(— OF SUCCESSION) SEQUENCE
(— OF WORSHIP) AGODUM
(— TOBACCO LEAF) CASE
(— TO LEVY MONEY) PRECEPT
(— TO RETURN) RECALL
(CIVIL —) EUNOMY
(COSMIC —) TAO RITA
(GOOD —) EUTAXY
(IN —) SOAS
(KIND OF —) GAG
(KNIGHTHOOD —) DANNEBROG
(LACKING —) AMISS MESSY MUSSY
ROUGH CHAOTIC UNKEMPT
CONFUSED
(LEGAL —) SIST STET WRIT DAYWRIT
SUMMONS SENTENCE SUBPOENA
(LOWER — OF MAN) ALALUS
(MARCHING —S) ROUTE
(MINOR CHURCH —) BENET
(MONASTIC —) SAMGHA SANGHA
ACOEMETI
(PROPER —) TRAIN
(RECURRENT —) ROTATION
(TAKE —S) WAITRESS
(TRAIN —) FLIMSY
(TURKISH —) MEDJIDIE
(UNIVERSAL —) KIND
(WRITTEN —) CHECK DRAFT BILLET
DRAUGHT
(PREF.) (REVERSE —) OB
(SUFF.) TACTIC TAXIS TAXY
(— OF ANIMALS) INI
ORDERED BANDBOX BESPOKE
REGULAR SCRAPED COHERENT
(WELL —) TRIM
ORDERLINESS METHOD SYSTEM
CLARITY DECORUM
ORDERLY AIDE DULY NEAT PEON
RULY SNOD TIDY TRIM CRISP SOWAR

SUWAR BATMAN BURSCH COSMIC
FORMAL MODEST ORDENE GRADELY
REGULAR SHAPELY DECOROUS
GALLOPER GRAITHLY OBEDIENT
PEACEABLE SHIPSHAPE
ORDINANCE LAW DOOM FIAT RITE
BYLAW EDICT ASSIZE DECREE
RECESS CONTROL MANDATE
SETNESS STATUTE WORKING
DECRETUM JUDICIAL REGIMENT
TAKKANAH DIRECTION
ORDINANT DIHELY DIHELIOS
DIHELIUM
ORDINARY LAY LOW SOS BEND
FESS LALA MEAN PALE PALL RUCK
BANAL CHIEF CROSS NOMIC PLAIN
PROSE USUAL CANTON COMMON
FILLET FLANCH MODERN NORMAL
PAIRLE SIMPLE VULGAR AVERAGE
MUNDANE NATURAL PROSAIC
ROUTINE SALTIRE SAUTIER TRIVIAL
VANILLA VULGATE EVERYDAY
FAMILIAR HABITUAL MEDIOCRE
MIDDLING PLEBEIAN RUMTYTOO
WORKADAY QUOTIDIAN SHAKEFORK
ORDINATE ORDER ORDAIN APPOINT
ORDERLY REGULAR MODERATE
TEMPERATE
ORDNANCE LAW ARMS GUNS
ARMOR ORGUE FALCON MINION
PETARD PEDRERO RABINET SERPENT
WEAPONS BASILISK PETERERO
ARTILLERY
ORDO ORDER ALMANAC DIRECTORY
ORDURE
(PREF.) SCAT(O) SCORI
ORE (ALSO SEE MINERAL) TIN CHAT
DISH DRAG FELL GOLD IRON LEAD
MINE POST PULP ROCK CRAZE
CRUDE FAVOR GLORY GRACE HONOR
MANTO MERCY METAL PRILL COPPER
CUPRITE FLOATER RESPECT
SEAWEED SMEDDUM URANITE
CLEMENCY KNOCKING CARBONATE
REVERENCE
(— CRUSHER) DOLLY
(— DEPOSIT) LODE SCRIN BONANZA
(— LAYER) SEAM STOPE
(— LOADING PLATFORM) PLAT
(— MASS) SQUAT
(— NOT DRESSED) WORK
(— WITH STONE ADHERING) CHAT
CHATS
(BEST —) CROP
(BROKEN —) DIRT
(CONCENTRATED —) MIDDLINGS
(COPPER —) BORNITE HORNITE
ATACAMITE MALACHITE
(CRUDE —) HEADS
(CRUSHED —) PULP SCHLICH
(CUBE —) SIDERITE
(EARTHY-LOOKING —) PACO

(HORSEFLESH —) BORNITE
(IMPURE —) SPEISS HALVANS
(IRON —) OCHER OCHRE MINION
IRONMAN LIMNITE MINETTE OLIGIST
TURGITE HEMATITE LIMONITE
SIDERITE TACONITE BLACKBAND
JACUTINGA
(LEAD —) BOOZE GALENA
ARQUIFOUX
(LUMP OF —) HARDHEAD
(MANGANESE —) WAD WADD
(MERCURY —) GRANZA CINNABAR
(SOLID —) RIB
(TIN —) ROWS CRAZE SCOVE WHITS
FLORAN TINSTUFF
(URANIUM —) COFFINITE
(WORTHLESS —) SLAG DROSS
MATTE
(ZINC —) SMITHSONITE
OREAD PERI NYMPH

OREGON
CAPITAL: SALEM
COLLEGE: REED PACIFIC LINFIELD
PORTLAND WILLAMETTE
COUNTY: LINN CROOK CURRY WASCO
CLATSOP KLAMATH MALHEUR
WALLOWA YAMHILL UMATILLA
INDIAN: ALSEA MODOC WASCO
CAYUSE CHETCO KUITSH TENINO
KLAMATH TAKELMA YAQUINA
LAKE: ABERT WALDO CRATER HARNEY
MCNARY KLAMATH MALHEUR
MOUNTAIN: HOOD WALKER WILSON
ELKHORN GRIZZLY JACKSON
RAINIER TIDBITS
MOUNTAIN RANGE: BLUE COAST
CASCADE
RIVER: ROGUE IMNAHA OWYHEE
POWDER UMPQUA BLITZEN
KLAMATH SILVIES COLUMBIA
DESCHUTES
STATE BIRD: MEADOWLARK
STATE FLOWER: GRAPE
STATE NICKNAME: BEAVER SUNSET
WEBFOOT VALENTINE
STATE TREE: FIR
TOWN: BEND MORO VALE NYSSA
CONDON EUGENE FOSSIL MADRAS
ASTORIA HEPPNER COQUILLE
PORTLAND CORVALLIS

OREGON TRAIL (AUTHOR OF —)
PARKMAN
(CHARACTER IN —) SHAW HENRY
QUINCY FRANCIS PARKMAN
CHATILLON DESLAURIERS
OREN (FATHER OF —) JERAHMEEL
ORE-PRODUCING QUICK
ORESTES (COMPANION OF —)
PYLADES
(FATHER OF —) AGAMEMNON

(FRIEND OF —) PYLADES
(MOTHER OF —) CLYTEMNESTRA
(SISTER OF —) ELECTRA IPHIGENIA
(WIFE OF —) HERMIONE
ORGAN CUP GILL LIMB PART CHELA
FLOAT GREAT HEART MEANS PAPER
REGAL SERRA ELATER FEEDER
FEELER HAPTOR MEDIUM SPLEEN
SUCKER CLASPER CONSOLE
JOURNAL ARMATURE EFFECTOR
ISOGRAFT MAGAZINE MELODEON
MELODICA MYCETOME OOGONIUM
EQUIPMENT HARMONIUM
NEWSPAPER PORTATIVE
(— GALLERY) LOFT
(— OF HEARING) EAR
(— OF SCORPION) PECTEN
(— OF SENSE) SENSE SENSORY
(— OF SIGHT) EYE
(— OF SILKWORM) FILATOR
(— OF SPIDER) CRIBELLUM
SPINNERET
(— OF TOUCH) TACTOR TACTUS
(— PIPE) REED FLUTE SCHWEGEL
(— STOP) ECHO HARP OBOE SEXT
TUBA VIOL ACUTA DOLCE FLUTE
GAMBA ORAGE QUINT TENTH VIOLA
BIFARA CURTAL CYMBAL DECIMA
DULCET FUGARA GEDACT NASARD
OCTAVE SCHARF TIERCE TROMBA
BASSOON BOMBARD BOURDON
CELESTE CLARION CREMONA
DOLCIAN DOUBLET DULCIAN
FAGOTTO GEDECKT MELODIA
PICCOLO POSAUNE SERPENT
TERTIAN TRUMPET TWELFTH
VIOLINA BOMBARDE CARILLON
CLARINET DIAPASON DIAPHONE
DULCIANA GEMSHORN REGISTER
TENOROON TROMBONE WALDHORN
BOMBARDON CORNOPEAN
DOUBLETTE HARMONICA PRINCIPAL
SAXOPHONE CLARABELLA
(— VIBRATO) TREMOLO
(ADHESIVE —) SUCKER
(BRISTLELIKE —) SETA
(CHINESE —) SANG CHENG
(CIRCUS —) CALLIOPE
(HAND —) SERINETTE
(INTROMITTENT —) VERGE
(KIND OF —) REED
(OLFACTORY —) NOSE
(PLANT'S —) HOLDFAST
(PORTABLE —) REGAL
(RESPIRATORY —) LUNG
(SMALL —) REGAL
(STINGING —) NEMATOCYST
(SWIMMING —) OAR CTENE
(VOCAL — OF BIRDS) SYRINX
(WASTE —) KIDNEY
(PREF.) (INTERNAL —) VISCER(I)(O)
ORGANELLE LYSOSOME

ORGANIC VITAL INBORN NATURAL
INHERENT
ORGANISM WOG BODY ECAD GERM
GUEST PLANT AEROBE ANIMAL
EMBRYO SYSTEM DIPLONT DISEASE
MACHINE PLANONT SUSCEPT
HEMAMEBA PATHOGEN PLANKTER
MESOPHILE POLYMORPH
(— CHARACTERISTIC) MIXIS
(COLD-BLOODED —) POIKILOTHERM
(COMPOUND —) STOCK
(FOSSIL —) EOZOON
(MINUTE —) AMEBA MONAD SPORE
(MODIFIED —) ECAD
(PELAGIC —S) NEKTON
(POLITICAL —) LEVIATHAN
(SIMPLE —) MONAD
(SMALL AIRBORNE —S)
AEROPLANKTON
(PL.) BENTHON BENTHOS HAYSEED
NEUSTON PLEUSTON
(PREF.) BIO ONT(O)
(SUFF.) ACEAN ONT PHORA
(SIMPLE —) MONAS
ORGANIZATION ART BIG ITO CLUB
FIRM KLAN CADRE FIDAC FORUM
HOUSE MAFIA SETUP AUMAGA
CHURCH OUTFIT SURVEY SYSTEM
CHARITY COMPANY CONCERN
DEMOLAY ECONOMY GIDEONS
MENORAH SOCIETY CONGRESS
PATRONAGE STRUCTURE
(— OF ACTORS) COMPANY
(— OF DEALERS) AUCTION
(— OF EXPERIENCE) SCHEMA
(— WITH MANY BRANCHES)
OCTOPUS
(ARMY —) LANDSTORM
(AUXILIARY —) AID SYNODICAL
(COLLEGE —) FRAT ALUMNA ALUMNI
ALUMNUS SORORITY
(COMMUNIST —) COMECON
(HARMONIOUS —) ORCHESTRATION
(HEALTH —) HMO
(JEWISH —) ITO MENORAH
(MARDI GRAS —) KREWE
(MUSICAL —) BAND COMBO CAPELLE
KAPELLE ENSEMBLE ORCHESTRA
(POLICE —) GESTAPO
(POLITICAL —) PARTY VEREIN
HETAERIA HETAIRIA APPARATUS
(SAMOAN —) AUMAGA
(SECRET —) WOW BPOE ELKS
MOOSE MASONS MIDEWIN
(SOCIAL —) POLICE
(WAR VETERANS —) AVC DAV GAR
SAR VFW FIDAC AMVETS
(WOMEN'S —) DAR WAF WRC WCTU
SORORITY
(YOUTH —) KOMSOMOL
ORGANIZE FORM EDIFY FOUND
MODEL ORDER RALLY DESIGN
EMBODY ARRANGE MODULIZE

REGIMENT UNIONIZE BLUEPRINT
INSTITUTE INTEGRATE STRUCTURE
COORDINATE
ORGANIZED FORMED ORGANIC
TOGETHER
(BADLY —) INCONDITE
ORGANIZER PROMOTER
ORGANZA GAZAR
ORGIASTIC BACCHIC SATURNALIAN
ORGY LARK RITE ROMP BINGE REVEL
SPREE FROLIC SHINDY REVELRY
WASSAIL CAROUSAL CEREMONY
SATURNALIA
(PL.) ORGIACS DEBAUCHERIES
ORIANA (FATHER OF —) LISUARTE
(HUSBAND OF —) MIRABEL
(LOVER OF —) AMADIS
ORIBI OUREBI ANTELOPE BLEEKBOK
PALEBUCK
ORIEL BAY CHAPEL DORMER RECESS
WINDOW BALCONY GALLERY
MIRADOR PORTICO CORRIDOR
ORIENT DAWN EAST ADAPT BUILD
PEARL PLACE SHEEN ADJUST
LEVANT LOCATE LUSTER RISING
GLOWING INCLINE RADIANT
SUNRISE LUSTROUS SPARKLING
ORIENTAL ASIAN PEARL BRIGHT
INDIAN ORTIVE RISING EASTERN
SHINING INDOGEAN LUSTROUS
PELLUCID PRECIOUS BRILLIANT
LEVANTINE
ORIENTATION ASPECT PHORIA
STRIKE COLORING LOCALITY
ORIFICE BUNG HOLE PORE PORT
VENT INLET MOUTH STOMA TREMA
BLOWER CAVITY OUTLET RICTUS
SIPHON THROAT CHIMNEY EARHOLE
FORAMEN OPENING OSCULUM
OSTIOLE APERTURE FUMAROLE
INTROITUS
(— IN VOLCANIC REGION) FUMAROLE
(— OF INFUNDIBULUM) LURA
(BREATHING —) SPIRACLE
(VOLCANIC —) BLOWER
(PREF.) TREMATO
(— OF STOMACH) PYLOR(O)
(SUFF.) PYL(E) TREMA(TA)
ORIGANUM ORGANY MARJORAM
ORGAMENT
ORIGILLE (FATHER OF —)
MONODANTE
(LOVER OF —) GRIFONE
(SISTER OF —) BRANDIMARTE
ORIGIN NEE GERM KIND RISE ROOT
SEED BIRTH CAUSE RADIX START
STOCK FATHER GROWTH NATURE
PARENT SOURCE SPRING EDITION
GENESIS LINEAGE UPSTART
NASCENCE UPSPRING BEGINNING
INCEPTION OFFSPRING PARENTAGE
PROVENANCE
(— ON EARTH) EPIGENE

(FOREIGN —) ECDEMIC
(POINT OF —) POLE
(PREF.) (ANCIENT —) PALAE(O)
PALAI(O) PALE(O)
(SUFF.) GENY
ORIGINAL NEW HOME SEED FIRST
FRESH NOVEL PRIME STOCK FONTAL
MASTER MOTHER NATIVE PRIMAL
PRIMER SAMPLE PIONEER PRIMARY
RADICAL SEMINAL CREATION
NASCENCY PRISTINE AUTHENTIC
AUTOGRAPH BEGINNING INVENTIVE
OFFSPRING PRIMITIVE
(NOT —) DERIVED
(PREF.) ARCH(AE)(AEO)(E)(EO)(I)
ORIGINALITY INGENUITY
ORIGINATE COIN COME DATE GROW
HEAD MAKE MOVE OPEN REAR RISE
SIRE ARISE BEGIN BIRTH BREED
CAUSE ENDOW FOUND HATCH RAISE
START AUTHOR CREATE DERIVE
DESIGN DEVISE FATHER INVENT
PARENT SPRING CAUSATE DESCEND
EMANATE PIONEER PROCEED
PRODUCE COMMENCE CONCEIVE
CONTRIVE DISCOVER GENERATE
INITIATE INSTITUTE
ORIGINATION MAKING DESCENT
GENESIS BREEDING ORIGINAL
COSMOGONY ETYMOLOGY
ORIGINATOR AUTHOR FATHER
CREATOR INVENTOR GENERATOR
PROGENITOR
ORIOLE PIROL BUNYAH LARIOT
LORIOT CACIQUE FIGBIRD PEABIRD
FIREBIRD GOLDBIRD HANGBIRD
HANGNEST TROUPIAL
ORION RIGEL ALGEBAR
(BELT OF —) ELLWAND
(FATHER OF —) HYRIEUS POSEIDON
(GUIDE OF —) CEDALION
(HOUND OF —) ARATUS
(SLAYER OF —) ARTEMIS
ORITHYIA (DAUGHTER OF —)
CHIONE CLEOPATRA
(FATHER OF —) ERECHTHEUS
(MOTHER OF —) PRAXITHEA
(SON OF —) ZETES CALAIS
ORKNEY ISLANDS (CAPITAL OF —)
KIRKWALL
(ISLAND OF —) HOY POMONA
ROUSAY SANDAY STRONSAY
ORLANDO (BELOVED OF —)
ROSALIND
ORLE ORLET BORDER FILLET WREATH
BEARING CHAPLET TRESSURE
ORLOP DECK ARLOUP
ORMENUS (FATHER OF —)
CERCAPHUS
(SON OF —) AMYNTOR
ORMER ABALONE
ORMOLU GILT GOLD ALLOY BRASS
VARNISH

ORNAMENT BOB DUB FLY FOB GAY
JOY PIN POT TAG TEE TOY URN BALL
BOSS CURL CUSP DICE ETCH FALL
FRET FROG GAUD GEAR HUSK KNOP
LEAF NULL OUCH RULE STAR TOOL
TRIM WALY WING ADORN BRAID
BULLA CHASE CROSS CROWN
DECOR EXORN FUSEE GRACE GUTTA
HELIX HONOR INLAY KNOSP LUNET
MENSK MENSO OVOID PATCH POPPY
PRUNT SPANG SPRAY SPRIG STALK
TRAIL TRICK WALLY AMULET ANKLET
ATTIRE BEDAUB BEDECK BILLET
BRANCH BROOCH BUTTON CIMIER
COLLAR DIAPER DOODAD EDGING
EMBOSS ENRICH FALLAL FINERY
FLORET FLOWER GORGET INSERT
LABRET LUNULA NIELLO OFFSET
PAMPRE PARURE PATERA ROCOCO
ROSACE RUNTEE SETOFF TABLET
TAHALI TEMPLE TIRADE AGREMEN'
AKROTER AMALAKA BIBELOT
BUCRANE CIRCLET COCARDE
CORBEIL CROCKET DIGLYPH
EARPLUG ECHINUS EMBLEMA
ENGRAVE ENHANCE FRIGGER
FURNISH GADROON GARNISH
NETSUKE RINCEAU ROSETTE
SEXFOIL STRIGIL TORSADE TREFOIL
TRINKET ACCOLADE ANAGLYPH
APPLIQUE BRELOQUE DECORATE
FLOURISH GIMCRACK LAVALIER
MORESQUE NOSERING PALMETTE
ROCAILLE SUNBURST SWASTIKA
POPPYHEAD
(— FOR HEAD) MIND TARGET
(— ON CHAIR) SPLAT
(— ON GLASS) PRUNT
(— ON SHIP) BADGE APLUSTRE
(ARCHITECTURAL —) GUTTA
(CHILD'S —) GAY
(CLAW-LIKE —) GRIFFE
(CRYSTAL —) SPAR
(DRESS —) FROG LACE JABOT
SEQUIN SPANGLE
(EXTRAVAGANT —) GROTESQUE
(FANTASTIC —) ANTIC
(GLITTERING —) SPANG
(HAIR —) POMPOM TETTIX
(HEAD —) TIARA TEMPLE
(HORSE COLLAR —) HOUNCE
(JAPANESE —) NETSUKE
(JEWELRY —) RONDEL
(LIP —) LABRET
(MATCHING SET OF —S) PARURE
(MUSICAL —) TURN MORDENT
BACKFALL PRALLTRILLER
(PENDANT —) BOB BULLA ANADEM
BANGLE TASSEL EARRING LAVALIER
(ROCK-CRYSTAL —) ALMOND
(ROOF —) ANTEFIX
(ROOFING —) ANTEFIX
(SCROLL—) ROCAILLE

(SHIP-SHAPED —) NEF
(SHOULDER —) EPAULET
(SPIRAL —) SCROLL
(STOCKING —) CLOCK
(SUPERFLUOUS —) FRILL FURBELOW
(TAWDRY —) GINGERBREAD
(PL.) FIGGERY KNAVERY
AGREMENS
ORNAMENTAL FANCY CHICHI
FRILLY LILYTURF BLUEBEARD
NASTURTIUM SEMPERVIVUM
ORNAMENTATION BOSS FOIL
ACORN DECOR ADORNO BABERY
CHICHI CILERY DICING BARBOLA
CUSPING ECHELLE LACWORK
STYLING ACANTHUS APPLIQUE
FROUFROU HEADWORK PURFLING
ROCAILLE STAFFAGE TRESSURE
(CHEAP —) TINSEL
(EXTRAVAGANT —) ROCOCO
(MUSICAL —) GRUPPO GRUPPETTO
SCHLEIFER
ORNAMENTED FIGURY FOILED
ORNATE TAWDRY ADORNED
FLOUNCY FROSTED TREFLEE
WROUGHT GOFFERED SINNOWED
ELABORATE STELLATED
ORNAMNET (NECK —) GORGET
(WATCHCHAIN —) BRELOQUE
ORNATE GAY FINE FANCY FUSSY
GIDDY SHOWY DRESSY FLORID
FLOSSY PURPLE SUPERB AUREATE
BAROQUE FLOWERY TAFFETA
MANDARIN OVERRIPE SPLENDID
ELABORATE UNNATURAL
(EXTREMELY —) GIDDY
ORNERY CONTRARY
ORNITHOLOGIST AUDUBON
BIRDMAN
AMERICAN CORY OBER ARBIB BEEBE
COUES MINER STONE BAILEY
BREWER BUTLER CASSIN KEELER
MILLER STROUD TORREY WILSON
XANTUS AUDUBON BRASHER
CHAPMAN FORBUSH FUERTES
HENSHAW NUTTALL RIDGWAY
SHUFELDT TOWNSEND
CANADIAN NASH
ENGLISH DIXON GOULD CLARKE
LATHAM SHARPE HOSKING KIRKMAN
FRENCH LEVAILLANT
GERMAN NAUMANN REICHENOW
KLEINSCHMIDT
INDIAN ALI
NEW ZEALAND BULLER
OROMO GALLA
OROONOKO (WIFE OF —) IMOINDA
OROTUND FULL CLEAR SHOWY
MELLOW STRONG POMPOUS
RESONANT SONOROUS BOMBASTIC
ORP FRET WEEP
ORPAH (HUSBAND OF —) CHILION
(SISTER-IN-LAW OF —) RUTH

ORPHAN PIP WAIF WARD
FOUNDLING STEPCHILD
ORPHANED ORBATE
ORPHEUS (BIRTHPLACE OF —) PIERIA
(FATHER OF —) APOLLO OEAGRUS
(MOTHER OF —) CALLIOPE
(WIFE OF —) EURYDICE
ORPHREY BAND BORDER
ORPIMENT ORPIN HARTAL SPIRIT
ARSENIC HARTAIL ZARNICH
ORPINE SEDUM LIVELONG
BAGLEAVES EVERGREEN
ORRA ODD IDLE ORROW WORTHLESS
ORRIS GIMP IRIS LACE BRAID ORRICE
GALLOON
ORSINO (WIFE OF —) VIOLA
ORT BIT END TAG CRUMB SCRAP
MORSEL REFUSE TRIFLE LEAVING
REMNANT FRAGMENT LEFTOVER
ORTHOCLASE ADULARIA
AMAZONITE
ORTHODOX GOOD GREEK SOUND
USUAL PROPER CANONIC CORRECT
ACCEPTED CATHOLIC STANDARD
CUSTOMARY
ORTHODOXY PIETY TRUTH
SOUNDNESS
ORTHOGRAPHY WRITING
ORTHOPTERON WALKER
ORTNIT (BROTHER OF —)
WOLFDIETRICH
ORTOLAN BIRD RAIL SORA BUNTING
BOBOLINK WHEATEAR
ORTSTEIN HARDPAN
ORYX BEISA PASANG PASENG
GAZELLE GEMSBOK ANTELOPE
LEUCORYX
OS BONE ESKAR ESKER MOUTH
OPENING ORIFICE
OSAGE ORANGE HEDGE OSAGE
BODOCK BOWWOOD
OSCILLATE LOG WAG HUNT ROCK
SWAY VARY SQUEG SWING WAVER
WEAVE SHIMMY FEATHER VIBRATE
FLUCTUATE
OSCILLATION HOWL WAVE SHOCK
SEICHE SHIMMY SQUEAL FLUTTER
LIBRATION VIBRATION
(— OF EARTH'S AXIS) NUTATION
(SUDDEN —) SURGE
OSCULATE BUSS KISS
OSCULATION TACNODE
OSCULATORY PAX
OSIER ROD WAND EDDER SALIX
SKEIN SPLIT WITHY BASKET SALLOW
WICKER WILLOW DOGWOOD
WILGERS REDBRUSH
(— CAGE) TUMBREL
(— WILLOW) TWIGWITHY
OSIRIS HERSHEF UNNEFER
(BROTHER OF —) SET SETH
(CROWN OF —) ATEF
(FATHER OF —) GEB KEB SEB

(MOTHER OF —) NUT
(SISTER OF —) ISIS
(SON OF —) HORUS ANUBIS
(WIFE OF —) ISIS
OSMANLI TURK TURKISH
OSPREY GLED HAWK OSSI GLEDE
PYGARG BALBUSARD OSSIFRAGE
OSSATURE SKELETON OSSEMENTS
OSSE DARE ATTEMPT PRESAGE
PROMISE VENTURE PROPHESY
RECOMMEND UTTERANCE
OSSEOUS BONE BONY SPINY LITHIC
OSTEAL
OSSIAN (FATHER OF —) FINN
OSSICLE BONE INCUS ADORAL
STAPES ALVEOLE BONELET
MALLEUS SCUTELLA
OSSIFICATION OSTOSIS UROSTEON
METOSTEON SIDEBONES
OSSIFIED SCLEROUS
OSSUARY URN TOMB GRAVE VAULT
OSSARIUM
OSTEND SHOW REVEAL EXHIBIT
MANIFEST
OSTENSIBLE NOMINAL SEEMING
APPARENT SPECIOUS
OSTENT AIR MIEN SIGN TOKEN
DISPLAY PORTENT
OSTENTATION DOG POMP PUFF
SHOW CLASS ECLAT FLARE GLITZ
PRIDE STRUT SWANK VAUNT
PARADE VANITY DISPLAY FLUTTER
PAGEANT PORTENT PRESAGE
FLOURISH FRIPPERY PRETENCE
PRETENSE SHOWINESS SPECTACLE
OSTENTATIOUS ARTY LOUD VAIN
GAUDY SHOWY SWANK FLASHY
SPORTY SWANKY TURGID FLAUNTY
GLARING OBVIOUS POMPOUS
SPLASHY SPLURGY FASTUOUS
ELABORATE
OSTERIA INN TAVERN
OSTIOLE PORE MOUTH STOMA
OPENING ORIFICE APERTURE
OSTRACISM TABU TABOO
PETALISM
OSTRACIZE BAN BAR CUT SNUB
EXILE BANISH PUNISH REJECT
ABOLISH BOYCOTT CENSURE
EXCLUDE BLACKBALL PROSCRIBE
OSTRACON SHELL FRAGMENT
POTSHERD
OSTRICH EMU RHEA NANDU
BREVIPEN STRUCION
(— FEATHER) BOO
(JERKED —) BILTONG
(PREF.) STRUTHI(O)(ONI)
OSTYAK KHANTY
OSWALD (FATHER OF —) ETHELFRITH
(SLAYER OF —) PENDA
OSWEGO TEA BALM
OTAHEITE TAHITI
(— APPLE) HEVI MACUPA MACUPI

OTALGIA EARACHE
OTARIOID SEAL SEALION
OTHELLO MOOR
(AUTHOR OF —) SHAKESPEARE
(CHARACTER IN —) IAGO BIANCA
CASSIO EMILIA MONTANO OTHELLO
GRATIANO LODOVICO RODERICO
BRABANTIO DESDEMONA
(ENSIGN OF —) IAGO
(FRIEND OF —) IAGO
(LIEUTENANT OF —) CASSIO
(WIFE OF —) DESDEMONA
OTHER HE MO HER HIM ELSE MORE
OTRA ALTER FORMER NOTHER
SECOND TIDDER TOTHER ALTERUM
FURTHER DISTINCT DIFFERENT
(— THAN) SAVE
(PL.) LAVE REST LUTRA
(PREF.) ALL(O) HETER(O)
OTHERNESS ALTERITY
OTHERS THEM THEY
OTHERWISE OR NOT ELSE ENSE
ALIAC ELLUS ALITER EXCEPT
BESIDES ELSEHOW ELSEWAYS
OTHERWORDLY FEY SPACY
OTHERWORLDLY EERIE
OTHNI (BROTHER OF —) CALEB
(FATHER OF —) KENAZ SHEMAIAH
(WIFE OF —) ACHSAH
OTIC AURAL AUDITORY ORACULAR
AURICULAR
OTIONIA (FATHER OF —)
ERECHTHEUS
(MOTHER OF —) PRAXITHEA
(SISTER OF —) PANDORA
PROTOGONIA
OTIOSE IDLE LAZY VAIN ALOOF
FUTILE OTIANT REMOTE STERILE
USELESS INACTIVE INDOLENT
REPOSING
OTOLITH SAGITTA LAPILLUS
OTOSTEON
OTOLOGIST AURIST
OTTAVINO PICCOLO
OTTER DOG FUR PUP FISH NAIR PELT
BITCH HURON LOUTRE SIMUNG
TACKLE ANNATTO PERIQUE
MAMPALON MUSTELIN PARAVANE
(— TAIL) POLE
(DEN OF — S) HOLT
(SEA —) KALAN
OTTOMAN (ALSO SEE TURKEY)
POUF SEAT SOFA TURK COUCH
DIVAN SQUAB STOOL FABRIC
OTHMAN POUFFE SULTANE
FOOTSTOOL
(— COURT) PORTE
(— GOVERNOR) PASHA
(— LEADER) OSMAN
(— PROVINCE) VII AYET
(— STANDARD) ALEM
(— SUBJECT) RAIA RAYAH
OUABE HOGNUT

OUAKARI ACARI UKARI MONKEY
UAKARI
OUBLIETTE DUNGEON
OUCH OH OW ADORN BEZEL CLASP
JEWEL NOUCH BROOCH FIBULA
NOUCHE BRACELET NECKLACE
ORNAMENT
OUGHT BIT BUD BUT MOW BOOD
BOOT MOTE MUST ZERO SHALL
BELONG CIPHER NAUGHT NOUGHT
SHOULD BEHOOVE
OUISTITI WISTITI MARMOSET
OUNCE URE OKET OKIA ONCA ONCE
ONZA OKIEH UNCIA CHEETAH
LEOPARD WILDCAT
(CHINESE —) LIANG
(EIGHT —S) CUPFUL
(HALF —) SEMUNCIA
(ONE-16TH OF —) DRAM
(ONE-20TH OF —) EASTERLING
(ONE-8TH OF —) DRAM
OUPHE ELF OOF OUF GOBLIN
OUR UR ORE URE WER WIR HORE
NOTRE UNSER
(— LORD) NS
(— SAVIOR) NSIC
(PREF.) NOSTRI
OURICURY LICURI LICURY
CABECUDO
OUR MUTUAL FRIEND (AUTHOR
OF —) DICKENS
(CHARACTER IN —) JOHN WEGG
WREN BELLA BETTY FANNY HEXAM
JENNY JESSE SILAS BOFFIN
EUGENE HARMON HIDGEN JULIUS
LIZZIE WILFER BRADLEY CHARLEY
CLEAVER HANDFORD WRAYBURN
HEADSTONE HENRIETTA
NICODEMUS ROKESMITH
OURSELVES USSELF USSELS
USSELVEN
OUR TOWN (AUTHOR OF —) WILDER
(CHARACTER IN —) JOE WEBB EMILY
GIBBS HOWIE SIMON WALLY
GEORGE CROWELL NEWSOME
REBECCA STIMSON GORUSLOWSKI
OUSIA NATURE ESSENCE
SUBSTANCE
OUST BAR BUMP FIRE SACK CHUCK
EJECT EVICT EXPEL BANISH DEBOUT
REMOVE CASHIER DISCARD DISMISS
SUSPEND DISSEIZE FORJUDGE
ELIMINATE
OUSTING AMOTION
OUT EX AWAY DOWN HORS DATED
FORTH ABSENT BEGONE ISSUED
OOTWITH OUTWARD EXTERNAL
PUBLISHED
(— AT ELBOWS) SCRUFFY
(— LOUD) BOST
(— OF) EX FROM DEHORS OUTWITH
(— OF BREATH) BLOWN
(— OF COMMISSION) BUNG

(— OF DATE) OLD DOWDY PASSE
OUTWORN TIMEWORN OVERDATED
(— OF DOORS) ABROAD FOREIGN
THEREOUT
(— OF EXISTENCE) AWAY
(— OF KILTER) ALOP AWRY CRANK
BROKEN
(— OF ONE'S MIND) FEY DAFT
DELEERIT
(— OF ORDER) AMISS KAPUT FAULTY
DEFICIENT
(— OF PLACE) AMISS INEPT
(— OF PLAY) DEAD FOUL
(— OF SIGHT) DOGGO INVISIBLE
(— OF SORTS) CROOK CROSS HUMPY
NOHOW SEEDY ROTTEN COMICAL
PEEVISH
(— OF THE WAY) BY BYE ASIDE BLIND
CLEAR CLOSE AFIELD GEASON
REMOTE
(— OF THIS LIFE) HYNE
(— OF TUNE) FALSE SCORDATO
(FARTHER —) UTTER
(NOT —) SAFE
(PREF.) E ECT(O) EXO PRO
(— OF) EC
OUTAGE VENT ULLAGE HEADSPACE
OUT-AND-OUT RANK STARK
PATENT REGULAR TEETOTAL
THOROUGH GROSS PLUMB SHEER
SWORN UTTER ARRANT DIRECT
WHOLLY REGULAR ABSOLUTE
COMPLETE CRASHING OUTRIGHT
OUTBID OVERCALL
OUTBREAK FIT ROW RASH RIOT
BURST SALLY EMEUTE PLAGUE
REVOLT RUCKUS TUMULT UPROAR
BOUTADE OUTCROP RUCTION
BLIZZARD ERUPTION OUTBURST
EXPLOSION
(— OF DISEASE) PANDEMIC
(— OF EMOTIONALISM) HYSTERIA
(— OF SELF-INDULGENCE) LOOSE
(— OF TEMPER) MOORBURN
(REVOLUTIONARY —) PUTSCH
(SUDDEN —) SPURT
(VIOLENT —) STORM
OUTBUILDING BARN SHED LODGE
PRIVY BARTON GARAGE HEMMEL
LEANTO OUTHOUSE SKEELING
SKILLING BACKHOUSE
OUTBURST BOUT CROW FLAW
FUME GALE GUST RAGE TEAR TIFF
AGONY BLAST BLAZE BLURT BREAK
BRUNT BURST FLARE FLASH GEARE
SALLY SPATE START STORM ACCESS
BLOWER BLOWUP ESCAPE FANTAD
FANTOD GOLLER TIRADE TUMULT
VOLLEY BLOWOUT BOUTADE
OUTCROP PASSION TANTRUM
TORRENT ERUPTION EXPLOSION
(— OF ANGER) FIT GERE GEARE
TATTER

(— OF APPLAUSE) OVATION
(— OF BIRD) SONG
(— OF FEELING) PASSION
(— OF ORATORY) SQUIRT
(— OF SPEECH) STRAIN
(— OF TEMPER) FUFF TIFF BLOWOUT
(— OF WORDS) VOLLEY
(SPACE —) SUPERNOVA

OUTCAST EXILE LEPER RONIN
SHREW ABJECT PARIAH WRETCH
AOUTLET ISHMAEL MISSILE
OUTWALE CASTAWAY CHANDALA
REJECTED VAGABOND DIALONIAN
(HOMELESS —) ARAB
(JAPANESE —) ETA RONIN
(PYRENEES —) CAGOT

OUTCOME END OUT FATE TERM
CLOSE EDUCT EVENT HATCH ISSUE
LOOSE PROOF UPSET BROWST
EFFECT EXITUS OUTLET PERIOD
RESULT SEQUEL UPSHOT EMANATE
PROGENY SUCCESS FATALITY
AFTERMATH
(UNPREDICTABLE —) CRAPSHOOT

OUTCROP CROP REEF LEDGE
BASSET INLIER BLOSSOM BLOWOUT
OUTBREAK OUTBURST

OUTCROPPING BULT SCABROCK

OUTCRY CAW CRY HUE YIP BAWL
BRAY DITE GAFF HOWL REAM ROAR
SCRY UTAS YARM YELL ALARM
BOAST DITTY NOISE OUTAS SHOUT
STINK WHAUP BELLOW CLAMOR
HOLLER RACKET SCREAM SHRIEK
STEVEN TUMULT CALLING EXCLAIM
PROTEST SCREECH SHILLOO
COMPLAINT PHILLILEW
(PUBLIC —) STINK

OUTDATED PASSE CRINOLINE

OUTDISTANCE DROP SKIN OUTGO
SURPASS OUTSTRIP

OUTDO CAP COB CAP COW POT TOP
BANG BEAT BEST BURN FLOG WHIP
EXCEL OUTGO REVIE TRUMP WORSE
DEFEAT OUTACT OUTMATCH NONPLUS
OUTPACE SURPASS OUTMATCH
OUTSHINE OVERCOME

OUTDOOR OPENAIR

OUTDOORS FORTH OUTBY OUTBYE
OUTSIDE

OUTER BUT OVER ALIEN ECTAD
ECTAL UPPER UTTER FOREIGN
OUTSIDE OUTWARD EXTERIOR
EXTERNAL FORINSEC
(PREF.) ECTO EPH EPI EXO

OUTER MONGOLIA (SEE
MONGOLIA)
(COIN OF—) MONGO TUGRIK

OUTERMOST FINAL UTTER
UTMOST EVEREST EXTREME
OUTWARD FARTHEST REMOTEST

OUTFACE DEFY RESIST SUBDUE
CONFRONT OVERCOME

OUTFIELDER GARDENER OUTSCOUT
(THROW BY —) PEG

OUTFIT KIT RIG TOG DRAG GANG
GARB REAR REEK SUIT TEAM UNIT
DRESS EQUIP GETUP HABIT TROUP
ATTIRE CONREY DUFFEL FITOUT
LAYOUT CLOTHES FURNISH
SHEBANG EQUIPAGE FURNITURE
GRUBSTAKE
(BRIDE'S —) TROUSSEAU
(CHINESE —) SAMFU SAMFOO
(INFANT'S —) LAYETTE
(SEWING —) HOUSEWIIFE
(SPARE —) CHANGE

OUTFLANK OUTWING OVERWING

OUTFLOW FLUX DRAIN ISSUE
OUTGO EFFLUX ESCAPE SPRING
OUTPOUR
(SEWAGE —) EFFLUENT

OUTGO EXIT EXCEL ISSUE OUTDO
EFFLUX EGRESS EXCEED OUTLAY
OUTLET OUTRUN OUTCOME
PRODUCT SURPASS OUTSTRIP

OUTGROWTH ALA BUD JAG ARIL
FOOT HAIR LEAF MOSS SPUR CLAMP
FRUIT HILUM HYPHA SCALE SPINE
ACULEA COCKLE CUPULE FIBRIL
ENATION FEATHER ISIDIUM VERRUCA
APPENDIX CARUNCLE EPIDERMA
FLOCCULE HAPTERON INDUSIUM
OFFSHOOT CARBUNCLE EMERGENCE
FLOCCULUS PROPAGULE
ROSTELLUM OSTEOPHYTE
(PLANTS —) OVULE

OUTGUESS PSYCH PSYCHE

OUTHOUSE SHED SKEO BIFFY
LODGE PRIVY BIGGIN LINHAY
OUTHUT LATRINE SKEELING
SKILLION
(PL.) STEADING

OUTING OUT SKIP STAY TRIP
JUNKET PICNIC COOKOUT HOLIDAY
CLAMBAKE VACATION WAYGOOSE
EXCURSION WAYZGOOSE

OUTLANDER ALIEN PARDESI

OUTLANDISH ALIEN KINKY OUTRE
EXOTIC REMOTE BIZARRE FOREIGN
STRANGE UNCOUTH PECULIAR
BARBAROUS FANTASTIC
GROTESQUE UNEARTHLY
(AMUSINGLY —) CAMPY

OUTLAST ELAPSE SURVIVE
OVERBIDE

OUTLAW BAN BAR CACO HORN
TORY EXILE EXLEX FLEME RONIN
ARRANT BADMAN BANDIT BANISH
BRUMBY COWBOY DACOIT UNLEDE
BANDIDO ISHMAEL FUGITATE
FUGITIVE PROHIBIT PROSCRIBE
PROSCRIPT
(IRISH —) WOODKERN
(JAPANESE —) RONIN
(PL.) MANZAS

OUTLAWED ILLEGAL ILLICIT LAWLESS

OUTLAWRY BAN EXILE UTLAGARY

OUTLAY COST MISE OUTGO EXPENSE PENSION

OUTLET BORE DRIP EXIT VENT ISSUE EGRESS ESCAPE EXITUS FUNNEL OUTAGE OPENING FUMEDUCT OVERFLOW SINKHOLE AVOIDANCE
(— FOR COASTAL SWAMP) BAYOU
(— FOR SMOKE) FEMERALL
(— OF CARBURETOR) BARREL
(— OF SPRING) EYE
(AIR —) GRILL GRILLE
(ELECTRIC —) POINT
(REGULATED —) SLUICE
(RETAIL —) MINILAB

OUTLIER KLIP KLIPPE

OUTLINE MAP BOSH EDGE ETCH FLOW FORM LINE PLAN PLAT BRIEF CHALK CHART DRAFT FRAME MODEL SHAPE TRACE AGENDA APERCU DESIGN DOODLE FIGURE FILLET LAYOUT SCHEMA SCHEME SCROLL SKETCH SURVEY CAPSULE CONTOUR CROQUIS DIAGRAM DRAUGHT ELEMENT EXTRACT FEATURE GABARIT ISOTYPE PROFILE SUMMARY CONTORNO DESCRIBE ESQUISSE SKELETON SYLLABUS SYNOPSIS DELINEATE GUIDELINE TREATMENT
(— HASTILY) SPLASH
(— OF ANIMAL'S BODY) UNDERLINE
(— OF A SCIENCE) GRUNDRISS
(— OF COLUMN) ENTASIS
(— OF PLAY) SCENARIO
(— SHARPLY) ITALICIZE
(CURVING —) SWING
(DOUBLE —) FRINGE
(SHADOWY —) GHOST

OUTLIVE OUTLAST OUTWEAR SURVIVE OVERBIDE

OUTLOOK MIND VIEW FRONK FRONT VISTA ASPECT CLIMATE LOOKOUT PURVIEW FRONTAGE OUTSIGHT PROSPECT MENTALITY
(BRASH —) FACE
(MEDICAL —) PROGNOSIS
(SELF-CONFIDENT —) SWAGGER

OUTLYING OUTBY FORANE OUTBYE OUTLAND

OUTMANEUVER HAVE OUTPLAY

OUTMODED COLD DATED KAPUT PASSE RUSTY BYGONE EFFETE ANTIQUE ELDERLY VINTAGE OBSOLETE

OUT-OF-DATE RINKYDINK

OUT-OF-DOOR GIPSY GYPSY

OUTPLAY HAVE

OUTPOST STATION FOREPOST OUTGUARD

OUTPOURING FLOW GALE GUSH FLOOD RIVER SPATE EARFUL LAVISH STREAM OUTFLOW TORRENT FUSILLADE

OUTPUT CUT GET CROP MAKE EXPEL GRIST POWER YIELD ENERGY UPCOME TURNOUT
(IRRELEVANT —) NOISE

OUTRAGE RAPE ABUSE INSULT OFFEND RAVISH ABUSION AFFRONT OFFENSE VIOLATE VIOLENCE INDIGNITY

OUTRAGEOUS ENORM GROSS OUTRE DAMNED UNHOLY HEINOUS OBSCENE UNGODLY FLAGRANT INFERNAL SHAMEFUL SHOCKING ATROCIOUS DESPERATE MONSTROUS

OUTRANK CAMP PREFER SURPASS

OUTRE ODD BIZARRE STRANGE ECCENTRIC

OUTREACH CHEAT EXCEED EXTEND OUTWIT SEARCH DECEIVE SURPASS OVERREACH

OUTRIDER HAYDUK HEIDUCK HEYDUCK
(PL.) SWING

OUTRIGGER BOOM PROA BUMKIN RIGGER SPIDER

OUTRIGHT RUN BALD CLEAN TOTAL WHOLE DIRECT ENTIRE OPENLY WHOLLY ABSOLUTE COMPLETE DIRECTLY ENTIRELY

OUTRIVAL WIN EXCEL OUTDO DEFEAT ECLIPSE SURPASS

OUTRUN BEAT COTE NICK PASS OUTGO EXCEED ATRENNE FORERUN OUTFOOT PREVENT

OUTRUSH GUST

OUTSET START OFFSET SETOUT BEGINNING THRESHOLD

OUTSHED SKIPPER

OUTSHINE BLIND EXCEL OUTDO STAIN DAZZLE DEFACE DISTAIN SURPASS OVERSHINE

OUTSIDE BUT OUT BOUT FREE RIND OUTBY UTTER AFIELD OUTFACE SURFACE EXTERIOR EXTERNAL
(— BOUNDS) ALOGICAL
(— OF) BESIDE
(— OF COCOON) FLOSS
(COMB. FORM) ECTO
(JUST —) FRINGE
(MERE —) SHELL
(PREF.) EC ECT(O) EXO EXTERO EXTRA EXTRO

OUTSIDER ALIEN OUTMAN BOUNDER ISHMAEL CIVILIAN EXOTERIC STRANGER EXTRANEAN FOREIGNER PHILISTER
(PL.) OUSTITI

OUTSKIRTS SIDE SKIRTS PURLIEU SUBURBS ENVIRONS PURLIEUS OUTSHIFTS

OUTSMART SLICK
OUTSPOKEN BOLD FREE LOUD
APERT BLUFF BLUNT BROAD FRANK
NAKED PLAIN ROUND VOCAL
CANDID DIRECT ARTLESS EXPRESS
EXPLICIT
(ROBUSTLY —) RABELAISIAN
OUTSTANDING ACE BIG ARCH
RARE SOME AMONG FAMED NOTED
SMASH SOCKO BANNER FAMOUS
GIFTED HEROIC MARKED SIGNAL
SNAZZY UNPAID EMINENT PALMARY
SALIENT STELLAR SUBLIME
SUPREME TOPPING FABULOUS
INSPIRED PREMIERE SEASONED
SKELPING SLAMBANG SMACKING
STANDOUT TOWERING BEAUTIFUL
PRINCIPAL PROMINENT UNSETTLED
MONUMENTAL NOTICEABLE
PREEMINENT
OUTSTAY TARRY
OUTSTRETCHED STENT EXPANDED
EXTENDED
OUTSTRIP CAP TOP WIN BEST COTE
LEAD LOSE PASS EXCEL OUTDO
STRIP EXCEED OUTRUN DEVANCE
SURPASS DISTANCE OVERCOME
TRANSCEND
OUTVIE SURPASS OUTSTRIP
OUTWARD ECTAD OUTER OVERT
DERMAD EXODIC EXTERN FORMAL
EXTREME VISIBLE APPARENT
EXTERIOR EXTERNAL OBSOLETE
OUTFORTH EXTRINSIC
(GROWING —) ENATE
OUTWARDS BUT OVER
OUTWEIGH WEIGH OUTPOISE
OVERBEAR OVERSHADE
PREPONDERATE
OUTWIT FOX POT BALK BEST DISH
FOIL HAVE BLOCK CHECK CROSS
ELUDE BAFFLE EUCHRE FICKLE
JOCKEY OVERGO THWART STONKER
OUTGUESS OUTSHARP CROSSBITE
OVERREACH CIRCUMVENT
OUTWORK BRAY JETTY FLECHE
TENAIL BULWARK RAVELIN
BARBICAN HORNWORK TENAILLE
HORSESHOE
OUTWORKER BONDAGER
OUTWORN WAPPENED
OUZEL PIET AMSEL COLLY OUSEL
OWZEL DIPPER THRUSH WHISTLER
OVAL O ELLIPSE STADIUM VESICAL
VULVATE AVELONGE NUMMULAR
VULVIFORM
OVARY CORAL GONAD GERMEN
OARIUM OOPHORON
(PREF.) OOPHOR(O) OV(I) OVARI(O)
OVATO
OVATION HAND APPLAUSE
OVEN OON UMU KILN LEAR LEER
LEHR OAST BAKER BENCH GLAZE
GLOOM HANGI KOHUA TANUR TILER
CALCAR MUFFLE CABOOSE
FURNACE KITCHEN TANDOOR
(— FORK) FRUGGAN FRUGGIN
(— MOP) SCOVEL
OVENBIRD BAKER FURNER
HORNERO TEACHER ACCENTOR
OVER BY BYE OER TOO ALSO ANEW
ATOP BACK DEAD DONE GONE PAST
UPON ABOVE AGAIN ALOFT ATOUR
ATURN CLEAR ENDED EXTRA VAULT
ABROAD ACROSS AROUND BEYOND
DESSUS EXCESS UPWARD SURPLUS
THROUGH FINISHED
(— AGAINST) FORNENT
(— AND ABOVE) ATOP ATOUR
BESIDES
(ALL —) NAPOO NAPOOH SURTOUT
(PREFIX) SUR SUPER SUPRA
(PREF.) EPH EPI HYPER OB PERI
SUPER SUR
OVERABUNDANCE WASTE
EXCESS SURPLUS PLETHORA
OVERABUNDANT LUXURIANT
OVERACT HAM EMOTE OUTDO
BURLESQUE
OVERACTING HAM
OVERADORNED FLORID
OVERALL (BABY'S —) CRAWLER
OVERALLS SLIP CHAPS JEANS
TONGS DENIMS
OVERANXIETY WORRY
OVERARCH COVE
OVERAWE COW ABASH BULLY
DAUNT BUFFALO CONCUSS
BROWBEAT
OVERBEARING HIGH PROUD
LORDLY OVERLY HAUGHTY
ARROGANT BULLYING DOGMATIC
INSOLENT PRUSSIAN SNOBBISH
IMPERIOUS MASTERFUL
OVERBLOUSE SHELL
OVERBLOWN RECHERCHE
OVERBURDEN COVER HOIST
PESTER CONGEST OVERLAY
ENCUMBER STRIPPING SURCHARGE
OVERBUSY FUSSY PRAGMATIC
OVERCAREFUL METICULOUS
OVERCAST DIM SEW BIND DARK
DULL GLUM GREY WHIP CLOUD
HEAVY SERGE CLOUDY DARKEN
GLOOMY LOWERY CLOUDED
NUBILOUS
OVERCHARGE GYP RUSH SOAK
CROWD GOUGE STICK STING
BURDEN EXCISE OPPRESS
EXTORTION
OVERCOAT MINO BENNY GREGO
JEMMY SHUBA BANGUP CAPOTE
RAGLAN SLIPON TABARD TOPPER
ULSTER PALETOT SPENCER
SURTOUT TOPCOAT BALMACAN
BENJAMIN COONSKIN TAGLIONI

COTHAMORE GREATCOAT
INVERNESS

OVERCOATING DUFFEL DUFFLE

OVERCOME DO AWE GET MOW
WAR WIN BEAT BEST DING LICK
LOCK MATE POOP SACK SUNK TAME
WAUR CHARM CRUCH DAUNT
DROUK DROWN FORDO MOPUP
STILL STOOP THROW APPALL
BEATEN BUSHED CRAVEN DEFEAT
EXCEED EXPUGN FOREDO HURDLE
MASTER MOIDER OUTRAY PLUNGE
SUBDUE VICTOR CONFUTE
CONQUER DEPRESS ENFORCE
RECOVER SMOTHER CONVINCE
OUTSTRIP SUPERATE SURMOUNT
SURPRISE PROSTRATE
(— DIFFICULTIES) SWIM
(— WITH FATIGUE) FORDO FOREDO
(— WITH WEARINESS) HEAVY
(BE — BY HEAT) SWELTER
(EASILY —) WEAK

OVERCONFIDENT SECURE
POSITIVE

OVERCROWD PESTER CONGEST
SURCHARGE

OVERDAINTY TAFFETA

OVERDECORATED GARISH

OVERDEVELOPED GAUDY

OVERDO EXCEED EXHAUST FATIGUE
PERCOCT OVERCOOK OVERWORK
BURLESQUE

OVERDONE FUSTIAN EXUBERANT

OVERDOSE OD SICKENER

OVERDRESS SAC SACK DIZEN
SACUE POLONAISE

OVERDRESSED FLOSSY

OVERDRIED SLEEPY

OVERDUE BACK LATE TARDY
UNPAID ARREARS BELATED DELAYED
EXCESSIVE

OVEREAGER ANTSY FEVERISH
FEVEROUS

OVEREAT GORGE SLOFF SATIATE
GOURMAND

OVERELABORATE NIGGLE
LABORED

OVEREMPHATIC MOUTHY

OVERENRICHED OPULENT

OVEREXACT PRECISE

OVEREXCITED HIGH
(GET —) GOAPE

OVEREXERT TORLE STRAIN TORFEL
OVERPLY

OVEREXPOSURE (— TO SUN)
HELIOSIS

OVERFASTIDIOUS SPRUCE

OVERFED RANK FULSOME

OVERFEED CRAM

OVERFLOW REE COME FLUX REAM
SLOP SWIM TEEM VENT BRIME
FLOAT FLOOD SPATE SPILL ABOUND
DEBORD OUTLET SPILTH OVERRUN

REDOUND BOILOVER EXUNDATE
INUNDATE OUTSWELL SUBMERGE
CATACLYSM
(— FROM MOLD) SPEW SPUE

OVERFLOWING FLOW AWASH
FLOAT DELAVY DELUGE ALLUVIO
COPIOUS FRESHET PROFUSE
INUNDANT EXUBERANT LANDFLOOD
SUPERFLUX

OVERFRIENDLY PALSY
PALSYWALSY

OVERGARMENT SMOCK BLOUSE
DUSTER

OVERGROWN FOZY RANK GAWKY
BRANCHY FULSOME SPRATTY
SPRITTY

OVERHAND WHIP

OVERHANG JUT BEND EAVE RAKE
BULGE JETTY BEETLE SHELVE
TOPPLE FANTAIL OVERLAP PROJECT
SUSPEND

OVERHANGING BEETLE SHELVY
HANGING PENDENT PENSILE
BEETLING IMMINENT OBUMBRANT
PENTHOUSE PRECIPITOUS

OVERHASTY RASH

OVERHAUL EXAMINE OVERHAIL
RENOVATE FOREREACH

OVERHEAD COST ABOVE ALOFT
BURDEN ONCOST UPKEEP EXPENSE
OVERTOP

OVERHEARTY ROBUST

OVERHEAT PARBOIL SCOUTHER

OVERINDULGE PAMPER
DEBAUCH

OVERINFUSE STEW

OVERLAP LAP RIDE SYPHER
SHINGLE IMBRICATE INTERSECT

OVERLAPPING JUGATE RIDING
EQUITANT OBVOLUTE IMBRICATE
(— IN FUGUE) STRETTA STRETTO

OVERLAVISH BAROQUE

OVERLAY CAP LAP CEIL COAT WHIP
APPLY COUCH COVER GLAZE PATCH
PLATE CEMENT CRAVAT SPREAD
STUCCO VENEER ENCRUST OPPRESS
OVERLIE SMOTHER APPLIQUE
TEMPLATE
(— WITH GOLD) BEAT GILD

OVERLOAD CRAM GLUT STUFF
SWAMP CHARGE ENCUMBER
SURCHARGE

OVERLOADED PLETHORIC
PLETHOROUS

OVERLOOK BALK MISS OMIT PASS
SKIP SLIP WINK BLINK ELIDE FORGO
ACQUIT EXCUSE FOREGO FORGET
IGNORE MANAGE OVERGO ABSOLVE
COMMAND CONDONE FORGIVE
INSPECT MISKNOW NEGLECT
CONFOUND DOMINATE DISREGARD
DISSEMBLE

OVERLOOKER GAITER

OVERLOOKING (INTENTIONAL —) AMNESTY

OVERLORD LIEGE DESPOT ISWARA SATRAP TYRANT ISHVARA SUZERAIN TYRANNIZE

OVERLY CAP TOO

OVERLYING JESSANT BROCHANT INCUMBENT

OVERMAN CHIEF LEADER ARBITER FOREMAN REFEREE OVERSEER SUPERMAN

OVERMANTLE (— TREATMENT) TRUMEAU

OVERMASTER GET

OVERMATCH BEST DEFEAT EXCEED SURPASS VANQUISH

OVERMODEST PRIM PRUDISH

OVERMUCH TOO EXCESS SURPLUS EXCESSIVE (PREF.) HYPER

OVERNICE FEAT FUSS SAUCY DAINTY QUAINT SPRUCE FINICKY PRECISE DENTICAL PRECIOUS SQUEAMISH

OVERPAINT CLOBBER (— ENAMEL) CLOBBER

OVERPLAY HAM

OVERPOWER AWE BEAT ROUT RUSH CRUSH DROWN QUELL SWAMP WHELM COMPEL DEFEAT DELUGE ENGULF MASTER OVERGO SUBDUE WRIXLE CONQUER CONTROL OPPRESS REPRESS CONVINCE OUTSCOUT SCUMFISH SURPRISE (— WITH HEAT) SWELT (— WITH LIGHT) DAZZLE

OVERPOWERING DIRE FIERCE KILLING DAZZLING STUNNING DESPERATE MONSTROUS

OVERPRAISE FLATTER OVERSELL

OVERPRECISE MIM PRISSY FINICKY CLERKISH NIGGLING PRECIEUSE

OVERREACH DO POT DUPE GRAB CHEAT COZEN CHOILE GREASE NOBBLE OUTWIT OVERGO DECEIVE

OVERREADY FORWARD

OVERREFINED QUAINT PRECIOUS

OVERRIDE SUPERSEDE

OVERRIPE FRACID SQUSHY SQUSHY

OVERRIPENESS SEED

OVERRULE NIX VETO GOVERN ABROGATE OVERCOME

OVERRULING GREAT PREDOMINANT

OVERRUN TEEM BESET CRUSH SWARM DELUGE EXCEED INFEST INVADE OVERGO RAVAGE SPREAD DESTROY

OVERSEAS OUTREMER

OVERSEE TEND WATCH DIRECT HANDLE MANAGE SURVEY EXAMINE INSPECT NEGLECT DISREGARD SUPERVISE

OVERSEER BAAS BOSS CORK JOSS EPHOR GRAVE REEVE BISHOP CENSOR DRIVER GAFFER GRIEVE KEEKER MIRDHA TINDAL WARDEN BAILIFF CAPATAZ CAPORAL CURATOR FOREMAN HEADMAN KANGANI MANAGER MANDOER MAYORAL OVERMAN PRISTAW TAPSMAN BANKSMAN CHAPRASI DECURION MARTINET SURVEYOR VILLICUS (— OF MACHINERY) TENTOR (— OF MINE) CAPTAIN (SPIRITUAL —) PASTOR PRIEST

OVERSENSITIVE TICKLISH

OVERSENTIMENTAL SOFT SLOPPY

OVERSHADOW DIM CLOUD COVER DWARF SHADE TOWER DARKEN EFFACE ECLIPSE OBSCURE UMBRAGE UPSTAGE BESCREEN DOMINATE OVERCAST

OVERSHOE GUM BOOT GUME ARCTIC GAITER GALOSH GOLOSH PATTEN RUBBER SANDAL FLAPPER EXCLUDER FOOTHOLD PANTOFLE

OVERSIGHT EYE CARE HOLE SLIP ERROR FAULT GAFFE LAPSE WATCH CHARGE BLUNDER CONTROL JEOFAIL MISTAKE OMISSION TUTELAGE DIRECTION (LEGAL) JEOFAIL

OVERSKIRT PEPLUM PANNIER

OVERSMART FLIP

OVERSOFT QUASHY

OVERSPREAD FOG CAST CLOT DECK PALL BATHE BREDE CLOUD COVER SMEAR STREW CLOTHE DELUGE DOODLE INDUCE SCATTER SUFFUSE BESPREAD

OVERSTATE MAGNIFY EXAGGERATE

OVERSTEP PASS EXCEED SURPASS TRANSGRESS

OVERSTEPPING FOOTFAULT

OVERSTIMULATED HYPER

OVERSTOCK SURCHARGE

OVERSTRAINED EPITONIC

OVERSUPPLIED RANK

OVERSUPPLY GLUT

OVERT OPEN PATENT PUBLIC OBVIOUS APPARENT MANIFEST

OVERTAKE PASS ATAKE CATCH ATTAIN BEFALL DETECT ENSNARE OVERHIE FOREHENT OVERHAUL (— BY DARKNESS) BENIGHT

OVERTASK DRIVE

OVERTAX HOIST EXCEED STRAIN STRESS

OVERTHROW TIP CAST DASH DOWN FALL FELL FOIL FOLD HURL RAZE ROUT RUIN RUSH WALT WEND ALLAY CRUSH EVERT FLING LEVEL QUASH UPSET WORST WRACK

WRECK DEFEAT DEJECT DEPOSE
REPUTE SLIGHT TOPPLE TUMBLE
UNSEAT WRITHE AFFLICT CONQUER
CONVELL DESTROY DISMISS
RUINATE SUBVERT UNDOING
UNHORSE WHEMMLE CONFOUND
DEMOLISH OVERCOME OVERTURN
REVERSAL SUPPLANT VANQUISH
CHECKMATE CONFUSION
OVERWHELM
(— BY TRIPPING) CHIP
OVERTONE PARTIAL HARMONIC
OVERTOP COW OVERREACH
OVERTURE OFFER PROEM ADVANCE
OPENING PRELUDE APERTURE
PROPOSAL SINFONIA VORSPIEL
(INDECENT —) ASSAULT
OVERTURN TIP CAVE COUP KEEL
TILT WALT WELT TERVE THROW
UPEND UPSET WELME WHALM
WHELM SLIGHT TIPPLE TOPPLE
WELTER CAPSIZE DESTROY PERVERT
REVERSE SUBVERT WHEMMLE
(— A WATCHMAN) BOX
OVERWEENING MISPROUD
PRESUMPTUOUS
OVERWEIGHT OUTGANG
OVERWHELM BOWL BURY SINK
SLAY AMAZE COVER CRUSH DROOK
DROUK DROWN FLOOD FLOOR SEIZE
SPATE SWAMP CUMBER DEFEAT
DELUGE ENGULF OBRUTE PLUNGE
QUELME QUENCH ASTOUND
BESIEGE BOMBARD CONFUTE
CONQUER ENGROSS FLATTEN
IMMERSE INFLOOD OPPRESS
SMOTHER ASTONISH DISTRESS
DOMINATE INUNDATE OVERCOME
SUBMERGE AVALANCHE
OVERWHELMED ACCABLE
OVERWORK HOIN TIRE TOIL SWEAT
STRAIN SURMENAGE
OVINE OVIN OVILE SHEEP SHEEPLIKE
OVIPOSITOR TEREBRA
OVOID OVATE OBOVOID
OVOLO OVAL THUMB BOLTEL
OVULE EGG NIT GERM SEED
EMBRYO OVULUM GEMMULE
SEEDLET
OVUM EGG OVAL SEED SPORE
OOSPERM OOSPHERE
OWAIA TREE BOBO
OWE DUE OWN REST AUGHT OUGHT
SHALL POSSESS ATTRIBUTE
OWED DUE
OWER DEBTOR
OWING INTHEHOLE
OWL ULE BUBO LULU MOMO RURU
SURN TYTO UTUM JENNY MADGE
NINOX PADGE SCOPS STRIX TAWNY
WEKAU AZIOLA HOOTER HOWLET
KETUPA MUCARO RAPTOR STRICH
VERMIN WHEKAU BOOBOOK

HARFANG KATOGLE WAPACUT
WOOLERT BILLYWIX COQUIMBO
MOREPORK
(— CALL) HOOT
(CRY OF —) HOOT WHOO TUWHIT
TUWHOO
(LIKE AN —) STRIGINE
(YOUNG —) UTUM OWLET
(PREF.) STRIGI
OWL PARROT KAKAPO
OWN AIN OWE AVOW FESS HAVE
HOLD HOWE MEET NAIN SELF ADMIT
AUGHT OUGHT MASTER CONCEDE
CONFESS POSSESS PROSPER
ACKNOWLEDGE
(PREF.)
(ONE'S —) IDIO
OWNER BEL MALIK WALLA HOLDER
DOMINUS HERITOR ODALLER
PROPRIETOR
(— OF ESTATE) ALIRD
(— OF FISHING PLANT) PLANTER
(— OF SLAVES) PATRON
(— OF YACHT) AFTERGUARD
(PLANTATION —) COLON
(SHEEP —) NABAL
OWNERSHIP ODAL UDAL AUGHT
TITLE CORNER SEIZIN SEIZURE
SEVERAL TENANCY DOMINIUM
PROPERTY COMMUNITY
POSSESSION
OX YAK ANOA AVER BEEF BUFF BULL
GAUR MUSK NAWT NEAT NEWT
NOWT OWSE REEM RUNT STOT
URUS ZEBU AIVER BISON BUGLE
GAYAL SANGA STEER TOLLY TSINE
BOVINE MITHAN ROTHER BANTENG
BUFFALO KOUPREY TWINTER
SELADANG TALLOWER
(CAMBODIAN —) KOUPREY
KOUPROH
(HORNLESS —) MOIL
(KIND OF —) MUSK
(SMALL —) RUNT
(TAME —) COACH
(WILD —) URE ANOA BUFF GAUR
REEM URUS BISON BUGLE BANTIN
BANTENG BUFFALO SELADANG
(YEARLING —) STIRK
(YOUNG —) STOT
(PREF.) BOVI BU
OXBLOOD KAZAK COPTIC KAZAKH
OXBOW INCIDENT (AUTHOR OF —)
CLARK
(CHARACTER IN —) GIL DREW ROSE
CANBY CROFT GRIER JOYCE MAPEN
TYLER CARTER DAVIES DONALD
GERALD MARTIN OSGOOD RISLEY
TETLEY FARNLEY KINKAID
OXEN NOWT OWSEN CATTLE
OXEYE BOCE GOLD ASTER CLOUD
DAISY GOLDE DUNLIN PLOVER
TARPON

OXFOOT (STEWED —) COWHEEL
OXFORD DOWN SHOE CLOTH
  OXONIAN SLIPPER
OXGANG OSKEN BOVATE OXGATE
  OXLAND PLOWGANG
OXIDATION RUST
OXIDATIVE AEROBIC
OXIDE EARTH FLOSS CADMIA HAFNIA
  MOILES ZAFFER CALCINE GUMMITE
  KERNITE LIMONITE DJALMAITE
  (— OF CALCIUM) LIME
  (— OF IRON) RUST COLCOTHAR
  MAGNETITE
OXLIP PAGLE PAIGLE PRIMULA
  MILKMAID PRIMROSE PRIMWORT
OXSHOE CUE
OXYGEN GAS OZONE OXYGENIUM
  (LIQUID —) LOX
  (PREF.) OXO
OXYGENATE AERATE VENTILATE
OXYGENATOR GILL
OXYSTER COPIS COUNT PINNA PLANT
  SHELL COTUIT HUITRE NATIVE
  REEFER BIVALVE MOLLUSK PANDORE
  RATTLER SHARPER BLUEPOINT
  GREENGILL LYNNHAVEN
  (— BED) PARK STEW LAYER SCALP

  CLAIRE SCALFE OYSTERAGE
  (— CATCHER) OLIVE PYNOT TIRMA
  KROCKET PIANNET REDBILL
  SCOLDER SHELDER PILWILLET
  SKELDRAKE
  (— CRAB) PINNOTERE
  (— FOSSIL) OSTRACITE
  (— MEASURE) WASH
  (— PLANT) SALSIFY
  (— SHELL) HUSK TEST SHUCK
  (— SMALLER THAN QUARTER)
  BLISTER
  (— SOLD BY POUND) COUNT
  (IRISH —) POWLDOODY
  (ROCK —) CHAMA
  (VEGETABLE —) SALSIFY
  (YOUNG —) SET SPAT
  (2,3, OR 4 —S) WARP
  (PREF.) OSTRE(I)(O)
OYSTER CATCHER SEAPIE
OYSTERFISH TAUTOG TOADFISH
OZARK STATE MISSOURI
OZEM (BROTHER OF —) DAVID
  (FATHER OF —) JESSE
OZNI (FATHER OF —) GAD
OZOCERITE MALTHA NEFTGIL
OZONE AIR

P

P PAPA PETER
PA DAD PAW FORT PAPA DADDY FATHER VILLAGE STOCKADE
PABULUM FOOD FUEL PROG CEREAL ALIMENT SUPPORT NUTRIMENT
PAC BOOT SHOE MOCCASIN
PACA CAPA CAVY LAVA LABBA AGOUTI RODENT
PACE FIG PAD RIP WAY BEMA CLIP GAIT LOPE PASS PELT RACK RATE STEP TEAR TROT WALK AMBLE BRAWL CANTO SLINK SPACE SPEED STEEK SWING TEMPO TRACE TREAD CANTER GALLOP STRAIT STRIDE CHANNEL CHAPTER DOGTROT MEASURE PASSAGE SCUTTLE
(FAST —) ROMP
(RAPID —) CLIP CRACKER
(SLOW —) JOG CRAWL CREEP
(PL.) MANAGE
PACER HORSE AMBLER SPANKER TRIPPLER
PACHISI LUDO UCKERS PARCHESI
PACHYDERM BABAR HIPPO RHINO ELEPHANT
PACIFIC CALM MEEK MILD IRENE IRENIC PLACID SERENE PEACEFUL TRANQUIL PEACEABLE
(— ISLAND PINE) IE KOU IEIE LEHUA
PACIFIER DUMMY COMFORTER
PACIFIST BOLO
PACIFY PAY CALM EASE LULL STAY ABATE ALLAY AMESE MEASE PEASE QUELL QUIET STILL PECIFY SERENE SETTLE SOFTEN SOOTHE APPEASE ASSUAGE MOLLIFY PLACATE QUALIFY STICKLE MITIGATE ALLEVIATE RECONCILE
PACK JAM PUN WAD BALE CADE CRAM DECK FILL GANG JAMB LADE LOAD PAIR ROUT STOW SWAG TAMP TOTE TUCK COUCH CRAME CROWD DRESS FLOCK HORDE SKULK SOMER STEVE STORE STUFF TRUSS BARREL BODDLE BOODLE BUDGET BUNDLE CARTON DUFFLE EMBALE ENCASE FARDEL HAMPER IMPACT PARCEL STEEVE THWACK TURKEY WALLET PANNIER PORTAGE RUMMAGE SUMPTER KNAPSACK
(— ANIMAL) ASS MULE BURRO CAMEL HORSE LLAMA DONKEY PACKER
(— BUILDER) GOBBER
(— JURY) WATER
(— LOOSELY) HOVER
(— OF BEARS) SLOTH
(— OF CARDS) STOCK
(— OF DOGS) CRY KENNEL
(— OFF) WAG SHANK TURSE
(— OF FOXES) GROUP SKULK
(— OF HOUNDS) CRY HUNT MUTE
(— ROAD) PACKWAY
(— TIGHTLY) STIVE
PACKAGE PAD BALE BOLT PAIR DUMMY TRUSS BINDLE BUNDLE PACKET PARCEL SAMPLE SEROON DORLACH
(— OF CIGARETTES) DECK
(— OF GOLDBEATER'S SKINS) SHODER
(— OF LEAF) BOOK
(— OF PEPPERS) ROBBIN
(— OF STAMPS) KILOWARE
(— OF VELLUM) KUTCH
(— OF VENEER) FLITCH
(— OF WOOL) BAG PAD BUTT FADGE
(YARN —) CONE CHEESE
PACKAGING (— MATERIAL) SARAN
PACKED THICK THRONGED CONGESTED SPOONWISE
PACKER BALER LINER ROPER CANNER
PACKET BOAT BOOK DECK ROLL SCREW BUNDLE PARCEL SACHET
(— OF A DRUG) BAG
(— OF VELLUM) CUTCH KUTCH
(FIVE DOLLAR DRUG —) NICKEL
PACKHORSE SOMER JAGGER PACKER SUMPTER
PACKHORSEMAN JAGGER
PACKING CUP RAGS GAUZE PAPER STRAW WASTE GASKET GROMMET STOWAGE STOPPING
(— MATERIAL) BALINE GASKET
(CLAY —) LUTE
(SEND —) EXPEL
PACKINGHOUSE MEATWORKS
PACKMAN HAWKER
PACKSACK KYACK
PACKSADDLE BAT BARDEL APAREJO
PACT MISE ACCORD CARTEL PACTUM TREATY BARGAIN COMPACT LOCARNO ALLIANCE CONTRACT COVENANT AGREEMENT CONCORDAT
PAD MAT WAD WAY BLAD BOSS DIGS FROG LURE MUTE PATH PUFF ROAD ROLL SHOE WALK WASE BLOCK INKER PERCH PILCH QUILT STENT STINT STUFF TABBY TRAMP BASKET BUFFER BUSTLE DAUBER HOLDER JOCKEY NUMNAH PADDLE PADNAG

PANNEL PILLOW SPONGE TABLET
TRUDGE VELURE WREATH BOLSTER
BOMBAST CUSHION FOOTPAD
PILLION SASHOON
(— FOR HORSE'S BACK) SADDLE
(— IN CRIB) BUMPER
(— OF ROPE) PUDDING PUDDENING
(— OF STRAW) SUNK WASE
(— ON HORSE'S FOOT) FROG
(— WORN AT THE WAIST) TOURNURE
(BOXER'S —) GUMSHIELD
(ETCHER'S —) DABBER
(FENCING —) PLASTRON
(HAIR —) RAT MOUSE TOQUE
(INKING —) INKER TOMPION
(KIND OF —) TOUCH
(MEDICAL —) PLEDGET
(PERFUMED —) SACHET
(POLISHING —) RUBBER VELOUR
VELOURS
(POOR —) HUT SHACK
(PROTECTIVE —) SHIELD
(SADDLE —) PANEL PILLOW PILLION
(PREF.) TYL(O)

PADADE CALLITHUMP
PADAUK CORAIL
PADDER MANGLE
PADDING TABBY CADDIS BOLSTER
BOMBAST BUSHING CADDICE
FILLING PACKING ROBBERY
WADDING MAHOITRE STUFFING
PADDLE OAR ROW SPUD WADE
ALOOF CANOE SLICE CRANK BUCKET
DABBLE PETTLE PUNISH STRIKE
THRASH TODDLE SPANKER SPURTLE
LUMPFISH
(— BOX) WHEELHOUSE
(— FOR FLOUR) SLICK
(TAILOR'S —) BEATER
PADDLEBOAT PEDALO
PADDLEFISH GANOID DUCKBILL
STURGEON POLYODONT SPADEFISH
SPOONBILL
PADDOCK LOT FROG PARK CLOSE
FIELD SLEDGE GARSTON LOANING
BIRDCAGE
PADDYMELON QUOKKA PADMELON
PADISHAH SULTAN PADASHA
POTSHAW
PADLOCK LOCK FASTEN SECURE
CLOSING FASTENER HORSELOCK
(— LINK) SHACKLE
PADRE MONK CLERIC FATHER PRIEST
CHAPLAIN
PADRONA LANDLADY MISTRESS
PADRONE BOSS CHIEF MASTER
PATRON LANDLORD INNKEEPER
PAEAN ODE HYMN SONG PRAISE
OUTBURST TRIUMPHAL
PAGAN ATA BUID BATAK BUKID
APAYAO BAGORO BANGON DILAAN
BONTOC ETHNIC PAYNIM SABIAN
ALANGAN DUMAGAT GENTILE

HEATHEN INFIDEL SARACEN
SUBANUN UNGODLY IDOLATOR
(— OF INDIA) GENTOO
PAGANDOM PAYNIM
PAGE BOY CALL LEAF MOTH SIDE
CHILD FACER FOLIO GROOM SHEET
DONZEL ERRATA SUMMON VARLET
BUTTONS CALLBOY FUNNIES
PAVISER SERVANT CHASSEUR
HENCHMAN ICHOGLAN
(— BOTTOM) TAIL
(BLANK —S) CANCEL
(FACING —S) SPREAD
(LADY'S —) ESCUDERO
(LAST FEW —S) BACK
(LEFTHAND —) VERSO
(NEWSPAPER —) OPED
(RIGHTHAND —) RECTO OUTPAGE
(TITLE —) TITLE UNWAN RUBRIC
(PL.) ODDMENTS
PAGEANT JEST POMP SHOW ANTIC
PARADE RIDING TABLEAU TAMASHA
TRIUMPH AQUACADE CAVALCADE
SPECTACLE WATERWORK
PAGEANTRY POMP PARADE
HERALDRY SPLENDOR
PAGER BEEPER
PAGIEL
(FATHER OF —) OCRAN
PAGLIACCI
(CHARACTER IN —) BEPPE CANIO
NEDDA TONIO SILVIO
(COMPOSER OF —) LEONCAVALLO
PAGODA PON TAA HOON WATT
TEMPLE VARELLA
(PART OF —) TEE ROOF TOPE STUPA
FINIAL BALCONY
PAHOUIN FAN FANG
PAHUTAN PAHO
PAID EVEN RESOLUTE
(— IN COIN) DRY
(— IN FULL) SATISFIED
PAIL CAN COG PAN SOA SOE BEAT
BOWK GAWN MEAL STOP TRUG
BOWIE COGUE CRUCK DANDY ESHIN
SKEEL STOOP BLICKY BUCKET
COGGIE HARASS KETTLE LEGLEN
NOGGIN PIGGIN SITULA THRASH
COLLOCK
(MILK —) KIT SOE TRUG ESHIN
LEGLEN
(ON WHEELS) DANDY
(PART OF —) EAR RIM BODY CURL
HANDLE
(POTTERY —) SEAU
(SMALL —) KIT BLICKY BLICKIE
(WOODEN —) COG COGUE LUGGIE
PIGGIN
PAIN GYP ACHE AGRA BALE CARE
CARK DOLE FRET GRUE HARM HURT
PANG SITE SORE TEEN TINE WARK
AGONY BEANS CRAMP DOLOR GRIEF
GRIPE PINCH PINSE SCALD SMART

**STING STOUN THRAW THROE
WOUND WRING BARRAT GRIEVE
MISERY SHOWER STITCH TWINGE
AFFLICT ALGESIS ANGUISH
EARACHE HURTING MYALGIA
OFFENCE PENALTY TORTURE
TRAVAIL TROUBLE AGGRIEVE
DISTRESS FLEABITE**
(— IN BACK) NOTALGIA SCIATICA
(— IN HAND) CHIRAGRA
(— IN SIDE) STEEK
(— IN THE NECK) PEST
(— OF MIND) AGONY
(— RELIEVER) OPIATE ANODYNE
ASPIRIN TYLENOL
(FILL WITH —) YEARN
(SHARP —) WRING
(STOMACH —) GRIPES GNAWING
(WRENCHING —) TORSION
(PL.) FASH LABOR WHILE EFFORT
TROUBLE
(PREF.) ALG(IO)(O) DOLORI NOCI
PENO
(SUFF.) AGRA ALGIA ALGIC ODYNE
ODYNIA
PAINFUL BAD ILL DIRE EVIL FELL SAIR
SORE SOUR TART ANGRY CRUEL
SHARP SORRY BITTER STICKY
TENDER THORNY BALEFUL GRIPING
HURTFUL IRKSOME LABORED
PENIBLE PUNGENT EXACTING
TERRIBLE TORTUOUS DIFFICULT
HARROWING
(PREF.) MOGI
PAINLESS EASY
PAINSTAKING BUSY LOVING
NARROW CAREFUL PENIBLE
DILIGENT EXACTING STUDIOUS
ASSIDUOUS ELABORATE
PAINT BICE BLOT COAT DAUB DRAW
FARD GAUD LIMN PENT PICT SOIL
COLOR FEIGN FUCUS GRAIN ROUGE
STAIN BEDAUB DAZZLE DEPICT
ENAMEL FRESCO OPAQUE SHADOW
SKETCH BESMEAR PORTRAY
PRETEND SCUMBLE AIRBRUSH
DECORATE DEPEINCT DESCRIBE
DISGUISE URFIRNIS CALCIMINE
(— A PIPE) SOIL
(— FACE OR BODY) FUCUS PARGET
(— HASTILY) SQUIGGLE
(— IN DOTS) STIPPLE
(— SKETCHILY) SPLASH
(— THROUGH PATTERN) STENCIL
(— WITH COSMETICS) POP POT FARD
(PREF.) PICTO
PAINTBRUSH WICKAWEE
NOSEBLEED
(PART OF —) HAIR CRIMP HANDLE
BRISTLE FERRULE
PAINTED PINTO FUCATE PASTOSE
PINTADO FUCOIDAL GOFFERED

(— BEAUTY) VANESSA
(— BUNTING) POP NONPAREIL
(— CUP) WICKAWEE PAINTBRUSH
(— WAKE-ROBIN) SARA
PAINTER BRUSH FAUVE ARTIST
DAUBER PICTOR PANTHER SIGNIST
SIGNMAN WORKMAN BRUSHMAN
LUMINIST MURALIST NAZARENE
STIPPLER DECORATOR TACTILIST
(PL.) ECLECTICS
AMERICAN AHL COX GAG LOW MAX
RAY RIX AMES BAER BEAL COLE
DABO DANA DEHN DINE DOVE GRAY
HART HAYS HELD HOWE HURD KOCH
KOST LOEB LUKS NEAL NEEL PAGE
PETO POOR REID THON UFER WEIR
WEST WOOD ABBEY AGATE AIKEN
ALDIS AVERY BACON BAKER BARSE
BEARD BEAUX BETTS BOGGS BROOK
BROWN BRUSH BUNCE CHASE CHILD
CRANE CURRY DAVIS DEWEY EATON
ENNIS FIENE FLAGG FOOTE GILES
GOLUB GORDY GORKY GRANT
GROLL GROSZ HEALY HENRI HICKS
HOMER INMAN IPSEN JONES LAHEY
LUCAS MARSH MINOR MOORE
MORAN MYERS ODGEN OKADA
PEALE PERRY POONS POORE RYDER
SHINN SLOAN SMITH SOYER TRYON
UPTON WALDO WAUGH WEBER
WEEKS WHITE WOOLF WYANT
WYETH YOUNG BENSON BENTON
BLYTHE BOGERT BOHROD BOUCHE
BROWNE CADMUS CHAPIN CHURCH
COLMAN COOPER COPLEY COTTON
CRANCH CURRAN DANIEL DANNAT
DAVIES DEARTH DECAMP DEMUTH
DEWING DUNLAP DURAND DURRIE
EAKINS EISEN FISCHL FORBES
FOSTER FOWLER GUERIN HAGGIN
HARVEY HASSAM HAYDEN HEATON
HERTER HOPPER INGHAM INNESS
JARVIS JOUETT KINNEY KNATHS
KNIGHT LAWSON LEUTZE LEVINE
LOOMIS MARTIN MAURER MAYHEW
MEIERE MILLER MOSLER MURPHY
NEAGLE NOLAND NOURSE OAKLEY
PARTON PEARCE PIPPIN POWELL
QUIDOR RIVERS ROTHKO SAMPLE
SAVAGE SINGER STELLA STUART
SYMONS TANGUY TANNER TAUBES
TURNER VEDDER WARHOL WRIGHT
ZORACH ADDISON ALLSTON
AUDUBON BANVARD BELLOWS
BINGHAM BRINLEY CAMERON
CARLSON CARROLL CASSATT
CHAPMAN CHRISTY CORBINO
COUDERT CROPSEY DOUGHTY
EDWARDS ELLIOTT FASSETT
FREEMAN GARNSEY GIFFORD
GRIFFIN GROPPER HARDING
HARNETT HIBBARD HIGGINS

HUBBARD HUBBELL JOHNSON
KARFIOL KENDALL KENSETT
LAFARGE LATHROP MACEWEN
MATHEWS MCENTEE METCALF
MUNSELL NAEGELE OKEEFFE
OLITSKI PARRISH PEIXOTO PROCTOR
RATTNER SAMARAS SCUDDER
SIMMONS SMIBERT SPENCER
STIMSON TWOMBLY TWORKOV
WATROUS WIGGINS ALAJALOV
ATCHISON BARTLETT BECKWITH
BICKNELL BILLINGS BOUGHTON
BRACKMAN BRADFORD BREVOORT
BRIDGMAN CORNWELL COSTIGAN
DUVENECK FAULKNER HAMILTON
HARRISON HOVENDEN HUTCHENS
JOHANSEN KRONBERG LOCKWOOD
MATTESON MELCHERS PHILLIPS
REINHART RICHARDS ROCKWELL
ROSSITER SHATTUCK SPEICHER
TRUMBULL WHISTLER WILMARTH
WOODBURY ALEXANDER
ARMSTRONG BEMELMANS
BERDANIER BERNSTEIN BIERSTADT
BITTINGER BLAKELOCK DAUGHERTY
DEKOONING HALLOWELL
HAWTHORNE KUNIYOSHI
REMINGTON ROTHERMEL SCHREIBER
TWACHTMAN VANDERLYN
WENTWORTH BLASHFIELD
BURCHFIELD CLINEDINST
EILSHEMIUS FARNSWORTH
HIRSHFIELD HUNTINGTON
MACCAMERON WHITTREDGE
BERNINGHAUS DELLENBAUGH
PRENDERGAST BLUMENSCHEIN
BRECKENRIDGE WAINGERFIELD
CROWNINSHIELD
ARGENTINIAN CENTURION
AUSTRIAN ALT KLIMT EHRLICH
FUHRICH AMERLING HAUSMANN
DANHAUSER DEFREGGER
KOKOSCHKA FRIEDLANDER
PETTENKOFEN
BELGIAN CLAYS ENSOR FOLON
NAVEZ VIGNE BEIFVE KEYSER
WIERTZ GALLAIT GUFFENS LALAING
PAUWELS STEVENS WAPPERS
WAUTERS WILLEMS BAERTSON
LAERMANS MAGRITTE BROUCKERE
EVENEPOEL TONGERLOO
BRAEKELEER CHAMPAIGNE
VERROECKHOVEN
BRAZILIAN VOLPI
CANADIAN AZIZ CARR COTE KANE
MILNE FORBES HARRIS LISMER
OBRIEN VARLEY WALKER WATSON
BORDUAS KURELEK MORRICE
COLVILLE
CHILEAN MATTA
CHINESE SHUBUN
COLOMBIAN BOTERO

CZECH KUPKA MANES MUCHA
BROZIK
DANISH JUEL BLOCH CARLSEN
DAISGAARD MARSTRAND
WIEGHORST WILLUMSEN
ZAHRTMANN ABILDGAARD
ECKERSBERG
DUTCH BOL DOU BECK BEGA CORT
CUYP GOES GOGH HAAS HALS HEDA
HEEM KALF LAAR LELY LOOY MAES
MEER NEER AELST APPEL BAUER
BOSCH BOUTS BRUYN CODDE DAVID
GOYEN HELST HOOCH KETEL MARIS
METSU NEEFS OVENS STEEN VELDE
VROOM WITTE BACKER DECKER
EGMONT ESCHER FLINCK GELDER
HEYDEN KESSEL KEYSER MANDER
MESDAG MIERIS MULIER OSTADE
POTTER RUYSCH SCOREL TOOROP
WEENIX AERTSEN AERTZEN
ASSELYN BERCHEM BEYEREN
CRABETH DOUFFET HOBBEMA
ISRAELS KONINCK LASTMAN
LIEVENS LOMBARD PATINIR
POURBUS VANGOGH VERMEER
WYNANTS AGRICOLA DOESBURG
DUJARDIN EECKHOUT GOLTZIUS
HUYSMANS JONGKIND KOEKKOEK
LAIRESSE MOREELSE RUYSDAEL
TERBORCH BLOEMAERT CORNELISZ
FABRITIUS HOEFNAGEL HONTHORST
HOUBRAKEN MIEREVELT
MONDRIAAN MOUCHERON
REMBRANDT STEENWILK
WOUWERMAN BACKHUYSEN
BERCKHEYDE CAMPHUYSEN
EVERDINGEN GESELSCHAP
LINGELBACH BREKELENKAM
HONDECOETER POELENBURGH
TERBRUGGHEN HOOGSTRAETEN
ENGLISH COX EGG FRY BIRD BONE
COLE COPE EAST ETTY EVES GILL
HAAG HOOK HUNT JOHN LEAR NASH
OPIE SWAN TAIT WARD WEIR BLAKE
BROCK BROWN CRANE CROME
CUNEO DAVIS DOYLE FRITH FURSE
LEWIS LOWRY LUCAS MOORE ORPEN
STARK STEER STONE TONKS UWINS
WATTS WELLS ABBOTT ASHTON
BARKER BOXALL BROOKS BROWNE
CARTER CHALON COATES COOPER
COSWAY COTMAN COWPER COZENS
CROFTS DEWINT DOBSON FILDES
GIRTIN GLOVER HACKER HAYDON
HOLMES KNIGHT LAVERY LAWSON
LEADER MARTIN MAYTER MCEVOY
MULLER NEWTON OLIVER OULESS
ROMNEY SEVERN SMIRKE STUART
STUBBS TURNER VARLEY WALKER
ANSDELL BAYLISS BEECHEY
BOMBERG CALVERT CAMERON
CLAUSEN COLLIER DANIELL DICKSEE

GILBERT GUEVARA HERBERT
HODGSON HOGARTH HOLIDAY
HOLROYD LINNELL MILLAIS
MORLAND POYNTER RIVIERE
RUSSELL SOLOMON ZOFFANY
ARMITAGE ATKINSON AUMONIER
BEAUMONT BRANGWYN CALDERON
CALLCOTT CORBOULD CRESWICK
EASTLAKE FIELDING HILLIARD
LANDSEER LEIGHTON MUNNINGS
REDGRAVE REYNOLDS RICHMOND
RICKETTS ROSSETTI STOTHARD
TOPOLSKI WATERLOW WHISTLER
AMSHEWITZ BEARDSLEY
BONINGTON BOURGEOIS
COLLINSON CONSTABLE
GREENAWAY NORTHCOTE
STANFIELD THORNHILL
BROCKHURST KENNINGTON
WATERHOUSE WOOLDRIDGE
ROTHENSTEIN GAINSBOROUGH
FINNISH EDELFELT
FLEMISH VOS BLES BRIL EYCK GOES
BALEN CLAUS CLEVE COXIE ORLEY
CAMPIN COQUES CRAYER MABUSE
MASSYS RUBENS WEYDEN
BLOEMEN BREUGEL BROUWER
BRUGHEL CANDIDO TENIERS
VANDYCK VANEYCK BRUEGHEL
CHRISTUS CRAESBEECK
FRENCH ZO ARP BIDA CAIN DORE
DUFY ETEX GROS HEIM HUET LAMI
TROY BIARD CAZIN CHERY CORNU
COROT DAVID DEGAS DENIS DOYEN
DUPRE FRERE JONAS LEGER LHOTE
MANET MONET MOROT PATER PUVIS
REDON STAEL VEBER VOUET
BAUDRY BERARD BERAUD BOILLY
BONNAT BONVIN BOUDIN BOUTON
BRAQUE BRETON BUFFET CALLOT
CARREY CARZOU CHABAS CHERET
CHERON CLOUET CORMON COTTET
COUDER COUSIN COYPEL DAUBAN
DERAIN DONGEN DOUCET DUBUFE
FAVORY FORAIN FORBIN FRIESZ
GERARD GEROME GERVEX GIGOUX
GRANET GREUZE GUERIN HEBERT
HELION HENNER INGRES LAHIRE
LATOUR LEBLON LEBRUN LELEUX
LEPINE LORJOU MARTIN MERSON
MILLET MIRBEL MOREAU MULLER
RENOIR SEURAT SIGNAC STELLA
TISSOT TROYON VANLOO VERNET
VIBERT WEERTS BALTHUS BARRIAS
BESNARD BONHEUR BONNARD
BOUCHER BOUCHOR BOURDON
CABANEL CEZANNE CHARDIN
CHARLOT COGNIET COURBET
COUTURE DAMERON DORIGNY
DROUAIS DUCHAMP FERRIER
FLANDIN FOUQUET GARNIER
GAUGUIN GENDRON GLEIZES
HARTUNG HEDOUIN HERSENT

JEANRON LAFOSSE LANCRET
LANSYER LAURENS LEBOURG
LEGRAND LEHMANN LEMOYNE
LESUEUR LORRAIN MAIGNAN
MARQUET MATISSE MICHAUX
MIGNARD MORISOT NATTIER
PICABIA POUSSIN PRUDHON
RESTOUT ROUAULT SOUTINE
UTRILLO VALADON WATTEAU
BELLANGE BERCHERE CARRIERE
CHARTRAN CONSTANT DAGUERRE
DALAUNAY DAUBIGNY DESCAMPS
DETAILLE DROLLING ESPAGNAT
FLANDRIN GALIMARD JOUVENET
KLINGSOR LANDELLE LATOUCHE
LEFEBVRE LENEPVEU LEPRINCE
OZENFANT PARROCEL PISSARRO
ROUSSEAU SCHEFFER STEINLEN
VUILLARD WILLETTE BOULANGER
CHATILLON CHENAVARD COUBERTIN
DEBUCOURT DEHODENCQ
DELABORDE DELACROIX DELAROCHE
DESPORTES FALGUIERE FRAGONARD
GERICAULT GLEISPACH GUILLEMET
HENNIQUIN LAURENCIN METZINGER
SCHUSSELE BARTHOLOME
BOUGUEREAU BOULLONGNE
BRASCASSAT CHASSERIAU
DESBROSSES GUILLAUMET
GUILLAUMIN HARPIGNIES
JACQUEMART MEISSONIER
BRACQUEMOND CARMONTELLE
LARGILLIERE DESVALLIERES
LOUTHERBOURG
GERMAN DIX MAX ADAM DIEZ HESS
JANK LENZ MARC MARR SOHN UHDE
VEIT ANTES BEGAS BEHAM BINCK
BRUYN DURER EBERS EMELE ERNST
FOLTZ FRIES FUGER GRAFF GROSZ
HOFER KNAUS KUEHL LEIBL MACKE
MENGS MEYER MUCKE NEHER
NOLDE OESER PECHT PENCZ STUCK
THOMA VOGEL BECKER BRACHT
BRAITH BUHLER BURGER EBERLE
ECHTER FITGER FRESE GEBLER
GUSSOW HECKEL HENSEL HERLIN
HERTEL HEYDEN HUBNER KELLER
KOBELL KRAFFT KRUGER LANGER
LOFFTZ MAREES MENZEL MULLER
RETHEL WERNER BALDUNG BARTELS
BLECHEN CORINTH CRANACH
FLICKEL GENELLI HOFMANN
HOLBEIN KLINGER KOPSICH KRELING
LENBACH LESSING LINDNER
LOCHNER PRELLER RICHTER
SCHWIND STEUBEN AGRICOLA
AMBERGER BECKMANN CARSTENS
DETTMANN FIORILLO GEBHARDT
GRUTZNER HABERLIN HENDRICH
KAULBACH KIRCHNER KOLLWITZ
KUGELGEN KULMBACH ROTTMANN
SCHIRMER SCHREYER ZEITBLOM
ACHENBACH AINMILLER ALTDORFER

BENDEMANN BLEIBTREU
BURGKMAIR CORNELIUS ELSHEIMER
ENGELHARD FRIEDRICH GRUNEWALD
HABERMANN KNACKFUSS
KRIEGHOFF MEYERHEIM
MODERSOHN PASSAVANT TISCHBEIN
ALDEGREVER BAUMEISTER
CAMPHAUSEN HECKENDORF
HILDEBRAND SCHONGAUER
SCHROEDTER WOHLGEMUTH
ZIMMERMANN CHODOWIECKI
HASENCLEVER HILDEBRANDT
HUCHTENBERG MORGENSTERN
SCHRAUDOLPH LINDENSCHMIT
ROTTENHAMMER WINTERHALTER
GREEK GYSIS AETION NICIAS ZEUXIS
APELLES PAUSIAS EUPOMPUS
ARISTIDES EUPHRANOR MELANTHUS
PAMPHILUS TIMANTHES
AGATHARCUS PARRHASIUS
POLYGNOTUS PROTOGENES
SPYROPOULOS
GUATEMALAN MERIDA
HUNGARIAN LOTZ ZICHY VADASZ
WAGNER SZINYEI MUNKACSY
IRISH BARRY DANBY BURTON
FORBES LAVERY PETRIE MACLISE
COSTELLO MULREADY ODOHERTY
ISRAELI AGAM RUBIN
ITALIAN CHIA FETI MOLA RENI ROSA
TURA VAGA BACCI BALLA CAFFI
CAMPI CARPI CARRA COSSA COSTA
DANTI DOLCI FERRI FETTI FOPPA
GATTI GENGA IORIS LIPPI LOTTO
LUINI MELZI PALMA PENNI PIERO
PISIS PRETI RICCI SANTI SARTO
SPADA VANNI VINCI ABBATE ALBANI
ALLORI AVANZO BATONI CALCAR
CECANI CIARDI COSIMO CRESPI
FRANCO GAULLI GIOTTO GUUIDO
MORONI NITTIS PASINI PISANO
PREDIS RICCIO ROMANO SACCHI
SIRONI SODOMA SOLARI SUARDI
TITIAN VASARI VERRIO AMIGONI
APPIANI BARBARI BAROCCI BARTOLI
BASSANO BELLINI BERNINI BOLDINI
BRUMIDI CENNINI CHIRICO CIGNANI
CORTONA FALCONE FRANCIA
GIORGIO GOZZOLI MARATTI MARTINI
MORELLI MUZIANO OGGIONO
PALIZZI PERUZZI RAPHAEL ROBERTI
STROZZI TIBALDI TIEPOLO UCCELLO
VECELLI ZUCCARO BACICCIO
BAGLIONI BARBIERE BOCCIONI
BONFIGLI CAGLIARI CARDUCCI
CARRIERA CASANOVA CASTELLO
CIPRIANI COGHETTI CORENZIO
GRIMALDI MAGNASCO MAINARDI
MANTEGNA MICHETTI MONTAGNA
POCCETTI PONTORMO SALVIATI
SEVERINI UBERTINI VAROTARI
VERONESE VIVARINI ASPERTINI
BECCAFUMI CAMUCCINI CANTARINI

CAVALLINI CORREGGIO FRANCESCA
GHISLANDI MAZZOLINO PIAZZETTA
SCHIAVONE SEGANTINI BELTRAFFIO
BOCCACCINO BORGOGNONE
BOTTICELLI CAMPAGNOLA
CARAVAGGIO LORENZETTI
MODIGLIANI PROCACCINI
SIGNORELLI SQUAREIONE
TINTORETTO VERROCCHIO
ZUCCARELLI ANGUISCIOLA
CASTIGLIONE GENTILESCHI
PRIMATICCIO ALBERTINELLI
BALDOVINETTI FRANCESCHINI
MICHELANGELO PARMIGIANINO
PINTURICCHIO
JAPANESE KANO OKYO BUSON
IWASA KORIN SAITO SOSEN TORII
GOSHUN KOETSU KYOSAI SESSHU
JAKUCHU JOSETSU SOTATSU
UTAMARO HARUNOBU KIYOMASU
KIYONAGA KIYONOBU MORONOBU
TOYOKUNI HIROSHEGE KIYOMITSU
TSUNETAKA
LITHUANIAN SOUTINE
MEXICAN CANTU MERIDA OROZCO
RIVERA TAMAYO SIQUEIROS
CASTELLANOS
NORWEGIAN DAHL GUDE KROHG
MUNCH LERCHE MUNTHE SINDING
FEARNLEY WERENSKIOLD
POLISH BENDA GERSON MATEJKO
GROTTGER CHELMINSKI
MARCOUSSIS WYSPIANSKI
PORTUGUESE FONSECA
RUSSIAN BAKST REPIN BENOIS
BERMAN GRABAR BURLIUK
CHAGALL ROERICH LARIONOV
LEVITSKI MALEVICH CHELISHEV
KANDINSKI LISSITZKY RODCHENKO
AIVAZOVSKI BOGOLYUBOV
BASHKIRTSEV VERESHCHAGIN
SCOTTISH BONE DYCE FAED HILL
ALLAN DAVIE GRANT PATON SCOTT
AIKMAN ARCHER BARKER BROUGH
DUNCAN GEDDES GORDON GRAHAM
HARVEY LAUDER LEITCH MANSON
MURRAY PETTIE RAMSAY WILKIE
DOUGLAS GUTHRIE LORIMER
MACBETH NASMYTH RAEBURN
THOMSON CHALMERS
MACTAGGART MACWHIRTER
ORCHARDSON
SPANISH ARCO CANO DALI GOYA
GRIS MAZO MIRO MOYA SERT
GRECO HAMEN MACIP CEREZO
COELLO PAREJA RIBERA RINCON
VARGAS ALVAREZ HERRERA IRIARTE
MADRAZO MORALES MURILLO
ORRENTE PACHECO PICASSO
RIBALTA ZULOAGA CESPEDES
PRADILLA ZAMACOIS ZURBARAN
VELASQUEZ ZUBIAURRE
BERRUGUETE

SWEDISH DAHL ZORN BERGH
ROSLIN LARSSON FAGERLIN
LUNDGREN HELLQUIST JOSEPHSON
LILJEFORS
SWISS KLEE LIPS MIND WITZ ASPER
DIDAY ITTEN MEYER BODMER
CALAME FUSELI GLEYRE HODLER
MANUEL BOCKLIN BUCHSER DISTELI
LIOTARD PETITOT VAUTIER
KAUFFMANN
WELSH JOHN
PAINTING ART OIL PAT DAUB PATA
DRAFT MURAL PIECE TABLE WATER
CANVAS CROUTE FRESCO MINERY
TITIAN BODEGON CAMAIEU
CARTOON COMBINE DAUBING
GRADINO GRAPHIC HISTORY
PAYSAGE FROTTAGE PREDELLA
SEAPIECE SYMPHONY AQUARELLE
MINIATURE TABLATURE
(— EQUIPMENT) OIL BRUSH EASEL
PAINT CANVAS PALLET
(— IN COLLOIDAL MEDIUM) TEMPERA
(— OF EVERYDAY LIFE) GENRE
(— OF FOLIAGE) BOSCAGE
(— ON PLASTER) SECCO FRESCO
(— ON VELVET) THEOREM
(— SCHOOL) ASHCAN
(— WITH OPAQUE COLORS)
GOUACHE
(ACTION —) TACHISM
(CIRCULAR —) TONDO
(EGG —) TEMPERA
(JAPANESE INK —) SUMIE
(JAPANESE STYLE OF —) YAMATO
(PREHISTORIC —) PICTOGRAM
PICTOGRAPH
(RELIGIOUS —) PIETA TANKA
(SCENIC —) SCAPE
(SMALL —) TABLET
(TEMPERA —) SECCO
(THREE PANEL —) TRIPTYCH
(PL.) GENRE
(SUFF.) CHROMY
PAIR DUO TWO ZYG CASE DIAD DUAD
DUAL DYAD MATE SIDE SPAN TEAM
TWIN YOKE BRACE MARRY MATCH
TWAIN UNITE COUPLE GEMINI
COUPLET DOUBLET JUMELLE
TWOSOME
(— OF FILMS) BIPACK
(— OF HORSES) SPAN
(— OF MILLSTONES) RUN
(— OF SHOTS) BRACKET
(— OF TONGS) GRAMPUS GRAPPLE
(— OF WINGS) SHEARS
(— ROYAL) PARIAL
(KIND OF —) COOPER
(ONE OF —) IMPAIR NEIGHBOR
(ONE OF A —) MATE
(PL.) GEMELS
(PREF.) GEMINI ZYG(O)(OTO)
(SUFF.) ZYGOUS

PAIRED GEMEL MATED JUGATE
ZYGOUS JUMELLE
PAISLEY PRINT SHAWL DESIGN
FABRIC
PAIUTE DIGGER
PAJAMAS JAMMIES SHALWAR
SLEEPER
PAKHT (HUSBAND OF —) PTAH

PAKISTAN

BAY: SOYMIANA
CANAL: NARA ROHRI
CAPE: FASTA JADDI JIWANI
CAPITAL: ISLAMABAD
COIN: ANNA PAISA RUPEE
DAM: TARBELA
LANGUAGE: URDU PUSHTU SINDHI
BALUCHI BENGALI PUNJABI
PORT: CHALNA KARACHI
PROVINCE: SIND PUNJAB
RIVER: NAL BADO RAVI ZHOB DASHT
INDUS CHENAB GANGES JAMUNA
JHELUM KUNDAR PORALI
STATE: DIR SWAT KALAT KHARAN
CHITRAL KHAIRPUR
TOWN: DACCA CHALNA KHULNA
LAHORE MULTAN QUETTA KARACHI
SIALKOT LYALLPUR PERSHAWAR
SARGODHA
WEIGHT: SEER TOLA MAUND

PAKTONG TUTENAG
PAL BO ALLY CHUM JACK PARD BILLY
BUDDY BUTTY CHINA CRONY LOUKE
COBBER COPAIN DIGGER FRIEND
COMRADE PARTNER COMPANION
PALACE SALE CHIGI COURT SERAI
STEAD CASTLE ELYSEE LOUVRE
PALAIS ALCAZAR EDIFICE LATERAN
MANSION PALAZZO TRIANON
VATICAN ZWINGER BASILICA
SERAGLIO WHITEHALL
(— OF SATAN) PANDEMONIUM
(FAIRY —) SHEE SIDHE
PALADIN HERO PEER ANSEIS ASTOLF
KNIGHT CHAMPION DOUZEPER
PALAL (FATHER OF —) UZAI
PALAMEDES (BROTHER OF —) OEAX
SFORZA ACHILLES
(FATHER OF —) NAUPLIUS
(MOTHER OF —) CLYMENE
(SLAYER OF —) CORINDA
PALAMON (RIVAL OF —) ARCITE
(WIFE OF —) EMELYE
PALANQUIN JAUN JUAN KAGE
KAGO DANDI DOOLI DOOLY PALKI
SEDAN DOOLIE LITTER PALKEE
TONJON NORIMON
PALATABLE SAPID SPICY TASTY
DAINTY SAVORY MOREISH DELICATE
LUSCIOUS PLEASING SAPOROUS
AGREEABLE DELICIOUS
TOOTHSOME

PALATAL SOFT FRONT VELAR
GUTTURAL
PALATALIZED MOUILLE
PALATE TASTE VELUM RELISH
GOURMET URANISCUS
(SOFT —) UVULA
(PREF.) URAN(O)(OSO)
PALATIAL LARGE ORNATE STATELY
SPLENDID
PALATINE CAPE OFFICER PALADIN
PALATIAL
PALAVER GASH SLUM TALK CAJOLE
DEBATE GLAVER JARGON PARLEY
CHATTER FLATTER WHEEDLE
CAJOLERY FLATTERY
PALE DIM WAN ASHY BLOC FADE
GREY GULL LILY PALL SICK THIN
WHEY ASHEN BLAKE BLATE BLEAK
CLOSE FAINT FENCE GREEN LIGHT
LINEN LIVID LURID MEALY STAKE
STICK VERGE WHITE ANEMIC
BLANCH CHALKY CHANGE DOUGHY
FALLOW FEEBLE PALLID PASTEL
PICKET REGION REMISS SICKLY
SILVER WATERY WHITEN DEFENSE
GHASTLY HAGGARD INSIPID
OBSCURE SHILPIT DELICATE
WATERISH
(— BY COMPARISON) STAIN
(IN —) HAURIENT
(PREF.) LIRO PALLIDI POLI(O)
PALEA PALET SQUAMELLA
PALENESS WAN PALLOR ACHRUMA
PALEONTOLOGIST AMERICAN HAY
GABB HALL LULL MEEK BERRY
GOULD MARSH CLARKE FOSTER
GNADAU HORNER OSBORN BEECHER
GREGORY MERRIAM WALCOTT
KNOWLTON SPRINGER WILLIAMS
SCHUCHERT WACHSMUTH
WILLISTON
AUSTRIAN SUESS HOERNES
MOJSISOVICS ETTINGSHAUSEN
ENGLISH TATE CAUTLEY MANTELL
DAVIDSON WOODWARD
BOWERBANK PARKINSON
FRENCH BOULE GAUDRY LARTET
BARRANDE TEILHARD
GERMAN ZITTEL BEYRICH
QUENSTEDT
SCOTTISH FALCONER
SOUTH AFRICAN BROOM
PALESTINE (SEE ISRAEL)
(CITY OF ANCIENT —) DAN
PALETOT COAT JACKET OVERCOAT
GREATCOAT
PALFREY HORSE PALFRY
PALIMPSEST TABLET PARCHMENT
PALINDROMIC SOTADIC
SOTADEAN
PALING PALE FENCE FLAKE LIMIT
PALIS STAKE PICKET FENCING
BLENCHING

PALISADE HAY BOMA PALE PEEL
CLIFF FENCE RIMER STAKE FRAISE
HURDIS PICKET BARRIER ENCLOSE
FORTIFY HURDIES STACKET
TAMBOUR ESPALIER
(MILITARY —) CIPPUS
(PL.) BAIL BARRIER
PALL FOG BORE CLOY PALE SATE
CLOAK CLOTH FAINT QUALM STALE
WEARY MANTLE NAUSEA SHROUD
DISGUST SATIATE ANIMETTA
MORTCLOTH
PALLET BED COT PAD COUCH QUILT
PADDLE BLANKET MATTRESS
PLANCHER
PALLIARD BEGGAR LECHER RASCAL
VAGABOND
PALLIATE EASE HIDE MASK VEIL
ABATE CLOAK COLOR COVER GLOSS
GLOZE LITHE BLANCH LESSEN
REDUCE SMOOTH SOFTEN SOOTHE
CONCEAL CUSHION SHELTER
DISGUISE MITIGATE
PALLID WAN ASHY PALE PALY BLEAK
MEALY WASHY WAXEN WHITE
SALLOW GHASTLY BLOODLESS
COLORLESS INNOCUOUS
PALL-MALL MAIL
PALLOR ASH WAN PALE ASHES
PALENESS
PALLU (FATHER OF —) REUBEN
(SON OF) ELIAB
PALM ADY DOM ITA ATAP BRAB BURI
BUSU COCO DATE DOUM FLAT HIDE
JARA KOKO LOOF NIOG NIPA PAWN
SAGO SLIP TARA ARCHA ARECA
ARENG ASSAI ATTAP BONGA BUNGA
CARRY COCOA COYOL CURUA DATIL
FOIST HOWEA INAJA JAGUA LOULU
MACAW MERUS NIKAU RATAN
SABAL SALAK TECUM TUCUM
UNAMO YAGUA YARAY ANAHAO
ASSAHY BACABA BURITI CHONTA
COHUNE COROJO COROZO GEBANG
GOMUTI GRUGRU JAMBEE JUPATI
KENTIA KITTUL LAWYER LONTAR
NIBONG PACAYA RAFFIA ROTANG
THENAR TOOROO TROPHY APRICOT
BABASSU BACTRIS CARANDA
CONCEAL COQUITO ERYTHEA
GEONOMA MORICHE PALMYRA
PUPUNHA SAGWIRE TALIPOT
TROOLIE URUCURI JACITARA
LATANIER MACAHUBA PIASSAVA
(— FERN) PONJA
(— FOOD) NUT COCO DATE NIPA
SAGO SURA ASSAI TAREE TODDY
COCONUT
(— JUICE) SURA
(— LEAF) OLA OLLA CAJAN FROND
(LILY) TI
(— OFF) COG FOB TOP SHAB FOIST
TRUMP

(— OF HAND) FLAT LOOF VOLA TABLE THENAR
(— OUT) APPAUME
(BETEL —) ARECA BONGA PUGUA PINANG
(CLIMBING —) RATTAN
(FEATHER —) HOWEA GOMUTI URUCURI
(KIND OF —) SAGO
(SLAPPING OF —S) SKIN
(SPINY —) PEACH GRIGRI GRUGRU
(PREF.) CYCAD(I)(O) PALMATO PALMI PALPI PALPO
PALMARY CHIEF PALMAR SUPERIOR
PALMATE FLAT BROAD LOBED WEBBED
PALMER LOUSE FERULE STROLL TRAVEL VOTARY WANDER FOISTER PILGRIM
PALMETTO CABBAGE PALMITO BIGTHATCH
(— STATE) SOUTHCAROLINA
PALMISTRY CHIROMANCY
PALMODIC JERKY
PALMYRA BRAB TALA LONTAR RONIER TADMOR BASSINE
(QUEEN OF —) ZENOBIA
PALP FEEL TOUCH CAJOLE FEELER HANDLE PALPUS FLATTER TENTACLE
PALPABLE BALD RANK PLAIN PATENT AUDIBLE EVIDENT OBVIOUS TACTILE APPARENT DISTINCT MANIFEST TANGIBLE CORPOREAL
PALPATE FEEL
PALPATION THROB TOUCH WALLOP DIPPING PITAPAT
PALPEBRA EYELID
PALPITATE PANT QUAP THROB FLACKER FLICKER FLUTTER PULSATE
PALPITATION BEAT DUNT PANT FLICKER FLUTTER PULSATION SALTATION THROBBING
(— OF HEART) THUMB
PALSIED SHAKY SHAKING PARALYZED TOTTERING TREMBLING TREMULOUS
PALSY PARLESIE PARALYSIS
PALTER FIB LIE BABBLE HAGGLE MUMBLE PARLEY TRIFLE BARGAIN CHAFFER CHATTER QUIBBLE SHAFFLE
PALTIEL **(FATHER OF —)** AZZAN
PALTRY BALD BARE BASE MEAN ORRA PUNY SCAB VILE WAFF CHEAP FOOTY MINOR PETTY SCALD SCALL SCRUB SILLY TRASH CHETIF FLIMSY JITNEY SHABBY SLIGHT TRASHY WOEFUL HILDING PELTING PIMPING PITEOUS PITIFUL ROYNISH RUBBISH SCABBED SCRUBBY TRIVIAL PICAYUNE PICKLING PIDDLING TRIFLING

PALUDAL MARSHY
PAMELA **(AUTHOR OF —)** RICHARDSON
(BROTHER OF —) PHILOCLEA
(CHARACTER IN —) JACOB DAVERS JERVIS JEWKES PAMELA ANDREWS SWYNFORD
(FATHER OF —) BASILIUS
PAMPA PLAIN PRAIRIE
PAMPAS **(— CAT)** KODKOD PAJERO
(— DEER) MAZAME
PAMPER PET BABY CRAM DELT GLUT POMP HUMOR SPOIL TUTOR WALLY CARESS COCKER CODDLE COSHER COSSET CUDDLE CUITER DANDLE FONDLE MAUNGE POSSET TIDDLE CHERISH COCKNEY FORWEAN GRATIFY INDULGE SATIATE SMOODGE SAGINATE
PAMPHLET JACK LEAD FLIER QUIRE SHEET TRACT FOLDER BOOKLET CATALOG LEAFLET NOVELET BROCHURE CHAPBOOK CIRCULAR WORKBOOK CATALOGUE NEWSLETTER
PAN FIT TAB VLY MELL PART PRIG VLEI WASH AGREE BASIN BATEA COVER GRAND ROAST SHEET UNITE CENSER FRACHE LAPPET PANKIN PATINA SPIDER VESSEL CRANIUM CREAMER HARDPAN PORTION ROASTER SKILLET SUBSOIL PANNIKIN RIDICULE
(— FOR COALS) BRAZIER
(— OF BALANCE) BOWL BASIN SCALEPAN
(— WITH 3 FEET) POSNET
(EARTHENWARE —) PANCHEON
(EVAPORATING —) ROOM COVER TACHE SALTPAN
(FRYING —) GRIDDLE
(GOD —) FAUNUS
(IRON —) YET FRACHE
(LONG-HANDLED —) PINGLE
(MILK —) LEAD
(OIL —) SUMP
(PREF.) PATELLI PATELLO
PANACEA CURE BEZOAR ELIXIR REMEDY SOLACE CUREALL GINSENG HEALALL NEPENTHE CATHOLICON
PANACHE STYLE

PANAMA
CAPITAL: PANAMA
COIN: BALBOA
COUNTY: DARIEN HERRARA
CROP: ABACA CACOA
GULF: DARIEN SANBLAS CHIRIQUI MOSQUITO
ISLAND: COIBA
LAKE: GATUN
MEASURE: CELEMIN

MOUNTAIN: CHICO GANDI COLUMAN
  SANTIAGO
MOUNTAIN RANGE: VERAGUA
PENINSULA: AZUERO
PORT: CRISTOBAL
PROVINCE: COCLE COLON CHIRIQUI
  VERAGUAS
RIVER: CHEPO SAMBU TUIRA BAYANO
  PANUGO CHAGRES
TOWN: COLON DAVID AZUERO
  BALBOA PANAMA PENONOME
  SANTIAGO
TREE: YAYA MARIA QUIRA ALFAJE
  CATIVO

PANAMA HAT JIPIJAPA
PANAMINT KOSO
PANCAKE BLIN FLAM AREPA CREPE
  FADGE FLAWN KISRA LEFSE TOURT
  BLINTZ FRAISE FROISE CHUMPET
  FLAPPER FLIPPER FRITTER HOTCAKE
  PIKELET CORNCAKE FLAPJACK
  FLIPJACK
  (PL.) LEFSEN
PANCREAS BUR NUT
PAND PAWN DRAPERY
PANDA WA WAH BEARCAT
PANDAREUS (DAUGHTER OF —)
  AEDON MEROPE CLEOTHERA
  (FATHER OF —) MEROPS
  (WIFE OF —) HARMOTHOE
PANDARUS (BROTHER OF —) BITIAS
  (FATHER OF —) LYCAON ALCANOR
PANDAVA BHIMA
PANDECT COMPENDIUM
PANDEMONIUM DIN HELL CHAOS
  NOISE BEDLAM TUMULT UPROAR
  DISORDER CONFUSION
PANDER BAWD PIMP BULLY CATER
  BROKER MICHER PURVEY RUFFIAN
  WHISKIN PROCURER BAWDSTROT
PANDION (BROTHER OF —)
  PLEXIPPUS
  (DAUGHTER OF —) PROCNE
  PHILOMELA
  (FATHER OF —) CECROPS PHINEUS
  ERICHTHONIUS
  (MOTHER OF —) CLEOPATRA
  (SON OF —) BUTES LYCUS NISUS
  AEGEUS PALLAS ERECHTHEUS
  (WIFE OF —) PYLIA
PANDORA BANDORE
  (BROTHER OF —) PROMETHEUS
  (HUSBAND OF —) EPIMETHEUS
PANDOWDY PIE DESSERT
PANDU (BROTHER OF —)
  DURYODHANA
  (FATHER OF —) DHRITARASHTRA
PANE GLASS GLAZE LOZEN PANEL
  QUIRK SHEET SHOCK SLASH
  QUARRY QUARREL SECTION
  PORTLIGHT

PANEGYRIC ELOGE ELOGY EULOGY
  PRAISE ORATION TRIBUTE
  ENCOMIUM LAUDATION
PANEL FIN PAN JURY SKIN BOARD
  GROUP LABEL TABLE ABACUS
  ASSIZE COFFER HURDLE MIRROR
  PADDLE PILLOW ROSACE TABLET
  TYMPAN CAISSON CONSOLE FLIPPER
  LACUNAR DECORATE MANDORLA
  MEDALLION
  (— IN FENCE) LOOP
  (— IN GARMENT) LAP STEAK
  (CIRCULAR —) ROUNDEL
  (GAUZE —) SCRIM
  (GLAZED —) LAYLIGHT
  (LEGAL —) ARRAY
  (REAR — ON STATION WAGON)
  LIFTGATE
  (RECESSED —) ORB COFFER
  LACUNAR
  (SUNKEN —) CAISSON CASSOON
  (3-PART —) TRIPTYCH
PANELLING WAINSCOT
PANFISH SCUP
PANG ACHE CRAM FILL GIRD PAIN
  STAB TANG AGONY PINCH PRONG
  SPASM STANG STOUN STUFF THROB
  THROE SHOWER STOUND TWINGE
  ANGUISH TRAVAIL
  (PL.) GNAWINGS
PANGLOSS (PUPIL OF —) CANDIDE
PANGOLIN MANID MANIS ANTEATER
  EDENTATE TANGILIN
PANGS MUNCHIES
  (HUNGER —) MUNCHIES
PANGWE FAN FANG
PANHANDLE BEG CADGE SKELB
  SKILDER
  (— STATE) WV WVA
PANIC FEAR FRAY FUNK WILD ALARM
  AMAZE CHAOS SCARE FRIGHT
  SCHRIK TERROR SWITHER
  CONSTERNATION
PANICKY FUNKY ALARMED
PANICLE JUBA WHISK ANTHELA
PANNIER BAG PED SERON BASKET
  CAJAVA CURAGH DORSEL DORSER
  DOSSAL DOSSER PANTRY CORBEIL
  CURRACK KAJAWAH KEDJAVE
PANOPE (FATHER OF —) NEREUS
  (MOTHER OF —) DORIS
PANOPEUS (BROTHER OF —) CRISUS
  (COMPANION OF —) AMPHITRYON
  (DAUGHTER OF —) AEGLE
  (FATHER OF —) PHOCUS
  (MOTHER OF —) ASTERIA
PANOPLY POMP ARMOR ARRAY
  UNIFORM
PANORAMA VIEW RANGE SCENE
  SWEEP VISTA NEORAMA PICTURE
  SCENERY CYCLORAMA
  POLYORAMA

PANPIPE SICU SIKU QUILL ANTARA
SYRINX ZAMPOGNA
PANSY FANCY PENSE VIOLA KISSES
PENSEE VIOLET TRINITY FANTASQUE
HEARTEASE
(PREF.) VIOL
PANT FAB ACHE BEAT BLOW FUFF
GAPE GASP HECH LONG PANK PECH
PEGH PINE PIPE PUFF TIFT FLAFF
HEAVE QUIRK STECH SUGGE THROB
YEARN ANHELE ASPIRE FRIESE
PANTLE PULSATE
PANTAGRUEL (COMPANION OF —)
PANURGE
(FATHER OF —) GARGANTUA
(MOTHER OF —) BADEBEC
PANTALOONS PANTS TROUSERS
PANTDRESS CULOTTE
PANTHEA (HUSBAND OF —)
ABRADATUS
PANTHEIST AMALRICIAN
PANTHEON AESIR TEMPLE
ROTUNDA VALHALL VALHALLA
PANTHER CAT PARD PUMA COUGAR
JAGUAR LEOPARD PAINTER PANTILE
(KIND OF —) GRAY
PANTIES SCANTIES
PANTILE TILE IMBREX BISCUIT
HARDTACK
PANTING ANHELOSE ANHELOUS
PANTOGRAPH EIDOGRAPH
POLYGRAPH
PANTOMIME PLAY PANTO
DUMBSHOW
PANTOMIMIST MUMMER
PANTRY CAVE STUE AMBRY COVEY
CUDDY CLOSET LARDER SPENCE
BUTLERY BUTTERY PANNIER
PANTLER SERVERY SPICERY
CUPBOARD
PANTS CORDS JEANS LEVIS BRIEFS
SLACKS DRAWERS JODHPUR
BREECHES BRITCHES KICKSIES
KNICKERS SNUGGIES TROUSERS
(— THAT REACH TO MID-CALF)
CLAMDIGGER
(— WITH WIDE BOTTOMS) BELLS
(KIND OF —) TAP CAPRI
(LEATHER —) CHAPS LEDERHOSEN
(WIDE-LEGGED —) PALAZZO
PANUELO COLLAR RUFFLE KERCHIEF
NECKCLOTH
PANURGE (COMPANION OF —)
PANTAGRUEL
PANZER TANK
PAOLO (LOVER OF —) FRANCESCA
PAP DUG TIT POBS TEAT NIPPLE
EMULSION FLUMMERY
PAPA PA DAD PAP PAW POP SIN BABA
EVIL DADDY LOVER PAPPY BABOON
FATHER POTATO PRIEST HUSBAND
VULTURE

PAPAL (ALSO SEE POPE) POPAL
PAPANE POPELY APOSTOLIC
PAPAW PAPA ASIMEN PAPAIO
ASIMINA CORAZON JASMINE
PAPAYA PAPAW LECHOSA
PAPER LIL WEB BILL BOND BLANK
BROKE ESSAY STUDY THEME
ASTHMA BINDLE CARTEL PAPIER
REPORT RETREE VESSEL CHEVIOT
EXHIBIT JOURNAL WRITING
YOSHINO DOCUMENT MONOGRAPH
NEWSPRINT ONIONSKIN
PARCHMENT VALENTINE
(— FOLDER) STROKER
(— MAKER) WASHERMAN
(— NAUTILUS) ARGONAUT
(— PULP) WATERLEAF
(— QUANTITY) PAGE REAM QUIRE
SHEET BUNDLE
(— SIZE) SIXMO
(ABSORBENT —) BLOTTER
TOWELLING
(ADVERTISING —) FLIER FLYER
SHOPPER
(ALBUMINIZED —) SAXE
(BUILDING —) FELT
(BUNDLE OF —S) DUFTER DOSSIER
(CHINESE —) INDIA
(COMMERCIAL —) PORTFOLIO
(DAMAGED —) BROKE CASSE SALLE
RETREE
(DEFECTIVE —) BROKES
(DIPLOMATIC —) NOTE
(DRAWING —) TORCHON
(FOLDED —) SADDLE AIRPLANE
(FRILLED —) PAPILLOTE
(GIVING AUTHORITY) POWER
(GLOSS —) GILL
(HARD —) PELURE
(HEAVY —) FELT
(LAVATORY —) BUMF
(LINING —S) SKIPS
(METAL-COATED —) FOIL
(NEGOTIABLE —) STIFF
(OFFICIAL —) TARGE HOOKUM
DOCUMENT
(PARCHMENT —) VELLUM
PERGAMYN
(PHOTOGRAPHIC —) SEPIA
(SIZE OF —) CAP COPY DEMI NOTE
POST PAST TOWN ATLAS CROWN
FOLIO JESUS LARGE LEGAL ROYAL
SIXMO ALBERT BILLET CASING
LETTER MEDIUM THIRDS BASTARD
CABINET EMPEROR THEOREM
ELEPHANT FOOLSCAP IMPERIAL
(SMALL PIECES OF —) CHAD
(STRIP OF —) TAPE
(STRONG —) MANILA MANILLA
(THIN —) FLIMSY PELURE TISSUE
ONIONSKIN
(THROWN —) CONFETTI

(TOILET —) BUMF
(TRANSPARENT —) GLASSINE
(UNCUT —) BOLT
(WALL —) TENTURE
(WATERMARKED —) BATONNE
(WRAPPING —) SKIP KRAFT SEALING
SCREENING
(WRITING —) FLAT LINEN WEDDING
(PREF.) PAPYRO
PAPERBARK CAJEPUT MILKWOOD
PAPERBOARD BENDER VENEER
CARDBOARD CHIPBOARD PULPBOARD
PAPER FACTOR JUVABIONE
PAPERWORK BUMF BUMPH
PAPIER-MACHE FLONG
PAPILLA CERAS DEIRID NIPPLE
PAPULA MAMMULA THELIUM
(PL.) CERATA
PAPILLOMA ANGLEBERRY
PAPIO MORMON
PAPIST TORY PAPANE CATHOLIC
POPELING
PAPPUS DOWN STIPE AIGRETTE
PARACHUTE THISTLEDOWN
PAPPY PA DAD PAW PAPA SOFT
MUSHY PULPY FATHER SUCCULENT
PAPRIKA PIMENTO PIMIENTO
PAPUA (BAY OF —) DYKE MILNE
ACLAND HOLNICOTE
(CAPITAL OF —) PORTMORESBY
(MONEY OF —) KINA
(RIVER OF —) FLY KIKORI PURARI
(TOWN OF —) LAE BUNA DARU
WEWAK GOROKA KIKORI MADANG
SAMARAI
PAPUAN ARAU BIAK HULA KATE
BUANG EKARI KIWAI KWOMA SIVAI
SULKA BAITSI BANARO IATMUL
KEREWA KOIARI ARAPESH DAINING
PAPULE WHELK PIMPLE
PAPYRUS REED PAPER SEDGE
BIBLOS GLUMAL SCROLL BULRUSH
(— STRIP) ORIHON
PAR BY NORM EQUAL NORMAL
AVERAGE EQUALITY
(ONE OVER —) BOGIE
(ONE UNDER —) BIRDIE
(TWO UNDER —) EAGLE
PARA FODDA PERAU PARRAH
PARABASIS ODE
PARABLE MYTH TALE FABLE STORY
APOLOG BYWORD MASHAL SAMPLE
BYSPELL PROVERB ALLEGORY
APOLOGUE FORBYSEN LIKENESS
SIMILITUDE
PARABOLA ARC CURVE ANTENNA
PARACETAMOL PANADOL
PARACHUTE SILK CHUTE BROLLY
DROGUE BALLUTE PATAGIUM
STREAMER
(— OF DOWN) PAPPUS
(FOLDED —) PACK

(SEND BY—) DROP
(SMALL—) BALLUTE
PARACHUTIST PATHFINDER
(PL.) STICK
PARACLETE AIDER HELPER PLEADER
ADVOCATE CONSOLER COMFORTER
PARADE JET TOP POMP SHOW WALK
MARCH STRUT FLAUNT MUSTER
REVIEW STROLL CORTEGE DISPLAY
EXHIBIT MARSHAL CEREMONY
EXERCISE FLOURISH GRANDEUR
SPLENDOR PAGEANTRY
(—GROUND) MAIDAN
(—OF BULLFIGHTERS) PASEO
(—OF WORDS) FLOURISH
(UNSUBSTANTIAL—) PAGEANT
PARADED AFFICHE
PARADISE EDEN JODO BLISS JENNA
AIDENN GOLOKA HEAVEN PARVIS
ELYSIUM NIRVANA
(—OF INDRA) SVARGA SWARGA
(—TREE) ACEITUNA STAVEWOOD
PARADOX KOAN ANTINOMY
PARADOXURE MUSANG PALMCAT
PALMCIVET
PARAFFIN ALKANE
PARAGON GEM HERO PINK TYPE
IDEAL MODEL PEARL APERSEE
PATTERN PEROPUS PHOENIX
NONESUCH NONPAR
(—OF KNIGHTHOOD) PALADIN
PARAGRAPH ITEM SIGN CAPUT
PAUSE CLAUSE NOTICE RUBRIC
ARTICLE INITIAL PILCROW SECTION
CAUSERIE MATERIAL PEELCROW
PERSONAL SUBLEADER
(—MARK) PILCROW
(UNIMPORTANT—S) BALAAM

PARAGUAY

CAPITAL: ASUNCION
COIN: GUARANI
DEPARTMENT: GUAIRA ITAPUA
OLIMPO CAAZAPA BOQUERON
LAKE: VERA YPOA YPACARAI
LANGUAGE: GUARANI
MEASURE:
PIE LINE LINO VARA LEGUA LINEA
CORDEL CUADRA CUARTA FANEGA
PLAIN: CHACO
RIVER: YPANE ACARAY PARANA
CONFUSO
TOWN: LUQUE PILAR CAACUPE
CAAZAPA TRINIDAD CONCEPCION
VILLARRICA
WEIGHT: QUINTAL

PARAGUAY TEA MATE
PARAKEET CONURE PARROT
WELLAT ROSELLA ARATINGA
KAKARIKI POPINJAY ROSEHILL
GREENLEEK

PARALLEL EVEN LIKE ALONG EQUAL MATCH SECOND EXAMPLE FRONTAL PARAGON PENDANT ANALOGUE LIKENESS MULTIPLE QUANTITY (PREF.) ORTH(O) PAR(A)

PARALLELEPIPED CUBOID

PARALLELISM PARITY ANALOGY

PARALLELOGRAM RHOMB OBLONG SQUARE RHOMBUS RHOMBOID RECTANGLE

PARALYSIS CRAMP PALSY POLIO SHOCK PARESIS DIPLEGIA PARAPLEGIA POLIOMYELITIS (SUFF.) LYSE LYSIS LYST LYTE LYTIC LYZE

PARALYZE DARE DAZE STUN PALSY SCRAM ASTONY BENUMB CONGEAL IMPALSY PETRIFY TORPEDO TORPEFY (— WITH EMOTION) TRANSFIX

PARALYZED NUMB PALSIED CRIPPLED

PARAMEDIC EMT

PARAMORPHINE THEBAINE

PARAMOUNT ABOVE CHIEF RULER SOVRAN CAPITAL SUPREME DOMINANT SUPERIOR SUZERAIN SOVEREIGN

PARAMOUR DOLL PRIM PURE LEMAN LOVER WOMAN WOOER AMORET FRIEND MASTER MINION FRANION GALLANT HETAERA RUFFIAN SERVANT SPECIAL SULTANA STALLION BOYFRIEND

PARAPET BUTT WALL BAHUT REDAN BARBET BONNET FLECHE PARPEN TRENCH BULWARK PLUTEUS RAILING RAMPART BARTIZAN ENVELOPE TRAVERSE

PARAPH RUBRIC

PARAPHERNALIA GEAR EQUIPAGE APPARATUS EQUIPMENT TRAPPINGS

PARAPHRASE FARSE REWORD TARGET TARGUM PREFACE THARGUM VERSION TRANSLATE

PARASITE BUG BUR FLY BURR MOSS SPIV TRYP CHARK DRONE LEECH SHARK TOADY VIRUS FEEDER FUNGUS GNATHO SHADOW SPONGE SUCKER THRIPS BLEEDER BYWONER SPONGER TAGTAIL DICYEMID ENTOZOON EPIPHYTE HANGERON SLAVERER INFESTANT POTHUNTER SACCULINA SPARGANUM SYCOPHANT TOADEATER TUBHUNTER (— ON TROUT) SUG (PL.) ECTOZOA ENTOZOA DRIFTWOOD (PREF.) (VEGETABLE —) PHYT(I)(O)

PARASITIC CYTOZOIC TRENCHER BIOPHILOUS (— JAEGER) SHOOI DIRTBIRD

PARASOL SHADE AOGIRI SHADOW ROUNDEL TIRESOL KITTYSOL SUNSHADE UMBRELLA (— MUSHROOM) LEPIOTA (PREF.) UMBELL(I)

PARATROOPER SKYMAN

PARAVANE OTTER

PARBOIL CODDLE

PARBOILED LEEPIT

PARCEL DAK LOT DAWK DEAD DEAL DOLE METE PACK PART WISP BULSE BUNCH GROUP PIECE BUNDLE DIVIDE FARDEL PACKET PASSEL CONACRE PACKAGE PORTION COMMODITY (— OF DIAMONDS) SERIES (— OF GROUND) LOT PICK CLOSE SOLUM SUERTE CONACRE PENDICLE (— OF HEMP FIBER) PIG (— OF JEWELS) BULSE (— OUT) ALLOT

PARCH DRY FRY BURN COOK SEAR ROAST TOAST PEARCH RIZZER SCORCH BRISTLE BRUSTLE GRADDAN SHRIVEL TORREFY TORRIFY (PREF.) TORRE XER(O)

PARCHED ARID HUSK SERE ADUST FIERY GIZZEN TORRID THIRSTY SCORCHED

PARCHING URENT

PARCHMENT LARK FOREL CHARTA MEZUZAH PAPYRIN SCYTALE DRUMHEAD SHEEPSKIN PALIMPSEST (— PAPER) DOCKET PERGAMYN (FINE —) VEL VELLUM (PIECE OF —) MEMBRANE (ROLL OF —) PELL SCROLL

PARD PAL CHUM TIGER FRIEND LEOPARD PANTHER PARTNER COMPANION

PARDON FREE CLEAR COVER GRACE MERCY REMIT SPARE ACQUIT ASSOIL EXCUSE SHRIVE ABSOLVE AMNESTY CONDONE FORGIVE OVERLOOK REPRIEVE TOLERATE EXCULPATE

PARDONABLE VENIAL VENIABLE EXCUSABLE

PARDONER QUESTOR QUAESTOR

PARE CUP CHIP COPE FLAY PEEL SKIN FRIZZ SHAVE SKELP SKIVE SLIPE SPADE CHISEL REDUCE REMOVE RESECT CURTAIL FLAUGHT WHITTLE (— LEATHER) SKIVE (— SOD) BURNBEAT (— STAVES) BUCK (— STONE) BOAST

PAREGORIC ANODYNE MITIGATING

PAREL PARELL APPAREL CLOTHING ORNAMENT

PARENCHYMA AMYLOM MESOPHYL

PARENT DAD DAM MAMA PAPA SIRE
DADDY ELDER MATER PATER
AUTHOR FATHER MOTHER ORIGIN
FORBEAR GENITOR ANCESTOR
BEGETTER FILICIDE GUARDIAN
PARENTAGE KIND BIRTH BROOD
FAMILY ORIGIN PROGENY
ENGENDURE
PARENTHESIS HOOK ASIDE PAREN
BRACKET TOENAIL INNUENDO
INTERVAL INTERLUDE
(PL.) HOOKS CURVES
PAREVE NEUTRAL
PARGET COAT GYPSUM PARIET
PLASTER DECORATE WHITEWASH
PARGO MUTTONFISH
PARHELION DOG SUN SUNDOG
PARIAH LEPER PAREA ISHMAEL
OUTCAST
PARIAN CHINA MARBLE PORCELAIN
PARIETAL SOMAL SOMATIC
PARI-MUTUEL TOTE TOTALIZER
PARING CHIP FOIL SHRED SPECK
GUBBIN PARURE PEELING
(FISH —S) GUBBINS
(PL.) BOXING
PARIS ALEXANDER
(— AIRPORT) ORLY
(FATHER OF —) PRIAM
(MOTHER OF —) HECUBA
(PALACE IN —) ELYSEE LOUVRE
TUILERIES
(RIVER OF —) SEINE
(STOCK EXCHANGE IN —) BOURSE
(SUBWAY IN —) METRO
(WIFE OF —) OENONE OENONE
PARISH CURE HOUSE TITLE CHARGE
SOCIETY PECULIAR OUTPARISH
(— HEAD) PASTOR PRIEST MINISTER
(— MEETING) VESTRY
PARISIAN LUTETIAN
PARISINA (BELOVED OF —) HUGO
(HUSBAND OF —) AZO
PARISON BLOW GATHERING
PARITY ANALOGY EQUALITY
LIKENESS GRAVIDITY
PARK HAY PEN HOLE STOP WAIT
GREEN LEAVE CIRCLE DAPHNE
GARDEN PRATER COMMONS
DIAMOND PADDOCK TERRACE
PARADISE TETRAGON
(AMUSEMENT —) FUNFAIR
(KIND OF —) THEME
PARKA PARCA ANORAK JACKET
PULLOVER
PARKING (KIND OF —) VALET
PARKLEAVES TUTSAN
PARLANCE TALK IDIOM SPEECH
DICTION DISCOURSE
PARLAY WAGER DOUBLE
PARLEY DODGE PARLE SPEAK TREAT
UTTER CONFER INDABA PALTER
PAROLI DISCUSS PALAVER PARLING

PARLANCE DISCOURSE TEMPORIZE
NEGOTIATION
PARLIAMENT DIET RUMP TING
COURT SENAT CORTES FANTAN
MAJLIS SAEIMA COUNCIL ESTATES
KNESSET LAGTING RIKSDAG
TYNWALD CONGRESS CONVERSE
STORTING VOLKSRAAD
SANDHEDRIN
(— HOUSE) DAIL SEANAD
(GREEK —) BOULE
(SCAND. —) THING
PARLIAMENTARIAN APRONEER
PARLOR BEN BOOR HALL SALON
FOREROOM LOCUTORY SNUGGERY
SOLARIUM
(COUNTRY —) SPENCE
(MILKING —) BAIL
PARLORMAID MATRON
PARLOUS KEEN RISKY CLEVER
SHREWD CUNNING CRITICAL
PERILOUS DANGEROUS HAZARDOUS
PARMASHTA (FATHER OF —)
HAMAN
PARMESAN GRANA
PARNACH (SON OF —) ELIZAPHAN
PAROCHIAL PETTY NARROW
PAROCHIAN SECTARIAN
PARODIST SPOOFER
PARODY RIB SKIT PUTON SPOOF
SATIRE SENDUP TRAVESTY
BURLESQUE IMITATION
PAROLE FAITH PLEDGE LICENSE
PROMISE
PARONOMASIA PUN
AGNOMINATION
PARONYCHIA FELON PANARIS
WHITLOW NAILWORT
PAROTITIS MUMPS
PAROXYSM FIT KINK PANG AGONY
COLIC QUIRK SPASM STORM STOUR
THROE ACCESS ATTACK FRENZY
ORGASM RAPTUS SHOWER
RAPTURE EPITASIS AGITATION
PARR PAR SAMLET SCEGGER
SKEGGER BRANDLIN BRANDLING
PARROT ARA HIA KEA COPY ECHO
JAKO KAKA LORO LORY POLL VAZA
ARARA CAGIT MACAW MIMIC POLLY
AMAZON CAIQUE CONURE KAKAPO
REPEAT TIRIBA CORELLA GRASSIE
ITERATE LORILET COCKATOO
LORIKEET LOVEBIRD PARAKEET
PICARIAN POPINJAY BROADTAIL
COCKATEEL BUDGERIGAR
(PREF.) PSITTAC(I)
PARROT FISH LORO SCAR LANIA
LAUIA SCAUR VIEJA COTORO
SCARUS LABROID MUDFISH
OLDWIFE BLUEFISH
PARRY FEND STOP WARD AVOID
BLOCK DODGE EVADE FENCE PRIME
QUART SIXTE OCTAVE PARADE

QUINTE SECOND THWART TIERCE
COUNTER DEFLECT EVASION
PARSE PACE PEARCE ANALYZE
DIAGRAM DISSECT CONSTRUE
ANATOMIZE
PARSEGHIAN ARA
PARSHANDATHA (FATHER OF —)
HAMAN
PARSI ZOROASTRIAN
(— **HOLY BOOK)** AVESTA
(— **PRIEST)** MOBED DASTUR
PARSIFAL (CHARACTER IN —)
KUNDRY TITUREL AMFORTAS
KLINGSOR PARSIFAL GURNEMANZ
(**COMPOSER OF —)** WAGNER
PARSIMONIOUS GARE MEAN NEAR
NIGH CLOSE MINGY NIPPY SCANT
SPARE TIGHT FRUGAL NARROW
SCARCE SCOTCH SKIMPY SORDID
STINGY STRAIT MISERLY SCRIMPY
SPARING COVETOUS GRASPING
GRUDGING SCREWING WRETCHED
MERCENARY NIGGARDLY
PENURIOUS RETENTIVE
ABERDONIAN
PARSLEY ACHE CUMIN UMBEL
CICELY CONIUM ELTROT KARPAS
CHERVIL HOGWEED FLUELLIN
PARSLEY CAMPHOR APIOL APIOLE
PARSNIP TANK WYPE UMBEL
CONIUM MADNEP CADWEED
HOGWEED SKIRRET BUNDWEED
QUEENWEED
(**WATER —)** SIUM
PARSON RECTOR CROAKER PATRICO
PERSONA MINISTER PREACHER
GUIDEPOST
(**COUNTRY —)** RUM
(**PL.)** PARSONRY
PARSONAGE GLEBE MANSE
RECTORY PASTORATE PASTORIUM
PARSON BIRD POE TUI KOKO TUWI
POEBIRD POYBIRD
PART DEL END LOT PAN DEAL DOLE
FECK GRIN HAET HALF HAND NECK
PANE ROLE ROVE SECT SHED SIDE
SOME TEAR TWIN AUGHT PARTY
PIECE QUOTA SEVER SHARE SHODE
SNACK SPLIT TWAIN BEHALF
CANTON CLEAVE DEPART DETAIL
DIVIDE FEEDER FINGER MEMBER
MINUTE MOIETY PARCEL PORTIO
QUORUM SECTOR SINGLE SUNDER
UNYOKE DISJOIN ELEMENT FEATURE
FRUSTUM PORTION SECTION
SEGMENT SEVERAL ALIENATE
DISSEVER DIVISION ELIQUATE
FRACTION LIRIPIPE
(— **HAIR)** SHADE
(— **OF ANIMAL'S TAIL)** DOCK
(— **OF BEEF)** CHUCK SKINK
(— **OF BLAST FURNACE)** BOSH BELLY

(— **OF BOW)** PEAK
(— **OF CAM WHEEL)** LOBE
(— **OF CANNON)** CHASE
(— **OF CHAIR)** SPLAT
(— **OF COMPASS)** FLY
(— **OF CONCERTO)** CEMBALO
(— **OF CONFIRMATION SERVICE)**
ALAPA
(— **OF CROSSBOW)** LATH
(— **OF DIAMOND)** BEZEL
(— **OF FLEECE)** LEECH
(— **OF FOWL'S COMB)** BLADE
(— **OF FURNACE)** HEARTH
(— **OF GUN SHIELD)** APRON
(— **OF HARBOR)** FAIRWAY
(— **OF HAWK'S BEAK)** CLAP
(— **OF HIDE)** RANGE
(— **OF HOOKAH)** CHILLUM
(— **OF HORSE)** FOREHAND
(— **OF JOINT)** TABLE
(— **OF MASS)** INTROIT
(— **OF POETIC FOOT)** ARSIS
(— **OF PORK LOIN)** GRISKIN
(— **OF RIVER)** FRESH
(— **OF SADDLE TREE)** FORK
(— **OF STAIR TREAD)** NOSING
(— **OF STAMEN)** ANTHER
(— **OF SWORD)** FORTE
(— **OF SWORD BLADE)** FOIBLE
(— **OF TEMPLE)** CELLA
(— **OF THROAT)** GULA FAUCES
(— **OF TONGUE)** DORSUM
(— **OF TURTLE)** CALIPEE
(— **OF VIOLIN BOW)** BAGUET
(— **OF WHEEL)** SPEECH
(— **THAT REVOLVES)** ROTOR
(— **THE LEGS)** STRADDLE
(— **WITH)** CEDE GIVE LOSE SELL
LEAVE DONATE ABANDON
(— **WITHIN)** INSIDE
(**ACCOMPANYING —)** BURDEN
OBBLIGATO
(**ARTIFICIAL —)** PROSTHESIS
(**ASSIGNED —)** QUOTA
(**ASSUMED —)** FIGURE
(**BAGLIKE —)** SAC
(**BEST —)** FAT YOLK CREAM FLOWER
MARROW
(**BRISTLELIKE —)** SETA
(**BROADEST — OF PLANK)** TOUCH
(**CENTRAL —)** HUB BODY CORE
HEART KERNEL
(**CHOICE —)** ELITE
(**CLEAR — OF LIQUID)** SWIM
(**CLOSING —)** HEEL
(**COARSE — OF FLAX)** HURDS
(**CONCLUDING —)** WRAPUP
(**CONICAL —)** BULLET
(**CONNECTING —)** NECK PONS
UNION
(**CURVED —)** START
(**DEPRESSED —)** HOLLOW

(DISTANT —S) FARNESS
(DUPLICATE —) SPARE
(EDIBLE — OF CLAM) CHEEK
(EIGHTH — OF CIRCLE) OCTANT
(ESSENTIAL —) PITH
(ESSENTIAL —S) STAMINA
(FIFTH —) QUINTUS
(FINAL —) LAST SHANK EPILOG
(FIRST —) FRONT PRIME VAUNT
INITIAL BEGINNING
(FOURTH —) FARDEL FORPIT FERLING
(FRONT —) VAUNT BREAST FORESIDE
(FURTHEST —) TIP
(GREATER —) HEFT SUBSTANCE
(HARDEST —) BRUNT
(HIGHEST —) CROP CROWN HEIGHT
(HUNDREDTH —) CENTESM
(IMPAIRING —) ALLOY
(IN —) HALVES
(INDETERMINATE —) PERCENTAGE
(INNERMOST —) FUND
(INNERMOST —S) PENETRALIA
(INSTRUMENTAL —) HAND
CONTINUO
(INTERLACED —) TWINE
(INTRODUCTORY —) PROTASIS
(LARGE —) FORCE
(LATERAL — OF HEAD) CHEEK
(LATTER —) HEEL SHANK
(LEAST —) STITCH
(LESS DESIRABLE —) RIDDLINGS
(LEVEL —) FLAT
(LOWER —) SECONDO
(LOWER — OF ROBE) BASES
(LOWEST —) FOOT BOTTOM
GROUND DESCENT
(MAIN —) BODY BULK SUBSTANCE
(MATERIAL —) GIST
(MIDDLE —) DEEP CENTER
(MIDDLE — OF NIGHT) HOWE
(MINOR —) BIT COG
(MINUTE —) PRICK TITTLE
(MISSING —) LACUNA
(MOST IMPORTANT —) EYE
FOREHAND
(MOST SERIOUS —) DICKENS
(NARROW —) STRAIT THROAT
(OF HORSE'S THIGH) GASKIN
(OVERDUE —) ARREAR
(PRINCIPAL —) BODY MAIN GROSS
(PRIVATE —) THING MEMBER
(PROJECTING —) ARM JAG JET JOG
APSE LOBE SPURN
(PROTUBERANT —) BOSS BULGE
(REJECTED —S) CHANKINGS
(REMAINING —) BUTT DREG HEEL
(REMOTEST —) EXTREMITY
(RINGLIKE —) ANNULUS
(ROOTLIKE —) RADICLE
(ROTATING —) ROTOR
(ROUNDED —) BULB
(SAWLIKE —) SERRA

(SECRET —) RECESS
(SLENDER —) NECK
(SMALL —) BIT ATOM FLOW TITHE
DETAIL MINUTE SNIPPET
(SMALLEST —) ATOM WHIT MINIM
(SOFT — OF BREAD) CRUMB
(SOFT — OF VEIN) LEATH
(SOLO —) CALL
(STAMEN —) ANTHER
(STATIONARY —) STATOR
(STILL — OF WATER) KELD
(SWINGING —) FLAIL
(TELLING —) POINT
(TENTH —) TITHE
(THIN —) LEAF
(THIN — OF WALL) ALLEGE
(THIRD —) THIRDENDEAL
(TOP —) HEADPIECE
(TWELFTH —) INCIA POINT UNCIAL
(UPPER —) CHIEF RIDGE OVERPARTY
(UPPERMOST —) TOP PEAK CHIEF
UPSIDE TOPSIDE
(VAUDEVILLE —) OLIO
(VITAL —) HEART
(WINGLIKE —) ALA
(WORST —) DEPTH
(WORTHLESS —) DREGS
(24TH —) CARAT
(360TH —) DEGREE
(PREF.) MER(I)(O) PARTI
(SUFF.) MER(E)(IC)(IS)(OUS)(Y) TOMA
TOME TOMIC TOMUUS TOMY
PARTAKE BITE PART SHARE DIVIDE
PARTEN PARTICIPATE
(— OF) EAT USE HAVE SHARE TASTE
TOUCH IMPART
PARTAN CRAB
PARTED PARTITE
PARTHAON (FATHER OF —)
AGENOR
(MOTHER OF —) EPICASTE
(SON OF —) OENEUS
(WIFE OF —) EURYTE
PARTHENIA (HUSBAND OF —)
ARGALUS
PARTHENIUS (BROTHER OF —)
PANDION
(FATHER OF —) PHINEUS
(MOTHER OF —) CLEOPATRA
PARTHENOGENETIC AGAMIC
AGAMOUS
PARTIAL HALF PART SEMI BIASED
UNFAIR COLORED HALFWAY
UNEQUAL HARMONIC INCLINED
PARTISAN PROPENSE SKELETON
FAVORABLE SEGMENTAL
PARTICULAR RESPECTIVE
(PREF.) DEMI MER(I)(O) MES(O) SEMI
PARTIALITY BIAS FAVOR RESPECT
AFFECTION SPECIALTY
PARTIALLY HALF HALFWAY
HALFWISE

PARTICIPANT BOOK ACTOR PARTY
MEMBER PARTNER DUETTIST
PARTABLE PARTISAN
(SUBORDINATE —) STOOGE
(PL.) FIELD
PARTICIPATE JOIN SIDE ENTER
SHARE ENGAGE ENLIST IMPART
COMPETE PARTAKE
(— IN) GO HAVE JOIN STAY STAND
TASTE COMMON STICKLE
PARTICIPATION HAND PLOT
SOCIETY INTEREST
(COMMON —) COMMUNITY
PARTICIPATOR
(SUFF.) STER STRESS
PARTICIPLE VERBID
PARTICLE ACE BIT DOT FIG GRU JOT
PSI RAY ATOM BETA CORN CROT
CURN DUST GRUE HAET IOTA KNIT
MITE MOTE SNIP SPOT STIM WHIT
ALPHA BOSON FLAKE FLECK GHOST
GRAIN MESON OMEGA POINT PRION
QUARK SHRED SIGMA SPECK STARN
STIME THRUM TWINT FILING GEIGER
LEPTON MOMENT PANGEN PARTON
RIZZOM SMIDGE SMITCH TITTLE
VIRION AMICRON FERMION
GEMMULE GRANULE NUCLEUS
PHOTINO PSYCHON SINGLET
SMIDGIN TACHYON ACCEPTER
GRAVITON NEUTRINO SMIDGEON
SYLLABLE MICROSOME POSITRINO
SCINTILLA
(— IN BLOOD) EMBOLUS
(— IN INTERNAL EAR) OTOCONIUM
(— OF FIRE) SPARK
(— OF GOLD) COLOR
(— OF QUARKS) HADRON
(— OF SOOT) ISEL IZLE SMUT
AIZLE
(—S IN BEER) FLOATERS
(—S OF GRAIN) CHOP
(— TO BIND QUARKS) GLUON
(ATOMIC —) ION MUON BARYON
HADRON LEPTON ELECTRON
(BINDING —) GLUON
(COLLECTION OF CHARGED —S)
PLASMA
(COMBINING —) ACCEPTOR
(ELECTRIFIED —) ION ANION PROTON
POSITRON THERMION
(ELEMENTARY —) MUON NEUTRON
NEUTRINO
(FINE ICY —S) SLEET
(GROUP OF —S) MESON
(HYPOTHETICAL —) QUARK
(JAGGED —) SPLINTER
(KIND OF —) ETA TAU
(LEAST POSSIBLE —) MINIM
(LINGUISTIC —) SERVILE
(MASSLESS —) GLUON
(MESON —) UPSILON

(MINUTE —) JOT ORT RAY ATOM
GRAIN SPECK RAMENT GRANULE
MOLECULE RAMENTUM CORPUSCLE
(NEGATIVE —) NOR NOT
(NUCLEAR —S) FALLOUT
(PHYSICS —) QUARK POSITRON
(POSITIVELY-CHARGED —) CATION
KATION
(PROTEIN —) PRION
(QUARK —S) HADRON
(SMALL —) NIP BLEB CORN MOTE
CRUMB GRAIN SPECK PROTON
AMICRON GRANULE SPRINKLE
SUBMICRON
(SUBATOMIC —) PION LAMBDA
(TINY —) ATOMY
(ULTIMATE —) PSYCHON
(UNCHARGED —) LAMBDA
(PL.) DUST FINES SWARF SIZINGS
CUTTINGS FURFURES
(SUFF.) PLAST
(OF A KIND) ID
PARTI-COLORED PIED FANCY
MOTLEY PARTED PIEBALD
BUTTERFLY HARLEQUIN
PARTICULAR AND ATOM FIXY ITEM
NICE SELF SOME FUSSY PARTY
POINT THING CHOOSY DAINTY
DETAIL MINUTE MOROSE REGARD
SINGLE STICKY ARTICLE CAREFUL
CERTAIN CORRECT FINICKY PRECISE
PRIVATE RESPECT SEVERAL SPECIAL
UNUSUAL CLERKISH CONCRETE
ESPECIAL PECULIAR PICKSOME
PRECIOUS SINGULAR SUBALTERN
RESPECTIVE
(NOT —) INCURIOUS
PARTICULARLY ONLY EXTRA
SINGLY SPECIAL EXPRESSLY
SPECIALLY
PARTING DEATH GOODBYE
FAREWELL
(— AS OF HAIR) SHED
PARTISAN PIKE SIDER STAFF BIASED
FACTOR FAUTOR MARIAN ZEALOT
CALOTIN DEVOTEE GUISARD
PARTNER ADHERENT CRISTINO
ESPOUSER FAVORITE FENNOMAN
FOLLOWER HENCHMAN JACOBITE
MOSSBACK SIDESMAN STALWART
URBANIST HIGHFLIER MAZZINIST
OCHLOCRAT OLIVERIAN SECTARIAN
TERRORIST
(NOT —) CATHOLIC
(PL.) FOLLOWING
(SUFF.) CRAT
PARTITION BAR CUT DAM FIN FLAG
SEPT WALL SHOJI SPEER STAGE
WITHE BAFFLE DIVIDE PARPAL
PARPEN SCONCE SCREEN SEPTUM
BARRIER CLOISON ENCLOSE
GRATING PINFOLD PORTION

SCANTLE BRATTICE BULKHEAD
CLEAVAGE DIVISION STOPPING
TRAVERSE DASHBOARD DAYABHAGA
ICONOSTAS MESENTERY
STOOTHING
(— **BETWEEN STALLS**) TRAVIS TREVIS
TRAVISS
(— **IN CHIMNEY**) WITH WITHE
(— **IN CORAL**) TABULA
(— **IN COTTAGE**) SPEER HALLAN
(— **IN FRUIT**) REPLUM
(— **IN LOUDSPEAKER**) BAFFLE
(— **IN WATERWHEEL**) WREST
(— **OF ESTATE**) BOEDELSCHEIDING
(— **OF LATH AND PLASTER**)
STOOTHING
(**HORIZONTAL** —) STAGE
(**MINING** —) SOLLAR BRATTICE
STOPPING
(**PL.**) CANCELLI
PARTLET HEN WOMAN PERTELOT
PARTLY WHAT PARCEL PARTIM
HALFLINGS
(**PREF.**) SEMI
PARTNER BOY PAL ALLY HALF MATE
PARD WIFE BUDDY BUTTY PARTY
FELLOW MARROW SHARER
COMRADE CONSORT HUSBAND
CAMARADA COPEMATE SIDEKICK
YOKEMATE
(— **OF DUMMY**) VIVANT
(**DANCING** —) GIGOLO CAVALIER
(**ROMANTIC** —) SQUEEZE
(**PREF.**) CO
PARTNERS INOUT ONOFF TOFRO
COMEGO HEMHAW HITRUN HUECRY
PROCON BILLCOO DOTDASH
DOWNOUT EBBFLOW FARWIDE
FIVETEN HAMEGGS HIGHDRY
HIGHLOW INSOUTS KITHKIN
PATMIKE PUTTAKE TOUCHGO
YINYANG AMOSANDY BECKCALL
GIVETAKE HANDFOOT HIDESEEK
HILLDALE MUCKMIRE MUTTJEFF
ODDSENDS RICKRACK ROCKROLL
SHOWTELL SPICSPAN TIMETIDE
ALASALACK BACKFORTH BALLCHAIN
FACTFANCY HITHERYON KNIFEFORK
LOSTFOUND READWRITE
ROOMBOARD THICKTHIN TRIEDTRUE
BAGBAGGAGE BITSPIECES
BLACKWHITE FUSSBOTHER
HALEHEARTY HOOTHOLLER
NOOKCRANNY SPITPOLISH
SWITCHBAIT TARFEATHERS
ALIVEKICKING ROMULUSREMUS
STARSSTRIPES ASSAULTBATTERY
PARTNERSHIP HUI AXIS FIRM
HOUSE FUSION CAHOOTS COMPANY
CONSORT SOCIETY SOCIETEIT
(**MUTUALLY BENEFICIAL** —)
SYMBIOSIS

PARTRIDGE HUN BIRD KYAH YUTU
LERWA RUDGE TITAR CHUKAR
REDLEG SEESEE CHEEPER PATRICK
SHRIMPI TINAMOU BOBWHITE
FRANCOLIN FRENCHMAN
TETRAONID
(— **NOISE**) JUCK
(**SAND** —) TEHOO
(**YOUNG** —) CHEEPER SQUEALER
PARTRIDGEBERRY BOXBERRY
COWBERRY EYEBERRY ONEBERRY
SNOWBERRY TWINBERRY
PARTS
(**PREF.**)
(**SIDE** —) ALI
PART-SONG MADRIGAL
PART-TIME PARCEL
PARTURITION EUTOCIA TRAVAIL
CHILDBED DELIVERY DYSTOCIA
(**SUFF.**) TOKY
PARTY DO BAL BEE CRY TEA CAMP
CLAN DRUM GALA SECT SIDE BINGE
BLAST BRAWL BUNCH CABAL COVEY
CRUSH FESTA GROUP LEVEE MIXER
COMITE FIESTA FROLIC FRONDE
GERMAN INFARE JUNKET PERSON
SETOUT SHINDY SHOWER BLOWOUT
CANTICO COMPANY FACTION
GREGORY PATARIA SHINDIG
CLAMBAKE DRINKING FENNOMAN
POTLATCH POUNDING SOCIABLE
SQUANTUM TERTULIA CONCISION
INCLINING MERRIMENT
(— **GIVEN AT HOME**) HUDDLE
(**AFTERNOON** —) TEA RECEPTION
(**BEACH** —) CLAMBAKE
(**BOISTEROUS** —) BASH HOOLEY
BLOWOUT JAMBOREE
(**BRIDAL** —) SEND SHOWER
(**DANCING** —) HOP GERMAN
CANTICO HOEDOWN RIDOTTO
FANDANGO
(**DRINKING** —) SPREE KNEIPE MOLLIE
POTATION SYMPOSIUM
(**DRUNKEN** —) BLIND
(**EVENING** —) BALL SOIREE GREGORY
ROCKING TERTULIA
(**FISHING** —) HUKILAU
(**HUNTING** —) FAID
(**INFORMAL** —) SOCIABLE TERTULIA
(**IRISH** —) HOOLEY
(**LARGE** —) ROUT
(**MASQUERADE** —) GUISE RIDOTTO
(**MEMBER OF YOUTH** —) YIPPIE
(**MEN'S** —) STAG SMOKER
(**MILITARY** —) COMMANDO
(**NOISY** —) BEANO SHIVOO
(**POLITICAL** —) SAM SIDE WAFD
HOOKS LABOR CAUCUS FRONDE
SWARAJ ZENTRUM MINSEITO
KENSEIKAI SQUADRONE
OPPOSITION

(POPULAR —) HOOKS
(ROWDY —) BASH BLAST BLOWOUT
WINGDING
(SCOUTING —) ESPIAL
(SEARCH —) QUEST
(SPINNING —) ROCKING
(SUPPLY —) BRIGADE
(TEA —) DRUM TEMPEST
(THIRD —) STRANGER
(TYPE OF —) MIXER
(WILD —) WINGDING WHINGDING
(WORKING —) SQUAD
PARUAH (SON OF —) JEHOSHAPHAT
PARULIS GUMBOIL
PARVENU SNOB ARRIVE UPSTART
ARRIVIST MUSHROOM ARRIVISTE
PARVIS PARADISE
PARZIFAL (FATHER OF —) GAMURET
(MOTHER OF —) HERZELOIDE
PASACH (FATHER OF —) JAPHLET
PASCH PACE PAQUE EASTER
PASSOVER
PASCHAL LAMB CANDLE SUPPER
PASSOVER
PAS DE DEUX DUET
PASE FAROL NATURAL VERONICA
PASEAH (FATHER OF —) ESHTON
PASEAR WALK AIRING EXCURSION
PROMENADE
PASHA DEY EMIR BASHAW
PASAHAW
PASHTO AFGHAN
PASIPHAE (BROTHER OF —) AEETES
(CHILD OF —) ARIADNE PHAEDRA
(DAUGHTER OF —) ARIADNE
PHAEDRA
(FATHER OF —) HELIUS
(HUSBAND OF —) MINOS
(MOTHER OF —) PERSA
(SISTER OF —) CIRCE
PASQUEFLOWER BADGER
GOSLING APRILFOOL
PASQUINADE PIPE SQUIB SATIRE
LAMPOON PASQUIL
PASS BY GO COL DIE END FIG GAP
SAG USE ABRA BEAL CEDE CHIT
COMP COVE DREE DROP FALL FARE
FLIT FOIN GATE GHAT GULF HALS
HAND HAVE JARK LANE LEAD PACE
RIDE ROLL SEEK SILE SLAP SLIP STEP
WADE WALK WEAR WEND WIND
ALLOW CANTO DREIE ENACT FLEET
GHAUT GORGE HALSE HURRY KOTAL
LAPSE LITHE NOTCH OCCUR
ORDER PAPER PUNTA REACH RELAY
SHAKE SHOOT SMITE SPEND STRIP
TRADE UTTER WASTE WHELM YODEL
BILLET CHALAN CONVEY COUPON
DEFILE DEMISE ELAPSE EXCEED
HAPPEN PASSUS PERMIT RAVINE
SPIRAL TICKET TRAVEL TWOFER
ABSOLVE ALLONGE APPROVE
BREATHE DESCEND DEVOLVE
DIFFUSE ENTREAT LATERAL
OVERGET PASSAGE UNDERGO
JUNCTURE REBOLERA PURWANNAH
SAFEGUARD
(— A BALL) FEED HEEL
(— ABRUPTLY) LEAP
(— ALONG) BANDY DERIVE
(— AWAY) DIE SET FLEE VADE WING
DEPART EXPIRE PERISH FORFARE
FORTHGO OVERDRIVE
(— BACK AND FORTH) FIG
CRISSCROSS
(— BAD COIN) SMASH
(— BETWEEN HILLS) BEAL SLAP
SLACK
(— BEYOND) TURN OVERSHOOT
(— BY) COTE OMIT SKIP VADE WEND
APASS CLEAR FORGO FOREGO
IGNORE OVERGO INTERMIT
OVERHEAVE
(— DISCONTINUOUSLY) SKIP
(— FURTIVELY) SNEAK
(— GRADUALLY) FADE
(— IDLY) TRIFLE
(— IMPERCEPTIBLY) SHADE
(— IN BULLFIGHT) SUERTE
(— IN POKER) BREATHE
(— IN SCRUTINY) PERUSE
(— INTO USE) ENURE INURE
(— JUDGMENT ON) DEEM DECERN
SENTENCE
(— LIGHTLY) BRUSH SKATE SKITTER
(— OFF) SHAM FOIST
(— ON) LEAK PACE DELATE
TRANSMIT PROPAGATE
(— ONE'S LIFE) TRADE
(— OUT) CONK DEBOUCH EXHAUST
(— OVER) DO HIP BALK FREE SKIM
SKIP SLIP COVER CROSS ELIDE
FLEET SCOUR SWEEP TRANCE
OVERHIP TRANSIT INTERMIT
OVERLOOK OVERPOST PROGRESS
TRAVERSE
(— OVER LIGHTLY) SKIM SWEEP
OVERSKIP
(— OVER QUICKLY) SCUD FLEET
(— QUICKLY) FLIT SPIN SPEED
STRIKE
(— THE NIGHT) LIE LODGE
(— THROUGH) CROSS REEVE TRACE
DIVIDE OVERGO PIERCE SUFFER
EXCURSE PERVADE OVERPASS
OVERRIDE PERMEATE PROGRESS
PENETRATE
(— THROUGH A BLOCK) REEVE
(— THROUGH HOLE) REEVE
(— THROUGH NARROW WAY) THRID
THREAD
(— TIME) DRIVE SPEND TRADE
(— UNHAPPILY) DREE
(— UP) REJECT DECLINE DISREGARD
(— WITH DIFFICULTY) WADE
(— WITH VIOLENCE) RAKE

(CUSTOMS —) CARNET
(FENCING —) FOIN BOTTE LUNGE
PUNTA
(FOOTBALL —) FLY FLARE FORWARD
LATERAL PITCHOUT
(FORWARD —) AERIAL
(FREE —) PAPER
(FREE —S) PAPER
(HIGH —) CHIP
(HILL —) SLAP
(HOCKEY —) CENTER
(KIND OF —) SPOT OUTLET
(LONG — IN FOOTBALL) BOMB
(MOUNTAIN —) COL GAP NEK SAG
GATE GHAT SLIP CLOVE GHAUT
KLOOF KLOTAL POORT SWIRE
SWIRL BEALACH
(NARROW —) ABRA GULF CLOSE
SLYPE DEFILE
(SHORT — IN FOOTBALL) FLARE
(SUDDEN —) LUNGE
PASSABLE FIT FAIR SOSO TOLLOL
GENUINE ADEQUATE MEDIOCRE
MODERATE POSSIBLE TRAVELED
PERMEABLE TOLERABLE
(PREF.) BATO
PASSABLENESS INDIFFERENCE
PASSABLY SEEMLY
PASSAGE CUT GAT GUT ROW VIA
WAY WRO ADIT BELT BORD DOOR
EXIT FARE FLUE FORD GANG GATE
HALL ITER LANE PACE PASS PAWN
RACE RAMP SLIP SLUM VENT WELL
AISLE ALLEY ALURE BAYOU BEARD
BOGUE CANAL CHOPS CHUTE CLOOT
CREEK CRUSH DRAFT DRIFT DRIVE
ENTRY FLYBY FORTE GLADE GORGE
GORGE INLET JETTY MEUSE PATCH
PORCH SHUNT SLYPE SOUND
ACCESS ADITUS APORIA ARCADE
ATRIUM AVENUE BRIDGE BURROW
BYPASS CAREER COURSE DEFILE
DROMOS EGRESS ELAPSE FAUCES
HIATUS MEATUS PARODE RELIEF
SCREEN SLUICE STRAIT TRAJET
TRANCE TRAVEL TUNNEL VOYAGE
ARCHWAY BALTEUS CHANNEL
CHAPTER CHIMNEY CONDUIT
COULOIR COUPURE DIAZOMA
DOGTROT DRAUGHT ESTUARY
EXCERPT FISTULA FRAUGHT
GALLERY GANGWAY GATEWAY
ISTHMUS JOURNEY MANHOLE
OFFTAKE OUTTAKE PARADOS
PROCESS TRANSIT APPROACH
AQUEDUCT CITATION CLOISTER
COMMERCE DEBOUCHE DELETION
PARADIGM PERICOPE SENTENCE
SHIPPING SINUSOID SPILLWAY
(— ACROSS) TRAVERSE
(— ACROSS WATER) WAFT
(— BACK) REGRESS
(— BETWEEN WALLS) SLYPE

(— FOR MOLTEN METAL) SPRVE
RUNNER
(— IN BOOK) WHERE EXCERPT
(— IN CRUIVE) SLAP
(— IN JEWISH SCRIPTURE)
PARASHAH
(— OF POETRY OR MUSIC) MORCEAU
(— OF THREAD) FLOAT
(—S OF LITERATURE) BEAUTIES
(— TO STOMACH) SWALLOW
(— TO TOMB) DROMOS SYRINX
(AIR —) FLUE THIRL WINDWAY
THIRLING VENTIDUCT
(ANATOMICAL —) ITER
(CENSORED —) CAVIAR
(CONTINUOUS —) LAPSE
(COVERED —) OPE PAWN PEND
(DIFFICULT —) APORIA
(LITERARY —) TEXT QUOTE EXCERPT
SNIPPET QUOTATION
(MINE —) RUN ADIT HEAD ROOF
SLUM DRIVE LEVEL SHAFT THIRL
AIRWAY OTENTON UNDERCAST
(MINUTE —) PORE
(MUSICAL —) CUE CODA LINK BREAK
FORTE INTRO STAVE ARIOSO
FUGATO LEGATO PRESTO REPEAT
CADENZA CODETTA FANFARE
STRETTO FLOURISH RITENUTO
SPICCATO STACCATO SYMPHONY
VOCALISE PIZZICATO RITARDANDO
RITORNELLO
(NARROW —) GUT HASS ALLEY
CREEP GORGE JETTY NOTCH SLYPE
SMOOT DEFILE GULLET NARROW
STRAIT
(OPENING —) INTRO INTRODUCTION
(SECRET —) BOLTHOLE
(SECURE — OF) CARRY
(SUBTERRANEAN —) POSTERN
(SWIFT —) FLIGHT
(THROUGH —) TRANCE
(UNDERGROUND —) SUBWAY
(VAULTED —) PEND
(VOCAL —) SPRECHSTIMME
(WATER —) TICKLE TICKLER
(PREF.) MEATO
(SUFF.) PLANIA PORA PORE
PASSAGE HAWK TARTARET
PASSENGER
PASSAGE TO INDIA (AUTHOR OF
—) FORSTER
(CHARACTER IN —) AZIZ ADELA CECIL
MOORE RONALD STELLA GODBOLE
HEASLOP QUESTED FIELDING
PASSAGEWAY (ALSO SEE
PASSAGE) BORD FLUE GANG HALL
LANE PACE PASS PEND PORT RACE
SHED SLIP WENT YAWN AISLE ALLEY
ALURE CHUTE DRIFT DRONG ENTRY
GOING LUMEN RAISE SHOOT SMOOT
STULM ACCESS AIRWAY AVENUE
COURSE DINGLE FUNNEL GUTTER

INTAKE MANWAY RUELLE RUNWAY
TRANCE ZAGUAN DOORWAY
GALLERY SLIPWAY TWITTEN
WALKWAY WAYGATE CALLEJON
CORRIDOR HATCHWAY
(CLEARED — IN CROWD) HALL
(COVERED —) ARCADE CLOISTER
(LOCKED —) CANAL
(MINE —) BORD BOARD DRIFT SLANT
STULM WINZE
(NARROW —) SLIP AISLE SMOOT
BOTTLENECK
(SLOPING —) RAMP
(UNDERGROUND —) CATACOMB
PASSANT PAST CURRENT CURSORY
PASSING EPHEMERAL
PASSE AGED PAST WORN DATED
FADED BELATED OBSOLETE
OUTMODED
PASSED GONE
PASSENGER FARE INSIDE
FERRYMAN TRAVELER WAYFARER
(— WHO AVOIDS PAYING FARE) NIP
STOWAWAY
(— WITHOUT TICKET) HARE
(AIRPLANE —) BIRDMAN
(UNBOOKED —) CAD
(PL.) WAYBILL
PASSEPARTOUT SPANDREL
PASSERBY PASSER PASSANT
BYPASSER SAUNTERER
PASSERINE OSCINE PERCHER
TANAGER
PASSIFLORA TACSO
PASSING DEATH DYING ELAPSE
CURSORY DIADROM PASSADO
RUNNING SLIDING ELAPSING
FLEETING ENACTMENT EPHEMERAL
WAYFARING
(— BETWEEN) INTERCURRENT
(— BY) COTE
(— INTO EACH OTHER) FONDU
(— OF HOURS) TIME
(— OF TIME) EFFLUX
(SLOWLY —) LAG
PASSION IRE WAX BATE FIRE FURY
HEAT LOVE LUST PASH RAGA RAGE
TEAR TIDE WILL ZEAL ANGER ARDOR
BLOOD BRAME CHAFE DEVIL ERROR
FLAME LETCH MANIA RAJAS SPUNK
WRATH AFFECT CHOLER DESIRE
FERVOR MOTHER PELTER SATTVA
SPLEEN TALENT WARMTH EARNEST
EMOTION EROTISM FEELING
OUTRAGE VULTURE APPETITE
DISTRESS VIOLENCE PADDYWACK
(— FOR DOING GREAT THINGS)
MEGALOMANIA
(— FOR MUSIC) MELOMANIA
(ANGRY —) FUNK
(ANIMAL —) KAMA
(EXALTED —) ALTITUDES

(PREF.) PASSI PATH(O)
(SUFF.) (—FOR) MANE MANIA(C)
PASSIONATE HOT FOND WARM
WILD FIERY GUTSY QUICK WHITE
ARDENT FERVID FIERCE FUMOUS
IREFUL STORMY SULTRY TORRID
AMOROUS FLAMING PEPPERY
THERMAL VIOLENT CHOLERIC
FRENETIC VASCULAR VEHEMENT
WRATHFUL DIONYSIAN IRASCIBLE
PASSIONATELY HASTILY FERVIDLY
PASSIONFLOWER MAYPOP
BULLHOOF
PASSIONLESS COLD FREDDO
APATHETIC
PASSIVE INERT STOIC PATHIC STOLID
SUPINE PATIENT FEMININE INACTIVE
SIGNLESS YIELDING APATHETIC
PASSIVENESS QUIETISM
PASSIVITY INERTIA
PASSOVER PESAH PHASE PASQUE
PESACH
(— FESTIVAL) SEDER
(JEWISH —) EASTER
PASSPORT CHOP PASS CONGE
CONGEE DUSTUK DUSTUCK
FURLOUGH TESCARIA TEZKIRAH
SAFEGUARD
PASSUS PACE PART PASS STEP
CANTO DIVISION
PASSWORD SIGN WORD TOKEN
DUSTUK TESSERA WATCHWORD
PAST BY AGO WAS GONE YOND YORE
AFTER AGONE APAST ASIDE ENDED
SINCE BEHIND BYGONE FOREBY
PRETER ANOTHER FOREGONE
PRETERIT COMPLETED
(LONG —) HIGH
(RECENTLY —) OTHER
(TIME IN THE —) LANGSYNE
(TIME NOT LONG —) YESTERDAY
(PREF.) PRETER RETRO
PASTA ORZO ZITI PENNE NOODLE
TUFOLI FUSILLI LASAGNA RAVIOLI
LINGUINE LINGUINI MACARONI
RIGATONI MANICOTTI SPAGHETTI
FETTUCELLE TORTELLINI
MOSTACCIOLI PERCIATELLI
TAGLIATELLE
(— BITS) PASTINA
(TUBULAR —) ZITI
(WAY TO COOK —) ALDENTE
PASTE HIT PAP BEAT BLOW DIKA
DUFF GLUE MISO PACK PATE CREAM
DOUGH FALSE GESSO HENNA
PUNCH STICK ATTACH BATTER
CERATE FASTEN GROUND PANADA
RASTIK STRASS BUCKETY CLOBBER
COLOGNE DRAWOUT FILLING
GORACCO GUARANA STICKUM
BADIGEON BARBOTINE
(— FOR CAULKING) BLARE

(— FOR LINING HEARTHS) BRASQUE
(— FOR SHOES, BOOTS) CLOBBER
BLACKING
(— FROM SESAME SEEDS) TAHINI
(— OF CLAY) BATTER
(— OF SESAME SEEDS) TAHINI
(— TO FILL HOLES IN WOOD AND
STONE) BADIGEON
(ALIMENTARY —) PUREE FEDELINI
SCUNGILLI SPAGHETTI
(AROMATIC —) PASTILE
(CHICK-PEA —) HOMMOS HUMMUS
(COLORING —) HENNA
(DRIED —) GUARANA
(EARTHY —) ENGOBE
(FISH —) BAGOONG
(MEDICATED —) ELECTUARY
(PORCELAIN —) PATE
(POTTER'S —) BARBOTINE
(TOBACCO —) GORACCO
(WEAVER'S —) SOWENS BUCKETY
PASTEBOARD CARD SHAM CARTON
FLIMSY TICKET MATBOARD
PASTEDOWN LINING
PASTEL WOAD LIGHT CRAYON
PICTURE DELICATE
PASTEL BLUE OADE WOAD
PASTEN HOBBLE TETHER PASTOUR
SHACKLE
PASTILLE CACHOU CANDLE
LOZENGE
PASTIME GAY TOY GAME PLOY
HOBBY SPORT GOSSIP OLEARY
SAILING PASTANCE AMUSEMENT
DIVERSION ABRIDGMENT
PASTOR HERD ANGEL RABBI CURATE
KEEPER PRIEST RECTOR DOMINIE
VICAIRE GUARDIAN MINISTER
SHEPHERD
PASTORAL POEM DRAMA RURAL
RUSTIC BUCOLIC CROSIER IDYLLIC
NOMADIC ROMANCE ARCADIAN
THEOCRITEAN
PASTORALIST SQUATTER
PASTRY PIE FLAN HUFF PUFF SOCK
TART TUCK CORNET DANISH ECLAIR
ABAISSE BRIOCHE CANNOLI
CARCAKE STRUDEL BAKEMEAT
EMPANADA NAPOLEON TALMOUSE
TURNOVER APPLEJACK
(— COOK) PASTLER
(— DOUGH) PHYLLO
(— SHELL) BOUCHEE DARIOLE
TIMBALE TALMOUSE
(— STRIPS) LATTICE
(— WHEEL) JAGGER
(KIND OF —) PUFF
(SWEET —) DOUCET
(PL.) PIROZKI PIROSHKI
PASTURAGE FEED GANG GATE
STRAY COLLOP EATAGE FORAGE
HERBAGE SHEEPGATE

PASTURE ALP FOG HAG HAM ING
LEA PEN TYE BENT FEED GAET GANG
GATE GISE GIST HAFT HALF HEAF
HOGA INGE KEEP PARK RAIK AGIST
DRIFT EJIDO GRASS GRAZE LAYER
LEASE RANGE VELDT INTAKE
MEADOW OUTRUN SAETER
COWGATE FOGGAGE GRAZING
HERBAGE LEALAND POTRERO
VACCARY VICTUAL HERDWICK
OUTFIELD SHEEPWALK
(— GRASS) TORE GRAMA
(— IN STUBBLE) SHACK
(— LAND) RAKE TACK LEASOW
(HILL —) HOGA
(MOUNTAIN —) SETER SAETER
SHIELING
(SHEEP —) HEAF EWELEASE
(SHETLAND I, —) SETER
(SUMMER —) AGOSTADERO
(WET —) SLINK
PASTURELAND BENT SOUM
PASTURING RELIEF PANNAGE
PASTY PIE PATE SLAB PATTY
DOUGHY FRACID SAMBOUSE
PAT APT DAB DIB TAP TIG BLOW CLAP
GLIB JUMP PALP TICK CHUCK FITLY
FIXED IMPEL THROW CARESS
DABBLE PRETTY SMOOGE SOOTHE
STRIKE STROKE TIMELY APROPOS
CHERISH FITTING PATAPAT READILY
SUITABLE PERTINENT SEASONABLE
PATAGIUM TEGULA TIPPET
SCAPULA PARACHUTE PTERYGODE
PATAGONIA (DEITY OF —) SETEBOS
(RODENT OF —) CAVY MARA
(TREE OF —) MANIU ALERCE ALERSE
PATAGONIAN HARE MARA
PATAMAR COURIER PATTAMAR
MESSENGER
PATAYAN YUMAN
PATCH BIT EKE FLY BOUT LAND
MEND SKIP SPOT SWAB SWOB VAMP
BLAZE BODGE CLOUT CLUMP COVER
FRIAR FUDGE PIECE SAVER SCRAP
SPECK SPLAT BLOTCH COBBLE
COOPER DOLLOP GORGET MOUCHE
PARCEL REVAMP SOLDER SPETCH
SWATCH TINKLE CLAMPER CLOBBER
INWEAVE PELIOMA REMNANT
(— AS ORNAMENT) MOUCHE
(— CLUMSILY) BOTCH CLOUT
CLAMPER
(— IN NEWSPAPER) FUDGE
(— OF COLOR) CLOUP DAPPLE
SPLASH SPECULUM
(— OF DARK HAIR) SMUT
(— OF DIRT) MIRE
(— OF FEATHERS) BIB CAP PTERYLA
(— OF ICE) RONE
(— OF LAND) RODHAM
(— OF LEATHER) SPECK

(— OF LIGHT) GLADE
(— OF PRINT) FUDGE
(— OF RUFFLED WATER) ACKER
(— OF SALIVA) SIXPENCE
(— OF TIRE) BOOT
(— ON BIRD'S BEAK) CERE
(— ON BIRD'S WING) SPECULUM
(— ON BOAT) TINGLE
(— ON HORSE) SNIP
(— ON PRINTED PAGE) FRIAR
(— ON THROAT) GORGET
(— TOGETHER) CONSARCINATE
(— UP) HEAL JUMP MEND FUDGE
SHUFFLE
(BALD —) AREA
(BLURRED —) FOG
(BOGGY —) LATCH LETCH
(CABBAGE —) KALEYARD
(ISOLATED —) POCKET
(KIND OF —) OIL
(LIVID —) PELIOMA
(OOZY —) SPEW SPUE
(OPEN — IN FOREST) CAMPO
(RANK —) DALLOP DOLLOP
(SHOULDER —) FLASH
PATCHOULI PACCIOLI PATCHLEAF
PATCHWORD WASTEWORD
PATCHWORK OLIO BOTCH CENTO
CENTON JUMBLE SCRAPS PATCHERY
FRAGMENTS PASTICCIO
PATE PIE TOP HEAD BROWN PASTE
PASTY PATTY BADGER NODDLE
NOGGIN COSTARD COXCOMB
PATELLA CAP PAN DISH VASE
ROTULA KNEECAP KNEEPAN
WHIRLBONE
PATEN ARCA DISC DISH DISK PLATE
PATINA PLATEN VESSEL
PATENT ARCA BALD OPEN BERAT
BROAD OVERT PLAIN SUNNUD
CHARTER EVIDENT LICENSE
OBVIOUS APPARENT ARCHIVES
MANIFEST PALPABLE PRIVILEGE
PATENTED BREVETE
PATER FATHER PRIEST
PATERFAMILIAS MASTER
PATERNAL FATHERLY
PATERNITY FATHER ORIGIN
PATESI ISHSHAKKU
PATH ARC PAD RIG RUN RUT TAN
WAY BERM FARE GATE LANE LEAD
LINE LODE RACE RACK ROAD TRIG
TROD WALK ALLEY BYWAY GOING
JETTY ORBIT PISTE ROUTE SPACE
TRACK TRACT TRADE TRAIL BOSTAL
BYPASS CAMINO CASAUN CIRCLE
COMINO COURSE GROOVE SLEUTH
SPHERE SWATHE TRENCH CHANNEL
ERGODIC FAIRWAY FOOTWAY
HIGHWAY LANDWAY MEANDER
PASSAGE RODDING SIDEWAY
TARIQAT TOWPATH TRAFFIC

TRUNDLE WAYGATE BORSTALL
CENTRODE CROSSCUT DRIFTWAY
TRAILWAY TWITCHEL CROSSWALK
(— BETWEEN HEDGES) TWITCHEL
(— CUT IN MOWING) SWATH
SWATHE
(— FOLLOWED BY ENERGY) ERGODIC
(— MADE BY ANIMAL) PIST PISTE
(— OF CELESTIAL BODY) ORBIT
(— OF CLOUDS) RACK
(— OF ELECTRIC CURRENT) CIRCUIT
(— OF MOVING POINT) CURVE
LOCUS
(— OF RACE) STRIP
(— OF SUN) ECLIPTIC
(— UP STEEP HILL) BOSTAL BORSTAL
BORSTALL
(BRIDLE —) SPURWAY
(BURIAL —) LICHWAY
(CLOSED —) CIRCUIT
(FORTIFICATION —) RELAIS
(GARDEN —) ALLEE
(NARROW —) BERM RACK TRIG
RODDIN TROCHA RODDING
(PHILIPPINE FOOT —) SENDA
(STEEP —) SLIDDER
(STONE-PAVED —) STEEN
(SUFI —) TARIQAT
(WINDING —) ESS
(WINDING —S) AMBAGES
(PREF.) HODO ODO
(SUFF.) ODE OID
PATHAN TURI AFRIDI SIVATI BAJOURI
BANGASH PAYTHAN DANGARIK
PATHETIC SAD SILLY TEARY TENDER
FORLORN PITIFUL DOLOROSO
PATETICO PITIABLE POIGNANT
STIRRING TOUCHING AFFECTING
PATHFINDER
(AUTHOR OF —) COOPER
(CHARACTER IN —) CAP DAVY MUIR
MABEL NATTY BUMPPO DUNHAM
JASPER MACNAB CHARLES
WESTERN SANGLIER ARROWHEAD
CHINGACHGOOK
PATHIC MORBID VICTIM PASSIVE
CATAMITE DISEASED SUFFERER
SUFFERING
PATHOGEN VIRUS
PATHOLOGICAL
(SUFF.)
(CONDITION) IA
PATHOLOGIST AMERICAN OPIE
ROUS SLYE EWING MOORE SMITH
WELCH MOHLER FLEXNER HEKTOEN
PRUDDEN WARTHIN WHIPPLE
RICKETTS GOODPASTURE
AUSTRALIAN POPPER
CANADIAN WESBROOK
DANISH FIBIGER
ENGLISH ADAMI BOYCE PAGET
ANNETT FLOREY WRIGHT SPILSBURY

GERMAN HENLE KLEBS TRAUBE
ZENKER VIRCHOW COHNHEIM
RECKLINGHAUSEN
IRISH STOKES
ITALIAN GUARNIERI
PATHOS BATHOS SNIVEL
POIGNANCY
PATHWAY (ALSO SEE PATH) RUN
LANE PATH RACK SLADE COURSE
RAMBLA RAMBLE RODDIN BORSTAL
RODDING
(RAISED —) CAUSEY CAUSEWAY
PATIENCE CALM THILD BEARANCE
STOICISM COMPOSURE ENDURANCE
FORTITUDE
PATIENT CASE CURE MEEK SOBER
BOVINE PASSIVE ENDURING
THOLEMOD SUFFERANT
(— OF ASYLUM) BEDLAM
(BE —) BEAR
(HYDROPATHIC —) WATERER
(MEDICAL —) CURE
PATIO COURT ATRIUM COURTYARD
PATOIS CANT GOMBO GUMBO
CREOLE JARGON PATTER DIALECT
GUERNSEY
(FRENCH —) JOUAL
PATOLA SARI GOURD
PATRIARCH JOB ABBA ENOS LEVI
NASI NOAH PAPA POPE ALDER ELDER
JACOB PITRI DESPOT JOSEPH
NESTOR ABRAHAM ANCIENT
VETERAN VENERABLE
(ETHIOPIAN —) ABUNA
PATRICIAN NOBLE EMPEROR
PATRICK MUELLMAN GENTLEMAN
PATRIMONY PORTION ANCESTRY
HERITAGE LONGACRE
PATRIOT LOVER AMATEUR
PATRIOTIC PUBLIC ENVELOPE
NATIONAL
PATRIPASSIAN NOETIAN
PATROCLUS (FATHER OF —)
MENOETIUS
(MOTHER OF —) PERIAPIS POLYMELE
STHENELE
(SLAYER OF —) HECTOR
PATROL GUARD SCOUT WATCH
STOOGE PATROLE PROTECT
PATROLMAN COP GUARD
FLATFOOT INSPECTOR
PATRON GOER BUYER GUEST STOOP
AVOWRY CLIENT FATHER FAUTOR
JAJMAN ACCOUNT PADRONE
PATROON PROCTOR SPONSOR
ADVOCATE CHAMPION CUSTOMER
DEFENDER GUARDIAN MAECENAS
(PL.) FOLLOWING
PATRONAGE AEGIS FAVOR AVOWRY
CUSTOM FAVOUR ACCOUNT
AUSPICE FOMENTO HEARING
AUSPICES BUSINESS PADROADO

(— AND CARE) AUSPICE
(— TO RELATIVES) NEPOTISM
(POLITICAL —) PAP
PATRONAL TITULAR
PATRONIZE USE DEIGN FAVOR
DEFEND FATHER PROMOTE PROTECT
EMPATRON FREQUENT
PATRON SAINT
(OF CRIPPLES) GILES
(OF ENGLAND) GEORGE
(OF FISHERMEN) PETER
(OF FRANCE) DENIS
(OF GOLDSMITHS) ELOY
(OF IRELAND) PATRICK
(OF LAWYERS) IVES
(OF NORWAY) OLAF
(OF PAINTERS) LUKE
(OF SAILORS) ELMO
(OF SCOTLAND) ANDREW
(OF SPAIN) SANTIAGO
(OF THIEVES) DISMAS
(OF WALES) DAVID
PATROON TRACT CAPTAIN
SUPPORTER
PATTEE FORMY FORMEE
PATTEN BASE CLOG FOOT SHOE
SKATE STAND STILT CHOPIN GALOSH
RACKET SANDAL CREEPER RACQUET
SUPPORT CIOPPINO SNOWSHOE
PATTER RAP CANT TALK TIRL ARGOT
LINGO HAPPER JARGON BLATHER
BLATTER CHATTER DIALECT
PATTERING PITAPAT
PATTERN CUT FUR SET BASE CAST
COMB COPY FORM GIMP IDEA LAUE
MOLD NORM PLAN SEME STAR
WAVE BISON BYSEN CHECK DECOR
DISME DRAFT EPURE GUIDE IDEAL
INLAY MODEL MOIRE MOULD NOTAN
PLAID SEMEE SHAPE WATER BASKET
BURELE CANVAS CHECKS DESIGN
DIAPER ENTAIL ETOILE FABRIC
FIGURE FLORAL FORMAT FORMER
LACERY MAGPIE MATRIX MIRROR
MODULE MUSTER ONDULE PATRON
POUNCE RANDOM RECIPE SAMPLE
SQUARE STRIPE SYSTEM ALLOVER
CHEVRON EXAMPLE FACONNE
FILLING FOLKWAY GESTALT GRIZZLE
HOBNAIL MEANDER MEANING
MULLION PARAGON PROJECT
SAMPLER SLEIGHT STENCIL
TEMPLET CALENDAR DENTELLE
DYNAMICS FILIGREE HATCHING
ILLUSION OVERSHOT PARADIGM
PLATFORM STRICKLE PROTOTYPE
(— AFTER) COPY
(— IN BRAIN) GYRATION
(— OF BEHAVIOR) HABIT DISPLAY
(— OF CADENCE) CURSUS
(— OF HINDU MUSIC) TALA
(— OF LARGE SQUARES) DAMIER

(— OF SCARS) KELOID
(— OF SEPARATE OBJECTS) SEME
(— OF STRESS) SUPERFIX
(— OF TARTAN) SET SEET SETT
SETTE
(— OF THOUGHT) GROUPTHINK
(— ON PAPER) BURELAGE
(— ON STAMP) GRILL GRILLE
(—S ON SILK) ARMURE
(— USED BY SILVERSMITHS) WORK
BOROON
(CHARACTERISTIC BEHAVIOR —) BIT
(CROSS-BARRED —) PLAID
(FABRIC —) PAISLEY
(FACIAL —) BLAZE
(FOOTBALL —) FLY
(FRET —) KEY
(GARMENT —) SLOPER
(HAT —) BLOCK
(KNITTING —) ARGYLE
(MASONRY —) SPICATUM
(MELODIC —) RAGA
(METRIC — OF HINDU MUSIC) TALA
(PORCELAIN —) FITZHUGH
(RUG —) AINALEH
(SCANNING —) RASTER
(SHOE —) FORME
(SKATING —) EDGE
(SOCIAL —) FAMILISM
(SPEECH —) IDIOLECT
(SPOTTED —) SEME
(SQUARED FABRIC —) TATTERSALL
(STRIPED —) BARRE
(SYMBOLIC —) MANDALA
(TAILOR'S —) PROTRACTOR
(TATTOO —) MOKO
(TREE —) HOM HOMA
(WEAVING —) DRAW
PATTERNED GOFFERED
PATTY TABLET BOUCHEE PRALINE
PATTYPAN VOLAUVENT
(— SHELL) DARIOLE TALMOUSE
CROUSTADE
PATTYPAN SQUASH CYMLING
PATULOUS OPEN SPREAD
DISTENDED
PAUCITY LACK DEARTH FEWNESS
EXIGUITY SCARCITY
PAUL PAOLO
(ASSOCIATE OF —) DEMAS SILAS
TITUS ARTEMAS BARNABAS
PAULDRON POLLET EPAULET
PALERON POLDRON POLLETTE
PAULINA (HUSBAND OF —) CAMILLO
ANTIGONUS
PAULLU (BROTHER OF —) MANCO
HUASCAR
PAULOPOST DEUTERIC
PAULOWNIA KIRI
PAUNCH TUN KITE KYTE BELLY
PENCH RUMEN ABDOMEN STOMACH
GUNDYGUT POTBELLY
PAUNCHY BLOATED

PAUPER BEGGAR INDIGENT
ROUNDSMAN
PAUPERISM BEGGARY
PAUSANIAS (FATHER OF —)
CLEOMBROTUS
PAUSE HO HEM HALT HANG HOLD
LULL REST RUFE STAY STOP WAIT
ABIDE BREAK CEASE CHECK COMMA
DELAY DEMUR DEVAL DWELL HOVER
LETUP LIMMA POISE SELAH TARRY
TENOR BREACH BREATH CORONA
CUTOFF FALTER HANKER HIATUS
PERIOD STANCE CAESURA FERMATA
RESPITE VIRGULE BREATHER
INTERVAL
(— BEFORE HURDLE) DWELL
(SUDDEN —) CHECK
(PL.) LIMMATA CAESURAE
PAUT PAW POKE POWT STAMP
FINGER
PAVANE DANCE PADUAN
PASSAMEZZO
PAVE LAY TAR PATH STUD TILE COVER
FLOOR CAUSEY COBBLE QUARRY
SMOOTH OVERLAY PREPARE
RUDERATE MACADAMIZE
(— WITH STONES) STEEN CAUSEY
PAVED COBBLED
PAVEMENT SARN SLAB HEARTH
PAEPAE TARMAC ASPHALT
MACADAM MADADAM TELFORD
ASAROTUM FLAGGING FLOORING
PATHMENT PEDIMENT PITCHING
SIDEWALK TROTTOIR WASHBOARD
PAVER CUBER PAVIOR
PAVID TIMID AFRAID FEARFUL
PAVILION BASE FLAG TELD TENT
FOLLY KIOSK PINNA ROYAL STAND
CANOPY ENSIGN HOWDAH LITTER
PANDAL PALLION COVERING
GLORIETTE
(— ON ELEPHANT) HOUDAH
HOWDAH
PAVILLON CHINOIS CRESCENT
PAVING FLAG SETT BLOCK BRICK
DALLE PAVER STEAN STEEN STONE
COBBLE TARMAC ASPHALT TELFORD
PITCHING PITCHSTONE
(SQUARE —) MITCHEL
PAVIS COVER PAVADE PAVOIS SHIELD
PROTECT
PAW PAT PUD TOE CLAW FOOT GAUM
GRAB HAND MAUL PATY PAUT PORT
FLAIL PATTE TRICK CLUTCH FUMBLE
HANDLE PATTEE CRUBEEN FLIPPER
FORELEG FOREFOOT
PAWKY SLY ARCH BOLD CANNY
SAUCY CRAFTY LIVELY SHREWD
CUNNING FROWARD SQUEAMISH
PAWL COG DOG BOLT HAND SEAR
STOP TENT TRIP CATCH CLICK
DETENT FINGER PALLET TONGUE
CLAWKER RATCHET

PAWN DIP POP WED FINE GAGE HOCK
SOAK VAMP WAGE SPOUT SWEAT
ENGAGE LUMBER OBLIGE PIGNUS
PLEDGE WADSET COUNTER
HOSTAGE PEACOCK CHESSMAN
MOSKENEER TRIBULATION
(PL.) PHALANX

PAWNBROKER MOUNT UNCLE
BROKER LUMBERER MONEYLENDER

PAWNEE PANEE SKIDI WATER
ALMOND BISCUIT PLEDGEE

PAWNIE PAWN PEACOCK

PAWNSHOP PAWN SPOUT LUMBER
LOMBARD POPSHOP
(UNLICENSED —) TIDDLYWINK

PAX BOARD PEACE TRUCE FRIEND
TABLET

PAXWAX WHITELEATHER

PAY DO BUY FEE POP TIP ANTE FOOT
FORK GIVE MEET RENT SOLD WAGE
BATTA CLEAR COUGH DOUSE PLANK
PUTUP REMIT SCREW SHEPE SOUND
WAGES YIELD ANSWER RETAIL
DEFRAY IMPEND PONYUP REWARD
SALARY SETTLE COMMUTE
DEADRAY HALVANS IMBURSE
REQUITE SATISFY SOULDIE STIPEND
TRIBUTE RECOMPENSE
(— ATTENTION) DIG SEE COME
GAUM HARK HEED TENT ADVERT
REGARD AUDIENT
(— COURT TO) NUT SUE GALLANT
(— DOWN) DOUSE
(— FLIRTATIOUS ADVANCES) QUEEN
(— FOR) ABY BUY BYE COUP ABIDE
COVER LLUUT STAND ABEGGE
(— FOR LIQUOR) BIRL
(— HEAVY PENALTY) SMART EXPIATE
(— HOMAGE) CHEFE CHEVE CHIVE
SALAAM ADULATE
(— IN ADVANCE) IMPRESS
(— MONEY) PINGLE
(— OFF) LIFT SINK ACQUIT
(— OF SOLDIER) SAWDEE
(— OUT) VEER BLEED SPEND STUMP
EXPEND DISBURSE
(— PART OF) DEFRAY
(— PENALTY) ABY ABYE
(— TAXES) GILD
(— UP) ANTE QUIT SETTLE
LIQUIDATE
(— WITH IOU) VOWEL
(ADVANCE —) IMPREST
(DAILY —) DIET
(EXTRA —) BATTA BONUS KICKBACK
(SMALL —) SCREW

PAYABLE DUE CARTAL

PAYEE HOLDER ENDORSER

PAYMASTER BAKSHI BUKSHI
PURSER BUKSHEE PAGADOR

PAYMENT CRO DUE FEE TAX DILL
CENS DOES DOLE DUTY ERIC FEAL
FINE GALE GILD HIRE LEVY MAIL

MISE TACK TOLL BONUS CANON
CLAIM GAVEL MAILL MENSE MODUS
PREST PRICE YIELD ANGILD BOUNTY
CHARGE LINAGE LOBOLA OUTLAY
PAYOLA PLEDGE REBATE RETURN
REWARD TARIFF ADVANCE ALIMONY
ANNUITY BENEFIT CUSTOMS
DEPOSIT FOOTAGE GARNISH
PANNAGE PENSION PRIMAGE
SOLUTIO STIPEND SUBSIDY SUBSIST
TREWAGE TUITION CASUALTY
FOREGIFT GRATUITY KICKBACK
MALIKANA MARITAGE MONEYAGE
TREASURY WOODGELD HEADPENNY
MALGUZARI
(— BY CLERGYMAN) SYNODAL
(— FOR INJURY) UTU
(— FOR LABOR) MEED
(— FOR OFFENSE) ENACH
(— FOR RELEASE) LOOSING
(— FOR RERUN) RESIDUAL
(— FOR USE) RENT
(— IN ADVANCE) PREST
(— IN GOODS) TRUCK
(— IN KIND) SPECIE
(— OF DEBT) SOLUTION
(— OF FEE) FEAL
(— OF MINERS) FOOTAGE YARDAGE
(— ON DELIVERY) COD
(— TO SECURE FAVOR) PAYOLA
(ADVANCE —) ANTE
(DEMAND —) DUN BILL
(EVADE —) BILK DEFAULT
(FIXED —) FARM MODUS
(HOMICIDE'S —) KELCHIN
(INSURANCE —) PREMIUM
(PARTIAL —) INSTALMENT
INSTALLMENT
(PERIODICAL —) GALE GAVEL
(RENT —) GALE
(SECRET —) PAYOLA

PAYNIM PAGAN PANIME HEATHEN
INFIDEL PAGANDOM

PAYOFF FIX SOP DRIBE CLIMAX
PROFIT REWARD DECISIVE
RECKONING

PDQ ASAP IMMEDIATELY

PEA DAL TUR DHAL GRAM LANG SEED
ARHAR CHICK CICER GANDUL
LEGUME PIGEON PODDER CARMELE
CATJANG KHESARI PODWARE
TANGIER GARVANRO MARROWFAT
(— DOVE) ZENAIDA
(— HARVESTER) VINER
(— PETAL) KEEL
(—S AND BEANS) PULSE
(EARLY —S) HASTINGS
(PARCHED —S) CARLS CARLINS
(PL.) POIS GRAIN
(PREF.) PISI

PEABIRD ORIOLE WRYNECK

PEACE PAX CALM EASE FINE LIOS
LISS REST AMITY FRITH GRITH LISSE

QUIET TRUCE REPOSE SAUGHT
SHALOM CONCORD HARMONY
REQUIEM SERENITY
(— MAKER) TREATY
(— OF MIND) ATARAXIA
(GODDESS OF —) IRENE
(SYMBOL OF —) DOVE TOGA OLIVE
(PREF.) PACI
PEACEABLE FAIR SOME CIVIL
DOUCE QUIET STILL GENTLE SILVER
ORDERLY PACIFIC SOLOMON
AMICABLE SACKLESS
PEACEFUL CALM SOME SOBER
STILL IRENIC PLACID SILVER
HALCYON ORDERLY PACIFIC
PEACE PIPE CALUMET
PEACH BLAB PAVY CLING PAVIE
SNEAK SPLIT TRUMP ACCUSE
BETRAY CARMAN CROSBY FOSTER
INDICT INFORM OREJON PEENTO
SALWEY BRUNION ELBERTA PERSIAN
PIENTAO WHITTLE CRAWFORD
ISABELLA RARERIPE ROSEWORT
NECTARINE VICTORINE
(— STATE) GEORGIA
(— STONE) PUTAMEN
PEACHBLOW FAKIR
PEACHY FINE DANDY
PEACOCK MAO PAON PAVO
PAWN POSE PEKOK STRUT PAJOCK
PAVONE POWNIE PEAFOWL
PHASIANID
(— TAIL) TRAIN
(CONGO —) AFROPAVO
(EYELIKE SPOT ON —) OCELLUS
PEACOCK BITTERN SUN
PEACOCK BUTTERFLY IO
PEACOCK FISH WRASSE
PEACOCK FLOWER FLAMBEAU
POINCIANA
PEA CRAB PINNOTERE
PEAG TAX TOLL BEADS PAAGE PEACK
PEAGE PEDAGE WAMPUM
PEAI PIAY PIACHE
PEA JACKET PEACOAT
PEAK ALP BEN NAB NOB PAP PIC TOP
TOR ACME APEX BEAK CIMA CUSP
DENT DOLT DOME KNOB KNOT PICO
PIKE TOLT BLOOM CREST CROWN
PIQUE PITCH PITON POINT SLINK
SNEAK SPIRE STEAL STUMP CLIMAX
CUPULA SHASTA SHRINK SUMMIT
ZENITH EPITOME MAXIMUM
PICACHO CENTROID
(— OF ANCHOR) PEE
(— OF CAP) SCOOP
(— OF ENERGY) NUCLEUS
(ICE —) SERAC
(ISOLATED —) TOLT
(SHARP —) HORN AIGUILLE
(SNOW-CAPPED —) DOME CALOTTE
(PREF.) ACR(O)

PEAKED WAN PALE THIN DRAWN
PIKED SHARP COPPED SICKLY
SLIMSY POINTED SLIMPSY
PEAKEDNESS KURTOSIS
PEAL CLAP RING TOLL CHIME CRACK
GRILSE SHOVEL MINNING RESOUND
SUMMONS THUNDER CARILLON
(— OF THUNDER) CLAP REEL
PEANUT BUR FLAX MANI MEAN
PETTY PINDA GOOBER LEGUME
PINDAL ARACHIS BEENNUT
ARACHIDE EARTHPEA GRASSNUT
KATCHUNG VALENCIA MONKEYNUT
(— DISEASE) TIKKA
PEA POD COB PYSE QUASH PESCOD
(POORLY FILLED —) POP
(UNRIPE —) SQUASH
PEAR BOSC BURY DIEGO MELON
NELIS SABRA BEURRE BURREL
COLMAR PANINI SECKEL WARDEN
WINTER KIEFFER PEPERIN PRICKLY
AMBRETTE BERGAMOT BLANQUET
MUSCATEL TASAJILLO
(PRICKLY —) TUNA NOPAL OPUNTIA
(PREF.) PIRI PIRO PYRI
PEAR HAW THORN
PEARL GEM MABE TERN GRAIN
NACRE ONION PICOT UNION
BOUTON OLIVET ORIENT BAROQUE
BLISTER PARAGON BDELLIUM
CATARACT MOONBEAM MARGARITE
(— WEIGHT) TANK
(IMITATION —) OLIVET
(IRREGULAR —) SLUG
(KIND OF —) MOBE
(MOCK —) OLIVET
(PIERCED —) WIDOW
(SEED —) ALIOFAR
(SMOKED —) MITRAILLE
(PREF.) PERLI
PEARL BLUE METAL
PEARL BLUSH ROSETAN
PEARL FISHERS, THE (CHARACTER
IN —) LEILA NADIR ZURGA
NOURABAD
(COMPOSER OF —) BIZET
PEARL MILLET KOUS BAJRA
CUMBU DUCHN DUKHN KOUSE
JONDLA DAGASSA
PEARLSIDES ARGENTIN
PEARLWEED SAGINA POVERTY
SEALWORT
PEARLY NACRY NACROUS
MARGARIC PRECIOUS
PEARLY EVERLASTING LIVELONG
MOONSHINE
PEAR-SHAPED FULL MELLOW
ROUNDED PYRIFORM
PEASANT TAO BOND BOOR HERA
HIND KERN KONO KOPI PEON RAYA
RYOT SERF BAIRU BOWER CHURL
KNAVE KULAK RAYAH SWAIN

CARLOT COTMAN COTTAR FARMER
FELLAH RASCAL RUSTIC BONDMAN
LABORER PAISANO VILLAIN
CHOPSTICK CONTADINO
(— CLASS) JACQUERIE
(— OF INDIA) RYOT KISAN RAIYAT
(ARABIC —) FELLAH
(IRISH —) KERN KERNE
(ITALIAN —) CONTADINO
(RUSSIAN —) KULAK MUZHIK
MUZJIK

PEASANTS (AUTHOR OF —)
REYMONT
(CHARACTER IN —) KUBA ROCH
ANTEK HANKA SIMON YAGNA YANEK
BORYNA NASTKA TERESA MATTHEW
MATTHIAS DOMINIKOVA

PEASCOD (UNRIPE —) SQUASH
PEASE CROW TERN
PEASHOOTER TRUNK BLOWER
PISTOL BLOWGUN

PEAT GOR PET SOD VAG COOM FUEL
MIST MOOR MUCK MULL TURF
COOMB YARFA LAWYER MINION
YARPHA DARLING FAVORITE
(— BOG) CESS YARPHA
(— CUTTER) PINER
(— SPADE) SLADE TUSKAR TWISCAR
(DRIED — FOR FUEL) VAG
(LAYER OF —) FLAW

PEA TREE KATURAI
PEATY KETTY
PEBA PEVA ARMADILLO
PEBBLE DIB FLAX JACK PLUM CHUCK
SCREE STONE BANTAM COGGLE
GIBBER GRAVEL QUARTZ SHILLA
SYCITE CHUCKIE CRYSTAL SHINGLE
STANNER JACKSTONE
(PL.) BEACH DREIKANTER
(PREF.) CALCULI CHALICO PSEPH(O)
THRIO

PEBBLY BEACHY
PECAN NOGAL PACANE
PECCADILLO FAULT OFFENSE
MISCHIEF
PECCANT FAULTY MORBID CORRUPT
SINNING DISEASED
PECCARY HOG SWINE JAVALI
WARREE TAGASSU TAYASSU
JAVELINA TAYASSUID
PECK DAB DOT JOB NIP BEAK BILL
CARP FOOD GRUB HOLE JERK KISS
PYKE PITCH PRICK STOCK THROW
HATFUL NIBBLE PEGGLE PICKLE
PIERCE STROKE CHIMBLE
(1-4TH OF —) LIPPY FORPET FORPIT
LIPPIE
PECKER BILL NOSE COURAGE
SPIRITS
PECTEN COMB MARSUPIUM
PECTORAL SANDPIPER JACK
PERT PEERT BROWNY BROWNIE

CHOROOK CREAKER FATBIRD
HAYBIRD KRIEKER SQUATTER
TRIDDLER JACKSNIPE
PECULATE STEAL MISUSE
EMBEZZLE
PECULIAR ODD VERY QUEER WEIRD
PROPER QUAINT UNIQUE CURIOUS
PRIVATE SEVERAL SPECIAL STRANGE
UNUSUAL SEPARATE SINGULAR
SPECIFIC
(— TO ONESELF) PRIVATE
(PREF.) IDIO
PECULIARITY KINK IDIOM QUIRK
TRAIT TRICK TWIST IDIASM ODDITY
AEOLISM ANOMALY FEATURE
IRISHRY CROTCHET HEADMARK
MANNERISM PROPRIETY
SINGULARITY
(— IN BOWL) BIAS
(— OF SPEECH) IDIOLOGISM
(CROTCHETY —) FIKE
PECUNIARY POCKET MONETARY
FINANCIAL
PED BASKET HAMPER PANIER
PEDAGOGUE TUTOR PEDANT
DOMINIE SQUEERS TEACHER
THWACKUM
PEDAGOGY SCHOOL DIDACTICS
EDUCATION
PEDAHEL (FATHER OF —) AMMIHUD
PEDAHZUR (SON OF —) GAMALIEL
PEDAIAH (BROTHER OF —)
SALATHIEL
(DAUGHTER OF —) ZEBUDAH
(FATHER OF —) PAROSH
(SON OF —) JOEL
PEDAL LEVER SWELL TREADLE
FOOTFEED PEDALIAN THROTTLE
(— COUPLER) TIRASSE
(BICYCLE —) RATTRAP
(KIND OF —) WAWA WAHWAH
(PIANO —) CELESTE
(PIANO SOFTENING —) CELESTE
PEDAL POINT DRONE
PEDANT PRIG DUNCE TUTOR
DORBEL PURIST TASSEL ACADEME
PEDAGOG GAMALIEL DRYASDUST
OLOFERNES
PEDANTIC BLUE STODGY BOOKISH
DONNISH ERUDITE INKHORN
TEACHING SCHOLASTIC
PEDDLE HAWK SELL CADGE SHOVE
TRANT TRUCK HIGGLE MEDDLE
PIDDLE RETAIL COLPORT
(— OVERPRICED TICKETS) SCALP
PEDDLER ARAB SMOUS BADGER
BODGER CRAMER JAGGER JOWTER
MUGGER STROLL WALKER YAGGER
CHAPMAN NIGGLER PACKMAN
ROADMAN SANDBOY SWADDER
TRUGGER TRUCKER HUCKSTER
BOXWALLAH DUSTYFOOT

(— OF DOPE) FIXER
(— OF DRESS PIECES) DUDDER
(— OF FISH) RIPIER RIPPIER
(— OF SHAM JEWELRY) DUFFER
(BOOK —) COLPORTEUR
(ITINERANT —) SMOUS SMOUSE
SMOUSER STROLLER
(MOHAM. —) BORA
(STREET —) CAMELOT
(WARES OF —) TROGGIN
PEDESTAL ANTA BASE BASIS BLOCK
SOCLE STAND PILLAR PODIUM
ROCKER AKROTER SUPPORT
PADMASANA ACROTERIUM
(— PART) DADO
PEDESTRIAN PED DULL FOOT SLOW
HIKER FOOTER HOOFER WALKER
FOOTMAN PROSAIC PLODDING
WINGLESS PONDEROUS
VOETGANGER PERIPATETIC
PEDICAB TRISHAW
PEDICEL RAY STEM SCAPE STALK
PEDUNCLE FOOTSTALK
PEDIGREE STEMMA DESCENT
LINEAGE ANCESTRY PETEGREU
PUREBRED
PEDIMENT FRONTAL FRONTON
FASTIGIUM
PEDIPALP
(PL.) LABIUM
PEDOMETER ODOGRAPH
WAYWISER
PEDRERO PERRIER PETRARY
PEDUNCLE STEM SCAPE STALK
STIPES PEDICEL EYESTALK
HYPOCARP
(PL.) CRURA
PEEK PEEP PIKE GLANCE GLIMPSE
PEEKABOO PEEP BOPEEP PEEPEYE
PEEL BARK HARL HULL HUSK PARE
RIND SKIN FLAKE FLIPE SCALE SLIPE
STAKE STRIP CORTEX SHOVEL
SPITTLE UNDRESS BARKPEEL
ORANGEADO
(— OFF) HARL CRAZE FLAKE SHUCK
(BAKER'S —) PALE SPITTLE
(ORANGE OR LEMON —) ZEST
ORANGEAT
PEELER CRAB BOBBY CORER
HUSTLER SHEDDER SPUDDER
PILLAGER
PEELING RIND SKIN PARING
PARURE
PEEN PIN PYNE RIVET
PEEP PIP PRY SPY COOK JEEP KEEK
KOOK PEEK PEER PINK PULE SKEG
STEP TOOT TOTE TOUT CHEEP CHIRP
DEKKO GLINT PIPIT SNOOP TWEET
DEGREE GLANCE SQUEAK SQUINNY
PEEKABOO
(— SHOW) RAREE
PEEPER EYE TOM FROG KEEK
VOYEUR

PEEPHOLE PEEP JUDAS EYELET
CREVICE
PEEPING NOSY PRYING
PEEPING TOM VOYEUR
PEER PRY DUKE EARL FEAR GAZE
LOOK LORD MATE PEEP PINK TOOT
TOUT BARON EQUAL GLINT GLOZE
MATCH NOBLE RIVAL STARE STIME
THANE TWIRE APPEAR FELLOW
OLIVER PINKER COMPERE
PEERAGE RANK DEBRETT DIGNITY
BARONAGE NOBILITY TENEMENT
PEER GYNT (AUTHOR OF —) IBSEN
(CHARACTER IN —) ASE BOYG GYNT
PEER ANITRA HEGSTAD SOLVEIG
PEERING SQUINNY
PEERLESS SUPREME MATCHLESS
NONPAREIL UNRIVALED
PEESWEEP FINCH PEWIT LAPWING
PEEWEEP
PEEVE IRK ANNOY GRUDGE NETTLE
IRRITATE
PEEVISH SOUR CROSS DORTY
PENSY SNACK TECHY TEENY TESTY
TETTY THRAW TIFFY WEMOD
CRUSTY FRANZY GIRNIE HIPPED
PATCHY SNARLY SNUFFY SULLEN
TATTER TOUCHY TWARLY TWAZZY
TWITTY UPPISH UPPITY VAPORY
CRABBED FRATCHY FRECKET
FRETFUL FROWARD GROUCHY
PETTISH SPLEENY TEDIOUS TIFFISH
WASPISH CAPTIOUS PERVERSE
PETULANT PHRAMPEL PINDLING
SANSHACH TWANKING
FRAMPOLD,PETULANT
PEEVISHLY CRUSTILY
PEEVISHNESS PET BILE
PETULANCE
PEEWEE BOOT RUNT TINY PEWEE
MARBLE LAPWING
PEG FIX HOB HUB NOB NOG PIN TEE
HOBB KING KNAG PLUG SCOB SHAG
SKEG STEP CLEAT DOWEL DRINK
NOTCH PERCH PITON PRONG SPELL
SPILE SPILL STAKE THOLE THROW
TOOTH WADDY DEGREE DOWELL
FAUCET MARKER NORMAN PICKET
REASON SPIGOT TAPOUN TIPCAT
PINNING PRETEXT SCOLLOP
SPERKET SUPPORT TRENAIL
(— FOR PLAYING GAME) CAT SPILIKIN
(— FOR SADDLES) SPERKET
(— OF FAUCET) SPIGOT
(— OF STRINGED INSTRUMENT)
CHEVILLE
(— OUT) DIE FAIL
(BELAYING —) KEVEL
(IRON —) PITON
(THATCH —) SCOB
PEGA REMORA
PEGALL BASKET PACKALL
PEGASUS QUAVIVER HYPOSTOME

PEG TOP PIRY PEERY PEERIE
PEG WOFFINGTON (AUTHOR
  OF —) READE
  (CHARACTER IN —) PEG RICH VANE
  HARRY MABEL CIBBER COLLEY
  CHARLES TRIPLET POMANDER
  WOFFINGTON BRACEGIRDLE
PEIGNOIR GOWN DRESS KIMONO
  NEGLIGEE
PEISE BLOW FORCE PASSE POISE
  POIZE IMPACT WEIGHT BALANCE
  POISURE
PEKAH (FATHER OF —) REMALIAH
  (SLAYER OF —) HOSHEA
PEKAHIAH (FATHER OF —)
  MENAHEM
  (SLAYER OF —) PEKAH
PEKAN WEJACK
PEKING MAN SINANTHROPUS
PELAGE FUR COAT HAIR PILAGE
PELAGIC MARINE AQUATIC OCEANIC
  PELAGIAN
PELAIAH (FATHER OF —) ELIOENAI
PELALIAH (FATHER OF —) AMZI
PELATIAH (FATHER OF —) BENAIAH
  HANANIAH
PELEG (BROTHER OF —) JOKTAN
  (FATHER OF —) EBER
PELET (FATHER OF —) JAHDAI
  AZMAVETH
PELETH (FATHER OF —) JONATHAN
  (SON OF) ON
PELEUS (BROTHER OF —) TELAMON
  (FATHER OF —) AEACUS
  (HALF BROTHER OF —) PHOCUS
  (MOTHER OF —) ENDEIS
  (SON OF —) PELIDES ACHILLES
  (WIFE OF —) THETIS ANTIGONE
PELF GAIN DOOTY LUCRE MONEY
  SPOIL TRASH PILFER PILFRE REFUSE
  RICHES WEALTH COMPOST
PELIAS (BROTHER OF —) NELEUS
  (DAUGHTER OF —) ALCESTIS
  (FATHER OF —) POSEIDON
  (MOTHER OF —) TYRO
  (SON OF —) ACASTUS
  (WIFE OF —) ANAXIBIA PHYLOMACHE
PELICAN DOVE ALCATRAS
  ONOCROTAL
  (— STATE) LOUISIANA
PELISSE POSTIN POSTEEN
PELL BEAT PELE PELT HURRY PEELE
  HASTEN
PELLAGRA MAIDISM PELAGRA
PELLEAS (BELOVED OF —)
  MELISANDE
  (BROTHER OF —) GOLAUD
PELLEAS ET MELISANDE
  (CHARACTER IN —) ARKEL GOLAUD
  YNIOLD PELLEAS ALLEMONDE
  GENEVIEVE MELISANDE
  (COMPOSER OF —) DEBUSSY
PELLES (DAUGHTER OF —) ELAINE

PELLET BB WAD BALL CAST PILL
  SHOT BOLUS PRILL STONE BEEBEE
  BULLET FECULA OGRESS PILULE
  CASTING GRANULE PALLION TRATTLE
  BUCKSHOT GUNSTONE HAILSTONE
  (RAIN —S) HAIL
  (SNOW —S) GRAUPEL
  (PL.) SHOT
PELLICLE FILM SCUM SKIN CRUST
  CUTICLE EPISTASIS
PELLINORE (SLAYER OF —) GAWAIN
  (SON OF —) TORRE DORNAR
  LAMEROK PERCIVAL AGGLOVALE
PELLITORY BERTRAM BERTRUM
  WALLWORT
PELL-MELL RUSH MELPELL
  DISORDER HEADLONG
PELLOCK PALACH PORPOISE
PELLUCID CLEAR BRIGHT LIMPID
  ORIENT CRYSTAL
PELMA TRACK
PELMET CORNICE VALANCE
  PALMETTE
PELOPONNESUS (CITY OF —)
  SPARTA
  (PEOPLE OF —) MOREOTE
  (RIVER GOD OF —) ALPHEUS
PELOPS (FATHER OF —) TANTALUS
  (SON OF —) ATREUS TROEZEN
  PITTHEUS THYESTES
  (WIFE OF —) HIPPODAMIA
PELORIA EPANODY
PELOTA (— BASKET) CESTA
PELT FUR KIT BEAR BEAT BLOW CAPE
  CAST CLOD COON DASH FELL HIDE
  HURL KITT PELL PUSH RACK SKIN
  BESET CHUNK FITCH HURRY SABLE
  SLASH SPEED STONE WHACK
  BADGER BEAVER FISHER PELTER
  PEPPER SERVAL SPRING BETHUMP
  COONSKIN
  (— OF SEAL, WITH BLUBBER) SCULP
  (— WITH MISSILES) BUM SQUAIL
  (— WITH STONES) LAPIDATE
  (BEAVER —) BLANKET
PELTAST SOLDIER TARGETEER
PELTATE SCUTATE
PELTER SKEET
PELTING SLASHING
PELTRY FURS SKINS
PELUDO POYOU ARMADILLO
PELVIS
  (PREF.) PELVI(O) PELYCO PYEL(O)
  (SUFF.) PELLIC
PEN BIC CAN COT CUB GET HOK MEW
  PAR PIN STY BOLT CAGE COOP CROO
  CROW FAUD FOLD JAIL STUB WALK
  YARD BUGHT CRAWL CREEP CUBBY
  HUTCH KRAAL POINT QUILL STYLE
  WRITE BOUGHT CORRAL CRUIVE
  FASTEN FLIGHT HURDLE INDITE
  RECORD STYLUS ZAREBA CONFINE
  WARKLOOM

(— BRAND) CLIC
(— CATTLE) STANCE
(— FOR CATTLE) CUB LOT CREW
CRUE LAIR REEVE
(— FOR ELEPHANTS) KRAAL
(— FOR HOGS OR SLAVES) CRAWL
(— OF CUTTLEFISH) GLADIUS
(— POINT) NEB NIB STUB
(— UP) FRANK STIVE
(AUTHOR'S —) STYLE STYLUS
(BALLPOINT —) BIRO
(FOUNTAIN —) STICK
(KIND OF —) POISON
(MUSIC —) RASTRUM
(REED —) CALAMUS
PENALIZE CHECK
PENALTY BETE CAIN COST DOOM
FINE LOSS PAIN BEAST JUISE MULCT
AMENDE AMERCE SOLACE FORFEIT
NEMESIS SURSIZE BLOODWIT
HARDSHIP SCAFFOLD
(DRINKING —) KELTIE
PENANCE TAP SORE SHRIFT
SORROW REMORSE SUFFERING
(DO —) ATONE
PEN CASE PENNER POPPET
PENCEL FLAG PENNON STREAMER
PENNONCEL
PENCHANT BENT TASTE FOIBLE
GENIUS LIKING LEANING FONDNESS
PENCIL PEN RED WAD BLUE LEAD
WADD LINER SHEAF SKETCH STYLUS
POINTEL CHARCOAL KEELIVINE
(PART OF —) CASE LEAD POINT
ERASER FERRULE SHOULDER
(SLATE —) CAM CALM SKAILLIE
(PL.) STATIONERY
(PREF.) PENCILLI PENICILLI
PENCILWOOD MORDORE
PEND HANG
PENDANT BOB JAG DROP FLAG
JAGG PEND TAIL AGLET BULLA
GUTTA POINT AIGLET LUSTER
PALAOA PLAYER TABARD TARGET
TASSEL EARDROP LANGUET
SUPPORT LAVALIER
PENDENNIS (AUTHOR OF —)
THACKERAY
(CHARACTER IN —) BELL AMORY
EMILY FANNY FOKER HELEN HENRY
LAURA ARTHUR BOLTON GEORGE
JEMIMA BLANCHE FRANCIS
ALTAMONT COSTIGAN CLAVERING
PENDENNIS WARRINGTON
THISTLEWOOD
PENDENT LOP BAGGED ICICLE
HANGING PROMISS
PENDICLE POFFLE
PENDING NISI
PENDULOUS LOP SLOUCH
HANGING NODDING PENSILE
CERNUOUS DROOPING

PENDULUM SWING PENDLE
SWINGEL SWINGLE VIBRATILE
(INVERTED —) NODDY
PENELOPE (FATHER-IN-LAW OF —)
LAERTES
(FATHER OF —) ICARIUS
(HUSBAND OF —) ULYSSES
ODYSSEUS
(MOTHER OF —) PERIBOEA
(SON OF —) TELEMACHUS
(SUITOR OF —) AGELAUS
PENEPLAIN STRATH ENDRUMPF
PENETRABLE PERVIOUS
PENETRATE CUT DIG DIP SEE BITE
BORE DIVE GORE PASS PINK SINK
STAB WADE BREAK DRILL DRIVE
ENTER IMBUE PROBE SEIZE THIRL
CLEAVE FATHOM FICCHE GIMLET
INVADE PIERCE RIDDLE SEARCH
STRIKE THRILL WIMBLE DISCERN
PERVADE PERCOLATE PERFORATE
(— MENTALLY) ENTER
(— ONE'S MIND) SOAK
PENETRATED (EASILY —) MELLOW
PENETRATING ACID KEEN ACUTE
LEVEL NASAL SHARP ASTUTE
DEADLY SHREWD SHRILL SUBTLE
GIMLETY INGOING INTRANT
KNOWING PUNGENT PERCEANT
PIERCING REACHING TRENCHANT
PENETRATION DEPTH ACUMEN
FATHOM INROAD INGOING INSIGHT
SEEPAGE INCISION INVASION
SAGACITY
(IMAGINATIVE —) INSIGHT
PENEUS (DAUGHTER OF —) DAPHNE
(FATHER OF —) OCEANUS
(MOTHER OF —) TETHYS
(SON OF —) HYPSEUS
PENGUIN AUK DIVER GENTU ADELIE
ARCTIC DIPPER GENTOO JOHNNY
PINWING BREVIPED MACARONI
ROCKHOPPER
(PL.) IMPENNES
(PREF.) SPHENISCI SPHENISCO
PENGUIN ISLAND (AUTHOR OF —)
FRANCE
(CHARACTER IN —) MAEL CLENA
CRRES DRACO OLIVE PYROT TALPA
AGARIC KRAKEN TRINCO VISIRE
EVELINE BOSCENOS CLARENCE
GREATANK JOHANNES OBEROSIA
CHATILLON MARBODIUS
PENINNAH (HUSBAND OF —)
ELKANAH
(SON OF —) SAMUEL
PENINSULA CAPE MULL NECK INDIA
BILAND BYLAND ISLAND PENILE
CHERSONESE
PENIS
(PREF.) BALAN(I)(O) PHALL(O)
POSTH(E)(IO)(O)

PENITENCE RUE REGRET SORROW
PENANCE PENANCY REMORSE
PENITENT RUER SORRY HUMBLE
WEEPER MOURNER STANDER
CONTRITE
(— OF 3RD STAGE) KNEELER
PENITENTIARY JUG PEN JAIL STIR
TENCH PRISON PENITENT
PENMAN CLERK AUTHOR SCRIBE
WRITER
PENMANSHIP HAND SCRIPT
PENSHIP WRITING
PENNANT FANE FLAG WHIP COLOR
ROGER BANNER BURGEE CORNET
ENSIGN PENCIL PENNON PENSIL
PINION PINNET MEATBALL REPEATER
STREAMER
PENNILESS POOR BROKE NEEDY
SKINT BANKRUPT INDIGENT
STRAPPED PLACKLESS
PENNON FLAG VANE WING ANVIL
BANNER PENCIL PENOUN PINION
FEATHER GONFANON

PENNSYLVANIA
CAPITAL: HARRISBURG
COLLEGE: JUNIATA URSINUS
LYCOMING
COUNTY: ELK ERIE PIKE YORK BERKS
BUCKS PERRY TIOGA LEHIGH
CAMBRIA JUNIATA LUZERNE
VENANGO WYOMING LYCOMING
MOUNTAIN RANGE: POCONO
ALLEGHENY
NATIVE: AMISH DUTCH
PRESIDENT: BUCHANAN
RIVER: LEHIGH CLARION JUNIATA
LICKING TOWANDA CALDWELL
DELEWARE SCHRADER ALLEGHENY
SCHUYLKILL MONONGAHELA
SUSQUEHANNA
STATE BIRD: GROUSE
STATE FLOWER: LAUREL
STATE NICKNAME: KEYSTONE
STATE TREE: HEMLOCK
TOWN: ERIE ETNA PLUM YORK AVOCA
MEDIA EASTON EMMAUS SHARON
ALTOONA EPHRATA HERSHEY
READING TOWANDA BRYNMAWR
SCRANTON SHAMOKIN BETHLEHEM
CHARLEROI GETTYSBURG
PITTSBURGH
UNIVERSITY: PITT DREXEL LEHIGH
TEMPLE BUCKNELL DUQUESNE
VILLANOVA

PENNON SPAR PEGGYMASTA
PENNY DY AES MEG RED SOU WIN
GILL WING WINN BROON BROWN
OULAP PENCE COPPER FOLLIS
SALTEE STIVER BROWNIE REDCENT
STERLING

(— DREADFUL) HORRIBLE
(DUTCH —) STIVER
(HALF —) HALFLIN
(OLD SCOTCH —) TURNER
(PL.) PENCE FOLLES
PENNYCRESS FANWEED
STINKWEED
PENNY-PINCHING STINGY
PENNYROYAL PULIOL HEDEOMA
HILLWORT TICKWEED SQUAWWEED
PENNYWEIGHT DWT PENNY
WEIGHT STERLING
PENNYWORT ROTGRASS
PENROD (AUTHOR OF —)
TARKINGTON
(CHARACTER IN —) CRIM JONES
SARAH PENROD MARJORIE
SCHOFIELD
PENSION WAGE PAYMENT STIPEND
SUBSIDY TRIBUTE GRATUITY
MALIKANA
PENSIONER COD RETIREE
PENSIVE MESTO MOODY PENSY
SOBER DREAMY MUSING PENCEY
WISTFUL THOUGHTY MELANCHOLY
PENT CAGED PENNED CONFINED
ENCLOSED RESERVOIR
PENTACLE STAR HEXAGRAM
PENTAGRAM
PENTAD QUINTAD
PENTASTICH POEM UNIT STANZA
STROPHE
PENTATEUCH TORAH THORAH
PENTECOST SHABUOTH
WHITSUNDAY
PENTHESILEA (SLAYER OF —)
ACHILLES
PENTHEUS (FATHER OF —) ECHION
(GRANDFATHER OF —) CADMUS
(MOTHER OF —) AGAVE
PENTHIA STARLIGHT
PENTHOUSE CAT PENT ROOF SHED
AERIE ANNEX HANGAR LOOKUM
SHADOW PLUTEUS BULKHEAD
SKEELING SKILLION APPENTICE
PENTOSAN ARABAN
PENTOSE APIOSE RIBOSE
PENTYL AMYL
PENUMBRA AURA
PENURIOUS MEAN POOR BARREN
SCANTY STINGY MISERLY WANTING
INDIGENT HIDEBOUND NIGGARDLY
PENURY WANT BEGGARY BORASCO
POVERTY SCARCITY INDIGENCE
PRIVATION
PEON HAND PAWN SERF SLAVE
PELADO THRALL FOOTMAN LABORER
PEASANT SOLDIER CONSTABLE
PEONY PINY MOUTAN
PEOPLE (ALSO SEE NATIVE AND
TRIBE) ARU FUL LOG MEN PUL TAT
VAI YAO AKRA ASHA BENI BUGI CHIN

CHUD EMIM FOLK FULA GARO GENS HERD HIMA HUMA IRON LAND LEDE LOLO LUBA LURI NOSU PHUD PHUL PHUT RACE RAIS REMI SAFI SARA SEBA SERE TEMA THEY TODA TOMA TULU USUN VITI VOLK WARE AFIFI AVARS BENIN BONGO CATTI CHAGA COURS DEMOS DUALA EDONI ELYMI FOLKS FULAH GENTE GOMER HAUSA JACKS KAREN LAITY LANAO LENDU LUREM MARSI MASAI NOGAI ORANG PUNAN QUADI RAMBO ROTSE SACAE SALAR SAURA SHAKA STOCK TAURI VOLTA WARUA WORLD ABABUA ACHUAS AFSHAR AISSOR ANGAMI ANGLES ARUNTA AVIKOM BAHIMA BAKELE BAKUBA BALUBA BELTIR BOSHAS BULLOM CIMBRI COMMON DAOINE GENTRY GILAKI GILEKI HAUSSA HERERO HERULI KANWAR KPUESI KRUMAN MANTZU MINYAE MOSCHI NATIÓN OVAMPO PAMIRI PUBLIC RAMUSI RUTULI SAFINY SAMBAL SATRAE SEMANG SHARRA TADJIK TAGAUR TELUGU TUNGUZ TURSHA VENETI VOLCAE WACAGO WAHIMA YNDOYS YUECHI ZAMBAL ACHANGO ASTOMOI BAGANDA BAGARRA BAKALAI BANGALA BANGASH BAROTSE BUNYORO DARDANI DENIZEN DURZADA FALISCI GAETULI GENERAL GEPIDAE GOAJIRO GUHAYNA INHABIT IRISHRY ISSEDOI ITALICI KINDRED KURANKO MAKONDE MESHECH MITANNI NABALOI PICENES PICTAVI PUKHTUN ROHILLA SAMBURU SENONES SILURES SUKKIIM TIRURAI VESTINI WABUNGA WACHAGA WAKAMBA WANGONI POPULATE

(— HAVING DISTINCT LANGUAGE) TONGUE
(— OF FASHION) FLOSS
(— OF GOOD BREEDING) GENTRY GENTILITY
(— WITH SIMILAR INTERESTS) MAFIA
(ABORIGINAL —) JAKUN KHMER KODAGU SEKHWAN
(ANCIENT —) CARA CHAM JUNG ELYMI GETAE HURRI ICENI SACAE SERES SICULI DARDANI FALISCI FIRBOLG KIPCHAK SEQUANI SILURES
(BEAUTIFUL —) GLITTERATI
(BIBLICAL —) ALUR IBAD IBAN MAGOG IBANAG SOMALI GADDANG
(CAVE-DWELLING —) HORITE
(COMMON —) DEMOS PLEBE VULGAR VULGUS TILIKUM SNOBBERY
(EXTINCT —) KOT CHONO COFAN COREE CHANGO CHATOT GUINAU HIBITO SAPONI SHIRINO

(FOREST —) SAKAI SAORA SAURA
(GROUP OF —) CAUCUS
(HONORABLE —) HONESTY
(LOWEST CLASS OF —) CANAILLE
(MARITIME —) LAMUT
(MOUNTAIN —) HUZUL HUTZUL
(NOMADIC —) SHUA HORDE IGDYR IHLAT SHUWA HABIRU SHAGIA SARACEN SHAMMAR SHORTZY SHUKRIA
(OLD —) ANCIENTRY
(ORDINARY —) LAYFOLK
(PAGAN —) IRAYA HANUNOO SUBANUN
(POWERFUL GROUP OF —) MAFIA
(PRIMITIVE —) DAFLA IRULA KADIR KURUKH CHENCHU
(WHITE —) ALBICULI
(PL.) MAKHZAN
(PREF.) DEM(O) ETHN(O) PLEBI POPULI
PEOPLED ABAD SETTLED POPULATE
PEORIA MASCOUTEN
PEP GO VIM ZIP DASH MOXIE VERVE VIGOR BOUNCE ENERGY GINGER ANIMATE QUICKEN ACTIVITY
(— UP) ENLIVEN
PEPLUM GOWN SKIRT TUNIC PEPLOS OVERSKIRT
PEPO GOURD MELON SQUASH PUMPKIN PEPONIDA PEPONIUM
PEPPER CAVA IKMO ITMO KAVA SIRI BETEL CHILI MANGO PIPER SIRIH MATICO TOPEPO CAYENNE PAPRIKA PIMENTA RELIENO JALAPENO KAVAKAVA
(JAVA —) CUBEB
(MEXICAN HOT —) SERRANO
(RED —) LADYFINGER
(PREF.) PIPERI PIPERO
PEPPER-AND-SALT JASPER
PEPPERGRASS CRESS CANARY ANOUNOU COCKWEED
PEPPERMINT MENTHE LABIATE
PEPPER TREE MOLLE HOROPITO PIMIENTO
PEPPERWORT DITTANDER
PEPPERY HOT FIERY SAUCY SPICY TOUCHY PIQUANT PUNGENT SPIRITED STINGING
PEPPY RAHRAH GINGERY
PEPTIDE KININ AMANITIN
PEPTIDOGLYCAN MUREIN
PEPTONE ASCARON
PER BY THE EACH THROUGH
PERADVENTURE HAP DOUBT MAYBE CHANCE MAPPEN MAYHAP HAPPILY PERHAPS POSSIBLY
PERAMBULATE ROAM WALK RAMBLE STROLL PERAMBLE TRAVERSE
PERAMBULATION WEND

PERAMBULATOR BUGGY WAGON
BASSINET VIAMETER WAYWISER
PEDOMETER
PERATE OPHITE
PERCEIVE SEE ESPY FEEL FIND
GAUM HEAR KNOW LOOK MIND
NOTE SCAN TWIG SCENT SENSE
SMELL TASTE TOUCH BEHOLD
COTTON DESCRY DIVINE FIGURE
NOTICE REMARK SURVEY COGNIZE
DISCERN OBSERVE REALIZE
SENSATE COMPRISE DESCRIBE
UNDERNIM RECOGNIZE
(—CRITICALLY) SAVOR
PERCENTAGE CUT AGIO PART
SHARE PROFIT PORTION RAKEOFF
SCALAGE CONTANGO DEFLATOR
PROPORTION
(INSURANCE —) FRANCHISE
(MINING —) LEY
PERCEPT IDEA
PERCEPTIBLE PUBLIC NOTABLE
TACTILE VISIBLE APPARENT
PALPABLE SENSIBLE TANGIBLE
TRACTABLE PERCEIVABLE
(— BY TASTE) SAPID
(FAINTLY —) SHADOWY
(HARDLY —) FAINT
(PREF.) ESTHETO
PERCEPTION RAY BUMP GAUM
TACT SAVOR SCENT SENSE SIGHT
ACUMEN VISION CLOSURE FEELING
GLIMMER NOSTRIL BEARINGS
DELICACY OUTSIGHT COGNITION
SENSATION SENTIMENT
(DIM —) GLIMMER
(MENTAL —) TACT TOUCH
SENSATION
(NICE —) TASTE
(SPIRITUAL —) WISDOM
(UNREAL —) HALLUCINATION
PERCEPTIVE ACUTE QUICK SHARP
SUBTLE KNOWING PIERCING
SENTIENT SENSITIVE
PERCH BAR BAS LUG PEG ROD SIT
BASS JOUK MADO OKOW PERK PIKE
POLE POPE RUFF SEAT BARSE BEGTI
BEKTI BLOCK LIGHT REACH ROOST
RUFFE STAFF STANG ALIGHT
ANABAS BUGARA CALLOP COMBER
PERCID SANDER SAUGER SETTLE
ZANDER ZINGEL ALFIONE HOGFISH
STATION ROCKFISH MARTENIKO
TRUMPETER MADEMOISELLE
(KIND OF —) NILE
(LOFTY —) AERIE
(2-YEAR OLD —) EGLING
(PREF.) PERCI
PERCHANCE HAPLY MAYBE
AUNTERS FORTUNE PERHAPS
POSSIBLY
PERCHER STAKER
PERCHTA BERTHA

PERCOLATE MELT OOZE PERK SEEP
SIFT SILT SIPE SOAK WEEP DRILL
EXUDE LEACH EXHALE FILTER
STRAIN
PERCOLATION SIPING SEEPAGE
LEACHING
PERCOLATOR SIPER BIGGIN
CAFETIERE DISPLACER
PERCUSSION (ALSO SEE DRUMS)
BLOW IMPACT STROKE TOMTOM
PNEUMATIC
(— IN MASSAGE) TAPOTEMENT
PERDITA (FATHER OF —) LEONTES
(MOTHER OF —) HERMIONE
PERDITION HELL LOSS RUIN
BOWWOWS BALLYWACK
DAMNATION
PEREGRINATE TOUR WALK TRAVEL
WANDER JOURNEY SOJOURN
TRAVERSE
PEREGRINE ALIEN NOMAD EXOTIC
ROVING PILGRIM STRANGE
IMPORTED
PEREGRINE FALCON SAKER
GENTLE TASSEL TERCEL
PEREGRINE PICKLE (AUTHOR
OF —) SMOLLETT
(CHARACTER IN —) TOM VANE PIPES
SALLY EMILIA HAWSER PICKLE
APPLEBY GRIZZLE GAMALIEL
GAUNTLET HATCHWAY HORNBECK
TRUNNION PEREGRINE
CADWALLADER
PEREMPT QUASH DEFEAT DESTROY
PEREMPTORY FLAT FINAL UTTER
EXPRESS HAUGHTY ABSOLUTE
DECISIVE DOGMATIC POSITIVE
ESSENTIAL MASTERFUL
PERENNIAL HERB CAREX LIANA
PEONY SEDUM BANANA CENTRO
BLUEWEED CONSTANT ENDURING
KNAPWEED TOADFLAX CONTINUAL
EVERGREEN PENNYWORT
PERPETUAL RECURRENT
PERESH (FATHER OF —) MACHIR
(MOTHER OF —) MAACHAH
PERFECT ALL AOK BACK BORN CURE
FILL FINE FULL HOLY HONE PURE
SURE TOAT EXACT FINAL FULLY
IDEAL PLAIN RIGHT RIPEN SHEER
SOUND TOTAL UTTER WHOLE
ENTIRE EXPERT FINISH MATURE
POLISH REFINE SPHERE TIPTOP
CERTAIN CONCOCT CONTENT
CORRECT CROWNED DEVELOP
GEMLIKE IMPROVE PLENARY
PRECISE SINLESS SPHERAL TYPICAL
COMPLETE COPYROOK FLAWLESS
INFINITE INTEGRAL REPLENISH
(— IN RIGHTEOUSNESS) HOLY
(— SCORE) MAX
(NOT —) IMMATURE
(PREF.) TEL(E)(EO)

PERFECTA EXACTA
PERFECTED EXACT SUMMED
FINISHED PERQUEIR
PERFECTION ACME BEST PINK
BLOOM IDEAL BEAUTY FINISH
PLENTY PARAGON FINALITY
FINENESS FULLNESS MATURITY
RIPENESS ERUDITION
(STATE OF —) SIDDHI
(TO —) NINE
(TYPE OF —) PARAGON
PERFECTIVE TELIC
PERFECTLY SPAN QUITE IDEALLY
PERQUEIR
PERFIDIOUS FALSE SNAKY DISLEAL
SNAKISH DISLOYAL SPITEFUL
FAITHLESS
PERFIDY DECEIT TREASON
FALSEHOOD FALSENESS TREACHERY
PERFORATE EAT DOCK HOLE DRILL
PRICK PUNCH SIEVE THIRL PIERCE
POUNCE RIDDLE THRILL PINHOLE
PUNCTURE PENETRATE TEREBRATE
(— A STAMP) CENTER
PERFORATED OPEN CRIBROSE
FENESTRAL PUNCTURED
PERFORATION BORE HOLE THIRL
TORET BROACH EYELET STIGMA
TRESIS FORAMEN PINHOLE SEPTULA
STENCIL FENESTRA DIABROSIS
PERTUSION
PERFORATOR (SURGICAL —)
TROCAR
PERFORM DO ACT CUT KIP CHAR
FILL FULL HAVE KEEP LAST MAKE
PLAY SHOW STEP CHARE DIGHT
ENACT EXERT FETCH PUTON THROW
ACQUIT COMMIT EFFECT FULFIL
RENDER ACHIEVE EXECUTE EXHIBIT
EXPLOIT FUNGIFY FURNISH
IWURCHE OPERATE PRESENT
PRESTATE PROSECUTE
(— AWKWARDLY) BOGGLE
(— BADLY) BOLLIX
(— BRILLIANTLY) STAR SPARKLE
(— CLUMSILY) THUMB BUNGLE
(— FANCY STUNTS) HOTDOG
(— FULLY) END
(— HASTILY) SKIMP SCAMP,
(— HURRIEDLY) SLUR
(— IN DANCING) FIGURE
(— PERFECTLY) DOTOAT
(— POORLY) CLUTCH
(— SLUTTISHLY) SOZZLE
(— SUCCESSFULLY) CUTIT
(FAIL TO —) CHOKE
(FAIL TO — EFFECTIVELY) CHOKE
PERFORMANCE ACT JOB DEED
FEAT GALA HAND SHOW TEST WORK
CAPER SLANG SPORT STUNT ACTING
ACTION BALLET EFFECT HORARY
MASQUE ACCOUNT ACROAMA
BENEFIT BOOKING CONCERT

EXPLOIT MATINEE MUMMERY
RELEASE SHOWING FAREWELL
FUNCTION PRACTICE STERACLE
OPERATION
(— FOR ONE) SOLO
(— OF DUTY) FEASANCE
(— OF OBLIGATION) SOLUTIO
(— VARIATIONS) COUNTER
(— WITH SENTIMENTALITY) DROOL
(ARAB —) FANTASIA
(BOISTEROUS —) KNOCKABOUT
(BRILLIANT —) BRAVURA
(CHRISTMAS EVE —) GOMBAY
(CLUMSY —) BUNGLE
(DISORDERLY —) SCRAMBLE
(DRAMATIC —) TOPENG PANTOMIME
(FIRST —) OPENING PREMIERE
(HILARIOUS —) HOOT
(INEPT —) BOMB
(MUSICAL —) LESSON RECITAL
DIVISION
(NO —) RELACHE
(PAST —) FORM
(RENEWED —) REVIVAL
(SHORT —) SPOT
(STAGE —) SCENE
(SURGICAL —) OPERATION
(TRAVELLING —) SLANG
(TRIAL —) AUDITION
(VOCAL —) SPRECHSTIMME
(VULGAR —) BLOWOFF
(WRONG —) MISPRISION
(SUFF.)
LOG(ER)(IA)(IAN)(IC)(ICAL)(IST)(UE)(Y
PERFORMER ACT DOER GEEK MOKE
STAR ACTOR SHINE ARTIST DANCER
KINKER LEADER PLAYER WORKER
ACROAMA ACROBAT ARTISTE
GAMBIST HORNIST HOTSHOT
SOLOIST EXECUTOR SPARKLER
HAMFATTER HEADLINER
(— ON SEVERAL INSTRUMENTS)
MOKE
(— WITH NEGRO DIALECT) HAMBONE
(BURLESQUE —) GRINDER
(CIRCUS —) LEAPER
(INFERIOR —) HAM SHINE
PERFUME ATAR BALM FUME MUSK
NOSE OTTO AROMA ATTAR CENSE
CIVET MYRRH SCENT SMELL SPICE
CARVOL CHYPRE EMBALM FLAVOR
IONONE BOUQUET CARVONE
DIAPASM ESSENCE INCENSE
JASMINE NOSEGAY ODORIZE
SWEETEN BERGAMOT MARECHAL
ORANGERY PATCHOULI
(— BASE) MUSK CIVET NEROL
NEROLI
(— CENTER) GRASSE
(POWDERY —) PULVIL
PERFUNCTORY CURSORY
CARELESS SLIPSHOD SLOVENLY
APATHETIC

PERGOLA ARBOR BOWER RAMADA
BALCONY TRELLIS
PERHAPS HAPS MAYBE ABLINS
BELIKE HAPPEN MAPPEN MAYHAP
ABLINGS AIBLINS LIGHTLY PERCASE
YIBBLES POSSIBLY PERCHANCE
PERI ELF FAIRY SPRITE
PERIAPT CHARM AMULET
PERICARP BUR BOLL BURR BLADDER
PERICHOLE, LA (CHARACTER IN —)
ABDRES PIQUILLO PERICHOLE
(COMPOSER OF —) OFFENBACH
PERICLES (AUTHOR OF —)
SHAKESPEARE
(CHARACTER IN —) BOULT CLEON
DIANA GOWER MARINA THAISA
CERIMON DIONYZA ESCANES
LEONINE PERICLES PHILEMON
THALIARD ANTIOCHUS HELICANUS
LYCHORIDA SIMONIDES
LYSIMACHUS
(FATHER OF —) XANTHIPPUS
(MISTRESS OF —) ASPASIA
(MOTHER OF —) AGARISTE
(SON OF —) PARALUS XANTHIPPUS
(TEACHER OF —) ZENO DAMON
PERICLYMENUS (BROTHER OF —)
NESTOR
(FATHER OF —) NELEUS POSEIDON
(MOTHER OF —) CHLORIS MELIBOEA
PERICOPE LESSON
PERICRANIUM HEAD BRAIN
PERIDOT OLIVINE
PERIDOTITE PICRITE EULYSITE
JOSEFITE SAXONITE WEHRLITE
PERIERES (FATHER OF —) AEOLUS
(MOTHER OF —) ENARETE
(SON OF —) APHAREUS LEUCIPPUS
(WIFE OF —) GORGOPHONE
PERIGEE EPIGEUM
PERIGYNIUM UTRICLE
PERIL RISK WERE WATHE CRISIS
DANGER HAZARD MENACE SCYLLA
THREAT THRONG TRANCE DISTRESS
JEOPARDY CHARYBDIS
PERILOUS KITTLE DOUBTFUL
DREADFUL INFAMOUS DANGEROUS
HAZARDOUS
PERIMETER RIM CIRCUIT OUTLINE
BOUNDARY PERIPHERY
PERIOD GO AGE DOT END EON ERA
AEON DATE LIFE RACE SPAN STOP
TERM TIDE TIME YEAR AVAIL CLOSE
CYCLE EPACT EPOCH LABOR LAPSE
PATCH POINT SPACE SPELL STAGE
CUTOFF GHURRY HEMERA MOMENT
PARODY PICTUN SEASON STOUND
ACCOUNT DICOLON FLORUIT
PASTIME SESSION STADIUM
STRETCH DURATION INDUCIAE
INSTANCE LIFETIME SENTENCE
(— ENDING FROST) FRESH
(— FOR WHICH ENJOYED) TENURE
(— IN DEVELOPMENT) STAGE
(— OF ACTION) GO BOUT
(— OF DECLINE) SUNSET EVENING
(— OF DRYNESS) DROUTH
DROUGHT
(— OF DUTY) WATCH
(— OF FAIR WEATHER) SLATCH
(— OF FESTIVITY) WAKES
(— OF FIVE YEARS) LUSTRE PENTAD
LUSTRUM QUINQUENNIUM
(— OF GLOOM) DEAD
(— OF GRACE) DAY
(— OF HAPPINESS) MILLENNIUM
(— OF HEAT) CALLING
(— OF HUMID WEATHER) SIZZARD
(— OF IMMATURITY) SWADDLE
(— OF INSTRUCTION) LESSON
(— OF ISOLATION) QUARANTINE
(— OF LEAVE) SABBATICAL
(— OF LIFE) AGE ELD SPAN
(— OF MILITARY SERVICE) HITCH
(— OF MOTILITY) SWARMING
(— OF MOURNING) SHIVA SHIRAH
(— OF NEW MOON) SYZYGY
(— OF PERFORMING) STANZA
(— OF PLAY) HALF CHUKKER
QUARTER
(— OF RAINFALL) FLUVIAL
(— OF RECREATION) HOLIDAY
VACATION
(— OF REMISSION) JUBILEE
(— OF REST) SMOKO BREATHER
(— OF REVOLUTION OF HEAVENLY
BODY) ORB
(— OF SERVICE) TOUR
(— OF TIME) DAY HOUR WEEK YEAR
MONTH DECADE MINUTE SECOND
(— OF WORK) SHIFT SPELL STINT
(— OF 10 YEARS) DECADE
(— OF 100 YEARS) AGE CENTURY
(— OF 1000 YEARS) CHILIAD MILLIAD
(— OF 14 MINUTES, 24 SECONDS)
CENTIDAY
(— OF 2 MONTHS) DIMESTER
(— OF 2 YEARS) BIENNIUM
(— OF 20 TUNS) KATUN
(— OF 20 YEARS) KATUN
(— OF 260 DAYS) TONALMATL
(— OF 4 YEARS) QUADRENNIUM
(— OF 5 DAYS) PENTAD
(— OF 5 YEARS) LUSTRE LUSTRUM
(— OF 50 YEARS) JUBILE JUBILEE
(— OF 7 DAYS) HEBDOMAD
(— OF 7 YEARS) SEPTENARY
(— PRECEDING IMPORTANT EVENT)
EVE
(CLASS —) HOUR
(CONTINUOUS —) RUN
(CULTURAL —) HORIZON
(DEFINITE —) MOMENT
(DISTINCTIVE —) EPOCH
(DULL —) SLACK
(EVOLUTIONAL —) HEMERA

(GEOLOGICAL —) JURA KAROO
EOCENE ALGOMAN HORIZON
NEOCENE CAMBRIAN DEVONIAN
JURASSIC SILURIAN TERTIARY
TRANSVAAL
(HAPPY —) MILLENIUM
(HYPOTHETICAL —) ACME
(JAPANESE —) MEIJI
(JAPANESE CULTURAL —) JOMON
(LONG —) EON AEON CYCLE
(MEETING —) SESSION
(MENSTRUAL —) TERMS
(OCCASIONAL —) SNATCH
(OF JAPANESE —) JOMON
(OF JAPANESE CULTURAL —) YAYOI
(PENITENTIAL —) LENT
(RECOVERY —) REHAB
(RECURRING —) EMBER
(SHORT —) BIT FIT BLINK SHAKE
SPELL SPURT SNATCH
(TELEVISION RATINGS —) SWEEP
(WAITING —) MORATORIUM
(WET —) PLUVIAL
(SUFF.) (OF A —) CHRONUS
PERIODIC ERAL ANNUAL CYCLIC
ETESIAN REGULAR FREQUENT
SEASONAL
(NOT —) LOOSE ACYCLIC
PERIODICAL DAILY ORGAN PAPER
SHEET ANNUAL DIGEST REVIEW
ETESIAN FANZINE JOURNAL
REGULAR TABLOID DREADFUL
EXCHANGE MAGAZINE EPHEMERIS
PICTORIAL
PERIODICALLY TERMLY
PERION (SON OF —) AMADIS
PERIPATETIC ROVING RAMBLING
ITINERATE
PERIPHERAL DEEP OUTER DISTAL
DISTANT EXTERNAL MARGINAL
PERIPHERY LIP RIM BRIM DOME
EDGE AMBIT LIMIT SKIRT AREOLA
BORDER BOUNDS FRINGE AMBITUS
CONTOUR SUBURBS SURFACE
CONFINES PERIMETER
PERIPHRASTIC AMBAGIOUS
PERISCOPE ALTISCOPE HYPOSCOPE
OMNISCOPE
PERISH DIE FADE FALL RUIN TINE
TYNE QUAIL SPILL SWELT WASTE
DEPART EXPIRE STARVE DESTROY
FORFARE MISCARRY
(— GRADUALLY) FADE
PERISHABLE SOFT DYING CADUKE
BRITTLE FUGITIVE
PERISHED MUSHY
PERISTOME FRINGE
PERITE SKILLED
PERITHECIUM ALVEOLA
PERITONEUM RIM SIPHAC
PERIWIG FLASH GALERA PERUKE
TOUPEE GALERUM PERWICK
CHEVELURE

PERIWINKLE PERY PIRE WINK PERRY
SNAIL MYRTLE WINKLE DOGBANE
PINPATCH SENGREEN BLUEBUTTON
PERJINK NEAT TRIM PRECISE
PERJURE FORSWEAR
PERJURED MANSWORN
PERK BRISK FRILL PERCH PREEN
PRINK FRESHEN SMARTEN
PERKY AIRY PERT COCKY JAUNTY
CHIPPER
PERMANENCE STAY STABILITY
PERMANENT FIXED STABLE
ABIDING DURABLE LASTING STATIVE
CONSTANT ENDURING REMANENT
STANDING INDELIBLE
PERMANENTLY KEEPS
PERMEABLE POROUS PERVIOUS
PERMEATE FILL SEEP SOAK BATHE
IMBUE DRENCH INFORM INVADE
ANIMATE PERVADE DOMINATE
SATURATE PENETRATE
PERMEATED SHOT
PERMEATION SATURATION
PERMIAN DYAS DYASSIC
PERMISSIBLE FREE VENIAL
POSSIBLE CONGEABLE
(NOT —) NEFAS
PERMISSION MAY FIAT LIEF PASS
CONGE DARST FAVOR GRACE GRANT
LEAVE ACCESS ACCORD PERMIT
CONSENT LIBERTY LICENSE
SANCTION
(— TO ACT) POWER
(— TO BE ABSENT) ABSIT
(— TO PRINT) IMPRIMATUR
(— TO PROCEED) GOAHEAD
(— TO USE) LOAN
(LETTER OF —) EXEAT
(WRITTEN —) PASS
PERMISSIVE TOLERANT
CONCESSORY
PERMIT LET CHIT CHOP GIVE LEVE
PASS ADMIT ALLOW CONGE EXEAT
FAVOR GRACE GRANT LEAVE SERVE
ACCORD BETEEM CEDULA DUSTUK
ENDURE ENTREE SUFFER CONCEDE
CONSENT DUSTUCK FACULTY
LICENSE PLACARD POMPANO
WARRANT DISPENSE
(— NEGATIVELY) TOLERATE
(— TO ENTER) INTROMIT
(— TO TAKE) SOAK
(CUSTOMS —) CARNET
PERMITTED FREE LOOT LICIT
ALLOWED INNOCENT SUPPOSED
(— BY LAW) LEGAL
PERMUTATION BARTER CHANGE
EXCHANGE
PERNICIOUS BAD ILL EVIL FATAL
QUICK SWIFT DEADLY MALIGN
WICKED BALEFUL BANEFUL
HARMFUL HURTFUL NOISOME
NOXIOUS RUINOUS

PERNIO CHILBLAIN
PERO (BROTHER OF —) NESTOR
  (FATHER OF —) NELEUS
  (HUSBAND OF —) BIAS
  (MOTHER OF —) CHLORIS
  (SON OF —) ASOPUS
PEROPUS PARAGON
PERORATION EPILOG PERIOD
  CLOSING PURLICUE
PEROXISOME MICROBODY
PERPEND JUMPER PARPEN PONDER
  REFLECT THROUGH
PERPENDICULAR SINE ERECT
  PLUMB SHEER ABRUPT NORMAL
  APOTHEM UPRIGHT BINORMAL
  CATHETUS EVENDOWN VERTICAL
  (MUTUALLY —) ORTHOGONAL
PERPENDICULARITY APLOMB
PERPENDICULARLY BOLT SHEER
  SHEERLY
PERPETRATE DO PULL COMMIT
  EFFECT PERFORM
PERPETUAL ETERN ENDLESS
  ETERNAL CONSTANT INFINITO
  UNENDING CONTINUAL PERENNIAL
PERPETUALLY EVER ALWAYS
  FOREVER
PERPETUATE CONTINUE ETERNIZE
  MAINTAIN
PERPLEX CAP MAR SET VEX BEAT
  CLOG DOIT DOZE FIKE MAZE STUN
  AMAZE BESET BI AIK STUMP TWIST
  BAFFLE BOGGLE BOTHER BUNKER
  CUMBER DARKEN FEAGUE FICKLE
  GRAVEL HAMPER HARASS HOBBLE
  KITTLE MAMMER MITHER MOIDER
  MUDDLE PLAGUE POTHER POTTER
  PUTTER PUZZLE RAFFLE RIDDLE
  TWITCH WILDER WRIXLE BEDEVIL
  BUMBAZE CONFUSE DIFFUSE
  EMBROIL FLUMMOX MYSTIFY
  NONPLUS PLUNDER STAGGER
  STUMBLE TORMENT BEWILDER
  CONFOUND SURPRISE WINDLASS
  BAMBOOZLE
PERPLEXED ASEA MAZY ATSEA
  ANXIOUS NONPLUS PUZZLED
  CONFUSED TROUBLED INTRICATE
  TOSTICATED
PERPLEXING HARD MAZY SPINY
  CRABBY KNOBBY KNOTTY CARKING
  COMPLEX CRABBED QUISCOS
  BAFFLING
PERPLEXITY FOG KNOT WERE
  BRAKE FOITER HOBBLE PUCKER
  PUZZLE TAKING TANGLE ANXIETY
  NONPLUS STICKLE TROUBLE
  POSEMENT SURPRISE CONFUSION
  LABYRINTH PUZZLEMENT
  (MENTAL —) STUDY
  (RELIEVE OF —) CLEAR
PERQUISITE FEE TIP LOCK PERK VAIL
  GOUPIN GOWPEN INCOME ADJUNCT

APANAGE VANTAGE CONQUEST
  GRATUITY
  (PL.) PICKING
PERRIER PEDRERO
PERRINIST LIBERTINE
PERSE BLUE
  (DAUGHTER OF —) CIRCE PASIPHAE
  (FATHER OF —) OCEANUS
  (HUSBAND OF —) HELIOS
  (SON OF —) AEETES PERSES
PERSECUTE VEX BAIT ANNOY
  CHASE HARRY HOUND WRACK
  WRONG HARASS PESTER PURSUE
  AFFLICT CRUCIFY DRAGOON
  OPPRESS TORMENT TORTURE
PERSECUTED JOB REFUGEE
PERSECUTOR TORQUEMADA
PERSEPHONE KORE DESPOINA
  PRAXIDIKE
  (DAUGHTER OF —) CORA KORE
  (FATHER OF —) ZEUS JUPITER
  (HUSBAND OF —) HADES PLUTO
  (MOTHER OF —) CERES DEMETER
PERSES (BROTHER OF —) AEETES
  (DAUGHTER OF —) HECATE
  (FATHER OF —) CRIUS HELIOS
  (MOTHER OF —) PERSE EYRYBIA
  (SISTER OF —) CIRCE PASIPHAE
PERSEUS RESCUER CHAMPION
  (FATHER OF —) ZEUS JUPITER
  (GRANDFATHER OF —) ACRISIUS
  (MOTHER OF —) DANAE
  (STAR OF —) ATIK ALGOL
  (VICTIM OF —) MEDUSA
  (WIFE OF —) ANDROMEDA
PERSEVERANCE GRIT MOXIE
  STAMINA INDUSTRY PATIENCE
  TENACITY CONSTANCY
  PERSISTENCE
PERSEVERE PEG CANK KEEP PLUG
  TORE ABIDE STICK HANGIN INSIST
  REMAIN PERSIST CONTINUE
PERSEVERING BUSY HARD STILL
  PATIENT RESOLUTE SEDULOUS
  ASSIDUOUS INSISTENT
PERSIA (SEE IRAN)
PERSIAN MEDE FARSI PERSE GILAKI
  HAJEMI IRANIC DURZADA HADJEMI
  IRANIAN MEMNONIAN
  (— RED DEER) MARAL
PERSICARY REDLEG REDLEGS
  REDSHANK HEARTEASE HEARTWEED
  PEACHWORT
PERSIFLAGE BANTER RAILLERY
PERSIMMON KAKI SIMON SIMMON
  ZAPOTE CHAPOTE HYAKUME
  TRIUMPH
  (— TREE) GAB GAUB LOTUS
PERSIST HOLD KEEP LAST URGE
  ADHERE ENDURE INSIST REMAIN
  PREVAIL SUBSIST CONTINUE
  PERSEVERE
PERSISTENCE GUTS

PERSISTENCY TENACITY
PERSISTENT SET DREE FIRM HARD
GREAT STOUT TOUGH DOGGED
DREECH GRITTY HECTIC SLEUTH
DURABLE RESTANT RESTIVE
CONSTANT ENDURING HOLDFAST
OBDURATE RESOLUTE SEDULOUS
STUBBORN ASSIDUOUS OBSTINATE
PERENNIAL PRIMITIVE RELENTLESS
PERSISTING
(PREF.) MENO
PERSON BOD CAT EGG EGO GUY
MAN ONE BABY BODY CHAL CHAP
COVE DUCK FISH FOOD FORM GINK
HOOK LEDE LIFE NABS PRIG SELF
SOUL BEING BLOKE BOSOM CHILD
COOKY GHOST HEART HUMAN PARTI
PARTY PIECE STICK THING WATCH
WIGHT ANIMAL BUGGER ENTITY
FELLOW GALOOT GAZABO JOHNNY
KIPPER NUMBER SINNER SISTER
SPIRIT SPRITE ARTICLE BLISTER
WAGTAIL SPECIMEN TILLICUM
(— ACTING FOR ANOTHER) PROXY
(— ASSOCIATED WITH WORK)
WALLAH
(— BEARING HEAVY BURDEN) CAMEL
(— BEHIND THE TIMES) FOGY FOGEY
(— BRINGING GOOD LUCK) MASCOT
(— FROM WHOM FAMILY IS
DESCENDED) STIRPS
(— INTERESTED IN FOOD FADS)
FOODIE
(— MEANLY CLAD) SCARECROW
(— NAMED) NOMINEE
(— NOT IN THE KNOW) LAME
(— NOT OF NOBLE BIRTH) ROTURIER
(— OF AGE) COOT FALDWORTH
(— OF CONSEQUENCE) BIGGIE
BIGWIG TALLBOY
(— OF COURAGE) SPARTAN
(— OF ENERGY) LIVEWIRE
(— OF HONOR) MENSCH
(— OF INFLUENCE) CAPTAIN
HEAVYWEIGHT
(— OF INTEGRITY) MENSCH
(— OF MEAN BIRTH) GUTTERBLOOD
(— OF NO REFINEMENT) SLOB
(— OF RANK) STATE MAGNATE
EMINENCE MAGNIFICO PERSONAGE
(— OF WEAK MIND) FOOL
(— OF WISDOM) SOLOMON
(— OPPOSED TO CHANGE) LUDDITE
(— PREJUDICED AGAINST ELDERLY)
AGIST AGEIST
(— PRETENDING INTELLIGENCE)
PSEUD
(— RESEMBLING ANOTHER) SOSIA
(—S IN AMBASSADOR'S SUITE)
COMES
(— TO BE IMITATED) EXEMPLAR
(— TOO STRONG FOR ASSAILANT)
TARTAR

(— TO SERVE WRIT) ELISOR
(— TRYING TO ATTRACT ATTENTION
SHOWBOAT
(— WANTING TO BE SOMEONE ELSE)
WANNABE
(— WHO DOESN'T FIT IN) GEEK
(— WHO HOARDS) SQUIRREL
(— WHO IS UP-TO-DATE) SWINGER
(— WHO LOCATES ANTIQUES)
PICKER
(— WHO PERFORMS MENIAL TASKS)
DOGSBODY
(— WHO TAKES AMPHETAMINES)
PILLHEAD
(— WHO TAKES CAPSULES)
PILLHEAD
(— WHO TALKS EXCESSIVELY)
MOTORMOUTH
(— WITH MENTAL TWIST) CRANK
(— WITH MILITANT ATTITUDE) HAWK
(— WITH NERVOUS DISORDERS)
NEUROTIC
(— WITHOUT EQUAL) NONPAREIL
(— WITHOUT STAMINA) JELLYFISH
(— WITH QUEER IDEAS) ROZUM
(— WITH SHORT HAIR) SKINHEAD
(ABJECT —) SLAVE CRAWLER
(ABSENT-MINDED —) MUSARD
(ACTIVE —) GOER
(ADMIRABLE —) GEM PIPPIN RIPPER
(AFFECTED —) POSEUR MINNICK
GIMCRACK
(AFFECTEDLY INTELLECTUAL —)
PSEUD
(AGGRESSIVE —) SHOVER HOTSHOT
(AMUSING —) COMIC
(ANNOYING —) FIEND NUDNICK
(ANTIQUATED —) MUMPSIMUS
(ARABIZED —) MOZARAB
(ARROGANT —) HUFF TENGU
(ATTRACTIVE —) DISH CUTEY CUTIE
KILLER KNOCKOUT
(AVARICIOUS —) YISSER
(AWKWARD —) PUT GAWP HICK
MUFF RUBE SLAM STAG STEG KLUTZ
STIFF GALOOT GUFFIN TUMFIE
HOOSIER LOBSTER SCHLEPP
KITHOGUE SHLEPPER SLOMMACK
SPELDRIN
(BAD —) UNSEL
(BALD —) BALLARD BALDHEAD
SKINHEAD BALDICOOT
(BANISHED —) WRETCH
(BAPTIZED —) MEMBER ILLUMINATO
(BASE —) CUT RASCAL CAITIFF
HILDING PUTTOCK
(BELOVED —) FLAME HEARTROOT
(BIG-BELLIED —) GORBELLY
(BLACK —) BLECK
(BOASTFUL —) BLOWER GASCON
(BOISTEROUS —) TEARER
(BOORISH —) GOOP
(BORING —) SCHMO

(BRUTAL —) RUFFIAN
(BUSTLING —) STIRABOUT
(CALLOW —) GORLIN SMARTY GOSLING
(CANONIZED —) SAINT
(CARELESS —) HASH TASSEL
(CASTRATED —) SPADO
(CERTAIN —) QUIDAM
(CHARMING —) SMASHER
(CHATTERING —) MAGPIE
(CHICKENHEARTED —) HEN
(CHILDISH —) BAUBLE WHIMLING
(CHUNKY —) JUNT
(CHURLISH —) TIKE TYKE
(CIRCLE OF —S) COTERIE
(CLEVER —) BIRD WHIZ WHIZZ MERCURY
(CLOWNISH —) BUFFOON HOBNAIL VILLAIN
(CLUMSY —) DUB LOB BOOB GAWK SLOB TIKE TYKE JUMBO KLUTZ STAUP STIFF DUFFER KEFFEL LUMMOX HODMADOD
(COARSE —) COW STIRK BABOON MUCKER
(COAXING —) WHILLY WHEEDLE
(COLD —) ICICLE
(COMBATIVE —) DRAGON GAMECOCK
(COMMONPLACE —) MUT MUTT BROMIDE
(CONCEITED) IT HUFF COXCOMB PRAGMATIC
(CONFUSED —) FOOSTERER
(CONSERVATIVE) HUNKER SQUARE MOSSBACK
(CONSPICUOUS —) LIGHT
(CONTEMPTIBLE —) YAP CRUD HEEL PUKE SCAB SKIN SWAB CATSO SHRUB SKITE SKUNK SNIPE TWERP INSECT SHICER STINKER BLIGHTER WHIFFLER PETTITOES
(COWARDLY —) WIMP FUGIE SISSY SLINK SQUIB
(CRAFTY —) TOD FILE SHARK JESUIT
(CRAZED —) NUT NUTTER PSYCHOPATH MESHUGGENAH
(CRINGING —) SNAKE SNOOL FLUNKY SPANIEL
(CRUEL —) LAMB FIEND MALISON
(CUNNING —) PIE
(CURIOUS —) RUBBERNECK
(DAINTY —) MIMMOCK
(DARK —) MOOR OUSEL OUZEL MELANO NIGNOG
(DEAD —) DEFUNCT DECEASED DECEDENT
(DEBAUCHED —) RAKEHELL
(DECREPIT —) CROCK WITHERLING
(DEDICATED —) OBLATE
(DEFORMED —) CRILE CALIBAN HODMADOD
(DENSE —) DUFFER

(DEPENDENT —) JUNKIE
(DEPRAVED —) SKATE
(DERANGED —) PSYCHE
(DESPICABLE —) SCAB HOUND SLAVE CAITIFF
(DESTITUTE —) PAUPER
(DEVILISH —) SHAITAN
(DIMINUTIVE —) BANTY MIDGE BANTAM MIDGET NIFFNAFF
(DIRTY —) SWEEP DRIVEL HOWLET
(DISABLED —) DUCK CRIPPLE INVALID
(DISAGREEABLE —) GOOP PILL QUAT SKITE RATBAG
(DISGRUNTLED —) SOREHEAD
(DISHONEST —) ROGUE ROTTER BEZONIAN
(DISLIKED —) WARLING
(DISREPUTABLE —) RIP QUANDONG
(DISSOLUTE —) RIBALD ROUNDER STRIKER
(DOLEFUL —) MISERY
(DOLTISH —) BLOCK SWINE
(DRUG-ABUSING —) BURNOUT
(DRUNKEN —) LUSH TUMBREL TUMBRIL
(DULL —) LOB BORE DODO DRIP GOON GOOP GRUB LUMP MOME MOPE SLOB CLUNK DROUD PRUNE SCHMO STICK STOCK LURDAM LACKWIT LOBCOCK NUDNICK OPACITY DEADHEAD
(DULL-WITTED —) DOPE GUMP DUNCE
(DUMB —) MUTE
(DUMPY —) HODDYDODDY
(DUPED —) GULL
(DWARFISH —) AGATE CROWL SHURF
(DYING —) MORIBUND
(ECCENTRIC —) COON GINK KOOK TIKE TYKE GAZABO GAZEBO FANTAST ODDBALL
(EDUCATED —) SCHOLAR LITERATE
(EFFEMINATE —) SOFTY SQUAW CODDLE SOFTIE WANTON BADLING SOFTLING SMOCKFACE
(ELDERLY —) SENIOR SOAKER GRAYHEAD GERIATRIC
(EMACIATED —) FRAME WASTREL SKELETON
(EMPTY-HEADED —) NITWIT
(ENERGETIC —) DYNAMO
(ENROLLED —) MEMBER
(ENTERTAINING —) COMEDIAN
(ENTHUSIASTIC —) FANATIC
(ESSENTIAL —) LINCHPIN
(EVIL —) QUED SCUM QUEDE SHREW
(EXALTED —) PERSONAGE
(EXPERIENCED —) EXPERT SOAKER STAGER
(EXPERT —) ACE DAB
(EXTORTIONATE —) SCREW
(EXTRAORDINARY —) ONER BUSTER

(FADED —) SHARGAR SHARGER
(FAINT-HEARTED —) HEN
(FAMOUS —) DON NOTORIETY
(FANTASTIC —) KICKSHAW
(FARSIGHTED —) PRESBYOPE
(FASHIONABLE —) GIMCRACK
(FASTIDIOUS —) MIMMOCK DELICATE
(FAT —) GURK BLIMP FATSO QUILT
SQUAB STOUT
(FATUOUS —) GOOP
(FAWNING —) COGGER SPANIEL
(FEEBLEMINDED —) FEEB IDIOT
MORON IMBECILE
(FEROCIOUS —) LAMB
(FICKLE —) ROVER MOONCALF
(FILTHY —) HOGG
(FINE —) WHIPPA
(FLABBY —) HUDDERON
(FLAKY —) SPACECADET
(FLASHY —) KID FLASHER
(FLIGHTY —) FLIBBERTIGIBBET
(FOOLISH —) FOP GIT BOZO COOT
GUMP HOIT JERK PUTZ BOOBY
SOFTY BAUBLE DOODLE DOOFUS
DOTARD DRIVEL HOWLET TURKEY
GOSLING GUBBINS HAVEREL
BUBBLEHEAD
(FORCELESS —) DRIP
(FORGETFUL —) SPACECADET
(FOUL —) DREVILL
(FRANK —) TELLTRUTH
(FRIVOLOUS —) HOBBYHORSE
FEATHERBRAIN
(FUSSY —) FAD FADDLE GRANNY
SPOFFY GRANNIE
(GAY —) GRIG HUZZA
(GIDDY —) SCATTERBRAIN
(GLOOMY —) SATURNIST
(GOOD-FOR-NOTHING —) KET PELF
TASSEL WASTER WANHOPE
WASTREL
(GOSSIPING —) SHULER SHUILER
(GOSSIPY —) BIGMOUTH QUIDNUNC
NEWSMONGER
(GOSSIP, TALKATIVE —) YENTA
(GRASPING —) SHYLOCK
(GRAVE —) SOBERSIDES
(GREEDY —) GORB GANNET
GRASPER PUTTOCK
(GROTESQUE —) GUY GOLLIWOGG
PUNCHINELLO
(GRUMPY —) SOURBELLY
(GULLIBLE —) JAY BOOB GULPIN
LOBSTER FLATHEAD SHLEMIEL
WOODCOCK
(GYPSY —) CHI CHAI
(HANDLESS —) SAMMY
(HARD —) MALISON
(HARD-HEADED —) NUT
(HATEFUL —) TOAD
(HEAVY —) STODGER
(HEAVY-SET —) LUMP

(HETEROSEXUAL —) STRAIGHT
(HOLY —) SAINT
(HOT-TEMPERED —) SPARK
(HUMPBACKED —) LORD
(HUNGRY —) HUNGARIAN
(HYPOCRITICAL —) PHARISEE
(IDENTICAL —) SELF
(IDLE —) BUMMLE RAGABASH
SLUGGARD
(IGNORANT —) BABE BOOB PORK
IDIOT IGNARO
(ILL-BRED —) BOOR CHURL CLOWN
(ILL-MANNERED —) GRUB SKUNK
(ILL-NATURED) PATCH CROSSPATCH
(ILL-NATURED —) CRAB HUNKS
PATCH
(ILL-TEMPERED —) CRAB ETTERCAP
TAISTREL
(ILLUSTRIOUS —) HERO
(IMMATURE —) BUD SQUAB GORLIN
(IMMORAL —) REP PERDU
IMPURITAN
(IMPASSIVE —) BLOCK
(IMPERTINENT —) PAUK PAWK SNIP
(IMPETUOUS —) HOTHEAD
(IMPISH —) SPRITE
(IMPORTANT —) NIB POT LION
HONOR MOGUL NABOB KINGPIN
MUGWUMP SOMEBODY
(IMPOTENT —) SPADO
(IMPRACTICAL —) IDEALIST
(IMPUDENT —) SAUCE SQUIRT
SAUCEBOX
(INACTIVE —) SLUGGARD
(INANE —) SHAUP
(INCOMPETENT —) BOZO SCHLEP
(INCONSTANT —) ROVER
(INDECISIVE —) INVERTEBRATE
(INEPT —) DWEEB KLUTZ
(INEXPERIENCED —) BABE INGENUE
BEGINNER
(INFAMOUS —) NITHING
(INFERIOR —) BATA SHRUB SHABBLE
(INFLEXIBLE —) RAMROD
(INFLUENTIAL —) MOGUL
(INSCRUTABLE —) SPHINX
(INSENSITIVE —) LOG PACHYDERM
(INSIGNIFICANT —) DAB MUT MUTT
NERD NURD QUAT BILSH CREEP
DWEEB JOKER SHURF SPRAT SQUIB
ABLACH PEANUT NEBBISH PINKEEN
WHIFFET GNATLING GRILDRIG
PIGWIGEON
(INSINUATING —) WHILLY
(INSURED —) LIFE
(INTRACTABLE —) BUCKIE TARTAR
HAGGARD HARDCASE
(IRASCIBLE —) TOUCHWOOD
(IRRESPONSIBLE —) PLAYBOY
FLYBYNIGHT
(IRRITATING —) BOT
(ISOLATED —) ISOLATO

(LAME —) VULCAN
(LANK —) TANGLE GANGEREL WINDLESTRAW
(LARGE —) CHUNK WHIPPA SKELPER STODGER STRAPPER
(LASCIVIOUS —) SUCCUBUS
(LAST — IN CONTEST) MELL
(LAZY —) BUM DAW HOIT POKE IDLER TRAIL LORDAN LURDAN BLELLUM LAZYLEGS SLUGABED SLUGGARD
(LEAN —) RIBE TANGLE SHARGER THINGUT
(LEARNED —) CLERK ERUDIT ACHARYA SCHOLAR LITERATO WISEACRE LITERATUS
(LECHEROUS —) SATYR
(LEFT-HANDED —) SINISTRAL
(LETHARGIC —) ZOMBI ZOMBIE
(LEWD —) WANTON GAMESTER
(LIGHTHEADED —) BEEHEAD
(LISTLESS —) MOPE
(LITERATE —) SCHOLAR
(LITTLE —) SMOLT SMOUT
(LIVELY —) GRIG BIRKIE HEMPIE WHISKER
(LONG-HAIRED —) HIPPY HIPPIE
(LOUD-VOICED —) STENTOR
(LOW —) PACK SCUM RASCAL BEASTMAN
(LOW-BORN —) GUTTERBLOOD
(LOW SOCIETY —) MUDSILL
(LUBBERLY) OAF
(LUMBERING —) PUMPKIN TUMBREL TUMBRIL
(LUMPISH —) DROUD
(LUSTY —) BILCH BILSH
(MAD —) MADLING
(MALICIOUS —) SERPENT
(MARRIAGEABLE —) PARTI
(MARRIED —) WIFE SPOUSE HUSBAND MATRIMONY
(MEAN —) RIP SCAB CHURL HOUND MISER SKATE SNEAK SHICER BASTARD DOGBOLT BEZONIAN HUCKSTER STINKARD EARTHWORM
(MEDDLESOME —) BREVIT HESSIAN
(MENTALLY DEFICIENT —) AMENT
(MENTALLY UNBALANCED —) MATTOID
(MISCHIEVOUS —) IMP LIMB PEST TOOL HEMPIE HELLION WHIPSTER
(MISERABLE —) SNAKE SWELP WRETCH
(MISERLY —) SKATE SCROOGE PINCHGUT PINCHBACK
(MONSTROUS —) WAMPUS
(MORAL —) PURITAN
(MORALLY ILL —) SICKO SICKIE
(MOST DISTINGUISHED —) FLOWER
(NAIVE —) JERK CLUCK GUNSEL INGENUE INNOCENT

(NASTY —) BLEEDER
(NEGLECTED —) TACKY TACKEY
(NIMBLE —) MERCURY
(NOISY —) YAP HOWLET
(OBJECTIONABLE —) CUR COYOTE FOUTER
(OBNOXIOUS —) CREEP
(OBSTINATE —) DONKEY STIFFNECK
(ODD —) GIG CURE GEEZER QUIZZY RATBAG CAUTION
(ODD-LOOKING —) QUIZ
(OFFENSIVE —) TICK SKITE SHOCKER STINKER HEDGEHOG
(OLD —) OLDY OLDIE
(OLD-FASHIONED —) FRUMP
(OPINIONATIVE —) PRAGMATIC
(ORACULAR —) PONTIFF
(ORDINARY —) PUNTER
(OVER-LEARNED —) PEDANT
(OVERGROWN —) FUSTILUGS
(OVERSLENDER —) SPINDLING
(PALTRY —) PELTER
(PAMPERED —) WANTON
(PASSIONATE —) FUME
(PATIENT —) JOB
(PECULIAR —) BIRD CASE
(PEEVISH —) GRIZZLER SPLENETIC
(PERNICKETY —) FIKE
(PERT —) PIE FLIRT
(PLODDING —) STODGE
(POLISHED —) SMOOTHY SMOOTHIE
(POMPOUS —) PUFFIN PUMPIST
(POT-BELLIED —) GORREL
(PRE-EMINENT —) STAR
(PRIGGISH —) PRUDE
(PRIVATE —) JUDEX
(PROMISING —) HOPEFUL
(PROSAIC —) PHILISTINE
(PRYING —) POKER PEEPER SMELLER
(PUDGY —) FATSO FATTY PODGE PUDGE ROLYPOLY
(PUGNOSED —) CAMUS CAMUSE
(PUNY —) SCART SHILP SHRIMP TITMAN
(PURITANICAL —) WOWSER
(QUEER —) RUM SKITE SKYTE GEEZER
(QUEER-LOOKING —) JIGGER
(QUERULOUS —) GRUMP JACKDAW
(QUICK-TEMPERED —) SPUNKIE WILDCAT SPITFIRE
(RAGGED —) ROTO SHAGRAG TATTERWAG
(RAPACIOUS —) SHARK CATERER
(RAWBONED —) SCRAG
(RECKLESS —) MADCAP RAMSTAM RANTIPOLE HELLBENDER
(RED-HAIRED —) BRIQUE
(REFRACTORY —) BUCKIE
(RELENTLESS —) HARDFACE
(REMARKABLE —) PHENOMENON
(RESOLUTE —) STALWART

(RESTLESS —) RAMPLER RAMPLOR RANTIPOLE
(RETICENT —) CLAM
(RICH —) MONEYBAGS
(RIDICULOUS —) GOOF HARE MONIMENT MONUMENT
(RIOTOUS —) ROARER
(ROBUST —) STRAPPER
(ROUGH —) TOWSER
(ROUGH-LOOKING —) RULLION
(RUDE —) HICK PORK RULE CHURL CLOWN GROBIAN
(RUSTIC —) COON KERN KERNE HAYSEED HOMESPUN
(SAINTLY —) SADDIK
(SANGUINE —) OPTIMIST
(SAUCY —) PIET
(SCRAWNY —) SCART SCRAG
(SECRETIVE —) OYSTER
(SELF-ASSERTIVE —) PUSHER
(SELF-CENTERED —) HEEL DEVIL FLANEUR
(SELF-RIGHTEOUS —) PHARISEE
(SELFISH —) HOGG
(SENSUAL —) SWING CARNALIST
(SENTIMENTAL —) MARSHMALLOW
(SEXY —) DISH
(SHAMEFUL —) BISMER
(SHIFTY—) SLICKER
(SHORT —) CRILE FADGE KNURL STUMP
(SHOWY —) FLASH FLASHER HOTSHOT
(SHREWD —) FILE YEPE HARDHEAD SNOLLYGOSTER
(SICK —) SICK MALADE PATIENT AEGROTANT
(SICKLY —) INVALID
(SILENT —) MUM MUMCHANCE
(SILLY —) FOP CAKE DITZ GUMP SOFT DOBBY GOOSE SOFTY SPOON CUCKOO NIMSHI SOFTIE GOOSECAP LIRIPIPE LIRIPOOP SOFTHEAD
(SILLY OR CRAZY —) DINGBAT
(SIMPLE —) DRIP LAMB IDIOT TURKEY PIGWIGEON
(SINGULAR —) ODDITY
(SKINNY —) SCRAE SCARECROW
(SLATTERNLY —) SLATE
(SLIM—) SWABBLE
(SLOTHFUL —) SLOWBELLY
(SLOVENLY —) HASH SLOB SLORP TRAIL STREEL SLOMMACK STREELER
(SLUGGISH —) LUMP DOLDRUM DRUMBLE LOBCOCK
(SLY —) COON SLYBOOTS SNECKDRAW SNICKDRAW
(SMALL —) GRIG TICH TICK AGATE DWARF SPRAT INSECT MORSEL POPPET SACKET GNATLING MUNCHKIN
(SOLEMN —) OWL

(SOPHISTICATED —) WELTKIND
(SPIRITED —) SPUNK SPUNKIE
(SPIRITLESS —) MOPE STICK
(SPITEFUL —) HELLCAT ETTERCAP
(SPRUCE —) SPRUSADO
(STIFF —) POKER STICK
(STINGY —) CHURL HAYNE STINGY
(STOCKY —) STUMP
(STOLID —) CLAM THICKSKIN
(STRANGE —) WAMPUS
(STRANGE OR ECCENTRIC —) WEIRDO
(STRAY —) WAIF
(STUBBORN —) BUCKY STOUT BUCKIE
(STUMPY —) SPUD SQUAB
(STUNTED —) URF SCRUNT SHARGAR
(STUPID —) ASS DIP DUB JAY MUT BETE BOOB DODO DOLT DOPE DRIP GAUM GAWP GOOF GUMP HASH HOIT JERK MOKE MUTT NERD PUTZ BLOCK BUCCA CLUCK CLUNK CUDDY DUMMY DUNCE HOBBY JUKES LOACH MORON SHEEP STIFF STIRK STOCK STUPE SUMPH SWINE THICK WAMUS ZOMBI BOODLE DAWKIN DIMWIT DODUNK DONKEY DOOFUS DUFFER DUMDUM GANDER GILLIE GRANNY GUNSEL LUMMOX LURDAN NITWIT NOODLE SACKET SHMUCK STUPEX TUMFIE TUMPHY TURKEY ZOMBIE AIRHEAD BLUNTIE DULLARD FATHEAD FUSSOCK HOWFING JACKASS JUGHEAD MUDHEAD PINHEAD SAPHEAD SCHMUCK SCHNOOK BONEHEAD BULLHEAD DOTTEREL DUMBBELL FLATHEAD GAMPHREL IRONHEAD MEATHEAD MOLDWARP MUMPHEAD STUNPOLL THICKWIT HODMANDOD MUMCHANCE THICKHEAD BUBBLEHEAD
(STUPID, FOOLISH —) YOYO
(STURDY —) LUMP CHUNK STALWART
(SUAVE —) SMOOTHIE
(SUBMISSIVE —) SLAVE
(SULKY —) GLUMP GRUMP SUMPH GROUCH
(SUPERLATIVE —) SMASHEROO
(SURLY —) CRUST HUNKS
(TACITURN —) OYSTER
(TALKATIVE —) GASSER BLELLUM BIGMOUTH
(TALL, AWKWARD —) GAMMERSTANG
(TENDER —) LAMBKIN
(THICKSET —) NUGGET
(THIN —) RAKE WRAITH BEANPOLE
(THIRD —) GOOSEBERRY
(THOUGHTLESS —) AIRLING SKIPPER BIRDBRAIN

(TIMID —) MOUSE RABBIT NEBBISH MILQUETOAST

(TIMID OR MEEK —) NEBBISH

(TINY —) KEEROGUE

(TIRESOME) PILL

(TIRESOME —) BORE PILL BROMIDE

(TOUGH —) STUD

(TRADITIONAL —) SQUARE

(TREACHEROUS —) JUDAS SNAKE VIPER GUNSEL SERPENT

(TRICKY —) SLYBOOTS

(TROUBLESOME —) COW PEST HELLION HESSIAN

(TRUSTWORTHY —) TRAIST STANDBY

(TRUSTY —) TROJAN

(TYRANNICAL —) SATRAP

(UNAPPRECIATIVE —) INGRATE

(UNATTRACTIVE —) DRIP GOON GRUB NERD NURD SCUG CREEP DWEEB

(UNBENDING —) STIFF

(UNCHASTE —) SHORTHEELD

(UNCIVILIZED —) VISIGOTH

(UNCOUTH —) APE PUT STIFF YAHOO BABOON SLOMMACK ROUGHNECK

(UNDERSIZED —) DURGAN SPARROW

(UNEMOTIONAL —) ICEBERG

(UNFAITHFUL —) INFIDEL

(UNGAINLY —) CLATCH

(UNGRACIOUS —) NEANY MEANIE

(UNHANDY —) FOUTER

(UNHAPPY —) UNSEL

(UNIMPORTANT —) MINNOW NOTHING SCHNOOK NONENTITY

(UNIQUE —) ONER

(UNKNOWN —) INCONNU STRANGER

(UNLUCKY —) SHLIMAZEL SCHLIMAZEL

(UNMARRIED —) MAIDEN SINGLE AGAMIST BACHELOR CELIBATE SPINSTER

(UNPLEASANT —) NERD NURD SCUMBAG

(UNPRACTICAL —) MUFF

(UNREASONABLE —) DUFFER

(UNRULY —) TURK

(UNSCRUPULOUS —) CATSO KNAVE

(UNSOPHISTICATED —) JAY HICK NYAS HAYSEED CORNBALL INNOCENT

(UNTHANKFUL —) INGRATE

(UNTIDY —) SLOVEN STREEL SLAISTER

(UNUSUALLY INTELLIGENT —) WHIZKID WHIZZKID

(UNWANTED THIRD —) GOOSEBERRY

(UNWIELDY —) FUSTILUGS

(USELESS —) POOP SWAB UNSEL BAUCHLE

(VALOROUS) HERO

(VENOMOUS —) SPITPOISON

(VIGOROUS —) SNEEZER

(VIOLENT —) DRAGON BANGSTER SPITFIRE

(VIRILE —) STUD

(VORACIOUS —) HUNGARIAN

(VULGAR —) MUCKER

(WANTON —) RIG FLIRT WHIPSTER

(WASTEFUL —) SCATTERGOOD SPENDTHRIFT

(WEAK —) WIMP SCART SHILP SOFTY PUSSYCAT WHIMLING

(WEAK-MINDED —) SAPHEAD TOTTYHEAD

(WEAK-WILLED —) PUTTY

(WEAK OR INEFFECTUAL —) WIMP

(WEALTHY —) MONEYBAGS

(WELL-BORN —) FREE

(WHITE —) FAY OFAY GRIFFIN EUROPEAN PALEFACE

(WICKED —) DEVIL SATAN SHREW UNLEAD UNLEDE SATANIST

(WILD —) HELLICAT RANTIPOLE

(WILY —) PIE

(WITHERED —) RUNT

(WITLESS —) WITHAM WITTOME SLABBERER

(WITTY —) WITSHIP SPARKLER

(WORNOUT —) HUSHEL

(WORTHLESS —) GIT YAP FILE GEAR HOIT JADE LOON SCUM TOOT CRUMB LOREL LOSEL SCOUT SHAND BAUBLE BUGGER FELLOW FOUTRA SHICER DUDMAGH GULLION BLIGHTER VAGABOND PHARMAKOS

(WRETCHED —) MISER MISERY

(YOUNG) CUB KID COLT LAMB CHILD HEMPY SMOLT SMOUT SPRIG YONKE GUNSEL HEMPIE JUNIOR CHICKEN CHOOKIE GRISTLE LAMBKIN JUVENILE STRIPLING

(PL.) FRY PERSONNEL

(PREF.) PROSOP(O)

(SUFF.) (FEMALE —) INE

PERSONABLE COMELY SHAPELY HANDSOME

PERSONAGE DON DUSE NIBS BLOKE FIGURE SHOGUN TYCOON

(EXALTED —) STATE

(GREAT —) MOGUL SOPHI SOPHY SUFFEE

(GROTESQUE —) PUNCHINELLO

PERSONAL SELF PRIVY DIRECT PRIVATE CHATTELS CORPORAL INTIMATE

(— EFFECTS) DUNNAGE

(PREF.) IDIO

PERSONALITY EGO AURA DRAW SELF SOUL BEING ETHOS HEART EGOITY FIGURE CONTROL FACULTY DEMIURGE PRESENCE SELFHOOD SELFNESS

(OF IMPATIENT —) TYPEA

PERSONATE ACT FEIGN MIMIC MASKED PERSON TYPIFY PRESENT

PERSONATION (SHAM —) IDOL
PERSONIFICATION SOUL GENIUS
  (— OF DIVINE VIRTUE) EON
  (— OF JUSTICE) THEMIS
  (— OF PRINCIPLES) AVATAR
PERSONIFY EMBODY INCARNATE
  PERSONIZE
PERSONNEL BLOOD STAFF KITCHEN
  PHYSIQUE
PERSPECTIVE ANGLE OPTICS
  DISTANCE TELESCOPE
PERSPICACIOUS KEEN ACUTE
  ASTUTE SHREWD
  (MAKE —) CLEAR
PERSPICACITY WIT ACUMEN
PERSPICUOUS CLEAR LUCID PLAIN
  PRECISE VISIBLE MANIFEST
  LIGHTSOME
PERSPIRATION DEW SUDOR SUINT
  SWEAT HIDROSIS OLIGIDRIA
  SUDORESIS
PERSPIRE PUG MELT BREAN SWEAT
  SWELTER TRANSPIRE
PERSUADE CON GET WIN COAX
  GAIN MOVE RULE SNOW TICE URGE
  WISE ARGUE BRING EDUCE SUADE
  SWADE WEISE ADVISE ARGUFY
  ASSURE CAJOLE ENGAGE ENTICE
  INDUCE REMOVE SUBORN CONVERT
  DISPUTE ENTREAT IMPRESS PREVAIL
  SATISFY CANOODLE INFLUENCE
  (— SUCCESSFULLY) SELL
PERSUADED PLIABLE GULLIBLE
  RESOLVED SENSIBLE
PERSUASION KIND SORT BELIEF
  OPINION SUASION JUDGMENT
  (AUTHOR OF —) AUSTEN
  (CHARACTER IN —) ANNE CLAY
  MARY CROFT ELLIOT LOUISA
  WALTER BENWICK CHARLES
  RUSSELL WILLIAM HARVILLE
  MUSGROVE ELIZABETH FREDERICK
  HENRIETTA WENTWORTH
PERSUASIVE COGENT WINNING
  INDUCTIVE PLAUSIBLE PROTEPTIC
  (PREF.) PITHANO
PERT BOLD CHIC FESS FLIP KECK
  SPRY TRIM ALERT ALIVE BARDY
  BRISK COCKY DONSY KISKY PEART
  PERKY PIERT QUICK SASSY SAUCY
  SMART TAUNT CHEEKY CLEVER
  COCKET COMELY DAPPER FRISKY
  SWASHY THWART BOBBISH
  PAUGHTY INSOLENT PETULANT
  (— TALK) CHELP
PERTAIN BE BEAR COME LONG
  BELIE TOUCH AFFEIR BEFALL BELIMP
  BELONG RELATE RETAIN CONCERN
  (— TO) RINE
PERTAINING (— TO ABDOMEN)
  ALVINE
  (— TO AFFAIRS OF STATE)
  PRAGMATIC

(— TO AGRICULTURE) GEORGIC
(— TO AIR) AURAL PNEUMATIC
(— TO ALL NATURE) PAMPHYSIC
(— TO ANIMALS) ZOIC
(— TO ANKLE) TARSAL
(— TO APOLLO) PYTHIAN PAEONIAN
(— TO APOSTLE) PETRINE
(— TO APPETITES) ORECTIC
(— TO ARMPIT) AXILLAR
(— TO ARMY) MARTIAL STRATONIC
(— TO ARROW) SAGITTAL
(— TO ART) TECHNICAL
(— TO ATHENA) PALLADIAN
(— TO BACK) DORSAL TERGAL
(— TO BATH) BALNEAL
(— TO BEAM) TRAGAL
(— TO BEARD) BARBAL
(— TO BED) THORAL
(— TO BEES) APIAN APIARIAN
(— TO BELLY) ALVIN ALVINE VENTRAL
VENTRIC
(— TO BIBLICAL LAW) LEVITIC
(— TO BIRDS) AVIAN AVINE ORNITHIC
VOLUCRINE
(— TO BIRTH) NATAL
(— TO BISHOP) LAWN
(— TO BITTER TASTE) PICRIC
(— TO BLACK SEA) PONTIC
(— TO BODIES AT REST) STATIC
(— TO BODY) SOMAL SOMATIC
(— TO BONE) OSSAL OSTEAL
(— TO BOSOM) GREMIAL
(— TO BRACELET) ARMILLARY
(— TO BRANCHES) RAMOUS
(— TO BREAD) PANARY
(— TO BREADMAKING) PANARY
(— TO BREAKFAST) ENTACULAR
(— TO BREAST) PECTORAL
(— TO BREASTBONE) STERNAL
(— TO BRISTLES) SETAL
(— TO BROTHEL) STEWISH
(— TO BUNCH) COMAL
(— TO CALF) VITULINE
(— TO CALF OF LEG) SURAL
(— TO CART) PLAUSTRAL
(— TO CARTHAGINIANS) PUNIC
(— TO CARVING) GLYPHIC
(— TO CAVE) SPELEAN SPELUNCAR
(— TO CHAIN) CATENARY
(— TO CHAMBER) CAMERAL
(— TO CHARIOTEER) AURIGAL
(— TO CHEEK) MALAR
(— TO CHESS) SCACCHIC
(— TO CHILDREN) PUERILE
(— TO CHINA) SINIAN SINISIAN
(— TO CITY) CIVIC URBAN
(— TO CLAN) SEPTAL
(— TO CLAY) BOLAR
(— TO CLOTHES) VESTIARY
VESTURAL
(— TO COAST) ORARIAN
(— TO COINS) NUMMARY
NUMISMATIC

(— TO COLOR) CHROMATIC
(— TO COMB) PECTINAL
(— TO CONSTRUCTION) TECTONIC
(— TO CONTESTS) AGONISTIC
(— TO CORK) SUBERIC SUBEROUS
(— TO COUGH) TUSSAL TUSSIVE
(— TO COURT) AULIC JUDICIAL JUDICIARY
(— TO CROCKERY) PIG
(— TO CROWN) CORONAL
(— TO DANCING) SALTATORY TRIPUDIAL
(— TO DAUGHTER OR SON) FILIAL
(— TO DAWN) EOAN
(— TO DEFENSE) PHYLACTIC
(— TO DESERTS) EREMIC
(— TO DIAPHRAGM) PHRENIC
(— TO DIGESTION) PEPTIC
(— TO DINNER) CENATORY PRANDIAL
(— TO DIVINATION) MANTIC
(— TO DOVE) COLUMBINE
(— TO DREAMS) ONEIRIC ONIROTIC
(— TO DRINKING) BIBITORY
(— TO DUNG) STERCORAL
(— TO EARTH) GEAL TELLURIC TERRANEAN
(— TO EARTHQUAKE) SEISMAL SEISMIC
(— TO EAST) EOAN
(— TO EGGS) OVAL
(— TO ESSENCE) BASIC
(— TO EUNUCH) SPADONIC
(— TO EVENING) VESPER
(— TO EYELIDS) BLEPHARAL
(— TO FACE) PROSOPIC
(— TO FAIR) NUNDINAL
(— TO FAITH) PIOTIC
(— TO FEET) PEDAL PEDARY
(— TO FERMENTATION) ZYMIC ZYMOTIC
(— TO FIELDS) AGRARIAN
(— TO FINGERS) DIGITAL
(— TO FISH) PISCINE
(— TO FISHING) HALIEUTIC
(— TO FLEAS) PULICENE PULICOSE
(— TO FLESH) SARCOUS
(— TO FLOCK) GREGAL
(— TO FLOOD) DILUVIAL DILUVIAN
(— TO FLOWERS) FLORAL ANTHINE
(— TO FOREARM) CUBITAL
(— TO FOREHEAD) METOPIC
(— TO FORM) MORPHIC
(— TO FOX) VULPINE
(— TO FRANCE) GALLICAN
(— TO FRESH WATER) LIMNETIC
(— TO FROGS) ANURAN RANINE
(— TO FRUIT) POMONAL POMONIC
(— TO FUNERALS) EXEQUIAL
(— TO FUNGUS) MYCETOID
(— TO FURNACE) FORNACIC
(— TO GALLOWS) PATIBULARY
(— TO GARDEN) HORTULAN
(— TO GARRISON) PRESIDIAL

(— TO GENTILES) ETHNIC
(— TO GLASS) VITREOUS
(— TO GOATS) CAPRIC
(— TO GOVERNMENT) ARCHICAL POLITICAL
(— TO GRANDPARENTS) AVAL
(— TO GRINDING) MOLINARY
(— TO GROIN) INGUINAL
(— TO GROUND) SOLARY
(— TO GROVE) NEMORAL
(— TO GULLS) LARINE
(— TO GUMS) ULETIC GINGIVAL
(— TO HAIR) PILAR CRINAL PILARY
(— TO HAND) CHIRAL MANUAL
(— TO HARE) LEPORINE
(— TO HAWKS) ACCIPITRINE
(— TO HEAD) CEPHALIC
(— TO HEALTH) HYGEIAN
(— TO HEAP) ACERVAL
(— TO HEART) CARDIAC
(— TO HEAT) CALORIC THERMAL THERMIC
(— TO HEAVEN) EMPYREAL EMPYREAN
(— TO HIPS) SCIATIC
(— TO HOLIDAY) FERIAL
(— TO HORIZON) MUNDANE
(— TO HORSE) EQUINE HIPPIC CABALLINE
(— TO HOSPITALITY) XENIAL XENIAN
(— TO HOUSE) DOMAL
(— TO HUNGER) FAMELIC
(— TO HUNTING) VENATIC VENERIAL CYNEGETIC
(— TO INCH) UNCIAL
(TO INTELLECT) NOETIC
(— TO INTESTINES) ALVIN ALVINE
(— TO JAW) MALAR GNATHAL GNATHIC
(— TO JOURNEY) VIATIC
(— TO KIDNEY) RENAL NEPHRIC
(— TO KNOWLEDGE) GNOSTIC
(— TO LAKES) LACUSTRINE
(— TO LAP) GREMIAL
(— TO LAUGHING) GELASTIC
(— TO LAUGHTER) RISORIAL
(— TO LEARNING) PALLADIAN
(— TO LEG) CRURAL
(— TO LICE) PEDICULAR
(— TO LIFE) VITAL ZOETIC
(— TO LINE) FILAR
(— TO LIPS) LABIAL
(— TO LIVER) HEPATIC JECORAL
(— TO LIVERPOOL) LIVERPUDLIAN
(— TO LOINS) LUMBAR
(— TO LOVE) EROTIC AMATORY
(— TO LUCK) ALEATORY
(— TO LUNGS) PULMONIC PNEUMONIC PULMONARY
(— TO MANCHESTER) MANCUNIAN
(— TO MANKIND) COMMON ANTHROPIC
(— TO MARBLE) MARMORIC

(— **TO MARKET**) NUNDINAL
(— **TO MARRIAGE**) MARITAL HYMENEAL
(— **TO MARS**) AREAN MAMERTINE MAVORTIAL
(— **TO MARSHES**) PALUDAL PALUDIC
(— **TO MASS**) MOLAR
(— **TO MASTER**) HERILE
(— **TO MEADOWS**) PRATAL
(— **TO MEAL**) PRANDIAL
(— **TO MECCA**) MECCAWEE
(— **TO MEDICINE**) IATRIC IATRICAL
(— **TO MEMORY**) MNESTIC MNEMONIC
(— **TO MIDDAY**) MERIDIAN
(— **TO MILK**) LACTARY LACTEAL
(— **TO MILL**) MOLINARY
(— **TO MIND**) MENTAL PHRENIC PSYCHIC PSYCHICAL
(— **TO MIRROR**) SPECULAR
(— **TO MOISTURE**) HYGRIC
(— **TO MONEY**) PECUNIARY
(— **TO MOON**) LUNAR SELENIC SELENIAN
(— **TO MORNING**) MATIN MATINAL MATUTINAL
(— **TO MOTION**) GESTIC KINETIC
(— **TO MOUNTAINS**) MONTANE
(— **TO MOUTH**) ORAL OSCULAR STOMATIC
(— **TO MUSCLE**) SARCOUS
(— **TO MUSES**) PIERIAN
(— **TO MUSIC**) HARMONIC
(— **TO MYSTERIES**) TELESTIC
(— **TO NAME**) ONOMASTIC
(— **TO NAMES**) ONOMASTIC
(— **TO NAVEL**) OMPHALIC
(— **TO NECK**) JUGULAR
(— **TO NEPHEW**) NEPOTAL
(— **TO NET**) RETIARY
(— **TO NEW ZEALAND**) ZELANIAN
(— **TO NIGHT**) NOCTURNAL
(— **TO NOSE**) NASAL RHINAL
(— **TO NUT**) NUCAL
(— **TO NUTRITION**) TROPHIC
(— **TO OAK**) QUERCINE ROBOREOUS
(— **TO OCEAN**) PELAGIC OCEANOUS THALASSIC
(— **TO OCEAN DEPTHS**) HADAL
(— **TO OLD AGE**) SENILE GERATIC GERONTIC
(— **TO OPEN SKY**) SUBDIAL
(— **TO PALACE**) PALATINE
(— **TO PALM**) VOLAR
(— **TO PARISH**) PAROCHIAL
(— **TO PARLOR**) BEN BOOR
(— **TO PARROTS**) PSITTACINE
(— **TO PASTURES**) PASCUAL
(— **TO PAWNBROKER**) AVUNCULAR
(— **TO PEACOCK**) PAVONINE
(— **TO PEARL**) MARGARIC
(— **TO PERSPIRATION**) SUDORIC

(— **TO PICTURE**) ICONIC
(— **TO PIGS**) PORCINE
(— **TO PINE**) WARRYN
(— **TO PLAGUE**) LOIMIC
(— **TO PLEASURE**) HEDONIC
(— **TO POETRY**) MUSAL IAMBIC
(— **TO POISON**) TOXIC
(— **TO POTTERY**) CERAMIC
(— **TO PRIESTS**) SACERDOTAL
(— **TO PRISON**) CARCERAL
(— **TO PULSE**) SPHYGMIC
(— **TO PUNISHMENT**) PENAL PUNITIVE
(— **TO PURIFICATION**) LUSTRAL
(— **TO QUEEN**) REGINAL
(— **TO RAIN**) HYETAL PLUVIAL
(— **TO RAINBOW**) IRIDAL
(— **TO REGISTER**) MATRICULAR
(— **TO REMOTE PLACE**) FORANE
(— **TO RESONANCE**) SYNTONIC
(— **TO RING**) ARMILLARY
(— **TO RISING**) ORTIVE
(— **TO RIVER**) AMNIC POTAMIC RIVERINE FLUMINOSE
(— **TO RIVER BANK**) RIPARIAN
(— **TO ROAD**) VIATIC
(— **TO ROCK**) PETREAN SAXATILE
(— **TO ROD**) BACULINE
(— **TO RUBBISH**) RUDERARY
(— **TO SABLES**) ZIBELINE
(— **TO SAIL**) VELIC
(— **TO SALVATION**) SOTERIAL
(— **TO SANDARAC**) THYINE
(— **TO SATURDAY**) SABBATINE
(— **TO SEAL**) PHOCINE SIGILLARY SPHRAGISTIC
(— **TO SEAM**) SUTURAL
(— **TO SEASHORE**) LITTORAL
(— **TO SEAWEED**) ALGOUS
(— **TO SENSE OF TASTE**) GUSTATIVE
(— **TO SEVEN**) SEPTIMAL
(— **TO SEWING**) SUTORIAL SUTORIAN
(— **TO SHEEP**) VERVECINE
(— **TO SHEPHERDS**) PASTORAL
(— **TO SHERIFF**) VICONTIEL
(— **TO SHIN**) CNEMIAL
(— **TO SHIP**) NAVICULAR
(— **TO SHOPMAN**) APOTHECAL
(— **TO SHOULDER**) ALAR SCAPULAR
(— **TO SIGHT**) VISUAL
(— **TO SIGNS**) SEMIC SEMANTIC
(— **TO SILVER**) LUNAR ARGENTAL
(— **TO SISTER**) SORORAL
(— **TO SKIN**) DERIC DERMAL CUTICULAR
(— **TO SLAVES**) SERVILE
(— **TO SLEEP**) SOMNIAL MORPHETIC
(— **TO SMELLING**) OLFACTORY
(— **TO SNAKE**) ANGUINE
(— **TO SNORING**) RHONCAL RHONCIAL

(— TO SNOW) NIVAL
(— TO SOFT PALATE) VELAR
(— TO SOIL) DAPHIC
(— TO SOLE) VOLAR
(— TO SONG) MELIC
(— TO SPECTACLE) THEORIC
(— TO SPEECH) PHEMIC
(— TO SPINAL CORD) MYELIC
(— TO SPRING) VERNAL
(— TO STARS) ASTRAL STELLAR SIDEREAL
(— TO STATE AFFAIRS) PRAGMATIC
(— TO STEPMOTHER) NOVERCAL
(— TO STOMACH) GASTRIC
(— TO STONE) LITHIC
(— TO STORKS) PELARGIC
(— TO SULPHUR) THIONIC
(— TO SUMMER) ESTIVAL AESTIVAL
(— TO SUN) SOLAR HELIAC
(— TO SUNDAY) DOMINICAL
(— TO SUNDIAL) SCIATHERIC
(— TO SUPPER) CENATORY
(— TO SURFACE OF ANYTHING) FACIAL
(— TO SWALLOWS) HIRUNDINE
(— TO SWEAT) SUDORIC
(— TO SWIMMING) NATATORY
(— TO SWINEHERD) SYBOTIC
(— TO TAIL) CAUDAL
(— TO TAILOR) SARTORIAL
(— TO TANNING) SC
(— TO TEACHER) MAGISTERIAL
(— TO TEARS) LACRIMAL LACHRYMAL
(— TO TEMPO) AGOGIC
(— TO THE BEAUTIFUL) ESTHETIC AESTHETIC
(— TO THIEVING) KLEPTISTIC
(— TO THIGH) CRURAL
(— TO THREAD) FILAR
(— TO THROAT) GULAR JUGULAR
(— TO THUNDER) FULMINEOUS
(— TO TILE) TEGULAR
(— TO TIN) STANNIC
(— TO TITHES) DECIMAL
(— TO TITMICE) PARINE
(— TO TOMB) TOMBAL
(— TO TONGUE) GLOSSAL LINGUAL
(— TO TORTOISES) CHELONIAN
(— TO TOUCH) TACTILE
(— TO TOWER) TURRICAL
(— TO TREES) DENDRAL ARBOREAL
(— TO TWENTY) VICENARY
(— TO UNCLE) AVUNCULAR
(— TO UNDERGROUND WATER) VADOSE PHREATIC
(— TO VESSEL) VASAL
(— TO VIRGIN) PARTHENIAN
(— TO VISION) OCULAR
(— TO VOW) VOTAL
(— TO WAGON) PLAUSTRAL
(— TO WALLS) MURAL PARIETAL

(— TO WAR) POLEMICAL
(— TO WASPS) VESPAL VESPINE
(— TO WAX) CERAL
(— TO WEAVING) TEXTORIAL
(— TO WEIGHT) BARIC PONDERAL PONDERARY
(— TO WELL) PHREATIC
(— TO WHALES) CETIC
(— TO WHEAT) VULGARE
(— TO WHEELS) ROTAL
(— TO WHETSTONES) COTICULAR
(— TO WIFE) UXORIAL
(— TO WILL) VOLITIVE
(— TO WIND) EOLIAN PNEUMATIC
(— TO WINE) VINIC VINOUS
(— TO WINE-MAKING) OENOPOETIC
(— TO WINGS) ALAR PTERIC EXRUPEAL PTEROTIC
(— TO WINTER) HIEMAL
(— TO WISDOM) PALLADIAN
(— TO WOMANKIND) MULIEBRAL
(— TO WOODPECKERS) PICINE
(— TO WOODS) SYLVAN NEMORAL
(— TO WORMS) VERMICULAR
(— TO WOUNDS) VULNERAL
(— TO WRIST) CARPAL
(— TO YESTERDAY) PRIDIAN
(— TO YEW) TAXINE
(SUFF.) (—TO) AL AR ORIOUS ORY

PERTINACIOUS FIRM STIFF DOGGED ADHERING STUBBORN OBSTINATE
PERTINENCE RELEVANCE
PERTINENCY FORCE
PERTINENT APT FIT PAT HAPPY COGENT PROPER TIMELY ADAPTED APROPOS GERMANE POINTED TELLING INCIDENT MATERIAL RELATIVE RELEVANT
PERTLY CROUSE
PERTURB BITE GRATE UPSET WORRY DISMAY AGITATE CONFUSE CONTURB DERANGE DISTURB TROUBLE
PERTURBATION DISMAY FLIGHT POTHER UNEASE POOTHER STICKLE TROUBLE TURMOIL EVECTION AGITATION
PERTURBED UNEASY
PERTUSSIS COUGH CHINCOF CHINCOUGH

PERU

CAPITAL: LIMA
COIN: SOL LIBRA DINERO CENTAVO
DEPARTMENT: ICA LIMA PUNO CUSCO CUZCO JUNIN PIURA TACNA ANCASH LORETO TUMBES
DESERT: SECHURA
ISLAND: CHINCHA
LAKE: TITICACA
LANGUAGE: AYMARA QUECHUA

MEASURE: TOPO VARA GALON
CELEMIN FANEGADA
MONEY: INTI
MOUNTAIN: HUAMINA COROPUNA
HAUSCARAN
PERIOD: RECUAY
RIVER: NAPU RIMAC SANTA TIGRE
MORONA YAGUAS YAVARI CURARAY
MARANON PASTAZA UCAYALI
AMAZONAS APURIMAC HUALLAGA
URUBAMBA
TOWN: ICA LIMA PUNO CUZCO PAITA
PISCO PIURA TACNA CALLAO
TUMBES IQUITOS AREQUIPA
CHICLAYO TRUJILLO
VOLCANO: MISTI YUCAMANI
WEIGHT: LIBRA QUINTAL

PERUKE WIG FLASH GALERA TOUPEE
GALERUM PERIWIG WIGGERY
PERUSAL SIGHT LECTURE SCRUTINY
PERUSE CON READ SCAN STUDY
HANDLE SEARCH SURVEY EXAMINE
INSPECT
(— QUICKLY) SKIM
PERUVIAN BARK CALISAYA
CINCHONA
PERVADE FILL BATHE IMBUE
DRENCH INSTIL OCCUPY THREAD
INSTILL PERMEATE TRAVERSE
PERVADED STIFF
PERVASIVE POIGNANT
PERVERSE AUK AWK CAM CAR
AWRY WOGH WRAW CROSS DONSY
GAMMY THRAW WROTH CUSSED
DIVERS LOUCHE THRAWN THWART
WICKED WILFUL WRAIST AWKWARD
CRABBED CROOKED DIVERSE
FORWARD FROWARD OBLIQUE
PEEVISH WAYWARD CAMSHACH
CRANKISH STUBBORN
PERVERSELY AUK AWK AWRY
ATHWART OVERWART
PERVERSION WREST ABUSION
(— OF TASTE) MALACIA
PERVERT WRY DRAW RACK RUIN
SKEW TURN WARP ABUSE CROOK
GLOSS TWIST UPSET WREST
DEBASE DETORT DIVERT GARBLE
INVERT MISUSE POISON VOYEUR
WRENCH WRITHE CONTORT
CORRUPT DEGRADE DEPRAVE
DEVIATE DISTORT MISTURN
SUBVERT TRADUCE VITIATE
MISWREST
PERVERTED BAD WICKED ABUSIVE
AWKWARD CORRUPT TWISTED
VICIOUS
PERVERTER WRESTER
PERVIOUS LEACHY PERVIAL
PERVADING
PES NEUME TENOR PODATUS

PESKY VERY PLAGUY ANNOYING
DEVILING EXTREMELY
PESO DURO CONANT DOLLAR
CAROLUS PATACAO
PESSIMISM WELTSCHMERZ
MISERABILISM
PESSIMIST ALARMIST JEREMIAH
WORRYWART
PESSIMISTIC GLOOMY ALARMED
BEARISH CYNICAL DOWNBEAT
PEST BOT BANE GNAT TICK WEED
APHIS MOUSE MYZUS TRAIK INSECT
MENACE PLAGUE SCHELM SORROW
VERMIN HASSLER NUDNICK
SCOURGE MEALYBUG SANDMITE
BUTTINSKY
(GARDEN —) APHID
PESTER DUN HOX NAG RAG RIB TIG
HAKE ANNOY DEVIL TEASE WORRY
BADGER BOTHER HARASS INFEST
MOLEST BEDEVIL TORMENT
TROUBLE OBSTRUCT PERSECUTE
PESTHOUSE LAZARET LAZARETTO
PESTICIDE ALAR BIOCIDE FUMIGANT
PESTILENCE LUES PEST DEATH
QUALM PLAGUE MURRAIN EPIDEMIC
MORTALITY
PESTILENT FATAL DEADLY VEXING
NOXIOUS
PESTLE MIX BRAY GRIND PESTL
PILUM STAMP BEETLE BRAYER
MULLER PISTIL CHAPPER POUNDER
STAMPER
PET TOY CADE COAX DAUT DEAR
DUCK HUFF LAMB NECK PEAT SNIT
SOCK SULK TIFF DRUNT DUCKY
HUMOR QUIET SPOIL SPOON TETCH
CARESS CODDLE COSHER COSSET
CUDDLE DANDLE DAUTIE DAWTIE
FADDLE FANTAD FANTOD FONDLE
GENTLE PAMPER PETKIN SMOOCH
SQUALL STROKE WANTON CHERISH
DARLING INDULGE PINKENY
TANTRUM TIDLING UMBRAGE
WHITHER CANOODLE FAVORITE
TIDDLING PADDYWACK
(— NICKNAME) DEARIE
PETAL ALA HELM HOOD LEAF WING
BANNER
(— IN PEA FLOWER) VEXILLUM
(— OF IRIS) STANDARD
(FLOWER —S) ALAE
(UPPER —) HOOD BANNER
(PL.) COROLLA
PETALIA NYCTERIS
PETARD PITTARD FIREWORK
PETATE BANIG
PETECHIA STIGMA
PETER P FADE FAIL PEAK SAFE WANE
CEASE PEDRO PIERS PIERRE SIGNAL
DWINDLE
(— OUT) FIZZLE

(BROTHER OF —) ANDREW
(FATHER OF —) JONAS
PETER GRIMES (CHARACTER IN —)
ELLEN PETER GRIMES ORFORD
BALSTRODE
(COMPOSER OF —) BRITTEN
PETER IBBETSON (AUTHOR OF —)
DUMAURIER
(CHARACTER IN —) DEANE MADGE
MIMSY PETER LINTOT GREGORY
PLUNKET IBBETSON PASQUIER
PETERMAN YEGG
PETER PAN (AUTHOR OF —) BARRIE
(CHARACTER IN —) PAN HOOK JOHN
NIBS SMEE PETER WENDY TINKER
DARLING MICHAEL TOOTLES
MARGARET SLIGHTLY
PETHAHIAH (FATHER OF —)
MESHEZABEEL
PETHEUL (SON OF —) JOEL
PETIOLE STEM SPINE STALK STIPE
PODEON PEDUNCLE PHYLLODE
LEAFSTALK
PETITE SMALL LITTLE MIGNON
MIGNONNE
PETITION ASK BEG SUE BILL BOON
PLEA PRAY SUIT VOTE WISH APPLY
ORATE PLEAD APPEAL DESIRE
INVOKE MOTION PLACIT PRAYER
STEVEN ADDRESS BESEECH
ENTREAT IMPLORE ORATION SOLICIT
ROGATION SUFFRAGE
(MAKE —) SUE
(PL.) PRECES
PETITIONER BEGGAR ORATOR
SUITOR BEADSMAN APPLICANT
ENTREATER PLAINTIFF
PETO WAHOO
PETREL BILL TITI CAHOW MITTY
NELLY PRION WITCH FULMAR
SPENCY TEETEE ASSILAG GLUTTON
KAEDING PINTADO SEABIRD
SEAFOWL STINKER ALLAMOTH
FORKTAIL STINKPOT ALLAMOTTI
MALLEMUCK NIGHTHAWK
PETRIFY DAZE APPAL SCARE APPALL
DEADEN STONIFY STUPEFY
FRIGHTEN LAPIDIFY FOSSILIZE
GORGONIZE
PETRIFYING STONY GORGON
PETROL GAS GASOLINE
PETROLATUM VASELINE
PETROLEUM OIL CRUDE PETROL
NAPHTHA
(— INDUSTRY) OILDOM
(CRUDE —) MAZOUT
PETRUCHIO (WIFE OF —) KATHERINE
PE-TSAI PECHAY
PETTED CADE DANDILY
PETTICOAT BAJO GORE KILT SLIP
SOUS DICKY GREEN JUPON PAGNE
SOUSE KIRTLE LUHINGA PLACKET

WHITTLE BALMORAL BASQUINE
WILYCOAT UNDERSKIRT
(— OF TARGET) GREEN
PETTIFOG FOG CAVIL BICKER
PETTIFOGGER FOGGER SHYSTER
LEGULEIAN
PETTINESS NAGGLE PARVINIMITY
PETTING COLLING
PETTISH DORTY HUFFY FRETFUL
PEEVISH PLAINTIVE
PETTY TIN BASE JERK MEAN ORRA
PUNY VAIN BANAL GRIMY MINOR
PETIT PUNEE SMALL MEASLY
MINUTE PALTRY PEANUT POKING
PUISNE PUSILL SNIFTY TWOBIT
KITLING PIMPING TRIVIAL TWATTLE
CHILDISH FIDDLING INFERIOR
NIGGLING NUGATORY PEDDLING
PICAYUNE PIFFLING SNIPPETY
TRIFLING PAROCHIAL
(PREF.) MICR(O)
(SUFF.) (—ONE) EEN
PETULANCE PROCACITY
PETULANT PERT CROSS SAUCY
SHORT TESTY TIFFY FEISTY SULLEN
WANTON WILFUL CRABBED FRETFUL
FROWARD HUFFISH PEEVISH
WASPISH PERVERSE SNAPPISH
PEULTHAI (FATHER OF —)
OBEDEDOM
PEUMUS BOLDU
PEW BOX PUE ROUT DESK PFUI PUGH
SEAT SLIP BENCH BUGHT STALL
BOUGHT
(— ATTACHMENT) KNEELER
PEWEE PEWIT PEEWEE PEEWIT
PEWIT PEESWEEP
PEWTER CUP BIDRI BIDRY ETAIN
MONEY PUDER BIDERY TRIFLE
PEAUDER SADWARE TUTENAG
(— MARK) TOUCHMARK
PEYOTE HIKULI MESCAL
PFENNIG PENNING
PHAEDRA (AUTHOR OF —)
RACINE
(CHARACTER IN —) ARICIA OENONE
PHAEDRA THESEUS HIPPOLYTUS
THERAMENES
(FATHER OF —) MINOS
(HUSBAND OF —) THESEUS
(MOTHER OF —) PASIPHAE
(SISTER OF —) ADRIADNE
(SON OF —) ACAMAS DEMOPHON
PHAETON DUKE FAETON SPIDER
STANHOPE
PHAETON BUTTERFLY
BALTIMORE
PHALANGER TAIT ARIEL TAPOA
CUSCUS TAGUAN OPOSSUM
PENTAIL SQUIRREL
PHALAROPE LOBIPED COOTFOOT
LOBEFOOT WHALEBIRD

PHALERA BEAD BOSS DISK STUD CAMEO
PHALTI (FATHER OF —) LAISH
PHANTASM DREAM FANCY GHOST VAPOR FIGURE SHADOW SPIRIT FANTASY PHANTOM SPECIES SPECTER SPECTRE
PHANTASMAL EERIE UNREAL SPECTRAL
PHANTASUS (BROTHER OF —) ICELUS MORPHEUS PHOBETOR THANATOS
(FATHER OF —) HYPNOS SOMNUS
(MOTHER OF —) NYX
PHANTASY FANCY FANTASY PHANTASIA
PHANTOM IDOL BOGEY BOGLE DUMMY GHOST IMAGE PHASM SHADE SHAPE UMBRA BOGGLE DOUBLE FANTOM IDOLON IDOLUM SHADOW SPIRIT BUGBEAR EIDOLON ELUSIVE FANTASY FEATURE SPECIES SPECTER ILLUSORY ADAMASTOR SIMULACRUM
PHANUEL (DAUGHTER OF —) ANNA
PHARAOH ALE FARO PHARO TYRANT BUSIRIS
PHARAOH'S HEN VULTURE
PHAREZ (BROTHER OF —) ZARAH
(FATHER OF —) JUDAH
(MOTHER OF —) TAMAR
PHARISEE MUGWUMP NICODEMUS
PHARMACEUTICAL MERCURIAL
(SUFF.) (—PRODUCT) EIN EINE IN INE
PHARMACIST CHEMIST DRUGGIST DISPENSER APOTHECARY
PHARMACY FERMACY DRUGSTORE
PHAROS CLOAK LIGHT TORCH BEACON LANTERN
PHARYNGEAL FAUCAL
PHARYNX MASTAX PROBOSCIS
(PREF.) LAEMO LEM(O)
PHASE EFT END LEG FAZE SIDE ANGLE FACET GRADE STAGE ASPECT AVATAR BACKLASH PASSOVER DICHOTOMY
(INITIAL —) BUD
(LOWEST —) BATHOS
(TRANSITORY —) STREAK
PHASM FANTOM METEOR PHASMA PHANTOM
PHEASANT CHIR GUAN ARGUS CHEER KALIJ MINAL MONAL COUCAL GROUSE LEIPOA MAGPIE MONAUL MOONAL PUKRAS KALLEGE FIREBACK ITHAGINE RINGNECK TRAGOPAN MACARTNEY
(BREEDING PLACE FOR —S) STEW
(BROOD OF —) NID NYE NIDE
(YOUNG —) POULT
PHEASANT CUCKOO COUCAL
PHEASANT DUCK PINTAIL MERGANSER

PHEASANT FINCH WAXBILL
PHEASANT'S-EYE ROSARUBY
PHEBE (HUSBAND OF —) SILVIUS
PHELLEM CORK SUBER
PHENOBARBITOL LUMINAL
PHENOCRYST INSET
PHENOL BHT LACCOL THYMOL ALOESOL CREOSOL DURENOL EUGENOL ORCINOL CHAVICOL RESORCIN CARVACROL
PHENOMENA
PHENOMENON FIRE ANOMY COLOR EVENT IMAGE ARTHUS EFFECT METEOR MIRAGE SHADOW ISOTOPY MIRACLE PARADOX PROCESS SYMPTOM ASTERISM PRAKRITI SIDERISM SUNQUAKE LANDSPOUT
(ATMOSPHERIC —) METEOR
(LUMINOUS —) FIREDRAKE
(METEOROGICAL —) STORM
PHENYLSALICYLATE SALOL
PHERES (BROTHER OF —) AESON AMYTHAON
(DAUGHTER OF —) IDOMENE PERIAPIS
(FATHER OF —) CRETHEUS
(MOTHER OF —) TYRO
(NEPHEW OF —) JASON
(SON OF —) ADMETUS LYCURGUS
PHIAL CUP FIAL VIAL CRUET BOTTLE VESSEL
PHILABEG KILT FILIBEG
PHILANDER FOOL WOLF DALLY FLIRT SMOCK
PHILANTHROPIC HUMANE
PHILANTHROPIST DONOR SHARER ALTRUIST HUMANITARIAN
AMERICAN DIX CASE DUKE FELS HOGG HOLT LICK LOEB MOTT RICE SAGE URIS VAUX YALE AVERY BACHE BRUCE DEPEW EVANS FRICK GERRY GETTY GRATZ HEINZ LENOX LEWYT MILLS ODGEN PEROT PRATT SMITH TRASK TULLY COOPER CRERAR DEDMAN EUSTIS FOLSON GEORGE GIRARD GURLEY HAYDEN HEARST LAMONT LASKER LEHMAN LOWELL MELLON MILLER MORGAN MURPHY PEPPER PHIPPS PUTNAM ROBERT SCHIFF STRAUS TAPPAN TULANE COCHRAN CORNELL DOREMUS FARNHAM GILBERT GRELLET HOPKINS LATHROP LAZARUS MILBANK PARRISH PEABODY RUTGERS RYERSON SHEPARD STEWART WARBURG CARNEGIE CORCORAN HARKNESS HARRIMAN LEWISOHN PHILLIPS ROBINSON STERLING JUILLIARD MEYERHOFF ROSENWALD SHEFFIELD CRITTENTON GUGGENHEIM SULZBERGER

VANDERBILT ABERCROMBIE
ROCKEFELLER
AUSTRIAN FRANKL
CANADIAN MCGILL
ENGLISH FRY GUY COBBE CORAM
  CORRY KYRLE MAYER SHARP
  WAUGH GURNEY KENYON SLOANE
  COWDRAY HIBBERT MONTAGU
  PEARSON RYLANDS CHRISTIE
  KINNAIRD MACAULAY SOMERSET
  FAITHFULL MONTEFIORE
  OGLETHORPE SHAFTESBURY
  WHITTINGTON WILBERFORCE
FRENCH MANCE GIRARD MARBEAU
  MONTYON MICHELIN MIRAMION
GERMAN FALK HIRSCH MULLER
  FLIEDNER
INDIAN JEEJEEBHOY
IRISH RICE GONNE MADDEN
ITALIAN KRIM
RUSSIAN NOVIKOV
SCOTTISH DALE HERIOT FINDLAY
  GUTHRIE
SWEDISH NOBEL
SWISS DUNANT
PHILANTHROPY CHARITY
  ALMSGIVING
PHILEMATOLOGY KISSING
PHILEMON (WIFE OF —) BAUCIS
PHILIP PIP PHLP SPARROW
PHILIPPIC SATIRE SCREED TIRADE
  ABUSIVE DIATRIBEU JOLO MATI
  ALBAY DAVAO DIGOS LAOAG PASAY
  VIGAN APARRI BAGUIO CAVITE
  ILAGAN ILOILO MANILA BACOLOD
  BASILAN DAGUPAN CALOOCAN

PHILIPPINES
ARCHIPELAGO: SULU
CAPITAL: DAGUIO MANILA
COIN: PESO PISO PESATA CENTAVO
  SENTIMO
FIBER: ERUC ABACA BUNTAL
ISLAND: CEBU BATAN BOHOL LEYTE
  LUZON PANAY SAMAR NEGROS
  MASBATE MINDORO PALAWAN
  ROMBLON MINDANAO
LAKE: TAAL LANAO
LANGUAGE: MORO BICOL IBANAG
  ILOCANO TAGALOG VISAYAN
MEASURE: LOAN BRAZA CABAN
  CAUAN CHUPA GANTA APATAN
  BALITA QUINON
MOUNTAIN: APO IBA MAYON PULOG
  BANAHAO
NATIVE: ATA ATI ITA TAO AETA ATTA
  ETAS MORO SULU BICOL TAGAL
  VICOL IGOROT TIMAUA BISAYAN
  TAGALOG FILIPINO
PROVINCE: ABRA CEBU SULU ALBAY
  CAPIZ DAVAO LANAO RIZAL BAATAN
  CAVITE IFUGAO ILOILO TARLAC
  SURIGAO

RIVER: ABRA AGNO MAGAT PASIG
  AGUSAN LAOANG CAGAYAN
  MINDANAO PAMPANGA
TOWN: IBA AGOA BOAC CEBU JOLA
  MATI ALBAY DAVAO DIGOS LAOAG
  PASAY VIGAN APARRI BAGUIO
  CAVITE ILAGAN ILOILO MANILA
  BACOLOD BASILAN DAGUPAN
  CALOOCAN
TREE: DAO IDA TUA TUI ACLE ANAM
  ATES BOGO DITA IPIL CUIJO LAUAN
  TICAO ALUPAG ANAHAU ARANGA
  ANONANG APITONG TINDALO
  ALMACIGA AMPALAYA
VOLCANO: APO TAAL MAYON
  BULOSAN CANLAON
WEIGHT: CATTY FARDO PICUL PUNTO
  LACHSA QUILATE CHINANTA

PHILISTINE BOOB GIGMAN MUCKER
  BABBITT GITTITE BOEOTIAN
  BARBARIAN BOURGEOIS
  HYPOCRITE
  (— CITY) GATH
  (PL.) PULESATI PURASATI
  CAPHTORIM
PHILOLOGIST LAVENGRO
  LINGUIST
AMERICAN BUCK COOK HART TODD
  WOOD ADLER BROWN CHILD CURME
  GIBBS HEMPL MARCH MARSH
  DENDER BRIGHT MARDEN PRINCE
  REEVES CHOMSKY EMERSON
  GEROULD GUDEMAN HOPKINS
  KENNEDY LEARNED SHELDON
  WHITMAN HARRISON TRUMBULL
  GREENOUGH KORZYBSKI
  BLOOMFIELD STURTEVANT
AUSTRIAN MINOR MULLER KARAJAN
  REINISCH SCHONBACH
COLOMBIAN CUERVO MARROQUIN
CZECH HANKA GEBAUER
  JUNGMANN DOBROVSKY
DANISH RAFN RASK VERNER
  HEIBERG MOLBECH THOMSEN
  JESPERSEN WESTERGAARD
DUTCH KATE KERN BRINK VRIES
  VREESE WINKEL HEINSIUS
  HEREMANS UHLENBECK
  HUYDECOPER VALCKENAER
  HEMSTERHUIS
ENGLISH WYLD ASTON EARLE ELLIS
  NARES SAYCE SKEAT TOOKE
  CONWAY CRAGIE GOWERS MORRIS
  MURRAY ONIONS THORPE WERNER
  WRIGHT ALLEGRO GARNETT
  GOMPERZ SKINNER WEEKLEY
  BOSWORTH CHADWICK STEPHENS
  WEYMOUTH COLERIDGE
  DONALDSON FURNIVALL
FINNISH SETALA CASTREN
FRENCH ADAM BREAL DOLET EGGER
  HENRY LEBAS MEYER RENAN

BRUNOT LAMBIN WAILLY BRACHET
BURNOUF MEILLET LEFEBVRE
VAUGELAS CHABANEAU QUICHERAT
HOVELACQUE DARMESTETER
GERMAN AST ABEL BIRT BOPP DIEZ
FICK HIRT JULG KERN MOGK PAUL
POTT WOLF BERGK BLANC BLASS
BOCKH EBERT GREIN GRIMM HAASE
HAGEN HAUPT HEYNE HEYSE JUSTI
KLOTZ KRAPF KRAUS KROLL LEHRS
MEYER NIESE PAULY ZEUSS BECKER
BEKKER BENFEY CHRIST FREUND
FRISCH HENZEN JACOBI JACOBS
KELLER KOCHLY MARTIN MULLER
PASSOW REISKE VAHLEN VIETOR
ADELUNG BARTSCH BERNAYS
BRANDIS BURSIAN CORSSEN
CREUZER CURTIUS DINDORF
DUNTZER GERLAND KIEPERT
KORTING LEPSIUS LESKIEN
MATZNER OSTHOFF RIBBECK
RITSCHL RUHNKEN SANDERS
SCHERER SIEVERS WEIGAND
WELCKER WISSOWA ZARNCKE
ZUPITZA AUFRECHT BEHAGHEL
BISCHOFF BOTTIGER BRUGMANN
FOERSTER GRAEVIUS HOFFMANN
HUMBOLDT MASSMANN SCHRADER
THIERSCH WEINHOLD WESTPHAL
XYLANDER ACIDALIUS BAUMSTARK
BERNHARDY BUSCHMANN
ETTMULLER FRISCHLIN GABELENTZ
HOLTZMANN KIRCHHOFF
KOSCHWITZ STEINTHAL
TRAUTMANN HOLTHAUSEN
MULLENHOFF STREITBERG
THURNEYSEN VOLLMOLLER
BARTHOLOMAE
HUNGARIAN REVAI HUNFALVY
DOBRENTEJ ENDLICHER
ICELANDIC JONSSON EGILSSON
MAGNUSSON VIGFUSSON
ITALIAN ASCOLI MONACI NOVATI
OVIDIO COMPARETTI CASTELVETRO
CASTIGLIONE
NORWEGIAN AASEN BUGGE KONOW
MUNCH
POLISH ZAMENHOF ROZWADOWSKI
PORTUGUESE COELHO
RUMANIAN HASDEU
RUSSIAN GROT VOSTOKOV
SCHIEFNER
SCOTTISH GRANT BAIKIE MURRAY
SPANISH MENENDEZ
SWEDISH IHRE LUNDELL AHLQUIST
SODERWALL ZACHRISSON
SWISS MAHLY ISELIN
PHILOLOGY SEMITICS
PHILOMACHUS MACHETES
PHILOMELA STOP FILOMEL
(FATHER OF —) PANDION
(RAVISHER OF —) TEREUS
(SISTER OF —) PROCNE

(SLAIN BY —) ITYS
(VICTIM OF —) ITYS
PHILOSOPHER WIT SAGE CYNIC
STOIC ARTIST IONIAN LEGIST
DOTTORE ELEATIC ERISTIC SCHOLAR
SOPHIST SUMMIST THINKER ZETETIC
ACADEMIC EPOCHIST MAGICIAN
VIRTUOSO ACADEMIST ALCHEMIST
DIALECTIC PHYSICIAN SCHOOLMAN
AMERICAN AYER HOOK HUME LADD
MEAD MORE ADLER ALBEE BOWEN
BOWNE DEWEY EDMAN FANON FISKE
JAMES LEWIS MOORE PAINE PERRY
QUINE ROYCE UPHAM WATTS DRAPER
HARRIS HICKOK HOFFER HYSLOP
JAEGER KALLEN LANGER NOZICK
PEIRCE SNIDER BARRETT CALKINS
EMERSON HOCKING HOWISON
LOVEJOY MARCUSE NEWBOLD
CALLAHAN WILLIAMS ALEXANDER
SANTAVANA SANTAYANA
ARAB AVICENNA
ARABIAN GHAZZALI
AUSTRIAN BUBER EXNER DEUBLER
MEINONG STEINER ZIMMERMANN
RATZENHOFER
BELGIAN MERCIER DELBOEUF
BRAZILIAN MAGALHAES
CANADIAN MURRAY STEWART
SCHURMAN
CHINESE MOTI LAOTZU MENCIUS
CONFUCIUS
CZECH MASARYK SMETANA
DANISH SIBBERN HOFFDING
KIERKEGAARD
DUTCH BOLLAND ERASMUS
HEYMANS SPINOZA OPZOOMER
EGYPTIAN ORIGEN PLOTINUS
ENGLISH AYER CASE JOAD MILL
MORE RYLE WARD BACON BROAD
COTES DUNNE GREEN GROTE
HOOKE HULME JONES LAIRD LEWES
LOCKE MOORE PALEY STOUT SULLY
BAYNES BIDDLE BUTLER FOWLER
GODWIN GURNEY HOBBES LATHAM
MCCABE NEWTON NORRIS OCKHAM
TAYLOR AINSLIE BALFOUR BENTHAM
BRADLEY COLLIER HALDANE
HARTLEY HERBERT HODGSON
INGELBY JACKSON RUSSELL
SPENCER STEPHEN STEWART
WHEWELL CONGREVE CORNFORD
COURTNEY CUDWORTH GLANVILL
HOBHOUSE MUIRHEAD SCHILLER
SIDGWICK BOSANQUET MACKENZIE
WHITEHEAD CUMBERLAND
HUTCHINSON SHAFTESBURY
FINNISH WESTERMARCK
FRENCH DROZ WEIL ALAIN BAYLE
CAMUS COMTE GUYAU HELLO
JANET LEROY LIARD MABLY RAMUS
REVEL SIMON TAINE BERARD
BONALD COUSIN GILSON GOBLOT

LEROUX MARCEL PASCAL QUESNE
RAYNAL SARTRE VALERY ABAUZIT
ABELARD BARTHEZ BERGSON
BURIDAN CABANIS CHARRON
DAMIRON DIDEROT FOURIER
GERANDO HOLBACH MAISTRE
MILHAUD REYNAUD ROMAINS
ALEMBERT BOURDEAU BOUTROUX
CHARTIER FOUCAULT FOUILLEE
GASSENDI GILLOUIN GOBINEAU
JOUFFROY LAFFITTE MARITAIN
MEYERSON ROUSSEAU TEILHARD
VACHEROT VOLTAIRE BALLANCHE
CONDILLAC CONDORCET DESCARTES
HELVITIUS LACHELIER SCHWEITZER
MONTESQUIEU LAROMIGUIERE
GERMAN BIEL HAYM KANT KRUG
MARX OKEN PREL BAUER CARUS
COHEN DREWS ENGEL FRIES GROOS
HEGEL LIPPS LOTZE MARBE MEYER
RIEHL STEIN UTITZ WAITZ WOLFF
BENEKE CARNAP CAROVE EUCKEN
FICHTE GABLER GEIGER GEYSER
GRUPPE HEINZE HERDER JACOBI
KRAUSE KRONER LASSON MAIMON
MESSER MULLER PRANTL RITTER
SIMMEL STUMPF ULRICI ZELLER
ZIEHEN BRUCKER BRUNNER
CRUSIUS DEUSSEN DILTHEY
DRIESCH DUHRING ECKHART
ERDMANN FECHNER HAECKEL
HENNING HERBART JUNGIUS
KNUTZEN LASAULX LAZARUS
LEIBNIZ PAULSEN STIRNER STRAUSS
VOLKELT CARRIERE CASSIRER
DROBISCH EBERHARD FORTLAGE
HARTMANN HERTLING LASSWITZ
LEIBNITZ MICHELET MICHELIS
PANNWITZ REINHOLD SPENGLER
AVENARIUS BILFINGER CORNELIUS
DIETERICI EHRENFELS FEUERBACH
GOCLENIUS HEIDEGGER LEISEGANG
NIETZSCHE SCHELLING THOMASIUS
TIEDEMANN VAIHINGER VORLANDER
BAUMGARTEN HILLEBRAND
KEYSERLING ROSENKRANZ
FRAUENSTADT MENDELSSOHN
SCHOPENHAUER TRENDELENBURG
SCHLEIERMACHER
GREEK BION ZENO CEBES DAMON
LYCON PLATO CRATES EUCLID
PHAEDO PYRRHO STRATO THALES
CRANTOR DEMONAX EUDEMUS
PROCLUS TIMAEUS ALCMAEON
APULEIUS CRATYLUS DIODORUS
DIOGENES EPICURUS MELISSUS
MENIPPUS NUMENIUS PHAEDRUS
PORPHYRY SOCRATES ARCHELAUS
ARISTOTLE CARNEADES CHARMIDES
CLEANTHES CRITOLAUS DAMASCIUS
EPICTETUS EUBULIDES FAVORINUS
HIEROCLES LEUCIPPUS MENEDEMUS
PANAETIUS PANTAENUS PHILOLAUS

ANAXAGORAS ANAXARCHUS
ANAXIMENES ARCESILAUS
ARISTIPPUS CHRYSIPPUS
DEMOCRITUS EMPEDOCLES
HERACLITUS IAMBLICHUS
METRODORUS PARMENIDES
PHERECYDES POSIDONIUS
PROTAGORAS PYTHAGORAS
SIMPLICIUS SPEUSIPPUS
XENOCRATES XENOPHANES
ANAXIMANDER ANTISTHENES
ARISTOXENUS CLITOMACHUS
DICAEARCHUS CALLISTHENES
PHILOSTRATUS THEOPHRASTUS
HUNGARIAN ERDELYI LAKATOS
INDIAN GHOSE IQBAL
KRISHNAMURTI
IRISH BERNARD ERIGENA BERKELEY
MOLYNEUX
ISRAELI BUBER
ITALIAN NIFO VERA VICO ABANO
BRUNO CONTI CROCE FERRI ARDIGO
FICINO PAPINI VANINI AQUINAS
CANTONI CARDANO FERRARI
FRANCHI GENTILE MAMIANI TELESIO
UBERWEG GIOBERTI GUARDINI
ALGAROTTI CESALPINO
CAMPANELLA FIORENTINO
POMPONAZZI BONAVENTURA
MACHIAVELLI PICCOLOMINI
JAPANESE SUZUKI
NORWEGIAN MONRAD
POLISH LIBELT WRONSKI
LUTOSLAWSKI
PORTUGUESE ACOSTA
ROMAN CICERO SENECA BOETHIUS
CORNUTUS PLOTINUS AUGUSTINE
LUCRETIUS
RUSSIAN BERDYAEV CHICHERIN
PLEKHANOV
SCOTTISH BAIN HOME HUME MILL
REID SETH CAIRD FLINT FRASER
VEITCH FERRIER STEWART WALLACE
BREWSTER FERGUSON HAMILTON
STIRLING HUTCHESON
CALDERWOOD MACKINTOSH
SPANISH VIVES BALMES ORTEGA
SUAREZ UNAMUNO AVERROES
MAIMONIDES
SWEDISH BOSTROM ATTERBOM
SWEDENBORG
SWISS WYSS AMIEL HILTY PREVOST
HABERLIN
PHILOSOPHER'S STONE ADROP
    MICROCOSM
PHILOSOPHIC SAGE
PHILOSOPHICAL DEEP
PHILOSOPHY YOGA ETHICS GOSPEL
    MAGISM SYSTEM TAOISM APRISMO
    COSMISM DUALISM INQUIRY
    MIMAMSA SANKHYA SCEPSIS
    ACTIVISM HINDUISM HUMANISM
    IDENTISM IDEOLOGY LEGALISM

OCCAMISM STOICISM ABSURDISM
NOUMENISM SOCRATISM
VEDANTISM
(— OF LIFE) LIGHTS
(NATURAL —) PHYSIC
PHILTER DRUG CHARM WANGA
FILTER POTION AMATORY
PHINEHAS (FATHER OF —) ELI
ELEAZAR
(GRANDFATHER OF —) AARON
PHINEUS (BROTHER OF —) CADMUS
CEPHEUS
(FATHER OF —) BELUS AGENOR
(MOTHER OF —) ANCHINOE ·
TELEPHASSA
(SISTER OF —) EUROPA
(WIFE OF —) IDAEA CLEOPATRA
PHLEBOTOMIZE BLEED VENESECT
PHLEBOTOMUS TATUKIRA
PHLEGM FLEM GLEET MUCUS
WATER FLEUME PITUITE MOUSEWEB
PHLEGMATIC CALM COOL DULL
SLOW INERT MUCOID SLEEPY
WATERY VISCOUS COMPOSED
SLUGGISH APATHETIC IMPASSIVE
PHLEGYAS (DAUGHTER OF —)
CORONIS
(FATHER OF —) ARES MARS
(MOTHER OF —) CHRYSE
(SLAYER OF —) APOLLO
(SON OF —) IXION
PHLOEM BAST LIBER LEPTOME
PHLOGISTIC FIERY HEATED
BURNING FLAMING
PHLOMIS SAGELEAF
PHLOX CYME FLOX ALBION BEACON
COBAEA
PHOCUS (FATHER OF —) AEACUS
ORNYTION
(HALF-BROTHER OF —) PELEUS
TELAMON
(MOTHER OF —) PSAMATHE
(SON OF —) CRISIUS PANOPEUS
(WIFE OF —) ANTIOPE
PHOEBE FEBE FIVE MOON DIANA
PEWEE ARTEMIS
(BROTHER OF —) CASTOR POLLUX
POLYDEUCES
(DAUGHTER OF —) LETO
(FATHER OF —) URANUS LEUCIPPUS
TYNDAREUS
(MOTHER OF —) GAEA LEDA
(SISTER OF —) HELEN
CLYTEMNESTRA
PHOEBUS SOL SUN APOLLO
PHOIBUS
PHOENICIA (COLONY OF —)
CARTHAGE
(GODDESS OF —) TANIT BALTIS
TANITH ASTARTE
(KING OF —) AGENOR
(TOWN OF —) ACRE TYRE SIDON
SAREPTA

PHOENIX FUM FUNG
(BROTHER OF —) CILIX CADMUS
THASUS PHINEUS
(FATHER OF —) AGENOR AMYNTOR
(MOTHER OF —) CLEOBULE
TELEPHASSA
(PUPIL OF —) ACHILLES
(SISTER OF —) EUROPA
PHOLAS PIDDOCK
PHONE CALL DIAL RING CALLUP
RINGUP
PHONEME MORPH TONEME
LARYNGAL
PHONEMIC BROAD
PHONOGRAM LOGOGRAM
SINOGRAM
PHONOGRAPH VIC PHONO
VICTROLA
(— RECORD) DISK PLATTER
PHONY FAKE JIVE SHAM BOGUS
FAKER FALSE BRUMMY BUNYIP
PHONEY PLASTIC IMPOSTOR
SPURIOUS
PHORONEUS (DAUGHTER OF —)
NIOBE
(FATHER OF —) INACHUS
(MOTHER OF —) MELIA
(SISTER OF —) IO
(SON OF —) APIS IASUS AGENOR
PELASGUS
(WIFE OF —) CERDO LAODICE
PHOSPHATE EHLITE FLOATS
APATITE CABOCLE CACOXENE
GRIPHITE MONAZITE
PHOSPHORESCENCE BRIMING
MARFIRE
PHOSPHORESCENT PHOSPHOR
NOCTILUCOUS
PHOTISM SYNOPSY
PHOTO PIC
(— FINISH) MAT MATT MATTE
(ART —) SEPIA
PHOTOENGRAVER
ZINCOGRAPHER
PHOTOENGRAVING HALFTONE
HELIOGRAPH
PHOTOGENE AFTERIMAGE
PHOTOGRAPH MUG PIC FILM LENS
SNAP CARTE IMAGE PANEL PHOTO
PINUP PRINT SHOOT STILL CANDID
GLOSSY MOSAIC RETAKE SCENIC
STEREO AIRVIEW MONTAGE PICTURE
TINTYPE LIKENESS PORTRAIT
POSITIVE SNAPSHOT TABLETOP
CYCLOGRAM MAMMOGRAM
(— OF RENAL EXCRETION)
RENOGRAM
(— SIZE) PANEL
(X-RAY —) SKIAGRAM
(PL.) PIX
PHOTOGRAPHER PHOTOG
LENSMAN CAMERIST CAMERAMAN
PAPARAZZO SHUTTERBUG

PHOTOGRAPHY STEREO CALOTYPE
PHOTOGENY
(— SESSION) SHOOT
(KIND OF —) KIRLIAN
PHOTOMETER LUCIMETER
PHOTOMONTAGE COLLAGE
PHOTON BOSON TROLAND
PHRASE CRY HIT MOT SET CRIB FUSS
HAVE IDEA TERM WORD COMMA
COUCH IDIOM LABEL LEMMA POINT
STATE STYLE TOPIC TROPE BYWORD
CLAUSE CLICHE DITTON DORISM
GRUPPO HOBNOB NOTION PNEUMA
PRAISE SAVING SLOGAN ATTACCO
DICTION EPITHET PASSAGE
CONCEIVE DIVISION DORICISM
FLATTERY IDEOGRAM IRISHISM
LATINISM LEITMOTIV
(— DIFFERENTLY) TURN
(— UNCTUOUSLY) DROOL
(CANT —) SHIBBOLETH
(JAZZ —) RIFF
(MUSICAL —) RIFF POINT ATTACCO
SUBJECT
(PET —) SHIBBOLETH
(PITHY —) LACONISM LACONICISM
(REDUNDANT —) CHEVILLE
(STOCK —) CANT
(TRITE —) CLICHE
(WELL-WORN —) STROKE
PHRASEOLOGY CANT STYLE
DIALECT DICTION WORDING
LOCUTION PARLANCE
PHRATRY CLAN
PHRENETIC PYTHIAN FRENETIC
PHRENIC MENTAL
(PL.) PSYCHOLOGY
PHRIXOS (FATHER OF —)
ATHAMUS
(MOTHER OF —) NEPHELE
(SISTER OF —) HELLE
PHRONTIS (BROTHER OF —) ARGUS
MELAS CYTISSORUS
(FATHER OF —) PHRIXUS
(HUSBAND OF —) PANTHOUS
(MOTHER OF —) CHALCIOPE
(SON OF —) EUPHORBUS
HYPERENOR POLYDAMAS
PHRYGIA (GOD OF —) ATYS ATTIS
SABAZIOS
(KING OF —) MIDAS
PHRYNIN BUFIDIN
PHTHISIS DECAY
PHUVAH (FATHER OF —) ISSACHAR
PHYLACTERY FILACTERY
(PL.) TEFILLIN TEPHILLIN
PHYLE TRIBE
PHYLLO FILO
PHYLOMACHE (DAUGHTER OF —)
ALCESTIS
(FATHER OF —) AMPHION
(HUSBAND OF —) PELIAS
(SON OF —) ACASTUS

PHYLUM HOKA CLASS HOKAN
NADENE BRYOZOA ANNELATA
ANNELIDA CHORDATA DIVISION
LIGNOSAE PORIFERA
PHYMA TUMOR
PHYSALIS POP POPPER TOMATILLO
PHYSETER CATODON
PHYSIC CURE HEAL FISIC PURGE
TRADE REMEDY MEDICAL NATURAL
RELIEVE DRUGGERY
PHYSICAL ILI LUSTY SOMAL BODILY
CARNAL DISTAL NATURAL SOMATIC
CORPORAL CURATIVE EXTERNAL
MATERIAL CORPOREAL
(PURELY —) BRUTE
PHYSICIAN ASA DOC PILL CURER
GALEN HAKIM LEECH MEDIC QUACK
ARTIST BAIDYA DOCTOR FELLOW
HEALER INTERN MEDICO DOTTORE
EMPIRIC SURGEON ALIENIST
RESIDENT SAWBONES SUNDOWNER
(— OF GODS) PAEAN
(— OF THE GODS) PAEAN
(PREF.) IATRO JATEO JATO
(SUFF.) IATRIST
AMERICAN ILG LEE RAY BARD COIT
DICK DREW FITZ HARE HOLT KING
LUST MUDD PARK ROCK ROUS SALK
SIMS APGAR APPEL BIGGS BRILL
BRUSH CABOT COHEN CROHN
DRAKE FLINT GOLER GUION KNOPF
KOLFF LILLY LOEWI LOGAN MARAT
MINOT SMITH SPOCK TONER TULLY
TYSON WHITE BARKER BATTEY
BENNET BROOKS CARTER CLARKE
DEVITA ENDERS FISHER FOSTER
GESELL GORGAS GORRIE HEISER
HOOKER HORNER HOSACK JACOBI
JARVIK JOSLIN KEELEY KNIGHT
KOPITS LAZEAR MILLER MIRKIN
MORGAN MORROW MURPHY
ODWYER PARRAN PINCUS SCHICK
STILES STILLE STORER STRONG
TILTON WALKER WATSON WELLER
ALVAREZ CAMMANN CHAPMAN
DARLING DICKSON FRANCIS
GERHARD GILBERT HAGGARD
HEPBURN HOPKINS JACKSON
JANEWAY ROBBINS TROLAND
TRUDEAU WHIPPLE BARTLETT
BILLINGS BOYLSTON CHANNING
FISHBEIN GUERNSEY GWATHMEY
HAMILTON KIRTLAND KNOWLTON
MITCHELL PETERSON RICHARDS
ROCKWELL SHATTUCK SPALDING
TOWNSEND WOODWARD
BLACKWELL BRAZELTON
STERNBERG CLENDENING
GOLDBERGER STEPHENSON
WATERHOUSE ZAKRZEWSKA
CASTIGLIONI WIGGLESWORTH
ARAB AVICENNA ABDALLATIF
ARGENTINIAN BUNGE

NICHOLS PENZIAS PURCELL RANDALL RENWIEK RICHTER ROWLAND SZILARD WHEELER ANDERSON BLODGETT BRATTAIN BRIDGMAN DAVISSON EINSTEIN HASTINGS HAUPTMAN LAWRENCE MILLIKAN SHOCKLEY STRATTON THOMPSON VANALLEN VANVLECK WINTHROP ZWORYKIN BITTINGER GOODSPEED HUMPHREYS INGERSOLL LAURITSEN MICHELSON RAINWATER SCHWINGER HOFSTADTER MENDENHALL RENTSCHLER RUTHERFURD SCHRIEFFER TROWBRIDGE CHAMBERLAIN OPPENHEIMER

ARGENTINIAN CERNUSCHI

AUSTRIAN HESS MACH RABI DOPPLER MEITNER PRECHTL BOLTZMANN SCHRODINGER SCHROEDINGER

BELGIAN PLATEAU

CANADIAN TORY HILLIER DEMPSTER HERZBERG

DANISH BOHR OERSTED MOTTELSON

DUTCH WAALS ZEEMAN HUYGENS LORENTZ ZERNIKE HARTSOEKER KAMERLINGH VANDERMEER MUSSCHENBROEK

ENGLISH EVE BORN LAMB LEES MOTT ASTON BOYLE BRAGG DEWAR DIRAC DYSON FUCHS GROVE JEANS JOULE LODGE NICOL SALAM AITKEN BARKLA CANTON DALTON DARWIN FRISCH KELVIN STOKES ANDRADE BARRETT BULLARD CROOKES DANIELL FARADAY FLEMING GILBERT GUTHRIE HARTREE MICHELL MOSELEY SIEMENS THOMSON TYNDALL APPLETON BLACKETT CHADWICK HAUKSBEE POYNTING RAYLEIGH SCHUSTER STURGEON CALLENDAR CAVENDISH COCKCROFT HEAVISIDE JOSEPHSON GLAZEBROOK RICHARDSON RUTHERFORD WHEATSTONE

FRENCH HIRN NEEL ARAGO CORNU FARRY JAMIN MALUS PAPIN PETIT PITOT WEISS BRANLY CARNOT CLAUDE COTTON DULONG FIZEAU FORTIN JOLIOT NIEPCE NOLLET PERRIN RAOULT SAVART VIOLLE BABINET BEUDANT BLONDEL BROGLIE CHARLES COULOMB FIZERAU FOURIER FRESNEL JOUBERT KASTLER MASCART PELTIER REAUMUR SAUVEUR AMONTONS ARSONVAL DESPRETZ FOUCAULT LANGEVIN LIPPMANN MARIOTTE POUILLET REGNAULT BECQUEREL BRILLOUIN CAILLETET GUILLAUME LISSAJOUS CHARDONNET

GERMAN MIE OHM BORN DOVE KORN LAUE LENZ REIS WIEN BETHE BOTHE BRAUN BUDDE DEBYE ERMAN HERTZ HOLTZ JOLLY KUNDT MAYER STARK VOIGT WEBER BALMER ELSTER GEIGER HANKEL JENSEN KOENIG LAMONT LENARD LUMMER MAGNUS NERNST PLANCK RIECKE RITTER ZEUNER AEPINUS BEDNORZ BRODHUN CHI ADNI FECHNER GEHRCKE HITTORF LAMBERT NEUMANN PLUCKER PRANDTL QUINCKE REGENER RUDOLPH SCAEFER SEEBECK TOEPLER WULLNER CLAUSIUS EINSTEIN GUERICKE ROENTGEN SCHUMANN FEDDERSEN GOLDSTEIN HALLWACHS KIRCHHOFF MOSSBAUER SCHEIBLER STEINHEIL WIEDEMANN BARKHAUSEN FAHRENHEIT KOHLRAUSCH PRINGSHEIM SCHWEIGGER SIEDENTOPF SOMMERFELD LICHTENBERG

GREEK CTESIBIUS

HUNGARIAN WIGNER

INDIAN BOSE SAHA RAMAN

IRISH JOLLY KELVIN STONEY WALTON ANDREWS TOWNSEND FITZGERALD

ITALIAN RIIS FERMI PORTA RIGHI VOLTA AI DINI NOBILI RUBBIA BORELLI CAVALLO GALILEI GALVANI MELLONI VENTURI AVOGADRO BECCARIA BELTRAMI BLASERNA CUDMARIS GRIMALDI PALMIERI BOSCOVICH PACINOTTI TORRICELLI

JAPANESE ESAKI YUKAWA TOMONAGA

NORWEGIAN GIAEVER BJERKNES HANSTEEN

POLISH INFELD WROBLEWSKI

RUSSIAN TAMM BASOV FRANK LANDAU KAPITZA LEBEDEV SAKHAROV CHERENKOV PROKHOROV

SCOTTISH KERR TAIT WATT BLACK DEWAR EWING NOBLE WILSON MAXWELL RANKINE STEWART BREWSTER

SWEDISH EDLEN ALFVEN EDLUND NILSON ANGSTROM SIEGBAHN ARRHENIUS BENEDICKS

SWISS WILD BLOCH EULER PAULI ARGAND LARIVE PICTET MUELLER PICCARD PREVOST ALLAMAND

WELSH GROVE

PHYSIC NUT TUBA CURCAS PIGNON TARTAGO

PHYSICS (— PARTICLE) QUARK

PHYSIOCRAT ECONOMIST

PHYSIOGNOMY MUG FACE PHIZ VIZNOMY PORTRAIT VISENOMY

PHYSIOLOGIST AMERICAN IVY
KEYS LUSK HOUGH CANNON
DALTON GASSER HARVEY HOWELL
CARLSON SCHALLY COURNAND
ECKSTEIN ERLANGER HARTLINE
MEYERHOF GUILLEMIN HENDERSON
OSTERHOUT
ARGENTINIAN HOUSSAY
AUSTRALIAN ECCLES
AUSTRIAN STEINACH
BELGIAN HEYMANS
CANADIAN BEST
CZECH PURKINJE
DANISH KROGH
DUTCH DONDERS EINTHOVEN
ENGLISH DALE HILL KATZ BEALE
HALES LOWER ADRIAN DARWIN
FOSTER HUXLEY RIVERS WALLER
BAYLISS EDWARDS HERRING
HODGKIN BARCROFT MARSHALL
STARLING ELLIOTSON SHERRINGTON
FINNISH GRANIT
FRENCH BERT MAREY RICHET
BEAUNIS BERNARD FLOURENS
MAGENDIE DUTROCHET POISEUILLE
GERMAN FICK VOIT BUDGE GOLTZ
KUHNE REMAK WUNDT HENSEN
HERING LUDWIG MULLER PREYER
WAGNER BEHRING BURDACH
PFLUGER SCHWANN VERWORN
WARBURG MEISSNER MEYERHOF
VALENTIN HELMHOLTZ
BLUMENBACH HEIDENHAIN
ITALIAN BOVET MOSSO
MANTEGAZZA
RUSSIAN CYON PAVLOV
SCOTTISH HALDANE MACLEOD
SWEDISH EULER GRANIT HOLMGREN
SWISS HESS
PHYSIOLOGY BIONOMY ZOONOMY
PHYSIOTHERAPY PATTERNING
PHYSIQUE BODY BUILD COOST
HABIT FIGURE STRENGTH
PHYSOCARPUS NEILLIA
OPULASTER
PHYSOSTIGMINE ESERE ESERINE
PHYTOMER PHYTON PODIUM
PI JUMBLE CONFUSE PREACHY
CONFUSION
PIA PI GABI GABGAB MARMOT
PIACLE SIN CRIME GUILT OFFENSE
PIAN YAWS FRAMBESIA
PIANETTE PYNOT PIANINO
PIANFORTE CEMBALO
PIANIST CEMBALIST CLAVIERIST
PIANO SOFT FLOOR GRAND GRANT
STORY FLUGEL GENTLY SOFTLY
SPINET SQUARE CLAVIAL CLAVIER
GIRAFFE PIANOLA QUIETLY UPRIGHT
MELOTROPE
(— SOFTENING PEDAL) CELESTE
(AFRICAN —) KALIMBA
(KIND OF —) THUMB

(PART OF —) ARM KEY LEG LID DESK
FALL HEEL LYRE PROP CHEEK PEDAL
STRING KEYSLIP KEYBOARD
(STYLE OF JAZZ —) STRIDE
(THUMB —) KALIMBA
PIASSAVA IYO JARA BAHIA PIACABA
PIASTER KURUS
PIATTI CYMBALS
PIAZZA PORCH SQUARE BALCONY
GALLERY PORTICO VERANDA
PIAZZETTA
PIC PEAK LANCE PHOTO PIQUE
PICADOR
PICA M EM LINE
PICARD PYKAR
PICARO KNAVE ROGUE TRAMP
BOHEMIAN VAGABOND
PICAROON ROGUE PICARO PIRATE
CORSAIR WRECKER
PICAYUNE PIC PETTY MEASLY
PALTRY TRIVIAL PISTAREEN
PICCADILL RABATA REBATE REBATO
PICCOLO BUSBOY JUKEBOX
FLAUTINO OTTAVINO
PICHICIAGO ARMADILLO
CHLAMYPHORE
PICK NAP NIB OPT, BILL CULL GAFF
HACK LIFT PIKE PILK SHOT WALE
ADORN BEELE BREAK CAVIL ELECT
FLANG LEASE PILCH PLUCK PRIDE
PRIME CHOICE CHOOSE GATHER
PICKAX PUDDLE TWITCH BARGAIN
CASCROM DIAMOND DRESSER
MANDREL
(— APART) TOW
(— KNOTS FROM) BURL
(— OUT) CULL SPOT TAKE WELE
CRONE GLEAN GARBLE SELECT
(— POCKETS) FIG FILE FOIST TOUCH
(— TOBACCO) STRIP
(— UP) SHARK
(FILLING —) ABB
PICKAX PIX BEDE BILL PIKE GURLET
TUBBER TWIBIL TWIBILL
PICKED PICK TRIM PIKED CHOSEN
DAINTY PEAKED SELECT ADORNED
POINTED
(PREF.) LECTO
PICKER COD HOPPER
(BERRY —) HURTER
(PEA —) VINER
PICKEREL JACK SNAKE DUNLIN
SAUGER SLINKER WALLEYE
PICKERELWEED TULE WAMPEE
PICKER-UP FINDER
PICKET PEG PALE POST TERN FENCE
STAKE FASTEN PALING TETHER
ENCLOSE FORTIFY OUTPOST
PICQUET PALISADE OUTPICKET
PICKLE BOX ALEC BIND DILL MESS
PECK ACHAR BRINE GRAIN MANGO
SAUCE SOUSE ATSARA CAPERS
DAWDLE HIGDON KERNEL KIMCHI

MUDDLE NIBBLE PIDDLE PILFER
PLIGHT TRIFLE CONDITE CONFECT
GHERKIN TROUBLE VITRIOL
MARINADE
(FISH —) ALEC
PICKLED DRUNK OILED UNSOBER
MURIATED POWDERED MARINATED
PICKLOCK LOCK PICKER
PICK-ME-UP TONIC BRACER SCREW
PICKUP
PICKPOCKET DIP FIG GUN NIP BUNG
FILE WIRE DIVER FILER FOIST BULKER
BUZZER CANNON DIPPER FIGBOY
HOOKER NIPPER RATERO FOISTER
MOBSMAN CLYFAKER CUTPURSE
KNUCKLER BUZZGLOAK
(HELPER OF —) STALL BULKER
PICKUP BRUSH TRUCK ARREST
BRACER ANACRUSIS
PICKWICK PAPERS
(AUTHOR OF —) DICKENS
(CHARACTER IN —) BOB SAM MARY
ALLEN EMILY TRACY ALFRED
HUNTER JINGLE PERKER SAWYER
TUPMAN WARDLE WELLER WINKLE
BARDELL RACHAEL SLAMMER
ARABELLA AUGUSTUS CLUPPINS
ISABELLA PICKWICK NATHANIEL
SMORLTORK SNODGRASS
PICNIC FRY BALL GIPSY GYPSY
BURGOO FROLIC JUNKET MAROON
OUTING SHOULDER SQUANTUM
SUMMERING WAYZGOOSE
(PRINTERS' —) WAYGOOSE
WAYZGOOSE
PICOT LOOP PEARL PERLE
PICOTAH SWEEP PACOTA
PICTOGRAPH GLYPH PICTOGRAM
PICTORIAL GRAPHIC
PICTURE GAY MAP OIL COPY DAUB
ICON IKON LIMN SIGN VIEW DECAL
FRAME IMAGE LINER PAINT PHOTO
PIECE PINAX PRINT SCENE SHAPE
STAMP STORY TABLE CACHET
CANVAS CHROMO CUTOUT DEPICT
EMBLEM MARINE PASTEL SEMBLE
SHADOW STEREO TABLET CUTAWAY
DIORAMA DIPTYCH EMBLEMA
ETCHING EXHIBIT FASHION FEATURE
GOUACHE GRAPHIC HISTORY
MIZRACH PAYSAGE PORTRAY
PORTURE RETRAIT SCENERY
TABLEAU VANDYKE AIRSCAPE
AUTOTYPE DESCRIBE DROLLERY
ENVISION IDEOGRAM KAKEMONO
LANDSKIP LIKENESS MAKIMONO
MONOTINT OVERDOOR PAINTING
PANORAMA PORTRAIT PROSPECT
RITRATTO SEASCAPE SINGERIE
SKYSCAPE TRIPTYCH VIGNETTE
ENCAUSTIC
(— IN BOOK) GAY
(— IN 3 COMPARTMENTS) TRIPTYCH

(— MAT) SPANDREL
(— OF MONKEYS) SINGERIE
(— ON ROLLER) KAKEMONO
MAKIMONO
(— PUZZLE) REBUS JIGSAW
(—S IN BOOKS) BABY
(— WOVEN IN SILK) STEVENGRAPH
(COMIC —) DROLLERY
(RELIGIOUS —) TANKA
(STEREOSCOPIC —) ANAGLYPH
(THREE-DIMENSIONAL —)
HOLOGRAM
(PREF.) PINAC(O)
PICTURE OF DORIAN GRAY
(AUTHOR OF —) WILDE
(CHARACTER IN —) ALAN GRAY VANE
BASIL HENRY JAMES SIBYL DORIAN
WOTTON CAMPBELL HALLWARD
PICTURESQUE VIVID EXOTIC
QUAINT SCENIC GRAPHIC IDYLLIC
ROMANTIC PICTORIAL
PICUL TAN PICO PIKOL
PIDDLE PICK PLAY DAWDLE PICKLE
PUTTER TRIFLE
PIDDLING JERK MEASLY PALTRY
TRIVIAL USELESS FOOTLING
TRIFLING JERKWATER
PIDDOCK DACTYL PHOLAD PHOLAS
PIDGIN LANGUAGE SABIR
PIE PAI FLAM FLAN HEAP MESS PATE
PILE TART DOWDY FLAWN PASTY
PATTY TORTA TOURT AFFAIR BRIDLE
CHEWET MAGPIE PASTRY TOURTE
COBBLER SMASHER STRUDEL
BAKEMEAT CRUSTADE FLAPJACK
PANDOWDY SURPRISE TURNOVER
SMASHOVER
(CUSTARD —) QUICHE
(GREEK —) SPANAKOPITA
SPANOKAPITA SPANAKOPITTA
(MEAT —) FLOATER
(MINCE —) SHREDPIE
(PL.) BAKEMEAT
PIEBALD PIE PIED PIET MIXED PIETY
PINTO CALICO MOTLEY SKEWBALD
PIECE BAT BIT COB CUT DAM FIG JOB
LAB LOG MAN TUT GIRL MIND PART
PISE PLAY BLYPE DAGON DRAMA
DWANG FLOOR PEZZO SCRAP SHARD
SHERD SHRED SLICE SNODE STEEK
STUCK THROW COLLOP FARDEL
FUGATO GOBBET PARCEL STITCH
CANTLET EXAMPLE FLINDER FLITTER
MORCEAU OPINION PICTURE
PORTION SEGMENT DUOLOGUE
EMBOLIUM FANDANGO PAINTING
(— AT END) HEELPIECE
(— FOR TWO) DUET DUOLOGUE
(— IN CHECKERS) DAM
(— IN ORGAN) THUMPER
(— LEFT) STUB
(— OF ARMOR) JAMB JAMBE
(— OF BAD LUCK) DIRDUM

(— OF BLANKET) DAGON
(— OF BLUBBER) BIBLE
(— OF CLOTH) REMNANT
(— OF DECEPTION) BEGUNK
(— OF DECORATED METAL) NIELLO
(— OF EIGHT) PIASTRE
(— OF FALSE HAIR) JANE
(— OF FIBER) NOIL
(— OF FIRED CLAY) TILE
(— OF FOOD) MORSEL
(— OF GOOD FORTUNE) GODSEND
(— OF GROUND SURROUNDED BY
WASTE) HOPE
(— OF HARD WOOD) MOOT
(— OF LAND) ERF HAM LOT BUTT
GORE PANE PARK PLOT CROFT LEASE
PATCH SPONG SQUAT ESTATE
GARDEN HUERTA RINCON SECTION
CLEARAGE METAIRIE PROPERTY
SOLIDATE PENINSULA
(— OF LIGHT ORDNANCE) ASPIC
(— OF LINEN) AMIT AMICE
(— OF LOG) SLAB
(— OF MAST) TONGUE
(— OF MATZOTH) AFIKOMEN
(— OF MEAT) EYE HEEL RAND
COLLOP EPIGRAM
(— OF METAL) JAG COIN JAGG
SPRAG
(— OF MISCHIEF) LARK
(— OF MONEY) COG SOU SHINER
(— OF NEEDLEWORK) SAMPLER
(— OF NEWS) NOVEL
(— OF NONSENSE) FUDGE
TRIMTRAM
(— OF ORE) CHAT
(— OF PROPERTY) CHOSE SUBJECT
(— OF SAIL) HULLOCK
(— OF SCENERY) FLAT
(— OF SEPARATED LAND) BUTT
(— OF SKIN) BLYPE
(— OF SKIN FOR GLOVE) TRANK
(— OF SLATE) SLAT
(— OF SOAP) BALL
(— OF SOMETHING EDIBLE) STULL
(— OF TIMBER) FISH COULISSE
FOREHOOK
(— OF TOAST) SLINGER
(— OF TOBACCO) FIG
(— OF TRACK) LEAD RUNBY
(— OF TRICKERY) CROOK CANTRIP
(— OF TURF) FLAG DIVOT SCRAW
SHIRREL
(— OF WOOD) KIP LATH APRON
BOARD CHUMP CHUNK PLANK
SPOON WADDY BILLET COMMON
STOWER TIMBER LIPPING
(— OF WORK) JOB CHAR TURN
(— OF WRITING) SCREED SCREEVE
(— OUT) EKE
(—S OF MACARONI) DITALI DITALINI
(— SPLIT OFF) SPLINT

(— TO PREVENT SLIPPING) CLEAT
(ARTILLERY —) DRAKE SAKER
LANTACA
(BACKGAMMON —) BLOT STONE
(BROAD —) SHEET
(BROKEN —) BRACK MAMMOCK
FRACTION
(BUTTING —) HURTER
(CHESS —) PIN KING PAWN ROOK
QUEEN BISHOP CASTLE KNIGHT
OFFICER
(DRAMATIC —) SKIT
(DREAMY —) REVERIE
(END — OF BUCKET) CANT
(FLAT —) FLAP FLAKE
(FUR —) PALATINE
(GOLD —) SLUG TALI
(IN —S) LIMBMEAL
(IRREGULAR —) SNAG
(KIND OF —) PERIOD
(LARDED — OF MEAT) DAUB
(LARGE —) HUNK MOLE STULL
DOLLOP
(LEFT-OVER —) SCRAP
(LITERARY —) CAMEO
(LITTLE —) STNEKI SCANTLING
(LONG —) STRIP
(MAH JONGG —) TILE
(MISCELLANEOUS —S) ODDS
(MOVABLE — IN VIOLIN BOW) NUT
(MUSICAL —) ITEM CHORO DANCE
ETUDE CHASER LESSON ALLEGRO
ANDANTE BLUETTE CANZONA
CANZONE CONCERTO DUOLOGUE
ENTRACTE OVERTURE PASTORAL
RHAPSODY BAGATELLE INVENTION
DIVERTIMENTO
(NARROW —) LABEL STAVE STRIP
(ODD — OF CARPENTRY) DUTCHMAN
(PIANO —) NOVELETTE
(PROJECTING —) TANG
(ROTATING —) CAM ROTOR SPINDLE
(SAMPLE —) SWATCH
(SHAPELESS —) DUMP MAMMOCK
(SIDE —) RIB JAMB JAMBE
(SINGLE —) LENGTH
(SLENDER —) SPILL SLIVER
(SMALL —) BIT BOB NOB PEA CHIP
SNIP TATE CRUMB PATCH PRILL
SCRAP SPECK MORSEL SIPPET
DRIBLET FLITTER PALLION
SPLINTER
(SMALL — OF FLESH) GIGOT
(SMALL — OF WOOD) KIP
(SMALL —S) MATCHWOOD
(STRENGTHENING —) DWANG
HURTER
(TAPERING —) GORE GUSSET
(THICK —) JUNK HUNCH
(THIN —) SHIM FLAKE SHIVE SLICE
(WEDGESHAPED — OF WOOD) GLUT
SHIM

(100-REAL GOLD —) ISABELLA
(25-CENT —) CUTER
(4-DOLLAR GOLD —) STELLA
(PL.) MATERIAL NOBLEMEN
PIECEWORK SETWORK TUTWORK
TASKWORK
PIECEWORKER JOBBER
PIECRUST BREAD COFFIN ABAISSE
PIED PINTO SHELD MAGPIED
PIEBALD
PIED ANTELOPE BONTEBOK
PIEDFORT PATAGON
PIED WAGTAIL COB COBB PEER PILE
PILLAR WAGGIE WASHER WATERIE
SEEDBIRD WASHDISH WASHTAIL
PIEPLANT RHUBARB RHAPONTIC
PIER COB ANTA BELT COBB DOCK
MOLE PILE QUAY TILT GROIN JETTY
JOWEL JUTTY LEVEE STILT WHARF
BRIDGE BUNDER MULLION STAGION
PIEDROIT STELLING
(— CAP) SUMMER
(HALF —) RESPONSE
PIERCE CUT DAD DAG DEG DIG JAB
JAG RIT BARB BEAR BITE BORE BROB
BROD CLOY DART DIRL GORE HOLE
HOOK LACE LACK PASS PINK POKE
PROB PROG RIVE ROVE STAB STOB
TAME TANG WHIP BREAK DRIFT
DRILL ENTER GOUGE GRIDE LANCE
PERCH PITCH POACH PREEN PROBE
PRONG SHEAR SNICK SPEAR SPIKE
STEEK STICK STING THIRL AI TAME
BROACH CLEAVE DAGGER EMPALE
FICCHE GIMLET IMPALE LAUNCH
PRITCH RIDDLE SEARCH SKEWER
STITCH STRIKE THRILL THRING
THRUST WIMBLE ASSAGAI JAVELIN
ENTHRILL LACERATE PUNCTURE
PENETRATE
(PREF.) FORAMINI
PIERCED AJOURE CRIBRAL PERTUSE
CRIBROSE PERFORATE
PIERCING SHY FELL HIGH KEEN
LOUD TART ACUTE CLEAR EAGLE
SHARP SNELL ARROWY BITTER
BORING SHREWD SHRILL SNITHE
SNITHY CUTTING GIMLETY POINTED
PUNGENT DRILLING INCISIVE
PERCEANT POIGNANT POUNCING
STABBING STICKING PENETRATIVE
PIERHEAD MOLEHEAD
PIET PYOT DIPPER MAGPIE
PIETIST LABADIST
PIETISTIC DEVOUT
PIETY HONOR LOYALTY PIETISM
DEVOTION SANCTION GODLINESS
PIFFLE RUFF FOLDEROL
PIG (ALSO SEE HOG, SWINE) COW FAR
HAM HOG SLIP SLOB BACON BONAV
BROCK CHEAT CHUCK GRICE INGOT
PIGGY SHOAT APEREA BONHAM

COCHON FARROW GUSSIE HOGGIE
PORKET PORKIN SUCKER TITMAN
WEANER BONNIVE GLUTTON
GRUMPHY HOGLING PIGLING
ROOKLER GRUNTLING
(— OUT) GORGE
(BROOD OF —S) TEAM
(CASTRATED —) BARROW
(CASTRATED MALE —) BARROW
(EIGHT —S) FODDER
(FEMALE —) SOW
(MALE —) BOAR
(PART OF —) EAR EYE HAM BUTT
HOCK JOWL LOIN POLL TAIL TEAT
FLANK SNOUT PICNIC FATBACK
FOREFOOT SHOULDER SPARERIB
TENDERLOIN
(SMALLEST — OF LITTER) DOLL
TITMAN ANTHONY DILLING
TANTANY TANTONY
(SUCKLING —) ROASTER
(UNDERSIZED —) RUNT TITMAN
TEATMAN
(YOUNG —) ELT FAR SLIP GRICE
GURRY
(YOUNG—) SHOAT SHOTE
(YOUNG —) BONEEN BONHAM
SQUEAKER
(YOUNG FEMALE —) GILT
(PREF.) HYO
(SUFF.) CHOERUS
PIG DEER DABIRUSA
PIGEON DOO NUN OWL TOY BARB
CLAY DOVE JACK KING KITE LUPE
RUFF RUNT SPOT BALDY DOWVE
FRILL HOMER KOKLA PIPER SQUAB
WONGA CULTER CULVER CUSHAT
DODLET DRAGON FEEDER HELMET
JEWING MAGPIE MANUMA MAUMET
MODENA POUTER PRIEST ROCKER
SHAKER TRERON TURBIT TURNER
WATTLE ANTWERP CARNEAU
CARRIER CROPPER FANTAIL FINIKIN
JACINTH JACOBIN MALTESE
PINTADO SWALLOW TIPPLER
TUMBLER BALDHEAD CAPUCHIN
FINIKING HORSEMAN MANUTAGI
RINGDOVE SASSOROL SQUABBER
SQUEAKER SQUEALER FRILLBACK
TOOTHBILL
(CLAY —) BIRD GYROPIGEON
(FLIGHTLESS —) SOLITAIRE
(STOOL —) PIG NARK
(YOUNG —) SQUAB
PIGEON BLOOD GARNET
PIGEON HAWK MERLIN
PIGEONHOLE BOX SLOT LABEL
SHELVE ANALYZE CELLULE CLASSIFY
CUBBYHOLE
(PL.) STOCK
PIGEON HOUSE COT DOOKET
DOVECOT COLUMBARY

PIGEON PEA DAL TUR TARE ARHAR DAHIL GANDUL TURNER TURNOR CATJANG

PIGEON WOODPECKER FLICKER

PIGGERY PIGS PIGSTY HOGGERY POTTERY SWINERY CROCKERY

PIGGIE TOE

PIGGIN HANDY PIPKIN

PIGHEADED WILLFUL PERVERSE STUBBORN OBSTINATE

PIGHTLE PIKLE PICKLE PIDDLE PIGTAIL

PIG IRON GRUNDY

PIGLET PORKLING

PIGLIKE SUIFORM SUILINE SWINISH

PIGMENT (ALSO SEE DYE, COLOR) BLUE HEME BROWN COLOR EARTH GREEN HUMIN MORIN MUMMY PAINT STAIN TONER BRONZE CEROID CERUSE IDAEIN LITHOL MALVIN ORANGE PURPLE SIENNA VIOLET BEZETTA GOUACHE PAINTRY PUCCOON STAINER TURACIN ALTHAEIN COLORANT EXTENDER GOSSYPOL MELANOID PAINTURE TINCTURE UROPHEIN VERDITER

  (— FOR WOODWORK) KOKOWAI
  (— IN BUTTERFLY WING) PTERIN
  (BLACK —) ABAISER MELANIN
  (BLUE —) BICE SMALT CYANIN ALTHEIN CERULEUM MARENNIN
  (BLUE-GREEN —) LEUCOCYAN
  (BROWN —) MUMMY SEPIA UMBER BISTER FUSCIN ASTERIN SINOPIA
  (BROWNISH-YELLOW —) SIENNA
  (GRAPE —) ENIN OENIN
  (GREEN —) VERDITER
  (MADDER-ROOT —) RUBIATE
  (ORANGE-RED —) REALGAR
  (PLANT —) CYANIN
  (RED —) HAEM LAKE ARUMIN PATISE SANDYX AMATITO KOKOWAI PUCCOON SCARLET SINOPIA CAPSUMIN URORUBIN URRHODIN VERMILION
  (RED-VIOLET —) TURACIN
  (WHITE —) CERUSE ANATASE LITHOPONE
  (YELLOW —) MORIN FLAVIN PURREE ETIOLIN FISETIN GAMBOGE PUCCOON CAROTENE DIATOMIN GALANGIN GENTISIN MASSICOT ORPIMENT UROBILIN
  (PREF.) CHROM(AT)(ATO)(I)(IDIO)(O)

PIGMENTATION COLOR LENTIL ARGYRIA LENTIGO JAUNDICE NIGRITES

  (SKIN —) ARGYRIA

PIGNUS PAWN PLEDGE

PIGNUT ARNOT ARNUT HOGNUT

PIGS' FEET CRUBEEN PETTITOES

PIGSKIN SADDLE FOOTBALL

PIGSNEY EYE DARLING

PIGSTY FRANK CRUIVE HOGCOTE HOGGERY PIGGERY SWINESTY

PIGTAIL BRAID PLAIT QUEUE COLETA

PIGWASH SWILL

PIGWEED QUINOA BEETROOT CARELESS GOOSEFOOT

PIK DRA PICKI PICKL ENDAZE ENDASEH

PIKA CONY HAIR HARE LEPORID LAGOMORPH

PIKE GED DORE DORY GADE GEDD JACK LUCE TANG TOUG TUCK HAKED LUCET SNAKE SNOOK STING VOUGE SALMON SAUGER JAVELIN WALLEYE BLOWFISH GLASSEYE JACKFISH NORTHERN PARTISAN PICKEREL POULAINE TURNPIKE MUSKELLUNGE

PIKELET CRUMPET

PIKEMAN PIKE WATTLEBOY

PIKE PERCH FOGASH PERCID SANDER SAUGER ZANDER

PIKER TRAMP VAGRANT TELLTALE TIGHTWAD VAGABOND

PILASTER ANTA PIER RIDGE ALETTE ALLETTE RESPOND TELAMON

PILCHARD FUMADO ALEWIFE SARDINE MENHADEN

PILCORN OAT

PILDASH (FATHER OF —) NAHOR
  (MOTHER OF —) MILCAH

PILE COP FUR LOT NAP PIE TIP BALE BANK BING BULK BUNG BURR COCK DASS DECK DESS DOWN HACK HAIR HEAP LEET LOAD PEEL PIER POLE POOK PYRE REEK RUCK SESS SHAG SPUD AMASS CANCH CLAMP CROWD FAGOT POINT SPILE SPIRE STACK STILT TOWER CASTLE FAGGOT FENDER FILLER GALGAL PILLAR RICKLE RUCKLE FORTUNE JAVELIN PYRAMID REACTOR SPINDLE CROWBILL INCREASE SANDPILE

  (— CROSSWISE) COB
  (— CURD) CHEDDAR
  (— OF BRICKS) HACK CLAMP
  (— OF CLOTH) LAY
  (— OF HAY) RICK SHOCK DOODLE HAYCOCK HAYRICK
  (— OF ICE) HUMMOCK
  (— OF LOGS) DECK
  (— OF PLATES) BUNG
  (— OF REFUSE) DUSTHEAP
  (— OF SALT FISH) BULK
  (— OF SEALSKINS) PAN
  (— OF SHEAVES) SESS
  (— OF SHEETS) LIFT
  (— OF STONES) ISLAND STONAGE WARLOCK
  (— OF TOBACCO) BULK
  (— OF WOOD) STRAND

(— TO BE BURNT) PYRE
(— UP) BIG BULK CORD RICK
COMPILE ACCUMULATE
(— WHEAT SHOCKS) STITCH
(IRON —) SPINDLE
(LITTLE —) HOT HOTT
(LOOSE —) RICKLE
(ROCK —) HOODOO
(SMALL —) COCK CANCH
(PL.) FIG DRIFT
PILEA ADICEA
PILEATED WOODPECKER
LOGCOCK WOODCOCK
PILE DRIVER TUP FISTUCA
HERCULES IMPACTER
(— DOLLY) FOLLOWER
(— WEIGHT) RAM TUP MONKEY
PILEUS CAP MITRA PILEOLUS
PILEWORT CRAIN CRANE FICARY
FIGWORT CELANDINE
PILFER NIM NIP ROB CRIB HOOK
PALM PELF PICK PILK PRIG SMUG
SNIG FILCH MICHE MOOCH PILCH
PROWL SHARP SLOCK STEAL SWIPE
FINGER MAGPIE MOOTCH NIBBLE
PICKLE SMOUCH SNITCH CABBAGE
MANAVEL PLUNDER PURLOIN
SNAFFLE UNHITCH PETTIFOG
SCROUNGE
PILFERER PRIG PIKER TAKER
SLOCKER FINGERER SLOCKSTER
PILFERING CRIB MICHING PICKING
THIEVISH
PILGRIM HADJ HAJI HADJI HAJJI
PALMER PELERIN PEREGRIN
WAYFARER
(MUSLIM —) HADJ
PILGRIMAGE TRIP TURUS VOYAGE
JOURNEY
(— TO MECCA) HADJ
(BRETON —) PARDON
PILGRIM BROWN FRIAR
PILGRIM'S PROGRESS (AUTHOR
OF —) BUNYAN
(CHARACTER IN —) POPE PAGAN
PIETY SLOTH PLIANT SIMPLE
CHARITY DESPAIR HOPEFUL SINCERE
APOLLYON FAITHFUL GOODWILL
PRUDENCE WATCHFUL CHRISTIAN
FORMALISM HYPOCRISY IGNORANCE
KNOWLEDGE OBSTINATE
DISCRETION EVANGELIST
EXPERIENCE PRESUMPTION
(LAND IN —) BEULAH
PILING SPILING STOCKADE
(PL.) STARLING
PILL PIL ROB BALL BARK GOLI PEEL
POOL CREEK CACHOU EXTORT
TABLET UNHAIR DESPOIL DIURNAL
GLOBULE GRANULE PARVULE
PILLULE PREFORM BASEBALL
GOOFBALL BLACKBALL CIGARETTE

(AROMATIC —) CACHOU
(LARGE —) BALI BOLUS
(LITTLE —) PILULA PILULE
(SLEEPING —) GOOFBALL
(SMALL —) MICRODOT
PILLAGE LOOT PEEL PILL PREY SACK
BOOTY FORAY HARRY REAVE RIFLE
SPOIL HARROW MARAUD PICORY
RAPINE RAVAGE DESPOIL PICKEER
PLUNDER RANSACK ROBBERY
BOOTHALE EXPILATE PURCHASE
SPOLIATE DEVASTATE
PILLAGER PEELER PILLER ROBBER
SACKER SPOILER SNAPHANCE
PILLAGING EXECUTION PREDATORY
PILLAR COG HERM JAMB PACK PIER
PILE POST PROP STUD TERM JAMBE
NEWEL SHAFT STELA STELE STOCK
STONE STOOP STUMP CIPPUS
COLUMN HERMES PILLER STAPLE
BEDPOST DEADMAN TRESTLE
TRUMEAU BOUNDARY MASSEBAH
PEDESTAL RESPONSE STANCHION
(— CAPPED WITH SLAB) BILITH
(— IN LARGE DOORWAY) TRUMEAU
(— IN MINE) STOOK STUMP
(— OF COAL) SPURN STOOK STOOP
(—S OF HERCULES) ABILA CALPE
(— SUPPORTING ARCH) RESPONSE
(— SURMOUNTED BY HEAD) HERMES
(BUDDHIST —) LAT
(CHANGED TO —) OLENUS
(EARTH —) HOODOO
(MAN-LIKE —) TELAMON
(ROCK —) STACK GENDARME
(SACRED —) ASHERAH
(SEMITE —) MASSEBAH
(STONE —) CIPPUS
(TEMPORARY —) DEADMAN
(UPRIGHT —) STANDARD
(4-SIDED —) OBELISK
(PL.) CRURA
(PREF.) CION(O) STELO STYL(I)(O)
PILLARIST STYLITE
PILLAS PILCORN PILKINS
PILLBOX SCATULA
PILLBUG ISOPOD KEESLIP MILLEPED
PILLWORM CHEESELIP
PILLED BALD SHAVEN TONSURED
PILLION PAD PILLOW SADDLE
CUSHION
PILLORY CANG THEW JOUGS TRONE
CANGUE CRUCIFY HALSFANG
PILLOW COD BOTT DAWN PEEL PILE
REST FLOAT WANGER BOLSTER
CUSHION FUSTIAN HEADING
OREILLER PULVINAR
(PREF.) PULVILLI PULVINI
PILLOWCASE COD BEAR PILL SHAM
PILLIVER
PILLOWY PULVINAR
PILM DUST

PILON BONUS LAGNIAPPE
PILOSE HAIRY HIRSUTE PILEOUS
PILOT ACE SPY JOCK KIWI COACH
GUARD GUIDE STEER AIRMAN
ESCORT MANAGE THAMUS AVIATOR
CAPTAIN CONDUCT HOBBLER
LODEMAN SHIPMAN WINGMAN
AIREDALE GOVERNOR HELMSMAN
NAVIGATE NAVIGATOR PALINURUS
WHEELSMAN COWCATCHER
(AUTHOR OF —) COOPER
(AUTOMATIC —) GEORGE
(CHARACTER IN —) TOM GRAY ALICE
JONES MERRY COFFIN DILLON
EDWARD HOWARD MANUAL
MUNSON CECILIA PLOWDEN
RICHARD GRIFFITH DUNSCOMBE
KATHERINE BARNSTABLE
CHRISTOPHER BORROUGHCLIFFE
(DUD —) PRUNE
(UNLICENSED —) HOBBLER
PILOT BIRD PLOVER
PILOT FISH ROMERO JACKFISH
AMBERFISH
PILOTHOUSE TEXAS CHARTHOUSE
CONNINGTOWER
PILUM PESTLE JAVELIN
PIMENTA MYRTAL
PIMENTO PIMENTA ALLSPICE
PIMIENTO
PIMP MACK BULLY CADET FAGOT
PONCE SNEAK MACRIO PANDER
MACKMAN RUFFIAN INFORMER
PROCURER PURVEYOR SCOUNDREL
SOUTENEUR
PIMPERNEL BURNET WAYWORT
EYEBRIGHT MARGELINE WINCOPIPE
PIMPLE GUM NOB PAP WEN ZIT BURL
KNOB PUSH QUAT SPOT BLAIN
BOTCH HICKY PLOOK PLOUK PLUKE
WHELK BLOTCH BOUTON BUTTON
PAPULA PAPULE TETTER BUBUKLE
PUSTULE PIMGENET WHEYWORM
(— ON NOSE) RUMBUD
(PREF.) CHALAZI CHALAZO PAPULI
PAPULO
PIN FID FIX HOB HUB LAG LEG NOG
PEG PEN ACUS APEX AXLE BANK
BOLT LILL MOOD PEEN POST PRIN
PROP PYNE RUNG STUD DRIFT
HUMOR KAYLE POINT PREEN SPILL
THOLE BOBBIN BODKIN BROACH
BROOCH CALIGO COTTER CURLER
FASTEN HATPIN JOGGLE NORMAN
PINNET SKEWER SPIGOT TEMPER
TENPIN TOGGEL TONGUE TRIFLE
BAYONET CONFINE ENCLOSE
GUDGEON HAIRPIN IMPOUND
LOCKPIN PUSHPIN SPINDLE TAMPION
TANGENT TUMBLER WOOLDER
FORELOCK PINNACLE
(— FOR FITTING PLANKS) SETBOLT
(— IN AXLETREE) LINCHPIN
(— IN RIFLE) TIGE
(— OF DIAL) STYLE GNOMON
(— OF LANTERN PINION) RUNDLE
(— OF WATCH) DART
(— ON CLAVICHORD KEY) TANGENT
(— TO HOLD BEDCLOTHES)
BEDSTAFF
(— USED AS TARGET) HOB
(BELAYING —) CAVIL
(BOWLING —) DUCKPIN HEADPIN
KINGPIN SLEEPER
(BOWLING —S) DEADWOOD
(CARPENTRY —) DOWEL
(COUPLING —) DRAWBOLT
(ENGAGING —) BAYONET
(HAIR —) BARRETTE
(HEADED —) RIVET
(JEWELED —) PROP
(NECKTIE —) TIETAC TIETACK
(OAR —) THOLE
(ORNAMENTAL —) AGLET AIGLET
(PIVOT —) PINTLE
(SMALL —) LILL MINIKIN MICROPIN
(SPLIT —) COTTER FORELOCK
(SURVEYOR'S —) ARROW
(TAPERED —) DRIFT
(TIRLING —) RISP
(WOODEN —) DOWEL SPILE
TRENAIL
(PL.) LEGS KAILS DEADWOOD
(PREF.) PERONEO PERONO
PINACOID BASE HEMIDOME
PINAFORE BRAT SLIP TIDE TIDY TIER
TYER DAIDLY PINNER SAVEALL
SLIPPER GABERDINE
PINBALL BAGATELLE
PINBALL MACHINE PACHINKO
PINCASE POPPET
PINCE-NEZ NIPPER LORGNON
NOSEPINCH
PINCER CLAW
PINCERS TEU TEW CLAM CHELA
TUARN PLIERS TURKIS WYNRIS
FORCEPS MULLETS NIPPERS
PINCHER PINSONS TWEEZERS
PINCH NAB NIP TAD TOP VEX WRY
BITE CLAM HURT POOK PUSH STOP
TAIT TATE TUCK CHACK CRIMP GRIPE
HINCH PUGIL SNUFF SQUAT STEAL
STINT TAPER THEFT TWEAK WRING
ARREST CLUTCH COLLAR EXTORT
HARASS NARROW SNITCH STRAIT
STRESS TWITCH SCRINCH SQUEEZE
JUNCTURE PRESSURE SHORTAGE
STRAITEN VELLICATE
(— OF SNUFF) SNEESH SNEESHIN
(— WITH COLD) NIRL
(— WITH HUNGER) CLAM CLEM
PINCHBECK SHAM CHEAP
SPURIOUS PRETENDED
PINCHED CHITTY WASTED HAGGARD
PUNGLED SQUINCH
PINCHING CHACK

PINCHPENNY CARL MISER
NIGGARDLY SKINFLINT

PINDARIC ODE WILD

PINE IE ARA LIM ACHE CHIL CHIR FADE
FLAG HALA HONE IEIE KAIL WANT
AGGAG DROOP DWAIN GRIEF KAURI
MATAI MATSU MOURN OCOTE PINON
THUJA WANZE WEARY WRIST YEARN
APACHE AROLLA DUSTER FAMINE
GRIEVE HUNGER LAMENT PANDAN
SHRINK SORROW STARVE TOATOA
TORFEL WITHER CYPRESS DAISING
DWINDLE FORPINE FOXTAIL JEFFREY
LAUHALA TARWOOD TORMENT
TORTURE AKAMATSU AUSTRIAN
GALAGALA LANGUISH LOBLOLLY
LONGLEAF PINASTER STAGHORN
TANEKAHA VANQUISH
(— AWAY) PEAK DROOP DWINE
SNURP WANZE WINDER FORPINE
MACERATE
(AUSTRALIAN —) BEEFWOOD
(GROUND —) FOXTAIL
(KIND OF —) MUGHO JEFFREY
(PITCH —) THYME
(PREF.) PINI PITYO

PINEAPPLE BOMB NANA PINA PINO
PITA ANANA ANANAS ABACAXI
GRENADE

PINE FINCH SISKIN

PINE MARTEN SABLE

PINE NEEDLE SHAT SPILL PINING
ALFILARIA
(PL.) TWINKLES

PINE TREE STATE MAINE

PINFEATHER PEN STUMP STIPULE

PINFISH CHUB SPOT JIMMY PORGY
SARGO

PINFOLD POUND

PING KNOCK

PING-PONG SHIFT BOUNCE

PINGRASS ALFILERIA

PINGUIN MAYA ANANAS AGUAMAS
PINUELA HUIPILLA

PINGUITUDE FATNESS OBESITY
OILINESS

PINING SICK LANGUOR HOMESICK
LOVELORN

PINION NOIL WING PINON QUILL
PENNON SARCEL SECURE LANTERN
PINACLE SHACKLE TRUNDLE
FLIGHTER WALLOWER

PINION WHEEL MOBILE

PINITOL SENNITE MATEZITE

PINK JAG PIP CYME DAWN DECK FADE
MICE PING STAB WINK ADORN BLINK
CORAL ELITE MOVED SWELL WOUND
AURORE BISQUE CHERUB FIESTA
HEIGHT MINNOW POUNCE SHRIMP
SILENE TATTOO ZEPHYR ANNATTO
ARBUTUS BEGONIA BERMUDA
BLOSSOM CAMPION EXTREME
PARAGON REVERSE SANDUST

TUSSORE CONFETTI COQUETTE
DECORATE DIANTHUS GILLIVER
LIMEWORT RADIANCE RECAMIER

PINKED JAGGED

PINKIE PIRLIE

PINKROOT REDROOT WORMWEED
STARBLOOM

PINNA EAR EARFLAP PINNULE
APHLEBIA AURICULA PAVILION

PINNACE BARK CROWN WOMAN
BARQUE PINNAGE MISTRESS

PINNACLE IT PIN TOP ACME APEX
CREST CROWN IDEAL SERAC SPIRE
THUMB FINIAL HEIGHT SUMMIT
GENDARME
(ICE —) SÉRAC
(ROCKY —) TOR HOODOO AIGUILLE
GENDARME

PINNATE WINGED

PINNER PINDER FLANDAN STICKER

PINNIPED SEAL

PINNULE FIN

PINOCHLE BINOCLE GOULASH
AIRPLANE
(— SCORE) MELD

PINPILLOW PIMPLO

PINPOINT ISOLATE
(— OF LIGHT) GLEAM

PINT O GULL PINNET SWIGGER
OCTARIUS
(FOURTH —) GILL JACK
(HALF —) CUP NIP GILL JACK CUPFUL
NIPPERKIN
(9-10THS —) MUTCHKIN

PINTADO CERO PIED SIER SEARER
SIERRA SPOTTED KINGFISH

PINTAIL DUCK SMEE SPIKE SPRIG
GROUSE SMETHE CRACKER
LADYBIRD LONGNECK PIKETAIL

PINTANO PILOT COCKEYE CHIRIVITA

PINTID EMPEINE

PINTO PAINT

PINTO BEAN ROSILLO

PINUP CHEESECAKE

PINWEED
(PL.) LECHEA

PINWHEEL WINDMILL

PINWORM NEMA OXYURID

PIN WRENCH SPANULE

PINZA EZIO

PION MESON

PIONEER BLAZE GUIDE MINER
GROPER HALUTZ SETTLE CHALUTZ
EXPLORE EARLIEST EMIGRANT
ORIGINAL RAWHIDER VOORTREKKER

PIONEERS (AUTHOR OF —) COOPER
(CHARACTER IN —) JOHN GRANT
HIRAM JONES NATTY BUMPPO
LOUISA OLIVER TEMPLE EDWARDS
RICHARD DOOLITTLE EFFINGHAM
ELIZABETH CHINGACHGOOK

PIOUS PI HOLY WISE FROOM GODLY
MORAL SEELY DEVOUT DIVINE

INWARD PIETIC CANTING DUTIFUL
GODDARD PITEOUS SAINTED
SAINTLY FAITHFUL REVERENT
RELIGIOUS

PIP DIE CHIP ECHO KILL PAIP PEEP
SEED SPOT SPECK ACINUS DEFEAT
PIPPIN BLACKBALL

PIPAL BO FIG

PIPE TD BIN GUN HUB TAP TEE BONG
BUTT CALL CANE DALE DRIP DUCT
FLUE HOSE LINE MAIN MUTE PULE
REED TILE TUBE WEEP WORM BLAST
BRAIL BRIAR BRIER CANAL CANEL
CINCH CRANE CROSS CUTTY HOOKA
PROBE PUNGI QUILL RIDER RISER
SPOUT STAND STRAW TEWEL
TRUMP TRUNK VOICE BRANCH
BURROW CALEAN CASING DUCTUS
DUDEEN FAUCET FILLER GEWGAW
HEWGAG HOGGER HOOKAH KINURA
NIPPLE NOTICE NOZZLE OFFLET
OFFSET POOGYE RANKET SLEEVE
SLOUCH SLUICE SUCKER TROWEL
TUBULE TUNNEL UPTAKE WEEPER
CHANNEL CHANTER CHIBOUK
CONDUIT DUCTURE FISTULA
HYDRANT SERVICE SPARGER
SPINDLE SUCTION TALLBOY
TWEEDLE WHISTLE CALIDUCT
DOWNTAKE GALOUBET LAMPHOLE
MIRLITON NARGHILE NARGILEH
PENSTOCK SEMIDOLE SUSPIRAL
TELLTALE THRIBBLE
(— AS NAVIGATION AID) SPINDLE
(— BENDER) HICKEY
(— BOWL) STUMMEL
(— FOR CONDUCTING WATER)
LEADER
(— JOINT) TURNOUT
(— OF ORE) BUNNY
(— OF PAN) SYRINX
(— OF QUEEN BEE) TEET
(— ON BAGPIPE) DRONE CHANTER
(— SUPPORT) CRADLE
(— TAB) TACK
(— TO MUFFLE TRUMPET) SORDINE
(— USED IN WELL) STRING
(— WITH SOCKET ENDS) HUB
(BOWL AND STEM OF —) STUMMEL
(CEREMONIAL —) CALUMET
(CLAMMING —) BRAIL
(CLEAN A —) REAM
(CONNECTING —) HOGGER
(FLUE —) LABIAL
(HEATING —) CALIDUCT
(IRISH —) DUDEEN
(KIND OF —) UILLEANN
(MUSICAL —) BODY GEWGAW
FISTULA SORDINE HORNPIPE
SCHWEGEL
(OATEN —) OAT
(ORGAN —) FLUE KINURA LABIAL
ERZAHLER SCHWEGEL TREMOLANT

(ORGAN —S) MONTRE
(PART OF —) BIT BOWL STEM SHANK
SHAPE SADDLE MOUTHPIECE
(PEACE —) CALUMET
(PROJECTING —) BRACKET
(RESIDUE IN OPIUM —) YENSHGEE
(SEWER —) SLANT
(SHEPHERD'S —) REED LARIGOT
CHALUMEAU
(SNAKE-CHARMER'S —) PUNGI
(TOBACCO —) GUN CLAY BRIAR
BRIER CUTTY HOOKA STRAW
CALEAN DUDEEN HOOKAH BULLDOG
CHIBOUK CHILLUM CORNCOB
BILLIARD CALABASH MEERSCHAUM
(TOY —) HEWGAG
(VERTICAL —) STACK LAMPHOLE
(WATER — FOR ENGINE) SLOUCH
(4 LENGTHS OF —) FOURBLE
(PREF.) AUL(O) SIPHON(O) SOLEN(O)
SYRING(O) TUBI TUBO TUBULI
TUBULO

PIPECLAY CAM CALM CAUM

PIPED DRUNK JETTED

PIPEFISH EARL LONGJAW
NEEDLEFISH

PIPELAYER YARNER

PIPESTEM STOPPEL STOPPLE

PIPETTE PIPET TASTER

PIPEWORT HATPIN WOOLWEED

PIPING HOSE SOFT VERY CRYING
ROULEAU WAILING WEEPING
TRANQUIL

PIPING CROW CASSICAN
FLUTEBIRD

PIPIRI PITIRRI

PIPISTRELLE BAT NOCTULE

PIPIT PEEP TEETAN WEKEEN CHEEPER
SKYLARK TIETICK TITLARK TITLING
WAGTAIL LINGBIRD TWITLARK

PIPPIN PIP APPLE PEPPIN RIBSTON

PIPSISSEWA EVERGREEN
WINTERGREEN

PIQUANCY SALT ZEST JUICE
FLAVOR GINGER TARTNESS

PIQUANT BOLD RACY JUICY NUTTY
SALTY SHARP SPICY TASTY ZESTY
LIVELY SEVERE CUTTING PEPPERY
PUNGENT POIGNANT STINGING
(SHARPLY —) ZINGY

PIQUE FRET GOAD PEAK PICK PIKE
PYKE TICK ANNOY PRISE SNUFF
SPITE STING HARASS MALICE
NETTLE PRITCH STRUNT CHIGGER
OFFENSE PROVOKE UMBRAGE
IRRITATE MARCELLA

PIRACY CAPTURE PIRATISM

PIRAGUA CANOE DUGOUT PIROGUE
PETTIAGUA

PIRANHA PIRAI CARIBE PIRAYA

PIRARUCU PAICHE ARAPAIMA

PIRATE CAPER ROVER ROBBER
VIKING CATERAN CORSAIR PICKEER

SCUMMER ALGERINE MAROONER
PICAROON BUCCANEER
SALLEEMAN
(— FLAG) ROGER BLACK JACK
PIRENE (FATHER OF —) ASOPUS
ACHELOUS
(MOTHER OF —) METOPE
(SON OF —) CENCHRIAS
PIRIPIRI BIRK BIRCH MAPAN
PIRL SPIN TWINE TWIST REVOLVE
PIRN QUILL BOBBIN PIRNIE SPINDLE
PIROGUE CANOE PERIOQUE
PIROPLASM BABESIA
PIROSHKI PIROGEN
PIROUETTE TURN
PISCINA POOL TANK BASIN SACRARY
LAVATORY SACRARIUM
PISE CAJON PISAY
PISHOGUE CHARM SPELL SORCERY
WITCHERY
PISMIRE ANT EMMET
PISOLITE PEASTONE
PISTACHIO PISTIC PISTICK
PISTIL CHIVE CARPEL UMBONE
POINTEL
(PL.) GYNECIUM
(PREF.) GYN(AE)(AEO)(F)(EO)(O)(O)
GYNAECO GYNANDRO GYNECO
PISTILLATE FEMALE
PISTOL DAG GAT GUN POP ROD BULL
COLT DAGG IRON TACK FLUTE RIFLE
STICK BARKER BUFFER BULDER
BULLER CANNON DRAGON HEATER
POTGUN RIFFLE ROSCOE BULLDOG
DUNGEON SHOOTER TICKLER
DERINGER PETRONEL REPORTER
REVOLVER PEPPERBOX
(TOY —) SPARKLER
PISTON BUCKET FORCER PALLET
SUCKER EMBOLUS PLUNGER
(— HUB) SPIDER
PIT PET POT PUT BURY CIST DELF
DELL DISC DISK FOSS HELL HOLE
KHUD KIST LAKE MINE PLAY PUTT
SEED SILO SINK SUMP SWAG TURN
WEEM WELL ABYSM ABYSS CRYPT
DELFT DITCH FOSSA FOVEA FROST
GRAVE LEACH MATCH PITCH PORUS
SLACK SLUIG TREAD AREOLE
BORROW BUNKER KERNEL OPPOSE
RADDLE WALLOW ABADDON
ALVEOLA AMPULLA BOTHROS
CHARPIT FOSSULA FOXHOLE
HANDLER LATRINE MEGARON
PINHOLE VARIOLE WINNING
CESSPOOL CYPHELLA DOWNFALL
FAVEOLUS FENESTRA POCKMARK
PUNCTULE WELLHOLE
(— FOR BAKING) IMU UMU
(— FOR OFFERINGS) BOTHROS
(— OF STOMACH) MARK WIND
ANTICARDIUM
(— OF THEATER) GROUND PARTERRE

(— ON COCKROACH HEAD)
FENESTRA
(— ON LICHENS) LACUNA CYPHELLA
(— SACRED TO DEMETER) MEGARON
(AUTHOR OF —) NORRIS
(BITTER —) STIPPEN
(BOTTOMLESS —) ABYSS ABADDON
BARATHRUM
(CHARACTER IN —) PAGE WESS
LAURA CURTIS GRETRY JADWIN
SHELDON CORTHELL CRESSLER
DEARBORN
(COAL —) HEUCH HEUGH WINNING
(COOKING —) IMU
(FODDER —) SILO
(MAORI —) RUA
(MIRY —) SLUIG
(RIFLE —) SANGAR
(ROOFED —) CIST KIOT
(SALT —) VAT PEZOGRAPH
(SAND —) BUNKER
(SMALL —) AREOLE LACUNA
STAPLE
(TANNING —) LIME LAYER LEACH
HANDLER LAYAWAY SUSPENDER
(PREF.) BOTHR(I)(IO)(O) FOVEI
PITA PITO YUCCA ARGHAN
PITCH GO DIP FIT KEY LAB MEL PIC
TAR BUCK CANT CHAT CODE COOK
DING FALL FORK HURL PECK PICK
PLUG RAKE TELL TONE TOSS ARODE
BOOST BUNCH CHUCK FLING LABOR
LURCH PLANT SLENT SLOPE SPIEL
THROW TWIRL BINDER CAREEN
DIRECT ENCAMP FILLER LENGTH
MALTHA MANJAK PLUNGE SQUARE
TOTTER TUMBLE VOLLEY WICKET
CURRENT NARRATE ALKITRAN
OVERHANG
(— AT A MARK) LAG
(— FROM FIR TREES) ALKITRAN
(— INSIDE) JAM
(— INTO TROUGH OF SEA) SEND
(— OF BIRD OF PREY) PLACE
(— OF HELIX) JAW
(— TENT) TELD
(— TENTS) CAMP
(ABOVE —) SHARP
(AUCTION —) SETBACK
(BASEBALL —) CURVE STRIKE
CRIPPLE SPITTER FADEAWAY
KNUCKLER SPITBALL BRUSHBACK
(BELOW —) FLAT
(COBBLER'S —) CODE
(FULL —) VOLLEY
(GLANCE —) MANJAK MANJACK
(HIGH —) BLOOPER
(HIGHEST —) PRIDE
(IDENTITY IN —) UNISON
(MINERAL —) BITUMEN
(PREF.) MISERI
PITCH APPLE COPEI CUPAY
PITCHBLENDE CLEVEITE

PITCHED SET
(PREF.) (— BELOW BASS) CONTRA
PITCHER JUG JACK OLLA PILL PRIG
BUIRE CROCK CRUET GALON GORGE
GOTCH AFTABA CROUKE GALLON
HURLER POURIE STRAIN URCEUS
CANETTE CHUCKER FLINGER
GROWLER STARTER STOPPER
TWIRLER URCEOLE AIGUIERE
ASCIDIUM OENOCHOE SOUTHPAW
MOUNDSMAN
(— AND CATCHER) BATTERY
(— FOR BEER) GROWLER
(— OF ORCHID) BUCKET
(— SHAPED LIKE MAN) TOBY
(— WITH ONE HANDLE) URCEUS
(BULGING —) GOTCH
(EARTHEN —) GEORG GORGE
(KIND OF —) RELIEF
(RELIEF —) FIREMAN
(RELIEF —S) BULLPEN
(REMOVE — FROM BASEBALL GAME)
DERRICK
(WIDEMOUTHED —) EWER
PITCHER PLANT BISCUIT FLYTRAP
FEVERCUP FOXGLOVE WATERCUP
NEPENTHES SKUNKWEED
PITCHFORK EVIL PICK PIKE PICKEL
SHEPPECK PITCHPIKE
(THATCHER'S —) GROOM
(PL.) HARD
PITCHHOLE CAHOT
PITCHMAN VENDER SALESMAN
PITCH PINE THYME
PITCH PIPE TUNER EPITONION
PITCHSTONE RETINITE
PITCHY BLACK
PITEOUS MEAN PALTRY PITIFUL
MERCIFUL MOURNFUL PIERCING
PITFALL PIT FALL TRAP SNARE
DANGER TRAPFALL
PITH JET PUT SAP CORE GIST MEAT
PULP PUTT SOLA HEART VIGOR
ENERGY KERNEL MARROW ESSENCE
EXTRACT MEDULLA NUCLEUS
PAPYRUS STRENGTH
(PREF.) MEDULLI METR(O) PULPE
PULPI PULPO
PITH HELMET TOPI TOPEE
PITHINESS BREVITY
PITHON (FATHER OF —) MICAH
PITH TREE AMBATCH
PITHY CRISP MEATY SAPPY TERSE
STRONG CONCISE LACONIC
MARROWY SUCCINCT
PITIABLE SAD POOR SEELY
WOFUL RUEFUL WOEFUL FORLORN
PITIFUL
PITIFUL MEAN MEEK RUTH SILLY
SORRY PALTRY RUEFUL TENDER
HANGDOG RUESOME RUTHFUL
MERCIFUL PATHETIC

PITILESS GRIM CRUEL STERN STONY
BRASSY SAVAGE RUTHLESS
UNPITIED MERCILESS
PITMAN GEORDIE
PITTANCE BIT ALMS DOLE GIFT MITE
SONG TRIFLE BEQUEST
PITTED FOVEATE OPPOSED
PUNCTATE ALVEOLATE
PITTER STONER
PITTHEUS (DAUGHTER OF —)
AETHRA
(FATHER OF —) PELOPS
(PUPIL OF —) THESEUS
PITURI BEDGERY PITCHERY
PIT VIPER- MOCCASIN
PITY RUE ACHE MEAN MOAN PETE
PITE RUTH MERCY PIETY REIVE
SCATH BEMOAN PATHOS MERCIFY
REMORSE WAESUCK CLEMENCY
SYMPATHY COMPASSION
PIVOT TOE AXIS CRUX SLEW SLUE
TURN HEART HINGE CENTER
SLOUGH WORDLE GUDGEON
TRAVERSE TRUNNION
PIVOTAL KEY POLAR CENTRAL
TROCHOID
(— POINT) KNUCKLE
PIVOTING DISHRAG
PIVOTMAN CENTER
PIVOT STAND PEDESTAL
PIXILATED DAFT DAFFY DOTTY
DRUNK FLAKY KOOKY PIXIE
BEMUSED PUCKISH TOUCHED
CONFUSED WHIMSICAL
PIXY ELF FAIRY PYGMY ROGUE
IMPISH RASCAL SPRITE PUCKISH
ROGUISH
PIZE OATH PISE CURSE
PLACABLE WEAK QUIET PACABLE
PEACEFUL YIELDING FORGIVING
PLACARD BILL POST TITLE POSTER
TICKET AFFICHE REDLINE
STOMACHER
PLACATE CALM GENTLE PACIFY
PLEASE SOOTHE APPEASE FORGIVE
PLACE L DO BIT FIX PUT SET AREA
HOLE LIEU PLAT PLOT POSE POST
RANK ROOM SEAT SITE SITU SPOT
STEL STEP STOW TEXT VICE YARK
BEING ESTER ESTRE HOUSE JOINT
LOCUS PLAZA POINT POSIT SCENE
SITUS STALL STATE STEAD STELL
STOUR WHERE BESTOW CHARGE
GROUND IMPOSE INVEST LAYOUT
LOCALE LOCATE OFFICE POSSIE
RECKON ROOMTH ALLODGE
ARRANGE DEPOSIT KITCHEN
STATION ABDITORY ALLOCATE
DIGGINGS EMPORIUM LOCATION
POSITION
(— ALONE) ISOLATE
(— ALTERNATELY) STAGGER.

(— APART) ENISLE
(— BEFORE) APPOSE PREFIX
(— BETWEEN) INTERPOSE
(— BY FORCE) PILI
(— CROSSWISE) THWART
(— DEDICATED TO GOD) TEMENOS
(— EXACTLY) PINPOINT
(— FISH IN SALTING BIN) KENCH
(— FOR CATTLE) CAMP
(— FOR DUMPING RUBBISH) SHOOT
(— FOR GAMES) GYMKHANA
(— FOR HAWKING) RIVER
(— FOR MILKING) LOAN
(— FOR MILKING COWS) LOAN
(— FOR MORTAR AND BRICK) FROG
(— FOR PHEASANTS) STEW
(— FOR PRAYERS) IDGAH
(— FOR RABBITS) WARREN
(— FOR RECEPTION) RECEIPT
(— FOR RUBBISH DEPOSITS)
LAYSTALL
(— FOR SEETHING) STEW
(— FOR SLEEPING) BED BUNK DOSS
FLOP LAIR LIBKIN
(— FOR STROLLING) PROMENADE
(— FOR TORTURE) CATASTA
(— FOR TRAINING HORSES) LONGE
(— FROM WHICH JURY IS TAKEN)
VENUE
(— IN) INNEST
(— IN COMPACT MASS) STOW
(— IN LINE) RANK
(— IN OFFICE) INVEST
(— IN ORDER) ARRAY ENRANK
(— IN WATERFALL) LEAP
(— MUCH FREQUENTED) RESORT
(— OF ABODE) LIBKEN
(— OF ACTION) GROUND
(— OF AMUSEMENT) GAFF
(— OF ASSEMBLY) AGORA CURIA
KGOTLA SYNAGOG
(— OF BEAUTY) TEMPE
(— OF BLISS) PARADISE
(— OF BLOODSHED) ACELDAMA
(— OF BURIAL) AHU KIL KILL LAIR
GRAVE LAYSTOW CATACOMB
CEMETERY GOLGOTHA LAYSTALL
(— OF BUSINESS) BANK AGENCY
KNACKERY
(— OF CARNAGE) SHAMBLES
(— OF CONCEALMENT) DEN BOMA
BLIND STALE HIDING HIDEOUT
HIDEAWAY
(— OF CONFINEMENT) BRIG CAGE
COOP LIMBO PRISON BULLPEN
(— OF CONFUSION) BABEL
TROYTOWN
(— OF CREMATION) GHAT GHAUT
(— OF CRUCIFIXION) GOLGOTHA
(— OF DEPARTED SPIRITS) SHEOL
(— OF DEPRAVITY) SODOM
(— OF DESTRUCTION) ABADDON

(— OF DETENTION) BAGNIO
(— OF DWELLING) WANE
(— OF EMPLOYMENT) SHOP
(— OF ENTERTAINMENT) INN JOINT
DANCERY HANGOUT HOSTELRY
(— OF EXERTION) ARENA
(— OF EXILE) PATMOS
(— OF FABRICATION) MINT
(— OF HAPPINESS) CAMELOT
(— OF HONOR) HEAD PRECEDENCE
(— OF IDYLLIC BEAUTY) XANADU
(— OF JUNCTION) SYMPHYSIS
(— OF MISERY) HELL
(— OF NETHER DARKNESS) EREBUS
(— OF NOISE) BABEL
(— OF PLEASURE) OASIS
(— OF PROTECTION) PORT SCUG
(— OF QUARANTINE) LAZARET
LAZARETTO
(— OF REFUGE) ARK BAST HOLD
ASYLUM ADULLAM HIDEOUT
(— OF RESIDENCE) SOIL DOMICILE
(— OF RESORT) PURLIEU
(— OF REST) OASIS REPOSE
(— OF RESTRAINT) LIMBO PINFOLD
(— OF REVERENCE) MECCA
(— OF SACRIFICE) ALTAR
(— OF SAFETY) GRITH HAVEN
WARRANT
(— OF SECLUSION) PRIVACY
(— OF SECURITY) GRITH ASYLUM
CORRAL HARBOR GARRISON
(— OF SHELTER) LEW HOLD JOUK
COVER
(— OF SUBMISSION) CANOSSA
(— OF THE DEAD) HELL
(— OF TORMENT) GOLGOTHA
(— OF TRADE) MART
(— OF WORSHIP) HEIAU BETHEL
CHAPEL CHURCH DESERT SHRINE
TEMPLE GURDWARA SYNAGOGUE
TABERNACLE
(— SIDE-BY-SIDE) JUXTAPOSE
(— SIDE BY SIDE) APPOSE
(— SPAWNING) REDD
(— STRUCK BY LIGHTNING)
BIDENTAL
(— UNDER RESTRICTIONS)
PROCLAIM
(— WHERE FOOD IS KEPT) LARDER
(— WHERE MEAT IS SMOKED) BUCAN
BUCCAN
(— WHERE OUTCASTS GATHER) HELL
(— WHERE ROADS CROSS) LEET
(— WHERE STREAM IS RAPID) SHARP
(— WHERE TROOPS HALT
OVERNIGHT) ETAPE
(— WHERE 4 OR MORE WAYS MEET)
CARFAX
(ABIDING —) GRANGE
(BARE —) GALL SCAR SCAUR
(BOGGY —) SLACK SLUMP

(BORING —) DULLSVILLE
(BREEDING —) NIDUS LOOMERY SEMINARY PELICANRY
(BUSHY —) SCROG
(CHAFED —) GALL
(CHIEF —) HEADSHIP
(CIRCULAR —) ORBELL
(CONCEALED —) HIDE
(CONFINED —) CRIB
(CONSECRATED —) HIERON
(COOKING —) GALLEY
(DARK —) GLOOM
(DEEP —) GULF DEPTH GULPH
(DELIGHTFUL —) ELYSIUM
(DILAPIDATED —) DUMP
(DISTASTEFUL —) FLEABAG
(DOME-SHAPED —) IGLOO
(DRINKING —) BOOZER MUMHOUSE
(DRY —) SEARING
(DWELLING —) BY BYE DEN SEE BAWN HAFT HIVE HOME ABODE BEING HOUSE HOWFF SOJOURN HABITACLE
(EATING —) CAFE GRUBBERY
(EMPTY —) BLANK SPACE
(ENCLOSED —) BIN HAY WORTH SEVERAL CLOISTER
(ESSENTIAL —) EYE
(EXOTIC —) XANADU
(FAMILIAR —) KITH
(FAULTY — IN THREAD) TRAP
(FILTHY —) STY
(FIRST —) BLUE LEAD STRAIGHT
(FLAT —) PLAT
(FORTIFIED —) LIS LISS CASTLE FASTNESS
(GARRISONED —) PRESIDIO
(GATHERING —) SHOP AGORA FOYER JOINT LESCHE
(GRASSY —) LAUND
(HALLOWED —) SHRINE
(HALTING —) MARAH
(HIDING —) MEW CACHE HIDEL HOARD STASH COVERT HIDDELS RETREAT STOWAWAY
(HIGH —) EMINENCE
(HIGHEST —) TOP
(HOLLOW —) GULF HOLE HOLL SCOOP CAVITY ALBERCA SINKHOLE
(IDYLLIC —) XANADU BRIGADOON
(IMAGINARY —) FANTASYLAND
(INHABITED —) ABADI
(LANDING —) GHAT HARD HITHE LEVEE SCALE BUNDER PALACE HELIPORT
(LEVEL —) PLANILLA
(LODGING —) CAMP LOGIS BIDING BILLET LIBKEN
(LONELY —) SOLITUDE
(LOOKOUT —) TOOT
(LURKING —) HOLD HOLE HOARD HULSTER
(LYING —) LAY LAIR

(MARKET —) AGORA TRONE MARKET RIALTO
(MARSHY —) SLEW SLOO SLUE SLUMP SLOUGH
(MEETING —) CLUB PNYX COURT FORUM GUILD TRYST TOLSEL TOLZEY AMBALAM KLAVERN TINWALD
(MIDDLE —) MEDIUM
(MUDDY —) SOIL
(NARROW —) NOOK STRAIT
(NESTING —) JUG NIDARY
(OPEN —) ENAJIM
(OTHERWORLDLY —) EMPYREAN
(PARTICULAR —) ROOM
(PASSING —) TURNOUT
(POLLING —) BOOTH
(PRECIPITOUS —) STEEP
(PRIVATE —) SECRET
(RAVELED —) FRAY
(REMOTE —) JERICHO
(RESTING —) LAY CAMP FORM GIST LAIR PARAO CRADLE
(ROCKY —) ROCHER
(SACRED —) HAREM HIERON CHAITYA SANCTUM
(SALTING —) SALADERO
(SECRET —) LAIR ADYTUM CORNER CRANNY
(SECURE —) REDOUBT
(SHADY —) GLOOM SWALE FRESCADE UMBRACLE
(SHELTERED —) NOOK SCUG SUCCOR
(SLEEPING —) ROOST
(SORE —) RAW
(SPAWNING —) REDD
(STARTING —) JUMPOFF
(STEEP —) PITCH
(STOPPING —) HALT MANZIL
(STORAGE —) DEPOT HOARD LODGE SPICERY STORAGE STOWAGE DOCKYARD
(STRONG —) STRENGTH
(SUNKEN —) SWALE
(SWAMPY —) FLUSH SOUGH
(THIRD —) SHOW
(TIGHT —) JAM JAMB
(UNEVEN —) RUB
(WALLOWING —) SOIL
(WATCH —) TOOTHILL
(WATERING —) ABREUVOIR
(WATERY —) SOIL FLUSH
(WEAK —) BLOT
(WET —) DANK
(WORN —) ABRASION
(WRETCHED —) DEN MISERY
(PL.) LOCI
(PREF.) CHOR(O) LOCO TOP(O)
(DRY —) XER(O)
(TAKES — OF) PRO VICE
(SUFF.) ESE THESIS THESTE THETIC TOPE TOPY

PLACEBO SOP TOADY VESPERS
PARASITE
PLACED FIXED BESTEAD
(— ON ITS SIDE) LAZY
PLACEHOLDER VARIABLE
PLACE-NAME TOPONYM
PLACENTA MAZA REPLUM
(PREF.) MAZ(O)
PLACENTAL MAZIC
PLACID CALM COOL EVEN MEEK
MILD SOFT DOWNY QUIET SUANT
SUENT GENTLE SEDATE SERENE
SMOOTH PACIFIC TRANQUIL
THROBLESS
PLACKET FENT SLIT SPARE WOMAN
CLOSING PETTICOAT
PLAGAL MODE
(PREF.) HYPO
PLAGIARISM CRIB PLAGIUM
PLAGIARIST TAKER COPYIST
PLAGIARIZE CRIB LIFT STEAL
PLAGUE DUN IMP POX VEX FRAB
FRET GNAW PEST TWIT RESET
CURSE DEATH DEUCE HARRY UHALM
TEASE TRAIK WEARY WORRY
WOUND BOTHER BURDEN HAMPER
HARASS INFEST PESTER PESTIS
SORROW WANION DESTROY
MURRAIN PERPLEX SCOURGE
TORMENT TORTURE TROUBLE
BEPESTER HANDICAP OUTBREAK
PESTILENCE
(PREF.) LEMO LOIMO PESTI PESTO
PLAGUY VERY PESKY VEXING
MURRAIN PESTFUL INFERNAL
PLAICE FLUKE FLATFISH FLOUNDER
PLAID CALM FAKE MAUD PLOD
TARTAN BRACKEN BRECHAN
(KIND OF —) GLEN
PLAIN DRY LOW BALD BARE CHOL
EASY EVEN FLAT OPEN PLAT RIFE
VEGA WALD WOLD BLAIR BLUNT
BROAD CAMPO CORAH FIELD FRANK
GREEN GROSS LAUND LEVEL LLANO
MOURN NAKED PAMPA PROSE
ROUND SEBKA SECCO SILLY SMALL
SOBER TALAO UNORN BEMOAN
DEWAIL CHASTE CUESTA GRAITH
HOMELY HONEST HUMBLE LENTEN
MACHAR MAIDAN PARAMO PUSZTA
RUSTIC SABANA SEVERE SIMPLE
SINGLE SMOOTH ARTLESS EVIDENT
GENUINE IDAVOLL LEGIBLE OBVIOUS
POPULAR SAVANNA TERRACE
UNARTED VANILLA APPARENT
CAMPAIGN DISTINCT EVERYDAY
EXPLICIT FAMILIAR HOMEMADE
HOMESPUN ITHAVOLL PALPABLE
PIEDMONT SEMPLICE STRAIGHT
(— AMONG TREES) LAUND
(— OF ARGENTINA) PAMPA
(— OF RUSSIA) STEPPE
(ALKALI —S) USAR

(ALLUVIAL —) APRON CARSE HAUGH
(ARCTIC —) TUNDRA
(DESOLATE —) CHOL
(HEATHY —) LANDE
(LOW-LYING —) MACHAR MACHAIR
(LUNAR —) MARE
(MARSHY —) BLAIR
(NOT —) MEALYMOUTHED
(SALINE —) SEBKA SEBKHA
(SALT —) SALADA
(SLOPING —) HOPE CUESTA
CONOPLAIN
(SMALL GRASSY —) CAMAS CAMASS
QUAMASH
(TREELESS —) BLED TUNDRA
SAVANNA SAVANNAH
(UNOCCUPIED —) DESERT
(PL.) VIZCACHA
(PREF.) LITI PEDI(O) PLAN(I)
PLAIN CHANT CF
PLAINCLOTHESMAN SPLIT
PLAINLY FAIR BARELY FAIRLY FLATLY
SIMPLY BROADLY FRANKLY DIRECTLY
PLAINNESS PROSE INNOCENCE
PLAINSMAN LLANERO
PLAINSONG GROUND
PLAINT WAIL PLANT LAMENT
COMPLAINT
PLAINTEXT CLEAR
PLAINTIFF SUER USEE ACTOR
ORATOR PURSUER QUERENT
PLAINTIVE SAD CROSS PINING
DOLENTE ELEGIAC FRETFUL
MOANFUL PEEVISH PETTISH
DOLOROSO MANGENDO PETULANT
WAILSOME SORROWFUL
PLAIN-VANILLA BASIC
PLAIT CUE PLY KNIT PAIR PLAT RUFF
TURN WALE WAND BRAID BREAD
CRIMP FETCH FITCH PEDAL PINCH
QUEUE QUILL QUIRK TRACE TRESS
WEAVE BORDER DOUBLE GATHER
GOFFER PLEACH PLIGHT RUMPLE
TUSCAN WIMPLE WRITHE CRIMPLE
FROUNCE PIGTAIL SCALLOM
COMPLECT
(— FOR HAT) DUNSTABLE
(— OF STRAW) MILAN TRACE
(SERIES OF —S) KILTING
PLAITED PLISSE DEVIOUS PLICATE
PLAITING PLISSE LEGHORN NATTIER
PLAN AIM ART LAY WAY CARD CAST
COUP DART FOOT GAME HANG IDEA
MIND MOOD PLAT PLOT REDE WENT
ALLOW BRIEF CHART DARTY DRAFT
DRIFT ETTLE FRAME HOBBY MODEL
REACH SHAPE TRACE ADVICE
AGENDA BEREDE BUDGET CIPHER
DECOCT DESIGN DEVISE ENGINE
FIGURE INTEND LAYOUT METHOD
MODULE ORDAIN PROJET SCHEMA
SCHEME SURVEY THEORY ARRANGE
CONCERT CONCOCT COUNSEL

DRAWING FORELAY NOSTRUM
OUTLINE PATTERN PROGRAM
PROJECT PURPOSE THOUGHT
COGITATE CONSPIRE CONTRIVE
ENGINEER FORECAST FOREGAME
LANDSKIP MEDITATE PLATFORM
PRACTICE SCHEDULE SKELETON
STRATEGY BLUEPRINT CALCULATE
(— AHEAD) FORECAST
(— OF FUTURE PROCEDURE)
PROGRAM
(— ON A FLOOR) EPURE
(— TOGETHER) CONCERT
(CUNNING —) WHEEZE
(GROUND —) TRACE GRUNDRISS
(INSURANCE —) TONTINE
(KIND OF —) KEOGH
(KIND OF RETIREMENT —) KEOGH
(5-YEAR —) PIATILETKA
PLANARIAN PLATODE TRICLAD
FLATWORM PLATYHELMINTH
PLANE BEAD DADO FACE FLAT HOLL
MILL AXIAL CHUTE CROZE FACET
GLIDE HOULE HOWEL LEVEL MESON
SHOOT STICK TABLE WHISK AEQUOR
AIRBUS BEADER HOLLOW REEDER
ROUTER SMOKER SNIBEL COURIER
INSHAVE JOINTER NONSKED
SURFACE WITCHET BULLNOSE
DECLINER LEEBOARD MERIDIAN
RECLINER SYCAMORE TRAVERSE
(— CURVE) ROSE
(— HANDLE) TOAT TOTE
(— OF CLEAVAGE) BACK
(— OF EARTH'S ORBIT) ECLIPTIC
(— OF ROCK) BED
(—S OF GUNNERY FIRE) SHEAF
(ENEMY —) BANDIT
(INCLINED —) RAMP SLIP
(MOLDING —) HOLL HOULE HOLLOW
(PERSPECTIVE —) TABLE
(RABBET —) PLOW RABAT PLOUGH
REBATE FILLETER
(SLOPING —) CUESTA
PLANER JOINTER SURFACER
PLANER TREE HORNBEAM
SYCAMORE
PLANET ORB SUN BODY IRIS JOVE
MARS MOON STAR EARTH GLOBE
HYLEG PLUTO SHREW VENUS
WORLD SATURN SPHERE URANUS
VULCAN ALMUTEN ANARETA
BENEFIC FORTUNE JUPITER
MERCURY NEPTUNE PRIMARY
CHASUBLE LUMINARY RECEPTOR
TERRELLA WANDERER
(— IN A NATIVITY) ALMUTEN
(BENEVOLENT —) FORTUNE
(CONTROLLING —) LORD
(FICTIONAL —) ORK KRYPTON
(HYPOTHETICAL —) VULCAN
(INNER —) MARS EARTH VENUS
MERCURY

(MALEFICENT —) SHREW
(MINOR —) VESTA PALLAS PSYCHE
(RULING —) DOMINATOR
(SMALL —) IRIS ASTEROID TERRELLA
PLANETARIUM ORRERY
PLANETOID UNDINE ASTEROID
PLANE TREE CHINAR PLATAN
COTONIER PLANTAIN SYCAMORE
PLANET-STRICKEN SIDERATED
PLANISPHERE ASTROLABE
METEORSCOPE
PLANK CLAM HOOD PATA PLAT RAIL
SOLE WAIR BOARD CLAMP PATTA
SHIDE SWALE THEAL DAGGER
FLITCH PLANCH ROOFER STRAKE
CLAPPER CROSSER DEPOSIT
MADRIER RIBBAND STEALER
FOREPOLE GARBOARD STRINGER
(— AS PROTECTION) SHOLE
(— OVER BROOK) CLAM
(—S IN BRIDGE) CHESS
(—S LESS THAN 6 FT.) DEAL
(— 6 FT. X 1 FT.) WARE
(CURVED —) SNYING
(ROUGHHEWN —) SLAB
PLANK DRAG RUBBER
PLANK END STUB
PLANKING GORE RACK HATCH
SWALE STRAKE CEILING LAGGING
BERTHING BRATTICE GARBOARD
WATERWAY
PLANKSHEER WATERWAY
PLANKTON KRILL DIATOM SESTON
(GROWTH OF —) BLOOM
PLANNED PREPENSE
(AS —) ONTRACK
PLANNING
(KIND OF —) ESTATE
(TECHNIQUE FOR —) PERT
PLANOMILLER SLABBER
PLANT AJI BED SET SOW ACHE ALGA
ARUM BURY CROP FAST HERB HIDE
MORE RAPE SALT SEED SEGO SLIP
TREE WORT ABACA AGAVE AJWAN
ARGEL AVENS CAMAS CAROA CHIVE
CLOTE CLOVE CUMIN EARLY FANCY
GRAFT HEATH INTER INULA JALAP
KEIKI ORACH PITCH PUTIN SEDUM
SHRUB YERBA ACACIA AJOWAN
AKELEY ALASAS ANNUAL BEDDER
CACOON CALALU CARROT CLOVER
COKERY COSMEA COTTON CUMMIN
DERRIS DIBBLE ESCAPE FICOID
FORCER GALAXY GROWTH KARREE
LENTIL LIGGER MALLOW MANUKA
MEDICK MESCAL ORPINE PEPINO
SESAME SETTLE SPRING ULLUCU
YARROW ABANDON ALKANET
ALYSSUM BREWERY BUGLOSS
CARAWAY CARDOON CHERVIL
CONCEAL CUTTING DAGGERS
ENCELIA GENTIAN GINSENG
HAEMONY IMPLANT JIKUNGU

LETTUCE PALMIET PICKERY
RAMBONG SAWMILL ABUTILON
AGERATUM AGRIMONY ANGLEPOD
BIENNIAL BLUEBELL CAMOMILE
CONSOUND DRAWLING DYEHOUSE
EMERGENT ENGINERY FOXGLOVE
FUMEROOT GASWORKS GERANIUM
GROMWELL HAWKWEED HONEWORT
JAPONICA KNAPWEED LARKSPUR
CHAMOMILE SPIKENARD
PHILODENDRON
(— BY SPADING) SPIT
(— DEEPLY) HEEL
(— DISEASE) NECROSIS
(— FIRMLY) BRACE
(— GROWING IN WATER) BILDERS
HYDROPHYTE
(— GROWTH MEDIUM) PERLITE
(— IN ROWS) DRILL
(— LIFE) BIOS BIOTA
(— NOT ATTACKED) NONHOST
(— NUTRIENTS) SIDEDRESS
(— OF MEADOWS) POOPHYTE
(— OF THE DEAD) ASPHODEL
(OUTGROWTH) OVULE
(— ROOTED IN GROUND) LIANA
LIANE
(— SUPPORTING PARASITES)
SUSCEPT
(— TEMPORARILY) SHEUCH
(— TREE) MOTCH
(— WITH A SPADE) SPIT
(— WITH NO DISTINCT MEMBERS)
THALLUS
(— WITH THREE PISTILS) TRIGYN
(— WITH THREE STAMENS)
TRIANDER
(— 2ND CROP) ETCH
(AIR —) FLOPPERS
(ANCIENT —) CYCAD
(AQUATIC —) ALISMA NUPHAR
SUGAMO TAWKEE AMBULIA
AWLWORT FROGBIT DUCKWEED
PONDWEED PICKERELWEED
(AROMATIC —) MINT NARD BASIL
CUMIN TANSY THYME AMOMUM
CUMMIN CARAWAY DITTANY
ALBAHACA CALAMINT LAVENDER
SPIKENARD
(AUSTRALIAN —) LILAC STYLO
LIGNUM LANCEPOD
(BULBOUS —) GALTONIA
(CENTURY —) PITA
(CLIMBING —) VETCH LAWYER
RUNNER ULLUCE ULLUCU CORALITA
(COMPOSITE —) SUCCORY
HAWKWEED SNEEZEWEED
(CONSECRATED —) HAOMA
(CREATED —) BARAMIN
(CREEPING —) IPECAC KAREAO
KAREAU PENNYWORT
(CROSSBRED —) HYBRID
(CRUSHING —) BREAKER

(DWARF —) CUMIN STUNT
(DYE —) WAD ANIL WOAD WOLD
WOALD MADDER
(E. INDIAN —) JATI
(ETIOLATED —) ALBINO
(FIBER —) ALOE FLAX HEMP PITA
CAJUN RAMIE SISAL
(FLOWERING —) HOP ROSE DAISY
HOLLY POPPY ORCHID VIOLET
HAWTHORN LARKSPUR POLYGALA
PRIMROSE SNOWDROP
(FORAGE —) RAPE ALFALFA DAINCHA
(FOSSIL —) CALAMITE
(GERMINATING —) SPIRE
(GRAIN —) TEFF
(HEDGE —) ESPINO
(HEMP —) FIMBLE
(IMMATURE —) KEIKI
(LEAFLESS —) ULEX DODDER
RESTIAD TRIURID
(MALE —) MAS MACRANDER
(MARSH —) CALL FERN RUSH CALLA
JUNCUS BULRUSH CATTAIL
BUCKBEAN MARSHMALLOW
(MEDICINAL —) ALOE HERB ERICA
ARNICA CATNEP CATNIP IPECAC
SIMPLE ACONITE BONESET GENTIAN
LOBELIA CAMOMILE
(MEDICINIAL —) SENNA
(NON-FLOWERING —) FERN
(NURSERY —) SEEDLING
(PEPPER —) ARA
(PHILIPPINE —) ABACA
(PISTILLATE —) FEMALE
(POISONOUS —) COWBANE DEATHIN
HENBANE MANDRAKE SAMNITIS
NIGHTSHADE
(POTTED —) BONSAI LANTANA
(POWER —) HYDRO
(PRICKLY —) BRIAR BRIER CACTUS
CARDON NETTLE TEASEL TEAZEL
PRICKFOOT
(PUNGENT —) PEPPER
(RAPIDLY-GROWING —) FILLER
(REEDY —) SPRIT
(RENDERING —) KNACKERY
(ROSACEOUS —) AVENS
(SENSITIVE —) MIMOSA
(SIBERIAN —) BADAN
(SPINOUS —) KANTIARA
(STAMINATE —) HUSBAND
(SUBMERGED —) ENALID
(SUCCULENT —) ALOE HERB
GASTERIA HAWORTHIA HOUSELEEK
(SWORD-LEAVED —) LEVERS
(THALLOPHYTIC —) LICHEN
(TRAILING —) ARBUTUS
(TUFTED —) DRYAS
(TWINING —) SMILAX WINDER
CLIMBER BINDWEED SCAMMONY
(UNIDENTIFIED —) HORDOCK
(WATER —) LIMU LOTUS AQUATILE
STARFRUIT

(WEEDY —) DOCK KNAWEL
(YOUNG —) SET SPRINGER
(PL.) FLORA
(PREF.) BOTAN(O) PHYT(I)(O)
(SUFF.) AD CHORE COCCUS OECIA
PHYTA PHYTE(S) PHYTIA PHYTIC
PHYTUM
PLANTAGENET ANGEVIN
PLANTAIN COCK PALA ABACA
ALISMA FINGER PISANG WABRON
BENTING NETLEAF RIBWORT SITFAST
BALISIER BUCKHORN FIREWEED
FLEAWORT ISPAGHUL PLANTANO
RATSBANE RIBGRASS ROADWEED
WAYBREAD
PLANTAIN EATER TOURACO
SPLITBEAK
PLANTAIN LILY HOSTA FUNKIA
PLANTATION PEN HOLT WALK
FINCA GROVE BOSKET BOWERY
COLONY ESTATE SHAMBA SPRING
YERBAL CAFETAL FAZENDA NOPALRY
PINETUM THICKET ARBUSTUM
HACIENDA TRAPICHE VINEYARD
(HEMP —) LATE
(WILLOW —) SALICETUM
PLANTED LISTED
PLANTER SNAG COLON SOWER
FARMER SETTLER PLANTATOR
PLANTING GROVE SATION
PLANTING STICK DIBBLE
PLANT LOUSE APHID PSYLLID
PUCERON HOMOPTER
PLANTS
(SUFF.) ACEAE ALES INEAE
PLAQUE CHIP PINAX PLATE PLATEAU
SARCOID NAMEPLATE STOMACHER
PLASH LIP DASH BLASH PLOSH
PLOUT PLEACH PUDDLE SPLASH
SPATTER SPECKLE
PLASMA LATEX PLASM
PLASTER CAST CEIL DAUB HARL
LEEP LOCK TEER CLEAM GATCH
PARGE SLICK SMALM STAFF TOPIC
TREAT CHARGE CHUNAM CLATCH
GAGING MORTAR PARGET SPARGE
STOOTH STUCCO BLISTER
MALAGMA DIACULUM DIAPALMA
SINAPISM VESICANT CATAPLASM
(— BETWEEN LATHS) CAT
(— OF PARIS) GESSO GYPSUM
(— WITH COW DUNG) LEEP
(COARSE —) GROUT
(COVER WITH —) CEIL
(MEDICAL —) SALVE TOPIC TREAT
CHARGE SPARADRAP
(MUSTARD —) SINAPISM
(2 COATS OF —) RENDERSET
PLASTERBOARD GYPSUM
DRYWALL
PLASTERED DRUNK SOUSED
SWACKED

PLASTERER DAUBER DAUBSTER
PARGETER SPREADER
PLASTERING KEY SETWORK
ROUGHCAST
PLASTIC ABS FOAM LOID RICH SIRUP
LABILE PLIANT ACETATE CATALIN
CRYSTAL DUCTILE FICTILE ORGANIC
PERSPEX CREATIVE FLEXIBLE
LAMINATE MELAMINE PHENOLIC
TECTONIC UNCTUOUS FORMATIVE
(—S BASE) RESIN
(FLEXIBLE —) SARAN
PLASTICIZER CAMPHOR
PLASTRON DICKEY CALIPEE
PLAT BED FLAT FOOD PLAN PLOT
SLAP BRAID LEVEL PLACE PLAIN
PLAIT BUFFET WATTLE ARRANGE
FLATTEN PLATEAU QUADRAT
PLATANIST SUSU
PLATANUS PLANE COTONIER
SYCAMORE
PLATBAND IMPOST LINTEL ERISTYLE
PLATE BAT CAP CUT DIP DOD EAR FIN
GIB WEB ANAL BACK BASE BRIN
CASE CAST CURB DIAL DISK DROP
FISH GILL GONG GULA HOME HOOF
LAME LEAF MOLD NAIL ORAL RETE
ROSE SHOE SHUT SLAB SOLE STUD
TACE TRAY AMPYX ANODE BASAL
BELLY BLADE CHAIR CLAMP CLEAT
CLOUT FACIA FENCE FLOOR FLUKE
FORCE GLAND GUARD GULAR
LAMEL PATEN PYGAL SCALE SCUTE
SHEET SHOLE SLICE STAMP STAVE
STRAP TABLE TASSE TERNE TRAMP
UNCUS WATER ADORAL BAFFLE
BRIDGE BUCKLE CASTER CIRCLE
CLICHE COLLAR COPPER COSTAL
CRUSTA DAMPER DASHER EPIGNE
FASCIA FILLER FOLIUM FRIZEL
GENIAL GNOMON GORGET GUSSET
LABIAL LAMINA LOREAL MASCLE
MATRIX MENTAL MENTUM MOTHER
PALLET PATTEN PLATEN RADIAL
SCREEN SCUTUM SEPTUM SERVER
SHEATH SHROUD SPLINT STAPLE
TARSUS TEGMEN TURTLE TYMPAN
VESSEL BESAGNE BOLSTER
BRACKET BRACTEA BUCCULA
BUCKLER CHARGER CLYPEUS
COASTER CORNULE CORONET
CRYSTAL DOUBLER ETCHING FRIZZLE
FRONTAL GRAVURE HUMERAL
INKBLOT MORDANT MYOTOME
NEPTUNE PETALON PRIMARY
ROSTRAL ROUNDEL SPANGLE
STEALER STEELER TERGITE TESSERA
VENTRAL ASSIETTE BEDPLATE
BIQUARTZ BRACHIAL CELLOCUT
DIASCOPE DRAWBACK ELECTRUM
EPIGYNUM EPIPROCT EPISTOME
FIREBACK FLOUNDER SKEWBACK

STAPLING STRINGER SUBPLATE
SURPRINT
(— COVERING KEYHOLE) DROP
(— COVERING MIDDLE EAR) TEGMEN
(— IN AIRPLANE WING) SPOILER
(— IN BATTERY) GRID
(— IN ORGAN PIPE) LANGUET
(— IN STEAM BOILER) SPUT DASHER
(— OF BALEEN) BLADE
(— OF BLAST FURNACE) TYMP
(— OF CTENOPHORE) COMB
(— OF GELATIN) BAT
(— OF GLASS) SLIDE
(— OF JAW) AURICLE
(— OF PRECIOUS METAL) BRACTEA
(— OF SOAP FRAME) SESS
(— OF SUNDIAL) GNOMON
(— ON FIREPLACE) BLOWER
(— ON LANCE SHAFT) VAMPLATE
(— ON PLOW) MOLDBOARD
(— ON SADDLE) SIDEBAR
(— ON SATCHEL STRAP) OLIVE
(— ON SHOE SOLE) SEG
(— ON THROAT OF FISH) GULAR
(— ON WATERWHEEL) SHROUD
(—S OF CARDING MACHINE) ARCH
(—S OF GUN CARRIAGE) FLASK
(— TO SUPPORT BEAM) TASSEL
TORSEL
(ARMOR —) SPLINT AILETTE
PALLETTE
(COLLECTION —) BROD
(COMMUNION —) PATEN
(DEEP —) MAZARINE
(DERMAL —) SCUTE
(DORSAL —) ELYTRUM ALINOTUM
(EARTHEN —) MUFFIN
(FASHION —) SWELL
(FIREPLACE —) IRONBACK
(FLAT —) APRON
(GOLD — ON FOREHEAD) PATA PATTA
(GROOVED TRAM —) GULLY GULLEY
(GUARD —) SHELL
(HINGED —) SHUT
(HOME —) DISH
(HOT —) GRILL GRILLE
(INSCRIBED —) TABLET
(IRON —) CLOUT STAVE LATTEN
MARVER LAPSTONE SKEWBACK
MOLDBOARD TURNPLATE
TURNSHEET
(LARGE —) DOUBLER
(LOCK —) SELVEDGE
(MELTED —) SOUP
(METAL —) ROVE CHROME
(NAME —) FACIA
(PERFORATED —) DOD GRID WORTLE
PINNULE
(PITCHER'S —) SLAB MOUND
(RIMLESS —) COUPE
(SIEVE —) LATTICE
(SIFTING —) TROMMEL

(SKELETAL —) SCLERITE
(THIN —) LAME LAMP LAMINA
LAMELLA
(THIN TIN —) TAIN LATTEN TAGGERS
(WALL —) PAN RASEN TORSEL
(WOODEN —) TRENCHER
(PREF.) ELASM(O) LAMELLI LAMIN(I)
PLAC(O)
(SUFF.) (COVERING —) STEGE
STEGITE
PLATEAU PI AT PUNA FJELD KAROO
KARST TABLE CAUSSE HAMADA
MESETA NIVEAU PARAMO SABANA
UPLAND ANASAZI PLATFORM
(PL.) BARRENS
PLATEHOLDER CASSETTE
PLATE-LIKE PLACOID
PLATEN ROLL
PLATER VATMAN CLAIMER
COLLARMAN
PLATFORM TOP BANK BEMA DAIS
DECK DRIP DROP DUCK FLAT GHAT
HEFL KITE PACE PLAT STEP WING
ALTAR APRON BENCH BLIND BLOCK
CHAIN DUKAN FLAKE FLOAT HEIAU
SOLEA STAGE STAND STOEP STOOL
STOOP STULL STUMP TOLDO
ARBOUR AZOTEA BRIDGE DESIGN
GANTRY HURDLE ISLAND MACHAN
PAEPAE PALLET PERRON PILLAR
PODIUM PULPIT RUNWAY SETTLE
SLEDGE ALMEMAR BALCONY
BATTERY CATWALK ESTRADE
FORETOP GALLERY LANDING
LOGEION PADDOCK PATTERN
ROLLWAY ROSTRUM SKIDWAY
SOAPBOX TRIBUNE BARBETTE
FOOTPACE HUSTINGS SCAFFOLD
STALLAGE MORTARBOARD
(— FOR ACTORS) LOGEION
THEOLOGIUM
(— FOR ALTAR) PREDELLA
(— FOR DRYING FISH) FLAKE
(— FOR PUBLIC SPEAKING) BEMA
PODIUM TRIBUNE
(— FOR STORING FOOD) WHATA
(— IN CHURCH) SOLEA
(— IN SYNAGOGUE) ALMEMAR
(— IN TEMPLE) DUKAN
(— IN TREE) MACHAN
(— OF GALLOWS) DROP
(— ON RUNNERS) SLEDGE
(— ON STEAMER) SPONSON
(— ON TOP OF HOUSE) AZOTEA
(— ON WHEELS) SKID DOLLY
FLOAT
(— TO SUPPORT MINERS) STULL
(BOARDING —) RAMBADE
(GUN —) BARBET SPONSON
BARBETTE
(LEADSMAN'S —) CHAIN
(MINE —) STULL SOLLAR SOLLER

(MOHAMMEDAN STONE —)
MASTABA
(MOUNTED —) SKID
(NAUTICAL —) FORETOP MAINTOP
ROUNDTOP
(ORE —) BUDDLE
(RAILROAD —) DOCK DOCKEN
TRAINWAY
(RAISED —) DAIS PYAL STAND STOEP
STOOL STOOP EXEDRA LISSOM
PANTALAN
(ROCK —) STANCE
(SLEEPING —) KANG
(STAIRCASE —) HALFPACE HATHPACE
(WOOD —) PLANCHER
PLATING ARMOR SKIRT
PLATINUM COSTLY PLATINA
PLATITUDE CLICHE TRUISM
BROMIDE DULLNESS STALENESS
TRITENESS
PLATONIST IDEIST
PLATOON SQUAD VOLLEY PELOTON
PLOTTON
PLATTER DISH DISK LANX ASHET
GRAIL PLATE RECORD CHARGER
TRENCHER
PLATY MOON MOONFISH
PLATYPUS DUCKBILL DUCKMOLE
MALLANGONG
PLAUDIT APPLAUD APPROVAL
ENCOMIUM
(PL.) PRAISE APPLAUSE
PLAUSIBILITY COLOR
PLAUSIBLE FAIR OILY SNOD SLEEK
GLOSSY SMOOTH AFFABLE POPULAR
CREDIBLE PROBABLE PROVABLE
SPECIOUS SUITABLE OSTENSIBLE
PLAY FUN JEU JIG RUN RUX TOY
AUTO BEAR COME DAFF DEAL DICE
DRAW FAIR GAME JEST LAKE MOVE
MUCK PLEE PUNT ROMP SPIN TUNE
WAKE CARRY CHARM DALLY DRAMA
ENACT FLIRT FROST HORSE SHOOT
SOTIE SOUND SPIEL SPORT STUCK
WREAK YEDDE ACTION COMEDY
COQUET DANDLE DIVIDE FILLER
FROLIC GAMBLE GAMBOL GAMING
GHOSTS MUSERY NUMBER PIDDLE
ROLLIX TRIFLE CONSORT CUTBACK
DISPORT EXECUTE EXPLOIT
GUIGNOL HISTORY HOLIDAY
MIRACLE PAGEANT PASSION
PERFORM PRELUDE STAGERY
VENTURE BURLETTA MORALITY
SKITTLES MELODRAMA
(— ABOUT) SPANIEL
(— A DOMINO) SET POSE
(— AGAINST) BUCK
(— AN INSTRUMENT) BOW BLOW
SWAY FINGER TWEEDLE
(— A PART) DO ACT ENTER GAMMON
GUIZARD
(— A PIPE) CHARM

(— AT COURTSHIP) FLIRT
(— BAGPIPE) SKIRL DOODLE DOUDLE
(— BY STROKES) STRIKE
(— FANFARE) FLOURISH
(— FAST AND LOOSE) PALTER
(— FIRST CARD) LEAD
(— FLORIDLY) DIVIDE
(— FOR TIME) STALL
(— GOLF BALL) DRIVE
(— IMPOSTER) MUMP
(— IN MUD) MUDLARK
(— IN POOL) BURST
(— IN STREAKS) FORK
(— IN TRIGGER) CREEP
(— JAZZ) BLOW
(— LEGATO) SUSTAIN
(— LOCATION) SET
(— LOOSELY) WAVE
(— LOUT) SWAB SLUBBER
(— MEAN TRICKS) SHAB
(— NERVOUSLY) FIDGET
(— OF COLORS) IRIS
(— OF FOAM) HOOD
(— OF LIGHT) GLORY
(— ON WORDS) PUN CLENCH CLINCH
PARAGRAM CALEMBOUR
PARONOMASIA
(— THE BUFFOON) DROLL
(— THE BULLY) BLUSTER
(— THE FOOL) HOIT
(— THE HYPOCRITE) FACE
(— THE TOADY) SUPE
(— TRICKS) COD JAPE JINK
(— TRUANT) KIP WAG JOUK MICHE
MOOCH MOUCH PLUNK TRONE
MOOTCH
(— UNSKILLFULLY) STRUM FOOZLE
(— WITH) DANDLE
(AMOROUS —) GAME
(BOISTEROUS —) ROMP
(BRIDGE —) COUP ECHO SIGNAL
SQUEEZE
(END —) SHAKE
(FARCICAL —) SOTIE
(FOOTBALL —) DOWN KEEP DELAY
SWING KEEPER SAFETY AUDIBLE
COUNTER CUTBACK ROLLOUT
SPINNER
(IN —) ALIVE
(JAPANESE —) NOH
(MASKED —) GUISE
(MIRACLE —) AUTO GUARY MIRACLE
(ONE-PERSON —) MONODRAMA
(RAPID CHESS —) SKITTLES
(SHORT —) ONELINER
(USED IN —) LUSORY
(PL.) THEATER VANGELI
PLAYA BEACH SEBKA SALINA
SEBKHA
PLAYBOY RAKE ROMEO LOTHARIO
LIBERTINE
**PLAYBOY OF THE WESTERN
WORLD (AUTHOR OF —)** SYNGE

(CHARACTER IN —) QUIN KEOGH
MAHON SHAWN PEGEEN CHRISTY
FLAHERTY MARGARET
CHRISTOPHER
PLAY-BY-PLAY DETAILED
PLAYER IT CAP END BACK DUCK SIDE
ACTOR BLACK COLOR GUARD
BANKER BUSKER FEEDER STAGER
STROLL TENTER ALTOIST FIELDER
FORWARD GAMBLER STRIKER
TRIFLER TURQUET BUDGETER
GAMESTER HORNSMAN STROLLER
(— IN CHESS) BLACK WHITE
(— IN CHOUETTE) CAPTAIN
(— OF JAZZ) CAT
(— WHO CUTS CARDS) PONE
(— WHO IS IT) HE
(— WHO SCORES ZERO) DUCK
(— WITH LOWEST SCORE) BOOBY
(BACKGAMMON —) TABLER
(BASEBALL —) SHORT SACKER
CATCHER FIELDER LEADOFF PITCHER
BACKSTOP
(BASKETBALL —) PIVOT CAGEMAN
HOOPMAN HOOPSTER PIVOTMAN
(BOWLING —) LEAD
(CARD —) EAST HAND PONE WEST
BLIND DUMMY NORTH OMBRE
SOUTH JUNIOR SENIOR BRAGGER
DECLARER
(CRICKET —) LEG BOWLER INNING
(CROQUET —) MALLET
(DICE —) SHOOTER
(FLUTE —) AULETE
(FOOTBALL —) END BACK GUARD
SLANT BUCKER CENTER TACKLE
BLOCKER FLANKER GRIDDER
SNAPPER FULLBACK HALFBACK
SCATBACK SLOTBACK
(INEPT CHESS —) PATZER
(KEY —) PIVOT
(LACROSSE —) HOME COVER POINT
ATTACK STICKMAN
(LEAPFROG —) BACK
(POKER —) AGE
(RUGBY —) SCRUM HOOKER
(SOCCER —) CAP INNER BOOTER
(STUPID —) HAM
(TENNIS —) SMASHER
(TWO OR MORE —S) PLATOON
(UNSKILLFUL —) DUB
(VOLLEYBALL —) SPIKER
(WEAK —) RABBIT
(PL.) CAST
PLAYFUL SLY ELFIN LUDIC MERRY
FRISKY GAMBOL JOCOSE LUSORY
TOYISH WANTON COLTISH GIOCOSO
JIGGISH JOCULAR TOYSOME
GAMESOME HUMOROUS
LARKSOME SPORTFUL SPORTIVE
KITTENISH
(EXTRAVAGANTLY —) MAD
(IRRESPONSIBLY —) MISCHIEVOUS

PLAYFULLY SCHERZANDO
PLAYFULNESS FUN BANTER
GAMMICK GAMMOCK
PLAYGROUND OVAL CLOSE TOTLOT
PLAYSTOW PLAYSTEAD
PLAYHOUSE HOUSE MOVIE CINEMA
THEATER
PLAYING FROLIC LAKING
(— CARD) ACE JACK KING TREY
DEUCE QUEEN TAROT
(— CARDS) DECK
(— LIGHTLY) LAMBENT
PLAYING FIELD PADANG
PLAYLET SKIT
PLAYTHING DIE TOY HOOP KNACK
PLAIK SPORT BAUBLE LAKING
SUCKER TRIFLE PLAYOCK
PLAYWRIGHT AUTHOR DRAMATIST
PLAYMAKER
AMERICAN ADE LEA BABE BAUM
DALY DELL EYEN HART HOYT INGE
KERR LOOS RABE RICE ROOT
SHAW UHRY AKINS ALBEE BARRY
COHAN DAVIS DOBIE FITCH FRIEL
GREEN HECHT HWANG LEWIS
LOGAN LORTZ MAMET ODETS
RIGGS RIVES SIMON SMITH STEIN
WILDE YOUNG ABBOTT BARAKA
BARKER BARRAS BEAHAN BOLTON
BOOTHE BROOKS COMDEN CROUSE
FLAVIN FRINGS GOLDEN HEGGEN
HOWARD HUGHES KRASNA
LAWSON LERNER LUDLAM MEGRUE
MILLER NUGENT OBOLER ONEILL
THOMAS TOTTEN WALKER WALTER
WEXLEY WILDER ZINDEL ANDREWS
BEHRMAN BELASCO BISSELL
BLOSSOM BURROWS CARROLL
COLLIER HELLMAN HOPWOOD
HURLBUT KAUFMAN LEBLANC
LINDSAY MOELLER NICHOLS
PEABODY RICHMAN RYSKIND
SAROYAN SHELDON SHEPARD
SHIPMAN SHULMAN SPEWACK
TEBELAK VEILLER ANDERSON
BOGOSIAN CARLETON CHODOROV
COLLISON CONNELLY KINGSLEY
KIRKLAND MITCHELL SCHISGAL
SCHWARTZ SHERWOOD TOTHEROH
WILLIAMS BALDERSON CHAYEFSKY
ISHERWOOD MACARTHUR
MIDDLETON MOREHOUSE
NICHOLSON STALLINGS
BOUCICAULT TARKINGTON
WEITZENKORN
AUSTRALIAN CHAMBERS
AUSTRIAN BLEI COLLIN MULLER
NISSEL WERFEL NEUMANN ZEDLITZ
CASTELLI WILDGANS SCHONTHAN
SCHNITZLER GRILLPARZER
HOFMANNSTHAL
BELGIAN CLAUS GHELDERODE
MAETERLINCK

CANADIAN BOLT COOK ROSE SLADE
COULTER DOHERTY HERBERT
TREMBLAY
CZECH HAVEL KLIMA JERABEK
JIRASEK
DANISH EWALD TANDRUP
BERGSTROM BUCHHOLTZ
OEHLENSCHLAGER
DUTCH FEITH HOOFT COSTER
EMANTS VONDEL BREDERO
ENGLISH BAX FRY GAY KYD LEE
BART BEHN BELL FORD HILL LEVY
LONG NASH ROWE SHAW SIMS TATE
TUKE BARRY BROME BYRON DUKES
FIELD FOOTE HOOLE JONES KEEFE
LEMON LEWIS LILLO LODGE MILNE
MOORE MUNRO ORCZY ORTON
PEELE SMITH STORY UDALL WOODS
ALBERY BOADEN BROPHY CANNAN
CASTLE CIBBER COWARD COWLEY
CROWNE DAVIES DEKKER DENNIS
DIBDIN DRYDEN DURFEY GRAHAM
GREENE GRILLO HOWARD JONSON
KENNEY LYTTON MANLEY MORTON
MUNDAY NABBES PINERO PINTER
PORTER PUDNEY ROWLEY SETTLE
STEELE STOREY TAYLOR TREECE
WESKER WILSON ABLEMAN
ACKLAND AMBROSE BAGNOLD
BARNETT BARRETT BENNETT
BURNAND CHAPMAN CHETTLE
EDWARDS FLECKER GILBERT
HARWOOD HEYWOOD HOUSMAN
JERROLD JOHNSON MARLOWE
MARMION MARSTON MERRICK
MITFORD MOTTEUX NICHOLS
OSBORNE PLANCHE PRESTON
SHIRLEY SIMPSON SITWELL
SOWERBY TRAVERS WEBSTER
BEAUMONT CLIFFORD CONGREVE
DAVENANT ETHEREGE FIELDING
FITZBALL FLETCHER HAMILTON
HOLCROFT HOUGHTON JELLICOE
JOHNSTON KNOBLOCK LONSDALE
MORRISON PHILLIPS RATTIGAN
ROBINSON SHADWELL THEOBALD
THURSTON TOURNEUR VANBRUGH
WILLIAMS ZANGWILL BOTTOMLEY
BRIGHOUSE GOLDSMITH
GREENWOOD ISHERWOOD
KILLIGREW MANKOWITZ MASSINGER
MIDDLETON MONCRIEFF
MONKHOUSE SIEVEKING
SOUTHERNE VANDRUTEN
WYCHERLEY BROADHURST
CARTWRIGHT DRINKWATER
GALSWORTHY PHILLPOTTS
SHAKESPEARE
ESTONIAN TAMMSAARE
FINNISH KIVI CHORELL
TAVASTSTJERNA
FRENCH BLUM HUGO JOUY KOCK
PYAT VADE BELOT BLOCH CAMUS

CAPUS CARRE CEARD COLLE CUREL
DUCIS DUMAS FABRE FEVAL FLERS
GENET GIONO JARRY PIRON VIGNY
WOLFF ACHARD AUGIER BAYARD
BECQUE BELLOY BRIEUX COLLIN
COOLUS COPEAU DONNAY DOUCET
FAVART HALEVY LESAGE MAIRET
MARCEL MONVEL MOREAU PAGNOL
PARODI PICARD RACINE RAYNAL
RENARD ROTROU SARDOU SARTRE
SCRIBE SOUMET ANCELOT ANOUILH
BARBIER BERNARD BORNIER
BOUILLY BOUVIER CLAUDEL
COCTEAU DENNERY FERRIER
FEYDEAU GRESSET HERVIEU
IONESCO LABICHE LAPLACE LARIVEY
LAVEDAN LEGOUVE MAURIAC
MEILHAC MEURICE MOLIERE
MORTIER NUITTER PONSARD
PREVOST ROSTAND SANDEAU
SARMENT SEDAINE VILDRAC
ANDRIEUX BARRIERE BATAILLE
BEAUVOIR BENJAMIN CROISSET
DANCOURT DUMANOIR FAUCHOIS
MARIVAUX MONTEPIN QUINAULT
VOLTAIRE BENSERADE BERNSTEIN
BOURSAULT CORNEILLE DELAVIGNE
DUVEYRIER LEMERCIER VACQUERIE
CAMPISTRON CLAIRVILLE
DESTOUCHES BEAUMARCHAIS
GERMAN BAB BABO BEER KIND LENZ
BLOEM ERNST HALBE JOHST LAUBE
SORGE UNRUH ZWEIG ANGELY
BRECHT DREYER GOETHE HEBBEL
KAISER KLEIST KORNER REUTER
TOLLER WEISSE BARLACH BENEDIX
BRONNEN GUTZKOW KLINGER
LESSING RAUPACH REDWITZ
VULPIUS BRENTANO GRYPHIUS
HOCHHUTH KATZEBUE KOTZEBUE
LISSAUER SCHILLER WEDEKIND
WOLZOGEN BEYERLEIN GANGHOFER
IMMERMANN SUDERMANN
UECHTRITZ WILBRANDT ZUCKMAYER
AUFFENBERG BLUMENTHAL
FEUCHTWANGER
GREEK ALEXIS SOPHRON THESPIS
CRATINUS PHILEMON RHINTHON
AESCHYLUS EURIPEDES SOPHOCLES
ANTIPHANES PHRYNICHUS
PHERECRATES ARISTOPHANES
HUNGARIAN TOTH DOCZI JOKAI
VAJDA MOLNAR ZILAHY BESSENYEI
KISFALUDY SZIGLIGETI
ICELANDIC KAMBAN LAXNESS
SIGURJONSSON
IRISH BEHAN COLUM KEANE KELLY
SYNGE WILDE WILLS YEATS ERVINE
MARTYN OCASEY TREVOR WELDON
BECKETT DUNSANY GREGORY
GRIFFIN LEONARD MATURIN
OKEEFFE SHEILDS ORIORDAN
SHERIDAN BICKERSTAFFE

ITALIAN FO BETTI CECCHI GIRAUD
ALFIERI ARETINO BENELLI CARRERA
GIACOSA GOLDONI MARENCO
PELLICO TORELLI RUCELLAI SABATINI
CHIARELLI NICCOLINI METASTASIO
PIRANDELLO
JAPANESE CHIKAMATSU
MEXICAN GAMBOA FUENTES
NORWEGIAN BOJER IBSEN HEIBERG
BJORNSON KIELLAND
POLISH ASNYK FREDRO SZUJSKI
ZAPOLSKA ZEROMSKI ZULAWSKI
NALKOWSKA WYSPIANSKI
BELCIKOWSKI BOGUSLAWSKI
KORZENIOWSKI
PORTUGUESE SILVA BIESTER
ROMAN SENECA NAEVIUS PLAUTUS
TERENCE PACUVIUS
RUMANIAN BEIN BLAGA
RUSSIAN ADAMOV KRYLOV
CHEKHOV KAPNIST KIRSHON
TOLSTOI BULGAKOV CHIRIKOV
FONVIZIN POTEKHIN SUMBATOV
ABLESIMOV BOBORYKIN
OSTROVSKY KNARITONOV
YUSHKEVICH KHMELNITSKI
LAZHECHNIKOV
SCOTTISH BEITH BARRIE BRIDIE
DAVIDSON ROBERTSON
SOUTH AFRICAN FUGARD
SPANISH CRUZ LARRA ROJAS RUEDA
CANETE ENCINA ESPRIU ZAMORA
ALARCON ARRABAL MACHADO
MORATIN CALDERON DIAMANTE
MARTINEZ CERVANTES FERNANDEZ
SWEDISH WEISS BESKOW EDGREN
BLANCHE HEDBERG MESSENIUS
LAGERKVIST STRINDBERG
SWISS ILG FAESI
WELSH ABSE EVANS HUGHES
WILLIAMS LLEWELLYN
PLAZA PLACE PLEIN SQUARE ZOCALO
(— DE TOROS) BULLRING
(— GIRL) ELOISE
PLEA BAR BID PLY MOOT NOLO SUIT
ALIBI CLAIM PLEAD ABATER APPEAL
EXCUSE REFUGE APOLOGY
CONTEND DEFENCE LAWSUIT
PRETEXT QUARREL DILATORY
ENTREATY PLACITUM PRETENSE
PLEACH PLAIT PLASH INTERLACE
PLEAD BEG SUE MOOT PLEA PRAY
PRIG SHOW URGE COUNT ORATE
ALLEGE APPEAL ASSERT PLAYTE
PURSUE ENTREAT IMPLORE SOLICIT
WRANGLE ADVOCATE LITIGATE
(— FOR) SOLICIT PETITION
PLEADER ACTOR VAKIL PATRON
SUITOR VAKEEL COUNTOR
ADVOCATE
PLEADING PLEA PAROL ANSWER
PAROLE ADVOCACY COGNOVIT
DEMURRER INTENDIT MEMORIAL

PLEASANT FUN GAY BEEN BIEN
BRAW FAIR FINE GLAD GOOD HEND
JOLI NEAT TRIM WEME AMENE BIGLY
BONNY CANNY COUTH CUSHY
DOUCE DRUNK DUCKY GREEN
HAPPY HENDE HODDY JOLLY LEPID
LISTY LUSTY MERRY NUTTY QUEME
SMIRK SUAVE SWEET TIPSY WALLY
WETHE COMELY DAINTY DULCET
GENIAL KINDLY PRETTY SAVORY
SMOOTH AFFABLE ELEGANT
FARRAND JANNOCK LEESOME
WINSOME DELICATE GLORIOUS
GRATEFUL HEAVENLY LIEFSOME
LIKESOME LOVESOME THANKFUL
TOWARDLY GEMUTLICH
(PREF.) HEDY
PLEASANTLY FAIR WINLY FAIRLY
AFFABLY SWEETLY GENIALLY
LIKINGLY
PLEASANTNESS GAIETY NAAMAN
AMENITY SUAVITY JOCUNDITY
PLEASANTRY WIT JEST JOKE
SPORT BANTER JESTING JOLLITY
WAGGERY
PLEASE PAY GAME LIKE LIST LUST
SUIT WANT WISH AGREE AMUSE
BITTE CHARM ELATE FANCY HUMOR
QUEME SAVOR TASTE ARRIDE KITTLE
OBLIGE REGALE SOOTHE TICKLE
AGGRATE APPLESE CONTENT
DELIGHT GLADDEN GRATIFY
PLACATE REJOICE SATISFY
(— FORWARD) FS
(— THE PUBLIC) TAKE
PLEASED FAIN FOND GLAD APAID
HAPPY PROUD BUCKED CONTENT
GLADSOME
(BE —) GAME
PLEASING AMEN COOL GLAD GOOD
LIEF NICE SOFT AMENE DICTY NIFTY
SOOTH SWEET CLEVER COMELY
DREAMY FACILE FLASHY GAINLY
LIKING LUSTLY MELLOW PRETTY
AMIABLE BLESSED CORKING
DARLING LIKABLE LIKEFUL TUNABLE
WELCOME CHARMING DELICATE
FAVOROUS FETCHING GRACEFUL
GRACIOUS GRATEFUL HEAVENLY
INVITING LIKESOME PLACABLE
PLAUSIVE SPECIOUS PLAUSIBLE
PERSONABLE
(— TO EAR) HARMONIC
(— TO EYE) EESOME
(— TO HEAR) FAIR
(VERY —) SNAZZY
PLEASURABLE GOOD JOLLY
ANIMAL MIRTHFUL
PLEASURE JO EST FUN JOY BANG
BOOT EASE ESTE GREE KAMA LIST
LUST PLAY WILL BLISS KICKS MIRTH
SAVOR SOOTH TASTE DAINTY
DEDUIT GAIETY GAYETY LIKING

LUXURY NICETY VOLUPT COMFORT
DELIGHT GRATIFY JOLLITY JOYANCE
VOLUPTY DELICACY FRUITION
GLADNESS HILARITY VOLUPTAS
(— BY INFLICTING PAIN) SADISM
(INTERJECTION TO EXPRESS —)
YUMYUM
(SELFISH —) LECHERY
(STOLEN —) STOUTH STOWTH
(PL.) DELICIAE
PLEASURE SEEKER FRANION
PLEAT SET FOLD KILT POKE RUCK
FLUTE FRILL PINCH PLAIT PRANK
GUSSET SUNRAY
PLEATED PLICATE SUNBURST
PLEBE PLEBS FRESHMAN
PLEBEIAN LOW BASE PLEB SNOB
COMMON HOMELY VULGAR
IGNOBLE LOWBORN POPULAR
BASEBORN EVERYDAY HOMESPUN
INFERIOR MECHANIC ORDINARY
ROTURIER RUPTUARY
PLEBISCITE VOTE DECREE
PLECTRUM PICK SPUR QUILL UVULA
MALLEUS POINTEL PLECTRON
(— OF HARP) FESCUE
PLEDGE LAY VAS VOW WAD WED
AFFY BAND CLAP EARL GAGE HAND
HEST HOCK OATH PASS PAWN WAGE
WOID WORD FAITH SIKER SPOUT
STAKE SWEAR SWEAT TOKEN TROTH
TRUTH WAGER ARREST BORROW
COMMIT ENGAGE IMPAWN IMPONE
LUMBER PAROLE PIGNUS PLEVIN
PLIGHT SICCAR SICKER VADIUM
WADSET BARGAIN BETROTH
CAUTION CREANCE EARNEST
HOSTAGE PROMISE BOTTOMRY
MORTGAGE SECURITY SPONSION
VADIMONY
(— IN DRINKING) PROPINE
(— ONESELF) UNDERTAKE
PLEDGED HIGHT SWORN ASSURED
ENGAGED PIGNORATE
(— TO MARRY) SURE
PLEDGET DOSSIL PENICIL
PLEIADES MAIA MEROPE ALCYONE
CELAENO ELECTRA STEROPE
TAYGETA
PLEIN-AIRIST LUMINIST
PLEISTHENES (FATHER OF —)
ATREUS
(MOTHER OF —) AEROPE
(SON OF —) MENELAUS
AGAMEMNON
PLENARY FULL ENTIRE PLENAL
PERFECT ABSOLUTE COMPLETE
PLENITUDE PLENITY PLEROMA
FULLNESS PLETHORA
ABUNDANCE
PLENTEOUS RICH COPIOUS FERTILE
AFFLUENT FRUITFUL GENEROUS
ABOUNDING EXUBERANT

PLENTIFUL OLD FULL RANK RICH
RIFE AMPLE HEFTY LARGE ROUTH
SONSY STORE ENOUGH FOISON
GALORE LAVISH SONSIE COPIOUS
FERTILE LIBERAL OPULENT PROFUSE
UBEROUS ABUNDANT FRUITFUL
NUMEROUS EXUBERANT
PLENTIFULLY RIFE FREELY GALORE
APLENTY
PLENTY WON BAIT COPY MANY
RAFF SONS AMPLE CHEAP COPIA
FOUTH PRICE ROUTH SONSE TEEMS
FOISON OODLES SCOUTH UBERTY
LASHINGS
(— OF) GALORE
(GREAT —) ABUNDANCE
PLEON TELSON ABDOMEN
PLEONASM ITERATION
MACROLOGY TAUTOLOGY
PLETHORA RASH EXCESS PLENUM
PLURISY FULLNESS PLEURISY
POLYEMIA PROFUSION REPLETION
PLETHORIC TUMID TURGID
SWOLLEN INFLATED
PLEURISY EMPYEMA
PLEURON SCAPULA
PLEXUS RETE GLOMUS NETWORK
PROPLEX GENIPLEX
PLIABLE WAXY WEAK LITHY WAXEN
DOCILE LIMBER PLIANT SEMMIT
SUPPLE BOWABLE FICTILE FINGENT
FLEXILE PLASTIC WINDING
CUSHIONY FLEXIBLE COMPLIANT
PLIANCY FLEXURE FACILITY
PLIANT APT FLIP SWAK AGILE
BUXOM LITHE SWACK YOUNG
DOCILE LIMBER SUPPLE WANDLE
DUCTILE FLEXILE PLASTIC PLIABLE
SLIPPER WILLOWY APPLIANT
FLEXIBLE SUITABLE WORKABLE
SEQUACIOUS
PLICA FOLD TRICHOMA
PLICATE FOLD PLEAT FOLDED
FANLIKE PLAITED
PLIERS BENDER FLEXOR GRATER
FLECTOR PINCERS
PLIGHT PLY FOLD ARRAY BRAID
DRESS PLAIT POINT STATE WOVEN
ATTIRE ENGAGE PICKLE PLEDGE
PLISKY STRAIT TAKING BETROTH
MISCHIEF QUANDARY
PLIGHTED ASSURATE
PLIM PLUM STOUT SWELL INFLATE
PLIABLE
PLIMSOLL (WHITE —S)
MUTTONDUMMIES
(PL.) RUBBERS
PLINTH ORLE ORLO BLOCK SOCLE
ABACUS PATAND QUADRA SUBBASE
FOOTSTALL SCAMILLUS
PLISTHENES (FATHER OF —)
ATREUS
(MOTHER OF —) CLEOLA

(SON OF —) MENELAUS
AGAMEMNON
(WIFE OF —) AEROPE ERIPHYLE

PLOD JOG GRUB PLOT SLOG STOG
TOIL TORE TROG VAMP POACH
TRAMP TRASH DRUDGE SLOUCH
TRUDGE PLUNTHER
(— ALONG) PEG TORE
(— THROUGH MUD) SLOUGH

PLODDER GRUB DIGGER SLOGGER

PLOIARIA EMESA

PLONK WINE

PLOP FLUMP PLUMP HEAVILY
(— DOWN) SIT

PLOT BREW CAST MARK PACK PLAN
PLAT CABAL DRIFT FRAUD GLEBE
GRAPH GREEN HATCH MODEL PLECK
SCALD STORY STUDY WATCH
ACTION BRIGUE CLIQUE DESIGN
DEVISE GARDEN MALIGN MYTHOS
SCHEME SHAMBA TAMPER AGITATE
COLLUDE COMPACT COMPASS
CONJECT CONNIVE CONTOUR
DRAUGHT FEEDLOT LAZYBED
MACHINE PRETEND QUADRAT
QUARTER SWIDDEN ARGUMENT
COGITATE CONSPIRE CONTRIVE
INTRIGUE PRACTICE PROTRACT
SEMINARY MACHINATE
(— OF GRASS) SONK
(— OF LAND) ERF LOT PLAT SHOT
FORTY MILPA PATCH PLECK SPLAT
COMMON PARCEL SCHERM SHAMDA
HAGGARD LAZYBED SEVERAL
(— OF 1-2 ACRE) ERF
(— SECRETLY) WHISPER
(GARDEN —) BED ERI QUINTA
QUARTER
(UNPRODUCTIVE —) HIRST

PLOTTER PACKER HATCHER JACOBIN
SCHEMER DESIGNER ENGINEER

PLOUK KNOB PIMPLE

PLOVER DROME KOLEA OXEYE PILOT
SANDY STILT KILDEE QUAILY TURNIX
COLLIER COURSER DOTTREL
LAPWING MAYCOCK OWLHEAD
PAPABOT WRYBILL BULLHEAD
DOTTEREL DULWILLY HILLBIRD
KILLDEER RINGNECK SPURWING
SQUEALER TOADHEAD WHISTLER
WIREBIRD SANDERLING

PLOW EAR ERE BOUT DISK FOIL HINT
LIST MOLE PLOD RIVE ROVE SLUG
STIR SULK SULL TILL BREAK FLUNK
SPLIT SULKY THROW ARAIRE
BUSTER DIGGER DIPPER FALLOW
FURROW GOPHER JUMPER LISTER
PLOUGH RAFTER ROOTER RUTTER
SULLOW BACKSET BREAKER
HUSBAND SCOOTER SULCATE
TWISTER FIREPLOW FURROWER
GANGPLOW SNOWPLOW
TURNPLOW

(— CROSSWISE) THORTER
(— HANDLE) STILT
(— LIGHTLY) SKIM RIFFLE
(— PART) PINHEAD
(— WITH SPACE BETWEEN
FURROWS) RIB RIVE
(MOTORIZED —) TRACTOR
(PL.) OUTSIGHT

PLOWBOY YOKEL

PLOWING ARDER EARTH ARDURE
ARATION CARUAGE STIRRING

PLOWLAND CARUE CARVE TILTH
CARUCATE TEAMLAND

PLOWMAN PLOWER TILLER
ACREMAN

PLOWSHARE LAY SLIP SOCK LAVER
REEST SHARE JUMPER
(— BONE) VOMER PYGOSTYLE
(PREF.) VOMERO

PLOY BENT BOWED SPORT RAMBLE
TACTIC PURSUIT ACTIVITY ESCAPADE

PLUCK GO PUG ROB TUG BOUT CROP
CULL DRAG GAME GRAB GRIT PELT
PICK PILL POOK PULL RACE RASE
RASH SAND TUCK ARBER ARBOR
BREAK DRAFT HANGE MOXIE NERVE
PILCH PLOAT PLUME RANCH SMITE
SPUNK STEAL STRIP AVULSE DECERP
EVULSE FLEECE GATHER PIGEON
PLITCH PLOUGH QUARRY SNATCH
SPIRIT TWINGE TWITCH COURAGE
DEPLUME PLUNDER BOLDNESS
DECISION DEMOLISH GAMENESS
GUMPTION VELLICATE PURTENANCE
(— APART) DIVELLICATE
(— AS A STRING) TIRL PINCH
(— FEATHERS) STUB
(— LEAVES) BLADE
(— OF SHEEP OR CALF) RACE
GATHER
(— UP COURAGE) CHEER
(— WOOL BY HAND) ROO

PLUCKED PLUMED PIZZICATO

PLUCKY GAMY SANDY BANTAM
GRITTY SPUNKY FIGHTING

PLUG BUG FID PEG PIN TAP TOP WAD
BLOW BONE BOTT BUNG FILL JADE
ROOT SHOT SLOG STOP SWAT SWOT
BOOST DOWEL DUMMY PILOT
PUNCH SHACK SKATE SPILE STUN
SWEAT BOUCHE BOXING BULLET
COMEDO DOSSIL DOTTLE FIDDLE
SPIGOT BOUCHON BUSHING
CHAMBER CHUGGER FERRULE
STOPPER STOPPLE DRIVECAP
FUSEPLUG PELELITH STOPCOCK
(— FOR CANNON) TAMPION
(— IN GRENADE) BOUCHON
(— IN ORGAN PIPE) STOPPLE
TAMPION
(— OF CLAY) BOTT
(— OF OAKUM) FID
(— OF VOLCANO) CORE

(— TO HOLD NAIL) DOOK
(— UP) CLAM STOP ESTOP
RAMFORCE
(FIRE —) HYDRANT
(FISHING —) BUG
(LIP —) LABRET
(NOSE —) TEMBETA TEMBETARA
(WASTE —) WASHER
(WATER —) HYDRANT
PLUG-IN JACK
PLUG-UGLY THUG ROWDY TOUGH
RUFFIAN ROUGHNECK
PLUM GAGE JOBO RISE ISLAY
JAMAN PRUNE SWELL BEAUTY
CHENEY DAMSEL DAMSON KELSEY
MUSSEL SAPOTE APRICOT BULLACE
BURBANK FORTUNE ORLEANS
QUETSCH PRUNELLO ROSACEAN
ROSEWORT VICTORIA WINDFALL
(COCO —) ICACO
(JAVA —) DUHAT JAMBUL JAMBOOL
JAMBOLAN
(WILD —) SKEG SLOE ISLAY
(PREF.) PRUNI
PLUMAGE ROBE RUFF FLUFF
HACKLE SHROUD FEATHER FLOCCUS
JUVENAL PENNAGE FEATHERS
PARADISE PTILOSIS
PLUMB BUNG SHEER BOTTOM
BULLET SINKER EXACTLY PLUMMET
UTTERLY ABSOLUTE COMPLETE
DIRECTLY ENTIRELY VERTICAL
PLUMBAGO LUSTER LUSTRE
GRAPHITE LEADWORT
PLUMB BOB PLUMMET
PLUMBISM SATURNISM
PLUMB LINE MERKHET
PLUM CURCULIO TURK WEEVIL
PLUME PEN TIP TUFT CREST EGRET
PRIDE PRUNE DEPRIVE DESPOIL
FEATHER PANACHE AIGRETTE
(— ON HELMET) CREST PANACHE
(— ON HORSE) PLUMADE
(— ON TURBAN) CULGEE
(EGRET —) OSPREY
(MILITARY —) PANACHE
PLUME NUTMEG SASSAFRAS
PLUMMET LEAD FLOAT PLUMB
WEIGHT
PLUMMING BRONZING
PLUMP FAT BOLD FAIR FLOP FULL
PLOP SLAP SOSS TIDY BLUNT
BONNY BUXOM CLUMP FLUMP
FUBBY FUBSY GROUP JOLLY PLUNK
PUDGY SAPPY SLEEK SMACK SONSY
SQUAB STOUT THICK BONNIE
CHUBBY CRUMBY CRUMMY DIRECT
FATTEN FLATLY FLESHY FODGEL
GAWSIE PLUNGE PUBBLE ROTUND
ZAFTIG ZOFTIG BLUNTLY BUNTING
CLUSTER DISTEND FULSOME
RIBLESS THRODDY CHOPPING
FLESHFUL

(— AND ROSY) BUXOM
(— AND ROUND) CHUBBY
(NOT —) ANGULAR
(PLEASINGLY —) ZAFTIG ZOFTIG
PLUM POCKET FOOL
PLUMULE BLASTUS FEATHER
GEMMULA GEMMULE GEOBLAST
ACROSPIRE
PLUNDER GUT ROB BOOT FANG
JUNK LOOT PILL POLL PREY RAID
RAPE REIF RIPE RUMP SACK SWAG
BEROB BOOTY CHEAT GAINS HARRY
PLUCK PREDE RAVEN REAVE RENNE
RIFLE SCOFF SHAVE SPOIL STRIP
BEZZLE BOODLE CREACH DACOIT
FLEECE FORAGE HARROW MARAUD
PANYAR PROFIT RAPINE RAVAGE
DESPOIL ESCHEAT FREIGHT PILFERY
PILLAGE RANSACK SACKAGE
SPREAGH SPULZIE BOOTHALE
FREEBOOT SPOLIATE
PLUNDERER THIEF BANDIT
BUMMER PEELER POLLER RAPTOR
ROBBER VANDAL ROUTIER SPOILER
MARAUDER RAPPAREE
PLUNDERING PREY SACK MARAUD
RAPINE ESCHEAT HERSHIP
PURCHASE RAVENOUS SPECHERY
SPOILFUL SPOILING PREDATORY
PLUNGE BET DIG DIP CAVE DIVE
DOOK DUCK DUMP JUMP PURL PUSH
RAKE RISK SINK SOSS BURST DOUSE
FLING PITCH PLUMP SOUSE SWOOP
FOOTER GAMBLE HEADER LAUNCH
SPLASH THRUST WALLOP BRAINGE
DEMERGE IMMERSE PLOUNCE
SUBMERGE
(— DEEPLY) WHELM
(— INTO) CLAP ENGULF IMMERGE
(— INTO WATER) ENEW
(BETTING —) RAKER
(GAMBLING —) RAKER
PLUNGER RAM SWAB FORCE
DUCKER POMMEL BLUNGER
STRIKER
PLUNGING FLING
PLUNK DIVE PLONK PLUCK PLUMP
DOLLAR SUPPORT SUDDENLY
PLUNTHER PLOD FLOUNDER
PLURAL
(SUFF.) IM
PLURALIST TOTQUOT
PLURALITY MAJORITY MORENESS
TRIALITY
(PREF.) POLY
PLURALIZER ESS
PLUS AND GAIN WITH EXTRA
BESIDES SURPLUS ADDITION
INCREASE POSITIVE
PLUSH EASY BEAVER VELOUR
SUPERIOR
PLUSHY SWANK SWANKY
PLUTEUS WAGON PARAPET

PLUTO DIS HADES ORCUS
  (BROTHER OF —) JUPITER NEPTUNE
  (FATHER OF —) SATURN
  (WIFE OF —) PROSERPINE
PLUTOCRAT NABOB RICHARD
PLUTONIC HYPOGENE INTRUSIVE
  VULCANIAN
PLUTUS (ASSOCIATE OF —) TYCHE
  EIRENE
  (FATHER OF —) IASION
  (MOTHER OF —) CERES DEMETER
PLY RUN BEAT BEND BIAS CORD CORE
  DRAM FOLD MOLD SAIL URGE ADAPT
  APPLY EXERT LAYER STEER TWIST
  WIELD YIELD COMPLY DOUBLE
  HANDLE TRAVEL EXERCISE
  (— NEEDLE) SEW
  (— WITH DRINK) BIRL ROSIN
  (— WITH DRUGS) HOCUS
  (— WITH QUESTIONS) HECKLE
  (OF ONE —) SINGLE
PLYWOOD (LIKE —) LAMINAR
PNEUMA NEUM SOUL NEUME
  BREATH SPIRIT
PNEUMATIC HAMMER GUN
PNEUMATOCYST FLOAT
PNEUMONIA PULMONITIS
POACH PUG RUB COOK DROP POKE
  PUSH SINK BLACK DRIVE FORCE
  POTCH STEAL BLEACH PLUNGE
  INTRUDE
POACHED EGGS MOONSHINE
POACHER BLACK POUGE SPOACH
  LURCHER STALKER WIDGEON
  BALDPATE BULLHEAD
  (SALMON —) REBECCA REBEKAH
  (PL.) BLACKS
POALES GLUMALES
POCAHONTAS (HUSBAND OF —)
  ROLFE
POCHARD DUCK SMEE DIVER POKER
  SCAUP DUNAIR DUNKER DUNBIRD
  REDHEAD WHINGER GOLDHEAD
  WHINYARD
POCHETTE KIT VIOLIN HANDBAG
POCKET BOX CLY FOB PIT CLAY KICK
  POKE PRAT BASIN BURSE MEANS
  POUCH PURSE STEAL ACCEPT
  BECKET CASING CANTINA PLACKET
  SWALLOW TROUSER ENVELOPE
  ISOLATED MONETARY PROFONDE
  SUPPRESS CONDENSED MINIATURE
  (— A WRONG) PURSE
  (— IN BOOK BINDER) STATION
  (— OF NET) BOWL
  (BILLIARD —) POT HOLE HAZARD
  (KIND OF —) BESOM HACKING
  KANGAROO
  (MAGICIAN'S —) PROFONDE
  (NOODLE —S) KREPLACH
  (ORE —) CHURN BONANZA
  (SMALL —) FOB
  (TROUSER —) PRAT BECKET

  (WATCH —) FOB
  (WATER —) TINAJA ALBERCA
  (PL.) KREPLACH
  (PREF.) PERO
POCKETBOOK BAG KICK SKIN
  PURSE INCOME READER WALLET
  HANDBAG LEATHER BILLFOLD
  NOTECASE
POCKET GOPHER TUZA QUACHIL
POCKETING COUP
POCKETKNIFE BARLOW PENKNIFE
  PIGSTICKER
POCKMARK PITHOLE
POD BAG COD GAM KID POP SAC
  BALL BEAN BOLL HULL HUSK POKE
  SWAD BOLLY BURSE CAROB FLOCK
  POUCH QUASH SHAUP SHELL SHUCK
  SNAIL WHAUP CHILLI LEGUME
  PESCOD SCHOOL HARICOT PEASCOD
  SILIQUA PEASECOD PODOCARP
  POTBELLY SEEDCASE TAMARIND
  (— FORMING) KID
  (— OF LEGUME) KID
  (— OF MESQUITE) HONEYPOD
  (BABLAH —S) NEBNEB
  (CASSIA —) PUDDINGPIPE
  (COILED —) STROMBUS
  (EXPLOSIVE —) SANDBOX
  (SUBTERRANEAN —) EARTHNUT
  (UNRIPE —) SQUASH
  (PL.) PIPI SLINT BADUL GARAD
  BABLAH GARRAT COWHAGE
  GONAKIE ALGAROBA DIVIDIVI
  (PREF.) SILIQUI
PODALIRIUS (BROTHER OF —)
  MACHAON
  (FATHER OF —) ASCLEPIUS
PODARCES (BROTHER OF —)
  PROTESILAUS
  (FATHER OF —) IPHICLUS
PODDED BOLLED
PODIUM DAIS FOOT WALL
  LECTERN
PODOCARP YACCA
PODWARE PODDER
PODZOL SPODOSOL
POEM GEM LAI LAY ODE DUAN EPIC
  GEST IDYL JOSE MELE POSY RUNE
  SONG CENTO DIRGE DITTY EDYLL
  GESTE HAIKU IWEIN METER STAFF
  VERSE AMHRAN AUBADE BALLAD
  CACCIA CARMEN CYCLIC DIXAIN
  EPOPEE EROTIC ESTRIF HEROID
  MELODY MONODY NOSTOS PIYYUT
  SESTET SONNET TENSON TERCET
  BUCOLIC CANTARE CANTATA
  CANZONE DESCORT DIZAINE
  ECLOGUE ELEGIAC FLITING GEORGIC
  SOTADIC TRIOLET VIRELAI VIRELAY
  VOLUSPA ACROSTIC AMOEBEUM
  BRINDISI CANTICLE DINGDONG
  DOGGEREL INVICTUS LIMERICK
  MADRIGAL TELESTIC THEOGONY

TRISTICH TROCHAIC VERSICLE
MONORHYME ROUNDELAY
(— **ABOUT DEBATE**) ESTRIF
(— **ABOUT SHEPHERDS**) ECLOGUE
(— **GREETING DAWN**) AUBADE
(— **OF LAMENTATION**) ELEGY
(— **OF RETRACTION**) PALINODE
(— **OF 10 LINES**) DIZAINE
(— **OF 14 LINES**) SONNET
(**AMATORY** —) EROTIC SONNET
(**EPIC** —) EPOS EPOPEE LUSIAD
THEBAID
(**HOMELY** —) DIT
(**IRISH** —) AMHRAN
(**JAPANESE** —) HAIKU RANKA TANKA
SENRYU
(**LITURGICAL** —) VIDDUI VIDDUY
SELIHOTH
(**LOVE** —) AMORETTO
(**LYRIC** —) LAI LAY ODE ALBA EPODE
GHAZEL RONDEL CANZONA
PARTIMEN
(**MUSICAL** —) RONDO
(**PART OF** —) PASSUS
(**PASTORAL** —) IDYL IDYLL BUCOLIC
(**PERSIAN** —) GHAZAL
(**RELIGIOUS** —) HYMN
(**RURAL** —) GEORGIC
(**SACRED** —) PSALM YIGDAL
(**SATIRICAL** —) IAMBIC KASIDA
(**SHORT** —) DIT DITTY EPILOG
RONDEL SONNET CANZONE
EPIGRAM RONDEAU EPILOGUE
EPYLLION
(**TONE** —) BALLADE
(**WELSH** —) CYWYDD
(**PL.**) AZAHROT MAKINGS
(**SUFF.**) STICH
POET OG RSI BARD FILE FILI FIRI LARK
MUSE SCOP SWAN ARION LAKER
LINOS LINUS LYRIC MAKAR MAKER
ODIST RISHI SAYER SCALD SKALD
FINDER GNOMIC IBYCUS LAKIST
LYRIST SHAPER SINGER DICHTER
ELEGIAC EPICIST IDYLIST IMAGIST
MUSAEUS ORPHEUS PROPHET
CONCRETE FERAMORZ GEORGIAN
LAUREATE LUTANIST MINSTREL
SONGSTER TROUVERE
MINNESINGER
(**INSPIRED** —) PROPHET
(**IRISH** —) FILI
(**MEDIOCRE** —) RIMER RHYMER
(**MINOR** —) BARDIE
ALBANIAN FISHTA
AMERICAN BLY LOW POE AGAR
AGEE BURR CARY CONE DALY HEAD
KEMP MARX NASH READ REED SAXE
SILL SNOW TABB TATE TOWN VERY
WARE ADAMS AIKEN AKINS ALLEN
AUDEN BACON BEERS BENET
BOGAN BROWN CLAPP CLARK COLES
CORSO CRANE DAMON DRAKE

ENGLE FAUST FICKE FIELD FINCH
FITTS FROST GUEST HAYNE HECHT
HOVEY JOLAS MOODY OPPEN PIATT
POUND PRIME RIDGE RILEY SIMIC
STORY TOWNE WELBY WILDE WYLIE
ARNOLD BARLOW BRALEY BRANCH
BROOKS BRYANT BURTON CARMER
CAWEIN CHENEY CIARDI CLARKE
COATES COFFIN CRANCH CULLEN
CUTTER DARGAN DUNBAR FISHER
GIBRAN GILDER GIORNO GUINEY
HOLMES HOOPER KEELER KILMER
LANIER LEDOUX LOWELL MILLAY
MILLER MONROE MORGAN MORTON
NORTON OSGOOD PARKER SAVAGE
SEEGER SEXTON SHANGE THOMAS
TIMROD TOOMER VIORST WILCOX
WRIGHT AINSLIE BABCOCK BRODSKY
CARRUTH CHIVERS CROWELL
EMERSON FEARING FRENEAU
HALLECK HILLYER JEFFERS
KNOWLES LAFARGE LAZARUS
LIFSHIN LINDSAY MARKHAM MIFFLIN
MOULTON PARSONS PATCHEN
PEABODY PROCTOR ROBERTS
RUSSELL SHAPIRO SHERMAN
STEDMAN TAGGARD THAXTER
VIERECK WAKOSKI WATTLES
WHITMAN BERRYMAN BRAINARD
CARLETON CONKLING CORNFORD
CUMMINGS DINSMOOR FISHBACK
FLETCHER GINSBURG HAGEDORN
MACLEISH NEIHARDT PETERSON
PHILLIPS PROKOSCH ROBINSON
RUKEYSER SANDBURG SCOLLARD
SPOFFORD STERLING STODDARD
TEASDALE THOMPSON TIETJENS
TRUMBULL WHEATLEY WHITTIER
AUSLANDER COOLBRITH DICKINSON
GUITERMAN HENDERSON
HOLLANDER HOPKINSON
KREYMBORG OPPENHEIM
TUCKERMAN WURDEMANN
COATSWORTH LONGFELLOW
BRAITHWAITE RITTENHOUSE
ARAB TARAFA
ARGENTINIAN ASCASUBI
ECHEVERRIA
AUSTRALIAN GORDON TURNER
AUSTRIAN VOGL KAFKA BACHER
FRANKL GRAZIE WERFEL NEUMANN
ZEDLITZ CASTELLI WILDGANS
WURZBACH ZINGERLE HAMERLING
HOFMANNSTHAL
BELGIAN CLAUS GILKIN GIRAUD
EEKHOUD ELSKAMP HASSELT
CAMMAERTS RODENBACH
VERHAEREN MAETERLINCK
BRAZILIAN GAMA COSTA AZEVEDO
BANDEIRA GUIMARAES MAGALHAES
BULGARIAN VAZOV BOTYOV
CANADIAN FISET PRATT SCOTT
SMITH BIRNIE CARMAN MACKAY

MCCRAE FERLAND JOHNSON
LAMPMAN SERVICE CAMPBELL
CRAWFORD DRUMMOND FRECHETTE
MACDONALD
CHILEAN NERUDA MISTRAL
CHINESE LU TU CHAO LIPO TUFU
POCHUI MEISHENG
COLOMBIAN ARBOLEDA
CUBAN VALDES
CZECH CECH GOLL ERBEN FRIDA
HALEK HANKA JEBAVY KVAPIL
MACHAR NERUDA SEIFERT
DANISH BOYE RODE EWALD HAUCH
KINGO PLOUG ARREBO JENSEN
RAHBEK BLICHER CLAUSEN
HOSTRUP KAALUND WINTHER
BAGGESEN BODTCHER INGEMANN
JACOBSEN AARESTRUP GRUNDTVIG
JORGENSEN GERSTENBERG
DUTCH CATS GOES KATE POOT
BEETS BERGH EEDEN FEITH HAREN
HOOFT DECKER EMANTS LENNEP
LOGHEM VERWEY VONDEL BELLAMY
BREDERO HELMERS TOLLENS
BARLEAUS SECUNDUS ACHTERBERG
BILDERDIJK HEEMSKERCK
HUYDECOPER BROEKHUIZEN
ECUADORIAN OLMEDO
ENGLISH BAX GAY MAY MEW PYE
BELL BIGG COOK CORY DYER GALE
GRAY HAKE HALL HILL HOOD HUNT
KOPS LEAR NOEL OWEN POPE ROWE
TATE VAUX ADAMS AUDEN BASSE
BLAKE BLUNT BROWN BRYAN
BYROM BYRON CAREW CAREY
CLARE COOKE DIXON DONNE DOYLE
GOOGE GOULD GOWER GREEN
JONES KEATS KEOWN LEWIS
MASON MERRY MILNE MINOT
MONRO MOORE MYERS NADEN
NOYES PAYNE PEELE PERCY PRAED
PRIOR SMART SMITH SWAIN WATTS
WAUGH WELLS WHITE WOLFE
WOODS WYATT YOUNG ABBOTT
ANSTEY ARNOLD AUSTIN BAILEY
BARKER BARLOW BARNES BARTON
BINYON BOWLES BRETON BRONTE
BROOKE BROWNE BUTLER CANTON
CAPERN CARTER CLOUGH CORBET
COTTON COWLEY COWPER CRABBE
DANIEL DAVIES DENHAM DOBELL
DOBSON DOMETT DOWSON DRYDEN
EUSDEN FENTON GIBSON GLOVER
GODDEN GODLEY GRAVES GREENE
HARVEY HAWKER HAYLEY HEMANS
HOWARD JONSON KENYON LANDON
LANDOR LARKIN LYTTON MACKAY
MARTIN MASSEY MCLEOD MILMAN
MILNES MILTON MORRIS MUNDAY
NESBIT ROGERS SAVAGE SCOGAN
SEWARD SISSON STRODE SYMONS
TAYLOR THOMAS TREECE TRENCH
WALLER WARNER WARREN WARTON

WATSON WITHER WOLCOT WOTTON
AINSLIE BAMFORD BARCLAY
BLUNDEN BRIDGES CAEDMON
CAMPION CHAPMAN CHAUCER
COKAYNE COLLINS COPPARD
CRASHAW DARYUSH DOUGHTY
DRAYTON ELLIOTT FAUSSET
FLATMAN FLECKER FRAUNCE
FREEMAN GIBBONS GIFFORD
GRIGSON HERRICK HEWLETT
HOPKINS HOUSMAN INGELOW
KENNEDY KIPLING LAYAMON
LYDGATE MANNYNG MARLOWE
MARVELL MEYNELL MONTAGU
NEWBOLT NICHOLS PATMORE
PEACOCK PHILIPS POMFRET
PROCTER QUARLES SASSOON
SEYMOUR SHELLEY SITWELL
SKELTON SKIPSEY SOUTHEY
SPENDER SPENSER SYMONDS
TICKELL TREVENA VAUGHAN
WEBSTER WOOLNER AKENSIDE
BEAUMONT BETJEMAN BLAGMIRE
BRANFORD BRERELEY BROWNING
BUCHANAN CAMPBELL CHALONER
CYNEWULF DAVENANT FALCONER
GASCOYNE GREVILLE HAMILTON
HOCCLEVE LANGLAND LOVELACE
MACNEICE MOULTRIE OVERBURY
ROSSETTI SHADWELL STERLING
SUCKLING TENNYSON THOMPSON
TRAHERNE WHISTLER ALDINGTON
ARMSTRONG BARNFIELD
BLANCHARD BOTTOMLEY
CALVERLEY CAMBRIDGE CHALKHILL
CHURCHILL CLEVELAND COLERIDGE
CONSTABLE GASCOIGNE
GOLDSMITH HABINGTON
LANGHORNE MASEFIELD
MONKHOUSE ROSCOMMON
SACKVILLE SHENSTONE SOUTHWELL
SWINBURNE SYLVESTER UNDERHILL
WHITEHEAD BLOOMFIELD
BOURDILLON BRATHWAITE
CHATTERTON DRINKWATER
FITZGERALD MONTGOMERY
SOMERVILLE WORDSWORTH
ABERCROMBIE SHAKESPEARE
TURBERVILLE CHAMBERLAYNE
OSHAUGHNESSY
FINNISH MANNINEN RUNEBERG
ARWIDSSON TAVASTSTJERNA
FRENCH NAU AIDE BAIF CHAR FORT
GHIL GRAS KAHN LABE VIAU ARENE
BOREL CARCO DIERX DORAT DUCIS
GACON GREGH GUYAU HARDY
LEGER LOUYS MAROT MURET PERET
PIRON RETTE SCEVE SULLY TASTU
VIGNY AICARD ARAGON ARTAUD
AUGIER AUTRAN BARTAS BELLAY
DERTIN BRETON BRUNET COPPEE
DANIEL DEREME DUPONT ELUARD
FRANCE GUERIN HUGUES JAMMES

LEBRUN MORICE MUSSET PARODI
PRADON RACINE REBOUL RICARD
RICTUS SAMAIN THIARD VALERY
VILLON ANCELOT AUBANEL BARBIER
BOCCAGE BOILEAU BONNARD
BORNIER BOUCHOR BOURGET
BRIZEUX CARRERE CAZALIS CHENIER
CLAUDEL COCTEAU DELTEIL
FEYDEAU GAUTIER GILBERT
GRESSET HENRIOT HEREDIA
JODELLE LAPRADE MATHIEU
MAYNARD MISTRAL MOLINET
PONSARD REGNIER RIMBAUD
RONSARD ROSTAND SCARRON
SEGRAIS VICAIRE VILDRAC AJALBERT
ANDRIEUX BEAUVOIR BERANGER
BERGERAT BERTRAND BOUILHET
CHARTIER CHAULIEU COLLERYE
CORBIERE GRECOURT GRINGORE
LAFORGUE MALHERBE MALLARME
PEROCHON PERRAULT QUILLARD
QUINAULT RABELAIS ROUSSEAU
VERLAINE BELMONTET BOUFFLERS
CHAPELAIN CREBILLON DELAVIGNE
DESCHAMPS LAMARTINE LEMERCIER
MONTREUIL PRUDHOMME
ARLINCOURT BARTHELEMY
BAUDELAIRE BOISROBERT
CHENEDOLLE DESPORITES
MALFILATRE CHANTAVOINE
GRANDMOUGIN DESHOULIERES
GERMAN UZ BAUM BOIE DACH HUCH
KLAJ LENZ RIST VOSS AYRER BOHME
BRANT BUSCH FRANK GLEIM HARDT
HEBEL HEINE HERTZ HOLTY LANGE
LOGAU OPITZ RAABE RILKE SACHS
SORGE STEIN UNRUH WEBER
BECKER BRECHT BROGER BURGER
DEHMEL FOLLEN GEORGE GOETHE
GOTTER GRABBE HAMMER HEBBEL
HERDER HESSUS JORDAN KARSCH
KERNER KLEIST KNEBEL KOBELL
KORNER LEFORT MORIKE MULLER
TIEDGE TOLLER UHLAND ULRICH
WALDIS WEISSE WERNER ALLMERS
BARLACH BARTHEL BOTTGER
BROCKES BUCHNER FONTANE
FORSTER GELLERT HARRIES HENRICI
KALBECK KASTNER KOPSICH
MALTITZ NEUMARK NOVALIS
REDWITZ RUCKERT VISCHER
WALTHER WIELAND BAUMBACH
BIERBAUM BRENTANO CLAUDIUS
ECKSTEIN FLEMMING FREIDANK
GERHARDT GRYPHIUS HAGEDORN
HOFFMANN JUNGHANS KAUFMANN
LISSAUER MAHLMANN OVERBECK
SCHEFFEL SCHILLER SCHUBART
STOLBERG WERNICKE ACIDALIUS
BECHSTEIN BULTHAUPT
HAUPTMANN HOLDERLIN
IMMERMANN KIRCHBACH
KLOPSTOCK MOSENTHAL NIETZSCHE

RODENBERG WILBRANDT
BODENSTEDT CREIZENACH
FASTENRATH HARDENBERG
KOSEGARTEN MATTHISSON
WECKHERLIN FREILIGRATH
KOLBENHEYER SCHNECKENBURGER
GREEK ION BION AGIAS ARION
HOMER ELYTIS ERINNA HESIOD
IBYCUS NONNUS PALLES PIGRES
PINDAR SAPPHO AGATHON ALCAEUS
ARCHIAS BIKELAS CORINNA EUPOLIS
HERODAS ISYLLUS LESCHES
MOSCHUS MUSAEUS PALAMAS
RHIANUS SOLOMOS THESPIS
ANACREON COLUTHUS DIAGORAS
HIPPONAX NICANDER PANYASIS
PHILETAS PISANDER STASINUS
THEOGNIS TYRTAEUS AESCHYLUS
EUPHORION LYCOPHRON SIMONIDES
SOPHOCLES TERPANDER
TIMOTHEUS PARTHENIUS
PHOCYLIDES SEFERIADES
THEOCRITUS ASCLEPIADES
BACCHYLIDES HERMESIANAX
STESICHORUS CHRISTOPOULOS
HINDU BHARTRIHARI
HUNGARIAN ADY TOTH AMADE
ARANY GARAY REVAI SZASZ JOZSEF
MADACH PETOFI BALASSA CZUCZOR
KOLCSEY MAILATH BACSANYI
GYONGYOSI KISFALUDY
VOROSMARTY
ICELANDIC EGILSSON GUNNARSSON
JOCHUMSSON THORODDSEN
HALLGRIMSSON SIGURJONSSON
INDIAN GHOSE OQBAL TAGORE
BILHANA
IRISH FILI BANIM COLUM DAVIS
JOYCE KEANE MOORE TIGHE TYNAN
WILDE WILLS WOLFE YEATS ANSTER
BROOKE CLARKE DARLEY DEVERE
FIGGIS GRAVES HEANEY MAGINN
MANGAN PEARSE SKRINE BARRETT
DRENNAN DUNSANY HIGGINS
MACGILL STARKEY CAMPBELL
FERGUSON FLECKNOE KAVANAGH
LEDWIDGE MCCARTHY STEPHENS
ALLINGHAM LARMINNIE
MACDONAGH
ISRAELI BIALIK
ITALIAN REDI ROSA VIDA ZENO BELLI
BERNI BETTI BONDI BOSSI CASTI
DANTE GUIDI MOLZA MONTI PORTA
PRAGA PRATI PULCI TASSO CIAMPI
GIUSTI GROSSI MAMELI MARINI
PARINI POERIO REVERE ALEARDI
ALFIERI ARIOSTO BERCHET BOIARDO
FOLENGO FRUGONI GUARINI
MANZONI MARRADI MAZZONI
MONTALE PASCOLI ZANELLA
ALAMANNI BACCELLI BIBBIENA
CARDUCCI CHIARINI COSTANZO
FILICAIA GUERRINI LEOPARDI

MARTELLI NENCIONI PETRARCH
RUCELLAI TANSILLO ARNABOLDI
BARBERINI BROFFERIO CALZABIGI
CESAROTTI CHIABRERA MARINETTI
QUASIMODO RAPISARDI ANGIOLIERI
CANNIZZARO FIRENZUOLA
METASTASIO PINDEMONTE
BRACCIOLINI CRESCIMBENI
FORTEGUERRI
JAPANESE BASHO AKAHITO
MASAOKA NOGUCHI
LITHUANIAN MAIRONIS
MEXICAN PAZ
NEW ZEALAND DUGGAN
NICARAGUAN DARIO
NORWEGIAN MOE KRAG IBSEN
AANRUD HANSEN GARBORG
BJORNSON WELHAVEN
PAKISTANI FAIZ
PERSIAN HAFIZ SAADI ANVARI
DAKIKI HATIFI NIZAMI FIRDAUSI
PERUVIAN CHOCANO
POLISH POL ASNYK LANGE POTOCKI
SZUJSKI UJEJSKI WITTLIN ZALESKI
KLONOWIC KRASICKI ZEROMSKI
ZULAWSKI GASZYNSKI KARPINSKI
KRASINSKI BRODZINSKI
DANILOWSKI KONOPNICKA
LOBODOWSKI MALCZEWSKI
MICKIEWICZ SARBIEWSKI
WIERZYNSKI WYSPIANSKI
KOCHANOWSKI LENARTOWICZ
SZYMONOWICZ
PORTUGUESE DEUS MELO QUITA
BOCAGE CAMOES CASTRO
GONZAGA QUENTAL RESENDE
RIBEIRO CASTILHO FERREIRA
JUNQUEIRO PALMEIRIM
NASCIMENTO
ROMAN CATO OVID CINNA LUCAN
VARRO ACCIUS BAVIUS ENNIUS
HORACE LIVIUS VERGIL VIRGIL
AVIENUS MARTIAL NAEVIUS STATIUS
TERENCE AFRANIUS CATULLUS
LUCILIUS SEDULIUS TIBULLUS
VALERIUS LUCRETIUS PROPERTIUS
RUMANIAN BLAGA TZARA
EMINESCU ALEXANDRI ALECSANDRI
THEODORESCU
RUSSIAN FET MEI BELY BLOK BUNIN
BUGAEV ESENIN IVANOV MAIKOV
RYLEEV BALMONT BRYUSOV
GNEDICH GUMILEV KAPNIST
KOLTSOV NIKITIN PUSHKIN
NEKRASOV POLONSKI TYUTCHEV
BESTUZHEV DERZHAVIN KHERASKOV
KHOMYAKOV LERMONTOV
LOMONOSOV PASTERNAK
ZHUKOVSKI BARATYNSKI
BATYUSHKOV EVTUSHENKO
MAYAKOVSKI PLESHCHEEV
BOGDANOVICH VOZNESENSKY
YEVTUSHENKO

SCOTTISH ADAM AIRD GRAY HOGG
LANG MURE THOM AYTON BRUCE
BURNS JACOB LOGAN SCOTT SHARP
SMITH YOUNG AYTOUN DUNBAR
GRAHAM HERVEY LEYDEN MALLET
MICKLE MILLER MURRAY NICOLL
POLLOK RAMSAY SPENCE WILSON
BAILLIE BARBOUR BARCLAY BEATTIE
CLELAND DOUGLAS GRAHAME
KENNEDY LINDSAY MACBETH
PRINGLE TENNANT THOMSON
ANDERSON CAMPBELL COCKBURN
DAVIDSON DRUMMOND HAMILTON
HENRYSON MACNEILL MAITLAND
ALEXANDER BELLENDEN
BLACKLOCK FERGUSSON GILFILLAN
MACDONALD STEVENSON
BALLANTINE CUNNINGHAM
MACDIARMID MOTHERWELL
MONTGOMERIE
SOUTH AFRICAN BREYTENBACH
LANGENHOVEN
SPANISH CRUZ MENA RUIZ VEGA
DURAN LORCA RIOJA CANETE
CETINA ESPRIU GARCIA VIRUES
ALCAZAR BECQUER GALLEGO
GONGORA HERRERA IRIARTE
JIMENEZ MORATIN SALINAS
AGUILERA BALBUENA CORONADO
FIGUEROA MANRIQUE VILLEGAS
CERVANTES ALEIXANDRE
CASTILLEJO CIENFUEGOS
ESPRONCEDA SANTILLANA
VILLAMEDIANA
SWEDISH DALIN BESKOW CREUTZ
LIDNER TEGNER WALLIN DALGREN
EKELUND LEOPOLD RYDBERG
SJOWALL ATTERBOM BELLMANN
BORJESON BOTTIGER BRINKMAN
KELLGREN LAGERLOF LENNGREN
LEVERTIN NICANDER ADLERBETH
KARLFELDT MARTINSON MESSENIUS
FAHLCRANTZ LAGERKVIST
STAGNELIUS STRANDBERG
WENNERBERG OXENSTIERNA
SWISS ILG AMIEL FAESI MEYER
BODMER GESSNER LAVATER
FROHLICH LEUTHOLD SPITTELER
SYRIAN GIBRAN
TURKISH NABI FUZULI
URUGUAYAN FIGUEROA
WELSH DAVID HUGHES SYMONS
THOMAS VAUGHAN WILLIAMS
YUGOSLAVIAN POPA
POETASTER BARDET BAVIAN
BAVIUS POETITO BARDLING
VERSEMAN SONNETEER
POETIC ODIC LYRIC STILTED
PEGASEAN POEMATIC
POETICAL (NOT —) PROSE
POETRY EPOS SONG BLANK MELIC
POEMS VERSE EPOPEE POESIS
SONIOU DOGGREL KALEVALA

(FINNISH —) RUNES
(GOD OF —) BRAGI
(HEROIC —) EPOS
(KIND OF —) CONCRETE
(MUSE OF —) ERATO THALIA
EUTERPE CALLIOPE
(PASSAGE OF —) MORCEAU
POGGE BULLHEAD
POGROM RIOT PILLAGE MASSACRE
POGY POGIE MENHADEN
POI (— INGREDIENT) TARO
POIGNANT APT HOME KEEN ACUTE
SHARP SMART BITING BITTER
MOVING SEVERE URGENT CUTTING
INTENSE POINTED PUNGENT SATIRIC
INCISIVE PIERCING PRESSING
STINGING STRIKING TOUCHING
AMAREVOLE
POINCIANA DELONIX FLAMBEAU
GULMOHAR FLAMBOYER
POINSETTIA BANNER FIREFLOWER
POINT AIM DOT JOT NAK NEB NIB
NUB PEG PIN RES WAY APEX BACK
BOKE CHAT CUSP FORK GAFF GAME
GOOD HEAD HOLD ITEM KNOT LACE
LOOK NAIL PEAK PICK PILE PINT
SPOT STOP WHET BEARD CHALK
DIGIT FOCUS INDEX LEVEL MUCRO
PITCH PRICK PUNCH PUNCT PUNTA
PUNTC REFER STAND TEACH THING
TOOTH ALLUDE BROACH CRAYON
CUSPIS CUTOFF DEGREE DIRECT
FLECHE JUGALE MATTER NOSING
PERIOD THESIS TITTLE VERTEX
ZYGION APICULA ARTICLE BENEFIT
CACUMEN CRUNODE ESSENCE
GATEWAY PUNCTUM PUSHPIN
SHARPEN TANJONG TRAGION
ANNOUNCE PUNCTULE STRIPPER
PARTICULAR
(— AIMED AT) SCOPE
(— AT ISSUE) BEEF CRUX
(— AT WHICH LEAF SPRINGS) AXIL
(— BEHIND EAR) ASTERION
(— FOR PHONOGRAPH RECORD)
STYLE
(— IN CAPSTAN) STRIPPER
(— IN CONSONANT) DAGHESH
(— IN DEBATE) ISSUE
(— IN GAME) SHY
(— IN ORBIT OF PLANET) AUGE APSIS
APOGEE SYZYGY APOJOVE PERIGEE
APASTRON APHELION
(— IN ORBIT OF SPACECRAFT)
PERILUNE
(— IN QUESTION) ISSUE
(— IN SEVEN-UP) GIFT
(— IN SOME GAMES) PUNT
(— NEAREST EARTH) PERIGEE
(— OF A BORDER) VANDYKE
(— OF ANCHOR) BILL
(— OF ANTLER) PRONG
(— OF ANVIL) HORN

(— OF CELESTIAL SPHERE) ANTAPEX
(— OF CHIN) BUTTON
(— OF CONTACT) EPHAPSE
(— OF CRESCENT MOON) CUSP
(— OF CURVE) SPINODE
(— OF CUTTING) STYLE
(— OF DECLINE) EBB
(— OF DEVELOPMENT) STAGE
(— OF DIVERGENCE) AXIL
(— OF ECLIPTIC) LAGNA SOLSTICE
(— OF ENERGY) CHAKRA
(— OF EPIGRAM) STING
(— OF FAITH) ARTICLE
(— OF HONOR) PUNDONOR
(— OF INTEREST) CLOU
(— OF INTERSECTION) FOOT
STAURION
(— OF JAVELIN) SAGAIE
(— OF JUNCTION) MEET BREGMA
LAMBDA
(— OF LABEL) LAMBEAU
(— OF LACE) TAG
(— OF LAND) ODD CAPE SPIT MORRO
HEADLAND
(— OF LEAF) MUCRO
(— OF LIFE) HYLEG
(— OF LIGHT) GLINT SPANGLE
(— OF LIGHTNING ROD) AIGRETTE
(— OF LIPS) CHEILION
(— OF MANGO) NAK
(— OF ONSET) BRINK
(— OF ORIGIN) HIVE SOURCE
FOUNTAIN
(— OF PEN) NEB NIB
(— OF PETAL) LACINULA
(— OF REFERENCE) STYLION
(— OF ROCK) NUNATAK
(— OF STAG'S HORN) START
(— OF STORY) KNOT
(— OF STYLUS) CUTTER
(— OF SUPPORT) BEARING
(— OF TEMPERATURE) SOLIDUS
(— OF TIME) DATE INSTANT
JUNCTURE
(— OF TOOTH) CUSP
(— OF UMBRELLA) FERRULE
(— OF VIEW) EYE ANGLE FRONT
SLANT COLORS CORNER GROUND
RESPECT FUTURISM
(— OF VIOLIN BOW) HEAD
(— OF WEAPON) ORD BARB
(— ON AUGER OR BIT) SPUR
(— ON BACKGAMMON BOARD)
FLECHE
(— ON BILLIARD TABLE) SPOT
(— ON CURVE) TACNODE
(— ON JAW) GONION
(— ON STAG'S HORN) BROACH
(— ON SUNDIAL) NODE
(— OUT) SHOW DIGIT INFER ASSIGN
DIRECT ENSIGN FINGER MUSTER
NOTIFY REMARK PRESAGE INDICATE
(APPROPRIATE —) PLACE

(ASTROLOGICAL —) INGRESS DESCENDANT
(AT THAT —) THEN THERE
(BARBED —) FORK
(BLUNT —) MORNETTE
(CARBON —) CRAYON
(CARDINAL —) EAST WEST HINGE NORTH SOUTH
(CARDINAL —S) CARDINES
(CENTRAL —) OMPHALOS
(CHIEF —S) SUM
(CHRONOLOGICAL —) ERA EPOCH
(COMPASS —) E N S W NE NW SE SW ENE ESE NNE NNW SSE SSW WNW WSW AIRT AIRTH RHUMB COURSE
(CRITICAL —) JUMP
(CROWNING —) CAPSHEAF CAPSTONE
(CRUCIAL —) CRUX
(CULMINATING —) HEAD COMBLE
(DOUBLE — OF CURVE) ACNODE CRUNODE
(END —) TERMINUS
(ESSENTIAL —) MAIN
(EXACT —) TEE
(EXCESS —S) LAP
(EXCLAMATION —) BANG SCREAMER
(EXTREME —) END
(FARTHEST —) APOGEE SOLSTICE
(FINAL —) UPCOME
(FIXED —) ABUTMENT
(GET THE —) SEE
(GLAZIER'S —) SPRIG
(HALFWAY — IN CRIBBAGE) CORNER
(HEBREW —) SHEVA
(HIGHEST —) TIP ACME APEX AUGE NOON PEAK CREST FLOOD APOGEE CLIMAX CULMEN HEIGHT PERIOD SUMMIT VERTEX ZENITH EVEREST MAXIMUM MERIDIAN SOLSTICE
(HIGHEST SAFE —) REDLINE
(KNOTTY —) CRUX NODUS
(LAST —) END
(LATERAL —) ALARE
(LOW —) TROUGH
(LOWEST —) NADIR BOTTOM BEDROCK
(LOWEST — OF HULL) BILGE
(MAIN —) JET SUM GIST
(MEDIAN —) HORMION
(NICE —) PUNCTILIO
(NO —S) LOVE
(ONE'S STRONG —) FORTE
(PEDAL —) DRONE
(PIVOTAL —) KNUCKLE
(PRECISE —) NICK
(PROJECTING —) CRAG PEAK BEARD
(SELLING —) HOOK
(SHARP —) JAG PRICK PRICKLE
(SIGNIFICANT —) MILESTONE
(SINGLE —) ACE
(SKULL —) TYLION
(SORE —) NERVE

(STARTING —) BASE ORIGIN SCRATCH
(STATIONARY —) SPINODE
(STRIKING —) SALIENCE
(STRONG —) FORTE
(TAPERING —) ACUMEN
(TENNIS —) LET CHASE BISQUE
(TENTH OF —) MOMENT
(TERMINAL —) GOAL BOURN BREAK AIRPORT
(TOP —) TUFT
(TO THE —) BLUNT COGENT
(TURNING —) CARDO EPOCH CRISIS
(UNIPLANAR —) UNODE
(UTMOST —) EXTREME SUBLIME
(VANTAGE —) TOWER
(VOWEL —) SERE SEGOL SEGHOL
(WEAK —) BLOT
(PREF.) KENTRO MUCRONI PUNCTATO PUNCTI PUNCTO STIGMATI STIGMEO STIGMO

POINT-BLANK BLUNT PLAIN POINT DIRECT WHOLLY EXPRESS DIRECTLY

POINT COUNTER POINT (AUTHOR OF —) HUXLEY
(CHARACTER IN —) JOHN LUCY MARK BURLAP ELINOR GILRAY PHILIP RACHEL SIDNEY WALTER WEBLEY BIDLAKE CARLING EVERARD QUARLES RAMPION BEATRICE MARJORIE SPRANDRELL TANTAMOUNT

POINTED SET ERDE HOME ACUTE EXACT FIXED PEAKY PIKED TANGY TERSE ACUATE FITCHE LIVELY OXEOTE PEAKED PECKED PICKED SPIRED ANGULAR FITCHEE LACONIC PRECISE SPICATE ZESTFUL ACICULAR ACULEATE COPATAIN CULTRATE DIACTINE PUNCTUAL STELLATE ACUMINATE
(PREF.) OXY

POINTEDNESS BARB

POINTER TIP YAD COCK HAND WAND ARROW DUBHE INDEX POINT FESCUE FINGER GUNDOG INDICE SILKER STYLUS FLUSHER INDICANT SIGNITOR
(— IN GREAT BEAR) DUBHE DUBBHE
(— ON ASTROLABE) ALMURY
(— ON GAUGE) ARM
(BUILDER'S —) RAKER
(TEACHER'S —) FESCUE
(PL.) MEN GUARDS YADAYIM

POINTLESS DRY ILL DULL FLAT INANE SILLY VAPID FRIGID STUPID INSIPID WITLESS MUTICOUS

POINTSMAN TRAPPER LATCHMAN SWITCHMAN

POISE PEE CALM HEAD REST SWAY TACT BRACE PEIZE APLOMB OFFSET PONDER BALANCE BEARING DIGNITY

OPPRESS POISURE DELIVERY
EASINESS SERENITY
(— RECIPROCAL) RHE
POISED SET FACILE HOVERING
NERVELESS
(BE —) LIBRATE
POISER HALTER
POISON FIG GAS BANE BIKH DRAB
DRUG GALL TUBA VERY ATTER TAINT
TOXIN VENOM VIRUS ANTIAR
DERRIS INFECT RANKLE TOXIFY
TOXOID ACONITE BABASCO
CORRUPT ENVENOM FLYBANE
MINERAL PERVERT PHALLIN
TANGHIN VITIATE ACQUETTA
DELETERY RATSBANE VENENATE
SAXITOXIN
(— IN DEATH CUP) PHALLIN
(ARROW —) HAYA INEE URALI URARE
URARI ANTIAR ANTJAR CURARE
CURARI DERRIS OURARI OUABAIN
(FISH —) AKIA CUBE TIMBO DERRIS
HAIARI BABASCO BARBASCO
(RAT —) ANTU
(VIRULENT —) BIKH TANGHIN
(PREF.) PHARMACO VENENI VENENO
VIRU
POISONED BUCKEYED TOXICATE
VENENATE VENOMOUS
POISONER SEPSIN CANIDIA VENEFIC
VENOMER
POISON HEMLOCK BUNK CICUTA
POISONING PYEMIA UREMIA
ARGYRIA GASSING JIMMIES
BOTULISM MYCETISM PLUMBISM
CROTALISM FLUOROSIS ICHTHYISM
LATHYRISM SATURNISM SELENOSIS
INTOXICATION
(ANTIMONY —) STIBIALISM
(LEAD —) SATURNISM
POISON IVY CLIMATH MARKERY
MERCURY MARKWEED
POISON OAK YEARA
POISONOUS ATTRY TOXIC ATTERY
VENENE VIROSE VIROUS BANEFUL
NOISOME NOXIOUS DELETERY
MEPHITIC TOXICANT VENENATE
VENOMOUS VIRULENT MALIGNANT
(PREF.) TOX(I)(IC)(ICO)(O)
POISON SUMAC BURTREE
DOGWOOD
POISON TOBACCO HENBANE
POISONWOOD BUMWOOD
POITREL ARMOR PECTRON
POKE BAG DAB DIG DUB HIT JAB JOG
PUG PUR TIG WAD BROD PAUT PORR
PROD PROG RAUK RUCK SACK SOCK
STAB STIR NIDGE POACH PROKE
PROTE PUNCH ROUSE STEER STOKE
COWBOY DAWDLE INCITE PIERCE
POCKET POUNCE POUTER PUGGLE
PUTTER WALLET PRODDLE

(— ABOUT) ROKE ROUT RUMMAGE
(— AROUND) ROOT SCROUNGE
(— FUN) COD
(— LIGHTLY) POTTER PUTTER
(— WITH FOOT) SCUFF
(— WITH NOSE) SNUZZLE
POKE-IN STRANDER
POKELOKEN BOGAN LOGAN
POKER DART DRAW FLIP POIT PORR
POTE STUD BLUFF BOGIE CURATE
GOBLIN STOKER ACEPOTS FRUGGAN
LOWBALL PASSOUT POCHARD
SHOTGUN BASEBALL COALRAKE
JACKPOTS MISTIGRI SHOWDOWN
(— ACTION) RAISE
(— CHIP) JETON JETTON
(— HAND) RUNT FLUSH SKEET
KILTER PELTER STRAIGHT
(— PLANT) TRITOMA
(FORM OF —) DRAW STUD
(HOT —) SALAMANDER
POKEWEED POKE POCAN SCOKE
COAKUM GARGET FOXGLOVE
INKBERRY REDBERRY
POKEY STIR
POKY DEAD DULL JAIL SLOW DOWDY
POKEY POKING SHABBY STODGY
STUFFY STUPID CRAMPED TEDIOUS
POLAK BALSA POLLAC

POLAND		
CAPITAL: WARSAW		
COIN: DUCAT GROSZ MARKA ZLOTY		
FENNIG HALERZ KORONA		
DANCE: POLKA MAZURKA		
KRAKOWIAK POLONAISE		
GENTRY: SZLACHTA		
LAKE: GOPLO MAMRY SNIARDWY		
MEASURE: CAL MILA MORG PRET		
LINJA SAZEN STOPA VLOKA WLOKA		
CWIERK KORZEC KWARTA LOKIEC		
GARNIEC		
MOUNTAIN: RYSY TATRA SUDETEN		
NAME: POLONIA SARMATIA		
NATIVE: SLAV MARUR SILESIAN		
PARLIAMENT: SEJM SEYM SENAT		
PROVINCE: OPOLE KIELCE		
RIVER: BUG SAN ALLE BRDA GWDA		
LYNA NYSA ODER STYR BIALA		
BZURA DRANA DWINA NOTEC		
SERTE WARTA WISTA NEISSE		
NIEMEN PILICA PRIPET PROSNA		
STRYPA WIEPRZ VISTULA WISTOKA		
DNIESTER		
TITLE OF ADDRESS: PAN PANI PANIE		
TOWN: LWO KOLO LIDA LODZ LVOV		
OELS BREST BYTOM CHELM POSEN		
RADOM SRODA TORUN VILNA		
GDAKNSK GDYNIA GRODNO		
KRACOW KRAKOW LUBLIN POZNAN		
TARNOW WARSAW ZABRZE		
BEUTHEN BRESLAU CHORZOW		

GARDCIN GLIWICE LEMBERG
LITOUSK WROCLAW GLEIWITZ
KATOWICE SZCZECIN TARNOPOL
WEIGHT: LUT FUNT UNCYA KAMIAN
CENTNER SKRUPUL

POLAR ARCTIC EMANANT PIVOTAL
DIRECTRIX
POLARIS ALRUCABA
POLARITY (WITHOUT —) ASTATIC
POLE BAR LAT LEG LUG POL POY ROD
SKY XAT BEAM BIND BROG COPE
FALL HOOK KENT MAST NEAP PALO
PERK PIKE PROP SKID SPAR TREE
UFER CABER FOCUS MASUR MAZUR
PERCH QUANT REACH SHAFT SPEAR
SPOKE STAFF STANG STILT STING
STODE SWAPE SWIPE BEACON
BORITY CROTCH FLOWER IMPOSE
JUFFER KILHIG RICKER RISSLE
RYPECK SPONGE STOWER TONGUE
BARLING HEAVENS TOWMAST
ALESTAKE FLAGPOLE FOOTPICK
POLANDER STANDARD
(— AS EMBLEM OF SOVEREIGNTY)
KAHILI
(— AS HOLDFAST FOR BOATS)
RYPECK
(— FOR BEARING COFFIN) SPOKE
(— FOR PROPELLING BOAT) POY
(— FOR TOSSING) CABER KEBAR
(— HOLDING SAIL) BOOM MAST
SPRIT
(— MARKING SAND DUNE) BALIZE
(— OF TIMBER WAGON) NIB
JANKER
(— OF VEHICLE) NEAP
(— ON TWO WHEELS) JANKER
(— SEPARATING HORSES) BAIL
(—S LIVING OUTSIDE POLAND)
POLONIA
(— USED AS SIGN) ALEPOLE
ALESTAKE
(— WITH BIRD DECOY) STOOL
(BOAT —) SPRIT
(CARRIAGE —) NIB BEAM
(COUPLING —) REACH
(FIR —) UFER UPHER JUFFER
(FISHING —) WAND
(FORKED —) CROTCH
(LOGGING —) JANKER KILHIG
KILLIG
(LONG —) PEW
(MANGROVE —) BORITY
(MINE —S) LAGGING
(NEGATIVE —) CATHODE
(PUNT —) QUANT STOWER
(RANGE —) FLAG
(SACRED —) ASHERAH
(SHEPHERD'S —) KENT
(SPRINGY —) BINDER
(STABLE —) BAIL

(STOUT —) KILHIG RICKER
(WATER-RAISING —) SWEEP
POLEAX STAFF POLEARM
POLECAT FITCH SKUNK ZORIL
FERRET FICHAT WEASEL FOUMART
FOULMART PERWITSKY SARMATIER
(— PELT) FITCH
POLE FLOUNDER SOLE
POLEHEAD TADPOLE
POLESTAR STAR GUIDE POLARIS
LODESTAR
POLICE MAN FUZZ HEAT GUARD
WATCH GOVERN CONTROL JEMADAR
OCHRANA POLIZEI PROTECT
TOXOTAE OPRICHNIK
(— CAR) PANDACAR
(— FINDING) MO
(— OFFICER) ROZZER
(— STATION) NICK
(SECRET —) CHEKA
POLICEMAN COP JOE KID NAB PIG
BOGY BULL FLIC FUZZ GRAB JACK
JOHN PEON SI OP TRAP ZARP
BOBBY BOGEY BULKY BURLY GAZER
PEACE RURAL SCREW SEPOY
ASKARI BADGER BOBBIE COPPER
FISCAL FLATTY HARMAN JOHNNY
PEELER REDCAP ROZZER RUNNER
SHAMUS SMOKEY CRUSHER
FOOTMAN GHAFFIR GUMSHOE
JEMADAR OFFICER SHOOFLY
TROOPER ZAPTIAH ZAPTIEH
BARGELLO BLUECOAT DOGBERRY
FLATFOOT GENDARME MINISTER
PATROLMAN
(CANADIAN —) MOUNTY MOUNTIE
(CLUB OF —) BILLY STAFF
SPONTOON TRUNCHEON
(MILITARY —) REDCAP SNOWDROP
(MOUNTED —) SOWAR
(PL.) FINEST
POLICE STATION THANA
BARGELLO KOTWALEE
POLICY WIT DEAL FRONT ORDER
GOVERN NUMBER TICKET WISDOM
AUTARKY COUNSEL CUNNING
FLOATER LEFTISM LOTTERY TONTINE
VOUCHER ACTIVISM ARTIFICE
SAGACITY STATEWAY PLURALISM
(CHOSEN —) COURSE
(SOVIET — OF DISCUSSION)
GLASNOST
(PL.) APRISMO
POLISH BOB LAP MOP RUB RUD BUFF
DUCO FILE POLE CLEAN COUTH
FRUSH GLAZE GLOSS GRACE RABAT
ROUND SHINE SLICK STONE AFFILE
BARREL LUSTER PUNISH REFINE
RUMBLE SHAMMY SLIGHT SMOOTH
STREAK BEESWAX BURNISH
CHAMOIS FURBISH LACQUER
PERFECT PLANISH VARNISH

ELEGANCE LEVIGATE SIMONIZE
URBANIZE SARMATIAN
(— WITH WAX) SIMONIZE
(FINGERNAIL —) ENAMEL
POLISHED FINE COMPT COUTH
ROUND SHINY SLICK TERSE BUFFED
FACETE GLOSSY INLAND POLITE
SMOOTH ELEGANT GALLANT
GENTEEL POLITIC REFINED
CULTURED
(NOT —) BLIND
POLISHER EMERY BUFFER GLAZER
WAGWAG WIGWAG DOLLIER
GLOSSER LAPIDARY SMOOTHER
POLISHING SANDING FROTTAGE
LIMATION
(— MATERIAL) RABAT
POLITE NEAT TIDY TRIM BLAND CIVIL
SUAVE GENTLE HUMANE SMOOTH
URBANE COURTLY GALLANT
GENTEEL DELICATE DISCREET
LUSTROUS ATTENTIVE COURTEOUS
POLITENESS FINISH TASHRIF
CIVILITY COURTESY ELEGANCE
URBANITY GENTILITY
POLITES (FATHER OF —) PRIAM
(MOTHER OF —) HECUBA
POLITIC WARY WISE SUAVE ARTFUL
CRAFTY CUNNING TACTFUL
DISCREET PROVIDENT
POLITICAL (— ASSN.) VEREIN
(— PARTY) GOP TORY WHIG LABOR
POLITICIAN BOSS STATIST
WARWICK PIPELAYER STATESMAN
POLITY SERFISM
POLIXENES (SON OF —) FLORIZEL
POLL COW DOD NOT POW ROB CHUB
COLL DODD HEAD NAPE NOTT PASH
CROWN SKULL STRIP CENSUS
FLEECE PARROT CANVASS DESPOIL
PILLAGE PLUNDER POLLARD
(KIND OF —) EXIT
POLLACK LOB GADE LAIT GADID
LYTHE BILLET LAITHE SAITHE
BADDOCK SILLOCK WALLEYE
BLUEFISH COALFISH GRAYFISH
LORICATE MOULRUSH
POLLARD CHU COW DOD BRAN POLL
STAG SHEEP CHEVAN DODDLE
DOTARD BOLLING LOPPARD
WOODSERE
POLLARD TREE DOTARD RUNNEL
POLLED NOT NOTT POLEY
HORNLESS
POLLEN DUST MEAL FLOUR FARINA
POWDER BEEBREAD
(— BEARER) ANTHER
(— BRUSH) SCOPA
(— TUBE) SPERMARY
POLLER VOTER BARBER POLLSTER
POLLEX THUMB
POLLINATE SELF FECUNDATE
FECUNDIZE FERTILIZE

POLLINATING SIBBING
POLLIWOG TADPOLE
POLLOCK PODLER
POLLSTER HEADCOUNTER
POLLUTE FOIL FOUL SOIL BLEND
DIRTY SMEAR TAINT BEFOUL DEFILE
INFECT MUDDLE RAVISH ADULTER
DEBAUCH PROFANE SLOTTER
VIOLATE CONTAMINATE
POLLUTED FOUL DRUNK TURBID
CORRUPT
POLLUTING FILTHY
POLLUTION STAIN SULLAGE
FOULNESS IMPURITY
POLLUX POL HERCULES
(BROTHER OF —) CASTOR
(MOTHER OF —) LEDA
POLO (PERIOD IN —) CHUKKER
POLONAISE POLACCA FACKELTANZ
POLONIUS CORAMBIS
(DAUGHTER OF —) OPHELIA
(SON OF —) LAERTES
POLT BLOW THUMP STROKE
POLTERGEIST GHOST SPIRIT
POLTROON IDLER COWARD CRAVEN
WRETCH DASTARD COWARDLY
SLUGGARD
POLUTANT PCB
POLYA RNA
POLYANDRIUM CEMETERY
POLYBUS (FATHER OF —) ANTENOR
(MOTHER OF —) THEANO
(WIFE OF —) MEROPE PERIBOEA
POLYDAMAS (BROTHER OF —)
EUPHORBUS HYPERENOR
(COMPANION OF —) HECTOR
(FATHER OF —) PANTHOUS
(MOTHER OF —) PHRONTIS
POLYDORE (BROTHER OF —)
CASTALIO
POLYDORUS (FATHER OF —) PRIAM
CADMUS HIPPOMEDON
(MOTHER OF —) HECUBA HARMONIA
(SLAYER OF —) POLYMNESTOR
(SON OF —) LABDACUS
(WIFE OF —) NYCTEIS
POLYESTER (— BRAND) DACRON
POLYGALA GAYWINGS
POLYGON DECAGON HEXAGON
NONAGON HEPTAGON PENTAGON
CHILIAGON MULTANGLE
POLYGRAPH KEELER
POLYHEDRON BEAD PRISM
PRISMATOID
POLYMER DIMER HYDROL MANNAN
MUREIN HEXAMER OLIGOMER
(— UNIT) MER

POLYNESIA
CHESTNUT: RATA
IMAGE: TIKI
ISLAND: COOK LINE SAMOA TONGA
EASTER ELLICE PHOENIX

ISLE: MOTU
KING: ALI ARII ARIKI
LANGUAGE: UVEA TAGALOG
MOUND: AHU
NATIVE: ATI MAORI KANAKA NIVEAN
  TONGAN NESOGAEAN
PRINCIPLE: TIKI
WOMAN: WAHINE

POLYNESIAN MAORI KANAKA
TONGAN FUTUNAN
POLYNICES (BROTHER OF —)
ETEOCLES
(FATHER OF —) OEDIPUS
(MOTHER OF —) JOCASTA
(WIFE OF —) ARGIA
POLYNOMIAL CUBIC
POLYP CORAL HYDRA TUMOR ZOOID
ISOPOD HYDRULA OCTOPOD
POLYPARY ZOARIUM
POLYPHONY ORGANUM FABURDEN
COUNTERPOINT
POLYPIDOM CORMUS
POLYSACCHARIDE LEVAN GELOSE
GLUCAN GLYCAN INULIN IRISIN
MANNAN AMYLOSE DEXTRAN
FUCOSAN HEXOSAN POLYOSE
GALACTAN GLYCOGEN LICHENIN
SECALOSE SINISTRIN
POLYTYPE CAST
POLYXENA (FATHER OF —) PRIAM
(MOTHER OF —) HECUBA
POLYZOAN POLYP CESTODE
RADIATE
POMACE MUST RAPE POMMY
STOCK STOSH CHEESE
POMADE CIDER POMATUM LIPSTICK
OINTMENT
POMANDER CASE POUNCET
POMATO TOPATO
POME BALL APPLE GLOBE
JUNEBERRY
POMEGRANATE GRENAT GRENADE
BALAUSTA
POMELO SHADDOCK GRAPEFRUIT
POMERANIA (CAPITAL OF —)
STETTIN
(CITY IN —) THORN TORUN ANKLAM
(ISLAND IN —) RUGEN USEDOM
(PROVINCE IN —) POMORZE
POMFRET BULLY HENFISH
POMME DE TERRE POTATO
POMMEL BOB FIB NOB BEAT HORN
KNOB PAIK PAKE TORE NEVEL
BRUISE BUFFET CRUTCH FINIAL
PLUMMET
POMP BRAG FARE WEAL BOAST
PRIDE STATE ESTATE PAMPER
PARADE RIALTY SCHEME SPRUNK
BOBANCE DISPLAY PAGEANT
PANOPLY SPLURGE CEREMONY
EQUIPAGE GRANDEUR SEMBLANT
SPLENDOR

POMPANO DART JUREL ALLICE
CARANX PERMIT ALEWIFE COBBLER
OLDWIFE CARANGID MACKEREL
(— CLAM) COQUINA
POMPOSITY TUMOR TUMOUR
BIGHEAD BIGNESS BOMBAST
POMPOUS BIG BUG BUDGE JELLY
LARGE SHOWY TUMID WIGGY
ASTRUT AUGUST TURGID BLOATED
BOMBAST FUSTIAN OROTUND
STILTED SWOLLEN TURGENT
BEWIGGED INFLATED MAGNIFIC
SWELLING TOPLOFTY IMPORTANT
PONTIFICAL PORTENTOUS
PONCEAU GRANAT
PONCHO MANGA RUANA
POND (ALSO SEE POOL) LAY LUM
DELF DIKE MOAT PULK SLEW STEW
TANK VLEI VLEY CANAL DECOY
DELFT LACHE LETCH STANK WAYER
CLAIRE LAGOON LAGUNA LAGUNE
LOCHAN PUDDLE SALINA SLOUGH
SPLASH STAGNE MULLETRY
(— DRY IN SUMMER) TURLOUGH
(— FOR OYSTERS) CLAIRE ·
(— MAN) JACKER
(ARTIFICIAL —) AQUARIUM
(DIRTY —) SOAL
(FISH —) VIVER GURGES PISCINA
(FISH STORING —) STEW
(SMALL —) KHAI
(STAGNANT —) DUB
(PREF.) LACO LIMN(I)(O)
PONDER CON CAST CHAW MUSE
PORE ROLL TURN BROOD STUDY
VOLVE WEIGH ADVISE EXPEND
REASON RECORD REMORD BALANCE
COMPASS EXAMINE IMAGINE
PERPEND REFLECT REVERIE REVOLVE
APPRAISE COGITATE CONSIDER
MEDITATE
PONDERABILITY WEIGHT
GRAVITY
PONDEROUS DULL SLOW BULKY
GRAVE HEAVY SOGGY AWKWARD
WEIGHTY UNWIELDY IMPORTANT
PONDEROUSNESS HEFT
POND HEN COOT
PONDMAN JACKER
PONDOKKIE HUT HOVEL
PONE CAKE LUMP WRIT PAUNE
PUDDING SWELLING
PONGEE PAUNCHE SHANTUNG
PONGID APE
PONIARD STAB BODKIN DAGGER
STYLET POINADO
PONOCRATES
(PUPIL OF —) GARGANTUA
PONT FERRY FLOAT BRIDGE
FERRYBOAT
PONTIANAC JELUTONG
PONTIC DUMMY
PONTICELLO BREAK MAGAS

PONTIFF POPE BISHOP PRIEST
PONTIFEX
PONTIFICAL AARONIC
PONTIL PUNTY
PONTOON FLOAT RHINO BRIDGE
PONY CAB RAW TAT CAVY TROT
YABU BIDET DALES GRIFF PAINT
PINTO POWNY TACKY TRICK WELCH
WELSH BASUTO BHUTIA BRONCO
CAYUSE EXMOOR GARRAN SHELTY
TANGUN TATTOO ENGLISH HACKNEY
MANIPUR MUSTANG SHELTIE
FORESTER GALLOWAY SHETLAND
(— NEW TO RACING) GRYFON
GRIFFIN GRIFFON GRYPHON
(STUDENT'S —) CRIB TROT BICYCLE
(USE A —) CRIB
(PL.) DALES
POODLE SHOCK BARBET
POOH TUSH POWWAW
POOK HEAP PICK PULL PLUCK STACK
POOKA PUCK GOBLIN SPECTER
POOL (ALSO SEE POND) CAR DIB DUB
LAY LUM PIT POL POT POW BANK
BOOK CARR DIKE DUMP FARM FLOW
JHIL LAKE LIDO LINN LLYN LUMB
MERE PANT PEEL PLUD POLK POND
PULE PULK RING SINK SLEW SOIL
SWAG TANK TARN WEEL BAYOU
BOWLY DECOY FLASH FLUSH FRESH
JHEEL KITTY LETCH LOUGH MEARE
PLASH PLUMB SLACK STANK STELL
STILL THERM TRUNK CARTEL
CHARCO FLODGE LAGOON LASHER
PLUNGE PUDDLE SILOAM SPLASH
STABLE CARLINE CATHOLE CUSHION
JACKPOT PLASHET SNOOKER
STAGNUM INTERLOT QUINIELA
(— AT JERUSALEM) BETHESDA
(— BELOW WATERFALL) LIN LINN
LLYN
(— IN BOG) HAG HAGG
(— OF MONEY) KITTY
(— WITHOUT OUTLET) STAGNUM
(— WITH SALMON NETS) STELL
(ARTIFICIAL —) CUSHION
(AUCTION —) CALCUTTA
(BATHING —) JACUZZI
(BETTING —) EXACTA PERFECTA
TRIFECTA
(DIRTY —) SUMP
(FISH —) TRUNK STEWPOND
(MEMBER OF —) STENO
(MOUNTAIN —) TARN
(MUDDY —) LETCH
(SWIMMING —) BATH LIDO PISCINA
NATATORIUM
(PREF.) LIMN(I)(O) STAGNI
POON DILO PEON PUNA DOMBA
KEENA TAMANU SIRPOON
MASTWOOD
POONGHIE RAHAN PRIEST PUNGYI
PHONGHI TALAPOIN

POOP DOCK FIRE GULP TOOT CHEAT
COZEN STERN BEFOOL ISLAND
DECEIVE EXHAUST HINDDECK
OVERCOME
POOR BAD OFF SAD BASE EVIL FOUL
LEAN LEWD PUNK SICK SOUR THIN
DINKY EXILE FOOTY GROSS JERRY
KETTY SCALY SEELY SILLY SOBER
SORRY UNORN FEEBLE HUMBLE
HUNGRY LEADEN MEAGER MEAGRE
MEASLY PILLED PORAIL PRETTY
SCANTY SHABBY STREET SUBPAR
CODFISH HAPLESS NAUGHTY
SCRAWNY SCRUBBY SQUALID
TRIVIAL UNLUCKY INDIGENT
ORDINARY PRECIOUS SCRANNEL
SNEAKING TERRIBLE UNTHENDE
PENNILESS PENURIOUS
(— BOY) HERO
(— MAN) PAUPER
(PREF.) MAL(E) PTOCHO
POORHOUSE MEASONDUE
POORLY ILL BADLY SADLY BARELY
FEEBLY SIMPLY SLIGHT SHABBILY
(PREF.) DYS
POOR SOLDIER FRIARBIRD
POORTITH POVERTY
POOR WHITE (AUTHOR OF —)
ANDERSON
(CHARACTER IN —) JIM JOE TOM
HUGH CLARA MCVEY SARAH STEVE
HUNTER SHEPARD WAINSWORTH
BUTTERWORTH
POP GO DOT GUN HIT TRY BLOW
DART HOCK JUMP PAWN SODA
BREAK CLOOP CRACK KNOCK SHOOT
ATTACK EFFORT FATHER POPPER
STROKE THRUSH ASSAULT ATTEMPT
CONCERT EXPLODE INSTANT
REDWING BACKFIRE SUDDENLY
POPDOCK FOXGLOVE
POPE LEO JOHN PAPA PAPE PAUL
PIUS RUFF CAIUS FELIX GAIUS PETER
URBAN ADRIAN BISHOP CLETUS
EUGENE JULIAN LUCIUS PUFFIN
SHRIKE SIXTUS VICTOR CLEMENS
GREGORY HADRIAN BENEDICT
BONIFACE INNOCENT PONTIFEX
FISHERMAN
(SPECIFIC —) LEO PAUL PIUS URBAN
GREGORY
(PREF.) PAPI PAPO POPO
POPERY POPEISM PAPISTRY
POPE'S-EYE NUT NOIX
POPGUN SCOOT PENGUN POTGUN
PLUFFER
POPINJAY PARROT PAPINGO
POPLAR ABBEY ABELE ALAMO
ASPEN BAHAN LIARD BALSAM
POPPLE BAUMIER ABELTREE
WHITEBARK
POPLIN TABINET
POPOLOCA CHOCHO

POPPY HEAD BLAVER CANKER COPROSE EARACHE PONCEAU REDWEED ARGEMONE BALEWORT BOCCONIA HEADACHE DANNEBROG SQUATMORE COQUELICOT
(CORN—S) SOLDIERS
(PREF.) MECON(O)

POPPYCOCK BOSH BULL BUNK PISH FOLLY STUFF HAVERS HUMBUG HOGWASH

POPPYFISH POMPANO

POPPY SEED MAW MOHNSEED

POPULACE MOB MASS CROWD DEMOS PLEBS MASSES MOBILE PEOPLE PUBLIC COUNTRY MULTITUDE
(PREF.) DEM(O) OCHLO

POPULAR LAY POP COMMON GOLDEN PUBLIC SIMPLE VULGAR CROWDED DEMOTIC VULGATE APPROVED FAVORITE PEOPLISH PLEBEIAN GANGBUSTERS
(EXTREMELY—) HOT REDHOT

POPULARITY VOGUE CLAPTRAP
(— OF BUSINESS) GOODWILL

POPULATE MAN BREED PLANT WORLD PEOPLE INHABIT

POPULATION DEME COLONY FLOTSAM KINDRED TOPODEME UNIVERSE
(— OF A SPECIES) MORPH
(PREF.) DEM(O)

POPULUS SALIX

PORATHA (FATHER OF —) HAMAN

PORBEAGLE LAMNA SHARK LAMNID LAMNOID

PORCELAIN JU KO TING CHINA MURRA SPODE BISQUE MURRHA NANKIN BISCUIT CELADON DRESDEN NANKEEN NANKING MANDARIN STEATITE WORCESTER
(FINE —) SPODE
(JAPANESE —) KUTANI
(VARIETY OF —) CAEN KUAN ARITA HIZEN IMARI KYOTO AMSTEL PARIAN SEVRES BUDWEIS DRESDEN LIMOGES MEISSEN SWANSEA COALPORT HAVILAND KAKIEMON CHANTILLY

PORCH HOOD STOA LANAI STOEP STOOP INGANG PARVIS PIAZZA PORTAL RAMADA BALCONY GALERIE GALILEE NARTHEX PASSAGE POIKILE PORTICO PRONAOS VERANDA ANTENAVE SOLARIUM TRANSEPT VESTIBLE
(FRONT —) ANTICUM

PORCUPINE QUILL URSON CAWQUAW COENDOU ERECTER ERICIUS PORKPEN HEDGEHOG HEDGEPIG
(PREF.) HYSTRICO

PORCUPINE ANTEATER ECHIDNA

PORCUPINE FISH ERIZO ATINGA BURFISH DIODONT

PORCUPINE GRASS SPINIFEX

PORE GAZE GLOSE GLOZE STARE STOMA STUDY TRYPA BROWSE PONDER ALVEOLA CINCLIS OSTIOLE TUBULUS BAJONADO JOLTHEAD LENTICEL POROSITY

PORGY TAI SCUP PARGO PLUMA POGGY BESUGO BRAISE MAMAMU PAGRUS SPARID MARGATE PINFISH MENHADEN SPADEFISH

PORK HAM HOG PIG LARD BACON BRAWN MONEY SWINE BALDRIB LARDOON MIDDLING
(— AND SALMON) LAULAU
(— CHOP) BALDRIB GRISKEN
(— SHOULDER) HAND
(DEEP-FRIED —) CUCHIFRITO
(FRIED CUBE OF —) CUCHIFRITO
(SALT —) BACON SPECK SOWBELLY

PORKFISH SISI CATALINETA

PORKY FAT GREASY

PORNOGRAPHIC LEWD ADULT CURIOUS OBSCENE

PORNOGRAPHY SMUT CURIOSA ESOTERICA

POROUS OPEN LIGHT LEACHY CELLULAR

PORPHYRY ELVAN EURITE ELVANITE GRORUDITE

PORPOISE WHALE PALACH PUFFER COWFISH DOLPHIN HOGFISH PELLOCK PULLOCK SNUFFER CETACEAN GAIRFISH

PORRECT EXTEND TENDER PRESENT

PORRET LEEK ONION PORETT SCALLION

PORRIDGE KHIR MUSH POBS SAMP ATOLE BROSE GROUT GRUEL BURGOO CROWDY SEPAWN SKILLY SOWENS TARTAN BROCHAN BURGOUT OATMEAL POBBIES POLENTA POTTAGE FLUMMERY SAGAMITE
(PREF.) POLTO

PORRINGER TASTER TRINKET

PORT GATE GOAL LEFT MIEN WICK WINE CARRY CREEK HAVEN HITHE SALLY SCALE STATE APPORT HARBOR INPORT REFUGE AIRPORT BEARING DIGNITY LIBERTY OUTPORT ANTEPORT DEMEANOR LARBOARD MALTOLTE PORTHOLE PRESENCE

PORTABLE LAPTOP MOBILE MOVABLE BEARABLE

PORTAGE PACK CARGO CARRY TARBET FREIGHT TONNAGE HAULOVER

PORTAL DOOR GATE ENTRY PORCH DOORWAY ENTRANCE

PORTAMENTO DRAG GLIDE SCOOP SLIDE PORTATO GLISSADE

PORTCULLIS BAR SHUT HERSE
ORGUE SARASIN CATARACT
SARRASIN
PORTE GATE
PORTE-MONNAIE PURSE
PORTEND BODE AUGUR DIVINE
EXTEND BESPEAK BETOKEN PREDICT
PRESAGE DENOUNCE FOREBODE
FORECAST FORETELL
PORTENT AYAH LUCK SIGN SOUND
TOKEN AUGURY MARVEL OSTENT
WONDER AUSPICE PREDICT
PRESAGE PRODIGY CEREMONY
DISASTER SOOTHSAY PROGNOSTIC
PORTENTOUS AWFUL GRAVID
BODEFUL DOOMFUL FATEFUL
OMINOUS POMPOUS DOOMLIKE
DREADFUL INFLATED SINISTER
PORTER ALE BEER MOZO CADDY
HAMAL STOUT TAMEN BADGER
BEARER CADDIE COOLIE DARWAN
DURWAN ENTIRE KHAMAL REDCAP
SUISSE DROGHER DVORNIK
HUMMAUL JANITOR PITCHER
REMOVER BADGEMAN BUMMAREE
CARGADOR CHAPRASI LODGEMAN
PORTITOR RECEIVER
(— AND STOUT) COOPER
(JAPANESE —) AKABO
(MEAT —) PITCHER
(MEXICAN —) TAMEN
PORTFOLIO BLAD
PORTIA (HUSBAND OF —) BRUTUS
(LOVER OF —) BASSANIO
(MAID OF —) NERISSA
PORTIA TREE MAHO BENDY MAHOE
PORTICO ANTA STOA WALK XYST
ORIEL PORCH XYSTA ZAYAT EXEDRA
PARVIS PIAZZA SCHOOL XYSTUS
BALCONY DISTYLE GALLERY
NARTHEX PARVISE PRONAOS
TERRACE VERANDA PORTICUS
POSTICUM VERANDAH PENTASTYLE
TETRASTYLE
PORTION BIT CUP CUT DAB JAG LAB
LOT PAN BLAD DALE DEAL DOLE
DOSE FATE FECK JAGG PART SIZE
WHAT DOWER PIECE RATIO SHARE
SLICE SNACK TASTE WHACK CANTLE
CANTON COLLOP DETAIL GOBBET
MATTER PARCEL RASHER REGION
EXCERPT PARTAGE SCANTLE
SECTION SEGMENT TODDICK
TRANCHE FRACTION FRAGMENT
PITTANCE QUANTITY SCANTLET
FODDERING SOMETHING
(— DRUNK) DRAFT DRAUGHT
(— OF ACTOR'S PART) LENGTH
(— OF ARROW) BREAST
(— OF BIRD SONG) TOUR
(— OF BREAD) TOKE
(— OF BREAD OR BEER) CUE
(— OF CITRUS RIND) ALBEDO

(— OF ESTATE) LEGITIM
(— OF FARMLAND) BEREWICK
(— OF FLOODPLAIN) BANCO
(— OF FODDER) JAG
(— OF FOOD) HELP GOBBET HELPING
(— OF HIDE) HEAD
(— OF LAND) BLOCK PATTI INTAKE
DIVISION DONATION
(— OF LIQUOR) STICK DIVIDEND
(— OF LITURGY) ANAPHORA
(— OF MAST) HOUSING HOUNDING
(— OF PASTURE) BREAK
(— OF POEM) STRAIN
(— OF RUG) GRIN
(— OF SERPENT'S BODY) TRAIN
(— OF STEM) BOON
(— OF STORY) SNATCH
(— OF STREAM) LAVADERO
(— OF TEA) DRAWING
(— OF TIME) SPAN DISTANCE
(— OF TOBACCO) CUD
(— OF TONGUE) BLADE
(ADDITIONAL —) RASHER
(ALLOTTED —) MOIRA SCANTLING
(BRIDE'S —) DOWRY
(CLOTTED — OF BLOOD) CRUOR
(COARSER —) BOLTINGS
(EARLY —) SPRING
(INHABITED — OF EARTH)
ECUMENE
(LARGE —) SKELP
(LATTER —) AUTUMN EVENING
(MAIN —) CORPSE
(MARRIAGE —) DOT DOTE TOCHER
(MINUTE —) GRAIN
(MOST VALUABLE —) CHIEF
(PERCEPTIBLE —) KENNING
(REPRESENTATIVE —) SAMPLE
(SIGNIFICANT —) CHAPTER
(SIZABLE —) DUNT
(SMALL —) BIT DAB DOT DRAM DROP
SOSH TAIT TATE CHACK SPICE
SPUNK SHADOW KENNING
MODICUM REMNANT SCANTLE
SMIDGEN SOUPCON SCANTLET
(SMALL — OF LIQUOR) DOLLOP
HEELTAP
(TRIFLING —) SMACK
(SUFF.) (BY A SPECIFIC—) MEAL
PORTLY FAT FULL AMPLE GAUCY
GAWCY GAWSY STOUT GAUCIE
GOODLY STATELY SWELLING
OVERBLOWN
PORTMANTEAU BAG HOOK VALISE
POCKMANKY
PORTRAIT BUST ICON IKON IMAGE
IMAGO MODEL PIECE PINUP KITKAT
STATUE VISAGE PORTRAY RETRAIT
RETRATE LIKENESS RITRATTO
VERONICA MINIATURE
(— ON COIN) EFFIGY
PORTRAIT OF A LADY (AUTHOR
OF —) JAMES

(CHARACTER IN —) MERLE PANSY
RALPH ARCHER CASPAR EDWARD
GEMINI ISABEL OSMOND ROSIER
GILBERT BANTLING GOODWOOD
TOUCHETT HENRIETTA STACKPOLE
WARBURTON

PORTRAY ACT GIVE LIMN LINE BLAZE
ENACT IMAGE PAINT CIPHER CLOTHE
DEPICT FIGURE SHADOW FEATURE
IMITATE PICTURE DECIPHER
DESCRIBE RESEMBLE ARO OVAR
BRAGA EVORA HORTA PORTO VISEU
GUARDA OPORTO COIMBRA
FUNCHAL SETUBAL BRAGANCA

PORTUGAL

BAY: SETUBAL
CAPE: ROCA MONDEGO ESPICHEL
CAPITAL: LISBON
COIN: JOE REI PECA REAL CONTO
COROA DOBRA INDIO ESCUDO
MACUTA TAPACA TESTAO VINTEM
CENTAVO CRUSADO MOIDORE
EQUIPAGA
COLONY: MACAO TIMOR ANGOLA
GUINEA PRINCIPE
DISTRICT: BEJA FARO BRAGA EVORA
HORTA PORTO VISEU LEIRIA LISBOA
ISLAND: TIMOR
ISLANDS: MADEIRA
MEASURE: PE ALMA BOTA MEIO MOIO
PIPA VARA ALMUND BRACA FANGA
GEIRA LEGOA LINHA MILHA PALMO
ALMUDE CANADA COVADO QUARTO
ALQUIER ESTADIO FERRADO
SELAMIN ALQUEIRE TONELADA
MOUNTAIN: ACOR GEREZ MARAO
MOUSA PENEDA ESTRALA
MONCHIQUE
RIVER: SOR TUA LIMA MINO MIRA
SADO SEDA TAGO TEJO DOURO
MINHO SABAR TAGUS VOUGA
ZATAS CAVADO CHANCA TAMEGA
ZEZERE MONDEGO GUADIANA
TOWN: BEJA FARO OVAR BRAGA
EVORA HORTA PORTO VISEU
GUARDA OPORTO COIMBRA
FUNCHAL SETUBAL BRAGANCA
UNIVERSITY: COIMBRA
WEIGHT: GRAO ONCA LIBRA MARCO
ARROBA OITAVA ARRATEL QUINTAL
WINE: PORT

PORTUGUESE
(PREF.) LUSO
PORTULACA MOSS PURSLANE
PORWIGLE TADPOLE
POSADA INN
POSAUNE TROMBONE
POSE ASK SET SIT HOARD MODEL
OFFER PLANT STICK BAFFLE STANCE
NONPLUS PEACOCK POSTURE
PRESENT PROPOSE POSITION

PRETENSE PROPOUND QUESTION
MANNERISM
POSEIDON NEPTUNE EARTHSHAKER
(BROTHER OF —) ZEUS
(FATHER OF —) KRONOS
(MOTHER OF —) RHEA
(WIFE OF —) AMPHITRITE
POSER FACER POSEUR PUZZLE
STAYER STICKER STUMPER TWISTER
EXAMINER STICKLER BANDARLOG
POSH RITZY SWANKY SWAGGER
POSING OPPOSAL
(— TECHNIQUE) PLASTIQUE
POSIT FIX PUT SET PLACE AFFIRM
ASSUME
POSITING PONENT
POSITION LAY LIE HANG LINE POSE
RANK SITE CENSE COIGN PLANT
POINT POSTE SIEGE SITUS STAND
STATE STEAD ASSIZE FIGURE HEIGHT
OCTAVE OFFICE STANCE UBIETY
VALGUS POSTURE STATION
ATTITUDE CAPACITY DOCTRINE
LOCATION STANDING VOCATION
PLACEMENT SITUATION
(— IN AUTO RACE) POLE
(— IN DISCOURSE) POINT
(— OF AFFAIRS) STATUS
(— OF BODY) AKIMBO
(— OF FEAR) GAZE
(— OF HEAVENLY BODY) HARBOR
(— OF VESSEL) GAUGE HEIGHT
(— OF WEAPON) PORT READY
PRESENT
(— WITH NO ESCAPE) IMPASSE
(— WITH NO RESPONSIBILITY)
SINECURE
(BALLET —) POINTE
(CHESS —) ZUGZWANG
(COMMANDING —) PRESTIGE
(CRICKET —) GULLY GULLEY
(CRITICAL —) PASS
(DEFENSIVE —) WARD OUTWORK
(DIFFICULT —) SPOT
(DISTINGUISHED —) HONOR
(EMBARRASSING —) FIX HOLE
LURCH CORNER
(ESTABLISHED —) TOEHOLD
(FENCING —) CARTE SIXTE SIXTH
QUARTE TIERCE SACCOON SECONDE
SEPTIME
(FIRST —) PRIMACY
(FOREMOST —) HEAD LEAD STEM
(FORTIFIED —) HEDGEHOG
(FRONT —) FOREHEAD
(HABITUAL —) SET
(HINDMOST —) REAR
(HORIZONTAL —) LEVEL
(INCLINED —) SLOPE
(INITIAL —) ANLAUT
(MEDIAL —) INLAUT
(MIDDLE —) MEAN
(NATURAL —) LEVEL

(NEAR —) NEIGHBORHOOD
(OBLIQUE —) SHEER
(OFFICIAL —) RANK
(OPPOSITE —) OPPOSITION
(RELATIVE —) RANK PLACE TERMS
BEARING FOOTING STANDING
(SEATED —) SESSION
(SKIING —) SNOWPLOW
(SOCIAL —) CASTE STATE VALOUR
(SYMBOLIC —) HASTA
(UNFORTUNATE —) PREDICAMENT
POSITIONAL SITUAL
POSITIVE POS POZ COOL DOWN
FLAT PLUS SURE BASIC SHEER
UTTER ACTIVE DIRECT THETIC
GENUINE HEALTHY ABSOLUTE
CONCRETE DECISIVE DEFINITE
DOGMATIC EXPLICIT INHERENT
RESOLUTE SIGNLESS THETICAL
(THREE —S) KROMOGRAM
POSITIVELY BUT POS FLAT PLUS
QUITE FAIRLY INDEED STRICTLY
POSITIVISM COMTISM CERTAINTY
DOGMATISM
POSITRON LEPTON
POSSESS GET OWE OWN HAVE
HOLD WALD BOAST BROOK OUGHT
REACH WIELD MASTER OBTAIN
OCCUPY BEDEVIL ENVELOP FURNISH
INHABIT INHERIT INSTALL INSTATE
SMITTLE ACQUAINT DOMINATE
INSTRUCT
POSSESSED MAD CALM COOL
OUGHT CRAZED JERUSHA ENTHEATE
(— BY EVIL SPIRIT) DEMONIAC
(AUTHOR OF —) DOSTOEVSKI
(CHARACTER IN —) BLUM DASHA
FEDKA MARIE MARYA PYOTR YULIA
SHATOV DROZDOV LIPUTIN NIKOLAI
STEPHAN VARVARA KIRILLOV
LIZAVETA LYAMSHIN PETROVNA
SHIGALOV LEBYADKIN STAVROGIN
VIRGINSKY KARMAZINOV
TIMOFYEVNA VERHOVENSKY
POSSESSION AVER HAND HOLD
YHTE AUGHT GRASP STATE CLUTCH
CORNER HAVIOR SASINE SEISIN
SEIZIN WEALTH CONTROL COUNTER
DEMESNE DEWANEE FINGERS
KEEPING MASTERY SEIZURE
TENANCY CONQUEST DEFIANCE
PROPERTY OCCUPANCY
OCCUPATION
(— BY INSPIRATION) ENTHUSIASM
(— OF COMMON FEATURES)
AFFINITY
(— OF KNOWLEDGE) SCIENCE
(— WITH QUIET ENJOYMENT) SEISIN
SEIZIN
(BURDENSOME —) ELEPHANT
(COMMON —) COMMUNION
COMMUNITY

(DEAREST —) EWELAMB
(EXCLUSIVE —) MONOPOLY
(LOST — OF BALL) TURNOVER
(OUTDOOR —S) OUTSIGHT
(PETTY —S) SPRECHERY
(RELIGIOUS —) POWER
(SATISFACTORY —) ENJOYMENT
(TEMPORAL —S) WORLD
(TEMPORARY —) LEND
(PL.) ALLS STORE STUFF WRACK
DOMAIN ESTATE GRAITH PROPER
CAPITAL FORTUNE HAVINGS LIVINGS
POSSET CURDLE PAMPER
POWSOWDY BALDUCTUM
MERRYBUSH
POSSIBILITY MAY MAYBE POSSE
CHANCE PROSPECT QUESTION
(— OF REFORM) RECLAIM
POSSIBLE ABLE RIFE MAYBE LIKELY
EARTHLY ELIGIBLE FEASIBLE
PROBABLE PROBABLY POTENTIAL
CONTINGENT PRACTICABLE
(BARELY —) OUTSIDE
POSSIBLY MAPPEN LIGHTLY
PERHAPS PERCHANCE
PERADVENTURE
POSSUM TAIT FEIGN PRETEND
POST DAK SET TIE BITT BOMA CAMP
CRIB DAWK DOLE FAST FORT MAIL
META POLE ROOM SPOT SPUD STOB
STUD TREE BERTH CHEEK CLOSH
CRANE NEWEL PLACE SETUP SPILE
SPRAG STAKE STAND STILT STING
STOCK STODE STOOP STULP STUMP
BILLET CIPPUS COLUMN CROTCH
FENDER GIBBET INFORM OFFICE
PICKET PILLAR SAMSON SCREEN
STAPLE STOOTH STOWER TRUNCH
ASHERAH BOLLARD COURIER
GARETTA PLACARD POSTAGE
POSTBOX QUARTER STATION
STUDDLE UPRIGHT BANISTER
DEADHEAD LEGPIECE MAKEFAST
PRESIDIO PUNCHEON QUINTAIN
STRADDLE STANCHION
(— AS RACE MARKER) META
(— ON PIER) FAST BOLLARD
DEADHEAD
(BOUNDARY —) TERM STOOP
TERMINUS
(CHIMNEY —) SPEER
(CUSTOMS —) CHOKEY
(DECK —) BITT
(DOOR OR GATE —) DURN
(ECCLESIASTIC —) BENEFICE
(FENCE —) DROPPER
(HANGING —) GIBBET
(INDIAN MILITARY —) TANA TANNA
THANA
(MILITARY —) FORT GARRISON
(MOORING —) BITT DOLPHIN
(OBSERVATORY —) CUPOLA

(SACRED —) ASHERAH
(SIGN —) PARSON
(PREF.) STELO
POSTAGE POST INDICIA STAMPAGE
POSTAGE-FREE FRANCO
POSTAGE STAMP DUE HEAD
STICKER
POSTBOY YAMSHIK YEMSCHIK
POSTILION
POSTCARD (— COLLECTOR)
DELTIOLOGIST
POST CHAISE JACK POCHAY
POSHCAY
POSTER BILL CLAP SIGN SNIPE
CLAPPE AFFICHE PLACARD SHOWING
STICKER STREAMER
POSTERIOR BACK REAR CAUDAL
DORSAL POSTIC RETRAL ADAXIAL
BUTTOCKS
(PL.) WHEERIKINS
(PREF.) OPISTH(O) UR(O)
POSTERIORLY RETRAD
POSTERITY SEQUEL KINDRED
FUTURITY
POSTERN SIDE CLOCKET KLICKET
PRIVATE POSTICUM
POSTHOUSE YAM MUTATION
POSTICHE WIG SHAM SWITCH
TOUPEE PRETENSE SPURIOUS
POSTIL HOMILY COMMENT
POSTILION COURIER POSTBOY
YAMSHIK
POSTLUDE SORTIE SORTITA
EPILOGUE
POSTMAN MAIL CORREO MAILBAG
MAILMAN
POST OFFICE BOMA CORREO
POSTHOUSE
POSTPONE OFF STAY WAIT DEFER
DELAY FRIST REFER REMIT WAIVE
FUTURE LINGER RELONG RETARD
ADJOURN DEGRADE OVERSET
PROLONG RESPECT SUSPEND
CONTINUE PROROGUE REPRIEVE
WITHHOLD
POSTPONED DEFERRED
POSTPONEMENT MORA STAY
DELAY RESPECT RESPITE
DEFERRAL
POSTRIDE COURIER POSTILION
POSTSCRIPT EKE ENVOI ENVOY
POST SUPPORT CROWFOOT
POSTULANT NOVICE
POSTULATE AXIOM CLAIM POSIT
ASSERT ASSUME DEMAND THESIS
PERHAPS PREMISE PETITION
PRINCIPLE
POSTULATION PREMISE
POSTURE SET POSE SEAT SITE
ASANA FRONT HEART PLACE SHAPE
SQUAT STATE LOUNGE SLOUCH
STANCE BEARING CROWHOP

STATION STATURE ATTITUDE
CARRIAGE POSITION
(— IN BED) DECUBITUS
(— OF DEFENSE) GUARD
(DANCE —) HOLD
(KNEELING —) SHIKO
POSY POESY TUTTY FLOWER
BOUQUET NOSEGAY ANTHOLOGY
(SMALL —) FLORET
POT BAG CAN COOP FOOL JUST LEAD
OLLA PINT POOL RUIN VASO CREWE
CROCK CRUSE DIXIE KITTY SHANT
SHOOT ALUDEL CHATTY CHYTRA
JORDAN JORDEN KETTLE MARMIT
MASLIN MONKEY OUTWIT PINGLE
PIPKIN POCKET POSNET BRAISER
CHAMBER CUVETTE DECEIVE
POTSHOT SEETHER SKILLET YETLING
FAVORITE JACKSHEA PRESERVE
MARIJUANA
(— FOR CATCHING FISH) COOP
(— FOR MEDICINE) GALLIPOT
(— OF BRASS) LOTA MASLIN
(— OF DRINK) SHANT
(— STICKER) DUMPLING
(— WITH 3 FEET) POSNET
(BOILING —) STEW
(BULGING —) OLLA
(BUSHMAN'S —) JACKSHAY
JACKSHEA
(CHAMBER —) JERRY JORDAN
JORDEN COMMODE JEROBOAM
(CHIMNEY —) CAN TUN
(EARTHEN —) OLLA CROCK CHATTY
PIPKIN
(FLOWER —) PLANTER
(INDIAN —) LOTA LOTAH
(LEATHER —) GISPIN
(LOBSTER —) COY TRUNK
(LONG-HANDLED —) PINGLE
(MELTING —) CREVET CRUCIBLE
(ORNAMENTAL —) PLANTER
(PART OF —) EAR LIP RIM ANTE BASE
BODY FOOT NECK SPOUT HANDLE
(PEAR-SHAPED —) ALUDEL
(SMALL ROUND —) LOTA LOTAH
(TEA —) TRACK
(THREE-LEGGED —) TRIVET
(12-GALLON —) DIXY DIXIE
POTABLE DRINK BEVERAGE
POTATORY
POTAGE SOUP BROTH
POTAMOGETON PONDWEED
PONDGRASS
POTASH KALI SALINE PEARLASH
POLVERINE
(— FACTORY) ASHERY
POTASSIUM K KALIUM POTASS
(— DICHROMATE) CHROME
POTASSIUM BICARBONATE
SALERATUS
POTASSIUM NITRATE GROUGH

POTATION POT DRAM DRAFT DRINK
LIBATION
POTATO PAP YAM CHAT PAPA SPUD
YAMP FLUKE IDAHO RURAL TATER
TUBER BATATA CAMOTE KUMARA
LUMPER MURPHY PRATEY SKERRY
BURBANK EPICURE SOLANUM
BLUENOSE
(— BALL) NOISETTE
(— CHIP) CRISP
(— MASHER) RICER CHAPPER
(—S AND CABBAGE) COLCANNON
(— SLICES) LATTICE
(— STATE) IDAHO MAINE
(BAKING —) IDAHO
(FRENCH FRIED —) CHIP
(FRENCH FRIED —S) GAUFRETTES
(JAPANESE —) IMO
(KIND OF —) COUCH
(MASHED —ES) MASH
(STEWED —S) STOVIES
(WITH —S) PARMENTIER
(PL.) WARE CHUNO
POT BEARER POTIFER
POTBELLIED KEDGE PODDY
STOMACHY ABDOMINOUS
POTBELLY PAUNCH TUNBELLY
POTBOY GANYMEDE
POTE KICK MOPE POIT POKE PUSH
NUDGE PLATE POKER SHOVE
THRUST
POTEEN POTHEEN WHISKEY
POTWHISKY
POTENCE STUD CROSS GIBBET
POTENCY FORCE POWER VIGOR
ORENDA VIRTUE EFFICACY
STRENGTH VITALITY OPERATION
(TRANSMUTING —) ALCHEMY
POTENT ABLE MAIN RICH STAY STIFF
CAUSAL COGENT CRUTCH MIGHTY
STRONG DYNAMIC SUPPORT
WARRANT FORCIBLE POWERFUL
PUISSANT VIGOROUS VIRTUOUS
VIRULENT
POTENTATE KING RULER HUZOOR
POTENT PRINCE SATRAP DICTATOR
DOMINION SOVEREIGN
POTENTIAL EH LATENT VIRTUAL
IMPLICIT INCHOATE POSSIBLE
PREGNANT
(— ENERGY) ERGAL
(ACTION —) SPIKE
(EXCESS —) OVERVOLTAGE
POTENTIALITY POSSE POWER
DUNAMIS DYNAMIS POTENCY
CAPACITY PREGNANCY
POTGUN PISTOL POPGUN
BRAGGART
POTHER ADO VEX FUSS STEW STIR
WORRY BOTHER BUSTLE HARASS
POTTER PUTTER PUZZLE PERPLEX
TURMOIL

POTHERB WORT CLARY WERTE
GREENS CHERVIL OLITORY POTWORT
QUELITE SPINACH TAMPALA
POTHOLE POT RUT KETTLE TINAJA
POTHOOK HAIK HAKE CROOK
HANGLE RACKAN SLOWRIE
TRAMMEL COTTEREL
POTHOUSE TAVERN ALEHOUSE
MUGHOUSE
POTION DOSE DRUG DRAFT DRINK
DWALE STUFF DRENCH POISON
AMATORY MIXTURE PHILTER PHILTRE
NEPENTHE
(PALM —) NIPA
POTIPHERAH (DAUGHTER OF —)
ASENATH
POTLATCH GIFT FEAST PARTY
POTLACH FESTIVAL
POT MARIGOLD GOLD GOLDE
SUNFLOWER
POTPOURRI HASH OLIO STEW
MASLIN MEDLEY POTPIE RAGOUT
FANTASIA PASTICHE JAMBALAYA
SALMAGUNDI BOUILLABAISSE
POTRO COLT
POTSHERD BIT PIG TEST CROCK
SHARD SHERD FRAGMENT
OSTRACON PANSHARD
POTTAGE SEW SOUP SOWL STEW
BERRY BROTH BRUET BREWIS
BROWET POTAGE OATMEAL
PULMENT
POTTED DRUNK CANNED
(— MEAT) RILLETT
POTTER FAD FUSS MUCK POKE
ANNOY DAKER TRUCK BOTHER
DABBLE DACKER DAIDLE DIDDLE
DISHER DODDER FIDDLE FOOTLE
FOTTER JOTTER KUMHAR MUDDLE
NANTLE NIGGLE PETTLE POUTER
TIDDLE TIFFIE TIFFLE TRIFLE
CLOAMER CROCKER DISTURB
FIGURER FOSSICK HANDLER
NAUNTLE PERPLEX PLOWTER
PRODDLE THROWER TROUBLE
CERAMIST TERRAPIN
(— OFFICIOUSLY) TEW
(MACHINE OF —) JOLLY
POTTERER TWIRLER
POTTERY POT BANK CHUN DELF
GROG WARE BIZEN CROCK DELFT
GLOST ROUEN SPODE BASALT FICTIL
KASHAN MIMPEI ASTBURY BELLEEK
BOCCARO BRISTOL DIPWARE
FIGMENT JETWARE KAMARES
POTBANK POTWARE POTWORK
REDWARE SATSUMA TICKNEY
TZUCHOU BUCCHERO CERAMICS
FIGULINE GRAYWARE SANTORIN
SLIPWARE BROWNWARE
(— CIVILIZATION) MINYAN
(— CULTURE) PUCARA

(— DECOR) MISHIMA
(— DECORATED WITH SCRATCHING) GRAFFITO
(ANCIENT —) KAMARES GRAYWARE
(BLACK —) BASALT BUCCHERO
(BLUE-AND-WHITE —) DELFT
(CHINESE —) KUAN YIHSING
(CRUSHED —) GROG
(HINDU —) UDA
(JAPANESE —) IMARI
(RICHLY COLORED —) MAJOLICA
(TURKISH —) IZNIK
(UNGLAZED —) BISCUIT
POTTERY TREE CARAIPE
POTTINGER COOK POTYCARY
POTTO LEMUR APOSORO KINKAJOU
POTTY CRAZY FOOLISH TRIVIAL SNOBBISH
POUCH BAG COD JAG POD SAC BELL
BOTA CYST POCK POKE BULGE
BURSA POKKE PURSE BUDGET
CAECUM CRUMEN GIPSER PACKET
POCKET PURSET SACHET ALFARGA
ALFORJA CANTINA CRUMENA
GIPSIRE MAILBAG MOCHILA OVICYST
SCROTUM SPORRAN SWALLOW
BURSICLE PROTRUDE SPEUCHAN
MARSUPIUM
(— OF FLY) AEROSTAT
(— ON DEER'S NECK) BELL
(— ON PETAL) SPUR
(PILGRIM'S —) SCRIP
(TOBACCO —) DOSS
(PREF.) PERO PHAOCO PHASCOL(O) THYLAC(O)
POUCHED SACCATE
POUCH OF DOUGLAS
(PREF.) CULDO
POUF PUFF OTTOMAN
POULAINE PIKE CRAKOW
POULPE POULP CUTTLE OCTOPUS
POULTICE QUILT STUPA STUPE
MALAGMA EPITHEME SINAPISM
CATAPLASM
POULTRY FOWL HENS DUCKS GEESE
PULLEN PEAFOWL PIGEONS PULLERY
TURKEYS CHICKENS PULLAILE
VOLAILLE
POUNAMU JADE PUNAMU NEPHRITE
POUNCE NAB CHOP CLAP JUMP
POKE SWAP SWOP FLECK PRICK
PUNCH SOUSE SWOOP TALON
EMBOSS PIERCE TATTOO BOBCOAT
DESCEND SPRINKLE
(— UPON) STOOP
POUND L LB BUM DAD LIB PIN PUN
SOV BEAT CHAP DRUB FRAM PELT
PIND POON POSS PUND QUID SKIT
SPCA THUD TRAP TUND CRUSH
FRAME KNOCK LABOR LIVRE NEVEL
STAMP THUMP TRAMP WEIGH

BATTER BRUISE HAMMER LUMBER
NICKER POUNCE PRISON THRASH
CONTUND CONTUSE PINFOLD
THUNDER LAMBASTE RESTRAIN
(— FINE) BRAY
(— SYMBOL) OCTOTHORP
(FISH —) KEEP MADRAGUE
(ISRAELI —S) LIROTH
(1-8TH OF —) HANDFUL
(100 —S) CENTAL CENTURY
(12 —S OF BUTTER) GAUN
(25 —S) PONY PONEY
(32, 56, OR 75 —S OF RAISINS) FRAIL
(500 —S) MONKEY
POUNDMASTER PINDER PINNER PONDER
POUR JAW RUN TUN YET BIRL BREW
DROP EMIT FILL FLOW GOSH GUSH
HELD LASH LAVE RAIN TEEM TOOM
VENT FLOOD FLUSH HEELD HIELD
POWER SLIDE SOUSE SPILL SPOUT
SWARM TRILL AFFUSE DECANT
SLUICE STREAM CASCADE CHANNEL
DIFFUSE SUFFUSE
(— AWAY) STAVE
(— BACK) REFUND
(— BEER OR WINE) BIRL
(— BETWEEN) INTERFUSE
(— CLUMSILY) SLOSH
(— COPIOUSLY) HALE
(— DOWN) RASH SILE SHOWER
DESCEND DISPLUNGE
(— FORTH) SHED TIDE VENT WELL
DISTILL OVERFLOW
(— FREELY) SWILL
(— FROM ONE VESSEL TO ANOTHER)
DECANT JIRBLE TRANSFUSE
(— IN) INFUSE INFOUND INHELDE
(— IN DROP BY DROP) INSTIL INSTILL
(— LIKE RAIN OR TEARS) LASH
(— MELTED WAX) BASTE
(— MOLTEN LEAD) YOTE
(— OFF) SLUICE
(— OIL UPON) ANOINT
(— OUT) FILL SEND SHED SKINK
STOUR UTTER EFFUSE LIBATE
DIFFUND DIFFUSE
(— OVER) PERFUSE SUFFUSE
(— TOGETHER) CONFUSE
(— UNSTEADILY) JIRBLE
(— UPON) AFFUSE
(PREF.) CHYMI
POURBOIRE TIP GRATUITY TRINKGELD
POURER TEEMER INFUSER
POURING AFFUSION EFFUSION
INFUSION LIBATION
(SUFF.) ENCHYSIS
POURPOINT GIPON JUPON QUILT DOUBLET
POUT BIB MOP MAID MOUE PUSS
SULK BLAIN BOODY GROIN BRASSY

BRASSIE CATFISH EELPOUT
BULLHEAD PROTRUDE
POUTERIA LUCUMA
POUTING BOUDERIE
POUTY DOUR GLUM MOROSE
SULLEN
POVERTY LACK NEED WANE WANT
DEARTH PENURY BEGGARY DEFAULT
MISEASE TENUITY DISTRESS
POORTITH PUIRTITH SCARCITY
WANDRETH NECESSITY
(SUFF.) PENIA
POVERTY PLANT HEATH HEATHER
LINGWORT
POVERTY-STRICKEN POOR NAKED
NEEDY SQUALID SHIRTLESS
POWDER BRAY DUST KISH MILL
MULL SAND CHALK CURRY ERBIA
FLOUR GRIND HEMOL KOSIN PICRA
STOUR CEMENT CHARGE CHINOL
DECAMP DERMOL EMPASM ESCAPE
FARINA FILITE GERATE KAMALA
KERMES KUMKUM MELLON PEYTON
PINOLE POUNCE RACHEL SMEETH
YTTRIA ALCOHOL BESTREW
BROCADE LUPULIN SCATTER
SMEDDUM SPACKLE SPODIUM
ALGAROTH CATAPASM DYNAMITE
FLUMERIN PALEGOLD
(— A SHIELD) GERATE
(— FOR BRONZING) BROCADE
(— FOR EYELIDS) KOHL
(— OBTAINED BY SUBLIMATION)
FLOWERS
(— TO MASK SWEAT ODOR) EMPASM
EMPASMA
(— USED IN CHOCOLATE) PINOLE
(ABRASIVE —) EMERY
(ANTHELMINTIC —) KOSIN
(ANTIMONY —) KOHL
(ANTISEPTIC —) EUPAD
(APERIENT —) SEIDLITZ
(ASTRINGENT —) BORAL
(BLEACHING —) CHEMIC CHLORIDE
(BROWNISH —) LIGNIN
(CATHARTIC —) KAMALA
(COLORING —) HENNA
(EFFERVESCENT —) SALINE
(FINE —) DUST POUNCE ALCOHOL
(FLUORESCENT —) FLUMERIN
(GOA —) ARAROBA
(GOLD —) VENTURINE
(GRAPHITIC —) KISH
(GRAY —) ANTU
(HAIR —) MUST
(MALT —) SMEDDUM
(PERFUMED —) ABIR PULVIL SACHET
(PINK —) CALAMINE
(POISONOUS —) ROBIN
(PURPLE —) CUDBEAR
(REDDISH —) ABIR KUMKUM
SIMMON

(ROSE-COLORED —) ERBIA
(SACHET —) PULVIL
(SILICEOUS —S) SILEX
(SMOKELESS —) FILITE PEYTON
CORDITE AMBERITE INDURITE
SOLENITE
(WHITE —) CHINOL YTTRIA HYPORIT
SCANDIA HALAZONE LANTHANA
PARAFORM
(YELLOW —) KOSIN DERMOL
MELLON LUPULIN MALARIN
SAMARIA TANNIGEN
(PREF.) PUMICI
POWDERED SEME SPICED PICKLED
SEASONED
POWDER PUFF PLUFF
POWDER ROOM BATHROOM
MAGAZINE
POWDERY MEALY PRUINOSE
PULVEROUS
POWER ARM ART JUS ROD SAY SUN
VIS BEEF BULK DINT GIFT GRIP HAND
HANK HEAP HORN IRON KAMI MAIN
MANA MAYA SOUP SWAY WALD
WILL AGENT CROWN DEMON DEVIL
FORCE GRACE HUACA HYDRO INPUT
LURCH MIGHT SINEW SKILL STEAM
VALUE VIGOR WAKON WIELD YARAK
AGENCY APPEAL BREATH CLUTCH
CREDIT DANGER DEGREE DOUGHT
EFFORT ENERGY FOISON IMPACT
MOLOCH MUSCLE SHAKTI STROIL
STROKE SWINGE TALENT VIRTUE
WEIGHT ABILITY BALANCE
BOSSDOM COMMAND CONTROL
DEMESNE DESTINY DUNAMIS
DYNAMIS ENTHEOS FACULTY
POTENCY VALENCY VOLTAGE
WAKONDA ACTIVITY AUTONOMY
CAPACITY CLUTCHES COERCION
DELEGACY DEMIURGE DISPOSAL
DOMINION INTEREST LEVERAGE
LORDSHIP SEIGNORY STRENGTH
PUISSANCE PREROGATIVE
(— FROM SUPREME BEING) EON
AEON
(— OF ACID) BASICITY
(— OF ATTORNEY) PROXY
(— OF ATTRACTION) ALLURE
(— OF CHOICE) LIBERTY
(— OF DETERMINING) VOLITION
(— OF DIVORCE) TAFWIZ
(— OF ENTRY) INGRESS
(— OF GIVING) PROPINE
(— OF HEARING) AUDITION
(— OF IMAGINATION) ESEMPLASY
(— OF KNOWING) JNANASHAKTI
(— OF LIVING) VITALITY
(— OF MANIFESTATION) MAYA
(— OF MOVING AT SEA) YARAGE
(— OF PERFORMING) ART
(— OF RESISTANCE) STAMINA

(— OF RETURNING) REGRESS
(— OF SELF-DETERMINATION)
FREEWILL
(— OF SPEECH) TONGUE
(— OF TRANSMUTATION) ALCHEMY
(— OF VISION) KEN
(— OF WINE) SEVE
(—S OF EVIL) HELL
(— TO ATTRACT) DUENDE
(— TO CHARM) DUENDE
(— TO CONVINCE) FORCE
(— TO ENTER) ENTRANCE
(AUTHOR OF —) FEUCHTWANGER
(CHARACTER IN —) REB KARL ISAAC
JOSEF MARIE NAEMI ANSELF
GABRIEL SIBYLLE LANDAUER
MAGDALEN ALEXANDER
SELIGMANN WEISSENSEE
OPPENHEIMER
(CIVIL —) CAESAR
(COERCIVE —) SWORD
(CURATIVE —) THERAPY
(DIVINE —) MOIRA
(ELEVATING —) LIFT
(EMOTIONAL —) STOMACH
(EXTRAPHYSICAL —) MANA
(FIFTH —) SURSOLID
(FOCAL —) DIOPTRY
(GRIPPING —) HOLD
(GROWTH —) BATHMISM
(HYPOTHETICAL —) FORTUNE
(IMPERSONAL —) WAKAN WAKON
WAKANDA
(INHERENT —) VIRTUE
(INTELLECTUAL —) WIT
(LEGAL —) JUS
(MAGIC —) ORENDA
(MAGNETIC —) MAGNES
(MENTAL —) HABITUS
(MILITARY —) SWORDCRAFT
(MORMON —) KEYS
(MOTIVE —) PRINCIPLE
(MYSTERIOUS —) MANA
(NATURAL —) OD
(OCCULT —) MAGIC
(PERSUASIVE —) RHETORIC
(PERUVIAN —) HUACA
(POLITICAL —) DOMINIUM
(RATIONAL —) EYE
(REFLECTIVE —) ALBEDO
(ROYAL —) RIAL
(ROYAL —S) REGALIA
(SACRED —) KAMI
(SECOND —) SQUARE
(SECRET —) MAGIC
(SOLE —) MONOPOLY
(SOVEREIGN —) SWAY THRONE
(SPIRITUAL —) NGAI
(STAYING —) STEEL BOTTOM
STAMINA
(STRIKING —) PUNCH
(SUPERNATURAL —) CHARISMA

(SUPREME —) EMPIRE HEAVEN
IMPERIUM
(THIRD —) CUBE
(UNLIMITED —) OMNIPOTENCE
(VITAL —) SPIRITS
(ZEST-GIVING —) RELISH
(PREF.) CRATO DYN(A)(AMI)(AMO)
(SUFF.) OD ODIC (RULING —) CRACY
CRAT(IC)
POWERBOAT SEDAN SKIFF GLIDER
CRUISER STINKPOT GASOLINER
POWERFUL BIG FAT ABLE DEEP HIGH
MAIN RANK RICH VERY FORTE HEFTY
HUSKY LUSTY STARK STOUT VALID
VIVID WIGHT WILDE COGENT HEROIC
MIGHTY POTENT SEVERE STRONG
CAPABLE FECKFUL INTENSE
POLLENT RICHARD SKOOKUM
STAVING VALIANT FORCIBLE
PUISSANT VIGOROUS
(PREF.) MEGA
POWERLESS WEAK FEEBLE UNABLE
HELPLESS IMPOTENT
POWWOW CHAT PAWAW CONFAB
FROLIC COUNCIL MEETING SESSION
CONJURER
POX ROUP CANKER PLAGUE VARIOLA
(FOWL —) SOREHEAD
(SHEEP —) OVINIA
POYOU PELUDO ARMADILLO
PRABHU LORD CHIEF WRITER
PRACTICABLE AGIBLE DOABLE
USABLE VIABLE FEASIBLE OPERABLE
POSSIBLE
PRACTICAL HARD UTILE ACTIVE
ACTUAL THINGY USEFUL OPERARY
VIRTUAL WORKING BANAUSIC
HOMESPUN PRACTIVE THINGISH
DOWNTOEARTH
(— JOKE) WAGGERY
(NOT —) PROFESSORY
PRACTICALLY ALMOST NEARLY
REALLY VIRTUALLY
PRACTICE ACT ISM LAW PLY SUE
TRY URE USE KEEP LIVE PLAN PLOT
ADOPT APPLY ASSAY DRILL FOUND
GUISE HABIT HAUNT TRADE TRAIN
TREAD USAGE CUSTOM EMPLOY
FOLLOW GROOVE OCCUPY PRAXIS
RECORD BRUSHUP ENHAUNT
KNOCKUP OPERATE PROCEED
PROFESS RANDORI USAUNCE
ACTIVISM ALARMISM EXERCISE
FREQUENT GALENISM REHEARSE
OBSERVANCE
(— CHEATING) FOIST
(— DECEPTION) DEACON
(— DILIGENTLY) PLY
(— EXERCISE) DRYRUN
(— FRAUD) SHARK
(— HANDED DOWN) TRADITION
(— HYPOCRISY) CANT

(— OF AN ART) PRAXIS
(— OF MEDICINE) GALENISM
(— QUIETLY) RECORD
(— ROWING) TUB
(— WITCHCRAFT) HEX
(BASEBALL —) FUNGO
(BINDING —) LAW
(CEREMONIAL —) RITE
(COMMUNAL —) SUNNA SCHEME
SUNNAH INTRIGUE
(CORRUPT —) ABUSE WHORE
(DIPLOMATIC —) ALTERNAT
(DISHONEST —S) CROSS
(EVIL —) MISUSAGE
(HORTICULTURAL —) CUTTAGE
(MEDICAL —) ALLERGY
(RELIGIOUS —) CULT CULTUS
(SUPERSTITIOUS —) FREET
(TENNIS —) KNOCKUP
(UNDERHAND —) JUGGLING
(VICIOUS —) MOLOCH
(SUFF.) CY ERY ICS ISM
PRACTICED EXPERT VERSED
PRACTIC SKILLED VETERAN
HACKNEYED
PRACTICING EXERCENT
PRACTITIONER ADEPT DOCTOR
HEALER LAWYER NOVICE LEARNER
EXERCENT FELDSHER HUMANIST
HERBALIST HOMEOPATH
NATUROPATH
(SUFF.) ICIAN PATH(IA)(IC)(Y)
PRAD HORSE
PRAENOMEN AULUS CAIUS GAIUS
TITUS GNAEUS LUCIUS MANIUS
MARCUS SEXTUS SERVIUS SPURIUS
MAMERCUS NUMERIUS TIBERIUS
PRAESEPE CRIB CRATCH MANGER
BEEHIVE
PRAGMATIC BUSY BUSYBODY
DOGMATIC MEDDLING OFFICIOUS
PRACTICAL
PRAGMATIST REALIST
PRAIRIE BAY BLED CAMAS PAMPA
PLAIN CAMASS MEADOW PLATEAU
QUAMASH
(— STATE) ILLINOIS
(AUTHOR OF —) COOPER
(CHARACTER IN —) ASA BUSH INEZ
PAUL WADE ELLEN HOVER NATTY
WHITE ABIRAM BUMPPO ESTHER
BATTIUS ISHMAEL HARDHEART
MIDDLETON
PRAIRIE BERRY TROMPILLO
PRAIRIE CHICKEN GROUSE
PRAIRIE DOG GOPHER MARMOT
PRAIRIE WOLF COYOTE
PRAISE CRY LOF FUME HERY LAUD
LOSE LOVE PRES ADORE ALLOW
ALOSE BLESS CAROL CHANT CRACK
DEIFY EXTOL GLORY HERSE HONOR
KUDOS PLAUD PRIZE ROOSE SALVE
VALUE WURTH ANTHEM BELAUD

EULOGY FRAISE HILLEL KUDIZE
LOANGE LOVING ORCHID SALUTE
TONGUE ACCLAIM ADULATE
APPLAUD COMMEND FLATTER
GLORIFY MAGNIFY NOSEGAY
PLAUDIT PUFFING TRIBUTE WORSHIP
ACCOLADE APPLAUSE BLESSING
DOXOLOGY ENCOMIUM EULOGIZE
PROCLAIM PANEGYRIC
(— BE TO GOD) LD
(— HIGHLY) MAGNIFY
(— INORDINATELY) FUME
(— IN THANKSGIVING) JOY
(— OF ANOTHER'S FELICITY)
MACARISM
(— TO GOD ALWAYS) LDS
(EFFUSIVE —) FUSS
(EXAGGERATED —) PUFFERY
(EXCESSIVE —) FLATTERY
ADULATION PANEGYRIC
(EXCLAMATION OF —) BRAVO
(EXTRAVAGANTLY —) PUFF
(INSINCERE —) CLART DAUBING
(PUBLIC —) PRECONY
(SING FALSE —S) CHANT
PRAISED JUDAH JUDITH LAURELED
(UNDULY —) BEPUFFED
PRAISEWORTHY WORTHY
AMIABLE GLORIOUS LAUDABLE
SPLENDID EXEMPLARY
PRAJAPATI KA PITRI
PRAKRIT PALI MAGADHI
PRAM BUGGY CARRIAGE HANDCART
PUSHCART STROLLER
PRANCE STIR BRANK CAPER DANCE
JAUNT PRANK CANARY CAREER
CAVORT CURVET GAMBOL JAUNCE
TITTUP TRANCE PRANKLE SWAGGER
CAKEWALK
PRANCER HORSE DANCER CAPERER
PRANK JIG RAG RIG DECK DIDO FOLD
GAME GAUD JEST LARK PLOY PRAT
REAK ADORN ANTIC CAPER FREAK
SHINE SKITE TRICK VAGUE BROGUE
CURVET FEGARY FIGARY FROLIC
GAMBOL SHAVIE VAGARY MARLOCK
SPANGLE ESCAPADE FREDAINE
PRANCOME RIGWIDDIE SHENANIGAN
MONKEYSHINE
(PL.) REX GAMES JINKS
PRANKISH TRICKSY
PRANKSTER JOKER FOOLER
(NUDE —) STREAKER
PRASINE LEEK
PRAT PUSH NUDGE TRICK
PRATE GAB BUCK BUKH BUKK CARO
CHAT CLAP CLAT TALK BLATE BOAST
CLASH SCOLD BABBLE CACKLE
CLAVER JANGLE SQUIRT TONGUE
BLATHER BLATTER BLETHER
CHATTER CLATTER PALAVER PRATTLE
TWATTLE
PRATING GAFF CHATTER

PRATIQUE CUSTOM PRODUCT

PRATTLE GAB CHAT CLACK BABBLE
GIBBLE CACKLE DRIVEL JANNER
JAUNER YATTER BLATTER CHATTER
CLATTER GABNASH JAUNDER
NASHGAB PRITTLE TRATTLE
TWADDLE CHITCHAT RAVARDAGE

PRATTLER RATTLE GABNASH
PRATTLEBOX

PRATTLING CHAVISH

PRAWN CARID NIPPER PENEID
SHRIMP SQUILLA CARIDEAN
CARIDOID CREVETTE MACRURAN
LANGOSTINO LANGOUSTINE

PRAWN KILLER SQUILLA

PRAXIS HABIT ACTION CUSTOM
PRACTICE

PRAY ASK BEG BID BLESS CRAVE
DAVEN SOUGH VOUCH INVITE
BESEECH ENTREAT IMPLORE
REQUEST WRESTLE INVOCATE
(— FOR) BOON

PRAYA BUND BEACH STRAND

PRAYER ACT AHA AVE CRY VOW
BEAD BENE BOON PLEA SUIT VOTE
AGNUS ALENU NAMAZ SALAT
SHEMA ABODAH APPEAL ECTENE
ERRAND LITANY MANTRA MATINS
ORISON STEVEN VESPER YIZKOR
BIDDING COMPLIN FATIHAH GAYATRI
GEULLAH KADDISH MEMENTO
ORATION PRECULE PREFACE
TAHANUN ANAPHORA APOLYSIS
CATHISMA DEVOTION KEDUSHAH
MISERERE PETITION SUFFRAGE
TEHINNAH REQUIESCAT
(— BEADS) ROSARY
(— BEFORE MEAL) GRACE
(— BOOK) MAHZOR MISSAL SERVICE
(— LEADER) IMAM
(— OF DISMISSAL) APOLYSIS
(— RUG) NAMAZLIK
(— SHAWL) TALLITH
(— STICK) BAHO PAHO
(— TOWER) MINARET
(CANONICAL —S) BREVIARY
(CHIEF MOHAMMEDAN —) NAMAZ
(DAILY —) CURSUS
(DEVOTIONAL —) ANGELUS
(HINDU —) GAYATRI
(INAUDIBLE —) SECRET
(INWARD —) ACT
(ISLAM CALL TO —) AZAN
(JEWISH —) ALENU ABODAH
GEULLAH HOSHANA KADDISH
(LAST — OF DAY) COMPLIN
(LONG —) CATHISMA
(LORD'S —) PATERNOSTER
(MUSLIM —) SALAH SALAT KHUTBAH
(MUSLIM CALL TO —) AZAN
(OPENING —) COLLECT
(REPETITIVE —) NOVENA
(SECRET —) BREATHING

(SHORT —) GRACE COLLECT
(SILENT —) SECRET
(TABLE —) GRACE
(PL.) HOURS NORITO TIKKUN
CHAPLET
(PREF.) EUCHO

PRAYER-BOOK (JEWISH —)
MAHZOR MACHZOR

PRAYING ORISON IMPRECANT
(— FIGURE) ORANT

PREACH EDIFY SOUGH TEACH
EXHORT GOSPEL SERMON DELIVER
HOMILIZE PREDICATE SERMONIZE

PREACHER KHATIB MAGGID
PARSON PASTOR TUBMAN
DARSHAN LOLLARD MARTEXT
PROPHET ROUNDER TEACHER
TUBBIST TUBSTER EXHORTER
KOHELETH MINISTER PARDONER
PULPITER QOHELETH SERMONER
SPINTEXT SWADDLER VARTABED
BOANERGES
(PL.) PULPIT

PREACHING SPELL PULPIT SERMON
HEARING KERYGMA KERYGMA
PROPHECY PULPITRY SPELLING

PREACHY DIDACTIC

PREAMBLE PREFACE WHEREAS

PREARRANGED SET

PREBEND CANONRY

PREBENDARY PROVEND

PRE-CAMBRIAN MOINE EOZOIC
ARCHEAN PRIMARY HURONIAN
TORRIDONIAN

PRECARIOUS NEAR DICKY RISKY
SHAKY CASUAL INFIRM NARROW
UNSURE DUBIOUS TRICKLE
CATCHING DELICATE INSECURE
PERILOUS UNSTABLE DANGEROUS
UNCERTAIN

PRECAUTION CARE GUARD CAUTEL
SAFEGUARD

PRECEDE LEAD FOREGO HERALD
FORERUN PREFACE PREVENT
ANTECEDE PREAMBLE

PRECEDENCE PAS LEAD PRIMACY
HERALDRY PRIORITY
(RIGHT OF —) PAS
(SOCIAL —) LEVEL

PRECEDENT LEAD SIGN MODEL
TOKEN USAGE INSTANCE ORIGINAL
SPECIMEN STANDARD AUTHORITY

PRECEDING OLD FORE WEST
BEFORE FORMER LEADING
ADJACENT PREVIOUS
(— ALL OTHERS) FIRST
(PREF.) ANTE

PRECENTOR CANTOR PSALMIST
LETTERGAE

PRECEPT LAW HEST LINE RULE TORA
WRIT ADAGE AXIOM BREVE CANON
MAXIM ORDER SUTRA SUTTA TENET
TORAH BEHEST DICTATE MANDATE

WARRANT DOCTRINE DOCUMENT
LANDMARK
PRECEPTIVE DIDACTIC MANDATORY
PRECEPTOR TUTOR MASTER
PRECINCT BEAT AMBIT BOUND
CLOSE VERGE DOMAIN HIERON
VIHARA COLLEGE LENAEUM SOCIETY
TEMENOS BANLIEUE DISTRICT
ENVIRONS
(PL.) AMBIT
PRECIOUS CUTE DEAR FINE LIEF
RARE VERY CHARY CHERE GREAT
HONEY CHICHI CHOICE COSTLY
DAINTY GOLDEN PEARLY POSING
SILVER TENDER PRECISE AFFECTED
ORIENTAL OVERNICE VALUABLE
WORTHFUL PRICELESS
PRECIOUSNESS PRICE
PRECIPICE LIN KHUD LINN LLYN PALI
CLIFF KRANS SCREE SHEER STEEP
KRANTZ CLOGWYN DOWNFALL
HEADWALL
PRECIPITATE GEL CURD HURL RAIN
RASH HASTY HURRY SHOOT SPEED
STEEP ABRUPT COAGEL HASTEN
SLUDGE SUDDEN TUMBLE UNWARY
DISTILL LYCOPIN SUBSIDE TRIGGER
CATALYZE HEADLONG PROCLIVE
SEDIMENT SETTLING
(— DYE) STRIKE
PRECIPITATELY HEADLING
HEADLONG SLAPDASH
PRECIPITATION HAIL MIST RAIN
SNOW HASTE SLEET VIRGA
PRECIPITOUS FULL RASH BRANT
BRENT HASTY STEEP ABRUPT CHICHI
STEEPY SUDDEN PRERUPT
HEADLONG
PRECIS JUNONIA SUMMARY
ABSTRACT
PRECISE DRY SET FLAT HARD JUMP
JUST NEAT NICE TIDY TRIG TRIM
TRUE VERY CLEAN CLOSE EXACT
PRESS RIGID SOUND FORMAL
NARROW RIGORE STARCH STRICT
BUCKRAM CAREFUL CERTAIN
CLERKLY CORRECT EXPRESS
PERFECT PERJINK STARCHY
ABSOLUTE ACCURATE DEFINITE
EXPLICIT HAIRLINE PINPOINT
PUNCTUAL RIGOROUS
PRECISELY BUT EVEN JUST CLEAN
SHARP FINELY JUSTLY STRAIT
EXACTLY
PRECISENESS RIGOR RIGOUR
PRIMNESS
PRECISIAN PRIG PURITAN
PRECISION NICETY CLARITY
ACCURACY DELICACY ELEGANCE
JUSTNESS
PRECISIONIST PEDANT
PRECLUDE BAR DENY STOP CLOSE
CROSS DEBAR ESTOP FORBID

HINDER IMPEDE OBVIATE PREVENT
SILENCE CONCLUDE INTERPEL
PROHIBIT ANTICIPATE
PRECOCIOUS PRECOX UNRIPE
FORWARD PREMATURE RATHERIPE
PRECONCEIVE IDEATE
PRECONCEPTION PRENOTION
PRECONDITION PRIUS
PRECURSOR USHER HERALD INITIAL
ANCESTOR PRODROME WAYMAKER
HARBINGER HEMIAUXIN
PROGENITOR
PREDACITY RAVEN RAVIN
PREDATOR COACTOR
PREDATORY HUNGRY HARMFUL
RAVENOUS
PREDECESSOR ANCESTOR
FOREGOER
(PL.) OLDERS
PREDELLA FOOTPACE
PREDESTINATION FATE DESTINY
ELECTION
PREDESTINE DOOM SLATE
FOREDOOM FOREPOINT
PREDETERMINE DESTINE
FORECAST
PREDICAMENT BOX FIX JAM NODE
SOUP SPOT CLASS LURCH STATE
STEAD PICKLE PLIGHT SCRAPE
DILEMMA IMPASSE CATEGORY
JUNCTURE QUANDARY
PREDICANT FRIAR PREACHER
DOMINICAN
PREDICATE BASE FOUND AFFIRM
ASSERT PRAISE PREACH COMMEND
DECLARE EXTREME PREDICT
PROCLAIM
PREDICT LAY BODE CALL DOPE READ
REDE SPAE AUGUR WEIRD HALSEN
FORESAY PRESAGE FOREBODE
FORECAST FORETELL PROPHESY
SOOTHSAY AUSPICATE
PROGNOSTICATE
(— EVIL) CROAK
PREDICTION DOPE WEIRD AUGURY
BODING BODWORD PORTENT
PRESAGE BODEWORD FORECAST
PROPHECY VATICINE
PREDILECTION BIAS HANG FANCY
FAVOR LIKING RELISH FONDNESS
PREDISPOSE BEND INCLINE
SUBJECT
PREDISPOSED PRONE PARTIAL
TENDING INCLINED
PREDISPOSITION ITCH
DIATHESIS
PREDOMINANCE MAJORITY
REGNANCY ASCENDANCY
PREDOMINANT GREAT RULING
CAPITAL REIGNING SUPERIOR
CULMINANT HEGEMONIC
PREDOMINATE RULE DOMINE
EXCEED GOVERN PREVAIL

PREE KISS PRIE TEST TASTE TRIAL PRYING SAMPLE PROVING TASTING

PREEMINENT BIG TOP ARCH HIGH STAR FIRST GRAND GREAT PALMARY PASSING STELLAR SUPREME FOREMOST PRECLARE SPLENDID SUPERIOR PARAMOUNT PREPOTENT (PREF.) ARCH

PREEMPT COLLAR

PREEN PIN PERK PICK TRIM WHET DRESS GLOAT PLUME PRIMP PRINK PRUNE SWELL TRICK BROOCH GODWIT SMOOTH REPLUME (— WINGS) WHET

PREFABRICATED IDENTIKIT

PREFACE FRONT PROEM USHER HERALD PRESAY EPISTLE PRECEDE PREPOSE EXORDIUM FORETALK FOREWORD PREAMBLE PROLOGUE

PREFATORY PROEMIAL PRELIMINARY

PREFECT WALI EPARC GRAVE EPARCH MONITOR PROVOST GOVERNOR PRESIDENT

PREFECTURE EPARCHY
(CHINESE —) FU
(JAPANESE —) KEN
(TIBETAN —) JONG

PREFER LAY LIKE LOVE BRING ELECT EXALT FAVOR OFFER CHOOSE PROFER SELECT OUTRANK PREFECT PRESENT PROMOTE PROPOSE SURPASS

PREFERABLE LIEF RIGHT RATHER ELIGIBLE

PREFERENCE GOO LIKE FAVOR CHOICE DESIRE LIKING RATHER DRUTHERS FAVORITE FOREHAND PRIORITY PRIVILEGE PROMOTION PRECEDENCE

PREFERMENT DIGNITY

PREFIGURE TYPE IDEATE SHADOW TYPIFY FORERUN FORESEE PREDICT FORESHOW PROPHESY ADUMBRATE

PREFIX DUN DOON PREPOSE

PREGNANCY CYESIS TROUBLE ACCYESIS FETATION OOCYESIS GESTATION

PREGNANT BIG GONE OPEN GREAT HEAVY QUICK READY BAGGED CAUGHT COGENT GRAVID PAROUS ENCEINT FERTILE GESTANT TEEMING WEIGHTY CHILDING FORCIBLE GERMINAL PREGGERS PRESSING
(— WITH HUMOR) RICH

PREHALLUX CALCAR

PREHEND SEIZE

PREHISTORIC OGYGIAN IMMEMORIAL

PREINDICATE PRESAGE FORESHOW

PREJUDICE BIAS DOWN HARM HURT KINK TURN AGISM DERRY AGEISM DAMAGE IMPAIR INJURY SEXISM SCUNDER SCUNNER JAUNDICE PREJUDGE
(— AGAINST ELDERLY) AGISM AGEISM

PREJUDICED BIGOTED INSULAR PARTIAL

PREJUDICIAL BIASED HURTFUL CONTRARY DAMAGING INIMICAL SINISTER

PRELATE CHIEF LEADER PRIEST HIERARCH ORDINARY SUPERIOR MONSIGNOR

PRELIMINARY PRIOR PRELIM PREFACE PRELUDE LIMINARY PREAMBLE PREVIOUS PREFATORY

PRELUDE PROEM VERSET DESCANT FORERUN INTRADA PREFACE ANTELUDE BORSPIEL OVERTURE RITORNEL VERSETTE VORSPIEL

PREMATURE RATH UNRIPE IMMATURE PREVIOUS TIMELESS UNTIMELY

PREMEDIATE FORNCAST PURPENSE

PREMEDITATED SET STUDIED PREPENSE

PREMIER CHIEF FIRST OLDEST LEADING EARLIEST

PREMISE LEMMA MAJOR ASSUME GROUND REASON SUMPTION

PREMISES (REAR —) BACKSIDE

PREMIUM USE AGIO BACK AWARD BONUS FANCY PRIZE SHAVE USURY BOUNTY DEPORT REWARD GRASSUM CONTANGO DONATIVE FOREGIFT GIVEAWAY
(UNDERCOVER —) ICE
(UNDERCOVER — FOR SEATS) ICE

PREMIXED INSTANT

PREMONITION OMEN HUNCH VIBES NOTICE BODWORD PRESAGE WARNING BODEWORD FORESCENT

PREMUNE SALTED

PRENATAL INUTERO

PREOCCUPATION HEART INSIGHT FIXATION

PRE-OCCUPIED ABSENTMINDED

PREOCCUPIED DEEP LOST RAPT CRAZY ABSENT FILLED INTENT CRACKED ABSORBED ENGROSSED

PREPARATION DIA FIG GEL BALM DIBS DOPE PREP CREAM FLASH GELEE GLAZE GLOSS JELLY READY ACETUM BLEACH BLUING DERRIS FACIAL LOTION MEGILP NEBULA PEPSIN SIMPLE ADDRESS APPREST CLEANER DIPPING EMANIUM ESSENCE ETHIOPS EXTRACT FITNESS FONDANT LINCTUS MELLITE PLACERO TRYPSIN VARNISH ABSTRACT CONSERVE COSMETIC FIXATURE GELOSINE INHALANT

LAUDANUM MEDICINE RACAHOUT
TRAINING MAKEREADY PROVISION
(— CONTAINING HONEY) MELLITE
(— FOR COLORING LIQUORS) FLASH
(— OF GRAPEJUICE) DIBS
(AROMATIC —) ELIXIR
(CHEESE —) FONDU FONDUTA
(CHEESELIKE —) YOGURT CROWDIE
YOGHURT
(COSMETIC —) HENNA
(ENZYME —) KOJI
(EYELID —) KOHL
(IMPURE RADIOACTIVE —) EMANIUM
(INTOXICATING —) BOZA GANJA
(MEDICAL —) STUFF
(OPIUM —) LAUDANUM
(SALINE —) LICK
(SLOPPY —) SLIBBERSAUCE
(SWEET —) DULCE
(UNCTUOUS —) CERATE
PREPARATORY PRIMAL PIONEER
PRELIMINARY
PREPARE DO FIT FIX GET LAY ABLE
BOUN BUSK COOK GIRD MAKE PARE
PLOT PREP TILL YARK ATTLE BLEND
BOWNE BRACE DIGHT DRAFT DRESS
EQUIP FRAME ORDER PREDY READY
TRAIN ADJUST DESIGN GRAITH
ORDAIN ADDRESS AFFAITE APPAREL
APPOINT CONCOCT CONFECT
DISPOSE EDUCATE PRODUCE
PROVIDE QUALIFY INSTRUCT
(— BANQUET) COVER
(— BEFOREHAND) PRECONDITION
(— BY BOILING) BREW DECOCT
(— BY HEAT) FRIT
(— CAPON) SAUCE
(— COCAINE) FREEBASE
(— FISH) CALVER
(— FLAX FOR LINEN) RET
(— FOOD) DO COOK
(— FOR BUILDING) FRAME
(— FOR BURIAL) EMBALM
(— FOR DISPLAY) DRESS
(— FOR MARKETING) PROCESS
(— FOR PUBLICATION) EDIT
(— FOR TAKEOFF) STRAPIN
(— HASTILY) RASH
(— HEMP) TAW
(— LAND) CURE
(— ONESELF) ADDRESS
(— TEASEL HEADS) CARP
(— TO DEPART) INSPAN
PREPARED UP APT BUN FIT SET
BAAN BOON BOUN BOWN GIRT RIPE
YARE ALERT BOUND PREST READY
GRAITH CURRIED EQUIPPED
TOGETHER
(— WITH GRAPES) VERONIQUE
(HASTILY —) EXTEMPORARY
(INCOMPLETELY —) GREEN
(QUICKLY —) RUNNING

PREPAREDNESS PROCINCT
PREPENSE DESIGN FORETHOUGHT
PREPONDERANCE MAJORITY
DOMINANCE
PREPONDERATE EXCEED INCLINE
SURPASS DOMINATE OUTWEIGH
PERSUADE
PREPOSSESS BIAS PREVENT
PREPOSSESSING WINNING
PREPOSSESSION BENT BIAS
FETICH FANTASY PREJUDICE
PREPOSTEROUS RICH INEPT
ABSURD FOOLISH LAPUTAN
GROTESQUE RIDICULOUS
PREPUCE
(PREF.) POSTH(E)(IO)(O)
PREROGATIVE GRACE HONOR
RIGHT ESNECY REGALE FACULTY
PECULIAR PRIVILEGE
PRESA LEAD
PRESAGE BODE HINT OMEN OSSE
SIGN ABODE AUGUR TOKEN
AUGURY BETIDE BETOKEN FORESEE
OMINATE PORTEND PREDICT
FOREBODE FORECAST FOREDOOM
FORETELL INDICATE PREAMBLE
PROPHESY
PRESBYTER ELDER PRIEST PRESTER
ANTISTES MINISTER
PRESBYTERIAN WHIG CLASSIC
WHIGGAMORE
PRESBYTERY CLASSIS SENIORY
EXERCISE PARSONAGE CONSISTORY
PRESCIENCE PRESAGE FORESIGHT
PREVISION
PRESCIND SEVER DETACH
PRESCRIBE SET TAX ALLOT GUIDE
LIMIT ORDER ASSIGN DEFINE DIRECT
ENJOIN INDITE ORDAIN APPOINT
CONFINE CONTROL DICTATE
RESTRAIN
PRESCRIBED SET BASIC THETIC
POSITIVE THETICAL FORMULARY
PRESCRIPT LAW COMMAND
MANDATE PRECEPT
PRESCRIPTION RX BILL FORM
CIPHER RECIPE DICTATE FORMULA
RECEIPT
PRESENCE EYE FACE SELF BEING
ASPECT BEARING COMPANY
ASSEMBLY INSTANCE
(— OF GOD) GLORY
(BODILY —) PERSON
(DIRECT —) IMMEDIACY
(DIVINE —) SHEKINAH SHECHINAH
PRESENT AIM BOX NOW BILL BOON
GIFT GIVE HAND HERE MEED NEAR
NIGH SAND SHOW BEING CUDDY
DOLLY ENTER FEOFF GRANT NONCE
OFFER PLACE RAISE READY STAGE
THERE ACCUSE ACTUAL ADDUCE
ALLEGE AROUND BESTOW BOUNTY

BROACH CADEAU CLOTHE CUMSHA
DONATE DURANT HANSEL KHILAT
LATTER MODERN NEARBY PREFER
REGALE REGALO RENDER XENIUM
COMMEND CUMSHAW DISPLAY
DOUCEUR ETRENNE EXHIBIT
EXPOUND FAIRING FURNISH
HANDSEL INSTANT LARGESS
PERFORM PORRECT PRETEND
PROPINE RELEASE RESIANT TASHRIF
BLESSING CONGIARY DONATION
GRATUITY INSTANCE OFFFRING
PESHKASH RESIDENT SOULCAKE
SPORTULA LAGNIAPPE
(— AS GIFT) DASH
(— FOR ACCEPTANCE) TENDER
(— FORMALLY) SERVE
(— FROM PUPIL TO TEACHER)
MINERVAL
(— IN DETAIL) DISCUSS
(— IN MIND) DEAR
(— OF MONEY) BAKHSHISH
BAKSHEESH BACKSHEESH
(— ONESELF) APPEAR
(— PROMINENTLY) FEATURE
(— TO SOLDIERS) CONGIARY
(— TO STRANGER) XENIUM
(— TO SUPERIOR) NUZZER
(— TO VIEW) YIELD
(— WITHOUT WARRANT) OBTRUDE
(ALWAYS —) CHRONIC
(BRIDEGROOM'S —) HANDSEL
(CEREMONIAL —) KHILAT
(NOT —) ABSENT
(SMALL —) STOCKINGFILLER
PRESENTATION BILL GALA GIFT
GLOW DROLL IMAGE DHARMA
MUSTER SCHEMA BILLING DISPLAY
EPITOME HOOKUPU MUSICAL
PRESENT SPECIES ANALYSIS
BESTOWAL DELIVERY DONATION
EXPOSURE CANDLEMAS
PERFORMANCE
(— IN ART) STUDY
(— TO VIEW) OBJECT
PRESENTIMENT FEELING PRESAGE
BODEMENT FOREFEEL PRENOTION
PREMONITION
PRESENTLY NOW ANON ENOW
SOON SHORTLY DIRECTLY
PRESERVATION FILING SAVING
KEEPING SERVATION
PRESERVATIVE SALT BORAX SPICE
SUGAR CONSERVE TREATMENT
(FOOD —) TINFOIL
PRESERVE CAN JAR CORN HAIN
HOLD KEEP SALT SAVE BLESS
GUARD SERVE SPARE SWEET WITIE
ATHOLD BOTTLE COMFIT DEFEND
EMBALM FREEZE GOGGLE POWDER
RETAIN SECURE SHIELD UPHOLD
CONDITE FORFEND KYANIZE

PROTECT RAISINE RESERVE
SUCCADE SUSTAIN CHOWCHOW
CONSERVE ENSHRINE MAINTAIN
MOTHBALL PARADISE WITHSAVE
(— BY BOILING WITH SUGAR) CANDY
(— BY SALTING) CORN CURE SALT
(— OF GRAPES) RAISINE
(— WOOD) KYANIZE PAYNISE
(GAME —) MOOR SHIKARGAH
(HUNTING —) WALK
(PL.) KONFYT
PRESERVED WET CONFECT
BRANDIED POWDERED
PRESERVES JAM JELLY
PRESIDE RULE GUIDE DIRECT
MODERATE
(— OVER) KEEP
PRESIDENCY MADRAS PRYTANY
PRESIDENT MIR FOUD PREX PREXY
PROXY REEVE DEACON RECTOR
PRAESES PREFECT
(— OF COLLEGE) PREX PREXY
(— OF GUILD) DEAN
(— OF LEGISLATURE) SPEAKER
(— OF SUPREME COURT) LAWMAN
(— OF TRADE) DEACON
PRESIGNIFY PRESAGE FORETOKEN
PRESLEY (MIDDLE NAME OF —)
ARON
PRESS FLY HUG JAM SIT BEAR BEND
CRAM DOME DROP DRUK HORN
HUSH IRON JAMB KISS PLOT SERR
THEW TUCK URGE VICE YERK ARGUE
BESET BRIZZ CHAFE CHIRT CRIMP
CROWD CRUDH DRIVE EXACT FORCE
KNEAD MIDST PRIZE SCREW SHREW
SMASH STAMP STUFF TWIST WEIGH
WRING ASSAIL CHISEL CLOSET
COARCT CRUNCH GOFFER HARASS
JOBBER KVETCH MANGLE NUDDLE
PREACE SQUASH STRAIN STRESS
THRAST THREAP THREAT THREEP
THRIMP THRING THRONG THRUST
AFFLICT ARMOIRE ATTEMPT
BESEECH BESIEGE CONCISE
CRUMPLE EMBRACE ENVIRON
FLATBED IMPRESS MACHINE
OPPRESS SCROOGE SCRUNGE
SQUEEZE THRUTCH AGGRIEVE
CALENDER COMPRESS PRESSURE
SCROUNGE SQUEEGEE SURROUND
(— AGAINST) CONTACT
(— CLOSE) NUDDLE
(— CLOSELY AND PAINFULLY) MASH
(— DOWN) QUAT
(— FORWARD) DRIVE BREAST
(— FOR WINE) TORCULAR
(— HARSHLY) GRIND
(— IN CHEESE VAT) CHISEL CHIZZEL
(— INTO) THRIMBLE THRUMBLE
(— INTO SERVICE) REQUISITION
(— ON ANVIL) HORN

(— ONWARD) STRETCH
(— OUT) EXTRUDE
(— PAINFULLY) PINCH
(— PAPER) COUCH
(— TOGETHER) PACK KNEAD SERRY
IMPACT CONSTRICT
(— UPON) ELBOW DOWNBEAR
(— WITH FOOT) TREAD
(— WITH HEAD OR HORNS) BOX
(— WITH NOSE) NOUSLE NUZZLE
(— WITH VIOLENCE) DRIVE
(PREF.) PIEZO PRESSI
(SUFF.) (—TOGETHER) ARCTIA
PRESS AGENT FLACK
PRESS-AGENTRY FLACKERY
PRESSED SERRIED
(— WITH BUSINESS) THRONG
(— WITH LEFTHAND FOREFINGER)
BARRED
PRESSES
(SUFF.) (—CLOSE) NASTIC
PRESSING RASH ACUTE CRYING
URGENT CLAMANT EARNEST
EXIGENT INSTANT SQUEEZE
CRITICAL PREGNANT NECESSITOUS
(— HARD) SEVERE
PRESSMAN PIG MINDER PROVER
PRINTER
PRESSURE JAM HEAD HEAT PEND
PUSH SWAY DRIVE FORCE IMAGE
PINCH STAMP BURDEN DURESS
STRESS THRONG WEIGHT BEARING
MERCURY PUSHING SQUEEZE
TENSION URGENCY EXACTION
EXIGENCY FUGACITY PRESSION
(— GROUP) LOBBY
(— OF CIRCUMSTANCE) NECESSITY
(— OF 1 DYNE) BARAD
(— ON INSTRUMENT STRING) STOP
(— UNIT) TORR MICRON
(LIQUID —) HEAD
(MANUAL —) TAXIS
(OSMOTIC —) TONICITY
(UNIT OF —) TORR OSMOL PASCAL
MICROBAR
(VAPOR —) FUGACITY
(PREF.) PIEZO TONO
PRESSURE COOKER STEAMER
AUTOCLAVE
PRESSWORK BACKUP
PRESTIDIGITATOR PALMER
JUGGLER PYTHONIC
PRESTIGE FACE MANA CASTE IKBAL
IZZAT KUDOS PLACE CACHET
STATUS STATURE ILLUSION
INFLUENCE
(HAVING —) STATUSY
PRESTO QUICKLY SPEEDILY
PRESUME BEAR DARE GROW IMPLY
INFER ASSUME EXPECT DARESAY
SUPPOSE ARROGATE
PRESUMED PUTATIVE
PRESUMING ARROGANT FAMILIAR

PRESUMPTION GALL JOLLITY
OUTRAGE PRESUME AUDACITY
SUCCUDRY SURQUIDY
PRESUMPTUOUS BOLD PERT
FRESH PROUD WICKED WILFUL
FORWARD HAUGHTY ARROGANT
ASSUMING FAMILIAR INSOLENT
FOOLHARDY
PRESUPPOSE IMPLY POSIT ASSUME
EXPECT PREMISE FORETAKE
PRESUPPOSITION PREMISE
PRETA PETA
PRETEND ACT LET FAKE MAKE MOCK
SHAM CLAIM FEIGN LETON AFFECT
ASPIRE ASSERT ASSUME GAMMON
INTEND OBTEND POSSUM RECKON
SEMBLE ATTEMPT PORTEND
PRESUME PROFESS SUPPOSE
VENTURE SIMULATE
(— IGNORANCE) CONNIVE
(— TO) FA
PRETENDED FAKE SHAM BOGUS
FALSE IRONIC PSEUDO UNREAL
ALLEGED ASSUMED COLORED
FEIGNED SEEMING SIMULAR
AFFECTED IRONICAL SIMULATE
PRETENDER FOP FAKE IDOL CHEAT
COWAN FAKER FRAUD POSER
QUACK PSEUDO SEEMER AEOLIST
CLAIMANT IMPOSTOR INTENDER
TARTUFFE MOUNTEBANK
(— TO LEARNING) SCIOLIST
PRETENDING FICTION
PRETENSE ACT AIR FACE GRIM
MASK MIEN PLEA RUSE SCUG SHAM
SHOW SIGN WILE CLOAK COLOR
COVER FEINT GLOSS GLOZE GUISE
STUDY EXCUSE HUMBUG VENEER
CHARADE DAUBERY FAITERY
FASHION FICTION GRIMACE PRETEXT
PURPOSE UMBRAGE ARTIFICE
DISGUISE POSTICHE POSTIQUE
SEMBLANT
(SUPERFICIAL —) VENEER
PRETENSION AIRS PARADE VANITY
PRETEXT
(—S TO KNOWLEDGE) SCIOLISM
(FALSE —) DISSIMULATION
PRETENTIOUS BIG ARTY BRAG
HIGH SIDY BRANK FLASH GAUDY
PUFFY SHOWY BRAGGY CHICHI
GEWGAW GLOSSY PUFFED ROCOCO
SHODDY TINSEL BOMBAST
POMPOUS STILTED TINHORN
TOPPING BRAGGART OVERBLOWN
RECHERCHE
PRETENTIOUSNESS SIDE SWANK
PRETERMIT OMIT NEGLACT
SUSPEND INTERRUPT
PRETERNATURAL GOUSTY
GOUSTIE STRANGE ABNORMAL
UNCOMMON UNEARTHLY
(— BEING) MARE

PRETEXT PEG FLAM MASK PLEA RUSE VEIL CLOAK COLOR COVER GLOSS SALVO STALL EXCUSE REFUGE SCONCE APOLOGY UMBRAGE OCCASION PRETENCE PRETENSE

PRETTIFY EYEWASH

PRETTINESS
(ARTFUL —) COQUETRY)

PRETTY APT GEY PAT ABLE BRAW CUTE DEFT FAIR FEAT FINE GAIN GENT GOOD JOLI MILD MOOI POOR TRIM BONNY DINKY JOLIE POOTY PURTY QUITE SWEET BONITA DIMBER FINELY INCONY MINION PRATTY RATHER TRETIS CLEMENT CUNNING DOLLISH GENTEEL BUDGEREE PRECIOUS
(— WELL) GAILY GAYLY

PRETTY-PRETTY KEEPSAKE

PREVAIL WIN BEAR BEAT REIGN WIELD INDUCE OBTAIN CONQUER PERSIST SUCCEED TRIUMPH DOMINATE
(— BECAUSE BEYOND CONTROL) RAGE
(— OVER) OVERRIDE OVERRULE SURMOUNT
(— UPON) GET FOLD LEAD ARGUFY ENTICE INDUCE OBTAIN ENTREAT OVERSWAY

PREVAILING RIFE GOING USUAL CURRENT DOMINANT

PREVALENCE RUN

PREVALENT UP RIFE BRIEF COMMON POTENT VULGAR CURRENT GENERAL POPULAR RAMPANT REGNANT CATHOLIC EPIDEMIC POWERFUL

PREVARICATE LIE EVADE STRAY SKLENT WANDER QUIBBLE SHUFFLE WHIFFLE

PREVARICATOR LIAR JESUIT

PREVENT BAR LET HELP KEEP NILL SHUN STAY STOP TENT WARN AVERT CHECK DEBAR DETER ESTOP ARREST DEFEND FORBID FORLET HINDER OUTRUN RETAIN REVOKE SECURE FORFEND FORLEIT IMPEACH INHIBIT OBVIATE OCCLUDE PRECEDE RETRACT RULEOUT ANTEVERT INTERPEL PARALYZE PRECLUDE PROHIBIT WITHHOLD
(— OPPONENT FROM SCORING) CHICAGO

PREVENTION PREFACE ESTOPPEL OBSTACLE PREJUDICE

PREVIEW SNEAK SCREEN FUTURAMA

PREVIOUS HASTY PRIOR BEFORE FORMER RATHER EARLIER LEADING FORFGONE PRECEDING

PREVIOUSLY ERE YET FRST FORE ONCE SUPRA BEFORE ALREADY

HASTILY PRIORLY FORMERLY HITHERTO

PREVISION FORESEE FORECAST FORESIGHT

PREY ROB FEED GAME SOYL TIRE BOOTY PREDE RAVEN RAVIN SPOIL QUARRY RAVAGE RAVINE VICTIM CAPTURE PILLAGE PLUNDER ROBBERY SPREATH VULTURE
(— OF HUNTER) GAME
(— UPON) DEVOUR PICAROON DEPREDATE
(HAWK'S —) PELT

PREYER KITE

PRIAM (DAUGHTER OF —) CREUSA POLYXENA CASSANDRA
(GRANDFATHER OF —) ILUS
(SLAYER OF —) PYRRHUS
(SON OF —) PARIS HECTOR TROILUS
(WIFE OF —) HECUBA

PRIAPISM TENTIGO

PRICE LAY ANTE COST FARE FEER FIAR FIER FOOT ODDS PRYS RATE BRIBE CHEAP CLOSE VALUE WORTH CHARGE FIGURE HANSEL TARIFF AVERAGE CATALOG CRANAGE EXPENSE FURNACE HANDSEL PRETIUM STORAGE CARRIAGE FERRIAGE INTEREST
(— FOR KEEPING GOODS) STORAGE
(— FOR PASTURING CATTLE) AGISTMENT
(— OF RECLAMATION) RANSOM
(ESTIMATED —) QUOTATION
(HIGH —) DEARTH
(KIND OF —) RETAIL STICKER
(LOW —) WANWORTH
(PROPER —) VALUE
(REDUCED —) SALE BARGAIN
(RISING —S) BOOM INFLATION

PRICELESS RARE COSTLY UNIQUE UNSALABLE

PRICEY DEAR STEEP

PRICK DOT JAG BROD BROG DROB FOIN GOAD JAGG PECK PING PROG SPUR STAB TANG URGE DRESS ERECT POINT PREEN PUNCH STEEK BROACH GALLOP INTENT LAUNCH POUNCE PRITCH SKEWER STITCH TARGET THRUST TWINGE ACANTHA POINTED BULLSEYE
(— OUT) SPOT
(— PAINFULLY) STING
(— WITH NAIL) CLY CLOY ACCLOY
(PREF.) STIGMATI STIGMEO STIGMO

PRICKED PIQUE
(— UP) ARRECT

PRICKER PROD NEEDLE STABBER

PRICKET DAG SNUFFER SPITTER

PRICKING SMART PUNGENT RETRACT POIGNANT POINTURE PUNCTION

PRICKLE PIKE SETA BRIAR BRIER
SPEAR SPINE THORN BASKET
ACANTHA ACULEUS PRINKLE
SPICULA STICKLE STIMULUS
(PREF.) ECHIN(O)

PRICKLY BURRY JAGGY SHARP
SPINY URCHIN BEARDED SPINOSE
SPINOUS STICKLY THISTLY
ACULEATE ECHINATE MURICATE
SCABROUS SCRATCHY SPICULAR
STICKERY STINGING VEXATIOUS
(PREF.) CHIN(O)

PRICKLY ASH RUEWORT

PRICKLY HEAT MILIARIA

PRICKLY PEAR TUN TUNA NOPAL
SABRA OPUNTIA PINPILLOW

PRICKLY-POINTED PUNGENT

PRICKLY POPPY ARGEMONE
COCKSCOMB

PRIDE HEAT HORN LUST POMP RUFF
ADORN CREST GLORY ORGUL PLUME
PREEN PRIME WLANK EXCESS
HUBRIS METTLE NOSISM VANITY
COMPANY CONCEIT DISDAIN
EGOTISM GLORIFY HAUTEUR
STOMACH SMUGNESS SURQUIDY
WLONKHEDE
(— ONESELF) PIQUE
(EXCESSIVE —) SWELLING
ARROGANCE
(MASCULINE —) MACHISMO
(SENSE OF MASCULINE —)
MACHISMO

PRIDE AND PREJUDICE (AUTHOR
OF —) AUSTEN
(CHARACTER IN —) JANE MARY
DARCY KITTY LUCAS LYDIA BENNET
GEORGE BINGLEY COLLINS
WICKHAM CAROLINE DEBOURGH
GARDINER CATHERINE CHARLOTTE
ELIZABETH FITZWILLIAM

PRIDEFUL FASTUOUS

PRIEST EN ABBE CURA CURE DEAN
EZRA IMAM MAGA CLERK COHEN
EPULO IMAUM ISIAC MOBED PADRE
PATER SABIO SARIP VICAR ZADOK
ABACES AMAUTA BHIKKU BISHOP
DASTUR DIVINE FALMEN FATHER
FLAMEN GALLAH GALLUS GELONG
GETSUL GOSAIN JETHRO KAHUNA
LEVITE POWWOW SHAMAN
ANANIAS ARBACES CALCHAS
CASSOCK CHANTER DESTOUR
DUSTOOR GALLACH LAOCOON
PANDITA PAPALOI PATENER PATRICO
PHINEAS POONGEE PRESTER
STOLIST TEACHER TOHUNGA
BABAYLAN BEROSSOS CHRYSEIS
HANANIAH KASHYAPA MINISTER
PANDARAM PENANCER PONTIFEX
POONGHIE SACERDOS SEMINARY
SOGGARTH SYRIARCH TALISMAN

VARDAPET ZADOKITE OFFICIANT
SHAVELING CHAMBERLAIN
((MISSIONARY —) REDEMPTORIST
(— OF APOLLO) CALCHAS CHRYSEIS
(— OF CYBELE) CORYBANT
(— OF RAMA) KASHYAPA
(— OF RHEA) CURETE
(BABYLONIAN —) BEROSSOS
(BUDDHIST —) LAMA BHIKKU
GELONG POONGEE POONGHIE
TALAPOIN
(BULGARIAN —) BOGOMIL
BOGOMILE
(CELTIC —) DRUID
(CHIEF —) SYRIARCH
(CHIEF — OF SHRINE) EN
(EGYPTIAN —) ARBACES CHOACHYTE
(ETRUSCAN —) LUCUMO
(EUNUCH —) GALLUS
(FRENCH —) PERE SULPICIAN
(GREEK —) PAPA
(GYPSY —) PATRICO
(HIGH —) ELI SARIP DASTUR KAHUNA
DESTOUR PHINEAS PONTIFF
PRELATE CAIAPHAS HIERARCH
JEHOIADA PONTIFEX
(HINDU —) PANDARAM
(IGNORANT —) LACKLATIN
(INCA —) AMAUTA
(INFERIOR —) LEVITE
(LAMAIST —) GETSUL
(MAORI —) TOHUNGA
(MORO —) SARIP PANDITA
(MOSLEM —) ALFAQUI TALISMAN
(NEW —) NEOPHYTE
(PAGAN —) BABAYLAN
(PARISH —) CURA CURE PAPA POPE
PARSON PERSON SECULAR
(PERSIAN —) MAGUS
(ROMAN —) EPULO FLAMEN
(TIBETAN —) LAMA
(VAISHNAVA —) GOSAIN
(VOODOO —) BOCOR BOKOR
(PL.) LUPERCI

PRIEST-DOCTOR SHAMAN
WABENO

PRIESTESS NUN ENTUM HORSE
MAMBO MAMBU BACBUC PYTHIA
DIOTIMA MAMALOI PHOIBAD
PHITONES PYTHONESS
(— OF APOLLO) PYTHIA PHOEBAD
(— OF THE BOTTLE) BACBUC
(BABYLONIAN —) ENTUM
(VOODOO —) HORSE

PRIESTFISH CHERNA ROCKFISH

PRIESTHOOD SALII SACERDOCY

PRIEST-KING PATESI

PRIESTLY AARONIC LEVITIC
SACERDOTAL

PRIG BEG FOP BRAD BUCK NAIL
SMUG DANDY FILCH PLEAD STEAL
THIEF FELLOW HAGGLE PERSON

PILFER TINKER ENTREAT PURITAN
QUIBBLE
PRIGGER THIEF
PRIGGISH PRUDISH
PRIM MIM NEAT TRIG TRIM MIMZY
DEMURE FORMAL MIMSEY PRISSY
PRIVET PROPER STUFFY MISSISH
PERJINK PRECISE PRIMSIE STARCHY
PRIMACY CHIEFTY PRIMITY
HEADSHIP
PRIMA DONNA DIVA STAR
PRIMARY CYAN MAIN BASIC CHIEF
FIRST PRIME CAUCUS DIRECT
FONTAL MANUAL MAGENTA
RADICAL ARCHICAL CARDINAL
HYPOGENE ORIGINAL PRIMEVAL
PRINCIPAL
(PREF.) ARCHI PROT(E)(EO)
PRIMATE BISHOP GALAGO LEADER
PREMAN PRINCIPAL PREHOMINID
PRIME MAY FANG FILL LOAD MAIN
CHIEF COACH FIRST PRIDE TONIC
YOUTH CHOICE FLOWER SPRING
CENTRAL LEADING LUSTFUL
PREPARE DOMINEER ORIGINAL
YOUTHFUL PRINCIPAL
(— A PUMP) FANG PHANG
(— OF LIFE) FLOWER
PRIME MINISTER DEWAN DIWAN
ATABEG PREMIER
(DEPUTY —) TANAISTE
(IRISH —) TAOISEACH
PRIMER ABC CAP DONAT WAFER
READER CORDERY HORNBOOK
PRIMEVAL OLD NATIVE ANCIENT
OGYGIAN PRIMARY PRISTINE
PRIMITIVE
PRIMING MORSING TWOPENNY
CLEARCOLE
PRIMING IRON DRIFT
PRIMING WIRE PICKER
PRIMITIVE DARK CRUDE EARLY
FIRST GROSS NAIVE PLAIN PRIME
FANTEE GOTHIC PRIMAL SAVAGE
SIMPLE ANCIENT ARCHAIC PRIMARY
PRISCAN BACKVELD BARBARIC
EARLIEST IGNORANT ORIGINAL
PRISTINE ABORIGINAL PRIMORDIAL
NEANDERTHAL ANTEDILUVIAN
(PREF.) ARCH(AE)(AEO)(E)(EO)(I)
PALAE(O) PALE(O)
PRIMNESS STARCH PRUDERY
PRIMORDIAL CRUDE FIRST PRIMARY
ARCHICAL EARLIEST PRIMEVAL
PRIMORDIUM BUD ANLAGE
BLASTEMA
PRIMP PRIM ADORN PREEN PRINK
DOLLUP
PRIMROSE GAY OXLIP SPINK
FLOWER SUNCUP COWSLIP
FLOWERY PRIMULA SCABISH
AURICULA PLUMROCK SCURVISH

AFTERGLOW PIMPERNEL
POLYANTHUS
PRIMULA OXLIP COWSLIP
PRIMWORT
PRINCE MIN RAS DUKE EARL EMIR
IMAM KHAN KING KNEZ LORD NASI
RAJA RANA RIAL SAID WANG
ALDER EBLIS EMEER FURST GEBIR
MIRZA PWYLL RAJAH SAYID
ARJUNA DESPOT DYNAST SHERIF
SOLDAN BHARATA ELECTOR
GLAUCUS HELENUS MONARCH
TANCRED TOPARCH ZERBINO
ARCHDUKE ATHELING CARDINAL
FLORIZEL HOSPODAR MAMILIUS
OROONOKO RASSELAS SARPEDON
PENDRAGON
(— OF ABYSSINIA) RAS RASSELAS
(— OF APOSTATE ANGELS) DEVIL
EBLIS
(— OF ARGO) DIOMED DIOMEDES
(— OF BOHEMIA) FLORIZEL
(— OF DARKNESS) DEVIL SATAN
(— OF DEMONS) BEELZEBUB
(— OF DYFED) PWYLL
(— OF SALERNO) TANCRED
(— OF SCOTLAND) ZERBINO
(— SOLD INTO SLAVERY) OROONOKO
(— WITH CHARLEMAGNE) ASTOLF
ASTOLFO
(ANGLO-SAXON —) ADELING
ATHELING
(ARAB —) SHERIF
(CHINESE —) WANG
(ETRUSCAN —) LUCUMO
(GERMAN —) FURST ELECTOR
(INDIAN —) RAJA RANA RAJAH
BHARATA AILUWALIA
(LYCIAN —) GLAUCUS SARPEDON
(MESHECH —) GOG
(MOHAMMEDAN —) SOLDAN
(MOSLEM —) IMAM SAID SAYID
SAYYID SHEIKH SOLDAN
(PETTY —) SATRAP VERGOBRET
(SERVIAN —) CRAL
(SLAVIC —) KNEZ
(TROJAN —) HELENUS
(WIFE OF — VALIANT) ALETA
PRINCE EDWARD ISLAND (BAY
OF —) ROLLA EGMONT ORWELL
MALPEQUE
(CAPITAL OF —) CHARLOTTETOWN
(TOWN OF —) ABNEY SOURIS
TIGNISH MONTAGUE GEORGETOWN
SUMMERSIDE
PRINCELY NOBLE ROYAL KINGLY
STATELY SOVEREIGN
PRINCE'S FEATHER LILAC
PILEWORT
PRINCESS AIDA ELSA OZMA RANI
DANAE PALLA RANEE SARAH
CREUSA GLAUKE ILDICO MADAME

PSYCHE ANTIOPE CORONIS PHYLLIS
DRAUPADI MAHARANI
(— CHANGED INTO CROW) CORONIS
(— MOTHER OF ZEUS) ANTIOPA
ANTIOPE
(— OF ARGOS) DANAE
(— OF CORINTH) CREUSA GLAUKE
(— WHO SLEW ATTILA) ILDICO
(MOHAMMEDAN —) BEGUM
(THRACIAN —) PHYLLIS
(TYRIAN —) DIDO
PRINCEWOOD CYP BARIA CYPRE
CERILLO CANALETE SALMWOOD
PRINCIPAL ARCH BOSS HEAD HIGH
LEAD MAIN STAR CHIEF FIRST
GRAND GREAT PRIME STOCK
AUCTOR CORPUS MASTER STAPLE
CAPITAL CAPTAIN CENTRAL CHATTEL
DECUMAN DOMINUS PREMIER
PRIMARY SALIENT STELLAR
CARDINAL ESPECIAL FOREMOST
OFFICIAL PRESTANT PRINCELY
(— OF SCHOOL) PRECEPTOR
HEADMASTER
(POLITICAL —) PLANK
(PREF.) ARCH PROT(O)
PRINCIPALITY ZUPA ARZAVA
ARZAWA ORANGE SATRAPY
APPANAGE DESPOTAT PRINCEDOM
PRINCIPE (MONEY OF —) DOBRA
PRINCIPLE JUS LAW RTA TAO BASE
FATE RITA RULE SEED YANG AGENT
AXIOM BASIS CANON CAUSE DATUM
ETHOS PRANA SPARK STUFF TENET
ANIMUS ARABIN CNICIN COGITO
CORTIN ELIXIR EMBRYO FAGINE
GOSPEL ARCHEUS BROCARD
BUFAGIN CLYSSUS ELEMENT
FORMULA GENERAL PRECEPT
QUASSIN RADICAL THEOREM
URGRUND DOCTRINE GOSSYPOL
INTIMISM LANDMARK NICOTINE
SANCTION SPECIFIC TINCTURE
(— ACCEPTED AS TRUE) CANON
(— FROM TOAD) BUFAGIN
(— IN BEECHNUTS) FAGINE
(— OF BLESSED THISTLE) CNICIN
(— OF COTTONSEED) GOSSYPOL
(— OF EXISTENCE) TATTVA
(— OF INDIVIDUATION) AHANKARA
(— OF KEY IN MUSIC) TONALITY
(— OF MENTAL LIFE) PSYCHE
(— OF PARTY) PLANK
(— OF REST) ADHARMA
(— UNDERLYING —) REASON
RATIONALE
(COSMIC —) HEAVEN URGRUND
PRAJAPATI
(DIVINE —) OVERSOUL
(DOGMATIC —) DICTUM
(ELEMENTARY —) BROCARD
(FEMALE —) YIN SAKTI

(FIRST —) ABC SEED ARCHE
(FUNDAMENTAL —) GROUNDSEL
(GERMINAL —) STAMEN
(GOVERNING —) HINGE
(GUIDING —) SQUARE POLESTAR
(KIND OF —) FICK PETER
(LIFE —) SOUL GHOST PRANA
(MALE —) YANG PURUSHA
(MOHAMMEDAN THEOLOGICAL —)
IJMA
(MORAL —) SCRUPLE
(NARCOTIC —) FAGINE
(ONTOLOGICAL —) DHARMA
(POISONOUS —) PICROTOXIN
(PRIMAL —) APEIRON
(PROMINENT —) KEY
(QUICKENING —) LIFE
(RHYTHMICAL —) ACCENT
(SANITARY — S) HYGIENE
(SPIRITUAL —) SOUL
(STOIC —) LOGOS
(SUMMARY OF —S) CREED
(VITAL —) JIVA SPIRIT STAMEN
ARCHAEUS
PRINK PERK PRIG WINK ADORN
PRICK PRIMP PRUNE BEDECK
SMUDGE
PRINT CUT GAY GUM RUN DRUK
MARK TYPE FUDGE PORTY PRESS
SEPIA STAMP BANNER BORDER
CARBON CARBRO ENFACE LETTER
STRIKE BROMOIL DROPOUT
DUOTYPE ENGRAVE GRAPHIC
GRAVURE IMPRESS PUBLISH
TRACING VANDYKE VESTIGE
WOODCUT AQUATONE CALOTYPE
CHLORIDE DRYPOINT HALFTONE
INSCRIBE LEIMTYPE MONOTYPE
POSITIVE URUSHIYE
PHOTOENGRAVING
(— OF WILD MAMMAL) PUG
(— OTHER SIDE) BACK
(— OVER) SURCHARGE
(— PROMINENTLY) SPLASH
(— SECOND SIDE) PERFECT
(— TO RIGHT) ADSCRIPT
(BLOCK —) LINOCUT
(SILK SCREEN —) SERIGRAPH
(UNEDITED —) RUSH
PRINTED FONTED
PRINTER TYPO TWICER PRESSMAN
IMPRIMENT
(AID TO —) DEVIL
(KIND OF —) LINE LASER INKJET
(PL.) TYPOTHETAE
AMERICAN DAY GOUDY GREEN
RUDGE AITKEN BEADLE DRAPER
DUNLAP HUNTER ROGERS SHOLES
THOMAS UPDIKE WILSON ZENGER
DEVINNE GARNETT ROLLINS
BRADFORD WOODWORTH
AUSTRIAN WELSBACH

DUTCH ROMBERG ELZEVIR ENSCHEDE
ENGLISH CAVE DAYE JONES WORDE BLOUNT BOWYER BULMER BUTTER CAXTON OGILBY RAIKES WALKER AWDELAY COPLAND CROWLEY GRAFTON HANSARD NICHOLS BRADSHAW ROYCROFT WOODFALL BASKERVILLE WHITTINGHAM
FRENCH DIDOT DOLET MOREL COLINES PLANTIN RICHARD ESTIENNE
GERMAN FUST ZELL KONIG LUFFT FROBEN MENTEL ZAINER ZENGER PFISTER RATDOLT AMERBACH GRYPHIUS SCHOFFER BREITKOPF GUTENBERG TAUCHNITZ
ITALIAN BODONI GIUNTA CASTALDI MANUTIUS
JAPANESE HARUNOBU
SCOTTISH SMELLIE BALLANTYNE
SWISS GERING
PRINTER'S DEVIL FLY
PRINTING TIRAGE EDITION VIGOREUX CHARACTER IMPRIMERY
(— CHARACTER) SWUNGDASH
(KIND OF —) DNA
(LAST —) THIRTY
PRION PETREL
PRIONID BEETLE
PRIONODON LINSANG
PRIOR ERE OLD FORE PAST EIGNE ELDER FORMER RATHER ALREADY EARLIER FARTHER ANTERIOR FOREHAND HITHERTO PREVIOUS PRECEDING
(PREF.) ANTE EPH EPI
(— TO) ANTE PRAE PRE SUPRA
PRIORITY PRIVILEGE PRECEDENCE PREFERMENT
(PREF.) PRAE PRE
PRIORY ABBEY NUNNERY CLOISTER PRIORATE
PRISCA (HUSBAND OF —) AQUILA
PRISM BLOCK NICOL CYLINDER SPECTRUM WERNICKE REFRACTOR
PRISMATIC SHOWY BRILLIANT
PRISON GIB JUG PEN BRIG COOP GAOL HELL HOCK HOLD HOLE JAIL KEEP LAKE NICK QUAD QUOD SHOP SLAM STIR WARD BAGNE CHOKY CLINK FLEET GRATE JOINT KITTY LIMBO LODGE POUND RATEL TENCH TRONK VAULT BAGNIO BAILEY BUCKET CARCEL CARCER COOLER JIGGER LUMBER RATTLE BASTILE BOCARDO BULLPEN COLLEGE COMPTER CONFINE COUNTER DUNGEON FREEZER GEHENNA KIDCOTE LUDGATE NEWGATE SLAMMER DARTMOOR HOOSEGOW

TOLBOOTH TRIBUNAL CALABOOSE PENITENTIARY
(— CAMP) GULAG OFLAG
(— IN ROME) TULLIANUM
(AUSTRALIAN —) TENCH
(IN —) INSIDE
(MILITARY —) GLASSHOUSE GUARDHOUSE
(POLITICAL —) GULAG
(SUBTERRANEAN —) MASSYMORE
(UNIVERSITY —) CARCER
PRISONER CON POW MUTE LIFER DETENU INMATE REMAND TERMER CAITIFF CAPTIVE CONVICT GAOLBIRD JAILBIRD LONGTIMER
(RELEASED —) EXCON
PRISONER OF ZENDA (AUTHOR OF —) HOPE
(CHARACTER IN —) ROSE SAPT FRITZ FLAVIA RUDOLF MICHAEL DEMAUBAN BURLESDON ANTOINETTE RASSENDYLL TARLENHEIM
PRISONER'S BASE CHEVY CHIVY
PRISSY PRIM FUSSY DAINTY FINICKY PRUDISH PRIGGISH SISSIFIED
PRISTINE NEW PURE FIRST FRESH UNTROD ANCIENT PRIMARY ORIGINAL PRIMEVAL PRIMITIVE UNSPOILED
PRIVACY RECESS SECRET PRIVITY RETREAT SECRECY DARKNESS INTIMACY INTIMITY SOLITUDE SECLUSION
(IN —) ASIDE
(PL.) VERENDA
PRIVATE SNUG ALONE CLOSE GUIDE INNER KHASS PRIVY SHARE CLOSET COVERT INWARD POCKET SECRET STANCH POSTERN SECRECY SEVERAL SOLDIER SQUADDY CIVILIAN DOMESTIC ESOTERIC HOMEFELT INTERNAL INTIMATE PERSONAL SINGULAR UMBRATILE
(BRITISH —) TOMMY
(PREF.) CRYPT(O) KRYPT(O) PRIVI
PRIVATEER CAPER MARQUE PIRATE ALABAMA CORSAIR CRUISER DUNKIRK PICKEER
PRIVATELY ASIDE INWARDLY SECRETLY
PRIVATION LOSS WANT PINCH PENURY PERISH ABSENCE POVERTY HARDSHIP
PRIVET PRIM HEDGE SKEDGE IBOLIUM PRIMWORT PRIMPRINT
PRIVILEGE UP PUT SOC BOTE DOWN HAND STAR TEAM CLAIM ENTRY FAVOR FRANK GRACE HONOR REGAL RIGHT THEAM EXCUSE INDULT MUNITY OCTROI OPTION PATENT WARREN CHARTER FALDAGE

FREEDOM LIBERTY MITZVAH
PASSAGE GRANDEZA STANDAGE
PERQUISITE PREROGATIVE
(— TO USE THINGS) BOTE
(ACQUIRED —) EASEMENT
(POKER —) EDGE
(POOL —) STAR
PRIVILEGED CURULE EXEMPT
LICENSED CHARTERED
(— PLACE) WARREN
PRIVY WC AJAX GONG REAR BIFFY
DRAFT DUNNY ISSUE JAKES PETTY
QUIET SIEGE CLOACA CLOSET
OFFICE SECRET DRAUGHT FOREIGN
LATRINE PRIVATE DONICKER
FAMILIAR INTIMATE OUTHOUSE
PERSONAL STEALTHY WARDROBE
(MONASTERY —) REREDORTER
PRIZE CUP FEE GEM PRY BELL BEND
GAME GREE PALM GONG PLUM PREY PRIX
RATE RISK AWARD BACON BOOTY
LEVER PLATE PLUME PRICE PURSE
STAKE VALUE WAGER ESTEEM
GLAIVE PRAISE PREMIO TROPHY
BENEFIT CAPTURE GARLAND
PREMIUM ESTIMATE LEVERAGE
PURCHASE REPRISAL TREASURE
(— FOR LAST) MELL
(FIRST —) BLUE
(LOTTERY —) LOT TERN
(THEATER —) OBIE
PRIZE CUP PEWTER
PRIZED DEAR CHARY VALUED
PRIZEFIGHT GO BOUT MILL MATCH
SCRAP BARNEY
PRIZEFIGHTER BOXER BLEEDER
FIGHTER SLUGGER PUGILIST
PRIZE MONEY GUNNAGE
PRO TO FOR FAVORING
PROA PARO PRAU PROW PAROO
PRAHU CARACOA
PROBABILISTIC STOCHASTIC
PROBABILITY ODDS SHOW CHANCE
PERCENTAGE
(STRONG —) PRESUMPTION
PROBABLE MAYBE LIKELY PROBAL
TOPICAL APPARENT FEASIBLE
POSSIBLE INTHECARDS
PROBABLY BELIKE LIKELY
PROBATION TEST PROOF TRIAL
PAROLE EVIDENCE
PROBATIONER STIBBLER
PROBE PICK SEEK SIFT STOG TENT
DELVE ENTER GROPE SOUND
FATHOM SEARCH SEEKER STYLET
THRUST TRACER ACCOUNT EXAMINE
INQUIRY SOUNDER GYROMELE
PROBITY HONESTY INTEGRITY
RECTITUDE
PROBLEM NUT SUM WHY BOYG
CRUX DUAL ISSE KNOT BLAIK HYDRA
POSER APORIA ENIGMA HANGUP
BUGBEAR DILEMMA FUNERAL

GORDIAN GRUELER TICKLER
EXERCISE HEADACHE JEOPARDY
QUESTION STICKLER SITUATION
(CHESS —) DUAL MOVER SUIMATE
MINIATURE
PROBLEMATICAL DUBIOUS
DOUBTFUL PUZZLING UNCERTAIN
UNDECIDED
PROBOSCIS NOSE SNOUT TRUMP
TRUNK ANTLIA LINGUA SIPHON
SYPHON TONGUE ROSTRUM
PROBOSCIS MONKEY KAHA
KAHUA
PROCACIOUS PREY SASSY SAUCY
PROCAINE NOVOCAINE
PROCAVIA HYRAX
PROCEDURE BIAS FORM HAVE VEIN
DRAFT ORDER TENOR TRACK AFFAIR
COURSE METHOD POLITY SYSTEM
DRAUGHT PROCESS PRODUCT
ACTIVITY PROTOCOL OPERATION
(PRESCRIBED —S) CEREMONY
(ROUNDABOUT —) CIRCUITY
(SECRET —) STEALTH
(STANDARDIZED —) BIT
(SURGICAL —) BYPASS
(UNWISE —) FOLLY
PROCEED DO GO BANG BEAR FAND
FARE FLOW FOND HAVE MAKE MARK
MOVE PASS ROAM ROLL SEEK STEP
TAKE TOOL TOUR WEAR WEND WIND
YEAD YEDE YEED AMBLE ARISE
DRESS FOUND FRAME ISSUE MARCH
REACH TRACE BREEZE INTEND
PURSUE RESULT SPRING STRAKE
STRIKE TRAVEL ADVANCE AGGRESS
DEVOLVE EMANATE FORTHGO
PRETEND STRETCH CONTINUE
PROGRESS
(— AIMLESSLY) CIRCLE
(— ALONE) SINGLE
(— AWKWARDLY) SHLEP SCHLEP
SCHLEPP
(— BY STEPS) RATCHET
(— CLUMSILY) FLOUNDER
(— INSIDIOUSLY) SAP
(— LINGERINGLY) LOITER
(— OBLIQUELY) CUT
(— RAGGEDLY) HALT
(— RAPIDLY) RAKE STRETCH
(— SECRETLY) MINE
(—S FROM GAMBLING) MOTZA
MOTSER
(— SLOWLY) INCH
(— SUCCESSFULLY) COOK
(— THROUGH) PLAY
(— UNSTEADILY) DRIDDLE
(— WITH) PLAY
(— WITH DIFFICULTY) STRUGGLE
(— WITH LITTLE EFFORT) CRUISE
(PL.) TAKE VAIL AVAILS INCOME
PROFITS PROVENT RETURNS
PREVENUE

PROCEEDING ACT DEED FARE PLOY
STEP AFFAIR AMPARO COURSE
DOMENT ISSUANT MEASURE
ONGOING PASSANT QUIETUS
TEMANET WARRANT CONCURSO
INSTANCE PLACITUM PRACTICE
(— BY THREES) TERNARY
(— FROM GOD) DIVINE
(— FROM THE EARTH) TELLURIC
(— STEP-BY-STEP) GRADATORY
(COURT —S) ACTA TRIAL ACTION
(INDIRECT —S) AMBAGES
(PARLIAMENTARY —S) HUSTINGS
(PREVIOUS —) PRECEDENT
(RECORDED —S) ACTA
(SECRET —) COVERTURE
(PL.) ONGOINGS
PROCERITY HEIGHT TALLNESS
PROCESS RUN FANG FOOT TINA
WRIT CREST FURCA HAMUS MUCRO
SPINA CALCAR CAPIAS CILIUM
COURSE CRUNCH FEELER HABEAS
INTEND METHOD REPORT ACCOUNT
BARBULE FURCULA GOBBING
HAMULUS ISOLATE LAMELLA
MANDATE SPATULA SUMMONS
ACROMION ACTIVITY APPENDIX
AUTOTYPE FILAMENT FRENULUM
GRAINING INSTANCE MANUBRIUM
OPERATION
(— OF BONE) HORN
(— OF CHANGE) ACTION
(— OF CREATING VACUUM)
EXHAUOT
(— OF DYEING) BATIK HANKING
(— OF METALPLATING) ACIFRAGE
(— OF PACKING) GOBBING
(— OF REASONING) ALGEBRA
(— OF SUPPLYING WANTAGE)
ULLING
(— ON FISH'S HEAD) LACINIA
(— PAPER) CONVERT
(— TO RECOVER LAND) DADENHUDD
(— TO REGAIN USE) RECYCLE
(ABRUPT —) MUCRO
(ALCHEMICAL —) CIBATION DIPLOSIS
(ARTISTIC —) FROTTAGE
(BRISTLE-LIKE —) STILET STYLET
(CALENDERING —) SWISSING
(CARBON —) AUTOTYPE
(CERAMIC —) FIRING
(COATING —) BLOOMING
(CURVED —) HAMUS
(DEVELOPMENTAL —) ANCESTRY
(EARLIKE —) AURICLE
(FALCONRY —) IMPING
(FINISHING —) BRUSHING CRABBING
(FORKED —) FURCA FURCULA
(HAIRLIKE —) VILLUS
(HELMETLIKE —) CASQUE
(HOOKLIKE —) HAMULUS
(HORNSHAPED —) CORNICLE
(INTELLECTUAL —S) COGITO

(KIND OF —) MARKEY MARKOFF
(KNOBLIKE —) BOSS
(LEGAL —) BAIL SUIT CAUSE ATTAINT
INSTANCE
(MATHEMATICAL —) ADDITION
DIVISION
(MENTAL —) COMPOUND
(MINING —) STOPING
(MOVIE-MAKING —) SLATING
(NERVE-CELL —) DENDRON
(NERVELIKE —) AXON AXONE
(PHOTOGRAPHIC —) CARBRO
(POINTED —) AWN SPINE STYLUS
LANGUET
(PRINTING —) OFFSET GRAVURE
STENCIL INTAGLIO
(REORGANIZATION —) HEMIXIS
(SMALL POINTED —) AWN
(SPINNING —) JACKING
(SPINOUS —) ACANTHA
(SPINY —) STYLOID
(TEXTILE —) DECATING
(WEAVING —) HATCHING
(WINGLIKE —) ALA FIN
(PREF.) TYP(I)(O)
(DRY —) XER(O)
(SUFF.) AL ANCE ANT ENCE ESIS IAL
ING ISATION ISM IZATION OSIS SIS
TH TYPAL TYPE TYPIC TYPY
(—OF BECOMING) ESCENCE
PROCESSED DOWN FINISHED
PROCESSION POMP WALK CORSO
DRIVE TRACE TRAIN BRIDAL EXEQUY
LITANY PARADE STREAM CORTEGE
FUNERAL THIASOS TRIONFO
TRIUMPH ENTRANCE MOHARRAM
PROGRESS MOTORCADE
(— OF THE HOLY CHRIST) SPIRATION
(BOISTEROUS —) SKIMMITY
(FUNERAL —) EXEQUY EXEQUIES
(IRISH CIVIC —) FRINGES
(MUSLIM —) MOHARRAM
MUHARRAM MUHARREM
PROCESSOR (KIND OF —) WORD
PROCLAIM BID CRY BAWL DEEM
HORN OYES OYEZ SCRY SING TOOT
TOUT BLARE BLAZE BOAST CLAIM
GREDE KNELL SOUND SPEAK
BLAZON BOUNCE DEFAME HERALD
INDICT OUTCRY CLARION DECLARE
DIVULGE PROTEST PUBLISH
TRUMPET ANNOUNCE DENOUNCE
RENOUNCE PROMULGATE
(— ALOUD) ROAR
(— PUBLICLY) PRECONIZE
(— WITH BIG TALK) BOUNCE
PROCLAMATION CRY HUE BANS
FIAT OYES OYEZ RERD SCRY BANDO
BANNS BLAZE EDICT UKASE
PLACARD PROGRAM PUBLICATION
ANNUNCIATION
PROCLIVITY BENT ANLAGE APETITE
APTNESS LEANING TENDENCY

PROCNE (FATHER OF —) PANDION
  (HUSBAND OF —) TEREUS
  (SISTER OF —) PHILOMELA
  (SON OF —) ITYS
PROCONSUL GALLIO PROVOST
PROCRASTINATE LAG TIME DEFER
  DELAY LINGER ADJOURN POSTPONE
  PROROGUE TEMPORIZE
PROCRASTINATION DELAY
  CUNCTATION
PROCREANT FRUITFUL
PROCREATE WIN SIRE BEGET
  ENGENDER GENERATE OCCASION
PROCREATION INCREASE
PROCREATOR AUTHOR
PROCRIS (FATHER OF —)
  ERECHTHEUS
  (HOUND OF —) LAELAPS
  (HUSBAND OF —) CEPHALUS
PROCTOR LIAR PROG ACTOR AGENT
  PROXY BEGGAR RECTOR MONITOR
  PROCUTOR
PROCUMBENT HUMIFUSE
  PROSTRATE
PROCURABLE PARABLE
PROCURATOR PROXY PILATE
  PROCTOR
PROCURE GET WIN FANG FIND GAIN
  GIVE HALE BRING INFER TOUCH
  EFFECT INDUCE OBTAIN ACHIEVE
  ACQUIRE COMPARE CONQUER
  CONTRIVE PURCHASE
  (— TO COMMIT PERJURY) SUBORN
PROCURER PIMP PROXENET
  PURVEYOR
PROCURESS AUNT BAWD HACK
  LENA PANDER COMMODE PINNACE
PROD DAB EGG GIG JAB JOB JOG
  BROD BROG GOAD HEEL POKE PROG
  URGE GOOSE HURRY NUDGE PROBE
  INCITE JOSTLE THRUST IRRITATE
  (— THE BUTTOCKS) GOOSE
PRODIGAL PROD FLUSH LARGE
  COSTLY LAVISH WANTON WASTER
  PROFUSE SPENDER WASTRIE
  WASTRIFE PROFLIGATE
PRODIGALITY WASTE WASTRY
  WASTRIFE PROFUSION
PRODIGIOUS HUGE VAST GIANT
  AMAZING IMMENSE STRANGE
  ABNORMAL ENORMOUS GIGANTIC
  MONSTROUS PORTENTOUS
PRODIGY OMEN SIGN MARVEL
  OSTENT WIZARD WONDER MIRACLE
  MONSTER PORTENT CEREMONY
PRODITION TREASON BETRAYAL
PRODUCE DO GO ANTE BEAR FORM
  GIVE GROW MAKE REAR SHOW TEEM
  WAGE BEGET BIRTH BREED BRING
  BROOD BUILD CARRY CAUSE DRIVE
  FORGE FRAME HATCH ISSUE PUTON
  RAISE SPAWN THROW TRADE YIELD
  APPORT CREATE EFFECT GROWTH

INCOME INVENT INWORK PARENT
  SECURE TURNIN ADVANCE ANIMATE
  COMPOSE DEPROME GIGNATE
  INSPIRE OUTWORK PRODUCT
  PROLONG PROVENT CONCEIVE
  CONFLATE ENGENDER GENERATE
  INCREASE LENGTHEN OFFSPRING
  (— A COPY OF) TYPE
  (— AN EFFECT) ACT AFFECT
  (— ANEW) REGENERATE
  (— AS PROFIT) NET NETT
  (— AUDIBLE EFFECT) SOUND
  (— BY GREAT EFFORT) GRIND
  (— CROPS) CARRY
  (— DULL APPEARANCE) CHILL
  (— EFFECT) OPERATE
  (— FREELY) PULLULATE
  (— FRUIT) TEEM
  (— HEAT) ENRAGE
  (— IN SPECIFIED FORM) FORMAT
  (— PAID FOR RENT) CAIN
  (— SHARP NOISE) CRINK
  (AGRICULTURAL —) PODWARE
  (FARM —) HUSBANDRY
  (GARDEN —) STUFF TRUCK
  (MINING —) LEY
PRODUCED (ARTIFICIALLY —)
  FORCED
  (SEXUALLY —) GAMIC
  (SUFF.) GENETIC
PRODUCER GASMAN BEARING
  SHOWMAN DIRECTOR GAZOGENE
  OUTPUTTER
  (— OF COMPUTER SYSTEMS) OEM
  (SUFF.) ARIAN EER
PRODUCING IN PROCREANT
  (PREF.) EXO
  (SUFF.) GENIC GEROUS GON(E)
  (IDIUM)(IMO)(Y) IGEROUS PARA
  PAROUS
PRODUCT HEIR ITEM BRAND CHILD
  FRUIT GROSS OUTGO SPAWN
  ALCLAD EFFORT FABRIC GROWTH
  RESULT UPCOME FALLOUT
  OUTTURN PRODUCE PROGENY
  TURNOUT OUTBIRTH OFFSPRING
  (— MADE IN INDIA) SWADESHI
  (— OF ROCK DECAY) LATERITE
  (—S OF LAND) ESPLEES
  (—S OF ORCHARD) BIKKURIM
  (ADDITION —) ADDUCT
  (CHEESE AND MILK —S) GERVAIS
  (CHOICE —) CAVIAR
  (COMPLETED —) TURNOFF
  (FISH —) SURIMI
  (LEGISLATIVE —) ACT
  (MATHEMATICAL —) SQUARE
  (MINERAL —) HUTCH
  (OXIDATION —) SUBSCALE
  (RESIDUAL —) LATERITE
  (SECONDARY —) CONGENER
  (SURPLUS —S) ARISINGS
  (TRANSFORMATION —) BAINITE

(WASTE —) RESIDUENT
(WORTHLESS —) CHAFF
(SUFF.) ADE
(COMMERCIAL—) INE
(MANUFACTURED—) ITE
PRODUCTION WORK FORGE FRUIT
GROSS PIECE YIELD GROWTH
OUTPUT EDITION GUIGNOL
PRODUCE ARTIFICE INDUCTION
OPERATION
(— OF MEDIUM) APPORT
(— OF YOUNG) INCREASE
(BEST – 6) FAT
(SUCCESSFUL —) HIT
(SUFF.) GENY POEIA POESIS POIESIS
POIETIC
PRODUCTIVE FAT RICH LOOSE
QUICK ACTIVE BATTLE PAROUS
STRONG CAUSING FERTILE GAINFUL
HEALTHY TEEMFUL TEEMING
CHILDING CREATIVE FRUITFUL
GERMINAL PLENTEOUS
(SUFF.) POEIA POESIS POIESIS
POIETIC
PROEM PREFACE PRELUDE PROHEIM
FOREWORD OVERTURE PREAMBLE
PROETUS (BROTHER OF —)
ACRISIUS
(DAUGHTER OF —) IPHINOE LYSIPPE
IPHIANASSA
(FATHER OF —) ABAS
(MOTHER OF —) OCALEA
(WIFE OF —) ANTEA
PROFANATION VIOLENCE
SACRILEGE
PROFANE LAY NOA BLUE FOUL
ARUSE COARSE DEBASE DEFILE
DEFOIL DEFOUL UNHOLY VULGAR
WICKED GODLESS IMPIOUS
POLLUTE SECULAR UNGODLY
VIOLATE WORLDLY TEMPORAL
UNHALLOW
PROFANITY OATH CURSE CURSING
LANGUAGE BLASPHEMY
PROFESS OWN AVOW ADMIT CLAIM
AFFECT AFFIRM ALLEGE ASSERT
ASSUME FOLLOW PRESUME
PRETEND PURPORT PRACTICE
(— TO BE) SUBSCRIBE
PROFESSION ART BAR LAW COAT
FEAT GAME WALK CRAFT FAITH
FORTE TRADE CAREER CHURCH
EMPLOY METIER MISTER CALLING
FACULTY QUALITY SERVICE
ADVOCACY BUSINESS COACHING
FUNCTION PEDAGOGY SOLDIERY
VOCATION
(— OF LETTERS) QUILL
(JOURNALISTIC —) PRESS
(SUFF.) SHIP
PROFESSIONAL PRO COLT PAID
HIRED EXPERT SKILLED TRAINED
FINISHED

PROFESSOR DON PROF HANIF
KHOJA LAWYER REGENT ADJOINT
ACADEMIC CIVILIAN EMERITUS
PROFESSORSHIP CHAIR FAUTEUIL
PROFFER BID CAP GIVE TEND TENT
DEFER DODGE ESSAY OFFER EXTEND
OPPOSE PREFER PROFRE TENDER
ATTEMPT PRESENT HESITATE
PROFICIENCY SIGHT SKILL ABILITY
APTNESS MAITRISE
PROFICIENT ADEPT EXPERT MASTER
SALTED VERSED PERFECT SKILLED
SKILLFUL
PROFILE FORM FLANK PURFLE
SKETCH CONTOUR OUTLINE
SECTION PSYCHOGRAPH
(— OF RIVERBED) THALWEG
(— OF RIVER BOTTOM) THALWEG
PROFIT AID GET NET WIN BOOT GAIN
MEND NOTE SKIN VAIL AVAIL EDIFY
FRAME GRIST LUCRE SCALP SPEED
BEHOOF INCOME MAKING PAYOFF
RETURN ACCOUNT ADVANCE
BENEFIT CLEANUP FURTHER
GETTING IMPROVE MILEAGE
PLUNDER REVENUE VANTAGE
WINNING CLEANING INCREASE
INTEREST PERCENTAGE PERQUISITE
(— BY) BROOK
(ILLICIT —) GRAFT
(INORDINATE —) BUNCE
(UNDERCOVER —) SQUEEZE
(PL.) TAKE GRAVY ISSUE AVAILS
JALKAR ESPLEES
PROFITABLE FAT GOOD UTILE
GOLDEN PLUMMY GAINFUL HELPFUL
PAYABLE BEHOVELY ECONOMIC
PROVABLE REPAYING VAILABLE
REWARDING
PROFITLESS BOOTLESS
PROFLIGATE ROUE ROVE DEFEAT
CORRUPT IMMORAL RIOTOUS
SPENDER VICIOUS WASTREL
DEPRAVED FLAGRANT OVERCOME
RAKEHELL WASTEFUL ABANDONED
PROFOUND DEEP HARD WISE
ABYSS DEPTH HEAVY OCEAN
SOUND THICK PITCHY STRONG
ABYSMAL INTENSE ABSTRUSE
COMPLETE PREGNANT REACHING
THOROUGH
PROFUNDITY ABYSS DEPTH
FATHOM DEEPNESS
PROFUSE FREE LUSH SLAB FRANK
GALORE LAVISH COPIOUS LIBERAL
OPULENT ABUNDANT GENEROUS
PRODIGAL SQUANDER WASTEFUL
LUXURIANT REDUNDANT
UNSPARING
PROFUSELY HEARTILY
PROFUSION RIOT WASTE EXCESS
LAVISH FLUENCY OPULENCE
REDUNDANCY

PROG FOOD GOAD POKE PROD
PROWL TRAMP BEGGAR FORAGE
PROCTOR
PROGENITOR BURI MANU ROOT
SIRE PITRI STOCK PARENT
ANCESTOR
PROGENY BED GET IMP KIN BURD
CLAN KIND SEED TEAM BROOD
CHILD FRUIT ISSUE STRAIN STRIND
INCROSS KINDRED LINEAGE
OUTCOME PRODUCT CHILDREN
FRUITAGE INCREASE OUTBIRTH
OUTCROSS OFFSPRING
(— OF WATER-BUFFALO AND YAK)
DZO
(— OF WITCH AND DEMON) HOLD
(INSECT —) SOCIETY
PROGNOSIS FORECAST PROPHASIS
PROGNOSTIC OMEN SIGN TOKEN
AUSPICE OMINOUS PRESAGE
PROPHECY
PROGNOSTICATE BODE AUGUR
SPELL BETOKEN CONJECT PREDICT
PRENOTE FOREBODE FORESHOW
FORETELL PROPHESY
PROGNOSTICATION RACE
PRESAGE FOREBODE FORECAST
PROGRESS PROPHECY
PROGNOSTICATOR SEER DOOMER
PROPHET HARUSPEX
PROGRAM CARD SHOW FORUM
AGENDA DESIGN SCHEME
AGENDUM PREFACE CLAMBAKE
FESTIVAL GIVEAWAY GUIDANCE
JAMBOREE PLAYBILL SCHEDULE
SEQUENCE SYLLABUS
(COMPUTER —) DOS EDITOR
FIRMWARE SPREADSHEET
(COMPUTER —S) SOFTWARE
(CURRENT AFFAIRS —) REALITES
(EMPLOYEE —) ESOP
(HEALTH —) MEDICAID MEDICARE
(PART OF COMPUTER —) BRANCH
(PARTY —) PLATFORM
(STOCK —) ESOP
(TELEVISION —) SITCOM
PROGRAMMA EDICT DECREE
PREFACE PROGRAM
PROGRESS WAY BIRL DENT FARE
GAIN GROW MOVE RACE RISE STEM
STEP TOUR WEAR WEND WENT
BUILD DRIFT FORGE GOING MARCH
SWING WEENT ASCENT BUFFET
COURSE GROWTH STREEK ADVANCE
DEVELOP FOOTING HEADWAY
IMPROVE JOURNEY ONGOING
PASSAGE PROCESS PROFICIENCY
(— CLUMSILY) SCRAMBLE
(— ERRATICALLY) FLAIL
(— FEEBLY) DODDER
(— INTELLIGENTLY PLANNED)
TELESIA TELESIS

(— NOISILY) CHORTLE
(— SLOWLY) CRAWL
(SINGLE —) THROUGH
PROGRESSED FAR
PROGRESSION WAY SWING
COURSE GALLOP ADVANCE
PASSAGE PROGRESS SEQUENCE
(— OF CHORDS) SWIPE
(MUSICAL —) SKIP
(SMOOTH —) SLIDE
PROGRESSIVE ACTIVE ONWARD
FORWARD GRADUAL LIBERAL
(NOT —) SLOW
PROGRESSIVELY STILL
PROHIBIT BAN BAR STOP VETO
BLOCK DEBAR ESTOP DEFEND
ENJOIN FORBID HINDER OUTLAW
FORFEND FORWARN INHIBIT
PREVENT DISALLOW PRECLUDE
SUPPRESS PROSCRIBE
PROHIBITED HOT TABU TABOO
ILLEGAL ILLICIT UNLAWFUL
VERBOTEN
PROHIBITING VETITIVE
PROHIBITION BAN NAY NON VETO
ORDER BARRIER DEFENCE DEFENSE
EMBARGO FORBODE ESTOPPEL
PROHIBITIONIST DRY PUSSYFOOT
PROJECT GAB GAG JET JUT LAP TUT
BEAM CAST GAME HURL IDEA PLAN
POKE PUSH DRIVE IMAGE JETTY
JUTTY SETUP SHOOT STICK THROW
BEETLE DESIGN DEVICE ESTATE
EXTEND FILLIP OUTJUT PROPEL
SCHEME SCREEN SHELVE EXTRUDE
GOSPLAN IMAGINE KNUCKLE
OUTCROP PATTERN BUSINESS
CONTRIVE OUTREACH OUTSHOOT
OVERHANG PROPOSAL PROTRUDE
SPANGHEW
(UNETHICAL —) SCHEME
(VISIONARY —) BABEL
PROJECTILE BALL BOLT CASE SHOT
SHAFT TRACER OUTCAST POUNDER
FIREBALL SHRAPNEL
(— DESIGNED TO SET FIRE TO
HOUSES) CARCASS
(EXPLOSIVE —) BOMB SHELL
(SMALL —S) MITRAILLE
(SUBMARINE —) TORPEDO
(PL.) LEAD SHOT SALVO STUFF
PROJECTING BEETLE SHELVY
EMINENT JUTTING OUTSHOT
PENDENT SALIENT SNAGGLED
PROMINENT OUTSTANDING
(PREF.) PRO
PROJECTION ARM CAM COG DOG
EAR FIN GIB JUT JOG JUT NAB NAG
NUT TAB TOE BEAK BOSS BROW
BUHR COAK COCK CROC CUSP HEEL
HORN KEEL KICK KINK KNAG KNOB

KNOP LOBE RIDE SAIL SNUG SPUD
SPUR TEAT WING BULGE CLEAT
EJECT ELBOW FENCE FURCA JUTTY
PRONG SALLY SCRAG SHANK SHOOT
SNOUT SPIKE TOOTH BRANCH
CALCAR CORBEL CROSET FUSULA
HEARTH ICICLE MENTUM NOSING
PALATE RELIEF RELISH TAPPET
BREAKER CONSOLE DRAWING
EPAULET EYEBROW FETLOCK
KNUCKLE LANGUET ORILLON
OUTSHOT PRICKER PRICKLE
RESSAUT AJUTMENT CASCABEL
DENTICLE EMINENCE FOOTLOCK
ORILLION OVERHANG OVERSAIL
SALIENCE SHOULDER SPROCKET
STERIGMA TRUNNION APOPHYSIS
OUTTHRUST PROMINENCE
(— CONNECTING TIMBER) COAK
(— EXTENDING BACKWARD) BARB
(— FROM CASTING) SPRUE
(— FROM SHIP'S KEEL) SPONSON
(— IN CLOCK) SQUARE
(— IN ORCHIDS) MENTUM
(— OF FOREHEAD) ANTINION
(— OF JAW) GNATHISM
(— OF PEAT) HAG
(— OF RAFTER) SALLY
(— OF TERRITORY) PANHANDLE
(— ON CANNON) CASCABEL
(— ON CHURCH SEAT) MISERICORD
(— ON FOOTWEAR) STUD
(— ON GUN) CROC LUMP
(— ON HARNESS) HAME
(— ON HORSE'S LEG) FETLOCK
(— ON HORSESHOE) STICKER
(— ON LOCK) FENCE STUMP
(— ON MAST) STOP
(— ON OVARY) STIGMA
(— ON POCKETKNIFE) KICK
(— ON SALMON JAW) GIB
(— ON WHEEL) GUB GROUSER
GROUTER
(— OVER AIR PORT) EYEBROW
(CARPENTRY —) TENON
(FIREPLACE —) HOB
(JAGGED —) SNUG
(NARROW —) STRAP TONGUE
(SHARP —) BARB FANG
(SUBMERGED —) KNOLL
(PL.) GRAIN BARLEY
PROJECTOR KINO LANTERN
PLANNER SCHEMER BIOSCOPE
EPISCOPE VITASCOPE
PROLAMIN ZEIN SEINE GLIADIN
HORDEIN KAFIRIN SECALIN
PROLAPSE PTOSIS BLOWOUT
FALLING
PROLETARIAN POPULAR
PROLETARIAT MASSES
PROLIFIC BIRTHY BREEDY BROODY
FECUND FERTILE PROFUSE

TEEMING ABUNDANT FRUITFUL
SPAWNING
(BE —) INCREASE
PROLIX LARGE WORDY DIFFUSE
LENGTHY PROSAIC TEDIOUS
VERBOSE TIRESOME WEARISOME
PROLIXITY REDUNDANCY
PROLOGUE BANS BANNS INDEX
PREFACE
PROLONG DREE LENG LONG SPIN
DEFER DELAY DRIVE ELONG TWINE
DILATE EXTEND LINGER SPREAD
DISPACE PRODUCE RESPITE
SUSTAIN CONTINUE ETERNIZE
LENGTHEN POSTPONE PROROGUE
PROTRACT
PROLONGATION BEAK AORTA
CONUS STIPE STYLE FERMATA
ACROSOME APPENDIX GYNOBASE
LABELLUM
PROLONGED GREAT PROLIX
DELAYED EXTENDED SOSTENUTO
PROMENADE BUND MAIL MALL
PIER PROM WALK CORSO FRONT
PASEO PRADO MARINA PARADE
PASEAR ALAMEDA GALLERY
FRESCADE GALLERIA SEAFRONT
BOULEVARD
(CARRIAGE —) TOUR
(GREEK —) STOA
PROMETHEUS (BROTHER OF —)
ATLAS MENOETIUS EPIMETHEUS
(FATHER OF —) IAPETUS
(MOTHER OF —) CLYMENE
PROMETHEUS UNBOUND
(AUTHOR OF —) SHELLEY
(CHARACTER IN —) ASIA IONE EARTH
JUPITER MERCURY PANTHEA
HERCULES DEMOGORGON
PROMETHEUS
PROMINENCE BUR NOB BOSS BURR
CUSP KNOB NOOP UMBO AGGER
BULLA CREST GRAIN OLIVA SWELL
TUBER TYLUS ACCENT CALCAR
NODULE TRAGUS BILLING BUTTOCK
CONDYLE FASHION HAMULUS
KNUCKLE LINGULA AMYGDALA
EMINENCE EMPHASIS GLABELLA
PULVINAR SALIENCE TUBERCLE
MONTICULE PROMONTORY
(PREF.) TUBERCULI TUBERCULO
TUBERI
PROMINENT BIG BOLD BEADY
BRENT GREAT HEAVY STEEP BEETLE
MARKED SIGNAL BLATANT BOLTING
CAPITAL EMINENT JUTTING LEADING
NOTABLE OBVIOUS SALIENT
AQUILINE BEETLING MANIFEST
STRIKING NOTICEABLE
CONSPICUOUS OUTSTANDING
(SOCIALLY —) SWELL
(UNDULY —) OBTRUSIVE

PROMISCUOUS LIGHT CASUAL RANDOM CARELESS
PROMISCUOUSLY TAGRAG
PROMISE VOW AVOW BAND HEST HETE HOPE HOTE OATH OSSE PASS PLEA SURE WORD FAITH GRANT HIGHT TRUTH ASSURE BEHEST ENGAGE FIANCE HALSEN INSURE PAROLE PLEDGE PLIGHT PROMIT BEHIGHT BETROTH WARRANT CONTRACT COVENANT GUARANTY BETROTHAL OBLIGATION
(— IN MARRIAGE) BETROTH ESPOUSE AFFIANCE
(— OF SUCCESS) LIKELIHOOD
(— RESULTS) PROSPECT
(— TO PAY) NOTE ACCEPT
(— TO TAKE IN MARRIAGE) AFFY
PROMISED VOTARY
(— IN MARRIAGE) SURE HIGHT ENGAGED
(— LAND) CANAAN
PROMISING APT FAIR ROSY BRIGHT LIKELY PROOFY TOWARD GRADELY TOWARDLY
PROMISSORY NOTE IOU HUNDI HOONDI TICKET
PROMONTORY HOE NAB BEAK BILL HEAD MULL NAZE NESS NOOK NOUP PEAK SCAW SKAW TOOT ELBOW MORRO POINT REACH SNOUT SALIENT FORELAND HEADLAND
PROMOTE AID FLOG HELP HYPE LOFT PLUG PUSH AVAIL BOOST EXALT NURSE RAISE SERVE SETON SPEED ASSIST EXCITE FOMENT FOSTER LAUNCH PREFER ADVANCE DIGNIFY ELEVATE FORWARD FURTHER IMPROVE PREFECT PRODUCE PROMOVE SUCCEED SUPPORT INCREASE SUBSERVE
PROMOTER AGENT FRIEND ABETTOR BOOSTER BUBBLER BROACHER HUMANIST PROJECTOR (SUFF.) ANT
PROMOTION LIFT REMOVE ADVANCE FLACKERY PROMOVAL
(— OF CONSUMER INTERESTS) NADERISM
PROMOTIONAL PROMO
(— PRONOUNCEMENT) PROMO
PROMPT APT CUE MOVE URGE YARE ALERT FRACK PREST QUICK READY SERVE SWIFT WILLY YEDER EXCITE INDITE MATURE NIMBLE SPEEDY SUDDEN ANIMATE FORWARD PROVOKE SUGGEST PUNCTUAL REMINDER
(— TO EVIL) SUGGEST
PROMPTER CUER CALLER MEMORIST ORDINARY SOUFFLEUR

PROMPTING CALL BEHEST BEHIND MOTIVE
(SPIRITUAL —) LEADING
PROMPTITUDE ALACRITY
PROMPTLY UP PAT TID TIT SOON TITE PRONTO YARELY BETIMES PRESTLY QUICKLY DIRECTLY SPEEDILY
PROMPTNESS ALACRITY CELERITY DISPATCH
PROMULGATE SPREAD DECLARE PUBLISH PROCLAIM
PRONAOS ANTICUM
PRONE APT BENT EASY FLAT FREE GRUF BUXOM GIVEN GROOF JACENT LIABLE SUPINE BEASTLY BESTIAL DORMANT SUBJECT ADDICTED COUCHANT DISPOSED DOWNWARD PROPENSE
(— TO TAKE UP FADS) ISMY
(NATURALLY —) PROLIVE
PRONENESS
(SUFF.)
(—TO) ITIS
PRONG NEB NIB PEG PEW BILL FANG FORK HOOK PUGH SPUR TANG TENG TINE TING GRAIN SPADE SPEAN SPRONG FOURCHE TICKLER GRAINING
(— FOR EXTRACTING BUNG) TICKLER
(— FOR FISH) PEW PUGH
(— OF ANTLER) KNAG TIND TINE POINT
(— OF FORK) SPEAN
PRONGHORN CABREE CABRIT MAZAME BERENDO BERRENDO
PRONOUN HE IT ME MY WE YE ANY HER HIM HIS ONE OUR SHE THY WHO YOU OURS THAT THEM THEY THOU WHAT WHOM YOUR THINE WHICH WHOSE ITSELF MYSELF HERSELF HIMSELF OURSELF WHOEVER YOURSELF OURSELVES
(GENDERLESS —) THON
PRONOUNCE SAY PASS ACUTE SPEAK UTTER PREACH RECITE TONGUE ADJUDGE BEHIGHT CENSURE MOUILLE ASPIRATE
(— FREE) ABSOLVE
(— GUILTY) CONDEMN
(— HOLY) BLESS
PRONOUNCED HIGH MARKED DECIDED HOWLING INTENSE MOVABLE
(— AS FRICATIVE) GRASSEYE
(— PALATALLY) MOUILLE
(NOT —) SOFT
PRONOUNCEMENT FIAT CURSE DICTUM DICTAMEN
PRONTO QUICK ATONCE QUICKLY PROMPTLY

PRONUNCIATION BROGUE
DICTION ETACISM LIAISON DELIVERY
ENCLISIS ORTHOEPY
(BAD —) CACOEPY CACOLOGY
LABDACISM
(BROAD —) PLATEASM
(CORRECT —) ORTHOEPY
(FAULTY —) CACOLOGY
(PLEASING —) EUPHONY EUPHONIA
(ROUGH —) BUR BURR
PROOF SAY MARK PULL SLIP TEST
ESSAY PREWE REPRO TOKEN TOUCH
TRIAL CLENCH GALLEY ORDEAL
REASON RESULT REVISE ATTEMPT
OUTCOME PROBATE SHOWING
UTTERLY VOUCHER WARRANT
ANALYSIS CACOLOGY DOCUMENT
EVICTION EVIDENCE GOODNESS
MONUMENT
(— AGAINST ATTACK)
IMPREGNABLE
(— OF WRONGDOING) GOODS
(— SPIRIT OF WINE) SVT
(ABSOLUTE —) APODIXIS
(CLEAR SHARP —) DUPE REPRO
(INDIRECT —) APAGOGE
(PL.) STRING WARRANTY
PROOFREADER MARK CAP DELE
STET CARET
PROP LEG BROB BUNT POST REST
SPUR STAY STUD TRIG APPUI BRACE
PERCH PUNCH RANCE SCOTE SHORE
SHOVE SOUSE SPRAG SPURN STAFF
STELL STOOP STULL COLUMN
CROTCH CRUTCH PILLAR SCOTCH
SHORER STAYER UPHOLD BOISTER
FULCRUM PINNING STUDDLE
SUPPORT DUSTAIN BUTTRESS
CROTCHET DUTCHMAN UNDERLAY
UNDERSET
(— AS TRAP) TEEL
(— FOR CART) NEAP
(— FOR ROOF OF MINE) GIB
(— UP) CUSHION SCAFFOLD
(PREF.) FULCI
PROPAGANDA BOLOISM AGITPROP
BALLYHOO
PROPAGATE BREED HATCH LAYER
EXTEND SPREAD STRIKE DIFFUSE
GEMMATE PRODUCE PUBLISH
ENGENDER GENERATE INCREASE
MULTIPLY POPULATE TRANSMIT
PROCREATE
(— BY LAYERING) PROVINE
PROPAGATION BREED BREEDING
DIVISION INCREASE LAYERAGE
OFFSPRING
PROPEL ROW CALL CAST FIRE FLIP
KENT POLE PUSH SEND URGE DRIVE
FLICK IMPEL KNOCK PRICK RANGE
SPANK THROW HURTLE LAUNCH
PROJECT
(— BALL) STROKE
(— BOAT) OAR ROW SET KENT POLE
SCULL BUSHWACK
(— BOAT WITH FEET) LEG
(— ONESELF) HAUL
(— PUCK) CARRY
(— SUDDENLY) ZAP
(— WITH FORCE) RIFLE
PROPELLANT LOX
PROPELLER FAN HELIX SCREW
AIRSCREW WINDMILL
PROPENSITY YEN BENT ITCH LURCH
APTNESS IMPULSE LEANING
PRONITY APPETITE FONDNESS
INTEREST TENDENCY
PROPER FIT OWN GOOD JUST
MEET TRUE WELL PREST RIGHT
UTTER COMELY DECENT HONEST
LAWFUL MODEST SEEMLY CAPITAL
CORRECT FITTING GRADELY
SEEMING SKILFUL THRIFTY
ABSOLUTE BECOMING CONGREVE
DECOROUS FORMULAR IDONEOUS
PECULIAR RIGHTFUL SORTABLE
SUITABLE VIRTUOUS
(APPARENTLY —) SPECIOUS
(BE — TO) BESEEM
(PREF.) CURIO ORTH(O)
PROPERLY DULY WELL FITLY TRULY
ARIGHT FAIRLY FEATLY GLADLY
MEETLY RIGHTLY
PROPERTY AVER BONA DHAN TOOL
WAIF ASSET AUGHT GOODS GRANT
MOYEN STATE STOCK THING WORTH
APPEAL DEVISE ESTATE HAVIOR
KELTER LIVING MUSHAA REALTY
TALENT USINGS WEALTH ACQUEST
APANAGE CHATTEL DEMESNE
ESCHEAT ESSENCE FACULTY
FITNESS HARNESS HAVINGS
QUALITY WARISON ALLODIAL
CATALLUM HOLDINGS PECULIUM
POSSESSION PARAPHERNALIA
(— BELONGING TO WOMAN)
STRIDHAN
(— FROM WIFE TO HUSBAND) DOS
(— GIVEN BY WILL) DEVISE
(— OF MATTER AT REST) INERTIA
(— SECURED DISHONESTLY) HARL
(— SEIZED BY FORCE) SPOIL
(ABSOLUTE —) ALODIUM
(BEQUEATHED —) DEVISE
(ENEMY —) HEREM
(LANDED —) DOMAIN ESTATE
DEMESNE PRAEDIUM
(MOVABLE —) GEAR CHATTEL
EFFECTS CATALLUM
(PERSONAL —) FEE BONA GOODS
STUFF INSIGHT PLUNDER
(PRIVATE —) SEVERAL
(RURAL —) FINCA
(STOLEN —) PELF MAINOR STEALTH

(THEATRICAL —S) PROPS
(WITHOUT —) LACKLAND
(SUFF.) ISM
PROPHECY SPAE WEIRD EXHORT
PREACH PREDICT BODEMENT
FORECAST FORESHOW SOOTHSAY
VATICINE SIBYLLISM PROGNOSTIC
PROPHESY OSSE SPAE AREAD
AUGUR DIVINE EXHORT PREACH
OMINATE PORTEND PREDICT
ARIOLATE FORETELL
PROPHET GAD AMOS JOEL SEER
ANGEL AUGUR DRUID ELIAS HOSEA
JONAH MICAH MOSES NAHUM SILAS
SYRUS ARIOLE BALAAM DANIEL
ELIJAH HAGGAI ISAIAH MERLIN
MORONI NATHAN ORACLE PYTHON
SAMUEL EZEKIEL MALACHI
SPAEMAN HABAKKUK JEREMIAH
(WEATHER —) PROGNOSTICATOR
(PL.) VATES NEBIIM
(PREF.) VATI
PROPHETE, LA (CHARACTER IN —)
JOHN FIDES BERTHA OBERTHAL
(COMPOSER OF —) MEYERBEER
PROPHETESS ANNA ANNE HULDA
SIBYL PYTHIA DEBORAH PHOIBAD
SEERESS VOLUSPA DRUIDESS
SPAEWIFE CASSANDRA PYTHONESS
PROPHETIC FATAL VATIC MANTIC
FATEFUL FATIDIC MANTIAN DELPHIAN
ORACULAR SIBYLLIC VATICINAL
(— OF DISASTER) APOCALYPTIC
(SUFF.) MANTIC
PROPINE TIP GIFT EXPOSE PLEDGE
PROFFER
PROPINQUITY KINSHIP AFFINITY
NEARNESS VICINITY PROXIMITY
PROPITIATE MILD ATONE PACIFY
APPEASE RECONCILE
PROPITIATORY HILASMIC
PROPITIOUS FAIR KIND HAPPY
LUCKY BENIGN DEXTER KINDLY
HELPFUL PRESENT FRIENDLY
GRACIOUS MERCIFUL TOWARDLY
FAVORABLE PROMISING AUSPICIOUS
PROPONENT BACKER ADVOCATE
SUPPORTER
PROPORTION END LOT DOSE SIZE
CHIME FRAME QUOTA RATIO SCALE
SHARE ACCORD DEGREE EXTENT
FORMAT QUOTUM ANALOGY
BALANCE COMPASS CONTENT
MEASURE EURYTHMY QUANTITY
SYMMETRY PERCENTAGE
(— OF CATTLE TO GIVEN AREA)
SOUM
(— OF MALT IN BREWING) STRAIK
(— OF REFLECTED LIGHT) ALBEDO
(ALLOTTED —) STENT STINT
(EXACT —) SQUARE
(SMALL —) TITHE

PROPORTIONAL TOSCALE
PROPORTIONATENESS CONTOUR
PROPOSAL BID KITE MOVE PLAN
PLEA VOEU GRACE OFFER PARTY
DEMAND FEELER MOTION MOTIVE
PROJECT PROPOSE PURPOSE
OVERTURE SCHEDULE SENTENCE
PROPOSITION
(— OF HEALTH) TOAST
(FORMAL —) RESOLUTION
(TENTATIVE —) SNIFF
PROPOSE FACE MOVE PLAN POSE
SHOW WISH OFFER ALLEGE DESIGN
INJECT INTEND MOTION ADVANCE
EXHIBIT IMAGINE PROPINE PURPOSE
SUPPOSE CONFRONT CONVERSE
PROPOUND
(— FOR DISCUSSION) MOOT
(— FOR ELECTION) NOMINATE
(— MARRIAGE) POP
(— RESOLUTION) FIRST
(— TENTATIVELY) SUGGEST
PROPOSITION R FACT AXIOM
MODAL OFFER THEME AFFAIR
CONNEX MEMBER PORISM GENERAL
INVERSE PREMISS PROBLEM
PURPOSE THEOREM TYCHISM
BUSINESS CONTRARY EMPIREMA
IDENTITY IRENICON JUDGMENT
NEGATION OVERTURE PROPOSAL
PROTASIS SENTENCE SINGULAR
SUPPOSAL
(— FOR PEACE) IRENICON
(— IN LOGIC) TERMAL OBVERSE
CONTRARY CONVERSE
(— LEADING TO CONCLUSION)
PREMISE
(PARTICULAR NEGATIVE —) O
(PRELIMINARY —) LEMMA
(UNIVERSAL NEGATIVE —) E
PROPOUND POSE OFFER POSIT
START STATE INVOKE PROPOSE
PURPOSE
PROPOUNDER HYLICIST
PROPRIETOR LORD LAIRD MALIK
OWNER MASTER PATRON TANIST
YEOMAN ESQUIRE PATROON
ABSENTEE BONIFACE SQUARSON
TALUKDAR YEOWOMAN
PROPRIETY GRACE IDIOM
MENSE ESTATE NATURE
REASON DECENCY DECORUM
ESSENCE FITNESS HOLDING
MODESTY CIVILITY PROPERTY
ETIQUETTE
PROPROCTOR RECTOR
PROPULSION DRIFT EJECTION
PROPULSIVE ELASTIC
PRORATE ALLOT ASSESS DIVIDE
APPORTION
PROROGUE DEFER ADJOURN
PROLONG POSTPONE PROTRACT

PROSAIC DRAB DULL FLAT FOOT PROSE PROSY PROLIX STODGY STOLID STUPID FACTUAL HUMDRUM INSIPID LITERAL TEDIOUS SOULLESS TIRESOME WORKADAY

PROSCENIUM FRAME STAGE

PROSCRIBE BAN TABU EXILE LIMIT TABOO FORBID OUTLAW REJECT PROHIBIT

PROSCRIPTION EXILE OUTLAWRY

PROSE CHAT PROSY GOSSIP PROSAIC TEDIOUS SEQUENCE ELOQUENCE

PROSECUTE LAW SUE HOLD URGE CARRY ENSUE ACCUSE CHARGE DEDUCE FOLLOW INDICT INTEND PURSUE IMPLEAD PROCESS

PROSECUTION PURSUANCE

PROSECUTOR DA FISCAL PURSUER SAKEBER PROMOTER QUAESTOR
(PUBLIC —) ACTOR

PROSELYTE CONVERT NICOLAS NEOPHYTE PURSUANT
(JEWISH —) GER

PROSER HAVERER GRATIANO

PROSODY METER METRICS

PROSPECT HOPE VIEW SCENE SPECK VISTA CHANCE CHIEVE FUTURE REGARD SEARCH SURVEY COMMAND EXPLORE FOSSICK HORIZON LOOKOUT OUTLOOK PROJECT RESPECT LANDSKIP OFFSCAPE
(— FOR GOLD) SPECK
(— OF FUTURE) PERSPECTIVE
(— WITHOUT SYSTEM) GOPHER
(FORBIDDING —) DESERT

PROSPECTING LOAMING

PROSPECTIVE VIEW WATCH LOOKOUT EXPECTED

PROSPECTOR SNIPER FOSSICKER SOURDOUGH
(LONE —) HATTER

PROSPECTUS PROGRAM

PROSPER DO DOW FAY HIE LIKE RISE THEE CHEVE CHIVE EDIFY FRAME LIGHT SPEED BATTEN THRIVE BLOSSOM SUCCEED WELFARE FLOURISH

PROSPERITY HAP BOOM GLEE GOOD SEEL SONS WEAL IKBAL SONSE HEALTH THRIFT FORTUNE SUCCESS THEEDOM WELFARE FLOURISH
(GOD OF —) FREY
(INCREASE IN —) FREY UPTICK

PROSPERO (DAUGHTER OF —) MIRANDA
(SERVANT OF —) ARIEL
(SLAVE OF —) CALIBAN

PROSPEROUS UP FAT BEEN BEIN BIEN BOON GOOD FELIX FLUSH HAPPY LUCKY PALMY SONSY

EUROUS GILDED SONSIE WELSOM HALCYON HEALTHY THRIFTY THRIVEN WEIRDLY SUNSHINE THRIVING WEALSOME

PROSTITUTE BAG BAT CAT COW DOG MOB AUNT BAWD DOXY DRAB HACK MAUX MISS MUFF PUNK SLUT STEW TART TRUG BROAD CRACK MAWKS PAGAN POULE PROSS STALE WHORE BULKER CALLET CHIPPY DEBASE GIRLIE HARLOT HOOKER LIMMER MUTTON PROSTY RANNEL TOMATO TRADER VIZARD BAGGAGE BROTHEL CRUISER CYPRIAN HACKNEY HETAERA HUSTLER PAPHIAN PINNACE POLECAT PROSSIE PROSTIE PUCELLE SELLARY BERDACHE COMMONER CUSTOMER HACKSTER MAGDALEN MERETRIX OCCUPANT RUMBELOW SLATTERN STRUMPET VENTURER COURTESAN
(PREF.) PORN(O)

PROSTITUTION BORDEL SACKING BORDELLO HARLOTRY PUTANISM

PROSTRATE LOW FELL FLAT GRUF RASE RAZE FLING GROOF PRONE STOOP THROW ATTERR CUMBER FALLEN REPENT WEAKEN FLATTEN DEJECTED HELPLESS OVERCOME PROSTERN DEPRESSED
(— ONESELF) HURKLE
(BECOME —) FALL

PROSTRATION SHOCK KOWTOW COLLAPSE
(BURMESE —) SHIKO

PROSY DRY DULL JEJUNE HUMDRUM INSIPID PROSAIC PROSISH TEDIOUS TIRESOME

PROTAGONIST HERO ACTOR LEADER PALADIN ADVOCATE ANTIHERO CHAMPION

PROTAMINE SALMINE STURINE CLUPEINE

PROTEAN EDESTAN VARIABLE

PROTECT CAP BANK BIEL BIND DIKE FEND FORT HILL KEEP REDE SAVE WARD WEAR BLESS CHAIN CLOUT COURE COVER FENCE GANGE GRATE GUARD HEDGE PAVIS SHADE SHEND UMBER ASSERT BORROW DEFEND SCREEN SHADOW SHIELD WARISH BULWARK CHERISH CUSHION FASCINE FORFEND SECLUDE SHELTER SUPPORT WARRANT BESTRIDE CHAMPION DEFILADE PRESERVE SAFEGUARD
(— AGAINST RAIN) FLASH
(— BY BINDING) KECKLE
(— BY COVERING) HILL
(— BY WINDING WITH WIRE) GANGE
(— FROM INTRUSION) TILE TYLE
(— IRON OR STEEL) BARFF

PROTECTED SAFE SHADY IMMUNE
CLOUTED GUARDED SHEATHED
SHIELDED
(PREF.) IMMUNO
PROTECTING TUTELAR TUTELARY
SECURELUL
PROTECTION LEE CARE EGIS HOLD
WARD WING AEGIS ARMOR BIELD
COVER GRITH GUARD SHADE TARGE
TOWER AMULET ASYLUM AVOWRY
CONVOY ESCORT FENDER REFUGE
SAFETY SCONCE SCREEN SHADOW
SHROUD AUSPICE CUSTODY
DEFENCE HOUSING MANTLET
SHELTER TUITION UMBRAGE
WARRANT BLINDAGE COVERAGE
DEFILADE PASSPORT SECURITY
TUTAMENT TUTELAGE WARDSHIP
SAFEGUARD
(— FOR SAILOR) HORSE
(— FROM LOSS) INDEMNITY
(— FROM RAIN) OMBRIFUGE
(— FROM SUN) HAVELOCK
(— FROM WEATHER) LEWTH
(— RIGHT) MUND
(ITEM FOR —) MACE
(VALUABLE —) EDMUND
(WISE —) RAYMOND
PROTECTIVE (— SURFACE) LAGGING
PROTECTOR BIB GUARD BRACER
FAUTOR KEEPER PATRON REGENT
WARRANT DEFENDER GUARDIAN
PECTORAL PRESIDENT
(— OF PROSTITUTE) BULLY
(— OF VINEYARDS) PRIAPUS
(CHEST —) BIB
PROTEGE WARD PUPIL SMIKE
PROTEIN ZEIN ABRIN ACTIN OPSIN
RICIN SOZIN AVIDIN CASEIN FIBRIN
GLOBIN MYOGEN ALBUMIN
AMANDIN ELASTIN GELATIN GLIADIN
HISTONE HORDEIN KERATIN LIVETIN
MUCEDIN PROTEID SERICIN TUBULIN
ALEURONE COLLAGEN COLLOGEN
FERRITIN GLOBULIN GLUTELIN
GORGONIN IPOMOEIN PROLAMIN
ELEDOISIN PROPERDIN PROTAMINE
(— IN CEREAL) GLUTENIN
(— PARTICLE) PRION
(POISONOUS —) ABRIN
(RICH IN —S) NARROW
PROTEINASE PAPAIN PEPSIN
PROTEOSE ALBUMOSE ELASTOSE
GELATOSE
PROTESILAUS (BROTHER OF —)
PODARCES
(FATHER OF —) IPHICLUS
(MOTHER OF —) ASTYOCHE
(SLAYER OF —) HECTOR EUPHORBUS
(WIFE OF —) LAODAMIA POLYDORA
PROTEST AVER BEEF FUSS HOWL
KICK BROCK CROAK DEMUR AFFIRM
ASSERT BOWWOW EXCEPT HOLLER

OBJECT OBTEST PLAINT SQUAWK
SQUEAL CONTEST INVEIGH PUBLISH
RECLAIM RHUBARB SCRUPLE
TESTIFY HARRUMPH PROCLAIM
(— A CHARGE) TESTIFY
(— AGAINST) ABHOR
(— AGAINST INJUSTICE) HARO
(FORMAL —) REMONSTRANCE
(ORGANIZED —) LIEIN
(TINY —) PEEP
PROTESTANT ALASCAN GENEVAN
GOSPELER HELVETIC HUGUENOT
MORAVIAN SWADDLER
PROTEUS OLM AMOEBA
PROTHESIS CREDENCE PARABEMA
PROTHORAX COLLAR CORSELET
MANITRUNK
PROTOCOL PROCEDURE
PROTOPINE FUMARINE
PROTOPLASM PLASMA PLASSON
SARCODE OVOPLASM PERIPLAST
SOLEPLATE
PROTOPLAST CELL ENERGID
PROTOTYPE IDEAL MODEL FATHER
EXAMPLE PATTERN ANTITYPE
EXEMPLAR
PROTOZOAN AMEBA FORAM
MONAD MONER AMOEBA AGAMETE
ARCELLA BABESIA BODONID CILIATE
PROTIST RADIATE STENTOR
DIDINIUM HYPOZOAN PARAMECIUM
(HYPOTHETICAL —) MONER
MONERON
(PL.) MICROZOA
PROTRACT DRAG DRAW DREE PLOT
SPIN DEFER DELAY DRIVE TRACT
TRAIL TRAIN DILATE EXTEND LINGER
SPREAD DETRACT PROLONG
CONTINUE LENGTHEN PROROGUE
PROTRACTED DREE LONG DREICH
PROLIX LENGTHY DRAGGING
EXTENDED
PROTRUDE BUG JUT LILL LOLL PEER
POKE POUT BLEAR BULGE BUNCH
POUCH SHOOT START STICK STRUT
SWELL EXSERT EXTEND EXTRUDE
KNUCKLE PROJECT PROTEND
HERNIATE OUTPOINT OUTREACH
OUTSHOOT
PROTRUDING STEEP ASTRUT
BUNCHY GOGGLE BLABBER
EMINENT JUTTING OBTRUSIVE
PROTRUDINGLY ASTRUT
PROTRUSION JAG LAP NOB BURR
KNOB POUT HERNIA SALIENCE
SHOULDER TYLOSOID PROJECTION
PROTUBERANCE BUD HUB JAG
NOB NUB WEN BEAN BOLL BOSS
BULB BUMP HEEL HUMP JAGG KNAP
KNOB KNOP KNOT LUMP NODE PUFF
SCAB SNAG STUB UMBO WART
BULGE BUNCH CAPUT GLAND
GNARL HUNCH KNURL SWELL

TORUS TUBER TUMOR BREAST
CALLUS HUBBLE PIMPLE POMMEL
CRANKLE EXTANCY PAPILLA
EMINENCE FLANKARD MAMELEON
NODOSITY SWELLING APOPHYSIS
PROJECTION
(— AT BASE OF BIRD'S BILL) CERE
SNOOD
(— BEARING SPINE) UMBO
(— FROM SWELLING) PUFF
(— IN SIDE OF DEER) FLANKARD
(— ON A CASTING) SCAB
(— ON BONE) CONDYLE EMINENCE
(— ON HAND) MOUNT
(— ON HORSE'S HOOF) BUTTRESS
(— ON MANDIBLE OF GEESE) BEAN
(— ON SADDLEBOW) POMMEL
(— ON SALAMANDER) BALANCER
(— ON TONGUE) PAPILLA
(KNOBLIKE —) CAPUT
(OCCIPITAL —) INION
(RAGGED —) JAG JAGG
(ROUGH —) HUB
(SKIN —) WEN MOLE WART PIMPLE
(PREF.) TORO
PROTUBERANT BULGY BUMPY
NODAL PROUD STRUT TUMID
BUCKED EXTANT GOGGLE BOTTLED
BULGING BUNCHED EMINENT
GIBBOUS SALIENT SWOLLEN
PROMINENT PROTRUSIVE
(REGULARLY —) CONVEX
PROUD FFSS GLAD HIGH IKEY LOFT
PERK RANK SIDE VAIN BRANT CHUFF
GELLY GREAT JELLY LOFTY NOBLE
ORGUL PRIDY SAUCY STEEP STIFF
STOUT VOGIE WINDY WLONK
COPPED ELATED FIERCE LORDLY
ORGUIL PENCEY QUAINT SKEICH
SKEIGH UPPISH UPPITY VAUNTY
CHUFFED HAUGHTY SUBLIME
SWOLLEN TOPPING ARROGANT
EXULTANT GLORIOUS IMPOSING
INSOLENT ORGULOUS SPLENDID
STOMACHY TOPLOFTY
OVERBEARING
(TOO — FOR) ABOVE
PROUDLY HIGH
PROVE TRY FAND FOND PREE SHOW
TEST ARGUE ASSAY EVICT TAINT
TASTE TEMPT ARGUFY EVINCE
SUFFER VERIFY BALANCE CONFESS
CONFIRM CONVICT DERAIGN
IMPROVE JUSTIFY CONCLUDE
CONVINCE EVIDENCE INDICATE
INSTRUCT MANIFEST
(— FALSE) BELIE BETRAY FALSIFY
(— GUILTY) ATTAINT
(— ONESELF) ACQUIT
(— OUT) SERVE
(— TITLE) DEDUCE
(— VALID) DEFEND
PROVED TRIED EXPERT PROBATE

PROVENCAL LANGUEDOC
ROMANESQUE
PROVENDER HAY CORN FEED FOOD
OATS STRAW PABULUM PROVAND
PROVIANT
PROVERB SAW SAY REDE WORD
ADAGE AXIOM CREED GNOME
MAXIM SOOTH BALLAD BYWORD
DITTON DIVERB MASHAL SAYING
SPEECH SYMBOL WHEEZE BYSPELL
IMPRESA NAYWORD PARABLE
APHORISM FORBYSEN PAROEMIA
SCHOLION SCHOLIUM SENTENCE
SOOTHSAY
(PREF.) PARAMIO PAROEMIO
PROVIDE DO FIT SEE FEND FILL FIND
GIRD LEND LOOK BLOCK CATER
ENDOW ENDUE EQUIP SPEED STOCK
STORE AFFORD FOISON PURVEY
SUBORN SUPPLY COMPARE EXHIBIT
FORESEE FURNISH INSTORE
PREPARE ACCOUTER APPANAGE
DISPENSE PURCHASE
(— AHEAD OF TIME) ADVANCE
(— AMUSEMENT) DISTRACT
(— BY STEALTHY MEANS) SUBORN
(— FOOD) GRUB CATER SCAFF
(— FOR) FEND SERVE CHEVEYS
CHEVISE PROVANT
(— STINGILY) SKINCH
(— SUPPORT) ESCOT
(— WITH) BESEE
(— WITH DOWRY) DOT
(— WITH HIP-ROOF) COOT
(— WITH LOAN) ACCOMMODATE
(— WITH MONEY) FUND
PROVIDED IF BODEN FIXED READY
SOBEIT PROVISO INSTRUCT
PREPARED
PROVIDENCE THRIFT ECONOMY
PRUDENCE
PROVIDENT WARY WISE FRUGAL
SAVING CAREFUL PRUDENT THRIFTY
PROVINCE LAN AREA NOME WALK
AIMAK BANAT FIELD MOUTH NATAL
NOMOS REALM SHENG SHIRE
SUBAH WORLD BANNAT EMPIRE
EYALET MALAGA MONTON OBLAST
REGION SIRCAR SPHERE SYSSEL
YAMATO DEMESNE DONGOLA
EPARCHY MUDIRIA PURVIEW
RECTORY VILAYET APPANAGE
DISTRICT FUNCTION MUDIRIEH
NOMARCHY TERRITORY
(PAPAL —) LEGATION
(ROMAN —) RAETIA RHAETIA
(RUSSIAN —) OBLAST
(SUBDIVISION OF EGYPTIAN —) KISM
(PL.) OUTLAND
PROVINCIAL HICK BORNE CRUDE
NARROW RUSTIC STUFFY INSULAR
MOFUSSIL SUBURBAN PAROCHIAL
PRESIDIAL

PROVINCIALISM LOCALISM
PROVISION BOARD CHECK GRIST
FODDER MATTER PURVEY STOVER
UNLESS WRAITH APPREST CAUTION
CODICIL DOWNSET KEEPING
SLEEPER VICTUAL WARNISH
WARNISON
(— FOR MAINTENANCE) APANAGE
APPANAGE
(—S FOR JOURNEY) VIATICUM
(BOUGHT —S) ACATES ACATERY
(SUBORDINATE —) ITEM
(PL.) CHOW FOOD JOCK KEEP LOAN
PROG BOUGE CATES CHUCK SCRAN
STORE TERMS TOMMY ANNONA
VIANDS VIVRES COMMONS
WARNAGE WAYFARE VICTUALS
PROVISO SALVO CAVEAT CLAUSE
CAUTION CONDITION
PROVOCATION TEEN APPEAL
INCENTIVE
PROVOCATIVE GUTTY SALTY
AGACANT PIQUANT IRRITANT
APPEALING
PROVOKE BOG EGG GIG IRE TAR VEX
BEAR DARE HUFF MOVE PICK STIR
TARR TEEN URGE WORK ANGER
ANGRY ANNOY EAGER EVOKE
FRUMP PIQUE TAUNT TEMPT APPEAL
ELICIT EVINCE EXCITE GRIEVE
HARASS INCITE KINDLE NETTLE
PROMPT SUMMON TICKLE AFFRONT
ILLICIT INCENSE INFLAME INSPIRE
VROTHER CATALYZE IRRITATE
(— AVERSION) REPEL
PROVOKER GADFLY
PROVOKING AGACANT
PROVOST JUDGE PRIOR REEVE
KEEPER WARDEN STEWARD
PROW BOW BEAK SPUR STEM PRORE
SNOUT SPERON STEVEN DIVIDER
GALLANT VALIANT
(— OF GONDOLA) FERRO
PROWESS FEAT PROW VALOR
NOBLEY BRAVERY COURAGE
PROWL OWL PROG ROAM LURCH
MOOCH MOUSE RAVEN BREVIT
RAMBLE
PROWLER WALKER SLASHER
TENEBRION
PROWLIKE PROREAN
PROWLING GRASSANT
PROXIMAL CLOSE
PROXIMATE NEXT CLOSE DIRECT
CLOSEST NEAREST PROXIME
IMMINENT PROXIMAL
PROXIMITY SHADOW NEARNESS
PRESENCE VICINITY PROPINQUITY
NEIGHBORHOOD
PROXY VICE AGENT VICAR BALLOT
MANDAT PROCTOR
(PL.) ELECTION

PRUDE PRIG COMSTOCK
PRUDENCE CARE METIS ADVICE
CAUTEL WISDOM CAUTION
COUNSEL SLEIGHT FORECAST
FORELOOK
PRUDENT FIT SAFE SAGE WARE
WARY WISE CANNY DOOSE DOUCE
SOLID SYKER VERTY FRUGAL
QUAINT SEKERE SICCAR POLITIC
THRIVEN CAUTIOUS DISCREET
PROVIDENT
(NOT —) ADVISED
PRUDISH NICE PRIM MIMZY MIMSEY
PRIGGISH PUDIBUND VICTORIA
PRUDISHNESS NICETY PUDENCY
PRUNE COW LOP TOP CLIP COLL
COUL GELD PLUM SNED SPUR TAME
TRIM CLEAN DRESS KNIFE PLUMB
PREEN PRIME PURGE SHEAR SHRAG
SHRED SHRUB TRASH TWIST
DEHORN REFORM SHRIDE SNATHE
SWITCH AMPUTATE CASTRATE
RETRENCH
(— SEVERELY) DEHORN
(IMPERFECTLY RIPENED —) FROG
PRUNING HOOK SARPE CALABOZO
HANDBILL
PRUNING KNIFE SERPETTE
PRUNING SHEARS SECATEUR
PRURIENCE ITCH
PRURIENT ITCHY
PRURITIS ITCH
PRUSSIA PRUCE SPRUCE
PRUSSIAN PRUTENIC
PRY GAG KEEK NOSE NOTE PEEK
PEEP PEER TEET TOOT JIMMY LEVER
PRIZE SNOOP BREVIT FERRET PIGGLE
POTTER PUTTER CROWBAR
GUMSHOE LEVERAGE
(— ABOUT) OWL MOUSE SNOOK
SCROUNGE
(— INTO) BREVIT
(— INTO AND REPEAT) RAVE
PRYING NOSY NOSEY PEERY
CURIOUS PEEPING
PSALM ODE HYMN SONG DIRGE
GATHA TRACT ANTHEM CANTATE
CHORALE INTROIT MISERERE
(LENTEN —) TRACT
(100TH —) JUBILATE
(95TH —) VENITE
(98TH —) CANTATE
PSALMS HALLEL
(BOOK OF —) PSALTER
PSALTERIUM BOOK LYRA OMASUM
PSALTER PSALTERY
PSALTERY GUSLA CITOLE SAUTREE
SAUTERIE
PSEUDO FAKE MOCK SHAM BOGUS
FALSE FEIGNED SPURIOUS
(PREF.) NE
PSEUDOCARP HIP

PSEUDOLOGIST LIAR
PSEUDONYM ALIAS ANONYM
  JUNIUS
PSHAW SHA DARN DRAT POOH
  SUGAR PHOOEY SHUCKS
PSITTACOSIS ORNITHOSIS
PSORIASIS ALPHOS
PSYCHE MIND SELF SOUL
PSYCHIATRIST SHRINK ANALYST
  ALIENIST
  AMERICAN LIDE BERNE BRILL KLINE
  MEYER SZASZ OLIVER REUBEN
  SALMON WILDER RADECKI SPITZKA
  ABRAMSON MENNINGER
  DUNBARMFRANK
  AUSTRIAN ADLER FRANKL
  GERMAN PERLS ZIEHEN JASPERS
  ISRAELI LEVY
  SCOTTISH LAING
  SOUTH AFRICAN COOPER
  SWISS JUNG BLEULER RORSCHACH
  BINSWANGER
PSYCHIC (— POWERS) PSI
PSYCHOANALYST FREUDIAN
PSYCHOLOGIST
  AMERICAN AMES HALL HOLT LADD
  MEAD SALK BRITT DODGE JANOV
  LAIRD LEWIN RHINE SEARS SIMON
  URBAN WELLS ANGELL BORING
  BRUNER GESELL GINOTT HAINES
  HUNTER KANNER KOFFKA MASLOW
  PRINCE STARCH STRONG TERMAN
  WATSON ALLPORT BAI DWIN
  BATESON CATTELL DOLLARD
  GODDARD NEWBOLD TROLAND
  BROTHERS LANGFELD MARSHALL
  SEASHORE WECHSLER PILLSBURY
  SCRIPTURE WOODWORTH
  CARRINGTON HOLLINGWORTH
  ARGENTINIAN INGENIEROS
  AUSTRIAN ADLER BETTELHEIM
  DANISH LANGE
  ENGLISH BURT WARD BUCKE ELLIS
  MYERS OGDEN STOUT SULLY
  GURNEY MORGAN AVELING
  BARTLETT MAUDSLEY
  FRENCH COUE BINET JANET SIMON
  BEAUNIS
  GERMAN KROH GEISE MARBE STERN
  WUNDT BENDER KOHLER MULLER
  PREYER RUBNER ZIEHEN JAENSCH
  MEUMANN KRONHAUSEN
  SCOTTISH BAIN
  SWISS JUNG PIAGET
PSYCHOLOGY HORMISM HEDONICS
  ANIMASTIC FORMALISM
PSYCHOPATH MATTOID
PSYCHOSIS INSANITY PARANOIA
  SENILITY MELANCHOLIA
  SCHIZOPHRENIA
PSYCHOTIC MAD CRAZY INSANE
PSYLLA DIMERAN

PSYLLIUM FLEAWORT
PTAH (— EMBODIED) APIS
  (ASSOCIATED WITH —) SEKHET
PTARMIGAN RYPE GROUSE
  LAGOPODE
PTEROCARPUS LINGOUM
PTEROID ALAR
PTEROSAUR DIAPSID
PTERYGIUM WEBEYE
PTERYGOID EXTERNUM
PTERYLA TRACT
PTISAN TEA TISANE
PTOLEMY SOTER
  (WIFE OF —) CLEOPATRA
PTOMAINE NEURIN SEPSIN SAPRINE
  GADININE PUTRESCINE
PTOUS (FATHER OF —) ATHAMAS
  (MOTHER OF —) THEMISTO
PUAH (FATHER OF —) ISSACHAR
  (SON OF —) TOLA
PUB BAR INN CAFE CAFF BISTRO
  BOOZER LOUNGE SHANTY TAVERN
PUBBLE FAT FULL PLUMP
PUB-CRAWL BARHOP
PUBERTY
  (PREF.) HEBE
PUBES
  (PREF.) EPISIO PUBI(O) PUBO
PUBESCENCE DOWN SCURF YOUTH
  TOMENT TOMENTUM
PUBESCENT HIRSUTE VILLOUS
  (PREF.) HEBE
PUBLIC KUNG OPEN TOWN APERT
  CIVIC OVERT WORLD COMMON
  SOCIAL VULGAR GENERAL OMNIBUS
  POPULAR EXTERNAL MATERIAL
  NATIONAL MULTITUDE
  (GENERAL —) GALLERY
PUBLICAN BUNG FARMER KEEPER
  TAVERNER ZACCHEUS CATCHPOLL
PUBLICATION BOOK ORDO BIBLE
  FOLIO ISSUE SHEET ANNUAL
  BLAZON DIGLOT SERIAL WEEKLY
  ALMANAC BOOKLET ELZEVIR
  JOURNAL MONTHLY WRITING
  BIWEEKLY BULLETIN DOCUMENT
  EMISSION EXCHANGE PRODROME
  EPHEMERIS PERIODICAL
  (KIND OF —) MIMEO NUDIE
PUBLIC HOUSE BAR INN PUB
  BOOZER PUBLIC SALOON HOSTELRY
  POTHOUSE
PUBLICIST AGENT SOLON WRITER
PUBLICITY AIR HYPE BLAZE
  ECLAT BUILDUP PUFFERY
  RECLAME BALLYHOO BROUHAHA
  DAYLIGHT FLACKERY HERALDRY
  PROMOTION
  (PROVIDE —) FLACK
PUBLICIZE CRY FLOG HYPE PLUG
  BLURB BREAK BRUIT HERALD
  BALLYHOO HEADLINE PROPAGATE

PUBLIC SQUARE PLAZA PLEIN
ZOCALO
PUBLISH AIR ASH BLOW CALL EDIT
EMIT VEND VENT CARRY ISSUE
PRINT SPEAK UTTER BLAZON
BROACH DEFAME DELATE EVULGE
EXPOSE SPREAD CENSURE DECLARE
DIFFUSE DIVULGE GAZETTE PROTEST
RELEASE DENOUNCE DISCLOSE
EVULGATE PROCLAIM PROMULGE
(— BANNS OF MARRIAGE) CRY SPUR
OUTASK
(— IN CHURCH) ASK
(— WITHOUT AUTHORIZATION)
PIRATE
PUBLISHER CRIER EDITOR ISSUER
PRINTER STATIONER
AMERICAN COX DOW LEA AMES
BONI CERF DODD FUNK GINN HOLT
HOYT KERN KNOX LOEB LUCE MACY
MUIR NAST OCHS ZIFF BOBBS
BOEHM BROWN CAREY ENGEL
ENOCH FODOR GODEY HECHT
HOBBY JONES KNOPF MCRAE SIMON
SMITH STERN ZEVIN BOWKER
CAPPER CHILDS COVICI CURTIS
DUTTON FARRAR FIELDS FORBES
GIROUX HARPER HARRIS HEARST
HEFNER KLOTZ LAFFAN LESLIE
LITTLE MOSHER MUNSEY NIEMAN
PAYSON PUTNAM RIDDER RODALE
SCHIFF STOKES THOMAS UPDIKE
VICTOR WALKER WILSON ZENGER
ATTWOOD BINGHAM CAHNERS
COLLIER CONNERS DRYFOOS
GANNETT GUPTILL LOTHROP
MIFFLIN POULSON PRESSER SADLIER
SCRIPPS SHUSTER TICKNOR
VERONIS WITMARK BANCROFT
BARTLETT HOUGHTON PULITZER
RINEHART SCHUSTER SCRIBNER
WAGNALLS DOUBLEDAY LIVERIGHT
MCCORMICK LIPPINCOTT
AUSTRALIAN SHEED MURDOCH
THEODORE
CANADIAN SWEET
DUTCH ELZEVIR
ENGLISH DAY BELL BOHN CAPE LANE
PAUL ALMON LUCAS MOXON MUDIE
UNWIN WARNE WOOLF AITKEN-
BOOSEY FROWDE HAWKES KNIGHT
LINTOT MILLAR NEWNES TONSON
TOTTEL BEMROSE BENTLEY
BRACKEN CASSELL CHAPMAN
DEBRETT DODSLEY JENKINS
METHUEN BRITTAIN NEWBERRY
QUARITCH RICHARDS WHITAKER
HEINEMANN PICKERING RIVINGTON
ROUTLEDGE VIZETELLY
WHITCHURCH BEAVERBROOK
FRENCH DIDOT HETZEL LEMERRE
LITOLFF PLANTIN HACHETTE
GALIGNANI

GERMAN COTTA MEYER FROBEN
ZENGER PERTHES TEUBNER
BAEDEKER SCHIRMER SPRINGER
ULLSTEIN BROCKHAUS TAUCHNITZ
IRISH BRACKEN
ITALIAN RICORDI SONZOGNO
SCOTTISH BLACK SMITH CADELL
CREECH NELSON CHAMBERS
BLACKWOOD CONSTABLE
MACMILLAN
SOUTH AFRICAN QOBOZA
WELSH BERRY
PUCCOON GROMYL ALKANET
GROMWELL BLOODROOT
PUCE FLEA
PUCK ELF IMP LOB PUG BLOW BUTT
DISK POKE POOK DEMON DEVIL
FAIRY PEWKE SPORT RUBBER SPRITE
STRIKE PUCKREL HOBGOBLIN
PUCKER DRAW FULL RUCK PURSE
REEVE RIVEL TIZZY COCKLE
COTTER FURROW LUCKEN RUCKLE
WRINKLE CONTRACT AGITATION
CONSTRICT
PUCKERED PURSY BULLATE
COCKLED ROUCHED WRINKLED
BULLIFORM
PUCKEREL IMP
PUCKFIST BRAGGART PUFFBALL
PUCKISH PUXY ELFIN IMPISH
WHIMSICAL
PUDDING DICK DUFF LINK SAGO
BOMBE DOWDY KUGEL MERIT
BURGOO FENDER HACKIN HAGGIS
HAUPIA JAUDIE SPONGE TANSEY
TARTAN DESSERT ADEQUACY
BLOODING HEDGEHOG LIVERING
PANDOWDY PLUMDUFF ROLYPOLY
STICKJAW WHITEPOT CHARLOTTE
(— CONTAINING KALE) TARTAN
(— INGREDIENT) TAPIOCA
(— OF FLOUR) DUFF
(BOILED —) HOY
(FRUIT —) HEDGEHOG
(HASTY —) MUSH SEPON SUPAWN
(HAWAIIAN —) HAUPIA
(KIND OF —) COTTAGE
(MEAT —) ISING CHEWET HACKIN
HACKING
(SUET —) KUGEL
PUDDINGWIFE PUDIANO
DONCELLA GLUEFISH
PUDDLE DUB PANT PLUD POOL
PULK ROIL SLAB SLOP SOSS SUMP
FLUSH PLANT PLASH PUDGE
CHARCO FLODGE KENNEL MUDDLE
PUDDER SPLASH TAMPER CONFUSE
PLASHET SLODDER SPUDDLE
BEFUDDLE
(MUD —) DUB SLOP LOBLOLLY
PUDDLEBALL LOOP
PUDDLER'S RABBLE STRIKE
PUDENCY MODESTY DELICACY

PUDGY MIRY BULKY MUDDY PODGY
SQUAT CHUBBY SPUDDY ROLYPOLY
ROLLABOUT
PUDU VENADA
PUEBLO ANASAZI
PUELCHE PAMPA TEHUELET
PUERILE WEAK SILLY BOYISH
JEJUNE TRIVIAL CHILDISH
IMMATURE YOUTHFUL

PUERTO RICO
BAY: SUCIA RINCON BOQUERON
AQUADILLA
CAPITAL: SANJUAN
ISLAND: MONA CULEBRA VIEQUES
LAKE: LOIZA CARITE CAONILLAS
MEASURE: CUERDA CABALLERIA
RIVER: CAMUY CANAS YAUCO
ANASCO DORADO MANATI ARECIBO
BAYAMON FAJARDO GUAYAMA
HUMACAO MAYAGUEZ

PUFF GUF POP BLOW BRAG DRAG
FLAM FLAN GASP GUFF GUST HUFF
PANT PECH SHOW WAFF WAFT
BLURB BLURT ELATE ERUPT EXTOL
FLUFF QUIFF SKIFF STECH SWELL
WHIFF CAPFUL EXPAND FLATUS
BLUSTER EXPLODE GRATIFY INFLATE
WHIFFET BRAGGART OVERRATE
WINDGALL BOUILLONE
(— FROM SHELL BLAST) BURST
(— OF WIND) FLAM TIFT SCART
SLANT FLATUS HUFFLE
(— ON MARIJUANA CIGARETTE)
TOKE
(— OUT) BELL BLUB VENT BLOUSE
BLUBBER EFFLATE INFLATE
(— OUT SMOKE) EFFUME
(— UP) BLOW HUFF RISE BLOAT
HEAVE BLADDER
(— VIOLENTLY) BLAST
(APPLE —) FLAPJACK
(CREAM —) DUCHESSE
(PASTRY —) PROFITEROLE
(SUDDEN —) FLAN FLAW GUST
PUFFBALL FIST FUZZ PUFF SMOKE
FUNGUS PUFFIN BULLFICE BULLFIST
PUCKFIST SNUFFBOX
PUFFBIRD BARBET MONASE
NUNLET DREAMER NUNBIRD
BARBACOU
PUFFED BLUB ROLLEN BLOATED
SOUFFLE SWOLLEN ARROGANT
INFLATED
(— OUT) BAGGY BOUFFANT
(— UP) RANK BOBBY ASTRUT
BLOATED SWOLLEN TURGENT
VENTOSE
(BE — UP) BELL
PUFFER ATINGA BALLER BLOWER
SLIMER TAMBOR BURFISH EGGFISH
BLOWFISH TOADFISH

PUFFIN LOOM PAPE POPE MARROT
MULLET MARROCK WILLOCK
COCKANDY PARAKEET TOMNODDY
TOMNORRY
(HAWAIIAN —) AO
PUFFY SOFT BAGGY BLOAT FAFFY
GUMMY GUSTY PURSY CHUBBY
FLUFFY PURFLY PURSIVE SWOLLEN
BLADDERY BOUFFANT DROPSICAL
PUG FOX IMP PET BOXER CHAFF
GOUGE SPOOR TRACK TRAIL
CAMOIS CAMUSE GOBLIN MONKEY
MISTRESS PUGILIST FOOTPRINT
PUGENCY TANG
PUGILIST PUG MILLER BRUISER
SLOGGER
PUGNACIOUS BELLICOSE
PUG-NOSED CAMUS CAMUSE
PUISNE PUNY LATER PETTY JUNIOR
YOUNGER INFERIOR
PUISSANCE ARMY FORCE POWER
CONTROL POTENCY PROWESS
DOMINION STRENGTH
PUJUNAN MAIDU
PUKKA GOOD REAL GENUINE
LASTING COMPLETE SUPERIOR
AUTHENTIC
PUKRAS PHEASANT KOKLAS
PULCHRITUDE GRACE BEAUTY
PULE CRY PEEP CHIRP COWRY WHINE
SNIVEL WHIMPER
PULING PULY GRINDLY WHINING
PULITZER PRIZE (— IN LETTERS)
BOK LEE NYE AGAR AGEE BATE
BUCK CARO COLT DOVE DUYN EDEL
FEIO GALE GRAU HART INGE LASH
LEVY MACK MOTT RICE TATE UHRY
VANN WOOD WOUK AIKEN AKINS
ALBEE AUDEN BAKER BEMIS
BENET BRUCE BRUCE BULEY CHASE
CLAPP CURTI DAVIS DRURY DUGAN
FRANK FROST GLUCK HECHT ISAAC
ISSAC JAMES KAMOW KIZER
KRAMM KUMIN LEECH LUKAS LURIE
MABEE MAMET MOSEL NEELY
OPPEN PLATH PLATH PUPIN PUSEY
SAGAN SIMIC SIMON SMITH STARR
TEALE TOOLE TYLER UNGER WELTY
WILLS ABBOTT BAILYN BAILYN
BECKER BELLOW BRANCH BUTLER
BUTLER CATHER CATTON CREMIN
CREMIN CROUSE DEGLER DONALD
DURANT FERBER FRINGS FULLER
GARROW GRAZIA HANDIN HARLAN
HENLEY HERSEY HORGAN KAMMEN
KENNAN KIDDER KIDDER KINNEL
LAPINE LARKIN LOWELL MAILER
MAILER MARNET MASSIE MASSIE
MCCRAW MILLAY MORRIS NAIFEH
NORMAN NORMAN OLIVER ONEILL
PULLER RHODES SHAARA SMILEY
TAYLOR TAYLOR TERKEL TOLAND
ULRICH UPDIKE UPDIKE WALKER

WALKER WARNER WILBUR WILDER
WILSON WILSON YERGIN ZINDEL
ASHBERY BURROWS CHEEVER
DILLARD ELLMANN ERIKSON
JUSTICE JUSTICE KAUFMAN
KENNEDY KENNEDY KINNELL
KUSHNER LAFARGE LINDSAY
LITWACK LITWACK LOESSER
MCFEELY MCFEELY NEMEROV
POLLOCK RODGERS SAROYAN
SHEEHAN SHEEHAN SHIPLER
TUCHMAN VIERECK BOORSTIN
FAULKNER HIJUELOS KINGSLEY
LELYVELD MACLEISH MARQUAND
MCMURTRY MEREDITH MICHENER
MORRISON SANDBURG SCHORSKE
SCHORSKE SCHUYLER SCHUYLER
SHERWOOD SINCLAIR SONDHEIM
VANDOREN WOODWARD
HEMINGWAY MAHARIDGE
MCDOUGALL MCPHERSON
SCHENKKAN SILVERMAN STEINBECK
HOFSTADTER HOFSTADTER
HOLLDOBLER MCCULLOUGH
WILLIAMSON WASSERSTEIN
(— IN MUSIC) RAN HUSA IVES TOCH
WARD CRUMB KUBIK MOORE PERLE
RANDS ROREM ROUSE ALBERT
BARBER BOLCOM CARTER HANSON
PISTON PORTER POWELL ARGENTO
BASSETT COPLAND MARTINO
MENOTTI SCHUMAN SOWERBY
THOMSON WERNICK ZWILICH
COLGRASS DRUCKMAN HARBISON
KIRCHNER PETERSON REYNOLDS
SESSIONS WUORINEN DELLOJOIO
DAVIDOVSKY DELTREDICI
SCHWANTNER
PULL IN PU EAR LUG POO POU RIG
RUG TIT TOW CHUG CLAW DRAG
DRAW DUCT HALE HARL HAUL HOOK
RUGG SWIG TIRE TREK TUSH TWIG
YANK BOUSE BREAK BUNCH CLOUT
DRAFT HEAVE HITCH IMPEL JUICE
PLUCK POLLE PROOF TRICE TWEAK
ASSUME COMMIT GATHER OBTAIN
PLITCH RUGGLE SCHLEP SECURE
TWITCH UPROOT WRENCH ATTRACT
EXTRACT
(— A BELL) SET
(— ABOUT) TEW SOOL TOSE TOZE
MOUSLE
(— APART) RAVE REND TEAR
DIVULSE
(— AWAY) AVEL AVELL WREST
REVULSE
(— BY EARS) SOLE SOWL
(— DOWN) UNPILE DESTROY
DEMOLISH
(— FOR) BACK
(— FORCIBLY) TUG
(— HERE AND THERE) TOOZLE
TOUSLE

(— IN PIECES) DIVELLICATE
(— NOSE) SNITE
(— OF DRUM) EAR
(— OFF) CROP DRAW STRIP AVULSE
(— ON CIGARETTE) TOKE
(— ON FISHING ROD) STRIKE
(— ON ROPE) BOWSE
(— OUT) RAX UPROOT EXTRACT
OUTBRAID
(— QUICKLY) YANK
(— ROUGHLY) WAP TOWSE WOUSE
(— SUDDENLY) TRICE
(— THE LEG) STRING
(— TOGETHER) KNOT ATTRACT
(— TRIGGER) SQUEEZE
(— UP) LOUK
(— UP BY THE ROOTS) ARACE
(— VIOLENTLY) WHAP WHOP WHANG
(— WITH A TWIST) WRENCH
(— WITH JERK) HOICK SWITCH
(ZIPPER —) SLIDER
PULLDEVIL SCROUGER SCRODGILL
PULLER KNOCKER
PULLER-IN CLICKER
PULLET HEN EAROCK EEROCK
EIRACK MABYER POULARD
POULAINE
PULLEY RIM CONE DRUM BLOCK
FUSEE FUZEE IDLER TRICE WHEEL
DRIVEN IDLEBY JOCKEY POLYVE
RIGGER SHEAVE SHIVER WHARVE
CAPSTAN FERRULE TIGHTER
TRUCKLE WHARROW PULLISEE
PURCHASE TROCHLEA
(PL.) TRISPAST JACKANAPES
PULLOVER JERSEY SWEATER
PULLULATE BUD TEEM BREED
SWARM MULTIPLY
PULMONATE LUNGED
PULMONIC PNEUMONIC
PULP MAG PAP PUG CHUM MUSH
BROKE JELLY NERVE SLUSH STOCK
STUFF MARROW SQUEEZE
SQUELCH
(FOOD —) CHYME
PULPIT PEW TUB AMBO BEMA DESK
WOOD CHAIR PREACH ROSTRUM
TRIBUNE
(— BOARD) TYPE
(— FOR CHOIR BOOKS) ANALOGION
(MOSLEM —) MIMBAR MINBAR
(OPEN-AIR —) TENT
PULPY SOFT SPEWY FLABBY FLESHY
SIDDER SIDDOW BACCATE
SQUELCHY
PULSATE BEAT BRIM FLAP PANT
PUMP THROB COURSE STRIKE
PALPITATE
PULSATION BEAT PANT BEATING
HEARTBEAT LIFEBLOOD VIBRATION
(— OF ARTERY) ICTUS
PULSE DAL EMP BEAT DOHL TAKT
URAD WAVE POUCE STUFF THROB

BATTUTA IMPULSE PULSIDGE
SPHYGMUS VITALITY
(PREF.) PALMO SPHYGMO
(SUFF.) CROTIC
PULSING VIBRANT
PULVERIZATION TRIPSIS
PULVERIZE BRAY BUCK DRAG FINE
MEAL MULL STUB BRAKE CRUSH
FLOUR GRIND POUND BRUISE
POWDER ATOMIZE DEMOLISH
VANQUISH COMMINUTE MICRONIZE
PULVERIZED FINE POWDERED
PULVERIZER MULLER
PULVERULENT DUSTY CRUMBLY
POWDERY
PULVILLUS PAD
PUMA COUGAR PAINTER PANTHER
PUME YARURA
PUMICE LAVA PUMEX PUMIE
(UNCOOLED —) LAVA
PUMMEL FIB BEAT DRUB PAIK SLAT
POUND SLATE THUMP POUNCE
PUMP GIN GUN FORK JACK COURT
FORCE HEART PLUMB SLUSH
DOCTOR DORSAY FORCER SINKER
VOLUTE BOOSTER DOWNTON
EJECTOR EVACTOR PITWORK
SLUDGER SYRINGE TOEPLER
BEERPULL ELEVATOR INFLATER
INJECTOR PULSATOR PULSOMETER
(— ON SHIPS) DOWNTON
(— UP) AERATE INFLATE
(GAS —) BOWSER
(HAND —) GUN
(MINE —S) SET
(SET OF —S) LIFT
PUMP DOCTOR GRATHEN
PUMPER RACKER
PUMPERNICKEL BOMBERNICKEL
PUMPKIN PEPO CHUMP GOURD
PEPON QUAGH CASHAW CITRUL
CUCURB CUSHAW SQUASH
QUASHEY CUCURBIT PEPONIDA
PUMPKINSEED RUFF SUNNY
FLATFISH FLOUNDER REDBELLY
PUN NICK WHIM ALLUDE CLINCH
GROANER QUIBBLE EQUIVOKE
PARAGRAM CALEMBOUR
PARANOMASIA ANNOMINATION
PUNCH DAB DIG FIB HUB JAB SET
BASH BELT BLOW BOFF BUST DECK
DING PLUG POKE SETT SLUG SOAK
SOCK TIFF BUMBO DOUSE DRIFT
FORCE GLOGG PASTE PENCH SHORT
SLOSH CANCEL INCUSE PATRIX
PAUNCH SHAPER STINGO STRIKE
TRACER MATTOIR PERLOIR SANGRIA
SHELLAC STARTER EMBOSSER
GROUNDER HAYMAKER PRITCHEL
PUNCTURE SWATCHEL THICKSET
(CHASING —) TRACER
(DOG OF —) TOBY
(ETCHER'S —) MATTOIR

(HORSESHOE —) PRITCHEL
(KIND OF —) RABBIT
(OVAL —) PLAISHER
(RUM —) RUMBO
(SWINGING —) ROUNDHOUSE
(WIFE OF —) JUDY
PUNCHBOARD PUSHCARD
PUNCH BOWL SNEAKER
PUNCHCARD (GROUP OF —S) DECK
PUNCH-DRUNK PUNCHY
SLAPHAPPY
PUNCHED PERTUSE
PUNCHEON CASK PULE SNAP
PUNCH
PUNCHER COWBOY SOCKER
PUNCHINELLO CLOWN BUFFOON
PUGENELLO
PUNCH PRESS BEAR DROP
PUNCHY POUNCY FORCEFUL
PUNCTILIO PIQUE PUNTO PUNCTO
PUNCTILIOUS NICE EXACT STIFF
FORMAL CAREFUL POINTED PRECISE
PUNCTUAL
PUNCTUAL DUE EXACT ONTIME
PROMPT CAREFUL PRECISE
ACCURATE DEFINITE DETAILED
EXPLICIT
PUNCTUALLY SHARP
PUNCTUATE MARK STOP POINT
EMPHASIZE
(— JAZZ SOLO) COMP
PUNCTUATION MARK DOT DASH
STOP BRACE COLON COMMA PRICK
SLASH HYPHEN PERIOD STIGME
BRACKET VIRGULE ELLIPSIS
SEMICOLON
PUNCTURE HOLE PICK PINK PROD
STAB DRILL POINT PRICK PUNCH
STICK NEEDLE PIERCE PIQURE
DEFLATE DESTROY PUNCTUM
CENTESIS PINPRICK
(SKIN —) NEEDLESTICK
PUNCTURED CRIBLE
PUNDIT GURU SAGE SVAMI SWAMI
CRITIC PANDIT TEACHER
PUNG SLED
PUNGENCY NIP HEAT SALT SNAP
ACRIMONY KEENNESS PIQUANCY
SALTNESS
PUNGENT HOT TEZ ACID BOLD FELL
KEEN RACY RICH SALT TART ACRID
ACUTE BRISK NIPPY QUICK SHARP
SMART SNELL SPICY TANGY ZESTY
BITING BITTER SHRILL SNAPPY
CAUSTIC MORDANT PEPPERY
PIQUANT POINTED TELLING
CAYENNED PIERCING POIGNANT
STABBING STINGING
(— QUALITY) ZAP
PUNGI BIN
PUNIC PUNICAL FAITHLESS
PUNISH FIT FIX PAY BUCK CANE
COLT COOK CUCK FINE FLOG GATE

SORT WIPE ABUSE BIRCH CURSE
ORDER SCOUR SHEND SLATE SPILL
STOCK STRAP TWINK WREAK
AMERCE AVENGE CAMPUS FERULE
FOLLOW IMMURE LESSON REFORM
SCHOOL STRAFE STRIKE CHASTEN
CONSUME CORRECT CORRIGE
DEPLETE PENANCE REQUITE
SCOURGE CARTWHIP CHASTISE
DISTRAIN CASTIGATE
(— BY BLOW ON PALM) PANDY
(— BY COMPENSATION) FINE
AMERCE
(— BY CONFINEMENT) GATE
(— BY FINE) MULCT
(— BY LASHING WRISTS) BUCK
(— IN PRISON) ISOLATE
PUNISHING HARD GRUELING
PUNISHMENT GIG FINE LASH PAIN
PINE RACK SACK WITE YARD BEANS
GRUEL LIBEL PANDY PEINE SMART
WRACK WREAK DESERT DIRDUM
FERULE LESSON PICKET EXAMPLE
GALLOWS GANTLET JANKERS
PAYMENT PENALTY PENANCE
PENANCY REVENGE SCOURGE
HERISSON JUDGMENT PUNITION
STOCKING SUPPLICE EXECUTION
(CAPITAL —) SCAFFOLD
(MILITARY —) JANKERS
(SCHOOL —) PANDY
PUNITIVE PENAL PUNITORY
PUNK BAD BOY MUG FUNK JERK
MONK POOR PUNG THUG CONCH
SPONK SPUNK AMADOU BUNKUM
NOVICE HOODLUM RUFFIAN
BEGINNER GANGSTER INFERIOR
NONSENSE STRUMPET TERRIBLE
TOUCHWOOD
PUNKIE MIDGE MIDGET
PUNNING ALLUSIVE BIVERBAL
PUNSCH ARRACK
PUNSTER WAG SPEED
PUNT BET HIT POY KENT KICK QUANT
GAMBLE GARVEY SKERRY
PUNTER BIDDER GAMBLER SCALPER
SERVITOR
PUNY WEAK DAWNY DEENY DWARF
FRAIL PETTY SCRAM WEARY JUNIOR
MAUGER NOVICE PUISNE RECENT
SICKLY SPROTY MANIKIN PIMPING
QUEECHY SHILPIT YOUNGER
DROGHLIN INFERIOR PINDLING
RECKLING
(— PERSON) TITMAN
PUP PUPPY WHELP
PUPA EGG NYMPH PUPPET TUMBLER
WIGGLER FLAXSEED WRIGGLER
CHRYSALIS
PUPIL BOY GYTE TYRO WARD BLACK
CADET CHILD ELEVE NORRY NURRY
RAPIN TUTEE ALUMNA GRADER
INFANT JUNIOR SENIOR LEARNER

PAULINE SCHOLAR SOJOURN
STUDENT ABSENTEE BLUECOAT
DISCIPLE RUGBEIAN SCHOOLER
(— AT HEAD OF CLASS) DUX
(— GOING TO UNIVERSITY)
ABITURIENT
(— IN STUDIO) RAPIN
(— OF CHRIST'S HOSPITAL)
BLUECOAT
(— OF EYE) BLACK PEARL SIGHT
(— WITH SOME AUTHORITY)
PREFECT PRAEFECT
(ANGLO-INDIAN —) CHELA
(BOARDED —) SOJOURN
(GERMAN —) ABITURIENT
(PREF.) COR(E)(O)
(SUFF.) CORIA
PUPILAGE (WARDSHIP PEDANTISM
PUPPET BABY DOLL DUPE IDOL
MOTE BABBY DROLL DUMMY
MAUMET MOTION POPPIN STOOGE
WAJANG WAYANG GUIGNOL
DROLLERY MARIONET MARIONETTE
(— PLAY) WAJANG
(— SHOW) VERTEP
(— THEATER) BUNRAKU
(PREF.) PUPI
PUPPETEER SARG
PUPPIS STERN
PUPPY FOP PUP DOLL DOUGH WHELP
PUPPET
(FEMALE —) GYP
(GREYHOUND —) SAPLING
PURBLIND BISME BISSON
PURCHASABLE VENAL CORRUPT
PURCHASE BUY WIN EARN FISH
GAIN KOOP WHIP BOOTY HEDGE
PRIZE DUPLEX EFFECT EMPTIO
TACKLE ACQUIRE BARGAIN EMPTION
PILLAGE PROCURE BARRATRY
(— AND FATTEN CATTLE) HIGGLE
PURCHASER BUYER EMPTOR
VENDEE CHAPMAN POULTER
SHOPPER CUSTOMER
PURE NET CAST EVEN FAIR FINE FREE
FULL GOOD HOLY MERE NEAT PUTE
TRUE CLEAN CLEAR FRESH MORAL
NAKED SHEER STARK SYCEE UTTER
WHITE WHOLE CANDID CHASTE
ENTIRE IMMIXT LIMPID PISTIC
SIMPLE VESTAL VIRGIN ANGELIC
CATHARI GENUINE PERFECT SINCERE
ABSOLUTE ABSTRACT COMPLETE
DOVELIKE INNOCENT PRISTINE
SERAPHIC SPOTLESS VIRGINAL
VIRTUOUS SPIRITUAL
(— IN COLOR) ORIENT
(PREF.) KATHARO
PUREE DAL SOUP CREAM BRANDADE
PURFLE ADORN
PURGATIVE PURGE SENNA
CALOMEL DIASENE DRASTIC
TURPETH ALOEDARY APERIENT

CLEANSER ELATERIN EVACUANT
CATHARTIC ABSTERSIVE
PURGATORY PAIN SWAMP
PURGE LAX RID FIRE FLUX SOIL
CLEAR RHEUM SCOUR DRENCH
PHYSIC REMOVE SEETHE SHRIVE
SPURGE CHISTKA CLEANSE DETERGE
ABSTERGE
PURIFICATION BAPTISM ELUTION
LUSTRUM VASTATION
PURIFIED WHITE
PURIFY TRY BOLT FINE PURE WASH
CLEAN PURGE SNUFF BLEACH DISTIL
FILTER REFINE SETTLE SPURGE
WINNOW BAPTIZE CHASTEN
CLEANSE EPURATE EXPIATE
LAUNDER MUNDIFY SUBLIME
SWEETEN DEPURATE EXORCISE
FILTRATE LUSTRATE SANCTIFY
SCAVENGE SPRINKLE
(— ORE) DILVE
(— SUGAR) CLAY
PURIFYING SMECTIC DEPURANT
PURIRI TEAK BULKEEDY IRONWOOD
PURIST PRIG PEDANT STICKLER
PURITAN PRIG SAINT CANTER
CROPPY BLUENOSE CATHARAN
GOSPELER PRECISIAN ROUNDHEAD
PURITANICAL BLUE STRICT
GENTEEL PRECISE
PURITANI, I (CHARACTER IN —)
ARTHUR ELVIRA TALBOT WALTON
HENRIETTA
(COMPOSER OF —) BELLINI
PURITY PURE ASSAY HONOR WHITE
CANDOR SATTVA VIRTUE FINESSE
CHASTITY FINENESS PURENESS
(— OF BREED) PEDIGREE
(— OF LUSTER) ORIENT
PURL RID EDDY KNIT PEARL UPSET
RIPPLE TOTTLE CAPSIZE OVERTURN
PURLIEU AREA HAUNT
(PL.) BOUNDS CONFINES ENVIRONS
PURLIN RIB
PURLOIN CAB CRIB WEED ANNEX
BRIBE FILCH STEAL SWIPE FINGER
PILFER PIRATE CABBAGE SNAFFLE
SURREPT ABSTRACT SCROUNGE
PURPLE GAY VIOL LILAC REGAL
SHOWY ARGYLE BLATTA BLOODY
CROCUS EVEQUE MIGNON ARDOISE
FUCHSIA FUCHSIN HEATHEN
LOGWOOD PETUNIA PONTIFF
PURPURE AMARANTH BURGUNDY
CAMERIER CYCLAMEN EGGPLANT
EMINENCE IMPERIAL MAUVETTE
MULBERRY WISTARIA
(BROWNISH —) PUCE
(DELICATE —) MAUVE
(PALE —) LILAC
(VISIBLE —) RHODOPSIN
(PREF) PORPHYR(O) PURPUREO
PURPURI PURPURO

PURPLE FISH MUREX
PURPLE GALLINULE SULTAN
SULTANA HYACINTH
PURPLE LAND (AUTHOR OF —)
HUDSON
(CHARACTER IN —) JOHN LAMB
ANITA MARCO COLOMA LUCERO
MARCOS MONICA SANTOS
ANSELMO BARBUDO CALIXTO
GANDARA HILARIO ISIDORA PAQUITA
PERALTA RICHARD DEMETRIA
MARGARITA CARRICKFERGUS
PURPLE LOOSESTRIFE KILLWEED
PURPLE MEDIC ALFALFA
PURPLE RAGWORT JACOBY
PURPLE SANDPIPER REDLEG
REDLEGS ROCKBIRD
PURPORT FECK GIST PORT DRIFT
SENSE TENOR DESIGN EFFECT
IMPART IMPORT INTEND INTENT
BEARING MEANING PROFESS
PURPOSE COVERING DISGUISE
STRENGTH
PURPOSE GO AIM END GOAL IDEA
MAIN MEAN MIND MINT PLAN SAKE
TALK TEND VIEW WEEN WILL ARTHA
CAUSE ETTLE HEART LEVEL POINT
SCOPE STUDY THINK DESIGN
DEVICE EFFECT INTEND INTENT
OBTENT PREFIX REASON SCHEME
COMPASS COUNSEL DESTINE
EARNEST IMAGINE MEANING
PROPOSE THOUGHT DEVOTION
FUNCTION PLEASURE PROPOUND
DISCOURSE
(ALLEGED —) PRETEXT
(FIXED —) HEART
(INSIDIOUS —) CAUTEL
(MORAL —) ETHOS
(PARTICULAR —) NONCE
(PRESENT —) NONCE
PURPOSEFUL AIMFUL POINTED
PURPOSELESS WASTE RANDOM
AIMLESS FECKLESS
PURPOSIVE TELIC HORMIC
PURPURA MUREX PURPLES
PELIOSIS
PURPURE GOLP GOLPE PURPLE
MERCURY
PURR MURR THRUM WHURL DUNLIN
PURSE BAG CLY JAN BUNG CLAY
CLOY FISC KNIT POKE PUSS SKIN
BULSE BURSE DUMMY FUNDS
MEANS POUCH SPUNG COMMON
FOLLIS GIPSER POCKET PUCKER
READER SHAMMY ALMONER GIPSIRE
LEATHER SPORRAN BUCKSKIN
BURSICLE CRUMENAL AUMONIERE
POCKETBOOK
(PREF.) BURSI
PURSE CRAB PAGURID
PURSER CLERK BURSAR BOUCHER
PINCHGUT NIPCHEESE

PURSING MIMP
(— OF MOUTH) PRIM
PURSLANE PURPIE PUSSLY
PIGWEED PUSSLEY PORTULACA
PURSLANE TREE SPEKBOOM
PURSUANCE SUING SEQUENCE
PURSUE BAY RUN SUE HUNT SEEK
CHASE CHEVY CHIVY ENSUE HOUND
QUEST SLATE STALK TRADE COURSE
FOLLOW GALLOP TRAVEL BEDEVIL
HOTFOOT CONTINUE PRACTICE
(— ZIGZAG COURSE) TACK
PURSUER FOLLOWER PLAINTIFF
QUESTRIST
PURSUIT FAD HUNT SUIT CAPER
CAUSE CHASE CHEVY CRAFT HOBBY
COURSE SEARCH ASSAULT ACTIVITY
ENTREATY PROSECUTION
(— OF PLEASURE) EPICURISM
(— OF WISDOM) PHILOSOPHY
(FAVORITE —) MEAT
PURSUIVANT BUTE MARCH FALCON
ORMOND ATHLONE CARRICK
ANTELOPE DINGWALL FOLLOWER
PURSY FAT OBESE PUFFY
ASTHMATIC
PURULENT PYIC ATTRY ATTERY
PURVEY CATER PANDER SUPPLY
FORESEE PROVIDE
PURVEYOR CATER TAKER ACHUAS
PROWER CATERER ACHATOUR
MANCIPLE
PUS WARE AMPER FESTER MATTER
WORSUM QUITTER
(PREF.) PURI PURO PY(O)
(CONTAINING — AND GAS)
PYOPNEUMO
PUSH CA DUB JAM JOG JUR PUT
BANG BIRR BOIL BOOM BORE BUNT
DING DUSH FLOG KENT PICK PILT
PING PORR POSS POTE SHOG STOP
BLITZ BOOST BRUSH BUNCH CROWD
CRUSH DRIVE DUNCH ELBOW GOOSE
HUNCH NUDGE PINCH POACH POUSE
SCAUT SHOVE SKELP STICK STOVE
EXTEND HURTLE HUSTLE JOGGLE
JOSTLE POTTER PROPEL THRING
THRONG THRUST ASSAULT IMPETUS
IMPULSE OPERATE PERPLEX
SHUFFLE THRUTCH CONTRUDE
INCREASE SHOULDER STRAITEN
DISMISSAL
(— ALONG) TUSH
(— APART) SPREAD
(— ASIDE) SHOG
(— BY STICK) KENT POLE
(— FORWARD) BUCKET ADVANCE
(— GENTLY) NUDGE
(— IN HASTE) RUSH
(— INTO) INVADE
(— INTO PROMINENCE) BOOM
(— MONEY) SPIFF
(— ON) BEAR YERK

(— OUT) DEBOUT LAUNCH
(— OUT LIPS) POUT
(— RUDELY) BARGE HORSE HUSTLE
(— TO FULL STRIDE) EXTEND
(— TOGETHER) CONTRUDE
(— UNDERNEATH) SUBDUCT
(— UP) BOOST
(— VIOLENTLY) WHANG
(— WITH ELBOW) ELBOW HUNCH
(— WITH FEET) DIG SCAUT
(— WITH HEAD) BUNT BUTT
(— WITHIN) INVAGINATE
(STRONG —) BEVEL
PUSH BUTTON PUSH PRESSEL
PUSHCART BARROW TROLLEY
PUSHER PLUNGER TRAILER
TRAMMER WHEELER
PUSHING OBTRUSIVE PROTRUSIVE
PUSHOVER SNAP SOFTY SUCKER
PUSHY FORWARD AGGRESSIVE
PUSILLANIMOUS WEAK TIMID
FEEBLE COWARDLY TIMOROUS
PUSS CAT FACE HARE CHEET CHILD
MOUTH RABBIT BAUDRONS
PUSSYCAT SOFTY
PUSTULE NOB BEAL BURL KNOB
POCK PUSH QUAT WART ACHOR
AMPER BLAIN WHEAL WHELK
BLOTCH FESTER PIMPLE TETTER
ANTHRAX BLISTER ERUPTION
WHEYWORM
PUT DO BET LAY PIT SET BANG BUTT
FILL GIVE GROW PILT REST URGE
ADAPT APPLY DIGHT DRIVE FOCUS
PLACE STALL STATE STEAD STEEK
STELL WAGER ASSIGN BESTOW
DECAMP IMPOSE INVEST PHRASE
REPOSE SPROUT THRUST DEPOSIT
EMPLACE EXPRESS INFLICT SUBJECT
(— AN END TO) DATE SNIB ABATE
NAPOO SNUFF SPIKE STASH STILL
STINT SOPITE STANCH ABOLISH
ASSUAGE EXPIATE SATISFY
ABROGATE DEMOLISH FINALIZE
SURCEASE
(— ANOTHER IN PLACE OF) RELIEVE
(— APART) DISPART
(— ASHORE) MAROON
(— ASIDE) BLOW HAIN SAVE SHUNT
REJECT SHUFFLE
(— ASUNDER) PART
(— AT REST) HUSH
(— AWAY) STOW COVER ELONG
HUTCH SHIFT RECOND SAVEUP
DIVORCE
(— BACK) REMIT REMISE
(— BACK INTO USE) RESTORE
(— BEFORE) PROFER ANTEPONE
(— DOWN) LAY DEMIT QUASH QUELL
DEPOSE SQUASH DEPRESS OPPRESS
REPRESS SILENCE DIMINISH
SUPPRESS
(— EDGE ON) TED

(— EVASIVELY) SHUFFLE
(— FLAX UPON A DISTAFF) DIZEN
(— FORTH) GEM BLOW CAST GIVE PUSH EXERT LANCE PROFER STRETCH
(— FORTH BLOSSOMS) GEM
(— FORWARD) RUN PLEAD TABLE PREFER PRESENT PROPONE PROPOSE SUGGEST OVERTURE
(— GRAIN IN BARN) END
(— IN) ENTER INSERT INTROMIT
(— IN AGONY) THROE
(— IN CHARGE) COMMIT
(— IN CLAIM) PRETEND
(— IN COMPETITION) PIT
(— IN CONDITION) TUNE
(— IN CUSTODY) REMIT
(— IN DANGER) SCUPPER
(— IN DREAD) ADRAD
(— INFORMATION INTO) ADDRESS
(— IN MOTION) AROUSE
(— IN OPERATION) LAUNCH
(— IN ORDER) DO SET REDD SIDE SORT TRIM DIGHT MENSE SHIFT TRICK ADJUST DAIKER GRAITH ORDAIN SETTLE ARRANGE CLARIFY DISPOSE REDRESS INSTRUCT
(— IN PLACE) POSE
(— IN POSSESSION) SEISE
(— IN PRISON) WARD
(— INTO ACTION) SERVE
(— INTO BARN) END
(— INTO CASE) SHEATHE
(— INTO CIRCULATION) EMIT SPRING
(— INTO ECSTASY) ENTRANCE
(— INTO EFFECT) EXECUTE SANCTION
(— INTO IRONS) BOLT
(— INTO RHYTHM) METER METRE
(— LIQUOR INTO CASK) TUN
(— OFF) DAFF DOFF HAFT DEFER DELAY DEMUR FOIST PARRY REMIT REPRY SHIFT TARRY THROW LINGER RETARD SHELVE ADJOURN FORSLOW PROLONG RESPITE POSTPONE PROROGUE PROCRASTINATE
(— ON) DON HYPE APPLY CRACK DRAPE ENDUE MOUNT STAGE ASSUME INVEST ADDRESS
(— ON AIRS) PROSS FINICK DEVEST
(— ON ALERT) ALARM
(— ON BOARD) LADE
(— ON COVER) HACKLE
(— ON GUARD) ALERT CAUTION
(— ON HAT) COVER
(— ON PRETENSE) AFFECT
(— ON RECORD) FILE REGISTER
(— ON SALE) SHOP
(— ON SHORT ALLOWANCE) SCRIMP
(— ON STAGE) PRODUCE
(— ON STRING) ENFILE

(— OUT) GET OUT DOUT OUST DOWSE EVICT EXERT OUTED SLAKE SLOCK RETIRE DISMISS EXCLUDE EXTINCT FORJUDGE
(— OUT BATSMAN) SKITTLE
(— OUT OF ACTION) HAMPER
(— RIGHT) AMEND
(— ROAD METAL ON) STEEN
(— SUDDENLY) CLAP
(— SURREPTITIOUSLY) STEAL
(— THROUGH A STRAINER) TAMMY
(— TO FLIGHT) AFLEY FEAZE FLEME GALLY
(— TOGETHER) ADD JOIN BUILD COMPILE COMPOSE CONCOCT CONFECT PREPARE ASSEMBLE COMPOUND
(— TO PROOF) TEST
(— TO RIGHTS) SORT DIGHT
(— TO SHAME) DASH ABASH SHEND UPRRAID
(— TO SLEEP) OPIATE SOPITE SOPORATE
(— TO THE TEST) SEARCH
(— TO TRIAL) TEMPT
(— TO USE) STOW APPLY BESTOW
(— TO WORK) HARNESS
(— UP) ANTE ERECT FLUSH DISPENSE
(— UP HAY) BOTTLE
(— UPON) GAMMON
(— UP WITH) GO BEAR BIDE HACK ABIDE BROOK ENDURE SUFFER COMPORT STOMACH SWALLOW TOLERATE
(— WITH ANOTHER) APPOSE
(SUFF.) STOLE
PUTAMEN PYRENE
PUTCHER PUTLOG PUTCHEN PUTLOCK
PUT-DOWN SLUR
PUT-ON HYPE
PUTREFACTION ROT DECAY SEPSIS
PUTREFACTIVE SEPTIC
(PREF.) SEPTICO
PUTREFIED ROTTEN
PUTREFY ROT ADDLE DECAY SWEAT FESTER POLLUTE PUTRESCE
PUTRESCENT PUTRID ROTTEN
PUTRID FOUL RANK SOUR VILE LOUSY ADDLED RANCID ROTTEN CORRUPT DECAYED FRIABLE VICIOUS DEPRAVED MALODOROUS
(PREF.) SAPR(O) SEPTI SEPTO
(SUFF.) SEPSIS SEPTIC
PUTT CLOWN BORROW GOBBLE
(SHORT —) GIMME TAPIN
PUTTEE PAT PATA GAITER BANDAGE LEGGING
PUTTER FUSS MESS MUCK POKE TRUCK CADDLE DAWDLE MUCKER MUCKLE PIDDLE TINKER FRIGGLE
PUTTY BEDDING

PUTTYROOT CRAWFOOT
PUTZ CRECHE
PUXY SWAMPY QUAGMIRE
PUZZLE CAP GET SET BEAT CRUX
DEAD LICK POSE BEFOG GRIPH
POSER QUEER REBUS STICK BAFFLE
BOTHER ENIGMA FICKLE FOITER
GLAIKS JIGSAW KITTLE RIDDLE
CONFUSE MYSTERY MYSTIFY
NONPLUS PERPLEX STICKER TAISSLE
TANGRAM TRANGAM ACROSTIC
BEFUDDLE BEWILDER CONFOUND
DISTRACT DUMFOUND ENTANGLE
INTRIGUE REMBLERE CROSSWORD
METAGRABOLIZE METAGROBOLIZE
(SOPHISTICAL —) SORITES
(TYPE OF —) JIGSAW
PUZZLED ASEA ATSEA PERPLEXED
PUZZLING KNOTTY CURIOUS
KNOTTED RIDDLING DIFFICULT
PROBLEMATIC
PYCNANTHEMUM KOELLIA
PYCNOGONID SPIDER
PYGARG ADDAX OSPREY
PYGIDIUM PODEX
PYGMALION (AUTHOR OF —) SHAW
(BELOVED OF —) GALATEA
(CHARACTER IN —) HILL LIZA CLARA
HENRY ALFRED FREDDY HIGGINS
EYNSFORD DOOLITTLE PICKERING
(FATHER OF —) BELUS MUTGO
AGENOR
(MURDERED BY —) SICHAEUS
(SISTER OF —) DIDO
(STATUE FASHIONED BY —) GALATEA
PYGMY ELF AKKA AMBA DOKO
ACHUA AFIFI ATOMY BATWA DWARF
GNOME PIXIE PIGMEW WOCHUA
ACHANGO ASHANGO MANIKIN
DWARFISH NEGRILLO VAALPENS
DANDIPRAT
PYGMY GOOSE GOSLET
PYGMY RATTLESNAKE
MASSASAUGA
PYGOSTYLE VOMER
PYKNIC SQUAT STOCKY STHENIC
MUSCULAR
PYLADES (COMPANION OF —)
ORESTES
(FATHER OF —) STROPHIUS

(MOTHER OF —) ANAXIBIA
(SON OF —) MEDON STROPHIUS
(WIFE OF —) ELECTRA
PYRAMID BENBEN HOPPER
TEOCALLI
(— OF CRAYFISH) BUISSON
(DOUBLE —) TWIN ZIRCONOID
(INVERTED —) HOPPER
PYRAMIDAL HUGE ENORMOUS
IMPOSING
PYRAMIDICAL TAPER
PYRAMUS (LOVER OF —) THISBE
PYRAZINE ALDINE PIAZIN DIAZINE
PYRE BALE PILE TOPHET BONFIRE
BALEFIRE
PYRIDOXIN ADERMIN
PYRITE BALE MUNDIC
(PL.) BRAZIL STANNITE FIRESTONE
MAGISTRAL MARCASITE
PYROCLES (BROTHER OF —)
CYMOCLES
(FATHER OF —) ACRATES
PYROLA LIMONIUM SHINLEAF
PYROMANIAC FIREBUG ARSONIST
PYRONE CUMALIN
PYROPHYLLITE PENCIL
PYROTECHNICS FIREWORKS
PYROXENE ACMITE AUGITE SALITE
SAHLITE AEGIRITE DIALLAGE
DIOPSIDE WOLLASTONITE
PYROXENITE ARIEGITE MARCHITE
OSTRAITE NIKLESITE
PYRRHIC DIBRACH
PYRRHULOXIA GROSBEAK
BULLFINCH
PYRRHUS (FATHER OF —) AEACIDES
(MOTHER OF —) PHTHIA
(SON OF —) PTOLEMY SOPATER
(WIFE OF —) ANTIGONE
PYRROLE AZOLE
PYTHON ADJIGER PEROPOD
ANACONDA
PYTHONESS WITCH PHITONES
PYTHONIC HUGE INSPIRED
ORACULAR MONSTROUS
PROPHETIC
PYX BOX CAPSA CASKET CHRISM
VESSEL BINNACLE CHRISMAL
CIBORIUM
PYXIDIUM CAPSULE

Q

Q KU CUE KUE QUEEN QUEUE QUEBEC
QATAR (CAPITAL OF —) DOHA
   (TOWN OF —) RUWAIS UMMSAID
QUA HERON QUABIRD
QUACK PUFF WHACK CROCUS
   SALVER SUBTLE EMPIRIC IMPOSTOR
   OPERATOR SANGRADO CHARLATAN
   (PREF.) PSEUD(O)
QUACKERY HUMBUG
QUADRAGESIMA LENT
QUADRANGLE QUAD CLOSE
   COURT TETRAGON
QUADRANT BOW RADIAL SQUARE
   QUARTER TETRANT ALTIMETER
QUADRATE SUIT AGREE IDEAL
   QUADER SQUARE PERFECT
   BALANCED
QUADRIC CONICOID
QUADRILATERAL TRAPEZIA
   TETRAGRAM
   (PL.) TESSARA
QUADRILLE CONTREDANSE
   (PL.) LANCERS
QUADRILLION
   (PREF.) ASTRA PETA QUEGA
QUADRILLIONTH
   (PREF.) FEMTO
QUADROON QUATERON TERCERON
QUADRUPED BABIRUSA
QUADRUPLE FOURDLE FOURFOLD
QUADRUPLED
   (PREF.) TETRAKIS
QUADRUPLET FOURLING
   QUARTOLE
QUAFF QUAX TOOT DRINK QUASS
   WAUCHT CAROUSE TRILLIL
QUAG BOG MARSH SHAKE QUIVER
QUAGMIRE BOG FEN GOG HAG QUA
   SOG LAIR PUXY QUAW MARSH
   MIZZY SWAMP MORASS PUDDLE
   SLOUGH BOGMIRE PUCKSEY
   WAGMOIRE
QUAHOG CLAM COHOG VENUS
   BULLNOSE
QUAIL COW LOWA WEET COLIN
   COWER DAUNT ORTYX QUAKE SPOIL
   WASTE BLENCH CURDLE FLINCH
   SHRINK TURNIX WITHER DECLINE
   HEMIPOD TREMBLE BOBWHITE
   (YOUNG —) SQUEALER
QUAINT DRY ODD TWEE FUNKY
   NAIVE BIZARRE STRANGE FANCIFUL
   HANDSOME PICTURESQUE
   (— IN APPEARANCE) FUNKY
QUAKE JAR QUOG RESE CHILL QUAIL
   SEISM SHAKE DITHER QUIVER

SHIVER WAMBLE FLUTTER SHUDDER
TREMBLE
   (PREF.) PALLO
QUAKER ASPEN HERON FRIEND
   OBADIAH WHACKER HICKSITE
   TREMBLER BEACONITE BROADBRIM
   SHADBELLY
   (— STATE) PENNA PENNSYLVANIA
QUAKER GRAY ACIER
QUAKING ASPEN QUAKY TREPID
   SHAKING TREMBLING
QUAKING GRASS BRIZA
   COWQUAKE WAGWANTS
QUALIFICATION NATURE RESERVE
   SHADING CAPACITY
QUALIFIED FIT ABLE MEET FITTED
   FITTEN LIKELY PASSED CAPABLE
   ELIGIBLE SUITABLE AUTHENTIC
   (DULY —) REGULAR
   (NOT —) INAPT INHABILE
QUALIFIER MODIFIER
QUALIFY FIT DASH ADAPT ALLAY
   ALLOY EQUIP HEDGE ENABLE
   MODIFY SOFTEN TEMPER ABSOLVE
   CERTIFY ENTITLE LICENCE PREPARE
   GRADUATE MODERATE RESTRAIN
   RESTRICT
QUALITIES
   (BUFF.) ERY ICS
QUALITY Y BRAN BUMP CHOP COST
   FEEL GUNA LEAD SORT COLOR
   GRACE STATE TRAIT ASSIZE BARREL
   FABRIC STRAIN THREAD TIMBER
   TIMBRE ADJUNCT CALIBER KINSHIP
   STATURE ACCIDENT MOVEMENT
   PROPERTY TONEBRAND
   (— OF MIND) CALIBER CALIBRE
   (— OF PERSONAL EMOTIONS)
   PATHOS
   (— OF PHOTOGRAPH) CONTRAST
   (— OF SOUND) TONE
   (— OF TONE) TIMBRE
   (— OF VOWELS) LENGTH
   (— PECULIAR TO ONESELF) SEITY
   (AESTHETIC —) TASTE
   (ARTISTIC —) VIRTU
   (ATTRACTIVE —) TAKE
   (BASIC —) GRAIN
   (BASIC —S) STUFF
   (CHARACTERISTIC —) TURN
   (CHIEF —) SPIRIT
   (COLOR —) TONE
   (ESSENTIAL —) ALLOY SPECIES
   SUCHNESS
   (GOOD —) THEW
   (HEREDITARY —) STRAIN

(IMPECCABLE —) FINISH
(IMPLICIT —) OVERTONE
(INCISIVE —) BITE
(INNATE —) LARGESS
(INTELLECTUAL —) BROW
(MELODRAMATIC —) SENSATION
(MORAL —) THEW
(NATURAL —) TARAGE
(OBJECTIONABLE —) ANILITY
(OF HIGH —) FRANK
(OF HIGHEST —) PRIMO
(OF LOW —) SHLOCK SCHLOCK
(OF POOR —) GROTTY
(PERVASIVE —) AROMA
(PHYSICAL —S) BOTTOM
(POSITIVE —) PLUS
(PRIMAL —) GUNA
(PUNGENT —) SNAP
(RELATIVE —) RATE
(SECONDARY —) OVERTONE
(SPATIAL —) MAGNITUDE
(SPRINGY —) SPINE
(STRUCTURAL —) TEXTURE
(SUBDUED —) SHADE
(SUBTLE —) BOUQUET
(SUPERIOR —) SUPER FINENESS
(TRIED —) TOUCH
(UNESSENTIAL —) ACCIDENT
(UNUSUAL —) SURD
(USEFUL —) ASSET
(WAVY — OF HAIR) FLIX
(SUFF.) ACITY ANCE ANCY CY ENCE
ENCY HEAD HOOD ICE ICITY ILITY ITY
MENT NESS SHIP TY
(—THAT FILLS) FUL FULL
(CHARACTERIZED BY—) SOME
QUALITY STREET (AUTHOR OF —)
BARRIE
(CHARACTER IN —) BROWN LIVVY
PATTY SUSAN BLADES PHOEBE
THROSSEL VALENTINE
QUALM CALM DROW PALL NAUSEA
SQUEAM SCRUPLE
QUALMISH TEWLY SICKISH
SQUEAMISH
QUAMOCLIT MOONFLOWER
QUANDARY FIX PUXY PUZZLE
TANGLE DILEMMA NONPLUS
SWITHER DOLDRUMS JUNCTURE
QUANDONG PEACH
QUANT RYPECK
QUANTIC NONIC OCTIC SEPTIC
SEXTIC QUADRIC QUINTIC
QUANTIFIER PREFIX
QUANTITATIVE METRIC
QUANTITY BAG JAG SUM SUP BODY
DEAL DISH DOSE FECK JAGG LIFT
MASK SOME SOUD WARE BATCH
BREAK CLASH GRIST KITTY SIEGE
TROOP WHEEN ACTION ADDEND
AMOUNT BAGFUL BOTTLE BUDGET
DICKER EFFECT FOTHER HANTLE
NUMBER PARCEL SCALAR SPINOR

THRAVE VOLUME CONTENT
FOOTAGE PORTION QUANTUM
GLASSFUL KNIFEFUL LADLEFUL
PARAMETER
(— OF ARROWS) SHEAF
(— OF BUTTER) CHURNING
(— OF CLOTHES) BUCKING
(— OF COTTONSEED) CRUSH
(— OF CUT TREES) FALL
(— OF DRINK) HOOP DRAFT
DRAUGHT
(— OF ELECTRICITY) FARADAY
(— OF EXPLOSIVE) CHARGE
(— OF FISH OR GAME) TAKE CATCH
DRAFT DRAUGHT
(— OF GRAIN) GAVEL
(— OF HAY) LOCK TRUSS
(— OF IRRIGATION WATER) DUTY
(— OF LAND) PLOUGHGATE
(— OF LIQUID) DROP JAUP SLASH
GOBBET JABBLE
(— OF LIQUOR) HEELTAP
(— OF LUMBER) RUN
(— OF MEAL) MELDER
(— OF METAL) BLOW
(— OF MUD) CLASH
(— OF NARCOTICS) BINDLE
(— OF PAPER) TOKEN
(— OF PRODUCE) BURY
(— OF RAISINS) FRAIL
(— OF THREAD) LEASE
(— OF WOOD) HAG FATHOM
(— PRODUCED) OUTPUT
(DIRECTED —) VECTOR
(EQUAL —) PART
(ESTIMATED —) WEY
(EXCESSIVE —) GLUT SPATE
(FIXED —) CONSTANT
(GREAT —) HOST MASS MORT MUCH RAFT
HIRST SHOAL SIGHT STORE BARREL
FOREST SLATHER TUMMELS
(INCREASED —) SPATE SPEAT
(IRRATIONAL —) SURD
(LARGE —) ACRE BOLT DEAL FECK
HEAP MASS PECK SCAD SLEW
FLOOD FORCE GRIST JORUM POWER
SCADS SHEAF STACK STORE
BUCKET BUSHEL DICKER DOLLOP
GALLON MATTER MELDER CLUTHER
SKINFUL HECATOMB MOUNTAIN
PLURALITY
(LEAST —) BEDROCK
(MINUTE —) DRAM DROP SHADE
SCRUPLE PARTICLE
(NOTEWORTHY —) CHUNK
(REGULATED —) QUOTA
(RELATIVE —) DEGREE
(SETTLED —) SIZE
(SIZABLE —) SCUMP
(SLIGHT —) SUSPICION
(SMALL —) ACE BIT SUP TOT CURN
DASH DUST HAET HAIR HARL IOTA
PEAK SOSH SPOT CANCH PRILL

SMACK SPICE SQUIB TOUCH TRACE
JOBBLE MORSEL PICKLE SAMPLE
SONGLE STIVER CAPSULE CURTSEY
DRIBBLE DRIBLET EPSILON HANDFUL
MODICUM SMICKET SPATTER
TODDICK FARTHING MOUTHFUL
PENNORTH SCANTLET SPRINKLE
PENNYWORTH SPRINKLING
THIMBLEFUL
(UNDIRECTED —) SCALAR
(UNLIMITED —) OCEAN
(VARYING —) SKID
(ZERO —) NOTHING
QUANTUM MAGNON PHONON
PHOTON ISOSPIN
(— OF ENERGY) PLASMON
QUAPAW KWAPA ARKANSAS
QUARANTINE DETAIN ISOLATE
SANCTION
QUARENTENE ROOD FURLONG
QUARK PARTICLE
(PARTICLE TO BIND —S) GLUON
(PROPERTY OF —S) FLAVOR
QUARREL JAR ROW WAP YED BEEF
CHIP DEAL FEUD FRAY FUSS JARL
JOWL MIFF NIFF ODDS PICK PLEA
SPAT TIFF WHID BRACK BRAWL
BRIGE BROIL FLITE FLUSK GRUFF
HURRY JOWER NOISE PIQUE RUNIN
SCOLD SCRAP SHINE STOUR UPSET
WRALL AFFRAY BARNEY BLOWUP
BREACH BREEZE BRIGUE DEBATE
DIFFER DUSTUP FRACAS FRATCH
GARROT JANGLE MATTER QUARRY
RIPPET SQUARE SQUEAL STRIFE
THREAP THREEP THWAIT DRABBLE
DRATTLE DISGUST DISPUTE FACTION
OUTCAST PRABBLE RUCTION
SIMULTY STASHIE SWAGGER TUILZIE
WRANGLE DISAGREE MOORBURN
SCRAFFLE SPLUTTER SQUABBLE
TRAVERSE
(— IN WORDS) JANGLE
(NOISY —) ROW FRACAS KICKUP
(PETTY —) MIFF SPAT TIFF
QUARRELING BICKER CONTEK
CHIDING CONTECK
QUARRELSOME RIXY UGLY ROWTY
FEISTY CURRISH SCRAPPY
DRAWLING FRAMPOLD FRATCHED
PETULANT PHRAMPEL BELLICOSE
BUMPTIOUS FRACTIOUS LITIGIOUS
CONTENTIOUS
(NOT —) AMICABLE
QUARRELSOMENESS SQUARING
WARIANCE
QUARRIED (NOT —) LIVE
(PREF.) ORYCTO
QUARRIER FACEMAN QUARION
QUARRY PIT DELF GAME LODE MEAT
CHASE DELFT DELPH PLUCK LATOMY
REWARD LATOMIA LOZENGE
(HAWK'S —) MARK

QUARRYMAN SCABBLER SCAPPLER
QUART SHANT WHART
(METRIC —) LITER
(ONE-HALF —) PINT
(TWO —S) MAGNUM
(1-8TH —) GILL
(2 —S) FLAGON
(4 —S) GALLON
QUARTE FOURTH
QUARTER AIRT PART STUD EAVER
GRITH TRACT BARRIO BEHALF
BESTOW CANTON COLONY FARDEL
HARBOR SECTOR TWOBITS
CONTRADA FAUBOURG FIERDING
STANDARD POBLACION
(— IN BATTLE) GRITH
(— OF A POUND) TRIPPET
(— OF BEEF OR MUTTON) BOUT
(— OF CITY) BLOCK GHETTO
(— OF COMPASS) PLAGE
(— OF FLAG) CANTON
(— OF HOUR) POINT
(— OF HUNDRED) FIERDING
(— OF YEAR) RAITH
(— ONESELF) SORN
(— UPON) LAY
(JEWISH —) ALJAMA
(NATIVE —) MEDINA
QUARTERBACK BOSS
QUARTERING LASKING
CHUMMAGE
QUARTER NOTE CROTCHET
QUARTER REST SOSPIRO
QUARTERS BOTHY BILLET BOTHIE
LIVERY MENAGE FARDELS
CHUMMERY DIGGINGS LODGMENT
(— FOR IMMIGRANTS) HOSTEL
(— OF CREW) FOCSLE FORECASTLE
(— OF SALVATION ARMY) BARRACKS
(GENERAL'S —) PRINCIPIUM
(HIGH —) AERY EYRY AERIE EYRIE
(JUNIOR OFFICERS' —) GUNROOM
(LIVING —) PAD
(MEN'S —) SELAMLIK
(MONASTERY —) FRATRY
(RELIGIOUS —) NOVICIATE NOVITIATE
(TEMPORARY —) CAMP
CANTONMENT
(WINTER —) HIBERNACLE
(WOMEN'S —) HAREM SERAGLIO
GYNAECEUM
QUARTET FOURSOME
QUARTILE SQUARE TETRAGON
QUARTO FOURS
QUARTZ IRIS ONYX SARD AGATE
CHERT FLINT PRASE TARSO TOPAZ
JASPER MORION PEBBLE PLASMA
SILICA ALENCON CITRINE CRYSTAL
RUBASSE SINOPLE AMETHYST
BASANITE SARDONYX SIDERITE
YENTNITE BUHRSTONE
BURRSTONE
QUARTZITE GANISTER SILCRETE

QUASH CASS CRUSH QUELL SPIKE SQUAT SOPITE CASSARE PEREMPT SUPPRESS
QUASI (PREF.) SEMI
QUASI-ATOM MUONIUM
QUAT FOUR GLUT SQUASH SATIATE UPSTART
QUATERNION TETRAD QUADRATE
QUATREFOIL TRESSURE
(DOUBLE —) EIGHTFOIL
QUAVER QUAP CROMA SHAKE TRILL WAVER CHROMA FALTER QUIVER WABBLE WOBBLE WRIBLE FREDDON VIBRATE
QUAVERY WARBLY UNSTEADY
QUAY KEY POW QUAI LEVEE BUNDER STRAND
QUEACH BOG FEN MARSH THICKET
QUEASINESS KECK SICKNESS
QUEASY NICE SICK SQUEEZY DELICATE NAUSEATED SQUEAMISH
QUEBEC (LAKE OF —) MINTO BIENVILLE MISTASSINI
(TOWN OF —) AMOS HULL AMQUI LAVAL MAGOG PERCE BASSIN VERDUN JOLIETTE MONTREAL LAPRAIRIE
QUEBRACHO BREAKAX AXMASTER IRONWOOD AXBREAKER
QUEBRADA BROOK GULLY RAVINE FISSURE
QUECHUA INCAN KICHUA
QUEEN ENA REG DAME FERS LADY MEDB RANI AEDON BEGUM FIERS RANEE ATOSSA REGINA ROXANA TAILTE TAMARA ARGANTE ATHALIA CANDACE JOCASTE OMPHALE PHEARSE STATIRA TITANIA BRUNHILD GERTRUDE GLORIANA GUINEVER MAHARANI
(— AND KING OF TRUMPS) BELLA
(— CITY) CINCINNATI
(— IN CHESS) FERS LADY FIERS
(— OF CLUBS) SPADILLA
(— OF DENMARK) GERTRUDE
(— OF EGYPTIAN GODS) SATI
(— OF ETHIOPIA) CANDACE
(— OF FAIRY LAND) MEDB GLORIANA
(— OF GEORGIA) TAMARA
(— OF GOTHS) TAMORA
(— OF HEARTS) ELIZABETH
(— OF HEAVEN) HERA
(— OF JUDAH) ATHALIA
(— OF LYDIA) OMPHALE
(— OF SHEBA) BALKIS BILKIS
(— OF SPADES) BASTA LIZZY
(— OF THE ADRIATIC) VENICE
(— OF THE ANTILLES) CUBA
(— OF THEBES) JOCASTA
(— OF THE EAST) ZENOBIA
(— OF THE MAY) MAYLADY MAYQUEEN
(— OF TRUMPS) HONOR

(FAIRY —) MAB ARGANTE TITANIA
(FORMER SPANISH —) ENA
(INDIAN —) RANI SUNK MAHARANI
(MOHAMMEDAN —) BEGUM
(NEIGHBOR OF —) KING BISHOP
QUEEN ANNE'S LACE UMBEL
QUEEN BEE KING
QUEEN ELIZABETH DIANA ORIANA CYNTHIA
QUEENFISH WAHOO CROAKER DRUMFISH
QUEENLY HAUGHTY REGINAL MAJESTIC
QUEENROOT YAWSHRUB
QUEEN'S-DELIGHT YAWSHRUB
QUEENSLAND HEMP SIDA JELLYLEAF
QUEER HEX ODD RUM HARM DICKY DIPPY DROLL FAINT FUNNY GIDDY NUTTY RUMMY COCKLE FIFISH HIPPED QUEASY QUISBY UNIQUE AMUSING COMICAL CURIOUS DISRUPT ERRATIC STRANGE TOUCHED WHIMSIC FANCIFUL OBSESSED PECULIAR
(— THING) QUOZ
QUEERNESS ODDITY
QUEEST RINGDOVE
QUELL DIE CALM FLOW HUSH KILL QUAY SLAY ABATE ALLAY CRUSH QUASH QUIET YIELD PACIFY PERISH REDUCE SOOTHE SPRING STANCH STIFLE KILLING REPRESS SQUELCH SUPPRESS
QUEME QUIM HANDY WHEAM COMELY PLEASE GRATIFY PLEASANT
QUENCH COOL DAMP SIND ALLAY CHECK CRUSH SLAKE SLOCK STILL STANCH STIFLE ASSUAGE SLOCKEN AUSTEMPER
QUENCHED EXTINCT
QUENCHER STANCH
QUENCHING FRITTING
QUENTIN DURWARD (AUTHOR OF —) SCOTT
(CHARACTER IN —) CARL CROYE LOUIS LESLEY PHILIP PIERRE TOISON BALAFRE CHARLES DURWARD EBERSON HERMITE LAMARCK LUDOVIC QUENTIN TRISTAN WILLIAM CRAWFORD HAMELINE ISABELLE HAYRADDIN JAQUELINE MAUGRABIN CREVECOEUR
QUERCINE OAKEN
QUERECHO VAQUERO
QUERELA AUDITA
QUERENT INQUIRER PLAINTIFF
QUERN KERN MILL METATE MILLSTONE
QUERULOUS WHINY FRETFUL PEEVISH NATTERED PETULANT IRRITABLE

QUERY ASK DOUBT DEMAND INQUIRE INQUIRY QUESTION
QUEST ASK BAY GAPE SEEK DEMAND EXAMINE PURSUIT SEEKING VENTURE
QUESTING OUTREACH
QUESTION ASK HOW SPY POSE QUIZ TALK ARGUE DOUBT DREAD QUERY ACCUSE CHANCE CHARGE DEMAND LEADER MATTER PONDER QUAERE REASON SHRIVE EXAMINE INQUIRE INQUIRY PROBLEM PURPOSE SCRUPLE OVERTURE RELEVANT RESEARCH STICKLER CATECHISE
(— AMBIGUOUSLY WORDED) RIDDLE
(— FRETFULLY) RAME
(BAFFLING —) POSER
(BUDDHIST —) KOAN
(CAPTIOUS —) QUIDDIT QUIDDITY
(DIFFICULT —) POSER
(PERPLEXING —) STUMPER
(RHETORICAL —) EROTEMA EROTESIS EROTESIS
(UNSOLVED —) CRUX
(ZEN —) KOAN
QUESTIONABLE FISHY QUEER SHAKY UNSAFE BATABLE CLOUDED DUBIOUS DOUBTFUL PROBLEMATIC
(NOT —) DECENT
QUESTIONER APPOSER INQUIRER
QUESTIONING DUBIOUS QUIZZICAL
QUESTION MARK QUERY QUAERE EROTEME
QUESTIONNAIRE POLL INVENTORY
QUETCH STIR TWITCH
QUETZAL QUESAL TROGON
QUEUE CUE COLA LINE DRAID PIGTAIL CROCODILE
QUEY KOY WHY WHEY HEIFER
QUIBBLE COG PUN BALK CARP QUIB QUIP CAVIL DODGE EVADE QUIRK SALVO AMBAGE BAFFLE BICKER HAFFLE PALTER SNATCH BRABBLE CAPTION CHICANE QUILLET QUIDDIT QUILLET SHUFFLE PETTIFOG QUIDDITY QUILLITY SCRAFFLE CONUNDRUM PREVARICATE
QUIBBLING CHICANERY
QUICA OPOSSUM SARIGUE
QUICK APT RAD YAP FAST FLIT GLEG KECK KEEN LISH LIST PERT RATH RIFE SNAP SOON WHAT WHIT WICK YARE AGILE ALIVE APACE BRISK CHEAP FLEET HASTY MERRY NIFTY NIPPY PREST RAPID READY SHARP SHORT SNACK SNELL SWIFT SWITH TOSTO TRICK VISTO YARRY ACTIVE CLEVER FACILE KITTLE NIMBLE PROMPT PRONTO SNAPPY SPEEDY SUDDEN DARTING SCHNELL SHUTTLE DEXTROUS TRIPPING CITIGRADE

(— AND NEAT) DEFT
(— AS A FLASH) WHIP
(— IN PERCEPTION) ACID
(— IN RESPONSE) GNIB
(— OF MIND) INTELLIGENT
(— TO DETECT) SMOKY
(— TO FLARE UP) GASSY
(— TO LEARN) APT
(— TO MOVE) YARE
(LIGHT AND —) VOLANT
(PREF.) OXY TACHEO TACHISTO TACHO TACHY
QUICKEN PEP MEND STIR WHET HURRY SPEED ACUATE AROUSE HASTEN INCITE KINDLE REVIVE VIVIFY ANIMATE ENLIVEN PROVOKE REFRESH SHARPEN EXPEDITE INSPIRIT ACCELERATE
QUICKENING FLICKER REVIVAL STIRRING
QUICKLY TID TIT ASAP CITO FAST RIFE SOON TIVY WHIP YARE APACE NEWLY RADLY RATHE SHARP SKELP SNACK SNELL SWITH TIGHT WIGHT YEPLY ASTITE BELIVE HOURLY PRESTO PRONTO RASHLY EFTSOON PRESTLY READILY SPEEDILY WIKIWIKI
(— AND WITH FORCE) SWAP
(MORE —) TIDDER TITTER STRETTO
QUICKNESS HASTE SPEED ACUMEN AGILITY SMEDDUM ACTIVITY CELERITY DISPATCH KEENNESS SAGACITY
(— OF DECISION) PROMPTITUDE
(MENTAL —) NOUS SLEIGHT LEGERITY
QUICKSAND FLOW SYRT SYRTIS SWALLOW
QUICK-SELLING LEEFTAIL
QUICKSILVER OREMIX MERCURY TIERRAS HEAUTARIT
QUICK-SPEAKING PROMPT
QUICK-TEMPERED DONCY DONSY PEPPERY IRASCIBLE
QUICK-WITTED APT SHARP SMART NIMBLE KNOWING
QUID FID CHAW CHEW SOVEREIGN
(— OF TOBACCO) CUD FID
QUIDDANY JELLY SYRUP CODINIAC
QUIDDITY QUIBBLE WHATNESS
QUIDNUNC GOSSIP BUSYBODY
QUIESCENCE KAIF REPOSE STASIS DORMANCY
QUIESCENT QUIET LATENT STATIC DORMANT RESTING INACTIVE
QUIET QT ST COY LAY CALM COSH DEAD DUMB EASE EASY HUSH LOUN LOWN LULL REST ROCK SNUG SOFT WEME ACCOY CANNY CIVIL DOWNY LEVEL PEACE PEASE QUATE QUELL QUEME RESTY SALVE SHADY SHUSH SILKY SLEEP SOBER SQUAT STILL SUANT WHIST DREAMY GENTLE

PACIFY PLACID RETIRE SAUGHT
SEDATE SERENE SETTLE SILENT
SMOOTH SOFTLY SOOTHE SOPITE
STEADY STILLY HUSHFUL ORDERLY
REQUIEM RESTFUL SILENCE
COMPOSED DECOROUS PEACEFUL
TRANQUIL UNRUFFLE
(— DOWN) DILL
(BE —) SSH
(MAKE —) ALLAY
(STEALTHILY —) SLINKY
QUIETEN SEDATE SOPITE SUBDUE
QUIETISM MOLINISM
QUIETLY LOW FAIR CANNY STILL
WINLY EVENLY GENTLY SOFTLY
TIPTOE
QUIETNESS REST REPOSE
SERENITY
QUIETUDE CALM INERTION
QUIETUS REST DEATH RELEASE
QUILL COP PEN RIB PIRN FLOAT
STALK BOBBIN FESCUE PINION
SLEEVE BRISTLE CALAMUS PRIMARY
TRUNDLE
(— FOR WINDING THREAD) COP
(— OF FEATHER) BARREL
(PORCUPINE —) PEN
QUILLBACK SAILFISH SKIMBACK
QUILLWORT ISOETES FERNWORT
QUILT BEAT GULP WALT WELT WHIP
DUVET REZAI CADDOW CHALON
PALLET THRASH SWALLOW
MATTRESS POULTICE COMFORTER
QUILTING MARCELLA
QUIMPER NICE
QUINCE SKEG COYNE ANGERS
SQUINCH JAPONICA
(BENGAL —) BEL BAEL BALE BHEL
QUINCE SEED CYDONIUM
QUININE KINA SPECIFIC
(PREF.) CHIN(O)
QUINK BRANT
QUINONE EMBELIN
QUINSY ANGINA PRUNELLA
QUINTAIN FAN
QUINTE FIFTH
QUINTESSENCE CREAM ELIXIR
CLYSSUS OSMAZOME
QUINTILLION
(PREF.) EXA NEBU
QUINTILLIONTH
(PREF.) ATTO
QUINTUPLE QUINARY FIVEFOLD
QUINIBLE
QUIP GIBE JAPE JEST JOKE CRACK
QUIRK SALLY SCOFF TAUNT RETORT
CONCEIT QUIBBLE
QUIRA CAOBA ROBLE HORMIGO
VENCOLA MACAWOOD
QUIRE CHOR SEXTERN
(20 —S) REAM
(PL.) INSIDES

QUIRK BEND KINK QUIP TURN CLOCK
CROOK TWIST CONCEIT QUIBBLE
FLOURISH PAROXYSM MANNERISM
PECULIARITY
(— OF BEHAVIOR) TIC
QUIRKY ZANY CRAZY DIPPY DOTTY
KINKY
QUIRQUINCHO PICHI PELUDO
QUIRT WHIP ROMAL
QUIS WOODCOCK
QUISLING APOSTATE
QUIT GO DROP NASH PART QUAT
AVOID BELAY CEASE DOUSE LEAVE
SHIFT SHOOT STASH WHITE BEHAVE
CIVITE DESERT DESIST FOREGO
RESIGN SECEDE VACATE ABANDON
FORSAKE RELEASE UNTENANT
QUITCH COUCH QUICK SCUTCH
TWITCH
QUITCLAIM DEED ACQUIT RELEASE
DISCHARGE
QUITE SO ALL BUT GEY BRAW EVEN
FAIR FREE FULL JUST PLAT WELL
CLEAR CLOSE FULLY SHEER STARK
CLEVER DAMNED ENOUGH JUSTLY
MERELY TOTALLY PERFECTLY
(NOT —) HARDLY
(PREF.) DE
QUITERIA (HUSBAND OF —)
CAMACHO
QUITRENT CANON
QUITS EVEN EVENS UPSIDES
QUITTER PUS SLAG PIKER COWARD
JUMPER SHIRKER TURNBACK
QUIVER DIRL QUAG QUOG BEVER
NIDGE QUAKE SHAKE TRILL WAVER
WIVER BICKER COCKER DIDDER
DINDLE SHEATH SHIMMY SHIVER
TREMOR WAMBLE DORLACH
FLUTTER FRISSON SHUDDER
TREMBLE TWIDDLE TWINKLE
TWITTER VIBRATE FLICHTER
WERSLETE
(PREF.) PALLO
QUIVERING ASPEN AGUISH DIDDER
DITHER QUAGGLE QUAKING
AGITATED ATREMBLE
QUIVER TREE KOKERBOOM
QUIXOTIC ERRANT IMAGINARY
VISIONARY
QUIZ ASK GUY EXAM HOAX MOCK
CHAFF QUEER EXAMINE QUESTION
RIDICULE
QUIZZICAL ODD QUEER QUIZZY
CURIOUS WHIMSICAL
QUO KA
QUOD JAIL QUAD PRISON
QUOIN COIN ANGLE GOIGN
CORNER LOZENGE KEYSTONE
VOUSSOIR
QUOIT CIST DISC DISH DISK LINER
DISCUS HOBBER CROMLECH

QUOMODO HOW WAY MEANS
   MANNER
QUONDAM OLD ONCE WHILE
   FORMER ONETIME SOMETIME
QUORATEAN KAROK
QUORUM CORAM HOUSE MINYAN
   MAJORITY
QUOTA PART BOGEY SHARE
   QUOTIENT PROPORTION
QUOTATION TAG PRICE QUOTE
   EXTRACT SNIPPET EPIGRAPH
   (— DEVELOPED INTO ESSAY) CHRIA
   (TRITE —) TAG
QUOTATION MARK GUILLEMET
QUOTE CITE COAT COTE MARK NAME
   NOTE ADDUCE ALLEGE RECITE

   REPEAT EXCERPT EXTRACT OBSERVE
   REHEARSE
   (— SARCASTICALLY) FLOUT
QUOTH CO KO CUTH QUAD QUOD
   SAID SPOKE UTTERED
QUOTIDIAN DAILY TRIVIAL
   ORDINARY
QUOTIENT QUOTE FRACTION
   MILLESIMAL
QUO VADIS (AUTHOR OF —)
   SIENKIEWICZ
   (CHARACTER IN —) ACTE NERO PAUL
   CHILO LYGIA PETER URSUS CROTON
   EUNICE GLAUCUS VINICIUS
   PETRONIUS TIGELLINUS
QUTB POLE

R

R AR ROGER ROMEO
  (UVULAR —) BURR
RA RE RAE SHU TEM ATMU BACIS
  HORUS MENTU KHEPERA SOKARIS
RAAMAH (FATHER OF —) CUSH
  (SON OF —) DEDAN SHEBA
RABBAN MASTER TEACHER
RABBET CHECK GROOVE BACKJOINT
  FILLISTER
RABBI TANA AMORA CACAM
  HAKAM TANNA MASTER SABORA
  KHAKHAM TEACHER GAMALIEL
  SABORAIM
  (PL.) AMORAIM TANNAIM
RABBIT BUN REX TAN BUNT CONY
  JACK POLE RACK BUNNY CAPON
  CREAM CUNNY DUTCH FRIER LAPIN
  ANGORA ASTREX CONEEN HAVANA
  OARLOP PARKER POLISH SILVER
  TAPETI WOOLER BEVEREN CONYNGE
  FLEMISH LEPORID SNOWSHOE
  WARRENER
  (— BURROW) CLAPPER
  (— FUR) CONY SCUT CONEY FLICK
  LAPIN FLITCH
  (— MEAT) LAPAN
  (— SKIN) RACK
  (— TAIL) SCUT
  (— WARREN) CONYGER
  (CASTRATED —) CAPON
  (FEMALE —) DOE
  (MALE —) BUCK
  (RELATIVE —) PIKA
  (YOUNG —) KITTEN
  (PL.) FLICK WARREN
RABBITFISH SPINY
RABBLE MOB TAG GING HERD RAFF
  ROUT SCUM FRAPE SCAFF SCUFF
  TRASH MEINIE RADDLE RAFFLE
  RAGTAG RASCAL TAGRAG DOGGERY
  PUDDLER RABBLER RANGALE
  TRAFFIC BRAGGERY CANAILLE
  RAGABASH RIFFRAFF VARLETRY
  RASCALITY CLAMJAMFRY
  (DISORDERLY —) HERD
RABBLE-ROUSER FIREBRAND
  DEMAGOG
RABID MAD RAGING FRANTIC
  FURIOUS RABIOUS RABITIC
  FRENZIED RAVENING VIRULENT
RABIES LYSSA MADNESS PIBLOKTO
  RAVENING
  (PREF.) LYSSO RABI
RACCOON COON COATI GUARA
  TEJON AGUARA MAPACH OLINGO
  WASHER AGOUARA ARCTOID
  RATTOON RINGTAIL CRABEATER
  (ANIMAL LIKE A —) OLINGO
  (HIMALAYAN —) PANDA
RACCOON DOG TANUKI
RACE CAP CUP LOG ROD RUN BENT
  CONE DASH DRAG GEST HUMP KIND
  LINE NAME RAIS RAZE RING RINK
  TEAM TRAM BLOOD BREED BROOD
  BRUSH CASTE CHEVY CORSO DERBY
  FLESH HOUSE ISSUE PLATE PURSE
  RATCH REACH ROUTE SPEED STAKE
  STAMM STIRP STOCK BROOSE
  CHEVVY COURSE FAMILY NATION
  PEOPLE PHYLON RUNOFF SPRING
  STIRPS STRAIN STRIND BIOTYPE
  CENTURY CLAIMER CLASSIC
  HACKNEY HUNDRED KINDRED
  LINEAGE MATINEE NURSERY
  PROGENY PROSAPY RACEWAY
  REGATTA STADIUM FUTURITY
  HANDICAP MARATHON WALKOVER
  MOTOCROSS OFFSPRING
  ORIENTEERING
  (— A HORSE) CAMPAIGN
  (— AT WEDDING) BROOSE BROUZE
  (— FOR BALL-BEARINGS) CONE
  (— OF BARLEY) BENT
  (— OF GODS) VANIR
  (— OF PEOPLE) VANS AMALS VANIR
  HAZARA SAKAIS YADAVA BAMBUTE
  FIRBOLG GIANTRY NISHADA
  RASENNA REPHAIM AMALINGS
  (— OF UNDERGROUND ELVES) DROW
  (— OF WINDMILL) CURB
  (FINAL —) RUNOFF NIGHTCAP
  (HORSE —) AGON DERBY PLATE
  SPRINT MATINEE FUTURITY
  WALKOVER
  (HUMAN —) MAN MANKIND SPECIES
  MORTALITY
  (IMPROMPTU —) BRUSH
  (JUMPING —) SCURRY
  (LENTEN —S) TORPIDS
  (LONG —) ENDURO
  (MILL —) LADE
  (MOTORCYCLE —) SCRAMBLE
  MOTOCROSS
  (PRELIMINARY —) HEAT
  (ROWING —) SCULLS REGATTA
  (RUNNING —) MILE RELAY SPRINT
  HUNDRED HURDLES
  (SHORT —) BICKER
  (SHORT-DISTANCE —) DASH SCURRY
  SPRINT
  (SKI —) SLALOM DAUERLAUF
  (TIDAL —) ROOST
  (PL.) FOURS
  (PREF.) ETHN(O) GEN(O) PHYL(O)

RACECOURSE LIST OVAL PIST RING
TURF EPSOM CAREER CIRCUS
CURSUS DROMOS STADIE STRETCH
GYMKHANA SPEEDWAY
(PREF.) DROM(O)
(SUFF.) DROME
RACEHORSE DOG PONY PACER
RACER CHASER SLEEPER TROTTER
BANGTAIL
(— THAT HAS NEVER WON) MAIDEN
(INFERIOR —) PLATER HAYBURNER
(2-YEAR OLD —) JUVENILE
(PL.) RUCK
RACEME STRIG PANICLE
RACEMOSE BOTRYOSE
RACER CRACK SNAKE RUNNER
BICYCLIST CINDERMAN
RACETRACK OVAL DROMOS
FURLONG AUTODROME
(— INFORMANT) SPIV TOUT
TIPSTER
RACEWAY CANAL TRACK GROOVE
CHANNEL FISHWAY
RACHEL POWDER
(FATHER OF —) LABAN
(HUSBAND OF —) JACOB
(SISTER OF —) LEAH
(SON OF —) JOSEPH BENJAMIN
RACHIS SPINE SPINDLE
(— OF HOP STROBILE) STRIG
RACHITIS RICKETS
RACIAL GENTILE GENTILIC
PHYLETIC
RACING (— BET) WIN SHOW PLACE
DOUBLE EXACTA PARLAY TRIPLE
PERFECTA QUINELLA TRIFECTA
(AUTO — PROBLEM) SPINOUT
(HORSE —) TURF
(MOTORCYCLE —) MOTOCROSS
RACIST COLOR
RACK GIN RAK RAT TUB BINK BUCK
CASE HACK HECK SHOG TACK
AMBLE BRAKE DRIER DRYER FLAKE
FRAME POKER THROW TOUSE TRAIN
WRACK WRECK WRING CIRCLE
CRATCH CUDGEL ENGINE NIPPER
PULLEY TREBLE WRENCH AFFLICT
AGONIZE PENRACK POTTARO
TORMENT TORTURE BARBECUE
EQUULEUS PINEBANK SAWHORSE
(— ATTACHED TO WAGON) SHELVING
OUTRIGGER
(— FOR BARRELS) JIB
(— FOR CHINAWARE) FIDDLE
(— FOR DISHES) BINK
(— FOR FEEDING) HACK HAYRACK
(— FOR FODDER) HECK CRATCH
(— FOR PLATES) CREEL
(— FOR STORAGE) FLAKE
(— IN THRESHER) SHAKER
(DRYING —) CRIB TREBLE
(PLATE —) BINK
(WOODEN —) BUCAN

RACKED WRUNG TORTURED
RACKET BAT DIN GAME RORT BANDY
MUSIC RAZOO CLAMOR CROSSE
DRIVER HUBBUB HUSTLE RAQUET
RATTLE BUSINESS REVELING
STRAMASH
(PART OF —) CAP BUTT CORD GRIP
HEAD HEEL TAPE YOKE CROWN
FLAKE SHAFT HANDLE PALLET
STRING THROAT BINDING SHOULDER
THROATPIECE
(TENNIS —) SCUFE
RACKETEER HOOD HUSTLER
GANGSTER
RACKETT CERVELAT CERVELAT
RACKING FIERCE
RACKMAN TOPMAN
RACON BEACON
RACONTEUR STORYTELLER
RACQUET CROSSE GAZELLE
RACY GAMY LEAN SEXY JUICY SALTY
SMART SPICY LIVELY RISQUE
PIQUANT PUNGENT ZESTFUL
SPIRITED MERACIOUS
RAD COOL MARV EAGER MARVY
QUICK READY AFRAID ELATED
FAROUT WAYOUT RADICAL
RADAR (— BEACON) RACON
(— NAVIGATION SYSTEM) LANAC
(— RECEPTION) ECHO
(SYSTEM) OBOE
RADARSCOPE PPI HSCOPE
RADDAI (BROTHER OF —) DAVID
(FATHER OF) JESSE
RADDLE PIT BEAT SCAR RAVEL
RUDDLE THRASH SEPARATOR
RADHA
(FOSTER SON OF —) KARNA
(HUSBAND OF —) ADHIRATHA
RADIAL RAY TIRE QUADRANT
(PREF.) RADIO
RADIANCE RAY GLOW LEAM GLARE
GLEAM GLINT GLORY LIGHT SHINE
LUSTER AUREOLA GLITTER
SPLENDOR
RADIANT BEAMY SHEEN SHINY
ABLAZE BRIGHT GOLDEN LUCENT
SHEENY AURORAL BEAMFUL
BEAMING FULGENT LAMBENT
GLORIOUS LUSTROUS RELUCENT
SPLENDID BRILLIANT
(— INTENSITY) J
(PREF.) STILPNO
RADIATE RAY BEAM POUR SHED
SHINE EFFUSE SPREAD EFFULGE
EMANATE ACTINOID
RADIATED PENCILED STELLATE
RADIATING DIADROM
RADIATION AURA LIGHT INFRARED
(— DOSAGE) REM REP REPP
(— UNIT) LANGLEY
(DEVICE TO GENERATE —) LASER
(ELECTROMAGNETIC —) PUMP

(SOURCE OF —) PULSAR
(UNIT OF —) RAD REM
RADIATOR HEATER EMANATOR
(— FLUID) COOLANT
(SET OF —S) STACK
RADICAL KEY SURD BASAL CRAZY
GROUP RADIX ROUGE ULTRA
CAPRYL HEROIC CAPITAL CAPROYL
DRASTIC EXTREME FORWARD
HERETIC JACOBIN LEFTIST LEVELER
LIBERAL PRIMARY CARDINAL
LOCOFOCO
(CHEMICAL —) ACYL AMYL CARYL
CETYL GROUP ACETYL ADENYL
CAPRYL PHENYL PHYTYL HALOGEN
LINALYL CARBAMYL QINNAMAL
(NOT —) FORMATIVE DERIVATIVE
RADICALISM EXTREMISM
JACOBINISM
RADICCHIO CHICORY CHICKORY
RADICEL ROOTLET
RADICLE (— THAT DEVELOPS IN
GRAIN) COME
RADIENT ORIENT
RADIO AIR SET WIRELESS
(— OPERATOR) HAM DEEJAY SPARKS
(— PIONEER) TESLA
(— PROGRAM) TALKSHOW
(— SYSTEM) TBS
(— WAVE EMITTER) QUASAR
RADIOGRAM FLIMSY
RADIOGRAPH EXOGRAPH
SKIAGRAM
RADIOISOTOPE TRACER
RADIO-WAVE (— EMITTER)
PULSAR
RADISH RUNCH DAEKON DAIKON
RIFART CADLOCK CRADLOCK
CRUCIFER CROSSWEED
RADIUS RAYON SPOKE SWEEP
THROW ADRADIUS
RADIX BASE ROOT ETYMON RADICLE
RADON NITON THORON ACTINON
EXRADIO
RADULA RIBBON TONGUE
RAFF LOW IDLE SCUM SWEEP TRASH
COMMON JUMBLE LUMBER RABBLE
RAFFLE RAGTAG SNATCH RUBBISH
RAFFISH RAKISH TAWDRY RACKETY
UNKEMPT
RAFFLE MOVE RAFF JUMBLE RABBLE
REFUSE RUBBISH
RAFT COW CRIB MOKI BALSA BATCH
FLOAT TABLE DINGEY DINGHY
JANGAR MOKIHI PIPERY RADEAU
JANGADA ZATTARE CATAMARAN
(— OF INVERTED POTS) GHARNAO
(— OF LOGS) BOOM CRIB
(— WITH CABIN) COW
(BAMBOO —) RAKIT
(FIRE —) CATAMARAN
(LUMBER —) BATCH
RAFT DOG RAKER

RAFTER HIP BALK BLAD FIRM SILE
SOIL SPAR SPUR VIGA BAULK BLADE
CABER RIDGE BOUGAR BULKER
COUPLE CARLINE CHEVRON
RAFFMAN SLEEPER
(— OF TURKEYS) FLOCK
RAFTY RAW DAMP FUSTY MUSTY
RANCID
RAG JAG LAP TAT HAZE HOAX JAGG
SAIL ANNOY CLOUT PRANK SCOLD
SCRAP SHRED WIPER GIBBOL LIBBET
RAGGLE TAGRAG TATTER FLITTER
REMNANT TORMENT RAGSTONE
STRAGGLE NEWSPAPER
(— GATHERER) TATTER
(— USED AS CANDLE) SLUT
(CURLING —) CRACKER
(FLAPPING —) WALLOP
(GLAD —S) GARB
(TARRED —) HARDS
(TARRED —S) HARDS HURDS
(PL.) DUDS CADDIS FITTERS
RAGGERY FLITTERS
RAGAMUFFIN MUFFLIN BEGGARLY
SHABROON TITMOUSE
RAGAU (FATHER OF —) PHALEC
RAGBAG CATCHALL
RAGE GO AWE FAD RAG WAX BAIT
BATE BEEF FARE FOAM FRET FUFF
FUME FUNK FUNX FURY GLOW GRIM
HEAT PELT RAMP RASE RESE TAVE
TEAR WOOD ANGER BRETH CHAFE
CRAZE FUROR PADDY STORM TEAVE
TEVEL VOGUE WRATH FRENZY
FURORE PELTER TYAUVE BLUSTER
FASHION MADNESS PASSION
RUFFIAN TEMPEST INSANITY
WOODNESS PADDYWACK
(BE IN A —) RANT
RAGFISH ICOSTEID
RAGGED DUDDY HARSH TATTY
FRAYED JAGGED SCOURY
UNEVEN SHAGRAG SHREDDY
TATTERY SCRAGGLY SCRATCHY
TATTERED
RAGGED ROBIN ROBIN CUCKOO
RAGGEE MAND RAGI MARUA
MANDUA KORAKAN ELEUSINE
RAGGLE-TAGGLE MOTLEY
RAGING HOT GRIM WILD YOND
RABID FIERCE FURIAL FERVENT
MADDING PELTING VIOLENT
FLAGRANT FURIBUND WRATHFUL
RAGOUT SALMI GOULASH HARICOT
TERRINE SALPICON CHIPOLATA
PULPATONE
(— OF GAME) SALMI SALMIS
RAGPICKER BUNTER RAGMAN
TATTER
RAGWEED HAYWEED HOGWEED
AMBROSIA IRONWEED KINGHEAD
KINGWEED RICHWEED
FRANSERIA

RAGWORT CUSHAG JACOBY
BENWEED CAMMOCK SEGGROM
LIFEROOT
RAHAM (FATHER OF —) SHEMA
(SON OF —) JORKOAM
RAID BUST RADE ROAD TALA FORAY
HARRY PINCH REISE REIVE BODRAG
CREACH FORAGE HARASS INROAD
MOLEST PANYAR RAZZIA SORTIE
BODRAGE BORDRAG CHAPPOW
DESCENT JAYHAWK OUTFALL
OUTRAKE OUTRIDE OUTROAD
SPREATH COMMANDO SPOILING
(— ORCHARDS) SCRUMP SKRIMP
SKRUMP
(AIR —) BLITZ
(BOMBING —) PRANG
(CATTLE —) SPREAGH SPREATH
(MAKE A — ON) BUST
(WARLIKE —) HERSHIP
RAIDER REDLEG BUSHWACK
(SEA —) VIKING
RAIL BAN BAR BULL COOT GIRD JEST
KOKO LIST MOHO RANT RAVE SKID
SORA TRAM WEKA WING CRAKE
EASER FENCE GUARD PLATE RAVEL
REILE SCOFF SCOLD SLENT STANG
STANK STEEL SWEAR BANTER
BEDWAY CALLET FENDER RUNNER
SKITTY TIKLIN BIDCOCK BILCOCK
COURLAN INVEIGH OARCOCK
RACKWAY TOPRAIL BULLHEAD
CANCELLI CORNBIRD PORTLAST
TOADBACK VIGNOLES BRANDRETH
BRANDRITH
(— AROUND A WELL) BRANDRETH
(— AT) JEST CURSE SCOFF RATTLE
REVILE BETONGUE
(— OF BED) STOCK
(— OF RAILWAY SWITCH) TONGUE
(— ON GUN PLATFORM) TRINGLE
(— ON HAY VEHICLE) THRIPPLE
(— ON SHIP) FIFE
(ALTAR —) SEPTUM
(ARCHED —) HOOPSTICK
(CHAIR —) LEDGE
(FENCE —) RIDER
(GROOVED —) GULLY GULLEY
(PART OF —) BED TIE FROG JOINT
SPIKE BALLAST SLEEPER CROSSTIE
BASEPLATE FISHPLATE
(SHUNTING —) SWITCH
(PL.) RAILING CANCELLI RAILROAD
(PREF.) RALLI
RAIL CHAIR CARRIAGE
RAILING BAR SEPT GRATE RAVEL
FENDER FIDDLE GITTER VEDIKA
BARRIER GALLERY PARAPET
CANCELLI ESPALIER HANDRAIL
PARCLOSE TRAVERSE
RAILLERY GAFF HASH JEST JOKE
RAGE CHAFF RALLY SPORT BANTER
BLAGUE HOORAY HURRAH SATIRE

TRIFLE MOCKERY RADINAGE
DICACITY RABULOUS RIDICULE
PERSIFLAGE
RAILROAD EL ROAD YARD STEEL
COALER FEEDER GRANGER
TRAMWAY CEINTURE ELEVATED
(— CAR) IDLER
(— FLARE) FUSEE
RAILROAD CHAIR SADDLE
RAILSPLITTER MAULER
RAILWAY ROAD TUBE COGWAY
SUBWAY COGROAD INCLINE
TRANVIA WIREWAY ASCENSOR
PLATEWAY TRAMROAD FUNICULAR
CREMAILLERE
(CARNIVAL —) ROLLERCOASTER
(KIND OF —) COG
(MOUNTAIN —) SWITCHBACK
(UNDERGROUND —) TUBE METRO
SUBWAY
RAIMENT RAY GARB CLOTH ATTIRE
APPAREL CLOTHES VESTURE
CLOTHING DRESSING WARDROBE
(SPLENDID —) SHEEN
(SUFF.) ESTHES
RAIN WET ISLE MIST SMUR ULAN
WEET BLASH STORM DELUGE
MIZZLE SERENE SHOWER SOAKER
DRIZZLE DOWNPOUR SPRINKLE
(— AND SNOW) SLEET
(— CHECK) TARP
(— HEAVILY) TEEM
(— LIGHTLY) SMUR SPIT SPRINKLE
(— OF SPARKS) SHOWER
(— SUDDENLY) PLUMP
(DRIZZLING —) DAG
(FINE —) MIST SEREIN SERENE
(FROZEN —) HAIL GRAUPEL
(GOD OF —) PARJANYA
(HARD —) SLEET
(HEAVY —) PASH SPOUT
(LIGHT —) SEREIN WEATHER
HEATDROPS
(SHORT —) SHOWER
(SMALL —) ROKE
(SUDDEN —) SKEW
(WHIRLING —) SKIRL
(WIND-DRIVEN —) SCAT
(PL.) VARSHA
(PREF.) HYET(O) OMBRI OMBRO
PLUVI(O)
RAINBIRD KOEL TOMFOOL
STORMBIRD
(— OF JAMAICA) HUNTER
RAINBOW ARC BOW ARCH IRIS
GAMUT METEOR SUNBOW ILLUSION
(AUTHOR OF —) LAWRENCE
(BROKEN —) WINDDOG WINDGALL
(CHARACTER IN —) TOM ANNA WILL
ANTON LYDIA LENSKY URSULA
BRANGWEN SKREBENSKY
(PREF.) IRID(O)
RAINBOW FISH GUPPY MAORI

RAINBOW RUNNER SKIPJACK
SHOEMAKER
RAINBRINGER KACHINA
RAIN CLOUD NIMBUS
RAINCOAT MAC MACK MINO OILER
PONCHO BURSATI OILSKIN SLICKER
GOSSAMER MACINTOSH
MACKINTOSH
RAINFALL PLOUT SKIFF SKIFT
ONDING STEMPLOW
RAIN GAGE UDOMETER
RAINGEAR MAC
RAINMAKER SEEDER
RAINSPOUT RONE
RAINSTORM WET SPATE
SCOWTHER
RAIN TREE SAMAN ZAMAN
GUANGO ZAMANG ALGAROBA
GENISARO MONKEYPOD
RAINY WET KICK FRESH JUICY RAYNE
SAPPY WEETY BLASHY DRIPPY
HYETAL PLUNGY SPONGY PLUVIAL
PLUVINE SHOWERY WEEPING
CLUTTERY PLUVIOUS SLATTERY
(— SEASON) VARSHA
RAISE END SET WIN BUMP BUOY
GROW HAIN HEFT HIGH HIKE HOVE
JACK KICK LEVY LIFT MAKE OVER
REAR ROOF STIR TELD TOSS AREAR
BLOCK BOOST BREED BUILD CAIRN
CHOCK CRANE DIGHT ELATE ENSKY
ERECT EXALT FORCE GREET HANCE
HEAVE HEEZE HEVEN HOISE HOIST
HORSE LEAVE MOUND MOUNT PRICK
PUTUP RISER ROUSE VOICE ARRECT
ASSIST BETTER CREATE DOUBLE
EMBOSS EXHALE GATHER LEAVEN
MUSTER NANTLE PREFER REMOVE
RISING UPHOLD UPLIFT ADDRESS
ADVANCE COLLECT ELEVATE
ENHANCE LIGHTEN NOURISH
PRESENT PROMOTE RECRUIT
UPSHOOT ANGELIZE HEIGHTEN
INSPIRIT RELEVATE
(— A BUMP) CLOUR
(— ALOFT) SPHERE
(— A NAP) MOZE TEASE TEASEL
TEAZLE
(— ANCHOR) CAT
(— A NESTLING) FLEDGE
(— A SIEGE) RISE RELIEVE
(— BRIDGE BID) JUMP
(— BY ASSESSMENT) LEVY
(— BY HAND) NOB
(— CLAMOR) BRAWL
(— IN PITCH) SHARP
(— OBJECTIONS) CAVIL BOGGLE
(— ONESELF) CHIN
(— TO A POWER) INVOLVE
(— TO HIGH DEGREE) STRAIN
(— TO 3RD POWER) CUBE
(— UP) BUOY AREAR ELATE EXALT
EXTOL ELEVATE CIVILIZE

RAISED HIGH UPSET ARRECT
HOGGED BULLATE EXALTED
ELEVATED MOUNTANT UPLIFTED
UPRAUGHT
(— A SEMITONE) SHARP
RAISIN FIG PASA PLUM LEXIA ZIBEB
REYSON CURRANT SULTANA
MUSCATEL
(PL.) SPICE
RAISING ATOLLENT
(— OF BELL) SALLY
(— OF CATTLE) GRAZING
(— OF SIEGE) REMOVE
(— OF TONE) ECBOLE
RAJ RULE REIGN
RAJA KING CHIEF RULER PRINCE
PANGLIMA
RAJAB MONTH
RAJAH FABRIC
RAJMAHAL CREEPER JITI CHITI
JETEE JEETEE
RAJPUT SAMMA SUMRA GAHRWAL
RAZBOOCH
RAKE GO HOE RIP WAY COMB PATH
RACK RAFF RAVE REAP ROAM ROUE
ROVE RUCK BLOOD CLAUT PITCH
SCOOP SCOUR SULKY TIGER
PLUNGE RABBLE ROLLER SEARCH
RANSACK SCRATCH LOTHARIO
SCRAPPLE
(— GRAIN) GAVEL
(— UP IN ROWS) HACK
(— WITH GUNFIRE) SCOUR STRAFE
ENFILADE
(— WITHOUT TEETH) LUTE
(BUCK —) SWEEP
(CRANBERRY —) SCOOP
(HORSE-DRAWN —) GLEANER
(OYSTER —) GLEANER
(PART OF —) BOW TANG TINE TOOTH
HANDLE FERRULE
RAKEHELL RASCAL IMMORAL
LIBERTINE
RAKER GUMMER ROOKER
RAKISH SLANG JAUNTY SPORTY
WANTON DASHING CARELESS
DEVILISH RANTEPOLE RANTIPOLE
RALE RATTLE SIFFLE SIBILUS
RHONCHUS
RALLENTANDO DRAG RITARD
RALLY KID DRAG JOKE MOCK RELY
STIR BULLY JOLLY QUEER BANTER
DERIDE REVIVE COLLECT REBOUND
CAMPOREE CLAMBAKE RIDICULE
SPEAKING
(KIND OF —) PEP
(POLITICAL —) CLAMBAKE
RAM PUN TIP TUP BUCK CRAM PACK
RAME STEM TEAP TOOP ARIES
CHOKE CRASH POACH ROGER SLIDE
BEETLE CHASER RANCID ROSTRUM
BULLDOZER WETHERHOG
WETHERTEG

(— OF WAR VESSEL) SPUR
(CASTRATED —) WETHER
(FATHER OF —) HEZRON JERAHMEEL
(SON OF —) AMMINADAB
(PREF.) CRIO
RAMA MELCHORA
(FATHER OF —) DASHARATHA
(MOTHER OF —) KAUSHALYA
(WIFE OF —) SITA
RAMADA ARBOR PORCH
RAMAGE WILD RAMMISH UNTAMED
RAMAGE HAWK BRANCHER
RAMBLE RAKE ROAM ROVE SKIR
WALK JAUNT PROWL RANGE TRACE
TROLL DODDER RUMBLE STROLL
VAGARY WAMBLE WANDER
ENRANGE EXCURSE SAUNTER
SPROGUE TROUNCE FLAGARIE
SCRAMBLE SPATIATE
(— AIMLESSLY) HAZE
(— IN TALK) DODDER
RAMBLING GAD RAISE VAGARY
CURSORY DEVIOUS WINDING
DESULTORY SCATTERED
RAMBUNCTIOUS RUDE WILD
ROUGH UNRULY UNTAMED
VIOLENT
RAMBUTAN SOAPWORT
RAMENTUM PALEA PALET SCALE
SHAVING
RAMIE BAST HEMP RHEA ORTIGA
RAMIFICATION ARM RAMUS
BRANCH OFFSHOOT OUTGROWTH
RAMIFY BRANCH SPRANGLE
RAMMAN ADAD ADDA ADDU
RAMMED EARTH PISE
RAMMEL TRASH RUMMLE RUBBISH
RAMMER TUP HEAD BOSER PUNNER
WORMER
RAMONA (HUSBAND OF —)
ALESSANDRO
RAMOSE CLADOSE BRANCHED
RAMOTH (FATHER OF —) BANI
RAMP ROB RUN BANK EXIT HOAX
RAGE RANK SLIP CREEP STORM
WAYON EASING FROLIC GARLIC
WAYOFF WAYOUT FOOTPAD
SLIPWAY SWINDLE GRADIENT
(AIRPORT —) JETWAY
RAMPAGE RAGE ROMP BINGE
SPRAY SPREE STORM RANDAN
RAMPAGEOUS UNRULY GLARING
RAMPANT VIOLENT
RAMPANT RANK PROFUSE SALIANT
SALIENT SEGREANT
RAMPART BRAY LINE WALL AGGER
ARGIN ABATIS VALLUM ABATTIS
BULWARK DEFENSE PARAPET
RAMPIER BARBICAN MUNITION
BARRICADE
RAMPER LAMPREY
RAMPIKE SNAG RAUNPICK ROUNSPIK
RAMROD FORMAL GUNSTICK

RAMSHACKLE RUDE UNRULY
RICKETY SHACKLY UNSTEADY
RAMSON RAMP GARLIC BUCKRAM
(PL.) RAMS
RAMSTAM RASH HEADLONG
RECKLESS
RAN ARN
(HUSBAND OF —) AEGIR
RANCEL SEARCH RANSACK
RANCH RUN FARM TEAR FINCA
CHACRA OUTFIT SPREAD WRENCH
STATION ESTANCIA HACIENDA
RANCHE NATURAL
RANCHER COWMAN HERDER
GRAZIER SHEEPMAN CATTLEMAN
RANCID RAM RANK SOUR FROWY
RAFTY RASTY REEST RESTY FROWZY
ODIOUS ROTTEN MALODOROUS
RANCOR BILE GALL HATE SPITE
ENMITY GRUDGE HATRED MALICE
ACRIMONY
RANCOROUS ACRID VENOMOUS
MALIGNANT ACRIMONIOUS
(NOT —) GOOD
RAND EDGE ROON RUND BORDER
HIGHLAND
RANDAN SPREE RANTAN UPROAR
RAMPAGE
RANDOM BANK FORCE LOOSE
STRAY CASUAL CHANCE CHANCY
AIMLESS RANDALL RENDOUN
SHOTGUN UNAIMED VAGRANT
ALEATORIC
(AT —) HOBNOB
(SOMEWHAT —) LONG
RANDY LEWD RUDE RUDAS SPREE
BEGGAR VIRAGO LUSTFUL RIOTOUS
CAROUSAL
RANGE KEN ROW ALLY AREA BEAT
GATE GAUT GHAT LINE RAIK RAKE
RANK ROAM ROVE SCUM SHOT
TOUR WALK ALIGN BLANK CARRY
FIELD GAMUT HILLS ORBIT REACH
SCOPE SCOUR SHOOT SPACE STAND
START STOVE SWEEP SWING VERGE
COURSE DANGER EXTEND EXTENT
LENGTH RADIUS RAMBLE SCOUTH
SPHERE STROLL WANDER BOWSHOT
COMPASS DEMESNE EARSHOT
GUNSHOT HABITAT HORIZON
PURVIEW CLASSIFY DIAPASON
EARREACH EYEREACH LATITUDE
PANORAMA
(— ABOUT) SCOUR
(— FOR FOOD) FORAGE
(— FOR GAME) QUARTER
(— OF ARROW) FLIGHT
(— OF BRICK) COURSE
(— OF BUILDINGS) CRESCENT
(— OF COLORS) PALETTE SPECTRUM
(— OF COLUMNS) PORTICO
COLONNADE PERISTYLE
(— OF FOOD) FARE

(— **OF FREQUENCIES**) BAND SPECTRUM
(— **OF GOVERNANCE**) DOMAIN
(— **OF GUN**) CARRY RANDOM GUNSHOT
(— **OF HEARING**) EARSHOT
(— **OF HILLS**) GAUT GHAT HUMP TIER CHAIN GHAUT RIDGE SIERRA SAWBACK BACKBONE
(— **OF MOVEMENT**) TRAVEL
(— **OF ORGANISM**) BIOZONE
(— **OF PASTURE**) GANG
(— **OF PLANKS**) STRING
(— **OF PRINTING TYPES**) SERIES
(— **OF SIGHT**) KEN SCAN EYESHOT KENNING
(— **OF TONES**) KEY SCALE GRADATION
(— **OF VISION**) EYE SIGHT KENNING
(— **OF WAVELENGTH**) BAND
(— **OVER**) SWEEP
(— **TOP**) COOKTOP
(— **WILDLY**) RAMP
(**ARCHERY** —) BUTTS GREEN
(**COOKING** —) KITCHENER
(**FREE** —) SCOUTH SCOWTH LIBERTY
(**MOUNTAIN** —) CHAIN SERRA SIERRA
(**PART OF** —) CAP DOOR FLUE HEAD KNOB OVEN RACK TRIM VENT GRATE GUARD GUIDE HINGE PANEL BURNER GASKET HANDLE WINDOW BROILER CONTROL GRIDDLE DRIPPLATE BACKSPLASH
(**SHOOTING** —) MES GALLERY
(**TEMPERATURE** —) CONE
RANGE FINDER STADIA MEKOMETER
RANGE POLE PICKET
RANGER ROVER ROBBER MONTERO FIREWARD
RANGOON SHERRY
RANGY OPEN ROOMY SPACIOUS
RANK RAY ROW SEE DANK FOOT FORM FOXY GOLE GREE LINE RAMP RATE ROOM SEED SOUR STEP TIER CENSE CHOIR CLASS FETID FRANK FUSTY GRADE GROSS HONOR LEVEL MARCH ORDER PLACE QUIRE RANGE ROWTY SIEGE SPACE STALL STAND STATE TCHIN TRAIN AFFAIR AGREGE DEGREE ERMINE ESTATE ESTEEM FIGURE LAVISH PARAGE RATING SPHERE STATUS STRONG CALIBER CALLING DIGNITY DUKEDOM EARLDOM FOOTING GLARING RAMMISH RAMPANT STATION WORSHIP ABSOLUTE EARLSHIP ENSIGNCY EQUIPAGE FLAGRANT GENTRICE LADYSHIP PALPABLE STINKING MALODOROUS
(— **AND FILE**) RUCK RANGALE
(— **OF GENTLEMEN**) GENTRY GENTILITY

(— **OF SERGEANT-AT-LAW**) COIF COIFFE
(**ACADEMIC** —) AGREGE
(**BOTTOMMOST** —) CELLAR
(**HIGH** —) PURPLE DIGNITY EMINENCE
(**LOWEST** —) SCOURING
(**MILITARY** —) GRADE AIRMAN CORNET CHAOUSH
(**NOBLE** —) ADELAIDE
(**ONE HIGHEST IN** —) SUPREMO
(**SAME** —) KIND
(**SOCIAL** —) CLASS ESTATE HERALDRY POSITION
(**SUFF.**) CY HEAD HOOD
RANKLE FRET CHAFE FESTER INJURE RANCOR DESTROY INFLAME
RANSACK RIG DRAG RAKE RIPE SACK SEEK RIFLE DACKER RANCEL SEARCH PLUNDER RUMMAGE
RANSOM FINE RAME REDEEM RESCUE RESGAT EXPIATE
RANSTEAD TOADFLAX
RANT CAVE HUFF RAIL RAND MOUTH REVEL ROUSE SCOLD SPOUT STEVEN BOMBAST CAROUSE DECLAIM FROTHING RODOMONTADE
(— **AND RAVE**) FAUNCH
RANTAN NOISE
RANTING RANTISM TEARCAT
RANTIPOLE WILD CARROT RAKISH SEESAW ROMPING
RANULA CYST FROGTONGUE
(**PREF.**) BATRACH(O)
RANUNCULUS MOSS GOLLAND CROWFOOT HEDGEHOG BUTTERCUP
RAOULIA HAASTIA
RAP BOB CON BLOW CHAP GRAB KNAP TIRL TUNK WRAP BLAME CLICK CLINK FLIRT KNOCK STEAL TOUCH BARTER CHARGE HANDLE YANKER
RAPACIOUS CRUEL GREEDY TAKING RAVENING RAVENOUS
RAPACITY RAVEN RAVIN CUPIDITY EXTORTION VULTURISM
RAPE COLE ABUSE COLZA FORCE NAVET NAVEW TOUCH ATTACK CANOLA FELONY RAPEYE TURNIP ASSAULT DESPOIL NAVETTE OPPRESS OUTRAGE PLUNDER RAPTURE STUPRUM VIOLATE COLESEED COLEWORT DISHONOR STUPRATE SUPPRESS
RAPE OF THE LOCK (**AUTHOR OF** —) POPE
(**CHARACTER IN** —) ARIEL BETTY PETRE PLUME SPLEEN BELINDA UMBRIEL CLARISSA THALESTRIS
RAPESEED COLZA RAVISON
RAPHA (**FATHER OF** —) BINEA
RAPHIA JUPATI
RAPHU (**SON OF** —) PALTI
RAPHUS DIDUS

RAPID GAY FAST CHUTE HASTY MOSSO QUICK ROUND SAULT SHARP SHOOT SHUTE TOSTO WINGY RIFFLE SPEEDY WINGED CURSIVE SCHNELL SKELPIN STICKLE TANTIVY SLAPPING SPEEDFUL OVERNIGHT
(—S IN RIVER) SAULT DALLES RIFFLE STICKLE CATARACT
(MORE —) STRETTO
(PREF.) TACHY

RAPIDITY HASTE SPEED RADEUR CELERITY VELOCITY

RAPIDLY APACE CHEAP FLEETLY HASTILY SPEEDILY QUICKFOOT

RAPIER TUCK TUKE BILBO ESTOC SHARP STOCK VERDUN TOASTER

RAPINE FORCE RAVIN PILLAGE PLUNDER VIOLENCE

RAPINI BROCCOLI

RAPPACCINI (DAUGHTER OF —) BEATRICE

RAPPAREE ROBBER CREAGHT VAGABOND

RAPPEE SNUFF

RAPPEL APPEIL

RAPPORT ACCORD HARMONY RELATION AGREEMENT
(ESTABLISH —) GROK

RAPSCALLION ROGUE RASCAL VILLAIN HOSEBIRD VAGABOND

RAPT LOST WRAP TENSE INTENT RAVISH TRANCE CARRIED ENGAGED RAPTURE ABDUCTED ABSORBED ECSTATIC

RAPTORES RAPACES

RAPTURE JOY BLISS DELIGHT ECSTASY PAROXYSM RHAPSODY

RAPTUROUS ECSTATIC RHAPSODIC

RARA AVIS PHENIX RARITY WONDER PHOENIX

RARE FINE REAL SELD THIN ALONE EARLY GREAT ANTRIN CHOICE GEASON INCONY SCARCE SEENIL SELDOM SINDLE SPARSE SUBTLE SULLEN UNIQUE ANTERIN CURIOUS TENUOUS UNUSUAL CRITICAL SELDSEEN SINGULAR UNCOMMON RECHERCHE
(PREF.) AREO MANO SPAN(I)(O)

RAREFACTION POROSIS

RAREFIED HIGH THIN SUBTILE ABSTRUSE AETHERED ESOTERIC

RAREFY THIN DILUTE EXTENUATE SUBTILIZE

RARELY SELDEN SELDOM

RARENESS RARITY TENUITY SCARCITY

RARITY SWAN CURIO RELIC RARIETY TENUITY RARENESS
(PL.) CURIOSA

RASCAL BUY CAD DOG IMP LOW RAP BASE DUCK FILE KITE LOON MEAN SHAG SMAK CATSO FILTH GANEF GIPSY KNAVE ROGUE SCAMP SHELM SLAVE SMAIK THIEF VIPER ABLACH BEGGAR BRIBER BUDZAT BUGGER COQUIN HARLOT LIMMER RABBLE RAGGIL RIBALD SCHELM SORROW TINKER BLEEDER CAMOOCH CULLION GLUTTON HALLION HESSIAN NEBULON PANURGE PEASANT RAPTRIL SHELLUM SKEEZIX SKELLUM VILLAIN BEZONIAN BLIGHTER HOSEBIRD LIDDERON PALLIARD PICAROON RAKEHELL RUBIATOR SCALAWAG SPALPEEN TAISTREL VAGABOND WIDDIFOW SCAPEGRACE SCARAMOUCH RAPSCALLION SCARAMOUCHE

RASCALITY FOIST RABBLE KNAVERY ROGUING RASCALRY

RASCALLY BASE MEAN ROOKY ARRANT GALLUS LIMMER GALLOWS KNAVISH RAGGILY SHAGRAG WIDDIFOW

RASE PULL RAIS RAZE ERASE PLUCK INCISE SNATCH

RASH ID CUT BRASH HARDY HASTY HEADY SLASH SLICE DARING SUDDEN UNWARY URGENT BULRUSH HOTSPUR RABBISH RAMSTAM ROSEOLA BLIZZARD CARELESS ERUPTION EXANTHEM HEADLONG HEEDLESS MADBRAIN OVERSEEN PRESSING RECKLESS TEMEROUS IMPETUOUS IMPULSIVE

RASHER SLICE COLLOP TRIFLE COLLOPE

RASHLY HEADILY HEADLONG

RASHNESS RAGE RESE HASTE ACRISY TEMERITY HEADINESS

RASKOLNIK POPOVETS

RASP RUB FILE RAPE ERUCT GRATE TOOTH RAPEYE RUBBER RUGINE RIFFLER DENTICLE
(SHOEMAKER'S —) FLOAT

RASPBERRY AKPEK BAZOO MOLKA AVARIN RASPIS PLUMBOG ARNBERRY BLACKCAP BOGBERRY CUTHBERT MULBERRY RESPASSE ROSACEAN SALMONBERRY

RASPING HARSH ROUGH STOOR STOUR HOARSE RASION RAZZLY GRATING RAUCOUS GUTTERAL
(PL.) SCOBS

RASPY HARSH GRATING SCREAKY SCRABBLY

RASSE CIVET WEASEL

RASSELAS (AUTHOR OF —) JOHNSON
(CHARACTER IN —) IMLAC PEKUAH NEKAYAH RASSELAS
(MENTOR OF —) IMLAC
(SISTER OF —) NEKAYAH

RAT BUCK DAMN DRAT FINK HEEL
NOKI ROTN SCAB VOLE KIORE LOUSE
METAD RATON SELVA ZEMMI ZEMNI
CRABER MURINE RODENT ROTTAN
SLEPEZ VERMIN YUNGAS CUSHION
CONFOUND INFORMER MYOMORPH
SQUEALER
(— ON) SING
(INDIAN —) KOK
RATAPLAN RATTAN RATTLE
RATCH RASH REND ROCH SPOT
NOTCH STREAK RATCHET STRETCH
RATCHET DOG PAWL CLICK DETENT
ROCHET
RAT CHINCHILLA ABROCOME
RATE LAY RAG SET CESS CHOP DEEM
EARN GAIT GIVE HAND KIND RANK
RATA ABUSE CULET CURVE PRIZE
RATIO REBUT SCOLD STENT STYLE
VALUE ZAKAT ASSIZE GALLOP
ACCOUNT BESHREW CARTAGE
DESERVE FASHION MILLAGE
REPROVE CLASSIFY ESTIMATE
QUANTIFY
(— HIGHLY) EXALT PRICE
(— OF ASCENT) GRADE
(— OF CHANGE) GRADIENT
(— OF DRAINAGE) FREENESS
(— OF EXCHANGE) BATTA
(— OF FLOW) FLUX DISCHARGE
(— OF INTEREST) COUPON DISCOUNT
(— OF MOTION) BAT SPEED
(— OF MOVEMENT) PACE TEMPO
(— OF RECKONING) FOOT
(— OF SPEED) BAT AGOGE
(— OF TAX) CENSE
(— OF TRANSFER) FLUX
(— OF TUITION) CULET
(— SCHEDULE) TARIFF
(AT ANY —) HURE
(BIRTH —) NATALITY
RATE BOOK STREET
RATEL BADGER BURIER
RATH CAR HILL REUT RUTH EARLY
MOUND QUICK REUTE SWIFT
BETIMES CHARIOT YOUTHFUL
RATHER Y BUT GEY ATAD LIKE SOON
LOURD QUITE ASTITE ATOUCH
BEFORE FAIRLY HELDER KINDLY
PRETTY RUTHER SEEMLY SORTOF
TIDDER TITTER EARLIER INSTEAD
MIDDLING SOMEWHAT
(— THAN) ERE BEFORE
RATIFICATION AMEN RATE
SANCTION
RATIFY AMEN PASS SEAL SIGN VISA
ENSEAL FASTEN OBSIGN APPROVE
CONFIRM SCEPTER CANONIZE
ROBORATE SANCTION VALIDATE
RATING RANK CENSE CLASS GRADE
WRITER STANDING
RATIO Q PI GAIN RATE SINE SLIP
INDEX RESON SETUP SHEAR ASPECT

CAMBER DECADE QUOTUM REASON
REYSON SECANT AVERAGE PORTION
CONTRAST SOLIDITY MULTIPLIER
PROPORTION
RATIOCINATION MACH LOGIC
THOUGHT REASONING
RATION DOLE ALLOT RATIO ALLOCATE
(— OF BREAD) TOMMY
(ANIMAL —) CHOW
(EXTRA —S) BUCKSHEE
(HOG —) SWILL
(PL.) FOOD BOUCH ETAPE COMMON
RATIONAL SANE LUCID SOBER
LOGICAL REASONAL SENSIBLE
THINKING
RATIONALISM (GERMAN —)
NEOLOGY
RATIONALIZE THOB EXPLAIN
RATITE EMU MOA EMEU KIWI RHEA
OSTRICH STRUTHIAN
RAT KANGAROO TUNGO POTOROO
SQUEAKER
RATOON SHOOT SPROUT SUCKER
RATTAIL MULE ARREST GRENADIER
RATTAN CANE SEGA ROTAN BEJUCO
ROTANG SWITCH RATTOON
RATTLE DIN BIRL BURL REEL RICK
TIRL CHINK CLACK CROTAL GRAGER
HENPEN HURTLE MARACA RACKLE
RICKLE RIFFLE ROTTLE RUCKLE
RUTTLE CHACKLE CLACKER CLAPPER
CLATTER CLICKET CREAKER GNATTER
GROGGER SHATTER SISTRUM
SKELLAT CAIXINHA CHOCALHO
COWWHEAT NOISEMAKER
(CRIER'S —) CLAPPER
(IRON —) SKELLAT SKILLET
(PREF.) CROTALI
RATTLEBRAINED MADCAP
RATTLER LIE ROMBLE RUMBLER
RATTLESNAKE BELLTAIL CASCABEL
CASCAVEL CROTALID MASSASAUGA
SIDEWINDER
(— PLANTAIN) NETLEAF RATSBANE
RATTLESNAKE ROOT BUGBANE
JOYLEAF
RATTLETRAP HEAP GEWGAW
JUNKER TRIFLE RICKETY
RATTLING REEL BRISK HUSKY
SLAPPING SPLENDID CREPITANT
RATTY NASTY SHABBY UNKEMPT
WORTHLESS
RATWA MUNTJAC
RAUCOUS LOUD HARSH COARSE
HOARSE SQUAWKY STRIDENT
RAUN ROE ROWN SPAWN
RAUPO CATTAIL
RAVAGE EAT PREY RIOT RUIN SACK
FORAY HARRY HAVOC SPOIL WASTE
FORAGE DESPOIL DESTROY
OVERRUN PILLAGE PLUNDER
DEFLOWER DESOLATE POPULATE
SPOLIATE

RAVANA (SISTER OF —)
SHURPANAKHA
RAVE MAD RAGE RAND WOOD AWEDE
BLURB CRUSH RATHE ROUSE STORM
TAVER DELIRE TAIVER WANDER
RAVEL FAG RUN FRAY FRET UNDO
REYLE SNARL EVENER LADDER
RADDLE RUNNER SLOUGH TANGLE
CONFUSE INVOLVE PERPLEX RAILING
UNWEAVE
RAVELIN RABLIN OUTWORK
DEMILUNE
RAVELING LINT
RAVEN DARK BLACK CRAKE RALPH
CORBEL CORBIE CORBIN FORAGE
RAVINE WAYBIRD
(BRIGHT —) BERTRAM
RAVENING CRUEL RABIES
RAVENOUS GREEDY LUPINE
TOOTHY WOLFISH RAPACIOUS
VORACIOUS
RAVINE DEN GAP GUT LIN DELL
DRAW GILL GULL KHOR KHUD LINN
LLYN OIKE WADI BREAK BUNNY
CHASM CHINE CLOVE COULE DONGA
FLUME GHYLL GLACK GORGE GOYAL
GOYLE GRIFF GRIKE GULCH GULLY
HEUCH KLOOF NULLA SLADE SLAKE
STRID ARROYO CLEUCH CLOUGH
COULEE DIMBLE DINGLE DUMBLE
GULLET GULLEY HOLLOW NULLAH
RAMBLA SHEUGH STRAIT
BARRANCA QUEBRADA
RAVING RAVERY DELIRANT FRENZIED
DELIRIOUS
RAVISH ROB RAPE ABUSE CHARM
FORCE HARRY SPOIL ABDUCT
ATTACK DEFILE AFFORCE CORRUPT
DELIGHT ENFORCE OPPRESS
OUTRAGE OVERJOY PLUNDER
POLLUTE VIOLATE VITIATE
DEFLOWER ENTRANCE STUPRATE
SUPPRESS UNMAIDEN
RAVISHER RAPTER RAVENER
RAVISHMENT ECSTASY RAPTURE
TRANSPORT
RAW RA RED ROW BRUT LASH REAR
RUDE BLEAK CHILL CRUDE FRESH
GREEN HARSH NAKED RAFTY SHARP
WERSH BITTER CALLOW COARSE
CUTCHA KUTCHA UNRIPE VULGAR
WAIRSH NATURAL NOUVEAU
UNBOUND VERDANT WEARISH
WEERISH IMMATURE RAWBONED
UNCOOKED UNEDITED VISCERAL
(— AND COLD) CRIMPY
(PREF.) OMO
RAWBONED RAW BONY LEAN
GAUNT LANKY SCRAG SCRAWNY
(— PERSON) SCRAG
RAWHIDE WHIP WHANG COWHIDE
COWSKIN GREENHIDE PARFLECHE
RAWNESS CRUDITY

RAY BEAM BETA DORN SOIL WIRE
ALPHA BRAND DRESS EQUIP FLAIR
FLAKE FLATH GLEAM GLEED MANTA
ORDER RAYON ROKER SKATE BATOID
CHUCHO OBISPO RADIAL RADIUS
RAIOID SEPHEN STREAM TRYGON
VISUAL BATFISH COWFISH
DEWBEAM DRILVIS FIDDLER
HOMELYN PLACOID RAIMENT
TORPEDO WAIREPO BRACHIUM
MOONBEAM NUMBFISH PLOWFISH
PYLSTERT STINGRAY STINGAREE
(— OF LIGHT) GLINT SPEAR GLANCE
SUNRAY SUNBEAM
(— OF STARFISH) ARM
(FEMALE —) MAID
(FIN —) SPINE
(KIND OF —) GAMMA
(WITHOUT —S) ABACTINAL
(PREF.) BATO
(ELECTRIC —) NARC(O)
RAYED
(PREF.) ACTIN(IO)(O)
(SUFF.) ACTIN(IO)(O)
(—WITH IMPAIRMENT) LEXIA
RAYON BEAM RADIUS DUCHESS
RAZE CUT FLAT RUIN ARASE ERASE
LEVEL STREW ARRACE EFFACE
SCRAPE SLIGHT UNPILE DESTROY
SCRATCH SUBVERT UNBUILD
DEMOLISH
RAZOR SHIV TUSK MUSSEL RASOIR
SHAVER RATTLER SLASHER
CUTTHROAT
(PREF.) XYR(O)
RAZORBACK STATE ARKANSAS
RAZORBILL MURRE
RAZOR-BILLED AUK FALK TINK
MURRE NODDY SCOOT SCOUT
SKOOT TINKER SKIMMER WILLOCK
ROCKBIRD
RAZOR CLAM PIROT RASOR SOLEN
SPOUT RASOIR
RAZZ BOO KID PAN HARRY TEASE
CHIACK HECKLE NEEDLE RIDICULE
RASPBERRY
RAZZIA RAID FORAY INCURSION
RAZZING RAZOO
RAZZLE-DAZZLE SHOWBIZ
RE RAY ANENT ACTION MATTER
REGARDING
REACH GO GET HIT RAX RUN WIN
BEAT COME FIND GAIN HAWK HENT
MAKE PUSH REEK REIK RYKE SHOT
SORT SPAN SPIT TEND BRACE CROSS
FETCH GRASP PERCH RANGE RETCH
TOUCH ADVENE ARRIVE ATTAIN
DANGER EXTEND FATHOM LENGTH
OBTAIN SNATCH STREEK STRIKE
ACHIEVE COMPASS CONTACT
GUNSHOT OVERGET POSSESS
RECOVER STRETCH
(— ACROSS) SPAN OVERSTRIDE

(— AN END) STAY
(— BEYOND) OVERREACH
(— BY EFFORT) ATTAIN
(— BY FIGURING) STRIKE
(— FORTH) EXTEND
(— GOAL) HAIL
(— HIGHER) OUTTOP
(— IN TOTAL) RUNTO
(— OF SIGHT) EYESHOT
(— OF WATER) LODE
(— OUT) UTTER SPREAD STRETCH
(— TO) LINE
(— TOTAL) AMOUNT
(— UNDERSTANDING) AGREE
(— WITH END) ABUT
(EXTREME —) PITCH STRETCH
(TRY TO —) ASPIRE
(ULTIMATE —) PITCH
REACHER INGIVER
REACT ACT BUCK BEHAVE RETROACT
REACTION BELT BUZZ KAHN WOHL
START WIDAL FAVISM RECOIL
BLOWOFF EMOTION FEELING
SETBACK BACKLASH BACKWASH
EXCHANGE GUARDING KICKBACK
RESPONSE RECEPTION
COUNTERBUFF
(— TIME) LATENCY
(ADVERSE —) BACKLASH
(ANGRY —) RISE
(DELAYED —) DOUBLETAKE
(KIND OF —) FEULGEN
(NUCLEAR —) SPALLATION
(VIOLENT —) SONG
REACTIONARY WHITE BOURBON
BACKWARD
REACTIVATED AWAKE ACTIVE
REACTIVATOR ACTIFIER
REACTOR PILE CHOKER FURNACE
INDUCTOR
(SHUTDOWN OF —) SCRAM
READ GO CON KRI QRI SEE CALL KERE
QERI TURN CHOKE JUDGE SOLVE
WRITE PERUSE RELATE FORESEE
LEARNED LECTION PREDICT
ABOMASUM DECIPHER FORETELL
INDICATE OVERLOOK
(— ALOUD) LINE DEACON
(— BAR CODES) SCAN
(— HERE AND THERE) BROWSE
(— MECHANICALLY) RETINIZE
(— OF) SEE
(— OFF) DICTATE
(— PROOF) HORSE
(— RAPIDLY) DIP SCAN SKIM GOBBLE
(— SLOWLY) SPELL
(— SYSTEMATICALLY) FREQUENT
(— WITH PROFOUND ATTENTION)
PORE STUDY
READER PURSE DIPPER LECTOR
LISTER MAFTIR GRANTHI PISTLER
DEVOURER
(CHILD'S —) TENPENNY

(CHURCH —) LECTOR ANAGNOST
(PUBLIC —) PRELECTOR
(VORACIOUS —) BIBLIOPHAGIST
(PL.) FOLLOWING
READILY PAT LIEF YERN APTLY PREST
YERNE EASILY GAINLY PROBABLY
SPEEDILY
READINESS ART EASE GIFT PRESS
SKILL BELIEF GRAITH ADDRESS
FLUENCY FREEDOM ALACRITY
FACILITY GOODWILL
(— TO LEARN) APTITUDE
(IN —) APOISE AGAINST
READING KRI QRE QRI KERE KERI
QERI KTHIB KETHIB LESSON LECTION
LECTURE PERUSAL SETTING
CORALENE
(— ANTIPHONALLY) ALTERNATION
(DOCTOR'S —) EEG EKG
(HEAVY —) TOME
(MARGINAL —) KRI
(PL.) PROCINCT
READING DESK AMBO LECTERN
READING ROOM ATHENEUM
READJUST MEND ADVANCE
(— TYPE) OVERRUN
READY UP APT BUN FIT RAD YAP
BAAN BAIN BOON BOUN BOWN FREE
GIRT GLIB GNIB RIFE RIPE TALL YARE
APERT EAGER FRACK HANDY HAPPY
ONTAP PREDY PREST PRIME QUICK
SWIFT THERE TIGHT ADROIT APPERT
FACILE GRAITH HEARTY PROMPT
PREPARE PRESENT RENABLE
WILLING CHEERFUL DEXTROUS
HANDSOME PREGNANT PREPARED
PROVIDED SKILLFUL
(— A COMPUTER) BOOT
(— FOR ACTION) ARM EXPEDITE
(— TO GO) ALLSET
(— WITH WORDS) FLUENT
(MAKE —) PREP
(NOT —) SET BOUND GROOM
FORWARD DISPOSED IMPROMPT
INCLINED
READY-MADE SALE STORE BOUGHT
REAGENT ETCHANT REACTOR
TITRANT ALTERANT REACTIVE
NINHYDRIN
REAIA (FATHER OF —) MICAH
REAL BODY FAIR GOOD LEAL LEVY
PURE RIAL TRUE VERY VRAI PAKKA
PUCKA PUKKA RIGHT ROYAL SOLID
SOOTH ACTUAL DINKUM ENTIRE
HONEST THINGY CORDIAL GENUINE
GRADELY SINCERE THINGAL
CONCRETE DEFINITE EXISTENT
GRAITHLY POSITIVE THINGISH
UNFEIGNED VERITABLE
(EXTERNALLY —) TANGIBLE
(HALF —) PICAYUNE
(NOT —) FACTITIOUS INSUBSTANTIAL
(1-8TH —) TLAC TLACO

REALGAR ARSENIC ROSAKER ZARNICH SANDARAC

REALISM VERITE VERITY REALITY LITERALISM NATURALISM

REALISTIC HARD SOBER VIVID EARTHLY LIFELIKE PROBABLE

REALITY FEAT TRUE BEING SOOTH THING TRUTH ACTUAL DASEIN EFFECT VERITY EARNEST SUBJECT IDENTITY OVERSOUL POSITIVE REALNESS TRUENESS
(LIMITED —) SOMEWHAT
(ULTIMATE —) GOD SOURCE DIVINITY SUBSTANCE
(PL.) REALIA

REALIZATION PASS SENSE CRUSHER FRUITION AWAKENING

REALIZE GET EARN GAIN KNOW FETCH LEARN SENSE EFFECT FULFIL ACQUIRE CONCEIVE RECOGNIZE
(— BEFOREHAND) ANTICIPATE

REALIZED BODILY
(FULLY —) COMPLETE

REALLY ARU WIS ARAH HALF JUST ARRAH TRULY WISHA FINELY INDEED SIMPLY SURELY VERILY ACTUALLY
(NOT —) ILL ALMOST

REALM AREA LAND SOIL BOURN CLIME RANGE REIGN REWME RICHE BOURNE CIRCLE DEMAIN EMPIRE HEAVEN REALTY REGION SPHERE DEMESNE GAELDOM KINGDOM NOTALIA ROYALME TERRENE CLUBLAND DEVILDOM DOMINION ELDORADO GHOSTDOM ELYSYIUM NOTOGAEA
(— OF DARKNESS) PO
(— OF FABULOUS RICHNESS) ELDORADO
(— OF THOR) THRUTHHEIM THRUTHVANG
(MARINE —) NOTALIA TROPICALIA
(VISIONARY —) CLOUDLAND
(ZOOLOGICAL —) NOTOGAEA
(SUFF.) DOM
(OF ANIMAL LIFE) ALIA

REALTY FEALTY REAUTE ROYALTY

REAM FOAM RIME SEED SKIM CHEAT CREAM FROTH FRAISE RHYMER STRETCH
(PL.) INSIDES OUTSIDES

REAMER BUR BURR SPUD DRIFT RIMER BROACH CHERRY FRAISE RANCER RHYMER RIMMER WIDENER

REANIMATE WAKE RENEW REVIVE RECREATE

REANIMATED AWAKE

REAP BAG CUT REP CROP RIPE GLEAN SHEAR GARNER GATHER SICKLE HARVEST

REAPER LORD COCKER TASKER WINNER CRADLER SHEARER SICKLER
(GRIM —) DEATH

REAPING HOOK SICKLE TWIBIL CROTCHET

REAPPEARANCE RENTREF EMERSION

REAR AFT BACK BUNT HIND HINT JUMP LIFT STEN TOSS BREED BUILD CARVE ERECT JUNCH STEND ACHTER AROUSE CRADLE FOSTER NURSLE SUCKLE APPREAR ARRIERE EDUCATE ELEVATE NOURISH NURTURE UPBRING BUTTOCKS HINDMOST REARWARD
(— CAREFULLY) TIDDLE
(NEARER THE —) AFTER
(TO THE —) BACK BEHIND
(TO THE — OF) ABAFT

REARED (— BY HAND) CADE
(DELICATELY —) SOYLED

REARHORSE MANTIS

REARING CABRE FRESNE PESADE FORCENE RAMPANT
(— UP) STEND

REARRANGE DO ALTER AMEND ADJUST JIGGER REORDER READJUST

REARRANGEMENT WAGNER DIAGENESIS

REARWARD AFT BACKWARD

REASON PEG WAY HOTI NOUS REDF SAKE TALK ARGUE CAUSE COLOR COUNT LOGOS PROOF RATIO SCORE SENSE SKILL THING THINK TOPIC EXCUSE GROUND MANNER MATTER MOTION NOESIS ACCOUNT PREMISE QUARREL SUBJECT TUITION ARGUMENT ENCHESON LOGICIZE VERNUNFT
(— AGAINST) OBJECTION
(— FALSELY) PARALOGIZE
(— FOR PRIDE) BOAST
(LACKING —) INEPT
(SUFFICIENT —) GROUND
(PREF.) RATI

REASONABLE FAIR JUST SANE SOBER NATURAL SKILFUL FEASIBLE MODERATE RATIONAL SENSIBLE

REASONABLENESS EPIKY EPIKIA FITNESS FAIRNESS SOBRIETY

REASONABLY SOON

REASONER (FALLACIOUS —) SOPHIST

REASONING LOGIC THOUGHT ERGOTISM RATIONAL
(CLUMSY —) ARGAL
(DEDUCTIVE —) SYLLOGISM
(FALLACIOUS —) CIRCLE SOPHISTRY PARALOGISM

REASSEMBLE RELY

REASSEMBLY RALLY

REASSUME REVOKE REPRISE

REAVE ROB REFE SEIZE SPLIT REMOVE DESPOIL PILLAGE PLUNDER UNRAVEL

REB RABBI REBEL MISTER

REBAB GUSLE

REBATE BLUNT CHECK LESSEN
REFUND RIBBET DIMINISH DISCOUNT
DRAWBACK KICKBACK
REBEC LYRE SAROD RIBIBE RUBIBLE
REBECCA (AUTHOR OF —)
DUMAURIER
(CHARACTER IN —) JACK BAKER
FRANK GILES MAXIM FAVELL JULYAN
CRAWLEY DANVERS BEATRICE
DEWINTER
(FATHER OF —) ISAAC
REBEKAH (BROTHER OF —) LABAN
(FATHER OF —) BETHUEL
(HUSBAND OF —) ISAAC
(SON OF —) ESAU JACOB
REBEL REB DEFY KICK RISE TURN
ARISE BRAND FAUVE ANARCH
CROPPY MUTINE REVOLT FRONDEUR
SOLECIST MALCONTENT
(— IN ART) FAUVE
(RELIGIOUS —) APOSTATE
(PL.) REBELDOM
REBELLION MUTINY PUTSCH
REVOLT MISRULE UPRISING
REBELLIOUS RUSTY ANARCHIC
MUTINOUS AUDACIOUS INSURGENT
REBIRTH REVIVAL
(SPIRITUAL —) REGENERATION
REBOANT AROAR
REBORN REDIVIVUS
REBOUND DAP HOP HANG KISS
STOT CANON CAROM STITE BOUNCE
CANNON CARROM RECOIL RESILE
RESULT BRICOLE REDOUND
RICOCHET SNAPBACK
(— ERRATICALLY) KICK
REBOUND CLIP RETAINER
REBUFF NO SLAP SNIB SNUB CHECK
FLING NOSER REPEL DEFEAT DENIAL
REBUKE REBUTE REFUTE REPULSE
SETDOWN
REBUILD MEND
REBUKE NIP WIG BAWL RATE REDD
SNEB SNIB SNUB TRIM BARGE
BLAME CHECK CHIDE DRESS SAUCE
SCOLD SNAPE SNEAP TOUCH
DIRDUM GANSEL LESSON PULLUP
RATING RATTLE REHETE REMORD
THREAP CENSURE CHIDING CORRECT
HOTFOOT LECTURE REPROOF
REPROVE SARCASM TICKOFF
BLESSING BUSINESS CHASTISE
KEELHAUL REPROACH SCORCHER
THREAPEN UNDERNIM CASTIGATE
REBUS BADGE ENIGMA PUZZLE
RIDDLE
REBUT REPEL RECOIL REFUTE
REPULSE RETREAT DISPROVE
RECALCITRANT UNRULY RENITENT
OBSTINATE RESISTANT
RECALL CITE BRING UNSAY REMAND
REMIND RETURN REVOKE UNLOOK
BETHINK RECLAIM RETRACE

RETRACT REVIVAL UNSHOUT
REMEMBER WITHCALL WITHDRAW
REPRODUCE
(— FONDLY) CHERISH
(— FROM BANISHMENT) REPEAL
(— OF PURSUERS) RETREAT
RECANT UNSAY ABJURE REVOKE
UNSING DISAVOW RETRACT
SWALLOW PALINODE RENOUNCE
RECANTATION PALINODE
RECAPITULATE SUM UNITE RECITE
REPEAT RECOUNT RESTATE
REHEARSE REITERATE SUMMARIZE
RECAPITULATION EPANODOS
RECAPTURE RETAKE RECOVER
REPRISAL
RECASTING (— OF LITERARY WORK)
RIFACIMENTO
RECEDE DIE EBB BACK FADE STEP
VARY RECUR DEPART DIFFER RETIRE
SHRINK DECLINE DIGRESS RETREAT
CONTRACT DIMINISH ELONGATE
WITHDRAW
RECEIPT CHIT RECU RESET APOCHA
BINDER RECIPE WARRANT
(PL.) GATE TAKE SALES INCOME
ENTRADA
RECEIPTS GATE TAKE
RECEIVE GET BEAR FALL GAIN HAVE
HOLD TAKE ADMIT AFONG CATCH
GREET GUEST LATCH RESET ACCEPT
ASSUME BORROW DERIVE GATHER
HARBOR RECULE BELIEVE CONTAIN
EMBRACE INHERIT SUSTAIN
UNDERFO PERCEIVE
(— A CRIMINAL) RESET
(— A DEGREE) GRADUATE
(— AS GUEST) FANG HOST VANG
GREET
(— AS MEMBER) INCEPT
(— AS REWARD) REAP
(— FROM LOTTERY) DRAW
(— INTO RELIGIOUS ORDER) PROFESS
(— PAYMENT) COLLECT
(— SHEETS) FLY
(— STOLEN GOODS) RESET
(— WITH KINDNESS) WELCOME
(— WITH PLEASURE) GRATIFY
(PREF.) RECIPIO
RECEIVER DONEE FENCE PHONE
PERNOR SINDICO CYMAPHEN
DONATARY REHEATER
(— IN BANKRUPTCY) SINDICO
(— OF INCOME) PERNOR
(— OF PROPERTY) ALIENEE
(— OF STOLEN GOODS) LOCK FENCE
(RADIO —) SET
(SECRET —) TAP
(TELEGRAPH —) INKER INKWRITER
(TELEPHONE —) PHONE CYMAPHEN
RECEIVING PERNANCY
RECENSION REVIEW SURVEY
CENSURE CRITIQUE

RECENT HOT NEW LATE PUNY
ENDER FRESH GREEN HOURLY
LATELY LATTER MODERN CURRENT
HOLOCENE NEOTERIC
(MOST —) LAST
(PREF.) CAEN(O) CEN(O) NE(O)
RECENTLY ANEW JUST LATE NEWLY
LASTLY LATELY FRESHLY LATTERLY
RECENTNESS YOUTH
RECEPTACLE ARK BIN BOX CAN CUP
DIP FAT PAN TIN TUB URN VAT BATH
BOAT BOWL CASE CELL CIST DOVE
DROP FACK FONT HELL HOLD INRO
LOOM RACK RECU SAFE SINK TIDY
TOUR ARBOR CARRY CREEL KIOSK
KITTY RESET SCOOP STEAN STEEN
TABLE TORUS BASKET BUCKET
BUTLER CARTON CUPULE DIPPER
DRAWER HAMPER HOPPER MORTAR
PITCHI POCKET SHRINE TABLET
TROUGH ASHTRAY CAPSULE
CARRIER CORBULA DUSTBIN
ENVELOP HEADBOX LATRINE
OMNIBUS OSSUARY PARISON
RECEIPT SANDBOX SETTLER
SOAPBOX STOWAGE TRAVOIS
BURSICLE CANISTER CESSPOOL
DUMPSTER FOREBOOT GYNOBASE
HONEYPOT LOCKFAST OSSARIUM
OVERFLOW PERFUMER SPITTOON
STOCKPOT SEPULCHER
(— FOR ABANDONED INFANTS) TOUR
(— FOR BONES) OSSUARY OSSARIUM
(— FOR BROKEN TYPE) HELL
(— FOR BUTTER) RUSKIN
(— FOR COAL) BUNKER
(— FOR CONVEYING) APRON
(— FOR DRY ARTICLES) FAT
(FOR FOUL THINGS) SINK
(— FOR GLASS BATCH) ARBOR
(— FOR HOLY WATER) FONT
(— FOR ORE-CRUSHING) MORTAR
(— FOR POKER CHIPS) KITTY
(— FOR SACRED RELICS) TABLE
SHRINE TABLET SEPULCHRE
(— FOR SAVINGS) SOCK
(— FOR SEWING MATERIALS) TIDY
(— FOR TREASURE) HANAPER
(— FOR TYPE CASES) RACK
(— FOR VOTES) SITULA
(— IN BOTTLE-MAKING MACHINE)
PARISON
(— OF CLAY OR STONE) STEAN STEEN
(— OF FLOWER) THALAMUS
(— ON WEIGHING SCALES) PAN
(— OVER ALTAR) DOVE
(CLAY —) BOOT
(DILATED —) GYNOBASE
(ELECTRICAL —) BASEPLUG
(INCENSE —) ACERRA
(OPEN —) TRAY
(PURSELIKE —) BURSICLE
(TAILOR'S —) HELL

(TRASH —) DUMPSTER
(WOODEN —) SEBILLA
RECEPTION TEA ROUT COURT
CRUSH DIFFA LEVEE SALON TREAT
ACCOIL DURBAR RUELLE SOIREE
SQUASH ACCUEIL COUCHEE
MATINEE OVATION PASSAGE
RECEIPT RECUEIL TEMPEST
WELCOME ASSEMBLY FUNCTION
GREETING PERNANCY REACTION
SOCIABLE ACCEPTANCE RECIPIENCE
RECIPIENCY
(— AT BEDTIME) COUCHEE
(— OF NATIVE PRINCES) DURBAR
(— OF SOUND) AUDIO
(ARABIC —) DIFFA
(CORDIAL —) WELCOME
(CROWDED —) SQUASH
(FASHIONABLE —) LEVEE SALON
(MORNING —) LEVEE RUELLE
(WEDDING —) INFARE
RECEPTIVE OPEN SENSORY
OPENHANDED
RECEPTOR STOCK RECEIVER
DOMINATOR
RECERCELEE SARCELLY
RECESS ALA ARK BAY BOX COD CUP
PAN BOLE BUNK COVE DEEP HOLE
NOOK TRAP AMBRY BOSOM BOWER
CANAL CAVUM CLEFT CREEK HAVEN
HITCH INI FT NICHE ORIEL PRESS
SINUS ALCOVE ANCONA CAVERN
CENTER CHAPEL CIRQUE CLOSET
COFFER CRANNY EXEDRA GROTTO
INDENT LOCULE RABBET REBATE
BEDSITE CONCAVE CREVICE
LOCULUS MANHOLE RETREAT
SINKING INTERVAL LOCKHOLE
OVERTURE TABLINUM TOKONOMA
TRAVERSE VACATION PIGEONHOLE
(— BETWEEN CAPES) BAY
(— FOR FAMILY RECORDS) TABLINUM
(— FOR HINGE LEAF) PAN
(— FOR PIECE OF SCULPTURE)
ANCONA
(— FOR URN) LOCULUS
(— IN CHURCH) APSE
(— IN CHURCH WALL) AMBRY
AWMRY AUMBRY AUMERY AWMRIE
(— IN COLON) HAUSTRUM
(— IN JAPANESE HOUSE) TOKONOMA
(— IN MOUNTAIN) CIRQUE
(— IN ROCK) HITCH
(— IN SIDE OF HILL) CORRIE
(— IN SIDE OF ROOM) ALA
(— IN WALL) BOLE NICHE ALCOVE
(— ON STAGE) CANOPY
(INMOST —) BOSOM
(PL.) FLASH
RECESSED SUNK SUNKEN
RECESSION BUST RETREAT
RECESSIVE BACKWARD RECEDING
RETIRING WITHDRAWN

RECHAB (SON OF —) MALCHIAH JEHONADAB

RECHERCHE RARE CHOICE EXOTIC CURIOUS PRECIOUS UNCOMMON EXQUISITE

RECIDIVIST REPEATER

RECIPE RX FORM RULE FORMULA RECEIPT

RECIPIENT HEIR DONEE ALMSMAN DONATEE DONATORY LAUREATE

RECIPROCAL CROSS COMMON MUTUAL SECANT SEESAW
(— OF A POISE) RHE
(— OF RADIUS) CURVATURE
(— OF VISCOSITY) FLUIDITY
(PREF.) COUNTER INTER

RECIPROCATE REPAY RETURN REQUITE RETROACT

RECIPROCITY SHU ISOPOLITY MUTUALITY

RECITAL TALE ASHRE CITAL RECIT STORY EXPOSE LITANY PARADE REPEAT TIKKUN READING RELATION REPETITION
(— OF PRAYER) GEULAH HAMOTZI KEDUSHAH
(UNTRUE —) TALE
(SUFF.) LOG(ER)(IA)(IAN)(IC)(ICAL) (IST)(UE)(Y)

RECITATION DHIKR READING RECITAL RHAPSODY

RECITATIVE SCENA CHANSON PARLANDO

RECITE SAY CARP TELL STATE INTONE RECKON RELATE RENDER REPEAT DECLAIM DECLINE DICTATE NARRATE RECOUNT REELOFF REHEARSE
(— AS ELOCUTION EXERCISE) DECLAIM
(— IN MONOTONE) INTONE
(— METRICALLY) SCAN
(— MONOTONOUSLY) CHANT CHAUNT
(— NUMBERS) COUNT
(— PRAYERS) BENSH DAVEN
(— TIRESOMELY) THRUM
(— WITH GREAT EASE) RUSH

RECITER SCALD SKALD ANTERI DISEUR CONTEUR DISEUSE HOMERIST ILIADIST RHAPSODE

RECITING CHARM

RECK RAK CARE DEEM PASS MATTER REGARD CONCERN CONSIDER ESTIMATE

RECKLESS RASH WILD BLIND FOLLE PERDU MADCAP RACKLE SAVAGE GALLOWS RAMSTAM CARELESS HEADLONG HEEDLESS TEARAWAY BLINDFOLD TEMERARIOUS DEVILMAYCARE

RECKLESSLY FAST BLIND RAMSTAM HEADLONG HEADFIRST

RECKLESSNESS BAYARD

RECKON RET ARET CAST DATE ITEM RATE RECK RELY TALE TELL TOTE ALLOT AUDIT CLAIM CLASS COUNT JUDGE PLACE RETTE SCORE TALLY THINK ASSIGN FIGURE IMPUTE NUMBER REPUTE TOTTLE ACCOUNT ASCRIBE COMPUTE INCLUDE PRETEND RECOUNT SUPPOSE SUPPUTE CONSIDER ESTIMATE
(— IN) INCLUDE
(— TOO HIGH) OVERCOUNT

RECKONING TAB BILL NICK POST SHOT TAIL TALE COUNT SCORE TALLY COMPOT LAWING REASON TAILYE TOTTLE ACCOUNT DAYTALE TAILZEE COMPUTUS
(TAVERN —) LAWING

RECLAIM IN TAME ADEEM ASSART OBJECT RECALL REDEEM REFORM RESCUE SUBDUE PROTEST RECOVER RESTORE
(— FOR AGRICULTURE) ASSART
(— FROM SAVAGE STATE) CIVILIZE

RECLAIMANT GOEL

RECLAME FAME

RECLINE LIE LIG LEAN LOLL REST COUCH ACCUMB RECUMB UPLEAN DISCUMB
(— AWKWARDLY) SPRAWL SPRADDLE
(— LANGUIDLY) GAULSH

RECLINING CUMBENT ACCUMBENT RECUMBENT ACCUBATION
(— ON COUCH) ACCUMBENT

RECLUSE NUN MONK CULDEE HERMIT REMOTE ASCETIC EREMITE INCLUSA INCLUSE ANCHORET INCLUSUS SECLUDED SOLITARY SCIOPHYTE SOLITAIRE
(BROWN —) SPIDER
(PL.) SECLUSE

RECLUSIVE HERMETIC

RECOGNITION FAME SPUR HONOR SENSE CREDIT STATUS FEELING KENNING KNOWING AGNITION SANCTION ANAGNOSIS
(— OF ACHIEVEMENT) LAUREL CITATION
(— OF ERROR) RESIPISCENCE
(HONORIFIC —) DISTINCTION
(SUFF.) GNOSIA GNOSIS GNOSTIC GNOSY

RECOGNIZE KEN SEE WIT ESPY FACE KNOW SPOT TELL ADMIT ALLOW BLINK CROWN HONOR KEETH KITHE KYTHE ACCEPT ACKNOW AGNIZE BEKNOW COUTHE REVISE CORRECT DISCERN REALIZE ACCREDIT
(— IN ANY CAPACITY) AGNIZE

RECOGNIZED GOOD CLEAR KNOWN CLASSIC FAMILIAR

RECOIL SHY BALK KICK TURN REBUT SHRUG SHUCK START STRAM

BLENCH BOUNCE FLINCH RECULE
RESILE RESULT RETORT SHRINK
REBOUND REDOUND REVERSE
BACKLASH REJOUNCE
(WITHOUT —) DEADBEAT
RECOLLECT RECALL RECORD
RETAIN BETHINK COMPOSE RECOVER
RECOLETO REMEMBER
RECOLLECTION MIND MEMORY
RECALL RECORD MINDING THOUGHT
MEMORIAL SOUVENIR ANAMNESIS
RECOMMENCE RENEW REOPEN
RESUME REPRISE
RECOMMEND MOVE OSSE PLUG
TOUT WISH ADVISE COMMIT PRAISE
PREFER COMMEND CONSIGN
COUNSEL ENTRUST ADVOCATE
RECOMMIT
RECOMMENDATION NAP CHIT
VŒU ADVISE COUNSEL TESTIMONY
(PARTY —) COUPON
(SERVANT'S —) CHIT
RECOMPENSE PAY MEED MEND
ATONE MENEE QUITS REPAY YIELD
AMENDS BOUNTY HADBOT RECOUP
REWARD SALARY GUERDON
IMBURSE PAYMENT PREMIUM
REQUITE RESTORE SATISFY SERVICE
RECONCILE GREE WEAN ADAPT
AGREE ATONE ACCORD ADJUST
SETTLE SHRIVE REUNITE HARMONIZE
RECONCILED FAIN VAIN SAUGHT
RECONCILIATION ATONE ACCORD
SAUGHT REUNION IRENICON
(— OF BELIEFS) SYNCRETISM
RECONDITE DARK DEEP HIGH
HIDDEN MYSTIC OCCULT SECRET
CRYPTIC CURIOUS OBSCURE RETINED
ABSTRACT ADSTRUSE ESOTERIC
RECONNAISSANCE RECCE RECCO
RECCY RECON SURVEY
RECONNOITER CASE SCOUT
RECALL SURVEY EXAMINE PICKEER
DISCOVER REMEMBER
RECONSIDER REVIEW FORTHINK
RECONSTRUCT RECAST REPAIR
REEVOKE REMODEL RESTORE
RECORD CAN CUT BOOK CARD DATE
DISC ITER MARK NICK PAGE ROLL
SING SLIP TAPE WICK ALBUM CHART
DIARY ENACT ENTER ENTRY FASTI
GRAPH JUMBO PRICK QUIPO QUIPU
SCORE SIJIL SLATE STYLE TITLE
WRITE ANNALS CHARGE DOCKET
LEGEND MEMOIR SCROLL SPREAD
WARBLE ACCOUNT CALENDS
CAPTURE CITATOR DUBBING
KALENDS LEXICON MENTION
MYOGRAM SHOWING TICKLER
TRACING ANAGRAPH ARCHIVES
CYLINDER ENTRANCE ERGOGRAM
HERDBOOK INSCROLL JUDGMENT
KYMOGRAM LAUEGRAM MARIGRAM

MELOGRAM MEMORIAL MEMORIZE
MONUMENT NOCTUARY
ONDOGRAM PANCHART PRESSING
REGISTER REMEMBER SCHEDULE
STUDBOOK INSCRIPTION
OBSERVATION OSCILLOGRAM
(— BY NOTCHES) SCORE
(— OF CAR MOVEMENTS) JUMBO
(— OF DOCUMENT) PROTOCOL
(— OF EVENTS) FASTI
(— OF FOOTPRINTS) STIBOGRAM
(— OF HUMANITY'S FATE) SIJIL SIJILL
(— OF JOURNEY) JOURNAL ITINERARY
(— OF LOAN) CHARGE
(— OF MUHAMMAD'S SAYINGS)
HADIT
(— OF MUSCULAR WORK) ERGOGRAM
(— OF PROCEEDINGS) ACTA ITER
JOURNAL MINUTES
(COMPUTER —) PRINTOUT
(COURT —) EYRE
(DAILY —) DIARY
(DEMONSTRATION —) DEMO
(FORMAL —) ACT
(HISTORICAL —) STORY
(MAGNETIC —) DISK FLOPPY
(PERSONAL —) BIO VITA RESUME
DOSSIER
(PHONOGRAPH —) DISC DISK MONO
SINGLE BISCUIT SHELLAC
(PLASTIC MAGNETIC —) DISK
(SHIP'S —) LOG
(TYPE OF —) CD HIFI MONO STEREO
MONAURAL
(PL.) LIBER ANNALS ARCHIVE
MEMORABILIA
(PREF.) DISC(I)(O)
(SUFF.) GRAM GRAPH(ER)(IA)(IC)(Y)
RECORDED TAPE TAPED ONTAPE
RECORDER VCR FLUTE BOOKER
FLAUTO NOTATOR GREFFIER
REGISTER FIPPLEFLUTE
(— AND CAMERA) PORTAFAX
PORTAPACK
(VIDEOTAPE —) VCR
RECORDING ALBUM ALIVE LABEL
VIDEO CUTTING VIDEODISC
VIDEODISK
(— AWARD) GRAMMY
(NARRATION —) VOICEOVER
(TELEVISION —) VIDEOTAPE
RECOUNT MING TELL COUNT
DEVISE RECITE REGARD RELATE
REPEAT SPREAD EXPRESS HISTORY
ITERATE NARRATE CONSIDER
DESCRIBE REHEARSE REITERATE
RECOUP DEDUCT REGAIN RECOVER
INDEMNIFY
RECOUPLING HOOKUP
RECOURSE SUIT ACCESS APPEAL
REFUGE RESORT STRING REGRESS
RESTAUR RISORSE
(HAVE —) RECUR

RECOVER DOW COUR COWR CURE FIRM HEAL KERE COVER RALLY REACH UPSET BOUNCE RECURE REGAIN RESCUE RESUME RETAKE RETIRE REVERT REVOKE WARISH DELIVER OVERGET OVERPUT OVERSET READEPT RECLAIM RECRUIT REPAREL REPRISE RESTORE RETRIEVE SNAPBACK
(**— LOST TERRITORY**) REVENDICATE
RECOVERER DIGESTER
RECOVERY CURE RECOUR RECURE REMEDY RETURN SALVAGE COMEBACK SNAPBACK RECLAMATION
(**— OF METAL**) CUPELLATION
(**— PERIOD**) REHAB
(**FORCIBLE —**) RESCUE
RECREANT FALSE CRAVEN YELLOW APOSTATE COWARDLY DESERTER RECRAYED
RECREATE AMUSE EVOKE REVIVE
RECREATION PLAY SPORT SOLACE RENEWAL ACTIVITY DIVERSION PALINGENY
(**PERIOD OF —**) HOLIDAY VACATION
RECREATIONAL AMUSIVE
RECREATIVE PLAYING
RECREMENT SLAG DROSS SCORIA
RECRUIT BLEU BOOT FRESH RAISE SPROG GATHER INTAKE MUSTER RECREW REPAIR REVIVE RECOVER REFRESH RESTORE ASSEMBLE BEZONIAN CONSCRIPT
(**RAW —**) ROOKY ROOKIE
RECTAL
(PREF.) ARCHO
RECTANGLE BOX SQUARE CHECKER
(**COTTON —**) HUIPIL
(**CURVILINEAR —**) TESSERA
(**EQUILATORAL —**) SQUARE
(**WOVEN —**) SINKER
RECTANGULAR OBLONG SQUARE BOXLIKE EMERALD
RECTIFICATION REFORM LIMATION
RECTIFIER DIODE VALVE COLUMN DETECTOR EXCITRON
RECTIFY AMEND EMEND RIGHT ADJUST BETTER DETECT REFORM REMEDY CORRECT IMPROVE REDRESS EMENDATE REGULATE
RECTITUDE DOOM EQUITY JUSTICE PROBITY
RECTOR RULER LEADER PARSON PERSONA INCUMBENT
RECTUM SIEGE TEWEL
(PREF.) ARCHO PROCT(O) RECTO
RECUMBENT IDLE PRONE JACENT CUMBENT LEANING RESTING INACTIVE REPOSING
RECUPERATE MEND RALLY REFETE REGAIN RECOVER RECRUIT RETRIEVE

RECUR ACTUP CYCLE REFER REPEAT RESORT RETURN REOCCUR REVOLVE REAPPEAR
(**— CONSTANTLY**) HAUNT
RECURRENCE RESORT RETURN ATAVISM REPRISE ITERANCE ITERANCY RECOURSE FLASHBACK
(**— OF SOUND**) CADENCE
(**REGULAR —**) RHYTHM
(SUFF.) LY
RECURRENT CYCLIC FREQUENT PERENNIAL
RECURRING ROLLING CONTINUAL
(**— ANNUALLY**) ETESIAN
(**— EVERY THIRD DAY**) TERTIAN
(**— EVERY 72 HOURS**) QUARTAN
(**— ON NINTH DAY**) NONAN NONANE
(**— ON SEVENTH DAY**) SEPTAN
(**CONSTANTLY —**) ETERNAL
(**CONTINUALLY —**) CONSTANT
(SUFF.) ENNIAL
RECURVED REFLEX ERICOID
RECUTTING FRESHING
RED (ALSO SEE COLOR) GOYA GULY PINK PUCE ROJO ROSY RUBY ANGRY CANNA CORAL FIERY JUDAS ROUGE RUDDY RUFUS ARCHIL AZALEA BLOODY CERISE FLORID FULGID GARNET HECTIC NECTAR ORCHIL ORIENT RAISIN RUBRIC TITIAN TRYPAN VERMIL WANTON CARMINE GLOWING NACARAT PIMENTO RADICAL RUBELLE RUBIOUS STAMMEL VERMILY ARMENIAN AUBUSSON BORDEAUX CARDINAL CHOLERIC COLORADO FLAGRANT MANDARIN MOROCAIN RUBICUND SANGUINE ARTILLERY RUBINEOUS COQUELICOT SANGDEBOEUF
(**— AND INFLAMED**) BLOODSHOT
(**— PLANET**) MARS
(**ANTIQUE —**) CANNA
(**BRICK —**) TESTACEOUS
(**BRIGHT —**) TULY CHERRY PUNICIAL VERMILION
(**BRILLIANTLY —**) FLAMING
(**DARK —**) CLARET
(**EUREKA —**) PUCE
(**FIERY —**) MINIUM
(**GRAYISH —**) AZALEA
(**HERALDIC —**) GULES
(**IRON OXIDE —**) AGATE TARRAGONA
(**ORANGE —**) NACARAT
(**PURPLISH —**) LAKE MURREY MAGENTA
(**SEE —**) GETMAD
(**WAX —**) COPPER
(**YELLOWISH —**) MAROON
(PREF.) ERYTHR(O) PHENIC(O) PHOENIC(O) PYRRH(O) PYRRO RHOD(O) RUBE RUBI RUBO RUBRI RUBRO RUFI RUFO
REDACT EDIT

RED ADMIRAL VANESSA
**RED AND THE BLACK (AUTHOR OF
—)** STENDHAL
  (CHARACTER IN —) SOREL FOUQUE
  JULIEN PIRARD DERENAL VALENOD
  MATHILDE
RED-BACKED SHRIKE POPE
**RED BADGE OF COURAGE
  (AUTHOR OF —)** CRANE
  (CHARACTER IN —) JIM HENRY
  WILSON CONKLIN FLEMING
RED BANEBERRY REDBERRY
  TOADROOT
RED BAY PERSEA
RED-BELLIED (— TERRAPIN) SLIDER
  SKILPOT
  (— WOODPECKER) CHAB
REDBREAST ROBIN RUDDOCK
RED-BREASTED BREAM FLATFISH
  FLOUNDER
RED-BREASTED KNOT GRAYBACK
  GREYBACK
REDBUD CERCIS JUNEBUD
RED CAMPION ROBIN SOLDIER
RED CEDAR SAVIN SABINA
  JUNIPER
RED CLOVER SAPLING TREFOIL
  TRIFOLY
RED CURRANT GOYA RIZZLE TIZZAR
REDD RID COMB OPEN LITTER
  NEATEN REFUSE RESCUE SETTLE
  ARRANGE DELIVER SMARTEN
  UNBLOCK UNRAVEL
RED DEER OLEN SPAY STAG
  (FEMALE —) HIND
  (MALE —) HART STAG
REDDEN RUD FIRE RUBY BLUSH
  FLUSH LIGHT ROUGE RUDDY
  BLOODY RUBIFY RUBRIC RUDDLE
  EMPURPLE
REDDISH REDDY RUDDY RUFUS
  FLUSHY GINGER RUFOUS
  COLORADO PYRRHOUS RUBICUND
RED DOG BLITZ
RED DRUM SPOT REDFISH
REDEAR SHELLCRACKER
REDEEM BUY WIN SAVE ALESE
  CLEAR LOUSE REPRY BORROW
  OFFSET RANSOM DELIVER FULFILL
  JUSTIFY RECLAIM WITHBEG
  AGAINBUY LIBERATE
REDEEMER GOEL SAVIOR
REDEEMING SAVING
REDEMPTION RANSOM REFORM
  SAFETY SALVATION
REDEYE BASS RUDD VIREO
RED-EYE CATSUP CICADA WHISKY
REDEYE SUNFISH
RED-EYED VIREO REDEYE
  GRASSET PREACHER
RED-FACED FLUSHED SCARLET
REDFIN DACE SHINER REDHORSE
  YELLOWFIN

REDFISH SALMON FATHEAD
  ROSEFISH
RED GOOSEFOOT PIGWEED
  SOWBANE
RED GROUPER MERO NEGRE
  REDBELLY
RED GROUSE GORHEN GORCOCK
  LAGOPODE MOORBIRD MUIRFOWL
RED GUM JARRAH EUCALYPT
RED GURNARD CUR ELLECK
  ROCHET SOLDIER
RED-HAIRED RUFUS CARROTY
REDHEAD DIVER FINCH POCHARD
  CARROTTOP KIZILBASH
RED HIND GRAYSBY GROUPER
  CABRILLA
REDHORSE REDFIN SUCKER
REDIA SPOROSAC
REDIRECT DISPLACE READDRESS
REDISTILL COHOBATE
REDISTRIBUTE FRESHEN REASSIGN
RED LAVER SLOKE
REDNESS RED RUD GLOW HEAT
  RUDD RUBOR ERYTHEMA RUBEDITY
  (— OF NOSE) GROGBLOSSOM
  (— OF SKIN) EFFLORESCENCE
  (— OF SKY) AURORA
REDO REDACT RESTYLE
  (— UNSKILLFULLY) BOTCH
RED OCHER TIVER ABRAUM RUDDLE
REDOLENCE BALM AROMA SCENT
REDOLENT RICH ODOROUS
  SCENTED AROMATIC FRAGRANT
  SMELLING
RED OSIER WILLOW REDBRUSH
REDOUBLE REECHO INTENSIFY
REDOUBT FEAR MASK DREAD
  SCHANZ SCONCE BULWARK
REDOUND TURN ACCRUE BILLOW
  CONDUCE REFLECT OVERFLOW
RED RASPBERRY CUTHBERT
REDRESS HEAL DRESS REDUB RIGHT
  AVENGE OFFSET REFORM RELIEF
  REMEDE REMEDY REPAIR ADDRESS
  CORRECT RECTIFY REFOUND RELIEVE
RED ROCKFISH TAMBOR
REDROOT PIGWEED
RED ROVER (AUTHOR OF —)
  COOPER
  (CHARACTER IN —) ARK FID DICK
  HENRY AFRICA DELACY SCIPIO
  WILDER WYLLYS BIGNALL GRAYSON
  GERTRUDE RODERICK
RED SAGE LANTANA
RED SALMON SOCKEYE
RED SANDALWOOD CHANDAM
REDSHANK CLEE TEUK SHAKE
  GAMBET REDLEG YELPER PELLILE
  TATTLER
REDSKIN RED ROJO TAWNY INDIAN
REDSTART YELPER BRANTAIL
  FIRETAIL WHITECAP FIREFLIRT
RED STOPPER EUGENIA IRONWOOD

RED-TAILED (— HAWK) REDTAIL
(— TROPIC BIRD) KOAE
RED TAPE CHICHI
RED-TAPISM BEADLEDOM
RED-THROATED LOON WABBY
REDTOP COUCH FIORIN FINETOP
FINEBENT FURZETOP BLUEJOINT
REDUCE CUT BATE CLIP DOCK DROP
EASE PARE PULL THIN ABASE ABATE
ALLAY APPAL BREAK DRAFT ELIDE
LOWER QUELL SCANT SHAVE SLAKE
SLASH SMELT ATTRIT DEDUCE
DEFALK DEJECT DELETE DEPOSE
DILUTE HUMBLE LESSEN REBATE
REDUCT SHRINK SUBACT SUBDUE
WEAKEN ABANDON ABRIDGE
ASSUAGE ATOMIZE CHANCER
CONQUER CURTAIL DEFLATE
DEGRADE DEPLETE DWINDLE
ECLIPSE FRITTER INHIBIT RESOLVE
RETREAT SCISSOR SHORTEN
SUBJECT ABSTRACT ATTEMPER
CONDENSE DECREASE DIMINISH
DOWNSIZE MINIMIZE
(— ACCORDING TO FIXED RATIO)
SCALE
(— ANGLE) CHAMFER
(— BULK) BLEND
(— LUMBER) SIZE
(— PROFITS) SQUEEZE
(— PURITY) ALLOY
(— SAIL) REEF
(— STONE BLOCKS) SPALL SPAWL
(— THE VALUE) DECRY BEGGAR
DEPRAVE
(— TO A MEAN) AVERAGE
(— TO ASHES) CREMATE
(— TO CARBON) CHAR
(— TO FINE PARTICLES) ATOMIZE
MICRONIZE
(— TO FLAT SURFACE) LEVEL
(— TO INSIGNIFICANCE) DROWN
(— TO LOWER GRADE) BREAK
DEMOTE DEGRADE
(— TO NIL) CLOSE
(— TO NOTHING) ANNUL
(— TO PASSIVITY) CHINAFY
PROSTRATE
(— TO POWDER) GRIND PULVERIZE
(PREF.) DE
REDUCED SUNK TAIL BROKEN
SHRUNK CURTATE DWARFED
DEGRADED SHRUNKEN WEAKENED
VESTIGIAL
(— TO HELPLESSNESS) PROSTRATE
REDUCING (— EXERCISES)
SLIMNASTICS
REDUCTION BUST LETUP SLASH
CUTBACK CUTDOWN DOCKAGE
SHAVING ANALYSIS DILUTION
DISCOUNT DRAWDOWN ABATEMENT
SHRINKAGE

(— IN FORCE) RIF
(— IN PITCH) DROP
(— IN PRICE) SAVING CONCESSION
(— OF POWER) SHUTDOWN
(— OF THICKNESS) OFFSET
(— TO ABSURDITY) APAGOGUE
(PREF.) LY(O)
(SUFF.) LYSE LYSIS LYST LYTE LYTIC
LYZE
REDUNDANCY EXCESS NIMIETY
SURPLUS PLEONASM PLETHORA
VERBIAGE MACROLOGY TAUTOLOGY
REDUNDANT WORDY LAVISH
PROFUSE SURPLUS VERBOSE
SWELLING EXCESSIVE
REDWING POP THRUSH WINDLE
GADWALL WINNARD
REDWOOD MAD AMBOYNA
BARWOOD FURIOUS SEQUOIA
MAHOGANY
RE-ECHO REWORD REBOUND
RESOUND REDOUBLE
REED NAL RIE RIX SAG SAX BENT
JUNK MILL OBOE PIPE PIRN RODE
SLEY TULE ARROW DONAX SPEAR
TWILL BENNEL RADDLE SAGGON
BASSOON CALAMUS FISTULA
WHISTLE WINDING ABOMASUM
CLARINET
(— FOR WARPING) WRAITHE
(— FOR WINDING THREAD) PIRN
SPOOL
(— IN ORGAN) VIBRATOR
(— OF LOOM) COMB
(— OF MUSICAL INSTRUMENT)
TONGUE
(FOXTAIL —) DOD
(GIANT —) DONAX
(MUSICAL —) OAT
(WEAVER'S —) SLAY SLEY RADDLE
SLEIGH
(PL.) SPEAR
(PREF.) ARUNDI CALAM(I)(O)
REED BENT CARRIZO
REEDBIRD BOBOLINK
REEDBUCK BOHOR NAGOR REITBOK
REED BUNTING RINGBIRD
REED CANARY GRASS SPIRE
DAGGERS
REED END TONGUE
REEDING GADROON MILLING
STRIGIL GRAINING
REED MACE RAUPO CATTAIL
MATREED
REED ORGAN MELODEON
HARMONIUM
REED PIPE MIRLITON
REED WARBLER PITBIRD
REEDY THIN WEAK FRAIL TWILLED
REEF CAY KAY KEY CAYO LODE RYFT
SCAR VEIN ATOLL LEDGE SHELF
STICK BOILER REEFER SADDLE

SKERRY BAGREEF BALANCE
BIOHERM MAKATEA TOMBOLO

REEFER CAR COAT STICK JACKET
MUGGLES

REEK FOG FUG EMIT FUME HEAP
MIST PILE RICK RISE VENT EQUIP
EXUDE FETOR ISSUE NIDOR SMEEK
SMOKE STEAM VAPOR EXHALE
OUTFIT EMANATE
(— WITH CORRUPTION) FESTER

REEL PIRN RANT ROCK SPIN STOT
SWAB SWIM TURN GIDDY SPOOL
SWIFT TRULL WAVER WHEEL WHIRL
WINCE WINCH BOBBIN RECOIL
SWERVE TOTTER TUMULT WAGGLE
WALTER WELTER WINDER WINDLE
WINNLE WINTLE BALLOON STAGGER
SWABBLE TITUBATE
(— FOR DRAWING SILK) FILATURE
(— FOR WARP DRYING) BALLOON
(— FOR WINDING YARN) PIRN
SWIFT
(— OFF A STORY) SCRIEVE
(— USED FOR YARN) CRIB
(DYEING —) WINCE
(FISHING —) TROW TROLL TRULL
WINCH
(HIGHLAND —) HOOLICAN
HOOLACHAN
(PL.) REVELS

REELER TWINER

REELING TURN AREEL LURCH
FILATURE STAGGERY WAMBLING

REEM MOAN URUS UNICORN

REEVE REE REFE THREAD BAILIFF
PROVOST STEWARD OVERSEER

REFECTION MEAL RELIEF REPAST
HOGMANAY
(NEW YEAR'S —) HOGMANAY

REFECTORY FRATER FRATRY

REFER DEFER LEAVE POINT ADVERT
ALLUDE APPEAL ASSIGN CHARGE
COMMIT DELATE DIRECT IMPUTE
PREFER RELATE SUBMIT ASCRIBE
PERTAIN REJOURN RELEGATE
(— TO) SEE CITE INTEND CONCERN
CONSULT MENTION INTIMATE
(— TO SOMETHING REPEATEDLY)
HARP

REFEREE ZEBRA BREHON UMPIRE
ARBITER AUDITOR

REFERENCE TAB FOLIO REMIT SIGIL
APPEAL REGARD RENVOI BEARING
MEANING RESPECT ALLUSION
HANDBOOK INNUENDO RELATION
(— WORK) OED ATLAS INDEX ROGET
ALMANAC LEXICON CATALOGUE
GAZETTEER
(BRITISH — WORK) OED
(OBLIQUE —) SQUINT
(SATIRICAL —) GLANCE

REFERENDUM POLL MANDATE

REFINE RUN TRY BOLT EDIT FILE FINE
PURE CUPEL EXALT PLAIN SLICK
SMELT AFFINE DECOCT EXCOCT
FILTER GARBLE SMOOTH CONCOCT
ELEVATE PERFECT SUBLIME
SWEETEN CIVILIZE HUMANIZE
URBANIZE
(— AS GOLD) TEST CARAT
(— PULP) JORDAN
(— SUGAR) CLAY
(— WINE) FORCE

REFINED FINE GENT NEAT NICE TRIE
ATTIC EXACT PURED TERSE CHASTE
EXCOCT INLAND NIMINY POLITE
QUAINT SUBTLE URBANE CLEANLY
COURTLY ELEGANT GENTEEL
PRECISE SCRAPED AUGUSTAN
DELICATE ELEVATED HIGHBRED
POLISHED PRECIEUX PRECIOUS
SERAPHIC RECHERCHE
SOPHISTICATED
(AFFECTEDLY —) FOPPISH
(NOT —) CRUDE
(TOO —) FINESPUN

REFINEMENT COUTH GRACE TASTE
NICETY POLISH CULTURE FINESSE
DELICACY ELEGANCE POLITURE
SUBTLETY URBANITY PRECIOSITY

REFINER TRIER JORDAN SMELTER
PURIFIER

REFINERY SMELTER

REFINING HUMAN FINING CULTURE
AFFINAGE

REFINISH ANTIQUE

REFLECT COW CHEW MUSE PORE
SHOW BLAZE FLASH GLASS GLINT
IMAGE SHINE STUDY THINK ADVISE
DAZZLE DEBATE MIRROR PONDER
RECORD REFLEX RELUCE RETORT
RETURN REVISE STEVEN EXPRESS
PERPEND REDOUND REFRACT
SHIMMER COGITATE CONSIDER
MEDITATE REDOUBLE RUMINATE
(— IRREGULARLY) SCATTER
(— UPON) SPECULATE

REFLECTED DERIVED MIRRORED
SPECULAR

REFLECTING
(SUFF.) ESCENT

REFLECTION ECHO FOLD IDEA BKIT
BLAME GHOST GLARE GNOME
IMAGE DEBATE MUSING PONDER
REFLEX RETURN SHADOW CENSURE
COUNSEL SPECIES THOUGHT
EYESHINE MOONPATH THINKING
(— OF SELF IN ANOTHER'S EYES)
BABY

REFLECTIVE PENSIVE THOUGHTFUL
(— POWER) ALBEDO

REFLECTOR DISH FLAT CRITIC
HASTER SHINER TAMPER HORIZON
DIFFUSER HASTENER SPECULUM

REFLEX COPY IMAGE TROPISM
ALLUSION
(NOT —) IDEOMOTOR
REFLUX EBB EBBING REFLOW
REFOREST REBOISE
REFORM MEND AMEND EMEND
PRUNE BETTER REBUKE REPAIR
CENSURE CORRECT DISBAND
RECLAIM RECTIFY REDRESS
REFORMATORY COLLEGE
MAGDALEN
REFORMER MOTT APOSTLE
UTOPIAN UTOPIAST JANSENIST
(DANISH-AMERICAN —) RIIS
(GREAT SOCIAL —) RIIS
REFRACT DIVIDE REFLECT REFRINGE
REFRACTION REBATE REBOUND
DIACLASIS
REFRACTOR PRISM
REFRACTORY TOUGH SULLEN
UNRULY WANTON ALUNDUM
FROWARD MULLITE RESTIVE VICIOUS
WAYWARD MUTINOUS PERVERSE
STUBBORN CAMSTEERY REBELLIOUS
REFRAIN BOB TAG CURB DOWN
KEEP SHUN AVOID FORGO SPARE
WONDE BURDEN CHORUS DESIST
FOREGO LUDDEN RETAIN THRAIN
ABSTAIN FORBEAR LULLABY REFREIT
REPRISE TORNADA FABURDEN
FALDERAL OVERCOME OVERWORD
REPETEND RESTRAIN WITHDRAW
TURNAGAIN
(— FROM) CAN HELP AVOID SPARE
WAIVE FOREGO RESIGN ABSTAIN
(— FROM EXACTING) REMIT
(— FROM INDULGENCE) ABSTAIN
(— FROM TELLING) LAYNE
(— FROM USING) BOYCOTT
(— OF SONG) BOB TAG DOWN
FOOT WHEEL BURDEN CHORUS
FALDEROL
(EPODIC —) HEMISTICH
(MEANINGLESS —) DERRY DUCDAME
(RECURRING —) REPETEND
REFRESH FAN COOL REST CHEER
FRESH SLAKE CAUDLE REFECT
REFETE REGALE REHETE REPOSE
REVIVE UNTIRE COMFORT FORTIFY
FRESHEN QUICKEN RECRUIT
IRRIGATE RECREATE
REFRESHING DEWY BALMY CRISP
FRESH TONIC CALLER LIVING
BRACING COOLING REFRIGERANT
REFRESHMENT BAIT LUNCH
CHARITY NUNCHEON REFRESCO
COLLATION
(PL.) FOURS
REFRIGERANT ICE FREON COOLER
AMMONIA COOLING CRYOGEN
REFRIGERATE CHILL
REFRIGERATION CRYOGENY

REFRIGERATOR FRIG FRIDGE
ICEBOX FREEZER CONDENSER
(— CAR) REEFER
REFUEL TANK FILLUP
REFUGE ARK DIVE HOLT HOME
PORT ROCK SOIL BIELD GRITH
HAVEN OASIS RESET ASYLUM
BILBIE COVERT HARBOR REFUTE
RESORT SPITAL SUCCOR ALSATIA
CRANNOG RESERVE RETREAT
SHELTER UMBRAGE WARRANT
BOLTHOLE CRANNOGE FORTRESS
HIDEAWAY MAGDALEN RESOURCE
SAFEHOLD
(FORTIFIED —) STRONGHOLD
(LAST —) SHEETANCHOR
(PLACE OF —) LAIR
(TAKE —) HOLEUP
REFUGEE REFFO COWBOY FUIDHIR
FUGITIVE
REFULGENT BRIGHT SHINING
RELUCENT BRILLIANT
REFUND REPAY UPSET REBATE
REFOUND RESTORE DRAWBACK
KICKBACK
REFURBISH DUST RENEW REVAMP
FRESHEN BRIGHTEN RENOVATE
REFUSAL NAY VEE WARN WONT
DENIAL MITTEN NAYSAY REPULSE
ACCISMUS DECLINAL NEGATION
NEGATIVE
(— TO SPEAK) APHRASIA
(SLANG —) NOWAY NODICE
(UNEXPECTED —) REBUFF
REFUSE ASH NAY NIL ORT SUD BALK
COOM DENY DUST JUNK KEMP NAIT
NILL NITE PELF PELT REDD SCUM
SKIM SOIL SUDS WARN BAVIN
COOMB CRAWN DEADS DRAST
DROSS EXPEL FLOCK NITTE OFFAL
RENAY REPEL SCRAN STENT STUFF
SWASH SWILL TRADE TRASH WAIVE
WASTE COLDER DANDER DEBRIS
FORBID LITTER LUMBER MIDDEN
NAYSAY PALTRY PELTRY RAFFLE
RAMMEL RECUSE REFUGE REJECT
SCRUFF SCULCH SHORTS SHRUFF
SORDES SORDOR SPILTH BACKING
BAGGAGE BROCKLE DECLINE
DETRACT DETRECT DISAVOW
DISOBEY FORSAKE GARBAGE
GUBBINS MULLOCK OFFSCUM
OUTCAST PRUNING RUBBISH
SOILAGE SULLAGE WITHNAY
WITHSAY CRASSIER DENEGATE
DISALLOW DISCLAIM GARBLING
LEAVINGS RIFFRAFF SWEEPAGE
WITHHOLD OFFSCOURING
(— ADMISSION) CLOSE
(— FROM CHARCOAL OR COKE)
BREEZE
(— FROM COFFEE BERRIES) TAILINGS

(— FROM CUTTING UP WHALE)
GURRY
(— FROM MELTING METALS) SLAG
DROSS SCORIA
(— FROM SIFTING COFFEE-BEANS)
TRIAGE
(— FROM THRESHING) HUSK COLDER
(— FROM WINE-MAKING) RAPE
(— GREASE) COOM COOMB
(— OF CROP) STOVER
(— OF FLAX) PAB POB HARDS HURDS
(— OF FRUITS) MUST
(— OF GRAIN) PUG BRAN
(— OF GRAPES) MARC
(— OF INSECT) FRASS
(— OF MALT) DRAFF
(— OF MINE) BING DEAD
(— OF OIL MILLS) SHODE
(— OF PLANTS) ROSS
(— OF SILK) STRASS
(— OF SPICES) GARBLE
(— OF WHALE) FENKS GURRY TWITTER
(— OF WOOL) BACKINGS
(— TO APPROVE) VETO
(— TO COMPLY) STONEWALL
(— TO GO) JIB BALK
(— TO MOVE) REEST REIST
(— TO RECOGNIZE) CUT
(— TO SUPPORT) BOLT
(— TO TALK) DUMMY
(BREWERY —) DRAFF
(FISH —) CHUM GUBBINS
(FOOD —) SWILL
(LEATHER —) SPETCHES
(PLANT —) SCROFF
(STREET —) PULLAGE SCAVAGE
REFUTATION DISPROOF ELENCHUS
HYPOBOLE REBUTTER
REFUTE DENY AVOID BELIF REBUT
REFEL ASSOIL CONFUTE CONVELL
CONVICT REPROVE REVINCE
CONFOUND DISPROVE INFRINGE
REDARGUE
REGAIN READEPT RECOVER
RETRIEVE RECAPTURE
(— SOMETHING LOST) RECOUP
REGAL REAL ROYAL KINGLY PURPLE
RIGGAL RIGOLE STATELY IMPERIAL
MAJESTIC PRINCELY REGALIAN
SPLENDID
REGALE FETE FEAST TREAT PLEASE
DELIGHT REFRESH
REGALIA KIT ROYALTY
REGALO GIFT BONUS TREAT
REGAN (FATHER OF —) LEAR
(HUSBAND OF —) CORNWALL
(SISTER OF —) GONERIL CORDELIA
REGARD CON CARE DEEM FIND
GAUM GAZE GIVE HEED HOLD LIKE
LOOK MARK MIND RATE RECK SAKE
TELL YEME ADORE COUNT FAVOR
HONOR TREAT WEIGH ADDEEM

ADMIRE ASPECT BEHOLD ESTEEM
FIGURE GLANCE HOMAGE IMPUTE
INTEND LIKING MOTIVE NOTICE
RECKON REMARK REWARD SURVEY
ACCOUNT ADJUDGE CONCERN
OBSERVE RESPECT RESPITE
CONSIDER ENVISAGE ESTIMATE
(— AS) SEE
(— AS HOPELESS) DEPLORE
(— AS OBJECT OF GREAT INTEREST)
LIONIZE
(— AS PROPER) ACCEPT
(— HIGHLY) ADMIRE CONSIDER
(— WITH PROFOUND RESPECT)
REVERE VENERATE
(— WITH REPUGNANCE) ABHOR
(ATTENTIVE —) EYE
(MENTAL —) EYE
(PL.) COMPLIMENTS
REGARDED (— WITH AFFECTION)
DEAR AFFECTED
REGARDING ABOUT ANENT
APROPOS
REGARDLESS DEAF CARELESS
HEEDLESS RECKLESS
(— OF THAT) BUT
REGATTA HENLEY LIBERTY
REGEM (FATHER OF —) JAHDAI
REGENCY RULE DOMINION
REGENERATE RENEW REFORM
REVIVE RECLAIM GRACIOUS
RENOVATE
(NOT —) CIVIL
REGENERATION REBIRTH
NEOGENESIS
(GOD OF —) SIVA
REGENT RULER RULING WARDEN
SHIKKEN GOVERNOR PANGERANG
PROTECTOR
(— DIAMOND) PITT
(— OF NORTH) KUBERA KUVERA
REGIME FASCISM CAFETERIA
REGIMEN CURE DIET KEEP RULE
REGIMENT
REGIMENT BUFF RULE COLOR
TERCIO GUIDANCE INFANTRY
SLASHERS
(BRITISH —) GRAYS GREYS
(COSSACK —) PULK
(FRAMEWORK OF —) CADRE
(INDIA —) PULTON PULTUN
(SPANISH —) TERCIO
(TURKISH —) ALAI
(28TH —) SLASHERS
REGION DO END ERD EYE GAU WON
AREA BELT KITH KNOT NECK PART
SOIL WONE WOON ZONE CLIME
COAST EARTH EXURB INDIA MARCH
PAGUS PLACE PLAGE REALM SHIRE
TRACT TROAD ALKALI BORDER
CENTER DESERT DOMAIN EXTENT
GILEAD GROUND GUIANA TATARY

CLIMATE CONFINE COUNTRY
DEMESNE ENCLAVE IMAMATE
KINGDOM MALABAR STATION
TARTARY CHIEFDOM CLUBLAND
DEMERARA DISTRICT ENVIRONS
EPISTOME FLATLAND FORTRESS
FRONTIER KRATOGEN LAKELAND
LATITUDE NAPHTALI PROVINCE
REGIMENT SERICANA STANNARY
TERRITORY
(— ABOVE MOUTH) EPISTOMA
EPISTOME
(— ADJACENT TO BOUNDARY)
MARCH
(— BEYOND ATMOSPHERE) SPACE
(— BEYOND DEATH) CANAAN
(— BORDERING ON HELL) LIMBO
(— FAR AWAY) STRAND
(— IN FIBER) MICELLE
(— NEAR EQUATOR) DOLDRUMS
(— NOTED FOR MANY CONFLICTS)
COCKPIT
(— OF AMPLITUDE) ANTINODE
(— OF CHROMOSOME) PUFF
(— OF CLOUDS) WELKIN
(— OF COLD AND DARKNESS)
NIFLHEL NIFLHEIM
(— OF DEAD) AMENTI UTGARTHAR
(— OF JAPAN) DO
(— OF MARS) LIBYA
(— OF OCEAN) COUNTRY
(— OF ORIGIN) CRADLE
(— OF PHOTOSPHERE) FACULA
(— OF SHIFTING SAND) ERG
(— OF SIMPLE PLEASURE) ARCADY
ARCADIA
(— OF SOURCE OF GOLD) OPHIR
(— OF TISSUE) FIELD
(— OUTSIDE CITY) EXURB
(— WITHOUT LAW) ALSATIA
(— WITHOUT WOODS) WOLD WEALD
(CELESTIAL —S) LANGI
(COASTAL —) LITTORAL
(CULTIVATED —) GARDEN
(DARKISH —S ON MARS) MARE
(DESERT —) ERG HAMADA
(DESERTED —) WASTE
(DESOLATE —) PUNA
(DISTANT —) THULE
(E. INDIAN —) DESH
(ELEVATED —) ALTITUDE
(FOREST —) TAIGA
(FORESTED —) MONTANA
(GEOGRAPHICAL —) BOWL SIDE
(HEAVENLY —) SPHERE
(IDEAL —) JINNESTAN
(INFERNAL —S) ABYSS TARTAR
TARTARUS
(LARGE —) COMPAGE
(LIMESTONE —) KARST
(MOUNTAINOUS —) SIERRA
(OPEN —) SAVANNAH
(ORIENTAL —) INDOGAEA

(STAGNANT —) EDDY
(SUPERIOR —) HIGH
(TREELESS —) HIGHMOOR
(UPPER —) HIGH LOFT
(UPPER —S) ETHER
(WOODED —) FOREST
(PL.) DIGGINGS
(PREF.) NESO
(SUFF.) DOM NESE NESIA(N) NESUS
REGIONAL LOCAL SECTIONAL
REGISTER PIE BEAR BOOK FREE LIST
MARK'PILE POLL READ ROLL STOP
ALBUM DIARY ENROL ENTER FASTI
GRILL SIJIL SLATE ANNALS BEHAVE
ENROLL LEDGER MUSTER RECORD
REGEST ALMANAC ASCRIBE
CALENDS CATALOG COUCHER
DIPTYCH INDORSE KALENDS NOTITIA
ROTULET ANAGRAPH ARCHIVES
CADASTER CALENDAR GREFFIER
INDICATE INSCRIBE MENOLOGY
PEDIGREE POLLBOOK TOLLBOOK
STROHBASS
(— OF JUDGMENTS) DOCKET
(LOWEST —) CHALUMEAU
(MIDDLE —) CLARINO
(OFFICIAL —) TABLEAU CADASTER
REGISTRAR GUARD BURSAR
ACTUARY PATWARI PUTWARI
GREFFIER RESIDENT
REGISTRY FLAG STUDBOOK
REGLET FILET BATTEN FILLET RIGLET
REGRATER HUCKSTER
REGRESS EGRESS RETURN
ANALYSIS RECOURSE
REGRET REW RUE RUTH GRIEF
DESIRE RELENT REPENT SORROW
DEPLORE REGRATE REMORSE
FORTHINK REPINING
REGRETFUL BAD SORRY REPINING
REGRETTABLE DIRTY DOLOROUS
REGULAR DUE SET EVEN FULL JUST
WEAK SOBER SUANT SUENT USUAL
FORMAL GIUSTO NORMAL SQUARE
STATED STEADY CANONIC CERTAIN
CORRECT NATURAL ORDERED
ORDERLY ORDINAL PERFECT TYPICAL
UNIFORM COMPLETE CONSTANT
DECOROUS FORMULAR HABITUAL
ORDINARY ORDINATE TESSERAL
(PREF.) SYM
REGULARITY METHOD SQUARE
SYSTEM EVENNESS SYNAPHEA
(— OF NATURE) LAW
REGULARLY DULY EVEN ORDERLY
PROPERLY STATEDLY
REGULATE SET PACE RATE RULE
WIND BOOST FRAME GUIDE ORDER
RIGHT SHAPE ADJUST ASSIZE
BEHAVE DIRECT GOVERN MASTER
RADDLE SETTLE SQUARE TEMPER
ARRANGE CONTROL DISPOSE
MEASURE MONITOR QUALIFY

RECTIFY ATTEMPER MODERATE •
MODULIZE
(— FOOD) DIET
(— PITCH) KEY STOP
REGULATED ORDENE ORDERED
ORDERLY
(NOT —) INCORRECT
(WELL —) ORDERLY
REGULATING BEHIND
REGULATION LAW RULE BYLAW
ORDER REGLE USUAL CURFEW
ZABETA CONTROL PRECEPT STATUTE
VOICING DISPOSAL STEERAGE
(— OF PRICE) ASSIZE
(DORMITORY —S) PARIETALS
REGULATOR GUIDE DISPOSER
GOVERNOR
(GROWTH —) GIBBERELLIN
REGULUS MATTE SLURRY KINGLET
REHABIAH (FATHER OF —) ELIEZER
(GRANDFATHER OF —) MOSES
REHABILITATE REABLE REPONE
RESTORE REINSTATE
REHASH RECHAUFFE
REHEARSAL CALL DRYRUN
HEARSAL HERSALL PREVIEW
CLAMBAKE NARRATION
REHEARSE TELL TRAIN DETAIL
RECITE RELATE DECLINE NARRATE
RECOUNT DESCRIBE PRACTICE
(— QUICKLY) RUNOVER
REHEAT FLASH
REHOB (SON OF —) HADADEZER
REHOBOAM ROBOAM
(FATHER OF —) SOLOMON
(MOTHER OF —) NAAMAH
REICHSTAG DIET
REIF PLUNDER ROBBERY
REIGN RING RULE REALM RICHE
EMPIRE GOVERN KINGDOM PREVAIL
REGIMENT REGNANCY
(— IN INDIA) RAJ
REIMBURSE PAY REPAY DEFRAY
RECOUP REFUND REBURSE
INDEMNIFY
REIN CURB STOP CHECK SWING
THONG GOVERN BABICHE LEATHER
PLOWLINE RESTRAIN
(PL.) LINES RIBBONS
REINCARNATION AVATAR REBIRTH
REINDEER REIN CERVID TARAND
CARIBOU CERVINE CERVOID
RANGIFER
REINDEER MOSS SWARD
REINFORCE BAR GUY BACK FACE
STAY BRACE FORCE INLAY STUFF
SUPER CRADLE DOUBLE GUSSET
HARDEN MUSCLE SUPPLY AFFORCE
BOLSTER BULWARK ENFORCE
GROMMET NERVATE STIFFEN
SUPPORT
(— ROAD) SKID
REINFORCED KEYED SPLICED

REINFORCEMENT CREW FUEL
STAY BRACE HURTER CUNETTE
SPLICING STRAINER
(PL.) SUCCOR SUPPLY
REINVIGORATE QUICK REVIVE
RECRUIT RENERVE
REISSUE REPRISE
REITERATE BACK DING REITER
REPEAT RESUME ITERATE
REHEARSE
REIVER CATERAN
REJECT BEG ORT CAST DEFY DENY
DICE FAIL JILT KICK NILL SPIN ABHOR
BANDY BELIE BRUSH CHECK EJECT
REFEL REPEL SCOUT SPURN WAIVE
ABJECT ABJURE DELETE DESERT
IGNORE RECUSE REFUSE REFUTE
RESPUE RETORT ABANDON CASHIER
CONTEMN DECLINE DISCARD
DISMISS FORSAKE PROJECT
REPROVE REPULSE ABNEGATE
ATHETIZE DESELECT DISALLOW
DISCLAIM FORSWEAR NEGATIVE
RENOUNCE THROWOUT
(— A STUDENT) PLUCK PLOUGH
(— COPY) SPIKE
REJECTED OFFCAST OUTCAST
CASTAWAY
(— BY GOD) REPROBATE
REJECTION SACK BRUSH SPURN
DENIAL MITTEN REBUFF REFUSAL
REPULSE DEFIANCE TURNDOWN
(— AS SPURIOUS) ATHETESIS
(— OF DOCTRINE) HERESY
(INTERJECTION TO EXPRESS —) YUK
YECH YUCK YECCH
REJOICE JOY FAIN GAME CHEER
ENJOY EXULT GLORY BLITHE PLEASE
DELIGHT GLADDEN MAFFICK
JUBILATE
REJOICING GLEE MIRTH OVATION
FESTIVITY
REJOIN REPLY TAUNT ANSWER
REUNITE
REJOINDER REPLY ANSWER
COUNTER RESPONSE
REJUVENATE UNOLD
REKEM (FATHER OF —) HEBRON
REKINDLE RELUME REVIVE
RELAPSE SINK WEED LAPSE RECIDE
RETURN BACKSET SUBSIDE
BACKCAST WITHDRAW RECIDIVISM
RELAPSING (— INTO CRIME)
RECIDIVISM
RELATE SAY ALLY BEAR JOIN READ
TELL PITCH REFER SPELL STATE
TOUCH ALLUDE ASSERT DELATE
DETAIL DEVISE RECITE REPORT
REPUTE COGNATE CONCERN
DECLARE INVOLVE NARRATE
PERTAIN RECOUNT CALABASH
DESCRIBE REHEARSE APPERTAIN
(— TO) TOUCH

RELATED KIN SIB AKIN ALLIED
AFFINED RELEVANT CONNECTED
CONSANGUINE
(— BY FATHER'S SIDE) AGNATE
(— INVERSELY) RECIPROCAL
(— ON MOTHER'S SIDE) ENATE
ENATIC COGNATE
(RECIPROCALLY) — CONJUGATE
(PREF.) (— BY REMARRIAGE) STEP
RELATING (ALSO SEE PERTAINING)
(— TO) AGAINST
(— TO A RECENT PAST) ERST
(SUFF.) (—TO) AL ATIVE IAL IC(AL) ILE
INE ISH ISTIC ITIC ITIOUS
RELATION KIN SIB TALE BLOOD FETII
AFFINE DATIVE REGARD ACCOUNT
BEARING HISTORY KINSHIP
KINSMAN RAPPORT RESPECT
SCHESIS TELLING AFFINITY
HABITUDE RELATIVE TENDENCY
REFERENCE REHEARSAL RISHTADAR
PROPORTION
(— BETWEEN SPECIES) AFFINITY
(— OF LIKENESS) ANALOGY
(BLOOD —) KIN SIB
(FIXED —) RATIO
(FRIENDLY —S) AMITY
(SYNTACTIC —) FUNCTION
(WORKING —) GEAR
RELATIONSHIP KIN BLOOD ACTION
AGENCY AMENITY AMITATE
ANALOGY ANGULUS BEARING
CONTACT KINDRED KINSHIP LIAISON
RESPECT SIBNESS SIBREDE SOCIETY
AFFINITY AGNATION CONTRAST
GOSSIPRY RELATIVE SYMPATHY
COGNATION FILIATION
(BUSINESS —) ACCOUNT
(CLOSE —) BOSOM AFFIANCE
INTIMACY BELONGING
(FRIENDLY —) ENTENTE
(HARMFUL —) DISOPERATION
(HARMONIOUS —) SYNC
(INHARMONIOUS —) OUTS
(MARITAL —) BED
(MATHEMATICAL —) PARITY
(MUTUAL —) TERMS SYMMETRY
(SEXUAL —) AFFAIR
(SOCIAL —) FOOTING
RELATIVE KIN ALLY BLOOD AFFINE
AGNATE ALLIED COUSIN GERMAN
KINDRED KINSMAN APPOSITE
COGNATUS RELATION RELEVANT
PERTINENT
(PL.) KIN SIB FOLK KINDRED KINFOLK
KINNERY KINSFOLK
RELAX LAX VEG GIVE REST ABATE
BREAK LOOSE REMIT SLACK DIVERT
INKINK LAXATE SOFTEN UNBEND
UNGIVE UNKNIT UNWIND DEBLOCK
RELEASE RESOLVE SLACKEN
UNPURSE MITIGATE UNBUCKLE
UNCLENCH WINDDOWN

RELAXANT (MUSCLE —) CURARE
CURARI
RELAXATION EASE LAZE REST
ATONY CREEP LETUP RELAX SOLACE
DETENTE LETDOWN RELACHE
BREATHER DIVERSION
(— OF MONASTIC RULES)
MISERICORD MISERICORDE
RELAXED LAX LASH LOOSE SLACK
SONSY REMISS SONSIE INFORMAL
RESOLVED TONELESS UNBENDED
UNBRACED GRASPLESS
RELAXING ANIMAL ANODYNE
DETENTE
(— POINT) SEAR
RELAY SPELL RELIEF REMUDA
AVANTLAY REPEATER
(— OF DOGS) VAUNTLAY
(— OF PALANQUIN BEARERS) DAK
RELEASE LES LET BAIL DROP EMIT
FREE LESE LIOS LISS SHED SLIP TRIP
UNDO ERUPT EXEEM LEISS LOOSE
MUKTI REMIT SLAKE ACQUIT ASSOIL
DEMISE EXCUSE EXEMPT LAUNCH
MOKSHA REMISE SPRING UNBEND
UNTACK UNWORK ABSOLVE APATHIA
DELIVER DETENTE DISBAND
FREEDOM QUIETUS SOLUTIO
UNSTICK DELIVERY DISPENSE
DISSOLVE LIBERATE DISCHARGE
RELINQUISH
(— AS DOGS) UNLEASH
(— DANCING PARTNER) BREAK
(— EMOTION) ABREAST
(— FROM CENSORSHIP) UNGAG
(— FROM CONFINEMENT) UNMEW
UNPEN SPRING STREET
(— FROM DEBT) FREITH
(— FROM MILITARY) INVALID
(— FROM SLAVERY) MANUMIT
(— ON ONE'S WORD) PAROLE
(PRESS —) HANDOUT
RELEASED OFF FREE EXEMPT
RELEGATE DOOM EXILE BANISH
COMMIT DEMOTE REJECT
DEGRADE
(— TO OBSCURITY) DOWN
RELEGATION (— OF LEGAL
DISPUTE) RENVOI RENVOY
RELENT COME MELT ABATE YIELD
REGRET REPENT LIQUEFY MOLLIFY
SLACKEN
RELENTLESS GRIM HARD HARSH
STERN STONY BITTER SAVAGE
STRICT AUSTERE PITILESS
RIGOROUS
RELEVANCE PRECISION
PERTINENCE
RELEVANT APT VALID GERMAN
APROPOS GERMANE APPOSITE
MATERIAL PERTINENT
RELEVANTLY ADREM
RELIABILITY STEEL CREDENCE

RELIABLE GOOD HARD SAFE SURE TRUE PUKKA SOLID SOUND THERE TRIED TRUST WHITE DINKUM STEADY TRUSTY CERTAIN FAITHFUL SOOTHFUL STRAIGHT

RELIANCE HOPE TRUST CREDIT AFFIANCE MAINSTAY
(— ON FAITH) FIDEISM

RELIC HUACO REMAIN ANTIQUE HALIDOM LEAVING MEMENTO RELIQUE VESTIGE SOUVENIR SURVIVAL
(LIFELESS —) SHELL
(PL.) CORPSE HALIDOM REMAINS
(PREF.) LIPSANO

RELICT WIDOW REMANIE RESIDUAL SURVIVOR EPIBIOTIC

RELIEF AID LAX SOB BOOT BOTE DOLE EASE HELP RELAY SCRUB SPELL SWING ESCAPE REMEDY SUCCOR COMFORT FEEDING REDRESS RILIEVO EASEMENT REPOUSSE
(— FROM SIEGE) RESCUE
(TEMPORARY —) HITCH
(SUFF.) LYSE LYSIS LYST LYTE LYTIC LYZE

RELIEVE ROB BEET EASE FREE HELP LIOS LISS ALLAY LIGHT LISSE LITHE RIGHT SLAKE SPARE SPELL ASSIST LESSEN PHYSIC REMEDY REMOVE RESCUE SOOTHE SUCCOR UNMAZE ASSUAGE COMFORT DELIVER DEPRIVE FRESHEN LIGHTEN REDRESS REFRESH SUCCEED SUPPORT SUSTAIN SWEETEN ALIGHTEN DIMINISH MITIGATE RELEVATE
(— A SAIL) SPILL
(— OF OFFICE) AX AXE
(— OF SIN) CONFESS

RELIEVED THANKFUL

RELIGIEUSE NUN CLERGESS

RELIGION BON DIN LAW SECT BONBO CREED DAENA FAITH OBEAH PIETY SOPHY DHARMA SHINTO SYSTEM TAOISM ELOHISM JAINISM JUDAISM MACUMBA ORPHISM PERSISM RELIGIO SIKHISM SYNAGOG BUDDHISM CAODAISM HINDUISM MAZDAISM PEYOTISM SANTERIA SHAMANISM
(— OF ABRAHAM) HANIFIYA
(— OF TIBET) BON
(— OF WITCHCRAFT) WICCA
(— PRACTICED IN CUBA) SANTERIA
(CHRISTIAN —) WAY
(FALSE —) SUPERSTITION
(GENTILE —) ETHNICISM
(UNORTHODOX —) CULT

RELIGIOSE PIETISTIC

RELIGIOUS PI HOLY EXACT GODLY PIOUS RIGID DEVOUT DIVINE SACRED FERVENT GHOSTLY ZEALOUS SPIRITUAL
(— HOUSE) KELLION
(MORBIDLY —) RELIGIOSE

RELINQUISH LAY LET CEDE DROP QUIT DEMIT FORGO GRANT LEAVE WAIVE YIELD CANCEL DESERT RESIGN ABANDON FORSAKE RELEASE ABDICATE ABNEGATE LINQUISH RENOUNCE

RELIQUARY ARCA CHEF CASKET CHASSE COFFER MEMORY SHRINE STEEPA TABLET CHORTEN HALIDOM MEMORIA FERETORY

RELISH CHOW DASH EDGE GOUT GUST LIKE SOUL SOWL TANG ZEST ACHAR ENJOY GUSTO RELES SAVOR SOWLE SPICE TASTE TRACE ATSARA DEGUST FLAVOR LIKING PALATE SAVOUR BOTARGO OUTWORK STOMACH APPETITE FONDNESS PICCALILLI
(— FOR FOOD) CHAW
(INTELLECTUAL —) TASTE
(MENTAL —) PALATE
(ROMAN —) GARUM
(SALT OR ACID —) ACHAR

RELUCENT RADIANT SHINING GLEAMING

RELUCT TARROW

RELUCTANCE GRUDGE AVERSION ANTIPATHY RENITENCE
(— UNIT) REL

RELUCTANT SET SHY CAGY LOTH NICE CHARY LOATH SWEER THRAW AFRAID AVERSE DAINTY FORCED SWEERT UNFAIN ASHAMED HALTING BACKWARD GRUDGING LOATHFUL RENITENT RETICENT THRAWART

RELY AFFY BANK BASE LEAN LITE REST STAY COUNT RALLY TRUST DEPEND GROUND RECKON REPOSE CONFIDE
(— ON) LIPPEN VENTURE

REMAIN LIE SIT BIDE REST STAY STOP ABIDE CLING DWELL LEAVE STAND TARRY THOLE BELIVE ENDURE MANENT RESIDE SUBSIST SURVIVE CONTINUE
(— ALOFT) HOVER
(— AWAKE) VIGILATE
(— FIRM) INHERE
(— IN DEADLOCK) HANG
(— MOTIONLESS) STAGNATE
(—S IN MASH TUN) GRAINS
(—S IN PIPEBOWL) TOPPER
(—S OF CANE) BEGASS BAGASSE
(—S OF FIRE) EMBER EMBERS
(—S ON STAGE) MANET
(— STATIONARY) FASTEN
(— UNDER HEAT TREATMENT) SOAK
(— UNDISTURBED AFTER HEAT TREATMENT) AGE

(— UNUSED) LIE
(— UPRIGHT) STAND
(ANIMAL —S) SPOILS
(FOSSIL —) EXUVIAE
(FOUL —S) SCURF
(PL.) CHAR DUST ASHES DECAY
DRAFF GHOST SHARD SHERD BURIAL
DEBRIS FOSSIL RELIEF CARCASS
REMNANT RESIDUE RELIQUIAE
(PREF.) MENO

REMAINDER NET HEEL LAVE REST
PLUGS ARREAR EXCESS RELIEF
BALANCE REMNANT RESIDUE
SURPLUS LEAVINGS LEFTOVER
RESIDUAL RESIDUUM
(— OF ATOM) CORE
(PL.) GARBLINGS LEFTMENTS

REMAINING OVER BIDING
REMNANT LEFTOVER REMANENT
RESIDUAL
(PREF.) MENO

REMALIAH (SON OF —) PEKAH

REMARK DIG SAY SEE GIRD HEED
NOTE WORD GLOSS STATE TOKEN
EARFUL GAMBIT NOTICE REGARD
COMMENT DESCANT DISCANT
OBSERVE PERCEIVE OBSERVATION
(— BRIEFLY) GLANCE
(ADVERSE —) STRICTURE
(AGGRESSIVE —) SHOT
(AMIABLE —) DOUCEUR
(AMUSING —) GAG
(BANAL —) PLATITUDE
(BITING —) BARB
(CLEVER —) QUIP NIFTY
(CONCLUDING —S) ENVOI
(CRITICAL —) SWIPE BRICKBAT
(CUTTING —) DIG SPINOSITY
(DULL —) BROMIDE
(EMBARRASSING —) BREAK
(EXPLANATORY —) SCHOLION
SCHOLIUM
(FOOLISH —) INANITY
(ILL-TIMED —) CLANGER
(INSULTING —) SLUR
(JEERING —) JEST SKIT
(LAUGH-PROVOKING —) GAG
(PITHY —) ONELINER
(SARCASTIC —) HIT GIRD SLANT
(SATIRICAL —) JEST SKIT SGAFT
(SHARP —) SWIPE GANSEL
STINGER
(SILLY —) FADAISE
(STAGE —) ASIDE
(STALE —S) BILGE
(TEASING —) NEEDLE
(UNCOMPLIMENTARY —) BRICKBAT
(UNKIND —) BARB
(WITTY —) MOT JEST CRACK ZINGER

REMARKABLE SOME FORBY GREAT
SIGNAL STRONG NOTABLE STRANGE
UNUSUAL FABULOUS MARKABLE
SINGULAR SPANKING STRIKING
UNCOMMON BODACIOUS
NOTICEABLE PHENOMENAL
(— ONE) LULU
(NOT —) INCURIOUS

REMARKABLY UNCO UNKO JOLLY
UNCOW DEUCED UNCOLY SIGNALLY

REMEDIAL BONEHEAD RELEVANT
SALUTARY

REMEDILESS BOOTLESS

REMEDY AID BOT BOOT BOTE CURE
GAIN HALE HEAL HELP REDE AZOTH
MANDS REDUB SHERE TOPIC PHYSIC
RECOUR RECURE RELIEF REPAIR
RESIDY URETIC ANTACID CORRECT
DRASTIC ICTERIC OTALGIC PLASTER
RECTIFY REDRESS RELIEVE
ANTIDOTE MEDICINE PHARMACY
RECOVERY REMEDIAL SPECIFIC
(— COUNTERACTING POISON)
TREACLE ANTIDOTE
(— FOR ALL DISEASES) PANACEA
CATHOLICON
(— FOR DIZZINESS) DINIC
(— FOR JAUNDICE) ICTERIC
(— TO REDUCE FEVER) FEBRIFUGE
(CHINESE —) SENSO
(EXTERNAL —) TOPIC
(FAVORITE —) NOSTRUM
(SECRET —) ARCANUM
(SOVEREIGN —) MAGISTERY
(TAPEWORM —) EMBELIA
(TOOTHACHE —) TONGA
(UNIVERSAL —) AZOTH CATHOLICON
(WITHOUT —) BOOTLESS

REMEMBER MEM MIN MEAN MIND
MINE MING IDEATE MEMBER RECALL
RECORD REMIND RETAIN REWARD
BETHINK MENTION RECOLLECT
(— REMORSEFULLY) REMORD

REMEMBRANCE MIN MIND
MEMORY RECORD MEANING
MINDING MINNING MEMORIAL
REMINDER SOUVENIR

**REMEMBRANCE OF THINGS
PAST (AUTHOR OF —)** PROUST
(CHARACTER IN —) MOREL SWANN
MARCEL ODETTE RACHEL ROBERT
VEDURIN GILBERTE VINTEUIL
ALBERTINE DECHARLUS
GUERMANTES

REMIND JOG MIN MIND MINE MING
IMMIND PROMPT REMEMBER

REMINDER CUE MEMO PROD TWIT
TOUCH PROMPT MINDING MONITOR
SOUVENIR REFRESHER

REMINISCENCE MEMORY RECALL
ANAMNESIS

REMISE RETURN RELEASE REPLACE
CARRIAGE

REMISS LAX LAZY MILD PALE FAINT
SLACK TARDY BEHIND DILUTED
LANGUID CARELESS DERELICT
DILATORY HEEDLESS NEGLIGENT

REMISSION CURE LIOS LISS
PARDON REMISE LOOSING REMITTAL
(— OF BUSINESS) RECESS
(— OF DEBT) ACCEPTILATION
(PARTIAL —) RELAXATION
REMISSNESS LACHES LASHNESS
REMIT SEND COVER LOOSE RELAX
CANCEL EXCUSE PARDON REMAND
REMISS RESIGN ABSOLVE FORGIVE
RELEASE SUSPEND ABROGATE
MITIGATE MODERATE
REMNANT END TAG BUTT DREG
FENT REST RUMP RUND RELIC
STUMP TRACE REMAIN LEAVING
REMAINS SURVIVOR
(— OF CLOTH) FENT
(— OF FOOD) CRUST
(— OF ROCK MASS) KLIP KLIPPE
(— OF VEIL) ANNULUS
(—S OF FILLETS) SCISSEL
(—S OF VEIL) CORTINA
(VESTIGIAL —) SHADOW
(PL.) EPIPLASM
REMODEL MEND RECAST CONVERT
REMONSTRANCE PROOF ADVICE
COUNSEL PROTEST REPROOF
EVIDENCE
REMONSTRANT ARMINIAN
REMONSTRATE ARGUE OBJECT
PROTEST REPROVE COMPLAIN
REMORA CLOG DRAG PEGA SUCKER
GUAICAN PEGADOR ECHENEID
LOOTSMAN STAYSHIP STOPSHIP
SUCKFISH
REMORSE HELL PITY RUTH PRICK
REGRET REMORD AYENBITE
PENITENCE
(— OF CONSCIENCE) GRUDGE
REMORSEFUL BAD PITIFUL
CONTRITE GUILTSICK
REMOTE FAR OFF BACK DEEP FERN
HIGH LONG ALOOF HOARY UTTER
ALENGE DISTAL ELENGE EXEMPT
OTIOSE SECRET DEVIOUS DISSITE
DISTANT EXTREME FAILING
FARAWAY FOREIGN OBSCURE
OUTSIDE ABDITIVE ABSTRUSE
ARMCHAIR BACKVELD INTERIOR
OUTLYING OUTWORLD SECLUDED
SOLITARY OUTLANDISH
(— FROM LIFE) SCHOOLISH
(MOST —) ULTIMA EXTREME
HINDMOST ULTIMATE
(PREF.) DIST(O) PALAE(O) PALE(O)
REMOTELY AFAR CLEAN DISTANTLY
REMOTENESS AWAYNESS
DISTANCE
REMOTER FARTHER ULTERIOR
REMOVABLE DATIVE REMOTIVE
REMOVAL AX AXE EXILE AMOTION
CLEANUP ERASION ABLATION
EXCISION EXERESIS OFFGOING
REMOTION

(— OF COAL) GETTING
(— OF ICE FROM GLACIER) ATTRITION
(— OF LAND) AVULSION
(DISTANT —) ELOIN ELOIGN
(SUFF.) CENOSIS
(SURGICAL—) ECTOMY
REMOVE GET PUT RID BATE COMB
DELE DRAW FILE FLIT FREE LIFT
MOVE PARE PEEL PULL QUIT RAZE
UNDO VOID WEED APART AUFER
AVOID BLAST BRUSH CLEAR EMITY
ERASE EVOID HEAVE HOIST LIGHT
PLANE RAISE REPEL SHIFT SHUCK
SLASH SLIPE STRIP SWEEP WAIVE
BANISH CANCEL CHANGE CONVEY
DEDUCT DEGREE DEPART DEPOSE
EFFACE ELOIGN EXEMPT EXPORT
MINISH RELLEVE REMBLE SPIRIT
ABOLISH AMOLISH DEPRIVE
DESCENT DISMISS DISPOST DIVORCE
EXCERPT RESCIND RETRACT
REVERSE STRANGE SUBDUCT
SUBLATE ABSTRACT ASPIRATE
DISPLACE DISPLANT ESTRANGE
EVACUATE RETRENCH SUPPLANT
TRANSFER WITHDRAW ELIMINATE
OBLITERATE
(— A FAULT) MEND
(— A STITCH) DECREASE
(— BARK FROM LOG) ROSS
(— BIT BY BIT) SCAMBLE
(— BY CUTTING) ABLATE
(— BY DEATH) SNATCH
(— BY SCRAPING) SHAVE
(— CLOTHING) DOFF STRIP
(— COLOR) BLEACH
(— CONTENTS) GUT
(— CORTEX) DECORTIGATE
(— COVER) UNCAP
(— DEFECTS) SCARF
(— DIRT) BLADE GARBLE
(— EXCESS METAL) CUT
(— FLOATING MATTER) SKIM
(— FROM CHECKER BOARD) HUFF
(— FROM OFFICE) DEPOSE RECALL
DISMISS
(— FROM REMEMBRANCE) COVER
(— FROM SHEATH) EVAGINATE
(— GILLS) BEARD
(— HAIR) DEPILATE
(— HUSKS AND CHAFF) GELD
(— IMPURITIES) PURGE
(— INSIDES OF FISH) GIB GIP
(— JUDGE) ADDRESS
(— LOWER BRANCHES) BRASH
(— MAST) UNSTEP
(— ORE) EXTRACT
(— PARTICLES OF GOLD LEAF) SKEW
(— PIECEMEAL) SCAMBLE
(— PITCHER FROM BASEBALL GAME)
DERRICK
(— POTATOES) GRABBLE
(— QUEEN BEE) DEMAREE

(— **QUIETLY**) ABSTRACT
(— **ROOTS**) GRUB
(— **SEED FROM FLAX**) RIBBLE
(— **SEEDS**) STONE
(— **SKIN**) HULL HUSK
(— **SOUND FROM TAPE**) BLIP
(— **SPROUTS FROM**) CHIT
(— **STALK FROM**) STRIG
(— **STAMENS**) CASTRATE
(— **SURGICALLY**) EXTIRPATE
(— **TABLECLOTH**) DRAW
(— **THE TOP OF**) COP
(— **TO A DISTANCE**) ELOIN
(— **TO AVOID TAX**) SKIM
(— **TROUSERS**) DEBAG
(— **WASTE TO FIBER**) GARNETT
(— **WOOL**) BELLY
(— **WORKS OF STOLEN WATCH**)
CHURCH
(— **WRONGFULLY**) MISTAKE
(PREF.) DE
REMOVED UP OFF AWAY ALIEN
ALOOF APART REMOTE DISTANT
SEMOTED ABSTRACT
REMOVER MOVER CROPMAN
KNOTTER
REMUDA CAVY CAVAYARD CAVYYARD
REMUNERATE PAY REPAY REWARD
GRATIFY SATISFY CONSIDER
REIMBURSE
REMUNERATION PAY REWARD
SALARY PAYMENT
REMUNERATIVE GAINFUL
REWARDING
REMUS (BROTHER OF —) ROMULUS
(FATHER OF —) MARS
RENAISSANCE NARA REBIRTH
REVIVAL
RENAL NEPHRIC NEPHRITIC
RENAME ANABAPTIZE
RENCOUNTER CLASH FIGHT
DEBATE CONTEST CONFLICT
REND PULL RENT RIVE TEAR TOIL
BREAK BURST DIVEL RATCH ROWEL
SEVER SPLIT WREST CLEAVE SCREED
WRENCH ABSCIND DIVULSE
RUPTURE WREATHE DISPIECE
DISTRAIN FRACTURE LACERATE
SPLINTER
(— **AND DEVOUR**) TIRE
RENDER DO PAY PUT TRY BEAR
DRAW ECHO EMIT MAKE RENT RIND
DEFER PRICK REPAY YIELD RECITE
REPEAT RETURN DELIVER PRECARY
REFLECT REQUITE RESTORE SERVICE
TALLAGE TRANSMIT
(— **ACID**) PRICK
(— **AGREEABLE**) DULCIFY
(— **AS LARD**) TRY
(— **ASSISTANCE TO SHIP**) FOY
(— **CAPABLE**) ACTIVATE
(— **CLEAR**) OPEN
(— **DEFECTIVE**) VITIATE

(— **DEFENSELESS**) DISARM
(— **DESTITUTE**) DISFURMSH
(— **FIT**) ADAPT
(— **GODLIKE**) DEIFY
(— **HEAVY WITH FOOD**) STODGE
(— **HOMAGE**) ATTORN
(— **IMMUNE**) FRANK VASTATE
(— **IMPASSIBLE**) STOP
(— **IMPERFECT**) LAME
(— **INEFFECTIVE**) VITIATE
(— **INSANE**) DEMENT DISTRACT
(— **KNOTTY**) GNARL
(— **OBLIQUE**) SPLAY
(— **OBSCURE**) DARKLE
(— **OF BOON WORK**) PRECARY
(— **PLAUSIBLE**) GLOSS
(— **PURE**) EXPURGATE
(— **QUIET**) ACCOY
(— **SENSELESS**) STUN ASTONISH
(— **SUDDENLY**) THROW
(— **TURBID**) ROIL
(— **UNFIT**) DENATURE
(— **UNSTABLE**) UNHINGE
(— **VERDICT**) PASS
(— **VOID**) CASS DEFEAT
(— **WATERTIGHT**) CALK CAULK
(— **WEAK**) EVIRATE
(— **LIABLE**) ENGAGE PREDISPOSE
(SUFF.) EN
RENDERED RENDU TRIED
RENDERING RENDU ENGLISH
VERSION RENDITION
(— **OF SCENE**) STUDY
RENDEZVOUS DATE HAUNT TRYST
REFUGE HANGOUT MEETING
RETREAT
(— **FOR SHIPS**) DOWN
(— **OF WITCHES**) SABBAT
RENDING SPLITTING
(— **ASUNDER**) DIVULSION
RENDITION ACCOUNT CONDUCT
DELIVERY
RENEGADE DORAX PERVERT
TRAITOR APOSTATE DESERTER
RECREANT RENEGADO RUNAGADO
RUNAGATE TURNCOAT
RENEGE BEG NIG DENY RENIG
DESERT REVOKE RETRACT
FAINAIGUE
RENEW NEW REST FRESH RECALL
REFORM RENOVE REPEAT RESUME
REVIVE INSTORE REBUILD REFRESH
REPLACE RESTORE OVERHAUL
REJUVENATE
(— **MORTAR**) REPOINT
(— **WINE**) STUM
RENEWAL RENEW REVIVAL
NOVATION
(SPIRITUAL-) REBIRTH
RENNET LAB RUEN VELL STEEP
RENNIN RUNNET EARNING
ABOMASUM YEARNING
CHEESELIP

RENOUNCE PUT CEDE DEFY DENY
QUIT DEVOW FORGO RENAY WAIVE
ABJURE DISOWN FORLET FORSAY
RECANT REFUSE REJECT RENEGE
RESIGN REVOKE ABANDON DECLARE
FORLEIT FORSAKE RETRACT
WITHSAY ABDICATE ABNEGATE
DISCLAIM FORSPEAK FORSWEAR
MANSWEAR PROCLAIM RELINQUISH
(— ALLEGIANCE) REVOLT
(— AUTHORITY) REBEL
(— PROMISE) RECEDE

RENOVATE DUST RENEW REVIVE
FURBISH REFRESH RESTORE
OVERHAUL RENOVIZE
(— HAT) MOLOKER MOLOCKER

RENOWN BAY BRAG FAME ECLAT
GLORY KUDOS PRICE RUMOR
ESTEEM LUSTER RENONE REPORT
EMPRISE SWAGGER WORSHIP
PRESTIGE NOTORIETY

RENOWNED FAMED NOBLE NOTED
FAMOUS EMINENT RENOMME
GLORIOUS MAGNIFIC RENOMMEE

RENT LET SET TAX FARM GALE GAPE
HIRE MAIL RACK RIME RIVE SLIT
TEAR TOLL TORN WAGE BREAK
CANON CENSO CUDDY ENDOW
GANCH GAVEL SPLIT BLANCH
BREACH BROKEN CENSUS CHASMA
CRANNY CUSTOM GAUNCH INCOME
SCHISM SCREED STRENT CHARTER
CHIEFRY CORNAGE CRACKED
CREVICE FISSURE MAILING
MOLLAND ONSTAND RENTAGE
REVENUE RUPTURE TRIBUTE
CHAMPART CHIEFERY HEADRENT
STALLAGE VECTIGAL WAYLEAVE
LANDGAFOL
(— BY BOAR'S TUSK) GANCH
GAUNCH
(— IN LIEU OF SUPPER) CUDDY
(— OF LAND PAID IN KIND) CAIN
(ANNUAL —) CANON
(EARTHQUAKE —) SCARLET
(GROUND —) CENSO CENSUS
(OATS IN LIEU OF —) AVENAGE

RENTAL KAIN PORT TONNAGE
TRIBUTE TUNNAGE

RENTED LETTEN

RENTER FARMER RANTER CHIPPER
BOXHOLDER
(— OF GRAZING LAND) AGIST

RENUNCIATION DENIAL APOSTASY
DEFIANCE DISAVOWAL REJECTION
SACRIFICE

REORGANIZE (— SCIENTIFICALLY)
RATIONALIZE

REP CANNELE DROGUET POPELINE

REPAIR DO EIK EKE FIX IMP HEAL
HELP MEND TINE AMEND BOTCH
DIGHT EMEND HAUNT RALLY REDUB
RENEW STORE TRADE UPSET
ASTORE BUSHEL COBBLE COGGLE
COOPER DOCTOR FETTLE RECURE
REDEEM REFORM REMEDY REPASS
RESORT RETURN UPKEEP CORRECT
INFAINT REDRESS REPAREL RESTORE
SERVICE FLOCKING OVERHAUL
RETRIEVE REVIVIFY RECONDITION
(— A SOCK) DARN
(— BOAT) CAREEN
(— CLUMSILY) BOTCH
(— FENCE) MOUND
(— ROAD) SKID
(— SHOE) FOX TAP

REPAIRED VAMPED

REPAIRER DOCTOR BOTCHER
COBBLER WOFFLER CEMENTER
(SHOE —) JACKMAN BENCHMAN
(TEXTILE —) SMASHER

REPAIRMAN FETTLER

REPARATION BOTE AMENDS
REMEDY REWARD DAMAGES
REDRESS REPAIRS REQUITAL
(— OF LESIONS) ANAPLASTY
(PL.) ATONEMENT

REPARTEE WIT KNACK REPLY
BANTER RETORT RIPOST RIPOSTE
BACKCHAT BADINAGE COMEBACK
GIFFGAFF

REPAST BAIT FEED FOOD MEAL
BEVER FEAST TREAT DRINKING
COLLATION
(— BETWEEN MEALS) BEVER
BRUNCH BANQUET
(HASTY —) SNACK
(LIGHT —) BAIT VOID VOIDEE
COLLATION

REPAY MEED QUIT APPAY TALLY
YIELD ACQUIT ANSWER AVENGE
REFUND RETORT RETURN REWARD
IMBURSE REQUITE RESTORE
REIMBURSE

REPEAL ANNUL CANCEL RECALL
REVOKE ABANDON ABOLISH
RESCIND REVERSE ABROGATE
DEROGATE DISENACT RENOUNCE

REPEAT SAY ECHO GAIT RAME RANE
SHOW TELL DITTO QUOTE RECUR
RENEW RESAY REVIE THRUM
ANSWER RENDER RESUME RETAIL
SECOND DECLINE DIVULGE ITERATE
PRESENT RECYCLE REPLICA REPRISE
DINGDONG REDOUBLE REHEARSE
REPLICATE
(— BY ROTE) PARROT
(— FROM MEMORY) RECORD
(— GLIBLY) SCREED
(— IN DETAIL) RETAIL
(— INSISTENTLY) PERSIST
(— LORD'S PRAYER) PATTER
(— MONOTONOUSLY) CUCKOO
DINGDONG
(— OF PATTERN) GAIT
(— TIRESOMELY) DIN

REPEATED OFTEN CONSTANT FREQUENT PERENNIAL
REPEATEDLY OFT EVERY THRICE
REPEATER GUN RIFLE WATCH PISTOL FLOATER HOLDOVER
REPEL FEND TURN WARD FENCE REBUT DEFEND PUTOFF REBEAT REBUFF REFUSE REFUTE REJECT REPUGN RESIST REVOLT DISGUST PELLATE REPULSE PROPULSE
REPELLANT REPUGNANT
REPELLENT DEET DOPE GRIM MACE HARSH CAMPHOR HATEFUL SQUALID
(INSECT —) DEET
REPELLING HARD SICKLY
REPENT REW RUE MOURN GRIEVE REGRET REPTANT CREEPING FORTHINK
REPENTANCE REW RUE PITY RUTH RUING REGRET SORROW PENANCE REMORSE
REPENTANT ATTRITE PENITENT
REPERCUSSION ECHO TENOR RECOIL REPULSE BACKWASH
REPERTORY REP BOOK LIST INDEX ARSENAL CATALOG
(PERFORMER'S —) REPERTOIRE
REPETITION BIS REP COPY ECHO REPP ROTE PLOCE REVIE TROLL DILOGY REPEAT MENTION RECITAL REPLICA REPRISE IDENTITY ITERANCE ITERANCY NEMBUTSU PALILOGY PARROTRY RECOVERY REDOUBLE REHEARSAL
(— IN REVERSE ORDER) EPANODOS
(— OF HOMOLOGOUS PARTS) MERISM
(— OF SPEECH FORMS) ROTE
(— OF WORD) ANAPHORA BATTOLOGY
(NEEDLESS —) REDUNDANCY
(SUCCESSIVE —) SEQUENCE
(UNINSPIRED —) STENCIL
(UNINTENTIONAL —) DITTOGRAPHY (PREF.)
(PATHOLOGICAL —) PALI
REPETITIOUS TATA
REPHAEL (FATHER OF —) SHEMAIAH
REPHAH (FATHER OF —) EPHRAIM
REPHAIAH (FATHER OF —) HUR TOLA BINEA
REPHAIM EMIM
REPINE FRET PINE WEAKEN COMPLAIN
REPINING MURMUR REGRET PLAINTIVE
REPLACE SWAP SWOP RENEW REPAY SHIFT STEAD CHANGE FOLLOW REFUND REMISE REPONE SUPPLY FRESHEN PREEMPT RESTORE SUCCEED DISPLACE SUPPLANT REPLENISH

REPLACEMENT CUT ERSATZ
(— FOR HAND) HOOK
(— OF CONSONANT) LENITION
REPLAY ECHO
REPLENISH CHUNK REFIT RENEW SUPPLY NOURISH PERFECT PLENISH REPLETE RESTORE SUFFICE
REPLETE FAT FULL RIFE SATED STOUT STUFF FILLED GORGED IMPLETE COMPLETE HONEYPOT
REPLETION FULTH FULNESS SURFEIT FULLNESS PLETHORA SATURITY
REPLICA BIS PUP COPY IDEA CHARM CLONE IMAGE REVIE FACSIMILE
REPLICATION ECHO REPLY ANSWER REJOINDER
REPLY CAP JAWAB KNACK RESAY ANSWER REJOIN RETORT RETURN REPLIAL RESOUND RESPOND REPARTEE REPLIQUE RESPONSE SIMILITER
(SECOND —) DUPLY
REPORT CRY POP SAY FAME ITEM NOTE TELL VENT VOTE WORD AUDIT BRUIT COVER CRACK NOISE REFER ROUND RUMOR SCALE SOUND STATE STORY VOICE BREEZE CAHIER CREDIT DELATE DETAIL FINGER GOSSIP RAPORT RECITE RELATE RENOWN REPUTE RETURN RUMBLE SPEECH STEVEN SURVEY THREAP ACCOUNT HANSARD HEARING HEARSAY INKLING KHUBBER NARRATE OPINION PROCESS RECITAL ADVISORY DECISION DESCRIBE HEMOGRAM VERBATIM GRAPEVINE
(— NEWS) COVER
(— OF GUN) CLAP
(— OF INFRACTION) GIG
(— OF PROCEEDINGS) CAHIER
(— OF TIMBER SURVEYOR) CRUISE
(ABSURD —) CANARD
(BELIEVED —) CREDIT
(CASUAL —) FABLE
(COMMON —) CRY FAME SPEECH
(FALSE —) SHAVE CANARD FURPHY SLANDER
(FLYING —) SOUGH
(HONORABLE —) TONGUE
(LAW —) CASE
(MILITARY —) STATE SITREP
(NEWS —) FLASH SCOOP
(NOISY —) RUMBLE
(OFFICIAL —) HANSARD
(POPULAR —) RUMOR RUMOUR
(PUBLIC —) FAME
(UNFAVORABLE —) SKIN
(UNVERIFIED —) VOICE GRAPEVINE
(VAGUE —) BREEZE

REPORTER LEGMAN PISTOL CREEPER NEWSMAN NEWSHAWK PRESSMAN STRINGER PAPARAZZO (SOCIETY —) JENKINS (YOUNG —) CUB

REPORTING BEAT COVERAGE

REPOSE RO BED LIE PUT AFFY CALM EASE RELY REST PEACE PLACE POISE QUIET SLEEP REPAST RECLINE EASINESS QUIETUDE SERENITY (— LAZILY) FROWST (DREAMY —) KEF

REPOSITORY ARK SAFE AMBRY CAPSA DEPOT HOARD VAULT ARMORY CASKET MUSEUM VESTRY ARCHIVE CABINET CAPSULE GENIZAH GRANARY HANAPER SPICERY ARCHIVES MAGAZINE TREASURY SEPULCHER STOREHOUSE (— FOR DEAD) URN (SECRET —) SECRETAIRE

REPOSOIR REPOSE

REPOSSESS PULL RECOVER

REPREHEND NIP WARN BLAME CHIDE REBUKE CENSURE REPRISE REPROVE CRITICIZE

REPREHENSIBLE ILL AMISS BLAMABLE CRIMINAL CULPABLE SCABROUS

REPREHENSION BLAME REBUKE CENSURE OBLOQUY REPROOF

REPRESENT GIVE LIKE LIMN SHOW TYPE SHADE DEPICT SEMBLE TYPIFY DISPLAY EXHIBIT FASHION PICTURE PORTRAY PROTEST TRADUCE DEFIGURE DESCRIBE RESEMBLE PERSONATE (— CONCRETELY) THING (— IN LANGUAGE) ACT BODY DRAW ENACT IMAGE SPEAK BLAZON CLOTHE EMBODY FIGURE SAMPLE BETOKEN EXPRESS DECIPHER (— ON GRAPH) PLOT (— ON STAGE) ACT

REPRESENTATION SUN BUST FORM ICON IDEA IDOL IKON SHOW SWAG ANGLE DRAFT FANCY IMAGE INSET LABEL MEDAL TABUT AVOWAL BUDDHA EFFIGY FIGURE FLEECE MODULE OBJECT SCHEMA SCHEME SKETCH SUNRAY WAYANG ANATOMY DIORAMA DRAUGHT DRAWING EPITOME EXPRESS EXTRACT FOLIAGE MAJESTY SCENERY TABLEAU BESTIARY BLAZONRY CREATION EPIPHANY EXTERIOR IDIOGRAM LIKENESS TYPORAMA SIMULACRUM RESEMBLANCE (— OF SERPENT) BASIL DRAGON BASILISK

(— OF SHRINE OF HUSAIN) TABUT (— OF VISION) AISLING (DIPLOMATIC —) DEMARCHE (FACSIMILE —) TYPORAMA (FAINT —) SHADOW (FUNERAL —) CADAVER (GRAPHIC —) CHART BISECT (HERALDIC —) LEOPARD LIONCEL (MENTAL —) FANCY IMAGE (MINIATURE —) MODEL (SYMBOLIC —) ALLEGORY

REPRESENTATIVE REP FAIR TYPE AGENT ENVOY VAKIL ASSIGN COMMON DEPUTY EMBLEM LEDGER SAMPLE VAKEEL BURGESS GRIEVER TRIBUNE TYPICAL DECURION DELEGATE EMISSARY EXPONENT FIELDMAN GASTALDO INTIMATE OBSERVER SALESMAN SPECIMEN (— AT FOREIGN COURT) RESIDENT (— OF ATMOSPHERE) AERIAL (— OF CLERGY) PROCTOR (LEGAL—) SYNDIC (MANUFACTURER'S —) BLOCKMAN (POPE'S —) INTERNUNCIO (PL.) COMMONS

REPRESS CURB HUSH BLUNT BRIDE CHAIN CHECK CHOKE CRUSH DAUNT DROWN QUELL SQUAT BRIDLE COERCE DEADEN REBUKE STIFLE SUBDUE CONTROL DEPRESS INHIBIT REPRIME SILENCE SWALLOW COMPRESS OVERBEAR RESTRAIN RESTRICT RETRENCH REVOCATE STRANGLE SUPPRESS WITHHOLD

REPRESSED SULLEN STIFLED

REPRIEVE DELAY GRACE ESCAPE REPRISE RESPITE SUSPEND POSTPONE

REPRIMAND WIG BAWL CALL CHEW JACK SKIN SLAP SLON SNEB SNIB TASK CHECK CREED SLATE SLOAN SPANK TARGE BOUNCE CARPET FARFUL REBUKE ROCKET STRAFE CENSURE CHAPTER LECTURE REPROOF REPROVE TICKOFF DRESSING WRAGGING

REPRINT COPY DEPRINT OFFPRINT REIMPOSE TAUCHNITZ

REPRISAL PRIZE MARQUE REPRISE REQUITAL RECAPTION

REPROACH ILL TAX BLOT GIBE JIBE LACK NOSE NOTE RAIL SLUR SPOT TEEN TWIT WITE ABUSE BLAME BRAID BRAND CHIDE SCOLD SHEND TAUNT WHITE AYWORD BISMER INFAMY REBUKE REVILE UPCAST VILIFY BLEMISH CENSURE CONDEMN REPROOF REPROVE SLANDER UMBRAID UPBRAID WITHNIM BETONGUE DISHONOR REDARGUE

REVILING CONTUMELY OPPROBRIUM REFLECTION

REPROACHFUL BITTER ABUSIVE SHAMEFUL

REPROBATE HARD LOST SCAMP DISOWN RASCAL REJECT SINNER ABANDON CENSURE CORRUPT EXCLUDE REPROVE DEPRAVED DISALLOW HARDENED SCALAWAG SKALAWAG

REPRODUCE BUD HIT COPY BREED SPORE RECITE REPEAT PORTRAY AUTOTYPE MULTIPLY REFIGURE REMEMBER PROCREATE
(— ONESELF) CLONE

REPRODUCTION CAST COPY REVI CLONE IMAGE PRINT ECTYPE RECALL STEREO EDITION ELECTRO EXOGAMY FISSION REPLICA REVIVAL APOMIXIS BLOCKOUT GAMOGAMY HOMOGAMY LIKENESS
(— BY FISSION) SCISSIPARITY
(— OF DESIGNS) SPATTERWORK
(— OF SOUND) AUDIO
(— WITHOUT SEX) MONOGENY
(SUFF.) GAM(AE)(IST)(OUS)(Y) GAMETE GON(E)(IDIUM)(IMO)(IUM)(Y)

REPRODUCTIVE PROLIFIC

REPROOF PROD RATE BLAME CHECK LESSON REBUKE CHIDING LECTURE SETDOWN JOBATION REPROACH REPROVAL SCOLDING TAXATION JAWBATION
(GENTLE —) ADMONITION

REPROVE RAG TAP BAWL FLAY FRIE JOBE RATE SNIB TRIM BLAME CHECK CHIDE CRAWL SCOLD SHEND SHENT SNEAP BERATE CHASTE REBUKE REFORM SCHOOL THREAT CENSURE CONDEMN CORRECT IMPROVE LECTURE UPBRAID WITHNIM ADMONISH CHASTISE KEELHAUL REDARGUE REPROACH UNDERNIM WITHTAKE

REPTILE LOW MEAN WORM GUANA SNAKE VIPER GAVIAL LIZARD MOLOCH TURTLE CRAWLER CREEPER DIAPSID GHARIAL PROTEUS SAURIAN SERPENT TUATARA BASILISK CREEPING CYNODONT DINOSAUR GALESAUR MESOSAUR MOSASAUR PLIOSAUR STEGOMUS SYNAPSID TORTOISE ALLIGATOR CROCODILE PELYCOSAUR PLESIOSAUR
(FLYING —) PTEROSAUR PTERANODON PTERODACTYL PTERODACTYLE
(PART OF —) EYE JAW PIT BODY FANG SCALE TOOTH BUTTON RATTLE SHEATH TONGUE SEGMENT
(PREF.) HERPET(I)(O)

REPTILIAN HERPETIC

REPUBLIC STATE SOVIET POBLACHT
(FRENCH —) MARIANNE
(IDEAL —) ICARIA
(IMAGINARY —) OCEANA

REPUBLICAN RED QUID STALWART SANSCULOT

REPUDIATE DEFY DENY ABJURE DISOWN RECANT REFUTE REJECT DECLINE DISAVOW DISCARD DIVORCE RETRACT DISCLAIM DISVOUCH RENOUNCE
(— DEBTS) NOCHEL NOTCHEL

REPUDIATING NAKIR

REPUGNANCE ENMITY HATRED HORROR DISGUST DISLIKE DISTASTE LOATHING

REPUGNANT ALIEN DIRTY NASTY ADVERSE HATEFUL OPPOSED INIMICAL OPPOSITE ABHORRENT OBNOXIOUS REPULSIVE

REPULSE FOIL ROUT RUSH CHECK FLING REBUT REFEL REPEL SMEAR DEFEAT DENIAL REBUFF REBUTE REFUSE REJECT

REPULSION UG DISLIKE AVERSION

REPULSIVE COLD DAIN EVIL LOTH UGLY VILE LOATH GREASY LAIDLY FULSOME HATEFUL LOATHLY SQUALID SCABROUS UNHONEST

REPURCHASE (— AGREEMENT) REPO

REPUTABLE GOOD HONEST WORTHY CREDIBLE ESTIMABLE

REPUTATION REP FAME LOSE NAME NOTE ODOR PASS GLORY HONOR IZZAT NOISE RUMOR SAVOR VOICE CREDIT ESTEEM RECORD RENOWN SHADOW LAURELS OPINION RESPECT WORSHIP STANDING
(EVIL —) INFAMY
(GOOD —) STANDING

REPUTE FAME ODOR RANK WORD NOISE SAVOR THINK RECKON REGARD STATUS OPINION RESPECT WORSHIP ESTIMATE JUDGMENT POSITION
(ILL —) SLANDER

REPUTED DIT PUTATIVE

REQUEST ASK BEG BOON CALL PLEA PRAY SEEK SUIT TELL WISH CLAIM LIBEL QUEST YEARN APPEAL BEHEST DEMAND DESIRE DIRECT ENCORE INVITE MOTION BESPEAK COMMAND ENTREAT INQUIRY REQUIRE SOLICIT ENTREATY INSTANCE PETITION ROGATION
(— FOR HELP) SOS
(— RECONSIDERATION) RECLAMA
(STRONG —) DUN DEMAND

REQUIEM HYMN MASS REST DIRGE PEACE QUIET REPOSE REQUIN

REQUIN SHARK TOMMY
REQUIRE ASK HAVE LACK NEED
TAKE WANT CLAIM CRAVE EXACT
FORCE GAVEL COMPEL DEMAND
DEPEND DESIRE ENJOIN ENTAIL
EXPECT GOVERN MISTER OBLIGE
BEHOOVE DICTATE INVOLVE
MANDATE SOLICIT STIPULATE
REQUIRED DUE SET SUPPOSED
NECESSARY REQUISITE OBLIGATORY
REQUIREMENT CALL MUST NEED
LEGAL ORDER BEHEST DEMAND
NECESSITY
(VEXATIOUS —) FIKE
(PL.) EXIGENCE EXIGENCY
REQUIRING
(PREF.) END(O)
REQUISITE DUE NEED NEEDY VITAL
NEEDFUL ESSENTIAL NECESSARY
REQUISITION ORDER DEMAND
IMPONT EMBARGO REQUEST
REQUITAL WAR APPAY MERIT REPAY
SERVE TALLY YIELD ACQUIT DEFRAY
REWARD GRATIFY PAYMENT
REVENGE CONSIDER FORYIELD
REPRISAL
REQUITE SERVE RECOMPENSE
RECIPROCATE
RERAILER DIAMOND
REREAD DOUBLE
RERECORD DUB
REREDOS SCREEN BRAZIER DRAPERY
RETABLO FIREBACK REARDOSS
REREMOUSE BAT
RERUN (PAYMENT FOR —)
RESIDUAL
RES POINT THING MATTER SUBJECT
RESCIND LIFT ANNUL CANCEL
REMOVE REPEAL REVOKE ABOLISH
RETRACT RETREAT ABROGATE
RESCRIPT EDICT ORDER DECREE
LETTER EPISTLE
RESCUE RID FREE HELP REDD SAVE
BORROW RANSOM REDEEM RESKEW
SUCCOR WARISH BAILOUT DELIVER
RECLAIM RECOVER RELEASE
SALVAGE DELIVERY LIBERATE
RECOURSE
(— OF PROPERTY) SALVAGE
RESEARCH ARBEIT SEARCH
ENQUIRY INQUIRY
RESECT EXCISE
RESEDA LEEK MENNUET MORILLON
RESELL (— AT INCREASED PRICES)
SCALP
RESEMBLANCE SWAP PARITY
SIMILE ANALOGY AFFINITY LIKENESS
PARALLEL VICINITY SIMILARITY
(DIM HAZY —) BLY
(SLIGHT —) BLUSH
RESEMBLE AGREE BRAID FAVOR
IMAGE LIKEN APPEAR DEPICT FIGURE

RECALL SEMBLE COMPARE IMITATE
PORTRAY ASSEMBLE SIMULATE
RESEMBLING LIKE SAME SEMBLE
SIMILAR SEMBLANT
(— AN EGG) OVULARIAN
(— COMB) PECTINAL
(— GOOSE) ANSERINE
(— HORSE) EQUOID
(— IVORY) EBURNEAN EBURNEOID
EBURNEOUS
(— LADDER) SCALARIFORM
(— SALT) HALOID
(— STAR) STELLATE
(— WALL) MURAL
(SUFF.) ACEOUS AR ARY EOUS FORM
FUL IFORM ITIC OIDAL
RESENT HATE MEAN INDIGN MALIGN
STOMACH SUGGEST
RESENTFUL HARD HURT BITTER
SULLEN ENVIOUS JEALOUS
STOMACHY
RESENTMENT HURT DEPIT PIQUE
SNUFF SPITE CHOLER ENMITY
GRUDGE HATRED MALICE RANCOR
DISDAIN DUDGEON OFFENCE
OFFENSE STOMACH UMBRAGE
JEALOUSY HEARTBURN
(CAUSE —) OUTRAGE
RESERVATION DIBS SALVO SPACE
SAVING UNLESS BOOKING CAUTION
KEEPING PROVISO RESERVE
FORPRISE RESERVAL
(MENTAL —) SALVO SCRUPLE
RESERVE BOOK CAVE FUND HOJU
HOLD KEEP SALT SAVE SPARE
BACKUP NICETY 3EPONE 3EPOSE
TRIARY BACKLOG CAUTION
CONTROL DIGNITY SEPOSIT
SHYNESS TENENUE COLDNESS
DISTANCE FALLBACK FORPRISE
IMMODEST WITHHOLD STOCKPILE
(HOME —S) LANDSTURM
(IN —) ONICE
(MILITARY —) HOJU YOBI TRIARY
TRIARII LANDWEHR
(MONETARY —) CUSHION
(PL.) FAT KOKUMIN STRENGTH
RESERVED COY DRY SHY COLD
UNCO ALOOF CHARY SAVED
BOOKED CLOSED DEMURE MODEST
SILENT STANCH COSTIVE DISTANT
RETIRED STRANGE RETICENT
RETIRING STANDOFF TACITURN
WITHHELD
(— FOR ROYAL USE) KHASS
(NOT —) COMMON
RESERVOIR DAM BOSS FONT KEEP
LAKE PENT SUMP TANK BASIN
FOUNT STANK STORE CENOTE
SIPHON SOURCE SYPHON CISTERN
CLEARER FAVISSA FOREBAY
IMPOUND PISCINA RECEIPT

AFTERBAY DEPOSITO FOUNTAIN
MAGAZINE STANDAGE
(— OF WEATHERGLASS) STAGNUM
RESET HELP ABODE ALTER RECEPT
RESORT SUCCOR RECEIPT REPLANT
SHARPEN WELCOME
RESHEPH (FATHER OF —) EPHRAIM
RESIDE BIG WIN BIDE BIGG HOME
LIVE STAY TELD WONT ABIDE DWELL
LODGE REMAIN CONSIST SOJOURN
HABITATE
(— TEMPORARILY) LIE STOP
RESIDENCE DUN WON DOON HALL
HOME SEAT SEMI STAY WENE WONE
ABODE COURT DAIRI DEMUR HOUSE
MAHAL MANSE YAMUN BIDING
DUKERY ELYSEE HOSTEL MANOIR
TENSER DEANERY DROSTDY
EMBASSY SOJOURN CURATAGE
DOMICILE DWELLING LEGATION
RESIANCE RESIANCY RESIDUUM
SEDIMENT SETTLING PREFECTURE
(— FOR STUDENTS) INN
(— OF ARCHBISHOP) PALACE
(— OF CHIEF OF VILLAGE) TATA
(— OF ECCLESIASTIC) MANSE PRIORY
DEANERY RECTORY CURATAGE
VICARAGE PARSONAGE
(— OF FRENCH PRESIDENTS) ELYSEE
(— OF MANDARIN) YAMEN YAMUN
(— OF MIKADO) DAIRI
(— OF PRIEST) CONVENTO
(— OF SOVEREIGN) PALACE
(— OF SULTAN) SERAGLIO
(FORTIFIED —) DUN
(HILL —) RATH
(OFFICIAL TURKISH —) KONAK
(RURAL —) SEAT FARMSTEAD
(SUMMER —) MAHAL
(TEMPORARY —) STAY
RESIDENT GER FIXED LEGER LIVER
INMATE LEDGER STABLE CITIZEN
DENIZEN DWELLER PRESENT
RESIANT RESIDER RESTING
HABITANT INHERENT KAMAAINA
MINISTER OCCUPANT
(— AT A UNIVERSITY) GREMIALE
(— OF HAWAII) KAMAAINA
(— OF NEWFOUNDLAND) LIVYER
(— OF WEST. AUSTRALIA) GROPER
(ALIEN —) GER METIC
(CHINESE — OF TIBET) AMBAN
(FOREIGN-BORN —) ALIEN
(OLD —) STANDARD
(TEMPORARY —) TRANSIENT
(SUFF.) ESE ITE
(—OF) ER IER YER
RESIDUAL RELICT REMANIE
REMANENT
RESIDUE ASH DREG FOOT GUNK
HEEL LAFE LAVE LEES REST SILT
SLAG UNIT MAZUT SHARD SHERD
BEGASS BORING BOTTOM GRUFFS

RELICS BAGASSE CINDERS REMAINS
HARDHEAD LEAVINGS LEFTOVER
REMANENT RESIDUUM SEMICOKE
TAILINGS
(— FROM DISTILLATION) VINASSE
(— FROM FAT) CRAP
(— FROM OLIVES) SANZA
(— FROM REFINING TIN) HARDHEAD
(— IN OPIUM PIPE) YENSHEE
(— IN STILL) BOTTOM BOTTOMS
(— OF COAL) COKE SEMICOKE
(— OF COKE) BREEZE
(— OF COMBUSTION) ASH
(— OF HONEYCOMB) SLUMGUM
(— OF PETROLEUM) MAZUT ASTATKI
(— OF SHINGLES) SPALT
(FRIABLE —) CALX
(INSOLUBLE —) MARC
(SMELTING —) SPEISS
(WORTHLESS —) SNUFF
(PL.) TANKAGE
RESIDUUM TAIL BOTTOM DEPOSIT
RESIDUE SEDIMENT
RESIGN QUIT DEMIT FORGO REMIT
YIELD PERMIT SUBMIT ABANDON
COMMEND DELIVER FORGIVE
ABDICATE RENOUNCE RELINQUISH
RESIGNATION PATIENCE
DEMISSION SURRENDER
RESILIENCE GIVE LIFE TONE
BOUNCE RECOIL SPRING REBOUND
BUOYANCY
RESILIENCY TONE
RESILIENT TOUGH BOUNCY LIVELY
SUPPLE WHIPPY ELASTIC SPRINGY
FLEXIBLE
RESIN ALK LAC BALM BATU BREA
HASH TOLU ALKYD AMBER ANIME
COPAL CUMAR ELEMI EPOXY GUGAL
GUGUL KAURI PITCH ROSEL ROSET
SIRUP SYRUP ANTIAR BINDER
CHARAS CONIMA DAMMAR GOOGUL
GUACIN HARTIN MASTIC STORAX
TAMANU ACOUCHI ACRYLIC
AMBRITE BENZOIN BISABOL DERRIDE
FLUAVIL GAMBOGE IONOMER
LADANUM PERSPEX SAGAPEN
SHELLAC ALKITRAN ALMACIGA
BAKELITE BDELLIUM CACHIBOU
CANNABIN COLOPHAN EUOSMITE
FORMVAIL GALAGALA GALLIPOT
GEDANITE GUAIACUM MALAPAHO
MELAMINE OPOPANAX PHENOLIC
SANDARAC SCAMMONY
(— DRAWN FROM TREES) CHIP
(— FROM HEMP) CHARAS
(— FROM NORWAY SPRUCE) THUS
(— OF FIR TREE) BLOB
(— PLASTIC) SARAN
(FLEXIBLE —) SARAN
(FOSSIL —) AMBER AMBRITE HARTITE
GEDANITE GLESSITE RETINITE
(GRADE OF —) SORTS

(GUM —) ELEMI GUGUL LASER
MYRRH ANTIAR BISABOL GAMBOGE
BDELLIUM SAGAPENUM
(NARCOTIC —) CHARAS CHURUS
(SYNTHETIC —S) TEFLON
(TURPENTINE —) ALK GALIPOT
COLOPHONY
(PREF.) RETIN(O)
RESINOID ALNUIN HELONIN LOBELIN
ASCLEPIN CERASEIN CHELONIN
TRILLIIN
RESINOUS ROSETY ROSETTY
RESIST BUCK DEFY FACE STAY REPEL
STAND DEFEND IMPUGN OPPOSE
REPUGN WITHER CONTEST DISPUTE
GAINSAY KNUCKLE RESERVE
WITHSET OUTBRAVE OUTSTAND
(— AUTHORITY) REBEL DEFORCE
(— SEPARATION) ATTRACT
RESISTANCE DRAG LOAD OHMAGE
REBUFF WITHER BALLAST ANTITYPY
BLOCKAGE FASTNESS FRICTION
HARDNESS OBSTACLE SEDITION
(— OF COTTON FIBERS) DRAG
(— OF KEYS) ACTION
(— THAT EXPLOSIVE MUST
OVERCOME) BURDEN BURTHEN
(— TO ATTACK) DEFENCE DEFENSE
(— TO CHANGE) INERTIA
(— TO COLOR CHANGE) FASTNESS
(— TO DISEASE) PREMUNITION
(— TO SLIPPING) BOND
(GREEK — GROUP) EDES ELAS
(PASSIVE —) SATYAGRAHA
(UNIT OF —) OHM
RESISTANT HARD STOUT STABILE
STUBBORN
(— TO CHANGE) FAST STICKY
(— TO HEAT) THERMODURIC
RESISTING OBSTANT RELUCTANT
RESISTOR BLEEDER DIVERTOR
RHEOSTAT
RESOLUTE BOLD FIRM GRIM BRAVE
FIXED HARDY MANLY STERN STIFF
STOUT GRITTY MANFUL PLUCKY
STABLE STANCH STEADY STUFFY
STURDY ANIMOSE ANIMOUS
DECIDED CONSTANT FAITHFUL
INTREPID POSITIVE STALWART
STUBBORN UNSHAKEN
(MAKE —) STEEL
RESOLUTELY TALLY FIRMLY
STOUTLY
RESOLUTION VOW SAND THEW
NERVE PARTY PLUCK POINT STARCH
ACUERDO BESLUIT CENSURE
COURAGE MANHEAD MANHOOD
PURPOSE RESOLVE THOUGHT
ANALYSIS DECISION DIERESIS
ENACTURE STRENGTH CONSTANCY
RESOLVE ACT BEND MELT REDE SOIL
UNDO LAPSE RELAX SALVE SOLVE
SOYLE UNTIE VOUCH ADJUST

ADVICE ASSOIL DECIDE DECREE
FACTOR INCIDE REDUCE SETTLE
STEVEN ABSOLVE ANALYZE APPOINT
BETHINK CONSULT PURPOSE
CONCLUDE DISSOLVE UNRIDDLE
UNTANGLE RECONCILE
(— GRAMMATICALLY) PARSE
(— INTO ELEMENTS) ANALYSE
ANALYZE
RESOLVED BENT BOUND INTENT
CERTAIN INTENSE RESOLUTE
(HALF —) GOOD
RESONANCE BODY EMPATHY
RAPPORT RESOUND SYNTONY
TYMPANY SONORITY VIBRANCY
MESOMERISM
RESONANT BIG BRASS RINGY
OROTUND RINGING SILVERY
VIBRANT CANOROUS PLANGENT
SONORANT SONOROUS SOUNDFUL
SOUNDING
RESORT GO RUN SPA BEAT DOME
HOWF LIDO SEEK TEEM TOUR TURN
CAUSE FRAME HAUNT HOWFF JOINT
RECUR RESET VISIT ESCORT FINISH
REPAIR RETURN REVERT THRONG
COMPANY PIMLICO RECOURSE
RESOURCE TEETOTUM
(— OF LEARNED) MUSEUM
(— TO) SEEK
(— TO DEVIOUS METHODS) FINAGLE
(— TO EXPEDIENTS) SHIFT
(BATHING —) PLAGE
(DISREPUTABLE —) KEN DIVE
(DRINKING —) DOGGERY
(EVIL —) ROOKERY
(LOW —) KEN DIVE ECHO STEW SPITAL
(MEANS OF —) REFUGE
(WORKINGMEN'S —) TEETOTUM
RESOUND DIN DUN ECHO PEAL
RING SOUND REECHO EXPLODE
REBOUND RESPEAK VIBRATE
REDOUBLE
RESOUNDING BRASS REVERB
REBOANT EMPHATIC FORCEFUL
PLANGENT RESONANT RUMOROUS
(— WITH TALK) ABUZZ
RESOURCE WON BOOT FUND WONE
MEANS SHIFT REFUGE RESORT
STOPGAP PURCHASE
(PL.) EASE FOND GAIN FUNDS
MEANS PURSE SINEW BOTTOM
FACULTY FOISONS PURCHASE
STRENGTH POCKETBOOK
RESOURCEFUL APT FENDY SHARP
SMART ADROIT CLEVER FACILE
SHIFTY PLANFUL
RESOURCEFULNESS SENSE SHIFT
AGILITY
RESPECT ORE WAY DUTY FACE HEED
HORE LOOK MARK DEFER DULIA
FRONT HONOR IZZAT PARTY VALUE
ASPECT BEHALF DETAIL ESTEEM

HALLOW HOMAGE NOTICE REGARD
CONCERN OBSERVE RESPITE
SUSPECT TASHRIF WORSHIP
CONSIDER HABITUDE RELATION
VENERATE
(PL.) DEVOIR

RESPECTABLE GOOD NICE SMUG
DOUCE DECENT PROPER FRUSANT
CULOTTIC

RESPECTFUL AWFUL CIVIL CAREFUL
DUTEOUS DUTIFUL HEEDFUL
REVERENT

RESPECTIVE SEVERAL

RESPIRATION SIGH EUPNEA
ANAPNEA DYSPNEA EUPNOEA
ROARING GRUNTING
(PREF.) PNEO PNEUM(A)(O)(ON)(ONO)
PNEUMATO SPIRO

RESPIRATOR MUZZLE CUIRASS
INHALER
(KIND OF —) DRINKER

RESPIRE BLOW LIVE REST EXHALE
REVIVE BREATHE SNUFFLE SUSPIRE

RESPITE SOB REST STAY TRUE
DELAY FRIST LETUP PAUSE BARLEY
BREATH LAYOFF REGARD REMISE
LEISURE RESPECT INTERVAL
REPRIEVE SURCEASE

RESPLENDENCE GLORY SHEEN
FULGENCE FULGENCY SPLENDOR

RESPLENDENT LUCID SHEEN
BRIGHT GILDED ORIENT SILVER
AUREATE SHINING GLORIOUS
GORGEOUS LUSTROUS SPLENDID
SUNSHINY

RESPOND FIELD REACT REPLY
ANSWER RETURN TRISAGION
(— TO LURE) STOOL
(— TO PROVOCATION) RISE
(— WARMLY) RISE

RESPONDENT ANSWERER APPELLEE

RESPONSE AMEN ECHO CHORD
REPLY SNAFF ANSWER EARFUL
VOLLEY INTROIT RESPOND
ANTIPHON BEHAVIOR INSTINCT
REACTION REANSWER RECEPTION
(— OF KEYS) ACTION
(— OF SHIP) STEERING
(— TO GRAVITY) GEOTAXIS
(INVOLUNTARY —) TIC
(LITURGICAL —) RESPONSORY
(NONCOMMITAL —) ISEE

RESPONSIBILITY BABY BALL CARE
DUTY ONUS WITE BLAME GUILT
TRUST CHARGE RACKET

RESPONSIBLE GOOD SOLID DIRECT
LIABLE AMENABLE
(JOINTLY —) SOLIDARY

RESPONSION REPLY ANSWER
(PL.) SMALLS

RESPONSIVE OPEN SOFT WARM
GUILTY MUTUAL NIMBLE SUPPLE

TENDER MEETING AMENABLE
SENSIBLE
(— TO BEAUTY) ESTHETIC
(— TO STIMULI) SENTIENT
(MUTUALLY —) ANTIPHONIC
(NOT —) IMMUNE

RESPONSIVENESS TOUCH FEELING
(ABNORMAL —) SENSITIVITY

RESPONSORY ANTHEM LIBERA
GRADUAL RESPOND

REST BED LAY LIE PUT SET SIT SOB
BASE BLOW CALM CAMP EASE HANG
HEEL LAIR LAVE LEAN LIOS LISS
PROP RELY RIDE RUST STAY STOP
COUCH FOUND LEATH LIEBY PAUSE
PEACE POISE QUIET RENEW ROOST
SLEEP SPELL STAND TRUST WREST
ANCHOR BOTTOM FAUCRE FEWTER
GROUND INSIST REMAIN REPOSE
SETTLE SIESTA STEADY UNTIRE
ADHARMA BALANCE BREATHE
CAESURA CLARION COMFORT
GALLOWS NOONING RECLINE
REFRESH RELACHE REMNANT
REQUIEM RESIDUE RESPITE SILENCE
SLUMBER SOJOURN SUFFLUE
SUPPORT SURPLUS AKINESIS
INTERVAL QUIETUDE STANDOFF
VACATION
(— FOR SPEAR OR LANCE) QUEUE
FAUCRE FEWTER
(— FOR SUPPORT) ABUT
(— FOR TYMPAN) GALLOWS
(— HORSE) WIND
(— IDLY) SLUG
(— LAZILY) FROWST
(— ON PLANER) SIDEHEAD
(— ON SUPPORT) BOTTOM
(— UPRIGHT) STAND
(HALF —) MINIM SOSPIRO
(LATHE —) STEADY
(LEG — ON SADDLE) CRUTCH
(MUSKET —) GAFFLE
(NOONDAY —) NAP SIESTA
(QUARTER —) SOSPIRO
(SHORT —) CATNAP
(PREF.) PAULO

RESTATE REHASH

RESTATEMENT SUMMARY

RESTAURANT CAFE DINER GRILL
HOUSE PLACE BISTRO BUFFET
EATERY AUTOMAT BEANERY
CABARET CANTEEN CANTINA
OSTERIA TEAROOM HIDEAWAY
BRASSERIE CHOPHOUSE TRATTORIA
(— KEEPER) BISTRO TRAITEUR
(SMALL —) CAFF

RESTAURANTEUR (FAMOUS —)
SARDI

RESTFUL COOL SOFT QUIET PLACID
EASEFUL RELAXED SOOTHFUL
TRANQUIL

RESTHARROW WHIN CAMMOCK
SITFAST LANDWHIN
RESTHOUSE KHAN SERAI
AMBALAM CHHATRI KHANKAH
RESTING DORMANT
(PREF.) STATO
RESTING PLACE
(ALSO SEE RESTHOUSE) FORM GIST
GITE STAGE CHHATRI DHARMSALA
RESTITUTION AMENDS RETURN
RECOVERY
(FINAL —) APOCATASTASIS
RESTIVE ANTSY BALKY FUDGY
ITCHY RESTY RUSTY FIDGETY
UNRESTY UNWAYED CONTRARY
INACTIVE RESTLESS SKITTISH
SLUGGISH STUBBORN UNWIELDY
RESTLESS ANTSY FIKIE FUDGY
ITCHY FITFUL HAUNTY HECTIC
ROVING UNEASY AGITATO ERETHIC
FIDGETY FLIGHTY FRETFUL INQUIET
RAMPLER RAMPLOR RESTIVE
TEWSOME TOSSING UNQUIET
UNRESTY VARIANT WAKEFUL
FEVERISH FEVEROUS STEERING
(— FLYCATCHER) GRINDER
RESTLESSNESS FIKE STIR FIDGET
UNREST DISQUIET ACATHISIA
AKATHISIA JACTATION
RESTORATION REPAIR RETURN
RENEWAL RESTORE REVIVAL
EXCHANGE RECOVERY REMITTER
RESTORAL RECLAMATION
RESTORATIVE ACOPON BALSAMIC
SALUTARY SANATIVE ANALEPTIC
RESTORE FIX CURE HEAL AMEND
BLOCK COVER REDUR REFER RENEW
REPAY STORE YIELD ASTORE
DOCTOR RECALL REDEEM REFORM
REFUND RELATE RENDER REPONE
REVERT REVIVE CONVERT ENSTORE
INPAINT REBUILD RECLAIM RECOVER
RECRUIT RECYCLE REFOUND
REFRESH REPLACE REVOLVE
DECOHERE REANSWER RECREATE
RESTITUE RETRIEVE RESURRECT
(— CONFIDENCE) REASSURE
(— TO CIVIL RIGHTS) INLAW
(— TO FORMER STATE) REHAB
(— TO HEALTH) CURE HEAL MEND
(— TO LIFE) REVIVIFY
(— TO OFFICE) REPONE
(— TO ORDER) STILL
(— YOUTH) REJUVENATE
RESTRAIN BAR BIT DAM BATE BIND
BOLT BUCK COOP CRIB CURB DAMP
GRAB GYVE HEAD HEFT KEEP REIN
SHUT SINK SNEB SNIB SNUB STAY
STEM STOP STOW BRANK CHAIN
CHECK COART CRAMP DETER GUARD
LEASH MINCE POUND REPEL SHUNT
SOBER STILL STINT TRASH ARREST

BOTTLE BRIDLE CHASTE COERCE
DETAIN ENJOIN FETTER FORBID
GOVERN HALTER HAMPER HINDER
KENNEL OBLIGE REBUKE RETAIN
RETIRE REVOKE STIFLE STRAIN
TEMPER TETHER ABRIDGE ABSTAIN
CHASTEN COHIBIT CONFINE
CONTAIN CONTROL ENCHAIN
EXCLUDE INHIBIT INJUNCT QUALIFY
RECLAIM REFRAIN REPRESS
RETRACT SHACKLE SNAFFLE
SWADDLE BULLDOZE COMPESCE
COMPRESS HANDCUFF IMPRISON
RESTRICT SIDELINE WITHDRAW
WITHHOLD
(— BY FEAR) OVERAWE
(— HAWK'S WING) BRAIL
(— MOTION) SNUB
(PREF.) ISCH(O)
RESTRAINED SOBER CHASTE
MODEST SEVERE ASHAMED
DISCREET RESERVED RITENUTO
RESTRAINER YOKE
RESTRAINT BIT BEND CLOG CURB
HEFT STAY STOP CHECK CRAMP
FORCE LEASH SPARE STENT STINT
TRASH ARREST BRIDLE DURESS
FETTER STAYER TETHER AWEBAND
BONDAGE CONTROL DURANCE
EMBARGO MANACLE SNEER
SNAFFLE TRAMMEL HEADREST
SOBRIETY
(— OF GOODS) HOCK
(BEYOND —) APE
(WITHOUT —) INSPADES
RESTRICT PEG TIE CURB HOLD
BOUND CHAIN COART FENCE HEDGE
STINT THIRL COARCT COERCE
CORRAL CORSET ENTAIL HAMPER
NARROW ASTRICT COHIBIT COMBINE
QUALIFY REPRESS SCANTLE
SWADDLE CONTRACT DEROGATE
DIMINISH RESTRAIN STRAITEN
(— MEANING) MODIFY
RESTRICTED CLOSE CRAMP LOCAL
CLOSED FINITE NARROW STRAIT
STRICT OBLIGATE PAROCHIAL
RESTRICTION STENT STINT
BURDEN DENIAL BARRIER CONFINE
RESERVE SQUEEZE BLACKOUT
CABOTAGE RESTRAINT
(LEGAL —) LIEN
(PROPERTY —) EASEMENT
(PL.) BARS SWADDLE
RESTRICTIVE SEVERE BINDING
STYPTIC COACTIVE LIMITARY
LIMITING CONFINING
RESTY LAZY RESTIVE INACTIVE
INDOLENT SLUGGISH
RESULT GO END OUT ECHO FALL
FATE FAVE GROW RISE TAKE BACON
BRING CHILD ENSUE EVENT FRUIT

FUDGE ISSUE PROOF EFFECT EFFORT
ENDING EVOLVE FINISH FOLLOW
GROWTH RECOIL REVERT SEQUEL
SPRING UPCOME UPSHOT ENTRAIN
FALLOUT FINDING OUTCOME
PROCEED PURPOSE REBOUND
REDOUND SUCCEED SUCCESS
FRUITAGE SEQUENCE OFFSPRING
(— FAVORABLY) SUCCEED
(— FROM) SUE
(ALGEBRAIC —) DUAL EXPANSION
(AS A —) AGAIN
(INCONCLUSIVE —) DOGFALL
(INEVITABLE —) NEMESIS
(PATHOLOGICAL —S) ALCOHOLISM
(REWARDING —) HAY
(SECONDARY —) SEQUELA
(PL.) AFTERINGS
(SUFF.) ISATION IZATION
RESULTANT CONCEPT OUTCOME
PROGENY
RESUME RENEW REOPEN
RECOVER SUMMARY CONTINUE
PURLICUE REASSUME RENOVATE
REOCCUPY
(PL.) EXCERPTA
RESURRECTION RISE RIST UPRIST
REBIRTH REVIVAL
RESURRECTION PLANT
FERNWORT
RESUSCITATE REVIVE QUICKEN
SUSCITE REVIVIFY
RESUSCITATION KATSU RENEWAL
REVIVAL
RET RAIT RATE SOAK DEWROT
RETABLE PREDELLA
RETAIL REGRATE HUCKSTER
(— OUTLET) MINILAB
(— STORE) WAREHOUSE
RETAILER DEALER CLOTHIER
HUCKSTER
RETAIN HAVE HEFT HOLD KEEP SAVE
CATCH ATHOLD CONTAIN RESERVE
CONTINUE MAINTAIN PRESERVE
(— MOMENTUM) DRIFT
RETAINER FEE FOOL HEWE LACKEY
MENIAL RIBALD SEQUEL YEOMAN
HOBBLER HUSCARL JACKMAN
LACQUEY PANDOUR SERVANT
TRAVERS EMPLOYEE FOLLOWER
HENCHMAN MYRMIDON
BURKUNDAZ PENSIONER
(ARMED —) GALLOGLASS
GALLOWGLASS
(JAPANESE —) SAMURAI
(PL.) FOLK
RETALIATE REPAY AVENGE RETORT
REQUITE RECIPROCATE
RETALIATION QUITS MARQUE
TALION REPRISAL REQUITAL
(MAKE —) TURN
(VINDICTIVE —) REVENGE
RETALIATORY COUNTER

RETARD LAG CHOP DAMP DRAG
SLOW STEM BRAKE DEFER DELAY
ELONG STUNT TARDY TARRY THROW
TRASH BACKEN BELATE DEADEN
DETAIN HINDER INHIBIT SLACKEN
ENCUMBER OBSTRUCT PROTRACT
RESTRAIN
RETARDANT (FIRE —) BORAX
RETARDATION LAG DRAG DELAY
ARREST
RETARDED DARK BEHIND LAGGED
SIMPLE OVERAGE
RETARDING LENTANDO
RETCH GAG BOKE KECK HEAVE REACH
VOMIT KECKLE RECCHE STRAIN
RETCHING HEFT
RETEM JUNIPER
RETENTION MEMORY RETAIN
HOLDING KEEPING RETINUE
RETIARIUS RETIARY GLADIATOR
RETICENCE RESERVE SECRECY
RESTRAINT
RETICENT ABED DARK SNUG CLOSE
SECRET SILENT MIMMOUD SPARING
BOUTONNE
RETICENTLY HEIMLICH
RETICULATE MESHED NETTED
RETICULE BAG CABAS SACHET
WORKBAG CARRYALL RIDICULE
RETICULUM NET MITOME
NETWORK MATTULLA
RETINOIC ACID TRETINOIN
RETINOL CODOL
RETINOPHORE VITRELLA
RETINUE CREW GING PORT ROUT
SUIT TAIL COURT MEINY SUITE TIRED
TRAIN FAMILY REPAIR RETAIN
COMPANY CORTEGE SOWARRY
EQUIPAGE TENDANCE BODYGUARD
(— OF CAVALRY) SOWARRY
(VILLAINOUS —) BLACKGUARD
RETIRE GO GET DRAW GIVE AVOID
LEAVE MICHE REBUT DEPART LOCATE
RECALL RECEDE RECESS RECOIL
SHRINK SURVEY PENSION REGRADE
RETRACT RETREAT WITHDRAW
(— IGNOMINIOUSLY) SLINK
(— IN CRICKET) BOWL
RETIRED QUIET SECRET DEVIOUS
OBSCURE OUTGONE PRIVATE
RETRAIT SECLUSE SHADOWY
ABSTRUSE EMERITUS SECLUDED
SOLITARY
(— FROM PLAY) DOWN
RETIREMENT SHADE RECESS
RETOUR SECESS PRIVACY PRIVATE
RETREAT FIRESIDE SOLITUDE
RETIRING SHY NESH TIMID DEMURE
MODEST FUGIENT RESERVED
UMBRATIC RECESSIVE
(— ROOM) RECAMERA
RETORT MOT QUIP RISE SNAP VENY
QUIRK REPAY REPLY SALLY ANSWER

REGEST RETURN RIPOST BOMBOLA
CORNUTE CRUSHER PELICAN
REFLECT RIPOSTE SQUELCH
BACKWORD BLIZZARD COMEBACK
MAGAZINE RECEIVER REPARTEE
(CURT —) SNAPHANCE
(GROUP OF —S) SETTING
(PUNNING —) CLINCH
(WITTY —) KNACK ZINGER
RETRACE RECALL FLYBACK RETREAT
UNTREAD BACKTRACK
RETRACT BACK UNSAY ABJURE
DISOWN RECALL RECANT RECEDE
REVOKE SHRINK UNLOOK RESCIND
RETREAT SWALLOW PALINODE
RENOUNCE WITHDRAW
RETRACTED INNER
RETRACTION PALINODE PALINODY
RETREAT DEN DOME DROP FADE
GIVE LAIR NEST ROUT ARBOR AVOID
BOWER LODGE NICHE QUAIL QUIET
SHADE START ASHRAM ASYLUM
BACKUP CASTLE HARBOR RECEDE
RECESS REFUGE RESILE RETIRE
REVOLT CABINET DESCEND PRIVACY
RETIRAL RETRACT SHELTER
ANABASIS CRAWFISH DISMARCH
FALLBACK FASTNESS NESTLING
RECOURSE RECULADE SOLITUDE
STAMPEDE WITHDRAW CREEPHOLE
KATABASIS
(— FOR FISH) HOD
(FORTIFIED —) REDUIT
(LAST —) REDOUBT
(RELIGIOUS —) ASRAM ASHRAM
(SECURE —) STRENGTH
(SHADY —) ALCOVE
(WINTER —) HIBERNACLE
RETRENCH OMIT EXCISE LESSEN
REDUCE ABRIDGE CURTAIL SHORTEN
RETRENCHMENT CUT RAMPART
EXCISION RETIRADE LESSENING
RETRIBUTION PAY PAYOFF RETURN
REWARD WISSEL MANNAIA PENALTY
REVENGE REQUITAL
RETRIBUTIVE VENGEFUL VINDICTIVE
RETRIEVE SHACK RECALL RECURE
REGAIN REPAIR RESCUE REVIVE
CORRECT RECOVER RESTORE
SALVAGE
RETRIEVER LAB FINDER GUNDOG
LABRADOR WATERRUG
RETROFLEX DEMAL CORONAL
CEREBRAL INVERTED REFLEXED
RETROGRADE RECEDE RETRAL
DECLINE INVERSE OPPOSED
REGRADE RETREAT BACKWARD
DECADENT REARWARD WITHDRAW
RETROGRESS SINK REGRESS
BACKSLIDE
RETROGRESSION SINK REGRESS
RETREAT FALLBACK
RETROSPECT REVIEW

RETUND DULL TURN BLUNT REFUTE
RETURN EBB GET COME ECHO TURN
VAIL RECUR REFER REPAY REPLY
VISIT YIELD AIRWAY ANSWER
HOMING REMISE RENDER REPAIR
REPASS REPORT RESORT RETIRE
RETORT RETOUR REVERT CLEANUP
PAYMENT REBOUND REDOUND
REFLECT REPRISE REQUITE RESTORE
REVENUE ATTOURNE DIVIDEND
ELECTION EPANODOS FEEDBACK
PICKINGS REACCESS REANSWER
RECOURSE RECOVERY REDITION
REFLECTION RECIPROCATE
(— FOR GOOD) REWARD
(— FROM DEATH) ARISE
(— LIKE FOR LIKE) RETALIATE
(— OF MERCHANDISE) COMEBACK
(— TENNIS BALL) RALLY
(— TO BAD HABITS) LAPSE
(— TO FORMER STATE) RELAPSE
(— TO ORIGINAL CONDITION)
RECYCLE
(— TO ZERO) FLYBACK
(GET IN —) REAP
(GROUNDED —) BOND
(TENNIS —) GET BOAST
(TRIFLING —) PEPPERCORN
RETURNING REDIENT REMEANT
REDITION
RETURN OF THE NATIVE
(AUTHOR OF —) HARDY
(CHARACTER IN —) VYE CLYM VENN
DAMON CANTLE JOHNNY DIGGORY
NUNSUCH WILDEVE EUSTACIA
THOMASIN CHRISTIAN YEOBRIGHT
REUBEN (FATHER OF —) JACOB
(MOTHER OF —) LEAH
REUEL (FATHER OF —) ESAU
(MOTHER OF —) BASHEMATH
(SON OF —) ELIASAPH
REUNE (ONE WHO —S) ALUM
ALUMNUS
REUNION COLLEGE ADHESION
HERENIGING
(— WITH BRAHMA) NIRVANA
REUNITE RALLY REUNE REJOIN
RECONCILE
REUSE RECYCLE
REVEAL BID BARE BLAB HINT JAMB
KNOW OPEN SHOW TELL WRAY
BREAK EXERT SPEAK SPLIT UNRIP
UNTOP UTTER YIELD ACCUSE
APPEAR BETRAY BEWRAY DESCRY
DETECT EVINCE IMPART OSTEND
PATEFY SPRING UNHELE UNLOCK
UNMASK UNVEIL UNWRAP BESPEAK
CLARIFY CONFESS DEVELOP DISPLAY
DIVULGE UNCLOAK UNCOVER
UNSHALE UNTRUSS DECIPHER
DISCLOSE DISCOVER INDICATE
MANIFEST UNBURDEN UNSHADOW
UNSHROUD

(— BY SIGNS) EXHIBIT
(— SECRETS) BABBLE
(— UNINTENTIONALLY) BETRAY
REVEILLE DIAN DIANA LEVET ROUSE
SIGNAL TRAVALLY
REVEIVER (DISTILLING —) BOLTHOLE
REVEL JOY MASK RANT RIOT BIZLE
COMUS FEAST GLOAT GLORY
WATCH BEZZLE FROLIC GAVALL
SPLORE TRESCA WALLOW WANTON
CAROUSE DELIGHT ROISTER
TRESCHE CAROUSAL DOMINEER
FESTIVAL WITHDRAW
(NOISY —) JAMBOREE
(PL.) REVELRY
REVELATION TORA TORAH EXPOSE
ORACLE REVEAL BATHKOL BATHQOL
SHOWING GIVEAWAY OVERTURE
APOCALYPSE
(— OF GOD'S WILL) LAW
(SUDDEN —) KICK
REVELER GREEK RANTER RIOTER
FRANION PIERROT ROISTER
BACCHANT CAROUSER
MERRYMAKER
REVELRY JOY ORGY RIOT RIOTISE
WASSAIL CARNIVAL CAROUSAL
FESTIVAL
REVENANT GHOST WRAITH SPECTER
REVENGE HELL WREAK WROIK
AVENGE ULTION REQUITE REQUITAL
REVANCHE
(MONTEZUMA'S —) TURISTA
REVENGED EVEN
REVENUE RENT JAGIR MANSE YIELD
INCOME ENTRADA FINANCE PROFITS
HACIENDA INCOMING
(— FROM WATER RIGHTS) JALKAR
(— REVENUE PAID TO POPE)
ANNAT
(CHURCH —) PATRIMONY
(GOVERNMENT —) JAGHIR
(GOVERNMENT —S) JAGIR JAGHIR
JAGHIRE
(STATE —) HACIENDA
REVERBERATE DIRL ECHO RING
REPEL RETORT REVERB REBOUND
REDOUND REFLECT RESOUND
REVERBERATING REBOANT
RESONANT SOUNDING
REVERBERATION ECHO REDOUND
REBOATION
REVERE ADORE HONOR ADMIRE
ESTEEM HALLOW RESPECT WORSHIP
VENERATE
REVERED
(PREF.) SEMNO
REVERENCE AWE ORE CULT FEAR
DREAD HONOR MENSK PIETY WURTH
HOMAGE REGARD WORSHIP
DEVOTION VENERANT VENERATE
WORTHING

(— FOR ANIMALS) ZOISM
(IRRATIONAL —) FETICH FETISH
(SHOW —) KNEEL
REVEREND SRI SHRI SHREE SVAMI
SWAMI PASTOR POTENT STRONG
(PREF.) SEBASTO
REVERENT DEVOUT STRONG
AWESOME DUTIFUL
REVERENTIAL PIOUS SOLEMN
REVERIE DUMP DWAM MUSE DREAM
DWALM STUDY PONDER MEMENTO
MOONING DAYDREAM TRAUMEREI
REVERSAL KNOCK CHANGE DOUBLE
SWITCH BACKCAST BACKFLIP
OVERTURN THROWBACK
TURNABOUT
(PREF.) ALL(O)
REVERSE BACK DOWN FACE FLOP
JOLT UNDO ANNUL CHECK UPSET
VERSO CHANGE DEFEAT INVERT
REPEAL RETURN REVERT REVOKE
BACKSET COUNTER INVERSE
PUTBACK RETREAT REVERSO
SETBACK SNIFTER SUBVERT
BACKCAST CONTRARY CONVERSE
OPPOSITE OVERRULE OVERTURN
RAMVERSE TRAVERSE WATERLOO
(— OARS) SHEAVE
(— OF COIN) PILE TAIL WOMAN
(— OF NOTE) BACK
(— PAGE OF BOOK) VERSO REVERSO
(PREF.) DE DIS DYS
(— ORDER) OB
REVERSED BACK INVERSE
REVERTED ROVESCIO
(NOT —) DIRECT
REVERSI QUINOLAS
REVERSION SCRAPS ATAVISM
ESCHEAT REMNANT FEEDBACK
REVERTAL REVERTER THROWBACK
REVERT ANNUL ADVERT RESORT
RESULT RETOUR RETURN REVOKE
ESCHEAT RESTORE RECOURSE
BACKSLIDE
(— TO A SUPERIOR) FALL
REVETMENT SODWORK
REVIEW HASH VIEW REVIE NOTICE
REVISE SURVEY BRUSHUP RECENSE
REJUDGE CRITIQUE REVIEWAL
REVISION
(— A FLOP) PAN
(— UNSPARINGLY) SLATE
(CRITICAL —) PAN
(ENTHUSIASTIC —) RAVE
(KIND OF —) RAVE
REVIEWER CRITIC
REVILE CALL RAIL ABUSE BLEIR
BRAWL REBUT SCOLD SHEND SHENT
SLANG MISSAY MISUSE VILIFY
INVEIGH MISCALL MISNAME
BACKBITE DISGRACE EXECRATE
REPROACH CLAPPERCLAW

REVILING ABUSE ABUSION ABUSIVE
BLASPHEMY
REVISE EDIT ALTER REDACT REFORM
REVIEW CORRECT RECENSE REFLECT
REVISIT OVERHAUL
REVISER REDACTOR REFORMER
REVIEWER
REVISION REVIEW SURVEY REVISAL
REVIEWAL EPANAGOGE
REVITALIZER BRACER
REVIVAL IMAGE PICKUP REBIRTH
REPRISE WAKENING
REVIVE DAW EBB WAKE FETCH
QUICK RALLY RENEW ROUSE
EXHUME GINGER RECALL RELIVE
REVERT REVOKE EKPHORE ENLIVEN
FRESHEN ENGLISH QUICKEN
REFRESH RESPIRE RESTORE
RECREATE REDIVIVE REKINDLE
RENOVATE RETRIEVE
(— FIRE) CHUNK
REVOCATION REPEAL REVERSAL
ADEMPTION
REVOICE ECHO
REVOKE LIFT ADEEM ANNUL
RENIG CANCEL RECALL RECANT
RENEGE REPEAL REVERT ABOLISH
COMMUTE FINAGLE RECLAIM
RESCIND RETREAT REVERSE
ABROGATE REVOCATE
(— A LEGACY) ADEEM
REVOLT ARISE REBEL REPEL START
MUTINY OFFEND RELUCT UPRISE
UPROAR MUTATION OUTBREAK
SEDITION UPRISING JACQUERIE
REBELLION
(RELIGIOUS —) APOSTASY
REVOLTING GARISH HORRID
BILIOUS FEARFUL HATEFUL HIDEOUS
DREADFUL
REVOLT OF THE ANGELS
(AUTHOR OF —) FRANCE
(CHARACTER IN —) MAX ZITA
ISTAR ARCADE AUBELS JULIEN
SOPHAR MAURICE GILBERTE
SARIETTE ESPARVIEU THEOPHILE
EVERDINGEN
REVOLUTION GYRE RIOT TOUR
TURN CYCLE WHEEL CHANGE
ANARCHY CIRCUIT REVOLVE
GYRATION MUTATION NOVATION
ROTATION SEDITION REBELLION
(RELIGIOUS —) REFORMATION
REVOLUTIONARY RED RADICAL
MUSCADIN ROTATING BOLSHEVIK
REVOLUTIONIST JACOBIN
REDSHIRT
REVOLVE BIRL GYRE PIRL ROLL SPIN
TIRL TURN WELT ORBIT PIVOT
THROW TREND TROLL TWINE VERSE
WHEEL WHIRL CENTER CIRCLE
GYRATE PONDER ROTATE SPHERE

SWINGE WAMBLE AGITATE VERSATE
CONSIDER OVERTURN REVOLUTE
(CAUSE TO —) TRUNDLE
REVOLVER GAT GUN ROD RIFLE
STICK CANNON CUTTER HEATER
HOGLEG PISTOL RIFFLE SIXGUN
BULLDOG DUNGEON
(PART OF —) ROD BORE BUTT GATE
GRIP SPUR BLADE FRAME GUARD
LATCH SIGHT SLIDE STRAP BARREL
HAMMER HANDLE MUZZLE
CHAMBER TRIGGER CYLINDER
BACKSTRAP
REVOLVING ORBY VOLUBLE
GYRATORY VOLUTION
(PREF.)
(—AROUND) CIRCUM
REVUE SHOW REVIEW FOLLIES
REVULSION FEAR REACTION
REWARD FEE PAY UTU GREE MEED
RENT SPUR WAGE AMEED BOOTY
BRIBE CROWN LOWER MERIT PLUME
SHEPE YIELD BOUNTY DESERT
GERSUM PAYOFF SALARY TROPHY
WEDFEE AUREOLE GUERDON
PREMIUM RENTAGE SOSTRUM
STIPEND WARISON CONSIDER
DIVIDEND EXACTION REMEMBER
REQUITAL ACKNOWLEDGE
(— FOR GOOD NEWS) ALDRICIAS
(— FOR INFORMATION ON CATTLE
THIEVES) TASCAL
(— OF VICTORY) CROWN
(— TO HAWK FOR KILL) QUARRY
(— TO HOUNDS) HALLOW
(ILLUSORY —) CARROT
(UNDERCOVER —) PAYOFF PAYOLA
(UNEXPECTED —) JACKPOT
(PREF.) LUCRI
REWARDED APAID BOUNTIED
REWARDING FAT PREMIANT
(FINANCIALLY —) JUICY
REWRITTEN PALIMPSEST
REZAI ROSEI COVERLET MATTRESS
REZON (FATHER OF —) ELIADAH
RHABDUS SCOPULA
RHADAMANTHUS (FATHER OF —)
JUPITER
(MOTHER OF —) EUROPA
RHAPSODIC CONFUSED EFFUSIVE
RAPTUROUS
RHAPSODY JUMBLE MEDLEY
BOMBAST ECSTASY RAPTURE
REVERIE
(— SECTION) LASSU
RHATANY LEGUME
RHEA EMU EMEU NANDU NANDOW
RATITE OSTRICH AGDISTIS AVESTRUZ
(DAUGHTER OF —) JUNO CERES
VESTA
(FATHER OF —) URANUS
(HUSBAND OF —) SATURN

(MOTHER OF —) GAEA
(SON OF —) PLUTO NEPTUNE
RHEBOK PEELE REHBOC
RHEINGOLD, DAS
(CHARACTER IN —) ERDA LOGE FREIA
WOTAN FAFNER FASOLT FRICKA
HUNDING ALBERICH SIEGMUND
SIEGLINDE
(COMPOSER OF —) WAGNER
RHENIUM BOHEMIUM
RHEOMETER STROMUHR
RHEOSTAT DIMMER
RHESA (FATHER OF —) ZOROBABEL
RHESUS BANDAR BUNDER MONKEY
BHUNDER MACAQUE
(FATHER OF —) EIONEUS STRYMON
(MOTHER OF —) CALLIOPE
RHETORIC SPEECH BOMBAST
PROSAIC ELOQUENCE
(ROLLING —) PERIODS
RHETORICAL FLORID PURPLE
AUREATE FORENSIC SWELLING
(FLORIDLY —) AUREATE
RHETORICIAN ORATOR RHETOR
RHEUM GORE TEARS CHOLER SPLEEN
RHINARIUM MUFFLE
RHINE REAN DITCH RUNNEL
RHINESTONE DEWDROP
(PL.) GLITTER
RHINO CASH MONEY PONTOON
RHINOCEROS FOW ABADA BADAK
RHINO BORELE KEITLOA UNICORN
UPEYGAN NASICORN
RHINOCEROS BEETLE UANG
SCARABAEID
RHINOCEROS HORNBILL TOPAU
RHINOPLASTY NOSEJOB
RHIPIDION FLABELLUM
RHIZOID RHIZINA ROOTLET
RHIZOME KAVA NARD ARUKE CAAPI
STOCK ARALIA ARNICA ASARUM
GINGER IPECAC STOLON BERBERY
CALAMUS CULVERS GENTIAN
SCOPOLA ZEDOARY ASPIDIUM
BARBERRY BERBERIS HELONIAS
KAVAKAVA TRILLIUM TRITICUM
VERATRUM
(PL.) INULA GERANIUM
RHODE (FATHER OF —) POSEIDON
(MOTHER OF —) HALIA
(SON OF —) PHAETHON

RHODE ISLAND
CAPITAL: PROVIDENCE
COLLEGE: BROWN BRYANT
COUNTY: KENT BRISTOL NEWPORT
INDIAN: NIANTIC
MOTTO: HOPE
NATIVE: GUNFLINT
NICKNAME: LITTLERHODY
RIVER: PAWTUXET PAWCATUCK
BLACKSTONE
STATE FLOWER: VIOLET
STATE TREE: MAPLE
TOWN: BRISTOL NEWPORT WARWICK
CRANSTON KINGSTON PAWTUCKET

RHODE ISLAND BENT FURZETOP
RHODE ISLANDER GUNFLINT
RHODESIA
(SEE ZIMBABWE)
RHODODENDRON ROSEBAY
SPOONHUTCH
(THICKET OF —) SLICK
RHOMB LOZEN WHEEL CIRCLE
LOZENGE
RHOMBUS DIAMOND LOZENGE
RHONCHUS RALE SNORE SNORT
WHEEZE
RHUBARB ROW FLAP RHEUM
HASSEL CITRINE DISPUTE YAWWEED
ARGUMENT PIEPLANT
RHYME CHIME CLINK VERSE CRAMBO
POETRY RHYTHM TINKLE MEASURE
(— ROYAL) TROILUS
(PL.) RIMUR
RHYOLITE LIPARITE
RHYTHM BEAT STOT TIME CHIME
METER PULSE SWING GROOVE
CADENCE RAGTIME BACKBEAT
MOVEMENT SEQUENCE
(BREEDING —) VOLTINISM
(DISTORTED —) RUBATO
RHYTHMICAL LILTED CADENCED
MEASURED NUMEROUS ACCENTUAL
(NOT —) RAGGED
RHYTINA SEACOW
RIA CREEK INLET
RIAL COIN RYEL ROYAL KINGLY
SPLENDID
RIALTO MART BRIDGE EXCHANGE
RIANT GAY RIDENT LAUGHING
MIRTHFUL
RIATA LASSO LARIAT
RIB FIN KID BULB CORD DIKE JAPE
JOKE PURL RIDE SLAT WALE WIFE
CORSE COSTA GROIN NERVE OGIVE
PEARL RIDGE TEASE VARIX VITTA
WHELP BRANCH LIERNE NEEDLE
PARODY RIPPLE SCROLL TIMBER
TONGUE BRISTLE FEATHER NERVURE
PLEURAL STRATUM FORMERET
SIDEBONE
(— IN GROINED ROOF) SPRINGER
(— OF INSECT WING) VEIN
(— OF LEAF) NERVE
(— OF SHIP) WRONG
(— OF STOCKING) RIDGE
(— OF VIOLIN) BOUT
(—S OF UMBRELLA) FRAME
(SHORT —S) CROP
(STRENGTHENING —) FEATHER
(VAULTING —) NERVE OGIVE LIERNE
TIERCERON

(PL.) SLATS
(PREF.) COST(I)(O) PLEUR(I)(O)
(SUFF.) COSTAL COSTATE PLEURA
PLEUROUS
RIBALD LEWD ROGUE COARSE
RASCAL VULGAR
RIBALDRY HASH HARLOTRY
RIBAND RIBBON SCROLL
RIBBED RIBBY CORDED COSTATE
RIBBING SPOOFERY
RIBBON BAR BOW FOB PAN BEND
COST PADS BRAID CORSE FILET
LABEL PADOU PIECE RUBAN
SHRED TASTE BENDEL CADDIS
CORDON FERRET FILLET LISERE
RADULA RECORD RIBAND SHOWER
STRING TAENIA TAWDRY TISSUE
TONGUE BANDING SAUTOIR
TORSADE BANDEROL BOOKMARK
FRAGMENT STREAMER TRESSURE
PETERSHAM
(— AS BADGE OF HONOR) CORDON
(— AS HEADDRESS) TRESSOUR
TRESSURE
(— FOR BORDER) LISERE
(— HANGING FROM CROWN) JESS
(— USED FOR GARTERS) CADDIS
CADDICE
(— WORN ON HOSE) FLASH
(COLORED —S) DIVISA
(CORDED —) PETERSHAM
(END OF —S) FATTRELS
(FLOATING —) PAN
(GATHERED —) QUILLING
(KNOT OF —S) SORTIE
(LINGUAL —) TONGUE
(RASPING —) RADULA
(SILK —) CORSE PADOU TASTE
(WATERED —) PADS
(PL.) REINS
(PREF.) TAENI(A)(O)
(SUFF.) TENE
RIBBON FERN PTERIS
RIBBONFISH GARFISH GUAPENA
AGUAVINA BANDFISH DEALFISH
RIBBONLIKE TAENIATE TAENIOID
TAENIFORM
RIBBON TREE AKAROA HOIHERE
HOUHERE LACEBARK
RIBGRASS WINDLES BUCKHORN
HARDHEAD PLANTAIN
RIBWORT KLOPS HEADMAN RATTAIL
SOLDIER WINDLES HARDHEAD
HEADSMAN PLANTAGO
RICCIARDETTO (SISTER OF —)
BRADAMANTE
RICE AUS AMAN BORO PADI PAGA
RISE SELA TWIG ARROZ BATTY
BIGAS CANIN CHITS GRAIN MACAN
PADDY PALAY PATNA BRANCH
CEREAL CONGEE SIDDHA ANGKHAK
MANOMIN RISOTTO

(— BOILED WITH MEAT) PILAF PILAU
PILAW
(— COOKED WITH MEAT) RISOTTO
JAMBALAYA
(— FIELD) SAWAH
(— IN HUSK) PALAY
(— OF 2ND OR 3RD GRADE) CHITS
(— POLISHINGS) DARAC
(BOILED —) CANIN KANIN
(COLD —) SUSHI
(HUSKED —) CHAL
(INFERIOR —) PAGA
(KIND OF —) DIRTY BASMATI
(LONG-STEMMED —) AMAN
(MOUNTAIN —) SMILO
(SHORT-STEMMED —) AUS
(SPRING —) BORO
(UNCOOKED —) BIGAS
(UNMILLED —) PADI PADDY
(WILD —) MANOMIN
(PREF.) ORYZ(I) RIZI
RICEBIRD BUNTING CACIQUE
SPARROW BOBOLINK
RICE FLOWER PIMELEA
RICEGRASS BARIT SACATE ZACATE
RICH FAT ABLE DEEP FAIR HIGH LUSH
OOFY WARM GLEBY OPIME PLUMP
RITZY ROUND TINNY VIVID BATFUL
COSTLY DAEDAL FRUITY HEARTY
PLUMMY PLUSHY PODDED SUPERB
ULRICA AMUSING BATTLE COPIOUS
FERTILE MONEYED OPULENT
PINGUID PLASTIC WEALTHY
ABUNDANT AFFLUENT GENEROUS
HUMOROUS LUSCIOUS
(— IN FAME) RODERICK
(— IN GIFTS) PREMIOUS
(— IN INTEREST) JUICY
(— IN MALT) HEAVY
(— IN METAL) HIGHGRADE
(— IN RESOURCES) STRONG
(— IN SILICA) ACID
(— IN TIMBRE) GOLDEN
(— MAN) DIVES
(— OF SOIL) PINGUID
(MAN —) NABOB
(NOT —) PLAIN
(OSTENTATIOUSLY —) RITZY
(VERY —) WALLOWING
RICHARD DICCON
RICHARD CARVEL (AUTHOR OF —)
CHURCHILL
(CHARACTER IN —) FOX JONES
CARVEL DOROTHY MANNERS
RICHARD WALPOLE
RICHARD II (AUTHOR OF —)
SHAKESPEARE
(CHARACTER IN —) JOHN ROSS
YORK BAGOT BUSHY GAUNT GREEN
HENRY PERCY EDMUND PIERCE
SCROOP SURREY THOMAS AUMERLE
HOTSPUR LANGLEY MOWBRAY

NORFOLK RICHARD STEPHEN
BERKELEY HEREFORD FITZWATER
LANCASTER SALISBURY
WILLOUGHBY BOLINGBROKE
NORTHUMBERLAND

RICHARD III (AUTHOR OF —)
SHAKESPEARE
(CHARACTER IN —) ANNE JOHN
YORK DERBY HENRY JAMES LOVEL
BLOUNT DORSET EDWARD GEORGE
MORTON OXFORD RIVERS ROBERT
SURREY THOMAS TYRREL WALTER
BRANDON CATESBY HERBERT
NORFOLK RICHARD STANLEY
TRESSEL URSWICK VAUGHAN
BERKELEY CLARENCE HASTINGS
MARGARET RATCLIFF RICHMOND
BOURCHIER ELIZABETH ROTHERHAM
BRAKENBURY BUCKINGHAM
GLOUCESTER CHRISTOPHER

RICHES GOLD PELF WEAL LUCRE
WORTH MAMMON TALENT WEALTH
FORTUNE OPULENCE RICHESSE
TREASURE

RICHLY HIGH AMPLY FATLY FULLY
DEARLY

RICHNESS BODY LUXE SUMEN
LUXURY ELEGANCE FECUNDITY

RICHWEED RAGWEED COOLWEED

RICK GOAF GOFE REKE CANCH RICKLE
SPRAIN WRENCH CORNRICK

RICKETS RACHITIS

RICKETY SHAKY SHACKY SHACKLY
UNSOUND RACHITIC SHATTERY
UNSTABLE TOTTERING
RAMSHACKLE

RICKMATIC CONCERN BUSINESS

RICOCHET SKIP SKITE GLANCE
REBOUND

RICTUS GRIN GRIMACE

RID FREE QUIT SHED SHUT ANOMY
CLEAR EGEST REDDE SCOUR SHIFT
ACQUIT ANOMIE REMOVE DELIVER
(— OF IMPURITIES) SCORIFY
(— OF INSECTS) BUG
(— OF LICE) CHAT
(— OF WEEDS) CLEAN
(— ONESELF OF) DOFF DEPOSIT
DISPATCH
(GET — OF) DITCH ERASE PALMOFF
PAWNOFF

RIDDANCE SHUT RELIEF DISPATCH

RIDDER SIFT SIEVE RIDDLE

RIDDLE SIFT BLAIK REBUS
DEBASE ENIGMA FOITER PUZZLE
RUDDLE SCREEN CORRUPT CRIBBLE
EXPLAIN GRIDDLE GRIPHUS MYSTIFY
PERPLEX PROBLEM CRATEMAN
PERMEATE
(— AS GRAIN) REE
(PL.) MURLEMEWES

RIDDLER CRATEMAN
(— OF OLD) SPHINX

RIDE GO NAG RIB BAIT DOSA HACK
HURL LAST LIFT PRIG SAIL TOOL
CROSS DRIVE TEASE BANTER
CANTER DEPEND DODGEM GALLOP
JUMBLE NEEDLE NOTICE SADDLE
HAYRIDE JOYRIDE OVERLAP SURVIVE
TANTIVY BESTRIDE
(— A WAVE) BODYSURF
(— FAST) PRICK POWDER
(— HARD) POUND BUCKET
(— IN HIRED VEHICLE) JOB
(— ON) MOUNT
(— ON A WAVE) BODYSURF
(— ON HORSE) BOOT LARK BURST
JOCKEY SCHOOL
(— RECKLESSLY) BRUISE
(— TO HOUNDS) GO
(AMUSEMENT PARK —) SWING
(CYCLE —) SPIN

RIDER TACK ANNEX CROSS HAZER
LABEL COWBOY JOCKEY SITTER
ALLONGE CODICIL NAGSMAN
PRICKER CAVALIER DESULTOR
HORSEMAN
(DUKEY —) BRAKEMAN
(DUMMY —) CROSS

**RIDERS TO THE SEA (AUTHOR OF
—)** SYNGE
(CHARACTER IN —) NORA MAURYA
BARTLEY MICHAEL

RIDGE AAS ARM BAR FIN RIB RIG RYG
BALK BAND BANK BARB BROW BULT
BURR BUTT COMB DRUM FRET FULL
HACK HILL KEEL LINK LIST PAHA
PUFF RAIN REAN ROLL SHIN SPUR
WALE WAVE WELT BARGH CHINE
COSTA CREST EARTH EAVES GONYS
GYRUS JUGUM KNURL LEDGE LINCH
RINGE RUDGE SCOUT SHANK SPINE
TORUS VARIX WHELP BRIDGE
CARINA COLLOP CREASE CRISTA
CUESTA CULMEN DIVIDE DORSUM
FRENUM RAFTER RIDEAU SADDLE
SELION SUMMIT ANNULET
APODEMA BREAKER BUCCULA
COLLINE COSTULA EYEBROW
EYELINE HOGBACK HUMMOCK
INTHROW PROPONS RIGGING
SOWBACK WINDROW WITHERS
WRINKLE YARDANG CATOCTIN
CINGULUM FOREDUNE HEADLAND
RESTBALK SHOULDER
(— BETWEEN FURROWS) STITCH
RESTBALK
(— IN BREASTPLATE) TAPUL
(— IN COAL SEAM) HORSEBACK
(— IN HORSE'S MOUTH) EAR
(— MADE BY PLOWING) HACK SELION
(— MADE BY TOOL) BUR BARB BURR
(— OF BIRD'S BILL) CULM CULMEN
(— OF BRAIN CORAL) COLLINE
(— OF BREASTBONE) KEEL
(— OF CLAY) DOWLE

(— OF EARTH) BALK
(— OF FLESH) COLLOP
(— OF HORSE'S NECK) CREST
(— OF LAND) BULT RAIN SELION STITCH HOGBACK
(— OF SAND IN WATER) REEF SANDBAR
(— OF SCAPULA) SPINE
(— OF SCREW) THREAD
(— OF SNOW) SASTRUGA ZASTRUGA
(— OF UNPLOWED LAND) LINCH LINCHET
(— OF WAVE) CREST
(— ON BOOK) HUB
(— ON CLOTH) WALE
(— ON CROWN OF TOOTH) CINGULUM
(— ON FINGERBOARD OF GUITAR) FRET
(— ON FISH SCALE) CIRCULUS
(— ON FRUITS OF CARROT FAMILY) JUGUM
(— ON GLUMES) CARINA
(— ON MOLLUSK SHELL) COSTULA
(— ON OVULE) RAPHE
(— ON SEA FLOOR) SWELL
(— ON SEASHORE) STANNER
(— ON SHEET METAL) BEAD
(— ON SIDE OF SADDLE) PUFF
(— ON SKIN) WALE
(— ON VIOLIN) NUT
(— PROTECTING CAMP) RIDEAU
(—S ON ROCK) LAPIES
(— WITH SHARP SUMMIT) HOGBACK
(ANATOMICAL —) CARINA
(BEACH —) FULL
(CHEWING —) ENDITE
(CONNECTING —) HAUSE
(CONVOLUTED —) GYRUS
(DRAINAGE —) BREAKER
(GLACIAL —) OS KAME PAHA ARETE ESKAR ESKER SERAC ESCHAR NUNATAK
(HAIRLIKE —) LIRA
(ICE —) SERAC
(ISOLATED —) BARGH
(LONG STONY —) RAND
(MOUNTAIN —) COMB CHINE SIERRA BACKBONE
(NARROW —) DRUM RAZORBACK
(PROJECTING —) HOE SCOUT
(RESIDUAL —) CATOCTIN
(ROCK —) CLEAVER
(SAND —) DUNE ESKER WAVEMARK
(SEEDED —) DRILL
(SHARP-CRESTED —) ARETE ARRIS
(SLIGHT —) PROPONS
(SNOW —) ZASTRUGA
(UNPLOWED —) BALK BAULK
(WOODED —) CHENIER
(PL.) OSAR KNURLING
RIDGED RIDGY SHARP MILLED PORCATE CARINATE

RIDGELING RIG REGALD RIDGIL RIGGOT RIGINAL
RIDGEPOLE ROOFTREE
RIDICULE DO FUN GUY MOB PAN RIG TAX GAME GIBE JEER JEST JIBE JOEY MOCK PLAY QUIZ RAZZ SKIT TROT TWIT BORAK CHAFF CLOWN HORSE IRONY MIMIC MOMUS QUEER RALLY ROAST SCOFF SCOUT SMOKE SNEER TAUNT RANTER DERIDE EXPOSE RAILLY SATIRE BUFFOON LAMPOON MOCKERY SARCASM DERISION RAILLERY SATIRIZE SPOOFERY BURLESQUE
RIDICULOUS DOTTY DROLL FUNNY SILLY ABSURD INSANE COMICAL FOOLISH MOCKING DERISIVE DERISORY FARCICAL INDECENT COCKAMAMY MONSTROUS COCKAMAMIE
RIDING AWHEEL LIVELY OVERLAP PRICKANT SHIVANEE TRITHING CHEVACHIE
(— ACADEMY) MANAGE MANEGE
(— CROP) ROD
(— WHIP) CROP QUIRT
RIDOTTO BALL REDOUTE
RIEM RHEIM RIMPI STRAP THONG
RIENZI (CHARACTER IN —) COLA IRENE PAOLO ORSINI RIENZI ADRIANO COLONNA STEFANO RAIMONDI
(COMPOSER OF —) WAGNER
RIFE EASY FULL RANK QUICK READY ACTIVE FILLED NIMBLE STRONG CURRENT REPLETE ABUNDANT INCLINED MANIFEST NUMEROUS
RIFF BIT SKIM ROUTINE
RIFFLE REEF RIFF WAVE RAPID RIPPLE SHUFFLE WATERFALL
RIFFRAFF MOB RAFF SCUM SCAFF TRASH RABBLE REFUSE RUBBISH CANAILLE POPULACE RAGABASH
RIFLE RIG ROB KRAG LOOT RIPE PIECE YAGER CARBIN JEZAIL JUZAIL RIFFLE SNIDER ARISAKA BULLPUP BUNDOCK BUNDOOK CARABIN CARBINE DESPOIL ENFIELD ESCOPET MARTINI PILLAGE PLUNDER RANSACK SPORTER BANDHOOK REPEATER SPLITTER STRICKLE TAKEDOWN CHASSEPOT
(— BALL CASING) THIMBLE
(— PIN) TIGE
(OPTICAL DEVICE ON —) SNIPERSCOPE
RIFLEMAN JAGER JAEGER
(PL.) RIFLERY
RIFT RIVE BELCH CHASM CRACK SPLIT CLEAVE DIVIDE BLEMISH FISSURE CREVASSE
(— IN TIMBER) LAG
RIG RI FIG REG HOAX JEST JOKE REEK SEMI WIND DRESS EQUIP GETUP

PRANK RIDGE SPORT STORM TRICK
BANTER CLOTHE GUNTER ROTARY
SADDLE SCHEME MARCONI
SPUDDER SWINDLE BACKSTAY
RIDICULE SEMITRAILER
(DRILLING —) JACKUP
(TRUCKING —) SEMI
RIGADOON DANCE RIGODON
RIGEL REGEL ALGEBAR
RIGGED (FULLY —) ATAUNT
RIGGER CLIMBER SLINGER SCAFFOLD
RIGGING NET GEAR ROOF RIDGE
TACKLE APPAREL CLOTHING
JACKSTAY TACKLING
RIGHT DUE FEE FIT IUS OFF REE SAY
SOC BANG DUTY FAIR FLOP GALE
GOOD HAND ITER JUST LIEN REAL
RECT REET SANE SLAP SOKE TEAM
TRUE WELL CLAIM DRESS DROIT
ENTRY EXACT FAVOR FERRY LEGAL
RICHT SOUND STRAY TECHT TITLE
ACTION ACTUAL ANGARY BALLOT
DEMAND DEXTER EATAGE EQUITY
PROPER PUTURE ANNUITY APANAGE
AUBAINE BENEFIT CORRECT
DERECHO DESIRED FACULTY
FALDAGE FITTING FOLDAGE
FREEDOM GENUINE HAYBOTE
LIBERTY LICENSE PRENDER RECTIFY
RELIEVE SLAPDAB UPRIGHT
WARRANT BANALITY BLOODWIT
FIREBOOT FORESTRY HEIRSHIP
INTEREST LIFERENT SEIGNORY
SLAPDASH STALLAGE STRAIGHT
SUFFRAGE SUITABLE THIRLAGE
PREROGATIVE
(— AND LEFT) HAY HEY
(— AS COMMAND TO HORSES) REE
(— EYE) OD
(— HAND) MD OPENBAND
(— IN A THING) INTEREST
(— IN WIFE'S INHERITED PROPERTY)
CURTESY
(— OF CHOICE) OPTION
(— OF CREDITOR) SECURITY
(— OF EXILE) POSTLIMINY
(— OF EXIT) ISH
(— OF FREE QUARTERS) CORODY
(— OF HOLDING COURT) TEAM
(— OF INQUIRY) SOKEN
(— OF OWNERSHIP) TITLE COMMONTY
(— OF PASTURAGE) FEED STINT
EATAGE COWGATE COMMONAGE
HORSEGATE
(— OF PRECEDENCE) PAS
(— OF PRESENTATION) ADVOWSON
(— OF PROTECTION) MUND
(— OF RETURNING) REGRESS
(— OF USING ANOTHER'S PROPERTY)
EASEMENT
(— OF USING GRASSLAND) EATAGE
(— SIDE) OFFSIDE
(— TIME) TID

(— TO COLLECT REVENUE) DIWANI
DEWANEE DEWANNY
(— TO COMMAND) IMPERIUM
(— TO CUT WOOD) VERT GREENHEW
(— TO DECIDE) SAY
(— TO DRAW WATER) HAUSTUS
(— TO DRIVE BEAST) ACTUS
(— TO PASS OVER LAND) ITER
(— TO PAYMENT) RECOURSE
(— TO REJECT) VETO
(— TO SEIZE PROPERTY) ANGARY
(— TO SHOOT FIRST) CAST
(— TO SUE) STANDING
(— TO WORK IN MINE) BEN
(ALL —) HUNK JAKE HUNKY
(EXACTLY —) PAT
(FEUDAL —) CUDDY THIRL MARITAGE
THIRLAGE
(FISHING —) PISCARY
(HUNTING —) WARDEN
(INDIAN LEGAL —) HAK HAKH
(JUST —) TOAT TOATEE
(LEGAL —) IUS JUS JURE DROIT
ACCESS APPEAL COMMON FISHERY
HYPOTHEC
(LEGAL —S) JURA
(MILLER'S —) SOKEN
(MINING —) GALE
(NOT —) AWRY ACUTE
(PROPERTY —) DOMINIUM
(TURN —) GEE
(WIDOW'S —) TERCE TIERCE
(PL.) DIBS JURA
(PREF.) DEXIO DEXTR(O) ORTH(O)
RECT(I)
(— HAND) DEXIO DEXTR(O)
RIGHT ANGLE RECTANGLE
(HUNDREDTH OF —) GRAD GRADE
RIGHTEOUS GOOD JUST GODLY
MORAL ZADOC ZADOK DEVOUT
FITTING PERFECT SKILFUL UPRIGHT
INNOCENT VIRTUOUS
RIGHTEOUSNESS DOOM DHARMA
EQUITY JUSTICE HOLINESS
JUDGMENT JUSTNESS MORALITY
RECTITUDE
RIGHTFUL DUE JUST TRUE LEGAL
KINDLY LAWFUL PROPER FITTING
RIGHTFULNESS JUSTICE
RIGHT-HANDED RIGHTY DEXTRAL
SKILLED DEXTROUS CLOCKWISE
RIGHT-HANDWISE DEASIL DESSIL
DEISEAL CLOCKWISE
RIGHTLY RITE FITLY ARIGHT FAIRLY
JUSTLY HANDILY PERQUEER
SUITABLY
RIGHTS (KIND OF —) MIRANDA
RIGHT WHALE BOWHEAD
BALAENID MYSTICETE NORDCAPER
RIGID SET ACID CARK FIRM HARD
HIGH FIXED SOLID STARK STERN
STIFF STONY STOUT TENSE TONIC
TOUGH FORMAL FROZEN MARBLY

SEVERE STARCH STICKY STRICT
AUSTERE IRONCLAD RIGOROUS
STRAIGHT INELASTIC STRINGENT
(— IN SELF-DENIAL) ASCETIC

RIGIDITY FROST RIGOR RIGOUR
BUCKRAM SETNESS HARDNESS
STIFFNESS

RIGMAREE COIN TRIFLE

RIGMAROLE RANE NOMINY RABBLE
RAGMAN SLAMPAMP SLAMPANT
AMPHIGORY RIDDLEMEREE

RIGOLETTO (CHARACTER IN —)
GILDA MANTUA MADDALENA
RIGOLETTO SPARAFUCILE
(COMPOSER OF —) VERDI

RIGOR TYRANNY ASPERITY
HARDNESS SEVERITY

RIGOROUS FIRM HARD CLOSE
CRUEL EXACT HARSH HEFTY RIGID
STERN STIFF TOUGH BITTER FLINTY
SEVERE STRAIT STRICT STRONG
AUSTERE DRASTIC PRECISE
SPARTAN DISTRICT DRACONIC
EXACTING IRONCLAD STRAIGHT
(MORALLY —) PURITANIC
(NOT —) INEXACT
(UNDULY —) HARSH

RIKSMAL BOKMAL

RILE VEX ROIL ANGER PEEVE TICKOFF
IRRITATE

RILL PURL SIKE CLEFT DRILL PRILL
GROOVE RUNLET RILLOCK RIVULET
DROOKLET RIVELING TRICKLET
ARROYUELO WATERSHUT

RILLSTONE VENTIFACT

RIM HEM LIP BEAD BRIM CURB EDGE
SHOE BEZEL BRINK CHIME EAVES
FELLY FRAME HELIX SKIRT BORDER
CALKER CHOANA FILLET FLANGE
MARGIN EXCIPLE
(— HOLDING WATCH CRYSTAL)
BEZEL BEZIL
(— OF BASKET) HOOP
(— OF COROLLA) ANNULUS
(— OF CRATER) SOMMA
(— OF EAR) HELIX
(— OF GEM) GIRDLE
(— OF HORSESHOE) WEB
(— OF INSECT'S WING) TERMEN
(— OF JELLYFISH) VELUM
(— OF SANIO) CRASSULA
(— OF TIN) LIST
(— OF WHEEL) FELLY FELLOE
STRAKE
(— ON CASK) CHIMB CHIME CHINE
(— ON CLOG) CALKER
(— SURROUNDING FLAGELLUM)
CHOANA
(EXTERNAL —) FLANGE
(PROTECTIVE —) BANK
(RAISED —) ROSS
(PREF.) AMBO

RIMA CHINK CLEFT RIMULA FISSURE

RIME RIM HOAR RIND RUNG CRACK
CRUST FROST ROUND CRANREUCH

RIMPLE FOLD RIPPLE WRINKLE

RINALDO (BELOVED OF —) ANGELICA
(COUSIN OF —) ORLANDO
(FATHER OF —) AYMON
(HORSE OF —) BAYARD

RIND BARK PEEL PILL RYND SKIN
CRUST FROST SWARD CITRON
SWARTH
(— OF HAM) SKIN
(— OF MEAT) SPINE
(— OF POMEGRANATE) GRANATUM
(— OF ROASTED PORK) CRACKLING
(PREF.) LEMMO LEPO
(SUFF.) LEMMA

RING GO BEE BOW BUR CUP DEE DIE
EKE FAM JOW ORB PIT RIM AMBO
BAIL BAND BELL BONG BURR BUZZ
CRIC CURB DING DIRL ECHO GYRE
HOOP JING LOOP MAIL PASS PEAL
RACE RINK RUSH SHUT SING TANG
TOLL VIRL WISP AMBON ANLET
ARENA BAGUE CAROL CHIME CHINK
CLANG CYCLE GRAIN GROUP GUARD
GUIDE JEWEL KNELL LUNET PISTE
RIGOL ROUND ROWEL TORUS VERGE
WAFER WITHE BANGLE BECKET
BROUGH BUTTON CIRCLE CIRCUS
CIRQUE CLIQUE COLLAR COLLET
DINDLE EYELET FAMBLE GIMMER
GIRDLE HARROW KEEPER LARIGO
LEGLET RINGLE RUNDLE RUNNELL
SIGNET TONGUE TURRET VIROLE
WASHER ANNULUS ARMILLA
CIRCLET CIRCUIT CLAPPER COMPASS
COUPLER CRINGLE DIAMOND
FAMELEN FERRULE GALLERY
GARLAND GROMMET GUDGEON
MANILLA NUCLEUS PACKING
RESOUND ROWLOCK SHACKLE
STIRRUP THIMBLE VIBRATE
BRACELET BULLRING CINCTURE
CORONULE DINGDONG DRAUPNIR
DUSTBAND ENCIRCLE FAIRLEAD
PACIFIER SONORITY SURROUND
TRAVELER
(— AROUND ARTICULAR CAVITY)
AMBON
(— AROUND MOON) BROCH
(— AROUND NIPPLE) AREOLA
(— AT EACH END OF CINCH) LARIGO
(— A TREE) FRILL
(— ATTACHED TO JIB) HANK
(— BELLS) FIRE
(— FOR CARRYING SHOT) LADLE
(— FORMING HANDLE OF KEY) BOW
(— FOR SECURING BIRD) VERVEL
(— FOR TRAINING HORSES) LONGE
(— OF ANNULATED COLUMN) BAGUE
(— OF BOILER) STRAKE
(— OF CILIA) TROCHUS
(— OF COLOR) STOCKING

(— OF DNA) PLASTID
(— OF DOTS AROUND EDGE OF COIN) GRAINING
(— OF LIGHT) GLORY
(— OF ODIN) DRAUPNIR
(— OF PILES) STARLING
(— OF RIDING SCHOOL) PISTE
(— OF ROPE) HANK BECKET GARLAND GROMMET SNORTER SNOTTER
(— OF SATURN) ANSA
(— OF SPINES) CORONULE
(— OF STANDING STONES) CAROL
(— OF TWO HOOPS) GEMEL GEMMEL
(— OF WAGONS) CORRAL LAAGER
(— ON BATTLEAX) BUR BURR
(— ON BIRD'S TIBIA) ARMILLA
(— ON DARTBOARD) TREBLE
(— ON DECK) CRANCE
(— ON GUN CARRIAGE) LUNET LUNETTE
(— ON HINGE) GUDGEON
(— ON LAMP) CRIC
(— ON LANCE) BURR
(— ON SPAR) TRAVELER
(— ON UMBRELLA ROD) RUNNER
(— SUPPORTING LAMPSHADE) GALLERY
(— SURROUNDING BUGLE) VIROLE
(— SUSPENDING COMPASS) GIMBAL
(— TO ENCLOSE DEER) TINCHEL TINCHILL
(— UNDER BEEHIVE) EKE
(— USED AS MONEY) MANILLA
(— USED AS VALVE) WAFER
(— WITH GROOVED OUTER EDGE) THIMBLE
(— WITH VIBRATION) DIRL
(BLACKSMITH'S —) BOLSTER
(BRIGHT —) HALATION
(CERVICAL —) TORQUE
(CURTAIN —) EYE
(FINGER —) HOOP
(FLESHY —) ANNULUS
(HARNESS —) DEE BUTTON LARIGO TERRET TORRET TURRET
(HAWK'S —) VERVEL
(INTERLINKED METAL —S) MAIL
(JOINED —) GIMMER GIMMOR
(KIND OF —) MOOD
(LITTLE —) ANNULET
(LUMINOUS —) BROUGH
(MOUNTAINEER'S —) KARABINER
(NECKERCHIEF —) WOGGLE
(NOSE —) PIRN
(OIL —) WIPER
(PACKING —) LUTE
(PART OF —) BAND CLAW PRONG SHANK STONE COLLET SETTING HALLMARK
(PLAITED —) RUSH WISP
(SURGICAL —) CURETTE
(SWIVEL —) TERRET TERRIT
(TAPERING SHANK —) BELCHER

(TARGET —) SOUS SOUSE
(TOOTHED IRON —) HARROW
(TOP OF —) BEZEL BEZIL
(PREF.) CRICO CYCL(O) GYRO
(HAVING OPENED —) SECO
RING AND THE BOOK (AUTHOR OF —) BROWNING
(CHARACTER IN —) PAUL GUIDO PIETRO GIUSEPPE POMPILIA VIOLANTE COMPARINI CAPONSACCHI FRANCESCHINI
RINGDOVE QUIST CUSHAT CUSHIE QUEEST TOOZOO ZOOZOO COWSHOT COWSHUT
RINGED GYRATE ZONATE ANNULAR ANNULOSE
RINGED SNAKE COLUBRID
RINGER CHEER YOUTH COWBOY CROWBAR STOCKMAN
RING FINGER ANNULAR
RINGGIT DOLLAR
RINGHALS COBRA
RINGING BELL BRIGHT FERVID JANGLE CLANGOR OROTUND SINGING DECISIVE RESONANT SONORANT SONOROUS TINNIENT TINNITUS
(— IN THE EARS) TINNITUS
(CHANGE —) CINQUES SINGLES
RINGLEADER FUGLEMAN
RINGLET CURL LOCK TRESS TENDRIL
(— ON FOREHEAD) FAVORITE
(PREF.) CIRRI(I)(O)
RING-NECKED TORQUATE
RING-NECKED DUCK DOGY SCAUP MOONBILL RINGBILL BLACKJACK
RING OUZEL AMSEL THRUSH WHISTLER
RING PLOVER SANDY COLLIER KILLDEE DULWILLY RINGNECK
RING-SHAPED ANNULAR CRICOID ANNULARY ANNULATE CIRCULAR
RINGTAIL CACOMIXL CACOMISTLE SERPIGO
RINGWORM TINEA KERION TETTER SERPIGO
RINGWORM BUSH SENNA
RINK ALLEY GLACIARIUM
RINSE NET SIND WASH RANGE RENCH RENSH RINGE SCIND SCOUR SWILL BLUING DOUCHE CLEANSE
RINSING NET SIND FLUSH RESIDUE
RIOT DIN HURL BRAWL REVEL WORRY ATTACK CLAMOR EXCESS JUMBLE MEDLEY RANTAN SPLORE TUMULT ANARCHY CONFUSE DESPOIL REVELRY BLOODWIT CAROUSAL TOHUBOHU
RIOTOUS ROID ROYD WILD NOISY RANDY RANTY HEMPIE RANDIE STORMY WANTON BACCHIC PROFUSE ROARING ABUNDANT BACCHIAN

RIP RIT COOP REAT TEAR BREAK SHARK SHRED SLITE UNSEW BASKET RIPPLE UNSEAM
(— OFF) ROB CHEAT FILCH STEAL DEFRAUD

RIPE RIT BOLD LATE DRUNK READY MATURE MELLOW SIDDER SIDDOW SMELLY DIGESTED FINISHED SEASHORE STINKING SUITABLE
(EARLY —) HASTY RARERIPE
(PREF.) HADR(O)

RIPEN AGE ADDLE AUGUST DIGEST MELLOW CONCOCT CRIMSON DEVELOP PERFECT COMPLETE MATURATE

RIPENESS MATURITY

RIPHATH (FATHER OF —) GOMER

RIP-OFF GYP THEFT IMITATION

RIPOSTE REPLY RETORT THRUST REPARTEE

RIPPER RIPSAW BOBSLED HUMDINGER

RIPPET FUSS TUMULT UPROAR DISPUTE QUARREL

RIPPING FINE GRAND SWELL CAPITAL TIPPING SPLENDID

RIPPLE CURL FRET PURL RIFF SEED WAVE ACKER CRISP TWINE COCKLE DIMPLE JABBLE LIPPER RIMPLE RUFFLE RUMBLE WIMPLE CRINKLE WAVELET WRINKLE
(— ALONG) DADE

RIPPLING BREAK BULGE JABBLE ARIPPLE
(— OF SEA) LIPPER
(— ON SURFACE) HORROR

RIPSAW RIPPER SPLITSAW

RIPSNORTER SNIFTER HUMDINGER

RISE COME DRAW GROW HEAD HIGH HIKE HILL HOIT HOVE LIFT PLUM SOAR ARISE BEGIN CANCH CHEER CLIMB ERECT HEAVE HOIST MOUNT OCCUR PITCH PLUFF PROVE RAISE ROUSE SCEND SOURD STAND START SURGE SWELL TOWER YEAST ASCEND ASCENT ASPIRE AURORA BILLOW EMERGE GROWTH HAPPEN HEIGHT ORIGIN RESULT RETORT SOURCE SPRING THRIVE UPDIVE UPREAR UPTICK ADVANCE APPLAUD HUMMOCK REDOUND UPHEAVE UPSHOOT EMINENCE FLOURISH HEIGHTEN INCREASE LEVITATE SCENSION UPSPRING
(— ABOVE) OVERLOOK SURMOUNT
(— ABRUPTLY) SKYROCKET
(— AGAIN) RESURGE
(— AND FALL) LOOM HEAVE WELTER
(— AS PRICE) MEND
(— GRADUALLY) LOOM
(— IN BLISTERS) YAW
(— IN CLOUDS) STOOR
(— IN MINE FLOOR) HOGBACK

(— IN PRICES) BULGE
(— IN VALUE) IMPROVE
(— OF CURVE) CAMBER
(— OF HAWK AFTER PREY) MOUNTY
(— OF SHIP'S LINES) FLIGHT
(— OF WATER) FLOOD
(— PRECIPITOUSLY) SKY
(— RAPIDLY) KITE
(— SHARPLY) BREAK
(— SUDDENLY) BOOM SPRING
(— SWIFTLY) BOIL
(— TO BAIT) TAKE
(— TO GREAT HEIGHT) TOWER
(— TO PEAK) SWELL
(— UP) FUME REAR ASCEND INSURRECT
(CURVED —) HANCE
(GIVE — TO) SPAWN
(SHARP —) HOGBACK

RISE OF SILAS LAPHAM (AUTHOR OF —) HOWELLS
(CHARACTER IN —) TOM COREY IRENE SILAS LAPHAM PERSIS ROGERS PENELOPE BROMFIELD

RISER HEAD RAISE FEEDHEAD INSURGENT

RISHI RSI POET SAGE SAINT DEVARSHI KASHYAPA MAHARSHI

RISIBLE FUNNY GELASTIC LAUGHABLE

RISING BOIL BULI RIET ARISE ARIST ORIENT PUTSCH SOURCE STRAKE UPREST UPWITH MONTANT PUSTULE SURGENT EMERGENT INCREASE MOUNTANT NAISSANT ONCOMING ASSURGENT EXCEEDING
(— ABOVE) SUPERIOR
(— ABRUPTLY) BOLD
(— AGAIN) REORIENT
(— AND FALLING) TIDAL
(— AS A BIRD) ROUSANT
(— AS OF HAWK) SOURCE
(— BY DEGREES) GRADIENT
(— FROM DEAD) RESURRECTION
(— GRADUALLY) SOFT
(— HIGH) AERIAL
(— SHARPLY) ABRUPT
(— STEEPLY) BLUFF
(— TO BREATHE) HAURIANT HAURIENT
(— WITH SUN) COSMICAL
(POPULAR —) EMEUTE

RISK GO RUN SET GAGE JUMP LUCK PAWN PERIL RISCO STAKE STAND THROW WAGER WATHE CHANCE DANGER GAMBLE HAZARD IMPAWN PLIGHT THREAT BALANCE IMPERIL VENTURE ENDANGER EXPOSURE
(PL.) COVERAGE

RISKY BOLD DICEY DODGY CHANCY DARING KITTLE RISQUE PARLISH PARLOUS TECHOUS TICKLISH

RISP BUSH RASP STEM TWIG STALK
BRANCH SCRATCH
RISQUE BLUE GAMY RACY SEXY
BROAD DARING SCABROUS
RISSOLE CROQUETTE
(PL.) CECILS
RISS-WURM NEUDECKIAN
RISURREZIONE (CHARACTER IN —)
DIMITRI KATUSHA SIMONSON
(COMPOSER OF —) ALFANO
RIT CUT RIP RUT REND SLIT TEAR
SCRATCH
RITE KEX ASAL BORA BRIS FORM
HAKO SOMA BRITH HONOR RIGHT
SRADH ABDEST AUGURY EXEQUY
FETISH OFFICE PANSIL PIACLE
POOJAH RITUAL BAPTISM FUNERAL
KATCINA LITURGY MYSTERY
OBSEQUY SRADDHA TASHLIK
CEREMONY HIERURGY HUSKANAW
MORTUARY PIACULUM OBSERVANCE
(FUNERAL —S) EXEQUY EXEQUIES
OBSEQUIES
(INITIATION —) BORA
(RELIGIOUS —) SYMBOL
(SECRET —) ORGY
(PL.) CULT SACRA SERVICE
RITUAL FORM RITE SOLEMN
AGENDUM HAGGADA LITURGY
OBSEQUY SERVICE CEREMONY
VISPARAD VISPERED
(PASSOVER —) AGADAH HAGGADA
HAGGADAH
(PRAYER —) PUJA
RITUALISTIC SACRAL
RITZY SWANKY HAUGHTY SNOBBISH
RIVAGE BANK RIVE COAST SHORE
RIVAL VIE EVEN PEER SIDE MATCH
COMPETE CORRIVE EMULATE
PARAGON CORRIVAL EMULATOR
OPPONENT
(PREF.) ANT(I) ANTH(O)
RIVALRY VIE GAME STRIFE PARAGON
JEALOUSY STRIVING EMULATION
RIVALS (AUTHOR OF —) SHERIDAN
(CHARACTER IN —) BOB JACK LUCY
ACRES JULIA LYDIA LUCIUS
ANTHONY ABSOLUTE BEVERLEY
LANGUISH MALAPROP MELVILLE
OTRIGGER FAULKLAND
RIVE RIP PLOW REND STAB TEAR
CRACK REAVE SEVER SPLIT WEDGE
CLEAVE SUNDER THRUST SHATTER
FRACTURE
RIVELING RULLION
RIVER EA LE LEE REE RIO TJI ALPH
AVON BAHR GEON ILOG KILL WADI
WADY BAYOU CREEK FLOOD GANGA
GIHON GJOLL GLIDE HABOR INLET
KIANG TCHAI BARCOO GUTTER
KHUBUR NYANZA STRAIT STREAM
CHANNEL COCYTUS ESTUARY
FROEMAN ILISSUS PHARPAR

RUBICON SENEGAL AFFLUENT
ERIDANUS PACTOLUS STAIRCASE
(— CHANNEL) ALVEUS
(— IN SPIRITUAL) JORDAN
(— NEAR GATE OF HEL'S ABODE)
GJOLL
(— OF ATTICA) ILISSUS
(— OF DAMASCUS) PHARPAR
(— OF HADES) STYX LETHE
(— OF LYDIA) PACTOLUS
(— OF PARADISE) GEON GIHON
(— OF QUEENSLAND) BARCOO
(— OF UNDERGROUND)
PHLEGETHON
(— OF UNDERWORLD) STYX LETHE
ACHERON COCYTUS FLEGETON
(AFRICAN —) NYANZA SENEGAL
(CHINESE —) HO KIANG
(EGYPTIAN —) BAHR NILE
(FULL —) BANKER
(JAVANESE —) TJI
(MINOR —) BAYOU
(SACRED —) ALPH GANGA
(SMALL —) BACHE TCHAI
(TIDAL —) ESTUARY
(PREF.) FLUVI(O) POTAM(O)
(SUFF.) POTAMIA POTAMUS
RIVERBANK RIPA RIPE
RIVERBED LAAGTE BATTURE
(DRY —) WADI WADY
RIVER BLINDNESS
ONCHOCERCIASIS
RIVERBOAT COG BARGE FOIST
PULWAR
RIVER DUCK TEAL MALLARD
WIDGEON GREENWING
RIVERINE (— FISH) HUCHO
RIVERWEED WATERWEED
RIVET STUD CLINK ROOVE PANHEAD
FLATHEAD
(— ATTENTION) GRIP
(— HEAD) CUPHEAD
RIVULET RUN BURN GILL LAKE
MOTH RILL SIKE BACHE BATCH
BAYOU BOURN BROOK GHYLL RITHE
RINDLE RUNLET RUNNEL STREAM
STRIPE STRYPE CHANNEL RIVERET
BROOKLET
RIXY TERN
RIZPAH (LOVER OF —) SAUL
(SON OF —) ARMONI MEPHIBOSHETH
RIZZAR DRY PARCH RASOUR RAZOUR
CURRANT HADDOCK
RIZZOM BIT EAR RISOM STALK
STRAW RISSOM
RNA POLYA
ROACH HOG BUTT ROCK SPOT
BRAISE BLATTID SUNFISH
ROAD LEG PAD TAO VIA WAY BELT
BORD CASH DRAG DRUN FARE GAET
GANG GATE LINE LODE LOKE PASS
PATH PAVE PIKE RADE RAID RIDE
RODE ROTE ROUT SLAB SPUR WENT

BARGH BLAZE BYWAY CLOSE DRIFT
DRIVE DROVE FORAY GAITE GOING
METAL PRAYA ROUTE TRACE TRACK
BYROAD CAMINO CAREER CAUSEY
CHEMIN COURSE DUGWAY FEEDER
RIDING ROUGHT RUNWAY SLOUGH
STREET TARMAC TRAJET BEELINE
CALZADA CARTWAY ESTRADA
GANGWAY HIGHWAY LANDWAY
OUTGANG PACKWAY PASSAGE
RAILWAY RAMPIRE ROADWAY
ROLLWAY SKIDWAY TELFORD
AUTOBAHN BEALLACH BLACKTOP
BROADWAY CHAUSSEE CORDUROY
FOOTRILL HORSEWAY OVERPASS
RIDGEWAY SPEEDWAY TRACKWAY
TRAMROAD TRAVERSE TURNPIKE
WAGONWAY ROADSTEAD
(— BORDERING SHORE) PRAYA
(— FOR LOGGING) SKIDWAY
CROSSHAUL
(— FOR SPACECRAFT) CRAWLERWAY
(— HAZARD) ESS
(— IN COAL MINE) BORD BOARD
FOOTRILL
(— ON CLIFF) CORNICHE
(— SCRAPER) HARL HARLE
(— SURFACE) TELFORD
(ALTERNATE —) DETOUR
(CEMENT OR CONCRETE —) SLAB
(COUNTRY —) BOREEN DRIFTWAY
(DESCENDING —) BAHADA BAJADA
(IMPASSABLE —) SLOUGH IMPASSE
(IMPROVED —) CASH
(MILITARY OR PUBLIC —) AGGER
(NARROW —) DRANG DRUNG
NODDIN
(PAVED —) CALZADA CHAUSSEE
(PRINCIPAL —) ARTERY
(PRIVATE —) LOKE DRIVE DRIVEWAY
(RAISED —) AGGER RAMPIRE
CAUSEWAY
(ROMAN —) ITER CAUSEY
(SIDE —) BRANCH SHUNPIKE
(STEEP —) BRAE PATH BARGH
SPRUNT
(TEMPORARY —) SHOOFLY
(UNIMPROVED —) DROVE
(ZIGZAG —) SWITCHBACK
(PREF.) ODO VIA
(SUFF.) ODE OID
ROADBED BALLAST BITUMEN
ROADBOOK MAP ITINERARY
ROAD DONKEY ROADER
ROADMAN PEDDLER SALESMAN
CANVASSER
ROADMASTER OVERSEER
ROAD RUNNER CUCKOO PAISANO
ROADSIDE HEDGE
ROADSTEAD RAID DOWNS
ROADSTER BUGGY TRAMP DRIVER
BICYCLE RUNABOUT RACEABOUT
SPEEDSTER

ROADWAY DECK EXIT STREET
MACADAM SLIPWAY TRUCKWAY
(— MANEUVER) UTURN
ROAM GO FRR RUN WAG RAKE RAME
RAVE ROIL ROLL ROVE WALK GIPSY
GYPSY KNOCK RANGE SCAMP SPACE
STRAY TAVER VAGUE WAVER
BANGLE RAMBLE STROLL SWERVE
TAIVER VAGARY WANDER GALLANT
PROCEED SQUANDER VAGABOND
(— FURTIVELY) PROWL
ROAMING ERROR NOMADIC
ROAMAGE FUGITIVE
(PREF.) PLAN(O)
ROAN HORSE GRIZZLE
ROANOKE WAMPUM
ROAR CRY BAWL BEAL BELL BERE
BOOM BRAY CAVE HOWL HURL RAIR
RARE RERD ROIN ROME ROOP ROUT
YELL BLARE BROOL CRACK RERDE
ROUST SHOUT SNORE BELLOW
BULDER BULLER CLAMOR GOLLAR
GOLLER RUMMES SCREAM SHRIEK
STEVEN BLUSTER RUMMISH
THUNDER ULULATE
(— AS BOAR) FREAM
(— LIKE WIND) HURL
(— OF SURF) ROTE
(LOW —) BROOL
ROARING RUT LOUD AROAR BRISK
ROUST BELLOW BOOMING RIOTOUS
THRIVING
ROARING BOY TWIBIL TWIBILL
ROARING GAME CURLING
ROARING MEG CANNON
ROAST RAZZ ROTI SOAK BREDE
BROWN PARCH ASSATE CODDLE
REMOVE TORREFY TORRIFY
BARBECUE RIDICULE
(— IN ASHES) BRY
(KIND OF —) RIB RUMP
(STUFFED —) FARCI
ROASTED ASADO
(NOT —) GREEN
ROASTER BURNER SCORCHER
ROASTING ASSATION
ROASTING JACK TURNSPIT
ROB COP PAD EASE FAKE FLAP MILL
NICK PEEL PELF PICK PILL POLL PREY
PULL RAMP RIPE ROLL TOBY BENIM
BRIBE FLIMP HARRY HEAVE HEIST
LURCH PINCH PLUCK PLUME PROWL
REAVE RIFLE ROIST SHAKE SPOIL
SPUNG STEAL STRUB TOUCH
HARROW HIJACK HUSTLE PILFER
RAVISH RIPOFF STRIKE THIEVE
BEREAVE DEPRIVE DESPOIL PLUNDER
RUMPADE SNAFFLE UNPURSE
DEFLOWER SPOLIATE
(— HOUSE) MILL
(— OF CHASTITY) DEFILE
(— OF FORCE) COOL
(— OF JOY) DESOLATE

(— **OF VIGOR**) ETIOLATE
(— **WITH VIOLENCE**) RAMP
ROBALO FISH PIKE SNOOK SNOWK
SERGEANT
ROBBED RUBATO
(**NOT** —) UNPILLED
ROBBER PAD CROOK FOMOR LARON
THIEF BANDIT BRIBER DACOIT
FORMOR HOLDUP LATRON RIFLER
BRIGAND CATERAN FOOTPAD
HEISTER LADRONE MOONMAN
PANDOUR PRANCER RAVENER
ROUTIER SPOILER TOBYMAN
BARABBAS FOMORIAN PILLAGER
RABIATOR BANDOLERO
(— **ON HIGH SEAS**) PIRATE
(— **WHO USES VIOLENCE**) RABIATOR
(**GRAVE** —) GOUL GHOUL
(**HIGHWAY** —) PAD FOOTPAD
TOBYMAN
(**INDIAN MURDEROUS** —) DACOIT
(**IRISH** —) WOODKERN
(**MOUNTAIN** —) CHOAR
(**NIGHT** —) MOONMAN
(**SEA** —) FOMOR FORMOR FOMORIAN
(**WANDERING** —) ROUTIER
(**PREF.**) LESTO
ROBBERY JOB JUMP REIF RIFE HEIST
SCREW STALE FELONY HOLDUP
STOWTH BRIBERY DACOITY
LARCENY PILLAGE PLUNDER
REAVERY STICKUP THUGGEE
PURCHASE SPOLIATION
(— **ON HIGH SEAS**) PIRACY
(**HIGHWAY** —) TOBY
ROBE GOWN TOGA VEST KANZU
STOLA CHIMER KIMONO KITTEL
MANTLE PEPLOS REVEST ARISAID
BUFFALO GALABIA SURCOAT
VESTURE PARAMENT WOLFSKIN
(— **FOR THE DEAD**) HABIT
(— **OF HONOR**) KHALAT KHILAT
KILLUT KELLAUT
(— **OF MONARCH**) PLUVIAL
(— **PRESENTED BY DIGNITARY**)
KHALAT KHILAT
(— **REACHING TO ANKLES**) TALAR
(**ACTOR'S** —) SYRMA
(**ARAB** —) ABA
(**BAPTISMAL** —) CHRISOM
(**BISHOP'S** —) CHIMER CHIMERE
(**CIRCULAR** —) CYCLAS
(**CORONATION** —) COLOBIUM
DALMATIC
(**DERVISH'S** —) KHIRKA KHIRKAH
(**EMPEROR'S** —) PURPLE
(**FUNERAL** —) SABLE
(**JEWISH** —) KITTEL
(**KING'S** —) DALMATIC
(**LOOSE** —) MANT CAMIS CAMUS
CYMAR SIMAR SYMAR MANTUA
CHIMERE MANTEAU
(**MASQUERADE** —) VENETIAN

(**MEXICAN** —) MANGA
(**MONK'S** —) HAPLOMA
(**OLD-FASHIONED** —) SAMARE
(**OUTER** —) JAMA
(**PRIEST'S** —) ALB
(**ROMAN** —) TOGA STOLA
(**TARTAN** —) ARISAID
(**TURKISH** —) DOLMAN
(**WHITE** —) CHRISOM
(**PL.**) ACADEMICALS
ROBERT DOB POP RAB DOBBIN
POPKIN
ROBERT OF LINCOLN BOBOLINK
ROBIN THRUSH PINFISH REDDOCK
RUDDOCK TOOTLER WINGFISH
REDBREAST
ROBIN GOODFELLOW ELF PUCK
FAIRY SPRITE HOBGOBLIN
ROBINIA LOCUST
ROBIN SANDPIPER KNOT
DOWITCHER
ROBORANT TONIC
ROBOT GELEM GOLEM AUTOMAT
TELEVOX
(**LIKE A** —) FACELESS
ROB ROY (**AUTHOR OF** —) SCOTT
(**CHARACTER IN** —) ROB OWEN
DIANA FRANK ANDREW MACFIN
MORRIS VERNON TRESHAM WILLIAM
CAMPBELL FREDERICK INGLEWOOD
MACVITTIE RASHLEIGH HILDEBRAND
FAIRSERVICE OSBALDISTONE
ROBUST ABLE FIRM HAIL HALE HARD
IRON RUDE BONNY HARDY HUSKY
LUSTY RENKY SOUND STARK STIFF
STOUR STOUT TOUGH VALID WALLY
HEARTY RUGGED SINEWY STRONG
STURDY HEALTHY NERVOUS
STHENIC VALIANT MUSCULAR
PITHSOME STALWART SWACKING
VIGOROUS STRAPPING
(**NOT** —) SLENDER
ROBUSTNESS VALIDITY
ROC BIRD BOMB RUKH ROQUE
SIMURG SIMURGH
ROCHET CLOAK SMOCK CAMISIA
ROCK CAP JOW LOG PAY RAG DAZE
HOST KLIP REEL RUKH SIAL SIMA
SWAY SWIG TOSS BRACK CLIFF
FLOOR GREET GRUSS HORSE LEDGE
ROACH ROQUE SHAKE SHOWD
SKARN STONE TRILL CRADLE FACIES
GROUND OOLITE PELITE TOTTER
BRECCIA COUNTRY FOLIATE GREISEN
CIMINITE PHYLLITE SILTSTONE
(— **AROUND DRILL HOLE**) COLLAR
(— **CHUNK**) KNUCKLE
(— **DEBRIS**) SCREE
(— **FRAGMENT**) CLAST
(— **GROUP FAN**) GROUPIE
(— **IN ANOTHER ROCK**) XENOLITH
(— **IN MINE**) CAPPING
(— **IN SEA**) STACK

(— SURFACE) KARREN
(— VIOLENTLY) STAGGER
(ARTIFICIAL —) GRANOLITH
(BALD —) SCALP
(BANDED —) BAR
(BARE —) SCARTH
(BASALTIC —) TEPHRITE
(CAP —) COVER
(COLUMN OF MOLTEN —) PLUME
(COMPACT —) BASEMENT
(CONGLOMERATE —) PSEPHITE
(COUNTRY —) RIDER ROCKABILLY
(CRUSHED —) GREET
(CRYSTALLINE —) ELVAN DUNITE
SCHIST DIORITE GREISEN ECLOGITE
(DECAY OF —S) GEEST LATERITE
(DECOMPOSED —) GOSSAN GOZZAN
(DENSE —) ADINOLE
(DISINTEGRATED —) SAPROLITE
(EXTRUSIVE —) DACITE SPILITE
ANDESITE CIMINITE
(FELDSPATHIC —) PETUNTSE
(FISSILE —) SHALE SHAUL
(FLUID —) LAVA
(FRAGMENTAL —) PSEPHITE
(FRAGMENT OF —) CLAST
(GABBROITIC —) EUCRITE
(GLASSY —) PITCHSTONE
(GRANULAR —) GABBRO OOLITE
DIORITE IJOLITE KOSWITE MYLONITE
PSAMMITE QUARTZITE
(GRANULATED —) GRUSS
(GREEN —) OPHITE
(HARD —) WHIN KIMGLE WHINSTONE
NOVACULITE
(HIGH —) SCOUT
(IGNEOUS —) BOSS SIAL SIMA TRAP
BASALT DUNITE GABBRO URTITE
FELSITE GRANITE MINETTE PICRITE
SYENITE UNAKITE DOLERITE
ESSEXITE RHYOLITE TONALITE
(IMPURE —) CHERT
(INSULAR —) SKERRY
(INSULATED —) SKERRY
(INTRUSIVE —) HORTITE MINETTE
MAENAITE
(IRON-BEARING —) GAL
(ISOLATED —) SCAR SCARR SCAUR
(JUTTING OF —) KIP
(MANTLE —) REGOLITH
(METAMORPHIC —) SKARN GNEISS
SCHIST BUCHITE GONDITE LEPTITE
ECLOGITE HORNFELS LIMURITE
(MICA-BEARING —) DOMITE
(MOLTEN —) MAGMA
(MOON —) KREEP
(MOTTLED —) SERPENTINE
(PLUTONIC —) TAWITE HOLLAITE
TURJAITE
(POROUS —) TUFA TUFF ARSOITE
(PROJECTING —) CLINT
(PULVERIZED —) FLOUR
(RARE —) ALNOITE

(ROUGH —) CRAG KNAR SCARTH
(ROUNDED —) ROGNON SHEEPBACK
(SAND —) PSAMMITE
(SEDIMENTARY —) CRAG IRONSTONE
SANDSTONE
(SHARP —) NEEDLE AIGUILLE
(SLATY —) PLATE SCHALSTEIN
(SOFT —) MALM
(SOLID —) GIBBER
(STUDY OF —S) LITHOLOGY
(SUBMERGED —) SHELF
(SURROUNDING —) GROUND
(UNDERLYING —) FLOOR
(UPRIGHT —) PILLAR
(VOLCANIC —) TUFA TUFF BASALT
DACITE DOMITE LATITE TAXITE
PEPERIN ANDESITE ASHSTONE
EUTAXITE RHYOLITE TEPHRITE
TRACHYTE
(WASTE —) MULLOCK
(WORTHLESS —) GANG GANGUE
(WORTHLESS — MATTER) GANGUE
(PL.) ROCHER
(PREF.) FELSO PETR(I)(O) RHYO RUPI
SAXI
(SUFF.) CLAST ITE LITE LITH(IC) LITIC
PHYRE PHYRIC
ROCKAWAY CARRIAGE
ROCK BADGER CONY HYRAX
ROCK BASS REDEYE CABRILLA
ROCK-BREAKER
ROCKBRUSH ROSILLA
ROCK CEDAR SABINO
ROCK CRESS ARABIS BICKLEPOD
ROCK DEBRIS TALUS
ROCK DOVE SOD
ROCK-DWELLING SAXATILE
ROCK ELM WAHOO
ROCKER CRADLE SHOOFLY
ROCKET DRAKE TITAN REBUKE
STREAK YELLOW CONGREVE
SKYLIGHT STARSHIP FIREDRAKE
(DYER'S —) WELD WOLD WOALD
WOULD
(SYSTEM OF SPACECRAFT —S)
RETROPACK
ROCKET SALAD ROQUETTE
ROCKFISH BASS JACK RENA REINA
VIUVA FLIOMA GOPHER RASHER
TAMBOR CORSAIR GARRUPA
GROUPER BOCACCIO CHINAFISH
GREENLING
ROCK HARE KLIPHAAS
ROCK HIND MERO AGAUJI
ROCKHOPPER PENGUIN
ROCK HOPPER MACARONI
ROCKLING BAUD GADE ROKER
SORGHE WHISTLER
ROCK NATIVE SNAPPER
ROCK OIL NAPHTHA PETROLEUM
ROCK PIPIT TIETICK
ROCK RABBIT PIKA HYRAX
HYRACOID

ROCKROSE CISTUS PINWEED
HUDSONIA ROCKCIST SAGEROSE
DAYFLOWER SUNFLOWER
ROCK SALT EMOL AMOLE HALITE
(BLOCK OF —) PIG
ROCK SANDWORT CYME
ROCKSHAFT SHAFT ROCKER
WEIGHBAR
ROCK TROUT BOREGAT GREENLING
ROCKWEED TANG FUCUS FUCOID
SEATANG SEAWEED
(PREF.) FUCI
ROCK WHITING KELPFISH
STRANGER
ROCKWORK ROCAILLE
(ARTIFICIAL —) ROCAILLE
ROCKY DAFT HARD STONY CLINTY
OBSCENE PETREAN PETROUS
UNCOUTH OBDURATE UNSTABLE
DIFFICULT RUPELLARY
(PREF.) TRACHY
ROCKY MOUNTAIN (— GOAT)
MAZAME
ROCOCO ORNATE QUAINT BAROCCO
BAROQUE OUTMODED
ROD BAR BOW CUE GAD GUY LUG
PIN TIE BOLT CALM CAME CANE
CORE FALL FORK GOAD GONG LINK
MACE POLE RAVE SCOB SNAP STEM
STUD WAND WHIP YARD ARBOR
BIRCH CATCH DOWEL LYTTA OSIER
PERCH POWER PUNCH REACH REBAR
ROUND SETUP SHOOT SPELK SPILL
SPOKE SPRAG STAFF STANG STEEL
STICK STING TEYNE TOMMY TRACE
VERGE WIPER BALEYS BROACH
CANARY CARBON CENTER CRUTCH
ETALON FERULA FINGER GLOWER
HANGER PISTOL PITMAN PODGER
RADDLE RAMMER SKEWER SPRING
STADIA SWITCH TOGGLE WATTLE
WICKER BACULUS CROPPIE
DRAWROD ELLWAND FEATHER
FESTUCA MANDREL PLUNGER
POINTER POTHOOK PRICKER
PROBANG PROLONG SCALLOM
SCEPTER SPINDLE STADIUM STICKER
TYRANNY VIRGULA WHISKER
WINDING AXOSTYLE BACKSTAY
BILBERRY BODSTICK BOWSTAVE
DIPSTICK JACKSTAY KINGBOLT
REVOLVER STRAINER TRAVELER
WEEDHOOK
(— AS SYMBOL OF OFFICE) VERGE
(— BEARING TRAFFIC SIGNAL)
STANCHION
(— FOR ALIGNING HOLES) PODGER
(— FOR CARRYING GLASS) FORK
(— FOR DISCIPLINE) YARD FERULA
FERULE
(— FOR FASTENING THATCH) SPELK
SPRINGLE
(— FOR FIREARM BORE) WIPER

(— FOR GLASS-MAKING) PUNTY
FASCET PONTEE PONTIL CROPPIE
(— FOR HOLDING MEAT) SPIT
(— FOR TRANSMITTING MOTION)
TRACE
(— IN ARC LAMP) CARBON
(— IN CRICKET) STUMP
(— IN INTERFEROMETER) ETALON
(— IN MINE PUMP) SPEAR
(— IN NERNST LAMP) GLOWER
(— IN SPINNING WHEEL) SPINDLE
(— OF CELLS) NOTOCHORD
(— OF FOUNDRY MOLD) LANCE
(— OF LOOM) SHAFT
(— OF WOOD) SCOB
(— ON DOG SLED) GEEPOLE
(— ON LOGGING TRUCK) RAVE
(— POINTED AT BOTH ENDS) SKEWER
(— SYMBOLIZING AUTHORITY)
BACULUS
(— TO BIND A CONTRACT) FESTUCA
(— TO FASTEN SAILS) JACKSTAY
(— TO IMMERSE SHEEP) CRUTCH
(— TO URGE BEAST) GOAD PROD
(— UPSET AT ONE END) SETUP
(— USED AS KEY) TOMMY
(— WITH ENDS AT RIGHT ANGLES)
STRAINER
(— WITH SPONGE ON END) PROBANG
(— WITH T-HEAD) TOGGLE
(AXIAL —) VIRGULA AXOSTYLE
(BASKETRY —) OSIER SLATH
(BUNDLE OF —S) DRIVER
(CARTILAGINOUS —) LYTTA
COLUMELLA
(CLAMMING —) BRAIL
(CONNECTING —) PITMAN
(CURTAIN —) TRINGLE
(DANCER'S —) CROTALUM
(DIVINING —) TWIG DOWSER
(FISHING —) GAD CALCUTTA
(FLEXIBLE —) RADDLE WATTLE
(FORKED —) CRUTCH
(GEM-CUTTING —) SETTER
(GRADUATED —) STADIA STADIUM
(IRON —) SNAP BETTY
(KNITTING —) NEEDLE
(LEAD —) CAME
(LOGGING —) CANARY
(MEASURING —) JUDGE SPILE
STADIA ELLWAND METEWAND
METEYARD
(PLIABLE —) WINDING
(SMALL —) LANCE
(STRENGTHENING —) RIB
(SUPPLE —) SWABBLE
(TETHERING —) STAKE
(THIN —) TEYNE SCALLOM
(TIE —) ANCHOR
(UMBRELLA —) STRETCHER
(WITHE —) BILBERRY
(PREF.) BACULI RHABD(O) RHAPIDO
VERGI

RODENT RAT CONY DEGU HARE
MARA MOCO MOLE PACA PIKA UTIA
VOLE CONEY COYPU GUNDI HUTIA
JUTIA LEROT MOUSE TUCAN ZOKOR
AGOUTI BEAVER BITING CURURO
GERBIL GLIRID GNAWER GOPHER
JERBOA MARMOT MURINE MUROID
RABBIT SOKHOR BIESMOL CHINCHA
DIPODID GEOMYID GNAWING
HAMSTER LEMMING LEVERET
MUSKRAT ABROCOME CAPIBARA
DORMOUSE LEPORIDE OCTODONT
SEWELLEL SPALACID SQUIRREL
TUCOTUCO VISCACHA VIZCACHA
ANOMALURE PORCUPINE

RODEO ROUNDUP

RODERICK RANDOM (AUTHOR
OF —) SMOLLETT
(CHARACTER IN —) TOM STRAP
OAKHUM RANDOM BOWLING
MELINDA SNAPPER CRAMPLEY
NARCISSA RODERICK WILLIAMS
QUIVERWIT

RODLIKE VIRGATE RHABDOID

RODMAN CLASHY CLASHEE
CHAINMAN

RODOMONTADE BRAG RANT
BOAST BLUSTER BOMBAST
BRAGGART

RODOMONTE (BELOVED OF —)
DORALICE
(VICTIM OF —) RUGGIERO

ROD-SHAPED RHABDOID
VIRGULATE

ROE RA DOE FRY PEA RAA RAE DEER
HIND KELK RAUN ROUN ROWN
CORAL TRUBU CAVIAR

ROEBUCK GIRL CHEVREUIL

ROGER RAM HODGE ROGUE

ROGUE BOY GUE IMP NYM HEMP
KEMP KITE LOON ROAG CATSO
CRACK CRANK DROLE GIPSY
GREEK GYPSY HEMPY KNAVE
SCAMP SHELM BEGGAR BORGER
BUGGER CANTER CHOUSE COQUIN
CURTAL HARLOT LIMMER PICARA
PICARO RASCAL SORROW TINKER
BLEEDER ERRATIC FOISTER HALLION
LADRONE PANURGE SHARPER
SKELLUM SWINGER VILLAIN
COMROGUE HEMPSEED
PICAROON SCALAWAG SWINDLER
WHIPJACK

ROGUE HERRIES (AUTHOR OF —)
WALPOLE
(CHARACTER IN —) ALICE DAVID
PRESS SARAH STARR DEBORAH
DENBURN FRANCIS HERRIES
MARGARET MIRABELL
OSBALDISTONE

ROGUERY ROPERY KNAVERY
LOONERY WAGGERY PATCHERY
PRIGGISM TRICKERY TRUANTRY

ROGUISH SLY ARCH HEMPY ROGUY
WICKED KNAVISH TRICKSY VAGRANT
WAGGISH ESPIEGLE SCAMPISH
DISHONEST

ROGUISHNESS KNAVERY
ARCHNESS

ROI DE LAHORE, LE (CHARACTER
IN —) ALIM SITA SCINDIA
(COMPOSER OF —) MASSENET

ROIL VEX FOUL RILE ANNOY AGITATE
BLUNDER DISTURB STUDDLE
BEWILDER DISORDER IRRITATE

ROILED TURBID

ROISTER REVEL ROIST SCOUR
CAROUSE GALRAVAGE

ROISTERER MUN GREEK HUZZA
BUSTER HECTOR RIOTER SCOURER
TWIBILL EPHESIAN

ROISTERING HOYDEN

ROKE FOG DAMP MIST REEK ROWK
STIR FOGGY SMOKE STEAM VAPOUR

ROKELAY ROCULO

ROLAND (BETROTHED OF —) AUDE
(COMPANION OF —) OLIVER
(HORN OF —) OLIVANT
(SWORD OF —) DURANDAL
(UNCLE OF —) CHARLEMAGNE

ROLE BIT JOB LEAD PART ROTE
HEAVY FIGURE CLOTHES BUSINESS
FUNCTION LIRIPIPE
(CHIEF —) LEAD
(SECONDARY —) COMPRIMARIO
(SMALL —) CAMEO

ROLL BAP BUN ROW WEB BOLT COIL
CURL FILE FLOW FURL LIST MILL
PASS REEL ROAM ROTA SWAG WELT
WIND WRAP BAGEL BIALY BREAD
BUILD DANDY DICKY ENROL FLUTE
ROYLE SPLIT TOMMY TRILL TROLL
WHELM BILLOW BUNDLE CIRCLE
ELAPSE ENFOLD GOGGLE GROVEL
KIPFEL LEGEND MUSTER PONDER
RECORD ROSTER ROTATE SCROLL
UPWIND VOLUME WAMBLE WANDER
WHELVE WINTLE WREATH BISCUIT
BOLILLO BRIOCHE CROCKET
ENVELOP MANCHET NOTITIA
REVOLVE ROTULET ROTULUS
ROULEAU STRETCH TERRIER
TRINDLE TRUNDLE TWISTER
BAGUETTE BROTCHEN CANNELON
CONSIDER CRESCENT JACKROLL
LAMINATE PORTEOUS REGISTER
SEDERUNT SPREADER VOLUTATE
(— A BALL) BOWL
(— ABOUT) WALTER SCAMBLE
(— ALONG) COAST TRUCK
(— AS A SHIP) SEEL LURCH
(— AS STONE) REEL
(— BY) WALK
(— CLOSELY) FURL
(— EYES) WALL WAUL WHAWL
GOGGLE

(— GLASS) MARVER
(— INTO A BALL) CLEW CLUE
(— OF BILLS) WAD
(— OF BREAD) BAP SEMMEL TAMMIE
(— OF CLOTH) BOLT DOSSIL WREATH
(— OF COINS) ROULEAU
(— OF DOUGH) TWIST
(— OF DRIED BARK) QUILL
(— OF DRUM) HURRY RATTAN
(— OF DUST) KITTEN
(— OF FIBERS) ROVING
(— OF HAIR) PUFF ROACH ROWEL
CROCKET
(— OF HAY) WAKE
(— OF LINT OR LINEN) TENT DOSSIL
(— OF LUGGAGE) SWAG
(— OF MINCED MEAT) RISSOLE
(— OF OFFENDERS) PORTEOUS
(— OF PAPER) SPILL STOMP STUMP
(— OF PARCHMENT) BOOK PELL
(— OF ROULETTE WHEEL) COUP
(— OF SPUN YARN) PRICK
(— OF TOBACCO) CAROT CIGAR
PRICK SEGAR CAROTTE
(— OF WALLPAPER) BOLT
(— OF WHEAT BREAD) MANCHET
(— OF WOOL) ROVE ROVING CARDING
(— ON CASTERS) TRUCKLE
(— ON LITTLE WHEELS) TRUNDLE
(— ONWARD) DEVOLVE
(— OVER) COMB JOLL WELTER
(— TOGETHER) CONVOLVE
(— TO RUB DOWN DRAWING) STUMP
(— UP) FURL STOW COLLAR
(— UP SLEEVES) REEVE
(BLANKET —) BINDLE SHIRALEE
(BREAKFAST —) BIALY DANISH
(DANDY —) DANCER
(HOLLOW —) CANNELON
(KIND OF —) KAISER
(LONG —) FLUTE
(ON A —) HOT
(PADDED —) BURLET
(PENNY —) TOMMY
(TWISTED — OF WOOL) SLUB
(WHIP —) BACKREST
(PREF.) HELI(C)(CO)
ROLLED (— IN SUGAR) SANDED
ROLLER FLY BOWL BRAY DRUM JACK
LEAD MILL PUCK RUBY WAVE BREAK
DANDY FINER GODET INKER RIDER
SHELL WAVER WINCH BRAYER
BREAST DOFFER DUCTOR FASCIA
MANGLE ROWLET RUNNER CARRIER
CLEARER MOIETER TRUCKLE
HEDGEHOG SQUEEGEE STRIPPER
TROUPAND
(— FOR MASSAGER) ROULETTE
(— IN HORSE'S BIT) CRICKET
(— IN ORGAN) TRUNDLE
(— IN STEELWORKS) COGGER
(— TO CLEAR FABRIC) MOIETER

(CARDING —) BREAST WORKER
SQUIRREL STRIPPER
(CHINESE —) SIRGANG
(DREDGING —) HEDGEHOG
(DROP —) DUCTOR
(GRINDING —) BREAK
(INKING —) BRAYER
(PLAYER ON — DERBY TEAM)
JAMMER
(PRINTING —) DANDY SHELL BRAYER
DAMPENER
(ROUND IN — DERBY) JAM
(STONE —) MAMMY TOTER
(SURGICAL —) FASCIA
(TOOTHED —) PRICK PRICKER
(TYPEWRITER —) PLATEN
ROLLER COASTER SWITCHBACK
ROLLER DERBY (ROUND IN —) JAM
ROLLERMAN BRAKER JACKMAN
LEVERMAN
ROLLER SKATE PEDOMOTOR
ROLLICK PLAY ROMP CAVORT FROLIC
ROLLIX
ROLLICKING GAY WILD MERRY
JOVIAL LIVELY
ROLLING CURL GOGGLE WHEELY
SWAYING TRILLED LURCHING
VOLUTION
(— OF SCROLL) GELILAH
(— OF SHIP) LABOR
(— OF STOMACH) WAMBLE
ROLLTOP TAMBOUR
ROLY-POLY TUBBY ROTUND
PUDDING TUMBLER SALTWORT
ROM RO GYPSY ROMANY
ROMAINE COS
ROMAN BRAVE LATIN NOBLE PAPAL
ANTIQUA UPRIGHT GOWNSMAN
(— COLLAR) RABAT
ROMAN CATHOLIC ROME ROMAN
PAPIST ROMIST JEBUSITE
BABYLONIC
ROMANCE WOO GEST ANTAR
FANCY FEIGN GESTE KATHA NOVEL
STORY AFFAIR ANTARA UTOPIA
FANTASY FICTION ROMANZA
ROMAUNT
(— LANGUAGE) FRENCH ITALIAN
SPANISH
ROMAN-FLEUVE SAGA

ROMANIA
CANAL: BEGA
CAPITAL: BUCHAREST
COIN: BAN LEI LEU LEY
COUNTY: OLT ARAD CLUJ DOLJ GORJ
IASI ARGES BACAU BIHOR BUZAU
ILFOV MURES NEAMT SALAJ SIBIU
TIMIS
DISTRICT: ALBA BANAT BIHOR
DOBRUJA DOBROGEA MARAMURES
LAKE: SINO

MOUNTAIN: BIHOR NEGOI CODRUL
   RODNEI CALIMAN PIETROSU
OLD NAME: DACIA
PASS: ROSUL
PROVINCE: ARDEAL MOLDAVIA
   WALACHIA
RIVER: ALT OLT JIUL PRUT ALUTA
   ARGES BUZDU MOROS MURES
   OLTUL SCHYL SIRET TIMIS TISZA
   VEDEA CRASNA DANUBE ARGESUL
   MURESUL SOMESUL BISTRITA
   IALOMITA
RIVER PORT: BRAILA GALATI GALATZ
TOWN: ARAD CLUJ IASI BACAU
   CERNA JASSY NEAMT SIBIU TURNU
   BRAILA BRASOV GALATI GALATZ
   LUPENI CRAIOVA FOCSANI PLOESTI
   SEVERIN CERNAVTI KISHENEF
   TEMESVAR KOLOZSVVAR

ROMANIST MISSARY
ROMANIZATION LATINXUA
ROMANSH LADIN
ROMANTIC AIRY WILD IDEAL
   ARDENT DREAMY GOTHIC POETIC
   UNREAL FERVENT FABULOUS
   FANCIFUL
ROMANY RO ROM GIPSY GYPSY
   ROMAN
ROMANY RYE (AUTHOR OF —)
   BORROW
   (CHARACTER IN —) DALE JACK BELLE
   ISOPEL JASPER URSULA BERNERS
   MURTAGH LAVENGRO SYLVESTER
   PETULENGRO
ROME (CHAPEL IN —) SISTINE
   (FOUNDER OF —) ROMULUS
   (HILL IN —) CAELIAN VIMINAL
   AVENTINE PALATINE QUIRINAL
   (OLD PORT OF —) OSTIA
   (RIVER IN —) TIBER
ROME HAUL (AUTHOR OF —)
   EDMONDS
   (CHARACTER IN —) BEN DAN JOE
   RAE SOL LUCY BERRY JACOB KLORE
   MOLLY WAMPY CALASH GURGET
   HARROW HECTOR JOTHAM JULIUS
   SAMSON TINKLE WEAVER WILSON
   FORTUNE LARKINS TURNESA
   WILLIAM FRIENDLY CASHDOLLAR
   BUTTERFIELD
ROMEO AND JULIET (AUTHOR OF
   —) SHAKESPEARE
   (CHARACTER IN —) JOHN PARIS
   PETER ROMEO JULIET TYBALT
   ABRAHAM CAPULET ESCALUS
   GREGORY SAMPSON BENVOLIO
   LAURENCE MERCUTIO MONTAGUE
   BALTHASAR
ROMOLA (AUTHOR OF —) ELIOT
   (CHARACTER IN —) DINO LUCA TITO
   BARDO CALVO TILLO MONNA PIERO

   TESSA MELEMA ROMOLA BRIGIDA
   NICCOLO BERNARDO BALDASARRE
ROMP REG RIG HEMP LARK PLAY
   ROIL FRISK SHIRL SPORT TRAIN
   FROLIC GAMBOL HOORAY HOYDEN
   HURRAH RIPPET COURANT
   GAMMOCK RAMMACK RUNAWAY
ROMPERS JUMPER JUMPERS
ROMPING ROYT HEMPY ROYET
ROMULUS (BROTHER OF —) REMUS
   (FATHER OF —) MARS
RONCADOR GRUNT CROAKER
   SCIAENID
RONDO ROTA
RONE BUSH BRAKE GUTTER THICKET
RONG LEPCHA
RONGA THONGA
RONSDORFER ZIONITE ELLERIAN
ROOD RUD REED ROPE CROSS
   SPAWN STANG CRUCIFIX
ROODLES RANGDOODLES
ROOF TOP ATAP DECK DOME
   FLAT ATTAP COVER HOUSE RAISE
   RISER SHELL THACK AZOTEA
   BONNET CUPOLA SUMMIT TECTUM
   CHOPPER CRICKET GAMBREL
   MANSARD RIGGING TECTURE
   BULKHEAD HOUSETOP SAWTOOTH
   SEMIDOME PENTHOUSE
   (— MEMBER) PURLIN
   (— OF CARRIAGE) IMPERIAL
   (— OF CAVERN) DOME
   (— OF MINING CAGE) BONNET
   (— OF MOUTH) PALATE
   (— OF NASOPHARYNX) VAULT
   (— OF RAILWAY CAR) DECK
   (— OF THE WORLD) PAMIR
   (— OVER DOOR) APPENTICE
   (— OVER STAGE) SHADOW
   (— PORTION) MONITOR
   (AUTOMOBILE —) FASTBACK
   (CLOTH —) CHUTT
   (FALSE —) CRICKET
   (FLAT —) LEADS AZOTEA TERRACE
   (STEEPLY TAPERING —) SPIRE
   (THATCHED —) ATAP ATTAP CHOPPER
   (TOWER —) SADDLEBACK
   (VAULTED —) DOME
   (PREF.) STEG(O) TECTI TECTO
   (SUFF.) STEGE STEGITE
ROOFING HEALING SHINDLE
   PANTILING TECTIFORM
ROOFTOP PEAK
ROOK GYP ROC CROW DUPE RUKH
   CHEAT CRAKE JUDGE TOWER
   BLACKY CASTLE DEFRAUD CASTILLO
   SWINDLER
   (NEIGHBOR OF —) KNIGHT
ROOKERY ROOST RUMPUS
   BUILDING
ROOKIE COLT DRONGO NOVICE
   RECRUIT BEGINNER

ROOM PAD WON AULA CAFE CRIB
FARM HALL KILN LIEU PLAY SALA
SEAT SLUM WAME WENE WONE
ATTIC BERTH CUDDY DIVAN EWERY
HOUSE LODGE OECUS PLACE SALLE
SCOPE SHACK SOLAR SPACE STALL
STOVE STUDY BELFRY BREAST
CAMERA CASINO CHAPEL ESTUFA
EXEDRA HAMMAM LEEWAY MARGIN
PARVIS SCOUTH SINGLE SMOKER
SOLLAR STANCE STANZA STUDIO
CABINET CAMARIN CHALMER
CHAMBER EPINAOS FREEZER
GALLERY HOLDING HYPOGEE
KITCHEN LAUNDRY LIBRARY SEMINAR
SERVERY SMOKERY SURGERY
AEDICULA ASSEMBLY BASEMENT
CAPACITY DRYHOUSE HOTHOUSE
HYPOGEUM LAVATORY NYMPHEUM
PLAYROOM SCULLERY SWEATBOX
TABLINUM THALAMUS PRESSROOM
(— ADJOINING SYNAGOGUE)
GENIZAH
(— BEHIND FACADE) ATTIC
(— BELOW STAGE) MEZZANINE
(— BETWEEN KITCHEN AND DINING
ROOM) SERVERY
(— CONTAINING FOUNTAIN)
NYMPHEUM
(— DUG IN CLIFF) HYPOGEE
HYPOGEUM
(— FOR ACTION) LEEWAY
(— FOR BATHING) HAMMAM
(— FOR CONVERSATION) EXEDRA
LOCUTORY
(— FOR DANCING) CASINO
(— FOR FAMILY RECORDS) TABLINUM
(— FOR KEEPING FOOD) LARDER
PANTRY
(— FOR PAINTINGS) GALLERY
(— FOR PIGEONS) LOFT
(— FOR PRIVATE DEVOTIONS)
ORATORY
(— FOR PUBLIC AMUSEMENTS)
CASINO THEATER
(— FOR STOWAGE) LASTAGE
(— FOR TABLE LINEN) EWERY
(— IN COAL MINE) BREAST
(— IN HAREM) ODA ODAH
(— IN KEEP) DUNGEON
(— IN PREHISTORIC BUILDING) CELL
(— IN REAR OF TEMPLE) EPINAOS
(— IN SIDE OF LARGER ROOM) ALA
(— IN TOWER) BELFRY
(— OF STUDENTS' SOCIETY) HALL
(— ON SHIP) CABIN STOKEHOLD
(— OVER CHURCH PORCH) PARVIS
(— OVER STAGE) SHADOW
(— TO ADVANCE) WAY
(— TOGETHER) CHUM
(— TO LIVE) LEBENSRAUM
(— UNDER BUILDING) CELLAR
(— UNDER ROOF) LOFT

(CHILDREN'S —) NURSERY
(COTTAGE —) END
(DINING —) CENACLE DINETTE
REFECTORY TRICLINIUM
(DRAWING —) SALON SALOON
(DRESSING —) SHIFT BOUDOIR
CAMARIN VESTUARY WARDROBE
TIREHOUSE
(DRYING —) HOTHOUSE
(ESKIMO ASSEMBLY —) KASHGA
(EXHIBITION —) THEATER
(GRINDING —) HULL
(HEATED —) STEW
(HIGH —) AERY EYRY AERIE EYRIE
(HOSPITAL —) WARD
(INNER —) BEN INBY INBYE SPENCE
THALAMUS
(INSULATED —) FREEZER
(KIND OF —) REC
(KITCHEN —) SCULLERY
(LECTURE —) AUDITORY
(LIVING —) HOUSE LANAI SALON
SERDAB SOLARIUM VOORHUIS
(MONASTERY —) CELL LAVABO
(NARROW —) CRIB
(OCTAGONAL —) TRIBUNA
(PORTER'S —) LODGE
(PRIVATE —) SNUG SCHOLA
SANCTUM CONCLAVE GARDEROBE
(PUBLIC —) SALOON
(PUEBLO ASSEMBLY —) ESTUFA
(READING —) ATHENEUM
(RECEPTION —) DIVAN PARLOR
KURSAAL MANDARAH
(REFRIGERATED —) COOLER
(RETIRING —) RECAMERA
(ROMAN —) ATRIUM AEDICULA
FUMARIUM
(ROUND —) ROTUNDA
(SEA —) BERTH
(SECLUDED —) DEN
(SECRET —) HOLE
(SERIES OF —S) SWEEP
(SITTING —) SEAT SITTER BOUDOIR
(SLEEPING —) DORMER BEDROOM
DORMITORY
(SMALL —) ALA CELL SNUG STEW
ZETA CUBBY CUDDY LOBBY CLOSET
CUBICLE SNUGGERY
(SMOKING —) DIVAN DIWAN TABAGIE
(SORTING —) SALLE
(STEAM —) STOVE
(STORAGE —) CAMARIN MAGAZINE
THALAMUS
(SWEATING —) SUDARIUM
SUDATORY LACONICUM
(THRONE —) AIWAN
(TOP —) GARRET IMPERIAL
(UPPER —) SOLAR
(VAULTED —) CAMERA
(WRITING —) SCRIPTORIUM
(PREF.) STEG(O)
(SUFF.) STEGE STEGITE

ROOMMATE CHUM ROOMY ROOMIE
ROOMY WIDE LARGE RANGY SPACY
ROOMSOME SPACIOUS CAPACIOUS
COMMODIOUS
ROOSE RUSE EXTOL PRAISE FLATTER
BOASTING BRAGGING
ROOST FVE SIT BAUK JOUK TIDE
PERCH GARRET HARBOR LODGING
ROOKERY SHELTER
ROOSTER COCK GAME GALLO
MANOC GAMECOCK
(CREST OF A —) COMB
ROOT DIG PRY ROI TAP BASE BULB
CHAY CHOY GRUB MOOR MOOT
MORE PLUG PULL RACE SPUR TAIL
CHEER FIBER FRUIT GROOT GROUT
HEART IREOS LAPPA RADIX STOCK
ALRAUN BOTTOM CARROT CATGUT
GROUND MUZZLE ORIGIN SENEGA
SETTLE SUMBAL SUMBUL ACONITE
ALKANET AZAFRAN BIACURU
BONIATA CALUMBA CHICORY
COLUMBO CRAMPON GINSENG
IMPLANT IPOMOEA NUNNARI
PAREIRA RADICAL RUMMAGE
TURPETH DEDENDUM EARTHNUT
PNEUMATOPHORE
(— BRANCH) TAPOUN
(— CONTAINING STARCH) KOONTI
(— DEEPLY) SCREW
(— OF GINGER) RACE
(— OF ORCHID) CULLIONS
(— OF TARO) EDDO
(— OF TOOTH) FANG
(— OF TREE) TANG SPURN
(— OF WORD) THEME
(— OUT) GRUB STUB STOCK EVULSE
DISPLANT DUPPLANT
(—S FOR SEWING CANOES) WATAP
WATAPEH
(—S OF ACONITE) BIKH NABEE
(— TUBERCLE) CLOG
(— WORD) ETYMON
(— YIELDING RED DYE) CHAY CHOY
CHAYA
(AROMATIC —) ORRIS
(CANDIED —) ERYNGO
(CUSCUS —S) VETIVER
(DRIED —) JALAP ALTHEA SENECA
BRYONIA KRAMERIA LICORICE
SCAMMONY
(DRIED —S) INULA IPECAC KRAMERIA
VERATRUM
(EDIBLE —) YAM BEET EDDO RADISH
TURNIP WASABI PARSNIP RUTABAGA
TUBERCLE
(FERN —) ROI
(FINE —) STRING
(FRAGRANT —S) VETIVER
(KIND OF —) LATENT
(MASS OF FIBROUS —S) SPONGE
(MEDICINAL —) JALAP LAPPA
GINSENG

(PROJECTING —) SPUR
(ROASTED BEET —) BONKA
(STUMP AND —) MOCK
(PL.) CULVERS
(PREF.) RADICI RHIZ(O)
(SUFF.) RHIZA RHIZOUS
ROOTCAP CALYPTRA SPONGIOLE
ROOTED FIXED CHRONIC
(DEEPLY —) BESETTING
ROOTER FAN PLUGGER
ROOTLESS ARRHIZAL
ROOTLESSNESS ANOMIE
ROOTLET VIVER CRAMPON RADICEL
RADICLE
(PL.) COME CULMS
ROOTSTOCK PIP ROI RACE TARO
CROWN ORRIS CASAVA DANNUM
GINGER ORIGIN PANNUM STOLON
BISCUIT MISHMEE TURMERIC
ORRISROOT
ROPE GAD GUY TIE TOW TUG CECI
COLT CORD FALL FAST OUSS HEMP
JEFF JUNK LIFT LINE ROOD SEAL
SOAM SPAN STAY TACK TAIL TAUM
TOME VANG WARP BRACE BRAIL
CABLE CABUL CHECK CHORD LASSO
LONGE SHANK STRAP STROP SWEEP
TRACE TWIST WANTY WIDDY WITHE
CABLET HALTER INHAUL LARIAT
LISSOM LIZARD MECATE PINION
RAPEYE RUNNER SHROUD SLATCH
STRAND STRING TETHER WARROK
AWEBAND BEDCORD BOBSTAY
CATFALL CRINGLE ENTRAIL HALYARD
HAYBAND LASHING LEEFANG
OUTHAUL PAINTER PAZAREE
PENDANT PIGTAIL SEAMING
SERPENT SERVICE STIRRUP SWIFTER
BACKBONE BACKSTAY BUNTLINE
CABESTRO CORDELLE DOWNHAUL
DRAGLINE FOREFOOT FORETACK
HALLIARD HAULYARD INHAULER
JACKSTAY LIFELINE NECKLACE
PASSAREE PROLONGE ROUNDING
SEQUENCE THRAMMLE BREECHING
(— A STEER) HEEL
(— COLLAR) PARRAL PARREL
(— CONNECTING NETS) BALK BAULK
(— COVERING) QUILTING
(— FOR FASTENING GATE) CRINGLE
(— FOR FISH) STRINGER
(— FOR TRAINING HORSE) LONGE
(— FOR TYING CATTLE) CEEL SEAL
AWEBAND
(— HANDLE) FETTLE SHACKLE
(— HOLDING RAFT TOGETHER) BRAIL
(— JOINT) TUCK
(— OF HAIR) CABESTRO
(— OF ONIONS) REEVE
(— OF STRAW) GAD SIME VINE
SIMON SUGAN FETTLE SIMMON
SOOGAN
(— OF 10 OR MORE INCHES) CABLE

(— ON DERRICK) TELEGRAF
(— ON FISHING NET) PINION
SEAMING
(— ORNAMENTATION) TORSADE
(— PASSING AROUND DEADEYE)
STRAP STROP
(—S IN RIGGING) CORDAGE
(— STOLEN FROM DOCKYARD)
RUMBO
(— WITH HOOK AND TOGGLE)
PROLONGE
(— WITH SWIVEL AND LOOP)
TOGGEL TOGGLE
(— WOUND AROUND CABLE)
KECKLING
(ANCHOR —) RODE VIOL VOYAL
(BELL —) TYALL HANGER
(CIRCUS —) JEFF
(COWBOY'S —) LASSO NOOSE RIATA
LARIAT
(DESCEND BY —) RAPPEL
(DRAFT —) SOAM
(DRAG —) GUSS
(FLAG-RAISING —) HALYARD
(FOOT —) HORSE
(GRASS —) SOGA
(GUIDE —) DRAGLINE
(HANDLE —) FETTLE
(HANGMAN'S —) HEMP TIPPET
(HARNESS —) TRACE HALTER
(HARPOON —) FOREGOER
(MOORING —) HEADFAST
(NAUTICAL —) TIE TYE COLT FANG
LIFT STAY VANG BRACE BRAIL SHEET
SLING STRAP STROP GILGUY
HAWSER INHAUL LACING RATLIN
SHROUD BOBSTAY BOWLINE
CATFALL GESWARP LANYARD
LEEFANG OUTHAUL PAINTER
PAZAREE PENDANT PENNANT
PIGTAIL RATLINE SNORTER SNOTTER
STIRRUP STOPPER SWIFTER TRIATIC
BACKBONE BACKSTAY BUNTLINE
DOWNHAUL FORETACK JACKSTAY
PASSAREE ROUNDING SELVAGEE
WOOLDING TIMENOGUY
(PART OF —) SLATCH
(SHORT —) SHANK
(SHORT CART —) WANTY
(SMALL HANDMADE —) FOX
(SMUGGLER'S —) LINGTOW
(TALLOWED —) GASKET
(TETHERING —) SPANCEL
(TOW —) CORDELLE
(WIRE —) HAULBACK JACKSTAY
(WORN OR POOR —) JUNK
(PL.) CORDAGE
(PREF.) FUN(I) RESTI SPIR(O)
ROPEBAND RABAND
ROPE-DANCER ACROBAT
ROPEDANCER ACROBAT
FUNAMBULIST
ROPEMAKER FOLLOWER RATLINER

ROPEWALKER FUNAMBULO
ROPEWAY TRAMWAY WIREWAY
CABLEWAY
ROPY SINEWY STRINGY VISCOUS
MUSCULAR GLUTINOUS
ROQUE CROQUET
ROQUELAURE CLOAK ROCOLO
ROCKLAY
RORIPA RADICULA
RORQUAL SEI FINBACK
ROSACEA ACNE
ROSADER (BELOVED OF —)
ROSALYNDE
(BROTHER OF —) TORRISMOND
ROSAMUNDA (FATHER OF —)
CUNIMOND
(HUSBAND OF —) ALBOIN
ROSARY BEADS CORONA TASBIH
BEADING PSALTER BEADROLL
(— BEAD) AVE GAUD GAUDY
(MOHAMMEDAN —) COMBOLOIO
ROSE ASH GUL KNOT MOSS ROIS
BRIAR BRIDE BUCKY FLUSH RHODA
CANKER OPULUS POMPON
BOURBON BURBANK GLAIEUL
HUGONIS LOZENGE MANETTI
MONTHLY OPHELIA RAMBLER
AGRIMONY COLUMBIA DOGBERRY
LOKELANI PEDELION
(COTTON —) CUDWEED
(DWARF —) POLYANTHA
(HYBRID —) NOISETTE
(KIND OF —) MOSS
(PREF.) RHOD(O) ROSEO ROSI ROSO
(SUFF.) RHODIN
ROSE ACACIA ROBINIA
ROSE APPLE JAMBO JAMBOS
JAMBOSA
ROSEATE SPOONBILL AJAJA
ROSE-BREASTED (— COCKATOO)
GALAH
ROSEBUSH ROSER BALWARRA
ROSE CAMPION LYCHNIS
ROSE-COLORED OPTIMISTIC
(— STARLING) PASTOR TILYER
ROSEFISH BRIM BREAM BERGYLT
REDFISH
(YOUNG —) SNAPPER
ROSE HIP CHOOP CHOUP
ROSELLE SORREL SABDARIFFA
ROSEMARY COSTMARY
MOORWORT ROSMARINE
ROSE MOSS PURSLANE PORTULACA
ROSENKAVALIER, DER
(CHARACTER IN —) OCHS SOPHIE
FANINAL MARIANDL OCTAVIAN
MARSCHALLIN
(COMPOSER OF —) STRAUSS
ROSET BRAZIL
ROSETTE CHOU KNOT ROSACE
ROSULA COCKADE
ROSEWOOD BUBINGA MOLOMPI
JACARANDA PALISANDER

ROSH (FATHER OF —) BENJAMIN
ROSIN FLUX ROSET COLOPHONY
(— SPIRIT) PINOLIN
ROSS SCALP
ROSSER BARKER PEELER SCALPER
SLIPPER
ROSTER LIST ROTA SCROLL REGISTER
ROSTRATE BEAKED
ROSTRUM PEW AMBE BEAK BEMA
GUARD SNOUT PULPIT ACROTER
TRIBUNE
ROSY ROSEN BLUSHY AURORAL
HEALTHY HOPEFUL AUROREAN
BLOOMING BLUSHFUL RUBICUND
ROT COE RET DOTE DOZE DROP FOUL
JOKE LEAK POKE SOUR WROX
DECAY SPOIL TEASE BLUING FESTER
MOLDER ROTTEN CORRUPT
HOOFRUT PUTREFY NONSENSE
STAGNATE
(— BY EXPOSURE) RET
(— OF GRAPES) SLIPSKIN
(APPLE —) FROGEYE
(FOOT —) FOUL
(FRUIT —) BLET LEAK
(LIVER —) COE
(PREF.) PYTHO
ROTA LIST ROLL ROSTER ROTULA
ROTARY CIRCLE GYRATORY
ROUNDABOUT
(PREF.) ROTO
ROTATE RUN BIRL GYRE ROLL SPIN
TURN PIVOT RABAT SCREW WHEEL
GYRATE REVOLVE TRUNDLE
ROTIFORM TURNOVER ALTERNATE
(— CAMERA) PAN
(— HIDE) GRIND
ROTATING VOLUBLE
(— PIECE) CAM
ROTATION SPIN TURN ROUND TWIRL
GYRATION SPINNING WHIRLING
(— ON BALL) STUFF
(DEVICE INDICATING SPEED OF —)
TACH
(KIND OF —) FARADAY
(STOP —) DESPIN
ROTCHE BULL RATCH ROTGE
DOVEKEY DOVEKIE BULLBIRD
ROTE CRWTH HEART ROTTA
REPEAT
ROTIFER POLYP LIPOPOD LORICATE
PLOIMATE
ROTIFORM TROCHAL
ROTL RATTEL WEIGHT ROTTOLO
(PL.) ARTAL ARTEL
ROTOGRAVURE ROTO COLOROTO
ROTOR IMPELLER
ROTTED PECKY
ROTTEN BAD FOUL PUNK ROXY
SOUR ADDLE DAZED MOSEY PUTID
ADDLED AMPERY FRACID MOOSEY
PUTRID DECAYED SPOILED
DEPRAVED UNSTABLE

(HALF —) DOTED DOATED
(PARTIALLY —) DRUXY
(PREF.) PUTRE PUTRI SAPR(O)
ROTTENSTONE TRIPOLI
ROTTER CAD LOUSE
(INDIAN —) BUDMASH
ROTTING SLEEPY CARIOUS
ROTTLERA KAMALA
ROTULA ROUND TROCHE KNEEPAN
PATELLA
ROTUND FAT PLUMP ROUND STOUT
CHUBBY SUBROUND
ROTUNDA PANTHEON
ROTURIER PEASANT PLEBEIAN
RUPTUARY
ROUE RAKE RAKEHELL DEBAUCHEE
ROUGE RED FARD BLUSH PAINT
FUCATE REDDEN RUDDLE CLINKER
SCRIMMAGE
(ANIMAL —) CARMINE
ROUGH RU ROW RUF BEAT FOUL
GURL HARD HASK LAMB ROID ROYD
RUDE THUG WILD ACRID ASPER
BLUFF BLUNT BRUTE CHURL CRUDE
DIRTY GOBBY GROFF GURLY HAIRY
HARSH HEFTY JAGGY LUMPY
REWCH ROUCH ROWDY RUGGY
RUVID STARK STEER STERN STOUR
TOUGH TOUSY WIGHT BORREL
BROKEN BRUSHY BURRED CHOPPY
COARSE COBBLY CRABBY CRAGGY
ELBOIC HACKLY HISPID HOARSE
HOBBLY HORRID HUBBLY INCULT
JAGGED KEELIE KNAGGY KNOTTY
NOGGEN RAGGED RAMAGE RASPED
ROBUST RUFFLE RUGGED RUMBLY
RUSTIS SEVERE SHAGGY SKETCH
STICKY TOOSIE TRYING UNEVEN
UNFEEL UNFELE UNFINE UNKIND
UNMILD UNRIDE ABUSIVE AUSTERE
BOORISH BRISTLY CRABBED HIRSUTE
INEQUAL INEXACT JARRING
RABBISH RAMMAGE RAPLOCH
RAUCOUS RUFFLED SCABRID
SCRAGGY STICKLE STICKLY
UNCOUTH UNKEMPT VICIOUS
ABRASIVE ASPERATE CHURLISH
DEPOLISH IMPOLITE LARRIKIN
OBDURATE SCABROUS SCRAGGED
STUBBORN TACTLESS UNGENTLE
UNTENDER MANHANDLE
SCABERULOUS
(— EDGES) FASH
(— IT) CAMP SIWASH
(— UP) MESS
(— UP ARROW FEATHERS) SPRANGLE
(MAKE —) SHAG
(PREF.) ASPERI DASI DASY TRACHY
ROUGHAGE FIBER FODDER
AVERAGE DALLAST BULKAGE
CELLULOSE
ROUGH-AND-READY BURLY
TOWSY TOWZIE MAKESHIFT

ROUGHCAST HARL PARGET SPARGE
ROUGHHEW SLAPDASH
ROUGH-EDGED JAGGED RAGGED
ROUGHEN CHAP FRET GAIG HACK
EMERY FEAZE FLOCK FROST SPRAY
TOOTH ABRADE CRISLE STIVER
CRIZZLE ENGRAIL SCRATCH SPREAZE
ASPERATE SPREATHE UNSMOOTH
(— BRICK WALL) STAB
ROUGHER BULLDOGGER
(PONY —) STRANDER
ROUGH-HOB
ROUGHING IT (AUTHOR OF —)
TWAIN CLEMENS
(CHARACTER IN —) HANK MARK
SLADE TWAIN YOUNG BRIGHAM
ERICKSON
ROUGHLY ABOUT
ROUGH-MILL GASH
ROUGHNECK ROWDY TOUGH
MUCKER UNCOUTH BANGSTER
ROUGHNESS GAFF GRAIN SCUFF
TOOTH RUFFLE CRIZZLE CRUDITY
ACRIMONY ASPERITY
(— OF SEA) LIPPER
(— OF SKIN) GOOSESKIN
GOOSEFLESH
(— OF WALL) KEY
ROUGHOMETER VIAGRAPH
ROULADE VOLATA ARPEGGIO
ROULETTE FILET FILLET TROCHOID
(HIGH — NUMBERS) PASSE
(TYPE OF —) RUSSIAN
(1-18 IN —) MANQUE
(13-24 IN —) MILIEU
ROUNCEVAL GIANT LARGE
MONSTER GIGANTIC
ROUND BALL BEAT BEND BOLD BOUT
FAST FULL GIRO HEAD RICH ROON
ROTA TOUR TRIM WALK ABOUT
AMPLE BEADY BRISK CATCH DANCE
GLOBE HAMBO HARSH LARGE
MOONY ORBED PLAIN ROMAN
RONDO SPOKE TROLL TUBBY CIRCLE
COURSE ENTIRE MELLOW NEARLY
ROTUND ROUNDY RUBBER RUNDLE
SPHERY SPIRAL STOWER STREAK
ZODIAC ANNULAR CIRCUIT SHAPELY
CIRCULAR COMPLETE CROSSBAR
ENCIRCLE GLOBULAR SONOROUS
LABIALIZE
(— EDGES OF TIMBER) BEARD
(— END OF LOG) SNIPE
(— FREQUENTLY GONE OVER) BEAT
(— IN BOWLING) FRAME
(— IN CARDS) GRAND
(— IN ROLLER DERBY) JAM
(— OF ACTIVITIES) SWING
(— OF APPLAUSE) HAND JOLLY
SALVO PLAUDIT
(— OF CHAIR) BALUSTER
(— OFF) TOP CROWN FILLET
(— OF KNITTING) BOUT

(— OF LADDER) STAVE
(— OF PLAY) LAP
(— OUT) ORB BELLY INTEGRATE
(— UP) CORRAL WRANGLE
SCROUNGE
(FINAL FOUR —S) SEMIS
(PENULTIMATE —) SEMI
(PLUMP AND —) CHUBBY
(SWEDISH —) HAMBO
(TRIAL —) HEAT
(PREF.) GLOBI GLOBO PERI ROTUNDI
ROTUNDO TROCH(I)(LEI)(O) VENTR(I)
(O)
ROUNDABOUT PLUMP DETOUR
ROTARY CURVING DEVIOUS
CAROUSEL CIRCULAR INDIRECT
TORTUOUS AMBAGIOUS
(— MOVEMENT) WINDLASS
ROUNDED FULL BOMBE BOWLY
CONVEX MELLOW ROTUND TERETE
WHELKY ARRONDI BUNTING
COMPAST CONCAVE GIBBOUS
SCUTATE SHAPELY COMPLETE
FINISHED HOOPLIKE SONOROUS
(— OUT) PLUM
(PREF.) TERETI
ROUNDEL HEURT PLATE POMME
PELLET FOUNTAIN
(— AZURE) HURT
(— GULES) TORTEAU TORTEAUX
(— OR) BEZANT BYZANT
(— PURPURE) GOLP GOLPE
(— SABLE) GUNSTONE
(— SANGUINE) GUZE
(— VERT) POMEY
ROUNDER SOAKER WASTREL
INFORMER
ROUNDERS TUT PATBALL TUTBALL
ROUNDHEAD SWEDE CROPPY
WEAKFISH
ROUND HERRING SHADINE
STRADINE
ROUNDHOUSE BARN POOP LOCKUP
ROUND-MOUTH HAG HAGFISH
ROUNDNESS ROTUND SPHERICITY
(— OF RIBS) SPRING
ROUND POMPANO PERMIT
PALOMETA
ROUND ROBIN ANGLER SERIES
PANCAKE SEQUENCE
ROUNDSMAN VANMAN
SWINGMAN WATCHMAN
ROUNDUP RODEO CAMBER GATHER
MUSTER
ROUNDWORM NEMA ASCARID
EELWORM GORDIAN HELMINTH
NEMATODE STRONGYL
ROUP ROLP ROOP CROAK CLAMOR
AUCTION SHOUTING
ROUSE DAW GIG HOP JOG BAIT BEET
CALL DRAW FIRK GOAD MOVE RANT
RAVE STIR WAKE WHET AMOVE
ERECT MOUNT RAISE START STEER

UPSET WAKEN ABRADE ABRAID
AROUSE BESTIR EXCITE FOMENT
KINDLE NETTLE RATTLE REVIVE
RUFFLE WECCHE AGITATE ANIMATE
DISTURB EKPHORE ENLIVEN
HEARTEN INFLAME STARTLE INSPIRIT
IRRITATE
(— TO ACTION) HIE ALARM ALARUM
BESTIR ALACRIFY

ROUSING LIVELY AWAKENING
INCITATION
(— OF GAME) BEATING

ROUSTABOUT LADER FLOORMAN
RAZORBACK

ROUT MOB MOW DRUM FUSS HERD
BRANT CHASE COHUE CROWD EJECT
FLOCK LURCH PASTE SMEAR SMITE
SNORE CLAMOR DEFEAT FLIGHT
NUMBER RABBLE SOIREE THRONG
UPROAR CONFUSE CONQUER
DEBACLE SCATTER SHELLAC
SPARPLE TEMPEST ASSEMBLY
CONFOUND DISTRESS VANQUISH
(BACCHIC —) THIASUS

ROUTE WAY BELT GATE GEST LINE
PASS PATH SEND TRACE TRACK
AIRWAY CAREER COURSE CUTOFF
SKYWAY TRAJET CHANNEL CIRCUIT
LANDWAY PASSAGE SHUTTLE
CORRIDOR DISTANCE LIFELINE
SHORTCUT TRAVERSE
(— MARKED OUT) ITER
(— TO DEFEAT) SKIDE
(CIRCUITOUS —) DETOUR
(MIGRATION —) FLYWAY
(OCEAN —) LANE
(OVERLAND —) LANDBRIDGE
(PREF.) ODO

ROUTH PLENTY ABUNDANT

ROUTINE RUT RIFF ROTA DRILL
GRIND HEIGH HOHUM ROUND
ROUTE SHTIK TROLL GROOVE
SCHTIK SHTICK HARNESS SCHTICK
EVERYDAY ORDINARY
(— LABOR) SCUTWORK
(COMPUTER —) BOOTSTRAP
(DOMESTIC —) HOMELIFE
(ENTERTAINMENT —) SHTICK
(SHOW BIZ —) SCHTICK
(THEATRICAL —) SCHTICK
(WEARISOME —) TREADMILL

ROVE RUN RAKE RAVE ROAM GUESS
KNOCK RANGE ROWAN SCOUR
SPACE STRAY FORAGE MARAUD
RAMBLE STROLL WANDER SPATIATE
STRAGGLE TRANSCUR
(— ON THE WING) FLIT

ROVER FLIRT HOYLE STAKE STRAY
MASHER RANGER VIKING GANGREL
SCUMMER MARAUDER SLIVERER
TRAVELER WANDERER COLORADAN

ROVING END SLUB NOMAD VAGUE
ARRANT ERRANT DEVIOUS NOMADIC

RAMPLER VAGRANT GADABOUT
RAMBLING RESTLESS SLUBBING
VAGABOND MIGRATORY RANTIPOLE
(— IN SEARCH OF KNIGHTLY
ADVENTURE) ERRANTRY

ROW LAY OAR RIG SET DUST FILE
LINE MUSS PULL RANK RULE TIER
ALLEY BRAWL CHESS FIGHT MOUTH
NOISE ORDER RAMMY RANGE RINGE
SCOLD SCRAP SCULL SWATH TRAIN
BARNEY BERATE COURSE DUSTUP
GARRAY KICKUP LISSOM PADDLE
POTHER RACKET RUCKUS RUMPUS
SHINDY STREET STROKE BOBBERY
BRULYIE QUARREL RUCTION
SHINDIG CATEGORY OUTBURST
REMIGATE SQUABBLE
(— BACKWARD) STERN
(— OF ARCHES) ARCADE
(— OF BENCHES) STACK
(— OF BUSHES) HEDGE
(— OF CASKS) LONGER
(— OF CORN, BARLEY, ETC.) RIG
(— OF DRY HAY) STADDLE
(— OF GRAIN) SWATH SWATHE
(— OF GRASS) HACK SWATH
(— OF GUNS) TIRE
(— OF HOUSES) CRESCENT
(— OF LAMPS) BATTEN
(— OF SEATS) BARRERA
(— OF SEED) DRILL
(— OF STAKES) ORGUE
(— OF STAMPS) STRIP
(— OF STONES) CORDON
(— OF TREES) SCREEN ESPALIER
(— OF VEGETABLES) RINGE
(—S OF BALCONY) MEZZANINE
(DISORDERLY —) RAG
(DOUBLE — OF TREES) AVENUE
(SHORT —) SPRINT
(PL.) EPEIRA
(PREF.) STICHO
(SUFF.) STICH(OUS)

ROWAN ASH RAN RED RODDIN

ROWAN TREE CARE SORB WICKY
WITCH RODDEN RODDIN WICKEN
WIGGEN QUICKEN RANTREE
WHITTEN WITCHEN ROUNTREE

ROWBOAT GIG OAR BARK OARS
PLAT BARIS COBLE DINGY FUNNY
KOBIL SCULL SKIFF BARQUE
CAIQUE DINGHY LURKER WHERRY
SCULLER
(— SEAT) TAFT
(CLINKER-BUILT —) FUNNY
(FLAT-BOTTOMED —) DORY
(PART OF —) RING SEAT STEM SOCKET
THWART GUNWALE OARLOCK
PAINTER ROWLOCK TRANSOM
(SMALL —) COG

ROWDY TOU BHOY CASH MONEY
RORTY ROUGH TOUGH TOMBOY
UNRULY VULGAR HOODLUM

RAFFISH BARRATER LARRIKIN
STUBBORN ROUGHNECK
ROWDYISM YAHOOISM
ROWEN EDGROW RAWING
AFTERMATH ROUGHINGS
ROWENA (FATHER OF —) HENGIST
(GUARDIAN OF —) CEDRIC
(HUSBAND OF —) IVANHOE
VORTIGERN
ROWER URGER GALIOT STROKE
OARSMAN STERNMAN CAIQUEJEE
(— ON UPPER SEATS) THRANITE
(OUTERMOST —) THALAMITE
(SECOND LEVEL —) ZYGITE
ROWING CREW
(— EQUIPMENT) OARAGE
ROWLOCK LOCK CRUTCH OARLOCK
RULLOCK
ROXANA (FATHER OF —) OXYARTES
(HUSBAND OF —) ALEXANDER
ROYAL EASY REAL RIAL ELITE REGAL
SMALT AUGUST KINGLY REGIUS
SOVRAN SUPERB BASILIC GLORIOUS
IMPERIAL IMPOSING MAJESTIC
PAVILION PRINCELY
(— MACE) SCEPTER SCEPTRE
ROYAL ANTELOPE MADOQUA
KLEENEBOC
ROYAL FERN OSMOND OSMUND
ROYALIST TORY ULTRA REGIAN
TANTIVY CAVALIER MUSCADIN
(PL.) CHOUANS
ROYALLY PURPLEY
ROYAL PALM COYAL
ROYALTY LOT ALII GALE BONUS
CROWN REGAL REALTY MAJESTY
PENALTY LORDSHIP NOBILITY
REGALITY
ROYET WILD HARSH UNRULY
ROMPING
RUB DUB BARK BILL FILE FRAY FRET
FRIG FROT RISP SHAB WIPE CHAFE
DIGHT FEEZE FRUSH GRATE GRAZE
GRIDE LABOR SCOUR SCRUB SMEAR
STONE FRIDGE RUBER STREAK
BEESWAX FRICACE FURBISH
MASSAGE
(— AS ANIMALS) SHAB
(— AS A ROPE) SNUG
(— AWAY) ERODE ABRADE
(— BOOT) BONE
(— DOWN) WIPE STRAP
(— ELBOWS) JOSTLE JUSTLE
(— GENTLY) STRIKE STROKE
(— HARD) SCOUR SCRUB
(— HARSHLY) GRIND
(— IN) HARPON
(— LIGHTLY) GRAZE
(— OFF) CROCK ABRADE ABRASE
(— OUT) ERASE EFFACE EXPUNGE
(— ROUGHLY) GRATE
(— SNUFF) DIP
(— THE SKIN OFF) SHAW

(— TOGETHER) FIDDLE
(— VELVET FROM ANTLERS)
BURNISH
(— WITH GREASE) DUB
(— WITH NOSE) NOUSLE NUZZLE
(— WITH OIL) ANOINT
(PREF.) TRIBO
RUBABOO SOUP
RUBBED TERSE
RUBBER BUNA FOAM PARA BUTYL
CREPE RASER ALASKA CAUCHO
DAPICO ERASER NIGGER RUNNER
BISCUIT BURUCHA EBONITE ELASTIC
GUAYULE RAMBONG BORRACHA
FRICTION NEOPRENE SERNAMBY
SERWAMBY SOVPRENE
(— CITY) AKRON
(HARD —) EBONITE
(RECLAIMED —) SHODDY
(PL.) SHAB
RUBBERIZE FRICTION
RUBBERNECK GAPE CRANE STARE
TOURIST SIGHTSEE
RUBBER TREE ULE MILKER
RAMBONG
RUBBING CHAFE CARESS ABRASION
FRICTION FROTTAGE FRICATION
RUBBISH KET BUNK CRAB CRAP
FLAM FLUM GEAR GWAG MULL
MUSH PELF PELT PUNK RAFF ROSS
TOSH TRAG BILGE BRASH BROCK
CRAWM CULCH OFFAL SCOWL
SLUSH STENT STUFF TRADE TRASH
TRIPE TRUCK WASTE COLDER DEBRIS
GARBLE KELTER LITTER PALTRY
PIFFLE RAFFLE RAMMEL REFUSE
RUBBLE SCULCH SHRUFF SPILTH
BAGGAGE BEGGARY FLANNEL
MULLOCK RUMMAGE SLITHER
TAFFIKE TRAFFIC FIRETRAP
NONSENSE RIFFRAFF TRASHERY
TRUMPERY CLAMJAMFRY
CLAMJAMPHRIE
(VEGETABLE —) WRACK
RUBBISHY POUCY PALTRY TRASHY
BAGGAGE RUMMAGY
RUBBLE BRASH STENT TALUS
RAMMEL BACKING MOELLON
SLITHER
RUBE JAY BOOR HICK JAKE YAHOO
JASPER BUMPKIN BUSHMAN
HAYSEED CORNBALL
RUBELLA ROTELN
RUBELLITE SIBERITE
RUBICUND RED ROSY RUDDY
FLORID FLUSHED
RUBIGINOUS RUSTY
RUBIK ERNO
RUBLE RO RUBLIS
(ONE-HALF —) POLTINIK
RUBRIC RED NAME CANON CLASS
TITLE CONCEPT CATEGORY
RUBRICATE MINIATE

RUBY AGATE BALAS RUBIN PYROPE
ANTHRAX SPARKLE VERMEIL
RUBY SPINEL BALAS ALMANDINE
RUCHING COQUILLE
RUCK RUT HEAP PILE RICK SLEW
CROWD SQUAT STACK TRASH
CREASE FURROW HUDDLE PUCKER
RUBBISH WRINKLE
RUCKUS ADO ROW FIGHT FRACAS
ROOKUS
RUCTION HURRY RUCKUS QUARREL
RUPTION FRACTION
RUDABAH (FATHER OF —) MIHRAB
(HUSBAND OF —) ZAL
(SON OF —) RUSTAM
RUDD REDEYE
RUDDER HELM STEER STERN TIMON
HELLIM RUTHER STEERER STEERAGE
GOVERNAIL
(— BACK) TALON
(— EDGE) BEARDING
(— OF WINDMILL) TAIL
(DIVING —) HYDROVANE
(PART OF —) STOCK
RUDDERFISH CHOPA OPALEYE
RUDDINESS RUBEDITY
RUDDLE RED ROLE KEEL SMIT ROUGE
RUDDY RED RODE RUDE FRESH VIVID
BLOWSY BLOWZY FLORID LIVELY
GLOWING RUDDISH BLUSHFUL
RUBICUND SANGUINE
(NOT —) PALE
RUDDY DUCK ROOK BOOBY NODDY
PADDY SPRIG BOBBER DUNBIRD
GREASER PINTAIL SLEEPER SPATTER
BLUEBILL BULLNECK HARDHEAD
WIRETAIL
RUDE ILL RAW BOLD IRON LEWD
WILD BLUFF BLUNT CRUDE GREEN
GROSS PLUMP ROUGH STOUR
SURLY UNORN ABRUPT BITTER
BORREL BRASSY CALLOW CHUFFY
CLUMSY COARSE DUDGEON GOTHIC
HOMELY HOYDEN INCULT RIBALD
ROBUST RUGGED RUSTIC SAVAGE
SHAGGY SIMPLE STORMY UNFEEL
UPLAND VULGAR ABUSIVE ARTLESS
BOORISH CARLAGE CARLISH INCIVIL
LOUTISH LOWBRED NATURAL
UNCOUTH UNHENDE CHURLISH
CLUBBISH HOMESPUN IMPOLITE
INSOLENT MECHANIC PETULANT
PORTERLY STUBBORN SYLVATIC
TACTLESS UNGENTLE UNPOLITE
YOKELISH GRACELESS TASTELESS
(— AND BOLD) HOIDEN HOYDEN
(NOT —) MANNERLY
RUDENESS GAFF
RUDIMENT GERM ANLAGE VESTIGE
BEGINNING PRIMORDIUM
(FIRST —) PRIMORDIUM
(PL.) ABC ALPHABET ELEMENTS
GRAMMATES

RUDIMENTARY BASIC GERMING
ABORTIVE INCHOATE ABECEDARY
ELEMENTAL EMBRYONIC PRIMITIVE
ABECEDARIAN
(MOST —) FIRST
(PREF.) LYO PRO
RUE RU REWE MOURN CATGUT
REGRET REPENT SORROW BORONIA
HARMALA TENTWORT
RUEFUL SAD RUELY WOEFUL
DOLEFUL PITIABLE
RUFF SET APEX FURY PAPE POPE
CREST PRIDE REEVE TEASE TEAZE
TRUMP COLLAR FRAISE RABATO
RUFFLE TIPPET ZENITH ELATION
PARTLET PASSION QUELLIO REBATER
ROTONDE PICKADIL
(FEMALE —) REE
RUFFED BUSTARD HOUBARA
RUFFED LEMUR VARI
RUFFIAN MUN LAMB PIMP PUNK
THUG TORY BRAVO BULLY DEVIL
ROUGH ROWDY TIGER TOUGH
APACHE BRUTAL COARSE CUTTER
CUTTLE MOHAWK MOHOCK NICKER
PANDER TOWSER HOODLUM
SWEATER TUMBLER HACKSTER
HOOLIGAN
RUFFLE VEX BAIT FRET HOOP ROOL
RUFF STIR BULLY CRISP FRILL GRAZE
JABOT PLEAT ROUGH ROUSE SHIRR
ABRADE ATTACK GATHER NETTLE
PEPLUM RIPPLE BLUSTER BRISTLE
DERANGE FLOUNCE FLUTTER
PANUELO STIFFEN SWAGGER
TROUBLE DISHEVEL DISORDER
DISTRACT FURBELOW IRRITATE
QUILLING SKIRMISH
(— THE TEMPER) ROIL
RUFFLED ROUGH UNKEMPT
**RUFFLING (— ON THE SURFACE OF
WATER)** HORROR
RUFUS (FATHER OF —) SIMON
RUG MAT RYA TUG BAKU COZY
HAUL MAUD PULL SNUG TEAR
WRAP BIJAR HERAT HEREZ HERIZ
JURUK KAZAK KHILA KONIA KULAH
KUMEH LADIK MECCA MELAS
MOSUL NAMDA SENNA SISAL
TEKKE TUZLA USHAK YURUK
ZOFRA AFSHAR BALUCH KANARA
KAROSS KASHAN KIRMAN
MOGHAN NAMMAD PERGAM
RUNNER SHIRAZ SMYRNA
TABRIZ TILPAH TOUPEE WILTON
BALUCHI BERGAMA BOKHARA
BUFFALO DERBEND DRUGGET
FERAHAN GIORDES GOREVAN
HAMADAN ISPAHAN SHEERAZ
SHIRVAN YARKAND AUBUSSON
DOMESTIC FOOTPACE PANDERMA
SARABAND SEDJADEH SERABEND
WOLFSKIN

(— FOR SADDLE) PILCH
(— OF SKINS) KAROSS WOLFSKIN
(GREEK —) FLOKATI
(KIND OF —) AREA SHAG NAVAJO
BRAIDED
(PERSIAN —) HEREZ
(PLAID —) MAUD
(PRAYER —) MELAS MELES
GHIORDES NAMAZLIK
(REVERSIBLE —) KILIM
(SCANDINAVIAN —) RYA
(SMALL —) MAT
RUGA FOLD CREASE WRINKLE
RUGBY FOOTER RUGGER FOOTBALL
(— PLAY) SCRUM
RUGGED RUDE WILD HAIRY HARDY
ROUGH STIFF COARSE CRAGGY
HORRID JAGGED KNAGGY KNOTTY
ROBUST SAVAGE STRONG STURDY
UNEVEN CRABBED GNARLED
OBDURATE SCRAGGED VIGOROUS
RUGGIERO (GUARDIAN OF —)
ATLANTE
(SISTER OF —) MARFISA
(SLAYER OF —) TISAPHERNES
(WIFE OF —) BRADAMANTE
RUIN DO MAR POT BANE BANG COOK
CRAB DAMN DASH DISH DOOM FALL
FATE FELL HELL JACK KILL LOSS
RASE RAZE SINK TALA BLAST BOTCH
BREAK CRUSH DECAY EXILE GUBAT
HUACA LEESE LEISS SHEND SHOOT
SMASH SPEED SPILL SPLIT SPOIL
SWAMP TRASH WRACK WRAKE
WRECK BANJAX BEDASH BLIGHT
CANCEL COOPER DAMAGE DEFACE
DEFEAT DIDDLE DISMAY FOREDO
INJURY JIGGER MANGLE RAVAGE
UNMAKE BOWWOWS CORRUPT
DESTROY FLATTEN FORLESE
FORWORK LEESING PERVERT
SCUPPER SHATTER SUBVERT
TORPEDO UNDOING BANKRUPT
COLLAPSE DEMOLISH DESOLATE
DISASTER DOWNFALL
(— AT GAMBLING) SHRUB
(SPIRITUAL —) FALL
(PL.) ASHES DEBRIS RELICS RUDERA
ZIMBABWE
RUINATION DOGS
RUINED FLAT GONE LORN BROKE
KAPUT BROKEN FALLEN NAUGHT
NOUGHT FORLORN BANKRUPT
DESOLATE
RUINER MARPLOT
RUINOUS DEADLY BANEFUL
DECAYED SHENDFUL WASTEFUL
CUTTHROAT
RULE LAW MAN RAJ WIN DASH KING
NORM SWAY WALD WARD YARD
AXIOM CANON GUIDE JUDGE MAXIM
NORMA ORDER POWER REGLE REIGN
RICHE RIGHT RULER SPILE STAFF

SUTRA SUTTA WIELD ALIDAD
CUTOFF DECIDE DECREE DITION
DOMINE EMPIRE ENTAIL GNOMON
GOVERN MANAGE MASTER METHOD
REGNUM REGULA SQUARE VASSAL
BROCARD COMMAND CONTROL
COUNSEL DICTATE DIETARY
FORMULA PLUMMET PRECEPT
PRESIDE REGENCY REGIMEN
THEOREM DICTAMEN DOCTRINE
DOMINATE FUNCTION LEGALISM
MODERATE ORDINARY OVERLEAD
PERSUADE REGIMENT REGNANCY
STANDARD TYRANNIS OBSERVANCE
(— BY UPSTARTS) NEOCRACY
(— OUT) EXCLUDE
(—S OF CONDUCT) ETIQUETTE
(—S OF DUELING) DUELLO
(— TYRANNICALLY) HORSE
(ABSOLUTE —) EMPERY AUTARCHY
(MOB —) OCHLOCRACY
(OPPOSING —) ANTINOMY
(PREF.) ARCH(AE)(AEO)(E)(EO)(I)
RULER (ALSO SEE CHIEF, TITLE,
LEADER) DEY GOG JAM MIN OBA
AMIR CZAR DAME DUKE EMIR INCA
KING LORD OBBA RULE TSAR TZAR
ALDER AMEER DECAN EMEER HAKIM
MPRET MWAMI NAGID NAWAB
SCALE SOPHI STEER SUBAH ZUPAN
APHETA ARCHON AUTHOR CAESAR
DESPOT DUARCH DYNAST EPARCH
FERULE GERENT HERSIR ISWARA
KABAKA KAISER MASTER NIMROD
PATESI PENLOP RECTOR REGENT
SATRAP SAWBWA SHERIF SOLDAN
SUFFEE SULTAN TYRANT ADMIRAL
ALIDADE BOURBON DEMARCH
FAIPULE ISHVARA KHEDIVE
MONARCH MORMAER PTOLEMY
RECTRIX REGULUS REIGNER
TOPARCH TRIARCH WIELDER
AUGUSTUS BASILEUS DRIGHTEN
EXILARCH GOVERNOR HEPTARCH
INTERREX OLIGARCH OVERLORD
PADISHAH PENTARCH PHYLARCH
REGINALD TARAFDAR WHIPKING
(— IN A NATIVITY) APHETA
(— OF ENCLOSURE) HENRY
(— OF UNIVERSE) PANTOCRATOR
(ALBANIAN —) MPRET
(CHIEF —) PADISHAH
(CURVED —) SWEEP
(DEIFIED —) THEOCRAT
(ELF —) AUBREY
(INCA —) CURACA
(INDIAN —) NIZAM MAHARAJA
MAHARAJAH
(JAPANESE —) SHOGUN
(JEWISH —) EXILARCH
(MONGOLIAN —) HUTUKTU
(MOSLEM —) SOLDAN
(NAME MEANING —) INCA

(STRONG —) REGINALD
(SUPREME —) SUZERAIN
(TATAR OR MOGUL —) CHAM
(WHITE —S) SERKALI
(PREF.) ARCH(AE)(AEO)(E)(EO)(I)
(SUFF.) ARCHIC ARCHY
RULING CALL CHIEF REGENT
SOVRAN CURRENT HOLDING
REGITIVE HEGEMONIC
RUM ODD ROME OCUBY QUEER
RUMBO TAFIA TAFFIA BACARDI
CACHACA JAMAICA PECULIAR
SWITCHEL EXCELLENT
RUMBLE CROWL DICKY GROWL
MELEE RUMOR SNORE BUMBLE
HOTTER HUMBLE LUMBER WAMBLE
GRUMBLE QUARREL
(— AS A GANG) BOP
RUMBLER VOLCANO
RUMBO RUM GROG LIQUOR
RUMEN CUD PAUNCH STOMACH
RUMINANT OX COW YAK BULL DEER
GOAT CAMEL LLAMA MOOSE SHEEP
STEER TAKIN ALPACA MAZAME
VICUNA GIRAFFE QUIDDER
ANTELOPE TUBICORN
RUMINATE CHAW CHEW MULL
MUSE PONDER CONCOCT REFLECT
SAUNTER CONSIDER
RUMINATION MERYCISM
RUMKIN RUMMER
RUMMAGE COMB GRUB POKE ROOT
ROUT SEEK BUSTLE FORAGE
POWTER TOUSLE UPROAR FOSSICK
RANSACK ROMMACK DISORDER
SKIRMISH UPHEAVAL
(— ABOUT FOR A PROFIT) FOSSICK
(— SALE) JUMBLE
RUMMY GIN RUM TUNK QUEER
CANASTA COONCAN DRUNKARD
OKLAHOMA
RUMOR CRY SAW BUZZ FAMA FAME
TALK WORD BRUIT MUDGE NOISE
SOUGH SOUND STORY VOGUE
VOICE BREEZE CANARD FURPHY
GOSSIP MURMUR POTGUN RENOWN
REPORT RUMBLE CLATTER HEARING
HEARSAY INKLING OPINION
WHISPER NORATION GRAPEVINE
SCUTTLEBUTT
(SCANDALOUS —S) GOSSIP
RUMORED AFLOAT
RUMP ASS FUD ARSE BEAM CULE
DOCK DOUP DUFF CROUP NACHE
NATCH PODEX STERN BOTTOM
CURPIN CROUPON CRUPPER
HURDIES KEISTER PLUNDER
BANKRUPT BUTTOCKS DERRIERE
(— OF BIRD) UROPYGIUM
(— OF HORSE) CROUP CROUPE
(PREF.) PYG(O)
(SUFF.) PYGAL PYGE PYGIA(N)
PYGOUS PYGUS

RUMPF CORE
RUMPLE FOLD MUSS WISP TOUSE
TOWSE MOUSLE ROMBLE CRUMPLE
SCRUNCH WRINKLE
RUMPUS RAG ROW BRAWL SHINE
CLAMOR FRACAS HUBBUB RUCKUS
SHINDY TOWROW UPROAR
BAGARRE BOBBERY ROOKERY
RUCTION ROWDYDOW
RUMSHOP BAR SALOON TAVERN
BARROOM TAPROOM DRUNKERY
RUN GO BYE ERN FLY FOG GAD HOP
JOG LAM LEG PLY RIN RUB URN
BUNK CALL FLOW FUSE HARE
HEAT HEEL HUNT IRNE KITE LEAD
LEAP MELT PASS PLAY RACE RAKE
RINN ROAM ROVE SCUD TEND TRIG
TRIP TROT TURN WALK WEEP WORK
ASSAY BLEND BREAK BRUSH CHASE
COAST EXTRA GOING HURRY NOTCH
POINT SCOUP SPEED SPEND STAND
TABLE TRACE BICKER CAREER
COURSE ELAPSE ESCAPE EXTEND
GALLOP HASTEN LADDER MANAGE
RESORT ROTATE SPRENT SPRINT
STREAM TUMBLE VOLATA ACCURRE
CONDUCT CONTAIN FLUTTER
LIQUEFY OPERATE PASSAGE
RETREAT SCUTTER SKELTER
STRETCH FUNCTION TRANSCUR
(— ADOUT) TIG FISK DISCURRE
(— ACROSS) STRIKE
(— AGAINST) JOSTLE
(— AGROUND) BEACH GRAVEL
HURTLE STRAND STRIKE
(— ALONG EDGE OF) SKIRT
(— AS DYE) BLEED
(— AS STOCKING) LADDER
(— AT HIGH SPEED) SCORCH
(— AT THE NOSE) SNIVEL
(— AT TOP SPEED) SPRINT
(— AWAY) FLY GUY FLEE HIKE JINK
JUMP SMUG ELOPE SCRAM SMOKE
DECAMP SCAMPER SCARPER
FUGITATE SKEDADDLE
(— AWAY FROM DEBTS) LEVANT
(— AWAY IN PANIC) STAMPEDE
(— BEFORE A GALE) SCUD
(— BEFORE A JUMP) FEAZE FEEZE
(— BETWEEN) INTERCUR
(— BLINDLY) SKITTLE
(— CLUMSILY) LOPPET TUMBLE
(— COUNTER) BELY BELIE CROSS
(— DOWN) SLUR TRASH OVERRUN
(— HARD) DIG
(— HIGH) FLOOD
(— IN CRICKET) BYE WIDE EXTRA
NOTCH
(— IN DROPS) WEEP
(— IN PLACE) IDLE
(— INTO) MEET INCUR
(— ITS COURSE) LAPSE
(— NAKED) STREAK

(— OBLIQUELY) SQUINT
(— OF CLAPBOARDING) STRAKE
(— OFF) BOLT FLEE SCADDLE
(— OF MULE CARRIAGE) DRAW
(— OF SHAD) SPURT
(— OF STAIRS) GOING
(— ON SKIS) SCHUSS
(— OUT) EXCUR ISSUE PETER
ELAPSE EXPIRE
(— OVER) HEAT TRAMP OVERFLOW
(— RAPIDLY) KITE RAKE SCUR SCOUR
SKIRR SPLIT CAREER
(— SHORT) STRAITEN
(— SOAP) FRAME
(— SPEEDILY) CHASE CAREER
(— SWIFTLY) HARE LEAP SCUD
CHEVY CHIVY
(— THE SHOW) EMCEE
(— THROUGH) PIERCE DISCURRE
(— TO) ACCURRE
(— TO EXERCISE HORSE) HEAT
(— TOGETHER) HERD MUDDY
CLUTTER
(— TRAINS) BLOCK
(— WILD) GAD ESCAPE STARTLE
(— WILDLY) STARTLE
(— WITH AFFECTED PRECIPITATION)
SCUTTLE
(— WITH SKIPS) SCOUP
(— WITH VELOCITY) DART
(BRIEF —) STREAK FLUTTER
(COMMON —) RUCK
(END —) SWEEP
(GLASS FURNACE —) BLAST
(HOME —) DINGER
(MUSICAL —) TIRADE ARPEGGIO
(OBSTACLE —) GYMKHANA
(RAPID MUSICAL —) TIRADE VOLATA
(SAILING —) STRETCH
(SHEEP —) SLAIT STATION
(SHORT —) FAIL BICKER SCURRY
FLUTTER RAMRACE SCUTTLE
(SKI —) PISTE SCHUSS LANGLAUF
(WILD —) LAMP
(PREF.) TRECHO TREKO
RUNAGATE APOSTATE FUGITIVE
RENEGADE RUNABOUT VAGABOND
WANDERER
RUNAWAY ROMP FUGIE RUNNER
DECISIVE DESERTER FUGITIVE
RUNAGATE
(PREF.) DRAPETO
RUNDI HUTU
RUNDLE DRUM RUNG STEP ORBIT
CIRCLE SPHERE WINDLASS
RUNDLET KEG BARREL
RUN-DOWN BAD
RUNDOWN INFO CHECK RECAP
SCOOP
RUN-DOWN SEEDY
RUNDOWN REPORT
RUN-DOWN SHODDY SQUALID

RUNDOWN SUMMARY ANALYSIS
RUN-DOWN DERELICT
RUNE WEN WYN AESE WYNN CHARM
OGHAM SPELL THORN SECRET
MYSTERY
RUNG RIM GREE RIME STEP ROUND
SCALE SPELL SPOKE STAFF STAIR
STALE STAVE STEAL TREAD WRUNG
DEGREE RUNDLE STOWER STREAK
CROSSBAR TRAVERSE
(— OF CHAIR) SPELL
(— OF LADDER) RIME STEP RANGE
SPOKE STALE RONDLE STREAK
(— OF ROPE WALK) STAKE
(PL.) STILE
RUNIC ALPHABET FUTHARK
FUTHORC
RUNIC LETTER THORN
RUNLET RUSH RINDLE RUNNEL
STREAM RIVELING
RUNNEL RILL BROOK RHINE RINDLE
RUNLET POLLARD RIVULET
STREAMLET
RUNNER RUG SOW GOER POST
SCUD SHOE SKID BLADE COBIA
FLOAT LOPER MILER RACER SABOT
SCARF SKATE SLIDE SPRAY TEDGE
CURSOR HEELER SPOKE KANARA
RENNER STOLON TOUTER CHANNEL
COURIER HARRIER NOMINEE
SARMENT CURSITOR SKIPJACK
TRAILING CANDIDATE
(— FOR GRINDING STONE) MARTIN
(— WHO SETS PACE) RABBIT
(BLUE —) HARDTAIL
(BOOKMAKER'S —) SPIV
(ERRAND —) CAD GOFER GOPHER
(FLUME —) HERDER
(PAIR OF —S) SLOOP
(RACE —) SCUTTLER
(SLED —S) BOB
(SLEDGE —) SLIP
(SLEDGE —S) SLIPES
(SNOW —) SKI
RUNNING RUN CARE EASY RACE
FLUID QUICK COURSE LIVING
COURANT CURRENT CURSIVE
FLOWING HOTFOOT SCUTTER
SLIDING FUGITIVE
(— ABOUT) COURANT CURSORY
(— ACROSS) DIAGONAL
(— AT SLOW PACE) JOGGING
(— BETWEEN) INTERCURRENT
(— DOWNWARD) DEFLUENT
(— FROM SIDE TO SIDE) SALLY
(— IN) INCURRENT
(— OF SHIPS TOGETHER) ALLISION
(— OVER) OVERFLOWING
(— SIDEWAYS) LATERIGRADE
(— TOGETHER) SLUR
(— TOWARD) APPULSE
(— VERTICALLY) DOWN

(FIRST —S) HEAD
(NOT —) DEAD
(SMOOTHLY —) SWEET
(PREF.) DROM(O)
(SUFF.) DROMOUS
RUNNING GEAR MOBILE
RUN-OF-THE-MILL SOSO AVERAGE
ORDINARY
RUNT BOOR SCRAG SCRUB SLINK
STEER STUMP STUNT HEIFER
PEEWEE SCRUMP SHRIMP TITMAN
URLING BULLOCK SHARGAR
SHARGER SLINKER RECKLING
RUNTY MEAN SURLY SCRUBBY
SCRUNTY STUNTED DWARFISH
RUNWAY RUN TIP DUCT STRIP TRAIL
TARMAC SLIPWAY AIRSTRIP
DOLLYWAY
(— OF HARE) FILE
RUPEE DIB CHIP SICCA ROUPIE
(ONE-SIXTEENTH —) ANNA
(TENS OF —S) RX
(10 MILLION —S) CRORE
(100,000 —S) LAC LAKH
RUPERT'S DROP IFAN
RUPIA RUPEE ERUPTION
(HALF —) PARDO PARDAO
RUPTURE BLOW REND RENT BREAK
BURST CRACK SPLIT BREACH DIVIDE
HERNIA RHEXIS DISRUPT RUPTION
DIVISION FRACTION FRACTURE
HERNIATE
(SUFF.) RHEXIS RRHEXIS
RUPTURED BROKEN
RURAL RUSTIC BUCOLIC COUNTRY
AGRESTIC ARCADIAN LANDWARD
MOFUSSIL PASTORAL PRAEDANT
PRAEDIAL VILLATIC
RUSE HOAX ROSE SHIFT STALL TRICK
WREST ARTIFICE TRICKERY
RUSH FLY FOG HIE RIP RIX RUB SAG
BANG BENT BOLT CLAP DASH DUSH
FALL FLAW GIRD HURL HUSH JUNK
KICK LASH LEAP LUSH PASH RACE
RACK RASH RESE RISH ROUT SCUD
SHOT SLUR SPUR SWIP TEAR TILT
WHIP WIND ADRUE CARRY CHASE
CHUTE DRASH DRIVE FEEZE FLASH
FLUSH FRAIL FRUSH HURRY ONSET
PIPES PREEL SCOUR SEAVE SHOOT
SPART SPATE SPEED SPRAT SPRIT
SPROT START STAVE STORM WHIRL
CHARGE DELUGE FESCUE HURTLE
JUNCUS POWDER RAMACK RANDOM
RAVINE STREAK THRESH THRILL
ASSAULT BRATTLE BULRUSH
DAILIES DEBACLE JUNCITE RAMMISH
RAMRACE SKELTER SMOTHER
SWITHER TANTIVY TORNADO
VIRETOT WHITHER CATARACT
DEERHAIR SALTWEED SPLATTER
VANQUISH

(— ABROAD) FLUSH
(— AGAINST) CHARGE
(— AWAY) BOLT FLEE SCUTTLE
(— DOWN) TRACE
(— FOR WEAVING) FRAIL
(— HEADLONG) BOIL RUIN SPURN
STAMPEDE
(— OF AIR) WAFT
(— OF LIQUID) HEAD FLUSH
(— OF WATER) FRESH SHOOT SPOUT
SWASH
(— OF WORDS) SPATE
(— ON FOOTBALL PLAYER) BLITZ
(— ON PASSER IN FOOTBALL)
BLITZ
(— OUT) SALLY
(CLUMP OF —S) RASHBUSS
(COMMON —) FLOSS
(DOWNWARD —) HURL
(FLAT —) SHALDER
(FORCEFUL —) JET
(NOISY —) OCUITER
(ONWARD —) BIRR SURGE
(PL.) REXEN
(PREF.) JUNCI THRYONO
RUSHED HECTIC
RUSHING HURL SCUD FURIOUS
HUDDLING IMPETUOUS
(— OF WIND) GUST
RUSHLIGHT SEAVE
RUSH NUT CHUFA
RUSK ZWIEBACK
RUSSELL'S VIPER DABOIA DADOYA
JESSUR KATUKALA KOLA CHIMEA
KARELIA KAMCHATKA

MOUNTAIN RANGE: ALAI URAL
CAUCASUS
NAME: CIS
PENINSULA: KOLA CRIMEA KARELIA
KAMCHATKA
PORT: EISK ANAPA ODESSA
REPUBLIC: ARMENIA BELARUS
MOLDOVA UKRAINE AZERBAIJAN
KAZAKHSTAN KYRGYZSTAN
TAJIKISTAN UZBEKISTAN
TURKMENISTAN
RUSSIANFEDERATION
RIVER: IK OB DON ILI KET NER OKA
ROS TAZ TYM UFA USA AMGA
AMUR KARA LENA NEVA OREL STYR
SURA SVIR URAL DESNA ISTRA
LOVAT MEZEN NADYM NEMAN
ONEGA TEREK TOBOL VOLGA
ABAKAN DONETS ENISEI IRTYSH
OLEKMA DNIEPER NEMUNAS
PECHORA YENISEI
SEA: ARAL AZOV KARA BLACK BAIKAL
OKHOTSK
TOWN: BAKU KIEV OMSK OREL PERM
RIGA GOMEL ISTRA KASAN KAZAN
KYZYL MINSK PENSA PSKOV TOMSK
FRUNZE IGARKA KERTCH KURGAN
NIZHNI ODESSA ROSTOV SARTOV
URALSK ALMAATA BATAISK
DONETSK IRKUTSK IVANOVO
KALININ KHARKOV RYBINSK
TALLINN KOSTROMA ORENBURG
SMOLENSK TAGANROG TASHKENT
VLADIMIR VORONEZH YAROSLAV
VOLCANO: ALAID SHIVELUCH

RUSSIAN IVAN RUSS SLAV VELIKA
MUSCOVITE
(— BRAID) SOUTACHE
(— HEMP) RINE
(— NOT ALLOWED TO EMIGRATE)
REFUSNIK REFUSENIK
(— POOL) CARLINE
(LITTLE —) RUSSENE RUTHENE
UKRAINIAN
RUSSIAN BANK CRAPETTE
RUSSIAN CALF FUDGESH KOLYMA
USSURI DNIEPER PECHORA
SUKHONA YENISEY VYCHEGDA
INDIGIRKA

RUSSIA FEDERATION (SEE ALSO
RUSSIA)
CAPITAL: MOSCOW
COIN: RUBLE
FORT: KREMLIN
ISLAND: KURIL SAKHALIN
NOVAYAZEMLYA
LAKE: CHANY ILMEN ONEGA BAYKAL
BELOYE BRATSK LADOGA PEIPUS
RYBINSK TOPOZERO VYGOZERO
MOUNTAIN: ELBRUS KORYAK
SREDINNY NARODNAYA

MOUNTAIN RANGE: URAL ALTAI
SAYAN BAIKAL KOLYMA CHERSKY
KHIBINY PUTORAN BAIKALIA
BYRRANGA CAUCASUS STANOVOY
BADZHALSKY DZHUGDZHUR
VERKHOYANSK
PENINSULA: KOLA CRIMEA KARELIA
KAMCHATKA
PORT: EISK ANAPA ODESSA
REPUBLIC: ARMENIA BELARUS
MOLDOVA UKRAINE AZERBAIJAN
KAZAKHSTAN KYRGYZSTAN
TAJIKISTAN UZBEKISTAN
TURKMENISTAN
RUSSIANFEDERATION
RIVER: IK OB DON ILI KET NER OKA
ROS TAZ TYM UFA USA AMGA
AMUR KARA LENA NEVA OREL STYR
SURA SVIR URAL DESNA ISTRA
LOVAT MEZEN NADYM NEMAN
ONEGA TEREK TOBOL VOLGA
ABAKAN DONETS ENISEI IRTYSH
OLEKMA DNIEPER NEMUNAS
PECHORA YENISEI
SEA: KARA BLACK JAPAN WHITE
ARCTIC BALTIC BERING LAPTEV
BARENTS CASPIAN CHUKCHI
OKHOTSK PACIFIC SIBERIAN
SWAMP: VASYUGANE
TERRITORY: ALTAI PRIMORYE
KRASNODAR STAVROPOL
KHABAROVSK KRASNOYARSK
TOWN: UFA AZOV ORSK PERM GORKY
KAZAN MOSCOW ROSTOV SAMARA
SARATOV MURMANSK VERONEZH
LENINGRAD VOLGOGRAD
STALINGRAD CHELYABINSK
NOVOSIBIRSK SVERDLOVSK
SAINTPETERSBURG
VOLCANO: KLYUCHEVSKAYA

RUSSIAN OLIVE OLEASTER
RUSSIAN THISTLE SALTWORT
TUMBLEWEED
RUSSIAN TURNIP RUTABAGA
RUSSIAN WOLFHOUND BORZOI
RUST CLOWN DROSS ROOST ROUST
UREDO AERUGO CANKER CORRODE
FERRUGO OXIDIZE
(— OF PLANTS) HEMIFORM
LEPTOFORM
(KNOT OF —) TUBERCULE
RUSTAM (FATHER OF —) ZAL
(HORSE OF —) RAKSH
(MOTHER OF —) RUDAPAH
(SON OF —) SOHRAB
(WIFE OF —) TAHMINAH
RUSTIC HOB JAY PUT BOOR CARL
CHAW HICK HIND JAKE JOCK RUBE
RUDE BACON BUSHY CARLE CHUFF
CHURL COLIN DAMON DORIC HODGE
ROUGH RURAL RURIC SILLY YOKEL
AGREST BORREL BUMKIN COARSE

FARMER GAFFER HONEST JOBSON RUSSET SAVAGE SCOLOC SCOLOG STURDY SYLVAN UPLAND ARTLESS BOORISH BORRELL BUCOLIC BUMPKIN BUSHMAN COUNTRY DAPHNIS FIELDEN GEORGIC HAYSEED HOBNAIL HOOSIER LANDMAN PAISANO PEASANT PLOWMAN THYRSIS WAYBACK AGRESTIC ARCADIAN BACKVELD CLOWNISH DAMOETAS GEOPONIC LANDWARD MOSSBACK CHAWBACON CLODHOPPER
(NOT —) CIVIL
(UNCOUTH —) JAKE
(YOUTHFUL —) SWAIN
(PL.) COUNTRYFOLK

RUSTLE TODO FISLE STEAL FISSLE FISTLE HIRSEL REESLE BRUSSEL BRUSTLE CRINKLE REESTLE SKITTER WHISTLE
(— OF SILK) SCROOP
(— UP) SNAVVLE

RUSTLER THIEF WADDY DUFFER WADDIE HUSTLER

RUSTLING ARUSTLE CRINKLY FROUFROU SOUGHING FRICATION SUSURROUS

RUSTY HOARY MOROSE ROOSTY SULLEN CANKERY OUTMODED

RUT RAT BRIM RACK RAIK RUCK TRACK TREAD CREASE FURROW GROOVE STRAKE SULCUS UPROAR CHANNEL OESTRUS WRINKLE
(— IN PATH) GAY

RUTABAGA BAGA SWEDE TURNIP

RUTH BABE PITY MERCY MISERY REGRET SORROW BAMBINO CRUELTY REMORSE SADNESS SYMPATHY

(HUSBAND OF —) BOAZ MAHLON
(MOTHER-IN-LAW OF —) NAOMI
(SON OF —) OBED JESSE

RUTHENIAN RUSSENE RUSSNIAK UKRAINIAN

RUTHLESS FELL GRIM CRUEL BRUTAL PITILESS CUTTHROAT ·

RUTILE NIGRINE SAGENITE

RUTTER PLOW DRAGOON GALLANT TROOPER

RUTTISH RANK LUSTFUL

RUY BLAS

RWANDA
CAPITAL: KIGALI
LAKE: KIVU
LANGUAGE: KIRUNDI SWAHILI
MOUNTAIN: KARISIMBI
MOUNTAIN RANGE: MITUMBA
PEOPLE: TWA HUTU TUTSI WATUSI
RIVER: KAGEREA AKANYARU
  LUVIRONZA
TOWN: BUTARE GABIRO NYANZA
  GISENYI
TRIBE: BATWA BAHUTU WATUSI
  BATUTSI

RYA RUG

RYE RAY RIE ERAY REYE SPELT WHISKY GENTLEMAN

RYEGRASS RAY EAVER DARNEL

RYMANDRA KNIGHTIA

RYND BAIL RHIND MILRIND

RYOT RAYAT FARMER RAIYAT TENANT TILLER PEASANT

RYUKYU ISLANDS (— ISLAND GROUP) AMAMI OKINAWA SAKISHIMA
(OTHER NAME FOR —) LUCHU LOOCHO NANSEI

S

S ESS SUGAR SIERRA
SAARINEN EERO ELIEL
SABBATH SUNDAY SABAOTH
SHABBAT SHABBOS
SABER KUKRI SABRE BANCAL
BASKET TULWAR ATAGHAN CIMETER
TULWAUR YATAGAN ACINACES
SCIMITAR
SABICU JIQUE JIQUI
SABINE (BROTHER OF —) CURIACE
SABLE DWALE SAPLE OGRESS
SATURN DIAMOND ZIBELINE
(ROUNDEL —) PELLET
SABLEFISH SKIL BESHOW COALFISH
SKILFISH
SABOTAGE MASTIC DESTROY
SABRA (FATHER OF —) PTOLEMY
(HUSBAND OF —) GEORGE
(SON OF —) GUY DAVID ALEXANDER
SABRINA (FATHER OF —) LOCRINE
(MOTHER OF —) ESTRILDIS
SABTAH (FATHER OF —) CUSH
SABTECHA (FATHER OF —) CUSH
SAC BAG GUT POD CYST SACK
ASCUS BURSA FLOAT POUCH THECA
VOLVA ACINUS AMNION SACCUS
VESICA AMPULLA BLADDER
CAPSULE CISTERN HYGROMA
UTRICLE VESICLE BROODSAC
FOLLICLE SACCULUS SPERMARY
(SPORE —) ASCUS
(PREF.) THEC(A)(I)(O)
SACAR (FATHER OF —) OBEDEDOM
(SON OF —) AHIAM
SACCHARIN SWEET STICKY
SUGARY GLUCOSE GLUSIDE
SACCHAROSE SUCROSE
SACERDOTAL HIERATIC PRIESTLY
SACHEM SAGAMORE
SACK AX AXE BAG BED CAN COT
MAT SAC FIRE LOOT MUID POCK
POKE BAYON GOOSE HARRY POUCH
SPOIL BUDGET POCKET RAVAGE
SACKET SACQUE DISMISS PILLAGE
PLUNDER RANSACK SACKAGE
SACKBAG DESOLATE PACKSACK
PEIGNOIR
(— OF PALM LEAVES) BAYONG
(— OF WOOL) SARPLAR
(MAIL —) BUM
(PACK —) KYACK
(SAD —) BOLO JERK SCHMO
(PREF.) THYLAC(O)
SACKBUT SAMBUKE TROMBONE
SACKING SACK GUNNY CROCUS
SACKEN HESSIAN POLDAVY
SOUTAGE

SACRAMENT RITE BAPTISM
MYSTERY NAGMAAL PENANCE
SACRARIUM PISCINA
SACRED HOLY TABU HUACA PIOUS
SACRE SAINT SANCT SANTO TABOO
DIVINE SACRAL HALLOWED
HEAVENLY NUMINOUS REVEREND
SACROSANCT
(PREF.) HAGI(O) HIER(O) HIERATICO
SACR(I)(O) SEMNO
SACRED FIG PIPAL
SACRED FISH KANNUME
SACREDNESS CHURINGA SANCTITY
TJURUNGA
SACRIFICE GIVE HOST LOSS OFFER
SPEND YAJNA CORBAN FOREGO
VICTIM EXPENSE CHILIOMB
IMMOLATE KAPPARAH LITATION
OBLATION OFFERING PASSOVER
SPHAGION PROPITIATION
(— OF CARGO) JETTISON
(— OF 100 OXEN) HECATOMB
(— OF 1000 OXEN) CHILIOMB
(PL.) HAGIGAH CHAGIGAH
SACRIFICIAL PIACULAR
SACRILEGE PROFANATION
SACRILEGIOUS IMPIOUS
SACRISTAN SEXTON SACRIST
SACRISTY SEXTRY SACRARY
VERGERY PARATORY SACRARIUM
SACROSANCT SACRED
SACRUM
(SUFF.) HIERIC
SAD LOW WAN DARK DOWY DRAM
BLACK DREAR DUSKY MESTO
MOODY SABLE SOBER SORRY
WEARY YEMER DREARY SOLEMN
SULLEN TRISTE WOEFUL BALEFUL
DOLEFUL DUMPISH FORLORN
FUNEBRE LUCTUAL MOANFUL
SOBERLY UNHAPPY DEJECTED
GROANFUL MOURNFUL MOURNING
PATHETIC PITIABLE SUBTRIST
TRISTIVE UNBLITHE DEPRESSED
MELANCHOLY
(PREF.) TRISTI
SADDEN SAD DUMP CLOUD GLOOM
GRIEVE ATTRIST CONTRIST
DISTRESS
SADDENED BROKEN
SADDENING LUCTUAL
SADDLE PAD RIG SAG TAG LOAD
SUNK CHINE PANEL PILCH SELLE
STICK BURDEN HEADER RECADO
PIGSKIN PILLION
(— AND BRIDLE) TACK
(— COVER) MOCHILA

(— FOR ONE-LEGGED RIDER)
SOMERSET
(— STUFFED WITH STRAW) SODS
(— WITH) STICK
(— WORKER) LORIMER
(LIGHT —) PILCH PILLION
(MOTORCYCLE —) PILLION
(PACK —) BAT
(PART OF —) HORN RING SEAT SKIRT
CANTLE FENDER JOCKEY POMMEL
STRING BINDING LEATHER STIRRUP
(STRAW —) SUNK SUGGAN
(WITHOUT A —) ASELLATE
(PREF.) SELLI
SADDLEBACK JACK JACKBIRD
SADDLEBAG ALFORJA CANTINA
SUMPTER TEETSOOK
(PL.) JAGS JAGGS
SADDLE BLANKET CORONA
SADDLEBOW BOW ARSON
SADDLECLOTH HOUSE NAMDA
HOUSING PADCLOTH SHABRACK
SADDLEMAKER FUSTER KNACKER
SADDLE MAT FLET
SADDLE PAD PANEL NUMNAH
PILLOW
SADDLER CODDER KNACKER
LORIMER WHITTAW
SADISM BRUTALITY
SADISTIC SICK CRUEL SADIC
BRUTAL
SADLY SAD ALAS UNWINLY
SADNESS DUMP RUTH DREAR
DUMPS GLOOM GRIEF UNWIN
SORROW DESPAIR
SAD SACK BOLO
SAFAWID SUFI
SAFE HUG CRIB PETE SURE WELL
AMBRY SALVA SIKER SOUND
SECURE SICCAR HEALTHY SYKERLY
COCKSURE SILVENDY
(— FOR MEAT) KEEP
(— TO DEAL WITH) CANNY
SAFEBLOWER PETEMAN
SAFEBREAKER YEGG YEGGMAN
PETERMAN
SAFE-CONDUCT JARK COWLE
GRITH CONDUCT NAVICERT
PASSPORT
SAFECRACKER YEGG BOXMAN
PETEMAN PETERMAN TORCHMAN
SAFEGUARD SAVE WARD GUARD
HEDGE SALVE DEFEND SAFETY
SECURE BASTION BULWARK
WARRANT FREEWARD PALLADIUM
PRECAUTION
SAFEKEEPING CUSTODY STORAGE
(IN —) ONICE
SAFELY SAFE SICCAR SICKER SURELY
SECURELY
SAFETY REFUGE SALUTE SURETY
WARRANT SECURITY
(PREF.) SOTERIO

SAFETY ZONE ISLET ISLAND
REFUGE
SAFFLOWER KUSUM ALAZOR
SAFFRON
SAFFRON CROCUS AZAFRAN
CROCEUS
(PREF.) CROCEO CROCO
SAFROLE SHIKIMOL
SAG BAG DIP TIE SWAG CREEP
DROOP PLANK SLUMP SAGGON
CURTAIN DEFLATE
SAGA EDDA EPIC MYTH TALE RIMUR
LEGEND NJALSAGA
SAGACIOUS DEEP ACUTE CANNY
SHARP ARGUTE ASTUTE SHREWD
CORDATE POLITIC PRUDENT SAPIENT
SAGACITY POLICY WISDOM
SMEDDUM YEPHEDE PRUDENCE
SAPIENCE
SAGAMORE SACHEM
SAGE RSI WARE WISE WITE CLARY
HAKAM IMLAC KATHA RISHI SABIO
SOLON SOPHY ABARIS DHARMA
NESTOR SALVIA SAULGE SAVANT
SHREWD WIZARD EYESEED
MAHATMA SAPIENT SOPHIST
TOHUNGA WISEMAN DEVARSHI
MAHARSHI WISEACRE
SAGEBRUSH SAGE HYSSOP
SAGEWOOD ARTEMISIA
SAGENESS SAPIENCE
SAGGER COFFIN SETTER CASSETTE
SAGGING DRAG SWAG PTOOIS
SAGITTA ARROW
SAGITTARIUS ARCHER
SAGO PALM CYCAD
SAGRADA CASCARA
SAGUARO SUAHARO SUWARRO
PITAHAYA
SAHIB SRI BWANA
SAHIDIC THEBAIC
SAIBLING TORGOCH
SAID DIT QUOTH STATED RELATED
SAIL JIB LUG RAG BEAT GALE HAUL
MAIN SCUN SLAT SWAN SWIM WING
DANDY FLEET FLIER FLOAT FLYER
JUMBO RAFFE SCALE SHEET
ACCOST CANVAS COURSE CRUISE
DRIVER JIGGER LATEEN MIZZEN
MUSLIN SINGLE ARTEMON LUGSAIL
SKYSAIL SPANKER SPENCER TRYSAIL
BACKWIND FORESAIL GAFFSAIL
HEADSAIL MAINSAIL MOONSAIL
NAVIGATE RINGTAIL STAYSAIL
STUNSAIL
(— ALONG COAST) COAST ACCOST
(— AROUND) TURN DOUBLE
(— BEFORE THE WIND) SPOON
(— BRISKLY) SPANK
(— BY THE WIND) STRETCH
(— CLOSE TO WIND) PINCH
(— DOWN) AVALE AWALE
(— FASTER) FOOT

(— **IN SPECIFIED DIRECTION**) STAND
(— **OF WINDMILL**) ARM AWE EIE FAN
VAN EIGHE FLIER FLYER SWEEP
SWIFT
(— **ON COURSE**) HAUL WORK
(— **QUIETLY**) GHOST
(— **RAPIDLY**) SCUR SKIRR
(— **SWIFTLY**) RAMP
(— **TO WINDWARD**) THRASH
(— **WITH WIND ABEAM**) LASK
(**FRAGMENT OF** —) HULLOCK
(**LIGHT** —) SHADOW
(**LOWEST** —) COURSE
(**PART OF** —) CLEW FOOT HEAD LUFF
SEAM SLAB TACK LEECH PANEL
POCKET WINDOW ZIPPER CRINGLE
TABLING TELLTALE HEADBOARD
(**REDUCE** —) REEF
(**SMALL** —) ROYAL
(**TRIANGULAR** —) RAFFE LATEEN
BENTINCK
(**WIND** —) BADGIR
(**3-CORNERED** —) JIB TRINKET
(**PL.**) VELA CLOTH KITES LINENS
SAILAGE CLOTHING
(**PREF.**) HISTI(O) ISTIO VELI
SAILBOARD (**RIDE A** —) WINDSURF
SAILBOAT CAT SAIL SCOW BULLY
DANDY NABBY SAPIT SCOUT SHARP
SKIFF SLOOP SNIPE CANGIA DINGHY
QUODDY SAILER SATTIE CATBOAT
SCOOTER SHALLOP SHARPIE
SUNFISH KEELBOAT SAILSHIP
SKIPJACK TRIMARAN
(**PART OF** —) JIB BOOM BUNK GATE
HEAD HELM KEEL MAST SINK SKEG
SOLE BERTH CLEAT FRAME HATCH
SALON TRUNK WHEEL WINCH
ANCHOR GALLEY JIBTOP LOCKER
PULPIT RUDDER SHROUD YANKEE
BULWARK COAMING COCKPIT
COUNTER GALLOWS PUSHPIT
TOPSAIL BACKSTAY BOWSPRIT
BULKHEAD FOREDECK FOREFOOT
FORESTAY HEADSTAY LIFELINE
MAINSAIL MASTHEAD OVERHEAD
SPREADER STAYSAIL TAFFRAIL
TRAVELER CUBBYHOLE MAINSHEET
PORTLIGHT STANCHION STATEROOM
COMPANIONWAY
(**WITCH'S** —) SIEVE
SAILFISH BOHO WOOHOO GUEBUCU
LONGJAW VOILIER VOLADOR
BILLFISH
SAILOR (**ALSO SEE NAVAL OFFICER**)
GOB TAR HAND JACK SALT SWAB
TOTY GUARD KLOSH LAKER LIMEY
CALASH CLASHY DAYMAN DECKIE
HEARTY MARINE MATLOW SEADOG
SEAMAN TARPOT TIERER TOPMAN
COLLIER MARINAL MARINER
MATELOT SHIPMAN SWABBER
WARRIOR YARDMAN CANOTIER

COXSWAIN DECKHAND FLATFOOT
GALIONJI GUNLAYER LANDSMAN
LITHSMAN MASTHEAD SHIPMATE
WATERDOG WATERMAN WATERRUG
YARDSMAN
(— **ON LEAVE**) LIBERTYMAN
(**CAPTIOUS** —) SEALAWYER
(**EAST INDIAN** —) LASCAR
(**INFERIOR** —) GREENHAND
(**OLD** —) SALT SHELLBACK
(**SCANDINAVIAN** —) KLOSH
(**TURKISH** —) GALIONGEE
SAILORLIKE TARRISH
SAILOR'S-CHOICE BREAM PIGFISH
PINFISH WHITING
SAIL YARD RAE
SAINFOIN ESPARCET
SAINT PIR RSI DADU HOLY QUTB
WALI ALVAR ARHAT RISHI SANTO
BHAGAT HALLOW PATRON SANTON
CANONIZE MARABOUT
(**CHINESE** —) IMMORTAL
(**PATRON** —) AVOWRY
(**PILLAR** —) STYLITE
(**PL.**) SS
(**PREF.**) HAGI
SAINT ELMO'S FIRE HERMO
CASTOR FUROLE HELENA
SAINT JOAN (**AUTHOR OF** —)
SHAW
(**CHARACTER IN** —) JOAN DUNOIS
ROBERT WARWICK BAUDRICOURT
ST-JOHN'S-BREAD CAROB
ST-JOHN'S-WORT AMBER TUTSAN
CAMMOCK
SAINT KITTS & NEVIS (**CAPITAL:**)
BASSETERRE
(**ISLAND:**) NEVIS SOMBRERO
SAINTCHRISTOPHER
SAINTLINESS HOLINESS SANCTITY
SAINT LUCIA (**CAPITAL OF** —)
CASTRIES
(**MOUNTAIN OF** —) GIMIE
(**MOUNTAINS OF** —) PITONS
CANARIES
(**VOLCANO OF** —) SOUFRIERE
SAINTLY DEVOUT ANGELIC SAINTED
BEATIFIC SAINTISH
(— **PERSON**) ZADDIK
ST REGIS RANERE
SAINT VINCENT (**CAPITAL OF** —)
KINGSTOWN
(**PART OF** —) UNION BEQUIA
GRENADINES
SAITH COALFISH
SAITHE SILLOC POLLACK SILLOCK
SAJ SAIN
SAKE SAKI SCORE ACCOUNT
(**SOURCE OF** —) RICE
SAKI BISA MONK COUXIA MONKEY
YARKEE
SALA (**FATHER OF** —) ARPHAXAD
(**SON OF** —) EBER

SALABLE VENAL SELLING SELLABLE VENDIBLE

SALACIOUS LEWD SALT RUTTISH SCARLET SCABROUS

SALAD SALLET COLESLAW TABBOULEH SILLSALLAT
(CORN —) MACHE FETTICUS
(KIND OF —) CAESAR
(LEBANESE —) TABOULI TABBOULEH
(TYPE OF —) TOSSED

SALADA SALINA

SALAL SHALLON

SALAMANDER EFT OLM SOW BEAR NEWT TWEEG GOPHER LIZARD TRITON AXOLOTL CRAWLER CREEPER DOGFISH MECODONT SALAMICH SHADRACH

SALAMI SAUSAGE
(KIND OF —) GENOA

SALAMMBO (AUTHOR OF —) FLAUBERT
(CHARACTER IN —) NARR GISCO HANNO HAVAS MATHO TAMIT HAMILCAR SALAMMBO SPENDIUS
(COMPOSER OF —) REYER

SAL AMMONIAC SPIRIT SALMIAC

SALARY PAY HIRE SCREW WAGES INCOME PACKET PENSION STIPEND

SALE FAIR VENT BREAK HEDGE TOUCH BOURSE VENDUE AUCTION MOHATRA SELLING HANDSALE KNOCKOUT PORTSALE
(— BY AUCTION) CANT ROUP BLOCK VENDUE OUTROOP
(— BY OUTCRY) ROUP ROWP HAMMER
(— OF OFFICE) BARRATRY
(— OF PERIODICAL) CIRCULATION
(— OF TOBACCO) BREAK
(— ON TRUST) CREDIT
(— TO CONSUMER) RETAIL
(PUBLIC —) AUCTION
(RUMMAGE —) JUMBLE

SALESMAN REP CLERK BAGMAN RUNNER SELLER BOOKMAN DRUMMER OUTRIDER PITCHMAN
(— IN FISH MARKET) BUMMAREE

SALESMANSHIP SELLING

SALESPERSON CLERK

SALESWOMAN WINSTER SHOPGIRL VENDEUSE

SALIENT SPUR BULGE CHIEF ARGINE BASTION SALTANT

SALIENTIA ANURA ANOURA ECAUDATA

SALINA SHOR SALINE

SALINE SALT BRINY SALAR SALTY MARINAL

SALIVA SPIT DROOL WATER DRIVEL SLAVER SPUTUM SPITTLE
(— FLOW) PTYALISM
(PREF.) PTYAL(O) SIAL(O)

SALIVARY SIALIC

SALIVATION PTYALISM SLOBBERS

SALLET SALADE

SALLOW WAN SALE SICK ADUST LURID MUDDY SALIX SAUCH SAUGH PALLID YELLOW

SALLY GRIP JERK PASS QUIP SAIL QUICK START ESCAPE GAMBIT SORTIE GAMBADE OUTFALL OUTLEAP DEMARCHE

SALM (BROTHER OF —) TUR IRAJ
(FATHER OF —) FARIDUN
(MOTHER OF —) SHAHRINAZ
(SLAYER OF —) MINUCIHIR

SALMAGUNDI OLIO SILLSALLAT

SALMON DOG LAX LOX SAM KETA MASU PINK AMOUT COHOE COUNT HADDO HOLIA SMOLT SMOOT SPROD TECON ALEVIN BAGGIT KIPPER LAUREL MYKISS SAMLET SAUQUI SILVER TAIMEN ANADROM ANNATTO BLUECAP BOTCHER CHINOOK DOGFISH GILLING GRAVLAX KAHAWAI KOKANEE NEWFISH QUINNAT REDFISH RUNFISH SAWMONT SHEDDER SOCKEYE BLUEBACK BRANDLIN GOLDFISH GRAVLAKS HUMPBACK LASPRING SALMONID SPRINGER OUANANICHE
(AFTER SPAWNING) KELT BAGGIT SHEDDER
(— BEFORE SPAWNING) GILLING GIRLING
(— ENCLOSURE) YAIR
(— IN 2ND OR 3D YEAR) SMOLT
(— IN 2ND YEAR) SPROD HEPPER GILLING
(— IN 3D YEAR) PUG MORT
(— ON FIRST RETURN FROM SEA) GRILSE
(BLUEBACK —) NERKA SAUQUI SOCKEYE
(CURED —) KIPPER GRAVLAX GRAVLAKS
(DOG —) CHUM KETA
(FATHER OF —) NAHSHON
(FEMALE —) RAUN BAGGIT
(HUMPBACK —) HADDO HOLIA
(MALE —) GIB BUCK COCK
(MILTER —) EKE
(NEWLY HATCHED —) PINK ALEVIN
(SMALL —) PEAL SKIRLING
(SON OF —) BOAZ
(SPENT —) JUDY SLAT LIGGER RUNFISH
(YOUNG —) FOG PARR PEAL SMOLT GRILSE HEPPER JERKIN SAMLET BOTCHER ESSLING SKEGGER LASPRING SPARLING

SALMONELLOSIS KEEL

SALMONEUS (BROTHER OF —) SISYPHUS

(DAUGHTER OF —) TYRO
(FATHER OF —) AEOLUS
(MOTHER OF —) ENARETE
(WIFE OF —) ALCIDICE
SALOME (FATHER OF —) HEROD
(HUSBAND OF —) PHILIP ZEBEDEE
ARISTOBULUS
(MOTHER OF —) HERODIAS
SALON HALL SALOON GALLERY
SALOON CAFE CUDDY DIVAN SALON
SHADE BARROOM CANTINA
RUMSHOP SCATTER DEADFALL
DRINKERY DRUNKERY EXCHANGE
BRASSERIE
(RAILWAY —) PULLMAN
SALPA SALP THALIA
SALSIFY GOATBEARD
SALT SAL TAR CORN KERN SAWT
BRINY ZIRAM AMIDOL AURATE
FOLATE GAMMON HALITE MALATE
OLEATE OSMATE POWDER SAILOR
SALIFY SALINE URANIN XENATE
KAINITE LACTATE MALEATE NIOBATE
PHYTATE TROPATE ABIETATE
BRACKISH HALINOUS PIMELATE
PLUMBITE SELENATE
(— FISH) ROIL
(— OUT) CUT GRAIN
(DOUBLE —) ALUM
(HAIR —) ALUNOGEN
(LUMP OF —) SALTCAT
(METAL —) SILICATE
(MIXTURE OF —S) REH USAR
(OLD —) SEADOG
(POISONOUS —) ARSENATE
(ROCK —) PIG HALITE
(ZINC —) ZIRAM
(PREF.) HAL(I)(O) SALI SALIN(I)(O)
(SUFF.) OATE
SALTATE JUMP
SALTATION LEAP
SALT BOILER WELLER
SALTBUSH BLUEBUSH
SALTCELLAR SALT CELLAR SELLER
SHAKER SALTFAT SALTFOOT
SALTED SALEE
SALTICID ATTID
SALT PAN PLAYA
SALTPETER NITER NITRE PETER
ANATRON CALICHE PRUNELLA
SALT PIT VAT WICH WYCH
SALT PORK SOWBELLY
SALTWORKS SALINA SALTERN
SALTERY SALTPANS
SALTWORT KALI BARILLA SALSOLA
KELPWORT
SALTY SALT BRINY SALINE SAVORY
HALINOUS
SALU (SLAYER OF —) PHINEHAS
(SON OF —) ZIMRI
SALUBRIOUS BENIGN HEALTHY
SALUTARY

SALUTARY GOOD BENIGN HEALTHY
HELPFUL BENEDICT
SALUTATION AVE HAIL ALOHA
SALUS MIZPAH SALAAM SALUTE
REGREET SLAINTE WELCOME
DIEUGARD GREETING HAEREMAI
(DRINKING —) SKOAL PROSIT
PROFACE WASSAIL
SALUTE CAP HAIL HEIL KISS MOVE
YULE CHEER DRINK GREET HALCH
HALSE HONOR SALUE SALVO
COLORS SALAAM EMBRACE
ACCOLADE CONGREET
(— TO DANCING PARTNER) COUPEE
(VICTORY —) VSIGN
SALVADOR BAHIA
SALVAGE SAVE SALVE RECOVERY
SCROUNGE
SALVAGER SALVOR
SALVATION BODAI MOKSHA SAFETY
NIRVANA KAIVALYA SAVEMENT
SOULHEAL
(— APPROACH) MARGA
SALVE SAW TAR SALVO SAUVE
NERVAL SUPPLE PLASTER UNGUENT
OINTMENT
SALVER TRAY SERVER WAITER
PLATEAU
SALVIA CHIA SAGE CLARY
MEJORANA MINTWEED
SALVO SALUTE SPREAD PROVISO
TRIBUTE STRADDLE
(PL.) LADDER
SAM (FATHER OF —) NARIMAN
(SON OF —) ZAL
SAMARA KEY CHAT
SAMARIA AHOLAH
SAMARITAN CUTHEAN CUTHITE
SAMBA CARIOCA
SAMBAR ELK DEER MAHA RUSA
SAME ID EAD ILK ONE IDEM LIKE
MEME SELF VERY DITTO EQUAL
SAMEN IDENTIC SELFSAME
(— AS) IQ
(— PLACE) IB
(MUCH THE —) ALIKE
(THAT —) THILK THICKE
(PREF.) AUT(O) AUTH(I) HOM(O)(OI)
HOME(O) HOMOE IPSI ISO TAUT(O)
SAMENESS ONENESS EQUALITY
IDENTITY MONOTONY
SAMLET PINK
SAMNITES SABELLI
SAMOA (CAPITAL OF —) APIA
PAGOPAGO
(COIN OF —) SENE TALA
(ISLAND OF —) OFU TAU ROSE
MANUA UPOLU SAVAII OLOSEGA
TUTUILA
(MOUNTAIN OF —) FITO SAVAII
MATAFAO
SAMOGITIAN ZHMUD

SAMOYED TUBA YURAK BELTIR KAIBAL KOIBAL NENTSI KAMASSIN

SAMPHIRE SALTWEED

SAMPLE DIP SIP CAST PREE CHECK ESSAY TASTE TRIAL CHANCE COUPON FLOWER MUSTER SWATCH TASTER EXAMPLE EXCERPT MONSTER PATTERN SAMPLER TASTING INSTANCE PULLDOWN SPECIMEN

(— OF METAL) DIET

SAMPLING SOUNDING

SAMSON (FATHER OF —) MANOAH

SAMSON ET DALILA

(CHARACTER IN —) PRIEST SAMSON DELILAH

(COMPOSER OF —) SAINTSAENS

SAMUEL (FATHER OF —) ELKANAH

(MOTHER OF —) HANNAH

SAMURAI BUSHI RONIN

SAN SAMPI

SANAD SUNNUD

SANBENITO SAMARRA

SAN BLAS TULE

SAN CARLOS ARIVAIPA

SANCTIFICATION HOLINESS

SANCTIFY BLESS SACRE SACRI DEDICATE

SANCTIMONIOUS PI DEVOUT PECKSNIFFIAN

SANCTION AMEN FIAT ALLOW PIETY ASSENT BISHOP RATIFY APPROVE ENDORSE JUSTIFY PASSAGE SUPPORT ACCREDIT APPROVAL CANONIZE COURTESY SUFFRAGE

SANCTIONED CANONICAL

SANCTITY SANTY HALIDOME HOLINESS

SANCTUARY ADYT BAST BEMA FANE HOLY SOIL ABBEY ALTAR BAMAH FRITH GIRTH GRITH SECOS SEKOS TOWER ADYTON ADYTUM ASYLUM CHAPEL HAIKAL REFUGE SENTRY SHRINE SACRARY SHELTER ARCHEION CABIRION DELUBRUM HALIDOME HOLINESS SACRARIUM

(— FOR LAWBREAKERS) ALSATIA

(AUTHOR OF —) FAULKNER

(CHARACTER IN —) LEE RED VAN REBA RUBY DRAKE GOWAN LAMAR TOMMY BENBOW HORACE POPEYE RIVERS SNOPES TEMPLE GOODWIN STEVENS

SANCTUM ADYT ADYTON ADYTUM

SAND DIRT GRIT ARENA GRAIL SONDE GRAVEL ISERINE ISERITE PARTING ASBESTIC BLINDING

(— FOR STREWING ON FLOORS) BREEZE

(— HILL) DENE DUNE

(— IN KIDNEYS) ARENA

(— MIXED WITH GRAVEL) GARD DOBBIN

(— ON SEA BOTTOM) PAAR

(BRAIN —) SABULUM ACERVULUS

(COLOR —) CHIP BEACH

(COLORED —) SMALT

(DEAUVILLE —) STUCCO

(VOLCANIC —) SANTORIN

(WATERY —) QUICKSAND

(PREF.) AMM(O) ARENI PSAMM(O)

SANDAL TIP BAXA FLAT SOCK ZORI TEGUA THONG CALIGA CHARUK PATTEN TATBEB RULLION SCUFFER FOOTHOLD GUARACHE HUARACHO

(JAPANESE —) GETA

(LOOSE —) SLIPSLOP

(RED SILK —) CALCEAMENTUM

(WINGED —) TALARIA

(WINGED —S) TALARIA

SANDAL TREE SANTOL

SANDALWOOD NAIO ALGUM ALMUG MAIRE CHANDAM SAUNDERS

SANDALWOOD TREE ILIAHI

SANDARAC TREE ARAR LIGNUM

SANDBAG CONK SANDCLUB

SAND BANK AIR CHAR MEAL SAND BATCH HURST HYRST KNOCK SHELF SHOAL

SANDBAR BALK LOOP SAND RARRA SHOAL TOMBOLO TOWHEAD

SANDBLASTER FROSTER BLASTMAN

SAND BORER SMELT

SANDBOX TREE ASSACU

SAND COLIC SABURRA

SAND DARTER SPECK

SAND DUNE TOWAN BARCHAN

SAND EEL GRIG SANDFISH

SANDEMANIAN GI ASSITE

SANDERLING OXBIRD

SAND FLEA SCREW SCROW SANDBOY

SAND-FLY BUSH TURMERIC

SAND GROUSE GANGA ROCKER ATTAGEN PINTAIL

SAND HOLE BUNKER

SANDIVER NATRON

SAND LAUNCE LANT SMELT WRIGGLE AMMODYTE SANDLING SCRIGGLE

SAND LILY SOAPROOT

SANDMAN DUSTMAN

SANDPAPER TREE CHAPARRO

SANDPIPER JACK KNOT PEEP RUFF STIB WEET OXEYE SNIPE STINT TEREK TIPUP WADER DUNLIN GAMBET OXBIRD PLOVER REDLEG TEETER TILTER TILTUP TRINGA BROWNIE CHOROOK CREEKER FATBIRD FIDDLER HAYBIRD KRIEKER MONGLER MONGREL REDBACK

TATTLER TIPTAIL GRAYBACK
LEADBACK PEETWEET REDSHANK
ROCKBIRD SANDPEEP SHADBIRD
SQUATTER SWEESWEE TELLTALE
TRIDDLER
(FEMALE —) REEVE
(FLOCK OF —S) FLING
SAND PIT BUNKER
SAND ROCKET FLIXWEED
SAND SHARK BONEDOG
SANDSTONE FAKE FLAG GRES GRIT
SAND GAIZE HAZEL ARCOSE ARKOSE
DOGGER KINGLE ARENITE HASSOCK
CARSTONE COCONINO GANISTER
PSAMMITE RUBSTONE SANDROCK
(BLOCK OF —) SARSEN
SANDSTORM BURAN HABOOB
TEBBAD
SANDUST VANITY
SANDWICH BLT SUB GYRO HERO
BUTTY HOAGY BURGER HOAGIE
REUBEN DAGWOOD FALAFEL
FELAFEL GRINDER WESTERN
(ITALIAN —) GRINDER
(SUFF.) BURGER
SANDWORT LONGROOT SANDWEED
SANDY DEEP GINGER GRISTY
SANDED ARENOSE PSAMMOUS
SABULINE SABULOUS
SANDY BROWN LARK
SANE SAFE WISE LUCID RIGHT
FORMAL NORMAL HEALTHY PERFECT
RATIONAL SENSIBLE
SANGA-SANGA ESSANG
SANGUINARY GORY CRUEL
BLOODY CRIMSON SANGUINE
SANGUINE FOND GUZE MURREY
HEMATIC HOPEFUL SARDONYX
SANHEDRIN GEROUSIA
SANICLE ALLHEAL SELFHEAL
SANIOUS ICHOROUS
SANITARY HYGIENIC
SANITY SENSE REASON WISDOM
BALANCE MARBLES LUCIDITY
SANENESS
SAN MARINO (CHURCH OF —) PIEVE
(DISTRICTS OF —) CASTELLI
(MOUNTAIN OF —) TITANO
(SUBURB IN —) BORGO
SANNUP SQUAW
SANSKRIT HINDU
(— SOUND OR SIGN) VISARGA
(— WORK) VEDANGA
SANS SERIF DORIC GOTHIC
SANTA MARIA TREE BIRMA
GALBA CALABA
SAN TOME (MONEY OF —) DOBRA
SANTONICA WORMSEED
SAO TOME AND PRINCIPE
(CAPITAL OF —) SAOTOME
(MONEY OF —) DOBRA
(NAME OF —) SAOTHOME
SAINTTHOMAS

SAP MUG GOON MINE OOZE RASA
SEVE DRAIN HUMBO KEEST LYMPH
SAPPER WEAKEN AIRHEAD ALVELOZ
FLUXURE JUGHEAD SAPHEAD
(— COURAGE) DAUNT
(— OF RUBBER TREE) LATEX
(FERMENTED PALM —) SURA
(PALM —) TODY TODDY
(POISONOUS —) UPAS
(SUGAR MAPLE —) HUMBO
SAPAJOU SAJOU WARINE
SAPANWOOD BOKOM BRAZIL
SIBUCAO
SAPEK DONG
SAPID SIPID FLAVORY
SAPIENT WISE SHREWD KNOWING
SAPI-UTAN ANOA
SAPLING SCOB PLANT SAPLE SPIRE
RUNNEL SPRING TILLER STADDLE
ASHPLANT SEEDLING SHILLALA
SPRINGER
(— AMONG FELLED TREES) WAVER
SAPODILLA GUM CHICA CHICO
DILLY ACHRAS MAMMEE SAPOTA
SAPOTE ZAPOTE NISPERO NISBERRY
NASEBERRY
SAPONIFYING KILLING
SAPONIN GITONIN SENEGIN
CYCLAMIN STRUTHIN
SAPONITE PIOTINE
SAPOTA MATASANO
SAPPHIRE SAFIR TOPAZ ADAMAS
ASTERIA ASTRION HYACINTH
SAPPHIRINE GURNARD TUB
SAPPHO (AUTHOR OF —) DAUDET
(CHARACTER IN —) JEAN ROSA
FANNY IRENE DEJOIE POTTER
CAOUDAL CESAIRE FLAMANT
GAUSSIN LEGRAND BOUCHEREAU
DECHELETTE LAGOURNERIE
SAPPY FRIM FRUM SAPFUL
SAPSAP PEPEREK
SAPUCAIA COCO COCOA KAKARALI
SAPWOOD SAP BLEA SPLENT SPLINT
GUAYABI LISTING ALBURNUM
SARA (— WOMAN) UBANGI
SARABAITES REMOBOTH
SARACEN CORSAIR
SARAH ATOSSA
(FATHER OF —) ASHER
(HUSBAND OF —) ABRAHAM
(SON OF —) ISAAC
SARAKOLLE WAKORE
SARASVATI VAC VACH BENTEN
SARCASM RUB GIBE WIPE FLING
IRONY TAUNT RUBBER SATIRE
BROCARD RIDICULE SCORCHER
SARCASTIC ACID ACRID WITTY
BITING IRONIC ACERBIC CUTTING
MORDANT PUNGENT INCISIVE
SARDONIC SATIRICAL ACRIMONIOUS
SARCASTICALLY DRILY DRYLY
ACIDLY

SARCOCARP FLESH
SARCOPHAGUS TOMB COFFIN
SARCOPSYLLA TUNGA
SARDINE BANG LOUR SARD SILD
　CLUPEID PILCHARD SARDELLE

SARDINIA
CAPITAL: CAGLIARI
CHEESE: ROMANO PECORINO
COIN: CARLINE
GREEK COLONY: OLBIA
GULF: OROSEI ASINARA CAGLIARI
　ORISTANO
MOUNTAIN: RASU FERRY LINAS
　GALLURA LIMBARA SERPEDDI
　VITTORIA
NAME: SARDEGNA
PROVINCE: NUORO SASSARI CAGLIARI
RIVER: MANNU TIRSO LASCIA
　SAMASSI COGHINAS FLUMENDOSA
STRAIT: BONIFACIO
TOWN: IERZU NUORO SASSARI
　THATARI CAGLIARI CARBONIA
　IGLESIAS

SARDONIC SARCASTIC
SARGASSUM GULFWEED
SARGO ZEBRA
SARI PATOLA TAMEIN
SAROD LUTE
SARONG PAU KAIN COMBOY KIKEPA
　TAMEIN
SARPEDON (BROTHER OF —) MINOS
　RHADAMANTHUS
　(FATHER OF —) ZEUS JUPITER
　(MOTHER OF —) LAODAMIA
SARSAPARILLA NUNNARI
　SHOTBUSH
SARUCH (FATHER OF —) REU
SASH BAR BELT BENN FAJA GATE
　TOBE SCARF TAPIS TOWEL VITTA
　FASCIA GIRDLE BALDRIC BURDASH
　CHASSIS TUBBECK CASEMENT
　CORSELET WAISTBAND
　CUMBERBUND CUMMERBUND
　(JAPANESE —) OBI
　(WINDOW —) CHESS
SASHAY WALK GLIDE STRUT CHASSE
　TRAIPSE
SASH BAR MUNTIN ASTRAGAL
SASKATCHEWAN (CAPITAL OF —)
　REGINA
　(LAKE OF —) ROUGE REINDEER
　ATHABASKA CHURCHILL
　WOLLASTON
　(RIVER OF —) WOOD MOOSE SOURIS
　FRENCHMAN
　(TOWN OF —) BIGGAR CLIMAX
　ESTEVAN MOOSEJAW ROSETOWN
　SASKATOON
SASQUATCH OMAH BIGFOOT
SASS LIP GUFF
SASSABY TSESSEBE

SASSAFRAS FILE SALOP SALOOP
　SAXIFRAX
SASSY FLIP KICKY LIPPY MOUTHY
　SPUNKY
SATAN ANGEL DEVIL EBLIS FIEND
　SHREW BELIAL LUCIFER SATANAS
　SHAITAN DIABOLUS SATANAEL
SATANIC SABLE INFERNAL
SATCHEL SCRIP HANDBAG KEESTER
SATE CLOY GLUT ACCLOY SATIATE
　SATISFY SATURATE
SATED SAD BLASE
SATEEN VENETIAN
SATELLITE MOON ARIEL LUNET
　DEIMOS MOONET OBERON PHOBOS
　ACOLYTE ACOLYTH LUNETTE
　ORBITER SPUTNIK TELSTAR
　TRABANT UMBRIEL COURTIER
　FOLLOWER
　(— LAUNCHER) AGENA
　(— OF JUPITER) IO EUROPA CALLISTO
　GANYMEDE
　(— OF NEPTUNE) NEREID TRITON
　(— OF SATURN) RHEA DIONE MIMAS
　TITAN PHOEBE TETHYS IAPETUS
　JAPETUS HYPERION
　(— OF URANUS) ARIEL OBERON
　MIRANDA TITANIA UMBRIEL
　(U.S. WEATHER —) ESSA
　(WEATHER —) TIROS
SATIATE CLOY FILL GLUT PALL QUAT
　SADE SATE FLESH GORGE SERVE
　STALL ENGLUT STODGE RASSASY
　SATISFY SURFEIT SATURATE
SATIATED SICK BLASE JADED
　SATED
SATIATING STODGY FULSOME
SATIETY FULNESS SURFEIT
　CLOYMENT
SATIN SAY RASH ATLAS PANNE
　CYPRUS MUSHRU COOTHAY
　CYPRESS SATINET
　(SILK —) DUCHESS
SATINFLOWER SAFFRON
SATINPOD HONESTY LUNARIA
SATINWOOD ZANTE HAREWOOD
SATIRE WIT GRIND IRONY IAMBIC
　LAMPOON SARCASM SOTADIC
　RIDICULE PASQUINADE
SATIRIC BITTER IRONIC ABUSIVE
　CAUSTIC CUTTING POIGNANT
　SLASHING
SATIRICAL IAMBIC INVECTIVE
SATIRIST GRIND NIPPER SATIRE
　JUVENAL PASQUIN SILLOGRAPH
　AMERICAN MENCKEN SANDERS
　ENGLISH HONE NIGEL SWIFT WAUGH
　WOLCOT MARVELL CHURCHILL
　GERMAN BORNE MURNER
　RABENER
　GREEK LUCIAN SOTADES
　ROMAN HORACE JUVENAL PERSIUS
　SPANISH LARRA

SATIRIZE SKIN SKIT GRIND EXPOSE
IAMBIZE LAMPOON PASQUIN
RIDICULE
(— UNFAIRLY) LIBEL
SATISFACTION CRO FIN PAY'UTU
EASE GREE BELLY ENACH TREAT
AMENDS ASSETH CHANGE
REASON COMFORT CONTENT
DELIGHT GLADNESS PLEASURE
REPLETION
(EXPRESSION OF —) VOILA
SATISFACTORILY SPROWSY
CLEVERLY
SATISFACTORY PAT FAIR GOOD
JAKE WELL DUCKY HUNKY CLEVER
DECENT NOMINAL ADEQUATE
LAUDABLE
(VERY —) COPACETIC
SATISFIED SAD FAIN FULL GLAD
PAID VAIN APAID CHUFF PROUD
ASSURED CHUFFED CONTENT
PERFECT GRUNTLED SENSIBLE
WILCWEME
SATISFY PAY EVEN FEED FILL MEET
SAIR SATE SUIT ADEEM AGREE
APPAY QUEME SERVE SLAKE SPEED
ANSWER DEFRAY PLEASE STODGE
SUPPLY ASSUAGE CONTENT
EXPLETE FULFILL GRATIFY GRUNTLE
RESPOND SATIATE STAUNCH
SUFFICE SATURATE
(— APPETITE) STAY
(— BY PROOF) CONVINCE
(— IN ADVANCE) PREVENT
(— NEEDS) DO ADJUST
SATISFYING DUE COOL AMPLE
SQUARE PERFECT REWARDING
SATURATE SOG GLUT SATE SOAK
DRAWK IMBUE SOUSE STEEP
DRENCH IMBIBE SEETHE SODDEN
DRUNKEN INGRAIN PERVADE
SATIATE SLOCKEN WATERLOG
(— WITH SYRUP) CANDY
SATURATED SOBBY SOGGY SOPPY
SODDEN SPONGY DRUNKEN
SATURATION CHROMA PURITY
SATURITY
SATURN (FATHER OF —) URANUS
(MOTHER OF —) GAEA
(RING OF —) ANSA
(SATELLITE OF —) RHEA DIONE
MIMAS TITAN TETHYS JAPETUS
HYPERION ENCELADUS
(SON OF —) JUPITER
(WIFE OF —) OPS CYBELE
SATURNINE SULLEN SATANIC
SATYAGRAHA GANDHISM
SATYR FAUN LECHER SAUMON
SALTIER WOODMAN WOODWOSE
SATYRIASIS TENTIGO
SAUCE MOLE SASS SOWL BERCY
CHILE CHILI CREAM CREME CURRY
GRAVY PESTO SALSA CATSUP
COULIS GANSEL MORNAY PANADA
ROBERT KETCHUP MARENGO
SOUBISE SUPREME TABASCO
VELOUTE BECHAMEL CHAWDRON
DRESSING DUXELLES MARINADE
MATELOTE POIVRADE RAVIGOTE
REMOLADE AVGOLEMONO
(CURRY —) SAMBAL
(FISH —) ALEC BAGOONG
(GARLIC —) AIOLI ROUILLE
(HOT —) SALSA
(ITALIAN —) RAGU PREGO
(KIND OF —) MORNAY NANTUA
MARINARA
(KIND OF —) HOLSIN
(SALAD —) DRESSING
(SAVORY —) DIP
(SOY —) TAMARI
(SPAGHETTI —) PESTO
(SPICY —) SALSA
(THICK —) LEAR
SAUCEDISH SAUCER BIRDBATH
SAUCEPAN CHAFER GOBLET
POSNET SKILLET STEWPAN
PANNIKIN
SAUCER BIRD PATERA PHIALE
CAPSULE PANNIKIN
(— OCCUPANT) ET
(FLYING —) UFO DISC
SAUCINESS SAUCE DICACITY
SAUCY BOG ARCH BOLD COXY PERT
BRASH DONSY DORTY FRESH LIPPY
PAWKY POKEY SASSY SMART
BANTAM COCKET COPPED CROUSE
THWART FORWARD PAUGHTY
FLIPPANT MALAPERT PETULANT
SANSHACH
SAUDI ARABIA: (CAPITAL OF —)
JIDDAH RIYADH
(COIN OF —) RIYAL HALALA
HALALAH
(DESERT REGION OF —) NEFUD
DAHANA ALNAFUD
(PLATEAU OF —) NEJD
(TOWN OF —) HAIL HOFUF JIDDA
MECCA MEDINA ALHOFUF
(WEIGHT OF —) OKE
SAUL (FATHER OF —) KISH
(SON OF —) JONATHAN
(UNCLE OF —) NER
SAUNTER IDLE ROAM ROVE TOIT
AMBLE MOSEY RANGE SHOOL SIDLE
STRAY TRAIK BUMMEL DACKER
DANDER FAFFLE LINGER LOITER
LOUNGE POTTER PUTTER RAMBLE
SOODLE STREEL STROLL TODDLE
WANDER SNAFFLE STAIVER
STRAVAGE
SAURA MAGA
SAUREL SCAD XUREL GASCON
BLUEFISH MACKEREL SKIPJACK
SAURY LONGJAW SKIPPER BILLFISH
GOWDNOOK SKIPJACK

SAUSAGE PUT LINK SNAG COPPA
GIGOT BANGER BOUDIN POLONY
SALAMI BOLOGNA BOLONEY
BOTARGO CHORIZO PUDDING
SAVELOY BLACKPOT CERVELAT
DRISHEEN KIELBASA LIVERING
ROLLICHE ANDOUILLE CHIPOLATA
COTECHINO
(KIND OF —) METT
(VIENNA —) WIENER WIENIE
(PREF.) ALLANT(O) BOTULI
SAUTE PANFRY
SAUTERNE YQUEM
SAVAGE ILL FELL GRIM RUDE WILD
BRUTE CRUEL EAGER FELON FERAL
STERN BRUTAL FIERCE GOTHIC
IMMANE BRUTISH FERVENT
HOWLING INHUMAN MANKEEN
MANKIND ROPABLE UNCIVIL
VIOLENT WILROUN CANNIBAL
PITILESS THEROID WARRAGAL
(PREF.) AGRIO
SAVAGELY FELLY UNMANLY
SAVAGERY FURY FERITY FEROCITY
SAVANNA CAMPO SAHEL SABANA
(— LANDS) LALANG
(— REGION) SAHEL
SAVANT ARTIST SCIENT SCHOLAR
VIRTUOSO
SAVE BAR WIN HAIN HELP KEEP SAFF
SALT STOP STOW AMASS PUTBY
SALVE SKIMP SPARE SPELL DEFEND
EXCEPT REDEEM RESCUE SAVING
SCRIMP UNLESS BARRING DELIVER
HUSBAND SALVAGE WARRANT
CONSERVE PRESERVE SALTAWAY
SETASIDE
(— FROM OBJECTION) SALVE
(— PENURIOUSLY) SCRAPE SNUDGE
(PREF.) SOZ(O)
SAVIN HEATH SABINE JUNIPER
SAVING FRUGAL THRIFT ECONOMY
SPARING THRIFTY PROVIDENT
SAVINGS FAT ADDLINGS
(— CLUB) MENAGE
SAVIOR LORD SAVER SOTER
REDEEMER
SAVOR EDGE SALT SAPOR SMACK
TASTE DEGUST FLAVOR RELISH
RESENT SAVOUR SEASON TASTEN
SAPIDITY
SAVORLESS FOND INSIPID WEARISH
SAVORY GUSTY MERRY SAPID
TASTY DAINTY SMERVY GUSTFUL
GUSTABLE TASTEFUL
SAVVY SABE
(— ABOUT) UPON
SAW SAG SEY WEB BUCK REDE
ADAGE FREIT GNOME SCEAR SPOKE
CLICHE JIGSAW PITSAW RIPSAW
SAYING SCRIBE BACKSAW BUCKSAW
CONVERT DRAGSAW FRETSAW
HACKSAW HANDSAW HEADRIG

HEADSAW PROVERB SLABBER
WHIPSAW CROSSCUT SENTENCE
(— INTO LOGS) BUCK
(— LENGTHWISE OF GRAIN) RIP
(— OF SAWFISH) SERRA
(— WITH TWO BLADES) STADDA
(CIRCULAR —) BUR BURR EDGER
DAPPER TRIMMER
(COMB-MAKER'S —) STADDA
(CROSSCUT —) BRIAR
(CYLINDER —) CROWN TREPAN
TREPHINE
(ENDLESS —) RIBBON
(SURGICAL —) TREPAN
(PREF.) PRI(O) PRION(O) SERRATI
SERRATO SERRI
(SUFF.) PRION
SAWAN SRABAN SHRAVAN
SAWBILL MOTMOT
SAWBUCK TENNER
SAWDUST COOM COOMB SCOBS
SAWINGS
(PREF.) SCOBI
SAW FERN DYGAL BUNGWALL
HARDFERN
SAWFISH RAY BATOID COMBFISH
(PREF.) PRIST(O)
SAWFLY CEPHID SECURIFER
SAW GATE FRAME
SAWHORSE BUCK JACK SETTER
SAWBUCK TRESTLE
SAWING
(PREF.) PRISO
SAW KERF SKAFF
SAWMILL RASPER
(— DEVICE) KICKER
(— WORKER) PONDMAN LEVERMAN
SAWYER WETA SAWER PITMAN
TOPMAN KNOTTER
SAXHORN ALTO TUBA ALTHORN
SAXTUBA BARITONE BARYTONE
SAXIFRAGE BAUERA BENNET
SESELI ASTILBE ROCKFOIL SELFHEAL
SENGREEN MITERWORT
PHILADELPHUS
SAXONIAN MINDEL
SAXOPHONE AX AXE SAX ALTO
TENOR SOPRANINO
SAY DEED MEAN MOVE TAKE TELL
SPEAK SPELL UTTER AUTHOR
QUETHE RELATE REMARK SAYING
REHEARSE PRONOUNCE
(— A BLESSING) BENSH
(— AGAIN) REPEAT ITERATE
(— FOOLISHLY) BLABBER
(— FURTHER) ADD
(— GLIBLY) SCREED
(— IN ANSWER) REPLY
(— INDISTINCTLY) MUMBLE
(— IN RETURN) REJOIN
(— NO TO) NAIT NICK
(— OVER AGAIN) REPEAT
(— REPEATEDLY) DECANTATE

(— SPITEFUL THINGS) BACKBITE
(— SUDDENLY) OUT
(— TOGETHER) CHORUS
(— TOO MUCH) SPILL OVERSAY
(—TRULY) MEAN
(— UNDER OATH) DEPOSE
SAYING DIT SAW SAY TAG DICT ITEM
REDE TEXT WORD ADAGE AXIOM
CHRIA DITTY FREIT MAXIM SPEAK
BALLAD BYWORD DICTUM DIVERB
LOGION DICTION PROVERB
APOTHEGM SENTENCE SPEAKING
(— LITTLE) DUMB
(—S OF JESUS) AGRAPHA
(—S OF RELIGIOUS TEACHER) LOGIA
(BRIEF —) APHORISM
(CLEVER —) QUIP
(COMMON —) CANT BYWORD
(CONCISE —) EPIGRAM
(CURRENT —) DICTUM
(HABITUAL —) OVERWORD
(NOTEWORTHY —) NOTABILIA
(OBSCURE —) ENIGMA
(PITHY —) GNOME MAXIM
APOTHEGM APOPHTHEGM
(QUICK —) JERK
(SENTENTIOUS —) REASON
(SILLY —) FADAISE
(TERSE —) EPIGRAM
(TRUE —) SOOTHSAW
(WISE —) SCHOLIUM
(WITTY —) MOT SALLY DICTERY
WITNESS
(WITTY —S) FACETIAE
(PL.) LOGIA
(SUFF.) LOGER LOGIA(N) LOGIC(AL)
LOGIST LOGUE LOGY
SCAB RAT ROIN SHAB SNOB CRUST
SCALD SCALL CANKER ESCHAR
RATTER GREENER RUBBERS
BLACKLEG BLACKNEB
(— ON HORSE'S HEEL) MELLIT
SCABBARD CHAPE SHEATH PILCHER
SCABBARD FISH HIKU
SCABBLE SCAB SCALP
SCABBY MANGY SCALD ROINISH
SCABIOUS
SCABIES ITCH SCAB PSORA
SCABIOSA KNAUTIA
SCABIOUS SCABIA BLUECAP
BUNDWEED PREMORSE
SCABROUS ROUGH SULTRY
ASPEROUS
SCAD COIN AKULE XUREL DOLLAR
GOGGLER QUIAQUIA
(PL.) ALOT LOTS TONS
SCAFFOLD CAGE PEGMA STAGE
BRIDGE GANTRY CATASTA HAYLOFT
STAGING HOARDING
(MOVABLE —) GANTRY
SCAFFOLDING DOCK STAGING
SCALARE ANGELFISH
SCALAWAG SCAMP

SCALD BURN LEEP PLOT SCAD BLAST
PLOUT SCAUD BLANCH SCALDER
AMBUSTION
SCALDFISH MEGRIM
SCALE PIP LEAF PELA PILL STEP TAPE
CLIMB FLAKE GAMUT GENUS GULAR
MOUNT PALEA PELOG PELOK PELTA
POISE SCUTE SHALE SHARD SHELL
SHERD SHIVE TRUNK ASCEND
CAUDAL CINDER COCCID FORNIX
GUNTER IMBREX KELVIN LABIAL
LADDER LAMINA LIGULE LOREAL
MENTAL NUCHAL OCULAR PERULE
RAMENT RONDLE RUSTRE SHIELD
SQUAMA STRIGA BALANCE CLINKER
ELYTRON FRONTAL FULCRUM
HUMERAL LATERAL NUCHALE
REAUMUR ROSTRUM VENTRAL
VERNIER ANALEMMA BRACHIAL
INDUSIUM LECANIUM LODICULE
MEALYBUG ODOPHONE RAMENTUM
SCRAMBLE SQUAMULE TEMPORAL
UROSTEGE
(— DOWN) DEGRADE
(— OF CORNSTALK) SHIVE
(— OF 7 TONES) SEPTAVE
(— ON BUTTERFLY) PLUMULE
(— ON MOTH) PATAGIUM
(— USED BY TAILORS) LOG
(GRADUATED —) RETE
(GREAT —) GAMUT
(KIND OF —) BRIX MOHS RICHTER
(SHAD —) CENIZO
(PL.) CHAFF DANDER
(PREF.) LEPID(O) LEPO PHOLID(O)
SQUAM(ATO)(ELLI)(I)(O)(OSO)(ULI)
(MUSICAL —) CHORD(O)
(SUFF.) LEPIS PHOLIS
SCALEBOARD SCABBARD
SCALEPAN BASIN
SCALER CULLER SOOTER
SCALES TRON TRONE BALANCE
SCALETAIL SQUIRREL
SCALLION PORRET
SCALLOP DAG CLAM GIMP MUSH
CRENA QUEEN SQUIN PECTEN
COQUILLE DOUGHBOY ESCALLOP
PECTINID
SCALLOPED INVECTED
(SUFF.) CRENATE
SCALP SCAUP SKELP ATTIRE
SCALPEL BISTOURY
SCALPER PUNTER
SCALY SCABBY SQUAMY LEPROSE
PALEATE LEPIDOTE SCABROUS
SQUAMOSE
SCALY ANTEATER PANGOLIN
SCAM DUPE BUNCO BUNKO CHEAT
STING BAMBOOZLE
SCAMP IMP LAD RIP LIMB SLIM
ROGUE SKEMP SKIMP THIEF BOOGER
BUGGER FRIPON NICKUM RASCAL
SINNER SORREL SORROW URCHIN

HALLION HESSIAN PEASANT
RAMMACK SKELLUM SLUBBER
SNOOZER BLIGHTER SCALAWAG
SLYBOOTS SPALPEEN VAGABOND
WIDDIFOW SCALLYWAG

SCAMPER DASH LAMP CHEVY
SCOUP SCOUR CHIVVY BRATTLE
SKITHER SKITTER

SCAN PIPE GLASS METER DEVISE
SURVEY EXAMINE
(KIND OF —) CAT

SCANDAL GUP CLASH CRACK ECLAT
SHAME CALUMNY OFFENSE
SCANMAG SLANDER NANNYGATE
WATERGATE

SCANDALIZE SHOCK
SCANDALMONGER CLAT
SCANDALOUS UNHOLY SHAMEFUL
SCANDINAVIAN DANE LAPP
NORSE SWEDE VIKING LOCHLIN
NORSEMAN NORTHMAN SCANDIAN
VARANGIAN
(PL.) OSTMEN

SCANT SHY JIMP LEAN MEET POOR
THIN SCAMP SHORT SKIMP SPLAY
BARISH GEASON LITTLE MEAGER
MEAGRE SCANTY SKINNY STINGY
STINTY SLENDER SCRATCHY
(PREF.) OLIG(O)

SCANTILY BARELY FEEBLY SMALLY
SCANTLY SPARSELY

SCANTINESS PENURY PARCITY
EXIGUITY SPARSITY

SCANTLING STUD FILLET JOIST
FILLET BOLSTER RIBBAND STUDDING

SCANTY BARE JIMP LANK LEAN
POOR SLIM EXILE GNEDL SCANT
SHORT SILLY SKIMP SPARE FRUGAL
MEAGER MEASLY SCRIMP SKIMPY
SLIGHT SPARSE SCRANNY SCRIMPY
SLENDER SPARING EXIGUOUS
PENURIOUS

SCAPEGOAT PATSY STOOGE
FALLGUY

SCAPEGRACE LIMB RASCAL
SCALLYWAG SKAINSMATE

SCAPHOID NAVICULAR
SCAPOLITE DIPYRE
SCAPULA BLADE OMOPLATE
SPADEBONE

SCAPULAR CUCULLA
SCAR ARR EYE WEM SEAM SEAR
WIPE CHALK FESTER KELOID RADDLE
STIGMA TRENCH CHELOID SCARIFY
CICATRIX SMALLPOX CICATRICE
(— ON SAWED STONE) STUN
(— ON SEED) HILUM
(— ON TREE) CATFACE

SCARAB ATEUCHUS
SCARCE DEAR RARE THIN SLACK
DAINTY GEASON CLASSIC
UNCOMMON
(PREF.) SPAN(I)(O)

SCARCELY ILL VIX JIMP SCANT
BARELY HARDLY MERELY ONETHE
SCARCE SCRIMP WENETH SCANTLY
UNEATHS UNNETHE

SCARCITY LACK WANT FAULT
SCANT DEARTH FAMINE RARITY
PAUCITY

SCARE COW BOOF BREE FAZE FEAR
FLEG FLIG FRAY GAST HUSH SHOO
ALARM APPAL GALLY GLIFF GLOFF
PSYCH SPOOK AFFRAY FRIGHT
GASTER POYCHE SCARIFY STARTLE
TERRIFY AFFRIGHT FRIGHTEN
(— BIRDS) KEEP
(— OFF) SCAT
(— WORD) BOO

SCARECROW BOGLE BUCCA
MOGGY SFWEL BOGGLE DUDMAN
MALKIN MAUMET MAWKIN
SCARER SHEWEL BOGGART
BUGABOO DEADMAN HODMADOD
SHAWFOWL

SCARED SCART SCARY AFRAID
GOOSEY STREAKED

SCAREMONGER ALARMIST
SCARF BARB HOOD SASH ABNET
ASCOT BARBE CLOUD CYMAR FICHU
LUNGI NUBIA PAGRI SHADE STOCK
STOLE TABLE THROW CRAVAT
PEPLOS HEBOZO SCREEN SQUARE
TAPALO TIPPET UPARNA BURDASH
DOPATTA FOULARD MANIPLE
MUFFLER NECKTIE ORARIUM
OVERLAY PUGGREE SAUTOIR
TALLITH CLAUDENT COINTISE
DOOPUTTY LIRIPIPE LIRIPOOP
MANTILLA MUFFETEE SLENDANG
(— AROUND HAT) PAGRI PUGGERY
PUGGREE PUGGAREE
(— ON BISHOP'S STAFF) ORARION
ORARIUM VEXILLUM
(— ON KNIGHT'S HELMET) COINTISE
(ARABIAN —) CABAAN
(FEATHER —) BOA
(PRAYER —) TALLIS TALLITH

SCARFING GRAFTING
SCARIFY LIFT
SCARLET LAC RED PINK TULY GRAIN
KERMES

SCARLET HAW HAWTHORN
SCARLET IBIS GUARA
SCARLET LETTER (AUTHOR OF —)
HAWTHORNE
(CHARACTER IN —) PEARL ROGER
ARTHUR HESTER PRYNNE
BELLINGHAM DIMMESDALE
CHILLINGWORTH

SCARLET LYCHNIS FIREBALL
NONESUCH

SCARLETT (LOVE OF —) RHETT
SCARLET TANAGER REDBIRD
FIREBIRD

SCARLIKE ULOID

SCARP CLIFF SCARF ESCARP
SCARLET
SCARY EERIE SPOOKY ALARMING
FEARSOME TERRIFYING
SCAT (— SINGER) ELLA
SCATHING MORDANT SCALDING
SCATHINGLY ROUNDLY
SCATOLOGICAL BARNYARD
SCATTER DAD SOW TED FLEE ROUT
SALT SCAT SEED SHED SPEW VOID
FLING SCALE SCHAL SEVER SHAKE
SKAIL SPRAY STREW STROW DISPEL
PEPPER SHOWER SKIVER SPARGE
SPARSE SPREAD SPRENG WINNOW
DIFFUSE DISBAND DISJECT FRITTER
RESOLVE SCAMBLE SHATTER
SKINKLE SKITTER SLATTER SPARKLE
SPARPLE SPATTER SWATTER
DISPERSE INTERSOW SEPARATE
SPLUTTER SPRINKLE SQUANDER
SQUATTER
(— BAIT FOR FISH) TOLE TOLL
(— CARELESSLY) LITTER
(— INK) SPLUTTER
(— OVER) BESTREW
(— WATER) SPLASH
SCATTERED LAX OPEN STRAY
DAIMEN SPARSE DIFFUSE SPOTTED
BESPRENT FUGITIVE SPARSILE
(PREF.) LAXI
SCATTERING SOWING DIASPORA
SCATTERY
SCATTERSHOT SHOTGUN
SCAUP DUCK DOGS DIVER DUCKER
DUNBIRD POCHARD BLUEBILL
GRAYBACK SHUFFLER
SCAVAGE SCEWING
SCAVENGE CLEANSE GARBAGE
SCAVENGER BUNGY RAKER
BHANGI BHUNGI MEHTAR REMOVER
SCAFFIE CORYDORA HALALCOR
RAMSHORN
SCAZON CHOLIAMB
SCEAT SKEAT STYCA
SCENARIO SCRIPT CONTINUITY
SCENE JOG SET CODA CYKE FLAT
SITE TODO VIEW ARENA STAGE
BRIDGE LOCALE VISION EPISODE
PAGEANT TABLEAU COULISSE
EXTERIOR INTERIOR PROSPECT
TABLETOP
(— IN OPERA) SCENA
(— OF ACTION) STAGE
(— OF ACTIVITY) BEEHIVE
(— OF CONFUSION) BABEL BEDLAM
(— OF HOSTILITIES) FRONT
(CLOSING —) FINALE
(FILM —) FLASHBACK
(FINAL —) CURTAIN EPILOGUE
(INTRODUCTORY —) INDUCTION
(NIGHT —) NOCTURNE
SCENERY DROP FLAT DECOR
CUTOUT NATURE IMAGERY PROFILE

(— CHANGER) TRIP
(PIECE OF —) MASKING
SCENESHIFTER GRIP
SCENT AIR DRAG NOSE ODOR VENT
WIND CIVET FAULT FLAIR FUMET
RELES SAVOR SMACK SMELL SNIFF
SNUFF SPOOR TASTE CHYPRE
ESSENCE INCENSE NOSEGAY
ODORIZE VERDURE FUMIGATE
MARECHAL PASTILLE REDOLENCE
(— OF ANIMAL FOLLOWED BY
HOUNDS) FEUTE
(— OF COOKING) NIDOR
(— OF FOX) DRAG
(— OF GAME) FUMET FUMETTE
(— OUT) SMOKE
(FALSE —) RIOT
(LOST —) FAULT
SCENTED OLENT ODORATE
PERFUMY ESSENCED
SCEPTER ROD WAND VERGE BAUBLE
CEPTER FERULA WARDER
SCHEDULE BOOK CARD HOLD LIST
SKED TIME PANEL SCRIP SCROW
SETUP SLATE TABLE SCROLL
CATALOG TABLEAU CALENDAR
REGISTER
(— OF COURT CASES) DOCKET
(— OF DUTIES) TARIFF
(— OF GAMES) SEASON
(TELEVISION —) LINEUP
SCHEDULED DUE
SCHEDULING (TECHNIQUE FOR —)
PERT
SCHEELITE TUNGSTEN
SCHEHERAZADE (HUSBAND OF —)
SCHAHRIAH
(SISTER OF —) DINARZADE
SCHEMA FORM
SCHEMATIC PLAN
SCHEME AIM GIN LAY WAY WEB
CAST DART GAME PLAN PLAT PLOT
REDE SWIM ANGLE BABEL CADRE
DODGE DRAFT DRIFT KNACK PINAX
REACH SCALE SETUP SHIFT TABLE
THINK TRAIN BRIGUE BUBBLE
CIPHER DESIGN DEVICE DEVISE
FIGURE HOOKUP POLICY SCHEMA
SYSTEM TAMPER THEORY UTOPIA
BUSTOUT COUNSEL DRAUGHT
GIMMICK IMAGINE KNAVERY
NOSTRUM PROJECT PURPOSE
CONSPIRE CONTRIVE FORECAST
GIMCRACK IDEOLOGY INTRIGUE
MANEUVER PLATFORM PRACTICE
TRIPOTER WINDMILL MACHINATE
(— FOR PEACE) IRENICON EIRENICON
(— OF ANCESTRY) PEDIGREE
(— OF RANK) LADDER
(ABORTIVE —) SOOTERKIN
(BETTING —) SYSTEM
(CONFIDENCE —) BUSTOUT
(DECEITFUL —) SHIFT

(DELUSIVE —) BUBBLE
(DIAGRAMMATIC —) PINAX
(FANCIFUL —) WINDMILL
(FAVORITE —) NOSTRUM
(KIND OF —) PONZI
(VERSIFICATION —) METER METRE
(VISIONARY —) BABEL
SCHEMER ARTIST DESIGNER
  ENGINEER SCHEMIST SLEEVEEN
SCHEMING SCHEMY PLANFUL
  SPIDERY FETCHING PRACTICE
SCHISM RENT DISUNITY SCISSION
  SCISSURE
SCHISMATIC HERETIC
SCHIST RAG AMPELITE MICACITE
  MYLONITE OLLENITE PHYLLITE
SCHIZONT MONONT AGAMONT
SCHIZOPHRENIA CATATONY
SCHLEP LUG
SCHMO JERK
SCHMOOZE CHAT
SCHNAPPER WOLLOMAI
SCHNOZZLE NOSE
SCHOLAR TUG DEMY GAON IMAM
  CLERK PUPIL DIVINE DOCTOR
  FELLOW JURIST LAMDEN MASTER
  PANDIT SABORA SAVANT SCOLOG
  SHEIKH BIBLIST BOOKMAN DANTIST
  LATINER LEARNER MAULANA
  STUDENT BOURSIER DISCIPLE
  HEBRAEAN HUMANIST ISLAMIST
  MASORITE TABERDAR THAUMASTE
  PHILOSOPHER
  (— OF QUEENS COLLEGE) TABERDAR
  (FOUNDATION —) BOURSIER
  (MOSLEM —) ULAMA ULEMA
  (PL.) CLERISY LITERATI
  AMERICAN LEWIS LOWES POUND
  BLYDEN CONANT GENUNG KELSEY
  MILLER NEWELL RIDDLE SARTON
  BABBITT GUMMERE SEYMOUR
  GOLDMANN HAMILTON HARKNESS
  PERCIVAL ROBINSON STERRETT
  LOUNSBURY
  AUSTRIAN SPANN
  CANADIAN MACMECHAN
  CHINESE YEN
  CZECH JIRACEK SAFARIK
  DANISH MADVIG GULDBERG
  DUTCH COBET BURMAN ERASMUS
  GROTIUS COORNHERT BILDERDIJK
  ENGLISH KER LEE BEDE BYNG LONG
  BYRON CROFT ELYOT JAMES LEWIS
  LOWTH MAYOR PALEY ROGET
  ROWSE YOUNG ALCUIN ALFORD
  BAXTER BODLEY BRIGHT BROOME
  BUTLER COWELL DASENT FARMER
  GARROD GODLEY GROCYN HARRIS
  JEVONS MURRAY NECKAM
  NEWMAN NICOLL YAHUDA ALDHELM
  ALDRICH BAINTON BUTCHER
  COGHILL DIODATI DUGDALE
  HOLLAND HOUSMAN LIDDELL

MACKAIL STANLEY CHRISTIE
GRIERSON HARRISON MCKERROW
PATTISON STRACHAN TUNSTALL
TYRWHITT CONINGTON NETTLESHIP
FINNISH LONNROT PORTHAN
KOSKENNIEMI
FLEMISH BLOMMAERT
FRENCH BUDE LAMY LUCE AMYOT
MAURY PARIS RASHI BAILLY BERARD
GAGUIN MAGNIN MENAGE MICHEL
DROSSES CAUMONT CHASLES
DELISLE LEFRANC LONGNON
SOURIAU DEMOGEOT ESTIENNE
JAUCOURT BONAPARTE SCALIGER
BARTHELEMY TAILLANDIER
GERMAN DIEZ BLEEK HEYNE KLOTZ
KROLL LEYEN STAHR FROBEN
KOCHLY RAUMER CONRING
GOEDEKE GOLTHER HEUSLER
LUDWICH MOMMSEN RIBBECK
RUHNKEN WILHELM AUFRECHT
BERNEKER BUTTMANN HAINISCH
PFEIFFER SPANHEIM WEINHOLD
KOSCHWITZ CAMERARIUS
GREEK DION GAZA CORAY PALLES
DIDYMUS MUSURUS RHIANUS
PORPHYRY ATHENAEUS CAECILIUS
EUPHORION ZENODOTUS
CALLIMACHUS CHRYSOLORAS
ERATOSTHENES
HUNGARIAN BEL
ICELANDIC BLONDAL SAEMUND
VIGFUSSON
INDIAN PATANJALI
IRISH BALL BUTLER TRENCH
MAHAFFY KEIGHTLEY
ITALIAN DONI PRAZ ZENO GNOLI
MAFFEI VARCHI ALEANDRO
MANUTIUS MARTELLI ROSSETTI
MARSILIUS NICCOLINI TIRABOSCHI
JAPANESE NITOBE MABUCHI
MEXICAN GAMA
PERUVIAN MENDIBURU
POLISH CIOLEK CHODZKO
RACZYNSKI OSSOLINSKI
ZDZIECHOWSKI
PORTUGUESE BRAGA
ROMAN PLINY VARRO AUSONIUS
CENSORINUS
RUSSIAN LAVROV CHUKOVSKY
LOMONOSOV DRAGOMANOV
MANDELSTAM
SCOTTISH LANG BLACKIE GROSART
LINDSAY CRICHTON BELLENDEN
MACDONALD
SPANISH CARO OCHOA CASTRO
VILLENA
SWEDISH MALMSTROM
STIERNHIELM
SWISS BODMER BREITINGER
PELLICANUS
SCHOLARLY CLERKLY ERUDITE
  LEARNED ACADEMIC

SCHOLARSHIP ART BOOK BURSE
BURSARY DEMYSHIP LEARNING
SCHOLASTIC PEDANTIC
SCHOOL GAM TOL EDDY PREP AGGIE
BOOKS ECOLE HEDER LYCEE NYAYA
SAKHA TEACH TRADE TRAIN TUTOR
ALJAMA CAMPUS CHEDER CHURCH
KUTTAB KYAUNG MADHAB MALIKI
RABFAK SCHOLA SCHULE SQUEEL
TRIPOS ACADEME ACADEMY
CRAMMER MADRASA PENSION
STUDIUM YESHIVA AUDITORY
DOCUMENT EXERCISE EXTERNAT
PEDAGOGY SEMINARY
(— FOR JUDO OR KARATE) DOJO
(— FOR SINGERS) MAITRISE
(— OF BLACKFISH) GRIND
(— OF BUDDHISM) CHAN RITSU
DHYANA SANRON
(— OF FISH) HERD SCALE SCULL
(— OF HINDU PHILOSOPHY) NYAYA
(— OF OPINION) SECT
(— OF PAINTING) GENRE
(— OF PHILOSOPHY) SECT ACADEMY
AUDITORY
(— OF VEDA) SAKHA SHAKHA
(— OF WHALES) GAM POD
(ART —) BAUHAUS LUMINISM
(AZTEC —) CALMECAC
(COMPARATIVE —) FOLKLORE
(DAY —) EXTERNAT
(ELEMENTARY —) GRADES
(HIGH —) HIGH ACADEMY COLLEGE
(KIND OF —) MAGNET
(MARTIAL ARTS —) DOJO
(MOSLEM —) HANAFI KUTTAB SHAFII
HANBALI
(PAINTING —) ASHCAN
(REFORM —) BORSTAL
(RELIGIOUS —) ALJAMA YESHIVA
(RIDING —) MANEGE
(SANSKRIT —) TOL
(SCOTCH —) SQUEEL
(SECONDARY —) LYCEE LYCEUM
COLEGIO
(WRESTLING —) PALESTRA
SCHOOLBOOK COCKER
SCHOOLBOY SCUG PETTY
CLERGION
SCHOOL FOR SCANDAL (AUTHOR
OF —) SHERIDAN
(CHARACTER IN —) MARIA MOSES
PETER JOSEPH OLIVER ROWLEY
TEAZLE CANDOUR CHARLES
PREMIUM SURFACE SNEERWELL
SCHOOLHOUSE PORTABLE
SCHOOLING LEARNING
SCHOOLMASTER BEAK CAJI CAXI
AKHUN KHOJA KHODJA MASTER
PEDANT AKHOOND DOMINIE
PEDAGOG ORBILIUS
SCHOOLROOM HOMEROOM
SCHOOL SHARK TOPE TOPER

SCHOOLWORK BOOKWORK
SCHOONER JACK TERN QUART
QUINT WUINT PUNGEY BALLAHOO
SCHORL COCKLE
SCHRADAN OMPA
SCHROTHER SHREDDER
SCHUSSBOOMER SKIER
SCHUYT SHOE SCOUT EELBOAT
SCIATICA BONESHAW
SCIENCE ART OLOGY SOPHY
MATHESIS SCIENTIA
(— OF ALGAE) ALGOLOGY
(— OF ANIMALS) ZOOLOGY
(— OF AQUEOUS VAPOR) ATMOLOGY
(— OF ARTILLERY) PYROBALLOGY
(— OF ATOMS) ATOMICS
(— OF BEING OR REALITY)
ONTOLOGY
(— OF BIOLOGICAL STATISTICS)
BIOMETRY
(— OF BREEDING) GENETICS
(— OF CAUSES) ETIOLOGY
(— OF CHARACTER) ETHOLOGY
(— OF CLASSIFICATION)
SYSTEMATICS
(— OF CLASSIFICATION OF
DISEASES) NOSOLOGY
(— OF COLORS) CHROMATICS
(— OF DISEASES) NOSOLOGY
(— OF DOSES) DOSOLOGY
POSOLOGY
(— OF DUTY) DEONTICS
DEONTOLOGY
(— OF EARTH'S FORMATION)
GEOGONY
(— OF EARTH MEASUREMENTS)
GEODESY
(— OF ELECTIONS) PSEPHOLOGY
(— OF ENVIRONMENT) ECOLOGY
(— OF ETHICS) DEONTICS
DEONTOLOGY
(— OF EXCHANGE) CAMBISTRY
(— OF FERMENTATION) ZYMOLOGY
(— OF FERNS) PTERIDOLOGY
(— OF FLOW OF MATTER) RHEOLOGY
(— OF FOOTPRINTS) ICHNOLOGY
(— OF FORMS OF SPEECH)
GRAMMAR
(— OF FRUIT GROWING) POMOLOGY
(— OF FUNDS MANAGEMENT)
FINANCE
(— OF GEMS) GEMMARY GEMOLOGY
(— OF GOD) DIVINITY
(— OF GOVERNMENT) POLITICS
(— OF HEALTH MAINTENANCE)
HYGIENE
(— OF HEAT) PYROLOGY
THERMOTICS
(— OF HISTORY OF EARTH) GEOLOGY
(— OF HUMAN BODY) SEMATOLOGY
(— OF HUMAN SETTLEMENTS)
EKISTICS
(— OF IDEAS) IDEOLOGY

(— OF IMAGINARY SOLUTIONS) PATAPHYSICS
(— OF INSECTS) ENTOMOLOGY
(— OF INTELLECT) NOOLOGY
(— OF INTERPRETATION) HERMENEUTICS
(— OF LANGUAGE) GRAMMAR PHILOLOGY
(— OF LAW) NOMOLOGY
(— OF LIFE) BIOLOGY
(— OF LIFE INFLUENCES) EUGENICS
(— OF LIFE OF TREES) SILVICS
(— OF LIGHT) OPTICS
(— OF LYING) PSEUDOLOGY
(— OF MEANING) SIGNIFICS
(— OF MEASURING TIME) HOROLOGY
(— OF MEDIEVAL CHEMISTRY) ALCHEMY
(— OF MIDWIFERY) TOKOLOGY
(— OF MIND) PSYCHOLOGY
(— OF MOLLUSCS) MALACOLOGY
(— OF MORAL DUTY) ETHICS
(— OF MOSSES) BRYOLOGY
(— OF MOTION) DYNAMICS
(— OF MOUNTAINS) OROLOGY
(— OF MUSCLES) MYOLOGY
(— OF NAVIGATION) NAUTICS
(— OF NUMBERS COMBINATIONS) ALGEBRA
(— OF PERSUADING A GOD) THEURGY
(— OF PLANTS) BOTANY
(— OF QUANTITY) POSOLOGY
(— OF RACIAL IMPROVEMENT) EUGENICS
(— OF REASONING) LOGIC
(— OF RECORDING GENEALOGIES) HERALDRY
(— OF REFRIGERATION) CRYOLOGY
(— OF REMEDIES) ACOLOGY
(— OF RIVERS) POTAMOLOGY
(— OF ROCKS) LITHOLOGY
(— OF SEA) THALASSOGRAPHY
(— OF SERUMS) SEROLOGY
(— OF SMELLS) OSMICS
(— OF SOILS) PEDOLOGY
(— OF SOUND) PHONICS ACOUSTICS
(— OF SPATIAL MAGNITUDES) GEOMETRY
(— OF STRUCTURE OF ANIMALS) ANATOMY
(— OF SUBSTANCES) CHEMISTRY
(— OF SUN) HELIOLOGY
(— OF SYMPTOMS) SEMEIOLOGY
(— OF TEACHING) PEDAGOGY
(— OF TEACHING ADULTS) ANDRAGOGY
(— OF THE EAR) OTOLOGY
(— OF TIDES) TIDOLOGY
(— OF TOUCH DATA) HAPTICS
(— OF VALUES) AXIOLOGY
(— OF VERSIFICATION) PROSODY
(— OF VIRTUE) ARETAICS

(— OF WEIGHT OR GRAVITY) BAROLOGY
(— OF WINES) ENOLOGY OENOLOGY
(— OF WORD MEANINGS) SEMANTICS
(BRANCH OF —) BIONICS
(ESOTERIC —) HERMETICS
(KIND OF —) LIFE
(LEGAL —) LAW
(MILITARY —) STRATEGY
(NATURAL —) STINKS PHYSICS
(PHYSICAL —) PHILOSOPHY
(RELIGIOUS —) THEOLOGY
(SUFF.) LOGER LOGIA(N) LOGIC(AL) LOGIST LOGUE LOGY OLOGY SOPH(ER)(IC)(IST)(Y)
(RELATING TO —) METRIC
SCIENTIST BOFFIN
(KIND OF RUSSIAN —) REFUSNIK REFUSENIK
SCIMITAR SAX SEAX TURK KHEPESH TULWAUR
SCINDAPSUS POTHOS
SCINTILLA ATOM
SCINTILLATE SNAP FLASH GLEAM GLANCE GLITTER SPARKLE TWINKLE
SCINTILLATION SPARKLE SPARKLET
SCION IMP ROD CION CYON HEIR ROOT SLIP GRAFT SPRIG BRANCH SPROUT SARMENT SETLING
SCISSORS SHEARS CLIPPER SECATEUR
(PREF.) FORFICI
SCLERITE TORMA LABIUM PLANTA PLAGULA AXILLARY EPIMERON
SCLERODERMA MORPHEA
SCLEROPROTEIN BRONGIN
SCLEROTIUM ERGOT SCLEROTE TUCKAHOE
SCOFF DOR GAB GALL GECK GIBE GIRD JEER JIBE MOCK RAIL CURSE FLEER FLOUT GLEEK SCARF SCORN SCOUT SNEER TAUNT DERIDE REPROVE RIDICULE
SCOFFER MOCKER ABDERITE
SCOLD JAW MAG MOB NAG RAG ROW WIG YAP BAWL CALL CAMP CANT DING FLAY FRAB FUSS HAZE JACK JOBE JOWL JUMP RAIL RANT RATE REDD RICK SHAW SNAG SNUB TUCK YAFF ABUSE BARGE BASTE BOAST CHIDE DRESS FLIRT FLITE PRATE RANDY SCALD SCORE SHORE SHREW SLANG STORM TARGE VIXEN BERATE BOUNCE CALLET CAMPLE CARPET HAMMER HOORAY HURRAH MAGPIE RATTLE REHETE REVILE TATTER THREAP TONGUE YAFFLE YANKIE CHANNER CHEWOUT REPROVE TRIMMER TROUNCE UPBRAID RALLYRAG BERATTLE BETONGUE CHASTISE CIDESTER DINGDONG RIXATRIX CLAPPERCLAW

SCOLDING JAW HURL JESSE SCOLD
DIRDUM JAWING RAKING RATTLE
SISERA FLITING HEARING LECTURE
RAGGING WIGGING BLESSING
CARRITCH JOBATION
SCOLEX HEAD
SCOLYTUS IPS
SCONCE SWAPE APPLIQUE
SCONE FARL FARLE
SCOOP BAIL BALE DRAG INFO ROUT
DIDLE GOUGE KEACH SHAUL SKEET
BUCKET DIPPER DISHER SHOVEL
WIMBLE SCRAPER SCUPPET
SKIMMER SKIPPET SCOOPFUL
(— FOR CANNON) LADLE
(— FOR DAMPENING CANVAS) SKEET
(— FOR GRAIN) WECHT
(— UP) LAP LAVE GATHER
(— WITH TONGUE) LAP
(CHEESE —) PALE
(GLASSMAKING —) PADDLE
(JAI ALAI —) CHISTERA
(LONG-HANDLED —) DIDLE
(SURGICAL —) CURET CURETTE
SCOOT ZIP DART SCOUT SKEET
SKYHOOT
SCOPE AIM AREA AMBIT POWER
RANGE REACH ROUND SCALE
SCOOP SWEEP VERGE SCOUTH
SPHERE TETHER BREADTH CIRCUIT
COMPASS OPERAND PURVIEW
CONFINES DIAPASON LATITUDE
(— OF VISION) COMMAND
(FREE —) SWING
SCOPOLINE OSCIN OSCINE
SCORBUTUS SCURVY
SCORCH BURN CHAR PLOT SCAM
SEAR ADURE ADUST BROIL PARCH
PLAUT REESE SCALD SCAUM SINGE
SWEAL SWELT BIRSLE BISHOP
DEGREE SMITCH SOTTER SPARCH
SWINGE SWITHE BLISTER BRISTLE
FRIZZLE SCORKLE SCOWDER
SWITHEN SWITHER TORRIFY
FIREFANG SCOUTHER SCOWTHER
SCORCHED ADUST LEEPIT
SCORCHER SIZZLER
(PREF.) SIRI(O)
SCORCHING BAKING FIRING
ADURENT SCALDING
SCORE ACE CUT LAW RIT RUN CARD
DEBT DROP GAME GOAL HAIL HOLE
MAKE MARK NICK POST RIDE SLOG
CHART CHASE CORGE COUNT EXTRA
NOTCH OPERA TALLY COOREE
FURROW SAFETY SCOTCH SCRIVE
SPADES STRING TARGET TICKET
TWENTY CONVERT SCORING
SCRATCH SQUEEZE GAMEBALL
PARTITUR PLACEKICK
(— FOR ALE) ALESHOT
(— HEAVILY AGAINST) SHELL

(— IN BRIDGE) BOARD BONUS
SWING
(— IN CRIBBAGE) GO PEG FIFTEEN
(— IN CRICKET) BLOB CENTURY
(— IN PIQUET) CAPOT REPIQUE
(— IN RUGBY) TRY
(— OF NOTHING) DUCK
(— OF 100) TON
(APTITUDE —) STANINE
(BASKETBALL —) HOOP
(BILLIARDS —) STRING
(BOWLING —) PINFALL
(GOLF —) ACE PAR BOGEY DEUCE
EAGLE BIRDIE BUZZARD
(INDEX —) APGAR
(KIND OF —) APGAR
(NO —) LOVE
(ORIGINAL MUSICAL —) URTEXT
(PINOCHLE —) LAST
(TENNIS —) CALL FIVE LOVE DEUCE
FORTY FIFTEEN
(THREE —) SHOCK SIXTY
(TIE —) HALVE DEADLOCK
(ZERO —) GOOSEEGG
(PL.) MUSIC
SCORED SULCATE SULCATED
SCOREKEEPER SCORER TALLIER
TALLYMAN
SCORER NIB MARKER NOTCHER
SCORIA SCUM SLAG CINDER
SULLAGE
SCORIFIER CAPSULE
SCORIFY SMELT
SCORN GECK LOUT HOKER
SCARN SPURN BISMER SLIGHT
CONTEMN DESPISE DESPITE
DISDAIN CONTEMPT DERISION
MISPRIZE
SCORNFUL SAUCY SCORNY SNIFFY
SNIFTY HAUGHTY FRUMPISH
INSOLENT SARDONIC
SCORNFULLY ASKEW ASWASH
SCORPION NEPA ALACRAN STINGER
UROPYGI ARACHNID PEDIPALP
WHIPTAIL
SCORPION FISH LAPON SERRAN
HOGFISH SCULPIN LORICATE
RASCACIO
SCORPION FLY PANORPID
SCOT
(ALSO SEE SCOTSMAN) CELT JOCK
KELT SANDY SAXON SCOTTY
BLUECAP SCOTSMAN
(PL.) SAWNY SAWNEY LALLANS
SCOTCH TRIG SCOAT SCOTS
SCOTTISH
SCOTCHMAN MAC GAUL SANDY
TARTAN SCOTCHY SCOTTIE
SCOTSMAN
SCOTER COOT FILK DIVER SCOUT
WHILK BASQUE DUCKER SURFER
PISHAUG SCOOTER SKUNKTOP

SCOTIA MOUTH
SCOTIST DUNCE
SCOTLAND ALBYN ALBANY ALBION
SCOTIA ALBAINN ALBANIA
(NORTHERN —) PICTLAND

SCOTLAND

BAY: SCAPA
CAPITAL: EDINBURGH
COIN: DEMY BODLE GROAT PLACK
RIDER BAWBEE
COUNTY: AYR BUTE FIFE ROSS ANGUS
BANFF MORAY NAIRN PERTH
ARGYLL LANARK ORKNEY BERWICK
KINROSS PEEBLES RENFREW
SELKIRK WIGTOWN ABERDEEN
AYRSHIRE CROMARTY DUMFRIES
ROXBURGH SHETLAND STERLING
FIRTH: LORN CLYDE FORTH MORAY
SOLWAY PENTLAND
ISLAND: RUM BUTE IONA JURA MULL
RHUM SKYE ARRAN BARRA ISLAY
LEWIS HARRIS ORKNEY SHETLAND
ISLANDS: ORKNEY HEBRIDES
SHETLAND
LAKE: TAY NESS MORAR LAGGAN
LINNHE LOMOND KATRINE
RANNOCH
LANGUAGE: ERSE I ALLAN LALLAND
MEASURE: CUP BOLL CRAN FALL MILE
PECK PINT ROOD ROPE SPAN CRANE
LIPPY FIRLOT AUCHLET CHALDER
CHOPPIN MUTCHKIN STIMPART
MOUNTAIN: HOPE ATTOW DEARG
NEVIS TINTO WYVIS CHEVIOT
MACDHUI
NATIVE: GAEL PICT SCOT
ORDER: THISTLE
REGION: FIFE BORDERS GRAMPIAN
RESORT: OBAN
RIVER: AYR DEE DON ESK TAY DOON
GLEN NITH NORN SPEY AFTON
ANNAN CLYDE FORTH GARRY
TWEED YTHAN AFFRIC TEVIOT
TUMMEL DEVERON FINDHORN
SEAPORT: ALLOA LEITH DUNDEE
ABERDEEN
TOWN: AYR DUNS OBAN WICK ALLOA
BRORA CUPAR ELLON LEITH NAIRN
PERTH SALEN TROON DUNDEE
GIRVAN HAWICK DUNKELD
GLASGOW PAISLEY ABERDEEN
DUMFRIES GREENOCK KIRKWALL
STIRLING
WATERFALL: GLOMACH
WEIGHT: BOLL DROP TRONE BUSHEL

SCOTSMAN SANDY SAWNY
BLUECAP
SCOTTISH SCOTCH SCOTLAND
SCOTTISH TERRIER DIEHARD
SCOTTIE VERMINER

SCOUNDREL RAP PIMP SCAB VILE
WARY BLECK FILTH KNAVE SCAMP
SHREW SMAIK SWEEP THIEF WHAUP
BRIBER LIMMER SLOVEN VARLET
CATAIAN GLUTTON HALLION
NITHING SCROYLE SKELLUM VILIACO
VILLAIN WARLOCK BEZONIAN
LIDDERON MASCHANT
SCOUNDRELLY VILLAIN
SCOUR ASH BEAT COMB RAKE SCUM
SEEK SIND SKIR SCOOR SCRUB
SKIRR SWEEP DRENCH SCURRY
SLUICE DEGRADE FURBISH
BACKWASH STONFFILE
(PL.) SKIT
SCOURER BLOOMER DOLLIER
PICKLER
SCOURGE EEL TAW LASH WHIP
CURSE FLAIL KNOUT SLASH SWING
BALEYS PLAGUE SWINGE SCORPION
SCOURGER WHIPSTER
SCOURING BEAT SCOUR HUSHING
SCRUBBING
SCOUT SPY BEAR LION SKIP ROVER
SPIAL VISOR ESPIAL GAYCAT
DESPISE MARINER PICKEER PIONEER
SCOURER WATCHER EMISSARY
OUTRIDER OUTSCOUT SCURRIER
SKIRMISH
(BOY —) CUB BOBCAT SCOUTER
WEBELOS EXPLORER
(CUB — SUBDIVISION) DEN
(GIRL —) DAISY
SCOW ACCON FLOAT GARVEY
SCOWL LOUR FROWN GLARE GLOOM
GLOUT LOWER SKIME GLOWER
VENNER GLOOMING
SCOWLING FROWNY GLARING
SCRABBLE PAW RAKE GROPE
CLAMBER SCRAMBLE
SCRAGGY WEEDY
SCRAM GIT HOP LAM BUNK SCAT
BUGGER BUGOFF SODOFF BUZZOFF
GETLOST
SCRAMBLE MUSS SPURL SCRAWM
SPRAWL CLAMBER LOUSTER
SCRABBLE SCRAFFLE SCRATTLE
SPRACHLE
SCRAP BIT END JAG ORT PIP CRAP
ITEM JAGG JUNK PICK SNAP BRAWL
GRAIN PATCH SCRAN SHRED THRUM
WASTE FRACAS TUSSLE DISCARD
MAMMOCK ODDMENT REMNANT
SNIPPET FRACTION SCRAPPET
SKERRICK SNATTOCK
(— FOR PATCHING) SPETCH
(— OF PAPER) SCRIP
(— OF SONG) CATCH
(— OF WRITING) SCRAPE
(FOOD —S) BROCK
(LEAST —) STITCH
(LITERARY —S) ANA

(METAL —) SCISSEL SCISSIL
(RAGGED —) SCART
(PL.) ORTS SCRAN RELICS SCROFF
GARBAGE GUBBINGS
SCRAPE LEG RUB CLAW COMB RAZE
CLAUT CURET ERADE ERODE GRATE
GRAZE GRIDE SCALP SCART SCUFF
SHAVE ABRADE HOBBLE RUGINE
SCREED SCROOP SPLORE CORRADE
CURETTE JACKPOT SCRATCH
SNAPPER TROUBLE SCRABBLE
(— ALONG) HARL HARLE SHOOL
(— GOLF CLUB ON GROUND) SCLAFF
(— OFF) SPUD
(— OUT) ERASE HOLLOW
(— SKINS) MOON SCUD FLESH
HARASS
(— TOGETHER) RAKE GLEAN
MUCKER SCAMBLE
(— WITH FEET) SCAUT
(PREF.) RAMENTI SCAPI
SCRAPED BRIGHT
SCRAPER PAN PIG HARL SLIP CURET
GLOVE HARLE QUIRL RASER SPOON
DOCTOR FRESNO GRADER GRATER
RASPER CURETTE FLANGER LEVELER
RACLOIR SLUSHER STRIGIL
GRATTOIR SCRAPPLE TERRACER
UNHAIRER
SCRAPING HARL GRIDE RASURE
(CRACKER —S) CUSH
(METAL —S) DIET
(PL.) RAMENTA
SCRAPMAN CHIPMAN
SCRAPPER BREAKER FIGHTER
SCRAPPLE PANHAS PONHAWS
SCRAPPY BITTY SNATCHY
SCRATCH RAT RIT CLAW CRAB RACE
RAIN RAKE RAPE RASE RAUK RAZE
RISP RIST SHAB SLUG STUN CHALK
CLAUT CLAWK CURRY FRUSH GRAZE
RANCH SCART SCLUM SCORE SCRAB
SCRAT SCROB SCRUB SHRUB SKELP
TEASE TOUCH BRUISE CANCEL
CRATCH RASURE RIPPLE SCORCH
SCOTCH SCRAPE SCRAWK SCRAWL
SCRAWM SCRAZE SCRIVE TORACE
DECLARE EMERIZE EXPUNGE
SCARIFY SCRABBLE SCRATTLE
SCRIBBLE
(— OUT MORTAR) POINT
(PREF.) RAMENTI
SCRATCHER RASER
SCRAWL SCRAWM SPRAWL
SCRATCH SCRABBLE SCRIBBLE
SQUIGGLE
SCRAWNY BONY LEAN SLINK
WEEDY SCRANK SCRAGGY SCRANKY
SCRANNY SCRAGGED
(— PERSON OR ANIMAL) RIBE
SCREAM CRY YAW REME WEAK
YARM YAUP YAWL YAWP YOWT
SKIRL SHRAME SHRIEK SHRILL

SQUALL SQUAWL YAMMER SCREECH
YELLOCH SKELLOCH
SCREAMER CHAJA ANHIMA
SCREAMING MEEMIES JITTERS
HYSTERIA
SCREECH QUAWK QUOCK SCREAM
SCREEK SCRITCH SKREIGH ULULATE
SKELLOCH
SCREECH OWL STRICH
SCREED BLAUD TIRADE HARANGUE
SCREEN TRY CAGE GOBO HARP HIDE
LAWN MASK PICK REJA SCUG SEPT
SIFT TENT VEIL ARRAS BLIND CHEEK
CHICK CLOAK CLOSE COVER FIGHT
GAUZE GRATE HOARD SHADE SHOJI
SIEVE SPEER SPIER TATTY BAFFLE
BASKET BORDER CANVAS DEFEND
ESCORT HALLAN MEDIUM PURDAH
RESEAU SCHERM SCONCE SHAKER
SHIELD SHROUD THREAD VQIDER
CEILING CONCEAL CRIBBLE CURTAIN
FLYWIRE GOGGLES GRIZZLY
REREDOS SECLUDE SHELTER
SHUTTER TESTUDO TROMMEL
BACKSTOP BESCREEN BLINDAGE
COVERING DIFFUSER ECLIPSER
EXCLUDER HOARDING OCCULTER
PARAVENT PARCLOSE PAVISADE
SCREENER SPLASHER STRAINER
TRAVERSE UMBRELLA
(— ALONGSIDE SHIP) PAVISADE
(— BEHIND ALTAR) REREDOS
(— FOR BATTING PRACTICE) CAGE
(— FOR SHIP'S COMBATANTS)
FIGHT
(— FOR SIZING ORE) GRATE
TROMMEL
(— FOR THEATER LIGHT) JELLY
MEDIUM
(— IN BASKETBALL) PICK
(— OF BAMBOO SLIPS) CHEEK
CHICK
(— OF BRUSHWOOD) SCHERM
(— OF FIRE) BARRAGE
(— OF SHIELDS FOR TROOPS)
TESTUDO
(— OF TAPESTRY) ARRAS CEILING
(— ON AUTOMOBILE) GRILL GRILLE
(— TO PROTECT LOOKOUTS)
DODGER
(— USED BY ARCHERS) PANNIER
(BULLETPROOF —) MANTA MANTEL
MANTELET
(CHANCEL —) JUBE
(FIRE —) FENDER
(KIND OF —) TOUCH
(MECHANICALLY ACTUATED —)
GRIZZLY
(PAPER —) SHOJI
(PL.) CANCELLI
SCREENED BLIND SECLUDED
SCREENINGS CULM SLACK SLECK
SCREENLAND FILMDOM

SCREENPLAY SCRIPT SCENARIO
SCREW HOB VISE WORM CRICK
  FEEZE SCROW WREST TEMPER
  TOGGLE COCHLEA AIRSCREW
  FLATHEAD SETSCREW THUMBKIN
  WINDMILL
  (KIND OF —) ALLEN MEANTIME
  (PART OF —) HEAD ROOT CREST
  PITCH POINT SHANK THREAD
  (PROPELLER —) FAN
SCREWBALL KOOK ZANY FLAKE
  ECCENTRIC NONSENSICAL
SCREW BEAN MESQUITE
  SCREWPOD TORNILLA
SCREWDRIVER (KIND OF —)
  PHILLIPS
SCREWED SQUINCH
SCREWER WORMER
SCREWMAN JACKMAN
SCREW PINE IE ARA HALA IEIE
  AGGAG PALMA VACOA VACONA
  LAUHALA PANDANUS
SCREW TREE TWISTY
SCRIBBLE GOUIB DOODLE SCRAWL
  SCRATCH REMARQUE SCRABBLE
  SQUIGGLE
SCRIBBLING GRAFFITO
  (PL.) GRAFFITI
SCRIBE EZRA CLERK THOTH BOOKER
  PENMAN SCRIVE SOPHER WRITER
  GRAFFER MASORET SCRIVAN
  NOVERINT PENCLERK SCRIPTOR
  SCRIVANO
  (PL.) SOPHERIM
SCRIMMAGE MAUL BULLY ROUGE
  SCRAP BICKER SPLORE SKIRMISH
SCRIMP HINCH SCREW SKIMP
SCRIP EXONUMIA
SCRIPT ROOK NEUM RONDE SERTA
  SERTO NASKHI NESKHI SCRITE
  SOOLOOS THULUTH BASTARDA
  GURMUKHI HIRAGANA KANARESE
  MAGHRIBI MAITHILI MEROITIC
  NASTALIQ SCENARIO
  (HINDI —) DEVANAGARI
  (KOREAN ALPHABETIC —) HANGUL
  (TYPE OF —) RONDE
SCRIPTURE WRIT AGAMA CHING
  SUTRA SUTTA TANTRA
  (HINDU —) VEDA
  (PL.) BIBLE GRANTH GRUNTH
  TANACH TENACH SHASTRA
SCRIVENER PENMAN WRITER
  GRAFFER SCRIVER NOVERINT
  TABELLION
SCROFULA EVIL CRUELS STRUMA
SCROLL BEND ROLL LABEL SCRIT
  AMULET ESCROL LEGEND SCRAWL
  STEMMA VOLUME VOLUTE EVOLUTE
  PAPYRUS RINCEAU BANDEROL
  CARTOUCH MAKIMONO
  (— AT END OF HANDRAIL)
  MONKEYTAIL

  (— AT MOUTH OF FIGURE)
  PHYLACTERY
SCROLL-LIKE TURBINAL
SCROPHULARIA FIGWORT
SCROTUM BAG COD PURSE
  (PREF.) OSCHE(O) SCROT(I)(O)
SCROUNGER SCAMBLER
SCRUB FILE ABORT SCOUR SCROG
  CANCEL COPPET MAQUIS SCODGY
  CLEANSE SCRUBBER YANNIGAN
SCRUBBY SHRUBBY
SCRUBLAND GARIGUE GARRIGUE
SCRUFF CUFF NAPE SCUFF SCROFF
SCRUFFY DOGEARED
SCRUPLE PASS DEMUR DOUBT
  FORCE POINT QUALM STAND STICK
  BOGGLE SCOTCH STRAIN STICKLE
  STUMBLE
SCRUPULOUS NICE SPICED TENDER
  CAREFUL FINICKY PRECISE DELICATE
  QUALMISH
SCRUTINIZE EYE PRY SEE DRY SCAN
  VIEW AUDIT PROBE SIGHT SOUND
  VISIT PERUSE SURVEY EXAMINE
  INSPECT ENSEARCH TRAVERSE
SCRUTINIZING NARROW
  SCANNING
SCRUTINY EYE SEARCH CANVASS
  EXAMINE HAWKEYE PERUSAL
  DOCIMASY
  (ELECTION —) CANVAS CANVASS
SCRYER SEER
SCUD RUN RACK RAMP SKID SKIM
  SKIP SCOOT SPOON
SCUDAMORE (LOVER OF —)
  AMORETTA
SCUDO FILIPPO
SCUFF SLAKE SLIDE SCLAFF SCUFFER
  SCUFFLE SHUFFLE
SCUFFLE HOE CUFF BUSTLE BUSTUP
  CLINCH CUFFLE TUSSLE WISTER
  BAGARRE BRULYIE SHAMBLE
  SHUFFLE SCRUFFLE
SCULL OAR FUNNY SHELL SKULL
  WHERRY
SCULLERY SINKROOM
SCULLION GIPPO SCULL SLUSH
  GALOPIN SWILLER CUSTROUN
  QUISTRON
SCULPIN COTTID GRUBBY JOHNNY
  BIGHEAD DRUMMER BULLHEAD
  BULLPOUT CABEZONE HARDHEAD
  LORICATE SCALAWAG
SCULPTOR CARVER GRAVER
  IMAGER MARBLER PLASTIC
  AMERICAN FRY BALL GABO HART
  IVES KECK LADD MEAD RUSH TAFT
  VOLK WARD ADAMS AKERS ANDRE
  BEACH BOEHM BROWN CLARK
  DOYLE EVANS GALLO GOULD HOXIE
  JONES KELLY KONTI MEARS MILLS
  PERRY PRATT SEGAL SERRA STONE
  STORY YOUNG AITKEN BARTHE

BENDER BITTER BUFANO CALDER
CLARKE COUPER CURTIS DALLIN
EAKINS EBERLE ELWELL FRASER
FRAZEE FRENCH GRAFLY GRIMES
HARVEY HOSMER HUGHES KASKEY
KEMEYS KINNEY KITSON LAWRIE
LEWITT MILLES MOZIER NAKIAN
NEWMAN PALMER POTTER POWERS
PUTNAM RIMMER ROGERS ROSZAK
RUMSEY SHRADY WALKER WARNER
ZORACH BARNARD BISSELL
BORGLUM BRENNER BRIGHAM
EDSTROM EZEKIEL GELLERT
GODDARD GREGORY HANCOCK
HARTLEY HOFFMAN JACKSON
JAEGERS KENDALL LAESSLE
LAURENT LIPPOLD LONGMAN
LUKEMAN MACNEIL MANSHIP
MARTINY MILMORE NIEHAUS
NOGUCHI OCONNOR PROCTOR
ROBERTS SCHULER SCUDDER
SIEVERS SIMMONS WHITNEY
AGOSTINI ALBRIGHT ATCHISON
BARTLETT BREWSTER CONNELLY
CRAWFORD DAVIDSON DECREEFT
DERIVERA FLANAGAN LACHAISE
LENTELLI MCCARTAN MULLIGAN
NADELMAN ODONOVAN PARAMINO
RINEHART CLEVENGER GREENOUGH
HUMPHREYS MACDONALD
REMINGTON RUCKSTULL VALENTINE
ARCHIPENKO MACMONNIES
PAPASHVILY PICCIRILLI ZIOLKOWSKI
ARGENTINIAN ALONZO
ATHENIAN ANTENOR
AUSTRIAN DONNER NATTER
TILGNER STRASSER
BELGIAN GEEFS FRAIKIN KESSELS
LALAING MEUNIER SIMONIS
STAPPEN LAMBEAUX TONGERLOO
CANADIAN HEBERT MACCARTHY
CZECH STRUSA MYSLBEK
DANISH BISSEN JERICHAU
WILLUMSEN THORVALDSEN
DUTCH VRIES SLUTER TASSAERT
DESJARDINS
ENGLISH BELL CARO FORD GILL
JOHN SWAN WARD WOOD ANGEL
BACON BAILY BANKS BATES BOEHM
COLIN DURST HESSE JONES MOORE
RHIND STONE TWEED WATTS
ARCHER DOBSON GIBSON JAGGER
KENNET LANDAU CHAROUX EPSTEIN
FLAXMAN GIBBONS GILBERT
STEVENS WOOLNER ARMITAGE
ARMSTEAD CHANTREY FRAMPTON
HEPWORTH SHERIDAN MACKENNAL
KENNINGTON WESTMACOTT
THORNYCROFT
FLEMISH BOLOGNE
FRENCH ARP ADAM ETEX RUDE UZES
BARYE BOSIO CHAPU CRAUK DALOU

DAVID DURET LEMOT PAJOU PILON
PUECH RODIN DANTAN DEJOUX
DUBOIS DUMONT GOUJON HOUDON
ISELIN LEGROS MERCIE MILLET
ROCHET ANGUIER BEGUINE
BOUCHER CARRIES CHAUDET
CLODION COLOMBE COUSTOU
DESPIAU FREMIET LEMAIRE
LEMOYNE MAILLET MAILLOL
PIGALLE PRADIER PREAULT RICHIER
CAFFIERI CARPEAUX CAVELIER
CHAPLAIN COYSEVOX FALCONET
FOYATIER GIRARDON GODEBSKI
JOUFFROY LEPAUTRE LIPCHITZ
SARRAZIN BARTHOLDI BEAUNEVEU
BOURDELLE CLESINGER FALGUIERE
INJALBERT LANDOWSKI ROUBILLAC
BARTHOLOME CASSEGRAIN
CHARPENTIER DELAPLANCHE
GERMAN HAHN KISS LENZ NAHL
BEUYS CAUER HAAKE KOLBE KRAFT
OESER RAUCH STOSS STUCK WOLFF
BANDEL BLASER GEIGER HABICH
HAHNEL HALBIG HERTER HOSAUS
WAGNER AFINGER BARLACH
BELLING KAUPERT KLIMSCH
KLINGER KRELING SCHADON
SCHAPER EBERHARD EBERLEIN
FERNKORN SCHLUTER ZUMBUSCH
DANNECKER ENGELHARD
LEHMBRUCK MAGNUSSEN
RIETSCHEL SIEMERING UECHTRITZ
LEINBERGER SCHWANTHALER
RIEMENSCHNEIDER
GREEK MYRON CHARES ONATAS
SCOPAS AGASIAS BOETHUS
BRYAXIS CALAMIS CRITIUS PHIDIAS
SCYLLIS AGELADAS CANACHUS
CRESILAS DAMOPHON LYSIPPUS
PAEONIUS SOCIBIUS AGESANDER
ALCAMENES ARCHERMUS
BATHYCLES EUPHRANOR
LEOCHARES PASITELES TAURISCUS
TIMOTHEUS POLYCLETUS
POLYCLITUS POLYEUCTUS
PRAXITELES AGORACRITUS
ATHENODORUS CALLIMACHUS
LYSISTRATUS CEPHISODOTUS
IRISH FOLEY MACDOWELL
FITZGERALD
ITALIAN VELA BANCO DANTI DUPRE
LEONI PORTA RIZZO VINCI CANOVA
GIOTTO MARINI PISANO ROBBIA
SOLARI ALGARDI BERNINI CELLINI
FIESOLE GIORGIO LAURANA
MAZZONI QUERCIA TRIBOLO
AGOSTINO AMMANATI ANTELAMI
BARBIERE BOCCIONI CAMPAGNA
CERACCHI CIVITALI GHIBERTI
LOMBARDO MARCHESI TENERANI
BARTOLINI BEGARELLI BORROMINI
DONATELLO SANSOVINO

GIACOMETTI MODIGLIANI
MONTEVERDE VERROCCHIO
DELLAROBBIA MICHELANGELO
NORWEGIAN VIGELAND
POLISH KALISH
ROMAN COSMATI
RUMANIAN BRANCUSI
RUSSIAN ZADKINS ORLOVSKI
ANTOKOLSKI
SPANISH CANO MENA SILOE
PICASSO CHILLIDA HERNANDEZ
BERRUGUETE
SWEDISH ZORN MILLES SERGEL
BYSTROM BORJESON FOGELBERG
SWISS HOERBST KISSLING TINGUELY
VENEZUELAN MARISOL
SCULPTURAL PLASTIC
SCULPTURE CAMEO DRAFT GRAVE
SCULP BRONZE ENTAIL GISANT
SCULPT CARVING DRAUGHT
ENGRAVE GRADINO IMAGERY
INSCULP STABILE MORTORIO
NATIVITY PORTRAIT PREDELLA
SCULLION
SCULPTURED GRAVEN GLYPHIC
SCUM BRAT FOAM GALL HEAD REAM
SCUD SILT SKIM SKIN DROSS FROTH
SCURF SLOAK SLOKE SLUSH SPUME
FLURRY MANTLE MOTHER REFUSE
RIDDAM SCRUFF BLANKET CACHAZA
OFFSCUM LAITANCE PELLICLE
SANDIVER SCOURING SCUMMING
(— OF THE PEOPLE) RIFFRAFF
(— ON FUSED GLASS) SANDIVER
(— ON LIQUOR) PELLICLE
(— ON MELTED METAL) SLAG
SCUP BREAM PORGY UPARID
SCUPPAUG
SCURF SCALD SCALL DANDER
FURFUR SCRUFF DANDRUFF
SCURFY SCALD SCURVY LEPROSE
SCRUFFY LEPIDOTE SCABROUS
SCABERULOUS
SCURRILITY ABUSE REPROACH
SCURRILOUS LOW FOUL VILE DIRTY
GROSS RIBALD VULGAR ABUSIVE
SCURRIL INDECENT
SCURRY HIE RUN ZIP BELT CRAB
SKIN CURRY HURRY SCOUR SKICE
SKURRY SCUFFLE SCUTTER SCUTTLE
SKELTER SKITTER
SCURRYING SKITTER
SCURVY SCALD SCUMMY SHABBY
ROYNOUS SCORBUCH SCORBUTE
UNLIKING
SCUT BUN
SCUTAGE ESCUAGE
SCUTATE CLYPEATE
SCUTCH SCOTCH SWINGLE
SCUTE PLATE SCUTUM SCUTELLA
SCUTELLATION SCALING
SCUTIFORM PELTATE

SCUTTLE HOD CRAB SINK SKEP
BEETLE MANHOLE SCUDDLE
SCUTTER SCRATTLE
SCUTTLEBUTT CASK RUMOR
GOSSIP FOUNTAIN
SCUZZY NASTY
SCYLLA (FATHER OF —) NISUS
TYPHON
SCYLLITOL INOSITOL
SCYPHUS PYXIS
SCYTHE SY LEA HOOK MEAK REAP
CRADLE
SCYTHIAN LAMB BAROMETZ
SEA MER BAHR BLUE BRIM FOAM
FRET GULF HOLM LAVE MAIN MARE
RACE TIDE WAVE BRINE BRINY FLOAT
FLOOD LOUGH OCEAN AEQUOR
PONTUS SEALET STRAND TETHYS
CHANNEL HYALINE NEPTUNE
BOSPORUS DEEPNESS SEAFLOOD
THALASSA
(— DIVINITY) TRITON
(— GOD) PROTEUS
(— LETTER) PASSPORT
(AT —) LOST PUZZLED
(HEAVY —) POPPLE
(HIGH —) MAIN
(MODERATE —) SEAWAY
(PREF.) HAL(I)(IO)(O) MARI MER
PELAG(O) THALASS(I)(IO)(O)
THALATTO
SEA ANCHOR DRAG DROGUE
SEA ANEMONE POLYP DAHLIA
OPELET ACTINIA VESTLET ACTINIAN
ZOANTHID
SEA BASS HANAHILL HUMPBACK
SERRANID TALLYWAG
SEA BEAR OTARIOID
SEABIRD HAGDON
SEA BISCUIT BREAD GALETTE
PANTILE
SEABOARD COAST
SEA BREAD HARDTACK
SEA BREAM TAI CARP CHAD PORGY
ROMAN BRAISE SARGUS SPARID
TARWHINE
SEA BREEZE DOCTOR
SEA BUTTERFLY PTEROPOD
SEACOAST BANK SEABOARD
SEASHORE
SEA COW SIREN DUGONG MANATEE
RHYTINA SIRENIAN
SEA CUCUMBER BALATE TREPANG
CUCUMBER SYNAPTID TEATFISH
SEADOG SALT FOGBOW FOGDOG
SAILOR
SEA DOVE DOVEKIE ICEBIRD
SEA DRAGON PEGASID QUAVIVER
SEA DUCK DIVER EIDER DIPPER
DUCKER SCOTER
SEA EAGLE ERN ERNE PYGARG
PYGARGUS

SEA-EAR ORMER ABALONE
SEAFARER SEAGOER
SEAFOOD (— AND STEAK)
SURFANDTURF
SEAFOOD)- ON SKEWERS)
YAKITORI
SEA FOX THRASHER
SEA GIRDLE CUVY CUTWEED
SEA GULL COB GOR MEW COBB
ANNET COBBE POPELER
(AUTHOR OF —) CHEKHOV
(CHARACTER IN —) NINA IRINA
TRIGORIN CONSTANTIN
SEA-GYPSY SELUNG
SEA HOLLY ERYNGO ERYNGIUM
SEA HORSE WALRUS HIPPODAME
HIPPOCAMPUS LOPHOBRANCH
SEA KALE COLE
SEAL CAN FIX FOB GUM BULL CHOP
CORK HARP HOOD JARK LUTE BLANK
BULLA CLOSE EAGLE PHOCA SIGIL
STAMP SWILE THONG UGRUG
URSUK WAFER ASSEAL BEATER
CACHET COCKET DOTARD ENSEAL
ENSIGN FASTEN GASKET MAKLUK
MATKAH OBSIGN PHOCID RANGER
SEALCH SECURE SIGNET CONFIRM
CONSIGN COWROID ENGLUTE
HOODCAP IMPRESS QUITTER
SADDLER SEALING SEALKIE
SIGNARY WEDDELL ADHESIVE
BACHELOR BEDLAMER BRELOQUE
CYLINDER MANDORLA PINNIPED
SECRETUM SEECATCH SIGILLUM
SIGNACLE TANGFISH VALIDATE
(— FOR WATCH CHAIN) ONION
BRELOQUE
(— OFF) CAP
(— OVER CORK) CAPSULE
(BEARDED —) URSUK MAKLUK
(CUSTOM-HOUSE —) COCKET
(EARED —) OTARY
(FEMALE —) MATKA
(GOLD —) BEZEL
(HARBOR —) DOTARD RANGER
TANGFISH
(HERD OF —S) PATCH
(IMMATURE —) BEDLAMER
(KIND OF —) HAIR MONK WEDDELL
(MALE —) WIG SADDLER BACHELOR
SEECATCH
(NEWFOUNDLAND —) SWILE
RANGER
(PAPAL —) BULL BULLA
(SHETLAND —) SILKIE
(YEARLING —) HOPPER
(YOUNG —) PUP BEATER JACKET
BLUEBACK
(3-YEAR OLD —) TURNER
(PREF.) PHOC(O) SIGILLO
SEA LACE WHIPLASH
SEA LAVENDER INKROOT STATICE

SEALED CLOSE
SEALER CAPPER GASKET
SEA LETTUCE LAVER SLAKE SLOKE
SEAWEED
SEA LILY CRINOID
SEA LION OTARY HAIRSEAL
PINNIPED PINNIPEDE
SEALSKIN SKIN SCULP MATARA
SAFARI
SEALSKIN COAT NETCHA
SEALYHAM TERRIER
SEAM DRY BAND DART FASH FELL
PURL REND DEVIL PEARL SPILL
FAGGOT INSEAM STREAK SUTURE
SEAMLET JUNCTURE OVERSEAM
(— IN INGOT) SPILL
(— IN SHIP'S HULL) DEVIL
(— OF COAL) RIDER SPLIT STREAK
(IRREGULAR —) FASH
SEAMAN SALT JACKY MATLO
ARTIST CALASH LUBBER SAILOR
MARINER MASTMAN SHIPMAN
SHIPPER SMASHER WAISTER
YOUNKER DESERTER SEASONER
SEAMARK MEITH
SEAMED SEAMY RUGGED
SEA MILE NAUT
SEA MONSTER ORC PHOCA
KRAKEN LEVIATHAN ROSMARINE
HIPPOCAMPUS
SEAMOUNT GUYOT
SEAMSTER TAILOR SEMPSTER
SEAMSTRESS SEAMER SEWSTER
NEEDLEWOMAN
SEANCE SITTING
SEA NETTLE BLUBBER
SEA OF GRASS (AUTHOR OF —)
RICHTER
(CHARACTER IN —) HAL JIM BRICE
BROCK HENRY LUTIE SARAH JIMMIE
BREWTON CAMERON CHARLEY
BREWSTER MCCURTIN
CHAMBERLAIN
SEA ONION SCILLA
SEA OTTER KID KALAN
SEA OXEYE SALTWEED SAMPHIRE
SEA PERCH GAPER COMBER
TRIPLETAIL
SEA PINK THRIFT SABBATIA
SEAPLANE HYDRO AIRBOAT
AEROBOAT
SEA PLANTAIN GIBBALS
SEA POACHER BULLHEAD
SEAPORT PARA PORT GROIN NATAL
HARBOR ENTREPOT MACASSAR
SEA PUSS OFFSET
SEAR BURN FIRE SERE FLAME FRIZZ
ENSEAR SCORCH SIZZLE FRIZZLE
SEA RAVEN SCULPIN
SEARCH FAN SPY BEAT COMB DRAG
DRAW FAND FISH FOND GAPE HUNT
LAIT RAKE RIPE ROUT SEEK SIFT

WAIT FRISK PRODE QUEST SCOUR
SNOOP VISIT DACKER DREDGE
FERRET FUMBLE RANCEL SLEUTH
ENQUIRE EXPLORE FOSSICK
INQUEST INQUIRE INSPECT
RANSACK SCRINGE ZETETIC
FINECOMB OUTREACH SCRABBLE
SCROUNGE SCRUTINY SHAKEDOWN
(— ABOUT) GRUB PROG GROPE
(— AMONG REFUSE) SCAVENGE
(— BY FEELING) GROPE
(— DEEPLY) TENT DELVE
(— DILGENTLY) SCOUR
(— EVERYWHERE) BUSK SCOUR
(— FOR) FORK HUNT LAIT SNOOK
REQUIRE SEEKOUT
(— FOR FOX'S TRAIL) CIPHER
(— FOR GAME) DRAW GHOOM
QUEST
(— FOR GOLD) FOSSICK
(— FOR KNOWLEDGE) OUTREACH
(— FOR PARTNER) CRUISE
(— FOR PROVISIONS) FORAGE
(— FOR SMUGGLED GOODS) DACKER
JERQUE
(FOR STOLEN GOODS) RANCEL
RANSEL RANZEL
(— FOR WEAPONS) FRISK
(— GROPINGLY) GLAMP
(— INTO) EXQUIRE INDAGATE
(— OUT) FERRET INVENT ROOTLE
EXQUIRE INDAGATE
(— SHIP) RUMMAGE
(— SYSTEMATICALLY) COMB
(— THROUGH) TURN
(— UNDERWATER) FISH
(CAREFUL —) RESEARCH
(SYSTEMATIC —) SWEEP
SEARCHER FINDER
SEARCHING HARD CLOSE SHREWD
CURIOUS GROPING
SEARED ADUST
SEARING CAUTERY
SEA ROBIN GURNARD WINGFISH
SEA ROVER VIKING SCUMMER
SEASAN NUDE
SEASCAPE MARINE SEAPIECE
SEA SCORPION COBBLER
SEA SERPENT ELOPS
SEASHELL PROP
SEASHORE SEA RIPE CLEVE COAST
PLAYA MARINE SEASIDE SEABEACH
SEABOARD SEACOAST
SEASICKNESS HILO NAUPATHIA
SEA SNAIL LIPARIAN
SEA SNAKE CHITAL KERRIL
SEASON BEEK CORN DASH FALL
PERT SALT SEEL TIDE TIME GRASS
INURE SAUCE SAVOR SHEMU SPICE
AUTUMN EASTER FLOWER HARDEN
HAYING MASTER SPRING STEVEN
STOUND SUMMER WINTER BUDTIME

FLYTIME HARVEST KITCHEN
OATSEED SEEDTIME
(— FOR HERRING FISHING) DRAVE
(— HIGHLY) DEVIL
(— IN THE SUN) HAZE
(— OF JOY) JUBILEE
(— OF MERRYMAKING) CARNIVAL
(CLOSED —) SHUTOFF
(DULL —) SLACK
(EGYPTIAN —) AHET PERT SHEMU
(HAYING —) HAYING HAYSEL
(LENTEN —) CAREME
(RAINLESS —) DRY
(RAINY —) KHARIF VARSHA
(REGULARLY RECURRING —) EMBER
(SPRING —) WARE APRIL GRASS
(THE RIGHT —) TID
SEASONABLE PAT TIDY TIMELY
TIDEFUL TIMEFUL VETERAN
TOWARDLY OPPORTUNE
SEASONABLY TIMELY APROPOS
BETIMES
SEASONED SAGY SALT SALTED
INDIENNE POWDERED
(MILDLY —) SWEET
SEASONER SURFACERER
SEASONING SALT SPICE SEASON
PAPRIKA SPICING OREGANUM
SEA SPIDER PYCNOGONOID
SEA SQUIRT ASCIDIAN
SEA SWALLOW TERN
SEAT BOX CAN SEE SET USH BANK
BOSS COSY DAIS FLOP FORM FROG
ROOM SILL SLIP SUNK TOIT ASANA
BENCH CELLE CHAIR DICKY PERCH
SELLA SELLE SETTE SIEGE SLIDE
STALL STOOL USHER BOUGHT
DODONA EXEDRA HUMPTY INSIDE
RUMBLE SADDLE SEATER SEGGIO
SETTEE SETTLE THWART BUTTOCK
CUSHION GRADINE GRADINO
INSTALL OTTOMAN SEATING
TABORET TRANSOM BLEACHER
ENTHRONE PULVINAR SEGGIOLA
SUBSELLA WOOLPACK
(— AT PUBLIC SPECTACLE) PULVINAR
(— FOR CLERGY) SEDILE
(— FOR GRINDER) HORSING
(— FOR PLANE IRON) FROG
(— FOR TWO) SOCIABLE
(— NEAR ALTAR) SEDILIUM
(— OF BIRTH) SIDE
(— OF CHAIR) BOTTOM
(— OF DIGNITY) STATE
(— OF EMOTIONS) CHEST SPLEEN
(— OF FEELINGS) STOMACH
(— OF HARE) FORM
(— OF INTELLECT) HEAD
(— OF KNOWLEDGE) RUACH
(— OF ORACLE) DODONA
(— OF PITY) BOWEL
(— OF POWER) SEE

(— OF REAL LIFE) SOUL
(— OF RESPONSIBILITY) SHOULDER
(— OF RULE) OGDOAD
(— OF THEATRE) STALL
(— OF TURF) SUNK
(— OF UNDERSTANDING) SKULL
(— ON ELEPHANT'S BACK) TOWER
CASTLE HOWDAH
(— ONESELF) LEAN PITCH
(— SLUNG ON POLES) HORSE
(— WITH BRAZIER BELOW) TENDOUR
(— WITHIN WINDOW OPENING)
CAROL
(AIRPLANE —) DORMETTE
(BACKLESS —) STOOL HASSOCK
(BISHOP'S —) APSE BISHOPRIC
FALDSTOOL FALDISTORY
SYNTHRONUS
(BUS —) KNIFEBOARD
(CANOPIED —) COSY COZY
(CARRIAGE —) DICKY
(CHIEF —) METROPOLIS
(CHIMNEY —) SCONCE
(CHURCH —) PEW DESK STALL
SEDILE
(COACH —) BOOT POOP
(COUNTRY —) TOWER GRANGE
QUINTA
(DILIGENCE —) BANQUETTE
(DRAPED —) MUSNUD
(DRIVER'S —) BOX DICKY COCKPIT
FORETOP
(ELEVATED —) PERCH
(FIXED —) DAIS
(GARDEN —) ALCOVE
(JUDGMENT —) TRIBUNAL
(KEY —) KEYWAY
(LONG —) BANK FORM BENCH
(MOTORCYCLE —) PILLION
(NIPPLE —) LUMP
(OARSMAN'S —) TAFT
(PORCH —) GLIDER
(RECLINING —) DORMEUSE
(ROMAN —) PULVINAR
(ROWER'S —) THWART
(ROYAL —) SIEGE STEAD THRONE
(STAGECOACH —S) BASKET
(STRAW —) BOSS
(TIER OF —S) TENDIDO
(TURF —) SUNK BUNKER
(UNRESERVED —S) BLUES
(PREF.) EDRI(O)
(SUFF.) HEDRAL
SEA TANGLE FURBELOW
SEATED (— IN MIND) INWARD
SEATING
(— AREA) LOGE
SEA TROUT SEWEN SMELT KIPPER
HERLING HIRLING BODIERON
(— AFTER SPAWNING) KELT
(YOUNG —) PEAL
SEA TURTLE RIDLEY CHELONID

SEA URCHIN WANA REPKIE
ARBACIA CIDARID ECHINID ECHINUS
RADIATE ECHINOID
(FOSSIL —) ECHINITE
(PREF.) ECHIN(O)
SEAWALL BULWARK
SEAWARD OFF MAKAI
SEAWEED ORE AGAR ALGA KELP
LIMU MOSS NORI OOZE REEK REIT
TANG WARE DRIFT DULSE KOMBU
LAVER SLAKE SLOKE VAREC VRAIC
WRACK DELISK FUCOID FUNORI
TANGLE HAITSAI OARWEED
OREWEED OREWOOD REDWARE
SEATANG SEAWARE CARAGEEN
GULFWEED HEMPWEED ROCKWEED
SARGASSO SEABEARD WHIPCORD
WHIPLASH CORALLINE NULLIPORE
(PL.) LUMUT
(PREF.) PHYC(O)
(SUFF.) PHYCEAE
SEA WOLF (AUTHOR OF —) LONDON
(CHARACTER IN —) HUMP MAUD
WOLF DEATH LEACH LOUIS LARSEN
JOHNSON BREWSTER HUMPHREY
JOHANSEN MUGRIDGE VANWEYDEN
SEA WORM PALOLO SABELLA
SEB (CONSORT OF —) NUT
(SON OF —) OSIRIS
SEBA (FATHER OF —) CUSH
SEBASTIAN (BROTHER OF —)
ALONSO
(SISTER OF —) VIOLA
SEBESTEN MYXA
SECANT SEC CHORD
SECCO FRESCO
SECEDE SPLINTER
SECESSIONIST SECESH SEPARATE
SECLUDE TACKLE ENCLOSE ISOLATE
RECLUSE CLOISTER SEQUESTER
SECLUDED COY SHY DEEP CLOSE
QUIET HIDDEN REMOTE SECRET
PRIVATE RETIRED RETRAIT SECLUSE
HIDEAWAY MONASTIC SEPARATE
SOLITARY UMBRATIC CLAUSTRAL
SECLUSION RECESS SHADOW
PRIVACY PRIVITY RETREAT SECRECY
SEQUEST SOLITUDE ISOLATION
(— OF WOMEN) PURDAH
SECOND AID SEC ABET BACK BETA
TICK OTHER VOUCH ASSIST LATTER
MOMENT TARTAN TIDDER TOTHER
ANOTHER INSTANT SUPPORT
SUSTAIN STICKLER
(— BASE) KEYSTONE
(— IN COMMAND) DEPUTY
(— IN HORSE RACE) PLACE
(— PERSON USE) TUISM
(MAJOR —) TONE
(1000TH OF A —) SIGMA
(60TH OF A —) THIRD
(PREF.) DEUT(O) DEUTER(O) SECUNDI

SECONDARY BY BYE SUB SLACK
DONKEY SECOND CUBITAL DERIVED
INFERIOR MIDDLING
(PL.) FLAGS
(PREF.) DEUT(ER)(ERO)(O) MES(O)
SECONDHAND USED
SECOND MRS TANQUERAY
(AUTHOR OF —) PINERO
(CHARACTER IN —) RAY HUGH PAULA
ARDALE AUBREY ELLEAN
CORTELYOU TANQUERAY
SECOND-RATE DIMESTORE
COMMON SHODDY INFERIOR
SECOND-RATER PIKER
SECRECY DERN HUSH HIDING
SECRET HIDLING HIDLINS PRIVACY
PRIVITY SILENCE DARKNESS
HIDLINGS SCUGGERY VELATION
SECLUSION HUGGERMUGGER
(STATE OF —) CLOSET
SECRET SLY DARK DERN INLY BLIND
CABAL CLOSE HUSHY PRIVY QUIET
ARCANE CLOSET COVERT HIDDEN
INWARD POCKET STOLEN ARCANUM
COUNSEL CRYPTIC EPOPTIC FURTIVE
MYSTERY PRIVACY PRIVATE PRIVITY
RECLUSE RESERVE RETIRED
SECRETA UNKNOWN ESOTERIC
HIDLINGS HUSHHUSH MYSTICAL
SNEAKING STEALTHY TETEATETE
HUGGERMUGGER
(PREF.) CRYPT(O) KRYPT(O) SUB
SECRETARY CLERK COPPY BARUCH
MUNSHI RAPTOR SCRIBE FAMULUS
MUNCHEE MOONSHEE
(SENIOR —) QUEENBEE
SECRETE HIDE CACHE NICHE RESET
SECERN SECRET CONCEAL SECLUDE
SALIVATE SEPARATE
(— MILK) LACTATE
(— ONESELF) HIVE
(— SALIVA) DROOL
(PREF.) ECCRINO
SECRETION INK LAC GOWL LAAP
LERP MILT SPIT WOOL HUMOR
LAARP MUCUS SEBUM SEPIA SLIME
SPADE CEMENT SALIVA SMEGMA
CERUMEN CHALONE FLOCOON
HORMONE SPITTLE AUTACOID
ENDOCRIN
(— OF MILK) LACTATION
(FATTY —) SEBUM
(GLAND —) SUCCUS
(OILY —) SEBUM
(THICKENED —) GUM
(VISCOUS —) SLIME
(WAXY —) LERP LAARP PRUINA
SECRETIVE SLY CAGY DARK SNUG
CAGEY CLOSE COVERT SECRET
SILENT INVOLVED
SECRETIVENESS SECRECY
SLYNESS

SECRETLY CLOSE DARKLY DERNLY
SECRET CLOSELY HIDLINGS
INWARDLY
SECRET, THE (CHARACTER IN —)
ROSE KALINA SKRIVANEK
(COMPOSER OF —) SMETANA
SECT SET ZEN BABI CLAN CULT JODO
KIND SHIN ALOGI BHORA ISAWA
PANTH BOHORA DONMEH HERESY
SCHISM SCHOOL CATHARI DHUNDIA
DOCETAE HASIDIM ISAWIYA
KHALSAH RINGATU SECTARY
SEQUELA SHAIKHI SHINGON
SIVAISM SUBSECT AGNOETAE
AHMADIYA AISSAOUA MURJIITE
NAASSENE SECTUARY SHAKTISM
BUCHANITES
(— MEMBER) DRUSE DRUZE
(LEBANESE —) DRUSE
(MEMBER OF —) KHLYST OPHITE
YEZIDI MOLOKAN NUSAIRI LINGAYAT
SECTARIAN CULTIST HERETIC
MAZHABI SECTARY SECTIST
SECTARY JESUIT HERETIC SECTIST
SECTUARY SEPARATE
SECTION CUT END AREA PACE PART
SECT UNIT CAPUT FRUST PIECE
SHARE TMEMA BILLET BRANCH
BRIDGE CANTON LENGTH MEMBER
PASSUS SECTOR ARTICLE CUTTING
HEADING SEGMENT TRANCHE
ADDENDUM DIVISION FRACTION
(— AROUND HOP KILN) CURB
(— OF A BODY) LAMINA
(— OF AVICENNA'S WORK) FEN
(— OF BLOOM) STAMP
(— OF BUILDING) ENTRY
(— OF FENCE) FLAKE
(— OF FILM) EXPOSURE
(— OF FILTER) LEAF
(— OF FISHING TACKLE) TRACE
(— OF GARMENT) GORE
(— OF GLASS) SHAWL
(— OF HIGH GROUND) DIVIDE
(— OF KORAN) SURA
(— OF LADDER) FLY
(— OF LOG) BOLT FLITCH
(— OF LOOM) LAY
(— OF MELODY) STRAIN
(— OF NET) DEEPING
(— OF NEWSPAPER) LEAD ROTO
(— OF PARLIAMENT) LAGTHING
(— OF PSALTER) CATHISMA
(— OF RHAPSODY) LASSU
(— OF ROOF) SEVERY
(— OF ROOTSTOCK) BIT
(— OF SHIP) STEERAGE
(— OF SONG) STOLLEN
(— OF THREE SHEETS) TERNION
(— OF TORAH) PARASHAH
(— OF TRENCH) BAY
(— OF VIOLIN) BOUT

(— OF WOOD) HAG
(— OF YARN) SLUB
(—S OF SCENERY) BOOK
(CONCLUDING —) ABGESANG
(CONIC —) PARABOLA
(DULL —) LONGUEUR
(LOWEST —) BOTTOM
(MINE —) BORASQUE BORRASCA
(MUSICAL —) CODA EPILOG FINALE
(NARROW —) STRIPE
(NATIVE —) KASBA CASBAH
(ONE-SIXTEENTH OF —) FORTY
(PERCUSSION —) BATTERY
(4-PAGE —) OUTSERT
(SUFF.) TOMA TOME TOMIC TOMOUS
TOMY
SECTIONALISM LOCALISM
SECTOR AREA GORE HOUSE
(45-DEGREE —) OCTANT
SECULAR LAIC CIVIL COMMON
EARTHLY PROFANE WORLDLY
TEMPORAL
SECULARIZE LAICIZE
SECURE FID GET GIB KEY POT
RUG SEW WIN BAIL BOLT BOND
CAUK COCK COLD EASY FAST
FIND FIRM FRAP GAIN GIRD HOOK
LAND MOOR NAIL SAFE SEAL SHOT
SNUG STAY SURE WARM BELAY
BLOCK CINCH CLEAT SLOUR
SOUND STRAP TIGHT TRUST
ANCHOR ASSURE BECKET BUTTON
CLINCH DEFEND ENSURE FASTEN
OBTAIN PLEDGE SETTLE SICCAR
SICKER STABLE STAPLE TRAIST
ACQUIRE BULWARK CONFINE
DUNNAGE FORFEND FORTIFY
RAMPIRE WARRANT GARRISON
PRESERVE
(— AGAINST INTRUSION) TILE
(— AID OF) ENLIST
(— A SAIL) TRICE
(— BAIT) EBB
(— FROM LEAKING) COFFER
(— IN ADVANCE) SCOOP
(— PROMPTLY) SNAP
(— WITH BARS) GRATE
SECURED BOUND SETTLED
SECURELY FAST SAFE SICCAR
SICKER STRAIT SURELY SOLIDLY
SOUNDLY
SECURITY PUP BAIL BAND EASE
GAGE MUNI SEAL WAGE FRITH
GRITH GUARD QUIET STOCK
BORROW CEDULA EQUITY PLEDGE
REFUGE SAFETY SCREEN SEVERE
SURETY VADIUM BULWARK CAUTION
CUSTODY DEFENSE DEPOSIT
FLOATER HOSTAGE SHELTER
SLEEPER WARRANT COLONIAL
COVENANT FASTNESS GUARANTY
HYPOTHEC STRENGTH VADIMONY
MUNICIPAL

(— DEVICE) SENSOR
(BELOW AVERAGE —) LAGGARD
(PL.) PERCENTS PORTFOLIO
SEDAN SEDIA JAMPAN SALOON
TONJON NORIMON TOMJOHN
BROUGHAM
SEDATE CALM COOL DOCE GRAVE
QUIET SOBER STAID SERENE
EARNEST SERIOUS SETTLED
COMPOSED DECOROUS
SEDATENESS SOBRIETY
SEDATIVE AMYTAL ACONITE
CALMANT CODEINE LUPULIN
BARBITAL LENITIVE QUIETIVE
SOOTHING
SEDENTARY STILL SESSILE
INACTIVE
SEDGE SAG LING RAIT REIT STAR
CAREX CHUFA TIKUG BHABAR
EHUAWA GLUMAL THATCH TOETOE
TOITOI BULRUSH MONOCOT
PAPYRUS SNIDDLE TUSSOCK
GALANGAL JIMSEDGE PIKERUSH
(PREF.) CARIC(O)
SEDGE FLY GRANAM GRANNOM
SEDGE WARBLER WREN
MOCKBIRD REEDBIRD
SEDGY SAGGY SEGGY TWILLED
SEDIMENT CARR DREG FAEX
FOOT GOBI LEES MULM SILT
WARP DRAST DREGS FECES
FOOTS MAGMA BOTTOM FECULA
SIMMON SLUDGE DREWITE
GROUNDS GRUMMEL SAPROPEL
SETTLING
(— OF BEER OR ALE) CRAP
(IRON —) CAR CARR
(REDDISH —) SIMMON
SEDITION REVOLT TREASON
SEDITIOUS RIOTOUS FACTIOUS
MUTINOUS
SEDUCE DRAW JAPE LOCK DECOY
TEMPT WRONG ALLURE BETRAY
ENTICE DEBAUCH ENSNARE
MISLEAD SUGGEST TRADUCE
INVEIGLE
(— WITH THE EYE) LEER
SEDUCER UNDOER LOTHARIO
SEDUCTION LURE BRIBE CHARM
SEDUCTIVE TEMPTING
SEDULOUS BUSY INTENT STUDIED
DILIGENT UNTIRING
SEDULOUSNESS INDUSTRY
SEDUM MOSS ORPINE SENGREEN
SEE LO EYE KEN SPY VID DATE ESPY
LOOK MIND NOTE PIPE SEAT SEGE
SPOT VIDE VIEW BESEE CATCH CHAIR
SIEGE SIGHT STOOL TENEZ WATCH
ATTEND BEHOLD DESCRY NOTICE
QUAERE REMARK SURVEY ARCHSEE
DISCERN GLIMPSE OBSERVE
WITNESS CATHEDRA CONCEIVE
PERCEIVE

(— AROVE) VS
(— BELOW) VI
(— FIT) CHOOSE
(— INTO) INSEE PENETRATE
(— THROUGH) RUMBLE
(— TO) FIX
(— VISIONS) SCRY
SEED REN MAW NIB PIP BEAN BOIL
CHAT CORN DIKA GERM KOLA LIMA
MOTE SETH TARE BEHEN BERRY
CACAO CARAT CARVY GRAIN LUPIN
SEMEN SPAWN SPERM SPORE
STONE ABILLA ACHENE ACINUS
ADZUKI BONDUC CACOON CARNEL
FENNEL KERNEL LEGUME LENTIL
NICKER NUTLET PIGNON PIPPIN
TILLEY ACHIOTE ACHUETE ALPISTE
ANISEED BUCKEYE CALINUT
FRIJOLE HARICOT HAYSEED
SEEDKIN SEEDLET SEMINAL
AMBRETTE COKERNUT CYDONIUM
DILLSEED FLAXSEED FLEASEED
HEMPSEED PIGNOLIA PRINCIPE
SEEDLING SEEDNESS PISTACHIO
PROPAGULE
(— COATING) TESTA
(— COVER) TESTA
(— OF MAPLE) SAMARA
(AROMATIC —S) ANISE
(COFFEE —) PEABERRY
(COLE —) COLZA
(EDIBLE —) PEA BEAN
(FENUGREEK —) HELBEH
(GRAPE —) ACINUS
(IMMATURE —) OVULE
(MUSTARD —) SENVY SINEWY
(NUTLIKE —) PEANUT
(OILY —) ARGAN ABILLA
(PALM —) COROZO
(POPPY —) MAW MOHNOEED
(SESAME —) JINJILI GINGELLY
(PL.) ANISE COFFEE SESAME ZERAIM
IGNATIA LARKSPUR
(PREF.) COCC(O) GON(O) OVULI
SEMINI SEMINULI SPERM(A)(ATI)
(ATIO)(ATO)(I)(IO)(O) SPOR(I)(IDI)(O)
(ULI)
(BEAK-LIKE —) RYNCO
(SUFF.) COCCAL CUCCIC SPERM(A)
(AE)(AL)(IA)(IC)(OUS)(UM)(Y) SPORA
SPORANGE SPORANGIATE
SPORANGIUM SPORE SPORIC
SPORIDIA SPORIUM SPOROUS
SPORY
SEEDCAKE WIG WIGG
SEEDCASE TEST TESTA THECA
SEED COAT ARIL TESTA SPIRICLE
SEEDED ARABLE
SEEDER SEEDMAN
SEEDLING FREE LINER
SEEDS
(PREF.) GRANI
SEEDY MANGY SCUFFY

SEEING SIGHT SIGHTED
(— THAT) SITH SINCE
SEEK ASK BEG SIC WOO BUSK FAND
FEEL FISH FOND FORK HUNT LAIT
LOOK SICK SIFT COURT DELVE ESSAY
FETCH SCOUR APPETE BOTTOM
FERRET FOLLOW FRAIST PURSUE
SEARCH FORSEEK INQUIRE
RANSACK REQUIRE RUMMAGE
SOLICIT ENDEAVOR
(— AFTER) SUE SUIT ENSUE
EXPLORE
(— AIMLESSLY) PROG
(— FAVOR) WISH
(— FOR) APPETE EXPLORE
(— IN MARRIAGE) WOO PRETEND
(— OUT) COMB ENSEARCH
(— TO ATTAIN) ASPIRE
(— URGENTLY) PRESS
SEEKER TRACER PETITOR ZETETIC
SEARCHER
(— AFTER FACTS) GRADGRIND
(— OF KNOWLEDGE) PHILONIST
(JOB —) CHANCER
(PLEASURE —) FRANION
SEEKING SOKE SOKEN ZETETIC
(SUFF.) PETAL
SEEM BID EYE SEE FARE LOOK PEER
SOUND APPEAR BESEEM REGARD
(— TO BE) LIKE
(IT —S) SEMBLE
SEEMING GUISE QUASI LIKELY
SEEMLY APPARENT SEMBLANT
(PREF.) QUASI
SEEMINGLY QUASI SEEMLY
SEEMING
SEEMLINESS GRACE DECENCY
DECORUM
SEEMLY FIT TALL CIVIL COMELY
DECENT LIKELY MODEST BECOMING
DECOROUS GRACEFUL
SEEP LEAK OOZE SIPE EXUDE
PERCOLATE
SEEPAGE SEEP SIPAGE SPRING
SEEPY WEEPY
SEER SIR SWAMI MOPSUS ORACLE
SCRYER PROPHET CHALDEAN
MELAMPUS
SEERBAND TURBAN
SEERESS SAGA SIBYL VOLVA
ALRUNE ALBRUNA PHOIBAD
SEESAW PUMP TILT DANDLE TEETER
TIDDLE TILTER TITTER TOTTER
SEETHE FRY JUG BOIL CREE ITCH
STEW WALL WALM BULLER HOTTER
SIMMER BLUBBER ELIXATE FERMENT
SEETHING ASEETHE BOILING
HUMMING ITCHING SCALDING
SEGMENT CUT LAP FALL HAND LITH
MERE PART BLANK CHORD ELITE
FEMUR FURCA SHARE SLICE TMEMA
CANTLE GLOSSA LENGTH SAMPLE
SYZYGY ARTICLE DIGITUS EXERGUE

FESTOON ISOMERE MYOMERE
MYOTOME SECTION SETIGER
ANTIMERE BRACHIUM COLUMNAL
DACTYLUS DIVISION GONOTOME
HYPOMERE INTERVAL MESOMERE
METAMERE MYOCOMMA NARICORN
(— OF CASK) CANT
(— OF CAULIFLOWER) FLOWERET
(— OF CIRCLE) SECTION
(— OF COMMUNITY) FACIES
(— OF EARTH'S CRUST) GRABEN
(— OF FIBER) BAND
(— OF INSECT'S LEG) FEMUR
TROCHANTER
(— OF IRIS) FALL
(— OF LEAF) LACINIA
(— OF MAXILLA) STIPES SUBGALEA
(— OF RATTLESNAKE'S RATTLE)
BUTTON
(— OF SPEECH) DOMAIN
(ABDOMINAL —) URITE UROMERE
PROPODEON
(BODY —) SOMITE
(HERALDIC —) FLANCH FLANCHE
(INSTRUCTIONAL —) LESSON
(MERE —) SNAPSHOT
(PEASANT —) HERA
(SUFF.) MERE TMEMA TMESIS
(— OF) ILE
SEGMENTAL MERISTIC
SEGMENTATION CLEAVAGE
(SUFF.) TOMA TOME TOMIC TOMOUS
TOMY
SEGMENTED INSECTED
SEGNO SIGN
SEGREGATE SHED SEVER INTERN
ISOLATE CLASSIFY INSULATE
SEPARATE
SEGREGATION APARTHEID
SEGUB (FATHER OF —) HIEL
HEZRON
SEIGNORAGE ROYALTY
SEIGNORY LORDSHIP
SEINE NET FARE TUCK TRAIN POCKET
SAGENE SPILLER MADRAGUE
(— SIGHT) ILE
SEISIN VESTURE
SEIZE BAG CAP CLY GET HAP NAB
NAP BEAK BONE CLAW CLUM FANG
GALL GLOM GRAB GRIP GRUP HAND
HENT HOOK JUMP KEEP LEVY NAIL
RAMP SMUG SNAP SPAN TAKE TIRE
YOKE CATCH CESSE CLASP CLEEK
CLICK CRIMP DRIVE GRASP GRIPE
LATCH PINCH RAVEN RAVIN REACH
REAVE SNACK ARREST ASSUME
ATTACH CLUTCH COLLAR EXTEND
FASTEN FREEZE GOBBLE NOBBLE
QUARRY SECURE SNATCH ASSEIZE
CAPTURE ENCLASP ENCLOSE
FORHENT GRABBLE GRAPPLE
IMPOUND POSSESS PREEMPT
PREHEND SCAMBLE SWALLOW

ARROGATE COMPRISE DISTRAIN
SPUILZIE SURPRISE UNDERNIM
(— AND HOLD FIRMLY) TRUSS
(— BAIT) STRIKE
(— BY NECK) SCRAG COLLAR SCRUFF
(— PREY) CHOP
(— SUDDENLY) NAB NIP SWOOP
SNATCH
(— UPON) ATTACK INFECT
(— WITH CLAWS) STRAIN
(— WITHOUT RIGHT) USURP
(— WITH TEETH) BITE
(— WITH WHOLE HAND) GLAUM
SEIZIN SASINE VESTURE
SEIZING FANG GRIP MARQUE
CAPTION SEIZURE
SEIZURE PIT BITE HOLD RAPE GRIPE
ICTUS SPELL ARREST EXTENT
PRISAL RAPTUS SNATCH TAKING
ANGARIA CAPTION CONCEIT
TELLACH DISTRESS STOPPAGE
(— IN RETALIATION) REPRISAL
(DRUG ADDICT'S —) WINGDING
(SUFF.) LEPSIA LEPSIS LEPSY LEPT(IC)
SELDOM RARE SELD RARELY
UNOFTEN
SELDOM-SEEN ANTRIN ANTERIN
SELECT ORT TAP TRY CULL PICK SIFT
SORT TAKE WALE DRAFT ELECT ELITE
PITCH TRIED ASSIGN BALLOT CHOICE
CHOOSE CLUBBY DECIDE DESUME
EXEMPT PREFER SAMPLE SINGLE
WINNOW DRAUGHT EMPANEL
EXCERPT EXTRACT OUTLOOK
EXIMIOUS HANDPICK SELECTED
(— A CAREER) GOINTO
(— BY LOT) DRAW
(— BY PATTERN) SWATCH
(— JURY) STRIKE
SELECTED DRAFT ELECT FANCY
DRAUGHT
SELECTING DRAFT GARBLING
SELECTION BLAD CHAP CULL ITEM
PICK CHOICE CHOOSE EXCERPT
EXTRACT ELECTION HAFTARAH
PERICOPE
(— OF PSALMS) HALLEL
(VERSE —) BLAUD SINGSONG
(SUFF.) ECLEXIS
SELECTIVE CHOOSY ECLECTIC
SELED (FATHER OF —) NADAB
SELENE (SISTER OF —) EOS
SELENIDE ZORGITE
SELF EGO SEL SEN JIVA SELL SOUL
DAENA NATURE PERSON PSYCHE
(INNER —) ANIMA
(OWN —) AINSELL NAINSEL
(SUPREME UNIVERSAL —) ATTA
ATMAN
(PREF.) AUT(O) AUTH(I) EGO
SELF-ACCUSATION GUILT
SELF-ACTING
(PREF.) AUT(O) AUTOMAT(O)

SELF-AGGRANDIZING IMPERIAL
SELF-ASSERTIVE BRASH PERKY
CHESTY BLUSTERY BUMPTIOUS
SELF-ASSURANCE CHEEK APLOMB
COOLNESS
SELF-ASSURED COCKY CALM
PERKY CONFIDENT
SELF-CENTERED SELFISH
SELF-CENTEREDNESS EGOTISM
SELFHOOD
SELF-COMMAND NERVE TEMPER
SELF-CONCEIT NOSISM
SELF-CONCEITED COXY PENSY
COCKSY PENCEY
SELF-CONFIDENCE CREST HUBRIS
HUTZPA CHUTZPA HUTZPAH JOLLITY
OPINION CHUTZPAH
SELF-CONFIDENT COCKSURE
FLUSH CHESTY
SELF-CONSCIOUS GAWKY
RASIIFUL
SELF-CONTAINED ABSOLUTE
SELF-CONTAINMENT CLOSURE
SELF-CONTRADICTORY ABSURD
SELF-CONTROL STAY WILL
ENCRATY MODESTY RETENUE
PATIENCE
(LOSE —) FLIP
SELF-DECEPTION FLATTERY
SELF-DEFENSE (ART OF—) AIKIDO
(ART OF —) KUNGFU
SELF-DENIAL DENIAL
SELF-DENYING ASCETIC
SELF-DESTRUCTION SUICIDE
SELF-DESTRUCTIVE SUICIDAL
SELF-DETERMINATION FREEDOM
AUTONOMY
SELF-DISCIPLINE ASCESIS
SELF-ENRICHMENT GROWTH
SELF-ESTEEM EGO PRIDE CONCEIT
SELFNESS
SELF-EVIDENT MANIFEST
SELF-EXALTATION NOSISM
ELATION
SELF-EXISTENT BEER INCREATE
UNCAUSED
SELF-FERTILIZATION AUTOGAMY
SELF-FULFILLMENT FREEDOM
SAMADHI
SELF-GENERATION AUTOGENY
SELF-GLORIFICATION VANITY
SELF-GOVERNMENT SWARAJ
SELF-HEAL ALLHEAL HOOKHEAL
HOOKWEED BLUECURLS
SELFHOOD SEITY EGOITY IPSEITY
OWNHOOD PROPRIUM SELFNESS
SELF-IDENTITY IPSEITY
SELF-IMPORTANT COXY PURDY
CHESTY COCKSY BIGGETY POMPOUS
BUMPTIOUS
SELF-INDULGENCE NICETY
PLEASURE
SELF-INDULGENT WANTON

SELFISH PIGGISH SELFFUL
DISSOCIAL
SELFISHNESS EGO SELF EGOTISM
SUICISM PHILAUTY SELFHOOD
SELFNESS
(MORBID —) PLEONEXIA
SELF-LOVE CONCEIT PHILAUTY
SELF-ORIGINATION ASEITY
SELF-POLLUTION ONANISM
SELF-POSSESSED COOL ASSURED
COMPOSED TOGETHER
SELF-POSSESSION PHLEGM COOL
POISE APLOMB COOLNESS
SANGFROID
SELF-PRODUCED
(PREF.) IDIO
SELF-REALIZATION FREEDOM
ENERGISM
SELF-RELIANT BOLD FREE
SELF-REPROACH GUILT REGRET
SELF-RESTRAINT HO HOO ASCESIS
CONTROL RESERVE RETENUE
HAVLAGAH
SELF-RIGHTEOUS STUFFY
SELF-SACRIFICING HEROIC
GALLANT
SELFSAME SAME VERY SELFSAID
IDENTICAL
SELFSAMENESS IDENTITY
SELF-SATISFIED SMUG STODGY
ASSURED
SELF SERVICE
(SUFF.) TERIA
SELF-SUFFICIENCY ASEITY
ASEITAS AUTARKY AUTARCHY
SELF-SUFFICIENT ABSOLUTE
SELF-TAUGHT PRIMITIVE
SELF-WILLED SET SENSUAL
STUBBLE WAYWARD CONTRARY
PERVERSE
SELION BUTT
SELL DO FLOG GIVE VEND CHEAP
PITCH SHAVE TRADE UTTER WRITE
AFFORD BARTER MARKET PEDDLE
AUCTION BARGAIN
(— A HORSE) CHANT
(— AT LOW PRICE) DUMP
(— BELOW COST) FOOTBALL
(— BY AUCTION) CANT ROUP
(— DRUGS ILLEGALLY) PUSH
(— FOR) BRING FETCH
(— FRAUDULENTLY) CHANT CHAUNT
(— IN SMALL QUANTITIES) RETAIL
(BUY AND —) CHOP
SELLER BOOMER BUSKER CADGER
VENDOR CHANTER FLESHER
CHANDLER
(— OF BEER) PINTPOT
(BEST —) CHARTBUSTER
(WINE —) ABKAR
SELLING
(SPECULATIVE —) AGIOTAGE
SELSYN SYNCHRO

SELVAGE EDGE LIST ROON GOUGE
FORREL LISTING STICKING
SEMACHIAH (FATHER OF —)
SHEMAIAH
SEMANTEME RHEME
SEMANTICS SEMOLOGY
SEMAPHORE FISHTAIL
SEMBLANCE FACE IDOL SHOW SIGN
COLOR GHOST GLOSS GUISE IMAGE
SCHEME VISAGE PRETEXT SEEMING
UMBRAGE LIKENESS SEMBLANT
SKERRICK SIMULACRUM
(— OF DIGNITY) FACE
(— OF REALITY) DREAM
(FALSE —) COLORING
SEME SEMY GUTTY HURTY FLEURY
GOUTTE GUTTEE BEZANTE
SEME-DE-LIS FLORETTY
SEMEI (SON OF —) MATTATHIAS
SEMELE (BROTHER OF —) POLYDORUS
(FATHER OF —) CADMUS
(MOTHER OF —) HARMONIA
(SISTER OF —) INO AGAVE AUTONOE
(SON OF —) BACCHUS
SEMEN SEED SPERM
(PREF.) GON(O) SPERM(A)(ATI)(ATIO)
(ATO)(I)(IO)(O)
(SUFF.) SPERM(A)(AE)(AL)(IA)(IC)
(OUS)(UM)(Y)
SEMESTER HALF
SEMI RIG
SEMIDARKNESS DUSK
SEMIDIAMETER RADIUS
SEMIDOME CONCHA
SEMIFLUID SOFT HUMOR
SEMIGLOSS EGGSHELL
SEMILIQUID SLAB
SEMINARY YESHIVA JUVENATE
SEMIOPAQUE HORNY
SEMIPORCELAIN GOMBROON
SEMIRAMIDE (CHARACTER IN —)
ASSUR ARSACE SEMIRAMIS
(COMPOSER OF —) ROSSINI
SEMIRAMIS (HUSBAND OF —) NINUS
(MOTHER OF —) DERCETO
SEMITE JEW ARAB HARARI SYRIAN
MOABITE SEMITIC SHEMITE
ARAMAEAN ASSYRIAN CHALDEAN
SEMITIC JEWISH
(— LANGUAGE) GAFAT
SEMITONE FEINT LIMMA DEMITONE
HEMITONE
SEMITRAILER ARTIC
SEMOLINA SUJI SEMOLA
SENAPO (DAUGHTER OF —)
CLORINDA
SENATE BOULE SENATO COUNCIL
SENATUS GEROUSIA SENATORY
(— AND PEOPLE OF ROME) SPQR
(— DIVISION) PRYTANY
SENATOR SOLON CONSUL FATHER
LAWMAKER
(PL.) ANZIANI

SENATORSHIP TOGA
SEND MIT FAST PACK SHIP ELATE
ENVOY SCEND THROW RENDER
THRILL ADDRESS CHANNEL
COMMAND CONSIGN DELIGHT
DELIVER FORWARD DISPATCH
TRANSMIT
(— ABOUT) TROLL
(— ALOFT) CROSS
(— AWAY) MAND SHIP AMAND
BANISH DISBAND DISMISS RELEGATE
(— BACK) ECHO FLING TURN WISE REMIT
REMAND REMISE RENVOY RESEND
RETURN REFRACT
(— BY MAIL) DROP
(— BY PARACHUTE) DROP
(— BY WIRE) FAX
(— DOWN) DEMIT DIMIT STRIKE
(— FOR) SUMMON
(— FORTH) BEAM BEAR CAST EMIT
MAND DIMIT FLING LANCH EFFUSE
LAUNCH OUTSEND EXPEDITE
FULMINATE
(— FORTH IN RAYS) RADIATE
(— HURTLING) SPIN
(— IN) IMMIT IMMISS INTROMIT
(— MESSAGE) TELEX BLINKER
(— OFF) POST WING
(— OFFICIALLY) ISSUE
(— OFF UNCEREMONIOUSLY) SHANK
(— OUT) BEAM EMIT AMAND SHOOT
SPEED DEDUCE DEPORT LAUNCH
DIFFUSE EXPEDITE
(— OVERSEAS) TRANSPORT
(— SWIFTLY) SPEED
(— TO JAIL) LAG MITTIMUS
(— TO PERDITION) CONFOUND
(— WITHIN) INTROMIT
(SUFF.) MISE MISS MIT
SENDING SAND
(— OF MONEY) REMITTANCE
(— OUT) EMISSIVE
(— WITHIN) INSERTION
INTROMISSION
SEND-UP PARODY TAKEOFF

SENILE DOLD ANILE DOTARD
SENILITY DOTAGE CADUCITY
PROGERIA
SENIOR AINE DEAN SIRE DOYEN
ELDER ANCIENT SUPERIOR

SENIORITY AGE ANCIENTY
SIGNEURY
SENNACHERIB (FATHER OF —)
SARGON
(SON OF —) ESARHADDON
SENNET SPET SIGNET
SENOR DON
SENORITA MISS SRTA SRITA
SENSATION FEEL ITCH SOUR STIR
SENSE TABET TASTE TIBBIT VEDANA
FEELING ESTHESIS EXPERIENCE
(— OF COLD) RHIGOSIS
(— OF FRIGHT) FRISSON
(— OF HEAT) HOTNESS
(— OF PAIN) ALGESIS
(ANTICIPATORY —) FOREFEEL
(BURNING —) ARDOR
(DARTING —) SHOOT
(IRRITATING —) ITCH
(STRONG —) CREEP
(SUBJECTIVE —) AURA
(TASTE —) GUST BITTER
(TINGLING —) DIRL
(VIBRATING —) FREMITUS
(VISUAL —) PHOSE PHOTOMA
(PREF.) AESTHESIO ESTHESIO
SENSATIONAL GORY BOFFO LURID
YELLOW SAFFRON SPLASHY
TABLOID THRILLY STUNNING
MELODRAMATIC
SENSATIONALISM BLARE
SENSISM
SENSE WIT FEEL SALT SMELL LETTER
MATTER REASON SCONCE WISDOM
FEELING HEARING MARBLES
MEANING SMEDDUM CARRIAGE
GUMPTION JUDGMENT
(— OF APPREHENSION) ANXIETY
(— OF DUTY) PIETY
(— OF HEARING) EAR
(— OF HUMOR) MUSIC
(— OF MOVEMENT) KINESTHESIA
KINESTHESIS KINAESTHESIS
(— OF MYSTERY) MYSTIQUE
(— OF ONENESS) KINSHIP
(— OF OUTRAGE) SHOCK
(— OF PANIC) JITTERS
(— OF RIGHT) GRACE
(— OF SHAME) PUDOR
(— OF SIGHT) VISION
(— OF SMELL) SCENT
(— OF STYLE) PANACHE
(— OF SUPERIORITY) EGOTISM
(— OF TASTE) GUST PALATE
GUSTATION
(— OF TOUCH) FEEL TASTE
(— OF WORD) ETYMON
(— ON ONE'S WORTH) PRIDE
(— THE MEANING OF) READ
(COMMON —) NOUS SALT BALANCE
GUMPTION
(DISCRIMINATING —) FLAIR
(GOOD —) MATTER

(LACKING —) INEPT
(MAKE —) ADDUP FOLLOW
(MORAL —) CONSCIENCE
(PLAIN —) ENGLISH
(RIGHT —S) MIND
(SOUND —) MATTER
SENSE AND SENSIBILITY
(AUTHOR OF —) AUSTEN
(CHARACTER IN —) JOHN LUCY
EDWARD ELINOR STEELE BRANDON
FERRARS MARIANNE WILLOUGHBY
SENSE-DATUM SENSUM
SENSELESS MAD COLD DUMB SILLY
FRIGID STUPID UNWISE WANTON
FOOLISH IDIOTIC PEEVISH SOTTISH
UNIDEAED POINTLESS REASONLESS
SENSIBILITY HEART SENSE FEELING
DELICACY ESTHESIA JUDGMENT
(PL.) FEELINGS
SENSIBLE SANE WISE AWARE PRIVY
WITTY ACTUAL FEELABLE MATERIAL
PASSIBLE RATIONAL SENSICAL
SENTIENT WISELIKE PERCEPTIBLE
SENSITIVE FINE KEEN SORE ALIVE
MIFFY QUICK KITTLY LIABLE NIMBLE
TENDER TETCHY FEELING NERVOUS
PRICKLY ALLERGIC DELICATE
EROGENIC SENSIBLE SENTIENT
SKINLESS TOUCHOUS
(— TO PAIN) TART
(NERVOUSLY —) TOUCHY
(TOO —) OVERSTRUNG
SENSITIVENESS SENSE TOUCH
ALGESIA DELICACY
SENSITIVE PEA HONEYCUP
SENSITIVE PLANT MIMOSA
SENSITIVITY FLESH ANTENNA
DELICACY FINENESS
SENSITIZER CYANINE
SENSORY SENSUAL AFFERENT
SENSUAL LEWD BRUTE MUDDY
CARNAL FLESHY SULTRY WANTON
BEASTLY BESTIAL BRUTISH FLESHLY
LESBIAN SWINISH PANDEMIC
SENSUOUS
SENSUALITY FLESH LIKING LUXURY
ANIMALISM
SENSUOUS SOFT LYDIAN SATINY
SENSAL FLESHLY SENSUAL
LUSCIOUS SENSIBLE
SENTENCE BAN DIT RAP SAW DAMN
DOOM TIME AWARD FUTWA JUISE
TENER TROPE ARREST ASSIZE
COMMIT DECREE DEPORT JUWISE
KERNEL REASON ADJUDGE
CENSURE CONDEMN FLOATER
IMPRESA LAGGING FOREDOOM
JUDGMENT VERSICLE PALINDROME
(— CONTAINING ALL LETTERS)
PANGRAM
(— CONTAINING EACH LETTER)
PANGRAM
(— INDICATING CHARACTER) MOTTO

(— OF TEN YEARS IN PRISON) DIME
(CONCISE —S) LACONICS
(IMPRISONMENT —) LAG RAP LIFE
LAGGING STRETCH
(KIND OF —) CLEFT
(MUSICAL —) PERIOD
(SERVE A —) DOTIME
(SHORT —) CLAUSE
(WITTY —) ATTICISM
SENTENTIOUS CONCISE LACONIC
SENTIENCE SENSE
SENTIENT AWARE FEELING SENSILE
SENSIVE SENSEFUL SENSIBLE
SENTIMENT MIND POSY ETHNOS
GENIUS HOBNOB NOTION PLEDGE
FEELING OPINION
(— IN DRINKING) HOBNOB
(EXCESSIVE —) SCHWARMEREI
(FALSE —) FALSETTO
(SLOPPY —) DRIP
SENTIMENTAL SLAB SOFT CORNY
GOOEY GUSHY MUSHY SAPPY
SOBBY SOPPY SOUPY TEARY FRUITY
SLUSHY SPOONY SUGARY SYRUPY
INSIPID MAUDLIN MAWKISH
ROMANTIC SCHMALZY SNIVELLY
MOONSTRUCK NOVELETTISH
(MORBIDLY —) WERTHERIAN
(OVERLY —) MUSHY
SENTIMENTALISM BATHOS
SCHMALZ SCHMALTZ
SENTIMENTALIST SOFTHEAD
SENTIMENTALITY GOO HAM
MUSH BLURB SIRUP SYRUP BATHOS
(INTOLERABLE —) TREACLE
(MAUDLIN —) GOO
SENTIMENTAL TOMMY (AUTHOR
OF —) BARRIE
(CHARACTER IN —) JEAN AARON
LOTTA NYLES TOMMY GRIZEL
ELSPETH
SENTINEL WAIT DEINO GUARD
WATCH BANTAY PICKET SENTRY
WARDEN PICQUET COCKATOO
PEPHEDRO WATCHMAN
(MOUNTED —) VEDET VEDETTE
(PL.) GRAEAE GRAIAE
SENTINEL BOX STATION
WATCHCASE
SENTRY KITE WATCH SENTINEL
SEPAL ALA LEAF HELMET LEAFLET
SEPARATE CUT TOM COMB CULL
CURD DEAL FALL FRAY FREE HAZE
PART REDD SERE SIFT SORT TEAR
TWIN ASIDE BLEED BREAK CALVE
ELONG FENCE FLAKE HEDGE PARTY
SCALE SEVER SIEVE SKILL SPLIT
TWAIN TWIST ABDUCT ABRUPT
ASSORT AVULSE BISECT CLEAVE
DECIDE DEPART DETACH DIGEST
DIVIDE DIVISI FILTER PROPER
REMOTE SCREEN SECERN SECRET
SEJOIN SETTLE SINGLE SOLUTE

SPREAD SUNDER SUNDRY SWATCH
UNLUTE WINNOW ABSCISE ABSCISS
BRACKET CONCERN DIALYZE
DISALLY DISCERP DISJOIN DISLINK
DISPAIR DISPART DIVERSE EXPANSE
FISSION ISOLATE SCATTER SCIOLTO
SECTION SEJUNCT SEVERAL
SWINGLE TAKEOUT ABSTRACT
BULKHEAD DECOUPLE DETACHED
DIFFRACT DISCRETE DISJOINT
DISSEVER DISSOLVE DISTINCT
DISTRACT DISUNITE DIVIDANT
DIVIDUAL FRACTION LAMINATE
LEVIGATE LIBERATE PECULIAR
SEVERATE SPORADIC UNMINGLE
UNSOLDER UNSTRING RESPECTIVE
(— BY BEATING) SCUTCH
(— BY CROSSWALL) ABJOINT
(— BY PICKING) LEASE LEAZE
(— COINS) JOURNEY
(— COMBATANTS) STICKLE
(— COPIES) DECOLLATE
(— FIBERS) HACKLE
(— FROM HERD) IMPRIME
(— GRAIN FROM CHAFF) FAN CAVE
WINNOW
(— HAIR) BLOCK
(— INTO COMPONENTS) STRIP
(— INTO FLOCKS) DRAFT DRAUGHT
(— INTO SHREDS) TEASE
(— ONESELF) ABDICATE
(— ORE) JIG SMELT DILLUE
(— SHEEP) DRAW
(— THREADS) SLEY SLEAVE
(PREF.) APH APO CHORI(ST)(STO)
ECCRINO IDIO
SEPARATED FREE ALONE BROKEN
REMOTE DISTANT DIVIDED
ABSTRACT ISOLATED RESOLVED
(— BY INTERVAL) OPEN
(PREF.) CHORI(ST)(STO) DIALY
SEPARATELY APART SINGLY
SUNDRY ASUNDER DIVISIM SEVERAL
SUNDERLY ABSOLUTELY
SEPARATING BETWEEN
SEPARATION GAP GULF PART RENT
SHED BREAK CHASM SPLIT SCHISM
BARRIER DIVORCE ELUTION PARTING
ANALYSIS AUTOTOMY AVULSION
CREAMING DECISION DIALYSIS
DISTANCE DISUNION DIVISION
INCISION SHEDDING SOLUTION
TWINNING SEQUESTER
(— OF BODY PARTS) ABDUCTION
(— OF COMPONENTS) RESOLUTION
(— OF LEAF) CHORISIS
(— OF MAN AND WIFE) ZIHAR
DIVORCE
(— OF METALS) DEPART
(— OF PIGMENT) FLOATING
(— OF SUSPENDED MATTER)
PRECIPITATION
(— OF WORD PARTS) TMESIS

(— OF YEAST IN BEER) BREAK
(ABNORMAL —) SOLUTION
(MENTAL —) PRECISION
(ORE —) FLOTATION
(PREF.) DE
SEPARATIST ZOARITE BIMMELER
SEPARATOR RAVEL PARTER
CREAMER SETTLER SEVERER
SUBSIDER
SEPARATRIX SLASH DIAGONAL
SEPHESTIA (FATHER OF —)
DAMOCLES
(HUSBAND OF —) MAXIMUS
(LOVER OF —) MENAPHON
(SON OF —) PLEUSIDIPPUS
SEPIA COCONUT SEPIARY
SEPOY PANDY TELINGA
SEPT KIN
SEPTEMBER 29 MICHAELMAS
SEPTET SEPTUOR
SEPTIC PURULENT
SEPTIOLITE MEERSCHAUM
SEPTIVALENT HEPTAD
SEPTUAGINT LXX
SEPTUM VITTA TABULA MYOTOME
PHRAGMA MYOCOMMA
SEPULCHER BIER GRAVE TITLE
CENOTAPH MONUMENT MORTUARY
SEPULCHRAL HOLLOW CHARNEL
TUMULARY
SEPULTURE BURIAL
SEQUEL SUITE EFFECT SEQUENT
BACKWASH SEQUENCE
(UNEXPECTED —) AFTERCLAP
SEQUENCE ROPE SUIT ORDER
TRACT TRAIN DOCKET ENTAIL
SEQUEL SERIES STRING CADENCE
CORONET SEQUENT SUCCESS
SPECTRUM STRAIGHT
(— IN ACID) EXON
(— IN MELODY) AGOGE
(— IN NUCLEIC ACID) INTRON
(— OF ARCS) PATH
(— OF BEHAVIOR) ACT
(— OF BILLIARD SHOTS) BREAK
(— OF CARDS) QUART TENACE
STRINGER
(— OF CHESS MOVES) DEFENCE
DEFENSE
(— OF EVENTS) CYCLE SCENARIO
(— OF MELODRAMA) CHASE
(— OF MESSAGES) QUEUE
(— OF ROCK UNITS) SECTION
(— OF SOUNDS) AFFIX
(— OF 3 NUCLEOTIDES) CODON
(ACTING —) EXTERIOR
(CUSTOMARY —) COURSE
(DNA —) HOMEOBOX
(FILM —) INTERCUT
(KIND OF —) CAUCHY
(LITURGICAL —) CANON
SEQUENT ENSUANT SEQUITUR
SEQUENTIAL SERIATE

SEQUESTER SINGLE ISOLATE
RECLUDE
SEQUESTERED LONELY PRIVATE
RECLUSE RETIRED SECLUDED
SOLITARY
SEQUIN CHICK SPANG VENTIN
ZEQUIN CHEQUIN CHEQUEEN
VENETIAN ZECCHINO
(PL.) GLITTER
SERAGLIO HAREM SERAI ZENANA
SERAH (FATHER OF —) ASHER
SERAI INN
SERAIAH (BROTHER OF —) BARUCH
OTHNIEL
(FATHER OF —) KENAZ NERIAH
HILKIAH TANHUMETH
SERAPHIC ANGELIC BEATIFIC
SERBOCROATIAN ILLYRIAN
SERE SEAR SERULE UNGREEN
HALOSERE
SERED (FATHER OF —) ZEBULUN
SERENADE AUBADE HORNING
ALBORADA NOCTURNE SERENATA
(MOCK —) SHIVAREE
SERENADER WAIT
SERENE CALM EVEN CLEAR LITHE
SEDATE SMOOTH HALCYON
DECOROUS
SERENITY CALM PEACE REPOSE
SERF BOND THEW CHURL HELOT
SLAVE THEOW THETE PENEST
SERVUS THRALL BONDMAN
COLONUS PEASANT VILLEIN
ADSCRIPT PRAEDIAL YANACONA
SERFDOM BONDAGE HELOTRY
SERFAGE SERVAGE HELOTISM
SERFHOOD SERFSHIP
SERGE SAY SAGATHY
SERGEANT NCO TOP SARGE CHIAUS
NONCOM DESKMAN SERVANT
TOPKICK HAVILDAR SERIAUNT
SERGEANT-AT-LAW COUNTOR
COUNTOUR
SERGEANT FISH LING CABIO COBIA
SNOOK BONITO CUBBYYEW
SERGEANT MAJOR PINTANO
SERIAL SEQUENTIAL
SERIALLY SERIATIM
SERIEMA CARIAMA GRUIFORM
SCREAMER
SERIES RUN SET ECCA RANK SUIT
TIRE CHAIN DRIFT DWYKA ORDER
SUITE TALLY TRACE COURSE
EOCENE SEQUEL STRING SYSTEM
BATTERY CASCADE CATALOG
BEADROLL SEQUENCE
PROGRESSION
(— GATHERED TOGETHER) SORITES
(— IN LINE) ROW
(— OF ABSTRACTS) SYLLABUS
(— OF ARCHES) ARCADE
(— OF BALLET TURNS) CHAINE
(— OF BALLS) OVER

(— OF BOAT RACES) REGATTA
(— OF CELLS) FILAMENT
(— OF CHARACTERS) CLINE
(— OF CHESS MOVES) COOK
(— OF CLASHES) CLATTER
(— OF COMMUNITIES) SERE
(— OF DANCE MOVEMENTS) ADAGIO
(— OF DRAIN TILES) FIELD
(— OF ELEMENTS) PERIOD
(— OF EVENTS) EPOS ACTION
(— OF EXTRACTS) CATENA
(— OF FORTIFICATIONS) CEINTURE
(— OF GAMES) RUBBER
(— OF IMAGES) DREAM
(— OF LEGENDS) SAGA
(— OF LIPS) GILL
(— OF MASSES) TRENTAL
(— OF MEETINGS) SESSION
(— OF METAL DISKS) PILE
(— OF MILITARY OPERATIONS)
CAMPAIGN
(— OF MOVEMENTS) DANCE
(— OF NEIGHBORING LOTS) COTE
(— OF NOTES) GAMUT GLISSADE
(— OF PASSES) FAENA
(— OF PILES) DRIFT
(— OF POEMS) DIVAN DIWAN
(— OF PRAYERS) COURSE SYNAPTE
(— OF RACES) CIRCUIT
(— OF REASONS) ARGUMENT
(— OF RINGS) COIL GIMMAL
(— OF ROOMS) SWEEP
(— OF SHOTS) BURST
(— OF SIMILAR STRUCTURES)
STROBILA
(— OF SLALOM GATES) FLUSH
(— OF SLIPS) DOCK
(— OF SOILS) CECIL
(— OF STAIRS) FLIGHT
(— OF STAMPS) SET
(— OF STEPS) STAIR STAIRS
(— OF STITCHES) STAY
(— OF STRAPS) LADDER
(— OF STRATA) KAROO MEASURES
(— OF STROKES) RALLY
(— OF TANKS) SOAPER
(— OF THIRTY MASSES) TRENTAL
(— OF THREADS) BINDER STUFFER
(— OF TONES) SCALE
(— OF TRAVELS) ODYSSEY
(— OF VERSES) ANTIPHON
(— OF WORDS) ACROSTIC ALPHABET
(CARD —) CORONET
(CONNECTED —) CATENA
(CONSECUTIVE —) STREAK
(DANCE —) DOUBLE
(GEOLOGICAL —) ECCA LIAS DWYKA
KENAI EOCENE MOLASSE KEEWATIN
(GRADUATED —) SCALE
(IMPRESSIVE —) ARRAY
(RADIOACTIVE —) FAMILY
(PREF.) HIRMO

SERIOUS RUM SAD DEEP HIGH
ACUTE GRAVE HEAVY SOBER SOLID
STAID DEMURE SEDATE SEVERE
SOLEMN SOMBER SOMBRE SULLEN
AUSTERE CAPITAL EARNEST
SERIOSO WEIGHTY GRIEVOUS
(PREF.) SERIO
SERIOUSLY BAD ILL DOWN SADLY
DEEPLY GRAVELY SOLIDLY
SERIOUSNESS EARNEST GRAVITY
SADNESS GRAVITAS SOBRIETY
SERMON SPELL SUTRA HOMILY
POSTIL ADDRESS FUNERAL
KHUTBAH SEREMENT SERMONET
PREACHMENT
(MUSLIM —) KHOTBAH KHOTBEH
KHUTBAH
SERMONIZE LECTURE
SERMONIZING MORALITY
SEROPURULENT SANIOUS
SEROUS ICHOROUS
SEROW THAR JAGLA SERAU
SERPENT
(ALSO SEE SNAKE) AHI SEPS WORM
ABOMA ADDER APEPI ATHER OPHIS
SIREN SNAKE TRAIN CHITAL DIPSAS
DRAGON GERARD HYDRUS PYTHON
APOPHIS PRESTER SCYTALE
JARARACA OPHIDIAN
(— WORSHIPER) NAASSENE
(FEATHERED —) GUCUMATZ
KUKULKAN
(HERALDIC —) REMORA
(NORSE —) GOIN
(SACRED —) AVANYU AWANYU
(SKY —) AHI
(PREF.) COLUBRI OPHI(O) SERPU
VIPERI
(SUFF.) OPHIS
SERPENTINE SNAKY SPIRY OPHITE
SNAKISH BOWENITE METAXITE
SCROLLED MARMOLITE
SERPENT STAR OPHIURAN
SERRANO PERCOID GITANEMUK
SERRATE SAWED ARGUTE RAFFLE
NOTCHED SERRIED
SERRATION SERRA DENTILE
SERUG (FATHER OF —) REU
SERUM WHEY FLUID BIOLOGIC
(PREF.) ORO ORRHO SERO
SERVANT BOY FAG KID MAN PUG
TAG AMAH BATA COOK DASI DAVY
HELP HIND JACK LUCE MATY MOZO
ALILA BAGOT BOOTS BOULT DAVUS
GILLY GROOM HAMAL MAMMY
SEWER SLAVE SOSIA SPEED USHER
ABDIEL ANDREW BATMAN BEARER
BILDAR BUTLER CHAKAR CLASHY
DORINE EWERER FEEDER FERASH
FLUNKY GILLIE GRUMIO HAIDUK
HARLOT KHAMAL MENIAL PAMELA
SIRCAR SKIVVY SLAVEY TEABOY

TEAGUE TRANIO VARLET VASSAL
VOIDER ANCILLA BOOTBOY
BOUCHAL COURIER DUFTERY
FAMULUS FEODARY FERRASH
FLUNKEY FOOTMAN GENERAL
GHILLIE MALCHUS PANDOUR
PANTLER PAPELON PIQUEUR
PISANIO WASHPOT ASSIGNEE
CHAPRASI CROMWELL DOMESTIC
FOLLOWER GRASSCUT HENCHMAN
HOUSEBOY MANCIPLE MINISTER
OUTRIDER PANTHINO PHILOTUS
PINDARUS SERGEANT SERVITOR
STANDARD TRENCHER VADELECT
WARDMAID KITCHENER OBSERVANT
(— IN CHARGE OF BREAD) PANTLER
(— IN CHARGE OF DAIRY) DEY
(— IN OFFICE) DUFTERY
(— OF SCHOLAR OR MAGICIAN)
FAMULUS
(— WHO CARVES) TRENCHER
(— WHO CLEARS TABLE) VOIDER
(— WHO RUNS BEFORE CARRIAGE)
PIQUEUR
(— WHO SERVES TABLE) SEWER
(ARMED —) PANDOUR
(ARMY —) BATMAN LASCAR
(BENGAL —) MEHTAR SIRCAR
(BODY —) VALET SIRDAR
(BOY —) BOY KNAVE CHOKRA
BOUCHAL
(CAMP —) BILDAR
(CLOWNISH —) SPEED LAUNCE
(COLLEGE —) GYP SKIP SCOUT
(FEMALE —) AMA NAN AMAH DASI
GIRL LASS MAID MAMMY NURSE
WENCH PAMELA SKIVVY ANCILLA
HANDMAID MUCHACHA WARDMAID
(GENERAL —) FACTOTUM
(HEAD —) BUTLER TINDAL
(HIGH PRIEST'S —) MALCHUS
(HINDU —) DAS DASI
(HOUSE —) COOK HEWE SEWER
DOMESTIC MATRANEE SCULLION
(INDIAN —) AYAH
(KITCHEN —) COOK WASHPOT
(LORD OR KING'S —) THANE
(LYING —) FAG
(MAID —) NAN DONNE
(MAN —) BOY JACK MOZO SWAIN
VALET ANDREW GILLIE KNIGHT
GHILLIE KHANSAMA MUCHACHO
SERVITOR
(MISCHIEVOUS —) TEAGUE
(NON-RESIDENT —) DAILY
(PETULANT —) DORINE
(PHILIPPINE —) BATA ALILA
(SCOTTISH —) JURR
(SOLDIER'S —) PAGE
(TRUSTY —) TROUT
(PL.) FOLK VOLK STAFF FAMILIA
NETHINIM

SERVE DO KA ACT AID HOP GIVE
HELP LEAP SHEW SLAP STAY TEND
TOSS WAIT COVER FRAME HORSE
SARRA STAND ANSWER ASSIST
FRIEND INTEND SAIRVE SARROW
SETTLE SPREAD SUCCOR WAITON
ADVANCE ASSERVE BESTEAD
CONVENT FORWARD FURTHER
SERVICE FUNCTION
(— A DISH) MESS
(— AS ESCORT) SQUIRE
(— AS HOST) GIVE
(— AS SUBSTITUTE) PASS
(— AS WELL AS) AVAIL
(— DRINK) SKINK
(— FOOD) HASH KITCHEN
(— FOR PASTURE) GRAZE
(— OBSEQUIOUSLY) LACKEY
LACQUEY
(— PERFECTLY) ACE
(SUFF.) (— FOR) ORY
SERVER SALVER TUREEN ACOLYTE
MINISTER
SERVICE AID FEE CENS DUTY HELP
RITE TIDE YOKE FAVOR MUSAF
STEAD DEVOIR EMPLOY ERRAND
FACTOR OFFICE YIZKOR BENEFIT
BONDAGE CHAKARI CORNAGE
FUNERAL LITURGY OBSEQUY
RETINUE SERVAGE SERVING
BREEDING EQUIPAGE FUNCTION
HEADWARD KINDNESS MINISTRY
ROUNDING TENDANCE SERVITIUM
(ASSIGNED —) MYOTERY
(BODYGUARD —) INWARD
(BREAKFAST —) DEJEUNER
(CHORAL —) MATIN
(CHURCH —) LAUDS CHAPEL
CHURCH HEARING STATION SYNAXIS
ASPERGES EVENSONG
(COFFEE —) CABARET
(COMMUNICATION —) TELEX
(COMPULSORY —) ANGARIA
(DOMESTIC —) CHAKARI
(FEUDAL —) BOON AVERA ARRIAGE
CORNAGE SEAWARD HEADWARD
(FUNERAL —) HERSE HEARSE
(MILITARY —) ARMS CAMP DUTY
ESCUAGE
(MILITIA —) COMMANDO
(RELIGIOUS —) AHA SEDER COMMON
(SECRET —) OGPU
(TENNIS —) ACE LET
SERVICEABLE UTILE USEFUL
DURABLE THRIFTY FRIENDLY
VAILABLE
SERVICEBERRY SHADDOW
SHADBUSH SASKATOON
SERVICE TREE SORB SORBUS
CHECKER SASKATOON
SERVILE BASE BOND ABJECT
MENIAL SUPINE VASSAL CAITIFF

SLAVISH VERNILE COISTREL
CRAWLING CRINGING SERVIENT
THEWLIKE
SERVILITY CRINGE
SERVING OBED SMACK DISHFUL
HELPING SERVIENT WHIPPING
(SUFF.) ATORY
(— FOR) ORIOUS ORY
SERVITOR FAG GROOM PUNTER
SERVANT PUNTSMAN
SERVITUDE USE VIA YOKE
BONDAGE PEONAGE SERVICE
SLAVERY SERVITUS THEOWDOM
THIRLAGE
SERVOMECHANISM SERVO
BOOSTER
SERVOMOTOR RELAY SERVO
SESAME TIL TEEL BENNE BENNI
SEMSEM VANGLO GINGILI OILSEED
WANGALA AJONJOLI BENISEED
SERGELIM
SESBANIA AGATI
SESQUITERPENE CEDROL
CLOVENE COPAENE HUMULENE
SESSION DAY BOUT DIET HOUR
SEAT COURT CLINIC SCHOOL
SEANCE ACUERDO HEARING
SEMINAR SITTING CONGRESS
SEDERUNT SEMESTER
(COURT —) HILARY
(HAVE A —) SIT
(JAM —) CLAMBAKE
(PL.) ASSIZES
(SUFF.) FEST
SESTERTIUS BRONZE
SESTINA SEXTAIN
SET DO DIP FIX GEL KIT LAY LOT MOB
PUT SIC SIT SOT CASE CREW CUBE
GAGE GANG GIVE JELL KNIT KNOT
NEST PAIR PICK PILT POSE REST SETT
SORT STEP STOW BATCH CLASS
CLOCK COVEY CROWD FIXED GAUGE
GLADE GROUP INFIX PAVER PLACE
POSIT READY STACK STAID STAND
STEAD STEEK STICK SUITE ADJUST
CIRCLE CLIQUE DEFINE FASTEN
FINALE FORMAL GLAZED GROUND
HARDEN IMPOSE PARCEL SERIES
SETTLE SPREAD SQUARE STATED
BATTERY BOILING COMPANY
COMPOSE CONFIRM COTERIE
DEPOSIT DISPOSE ENCHASE
FACTION IMPLANT INSTATE
PLATOON SERVICE STATION STIFFEN
STRATUM EQUIPAGE PANTALON
SEQUENCE SOLIDIFY STANDARD
(— ABOUT) FALL FANG GANG BEGIN
ADDRESS
(— ACROSS) TRANSVERSE
(— AFLOAT) LAUNCH
(— APART) MARK SHED DEMARK
DESIGN DEVOTE EXEMPT SACRED
SEPONE SEPOSE APPOINT ISOLATE

RESERVE ALLOCATE DEDICATE
INSULATE SEPARATE SEQUESTER
(— A PERIOD) DATE
(— A PRICE) ASK
(— ARMOR) GARNITURE
(— ARROWS IN ORDER) FRUSH
(— ASIDE) BAR DISH DROP HAIN SIDE
SINK SLIP BURKE KAPUT SEPOSE
BRACKET EARMARK PURLOIN
RESERVE SUSPEND ABROGATE
DISPENSE OVERRIDE OVERRULE
REVERSED
(— AS ONE'S SHARE) ALLOT
(— AT DEFIANCE) BEARD
(— AT LIBERTY) FREE RELEASE
LIBERATE
(— BACK TO BACK) ADDORSED
ADDOSSED
(— BEFORE) PRESENT
(— BOUNDS) PRESCRIBE
(— CLOSE TOGETHER) PAVEED
(— DOG ON) SIC SLATE
(— DOWN) JOT LAY GIVE LAND
PLANK SCORE EXPONE DEPOSIT
(— DOWN IN WRITING) SUBSCRIBE
(— DOWN UNDER NAME) TITLE
(— EDGEWISE) SURBED
(— ERECT) COCK
(— FIRMLY) FIRM STEM EMBED
IMBED PLANT POSIT
(— FORTH) DRAW ETCH SHOW GIVEN
STATE DEPART DEPICT EXPOSE
SPREAD ARTICLE DISPLAY ENOUNCE
EXHIBIT EXPOUND PRESENT
PROPONE PROPOSE PURPOSE
PROPOUND
(— FORWARD) PREFER ADVANCE
(— FREE) BAIL EASE REMIT SKILL
SOLVE ACQUIT ASSOIL ABSOLVE
DELIVER ENLARGE UNLOOSE
WINFREE ABSTRICT DISPLACE
DISSOLVE EXPEDITE UNVASSAL
(— GOING) INITIATE
(— IN ACCORD) SORT
(— IN ACTION) TRIGGER
(— IN EARTH) STRIKE
(— IN FROM MARGINS) INDENT
(— IN FRONT) PREFER
(— IN MOTION) SOW
(— IN OPERATION) DRIVE
(— IN OPPOSITION) PIT
(— IN ORDER) ARRAY FRUSH PITCH
ADIGHT DAIKER FETTLE INFORM
ADDRESS
(— IN POSITION) PLANT POSIT
STAND STICK POSITION
(— IN ROWS) RANGE
(— INTO) INLAY
(— INTO A GROOVE) DADO
(— LIMITS TO) SPAN BOUND
(— OF ACTORS) CAST
(— OF ANIMALS) TEAM
(— OF ARMS) CONVEYER

(— OF BARS) CONCAVE
(— OF BELIEFS) CREDO
(— OF BELLS) RING CHIME CARILLON
(— OF BOOKCASES) STACK
(— OF BOOKS) PLENARY
(— OF CARDS) DECK PACK
(— OF CARS) DRAG
(— OF CHARACTERS) FIELD
(— OF CHIMES) DOORBELL
(— OF CIRCUMSTANCES) CASE EGIS FRAME
(— OF CONDITIONS) REGIMEN
(— OF CORDS) SIMPLE
(— OF DISHES) GARNISH SERVICE CUPBOARD
(— OF EIGHT) OGDOAD
(— OF EXERCISES) KATA
(— OFF) FOIL MENSE SEVER SHOOT ACCENT BUNDLE BALANCE COMMEND EMBLAZE CONTRAST DECORATE EMBLAZON
(— OF FACTS) BOOK
(— OF FALSE CURLS) FRONT
(— OF FISH NETS) DRIFT
(— OF FIVE) PENTAD QUINTUPLET
(— OF FOLDED SHEETS) QUIRE
(— OF FOUR) WARP QUATENARY QUATERNION QUATERNITY
(— OFF TO ADVANTAGE) ADORN COMMEND
(— OF FURNITURE) SUITE DINETTE
(— OF GARMENTS) SUIT
(— OF GEARS) GEARSET
(— OF HIDES) KIP
(— OF HORSES) STABLE
(— OF HOUNDS) VANLAY VAUNTLAY
(— OF IDEAS) SYSTEM
(— OF JEWELLED ORNAMENTS) PARURE
(— OF LEAVES) COROLLA
(— OF LETTERS) ALPHABET
(— OF MUSICAL INSTRUMENTS) CONSORT
(— OF NETS) SHOT
(— OF NOTES) ACCORD
(— OF OPINIONS) CREDO
(— OF ORGAN PIPES) STOP
(— OF ORGANS) ARMATURE
(— OF ORNAMENTS) PARURE
(— OF PINS) KAILS KNOCKOUT
(— OF POINTS) INTERVAL
(— OF PUMPS) LIFT
(— OF QUADRILLES) LANCERS
(— OF RADIATORS) STACK
(— OF RAYS) PENCIL
(— OF ROOMS) STORY
(— OF RULES) CODE EQUITY DECALOG
(— OF SAILS) CANVAS
(— OF SHELVES) STAGE BUFFET DRESSER WHATNOT
(— OF SKI FASTENINGS) BINDING
(— OF SKINS) SHODER

(— OF STAVES) SHOOK
(— OF STEPS) LADDER
(— OF SYMBOLS) KATAKANA
(— OF TABLES) COMPUTUS
(— OF TEETH) DENTURE
(— OF TEN) DECADE
(— OF THREE) BALE TERN LEASH
(— OF TOOLS) STRING
(— OF TRAMS) JOURNEY
(— OF TWELVE) ZODIAC
(— OF TWENTY) SCORE
(— OF TYPEFACES) FAMILY
(— OF VALUES) CURRENCY
(— OF VARIATIONS) PARTITA
(— OF VATS) SOLERA
(— OF VERSES) STAVE
(— OF VOWELS) SERIES
(— OF WARP THREADS) LEA
(— OF 3 ANIMALS) LEASH
(— ON) TAR SLATE
(— ON END) UPEND
(— ONESELF) GO
(— ON FIRE) SPIT TIND LIGHT ACCEND IGNIFY IGNITE KINDLE ENFLAME INFLAME ENKINDLE
(— OUT) BOUN MAKE BOWNE FOUND SALLY START INTEND STARTLE
(— OVER) COUCH
(— RIGHT) REDD ADJUST SCHOOL SQUARE CORRECT REDRESS
(— SNARE) TAIL TILL
(— SOLIDLY) EMBED
(— STRAIGHT) DRESS
(— THICKLY) STUD
(— TO MUSIC) AIR DITTY
(— TO WORK) YOKE
(— TRAP) TELD
(— TYPE) KEYBOARD
(— UP) RIG ROAR AREAR ERECT PITCH RAISE ROUSE IMPOSE SETTLE INSTALL UPDRESS ACTIVATE ESTABLISH INSTITUTE
(— UP IN COLUMNS) TABULAR
(— UPON) BESET ATTACK AGGRESS BROWDEN
(— UPRIGHT) ERECT STAND ARRECT
(— UPSIDE DOWN) TURN
(— VALUE) APPRAISE
(— WITH BRISTLES) STRIGOSE
(— WITH GEMS) CHASE
(ANTIGEN —) SEROTYPE
(BECOME —) STRIKE
(CHESS —) MEINY MEINIE
(CHROMOSOME —) GENOME COMPLEX
(COMPLETE —) STAND
(CONSTRUCTION —) ERECTOR
(INFINITE —) FAMILY
(MATHEMATICAL —) LATTICE MANIFOLD
(MINIATURE —) DIORAMA
(RADIO —) BLOOPER

(SMART —) TON
(STAGE —) SCENE
(TELEVISION —) TUBE
(UNALTERABLY —) STOUT
(PL.) DECOR
(SUFF.) STOLE THESIS THETE THETIC
SETA STALK WHISK CHAETA SETULA
SETULE CROTCHET PODETIUM
SETBACK DASH JOLT SNAG KNOCK
LURCH BLIGHT BACKSET LICKING
PUTBACK RELAPSE REVERSE
BUSINESS COMEDOWN HAYMAKER
CONTRETEMPS
(TEMPORARY —) HICCUP
SETH (BROTHER OF —) ABEL CAIN
(FATHER OF —) ADAM
(MOTHER OF —) EVE
(SON OF —) ENOS
SETHUR (FATHER OF —) MICHAEL
SETLINE GEAR TRAWL BULTOW
OUTLINE TROTLINE
SETTEE SETTLE OTTOMAN WINDSOR
SETTER SOFA GUNDOG DROPPER
FLUSHER SETTLER
SETTERWORT PIGROOTS
SETTING SET FALL PAVE VAIL CHASE
MIDST SCENE SETUP CHATON
MILIEU FERMAIL MONTURE SITTING
INTERIOR MARQUISE MOUNTING
SHOWCASE BRILLIANT BRIOLETTE
(— APART) BETWEEN
(— FORTH) RECITAL PRESENTATION
(— FREE) SOLUTION
(— OF GEM) FOIL OUCH CHASE
GALLERY
(— OF REED) CAAMING
(— OF WHEELS) CAMBER
(CAMERA —) BULB
(FAMILIAR —) HOME
(MUSICAL —) CREDO BALLAD
BALLADE
(SHUTTER —) TIME
(STAGE —) SCENE
SETTLE BED FIT FIX ICE PAY SAG SET
SIT TAX BANK BIND CALM DAIS DEAS
FAST FIRM HAFT LEND NEST REST
ROOT SEAT SINK SNUG TOIT AGREE
CLEAR COUCH ISSUE LIGHT LODGE
ORDER PITCH PLACE PLANT QUIET
SQUAT STATE STILL ACCORD
ADJUST ALIGHT ASSIGN CLINCH
DECIDE DECREE ENCAMP LOCATE
NESTLE PURIFY RESIDE SCREEN
SECURE SOOTHE SOPITE SQUARE
ACCOUNT APPEASE APPOINT
ARRANGE BALANCE CLARIFY
COMPONE COMPOSE CONCERT
CONFIRM DEPOSIT DERAIGN INHABIT
PIONEER RESOLVE SUBSIDE
COLONIZE REGULATE SQUATTLE
CONJOBBLE RECONCILE
(— ACCOUNTS) WHACK
(— A FINE) AFFEER

(— AMICABLY) COMPOUND
(— AN ACCOUNT) PONYUP
(— BUSINESS) FEEZE PHEESE
PHEEZE
(— DOWN) CAMP SLUMP STEADY
DESCEND
(— ITSELF) INVEST
(— LANDS ON A PERSON) ENTAIL
(— ON) POINT
(— UP) PONY PONEY
(— UPON) AFFIX AGREE TIGHT
(— VERTICALLY) SQUASH
SETTLED SAD SET FIRM FIXED QUIET
STAID FORMED RANGED SEATED
SEDATE SQUARE STAPLE STATED
CERTAIN DECIDED EMPIGHT STATARY
DECOROUS RESOLVED STANDING
SEDENTARY
(NOT —) FARROW
SETTLEMENT AUL DEAL FINE FORK
MISE PACT POST BARRIO COLONY
DIKTAT MOSHAV WINDUP ACCOUNT
BIVOUAC FINANCE MAABARA
OUTPOST STATION CLERUCHY
DECISION DISPATCH JOINTURE
KEVUTZAH PRESIDIO SETTLING
SHOWDOWN TOWNSHIP
PLANTATION
(— OF JERRY-BUILT DWELLINGS)
BIDONVILLE
(— OF MONKS) SCETE SKETE
(— OF SHACKS) FAVELA FAVELLA
(— ON OUTSKIRTS) BIDONVILLE
(COLLECTIVE —) KVUTZA MOSHAV
KIBBUTZ
(HARSH —) DIKTAT
(INDIAN —) BUSTEE
(MARRIAGE —) MAHR ARRAS
DOWNSET
(NEW ZEALAND —) PA PAH
(RAPID —) BOOM
(UPLAND —) BOOLEY
SETTLER METIC SAHIB LIVYER
NESTER GRUELER PEOPLER PILGRIM
PIONEER TRIMMER FINISHER
GACHUPIN HABITANT SHAGROON
SIBERSKI SIBERYAK
(— IN AUSTRALIA) GROPER
(— IN NEW ZEALAND) SHAGROON
(DANISH —S) OSTMEN
SETTLING SIT
(— OF ESTATE) ENTAIL
(PL.) LEES SEDIMENT
SET-TO ROW MELEE BOUT TURN
PLUCK FETTLE TURNUP BRANGLE
SETUP SET SITTER ENTRAPMENT
SEVEN SEPT ZETA ZAYIN HEPTAD
SEPTET HEBDOMAD SEPTETTE
(— OF DIAMONDS) POPE
(— OF TRUMPS) MANILLA
(GROUP OF —) PLEIAD
(PREF.) HEPT(A) SEPT(I) SEPTEM
SEVENFOLD SEPTUPLE

SEVENTEEN (AUTHOR OF —)
TARKINGTON
(CHARACTER IN —) MAY JANE PRATT
BAXTER GEORGE JOHNNY WATSON
GENESIS PARCHER WILLIAM
CLEMATIS
SEVEN-UP PEDRO PITCH SLEDGE
SEVER AX AXE CUT BITE DEAL HACK
REND SLIT TWIN SHEAR SHRED
CLEAVE CUTOFF DEPART DETACH
DIVIDE SAWOFF SUNDER
DISALLY DISCERP DISCIDE DISJOIN
OUTRIVE DISSEVER PRESCIND
SEPARATE SEVERIZE
(PREF.) TEMNO
SEVERAL ODD TEN SERE WHEEN
DIVERS SUNDRY DIVERSE VARIOUS
DISTINCT MULTIPLE
(PREF.) PLURI POLY
SEVERALLY APIECE SEVERAL
SEVERANCE SUNDER SOLUTION
(— OF RELATIONSHIPS) AIR
SEVERE BAD DRY ACID BLUE
DEAR DOUR DURE FIRM HARD IRON
KEEN ROID RUDE SALT SIDE SORE
TART TAUT ACUTE BREME CRUEL
EAGER GRUFF HARSH RETHE RIGID
ROUGH SHARP SMART SNELL SOBER
SOUND STARK STEER STERN STIFF
STOUR TOUGH BITING BITTER
BRUTAL CHASTE COARSE FROSTY
HETTER SIMPLE SOLEMN STRICT
TORVID UNKIND UNMILD ACERBIC
ASCETIC AUSTERE CAUSTIC
CHRONIC CONDIGN CRUCIAL
CUTTING DRASTIC SERIOUS
SPARTAN TORVOUS UNCANNY
VICIOUS VIOLENT WEIGHTY
ACERBATE ACULEATE CATONIAN
EXACTING GRIEVOUS GRINDING
HORRIBLE IRONCLAD IRONHARD
RIGOROUS SCATHING STALWART
STRAIGHT TERMINAL TERRIBLE
STRINGENT
(MOST —) EXTREME
(VERY —) SPLITTING
SEVERELY BAD HARD BADLY STARK
STIFF HARDLY SORELY STRONG
HEAVILY ROUGHLY SMARTLY
SOUNDLY STITHLY SHREWDLY
SEVERIAN AGNOETE AGNOITE
SEVERING
(PREF.) PRISO
SEVERITY FROST RIGOR CRUELTY
TORVITY TYRANNY ACRIMONY
ASPERITY FERVENCY HARDNESS
RIGIDITY SORENESS VIOLENCE
SEW SUE FELL SEAM SLIP PREEN
STEEK NEEDLE STITCH OVERSEW
THIMBLE OVERCAST OVERHAND
(— A CORPSE) SOCK
(— LOOSELY) BASTE
(— TO REINFORCE) BAR

(— UP FERRET'S MOUTH) COPE
(— WAVED PATTERN) DICE
SEWAGE SOIL WASTE SOILAGE
SULLAGE AFFLUENT DRAINAGE
SEWERAGE WASTEWATER
SEWELLEL BEAVER BOOMER
SEWER SINK SIRE DRAFT DRAIN
FLEET ISSUE MAKER SHORE CLOACA
KILTER TACKER VENNEL BELTMAN
COPYIST CULVERT DRAUGHT
GULLION JAWHOLE SHIRRER
PIQUIERE
SEWING TACK SUTURE SEMPSTRY
(SUFF.) RHAPHY RRHAPHY
SEX KIND SECT GENDER
(FEMALE —) SMOCK
(KIND OF —) SAFE
(MALE —) WEPMANKIN
(PREF.) GEN(O)
SEX APPEAL IT OOMPH
SEXLESS NEUTER EPICENE
SEXT MIDDAY
SEXTANT (PART OF —) ARC ARM
DRUM LIMB MARK FRAME GLASS
INDEX LEVER HANDLE MIRROR
SUNSHADE TELESCOPE
SEXTET SESTET SEXTUOR
SESTETTO
SEXTON SAXON BEADLE SHAMUS
WARDEN SACRIST SHAMAOH
SHAMMES VESTURER SACRISTAN
SEXTUPLE SENARY
SEXTUPLET SESTOLE SEXTOLE
SESTOLET SEXTOLET
SEXUAL GAMIC CARNAL INTIMATE
(PREF.) GAM(ETO)(O) GON(O)
SEXY FOXY FREUDIAN
SEYCHELLES (CAPITAL OF —)
VICTORIA
(ISLAND OF —) MAHE LADIGUE
PRASLIN
SGANARELLE (BROTHER OF —)
ARISTE
(DAUGHTER OF —) LUCINDE
(WARD OF —) LEONORE ISABELLE
(WIFE OF —) MARTINE
SHA YASHIRO
SHAAPH (FATHER OF —) CALEB
JAHDAI
(MOTHER OF —) MAACHAH
SHAB RUBBERS
SHABBINESS WAFFNESS
SHABBY BASE MEAN POKY WORN
DINGY DIRTY DOWDY MANGY OURIE
POKEY RATTY SCALD SEEDY SORRY
TACKY CHEESY FROWZY GROTTY
GRUBBY GRUNGY SCABBY SCOURY
SCUFFY SCURVY SHODDY SHROVY
SLEAZY TAGRAG BUNTING MESQUIN
SCAILED SCRUBBY SCRUFFY
SCUFFED SHABBED SQUALID
PALTERLY SLIPSHOD WAFFLIKE
SHABUOTH PENTECOST

SHACHIA (FATHER OF —)
SHAHARAIM
(MOTHER OF —) HODESH
SHACK COE HUT CRIB SHAG HUMPY
HUTCH SHANTY
SHACKLE COP TIE BAND BIND BOLT
BOND GYVE LOCK STAY BASIL BILBO
CLAMP COPSE CRAMP CRANK
HUMPY TRASH TRAVE FETTER
GARTER HAMPER PINION SHANGY
STAYER SWATHE COTTAGE COUPLER
FETLOCK MANACLE MOUSING
PASTERN SHEBANG SNACKLE
TRAMMEL RESTRAIN
(PL.) IRONS
SHACKLER SLOTTER
SHAD BUCK CHAD ALLIS ALOSE
TRABU ALLICE TWAITE ALEWIFE
ANADROM CLUPEID FLATFISH
SAWBELLY
SHADBUSH DOGWOOD SERVICE
SERVICEBERRY
SHADDOCK LUCBAN POMELO
POMPION PAMPELMOUSE
POMPELMOOSE
SHADE EYE CAST DULL SCUG SHED
TONE VEIL BLEND COLOR ENNUE
GHOST GLIDE GLOOM GRAIN SCAUM
SCOUG SWALE SWILL TASTE TINCT
TINGE TRACE UMBER UMBRA
DEGREE FRESCO SHADOW SHIELD
SHROUD SPRITE STRAIN STRIPE
TONING CURTAIN ECLIPSE GRADATE
HACHURE KENNING PROTECT
SECTION SHADING UMBRAGE
BONGRACE HALFTONE UMBRELLA
(— OF COLOR) EYE CAST TONE
(— OF DIFFERENCE) NUANCE
(— OFF) GRADUATE
(— OF LINEN) ECRU
(— ON HAT) UGLY
(EYE —) UGLY
(NEUTRAL —) TAUPE
(OVERHANGING —) CANOPY
(WINDOW —) STORE
(PREF.) UMBRI
SHADED OMBRE SHADY DRUMLY
SOMBER SOMBRE DARKLING
SHADINESS GLOOM
SHADING FLUTING LAYERING
SHADOW DOG FOX BLOT SCUG TAIL
CLOUD SCOUG SHADE TRAIL UMBER
UMBRA CLEEKS DARKEN FINGER
SHROUD TAILER ISOGYRE PHANTOM
SCARROW SUGGEST UMBRAGE
UMBRATE PENUMBRA PHANTASM
SHEPHERD
(PREF.) SCI(A)(O) SKIA SKIO TENEBRI
UMBRI
SHADOWED DARKLING
SHADOWINESS GLOOM
SHADOWLESS ASCIAN WHITEOUT

SHADOWS ON THE ROCK
(AUTHOR OF —) CATHER
(CHARACTER IN —) LAVAL CECILE
HECTOR PIERRE AUCLAIR BLINKER
CHARRON EUCLIDE SAINTCYR
FRONTENAC
SHADOWY MISTY VAGUE GLOOMY
GHOSTLY OBSCURE
SHADRACH ANANIAS HANANIAH
SHADY DARK BOSKY BOWERY
CLOUDY LOUCHE SHADOWY
SHADOWY UMBROSE ADUMBRAL
SHAFT BAR NIB ROD AXLE BALK
BARB BOLT DART FUST HOLE PILE
POLE TRAM WELL ARBOR HEUGH
QUILL REACH SCAPE SHANK SHOOT
SNEAD SPRAG STAFF STALE STANG
STAVE STEAL STELE STILT STING
THILL TRUNK BOLTEL CANNON
COLUMN GNOMON SCAPUS STAPLE
TILLER TUNNEL UPRISE VAGINA
BOWTELL CHIMNEY INCLINE
MANDREL SPINDLE CAMSHAFT
DOWNCAST ESCONSON HOISTWAY
LAMPHOLE MISTREAT SHAFTWAY
STANDARD WEIGHBAR WELLHOLE
(— CONNECTING WHEELS) AXLE
(— IN GLACIER) MOULIN
(— IN WATCH) STEM
(— OF CANDLESTICK) BALUSTER
(— OF CARRIAGE) FILL SILL THILL
(— OF CART) ROD TRAM SHARP
STANG
(— OF CAVERN) DOME
(— OF CHARIOT) BEAM
(— OF CLUSTERED PIER) BOLTEL
(— OF COLUMN) FUST TIGE SCAPE
TRUNK VERGE
(— OF FEATHER) SCAPE SCAPUS
AFTERSHAFT
(— OF MINE) PIT WORK GRUFF
HEUCH HEUGH RAISE SLOPE STULM
WINZE GROOVE STAPLE INCLINE
WINNING
(— OF PADDLE) LOOM ROUND
(— OF SPEAR OR LANCE) TREE STALE
(— OF WAGON) STAVE THILL LIMBER
(HARNESS —) HEALD
(HOLLOW —) CANNON
(MAIN —) ARBOR
(ORNAMENTAL —) VERGE
(SCYTHE —) SNEAD
(STAIRWAY —) VICE
(TWISTED —) TORSO
(VENTILATION —) UPCAST UPTAKE
WINDHOLE
(PREF.) DORY SCAPI
SHAG PILE
SHAGE
(SON OF —) JONATHAN
SHAGGY SHAG SWAG HARSH NAPPY
ROUGH SHOCK TATTY TOUSY

BRUSHY COMATE HAGGED TOOSIE
HIRSUTE SHAGRAG SQUAMS
SWAGGED THRUMMY HIRSUTE
TATTERED
(REEKING) DASY LASI
SHAGREEN GALUCHAT
SHAGROON PILGRIM
SHAKE BOB DAD JAR JOG ROG WAG
WAP JOLT JOWL PLUM QUAG RESE
ROCK SHOG STIR SWAY TOZE WEVE
WHAP WHOP HOTCH JAUNT KNOCK
NIDGE QUASH SHOCK SWING TRILL
DIDDER DITHER DODDER DODDLE
EXCUSS GOGGLE HOTTER HUSTLE
JOGGLE JOUNCE JUMBLE QUATCH
QUAVER QUITCH QUIVER ROGGLE
RUFFLE SHIMMY SHIVER TOTTER
WAMBLE WANGLE WARBLE WEAKEN
WOBBLE AGITATE BRANDLE
CHOUNCE CONCUSS ROULADE
SHUDDER STAGGER SUCCUSS
TREMBLE TWITTER WHIFFLE
WHITHER BRANDISH CONVULSE
ENFEEBLE
(— A PURSUER) LOSE
(— FEATHERS) ROUSE
(— HERRING) SCUD
(— LIGHTLY) LIFT
(— OFF) ARISE EXCUSS
(— TO SEPARATE) HOTCH
(— UP) JABBLE JUMBLE RATTLE
(WIND —) ANEMOSIS
SHAKER DUSTER SIFTER DREDGER
JUMBLER POUNCET SANDBOX
SHAKING ASPEN ASHAKE TREMOR
JARRING AGITATED
(— OF AIRPLANE) BUFFET
SHAKTI TARA PRAKRITI
SHAKTIS MATRIS
SHAKUNTALA (FATHER OF —)
VISHVAMITRA
(FOSTER FATHER OF —) KANVA
(HUSBAND OF —) DUSHYANTA
(MOTHER OF —) MENAKA
(SON OF —) BHARATA
SHAKY CRANK DICKY QUAKY ROCKY
TIPSY TOTTY WONKY WOOZY
AGUISH COGGLY CRANKY GROGGY
INFIRM WAMBLY CASALTY DWAIBLE
DWEEBLE PALSIED RICKETY
SHOGGLY TITTUPY TOTTERY
COGGLEDY INSECURE
SHALE BAT BASS BONE CLOD FLAG
KOLM TILL BLAES FAKES METAL
PLATE XALLE KILLAS SHILLET
MUDSTONE SLIGGEEN TORBANITE
PORCELLANITE KUPFERSCHIEFER
SHALL SE MAY MUN MUST SALL
(— NOT) SANNA SHANT SHANNA
SHALLOON CUBICA
SHALLOT CIBOL ALLIUM ESCHALOT
SCALLION

SHALLOW EBB BANK FLAN FLAT
FLUE GLIB FLEET INANE SHOAL SILLY
SMALL FLIMSY FROTHY LITTLE
RIFFLE SLIGHT UNDEEP CRIPPLE
CURSORY TRIVIAL MAGAZINY
(PL.) FORD
SHALLOW BECOME A —) SHOAL
SHALLOWNESS INANITY
SHALLUM (FATHER OF —) BANI
KORE SHAUL JARESH JOSIAH
HOLOHESH NAPHTALI
(NEPHEW OF —) JEREMIAH
(SON OF —) HOLOHESH MAASEIAH
JEHIZKIAH
(WIFE OF —) HULDAH
SHALLUN (FATHER OF —) COLHOZEH
SHAM BAM FOB FOX GIG FAKE HOAX
MOCK PUFF BLUFF BOGUS CHEAT
DUMMY FALSE FEIGN FEINT FRAUD
LETON QUEER SHUCK SNIDE
ASSUME BRUMMY BUNYIP CHOUSE
DECEIT DUFFER HUMBUG PSEUDO
SHODDY STUMER FALSITY FORGERY
GRIMACE MOCKISH PLASTER
PRETEND STUMOUR POSTICHE
PRETENSE SPURIOUS BRUMMAGEM
PASTEBOARD SIMULACRUM
(PREF.) PSEUD(O)
SHAMAN PEAI CUREK MACHI
KAHUNA WABENO ANGEKOK
TOHUNGA CONTRARY WITCHMAN
SHAMARIAH (FATHER OF —)
REHOBOAM
SHAMASH (FATHER OF —) DIN
(SISTER OF —) ISHTAR
(WIFE OF —) AA AYA
SHAMBLE SHALE SHOOL CLOUCH
BAUCHLE SCAMBLE SHACHLE
SHACKLE SKEMMEL ABATTOIR
SHAMMOCK
(PL.) BUTCHERY
SHAMBLING SHACKLY
SHAME SISS ABASH AIDOS SHEND
SPITE ASHAME BISMER REBUKE
MORTIFY PUDENCY SCANDAL
SLANDER CONTEMPT DISGRACE
DISHONOR REPROACH SHENDING
VERGOYNE VITUPERY
(— BY CENSURE) TOUCH
SHAMED (FATHER OF —) ELPAAL
SHAMEFACED SHY
SHAMEFACEDNESS PUDENCY
SHAMEFUL BASE FOUL MEAN
GROSS HONTOUS IGNOBLE
FLAGRANT IMPROPER INFAMOUS
SHAMELESS HARD BRASH ARRANT
BRAZEN BASHLESS BROWLESS
IMMODEST IMPUDENT
SHAMELESSNESS BRASS
SHAMGAR (FATHER OF —) ANATH
SHAMIR (FATHER OF —) MICAH
(GRANDFATHER OF —) UZZIEL

SHAMMA (FATHER OF —) ZOPHAH
SHAMMAH (BROTHER OF —) DAVID
(FATHER OF —) JESSE REUEL
SHAMMAI (FATHER OF —) ONAM
REKEM
SHAMMES BEADLE
SHAMMUA (FATHER OF —) DAVID
ZACCUR
(MOTHER OF —) BATHSHEBA
(SON OF —) ABDA
SHAMPOO TRIPSIS
(— INGREDIENT) ALOE
SHAMPOOING TRIPSIS
SHAMROCK OCA SEAMROG
SHAMROOT
SHAMUS TEC SEXTON DETECTIVE
SHANK BODY CRUS GAMB JAMB
TANG FEMUR GAMBE CANNON
NIBBLE TARSUS KNUCKLE
(THREAD —) STEM
SHANNY BULLY
SHANTY SLED BOIST HUMPY HUTCH
SHACK SHEBANG CHANTIER
DOGHOUSE
SHAPE AX ADZ AXE CUT DIE HUE
ADZE BEAT BEND CAST COLE COPE
DRAW FACE FAIR FORM HACK MOLD
NICK BEVEL BLOCK BOAST BUILT
COLOR DRAPE DRESS FEIGN FORGE
FRAME GUISE HORSE JOLLY LATHE
MODEL MOULD SWAGE BROACH
CHISEL CUTOUT EFFORM FIGURE
FORMER FRAISE HAMMER JIGGER
SQUARE CHANNEL CONFORM
CONTOUR FASHION FEATURE
GESTALT INCLINE OUTLINE PATTERN
TONNEAU CONTRIVE LIKENESS
(— BY HAMMERING) SMITH
(— DIAMOND) BRUTE
(— GARMENTS) BOARD
(— LIKE AN EGG) OVOID
(— METAL) SWAGE EXTRUDE
(— OF BUST) TAILLE
(— OF ENVELOPE FLAP) KNIFE
(— ONE'S COURSE) ETTLE
(— ON POTTER'S WHEEL) THROW
(— RIGHTLY) FIT
(— ROUGHLY) BOAST SCABBLE
SCAPPLE
(— ROUGHLY WITH CHISEL) BOAST
(— STONE) BROACH SCABBLE
(CLAY —) FLOATER
(CONICAL —) BEEHIVE
(GEM —) BAGUET BAGUETTE
(GLOVE —) TRANK
(LIKE A DOUGHNUT) TORIC
(SPIRALLING —) SWIRL
(SURFACE —) GEOMETRY
(UNBLOCKED —) HOOD
(PREF.) MORPH(O)
SHAPED BUILT FITTED BLOCKED
FEATURED

(— LIKE A DOUGHNUT) TORIC
(— LIKE A HORN) LYRATE
(— LIKE ALMOND) AMYGDALOID
(— LIKE ANVIL) INCUS
(— LIKE ARROW) SAGITTAL
SAGITTATE
(— LIKE BASIN) PELVIFORM
(— LIKE BEAN) FABIFORM
(— LIKE BERRY) BACCIFORM
(— LIKE BOAT) SCAPHOID
NAVICULAR
(— LIKE BUCKLER) SCUTATE
(— LIKE CAKE) PLACENTIFORM
(— LIKE CAP) PILEATE PILEATED
(— LIKE CLUB) CLAVATE CLUBBED
(— LIKE COIN) NUMMULAR
(— LIKE COMB) CTENOID
(— LIKE CONE) CONIFORM
(— LIKE CUP) SCYPHATE
(— LIKE DOME) DOMAL
(— LIKE EAR) AURIFORM
(— LIKE FAN) RHIPIDATE
(— LIKE FEATHER) PINNATE
PINNATED PENNIFORM
(— LIKE FIDDLE) PANDURATE
(— LIKE FUNNEL) INFUNDIBULAR
(— LIKE HALBERD) HASTATE
(— LIKE HAMMER) MALLEIFORM
(— LIKE HEART) CORDATE
CORDIFORM
(— LIKE HOOK) ANKYROID
(— LIKE HORN) CORNIFORM
(— LIKE HORSESHOE) HIPPOCREPIAN
(— LIKE KEEL) CARINATE
(— LIKE KIDNEY) NEPHROID
RENIFORM
(— LIKE LEAF) FOLIATE
(— LIKE LENS) LENTOID PHACOID
(— LIKE LENTIL) PHACOID
PHACOIDAL
(— LIKE NEEDLE) ACUATE
(— LIKE ORANGE) OBLATE
(— LIKE PEA) PISIFORM
(— LIKE PEAR) PYRIFORM
(— LIKE PITCHER) ARYTENOID
ARYTAENOID
(— LIKE POUCH) BURSIFORM
(— LIKE PULLEY) TROCHLEAR
(— LIKE RING) ANNULAR
(— LIKE ROD) BACILLAR
(— LIKE S) SIGMATE
(— LIKE SAUCER) PATELLATE
(— LIKE SAUSAGE) ALLANTOID
(— LIKE SCIMITAR) ACINACIFORM
(— LIKE SHELL) CONCHATE
CONCHIFORM
(— LIKE SHIELD) ASPIDATE
CLYPEATE
(— LIKE SICKLE) FALCULAR
(— LIKE SLIPPER) CALCEIFORM
CALCEOLATE
(— LIKE SNAKE) ANGUIFORM

(— LIKE SOCKET) GLENOID
GLENOIDAL
(— LIKE SPINDLE) FUSOID FUSIFORM
(— LIKE SPUR) CALCARINE
(— LIKE STAR) ASTROID
(— LIKE STRAP) LIGULATE
(— LIKE SWORD) GLADIATE
(— LIKE THREAD) FILIFORM
(— LIKE TURNIP) NAPIFORM
(— LIKE WATCH GLASS) MENISCOID
(— LIKE WEDGE) CUNEAL CUNEATE
(— LIKE WHEEL) ROTATE
(— LIKE X) SALTIRE
(— WITH AX) HEWN
SHAPED)- LIKE BELL)
CAMPANIFORM
SHAPELESS DUMPY CLUMPY
DEFORM DUMPTY INFORM
FORMLESS INDIGEST UNSHAPED
AMORPHOUS
SHAPELINESS DELICACY
SHAPELY GENT TIDY TRIM CLEAN
TIGHT DECENT FORMAL GAINLY
FEATOUS FORMFUL SHAPABLE
SHAPHAT (FATHER OF —) HORI
ADLAI SHEMAIAH
(SON OF —) ELISHA
SHAPING DESCENT
SHARAI (FATHER OF —) BANI
SHARAR (SON OF —) AHIAM
SHARD SCAUR SHERD SHRED SLIVER
(PL.) PITCHER
SHARE CUT END LOT RUG CANT
DALE DEAL DOLE HAND PART PLOT
RENT SCOT SNIP DIVVY ENTER
PARTY QUOTA RATIO SHEAR SHIFT
SLICE SNACK SNICK SNUCK SPLIT
WHACK COMMON COPART DEPART
DIVIDE FINGER IMPART RATION
SHOVEL PARTAGE PARTAKE PORTION
DIVIDEND DIVISION INTEREST
PURPARTY PERCENTAGE
PROPORTION
(— A BED) BUNK
(— DWELLING) STALL
(— EQUALLY) HALVE
(— IN ACTIVITY) PIECE
(— OF CHURCH REVENUE) PREBEND
(— OF EXPENSES) LAW CLUB
(— OF LAND) DAIL DALE FREEDOM
RUNDALE
(— OF PROFIT) LAY
(— OF STOCK) STOCK ACTION
(— QUARTERS) CHUM
(— SECRETS) CONFIDE
(ALLOTED —) DOLE
(ANCESTRAL —) PATTI
(EQUAL —) PROPORTION
(FULL —) SKINFUL
(GREATER —) FECK
(LEGAL —) HAK
(MINING —S) KANGAROOS

(ONE'S —) AFFERE
(PROPORTIONAL —) QUOTA
(SMALL —) MOIETY
(PL.) STOCK
(PREF.) MER(I)(O) MERISTO
(SUFF.) MER(E)(IC)(IS)(OUS)(Y)
SHARECROPPER RENTER
BYWONER CROPPER
SHARED JOINT BETWEEN
(PREF.) CO
SHAREHOLDER (THEATRE —)
RENTER
SHAREZER (BROTHER OF —)
ESARHADDON ADRAMMELECH
(FATHER OF —) SENNACHERIB
SHARING INON
(— OF EXPENSE) CLUB
(— VICARIOUSLY) ARMCHAIR
SHARK FOX GATA HAYE KULP MAKO
MANO TOPE GUMMY HOMER
HOUND LAMIA TIGER TOMMY TOPER
BEAGLE DAGGAR GALEID PALOMA
REQUIN WHALER ACRODUS
BONEDOG DOGFISH FOXFISH
HUNFYSH PLACOID REQUIEM
SLEEPER SOUPFIN SQUALID
SUNFISH TIBURON TIGRONE
TUBARON BULLHEAD HYBODONT
ROUSETTE SAILFISH SEAHOUND
SKAAMOOG SPEAREYE SQUATINA
THRASHER THRESHER PORBEAGLE
SEAI AWYER SELACHIAN
WOBBEGONG SHOVELHEAD
(KIND OF —) LOAN MAKO NURSE
(YOUNG —) COB SHARKLET
(PREF.) SQUALI SQUALO
SHARP DRY SHY ACID ACRE CHIC
CUTE EDGY FELL FINE GAIR GASH
GLEG GNIB HARD HIGH KEEN PERT
SALT TART ACERB ACRID ACUTE
ALERT BRASH BREME BRISK CRISP
DOWNY EAGER EDGED FALSE
HARSH NASAL NEBBY NIPPY PEERY
QUICK SMART SNELL SQUAB
STEEP STIFF VIVID YAULD ACIDIC
ACUATE ARGUTE ASTUTE BITING
BITTER BRIGHT CRISPY DIESIS
GLASSY JAGGED PLUCKY SEVERE
SHREWD SHRILL SNELLY SNITHE
STINGY TOOTHY TWEAKY UNRIDE
ANGULAR AUSTERE BRITTLE
CAUSTIC CUTTING GINGERY
NIPPING PIQUANT POINTED
PRECISE PUNGENT SHARPEN
SLICING SPINOUS VARMINT
VIOLENT HATCHETY INCISIVE
POIGNANT ACIDULOUS IRRITABLE
ASTRINGENT ACRIMONIOUS
(NOT —) MILD
(SHAPED AS —) OCTOTHORP
(PREF.) ACE I (O) ACUT(I)(O) OXY
SHARP-EDGED VORPAL CULTRATE

SHARPEN EDGE FILE FINE HONE KEEN WHET BRISK FROST GRIND POINT RAISE SHARP SLYPE STONE STROP ACCENT AFFILE STROKE ENHANCE QUICKEN SMARTEN EXACUATE HEIGHTEN
(— HORSESHOE) FROST

SHARPENED ACUATE

SHARPENER SHARPER STROPPER
(SCYTHE —) RIP RIFLE

SHARPENING (— OF PITCH) RISE

SHARPER GUE GYP BITE KITE ROOK SKIN SNAP BITER CHEAT CROOK GREEK ROGUE SHARK SHARP BESTER COGGER NICKUM PICARO ROOKER SHARPY BARNARD CATALAN GAMBLER SHARKER SPIELER BLACKLEG DECEIVER PIGEONER SWINDLER

SHARPLY DAB SHARP SNACK ACIDLY ROUNDLY SHEERLY SMARTLY STEEPLY

SHARPNESS WIT EDGE SALT WHET PLUCK ACRITY ACUITY ACUMEN ACIDITY ACERBITY ACRIDITY ACRIMONY ASPERITY EDGINESS PUNGENCY

SHARP-POINTED ACUATE ACULEATE
(PREF.) ACUT(I)(O)

SHARPSHOOTER JAGER DEADEYE VOLTIGEUR TIRAILLEUR BERSAGLIERE

SHARP-SIGHTED SIGHTY LYNCEAN

SHARP-TAILED GROUSE PINTAIL

SHARP-WITTED ACUTE CANNY SNELL SHREWD

SHASHAI (FATHER OF —) BANI

SHASHAK (FATHER OF —) ELPAAL

SHASTRA PURANA SASTRA
(— CLASS) SRUTI

SHATTER BLOW DASH DICE BLAST BREAK BURST CRASH CRAZE CREEM FRUSH SMASH SMOKE SPLIT WRECK SHIVER SPIDER BEGUILE CHATTER CONVELL EXPLODE SMATTER TORPEDO DEMOLISH DYNAMITE SPLINTER
(— CLAY TARGET) KILL

SHATTERED BROKEN BROOZLED DODDERED

SHAUL (FATHER OF —) SIMEON

SHAVE BARB BITE DRAW PARE RAZE GLACE GRAZE SKIVE SCHAWE SCRAPE FLATTEN UPRIGHT

SHAVED POLLED SHAVEN

SHAVEN NOT NOTT PILLED TONSURED

SHAVER PLANE PLANER

SHAVING SHAVE SHRED SPALE SPELL RAMENT RAMENTUM
(LATHE —S) TURNINGS
(PL.) COOM COOMB SCOBS MOSLINGS

SHAWL MAUD WRAP LAMBA MANTA MANTO NUBIA PATTU RUMAL SCARF TOZIE AFGHAN ANGORA KAMBAL PEPLOS PEPLUM PEPLUS PUTTOO SARAPE SERAPE TAPALO TOILET TONNAG ZEPHYR AMLIKAR CHUDDAR PAISLEY WHITTLE WRAPPER ALGERINE CASHMERE EPIBLEMA KAFFIYEH SLENDANG TURNOVER
(COARSE —) KAMBAL
(COTTON —) FARDA
(PLAID —) MAUD
(TASSELED —) TALLITH

SHAWM WAIT SHALM BOMBARD SCHALMEI
(KIN OF —) OBOE

SHE A HE HEO HER SHU ELLE HAEC SCHO
(AUTHOR OF —) HAGGARD
(CHARACTER IN —) JOB LEO SHE HOLLY AYESHA LUDWIG USTANE VINCEY BILLALI MAHOMED KALLIKRATES

SHEAF TIE BEAT BUNG GAIT GERB OMER FLASH GAVEL GERBE GLEAN BATTEN THRAVE DORLACH HATTOCK CAPSHEAF CORNBOLE
(— LEVIED AS TAX) CORNBOLE
(— OF ARROWS) FLASH
(— OF FLAX OR HEMP) BEAT BEET GLEAN
(— OF GRAIN) GAIT GARB HOSE GARBAGE
(LAST — OF CORN) NECK
(LAST — OF HARVEST) KIRN
(PROTECTING —) HATTOCK
(UNBOUND —) REAP GAVEL

SHEAL (FATHER OF —) BANI

SHEALTIEL (SON OF —) ZERUBBABEL

SHEAR COW CUT DOD LIP NOT CLIP CROP NOTT TRIM BREAK FORCE SHARE SHEER SHIRL SLIDE STRIP FLEECE STRESS

SHEARER SNAGGER

SHEARIAH (FATHER OF —) AZEL

SHEARLING SHEARHOG
(PL.) ALPACA

SHEARS LEWIS SNIPS FORFEX SHEARER SNOUTER SECATEUR
(PREF.) FORFICI

SHEARWATER HAG CREW COHOW HAGDON HAGLET PETREL PUFFIN SCRABE PIMLICO SCRABER SEABIRD HACKBOLT

SHEATFISH WELS DORAD WALLER CATFISH SILURID

SHEATH COT HOT BOOT CASE CYST HOSE HOTT ARMOR CHAPE FOREL GAINE OCREA SHADE SHEAF SPILL THECA VOLVA COCOON CONDOM FORREL MYELIN OCHREA QUIVER

SLOUGH VAGINA AXILEMMA EPILEMMA SCABBARD STANDARD VAGINULA NEURILEMMA
(— FOR BOOK) FOREL FORRIL
(— FOR FINGER) STALL
(— FOR GAMECOCK'S SPUR) HOT HOTT
(— OF CIGARETTE) SPILL
(— OF PLOW) STANDARD
(— OF TISSUE) PERIBLEM
(MEDULLARY —) CORONA
(PREF.) COLE(O) COLI(O) ELYTR(O)
(SUFF.) LEMMA THECA THECIUM
SHEATHBILL PADDY
SHEATHE CLAD COPPER MUZZLE IMPLATE
SHEATHED THECATE
SHEATHING SKIN ARMOR COPPER FACING SHEATH INLAYER SHIPLAP SLITWORK
SHEA TREE KARITE KARITI
SHEAVE SHEAF SHIVER HATTOCK TRUCKLE
(24 —S OF GRAIN) THRAVE THREAVE
SHEBA (FATHER OF —) BICHRI
SHEBANG HUT
SHEBER (FATHER OF —) CALEB
(MOTHER OF —) MAACHAH
SHEBUEL (FATHER OF —) HEMAN
SHECHANIAH (FATHER OF —) ARAH JEHIEL
(SON OF —) SHEMAIAH
SHED BOX CUB SOW ABRI CAST COTE DROP HELM HULL KILN MOLT PEEL POUR SHUD SKEO SLIP BOOTH HIELD HOVEL MOULT SCALE SHADE SPILL THROW VINEA ZAYAT BELFRY BROACH DINGLE EFFUSE GARAGE HANGAR HEMMEL INFUSE LINHAY MISTAL PANDAL SLOUGH CHOLTRY COTTAGE DIFFUSE DISCARD MUSCLE RADIATE SKIPPER EXUVIATE SKEELING SKILLION WOODSHED PENTHOUSE
(— BLOOD) BROACH
(— DROPS) DRIZZLE
(— FEATHERS OR HORNS) MEW
(— FOR LIVESTOCK) SHIPPEN
(— FOR SHEEP) SHEALING
(— LIGHT) ENLIGHT ENLIGHTEN IRRADIATE
(— OVER MINE SHAFT) COE
(— TEARS) GIVE
(— TO PROTECT SOLDIERS) TESTUDO
(CATTLE —) CUB HELM LAIR BELFRY
(MOVABLE —) SOW BAIL MUSCLE
(READILY —) FUGACIOUS
(TEMPORARY —) PANDAL
(WEATHER —) DINGLE
SHEDDING FALL SPILTH ECDYSIS APOLYSIS
(— TEARS) LACHRYMOSE
SHE-DEMON LAMIA

SHEDEUR (SON OF —) ELIZUR
SHEEN GLAZE SHINE LUSTER LUSTRE SHIMMER
SHEEP SNA TEG DOWN LAMB LONK MUGS SHIP SOAY URIN ZENU ANCON BOVID DUMBA HEDER HUNIA MUGGS OVINE SAIGA SHORN TAGGE AOUDAD ARGALI BARHAL BHARAL BIDENT CHURRO DECCAN DORPER DORSET EXMOOR HIRSEL MARKER MASHAM MERINO MUTTON NAYAUR OXFORD PANAMA PAULAR ROMNEY WETHER WOOLIE WOOLLY BIGHORN BLEATER BRAXIES CHEVIOT CRIOLLA DELAINE DISHLEY FREEZER FRONTER JUMBUCK KARAKUL LINCOLN POLLARD SUFFOLK TARGHEE TWINTER VERMONT BIKANERI COMEBACK COTSWOLD DARTMOOR HERDWICK LONGWOOL LUGHDOAN RUMINANT SHEARHOG MONTADALE TALLOWER THRINTER MONTADALE ROMELDALE SHROPSHIRE
(— DIFFICULT TO HANDLE) COBBLER
(— IN 2ND YEAR) HOB TAG TEG TAGGE TWINTER
(— THAT HAS SHED PORTION OF WOOL) ROSELLA
(— TO BE SHEARED) BOARD
(DEAD —) MORT BRAXY MORLING
(FEMALE —) EWE GIMMER SHEDER
(HORNLESS —) NOT NOTT
(LOST —) WAIF
(MALE —) RAM TUP BUCK HEDER DINMONT
(MOUNTAIN —) IBEX
(OLD —) GUMMER
(PART OF —) EAR EYE LEG RIB BACK DOCK FACE LOIN NECK RACK RUMP FLANK SHANK BREAST MUZZLE BRISKET FORELEG PASTERN WITHERS FOREHEAD SHOULDER FORESHANK
(THICK-WOOLED —) MUG
(UNSHORN —) HOG TEG
(WILD —) SHA ARGAL AUDAD RASSE URIAL AOUDAD ARGALI BHARAL SHAPOO BURRHEL MOUFLON
(YOUNG —) HOG HOGG HOGGEREL
(3-YEAR-OLD —) THRINTER
SHEEPBERRY ALISIER VIBURNUM
SHEEPCOTE SHEPPEY
SHEEPDOG PULI KELPIE SHELTY BOBTAIL MALINOIS SHETLAND
(PL.) PULIK PULIS
SHEEP FLY FAG
SHEEPFOLD REE COTE FANK KRAAL REEVE STELL BOUGHT BARKARY SHEPPEY SHEEPCOT
SHEEPHERDER SNOOZER STOCKMAN
SHEEPISH SHY

SHEEP LAUREL IVY HEATH WICKY
KALMIA LAUREL CALFKILL LAMBKILL
SHEEPLIKE OVINE
SHEEPMAN HOBBER
SHEEP PLANT RAOULIA
SHEEP ROT CAW
SHEEP RUN STATION
SHEEPSHEAD JAMES JEMMY
JIMMY PARGO PORGY TAUTOG
FATHEAD PERCOID SPAROID
SHEEPSHEARER GUN
SHEEPSKIN ROAN SLAT MOUTON
SOLDIER CAPESKIN LAMBSKIN
WOOLFELL SOLDIER
(— TANNED WITH BARK) BASAN
BASIL
(— THAT SWEATS UNEVENLY)
SOLDIER
(— WITHOUT WOOL) SLAT
(ROUGH-TANNED —) CRUST
SHEEP SORREL SOURWEED
SHEEP TICK FAG KEB KED KADE
SHEEPWALK SLAIT
SHEER BOLD FINE MAIN MERE PURE
BLANK BRANT CRUDE FRANK NAKED
STARK STEEP SIMPLE CLOTTED
GAZETTE EVENDOWN
(MADE OF — FABRIC) PEEKABOO
SHEET FIN CARD FILM FINE FLAT FOIL
LEAF SILL BLANK FLONG FOLIO
NAPPE CANVAS CIRCLE DOUBLE
FASCIA FENDER FLIMSY SHROUD
SINDON BLANKET CHUDDAH
CHUDDER FLOGGER FRISKET
LEAFLET PALLIUM PAPYRUS
WRAPPER AIRSHEET EIGHTEEN
FOLLOWER HANDBILL INTERLAY
SHEETLET
(— ADDED TO DEED) FOLLOWER
(— ATTACHED TO INVOICE) APRON
(— FOR BRIDGE SCORES) FLOGGER
(— OF CELLULOID) CEL CELL
(— OF CLOUDS) PALLIUM
(— OF DOUGH) STRUDEL
(— OF FIBER) BAT LAP BATT
(— OF ICE) GLARE GLAZE
(— OF IRON) CRAMPET CRAMPIT
(— OF LAVA) COULEE
(— OF LEAD) SOAKER
(— OF LEATHER) BUFFING
(— OF MICA) FILM
(— OF MICROFILM) FICHE
(— OF MUSCLE) PLATYSMA
(— OF PAPER) FLAT FOLIO FRISKET
LEAFLET HANDBILL
(— OF PARCHMENT) SKIN FOLLOWER
(— OF RUBBER) DAM
(— OF STAMPS) PANE
(— OF STRAW) YELM
(— OF SUGAR) SLAB
(— OF TISSUE) FASCIA
(— OF TOBACCO) BINDER
(— OF WATER) NAPPE

(— USED FOR MATRIX) FLONG
(HEATED —) CAUL
(METAL —S) LATTENS
(NEWS —) GAZETTE
(ORGANIZATION —) BILL
(PERFORATED —) SIEVE
(PROTECTIVE —) CURTAIN
(THEATRICAL —) SIDE
(THIN —) LAMINA
(THIN —S OF IRON) DOUBLES
(TRANSPARENT —) GELATINE
(WINDING —) SINDON SUDARY
(PREF.) PALLIO
SHEETING PERCALE DOMESTIC
AMERIKANI
SHEHARIAH (FATHER OF —)
JEHORAM
SHEKEL (HALF —) BEKAH
SHEKINAH GLORY
SHELAH (FATHER OF —) JUDAH
SHELDRAKE SHELDER BARGOOSE
BERGANDER
SHELEMIAH (FATHER OF —) BANI
ABDEEL
(SON OF —) IRIJAH JEHUCAL
HANANIAH
SHELEPH (FATHER OF —) JOKTAN
SHELESH (FATHER OF —) HELEM
SHELF BANK BERM BINK DECK DESS
STEP TACK BENCH LEDGE SKELF
STAGE STOOL MANTEL SCONCE
SETTLE SHELVE BACKBAR BRACKET
COUNTER PLATEAU CREDENCE
CUPBOARD
(— BEFORE STOVE) HEARTH
(— BEHIND ALTAR) GRADINE
GRADINO RETABLE
(— IN MINE) BUNNING
(— OF ROCK) CAR LENCH LENCHEON
(ALTAR —) BUTSUDAN
(CONTINENTAL —) PLATFORM
(FIREWORKS —) BALLOON
(RAISED —) SETTLE
SHELL ARD HUD PEN POD BAND
CASK CHOU CLAM CONE HARD HOOF
HULL HUSK MAIL OBUS PELL PILL
PIPI PUKA PUPA SKIN SWAD UMBO
UNIO BALAT CHANK CHINK CONCH
COPIS CRUMP CRUST DRILL FRITZ
GOURD MITER MITRA MUREX
ORMER OVULA SCAUP SHALE
SHARD SHEAL SHERD SHOCK SHUCK
TESTA TIARA TROCA TURBO VALVE
VENUS ANOMIA ARCHIE BUCKIE
BULLET BURGAU CAPSID CERION
COCKLE CONKER COWRIE CRUSTA
DENTAL DOLIUM ECLAIR JINGLE
LORICA MAROON NOUGAT NUCULA
PULLET PURPLE SANKHA SINGLE
SLOUGH STROMB TRITON TURBAN
VANNET VENTER VOLUTE WINKLE
BALANUS BALLOON CARACOL
CARCASS COCONUT DARIOLE

DISCINA GLADIUS LIMACEL MARINER
PAPBOAT PHILINE PROJECT SCALLOP
SPICULE SPINDLE SPONDYL
TEREBRA THIMBLE TOHEROA
TORPEDO TOXIFER TROCHID
TRUMPET UNICORN BACULITE
BACULOID CARAPACE CONCHITE
COQUILLE CYLINDER DUCKFOOT
EGGSHELL ENVELOPE ESCALLOP
FIGSHELL FOCALOID FRUSTULE
HELICINA MERINGUE OLIVELLA
PUPARIUM SEASHELL SOLARIUM
STROMBUS UNIVALVE VELUTINA
VERMETID VERMETUS WARRENER
WHIZBANG WOODCOCK
(— CONTAINING MEDICINE) CAPSULE
(— OF DIATOM) FRUSTULE
(— OF OYSTER) HUSK SHUCK
(— OF SHIP) HULK SKIN
(— OF SLUG) LIMACEL
(— OF THE EARTH) SIAL
(—S FROM GUN) STUFF
(— SYSTEMATICALLY) COMB
(ANTIAIRCRAFT —) FLAK ARCHIE
(CARTRIDGE —S) BRASS
(CAST —S) EXUVIAE
(CUSTARD-FILLED —) ECLAIR
DARIOLE
(EMPTY —) DOP
(FOSSIL —) DOLITE AMMONITE
BACULITE BALANITE CONCHITE
(HOWITZER —) OBUS
(MATHEMATICAL —) HOMEOID
(OYSTER —S) CULCH CULTCH
(PART OF —) EAR LIP RIB TIP APEX
WING HINGE SPIRE VALVE WHORL
MUSCLE SUTURE ADDUCTOR
APERTURE
(PASTA —) TUFOLI
(PASTA —S) MANICOTTI
(PASTRY —) CORNET QUICHE
DARIOLE TIMBALE TALMOUSE
(PROTEIN —) CAPSID
(SNAIL —) CONKER HODMADOD
(SPIRAL —) CHANK
(TORTOISE —) HOOF
(VEGETABLE —) DOLMA
(PREF.) CHITINO CHITO CONCH(O)
LOPO OECO OSTRAC(O) TESTI
(SUFF.) OECA OECIA OSTRACA
SHELLED VINED
SHELLFISH ORM COCK BUCKY
NACRE PIROT BUCKIE LIMPET
WIGGLE MOLLUSK PERIWIG
ASTACIAN
(PART OF —) EYE FAN LEG CLAW TAIL
SHELL TOOTH FEELER RIPPER
TELSON UROPOD ABDOMEN
ANTENNA CRUSHER CARAPACE
SHELLING RATTLES
SHELL-LESS OON
SHELL MONEY UHLLO WAKIKI
SHELOMI (FATHER OF —) ABIHUD

SHELOMITH (FATHER OF —) DIBRI
ZERUBBABEL
SHELTER CAB HUT LEE LOO ABRI
BURY EAVE GIDE GITE HERD HIDE
HIVE JOKE JOUK LOWN ROOF SCOG
SCUG BARTH BELEE BENAB BERRY
BIELD BOIST BOOTH BOTHY BOWER
CABIN CLEAD CLOAK COVER EMBAY
HAVEN HOARD HOUSE HOVEL HOVER
HOWFF HUTCH LEWTH LITHE RESET
SCOUG SHADE SHEAL ASYLUM
AWNING BELFRY BILBIE BOOLEY
BOUGHT BURROW COVERT CRADLE
DEFEND DUGOUT GABION GUNYAH
HANGAR HARBOR HOSTEL PANDAL
REFUGE ROOFING TABERNA
UMBRAGE WANIGAN WICKIUP
BESCREEN DOGHOUSE ENSCONCE
LODGMENT PALLIATE SECURITY
SHIELING SNOWSHED WAYHOUSE
PESTHOUSE
(— FOR CATTLE) HELM BOOLY STELL
HEMMEL
(— FOR CROP WATCHERS) KISI
(— FOR DANCES) ENRAMADA
(— FOR SENTRY) GUERITE
(— FROM WEATHER) LEWTH
(— OVER BEEHIVE) HOOD
(BIRD HUNTER'S —) BLIND
(BULLETPROOF —) MANTLET
MANTELET
(CONCRETE-AND-STEEL —)
PILLBOX
(CRAMPED —) HUTCH
(FISH —) CROY
(LEAFY —) LEVESEL
(MINING —) TALPA
(PICNIC —) RAMADA
(PORTABLE —) MANTA CABANA
(ROCK —) KRAPINA
(ROUGH —) JACAL
(TEEPEELIKE —) CHUM
(TEMPORARY —) HALE HOLD CABIN
BIVOUAC
SHELTERED LEE LEW COSY COZY
LOUN LOWN SNUG BIELD LITHE
LOUND LOWND SHADY COVERT
(— SPACE) KILLOGIE
SHELTERED LIFE (AUTHOR OF —)
GLASGOW
(CHARACTER IN —) EVA BENA CORA
ETTA JOHN DELIA JENNY WELCH
BARRON GEORGE JOSEPH PEYTON
CROCKER ARCHBALD BIRDSONG
ISABELLA
SHELTERING BIELDY SHADING
SHELTERLESS HOMELESS
ROOFLESS

SHELUMIEL (FATHER OF —) ZURISHADDAI
SHELVE DISH BURKE SHELF SHUNT TABLE PIGEONHOLE
SHELVES STAGE ETAGERE
SHEM (BROTHER OF —) HAM JAPHET
(FATHER OF —) NOAH
SHEMA (FATHER OF —) ELPAAL
SHEMAIAH (FATHER OF —) JOEL HARIM DELAIAH HASSHUB ADONIKAM OBEDEDOM ELIZAPHAN NETHANEEL SHECHANIAH
(SON OF —) ABDA DELAIAH OBADIAH
SHEMARIAH (FATHER OF —) BANI
SHEMIDA (FATHER OF —) GILEAD
SHEMUEL (FATHER OF —) TOLA
SHENANIGAN ANTIC ESCAPADE
SHENAZAR (FATHER OF —) JECONIAH
SHENG SANG CHENG SHING
(ONE-HUNDREDTH —) CHAO
SHEOL HELL HADES
SHEPHATHIAH (SON OF —) MESHULLAM
SHEPHATIAH (FATHER OF —) DAVID JEHOSHAPHAT
SHEPHERD HERD SHEP TEND COLIN CORIN GADDI GYGES SWAIN FEEDER PASTOR TARBOX CORYDON DAPHNIS DRAFTER GADARIA KURUMBA THYRSIS TITYRUS MELIBEUS MENALCAS PASTORAL SHEEPMAN STREPHON
(GERMAN —) ALSATIAN
SHEPHERDESS DELIA MOPSA PHEBE DORCAS BERGERE GALATEA PASTORA PERDITA AMARYLLIS
SHEPHERD KING, THE
(CHARACTER IN —) ELISA AMINTA TAMIRI AGENORE ALESSANDRO
(COMPOSER OF —) MOZART
SHEPHERD'S-PURSE TOYWORT CASEWEED COCOWORT
SHEPHI (FATHER OF —) SHOBAL
SHERAH (FATHER OF —) EPHRAIM
SHERBET ICE GLACE SHRAB SORBET GRANITA SOUFFLE
SHERD SCARTH
SHERESH (FATHER OF —) MACHIR
(MOTHER OF —) MAACHAH
SHERIFF FOUD FOWD SCULT XERIF DEPUTY GRIEVE SCHOUT SHIRRA BAILIFF SHREEVE SHRIEVE ALGUACIL HUISSIER SHIREMAN VISCOUNT
SHERRY FINO CLOVE JEREZ XERES DOCTOR MANCHU SOLERA OLOROSO RANGOON SHERRIS MONTILLA MANZANILLA
SHERRY BROWN CLOVE
SHESHAI (FATHER OF —) ANAK
SHE STOOPS TO CONQUER
(AUTHOR OF —) GOLDSMITH

(CHARACTER IN —) KATE TONY MARLOW CHARLES LUMPKIN NEVILLE HASTINGS PEDIGREE CONSTANCE HARDCASTLE
SHEVA (FATHER OF —) CALEB
(MOTHER OF —) MAACHAH
SHEVRI SESBAN
SHIATSU MASSAGE
SHICER DUFFER
SHIELD ECU EGIS HIDE PELT AEGIS APRON BIELD BOARD CLOAK COVER FENCE GUARD GULAR MULGA PATCH PAVIS PELTA PYGAL SCUTE SHEND TARGE YELDE ANCILE ANGARA BLAZON CASQUE DEFEND FENDER GUNTUB GYROMA LINDEN MENTAL OCULAR PAUNCH RONDEL SCREEN SCUTUM SECURE TARGET BUCKLER CLIPEUS CLYPEUS CONCEAL LOZENGE PANNIER PAVISSE PRIDWIN PROTECT ROSTRAL ROTELLA ROUNDEL SHELTER SUPPORT TESTUDO CARTOUCH CUCULLUS HIELAMEN INSULATE MARGINAL PRESERVE RONDACHE STERNITE SUNSHADE BREASTING
(— BELOW A DAM) APRON
(— FOR ARCHERS) PANNIER
(— FOR CAMERA) GOBO
(— FOR HORSE) BIB
(— FOR LAMP) BONNET CHIMNEY
(— FOR MICROPHONE) GOBO
(— OF ABORIGINES) MULGA HIELAMEN
(— OF A STIRRUP) HOOD
(— OF CONTINENT) CORE
(— OF HIDE) SKILDFEL
(— OF SOMITE) STERNITE
(— OF TRILOBITE) CEPHALON
(— ON MAST) PAUNCH
(— ON THROAT OF FISH) GULAR
(— OVER BASE OF FAN) CANOPY
(— WITHOUT ARMS) ALBERIA
(BONY —) CARAPACE
(BULLETPROOF —) MANTA MANTLET MANTELET
(HERALDIC —) BLAZON
(KING ARTHUR'S —) PRIWEN PRIDWIN
(LEATHER —) CHAFE
(PART OF —) RIB BOSS ORLE UMBO ANTIA
(SACRED —) ANCILE
(SIBERIAN —) ANGARA
(WICKERWORK —) SCIATH
(PREF.) ASPID(O) CLYPEI CLYPEO PELTATI PELTATO SCUT(I) SCUTATI SCUTELLI
(SUFF.) ASPIS
SHIELDBEARER SQUIRE ESQUIRE PELTAST ESCUDERO SCUTIFER
SHIELD BUG STINKBUG
SHIELD FERN FERNGALE

SHIELDMAKER TYCHIOS
SHIELD-SHAPED PELTATE SCUTATE
  THYROID
SHIFT JIB BACK CHOP CORE FEND
  FLIT HAUL MOVE RUSE SHIP TACK
  TOUR TURN VARY VEER WEND
  BREAK BUDGE CREEP CYMAR DRIFT
  HOTCH QUIRK SHIRK SHUNT SIMAR
  SKIFT SLIDE SMOCK SPELL TRICK
  BAFFLE CHANGE DENIAL DEVICE
  DOUBLE PALTER SKYFTE SWERVE
  SWITCH CHEMISE CUTBACK EVASION
  FRESHEN SHUFFLE SLEIGHT WHIFFLE
  ARTIFICE DISLODGE DISPLACE
  DOGWATCH DOUBLING MUTATION
  PINGPONG RESOURCE REVIRADO
  TRANSFER TRAVERSE TURNOVER
  WINDLASS
  (— ABOUT AS THE WIND) LARGE
  (— ABRUPTLY) JUMP
  (— IN DANCING) BALANCE
  (— IN TACKING) JIB
  (— ORDER OF BELLS) HUNT
  (— RAILROAD EQUIPMENT) DRILL
  (— SUDDENLY) FLY CHOP GYBE JIBE
  (— WEIGHT) WING
  (KIND OF —) STICK
  (MINING —) CORE
SHIFTINESS LUBRICITY
SHIFTING FLUID QUICK AMBULANT
  CHOPPING DRIFTING FLOATING
  SLIPPAGE VARIABLE VEERABLE
  (— BACK AND FORTH) YOYO
SHIFTLESS DRIFTY SOZZLY
  DRIFTING FECKLESS HAVELESS
SHIFTLESSNESS SLOUCH
SHIFTY GREASY DEVIOUS EVASIVE
  HANGDOG SLIDING SLIPPERY
SHIITE SHIAH SECTARY SHAIKHI
  TWELVER
SHILHA SHLU CHLEUH
SHILHI (DAUGHTER OF —) AZUBAH
SHILL STICK BONNET CAPPER
  BOOSTER
SHILLEM (FATHER OF —) NAPHTALI
SHILLING BOB HOG ORA CHIP HOGG
  LEVY PREST DEENER HARPER
  TESTON TEVISS THIRTEEN
  (20 —S) POUND
  (21 —S) GUINEA
  (5 —S) CROWN DECUS
SHILLY-SHALLY HEDGE BACK
  BOGGLE
SHILSHAH (FATHER OF —) ZOPHAH
SHIM GLUT LINER SHIMMER
SHIMEA (FATHER OF —) DAVID
SHIMEATH
  (SON OF --) ZABAD JOZACHAR
SHIMEI (BROTHER OF —) CONONIAH
  ZERUBBABEL
  (FATHER OF —) BANI GERA KISH
  JAHATH GERSHON PEDAIAH
  JEDUTHUN

SHIMMA (BROTHER OF —) DAVID
  (FATHER OF —) JESSE
SHIMMER FLASH GLIMMER SHIMPER
  SKIMMER
SHIMRI (FATHER OF —) SHEMAIAH
  (SON OF —) JEDIAEL
SHIMRITH (SON OF —) JEHOZABAD
SHIMRON (FATHER OF —) ISSACHAR
SHIN SHANK SKINK SWARM CNEMIS
  SHINNY
SHINBONE TIBIA
  (SUFF.) CNEMA CNEMIA CNEMIC
  CNEMUS
SHINDIG SHINDY SHIVOO
SHINDY ROW BOBBERY
SHINE RAY SUN BEAM BUFF GLOW
  LAMP LEAM LINK STAR BLARE BLICK
  BLINK BLOOM EXCEL GLAIK GLARE
  GLEAM GLEIT GLENT GLINT GLISS
  GLORE GLORY GLOSS GLOZE SHEEN
  SKYRE STARE BEACON DAZZLE
  GLANCE LUSTER LUSTRE POLISH
  SCANCE EFFULGE GLIMMER GLISTEN
  GLITTER RADIATE REFLECT SHIMMER
  SPARKLE RUTILATE
  ((— IN DARK) PHOSPHORESCE
  (— BRIGHTLY) BEEK FLAME LIGHT
  (— FAINTLY) SCARROW
  (— UPON) SUN SMITE
SHINER CHUB DACE BREAM MOUSE
  REDFIN CYPRINID WINDFISH
SHINER-UP PATCHER
SHINGLE SHIM BEACH SHAKE SHIDE
  SLATE ASTYLL CHESIL KNOBBLE
  STARTER
SHINGLER NOBBLER
SHINGLES ZONA ZOSTER
  (PREF.) ZOSTERI ZOSTERO
SHININESS GLARE GLAZE GLOSS
SHINING GLAD NEAT CLEAR GLARY
  LIGHT LUCID NITID SHEER WHITE
  ARDENT ARGENT ASHINE BRIGHT
  FULGID GLOSSY GOLDEN LUCENT
  MARBLE NITENT ORIENT SERENE
  SHEENY SPUNKY STARRY ADAZZLE
  BURNING FULGENT GLARING
  GLIMMER LAMPING FLASHING
  GLEAMING LUCULENT LUSTRANT
  LUSTROUS NITIDOUS RELUCENT
  RUTILANT SPLENDID STARLIKE
  SUNBEAMY SUNSHINY
  (— THROUGH) TRANSLUCENT
  (PREF.) STILPNO
SHINLEAF PYROLA
SHINNY PEG SHINTY
SHINTO
  (— SECT) RYOBU
SHINTY CAMANACHA
SHIP (ALSO SEE BOAT AND VESSEL)
  ARK CAT COG HOY NAO BARK BOAT
  BOOM GRAB HAND HULK KEEL LADE
  NAVY PAHI PINE PINK SAIL SEND
  SNOW TREE WOOD ZULU CHECK

LAKER OILER PINTA PRORE RAZEE
SCOUT SCREW SKIFF WHELP
ANDREW ARGOSY BARKEY BARQUE
BOTTOM CARTEL CASTLE CHASER
COALER CODMAN DECKER DIESEL
GALIOT GALLEY HOLCAD HOPPER
LANCHA LATEEN LORCHA MASTER
MISTIC MOTHER PACKET PUFFER
RUNNER SAILER SALVOR SEALER
SMOKER TONNER TRAVEL VESSEL
ADMIRAL CARRACK CLIPPER COLLIER
CONSORT DROMOND FACTORY
FELUCCA FOREIGN FRIGATE FRUITER
GABBARD GALLEON GUNBOAT
INVOICE MACHINE MULETTA
ONERARY PATAMAR PINNACE
POLACRE SHALLOP SHIPLET SPITKIT
STEAMER BALANDRA BALINGER
BILANDER CAPITANA CUNARDER
DRUMBLER FLAGSHIP GALLEASS
GAYDIANG INDIAMAN JAPANNER
LANCHARA MAGAZINE PESSONER
PIPPINER REPEATER SAILSHIP
SCHOONER SMUGGLER SPANIARD
LEVIATHAN BRIGANTINE
MERCHANTMAN
(— BUILT FROM NAILS OF DEAD)
NAGLFAR
(— FITTED AS CHURCH) BETHEL
(— IN LIQUOR TRADE) COPER
(— OF ARGONAUTS) ARGO
(— OF NORSEMEN) KEEL
(CLUMSY —) TUB HULK
(DEPOT —) TENDER
(ESCORT —) CORVETTE
(FLEET OF —S) ARMADA
(JAPANESE —) MARU
(MALAY —) COUGNAR
(NOVA SCOTIAN —) BLUENOSE
(OBJECT SHAPED LIKE A —) NEF
(PART OF —) BOW CAP GUY RUN
BEAM BOOM GAFF JACK LIFT MAST
RAIL STAY VANG YARD BRACE CHAIN
ROYAL SHEET TRUCK JUMPER
RUDDER SHROUD STRAKE BOBSTAY
BULWARK BUMPKIN COUNTER
FORETOP JIBSTAY MAINTOP
NETTING PENDANT RATLINE
RIGGING SKYSAIL SPANKER STIRRUP
STRIKER SWIFTER TOPMAST
BACKROPE BACKSTAY CUTWATER
FOOTROPE FOREMAST LIFELINE
MAINMAST MAINSTAY STUDDING
CROSSTREE FORESHEET MAINSHEET
NAMEBOARD WATERLINE
MARTINGALE MIZZENMAST
TOPGALLANT
(PIRATE —) GALLIVAT
(PRIZE —) CAPTURE
(QUARANTINE —) LAZARET
(RECEIVING —) GUARDO
(REMOTE-CONTROLLED —) DRONE
(SLOW —) BUCKET

(STORE —) FLUTER
(SUPPLY —) COPER COOPER
(UNTRIM —) BALLAHOO
(VIKING —) DRAKE
(PL.) NAVY MARINE SEACRAFT
SHIPPING
(PREF.) NAU(TI) NAV(I)
SHIPFITTER FITTER ERECTOR
SHIPHI (SON OF —) ZIZA
SHIPHTAN (SON OF —) KEMUEL
SHIPMASTER PADRONE
SHIPMENT CARLOT RAILING
DISPATCH SHIPPAGE
SHIPPING (— UNIT CARLOAD
SHIPSHAPE NEAT TAUT TIDY TRIM
CIVIL TIGHT ATAUNT ORDERLY
SHIP-SHAPED (— UTENSIL) NEF
SHIP SWEEPER TOPASS TOPIWALA
SHIPWAY BERTH
SHIPWORM ARTER BORER COBRA
TEREDO PILEWORM WOODWORM
SHIPWRECK WRACK NAUFRAGE
SHIPWRIGHT WAYMAN BUILDER
SHIRE DERBY SHEER COUNTY
SHIRK BALK FUNK GOOF MIKE BAULK
BLINK BUDGE DODGE EVADE FEIGN
FUDGE SKULK SLACK RODNEY
FINAGLE SHACKLE SHAFFLE SOLDIER
SHAMMOCK
SHIRKER FUNK PIKER SOGER
FUNKER ROTTER BLUDGER
SLACKER SLINKER SUGARER
COBERGER CUTHBERT EMBUSQUE
SCOWBANK
SHIRLEY (AUTHOR OF —) BRONTE
(CHARACTER IN —) JOE DONNE
EMILY LOUIS MOORE PRYOR SCOTT
MALONE ROBERT KEELDAR SHIRLEY
CAROLINE HELSTONE HORTENSE
SWEETING MATTHEWSON
SHIRR SMOCK
SHIRT TOB TOP JUPE SARK TANK
TOBE BLUEY HAIRE JUPON KAMIS
SHIFT BANIAN BANIYA CAMISA
CAMISE PALAKA PARTLET UNDERGO
VAREUSE·KAMLEIKA
(— FRONT) DICKY DICKEY
(COLLARLESS —) KURTA KHURTA
(FUR —) PARKA
(HAIR —) HAIRE CILICE
(ROMAN —) SUBUCULA
(SLEEVELESS —) FECKET
(SPORT —) IZOD GUAYABERA
(WORKMAN'S —) FROCK
(WORNOUT —) DICKY
SHIRTING CHEVIOT HARVARD
HOLLAND SARKING
SHIRTWAIST BLOUSE GARIBALDI
SHISHA (SON OF —) AHIAH
ELIHOREPH
SHISH KEBAB SOUVLAKI
SOUVLAKIA
SHITTIMWOOD BOXWOOD

SHIVA (SON OF —) GANESHA KARTTIKEYA
(WIFE OF —) KALI DURGA
SHIVAREE BELLING CHIVARI HORNING SERENADE
SHIVER JAR GIRL GRUE BEVER BREAK CHILL CREEM CREEP FRILL GROWS QUAKE SHRUG SLICE CHIVER DITHER DUDDER GROOSE HOTTER NIDDER NITHER QUIVER SHRIMP SPLINT TREMOR CHITTER FLICKER FRISSON SHATTER SHITHER SHUDDER TREMBLE KAMLEIKA SPLINTER
(THE —S) AGUE
(PL.) SMITHERS SMITHEREENS
SHIVERING AGUED CHILL OURIE TREMOR ASHIVER
SHIZA (SON OF —) ADINA
SHNOOK TWERP
SHOAL BAJO BANK FLAT REEF SPIT BARRA DRAVE FLOTE SCULL SHELF SCHOOL SHALLOW TOWHEAD
SHOAT GURRY SHOOT SHOTT
SHOBAB (FATHER OF —) CALEB DAVID
(MOTHER OF —) AZUBAH BATHSHEBA
SHOBAL (FATHER OF —) SEIR CALEB
SHOBI (FATHER OF —) NAHASH
SHOCK COP JAR BLOW BUMP DINT JOLT RACK SHOG STUN TURN APPAL BRUNT GAVEL GLIFF GLOFF SHAKE STOOK STOUR DISMAY FRIGHT IMPACT JOSTLE JUMBLE REJOLT RICKLE ROLLER STRIKE TRAUMA ASTOUND CANVASS DISGUST HATTOCK HORRIFY STAGGER STARTLE STUPEFY TERRIFY DISEDIFY GLIFFING SURPRISE
(— OF CORN) STOOK STOUT STITCH
(MENTAL —) TRAUMA
(TYPE OF —) HAIR MANE
SHOCK ABSORBER SHOCK BUFFER DAMPER DASHPOT SNUBBER
SHOCKED AGHAST
SHOCKER RICKER STOOKER
SHOCKING GRIM AWFUL LURID HORRID UNHOLY BURNING FEARFUL FEARING GHASTLY HIDEOUS DREADFUL ENORMOUS HORRIBLE DESPERATE SCANDALOUS
SHOD CALCED
SHODDY SOFT CHEAP FOOTY MUNGO RATTY SOFTS TACKY SLEAZY TICKYTACKY
SHOE BAL CUE PAN BOOT BROG CLOG DRAG FLAT HALF SKID SOCK TURN BLAKE DERBY KLOMP MOYLE ROMEO SABOT SCRAE SLING SPIKE STOGA STOGY STRAP ANKLET BEAKER BROGAN BROGUE BUSKIN CALIGA CALIGO CHOPIN COBCAB

COCKER CRAKOW CREOLE DORSAY GAITER GALOSH GILLIE KILTIE LOAFER MULLER PATTEN PINSON POLISH SADDLE SANDAL SECQUE BAUCHLE BLUCHER BOTTINE CALCEUS CHOPINE COWHIDE FLIPPER GHILLIE OXONIAN RULLION SHOEPAC SLIPPER SNEAKER WINGTIP BALMORAL BRODEKIN CALCEATE COLONIAL PLATFORM PLIMSOLL SABOTINE SANDSHOE SKEWBACK SLIPSLOP SOLLERET
(— FOR GRINDING) MULLER
(— FOR MULE) PLANCHE
(— IN TRUSS OR FRAME) SKEWBACK
(— NOT FASTENED ON) PUMP
(— OF AN OX) CUE
(— OF A SLEDGE) HOB
(— OF COMIC ACTOR) BAXA
(— OF SUBWAY CAR) PAN
(— REPAIRER) JACKMAN
(—S AND STOCKINGS) FEET
(— STYLE) OPENTOE
(— TO CHECK WHEEL) DRAG SKID
(— USED AS BRAKE) SKATE
(— WITH A LONG TONGUE) KILTY KILTIE
(— WITH POINTED TOE) WINKLEPICKER
(— WORN ON EITHER FOOT) STRAIGHT
(ARMORED —) SABBATON
(BABY'S —) CACK
(DOWN-AT-HEEL —) SHAUCHLE
(HOBNAILED —) TACKET
(LARGE —S) GUNBOATS
(LOW-CUT —) SOCK GILLY ANKLET BUSKIN SLIPPER COLONIAL
(MILITARY —) CALIGA
(OLD —) BAUCHLE
(PART OF —) TIP TOE ARCH FLAP HEEL LIFT SOLE VAMP WELT AGLET SHANK COLLAR EYELET FOXING INSTEP LINING THROAT TONGUE COUNTER OUTSOLE QUARTER MUDGUARD PLATFORM SHOELACE BREASTING
(PIKED —) BEAKER
(RAWHIDE —) HIMMING VELSKOEN
(SPORT —S) NIKES
(SPORTS —S) GILLIES
(STEEL —) SOLLERET
(TENNIS —) TENNIES SNEAKERS
(THIN —) PINSON SCLAFF
(WINGED —S) TALARIA
(WOODEN —) KLOMP SABOT PATTEN RACKET RACQUET
(WORN —) SCRAE
(PL.) SHEEN SHOON SHUNE SCHONE CASUALS FOOTGEAR
(PREF.) CALCEI
SHOEMAKER SNOB FOXER SOLER ARCHER CHAMAR CODGER COZIER

FUDGER GOUGER SOOTER SOUTER
VAMPER COBBLER CRISPIN
CROWNER SHOEMAN SNOBBER
UPPERER CORVISER SNOBSCAT
CORDWAINER
SHOEMAKING SNOBBING
SHOESTRING LACE LACET
SHOGI (EXPERT LEVEL IN —) DAN
SHOGUN TYCOON
SHOHAM (FATHER OF —) JAAZIAH
SHOMER (SON OF —) JEHOZABAD
SHOO HOOSH DISPEL
SHOOK PACK BLANK SHAKE
SHOOT DAG GUN IMP PAY POT PUT
ROD TIP BANG BOLT BROD CANE
CHIT CION DRAW LEAF PLUG SLIP
WEFT ARROW BLAST BLAZE BROWN
DRILL DRIVE EXPEL FLUSH FROND
GEMMA GLEAM LANCE LAYER PLUFF
SCION SHEET SOBOL SPEAR SPIRE
SPRAY SPRIG SPRIT SPURT SQUIB
STICK STOOL TUBER TURIO VIMEN
BRANCH FLIGHT FLOWER GERMEN
GROWTH HEADER HURTLE LAUNCH
LEADER OFFSET RATOON SALLOW
SOBOLE SPRING SPROUT STOLON
STOUND STOVEN STRIKE SUCKER
TILLER TURION BUDLING CHIMNEY
DROPPER SCOURGE SPRING
TENDRIL TENDRON THALLUS
ANAPHYTE APOBLAST CATAPULT
TRAILING
(— A MARBLE) LAG TAW KNUCKLE
(— ASIDE FROM MARK) DRIB
(— AT LONG RANGE) SNIPE
(— A WHALE) STRIKE
(— DOWN) SPLASH
(— DUCKS) SKAG
(— FORTH) JET GLEAM SPIRE DARTLE
(— FROM DEER'S ANTLER) SPELLER
(— INDISCRIMINATELY) BROWN
(— MOOSE OR DEER) YARD
(— OF A TREE) STOW WHIP LANCE
BRANCH
(— OUT) JUT CHIT DART ERADIATE
(— SEAL) SWATCH
(—S USED AS FODDER) BROWSE
(— UP) SPIRE SPURT
(FIRST —S) BRAIRD
(FLEXIBLE —) BINE
(LATERAL —) ARM
(ORE —) BONANZA
(PAWNBROKER'S —) SPOUT
(SUGARCANE —) LALO
(TENDER —) FLUSH
(WILLOW —) SALLOW
(PREF.) BLAST(O) SOBOLI STOLONI
THALL(I)(O)
(SUFF.) BLAST(IC)(Y) SPERM(A)(AE)
(AL)(IA)(IC)(OUS)(UM)(Y)
SHOOTER SCOOT BLASTER
GUNSTER PLUFFER SHOTMAN
SKEETER

SHOOTING COCKING GUNNING
GUNPLAY HUNTING POTTING
SHOOTING STAR METEOR
COWSLIP SHOOTER PRIMWORT
SHOP CRIB TOKO BOOTH BURSE
STORE TRADE KOSHER PARLOR
SHOPPE TIENDA WINKEL ALMACEN
APOTHEC BOTTEGA CABARET
MERCERY SHEBANG SPICERY
TABERNA TURNERY BOUTIQUE
COOKSHOP CREMERIE EMPORIUM
ESPRESSO EXCHANGE MAGAZINE
SHOWSHOP SLOPSHOP TENDEJON
WAREROOM PERFUMERY
HABERDASHERY
(BARBER —) BARBERY
(BLACKSMITH —) SMITHY
(BUTCHER —) CHARCUTERIE
(DRINKING —) BOUSINGKEN
(DRUGGIST'S —) PHARMACY
(HERB —) BOTANICA
(KIND OF —) HEAD
(LIQUOR —) SALOON
(OLD CLOTHES —) FLIPPERY
(PASTRY —) PATISSERIE
(PAWNBROKER'S —) LUMBER
SPROUT
(REPAIR —) GARAGE
(SUTLER'S —) CANTEEN
(WINE —) BODEGA CANTINA
SHOPKEEPER CIT ARAB BAKAL
BANIAN CHETTY SOUDAGUR
SHOPLIFT BOOST
SHOPLIFTER BOOSTER
SHORE GIB TOM BANK RIPE RIVE
SAND SIDE TRIG BEACH BENCH CLIFF
COAST MARGE RAKER RANCE
SHOAR WARTH RIVAGE STRAND
SEASIDE BUTTRESS DOCKSIDE
LANDFALL LANDSIDE SEACOAST
SHOREBIRD AVOCET TATTLER
WRYBILL SURFBIRD PHALAROPE
SANDPIPER
SHORE CRAB OCHIDORE
SHOREFISH OPALEYE
SHORER BRACER CRIBBER
SHORN NOT NOTT POLLED
TONSURED
SHORT AIM LAG LOW SHY BAIN
CURT NEAR NIGH SOON BLUFF BRIEF
BUNTY CLOSE CRISP CUTTY FUBBY
FUBSY PUNCH SQUAB UNDER
ABRUPT CRISPY SCANTY SCARCE
STUGGY STUNTY SUDDEN ULLAGE
BOBTAIL BRUSQUE CURTATE
LACONIC SQUIDGY STUBBED
SUMMARY SNAPPISH SUCCINCT
(— AND FLAT) CAMUS
(— AND THICK) CHUNKY STOCKY
STUBBY STUMPY TRUNCH
TRUNCHED
(— AND THICKSET) NUGGETY
(— AS OF WOOL) FRIBBY

(— IN PAYMENT) SHY
(— OF MONEY) HARDUP PUSHED
IMPECUNIOUS
(— PERSON OR ANIMAL) PUNCH
(BRIEF —S) MONOKINI
(STOUT AND —) BUNTY CHUFFY
PLUGGY THICKSET
(PL.) BERMUDAS
(PREF.) BRACHI(O) BRACHY BREVI
(SUFF.) BRACH(ISTO)(Y)
SHORTAGE WANT CRUNCH FAMINE
DROUGHT WANTAGE UNDERAGE
SHORT-BREATHED PURSY
SHORTCHANGE FLUFF SHORT
SHORTCOMING SIN FLAW DEBIT
FAULT DEFECT FOIBLE DRAWBACK
SHORT-COUPLED CHUFFY
SHORTCUT CUTOFF
SHORT-EARED OWL MOMO
SHORTEN CUT CLIP STAG ELIDE
SLASH REDUCE ABRIDGE CURTAIL
EXCERPT SCANTLE CONTRACT
DIMINISH RETRENCH ABBREVIATE
(— AND THICKEN IRON) JUMP
(— A SAIL) REEF
(— GRIP) CHOKE
SHORTENED CURTED BOBTAIL
CURTATE ABRIDGED
SHORTENING LARD
(— IN PRONUNCIATION)
CORRECTION
(— OF SYLLABLE) SYSTOLE
(— OF WORD) APOCOPE
SHORTEST LEAST
SHORTFALL NEED
SHORTHORN DURHAM
TEESWATER
SHORT-LIVED FRAGILE
SHORTLY SOON INABIT DUMPILY
DIRECTLY PRESENTLY
SHORT-NAPPED RAS
SHORTNESS BREVITY CURTNESS
UNLENGTH
(— OF BREATH) ANHELATION
(— OF SIGHT) MYOPIA
(— OF SOUND) QUANTITY
SHORT-RANGE TACTICAL
SHORT-SIGHTED SANDED
PURBLIND
SHORTSIGHTEDNESS MYOPIA
SHORT-TEMPERED CROTCHETY
CROTCHETED CRUSTY SNIPPY
SNUFFY
SHORT-TERM FLOATING
SHORT-WINDED PURSY PURFLY
PURFLED PURSIVE
SHOSHONEAN UTE
SHOT POP SET BLUE CASE JOLT
OVER PLUG SETT SLUG BLANK FLIER
FLING FLUFF FLYER OUTER PLUFF
SHOOT TOWEL WHITE CARTON
CENTER CENTRE FOLLOW MUDCAP
REBOTE ALIIPOE BOMBARD

CUTAWAY DEADEYE GUNSHOT
LANGREL PELICAN SIGHTER
BLIZZARD BUCKSHOT HAILSHOT
LANGRAGE MARKSHOT SCORCHER
(— BEYOND TARGET) OVER
(— FOR CULVERIN) PELICAN
(— IN FIFTH CIRCLE) WHITE
(— IN FOURTH CIRCLE) BLACK
(— IN THIRD CIRCLE) BLUE
(— OF NARCOTIC) FIX
(— STRIKING BULL'S-EYE) CARTON
(— THAT HITS) CLOUT
(ARCHERY —) GREEN
(BADMINTON —) CLEAR
(BASKETBALL —) BOMB JUMPER
(BIG —) VIP
(BILLIARD —) DRAG STAB CAROM
MASSE SCREW FOLLOW SAFETY
SPREAD BRICOLE SCRATCH
(BOW —) DRAFT
(CAMERA —) PAN INTERCUT
(CROQUET —) SPLIT FOLLOW
(CURLING —) INWICK OUTWICK
(DROP —) DINK
(DUNK —) STUFF
(EASY —) SITTER
(FAULTY —) MISTAKE
(FINAL —) UPSHOT
(FREE —) CORNER MULLIGAN
(GOOD —) SCREAMER
(HIGH —) CHIP
(KIND OF —) MUG
(KIND OF BILLIARD —) BANK CAROM
(PISTOL —) BARK
(POOL —) BREAK
(SHORT —) HYPO
(SIZE OF —) F T BB FF TT BBB DUST
BUCKSHOT
(SMALL —) PELLET MITRAILLE
(SNOOKER —) POT
(TENNIS —) ACE LOB DINK SERVE
SMASH
(VOLLEY OF —S) BLIZZARD
SHOTGUN DOUBLE TUPARA
PEPPERER SCATTERSHOT
SHOULD MOW SUD WANT OUGHT
(— NOT) SHUDNA SHOULDNA
SHOULDNT
SHOULDER DOD AXLE CLOD DODD
GAIN HUMP SHIP STEP SULD BOUGH
PITCH SPALL SPULE VERGE AXILLA
EPAULE RELISH SCOTCH SPAULD
KNUCKLE RIMBASE SHOUTHER
(— AROUND TENON) RELISH
(— OF BOLT) NAB
(— OF FIREARM STOCK) RIMBASE
(— OF FLY) CHEEK
(— OF LAMB) BANJO
(— OF PORK) HAND PICNIC
CUSHION
(— OF RABBIT OR HARE) WING
(— OF ROAD) BERM BERME HAUNCH
QUARTER

(— PAIN) OMODYNIA
(BEVELED —) GAIN
(PL.) FOREBOWS
(PREF.) OM(O)

SHOULDER BLADE SPALD SPEAL
SCAPULA OMOPLATE
(PREF.) SCAPUL(I)(O)

SHOUT BAY BOO CRY HOY HUE
BAWL CALL CROW GAPE HAIL HOCH
HOOP HOOT REME ROOT ROUP ROUT
SCRY TOOT YELL BRAWL CHEER
CLAIM CLEPE CRACK GREDE HALLO
HAVOC HOLLO HUZZA REERE
WHEWT WHOOP ABRAID BOOHOO
CLAMOR GOLLAR GOLLER HALLOO
HOLLER HURRAH HUZZAH STEVEN
YAMMER ACCLAIM SHILLOO
GARDYLOO LULLILOO SCRONACH
(— AS CHILDREN) BELDER
(— DERISIVELY) BARRACK
(— FOR OR AGAINST) BARRACK
(— OF APPROVAL) BRAVO
(— OF ENCOURAGEMENT) HARK
(— OF HIGHLAND DANCER) HOOCH
(— OF JOY) IO
(HIGHLAND DANCER'S —) HOOCH
(HUNTING —) CHEVY
(SEAMAN'S —) AHOY

SHOUTING HUE GLAM ROUP ROUT
HOLLO CLAMOR HOLLOA JUBILEE

SHOVE JUT PUT BUNT DUSH FEND
MUCK PICK POTE PUSH SHOG SHUN
BOOST CROWD DUNCH ELBOW
HUNCH SHIVE SHUNT HUSTLE
JOSTLE JUSTLE MUSCLE THRUST
SCAMBLE
(— CARELESSLY) BUNG
(— IN MARBLES) FULK

SHOVEL FAN VAN CAST PEEL SPUD
SCOOP SHOOL SPADE SPOON
BLUNGER SCOPPET SCUPPIT
SLUDGER DUCKBILL DUCKFOOT
STROCKLE
(— FOR COIN) MAIN
(— FOR DRESSING ORE) VAN
(BAKER'S —) PEEL
(BANKER'S —) MAIN
(BRICKMAKING —) CUCKHOLD
(CASTING —) SCUTTLE
(CHARCOAL BURNER'S —) RABBLE
(FIRE —) PEEL SLICE
(GRATED —) HARP
(MINER'S —) BANJO
(PERFORATED —) SKIMMER

SHOVELER SCOOPER WHINGER
BLUEWING SHOULERD WHINYARD

SHOW DO SAY SEE WIS BOSH CALL
DASH HAVE ITEM LEAD MARK MIEN
SCAW SEEM SHEW TENT VIEW WEAR
WISE ARGUE ASSAY EXERT FLASH
GLOSS GLOZE KITHE PRIDE PROVE
SHINE SIGHT SLANG SPORT TEACH
ACCUSE ASSIGN BETRAY BLAZON

CHICHI COUTHE DENOTE DETECT
DEVICE DIRECT ENSIGN ESCORT
EVINCE EXPOSE FIGURE FLAUNT
GAIETY GAYETY LAYOUT MUSTER
OBJECT PARADE REVEAL SCHEME
SPREAD SPRUNK VANITY ADVANCE
ANALYZE BALLOON BESPEAK
BETOKEN BRAVURA BREATHE
DECLARE DISPLAY DIVULGE EXHIBIT
EXPRESS FASHION MONSTER
PRESAGE PRODUCE PROPOSE
SELLOUT SHOWING SIGNIFY
TAMASHA TRIUMPH COLORING
CONCLUDE EVIDENCE FLOURISH
FORESHOW INDICATE MANIFEST
PRETENCE PROCLAIM SEMBLANT
SIDESHOW
(— APPROVAL) CLAP APPLAUD
(— BRIEFLY) FLASH
(— CONTEMPT) SCOFF
(— DISCONTENT) GROUCH
(— DISPLEASURE) POUT
(— DOGS) BENCH
(— ENTHUSIASM) DROOL
(— FORTH) BLAZE CIPHER
(— IN PUBLIC CELEBRATION)
PAGEANT
(— ITSELF) APPEAR
(— MERCY) SPARE
(— OFF) FLASH PRANK SPORT
SWANK HOTDOG PARADE SWAGGER
SHOWBOAT
(— OF INDIA) TAMASHA
(— OF LEARNING) SCIOLISM
(— OF LIGHT) BLINK
(— OF REASON) COLOR
(— OF VANITY) AIR
(— ONESELF) BE
(— POSITION OF) MEITH
(— PROMISE) FRAME SHAPE
(— RESPECT FOR) REGARD
(— REVERSE TREND) REACT
(— SIGNS OF GIVING WAY) WAVER
(— SIGNS OF ILLNESS) GRUDGE
(— SPIRIT) SPUNK
(— THE BOTTOM) KEEL
(— THE SIGHTS) LIONIZE
(— THE TEETH) GIRN GRIN
(— THE WAY) LEAD CONDUCT
(— TO BE FALSE) BELIE DISPROVE
(— UNKINDNESS) WAIT
(— WITHOUT SUBSTANCE) FORM
(ARTFUL —) GRIMACE
(CALL-IN RADIO —) PHONEIN
(CINEMA —) FILM MOVIES PICTURES
(DAZZLING —) RAZZLEDAZZLE
(DUMB —) PANTOMINE
(EXTERNAL —) GLOSS
(FALSE —) COLOR FUCUS BUBBLE
TINSEL ILLUSION PRETENCE
(FLEETING —) PAGEANTRY
(FLOOR —) CABARET
(GAUDY —) HOOPLA BRAVERY

(KIND OF —) TRUNK
(MERE —) PHANTOM
(MOMENTARY —) FLASH
(ORNATE —) FLUBDUB
(OSTENTATIOUS —) SPRUNK
DISPLAY
(OUTSIDE —) VARNISH
(OUTWARD —) FUCUS VISAGE
(PUBLIC —) EXPO
(PUPPET —) DROLL MOTION
WAJANG WAYANG GUIGNOL
(RIDICULOUS —) FARCE
(RUDIMENTARY —) SATURA
(RUN THE —) EMCEE
(SPECIOUS —) GLOZE VARNISH
(STREET —) RAREE
(SUPERFICIAL —) GLOSS VENEER
(TELEVISION —) PILOT
(TRAVELLING —) SLANG
(PREF.) PHAENO PHANER(O) PHANTA
PHANTO PHENO
(SUFF.) PHANY
SHOW BOAT (AUTHOR OF —)
FERBER
(CHARACTER IN —) KIM ANDY ELLY
HAWKS JULIE PARTHY GAYLORD
RAVENAL MAGNOLIA SCHULTZY
SHOWCASE ISLAND VITRINE
SHOWER WET HAIL RAIN SCAT
SUMP AUGER BATHE BLASH SKITE
SOUSE FLURRY PELTER PEPPER
SHEWER DRIBBLE SHATTER
WEATHER COMMORTH SCOUTHER
(CONCENTRATED —) BARRAGE
(HEAVY —) SUMP
(RAIN —) RASH
(SUDDEN —) SCUD SKIT BRASH
PLUMP
SHOWERY BRASHY CLASHY SCATTY
SHOWILY GAILY BRAVELY GAUDILY
SHOWINESS DASH GLARE GLITZ
PAZAZZ PIZAZZ GLITTER PIZZAZZ
FLOURISH GEWGAWRY SPLENDOR
SHOWING SPRANK SPARKLE
(— OFF) EXHIBITION
(— SAME NATURE) AKIN
(— THROUGH THE SKIN) RAW
(ADVANCE —) PREVIEW
(PUBLIC —) EXPO
(SUPERFICIAL —) FACE
(PREF.) PHAEN(O) PHAINO
SHOWMAN IMPRESARIO
SHOWMANSHIP RECLAME
SHOW-ME STATE MISSOURI
SHOW-OFF HAM HOTDOG CUTUP
SHOWY GAY FINE LOUD NICE RORY
VAIN DASHY FLARY FLASH FRESH
GAUDY GIDDY GRAND JAZZY NOBBY
SPICY SWANK TOPPY VAUDY VIEWY
BRANKY BRAZEN BRUMMY CHICHI
DRESSY FLASHY FLOSSY GARISH
GEWGAW GLOSSY JAUNTY PURPLE
SHANTY SKYRIN SPANKY SPORTY

TAWDRY DASHING FLAUNTY
GALLANT GAUDFUL HOTSHOT
POMPOUS SHOWFUL SHOWISH
SPLASHY SPLURGY CLAPTRAP
FASTUOUS GIMCRACK GORGEOUS
ORGULOUS SPARKISH SPECIOUS
SPLENDID TRUMPERY CLINQUANT
OBTRUSIVE
(NOT —) CIVIL LENTEN DISCREET
SHOYU SOY
SHRED DAG HOG JAG RAG ROND
ROON SNIP TEAR WISP BLYPE CLOUT
GRATE PATCH SHRAG SHRIP CULPON
SCREED SLIVER TARGET FRAZZLE
FRITTER MAMMOCK SHATTER
FILAMENT
(— FISH) SCROD
(— OF CLOTHES) TACK
(— OF FLESH) TAG AGNAIL
(— OF HAIR) TAIT
(PL.) TAVERS CADDICE TAIVERS
SHREDDED CUT
SHREDDER DEVIL
SHREW ERD JES NAG TANA PRESS
RANNY SOREX VIXEN CALLET
JUMPER MIGALE TARGER TARTAR
TUPAIA VIRAGO BLARINA HELLCAT
MUSKRAT PENTAIL SCYTALE TUPAIID
SINSRING SORICINE SORICOID
UROPSILE XANTHIPPE
(TREE —) BANXRING
(PREF.) HYDRAC(O) SORICI
SHREWD DRY SLY ACID ARCH CUTE
FELL GASH SAGE TIDY WARE WISE
ACUTE CAGEY CANNY HEADY LOOPY
PAWKY POKEY SHARP SMART
SWACK ARGUTE ARTFUL ASTUTE
CALLID CLEVER CRAFTY SPRACK
SUBTLE CUNNING GNOSTIC
KNOWING PARLISH PARLOUS
POLITIC PRACTIC SAPIENT
SAGACIOUS PERSPICACIOUS
(— PERSON) FILE
SHREWDLY SLILY CANNILY
ASTUTELY
SHREWDNESS NOUS SAVVY
ACUMEN POLICY SLYNESS
GUMPTION PRUDENCE SAGACITY
CALLIDITY
SHREWISH CURST CURSED SHREWD
VIXENISH
SHREWMOUSE MYGALE SCYTALE
SHRIEK CRY YIP YARM YELL CHIRK
SKIRL SCREAM SCRIKE SHRIKE
SKRIKE SPRAICH
SHRIKE POPE BATARA BOUBOU
BRUBRU FISCAL FLASHER FLUSHER
LOGHEAD MIGRANT MINIVET
TRILLER BELLBIRD FALCONET
PUFFBACK WOODCHAT
SHRILL HIGH KEEN THIN ACUTE PIPEY
SHARP SHILL SHIRL ARGUTE BRASSY
GLASSY PIPING SQUEAK TREBLE

HAUTAIN MINIKIN SCREAKY
PIERCING STRIDENT
(MAKE — NOISE) POTRACK
(PREF.) OXY
SHRIMP GRIT RUNT APANG CARID
MYSID PARVA PRAWN NIPPER
PANDLE SCAMPI ARTEMIA BROWNIE
CAMARON DECAPOD POLYPOD
REDTAIL SPECTER SPECTRE
CARIDEAN CRAWFISH CREVETTE
MACRURAN
(KIND OF —) TIGER
(SUFF.) CARIS
SHRINE ADYT NAOS GUACA HUACA
ISEUM MAZAR SEKOS STUPA ZIARA
ADYTON ADYTUM CHASSE DAGABA
DAGOBA DURGAH HALLOW HIERON
MEMORY SAMADH VIMANA ZIARAT
CHAITYA CHAPLET CHORTEN
EDICULE FANACLE MARTYRY
MEMORIA SACRARY TEMENOS
THESEUM AEDICULA DELUBRUM
FERETORY FERETRUM GURDWARA
LARARIUM MARABOUT PANTHEON
VALHALLA RELIQUARY
(— FOR MEDITATION) ZENDO
(— STUDY) NAOLOGY
(PREF.) PASTO
SHRINK COY SHY DARE DUCK FULL
FUNK GIVE NIRL PEAK ABHOR ARGHE
CLING COWER CRINE QUAIL RELAX
RIVEL SHRAM SHRUG SHUCK START
WINCE BLANCH BLENCH BOGGLE
COTTER CRINGE FLINCH LESSEN
RECOIL SCRUMP SETTLE SHRIMP
WEAZEN ANALYST CRIMPLE
CRUMPLE DWINDLE SCUNNER
SHRIVEL COLLAPSE CONTRACT
(— FROM DRYNESS) GIZZEN
SHRINKAGE LOSS SETTLE SHRINK
SINKAGE
(— OF TYPE) SQUEEZE
SHRINKING COY SHY TIMID BLETHE
CREEPS DASTARD FULLING
LOATHFUL TIMOROUS
(— FROM REFERENCE TO SELF)
AUTOPHOBY
SHRIVE SHRIFT CONFESS SHRIEVE
SHRIVEL NIRL SEAR WELK BLAST
CLING CRINE PARCH RIVEL SHRAM
SNERP WIZEN BLIGHT COTTER
GIZZEN SCORCH SCRUMP SHRINK
WEAZEN WITHER CROZZLE
SHRIVELED WEDE CLUNG CORKY
THIRL GIZZEN STARKY PUNGLED
SHIRPIT WIZENED WRITHEN
SHRAMMED WRIZZLED
SHROPSHIRE SALOP
SHROUD HIDE PALL SARK CLOAK
CRAPE DRAPE HABIT SHEET SWIFT
EMBOSK HEARSE KITTEL MUFFLE
SCREEN SHADOW SINDON SUDARY

BENIGHT CONCEAL CURTAIN
INVOLVE SWIFTER CEREMENT
(PL.) PUTTOCK
SHROVETIDE SHROVE GUTTIDE
CARNIVAL
SHROVE TUESDAY FASTENS
GUTTIDE
SHRUB TI BAY HAW KAT MAY QAT
TOD AKIA ALEM BUSH COCA HOYA
INGA ITEA KARO KEUR KHAT MUSK
ULEX AKALA AKELA ALDER ALISO
ARUSA BOCCA BROOM BUAZE CEIBO
CUMAY ELDER GOOMA GORSE
GOUMI HAZEL HENNA IXORA LEDUM
LEMON LILAC MAQUI MARIA MUDAR
RETEM SALAL SHROG SUMAC
THUJA TOYON ZILLA ABELIA AGRITO
AKONGE AMULLA ANAGUA ANILAO
ARALIA ARUSHA AUCUBA AUPAKA
AZALEA BLOLLY CENIZO CHEKAN
CHERRY CISTUS CORREA DAPHNE
DHAURI DRIMYS FEIJOA FRUTEX
JACATE JOJOBA KARAMU KOWHAI
LABRUM LARREA LAUREL MATICO
MYRTLE NARRAS PENAEA PITURI
RAETAM SAVINE STORAX STYRAX
ACEROLA AFERNAN AGARITA
AMORPHA ARBORET ARRAYAN
ARRIMBY AZAROLE BANKSIA
BORONIA BUCKEYE BULLACE
CANTUTA CHACATE CHAMISE
CHANCHE DEUTZIA EHRETIA ENCELIA
EPACRID EPHEDRA FUCHSIA
GUMWOOD GUTWORT HOPBUSH
HOPSAGE JASMINE JETBEAD
JEWBUSH JOEWOOD KUMQUAT
LANTANA MAHONIA NUNNARI
PAVONIA PEABUSH PEARHAW
PIMELEA RHODORA SPIRAEA
TARBUSH THEEZAN ABELMOSK
ALLTHORN BARBERRY CAMELLIA
CARAGANA COMEBACK COPALCHE
DRACAENA GOATBUSH GOWIDDIE
GRAVILEA HARDHACK HARDTACK
HAWTHORN HIBISCUS IRONWOOD
KEURBOOM KOROMIKO MOORWORT
NINEBARK OCOTILLO OLEASTER
OSOBERRY PIPEWOOD PONDBUSH
ROSEBUSH ROSEMARY SANDSTAY
SANDWOOD SASANQUA SHRUBLET
SNOWBALL SNOWBELL SNOWBUSH
SOAPBARK STANDARD MISTLETOE
POINCIANA PHILADELPHUS
(AROMATIC —) THYME CLUSIA
BORONIA HOGBUSH ALLSPICE
(AUSTRALIAN —) GOOMA BUDDAH
DRIMYS GEEBUNG WARATAH
MILKBUSH SANDSTAY
(CHINESE —) KERRIA
(CLIMBING —) CATCLAWS
SOLANDRA
(DESERT —) AFERNAN

(EVERGREEN —) BOX BAGO ILEX TITI BOLDO ERICA FURZE HEATH HOLLY KOSAM PYXIE SALAL SAVIN TOYON BAUERA DAHOON KALMIA LAUREL PEPINO PROTEA RUSCUS SAKAKI ARDISIA BARETTA JASMINE JUNIPER MADRONA MAHONIA CALFKILL CARAUNDA EVONYMUS OLEANDER SASANQUA MANZANITA
(FRAGRANT —) JASMINE HUISACHE MEJORANA MEZEREON ROSEMARY
(HAWAIIAN —) AKALA AKELA ILIMA KOKIO OLONA
(LOW —) AYAPANA
(MEXICAN —) BLUEBUSH
(NEW ZEALAND —) KARO KAWA TUTU KARAMU KIEKIE KAWAKAWA KOROMIKO
(PASTURE —) COWBERRY
(PHILIPPINE —) IPILIPIL
(POISONOUS —) GIF CUBE LITHI SUMAC GIFBLAAR LABURNUM
(PRICKLY —) CAPER COLIMA BRAMBLE CATCLAWS
(SPINY —) ULEX AROMA GORSE JUNCO ESPINO BUMELIA CARISSA CYTISUS GENISTA GOATBUSH GRANJENO GUAJILLO HUAJILLO
(STRONG-SMELLING —) SALTWORT
(STUNTED —) SCRAB SCROG SCRUB
(THORNY —) CHANAR HAWTHORN
(TREELIKE —) ARBUSCLE
(TROPICAL —) INGA MAJO HENNA CAMARA DERRIS MOMBIN OLACAD PERSEA HAMELIA JEWBUSH LANTANA SOAPBARK
(WEST INDIAN —) ANIL RATWOOD MILKWOOD
(XEROPHYTIC —) SAXAUL
(PREF.) THAMN(O)
SHRUBBERY MOGOTE ARBORET
SHRUG SHUG HURKLE SHRINK
SHRUNK WEARISH
SHRUNKEN LANK CLUNG PUNGLED SLUNKEN WIZENED CONTRACT
(— HEAD) TSANTSA
SHTICK ACT BIT GAG GIMMICK ROUTINE
SHUAH (FATHER OF —) ABRAHAM
(MOTHER OF —) KETURAH
SHUAL (FATHER OF —) ZOPHAH
SHUBAEL (FATHER OF —) HEMAN GERSHON
SHUCK HULL HUSK SHACK SHELL SHOCK
SHUCKS DARN DRAT NUTS RATS PSHAW PHOOEY
SHUDDER GRUE CREEP GRISE HIRCH QUAKE SHRUG AGRISE GROOSE HIRTCH HOTTER HURKLE SHIVER FRISSON TREMBLE
SHUDDERING RIGOR

SHUFFLE JANK MAKE MILK SLUR MOSEY SCUFF SHALE SHIFT SHOOL JUGGLE RIFFLE RUFFLE SCLAFF SHOVEL DRAGGLE QUIBBLE SHACKLE SHAFFLE SHAMBLE SLIPPER SLUTHER
(— CARDS DISHONESTLY) PACK STACK
(— DISHONESTLY) PACK
SHUHAM (FATHER OF —) DAN
SHUN FIN SHY BALK FLEE TABU VOID WARE ABHOR AVOID EVADE EVITE SHUNT TABOO ASTART DEVOID ESCAPE ESCHEW REFUSE SHRINK DECLINE FORBEAR FORSAKE
SHUNI (FATHER OF —) GAD
SHUNT AYRTON BRIDGE BYPASS SWITCH
SHUSH HUSH WHISH SUPPRESS
SHUSWAP ATNAH
SHUT FAST HASP MAKE SEAL SHOT SLAM SLOT SPAR TAKE TEEN TINE CLOSE LATCH STEEK STICK CLOSED CABINET OCCLUSE UPCLOSE
(— DOWN) SCRAM
(— EYES) WINK
(— IN) BAR LAP CAGE COPSE EMBAR EMBAY FORBAR PENTIT TACKLE BELOUKE ENCLAVE
(— OFF) SCREEN SECLUDE SEPARATE
(— OUT) BAR DEBAR REPEL SKUNK HINDER DEPRIVE EXCLUDE OCCLUDE OUTSHUT PRECLUDE
(— SUDDENLY) SNAP
(— TOGETHER) CLASP
(— UP) BAR CUB MEW PENT STOP CHOKE FRANK STIVE STOVE CLOSET EMBOSS ENJAIL IMMURE IMPARK CONDEMN CONFINE DUNGEON ENCLOSE IMPOUND INCLUDE OCCLUDE OPPRESS PARROCK RECLUSE SECLUDE CONCLUDE PRECLUDE
(HALF —) PINK
(PREF.) OCCLUSO
SHUTDOWN LAYOFF
(— OF REACTOR) SCRAM
SHUT-EYE NAP SLEEP
SHUTOUT SKUNK
SHUTTER LID DROP SHUT BLIND SHADE CUTOFF DAMPER DOUSER SLUICE AUTOMAT BUCKLER SHUTTLE JALOUSIE
(— IN ORGAN) SHADE
(— OF TRIPTYCH) VOLET
SHUTTERBUG SNAPPER
SHUTTING CLAUDENT
SHUTTLE FLY FLUTE SHUNT BROCHE LOOPER SWIVEL SHITTLE
SHUTTLECOCK BIRD PETECA VOLANT

SHVANDA THE BAGPIPER
  (CHARACTER IN —) DEVIL BABINSKY
  ICEHEART SCHVANDA
  (COMPOSER OF —) WEINBERGER
SHY COY JIB MIM SCAR SHAN SHUN
  SKIT UNKO WILD BLATE CAGEY
  CHARY DEMUR FLING PAVID SCARE
  SHUNT SQUAB TIMID UNCOW
  BOGGLE BOOGER DEMURE MODEST
  SHANNY SKIEGH TARTLE BASHFUL
  GAWKISH RABBITY STRANGE
  TREMBLY UPSTAGE BACKWARD
  COCKSHOT DAPHNEAN FAROUCHE
  RETIRING SHEEPISH SKITTISH
  SWAIMOUS VERECUND WILLYARD
SHYLOCK (DAUGHTER OF —)
  JESSICA
SHYNESS COYNESS MODESTY
  RESERVE TIMIDITY
SHYSTER PETTIFOGGER
SIALAGOGUE SALIVANT
SIAM (SEE THAILAND)
SIAMANG APE UNGKA GIBBON
SIB SEPT AYLLU SIBLING SIBSHIP
  CALPULLI
SIBERIA (GULF IN —) OB
  (MOUNTAIN RANGE IN —) URAL
  ALTAI
  (NATIVE IN —) YAKU SAGAI TATAR
  KIRGIZ TARTAR KIRGHIZ YUKAGIR
  (RIVER IN —) OB ILI KET PUR TAZ TYM
  AMGA AMUR LENA MAYA ONON
  UCUR ALDAN ISHIM NADYM SOBOL
  TOBOL ANGARA IRTYSH OLEKMA
  VILYUY
  (TOWN IN —) OMSK CHITA KYZYL
  TOMSK IGARKA KURGAN BARNAUL
  IRKUTSK LENINSK YAKUTSK
SIBERIAN SQUILL SCILLA
SIBILANT HISS
SIBLING TWIN SISTER BROTHER
SIBYL SYBIL SIBYLLA VOLUSPA
  AMALTHEA
SIC SOOL
SICILIAN
  (PREF.) SICULO
SICILIAN VESPERS, THE
  (CHARACTER IN —) ELENA ARRIGO
  MONTFORT FREDERICK
  (COMPOSER OF —) VERDI

SICILY
CAPE: BOEO FARO PASSARO
CAPITAL: PALERMO
CATHEDRAL: MONREALE
COIN: LITRA UNCIA
GULF: NOTO CATANIA
ISLAND: EGADI LIPARI USTICA
MEASURE: SALMA CAFFISO
MOUNTAIN: EREI ETNA MORO SORI
  IBREI NEBRODI
NATIVE: ELYMI SICEL SICANI SICULI
OLD NAME: TRINACRIA TRIQUETRA

PROVINCE: ENNA RAGUSA CATANIA
  MESSINA PALERMO TRAPANI
  SIRACUSA
RIVER: SALSO TORTO BELICE SIMETO
  PLATANI
SEAPORT: ACI CATANIA MARSALA
  MESSINA PALERMO TRAPANI
TOWN: ENNA NOTO RAGUSA CATANIA
  MARSALA MESSINA TRAPANI
  SYRACUSE
VOLCANO: ETNA AETNA

SICK BAD ILL BADLY CRONK CROOK
  MORBID MAWKISH SEASICK
  UNWHOLE CROPSICK MALADIVE
  PHYSICAL STREAKED
SICKEN TIRE TURN WEARY SUNDER
  SUNNER WEAKEN DISGUST
  SCUNNER SURFEIT NAUSEATE
SICKENING FELL SICKLY FULSOME
  MAWKISH SICKISH NAUSEOUS
  VOMITOUS
SICKISH DAUNCY
SICKLE HOOK CROOK
  (PREF.) DREPANI FALCI ZANCIO
SICKLY WAN FLUE FOND PALE PUKY
  SICK DAWNY DONCY FAINT GREEN
  PEAKY SILLY TEWLY WEARY WERSH
  WISHT AMPERY ANEMIC CLAMMY
  CRANKY FEEBLE INFIRM PUKISH
  PULING WANKLY WEAKLY INVALID
  LANGUID MAWKISH PEAKING
  PEAKISH PIMPING QUEECHY SHILPIT
  SICKISH WEARISH WEERISH
  DELICATE DISEASED MALADIVE
  PINDLING
SICKLY-LOOKING SHILPIT
SICKNESS (ALSO SEE DISEASE) MAL
  SICK SORE TAKING AILMENT
  DISEASE ILLNESS MALAISE SURFEIT
  DISORDER
  (INTESTINAL —) TURISTA
  (MILK —) SLOWS TIRES
  (MOTION —) KINETOSIS
  (MOUNTAIN —) PUNA SOROCHE
  (SUDDEN —) DWALM
SIDA ILIMA ESCOBA
SIDE CAMP COST EDGE FACE HALF
  HAND KANT LEAF PANE PART BOARD
  CHEEK FLANK LATUS PARTY PHASE
  SITHE BEHALF PTERON ENGLISH
  PENDANT FORESIDE SIDELONG
  (— BY SIDE) ACCOLE ABREAST
  ACCOSTED PARALLEL
  (— OF ATTIC) SKEELING SKILLING
  SKILLION
  (— OF BIRD'S HEAD) LORE
  (— OF BOOM JAW) HORN
  (— OF BOW) BELLY
  (— OF BUILDING) WALL
  (— OF CAVITY) WALL
  (— OF DECK) GANGWAY
  (— OF DITCH) SCARP

(— OF DIVIDERS) LEG
(— OF FACE) CHEEK
(— OF GATE) FOLD
(— OF GEM) BEZEL
(— OF HEAD) HAFFET
(— OF HEARTH) BREAST
(— OF HILL) BRAE SCUG SLOPE
(— OF HOG) FLITCH
(— OF HORSESHOE) BRANCH
(— OF LACE) FOOTING
(— OF LAMB) CONCERTINA
(— OF LOG) RIDE
(— OF NAVE) AISLE
(— OF OPENING) JAW JAMB
(— OF PIG) BACON
(— OF QUADRANGLE) PANE
(— OF RABBET) LEDGE
(— OF RACECOURSE) STRETCH
(— OF RECTANGLE) SQUARE
(— OF ROOF) CATSLIDE
(— OF SHIP) BEAM WALE BOARD
BULWARK LARBOARD SEABOARD
(— OF STAGE) WING
(— OF TENNIS RACKET) ROUGH
SMOOTH
(— OF THEATER GALLERY) SLIP
(— OF TRIANGLE) LEG
(— OF TYPE) BEARD
(— OF VALLEY) COTEAU
(— OF VIOLIN) RIB
(— OF WAGON) RAVE
(— PIECE) RAVE
(— SHELTERED FROM WIND) LEE LEW
LEEWARD
(—S OF FIREPLACE) COVING
(—S OF GALLERY) SLIPS
(— WITH) SUFFRAGE
(BACK —) REAR BEHIND BACKSIDE
(BY THE —) ALONG
(DRESSED —) FACE
(FAR —) OFFSIDE
(FLAT —) PANE
(FOR EACH —) ALI
(LEFT —) PORT
(MOUNTAIN —) PUNA VETA
SOROCHE
(OUTER — OF SKIN) GRAIN
(RIGHT —) FACE
(RIGHT — OF SWORD) INSIDE
(UNDERNEATH —) BOTTOM
(WINDWARD —) AWEATHER
(PREF.) LATER(I)(O) PLEUR(I)(O)
(— BY —) PAR(A)
(— PARTS) ALI
(BY THE — OF) JUXTA
(ON THIS —) CIS CITRA
(SUFF.) PLEURA PLEUROUS
STICH(OUS)
SIDEBAR HOUND
SIDEBOARD ABACUS BUFFET
SERVER COMMODE DRESSER
CELLARET CREDENCE CREDENZA
SIDE-BY-SIDE ACCOLLE

SIDED
(SUFF.) MER
SIDE DISH OUTWORK
SIDEKICK CRONY
SIDEPIECE BAR BOW JAMB WING
CHEEK GUSSET EARPIECE LANDSIDE
SIDES
(PREF.)
(ON ALL —) CIRCUM
SIDESLIP SKID DRIFT DRILL
SIDESMAN HOGGLER QUESTMAN
SIDESPLITTER RIOT
SIDESTEP BEG AVOID DODGE
SIDETRACK SHUNT
SIDEWALK WALKWAY PAVEMENT
TROTTOIR BANQUETTE
SIDEWAYS ASKANT ASKANCE
EDGEWAYS EDGEWISE SIDELONG
SIDEWISE ASIDE ASIDEN
SIDING CURB SPUR GARAGE
SIDLE EDGE SLIVE PASSAGE
SAUNTER
SIDRA PARASHAH
SIEGE BOUT SEDGE ASSIEGE
JOURNEY LEAGUER
(— ENGINE) WARWOLF
SIEGFRIED (CHARACTER IN —) MIME
WOTAN FAFNER SIEGFRIED
BRUNNHILDE
(COMPOSER OF —) WAGNER
(SLAYER OF —) BRUNHILD
(WIFE OF —) KRIEMHILD
SIERRA CERO SERRA SAWBACK
KINGFISH

SIERRA LEONE
CAPITAL: FREETOWN
COIN: LEONE
LANGUAGE: KRIO MENDE TEMNE
MEASURE: LOAD KETTLE
MOUNTAIN: LOMA
NATIVE: VAI KONO LOKO SUSU KISSI
LIMBA MENDE TEMNE FULANI
GALLINA SHERBRO MANDINGO
RIVER: MOA JONG SEWA MUNGO
ROKEL ROKKEL SCARCY WAANJE
SEAPORT: HEPEL BONTHE SULIMA
TOWN: BO DARU MANO KISSI LUNGI
KENEMA MAKENI

SIESTA NAP MERIDIAN
SIEVA BEAN
SIEVE FRY TRY BOLT BUNT DRUM
HARP LAWN PREE SCRY SHOE SIFT
SILE SIZE TEMS GRATE RANGE
SCALP TAMIS TAMMY TEMSE
BOLTER RANGER RIDDER RIDDLE
SEARCE SEARCH SEMMET SIFTER
WEIGHT BOULTEL CHAFFER CRIBBLE
DILLUER PRICKLE TIFFANY TROMMEL
COLANDER SEARCHER STRAINER
(— FOR MILK) MILSEY
(PREF.) COSCINO CRIBRI ETHMO

SIF (HUSBAND OF —) THOR
SIFT REE TRY BOLT DUST SCRY
RANGE SCALP SIEVE TEMSE DREDGE
GARBLE RIDDER RIDDLE SCREEN
SEARCE WINNOW CANVASS CRIBBLE
DRIBBLE SIFTAGE CRIBRATE
(— **FLOUR**) DRESS
(— **IN**) INFILTER
(— **IN MINING**) LUE
(— **MEAL**) BUNT
(— **SHOT**) TABLE
(— **WHEAT**) SCALP
SIFTER SIEVE BOLTER CASTER
SIEVER WINNOWER
SIFTING DRIFT GARBLING
(**PL.**) BOLTING FANNINGS SIEVINGS
SIGH SOB PECH SIFE SOCK WIND
MOURN SIGHT SITHE SOUGH TWANK
BEMOAN BEWAIL SORROW SUTHER
DEPLORE SINGULT SUSPIRE
SIGHT AIM EYE KEN RAY BONE ESPY
FACE GAZE PEEP SEET VIEW FERLY
RAISE SCENE SCOPE SICHT TRACK
VISIE VIZZY BEHOLD DESCRY OBJECT
TICKET VISION DISCERN DISPLAY
EYESHOT GLIMPSE MONSTER
CONSPECT DISCOVER EYESIGHT
GUNSIGHT
(— **FOR GUN**) BEAD LEAF PEEP
SCOPE VISIE VIZZY HAUSSE
GUNSIGHT
(— **OF COMPASS**) VANE
(— **ON SURVEYOR'S STAFF**) TARGET
(—**S OF CITY**) LIONS
(— **TO SEE IF LEVEL**) BONE
(**AMAZING** —) STOUND
(**IMAGINARY** —) VISION
(**IMPRESSIVE** —) PICTURE
(**OFFENSIVE** —) EYESORE
(**OUT OF** —) HID
(**PITIFUL** —) RUTH
(**SECOND** —) TAISH TAISCH
DEUTEROSCOPY
(**SORRY** —) BYSEN
(**STRANGE** —) FERLY FERLIE
(**SUFF.**) OPSIA OPSIS OPSY OPTIC
OPTICON ORAMA
SIGHTER ALINER ALIGNER
SIGHTING LANDFALL
(— **DEVICE**) ALIDADE
SIGHTLY VIEWLY EYEABLE
SIGHTSEE RUBBERNECK
SIGLOS DARIC
SIGN INK AYAH DASH FIRM HINT HIRE
MARK NOTE OMEN TYPE BADGE
COLON FRANK GHOST GUIDA
HAMZA INDEX SEGNO SIGIL SINGE
SPOOR STAMP TOKEN TRACE
ASSIGN AUGURY CARACT EFFECT
EMBLEM ENGAGE ENSIGN FUGLER
INDICE MOTION NOTICE PARAPH
REMARK SIGLUM SIGNAL SIGNET
SIGNUM SYMBOL TITTLE WITTER

ALEBUSH AUSPICE CHECKER
CHEQUER CONSIGN EARMARK
ENDORSE INDICIA INSIGNE
KNOWING PORTENT PRESAGE
PRODIGY PROFFER SHINGLE
SHOWING SIGNARY SURMISE
SYMPTOM VESTIGE WARNING
CEREMONY INDICANT INSTANCE
MONUMENT PROCLAIM SIGNACLE
SYLLABIC TELLTALE
(— **DOCUMENT**) FIRM
(— **FOR KEYNOTE**) ISON
(— **OF A COVENANT**) SACRAMENT
(— **OF ALEHOUSE**) LATTICE
(— **OF AN IDEA**) EMBLEM
(— **OF APPROVAL**) CACHET
(— **OF CONTEMPT**) FIG
(— **OF DANGER**) SEAMARK
(— **OF GLOTTAL STOP**) HAMZA
HAMZAH
(— **OF MULTIPLICATION**) DOT
(— **OF ZODIAC**) LEO RAM BULL CRAB
GOAT LION ARIES HOUSE LIBRA
TWINS VIRGO ARCHER CANCER
FISHES GEMINI PISCES TAURUS
VIRGIN BALANCE SCORPIO
AQUARIUS SCORPION
(— **ON MAP**) ICON .
(**ASTROLOGICAL** —) CIPHER
(**CHARACTERISITC** —) SYMPTOM
(**DIACRITICAL** —) TILDE UMLAUT
(**GLOTTAL STOP** —) HAMZA HAMZAH
(**MATHEMATICAL** —) NAME FUNCTOR
(**MUSICAL** —) CLEF FLAT REST GUIDA
NEUME PRESA SEGNO SHARP SWELL
SIMILE FERMATA NATURAL
(**OUTWARD** —) EVIDENCE
(**ROAD** —) MERGE
(**SANSKRIT** —) ANUSVARA
(**SHILLING** —) SOLIDUS
(**SHORTHAND** —) DIPHONE
(**SLIGHT** —) SURMISE
(**SUBSCRIPT** —) SUBFIX
(**SUPERSTITIOUS** —) GUEST
(**TAVERN** —) BUSH ALEBUSH
ALEPOLE CHECKER CHEQUER
ALESTAKE
(**TRAMP'S** —) MONICA MONIKER
(**VOWEL** —) SEGOL SEGHOL
(**PL.**) INDICIA INSIGNIA
(**PREF.**) SEMA SEMANT(O) SEMASI(O)
SEMATO SEMEIO SEMIO SEMO
SYMBOLO
(**SUFF.**) SEME
SIGNAL OS CUE GUN PST WAG BALK
BECK BELL BUZZ CALL COND FLAG
GATE HASH SIGN WAFF WAFT WAVE
WINK ALARM ALERT BLINK FLARE
FUSEE FUZEE LIGHT SHAPE SHORT
SPEAK TOKEN WHIFF ALARUM
BANNER BEACON BECKON BUZZER
ENSIGN HERALD MARKER OFFICE
RECALL SIGNET TARGET WAVING

WIGWAG BLINKER CHAMADE
COMMAND EMINENT GRIFFIN
NOTABLE RETREAT TURNOUT
ASSEMBLY CRANTARA DIAPHONE
FLAGFALL LOGOGRAM STANDARD
STRIKING
(— FISHERMEN) BALK
(— FOR A PARLEY) CHAMADE
(— FOR PLUNDER) HAVOC
(— FOR WHALERS) WAIF
(— IN WHIST) ECHO PETER
(— OF DISTRESS) SOS
(— ON HORN) SEEK BLAST STRAKE
(— ON RADARSCOPE) BLIP
(— TO ATTACK) CHARGE
(— TO BEGIN ACTION) CUE
(— TO RETREAT) RETIRE
(— TO RETURN) RECALL
(— WITH FLAGS) WIGWAG
(AUDIO —) HUM
(BOAT'S —) WAFF WAFT
(DANGER —) RED SEAMARK
(DEATH —) KNELL
(DISTRESS —) FLARE
(FOG —) FOGHORN TORPEDO
DIAPHONE
(HUNTER'S —) SEEK PRIZE GIBBET
STRAKE
(MILITARY —) FLARE TURNOUT
ASSEMBLY
(NAVAL —) SECURE VERYLIGHT
(RADIO —) BEAM
(RAILROAD —) BANJO BOARD FUSEE
FUZEE TARGET HIGHBALL
SEMAPHORE
(TRAFFIC —) ROBOT
(WARNING —) RED ALARM KLAXON
TOCSIN REDFLAG REDLIGHT
(WEATHER —) CONE STORMCONE
STORMDRUM
SIGNALIZE MARK
SIGNALLING TICKTACK
SIGNALMAN FLAGS BELLBOY
BELLMAN
SIGNATE SENNET
SIGNATORY SIGNEE SIGNER
SIGNATURE BOLT FIRM HAND VISA
FRANK SHEET SIGIL THEME SIGNUM
TUGHRA SECTION HANDWRIT
SIGNATOR
SIGNBOARD SIGN SHINGLE
SIGNET SEAL SIGIL
SIGNIFICANCE WIT BODY PITH
SOUND AMOUNT IMPORT INTENT
LETTER STRESS WEIGHT BEARING
CONTENT GRAVITY MEANING
SENTENCE STRENGTH
(DEVOID OF —) JEJUNE
(HIDDEN —) HYPONOIA
(LACKING —) INANE
(MORAL —) ETHOS
SIGNIFICANT REAL RICH GREAT
MEATY AUGURAL EPOCHAL

OMINOUS POINTED SERIOUS
SENSEFUL SPEAKING PERTINENT
SIGNIFICANTLY SENSIBLY
SIGNIFICATION SENSE VALOR
VALUE ETYMON IMPORT MOMENT
NOTION MEANING CARRIAGE
SIGNIFIE
SIGNIFICS SENSIFICS
SIGNIFY BE SAY BEAR GIVE MAKE
MEAN NOTE SIGN WAVE AUGUR
IMPLY SKILL SOUND SPEAK SPELL
TOKEN UTTER AMOUNT ARGUFY
ASSERT BEMEAN DENOTE EMPLOY
IMPORT INTEND MATTER SIGNAL
BESPEAK BETOKEN CONNOTE
DECLARE EXPRESS PORTEND
PRETEND DESCRIBE INDICATE
INTIMATE MANIFEST
SIGNIFYING DOZENS GOADING
NEEDLING
SIGNOR BRUSCHINO, IL
(CHARACTER IN —) SOFIA
BRUSCHINO FLORVILLE
GAUDENZIO
(COMPOSER OF —) ROSSINI
SIGNPOST GUIDE MERCURY
WAYMARK HANDPOST
SIGURD (HORSE OF —) GRANI
(SLAIN BY —) FAFNIR
(SLAYER OF —) HOGNI
(VICTIM OF —) FAFNIR
(WIFE OF —) GUDRUN
SIGYN (HUSBAND OF —) LOKI
SIKH AKALI SINGH UDASI MAZHABI
SIKKIM (CAPITAL OF —) GANGTOK
(NATIVE OF —) RONG BHOTIA
LEPCHA
(RIVER OF —) TISTA
SIKSIKA SIHASAPA
SILAS MARNER (AUTHOR OF —)
ELIOT
(CHARACTER IN —) CASS AARON
DOLLY EPPIE NANCY SILAS MARNER
DUNSTAN GODFREY LAMMETER
WINTHROP
SILENCE GAG MUM CALK CLUM HIST
HUSH REST CHOKE FLOOR PEACE
QUIET SHUSH SQUAT STILL CLAMOR
MUFFLE SETTLE STIFLE WHISHT
CONFUTE SQUELCH DUMBNESS
PRECLUDE SUPPRESS
(— OF CONSONANT) QUIESCENCE
(CODE OF —) OMERTA
SILENCED STILL
SILENCER SOURDINE
SILENT MUM CLUM CLAM HUSH HUST
MUET MUTE SNUG CLOSE MUTED
STILL TACIT WHIST MUETTE SOPITE
SULLEN TIPTOE WHISHT APHONIC
UNWORDY ASPIRATE RESERVED
RETICENT TACITURN
SILENT DON (AUTHOR OF —)
SHOLOKHOV

(CHARACTER IN —) DARIA DUNIA MAURA GREGOR PIOTRA STEPAN AKSINIA DENIKIN MELEKHOV ILINICHKA PROKOFFEY PANTALEIMON

SILHOUETTE SHADE ISOTYPE OUTLINE SKYLINE

SILICA FLINT SILEX SINTER COESITE TRIPOLI TRIDYMITE

SILICATE MICA ALVITE CERITE IOLITE PINITE EUCLASE ILVAITE LOTRITE ZEOLITE CALAMINE ERIONITE WELLSITE

SILICEOUS SHELLY

SILICLE POD POUCH SILICULE

SILICON (THIN SLICE OF —) WAFER

SILICOSIS CON

SILIQUE POD

SILK SAY SOY CRIN ERIA LOVE MUGA ATLAS FLOSS GREGE HONAN JAPAN TABBY BLATTA CRACKS CULGEE DUCAPE FRISON MANTUA PONGEE RADIUM SENDAL SHALEE SHILLA SOUPLE TUSSAH ALAMODE CHIFFON HABUTAI PERSIAN SCHAPPE SQUEEZE TIFFANY TSATLEE TUSSORE YAMAMAI ARMOZEEN ARMOZINE LUSTRINE MILANESE **(— FOR LININGS)** SARSNET SARCENET **(— TREE)** MIMOSA **(CORDED —)** PADUASOY **(HEAVY —)** CRIN ARMOZINE **(RAW —)** GREIGE MARABOU TAYSAAM TSATLEE MARABOUT **(REFUSE —)** BUR BURR **(TWILLED —)** SURAH TOBINE FOULARD LOUSINE **(UNDYED —)** CORAH **(UNTWISTED —)** SLEAVE **(UPHOLSTERY —)** TABARET **(WASTE —)** KNUB NOIL FRISON **(PREF.)** SERI(CEO)(CI)(CO)

SILK COTTON KAPOK

SILK-COTTON TREE BULAK SEMUL SIMAL BOMBAX YAXCHE BENTANG MUNGUBA POCHOTE

SILKEN SILL SERIC SILKY SUAVE SEREAN

SILK GRASS KARATAS

SILK GUM SERICIN

SILK OAK LACEWOOD

SILKSMAN SCALPER

SILK TREE SIRIS

SILKWORM ERI ERIA SINA BOMBYX TUSSAH TUSSORE YAMAMAI BOMBYCID

SILKY GLOSSY SILKEN

SILKY CORNEL REDBRUSH

SILKY TAMARIN MARIKINA

SILL GIRD SOLE PLATE PATAND PATTEN SADDLE MUDSILL DOORSILL

SILLINESS BOSH FOLLY BETÍSE GOOSERY INANITY PORANGI SIMPLES IDLENESS NONSENSE ABSURDITY SIMPLICITY

SILLY TID BETE DAFT FOND FOOL NICE VAIN APISH BALMY BATTY BUGGY CAKEY DENSE DILLY DITSY DITZY DIZZY GIDDY GOOFY INANE KOOKY LOONY SAPPY SEELY WACKY BLASHY CRANKY CUCKOO DAWISH DOTARD DOTTLE FOOTLE FRUITY GUCKED MOPOKE PAULIE SAWNEY SHANNY SIMPLE SINGLE SKIVIE SLIGHT SPOONY VACANT ASININE FATUOUS FOOLISH FOPPISH FRIBBLE GLAIKET PEEVISH PUERILE SCRANNY SHALLOW UNWITTY ANSERINE FEATLESS FOOTLING FOPPERLY **(BE —)** DRIVEL **(PREF.)** MORO

SILO (PART OF —) BIN DOME PIPE TANK MELON INTAKE LADDER PUMPKIN UMBRELLA PARACHUTE

SILOXANE SILICON

SILPHIUM LASER

SILT DREGS SLEECH DEPOSIT RESIDUE SULLAGE BULLDUST

SILVER LUNA MOON PINA DIANA PLATE SYCEE WEDGE WHITE ALBATA ARGENT SILLER BULLION VERMEIL ARGENTUM STERLING ARGENTINE **(— INGOT)** SYCEE **(— STATE)** NEVADA **(DEBASED —)** VELLON **(GERMAN —)** ALBATA **(GILDED —)** VERMEIL **(NICKEL —)** PAKTONG **(PREF.)** ARGENT(O) ARGYR(O)

SILVER BELL HALESIA BELLWOOD COWLICKS

SILVERFISH SHINER SLICKER FISHTAIL WOODFISH

SILVERING BACKING

SILVERSIDES IAO BRIT TINK BRITT FRIAR SMELT TAILOR TINKER GRUNION ATHERINE PEIXEREY PEJERREY SKIPJACK

SILVERSMITH SONAR

SILVERTIP BEAR

SILVER TREE IRONWOOD

SILVER TREE FERN PITAU

SILVERVINE CATVINE

SILVERWEED TANSY

SILVERWING CINDER

SILVERY WHITE ARGENT SILVER SILVERN **(PREF.)** GLAUCO

SILVIA (FATHER OF —) BALLANCE **(LOVER OF —)** VALENTINE

SILYBUM MARIANA

SIMAR CYMAR SYMAR ZIMARRA

SIMEON (FATHER OF —) JACOB
  (MOTHER OF —) LEAH
SIMILAR AKIN LIKE SAME SUCH
  ALIKE METOO EVENLY LIKELY SIMILE
  COGNATE KINDRED SEEMABLE
  SELFLIKE SUCHLIKE SUITABLE
  SEMBLANCE
  (PREF.) HOL(O) HOM(E)(EO)(O)(OE)(OI)
  (SUFF.)
  (MAKE — TO) FY IFY
SIMILARITY SIMILE ANALOGY
  HOMOLOGY HOMOTAXY LIKENESS
  PARALLEL SAMENESS
SIMILARLY EQUALLY LIKEWISE
SIMILE ICON IKON IMAGE FIGURE
  SUIVEZ COMPARE
SIMILITUDE IMAGE FIGURE
  ANALOGY PARABLE PORTRAIT
SIMMER FRY CREE SILE STEW
  SIMPER SOTTER TOTTLE
SIMON ZELOTES
  (BROTHER OF —) JESUS
  (FATHER OF —) MATTATHIAS
  (SON OF —) JUDAS
SIMON BOCCANEGRA
  (CHARACTER IN —) MARIA PAOLO
  SIMON ADORNO AMELIA ANDREA
  FIESCO GABRIELLE BOCCANEGRA
  (COMPOSER OF —) VERDI
SIMONY BARRATRY
SIMOOM SAMUM SAMIEL KHAMSIN
SIMPER MINCE SMIRK BRIDLE
SIMPLE LOW BALD BARE EASY FOND
  MERE NICE ONLY PURE RUDE SNAP
  VERY WEAK AFALD BLEAK DIZZY
  GREEN NAIVE NAKED PLAIN SEELY
  SILLY SMALL SOBER AEFALD CHASTE
  GLOBAL HOMELY HONEST HUMBLE
  NATIVE OAFISH RUSTIC SEMPLE
  SEVERE SINGLE STUPID VIRGIN
  ARTLESS ASININE AUSTERE BABYISH
  FATUOUS FOOLISH ONEFOLD
  POPULAR SIMPLEX SPECIES
  ARCADIAN EXPLICIT HOMEMADE
  HOMESPUN INNOCENT INORNATE
  SACKLESS SEMPLICE SOLITARY
  (VEGETABLE —) GALENIC
  (PREF.) APL(O) HAPL(O) LITI
SIMPLE-MINDED SEELY SILLY
  INNOCENT
SIMPLETON AUF AWF COX DAW
  FON NUP OAF SAP SOT BABE BABY
  BOOB CAKE COOT CULL FLAT FOOL
  GABY GAUP GAWP GOFF GOUK
  GOWK GOWP GUFF PEAK ROOK SIMP
  SOFT TONY TOOT ZANY COKES
  GALAH GOOSE IDIOT IKONA JACOB
  LOACH NINNY NODDY PRUNE
  SAMMY SMELT SNIPE SPOON
  TOMMY BADAUD DAUKIN FONDLE
  GANDER GAUPUS GAWNEY
  GOTHAM GREENY GULPIN JOSSER

NINCUM NOODLE NUPSON SAWNEY
  SIMKIN SIMPLE DAWPATE GOMERAL
  GUBBINS JUGGINS MAFFLIN
  MUGGINS WIDGEON ABDERITE
  FLATHEAD FONDLING INNOCENT
  JEANJEAN JOCRISSE KNOTHEAD
  MOONCALF MOONLING OMADHAUN
  PEAGOOSE SILLYTON SOFTHEAD
  WISEACRE WOODCOCK
  NINCOMPOOP
SIMPLICITY NICETY PURITY
  MODESTY NAIVETE ELEGANCE
SIMPLIFY CLARIFY EXPOUND
SIMPLY JUST ALONE FONDLY
  MERELY PLATLY CRUDELY QUIETLY
  NATIVELY
SIMULACRUM ICON SHAM IMAGE
  IMITATION
SIMULATE ACT FAKE MOCK FEIGN
  MIMIC AFFECT ASSUME SEMBLE
  SIMULE SKETCH
SIMULATED FAINT FAKED ERSATZ
  FICTIOUS
SIMULATION ACTING ANALOGUE
  PRETENCE PRETENSE
SIMULTANEOUS CONJOINT
  CONJUGATE
SIMULTANEOUSLY ONCE
  TOGETHER
SIN ERR CULP DEBT ENZU EVIL HELL
  PAPA VICE BLAME CRIME ERROR
  FAULT FULLY GUILT SLOTH WATHE
  WRONG AGUILT COMMIT FELONY
  NANNAR OFFEND PIACLE PLIGHT
  VENIAL FRAILTY OFFENSE HAMARTIA
  INIQUITY PECCANCY QUEDSHIP
  TRESPASS
  (DAUGHTER OF —) ISHTAR
  (DEADLY —) ACEDIA
  (ORIGINAL —) ADAM
  (SEVEN DEADLY —S) ENVY LUST
  ANGER PRIDE SLOTH GLUTTONY
  COVETOUSNESS
  (SON OF —) NESKU SHAMASH
  (WIFE OF —) NINGAL
  (PREF.) HAMARTIO
SINCALINE CHOLINE
SINCE AS AGO FOR FRO NOW GONE
  SETH SITH SYNE BEING WHERE
  FORWHY BECAUSE SITHENS
  WHEREAS INASMUCH SITHENCE
  (PREF.) CIS CITRA
SINCERE GOOD REAL TRUE AFALD
  FRANK CANDOR DEVOUT ENTIRE
  HEARTY HONEST SIMPLE SINGLE
  CORDIAL EARNEST GENUINE
  ONEFOLD UPRIGHT FAITHFUL
  PRAYERFUL
  (NOT —) LIP PLASTIC SYNTHETIC
  SYNTHETICAL
SINCERELY TRULY SIMPLY SINGLY
  DEVOUTLY ENTIRELY HEARTILY

SINCERITY FAITH HEART CANDOR
VERITY HONESTY REALITY
SINDON CORPORAL
SINE SAGITTA
(VERSED —) SAGITTA
SINECURE SNAP
SINEW THEW BRAWN FIBER FIBRE
FORCE NERVE POWER LEADER
SINNER TENDON
SINEWY WIRY NERVY THEWY
ROBUST FIBROSE FIBROUS
NERVOUS STRINGY TENDINAL
SINFONIA SYMPHONY
SINFUL BAD EVIL VILE NEFAS
WRONG WICKED PECCANT UNGODLY
VICIOUS PIACULAR
SING HUM JIG LIP CANT CARP GALE
HYMN LILT TUNE CAROL CARRY
CHANT CHIRL CROON DIRGE DITTY
DRING FEIGN LYRIC RAISE TOUCH
TROLL YEDDE CHAUNT CHORUS
DIVIDE INTONE MELODY RECORD
RELISH STRAIN WARBLE CHORTLE
COUNTER DESCANT GRIDDLE
SINGING TWEEDLE CHERUBIM
FALDERAL MODULATE SINGSONG
VOCALIZE
(— ABOUT) BESING
(— ABOVE TRUE PITCH) SHARP
(— AS A BEGGAR) GRIDDLE
(— BRISKLY) KNACK
(— CHEERFULLY) LILT
(— FLORIDLY) DIVIDE
(— HARSHLY) SCREAM
(— IN A CRACKED VOICE) CRAKE
(— IN CHORUS) CHOIR
(— IN LOW VOICE) CROON
(— IN SWISS MANNER) YODEL
(— LOUDLY) BELT TROLL TROLLOL
(— PRAISES) LAUD
(— ROMANCES) GEST GESTE
(— SECOND PART) SURCENT
(— SOFTLY) SOWF SOWTH
(— TO THE MOON) BAY
(— WITH FLOURISHES) ROULADE
(— WITH MEANINGLESS SYLLABLES)
SCAT
SINGAPORE (RIVER IN —) SUNGEI
SELETAR
(STRAIT OF —) JOHORE SEMBILAN
SINGE GAS BURN CHAR SEAR SWEAL
GENAPP SCORCH SWINGE SCOWDER
SWITHEN FIREFANG
SINGER ALTO BARD DIVA LARK
SWAN BASSO BUFFA BUFFO SKALD
VOICE BULBUL BUSKER CANARY
CANTOR LYRIST SONGER BASSIST
CHANTER CROONER PRIMOMO
SOLOIST SONGMAN SOPRANO
TROLLER WARBLER BAYADERE
CANTADOR CASTRATO CHANTEUR
FALSETTO GRIDDLER MELODIST

MONODIST THAMYRIS VOCALIST
CITYBILLY
(— OF FOLK SONGS) CANTADOR
(— OF ROCK MUSIC) ROCKER
(— OF THE GODS) GANDHARVA
(BEWITCHING —) SIREN
(COUNTRY MUSIC —) CITYBILLY
(FEMALE —) SONGBIRD
(MENDICANT —) BUSKER
(PRINCIPAL —) PRIMOMO
(PROVENCAL —) MUSAR
(STROLLING —) CANTABANK
SINGING CANT SCAT CHANT LYRIC
HYMNODY CANOROUS JONGLERY
(— ANTIPHONALLY) ALTERNATION
(— CAROLS) PLYGAIN HODENING
(— COACH) REPETITEUR
(ALTERNATE —) ANTIPHON
(CANTORIAL —) HAZANUTH
HAZZANUT
(JAZZ —) SCAT
(SIMULTANEOUS —) CHORUS
SINGLE ODD ONE LAST ONLY SOLE
UNAL AFALD ALONE AEFALD SIMPLE
SOLEIN SULLEN UNIQUE VERSAL
ALONELY AZYGOUS ONEFOLD
SEVERAL SIMPLEX TWOSOME
PECULIAR SEPARATE SINGULAR
SOLITARY SPORADIC PARTICULAR
(— OUT) CUT NAP SPOT ISOLATE
SEPARATE
(PREF.) APL(O) HAPL(O) MANI MON(O)
UNI
SINGLE-FOOT RACK
SINGLEHANDEDLY SINGLY
SINGLE-MINDED AFALD ONEFOLD
DEDICATED
SINGLENESS UNITY ONENESS
SINGLETON ONER UNIT
(— LEAD) SNEAK
SINGLY SINGLE SOLELY SLONELY
SINGPHO CHINGPAW
SINGSONG CANT SOUGH
CHANTING
SINGULAR ODD RARE FERLY QUEER
QUAINT SEENIL SINGLE CURIOUS
STRANGE PECULIAR
SINGULARISM HENISM
SINGULARITY DOUBLET ONENESS
ONLINESS
SINHALESE SINHALA
SINISTER AWK CAR KAY DARK DIRE
FELL GRIM DISMAL LOUCHE MALIGN
AWKWARD OBLIQUE OMINOUS
SINISTRAL REVERSED
SINK DIP DOP EBB LUM SAG SET SYE
BORE DRAU DRAW DROP FADE FAIL
FALL GOWT HELD KILL LUMB SILE
SWAG AVALE DRAFT DRAIN DROOP
DROWN HIELD LAPSE LOWER MERGE
POACH SQUAT STOOP SWAMP
VERGE CLOACA DEVALL DOLINA

DOLINE DRENCH GUTTER JAWBOX
PLUNGE PUDDLE RESIDE SETTLE
COMMODE DECLINE DESCEND
DRAUGHT FOUNDER GULLION
IMMERSE RELAPSE SCUPPER
SCUTTLE SUBSIDE SWALLOW
DECREASE SINKHOLE SOAKAWAY
(— AND FALL) TWINE
(— AS IN MUD) LAIR
(— A WELL) DRILL
(— DOWN) BOG AVALE STOOP
DECLINE
(— FANGS INTO) STRIKE
(— FOR MIXING DRINKS) WETBAR
(— INTO OOZE) WASEL
(— NAILHEAD) SET
(— SUDDENLY) SLUMP
(— UNDER TRIAL) QUAIL
SINKBOX BOX SINK BATTERY
SINKER BUR BURR SINK DIPSY
DONUT PLUMB BULLET
SINKHOLE SINK PONOR UVALA
CENOTE COLLECT
SINKING GONE SINKAGE
(— DOWN) FONDU
SINKIUSE COLUMBIA
SINLESS INNOCENT
SINLESSNESS HOLINESS
SINNER DEBTOR PECCANT
SINNING PECCANT
SINUATE GYROSE
SINUOSITY WRIGGLE
SINUOUS WAVY SNAKEY SINUATE
SNAKISH TORTILE WINDING
INDENTED SWANLIKE
SINUS BOSOM ANTRUM RECESS
LOCULUS TEARPIT
(PL.) ANTRA
SINUSITIS ROUP
SIOUAN OTOE ABANIC DAKOTA
SANTEE SAPONI CATAWBA
DACOTAH
SIOUX (— FORCE) WAKAN WAKON
SIP BIB NIP SUP BLEB SEEP SLUP
SUCK TIFF KEACH NURSE SNACK
WHIFF TIPPLE TICKLER DELIBATE
SIPHON CRANE THIEF VALINCH
FLINCHER
SIPPING LIBANT
SIPUNCULOIDEA ACHAETA
INERMIA
SIR PO DAN DEN DON PAN AZAM
BAAS HERR MIAN STIR TUAN
BWANA SAHIB SENOR SEYID SIEUR
MESSER SAYYID SIGNOR SIRREE
BARONET DOMINUS EFFENDI
MESSIRE SIGNIOR SIGNORE
GOSPODIN GOVERNOR
(PL.) LORDINGS
SIRCAR BANIAN
SIRE KING BEGET THROW FATHER
GETTER

SIREN BUMMER HOOTER LIGEIA
LIGYDA ENTICER LORELEI MERMAID
SIRENIAN
SIRENIAN COWFISH MUTILATE
SIRENOMELUS SYMPUS SYMMELUS
SIRICID UROCERID
SIRIS KOKO LEBBEK
SIRIUS SOTHIS TISHIYA CANICULA
SIRLOIN SEY BACKSEY
SIRMUELLERA BANKSIA
SIRUP WAX LICK GOLDY SYRUP
GOWDIE GREENS ORGEAT RUNOFF
ANTIQUE CLAIRCE ECLEGMA
LIQUEUR MOLASSES QUIDDANY
SIRWASH SIDELINE
SISAL RUG CABUYA SISALANA
SISKIN TARIN ABERDEVINE
SISSIFIED PRISSY
SISSOO TALI SHISHAM
SISSY SIS CISSIE SISTER CHICKEN
PANTYWAIST
SISTER NUN SIB SIS GIRL NURSE
SISSY SOEUR TITTY WOMAN
EXTERN PERSON
(YOUNGER —) CADETTE
(PL.) SISTERN SISTREN
(PREF.) SORORI
SISTERHOOD BEGUINES SORORITY
SISTERLY SORORAL
SISYPHUS (BROTHER OF —)
ATHAMAS SALMONEUS
(FATHER OF —) AEOLUS
(MOTHER OF —) ENARETE
(SON OF —) SINON GLAUCUS
ORNYTION
(WIFE OF —) MEROPE
SIT SET LEAN SEAT BENCH PRESS
ROOST SQUAT WEIGH BESTRIDE
(— ABRUPTLY) CLAP
(— ASTRIDE) CROSS HORSE
STRADDLE
(— ERECT LIKE A DOG) BEG
(— FORCIBLY) DOSS
(— IN JUDGMENT) DEEM
(— ON) BROOD COVER
(— OVER EGGS) RUCK BROOD CLOCK
(— UPRIGHT) PERK
SITA (FATHER OF —) JANAKA
(HUSBAND OF —) RAMA SOMA
SITATUNGA NAKONG
SITE AREA PLOT SEAT SITU SOLE
SPOT TOFT FIELD PLACE SITUS
STAND STANCE BIVOUAC DAMSITE
HABITAT STEADING
(— OF BIRD SEXUAL DISPLAY) LEK
(— OF HUNT) DRIVE
(— OF SMELTER) BOLE
(ARCHAELOGICAL —) EXCAVATION
(BUILDING —) STANCE
(EXCAVATION —) DIG
(FORTIFIED —) KAIM KAME
(THRESHING —) SETTING

SITTER DOLLY DOLLIE INSESSOR
SITTING DIET SEAT ASSIS CLUTCH
SEANCE SEDENT SEJANT SESSION
CONGRESS SEDERUNT
SITUATE PLACE POSITION
SITUATED SET SEATED STATURED
(— OPPOSITE) COUNTER
(GET —) ORIENT
SITUATION JOB LIE CASE CRIB PASS
PLOT PLACE SEAT SITE SPOT BERTH
SIEGE SITUS STATE STEAD ASSIZE
CHANCE ESTATE OFFICE PLIGHT
STATUS EPISODE PICTURE PORTENT
POSTURE STATION INCIDENT
INSTANCE POSITURE STANDING
UBIQUITY
(— BESET BY DIFFICULTIES) SCRAPE
(— IN CRIBBAGE) GO
(— IN FARO) CATHOP
(— IN OMBRE) CODILLE
(— OF PERPLEXITY) HOBBLE STRAIT
(AMUSING —) BAR
(AWKWARD —) SCRAPE JACKPOT
(BAD —) SCENE
(CRITICAL —) CLUTCH
(DIFFICULT —) BOX PUXY BOGGLE
NINEHOLES PREDICAMENT
(DISTRESSING —) STYMIE
(EXECRABLE —) ATROCITY
(FAVORABLE —) BREAK
(FINAL — OF ACT) CURTAIN
(HIGH —) AERY AERIE
(HOPELESSLY DOOMED —) RATTRAP
(NECESSITOUS —) BREACH
(PAINFUL —) DISTRESS
(RELATIVE •) BEARING
(TIGHT —) CRUNCH
(TRYING —) COW
(UNPLEASANT —) BUMMER
(UNSATISFACTORY —) DILEMMA
(VEXATIOUS —) HEADACHE
(VILE —) DUNGHILL
(ZODIACAL —) HAYZ
SITZ BATH SITZBAD SEMICUPE
SITZMARK BATHTUB
SIVA RUDRA SHIVA ISVARA SHAMBU
BHAIRAVA MAHADEVA NATARAJA
(SYMBOL OF —) LINGA LINGAM
(WIFE OF —) KALI
SIX VAU WAW SICE SISE HEXAD
HEXADE SENARY SEXTET STIGMA
DIGAMMA SIXSOME
(PREF.) HEX(A) SEX(A)(I) SEXTI
SIXFOLD SEXTUPLE
SIX-FOOTED HEXAPOD
SIXMO SEXTO
SIXPENCE HOG PIG BEND KICK ZACK
SIMON SPRAT TIZZY BENDER FIDDLE
TANNER TESTON CRIPPLE FIDDLER
TESTRIL
SIXTEENTH ANA ANNA
SIXTH
(PREF.) SEXTI

SIXTIETH (— PART OF DAY) GHURRY
SIXTY SAMECH SAMEKH
SIZABLE SNUG HEFTY LARGE
HANDSOME
SIZE WAX AREA BIND BULK MARK
MASS DRESS GIRTH MOUND PLANK
SCALE EXTENT FORMAT GROWTH
MICKLE MOISON PICNIC SIZING
BIGNESS CONTENT CORSAGE
FITTING THIRTEEN TWELVEMO
(— OF BOOK) FOLIO OCTAVO
QUARTO
(— OF BULLET) CALIBER
(— OF CARDS) TOWN LADIES
(— OF HOLE) BORE
(— OF HOSIERY) POPE
(— OF PAGE) OCTAVO
(— OF PAPERBOARD) LARGE
(— OF PARTICLE) GRIND
(— OF ROPE) GRIST
(— OF SLATE) PEGGY IMPERIAL
(— OF TYPE) GEM PICA RUBY AGATE
CANON ELITE PEARL MINION PRIMER
BREVIER DIAMOND EMERALD
ENGLISH PARAGON COLUMBIAN
(— YARN) SLASH
(CLOTHING —) LONG SHORT STOUT
JUNIOR PETITE
(EXTRA LARGE —) SUPER
(GREAT —) MAGNITUDE
(MEASURED —) SCANTLING
(PAPER —) SIXMO
(RELATIVE —) SCALE
(UNUSUAL —) OUTSIZE
SIZEABLE HEFTY
SIZING DRESSING SLASHING
(— LIQUID) GLAIR
SIZZLE FRIZZ
SKADI (FATHER OF —) THJAZI
(HUSBAND OF —) NJORD
SKAG SCAG HEROIN
SKANDA (BROTHER OF —) GANESHA
(FATHER OF —) SHIVA
(WIFE OF —) DEVAYANI VALLIAMMAN
SKASTING (— JUMP) SALCHOW
SKAT CAT NULL TOURNEE
SKATE BOB RAY TUB RAJA RINK SKIT
TINK TUBE FLAIR SCULL BATOID
DOCTOR FLATHE PATENT PATTEN
ROCKER ROLLER RUNNER SKETCH
TINKER CHOPINE FLAPPER PLACOID
SKETCHER
(— MARK) CUSP
(FEMALE —) MAID
(PREF.) BATO
SKATER PATTENER SKETCHER
SKEDADDLE LAM RUN BUNK FLEE
SCAT SCOOT
SKEET FLEE KELTER KILTER PELTER
SKEIN RAP HANK HASP SCAN
BOTTOM SLEAVE SELVAGE
SKEINER RANDER SLIPPER
SKELETIN SPONGIN

SKELETON CUP CAGE MORT RAME
ATOMY BONES FRAME LOOFAH
SICULA SKELET ANATOMY CARCASS
RAWBONE ARMATURE CORALLUM
MANDIBLE OSSATURE
(— OF DRAMATIC WORK) SCENARIO
SKELETON KEY GILT SCREW
TWIRLER
SKELP SCUD
SKEPTIC DOUBTER INFIDEL ZETETIC
APIKOROS APORETIC
SKEPTICAL ACADEMIC APORETIC
DOUBTFUL
SKEPTICALLY ASKANCE
SKEPTICISM HUMISM UNBELIEF
SKETCH BIT DASH DRAW LIMN PLAN
VIEW VITA DRAFT ENTER PAINT
TRACE APERCU DESIGN DOODLE
SCHEME SPLASH BOZZETO CROQUIS
DRAUGHT DRAWING EBAUCHE
ETCHING OUTLINE SCHIZZO
ESQUISSE MONOGRAM PROFIELE
PROSPECT REMARQUE VIGNETTE
(— BEFOREHAND) INDICATE
(AUTOBIOGRAPHICAL —) VITA
(BIOGRAPHICAL —) ELOGY ELOGIUM
(FIRST —) ESQUISSE
(HERALDIC —) TRICK
(OUTDOORS —) LANDSKIP
(PRELIMINARY —) DRAFT ABBOZZO
MAQUETTE
(ROUGH —) NOTE CROQUIS
POCHADE ESQUISSE
(SATIRICAL —) SKIT
(THUMBNAIL —) BIO
SKEW ASKEW GAUCHE
SKEWBACK SPRINGER
SKEWBALD PINTO PIEBALD
SKEWED ALOP
SKEWER PIN PROD PROG SPIT STAB
PRICK SPEAR TRUSS SKIVER TASTER
BROCHETTE
SKEWERER TUBER
SKI SKEE SNOWSHOE
(— DOWN AT HIGH SPEED) SCHUSS
(— DOWNHILL) WEDEL
(— DOWN SLOPE) SCHUSS
(— METHOD) PASSGANG
(— MOVEMENT) RUADE
(— POSITION) VORLAGE
(— RACE) SLALOM
(— RACING) LANGLAUF
(— SITE) VAIL
(— STYLE) WEDELN
(— TURN) TELEMARK
(— WITH ROLLERS) TURFSKI
(CROSS-COUNTRY RACING ON —S)
LANGLAUF
(ONE WHO —S) SCHUSSBOOMER
(ONE WHO —S DOWNHILL)
SCHUSSBOOMER
(PART OF —) TIP EDGE TAIL SHOVEL
BINDING

(RELATING TO — EVENTS) NORDIC
(TYPE OF —) SNOWBOARD
(PL.) BOARDS
SKID DOG DRAG SLEW SLUE TRIG
DRIFT DRILL SLOUGH SKIDPAN
SLIPPER TRIGGER FISHTAIL SIDESLIP
(— LOGS) SNAKE TWICH TRAVOY
TWITCH
(— ON RAIL) SKATE
(AUTOMOBILE —) SPINOUT
(FENDER —) GLANCER
(IRON —) SABOT
(ROTATIONAL —) SPINOUT
SKIDDER SNAKER
SKIDI LOUP
SKIDWAY PIT
SKIER KANONE SNOWBIRD
LANGLAUFER SCHUSSBOOMER
(— POSITION) VORLAGE
SKIFF CANOE SHELL SKIFT CAIQUE
DINGHY SAMPAN CURRANE SKIPPET
JOHNBOAT
SKIING TOURING LANGLAUF
(— TURN) TELEMARK
(CROSS-COUNTRY —) LANGLAUF
(DOWNHILL —) WEDELN
(STYLE OF —) WEDELN
SKIL BESHOW SKILFISH
SKILL ART CAN WIT FEAT FEEL HAND
PATE TACT CRAFT DRAFT HAUNT
KNACK TRICK ENGINE TECHNE
ABILITY ADDRESS APTNESS
CUNNING FINESSE MASTERY
MYSTERY PROWESS SCIENCE
SLEIGHT ARTIFICE CAPACITY
CHIVALRY DEFTNESS FACILITY
INDUSTRY LEARNING
(— IN COMMUNICATION) ORACY
(DIPLOMATIC —) TACT
(INTELLECTUAL —) INTELLIGENCE
(LACK OF —) INERTIA
(NAVIGATION —) SEACRAFT
(PREF.) TECHNI TECHNO
(SUFF.) ICS SHIP TECHNIC TECHNY
SKILLED OLD SEEN WISE ADEPT
ASTUTE MASTER PERITE SCIENT
SKILLY VERSED HOTSHOT PRACTIC
EDUCATED SKILLFUL
SKILLET PRIG SPIDER
SKILLFUL APT SLY ABLE DEFT FEAT
FILE FINE GOOD HEND PERT TIDY
WISE ADEPT CANNY FITTY HANDY
HENDE READY SLICK SWEET ADROIT
ARTFUL CLEVER CRAFTY DAEDAL
EXPERT HABILE SCIENT SKILLY
SOLERT SUBTLE CUNNING POLITIC
SKILLED DEXTROUS PRACTIVE
SLEIGHTY TACTICAL PROFICIENT
SKILLFULLY DEFTLY YARELY
CRAFTILY
SKILLFULNESS CRAFT
SKIM TOP RIFF SCUD SCUM SCUN
SCUR SILE SKIP FLEET GRAZE SCALE

SKIFF SKIRR SKIVE BROWSE RABBLE
SAMPLE DESPUME SKITTER
(— ON WATER) SCHOON
SKIMMED FLAT FLET
SKIMMER FALK LARI SKEP SCOOP
LINGEL SCUMMER CUTWATER
SKIMMINGS SCRUFF
SKIMP JIMP SLUR SCAMP SKINCH
SKIMPY JIMP CHARY SPARE MEAGER
MEAGRE SCANTY STINGY
SKIN KIP KIT BACK BARK CASE CAST
DERM FELL FLAY FLEA HIDE HILD
KITT MORT PEAU PEEL PELT RIND
BALAT BLYPE BRAWN FLOAT GENET
SLUFF STRIP SWARD CORIUM
PELTRY SWARTH UNCASE CUTICLE
DOESKIN ENDERON KIDSKIN
LEATHER PELLAGE SKIMMER
BUCKSKIN DRUMHEAD LAMBSKIN
PARADERM PELLICLE SEALSKIN
TEGUMENT VITILIGO WOOLFELL
(— AROUND BIRD'S EYE) ORBIT
(— AROUND NAIL) PERIONYCHIUM
(— BETWEEN TOES) WEB
(— FOR BOOKBINDING) BASAN
(— FOR HOLDING WATER) KIRBEH
(— FOR WATER) KIRBEH
(— OF BACON) SWARD
(— OF BOARDS) CARPET
(— OF FRUIT) PEEL
(— OF GOOSE) APRON
(— OF INSECT) CAST
(— OF PLANT) CORTEX
(— OF POTATO) JACKET
(— OF POULTRY NECK) HELZEL
(— OF RABBIT) RACK CONEY
(— OF SEAL) SCULP
(— OF SHARK) SHAGREEN
(— OF THE HEAD) SCALP
(— OF WALNUT) ZEST
(— OF YOUNG CALF) SLINK DEACON
(— WITH WOOL REMAINING ON IT)
WOOLFELL
(BARE —) BUFF
(BEAVER —) PLEW
(BOAR'S —) SHIELD
(CAST —) SPOIL SLOUGH EXUVIAE
(CHAFED OR SORE —) IRE
(CHAMOIS —) FURWA
(DEEP LAYER OF THE —) CUTIS
(DRIED —) PARFLECHE
(FAWN —) NEBRIS
(INNER PART OF THE —) DERMA
(LAMB — PREPARED LIKE FUR)
BUDGE
(OUTER —) HUSK
(PENDULOUS FOLD OF —) DEWLAP
(ROUGHTANNED —) CRUST
(SHARK —) SHAGREEN
(SHEEP —) BASIL
(SQUIRREL —) VAIR
(SURFACE —) SCARFSKIN
(THICKENED —) BRAWN

(THIN —) FILM PELLICLE STRIFFEN
(TRUE —) ENDERON
(60 —S) TURN
(PREF.) CUT(I)(O) CUTANEO DERM(AT)
(ATO)(O) DERO EPIDERM(O) SCYT(O)
(SUFF.) DERM(A)(ATOUS)(IA)(IS)(Y)
SKIN FLICK NUDIE
SKINFLINT SKIN FLINT MISER PIKER
SCREW HUDDLE PELTER SCRAPER
SCROOGE SKEEZIX TIGHTWAD
CHEESEPARER
SKINK ADDA SCINCID SCORPION
(PREF.) SCINCI SCINCO
SKINNY BONY LEAN THIN SLINK
SKIOLD (FATHER OF —) ODIN
SKIP DAP HIP BALK BOUT FOOT JUMP
LEAP SLIP TRIP BOUND CAPER
DANCE ELIDE FRISK SALTO SCOON
SCOPE SCOUP SKITE SMOKE VAULT
GAMBOL GLANCE LAUNCH SPRING
GUNBOAT SALTATE SKIPPER SKITTER
TRIPPLE PORPOISE RICOCHET
(— SCHOOL) TIB
(MINING —) SLIPE
SKIPJACK FOP SKIP BONITO
ALEWIFE SKIPPER
SKIPPER IHI SKIP LAODAH LOWDAH
SERANG SHIPPER
SKIRMISH FRAY BRUSH CLASH
MELEE SKIRM BICKER HASSLE
TUSSLE PICKEER RUNNING
FIREFIGHT
SKIRMISHER HUSSAR TIRALLEUR
SKIRMISHING SPARRING
SKIRT CUT HUG LAP BANK BASE
COAT ENGI JUPE MIDI MINI SAYA
TUBE TUTU COAST JUPON LABIE
PAREU PASIN STRIP TREND TWIST
BASQUE DIRNDL HOBBLE JUMPER
KIRTLE PEPLUM SARONG TAMEIN
QUARTER BASQUINE PULLBACK
SKIRTING
(— STYLE) ALINE
(ARMOR —) TASSES LAMBOYS
(BALLET —) TUTU
(DIVIDED —) CULOTTE
(HOOP —) CRINOLINE
(HOOPED —) TUBTAIL
(LONG —) MAXI
(TARTAN —) KILT ARISAID
(PL.) DOCK DOCKEN
SKIRTING DADE SKIRT PLINTH
(PL.) BROKES
SKIT BLACKOUT
SKITTAGETAN HAIDA
SKITTISH SHY CORKY GOOSY WINDY
FLISKY KITTLE SKEIGH SPOOKY
FLIGHTY SCADDLE SKADDLE
STARTLY BOGGLISH SKITTERY
STARTFUL
SKITTLES BOWLS KAYLES KITTLES
SQUAILS
SKIVE PARE

SKUA BONXIE JAEGER TEASER
TULIAC SEAHAWK STINKPOT
WHIPTAIL
SKULDUGGERY JOUKERY
PAWKERY
SKULK DERN JOUK LURK LUSK
MICHE MOOCH SCOUT SHOOL
SKULL OAR ROW BEAN POLL CRANY
MOOCH SCALP SCAUP VAULT
COBBRA MAZARD PALLET SCONCE
CRANIUM HARNPAN HEADMOLD
PANNICLE
(— BONE) VOMER
(— POINT) TYLION
(BACK OF —) OCCIPUT
(INCOMPLETE —) CALVARIA
(PART OF —) INION
(UPPER HALF OF —) SINCIPUT
(PREF.) CRANI(O)
(SUFF.) CRANIA(L)
SKULLCAP COIF PIXY PIXIE SKULL
VAULT BEANIE COIFFE CALOTTE
CAPELINE HOODWORT
(ARABIAN —) CHECHIA
(JEWISH —) YAMILKE YARMULKE
(STEEL —) SECRET
SKUNK ANNA ATOC ATOK PUSS
HURON SKINK SNIPE ZORIL CHINCHA
POLECAT SEECAWK SMELLER
CONEPATE CONEPATL MUSTELID
PHOBYCAT ZORRILLO
(CARTOON —) LEPEW
(JAVANESE —) TELEDU
SKUNK CABBAGE COLLARD
POCKWEED
SKY BLUE HIGH LIFT LOFT POLE TIEN
AZURE CARRY DYAUS ETHER LANGI
VAULT CAELUS CANOPY HEAVEN
REGION WELKIN ELEMENT HEAVENS
OLYMPUS TENGERE WEATHER
(ICE —) ICEBLINK
(PREF.) CAELI CAELO COELI COELO
URAN(I)(O) URANOSO
SKY-BLUE AZURE
(PREF.) CERULEO
SKYLARK LARK YERK
SLAB BAT CANT CLAM LECH PARE
SLAT BLADE BOARD DALLE LINER
PANEL PLANK SLATE STELA STELE
TABLE WADGE ABACUS FLITCH
MARVER MIHRAB PAVIOR RUNNER
SHEAVE TABLET FLAPPET PLANCHE
SHINGLE PORPHYRY PUNCHEON
SLABWOOD
(— BESIDE SINK) BUNKER
(— BY SINK) BUNKER
(— INDICATING MECCA) MIHRAB
(— OF CLAY) BAT
(— OF COAL) SKIP SLIP
(— OF GLASS) PANE
(— OF ICE) SCONCE
(— OF LIMESTONE) BALATTE
(— OF MARBLE) DALLE

(— OF PEAT) SCAD
(— OF SANDSTONE) COMAI
(— OVER BROOK) CLAM
(ARCHITECTURAL —) METOPE
(BROKEN-OFF —) BLAUD
(FLOATING —) ICEPAN SCONCE
(GAME —) BOARD
(GRAVE —) LEDGER LEIDGER
(GRINDING —) MULLER
(HOPSCOTCH —) PEEVER
(MEMORIAL —) LEDGER
(PAINTER'S —) SLANT
(PLASTERER'S —) HAWK
(ROOFING —) SLATE
(SQUARE —) QUARRY
(STONE —) PLANK STELA STELE
INKSTONE
SLACK DRY LAX OFF CULM DUFF
LASH NESH SLOW SOFT VEER CHECK
CRANK FLOWN LOOSE SLAKE TARDY
ABATED FLABBY FLAPPY REMISS
SUPINE UNGIRT BACKING MAKINGS
RELAXED SLACKEN SMEDDUM
CARELESS DILATORY INACTIVE
SLOBBERY NEGLIGENT
(— IN TRIGGER) CREEP
(— OF ROPE) SLATCH
(— SHEET OF SAIL) FLOW
(— SUDDENLY) SURGE
(COAL —) COOM COOMB
(PL.) BAGS
SLACKEN LAG PAY EASE FLAG SLOW
DELAY DOWSE LOOSE QUAIL RELAX
REMIT SLACK SLAKE START SURGE
ASLAKE EXOLVE RELENT UNBEND
(— SPEED) HANG
SLACKENING LETUP DETENTE
LETDOWN SLACKAGE
SLACKER SPIV ROTTER COUCHER
SLINKER EMBUSQUE
SLACKNESS LACHES LASHNESS
SLADE SOLE
SLAG SCAR DROSS CINDER DANDER
SCORIA SLAKIN THOMAS QUITTER
SLACKEN
SLAIN FALLEN
SLAKE ABATE SLACK LESSEN
QUENCH REFRESH SATISFY
SLAKING FAT
SLAM CLAP DASH FLUB SLOG SLOT
VOLE CLASH GRAND PLANK SLOSH
STRAM CHELEM FLOUNCE
SLAMMER JAIL STIR PRISON
SLANDER CANT BELIE LIBEL NOISE
SMEAR BEFOUL DEFAME INJURE
MALIGN MISSAY VILIFY ASPERSE
CALUMNY OBTRECT SCANDAL
TRADUCE TRUMPET BACKBITE
DEROGATE STRUMPET ASPERSION
BESPATTER
SLANDERER JUROR BLAZONER
SLANDEROUS FAMOUS SCURRIL
SCURRILE VILIPEND SCURRILOUS

SLANG CANT ARGOT FLASH JARGON
DIALECT
(THIEVES' —) FLASH
SLANT TIP BIAS CANT FLUE SKEW
TILT BEVEL DRAFT SLOPE SPLAY
STOOP FLANCH SKLENT DRAUGHT
COLORING DIAGONAL
(PREF.) CLIN(O)
SLANTED CANTED BEVELED
COLORED COCKEYED
SLANTING AWRY BIAS CANT SKEW
BEVEL SLOPE ASLANT ASLOPE
SKLENT SQUINT LOXOTIC OBLIQUE
SLOPING AVELONGE COLORING
OVERWART SIDELONG
SLANTINGLY AHOO ASWASH
SLANTLY
SLANT LINE VIRGULA VIRGULE
SLANTWISE
(PREF.) LECHRI(O)
SLAP BOX DAB BAFF BLIP BLOW CLAP
CUFF FLAP LICK PLAT SCUD SLAT
SNUB SPAT TACK BLIBE CLINK CLOUT
CRACK PANDY POTCH SKEEG SKELP
SKITE SMACK SPANK TWANG
TWANK BLEEZE BUFFET SCLAFF
SLIGHT STRIKE TINGLER WHERRET
BACKSLAP
(— HARD) BLAD
(RANDOM —) FLAY
SLAPDASH BUCKEYE
SLASH CAG CUT JAG COUP GASH
HASH PANE RACE RASH SLIT TOPS
KNIFE MINCE SCORE SKICE SLISH
RAMMEL SCORCH STREAK SLITTER
DIAGONAL SLASHING
SLASHED JAGGED DECOPED
TATTERED
SLASHING ABATIS
SLAT BOW LAG FLAT PALE SLOT
WAND BLADE SCLAT SLOAT STAVE
RIFFLE SPLINE EUPHROE BEDSTAFF
(— IN SLUICE) RIFFLE
SLATE RAG SLAT FRAME KILLAS
TABLET TICKET SHALDER SHINDLE
SLATING
(— IN SMALL IRREGULAR PIECES)
SCANTLE
(— OF COURT CASES) DOCKET
(BLUE —) SHIVER SKAILLIE
(CLAY —) KILLAS
(EXPOSED PART OF ROOFING —)
BARI
(SIZE OF —) PEGGY QUEEN DUCHESS
COUNTESS IMPERIAL PRINCESS
MARCHIONESS
(SURFACE —) BONE
SLATER HELER HELLIER SLATTER
SKIMMITY
(TOOL OF —) STAKE
SLATTERN DAB DAW MAB FROW
MAUX SLUT TRUB DOLLY FAGOT
MAWKS MOGGY MOPSY BLOUSE

CLATCH DOLLOP MALKIN SLOVEN
STREEL TRAPES LADRONE TROLLOP
HUCKMUCK SLUMMOCK
SLATTERNLY DOWDY BLOWSY
DAWISH FROWZY SORDID BLOWZED
TRAPISH SLATTERN SLOVENLY
SLAUGHTER WAL FELL KILL SLAM
SLAY BUTCH HALAL QUELL BATTUE
MURDER STRAGE BUTCHER
CARNAGE KILLING SCUPPER
SHAMBLE BUTCHERY MASSACRE
OCCISION SHECHITA HOLOCAUST
(— ACCORDING TO MOSLEM LAW)
HALAL
(— OF LARGE NUMBER) HECATOMB
(WHOLESALE —) QUELL
SLAUGHTERER KILLER SHOHET
KNACKER SHOCHET
(HORSE —) KNACKER
SLAUGHTERHOUSE ABATTOIR
BUTCHERY MATADERO SHAMBLES
(— WORKER) LIMEMAN
SLAUGHTERING SHEHITA
SHECHITA
SLAV VEND WEND CZECH HUNKS
HUNKY SLAVE USKOK CROATIAN
MORAVIAN POLABIAN
SLAVE BOY DAS ARDU BOND DASI
DUPE ESNE MOIL SERF DAVUS
HELOT SWINK THEOW ABJECT
ALIPIN ALLTUD CUMHAL FORSAR
GUINEA HIEROS MAMLUK SLAVEY
THRALL VASSAL BONDMAN CAPTIVE
CHATTEL FORSADO HACKNEY
PEDAGOG SERVANT SLAVISH
BONDMAID LORARIUS MAMELUKE
MANCIPLE MORGIANA PRAEDIAL
SLAVELET THEOWMAN ODALISQUE
(— IN TEMPLE) HIEROS
(— OWNER) PATRON
(— WHO WHIPS OTHERS) LORARIUS
(DEFORMED —) CALIBAN
(FREED —) CLIENT
(FUGITIVE —) MAROON CIMMARON
(GALLEY —) FORSAR FORSADO
SFORZATO
(HAREM —) ODA ODAH ODALISK
ODALESQUE
(HINDU —) DAS DASI
(REFUGEE —) CONTRABAND
(SLAVE'S —) GIBEONITE
(TEMPLE —) HIERODULE
(PL.) CHIURM COFFLE HELOTRY
TOXOTAE
SLAVEDRIVER RUSHER
SLAVER DROOL FROTH DRIVEL
DRIBBLE SLABBER SLOBBER
SALIVATE
SLAVERY YOKE THRALL BONDAGE
HELOTRY MIZRAIM THRALDOM
SERVITUDE
SLAVEY DRUDGE
SLAVISH MEAN MENIAL

SLAVONIC (— BEING) VILA
SLAY DOIN KILL SMITE SPILL MURDER
STRIKE BUTCHER EXECUTE
STRANGLE SLAUGHTER
SLAYER BANE HOGNI KILLER
MURDERER
(— OF INFIDELS) GHAZI
(SUFF.) CTONUS
SLEAZY FLIMSY TICKYTACKY
SLED LUGE PUNG TODE JUMBO
SCOOT SLIDE SLIPE SLOOP HURDLE
JUMPER SLEDGE SLEIGH BOBSLED
CLIPPER COASTER DOGBOAT
DOGSLED KOMATIK MONOSKI
POINTER SLIPPER TRAILER TRAVOIS
HANDSLED SKELETON TOBOGGAN
(— RIDER) BOBBER
SLEDGE DAN DRAG DRAY LUGE
PULK SLED GURRY PULKA SLIDE
SLIPE TRAIL TRAIN TROLL TRUNK
SLEIGH KIBITKA KOMATIK PADDOCK
TROLLEY TRAINEAU
(— FOR CRIMINALS) HURDLE
(— FOR STRAIGHTENING RAILS)
GAG
(LOG —) SLOOP TIEBOY
(MINER'S —) MALLET
SLEDGEHAMMER SMASHER
SLEEK SNOD SOFT CLOSE JOLLY
SILKY SLICK TRICK SILKEN SLEEKY
SLIGHT SMARMY SMOOTH SVELTE
SLEEKIT SOIGNEE SLIPPERY
SLEEKNESS GLOSS
SLEEP BED KIP LIB LIE NAP CALK
CAMP DORM DOSS DOZE HALE REST
WINK BALMY CRASH DORSE ROOST
SWOON DROWSE SIESTA SNOOZE
SOMNUS SWEVEN SHUTEYE
SLUMBER WINKING
(— BROKEN BY SNORING) GRUFF
(— ON A PERCH) JOUK
(— PROBLEM) APNEA
(DEEP —) SOPOR SWOON STUPOR
(KIND OF —) REM
(LIGHT —) SLOOM
(PRETENDED —) DOGSLEEP
(PROFOUND —) SOPOR
(SHORT —) NAP SIESTA SNOOZE
(PREF.) HYPN(O) SOMNI SOPOR
(DEEP —) NARC(O)
SLEEPER TIE MOLE FENDER
DORMANT CROSSTIE DORMEUSE
ELEOTRID STRINGER
SLEEPINESS SOPITION
SLEEPING BED ASLEEP DORMANT
DORMIENT
(— IN HOLY PLACE) INCUBATION
(— TABLET) DALMANE
SLEEPING CAR PULLMAN
SLEEPLESS LIDLESS WAKEFUL
RESTLESS WATCHFUL
SLEEPLESSNESS WATCH
INSOMNIA

SLEEPY DOZY HEAVY NODDY PEEPY
DROWSY GROGGY MORPHIC
SLEEPISH SLUMBERY SOMNIFIC
SLUMBEROUS
(— ONE) NODDER
SLEET STORM
SLEEVE ARM BAND POKE ARMLET
MANCHE MOGGAN BUSHING
CATHEAD CUBITAL HOUSING
THIMBLE
(— ON A SHAFT) CANNON
(— ON GUN) BAND
(CANVAS —) DROGUE
(HANGING —) TAB
(LEG-OF-MUTTON —) GIGOT
(LONG —) POKE
(ROOMY —) RAGLAN
(TAPERED —) SKEIN
SLEIGH SLO PUNG SLED BOOBY
SLIPE TRAIN BERLIN CUTTER SLEDGE
CARIOLE TRAINEAU
(MOTORIZED —) SNOWMOBILE
SLEIGHT ARTIFICE
SLEIPNER (OWNER OF —) ODIN
SLENDER FINE HAIR JIMP LANK
LEAN PRIN SLIM THIN DELIE EXILE
FAINT LATHY REEDY SLANK SLEEK
SMALL SPIRY SWAMP WISPY FILATE
SCANTY SEMMIT SLIGHT SPINNY
SPIRED STALKY SVELTE TENDER
GRACILE LISSOME SLIVERY SPIRLIE
SQUINNY TENUOUS THREADY
WASPISH ACICULAR ETHEREAL
HAIRLIKE PILIFORM SPINDLED
ATTENUATE
SLENDERNESS EXILITY TENUITY
SLEUTH TEC DETECTIVE
SLEW LOT ALOT RAFT SLUE STROKE
SLICE CUT BITE CHIP CHOP FLAG
FLAP JERK SHED STOW CANCH
CAPER GIGOT LEACH SHARE SHAVE
SHIVE SKELB SLIPE SLIVE CANTLE
COLLOP CORNET CULPON SHIVER
SLIVER TARGET THIBLE TRENCH
SECTION SHAVING TRANCHE
COSSETTE TURNOVER
(— CUT IN PLOWING) FLAG
(— OF BACON) BARD BARDE LARDON
RASHER
(— OF BREAD) BUTTY WHANG
CROUTE TRENCHER
(— OF CHEESE) KEBBOC
(— OF COAL) SKIP
(— OF FISH) COBBIN
(— OF MEAT) STEAK COLLOP CUTLET
SCALLOP TAILZIE
(— OF MEAT OR FISH) PAUPIETTE
(— OF SMOKED SALMON) CORNET
(— OF TOAST) ROUND
(— OF VEAL) FRICANDEAU
(— REMOVED FROM ROADWAY)
CANCH
(—S OF APPLES) CHOPS

(—S OF VEAL) GRENADINE
SCALLOPINI
(— WITH MOTIONS) SAW
(LARGE —) BLAD DODGE
(POTATO —) SCALLOP
(ROLLED — OF MEAT) ROULADE
(THICK —) SLAB WHANG
(THIN —) CHIP WAFER SECTION
(THIN —S OF MEAT) PICCATA
SLICED CUT
SLICK LOY MAG GLIB OILY SNUG
SLEEK CLASSY GLOSSY SMOOTHY
SLIDDERY
SLICKER FLOAT SLICK SMOOTH
SLEEKER SMOOTHER
SLIDE SCLY SKID SLEW SLIP SLUR
BALOP CHUTE COAST COULE CREEP
GLIDE HURRY MOUNT SCOOT SHIRL
SLADE FINDER SLOUGH SLIDDER
SLITHER SLUTHER FADEAWAY
GLISSADE SLIDEWAY TOBOGGAN
SCHLEIFER
(— A DIE) SLUR
(— ALONG) SHOOT
(— BACK) RELAPSE
(— CARDS) SKIN
(— DOWN) RUSE SLUMP
(— FOR LOWERING CASKS)
POLEYNE
(— ON DRUMHEAD) BRACE
(— SIDEWISE) SKID SLUE
(TENT —) EUPHROE
SLIDER REGISTER
SLIDEWAY PULLEY
SLIDING COULE
SLIGHT CUT OFF EASY FINE HURT
POOR PUNY SLAP SLIM SLUR SNUB
THIN WEAK FILMY GAUZY LIGHT
MINOR SCANT SMALL SOBER
FLIMSY FORGET LACHES LITTLE
MINUTE REMOTE TWIGGY CONTEMN
FRAGILE GRACILE NEGLECT
NOMINAL SHALLOW SKETCHY
SLENDER SLIGHTY THREADY VILLAIN
DELICATE MISPRIZE OVERLOOK
SCRANNEL VILIPEND
SLIGHTER LESS
SLIGHTEST FIRST LEAST
SLIGHTINGLY LIGHTLY
SLIGHTLY FAINTLY SOMEWHAT
(PREF.) MI(O)
(SUFF.) ESCENT ULOUS
SLIGHTNESS DELICACY GRACILITY
SLIM THIN GAUNT WANDY SLIGHT
SLENDER TENUOUS
SLIME GLIT GORE OOZE SLAB SLIP
SLUM GLEET SLAKE SLOAK SLOKE
SLEECH SLUDGE SCHLICH SLUBBER
SLUTHER
(PREF.) MUC(I)(O) MUCOSO MYX(O)
(SUFF.) MYXA
SLIMMER DIETER

SLIMY EELY OOZY SLAB MUCID
GLAIRY GLEETY GLETTY LIMOUS
MUCOUS SNOTTY SLEECHY
MUCULENT
SLINE JOINT
SLING DUST LOOP FLING HONDA
SLUNG BRIDGE BRIDLE HALTER
SLACKIE
(— FOR HAULING GAME) TUMPLINE
(— OF BRAIDED FIBERS) MA
(PREF.) FUNDI
SLINGER FUNDITOR
SLINGSHOT SLING SLAPPY
TWEAKER CATAPULT SHANGHAI
SLINK SLY CAST HINT LEER LOOP
LURK PEAK MICHE SHIRK SLING
SLUNK SNEAK SLINKY
(— AWAY) SHAG SLOKE FLINCH
MIZZLE SHRINK
SLIP DIP IMP NOD SLY BALK CARD
CHIT DOCK FALL JINK LOOP RUSE
SKEW SKID SLEW SLUR SPEW
BEWET BEWIT BONER CHECK DAGGE
ERROR FLIER FLYER GLIDE LABEL
LAPSE SCAPE SCION SHIFT SHIRL
SKATE SKITE SLICK SLIDE SLIPE
SLIVE SLUMP STALK SURGE COUPON
ENGOBE LAPSUS MISCUE SLOUGH
SLURRY TICKET UNSLIP DELAPSE
FOUNDER ILLAPSE MISSTEP
MORTISE SLIDDER SLUTHER
SNAPPER STUMBLE BOOKMARK
GERTRUDE GLISSADE HEADBAND
QUICKSET SCHEDULE SIDESLIP
SLIPPAGE SLIPPING
(— AWAY) GO BILK SKIN WISE EVADE
ELAPSE
(— BY) ELAPSE
(— FROM A PLANT) STALLON
(— OFF COURSE) SLEW SLOUGH
(— OF FISH) RAND
(— OF PAPER) ALLONGE
(— OF PARCHMENT) PANEL
(— OF WOOD) SPILL REGLET
(— ON CARELESSLY) SLIVE
(— OUT) TIB
(— SECRETLY) CREEM
(— SMOOTHLY) SWIM
(— UP) BLUNDER
(CERAMICS —) SLOP ENGOBE
(INFANT'S —) GERTRUDE
(KIND OF —) FREUDIAN
(PILLOW —) BIER
(PREF.) CLAD(O)
(SUFF.) CLADOUS
SLIPCASE CASE FOREL FORREL
SLIPKNOT BOW SNITTLE
DRAWKNOT
SLIPMAN JACKER
SLIPOVER OVERSLIP
SLIPPER FLAT MULE NEAP PUMP
SOCK TURN GLAVE MOYLE ROMEO

SCUFF BALLET BOOTEE DORSAY
JULIET PANTON PINSON SANDAL
SCLAFF SCLIFF BAUCHLE CHINELA
CRAKOWE EVERETT SCUFFER
BABOUCHE FEWTERER PANTOFLE
SCLAFFER SLIPSHOE
(PREF.) CALCEI

SLIPPERINESS SLIDDER

SLIPPERY EELY GLEG GLIB SLID
GLARY GLINT SLAPE SLEEK SLICK
SOAPY SWACK CRAFTY GLINSE
GREASY LUBRIC SHIFTY SLIPPY
ELUSIVE EVASIVE GLIDDER SHUTTLE
SLIDDRY SLIDING SLITHER GLIBBERY
SLABBERY SLICKERY SLIDDERY
SLITHERY
(PREF.) LUBRI

SLIPPERY DICK DONCELLA

SLIPSHOD JERRY RAGGED
SLOPPY UNKEMPT SLAPDASH
SLOVENLY

SLIPSTREAM RACE

SLIPUP FLUFF MISTAKE

SLIT CUT EYE JAG KIN NAG RIT FENT
GATE NICK PORT RACE RENT SCAR
SLOT VENT CRACK SPARE BOUCHE
CRANNY OSTIUM STRENT FISSURE
PERTUSE PLACKET SLITTED
SLOTTEN WINDWAY APERTURE
BOTHRIUM
(— HIND LEG) HARL
(— IN EDGE OF SHIELD) BOUCHE
(— IN ORGAN PIPE) MOUTH
(— IN SKIRT) SPARE
(— IN STONE) GRIKE
(— IN TIRE TREAD) SIPE
(— IN WALL) LOOP
(— MADE BY CUT) KERF
(ORNAMENTAL —) SLASH

SLITHER SLIDE HIRSEL SLIDDER
SLUTHER

SLIVER TOP SHAVE SKELF SLICE
SPELK SPELL SHIVER DELIVERY
SPLINTER
(— OF WOOL) ROLL ROVE
(SPINNING —) END RIBBON
DELIVERY

SLOB JOKER SLUDGE SLOBBER
SLOMMACK LITTERBUG

SLOBBER SLOP SLUP SMALM
SMARM SLAVER SLABBER SLATHER
SLIVVER BESLAVER

SLOBBERY SLOBBY SMARMY
SLAVERY

SLOE SLA SNAG SLONE

SLOG PLOD SLOSH STRIKE

SLOGAN CRY CACHET CUTTER
PHRASE CATCHCRY GRAFFITO
SLUGHORN WARDWORD
CATCHWORD SHIBBOLETH

SLOOP STAR BOYER COMET SMACK
SCHUIT HOOGAARS

SLOP SLAP SOSS SQUAB SWILL
SOSSLE SOZZLE HOGWASH SLATTER
(— AROUND) SLAISTER
(PL.) SLIVERS SLIPSLOP SLOPPAGE

SLOPE UP DIP LIE BAND BANK BENT
BRAE CANT CAST CURB DROP FALL
HANG HILL LEAN PALI RAKE RAMP
RISE SIDE SINK TILT BEVEL CLIFF
COAST GAMMA HIELD PINCH PITCH
SCARP SLANT SLENT SLOOP SPLAY
STEEP TALUS VERGE YUNGA
ASCENT BAJADA BATTER BREAST
BROACH ESCARP GLACIS HADING
SHELVE TUMBLE UPBROW UPRISE
CUTBANK DESCENT DOWNSET
FORESET HANDING INCLINE
LEANING PENDANT UPGRADE
VERSANT WEATHER BANKSIDE
DRIPPING GLISSADE GRADIENT
SHOULDER SIDELING SNOWBANK
ACCLIVITY ESCARPMENT
(— BACK) BATTER
(— DOWN) SHED
(— OF CUESTA) INFACE
(— OF ROOF) CURB
(— OF STERNPOST) RAKE
(— ON GOLF GREEN) BURROW
(— UPWARD) CLIMB ASCEND BATTER
(DOWNWARD —) HANG DEVALL
DECLINE DESCENT HANGING
DOWNHILL
(GENTLE —) GLACIS
(MARGINAL —) CESS
(MOUNTAIN —) ADRET
(SKIING —) SCHUSS
(STEEP —) BROW HEADWALL
(TOBOGGANING —) ICEHILL
(SUFF.) CLINAL CLINE

SLOPING CANT DEVEX SLANT SLOPE
SLOPY ASLOPE SHELVY DECLIVE
SCARPED DOWNHILL SIDELING
(— ABRUPTLY) BOLD
(— BACKWARD) SUPINE
(STEEPLY —) RAPID
(SUFF.) CLINAL

SLOPPINESS BLURB

SLOPPY JUICY MESSY SOPPY
SLABBY SOZZLY SPLOSHY SLABBERY
SLAPDASH SLATTERN SLATTERY
SLIPSHOD WATERISH

SLOSH DOWSE SLASH SLUSH SOUSE
SQUDGE SPLODGE

SLOT COVE DROP SCROLL SPLINE
KEYHOLE GUIDEWAY

SLOTH AI UNAU TARDO ACEDIA
IGNAVY ACCIDIE IGNAVIA
BRADYPOD EDENTATE PIGRITIA
SLUGGING

SLOTH BEAR BHALU ASWAIL

SLOTHFUL FAT ARGH IDLE LAZY
INERT LITHER THOKISH UNLUSTY
DELICATE INDOLENT SLUGGISH

SLOUCH LOUCH LARRUP LOLLOP
LOUNGE SLIDDER TROLLOP
SHAMMOCK SLOUCHER
SLOUCH HAT SMASHER
SLOUGH CORE SHED SLEW SLUE
BAYOU RAVEL SHUCK SLONK SLUFF
SPOIL SWAMP ESCHAR DISCARD
LAMMOCK

SLOVAKIA (ALSO SEE CZECH
REPUBLIC)
CAPITAL: BRATISLAVA
COIN: CROWN DUCAT HALER HELLER
KORUNA
DANCE: POLKA REDOWA FURIANT
MEASURE: LAN SAH MIRA KOREC
LATRO STOPA MERICE STRYCH
MOUNTAIN: GERLACHOVSKY
MOUNTAIN RANGE: ORE TATRA
BESKID BESKYDY JAVORNIKY
CARPATHIAN NIZKETATRY
VYSOKETATRY BIELEKARPATY
NAME: SLOVENSKA
RIVER: UH UZH VAG VAH HRON IPEL
WAAG DUNAJ MARCH NITRA SLANA
BODROG DANUBE HORNAD
MORAVA ONDAVA POPRAD TORYSA
LABOREC
TOWN: NITRA BANSKA KOSICE
MARTIN PRESOV TRNAVA ZILINA
ZVOLEN BYSTRICA NOVADUBNICA
PARTIZANSKE

SLOVEN BESOM CLART SLUSH
TROLLY GROBIAN HALLION TRACHLE
HUDDROUN

SLOVENIA (ALSO SEE YUGOSLAVIA)
CAPITAL: LJUBLJANA
COIN: TOLAR
GULF: VENICE
LAKE: BLED BOHINJ
LANGUAGE: SLOVENE
MOUNTAIN: TRIGLAV
MOUNTAIN RANGE: SAVA DRAVA
KARST JULIAN KAMNIK POHORJE
SAVINJA HIGHALPS KARAVANKE
KARAWANKEN
NAME: SLOVENIJA
PORT: KOPER CAPODISTRIA
RIVER: MURA SAVA SOCA DRAVA
TOWN: CELJE KOPER KRANJ
MURSKA SOBOTA MARIBOR
NOVOMESTO NOVAGORICA
CAPODISTRIA

SLOVENLY DOWDY GAUMY MESSY
BLOWZY CLATTY FROWZY GRUBBY
SHABBY SLOPPY SLOVEN TRAILY
UNTIDY BUNTING RAUNCHY SLIVING
SLOUCHY UNSONCY CARELESS
HUDDROUN SLIPSHOD SLOBBERY
SLUBBERY SLUTTISH TROLLOPY

SLOW BOG LAG LAX LEK WET ARGH
DREE DULL LASH LATE LAZY LENT
SKID SLUG SOFT SULK BLUNT
DUNCH DUNNY HEAVY HOOLY INERT
POKEY SLACK SLOTH SWEER TARDE
TARDO TARDY UNAPT ARREST
BEHIND DRIECH DUMMEL HINDER
RETARD SLOOMY SOODLY TRAILY
COSTIVE DRONISH HALTING
LAGGARD LANGUID SLACKEN
SOAKING STRANGE TARDANT
TEDIOUS UNREADY DILATORY
INACTIVE LATESOME SLUGGISH
(— DOWN) SEIZE
(— DOWN SPACECRAFT) DEBOOST
(— IN BURNING) SOFT
(— IN MOVEMENT) GRAVE INERT
SULKY
(— OF LEARNING) DULL
(— OF MIND) STUPID
(— TO LEARN) BACKWARD
(— TO RESPOND) GROSS
(— UP) SLACK SLACKEN
(MODERATELY —) ANDANTE
(MUSICALLY —) LENTO
(PLEASANTLY —) SOFT
(VERY —) LARGO
(PREF.) BRADY TARDI
SLOW-BURNING PUNKY
SLOWED STIFF
SLOWER LATTER CALANDO
SLOWING RELENT LENTANDO
RITARDANDO RALLENTANDO
(SUFF.) STASIA STASIS
SLOW LORIS KOKAN
SLOWLY SLOW DULLY GRAVE HOOLY
LENTO ADAGIO GENTLY HEAVILY
SLOW-MOVING SLEEPY DORMANT
DRAWLING SLUGGISH
SLOWNESS LAG SLOTH LENTOR
TARDITY LATENESS
SLOWPOKE SNAIL TURTLE
ALSORAN DAWDLER
SLOW-WITTED FAT DENSE STUPID
SLOWWORM HAGWORM
SLUDGE GUNK OOZE SLOB
SLUE SLEW PIVOT SWAMP SLOUGH
SLUG BUST LINE MILL PLOW SHOT
SNAG STEW ARION CLUMP LIMAX
SNAIL RATTLE STRIKE SNIFTER
TREPANG GEEPOUND
(PREF.) LIMACI
SLUGGARD DAW SLOW SLUG
DRONE BUZZARD CAYNARD
LUGGARD SWINGER SLOWBACK
SLUGABED
SLUGGISH LAG DOZY DULL FOUL
LATE LAZY LOGY SLOW SOFT BROSY
DOPEY DRONY FAINT HEAVY INERT
LEADY LOURD RESTY SULKY BOVINE
DRAGGY DROWSY JACENT LEADEN
SLEEPY SLOOMY SLUGGY SUPINE
TORPID COSTIVE DORMANT

DRONISH LAGGARD LANGUID
LENTOUS LUMPISH RESTIVE
DILATORY INACTIVE INDOLENT
LOURDISH SLOTHFUL SLOTTERY
SLUGGARD
(PREF.) BRADY

SLUGGISHNESS LEAD SLOTH
APATHY LENTOR PHLEGM INERTIA
LANGUOR

SLUICE CLOW GOOL GOTE GOUT
SASSE SLUSH TRUNK CLOUGH
FENDER LAUNDER PENSTOCK
WASTWEIR

SLUICEGATE ABOIDEAU

SLUICEWAY FLASH

SLUM BUSTI BUSTEE WARREN

SLUMBER DORM DOVE DOZE JOUK
REST ROUT SLEEP SLOOM DROWSE

SLUMP FALL FLOP SOSS SLOUCH
LETDOWN TROLLOP

SLUR BIND SLIM COULE GLIDE SLIME
SCRUFF SLIGHT SLUBBER LIGATURE
(— IN PRINTING) SHAKE

SLURRY SLIP

SLUSH MIRE POSH SIND SLOP FLUSH
SLOSH SPOSH STUFF SWASH
SWOSH LOPPER SLUDGE SLUTCH
SLOBBER SLODDER

SLUSHY SLASHY SLOPPY SLOSHY
SLUDGY STICKY SPLASHY SLOBBERY

SLUT MAUX BITCH FILTH QUEAN
DOLLOP DRAZEL DRAZIL MALKIN
DROSSEL PUCELLE SLAMKIN
SLATTERN

SLUTTISH DRABBY SLUTTY
SORDID

SLY ARCH CUTE FOXY SLEE QUID SLIM
CANNY COONY LLERY LOOPY PAWKY
PLITY POKEY SLOAN SNAKY ARTFUL
ASTUTE CRAFTY FELINE SUBTLE
SUPPLE CUNNING EVASIVE FOXLIKE
FURTIVE LEERING POLITIC SUBTILE
UNFRANK GUILEFUL SLEIGHTY
SNEAKING STEALTHY THIEVISH
CLANDESTINE

SLYNESS CUNNING PAWKERY
STEALTH ARCHNESS

SMACK BANG BARK BIFF BUSS KISS
SALT SCAT SLAP TANG TROW VEIN
WHAM BAWLY GOUFF SAVOR SNACK
SPANG SPICE TASTE TWANG
BARQUE BAWLEY FLAVOR SMATCH
SMACKEE SPANKER BRAGOZZO
SLAPDASH TINCTURE
(— OF) RELISH

SMACKING SKELPING

SMALL BIT SMA WEE BABY MEAN
PINK SEED SLIM TINY WEAK BIJOU
BITTY DAWNY DEENY DINKY ELFIN
PETIT PETTY PINKY POKEY RUNTY
TEENY WEENY BANTAM FRIBBY
GRUBBY INSECT LITTLE MIDGET
MINUTE NARROW PEANUT PETITE

SCANTY SLIGHT SMALLY CAPSULE
MINIMAL NAGGISH NANITIC
NOMINAL PICCOLO QUEECHY
SCRIMPY SLENDER THRIFTY
PEDDLING PILULOUS SNIPPETY
MINIATURE MINISCULE
(— AND NUMEROUS) MILIARY
(— AND THICK) DUMPY DUMPTY
(— BUT TANGIBLE) CERTAIN
(— PORTION) MODICUM
(CONTEMPTIBLY —) MEASLY
(DAINTILY —) MIGNON
(EXCESSIVELY —) BOXY
(NOT —) GOOD
(VERY —) WEE FINE TINY DWARF
MICRO PUSIL PYGMY TEENY MINUTE
MINIKIN TIDDLEY DWARFISH
(PREF.) LEPT(O) MICR(O) OLIG(O)
PARV(I) PAURO TAPIN(O)
(SUFF.) (— ONE) EL ET IUM LING OCK
ULA ULE ULUM ULUS

SMALLAGE MARCH

SMALLCLOTHES SHORTS SMALLS

SMALL CRANBERRY FENBERRY

SMALLER LESS MINOR LESSER
(PREF.) MEIO MI(O) MINI

SMALLEST FIRST LEAST MINIM
TITMAN MINIMUS

SMALLHOLDER TOFTMAN

SMALL-MINDED PETTY PICAYUNE

SMALLNESS NANISM EXILITY
FEWNESS PAUCITY EXIGUITY
SCARCITY

SMALLPOX POX VARIOLA
ALASTRIM
(PREF.) VARIOLI VARIOLO

SMALL-SCALE MINI

SMALL-TIME PETTY TWOBIT
RINKYDINK INSIGNIFICANT

SMALT ROYAL ESCHEL SMALTZ
ZAFFER ASMALTE

SMART NIP YEP BRAW FESS FLIP
FOXY GNIB NICE PINK POSH RACY
SNAP SPRY SWAG TRIG ACUTE
BRISK CLEAN DINKY FLASH HEADY
JIMMY KIPPY NIFTY NOBBY NUTTY
PEERT PRANK PRIDY RITZY SASSY
SAUCY SHARP SLEEK SLICK SMIRK
SMOKE SMUSH SPICY SPRIG STING
SWANK SWISH TIGHT TIPPY TOFFY
TRICK AKAMAI BRAWLY BRIGHT
CHEESY CLEVER DAPPER GIGOLO
JAUNTY KITTLE PERTLY SHREWD
SPANKY SPIFFY SPRINK SPRUCE
STOUND SWANKY SWIDGE TIDDLY
KNOWING PUNGENT SWAGGER
TOFFISH VOGUISH BRUSHING
SPIFFING
(— IN APPEARANCE) POSH
(— IN DRESS) CHIC CLASSY DRESSY
GALLANT
(AFFECTEDLY —) SMUG
(IMPOSINGLY —) STYLISH

SMART ALECK FLIP SMARTY WISEASS WISEGUY WISEACRE WISENHEIMER

SMART-ALECKY CUTE

SMARTEN FINE PUSS SMUG GROOM PRINK SLICK TITIVATE

SMARTLY SMACK SMART SNACK YEPLY TIDELY

SMARTNESS TON SNAP SMART SPIFF SWISH

SMARTWEED CULERAGE REDKNEES

SMASH GIT BASH BUMP CAVE DASH PASH RUSH SCAT TRAP BREAK CRACK CRASH CRAZE PRANG SOCKO STAVE TRASH WRECK BANJAX CRACKER SHATTER SMASHUP DEBRUISE DEMOLISH OVERHEAD STRAMASH
(— A GAP) BREACH

SMASHED BUNG KAPUT STOVEN BROOZLED

SMASHING CRACKING

SMASHUP STRAMASH

SMATTERING TANG SMACK SMATCH SMATTER

SMEAR DAB DOPE RUB BLOT BLUR CLAM DAUB DOPE GAUM GLOB GORM MOIL CLEAM DITCH GLAIR SLAKE SLARE SMALM SMARM SULLY BEDAUB BESLAB DEFILE PLATCH SLAVER SLURRY SMIRCH SMOOCH SMUDGE SPREAD STREAK STRIKE BEPAINT BESMEAR PLASTER POLLUTE SPLOTCH SLAISTER
(— OVER) ENGLUTE
(— WITH BLOOD) GILD
(— WITH EGG WHITE) GLAIR
(— WITH MUD) CLART SLIME
(— WITH SOMETHING STICKY) GAUM GORM LIME
(— WITH TAR) PAY
(— WITH WAX) CERE

SMEAR DAB FLATFISH MARYSOLE

SMEARED FOUL BROSY MUSSY SCOVY BLOODY SMUDGY BLURRED BEGUMMED

SMEARING (— WITH OINTMENT) INUNCTION

SMEARY DAUBY GAUMY

SMEDDUM SMITHUM

SMELL FUNK FUST GUSH NOSE ODOR VENT AROMA FETOR FLAIR SAVOR SENSE USE SMACK SNIFF SNOOK SNUFF STIFE TASTE OLFACT RESENT SMEECH BREATHE PERFUME REFLAIR VERDURE
(— AFTER PREY) BREVIT
(— OFFENSIVELY) REEK
(BITING —) TANG
(DAMP FUSTY —) RAFT
(DISAGREEABLE —) GOO PONG STENCH
(HAVING PLEASANT —) SNIFTY

(MUSTY —) FUST
(OFFENSIVE —) FUNK FETOR STINK MEPHITIS
(PLEASANT —) INCENSE
(STRONG —) HOGO
(SWEET —) SWEET
(PREF.) BROM(O) ODIO ODORI ODORO OLFACTO OSM(O) OSMIO OSPHRESIO OZO(NI)(NO)
(SENSE OF —) OSPHRESIO
(SUFF.) OSMA
(SENSE OF —) OSPHRESIA

SMELLY OLID RIPE FETID FUGGY WHIFFY SMELLFUL

SMELT DECOCT INANGA EPERLAN ICEFISH ELIQUATE SALMONID SPARLING SPERLING
(FRY OF —) PRIM

SMEW NUN PIED SMEE DIVER SMETHE

SMIDGEN BIT DAB JOT SKOSH SLOSH

SMIDGEON (— OF TEA) SPOT

SMILAX LILY SARSA LILIUM

SMILE BEAM GRIN FLASH FLEER SMEER ARRIDE SMUDGE SMIRKLE
(— AMOROUSLY) SMICKER
(AFFECTED —) SMIRK
(SELF-CONSCIOUS —) SIMPER

SMILING GOOD BONNY RIANT SMILY BONNIE RIDENT SMIRKY TWINKLY SMILEFUL

SMIRCH SMIT SOIL SMEAR SULLY SLURRY SOILURE TARNISH

SMIRCHED DINGY

SMIRK DRAD YIRN SIMPER SMICKER SMIRKLE SMURTLE

SMITE DUNT FRAP GIRD SLAY FLING SKITE STRIKE
(— WITH LIGHTNING) LEVEN

SMITH MIMIR REGIN BOSSER FORGER SMITHY FARRIER GLUTTER SMITHER STEELER WAYLAND FLOORMAN FORGEMAN PANSMITH

SMITHSONITE CALAMINE

SMITHY FORGE SMIDDY STITHY STUDDIE FARRIERY

SMITTEN EPRISE INLOVE STRICKEN

SMOCK BRAT SLOP CAMIS KAMIS SMOKE JIBBAH JUMPER CHEMISE SMICKET

SMOG FOG HAZE

SMOKE PEW USE BLOW FLAN FOGO FUFF FUME FUNK HAVE LUNT NAVE PIPE REEK ROKE TOVE DRINK REECH SMEEK SMORE SMUSH STIVE VAPOR WHIFF BREATH BUCCAN POTHER SMEECH SMUDGE INCENSE SMOLDER SMOTHER BACONIZE
(— MARIJUANA) BLAST
(AUTHOR OF —) TURGENEV
(CHARACTER IN —) IRINA TANYA OSININ GRIGORY POTUGIN TATYANA

BAMBAEFF SHESTOFF BINDASOFF GUBARYOFF LITVINOFF RATMIROFF KAPITOLINA REISENBACH
(FROST —) BARBER
(HAZE AND —) SMAZE
(OFFENSIVE —) FUNK
(TOBACCO —) BLAST
(PREF.) ATMID(O) CAPNO FUMAR(O) FUMI

SMOKE-AND-MIRRORS DISGUISE
SMOKE BROWN ASPHALT
SMOKEHOUSE FUMATORY
SMOKEJACK STACKMAN
SMOKER STAG FUNKER NICOTIAN
(MARIJUANA —) VIPER
SMOKESTACK STACK FUNNEL TUNNEL CHIMNEY
SMOKE TREE ZANTE FUSTET FUSTIC SCOTINO
SMOKING ROOM DIVAN TABAGIE
SMOKY HAZY ROKY DINGY FUMID REEKY FUMISH FUMOSE REECHY REEKIE SMUDGY SMUISTY
SMOLDER SMUSH SMOTHER
SMOLDERING PUNKY
SMOLT SMELT SMOUT SPROD
SMOOCH PET BUSS KISS NECK SMUDGE LALLYGAG LOLLYGAG
SMOOTH DUB FAT LAP NOT BOSS COMB DRAG EASE EASY EVEN FACE FAIR FILE FLAT GLAD GLEG GLIB HONE IRON LENE NOTT REET SLID SNOD SOFT TRIM BLAND BRENT CLEAR COUTH DARBY DIGHT DOLCE DRESS EMERY FLOAT FRAZE GLARE GOOSE HOWEL LEVEL LITHE NAKED PLAIN PLANE PRESS QUIET SCARF SILKY SLAPE SLEEK SLICK SMOLT SNUFF SOAPY SUANT SUAVE SUENT TERSE ABRASE BUFFED CREAMY EQUATE EVENLY FETTLE FLUENT GLOSSY GREASE GREASY LEGATO LIMBER MANGLE POLITE SCREED SILKEN SLIGHT STREAK STRIKE STROKE SVELTE UNFRET BOULDER ERUGATE FLATTEN SLEEKIT EXPLICIT GLABRATE GLABROUS GLIBBERY GRAZIOSO LEVIGATE SARSENET SLIDDERY SQUEEGEE STRICKLE UNRUFFLE
(— BY BREAKING LUMPS) BILDER
(— MARBLE) GRIT
(— ONESELF UP) PREEN
(— OVER) GLOZE PLASTER
(— TYPE) KERN
(HYPOCRITICALLY —) SLEEK
(PHONETICALLY —) LENE LENIS
(PREF.) HOMAL(O) LEIO LEUR(O) LIO LISS(O) LITI OXY
SMOOTHER GLAZER
SMOOTHLY SLICK EASILY EVENLY GLIBLY SMOOTH SPROWSY SWEETLY POLITELY

SMOOTH-MANNERED URBANE
SMOOTHNESS EASE FLUENCY
SMOOTH-RUNNING SWEET
SMOOTH-TONGUED WHILLY
SMOOTH WINTERBERRY CANHOOP
SMOTHER BURKE CHOKE SMEAR SMOKE SMORE MOIDER SMUDGE STIFLE FLASKER OPPRESS QUEASON QUEAZEN SMOLDER SMUDDER
SMOTHERED ETOUFFE STIFLED
SMUDGE BLUR GAUM SLUR SMUT SOIL SOOT CROCK SMEAR SMOKE SMOOCH SMUTCH SMOLDER SMOTHER SOILURE
SMUDGED BLOTTY SMUTCHY
SMUG SLEEK SMUSH SUAVE SMUDGE
SMUGGLE RUN STEAL BOOTLEG SHUFFLE
SMUGGLER OWLER COYOTE RUNNER SPOTSMAN
(— OF DRUGS) MULE
(— OF IMMIGRANTS) COYOTE
(DOPE —) MULE
(DRUG —) MULE
SMUGGLING OWLING
SMUGLY FATLY
SMUT BUNT COOM PORN BLACK BLECK COLLY COOMB CROCK GRIME SMOOT SMITCH SMUTCH SMATTER COLBRAND
SMUTCH BLOT SMIRCH SMITCH SMOUCH SMUDGE
SMUT GRASS TUSSOCK
SMUTTINESS RAUNCH
SMUTTY BAWDY DIRTY SOOTY SULTRY RAUNCHY BARNYARD FREUDIAN
SMYRNA USHAK
SNACK BIT CUT BAIT BITE GORP NOSH SNAP TAPA BEVER BUTTY CHACK CHECK NACHO SHARE SNICK TASTE GOUTER MUNGEY NACKET SNATCH ZAKUSKA ANTOJITO MUNCHIES NUNCHEON
(— SPOT) TEAROOM
(CHOCOLATE —) OREO
SNAFFLE BIT GAG BRIDOON
SNAG KNAG SNUG STUB POINT GLITCH IMPASSE PLANTER SNAGGLE
(PL.) EMBARRAS
SNAIL HUA PILA SNAG CHINK DRILL HELIX OLIVA OVULA PHYSA SHELL THAIS TURBO WHELK CERION CONKER DODMAN NATICA NERITA NERITE PHYSID PURPLE TRITON WINKLE RISSOID UNICORN VERTIGO ZONITID CASSIDID ESCARGOT HODMADOD JANTHINA LYMNAEID MELANIAN NATICEID NERITOID RAMSHORN SOLARIUM WALLFISH PERIWINKLE

(PREF.) STROMBI STROMBULI
(SUFF.) COCHLEI COCHLI(O) COCHLO
SNAILFLOWER CARACOL
SNAKE (ALSO SEE SERPENT AND
REPTILE) ASP BOA BOM ESS NAG
APOD BOBA BOID BOMA JUBO NAGA
NAJA SEPS SNIG ABOMA ASPIC
COBRA CONGO CRIBO DRILL JIBOA
KRAIT MAMBA PTYAS RACER SNECK
TIGER VIPER BOIGID BONGAR CANTIL
CHITAL DABOIA DIPSAS ELAPID
GOPHER HISSER JESSUR KERRIL
PYTHON ROLLER RUNNER TAIPAN
URAEUS WENONA ADJIGER ANILIID
BOKADAM CAMOODI CRAWLER
CREEPER CULEBRA DIAPSID
HAGWORM HOGNOSE LABARIA
LANGAHA PRESTER RATTLER
REGULUS REPTILE SCYTALE
SERPENT SPITTER WALPAPI
ANACONDA BONETAIL BUNGARUM
CASCAVEL CERASTES CROTALID
EGGEATER FLATHEAD HAIRWORM
JARARACA KEELBACK MOCCASIN
OPHIDIAN RINGHALS SNAKELET
VIPERINE
(— OIL) BUNKUM POPPYCOCK
(TREE —) BOOMSLANG
(TWO-HEADED —) AMPHISBAENA
(PREF.) OPHI(O) SERPU
(SUFF.) OPHIS
SNAKEBARK IRONBARK
SNAKEBIRD DARTER PLOTUS
ANHINGA DUCKLAR
SNAKEHEAD MURRAL
SNAKELIKE ANGUINE VIPEROUS
SNAKE MACKEREL ESCOLAR
SNAKEMOUTH POGONIA
SNAKEPIECE POINTER
SNAKEROOT STEVIA BABROOT
BUGBANE SANGREL SANICLE
SAWWORT POOLWORT RICHWEED
WHITETOP
SNAKESKIN SPOIL HACKLE SLOUGH
(CASTOFF —S) EXUVIAE
SNAKEWEED BISTORT
SNAP SET ZIP BARK BITE CHOP GNAP
HUFF JERK KNAP LIRP PIPE SETT
BREAK CLACK FILIP FLICK GANCH
KNACK KNICK PHOTO SMACK SNACK
BLUDGE SNAPPY SNATCH FASTENER
PUSHOVER SNAPHEAD CREPITATE
(— AT) HANCH
(— LIGHTLY) KNICK
(— OFF) SNIP
(— TOGETHER) CRASH
(— UP) SNUP SNAFFLE
(— WITH FINGER) LIRP FILIP THRIP
FILLIP
SNAPBACK PASSBACK
SNAPDRAGON BULL SNAPS
BULLER BULLDOG DOGMOUTH
SNAPE FLINCH

SNAPPER UKU BRIM JOCU SESI
BREAM PARGO VORAZ CUBERA
HUSSAR JENOAR LAWYER NATIVE
TAMURE ULAULA COCKNEY
CRACKER BIAJAIBA CACHUCHO
FLAMENCO GNATSNAP LUTIANID
WOLLOMAI SCHNAPPER
MUTTONFISH SHUTTERBUG
SNAPPING CHACK DOGGISH
SNAPPING BEETLE ELATER
SKIPPER SNAPPER ELATERID
SKIPJACK
SNAPPING TURTLE LOGHEAD
SHAGTAIL
SNAPPISH CRUP EDGY PUXY CROSS
SNACK TESTY WASPY CUTTED
SNAGGY SNAPPY SNARKY SNIPPY
DOGGISH PEEVISH
SNAPPY CRISP JEMMY NIPPY ZIPPY
SNAPSHOT PRINT
SNARE BAG GIN HAY NET PIT SET
BAIT BUKE FANG GIRN GRIN HOOK
LACE LIME TOIL TRAP WAIT WIRE
BRAKE CATCH FRAUD GNARE LATCH
LEASH SINEW SNARL SNIRL STALE
SWEEK TRAIN COBWEB GILDER
PANTER SNATCH SPRINT TREPAN
TUNNEL ENSNARE MANTRAP
OVERNET PITFALL SETTING SNICKLE
SNIGGLE SPRINGE BIRDLIME
INVEIGLE LIMEBUSH SPRINGLE
TENDICLE MOUSETRAP
(— DEER) WITHE
(— FOR ELEPHANTS) KEDDAH
(— FOR FISH) WEEL
(FISH —) WEEL
SNARL ARR BITE CARL GIRN GNAR
GURR HARL HURR NARR TWIT WAFF
YARR GNARL GNARR GRILL KNURL
RAVEL SNIRL TWINE BOWWOW
BUMBLE GAUNCH MUCKER TANGLE
VENNER GRIZZLE GRUMBLE
SNARLED SNAFU
SNARLER CYNIC
SNARLING LATRANT
SNATCH HAP NAB NIP RAP GRAB
HINT RACE RASE SNAP SNIP WHIP
WRAP YERK YUCK BRAID CATCH
CLAWK CLICK EREPT GANCH GRASP
GRIPE PLUCK SNACK STRIP SWIPE
SWOOP TWEAK WHIFT WREST
SNITCH STRIKE TWITCH WRENCH
CLAUGHT GRABBLE SCAMBLE
VULTURE
(— MOMENTARY VIEW) GLANCE
SNAZZY CHIC COOL FANCY
SNEAK BLAB GRUB LEER LOOP LOUT
LURK PEAK PIMP SHUG SNIG LURCH
MEECH MOOCH SCOUT SHARK
SHIRK SKULK SLIDE SLINK SLIPE
SLIVE SLOKE SNEAP SNICK SNOOK
BLIFIL MICHER WEASEL SLOUNGE
SNIGGLE SNEAKSBY

(— AWAY) SLIPE
(— OFF) MAG SHAB MIZZLE
(PRYING —) SNOOP
SNEAKER CREEPER GUMSHOE
TENNIES
SNEAKERS TENNIES
SNEAKING HANGDOG PEAKING
SLIVING
SNEAKY FURTIVE MEECHING
SNEER SHY FLON GIBE GIRD GIRN
GULE JEER JERK JIBE MOCK FLEER
FLING FLOUT GLEEK JAUNT SCOFF
SCOUT SLARE SLEER SNIFF SNIRT
SNORT GIZZEN SNEEST TWITCH
WRINKLE RIDICULE
SNEERING FRUMPERY
SNEEZE NEESE NEEZE ARREST
(— AT) CONDEMN DESPISE
SNEEZEWEED ALANT ROSILLA
HELENIUM
SNEEZEWOOD NIESHOUT
SNEEZEWORT HARDHEAD
PTARMICA
SNEEZING PTARMIC
SNELL SNOOD TIPPET GANGING
SNICK TIP SNECK
SNICKER TEEHEE TITTER SMIRKLE
SNIGGER SNIGGLE
SNIDE ORNERY
SNIFF NOSE TIFT VENT WIND SCENT
SMELL SNAFF SNIFT SNUFF SNIVEL
SNAFFLE SNIFFLE SNOTTER
SNIFTER SLUG BALLOON INHALER
SNIGGER NICKER WHICKER
SNIGGLE BRAGGLE
SNIP CUT CLIP CROP MINX NICK
SHRED SNICK SCISSOR
SNIPE JACK NICK WISP SCAPE SNITE
WADER WILLET BLEATER BLITTER
DOWITCH HUMILITY LONGBILL
SHADBIRD WOODCOCK
SNIPER TEASER BUSHWACK
SNIPPET BIT
SNIPPINESS SASS
SNIVEL WHINE BUBBLE SNIFFLE
SNIFTER SNOTTER SNUFFLE
SNIVELY TEARY TEARFUL
SNOB SNAB SNOOT FLUNKY
SHONEEN SNOBBER
SNOBBERY ELITISM
SNOBBISH RITZY DICKTY OFFISH
SNOBBY SNOOTY UPPISH HAUGHTY
UPSTAGE
SNOOK SNOOT ROBALO
SNOOKER CON HOODWINK
SNOOP PRY PEEK PEEP PRIER SNEAK
BREVIT PIROOT GUMSHOE
SNOOPER CREEP BUSYBODY
SNOOPY CURIOUS
SNOOZE NAP NOD DOVER SLEEP
SNOOZLE
SNORE ROUT SNARK SNORK SNORT
SNOCKER SNOTTER

SNORING STERTOR RHONCHUS
SNORT BLOW ROUT SNUR TOOT
VENT BLURT FNESE SNARK SNEER
SNORE SNORK WHOOF EXCLAIM
SNIFTER SNOCKER SNORKEL
SNORTLE SNOTTER
SNOUT NEB SAW BEAK BILL NOSE
WROT GROIN SERRA SNOOT MUFFLE
MUZZLE NOZZLE GRUNTLE
ROSTRUM
(PREF.) PROBOSCI(DI) RHYNCH(O)
(SUFF.) RHYNCHUS RHYNCUS
SNOUT BEETLE CURCULIO
SNOUT MITE BDELLID
SNOW CORN DRIP GRUE COVER
SPOSH STORM SUGAR WHITE
POWDER COCAINE GRAUPEL
RAMPART WEATHER SCOUTHER
WINDSLAB
(— PELLETS) GRAUPEL
(— SLIGHTLY) SPIT
(— UP) STALL
(DISSOLVING —) FLUSH
(DRIFTED —) WINDLE
(GLACIER —) FIRN NEVE BLIZZ
(HEAVY FALL OF —) PASH
(MELTING —) SLUSH
(MUSHY —) SLOB
(NEW-FALLEN —) MANNA
(PARTLY MELTED —) SLUSH
(WHIRLING —) SKIRL
(PREF.) CHIO CHION(O) NIVI
SNOWBERRY MOXA WAXBERRY
SNOWBIRD JUNCO
SNOW BUNTING OATFOWL
SNOWBIRD SNOWFOWL
SNOW COCK JERMONAL
SNOWDRIFT WREATH YOWDEN
SNOWDROP TREE BELLWOOD
COWLICKS TISSWOOD
SNOWFALL PASH SKIFF SKIFT
FLURRY ONDING
SNOWFLAKE FLAG FLAUCHT
SNOW FLEA PODURAN PODURID
SNOW GOOSE WAVY
(— GENUS) CHEN
SNOWINESS NIVOSITY
SNOW LEOPARD IRBIS OUNCE
SNOWLESS GREEN
SNOW MAIDEN, THE
(CHARACTER IN —) LEL BOBYL
KUPAVA MIZGIR SPRING BERENDEY
BOBYLIKHA SNEGUROCHKA
(COMPOSER OF —)
RIMSKYKORSAKOV
SNOWMAN YETI
SNOW MOUNTAIN JOKUL
SNOWSHOE WEB PATIN PATTEN
RACKET RACQUET
SNOWSTORM PURGA DRIFTER
BLIZZARD
SNOWY NIVAL WHITE NIVEOUS
SNUB AIR RITZ SLAP SNIB FRUMP

SNEAP SWANK REBUFF REBUTE
SIMOUS SLIGHT SNOUCH SNUBBY
SETDOWN
SNUBBING MAIL
SNUBBY PUGGISH
SNUB-NOSED SIMOUS
(PREF.) SIMO
SNUFF TOP VENT MUSTY SNIFF
SNUSH TABAC COHOBA PULVIL
RAPPEE SNEESH STIFLE SNUFFLE
BERGAMOT MACCABOY ORANGERY
SMUTCHIN
(UP TO —) ABLE
SNUFFBOX MILL MULL
SNUFFBOX BEAN CACOON
SNUFFER PRICK DOUTER TOPPER
PRICKER
SNUFFLE SNIVEL SNAFFLE SNIFFLE
SNIFTER
SNUG LEW RUG BEIN BIEN COSH
COSY COZY NEAT SNOD TAUT TEAT
TOSH TOSY CANNY CLOSE COMFY
COUTH POVIE QUEME TIGHT PENTIT
COUTHIE SNUGGERY SNUGGISH
SNUGGLE SNUG BURROW CUDDLE
NESTLE SNUDGE CROODLE SNUZZLE
SNUGLY SHORT COSILY
SO SAE SUCH THAT THIS THUS
THISSEN INSOMUCH SUCHWISE
THUSWISE
(— AM I) LIKEWISE
(— BE IT) AMEN
(— FAR AS) QUOAD
(— TO SPEAK) FAIRLY
(NOT —) SECUS
(QUITE —) EXACTLY
SOAK RET SOB SOD SOG SOP WET
BOWK BUCK SIPE BINGE DROUK
DROWN SOUSE STEEP STING TOAST
DRENCH EMBAIN IMBIBE IMBRUE
SEETHE SODDEN SPONGE INSTEEP
MICKERY SWELTER SATURATE
(— A CASK) GROG
(— FLAX) RET RATE
(— IN) SOP FEATHER
(— UP) SOP
SOAKED SOGGY SOPPY SOBBED
SODDEN WATERY DRUNKEN
SOBBING DRAGGLED
SOAKING BATH SUING SOGGING
INFUSION
SOAP SAPO SUDS CHIPS STOCK
CASTILE TALLATE WINDSOR
SANDSOAP SAVONETTE
(— OPERA) SUDSER
(— SUBSTITUTE) AMOLE
(— UNIT) CAKE
(CAKE OF —) TABLET TABULATE
(LIQUID —) FIT
(PREF.) SAP(O) SAPONI
SOAPBARK QUILLAI SOAPWOOD
SOAPFISH JABON

SOAP PLANT AMOLE PALMILLO
SOAPROOT SOAPWEED
SOAPSTONE TALC ALBERENE
POTSTONE STEATITE
SOAPSTONER TALCER
SOAPWORT BORITH COWHERB
SAPONARY SOAPROOT SOAPWEED
SOAR FLY STY KITE FLOAT MOUNT
PLANE SPIRE TOWER ASCEND
ASPIRE AIRPLANE
SOARING ALOFT FLIGHT ICARIAN
SPIRING ESSORANT
SOB YEX SIKE SNOB SNUB SOUGH
BLUBBER SINGULT
SOBBING GREET
SOBER SAD CALM COOL SAGE CIVIL
FRESH GRAVE QUIET STAID DOULCE
SEDATE SEVERE SOLEMN SOMBER
STEADY EARNEST PENSIVE REGULAR
SERIOUS UNFOXED DECOROUS
MODERATE ABSTEMIOUS
SOBRIETY DRYNESS GRAVITY
ABSTINENCE
SOBRIQUET BYNAME HAWKEYE
SO-CALLED ALLEGED
SOCCER FOOTER FOOTBALL
(— NAME) PELE
(— PLAYER) SWEEPER
SOCIABLE COSY CHUMMY CLUBBY
FOLKSY SOCIAL AFFABLE AMIABLE
INNERLY CLUBABLE FAMILIAR
FELLOWLY INFORMAL
SOCIAL TEA DISTAL PUBLIC SOIREE
SUPPER SOCIABLE SOCIETAL
CONVIVIAL
(— WORKER) ALMONER
SOCIALISM ETATISM MARXISM
GUESDISM
SOCIALIST FABIAN NIHILIST
SOCIALISTIC PINK
SOCIALIZE CIVILIZE
SOCIETY BUND HALL HERD SANG
GUILD MONDE POLIS SABHA SAMAJ
SANGH SOKOL ADMASS MENAGE
NANIGO PARISH SYSTEM VEREIN
ACADEMY COLLEGE COLORUM
COMPANY COUNCIL KINGDOM
SOCIETE THIASOS EXCHANGE
HETAERIA PRECINCT SOCIETAS
SODALITY SORORITY
(— OF RELIGIOUS FANATICS)
COLORUM
(CHORAL —) CHOIR
(CLOWN —) KOSHARE KOYEMSHI
(CRAFT —) ARTEL
(CRIMINAL —) MAFIA MAFFIA
(DEBATING —) POP
(GENTEEL —) FASHION
(GYMNASTIC —) SOKOL
(HIGH —) SWELLDOM
(LITERARY —) HALL
(MEMBER OF CRUDE —) LUMPEN

(POLITICAL —) TAMMANY
(RELIGIOUS —) CHURCH
(SECRET —) HUI EGBO HOEY PORO
TONG LODGE MAFIA OGBONI
PURRAH CAMORRA
(STUDENT —) CORPS
(UTOPIAN —) ANARCHY
(WHITE —) MAN
(PREF.) SOCIO
SOCIETY ISLANDS (CAPITAL OF —)
PAPEETE
(ISLAND OF —) TAHITI
SOCINIAN RACOVIAN
SOCIOLOGIST
  AMERICAN HUNT LYND ODUM ROSS
WARD BALCH CAREY BARNES
BOGART DEVINE DUFFEY HUNTER
SUMNER VEBLEN COLLIER DUGDALE
ELLWOOD ETZIONI FRAZIER NEARING
STEIZLE WILLARD ZUERLIN
BOGARDUS GIDDINGS YANKELOVICH
GOLDENWEISER
  ENGLISH KIDD WEBB GLASS GEDDES
TOYNBEE
  FRENCH TARDE DURKHEIM
  GERMAN LANGE WEBER FREYER
SIMMEL MICHELS SCHAFFLE
THURNWALD
  GREEK BARDIS
  HUNGARIAN MANNHEIM
  ITALIAN LORIA
  SCOTTISH GEDDES MCLENNAN
  SWEDISH MYRDAL
SOCIOLOGY DEMOTICS
SOCK DOP ONE BIFF BUST HOSE
VAMP ANKLET ARGYLE VAMPEY
STOCKING
(— OF GOAT'S HAIR) UDO
(INFANT'S —) BOOTEE BOOTIE
(JAPANESE —) TABI
SOCKET BOX CUP PAD POD BUSH
CELL HOSE LEAD NOSE SHOE CHAIR
POINT SHANK BUCKET BUDGET
COLLET EYEPIT NOZZLE POCKET
SAUCER SCONCE ALVEOLE COCKEYE
FERRULE FUTCHEL GUDGEON
THIMBLE TORULUS ALVEOLUS
DRAWHEAD
(— FOR BIT) POD
(— FOR CARBINE) BUDGET
(— FOR GEM) OUCH
(— FOR LANCE) PORT
(— FOR LENS) CELL
(— FOR MAST) TABERNACLE
(— FOR MOUTHPIECE) BIRN
(— IN GOLF CLUB HEAD) HOSE
HOSEL
(— OF BONE) POT
(— OF GEM) OUCH
(— OF HINGE) PAN
(— OF LOCK) KEEPER
(— OF MILLSTONE) INK COCKEYE

(— OF WATER PIPE) BELL
(BIT —) POD
(PREF.) GLENO TORMO
SOCKEYE NERKA KOKANEE
BLUEBACK
SOCLE ZOCCO
SOCRATES (— METHOD) MAIEUTIC
(DISCIPLE OF —) XENOPHON
SOD HUB BEAT DELF FAIL FLAG SCAD
SONK TURF DELPH GAZON GLEBE
SCRAW SWARD CLOWER TERRON
SODDING
SODA POP BARILLA
(— FOUNTAIN) SPA
SODA POP TONIC
SODDEN SAMMY SAPPY SOGGY
POACHY DRAGGLED
SODI (SON OF —) GEDDIEL
SODIUM NA SODA NATRIUM
(PREF.) NATR(O)
SODIUM BICARBONATE SODA
BICARB
SODIUM BORATE BORAX
SODIUM CARBONATE SODA
TRONA NATRON ANATRON BARILLA
SALSODA
SODIUM CHLORIDE SALT HALITE
SODIUM THIOSULFATE HYPO
SODOMITE DOG BUGGER SPINTRY
ROUGERON
SOEVER SOME
SOFA ROIST COUCH DIVAN SQUAB
CANAPE LOUNGE SETTEE CAUSEUSE
SOCIABLE
(— IN RESTAURANT) BANQUETTE
SOFFIT GATHER PLAFOND INTRADOS
PLANCIER
SOFRONIA (LOVER OF —) OLINDO
SOFT COY LID FEIL LASH LIMP LUSH
MILD MURE NASH NESH PLUM SART
SLOW TOSY WAXY WEAK BALMY
BLAND CUSHY DABBY DOLCE
DOWNY FAINT GIVEY HOOLY LENIS
LIGHT MALMY MEALY MELCH
MUSHY MUTED PADDY PAPPY PIANO
PLIFF SILKY SLACK SMALL SOAPY
SOOTH SWASH SWEET WAXEN
WETHE YAPPY CASHIE CREAMY
EFFETE FLAGGY FLOSSY FLUFFY
GENTLE LITHER LYDIAN MELLOW
PIPING PLACID SAMMEL SIDDER
SIDDOW SILKEN SLOPPY SMOOTH
SOFTLY SPONGY SPOONY TENDER
UNDURE CLEMENT COTTONY
CRUMBLY DUCTILE FLESHLY LENIENT
SQUASHY CUSHIONY FEMININE
FLEXIBLE HOTHOUSE LADYLIKE
SARCENET SLUGGISH SQUELCHY
TRANQUIL
(— AND BRITTLE) FROWY FROWIE
FROUGHY
(— AND FLEXIBLE) FLOPPY

(— **AND LIFELESS**) DOUGHY
(— **IN SOUND**) SMALL
(— **IN TEXTURE**) SUPPLE
(**VERY** —) SQUASHY
(PREF.) LENI MALAC(O) MOLLI
SOFT-COVER PAPERBACK
SOFTEN CUT CREE MELT SOAK SOFT
TAME ALLAY BATCH BREAK FRIZZ
LITHE MALAX TOUCH WOKIE DIGEST
GENTLE LENIFY PACIFY RELENT
SOOTHE SUBDUE SUBMIT TEMPER
WEAKEN APPEASE ASSUAGE
CUSHION LENIATE MOLLIFY QUALIFY
SWEETEN UNSTEEL AMOLLISH
ATTEMPER ENFEEBLE HUMANIZE
MITIGATE MODULATE PALLIATE
PRETTIFY
(— **BY BOILING**) CREE
(— **BY KNEADING**) MALAX
MALAXATE
(— **BY STEEPING**) MACERATE
(— **COLOR**) CUT SCUMBLE
(— **FIBERS**) BREAK
(— **GRADUALLY**) SQUAT
(— **JUTE**) BATCH
(— **LEATHER**) BREY FRIZ FRIZZ
(— **METAL**) ALLAY
(— **TONE**) SURD
SOFTENED ROXY ANODYNE
MOUILLE FLEXUOUS
SOFTENER (**WATER** —) CALGON
SOFTENING LENIENT MALACIA
BLETTING
(— **OF ARTICULATION**) LENITION
SOFTER MANCANDO
SOFTHEARTED TENDER
SOFTLY LOW BAJO SOFT HOOLY
FAIRLY GENTLY SWEETLY CREAMILY
TENDERLY
SOFTNESS SOFT MOLLITIES
(— **IN COAL SEAM**) LUM LUMB
(**TENDER** —) LANGUOR
(SUFF.) MALACIA
SOFT-POINTED HEBETATE
SOFT-SHELLED TURTLE FLAPPER
FLIPPER FLAPJACK
SOFT-SOAP CON FLANNEL
SOFT-SPOKEN MEALY
SOFTWARE (**COMPUTER** —) DRIVER
MONITOR
(**DESKTOP — DISPLAY** WYSIWYG
(**OF — DISPLAY**) WYSIWYG
SOFTY PUSSYCAT
SOGGY SAD DUNCH SOBBY SODDEN
SPONGY WATERY
SOIGNE TRIM SLEEK MODISH
SOIL DAG DUB MUD RAY SOD BLOT
BLUR CLAY CLOD DAUB DIRT DUST
FOIL FOUL GRIT LAND MIRK MOOL
MOSS MUCK MURK MUSS SAUR
SILE SLUR SMUT SOOT TASH BULLI
CROCK EARTH GLEBE GRIME GUMBO
LAYER MUCKY ROSEL SLUSH SMEAR

SOLUM SOULE SPARK STAIN SULLY
BARING BEDAUB BEFOUL BEMIRE
BEMOIL GROUND PODZOL SLURRY
SMIRCH SMOOCH SMUDGE SPLASH
SUDDLE BEGRIME BENASTY
BESMEAR BESMOKE BETHUMB
FEWMAND PEDOCAL POLLUTE
REGOSOL SEEDBED SLUBBER
TARNISH TRACHLE AGROTYPE
ALLUVIAL BEDABBLE BESMIRCH
BUCKSHOT FLYSPECK LATERITE
PEDALFER PLANOSOL RENDZINA
WOODCOCK SOLONCHAK
CONTAMINATE
(— **ABOVE CLAY**) KELLY
(— **AGGREGATE**) PED
(— **DEPOSITED BY WIND**) ELUVIUM
(— **FORMED BY DECAY**) GEEST
(— **INTERMEDIATE BETWEEN SAND
AND CLAY**) ROSEL
(— **PREPARED FOR SOWING**) TILTH
(— **REMOVED FROM ORE**) BARING
(— **WITH GREASE**) LARD
(**AGGREGATE** —) PED
(**ALKALINE** —) SOLONETZ
(**ASHLIKE** —) PODSOL PODZOL
(**AZONAL** —) REGOSOL
(**CLAYEY** —) GALT MALM MAUM
ADOBE SOLOD SOLOTH
(**COTTON** —) REGUR
(**DRY** —) GROOT
(**FRIABLE** —) CRUMB
(**GRAVELLY** —) ROACH GROWAN
(**HARD** —) RAMMEL
(**INFERTILE** —) GALL
(**LEACHED** —**S**) LATOSOL
(**PEATY** —) YARFA YARPHA
(**PLUMBER'S** —) SMUDGE
(**POROUS** —) SPONGE
(**POTTING** —) COMPOST
(**PRAIRIE** —) BRUNIZEM
(**RED** —) LATERITE
(**SILTY** —) GUMBO
(**SPRINGY** —) WOODSERE
(**ZONAL** —) SEROZEM SIEROZEM
(PREF.) AGRI AGRO GE(O) PED(O)
SOLI
SOILAGE SOIL SMUDGE SOILING
SOILED FOUL BLACK DINGY DIRTY
MUSSY SOOTY TARRY SMUDGY
SMUTTY SNUFFY THUMBED
DRAGGLED SHOPWORN
SOIL-EXPOSING EROSIVE
SOIREE EVENING
SOJOURN LIE BIDE STAY STOP
ABIDE ABODE TARRY VISIT
RESIDE ALLODGE MANSION
STATION
(— **ABROAD**) PEREGRINATION
SOJOURNER PILGRIM
SOKOL FALCON
SOL SOH SOU ALCOSOL EMULSOID
HYDROSOL SOLUTION

SOLA SHOLA PAUKPAN
SOLACE CHEER CHEERER COMFORT
CONSOLE SWEETEN SOLATION
SOLAR HELIAC SOLLER HELIACAL
SOLARIUM
(— REFLECTOR) HELIOSTAT
(— SYSTEM APPARATUS) ORRERY
SOLAR DISK ATEN ATON
(CENTER OF —) CAZIMI
SOLAR ENERGY
(PREF.) HELI
SOLD SELT BOOKED
(ILLICITLY —) BOOTLEG
SOLDER PALE BRAZE FLOAT SOWDER
SPELTER
SOLDERER BROGUER
SOLDERING IRON COPPER
DOCTOR
SOLDIER GI SON TAP BLEU BOLO
GOUM GUGU KERN LEVY SHOT
SWAD TULK WART BERNE CROAT
FRITZ GUARD GUFFY KHAKI LANCE
LIMEY LINER MINER NIZAM PERDU
PIKER PIVOT POILU PONGO SAMMY
SWEAT TOLKE TOMMY TOPAS
ASKARI BONAGH BUMMER DARTER
DIGGER EXPERT GALOOT GUNNER
GURKHA HAIDUK HEINIE HOSTER
LANCER MARKER PIETON REITER
SENTRY SKIEUR SOLDAT SWADDY
THRASO WEAPON ZOUAVE BAYONET
BILLJIM BLIGHTY BRIGAND CARABIN
CATERAN CORSLET DARTMAN
DOGFACE DRAGOON FEDERAL
FEEDMAN FIGHTER GENETOR
GOUMIER HOBBLER INVALID
JACKMAN MATRONN ONDERLY
PAHHAN PANDOUR PAVISOR PELTAST
PIKEMAN PRIVATE REDCOAT
REGULAR REISTER SCARLET
SLINGER SOLDADO STRIKER
TROOPER VETERAN WARRIOR
ARQUEBUS BEZONIAN BLUECOAT
BUCKSKIN BUFFCOAT CAMELEER
CAVALIER DESERTER FENCIBLE
FUGLEMAN FUSILIER GALLOPER
GENDARME GRAYBACK GRAYCOAT
IRONSIDE JANIZARY KHANDAIT
LANCEMAN LINESMAN MILITANT
MIQUELET MUSTACHE PIOUPIOU
RAPPAREE SENTINEL SERVITOR
SILLADAR SPEARMAN SWORDMAN
TOLPATCH TRANSFER TRIARIAN
WARFARER WHIFFLER YARDBIRD
CATAPHRACT
(— OF MUSCOVITE GUARD) STRELITZ
(— ON GUARD) SENTRY
(— WITH SIDE WHISKERS) BADGER
(ALBANIAN —) PALIKAR
(ALGERIAN —) ARBI
(AMERICAN —) SAMMY
(ANT —) MAXIM
(ARMY OR MARINE FOOT —) GRUNT

(ASIAN —) GOOK
(AUSTRALIAN —) ANZAC DIGGER
BILLJIM
(BOMBAY —S) DUCKS
(BRITISH —) LIMEY TOMMY BLIGHTY
LOBSTER REDCOAT ROOINEK
(BRUTAL —) PANDOUR
(CAREER —) LIFER
(CAVALRY —) REITER TROOPER
(COWARDLY —) CAPITANO
(DISBANDED —) REFORMADO
(EGYPTIAN —) GIPPO GIPPY GYPPO
GYPPY GYPPIE
(FEMALE —) AMAZON
(FILE OF 6 —S) ROT
(FILIPINO —) GUGU
(FOOT —) KERN PAGE PEON GRUNT
PIETON FOOTMAN TOLPATCH
(GERMAN —) HUN FRITZ HEINE
KRAUT HEINIE
(GREEK —) EVZONE HOPLITE
(HORSE —) RUTTER CUIRASSIER
(INCOMPETENT —) BOLL
(INDIAN —) PEON JAWAN SEPOY
GURKHA
(INEPT —) SADSACK
(INVALID —) FOGY FOGEY
(IRREGULAR —) CROAT CATERAN
JAYHAWK SEBUNDY MIQUELET
RAPPAREE SILLADAR
(MERCENARY —) RUTTER HESSIAN
LANSQUENET LANDSKNECHT
(MOROCCAN —) ASKARI
(MOSLEM —) NIZAM
(MOUNTED —) LANCER DRAGOON
GENETOR LOBSTER TROOPER
VEDETTE CAVALIER
(NEW —) RECRUIT
(NEW ZEALAND —) ANZAC
(NEW ZEALAND OR AUSTRALIAN —)
DIGGER
(OLD —) GROGNARD
(PROFESSIONAL —) SAMURAI
(REVOLUTIONARY —) REDCOAT
BUCKSKIN
(ROMAN —) FOEDERATUS
(ROMAN —S OF THIRD LINE) TRIARY
TRIARII
(RUSSIAN —) IVAN
(SCOTTISH —) JOCK
(SMALL —) BANTAM
(TERRITORIAL —) TERRIER
(TURKISH —) NIZAM REDIF
(U.S. FOOT —) GRUNT
(UNTRAINED —) YARDBIRD
(PL.) FOOT ELITE TERZO TROOP
TERTIA CATERVA ENOMOTY MILITIA
VELITES FORAGERS INFANTRY
SOLDIERY
AMERICAN DIX LEA LEE ORD POE
AMES DELL BUTT CARR CLAY DEAN
DRUM FISK FORD HAIG HILL HOOD
HULL KNOX LANE LEAR LONG LORD

STEWART SWINTON TORRENS
VENNING VINCENT WANTAGE
WINGATE ALDERSON ANDERSON
AUCHMUTY BECKWITH BENTINCK
BLAKENEY BRADDOCK BRANCKER
BROWNING BURGOYNE CALLWELL
CAMPBELL CARDIGAN CARLETON
CATHCART CHETWODE COLBORNE
CONGREVE CROMWELL FERGUSON
GLEICHEN GREVILLE HAMILTON
HARDINGE HASTINGS HAVELOCK
HORROCKS LAWRENCE LIGONIER
LINDSELL LOCKHART MAITLAND
MONTFORT POYNINGS SHRAPNEL
STANHOPE TARLETON ALEXANDER
BEAUCHAMP BERESFORD
BROWNRIGG CONSTABLE
HARINGTON HENDERSON
KITCHENER MACDONALD
OCTERLONY POTTINGER REPINGTON
ROBERTSON WILKINSON WOODVILLE
AUCHINLECK CODRINGTON
CORNWALLIS DESBOROUGH
MACDOUGALL MONTGOMERY
SHENBROOKE WELLINGTON
BRACKENBURY WINTRINGHAM
FINNISH MANNERHEIM
FRENCH FAY FEY NEY BUAT FOCH
JUIN NIEL SAXE AMADE ANDRE
CONTI COSSE DOUAY DUMAS FOREY
HENRY HULIN JUNOT LALLY LEVIS
LOBAU MENOU MINIE MITRY MURAT
TRACY BAYARD BELLAY ROUDET
CHABOT CHANZY CISSEY CLARKE
CLOSSE DAUMAS DAVOUT DEJEAN
DROUOT DUCROT DUNOIS FABERT
FAILLY FAVRAS FLEURY FOLARD
FRIANT GERARD GIRAUD GOBERT
JARNAC JOFFRE KLEBER LACLOS
LANNES LATUDE LAUNAY LAUZUN
MAGNAN MAISON MANGIN MARBOT
MASSUE MONCEY MOREAU PETAIN
ROVIGO SUCHET TROCHU BAZAINE
BOICHUT BOSQUET BOUILLE
CATINAT CATROUX CHAMILLY
CHARRAS CHAUVIN CLAUSEL
CLISSON CRILLON CUSTINE
DEBENEY DREYFUS FABVIER
GAMELIN GASSION GOURAUD
GROUCHY GUIBERT JOUBERT
JOURDAN LABORDE LASALLE
LEBOEUF LECLERC LEJEUNE
LUCKNER LYAUTEY MARCEAU
MARMONT MAURICE MOLITOR
MONTLUC MORTIER NIVELLE
RENAULT REYNIER TALLARD
TURENNE VALENCE VENDOME
WEYGAND AUGEREAU BARATIER
BOURBAKI CHAMBRUN CHAUCHAT
CHOISEUL CLUSERET CONTADES
DEGAULLE DEGOUTTE ESTIENNE
GALLIENI GOURGAUD GOURGUES
GRAZIANI HARCOURT LAMARQUE

LANGLOIS LANREZAC LARMINAT
LEFEBVRE LORENCEZ MAUNOURY
MONTCALM PICHEGRU TAVANNES
VANDAMME AIGUILLON ANDREOSSY
BERTHELOT BOISSOUDY
BOULANGER CANROBERT
DAMPIERRE FALDHERBE GROSSETTI
GUEBRIANT HUNTZIGER LAFAYETTE
LALLEMAND LAURISTON
MACDONALD MONTHOLON
NIVERNAIS PELISSIER SCHOMBERG
CHASTELLUX GUILLAUMAT
KELLERMANN MONTGOMERY
ROCHAMBEAU WESTERMANN
CHANGARNIER JACQUEMINOT
MONTMORENCY CAULAINCOURT
LESDIGUIERES
GERMAN EPP JODL KALB ARNIM
BOEHN BULOW KLUCK KUNDT
HALDER HAUSEN HUTIER KEITEL
MOLTKE PAULUS ROMMEL SEECKT
BISSING BLUCHER CAPRIVI FISCHER
FRITSCH GROFNER JOCHMUS
SPEIDEL STEUBEN BERNHARD
BLOMBERG GALLWITZ GERHARDT
GUDERIAN HAESELER HARTMANN
LITZMANN RIEDESEL SCHWERIN
ZEITZLER ALDRINGEN HAUSHOFER
HEERINGEN HINDERSIN LINSINGEN
MACKENSEN MANSFIELD
REINHARDT RUNDSTEDT THEILMANN
WALDERSEE FRUNDSBERG
HINDENBURG KESSELRING
LUDENDORFF SCHLEICHER
SCHLIEFFEN BRAUCHITSCH
FALKENHORST FALKENHAUSEN
STAUFFENBERG
GREEK ARATUS KALERGES
KONDYLES PANGALOS PELOPIDAS
ALCIBIADES HIERONYMUS
EPAMINONDAS THEMISTOCLES
GUATEMALAN CHACON ORELLANA
HAITIAN PETION RIGAUD SALOMON
GEFFRARD
HUNGARIAN GORGEY HUNYADI
DAMJANICH SZECHENYI
IRISH LACY WADE COLLEY ODUFFY
CADOGAN COLLINS OREILLY
OHIGGINS PAKENHAM ALANBROOKE
IRTISH DILL BARRY CUNNINGHAM
ISRAELI ALLON DAYAN ELAZAR
NETANYAHU
ITALIAN BIXIO FANTI CANEVA
COSENZ DAVILA DOUHET GORGIA
NOBILE ABRUZZI CAPELLO
BADOGLIO CAVIGLIA CIALDINI
COLLEONI GIARDINO GRAZIANI
MARSIGLI RAMORINO BARATIERI
CAVALLERO DANNUNZIO GARIBALDI
LAMARMORA PICCULOMINI
JAPANESE ABE OKU TOJO ARAKI
KOISO NODZU SAITO TAMAI
KODAMA KUROKI DOIHARA FUSHIMI

KATSURA HASEGAWA SUGIYAMA
TERAUCHI FUKUSHIMA HASHIMOTO
HIDEYOSHI TAMASHITA
KOREAN PARK
LEBANESE HADDAD
MEXICAN MEJIA ALDAMA ARISTA
CALLES HUERTA ALMAZAN
ALMONTE ALVAREZ AMPUDIA
CAMACHO MIRAMON MORELOS
OBREGON VALLEJO ZULOAGA
CANALIZO CARDENAS ESCOBEDO
GONZALEZ GUERRERO ITURBIDE
VICTORIA BUSTAMANTE
NEW ZEALAND CHAYTOR FREYBERG
NIGERIAN GOWON
PARAGUAYAN MORINIGO
ESTIGARRIBIA
PERSIAN ARTAPHERNES
PERUVIAN BALTA PRADO CACERES
GAMARRA PIEROLA CASTILLA
IGLESIAS SALAVERRY
POLISH BEM PASEK HALLER PULASKI
CHLOPICKI DEMBINSKI KOSCIUSKO
PILSUDSKI DOMBROWSKI
MALCZEWSKI SOSNKOWSKI
KRUKOWIECKI
PORTUGUESE ALMEIDA PEREIRA
SALDANHA TEIXEIRA
PRUSSIAN GNEISENAU CLAUSEWITZ
ROMAN SULLA AETIUS ANTONY
BURRUS CAEPIO CAESAR GALLUS
POLLIO POMPEY SCIPIO AGRIPPA
ALBINUS CAECINA CALENUS
CASSIUS CHAEREA CRASSUS
FANNIUS LEPIDUS PLANCUS
AFRANIUS AGRICOLA CEREATIS
DENTATUS DUILLIUS LUCULLUS
FABRICIUS FLAMINIUS PASKEVICH
SERTORIUS CORIOLANUS
CINCINNATUS
RUMANIAN ILIESCU ANTONESCU
RUSSIAN CUI BERK GURKO KONEV
GLINKA NEVSKI PLATOV ZHUKOV
BLUCHER BUDENNY CHAPAEV
CHUIKOV DENIKIN KALEDIN
KAMENEV KUTUZOV SUVOROV
VATUTIN WRANGEL ZHDANOV
ALEKSEEV AVERESCU BOBRIKOV
BRUSILOV GOLITSYN GORBATOV
KAULBARS KORNILOV LINEVICH
MILYUTIN SAMSONOV SKOBELEV
YUDENICH BAGRATION BENNIGSEN
GORCHAKOV LECHITSKI MENSHIKOV
CHERNYAIEV CHERNYSHEV
DRAGOMIROV KUROPATKIN
ROSTOPCHIN TIMOSHENKO
VOROSHILOV ROKOSSOVSKY
SHAPOSHNIKOV
SALVADORAN REGALADO
SCOTTISH HAIG URRY BAIRD MUNRO
ELIOTT RUTHVEN DRUMMOND
IRONSIDE MIDDLETON

SOUTH AFRICAN BOTHA SMUTS
HERTZOG PRETORIUS
SPANISH CID ALVA ELIO MINA MOLA
RADA CROIX GARAY OSUNA ULLOA
AVALOS GUZMAN TOLEDO
ALMAGRO CORDOBA FARNESE
MONCADA NARVAEZ NAVARRO
ODONOJU PORTOLA ALVARADO
CANTERAC CARVAJAL CASTANOS
CASTILLO ESPINOSA MANRIQUE
MUNTANER ORELLANA VALDIVIA
PEDRARIAS REQUESENS VELASQUEZ
CASTELLANOS
SWEDISH HORN TOLL BANER BRAHE
ARMFELT LEWENHAUPT
TORSTENSON ADLERCREUTZ
ADLERSPARRE
SWISS DUFOUR ERLACH JENATSCH
TURKISH BABUR ENVER EVREN
ATATURL
URUGUAYAN ORIBE FLORES
VENEZUELAN PAEZ GOMEZ CASTRO
FALCON MONAGAS
YUGOSLAV ZIVKOVIC MIHAJLOVIC
SOLDIERLY WARLIKE
SOLDIERY HORSE MILITIA SEBUNDY
MILITARY SIBBENDY
SOLE CORK FACE GADE MERE ONLY
SLIP SOCK SPUR AFALD ALONE
CLUMP LEMON OLEPI PELMA WHOLE
GADOID INSOLE ONLEPY PLANTA
SINGLE SOLEYN SULLEN THENAR
TONGUE UNIQUE ANACANTH
FLATFISH HOGCHOKE MARYSOLE
SINGULAR SOLITARY
(— A SHOE) SPECK
(— FOR WALKING OVER SAND)
BACKSTER
(— OF BIRD'S FOOT) PTERNA
(— OF FOOT) PLAT VOLA PELMA
PLANT
(— OF PLANE) FACE
(— OF PLOW) SLADE
(— WITH WOOD) CLOG
(HALF —) SHOULDER
(KIND OF —) DOVER
(TOWARD THE —) PLANTAD
(PREF.) PEDI(O) PELMATO
(SUFF.) PELMOUS
SOLELY SOLE ALONE SIMPLY SINGLY
WHOLLY SHEERLY ENTIRELY
SOLEMN DEEP SAGE AWFUL BUDGE
SOBER DEVOUT FORMAL RITUAL
EARNEST SERIOUS WEIGHTY
FUNEREAL PORTENTOUS
(STUPIDLY —) POFACED
SOLEMNITY OBIT RITE SACRE
GRAVITY SEVERITY
SOLEMNIZE KEEP SEAL
SOLEMNLY GRAVE HIGHLY
SOLENODONT AGOUTA ALMIQUE
SOLEPIECE SOLE GIRDER

SOL-FA SOLMIZATE
SOLICIT ASK BEG SUE WOO DRUM
MOVE SEEK THIG TOUT URGE APPLY
COURT CRAVE TREAT ACCOST
HUSTLE INVITE INVOKE BESEECH
CANVASS ENTREAT IMPLORE
INSTANT PROCURE REQUEST
APPROACH PETITION
SOLICITATION SUIT QUEST
CANVASS INSTANT REQUEST
SOLICIT ENTREATY INSTANCE
SOLICITOR AVOUE LAWYER WRITER
ADVOCATE ATTORNEY TRAMPLER
SOLICITOUS URGENT CAREFUL
CURIOUS JEALOUS DESIROUS
CONCERNED
SOLICITUDE CARE CARK FEAR HEED
PAIN YEME HEART WORRY ANXIETY
CONCERN BUSINESS JEALOUSY
SOLID DRY SAD CONE CUBE FAST
FIRM FULL HARD CHAMP CUBIC
LEVEL MASSY MEATY SOUND STIFF
STOUT THICK TIGHT SECURE STABLE
STODGY STRONG STURDY
COMPACT CUPRENE UNIFORM
CONSTANT GROUNDLY MATERIAL
STERLING
(GEOMETRICAL —) CONE CUBE
PRISM CONOID CUPROID FRUSTUM
POLYHEDRON
(NOT —) BUBBLE
(THEORETICAL —) HYPERCUBE
(PL.) POCHE
(PREF.) STERE(O)
SOLIDARITY CIVILITY
SOLIDIFIED SOLID HARDENED
(READILY —) GLACIAL
SOLIDIFY DRY SET CAKE JELL
SHOOT GELATE HARDEN COMPACT
CONGEAL STIFFEN CONCRETE
SOLIDITY SADNESS FASTNESS
FIRMNESS HARDNESS
SOLIDLY FIRMLY SQUARE STOUTLY
GROUNDLY
SOLIDUS BEZANT NOMISMA
DIAGONAL HYPERPER
(HALF —) SEMIS
SOLIPSISM EGOISM
SOLITAIRE CLARINO CANFIELD
KLONDIKE NAPOLEON PATIENCE
SOLITARY
SOLITARY ODD WAF LONE ONLY
SOLE ALONE ELYNG LONELY
ONLEPY SAVAGE SINGLE SOLEYN
SULLEN DERNFUL EREMITE PRIVATE
RECLUSE UNCOUTH WIDOWED
DESOLATE EREMITIC ISOLATED
LONESOME PEGBOARD SECLUDED
SEPARATE
(PREF.) EREM(O)
SOLITUDE PRIVACY RETREAT
SOLITARY

SOLLERET SABBATON
SOLO ARIA CALL ALONE ARIOSO
CAVATINA SPADILLA
SOLOIST (BASS —) SUCCENTOR
SOLOMON SAM KOHELETH
(BROTHER OF —) ADONIJAH
(FATHER OF —) DAVID
(MOTHER OF —) BATHSHEBA
SOLOMON ISLANDS (CAPITAL:)
HONIARA
(CAPITAL OF —) HONIARA
(ISLAND:) GIZO SAVO FLORIDA
MALAITA RENDOVA CHOISEUL
SANJORGE NEWGEORGIA
GUADALCANAL SANTAISABEL
(ISLAND OF —) BUKA GIZO SAVO
TULAGI FLORISA MALAITA RENDOVA
RUSSELL CHOISEUL GUADALCANAL
BOUGAINVILLE
SOLOMON'S SEAL LILY
SEALWORT
SOLON SAGE GNOMIC GNOMIST
SENATOR LAWMAKER
SOLPUGID TARANTULA
SOLSTICE SUNSTAY SUNSTEAD
SOLUBLE FRIM FRUM FIXED SOLUTE
SOLVABLE
SOLUTION IT LYE AQUA EUSOL
STAIN TINCT ACETUM ANSWER
ASSOIL DOCTOR ERASER SALINE
EXTRACT EYEWASH LACQUER
RESOLVE SOLUTIO WORKING
ANALYSIS LEACHATE TINCTURE
(— ADDED FOR GOOD MEASURE)
INCAST
(— OF CHESS PROBLEM) COOK
(— OF FERMENTED BRAN) DRENCH
(— OF GUM TRAGACANTH) BED
(ACID —) SOUR
(ALCOHOLIC —) ESSENCE
(ANTISEPTIC —) EUSOL
(COLLOIDAL —) GEL
(CORROSIVE —) OLEUM
(PICKLING —) SOUSE
(PRESERVING —) BOLIN
(SALINE —) BRINE
(SOAP —) NIGRE
(SOLID —) AUSTENITE
(STERILE —) JOHNIN
(TEMPORARY —) QUICKFIX
(VISCOUS —) GLUE
(WATERY —) EAU SAP
SOLVE DO FIX READ UNDO WORK
BREAK CRACK LOOSE SALVE
ANSWER ASSOIL CIPHER FIGURE
REDUCE RIDDLE SOLUTE RESOLVE
UNRAVEL DECIPHER DISSOLVE
SOLVENT ETHER SOUND CETANE
ELUANT ELUENT SPIRIT TOLUOL
ACETONE ALCOHOL BENZINE
COUPLER DILUENT REMOVER
SPOTTER TOLUENE CARBITOL

PICOLINE SOLVABLE STRIPPER
TEREBENE TETRALIN MENSTRUUM
(UNIVERSAL —) ALKAHEST
SOLVER (PROBLEM —) HACKER
SOMALI SOMAL SHUHALI
(PL.) ASHA
SOMALIA (CAPITAL OF —)
MOGADISHU
(COIN OF —) BESA
(DIVISION OF —) HAWIYA
(MEASURE OF —) TOP CABA CHELA
DARAT TABLA CUBITO
(MOUNTAIN OF —) SURUDAD
(MOUNTAIN RANGE OF —) GUBAN
(NATIVE OF —) GALLA HAWIYA
ISBAAK SOMALI DANAKIL
(RIVER OF —) JUBA NOGAL SCEBELI
(TOWN OF —) MERCA BERBERA
KISMAYU HARGEISA
(WEIGHT OF —) PARSALAH
SOMATIC SOMAL BODILY
SOMBER SAD DERN DULL GRAVE
MORNE SOBER GLOOMY LENTEN
SOLEMN SOMBRE SULLEN AUSTERE
SERIOUS DARKSOME SOMBROUS
SOME ANY ODD AFEW THIS CERTAIN
SOMEBODY QUIDAM SOMEONE
SOMEDAY ONCE
SOMEHOW HOW ONEHOW
SOMEWAY SOMEGATE
SOMEONE SUCH
SOMERSAULT FLIP TOPPLE FLIFFUS
SPOTTER TWISTER BACKFLIP
SOMERSET
SOMETHING WHAT ALIQUID
WHATNOT SOMEWHAT
(— ABNORMAL) FREAK
(— ADDED) IMP EXTRA DOCTOR
(— AMUSING) HOOT
(— ATTRACTIVE) DUCK
(— BELIEVED) CREDIT
(— BIG) BOUNCER
(— BRIGHT RED) CORAL
(— CHERISHED) APPLE
(— COMMONPLACE) DROSS
(— CONSECRATED) SACRUM
(— CONTRARY TO LOGIC) ALOGISM
(— CORRUPT) CARRION
(— COUNTERFEIT) DUFFER
PINCHBECK
(— DIFFICULT) STINKER
(— DISLIKED) DOGMEAT
(— DONE) GERENDUM
(— EASILY ACHIEVED) GIMME
(— EASY) PIPE CAKEWALK
(— ELABORATE) DEVICE
(— ELUSIVE) FUGITIVE
(— EXCELLENT) DANDY
(— EXCESSIVE) LUXUS
(— EXTRAORDINARY) SNORTER
(— FALSE) HOOEY
(— FAMILIAR) KNOWN
(— FIRST-RATE) CHEESE

(— FLAWED) CRIPPLE
(— FOOLISH) IDIOCY FATUITY
(— FORGOTTEN) CORPSE
(— FORKED) CORNUTE
(— FRAUDULENT) CROSS
(— GIVEN WITHOUT CHARGE)
FREEBEE FREEBIE
(— HORRIFYING) SHOCKER
(— IDENTICAL) ISOMORPH
(— ILL-DEFINED) BLOB
(— IN ADDITION TO ORDINARY)
BONUS
(— INCOMPLETE) END
(— INFERIOR) DOG CULL LESS
CAGMAG
(— INJURIOUS) ENEMY
(— INSIGNIFICANT) STRAW FEATHER
SNICKET FRAGMENT
(— INTRICATE) KNOT
(— LARGE) GIANT SMASHER
(— MADE UP) FIGMENT
(— NOTABLE) DEUCE
(— NOT ESSENTIAL) FRILL
(— NOT EXPLAINED) MYSTERY
(— OFFERED FOR LOAN) PREMIUM
(— OF GREAT VALUE) EYETOOTH
(— OF LITTLE VALUE) SHUCK FOUTER
FOUTRA MAKEWEIGHT
(— OF NO VALUE) HAW DAMN
BAUBEE DOCKEN
(— OR OTHER) ANYTHING
(— OUTSTANDING) BROTH DOYEN
GASSER STANDOUT
(— PAINFUL) GAFF
(— PATCHED UP) VAMP
(— POOR) FLUMMERY
(— PRECIOUS) DUMPLING
(— PREJUDICIAL) FOE
(— PROVOKING) DEVIL
(— REPELLENT) SPINACH
(— RISKED) HAZARD
(— SHAPELESS) DUMP
(— SHOWY) FLOSS
(— SHRIVELED) SCRUMP
(— SMALL) DOT SNIP
(— SPECTACULAR) DILLY
(— STICKY) CAB
(— STOLEN) CRIB
(— STRANGE) FANTASIA
(— SUPERLATIVE) DARB
(— TAUGHT) DOCUMENT
(— THAT IS LIGHT) SKIFF SKIFT
(— THAT WHIRLS) GIG
(— TO BIND BARGAIN) EARNEST
(— TRIVIAL) CHIP FLUFF
(— UNDECIDED) ACRISY
(— UNINTELLIGIBLE) GREEK
(— UNPLEASANT) GUCK SOUR
(— UNSPECIFIED) ITEM
(— UNSUBSTANTIAL) FROTH
(— UNTRUE) HOKUM
(— USELESS) CRAP BLANK
(— VILE) DUNG

(— **WORTHLESS**) BOTH DUST HOKUM
DUFFER AMBSACE
(— **WRITTEN**) SCRIPT
SOMETIME FORMER SOMDEL
WHILOM ANCIENT QUONDAM
SOMEDEAL SOMEPART SOMEWHEN
SOMETIMES NOW TOO WHILE
PERDIE WHILES UMQUHILE
OCCASIONALLY
SOMEWHAT BIT ATAD POCO SOME
ATOUCH PRETTY RATHER SLIGHT
SUMMAT ALIQUID SOMEDEAL
(PREF.) SEMI
SOMEWHERE SOMERS SOMEGATE
SOMITE ZONITE SEGMENT TERGITE
GONOTOME MEROSOME MESOMERE
SOMATOME
SOMMER ELKA
SOMNIFEROUS OPIATE SOMNIFIC
SOMNUS HYPNUS
SON BEN BOY LAD ANAC FILS FITZ
ZONE CHILD KIBEI MOPSY FILIUS
JUNIOR REUBEN EPAPHUS
EPIGONUS MONSIEUR
(— **OF CHIEF**) OGTIERN
(— **OF KING OF FRANCE**) DAUPHIN
(— **OF NISEI**) SANSEI
(— **OF PEER**) MASTER
(— **OF SUDRA**) CHANDALA
(**DAVID'S FAVORITE** —) ABSALOM
(**FIRST-BORN** —) HEIR
(**FOURTH** —) MARTLET
(**FREEMASON'S** —) LEWIS
(**ILLEGITIMATE** —) NEPHEW
(**NISEI** —) SANSEI
(**PRIEST'S** —) NEPHEW
(**YOUNG** —) MOPSY
(**YOUNGER** —) CADET
(**YOUNGEST** —) CADET BENJAMIN
(PREF.) AP FILI(O)
SONANT VIBRANT
SONAR ASDIC
(— **BLIP**) ECHO
(**KIND OF** —) SIDESCAN
SONCHUS DINDLE
SONG AIR DIT FIT JIG LAY UTA CANT
DUAN FOLK GATO GLEE LEED MELE
NOTE RANT RUNE SANG TUNE
BLUES CANSO CAROL CHANT
CHARM CROON DILDO DITTY MELOS
MOLPE OLDIE PAEAN VOCAL BALLAD
BRANLE BUBBLE CANTIC CANZON
CARMEN CHANTY CHORUS HIMENE
JINGLE MELODY ORPHIC SHANTY
STRAIN VINATA WAIATA WARBLE
BACCHIC BALLATA CANCION
CANTION CHANSON COMIQUE
DESCANT MELISMA MELODIA
REQUIEM REVERDI ROMANCE
SCOLION SONGLET THRENOS
BIRDSONG BRINDISI CANTICLE
CANZONET COONJINE FLAMENCO
JUBILATE PALINODE RHAPSODY

SERVENTE SINGSONG ZORTZICO
ROUNDELAY
(— **ACCOMPANYING TOAST**)
BRINDISI
(— **FOR TWO VOICES**) GYMEL
(— **IN GREEK DRAMA**) STROPHE
(— **OF BASQUES**) ZORTZICO
(— **OF BIRD**) LAY KOLLER
(— **OF JOY**) CAROL PAEAN JUBILATE
(— **OF LAMENTATION**) THRENE
THRENODY
(— **OF MINSTREL**) YEDDING
(— **OF OCEANIA**) HIMENE
(— **OF PRAISE**) HYMN CAROL
ANTHEM CHORALE
(—**S OF BIRDS**) RAMAGE
(— **UNACCOMPANIED**) GLEE
(— **WITH MONOTONOUS RHYME**)
VIRELAI VIRELAY
(**ANDALUSIAN** —) SAETA
(**ART** —) LIED
(**BOAT** —) JORRAM
(**CEREMONIAL** —S) AREITO
(**CRADLE** —) HUSHO
(**CUBAN** —) GUAJIRA COMPARSA
(**DANCE** —) BALLAD BAMBUCO
(**DRINKING** —) BACCHIC SCOLION
SKOLION WASSAIL
(**EVENING** —) SERENA EVENSONG
SERENATA
(**FOLK** —) SON FADO FOLK BLUES
DOINA BYLINA CANTIGA JUBILEE
STORNELLO
(**FUNERAL** —) DIRGE MONODY
EPICEDE THRENODY
(**FUNEREAL** —) ELEGY
(**GAY** —) LILT
(**GERMAN** —) LIED
(**GYPSY** —) FLAMENCO
(**HAWAIIAN** —) MELE
(**HEBREW** —) ELIELI HATIKVAH
(**IMPROMPTU** —) SCOLION
(**JAPANESE** —) UTA
(**LOVE** —) ALBA CANSO CANZO
FANCY TORCH AMORET AUBADE
SERENA SERENATA
(**MELISMATIC** —) DIVISION
(**MOCKING** —) JIG
(**MORNING** —) MATIN AUBADE
(**MOURNFUL** —) DUMP PLAINT
ENDECHA
(**MYSTIC** —) RUNE
(**NEW ZEALAND** —) WAIATA
(**NIGHT** —) COMPLIN
(**NO** —S) UTAI
(**NUPTIAL** —) HYMEN
(**PART** —) CHACE TROLL CACCIA
CANZONE FROTTOLA MADRIGAL
(**PASTORAL** —) OAT
(**PLAIN** —) GROUND
(**PORTUGUESE** —) FADO
(**RELIGIOUS** —) HYMN CAROL PSALM
SHOUT ANTHEM POLYMNY SIRVENT

(REVOLUTIONARY —) CARMAGNOLE
(ROUND-) TROLL
(SACRED —) MOTET
(SAILOR'S —) CHANTY SHANTY
(SANSKRIT —) GITA
(SINGLE —) CUT
(SINGLE — ON RECORD) CUT
(SPIRITED —) LILT
(STUPID —) STROWD
(VINTAGE —) VINATA
(WORK —) HOLLER
(PL.) ZEMMI AREITO
(PREF.) MELO
(SUFF.) ODE ODIC ODIST ODY
SONGBIRD CHAT IORA LARK WREN
MAVIS ROBIN SABIA SHAMA SIREN
VEERY VIREO BULBUL CANARY
LINNET MOCKER ORIOLE SINGER
THRUSH CATBIRD GRASSET
TANAGER WARBLER ACCENTOR
BENGALEE BLUEBIRD BOBOLINK
CARDINAL SONGSTER
MEADOWLARK
SONGLIKE ARIOSE
SONG OF BERNADETTE (AUTHOR
OF —) WERFEL
(CHARACTER IN —) LOUISE THERESE
FRANCOIS PEYRAMALE SOUBIROUS
BERNADETTE
SONG OF HIAWATHA (AUTHOR OF
—) LONGFELLOW
(CHARACTER IN —) KWASIND
NOKOMIS WENONAH HIAWATHA
CHIBIABOS MINNEHAHA
MUDJEKEEWIS
SONG OF ROLAND (AUTHOR OF —
) UNKNOWN
(CHARACTER IN —) ALDA ALORY
MILON OGIER BERTHA FERRAU
GERARD MEDORO MORGAN OBERTO
OLIVER ROLAND SADONE ARGALIA
CHARLOT GANELON GODFREY
MALAGIS REINOLD ASTOLPHO
KARAHEUT BRADAMANT
GLORIANDA CHARLEMAGNE
MANDRICARDO
SONGSTER SINGER WARBLER
SONG THRUSH MAVIE MAVIS
SON-IN-LAW GENER MAUGH
SONNAMBULA, LA
(CHARACTER IN —) LISA AMINA
ELVINO TERESA RODOLFO
(COMPOSER OF —) BELLINI
SONNET AMORET
(— PART) SESTET
(LOVE —) AMORET
SONOGRAPHY ULTRASOUND
SONORITY RESONANCE
SONOROUS ROUND SHILL TONOUS
OROTUND VIBRANT RESONANT
SOUNDFUL SOUNDING
RESOUNDING
SONOROUSLY DEEPLY

SONS AND LOVERS (AUTHOR OF
—) LAWRENCE
(CHARACTER IN —) LILY PAUL ANNIE
CLARA DAWES MOREL ARTHUR
BAXTER MIRIAM WALTER LEIVERS
WILLIAM GERTRUDE
SONSHIP FILIETY
SONYA (FATHER OF —)
MARMELADOV
SOOLOOS THULUTH
SOON ERE ANON CITO TITE EARLY
NEWLY RADLY RATHE BELIVE INABIT
SUDDEN TIMELY BETIMES ERELONG
PRESTLY SHORTLY DIRECTLY
SPEEDILY PRESENTLY
(AS — AS POSSIBLE) ASAP
SOONER ERE ERER ERST OKIE FIRST
BEFORE TITTER
(— STATE) OKLAHOMA
(— THAN) OR ERE
SOONEST ERST RATHEST
SOOT COOM IZLE SMUT STUP SUMI
BLECK BROOK COLLY COOMB CROCK
GRIME SOTIK FULIGO SMOUCH
SMUTCH SPODIUM
(— ON GRATE BAR) STRANGER
SOOTHE COY DEW BALM CALM
COAX DILL EASE HUSH LULL ACCOY
ALLAY CHARM DULCE HUMOR
QUELL SALVE SLEEK STILL BECALM
PACIFY SETTLE SMOOTH SOLACE
STROKE SUPPLE ADDULCE APPEASE
ASSUAGE COMFORT COMPOSE
CONSOLE DEMULCE FLATTER
GRUNTLE LULLABY MOLLIFY
PLASTER QUALIFY ATTEMPER
BLANDISH MITIGATE UNRUFFLE
SOOTHER BALM BALSAM ANODYNE
SOOTHING MILD BALMY BLAND
DOWNY DULCE STILL SWEET ANETIC
ANIMAL DREAMY DULCET GENTLE
SMOOTH ANODYNE BALSAMIC
SEDATIVE
SOOTHSAY SORT
SOOTHSAYER SEER AUGUR WEIRD
ARIOLE DIVINE PYTHON ARUSPEX
DIVINER CHALDEAN HARUSPEX
TIRESIAS
SOOTY COLLY REECHY SMUTTY
BROOKIE COLLIED
SOOTY ALBATROSS NELLIE
QUAKER STINKER BLUEBIRD
STINKPOT
SOOTY SHEARWATER TITI
SOP BERRY SIPPET SOAKUP SPONGE
SUGARSOP SWEETSOP BREADBERRY
SOPATER
(FATHER OF —) PYRRHUS
SOPHER SCRIBE
SOPHISM FETCH ELENCH FALLACY
SOPHEME
SOPHIST SOPH DUNCE
SOPHISTICATE GARBLE MONDAINE

SOPHISTICATED WISE BLASE CIVIL SALTY SVELTE URBANE WORLDLY
SOPHISTICATION CHIC
SOPHISTRY DECEIT FALLACY SOPHISM CHICANERY
SOPHOCLES (— TRAGEDY) AJAX
SOPHONISBA
(BROTHER OF —) HANNIBAL
(FATHER OF —) HASDRUBAL
(HUSBAND OF —) SYPHAX
SOPORIFIC DWALE DROWSY HYPNIC OPIATE SLEEPY HYPNOTIC NARCOTIC SOMNIFIC
SOPPING SQUASHY
SOPPY JUICY SOAKY
SOPRANO CANARY TREBLE DESCANT CASTRATO
SORA ORTOLAN
SORB OCCLUDE LUSATIAN
SORBIAN WENDISH
SORBOSE ACROSE
SORCERER MAGE BOYLA BRUJO WITCH BOOLYA NAGUAL VOODOO WIZARD KORADJI WARLOCK WIELARE FETISHER MAGICIAN WITCHMAN
(PL.) GOETAE
SORCERESS BRUJA CIRCE LAMIA SIBYL WITCH ARMIDA HECATE BABAJAGA KORRIGAN WALKYRIE
SORCERY OBI MAGIC OBEAH SPELL MAKUTU PISHOGUE PRESTIGE SORTIARY WIGELING WITCHERY WITCHING NECROMANCY
(VOODOO —) OBEAH WANGA OUANGA
SORDES SABURRA
SORDID RAW BASE GAMY MEAN VILE DIRTY DUSTY MUCKY SEAMY CHETIF GRUBBY SODDEN MESQUIN SQUALID CHURLISH
SORDOR LEES
SORE BUM FOX PET BUBA CHAP DEAR GALL KIBE KYLE OUCH SAER BLAIN BOTCH GAMMY AGNAIL BITTER BOUBAS CANKER FESTER MELLIT MORMAL RANKLE TAKING CATHAIR CHANCRE SORANCE SCALDING
(— ON HORSE'S FOOT) MELLIT QUITTER
(ARTIFICIAL —) FOX
(SUMMER —S) CALORIS LEECHES
SO RED THE ROSE (AUTHOR OF —) YOUNG
(CHARACTER IN —) HUGH LUCY MARY VEAL ZACH AGNES SARAH AMELIE DUNCAN EDWARD BALFOUR BEDFORD CHARLES FRANCES LUCINDA MALCOLM MCGEHEE SHELTON VALETTE WILLIAM HARTWELL MIDDLETON TALIAFERRO
SORE MOUTH ORF

SORENESS FROG
(— OF EYES) LIPPITUDE
SORGHUM CANE CUSH MILO BATAD DARSO DURRA SORGO CHOLAM HEGARI IMPHEE KAFFIR SHALLU FETERITA KAOLIANG
SOROCHE PUNA
SORREL OCA OKA ROAN SORE CUCKOO HEARTS OXALIS RUBICAN SOUROCK ALLELUIA STABWORT
SORREL TREE TITI ELKWOOD SOURWOOD
SORROW WO RUE WOE BALE CARE DOLE HARM MOAN RUTH SORE TEEN DOLOR GRAME GRIEF MOURN RUING SARRA UNWIN GRIEVE LAMENT MISERY REGRET STOUND UNLUST ANGUISH CONDOLE DEPLORE PENANCE REGRATE REMORSE THOUGHT TROUBLE WOEFARE CALAMITY DISTRESS DOLEANCE DREARING EGRIMONY MOURNING
(— AUDIBLY) WAIL
(— FOR SIN) ATTRITION
(PREF.) LUCTI
SORROWFUL BAD SAD WAN BLUE GLUM CHARY DREAR TRIST WOFUL DISMAL DOLENT DREARY RUEFUL BALEFUL CAREFUL DOLEFUL LUCTUAL RUESOME UNHAPPY WAILFUL CONTRITE DESOLATE DOLESOME DOLOROSO GRIEFFUL MOURNFUL PITIABLE
SORROWFULLY SADLY WRATH DERNLY HEAVILY
SORRY BAD SAD WOE HURT VEXED UNFAIN PITIFUL CONTRITE PENITENT WRETCHED
SORT ILK KIN LOT BRAN COMB GERE HUMP KIND RANK SIFT SUIT WING WORK BRACK BREED GENUS GRADE SAVOR SPICE ASSORT BARREL DILLUE GARBLE GENDER KIDNEY MANNER MISTER NATURE STRAIN STRIPE FASHION SPECIES SPECKLE VARIETY CLASSIFY SEPARATE
(— CHICKS) SEX
(— COTTON BY STAPLE) STAPLE
(— MAIL) CASE
(— MERCHANDISE) BRACK
(— OF) INAWAY
(— OF PERSON) LIKE
(ATHLETIC —) JOCK
(OUT OF —S) GRUMPY
SORTER SHALEMAN
SORTIE RAID ISSUE SALLY ATTACK OUTFALL
SORTILEGE LOT
SORTING GARBLING
(— ROOM) SALLE
SORTITA ARIA
SORUS AECIUM TELIUM
SORVA BORRACHA

SOT LUSH SOAK DRUNK LOURD
TOPER LOURDY BLOTTER DASTARD
TOSSPOT DRUNKARD
SOTHO SUTO SESUTO
SOTIK SOOT
SOUFFLE FONDU FONDUE
SOUGH MOAN
SOUGHT QUESITED
SOUL BA AME EGO ALMA ANIMA
ATMAN GHOST HEART SHADE
BUDDHI DIBBUK NATURE PNEUMA
PSYCHE SPIRIT SPRITE NEPHESH
PURUSHA INTERNAL
(—S OF THE DEAD) LEMURES
(ANIMAL — IN MAN) NEPHESH
(DISEMBODIED —) KER
(EGYPTIAN IMMORTAL —) BA
(INDIVIDUAL —) JIVA
(LIBERATED —) KEVALIN
(UNIVERSAL —) HANSA
(WANDERING —) DIBBUK DYBBUK
(PREF.) PSYCH(O) THYM(O)
(SUFF.) PSYCHE
SOULFULLY GEISTLICH
SOULLESS TURNIPY
SOU MARQUE STAMPEE
SOUND GO CRY FIT BLOW DING DRIP
FAST FERE FIRM FLOG FLOW GLUG
GOOD HAIL HALE KYLE NOTE RING
SAFE SANE TEST TONE TRIG WISE
AFFIX BLAST BUGLE CHEEP DREAM
FLICK FRESH GLIFF GLUCK GRIND
GROPE HODDY NOISE PLANG PLUMB
PROBE RIGHT SLUSH SOLID SPANG
SPANK SPEAK SWASH VALID WHOLE
BICKER BIRDIE DORSAL ENDING
ENTIRE FATHOM FAUCAL HEARTY
INTACT LABIAL LAGOON ROBUST
SIGNAL SINGLE SONANT SPLASH
STABLE STRAIN STURDY HEALTHY
HEARING HURLING PERFECT
PHONEME PLUMMET SCRATCH
SONANCE VOCABLE FLAWLESS
FOOTFALL GRINDING GROUNDLY
LAUGHTER RELIABLE SEARCHER
SYLLABIC WAKELESS
(— A BAGPIPE) DOODLE
(— AS IF BY GUN) ZAP
(— BELL) PEAL RING KNELL KNOLL
(— BY PERCUSSION) STRIKE
(— DRUM OR TRUMPET) TUCK
(— FORTH) BOOM
(— INDEPENDENTLY OF THE PLAYER)
CIPHER
(— INDISTINCTLY) SLUR
(— IN GREEK AND LATIN) AGMA
(— IN MIND) FORMAL
(— LESS LOUD) FALL
(— LIKE THUNDER) BRONTIDE
(— LOUDLY) TANG LARUM
(— MELODIOUSLY) CHARM
(— OF BAGPIPE) DRONE
(— OF BEATING) RATAPLAN

(— OF BELL) DING PEAL RING KNELL
STROKE DINGDONG TINGTANG
(— OF BIRD) JUG CHURR
(— OF BULLET) ZIP
(— OF CICADA) CHIRR
(— OF CONTEMPT) HUMPH
(— OF CORK) CLOOP CLUNK
(— OF COW) MOO LOWING
(— OF DISAPPROVAL) BOO HOOT
BAZOO
(— OF DOG) ARF YIP BARK BOOK
WOOF YELP YIPE
(— OF DYING PERSON'S VOICE)
TAISCH
(— OF ENGINE) CHUG
(— OF EXPLOSION) BOUNCE
(— OF F) DIGAMMA
(— OF FLUTE) TOOTLE
(— OF FOOTSTEPS) TRAMP
(— OF GLOTTAL STOP) HAMZA
HAMZAH
(— OF HEN) CLUCK
(— OF HOG) OINK GRUNT SQUEAL
(— OF HOOF) CLOP
(— OF HORN) BEEP TOOT
(— OF HORSE) NEIGH SNORT
BLOWING
(— OF KNOCK) RAP
(— OF PLUCKED STRING) TUM
(— OF POURING LIQUID) GLUG
GLUGGLUG
(— OF RAIN) SPAT
(— OF RENDING) SCAT
(— OF REPROACH) FIE
(— OF SCISSORS) SNIP
(— OF SHEEP) BAA BLEAT
(— OF SLAP) SCLAFF
(— OF STEAM ENGINE) CHUFF
(— OF STRAW OR LEAVES) RUSTLE
(— OF SURF) ROTE
(— OF THUNDER) CLAP
(— OF TRUMPET) CLARION
(— OF WIND IN TREES) WOOSH
(— OUT) FEEL
(—S HAVING RHYTHM) MUSIC
(— TO AWAKEN TROOPS) REVEILLE
(ABNORMAL —→ BRUIT
(ADVENTITIOUS —) RALE
(BLOWING —) SOUFFLE
(BRAWLING —) CHIDE
(BREATHING —) RALE
(BRONCHIAL —) RHONCHUS
(BUBBLING —) BLATHER
(BUZZING —) Z WHIR WHIRR
(CHARACTERISTIC —) SONG
(CLASHING —) SWASH
(CLICKING —) SNECK
(CONSONANT —) ALVEOLAR
(COOING —) CHIRR TURTUR
(CRACKLING —) RISK
(CRISP —) BLIP
(CRUNCHING —) CRUMP SCRUNCH
(DELICATE —) TINK TINKLE

(DISCORDANT —) JAR BRAY JANGLE
(DISTINCTIVE —) SONG
(DRUMMING —) RATAPLAN
(DULL —) BUFF THUD CLONK CLUNK
FLUMP SQUELCH
(ELECTRONIC — APPARATUS) SYNTH
SYNTHESIZER
(EXPLOSIVE —) POP BARK CHUG
PUFF SNORT REPORT
(FAINT —) PEEP GLIFF WHISHT
INKLING
(FINAL —) AUSLAUT
(FINANCIALLY —) SOLID
(FLAT —) PLAP
(GENTLE —) TAP
(GROWLING —) SNARL
(GULPING —) GLUCK
(GUTTURAL —) GROWL
(HARSH —) JAR BRAY BLARE CLASH
CRANK TWANG SCROOP DISCORD
STRIDOR
(HEAVY —) DUMP
(HIGH-PITCHED —) BLIP TING BLEEP
(HISSING —) FIZZ SIZZ SWISH SIZZLE
(HOARSE —) ROOP
(HOLLOW —) CHOCK THUNGE
(HUMMING —) HUM BURR SUUM
DRONE SINGING
(INDISTINCT —) BLUR SURD
(INITIAL — OF WORDS) ANLAUT
(JINGLING —) SMIT
(KNOCKING —) RATTAT
(LAPPING —) SLOOSH
(LIGHT REPEATED —) PITAPAT
(LOUD —) PEAL BLARE CLANG
CRASH CLANGOR
(LOW —) WHISPER
(LOW-PITCHED —) BASS
(MEANINGLESS —S) GABBLE
(MEDIAL —) INLAUT
(MENTALLY —) SANE WISE
(MOANING —) SUUM SOUGH
(MOURNFUL —) GROAN
(MUFFLED —) MUFFLE
(MUSICAL —) CHIME
(NASAL —) ANUSVARA
(NON-SIGNIFICANT —) GLIDE
(NONVIBRATORY —) PRICTION
(PLEASING —) EUPHONY EUPHONIA
(QUADRAPHONIC —) QUAD
(RASPING —) BUZZ SKIRR SCROOP
(REPEATED —) ECHO
(RESONANT —) BONG
(REVERBERATING —) PLANG
(RINGING —) CLANG CLANK CLING
TWANG RINGLE DINGDONG
(ROARING —) BEAL
(RUSHING —) SWOOSH HURLING
(RUSTLING —) FISSLE FISTLE
(SCRAPING —) GRIDE
(SCRATCHY —) SCRAICH SCRAIGH
(SHARP —) POP PING SNAP CHINK
CRAKE KNACK SPANG SQUIRK

(SHORT, HIGH-PITCHED —) BLEEP
(SHRILL —) CHEEP KNACK SKIRL
SCREED SQUEAK STRIDOR
(SHUFFLING —) SCUFFLE
(SIBILANT —) HISS SHISH SHUSH
(SLAPPING —) CLATCH
(SLIGHT —) SWISH
(SNORING —) SNORK
(SOBBING —) YOOP
(SPEECH —) SURD DOMAL TENUE
VOWEL APICAL PHONEME CEREBRAL
(SPLASHING —) LAP CHUNK FLURR
SPLAT SWASH
(SPOKEN —) BREATH
(SQUEAKY —) CREAK
(SQUELCHING —) SQUASH
(STRANGLED —) GLUB GLUG
(SWISHING —) SCHLOOP
(TAPPING —) TACK
(TELEPHONE —) SIDETONE
(TINKLING —) PINK
(TRAMPING —) STUMP
(TREMULOUS —) TRILL
(TRILLING —) CHIRR CHIZZ HIRRIENT
(TUNEFUL —) HARMONY
(UNPLEASANT —) BLOOP
(VIBRATING —) TIRL
(VOWEL —) SHWA SCHWA
(WARNING —) ALARM SIREN
ALARUM TOCSIN
(WHIRRING —) BIRR FLURR SKIRR
(WHISPERING —) SUSURRUS
(WHISTLING —) STRIDOR
(PREF.) AUDIO AUDIT ECHO PHON(O)
SON(I)(O) SONORI SONORO TONICO
TONO
(SUFF.) PHON(E)(IA)(Y) SONANCE
SONANT SONOUS TONE TONIA
TONIC TONOUS TONY
SOUND-ABSORBENT ACOUSTIC
SOUND AND THE FURY (AUTHOR
OF —) FAULKNER
(CHARACTER IN —) HEAD JASON
DILSEY SYDNEY CANDACE
COMPSON QUENTIN BENJAMIN
SOUNDBOARD BELLY
SOUNDED (NOT —) QUIESCENT
SOUNDER TICKER LEADMAN
SOUNDING RAWIN SONANT
INKLING SONDAGE SONATION
(— HARSH) BRAZEN
(— OF BELL) CURFEW
(— OF MUSICAL INSTRUMENT)
SPEECH
(— OF ORGAN PIPE) CIPHER
(— WITH REVERBERATIONS)
PLANGENT
SOUNDLY FAST TIGHT FIRMLY
SOUNDNESS HEAL SANITY FITNESS
SOBRIETY STRENGTH VALIDITY
SOUP BREE KAIL KALE SOPA BRODO
BROTH GUMBO POSOL BISQUE
BORSCH BURGOO CALALU JOUTES

POTAGE POZOLE BILLIBI BILLYBI
BORSCHT CALALOO GARBURE
MARMITE RUBABOO CALLALOO
CALLALOU CONSOMME GAZPACHO
MINESTRA MORTREUX
AVGOLEMONO MINESTRONE
COCKALEEKIE MULLIGATAWNY
MULLIGATAWNEY
(— UP) SUPE
(BARLEY —) SMIGGINS
(BEEFSKIN —) SKINK
(CABBAGE —) SHCHI STCHI
(CLEAR —) CONSOMME JULIENNE
(COLD —) SCHAV
(HAWAIIAN NOODLE —) SAIMIN
(JAPANESE NOODLE —) RAMEN
(JELLIED —) GAZPACHO
(LARGE QUANTITY OF —) SLASH
(NOODLE —) SAIMIN
(POTATO —) TATTIECLAW
(SHINBONE —) SKINK
(THICK —) BISK GUMBO HOOSH
PUREE BISQUE BURGOO CHOWDER
GARBURE POTTAGE HOTCHPOT
MORTREWES
(THIN —) BROTH SKILLY
(VEGETABLE —) PISTOU
SOUR AWA DRY YAR ACID ASIM CRAB
DOUR FOXY GRIM GRUM HARD TART
TURN ACERB ACRID AIGRE EAGER
GOURY GRUFF MUSTY TEART
ACETIC ACIDIC BITTER CRUETY
CURDLE PONTIC RANCID RUGGED
SULLEN TORVID ACETOSE ACIDIFY
AUSTERE SUBACID ACERBATE
VINEGARY
(SLIGHTLY —) BLINK BLINKY
ACESCENT
SOURCE FONS FONT HAND HEAD
HIVE MINE RISE RIST ROOT SEED
FOUNT RADIX SPAWN SURGE
AUCTOR AUTHOR BOTTOM CENTER
FATHER FONTAL ORIGIN PARENT
RESORT STAPLE WHENCE EDITION
FOUNTAIN WELLHEAD PROVENANCE
(— OF ADVANTAGE) OYSTER
(— OF AID) RECOURSE
(— OF ANCESTRAL LINE) STOCK
(— OF ANNOYANCE) BOGY BOGIE
HARROW BUGBEAR
(— OF ASSURANCE) FORTRESS
(— OF CONCERN) BUGABOO
(— OF CONFIDENCE) ANCHOR
(— OF DANGER) THREAT
(— OF DISPLEASURE) DISGUST
(— OF ENERGY) STEAM TAPAS
(— OF ENLIGHTENMENT) TORCH
(— OF GRATIFICATION) TREAT
(— OF HAPPINESS) SUNSHINE
(— OF HARM) CURSE
(— OF HELP) RESOURCE
(— OF HONOR) CREDIT
(— OF INCOME) TITLE REVENUE

(— OF INFORMATION) CHECK
(— OF INSPIRATION) CASTALIA
CASTALIE
(— OF INSTRUCTION) BOOK
(— OF JOY) NUTS
(— OF LAUGHTER) SPLEEN
(— OF LIFE) SPRING
(— OF LIGHT) LAMP
(— OF MERRIMENT) FUN
(— OF MONEY) FUND
(— OF NOURISHMENT) BREAST
(— OF PERPLEXITY) PROBLEM
(— OF POWER) STRENGTH
(— OF QUOTATIONS) QUOTATIVE
(— OF RADIATION) PULSAR
(— OF REGRET) SCATH SCATHE
(— OF STREAM OR RIVER) FILL
(— OF STRENGTH) HORN
(— OF SUPPLY) SHOP FEEDER
ARSENAL
(— OF TROUBLE) HEADACHE
(— OF WATER) BRON SPRING
(— OF WEALTH) GOLCONDA
KLONDIKE
(— OF WORK OF ART) PROVENANCE
PROVENIENCE
(— OF WORRY) HEADACHE
(ABUNDANT —) CORNUCOPIA
(BE THE — OF) SPAWN
(ENCLOSED —) FLOW
(FROM ANOTHER —) ALIUNDE
(GENERATING —) LOINS
(MALIGNANT —) CANCER
(PHYSICAL —) MOTHER
(PRIMARY —) RADIX
(PRIMITIVE —) PRIMORDIUM
(RADIO —) QUASAR
(RICH —) MINE
SOURDOUGH LEAVEN
SOURED FOXY QUARRED
SOURING ACESCENCE
SOURNESS ACIDITY ACERBITY
ACRIMONY ASPERITY TARTNESS
VERJUICE
SOURPUSS CRAB CRANK GROUCH
SOURSOP CORRESOL GUANABANA
SOURWOOD TITI ELKWOOD
SOUSE DIP DUCK TOSH PLUMP
STOOP PLUNGE SOZZLE TOSSPOT
SOUTANE SIMAR ZIMARRA
SOUTH MIDI AUSTER DECANI
MIDDAY MERIDIAN
(FARTHER —) BELOW
(PREF.) AUSTR(O) NOT(O)

SOUTH AFRICA		
BAY: ALGOA FALSE		
CAPE: AGULHAS		
CAPITAL: CAPETOWN PRETORIA		
COIN: CENT RAND POUND FLORIN		
KRUGERRAND		
LANGUAGE: BANTU HINDI TAMIL		
TELUGU BUJARATI		

MOUNTAIN: AUX KOP KATHKIN
  INJASUTI
NATIVE: YOSA BANTU NAMAS PONDO
  DAMARA SWAHILI BECHUANA
  HOTTENTOT
PROVINCE: NATAL TRANSVAAL
RIVER: MODDER MOLOPO ORANGE
  KURUMAM LIMPOPO OLIFANTS
TOWN: AUS MARA STAD BENONI
  DURBAN SEVERN UMTATA KOKSTAD
  SPRINGS MAFEKING GERMISTON
  JOHANNESBURG
WATERFALL: HOWICK TUGELA
  AUGRABIES

SOUTH AMERICA (ALSO SEE SPECIFIC COUNTRIES)
LAKE: MIRIM POOPO TITICACA
  MARACAIBO LLANQUIHUE
MOUNTAIN: BAIA ANDES GOIAZ
  PARIMA ACARAHY TUMUCHUMAC
NATION: PERU CHILE BRAZIL GUYANA
  BOLIVIA ECUADOR URUGUAY
  COLOMBIA PARAGUAY SURINAME
  ARGENTINA NICARAGUA
  VENEZUELA
RIVER: NEGRO AMAZON CHUBUT
  PARANA SALADO ORINOCO
  RIONEGRO ESSEQUIBO
  MAGDALENA

SOUTH CAROLINA
CAPITAL: COLUMBIA
COLLEGE: COKER FURMAN LANDER
  CITADEL CLAFFIN CLEMSON
  ERSKINE WOFFORD
COUNTY: AIKEN HORRY DILLON
  JASPER OCONEE SALUDA
FORT: SUMTER
INDIAN: PEDEE SEWEE CUSABO
  SANTEE WAXHAW CATAWBA
  SUGEREE WATEREE CONGAREE
ISLAND: EDISTO PARRIS HILTONHEAD
LAKE: MARION MURRAY CATAWBA
  WATEREE HARTWELL MOULTRIE
MOUNTAIN: SASSAFRAS
NATIVE: WEASEL PALMETTO
NICKNAME: PALMETTO
PLATEAU: PIEDMONT
PRESIDENT: JACKSON
RESERVOIR: SANTEE PINOPOLIS
RIVER: BROAD EDISTO PEEDEE
  SALUDA SANTEE ASHEPOO
  TUGALOS WATEREE CONGAREE
  SAVANNAH
STATE BIRD: WREN
STATE FLOWER: JASMINE
STATE TREE: PALMETTO
TOWN: AIKEN GREER UNION BELTON
  CAMDEN CHERAW CONWAY DILLON
  SALUDA SENECA SUMTER

BAMBERG LAURENS MANNING
  BEAUFORT FLORENCE NEWBERRY
  WALHALLA GREENVILLE
  SPARTANBURG

SOUTH CAROLINIAN WEASEL
  PALMETTO

SOUTH DAKOTA
BUTTE: MUD CROW SULLY FINGER
  SADDLE THUNDER DEERSEARS
CAPITAL: PIERRE
COLLEGE: HURON YANKTON
COUNTY: DAY HYDE BRULE MINER
  MOODY SPINK SULLY TRIPP CUSTER
  JERAULD YANKTON MELLETTE
INDIAN: BRULE SIOUX DAKOTA
  CHEYENNE
LAKE: OAHE BIGSTONE TRAVERSE
MONUMENT: RUSHMORE
MOUNTAIN: BEAR SHEEP TABLE
  CROOKS HARNEY MOREAU
NICKNAME: COYOTE SUNSHINE
RIVER: JAMES MOREAU CHEYENNE
  MISSOURI
STATE BIRD: PHEASANT
STATE FLOWER: PASQUE
STATE TREE: SPRUCE
TOWN: LEAD HAYTI HURON LEOLA
  ONIDA CUSTER DESMET EUREKA
  KADOKA LEMMON MILLER WINNER
  STURGIS WEBSTER YANKTON
  ABERDEEN DEADWOOD SISSETON

SOUTHERLY AUSTRINE
SOUTHERN SUDIC AUSTRAL
  MERIDIAN SOUTHRON MERIDIONAL
  (PREF.) NOTIO
SOUTHERN CROSS CRUX CROSS
  CROSIER
SOUTHERNER CAVALIER
  SOUTHRON
SOUTHERN FRANCE MIDI
SOUTHERN ILLINOIS EGYPT
SOUTHERN INDIA DRAVIDA
SOUTHERNWOOD APPLERINGIE

SOUTH KOREA
BAY: KANGHWA
CAPITAL: SEOUL
COIN: WON CHUN HWAN
MONEY: JUN CHON JEON
MOUNTAIN: CHIRI
PROVINCE: CHEJU CHOLLA KANGWON
  KYONGGI
RIVER: HAN KUM PUKHAN SOMJIN
  NAKTONG YONGSAN
TOWN: CHEJU MASAN MOKPO PUSAN
  SUWON TAEGU WONJU CHINJU
  CHONJU INCHON KUNSAN TAEJON
  CHONGJU KWANGJU CHUNCHON

SOUTHLAND AUSTER

SOUTH SEA ISLANDER KANAKA
SOUTHWESTER SQUAM
SOUTH YEMEN (CAPITAL OF —)
ADEN
(ISLAND OF —) PERIM KAMARAN
SOCOTRA
(MONEY OF —) DINAR
(TOWN OF —) SEIYUN MUKALLA
SOUVENIR CURIO RELIC TOKEN
FAIRING NICKNACK
SOVEREIGN BEY SIR SOV BEAN
CHAM CHIP FREE KHAN QUID SHAH
SKIV CROWN JAMES NEGUS NIZAM
QUEED RULER CHAGAN COUTER
GUINEA KAISER KINGLY MASTER
PRINCE SAMORY SHINER SOLDAN
SOVRAN SULTAN CROWNED
MONARCH ZAMORIN AUTOCRAT
DOMINANT IMPERIAL SUFFRAIN
SUZERAIN
(DIVINELY —) THEARCHIC
(FELLOW —) COUSIN
(HEAVENLY —) TENNO HEAVEN
(MOSLEM —) SOLDAN
SOVEREIGNTY SWAY CROWN
REIGN DIADEM EMPERY EMPIRE
THRONE DEMESNE DYNASTY
KINGDOM MAJESTY SCEPTER
SCEPTRE AUTARCHY DOMINION
IMPERIUM MONARCHY REGALITY
REGNANCY SOVRANTY
(— OF REASON) AUTONOMY
(JOINT —) SYNARCHY
SOVEREIGN DYNAST
SOVIET (ALSO SEE RUSSIA) VOLOST
COUNCIL GUBERNIA
(— POLICY OF DISCUSSION)
GLASNOST
SOW ELT HOG GILT SEED SHED YELT
YILT DRILL PLANT PLUMP STREW
CHANNEL GRUMPHY IMPLANT
OVERSOW SCATTER ENGENDER
INTERSOW SEMINATE
(PREF.) HYO SCROFUL(O)
(SUFF.) CHOERUS
SOWAR SILLADAR
SOW BUG ISOPOD SLATER
ISOPODAN
SOWENS SONS SWEENS FLUMMERY
WASHBREW
SOWER SEEDER SEEDMAN
SEEDSTER SEMINARY
SOWING SATION SEMENCE
SEEDNESS
(PREF.) SPOR(I)(IDI)(O)(ULI)
(SUFF.) SPORA SPORE SPORIC
SPORIDIA SPORIUM SPOROUS SPORY
SOWN SEME SATIVE SEEDED
SEMEED
SOW THISTLE DINDLE GUTWEED
HOGWEED MILKWEED
SOY SHOYA SHOYU
(— SAUCE) TAMARI

SOYBEAN SOJA SOYA
SPA BATH CURE EVIAN HYDRO
SPACE GAP AREA BLUE CORD COSO
DENT FACE LUNG PALE RANK ROOM
SIDE VOID ABYSS BLOCK CHINK
CLEFT FIELD PLACE RANGE CANTON
HIATUS INDENT MATTER ROOMTH
ARRANGE COMPASS FOREIGN
GUNNIES LEGROOM ROOMAGE
SPACING SPATIUM DIASTEMA
DISTANCE EXOCOELE INTERVAL
(— ABOVE EARTH) AIRSPACE
(— AMONG MUSCLES) SINUS
(— AROUND HOUSE) AMBIT
(— AT WHARF) BERTHAGE
(— BEFORE KILN) LOGIE KILLOGIE
(— BEHIND ALTAR) FERETORY
(— BETWEEN ARCHES) SPANDREL
SPANDRIL
(— BETWEEN BED AND WALL)
RUELLE
(— BETWEEN BRIDGE PIERS) LOCK
(— BETWEEN CASKS) CONTLINE
(— BETWEEN COLUMNS) BAY
(— BETWEEN CONCENTRIC CIRCLES)
ANNULUS
(— BETWEEN DECKS) LAZARET
(— BETWEEN DOCKS) SLIPWAY
(— BETWEEN EYE AND BILL) LORE
(— BETWEEN FEATHERS) APTERYLA
(— BETWEEN FLOOR TIMBERS)
SPIRKET
(— BETWEEN FLUTINGS) FILET FILLET
GORGERIN
(— BETWEEN FURROWS) RIG
(— BETWEEN PAGES) GUTTER
(— BETWEEN RAILROAD TIES) CRIB
(— BETWEEN SAW TEETH) GULLET
**(— BETWEEN SHIP'S BOWS AND
ANCHOR)** HAWSE
(— BETWEEN STRANDS) CANTLINE
(— BETWEEN TEETH) DIASTEMA
**(— BETWEEN THUMB AND LITTLE
FINGER)** SPAN
(— BETWEEN TIMBERS) SPIRKET
(— BETWEEN TWO WIRES) DENT
(— BETWEEN VEINS OF LEAVES)
AREOLA
(— DEVOID OF MATTER) VACUUM
VACUITY
(— FOR SECRETION) BAG
(— IN CHURCH) KNEELING
(— IN COIL OF CABLE) TIER
(— IN FOREST) GLADE
(— IN MINE) GOB
(— IN THEATER) BOX
(— IN TYPE) CORE
(— OCCUPIED) VOLUME
(— OF THREE DAYS) TRIDUUM
(— OF TIME) DAY PULL STEAD
GHURRY STITCH INTERVAL
(— ON BILLIARD TABLE) BALK BAULK
(— ON COIN) EXERGUE

(— OVERHEAD) HIGH
(— OVER STAGE) FLIES
(— TRANSMITTER) TIROS
(— UNDER STAGE) DOCK
(— USED AS LIVING-ROOM) LANAI
(— WITHIN LIMITS) CONTENT
(AD —) LINAGE
(AIR —) CENTRUM
(ARCHITECTURAL —) METOPE
PEDIMENT SACELLUM
(BACKGAMMON —) POINT
(BARE — ON BIRD) APTERIUM
(BLANK —) GAP ALLEY LACUNA
(BOUNDLESS —) INFINITE
(BREATHING —) BARLEY
(CLEAR —) FAIRWAY HEADWAY
DAYLIGHT
(COUNTER —) BACKBAR
(CRAMPED —) CUBBY
(EMPTY —) AIR BLANK VACUUM
CAPACITY
(ENCLOSED —) AREA BOWL HATCH
VERGE PARVIS CHAMBER CIRCUIT
CLOSURE COMPASS PARVISE
PTEROMA CLOISTER CONFINES
(EUCLIDEAN —) FLAT
(FLAT —) HOMALOID
(KIND OF —) HILBERT
(LEVEL —) PLATEA PARTERRE
(NARROW —) SLOT STRAIT
(OPEN —) OUT LAWN ALLEY COURT
LAUND TAHUA MAIDAN AREAWAY
FAIRWAY LOANING APERTURE
DAYLIGHT KNEEHOLE
(OPEN — OF WATER) WAKE
(OVERHANGING —) DOME
(POPLITEAL —) HAM HOCK
(ROOF —) CELL
(RUSSIAN — STATION) MIR
(SEATING —) CAVEA
(SHELTERED —) KILLOGIE
(SMALL —) AREOLA
(STORAGE —) ATTIC
(TRIANGULAR —) SPANDREL
(UNFILLED —) GAP GAPE CAVITY
HOLLOW BREAKAGE
(VAULTED —) ALCOVE
(VERTICAL —) HEADROOM
(WORKING —) COUNTER
(PREF.) SPATIO
SPACECRAFT BUS SHIP CAPSULE
ORBITER
(CHANNEL SENDING TO —) UPLINK
(PROCESS OF SLOWING DOWN —)
DEBOOST
(SLOW DOWN A —) DEBOOST
(SYSTEM OF — ROCKETS) RETROPACK
SPACED MEATIC
SPACER QUAD
SPACEWALK EVA
SPACIOUS ROOM SIDE WIDE AMPLE
BROAD RANGY ROOMY GOLDEN
BARONIAL SCOPIOUS

SPADE DIG LOY FECK LILY PEEL PICK
SPIT SPUD DELVE DIDLE GRAFF
SLADE SLANE TRAMP DIGGER
PADDLE PATTLE SERVER SHOVEL
TUSKAR GRAFTER SCAFFLE SCUPPIT
SPADDLE SPITTER TWISCAR
(LONG NARROW —) LOY
(PART OF —) FROG STEP BLADE
HANDLE SOCKET SHOULDER
(PEAT —) SLADE SLANE TUSKAR
(PLASTERER'S —) SERVER
(TRIANGULAR —) DIDLE
SPADEFISH POGY PORGY
MOONFISH
SPADEFUL SPIT SPITFUL
SPAGHETTI PASTA SLEEVING
(— SAUCE) RAGU PREGO
SPAGNUOLO LADINO

SPAIN

CAPE: AJO NAO GATA CREUS MORAS
PALOS PENAS PRIOR DARTUCH
ORTEGAL SALINAS TORTOSA
ESPICHEL MARROQUI SACRATIF
CAPITAL: MADRID
COIN: COB DURO PESO REAL DOBLA
CUARTO DINERO DOBLON ESCUDO
PESETA ALFONSO CENTIMO
PISTOLE REALDOR DOUBLOON
DIALECT: BASQUE CATALAN GALICIAN
ISLAND: IBIZA PALMA GOMERA
HIERRO ALBORAN MAJORCA
MINORCA MALLORCA TAGOMAGO
TENERIFE
ISLANDS: CANARY BALEARIC
MEASURE: PIE CODO COPA DEDO
MOYO PASO VARA ALMUD BRAZA
CAFIZ CAHIZ CARGA LEGUA LINEA
MEDIO MILLA PALMO SESMA
ARROBA CORDEL CUARTA ESTADO
FANEGA RACION YUGADA
AZUMBRE CANTARA CELEMIN
ESTADEL PULGADA ARANZADA
FANEGADA
MOUNTAIN: GATA ANETO ROUCH
TEIDE ESTATS NETHOU TELENO
BANUELO CERREDO PERDIDO
ALMANZOR MONTSENY MULHACEN
PENALARA
MOUNTAIN RANGE: CUENCA GREDOS
MORENA TOLEDO ALCARAZ
DEMANDA MONCAYO MALADETA
MONEGROS PYRENEES
NAME: ESPANA IBERIA HISPANIA
NATIVE: CATALAN IBERIAN
PORT: ADRA NOYA VIGO CADIZ GADES
GADIR GIJON PALOS ABDERA
CORUNA MALAGA ALMERIA
ALICANTE BARCELONA
PROVINCE: JAEN LEON LUGO ALAVA
AVILA CADIZ SORIA BURGOS
CORUNA CUENCA GERONA HUELVA
HUESCA LERIDA MADRID MALAGA

MURCIA ORENSE OVIEDO TERUEL
TOLEDO ZAMORA ALMERIA
BADAJOZ CACERES CORDOBA
GRANADA LOGRONO NAVARRA
SEGOVIA SEVILLA VIZCAYA
ALBACETE ALICANTE BALEARES
PALENCIA VALENCIA ZARAGOZA
REGION: LEON ARAGON BASQUE
MURCIA CASTILE GALICIA NAVARRE
ASTURIAS CASTILLA VALENCIA
RIVER: SIL TER CEGA EBRO ESLA LIMA
MINO TAJO ULLA ADAJA CINCA
DOURO DUERO GENIL JALON
JUCAR NAVIA ODIEL RIAZA SEGRE
TAGUS TINTO TURIA ALAGON
ARAGON ERESMA HUERVA JARAMA
ORBIGO SEGURA TOROTE ALMERIA
ALMONTE ARLANZA BARBATE
CABRIEL DURATON GALLEGO
HENARES MIJARES PERALES
GUADIANA
TOWN: ROA ASPE BAZA ELDA HARO
IRUN JAEN LEON LUGO OLOT REUS
ROTA SAMA VIGO BAENA BEJAR
CADIZ CIEZA CUETA ECIJA EIBAR
ELCHE GIJON IBIZA JEREZ JODAR
LORCA OLIVA PALMA RONDA SIERO
UBEDA XERES YECLA ZAFRA AVILES
AZUAGA BILBAO BURGOS DUENCA
GANDIA GERONA GETAFE GUADIX
HELLIN HUELVA HUESCA JATIVA
LERIDA LUCENA MADRID MALAGA
MATARO MERIDA MURCIA ORENSE
OVIEDO TERMEL TOLEDO UTRERA
ZAMORA BADAJOZ CORDOBA
DAIMIEL GRANADA JUMILLA
LINARES LOGRONO MANRESA
SEGOVIA SEVILLA TARRASA VITORIA
BADALONA FIGUERAS PAMPLONA
SABADELL SANTIAGO TORRENTE
VALENCIA ZARAGOZA
WEIGHT: ONZA FRAIL GRANO LIBRA
MARCO TOMIN ADARME ARROBA
DINERO DRACMA OCHAVA ARIENZO
QUILATE QUINTAL CARACTER
TONELADA
WINE: RIOJA SHERRY

SPALL CHIP SCALE SPAWL GALLET
SPAN ARCH BEAM PAIR CHORD
SPANG SWING BRIDGE EXTEND
SPREAD OPENING QUARTER
BESTRIDE
(— OF TIME) PIECE
(— WITH FINGERS) SPEND
(UNSUPPORTED —) BEARING
SPANDREL GROIN ALLEGE SPANDLE
SPANGLE AGLET BEGEM PRANK
SPANG INSTAR SEQUIN CHEQUEEN
SPANGLET ZECCHINO PAILLETTE
SPANGLED POWDERED SPANKLED
SPANIARD DON DIEGO MULADI
(CHRISTIAN —) MOZARAB

SPANIEL TRASY COCKER SUSSEX
CLUMBER BLENHEIM PAPILLON
SPRINGER WATERRUG
SPANISH ALJAMIA HISPANIC
(PREF.) HISPANO
SPANISH-AMERICAN LADINO
CHINO LADINO
SPANISH BAYONET IZOTE YUCCA
SPANISH BROOM SPART RETAMA
SPANISH FLY CANTHARIS
SPANISH HOGFISH LADYFISH
SPANISH JACINTH SCILLA
SPANISH JASMINE MALATI
SPANISH MACKEREL SIERRA
SPANISH PLUM SIRUELAS
SPANISH STOPPER IRONWOOD
SPANK PRAT SCUD SKELP PADDLE
THRASH SLIPPER
SPANKER DRIVER MIZZEN
SPANKING SMACKING
SPANNER KEY WRENCH
SPANNING ASTRIDE
SPAR BEAM BOOM CAUK CLUB GAFF
MAST RAFT SPUR YARD CABER
SPAAD SPATH SPELK SPRIT STODE
BOUGAR BUMKIN RICKER STEEVE
BASTITE BUMPKIN DERRICK DOLPHIN
JIBBOOM RIBBAND BOWSPRIT
CRYOLITE LAZULITE OUTRIGGER
MARTINGALE
(BITTER —) DOLOMITE
(HEAVY —) CAUK BARITE BARYTE
SPARE BONY FAIK GASH HAIN LEAN
NICE SAVE SLIM THIN FAVOR LANKY
SPELL LENTEN MEAGER MEAGRE
SKIMPY RESERVE SLENDER
PRESERVE
SPARGE PIPE WEEPER
SPARING CHARY GNEDE SCANT
SPARE DAINTY FRUGAL STINGY
ENVIOUS ECONOMIC SPAREFUL
PENURIOUS ABSTEMIOUS
(— IN COMMUNICATION) RETICENT
(— OF WORDS) CURT
(NOT —) HANDSOME
(PREF.) PARCI
SPARINGNESS PARCITY SCARCITY
SPARK FUNK IZLE AIZLE GRAIN LIGHT
PURSE SPERK SPUNK BLUETTE
FLANKER FLAUGHT SPARKLE
SPUNKIE SPARKLET SCINTILLA
(—S OF MOLTEN IRON) NILL
(VITAL —) GHOST LIGHT
(PREF.) SCINTILLO
SPARKER IGNITER
SPARKLE FUNK SNAP WINK BLINK
FLASH GLENT GLINT SHINE SPARK
GLANCE KINDLE SIMPER CRACKLE
EMICATE FLANKER GLIMMER
GLISTEN GLISTER GLITTER RADIATE
SHIMMER SKINKLE SPANGLE
TWINKLE OPALESCE SPRINKLE
CORUSCATE

SPARKLER TWINKLER
SPARKLING DEWY CRISP QUICK
  SUNNY BRIGHT SPUNKY STARRY
  CREMANT DIAMOND SHINING
  TWINKLY MOUSSEUX SMIRKING
  SPERLING BRILLIANT OPALESCENT
  SCINTILLANT
  (MAKE —) AERATE
  (NOT —) STILL
  (SLIGHTLY —) PETILLANT
SPARK PLUG (PART OF —) CAP GAP
  SHELL GASKET BUSHING TERMINAL
  ELECTRODE INSULATOR
SPARLING SMELT
SPARROW SPUG DICKY DONEY
  FINCH HEMPY ISAAC PADDA PADDY
  SPRIG SPRUG CHIPPY PHILIP
  SPRONG TOWHEE CHANTER CHIPPIE
  DUNNOCK FIELDIE HAYSUCK
  PINNOCK SPADGER SPURDIE TITLENE
  TITLING TITTLIN ACCENTOR FIRETAIL
  HAIRBIRD WHITECAP
  (PREF.) PASSERI
SPARROW HAWK MUSKET
  SPARHAWK
SPARSE BALD THIN MEAGER
  MEAGRE SCANTY THRIFTY
SPARTAN GREEK LACONIC
SPASM PANG CRICK QUALM TONUS
  CLONUS ENTASIA FLUTTER RAPTURE
  SPASMUS MYOTONIA PAROXYSM
  (— OF EYELID) BLEPHARISM
  (— OF FOOT) PODISMUS
  (— OF IRIS) HIPPUS
  (— OF PAIN) GRIP
  (— OF THE IRIS) HIPPUS
  (—S OF WHALE) FLURRY
  (MUSCLE —) TRISMUS
  (TONIC —) HOLOTONY
  (PREF.) CLONICO
SPASMODIC FITFUL SNATCHY
  SPASMIC SPASTIC SPURTIVE
SPAT SEED TIFF BROOD JOWER
  GAITER LEGGING BOOTHOSE
  BOOTIKIN
SPATE ONRUSH SLUICE RAINSTORM
SPATHE CYMBA SHEATH
SPATHIC SPARRY SPATHOSE
SPATIAL LOCAL STERIC
SPATIATE ROVE RAMBLE STROLL
SPATTER DASH JAUP BERAY SKIRP
  SLART SPARK SPURT DABBLE
  SPLASH SQUIRT BESPAWL DESPETE
  SHATTER SMATTER SPATTLE SPIRTLE
  SPLATTER SPRINKLE
  (— WITH FOAM) EMBOSS
  (— WITH MUD) JAP BEMUD SPARK
SPATTERDASH SPAT BONNET
  GAITER CUTIKIN LEGGING
  BOOTHOSE BOOTIKIN
SPATTERDOCK DUCK CLOTE TUCKY
  WOKAS NUPHAR BONNETS
  CANDOCK

SPATTERING JAP JAUP SPAT
  SQUATTER
SPATULA SPAT SLICE THIBLE THIVEL
  CESTRUM SPATTLE SPLATTER
SPAVIN JACK SPAVIE VARISSE
SPAWN RUD BLOT RAUN REDD RUDD
  SILE SPORE TODDER GENERATE
  (— OF SHELLFISH) SPAT
  (OYSTER —) CULCH CULTCH
SPAWNEATER SHINER
SPAWNING SICK MILKY SEEDING
SPAY FIX GELD ALTER DESEX SPADE
  CHANGE DOCTOR SPEAVE
  CASTRATE
SPEAK ASK CUT SAY CANT CARP
  MEAN MOOT MOVE TALE TALK TELL
  WORD BREAK MOUTH NEVEN ORATE
  PARLE SOUND SPELL SPIEL UTTER
  ACCENT INTONE PARLEY PATTER
  QUETHE SERMON SPEECH SQUEAK
  TONGUE ADDRESS BESPEAK
  DECLAIM DELIVER EXCLAIM PARRALL
  CONVERSE REHEARSE
  (— ABUSIVELY) JAW
  (— AFFECTEDLY) MIMP KNACK
  (— AGAINST) ACCUSE GAINSAY
  FORSPEAK
  (— ANGRILY) ROUSE CAMPLE
  (— AT LENGTH) DISSERT ENLARGE
  (— BROKENLY) FALTER
  (— CAJOLINGLY) COLLOGUE
  (— CONFUSEDLY) HATTER CLUTTER
  SPLATHER
  (— CONSTANTLY) YAP
  (— CONTEMPTUOUSLY) SCOFF
  (— CRITICALLY) LAUNCH
  (— CURTLY) BIRK SNAP
  (— EVIL) BLACKEN
  (— FAIR) PALP
  (— FALSELY) ABUSE
  (— FAMILIARLY) HOBNOB
  (— FIRST TO) ACCOST
  (— FOOLISHLY) PRATE GIBBER
  JABBER
  (— HALTINGLY) HACK HAMMER
  STAMMER
  (— HESITANTLY) STAMMER
  (— HOARSELY) CROAK CROUP
  (— ILL OF) KNOCK DEPRAVE
  DETRACT
  (— IMPERFECTLY) LISP
  (— IMPUDENTLY) CHEEK
  (— IMPULSIVELY) BLURT
  (— INDISTINCTLY) FUMBLE JABBER
  MUFFLE MAUNDER SPLUTTER
  (— IN DRAWL) DRANT DRAUNT
  (— INEPTLY) BUMBLE
  (— IN JEST) FOOL
  (— IN ONE'S EAR) HARK
  (— IN POINTLESS MANNER) DROOL
  (— INSOLENTLY) SNASH
  (— IN STUMBLING WAY) STUTTER
  (— IN UNDERTONE) WHISPER

(— IN WHINING VOICE) CANT
(— LOUDLY) TANG
(— LOW) WHISPER
(— MINCINGLY) NAB MIMP
(— MONOTONOUSLY) DROLL
(— OBSCURELY) RIDDLE
(— OF) CALL NEVEN MENTION
(— ONE'S MIND) SHOUT
(— OUT) LEVEL SHOOT
(— PLAYFULLY) BANTER
(— POMPOUSLY) CRACK
(— PROFUSELY) PALAVER
(— QUERULOUSLY) CREAK
(— RAPIDLY) TROLL GIBBER JABBER
SQUIRT CHATTER
(— RESENTFULLY) HUFF
(— RHETORICALLY) DECLAIM
(— SARCASTICALLY) GIRD
(— SHORTLY) JERK
(— SLIGHTINGLY OF) BELITTLE
(— SLOWLY) DRAWL
(— SNARLINGLY) SNARL
(— TARTLY) SNAP
(— TEDIOUSLY) PROSE
(— THROUGH THE NOSE) SNAFFLE
(— TO ONESELF) SOLILOQUIZE
(— TRUTH) SOOTHSAY
(— WITH EMPHASIS) DWELL
(— WITH LIPS CLOSED) MUMBLE
(— WITH THE HANDS) SIGN
(— WITH UNCERTAINTY) QUAVER
SPEAKEASY SHEBEEN
SPEAKER TRIS VOICE BRYTHON
LOCUTOR MOUTHER STYLIST
EPILOGUE SPEECHER
(— IN POEM) PERSONA
(OBSCENE —) RIBALD
(ORATORICAL —) SPOUTER
(PUBLIC —) ORATOR STUMPER
SPEAKING STEVEN LOQUENT
PARLANCE SPELLING
(— ARTICULATELY) MEROP MEROPIC
(— MANY LANGUAGES) POLYGLOT
(— POMPOUSLY) MAGNILOQUENT
(— WITHOUT SOUND)
MUSSITATION
(EVIL —) PRATING
(INDISTINCT —) JABBER
(PUBLIC —) PLATFORM
(SUFF.) LOGER LOGIA(N) LOGIC(AL)
LOGIST LOGUE LOGY LOQUENCE
LOQUENT LOQUY
SPEAR GAD DART FRAM GAFF PIKE
GRAIN LANCE REJON SHAFT STAFF
VALET AMGARN BORDUN BROACH
FIZGIG FRAMEA GIDJEE GLAIVE
WASTER ASSEGAI BOURDON
HARPOON IMPALER JAVELIN
TRIDENT VERUTUM EELSPEAR
GAVELOCK LANCEGAY STANDARD
WALSPERE
(BROKEN —) TRUNCHEON
(EEL —) ELGER PILGER

(FISH —) GIG GAFF TREN POACH
FIZGIG GRAINS FISHGIG LEISTER
SNIGGER
(SALMON —) WASTER
(PREF.) DORI ENCHO HASTATO LANCI
SPEARFISH AGUJA GOGGLE
MARLIN BILLFISH LONGJAWS
SPEAR GRASS SPANIARD
SPEARHEAD BUNT GAFF SPUD
PRONG CORONAL
SPEARMINT MENTHE LABIATE
SPEAR-SHAPED HASTATE
SPEAR THROWER ATLATL
WOMMALA WOOMERAH
SPEARWORT BANEWORT
SPECIAL VERY EXTRA KHASS
CONCRETE ESPECIAL PECULIAR
SPECIFIC REDLETTER
(NOT —) GENERAL
SPECIALIST SWELL EXPERT HERALD
LEGIST ALTAIST ARABIST FAUNIST
FEUDIST GRECIAN OLOGIST
SURGEON AQUINIST ARBORIST
BANTUIST BOTANIST ETHICIST
GEMARIST GEOGNOST GEOMETER
HEBRAIST HOMERIST LATINIST
URBANIST PHYSICIST PEDIATRIST
PATHOLOGIST
(SUFF.) ICIAN LOG(ER)(IA)(IAN)(IC)
(ICAL)(IST)(UE)(Y)
SPECIALIZE MAJOR
SPECIALTY BAG THING
SPECIES FOLK FORM KIND SORT
BROOD CLASS EIDOS GENRE ESPECE
MANNER MISTER APOMICT FEATHER
SPECIAL ANALOGUE GENOTYPE
INDIGENE
(— VARIANT) MORPH
(ATOMIC —) DAUGHTER
SPECIFIC EXPRESS SPECIAL TRIVIAL
CONCRETE ESPECIAL
SPECIFICALLY NAMELY
SPECIFICATION MENTION
(WRITE —S) SPEC
SPECIFICITY HECCEITY
SPECIFIED SET GIVEN
SPECIFY ASSIGN DESIGN DETAIL
ARTICLE EXPRESS MENTION
INDICATE NOMINATE PRESCRIBE
SPECIMEN CAST TEST ESSAY FACER
MODEL SPICE CHANCE SAMPLE
SWATCH EXAMPLE ICOTYPE ISOTYPE
NEOTYPE PATTERN SAMPLER
ALLOTYPE EXEMPLAR HOLOTYPE
HYPOTYPE IDEOTYPE INSTANCE
REPRESENTATIVE
(— OF WORK) PIECE
(ADDITIONAL —) COTYPE
(ANATOMICAL —) PREPARATION
(EXCELLENT —) RATTLER
(EXTRAORDINARY —) BENDER
(FEMALE —) GYNETYPE
(FINEST —) PEARL

(LARGE —) ELEPHANT
(MISERABLE —) RAT
(POOR —) APOLOGY
(SMALL —) SPRIG
SPECIOUS GAY FAIR FALSE WHITE
FACILE GLOSSY HOLLOW TINSEL
PAGEANT PLAUSIVE PROBABLE
SPURIOUS PLAUSIBLE
MERETRICIOUS
SPECIOUSNESS DISGUISE
SPECK DOT JOT PIN PIP MOTE SPOT
TICK WHIT BLACK GI EBE PLECK
APHTHA SPECKLE FLYSPECK
NUBECULA
(— IN LINEN) SPRIT
(— ON FINGERNAIL) GIFT
(BLACK —) DARTROSE
SPECKLE FLECK GARLE SPECK
MIZZLE PECKLE STIPPLE
SPECKLED SHELD FIGGED MAILED
MENALD SANDED BLOBBED
BRACKET PECKLED SPECKED
SPECKLY FRECKLED IRONSHOT
IRRORATE JASPERED STIPPLED
SPECTACLE POMP SHOW SPEC
BYSEN SIGHT CIRCUS DEVICE
OBJECT EYEMARK PAGEANT SPECIES
TAMASHA MONUMENT NAUMACHY
STERACLE NAUMACHIA
(DEPLORABLE —) OBJECT
(ODD —) TRACK
(POMPOUS —) PAGEANTRY
(SORRY —) BIZEN BYSEN DYZEN
(WATER -) AQUACADE
(PL.) LUDI
(SUFF.) CADE ORAMA
SPECTACLES PAIR SPECS BRILLS
LUNETS PEEPER SIGHTS GLASSES
GOGGLES WINKERS ANAGLYPH
CHEATERS BARNACLES
SPECTACULAR VIEWY PAGEANT
SPECTATOR FAN VIEWER WITNESS
BEHOLDER OBSERVER OVERSEER
RAILBIRD VIEWSTER SCAFFOLDER
(PL.) DEDANS
SPECTER BUG BOGY MARE BOGIE
BOGLE GHOST LARVA POOKA SPOOK
TAIPO BOGGLE EMPUSA PHOOKA
REDCAP SHADOW SPIRIT SPOORN
WRAITH BOGGARD BOGGART
BUGBEAR PHANTOM RAWHEAD
REDCOWL SPECTRE GUYTRASH
PHANTASM PRESENCE REVENANT
SPECTRUM
(BROKEN —) GLORY
SPECTRAL SPOOKY GHOSTLY
SHADOWY
SPECULATE JOB BEAR RISK STAG
GAMBLE PONDER WONDER
CONSIDER RUMINATE THEORIZE
(— IN STOCKS) SCALP
SPECULATION THEORY THEORIC
VENTURE GAMBLING IDEOLOGY

(ABSTRACT —) IDEOLOGY
(DISHONEST —) BUBBLE
(VAGUE —) MYSTICISM
SPECULATIVE ACADEMIC
SPECULATOR PIKER GAMBLER
PLUNGER SCALPER BOURSIER
BUMMAREE OPERATOR
SPECULUM METAL MIRROR DILATER
DIOPTER DIOPTRIC
SPEECH GOB LIP SAW SAY TAT TOY
COAX LEED REDE RUNE TALE DUALA
FRUMP GLOZE LEDEN LINGO PARLE
SERMO SPEAK SPELL SPIEL SPOKE
SQUIB VOICE BREATH DILOGY
EPILOG GAELIC GASCON GILAKI
JARGON LEDDEN LEMOSI ORISON
REASON SALUTE STEVEN TONGUE
ACCENTS ADDRESS BROCARD
EASTERN MEITHEI ORATION
PALABRA VULGATE EPILOGUE
GALICIAN HARANGUE LANGUAGE
LOCUTION LOQUENCE MORAVIAN
PARLANCE QUESTION SONORITY
SPEAKING
(— CHARACTERIZED BY SLURRING)
SLURVIAN
(— FORM) LEXEME
(— IN GREEK DRAMA) RHESIS
(— IN PLAY) SIDE
(— REDUCER) VOCODER
(ABUSIVE —) REVILEMENT
(AFFECTED —) CANT
(AUSTRALIAN —) STRINE
(BITTER —) DIATRIBE
(BOASTFUL —) BLUSTER
(BOMBASTIC —) SQUIRT HARANGUE
(CHILDISH —) LALLATION
(COARSE —) HARLOTRY
(COCKNEY —) LONDONESE
(CONFUSED —) SPUTTER SPLUTTER
(CONTEMPTUOUS —) FRUMP
(CONVERSATIONAL —) PURPOSE
(DULL IN —) PROSY
(EXTEMPORE —) IMPROMPTU
(IMPUDENT —) SASS
(INCOHERENT —) WORDSALAD
(INDIGENOUS —) VERNACULAR
(INTRODUCTORY —) PROLOGUE
PROLOCUTION
(IRRITABLE —) SNAP
(JAVANESE —) KRAMA
(KIND OF —) CUED
(LONG —) MONOLOG
(LONG-DRAWN —) TIRADE
(MISLEADING —) PALAVER
(MOCKING —) TRIFLE
(MONOTONOUS —) DRONE
(NASAL —) RHINOLALIA
(OBSCURE —) ENIGMA
(OFFENSIVE —) INJURY
(PERSUASIVE —) ELOQUENCE
(PERT —) DICACITY
(PRETENTIOUS —) FUSTIAN

(ROUNDABOUT —) CIRCUIT
(SANCTIMONIOUS —) SNUFFLE
(SINGSONG —) CANT
(SLANDEROUS —) EVIL
(SLURRED —) SLURVIAN
(STAGY —) HISTRIONICS
(UNINTELLIGIBLE —) HEBREW
(VAPID —) WASH
(PREF.) LALO LEXI LOG(O) PHON(O)
(SUFF.) ESE LEXIA PHASIA PHEMIA
PHEMISM PHEMISTIC PHRASEO
PHRASIA PHRASIS
(— DISORDER) LALIA
SPEECHIFIER SPOUTER
SPEECHLESS DUMB MUTE SILENT
SPEECHMAKING SPOUTING
(— TO GAIN APPLAUSE) BUNKUM
BUNCOMBE
SPEED BAT HIE REV RIP RUN ZIP FLEE
FOOT GAIT HARE HIGH PACE PELT
PIKE PIRR POST TEAR TILT ZING
BLAST HASTE HURRY SMOKE WHIRL
ASSIST CAREER FOURTH HASTEN
STREAK QUICKEN WHIZZLE
AIRSPEED CELERITY DISPATCH
ESCALATE EXPEDITE FASTNESS
MOMENTUM RAPIDITY VELOCITY
ACCELERATE
(— OF NAUTICAL MILE) KNOT
(— OF PITCH) STUFF
(— OF 100 MILES PER HOUR) TON
(— RELATIVE TO SOUND) MACH
(— UP) HASTEN CATALYZE EXPEDITE
(AT FULL —) AMAIN
(AUTOMOTIVE —) LOW HIGH DRIVE
FIRST THIRD FOURTH SECOND
REVERSE
(DRIVING —) SWING
(FULL —) RANDOM RANDON
(GOOD —) BONALLY
(HIGH —) CLIP MACH
(UNIT OF —) BAUD
(PREF.) DROM(O) TACHO
SPEEDBOAT HYDRO
SPEEDILY CITO SOON APACE RATHE
BELIVE PRESTO BETIMES HYINGLY
QUICKLY TANTIVY
SPEEDING HURTLING
SPEEDWELL CATEYE HENBIT
FLUELLEN NECKWEED NICKWELL
BROOKLIME
SPEEDY FAST SOON HASTY QUICK
RATHE SWIFT RAKING SUDDEN
POSTING TANTIVY EXPEDITE
METEORIC SPEEDFUL SPINNING
POSTHASTE
SPELEOLOGIST CAVEMAN
SPELL GO FIT HEX JAG HACK JINX
MOJO PULL RUNE SCAT TACK TAKE
TIFF TIME TOUR TURN BRIEF CHARM
CRAFT CRASH MAGIC PATCH SPACE
WANGA WEIRD WHEEL ACCESS
GLAMOR GOOFER GRIGRI GUFFER

MAKUTU MANTRA PERIOD SNATCH
STREAK CANTRIP SORCERY SPELDER
CANTRAIP EXORCISM GREEGREE
MALEFICE PISHOGUE
(— OF ACTIVITY) BOUT
(— OF EVIL EYE) JETTATURA
(— OF EXERCISE) BREATHER
(— OF INSTRUCTION) LESSON
(— OF LISTLESSNESS) DOLDRUMS
(— OF PROSPERITY) UP
(— OF SHIVERING) AGUE
(— OF WEATHER) SNAP SLANT
SEASON
(— OF WEEPING) GREET
(— OF WORK) SLOG
(BREATHING —) BLOW
(BRIEF —) SNATCH
(COLD —) SNAP
(CONTINUOUS —) RUN
(DRINKING —) FUDDLE
(EVIL —) JINX
(FAINTING —) DROW DWALM
(MYSTIC —) RUNE
(NIPPING —) SNAPE
(SHORT —) WINK SPURT SNATCH
(STORMY —) FLAW
(VOODOOISTIC —) WANGA
(WITCH'S —) CANTRIP
SPELLBIND ENCHANT
SPELLBINDING BASILISK
SPELLBOUND HEXED
SPELLING GRAPH WRITING
PHONOGRAPHY
(BAD —) CACOGRAPHY
(UNSATISFACTORY —)
PSEUDOGRAPHY
SPELT FAR EMMER FITCH SPELTZ
SPELTZ EMMER
SPENCER TRYSAIL
SPEND USE BIRL COST DREE DROP
LEAD PASS STOW WARE WEAR
DALLY DREIE SERVE SHOOT TRADE
BESTOW BEWARE EXPEND LAVISH
MOIDER OUTRUN CONSUME
DISPEND EXHAUST UNPURSE
CONFOUND CONTRIVE DISBURSE
(— FRUITLESSLY) DAWDLE
(— IN IDLENESS) DRONE
(— LAVISHLY) BLUE SPORT DEBAUCH
(— MONEY) MELT
(— RECKLESSLY) BLOW LASH
(— SUMMER) ESTIVATE
(— TIME) DREE FOOL DREIE ENTREAT
(— TIME TEDIOUSLY) DRANT
(— WASTEFULLY) SPILL SQUANDER
SPENDTHRIFT WASTER PANURGE
ROUNDER SPENDER WASTREL
PRODIGAL PROFLIGATE
SCATTERGOOD
SPENSER IMMERITO
SPENT DONE WEARY EFFETE
OVERWORN
SPERM SEED SEMINIUM

SPERMACETI SPERM CETACEUM
SPERMOGONIUM PYCNIUM
SPERMOPHILE MARMOT SUSLIK
SPERM WHALE CACHALOT
PHYSETER
SPET SIGNET SINNET
SPEW PUKE SPUE VOMIT
SPHAERIUM CYCLAS
SPHAGION HIERA
SPHAGNUM MUSKEG
SPHALERITE JACK BLENDE
BLACKJACK
SPHENODON TUATARA HATTERIA
SPHERE ORB AREA BALL BOWL LOKA
SHOT FIELD GLOBE ORBIT RANGE
REALM SCOPE CIRCLE CROTAL
DOMAIN HEAVEN REGION RUNDLE
COUNTRY ELEMENT GLOBOID
KINGDOM ORBICLE PURVIEW
EARTHKIN EMPYREAL EMPYREAN
MOVEABLE PROVINCE TERRITORY
(— OF ACTION) AMBIT ARENA
WORLD DOMAIN
(— OF ACTIVITY) FIELD FRONT
(— OF AUTHORITY) DIOCESE
(— OF CELLS) BLASTULA
(— OF INFLUENCE) DOMAIN
SATRAPY
(— OF LIFE) EARTH WORLD STATION
(— OF OPERATION) AREA AMBIT
SCOPE THEATER THEATRE
(— OF WORK) TITLE
(CELESTIAL —) CYCLE ELEMENT
(ENCOMPASSING —) AMBIENT
(HOLLOW —) SHELL
(MAGNETIZED —) EARTHKIN
TERRELLA
(METAL —) HAMMER
(SMALL —) ORBICLE SPHERULE
(SUBMERSIBLE —) BENTHOSCOPE
(TINKLING —) CROTAL
(PREF.) GLOBO SPHAER(O) SPHER(O)
SPHERICAL ORBIC GLOBAL ROTUND
GLOBATE GLOBOSE ORBICAL
SPHERIC GLOBULAR ORBICULAR
(PREF.) GLOBO
SPHEROID QUANTASOME
SPHERULE GLOBULE VARIOLE
SPHINX MUSTANG COLOSSUS
HAWKMOTH
(SITE OF —) GIZA
SPICA AZIMECH
SPICCATO PIQUE
SPICE MACE VEIN ZEST AROMA
CLOVE EPICE TASTE GINGER
NUTMEG PEPPER SEASON STACTE
SPICERY SPICING ALLSPICE
CINNAMON SEASONER
(ADD — TO) ENLIVEN
(PL.) GARAMMASALA
SPICEBUSH BENZOIN SNAPWOOD
SPICED SPICY POWDERED
SPICKNEL MEW SCLERE BEARWORT

SPICULE OXEA TOXA ASTER CHELA
CYMBA DESMA DIACT SIGMA SPINE
STYLE ACTINE ANCHOR MONACT
SCLERE STYLUS TRIACT TRIPOD
TYLOTE CALTROP DIACTIN EUASTER
HEXAXON MONAXON PINULUS
RHABDUS SPICKLE SPIRULA
TETRACT TORNOTE TRIAENE
TRIAXON TYLOTUS HEXASTER
ISOCHELA OXYASTER POLYAXON
SCLERITE SPHERULA SPICULUM
STRONGYL TETRAXON TRICHITE
TYLASTER
(SUFF.) AENE
SPICY RACY SEXY GAMEY NUTTY
SWEET SPICED GINGERY PEPPERY
FRAGRANT SPICEFUL
SPIDER BUG COB ARAIN ATTID
COBBE COPPE LOPPE NANCY TAINT
ANANSI ARRAND EPEIRA HUNTER
KATIPO TRIVET WEAVER ARANEID
CREEPER DRASSID EPEIRID JAYHAWK
KNOPPIE POKOMOO RETIARY
SERPENT SKILLET SOLDIER SPINNER
ARACHNID ATTERCOP CTENIZID
DICTYNID ETTERCAP KARAKURT
ORBITELE PHALANGE PHALANGY
PHOLCOID SALTICID SOLPUGID
TELARIAN ULOBORID VENANTES
WANDERER TARANTULA
(PART OF —) EYE CLAW COXA FEMUR
TIBIA TARSUS ABDOMEN PATELLA
PEDICEL SCOPULA SPINNERET
METATARSUS PEDIPALPUS
TROCHANTER CEPHALOTHORAX
(PREF.) ARACHN(O)
SPIDER CRAB MAIAN MAIID
SPIDERFLOWER QUARESMA
SPIDER MONKEY SAJOU COAITA
SAPAJOU
SPIDERWORT TRINITY
SPIEL LINE SPEECH
SPIELER BARKER
SPIFF (— UP) ENLIVEN
SPIGNEL MEU
SPIGOT TAP SPILE DOSSIL DOZZLE
STOPCOCK
SPIKE GAD BARB BROB PICK PIKE PILE
SPUR TINE PITON POINT ROUGH
SPEAR SPICA SPICK MOOTER PRITCH
SPADIX SPIKER TENTER ALICOLE
GADLING PRICKER PRICKET TRENAIL
TURNPIN SPIKELET STROBILE
WHEATEAR
(— A CANNON) CLOY
(— AS CANDLESTICK) PRICKET
(— OF CEREAL) EAR
(— OF FLOWER) SPIRE
(— ON GAUNTLET) GADLING
(BRACTED —) AMENT
(DRIED —S) CANNABIS
(WILLOW —) CATKIN
SPIKED SPICATE SPINDLED

SPIKELET CHAT ALICOLE LOCUSTA
SPICULE
SPIKENARD PHU NARD ARALIA
SUMBUL ARALIAD IVYWORT
SPIGNET SPIGNUT
SPILE TAP SPILL FOREPOLE
SPILL LET DRIP DUMP SHED SLOP
TELL FLOSH SCALE SKAIL SPILE
SQUAB STAVE JIRBLE PURLER
SLATTER SLOBBER TURNOVER
(— FOR LIGHTING PIPES) FIDIBUS
SPIN CUT BIRL DRAW GYRE HURL PIRL
PURL REEL SCREW SPONE TWIRL
TWIST WEAVE WHIRL FOLLOW
GYRATE VRILLE WAMBLE TWIZZLE
TEETOTUM
(— AND MAKE HUM) BUM
(— AROUND) SWING
(— ON BASEBALL) STUFF
(— ON BILLIARD BALL) SIDE
(— OUT) SHOOT
(— SILK) THROW
(— SMOOTHLY) SLEEP
(— UNEVENLY) TWITTER
SPINACH SAVOY EPINARD OLITORY
POTHERB
SPINAL CORD AXION NUCHA
MYELON
(WHITE MATTER OF —) ALBA NUKE
(PREF.) MYEL(O)
(SUFF.) MYELIA
SPINDLE PIN AXLE HASP PIRN SPIT
STEM STUD ARBOR FLOAT QUILL
SPIKE SPILL VERGE BOBBIN BROACH
CANNON FUSEAU BOLSTER
MANDREL SPINNEL TRENDLE
WHARROW
(AXLE —) ARM
(FOURTH OF —) HASP
(ONE 24TH OF —) HEER
(PREF.) FUSI
SPINDLE TREE GAITER DOGWOOD
PEGWOOD EUONYMUS
SPINDLING SPEARY SPINDLY
SPIRLIE
SPINDLY LEGGY PULING
SPINE HORN PIKE PILE SETA SPUR
CHINE PRICK QUILL SPEAR SPIKE
SPINA THORN ACUMEN CHAETA
RACHIS ACANTHA ACICULA
FULCRUM GLOCHIS PAXILLA PRICKER
PRICKLE ROSTRUM SPINULE STICKLE
ACICULUM BACKBONE ILLICIUM
PAXILLUS PELELITH SPICULUM
SPINELET
(— OF FIN) RAY
(— OF SURGEON FISH) TUCK
(CURVATURE OF —) LORDOSIS
(PREF.) ACANTH(O) RACHI(O)
RHACHI(O)
(SUFF.) ACANTHUS CHAETA CHAETES
CHAETUS RACHIDIA RHACHIS
RRHACHIS

SPINEL BALAS CANDITE ESPINEL
GAHNITE VERMEIL PICOTITE
SPINELLE CEYLONITE RUBICELLE
SPINELESS SLAVISH
SPINET PIANO ESPINET GIRAFFE
OCTAVINA SOURDINE VIRGINAL
SPINNER LURE ROTOR
(THREAD OF LIFE —) CLOTHO
SPINNERET GALEA MAMMULA
SPINNER
SPINNING AREEL STROBIC
LANIFICE
(— WEB) TELARIAN
SPINNING JENNY MULE JENNY
SPINNING MULE IRONMAN
SPINNING WHEEL TURN CHARKHA
CHURRUCK
(PART OF —) BAND FLYER WHEEL
BOBBIN DISTAFF SPINDLE TREADLE
STANDARD
SPINSTER TABBY VIRGIN
SPINULE
(PL.) CTENII
SPINY PICKED THORNY
(PREF.) ACANTH(O) CENTR(I)(O)
ECHIN(O)
SPINY OYSTER SPONDYLE
SPINY RAT OCTODONT
SPIRACLE STOMA STIGMA
BLOWHOLE
SPIRAEA MAY ROSACEAN
MEADOWSWEET
SPIRAL COIL CURL GYRE SPIN HELIX
SCREW SNARE SPIRE BUTTON
GURGES LITUUS SCREWY SCROLL
SPIRED TWIRLY VOLUTE HELICAL
ROLLING SPIROID STROPHE
WINDING WREATHY GYROIDAL
HELICINE HELICOID
(— OF WIRE) GRID
(LACEWORK —) PURL
(PREF.) GYR(O) HELI HELIC(O)
SPIRANT VAU WAW HISS OPEN
DURATIVE
SPIRANTHES IBIDIUM
SPIRE CROWN SHAFT SIKAR SPEAR
TAPER TOLLY BROACH FLECHE
PRICKET SHIKARA SIKHARA SPIRALE
SPIRELET
SPIRE-BEARER SPIRIFER
SPIREME SKEAN SKEIN
SPIRIT GO AME FLY NAG PEP VIM
AITU AKUA ALMA ATUA BRIO DASH
DOOK ELAN FIRE GALL GIMP HYLE
JINN LIFE MARC MARE MIND MOOD
SOUL TONE ZEMI ZING AGIEL ARDOR
ARIEL ASURA AZOTH CHEER DEMON
DHOUL DJINN DOBBY ETHOS FLING
GEIST GHOST GORIC GUACA GUSTO
HAUNT HEART HOLDA HUACA JINNI
LARVA MOXIE NUMEN PLUCK POWER
PRETA RALPH SAINT SHADE SHRAB
SPOOK SPUNK VERVE ASTRAL

ASUANG BOTTOM BREATH CHULPA COURIL DAEMON ESPRIT TAINTS FLECHE FYLGJA GENIUS GINGER INWARD KOBOLD LESHEY METTLE MORALE ORISHA PAZAZZ PECKER PIZAZZ PNEUMA PYTHON SPRAWL SPRITE TAFFIA WRAITH ALCOHOL BRAVERY CONTROL CORDIAL COURAGE ENTRAIN EUDEMON KNOCKER MANITOU PISACHI PIZZAZZ PURUSHA RAPPIST SMEDDUM STOMACH CALVADOS ERDGEIST FAMILIAR FOLLETTO PHANTASM SPIRACLE SPIRITUS
(— DWELLING IN JEWEL) AZOTH
(— DWELLING IN MINES) KNOCKER
(— HAUNTING PRINTING HOUSES) RALPH
(— OF DEAD) CHINDI CHINDEE
(— OF DEATH) CHULPA
(— OF DECEASED) AKH
(— OF ENTERPRISE) ADVENTURE
(— OF FERTILITY) YAKSA YAKSHA YAKSHI
(— OF HOSTILITY) ANIMUS
(— OF LOYALTY) PIETAS
(— OF MAN) AKH
(— OF ONE WHO HAS MET VIOLENT DEATH) PISACHI
(— OF PHYSICAL HEART) AB
(— OF PRIESTHOOD) SACERDOTALISM
(— OF THE AGE) ZEITGEIST
(— OF THE AIR) SYLPH
(— OF TRAGEDY) COTHURN
(— OF UNBAPTIZED BABE) TARAN
(—S OF LOWER WORLD) INFERI
(—S OF THE DEAD) MANES
(— WHICH ACTUATES CUSTOMS) ETHOS
(ANCESTRAL —) ANITO KATCHINA
(ARDENT —) RAK RACK ARRACK
(ASTRAL —) AGIEL ASTRAL JOPHIEL UUCHATON
(AVENGING —) FURY ALECTO ALASTOR MEGAERA
(CHARACTERISTIC —) VIBE
(COMBATIVE —) SWORD
(DISEMBODIED —) KUFI KWEI SOUL GHOST LARVA SHADE ASUANG SPECTER SPECTRE
(DIVINE —) ISVARA ISHVARA
(EARTH —) ERDGEIST
(EFFULGENT —S) ARDORS
(EMANCIPATED —) MUKTATMA
(EVIL —) DEV DIV HAG IMP OKI BAKA BENG BOKO BOLL DEVA DUSE MARA OKEE ASURA BUGAN DAEVA DEMON DEVIL JUMBY OTKON DAITYA DIBBUK DYBBUK LILITH AHRIMAN BUGGANE CASZIEL INCUBUS KANAIMA RAKSHAS SHAITAN SHEITAN SKOOKUM WINDIGO

ASMODEUS BAALPEOR BEELPEOR HOBOMOCO SUCCUBUS NIGHTMARE
(FAMILIAR —) FLY GENIUS HARPIER
(FEMALE —) DUFFY DUPPY DUSIO HOLDA UNDINE BANSHEE ATAENSIC BABAJAGA BELFAGOR BELFAZOR
(FIGHTING —) DEVIL
(FOREST —) MIMING
(FULL OF —) CRANK
(FULL OF —S) BRAG
(GOOD —) DEVA EUDEMON
(GOVERNING —) ANIMUS
(GUARDIAN —) ANGEL TOTEM FYLGJA NAGUAL
(HIGH —) GINGER COURAGE
(HIGH —S) CREST GAIETY HEYDAY ELATION
(HOSTILE —S) LEMURES
(HOUSEHOLD —S) LARES PENATES
(HUMAN —) JIVATMA
(IMPISH —) PO
(IMPURE —) FAINTS
(INDIAN —) MANITO
(IN VIGOROUS —S) FIERCE
(LOW —S) DUMP BLUES MEGRIM DISMALS
(MALEVOLENT —) BHUT GORIC LARVA
(MALICIOUS —) DOBBY
(MALIGNANT —) IMP KER GYRE DEMON
(MANLY —) SPLEEN
(MISCHIEVOUS —) KOBOLD TIKOLOSH
(MOUNTAIN —) RUBEZAHL
(MOVING —) SOUL
(MUSICAL —) BRIO
(NATURE —) NAT
(NIGHT —) TENEBRIO
(PARTY —) FACTION
(REFINED —) ELIXIR
(RENEWED —) REFRESHMENT
(RESOLUTE —) SPRAWL
(ROVING —) RAMPLER
(SEA —) TANGIE
(SENSED —) KARMA
(SOOTHSAYING —) PYTHON
(SUPERNATURAL —) FAMILIAR
(SYLVAN —) LESHY SYLVAN
(TRICKSY —) ARIEL
(TUTELARY —S) DIS LARES
(VITAL —) TUCK
(VOLATILE —) ESSENCE
(WATER —) ARIEL KELPY ONDINE UNDINE
(WICKED —) IMP THURSE
(PL.) GENII IGIGI DAUBER
(PREF.) PNEUMAT(O) PSYCH(O) THYM(O)
(SUFF.) THYMIA
SPIRITED BRAG FELL GOGO RACY TALL BEANY BIRKY CRANK EAGER FIERY FLUSH KEDGE KINKY LIFEY

PEPPY PROUD SASSY SEEDY SMART
SPICY VIVID AUDACE FIERCE GINGER
LIVELY METTLE PLUCKY SKEIGH
SPRUCE SPUNKY VIVACE ANIMATO
DASHING FORWARD HUMMING
NERVOUS PEPPERY SPIRITY
DESIROUS FRAMPOLD GENEROUS
PHRAMPEL SLASHING STOMACHY
VASCULAR METTLESOME
SPIRITEDLY GAMELY
SPIRITLESS DEAD DOWF MEAN
MEEK POOR TAME AMORT FAINT
MILKY MUSTY SEEDY SOGGY VAPID
ABJECT ANEMIC CRAVEN DREEPY
FLASHY JEJUNE LEADEN MOPISH
SODDEN SOFTLY WOODEN HILDING
INSIPID LANGUID FECKLESS
FLAGGING LISTLESS THEWLESS
SPIRITLESSLY DAVIELY
SPIRITLESSNESS LANGUOR
SPIRITLIKE ETHEREAL
SPIRITS LACE RĀKI HOOCH MANES
METHS FETTLE PECKER FEATHER
LEMURES SAMSHOO WAIPIRO
SPIRITUAL ABOVE DEVOUT INWARD
MISTLY GHOSTLY CHURCHLY
INTERNAL NUMINOUS SUPERIOR
PNEUMATIC
(— LEADER) ZADDIK
SPIRITUALISM SPOOKISM
SPIRITUALITY HEAVEN
SPIRITUALIZE REFINE
SPIRITUOUS HARD
SPIROCHETE BORRELIA
SPIT YEX FUFF RACK FROTH REACH
SPAWL BROACH SPITTLE SANDSPIT
SPITTING
(— AND POLISH) BULL
(— OF LAND) HOOK
(SUFF.) PTYSIS
SPITE ENVY ONDE DEPIT LIVOR
PIQUE VENOM HATRED MALICE
MAUGRE RANCOR SPLEEN DESPITE
AMBITION
SPITEFUL MEAN CATTY NASTY
NEBBY PETTY SNAKY ELVISH
MALIGN SULLEN WANTON WICKED
CATTISH ENVIOUS PEEVISH SNAKISH
VICIOUS WASPISH CANKERED
KNAPPISH VENOMOUS
SPITFIRE CACAFOGO PEPPERBOX
(TYPE OF —) VOLCANO
SPITTING FUFF EMPTYSIS
SPITTING SNAKE RINGHALS
SPITTLE SPIT SPAWL SPUTUM
SLOBBER
(PREF.) PTYAL(O)
SPITTLEBUG FROGHOPPER
SPITTOON GABOON PIGDAN
SPITBOX CRACHOIR CUSPIDOR
SPIV RORTER
SPLAKE MENDIGO
SPLANCHNIC VISCERAL

SPLASH JAW LAP DASH GLOB GOUT
JAUP LOSH LUSH SKIT SOSS SPAT
WASH BLASH FLASH FLICK FLOOD
FLOSH PLASH PLOUT QUASH SKIRP
SLART SLASH SLOSH SLUSH SQUAT
SWILK BEDASH DABBLE DOLLOP
FLOUSE JABBLE LABBER PLATCH
SLUNGE SOZZLE SPLOSH SPRENT
SQUIRT PLOUTER SPATTER SPIRTLE
SPLODGE SPLURGE SWATTER
SPLAIRGE SPLATHER SPLATTER
SPLOTHER SPLUTHER SPLUTTER
(— OF COLOR) GOUT
(SLIGHT —) GILP
SPLASHBOARD FENDER SPLASHER
SPLASHING SWASH FLASHY
JABBLE DASHING SPATTER
SPLUTTER SWASHING
SPLASHY BLASHY GLITZY SLOPPY
SPRAWLY
SPLATTER DASH BLASH SPLAIRGE
SPLAY FLAN
SPLAYED FLEW FLUE
SPLAYFOOT FLATFOOT
SPLEEN IRE PIP BILE LIEN MELT MILT
RHEUM MALICE STOMACH
(PREF.) LIEN(O) SPLEN(I)(O)
(SUFF.) SPLENIA
SPLEENY PEEVISH
SPLENDID GAY BRAW FINE NEAT
RIAL BRAVE GRAND JOLLY NOBLE
PROUD REGAL ROYAL SHEEN
SHOWY STOUT TOUGH WALLY
WLONK CANDID COSTLY SIGHTY
SOLEMN SPIFFY SUPERB ELEGANT
GALLANT SHINING SUBLIME
TEARING BARONIAL CHAMPION
CLINKING COLOSSAL GLORIOUS
GORGEOUS MAJESTIC ORGULOUS
RATTLING SLASHING SPANKING
STUNNING TERRIFIC
(CHEAPLY —) TINNY
SPLENDIDLY FINE FINELY SPROWSY
SPLENDOR SUN UMA GITE LUXE
POMP BLAZE ECLAT GLARE GLEAM
GLORY SHEEN SHINE FULGOR
LUSTER LUSTRE PARADE RUFFLE
CLARITY DISPLAY JOLLITY PANACHE
GRANDEUR RADIANCE SUMPTURE
SPLENETIC SULLEN VAPORY
PEEVISH
SPLENIC LIENAL
SPLICE FOOT JOIN SCAB PIECE
SCARE SKELB CROTCH PIECEN
SPLICING
SPLICER STRAPPER
SPLINE FIN SLAT FEATHER
SPLINT SCOB FANON MATCH SPELK
SPELL TASSE SPLENT THOMAS
CALIPER SPLINTER
(— FOR FRACTURE) JUNK
SPLINTER BROOM BURST PURSE
SHAKE SHIDE SHIVE SKELB SKELF

SLICE SPAIL SPALE SPALL SPALT
SPEEL SPELK SPELL SPILE SPILL
SPLIT SPOON SLIVER SPLEET SPLINT
FLINDER SHATTER SLITHER SPLITTER
SPLINTERY SKELVY
SPLINTWOOD ALBURNUM
SPLIT AX AXE CUT RIT BUCK CHAP
CONE DUNT GAIG MALL MAUL RASH
REND RENT RIFT RIVE SKAG SLAT
TEAR BLAST BREAK BURST CHECK
CHINE LEAVE SHAKE SHEAR SKIVE
SLENT SLIVE SMASH SPALD SPALL
SPLAT CLEAVE CLOVEN CREASE
DEPART DIVIDE FLAGGY FLERRY
GOAWAY SCHISM SPRING SUNDER
BIVALVE SHATTER SLITHER
CREVASSE SCISSION SCISSURE
SPLINTER
(— FISH) SCROD
(— IN BOWLING) BEDPOSTS
(— OFF) SPALL SPAWL SCREEVED
(— TICKET) SCRATCH
(KIND OF —) STOCK
(PREF.) SCHISTO SCHIZ(O)
SPLITTERMAN BOLTER
SPLITTING FLAGGY FISSION
SCISSION
(— OF PERSONALITY) DISSOCIATION
(— OF WORD) TMESIS
(READILY —) SCISSILE
(PL.) FILMS
(SUFF.) RHEXIS RRHEXIS
SPLOTCH DAB BLOB DASH HALO
SPOT FLICK SMUDGE SPECKLE
SPLATCH SPLURGE
SPLURGE BINGE SPEND SPRAY
SPREE SPLASH
SPLUTTER FUFF GLUTTER SPATTER
SPUTTER SPLOTHER
SPODOPTERA LAPHYGMA
SPODUMENE KUNZITE TRIPHANE
SPOIL MAR MUX ROT BLOT BOOT
COOK DAZE FANG FOIL FRAB GAIN
KILL MANK PELF PREY ADDLE BITCH
BLEND BLUNK BOOTY BOTCH CROSS
DECAY LOUSE QUAIL QUEER SHEND
SPILL STAIN STRIP TOUCH TRASH
WALLY BOODLE BUGGER CODDLE
COOPER CORPSE COSSET CURDLE
DEFACE DEFORM FORAGE INJURE
MANGLE PERISH RAVAGE TIDDLE
BAUCHLE BEDEVIL BLEMISH
CONNACH CORRUMP CORRUPT
ESTREPE INDULGE MULLOCK
PILLAGE PLUNDER SPOLIUM
TARNISH VIOLATE BANKRUPT
CONFOUND DISGRACE MISGUIDE
SPOLIATE
(— BY SOAKING) RET RAIT RATE
SPOILED BAD BLOWN DAZED MUSTY
CADISH STICKIT BRATTISH
(— BY USE) OVERWORN
(EASILY —) GINGER

SPOILER HARROWER
SPOILERS (AUTHOR OF —) BEACH
(CHARACTER IN —) ROY BILL HELEN
CHERRY DEXTRY STRUVE CHESTER
MALOTTE MCNAMARA STILLMAN
GLENISTER
SPOILFIVE MAW
SPOILS BAG LOOT SKIN SWAG
BOOTY FORAY SPOLIA PILLAGE
PLUNDER PICKINGS
SPOILSPORT NARK PILL GRINCH
LETGAME
SPOILT MARDY
SPOKE RUNG QUOTH SPACK SPAKE
LOWDER SPONDIL SPONDYL
(— OF WHEEL) RADIUS
SPOKEN ORAL SAID VERBAL
VOICED
SPOKESMAN MOUTH HERALD
PROPHET SPEAKER TRUMPET
MOUTHPIECE
(— OF DEITY) PROPHET
SPOKEWISE RADIAL
SPOLIATION REIF SPOIL RAPINE
PILLAGE PLUNDER SPOILING
SPONGE BOT FORM MUMP POLE
SILK SORN SWAB ASCON CADGE
GRASS LUFFA SCAFF SHARK SHIRK
SHOOL SYCON ASCULA BUMMER
COSHER LEUCON LOOFAH MALKIN
MOPPET RHAGON ROLLER YELLOW
BADIAGA BLEEDER GELFOAM
RADIATE SCOURER SCRUNGE
SYCONID ZIMOCCA DEADBEAT
FREELOAD HARDHEAD HEDGEHOG
MANDRUKA OLYNTHUS REDBEARD
SCROUNGE SILICEAN SPHERIDA
SUBERITE ZOOPHYTE PORIFERAN
(TAKE UP LIKE A —) SORB
(YOUNG —) SEEDLING
(SUFF.) AENE
SPONGER BOT BUM TRAMP
BUMMER CADGER SPONGE
SCAMBLER SMOOTHER
SPONGINESS FOZINESS
SPONGING TRENCHER
SPONGY FOZY FUZZY POACHY
QUAGGY FUNGOUS BIBULOUS
SPONSOR COACH GOSSIP SURETY
ENDORSE WITNESS
(— AT BAPTISM) HEAVE
SPONSORSHIP EGIS AEGIS
SPONTANEOUS FREE CARELESS
FREEWILL UNBIDDEN UNTAUGHT
VOLUNTARY
SPONTANEOUSLY KINDLY SELFLY
PUTON
SPOOF PUTON
SPOOK GYRE GHOST HAUNT SCARE
SPOOL COB COP PIRN REEL QUILL
SPILL SPULE TWEEL TWILL BOBBIN
BROACH CHEESE COPPIN CARRIER
(— FOR NETS) GURDY
(HERALDIC —) TRUNDLE

SPOON HORN NECK CUTTY LABIS
SHELL COCHLEA JUMBLER MUDDLER
SKIMMER SPINNER STIRRER
BARSPOON COCHLEAR GOBSTICK
(EUCHARISTIC —) LABIS
(FISHING —) TROLL
(FLATTENED —) SPATULA
(LONG-HANDLED —) LADLE
(SKIMMING —) LINGEL SKIMMER
(SNUFF —) PEN
(PREF.) COCHLEARI LIGUL(I)
SPOONBILL AJAJA SPOONY
POPELER CICONIID
(PREF.) PLATALEI
SPOONERISM MARROWSKY
SPOONFUL COCHLEARE
SPOON-SHAPED COCHLEAR
SPATULAR
SPOONY SILLY FOOLISH
SPOOR SIGN SPUR PISTE
SPORADIC POPPING ISOLATED
SPORANGIUM THECA OOTHECA
SPORE CYST SEED SPORID TELIUM
AGAMETE AKINETE BISPORE
ISOLANT ISOLATE OOSPORE
SEEDLET SPORULE SWARMER
CONIDIUM EXOSPORE GONIDIUM
PROPAGULE
(— SAC) ASCI ASCUS
SPORES
(PREF.) CONI(DI)
SPOROCYST ZOOCYST SPOROSAC
SPORT FUN GIG KID MUM RIE RUX
SEE TOY ALSO GAME GAUD GLEE
JEST JOKE LAKE LARK PLAY PLOY
RAGE TAIT BOURD BREAK DALLY
DROLL FREAK MIRTH FROLIC
LAUGHS POPJOY RACING SHIKAR
SKIING BOATING CAMOGIE DISPORT
DUCKING FOWLING MARLOCK
PASTIME ROLLICK ROUNDER SAILING
SPANIEL FALCONRY PLEASURE
SKYDIVING MOUNTAINEERING
(— OF HAWKING) RIVER
(BOISTEROUS —) HIJINKS
(JAPANESE —) KENDO AIKIDO
(ONE-ON-ONE) EPEE
(ROUGH —) ROMP
(WATER —S) NAUTICS AQUATICS
(WINTER —) SKIJORING
(PREF.) LUDI
SPORTING VARMINT SPORTIVE
SPORTIVE GAY TAIT LARKY MERRY
FRISKY JOCUND LIVELY LUSORY
TOYFUL TOYING WANTON COLTISH
FESTIVE GAMEFUL JESTING
JOCULAR PLAYFUL TOYSOME
TRICKSY WAGGISH FROLICKY
GAMESOME PLAYSOME PLEASANT
SPORTFUL
SPORTIVENESS HELL KNAVERY
SPORTS (— OFFICIAL) REF ZEBRA
REFEREE

SPORTSMAN SPORT ATHLETE
SHIKARI
SPORTSMANLIKE CLEAN SPORTY
SPORTY FLASH RORTY FLASHY
RAKISH
SPORULE GRANULE
SPOT BIT DAB PIP SEE WEM BLOT
BLUR CHUB DIRT DRAB FLAW GALL
MAIL MOIL MOLE PLOT SCAM SITE
SKIP SLUR SMUT SOIL SPAT TICK
AMPER BLACK CLOUD FLECK GARLE
GOODY GUTTA HATCH JIMMY
MACLE PATCH PLACE PLECK POINT
ROACH SMEAR SPLAT STAIN SULLY
TACHE TAINT WHERE BLANCH
BLOTCH DAPPLE FOGDOG GERATE
LOCALE MACULE MAZUCA MOTTLE
SMUDGE SMUTCH SPLECK STIGMA
BLEMISH CHARBON CHECKER
FLECKER FRECKLE GUTTULA
MASOOKA OCELLUS OLDWIFE
SMATTER SMITTER SPATTER
SPECKLE SPLOTCH SPOTTLE
STATION STIPPLE TERRAIN
FENESTRA LOCALITY MACULATE
PUNCTULE SPARKLET SPRINKLE
(— A SHIELD) GERATE
(— IN CLOTH) YAW
(— IN MARBLE) TERRACE
(— IN MINERAL) MACLE
(— IN PAPER) SHINER
(— IN SAW BLADE) BLOB
(— IN STEEL) STAR
(— IN WOOD) WEM
(— IN YARN) MOTE
(— OF INK) MONK
(— OF PAINT) DAUB
(— OF QUICKSAND) SUCKHOLE
(— ON CAT) BUTTON
(— ON CAT'S FACE) LAVALIER
(— ON EGG) EYE
(— ON FINGERNAIL) GIFT
(— ON FOREHEAD) TILAK TILAKA
(— ON HAWK) GOUT
(— ON HORSE) RACE SNIP STAR
RACHE
(— ON HORSE'S TOOTH) CHARBON
(— ON INSECT WINGS) BULLA
(— ON MOTH'S WINGS) FENESTRA
(— ON PLAYING CARD) PIP
(— ON SUN) FACULA GRANULE
SUNSPOT
(—S IN BOOKS) FOXING
(— WITH MIST) ATOMIZE
(BARREN —) GALL
(BLIND —) SCOTOMA SCOTOSIS
(BROWN —) SPRAIN SPRAING
(CRUSTY —) SCAB
(ESSENTIAL —) EYE
(EYELIKE — ON PEACOCK) OCELLUS
(FERTILE —) OASIS
(FIRM — IN BOG) HAG
(GREEN — IN VALLEY) HAW

(HALLOWED —) BETHEL
(INFLAMED —) AMPER
(LEAF —) TIKKA BLACKARM
(LIVER —S) CHLOASMA
(LIVID —) TOKEN
(LOW —) DIP SWAMP HOLLOW
(MARSHY —) SPEW SPUE
(PAINFUL —) SORE
(PLAGUE —) TOKEN
(RED —) FLEABITE
(RETIRED —) SHADE
(ROUGH — IN WOVEN GOODS) FAG
(ROUND —) BLOB
(SCABBY —) SCALD
(SECLUDED —) ALCOVE CLOISTER
(SHADY —) SWALE
(SKIN —) MOLE BLISTER FRECKLE
LENTIGO PETECHIA
(SMALL —) DOT PLECK STIGMA
LUNULET SPARKLET
(SOILED —) SLOP
(SORE —) BUBU BOTCH
(SPARKLING —) SPANGLE
(SWAMPY —) FLAM
(TIGHT —) JAM JACKPOT
(WEAK —) GALL HOLE CHINK NERVE
(WORN —) FRAY FRET
(PL.) MOONING
(PREF.) MACUL(I)(O) SPIL(O)
SPOTLESS FAIR PURE WEMLESS
INNOCENT
SPOTLIGHT ARC SPOT DEUCE
SPOTTED PIED MARLY SCOVY SHELD
CALICO FIGGED HAWKED MACLED
MAILED MARLED MIRLED PARDED
SPOTTY TICKED BRACKET BROOKED
FINCHED GUTTATE MOTTLED
PARDINE PIEBALD PINTADO SPARKED
SPECKED SPECKLY TIGROID
FRECKLED LITURATE MACULOSE
SPECKLED STIPPLED
(SUFF.) MACULATE
SPOTTED EAGLE RAY MILLER
OBISPO
SPOTTED FLYCATCHER COBWEB
RAFTER WALLBIRD
SPOTTED GUM EUCALYPT
SPOTTED JEWFISH GUASA
SPOTTED SANDPIPER TIPUP
TILTUP CREEKER TIPTAIL PEETWEET
SPOTTED SPURGE DOVEWEED
SPOTTED WINTERGREEN
RATSBANE
SPOTTED WOODPECKER PICUS
WITWALL
SPOTTER DOTTER
SPOTTING (— OF LEAVES)
HELIOSIS
SPOTTY MEALY PATCHY PLATTY
SCABBY SPOTTED
SPOUSE EX FERE MAKE WIFE BRIDE
MATCH PARTY FELLOW MARROW
CONSORT ESPOUSE HUSBAND

SPOUT JET LIP BEAK DALE GEAT
GUSH NOSE SHOE ORATE SPILE
SPUME SPURT NOZZLE RIGGOT
SPLOIT SPROUT STRONE STROUP
BUBBLER FOUNTAIN GARGOYLE
(RAIN —) RONE
SPOUTER VAPORER
(MEDITERRANEAN —) ETNA
SPOUTING BLOW SALIENT
SPRAG PROP TRAILER
SPRAGGER SCOTCHER
SPRAIN RICK CHINK STAVE THRAW
THROW WRAMP WREST WRICK
STRAIN WRENCH STREMMA
SPRAT SMY BLAY BRIT BRITT SPRET
SPRIT GARVIE ALFIONE GARVOCK
BRISLING
(—S CAUGHT EARLY IN SEASON)
DROVE
SPRAWL LOLL TAVE SPURL SCRAWL
GRABBLE SCAMBLE SPARTLE
SPELDER SCRAMBLE SPRADDLE
SPRANGLE STRADDLE
SPRAWLING SPRANGLY
SPRAY FOG HOSE SCUD SPRY STEW
SPREE STOUR SWISH TRAIL TWIST
WATER HONEST SHOWER SPARGE
SPLASH SPRANG SPRITZ CURTAIN
SPAIRGE SYRINGE INHALANT
SPRANGLE
(— BEHIND MOTORBOAT)
ROOSTERTAIL
(— FROM SMALL WAVES) LIPPER
(— MASH) SPANGE
(— OF GEMS) AIGRETTE
(REDUCE TO —) NEBULIZE
SPREAD BED FAN LAY RUN COAT
DRAW FLUE SPAN TEER TELD TUCK
VEIN WALK APPLY CLEAM CREEP
FLARE KILIM PASTE SCALE SLICE
SPEND SPLAT SPLAY STALK STREW
WIDEN BUTTER EXTEND FLANGE
LARDER LAYOUT MANTLE SETOUT
THRUST UNFOLD UNFURL BROADEN
CANVASS DIFFUSE DISPLAY
DISTEND EXPANSE EXPLAIN
FEATHER OPENING SCATTER
SLATHER STRETCH DIASPORA
DISPENSE DISPERSE HUMIFUSE
INCREASE MULTIPLY SPLATHER
STRAGGLE
(— ABROAD) TOOT BLAZE DELATE
SPRING DIVULGE EMANATE
(— APART) GAPE
(— AS GOSSIP) BUZZ
(— BY REPORT) BLOW NOISE
NORATE
(— DEFAMATION) LIBEL
(— FOR DRYING) TED
(— INTO) INVADE
(— LIKE GRAIN) FLOOR
(— NEWS) HORN
(— ON THICK) COUCH SLATHER

(— **OUT**) FAN FLOW OPEN ROLL SPAN
ASPAR BREDE SPLAT SPLAY SPRAY
EXPAND FLANGE FRINGE MANTLE
OUTLAY SPRAWL UNLOCK DIFFUSE
DISPAND DISTENT EXPLAIN FEATHER
DIFFUSED SPRADDLE SPRANGLE
STRAGGLY
(— **OUTWARD**) FLARE
(— **OVER**) LAP DASH COVER
SUFFUSE
(— **PAINT**) KNIFE
(— **RAPIDLY**) MUSHROOM
(— **RUMORS**) WHISPER
(— **SECRETLY**) BUZZ
(— **THE NEWS**) BRUIT
(— **THE WORD**) TELL
(— **THINLY**) BRAY DRIVE TOUCH
SCANTY
(— **TO**) CATCH
(— **TO THE WIND**) SET
(— **WIDE**) SPELD SPELDER
(**EVENLY**) SUANT
(**TAPESTRY-WOVEN** —) KILIM
(PREF.) STRATO
(SUFF.) CHORE
SPREADER PLOW PLOUGH SANDER
(**HAY** —) TEDDER
SPREADING FLAN BUSHY FLANGE
PATENT ASPREAD DIFFUSE FLARING
SPRAYEY PATULENT PATULOUS
SPRANGLY
(— **OF LIGHT**) HALATION
(— **RAPIDLY**) RUNNING
(**NOT** —) ERECT
(**SLOW** —) CREEPAGE
SPREE BAT BUM JAG BLOW BUST
GELL LARK RANT SOAK TEAR TIME
TOOT BEANO BINGE BOOZE BURST
DRINK DRUNK SOUSE SPRAY
BENDER BUSTER HOORAY HURRAH
JUNKET RANDAN RANTAN RAZZLE
SPLORE BLOWOFF JAMBOREE
WINGDING
SPRIG POINT
(—**S FOR MOURNING**) CYPRESS
SPRIGGER STRIPPER
SPRIGHTLINESS GAIETY AIRINESS
ALACRITY BUOYANCY VIVACITY
SPRIGHTLY GAY TID AIRY GNIB PERT
WARM ALIVE BRISK CANTY CRISP
DESTO MERRY PERKY QUICK ALEGER
BLITHE BREEZY JAUNTY LIVELY
SPANKY SPRACK WIMBLE CHIPPER
DELIVER JOCULAR SPARKLY
LIFESOME PLEASANT
SPRING EN AIN BUG EYE FLY HOP
JET OJO URN VER WAX BATH BOLT
BOUT BUCK BUNT DART FLOW FONT
GEON HAIR HEAD JUMP KELD LEAP
PERT RISE SEEP SKIP SOAK STEM
URNA WALM WARE WELL WIND
YOAR ARISE BOUND DANCE FLIRT
FOUNT FRESH GIHON GLENT GRASS

ISSUE LYMPH PRIME QUELL SALLY
SOURD SPEND SPOUT START STEND
SURGE THROW VAULT BOUNCE
CHARCO DERIVE GAMBOL GEYSER
JUMPER LOCKET ORIGIN PIRENE
RESORT RESULT SILOAM SOURCE
SPRINT VENERO BUDTIME EMANATE
ESTUARY FLOUNCE GAMBADO
PROCEED REBOUND WRAPPER
BACKSTAY BANDUSIA CASTALIA
FOUNTAIN SPANGHEW ORIGINATE
PRINTEMPS
(— **AWKWARDLY**) KEVEL
(— **BACK**) RECOIL RESULT RETORT
REBOUND
(— **DOWN**) ALIGHT
(— **FORWARD**) LAUNCH
(— **FROM**) DESCEND
(— **IN MARSH**) WELLHEAD
(— **INTO BEING**) AWAKEN
(— **OF HORSE**) GAMBADO
(— **OF THE YEAR**) VER VOAR
(— **ON SHEARS**) BACKSTAY
(— **SEASON**) APRIL GRASS BUDTIME
(— **SUDDENLY**) FLY BOUNCE
(— **TO FASTEN NECKLACE**) LOCKET
(— **UP**) ARISE SHOOT SPROUT
BURGEON UPSPRING
(**BOILING** —) TUBIG
(**CARRIAGE** —) ROBBIN
(**ERUPTIVE** —) WALM GEYSER
(**FROM A** —) FONTAL
(**GUSHING** —) CHARCO
(**HOT** —) SPRUDEL
(**INTERMITTENT** —) NAILBOURN
(**INTERMITTENT** —S) GIPSIES
GYPSIES
(**LAND** —) LAVANT
(**MECHANICAL** —) RESORT RESSORT
(**MINERAL** —) SPA BALNEARY
(**SALT** —) LICK SALINE
(**WARM** —S) THERMAE
(**WATCH** —) SLEEVE
(PREF.) CREN(O) CROUNO PEGO
(SUFF.) CRENE
SPRING BEAUTY LETTUCE
SPRINGBOARD BATULE TREMPLIN
SPRINGBOK GAZELLE SPRINGER
SPRING CHAPLET JAMMER
SPRINGE TRAP NOOSE SNARE
SPRINGILY BOUNCILY SPONGILY
SPRINGINESS GIVE LIFE
SPRINGING LAUNCH SALIENT
(— **BACK**) RESULT ELASTIC
(— **FROM STEPS**) GRADY
SPRINGLIKE VERNAL
SPRING ORANGE STYRAX
SPRINGTAIL PODURA FURCULA
PODURID SKIPTAIL
SPRINGTIME VER WARE GERMINAL
SPRINGY WHIPPY ELASTIC FLEXIBLE
SPRINKLE ASH DAG DEG BLOW
DAMP DUST SHED SPIT FLASH

SHAKE SPURT WATER BEDROP DABBLE POUNCE SPARGE SPRENT SPRINK SQUIRT ARROUSE ASPERGE ASPERSE DRIZZLE RANTIZE SCATTER SKINKLE SKITTER SPAIRGE SPARKLE SPARPLE SPATTER SPATTLE SPERPLE SPURTLE DISPUNGE INTERSOW SPITTING SPRINGLE STRINKLE
(— IN BAPTISM) RANTIZE
(— OF RAIN) SPIT
(— OF SNOW) SCOWDERING SCOUTHERING
(— SEED) SPRAIN
(— TOBACCO) BLOW
(— WITH FLOUR) DREDGE
(— WITH POWDER) DUST
(— WITH SALT) CORN
(— WITH SAND) SAND
SPRINKLED SEEDED SPRENT
(— OVER) BESPRENT
SPRINKLER SPARGER SPRAYER WATERER DAMPENER STRINKLE
(HOLY WATER —) HYSSOP
SPRINKLES JIMMIES
SPRINKLING SEME LACING SPARGE STRANK RANTISM STIPPLE STOURING
(— OF PEOPLE) SALT
SPRINT DASH RACE BICKER SPRENT SPRUNT
SPRITE ELF HOB IMP PUG PIXY PUCK ARIEL BUCCA DOBBY FAIRY HOLDA PIXIE GOBLIN PILWIZ SPIRIT SPOORN UMBRIEL COLTPIXY GLAISTIG WATERMAN
(WATER —) NIX NECK NIXIE NICKER
SPRITELY WIMBLE
SPROCKET WHELP
SPROUT BUD LAD PUT BROD CHIT CHUN CION DRAW TOOT CATCH CHICK SCUTE SHOOT SPEAR SPIRE SPRIT SPURT BRAIRD GERMEN RATOON SIRING STOVEN TELLER TILLER BURGEON COPPICE SPURTER TENDRON BOURGEON PULLULATE
(— OF BARLEY) TAIL
(FIRST —S) BREER BRAIRD BREIRD
(STUMP —) TILLER
(PREF.) BLAST(O) CLAD(O) CYM(I)(O)
(SUFF.) BLAST(IC)(Y) CLADOUS SPERM(A)(AE)(AL)(IA)(IC)(OUS)(UM)(Y)
SPRUCE GIM DEFT JIMP NEAT POSH SMUG SPRY TRIG TRIM BRISK COMPT CRISP DINKY FRESH JEMMY JIMMY NATTY NIFTY SLICK SMART SMIRK SPIFF SPRIG DAPPER PICKED FOPPISH SMARTEN SMICKER SPRUNNY EPINETTE SPIFFING TITIVATE
(KIND OF —) SITKA
(TRIMMED —) LOBSTICK

SPRUE RUNNER PSILOSIS
SPRUER GATER
SPRY AGILE BRISK QUICK NIMBLE BOBBISH
SPUD SPADE TATER BARKER PADDLE POTATO WEEDER SPUDDER
SPUME EST BEES FOAM FROTH YEAST
SPUNK GUTS GETUP PLUCK SPRAWL SMEDDUM GUMPTION
SPUNKY GAME GUTSY
SPUR ARM GAD GIG EDGE GAFF GOAD KNAG MOVE STUD TANG ARETE DRIVE PRICK PRONG ROWEL SPICA SPURN BROACH CALCAR DIGGER EXCITE FILLIP FOMENT GAFFLE GRIFFE INCITE MOTIVE OFFSET RIPPON SICKLE SPERON WEAPON BICYCLE GABLOCK INCITER LORMERY SCRATCH COCKSPUR GAVELOCK
(— OF BIRDS) SPICA
(— OF COCK) HEEL
(— OF GAMECOCK) GAFF
(— ON HORSESHOE) CALK
(—S OF COCK) WEAPON
(— TO ACTION) GOOSE
(PART OF —) BAND CHAIN ROWEL BUTTON
(PREF.) CALCARI
SPURGE BALSAM INTISY RICINUS SUNWEED CATEPUCE DOVEWEED FLUXWEED MILKBUSH MILKWEED TITHYMAL WARTWEED WARTWORT POINSETTIA
SPURIOUS BAD DOG TIN FAKE SHAM BOGUS FUNNY PHONY QUEER SHICE SNIDE NOTHAL PSEUDO BASTARD NOTHOUS POSTICHE PINCHBECK SYNDIETIC
(PREF.) NOTH(O) PSEUD(O)
SPURN FOOT TACK REPEL SCORN REFUSE REJECT CONSPUE CONTEMN DECLINE DESPISE DISDAIN
SPURRY YARR FRANK COWQUAKE SANDWEED
SPURT JET GILP GIRD GOUT JAUP SPAR SPIN BURST CHIRT FLASH PULSE SALLY SPOUT GEYSER RANDOM SPLURT SPRING SPROUT SQUIRT SPATTER
SPUTTER SPIT FIZZLE SOTTER SPATTER SPLUTTER
SPUTUM SPIT
SPY FLY PRY ESPY MOLE NARK NOSE STAG TOOT TOUT WAIT WORM AGENT CALEB LOWER NINJA PERDU PLANT SCOUT SNEAP SPIAL SPION SPOOK WATCH BEAGLE BEHOLD DESCRY GAYCAT MOUTON PEEPER PERDUE SEARCH SHADOW SPIRAL TOUTER WAITER EXAMINE LURCHER

SPY OTACUST SMELLER SPOTTER
WATCHER DISCOVER EMISSARY
HIRCARRA MOUCHARD
(— ON RACEHORSES) TOUT
(— UPON) LAY
(AUTHOR OF —) COOPER
(BIBLICAL —) CALEB
(CHARACTER IN —) JACK BIRCH
HENRY SARAH CAESAR HARPER
HARVEY LAWTON PEYTON FRANCES
WHARTON ISABELLA JEANETTE
THOMPSON DUNWOODIE
SINGLETON WELLEMERE
(PLANTED —) STOOGE
(POLICE —) SETTER
SPYBOAT VEDET VEDETTE
SQUAB PIPER SQUABBY SQUEAKER
SQUEALER SQUILGEE
SQUABBLE MUSS TIFF BRAWL
SCRAP BICKER HASSLE JANGLE
SQUALL BOBBERY BRABBLE
BRANGLE CONTEND PRABBLE
QUARREL SWABBLE
SQUAD CREW DECURY TWENTY
PLATOON
(— OF DETECTIVES) HOMICIDE
SQUADRON BLUE SOTNIA
SQUADER
(— OF AIRCRAFT) ESCADRILLE
(CAVALRY —) RESSALAH
(THREE —S) WING
SQUALID DINGY DIRTY MANGY
NASTY SEEDY FILTHY FROWZY
SCUZZY SHODDY SLEAZO SLEAZY
SORDID SCABROUS SLOTTERY
SQUALL DROW FRET GUST MEWL
ROAR SCAT WAUL BARAT FRESH
PERRY SKELP BAYAMO FLURRY
SQUAWK BORASCA SUMATRA
TORNADO BLIZZARD BORASQUE
CHUBASCO
SQUALOR DIRT
SQUAMA ALULA TEGULA
SQUANDER SOT BLOW BLUE BURN
GAME LASH WARE SPEND SPILL
SPORT WASTE BEZZLE LAVISH
MAFFLE MUDDLE PADDLE PALTER
PERISH PLUNGE TIPPLE BRANGLE
CONSUME DEBAUCH DEBOISE
DISPEND PROFUSE SCAMBLE
SCATTER SKITTLE SLATHER
SWATTER EMBEZZLE MISSPEND
SQUATTER
SQUANDERER PRODIGAL
SQUANDERING WASTEFUL
(UNRESTRAINED —) RIOT
SQUARE FIX EDGE EVEN FOUR FULL
LAME NERD NURD POST QUAD SUIT
AGREE CHECK CROSS FRAME HUNKY
NERDY PLACE PLAIN PLAZA SUPER
BLOCKY DINKUM ISAGON MICKEY
PIAZZA QUARRY ZENZIC ZOCALO
CARREAU CHECKER COMMONS

EMERALD UPRIGHT QUADRANT
QUADRATE SQUADRON TETRAGON
(— A STONE) PITCH
(— FOR BOWLING SCORE) FRAME
(— OF CANVAS) SKATE
(— OF CLOTH) PANE
(— OF DOUGH) KNISH
(— OFF) BUTT
(— OF FRAMING) PAN
(— OF GLASS) QUARREL
(— OF LINEN) PALL
(— OF TARTAN) SET SETT
(— OF TURF) DIVOT QUADREL
(— ON BILLIARD TABLE) CROTCH
(— ON CHESSBOARD) HOUSE POINT
(BUILDINGS FORMING —) INSULA
(CARPENTER'S —) NORMA MITER
(CENTER — IN GAME) TAC
(CHURCH —) PARVIS
(FROM — ONE) ANEW
(KIND OF —) PUNNETT
(LINEN —) SUDARIUM
(NOT —) HEP HIP
(ONE-MILE —) SECTION
(PATTERN OF —S) DAMIER
(WOVEN —) SINKER
(PREF.) QUADR(ATO)(I)(U)
SQUARED HEWN QUARTO SQUARE
SQUARE DANCE TUCKER
SQUARE-DEALING WHITE
SQUARELY BUNG FAIR FULL FLUSH
SPANG FAIRLY DIRECTLY SMACKDAB
(— AND SHARPLY) SMACK
SQUARISH BOXY
SQUASH PEPO QUAT GOURD SQUAB
CASHAW CUCURB CUSHAW
MARROW SIMNEL SQUISH SQUOSH
TURBAN CYMLING HUBBARD
PUMPKIN CUCURBIT CYMBLING
PEPONIUM ZUCCHINI
SQUASH BUG STINKBUG
SQUASHY SWASHY SQUUSHY
SQUAT QUAT RUCK STUB SWAT
SWOT COWER DUMPY FUBSY
HUNCH PUDGY SQUAB FODGEL
HUNKER HURKLE QUATCH STOCKY
STUBBY SQUATTY TAPPISH
SQUATTLE THICKSET
SQUATINA RHINA
SQUATTER NESTER BYWONER
SQUAW JACK WEBB HOUND WENCH
MAHALA SQUARK
SQUAWBUSH SHOVAL
SQUAWFISH CHUB BOXHEAD
BIGMOUTH CHAPPAUL
SQUAWK SCRAWK SQUALL SQUARK
SQUAWL COMPLAIN
SQUAWROOT CLAPWORT ELOTILLO
SQUEAK GIKE PEEP WEAK CHEEP
CHIRK QUEAK SCRAWK SCROOP
SQUEAL
SQUEAKING SCRANNEL
SQUEAKY CREAKY

SQUEAL PIP RAT FINK HOWL SING
SWEEL SCREAK TATTLE WHISTLE
SQUEALER FINK CANARY
SQUEAMISH HELO NICE NAISH
PAWKY PENSY DAINTY DAUNCH
PENCEY QUAINT QUEASY SPICED
TICKLE WAIRCH WAMBLY FINICAL
MAWKISH WEARISH NAUSEOUS
OVERNICE
SQUEAMISHNESS NICETY
DISGUST MALAISE DELICACY
SQUEEZE EKE HUG JAM NIP CLAM
MULL MURE VISE ZEST BIRSE BUNCH
CHIRT CREEM CROWD CRUSH PINCH
PRESS SQUAB SQUAT WRING
GRUDGE QUEASE SCRUMP SCRUZE
SQUASH STRAIN THRIMP THRING
THRONG TWEEZE TWITCH SCRINGE
SCROOGE SCROUGE SCRUNCH
SCRUNGE SQUEEGE SQUINCH
COMPRESS CONTRACT PRESSURE
SHOEHORN THRIMBLE THRUMBLE
(— FROM) SPONGE
(— IN) FUDGE
(— INTO) THRIMBLE
(— MONEY FROM) SWEAT
(— OUT) PINCH STRAIN
(ECONOMIC —) CRUNCH
(PREF.) PRESSI
SQUEEZED STRETTA STRETTO
SQUEEZER REAMER ALLIGATOR
SQUELCH QUELCH SQUASH SQUISH
SQUIDGE SLAPDOWN
SQUELCHER BLIZZARD
SQUETEAGUE DRUM DRUMMER
SQUETEE BLUEFISH CHICKWIT
WEAKFISH
SQUIB MOTT SKIT FILLER EXPLODER
SQUID PLUG CALAMARI CALAMARY
SQUIFFED DRUNK BLOTTO
STONED
SQUIGGLE SCRIGGLE
SQUILL SCILLA SLANGKOP
(PREF.) SCILLI
SQUINT AWRY GLEE GLEG SKEN
SKEW BAGGE GLENT GLEDGE
GOGGLE SHEYLE SKELLY SQUINCH
SQUINNY STRABISM STRABISMUS
SQUINT-EYED GLEE GLEED
SQUINTING LOUCHE
SQUIRE SWAIN DONZEL JUNKER
TIMIAS ARMIGER ESQUIRE SQUIRET
YOUNKER HENCHMAN SCUTIGER
SERVITOR SQUARSON SQUIREEN
SQUIRM CURL WIND TWINE WRING
WRITHE WRESTLE WRIGGLE
SCRIGGLE SQUIGGLE
SQUIRREL BUN CON BUNT LEAD
SCUG BUNNY XERUS BOOMER
CHIPPY GOPHER RODENT TAGUAN
ARDILLA SCHILLU SCIURID
CHIPMUNK EGGEATER GRAYBACK
JELERANG RATATOSK CHICKAREE

(— SKIN) VAIR
(FLYING —) TUAN TAGUAN
ASSAPAN
(PREF.) SCIURO
SQUIRRELFISH ALAIHI MARIAN
MOJARRA SERRANO SOLDIER
SANDFISH WELSHMAN
SQUIRREL MONKEY TITI SAIMIRI
TAMARIN
SQUIRREL SHREW TANA TUPAIA
PENTAIL
SQUIRT CHIRT SCOOT SKITE SLIRT
SPIRT SPOUT SPURT SQUIB SQUIT
SPLOIT SPRENT SPRITZ SCOOTER
SQUITTER
SRI BWANA SAHIB

SRI LANKA
CAPITAL: COLOMBO
COIN: CENT RUPEE
FORMER NAME: CEYLON
GULF: MANNAR
LANGUAGE: SINHALA
MEASURE: PARA PARAH AMUNAM
PARRAH
POINT: PEDRO
STRAIT: PALK
TOWN: GALLE KANDY JAFFNA
MANNAR MATARA BADULLA
COLOMBO PUTTALAM
TREE: HORA PALU

S-SHAPED
(PREF.) SIGMO SIGMOID(O)
ST.CROIX (NATIVE OF —) CRUZAN
STAB DAB DAG JAB JAG JOB DIRK
GORE PINK POKE PROB SHIV STOB
STOG STUG YERK CHIVE KNIFE
POACH PRICK PRONG STICK STOKE
BROACH DAGGER PIERCE POUNCE
SLIVER STITCH THRUST BAYONET
STAGGER PRICKADO STILETTO
STOCCADO STOCCATA
(— IN MIDBREAST) SLOT
STABBING THORNY JABBING
PUNGENT STICKING
(SUFF.) NYXIS
STABILITY POISE FIXURE BALANCE
SADNESS FIRMNESS SECURITY
CONSTANCY
STABILIZE FIX SET EVEN TRIM POISE
SCHOOL STEADY BALANCE BALLAST
STIFFEN
STABILIZER ACARDITE
STABLE BYRE FAST FIRM SURE
HARAS HEMEL SOLID SOUND STALL
STIFF STOUT TAMBO LINTER LIVERY
SECURE SICKER STATIC STEADY
STRONG STURDY DURABLE
EQUERRY LASTING OXHOUSE
SETTLED SHIPPEN STABILE
BALANCED IMMOBILE RESIDENT
STANDING PERMANENT

(EMOTIONALLY —) TOGETHER
(ROYAL —S) MEWS
(PREF.) MONIMO
STABLEBOY LAD MAFU MAFOO
JACKBOY
STABLEMAN OSTLER HOSTLER
STACCATO TUT SECCO DETACHE
SALTATO RICOCHET SALTANDO
(NOT —) LEGATO TENUTO
STACK COB MOW SOW BIKE DESS
LEET PACK PILE POKE RICK CANCH
CLAMP GOAVE POAKE SCROO
SHOCK STAKE STALK STOCK
COLUMN FUNNEL RICKLE CALENDER
STACKAGE
(— BRICKS) CLAMP SCINTLE
(— IN KILN) BOX
(— LUMBER) STICK
(— OF ARMS) PILE
(— OF BRICK) LIFT
(— OF CERAMICS) BUNG
(— OF CHLOROPHYLL) GRANUM
(— OF CORN) SHOCK
(— OF FISH) BULK
(— OF GRAIN) RICK
(— OF HIDES) BED
(— OF PANS) SWEATER
(— OF SHEETS) BOOK
(HAY OR CORN —) HOVEL
(SMALL —) COB CANCH RICKLE
(TILE —) WELL
STACKER CROWDER PITCHER
STACKMAN
STACKING (— OF AIRCRAFT)
HOLDING
STACKYARD MOWIE MOWHAY
HAGGARD
STADIUM BOWL DOME STADE
STAGE FURLONG STADION
COLISEUM
(PRIVATE SEATS IN —) SKYBOX
(ROOFED —) DOME
STAFF MAN PIN ROD TAU TAW CANE
CLUB KENT LIMB MACE MALL MAUL
PIKE POLE RUNG TREE VARE YARD
BATON CROOK CROSS KEVEL NIBBY
PEDUM PERCH STAVE STICK SUITE
VERGE BASTON CADUCE CEPTER
CLEEKY CROCHE CRUTCH FAMILY
FERULE GROUND LITUUS MULETA
POTENT PRITCH RADIUS RISSLE
TAIAHA THYRSE WARDER BACULUS
BOURDON CAMBUCA CROSIER
CRUMMIE DISTAFF FESTUCA
PALSTER SCEPTER SCEPTRE
STADDLE THYRSUS CADUCEUS
CRUMMOCK PARTISAN PASTORAL
PLOWFOOT TIPSTAFF
(— AT END OF NET) BRAIL
(— OF AUTHORITY) VARE VERGE
(— OF COOKS) BOUCHE
(— OF OFFICIALS) OMLAH
(— WITH CROSSPIECE) POTENT

(BISHOP'S —) BAGLE BACULUS
CROSIER CROZIER PASTORAL
(FIELD MARSHAL'S —) BATON
(FORKED —) LINSTOCK
(GRADUATED —) LIMB
(HOTTENTOT —) KIRVI
(MAGICIAN'S —) RHABDOS
(NEWSPAPER —) DAYSIDE
(NUBIAN —) KURRI
(PILGRIM'S —) BURDEN
(PLASTERER'S —) BEATER
(SHEPHERD'S —) KENT CROOK
(SPARTAN —) SCYTALE
(TEACHING —) FACULTY
(THIEVES' —) FILCH
(PREF.) LITUI SCEPTRO
STAG HART ROYAL SPADE STAIG
WAPITI BULLOCK KNOBBER POINTER
KNOBBLER
(— OF THE 3D YEAR) SPIRE
(— OF 2ND YEAR) BROCKET
(— OF 8 YEARS OR MORE) ROYAL
(— THAT HAS CAST HIS ANTLERS)
POLLARD
(DEAD —) MORT
(HORNLESS —) HUMMEL
(TURNED TO —) ACTAEON
(12-POINT —) ROYAL
(3-YEAR OLD —) SPADE
(PREF.) ELAPH(O)
STAG BEETLE LUCANID
STAGE LEG BANK GEST POST STEP
TREK APRON DUMMY ETAGE FLAKE
GRADE PEGME PHASE POINT SCENE
STAIR STATE BOARDS DEGREE
HEMMEL PERIOD PHASIS STRIDE
CATASTA MANSION ROSTRUM
STADIUM INSTANCE PLATFORM
SCAFFOLD PROSCENIUM
(— DIRECTION) EXIT ENTER SOLUS
(— FOR DRYING FISH) FLAKE
(— FOR HAY) HEMMEL
(— IN DELIRIUM) TILMUS
(— IN FEVER) FLUSH
(— IN PORCELAIN FURNACE)
HOWELL
(— IN TRAVELING) GEST
(— MANAGER) REGISSEUR
(— OF CUPOLA) LANTERN
(— OF DEVELOPMENT) ERA
BLOSSOM
(— OF FUNGUS) OIDIUM
(— OF GLACIATION) RISS WURM
ACHEN MINDEL
(— OF INSECT) INSTAR
(— OF LIFE) AGE ASRAMA ASHRAMA
(— OF MITOSIS) ANAPHASE
PROPHASE
(— OF PERSONALITY) LATENCY
(— OF ROCKET) BOOSTER
(— OF THEATER) SCAENA THEATRON
(— WHERE SLAVES WERE SOLD)
CATASTA

(BOTTOMMOST —) CELLAR
(COMIC —) SOCK
(EARLIEST —) PRIME
(FINAL —) CLOSE FINISH STRETCH
(FIRST —) YOUTH SPRING
(FLOATING —) DUMMY
(FLOOD —) CREST
(GEOLOGICAL —) GUNZ GLACIAL
SENONIAN
(GLACIATION —) WURM
(INITIAL —) INFANCY
(LANDING —) STAIR BRIDGE STAITH
STELLING
(MOVING —) PEGMA PEGME
(PART OF —) FLY ARCH DROP FLAT
WING APRON DRAPE BATTEN
BORDER BRIDGE CENTER RETURN
TEASER CURTAIN ENTRANCE
TORMENTOR PROSCENIUM
(RADIO —) STEP
(THIRD —) AUTUMN
(PREF.) SCENO
STAGECOACH DILLY STAGE
STAGEHAND GRIP DAYMAN GAFFER
STAGER SOAKER
STAGGER REEL ROLL STOT DAVER
DODGE HODGE LURCH PITCH STITE
STOIT DACKER DAIDLE FALTER
GOGGLE STAVER STIVER SWAVER
TOTTER WALTER WAMBLE WELTER
WIGGLE WINTLE MEGRIMS STACHER
STACKER STAMMER STOITER
STOTTER STUMBLE SWAGGER
VANDYKE WAUCHLE TITUBATE
(— BACK) RECOIL
STAGGERBUSH LAMBKILL
STAGGERED STURTAN STURTIN
STAGGERING AREEL
STAGGERS DUNT GOGGLES
MEGRIMS STAVERS VERTIGO
STAGHEAD SPIKETOP
STAGING STAGE CRIPPLE DERRICK
HURRIES
STAGNANCY STASIS
STAGNANT DEAD DULL INERT STILL
STATIC COBWEBBY SLUGGISH
STAGNATE STANDING
STAGNATION STASIS TORPOR
LANGUOR
STAID SET CIVIL GRAVE SOBER
DEMURE STEADY EARNEST SERIOUS
DECOROUS
STAIN DYE LIT WEM BLOT BLUR BUFF
DIRT DRAB FILE FOIL HURT MEAL
MOLE RUST SCAM SLUR SMAD SMIT
SMUT SOIL SPOT TASH BLACK
BLEND BRAND CLOUD DIRTY HATCH
PAINT PLECK SMEAR SPECK SULLY
TACHE TAINT TINGE WEMMY BREATH
GIEMSA IMBRUE INFAMY INFECT
MACULA SMIRCH SMUDGE SMUTCH
SPLASH STIGMA SUDDLE ATTAINT
BESTAIN BLEMISH DEPAINT DISTAIN

SLUBBER SOILURE SPATTER
SPLOTCH STADDLE TARNISH
BESMIRCH CARMALUM DISCOLOR
DISGRACE DISHONOR FLYSPECK
MACULATE PYRONINE TAINTURE
(— BLACK) EBONIZE
(— IN LINEN) MELL
(— ON BRICK) SCUMMING
(— WITH BLOOD) ENGORE
(PREF.) MACUL(I)(O) SPIL(O)
STAINED FOXY RUSTY SMUDGY
BLOTCHY SMUTCHY
(— BY DECAY) DOATY
(— WITH BLOOD) BLOODY IMBRUED
STAINED GLASS VITRAIL
STAINER TRACER
STAINLESS PURE CHASTE
INNOCENT
STAIR STY GREE RUNG STEP DEGREE
COCHLEA ESCALIER
(LANDING —) GHAT GHAUT
(MINING —) LOB
(WINDING —) VICE VISE CARACOL
CARACOLE TURNPIKE
(PL.) PAIR PITCH FLIGHT DANCERS
ESCALIER
STAIRCASE SCALE ESCALIER
(PART OF —) MOLD POST RAIL
NEWEL RISER TREAD NOSING
LANDING BALUSTER BANISTER
HANDRAIL BALUSTRADE
(SHIP'S —) COMPANIONWAY
(SPIRAL —) SPIRAL CARACOLE
STAIRWAY STOOP GREESE PERRON
DESCENT ESCALIER
(— ON RIVER BANK) GHAT
(CURVED —) SWEEP
(SHIP'S —) LADDER
(WINDING —) VICE TURNPIKE
STAITH TIP
STAKE BET HOB LAY SET TAW VIE
WAD WED ANTE BENT GAGE MAIN
PALE PAWN PEEL POOL PUNT RISK
STAB STOB TREE WAGE PITCH SPILE
SPOKE SPRAG STOCK STOOP STOUR
WAGER BAIKIE CAULIS CHANCE
CORNER CROTCH ENGAGE GAMBLE
HAZARD IMPONE LOGGAT LOGGET
PALING PICKET STOWER TRUNCH
WEDFEE STOATER STUCKEN
VENTURE INTEREST PALISADE
PEASTICK STUCKING
(— HIGHER) REVIE
(— IN PRIMERO) REST
(— SUPPORTING FOUNDATION) PILE
(CART —) RUNG
(COMPULSORY — IN POKER) BLIND
(GAMBLING —) BET MISE WAGER
(POINTED —) SOULE SOWEL PICKET
(SURVEYORS' —) HUB
(TETHERING —) PUTTO
(TINSMITH'S —) TEEST
(PL.) POOL JACKPOT

STAKE-SHAPED SUDIFORM
STALACE COLUMELLA
STALE OLD COLD FLAT HOAR PALL
SICK WORN BLOWN DATED DUSTY
FROWY HOARY MOLDY MUSTY
RAFTY SANDY TRITE FROWZY
MOULDY STUFFY EXOLETE
FROUGHY INSIPID OVERWORN ·
STAGNANT TIMEWORN
(DAMP AND —) WAUGH
STALEMATE PATT STALE
STALK BUN RAY CORN HAFT MOTE
POLE RISP STAM STEG STEM TIGE
QUILL SCAPE SHANK SPEAR SPIRE
STAKE STALE STEAL STIPE STUMP
WRIDE COULIS RATOON STIPES
CASTOCK FUNICLE PEDICEL PETIOLE
SPINDLE CAUDICLE FILAMENT
PEDUNCLE PODETIUM STALKLET
STERIGMA PETIOLULE
(— OF BUCKWHEAT) STRAW
(— OF CRINOID) COLUMN
(— OF GRAIN) RESSUM RIZZOM
(— OF GRASS) BENT SPEAR
(— OF HAY) RISP
(— OF MOSS CAPSULE) SETA
(— OF OVULE) FUNICLE
(— OF PLANT) SPINDLE TENACLE
(— OF SPORE) STERIGMA
(— OF SPOROGONIUM) SETA
(— OF STAMEN) FILAMENT
(— OF SUGAR CANE) RATOON
(— OF UMBEL) RAY
(—S OF GRAIN) KARBI STRAW
(CABBAGE —) CASTOCK
(CROSSBOW —) TILLER
(DRY —) KEX KECK BENNET
(FLOWER —) SCAPE
(HOLLOW —) BUN KEX KECK
(PL.) HAULM STRAW WRIDE IWAIWA
(PREF.) CAUL(I)(O) CULMI
STALKLESS SESSILE
STALKY AND COMPANY
(AUTHOR OF —) KIPLING
(CHARACTER IN —) JOHN MTURK
ARTHUR BEETLE STALKY CORKRAN
GILBERT
STALL BAY BIN BOX CUB PEW BULK
CRIB SPAR STAW BOOSE BOOSY
BOOTH CRAME PITCH STAND STASH
CARCER CARREL STANCE TRAVIS
WICKET BALAGAN CABINET
SHAMBLE SHIPPEN BUTCHERY
STANDING TRAVERSE
(— FOR TIME) HAVER STRETCH
(— IN CLOISTER) CAROL
(— IN COAL MINE) BREAST WICKET
(— IN MUD) STOG
(— IN ROMAN CIRCUS) CARCER
(BISHOP'S —) TRIBUNE
(CHURCH —) PEW
(THEATER —) LOGE FAUTEUIL
STALLED STOODED

STALLION SIRE STAG STUD ENTRE
HORSE COOSER CUSSER ENTIRE
CUISSER STALLAND STONEHORSE
STALWART RUDE STARK STIFF
WIGHT STRONG STURDY BUIRDLY
VALIANT
STAMEN TAMIN STAMMEL
(PART OF —) ANTHER
(PL.) ANDROECIUM
(PREF.) ANDR(O)
(SUFF.) STEMONOUS
STAMINA GUTS SAND BOTTOM
STAMMER FAM HACK MANT STOT
STUT GANCH WLAFF FAFFLE FALTER
FAMBLE HACKER HAFFLE HAMMER
HOCKER HOTTER MAFFLE MAMMER
YAMMER FRIBBLE STUMBLE
STUTTER HESITATE SPLUTTER
TITUBATE
STAMMERING HACK PSELLISM
TRAULISM BALBUTIES
STAMP DIE CHOP COIL DRUB FAKE
MARK NIXY PAUT POSS RUFF SEAL
SNAP TYPE APPEL BLOCK DOLLY
ERROR FRANK LABEL LOCAL NIXIE
PRINT PUNCH STOCK STOMP STUNT
TENOR TOUCH WRITE ACCENT
CACHET CLICHE DOCKER FULLER
INCUSE INCUTE INDENT LOCKUP
PASTER POUNCE SCRIBE SHAPER
SIGNET STRAMP STRIKE CARRIER
CHARACT EDITION IMPRESS IMPRINT
MINTAGE POUNDER REPRINT
SEEBECK SPECIAL SQUELCH
STICKER TAXPAID WRAPPER
HALLMARK ORIGINAL PRESSURE
PUNCHEON
(— AFTER ASSAY) TOUCH
(— BOOK COVER) BLIND
(— FOR CUTTING DOUGH) DOCKER
(— HERRING BARREL) DUNT
(— HIDES) STOCK
(— HOLES) STOACH
(— OUT) SCOTCH
(— WITH DIE) DINK
(BOOKBINDING —) BLOCK FILLET
(CANCELLING —) KILLER
(HALF OF —) BISECT
(HAND —) CANCELER
(OFFICIAL —) CHOP
(POSTAGE —) AIR DUE CAPE FAKE
HEAD ERROR LABEL LOCAL BUREAU
INVERT AIRMAIL BICOLOR CHARITY
CLASSIC REPRINT STICKER ADHESIVE
COLONIAL ORIGINAL SPECIMEN
PRECANCEL
(REVENUE —) FISCAL TAXPAID
(RUBBER —) YESMAN
(SMART —) APPEL
(PL.) MIXTURE KILOWARE
(PREF.) TIMBRO
STAMP-COLLECTING PHILATELY
TIMBROLOGY

STAMPEDE RUSH BLITZ CHUTE
DEBACLE STAMPEDO
STAMPER FANCIER STOMPER
STAMPING TITLING
STANCE STATION STANDING
(— OF GOLFER) ADDRESS
(— OF HORSE) GATHER
STANCH FIRM STEM STIFF STOUT
HEARTY TRUSTY STAUNCH FAITHFUL
RESOLUTE
STANCHION BAIL PITON CROTCH
CRUTCH STENCIL STANCHEL
STANCHER
STAND GO JIB SET BANK BEAR BIER
DESK HALT RACK RANK REST STAY
STEL ZARF BIPOD BLOCK ERECT
FRAME FRONT KIOSK STALL STICK
STONE STOOL CASTER COLORS
ENDURE HASTER INSIST PATTEN
PILLAR SMOKER STANCE STANZA
STOUND STRIKE TEAPOY TRIPOD
TRIVET CONSIST DIOPTER EPERGNE
FOURBLE LECTERN STATION
TABORET TRESTLE TROLLEY
ATTITUDE BLEACHER COATRACK
CROWFOOT FRIPPERY GUERIDON
HASTENER INKSTAND POSITION
SCAFFOLD STALLAGE STANDING
STANDISH STILLAGE STILLING
STILLION
(— AS SPONSOR) FANG HEAVE
CHRISTEN
(— AT AN ANGLE) CATER
(— AT ATTENTION) BACK
(— BACK) BACCARE BACKARE
(— BEFORE A FIRE) FOOTMAN
(— BEHIND) COVER
(— BY) SERVE STICKTO
(— CLOSE) CROWD ENVIRON
(— DRINKS) SHOUT TREAT
(— ERECT) ROUSE
(— FAST) SUBSIST
(— FASTENED TO MESS TABLE)
CROWFOOT
(— FIRM) STAY
(— FOR) MEAN DENOTE
(— FOR AUCTIONING) BLOCK
(— FOR BARRELS) JIB THRALL
(— FOR COFFIN) BIER
(— FOR COMPASS) BINNACLE
(— FOR CONFINING HEAT) HASTER
HASTENER
(— FOR DRESSES) FRIPPERY
(— FOR DRILL PIPE) FOURBLE
(— FOR FINJAN) ZARF
(— FOR TILES) CRISS
(— FOR WRITING MATERIALS)
STANDISH
(— GUARD) COVER
(— IDLY) LOAF
(— IN AWE) FEAR
(— OFF) AROINT
(— OF FOREST) GROWTH

(— OF PLANTS) STOOL
(— ON AND OFF SHORE) BUSK
(— ON END) STARE UPEND
(— ON HIGH) TOWER
(— ON TWO FEET) BIPOD DUOPOD
(— OUT) CUT TOOT FLAUNT
(— READY) ABIDE
(— STIFFLY) STRUT
(— STILL) HO HOO HALT STAY
(— TO SHOOT) ADDRESS
(— TREAT) MUG SHOUT
(— UNMOVING) FREEZE
(— UNSTEADILY) STAGGER
(— UP) RARE
(— UP FOR) STICKLE
(— UP STIFF) STIVER
(— UP TO) CONFRONT
(— WITH LEGS APART) STRIDE
(BRANCHING —) TREE
(CAKE —) CURATE
(CHEMICAL —) RINGSTAND
(CONCESSION —) JOINT
(FIRECLAY —) CRANK
(HEARTH —) FOOTMAN
(ONE-NIGHT —) GIG
(PRINTER'S —) BANK FRAME
(PULPIT-LIKE —) AMBO
(RAISED —) PERGOLA
(REVOLVING —) KLINOSTAT
(SCULPTOR'S —) CHASSIS
(SHOOTING —) BUTT
(THREE-LEGGED —) TRIVET
STANDARD PAR ALEM DICK FIAR
FLAG GAGE IDEA MARK NORM
SIGN TEST TOUG ALLOY BOGEY
CANON CHECK DOLLY DRAKE
EAGLE GAUGE IDEAL JEDGE MODEL
NORMA SCALE STAND STOOL
AQUILA ASSIZE BANNER CORNET
DOLLIE FILLER NORMAL SOCKET
SQUARE STAPLE TIPONI TRIPOD
VIOLLE ANCIENT CLASSIC
DECORUM DRAPEAU LABARUM
MODULUS STANDER BRATTACH
GONFALON MOUNTING ORIFLAMB
ORTHODOX VEXILLUM
(— IN GATE) STRIKE
(— OF ACCURACY) COCKER
(— OF CONDUCT) LINE GNOMON
(— OF PERFECTION) IDEAL
(— OF PERFORMANCE) BOGY BOGEY
BOGIE
(— OF PITCH) DIAPASON
(— OF QUALITY) GRADE
(—S OF BEHAVIOR) ETHICS
(CONVENTIONAL —) PIETY
(LIGHT —) CARCEL
(NOT —) BASTARD
(TURKISH —) ALEM TOUG
(PL.) LIGHTS HOLSTERS
STANDARD-BEARER CORNET
ENSIGN ALFEREZ ANCIENT STALLER
SIGNIFER STANDARD VEXILLARY

STANDARDIZE FORDIZE MACHINE
CALIBRATE
STANDEL STORER
STAND-IN SUB STUNTMAN
STANDING RANK BEING ERECT
STATE CREDIT ESTEEM REGULAR
RESPECT PRESTIGE STAGNANT
PERPENDICULAR
(— ALONE) SEPARATE
(— BY ITSELF) ABSOLUTE DETACHED
(— ERECT) HORRENT
(— FIRM) STABLE
(— INCOORDINATION) ASTASIA
(— IN PROFILE) RAMPANT
(— ON STEPS) DEGRADED
(— OUT) BOLD PROUD EXTANT
RELIEF SALIENT PROMINENT
(— OUT CLEARLY) EMINENT
(— POSITION) OFFHAND
(— UPRIGHT) STANDARD
(HIGH —) RANK WORSHIP POSITION
(MODE OF —) STANCE
(SOCIAL —) LEVEL ESTATE FASHION
STATION
(PREF.) STAT(O)
(— IN SECOND PLACE BEYOND) DVI
EKA
(SUFF.) STASIA STASIS STAT STATIC
STATICS
STANDPATTISM TORYISM
STANDPOINT STANCE
STANDSTILL JIB SET HALT REST
STAY STAND STANCE
STANZA CALL RANN ENVOI ENVOY
STAFF STAND STAVE VERSE BASTON
DIXAIN DIZAIN OCTAVE SEPTET
SESTET SEXTET SIXAIN STANCE
STANZO HUITAIN SESTINA SEXTAIN
STROPHE TRIOLET TROILUS
CINQUAIN OCTONARY QUATRAIN
QUINTAIN RISPETTO SETTAINE
TRISTICH TROPARION
(SUFF.) STICH
STAPES STIRRUP
STAPLE LOOP FLOSS STITCH
SHACKLE STEEPLE VERVELLE
(PL.) BROKES
STAR COR SUN BEID FIRE LAMP
ASTER COMES DWARF EXCEL GIANT
MOLET RISHI SHINE STARN ALNATH
ASTRAL BINARY COUPLE DOUBLE
ETOILE LUCIDA MULLET NITHAM
SHINER SPHERE STELLA BENEFIC
DINGBAT ESTOILE GEMINID STARLET
STARNIE ASTERISK ASTEROID
HEXAGRAM MALEFICE PENTACLE
SUBDWARF SUBGIANT VARIABLE
(COMPANION —) COMES
(DOG —) ASTA SEPT SOPT TOTO
SEPTI LASSIE SIRIUS RINTINTIN
(EVENING —) VENUS HESPER
VESPER EVESTAR HESPERUS
(FEATHER —) COMATULA

(FILM —) VEDETTE
(FUTURE —) COMER
(GUIDING —) LOADSTAR LODESTAR
(KIND OF —) BETA
(MORNING —) VENUS DAYSTAR
PHOSPHOR
(NEW —) NOVA
(OFFICER'S —) PIP
(OF THE —S) SIDEREAL
(PULSATING —) CEPHEID
(RED —) ANTARES
(SHOOTING —) BOLIDE LEONID
METEOR COWSLIP SHOOTER
(SPECIFIC —) YED ADIB ALYA ATIK
CAPH ENIF ENIR IZAR KIED MAIA
NAOS PHAD SADR VEGA WEGA
ACRAB ACRUX AGENA ALCOR
ALGOL ALKES ANCHA ARNEB CHARA
DABIH DELTA DENEB DUBHE GIEDI
GUIAM GUYAM HAMAL HAMUL
JUGUM MERAK MIZAR NIBAL NIHAI
PHACD PHAET RIGEL SAIPH SPICA
TEJAT WASAT WEZEN ZOSMA
ADHARA ALHENA ALIOTH ALKAID
ALMACH ALTAIR ALUDRA APOLLO
ARIDED CASTOR CELENO CHELEB
DIPHDA ELNATH ETAMIN GIENAH
HYADES KOCHAB LESUTH MAASYM
MARKAB MARKEB MARSIC MEGREZ
MENKAR MENKIB MEROPE MIRACH
MIRFAK MIRZAM NEKKAR PHECDA
POLLUX PROPUS RANICH SCHEAT
SHEDIR SIRIUS THABIT THUBAN
ACUBENS ALBIREO ALCHIBA
ALCYONE ALGENIB ALGIEBA
ALGORAH ALMAACK ALNILAM
ALNITAK ALPHARD ALPHIRK ALSHAIN
ANTARES AZIMECH BUNGULA
CANOPUS CAPELLA ELECTRA
GIANSAR GOMELZA GRUMIUM
MEBSUTA MELUCTA MENCHIB
MINTAKA MUFRIDE POLARIS
PROCYON REGULUS ROTANIM
RUCHBAR SCHEDAR SEGINUS
SHELLAK STEROPE TARAZED
TAYGETA TEGMINE THEENIM
ACHERNAR ALPHECCA ARCTURUS
ASTERION DENEBOLA GRAFFIAS
HERCULES MULIPHEN PRAESEPE
SCALOOIN SCHEMALI SHERATAN
(THREE —S) KIDS ELLWAND
TRIANGLE
(7 —S OF GREAT BEAR) CAR
(PREF.) ASTER(O) ASTR(I)(O) SIDERO
STELLI
(SUFF.) ASTER ID
STAR APPLE CAIMITO
STARCH AMYL ARUM SAGO STIFF
TIKOR AMYDON AMYLUM CONJEE
FARINA FECULA CASSAVA CURCUMA
FAECULA MARANTA TALIPOT
AMIDULIN DRESSING FIXATURE
GLUCOSAN

(— IN SOLUTION) AMIDIN
(ANIMAL —) GLYCOGEN
(PREF.) AMYL(!)(O)
STARCHED FORMAL
STARE EYE BORE DARE GAPE GAUM
GAUP GAWK GAWP GAZE GOVE
GYPE KIKE LOOK PORE GLARE GLORE
GLOWER GOGGLE EYEBALL
(— DOWN) OUTFACE
(— IDLY) GOVE GOAVE
(— IMPERTINENTLY) OGLE
(— VACANTLY) GOWK
(COLD —) FISHEYE
STARFISH PAD STAR ASTERID
RADIATE ASTEROID OPHIURAN
(PART OF —) ARM ANUS DISC SPINE
EYESPOT TENTACLE MADREPORITE
STARFLOWER ASTER
STAR FRUIT CARAMBOLA
STARING STEEP ASTARE GOGGLE
GOOGLY HAGGARD
STAR JELLY STARSHOT
STARK BUCK CARK FAIR HARD CRUDE
HARSH NAKED STIFF STARCH
DESOLATE METALLIC
STARLIKE ASTRAL SPHERY
STARLING SALI STARE BEAVER
PASTOR TILYER SPREEUW STARNEL
STAYNIL CHEPSTER CUTWATER
SHEPSTER
STARRED LIZARD HARDIM
STARRING FEATURED
STARRY ASTRAL STARNY STELLED
SIDEREAL
STAR SAPPHIRE ASTERIA ASTRION
ASTROITE
STAR-SHAPED ASTROID
START DIG SET BOLT BOUN DART
DASH HEAD JERK JUMP OPEN TURN
WHIP ARISE BEGIN BIRTH BRAID
BREAK BUDGE ENTER FLIRT GLENT
ONSET RAISE ROUSE STORT THROW
ABRADE BOGGLE BROACH FLINCH
INTEND OFFSET OUTSET SETOFF
SETOUT STRIKE TEEOFF TWITCH
GETAWAY OPENERS OPENING
STARTLE SUNRISE COMMENCE
CONCEIVE INCHOATE OUTSTART
(— A HORSE) WINCE
(— ASIDE) SHY SKIT DODGE
(— A TRIP) EMBARK
(— BACK) RECOIL RESILE
(— BURNING) SPIT KINDLE
(— FERMENTATION) PITCH
(— OF BIRD'S FLIGHT) SOUSE
(— OF FLIGHT) HOPOFF TAKEOFF
(— OF PLAY) ACTONE SCENE1
(— OUT) FRAME INTEND
(— SUDDENLY) SPRING
(— UP) JUMP ASTART ASTERT
(— WITH FEAR) STURT
(FROM THE —) ABOVO
(SUDDEN —) SHY SQUIRT

STARTER KOJI OPENER
(BUNG —) FLOGGER
STAR THISTLE CALTROP CALTHROP
STARTING INCOMING
STARTLE JAR SOHO ALARM SCARE
SHOCK START STURT AFFRAY
BOGGLE BOOGER FRIGHT FRIGHTEN
SURPRISE
STARTLING LURID ALARMING
SHOCKING
STARVATION LACK PINE FAMINE
STARVE CLEM FAST FAMINE FAMISH
AFFAMISH
STARVED MEAGER MEAGRE
STARVEN
STARVED-LOOKING SLINK
STARVELING SHARGAR SHARGER
STARVING CLUNG
STARWORT ASTER ASTROFEL
ASTROPHEL
STASH QUIT STOP HOARD STORE
STATE WU LAY PUT SAY CASE ETAT
MODE NAME POMP PORT TERM TIFF
COVIN ESTER ESTRE POLIS SPEAK
STADE TERMS TUATH WHACK
AFFIRM AGENCY ASSERT ASSURE
CAESAR EFFEIR EMPIRE ESTATE
IMPORT NATION PLIGHT POLICY
POLITY RENDER RIALTY SOVIET
STATUS STEVEN CIVITAS DECLARE
DESERET DUKEDOM ENOUNCE
EXPOUND EXPRESS KINSHIP
PROPOSE SPECIFY STATION TERMINE
CEREMONY DEVACHAN DOMINION
FRANKLIN HEGEMONY INDICATE
KINGSHIP REPUBLIC STATELET
PREDICAMENT
(— EXPLICITLY) DEFINE
(— FIRST) PREMISE
(— FORMALLY) ENOUNCE
(— IN NORTH CAROLINA) FRANKLIN
(— OF AFFAIRS) CASE ARRAY STATUS
(— OF ALARM) GAST FEEZE SCARE
(— OF AMAZEMENT) STOUND
(— OF ANGER) FUME
(— OF APATHY) STUPOR
(— OF BEING) MODE
(— OF BEING CUT) SCISSION
(— OF BEING DRAWN) TRACTION
(— OF BEING OVERFULL) PLETHORA
(— OF BEING POISONOUS) TOXICITY
(— OF BEING WORSE) PEJORITY
(— OF BLISS) NIRVANA
(— OF CONCENTRATION) DHARANA
SAMADHI
(— OF CONFUSION) FOG FLAP HACK
MUSS CHAOS SWIRL HASSLE
HUBBUB FLUMMOX TROYTOWN
(— OF CONSECRATION) IHRAM
(— OF COOPERATION) HOOKUP
(— OF DISASTER) SMASH
(— OF DISORDER) HELL MUSS
FANTAD ANARCHY

(— OF DISSENSION) SCISSION
(— OF DISTRESS) KATZENJAMMER
(— OF DISTURBANCE) GARBOIL
(— OF DOUBT) MIST
(— OF EAGERNESS) HURRY
(— OF ECSTASY) SWOON
(— OF ENCHANTMENT) SPELL
(— OF ENLIGHTENMENT) BODHI
(— OF EQUALITY) PAR
(— OF EXALTATION) FURY ECSTASY
(— OF EXCITATION) FOMENT
(— OF EXCITEMENT) FRY FLAP GALE
HIGH SNIT STEW FEEZE HOIGH
DITHER DOODAH HUBBUB FANTEEG
FLUSTER KIPPAGE SWELTER
FANTIGUE
(— OF EXHAUSTION) GONENESS
(— OF FEAR) FUNK JELLY SCARE
(— OF HAPPINESS) ELYSIUM
PARADISE
(— OF HEALTH) EUCRASIA
(— OF HUMILIATION) DUST
(— OF IDEAL PERFECTION) UTOPIA
(— OF IMPERFECTION) SCARCITY
(— OF INACTION) DEADLOCK
(— OF INCIPIENCE) EMBRYO
(— OF INTENSITY) BUILD
(— OF IRRITABILITY) FUME GALL
FANTAD
(— OF JOY) JUBILEE
(— OF MELANCHOLY) GLOOM
(— OF MENTAL INACTIVITY) TORPOR
(— OF MENTAL READINESS)
ATTITUDE
(— OF MIND) CUE HIP CASE MOOD
HUMOR FETTLE CARAPACE
(— OF MISERY) HELL GEHENNA
(— OF NEGLECT) LIMBO
(— OF OPPOSITION) DEFIANCE
(— OF ORDER) HARMONY
(— OF OSTRACISM) COVENTRY
(— OF PERFECTION) SIDDHI
(— OF PERTURBATION) CRISE
(— OF PREOCCUPATION) CARE
(— OF QUIET) PEACE
(— OF READINESS) GUARD
(— OF REALITY) ACT
(— OF REJECTION) GATE
(— OF REPOSE) KEF CALM
(— OF RETIREMENT) GRASS
(— OF REVERIE) DUMP
(— OF SENSITIVITY) NERVES
(— OF SLUGGISHNESS) COMA
(— OF SUBDIVISION) FINENESS
(— OF SUFFERING) PURGATORY
(— OF SUSPENSE) TRANCE
(— OF SUSPENSION) ABEYANCE
(— OF TENSION) FANTEEG STRETCH
FANTIGUE
(— OF THE SOUL) BARDO
(— OF THINGS) FARE PASS
(— OF TRANQUILLITY) KEF KIF PEACE
(— OF UNCERTAINTY) FOG FLUX

(— OF UNREST) FERMENT
(— OF WEATHER) FREEZE
(— OF WORRY) TEW SWEAT FANTAD
(— POSITIVELY) AFFIRM
(— PRECISELY) FORMATE
(— UNDER OATH) ALLEGE DEPONE
TESTIFY
(AGITATED —) FUSS SNIT STIR
CHURN STORM LATHER SWIVET
(BLISSFUL —) NIRVANA
(BUFFER —) GLACIS
(CHINESE —) WU SHU WEI
(DAMAGED —) RUIN RUINS
(DAZED —) DAMP
(DEPRESSED —) GLOOM WALLOW
(DISTURBED —) STIR STORM UNREST
(DOMINANT —) SUZERAIN
(DROWSY —) DOVER
(EMOTIONAL —) FEVER FEELING
(EVIL —) PLIGHT
(FEUDAL —) WEI
(FICTITIOUS —) FABLE
(FILTHY —) DIRT
(FLUSTERED —) JITTERS
(FREE —) SAORSTAT
(GERMAN —) REICH
(GLOOMY —) DUMP
(HIGHEST —) SUPREME
(HOLY —) IHRAM
(HORIZONTAL —) LEVEL
(IMPAIRED —) SHATTER
(INDONESIAN —) NEGARA
(INTERMEDIATE —) LIMBO
(IRISH —) TUATH
(LIQUID —) FLUOR FLUIDITY
(LOWEST —) BEDROCK
(MARRIED —) SPOUSAL
(MENTAL —) EARNEST DELUSION
(MIDDLE —) MEAN
(MIXED —) PI PIE
(MORBID —) HIP IODISM
(MORMON —) DESERET
(NEUTRAL —) BUFFER
(ORDINARY —) NORM
(OVERHEATED —) STEW
(PECUNIARY —) FACULTY
(PERMANENT —) STAY
(PERTURBED —) DEVIL
(PROFOUND —) DEPTH
(PROSPEROUS —) WEAL
(RIGID —) RIGOR
(ROYAL —) MAJESTY
(RUDIMENTARY —) INCHOATION
(SHELTERLESS —) EXPOSURE
(SOCIAL —) LIFE
(SOUTHWESTERN —S) SUNBELT
(SOVEREIGN —) INDEPENDENCY
(SPOTTED —) FOXINESS
(STUPEFIED —) NOD
(SUBORDINATE —) SATELLITE
(SWEATY —) STEW
(SWISS —) CANTON
(TROUBLESOME —) HOWDYDO

(ULTIMATE —) END
(UNCERTAIN —) LIMBO
(UNCONTROLLED —) RANDOM
RANDON
(UNCULTIVATED —) FERITY
(UNDECIDED —) PENDENCY
(UNFAVORABLE —) FOULNESS
(VERIFIED —) FACT
(WORST —) PESSIMISM
(PREF.) CRATO TYP(I)(O)
(SUFF.) ANCE ANCY ANDRA ANDRIA
ATE ATION CY DOM ENCE ENCY ERY
HEAD HOOD ION ISATION ISM ITY
IZATION MENT NESS OSIS SHIP TH
(CHARACTERIZED BY —) SOME
(DISEASED —) SIS
(MORBID —) IASIS
STATED GIVEN CERTAIN
(DIRECTLY —) EXPRESS
(DISTINCTLY —) EXPLICIT
**STATE DEPARTMENT (—
EMPLOYEE)** ATTACHE
STATE FAIR (AUTHOR OF —) STONG
(CHARACTER IN —) PAT ABEL WARE
EMILY FRAKE HARRY MARGY WAYNE
ELEANOR GILBERT MELISSA
STATEHOUSE CAPITOL
STATELINESS STATE DIGNITY
MAJESTY GRANDEUR
STATELY DATE BURLY GRAND LARGO
LOFTY NOBLE PROUD REGAL STATE
STOUT AUGUST COUPON PORTLY
SOLEMN SUPERB TOGATE GALLANT
BARONIAL IMPOSING MAESTOSO
MAJESTIC PALATIAL STATEFUL
STATEMENT SAY BILL VOTE WORD
AXIOM BRIEF COUNT DIXIT LIBEL
STATE STORY BELIEF DICTUM
DOCKET EXPOSE FACTUM RETURN
SAYING SPEECH ACCOUNT ADDRESS
ANALOGY DISSENT EPITAPH
EPITOME FORMULA INVOICE
MENTION SHOWING ABSTRACT
ANTINOMY ARGUMENT AVERMENT
BULLETIN DELIVERY EQUATION
EXPLICIT JUDGMENT PROPOSAL
SCHEDULE SENTENCE SPEAKING
SYNGRAPH SYNOPSIS
(— AS PRECEDENT) AUTHORITY
(— OF FACTS) REPORT
(— OF GRIEVANCE) PLAINT
(— OF OPINION) CHANT
(— OF RELATIONS) THEOREM
(— ON DRUG LABEL) LEGEND
(AUTHORITATIVE —) DICTUM
(CASUAL —) REMARK
(CONCISE —) SCHEME APHORISM
(CONDENSED —) RESUME SYNOPSIS
(DEFAMATORY —) LIBEL
(EXAGGERATED —) STRETCH
(FABRICATED —) CANARD
(FINAL — OF ACCOUNT) AUDIT
(FINANCIAL —) BUDGET

(FOOLISH —) INANITY
(FORMAL —) CITATION
(IRRATIONAL —) ALOGISM
(OBSCURE —) ENIGMA
(PLAINTIFF'S —) BODY
(POMPOUS —) BRAG
(PUBLIC —) OUTGIVING
(SELF-CONTRADICTORY —) PARADOX
(SOOTHING —) SALVE
(UNTRUE —) LIE
STATER COLT TURTLE PEGASUS
CYZICENE
STATEROOM BIBBY CABIN
STATESMAN GENRO SOLON
FATHER STATIST WARWICK
JACOBEAN WEALSMAN
(UNPRINCIPLED —) MACHIAVELLIAN
AMERICAN DIX HAY JAY LEE AMES
BURR CASS CLAY FISH GREW HALE
HULL OTIS POLK REED ROOT RUSK
ADAMS BAKER BLAIR BLAND BORAH
DAWES CHASE GENET GERRY
GLASS HENRY LODGE MARCY
OLNEY WYTHE BARUCH BIDDLE
BLAINE BOWLES BROOKE BUNCHE
CARTER EVARTS FOSTER GORHAM
HURLEY MCKEAN MORRIS NORRIS
RODNEY SEWARD SUMNER TOOMBS
WALTON ACHESON ALDRICH
BARBOUR BULLITT CLINTON
CUMMINS DANIELS EVERETT
GADSDEN HANCOCK HOUSTON
KELLOGG LANSING LAURENS
LINCOLN MORRILL SHERMAN
STANTON TIMSON WEBSTER
FRANKLIN GALLATIN HAMILTON
HARRIMAN MILLEDGE PINCKNEY
RANDOLPH RUTLEDGE SCHUYLER
TRUMBULL DICKINSON ELLSWORTH
FULBRIGHT PICKERING
WASHINGTON SCHUSCHNIGG
BRECKENRIDGE
ARGENTINIAN MITRE ALBERDI
CARCANO DORREGO FRONDIZI
RIVADAVIA
ATHENIAN SOLON
AUSTRALIAN SEE COOK BRUCE
EVATT LYONS PRICE BARTON DEAKIN
FISHER HOLDER HUGHES ISSACS
LAWSON PARKES SCULLIN
NICHOLSON
AUSTRIAN BACH RAAB BRUCK
KHESL RAMEK UNGER BADENI
GLASER PLENER RENNER SEIPEL
TAAFFE BURESCH FIRMIAN HELFERT
KAUNITZ KOERBER SCHOBER
STADION BELCREDI DOLLFUSS
HAYMERLE HUSSAREK LAMMASCH
WALDHEIM EGGENBERG
BELLEGARDE METTERNICH
SCHMERLING BARTENSTEIN
GOLUCHOWSKI PILLERSDORF
STARHEMBERG

BELGIAN SPAAK DEVAUX HYMANS
JACOBS JASPAR MERODE ROGIER
ANETHAN NOTHOMB THEUNIS
ZEELAND DECHAMPS BEERNAERT
DELACROIX SCHOLLAERT
VANDERVELDE
BOLIVIAN FRIAS MONTES
BALDIVIESO
BRAZILIAN ABREU FEIJO CAXIAS
BERNARDES MAGALHAES
BULGARIAN DANEV SAVOY MALINOV
TSANKOV LIAPCHEV KARAVELOV
STAMBOLOV RADOSLAVOV
STAMBOLISKI
BURMESE THANT
CANADIAN KING GOUIN JETTE
LEGER SCOTT TACHE VIGER BORDEN
BOWELL FISHER FOSTER HUGHES
MANION SIFTON TUPPER BALDWIN
BENNETT BRODEUR CARTIER
CHAPAIS DOHERTY LAURIER
MEIGHEN PEARSON RALSTON
TRUDEAU MICHENER THOMPSON
MACDONALD MACKENZIE PELLETIER
CARTWRIGHT LAFONTAINE
DIEFENBAKER FITZPATRICK
CHILEAN CRUZ RIOS EGANA MONTT
FREIRE CRUCHAGA OHIGGINS
BALMACEDA ALESSANDRI
CHINESE WU HUA KOO YEN KUNG
SOONG
COLOMBIAN ZEA HERRAN
COSTA RICAN CASTRO
CUBAN PALMA
CZECH BENES HACHA HODZA
KRAMAR RIEGER SVEHLA UDRZAL
MASARYK
DANISH HALL ZAHLE BLUHME
ESTRUP MONRAD RANTZAU
GULDBERG STAUNING NEERGAARD
GRIFFENFELD
DUTCH CATS COEN FOCK ASSER
DOUSA FAGEL HAREN COLIJN
DEWITT KUYPER GROTIUS HEINSIUS
KLEFFENS HEEMSKERK KARNEBEEK
VANDIEMEN BARNEVELDT
BEEREENBROUCK
ECUADORIAN FLORES
EGYPTIAN SADAT ZIWAR
ENGLISH FOX LAW PYM EDEN HOPE
HYDE LAMB LONG MORE PEEL PITT
VANE WEBB WOOD AMERY BACON
BEVAN BURKE CECIL CLIVE ELIOT
HEATH HOARE JUXON LEWIS NIGEL
PAGET SYKES BLOUNT BRIGHT
COBDEN CRIPPS CURZON GEDDES
GIBSON GRAHAM HARLEY HATTON
HEATON HOLLES MILNER MORELY
MORTON SAVILE SELDEN SIDNEY
SOMERS TEMPLE WOLSEY ASQUITH
BALDWIN BALFOUR CADOGAN
CANNING FAWCETT FORSTER
GERMAIN GIFFARD GOSCHEN

HALDANE HALIFAX HAMPDEN
HERRIES LAMBTON NORWICH
OSBORNE RAFFLES READING
RUSSELL STANLEY STEWART
SWINTON WALDOCK WALPOLE
WINDHAM WYKEHAM WYNDHAM
ADDERLEY ANNESLEY BEAUFORT
CARTERET COURTNEY CROMWELL
DISRAELI GARDINER GOULBURN
HAMILTON HARCOURT HASTINGS
MACAULAY MONTFORT ROBINSON
STANHOPE VILLIERS ADDINGTON
BLEDISLOE CAVENDISH CHURCHILL
CUSHENDUN FITZNEALE FITZPETER
FORTESCUE GAITSKELL GLADSTONE
GLANVILLE GODOLPHIN
GREENWOOD GRENVILLE
HUSKISSON KIMBERLEY
LANSDOWNE LIVERPOOL
MACDONALD NORTHCOTE
STRAFFORD WAKEFIELD
BIRKENHEAD PALMERSTON
ROCKINGHAM WALSINGHAM
WELLINGTON WHITELOCKE
WILLINGDON BOLINGBROKE
CHAMBERLAIN FITZWILLIAM
SHAFTESBURY SOUTHAMPTON
CHESTERFIELD
ESTONIAN PATS STRANDMAN
FINNISH KALLIO TANNER CAJANDER
MECHELIN RELANDER STAHLBERG
MANNERHEIM
FRENCH BLUM COTY DARU MOLE
DUPUY FAURE FAVRE FERRY FOULD
MARET MONIS PASSY RIBOT SIMON
SUGER SULLY AVENOL BARROT
BERNIS BIGNON BRIAND CARNOT
CASSIN DOUMER DUPRAT FLEURY
FOUCHE GUIZOT LOUBET MELINE
NECKER PERIER PETAIN ROUHER
THIERS TURGOT COLBERT DECAZES
GRAMONT HERRIOT MAISTRE
MARIGNY MAUPEOU MAZARIN
MOLLIEN NOGARET REGNIER
ROUVIER SCHUMAN SEGUIER
VILLELE VIVIANI CHOISEUL
CONSTANS DALADIER DELCASSE
FONTANES FRANCOIS GAMBETTA
HANOTAUX LHOPITAL MIRABEAU
PAINLEVE POINCARE POMPIDOU
PORTALIS BONAPARTE BOURGEOIS
CHAMPAGNY CLEMENTEL
DALHOUSIE DOUMERGUE FALLIERES
LAFAYETTE MILLERAND RICHELIEU
VERGENNES BARTHELEMY
CLEMENCEAU TALLEYRAND
WADDINGTON BASSOMPIERRE
CHATEAUBRIAND
GERMAN BLOS CUNO FALK MARX
SOLF BEUST JAGOW NOSKE PAPEN
BRANDT GERBER KRANTZ LUTHER
MAURER MIQUEL MOLTKE WORNER
BRUNING CAPRIVI CURTIUS FABRICE

GESSLER STEPHAN ADENAUER
BISMARCK HAINISCH HERTLING
HOLSTEIN KUHLMANN SEVERING
SPANHEIM BENNIGSEN ERZBERGER
HALLSTEIN MICHAELIS BERNSTORFF
FEHRENBACH HILFERDING
RICHTHOFEN SCHLEICHER
STRESEMANN WINDTHORST
ZIMMERMANN SECKENDORFF
GREEK ZAIMES KANARES KORIZES
RANGABE RHALLES BULGARIS
GOUNARES KONDYLES PANGALOS
PERICLES TIMOLEON ARISTIDES
·DINARCHUS DRAGOUMES
HYPERIDES PERIANDER TIMOTHEUS
TRIKOUPES TSALDARES TSOUDEROS
VENIZELOS ALCIBIADES
SKOULOUDES THEMISTIUS
THERAMENES DEMOSTHENES
THRASYBULUS THEMISTOCLES
KOUMOUNDOUROS
MAVROKORDATOS
MICHALAKOPOULOS
HUNGARIAN DEAK NAGY VASS
CSAKY SZELL TISZA BANFFY
BAROSS EOTVOS GOMBOS
HORTHY LONYAY TELEKI BETHLEN
HORVATH HUNYADI KOSSUTH
WEKERLE ANDRASSY SZECHENYI
MARTINUZZI
ICELANDIC HAFSTEIN SIGURDSSON
INDIAN NOON GUPTA NEHRU SINHA
BAJPAI GANDHI SASTRI
IRISH HYDE ANDREWS GRATTAN
MCNEILL COSGRAVE DEVALERA
MACBRIDE CRAIGAVON
ISRAELI ALLON DAYAN RABIN
ITALIAN BALBO BERTI CIANO CROCE
DORIA FACTA LANZA MANIN NITTI
ROCCO ROSSI SELLA VOLPI BONGHI
CAVOUR CRISPI FEDELE GRANDI
PEPOLI RUDINI SFORZA ADRIANI
ALFIERI AZEGLIO CADORNA CAIROLI
DURANDO GASPERI GRAVINA
MAMIANI MANCINI ORLANDO
PELLOUX PONTANO SONNINO
TANUCCI TITTONI VILLARI ALBERONI
CIBRARIO CORRENTI DEPRETIS
GIOLITTI LAFARINA LUZZATTI
MATTIOLI MENABREA NICOTERA
RATTAZZI RICASOLI SALANDRA
SCIALOIA ANTONELLI FEDERZONI
GARIBALDI GUERRAZZI LAMARMORA
MINGHETTI MONTANELLI
ZANARDELLI MACHIAVELLI
LAMBRUSCHINI
JAPANESE ITO GOTO HARA KATO
SATO MUTSU OKUBO OKUMA
INOUYE KANEKO KOMURA MAKINO
TANAKA HAYASHI ITAGAKI IWAKURA
IYEYASU KATSURA SAIONJI
HIRANUMA KIYOMORI MATSUOKA
NOBUNAGA TERAUCHI YAMAGATA

YAMAMOTO HAMAGUCHI HIDEYOSHI
MATSUKATA WAKATSUKI
KOREAN RHEE
LATVIAN KVIESIS ULMANIS
MEIEROVICS
LEBANESE MALIK
LIBERIAN TUBMAN TOLBERT
LITHUANIAN SMETONA
VOLDEMARAS
MEXICAN DIAZ ALAMAN CALLES
OBREGON ZULOAGA IGLESIAS
NEW ZEALAND FOX HALL WARD
ALLEN VOGEL COATES FORBES
FRASER MASSEY SEDDON ATKINSON
STAFFORD
NORWEGIAN BULL KOHT FALSEN
HAMBRO NANSEN HAGERUP
KNUDSEN SVERDRUP MICHELSEN
MOWINCKEL NYGAARDSVOLD
PERUVIAN PRADO CORNEJO
CADLERON BENAVIDES MENDIBURU
PHILIPPINE ROXAS OSMENA
QUEZON ROMULO
POLISH BECK WITOS DMOWSKI
ZALESKI ZALUSKI SIKORSKI
SKRYNSKI KOSCIUSKO PILSUDSKI
PADEREWSKI WOJCIECHOWSKI
PORTUGUESE PAES COSTA POMBAL
ALMEIDA ARRIAGA CARMONA
MACHADO SALAZAR CARVALHO
SALDANHA SANTAREM
PRUSSIAN BULOW
ROMAN CATO CINNA PLINY CAESAR
CICERO POMPEY SENECA AGRIPPA
LAELIUS RUFINUS CAMILLUS
CATILINE GRACCHUS MAECENAS
STILICHO FABRICIUS FLAMINIUS
SERTORIUS SYMMACHUS
CASSIDORUS HORTENSIUS
ROMANIAN CARP MANIU IONESCU
CATARGIU MIRONESCU TITULESCU
MARGHILOMAN KOGALNICEANU
RUSSIAN BIRON GIERS WITTE
BLUDOV CANCRIN KALININ
MOLOTOV MUNNICH SIEVERS
TOLSTOI AVERESCU CHICHKOV
DMITRIEV GOLITSYN IZVOLSKI
LAMSDORF LITVINOV POTMEKIN
STOLYPIN CALINESCU CHICHERIN
GORCHAKOV GOREMYKIN
GRIBOEDOV MENSHIKOV SPERANSKI
NESSELRODE PROTOPOPOV
SCOTTISH HUME KNOX BEATON
GORDON MURRAY JAMESON
MAITLAND RANDOLPH HORSBRUGH
WARRISTON ELPHINSTONE
SERBIAN GRUIC
SOUTH AFRICAN BOTHA BRAND
REITZ SMUTS STEYN KRUGER
SPRIGG COGHLAN HERTZOG
MERRIMAN
SPANISH LUNA ALAVA GODOY
OSUNA PEREZ GALVEZ MANUEL

TORENO ABASCAL ALARCON
ISTURIZ MENDOZA NARVAEZ
SAGASTA SILVELA ENSENADA
ESCOSURA MANRIQUE OLIVARES
QUINTANA ZORRILLA CALOMARDE
ESCOIQUIZ ESPARTERO REQUESENS
JOVELLANOS MIRAFLORES
SWEDISH EDEN GEER HORN TOLL
BRAHE ESSEN UNDEN HANSSON
LINDMAN SANDLER BRANTING
FORSSELL EHRENSVARD
GYLLENBORG WENNERBERG
OXENSTIERNA OXENSTJERNA
HAMMARSKJOLD
SWISS ADOR DROZ FAZY KERN
MUSY FURER GOBAT MEYER MOTTA
BLUMER ESCHER MINGER MULLER
DEUCHER BLUNTSCHLI SCHULTHESS
TURKISH INONU SARACOGLU
URUGUAYAN RIVERA
VENEZUELAN VARGAS BOLIVAR
MONAGAS BETANCOURT
YUGOSLAV PASIC PROTIC ZIVKOVIC
DAVIDOVIC MARINKOVIC PRIBICEVIC
STATICE ARMERIA LIMONIUM
STATION BY BYE FIX ORB RUN SET
BASE GARE POST RANK ROOM SEAT
STOP BEING BERTH CHOKY DEPOT
PLACE POSTE SIEGE STAGE STALL
STAND STATE DEGREE LOCATE
STANCE CONTROL CUARTEL DIGNITY
HABITAT OUTPOST GARRISON
PILTDOWN POSITION STANDING
TERMINAL TERMINUS TRANSFER
(— IN BASEBALL) BASE
(— IN LIFE) BEING CALLING
(— OF HERON) SEDGE SIEGE
(ANIMAL'S —) LIE
(ASSIGNED —) QUARTER
(CONCEALED —) AMBUSH
(CUSTOMS —) CHOKEY
(EXALTED —) PURPLE
(HEALTH —) SANATORIUM
SANITARIUM
(MILITARY —) CAMP
(POLICE —) NICK TANA TANNA
THANAH KOTWALEE
(POST —) DAK
(RADIO —S) CHAIN NETWORK
(RAILWAY —) GARE CABIN
(RUSSIAN SPACE —) MIR
(SAILING —) MARINA
(SIGNALLING —) BANTAY BEACON
(SURVEYING —) STADIA
(TELEVISION —) CHANNEL
(TOLL —) CHOKY CHOKEY
(TRADING —) FACTORY
(WAY —) TAMBO
STATIONARY SET FAST FIXED STILL
ATREST LEDGER STATIC DORMANT
SITFAST STABILE STATARY IMMOBILE
STATIONERY PAPER PAPETERIE

STATION WAGON WOODY
WOODIE MICROBUS SUBURBAN
STATISTICIAN ANALYST STATIST
STATOBLAST SPORE
STATUARY IMAGERY
STATUE HERM ICON IDOL IKON TERM
BUSTO HERMA IMAGE MOSES
AGALMA BRONZE HERMES MEMNON
STATUA WEEPER XOANON ILISSUS
PASQUIN PICTURE STATURE
STATUTE ACROLITH CARYATID
MARFORIO MONUMENT PANTHEUM
PORTRAIT VICTORIA
(— ENDOWED WITH LIFE) GALATEA
(— OF ATHENA) PALLADIUM
(— OF GIGANTIC SIZE) COLOSSUS
(COLOSSAL —) GOG MAGOG
STATUETTE WAX CLIO EMMY
OSCAR WINNIE TANAGRA FIGULINE
FIGURINE SIGILLUM
(— AWARD) REUBEN
(AWARD —) GRAMMY
STATURE PITCH GROWTH HEIGHT
INCHES WASTME CAPACITY
STATUS RANK SEAT PLACE STATE
ASPECT FOOTING STATURE
POSITION STANDING SITUATION
(— OF YOUNGER SON) CADENCY
(HIGH —) CACHET
(LEGAL —) CAPUT
(SECONDARY —) BACKSEAT
STATUTE ACT LAW LEX DOOM EDICT
ASSIZE DECREE SETNESS SITTING
STATUTUM TANZIMAT
(— FAIR) MOP
STATUTORY LEGAL
STAUNCH FAST STOUT TRUSTY
FAITHFUL STALWART
STAVE LAG SLAT STAP SHAKE STAFF
STOVE VERSE BASTON STANZA
WATTLE
(— IN) BILGE BULGE
(SET OF —S) SHOOK
(PL.) LAGGEN LAGGIN STICKS
STAVING
STAY DAY GET LIE BASE HOLD LEND
PROP REST SIST STOP WAIT ABIDE
ABODE APPUI DEFER DELAY DEMUR
DWELL LEAVE STINT TARRY THOLE
ARREST ATTEND BIDING DETAIN
EXPECT GUSSET POTENT REMAIN
TIMBER UPHOLD EMBASSY JIBSTAY
LAYOVER MANSION SOJOURN
SUSPEND BACKSTAY CONTINUE
FORESTAY HORNSTAY MAINSTAY
MARTINGALE
(— AWAY) SKIP
(— BEHIND) LAG
(— CLEAR) AVOID
(— FOR) AWAIT
(— IN BED) LIEIN SACKIN
(— THE NIGHT) BUNK HOSTLE

(— WITH) STICK
(PRIEST'S —) STATION
(SHORT —) VISIT
(TAILORING —) BRIDLE
(PL.) JUMPS JUPES BODICE
STAY-AT-HOME HOMEBODY
HOMESTER
STAYER BONER
STAYLACE AGLET AIGLET
STAYSAIL JUMBO
STEAD LIEU ROOM VICE PLACE
BEHALF
STEADFAST PAT SAD FAST FIRM
SURE TRUE ROCKY STAID STEER
STABLE STANCH STEADY CERTAIN
EXPRESS SETTLED STAUNCH
VALIANT CONSTANT FAITHFUL
RESOLUTE STALWART
STEADFASTLY FIRM FIRMLY
INTENTLY
STEADILY SAD FAST STEADY
STEADINESS NERVE BALANCE
STEADING ONSET ONSTEAD
STEADY GUY SAD BEAU EVEN FIRM
SURE TRIG TRUE CANNY FRANK
LEVEL SOBER STUDY SUANT TIGHT
SICCAR SMOOTH STABLE STANCH
BALLAST EQUABLE STABILE
STATARY STAUNCH CONSTANT
DECOROUS DILIGENT FAITHFUL
RESOLUTE TRANQUIL UNSHAKEN
(— AT ANCHOR) HOLSOM
STEAK BROIL SHELL FLITCH TUCKET
FLANKEN GRISKIN PORTERHOUSE
(CLUB —) CONTREFILET
(KIND OF —) SHELL SKIRT TBONE
(LOIN —) FILET FILLET TOURNEDOS
STEAL BAG CAB CLY COP FOX GYP
LAG MAG NAP NIM NIP RAP RIG
BONE CHOR COON CRIB FAKE GLOM
HOOK KNAP LIFT LURK MAGG MAKE
MILL NAIL NICK PEAK PICK PRIG SLIP
SMUG ANNEX BOOST BRIBE CLOUT
CREEP FETCH FILCH FLIMP FRISK
GLIDE HARRY HEIST HOIST LURCH
MOOCH MOUCH PINCH PLUCK
POACH SCOFF SHAKE SHARP SHAVE
SLIDE SNAKE SNARE SNEAK STALK
SWIPE TOUCH TRUFF COLLAR
CONVEY FINGER HIJACK MOOTCH
NOBBLE PILFER RIPOFF SNITCH
STRIKE THIEVE TWITCH BESTEAL
CABBAGE PLUNDER PURLOIN
SCHLEPP SKYUGLE SNABBLE
SNAFFLE SURREPT ABSTRACT
CRIBBAGE EMBEZZLE LIBERATE
MANARVEL PECULATE SCROUNGE
SHOPLIFT PLAGIARIZE
(— A GLANCE) GLIME
(— ALONG) SLIME SLINK
(— A WATCH) FLIMP
(— AWAY) LOOP SLINK

(— BY ALTERING BRANDS) DUFF
(— CALVES) NUGGET
(— CATTLE) DUFF RUSTLE
(— COPPER FROM VESSEL'S
BOTTOM) TOSH
(— OFF) RUN
(— SLYLY) SCROUNGE
STEALER (CATTLE —) DUFFER
ABACTOR
STEALING STALE
(PREF.) KLEPT(O)
STEALTHILY SIDLINS THIEFLY
SIDELINS
STEALTHY CATTY PRIVY ARTFUL
FELINE TIPTOE CATLIKE FURTIVE
SNEAKING THIEVISH
STEAM IRE OAM ROKE STEM ANGER
BLAST SMOKE SWEAT VAPOR
BREATH POTHER CUSHION TICKOFF
(PREF.) ATM(O) ATMID(O)
STEAMBOAT KICKUP STEAMER
STEAMER CLAM LINER TENDER
CUNARDER
STEAMER DUCK RACER LOGHEAD
STEAMSHIP SCREW STEAM
STEAMER SEATRAIN SHOWBOAT
(— OF VENICE) VAPORETTO
STEAM SHOVEL NAVVY NAVVIE
STEATIN MULL
STEATITE LARDITE POTSTONE
SOAPROCK
STEATOPYGOUS RUMPY
STEED NAG ROIL HORSE MOUNT
STEAD PEGASUS SLEIPNER SLEIPNIR
STEEL RAIL BLOOM BRACE FUSIL
TERNE WEAPON WHITTLE FLEERISH
(— FOR STRIKING FIRE) ESLABON
(— FOR USE WITH FLINT) FUSIL
FURISON FLEERISH
(— INLAID WITH GOLD) KOFT
KOFTGARI
(DAMASCUS —) DAMASK
(INDIAN —) WOOTZ
(KIND OF —) MILD PEDAL
(MOLTEN —) HEAT
STEELER BONER
STEELING ACIERAGE
STEELWORKER HOOKER STICKMAN
STRANDER STRANNER
STEELYARD BISMAR BISMER
DESEMER DOTCHIN STATERA
STEENBRAS BISKOP
STEEP RET SOP BATE BOLD BOWK
BREW BUCK DEAR DRAW DUNG ELIX
LIME MASH MASK SOAK STAY STEW
STEY BLUFF BRANT BRENT HATCH
HEAVY HILLY QUICK SHARP SHEER
SOUSE STIFF ABRUPT BLUFFY CLIFFY
CLIFTY DECOCT IMBIBE INFUSE
SPRUNT STEEPY ARDUOUS
BRASQUE CLIVOSE INSTEEP
PRERUPT STICKLE HEADLONG

MACERATE SATURATE SIDELING
STIFFISH STRAIGHT PRECIPITOUS
(— IN VERY HOT WATER) PLOT
STEEPED SODDEN
STEEPING SOUSE INFUSION
STEEPLE SPEAR SPIRE
STEEPLEBUSH HARDHACK
STEEPLECHASE CHASE GRIND
STEER COX PLY AIRT BEEF BULL
HELM LEAD STEM STOT GUIDE
SPADE SPADO STERN TOLLY CANNER
RUDDER BULLOCK STOCKER
COWBRUTE MOSSHORN NAVIGATE
(— VEHICLE) DRIVE
(FAT —) BEAST
(HORNLESS —) NOT NOTT
(VICIOUS —) LADINO
(WILD —) YAW YEW COWBRUTE
(YOUNG —) STOT STOTT
STEERAGE STERN
STEERER SLUER CAPPER
STEERSMAN COX PILOT WHEEL
PATRON SLEWER CANOPUS
SHIPMAN STEERER COXSWAIN
HELMSMAN SEACUNNY STERNMAN
WHEELMAN COCKSWAIN
STEGOMYIA AEDES
STEIN MUG SHANT
STEINBOCK BOUQUETIN
STELE SHAFT EUSTELE OBELISK
STELLAR STARRY
STELLATE ASTROSE
STEM BUN BASE BEAK BEAM BINE
BIRN CANE CULM CURB NOSE PIPE
PROW RISP ROOT RUNT SHAW STUD
ARISE FILUM HAULM SCAPE SCREW
SHAFT SHANK SHOOT SPIRE STALE
STALK STEAL STICK STIPE STOCK
STRAW THEME TRUNK TUBER
BRANCH CAUDEX CAULIS DERIVE
SCAPUS SPRING CAULOME CONTAIN
FULCRUM HOPBINE HOPVINE
PEDICEL PETIOLE PLASHER SARMENT
SPINDLE STEMLET TIGELLA
CAULICLE ENGENDER EPICOTYL
FORESTEM PEDUNCLE PIPESTEM
TIGELLUM
(— OF ARROW) SHAFT
(— OF BANANAS) COUNT
(— OF GLASS) BALUSTER
(— OF GRAPES) RAPE
(— OF HOOKAH) SNAKE
(— OF MATCH) SHAFT
(— OF MUSHROOM) STIPE
(— OF MUSICAL NOTE) TAIL FILUM
VIRGULA
(— OF PIPE) STAPPLE
(— OF PLANT) AXIS RUNT CAULIS
(— OF SHIP) PROW STEMPOST
(— OF TREE) BOLE CAUDEX
(—S OF CULTIVATED PLANTS) HAULM
(BULBLIKE —) CORM

(DRY WITHERED —) BIRN
(EDIBLE —) EDDO
(GRIEF —) KELLY
(MAIN — OF DEER'S ANTLERS) BEAM
(ORNAMENTAL —) STAVE
(PITHY JOINTED —) CANE
(THORNY —) LAWYER
(TWINING —) BINE
(PREF.) CAUL(I) CORM(O) CULMI
SCAPI STIRPI
(SUFF.) DENDRON OME
STEMLESS ACAULINE
STEMMA OCELLUS OCELLANA
PEDIGREE
STEMMER STRIPPER
STEMWARE CRYSTAL
STENCH FOGO HOGO FETOR SMELL
STINK WHIFF FOETOR MEPHITIS
STENCIL THEOREM
(— PROCESS) POCHOIR
STENCILED GOFFERED
STENO TEMP
STENOGRAPHY SHORTHAND
STENOSIS SMALLING
STEP CUT FIT JOG PEG PIP BEMA
DESS FOOT GREE LINK PACE PASO
PEEP RUNG STAP BRASS CORTE
DODGE FLIER FLYER GRECE NOTCH
POINT STAGE STAIR TOOTH TRACE
TREAD DEGREE GRADIN RUNDLE
STRIDE WINDER CURTAIL DESCENT
FOOTING GRADINE GRADING
COONJINE DEMARCHE DOORSTEP
FOOTPACE FOOTSTEP FORESTEP
PREDELLA STRATLIN
(— ASIDE) DIGRESS
(— BACKWARD) DODGE
(— BY STEP) GRADATIM
(— DOWNWARD) DESCENT
(— FOR GEM MOUNTING) KITE
(— FORWARD) ADVANCE
(— IN A BEARING) BRASS
(— IN BELL RINGING) DODGE
(— IN DOCK) ALTAR
(— IN SELF-ESTEEM) PEG
(— IN SEQUENCE) PLACE
(— IN SHAFT) STEMPEL STEMPLE
(— IN SOCIAL SCALE) CUT
(— IN TRENCH) BANQUETTE
(— LIVELY) SKELP
(— OF LADDER) RIME RUNG ROUND
RUNDLE
(— OF TUSK) TOOTH
(— OUT) DIE
(— PERFORMED BY COMPUTER)
OPERATION
(—S OF BOWLER) APPROACH
(— SUPPORTING MILLSTONE)
TRAMPOT
(ALTAR —S) GRADUAL
(BALLET —) PLIE FOUETTE SISSONE
SISSONNE

(BALLET —S) ALLEGRO
(BOUNDING —) SKIP
(CLUMSY —) STAUP
(DANCE —) DIP PAS SET BUZZ DRAG
DRAW FLAT SHAG SKIP BRAWL
CHASS COULE GLIDE IRISH STOMP
BRANLE CANTER CHASSE DOUBLE
INTURN STRIDE BRANSLE BUFFALO
FISHTAIL GLISSADE PIGEONWING
(FALSE —) HOB SLIP SPHALM
SNAPPER SPHALMA STUMBLE
(FIRST —) STARTER RUDIMENT
(FLIGHT OF —S) GRECE GRICE
PERRON GEMONIES
(GLIDING —) CHASSE
(HALF —) HALFTONE SEMITONE
(LIGHT —) PITAPAT
(MINING —) LOB STEMPEL STEMPLE
(POMPOUS —) STRUT
(PRIM —) MINCE
(PROCEED BY —S) RATCHET
(SET OF —S) STILE
(STATELY —) STALK
(PL.) STY GHAT GHAUT STILE
LADDER
STEPFATHER FATHER STEPSIRE
STEPLADDER TRAP STEPS
(PART OF —) RAIL REST RUNG SHOE
STEP BRACE SPREADER
STEPMOTHER MOTHER HANGNAIL
STEPDAME
(RELATING TO —) NOVERCAL
STEPPE PUSZTA
(— REGION) SAHEL
(ARID REGION OF —) POECHORE
STEPPED STOPEN
STEPPENWOLF (AUTHOR OF —)
HESSE
(CHARACTER IN —) HARRY MARIA
HALLER HERMINE
STEPPING
(SUFF.) GRADE
STEREOISOMER ANOMER EPIMER
STEREOTYPE CAST LABEL CLICHE
STEREO TYPECAST
STEREOTYPED CHAIN STAGE TRITE
USUAL STEREO IDENTIKIT
STERILE DRY DEAD DEAF GELD POOR
AXENIC BARREN GALLED MEAGER
MULISH OTIOSE ASEPTIC ACARPOUS
BANKRUPT IMPOTENT
(PREF.) STEIRO
STERILITY ATOCIA APHORIA
STERILIZE INSULATE
STERILIZING BURNING
STERLING SOUND
(100,000 POUNDS —) PLUM
STERN GRIL GRIM HARD POOP ASPER
CRUEL GRUFF HARSH RIGID ROUGH
ROUND STARK STOUR FLINTY
GLOOMY GRIMLY SEVERE SHREWD
STRICT SULLEN TORVID UNKIND

WICKED AUSTERE TORVOUS
STEERAGE STERNFUL STRAIGHT
(— OF SHIP) DOCK APLUSTRE
(TOWARD THE —) ABAFT
STERNFAST PROVISO
STERNNESS RIGOR TORVITY
SEVERITY
STERNPOST POST STEM
MAINPOST
STERNUTATIVE ERRHINE PTARMIC
STERNUTATOR ERRHINE
STEROL AMYRIN STERIN AMBRAIN
STEROPE (FATHER OF —) ATLAS
(MOTHER OF —) PLEIONE
(SON OF —) OENOMAUS
STERTOR SNORE
STEVEDORE STOWER TRIMMER
WHARFIE CARGADOR DOCKHAND
STEVENSON, R.L. TUSITALA
STEW JUG FRET ITCH SLUM SNIT
SWOT BREDI CIVET CURRY DAUBE
SALMI STIVE STOVE SWEAT BRAISE
BURGOO HODDLE MUDDLE PAELLA
SCOUSE SEETHE SIMMER BROTHEL
CALDERA GOULASH HARICOT
NAVARIN PUCHERO STOVIES
TERRINE BOURRIDE ETOUFFEE
FRIJOADA HOTCHPOT MORTREUX
MULLIGAN STEWPOND STUFFATA
WATERZOOI CARBONNADE
RATATOUILLE SLUMGULLION
(— A HARE) JUG
(— IN A SAUCE) DAUBE
(— MADE IN FORECASTLE) HODDLE
(— OF TRAMPS) MULLIGAN
(CAJUN —) ETOUFFEE
(FISH —) STODGE CHOWDER
MATELOTE
(GAME —) SALMI
(IN A —) UPSET
(IRISH —) STOVIES
(MUTTON —) NAVARIN
(POT FOR —) OLLA
STEWARD HIND VOGT DEWAN
DIWAN GRAFF GRAVE REEVE
COMMIS FACTOR FARMER GRIEVE
LOOKER SIRCAR SIRDAR BAILIFF
CURATOR DAPIFER FLUNKEY
GRANGER HUSBAND MAORMOR
MORMAOR PESHKAR PROCTOR
PROVOST SPENCER SPENDER
APPROVER BHANDARI CELLARER
CONSUMAH GASTALDO HERENACH
KHANSAMA LARDINER MALVOLIO
MANCIPLE PROVISOR STEADMAN
VILLICUS MAJORDOMO
(JOCKEY CLUB —) STIPE
STEWED SODDEN
STEWING ITCHING
STEWPAN STEW COCOTTE SKILLET
STHENELUS (FATHER OF —)
PERSEUS CAPANEUS ANDROGEOS

(MOTHER OF —) EVADNE ANDROMEDA
(SON OF —) EURYSTHEUS
(WIFE OF —) NICIPPE
STHENOBOEA (FATHER OF —) IOBATES
(HUSBAND OF —) PROETUS
STIBNITE SURMA STIBIUM ANTIMONY
STIBOPHEN FUADIN
STICHIC SERIAL
STICK CAT CLA DIP GAD HEW LUG WAN BROG BUFF CHOP CLAG CLAM CLUB CRAB GLUE HANG HURL PALE PALO PICK POLE POTE RICE RUNG STAY TREE YARD BATON BRAIL CAMAN CLAME CLAVE CLEAM CLING CROME DEMUR HURLY PASTE PRICK SPELK STAFF STAKE STANG STAVE STEND STING STOCK STOKE VALET VERGE WADDY ADHERE ATLATL BALLOW BATLER BATLET BATTLE BILLET BROACH BULGER CEMENT CLEAVE CLEEKY COHERE CUDGEL FESCUE HOCKEY INHERE KIERIE KIPPIN LIBBET MALLET RADDLE RAMMER RISSLE STRIKE STRING THIVEL TWITCH BACKSET BATLING CAMMOCK CUMMOCK GAMBREL HURLBAT KILNRIB KIPPEEN MOLINET NOBBLER SHANGAN SPURTLE WOOLDER ASHPLANT BLUDGEON BRINGSEL BRINSELL CATPIECE CATSTICK CRUMMOCK DIPSTICK DUTCHMAN GIBSTAFF GOBSTICK KILNTREE POTSTICK SPREADER
(— AS ARCHERY MARK) WAND
(— AS VIETNAM WEAPON) PUNJI
(— FAST) JAM JAMB SEIZE FITCHER
(— FASTENED TO DOG'S TAIL) SHANGAN
(— FOR ADMITTING TENANTS) VERGE
(— FOR DRIVING OXEN) OXGOAD
(— FOR FIRING CANNON) LINSTOCK
(— FOR KILLING FISH) NOBBLER
(— FOR MAKING FENCE) RADDLE
(— FOR MIXING CHOCOLATE) MOLINET
(— FOR MIXING MORTAR) RAB
(— FOR SNUFF) DIP
(— FOR THATCHING) SPAR GROOM SPELK SPRINGLE
(— IN MUD) STODGE
(— IN OPERATION) FREEZE
(— IT OUT) LAST
(— OF A FAN) BRIN
(— OF CANDY) GIBBY
(— OF CHALK) CRAYON
(— OF ORCHESTRA LEADER) BATON
(— OUT) BUG POKE BULGE SHOOT EXSERT EXTEND EXTRUDE PROTEND

(— REGULATING SLUICEWAY) CATPIECE
(— SEPARATING LUMBER PILES) STICKER
(— TO BEAT CLOTHES) BATLER BATLET
(— TO DISTEND CARCASS) STEND BACKSET
(— TOGETHER) CLOT BLOCK CLING BALTER CEMENT COHERE COAGMENT
(— TO HOLD BOW) TILLER
(— TO HOLD LOG LOAD) DUTCHMAN
(— TO KEEP ANIMAL QUIET) TWITCH
(— TO MARK CROSSING) BROG
(— TO POKE WITH) POTE
(— TO REMOVE HOOK FROM FISH) GOBSTICK
(— TO STRETCH NET) BRAIL
(— TO STUFF DOLLS) RAMMER
(— TO THROW AT BIRDS) SQUAIL
(— TO TIGHTEN KNOT) WOOLDER
(— UP) COCK
(— USED AS POINTER) FESCUE
(BAMBOO —) LATHI LATHEE
(BASKETRY —) LEAGUE
(BENT —) RIFLE
(COLD —) ICICLE
(FIELD HOCKEY —) BULGER CAMMOCK
(FISHING —) GAD
(FORKED —) GROM GROOM
(HOCKEY —) CAMAN HURLY HOCKEY HURLEY SHINNY CAMMOCK CUMMOCK DODDART
(IRON-POINTED —) VALET
(KIND OF —) PUGIL
(KNOBBED —) BILLET
(LACROSSE —) CROSSE
(LARGE —) MOCK
(MARKING —) LEAD
(NOTCHED —) TALLY
(ODD —) JAY
(POLISHING —) BUFF
(PRAYER —) PAHO
(PRINTER'S —) SHOOTER
(RANGE-FINDING —) STADIA
(ROUND —) DOWEL SPINDLE
(STIRRING —) MUNDLE POOLER SPURTLE POTSTICK SWIZZLER
(STOUT —) BAT COSH LOWDER
(TALLY —) TAIL
(THROWING —) ATLATL HORNERAH
(TOBACCO —) LATH
(WALKING —) CANE KEBBY WADDY JAMBEE JOCKEY KEBBIE WHANGEE ASHPLANT GIBSTAFF
(PREF.) RHABD(O)
STICKER HINGE LABEL STRIP WAFER HOPPER PASTER BLEEDER CROSSER MOPSTICK STICKLER
STICK-IN STRANDER
STICKINESS GAUM TACK ROPINESS

STICKING ADHERENT ADHESION COHESION COHESIVE

STICKLE DEMUR BOGGLE HAGGLE HIGGLE

STICKLEBACK BAGGIE BANDIE HACKLE GHOSTER PINFISH

STICKLER
(— FOR FORMALITY) TAPIST

STICKMAN DEALER

STICKS BOONIES BOONDOCKS

STICKUM GLUE PINETAR

STICKY CAB CLAM CLIT ICKY DABBY FATTY GAUMY GLUEY GOOEY GUMMY JAMMY MALMY PUGGY SHORT TACKY TOUGH CLAGGY CLAMMY CLARTY CLINGY CLOGGY GLOPPY PLUCKY SMEARY VISCID VISCOUS ADHESIVE TENACIOUS
(PREF.) GLOEO GLOIO

STIFF BUM SAD CARK HARD NASH TRIG BUDGE CLUNG RIGID SOLID STARK STEER STITH STOUR THARF TOUGH BOARDY CLEDGY CLUMSY CLUNCH FORMAL FROZEN PLUGGY STARKY STEEVE STICKY STILTY STOCKY STURDY UNEASY WOODEN ANGULAR BUCKRAM COSTIVE STARCHY STILTED RAMRODDY RIGOROUS STAFFISH
(SOMEWHAT —) CARKLED
(PREF.) ANKYL(O) TORPI TORPORI

STIFFELIO (CHARACTER IN —) LINA STANKAR RAFFAELE STIFFELIO
(COMPOSER OF —) VERDI

STIFFEN GUM SET SIZE BRACE STARK STIFF STRUT TRUSS HARDEN STARCH STOVER CONGEAL STARKEN
(— PRICE) HARDEN

STIFFENED FUSED CARKLED

STIFFENER KNEE COUNTER

STIFFENING PUFF DRESS

STIFFNESS KINK RIGOR STARCH BUCKRAM PRIMNESS RIGIDITY SEVERITY
(SYMBOL OF —) RAMROD

STIFLE DAMP FUNK SLAY CHOKE CRUSH STIVE STUFF MUFFLE QUENCH FLASKER QUERKEN SMOTHER SCOMFISH STRANGLE SUPPRESS THROTTLE

STIFLED DEAF ETOUFFE

STIFLING CLOSE STIVY SMUDGY POTHERY SMOTHERY

STIGMA BLOT FOIL NOTE SLUR SPOT BRAND ODIUM STAIN TAINT BLOTCH BLEMISH

STIGMATIZE BLOT BRAND DENOUNCE

STILBITE DESMINE

STILE STY STICK TIMBER

STILETTO BODKIN STYLET PIERCER POINTEL

STILL BUT COY LAY YET BODY CALM COSH HUSH LOWN LULL WORM ACCOY CHECK QUIET WHIST HOWEER HUSHED PACIFY QUENCH SETTLE SILENT SOOTHE STATIC SUBDUE WITHAL ALEMBIC CORNUTE DORMANT HOWEVER PELICAN SILENCE CUCURBIT RECEIVER RESTRAIN STAGNANT STILLERY SUPPRESS
(— PART) KELD
(PART OF —) HEAD TUBE RETORT CONDENSER

STILLAGE SLOP STILLING STILLION

STILL-HUNT STALK

STILLNESS CALM HUSH REST PEACE LANGUOR SILENCE STATION

STILT KAKI POGO TILT LAWYER PATTEN SCATCH YEGUITA LONGLEGS STILTIFY TRIANGLE

STILTED LOFTY STIFF FORMAL POETIC STILTY POMPOUS

STIMULANT COCA STIM INULA BRACER CINDER FILLIP GINGER HARMAL PHYTIN CAMPHOR CARDIAC OUABAIN REVIVER ADONIDIN AMMONIAC EXCITANT INCITANT LOBELINE PEMOLINE STIMULUS SASSAFRAS WHETSTONE

STIMULATE FAN HOP KEY PEP FUEL GOAD HYPE HYPO MOVE SEED SPUR STIR URGE WHET FILIP IMPEL PIQUE PRIME ROUSE SPARK STING AROUSE BESTIR EXCITE FILLIP INCITE SPIRIT TICKLE UPSTIR ANIMATE ENLIVEN INNERVE INSPIRE PROVOKE QUICKEN SHARPEN ACTIVATE FARADIZE IRRITATE MOTIVATE TITILLATE
(FAIL TO —) UNDERWHELM

STIMULATED (ARTIFICIALLY —) HOPPEDUP

STIMULATING PERT SEXY BRISK BRACING BANGING EROGENIC EXCITING GENEROUS INCITANT POIGNANT STIRRING
(— ANGER) ADRENAL
(PREF.) AUXO EXCITO

STIMULATION GINGER IMPETUS
(MENTAL —) SPRITE

STIMULUS CUE AURA BROD EDGE GOAD HYPO SPUR STIM STING FILLIP MOTIVE SOURCE BAHNUNG IMPETUS OESTRUS STRESSOR

STING NIP BARB BITE BURN FOIN GOAD SOAK TANG ATTER DEVIL PIQUE PRICK SMART STANG TOUCH NETTLE ACULEUS BUGBITE PIERCER IRRITATE STIMULUS

STINGILY STRAIT SCARCELY

STINGINESS PARSIMONY

STINGING KEEN SMART PEPPERY PIQUANT POINTED PRICKLY PUNGENT ACRIMONY ACULEATE

NETTLING POIGNANT SCALDING
URTICANT
STINGING ANT KELEP
STINGRAY ANGLER OBISPO SEPHEN
TRYGON BATFISH LOPHIID STINGER
WAIREPO
STINGY DRY DREE GAIN GAIR HARD
MEAN NEAR NIGH CHEAP CLOSE
MINGY SCALY TIGHT CHEAPO
DRIECH GRIPPY HUNGRY MEASLY
NARROW SCABBY SCARCE SCRIMY
SKIMPY SKINNY SNIPPY STRAIT
CHINCHY CHINTZY COSTIVE MISERLY
NIGGARD PENURIOUS
PARSIMONIOUS
STINK FOGO GOAD NIFF PONG STEW
SUCK SMELL SMEECH STENCH
MEPHITIS
(PREF.) BROM(O)
STINKBIRD HOACIN HOATZIN
STINKER RAT BUMMER
STINKING FOUL HIGH FETID PUTID
STINKY MALODOROUS
STINKWOOD DOGWOOD
STINT TASK GRIST PINCH SCANT
SNAPE SCRIMP SKINCH STINGY
TANTUM SCANTLE
(SHORT —) SNATCH
(WITHOUT —) FREELY
STIPE STEM STALK
STIPEND ANN HIRE ANNAT WAGES
SALARY PENSION PREBEND
PROVEND COMMENDA
STIPENDIARY BEAK
STIPPLE SPONGE
STIPPLED DOTTED
STIPULATE ARTICLE PROTEST
PROVIDE COVENANT
STIPULATION IF ANNEX CLAUSE
ARTICLE PREMISE PROVISO STRINGS
COVENANT
(PL.) TERMS
STIPULE SPINE SHEATH STIPEL
STIPULA TENDRIL
STIR DO ADO FAN GOG JEE PUG WAG
BEET BUZZ CARD FUSS MOVE PEAL
POKE RAUK ROKE TODO WAKE
AMOVE BUDGE CHURN CREEP ERECT
FUROR HURRY MUDGE POACH
QUICH RAISE ROUST SLICE SPARK
STING STOOR STURT TEASE TOUCH
AROUSE AWAKEN BUBBLE BUSTLE
COOLER CRUTCH EXCITE FLURRY
GINGER HUBBUB JUMBLE KIAUGH
MUDDLE PADDLE POUTER QUINCH
QUITCH REMBLE REMOVE ROUNCE
STODGE SUMMON TATTER ACTUATE
ANIMATE BLATHER CLUTTER
COMMOVE FLUTTER PROVOKE
STARKLE SWIZZLE TROUBLE
SPLUTTER
(— ABOUT) KNOCK
(— CALICO COLORS) TEER

(— DRINK) MUDDLE SWIZZLE
(— LIQUID) ROG
(— SOIL) CHISEL
(— UP) FAN MIX BUZZ DRUM FUSS
MOVE PROG ROIL TOSS AMOVE
AREAR AWAKE ERECT QUICK ROUSE
SNURL SPOOK STOKE TARRY BESTIR
BOTHER CHOUSE EXCITE INCITE
JOSTLE KINDLE PUDDLE RUMBLE
TICKLE UPSTIR AGITATE ANIMATE
COMMOVE DISTURB PRODDLE
PROVOKE STUDDLE TORMENT
UNQUEME DISTRACT ENKINDLE
(— UP WITH YEAST) BARM
STIRRER HOG DOLLY ROUSER
RUMMAGER
STIRRING RACY ASTIR DEEDFUL
ROUSING THRILLY EXCITING
PATHETIC
STIRRUP IRON CHAPELET
STEELBOW
(PART OF —) EYE PAD TREAD
BRANCH
(PREF.) STAPED(I)(IO)
STITCH BAR RUN SEW KNIT LOOP
PURL WHIP CABLE CLOSE POINT
PREEN PUNTO STEEK ACCRUE
FESTON SUTURE TRICOT CROCHET
POPCORN FAGOTING
(— IN) QUILT
(— OF CLOTHES) TACK
(KIND OF —) FLAME
(NEEDLEPOINT —) BARGELLO
(SWEATER —) CABLE FAGGOT
(TEMPORARY —) TACK
(PL.) JOURS FILLING PINWORK
STITCHBIRD IHI
STITCHDOWN SEWROUND
STITCHED BROCHE
STITCHER WHIPPER
STITCHING SERGING FAGOTING
STOATING WHIPPING
(SUFF.) RHAPHY RRHAPHY
STITCHWORT PAIGLE ALLBONE
SNAPPER HEADACHE SNAPJACK
SNAPWORT
STITHY STUDY SMITHY STIDDY
STUDDY
STOAT VAIR ERMINE WEASEL
CLUBSTER FUTTERET WHITRACK
STOCK COP DOG KIN ROD CANT
CROP FILL FOND FUND SEED SELL
STEM TRIP BLOND BLOOD BROTH
CASTE CREAM FLESH HOARD ISSUE
PLANT STALE STIRP STORE STUFF
TALON BUDGET CHOKER COMMON
FUTURE KAFFIR SHARES STOVEN
STRAIN SUPPLY CAPITAL DESCENT
PILLORY PROSAPY PROVIDE REPLETE
RESERVE BONEYARD BOUTIQUE
CROSSBAR DIESTOCK GILLIVER
GUNSTOCK MAGAZINE MERCHANT
ORDINARY SECURITY PROVISIONS

(— OF ANCHOR) CROSS
(— OF BREEDING MARES) STRUDE
(— OF FOOD) FARE
(— OF GRAIN) COP
(— OF INDIVIDUALS) CLONE
(— OF MORPHEMES) LEXICON
(— OF WEAPONS) ARSENAL
(— OF WHIP) CROP
(— OF WINE) CELLAR
(— SOLD SHORT) BEAR
(— UNIT) SHARE
(FARM —) BOW
(LANGUAGE —) SALISH SIOUAN
BOROTUKE
(MEAT —) BLOND BOUILLON
(PLASTIC —) BISCUIT
(RAILROAD —) GRANGER
(PL.) FOODS CIPPUS HARMAN
TIMBER CATASTA KAFFIRS
(PREF.) STIPI(T)(TI) STIPULI STIRPI
(SUFF.) STIPULAR STIPULATE
STOCKADE BOMA PEEL ETAPE
ZAREBA BARRIER TAMBOUR
STOCKADO
STOCK EXCHANGE BOURSE
COULISSE
STOCKFISH STOCK LUTFISK TITLING
SPELDING SPELDRON
(PREF.) SALPI
STOCKING HOSE SOCK SHANK
STOCK CALIGA MOGGAN SCOGGER
SHINNER BOOTHOSE
(— PATTERN) ARGYLE
(FOOTLESS —) HOGGER HUSHION
(PROTECTIVE —) SPATTEE
(SOLELESS —) TRAHEEN
(PL.) HOSE NYLONS BUSKINS
DOUTHOSE
STOCKJOBBING AGIOTAGE
STOCKWORK CARBONA
STOCKY FAT COBBY DUMPY GROSS
SQUAT STOUT CHUMPY CHUNKY
DUMPSY STUBBY STUGGY STUNTY
BUNTING COMPACT HEAVYSET
STOCKISH THICKSET
STODGY STUFFY STUGGY
BOURGEOIS
STOGIE CIGAR
STOIC STOLID APATHETIC IMPASSIVE
STOKEHOLD FIREROOM
STOKER FIREMAN BLOCKMAN
STOLE BOA FUR STAW ARMIL ORARY
ARMILLA ORARION PALATINE
STOLEN HOT BENT INOME STOUN
FURTIVE
(— GOODS) MAINOUR
STOLID BEEFY BOVINE CLUMSE
STUPID WOODEN CLUMPST
DEADPAN PASSIVE
STOLIDITY MORGUE
STOLON WIRE SOBOL SOBOLE
SOLENIUM
STOMA PORE OPENING OSTIOLE

STOMACH MAW CROP GUTS KYTE
MARY POKE READ TANK WAME
WOMB BINGY BROOK GORGE GROUF
HEART TUMMY BINGEE BINGEY
BONNET CROPPY GEBBIE PECHAN
VENTER CONCOCT CRAPPIN GIZZARD
ABOMASUM
(— OF ANIMAL) CRAW
(— OF CALF) VELL
(— OF FOWLS) CRAW
(— OF RUMINANT) READ RUMEN
BONNET OMASUM PAUNCH
ABOMASUM MANIFOLD RODDIKIN
RETICULUM
(PIG'S —) JAUDIE
(PREF.) GASTER(O) GASTR(I)(O)
RUMENO
(SUFF.) GASTER GASTRIA
STOMACHACHE FANTAD GULLION
STOMACHER GIMP TRUSS ECHELLE
PLACARD POITREL FOREPART
STOMACHIC COTO CORNUS
BITTERS CALUMBA GENTIAN
LUPULIN ANTHEMIS
STOMATITIS NOMA
STONE DAM GEM RAG BOND DUCK
FLAG HERD KLIP KNAR MARK PELT
ROCK STEN TRIG RAUTA CAPEL
CHUCK DRAKE GUARD LAPIS PAVER
PITCH SCRAE SCREE SNECK STANE
ASHLAR BEDDER BENBEN CEPHAS
CHATON CLOSER COBBLE GAMAHE
GIBBER HEADER JUMPER LEDGER
MARVER METATE MULLER NUTLET
PEEVER PINNER RUNNER SUMMER
TORSEL ANGRITE CALLAIS DINGBAT
DONNOCK DORNICK GLIDDER
KNEELER KNICKER PERPEND PITCHER
PUTAMEN RATCHEL STANNER
SURFACE THROUGH BAETULUS
CABOCHON DENDRITE EBENEZER
HAGSTONE LAPIDATE LAPILLUS
LAPSTONE MACEHEAD MONOLITH
NAKHLITE SKEWBACK TOPSTONE
(— ADHERING TO LEAD ORE) KEVEL
(— AS AMULET) HAGSTONE
(— AS IT COMES FROM QUARRY)
RUBBLE
(— AS ROAD MARKER) LEAGUE
(— AT DOOR) RYBAT
(— BLOCK) ASSIZE
(— FOR GLASS-ROLLING) MARVER
(— FORMING CAP OF PIER) SUMMER
CUSHION
(— FOR MOUNTING HORSE)
MONTOIR
(— HARD TO MOVE) SITFAST
(— HEAP) MAN CAIRN
(— IN BLAST FURNACE) DAM
(— IN MEMORY OF DEAD)
MONUMENT
(— IN SMALL FRAGMENTS) RATCHEL
(— IN WALL) PARPEN

(— MARKING CENTER OF WORLD) OMPHALOS
(— OF FRUIT) COB PIT PAIP COBBE NUTLET PYRENE PUTAMEN
(— OF PYRAMID SHAPE) BENBEN
(— PROVIDING CHANGE OF DIRECTION) KNEELER
(— RELIC) NEOLITH
(— SET IN RING) CHATON
(—S FROM CRUSHER) TAILINGS
(— SHAPED BY WIND) VENTIFACT
(— SHOT FROM STONE-BOW) JALET
(—S IN WATER) STANNERS
(— TO DEATH) LAPIDATE
(— USED AS MONUMENT) MEGALITH
(— USED IN GAME) DUCK DRAKE
(— WITH INTERNAL CAVITY) GEODE
(ARTIFICIAL —) ALBOLITE
(BINDING —) PERPEND THROUGH PIERPONT
(BOND —) GIRDER KEYSTONE
(BOTTOM — OF ARCH) SPRINGER
(BOUNDARY —) TERM MONUMENT TERMINUS MERESTONE
(BROKEN —) RIPRAP
(BROKEN — USED FOR ROADS) BALLAST MACADAM
(BUILDING —) ASHLAR SUMMER MITCHEL SPERONE
(CARVED —) CAMEO CUVETTE
(CASTING —) TYMP
(CHINA —) PETUNSE
(CLAY —) LECH
(COPING —) SKEW TABLET TABLING CAPSTONE
(CURLING —) HOG HERD GUARD LOOFIE POTLID
(CYLINDRICAL —) TAMBOUR
(DESERT —) GIBBER
(DRUID —) SARSEN
(DRYING —) STILLAGE
(EDGING —) SETTER
(FLAT —) PLAT DRAKE LEDGER
(FOUNDATION —) BEDDER
(GLASSY —) TEKTITE
(GLITTERING —) DAZE
(GRAVE —) BAUTA STELE
(GREEN —) CALLAIS
(GRINDING —) METATE MULLER
(HOLY —) BEAR BAETYL
(HOPSCOTCH —) PEEVER PALLALL
(IMAGINARY —) ADAMANT
(KIDNEY —) NEPHRITE
(LAST — IN COURSE) CLOSER
(LOOSE —) GLIDDER
(MAGICAL —) BAETYL
(MEMORIAL —) BAUTA EBENEZER
(METEORIC —) ANGRITE AEROLITE AEROLHITE NAKHLITE
(MIDDLE —) HONEY
(MIDDLE — OF ARCH) KEY
(MONUMENTAL —) LECH

(PAVING —) SET SETT PAVER REBATE PITCHER
(PHILOSOPHER'S —) ADROP MAGISTERY TINCTURE
(POLISHING —) SLEEKSTONE
(PRECIOUS —) GEM OPAL RUBY EWAGE JEWEL TOPAZ ADAMAS LIGURE SHAMIR ASTERIA ASTRION CRAPAUD CUVETTE DIAMOND DIONISE EMERALD GELATIA JACINTH OLIVINE SARDINE SARDIUS AMETHYST ASTROITE HYACINTH PANTARBE SAPPHIRE YDRIADES
(PRECIOUS —S) PERRIE
(REFUSE —) ROACH
(ROCKING —) LOGAN
(SACRED —) BAETYL BAETULUS
(SEMIPRECIOUS —) ONYX SARD MURRA GARNET CITRINE TIGEREYE
(SHARPENING —) HONE WHET
(SHOEMAKER'S —) LAPSTONE
(SMALL ROUND —) JACK PEBBLE PELLET
(SOFTENED —) SAP
(STEPPING —) GOAT SARN
(STRATIFIED —) FLAG SLAB
(TALISMANIC —) GAMAHE
(TRANSPARENT —) PHENGITE
(UNSQUARED —) BACKING
(UPRIGHT —) BAUTA MENHIR MASSEBAH
(PL.) LAPIDES LAPILLI
(PREF.) LAPIDI LAPILLI LITH(O)
(— OF FRUIT) PYREN(O)
(SUFF.) LITE LITH(IC) LITIC
STONEBASS BAFARO WHAPUKU
STONEBOAT DRAY
STONEBOW RODD
STONECHAT CHAT SMICH SAXICOLA WHEATEAR
STONECROP ORPIN SEDUM ORPINE PRICKET WALLWORT
STONE CURLEW BUSTARD
STONECUTTER MASON JADDER LAPICIDE LAPIDARY SCABBLER SCAPPLER SQUAREMAN
STONED HIGH DRUNK RIPPED WRECKED
STONEFLY NAIAD
STONEHAND LOCKUP
STONELIKE LITHOID
STONEMAN IMPOSER
STONE MARTEN FOIN
STONEMASON DORBIE
STONE PARSLEY HONEWORT
STONE PINE PINON AROLLA CEMBRA
STONE ROLLER MAMMY MOMMY TOTER
STONE TOTER CUTLIPS
STONEWALLER STICKER
STONEWARE GRES BASALT JASPER BASALTES CANEWARE CHIENYAO

STONEWORKER MASON
STONINESS LAPIDITY PETREITY
STONY RIGID COBBLY PETROUS
LAPIDOSE PETROSAL
STOOGE (THREE —S) MOE CURLY
LARRY
STOOL FORM MORA SEAT STAB
COPPY CROCK HORSE STOLE TREST
BUFFET CREEPY CURRIE TRIPOD
TUFFET COMMODE CREEPIE
KNEELER SHAMBLE TABORET
TRESTLE TUMBREL BARSTOOL
STILLAGE
(CLOSE —) TOM
(CUCKING —) THEW
(LOW —) COPPY SUNKIE CREEPIE
CRICKET
(3-LEGGED —) BUFFET THRESTLE
STOOLBALL TUTBALL
STOOL PIGEON NARK SNITCH
STOOGE STOOLIE DIVULGER
STOOP BOW BEND CURB LEAN LOUT
POKE SINK COUCH COURB DEIGN
STOPE STULP COORIE CROUCH
HUCKLE BALCONY DECLINE
DESCEND RUCKSEY SUCCUMB
(— OF HAWK) SOUSE
STOOPING DUCK ASTOOP DESCENT
(PREF.) CYPH(O)
STOP HO BAS COG CUT DAM DIE DIT
DOG END HOO KEP LIN MAR NIX SET
BALK BODE BUNG CALK CALL COOI
DROP EASE HALT HELP HOLD HOOK
KILL QUIT REED REST SIST SNUB
OOFT STAP STAY STEM STOW TEAT
TENT TOHO TRIG VIOL WEAR WHOA
ABIDE ABORT AVADT BASTA BELAY
BLOCK BRAKE BREAK CAULK CEASE
CHECK CHOKE CHUCK CLAMP CLOSE
DELAY EMBAR HITCH LEAVE MEDIA
PAUSE PEACE POINT QUINT REEST
SCOTE SLAKE SPARE SPRAG STAND
STASH STEEK STICK STINT VIOLA
AEOLIN ANCHOR ARREST ASTINT
BIFARA BOGGLE BORROW CHEESE
CLAMOR COLLAR DESIST DETAIN
DEVALL FREEZE GRAVEL INSTOP
LAYOFF MONTRE NASARD PERIOD
SCOTCH SQUASH STANCE STANCH
STIFLE TENUIS TROMBA BASSOON
CAESURA MELODIA MUSETTE
OPPRESS SOJOURN SQUELCH
STATION TERTIAN TWELFTH
ASPIRATA BACKSTOP BOMBARDE
PRECLUDE RECORDER STOPOVER
STOPPAGE SUPPRESS SURCEASE
TENOROON WALDHORN WITHSPAR
(— AS IF FRIGHTENED) BOGGLE
(— BLAST) DAMP
(— FLOW) BAFFLE STANCH
(— FOR FOOD) BAIT
(— FOR HORSE) BLOW
(— FROM FERMENTING) STUM

(— GROWTH) BLAST
(— GUN BREECH) OBTURATE
(— IN EARLY STAGES) ABORT
(— IN SPEAKING) HAW
(— LEAK) CALK CAULK FOTHER
(— LIGHT) RED
(— ROWING) EASY
(— SHORT) JIB
(— SPEAKING) SHUTUP
(— SWINGING) SET
(— UNDESIREDLY) STALL
(— UP) DAM CALK CLOG CLOY FILL
PLUG CHINK ESTOP STUFF STANCH
OCCLUDE STAUNCH OPPILATE
(— USING) SINK
(— WITH CLAY) PUG
(— WORK) SECURE
(BRIEF —) CALL
(GLOTTAL —) STOD CATCH STOSS
PLOSIVE STOSSTON
(HARPSICHORD —) LUTE
(ROUGH —) ASPIRATA
(SUCTION —) CLICK
(TEMPORARY —) PAUSE SUSPEND
(VOICELESS —) TENUIS
(WILL NOT —) RUNON
(PL.) REEDWORK
(PREF.) ISCH(O)
STOPCOCK BIB BIBB BIBCOCK
BALLCOCK TURNCOCK
STOPGAP RESOURCE
STOPLIGHT IMPEDER
STOPOVER LAYOVER
STOPPAGE JAM BLIN ALLAY CHECK
HITCH LEATH STICK STINT ARREST
DEVALL STASIS EMBARGO GAOLUCK
REFUSAL SHUTOFF STOPPLE
ASTYLLEN SHUTDOWN STOPWORK
CESSATION
(— OF BLOOD) REMORA
(— OF DEVELOPMENT) ATROPHY
(WORK —) BUND HARTAL LOWSIN
STRIKE
(PREF.) ISCH(O) STASI
(SUFF.) STASIA STASIS
STOPPED PILEATA
(— WITH HAND) BOUCHE
STOPPER WAD BUNG CORK PLUG
STOP VICE CHECK FIPPLE STANCH
BOUCHON CLOSURE SHUTOFF
STOPGAP STOPPLE TAMPION
STOPCOCK
STOPPERED BOUCHE
STOPPING STAY HOLDUP PHASEOUT
STOPPAGE
(GRADUAL — OF OPERATIONS)
PHASEOUT
STOPPING-PLACE HALT PULLIN
OUTSPAN
STORAGE STORE STOWAGE
BESTOWAL
STORAX COPALM STACTE STYRAX
LORDWOOD

STORE CAVE CRIB DECK FOND FUND
HOLD KEEP MART MASS SAVE SHOP
STOW TOKO CACHE DEPOT HOUSE
HUTCH STASH STOCK UPLAY
BAZAAR CELLAR GARNER GIRNEL
RECOND STEEVE SUPPLY TIENDA
WINKEL ARSENAL BHANDAR
BOOTERY GROCERY HARVEST
HUSBAND IMBURSE REPOSIT
RESTORE SHEBANG BOUTIQUE
EMPORIUM EXCHANGE GARRISON
MAGAZINE TENDEJON WAREROOM
WARNISON
(— BEER) AGE LAGER
(— CROP) BARN
(— FODDER) ENSILE
(— IN A MOW) GOVE
(— IN LUMBER CAMP) VAN
(— IN MOUND) HOG
(— KEPT BY CHINESE) TOKO
(— OF COMPUTER DATA) PUSHDOWN
(— OF FOOD) LARDER
(— OF WEALTH) FORTUNE
(— POTATOES) HOG
(— UP) FUND POWDER IMBURSE
SQUIRREL
(ABUNDANT —) MINE
(BREAD —) PANARY
(HIDDEN —) BIKE
(LARGE —) RAFF ANCHOR
(LIQUOR —) GROGGERY
(MARINE —) DOLLYSHOP
(MILITARY —) DUMP
(MILITARY —S) DUMP MUNITIONS
AMMUNITION
(READY-TO-EAT FOOD —) DELI DELLY
(RESERVE —) SLUICE
(RICH —) ARGOSY
(SECRET —) STASH
(SMALL —S) SLOPS
(SUPPLEMENTARY —) RELAY
(PL.) SAMAN SUPPLY
STORE CHEESE CHEDDAR
STOREHOUSE BIKE GOLA CACHE
DEPOT ETAPE STORE ARGOSY
ARMORY BODEGA GODOWN PALACE
PANARY STAPLE VINTRY ARSENAL
BHANDAR CAMALIG CAMARIN
GRANARY STORAGE ENTREPOT
MAGAZINE SADDLERY TREASURE
(— FOR BREAD) PANARY
(— OF KNOWLEDGE) THESAURUS
(RAISED —) WHATA FUTTAH PATAKA
(UNDERGROUND —) PALACE
MATTAMORE
STOREKEEPER MERCHANT
STOREMAN
STOREROOM CAVE GOLA WARD
GOLAH BODEGA CELLAR DINGLE
BOXROOM BUTTERY GENIZAH
LAZARET POULTRY THALAMUS
(PAWNBROKER'S —) LUMBER
STORESHIP FLUTE

STOREY ETAGE ENTRESOL
STORK WADER ARGALA JABIRU
SIMBIL HURGILA MAGUARI
MARABOU ADJUTANT CICONIID
MARABOUT OPENBEAK OPENBILL
(PREF.) CICONI PELARGO
STORKLIKE PELARGIC
STORKSBILL ERODIUM
STORM RIG WAP BLOW HAIL HUFF
RAGE RAMP RAND RAVE WIND BLIZZ
BLOUT BRASH DEVIL DRIFT FORCE
ORAGE STOUR ATTACK BARBER
EASTER EXPUGN WESTER BLUSTER
BRAVADO CYCLONE DUSTING
EQUINOX GAUSTER PISACHI
SHAITAN SNIFTER TEMPEST
TORMENT WEATHER BLOWDOWN
CALAMITY ERUPTION UPHEAVAL
WILLIWAW
(— OF BLOWS) STOUR
(— OF RAGE) PELT
(DUST —) DEVIL DUSTER HABOOB
KHAMSIN PEESASH SHAITAN
(FURIOUS —) TEMPEST
(HAWAIIAN —) KONA
(SEVERE —) PEELER SNIFTER
(VIOLENT —) FLAW TUFAN CYCLONE
SNORTER
STORM DOOR DINGLE
STORMY FOUL GURL RUDE WILD
DIRTY DUSTY GURLY GUSTY STARK
WINDY WROTH COARSE RUGGED
UNFINE WINTRY FURIOUS NIMBOSE
RIOTOUS SQUALLY TROUBLE
VIOLENT AGITATED BLUSTERY
CLUTTERY ORAGIOUS TEMPESTY
BOISTEROUS
STORMY PETREL MITTY WITCH
SPENCY
STORY GAG SAW DECK DIDO FLAT
LORE REDE TALE TEXT YARN ATTIC
CRACK ETAGE FABLE FLOOR KATHA
PITCH PROSE RECIT SOLAR SPELL
SPIEL STAGE STORE CUFFER FABULA
FLIGHT PISTLE SCREED SOLLAR
ADVANCE HAGGADA HISTORY
MANSARD MARCHEN PROCESS
RECITAL ANECDOTE DREADFUL
ENTRESOL TREATISE NARRATIVE
(— FROM THE PAST) LEGEND
(— OF BEEHIVE) SUPER
(— OF BUILDING) DECK FLAT ATTIC
CHESS ETAGE FLOOR PIANO SOLAR
STAGE FLIGHT SOLLAR MANSARD
ENTRESOL MEZZANINE
(— OF HEROES) SAGA
(ABSURD —) CANARD
(ADVENTURE —) YARN
(AMUSING —) BAR DROLLERY
(BIRTH —) JATAKA
(CORNY —) GROANER
(DOLEFUL —) JEREMIAD
(EERIE —) CHILLER

(EXCITING —) THRILLER
(FAKE —) STRING
(FALSE —) SHAVE CANARD WHOPPER
(FISH —) YARN
(KIND OF —) WAR
(LIFE —) BIO BIOG
(LONG, INVOLVED —) MEGILLA
MEGILLAH
(LOWER —) DOWNSTAIRS
(MADE-UP —) FUDGE
(MONSTROUS —) BANGER
(MORBIDLY SENSATIONAL —)
DREADFUL
(MYSTERY —) WHODUNIT
(NEWS —) SIDEBAR
(NEWSPAPER —) LEAD FEATURE
(NOTED WAR —) ILIAD
(OLD —) DIDO
(POMPOUS —) BRAG
(PREPOSTEROUS —) CUFFER
(RIBALD —) HARLOTRY
(SAD —) TRAGEDY
(SATIRICAL —) SKIT
(SHORT —) CONTE NOVELLA
(STALE —) CHESTNUT
(UPPER —) ATTIC GARRET BARBECUE
HYPEROON CLERESTORY
(PL.) LEGENDA
STORY BOOK TALEBOOK
STORY OF A BAD BOY (AUTHOR
OF —) ALDRICH
(CHARACTER IN —) BEN TOM BILL
EZRA PHIL SETH ADAMS BINNY
KITTY MEEKS NELLY SILAS CONWAY
MARDEN NUTTER PEPPER ROGERS
ABIGAIL ALDRICH CHARLEY COLLINS
WALLACE WINGATE GRIMSHAW
WHITCOMB TREFETHEN
GLENTWORTH
STORY OF AN AFRICAN FARM
(AUTHOR OF —) SCHREINER
(CHARACTER IN —) EM ROSE TANT
WALDO SANNIE GREGORY LYNDALL
BLENKINS BONAPARTE
STORYTELLER LIAR FIBBER
CONTEUR DISCOUR DISSOUR
STOUP STOOP BENITIER
STOUT ALE FAT SAD FIRM STUT
TRIM BOSH BROSY BULKY BUNTY
BURLY COBBY FRACK FRECK GREAT
HARDY KEDGE OBESE PLUMP
PODDY PUNCH STARK STERN
BONNIE FLESHY PORTER PORTLY
PRETTY PYKNIC ROTUND SQUARE
STRONG STUFFY STURDY BOWERLY
REPLETE FORCIBLE PLUMPISH
POWERFUL ROBOREAN STALWART
THICKSET
(— PERSON) GURK
STOUTHEARTED GOOD VALIANT
STOUTLY FAST HARDILY
STOUTNESS STRENGTH
CORPULENCE

STOVE HOD STOW BOGEY CHULA
PEACH PLATE CHULHA COCKLE
COOKER HEATER PRIMUS BRASERO
CHAUFFER FRANKLIN POTBELLY
SALAMANDER
(— FOR DRYING GUNPOWDER)
GLOOM
(— ON SHIP) GALLEY
(PORTABLE —) SALAMANDER
(RUSSIAN —) PEACH
(WARMING —) KANGRI
STOVER OVENSMAN
STOW BIN BOX SET CRAM LADE
MASS CROWD DOUSE STORE
BESTOW COOPER STEEVE DUNNAGE
RUMMAGE
STOWAGE BURTON REMBLAI
RUMMAGE
STOWAWAY HIDER
STOWED IN
STOWER TOPPER
STOWING BINNING GOBBING
STP DOM
STRABISMUS CAST CROSS SQUINT
TROPIA ANOPSIA COCKEYE WALLEYE
STRADDLE SADDLE SPREAD STRIDE
BESTRIDE SPRADDLE STRIDDLE
STRADDLER HOE
STRADDLING ATOP
STRAGGLE GAD ROVE TRAIL
RAMBLE RANGLE SPRAWL STREEL
TAGGLE WANDER DRAGGLE
MEANDER SCRAMBLE SPRANGLE
STRAGGLER STRAY BUMMER
STRAGGLING RAGGED RAGGLED
SPRAYEY SCRATCHY VAGULOUS
STRAIGHT BOLT FAIR FULL GAIN
NEAT BRANT CLEAN DOGGY FLUSH
RIGHT SHORT SPANG ARIGHT DIRECT
HONEST STRAIT STRICT BOBTAIL
REGULAR UPRIGHT DIRECTLY
SEQUENCE
(— AHEAD) ANON PLUMP OUTRIGHT
(— ON) ENDLONG
(— SKINNY) INFO
(— UP AND DOWN) SHEER CLEVER
EVENDOWN
(NOT —) WRY AWRY CRAZY
(PREF.) EUTHY ITHO ITHY ORTH(O)
RECT(I)
STRAIGHTEDGE LUTE RULE RULER
STRICKLE
STRAIGHTEN GAG CONK ORDER
STENT EXTEND SQUARE UNKINK
COMPOSE RECTIFY STRETCH
(— BY HEATING) SET
(— HAIR) CONK
(— NEEDLE) RUB
(— RAILS) GAG
STRAIGHT-FIBERED BROAD
STRAIGHTFORWARD EVEN PLAT
APERT FRANK LEVEL NAKED PLAIN
ROUND CANDID DEXTER DIRECT

STRAIGHTFORWARD HONEST SIMPLE SQUARE JANNOCK
SINCERE EVENDOWN HOMESPUN
OUTRIGHT STRAIGHT OPENHEARTED
(NOT —) CROOKED PLAITED
(PREF.) LITI
STRAIGHTFORWARDLY SINGLY
SQUARE STRAIGHT
STRAIGHT-THINKING CLEAR
STRAIGHTWAY ANON AWAY RIGHT
ARIGHT BEDEEN BEDENE DIRECTLY
STRAIN FIT LAG RAX SIE TAX TRY
TUG ACHE BEND CALL DASH DRAG
HEAT HEFT LAWN NOTE PULL RACK
RANN RICK SILE SINE SOLO SONG
VEIN WORK BRUNT CHAFE DEMUR
DRAIN FORCE HEAVE PRESS RETCH
SHADE SHEAR SIEVE STOCK SURGE
TAMMY TOUCH WREST WRICK
CLENCH EFFORT EXTEND EXTORT
FILTER INTEND KVETCH SPRAIN
SPRING STREAK STRESS STRIND
THRONG DESCANT DISCANT
EUPLOID FATIGUE STRAINT
STRETCH STROPHE TENSION
TORMENT COLANDER DIAPASON
DIATRIBE DIHYBRID FILTRATE
SUBBREED
(— EYES) GOGGLE
(— FROM TWISTING) TORSION
(— MILK) SIE SYE
(— OF AN ARCH) THRUST
(— OF CHICKENS) ANCOBAR
(— OF EXCITEMENT) RACKET
(— OF RAILING LANGUAGE) DIATRIBE
(— ON BUGLE) MOT
(— ON HORN) RECHASE RECHEAT
(— THROUGH COLANDER) COIL
(CONCLUDING —) CADENCE
(MELANCHOLY —) DUMP
(MUSICAL —) FIT SOLO POINT
(MUSICAL —S) TOUCH
(MUTANT —) SALTANT
(PREF.) STREMMATO
STRAINED PENT TENSE INTENSE
LABORED INTENDED
STRAINER CAGE ROSE SILE RENGE
SIEVE STRUM TAMIS TAMMY THEAD
SEARCE SEARCH CRIBBLE COLATORY
COLATURE SEARCHER
(— OF TWIGS) HUCKMUCK
(COFFEE —) GRECQUE
(MILK —) SAY MILSEY MILSIE
(WICKER —) THEAD THEDE
(PREF.) COLI ETHMO
STRAINING CUTE COILED ASTRAIN
INTENSE COLATURE
STRAIT CUT GUT BAND BELT FRET
KYLE NECK PACE BRAKE CANAL
PHARE PINCH SHARD SOUND
ANGUST FRETUM NARROW PLUNGE
CHANNEL EURIPUS BOSPORUS
JUNCTURE

(IN —S) SET
(LAST —) EXIGENT
(NEWFOUNDLAND —) TICKLER
(PL.) CHOPS PRESS EXTREMES
STRAITEN PINCH SCANT STRAIT
STRAITENED CRIMP NARROW
CRIMPED
STRAITJACKET CAMISOLE
STRAITLACED STIFF STUFFY
BLUENOSED
STRAKE SHEER COURSE RISING
STREAK COAMING SAXBOARD
(PL.) TIRE
STRAMONIUM DEWTRY
STRAND PLY TOP BANK CORE FLAT
TOWT WISP BEACH BRAID CLIFF
PRAYA READY SHORE LISSOM
MAROON SINGLE SLIVER STRAIN
STRIKE SUTURE HAIRLINE
(— OF FIBERS) ROVING
(— OF HAIR) LICK SWITCH
(— OF PROTOPLASM) BRIDGE
(— OF TEXTILE) ROVE
(PREF.) CROCO
STRANDED AGROUND ISOLATED
STRANDER EDGER
STRANGE ODD RUM EERY FELL
FREM NICE RARE UNCO ALIEN EERIE
FREMT FUNNY KINKY NOVEL QUEER
UNKET UNKID WOOZY ALANGE
FERLIE QUAINT UNIQUE UNKENT
UNKIND CURIOUS ERRATIC
HEATHEN ODDBALL UNHEARD
UNKNOWN UNUSUAL FANCIFUL
INSOLENT INSOLITE PECULIAR
SELCOUTH SINGULAR UNCOLIKE
UNCOMMON UNKENNED UNKINDLY
MONSTROUS
(— TO SAY) ODDLY
(PREF.) XEN(O)
STRANGENESS ODDITY
STRANGER COME UNCO UNKO
ALIEN GUEST FRENNE GANGER
INCOME INMATE FUIDHIR INCOMER
UNCOUTH MALIHINI OUTCOMER
PEREGRIN OUTLANDER
(SUFF.) XENE XENOUS XENY
STRANGLE CHOKE GRAIN GRANE
SNARL WORRY STIFLE GARROTE
QUACKLE GARROTTE JUGULATE
THROTTLE
STRANGLEHOLD CHANCERY
STRANGUL
STRANIERA, LA (CHARACTER IN —)
ALAIDE ARTURO ISOLETTA
VALDEBURGO
(COMPOSER OF —) BELLINI
STRAP BAR TUG BAND BELT CLIP
CURB GIRD HASP RIDE RIEM BRACE
CHEEK GIRTH GUIGE PATTE RIDER
RISER SABOT SLING STROP THONG
TRACE VITTA ANKLET BACKER BILLET

COLLAR ENARME GARTER HALTER HANGER LAINER LATIGO SANDAL TOGGLE WARROK BABICHE BOWYANG CRIBBER DOLPHIN LANYARD LATCHET LEATHER RIEMPIE STIRRUP TICKLER WEBBING BACKSTAY BRETELLE SQUILGEE TURNBACK WRISTLET
(— **AROUND HORSE'S THROAT**) CRIBBER
(— **AROUND MAST**) DOLPHIN
(— **FOR SHIELD**) GUIGE ENARME BRETELLE
(— **IN FLAIL**) TAPLING
(— **OF BRIDLE**) REIN
(— **OF SENNIT**) BACKER
(— **ON HAWK'S LEAD**) JESS JESSE SENDAL
(— **WITH SLIT END**) TAWS TAWSE
(**ANKLE** —) BRACELET
(**CARRYING** —) METUMP TUMPLINE
(**DOOR** —) HASP
(**HARNESS** —) TRACE
(**MINER'S** —) BYARD
(**SHOE** —) BAR
(**STIRRUP** —**S**) CHAPELET
(**TIE** —) SHANK
(**U-SHAPED** —) STIRRUP
(**PL.**) LADDER
(**PREF.**) LIGUL(I)
STRAP FERN LONGLEAF
STRAPHANGER STANDEE COMMUTER
STRAPPER SPLICER
STRAPPING SWANK BOUNCING CHOPPING SLAPPING SWANKING
STRAP-SHAPED LORATE LIGULAR LIGULATE
STRATA EOCENE TERRANE UNDERAIR
(— **OF COAL**) MEASURES
STRATAGEM JIG COUP LOCK RUSE TRAM TURN WILE ANGLE DRAFT FETCH FRAUD GUILE JOKER KNACK TRAIN TRICK WREST BLENCH DECEIT DEVICE HUMBUG POLICY TRAPAN TREPAN WOIDRE WRENCH FINESSE SLEIGHT ARTIFICE CONTOISE FARFETCH INTRIGUE LIRIPIPE LIRIPOOP PRACTICE PRACTISE QUENTISE STRATEGY TRICKERY MOUSETRAP
(**INDIRECT** —) FEELER
STRATEGY GAME FINESSE
(**MANUFACTURING** —) KANDAN
STRATIFICATION BEDDING
STRATIFIED BEDDED VARVED
STRATIFORM LAYERED
STRATONICE (**FATHER OF** —) DEMETRIUS
(**HUSBAND OF** —) SELEUCUS
(**MOTHER OF** —) PHILA

STRATUM BED CAP CUT LAY RIB FAST LAIN SEAM TIER COUCH ELITE FLOOR LAYER LEDGE SHELF TABLE COUCHE GIRDLE GRAVEL LAYING LISSOM PINNEL AQUAFER AQUIFER ENTIRIS FISHBED SUBSOIL UPRIGHT AQUIFUGE FAHLBAND SUBGRADE
(— **OF COAL**) BENCH
(— **OF FIRECLAY**) THILL
(— **OF PALE COLOR**) FAHLBAND
(— **OF SANDSTONE**) PINNEL
(— **OF SOIL**) SOD
(— **OF STONE**) GIRDLE
(**SOCIAL** —) CUT
(**THIN** —) SEAM LENTIL
STRAW BAKU GLOY MOTE REED RUSH TOYO WASE HAULM PEDAL SHILF STALK STREW YEDDA FESCUE FETTLE PANAMA RIZZOM SIPPER TUSCAN BANGKOK SABUTAN STUBBLE WINDLIN STRAMMEL
(— **CUT FINE**) CHAFF
(— **FOR MAKING HATS**) SENNIT BANGKOK LEGHORN SABUTAN
(— **FOR THATCHING**) YELM
(— **MEASURE**) KEMPLE
(— **TO PROTECT PLANTS**) MULCH
(**BROKEN** —) BHUSA BHOOSA
(**COOKERY** —**S**) PAILLES
(**PLAITED** —) SENNIT
(**WAXED** —) STRASS
(**PREF.**) CARPHO
STRAWBERRY BERRY DUNLAP FRAISE RUNNER HAUTBOY FRUTILLA HAUTBOIS KLONDIKE ROSACEAN
(— **JAR**) PLANTER
STRAWBERRY BUSH WAHOO EUONYMUS EVONYMUS FISHWOOD
STRAWBERRY FINCH AMADAVAT AVADAVAT
STRAWBERRY SHRUB BUBBY COWBERRY
STRAWBERRY TOMATO PHYSALIS BLADDERCHERRY
STRAWBERRY TREE ARBUTUS
STRAY ERR ODD FALL RAVE ROVE WAFF WAIF WALK DRIFT RANGE TRAIK VAGUE WAVER ESTRAY RANGLE SWERVE VAGARY WANDER WILDER DEVIATE FORLORN STRAYER DIVAGATE MAVERICK STRAGGLE
STRAYING ASTRAY ERRANT ABERRANT VAGATION
STREAK PAY RAY BAND SEAM VEIN WALE FLAKE FLECK FLICK FREAK GARLE GLADE SLASH FACULA SMUDGE STRAIN STRAKE STREAM STRIPE FLECKER SPRAING STIPPLE DISCOLOR TRAVERSE
(— **CAUSED BY BLOOD**) VIBEX
(— **IN FABRIC**) CRACK SHINER

(— IN GLASS) SKIM
(— IN HAIR) BLAZE
(— IN SKY) ICEBLINK
(— IN WOOD) ROE
(— OF BLUBBER) BLANKET
(— OF LIGHT) STREAM
(— ON BEAST'S FACE) RACE RATCH
(— ON SURFACE OF SUN) FACULA
(—S FROM PLANE) CONTRAIL
(—S IN ROCK) SCHLIEREN
(— WITH FINE STRIPES) LACE
(BACTERIOLOGICAL —) STROKE
(LOSING —) SLUMP
(RAISED —) WEAL
(THEATRICAL —) HAM
(WHITE —) SHIM
STREAKED ROWY LACED HAWKED
SMEARY BRINDLE BROCKED
BROOKED FINCHED SPARKED
STRIPED WHIPPED BRINDLED
IRONSHOT PINROWED
STREAKY ROWY SCOVY STREAKED
STREAM EA PUP RIO RUN BECK
BURN FLOW FLUX FORD GILL GOTE
KHAL KILL LAKE OOZE POUR PUIT
PURL RILL SICK SIKE SILE SPIN TIDE
BACHE BATCH BAYOU BOGUE
BOURN BROOK CREEK DRILL DRINK
FLARE FLASH FLEAM FLOOD FLOSS
FLUOR FRESH GHYLL NYMPH PRILL
RITHE RIVER SWAMP TCHAI TRAIN
ARROYO CANADA BOURNE BRANCH
BURNIE CANADA COULEE FILLER
FLUENT GUZZLE OUTLET PIRATE
RANDOM RUNDLE RUNNEL SLUICE
SPRUIT STRAND STRONE CHANNEL
CURRENT DRIBBLE FLUENCE
FRESHET RIVULET TRICKLE
AFFLUENT INFLUENT MILLSTREAM
(— ALONG) SLIDE
(— FULL TO TOP) BANKER
(— OF AIR OR SMOKE) PEW
(— OF ELECTRODES) BEAM
(— OF LAVA) COULEE
(— OF SIRUP) THREAD
(— OF SPEECH) STRAIN
(— OUT) BREAK
(FLOWING —) NYMPH
(HIGH-SPEED —) JET
(MYTHOLOGICAL —S) ELIVAGAR
(SLOW —) OOZE
(SLOW-MOVING —) POW
(SLUGGISH —) LANE
(SMALL —) BECK LAKE SIKE DRAFT
RITHE COULEE SICKET SQUIRT
STRIPE DRAUGHT GRINDLE
(THIN —) TRICKLE TRICKLET
(TIDAL —) COVE SEAPOOSE
(TRANSIENT —) RILL
(TRICKLING —) DRILL
(TURBID —) DRUVE
(UNDERGROUND —) AAR SWALLET

(VIOLENT —) TORRENT
(WEAK —) DRIP
(PREF.) AMNI FLUVI
(— OF LAVA) RHYACO
STREAMER FLAG VANE FALLAL
GARTER GUIDON LAPPET PENCEL
PENNON PINNET SCROLL SIMPLE
WIMPLE BANDEROL FILAMENT
(— OF MOSS) WEEPER
(— ON HEADDRESS) LIRIPIPE
(PAPER —S) CONFETTI
STREAMING SLUICY ASTREAM
CRINITE CYCLOSIS DOWNPOUR
STREAMLET RILL RILLET RUNDLE
RUNLET RUNNEL RIVULET
STREAMLINE SIMPLIFY
(— FLOW) LAMINAR
STREAMLINED CLEAN SLEEK
STREET ROW RUE WAY CHAR DRUM
GATE PAVE STEM TOBY BLOCK
BORGO CALLE CANON CHAWK
CORSO DRIVE PASEO AVENUE
BOWERY CANYON CAUSEY CIRCLE
RAMBLA POULTRY TERRACE
THROUGH ARTERIAL BROADWAY
BYSTREET CHAUSSEE CONTRADA
PROSPECT
(— IN BARCELONA) RAMBLA
(— IN FLORENCE) BORGO
(MAIN —) CHAWK CHOWK
TOWNGATE
(NARROW —) CHAR ALLEY CHARE
RUELLE
(PRINCIPAL —) ARTERY
(QUIET —) CULDESAC
(SIDE —) HUTUNG
STREETCAR TRAMCAR TRAMWAY
ELECTRIC
STREET CLEANER ORDERLY
CLEANSER
STREET CLEANING SLOPPING
STREET SCENE
(AUTHOR OF —) RICE
(CHARACTER IN —) SAM ROSE
FRANK STEVE KAPLIN SANKEY
WILLIAM MAURRANT
STREETWALKER BULKER CRUISER
STRENGTH EL ARM VIR BEEF DRAW
GRIP GUTS HEAD HORN IRON MAIN
THEW BRAWN CRAFT ETHAN FIBER
FIBRE FORCE HEART JUICE MIGHT
NERVE POWER SINEW VIGOR
ENERGY FOISON MAUGHT MUSCLE
STARCH VIRTUE ABILITY AFFORCE
COURAGE PROWESS STAMINA
STHENIA CAPACITY FIRMNESS
VALIDITY PUISSANCE
(— OF ACID OR BASE) AVIDITY
(— OF ALE) STRIKE
(— OF CARD HAND) BODY
(— OF CHARACTER) GRISTLE
(— OF CURRENT) AMPERAGE

(— OF GRASP) GRIP
(— OF SOLUTION) TITER TITRE
(— OF SPIRITS) PROOF
(— OF TEA) DRAW
(— OF WILL) BACKBONE
(— OF WINE) SEVE
(SUPERIOR —) PREVALENCE
(PREF.) CRATO DYNAM(I)(O) ISCHY(O)
(SUFF.) DYNAMIA DYNAMOUS
STRENGTHEN IMP ABLE BACK
BIND FIRM FRAP HELP PROP SOUD
STAY BRACE CLEAT FORCE SINEW
STEEL THRAP TONIC TRUSS
ANNEAL ASSURE DEEPEN ENDURE
ENFIRM ENFORT GABION HARDEN
INTEND MUNIFY MUNITE NEEDLE
SETTLE STRING STRONG AFFORCE
BUCKRAM COMFORT CONFIRM
ENFORCE FASCINE FORTIFY
NERVATE QUICKEN RAMPIRE
SUPPORT THICKEN BUTTRESS
ENERGIZE ENTRENCH HEIGHTEN
ROBORATE
STRENGTHENED BULLED
BRANDIED
STRENGTHENING BRACING
ROBORANT
STRENGTHLESS DOWLESS
STRENUOUS HARD EAGER
ARDUOUS WILLING VIGOROUS
STREPHON (BELOVED OF —) CHLOE
STREPSIPTERON STYLOPS
STRESS HIT BIRR BRUNT ICTUS
PINCH SHEAR ACCENT STRAIN
THRONG TENSION CENTROID
DOWNBEAT EMPHASIS PRESSURE
(— OF SOUND) LENGTH
(METRIC —) BEAT
(SYLLABIC —) ARSIS
STRESSED TONIC STRONG
STRETCH EKE LAG LIE RAX RUN
BEAT DRAW LAST MAIN PASS RACK
REAM ROLL RYKE SPAN TEND BOARD
BURST FETCH RATCH RETCH SIGHT
SPELL STENT SWAGE VERGE
EXTEND LENGTH SMOOTH STRAIN
STRAKE STREEK DISPLAY DISTEND
EXPANSE SPELDER ELONGATE
LENGTHEN STRAIGHT
(— CLOTH) TENTER
(— FORCIBLY) RACK
(— FORTH) REACH PORRECT
PRETEND PROTEND
(— INJURIOUSLY) SPRAIN
(— IRREGULARLY) TRAIL
(— LEATHER) DRAFT STAKE
DRAUGHT
(— METAL) FORM
(— OF ARMS) FATHOM
(— OF BROKEN WATER) RIP
(— OF GROUND) BRECK
(— OF INTERVALE) CARSE

(— OF LAND) SWALE COMMON
GALLOP PARCEL COMMONS
(— OF OPEN COUNTRY) RANGE
(— OF ROAD) SIGHT
(— OF SEA) CHOP
(— OF TIME) TIFF
(— OF WALL) CURTAIN
(— OF WATER) GLIDE LEVEL LOGIN
FAIRWAY
(— OF WORK) YOKE
(— OUT) GROW SPIN REACH STENT
STRUT TWINE INTEND OUTLIE
SPRAWL SPREAD SPRING DISTEND
OUTSPAN PORTEND ELONGATE
(— ROPE) WARP
(— SPRAWLINGLY) STRAGGLE
(— THE NECK) CRANE
(— THE WINGS) MANTLE
(CONTINUOUS —) RUN
(GRASSY —) DRINN
(LEVEL —) LAWN
(PREF.) TANY TASI TEN(O) TENONT(O)
TETANI TETANO TINO
(SUFF.) EURYSIS
STRETCHABLE TENSILE
STRETCHED PROSTRATE
(— OUT) PORRECT PROJECT
PROLATE ELONGATE EXTENDED
(TENSELY —) TAUT TORT STIFF
STRETCHER COT STENT GURNEY
LITTER ANGAREP TROLLEY
ANGAREEB BRANCARD STRAINER
STRETCHING
(SUFF.) ECTASIA ECTASIS
STREW BED SOW CLOT DUST LARD
SPEW BESET STRAW STRAY STROW
CARPET LITTER SPREAD BESTREW
SCATTER SKINKLE SPARKLE
(— WITH BULLETS) SPRAY
STREWED BESPRENT
STREWING SEME
STREWN DOTTED BESPRENT
STRIA CORD STRIOLA DRAGLINE
STRIOLET
STRIATE VEIN
STRIATION STREAK STRIGA
STRICKEN STREAKED
STRICKER TIPPLER
STRICKLE SWEEP STRIKER
STRICT HARD TAUT TRUE CLOSE
EXACT HARSH RIGID STARK STERN
TIGHT GIUSTO SEVERE STRAIT
STRONG ASCETIC AUSTERE PRECISE
REGULAR DISTRICT RESTRICT
RIGOROUS STRINGENT
(NOT —) LAX SCIOLTO
STRICTLY NARROW STRAIT CLOSELY
PROPERLY
STRICTNESS RIGOR RIGIDITY
RIGORISM SEVERITY
STRIDE LAMP SAIL STEP FLOAT
SKELP SPANG STEND STRUT

LAMPER STROAM STROKE STROME
BESTRIDE POINTING STRIDDLE
(— ALONG) LAMP
(— EXULTANTLY) GALUMPH
GALLUMPH
(— LOFTILY) STALK
(— PURPOSEFULLY) SLING
STRIDENT HARD HARSH BRASSY
GLASSY SHRILL GRATING RAUCOUS
YELLING GRINDING
STRIDULATE CHIRP PITTER
STRIFE TUG WAR WIN BATE FEUD
HOLD PLEA BRIGE FLITE FLITE
JEHAD JIHAD NOISE STOUR STROW
STRUT STURT BARRAT BICKER
BRIGUE DEBATE ESTRIF MUTINY
STRIVE BARGAIN CONTECK CONTEST
DISCORD DISPUTE HURLING
QUARREL CONFLICT CONTRAST
DISPEACE STRUGGLE CONTENTION
(AUTHOR OF —) GALSWORTHY
(CHARACTER IN —) ENID JOHN
ANNIE DAVID EDGAR SIMON
ANTHONY FRANCIS HARNESS
ROBERTS UNDERWOOD
(CIVIL —) STASIS
STRIGIL COMB SCRAPER
STRIKE GO BAT BOB BOP BOX BUM
COB CUE DAD DUB GET HAB HIT JOB
JOW LAM LAY PUG RAP WAP ABRE
BAFF BEAK BEAT BELT BIFF BILL
BLAD BLIP BUFF BUMP CHAP CLUB
COIN COPE COSH CUFF DING DINT
DONG DUNT FALL FANG FIRK FLAP
FLOG FRAP GIRD GOWF GRAB HACK
HURT HEW KILL KNEE LASH LILT
LUSH MARK NAIL PAIK PASH PLAT
PUCK ROUT SLAM SLAP SLAT SLAY
SLOG SLUG SOCK SPAR SPAT SWAP
SWAT SWIP TAKE WHAP WHOP WIPE
ZONK ANGLE BATON CATCH CHECK
CHIME CHINK CLOUT CLUNK CRACK
CRUNT DEVEL DOUSE DOWSE DRIVE
DUNCH FETCH FILCH FILIP FLAIL
KNOCK PANDY PASTE POKER POTCH
SABER SKELP SKITE SLOSH SMACK
SMITE SNICK SOUND SPANK SQUAP
STAMP STEEK SWACK SWEEP SWIPE
SWISH THROW WHALE WHANG
ACOUPE AFFECT AFFRAP ALIGHT
ATTAIN BATTER BOUNCE BUFFET
COURSE DUNDER FETTLE FILLIP
HAMMER INCUSE INCUTE KEEPER
SLOUGH STOUSH STRICK STRIPE
SWITCH THRASH WALLOP BEARING
FLYFLAP IMPINGE KNUCKLE
PERCUSS STRIKER TURNOUT
WHAMPLE WILDCAT STOPPAGE
STOPWORK STRAMASH STRICKLE
(— ABOUT) FLOP
(— AGAINST) RAM BANG STUMP
ASSAULT COLLIDE
(— AND REBOUND) CAROM

(— A WICKET) BREAK
(— CRICKET BALL) EDGE
(— DOWN) LAY FALL SLAY WEND
FLASH FLOOR AFFLICT SIDERATE
(— DUMB) DUMFOUND
(— FEET TOGETHER) HITCH
(— FORCIBLY) GET CLOUT DEVEL
SLASH
(— GENTLY) PAT
(— GOLF BALL) HOOK DRIVE SCLAFF
(— GROUND IN GOLF) BAFF DUFF
(— HEAVILY) BASH DUNT DUSH FLOP
SLUG CLUMP SLOUGH CLOBBER
(— IN CURLING) WICK
(— LIGHTLY) BOB DAB SPAT FLICK
(— OF LOCK) KEEPER STRIKER
(— ON HEAD) COP NOBBLE
(— OUT) FAN DELE POKE TAKE
CROSS ELIDE CANCEL DELETE
EXPUNGE OUTLASH EXCUDATE
(— REPEATEDLY) DRUM LICK
(— SHARPLY) CUT SNICK
(— SMARTLY) NAP RAP KNAP
(— TEETH TOGETHER) GNASH
(— TOGETHER) CLASH KNACK
(— UP) LILT YERK RAISE
(— VIOLENTLY) RIP BASH DING PASH
SOUSE BENSEL
(— WITH AMAZEMENT) CONFOUND
(— WITH BAT) DRIVE
(— WITH FEAR) ALARM ASTONISH
(— WITH FIST) PLUG NODDLE
(— WITH FOOT) KICK BUNCH SPURN
STAMP
(— WITH HAMMER) CHAP JOWL
MELL
(— WITH HORNS) BUNT BUTT HOOK
(— WITH SHAME) ABASH
(— WITH SPEAR) STICK
(— WITH STICK) SQUAIL
(— WITH WHIP) JERK LASH QUIRK
(— WITH WONDER) SURPRISE
(BOWLING —S) DOUBLE
(HUNGER —) ENDURA
(LABOR —) STEEK STICK TURNOUT
WALKOUT
(LUCKY —) BONANZA
(MINING —) TREND
(THREE —S) TURKEY
(PREF.) PLESSI PLEXI TYPTO
STRIKEBREAKER FINK BLACKLEG
STRIKER BATMAN DRUMMER
TURNOUT PULSATOR
STRIKER-OUT SETTER
STRIKING FITTY FRESH SHOWY VIVID
DARING SIGNAL STRONG SALIENT
SKELPIN TELLING COLORFUL
CONFLICT DRAMATIC FRAPPANT
KNOCKOUT SENSIBLE SIZZLING
SPANKING SPEAKING NOTICEABLE
PERCUSSION PHOTOGENIC
STRING LAG BAND BEND CORD FILE
LACE MEAN PAIR SLIP TAPE TAUM

BRAID BRIDE CHORD POINT SINEW
SNEAD STRAP TWINE CORDON
STRAND TREBLE MINIKIN LIGATURE
RHAPSODY
(— IN BIRD'S EGG) CHALAZA
(— OF BEADS) ROSARY CHAPLET
NECKLACE
(— OF CASH) QUAN TIAO
(— OF DRUM) SNARE
(— OF FIDDLE) THARM
(— OF FLAGS) HOIST
(— OF INVECTIVE) TIRADE
(— OF LOCK) KEEPER
(— OF LYRE) MESE NETE TRITE
HYPATE PARAMESE PARAMETE
(— OF MUSICAL INSTRUMENT) WIRE
CHORD DRONE THAIRM CATLING
MINIKIN LICHANOSE
(— OF ONIONS) REEVE TRACE
(— OF PHRASES) CENTO
(— OF PROPOSITIONS) SORITES
(— OF RAILWAY CARS) SET
(— OF SUGAR CRYSTALS) COB
(— OF VEGETABLES) STRAP
(— OF VERSES) LAISSE
(— OF VIOL) MEAN
(— OF WAGONS) RAKE
(— TOBACCO) SEW
(— UP) KILT
(BONNET —) BRIDE
(E —) QUINT
(LEADING —) BAND
(OAKUM —) PLEDGET
(ORNAMENTAL —) CORDON
(PULL —S) PLUCK
(SURGICAL —) LIGATURE
(VIOLIN —) THAIRM VIBRATOR
(WEAVING —) LEASH
(SUFF.) CHORD(AL)
STRING BEAN SNAP HARICOT
SNAPPER
STRINGCOURSE LEDGE TABLE
CORDON STRING
STRINGENCY RIGOR
STRINGENT HARD RIGID TIGHT
SEVERE STRICT EXTREME
STRINGER BALK BAULK
STRINGHALTED CRAMPY
STRINGY ROPY WOOLY SINEWY
THONGY WOOLLY GARGETY
SINEWED THREADY
STRIP BAR LAG TAG BAND BARE
BEAD BELT BEND BUSK DRIP FUSE
GAGE GAIR HILD HUSK LIST MALL
NAKE NUDE PEEL RAND ROLL SACK
SHIM SKIN TIRL TIRR WELT CLEAN
DRIVE EXUTE FILET FLAKE FLYPE
GAUGE GLEAN GUARD HARRY LABEL
LINER LYNCH PANEL PLUME REEVE
SHEAR SHRED SKELP SLIPE SPEEL
SPOIL STRAP STROP STRUB SWATH
UNGUM UNRIG BORDER BOXING
BRIDGE COLLAR CULPON DENUDE

DEVEST DIVEST FEELER FILLET
FLEECE LIBBET MATRIX PANUNG
REGLET RUNWAY SCROLL SPLINE
STREAK STRIPE TARGET UNBARE
UNBARK UNCASE BANDAGE
BEREAVE CHANNEL DEPLUME
DEPRIVE DESPOIL DISROBE FEATHER
FLOUNCE LAMBEAU LANGUET
NAILROD PINRAIL PLUNDER
UNCLOAK UNCOVER UNDRESS
BOOKMARK COSSETTE DISARRAY
DISENDOW DISTRUSS FOOTBAND
SEPARATE
(— ACROSS SAIL) REEFBAND
(— A PLANT) SPRIG
(— BARK) PILL
(— BINDING STALKS TO WALL) TACK
(— BLUBBER FROM WHALE) FLENSE
(— EAR OF CORN) SILK
(— FOR DRAWING CURVED LINES)
SPLINE
(— FOR GUIDING PLASTER) BEAD
(— FOR MAKING TUBE) SKELP
(— HANGING AROUND SKIRT)
FLOUNCE
(— IN BASKETMAKING) INSIDES
(— IN BEEHIVE) STARTER
(— IN CANING) SPLENT SPLINT
(— IN TYPEWRITER) DRAWBAND
(— OF ARABLE LAND) RIDGE
(— OF BACON) LARDON LARDOON
(— OF CANVAS) FOOTBAND
(— OF CLOTH) LIST PATA RIND ROON
GUARD BANNER DUTCHMAN
(— OF CORK) SPREADER
(— OFF) TIRL FLIPE FLYPE SLIPE
(— OF FABRIC) FLIPPER
(— OF FAT) FATBACK LARDOON
(— OF FEATHERS) PLUCK PLUME
(— OF FIELD HOCKEY AREA) ALLEY
(— OFF SKIN) CASE FLAY
(— OF FUR) GROTZEN
(— OF GRASS) VERGE
(— OF HIDE) SPECK DEWLAP
(— OF LAND) BUTT LAND RAIK RAIN
RAKE TANG BREAK CREEK SLANG
SLIPE SPONG SCREED SELION
STRAKE STRIPE FURLONG ISTHMUS
CORRIDOR SIDELING
(— OF LEATHER) LAY RAND WELT
APRON RANGE THONG BACKSTAY
(— OF LEAVES) TWIST
(— OF LINEN) SETON
(— OF MASONRY) ARCHBAND
(— OF OFFICE) BREAK
(— OF OSIER) SKEIN
(— OF PALM LEAF) CADJAN CAJANG
(— OF PASTRY) STRAW
(— OF PLANKING) APRON
(— OF PLASTER) SCREED
(— OF PRAIRIE) COVE
(— OF PROVISIONS) FORAGE
(— OF RANK) DEGRADE

(— OF RED CLOTH) COXCOMB
(— OF ROADWAY) LANE
(— OF RUBBER) CUSHION
(— OF SHORE) LITTORAL
(— OF TERRITORY) PANHANDLE
(— OF TURF) PARKING
(— OF UNPLOWED LAND) GAIR HADE
HEADLAND
(— OF WATER) INLET
(— OF WOOD) LAG LAT LATH LIST
SHAW SLAT WELT CHINK CLEAT
STAVE BATTEN INWALE RADDLE
REEPER REGLET SPLINE SPLINT
FOOTING FURRING STICKER
TRACKER FOOTLING SPLINTER
(— ON FOLDING DOORS) ASTRAGAL
(— ON PRINTER'S GALLEY) LEDGE
(— ON SQUASH COURT) TELLTALE
(— ON TIRE) CHAFER
(— SEPARATING LINES OF TYPE)
LEAD REGLET
(— WORN ON ARM) MANIPLE
(ARMOR —) SPLENT SPLINT
(BOUNDARY —) PERIMETER
(CAMOUFLAGING —) GARLAND
(COMIC —) FUNNY
(CONSTRUCTION —S) LAGGING
(CORSET —) BUSK
(DEPENDENT —) LAMBEAU
(DIVIDING —) CLOISON
(ELECTROPHORETIC —) ZYMOGRAM
(FASTENING —) TACK
(FRIED —) POPADUM POPPADUM
(HORSESHOE-SHAPED —) BAIL BALE
(IRON IN —S) NAILROD
(LANDING —) RUNWAY
(MARINATED —) FAJITA
(MEDIAN —) MALL
(NARROW —) SEAM SLAT SLIP TAPE
REEVE STRAKE
(PAPER —) ORIHON
(PERFORATED —) LAG
(PROJECTING —) FEATHER
(RAISED —) RIDGE
(SPACING —) REGLET
(STRENGTHENING —) BEND
(THATCHING —) LEDGER
(UNPLOWED —) BALK LINCH LINCHET
LYNCHET
STRIPE BAR RAY BAND BEND LIST
PALE SLAT TRIM WALE WEAL WELT
ZONE FLECK PLAGA STRIA STRIP
SWATH VITTA WHEAL BORDER
CLAVUS COTICE FRENUM LADDER
RIBBON STRAKE STREAK STREAM
COTTISE SPRAING MUSTACHE
TRAVERSE
(— OF CHEVRON) ARC
(— OF COLOR ON CHEEK) FRENUM
FRAENUM
(— ON ANIMAL'S FACE) SNIP BLAZE
(— ON FABRIC) CROSSBAR
(— ON MILITARY SLEEVE) SLASH

(— ON ROMAN TUNIC) LATICLAVE
(— ON SHIELD) ENDORSE
(ENCIRCLING —) ZONE
(PURPLE —) CLAVUS
(SET OF —S) BAR
STRIPED BANDY PALED PIRNY
RAWED RAYED ROWED WALED
ZONED BARRED CORDED LISTED
PIRNED BROCKED TIGROID VITTATE
FASCIATE STRIPPED
(— CROSSWISE) BAYADERE
STRIPED BASS ROCKFISH
SERRANID
STRIPED MAPLE DOGWOOD
STRIPING HAIRLINE
STRIPLIGHT BORDER
STRIPLING LAD SLIP STIRRA
YONKER SPAUGHT YOUNKER
SKIPJACK SPRINGAL SHAVELING
STRIPPED BARE NUDE NAKED
HUSKED PICKED PLUMED UNPEELED
STRIPPER STEMMER SPRIGGER
STRIPPING STROKINGS
(PL.) JIBBINGS
STRIPTEASE (RELATING TO —)
EXOTIC
STRIPTEASER STRIPPER ECDYSIAST
STRIVE AIM HIE TEW TRY TUG DEAL
FEND PAIN TOIL WORK BANDY DRIVE
EXERT FIGHT FORCE LABOR PRESS
BRIGUE BUCKLE BUFFET DEBATE
INTEND PINGLE STRAIN STRIKE
AGONIZE BARGAIN CONTEND
CONTEST DISPUTE ENFORCE
SCUFFLE CONTRAST ENDEAVOR
PURCHASE STRUGGLE
(— AFTER) SEEK FOLLOW CANVASS
(— AGAINST) RESIST
(— FOR SUPERIORITY) VIE KEMP
(— IN OPPOSITION) RIVAL CONTEND
(— TO EQUAL) EMULATE
(— TO OBTAIN) FOLLOW
(— TO OVERTAKE) ENSUE
STRIVING NISUS HORMIC STRIFT
CONATUS CONATION
STRIX SYRNIUM
STROBILE BUR BELL BURR CHAT
CONE BRUSH
STROKE BAT COY CUT DAB FIT JOW
ODD PAT PET POP RUB BAFF BEAT
BLOW CHAP CHOP CLAP COUP CUFF
DASH DENT DING DINT DRAW
DUNT EDGE FIRK FLAP FLEG FLIP
FLOP FUNG GOWF HAND HURT JERK
JOWL KERF LASH LICK NACK PAIK
PEAL PECK SHOT SMIT SWAP TILT
TIRE TUCK WELT WHAP WIPE BRUSH
CHASE DOUSE DOWSE DRAFT FLACK
FLICK FORCE HATCH ICTUS MINIM
PANDY PULSE SHOCK SLASH SLING
SLIVE SLOSH STRIP SWEEP SWING
SWIPE THROW TOUCH TRAIT TRICE
WHACK CARESS CENTER FONDLE

FOOZLE GENTLE GLANCE PLAGUE
PLUNGE SMOOTH STRAIK STRAKE
STRIKE STRIPE DRAUGHT OUTLASH
SOLIDUS VIRGULE APOPLEXY
BACKHAND DRUMBEAT FOREHAND
INSTROKE SCORCHER
(— IN KEEPING TIME) TACT
(— IN PAINTING) HAND
(— IN PENMANSHIP) MINIM
(— IN TENNIS) LET LOB BOAST
CHASE SMASH BRICOLE BACKHAND
FOREHAND OVERHAND
(— OF A LETTER) DUCT STEM SERIF
POTHOOK CROSSBAR
(— OF ART) TOUCH
(— OF BAD FORTUNE) CLAP
(— OF BELL) JOW BELL JOWL KNELL
TELLER
(— OF BOW) SCRAPE
(— OF FORTUNE) CAST BREAK
BONZER FELICITY
(— OF LUCK) HIT FLUKE STRIKE
TURNUP CAPTION
(— OF MISFORTUNE) SISERARY
(— OF SCYTHE) SWATH SWATHE
(— OF SHEARS) SNIP
(— OF WIT) FLIRT
(— OF WORK) BAT CHAR
(— ON THE PALM) LOOFIE
(— WITH CLAW) CLOYE
(BILLIARDS —) SPOT STUN FLUKE
FORCE MASSE HAZARD
(CONNECTING —) LIGATURE
(CRICKET —) CUT GLANCE
(CROQUET —) ROQUET
(CURLING —) INWICK
(CUTTING —) GIRD
(DOUBLE SPINNING —) DRAW
(DRUM —) DRAG
(FINISHING —) NOBBLER
(GOLF —) ODD BAFF BISK HOOK LIKE
BLAST SLICE BISQUE FOOZLE
SCLAFF APPROACH
(HOCKEY —) JOB SCOOP
(JERKY —) STAB
(LIGHTNING —) BOLT
(MEDICAL —) ICTUS APOPLEXY
(MUSICAL —) TACT
(ORNAMENTAL —) FLOURISH
(QUICK —) FLIP
(SKATING —) EDGE MOHAWK
CHOCTAW
(SMART —) FIRK
(SOOTHING —) COY
(SWIMMING —) CRAWL TRUDGEN
BUTTERFLY DOGPADDLE SIDESTROKE
(SWINGING —) HEW
(SWORD —) MONTANTO
(PREF.) BOLO PLEGA PLEGO
(SUFF.) BOLA BOLE BOLIC BOLISM
BOLIST PLEGIA PLEGY PLEXIA
STROLL JET IDLE ROAM ROVE
AMBLE ANTER JAUNT RANGE STRAY

TRAIK BUMMEL DACKER DANDER
GANDER LOUNGE PALMER RAMBLE
SOODLE STROAM STROME TODDLE
WANDER SAUNTER TURNOUT
SPATIATE STRAVAGE STRAVAIG
PERAMBULATE
STROLLER SULKY TRAMP SHULER
FLANEUR SHUILER VAGRANT
BOHEMIAN PUSHCHAIR
STROLLING FLANERIE FUGITIVE
STROMA ECOID OECOID
STRONG FAT FIT HOT FELL FERE
FIRM FORT HALE HANG HARD HIGH
IRON KEEN RANK SURE TRIG TRIM
ACRID BONNY FORCY FRECK FRESH
HARDY HEAVY HOGEN HUSKY JOLLY
LUSTY NAPPY NERVY ORPED PITHY
SHARP SMART SOLID SOUND STARK
STEER STERN STIFF STOUR STOUT
SWITH THEWY VALID VIVID WIGHT
YAULD ARDENT BRAWNY BUCKRA
BUNKUM FEIRIE FIERCE MIGHTY
POTENT PRETTY ROBUST RUGGED
SECURE SEVERE SINEWY STABLE
STANCH STARCH STURDY WIELDY
BOARDLY BUIRDLY DOUGHTY
DURABLE EXALTED FECKFUL
HUFFCAP HUMMING INTENSE
LUSTFUL NERVOUS POLLENT
SKOOKUM STHENIC ATHLETIC
BIDDABLE MUSCULAR REVERENT
ROBOREAN SPANKING STALWART
STIFFISH VIGOROUS MERACIOUS
(PREF.) TRACHY VALE
STRONGBOX ARCA PETE COFFER
DEEDBOX
STRONGEST EXTREME
STRONGHOLD HOLD KEEP PEEL
PIECE PLACE TOWER CASTLE
WARDER BASTION CITADEL KREMLIN
REDOUBT FASTHOLD FASTNESS
FORTRESS FRONTIER MUNIMENT
STRENGTH
(— ON STEEP PLACE) AERY EYRY
AERIE EYRIE
STRONGLY BUT SAD BADLY SWITH
FIRMLY STRONG DURABLY FRESHLY
HEFTILY SOLIDLY STITHLY STOUTLY
HEARTILY
STRONG-SCENTED HIGH RANK
STRONG-SMELLING FOXY
STRONTIUM SULPHATE
ACANTHIN
STROP RIP STRAP
STROPHE ALCAIC LAISSE STANZA
SAPPHIC
STROPHIC MELIC
STROPHIUS (FATHER OF —)
CRISSUS
(MOTHER OF —) ANTIPHATIA
(SON OF —) PYLADES
(WIFE OF —) ANAXIBIA ASTYOCHIA
CYDRAGORA

STRUCK (— SHARPLY) SMITTEN
(— WITH AMAZEMENT) AGAZED
AGHAST
(— WITH FEAR) AFRAID
STRUCTURAL ORGANIC ANATOMIC
TECTONIC
(— UNIT) IDANT
STRUCTURE CAGE FALX FORM
MAKE ANNEX BOOTH CABIN FLOAT
FRAME GETUP HOUSE KIOSK PEGMA
SETUP SHAPE STOCK BRIDGE
CAGEOT FABRIC GANTRY GIRDER
ISOGEN KELSON PREFAB TIMBER
COTTAGE EDIFICE FAIRING FEATURE
GATEWAY GESTALT KEELSON
MANSION NURAGHE OUTCAST
PAGEANT STADIUM TURNOUT
ZEUGITE AEDICULA AIRCRAFT
AIRFRAME BUILDING BUTTRESS
COMPAGES CRIBWORK DOMATIUM
ENDOCONE ESCORIAL HEADWORK
MOUNTURE NEOMORPH SKELETON
STANDARD
(— ALONG WALK) PERGOLA
(— BUILT IN WATER) PIER
(— CONTAINING KILN) HOVEL
(— EXTENDED INTO SEA) JETTY
(— FOR PIGEONS) COTE
(— FRAMING SHIP) KEELSON
(— IN ROCKS) FLASER
(— OF CARTRIDGE) ANVIL
(— OF EYE) LENS
(— OF PRETENSION) PERRON
(— ON ROOF) CUPOLA FEMERELL
(— ON SHIP) BLISTER
(— ON STEAMER) TEXAS
(— OVER MINE SHAFT) HEADFRAME
(— OVER WELL) WELLHEAD
(— PRODUCING SMOOTH OUTLINE)
FAIRING
(— SHELTERING INSECTS)
DOMATIUM
(— SUPPORTING AIRSHIP
PROPELLER) PYLON
(— TO DEFLECT CURRENT) SPUR
(— WITHIN SHELL) ENDOCONE
(ANATOMICAL —) BUD APRON
CARINA CRESCENT
(ANTICLINAL —) SWELL
(ARCHED —) FORNIX
(ARTISTIC —) MOBILE
(BELL-SHAPED —) PETTICOAT
(BODILY —) FRAME PHYSIQUE
(BRICK —) KANG HOVEL
(BRISTLELIKE —) ARISTA
(BRONZE AGE —) HENGE
(CABINLIKE —) CABANA
(CLIMBING —) LADDER
(COAL-SHIPPING —) STAITH STAITHE
(COMPLEX —) EMBOLUS
(CONELIKE —) PYRAMID
(CONICAL —) BULLET
(CREMATION —) DARGA

(CROWNLIKE —) CORONA
(CRYSTAL —) POLYTYPE
(CYLINDRICAL —) SILO
(DEADENING —) BAFFLE
(DEFENSIVE —) CAT
(FLATTENED —) TABULA
(FORTIFIED —) CAVALIER
(FRAIL —) SHELL
(GENERAL —) GETUP
(GEOLOGICAL —) CAMBER
(GRAMMATICAL —) SYNTAX
(HIGH —) TOWER
(HOLLOW —) SHELL
(KNEE-LIKE —) GENU
(LATTICEWORK —) TRELLIS
(LENS-SHAPED —) LENTOID
(LOFTY —) BABEL STEEPLE
(LOGICAL —) EIDOS
(MEGALITHIC —) HENGE
(ORGANIZED —) BULK
(ORIENTAL STORIED —) PAGODA
(ORNAMENTAL —) KIOSK
(PLANT —) DISC DISK
(POINTED —) BEAK
(PROTECTIVE —) SHEATH
(PUEBLO —) KIVA
(RAISED —) CIMBORIO
(RAMSHACKLE —) COOP
(RINGLIKE —) ANNULUS
(RODLIKE —) RIB
(RUDE STONE —S) SPECCHIE
(SACRIFICIAL —) ALTAR
(SENTENCE —) SYNTAX
(SHELTERING —) COT
(SHIELDING —) SHELTER
(SICKLE-SHAPED —) FALX
(SLENDER —) HAIR
(SPIRY —) PINNACLE
(STEMLIKE —) STOLON
(STONE —) TAULA
(TEMPORARY —) HUT
(THEATER —) SKENE
(TIERED —) STAGE
(UNDERLYING —) BOTTOM
(UNSTABLE —) COBHOUSE
(VEHICLE —) MONOCOQUE
(WATERTIGHT —) CAMEL
COFFERDAM
(WHITE —) ALBEDO
(PREF.) MORPH(O)
(RADIATED —) ACTIN(O)
(SUFF.) (— OF A KIND) ID
(SUFF.) (— UNIT) EME
STRUDEL (PASTRY KIN TO —)
STOLLEN
STRUGGLE IT TEW TUG VIE WIN
AGON CAMP COPE DEAL FEND FICK
FRAB GAME PULL TAVE TOIL AGONY
FIGHT FLING HEAVE LABOR STRAY
SWORD TEAVE TWEIL WORRY WRELE
BATTLE BUCKLE BUFFET BUSTLE
COMBAT EFFORT HASSLE JOSTLE
JUSTLE PINGLE RELUCT SEESAW

SPRAWL SPRUNT STIVER STRIFE STRIVE TERVEE TUSSLE WARSLE WIDDLE AGONIZE CLAMBER CONTEND CONTEST DISPUTE FLOUNCE GRAPPLE SCUFFLE TUILYIE WARFARE WAUCHLE WRESTLE CONFLICT ENDEAVOR FLOUNDER SCRAFFLE SCRAMBLE SLUGFEST SPRANGLE SPRATTLE
(— ALONG) HOBBLE
(— CONVULSIVELY) SPRAWL
(— FOR LARGESS) SCAMBLE
(— FORTH) ELUCTATE
(— ON) POUND
(— TO GAIN FOOTING) SCRABBLE SPROTTLE
(AGONIZED —) THROE
(CLOSE —) HANDGRIPS
(CONFUSED —) MUSS
(DEATH —) AGONY
(HAND-TO-HAND —) GRAPPLE
(HAPHAZARD —) SCUFFLE
(SPIRITUAL —) PENIEL
(UNCEREMONIOUS —) SCRAMBLE
STRUGGLER LAOCOON
STRUM THRUM
STRUMA GOITER GOITRE
STRUMPET BRIM PUNK BIMBO TRULL WENCH WHORE BLOWEN BULKER STIVER TOMBOY TOMRIG COCOTTE SUCCUBA DOLLYMOP PUNKLING SUCCUBUS VENTURER
(WORN-OUT —) HARRIDAN
STRUT JET BRAG COCK POMP SPUR BRANK CORSO MAJOR PRINK RANCE SWANK SASHAY SCOTCH STRIDE STROKE STROOT STRUNT NAUNTLE PEACOCK STEMPLE SWAGGER TRANSOM
(KIND OF —) MACPHERSON
STRUTTER HAM
STRUTTING COCKING
STUB BUTT SNAG SPUD STOB STUD CHECK ERGOT GUARD HINGE STUMP SPRUNT
STUBBLE BUN ETCH MANE SHACK ARRISH EDDISH STOVER STUMPS EEGRASS GRATTEN STIBBLE
STUBBORN SOT BALKY ROWDY RUSTY STIFF STOUT STUNT THRAW TOUGH MULISH STURDY THWART BULLDOG PEEVISH PIGGISH RESTIVE WAYWARD WILLFUL OBDURATE PERVERSE STUNKARD THRAWART OBSTINATE PIGHEADED TENACIOUS REFRACTORY
STUBBORNNESS STOMACH ADAMANCY
STUBBY STUB CUTTY SQUAT STOCKY STUMPY STUBBED
STUCCO ALBARIUM
STUCK FAST MIRED INARUT MASHED WEDGED STICKIT STOODED

STUCK-UP BUG FROSTED
STUD SET BOLT BOSS KNOB KNOP KNOT NAIL RACE SLUG SPOT BESET BULLA CLOUT HARAS JOIST WRIST ASHLAR ENSTAR INSTAR STOOTH STRING CONTACT POTENCE QUARTER STUDDLE PUNCHEON STANDARD STUDDERY
(— FARM) HARAS
(— IN BOOT SOLE) SLUG
(— IN WATCH) POTENCE
(— SHOES) HOBNAIL
(— WITH NAILS) CLOUT
(INTERMEDIATE —) PUNCHEON
(ORNAMENTED —) AGLET AIGLET
STUDDED BOSSY BILLETY STELLED BILLETTE
STUDDLE POST ROIL
STUDENT BOY DIG WIT COED PLUG PREP SMUG SOPH AGGIE BAHUR BEJAN ELEVE FUCHS GRIND MEDIC PUPIL SIZAR SPOON BOCHER BURSAR BURSCH INTERN JUNIOR JURIST MEDICO OPTIME PREMED PRIMAR PRIMER PUISNE SCOLOG SENIOR ADVISEE CHRONIC CLASSIC DANTEAN EDUCAND ETONIAN FAILURE GOLIARD GRECIAN INTERNE INTRANT LEARNER MIDDLER MOOTMAN OPPIDAN PASSMAN PHARMIC PLUGGER SCHOLAR STUDIER TEMPLAR THEOLOG BOTANIST CABALIST COLLEGER DEMOTIST DISCIPLE EDUCATOR FEMINIST HOMERIST HOSTELER ISLAMIST PREMEDIC REPEATER SECONDAR SUBSIZAR TRANSFER
(— IN TALMUDIC ACADEMY) BAHUR
(— LAST IN CLASS) SPOON
(— OF LOW RANK) TERNAR TERNER
(— WHO LIVES IN TOWN) OPPIDAN
(ABNORMALLY ABSORBED —) SAP
(AFTER-DEGREE —) POSTDOC
(DAY —) EXTERN EXTERNE
(DIVINITY —) STIBBLER
(DRUDGING —) PLUG
(ENGLISH SCHOOL —) BLUE SWOT ETONIAN OXONIAN SWOTTER BATTELER
(GRADUATE —) FELLOW
(LAW —) PUNEE JURIST LEGIST PUISNE TEMPLAR STAGIARY
(MILITARY —) CADET
(MOSLEM —) SOFTA
(NON-COLLEGIATE —) TOSHER
(PLODDING —) DIG SMUG
(WANDERING —) GOLIARD
(1ST-YEAR —) FUCHS
(3RD-YEAR —) JUNIOR TERTIAN
(PL.) GOWN CLASS HOUSE SEMINAR
(SUFF.) LOG(ER)(IA)(IAN)(IC)(ICAL)
(IST)(UE)(Y)
STUDIED COOL VOULU STUDIOUS

STUDIO LOT SHOT ATELIER BOTTEGA
GALLERY
STUDIOUS BOOKY BOOKISH
CLERKLY DILIGENT SEDULOUS
STUDY CON BEAT BONE BOOK CASE
MUZZ PORE ROOM SIFT STUD GRIND
ESTUDY EXAMEN LESSON MUSEUM
SCOLEY SURVEY ABBOZZO
ACCOUNT ANALYZE CANVASS
CROQUIS POCHADE REVOLVE
SANCTUM ANALYSIS BOOKWORK
CONSIDER EXERCISE MEDITATE
SCRUTINY TYPOLOGY
(— ANEW) REVISE
(— BY LAMPLIGHT) LUCUBRATE
(— HARD) DIG MUG SAP BONE CRAM
PORE SMUG STEW SWOT
(— OF ALGAE) PHYCOLOGY
(— OF BLINDNESS) TYPHLOLOGY
(— OF BRAMBLES) BATOLOGY
(— OF CLOUDS) NEPHOLOGY
(— OF CODES) CRYPTOLOGY
(— OF CREEDS) SYMBOLICS
(— OF DREAMS) ONEIROLOGY
(— OF EARTHQUAKES) SEISMOLOGY
(— OF EXCREMENT) SCATOLOGY
(— OF FEVERS) PYRETOLOGY
(— OF FLYING OBJECTS) UFOLOGY
(— OF GRASSES) AGROSTOLOGY
(— OF INSECTS) ENTOMOLOGY
(— OF LAKES) LIMNOLOGY
(— OF MOUNTAINS) OROLOGY
OREOLOGY
(— OF MOUTH) STOMATOLOGY
(— OF MUSCLES) MYOLOGY
(— OF ONESELF) AUTOLOGY
(— OF PEACE) IRENOLOGY
(— OF PLACE NAMES) TOPONYMY
(— OF PRIMITIVE CUSTOMS)
AGRIOLOGY
(— OF PUNISHMENT) PENOLOGY
(— OF RELIGIOUS FEASTS)
HEORTOLOGY
(— OF SACRED EDIFICES) NAOLOGY
(— OF SNOW AND ICE) CRYOLOGY
(— OF SOILS) PEDOLOGY
(—OF SPORES) PALYNOLOGY
(— OF TREES) DENDROLOGY
(— OF VALUES) AXIOLOGY
(— OF VERSIFICATION) PROSODY
(— OF WEAPONS) HOPLOLOGY
(— STEADILY) PLOD
(— UNDER PRESSURE) CRAM
(ART —) ABBOZZO CROQUIS
POCHADE
(BROWN —) MEMENTO REVERIE
(CLAY —) BOZZETTO
(LABORIOUS —) GRIND
(MUSICAL —) ETUDE
(PRELIMINARY —) SKETCH
(UNINTERESTING —) GRIND
(SUFF.) ICS SOPH(ER)(IC)(IST)(Y)

**STUDY IN SCARLET (AUTHOR OF
—)** DOYLE
(CHARACTER IN —) HOPE JOHN LUCY
HOLMES TOBIAS WATSON FERRIER
GREGSON LESTRADE SHERLOCK
STAMFORD JEFFERSON
STANGERSON
STUFF PAD RAM WAD CRAM CRAP
GAUM GEAR JAZZ PANG SATE STOP
TACK TRIG TUCK WHAT CROWD
DUROY FARCE FORCE KEDGE METAL
PASTE SQUAB TRADE FABRIC GRAITH
KIBOSH MATTER PAUNCH STEEVE
STODGE TACKLE TIMBER BOMBARD
BOMBAST DRUGGET ELEMENT
ENFARCE DIAPHANE MARINATE
MATERIAL SPLUTTER WHIPPING
(— AND NONSENSE) HAVERS PICKLE
PIFFLE
(— FILLET OF VEAL) BOMBARD
(— FULL) STODGE
(— OF POOR QUALITY SILK) RASH
(— ONESELF) MAST
(— POULTRY) FARCE MARINATE
(— WITH DRESSING) QUILT
(CLAGGY —) STODGE
(COTTON —) CALICO
(HOUSEHOLD —) GEAR
(INFERIOR —) MOCKADO
(PALTRY —) TRASH
(POOR —) TRIPE
(SILKEN —) TARS TARSE DIAPHANE
(SLOPPY —) SLIPSLOP
(STICKY —) GOOK
(TASTELESS —) GLOP
(THIN —) CRAPE
(THIN SILK —) LOVE
(WATERY —) BLASH
(WISHY-WASHY —) BLASH
(WOOLEN —) SAY DUROY TWILLY
DRUGGET SAGATHY SHALLOON
(WORSTED —) BUNTING
(WORTHLESS —) GEAR GLOP
HOGWASH
STUFFED PANG TRIG BLOAT FARCI
STODGY BLOATED BOMBAST
(— DELICACY) DERMA
STUFFING PAD TAR FARCE KAPOK
STECH STUFF BOMBAST FARCING
SAWDUST SALPICON STUFFAGE
(— FOR MATTRESS) PULU
STUFFY POKY CLOSE FUBBY FUBSY
FUGGY STIVY WOOLY WOOLLY
AIRLESS FROUSTY
STULTIFY SOT PUPPIFY
STUMBLE CHIP FALL HAMP PECK
STOT TRIP HAMEL LURCH SPURN
STOIT STUMP BUMBLE CHANCE
FALTER HALPER HAMBLE HAPPEN
LUMPER OFFEND STEVEL TUMBLE
WAGGER BLUNDER FOUNDER
MISSTEP SCAMBLE SNAPPER

STAMMER STAMPLE STOITER
STOTTER STUMMER FLOUNDER
THRUMBLE

STUMBLING HACK HURTING
OFFENCE OFFENSE

STUMP CAG GET JOB NOG SET BUTT
DOCK GRUB LUMP MORE RUNT
SNAG STAB STAM STOB STUB STUD
CHUNK ORATE SCRAB SCRAG STICK
STOCK STOMP STOOL STOOP
STOWL DOTARD NUBBIN SCRUNT
SPRONG STOVEN WICKET DODDARD
RAMPICK RAMPIKE ST EDER
STUMMEL BALDHEAD HUSTINGS
STUBBLES
(— AND ROOT) MOCK
(— OF TAIL) STRUNT
(CIGAR —) TOPPER
(CRICKET —) STICKS
(DEAD —) RUNT
(TREE —) MOCK STOW STOCK STOOP
ZUCHE DOTARD NUBBIN STOVEN
DODDARD
(WALNUT —) BUTT

STUMPY SNUB BUNTY SNUBBED

STUN DIN BOWL DAZE ROCK ZONK
DAUNT DAVER DEAVE DOVER DOZEN
DROWN STONY ASTONY BEDAZE
BENUMB DEADEN DEAFEN DEVVEL
NOBBLE STOUND WITHER ASTOUND
DAMMISH SANDBAG SILENCE
STUPEFY STUPEND ASTONISH
PARALYZE
(— BY A SHOT) CREASE

STUNNED SILLY STUPENT
ASTONIED

STUNNER KNOCKER THUMPER
TRIMMER

STUNNING CRASHING SHOCKING

STUNT GAG KIP FEAT NIRL BLAST
CANOE CROWL DWARF STINT STOCK
BARANI BARONI CRADDY DOLPHIN
BACKBEND CATALINA CRUCIFIX
PORPOISE PRATFALL SUPPRESS
(PUBLICITY —) HYPE
(SWIMMING —) SHARK SPIRAL

STUNTED URLED GRUBBY RUNTISH
SCROGGY SCRUBBY SCRUFFY
SCRUNTY WANTHRIVEN

STUPA TOPE CHORTLN

STUPEFACTION STOUND STUPOR

STUPEFIED MAD DAMP DAZED
DRUNK MAZED SILLY SOTTED
ZONKED BEMAZED BEMUSED
DONNERT DOZENED DOZZLED
STUPENT BESOTTED DATELESS
MINDLESS

STUPEFIER OPIUM

STUPEFY FOX BAZE DAMP DAZE
DOZE DRUG DULL GOOF MAZE MULL
STUN ZONK BESOT DAUNT DAVER
DEAVE DIZZY DOZEN SHEND SMOKE

STONY ASTONE ASWEVE BEMUSE
BENUMB DUDDLE FUDDLE MOIDER
MUDDLE STOUND ASTOUND
CONFUSE FORDULL SLUMBER
STUPEND ASTONISH BEFUDDLE
BEMUDDLE BEWILDER CONFOUND
MORPHINE PARALYZE SOMNIATE
SOPORATE

STUPEFYING STONY

STUPENDOUS GREAT IMMENSE
ENORMOUS MONSTROUS

STUPID FAT JAY BETE DOWF DULL
DUMB DUNT FOOL HAZY LEWD NICE
NUMB SLOW BLUNT BOOBY BRUTE
CRASS DENSE DORKY DOTED DUNNY
GLAKY GOOSY GROSS HEAVY INERT
MOSSY MUZZY SILLY THICK ASSISH
BARREN BOVINE CUCKOO DAWKIN
DOITED DROWSY DUMMEL HEBETE
LOGGER LURDAN OBTUSE OPAQUE
SIMPLE SODDEN STOLID STULTY
STURDY SUMPHY TAVERT URLUCH
WOODEN ASININE BRUTISH CHUCKLE
DOLTISH DONNARD DONNERD
DOWFART DUFFING DUMPISH
FATUOUS FOOLISH FOPPISH
GAWKISH GLAIKIT GULLISH INSULSE
LUMPISH LURDANE PEAKISH
PINHEAD PROSAIC SOTTISH TAIVERT
TOMFOOL VACUOUS WITLESS
ANSERINE BAYARDLY BESOTTED
BLOCKISH BOBBYISH BOEOTIAN
CLODDISH DONNERED DUNCICAL
FOOTLESS GAUMI FOO HEADLESS
IMBECILE STUCKISH PINHEADED
BENSELESS
(— PERSON) HOIT NERD JUKEO
SUMPH LUMMOX TUMFIE KALLIKAK
(PREF.) MORO

STUPIDITY BETISE TORPOR
BOBBERY DENSITY DUNCERY
FATUITY DULLNESS DUMBNESS
HEBETUDE STOLIDITY

STUPOR FOG SOG COMA DAMP
DOTE SOPOR SWARF STOUND
TORPOR TRANCE NARCOMA
LETHARGY NARCOSIS
(PREF.) NARC(O) TYPH(O)

STURDILY BUFF TOUGH

STURDY GID BUFF DUNT RUDE TALL
THRO BURLY CRANK FELON HARDY
HUSKY LUSTY SOLID SOUND STARK
STERN STIFF STOUT VAUDY WALLY
FEERIE PLUGGY ROBUST RUGGED
RUSTIC SQUARE STABLE STEADY
STEEVE STOCKY STRONG STUGGY
VIRILE FECKFUL UPRIGHT VALIANT
STALWART STUBBORN VIGOROUS
YEOMANLY

STURGEON HUSO ELOPS BELUGA
GANOID MAMMOSE OSSETER
STERLET

STUTTER FAM BUFF HACK MANT
STOT STUT GANCH FAMBLE HABBER
HABBLE STAMMER
STUTTERER RATTLER
STUTTERING TRAULISM
BALBUTIENT
STY PEN QUAT STYE WEST FRANK
CRUIVE PIGPEN STITHE
HORDEOLUM
STYLE AIR CUT DUB PEN SAY TON
WAY CHIC FACE FORM GARB HAND
KIND MODE MOLD NAME PILE RATE
TWIG VEIN GENRE GETUP GUISE
IDIOM SHAPE STATE SWANK TASTE
FESCUE FORMAT GNOMON GOTHIC
PHRASE STEELE STRAIN STYLUS
UMBONE COSTUME DIALECT
DICTION FASHION INSTYLE QUALITY
EQUIPAGE LANGUAGE MARINISM
NARRANTE PULLBACK
PHRASEOLOGY
(— HAIR) CORNROW
(— OF ARCHITECTURE) ORDER
DRAVIDA GEORGIAN
(— OF COOKING) CUISINE
(— OF DRESS) GUISE
(— OF GEM SETTING) BOX
(— OF HANDWRITING) CHANCERY
SCRIPTION
(— OF HAT) BLOCK
(— OF MOUNTING) SETTING
(— OF MUSIC) BOOGIE
(— OF PAINTING) GENRE
(— OF PENMANSHIP) HAND
(— OF PRINTING) CAMAIEU
(— OF SPEAKING) ADDRESS
(— OF SWIMMING) STROKE
(— OF WRESTLING) SAMBO
(AFFECTED —) EUPHUISM
(ARTISTIC —) GUSTO GOTHIC
ARTIFICE DANDYISM MANNERISM
(BOOKBINDING —) ALDINE MAIOLI
MAJOLI FANFARE GROLIER
ETRUSCAN HARLEIAN ROXBURGH
(CUSTOMARY —) GATE
(DECORATIVE —) ARTDECO
(DISTINCTIVE —) CLOTHES
(FAVORED —) GROOVE
(HAIR —) CROP TETE
(INFLATED —) FUSTIAN
(JAZZ —) TAILGATE
(LACKING —) FUNKY
(LATEST —) KICK
(OF PAST —) RETRO
(PRETENTIOUS —) BOMBAST
(PROPER —) WEAR
(THEATRICAL —) LYCEUM
(WRITING —) MINUSCULE
(SUFF.) (IN THE — OF) ESQUE
STYLET SPEAR STILET STYLUS
TROCAR MANDRIN STILETTE
STYLIDIUM CANDOLEA

STYLISH FLY CHIC DOSS POSH TONY
DOGGY NIFTY NOBBY RITZY SASSY
SHARP SMART SWELL TIPPY TOPPY
CHEESY CLASSY DAPPER DRESSY
FLOSSY JAUNTY SWANKY TONISH
DASHING DOGGISH GENTEEL
KNOWING SWAGGER TOFFISH
STYLOBATE PODIUM
STYLOID BELONOID
STYLUS GAD PEN STYLE CUTTER
GREFFE TRACER HARPAGO POINTEL
PYROPEN
STYMPHALUS (FATHER OF —)
ELATUS
(MOTHER OF —) LAODICE
STYPTIC ALUM AMADOU MATICO
BAROMETZ STANCHER
STYRENE STYROL CINNAMOL
STYX (— FERRYMAN) CHARON
(FATHER OF —) OCEANUS
(HUSBAND OF —) PALLAS
(MOTHER OF —) TETHYS
SUAEDA DONDIA
SUAH (FATHER OF —) ZOPHAH
SUAN PAN SOROBAN
SUAVE COOL OILY SMUG SOFT
BLAND SOAPY SVELT GLOSSY
SILKEN SMOOTH URBANE FULSOME
POLITIC DEBONAIR UNCTUOUS
SUAVELY CREAMILY
SUAVITY COMITY URBANITY
SUB GRASS UBOAT
SUBALTERN WART
SUBBASE PLINTH
SUBCINCTORIUM BALTEUS
BALTHEUS
SUBCLASS GENDER BRYALES
CESTODA CYCLIAE DIGENEA SPECIES
AMOEBAEA ANAPSIDA CESTODES
COPEPODA GANOIDEI SELACHII
SUBCOMPACT MINICAR
SUBCULTURE HIPHOP
SUBCUTANEOUS DEEP
SUBDEACON MINISTER
SUBDIVIDE CARVE MINCE
SUBDIVISION DEN OBE SEX BEAT
CAZA DHER HAPU ITEM TASU BUNDA
CORPS CURIA DEKAN DHERI FERAE
FORTY HSIEN IOWAN NAHIE OKRUG
PHYLE SITIO STAGE TALUK TARAF
TURMA UINTA ALBIAN ARENIG
BANNER BRANCH BUREAU CERCLE
CIRCLE CLAUSE COHORT COLUMN
COMMOT DAKOTA DANIAN DOGGER
FACIES GUELPH HEMERA IMBREX
LENGTH LUDLOW MARKAZ NAHIYE
OBLAST ONEIDA SANJAK SECTOR
SERIAL SHIRAZ STRAIN SUBAGE
TAHSIL TASSOO TEHSIL BUKEYEF
CENTURY CHEMUNG CHIRIPA
COCHITI COMARCA ECOTYPE
ELEMENT EPARCHY EPISODE

GENESEE MANIPLE MONTANA
ORBITAL PHRATRY RONDOUT
3ASTEAN SECTION SEEDBED
SUBAREA SUBLINE SUBPLAT
SURPLOT SUBRACE SUBZONE
SUPPORT TRENTON TRINITY
WASATCH WASHITA WENLOCK
WICHITA BANOVINA DISTRICT
DIVISION DJAGATAY ENDBRAIN
FLOTILLA GUBERNIA LOCATION
MONTEREY NAUCRARY PARTICLE
PRECINCT STOCKTON SUBCASTE
SUBORDER SUBSTAGE SUBTRIBE
TOWNSHIP PARAGRAPH
(— OF SCOUTS) CREW
(EGYPTIAN —) KISM
(SPARTAN —) ENOMOTY
SUBDOMINANT FOURTH
SUBDUE BOW COW ADAW BEAT
BEND QUAY TAME ACCOY ALLAY
AMATE CHARM CRUSH DAUNT
DOMPT QUAIL QUASH QUELL
SOBER STILL ADAUNT BRIDLE
CHASTE DEBELL DISMAY EVINCE
GENTLE MASTER QUENCH
REDUCE SUBACT SUBMIT UNWILD
ABANDON AFFAITE CAPTURE
CHASTEN CONQUER DAUNTON
OVERAWE REPRESS REPRIME
SUCCUMB CONVINCE OVERCOME
SUPPEDIT SUPPRESS SURMOUNT
VANQUISH
SUBDUED MAK SOFT TAME MUTED
SOBER STILL UNDER BROKEN
CHASTE GENTLE ASHAMED
SUBMISS SOURDINE
SUBFAMILY KHOISAN CUSHITIC
ACHAEINAE
SUBGROUP BAND FAMILY
SUBHEAD BOXHEAD SIDEHEAD
SUBIMAGO DUN
SUBINDEX SUFFIX
SUBIRRIGATE SUB SUBWATER
SUBIRRIGATION SUBBING
SUBJECT DUX PUT ABLE ALLY RODY
BONE ITEM OPEN TEXT HOBBY
PLACE STOOP STUDY TESTO THEMA
THEME TOPIC GROUND IMPOSE
LIABLE PATHIC REDUCE SACOPE
SUBDIT SUBMIT THRALL VASSAL
CAITIVE CITIZEN FEODARY FEUDARY
OBVIOUS PROBAND SERVILE
AMENABLE ELFCTIVE INCIDENT
INFERIOR OBEDIENT OCCASION
SENTENCE SUBJUGAL
(— OF DISCOURSE) NOUN
(— OF FUGUE) GUIDA
(— OF PROPOSITION) EXTREME
(— TO ABUSE) REVILE
(— TO ARGUMENT) MOOT
(— TO BAD TEMPER) MOODY
(— TO CHANGE) MUTABLE FUGITIVE

(— TO CRITICISM) SCOURGE
(— TO FATE) FIE
(— TO PERCOLATION) DISPLACE
(— TO SOME ACTION) TREAT
(CONTROVERTED —) ISSUE
(LOYAL —) LIEGE
(PL.) FOLK
SUBJECTION SLAVERY SERVITUS
THIRLING
SUBJECTIVE IMMANENT INSEEING
INTERNAL PECTORAL EPISTEMIC
SUBJOIN AFFIX ANNEX
SUBJUGATE COW ENSLAVE
SUBJUGATION BONDAGE
SERVITUDE
SUBKINGDOM PHYLUM
ANNULOSA CHORDATA
SUBLEADER HEADMAN
SUBLEASE FARMOUT SUBTACK
SUBLET JOB SUBSET CONACRE
SUBLEASE
SUB-LIEUTENANT CORNET
SUBLIMATE FLOWER ALCOHOL
SUBLIME
SUBLIME BIG FUME GRAND LOFTY
NOBLE AUGUST REFINE SOLEMN
WINGED DANTEAN ELEVATO
EXALTED EMPYREAL EMPYREAN
MAGNIFIC MAJESTIC SERAPHIC
SPLENDID MAGNIFICENT
(— IN STYLE) MILTONIC
(FALSELY —) TUMID
SUBLIMITY GRANDEUR
SUBLUNARY EARTHLY
SUBMARINE SUB BOAT HERO DIVER
EBOAT FRITZ GUPPY HOAGY UBOAT
HOAGIE SUBSEA PIGBOAT POORBOY
TIDDLER
(GERMAN —) UBOAT
(PART OF —) DECK SAIL PLANE
TOWER BRIDGE RUDDER PROPELLER
SAILPLANE TURTLEBACK
FAIRWEATHER
SUBMEDIANT SIXTH
SUBMERGE BOG DIP BURY DIVE
DUNK HIDE SINK SOAK TAKE DROWN
SOUSE SWAMP WHELM DELUGE
DRENCH ENGULF DEMERGE
IMPLUNGE INUNDATE SUBMERSE
SURROUND OVERWHELM
SUBMERGENCE ONLAP
SUBMISSION VAIL STOOP
PATIENCE
SUBMISSIVE MEEK BUXOM DEMISS
DOCILE DUTIFUL PASSIVE SERVILE
SLAVISH SUBJECT SUBMISS
UNERECT AMENABLE OBEDIENT
RESIGNED YIELDING
(— TO WIFE) UXORIOUS
SUBMISSIVENESS SLAVERY
SUBMIT BOW EAT ABOW BEND
CAVE LEAN OBEY TAKE VAIL AVALE

DEFER HIELD STAND STOOP YIELD
ASSENT CRINGE DELATE RESIGN
CONSIGN KNUCKLE SUBJECT
SUBMISE SUCCUMB TRUCKLE
PROPOUND
(— FOR CONSIDERATION) REMIT
(— TAMELY) EAT
(— TO) ABIDE STAND SUFFER
SUBNORMAL OFF SICK ABNORMAL
SUBORDER LARI ALCAE APODA
APODI GALLI GRUES ARDEAE
COHORT CUCULI SAURIA AGLOSSA
ANSERES ARCACEA ASCONES
CORACII COSTATA SARCURA
SYCONES ACRASIDA ADEPHAGA
BATOIDEI COLUMBAE CORACIAE
CURSORIA ENOPLINA EUSUCHIA
FALCONES FREGATAE SELACHII
SUBORDINARY ENDORSE
ROUNDEL
SUBORDINATE SUB SINK PETTY
SCRUB UNDER EXEMPT MINION
PUISNE SECOND YEOMAN PARTIAL
SERVANT SERVILE SUBJECT
HENCHMAN INFERIOR MYRMIDON
PARERGAL POSTPONE SERVIENT
ANCILLARY SUBALTERN
(PREF.) (— TO) VICE
SUBORN HAVE BRIBE
SUBOVAL PETALOID
SUBPHYLUM EUCHORDA
SUBPOENA SUMMONS
SUBRACE STOCK
SUB ROSA COVERTLY SECRETLY
PROVATELY
SUBSCRIBE SIGN ASSENT ASCRIBE
CONSIGN SUBSIGN
(— AGAIN) RENEW
SUBSCRIBER RAILBIRD
SUBSCRIPT INFERIOR
SUBSCRIPTION APPROVAL
SIGNATURE ABONNEMENT
SUBSEQUENT AFTER LATER
FUTURE PUISNE ENSUING
POSTNATE
(PREF.) POST
(— TO) CIS
SUBSEQUENTLY SO LATER SINCE
SUBSERVIENT OILY UNDER
VASSAL DUTEOUS SERVILE SLAVISH
OFFICIAL
SUBSHRUB STOCK GUAYULE
COLUMNEA PERIWINKLE
SUBSIDE DIE EBB LAY LIE ADAW
CALM FALL LULL SILE SINK VAIL
ABATE ALLAY LAPSE RESIDE SETTLE
ASSUAGE RELAPSE UNSWELL
WITHDRAW
SUBSIDENCE FALL SETTLING
SUBSIDIARY CHILD DONKEY
SUBSIDY ACCESSORY
SUBSIDIZE AID HELP BONUS

SUBSIDY AID BONUS BOUNTY
POUNDAGE
SUBSILICIC BASIC
SUBSIST BE LIVE RELY
SUBSISTENCE DOLE BEING LIVING
SUBSISTENT ENTITY
SUBSOIL PAN LECK SOLE SHRAVE
RATCHEL
SUBSTAGE CARY GUNZ IOWAN
MANKATO STADIAL TAZEWELL
SUBSTANCE FAT SUM BODY CORE
FECK GIST GITE MEAT TACK WHAT
ADROP AGENT ALLOY ARCHE BEING
FOMES GREAT KEEST METAL MOYEN
OUSIA PROOF SENSE STUFF THING
BOTTOM GADUIN GETTER IMPORT
MATTER STAPLE WEALTH AEROSOL
AGAROID ANTIGEN COLICIN COLLOID
CONTENT ELEIDIN EMANIUM
ERGUSIA ESSENCE HYALINE
MEANING PURPORT REAGENT
SUBJECT SUPTION ACCEPTOR
ADDITIVE ADHESIVE ALLERGEN
AMBEROID ANTIFOAM BASSORIN
HARDNESS MATERIAL PSORALEN
(— CAPABLE OF EXPANSION)
DILATANT
(— FORMED IN VINEGAR) MOTHER
(— FROM CRUSHED APPLES)
POMACE
(— IN BLOOD) ALEXINE ABLASTIN
(— IN LIGHT BULBS) GETTER
(— IN WOODY TISSUE) LIGNIN
(— OF DENTINE) IVORY
(— OF EXTREME HARDNESS)
ADAMANT DIAMOND
(— PRODUCING POISONOUS
ATMOSPHERE) GAS
(— SURROUNDED BY FOREIGN
TISSUE) ENCLAVE
(— THAT INDUCES MITOSIS)
MITOGEN
(— THAT STOPS LOCOMOTION)
ARRESTANT
(— TO ADD STABILITY) BALLAST
(— TRANSPORTING GERMS) FOMES
(— USED AS HYPNOTIC) URAL
(— USED IN DETECTING OTHERS)
REAGENT
(— WITH MOLDY ODOR) CHARACIN
(ADHESIVE —) GLUE GLOEA PASTE
CEMENT STICKER
(AMORPHOUS —) GLASS RESIN
LIGNIN PECTIN FERRITE SAPONIN
(AROMATIC —) BALSAM
(ASTRINGENT —) ALUM CATECHU
(BITTER —) ALOIN LININ ILICIN
(BLACK —) SOOT BLECK
(CLEANSING —) LYE
(COLLOIDAL —) ALGIN EXPANDER
(COMBUSTIBLE —) COAL
(CONDENSED —) PITH

(CORROSIVE —) CAUSTIC
(CRYSTALLINE —) LAURIN ALANINE
HELENIN ELATERIN
(DARK —) ATRAMENT
(DISSOLVED —) SOLUTE
(ETERNAL —) DHARMA ADHARMA
(FATLIKE —) DEGRAS LIPOID
ERGUSIA
(FATTY —) SMEAR SUBERIN
(FERMENTATION —) LEAVEN
(FIBROUS —) COTTON
(FILAMENTOUS —) HARL
(FILMY —) GOSSAMER
(FIRST —) YLEM
(GENERATIVE —) SPERM
(GRINDING —) ABRASIVE
(GROWTH-PROMOTING —) AUXIN
(GUMMY —) GUM GURRY AMYLOID
GLACTAN
(HARD ANIMAL —) BONE ENAMEL
(HORNY —) BALEEN CHITIN
CHONDRIN
(HYPOTHETICAL —) FLUID INOGEN
PROTYL
(IDEAL —) CONTINUUM
(INFLAMMABLE —) BITUMEN
(INSOLUBLE —) CARRIER
HYALOGEN
(LIVERLIKE —) HEPAR
(NARCOTIC —) DRUG
(NITROGENOUS —) LACTENIN
(POISONOUS —) ARSENIC PHRYNIN
EXOTOXIN
(POWDER OF ANY —) FLOUR
(POWDERY —) STOUR
(PREDOMINATING —) BASE
(RESINOUS —) LAC COPAL CARANNA
CARAUNA COPALINE COPALITE
(SELF-DEFENSIVE —) ACRAEIN
(SEMISOLID —) GEL
(SOUR —) ACID
(STICKY —) GOO GOOP SIZE STICK
GLUTEN BIRDLIME
(SUBTLE —) SPIRIT
(SWEET —) SUGAR
(SYNTHETIC —) HORMONE
(TRANSLUCENT —) HYALINE
CHONDRIN
(UNBREAKABLE —) ADAMANT
(UNCREATED —) ADHARMA
(VISCOUS —) GLAIR GREASE
SLUBBER
(VITAL —) KEEST
(WAXY —) CERIN PARAFFIN
SUBERINE
(PREF.) HYL(O)
(SUFF.) (— HAVING FORM) PHANE
(— PRODUCED THRU PROCESS)
STATE
SUBSTANDARD BAD BAUCH
SUBSTANTIAL FAT FIRM MEATY
PUKKA STOUT ACTUAL BODILY

HEARTY SQUARE STABLE STANCH
STUFFY STURDY MASSIVE MATERIAL
SUBSTANT TANGIBLE
SUBSTANTIATE BACK CONFIRM
SUPPORT VALIDATE
SUBSTANTIVE DIRECT
SUBSTITUTE SUB MOCK TEMP VICE
AKORI EXTRA PINCH PROXY VICAR
BACKUP BEWITH CHANGE DEPUTY
DOUBLE ERSATZ STOOGE COMMUTE
REPLACE RESERVE STANDBY
STANDIN STOPGAP SUBDEAN
SUFFECT SUPPOSE DISPLACE
EMERGENT MAKESHIFT
SURROGATE
(— FOR SIGNATURE) MARK
(— FOR TEA) TIA FAHAM
(— FRAUDULENTLY) SUPPOSE
(NOT —) FULL
(POOR —) APOLOGY
(SOAP —) AMOLE
(TOOTH —) CROWN
(USE OF GRAMMATICAL —)
CATAPHORA
(PREF.) PSEUD(O)
(SUFF.) ETTE
SUBSTITUTING
(PREF.) (— FOR) PRO
SUBSTITUTION SHIFT CHANGE
ERSATZ ENALLAGE EXCHANGE
NOVATION REPLACEMENT
(— OF SOUNDS) LALLATION
SUBSTRATUM SUB GROUND
SUBBING SUBJECT
SUBSTREAM MATTER
SUBSTRUCTURE PODIUM
FOOTING CENTERING
(— OF DOME) THOLOBATE
SUBSUME COVER EXPLAIN
INCLUDE
SUBSUMING GENERIC
SUBTENANT VAVASOUR
SUBTERFUGE MASK BLIND CROOK
QUIRK SHIFT TRICK WRINK AMBAGE
CHICANE ARTIFICE PRETENCE
TRAVERSE VOIDANCE
SUBTILE SUBTLE TENUOUS
SUBTILIZE EXALT
SUBTITLE TITLE LEADER CAPTION
SUBTLE SLY FINE NICE WILY WISE
ACUTE ARGUTE ASTUTE CRAFTY
SHREWD CUNNING FRAGILE SUBTILE
CLERGIAL
(FALLACIOUSLY —) SOPHISTIC
(TOO —) FINESPUN
SUBTLETY NICE FRAUD DECEIT
NUANCE EXILITY FINESSE QUILLET
DELICACY FINENESS QUIDDITY
QUODLIBET REFINEMENT
(— IN ARGUMENT) QUILLET
(CRITICAL —) NICETY
SUBTLY FINE SLILY SLYLY

SUBTRACT BATE PULL TAKE SHAVE
DEDUCE DEDUCT DETRACT SUBDUCE
SUBDUCT SUBTRAY DIMINISH
SUBTRIBE HAPU SENAAH
SEMNONES
SUBURB ANNEX BORGO BARRIO
PETTAH BANLIEU ENDSHIP
FAUBOURG
(POORLY CONSTRUCTED —) SLURB
(PL.) BURBS SKIRTS ENVIRONS
OUTPARTS SUBTOPIA SUBURBIA
SUBURBIA VILLADOM
SUBVERSION FALL SABOTAGE
SUBVERSIVE RUINOUS
SUBVERT SAP KILL RAZE RUIN
EVERT UPSET GAINSAY OVERSET
REVERSE RUINATE OVERTURN
SUBVERTED LOST
SUBWAY BMT IND IRT DIVE TUBE
METRO
SUCCEED GO FAY HIT FARE RISE
WORK CLICK ENSUE FADGE PROVE
SCORE SPEED COTTON FOLLOW
MAKEIT OBTAIN PANOUT SECOND
THRIVE ACHIEVE INHERIT PREVAIL
PROSPER THROUGH TURNOUT
FLOURISH SUPPLANT
(— IN REACHING) RECOVER
(— TO THRONE) ACCEDE ASCEND
SUCCEEDING VICE AFTER CHANGE
ULTERIOR
SUCCESS DO GO HIT MAX WIN
WOW BANG CESS LUCK SMASH
SPEED THRIFT EXPLOIT FORTUNE
FURTHER PROWESS THEEDOM
FELICITY GODSPEED
(— IN A MATCH) GAME
(ACCIDENTAL —) FLUKE
(BRILLIANT —) ECLAT
(ECONOMIC —) BOOM
(FINANCIAL —) SELLER
(NOT LIKELY TO BE A —) NOWIN
(SUDDEN —) KILLING
(UNEXPECTED —) JACKPOT
(WORLDLY —) ARTHA
SUCCESSFUL HOT MADE SOCK
BOFFO LUCKY SPEEDFUL THRIVING
GANGBUSTERS
(BARELY —) NARROW
(HIGHLY —) RUNAWAY
SUCCESSFULLY GREAT HAPPILY
PROUDLY
SUCCESSION RUN SUIT ROUND
SUITE TRACK ASSISE COURSE
SEQUEL SERIES STREAM
STRING HEIRDOM SUCCESS
ANCESTRY DIADOCHE MUTATION
SEQUENCE
(— OF CHANGES) FLUX
(— OF CHORDS) CADENCE
(— OF CRUSTS) CALICHE
(— OF LUCK) STREAK
(— OF STAGES) CASCADE

(— OF WAVES) CRIMP
(— RULERS) DYNASTY
SUCCESSIVELY AROW
SUCCESSOR HEIR CALIF HERES
CALIPH HAERES EPIGONUS
(— OF CHIEFTAIN) TANIST
(— OF MUHAMMAD) CALIF CALIPH
(ECCLESIASTICAL —) COARB
COMARB
(PL.) DIADOCHI
SUCCINCT BRIEF PITHY SHORT
TERSE CONCISE LACONIC
SUMMARY
SUCCINIC DIACETIC
SUCCOR AID HELP RESET SERVE
SPEED ASSIST RELIEF RESCUE
SUPPLY UPTAKE COMFORT DELIVER
PRESIDY RELIEVE SECOURS SUSTAIN
BEFRIEND
SUCCORY CHICORY
SUCCULENT FRIM FRUM LUSH
JUICY LUSHY PAPPY PULPY SAPPY
YOUNG CASHIE FLESHY TENDER
WATERISH
SUCCUMB BREAK QUAIL STOOP
TRAIK YIELD
SUCH SIC SICK THAT SWICH
SUCHNESS TATHATA
SUCK SOUK SWIG SWOOP SUCKLE
(— DRY) SOAK
(— UP) DRINK ABSORB TIPPLE
(SUFF.) MYZA MYZON
SUCKEN THIRL
SUCKER CHUB FISH GULL CUIUI
PATSY SOBOL THIEF CHUPON
CUPULE MULLET RATOON REDFIN
SOBOLE SPROUT SQUARE STOLON
SUPPER TILLER CUTLIPS GONOTYL
LOCULUS OSCULUM PEDICEL
SCOURGE BOTHRIUM HUMPBACK
LOLLIPOP PUSHOVER REDHORSE
SURCULUS QUILLBACK
(PREF.) BDELL(O) BOTHR(I)(IO)(O)
MYZO STOLONI SURCULI
(SUFF.) BDELLA
SUCKLE FEED MILK SUCK LACTATE
NOURISH
SUCKLING SUCKER LACTANT
SUCKLER TEATLING
SUCTION INTAKE
(SUFF.) MYZA MYZON
SUCTORIA ACINETAE

SUDAN

CAPITAL: KHARTOUM
DESERT: NUBIAN
LANGUAGE: GA EWE IBO KRU EFIK
  MOLE TSHI YORUBA MANDINGO
MEASURE: UD
MOUNTAIN: KINYETI
NATIVE: DAZA GOLO NUER SERE
  DINKA FULAH HAUSA MOSSI
  NUBIYIN

PROVINCE: DARFUR KASSALA
KORDOFAN
REGION: DARFUR KASSALA
KORDOFAN
RIVER: NILE PIBOR
TOWN: WAU JUBA KOSTI MEROE
ATBARA ALUBAYD KASSALA
MALAKAL OMDURMAN
WEIGHT: HARBA

SUDANESE FULA FULAH
SUDAN GRASS GARAVA GARAWI
SUDDEN BRASH FERLY HASTY ICTIC
SWIFT ABRUPT FIERCE SNAPPY
SPEEDY PRERUPT HEADLONG
SPURTIVE SUBITANY SUBITOUS
OVERNIGHT PRECIPITATE
SUDDENLY BOB POP BOLT
FLOP SLAP AMAIN SHORT SKELP
SOUSE ASTART BOUNCE PRESTO
SUBITO ASUDDEN UNAWARES
HEYPRESTO
SUDDENNESS ATTACK SUDDENTY
SUDORIFIC SWEAT SWEATER
HIDROTIC SUDATORY
SUDRA HINDU VELLALA
SUDS BUCK FOAM SAPPLES
SOAPSUDS
SUE LAW WOO SUIT IMPLEAD
TROUNCE
SUET TALLOW
(PREF.) STEAR(I)(O) STEAT(O)
(SUFF.) STEARIN
SUFFER BYE GET LET BEAR BIDE
DREE FIND GAIN HURT DAIN PINE
ALLOW DREIE INCUR LABOR PROVE
SMART SMOKE STAND THOLE
ABEGGE BETEEM ENDURE PERMIT
AGONIZE SUPPORT SUSTAIN
UNDERGO TOLERATE
(— AGONY) THROE
(— A PENALTY) PAY
(— AT STAKE) SMOKE
(— DEFEAT) BOW
(— FOR) ABY ABYE ABIDE
(— FROM HEAT) SWELTER
(— FROM TIME) AGE
(— GREAT AFFLICTION) GROAN
(— HUNGER) CLEM STARVE
AFFAMISH
(— LOSS OF) GIVE
(— PAIN) STOUND ANGUISH
(— PENALTY) SWEAT
(— REMORSE) RUE
(— RUIN) WRECK
(— SHIPWRECK) SPLIT
(— SYNCOPE) FAINT
(— THE CONSEQUENCES) ANSWER
(— THROUGH) PASS
(— TO ENTER) ADMIT
SUFFERABLE PATIBLE
SUFFERANCE PAIN MISERY
PATIENCE THOLANCE

SUFFERER MARTYR AMNESIC
DOORMAT PATIENT
(SUFF.) PATH(IA)(IC)(Y)
SUFFERING BALE COST DREE HURT
PAIN PINE RACK AGONY DOLOR
GRIEF SMART WRAKE PATHIC
PATHOS THRALL INVALID LANGUOR
PASSION PASSIVE TRAVAIL DISTRESS
HARDSHIP MARTYRDOM
(— FROM HANGOVER) CHIPPY
(— FROM ILL HEALTH) DOWN
(— OF MIND) CARE
(—S OF CHRIST) AGONY
(SUFF.) PATH(IA)(IC)(Y)
(— OF) ITIS
SUFFICE DO LAST COVER REACH
SERVE SATISFY
SUFFICIENCY ENOUGH PLENTY
ADEQUACY BELLYFUL ABUNDANCE
PLENITUDE
SUFFICIENT DUE FAIR GOOD AMPLE
DECENT ENOUGH PRETTY BASTANT
ABUNDANT ADEQUATE RELEVANT
COMPETENT
(— LEGALLY) RELEVANT
(BARELY —) SCANT SKIMP NARROW
SCRIMPY
(BE — FOR) COVER
SUFFICIENTLY DULY WELL ENOUGH
SUFFIX POSTFIX
(SLANG —) AROO
SUFFOCATE CHOKE DROWN SMOOR
STIVE STUFF SWELT SLOKEN STIFLE
OVERLIE QUACKLE SMOLDER
SMOTHER SCUMFISH STRANGLE
THROTTLE
SUFFOCATION APNEA APNOEA
ASPHYXIA
SUFFRAGE VOTE VOICE TONGUE
VERSICLE
SUFFRAGETTE CATT
SUFFUSE DIP FILL BATHE EMBAY
TINGE INFUSE MANTLE
SUFFUSION COLOR
SUGAR CANDY DIOSE IDOSE MELIS
PIECE SUCRE THIRD ACROSE ALDOSE
ALLOSE FUCOSE GULOSE HEXOSE
INVERT KETOSE LYXOSE OCTOSE
PANELA TALOSE TRIOSE XYLOSE
AGAVOSE ALTROSE BASTARD
CHITOSE GLUCOSE GLUTOSE
GLYCOSE LACTOSE MALTOSE
MANNOSE PAPELON PENOCHI
PENTOSE PENUCHE SORBOSE
SUCROSE SWEETEN TETROSE
THREOSE BROWNING CONCRETE
CYMAROSE DEXTROSE FRUCTOSE
FURANOSE LEVULOSE PYRANOSE
RHAMNOSE RHODEOSE SECALOSE
TURANOSE
(BROWN —) CARAIBE JAGGARY
DEMERARA JAGGHERY
(COARSE —) RAAB PANOCHA

(CRUDE —) GUR HEAD MELADA
CONCRETE
(INFERIOR —) BASTARD
(SIMPLE —) OSE
(UNREFINED —) CASSONADE
MUSCOVADO
(PREF.) GLUC(O) GLYC(O) LYXO
SACCHAR(I)(O) SUCR(O) THREO
(SUFF.) ULOSE
SUGARCANE CANE GRAIN GLUMAL
RATOON MATTRESS
(— SAP) LIQUOR
SUGARHOUSE
(PART OF —) PURGERY
SUGARLESS DRY
SUGARPLUM KISS
SUGARY FAT SUGAR SWEET
OVERRIPE
SUGGEST JOG BEAR GIVE HINT
MINT IMPLY OFFER POSIT SPEAK
ADVISE ALLUDE HINTAT INDITE
INFUSE MOTION PROMPT
RESENT SUBMIT CONNOTE DICTATE
INSPIRE INDICATE INTIMATE
PROPOUND
(— DRINKING) PROPOSE
(— INSIDIOUSLY) INFUSE
(— STRONGLY) ARGUE
SUGGESTIBLE SOFT
SUGGESTION CUE CAST HINT
TANG WIND GLIFF TWANG ADVICE
BREATH MOTION SMATCH INKLING
LEADING POINTER PROFFER
REMNANT SOUPCON WRINKLE
INNUENDO INSTANCE PROPOSAL
SUGGESTIVE RACY SEXY RISQUE
ANICONIC PREGNANT REDOLENT
(— OF MELODY) CANOROUS
SUICIDAL KAMIKAZE
SUIT DO GO APT DOW FIT GEE HIT
SET SIT ACTO LIKE LIST PAIR SEEM
SORT VINE ADAPT AGREE APPLY
BEFIT BLEST CLUBS COLOR DRAPE
DRESS FADGE FANCY FRAME HABIT
LEVEL MATCH PLEAD QUEME SAVOR
SERVE SHAPE STAND SUING TALLY
AFFEIR ANSWER BECOME COHERE
COMPLY DITTOS EFFEIR HEARTS
PRAYER SPADES SPEECH SQUARE
BEHOOVE COMPORT COSTUME
COULEUR FASHION PURSUIT
REQUEST SEERPAW DIAMONDS
INSTANCE QUADRATE SKELETON
STANDARD TAILLEUR TROPICAL
PINSTRIPE
(— AT LAW) ACTO CASE LAWSUIT
(— OF ARMOR) PANOPLY
(— OF MAIL) CATAPHRACT
(DIVER'S —) SCAPHANDER
(KIND OF —) ZOOT
(SWIMMING —) BATHER BIKINI
MAILLOT

SUITABILITY (MUTUAL —) DECENCY
IDONEITY SYMPATHY
SUITABLE APT FIT PAT ABLE FEAT
GAIN GOOD JUMP JUST MEET TALL
WELL WEME DIGNE EQUAL FITTY
QUEME RIGHT SUITY COMELY FITTEN
GAINLY GIUSTO HABILE HONEST
LIABLE LIKELY PROPER SUITLY
AVENANT COMMODE CONDIGN
CONGRUE FITTING IDONEAL PLIABLE
SEEMING BECOMING DECOROUS
ELIGIBLE FEASIBLE HANDSOME
IDONEOUS SORTABLE ACCORDING
OPPORTUNE
(— FOR MALE AND FEMALE)
UNISEX
(— FOR STAGE PERFORMANCE)
ACTING
(EXACTLY —) VERY
(NOT —) UNFIT IMPROPER
SUITABLENESS APTNESS
HONESTY APTITUDE PROPERTY
SUITABLY FITLY MEETLY TIDELY
APROPOS GRADELY
SUITCASE BAG CAP GRIP
CAPCASE DORLACH KEESTER
PULLMAN
SUITE SET SUIT TAIL SWEEP SWEET
TRAIN SERIES PARTITA RETINUE
ENSEMBLE EQUIPAGE
(— OF MOLDINGS) LEDGMENT
(— OF ROOMS) FLAT CHAMBER
SUITED FIT ADAPT SEEMLY ADAPTED
ASSORTED CONGENIAL
(POORLY —) CROOK
(SUFF.) (— FOR) ILE
SUITING COVERT CHEVIOT
SHARKSKIN
SUITOR MAN BEAU SUER SWAIN
WOOER GALLANT SERVANT
SUKU WASUKUMA
SULCUS RUT FURROW GROOVE
SULFATE DEX
SULFIDE GLANCE CUBANITE
SULFURET COVELLITE
SULFUR BRIMSTONE
(PREF.) THI(O)
SULK DOD PET CHAW CRAB DORT
GLUM POUT SULL BOODY FRUMP
GLUMP GROUT GRUMP GROUCH
SNUDGE THURMUS
(PL.) GEE HUMP GLOUT MUMPS
FRUMPS SULLENS BOUDERIE
SULKER MUMPER
SULKINESS DORT GRUMP
SULKING PET BOUDERIE
SULKY BIKE CART CHUFF DODDY
DORTY GOURY HUFFY HUMPY
CHUFFY GLUMPY GROUTY JINKER
SNUFFY STUFFY SULLEN SUMPHY
DOGGISH HUFFISH MUMPISH
(NOT —) GOOD

SULLEN DOUR FOUL GLUM GRIM
SOUR BLACK CHUFF CROSS DUMPY
FELON GRUFF HARSH MOODY
RUSTY STERN SULKY SURLY
WEMOD CRUSTY DOGGED GLOOMY
GLUMMY GLUMPY GLUNCH
GROUTY MOROSE MULISH SOMBER
SOMBRE STUFFY AUSTERE
CRABBED CYNICAL FRETFUL
LOURING LUMPISH MUMPISH
PEEVISH CHUMPISH CHURLISH
FAROUCHE LOWERING PETULANT
SPITEFUL STUNKARD
SULLENNESS GEE DORT GLUM
MUMPS STOMACH
SULLIED DIRTY SPOTTED
SULLY BLOT BLUR DASH FOUL
SLUR SMIT SMUT SOIL CLOUD
DIRTY GRIME SMEAR SMOKE STAIN
TAINT BEFOUL DARKEN DEFILE
SMIRCH SMUTCH ATTAINT BEGRIME
BESMEAR BLEMISH CORRUPT
DISTAIN ECLIPSE POLLUTE
SLUBBER TARNISH BESMIRCH
BEDPATTER
SULPHATE ALUM BARITE ILESITE
LOWEITE SULFATE VITRIOL
KRAUSITE
SULPHIDE HEPAR GLANCE ZARNEC
SULFIDE ZARNICH CUBANITE
(PL.) MATTE
SULPHUR ORE SPIRIT SULFUR
YELLOW QUEBRITH BRIMSTONE
SULPHURIC ACID VITRIOL
SULTAN SOLDAN
(— OF MOROCCO) SHERIF SHEREEF
SULTANATE SULTANY ZANZIBAR
SULTANESS SOWDONES
SULTRY CLOSE FLUSH FAINTY
SMUDGY POTHERY PUTHERY
SWELTRY FEVERISH
SUM ALL GOB AGIO CASH DRAB
DUMP FUME HINE FOOT FUND MASS
TALE DEDIT GROSS KITTY SUMMA
TOTAL WHOLE AMOUNT DEMAND
DYADIC FIGURE NUMBER DECUPLE
INGOING MANBOTE SUBSIDY
SUMMARY SUMMATE ENTIRETY
OCTONION QUANTITY MOUNTANCE
OVERDRAFT POLYNOMIAL
(— AND SUBSTANCE) TOUR SHORT
UPSHOT
(— AS COMPENSATION FOR KILLING)
MANBOTE
(— FOR REENLISTMENT) GRATUITY
(— FOR SCHOLARSHIP) BURSARY
(— IN BASSET) SEPTLEVA
(— OF) SIGMA
(— OF DETERMINANTS) STIRP
(— OF EXPONENTS) DEGREE
(— OF FACTORS) COMPLEX
(— OF GOOD QUALITIES) ARETE

(— OF MONEY) POT BANK PILE
COVER PURSE STOCK BUNDLE
ACCOUNT DEPOSIT GRASSUM
STIPEND
(— OF 25 POUNDS) PONY PONEY
(— OF 3 FARTHINGS) GILL
(— OF 500 POUNDS) MONKEY
(— PAYABLE AT FIXED INTERVALS)
FARM
(— RISKED) STAKE
(— UP) ADD TOT FOOT RECAP
ASSESS RECKON SUBSUME
SUMMATE COMPRISE CONCLUDE
PERORATE
(COMPLETE —) SOLIDUM
(ENTIRE —) SOLIDUM
(EXCESS —) BONUS
(FORFEITED —) DEDIT
(GREAT —) PLUNK SIGHT MICKLE
(LARGE —) GOB SCREAMER
(PETTY —) CENT DIME DRAB
(SMALL — OF MONEY) SPILL DRIBBLE
DRIBLET SHOESTRING
(TRIFLING —) HAY GROAT
(UNEXPENDED —S) SAVINGS
(VAST —) MINT
(VECTOR —) GRADIENT
(PL.) BATTELS
SUMAC FUSTET KARREE SUMACH
ANACARD BURTREE SCOTINO
SHOEMAKE
SUMATRA (ISLAND NEAR —) NIAS
(LANGUAGE IN —) NIAD
(MEASURE OF —) PAAL
(MOUNTAIN IN —) LEUSER
KERINTJI
(RIVER IN —) HARI MUSI ROKAN
DJAMBI
(TOWN IN —) ACHIN KUALA MEDAN
NATAL SOLOK DJAMBI LANGSA
PADANG RENGAT BENKULEN
SUMBUL SAMBUL MUSKROOT
SUMERIAN ACCADIAN AKKADIAN
SUMITRA (HUSBAND OF —)
DASHARATHA
(SON OF —) LAKSHMANA
SHATRUGHNA
SUMMARIZE RECAP PRECIS
RESUME WRAPUP ABSTRACT
SUMMARY SUM CURT LEAD BRIEF
CHART RECAP SCORE SHORT
SUMMA TOTAL APERCU DIGEST
PRECIS RESUME SUMMAR CHAPTER
CONCISE EPITOME EXTRACT
MEDULLA OUTLINE RUNDOWN
VIDIMUS ABSTRACT ARGUMENT
BREVIARY BREVIATE DRUMHEAD
HEADNOTE OVERVIEW SUCCINCT
SYNOPSIS
(— OF FAITH) SYMBOL
(— OF PRINCIPLES) CREED
(CONCISE —) PRECIS

SUMMATION SUM DIGEST
SUMMARY
SUMMER ETE SHEMU SOMER
AESTAS SIMMER DORMANT
(OF —) ESTIVAL
(PREF.) ESTIVO
SUMMER CYPRESS KOCHIA
SUMMER FLOUNDER PLAICE
SUMMERHOUSE FOLLY KIOSK
MAHAL TUPEK ALCOVE CASINO
GAZEBO PAGODA CABINET
BELVEDERE
SUMMER HYACINTH GALTONIA
SUMMER TANAGER REDBIRD
SUMMERWOOD LATEWOOD
SUMMIT CAP DOD SUM TIP TOP VAN
ACME APEX BALD CRAP DODD HELM
KNAP KNOT PEAK ROOF CREST
CROWN SPIRE COMBLE CULMEN
HEIGHT VERTEX ZENITH CALOTTE
SUMMARY SUMMITY PINNACLE
MOUNTAINTOP
(— OF TUBE) MOUTH
(— WITHOUT FOREST) BALD
(ROCKY —) KNOT
(ROUND —) DOD DODD
(SNOW-CAPPED —) CALOTTE
(PREF.) APICO CORY(PH)(PHO)
(SUFF.) ACE
SUMMON BAN CRY BUZZ CALL CITE
DRUM HAIL SIST BUGLE CHARM
CLEPE EVOKE HIGHT KNELL SOUND
VOUCH ACCITE ADVOKE BECALL
BECKON COMPEL DEMAND SOMPNE
VOCATE ACCERSE COMMAND
CONJURE CONVENE CONVENT
CONVOKE PROVOKE SUMMONS
WHISTLE ASSUMMON EXORCISE
(— FOR HIRING) YARD
(— INTO COURT) DEMAND
(— TOGETHER) BAND MUSTER
ASSEMBLE
(— UP) FIND GATHER COLLECT
SUMMONER SUMNER LOCKMAN
SOMPNER OUTRIDER
SUMMONING CALL ARRAY
(— OF KING'S VASSALS) BAN
SUMMONS CRY CALL BREVE CITAL
TICKET BIDDING CALLING STICKER
WARNING WARRANT CITATION
MONITION VOCATION
(— TO GET UP) REVEILLE
(FALCONER'S —) WO
SUMP SINK STANDAGE
SUMPTUOUS RICH GRAND SHOWY
WLONK COSTLY DELUXE SOLEMN
SUPERB COSTLEW ELEGANT
MAGNIFIC SPLENDID MAGNIFICENT
SUMPTUOUSNESS LUXE DAINTY
SUMPTURE
SUN ORB SOL ATEN ATON BASK INTI
LAMP STAR SENGE SURYA TITAN

SUNLET DAYSTAR IOSKEHA
PHOEBUS SAVITAR JOUSKEHA
(— MOON AND STARS) HOST
(MOCK —) PARHELION
(RISING —) HERAKHTI
(PREF.) HELI(O) SOLARO SOLI
(SUFF.) HELION
SUN ALSO RISES (AUTHOR OF —)
HEMINGWAY
(CHARACTER IN —) BILL COHN JAKE
MIKE BRETT CLYNE PEDRO ASHLEY
BARNES GORTON ROBERT ROMERO
FRANCES MICHAEL MONTOYA
CAMPBELL GEORGETE
SUNAPEE TROUT SAIBLING
SUNBATHE GETATAN APRICATE
SUNBATHER BAKE
SUNBEAM BANANA
SUN BEAR BRUANG
SUNBIRD MAMO CADET FINFOOT
SUN BITTERN CARLE CAURALE
SUNBIRD
SUN BLIND CHICK UMRELLA
SUNBONNET TILT UGLY CRESIE
KAPPIE SHAKER
SUNBURN GREENING HELIOSIS
(— REMEDY) ALOE
SUNBURNED BRONZED
SUNBURNT ADUST BROWN
TANNED
SUNBURST SUNRAY SUNBREAK
SUNSHINE
SUNDAE GEDUNK
SUNDA ISLANDS (GREATER —)
JAVA BORNEO CELEBES SUMATRA
(LESSER —) BALI TIMOR
SUNDAY EXAUDI JUDICA GAUDETE
TRINITY
(FIFTH — AFTER EASTER) ROGATE
(FIRST — AFTER EASTER)
QUASIMODO
(FIRST — IN LENT) QUADRAGESIMA
(FOURTH — IN LENT) LAETARE
(LOW —) QUASIMODO
(SECOND — BEFORE LENT)
SEXAGESIMA
(THIRD — AFTER EASTER) JUBILATE
SUNDER PART RIVE TWIN BREAK
SEVER TWAIN TWINE DEPART DIVIDE
SINDER ASUNDER DISALLY DISJOIN
DIVORCE DISSEVER SEJUGATE
SEPARATE UNSOLDER
SUNDEW DROSERA EYEBRIGHT
SUNDIAL DIAL GHURRY HOROLGE
SCAPHION SOLARIUM
(PART OF —) DIAL LINE PLATE
GNOMON DIAGRAM
SUN DISK ATEN ATON CAKRA
CHAKRA
SUNDOG WINDGALL PARHELION
SUNDOWNER HOBO DRINK TRAMP
WHALER TUSSOCKER

SUN-DRIED TILED
SUNDROPS SCABISH
SUNDRY DIVERS DIVERSE
  SEVERAL
SUNFISH SUN HURO MOLA OPAH
  RUFF BREAM FLIER FLYER ROACH
  SUNNY KIVVER MOLOID REDEAR
  REDEYE CRAPPIE CROPPIE PANFISH
  PERCOID BLUEGILL FLATFISH
  FLOUNDER HEADFISH MOONFISH
  PONDFISH WARMOUTH REDBREAST
  PUMPKINSEED
SUNFLOWER GOLD HELIO CANADA
  GOLDEN SUNFOIL GIRASOLE
  TURNSOLE
  (— STATE) KANSAS
SUNGLASSES SHADES
SUN-GREBE FINFOOT SUNBIRD
  GRUIFORM
SUNK SUNKEN
  (— TO LOW STATE) ABJECT
SUNKEN SUNK LAIGH HOLLOW
SUNKEN BELL
  (CHARACTER IN —) MAGDA HEINRICH
  RAUTENDELEIN
  (COMPOSER OF —) RESPIGHI
SUNLESS BLAE
SUNLIGHT GLARE
SUNN SAN SANN DAGGA SANAI
  JANAPA MADRAS JANAPAN
  SANNHEMP
SUNNITE IHLAT SUNNI SUNNIAH
SUNNY GOOD SUNSHINE
SUN PARLOR SOLARIUM
SUNRISE ARIST SUNUP ORIENT
  (KIND OF —) TEQUILA
  (TEQUILA —) COCKTAIL
SUNSET SUNFALL
  (— STATE) OREGON ARIZONA
SUNSHADE PARASOL ROUNDEL
  TIRESOL SOMBRERO
SUNSHINE SUN SHINE SUNLIGHT
  (— STATE) FLORIDA
SUNSPOT SPOT FACULA MACULA
SUNSPURGE SUNWEED TURNSOLE
  WARTWEED WARTWORT
SUNSTROKE HELIOSIS SIRIASIS
SUNTAN MERIDA
SUN TREE HINOKI
SUNWISE DEASIL DESSIL
SUNYATA VOID
SUP EAT DINE SOWP FEAST
  CONSUME SWAI LOW
SUPAWN MUSH
SUPER COOL FINE GRAND GREAT
  NEATO NIFTY
SUPER-
  (PREF.) HYPER
SUPERABOUND OVERFLOW
SUPERABUNDANCE FLOOD
  EXCESS CATARACT PLEONASM
  PLETHORA PLEURISY PLURISIE

SUPERABUNDANT RANK LAVISH
  PROFUSE
SUPERALTAR PREDELLA
SUPERANNUATE RETIRE
  OVERYEAR
SUPERB GRAND GOLDEN CLIPPING
  GORGEOUS SPLENDID
SUPERCARGO MERCHANT
SUPERCILIOUS GRAND POTTY
  PROUD OVERLY SNIFFY SNIPPY
  SNOOTY SNOTTY SNUFFY HAUGHTY
  ARROGANT CAVALIER SNIFFISH
  SUPERIOR
SUPERCLASS AGNATHA
SUPERCONSCIOUSNESS
  SAMADHI
SUPERCOOL SUBCOOL SURFUSE
SUPERFAMILY APINA APOIDEA
  BOVOIDEA
  (SUFF.) OIDA OIDEA OIDEI
SUPERFICIAL GLIB ECTAL SUPER
  FACIAL FACILE FLIMSY FORMAL
  FROTHY GLASSY OVERLY SLIGHT
  CURSORY OUTSIDE OUTWARD
  PASSING SHALLOW SKETCHY
  SLIGHTY SURFACE SURFACY
  COSMETIC EXTERNAL MAGAZINY
  SMATTERY DEPTHLESS
SUPERFICIALLY FLEET
SUPERFICIES TERM EXTENT
SUPERFLUITY FAT FRILL LUXUS
  EXCESS OVERSET SURFEIT
  PLETHORA REDUNDANCY
  (CONFUSING —) FLUTHER
SUPERFLUOUS SPARE OTIOSE
  USELESS NEEDLESS REDUNDANT
SUPERFRONTAL FRONTLET
SUPERHEATED GASEOUS
SUPERHIGHWAY MOTORWAY
  (AVOID —) SHUNPIKE
SUPERHUMAN DEMON DAEMON
  DIVINE INHUMAN UNHUMAN
SUPERIMPOSE LAY OVERLAY
  SURPRINT
SUPERIMPOSING DISSOLVE
SUPERINTEND CON CONN GUIDE
  OVERSEE PRESIDE
SUPERINTENDENCE CARE
  CONTROL EPISCOPY GUIDANCE
SUPERINTENDENCY EDILITY
  AEDILITY
SUPERINTENDENT BOSS SUPE
  EPHOR SUPER EDITOR VENEUR
  VIEWER WARDEN CAPTAIN CURATOR
  EPHORUS MANAGER DIRECTOR
  OVERSEER SURVEYOR SWINGMAN
SUPERIOR JOE AYNE COOL FINE
  MORE OVER TRIE ABBOT ABOVE
  CHIEF CREAM EIGNE ELDER ELITE
  EXTRA FANCY FRANK GREAT LIEGE
  PRIOR PUKKA SWANK UPPER
  ABBESS BETTER COCKUP CUSTOS

DOMINA FATHER FORBYE MAHANT
SELECT SENIOR STRONG FORTHBY
PALMARY RANKING ABNORMAL
DOMINANT GUARDIAN SINGULAR
SPLENDID SUPERIAL MARVELOUS
PARAMOUNT
(— IN MANNER) SUPERCILIOUS
(— OF CONVENT) HEGUMEN
(— ONE) LAMA
(— TO) ATOP BEFORE
(PREF.) SUPER
SUPERIORITY DROP GREE PRICE
HEIGHT MASTERY PROWESS
EMINENCE PRIORITY
(MENTAL —) GENIUS
SUPERLATIVE RAVING CURIOUS
ROUSING CRASHING OLYMPIAN
PEERLESS SWINGING ULTIMATE
(ABSOLUTE —) ELATIVE
(SUFF.) EST
SUPERLATIVELY CRACKING
SWINGING
SUPERMAN OVERMAN
OBERMENSCH
SUPERNATURAL FEY ARCANE
DIVINE NUMINOUS SUPERIOR
MARVELOUS PARANORMAL
(— FORCE) WAKANDA
SUPERNUMERARY ORRA
(PREF.) POLY
SUPERORDER GLIRES
SUPERPOSE APPLY
SUPER-REMEDY CUREALL
SUPERSCRIBE DIRECT
SUPERSCRIPT SUPERIOR
SUPERSEDE REPLACE OVERRIDE
SUPPLANT
SUPERSTITION FREIT IDOLATRY
ABERGLAUBE
SUPERSTITIOUS FREITY
SUPERTONIC SECOND
SUPERVENE BEFALL FOLLOW
SUPERVISE BOSS GUIDE DIRECT
GOVERN HANDLE SURVEY FOREMAN
OVERSEE PROCTOR ENGINEER
OVERLOOK CHAPERONE
SUPERVISION EYE CARE DUTY
HAND CHECK CHARGE OVERSIGHT
SUPERVISOR BOSS BULL EPHOR
GUIDE SUPER CENSOR GASMAN
RUNMAN SOURER WARDEN
DESKMAN PROCTOR ALYTARCH
CHAIRMAN FLOORMAN FOREHAND
KNIFEMAN LEACHMAN MASHGIAH
OVERSEER
(— OF STUDENT DISCIPLINE)
HEBDOMADAR HEBDOMADER
SUPINE INERT DROWSY LANGUID
SERVILE UPRIGHT CARELESS
INACTIVE INDOLENT LISTLESS
SLUGGISH
SUPPER CENA MEAL CUDDY HOCKEY
PASCHAL

(— AT HOME) EATIN
(HARVEST-HOME —) HOCKEY
(LAST —) MAUNDY
(LORD'S —) NAGMAAL
SUPPING CENATION
SUPPLANT FOLLOW REMOVE
REPLACE DISPLACE DISPLANT
SUPPLE BAIN FLIP OILY SOFT WIRY
LINGY LITHE SLAMP SWACK AJOINT
LIMBER LITHER LUTHER PLIANT
SUMPLE SVELTE SWANKY WANDLE
LISSOME PLIABLE SPRINGE FLEXIBLE
SUPPLEJACK SOAPWORT
SUPPLEMENT ARM EKE MEND
TACK ANNEX SUPPLY BOLSTER
CODICIL ADDENDUM APPENDIX
BOUNTITH
(PL.) FIXINGS
SUPPLEMENTAL SPECIAL
PIGGYBACK
SUPPLEMENTARY ADDED SECOND
RIPIENO REMANENT PERIPHERAL
SUPPLENESS WHIP
SUPPLIANT ASKER PLEADING
SUPPLICATE BEG PRAY CRAVE
PLEAD INVOKE OBTEST SUPPLY
BESEECH ENTREAT IMPLORE
REQUEST SOLICIT PETITION
SUPPLICATION CRY VOW BEAD BILL
LIBEL VENIE APPEAL LITANY PRAYER
CRAVING SYNAPTE ENTREATY
PETITION PLEADING ROGATION
ROGATIVE SUFFRAGE
SUPPLICATORY EUCTICAL
SUPPLIED (— WITH FOOD) THORN
(AMPLY —) ABUNDANT
(SCANTILY —) BARE
SUPPLIER SOURCE
SUPPLIES STOCK STUFF DUFFEL
STORES VICTUAL ESTOVERS
ORDNANCE
SUPPLY FEED FILL FIND FRET FUND
GIVE HEEL LEND LINE ARRAY CATER
ENDUE EQUIP INDUE OFFER SERVE
STOCK STORE STUFF YIELD BUDGET
DONATE EMPLOY FOISON LAYOUT
POCKET RENDER SUBMIT ADVANCE
FORTIFY FRAUGHT FURNISH
LISSOME PROVIDE ACCOMMODATE
(— ABUNDANTLY) SWILL
(— ARRANGED BEFOREHAND) RELAY
(— EXCESSIVELY) FLOOD
(— FOR AN OCCASION) GRIST
(— FULLY) SATISFY
(— LIQUOR BY SHIP) COPER COOPER
(— OF FOOD) BOARD
(— OF HORSES) RELAY REMUDA
REMOUNT
(— OF MONEY) BANKROLL
(— OF POTENTIAL JURORS) TALES
(— OF REMOUNTS) REMUDA
(— OF SOLDIERS) GARRISON
(— OF TIN) SERVING

(— **PROVISIONS**) PURVEY
(— **THE NEED**) FOR
(— **WITH CLOTHES**) INFIT
(— **WITH FOOD**) FODDER
(— **WITH FUEL**) STOKE
(— **WITH LIQUOR**) LUBRICATE
(— **WITH MONEY**) GILD
(— **WITH OXYGEN**) AERATE
(— **WITH WATER**) FANG
(**CACHED** —) CAVE
(**CONSTANT** —) STREAM
(**EXTRA** —) RESERVE
(**FRESH** —) RECRUIT
(**FULL** —) PLENTY
(**HIDDEN** —) HOARD
(**INADEQUATE** —) DEARTH
(**LARGE** —) TON PILE
(**NEW** —) RECRUIT
(**OVERABUNDANT** —) SURFEIT
(**PLENTIFUL** —) CHOICE
(**RENEWED** —) RECRUITAL
(**RESERVE** —) CUSHION
(**RICH** —) ARGOSY
(**SCANTY** —) SCANT
(**SECRET** —) CACHE
SUPPORT AID ARM BAY BED BOW
KAI LEG PEG RIB TIE TOM ABET ABUT
AXIS BACK BASE BEAM BEAR BUOY
CRIB DADE FEND FIND FIRM FORK
FUEL HAVE HELP HOLD JAMB KEEP
KILP LIFT POST PROP RACK REST
ROCK SALT SIDE STAY STEM STUD
TRIG ADOPT AEGIS ANGEL APPUI
ATLAS BIPOD BLOCK BRACE BROOK
CARRY CHAIR CHEER CHOCK CLEAT
CRANK FAVOR FLOAT FRAME OXTER
PLUNK POISE RANCE SALVE SHORE
SPURN STAFF STAKE STEAD STELL
STIPE STOCK STOOP STRUT STULL
TOWER VOUCH WEIGH ANCHOR
ASSERT ASSIST BARROW BEHALF
CHEVAL COLUMN CORSET CRADLE
CRUTCH DEFEND DONKEY DUOPOD
GARTER PATTEN PILLAR POTENT
PULPIT PUTLOG SADDLE SECOND
SHIELD SOCKET SPLINT STAYER
STEADY SUFFER TASSEL TIMBER
TINGLE TORSEL UPHAND UPHOLD
UPKEEP UPTAKE WHIMSY ALIMENT
ARMREST BACKING BOLSTER
COMFORT CONFIRM CRIPPLE
DEADMAN ENDORSE ESPOUSE
FINDING FULCRUM GROMMET
HOUSING JACKLEG JUSTIFY
KEEPING KNUCKLE NOURISH
NURTURE PABULUM PROTECT
RADICAL SPIRALE SPONSOR
SQUINCH STADDLE STANDER
STIFFEN STIRRUP SUBSIST SUSTAIN
THICKEN TRESTLE ADJUMENT
ADVOCATE BALUSTER BEFRIEND
BESTRIDE BOOKREST BUTTRESS
CAPSHORE FAIRLEAD FOOTREST

FORESTAY FORTRESS HANDREST
HOLDFAST JACKSTAY KEYSTONE
MAINSTAY MAINTAIN MOUNTING
NEEDLING ORTHOTIC OVERCAST
PEDESTAL PEDIMENT STANDARD
STILLAGE STOCKING STRENGTH
SYMPATHY UNDERLIE UNDERPIN
UNDERSET PATRONAGE
MAINTENANCE
(— **FINANCIALLY**) BANKROLL
(— **FOR ANVIL**) STOCK
(— **FOR BELL CLAPPER**) BALDRIC
(— **FOR CANDLE**) STICK
(— **FOR CANOPY**) BAIL TESTER
(— **FOR CATALYST**) CARRIER
(— **FOR COLUMN**) SOCLE
(— **FOR CORSET**) BUSK
(— **FOR HEAVY MACHINERY**)
BUNTING
(— **FOR KNEES**) STOOL
(— **FOR LAUNCHING SHIP**) POPPET
(— **FOR LEVER**) BAIT
(— **FOR LIFE-CAR**) BAIL
(— **FOR MAST**) STEP
(— **FOR MILL**) LOWDER
(— **FOR MINE PASSAGE**) OVERCAST
(— **FOR OARLOCK**) OUTRIGGER
(— **FOR PICTURE HOOKS**) CORNICE
(— **FOR PIPE**) CHAPLET
(— **FOR PLATFORM**) STEMPEL
STEMPLE
(— **FOR SHAFT**) STEMPEL STEMPLE
(— **IN A LATHE**) DOCTOR
(— **IN PAPERMAKING TUB**) DONKEY
(— **OF COLUMN**) SOCLE PLINTH
(— **OF COPING**) KNEELER
(— **OF MOLD CORE**) ARBOR ARBOUR
(— **OF RAIL**) CHAIR BALUSTER
(— **THROUGH BIT AND BRIDLE**) APPUI
(**CRUTCHLIKE** —) DEADMAN
(**ELBOW-SHAPED** —) CRANK
(**EMBEDDED** —) SPURN
(**FIREPLACE** —) ANDIRON
(**GIVE** —) FEED
(**INCLINED** —) RIDER
(**LACKING** —) FOOTLESS
(**LOSE** —) ERODE
(**MINING** —) CAP FRAME
(**PORTABLE** —) STOOL
(**PRINCIPAL** —) BACKBONE
(**SHOE** —) TREE
(**TEMPORARY** —) NEEDLING
(**UPRIGHT** —) POPPET BANISTER
(**WHEELED** —) CARRIAGE
(PL.) SHIPWAY
SUPPORTED BASED BLOCKED
ACCOSTED SUCCINCT
(— **BY EVIDENCE**) PROBABLE
SUPPORTER ALLY JOCK ATLAS
STOOP COHORT DRAGON SATRAP
APOSTLE BOOSTER DEVOTEE
FAVORER FOUNDER LAUDIAN
PATROON PROPPER SUPPORT

ADHERENT ASSERTER ERASTIAN
ESPOUSER FAVORITE HENCHMAN
STALWART UPHOLDER CHURCHITE
(ATHLETIC —) CUP JOCK
(CHIEF —) STOOP PILLAR
(PL.) SECOND
(SUFF.) CRAT ITE
SUPPORTING BEHIND BEARING
SUPPORTIVE ENGAGE
SUPPOSE SAY SEE SET WIS WIT
DEEM POSE READ TAKE TROW WEEN
ALLOW COUNT ETTLE FANCY GUESS
JUDGE OPINE SEPAD THINK ASSUME
DEVISE DIVINE EXPECT RECKON
BELIEVE CONCEIT DARESAY IMAGINE
PRESUME PROPOSE SUPPONE
SURMISE CONCEIVE CONCLUDE
CONSIDER OPINIATE
SUPPOSED ALLEGED ASSUMED
PUTATIVE
SUPPOSING IF
SUPPOSITION IDEA FICTION
SURMISE WEENING
SUPPOSITORY BOUGIE CANDLE
PESSARY
SUPPRESS LAY DOWN GULP HIDE
HUSH SINK SLAY SNUB STOP BLACK
BURKE CHOKE CRUSH ELIDE QUASH
QUELL SHUSH SMORE SPIKE STILL
CANCEL QUENCH SQUASH STIFLE
CONTAIN CUSHION INHIBIT OPPRESS
REPRESS SILENCE SMOLDER
SMOTHER SQUELCH RESTRAIN
STRANGLE SUPPRIME VANQUISH
(— A SYLLABLE) ELIDE
(— IN SPEAKING) MINCE
SUPPRESSED BLIND CENSORED
SUPPRESSION ABEYANCE
AMEIOSIS BLACKOUT
(— OF VOWEL) ELISION
(— OF WORD SOUNDS) SYNCOPE
ECLIPSIS
(PREF.) ISCH(O)
(SUFF.) SCHESIS SCHETIC
SUPPURATE RUN BEAL WHEAL
DIGEST MATTER QUITTER
MATURATE
SUPPURATING
(PREF.) EMPYO
SUPPURATION PYOSIS BEALING
COCTION
SUPPURATIVE DIGERENT
SUPRACLAVICLE SCAPULA
SUPREMACY PALM PRIMACY
DOMINION OVERRULE
SUPREME HIGH LAST CHIEF VITAL
SUBLIME SUMMARY TOPLESS
FOREMOST GREATEST PEERLESS
SURA FATIHA FATIHAH
SURCHARGE PACK
SURCINGLE WANTY ROLLER
SURCOAT JUPON CYCLAS KABAYA
SURD SHARP ATONIC FLATED

SURE COLD SAFE BOUND SECURE
SICCAR SICKER STEADY WITTER
ASSURED CERTAIN PERFECT
COCKSURE POSITIVE UNERRING
SURELY WIS FINE IWIS SURE PARDY
REDLY ATWEEL PARDIE
SURENESS SURETY SECURITY
SURETY VAS ANDI BAIL BAND
BORROW CAUTION ENGAGER
SOVERTY SPONSOR BAILSMAN
SECURITY
SURETYSHIP SPONSION
SURF BREACH KALEMA
(— NOISE) RUT ROTE
SURFACE DAY AREA FACE ORLO
PLAT RYME SIDE ARISE BOSOM
FLOOR STONE SWARF CHROME
EMERGE FINISH GROUND SCRUFF
ASPHALT BLANKET COUNTER
ENVELOP OUTFACE OUTSIDE
STRETCH ADHEREND CONCRETE
EXTERIOR PLATFORM
(— BESIDE FIREPLACE) HOB
(— BETWEEN FLUTES OF SHAFT)
ORLO
(— BETWEEN TRIGLYPH CHANNELS)
MEROS
(— IN BEATER) BACKFALL
(— OF A GEM) BEZEL
(— OF ARCH) INTRADOS
(— OF BEAM) BACK
(— OF BODY) FLESH HABIT
(— OF CLOTH) PILE
(— OF COAL) BUTT
(— OF CRICKET FIELD) CARPET
(— OF DIAMOND) SPREAD
(— OF EARTH) DUST GROUND
TERRENE PENEPLAIN PENEPLANE
(— OF ESCUTCHEON) FIELD
(— OF GEM) FACET TABLE
(— OF GROUND OVER MINE) DAY
(— OF HAND) PALM
(— OF LIQUID) MENISCUS
(— OF MINE) GRASS
(— OF PARACHUTE) CANOPY
(— OF RECESS) REVEAL
(— OF RIFLE BARREL) LAND
(— OF ROOT) RHIZOPLANE
(— OF SAWED LUMBER) FUR
(— OF SHIELD) FIELD
(— OF TOOTH) TRITOR
(— OF VAULT) GROIN
(— OF WATER) RYME SCRUFF
(— WITHIN EARTH) GEOID
(AIRPLANE CONTROL —) ELEVEN
(BOUNDING —) PERIPHERY
(COBBLESTONE —) PITCHING
(CONCAVE —) LAP
(CONCRETE —) PAD
(CONTROL —) RUDDER
(CONVEX —) EXTRADOS
(CURVED —) BELLY
(DULL —) MAT MATTING

(EXTERNAL —) PERIPHERY
(FLAT —) BED FLAT AEQUOR PAGINA
(FLOOR —) BOWL
(FRONTAL —) METOPE
(GEOMETRIC —) TORE CONOID
SPHERE QUARTIC CONICOID
CYLINDER HELICOID PARABOLOID
(GLASSY —) HYALINE
(GLOSSY —) GLAZE
(GRASSY —) SWARD
(GROOVED —) DROVE
(HAIRY —) NAP
(HORIZONTAL —) LEVEL
(INCLINED —) CANT DESCENT
(MINERAL —) DRUSE
(PAVED —) FOOTWALK
(PILE —) FRIEZE
(PLANE —) AREA FACET
(PRINCIPAL —) FACE
(PRINTING —) CUT
(PROTECTIVE —) LAGGING
(REFLECTING —) MIRROR HORIZON
(ROAD —) MACADAM CORDUROY
(ROUGH —) KEY CRIZZLE STUBBLE
(ROUGHENED —) MAT FOOTGRIP
(SLIPPERY —) GLARE
(SLOPING —) SHELVING
(STRIKING —) BLADE
(UNDER — OF SKI) PALM
(UNGLOSSY PAINT —) FLAT
(UPPER —) NOTAEUM
(UPRIGHT —) JAMB
(WOOLLY —) NAP
(PREF.) (BENT —) SINU SINUATO
SURFACER SEASONER
SURFBOARD GUN
(LONG —) GUN BIGGUN
SURF DUCK COOT SCOTER
SURFEIT CLOY FILL GLUT SATE
STAW STALL STUFF AGROTE
ENGLUT SICKEN SATIATE SATIETY
SURCLOY SATURATE REPLETION
SATURATION
SURFEITED SAD SICK BLASE JADED
WEARY REPLETE SATIATED
SURFER GREMMY GREMLIN
GREMMIE
(GIRL —) WAHINE
(INEXPERIENCED —) GREMMY
GREMMIE
SURF FISH PERCH ALFIONA
SURFING (— MANEUVER) CUTBACK
SURF SCOTER COOT SCOTER
SURFER PISHAUG SKUNKTOP
SURF SHINER SPARADA
SURGE JAW GUST TIDE WASH DRIVE
GURGE LUNGE SPURT SWELL
BILLOW BREACH COURSE ONRUSH
SEETHE WALLOW WALTER ESTUATE
REDOUND AESTUATE UNDULATE
(— OF ELECTRIC POWER) GLITCH
(SHOREWARD —) SUFF
(TIDAL —) EAGRE

SURGEON (AMERICAN) WOOD
COOLEY DEVRIES OCHSNER
THEOREK SEAGRAVE SLAUGHTER
SURGEON (ALSO SEE PHYSICIAN
AND DOCTOR) LEECH ARTIST INTERN
MEDICO OPERATOR SAWBONES
(TREE —) TREEMAN
AMERICAN EVE BULL KEEN LONG
MAYO MOTT REED WOOD AGNEW
COLEY CRILE FLINT GROSS LAHEY
CARREL COOLEY FINNEY KELMAN
KOPITS LAWLER MORRIS MORTON
SHRADY ASHFORD BLALOCK
CUSHING DEVRIES HALSTED
HARTLEY HUGGINS KELLOGG
LAPLACE OCHSNER THEOREK
BEAUMONT MCBURNEY MCDOWELL
METTAUER SEAGRAVE SLAUGHTER
CANADIAN BETHUNE BIRKETT
ENGLISH POTT REID BRAID HADEN
PAGET BARKER BEDDOE BOWMAN
CHEYNE COOPER FAYRER LISTER
CHARNLEY ERICHSEN MOYNIHAN
ABERNETHY BRIFFAULT CHESELDEN
PARKINSON
FRENCH ANEL PARE BOYER BROCA
PETIT BECHAMP CHOPART CIVIALE
DESAULT NELATON CHAULIAC
CHASSAIGNAC
GERMAN GRAEFE ESMARCH
BILLROTH FORSSMANN
GREEK AMMONIUS
IRISH MADDEN OMEARA
ITALIAN FABRICIUS
RUSSIAN VISHNEVSKY
SCOTTISH BELL SYME BANKS
HUNTER LISTON MACEWEN
SOUTH AFRICAN BARNARD
SPANISH CASTROVIEJO
SWISS KOCHER
SURGEONFISH TANG TANGE
DOCTOR MEDICO BARBERO
SURGEON SAWBONES
SURGERY KNIFE
(VETERINARY —) ZOIATRIA
(SUFF.) CHIRURGIA
SURGING WALE ESTURE ESTUOUS
SURICATE ZENICK MEERKAT
SURINAM (CAPITAL OF —)
PARAMARIBO
(RIVER OF —) ITANY MARONI
COPPENAME SARAMACCA
COURANTYNE
(TOWN OF —) ALBINA KWATTA
TOTNESS LELYDORP
SURINAME (LANGUAGE IN —)
SRANAN
SURINAMINE ANDIRINE ANGELINE
SURINAM TOAD PIPA PIPAL
SURLINESS CYNICISM MOROSITY
SURLY BAD ILL GRUM LUNT BLUFF
CHUFF CYNIC GRUFF GURLY PURDY
ROUGH RUNTY RUSTY CHUFFY

SURLY CRUSTY GRUFFY GRUMPY MOROSE RUGGED SNARLY SULLEN DOGGISH CHURLISH

SURMISE DEEM REDE GUESS INFER TWANG SURMIT JALOUSE SUSPECT WEENING MISTRUST

SURMOUNT TOP BEAT TIDE CROWN ENSIGN HURDLE MASTER OUTTOP OVERGO SUBDUE CONQUER SURPASS OVERCOME SUPERATE
(— DIFFICULTIES) SWIM

SURMOUNTING ATOP BROCHANT

SURNAME BYNAME SURNOUN COGNOMEN OVERNAME SURSTYLE

SURPASS CAP COB TOP WAR BANG BEAT CAMP COTE DING FLOG FOIL HEAD PASS SHED WHAP WHOP EXCEL OUTDO OUTGO TRUMP ATREDE BETTER EXCEED OUTRAY OUTRUN OUTVIE OUTWIT OVERDO PRECEL ECLIPSE FORPASS OUTPEER OVERTOP PARAGON PRECEDE ANTECEDE DISTANCE DOMINATE OUTCLASS OUTMATCH OUTRANGE OUTREACH OUTSHINE OUTSTRIP OUTWRITE SURMOUNT

SURPASSING BEST FINE ABOVE PASSANT PASSING DOMINANT FRABJOUS TOWERING
(PREF.) PRETER SUPER

SURPLICE SARK COTTA EPHOD STOLA CHRISOM
(PL.) WHITES

SURPLUS ODD OVER PLUS REST EXCESS LUMBER SPILTH VELVET OVERAGE OVERRUN OVERSUM ARISINGS LEFTOVER OVERCOME OVERFLOW OVERMUCH OVERPLUS

SURPRISE CAP SHED SWAN YACH AMAZE SHOCK SNEAK FERLIE WAYLAY WONDER ASTOUND GLOPPEN PERPLEX STARTLE ASTONISH BEWILDER CONFOUND DUMFOUND
(BY —) ABACK
(CRY OF —) ACK
(EXCLAMATION OF —) QUOTHA
(EXPRESS —) MIRATE
(INTERJECTION EXPRESSING —) OOPS WOOPS
(SUDDEN —) KICK

SURPRISING FERLIE STRIKING

SURRA MBORI

SURREJOINDER TRIPLY

SURRENDER HEM LET PUT CEDE CESS DING FALL QUIT TAKE REMIT YIELD ADDICT REMISE RENDER RESIGN SUBMIT ABANDON CONCEDE DELIVER FORSAKE KAMERAD ABDICATE ABNEGATE DEDITION DELIVERY RENOUNCE UNDERLIE CAPITULATE
(— BY DEED) REMISE
(— OF CLAIM) REMISE

SURREPTITIOUS COVERT SECRET BOOTLEG FURTIVE SNEAKING

SURROGATE PROXY DEPUTY SUBSTITUTE

SURROUND HEM LAP ORB BELT DIKE DYKE FOLD GIRD GIRT HOOP WRAP BESET BRACE CLASP EMBAY EMBED FENCE HEDGE IMBED INARM ROUND BECLIP BEGIRD BEGIRT CIRCLE COLLET CORRAL ENFOLD ENWRAP FORSET GIRDLE IMPALE INCASE INVEST SPHERE SWATHE ARROUND BESIEGE BESTAND COMPASS EMBOSOM ENCLAVE ENCLOSE ENFEOFF ENROUND ENVELOP ENVIRON INVOLVE WREATHE CLOISTER ENCIRCLE ENTRENCH STOCKADE
(— WITH BOOM) CRIB
(— WITH CORD) GIRT
(— WITH MORTAR) GROUT

SURROUNDED AMID AMONG AMIDST AMONGST BETWEEN
(— BY WATER) INSULAR

SURROUNDING MIDST ROUND CIRCUM AMBIENT
(PL.) SCENE HARNESS ENVIRONS
(PREF.) CIRCUM PERI

SURROYALS CROWN

SURVEILLANCE WATCH SCRUTINY STAKEOUT OVERSIGHT
(— SYSTEM) AWACS

SURVEY EYE SEE DIAL POLL SCAN VIEW AVIEW STOCK STUDY PERUSE REGARD REVIEW SEARCH CANVASS CAPSULE OVERSEE SURVIEW TERRIER THEORIC EPISCOPY LUSTRATE OVERLOOK OVERVIEW PROSPECT SURVEYAL TRAVERSE RECONNAISANCE
(— RAPIDLY) GLANCE
(— TIMBER) SKYLOOK
(BRIEF —) APERCU

SURVEYING GEODESY GROMATICS
(MINE —) LATCHING

SURVEYOR BOLO ARTIST DIALER DIALLER NOTEMAN CHAINMAN GROMATIC LEVELMAN

SURVIVAL ECHO RELIC RELICT
(ANACHRONISTIC —) LEFTOVER
(USELESS —) SNUFF

SURVIVE LAST GETBY BILEVE OUTLAST OUTLIVE

SURVIVOR RELICT

SURYA (FATHER OF —) ADITI DYAUS
(MESSENGER OF —) PUSHAN
(WIFE OF —) USHAS

SUSCEPTIBILITY CAVIL SENSE EMOTION FEELING FRAILTY
(— TO ILL-HEALTH) DELICACY

SUSCEPTIBLE EASY SOFT LIABLE
FEELING PATIENT SENSIBLE
TOLERANT
(— TO CHANGE) CASALTY
SUSIAN FLAMITE
SUSLIK SISEL ZIZEL MARMOT
SUSPECT FEAR DOUBT FANCY
GUESS SMOKE THINK BELIEVE
ENDOUTE JALOUSE MISDEEM
SUPPOSE DISTRUST JEALOUSE
MISDOUBT MISTRUST
(NOT —) COLD
SUSPECTED SPOTTED SUSPECT
SUSPEND CALL HALT HANG OUST
SHUT SIST STAY BREAK CLOSE
DEBAR DEFER DEMUR EXPEL POISE
REMIT SLING SWING APPEND
DANGLE ADJOURN EXCLUDE
FLUIDIZE INTERMIT OVERHANG
PROROGUE REPRIEVE SCAFFOLD
SUSPENSE PRETERMIT
(— ANCHOR) COCKBILL
(— FROM ACTIVITY) SIDELINE
(— IN FLUID) ENTRAIN
SUSPENDED SWING AFLOAT
LATENT HANGING PENDANT
PENDENT PENSILE HOVERING
SUSPENSE
(NOT —) VESTED
SUSPENDER GALLUS GARTER
BRETELLE
(PL.) BRACES GALLOWS GALLUSES
SUSPENSE DEMUR POISE
SUSPENSION FOG BREI FUME SIST
STAY STOP DELAY DOUBT MAGMA
SMOKE BREACH CUTOFF SLURRY
AEROSOL FAILURE RESPITE
ABEYANCE BACTERIN EMULSION
INFUSION SHUTDOWN SUSPENSE
WISHBONE
(— OF JUDGMENT) EPOCHE
(— OF NOISE) HUSH
(— OF RESPIRATION) SYNCOPE
(— OF SENTENCE) REPRIEVE
PROBATION
SUSPENSIVENESS DRIVE
SUSPENSORY SUPPORT
SUSPICION HINT DOUBT SOUPCON
SURMISE SUSPECT UMBRAGE
DISTRUST JEALOUSY MISDOUBT
MISTRUST TINCTURE
(IRRATIONAL —) PARANOIA
(SNEAKING —) IDEA
SUSPICIOUS SHY CHARY FISHY
LEERY PEERY QUEER SMOKY
SHODDY JEALOUS SOUPCON
SUSPECT DOUBTFUL WAFFLIKE
SUSPICIOUSLY ASKANCE
SUSQUEHANNA CONESTOGA
SUSTAIN ABET BACK BEAR BUOY
DURE HELP HOLD LAST PROP STAY
ABIDE CARRY FAVOR SINEW SPRAG

STAND ASSIST CONVEY ENDURE
FOSTER SECOND SUCCOR SUFFER
UPHOLD UPSTAY ALIMENT BOLSTER
CONTAIN NOURISH OUTBEAR
PROLONG SUPPORT UNDERFO
BEFRIEND BUTTRESS CONTINUE
MAINTAIN PRESERVE SCAFFOLD
(PREF.) CO
SUSTAINED TENUTO SOUTENU
SUSTENANCE GEAR MEAT SALT
BREAD FOISON LIVING RELIEF
ALIMENT PABULUM TABLING
SUSU GERIP SOOSOO DOLPHIN
SUSURRUS WHISPER
SUTLER PROVANT VIVANDIER
SUTTEE SATI
SUTURE SEW SEAM RAPHE SETON
STITCH HARMONY PTERION
(SUFF.) RHAPHY RRHAPHY
SVANTOVIT TRIGLAV
SVELTE CHIC TRIM LITHE SLEEK
SUAVE SMOOTH URBANE SLENDER
SVENO (SLAYER OF —) SOLIMANO
SWAB GOB MOP WAD BOSH QTIP
SWOB WIPE PATCH DOSSIL SPONGE
EPAULET SWABBER SQUILGEE
SWABBIE GOB TAR
SWADDLE BIND SWEEL SWATHE
SWAG DRUM GAME LOOT BOOTY
LUCRE MONEY BOODLE FESTOON
MATILDA
SWAGE BOSS MOUTH UPSET FULLER
JUMPER SHAPER SWAGER SWEDGE
FLATTER
(PL.) OLIVER
SWAGGER JET ROY BRAG COCK
FACE ROLL BOAST BRANK BRAVE
NUTTY STRUT SWANK SWASH
BLAGUE BOUNCE GOSTER HECTOR
PARADO PRANCE RENOWN RUFFLE
SPROSE BLUSTER BRAVADO
GAUSTER PANACHE ROISTER
SOLDIER DOMINEER TIGERISM
SWAGGERER HUFF SWAG BUCKO
FACER TIGER CUTTLE JETTER PISTOL
BRAVADO HUFFCAP RUFFLER
FANFARON WHIFFLER
SWAGGERING HUFFY FACING
GASCON HUFFCAP TEARCAT
BLUSTERY TIGERISH
SWAGMAN WHALER DRIFTER
DRUMMER TRAVELER
SWAIN BEAU COLIN CUDDY RUSTIC
STREPHON
SWAINSONA INDIGO
SWALE SLASH
SWALLOW OFF SUP BOLT DOWN
DROP GAUP GAWP GLUT GULP SINK
SWIG TAKE CLUNK DRINK GORGE
GURGE POUCH QUILT SLOCK SWOOP
ABSORB ENGLUT ENGULF GLUTCH
GOBBET GOBBLE GODOWN GUZZLE

IMBIBE INGEST MARTIN POCKET
PROGNE SWELLY CONSUME
ENGORGE ARUNDELL WITCHUCK
(— AGAIN) REGORGE
(— GREEDILY) BEND SLUP GORGE
GULCH SWILL WORRY INHALE
(— HASTILY) SWAP SWOP GLOUP
SLUMMOCK
(— IN AGAIN) RESORB
(— OF LIQUOR) SLUG
(— UP) GULF SWAMP ABSORB
DEVOUR
(— WITH GREEDINESS) ENGORGE
(LOSS OF ABILITY TO —) APHAGIA
(NOISY —) SLURP
(WOMAN TURNED INTO —) PROCNE
(PREF.) CHELID(O)
SWALLOWTAIL TROILUS
SWALLOWWORT CELANDINE
SWAMP BOG FEN FLAT FLOW MIRE
MOSS SLEW SLUE SOAK SUMP VLEI
VLEY WHAM WHIN FLUSH LERNA
LETCH MARSH SWALE SWANG
URMAN DELUGE DISMAL ENGULF
MORASS MUSKEG SLOUGH
CIENAGA POCOSIN GREENING
INUNDATE QUAGMIRE
SWAMP COTTONWOOD LIAR
SWAMPER BUSHER GOPHER
SWAMPHEN COOT
SWAMP LOOSESTRIFE PEATWEED
PEATWOOD
SWAMP MAHOGANY GUNNUNG
SWAMP MILKWEED DAGGA
SWAMPY PUXY BOGGY POOLY
CALLOW POACHY QUASHY QUEASY
SLUMPY MOORISH PALUDAL
ULIGINOUS
SWAMPY CREE MASKEGON
SWAN COB ELK PEN OLOR CYGNET
HOOPER SWANNET WHOOPER
(FEMALE —) PEN
(FLOCK OF —S) GAME MARK
(KIND OF —) MUTE
SWANFLOWER SWANWORT
SWANHILD (FATHER OF —) SIGURD
(MOTHER OF —) GUDRUN
SWANK CHIC POSH TONY RITZY
SWANKY POSH SWASH SPIFFY
SWAP CHOP SWOP TRADE TRUCK
DICKER EXCHANGE
SWARD SOD TURF SPINE SWARF
SWATH SWARTH
SWARM FRY SNY BIKE CAST FARE
HIVE HOST KNIT NEST SORT SWIM
TEEM CLOUD CROWD FLOCK FLUSH
FRACK HORDE SNARL FLIGHT
HOTTER RABBLE SWARVE THRONG
OVERRUN SUBCAST PULLULATE
(— IN) FILL
(— OF BEES) BIKE HIVE
(— OF INSECTS) BAND FLIGHT

(— OF PEOPLE) BIKE DRIFT
(THIRD — OF BEES) COLT
SWARMING ALIVE ASWARM
SWARMY
SWARTBACK SWARBIE
SWARTHY DUN DARK BLACK
BROWN DUSKY GRIMY MOORY
SWART MORIAN SWARTH BISTRED
BISTERED
SWASH SWIG SWILL SWATCH
SWABBLE SWASHWAY
SWASHBUCKLER SWASH GASCON
SLASHER SWASHER
SWASTIKA FYLFOT GAMMADION
GAMMATION HAKENKREUZ
SWAT SWOT DEHGAN STRIKE
SWATH SWIPE STADDLE
SWATHE LAP BIND WRAP SWARF
ENWRAP INWRAP SWADDLE
WINDROW
SWATTER FLYSWAT
SWAY NOD WAG BEAR BEND BIAS
FLAP HIKE LILT ROCK ROLL RULE
SHOG SWAB SWAG SWIG TILT TOSS
WALD WAVE CARRY CHARM LURCH
POWER REIGN SHAKE SWALE SWING
WAVER WHEEL AFFECT ALLURE
CAREEN DIRECT EMPIRE TOTTER
WAGGLE COMMAND SHOGGIE
STAGGER SWABBLE SWIGGLE
(— IN WALKING) WADDLE
(SUFF.) CRACY CRAT(IC)
SWAYBACK WARFA LORDOSIS
RENGUERA
SWAYING ASWAY ROLLING
SWAZILAND (CAPITAL OF —)
MBABANE
(COIN OF —) RAND EMALANGEN
(LANGUAGE OF —) SISWATI
(MONEY OF —) LILANGENI
(RIVER IN —) USUTU KOMATI
MHLATUZE UMBULUZI
(TOWN OF —) STEGI GOLLEL
MANZINI PIGGSPEAK
SWEAR VOW VUM DAMN SINK
SNUM SWAN SWOW TAKE CURSE
ADJURE AFFIRM BEDAMN DEPONE
DEPOSE OBJURE CONJURE
DEJERATE EXECRATE FORSWEAR
(— FALSELY) RAP MOUNT
FORSWEAR MANSWEAR
SWEARING JURANT JURATION
(FALSE —) PERJURY
SWEARWORD CUSS
SWEAT DEW WET STEW WASH
BREAN MADOR SUDOR SUDATE
LAUNDER PARBOIL SWELTER
SWIVVET TRANSUDE PERSPIRATION
(— SKINS) STALE
(DYNAMITE —) LEAK
(PREF.) HIDR(O) HYDR(O) SUDORI
(SUFF.) IDROSIS

SWEATBOX HOTBOX
SWEATER FROCK GANSEY
 JUMPER WOOLLY CARDIGAN
 SLIPOVER
 (CLOSE-FITTING —) POORBOY
 (WOMAN'S SHORT —) SHRINK
SWEATHOUSE TEMESCAL
SWEATING TUB ASWEAT SWELTRY
 SUDATION SUDATORY
SWEATY PUGGY ASWEAT PERSPIRY
 SUDOROUS SWEATFUL

SWEDEN
CAPITAL: STOCKHOLM
COIN: ORE KRONA SKILLING
COUNTY: KALMAR OREBRO UPPSALA
DIVISION: AMT LAEN SKANE OREBRO
 UPPSALA GOTALAND JAMTLAND
 SWEALAND
GULF: BOTHNIA
ISLAND: OLAND GOTALAND
LAKE: SILJA VANERN MALAREN
 VATTERN DALALVEN STORAVAN
 HJALMAREN
MEASURE: AM ALN FOT MIL REF TUM
 FAMN STOP FODER KANNA KAPPE
 LINJE NYMIL SPANN STANG TUNNA
 FATHOM JUMFRU KOLLAST
 OXHUVUD TUNLAND FJARDING
 KAPPLAND KOLTUNNA
MOUNTAIN: SAHV AMMAR OVIKS
 HELAGS SARJEK
PROVINCE: KALMAR OREBRO
 GOTLAND HALLAND UPPSALA
 ALVSBORG BLEKINGE ELFSBORG
 JAMTLAND MALMOHUS
 WERMLAND
RIVER: DAL UME GOTA KLAR LULE
 KALIX PITEA RANEA LAINIO
 LJUSNE TORNEA WINDEL
 ANGERMAN
TOWN: UMEA BODEN RORAS EDANE
 FALUN GAVLE LULEA MALMO PITEA
 VISBY YSTAD ARVIKA OREBRO
 LUDVIKA UPPSALA GOTEBORG
 NYKOPING VASTERAS
WATERFALL: HANDOL TANNFORSEN
WEIGHT: ASS LOD ORT MARK PUND
 STEN UNTZ NYLAST LISPUND
 SKEPPUND

SWEDISH CLOVER ALSIKE
SWEEP OAR BUCK DUST RAFF SOOP
 SWAY TILT BESOM BROOM DIGHT
 DRIFT FETCH SCOPE SKIRL SWIPE
 SWOOP BREADTH CLEANSE PICOTAH
 SHADOOF STRICKLE
 (— A NET) BEAT
 (— MAJESTICALLY) SWAN
 (— OFF) SLIPE
 (— OF SCYTHE) SWATH SWATHE
 (— ON CULTIVATOR) SKIN

 (CHIMNEY —) CHUMMY SWEEPY
 RAMONEUR
 (HAY —) BUCK
SWEEPBOARD STRICKLE
SWEEPER BESOM BUNGY SWEEP
 TOPAZ BHANGI BHUNGI MEHTAR
 PRYLER ROADER SOOPER TOPASS
 BROOMER TUBEMAN BHUNGINI
 MATRANEE SCRUBBER
SWEEPING SURGE RASANT SWEEPY
 (— FOR FISH) DRAFT DRAUGHT
 (— OF CURVE) NUTATION
 (PL.) DUST FULVIE FULZIE RIFFRAFF
SWEET DOUX DUMP FOOT SOOT
 SUCK CREAM DILIS DOUCE DULCE
 FRESH HONEY MERRY SOOTH SPICY
 SPLIT BREEZE DULCET FRUITY
 GENTLE SILKEN SILVER SIRUPY
 SUGARY DARLING FAIRING HONEYED
 INSIPID MUSICAL PANDROP
 SUGARED SWEETLY WINNING
 WINSOME AROMATIC ENGAGING
 FLUMMERY LIEBLICH LUSCIOUS
 NECTARED PLEASANT
 (SICKLY —) ICKY
 (SLIGHTLY —) SEC
 (PREF.) DULCI GLYCERO GLYCO HEDY
 SUAVI
SWEET BAY BREWSTER MAGNOLIA
SWEETBREAD BUR BURR
 PANCREAS
 (— OF DEER) INCHPIN
SWEETBRIER BEDEGUAR
 EGLANTINE
SWEET CALABASH KURUBA
SWEET CASSAVA AIPI AIPIM
SWEET CHERRY MAZZARD
SWEET CICELY MYRRH
SWEET CLOVER LOTUS MELILOT
SWEET COLTSFOOT LAGWORT
SWEETEN CANDY HONEY SUGAR
 SWEET PURIFY ADDULCE CLEANSE
 DULCIFY FRESHEN MOLLIFY
 PERFUME MITIGATE
SWEETENER SACCHARIN
SWEET FENNEL FINOCHIO
 FLORENCE
SWEET FERN FERNGALE
SWEETFISH AYU
SWEET FLAG SEDGE BEEWORT
 CALAMUS
SWEET GALE GOLD GAGEL
 BAYBUSH FLEAWOOD GALEWORT
 GALLBUSH
SWEET GUM AMBER COPALM
 STORAX BILSTED
SWEETHEART JO BOY GRA HON
 JOE LAD PET PUG SIS AGRA AMIE
 BABY REAU DEAR DOLL DOXY DUCK
 FAIR GILL GIRL JILL LADY LASS LIEF
 LOVE MASH MORT POUT AGRAH
 BULLY BUSSY CHERI COOKY DOLLY

DONAH DONEY DONNA DRURY
FLAME LEMAN LOVER PUGGY SPARK
SWEET COOKIE EMILIA FELLOW
FRIEND MOPSEY PIGEON STEADY
WAHINE AMOROSA BELOVED
PHYLLIS PIGSNEY QUERIDA
SPRUNNY SWEETIE TOOTSIE
DOWSABEL DULCINEA FOLLOWER
LADYBIRD LADYLOVE LIEBCHEN
LOVELASS MISTRESS SWEETING
TRUELOVE
(— OF HARLEQUIN) COLUMBINE
SWEETIE
(— PIE) HON DEAR HONEY DEARIE
SWEETLEAF DYELEAVES
SYMPLOCOS
SWEET MARJORAM OREGANO
SWEETMEAT DROP DUMP KISS
DULCE FUDGE GOODY PASTE PLATE
SPICE TOFFY BONBON BUCAYO
COMFIT DRAGEE DREDGE JUNKET
ALCORZA BANQUET CARAMEL
CARAWAY CLAGGUM CONFECT
LOUKOUM PENUCHE SUCCADE
CONSERVE HARDBAKE MARZIPAN
PASTILLE
(PL.) BALUSHAI CONFETTI
SWEETNESS DULCE HONEY SIRUP
SYRUP DULCOR DOUCEUR DULCITY
SUAVITY FLORIMEL WORDNESS
SWEET ORANGE CHINA CHINO
SWEET PEA CATGUT LATHYRUS
SWEET PEPPERBUSH CLETHRA
SOAPBUSH
SWEET POTATO YAM SWEET
BATATA CAMOTE KUMARA
OCARINA
SWEET RUSH SQUINANT
SWEET-SMELLING AROMATIC
SWEETSOP ANON ATES ATIS ATTA
CORAZON SWEETING
SWEET-SOUNDING MERRY
SWEET-TALK ENAMOR
SWEET VIOLET FINELEAF
SWEET WILLIAM DIANTHUS
SWELL BAG DON NIB NOB BEAL BELL
BLAB BLOW BLUB BOLL BULB BULK
BUMP BUOY DOME FILL FINE GROW
HOVE HUFF HUSH PINK PLIM RISE
SWAG TOFF TONY WAVE BELLY
BERRY BLAST BLOAT BULGE BUNCH
DANDY FLASH NIFTY PLUFF PREEN
SMART STOCK STRUT SURGE TULIP
BILLOW BOWDEN DILATE EXPAND
GROWTH LOVELY SPRING STROUT
TUMEFY UPRISE AUGMENT BLUBBER
BURGEON DISTEND INFLATE
REGULAR SWAGGER OVERBLOW
TURGESCE
(— OF GUN MUZZLE) TULIP
(— OF WATER) HUSH SURF FLOOD
SURGE

(— OUT) BAG POD BUNT DRAW POUT
BOSOM BILLOW SPONGE BALLOON
BLADDER
(HEAVY —) RUN SEA
(SEA —) WALLOW BACKWATER
(PREF.) OEDE OEDI TUME
SWELLDOODLE EGGFISH
SWELLED BIAS BLOWN
SWELLFISH BLOWER PUFFER
TAMBOR
SWELLING BIG BUR NOB PAP PIN
BLAB BOLL BUBO BUMP BURR CLAP
COWL CURB FROG FULL GALL KNOB
KNOT NODE POKE PONE PUFF
AMPER BLAIN BOTCH BOUGE BULGE
BUNCH BUNNY CLOUR EDEMA
JETTY MOUSE PROUD SURGE SWELL
TUBER TUMOR ANCOME ASWELL
BOSOMY BUNCHY CALLUS FLATUS
GIBBER GROWTH KERNEL PIMPLE
RANULA STRUMA SWELTH TURGID
WARBLE AMPULLA BOSSING
CAPELET CHAGOMA CUSHION
GOUNDOU HAPTERE PUSTULE
SURGENT TURGENT UREDEMA
UROCELE APOSTEME BULLNECK
CHEMOSIS DACRYOMA FURUNCLE
GLANDULE GOURDING HAPTERON
HEMATOMA MUCOCELE NODOSITY
PULVINUS PUMPKNOT QUELLUNG
SCIRRHUS STYLOPOD VESSICNON
TUMESCENCE
(— IN HORSE'S CHEST) ANTICOR
(— IN HORSE'S MOUTH) LAMPAS
LAMPASSE
(— IN PLASTER) BLUB
(— OF PLANT TISSUE) GALL
(— OF THE CHEEK) HONE
(— ON ANIMAL'S JOINTS) BUNNY
CAPELLET
(— ON HEAD) COWL
(— ON SPLEEN) AGUECAKE
(DISCOLORED —) MOUSE
(EYE —) STY STYE
(ROUNDED —) TUBER
(PREF.) GANGLI GANGLO STRUMI
(SUFF.) EMATOMA PHYMA
SWELTER BAKE BOIL STEW SWELT
SWELTERING STEWY SULTRY
SWELTRY
SWERVE BOW CUT LUG YAW BIAS
FADE JOUK SKEW VARY VEER WARP
SHEER STRAY DEPART DEVIATE
DIGRESS DIVERGE INSWING
SWIDDEN CAINGIN KAINGIN
SWIFT CRAN FAST FLIT MAIN VITE
FLEET HASTY LIGHT QUICK RAPID
SNELL SWITH WIGHT WINDY
ARROWY MARLET NIMBLE RAKING
SOUPLE SPEEDY STRICT SUDDEN
SWIFTY TOTTER WINGED COLLIER
DEVELIN FLIGHTY POSTING

SWALLOW TANTIVY DEVELING
HEPIALID PEGASEAN SCREAMER
SCUTTLER SQUEALER SWIFTLET
SALANGANE
(PREF.) CITI CYPSELO OCY TACHEO
TACHISTO TACHO TACHY

SWIFTLY FAST SWAP APACE
SNELL SNELLY LIGHTLY STEEPLY
TANTIVY

SWIFTNESS FOOT HASTE SPEED
CELERITY FASTNESS VELOCITY

SWIG SCOUR SNORT SWILL SWING
SWIGGLE

SWILL SOSS BROCK SLOSH SLUICE
HOGWASH PIGWASH SWILLING

SWIM DIP COWD SAIL SOOM
SPAN TEEM BATHE CRAWL FLEET
FLOAT GLIDE SWARM PLUNGE
OVERFLOW
(— IN NEW DIRECTION) MILL
(— IN NUDE) SKINNYDIP
(— IN SHOALS) RUN
(— TOGETHER) SCHOOL
(— TRUNKS) JAMS
(PREF.) NECT(O)
(SUFF.) NECTAE NECTES

SWIMMER NAIAD BATHER NATATOR
BUTTERFLYER

SWIMMERET PLEOPOD

SWIMMING ASWIM NATANT
FLOTANT NATATION
(— APPARATUS) SCUBA
(— DEVICE) SNORKEL
(— STUNT) MARLIN WALKOVER

SWIMMING POOL POOL THERM
PLUNGE THERME PISCINA NATATORY
(— ON LINER) LIDO

SWIMSUIT MAILLOT

SWIN
(— IN NUDE) SKINNYDIP

SWINDLE CON GIP GYP JOB RIG BILK
BURN DUPE FAKE FLAP HAVE MACE
PULL RAMP ROOK ROPE SCAM SWIZ
BUNCO BUNKO CHEAT COZEN FLING
FOIST GOUGE GRIFT LURCH MULCT
PLANT PONZI ROGUE SHARK SHARP
SHAVE SHUCK SLANG SPOOF STING
SWIZZ UNCLE BOODLE BUBBLE
BUCKET CHISEL CHOUSE DIDDLE
FIDDLE FLEECE GAZUMP HUSTLE
INTAKE NOBBLE SUCKER TREPAN
DEFRAUD FINAGLE SKELDER
THIMBLE VERNEUK FLIMFLAM
BAMBOOZLE

SWINDLER DO FOB GYP LEG BILK
FYNK HAWK ROOK SKIN CHEAT
CROOK ESROC FAKER GANEF GREEK
HARPY KNAVE MACER ROGUE
CHIAUS GOUGER INTAKE RINGER
ROOKER SALTER SHAVER VERSER
BUBBLER GRIFTER HUSTLER
MACEMAN MAGSMAN NOBBLER

SHARPER SKELDER SLICKER SPIELER
BARNACLE BLACKLEG CHISELER
FINAGLER GILENYER LUMBERER
PIGEONER SHELLMAN TRAMPOSO
(DECOY —) BARNARD

SWINDLING MACE BUNCO BUNKO
GRAFT ROOKY SHARK GYPPERY
JOUKERY CHEATERY JOOKERIE

SWINE HOG OIC PIG SOW BOAR GALT
GILT PORK SUID YILT DUROC ESSEX
SWIPE WHITE GUSSIE POLAND
PORKER PORKET BUSHPIG LACOMBE
OINKERS PECCARY SUFFOLK
SUIDIAN CHESHIRE HYOTHERE
LANDRACE TAMWORTH
(— AND FOOD) PANNAGE
(— AND MAN) OMNIVORA
(PREF.) HYO

SWINEHERD GURTH HOGMAN
EUMAEUS HOGHERD HOGWARD

SWINE-LIKE GADARENE

SWING GO COOK HIKE JUMP LILT
SCUP SHOG STOT SWAY SWEE
TURN SHAKE SHOWD SLING SWALE
TREND DANGLE GYRATE HANDLE
SWINGE SWITCH SWIVEL TOTTER
JUMPING SHOGGIE SWINGEL
WAMPISH BRANDISH FLOURISH
OSCILLATE
(— AROUND) JIB SLEW SLUE
SLOUGH
(— A SHIP) SPRING
(— BY BATTER) CUT
(— FROM POSITION) CANT
(— FROM SIDE TO SIDE) JOW
(— FROM THE TIDE) TEND
(— OF PENDULUM) BEAT
(— OF SAIL) GYBE JIBE
(— OF SWORD) MOULINET
(— OUT OF LINE) SWAG
(— THE FOREFEET) DISH
(RHYTHMICAL —) LILT
(WILD —) HAYMAKER
(PREF.) OSCILLO

SWINGER HINGE

SWINGING BANK ASWING
SWINGY

SWINGLE SWORD SCUTCH
SWIPPLE

SWING SEAT TRANSOM

SWINISH SOWISH HOGGISH
PORCINE SUILLINE

SWIPE COP CHOP GLOM SLOG WIPE
SNAKE STEAL VULTURE

SWIRL BOIL EDDY GULF HURL PURL
WALM GURGE SWALE SWEEL
SWORL SWOOSH WREATHE
TOURBILLION
(— OF SALMON) BULGE

SWIRLING VORTICAL

SWISH HISH WHIP SMART SWILL
WHISH

SWISS SWISSER HELVETIC
(— PINE) MUGHO
SWISS FAMILY ROBINSON
(AUTHOR OF —) WYSS
(CHARACTER IN —) JACK EMILY FRITZ
ERNEST FRANCIS MONTROSE
ROBINSON
SWITCH GAD TAN LASH TWIG WAND
AZOTE BIRCH BREAK SHUNT SWISH
CHANGE CUTOUT DERAIL DIPPER
FERULA FERULE LARRUP RATTAN
SCUTCH SILENT SPRING HICKORY
KIPPEEN SCOURGE SQUITCH
CRYOTRON HAIRWORK POSTICHE
(— FOCUS) FADE
(AUTO —) DIMMER
(ELECTRIC —) KEY
(RAILROAD —) GATE POINT
SWITCHBOARD (PRIVATE PHONE
—) PBX
SWITCH ENGINE GOAT
SWITCHMAN SHUNTER SWITCHER

SWITZERLAND
BAY: URI
CANTON: ZUG BERN JURA VAUD
BASEL AARGAU GENEVA GLARUS
LUZERN SCHWYZ TICINO VALAIS
ZURICH GRISONS THURGAU
FRIBOURG OBWALDEN
CAPITAL: BERN BERNE
COIN: FRANC RAPPE RAPPEN
ANGSTER DUPLONE BLAFFERT
LAKE: URI ZUG THUN AGERI LEMAN
MORAT BIENNE BRIENZ GENEVA
LUGANO SARNEN WALLEN ZURICH
HALLWIL LUCERNE LUNGERN
VIERWALD
MEASURE: IMI POT AUNE ELLE FUSS
IMMI MUID PIED SAUM ZOLL LIEVE
LIGNE LINIE MAASS MOULE POUCE
SCHUH STAAB TOISE PERCHE
SETIER STRICH JUCHART KLAFTER
VIERTEL
MOUNTAIN: JURA RIGI ROSA BLANC
CENIS KARPF LINARD PIZELA
BERNINA BEVERIN GRIMSEL
PILATUS ROTONDO BALMHORN
JUNGFRAU
MOUNTAIN PASS: CENIS FURKA
ALBERG MALOJA BRENNER
GRIMSEL SIMPLON SPLUGEN
LOTSCHEN
NAME: HELVETIA
RIVER: AAR INN AARE THUR BROYE
DOUBS LINTH REUSS RHINE RHONE
MAGGIA SARINE TICINO PRATIGAU
TOWN: BALE BERN BIEL BRIG CHUR
SION AARAU BASEL VEVEY GENEVA
GLARUS LUZERN SCHWYZ ZURICH
FYZABAD HERISAU LUCERNE
LAUSANNE MONTREUX
VALLEY: AAR ZERMATT ENGADINE

WATERFALL: SIMMEN HANDEGG
IFFIGEN DIESSBACH GIESSBACH
STAUBBACH TRUMMELBACH
WEIGHT: PFUND CENTNER QUINTAL

SWIVEL LOPER SWAPE SWIPE
CASTER FIDDLE TIRRET TOGGLE
TONGUE TRAVERSE TRUNNION
SWIVET STEW
SWIZZLE STIR
SWOLLEN BLUB FULL PLIM RANK
BLOWN CHUFF GOUTY GREAT
GUMMY POBBY PROUD PUFFY
TUMID BOLLEN BRAWNY BULLED
GOURDY TURGID BESTRUT BLOATED
BLUBBER BULBOUS GIBBOSE
GIBBOUS GOURDED GOUTISH
STICKLE TURGENT BEPUFFED
BLADDERY TUMOROUS
(PREF.) PHYS(O)
SWOON KEEL SWEB SWIM DOVER
DROWN DWALM FAINT SLOOM
SOUND SWARF SWELT STOUND
SWOUND TRANCE ECSTASY
SWITHER SYNCOPE SWOONING
SWOONING ASWOON SYNCOPE
SWOOP CHOP DIVE JOUK SWAP
SWOP SOUSE STOOP SWOPE
POUNCE SOURCE DESCEND
(KIND OF —) FELL
SWOOPING SOUSE
SWORD FOX SAX BILL DIRK FALX
GRAM IRON PATA SAEX SEAX SPIT
TOOL TUCK TURK BILBO BLADE
BRAND DEGEN DIEGO ESTOC GULLY
KNIFE KUKRI PRICK RIPON SABER
SABRE SHARP STEEL ANDREW
BARONG BILBOA CATTAN DAMASK
DUSACK FLORET GLAIVE HANGER
KHANDA KUKERI MIMING PARANG
PINKER PORKER RAPIER SMITER
SPATHA TILTER TIZONA TOLEDO
WAFTER BALMUNG BRANDON
CURTANA CUTLASH CUTLASS
ESPADON ESTOQUE FERRARA
FLEURET IMPALER JOYEUSE
MALCHUS MORGLAY SHABBLE
SLASHER SNICKER SPURTLE
TOASTER WHIFFLE WHINGER
ACINACES BASELARD CAMPILAN
CLAYMORE DAMASCUS DURENDAL
FALCHION FLAMBERG SCHLAGER
SCIMITAR SPADROON SPITFROG
WACADASH WHINYARD
(— OF CHARLEMAGNE) JOYEUSE
(— OF CID) TIZONA
(— OF HERMES) HARPE
(— OF LANCELOT) ARONDIGHT
(— OF ROLAND) DURENDAL
(— OF SIEGFRIED) GRAM BALMUNG
(— OF SIR BEVIS) MORGLAY
(— OF ST. GEORGE) ASCALON
ASKELON

(— USED BY ST. PETER) MALCHUS
(BLUNT —) WAFTER SCHLAGER
(CELTIC —) SAX SAEX
(CURVED —) SCIMITAR
(DOUBLE-EDGED —) KEN PATA
KHANDA SPATHA
(DUELLING —) EPEE SHARP
(DYAK —) PARANG
(FENCING —) EPEE FOIL SABER
SABRE RAPIER
(HALF OF —) FORTE
(JAPANESE —) CATAN CATTAN
KATANA WACADASH
(LONG —) SPATHA WHIFFLE
(MATADOR'S —) ESTOQUE
(MORO —) BARONG CAMPILAN
(NARROW —) TUCK
(NORMAN —) SPATHA
(PERSIAN —) ACINACES
(POINTLESS —) CURTANA CURTEIN
(RUSTY —) SHABBLE
(SHORT —) DIRK ESTOC KUKRI
SKEAN CREESE HANGER CURTAXE
WHINGER FALCHION WHINYARD
(THRUSTING —) ESTOC STOCK
(TWO-HANDED —) ESPADON
SPADONE CLAYMORE
(WOODEN —) WASTER STRICKLE
SWORD-BEARER VERGER SELICTAR
PORTGLAVE
(PL.) ENSIFERI
SWORD DANCER MATACHIN
SWORDFISH AU ESPADA ESPADON
XIPHIAS ALBACORA BILLFISH
BOATBILL FORKTAIL XIPHIOID
SCOMBROID
(PREF.) XIPH(O)
SWORD-LIKE
(PREF.) XIPH(I)(O)
SWORDPLAY SPADROON
(STYLIZED —) KENDO
SWORD-SHAPED ENSATE
ENSIFORM GLADIATE
SWORDSMAN BLADE BLADER
FENCER SLASHER SWORDER
THRUSTER
SWORDSMANSHIP KENDO
SWORDTAIL HELLERI
SWORN AVOWED
SWOT GRI MUG
SYAGUSH SHARGOSS
SYBARITE EPICURE
SYBARITIC SENSUOUS
SYCAMORE MAY DAROO COTONIER
LACEWOOD PLANTAIN
SYCEE SHOE
SYCOPHANCY FAWNERY
SYCOPHANT TOADY COGGER
FAWNER GNATHO HANGBY TAGTAIL
CLAWBACK PARASITE PICKTHANK
SATELLITE
SYCOPHANTIC FAWNING SERVILE
SLAVISH OBEDIENT TRENCHER

SYCORAX (SON OF —) CALIBAN
SYCOSIS MENTAGRA
SYENITE APPINITE TRACHYTE
SYLLABARY KANA IROFA IROHA
KATAKANA
SYLLABIC SONANT CENTROID
SONANTIC
SYLLABLE ARSIS BREVE GROUP
SHORT DISEME SYLLAB THESIS
TRISEME ASSONANT
(— DENOTING ASSENT) OM
(BOBIZATION —) BO CE DI GA GE LO
MA NI
(IMPROVISE NONSENSE —S) SCAT
(LAST —) ULTIMA
(LAST — BUT ONE) PENULT
(LONG —) LONG
(MUSICAL —) DI DO FA FI LA LE LI ME MI
RA RE RI SE SI SO TA TE TI TO UT SOL
(REFRAIN —) DILDO
(SHORT —) MORA SHORT
(STRONG —) STRESS
(TERMINAL —) ENDING
(UNACCENTED —) OUTRIDE
(UNACCENTED —S) THESIS
(UNSTRESSED —) OUTRIDE
SYLLABUS PROGRAM VIDIMUS
HEADNOTE SYNOPSIS PROGRAMME
SYLLOGISM BARBARA ABDUCTION
ENTHYMEME
(SERIES OF —S) SORITES
SYLPH ARIEL SYLPHID
SYLPHID ARIEL SYLPHID
SYLVAN WOODY FOREST SILVAN
WOODEN WOODISH SYLVATIC
SYLVITE HARDSALT
SYMBIOSIS LICHENISM MUTUALISM
NUTRICISM
SYMBOL KEY CODE FISH FOUR ICON
IDOL IKON MARK NEUM SEAL SIGN
TYPE BADGE CREST CROSS EAGLE
IMAGE INDEX PRIME TOKEN CARACT
CIPHER EMBLEM ENSIGN FIGURE
LETTER PNEUME SHADOW SIGNAL
FACIEND MANDALA PALATAL
CEREMONY CONSTANT DIRECTOR
EXPONENT GUTTURAL IDEOGRAM
LIGATURE LOGOGRAM OPERATOR
SWASTIKA SYMBOLUM TRISKELE
IDEOGRAPH METOBELUS
OCTOTHORP ORIFLAMME
PICTOGRAPH PHRASEOGRAM
(— AS ROAD SIGN) GLYPH
(— FOR WAVELENGTH) LAMBDA
(— OF AUTHORITY) MACE
(— OF DEATH) CYPRESS
(— OF DISTINCTION) BELT HONOR
(— OF FAITHFUL DEAD) ORANT
(— OF FRANCE) LILY
(— OF LIFE) ANKH
(— OF MONK) COWL
(— OF PHYSICIAN) CADUCEUS
(— OF RAILROAD) HERALD
(— OF RESURRECTION) PHOENIX

(— OF SOMETHING SPIRITUAL)
SACRAMENT
(— OF SOVEREIGNTY) ASP URAEUS
(— OF SPRING) KARPAS
(— OF STRENGTH) HORN
(— OF SUN) DISC DISK
(— OF UNIVERSE) MANDALA
(— ON UNCHANGEABLENESS)
LEOPARD
(— REPRESENTING THE ABSOLUTE)
TAIKIH
(ALGEBRAIC —) EXPONENT
(CLAN —) TOTEM
(CRICKET —) ASHES
(CRUSADERS' —) CROSS
(CURVED —) HOOK
(EFFICIENCY —) ETA
(EGYPTIAN —) ANKH SCARAB
(INFORMATION —) GLYPH
(INTERSECTION —) CAP
(KOREAN —) TAHGOOK
(MAGIC —) CARACT
(MATHEMATICAL —) KNOWN FACTOR
OBELUS FACIEND OPERAND
PLACEHOLDER
(PHALLIC —) LINGA LINGAM
(PICTOGRAPHIC —) ISOTYPE
(PRINTING —) DIAGONAL
(PRONUNCIATION —) ENG
(RELIGIOUS —) CROSS LABRYS
(UNION —) CUP
(8 POINTS ON CIRCUMFERENCE —)
OCTOTHORP
(PL.) KATAKANA
SYMBOLIC GRAPHIC SHADOWY
ANICONIC
SYMBOLICAL ALLUSIVE
MYSTICAL
SYMBOLISM ICONOLOGY
SYMBOLIZE BODY SIGN TOKEN
FIGURE SAMPLE SHADOW SYMBOL
TYPIFY BETOKEN EXPRESS PORTEND
SIGNIFY RESEMBLE
SYMMETRICAL FORMAL DIMERIC
REGULAR SHAPELY SPHERAL
BALANCED
(NOT —) SKEW
SYMMETRY MEASURE
SYMPATHETIC AKIN FERE SOFT
WARM HUMAN FELLOW KINDLY
TENDER PIETOSO SIMPATICO
SYMPATHIZER FABIAN BLACKNEB
SHAYSITE
SYMPATHY PITY RUTH FLESH PHILIA
CONSENT EMPATHY RAPPORT
AFFINITY KINDNESS
SYMPHONY SINFONIA
(BEETHOVEN'S THIRD —) EROICA
SYMPOSIUM POTATION
SYMPTOM MARK NOTE SIGN
SHOWER STIGMA INSTANCE
PRODROME
(DISEASE —) MERCYISM

SYNAGOGUE SHUL SCHUL ALJAMA
PROSEUCHA
SYNAPSIS PAIRING
SYNAPTE ECTENE EKTENE
SYNARTHROSIS SUTURE
SYNCHRO SELSYN
SYNCHRONIZE MESH
SYNCHRONIZER SPEEDGUN
SYNCLINE DOWNFOLD ISOCLINE
SYNCOPATED ZOPPA ABRIDGED
SYNCOPE SWOON COTYPE
FAINTING
SYNDICATE HUI GROUP CARTEL
COMBINE
(UNIT OF CRIME —) FAMILY
SYNDICATED CANNED
SYNDROME
(KIND OF —) FANCONI
SYNECDOCHE MERISM
SYNERGIST BOOSTER SESAMIN
SYNOD SOBOR
SYNODAL SENAGE
SYNONYM ANTONYM HOMONYM
EUPHONYM POLYONYM
SYNOPSIS BRIEF TABLE EPITOME
OUTLINE SUMMARY ABSTRACT
ANALYSIS SCENARIO SYLLABUS
ABRIDGMENT
SYNSACRUM SACRARY
SYNTACTICAL FORMAL
SYNTHESIS SUMMA FUSION
SYSTASIS
SYNTHESIZER MOOG
SYNTHETASE LIGASE
SYNTHETIC ERSATZ PLASTIC
SYSTATIC ARTIFICER
SYPHAX (WIFE OF —) SOPHENISBA
SYPHILIS PIP POX LUES SYPH
CRINKUM GRINCOME

SYRIA

CAPITAL:	DAMASCUS
COIN:	POUND TALENT PIASTER
DISTRICT:	ALEPPO HAURAN
LAKE:	DJEBOID TIBERIAS
MEASURE:	MAKUK GARAVA
MOUNTAIN:	HERMON LIBANUS
NAME:	ARAM
NATIVE:	DRUSE ANSARIE SARACEN ANSARIEH
RIVER:	ASI BALIKH BARADA JORDAN KNABUR ORONTES EUPHRATES
TOWN:	ALEP HAMA HOMS NAWA BUSRA CALNO DERRA HALAB HAMAH IDLIB JERUD RAQQA ALEPPO BALBEL LATAKIA SELEUCIA
WEIGHT:	COLA ROTL ARTAL ARTEL RATEL TALENT

SYRINGA PHILADELPHUS
SYRINGE GUN HYPO ENEMA SCOOT
DOUCHE FILLER SQUIRT SCOOTER
SERRING

SYRINGIN LILACIN
SYRINX PANPIPE
SYRNIUM STRIX
SYRUP DIBS LICK SIRUP ORGEAT
  ANTIQUE ECLEGMA FALERNUM
  QUIDDANY
  (FRUIT —) ROB
  (STARCH —) GLUCOSE
SYRUPY FRUITY
SYRYENIAN SYRYAN ZYRIAN
  (PL.) KAMI KOMI
SYSTEM ISM AREA CREDO FRAME
  ORDER CIRCLE METHOD SCHEME
  STEREO SYNTAX COMPLEX DUALISM
  ECONOMY FAGGERY NAVARHO
  REGIMEN ENSEMBLE GALENISM
  OVERRIDE RELIGION UNIVERSE
  (— FOR ROMANIZING IDEOGRAMS)
  PINYIN
  (— OF BARS) LATTICE
  (— OF BELIEFS) FAITH
  (— OF BELL CHANGES) CATERS
  QUATERS STEDMAN
  (— OF CORDS) BRIDLE
  (— OF CROSSING THREADS) LEASE
  (— OF DIET) BANTING
  (— OF ETHICS) SELFISM
  (— OF EXCHANGE) KULA
  (— OF EXERCISES) AEROBICS
  (— OF FAITH) CREED
  (— OF GEARS) COMPOUND
  (— OF JOINTS) CLEAT
  (— OF LANGUAGE SIGNS) SIGNARY
  (— OF LAW) EQUITY
  (— OF LINES IN EYEPIECE) RETICLE
  RETICULE
  (— OF LOGIC) RAMISM
  (— OF MANUAL TRAINING) SLOJD
  SLOYD
  (— OF MARKETING) ADMASS
  (— OF MEANING) SEMANTIC
  (— OF MEDICINE) AYURVEDA
  (— OF MONEY TRANSFER) GIRO
  (— OF NUMERALS) ALGORISM
  (— OF OCCULT THEOSOPHY) CABALA
  (— OF PHILOSOPHY) HUMISM
  COMTISM HOBBISM SAMKHYA
  SANKHYA STOICISM
  (— OF PHONETIC NOTATION) ROMIC
  (— OF PRINCIPLES) CODE
  (— OF RAYS) ASTER
  (— OF ROCKS) CENOZOIC DEVONIAN
  SILURIAN
  (— OF RULE) REGIME
  (— OF RULES) ART
  (— OF SOLMIZATION) FASOLA
  (— OF SPACES) LACUNOME
  (— OF SUPPRESSING LITERATURE)
  SAMIZDAT
  (— OF SYMBOLS) CODE
  (— OF TENANCY) CROFTING

  (— OF TRANSPORTATION) AIRLINE
  AIRMAIL
  (— OF TRUSSING) CABANE
  (— OF VALUES) ETHOS
  (— OF WEIGHTS) TROY
  (— OF WIRES) HARNESS
  (— OF WORSHIP) CULT CULTUS
  (— OF WRITING) KANJI BRAILLE
  ALPHABET
  (— TO LOCATE AN OBJECT) LIDAR
  (ACOUSTICAL —) SODAR
  (AGRICULTURAL —) KOLKOZ
  KOLKHOS
  (ALARM —) BUG
  (BANKING —) GIRO
  (BETTING —) ALEMBERT PERFECTA
  QUINELLA MARTINGALE
  (COLLOIDAL —) SOL
  (COMMUNICATION —) BLOWER
  CIRCUIT
  (COMPUTER —) KLUGE KLUDGE
  TRSDOS
  (COMPUTER DISK OPERATING —)
  MSDOS PCDOS
  (CULTURAL —) ISLAM
  (DEFENSE —) SAGE
  (DISK OPERATING —) DOS
  (DISPERSE —) GEL
  (ELECTRICAL —) SELSYN
  (ELECTRONIC —) TELETEXT
  (GEOLOGICAL —) EOCENE
  CAMBRIAN DEVONIAN KEEWATIN
  TERTIARY
  (HAULING —) DILLY
  (HAVERSIAN —) OSTEON
  (IRRIGATION —) KAREZ
  (LANGUAGE —) LATINXUA
  (LOCATING —) LIDAR
  (NAVIGATING —) TACAN
  (NAVIGATION —) GEE DECCA LANAC
  TACAN NAVAID SHORAN NAVARHO
  OMNIRANGE
  (PENAL —) GULAG
  (RELIGIOUS —) LAW CULT CULTUS
  SHIISM SUNNISM DRUIDISM
  (RHYTHMIC —) STROPHE GLYCONIC
  (ROMANIZING —) PINYIN
  (SING-SONG VOWEL —) ABLAUT
  (SOCIAL —) CASTE
  (STAR —) GALAXY
  (TECHNOLOGICAL —) FORDISM
  (TELEVISION —) SCOPHONY
  (TRIANGULATION —) SOFAR
  (TRUCK —) TOMMY
  (WORK —) FLEXTIME FLEXITIME
SYSTEMATIC ORDERLY REGULAR
  METHODIC
SYSTEMATIZE ORDER CODIFY
  ORGANIZE METHODIZE
SYSTEMATIZED CODED ORGANIC
SYSTEMIC DEMETON

T TEE TARE TANGO

TAAL AFRIKAANS

TAB JAG PAN TAG BILL COST FLAP
CHECK FLASH PRICE TALLY WATCH
EARTAB EARTAG SIGNAL TOEPLATE

TABANID GADFLY

TABARD CHIMER CHIMERE

TABARRO, IL
(CHARACTER IN —) LUIGI MICHELE
GIORGETTA
(COMPOSER OF —) PUCCINI

TABERNACLE PIX PYX HOVEL
SACRARY

TABES WASTING

TABETIC MARCID

TABITHA DORCAS

TABLATURE LYRAWAY PICTURE
PAINTING

TABLE KEY PIE PYE RUN BANK BUCK
DAIS DESK FORM MESS BELLY
BENCH BOARD CANON CHART PINAX
PLANK SCALE STALL STAND STONE
WAGON COMMON SCHEME SHELVE
TABLET TABULA TARIFF TEAPOY
TRIPOD VANNER CABARET CAMBIST
CONSOLE COUNTER DIAGRAM
DIPTYCH DRESSER PROJECT
SHAMBLE TABLEAU TESSERA
TROLLEY WHIRLER CALENDAR
CREDENCE GUERIDON PEDIGREE
PEMBROKE REGIMENT SETASIDE
SPECULUM STILLAGE TOILETTE
VANITORY NIGHTSTAND
(— DECORATION) DOILY
(— FOR BOWING HAT-BODY) HURL
(— FOR GLAZING LEATHER) BANK
(— FOR ORNAMENT) CARTOUCH
(— FOR PHOTOGRAPHIC PLATES)
WHIRLER
(— FURNISHED WITH MEAL) SPREAD
(— IN STORE) COUNTER
(— OF ANCESTORS) PEDIGREE
(— OF CONTENTS) INDEX METHOD
(— OF DECLINATIONS) REGIMENT
(— TOP) AMOEBA
(— USED IN FELTING A HAT) BASON
(— WITH BRAZIER BENEATH)
TENDOOR TENDOUR
(ARITHMETIC —) TARIFF
(ASTROLOGICAL —) SPECULUM
(BOTANIC —) KEY
(CIRCULAR —) ROUNDEL
(COMMUNION —) ALTAR CREDENCE
(DINING —) MAHOGANY
(DRESSING —) TOILET VANITY
TOILETTE

(EUCHARISTIC —) PROTHESIS
(FOLDING —) SERVETTE
(INNER —) HOME
(KIND OF —) PARSONS PERIODIC
(MASSAGE —) PLINTH
(MUSICAL —) DIAGRAM
(NIGHT —) SOMNO
(ONE-FOOTED —) MONOPODE
(PRINCIPAL —) DAIS
(PRINTER'S —) STONE
(PROFUSELY ORNAMENTED —)
PEMBROKE
(SECTIONAL STUDY —) CARREL
(SERVING —) WAGON
(SHAKING —) SLIMER
(SMALL —) KURSI STAND TABORET
TABOURET
(STONE —) DOLMEN
(TEA —) TEAPOY
(WRITING —) DESK

TABLEAU LAYOUT PAGEANT
PICTURE

TABLECLOTH CLOTH COVER
CARPET

TABLE D'HOTE DINNER

TABLELAND PLAT PUNA PUNO
KAROO TABLE KARROO PLATEAU
BALAGHAT

TABLET PAD PAX BRED ALBUM FACIA
PIECE PINAX SLATE TABLE ABACUS
CAPLET TABULA TABULE TROCHE
ASPIRIN CODICIL DIPTYCH PALETTE
PREFORM TABLING CARTOUCH
CHURINGA TABULATE TRIPTYCH
MEDALLION
(— BEARING SYMBOL OF CHRIST)
PAX
(— FOR PUBLISHING LAWS)
PARAPEGM
(— OVER SHOP FRONT) FACIA FASCIA
(AMPHETAMINE —) BENNY
(DRUG —) QUAALUDE
(MEDICATED —) ASPIRIN JELLOID
TABELLA
(MEDICINAL —) DISC DISK TROCHE
(MEMORIAL —) BRASS TABUT
(PAINTER'S —) PALETTE
(SLEEPING —) DALMANE
(SQUARE —) ABACK
(UPRIGHT —) STELA STELE
(VOTIVE —) PINAX
(WRITING —) CODICIL TRIPTYCH
(PREF.) PINA PINAC(O) PLAC(O)

TABLEWARE CHINA FLATWARE
HAVILAND
(WOODEN —) TREEN

TABOO KAPU TABU TAPU FORBIDDEN
  INEFFABLE
TABOR ATABAL TADREI TIMBRE
  TABORIN TIMBREL
TABULATION SCALE SCHEME
  TABLING
TABUT TAZIA TAZEEA
TACHOMETER CUTMETER
TACHYGLOSSUS ECHIDNA
TACIT SILENT IMPLICIT
TACITURN DUMB STILL SILENT
  LACONIC RESERVED RETICENT
TACK LAY BEAT CAST STAY BASTE
  BOARD FETCH ENTAIL LAVEER
  TACKET TINGLE SADDLERY
  (GLAZIERS' —) BRAD
TACKER GUN SPREADER
TACKLE CAT RIG TAW GEAR SWIG
  TACK YOKE ANGLE FALLS ATTACK
  BURTON COLLAR GARNET JIGGER
  LEDGER RUNNER STEEVE TAGLIA
  TEAGLE DERRICK HALYARD HARNESS
  RIGGING FISHFALL PURCHASE
  TACKLING
  (— BY NECK) SCRAG
  (— FOR RAISING BOAT) FALLS
  (— TO HOIST ANCHOR) CAT
  (COMBINATION OF —S) JEER
  JEERS
  (FISHING —) TEW LEGER OTTER
  LEDGER
TACO FLAUTA TAQUITO
TACT TOUCH ADDRESS CONDUCT
  DELICACY
TACTFUL POLITIC DISCREET
  GRACEFUL
TACTFULLY HAPPILY
TACTIC GAME PLOY
TACTICAL THEATER
TACTICS FOOTWORK
TACTLESS BRASH GAUCHE
TAD LAD MOPPET SHAVER SPROUT
TADPOLE POWHEAD BULLHEAD
  POLEHEAD POLLIWOG POLLYWOG
  PORWIGLE
TAEL LIANG
TAENNIN KOSIN KOUSIN
TAFFETA TABBY ARMOZEEN
  FLORENCE
TAFFY GUNDY TOFFY TOFFEE
  CLAGGUM
TAG HE DAG EAR TAB TIG TAIL TICK
  AGLET DAGGE LABEL TALLY TOUCH
  AIGLET EARTAB EARTAG FOLLOW
  SWATCH TAGGLE TAGRAG TICKET
  TIGTAG HANGTAG
  (— OF A LACE) AGLET AIGLET
  (ANGLING —) TOUCH
  (ORNAMENTED —S) FANCY
TAGALOG PULAHAN
TAGETES MARIGOLD
TAGRAG SHAGRAG
TAHATH (FATHER OF —) BERED

TAHITI (CAPITAL OF —) PAPEETE
  (FORMER NAME OF —) OTAHEITE
  (MOUNTAIN IN —) OROHENA
TAHMURATH (BROTHER OF —) YIMA
  (FATHER OF —) VIVANGHAO
  (SLAYER OF —) AHRIMAN
TAHR KRAS JHARAL
TAHSILDAR TALUKDAR
TAI LI AHOM SHAM THAI PORGY
  KHAMTI
TAIGA URMAN
TAIL BOB BUN CUE BUNT BUSH CLUB
  FLAG POLE SCUT BRUSH CAUDA
  SNAKE START STERN TRAIN TWIST
  FLIGHT FOLLOW RUMPLE SHADOW
  SWITCH TAILET TAIL LE FANTAIL
  FOXTAIL RATTAIL
  (— OF ARTIFICIAL FLY) TOPPING
  (— OF BEAST) QUEUE
  (— OF BELL CLAPPER) FLIGHT
  (— OF BIRD) FAN
  (— OF BIRD OR ANIMAL) CUE POLE
  START
  (— OF BOAR) WREATH
  (— OF CART) ARSE
  (— OF COAT) DOCK
  (— OF COMET) BEARD STREAM
  STREAMER CHEVELURE
  (— OF DEER) FLAG SINGLE SHINGLE
  (— OF DOG) FLAG STERN
  (— OF FISH) UROSOME
  (— OF FLY) WHISK
  (— OF FOX) BUSH DRUSH FOXTAIL
  (— OF HARE OR RABBIT) BUN FUD
  BUNT SCUT
  (— OF HOOD) LIRIPIPE LIRIPOOP
  (— OF HORSE) BOB
  (— OF MAN'S TIED HAIR) CLUB
  (— OF METEOR) TRAIN
  (— OF MUSICAL NOTE) QUEUE
  (— OF PUG DOG) TWIST
  (— OF SQUIRREL) BUN
  (— OF STANZA) CODA
  (DRAGON'S —) KETU
  (STUMP OF —) STRUNT
  (TIP OF —) TAG
  (PREF.) CAUD(I)(O) CERC(O) ONCHO
  UR(O)
  (SUFF.) CERCAL CERCY URA URE
  UROUS URUS
TAILBAND FOOTBAND
TAILBOARD ENDGATE ENDBOARD
  ENDPIECE
TAILED CAUDATE CAUDATED
  (PREF.) UR(O)
  (SUFF.) URA URE UROUS URUS
TAILING CHAT
  (PL.) SAND TAIL GRUFFS
TAILLE TALLY
TAILLESS ACAUDAL ANUROUS
  ACAUDATE ECAUDATE
TAILOR SLOP SNIP BUILD DARZI
  GORER SHRED CUTTER DARZEE

FULLER SARTOR SNYDER STITCH
BOTCHER CABBAGE SNIPPER
TIREMAN CLOTHIER SEAMSTER
SEMPSTER SHEPSTER
(ITINERANT —) CARDOOER
TAILORBIRD DARZEE
TAILPIECE QUEUE ANQUERA
TAILRACE AFTERBAY
TAILSPIN FLICKER NOSEDIVE
TAILSTOCK DEADHEAD
TAINO HAITIAN
(— BELIEFS) ZEMIISM
TAINT HAUL HOGO MOIL SMUT SPOT
VICE CLOUD STAIN TOUCH DARKEN
INFECT REMORD SMIRCH SMUTCH
ATTAINT BLEMISH CORRUPT
DEBAUCH ENVENOM FLYBLOW
FORRUMP POLLUTE TARNISH
VITIATE EMPOISON TAINTURE
CONTAMINATE
TAINTED BAD OFF GAMY HIGH
BLOWN PINDY SAPPY TAINT WEMMY
RANCID ROTTEN SINFUL SMUTTY
CORRUPT FOUGHTY FLYBLOWN
TAIWAN (CAPITAL OF —) TAIPEI
(ISLAND GROUP OF —) MATSU
PENGHU QUEMOY
(MOUNTAIN IN —) TZUKAO YUSHAN
HSINKAO
(OTHER NAME OF —) FORMOSA
(RIVER IN —) WUCHI TACHIA
CHOSHUI HUALIEN TANSHUI
(TOWN IN —) CHIAL TAINAN TAIPEI
CHILUNG KEELUNG PINGTUNG
TAICHUNG

TAJIKISTAN
(ALSO SEE RUSSIA)
CAPITAL: DUSHANBE STALINABAD
COIN: RUBLE
LAKE: SAREZ KARAKUL ISKANDERKUL
MOUNTAIN: LENIN COMMUNISM
MOUNTAIN RANGE: KURAMA
  MOGOLTAU TIENSHAN PAMIRALAY
  TURKESTAN ZERAVSHAN
  GISSARALAY
NAME: TAJIK TADZHIK TOJIKISTON
  TADZHIKISTAN
RIVER: PANJ MURGAB VAKHSH
  AMUDARYA SYRDARYA KAFIRNIGAN
TOWN: NUREK REGAR KHOROG
  KULYAB KHUDZAND URATUYBE
  KAYRAKKUM KHUDZHAND
  LENINABAD TURSUNZADE
VALLEY: PANJ GISSAR HISSAR
  VAKHSH FERGANA OBIKIIK PYANDZH
  YAVANSU KAFIRNIGAN KAFIRNIHAN

TAJIN TOTONAC
TAJ MAHAL (SITE OF —) AGRA
TAKE COP HIT NIM NIP NOB BEAR
BONE DRAW FANG GLOM HAVE LEAD
TACK TEEM TOLL ADOPT AFONG

BRING CARRY CATCH CREEL FETCH
GRASP GRIPE LATCH SEIZE SNAKE
ACCEPT CLUTCH COTTON DERIVE
EXTEND FERRET FINGER RECIPE
SNATCH TAKING ATTRACT CABBAGE
CAPTURE RECEIVE UNPURSE
UNDERNIM
(— A BATH) TOSH
(— A CERTAIN POSITION) SIT
(— ACROSS) TRAJECT
(— ACTION) ACT
(— A DIRECTION) STEER
(— A DRINK) PULL SMILE
(— ADVANTAGE) DO ABUSE BLUDGE
CLUTCH EXPLOIT
(— AFTER) BRAID FOLLOW
(— AIM) BEAD
(— A LITTLE) DELIBATE
(— A NAP) DOSS
(— APART) UNRIG
(— ASIDE) SINGLE
(— AS ONE'S OWN) ADOPT
(— A STAND) ASSERT
(— AWAY) BATE EASE HENT LIFT
TOLL WISP ADEEM BENIM BLEED
HEAVE REAVE STEAL ABDUCT
CONVEY DEDUCE DEDUCT DEMISE
DEPOSE DEVEST DIVEST ELOIGN
EXEMPT REMOVE UNVEST ABJUDGE
BEREAVE DEPRIVE DETRACT
FORTAKE RETRACT SUBDUCE
SUBLATE ABSTRACT DEROGATE
DIMINISH SUBTRACT
(— BACK) RECALL RECANT RECOUP
REGAIN REVOKE RETRACT
RECAPTURE
(— BACK TO ONESELF) RESUME
(— BY ASSAULT) STORM
(— BY FORCE) SPOIL
(— BY FRAUD) BOB
(— BY LEVY) ESTREAT
(— BY STEALTH) HOOK SNITCH
(— BY STORM) EXPUGN INVADE
SURPRISE
(— CARE) FIX SEE GARE KEEP MIND
TEND WARD YEME NURSE BEWARE
GOVERN INTEND CUIDADO
HUSBAND CHAPERON
(— CENSUS OF) MUSTER
(— CHANCE) DICE RISK
(— CHARGE) ATTEND
(— CHARGE OF) CURE SOLICIT
(— COVER) COOK
(— DAMAGE) BANGE
(— DINNER) DINE
(— DOWN) STOOP STRIKE
(— DRUGS ORALLY) POP
(— EXCEPTION) DEMUR STRAIN
(— FIRE) SPUNK
(— FOOD) EAT DINE GRUB
(— FORCIBLY) USURP
(— FOR GRANTED) BEG ASSUME
PRESUME

(— FORM) FORM INFORM
(— FOR ONESELF) CAB
(— FOR RESALE) FLOG
(— FRAUDULENTLY) STEAL STRIKE
(— FRIGHT) BOOGER
(— FROM) DETRACT
(— FROM DEPOSIT) DRAW
(— GOLFING STANCE) ADDRESS
(— GREAT DELIGHT) REVEL
(— HEART) BRACE
(— HEED) RECK TENT
(— HOLD) GET BITE GRAB PINCH
SEIZE ARREST BEGRIPE
(— HOLIDAY) LAKE
(— IN) IN EAT SUP BITE HOAX KEEP
DOWSE DRINK ABSORB DEVOUR
ENFOLD GATHER HARBOR INCEPT
INGEST INSORB INSUME INTAKE
MUZZLE BEGRIPE EMBRACE INCLUDE
(— IN BY LEAKING) LADE
(IN LIVESTOCK) AGIST
(— IN SAIL) BRAIL
(— INTO HANDS) TOUCH EMBRACE
(— LEGALLY) ATTACH
(— LEVEL OF) BONE
(— LUNCH) TIFFIN
(— MEALS) BOARD
(— NOTE OF) NB COUNT SMOKE
NOTICE WITNESS
(— OATH) ABJURE
(— OFF) OFF ROB DOFF EXIT LIFT VAIL
DOUSE SHUCK STRIP DEDUCT
(— OFFENSE) DONT HUFF
(— ON) HIRE ADOPT MOUNT START
(— ONE'S LEAVE) CONGEE
(— ONESELF) BETAKE
(— OUT) DELE KILL EXCERPT
AIRBRUSH
(— OUT OF EARTH) EXTER
(— OVER) ABSORB SUBSUME
(— PAINS) BOTHER
(— PART) LEAD FIGHT ENGAGE
(— PLACE) BE DO GO COME GIVE
PASS ARISE BEFALL HAPPEN
(— PLEASURE IN) ENJOY ADMIRE
(— PORTION OF) PARTAKE
(— POSITION) STAND
(— POSSESSION) GRIP ANNEX BESET
SEIZE SPOIL EXTEND CONQUER
INHERIT DISTRAIN
(— REFUGE) HIDE SOIL EVADE HAVEN
WATCH
(— ROOT) MARE MORE ENROOT
STRIKE
(— SHAPE) JELL
(— SHELTER) HOWF NESTLE SHROUD
(— SUPPER) SUP
(— THE PLACE OF) ENSUE SECOND
SUPPLY DISPLACE SUPPLANT
(— THOUGHT) ADVISE
(— TO BE TRUE WITHOUT PROOF)
PRESUME
(— TO TASK) JACK CARPET CHAPTER

(— TO WING) FLUSH
(— UNAWARE) DECEIVE
(— UP) SORB ENTER MOUNT
ADSORB ASSUME GATHER HANDLE
STRIKE ELEVATE
(— UP AGAIN) RESUME
(— UP WITH) ALL
(— WELL OR ILL) RESENT
(— WIND ON OPPOSITE QUARTER)
JIBE
TAKEN TON TAIN
(— ABACK) BLANK
(— AWAY) ADEMPT
(— OUT) EXEMPT
TAKEOFF JATO VTOL SPOOF SENDUP
SCRAMBLE
(PREPARE FOR —) STRAPIN
TAKEOUT STACK
(FOR —) TOGO
TAKER PERNOR
TAKING HOT TAKY CAPTION
ADOPTION PERNANCY PREEMPTION
(— A VOTE) DIVISION
(— BACK) RECAPTION
(— EVERYTHING INTO ACCOUNT)
OVERALL
(— LIBERTIES) PRESUMPTUOUS
(— OF LIFE) BLOOD
(— PLACE) AGATE
(— POSSESSION) ENTRY
(PREF.) (— IN) END(O)
(SUFF.) LEPSIA LEPSIS LEPSY LEPT(IC)
TALAK AHSAN
TALARI PATACA PATACOON
TALAUS (FATHER OF —) BIAS
(MOTHER OF —) PERO
(SON OF —) ADRASTUS
(WIFE OF —) LYSIMACHE
TALC SPAAD TALCUM AGALITE
STEATITE SOAPSTONE
TALE SAW DIDO JEST LEED REDE
TELL BOURD CONTE CRACK FABLE
RECIT SPELL SPOKE STORY WINDY
AITION FABULA LEGEND PISTLE
PURANA FARLIAU FICTION HISTORY
MARCHEN ROMANCE WHOPPER
ANECDOTE FOLKTALE SPELLING
TREATISE
(— OF ACHIEVEMENTS) GEST GESTE
(— OF ADVENTURE) CONTE
(— OF CHIVALRY) ROMAN ROMANCE
(— OF FATE) WEIRD
(— OF FOUR) WARP
(— OF GOLD COAST NEGROS)
NANCY
(— OF GRIEF) JEREMIAD
(— OF TERROR) HAIRRAISER
(COMIC COARSE —) FABLIAU
(DEVISED —) AITION
(EPIC —) TAIN
(FALSE —) BAM VANITY SLANDER
(FATEFUL —) WEIRD
(FOLK —) NANCY THRENE

(FOLK —S) LORE
(HUMOROUS —S) FACETIAE
(ICELANDIC —) SAGA
(MEDIEVAL —) LAI
(MERRY —) BOURD
(METRICAL —) FABLIAU
(PITIFUL —) SOBSTORY
(POETIC NARRATIVE —) SAGA
(SENSATIONAL —) BLOOD SHOCKER
(SHORT —) LAI CONTE
(PREF.) STORIO
TALEBEARER BUZZER GOSSIP
TATTLER TALEPYET TELLTALE
TALEBEARING TALEWISE
TALENT GIFT HEAD NOUS VEIN
DOWER DOWRY VERVE CICHAR
GENIUS ABILITY CHARISM FACULTY
CAPACITY CHARISMA
TALENTED ABLE CLEVER GIFTED
TALE OF TWO CITIES (AUTHOR OF
—) DICKENS
(CHARACTER IN —) JOHN JERRY
LORRY LUCIE PROSS BARSAD
CARTON DARNAY JARVIS SYDNEY
CHARLES DEFARGE GASPARD
MANETTE STRYVER CRUNCHER
EVREMONDE
TALER ORT THALER
TALES OF HOFFMANN
(CHARACTER IN —) ANDRES LUTHER
STELLA ANTONIA CRESPEL LINDORF
MIRACLE OLYMPIA HOFFMANN
SCHLEMIL COPPELIUS GIULIETTA
NICALUSSE DAPERTUTTO
SPALANZANI PITICHINACCHIO
(COMPOSER OF —) OFFENBACH
TALIPES CLUBFOOT
TALISMAN ANGLE CHARM IMAGE
OBEAH SAFFI AMULET GRIGRI
SAPHIE SCARAB TELESM ICHTHUS
ICHTHYS GREEGREE
(AUTHOR OF —) SCOTT
(CHARACTER IN —) DAVID EDITH
PHILIP KENNETH RICHARD SALADIN
BERENGARIA MONTFERRAT
PLANTAGENET
TALK GAB GAS JAW JIB RAP SAW
SAY YAP BLAT BUCK BUKH CANT
CARP CHAT CHIN GAFF GIVE GUFF
KNAP MEAN TALE TOVE WORD
CRACK FABLE MOUTH PARLE PITCH
SPEAK SPELL SPIEL SPOKE TUTEL
COMMON GAMMON INDABA
KORERO PATTER SERMON SPEECH
STEVEN TONGUE YABBER ADDRESS
CHINWAG DISCUSS JAWBONE
LIPWORK PALABRA PALAVER
PARRALL PURPOSE WINDJAM
CAUSERIE COLLOQUY CONVERSE
LANGUAGE PARLANCE QUESTION
SCUTTLEBUTT
(— ABOUT) HASH
(— AT LENGTH) RUNON

(— BACK) SASS
(— BIG) SWANK BOUNCE
(— BOASTFULLY) GAS BLATTER
(— BOMBASTICALLY) BEMOUTH
(— CASUALLY) DISH
(— CONFIDENTIALLY) CUTTER
(— CONFUSEDLY) HOTTER
(— DELIRIOUSLY) RAVE
(— DISMALLY) CROAK
(— DRUNKENLY) SLUR
(— EMPTILY) BLOW
(— EXTRAVAGANTLY) ROMANCE
(— FAMILIARLY) TOVE CONFAB
(— FATUOUSLY) BABBLE
(— FONDLY) COO
(— FOOLISHLY) YAK BLAT FLAP YACK
HAVER BABBLE DRIVEL FOOTER
FOOTLE GABBLE GIBBER SAWNEY
TOOTLE BLATHER BLETHER
(— GLIBLY) PATTER SCREED
(— IDLY) GAB GAS BLAB CHAT CHIN
GASH YACK FABLE GARBLE JANGLE
RABBIT TATTLE CHATTER GNATTER
PRATTLE
(— IMPUDENTLY) SASS
(— INACCURATELY) BLAGUE
(— INARTICULATELY) CHUNNER
CHUNTER
(— INCESSANTLY) YANK BURBLE
RABBIT WAFFLE CHATTER
(— INCOHERENTLY) BABBLE BURBLE
HOTTER MITHER MOIDER
(— INCONSIDERATELY) BLAT
(— INDECISIVELY) WAFFLE
(— INFORMALLY) HOBNOB
(— INSOLENTLY) SNASH
(— INTENDED TO DECEIVE) GAMMON
PALAVER
(— IRRATIONALLY) RAVE
(— JARGON) JIVE
(— MONOTONOUSLY) DRONE
(— NEEDLESSLY) PALAVER
(— NOISILY) CLAP BLATTER BRABBLE
(— NONSENSE) GAS ROT BLEAT
DROOL FUDGE HAVER
(— OFFICIOUSLY) BLEEZE
(— PEEVISHLY) WITTER
(— PERTLY) CHELP
(— PRIVATELY) COLLOGUE
(— RAPIDLY) GABBLE JABBER
GNATTER
(— SCANDAL) HORN
(— SNAPPISHLY) KNAP
(— SPORTIVELY) DAFF
(— SUPERFICIALLY) SMATTER
(— TEDIOUSLY) DINGDONG
(— THOUGHTLESSLY) BLAB
(— TOGETHER) DEVISE
(— VAGUELY) WOOZLE
(— VOLUBLY) CHIN PATTER
(— WEAKLY) DRIVEL
(— WITH) CONTACT
(— WITHOUT MEANING) GABBLE

(— WITTILY) SCINTILLATE
(ABSURD —) BOSH
(ABUSIVE —) HOKER JAWING
(ARROGANT —) GUM BRAG
(BACK —) LIP SASS
(BAWDY —) SCULDUDDRY
SCULDUDDERY SKULDUDDERY
(BOASTFUL —) BULL GAFF
(BOMBASTIC —) FLASH
(COMMON —) FAME FABLE NOISE
HEARSAY
(CONCEITED —) BLAGUE
(CONTINUAL —) CLACK
(COUNTRY —) CLASH
(DECEPTIVE —) GAMMON
(DIFFUSE —) POTTER
(DRIVELLING —) MAUNDERING
(EMPTY —) GAS BOSH GASH FRASE
GLOZE FRAISE BLAFLUM GASSING
PRATTLE BALLYHOO GALBANUM
MOONSHINE POPPYCOCK
PRITTLEPRATTLE
(ENTHUSIASTIC —) JAZZ
(EVASIVE —) FLANNEL
(FALSE —) BALLYHOO
(FAMILIAR —) CONFAB CHITCHAT
(FANTASTIC —) GUYVER
(FLATTERING —) FLANNEL
(FLIP —) SASS
(FOOLISH —) GUP GAFF JIVE
BLEAT CLACK FABLE BLETHERS
COBBLERS
(FORMAL —) ADDRESS
(FRESH —) LIP
(FRIVOLOUS —) PERSIFLAGE
(FUSSY —) PHRASE
(GENERAL —) RUMOR REPORT
RUMOUR
(GLIB —) JIVE
(IDLE —) GAB YAK BLAB BUFF CHAT
GAFF GEST GUFF YACK FABLE GESTE
BABBLE CLAVER GOSSIP JANGLE
CHATTER CLATTER PALAVER
TWATTLE BABBLING BATTOLOGY
BALDERDASH BIBBLEBABBLE
(IMPUDENT —) PRATE SLACK
(INCOHERENT —) GABBER JABBER
(INFORMAL —) CAUSERIE
(INSINCERE —) JAZZ CROCK
BUNKUM MALARKEY
(JESTING —) CHAFF JAPERY
(LIGHT —) TRIFLING
(MEANINGLESS —) SLIPSLOP
(NONSENSICAL —) BLABBER
BLATHER FOLDEROL
(ORDINARY —) PROSE
(PIOUS OR SANCTIMONIOUS —) PI
(PUBLIC —) NOISE
(RAPID —) GABBLE JABBER CHATTER
CLATTER
(SALES —) PITCH
(SCOLDING —) HARANGUE
(SENSELESS —) TWADDLE

(SILLY —) BLAH BUFF CLART CACKLE
FOOTLE TWADDLE
(SMALL —) CHAT BACKCHAT
CHITCHAT
(SMOOTH —) GLOZE BLARNEY
(STUPID —) MOROLOGY
(TRIFLING —) PRATTLE CHITCHAT
(UNRESTRAINED —) JAWING
(USELESS —) WASTE
(VIOLENT —) BLUSTER
(WEAK —) SLIPSLOP
(WHINING —) BLEAT
(WILD —) RANT
(WORTHLESS —) PIFFLE
(SUFF.) LALIA LOG(ER)(IA)(IAN)(IC)
(ICAL)(IST)(UE)(Y)
TALKATIVE COSY GASH GLIB NAWY
BUZZY GABBY TALKY CHATTY
CLASHY CRACKY FLUENT FUTILE
SOCIAL VOLUBLE BIGMOUTH
FLIPPANT TELLSOME LOQUACIOUS
TALKATIVENESS FUTILITY
TALKER YENTA CAMPER POTGUN
CAUSEUR SPIELER
(IDLE —) WHIFFLER
(NOISY —) BLELLUM
(PROFESSIONAL —) JAWSMITH
(SENSELESS —) RATTLE
TALKING
(IDLE —) GASSING
(LOUD —) NORATION
TALKING-TO EARFUL LECTURE
TALKY GABBY
TALL HIGH LANKY LOFTY RANGY
STEEP WANDY CRANEY PROCERE
(— AND FEEBLE) TANGLE
(VERY —) TAUNT
TALLAGE CUTTING
TALLER DOMINANT
TALLNESS PROCERITY
TALLOW SUET SEVUM ARMING
TAULCH CHERVICE
(PREF.) SEBI SEBO STEAR(O)
STEAT(O)
(SUFF.) STEARIN
TALLY TAB JUMP NICK SUIT AGREE
CHECK COUNT SCORE STICK STOCK
CENSUS STRING SWATCH TAILYE
COMPORT TAILZIE
TALMAI (FATHER OF —) AMMIHUD
TALMUD GEMARA
TALON FANG SERE UNCE CLUTCH
POUNCE UNGUIS WEAPON
(— OF TOOTH) HEEL
TALONID HEEL
TALPA TESTUDO
TALTHIB GLAGA GLAGAH
TALUS SCREE RUBBLE ASTRAGAL
TAMANDUA ANTEATER
TAMAR (AUTHOR OF —) JEFFERS
(CHARACTER IN —) LEE WILL DAVID
JINNY TAMAR STELLA ANDREWS
MORELAND CAULDWELL

(FATHER OF —) DAVID ABSALOM
(HUSBAND OF —) ER ONAN
(MOTHER OF —) MAACHAH
(SON OF —) ZARAH PHAREZ
TAMARACK LARCH LARIX
EPINETTE
TAMARIN PINCHE JACCHUS
LEONCITO MARIKINA MARMOSET
TAMARIND SAMPALOC
TAMARISK ATLE JHOW HEATH
MYRICA
TAMASHEK TUAREG
TAMBOURINE RIKK TAAR DAIRA
TAMBO TABOUR TIMBER TABORIN
TIMBREL
(PART OF —) HEAD TACK SHELL
JINGLE
TAMBURLAINE THE GREAT
(AUTHOR OF —) MARLOWE
(CHARACTER IN —) ALMEDA
AMYRAS COSROE ZABINA MEANDER
MYCETES ORCANES BAJAZETH
CALYPHAS MENAPHON CALLAPINE
CELEBINUS SIGISMUND TECHELLES
ZENOCRATE THERIDAMAS
USUMCASANE TAMBURLAINE
TAME MAN CADE DEAD MEEK MILD
PACK ACCOY ATAME BREAK DAUNT
MILKY SPAKE CADISH ENTAME
GENTLE INWARD MEEKEN UNWIFE
AFFAITE AMENAGE CORRECT INSIPID
SUBDUED CICURATE DOMESTIC
MANSUETE
(— FALCON) MAN RECLAIM
TAMED BROKE GENTLE
TAMENESS MANSUETUDE
TAMER
(HORSE —) HIPPODAMIST
TAMIL VELLALA
TAMING OF THE SHREW
(AUTHOR OF —) SHAKESPEARE
(CHARACTER IN —) SLY BIANCA
CURTIS GREMIO GRUMIO TRANIO
BAPTISTA LUCENTIO BIONDELLO
HORTENSIO KATHARINA PETRUCHIO
VINCENTIO CHRISTOPHER
TAMMUZ
(FATHER OF —) NINGISHZIDA
TAMMY TAMIS STAMIN
TAMONEA MICONIA
TAM-O-SHANTER TAM TAMMY
TAMP PUG STEM
TAMPER FIX COOK FAKE FOOL GAFF
TOUCH DABBLE FIDDLE MEDDLE
MONKEY POTTER PUDDLE PUTTER
TEMPER FALSIFY TRINKLE
(— WITH HORSE'S TEETH) BISHOP
TAMPION TOMKIN TAMPOON
TAM-TAM GONG
TAN FAN ARAB BARK ADUST ASCOT
DRESS TANKA TAWNY ORIOLE
COCONUT EMBROWN LEATHER
SUNBURN

(BEACH —) SEDGE
(TROTTEUR —) BAY
(PREF.) TANN(I)(O)
TANACETYL THUJYL
TANAGER YENI LINDO REDBIRD
WARBIRD CARDINAL EUPHONIA
FIREBIRD ORGANIST
TANBARK BARK TAWN AVARAM
TURWAR ALGERIAN ALGERINE
TANCRED
(FATHER OF —) OTHO
(LOVER OF —) ERMINIA CLORINDA
(MOTHER OF —) EMMA
TANDAN EELFISH
TANEKAHA TOATOA
TANG NIP BITE FANG ODOR TING
VEIN SHANK STING STRAP TASTE
TWANG RELISH TANGLE TONGUE
SEATANG FAREWELL
TANGELO UGLI
TANGENCY CONTACT
TANGENT SLOPE
TANGERINE NAARTJE MANDARIN
TANGIBLE ACTUAL TACTILE
CONCRETE MATERIAL PALPABLE
TANGIER (NATIVE OF —) TANGERINE
TANGLE COT ELF ORE TAT FANK
FOUL HARL SHAG TAUT HARLE
KNURL SKEIN SNARL SNIRL THRUM
TWINE WOPSE BALTER BURBLE
ENTRAP FANKLE HANGER JUNGLE
MOMBLE MUCKER RAFFLE SLEAVE
TAFFLE TARDLE TAUGHT TEIHTE
BRANGLE TAISSLE THICKET
FURBELOW SCROBBLE
(PL.) COBWEB
TANGLED AFOUL TOUSY MESHED
SNARLY TAUTED IMPLICIT INTORTED
INVOLVED CESPITOSE
(— UP) HAYWIRE
TANGLEHEAD PILI
TANGUE TENREC
TANGY BRISK
TANHA TRISHNA
TANK DAM DIP TAL VAT BOSH SUMP
BASIN MIXER STANK STEEP TRUNK
BLOWUP BOILER HOPPER PANZER
TROUGH BATTERY BLOWPIT
BREAKER CISTERN FLUSHER PISCINA
PLUNGER POACHER SETTLER
STEEPER BLEACHER DIGESTOR
LANDSHIP SUBSIDER
(— FOR DYE OR SOAP) BECK
(— FOR FISH) STEW TRUNK PISCINA
AQUARIUM STEWPOND
(— IN SHIP) FOREPEAK
(— ON CANOE) SPONSON
(ARMORED —) FLAIL PANZER
WHIPPET LANDSHIP
(KIND OF —) DRUNK SCUBA THINK
SEPTIC
(PAPER MANUFACTURING —)
POACHER

(PHOTOGRAPHIC —) CUVETTE
(POTTER'S —) PLUNGER
(RECTANGULAR —) BOWLY
(SALT MANUFACTURING —) GRAINER
(SPEEDY —) WHIPPET
(STORAGE —) CHEST
(SUGAR REFINING —) TIGER BLOWUP
(TANNING —) FLOATER
(PL.) HEAVIES
(PREF.) LACO
TANKAGE AMMONATE
TANKARD GUN MUG JACK FACER
STOOP STOUP PEWTER POTTLE
TANKER GODDARD
TANKER ULCC VLCC BOWSER
(CRUDE-OIL —) ULCC
TANNED BROWN RUDDY TAWNY
REECHY BRONZED
(NOT —) RAW
TANNER EGGER SAMAR BARKER
STAKER PERCHER
TANNHAUSER (CHARACTER IN —)
VENUS HERMANN WOLFRAM
ELISABETH TANNHAUSER
(COMPOSER OF —) WAGNER
TANNING PASTING
(— SOLUTION) PLUMPER
TANSY COSTMARY
TANSY MUSTARD FLIXWEED
FLUXWEED
TANSY RAGWORT RAGWEED
TANTALIZE GRIG JADE MOCK TEASE
HARASS
TANTALUS (- CAPTIVE) IXION
(DAUGHTER OF —) NIOBE
(FATHER OF —) AMPHION JUPITER
THYESTES
(MOTHER OF —) NIOBE PLUTO
(SON OF —) PELOPS
(WIFE OF —) DIONE CLYTIA EUPRYTO
TAYGETE
TANTAMOUNT SAME
TANTARA BLARE
TANTRA AGAMA
TANTRUM SNIT HISSY SCENE
TIRADE TIRRIVEE WINGDING

TANZANIA
CAPITAL: DARESSALAAM
COIN: SENTI SHILINGI
ISLAND: MAFIA PEMBA ZANZIBAR
LAKE: RUKWA
NATIVE: BANTU SUKUMA MAKONDE
SWAHILI
REGION: MARA MBEYA PEMBA PWANI
TANGA MWANZA RUVUMA TABORA
SINGIDA
RIVER: RUVU WAMI RUAHA KAGERA
RUFIJI RUVUMA PANGANI
MBENKURU
TOWN: WETE KILWA MBEYA MOSHI
TANGA ARUSHA DODOMA IRINGA
KIGOMA MTWARA MWANZA

TABORA MTAWARA MOROGORO
ZANZIBAR
VOLCANO: KIRO KILIMANJARO
WATERFALL: KALAMBO
WEIGHT: FARSALAH

TAO MAN PEASANT
(— PRACTICE) WUWEI
TAP BOB DAB PAT TAT TIP TIT TOP
BEAT COCK DRUB FLIP JOWL PENK
TICK TIRL TUCK TUNK APPEL FLIRT
QUILL SNOCK START TOUCH ALETAP
BROACH CANNEL DABBLE FAUCET
NATTLE SPIGOT TAPLET BIBCOCK
BLENDER DRAWOFF HEELTAP
PERCUSS
(— A CASK) QUILL STRIKE
(— A DRUM) TUCK
(— FOR A LOAN) TIG
(— ON SHOE) CLUMP UNDERLAY
(— ON THE SHOULDER) FOB
(— REPEATEDLY) DRUM
(— THE GROUND) BEAT
(FENCING —) BEAT
(MASTER —) HOB HUB
(SMART — OF THE FOOT) APPEL
TAPA KAPA SIAPO KIKEPA
TAPACOLO TURCO
TAPE LEAR FERRET GARTER SCOTCH
TAPERY YNKELL BINDING MEASURE
TAPELINE TELETAPE
(— CARTRIDGE) CASSETTE
(DEMONSTRATION —) DEMO
(FISH —) SNAKE
(KIND OF —) DUCT REELTOREEL
(LAMP —) WICK
(LINEN —) INKLE
(METALLIC —) GALLOON
(NARROW —) TASTE
(PUT ON —) RECORD
(RED —) WIGGERY
(TV —) VIDEO
TAPE GRASS EELGRASS
TAPEMAN CHAINMAN
TAPER DRAW RISE RUSH DRAFT
GAUDY PINCH SCARF SNAPE SWAGE
CIERGE DRAUGHT LIGHTER PRICKET
SHAMMES TRINDLE DIMINISH
ACUMINATE
(— OF A SPRING) DRAW
(— OFF) CEASE TONGUE
(— OF PATTERN) STRIP
TAPERED BARRELED BOATTAIL
GRADUATED
(SLIGHTLY —) TERETE
TAPERING SHARP SPIRY SPIRAL
SPIRED TERETE SPIRING FUSIFORM
SUBULATE ATTENUATE
TAPER ROD PODGER
TAPESTRY ARRAS TAPET TAPIS
CUSTER DORSER DOSSER CEILING
GOBELIN HANGING SUSANEE
VERDURE AUBUSSON MORTLAKE

TAPEWORM TAPE LIGULA TAENIA
CESTODE CESTOID COENURE
HYDATID PLATODE BANDWORM
COENURUS DAVAINEA FLATWORM
HELMINTH STROBILA
(— LARVA) MEASLE
(PL.) CYSTICA
(PREF.) TAENI(A)(O)
TAPHATH (FATHER OF —) SOLOMON
TAPHOLE TAP FLOSS MOUTH
TAPIOCA CASSAVA
TAPIR ANTA KUDA DANTA TENNU
TAPIROID
TAPPED ABROACH
TAPPET CAM WIPER
TAPROOM TAP SALOON BARROOM
BUVETTE TAPHOUSE
TAPSTER NICKPOT SKINKER
TAPUYAN GE GES GHES BUGRE
GESAN JUYAS CAYAPO GOYANA
CAMACAN CARAHOS COROADO
TIMBIRA APINAGES BOTOCUDO
CAINGANG CHAVANTE
TAR PAY BREA LIMEY BINDER SAILOR
SEADOG ALKITRAN CREOSOTE
(BIRCH —) DAGGETT
(MINERAL —) MALTHA
TARA DOLMA
TARADIDDLE LIE
TARANTULA HUNTER JAYHAWK
MYGALID
TARAS BULBA (AUTHOR OF —)
GOGOL
(CHARACTER IN —) BULBA OSTAP
TARAS ANDRII YANKEL KIRDYAGA
TARBOOSH FEZ
TARDIGRADA ARCTISCA
TARDILY SLOWLY
TARDINESS SLOTH TARDITY
TARDY LAG LAX DREE LATE SLOW
SLACK DREIGH LAGGED REMISS
LAGGING OVERDUE DILATORY
LATESOME
TARE TINE VETCH LEAKAGE
(PL.) FILTH
TAREA (FATHER OF —) MICAH
TARES ZIZANY
TARGE BUCKLER
TARGET AIM MOT BUTT MARK
WAND CLOUT LEVEL PRICK ROVER
SCOOP SCOPE TARGE WHITE
BANNER NIVEAU OBJECT SLEEVE
COCKSHY INCOMER OUTGOER
SARACEN POPINJAY
(— OF KNEELING FIGURE) SQUAW
(— OF LEVELING STAFF) VANE
(— OF RIDICULE) GAME
(— RING) SOUS
(EASY —) SITTER
(PIECE OF —) SCAB
(RAILROAD SWITCH —) BANNER
(STRIKE A —) KEYHOLE
(THROWN —) COCKSHY COCKSHUT

(TOWED —) DROGUE
(UNIDENTIFIED —) SKUNK
TARHEEL STATE NORTH
CAROLINA
TARIFF ZABETA AVERAGE TRIBUTE
TARNISH DIM BLOT SMIT SOIL
CLOUD DIRTY STAIN SULLY TACHE
TAINT BREATH DARKEN DEFILE
INJURE SMIRCH ASPERSE BEGRIME
BESMEAR BLEMISH OBSCURE
BESMIRCH DISCOLOR
TARO COCO DALO EDDO GABE KALO
MASI TALO COCCO KAROU TANIA
TANYA COCKER TARROW YAUTIA
COCOYAM DASHEEN MALANGA
COCOROOT EDDYROOT
(— PRODUCT) POI
TAROT NAIB TAROCCO
TARPON SABALO
TARRAGON TARCHON ESTRAGON
TARRY BIDE LENG STAY STOP ABIDE
DALLY DEMUR PAUSE ARREST
LINGER PITCHY REMAIN SOJOURN
TARSIER LEMUR MALMAG
TARSOMETATARSUS SHANK
TARSUS HAND ANKLE DIGITAL
(BIRD'S —) SHANK
TART ACID FLAN SOUR ACERB
BOWLA CUPID EAGER SHARP SNIPPY
SUNKET PIQUANT POLYNEE
PUNGENT SUBACID TARTLET
TURNOVER
TARTAN PLAID
(— PATTERN) SETT
TARTAR ARGAL ARGOL CALCULUS
TARTARIN OF TARASCON
(AUTHOR OF —) DAUDET
(CHARACTER IN —) BAIA BRAVIDA
GREGORY BEZUQUET TARTARIN
BARBASSOU
TARTNESS ACRITY ACIDITY
VERDURE ACERBITY ASPERITY
VERJUICE
TARTUFFE (AUTHOR OF —) MOLIERE
(CHARACTER IN —) ARGAS DAMIS
ORGON DORINE ELMIRE VALERE
CLEANTE MARIANE PERNELLE
TARTUFFE
TASHMET (HUSBAND OF —) NEBO
TASK FAG JOB TAX CHAR DARG TOIL
CHARE CHORE GRIND KNACK LABOR
NULLO STINT CHARGE DEVOIR
NIYOGA PENSUM RAMSCH TOURNE
FATIGUE SWEATER TRAVAIL
BUSINESS EXERCISE TRAUCHLE
(— AS PSYCHOLOGICAL TEST)
AUFGABE
(ASSIGNED —) STENT STINT DEVOIR
(DIFFICULT —) BUGGER
(EASY —) PIPE SNAP SETUP PICNIC
CAKEWALK
(EXAMINATION —) QUESTION
(ONEROUS —) CORVEE

(ONE WHO PERFORMS MENIAL —S)
DOGSBODY
(ROUTINE —) DRUDGE
TASKMASTER DRIVER TASKER
RAWHIDER
(BRUTAL —) LEGREE
TASMANIA (CAPITAL OF —) HOBART
(LAKE IN —) ECHO SORELL
(MOUNTAIN IN —) DROME NEVIS
BARRON CRADLE LOMOND
HUMBOLDT
(RIVER IN —) ESK HUDN TAMAR
GORDON JORDAN PIEMAN DERWENT
(TOWN IN —) BURNIE HOBART
TASMANIAN DEVIL DASYURID
TASMANIAN WOLF HYENA TIGER
THYLACINE
TASSEL TAG TUFT LABEL THRUM
TARCEL TARGET TOORIE CORDELLE
(PL.) ZIZITH
(PREF.) THYSAN(O)
TASSEL)PL.) TZITZIS TZITZIT
TASTABLE GUSTABLE
TASTE EAT GAB GOO LAP SIP CAST
DASH GOUT GUST HINT PREE RASA
SALT TANG TEST TINT WAFT ASSAY
DRINK FANCY GUSTO HEART PROVE
RELES SAPOR SAVOR SHADE SKILL
SMACK SNACK SPICE TOOTH TOUCH
DEGUST FLAVOR GENIUS LIKING
PALATE RELISH SAMPLE SMATCH
ATTASTE PREGUST SOUPCON
THOUGHT APPETITE JUDGMENT
PENCHANT SAPIDITY
(— AFTER SWALLOWING) FINISH
(— COMBINED WITH APTITUDE)
FLAIR
(— IN MATTERS OF ART) FANCY
(— OF THE CAKE) FUST
(BAD —) GOTHISM
(DECIDED —) PENCHANT
(DELICATE —) BREED
(DISCRIMINATING —) SKILL
(GOOD —) DECORUM ELEGANCE
(OF MIDDLE-CLASS —) POLYESTER
(SLIGHT —) TINCTURE
(SOUR —) FOXINESS
(STRONG —) GOO
(PL.) MERIDIAN
(PREF.) SAPORI
(SUFF.) GEUSIA
TASTEFUL NEAT ELEGANT
GUSTOSO
TASTELESS DEAF FLAT FLASH
MALMY VAPID WERSH WALLON
FATUOUS INSIPID INSULSE WEARISH
UNSAVORY GRACELESS
TASTER TRIER
TASTING ASSAY
(— OF MALT) CORNY
TASTY SAPID YUMMY GUSTABLE
TASTEFUL PALATABLE DELECTABLE
TA-TA TOODLEOO

TATA BYE CIAO LATER CHEERIO
TATAR KIN JUNG KHAN KITAN SOYOT
CHAZAR KHAZAR KHITAN KHOZAR
SHORTZY MELETSKI
(PL.) HU
TATER SPUD POTATO
TATOUAY CABASSOU
TATTER JAG RAG TAG SHRED FITTER
LIBBET TAGRAG TARGET FLITTER
TROLLOP
(PL.) DUDS TAVERS FITTERS RIBBONS
TAIVERS FLITTERS
TATTERED DUDDY BEATEN TAGGED
FORWORN TATTERY TOTTERED
TATTERSALL WINDOWPANE
TATTING LACE
TATTLE BLAB GASH CHEEP CLASH
CLYPE PEACH SNEAK TUTEL GOSSIP
QUATCH SNITCH TATTER TITTLE
CLATTER
TATTLER LAB CLASH SNIPE FABLER
GAMBET GOSSIP TUTLER YELPER
STOOLIE TITTLER TELLTALE
TATTLETALE REVEALER
TATTLING LEAKY FUTILE
TATTOO TAT MOKO PINK POUNCE
RATAPLAN
TATTOOED PINKED
(— MAN) YUN
TATTOOING MOKO
TAUGHT MAK TEACHED INSTRUCT
(EASILY —) DOCIBLE
TAUNT BOB DIG MOB CHIP GIBE GIRD
JAPE JEER JEST MOCK PROG SKIT
TWIT CHECK FRUMP GLAIK JAUNT
SCOFF SCORN SLANT SLARE SLART
DERIDE SNEEST UPCAST SARCASM
TWITTER RIDICULE
TAUNTING RAIL SARCASTIC
TAUPE MOLESKIN
TAUROTRAGUS OREAS ORIAS
TA-URT THOUERIS
TAUT SNUG TORT STIFF TENSE TIGHT
CORDED
TAUTEN SNUB STIFFEN SWIFTER
TENSION
TAUTOG CHUB MOLL LABROID
TAVERN BAR INN BUSH HOWF VENT
FONDA MITER MITBE TAMBO BISTRO
CABACK KNEIPE BUVETTE CABARET
CANTEEN OSTERIA TABERNA
GASTHAUS ORDINARY POTHOUSE
TAPHOUSE
TAW TER ALLY ALLEY SCORE MARBLE
GLASSIE SHOOTER
TAWDRY CHEAP GAUDY NASTY
GILDED TINSEL RAFFISH DIMESTORE
TAWNY FUSC BRUSK DUSKY FULVID
TANNED FULVOUS JACINTH
MUSTELINE
(PREF.) CIRRO FUSCO PYRR(O)
PYRRH(O)
TAWNY BROWN TENNE CHAMOIS

TAW-SUG SULU

TAX FET LAY LOT TRY CAST CESS
DUTY GELD GELT GILD KAIN LEVY
POLL RATE SCAT SCOT SESS TAIL
TASK TOLL ABUSE AGIST DONUM
FINTA HANSA HANSE LEKIN MAILL
OBROK QUINT SCATT STENT TOUST
VERGI WATCH ZAKAH ZAKAT ABKARI
ASSESS AVANIA BURDEN CEDULA
DEMAND EXCISE EXTENT HIDAGE
IMPOST JEZIAH KHARAJ MURAGE
OCTROI OCTROY PAVAGE PURVEY
SENSUS STRAIN SURTAX VINAGE
BOOMAGE BOSCAGE CHANCER
CHEVAGE CHIVAGE CONDUCT
FINANCE GABELLE LASTAGE
PATENTE PENSION POLLAGE
PONTAGE SCUTAGE STIPEND
TAILAGE TERRAGE TOLLAGE
TRIBUTE ALCABALA AUXILIUM
BONAUGHT CARUCAGE CORNBOLE
DANEGELD EXACTION EXERCISE
KERNETTY MALTOLTE OBLATION
PESHKASH ROMESCOT ROMESHOT
STACKAGE SUPERTAX TAXATION
WHEELAGE CAPITATION
(— AT HARVESTTIME) CORNBOLE
(— FOR STORING LOGS) BOOMAGE
(— OF ONE-FIFTH) QUINT
(— ON EVERY PLOW) CARUCAGE
(— ON HERRING CATCH) LASTAGE
(— ON LIQUOR) ABKARI
(— ON SALT) GABELLE
(— ON UNBELIEVERS) KHARAJ
(— ON WALLS) MURAGE
(— ON WOOD) BOSCAGE
(— ON WOOL) MALETOTE MALTOLTE
(— TO PETTY PRINCES) KERNETTY
(— TO SYNAGOGUE) FINTA
(— TO TENTH AMOUNT) TITHE
(— UNDULY) STRAIN
(CAPITATION —) JIZYA JIZYAH
(CHINESE —) LEKIN LIKEN LIKIN
(EXCISE —) USERFEE
(EXTRAORDINARY —) AUXILIUM
(FEUDAL —) AID
(IRISH —) BONAGHT
(KIND OF —) SIN
(MOHAMMEDAN —) JEZIAH
(PARISH —) PURVEY
(PHILIPPINES —) CEDULA
(POLL —) TOLL CENSUS
(RUSSIAN —) OBROK
(SPANISH —) ALCABALA ALCAVALA
(TURKISH —) VERGI AVANIA

TAXABLE LISTABLE

TAX COLLECTOR TITHER
GABELLER

TAXGATHERER POLLER TAXMAN

TAXI CAB JIXIE CRAWLER
(SMALL —) MINICAB
(THREE-WHEELED —) CYCLO
(3-WHEELED —) CYCLO

TAXICAB CAB HACK CRUISER
MOTORCAB

TAXIDERMY NASSOLOGY

TAXING SEVERE GRUELING

TAXON MONERA

TAXONOMIC
(SUFF.)
(— DIVISION) IA

TAXONOMIST LUMPER CLADIST
SPLITTER

TAXPAYER FILER

TAYASSU PECARI

TAYGETE (FATHER OF —) ATLAS
(MOTHER OF —) PLEIONE
(SON OF —) EUROTAS LACEDAEMON

TAYRA GALERA

TCHAMBULI CHAMBERI

TEA CHA CHAR CHIA TCHA THAM TSIA
ASSAM CAPER CHAIS CONGO
FAHAM HYSON MIANG PEKOE STEEP
CONGOU KEEMUN OOLONG PTISAN
SUNGLO LAPSANG REDROOT
TWANKAY AUTUMNAL EARLGREY
GOWIDDIE SOUCHONG WORMSEED
(AFRICAN —) CAT KAT QAT KHAT
QUAT
(BLACK —) BOHEA CONGO OOPAK
CONGOU OOPACK SYCHEE
(COARSE —) BANCHA
(CUP OF —) CUPPA
(GREEN —) TWANKAY
(HIGH-GRADE —) GYOKURO
(INFERIOR —) BOHEA
(KIND OF —) OSWEGO
(MEDICINAL —) TISANE
(MEXICAN —) BASOTE APASOTE
(POOR —) BLASH
(WEAK —) MISERABLE
(PREF.) THEI

TEA BOWL CHAWAN

TEACAKE LUNN SCONE

TEACH ARAL LEAR READ SHOW TECH
TENT BREED CARRY COACH EDIFY
ENDUE LEARN SPELL TRAIN TUTOR
WISSE INFORM PREACH SCHOOL
BITECHE EDUCATE EXAMPLE
EXPOUND GRAMMAR AMAISTER
DISCIPLE DOCUMENT INSTRUCT
PUPILIZE
(— TO FIGHT) SPAR

TEACHABLE APT DOCILE DOCIBLE

TEACHABLENESS DOCITY
DOSSETY

TEACHER RAB ALIM GURU AKHUN
BIDDY CADET GUIDE MOLLA RABBI
REBBE TUTOR USHER AKHUND
AMAUTA DOCENT DOCTOR DOZENT
FATHER MADRIH MAULVI MENTOR
MULLAH PANDIT PUNDIT RABBAN
READER REGENT RHETOR SUPPLY
ACHARYA ALFAQUI DOMINIE
MAESTRA MAESTRO MOOLVIE
MUNCHEE MURSHID PEDAGOG

SHASTRI SOPHIST SPONSOR
STARETS TRAINER ALFAQUIN
AYUDANTE DIRECTOR EDUCATOR
EXTENDER GAMALIEL MAGISTER
MELAMMED MISTRESS MOONSHEE
MUJTAHID MAHARISHI PEDAGOGUE
PRECEPTOR ABECEDARIAN
PRIVATDOCENT
(— **OF ELOQUENCE)** RHETOR
(— **OF EMINENCE)** MAESTRO
(— **OF HIGH LEARNING)** SOPHIST
(— **OF KORAN)** ALFAKI ALFAQUIN
(— **OF PAUL)** GAMALIEL
(**INCA** —) AMAUTA
(**LANGUAGE** —) MUNSHI MOONSHEE
(**MOHAMMEDAN** —) COJA HODJA
  KHOJA KHOJAH
(**MOSAIC** —) SCRIBE
(**RELIGIOUS** —) STARETS STARETZ
(**UNIVERSITY** —) SCHOLASTIC
(**WALDENSIAN** —) GARBE
TEACHING LAW DHARMA DOCENT
LESSON LORING ACROAMA TUITION
BUDDHISM DIDACTIC DOCTRINE
DOCUMENT TUTELAGE
(— **ACTIVITY)** REALIA
(— **OBJECTS)** REALIA
(— **OF CHRIST)** GOSPEL
(**PL.**) ACOUSMA BROWNISM
  CACODOXY DIDACTICS
TEAK SAJ DJATI EBONY
TEAKETTLE SUKE SUKEY CHAFER
  KETTLE POURIE CRESSET
TEAL CRICK BLUEWING GARGANEY
  SARCELLE
TEAM SET FIVE PLOW SIDE SPAN
YOKE DRAFT SWING EQUIPE
PLOUGH SEXTET DRAUGHT
CARTWARE
(— **HARNESSED ONE BEFORE**
  ANOTHER) TANDEM
(— **OF CARS)** ECURIE
(— **OF GLASSWORKERS)** SHOP CHAIR
(— **OF OXEN)** SPAN
(— **OF 3 HORSES ABREAST)** TROIKA
(— **THAT FINISHES LAST)** DOORMAT
(— **2 ABREAST, 1 LEADING)** SPIKE
  UNICORN
(**ATHLETIC** —) CLUB
(**BASEBALL** —) NINE
(**BASKETBALL** —) FIVE
(**FOOTBALL** —) ELEVEN
(**2-HORSE** —) PODANGER
(**3-HORSE** —) RANDOM
TEAMSTER CARTER TEAMEO
  CARTMAN SKINNER TEAMMAN
TEAPOT TRACK TRACKPOT
TEAR HIE RIP RIT RUG TUT CLAW PILL
PULL RACE RASE RASH RAVE REND
RIVE RUGG SKAG SNAG STUN
BREAK CLAUT LARME PEARL RANCH
SHARK SLENT SPALT SPLIT SPREE
TOUSE CLEAVE HARROW RANCHE

RIPPLE SCHISM SCREED WRENCH
CHATTER CONVELL DISCIND
EYEDROP SCRATCH DISTRAIN
FRACTURE LACERATE LACHRYMA
TEARDROP
(— **APART)** REND TEASE DISCERP
  DIVULSE
(— **A STRIP OFF)** SCOLD
(— **ASUNDER)** DIVEL
(— **AWAY)** AVULSE
(— **DOWN)** UNPILE DESTROY
  DEMOLISH
(— **IN NEGATIVE)** SLUG
(— **INTO)** LAMBAST LAMBASTE
(— **INTO PIECES)** DRAW TOLE DEVIL
  SHRED TEASE LANIATE MAMMOCK
(— **INTO SHREDS)** HOG DEVIL TATTER
(— **OFF)** STRIP ABRUPT DISCERP
(— **OPEN)** PROSCIND
(— **TO SHREDS)** RIPUP
(— **UP BY THE ROOTS)** ARACHE
(**PL.**) DEW BRINE RHEUM EYEWATER
(**PREF.**) DACRY(O) LACHRYMI
  LACHRYMO SPARASSO
TEARDROP EYEWATER
TEARFUL SOFT TEARY WEEPY
LIQUID WATERY WEEPLY FLEBILE
MAUDLIN SHOWERY SNIVELY
SNIVELLY
TEARING SCREED
(— **AWAY)** AVULSION
TEARLESS DRYEYED
TEARPIT CRUMEN LARMIER
TEASE COD FUN MAD RAG RIB ROT
TAR TRY TUM VEX BAIT CHIP DRAG
FASH FRET GRIG HARE HOCK JADE
JIVE JOSH LARK NARK RAZZ RIDE
SOOL TARR TOUT TWIT WORK CHAFF
CHEEK CHEVY CHIAK CHYAK DEVIL
FEEZE RALLY TARIE TAUNT TOOSE
WRACK BANTER BOTHER CADDLE
CHIVVY HARASS HOORAY HURRAH
MOLEST MURDER NEEDLE PESTER
PLAGUE HATCHEL NEEDLER TERRIFY
TORMENT WHERRET
TEASEL KING TASSEL TEASLE
  MANWEED
TEASELER GIGGER TEASER
TEASELING MOZING
TEASER COMEON TIZEUR
TEASING CHAFF MERRY BANTER
  DEVILING QUIZZING
TEAT DUG PAP TIT DIDDY SPEAN
  NIPPLE SUCKLE
TEA TREE TI MANUKA
TEBAH (FATHER OF —) NAHOR
TEBALIAH (FATHER OF —) HOSAH
TECHIQUE SKILL
TECHNICIAN TECHIE SWITCHER
(**MEDICAL** —) EMT
TECHNIQUE FEAT GATE WRINKLE
COQUILLE INDUSTRY SPICCATO
(**BILLIARD** —) FOLLOW

(DANCE —) HEELWORK
(DECORATION —) IKAT
(DRAMATIC —) METHOD
(JUMPING —) SCISSORS
(PIANO —) PIANISM
(PLANNING —) PERT
(SOFT —) JUJITSU
(WEAVING —) SPRANG
(WRESTLING —) GLIMA
(WRITING —) CUBISM
(SUFF.) URGE URGIC URGY
TECHNOLOGY FISHERY TECHNIC
CERAMICS
TECMESSA (FATHER OF —)
TELEUTAS
(HUSBAND OF —) AJAX
(SON OF —) EURYSACES
TECOMIN LAPACHOL
TECTRIX COVERT
TEDDER KICKER
TEDIOUS DEAD DREE DULL LATE
LONG POKY PROSY WEARY ALENGE
BORING DREECH DREIGH ELENGE
MORTAL PROLIX STODGY IRKSOME
OPEROSE PREACHY PROSAIC
VERBOSE BORESOME DRAGGING
TIRESOME WEARIFUL
TEDIUM IRK YAWN ENNUI BOREDOM
TEE COCK TIGHT TOZEE WITTER
BULLHEAD
TEEM SNY FLOW SWIM SWARM
ABOUND BUSTLE SCRAWL
PULLULATE
TEEMER SHOOTMAN
TEEMING BIG ALIVE TUMID FERTILE
GUSHING TEEMFUL ABUNDANT
BRAWLING PREGNANT SWARMING
TEENAGER TEENY TEENYBOPPER
TEENY SMALL
TEESWATER MUGS MUGGS
TEETER ROCK WAVER JIGGLE QUIVER
SEESAW WOBBLE TREMBLE
TEETH CTENII CHOPPERS CRACKERS
GRINDERS
(HAVING —) IVORIED
(PETRIFIED —) BUFONITE
(SET OF —) DENTURE
(WHEEL —) COGS
(PREF.) DENT(ATO)(I)(INO)(O)
(SUFF.) ODON
TEETHRIDGE ALVEOLE ALVEOLUS
TEETOTUM TOTUM WHIRLIGIG
TEGETICULA PRONUBA
TEGMENTUM ROOF
TEGULA SQUAMA EPAULET
SCAPULA PATAGIUM SQUAMULA
TEGUMENT COAT TEGMEN
TEHUELCHE PATAGON
TEJU TEIOID JACUARU TEGUEXIN
TELAMON ATLAS
(BROTHER OF —) PELEUS
(FATHER OF —) AEACUS
(MOTHER OF —) ENDEIS

(SON OF —) AJAX TEUCER
(WIFE OF —) GLAUCE HESIONE
TELAMONES ATLANTES
TELEDU BADGER STINKARD
TELEGONUS (FATHER OF —)
ULYSSES
(MOTHER OF —) CIRCE
(SON OF —) ITALUS
(WIFE OF —) PENELOPE
TELEGRAM TAR WIRE FLASH FLIMSY
TELEGRAPH SEND WIRE CABLE
BUZZER TELEGRAM TELOTYPE
(BUSH —) GRAPEVINE
TELEMACHUS (FATHER OF —)
ULYSSES
(MOTHER OF —) PENELOPE
(SON OF —) LATINUS
TELENCEPHALON ENDBRAIN
TELEOLOGICAL TELIC FINALIST
TELEOLOGY FINALITY
TELEPHASSA (DAUGHTER OF —)
EUROPA
(HUSBAND OF —) AGENOR
(SON OF —) CADMUS PHOENIX
TELEPHONE CALL DIAL RING PHONE
BLOWER HANDSET
(KIND OF —) CORDLESS
(PART OF —) PAD BASE CORD DIAL
HOLE STOP PLATE CRADLE HANDLE
HANDSET PLUNGER SPEAKER
EARPIECE RECEIVER MOUTHPIECE
TRANSMITTER
TELEPHOTE DIAPHOTE
TELEPHUS (FATHER OF —)
HERCULES
(MOTHER OF —) AUGE
(WIFE OF —) ARGIOPE LAODICE
ASTYOCHE
TELEPRINTER CREED
TELESCOPE TUBE COUDE GLASS
SCOPE TRUNK ALINER FINDER
SECTOR ALIGNER BINOCLE TRANSIT
PROSPECT SPYGLASS REFRACTOR
PERSPECTIVE
(PART OF —) LEG CELL LENS TUBE
CLAMP GUIDE MOUNT SCOPE
CRADLE DEWCAP SLEEVE TRIPOD
DIAGONAL DRAWTUBE EYEPIECE
MOUNTING SUNSHADE
VIEWFINDER
(SURVEYOR'S —) LEVEL
TELEVISION TV AIR BOX TELLY
VIDEO VIDEOLAND SMALLSCREEN
(— AFTERNOON FARE) SOAP
(— BAND) UHF
(— COMEDY PROGRAM) SITCOM
(— PROGRAM) TALKSHOW
(— PROGRAM FOR CHILDREN) KIDVID
(— RATINGS PERIOD) SWEEP
(— SERVICE) PAYTV
(— SET) BOX TUBE BOOBTUBE
(— SHOW) RERUN SITCOM
(— STATION) CHANNEL

(CHILDREN'S —) KIDVID
(EDUCATIONAL —) ETV
(ELEMENT ON — SCREEN) PIXEL
(PERSON FOND OF —) VIDEOPHILE
TELIOSPORE TELEUTO
TELL HIP SAY DEEM MAKE MEAN
MOOT READ SHOW TALE AREAD
AREED BREAK BREVE COUNT NEVEN
PITCH SPELL STORY TEACH UTTER
AUTHOR DEVISE IMPART INFORM
MUSTER QUETHE RECITE RELATE
REPEAT REPORT REVEAL CONFESS
DIVULGE NARRATE PARTAKE
RECOUNT ACQUAINT REHEARSE
(— CONFIDENTIALLY) CONFIDE
(— CONFUSEDLY) SPLATHER
(— EARNESTLY) ASSURE
(— IN ADVANCE) FORESAY
(— LIES) BELY LIGE BELIE
(— OFF) JAR
(— ON) RAT
(— ROMANCES) GEST GESTE
(— SECRETS) CHEEP CLYPE SPILL
BABBLE
(— STRIKINGLY) CRACK
(— TALES) BLAB CANT PEACH
(HOME TO WILLIAM —) URI
TELLER CASHIER SPINNER STORIER
TALLIER FABLEIST FABULIST
SENACHIE
TELLING REDE PUNGENT POWERFUL
STINGING
(— OF SECRETS) BLAB
TELLTALE CLASH TATTLER TITTLER
REGISTER
TELL-TALE
(— SIGN) TIPOFF
TELLURIDE ALTAITE
TELSON PLEON
TELUGU GENTU GENTOO TELINGA
TEM TUM ATMU ATUM
TEMA (FATHER OF —) ISHMAEL
TEMAN (FATHER OF —) ELIPHAZ
(MOTHER OF —) ADAH
TEMENI (FATHER OF —) ASHUR
(MOTHER OF —) NAARAH
TEMERITY GALL CHEEK NERVE
AUDACITY RASHNESS
TEMP STENO
TEMPER CUE MAD BAIT BATE COOL
DASH DRAW MOOD MULL NEAL
PADD SCOT TONE ALLOY BIRSE
BLOOD CREST DELAY FRAME GRAIN
HUMOR IRISH SAUCE SOBER TRAMP
ADJUST ANIMUS ANNEAL DANDER
MASTER MONKEY SEASON SPIRIT
SPLEEN STRAIN SUBMIT CHASTEN
CLIMATE COURAGE HACKLES
QUALIFY STOMACH EBENEZER
GRADUATE MITIGATE MODERATE
MOORBURN
(— CLAY) TAMPER
(— METAL) ALLAY

(— OF MIND) CUE SPIRIT
(CAPRICIOUS —) SPLEEN
TEMPERAMENT BLOOD GEMUT
HEART HUMOR CRASIS KIDNEY
NATURE TEMPER STOMACH
SANGUINE
TEMPERAMENTAL FITIFIED
TEMPERANCE MEDIETY SOBRIETY
TEMPERATE CALM COOL MILD SOFT
GREEN SOBER STEADY TEMPRE
MODERATE ORDINATE ABSTINENT
CONTINENT LYSOGENIC
ABSTEMIOUS
TEMPERATURE SUN HEAT TEMP
HOTNESS DEWPOINT
(— FACTOR) WINDCHILL
(— UNIT) KELVIN
TEMPERED HARD MILD SOBER
SARCENET
TEMPERING MODULATION
TEMPEST GALE THUD WIND ORAGE
STORM TUMULT TORMENT TURMOIL
WEATHER
(AUTHOR OF —) SHAKESPEARE
(CHARACTER IN —) IRIS JUNO ARIEL
CERES ADRIAN ALONSO ANTONIO
CALIBAN GONZALO MIRANDA
TINCULO PROSPERO STEPHANO
FERDINAND FRANCISCO SEBASTIAN
TEMPESTUOUS WILD GUSTY
STERN WINDY RUGGED STORMY
VIOLENT STALWART
TEMPLATE CURB NORMA TEMPLET
PADSTONE STRICKLE
TEMPLE VAT WAT DEUL FANE NAOS
RATH CANDI GUACA HUACA KIACK
KOVIL MARAE RATHA CHANDI
HAFFET HERION MANDIR SACRUM
SHRINE TEOPAN TJANDI VIHARA
HERAEUM HERAION TEMPLET
TEMPLUM VARELLA OLYMPIUM
PANTHEON RAMESEUM TEOCALLI
VALHALLA PARTHENON
(— AREA) MANDAPA
(CAVE —) SPEOS
(FIJI —) BURE
(HAWAIIAN —) HEIAU
(JAPANESE —) SHA
(PART OF —) PRONAOS
(SHINTO —) SHA JINJA JINSHA
YASHIRO
(STUDY OF —S) NAOLOGY
(TOWERLIKE —) ZIGGURAT
(PREF.) NAO
TEMPLES
(PREF.) TEMPORO
TEMPLET FORMER STRICKLE
TEMPO TAKT TIME AGOGE
MOVEMENT
TEMPORAL LAIC CIVIL CARNAL
TIMELY EARTHLY PROFANE SECULAR
TEMPORARY ACTING FLYING
INTERIM STOPGAP WHILEND

EPISODAL EPISODIC TEMPORAL
PROVISIONAL
(PREF.) PSEUD(O)
TEMPORIZER DRIFTER POLITIC
TEMPT EGG BAIT FAND FOND LURE
TEMP TENT ASSAY COURT ALLURE
ASSAIL ENTICE INVITE SEDUCE
ASSAULT ATTEMPT SOLICIT
SUGGEST
TEMPTATION BAIT TRIAL ATTEMPT
TESTING SEDUCTION
TEMPTER DEVIL
TEMPTING ALLURING INVITING
TEMPTRESS SIREN DELILAH
TEN ICRE IOTA CHANG DIKER CHEUNG
DECADE DENARY DICKER ARTICLE
BRISQUE
(— OF TRUMPS) GAME
(PREF.) DEC(A)(I)(U) DECEM DEK(A)
(SUFF.) TY
TEN'A KOYUKON
TENACE FORK
TENACIOUS FAST ROPEY STIFF
TOUGH CLAGGY CLEDGY DOGGED
GRIPPY PLUGGY STICKY STRONG
VISCID GRIPPLE VISCOUS ADHESIVE
GRASPING HOLDFAST RETENTIVE
PERTINACIOUS
TENACIOUSNESS TENACY
FASTNESS
TENACITY LENTOR COURAGE
TENACULUM CLASP
TENANCY CONACRE JOINTURE
TENANT KMET LEUD SAER BARON
CEILE DRENG LAIRD BORDAR
COTTAR COTTER DRENGH GENEAT
HOLDER INMATE LESSEE MOLMAN
RADMAN RENTER SOCMAN VASSAL
CHAKDAR COTTIER FEODARY
FEUDARY GAVELER HOMAGER
SOCAGER SOKEMAN VAVASOR
COLIBERT CUSTOMER SERGEANT
SUCKENER
(— OF CROWN) THANE
(— OF THE CROWN) THANE
(FARM —) CROFTER
(LIFE —) LIVIER LIVEYER
(NEW —) INCOME INCOMER
TENCH CYPRINID
TEN COMMANDMENTS DECALOG
TEND HOP NOD RUN SET WRY BABY
BEND DRAW GROW KEEP MAKE
MIND MOVE TENT DRESS GROOM
NURSE OFFER SOUND TREND VERGE
WATCH AFFECT GOVERN INTEND
CHERISH CONDUCE DECLINE INCLINE
PROPEND
(— A FIRE) STOKE
(— IN A CERTAIN DIRECTION) LEAD
(— TO) NURSE
(— TO ONE POINT) CONVERGE
(— TOWARD) AFFECT
(— WHILE AT PASTURE) GRAZE

TENDENCY SET BENT BIAS HAND
TONE VEIN DRAFT DRIFT DRIVE
HABIT KNACK TENOR TREND TWIST
ANIMUS COURSE EONISM GENIUS
MOTION APTNESS CONATUS
DRAUGHT IMPULSE LEANING
NITENCY SAMKARA APTITUDE
INSTINCT STEERING VERGENCY
(— IN NATURE) KIND
(— TO APPROACH) ADIENCE
(— TO GOOD OR EVIL) PROPENSITY
(— TO STICK TOGETHER) CLANSHIP
(— TO WITHDRAW) ABIENCE
(— TO WRATH) TIDE
(INHERITED —) STRAIN
(SUFF.) (— TOWARD) PHIL(A)(AE)(E)
(IA)(ISM)(IST)(OUS)(US)(Y)
TENDER RAW TID BEAR COCK FINE
FOND FRIM FRUM KIND NESH SOFT
SORE TAKE TART TENT WARM CAGER
DEFER FRAIL GREEN MUSHY OFFER
PAPPY DELATE DRIVER GENTLE
GIMPER GINGER HUMANE LOVELY
RAISER SILKEN ADVANCE AMABILE
AMOROSO AMOROUS CONCHER
CRAMPER FLESHLY MASHMAN
OBLATIO PATACHE PINNACE PITEOUS
PITIFUL PORRECT PROFFER RUTHFUL
STENTER CAMELEER COLDBOAT
EFFETMAN FEMININE HEATSMAN
HERDSMAN LADYLIKE MERCIFUL
MORTISER SPREADER
(KIND OF —) LEGAL
(PREF.) ABRO HABRO
TENDERFOOT DUDE INNOCENT
CHEECHAKO
TENDERHEARTED HUMAN PITIFUL
TENDERIZER PAPAIN
TENDERLOIN FILET PSOAS FILLET
UNDERCUT
TENDERLY FONDLY GENTLY
AMOROSO
TENDERNESS CHERTE TENDER
DELICACY FONDNESS KINDNESS
SYMPATHY TENERITY YEARNING
(— OF FEELING) FLESH
TENDING
(SUFF.) CLINIC CLINOUS
(— TO) ABLE ATIVE ATORY BOND
BUND CUND FUL IBLE
TENDINOUS SINEWY
TENDON CORD TAIL CHORD NERVE
SINEW TENON LEADER PAXWAX
STRING
(PREF.) TENO
TENDRIL CURL CLASP CROOK TWIST
CIRRUS WINDER CAPREOL CIRRHUS
CLASPER TENTACLE
(PREF.) PAMPINI PAMPINO
TENEMENT LAND RENT TACK
CHAWL DECKER LIVING WARREN
HOLDING LETTING ROOKERY
BUILDING PRAEDIUM

TENES (FATHER OF —) CYNCUS
(MOTHER OF —) PROCLEA
PHILONOME
(SISTER OF —) HEMITHEA
(SLAYER OF —) ACHILLES
TENET ISM ADOXY CREDO CREED
DOGMA BELIEF GNOMON HOLDING
MISHNAH PARADOX DOCTRINE
(PL.) FAITH FAMILISM
TENFOLD DENARY DECUPLE
TENNANTITE FAHLERZ FAHLORE
TENNE TAWNY ORANGE HYACINTH

TENNESSEE
CAPITAL: NASHVILLE
COLLEGE: FISK LANE SIENA BETHEL
BELMONT LAMBUTH LEMOYNE
MILLIGAN TUSCULUM
VANDERBILT
COUNTY: DYER KNOX RHEA COCKE
GILES HENRY MEIGS OBION COFFEE
GRUNDY MCMINN SEVIER UNICOI
BLEDSOE FENTRESS
DAM: WILSON WHEELER
INDIAN: SHAWNEE CHEROKEE
CHICKASAW
LAKE: DOUGLAS CHEROKEE
REELFOOT WATTSBAR
MOUNTAIN: GUYOT LOOKOUT
MOUNTAIN RANGE: SMOKY
NATIONAL PARK: SHILOH
NATIVE: WHELP
NICKNAME: VOLUNTEER
PRESIDENT: POLK JACKSON
RIVER: ELK DUCK CANEY HOLSTON
HIWASSEE CUMBERLAND
STATE BIRD: MOCKINGBIRD
STATE FLOWER: IRIS
STATE TREE: POPLAR
TOWN: ERIN ALAMO ALCOA ERWIN
PARIS CAMDEN CELINA JASPER
SELMER SPARTA BOLIVAR DICKSON
JACKSON MEMPHIS PULASKI
GALLATIN KNOXVILLE
CHATTANOOGA

TENNIES SNEAKERS
TENNIS (— LET) DOOVER
(— NAME) ASHE ILIE
(— PERSONALITY) ASHE ILIE
(— PLAY) RALLY
(— PLAYER) DOD ASHE BETZ BORG
GORE GRAF KING BUDGE BUENO
COURT EVERT LAVER LENDL LLOYD
MOODY MOORE PERRY SEARS SELES
VILAS WILLS WRENN AGASSI
AUSTIN BECKER BROUGH BROWNE
COOPER DUPONT EDBERG JACOBS
LARNED MARBLE STERRY TILDEN
CONNORS COURIER DOHERTY
EMERSON ENGLEN MALLORY
MCENROE NASTASE RENSHAW
SAMPRAS VICARIO WHITMAN
WILDING ATKINSON BADDELEY
CAMPBELL CAPRIATI CHAMBERS
CONNOLLY GONZALES HILLYARD
NEWCOMBE ROSEWALL WILANDER
BJURSTEDT WRIGHTMAN
NAVRATILOVA
(— SCORE) ADIN LOVE ADOUT
DEUCE FORTY THIRTY FIFTEEN
(— SHOT) AD ACE LET LOB ADIN
DINK DROP ADOUT SMASH
(— UNIT) SET GAME MATCH
(ANCIENT —) BANDY
(NAME IN —) WADE
(PERFECT SERVE IN —) ACE
(TABLE —) PINGPONG
TENON COG PIN COAK STUB TUSK
LEWIS TOOTH TABLING DOVETAIL
LEWISSON
(KIND OF —) TUSK
TENOR PES FECK TONE VEIN COURSE
EFFECT TAILLE TENURE CURRENT
PURPORT STRENGTH TENDENCY
TENORINO
TENOROON FAGOTTINO
TENOR VIOL VIOLET
TENOR VIOLIN ALTO
TEN-PERCENTER AGENT
TENPINS BOWLS NEWPORT
TENPOUNDER AWA CHIRO MACABI
BONEFISH BONYFISH LADYFISH
SKIPJACK SPRINGER
TENREC TANGUE CENTETES
CENTETID HEDGEHOG HEDGEPIG
TENSE EDGY RAPT TAUT STIFF
WIRED AORIST CORDED FLINCH
FUTURE INTENT NARROW STRAIT
STRICT BRITTLE INTENSE PRIMARY
FRENETIC PRETERIT STRAINED
SYNTONIC
TENSION BENT HEAT DRIVE STEAM
SATTVA SPRING STRAIN STRESS
TROPPO BALANCE STRAINT
TENSURE ISOTONIA
(STATE OF NERVOUS —) YIPS
TENT AUL TOP HALE PAWL TAWN
TELD TILT TIPI CABIN CRAME LODGE
TEPEE TOPEK TUPIK CANNAT
CANVAS DOSSIL SEARCH TEEPEE
WIGWAM BALAGAN CABINET
KIBITKA MARQUEE SPARVER
TABERNA TENTLET TENTORY
ZDARSKY PAVILION SHAMIANA
TENTICLE TENTWORK
SHOOLDARRY
(— FOR WOUNDS) PENICIL
(— WHERE GOODS ARE SOLD)
CRAME
(CIRCULAR —) YURT YOURT YURTA
KIBITKA
(GENERAL'S —) PRAETORIUM
(INDIAN —) TEPEE WIGWAM
(SAMOYED —) CHUM
(SOUTH AMERICAN —) TOLDO

TENTACLE HORN SAIL PACLE FEELER
  BRACHIUM
TENTATIVE GINGERLY
TENT CATERPILLAR WEBWORM
TENTERER RACKER RATCHER
TENTH DIME DISME TITHE DECIMA
  (— OF CENT) MILL
  (— OF LINE) GRY
  (PREF.) DECI
TEN THOUSAND
  (PREF.) MYRIA MYRIO
TENTWORT RUE
TENUITY EXILITY DELICACY
TENUOUS SLIM FILMY FOGGY FRAIL
  SUBTLE TENDER FRAGILE GASEOUS
  SLENDER SUBTILE ETHEREAL
  GOSSAMER
  (TOO —) FINESPUN
TENUOUSNESS FRAILTY
TENURE FEU SORN TACK TAKE TERM
  GAVEL JAGIR BARONY CAPITE
  JAGHIR RUNRIG SOCAGE SORREN
  ALMOIGN BONDAGE BORDAGE
  BURGAGE CENSIVE CORNAGE
  CURTESY FARMAGE JAGHEER
  SOCCAGE SOREHON COPYHOLD
  DRENGAGE FREEHOLD OVERLAND
  SOCMANRY SUITHOLD VAVASORY
  VENVILLE
  (LAND —) RUNRIG SOCAGE
  RUNDALE SOCCAGE
TEPEE CHUM TENT TIPI HOGAN
  LODGE TEEPEE WICKIUP
TEPHROSIA CRACCA
TEPID LEW WARM WLACH WLECH
  LUKEWARM
TEQUISLATEC CHONTAL
TERAH (SON OF —) HARAN NAHOR
  ABRAHAM
TERATOMA EMBRYOMA
TERCET TRISTICH
TEREBINTH TEIL TURPENTINE
TEREDO BORER WOODWORM
TERENTIA (HUSBAND OF —) CICERO
TERETE CENTRIC
TEREUS (FATHER OF —) MARS
  (SON OF —) ITYS
  (WIFE OF —) PROCNE
TERGITE TERGUM PYGIDIUM
TERGIVERSATION DECEIT
TERGUM PYGIDIUM
TERM HALF NAME NOME WORD
  LEASE RHEMA SPEAK STYLE TRYST
  ABBACY GNOMON HILARY NOTION
  PARODY EPITHET EXTREME SESSION
  SUBJECT SUMMAND TERMINE
  VOCABLE EQUIVOKE HEADWORD
  MAHALATH POCHISMO SEMESTER
  TERMTIME
  (— IN JAIL) JOLT
  (— IN LOGIC) CONSTANT
  (— IN PROGRESSION) MEAN
  (— OF ABUSE) CUSSWORD

(— OF ADDRESS) SIRRAH MADONNA
(— OF CONTEMPT) SLIPE PILCHER
  TITIVIL
(— OF DEFERENCE) AHUNG
(— OF ENDEARMENT) HON LOVE
  PEAT ASTOR CHUCK COCKY HONEY
  JARTA LOVEY MOPSY MOUSE
  SUGAR YARTA ASTHORE MACHREE
  STOREEN POSSODIE POWSOWDY
  PRECIOUS
(— OF IMPRISONMENT) LAG
  LAGGING STRETCH
(— OF PROPOSITION) REFERENT
(— OF PUNISHMENT) JOB
(— OF RATIO) EXTREME
(— OF REPROACH) GIB BESOM
  MINGO RONYON
(— OF RESPECT) SAHIB
(— OF SYLLOGISM) EXTREME
  ARGUMENT
(—S OF REFERENCE) REMIT
(ARITHMETICAL —) NOME
  GNOMON
(COURT —) HILARY
(DESCRIPTIVE —) EPITHET
(FINAL —S) ULTIMATUM
(HYPHENED —) COMPOUND
(LITERAL —S) LETTER
(POSITIVE —) PLUS
(SOCIAL —S) FOOTING
(UNIVERSAL —) CONCEPT
(PL.) LAY MEANS
(PREF.) HORO
TERMAGANT JADE RUDAS SHREW
  VIXEN VIRAGO
TERMINABLE FINITE
TERMINAL JACK LAST POLE ANODE
  DEPOT IMPUT INPUT MUCRO
  CATHODE POTHEAD DESINENT
  (ELECTRIC —) POLE
TERMINATE CUT END ABUT CALL
  HALT KILL ABORT BLEED CEASE
  CLOSE ISSUE LAPSE EXPIRE FINISH
  FOREDO RESULT INCLUDE TERMINE
  COMPLETE CONCLUDE DISSOLVE
  (— A SESSION) PROROGUE
TERMINATED EXPIATE
TERMINATING FINAL
  (— ABRUPTLY) BLIND
  (SUDDENLY —) ABRUPT
TERMINATION END ISH DATE TERM
  ABORT CLOSE EVENT ISSUE ENDING
  EXITUS EXPIRY FINALE PERIOD
  UPSHOT TERMINUS
  (— OF CHURCH CHOIR) CHEVET
  (— OF FURNITURE LEGS) FOOT
  (— OF RIGHT) LAPSE
  (PROSPEROUS —) SUCCESS
TERMINATIVE FINITIVE
TERMINOLOGY JARGON
TERMINUS END FLAT
  (— IN FINGERPRINT) DELTA
  (— OF PERIOD) TIME

TERMITE ANAI ANAY KING NASUTE
WORKER POLILLA
TERMITOPHILE SYMPHILE
TERN KIP DARR INCA LARI NOIO PIRL
PIRR RIXY LARID NODDY PEARL
SCRAY SKEER SKIRR STERN CHIRRE
KERMEW PICKET GOELAND MEDRICK
PIRRMAW RITTOCK SCURRIT
SEAFOWL STRIKER TARRACK
TERNLET MANUSINA SPARLING
TIRRACKE
TERPENE CARENE PINENE
BORNANE SANTENE THUJENE
CAMPHENE FENCHENE LIMONENE
NOPINENE
TERRA GE GAEA TELLUS
(DAUGHTER OF —) RHEA THEA
PHOEBE TETHYS THEMIS
MNEMOSYNE
(HUSBAND OF —) URANUS
(SON OF —) OCEANUS
TERRACE POY DAIS PNYX STEP
XYST BEACH BENCH HEIAU LINCH
PATIO OFFSET PERRON LINCHET
VERANDA BARBETTE CHABUTRA
VERANDAH
(— AT ENTRANCE) PERRON
(LOUNGING —) LANAI
(NATURAL —) MESA
(SEA-FRONT —) PROMENADE
TERRA JAPONICA GAMBIR
GAMBIER
TERRAPENE CISTUDO
TERRAPIN EMYD COUNT COODLE
POTTER SLIDER TURPIN TURTLE
EMYDIAN FEUILLE SKILPOT
REDBELLY TORTOISE
(FEMALE —) HEIFER
(MALE —) BULL
TERRARIUM VIVARIUM
TERRELLA EARTHKIN
TERRENE EARTHLY
TERRESTRIAL EARTHY EARTHLY
TERRENE PLANETAL SUBLUNAR
SUBSOLAR TELLURIC PLANETARY
SUBASTRAL
TERRET CRINGLE
TERRIBLE DIRE UGLY AWFUL GHAST
LURID DEADLY PRETTY TARBLE
TRAGIC TURBLE CHRONIC DIREFUL
FEARFUL FERDFUL GHASTLY
HIDEOUS ALMIGHTY BHAIRAVA
FLEYSOME HORRIBLE TERRIFIC
TIMOROUS TRAGICAL
(PREF.) DEIN(O) DIN(O)
TERRIBLY FELLY FIERCE GRISLY
CONSARN
TERRIER SKYE LHASA SILKY BOSTON
DANDIE RATTER SCOTTY DIEHARD
SCOTTIE ABERDEEN AIREDALE
RATTONER SEALYHAM VERMINER
WIREHAIR
(YORKSHIRE) YORKIE

TERRIFIC FINE SWEET GORGON
AWESOME FEARFUL DYNAMITE
GORGEOUS
TERRIFIED AFRAID AGHAST
GHASTLY
TERRIFY AWE COW HAG BREE DARE
FEAR FLAY FLEY APPAL DREAD
GALLY SCARE ADREAD AFFRAY
AGRISE AWHAPE DISMAY FLIGHT
FREEZE FRIGHTEN
TERRIFYING GHASTLY HIDEOUS
FEARSOME FLEYSOME TERRIBLE
TERRITORIALISM ITOISM
TERRITORY FEE GOA HAN SOC AREA
MARK PALE SOKE BANAT DUCHY
FIELD MARCH STATE TUATH BORDER
COLONY DOMAIN EMPERY EMPIRE
GROUND APANAGE CONFINE
COUNTRY DEMESNE DUKEDOM
EARLDOM ENCLAVE EPARCHY
REGENCY SATRAPY APPANAGE
CASTLERY CONFINES CONQUEST
DISTRICT DOMINION IMPERIUM
LIGEANCE LUCUMONY PARMESAN
PASHALIK REGALITY SEIGNORY
(FOREIGN —) POSSESSION
(MONASTIC —) ABTHANE
TERROR AWE FEAR FRAY ALARM
APPAL DREAD PANIC AFFRAY
ALARUM APPALL FRIGHT HORROR
DRIDDER AFFRIGHT DREDDOUR
SURPRISE
TERRORISM NIHILISM
TERRORIST GOONDA ALARMIST
SICARIUS
TERRORIZE FRIGHTEN
TERROR-STRICKEN AWFUL
TERSE CURT SINEWY COMPACT
CONCISE LACONIC POINTED
SUMMARY UNWORDY SUCCINCT
TERSENESS BREVITY LACONISM
TERTIARY NEOZOIC PALAEIC
TESSELLATED MOSAIC
TESSELLATION AREOLE
TESSERA TILETTE ABACULUS
TESSELLA
TESS OF DURBERVILLES
(AUTHOR OF —) HARDY
(CHARACTER IN —) ALEC JACK TESS
ANGEL CLARE DURBERVILLE
DURBEYFIELD
TEST CON SAY TRY FAND FEEL FOND
QUIZ SEMI TASK TENT ASSAY AVENA
CANON CHECK ESSAY GROPE ISSUE
PROBE PROOF PROVE SENSE SOUND
TASTE TEMPT TESTA TOUCH TRIAL
SAMPLE TIENTA APPROOF APPROVE
AUSSAGE CONTROL EXAMINE
GANTLET PLUMMET TESTATE
BIOASSAY EXERCISE GAUNTLET
SEROLOGY STANDARD
(— CHEESE) PALE
(— EGGS) CANDLE

(— FOR MESSAGES) POLL
(— FOR WEIGHT AND FINENESS) PYX
(— GROUND) BOSE
(— OF COURAGE) SCRATCH
(— OF CRINOID) CALYX
(— OF GUILT) CORSNED
(— OF ORE) VAN
(ASSAY —) ELISA
(COLLEGE —) MIDTERM
(COLLEGE ENTRANCE —) PSAT
(KIND OF —) AMES ORAL MEANS
SWEAT DRAIZE LITMUS SCHICK
INKBLOT MANTOUX RORSCHACH
(SEROLOGICAL —) COGGINS
(SEVERE —) CRUCIBLE
(SYPHILIS —) KOLMER
(PREF.) DOCIMO OECO
(SUFF.) OECA OECIA
TESTA TEST LORICA EPISPERM
TESTACEOUS SHELLY
TESTAMENT TEST QUETHE
WITWORD COVENANT
TESTAR TETARD
TESTATOR LEGATOR
TESTED FIRED TRIED WEIGHED
TESTER TRIER CONNER PROVER
SPARVER DENIERER TESTIERE
(BUTTER —) SEARCHER
TESTES
(SUFF.) ORCHISM
TESTICLE STONE BALLOCK
DIDYMUS GENITOR
(PREF.) ORCHI(O) ORCHID(O) ORCHO
TESTICLES
(SUFF.) ORCHISM
TESTIFY SPEAK SWEAR AFFIRM
DEPONE DEPOSE WITTEN WITNESS
EVIDENCE
(— FALSELY) MOUNT
(— TO) BESPEAK
TESTIMONIAL CHIT SCROLL
CHARACTER
TESTIMONY TEST ATTEST AVOUCH
PROBATE TESTATE TESTIFY WITNESS
EVIDENCE
TESTING ASSAY CRUCIAL
SHAKEDOWN
(KIND OF —) DNA
TESTIS BALL GONAD STONE
BALLOCK CULLION KNOCKER
SPERMARY
(PL.) COBS CODS COJONES
DOWSETS
TEST TUBE PROOF TESTER PROBATE
TESTUDINATA CHELONIA
TESTUDO SNAIL GALAPAGO
TORTOISE
TESTY DONCY MUSTY TUTTY
CRANKY DONSIE PATCHY SPUNKY
PEEVISH TETTISH TOUSTIE WASPISH
SNAPPISH
TETANIC LOCKJAW SPASTIC
TRISMUS

TETANUS LOCKJAW HOLOTONY
TETE-A-TETE CHAT TWOSOME
CAUSEUSE
TETHER BAND LEASH STAKE PICKET
TEDDER TOGGLE PASTERN
CABESTRO
(— A HAWK) WEATHER
TETHYS APLYSIA
(DAUGHTERS OF —) OCEANIDES
(FATHER OF —) URANUS
(HUSBAND OF —) OCEANUS
(MOTHER OF —) TERRA
TETHYUM CYNTHIA
TETRA-
(PREF.) QUATER
TETRACHORD GENUS HYPATON
LICHANOS
TETRACTYS TETRAD
TETRAD FOURFOLD
TETRADRACHMA OWL
TETRAGONAL DIMETRIC
TETRAHEDRITE FAHLERZ FAHLORE
PANABASE
TETRAHEXAHEDRON FLUOROID
TETRAHYDRIDE GERMANE
STANNANE
TETRASACCHARIDE LUPEOSE
TETTER DARTRE
TETTIX ACRYDIUM
TEUCER (DAUGHTER OF —)
ASTERIA
(FATHER OF —) TELAMON
SCAMANDER
(HALF-BROTHER OF —) AJAX
(MOTHER OF —) IDAEA HESIONE
(WIFE OF —) EUNE
TEUTON GOTH LOMBARD
TEUTONIC GOTHIC GERMANIC
GOTHONIC

TEXAS

CAPITAL: AUSTIN
COLLEGE: SMU TCU RICE WILEY
BAYLOR
COUNTY: BEE CASS COKE JACK REAL
RUSK VEGA WEBB WISE BEXAR
DELTA ECTOR ERATH GARZA RAINS
FANNIN GOLIAD YOAKUM ZAPATA
ZAVALA HIDALGO REFUGIO
ATASCOSA
FORTRESS: ALAMO
INDIAN: LIPAN BILOXI KICHAI SHUMAN
HASINAI COMANCHE TONKAWAN
LAKE: FALCON TEXOMA AMISTAD
MOUNTAIN: GUADALUPE
NATIVE: TEJANO
NICKNAME: LONESTAR
PRESIDENT: JOHNSON EISENHOWER
RIVER: RED PECOS BRAZOS NUECES
TRINITY
STATE BIRD: MOCKINGBIRD
STATE FLOWER: BLUEBONNET
STATE TREE: PECAN

TOWN: GAIL VEGA WACO BRYAN
MARFA OZONA PAMPA TYLER
BORGER DALLAS DENTON ELPASO
KILEEN LAREDO ODESSA QUANAH
SONORA ABILENE HOUSTON
LUBBOCK AMARILLO BEAUMONT
FLOYDADA GALVESTON

TEXAS BUCKTHORN LOTEBUSH
TEXAS FEVER TRISTEZA
TEXT BODY MIQRA PLACE SAKHA
TESTO WORDS PURANA SCRIPT
SHAKHA TEXTUS TEXTLET
ANTETHEM PERICOPE VARIORUM
(— OF ADVERTISEMENT) COPY
(— OF OPERA) LIBRETTO
(— OF PLAY) SCRIPT
(— SET TO MUSIC) ORATORIO
(BIBLICAL —) SCRIPTURE
(REVISED —) RECENSION
(SACRED —) MANTRA
(SHASTRA —) SRUTI SHRUTI
TEXTBOOK DUNCE TUTOR
GENETICS
TEXTILE (ALSO SEE FABRIC) SABA
STUFF GREIGE MOCKADO SAGURAN
SINAMAY TEXTURE TIFFANY
(— MACHINE) WILLOW
(PL.) DRAPE
TEXTURE WEB BONE HAND KNIT
WALE WOOF FIBER GRAIN COBWEB
FABRIC WEFTAGE FRACTURE
(— OF SOAP) FIT
(— OF STONE) GRIT
THADDEUS OF WARSAW
(AUTHOR OF —) PORTER
(CHARACTER IN —) MARY ROSS
SARA DIANA BUTZOU ROBSON
VINCENT BEAUFORT EUPHEMIA
PEMBROKE SOBIESKI SOMERSET
THADDEUS CAVENDISH KOSCIUSKO
SACKVILLE TINEMOUTH
CONSTANTINE
THAHASH (FATHER OF —) NAHOR
(MOTHER OF —) REUMAH
THAI LAO SIAMESE

THAILAND

CAPITAL: BANKOK BANGKOK
COIN: AT ATT BAHT FUANG TICAL
PYNUNG SALUNG SATANG
FORMER NAME: SIAM
ISLAND: PHUKET
ISTHMUS: KRA
LANGUAGE: SHAN
MEASURE: WA KEN NIV NMU RAI SAT
SEN SOK WAH YOT KEUP NGAN
TANG YOTE KWIEN LAANG SESTI
TANAN KABIET KAMMEU CHAIMEU
ROENENG CHANGAWN
MOUNTAIN: KHIEO MAELAMUN
MOUNTAIN RANGE: DAWNA
BILAUKTAUNG

NATIVE: LAO THAI
PLAIN: KHORAT
RIVER: CHI NAN PING MENAM
MEKONG MEPING
TOWN: UBON PUKET RANONG
AYUDHYA AYUTHIA BANGKOK
LOPBURI RAHAENG SINGORA
SONGKLA KHONKAEN KIANGMAI
THONBURI
WEIGHT: HAP PAI SEN SOK BAHT HAPH
KLAM KLOM CATTY CHANG COYAN
PILUL FLUANG SALUNG SOMPAY
TAMLUNG

THAIS (CHARACTER IN —) THAIS
ATHANAEL
(COMPOSER OF —) MASSENET
THAISA (FATHER OF —) SIMONIDES
(HUSBAND OF —) PERICLES
THALABA (WIFE OF —) ONEIZA
THALER DALER
THALLOGEN AMPHIGEN
THALLOID FRONDOSE
THALLUS FROND THALAMUS
THAMNIUM
THAMNOPHIS EUTAENIA
THAMYRAS (FATHER OF —)
PHILAMMON
(MOTHER OF —) ARGIOPE
THAN AS NA NE OR TO AND BUT NOR
THEN TILL
THANE THEGN BANQUO GESITH
ABTHAIN MACDUFF
THANK GRACE MERCY AGGRATE
REGRACY REMERCY
THANKFUL GRATEFUL
THANKLESS INGRATE SLOWFUL
THANKS TA DANKE GRACE MERCI
MERCY GRACIAS GRAMERCY
THANKSGIVING GLORY
DOXOLOGY
THANK-YOU-MA'AM CAHOT
THAT AS AT SE BUT HOW THE THO
WHO YAT LEST THAM THIK THON
WHAT YOND THICK THILK THOUGH
BECAUSE
(— IS) IDEST
(— IS TO SAY) NAMELY
(— ONE) ILLE
(— WHICH HAS TO BE PROVED)
IQED
(— YONDER) THON
THATCH NIPA DATCH SIRKI SIRKY
STING THRUM CADJAN
(— OVER BEEHIVE) HOOD
THATCHED THACK REEDED
THATCHER HELER CROWDER
HELLIER THACKER
THAUMAS (DAUGHTER OF —) IRIS
AELLO HARPY OCYPETE
(FATHER OF —) PONTUS NEPTUNE
(MOTHER OF —) GAEA TERRA
(WIFE OF —) ELECTRA

THAUMATURGIST
(PL.) GOETAE
THAUMATURGY MAGIC
THAW GIVE MELT FRESH UNTHAW
DEFROST
THE LA LE SE TA THI THAM THEY YARE
THERE
(PREF.) AL
THEA CAMELLIA
(FATHER OF —) URANUS
(HUSBAND OF —) HYPERION
(MOTHER OF —) TERRA
THEANO (FATHER OF —) CISSEUS
(HUSBAND OF —) ANTENOR
METAPONTUS
(MOTHER OF —) TELECLIA
(SISTER OF —) HECUBA
(SON OF —) ACAMAS AGENOR
POLYBUS HELICAON IPHIDAMAS
ARCHELOCHUS
THEATER CINE GAFF KINO NABE
CAVEA HOUSE LEGIT ODEUM SCENE
STAGE CINEMA OZONER ADELPHI
COCKPIT GUIGNOL ORPHEUM
THEATRE BIOSCOPE COLISEUM
PANTHEON SHOWSHOP SPELLKEN
STRAWHAT THEATRON PLAYHOUSE
NICKELODEON
(— DISTRICT) RIALTO
(CLASSICAL —) ODEUM
(FULL —) SRO
(HARLEM —) APOLLO
(JAPANESE —) NOH BUNRAKU
(LOCAL —) NABE
(NEIGHBORHOOD —) NABE
(PUPPET —) BUNRAKU
THEATRICAL CAMP HAMMY STAGY
DRAMATIC SCENICAL SINGSONG
THEATRICALITY HAM PANACHE
THEBAN LAIUS NIOBE AMPHION
CADMEIA JOCASTA OEDIPUS
PENTHEUS
THEBE (FATHER OF —) ASOPUS
(HUSBAND OF —) ZETHUS
(MOTHER OF —) METOPE
(SISTER OF —) AEGINA
THECA CUP URN CELL VAGINA
CAPSULE PYXIDIUM VAGINULE
THEELIN ESTRONE FEMININ OESTRIN
THEFT CRIB LIFT HEIST PINCH SCORE
STALE STEAL FURTUM RIPOFF
STOUTH BRIBERY LARCENY MICHERY
PICKING PILFERY ROBBERY STEALTH
BURGLARY STEALAGE STEALING
(LITERARY —) PIRACY
(PETTY —) CRIB PICKERY
(PREF.) KLEPT(O)
(SUFF.) KLEPT
THEINE CAFFEINE
THEIR ARE HER ORE HORE YARE
THEIRS HERN THEIRN
THEM A EM HI UM HEM MUN HEMEN

THEME DUX BASE IDEA TEMA TEXT
DITTY HOBBY LEMMA MOTIF PLACE
SCOPE TESTO THEMA TOPIC URLAR
MATTER MYTHOS SUBJECT
ANTETHEM
(— OF FUGUE) DUX
(HACKNEYED —) CLICHE
(MAIN —) BURDEN
(RECURRING —) BURDEN
(STOCK —) TOPOS
THEMIS (DAUGHTER OF —) DICE
IRENE EUNOMIA
(FATHER OF —) URANUS
(HUSBAND OF —) JUPITER
(MOTHER OF —) TERRA
THEMSELVES HEM HEMSELF
THEN SO AND POI THO ANON SYNE
ALORS
THENCE AWAY THEN THEREFRO
THEOCRACY KHALSA
THEODELINDE (FATHER OF —)
GARIBALD
(HUSBAND OF —) AGO AUTHARI
THEODOLITE TAIPO DIOPTER
TRANSIT TRANSEPT
THEOLOGIAN FAQIH ULEMA DIVINE
MUJTAHID
AMERICAN COX BROWN HATCH
NEVIN SMITH TYLER WOODS
BURTON CURRAN ELIADE FOSTER
GLUECK KOHLER MACHEN SCHAFF
STUART TAYLOR EDWARDS EVERETT
HOPKINS MCCLURE MOFFATT
NIEBUHR PEABODY SEABURY
TILLICH VINCENT MCGIFFERT
WORCESTER
AUSTRIAN MOHR RAHNER BRUNNER
DENIFLE JELLINEK
BELGIAN BAIUS
BRAZILIAN BOFF
CZECH COMENIUS
DANISH MONRAD MULLER MYNSTER
PEDERSEN GRUNDTVIG
PONTOPPIDAN
DUTCH HAAR VOET WITS BEKKER
JANSEN KUENEN KUYPER
GOMARUS ARMINIUS
BOGERMAN LIMBORCH SCHOLTEN
EPISCOPIUS
ENGLISH BEDE BULL DODD HORT
OWEN WARD BLUNT COLET HATCH
PALEY PUSEY SWETE WATTS ALCUIN
BUTLER FERRAR HARRIS HOOKER
NEWMAN PECOCK STERNE WESLEY
LANGTON MARBECK MAURICE
PEARSON WHATELY WHISTON
CARDWELL DRUMMOND PELAGIUS
WYCLIFFE CHADERTON GUILLAUME
LIGHTFOOT STAPLETON
WARBURTON GROSSETESTE
CHILLINWORTH
FLEMISH JANSEN

FRENCH BEZE GURY AILLY FAVRE
PAJON SIMON CALVIN GERSON
GLAIRE GOGUEL JURIEU PASCAL
PORREE RICHER SORBON ABELARD
AMYRAUT BASNAGE BAUTAIN
BOCHART CHARRON FENELON
QUESNEL BERENGAR CASAUBON
COURAYER SABATIER CASTELLIO
BOURDALOUE LICHTENBERGER
LABERTHONNIERE
GERMAN ECK ESS ADAM ARND
BAUR DUHM EBER GASS HEIM MERX
RUPP ZAHN AMMON BAUER BUDDE
CALOV EMSER FRANK GOEZE HAUCK
HENKE KNAPP KRAUS LANGE MAJOR
ROTHE STORR WALCH WEBER WEISS
ALSTED ANDREA BAHRDT BENGEL
CRAMER DALMAN DIPPEL DORNER
EBRARD FICKER GEIGER HEILER
HERMES HERZOG HEUSSI HIRSCH
MOHLER NATORP PEUCER PLANCK
REUSCH SEMLER SPENER UHLICH
ZELLER ZIMMER AGRIPPA AMSDORF
BOUSSET CASPARI CRUSIUS
ECKHART EHRHARD ERNESTI
FORSTER GERHARD HAERING
HARNACK HOFMANN KOSTLIN
LECHLER MOSHEIM MUNSTER
NAUMANN NEANDER NIPPOLD
RITSCHL STRAUSS TILLICH
ULLMANN URSINUS WILHELM
BULTMANN CALIXTUS CANISIUS
CHEMNITZ COCCEIUS CRUCIGER
DIBELIUS DILLMANN EBERHARD
EICHHORN FLIEDNER GERHARDT
GESENIUS HAUSRATH KAUTZSCH
KLIEFOTH MICHELIS MYCONIUS
OETINGER OSIANDER REIMARUS
SCHENKEL AURIFABER BEYSCHLAG
BUSEMBAUM DELITZSCH DOLLINGER
FABRICIUS FREIDRICH JABLONSKI
MICHAELIS NIEMOLLER OLEVIANUS
OLSHAUSEN PFEIDERER
BAUMGARTEN BONHOEFFER
FANNENBERG MARHEINEKE
NEUMEISTER WISLICENUS
TISCHENDORF FROHSCHAMMER
BRETSCHNEIDER SCHLEIERMACHER
GREEK ALLACCI CLEMENT
EUSEBIUS
HUNGARIAN BALLAGI
IRISH DODWELL PLUNKET TYRRELL
ITALIAN OCHINO AQUINAS
LOMBARD PERRONE SOCINUS
PASSAGLIA BELLARMINE
JEWISH HIRSCH
NORWEGIAN MOE
PORTUGUESE ABARBANEL
RUSSIAN BERDYAYEV SCHMEMANN
SCOTTISH CAIRD EADIE BURNET
ALESIUS CAMERON ROLLOCK
TULLOCH CAMPBELL CHALMERS

FAIRBAIRN CUNNINGHAM
RUTHERFORD
SPANISH CANO MOLINA SUAREZ
VALDES ENZINAS CARRANZA
EYMERICO SERVETUS MALDONADO
SEPULVEDA
SWEDISH FRYXELL SODERBLOM
FAHLCRANTZ
SWISS KUNG BARTH GODET VINET
ISELIN BRUNNER DIODATI ERASTUS
LAVATER LECLERC BUCHMANN
HEIDEGGER
SYRIAN AETIUS
THEOLOGY KALAM IRENICS
DIVINITY POIMENIC POLEMICS
THEONOE (BROTHER OF —)
CALCHAS
(FATHER OF —) PROTEUS THESTOR
(MOTHER OF —) LEUCIPPE
PSAMATHE
THEORBO LUTE ARCHLUTE
THEOREM DUAL LEMMA CONVERSE
THEORETIC PURE
THEORETICAL BOOK PURE CLOSET
THEORIC ABSTRACT ACADEMIC
ARMCHAIR NOTIONAL PLATONIC
THEORIST MUSER OPINATOR
THEORIZE SUGGEST
THEORIZING IDEOLOGY
THEORY ISM OVISM EROTIC ETHICS
HOLISM LAXISM SYSTEM AGOGICS
ANIMISM ATOMISM BAASKAP
BIGBANG CAMBISM DUALISM
FORMISM HOBBISM PEELISM
PLENISM THEORIC TYCHISM
ACOSMISM AXIOLOGY DITHEISM
DYNAMISM ENERGISM ESTHETIC
ETIOLOGY FEMINISM FINITISM
GHOSTISM GOBINISM HEDONICS
IDEALISM IDEOLOGY MOLINISM
MONADISM ONTOLOGY PROGRESS
SEMANTIC SEMIOTIC SPERMISM
(— OF GAMES) AGONISTICS
(— OF THE UNIVERSE) SYSTEM
(KIND OF —) DOMINO GALOIS
(METRICAL —) STICHOLOGY
(PHYSICS —) BOHRS
(SUFF.) ISM LOGER LOGIA(N)
LOGIC(AL) LOGIST LOGUE LOGY
OLOGY
THEOW SERF THRALL THEOWMAN
THERAPEUTICS ACEOLOGY
THERAPY PHYSIATRICS
(SUFF.) PATH(IA)(IC)(Y)
THERAVADA HINAYANA
THERE ERE YARE ALONG VOILA
WHERE YONDER THEASUM THITHER
THEREABOUTS NEARBY
THEREAFTER UPON THENCE
THEREFORE SO ERGO THEN ARGAL
HENCE FORTHY IGITUR THENCE
THEREON UPON

THEREUPON SO SINCE WITHAL
THEREON THEREUP
THEREWITH MIT WITH
THERIACA GALENA
THERMOMETER GLASS HYDRA
CELSIUS REAUMUR
(PART OF —) BORE BULB LENS SCALE
COLUMN GRADUATIONS
CONSTRICTION
THERMOPLASTIC SARAN
THERMOSTAT DETECTOR PYROSTAT
THERSANDER (FATHER OF —)
POLYNICES
(MOTHER OF —) ARGIA
(SLAYER OF —) TELEPHUS
THESAURUS TREASURE
THESE THIR THIS THEASUM
THESEUS
(FATHER OF —) AEGEUS
(MOTHER OF —) AETHRA
(SON OF —) HIPPOLYTUS
(WIFE OF —) PHAEDRA
THESIS ACT PAPER THEMA
DOWNBEAT LOGICISM THESICLE
THESTIUS (DAUGHTER OF —)
ALTHAEA
(FATHER OF —) PARTHAON
(MOTHER OF —) EURYTE
(SON OF —) TOXEUS PLEXIPPUS
THESTOR (DAUGHTER OF —)
THEONOE LEUCIPPE
(FATHER OF —) IDMON APOLLO
(MOTHER OF —) LAOTHOE
(SON OF —) CALCHAS
THETIS (FATHER OF —) NEREUS
(HUSBAND OF —) PELEUS
(MOTHER OF —) DORIS
(SON OF —) ACHILLES
THEY A HI THO THEI ELLAS ELLOS
(— READ) LEG
THIAMINE ANEURIN
THICK FAT SAD HAZY SLAB BLIND
BROAD BURLY BUSHY CLOSE CRASS
DENSE FOGGY GREAT GROSS
MURKY SOLID SQUAB STIFF STOUT
CHUMPY COARSE GREASY LUBBER
SLABBY SPISSY STOCKY STODGY
TURBID BLUBBER GRUMOUS
FAMILIAR LUTULENT MOTHERED
(— OF A FIGHT) PRESS
(— WITH SMOKE) SMUDGY
(SHORT AND —) SQUAT
(11 POINTS —) HEAVY
(PREF.) CRASSI DASI DASY HADR(O)
PACHY ULO
(— WITH HAIR) DASI DASY
THICKEN GEL BODY CLOT FULL
BREAK KEECH LITHE DEEPEN
HARDEN ENGROSS STIFFEN
(— HEDGE) PLASH
THICKENED BODIED BULLED
FURRED CALLOUS CLUBBED
SPISSATED

THICKENER NAPALM
THICKENING FALX LEAR ROUX
SWELL CALLUS CLAVATE LIAISON
PLACODE ATHEROMA CLUBBING
CRASSULA PYCNOSIS EPHIPPIUM
(— OF ARTERIES) ATHEROMA
(— OF COAL SEAM) SWELLY
(— OF LETTER STROKE) STRESS
THICKET COP BOSK RONE SHAG
SHAW BLUFF BRAKE CLUMP COPSE
COVER DROKE HEDGE QUICK SHOLA
SLICK THICK BOSKET BUSHET
COVERT GREAVE JUNGLE MALLEE
QUEACH SPINNY BOSCAGE
BOSQUET BRUSHET COPPICE
CORYLET SPINNEY WOODRIS
CHAMISAL FERNSHAW QUICKSET
SHINNERY THICKSET SALICETUM
THICK-HEADED OPAQUE
THICKHEADED DULL DENSE
THICKHEADED FLY CONOPID
THICK-KNEE CURLEW DIKKOP
BUSTARD
THICKLY STEFLY
THICKNESS PLY BODY LAYER
DIAMETER
(— OF CHIP) CUT FEED
(— OF CLOTH) LAY
(— OF METAL) GRIP
(— OF PAPER) BULK CALLIPER
UNDERLAY
(ONE — OVER ANOTHER) LAYER
(SECOND —) DOUBLING
THICKSET STUB BEEFY PUNCH
SQUAT STOUT THICK CHUMPY
CHUNKY HUMPTY PLUGGY ROBUST
STOCKY STUBBY STUGGY NUGGETY
SQUATTY
THIEF GUN NIP PAD CHOR GILT LIFT
MILL PRIG BUDGE CREEP CROOK
FAKER GANEF PIKER SNEAK TAKER
TILER ANGLER BULKER CANNON
CLOYER DISMAS GONOPH HOOKER
KALLAN LIFTER MICHER NIMMER
NIPPER PICKER PIRATE RATERO
ROBBER SNATCH TOSHER WASTER
BOOSTER COLLERY FOOTMAN
GORILLA GRIFTER HARRIER HEISTER
LADRONE LURCHER MEECHER
MERCURY PRIGGER PRIGMAN
PROLLER PROWLER SNAPPER
SPOTTER STEALER THIEVER
CLYFAKER CONVEYER CUTPURSE
FINGERER HARROWER LARCENER
PETERMAN PICAROON PICKLOCK
PILFERER PRIGSTER SNATCHER
(— AT A MINE) CAVER
(CATTLE —) ABACTOR BLOTTER
PLANTER RUSTLER
(CLEVER —) KID CANNON
(CRUCIFIED —) DISMAS
(FLASHY —) KIDDY
(MOUNTAIN —) CHOAR

(NIGHT —) SCOURER
(PETTY —) HOOKER SLOCKER
(RIVER —) ACKMAN LUMPER
(SNEAK —) LURCHER
(VAGABOND —) WASTER
(WHARF —) TOSHER
(PREF.) KLEPT(O)
(SUFF.) KLEPT
THIEVE MAG NIM
THIEVERY PRIGGERY
THIEVING LAW SHARK PUGGING
PROGGERY STEALING
THIEVING MAGPIE, THE
(CHARACTER IN —) NINETTA
PODESTA GIANETTO
(COMPOSER OF —) ROSSINI
THIEVISH STEALY FURTIVE KLEPTIC
SCADDLE PRIGGISH
THIEVISHNESS PRIGGISM
THIGH HAM HOCK FEMUR FLANK
GAMMON
(— PAIN) MERALGIA
(PREF.) CRURO FEMORO MER(O)
(SUFF.) MERUS
THILL FILL SILL BLADE SHAFT
LIMBER
THIMBLE SKEIN BUSHEL GOBLET
SLEEVE CRINGLE
THIMBLEBERRY MULBERRY
THIN HOE LEW BONY FINE FLUE FUSE
LANK LEAN LIMP PRIN RARE SLIM
WEAK WHEY EXILE FRAIL GAUNT
GAUZY LATHY PEAKY SHEER SLINK
SMALL SPARE SWAMP THIRL WASHY
WIZEN AERIAL BLASHY DILUTE
FLUTED HOLLOW MAUGER MEAGER
MEAGRE PEAKED SCRANK SEROSE
SEROUS SHELLY SKINNY SLEAZY
SLIGHT SPARSE SPINNY SUBTLE
TENDER TWIGGY WATERY WEAKEN
COVERED FOLIOUS FRAGILE GRACILE
HAGGARD SANIOUS SCRAGGY
SCRAILY SCRANKY SCRAWNY
SHALLOW SHILPIT SLENDER SPIDERY
SPINDLY TENUOUS THREADY
ARANEOUS CACHETIC EGGSHELL
HAIRLINE ICHOROUS MACILENT
SCRAGGED SCRANNEL SKINKING
VAPORISH WATERISH ATTENUATE
SPINDLING
(— AND PINCHED) CHITTY
(— LEATHER) DOLE
(— OUT) HOE CHOP DISBUD FEATHER
(— SEEDLINGS) SINGLE
(— THE WALLS) IRON
(MAKE —) EMACIATE
(PREF.) AREO LEPT(O) MANO TENUI
THINE TUUM
THING JOB RES BABY ITEM SORT
WHAT CHEAT CHOSE AFFAIR ANIMAL
DINGUS FELLOW GILGUY MATTER
ARTICLE DINGBAT MINIKIN SHEBANG
WHATNOT THINGLET

(— DONE) FACT ACTUS
(— FOUND) TROVE
(— OBSERVED) OBJECT
(— OF LITTLE ACCOUNT) GEWGAW
(— OF LITTLE VALUE) NIFLE TRIFLE
TRINKET
(— OF LITTLE WORTH) STIVER
(— SEEN) REGARD
(—S PROHIBITED) VETANDA
(— TO BE REGRETTED) DAMAGE
(— TO EXHIBIT) BRAVERY
(ADMIRABLE —) GEM
(ANOTHER —) ALIUD
(BIG —) SWAPPER SWOPPER
(CONSECRATED —) ANATHEMA
(CORRECT —) CHEESE
(CREEPING —) SERPENT
(DISAGREEABLE —) STINKER
(EASY —) PIE PUSHOVER
(ENORMOUS —) MONSTER
(ENTIRE —) INTEGRAL
(EXTRAORDINARY —) ONER
(FAIR —) POTATO
(FIT —) CHECKER
(FLAT —) PLAT
(FOOLISH —) FOLLY
(GOOD —) WELFARE
(HOLY —) HALIDOM
(HOLY —S) HAGIA KODASHIM
(IMPORTANT —) ACE
(INSIGNIFICANT —) SCRAT
(INSIGNIFICANT —S) SMATTER
(JEWISH —S) JUDAICA
(LITTLE —S) FEWTRILS
(LIVING —S) BIOTA
(MISSHAPEN —) ABORTION
(NEW —) NEWEL
(OUTMODED —) SNUFF
(PETTY —) SHABBLE
(PRECIOUS —) JEWEL
(PRECISE —) POINT
(REMARKABLE —) UNCO
PHENOMENON
(RIDICULOUS —) MONUMENT
(RIGHT —) POTATO
(ROTTEN —) RUTTOCK
(SAD —) RUTH
(SILLY —) TRIMTRAM
(SINGLE —) UNIT
(SINGULAR —) ODDITY
(SMALL —) SNIPPET
(STRAY —) WAIF
(STUNTED —) SCRUNT SNEESHIN
(SURE —) CERT SNIP
(TERRIFYING —) BOGEYMAN
(TROUBLESOME —) PEST TRIAL
PLAGUE
(UNEXPECTED —) GODSEND
(UNIQUE —) ONER UNICUM
(UNREAL —) NOMINAL
(UNSPECIFIED —S) JAZZ
(UNSUBSTANTIAL —) PUFF
(WITHOUT EQUAL —) NONPAREIL

(WORLDLY —S) EARTH
(WORNOUT —) SNUFF HUSHEL
(PL.) GEAR REALIA SQUARES
(PREF.) REI
(SUFF.) ORIUM ORY SOME
(— USED) ANT
(— USED FOR) ORIUM
THINGAMAJIG GIZMO
THINGAMY DOODAD
THING-IN-ITSELF THINGY
NOUMENON
THINGS
(SUFF.) IA
THINGUMBOB DODAD DINGUS
DOODAD JIGGER THINGUM
THINGAMAJIG
THINGUMMY GISMO GIZMO
THINGAMAJIG
THINK LET SEE WIS WIT DEEM FEEL
HOLD MAKE MEAN MINT MULL
MUSE READ TROW WEEN ALLOW
CENSE FANCY GUESS JUDGE LOUSE
OPINE PANSE SEPAD ESTEEM
EXPECT FIGURE IDEATE REASON
RECKON REPUTE BELIEVE CONCEIT
IMAGINE REFLECT SUPPOSE
SURMISE COGITATE CONSIDER
ENVISAGE
(— BEST) SEEM
(— DIFFERENTLY) DISSENT
(— HARD) YERK
(— HIGHLY OF) RATE
(— IDLY) DREAM
(— ILL) MISDEEM
(— LOGICALLY) DEDUCE
(— OF) MIND PURPENSE
(— OF AS) ACCOUNT
(— OUT) STUDY REASON
(— OVER) BETHINK
(— UP) INVENT
(— UPON) BROOD
(— WELL OF) APPROVE
(— WRONGLY) MISTAKE
THINKER SOPHIST PHILOSOPH
PHILOSOPHER
(CHINESE —) LEGALIST
THINKING CONCEIT THOUGHT
(CLEVER —) HEADWORK
THINLY AIRILY SPARSE SPARSELY
THINNESS RARITY EXILITY FINESSE
TENUITY EXIGUITY
THINNING BALK BAULK PINCH
CLEANING
THIOL MERCAPTAN
THIRD FACE GAMMA TERCE THREE
DITONE TERTIA TIERCE
(PREF.) TRIT(O)
THIRDLY TERTIO
THIRD-RATE C3 HEDGE
THIRD-RATER PIKER
THIRST DRY ADRY CLEM DRYTH
APOSIA DROUTH THRIST DROUGHT
DIPSOSIS POLYDIPSIA

(EXCESSIVE —) POLYDIPSIA
(LOSS OF —) ADIPSIA
(PREF.) DIPS(O)
THIRSTING SITIENT
THIRSTY DRY ADRY ATHIRST
DROUGHTY
THIRTEEN
(YOUNGER THAN —) PRETEEN
THIS HE SO ESTA ESTO THIK DIESE
THILK
THIS ABOVE ALL (AUTHOR OF —)
KNIGHT
(CHARACTER IN —) PRUE CLIVE
MONTY BRIGGS CATHAWAY
PRUDENCE
THISTLE PUHA HOYLE CARDON
DASHEL DINDLE FISTLE TEASEL
CALTROP CARDUUS CARLINA
GUTWEED RAURIKI WARATAH
BEDEGUAR CALTHROP COMPOSIT
ECHINOPS MILKWEED
(PREF.) CARDO
THITHER TO YON YOND THERE
YONDER ULTERIOR YONDWARD
THOAS (BROTHER OF —) EUNEUS
(DAUGHTER OF —) HYPSIPYLE
(FATHER OF —) BACCHUS
ANDRAEMON
(MOTHER OF —) GORGE ARIADNE
HYPSIPYLE
(SON OF —) SICINUS
(WIFE OF —) MYRINE
THOMIST AQUINIST
THOMSONITE MESOLE MESOTYPE
OZARKITE
THONG LORE RIEM BRAIL GIRTH
LASSO LEASH ROMAL STRAP THUNK
WHANG WHANK LACING LINGEL
STRING TWITCH AMENTUM BABICHE
LANIARD LANYARD LATCHET RIEMPIE
(— ON JAVELIN) AMENTUM
(HAWK'S —) BRAIL
(PREF.) HIMANTO
THOR THUNAR THUNOR
(FATHER OF —) ODIN
(HAMMER OF —) MJOLLNIR
(MOTHER OF —) JORDH
THORACIC DORSAL
THORAX CHEST TRUNK BREAST
PEREION ALITRUNK CORSELET
FOREBODY
THORITE ENALITE ORANGITE
THORN BROD BUSH GOAD PIKE STOB
STUG BRIAR BRIER DOORN PRICK
SPIKE SPINE FUSTIC JAGGER
ACANTHA PRICKER STICKER
COCKSPUR THORNLET
(PL.) SPEAR HAYBOTE
(PREF.) ACANTH(O) SPINI SPINO(SO)
SPINULI SPINULOSO
(SUFF.) ACANTHUS SPINOSE
THORN APPLE HAW METEL
STAMONY

THORNBACK RAY DORN ROKER
THORNBILL TOMTIT
THORNY HARD SPINY PRICKLY
SCROGGY SPINOUS THISTLY
THORNED
THORON RADON
THOROUGH RUN DEEP FIRM FULL
SOUND ERRANT HOLLOW STRICT
HOTSHOT INGOING REGULAR
COMPLETE GROUNDLY INTIMATE
PRECIOUS
THOROUGHBRED HOTBLOOD
THOROUGHFARE BUND DRUM
ROAD ALLEY AVENUE STREET
BIKEWAY HIGHWAY PARKWAY
WHITEHALL
THOROUGH-GOING WHOLEHOG
THOROUGHGOING PAKKA
ARRANT ERRANT HEARTY PROPER
PUREDEE RADICAL ABSOLUTE
PROFOUND TRUEBRED
THOROUGHLY BUT FULL GOOD
INLY CLEAN FULLY PROOF DEEPLY
GAINLY KINDLY PROPER RICHLY
RIPELY WHOLLY ROUNDLY SOAKING
SOBBING SOGGING SOUNDLY
DRIPPING GROUNDLY HEARTILY
INWARDLY
(PREF.) E
THOROUGHWORT BONESET
THOSE THEM THEY YOND
THOTH DHOUTI
THOUGH AS AND SET YET ALTHO
ALTHOUGH
THOUGHT CARE IDEA MOOD VIEW
FANCY TASTE TRACE NOTION
RINDLE CONCEIT CONCEPT
COUNSEL OPINION SURMISE
PEMMICAN RUMINATE
(— EXPRESSED IN WORDS)
SENTIMENT
(— OUT) ADVISED
(CAREFUL —) ADVICE ACCOUNT
(CONTROLLING —) KEYNOTE
(DEEP —) MUSE MEDITATION
(FANCIFUL —) CONCEIT
(HIGHEST —) IDEE
(INMOST —) CONSCIENCE
(INNERMOST —S) PRIVITY
(ORIGINAL —) BRAINCHILD
(REASONED —) STUDY
(UNCLEAN —) SEWERAGE
(WELL-EXPRESSED —) STROKE
(PREF.) LOG(O)
THOUGHTFUL EARNEST PENSIVE
SERIOUS STUDIED STUDIOUS
THOUGHTY
THOUGHTFULNESS GRACE
COUNSEL
THOUGHTLESS RASH VAIN DIZZY
GLAKY SUPINE VACANT ETOURDI
GLAIKET RAMSTAM HEEDLESS
RECKLESS

THOUSAND CHI MIL GRAND MILLE
CHILIAD
(FIVE —) EPSILON
(SIX —) DIGAMMA
(TEN —) TOMAN
(10 —) MYRIAD
(100 —) LAC LAKH
(PREF.) CHILI(A) KILO MILLE MILLI
(TEN —) MYRIA MYRIO
THOUSANDTH
(— OF CUBIC CENTIMETER) LAMBDA
(— OF INCH) MIL
(HUNDRED —) SSU
(PREF.) MILLI
THRACIAN GETE GETAN GETIC
THRAX
THRALL SERF GURTH SLAVE CAPTIVE
THRALLDOM BONDAGE SLAVERY
THIRLAGE
THRASH DAD LAM PAY TAN BANG
BEAT BELT COMB DING DRUB DUST
FLAX JERK LACE LICK LOUK MILL
PAIL SOCK SOLE SOWL SWAP SWOP
TOSE TRIM WALK WHAP WHIP WHOP
YERK BASTE BELAM BLESS CREAM
CURRY DRASH FLAIL FRAIL LINCH
LINGE NOINT PASTE SLATE SLOSH
SWACK SWING TABOR TARGE
THUMP TOWEL TWINK WHALE
WHANG ANOINT BUMFEG CUDGEL
FETTLE JACKET LARRUP LATHER
MUZZLE RADDLE STOUSH SWINGL
TANCEL THREAP THRESH THWACK
WALLOP LAMBACK LEATHER
SWADDLE TROLLOP TROUNCE
BETHWACK RUMBASTE LAMBASTE
LAMBSKIN RIBROAST SPIFLICATE
THRASHER THREAPER THRESHER
SICKLEBILL
THRASHING LICK TOCO LALDY
HIDING WIPING BELTING LAMMING
LICKING WARMING WHALING
DRUBBING STRAPPING
THRASYMEDES (FATHER OF —)
NESTOR
(MOTHER OF —) ANAXIBIA
THREAD BAR END BAVE CHIP CLEW
CLUE CORD DOUP FILE FILM GIMP
GOLD LACE LINE POIL PURL ROON
SILK TRAM WIRE WORM BRIDE CHIVE
FIBER FIBRE FLOAT FLOSS HYPHA
INKLE LISLE LUREX REEVE SCREW
SETON SHIVE SHOOT SHUTE STEEK
THRUM TWFER TWIRE TWIST WATAP
BOTTOM COBWEB COTTON ENFILE
FIBRIL INFILE SINGLE STAMEN
STITCH STRAIN STRAND STRING
TASLAN TISSUE RABICHE BASTING
DOUPING SLUBBER SPIREME
TWITTER WARPING ACONTIUM
FILAMENT GOSSAMER LIGATURE
PICKOVER RAVELING SPINNING
SPIRICLE

(— AROUND BOWSTRING) SERVING
(— IN SEED COATING) SPIRICLE
(— LEGS OF RABBIT) HARL HARLE
(— OF SCREW) WORM
(— OF WAX) SWARF
(—S THAT CROSS WARP) WEFT
WOOF
(— USED FOR COCOON) BAVE
(BADLY TWINED —) SLUBBER
(BALL OF —) CLEW CLUE CLOWE
GLOME
(BUTTONHOLE —S) BAR
(COARSE) GIRD
(COARSEST — IN LACE) GIMP
(COILED —) COP
(FILLING —) PICK
(FINE COTTON —) LISLE
(FLOATING —) PICKOVER
(HARD —) LISLE
(LINEN —) LINE INCLE INKLE
(LOOSELY TWISTED —S) BUMP
(METAL —) LAME WIRE
(OAKUM —) PLEDGET
(PULLED —) SNAG
(REFUSE —S) BUR BURR
(SHOEMAKER'S —) END LINGEL
LINGLE
(SILK —) TRAM TRAME DOUPIONI
(SOFT SHORT —) THRUM
(STRONG —) GOUNAU
(SURGICAL —) SETON
(WARP —) END STAMEN
(WAXED —) TACKER
(WEFT —) PICK SHOT
(40 —S) BEER BIER
(PL.) FLOSS
(PREF.) FILI(CI) MIT(O) NEM(A)(O)
NEMAT(O) STAMIN(I)
(SUFF.) NEMA NEME STEMONOUS
THREADBARE BARE SEAR SERE
USED TRITE PILLED SHABBY
NAPLESS
THREADFIN SEER SEIR SULEA
BARBUDO KINGFISH SEERFISH
THREADFISH COBBLER SUNFISH
THREADING SCREW STRINGING
THREADLIKE FILATE FILOSE
FILIFORM
THREADWORK MACRAME
(KNOTTED —) MACRAME MACRAMI
THREASHOLD BRINK VERGE
THREAT ATTACK MENACE
THUNDER
(BOASTFUL —) BRAVADO
(PL.) MINES
THREATEM (— TO RAIN) SCOWDER
SCOUTHER SCOWTHER
THREATEN BODE BRAG FACE MINT
BOAST SHORE ATTACK IMPEND
MENACE ENDANGER MINATORY
OVERHANG
(— TO RAIN) SCOUTHER
THREATENED FRAUGHT

THREATENING BIG GLUM UGLY
ANGRY BOAST NASTY SABLE SHORE
GREASY BANEFUL BODEFUL
OMINOUS RAMPANT MINATORY
MINITANT MINACIOUS
(— TO RAIN) HEAVY
THREE TREY GIMEL LEASH TRIAS
TERNARY TERNION
(— CENT PIECE) TRIME
(— IN ONE) TRIUNE
(— MILES) LEAGUE
(— OF A KIND) GLEEK BRELAN
TRIPLET
(GROUP OF —) TRIO TRIAD TRIPLE
TROIKA
(SET OF —) TERN PAIRIAL
(PREF.) TER TERNATI TERNATO TRE
TRI(S)
(— DIMENSIONS) STERE(O)
(SUFF.) TERNATE
THREE BLACK PENNIES (AUTHOR
OF —) HERGESHEIMER
(CHARACTER IN —) HOWAT JAMES
PENNY SUSAN EUNICE JANNAN
JASPER POLDER BRUNDON
MARIANA LUDOWIKA WINSCOMBE
THREE-CORNERED HAT (AUTHOR
OF —) ALARCON
(CHARACTER IN —) LUCAS WEASEL
EUGENIO MERCEDES FRASQUITA
THREE-DIMENSIONAL CUBIC
CUBICAL
THREEFOLD TERN TRINE TERNAL
TREBLE TRINAL TRIPLE TERNARY
TRIFOLD TRIPLEX THRIBBLE
THREE-FORKED TRISULC
THREE MUSKETEERS
(AUTHOR OF —) DUMAS
(CHARACTER IN —) ATHOS ARAMIS
WARDES PORTHOS DEWINTER
PLANCHET BONACIEUX CONSTANCE
DARTAGNAN RICHELIEU
THREEPENCE JOEY TREY THRIP
THRUM TICKEY TICKIE
THREE SISTERS (AUTHOR OF —)
CHEKHOV
(CHARACTER IN —) OLGA IRINA
MASHA ANDREY SOLENI KULIGIN
NATASHA PROSOROV VERSHININ
THREE SOLDIERS (AUTHOR OF —)
DOSPASSOS
(CHARACTER IN —) DAN RED ANDY
JOHN MABE YVONNE ANDREWS
FUSELLI ANDERSON GENEVIEVE
CHRISTFIELD
THRENODY DIRGE HEARSE THRENE
THRESH COB BEAT CAVE LUMP WHIP
BERRY FLAIL FRAIL SPELT STAMP
THRASH
THRESHEL DRASHEL
THRESHER TASKER
THRESHER SHARK FOX FOXFISH
WHIPTAIL

THRESHOLD HEAD SILL SOLE
DEARN LIMEN DRASHEL DOORSILL
(— OF CONSCIOUSNESS) LIMEN
THRIFT SAVING VIRTUE ECONOMY
SEAPINK STATICE THEEDOM
PARSIMONY
THRIFTILY NEAR
THRIFTLESS WASTEFUL
THRIFTY CANNY FENDY PUIST
FRUGAL SAVING CAREFUL SPARING
THRILL JAG WOW BANG DIRL GIRL
KICK RUSH SEND FLUSH SHOOT
THIRL DINDLE STOUND TICKLE
TINGLE TREMOR ENCHANT FRISSON
VIBRATE FREMITUS
(PROVIDING A —) KICKY
(SHARP —) ZING
THRILLING TINGLY VIBRANT
PLANGENT TINGLING
THRINTER FRONTER
THRIPID PHYSOPOD
THRIPS BLACKFLY PHYSOPOD
THRIVE DOW GROW LIKE RISE THEE
ADDLE FADGE MOISE PROVE
THRAM BATTEN BATTLE CATTER
CHIEVE PROSPER STORKEN
SUCCEED WELFARE FLOURISH
THRODDEN
(— IN) LOVE
THRIVING BIEN GRUSHIE ROARING
THRIFTY BLOOMING TOWARDLY
THRIVINGLY GAILY GAYLY
BRAVELY
THROAT MAW CRAG CROP GOWL
GULA HALS HASS LANE GORGE
HALSE SWINE FAUCES GARGET
GULLET GUTTUR GUZZLE RICTUS
CHANNEL JUGULUM STOMACH
SWALLOW WEASAND THRAPPLE
THRUPPLE THROTTLE
(— AILMENT) STREP
(— OF ANCHOR) CLUTCH
(— OF COROLLA) FAUCES
(— OF FROG) KNEE
(CLEAR —) HARRUMPH
(KIND OF —) STREP
(MOUTH AND —) WHISTLE
(SORE —) HOUSTY PRUNELLA
(PREF.) BRONCH(I)(IO)(O) DER(O)
GUTTERO
THROATLATCH FIADOR
THROATY THICK GUTTURAL
THROB ACHE BEAT BELK DRUM
DUNT LEAP PANG PANT QUOP WARK
FLACK PULSE STANG WARCH
STOUND STRIKE STROKE TINGLE
WALLOP FLACKER PULSATE VIBRATE
FLICHTER PALPITATE
(— IN PAIN) SHOOT
(RAPID —S) FRIMITTS
THROBBING DUNT ATHROB THRILL
BEATING PITAPAT VIBRANT
PULSATORY

THROE PANG PULL STOUR SHOWER
PAROXYSM
(—S OF DEATH) AGONY
THROMBIN PLASMASE
THROMBOPLASTIN COAGULIN
CYTOZYME
THROMBOSIS SHOCK CORONARY
THRONE GADI SEAT ASANA GADDI
GADHI SELLE SIEGE STALL STATE
STEAD STOOL MUSNUD SEGGIO
SHINZA TRIBUNE CATHEDRA
SEGGIOLA SINHASAN
(— OF GOD) MERCYSEAT
(BISHOP'S —) SEE APSE CATHEDRA
(INDIAN —) GADI
THRONE ROOM AIWAN
THRONG CREW HEAP HOST ROUT
CHIRT CROWD FLOCK FRACK HORDE
POSSE PRESS SHOAL SWARM
RESORT THRAVE THREAT THRIMP
THRUOT COMPANY TEMPEST
THRUTCH SURROUND
(— OF SEAFOWL) SAVSSAT
(CONFUSED —) LURRY
THRONGED ALIVE FREQUENT
NUMEROUS
THROTTLE GUN CHOKE SCRAG
STIFLE GARROTE STRANGLE
THROPPLE
THROUGH BY PER DONE THRU WITH
ROUND AROUND
(— AND THROUGH) INGRAIN
INGRAINED
(RIGHT —) TILL
(PREF.) DIA PER
THROUGHOUT OVER ABOUT
ROUND ABROAD BEDENE BIDENE
DURING ENTIRE PASSIM SEMPRE
OVERALL THRUOUT
(PREF.) HOL(O)
THROW GO DAB DAD HIP HIT PAT
PEG PUT SHY ACES BIFF BUCK
BUNG CALE CAST CHIP CLOD COOK
CUCK DART DASH DROW DUMP HAIL
HANK HIPE HULL HURL HYPE JERK
LACE MILL PECK PICK PURL SEND
SKIM SLAT SOSS TOSS TURF VANG
WARP WURP YEND CHUCK CHUNK
DOUSE FLICK FLING FLIRT FLURR
HEAVE PITCH SLING SPANG DEVEST
ELANCE HAUNCH HURTLE INJECT
LAUNCH SLIGHT THRILL BLUNDER
BUTTOCK COCKSHY MANGANA
UPTHROW VIBRATE CATAPULT
JACULATE
(— A BASEBALL PITCH) HANG
(— ABOUT) BOUNCE
(— ASIDE) DEVEST
(— AT HAZARD) NICK
(— AWAY) DICE DOFF BANDY SCRAP
WAIVE PROJECT JETTISON
SQUANDER
(— BACK) REPEL

(— BASEBALL) BURN
(— BY KICKING) WINCE
(— CARELESSLY) COB
(— DICE) JEFF
(— DOWN) DUSH EVEN PILE FLUMP
LODGE ABJECT DETURB THRING
FLATTEN
(— FORTH) EJECT
(— FORWARD) LAUNCH
(— HEAVILY) LOB
(— HEEDLESSLY) SLIGHT
(— IN CRAPS) CRAP PASS CRABS
BOXCARS NATURAL
(— IN QUOITS) RINGER
(— INTO CONFUSION) CLUB EMBROIL
FLUTTER CONFOUND CONVULSE
(— INTO DISORDER) PIE ADDLE
BOLLIX DERANGE DISRANK DISRUPT
EMBROIL DISARRAY
(— INTO PERPLEXITY) FLUMMOX
(— INTO WASTE) BACK
(— JERKILY) FLIRT
(— LIGHT UPON) ILLUME
(— LIQUID) JAW
(— OF A STEER) DOGFALL
(— OFF) CANT CAST EMIT SLIRT
SPILL SLOUGH CONFUSE
UNBURDEN
(— OFF COURSE) EMIT SHED DERAIL
(— OF SHUTTLE) SHOT SHOOT
SHUTE
(— OF THREES) COCKEYES
(— ONESELF) CLAP
(— OPEN) DISPARK
(— OUT) FIRE HOOF LADE BELCH
EJECT ERUPT SPOUT DETURB
IGNORE EXTRUDE
(— OVER) JILT
(— QUICKLY) LASH
(— REPEATEDLY) PELT
(— ROUGHLY) WAP
(— SIDEWISE) SHY
(— SILK) THROWST
(— SMARTLY) SLAT
(— STEER) BUST
(— STICKS) SQUAIL
(— STONES) ROCK
(— TOGETHER) HUDDLE
(— UNDER) SUBJECT
(— UP) BARF CAVE PICK VOMIT
(— VIOLENTLY) BUZZ DING PASH
SOCK WHAP WHOP SMASH HURTLE
WUTHER WHITHER SPANGHEW
PRECIPITATE
(— WITH A JERK) JET CANT SQUIRR
FLOUNCE
(— WITH GREAT FORCE) BUZZ
SWACK
(— WITHOUT VIOLENCE) HURL
(CHEATING — OF DICE) KNAP
(FOOTBALL —) GROUND
(FREE —) FOUL
(LARIAT —) HOOLIAN

(LOWEST — AT DICE) AMBSACE
AMESACE
(WRESTLING —) HANK HIPE HYPE
BUTTOCK BACKHEEL
(SUFF.) JECT
THROWAWAY DODGER
THROWBACK ATAVISM ATAVIST
THROWER TRAMMER THROWSTER
(SPEAR —) ATLATL
THROWING DARTING
THROWING-STICK ATLATL
WOMMERA WOOMERA HORNERAH
TROMBASH TRUMBASH
THROWN
(— AWAY) CASTAWAY
(— DOWN) DEJECTED
(PREF.) (— OUT) RHIPTO
THROWSTER TWISTER
THRUM FUM STRUM THUMB FRINGE
THRUSH POP OMAO SOOR APTHA
BREVE FRUSH GRIVE MAVIS OUZEL
PITTA SABIA SHAMA SHIRL SPREW
UZZLE VEERY APHTHA DRAINE
JAYPIE KICKUP MISSEL OLOMAO
PULISH SHRITE JAYPIET REDWING
WAGTAIL BELLBIRD CHERCOCK
FORKTAIL PRUNELLA SHAGBARK
THRASHER THROSTLE THRUSHEL
THRUSTLE URTICATE WOODCHAT
SOLITAIRE MONILIASIS NIGHTINGALE
THRUSHLIKE TURDOID
THRUST DAB DEG DIG DUB JAB JAG
JAM JOB POP PUG BANG BEAR BIRR
BOKE BORE BUCK BUTT CANT CHOP
CRAM DART DASH DUSH FOIN HURL
KICK LICK MURE PASS PICK PILT
POKE PORR POSS POTE PROD PUSH
SEND SINK SPAR STAB STOP TILT
VENY WHAP WHOP BREAK DRIFT
DRIVE EXERT HUNCH LUNGE POACH
POINT PROKE PUNCH SHOOT SPANK
STAVE STICK STOKE STUFF THROW
DARTLE PLUNGE POUNCE STITCH
STRAIN STRESS STRIKE STRIPE
BEARING IMPULSE PRESSURE
SHOULDER STOCCADO
(— A LANCE) AVENTRE
(— ALONG) SLIDE
(— ASIDE) DAFF SHUFFLE
(— AWAY) DOFF SHOVE DETRUDE
ABSTRUDE
(— DOWN) THRING DEPULSE
DETRUDE
(— IN) INSERT STRIKE INTRUDE
(— OF ARCH) DRIFT
(— OF EXPLOSION) BLOWOUT
(— ONESELF) CHISEL
(— ONWARD) STAVE
(— OUT) POUT REACH STRUT
EXSERT DETRUDE EXTRUDE
OBTRUDE PROTRUDE OBTRUSIVE
(— SUDDENLY) STRIKE
(— THROUGH) ENFILED

(— WITH ELBOW) HUNCH
(— WITH GREAT FORCE) BUZZ
(— WITH NOSE) NUDDLE
(— WITH WEAPON) FOIN SHOVE
(DAGGER —) DAG
(FENCING —) PASS VENY BOTTE
PUNTO VENUE REMISE REPOST
TIMING PASSADO RIPOSTE
STOCCADO STOCCATA
(HOME —) HAI HAY
(MATADOR'S —) ESTOCADA
(SARCASTIC —) GIRD
THUD BAFF DUMP PHUT PLOD SWAG
DOYST FLUMP POUND BOUNCE
SQUELCH
THUG MUG GOON PUNK GOONDA
RODMAN GORILLA HOODLUM
MOBSTER GANGSTER
(LIKE A —) GOONY
(SOUTH AFRICAN —) TSOTSI
THUJA BIOTA
THUJONE SALVIOL
THULUTH SOOLOOS
THUMB THOOM POLLEX THENAR
(— THROUGH) SKIM
(BALL OF —) THENAR
THUMBHOLE BACKLILL
THUMBSTALL POUCER POUSER
THUMP COB DAD DUB BANG BEAT
BLOW BUMP DING DIRD DRUB DUNT
KNUB LUMP PAIK PAKE POLT SOSS
THUD TUND TUNK YARK YERK BLAFF
BLIBE BUNCH CLOUR CLUNK CRUMP
KNOCK POUND TABOR THACK
WHELK BOUNCE HAMMER PUMMEL
THUNGE
THUMPING WHAPPING WHOPPING
THUNDER ROAR SULFUR BRATTLE
FOULDRE SULPHUR INTONATE
(PREF.) BRONT(E)(O) CERAUN(O)
KERAUN(O)
THUNDERBOLT BOLT FIRE VAJRA
FULMEN FOULDRE ARTIFACT
FIREBOLT
(SHOOTER OF —S) THOR
(PREF.) CERAUN(O) KERAUN(O)
THUNDERING TONANT
THUNDERSQUALL BAYAMO
VENDAVAL
THUNDERSTONE ARTIFACT
THUNDERSTORM HOUVARI
TEMPEST TORNADO
THURIBLE CENSER
THUS AS SIC DYCE THUSLY THISWISE
THUSGATE
THWACK BLOW DUNT LICK CRUMP
SOUSE
THWART BALK FOIL WART BENCH
CROOK CROSS SPITE THRAW THROW
ZYGON BAFFLE SCOTCH STYMIE
SNOOKER CONTRAIR CONTRARY
TRAVERSE
THWARTING CROSS CROSSING

THYESTES (BROTHER OF —) ATREUS
(FATHER OF —) PELOPS
(MOTHER OF —) HIPPODAMIA
THYIA (FATHER OF —) CASTALIUS
CEPHISSEUS
(SON OF —) DELPHUS
THYINE THUGA THUYA
THYLACINE YABBI
THYME MARUM PELETRE HILLWORT
SERPOLET
TI KI TOI TITI
TIAMAT (HUSBAND OF —) APSU
(SLAYER OF —) MARDUK
TIARA MITER REGNUM CIDARIS
TIARELLA
TIBBU DAZA TEDA
TIBET (CHINESE NAME:) SITSANG

TIBETAN BALTI DRUPA BHOTIA
BHUTIA CHAMPA DROKPA KHAMBA
KHAMBU PANAKA SHERPA TANGUT
BHOTIYA BHUTANI GYARUNG
TIBIA SHIN SHANK CNEMIS
SHINBONE
(SUFF.) CNEMA CNEMIA CNEMIC
CNEMUS
TIBOURBOU CORTEZ
TIC FIXATION
(ONE SUBJECT TO —) TIQUEUR
TICAL BAHT
TICK FAG JAR KEB KED BEAT KADE
NICK PEAK PICK PIKE CHALK CHICK
CRIKE PIQUE STRAP ACARID IXODID
PALLET TALAJE TAMPAN ACARIAN
ARGASID BEDTICK IXODIAN PINOLIA
ARACHNID CARAPATO GARAPATA
GARAPATO TURICATA
(— OFF) IRK MIFF RILE STEAM
(— OF TIME) MOMENT
(PREF.) ACAR(I)(O) CRUTO
TICKED MACKEREL
TICKET LOT TAG COMP BLANK CHECK
DUCAT FICHE TOKEN BALLOT BILLET

COUPON DOCKET PIGEON POLICY
RETURN BENEFIT ETIQUET
CONTRACT DEADHEAD STOPOVER
TRANSFER PASTEBOARD
(— GIVEN WITHOUT CHARGE)
FREEBEE FREEBIE
(COMMISSION —) SPIFF
(FREE —) PASS FREEBEE FREEBIE
(HOT —) RAGE
(LOTTERY —) BLANK HORSE BENEFIT
(SALES —) TRAVELER
(SEASON —) IVORY
(PL.) PAPER
TICKET WINDOW GUICHET
TICKING KISS TICK BEDTICK
TICKLE AMUSE TEASE EXCITE KITTLE
PLEASE THRILL TIDDLE CUITTLE
TICKLISH RISKY GOOSEY KITTLE
KITTLY QUEASY TENDER TOUCHY
TRICKY KITTLISH
TICKSEED COREOPSIS
TICK TREFOIL BEDSTRAW SAINFOIN
TICKSEED
TIDBIT NOSH TRACE SAYNETE
BEATILLE KICKSHAW
TIDDLEYWINK SQUAIL
TIDE FLOW NEAP WAVE AGGER
EAGRE ROUST SPRING OVERTIDE
SEAFLOOD
(— MOVEMENT) LAKIE
(CRIMSON —) BAMA
(KIND OF —) YULE
(PREF.) (HIGH —) PLEMYRA
TIDINGS NEWS WORD RUMOR
SOUND UNCOW ADVICE MESSAGE
(GLAD —) GOSPEL
TIDY RID COSH MACK NEAT SIDE
SMUG SNOD SNUG TAUT TOSH TRIG
WEME CHART DONCY DONSY DOUCE
NATTY NIFTY QUEME TIGHT DONSIE
FETTLE POLITE SPOONY ORDERLY
ALLIGATE MACKLIKE MENSEFUL
SHIPSHAPE
TIE BOW LAP TYE BAND BEND BIND
BOND CAST DRAW KILT KNOT LACE
LASH LOCK ROOT WASH WISP YOKE
ASCOT BRACE CADGE LEASH NEXUS
POINT THRAP THROW TRICE TRUSS
ATTACH BUNDLE CONNEX COPULA
COUPLE FASTEN LIGATE SECURE
DOGFALL FOULARD JAZZBOW
NECKTIE SHACKLE SLEEPER
SPANCEL TABLEAU CROSSTIE
DEADLOCK INTERTIE LIGATURE
STANDOFF STRINGER VINCULUM
(— BENEATH) SUBNECT
(— IN TENNIS) DEUCE
(— IN WRESTLING) DOGFALL
(— KNOT) CAST
(— LEGS) HOBBLE
(— ONIONS) TRACE
(— SCORE) PEELS
(— THE SCORE) EQUALIZE

(— TOGETHER) KNIT LEASH
CONNECT HARNESS
(— UP) SNUB TRAMMEL LIGATURE
TWITCHEL
(— UP SHORT) SNUB
(LEATHER —) WANTY
(MADE-UP —) TECK
(NEEDLEWORK —) BRIDE
(STRING —) BOLO
(PL.) GILLIES
TIE BEAM BALK BAULK BINDER
TIED EVEN FAST KNIT EVENED
SQUARE
TIEPIN PROP SCARFPIN STICKPIN
TIE PLATE TURTLE
TIER ROW BANK DECK RANK CHESS
STORY WITHE DEGREE PINAFORE
(— OF CASKS) RIDER
(— OF GUNS) TIRE
(— OF SEATS) CIRCLE
(— OF SHELVES) STAGE
TIERCE LEASH THIRD UNDERSONG
TIFF MIFF SPAT TIFT
TIFFIN CONDOR
TIGER SHER SHIR TIGRE TIGERKIN
(PREF.) TIGRO
TIGER CAT CHATI MARGAY
TIGERFOOT IPOMOEA
TIGER SHARK DEMOISELLE
TIGER SNAKE ELAPID ELAPOID
TIGHT WET FULL HARD NEAR PANG
SNUG TAUT TIDY TRIG CLOSE DENSE
DRUNK STENT TENSE STINGY
STRAIT STRICT AIRTIGHT
TIGHTEN JAM CALK FIRM FRAP
BRACE CAULK CINCH CLOSE FEEZE
SCREW THRAP WRENCH STRAITEN
(— WITH ROPE) SWIFT
TIGHTFISTED NARROW STINGY
TIGHT-LIPPED SILENT
TIGHTLY FAST HARD SHORT STRAIT
CLOSELY
TIGHTS MAILLOT LEOTARDS
TIGHTWAD FIST MISER PIKER STIFF
TIKVAH (SON OF —) SHALLUM
JAHAZIAH
TILDE TIL WAVE TITTLE
(HAVING A —) CURLY
TILE LUMP SLAT FAVUS KASHI LATER
SLATE IMBREX LAPPET PAMENT
QUARRY SLATER TEGULA AZULEJO
CARREAU CONDUIT PANTILE
QUARREL STARTER MAINTILE
(— IN HOPSCOTCH) PEEVER
(— USED IN MOSAIC) ABACULUS
(HEXAGONAL —) FAVUS
(HOLLOW —) BACKING
(HOPSCOTCH —) PEEVER
(LARGE —) DALLE QUARL QUARLE
(MAH JONG —) HONOR SEASON
(ONE-HALF —) HEAD
(PERSIAN —) KASHI
(ROUNDED —) CREASE

(SMALL —) TILETTE
(SQUARE —) QUADREL QUARREL
(TURKISH —) IZNIK
(PREF.) OSTRAC(O) PLINTHI
TILER HELER HELLIER
TILL TO EAR FIT LOB CASH FARM
PLOW TEAL TOIL DRESS LABOR
UNTIL WHILE FURROW MANURE
PLOUGH TILLER WHILST HUSBAND
SHUTTLE DUCKFOOT OXHARROW
TILLABLE EARABLE
TILLAGE GAINOR MANURE ARATION
CULTURE TILTURE
TILLED GEOM TOILED
TILLER HELM STERN STOOL
HUSBAND KILLIFER
TILLING EARTH FALLOW
TILON
(FATHER OF —) SHIMON
TILT DIP TIP TOP BANK CANT CAVE
COCK HEEL LIST PEAK SWAG TRAP
BRASH HEELD HIELD JOUST STOOP
TIPUP CASTER TILTER TOPPLE
CURRENT TOURNEY ATTITUDE
COCKBILL QUINTAIN
(— BRICK) HACK
(— IN WATER) DABBLE
(— OF BOWSPRIT) STAVE
(— OF NOSE) KIP KIPP
TILTED ACOCK ASTOOP
TILT HAMMER OLIVER
TILTING DIP JOUSTING
TIMANDRA (FATHER OF —)
TYNDAREUS
(HUSBAND OF —) ECHEMUS
PHYLEUS
(MOTHER OF —) LEDA
(SISTER OF —) HELEN
CLYTEMNESTRA
TIMBAL DRUM TYMBALON
TIMBER CAP LOG RIB BEAM BIBB
BUNK BUNT CLOG DRAM FELL FISH
FROG GIRT PUMP RAFF SKID SPAR
SPUR TREE WOOD CAHUY CAVEL
CRUCK FLOOR GRIPE JOIST KEVEL
LEDGE ORGUE PLATE RIDER SISSU
SPALE STICK BEARER BRIDGE
BUMPER CAMBER CORBEL DAGGER
FENDER FOREST KNIGHT LIZARD
ROOFER SISSOO SUMMER TIMMER
BOLSTER CARLING DEADMAN
DIVIDER FALLAGE FUTCHEL FUTTOCK
GROUSER PARTNER PITWOOD
RIBBAND TRANSOM CORDWOOD
COULISSE DOGSHORE FOREHOOK
STRINGER STUMPAGE TRIPSILL
WOODFALL
(— BETWEEN TRIMMERS) HEADER
(— CUT TO LENGTH) JUGGLE
(— IN MINE) COG STULL LIFTER
DIVIDER JUGGLER
(— KEPT DRY) BRIGHT
(— ON SCAFFOLD) LIGGER PUTLOG

(— ON SLED) BUNK
(— PIECE) PUTLOG
(— SAWED AND SPLIT) LUMBER
(— SUPPORTING CAP) LEGPIECE
(— SUSTAINING YARDS) MAST
(— TO PROP COAL) BROB
(CONVEX —) CAMBER
(CURVED —) CRUCK
(CUT —) FELL
(FELLED —) HAG
(FLOOR —) JOIST SUMMER
(FLOORING —) BATTEN
(FOUNDATION —) PILE
(FRAMING —) PUNCHEON
(HORIZONTAL —) REASON
(NORWEGIAN —) DRAM
(PHILIPPINE —) LAUAN
(PRINCIPAL — OF VESSEL) KEEL
(ROOF —) LEVER RAFTER
(ROOFING —S) SILE
(SHIP'S —) CANT KEEL KNEE RUNG
SPUR APRON LEDGE WRONG
DAGGER HARPIN LACING SCROLL
BRACKET FUTTOCK STEMSON
DOGSHORE STANDARD
(SHIPBUILDING —S) STOCKS
DEADWOOD HARPINGS
(SLABBED —) CANT
(SQUARED —) BALK
(SUPPORT —) SILL GIRDER LEDGER
PUNCHEON STRINGER
(SYSTEM OF —S) BOND
(UNCUT —) STUMPAGE
(WEATHERBEATEN —) DRIKI
TIMBERLAND STICKS WOODLAND
TIMBERMAN BRACER
TIMBO CUBE AJARI
TIMRRE TUNE CLANG COLOR KLANG
COLORING
TIMBREL TABOR TABOUR
TIME DAY ELD BELL BOUT HINT HOUR
SELE SITH TIDE WHET ABYSS CHARE
EPOCH FLASH FRIST KALPA SITHE
SPACE STOUN STOUR TEMPO TEMPS
VOLTA WHACK WHILE COURSE
KAIROS PERIOD SEASON STOUND
TEMPUS CADENCE DEWFALL
SESSION MOVEMENT
(— AFTER) POST
(— ALLOWED FOR PAYMENT)
USANCE
(— AND — AGAIN) OFTEN
(— BEFORE WITHDRAWAL) FLOAT
(— BEING) NONCE
(— FOR PAYING) KIST
(— FOR PAYMENT) CREDIT
(— GRANTED) FRIST
(— HENCE) MORROW
(— IN GRAMMAR) TENSE
(— IN SERVICE) AGE
(— INTERVAL) WINDOW
(— INTERVENING) INTERIM
MEANTIME

(— IN THE PAST) LANGSYNE
(— LONG SINCE PAST) YORE
(— OF BEAUTY) BLOOM
(— OF BEGINNING) SPRING
(— OF CRISIS) EXIGENT
(— OF CURRENCY) TENOR
(— OF DYING) LAST
(— OF ELEVENTH ZONE) SAMOA
(— OF EXPIRY) ISH
(— OF EXUBERANCE) CARNIVAL
(— OF FASTING) LENT
(— OF FEASTING) GUTTIDE
(— OF HAPPINESS) CAMELOT
(— OF HIGHEST STRENGTH)
HEYDAY
(— OF INACTIVITY) INTERIM
NONTERM
(— OF LIGHT) DAY
(— OF MATURITY OR DECLINE)
AUTUMN
(— OF MAXIMUM USE) PEAK
(— OF NEWS STORY) BREAK
(— OF OLD AGE) SUNSET
(— OF QUIET) DEAD
(— OF REST) BREATH SABBATH
(— OF TRIAL) PROBATION
(— OF WOE) WOSITH
(— TO COME) FUTURITY
(ANOTHER —) AGAIN
(AT ANOTHER —) ALIAS
(BRIEF —) TINE FLASH THROW
(BY THE —) AGAINST
(CRITICAL —) PINCH
(EACH —) ONCE
(ENDLESS —) PERPETUITY
(EXTENDED —) TRAIN
(FAST —) LENT
(FIT —) TID
(FIXED —) HOUR STEVEN
(FUTURE —) MANANA
(GAY —) FRISK WHOOPEE
(GOOD —) BALL BASH BEANO JOLLY
BARNEY FROLIC HOLIDAY
(HARD —) GYP BUSINESS
(IMMEASURABLY LONG PERIOD OF —
) EON AEON
(INFINITE —) ABYSS
(INTERVENING —) MEANTIME
MEANWHILE
(KIND OF —) PRIME
(LONG —) AGE YEARS
(MUSICAL —) METER METRE
(OLD —S) ELD
(OPPORTUNE —) SEAL SEEL SEIL
SELE
(PAST —) FORETIME
(POINT OF —) MOMENT
(PRESCRIBED —) LIMIT
(QUIET —) SLACK
(RIGHT —) TID
(SECOND —) YET EFTSOON
EFTSOONS
(SET —) TRYST

(SHORT —) TIFF SPACE START
MINUTE STOUND
(SINGLE —) ONCE
(SPARE —) TOOM LEISURE
(SPECIAL —) OCCASION
(STRICT —) MEASURE
(TRIPLE —) TRIPLA
(UNENGAGED —) LEISURE
(UNIT OF —) AEON
(WORKING —) CORE
(PL.) SYSE
(PREF.) CHRON(O) HORO
(SUFF.) AD CHRONE CHRONOUS
SEMIC
TIMEAUS (SON OF —) BARTIMAEUS
TIME CLOCK BUNDY TELLTALE
TIME-HONORED VINTAGE
TIMELESS AGELESS ETERNAL
DATELESS ATEMPORAL
TIMELESSNESS ETERNITY
TIMELY PAT DULY TIDY COGENT
TIMEFUL TIMEOUS TOWARDLY
SEASONABLE TEMPESTIVE
TIME OF YOUR LIFE (AUTHOR OF
—) SAROYAN
(CHARACTER IN —) JOE TOM NICK
KITTY MCCARTHY
TIMEPIECE DIAL CLOCK TIMER
VERGE WATCH GHURRY PENDULE
HOROLGE HOROLOGY
TIMETABLE BRADSHAW SCHEDULE
TIME-WORN RUSTY
TIMID SHY ARGH EERY NESH SELY
SHAN BAUCH BLATE EERIE FAINT
PAVID SCARE SCARY AFRAID
COWARD ASHAMED BASHFUL
CHICKEN FEARFUL FRIGHTY NEBBISH
NERVOUS RABBITY SCADDLE
STRANGE TREMBLY COWARDLY
FEARSOME GHASTFUL RETIRING
TIMOROSO TIMOROUS
PIGEONHEARTED
TIMIDITY SHYNESS TIMERITY
FUNKINESS
TIMIDLY SMALL
TIMNA (BROTHER OF —) LOTAN
(LOVER OF —) ELIPHAZ
(SON OF —) AMALEK
TIMOLEON (FATHER OF —)
TIMODEMUS
(MOTHER OF —) DEMARISTE
TIMON OF ATHENS (AUTHOR OF —
) SHAKESPEARE
(CHARACTER IN —) CUPID TIMON
TITUS CAPHIS LUCIUS FLAVIUS
PHRYNIA LUCILIUS LUCULLUS
PHILOTUS TIMANDRA APEMANTUS
FLAMINIUS SERVILIUS VENTIDIUS
ALCIBIADES HORTENSIUS
SEMPRONIUS
TIMOR (CAPITAL OF —) DILI
(COIN OF —) AVQ PATACA
(ISLAND OF —) MOA LETI LAKOR

(LANGUAGE OF —) TETUM
(TOWN IN —) KUPANG ATAMBUA
TIMOROUS ASPEN FAINT MILKY
TIMID AFRAID COWISH TREPID
FEARFUL FERDFUL MEACOCK
NERVOUS FEARSOME SHEEPISH
TEMEROUS TIMOROSO
TIMOTHY (COMPANION OF —) PAUL
(WIFE OF —) SIF
TIN SN DIXY DIXIE JOVE DIXIE KATIN SWELL
TINNY KHATIN JUPITER PILLION
STANNUM PRILLION TINGLASS
(MFSS —) DIXY DIXIE
(RELATED TO —) STANNIC
(ROOFING —) TERNE
(SHEET —) LATTEN LATTIN
(TIE — CAN TO TAIL) TAILPIPE
(PREF.) STANN(I)(O)
TINAMOU YUTU MACUCA YNAMBU
TATAUPA MARTINET
TINCAL ALTINCAR
TINCTURE BUFO DRUG COLOR
IMBUE SMACK STAIN TAINT TENNE
TINCT ARGENT ARNICA ELIXIR
SATURN DIAMOND SERICON
ARAMAIZE INFUSION LAUDANUM
TAINTURE PAREGORIC
TINDER SPUNK AMADOU TENDRE
FIREBOX
TINE BAY KNAG SNAG TANG GRAIN
OFFER POINT PRONG RIGHT TOOTH
GRAINING TINETARE TINEWEED
(ANTLER'S —) RIGHT CROCKET
SURROYAL
TIN FOIL TAIN
TINGE DYE EYE HUE CAST DASH HINT
TANG TINT WOAD COLOR FLUSH
IMBUE PAINT SAVOR SHADE STAIN
TAINT TINCT TOUCH SEASON
SMUTCH DEPAINT DISTAIN GLIMPSE
DISCOLOR TINCTION TINCTURE
TINGED FLORID GILDED
TINGGIAN ITNEG ITANEG
TINGLE SOO BURN DIRL GELL GIRL
THIRL DINDLE SWIDGE TINKLE
PRINGLE PRINKLE TRINKLE VIBRATE
TINGLY AGOG
TING YAO PORCELAIN
TINHORN ARTY
TINKER PRIG TINK CAIRD FIDDLE
FIDGET MUGGER KETTLER PROJECT
TRAVELER
TINKLE TINK DINDLE DINGLE TINGLE
TRINKLE TWINKLE
TINKLING THIN
TINNER TINKER
TINSEL GAUDY TINSY TINNET
CLINQUANT
TINT DYE EYE COLOR ENNUE GRAIN
SHADE TINCT TINGE SPRAING
(— IN HORSE'S COAT) BLOSSOM
(— WITH COSMETICS) SURFLE
(CLANG —) TIMBRE

TINTED TINCT
TINWORKS STANNARY
TINY TINE BITSY BITTY DEENY SMALL
TEENY TIDDY WEENY ATOMIC BITTIE
WEESHY MINIKIN ATOMICAL
TIP CAP DIP END FEE NER TOP APEX
CANT CAVE COCK DUMP HEEL HELD
HORN KEEL LEAD LIST PALM PIKE
PILE SWAG TILT TYPE VAIL GRIFF
HEELD MUCRO POINT POUCH SPIRE
SPURE STEER CAREEN CENTER
CENTRE TICKLE TIPLET TIPPLE
TOPPLE WHEEZF APICULA
CUMSHAW DERTRUM DOUCEUR
GRIFFIN POINTER PROPINE WRINKLE
APICULUS BONAMANO ENTOMION
FOOTHOLD GRATUITY BAKSHEESH
BACKSHEESH PERQUISITE
(— AT A CASINO) TOKE
(— OF ANTENNA) ARISTA
(— OF BILLIARD CUE) LEATHER
(— OF BIRD'S BILL) DERTRUM
(— OF CHIN) POINT
(— OF CRESCENT) HORN
(— OF ELBOW) NOOP
(— OF FOX'S BRUSH) CHAPE
(— OF SKI) SHOVEL
(— OF SPIDER) BULB
(— OF STAMP) SHOE
(— OF TAIL) TAG
(— OF TOE) POINTE
(— OF TONGUE) CORONA
(— OF UMBO) BEAK
(— OF WHEAT KERNEL) BRUSH
(— OF WHIP) SNAPPER
(— ON ORGAN PIPE) TOE
(— OVER) TOP PURL UPEND
OVERSET
(— UP) CANT COUP COWP
(ABRUPT —) MUCRO
(BOW —) HORN
(GAMBLING —) TOKE
(INWARD —) BANK
(LARGE —S) LARGESS LARGESSE
(RACING —) NAP
(RUBBISH —) TOOM
(PREF.) ACR(O) APIC(O)
TIPCART COUPE COCOPAN
TUMBREL
TIPCAT CAT PIGGY PUSSY KITCAT
PIGGIE
TIPPED BANKED
(EASILY —) CRANK
TIPPER DUMPER THROWER TIPPLER
TIPPET FUR AMICE SCARF STOLE
ALMUCE SINDON LIRIPIPE LIRIPOOP
PELERINE VICTORINE
TIPPLE BIB NIP POT SOT DRAM GILL
BIBBER RIBBLE HUDDLE PUDDLE
SIPPLE TIPPLER TOOTHFUL
TIPPLER SOT SOUSE TOAST WINER
BIBBER BOLLER BOOZER BUBBER
DRAMMER PANURGE POTATOR

TUMBLER WHETTER ALESTAKE MALTWORM

TIPPLING POTTING BIBACITY BIBATION

TIPSTER TOUT PROPHET

TIPSY CUT BOSKY DRUNK FRESH MUSED MUZZY NAPPY OILED ROCKY SLUED TIGHT TOTTY TOZIE BUMPSY GROGGY SCREWY SLEWED SPRUNG SQUIFF EBRIOSE EBRIOUS EXALTED SQUIFFY ELEVATED MUCKIBUS OVERSEEN PLEASANT SQUIFFED

TIPTOE CREEP

TIP-TOP SWELL TIPPY REGULAR TOPPING

TIRADE LAISSE SCREED STOUSH JEREMIAD INVECTIVE PHILIPPIC

TIRAS (FATHER OF —) JAPHETH

TIRE DO FAG HAG LAG SAG BORE CORD FLAT FLOG JADE KILL MOIL SHOE LABOR SPARE WEARY CASING HAGGLE HARASS SICKEN TIRING TUCKER BALLOON EXHAUST FATIGUE FRAZZLE TRACHLE WEAROUT CLINCHER FORSPEND **(— OUT)** HAG FLOG THEAD BEJADE HARASS OVERWEARY **(BURST —)** FLAT BLOWOUT **(KIND OF —)** SNOW RADIAL **(SMOOTH —)** SLICK **(USED —)** REMOULD RETREAD **(WORN —)** CARCASS

TIRED SAD TAM BEAT BOEG DEAD TIRY BLOWN WEARY AWEARY BLEARY BUSHED PLAYED POOPED TAVERT FORWORN SHAGGED TAIVERT FATIGATE FORWAKED

TIREDNESS FATIGUE

TIRESIAS (FATHER OF —) EVERES **(MOTHER OF —)** CHARICLO

TIRESOME DRY DREE FAGGY ALANGE BORING DREICH PROLIX IRKSOME PROSAIC TEDIOUS BORESOME BROMIDIC ENNUYANT LONGSOME **(BECOME —)** CLOY WEAR

TIRHANAH (FATHER OF —) CALEB **(MOTHER OF —)** MAACHAH

TIRIA (FATHER OF —) JEHALELEEL

TIRING DRUDGING

TIRL RISP

TIRO TYRO NEOPHYTE

TIRTHANKARA JINA

TIRZAH (FATHER OF —) ZELOPHEHAD

TISAMENUS (FATHER OF —) ORESTES THERSANDER **(MOTHER OF —)** HERMIONE

TISANE PTISAN TILLEUL

TISSUE FAT WEB CORK FOIL PITH TELA TEXT FACIA GLEBA GRAFT SUBER TRAMA CALLUS DARTOS DIPLOE FABRIC FASCIA LIGNUM PANNUS PHLOEM SHEATH TEXTUS ADENOID ALBUMEN BINDWEB CAMBIUM CLYPEUS EPITELA EXPLANT HYDROME KLEENEX MESTOME NEURINE PHLOEUM TEXTURE TWITTER ADHESION BLASTEMA DESMOGEN ECTODERM ENDODERM EPIPLOON HISTOGEN HYPODERM ISOGRAFT MERISTEM OSTEOGEN PERIDERM PERIDESM POLYPARY STEREOME **(— IN PLANT)** STEREOME **(— IN SEED)** PERISPERM **(— OF FUNGUS)** CENTRUM **(— OF SILK)** SARSNET SARCENET SARSENET **(— OF SKULL)** DIPLOE **(— SURROUNDING TEETH)** GUM **(ADIPOSE —)** FATDEPOT **(BLACK —)** CLYPEUS **(BOTANICAL —)** TRACE **(CELL —)** CORK **(CONNECTING —)** WEB STROMA TENDON LIGAMENT MESENCHYME **(CORK —)** SUBER **(DEAD —)** SLOUGH **(FATTY —)** LARD GREASE **(HARD —)** BONE **(HYPOTHETICAL —)** COAGULIN **(LYMPHOID —)** TONSIL **(NERVE —)** GANGLION **(SOFT —)** FLAB **(VEGETABLE —)** ARMOR **(WOOD —)** LIGNUM VITRAIN **(PL.)** CHIRATA CHIRETTA MESODERM **(PREF.)** FASCIO HIST(I)(IO)(O) HIST(O) HYPHO **(FATTY —)** ADIP(O) **(FIBROUS —)** FIBR(I)(ILLI)(INO)(O) (OSO) IN(O)

TISWIN TESVINO TEXGUINO

TIT TID MESIA TITTY BLUECAP COLETIT MUFFLIN PINNOCK

TITAN BANA LETO MAIA ASURA ATLAS COEUS CREUS CRIOS DIONE THEIA CRONOS CRONUS PALLAS PHOEBE TETHYS THEMIS IAPETUS OCEANUS HYPERION **(AUTHOR OF —)** DREISER **(CHARACTER IN —)** FRANK PETER AILEEN BUTLER PLATOW FLEMING BERENICE LAUGHLIN STEPHANIE COWPERWOOD

TITANESS TETHYS

TITANIA (HUSBAND OF —) OBERON

TITANIC HUGE GREAT TITAN IMMENSE COLOSSAL GIGANTIC

TITANITE SPHENE GROTHITE LEDERITE LIGURITE

TITANIUM DIOXIDE ANATASE

TITA ROOT MISHMI MISHMEE

TITHE DIME DISME TEIND TENTH DECIMA PREBEND TITHING

TITHING BORGH BORROW DECIME DENARY DECENARY

TITHINGMAN DEAN DECURION TUTTIMAN

TITHONUS (FATHER OF —) LAOMEDON
(MOTHER OF —) STRYMO

TITI ORA TEETEE WISTIT SAIMIRI WISTITI IRONWOOD MARMOSET ORABASSU OUISTITI

TITILLATE AMUSE KITTLE TICKLE

TITILLATING GAMY SEXY GAMEY

TITIVATE PRIMP

TITLARK PIPIT TEETING

TITLE (ALSO SEE LEADER, CHIEF, GOVERNOR, RULER) AGA AYA BAN BEG BEY DAN DOM DUE FRA JAM LAR MIR PAN SAG SIR ABBA ABBE AGHA AMIR ANBA BABU DAME DEVI EMIR FRAY GAON GRAF HAJI HERR KHAN KNEZ LARS NAME PANI SIDI SLUG ABGAR ABUNA AMEER BABOO BEGUM CCOYA CLAIM CROWN EMEER FRATE GHAZI GOODY GRACE HADJI HAJJI HAKAM HANUM HONOR KNIAZ KNYAZ LEMMA MIRZA MPRET NAWAB NEGUS NIZAM PANNA PASHA RABBI RIGHT SINGH SOPHI SOPHY THANE UNWAN BASHAW BEGANI COUSIN DEGREE DEMAND DESPOT DOMINE EPONYM EXARCH HANDLE HUZOOR LEGEND MADAME MASTER MEHTAR MISTER PESHWA PREFIX SHERIF SQUIRE SUFFEE TITULE VIDAME ALFEREZ ALTESSE ALTEZZA BAHADUR BARONET CANDACE CAPTION CONVITO CRAWLER DIGNITY EFFENDI EPITHET ESQUIRE FIDALGO GAEKWAR GRAVITY HEADING HIDALGO INFANTE KHEDIVE MAHARAO MESSIRE RABBONI SHAREEF TITULUS VOIVODE BANNERET BASILEUS COMMENDA CONVIVIO EMINENCE GOSPODIN HIGHNESS HOLINESS HOSPODAR INTEREST LOKINDRA MAGISTER MAHARAJA MAHARANA MAHARSHI MISTRESS MONSIEUR PADISHAH PRINCIPE RAUGRAVE SUBTITLE TAMBURAN TITULADO
(— ACQUISITION) USUCAPT
(— HOLDER) OWNER
(— OF BOOK) QUARE
(— OF MEMBER OF PRIMROSE LEAGUE) KNIGHT
(— OF RESPECT) SIR SRI COJA LIEF MIAN SHRI SIDI BURRA HODJA KHAJA KHOJA MADAM SAHIB SIEUR KHOJAH MADAME MILADY
(BENEDICTINE —) DOM
(MOCK —) IDLESHIP

TITMOUSE MAG NUN TIT MAGG OXEYE PARUS SPICK FUFFIT HEFFEL PUFFER TOMTIT VERDIN BLUECAP BUSHTIT COLETIT COLMOSE GOLDTIT GRIGNET HAGMALL JACKSAW MUFFLIN PINCHEM PINNOCK TINNOCK TITMALL TOMNOUP CHICADEE HACKMALL OVENBIRD REEDLING SHABROON SHARPSAW

TITTER GIGGLE CHORTLE SNICKER TWITTER WHICKER

TITTLE DOT JOT IOTA TITLE MINUTE

TITUBATE REEL STAGGER

TITULAR LEGAL NOMINAL HONORARY

TITUS ANDRONICUS (AUTHOR OF —) SHAKESPEARE
(CHARACTER IN —) AARON CAIUS TITUS CHIRON LUCIUS MARCUS MUTIUS TAMORA ALARBUS LAVINIA MARTIUS PUBLIUS QUINTUS AEMILIUS BASSIANUS DEMETRIUS VALENTINE SATURNINUS SEMPRONIUS

TITYUS (FATHER OF —) TERRA JUPITER
(MOTHER OF —) ELARA

TIU ER EAR TIW TYR ZIO ZIU TIWAZ SAXNOT

TIV MUNCHI

TIZZY FLAP SNIT STEW PUCKER SWIVET SWIVVET

TLAKLUIT ECHE LOOT WISHRAM

TLEPOLEMUS (FATHER OF —) HERCULES
(MOTHER OF —) ASTYOCHIA
(SLAYER OF —) SARPEDON

TLINGIT SITKA KOLUSH SUMDUM CHILCAT CHILKAT STIKINE

TMESIS DIACOPE

TNT TROTYL

TO A AD FOR INTO TILL UNTO UPON
(— A CONCLUSION) OUT
(— BE) IBE
(— BE SURE) EVEN
(— COME) BEHIND
(— COMPLETION) DOWN
(— IT) TOOT SESSA
(— PRESS) DOWN
(— SUCH DEGREE) EVEN
(— THAT TIME) UNTIL
(— THE END) AF
(— THE OPPOSITE SIDE) ACROSS
(— THE REAR) ABAFT ASTERN
(— THIS) HERETO
(— THIS PLACE) HERE HITHER
(— VICTORY) ABU ABOO
(— WHAT) WHERETO
(— WIT) NAMELY INNUENDO SCILICET
(PREF.) AC AD AF AG AL AP AS AT INTRO OB

TOAD PAD AGUA BUFO FROG HYLA PIPA PODE HYLID PADDO PADDY PIPAL PIPID TOADY ANURAN CRAPON PEEPER BUFONID CHARLIE CRAPAUD CRAWLER CREEPER FROGLET GANGREL HOPTOAD PADDOCK PODDOCK PUDDOCK QUILKIN REPTILE SERPENT GANGEREL (PREF.) BATRACH(O) PHRYN(O) (SUFF.) BATRACH(O)(US)

TOADFISH SAPO SARPO TOAD GRUBBY SLIMER CABEZON FROGFISH LORICATE SCORPION

TOADFLAX FLAX FLAXWEED FLAXWORT FLUELLEN GALLWEED GALLWORT RAMSTEAD

TOAD RUSH SALTWEED

TOADSTONE BUFONITE

TOADSTOOL CANKER FUNGUS

TOADY FAWN SUCK TOAD ZANY COTTON EARWIG FAWNER FLUNKY GREASE HEELER LACKEY MUCKER YESMAN FLUNKEY JENKINS LACQUEY PLACEBO SHONEEN TRUCKLE BOOTLICK CLAWBACK LICKSPIT PARASITE SYCOPHANT

TOADYING GNATHONIC

TOADYISM FLUNKYISM

TOAST WET TOSS BREDE PROST ROUSE SANTE SKOAL TRINQ BIRSLE BUMPER CHEERS HEATH PLEDGE PROSIT BRISTLE CAROUSE CHEERIO FRIZZLE LEHAYIM PROFACE PROPINE RESPECT SLAINTE WASSAIL BRINDISI SCOUTHER
(— AND ALE) SWIG
(— ONESELF) LEEP
(— TO HEALTH) PROSIT
(DISH WITH —) RAREBIT
(JACOBITE —) LIMP

TOBACCO CANE CAPA HAND LEAF LUGS NAVY POAK POKE QUID ROLL SHAG WEED BACCO BACCY BACKY BROKE CUBAN DARKS FOGUS PETUN REGIE SMOKE SNOUT TABAC TWIST BACKER BRIGHT BURLEY COLORY COWPEN FILLER HAVANA RETURN TOMBAC TUMBAK CAPORAL CRACCUS GAGROOT GORACCO KNASTER LATAKIA NAILROD NICOTIA ORONOKO PERIQUE PIGTAIL SOTWEED UPPOWOC CANASTER HONEYDEW MAKHORKA MARYLAND NICOTIAN ORONOOKO SEEDLEAF VIRGINIA MUNDUNGUS NICOTIANA
(— AND PAPER) MAKINGS
(— CAKED IN PIPE BOWL) DOTTEL DOTTLE TOPPER
(— HAVING OFFENSIVE SMELL) MUNDUNGO
(— IN ROPES) BOGIE
(— JUICE) AMBEER PRAISS
(— MOISTENED WITH MOLASSES) HONEYDEW
(— MOSAIC) WALLOON
(— PASTE) GORACCO
(— ROOM) PRIZERY
(— WORKER) LOOPER LEAFBOY LEAFGIRL
(CAKED —) HEEL
(COARSE —) SHAG SCRAP CAPORAL
(CUT —) CANASTER PICADURA
(DRIED —) TABACUM
(HARD-PRESSED —) NAILROD
(HATING —) MISOCAPNIC
(INDIAN —) GAGROOT PUKEWEED EYEBRIGHT
(INFERIOR —) LUGS
(LADIES' —) CUDWEED
(LOWER LEAVES OF —) FLYING
(MILD —) RETURN
(PERSIAN —) SHIRAZ TUMBEK TUMBEKI
(PERUVIAN —) SANA
(POOR QUALITY —) DOGLEG
(PULVERIZED —) SNUFF
(QUID OF —) CUD
(RAW —) LEAF
(ROLLED —) CARROT
(SMALL PIECE OF —) FIG
(VIRGINIA —) COWPEN VIRGINIA

TOBACCO BROWN TABAC

TOBACCO ROAD (AUTHOR OF —) CALDWELL
(CHARACTER IN —) ADA LOV DUDE RICE ELLIE PEARL BENSEY BESSIE JEETER LESTER

TOBACCO WORM HORNWORM

TOBOGGAN COAST CARIOLE CARRIOLE

TOCHARIAN A AGNEAN

TOCHARIAN B KUCHEAN

TOCSIN ALARUM

TODAY DAY NOW HEUTE NOWADAYS

TODDLE TOT FADGE DADDLE DIDDLE DODDLE PADDLE TOTTLE WADDLE

TODDLER TROT TYKE GANGREL TROTTIE

TODDY TOD TUBA TERRY SAGWIRE

TO-DO FUROR HOOHA SCENE BROUHAHA HULLABALOO ADO FUSS STIR WORK STINK DOMENT HOOPLA FLUSTER FOOSTER FOOFARAW TRAVALLY

TODY ROBIN

TOE TER DIGIT DACTYL HALLUX PIGGIE MINIMUS TOENAIL TRIPPET POULAINE
(— OF BIRD) HEEL
(LITTLE —) MINIMUS
(RUDIMENTARY —) DEWCLAW
(PL.) TUN TAIS TOON
(PREF.) DACTYL(O) DACTYLIO DIGITI DIGITO

TOENAIL
(SUFF.) ONYCHA ONYCHES ONYCHIA
ONYCHIUM ONYCHUS ONYX
TOEPLATE SHOD
TOFF NOB GENT
TOFFEE TAFFY HARDBAKE
BUTTERSCOTCH
TOGA GOWN ROBE TOGUE TRABEA
TOGETHER ONCE SAME ATONE
YFERE BEDENE INSAME JOINTLY
ENSEMBLE
(— WITH) AND INTO
(PREF.) CO COL COM CON COR SYM
SYN
TOGGERY DUDS
TOGGLE COTTAR COTTER TOGGEL
NETSUKE
TOGO (CAPITAL OF —) LOME
(LANGUAGE OF —) EWE TWI MINA
HAUSA KABRAIS LOTOCOLI
(MOUNTAIN IN —) AGOU
(NATIVE OF —) EWE MINA CABRAI
KABRAI OUATCHI
(RIVER IN —) OTI ANIE HAHO MONO
(TOWN IN —) KANDE ANECHO
PALIME SOKODE TSEVIE ATAKPAME
TOHUBOHU RIOT CHAOS DISORDER
CONFUSION
TOI (SON OF —) JORAM
TOIL FAG TUG DARG GRUB HACK
MOIL MUCK PLOD TASK WORK
LABOR SCRAT SLAVE SWINK TWEIL
YAKKA BILDER DRUDGE EFFORT
HAMMER KIAUGH MITHER MOIDER
STRIVE UNRUFE YACKER FATIGUE
TRAVAIL TURMOIL DRUDGERY
INDUSTRY
TOILER PROLE SLAVE MOILER
WORKER
TOILET BOG CAN LOO HEAD JOHN
BIFFY DUNNY PRIVY CRAPPER
BASEMENT BATHROOM DONNIKER
LAVATORY PLUMBING DONNICKER
TOILING WORKADAY
TOILSOME HARD SWEATY
ARDUOUS TOILFUL MOILSOME
SWEATFUL
TOJOLABAL CHANABAL
TOKAY TUCKTOO
TOKEN BUCK CENT HARP SIGN TYPE
BADGE CHECK INDEX SCRIP BEAVER
CASTOR COLLAR COPPER COUPON
DOLLAR EMBLEM JETTON MARKER
OSTENT REMARK SIGNAL TICKET
WITTER AUSPICE COUNTER EARNEST
INDICIA MEMENTO PRESAGE
SYMPTOM TESSERA BUNGTOWN
COINTISE EVIDENCE FOOTSTEP
FORBYSEN INSTANCE KEEPSAKE
MONUMENT SHILLING SIGNACLE
(— OF A COVENANT) SACRAMENT
(— OF LUCK) HANSEL HANDSEL

(— OF POSSESSION) SEISIN
(— OF RESPECT) SALUTE
(— OF SUPERIORITY) PALM
(— OF VICTORY) LAUREL
(CANADIAN —) HARP
(CONFIRMING —) SEAL
(LOVE —) DRURY AMORET
(PORCELAIN —S) PI
(WARNING —) MONUMENT
(PL.) EXONUMIA
TOKHARI KUCHEAN
TOK PISIN CREOLE
TOKYO (— STREET) GINZA
(FORMER NAME OF —) EDO YEDO
TOLA (FATHER OF —) ISSACHAR
TOLD (— PRIVATELY) AURICULAR
TOLERABLE GAY SOSO PRETTY
TARBLE LIVABLE PATIBLE BEARABLE
PASSABLE PORTABLE
TOLERABLY GAIN GEYAN FAIRLY
MEETLY MEETERLY MIDDLING
TOLERANCE MERCY SHERE LEEWAY
REMEDY
TOLERANT SOFT BROAD BENIGN
PATIENT PLACABLE PERMISSIVE
TOLERATE GO BEAR BIDE HACK
HAVE ABEAR ABIDE ALLOW BROOK
SPARE STAND STICK THOLE ACCEPT
ENDURE PARDON PERMIT SUFFER
COMPORT STOMACH SUPPORT
SUSTAIN
TOLERATION WITHGANG
TOLKIEN (— CREATURE) ENT AROD
TOLL JOW TAX JOWL PIKE RENT
KNELL PEAGE CAPHAR EXCISE
OCTROI PEDAGE PESAGE BOOMAGE
KEELAGE LASTAGE LOCKAGE
MULTURE PASSAGE PICCAGE
PIERAGE PONTAGE SCAVAGE
SUMMAGE TERRAGE TOLLAGE
TRONAGE BERTHAGE STALLAGE
WEIGHAGE WHEELAGE
(PL.) CUSTOMS RAHDARI RATTAREE
TOLLHOUSE TOLLERY
TOLLIKER DUMMY
TOLSEN FOOTSTEP
TOLUENE DILUENT
TOLYL CRESYL
TOMAHAWK HATCHET NEOLITH
TOMATO TOM BERRY BURBANK
TOMB PIR BIER CIST MOLE GRAVE
GUACA HUACA MAZAR SPEOS
TABUT THOLE TURBE BURIAL
CHULPA DARGAH DURGAH GALGAL
HEARSE HEROON SAMADH SHRINE
SYRINX THOLOS TROUGH TURBEH
CHULLPA MASTABA OSSUARY
TOMBLET TRITAPH CENOTAPH
CISTVAEN CUBICULO HALLCIST
HYPOGEUM KISTVAEN MARABOUT
MASTABAH MONUMENT TREASURY
MAUSOLEUM SEPULCHER

(— IN CHURCH) SACELLUM
(— OF MOSLEM SAINT) ZIARA ZIARAT
(CAVE —) SPEOS
(PREHISTORIC —) KURGAN
TOMBAC ORSEDE ORSEDUE
TOMBOY HEMP RAMP GAMINE
HOYDEN MADCAP TOMRIG
TOMBSTONE SLAT TITLE THROUGH
TOMCAT GIB TOMMY PODGER
THOMAS
TOMCOD GADE GADID SMELT
GADOID WHITING TOMMYCOD
TOMENTUM WOOL
TOMFOOLERY HELL HORSE
TOM JONES (AUTHOR OF —)
FIELDING
(CHARACTER IN —) TOM BETTY
JENNY JONES NANCY BLIFIL
GEORGE SOPHIA SQUARE WATERS
BRIDGET WESTERN THWACKUM
ALLWORTHY BELLASTON PARTRIDGE
FITZPATRICK NIGHTINGALE
TOMMY FOOL PODGER REQUIN
TOMMYROT WAHOO BALONEY
TOMMY TALKER KAZOO
TOMORROW MANANA MORROW
TOMORN
TOM SAWYER (AUTHOR OF —)
TWAIN CLEMENS
(CHARACTER IN —) AMY JOE SID
TOM FINN HUCK MARY MUFF BECKY
POLLY HARPER POTTER SAWYER
DOUGLAS LAWRENCE ROBINSON
THATCHER
TOMTATE CAESAR
TON TUN TOUN STYLE
TONALAMATL TZOLKIN
TONALITY KEY
TONE A F DO FA LA MI RE SI SO TI
DOH KEY SOH SOL CALL FLAT NOTE
COLOR COUAC DRONE FIFTH FORTE
PRIME SHARP SIXTH SOUND STYLE
TONUS ACCENT DEGREE FOURTH
SECOND FORMANT MEDIANT
PARTIAL DEMITINT ELEVENTH
FORENOTE HARMONIC HEADNOTE
PARAMESE PARANETE SONORITY
(— A DRAWING) STUMP
(— DOWN) DRAB TAME SOFTEN
SUBDUE
(— OF TETRACHORD) TRITE
(— UP) BRACE
(ACCENTED —) SFORZANDO
(BROKEN —) CRACK
(COMPLEX —) KLANG
(DEEP —) BASS
(DOMINANT —) ANIMUS
(DRAWLING —) DRANT DRAUNT
(HIGH-PITCHED —) PIP
(KEY —) KEYNOTE
(KIND OF —) FUZZ
(LOUD —) FORTE

(LOW —) SEMISOUN
(MONOTONOUS —) DRONE
(SHARP NASAL —) TWANG
(SIGNIFICANT —) ACCENT
(SINGLE UNVARIED —) MONOTONE
(STRIDENT —) COUAC
(WHINING —) GIRN
(PREF.) PHON(O)
TONGA (CAPITAL OF —) NUKUALOFA
(COIN OF —) PAANGA SENITI
(ISLAND GROUP OF —) TOFUA VAVAU
HAAPAI NIUAFOO TONGATAPU
NIUATOBUTABU
(ISLAND OF —) ONO TOFUA VAVAU
HAAPAI
(TOWN OF —) NEIAFU
TONGS SNAPS SERVER FORCEPS
GRAMPUS TUEIRON SCISSORS
TONGUE COG GAB CHIB CLAP KALI
NEAP PAWL POLE REED CLACK IDIOM
LADIN VOICE GADABA GLOSSA
KABYLE KALIKA LADINO LANGUE
LINGUA SPEECH CLAPPER DIALECT
FEATHER ILOKANO LANGUET
DOVETAIL LANGUAGE LORRIKER
PLECTRUM
(— IN FLOORING) SPLINE
(— OF BELL) CLAPPER
(— OF JEW'S-HARP) TANG
(— OF LAND) DOAB REACH LANGUE
LANGUET
(— OF MOLLUSC) RASP RADULA
(— OF OXCART) COPE
(— OF SHOE) FLAP KILTY KILTIE
(— OF VEHICLE) NEAP SHAFT
(BELLOWS —) GUSSET
(CELTIC —) BRETON
(GIVE —) PRATE
(GOSSIPING —) CLACK CLACKER
(PART OF —) BUD UVULA FAUCES
LINGUA SEPTUM
(PIVOTED —) PAWL
(ROMANY —) ROMANES
(PL.) GAURA
(PREF.) GLOSS(O) GLOTT(I)(O)
LIGUL(I) LINGU(I)(LI)(O)
(SUFF.) GLOSSA GLOSSIA GLOT
TONGUEFISH SOLE
TONGUE-LASH SCOLD
TONGUE-LASHING RAT TOCO
BUSINESS
TONGUELESS AGLOSSAL
TONGUE-TIED SILENT
TONIC DO DOH ALOE KEEP PICHI
PRIME BRACER SAMBUL SONANT
SUMBUL BONESET CALAMUS
CALOMBO CHIRATA COLOMBA
DAMIANA FUMARIA GENTIAN
KEYNOTE NERVINE SALICIN TONICAL
ANTHEMIS BARBERRY BERBERRY
HELONIAS ROBORANT TRILLIUM
PIPSISSEWA

TONICITY MYOTONIA
TONKA BEAN GAIAC CUMARU
GUAIAC COUMAROU
TONNA DOLIUM
TONNAGE PORTAGE
TONO-BUNGAY (AUTHOR OF —)
WELLS
(CHARACTER IN —) RINK EFFIE FRAPP
GROVE MOGGS SUSAN ARCHIE
EDWARD GEORGE MANTEL MARION
OSPREY GARVELL RAMBOAT
BEATRICE NORMANDY NICODEMUS
PONDEREVO
TONSIL ALMOND KERNEL ADENOID
AMYGDAL AMYGDALA
(PREF.) AMYGDAL(O)
TONSILITIS QUINSY
TONSURE CROWN SHAVE SHEAR
CORONA DIKSHA RASURE
TONSURED PEELED PILLED SHAVED
TOO SO ALSO OVER TROP LUCKY
OVERLY LIKEWISE
(PREF.) OVER
TOOL (ALSO SEE IMPLEMENT AND
INSTRUMENT) AX ADZ AWL AXE BIT
BUR DIE DIG GIN GUN HOB HOE KEY
LAP LOY RIP SAW SAX TAP TIT VOL
ZAX ADZE BORE BRAY BURR CLAW
COMB DADO DISC DISK DUPE EDGE
FILE FLAY FROE FROG FROW GAGE
HACK HAWK HONE LEAF LOOM
MAUL MILL PICK RASP ROLL SATE
SEAX SLED SNAP SPID SPUD GTOP
TAMP TIER VISE AUGER BLADE
BORAL BORER BRAKE BRAND BREAK
BRUSH BURIN CROZE DARBY DOLLY
DRIFT DRILL DUMMY EDGER FLAKE
FLOAT FLUTE GAUGE GOUGE GUIDE
HARDY HORBY HOWEL KNIFE KNURL
LEVEL MAKER MISER MODEL PLANE
POINT PRUNT PUNCH QUIRK SABER
SABRE SCREW SHAVE SHELL SLICE
SLICK SNIPE SPADE SPEAR SPLIT
STAKE STAMP STING STOCK STRIG
STYLE SWAGE TEWEL TOYLE UPSET
VALET WAGON BEADER BEATER
BIDENT BIFACE BLADER BODKIN
BROACH BUDGER BUFFER CALKER
CHASER CHISEL CLEAVE COGGLE
COLTER CRADLE CRANNY CUTTER
DEVICE DIBBLE DIGGER DOCTOR
DRIVER ENGINE FASCET FERRET
FILLET FLANGE FLORET FLUTER
FORMER FRAISE FULLER GIMLET
GLAZER GOFFER GRAVER GUMMER
HACKER HAMMER HEMMER HOGGER
HOLDER HULLER JIGGER JUMPER
LADKIN LASTER LIFTER NIBBER
PALLET PARTER PICKAX PICKER
PLENCH PLIERS PROPER PUPPET
REAMER RIPPER ROCKER RUNNER
SANDER SAPPER SCRIBE SCUTCH

SEATER SHAPER SHAVER SHEARS
SHOVEL SKIVER SLATER SOCKET
SQUARE STYLET STYLUS SWIVEL
TAGGER TASTER TONGUE TREPAN
TURNER TURREL TWILLY VEINER
WAGGON WIGWAG WIMBLE
WORDLE WORMER YANKEE
ABRADER BLOCKER BRADAWL
CALIPER CAULKER CHAMFER
CHIPPER CHOPPER CLEANER
CLEAVER COULTER CREASER
DIAMOND DOLABRA DRESSER
FISTUCA FLANGER FREEZER
FROTTON GRAINER GROOVER
GRUBBER GUDGEON JOINTER
KNOTTER LOGHEAD MITENER
OUSTITI POINTEL POINTER PROFILE
RIVETER ROUGHER ROUNDER
SCAUPER SCORPER SCRIBER
SCRIVER SCURFER SLASHER
SLEEKER SLICKER SPLAYER
SPUDDER STEMMER STRIKER
STROKER TICKLER TREBLET TWIBILL
UPRIGHT WRAITHE AIGUILLE
BIFACIAL BILLHOOK BOOTJACK
BURGOYNE CALLIPER CREATURE
CRIPPLER CROSSCUT CROWFOOT
DUCKFOOT ELEVATOR EXPANDER
FLOUNDER GRAVETTE GRIFFAUN
POLISHER PRITCHEL PROPERTY
PUNCHEON RAVEHOOK RECAPPER
SCRAPPLE SCULPTOR SPLITTER
STIPPLER STRICKLE STRINGER
SURFACER THWACKER TOLLIKER
WARKLOOM WORKLOOM
SCRATCHER
(— A BOOK) FINISH
(BORING —) TREPAN
(CHEF'S —) WHISK SPATULA
(PL.) TEW FISH GEAR TRADE
CUTLERY GIBBLES PIONERY
ENGINERY
TOOLED GOFFERED
(— WITHOUT GILDING) BLIND
TOOLHOLDER TURRET MONITOR
TOOLHOUSE COPHOUSE
TOOLING (— ON BOOK) GOFFERING
TOOLSHED DOGHOUSE
TOON LIM CEDAR TOONWOOD
TOOT BLOW TOWT BINGE BLAST
SOUND SPREE TRUMPET
TOOTH BIT COG GAM JAG PEG DENS
DENT FANG LEAF RASP SNAG TIND
TINE TUSH TUSK CRENA IVORY
MOLAR PEARL PRONG RAKER TENON
BROACH CANINE CUSPID CUTTER
DENTAL INDENT JOGGLE TRIGON
TRITOR DENTILE DIVIDER GRINDER
INCISOR LATERAL SURIDENT
UNCINUS ABUTMENT BICUSPID
BLEPHARA DENTICLE EYETOOTH
GAGTOOTH MARGINAL PREMOLAR

SAWTOOTH SPROCKET TOOTHLET
TRIGONID CARNASSIAL
(— OF A MOSS) BLEPHARA
(— OF HORSE) DIVIDER
(— OF MOLLUSC) MARGINAL
(— OF PINION) LEAF
(— OF RADULA) UNCINUS
(— ON ROTATING PIECE) WIPER
(ARTIFICIAL —) DUMMY PONTIL
(CANINE —) CUSPID HOLDER
LANIARY CYNODONT DOGTOOTH
EYETOOTH
(GEAR —) COG GUB DENT
ADDENDUM SPROCKET
(HARROW —) TINE
(MOLAR —) WANG
(OF SURFACE OF A —) MESIAL
(PART OF —) GUM NECK PULP ROOT
CROWN DENTIN ENAMEL
CEMENTUM
(UPPER SURFACE OF —) TABLE
(PREF.) DENT(ATO)(I)(INO)(O)(ODO)
ODONT(O)
(SUFF.) DENT(ATE) ODON(T)(TA)(TES)
(TIA)(TY) ODUS
TOOTHACHE WORM DENTAGRA
TOOTHED SERRATE VIRGATE
SERRATED PECTINATE
(SUFF.) ODON ODUS
TOOTHLESS GUMMY
TOOTHPICK QUILL ARKANSAN
TOOTHSOME SAVORY PALATABLE
TOOTHWORT CROWTOE
COOLWORT DENTARIA PEPPERROOT
TOO-TOO ULTRA LADIDA
TOP CAP COP GIG NUN TAP TIP ACME
APEX BEAT COCK CULM HEAD HELM
ROOF SKIM STOP BLOOM CHIEF
COVER CREST CROWN FANCY GIGGE
OUTDO PITCH RIDGE SHIRT SPIRE
STRIP TOTUM TRUMP UPPER
CALASH CAPOTE CULMEN SUMMIT
UPWARD VERTEX CACUMEN
SPINNER ROUNDTOP SURMOUNT
TEETOTUM CULMINATION
(— FOR CHIMNEY OR PIPE) COWL
HOOD
(— FOR PEDESTAL) DADOCAP
(— OF ALTAR) MENSA
(— OF AUTOMOBILE) HEAD HOOD
(— OF BIRD'S HEAD) PILEUM
(— OF CAPSTAN) DRUMHEAD
(— OF FURNACE) ARCH
(— OF GLASS) PRETTY
(— OF HEAD) MOLD PATE MOULD
SCALP VERTEX
(— OF HELMET) SKULL
(— OF HILL) KNAG KNAP KNOLL
(— OF INGOT) CROPHEAD
(— OF MINING SHAFT) PITHEAD
(— OF MOUNTAIN) MAN
(— OF PLANT OR TREE) CROP

(— OF ROOF) DECK
(— OF SPINDLE) COCKHEAD
(— OF THE LINE) AONE
(— OF THUNDERCLOUD) INCUS
(— OF WAVE) COMB
(— OF WOODEN STAND) CRISS
(—S OF CROP) SHAW
(BLOW ONE'S —) SPEW
(BOOT —) RUFF
(BOX —) COUPON
(CARRIAGE —) CALASH
(PEG —) PEERIE
(RESEMBLING A —) STROBIC
(SITUATED AT —) APICAL
(SPINNING —) PEERY PEERIE
(PREF.) ACR(O)
(SPINNING —) RHOMB(O)
TOPAZ PYCNITE PYCNIUM
PHSALITE
TOPCOAT OVERCOAT SIPHONIA
TOPE SOT DHER DHERI STUPA
DAGOBA SOUPFIN
TOPER BOUSER CUPMAN POTMAN
POTTER SIPPER SOAKER SUPPER
TROUGH BOMBARD POTLING
SWILLER TOSSPOT BLACKPOT
DRUNKARD MALTWORM
TOPI TIANG
(MATERIAL FOR —) PITH
TOPIC HARE ITEM TEXT HOBBY
THEMA THEME BURDEN GAMBIT
GROUND MATTER SUBJECT
OCCASION
(STOCK —) TOPOS
TOPKNOT TUFT CREST ONKOS
TOPPING
TOPMAN COB
TOPMINNOW GUPPY LIMIA
GULARIS HELLERI SAILFIN
GAMBUSIA MOLLIENSIS
TOP-NOTCH APLUS
TOPOGRAPHIC TERRAIN
TOPPER CAP FEZ HAT LID TAM BERET
TOPPLE TIP TOP TILT LEVEL UPEND
TOTTLE
TOPS AONE
TOPSAIL RAFFE RAFFEE
TOPSOIL KELLY
TOPSTONE CAPSTONE
TOPSWARM TOPCAST
TOPSY-TURVY COCKEYED
REELRALL
TOQUE ZATI MUNGA MACACO
RILAWA MACAQUE
TOQUILLA JIPIJAPA
TOR CRAG
TORCEL BURN BERNE BORNE
TORCH DUCK JACK LAMP LINK LUNT
PINE TEAD WASE WISP BLAZE
BRAND FLARE LIGHT MATCH FOCKLE
LAMPAD MASHAL MUSSAL
BRANDON CRESSET GRIDDLE

LUCIGEN ROUGHIE (BROIL)
FLAMBEAU
(KIND OF —) PLASMA
(PREF.) DAD(O) LAMPADE
TORCHBEARER KERYX LINKBOY
LINKMAN DADUCHUS TORCHMAN
TOREADOR TORERO CAPEADOR
TORII (PART OF —) NYKI DAIWA
KASAGI KUSABI LINTEL GAKUZUKA
CROSSPIECE
TORIL CHIQUERO
TORMENT WO RAG TAW TRY WOE
BAIT BALE FRET MOIL PAIN PANG
PINE RACK SOOL TEAR TUCK CHEVY
CURSE DEVIL GRILL HARRY SCALD
TEASE TWIST WRING CHIVVY
HARASS HARROW HECTOR INFEST
NEEDLE PLAGUE TRAVEL AFFLICT
ANGUISH BEDEVIL CRUCIFY HAGRIDE
HATCHEL MALISON PERPLEX
PINDING TERRIFY TORTURE TRAVAIL
CRUCIATE DISTRAIN LACERATE
MACERATE
(EXTREME —) AGONY
TORMENTED RODE CRUCIATE
TORMENTIL SEPTFOIL
TORMENTING PLAGUY
TORMINA TORSION
TORN RENT BROKEN RAGGED
BLASTED LACERATE LACERATED
TORNADO VORTEX CYCLONE
TRAVADO TWISTER
TORPEDO FISH SHELL SQUIB BATOID
HOAGIE
TORPID FOUL NUMB BROSY INERT
SODDEN STUPID TOGGER LANGUID
TORPENT COMATOSE COMATOUS
SLUGGISH
TORPIFY DAZE ETHERIZE
TORPOR COMA SLEEP SWOON
ACEDIA ACCIDIE SLUMBER
LETHARGY
(PREF.) NARC(O)
TORQUE BEE SARPE TWIST
TORREFY PARCH
TORRENT FLOW RUSH FLOOD SPATE
STREAM NIAGARA CATARACT
(— OF WORDS) BLATTER
TORREYA SAVIN TUMION
TORRID HOT SULTRY AUSTRAL
BOILING
TORSALO BERNE
TORSION STRESS DIDROMY
TORSK CUSK
TORT LIBEL WRONG
TORTE DOBOS
TORT-FEASOR ACTOR
TORTICOLLIS WRYNECK
TORTILLA TACO BREAD BURRITO
TOSTADO ENCHILADA QUESADILLA
(— CHIP) NACHO
(FRIED —) TACO

TORTOISE EMYD BEKKO GAPER
COOTER GOPHER TURTLE EMYDIAN
HICATEE MUNGOFA TESTUDO
GALAPAGO KASHYAPA SHELLPAD
SHELLPOT TERRAPIN
(PREF.) CHEL(O)(Y)
TORTOISESHELL CAREY
TORTUOUS CRANKY SCREWY
SINUATE WRIGGLY SINUATED
TORTURE GYP TAW BOOT CARD FIRE
PAIN PANG PINE RACK AGONY
SCREW TWIST ENGINE EXTORT
IMPALE MARTYR AFFLICT AGONIZE
ANGUISH BOOTING CRUCIFY
PERPLEX TORMENT MARTYRDOM
STRAPPADO
(METHOD OF —) FALANGA
TORTURER BOURREAU
TORUS CORK TORE DONUT BASTON
BOLTEL BOUTELL BOWTELL
DOUGHNUT THALAMUS
TORY BANDIT OUTLAW ROBBER
PEELITE TANTIVY ABHORRER
LOYALIST
TOSS BUM COB LAB SHY BUNG
CANT CAST CAVE DOSS FLAP FLIP
HIKE PASS SHAG SLAT TOUT CHAFE
CHUCK FLICK FLING FLIRT FLURR
HEAVE PITCH TEAVE THROW
BETOSS BOUNCE DANDLE
TOTTER WALTER WELTER WENTLE
BLANKET TURMOIL WAMPISH
WHEMMEL
(— ABOUT) VEX SWAB TAVE STREW
POPPLE THRASH THRESH TORFLE
WAMPISH
(— A COIN) SKY
(— A JACK) LAG
(— ASIDE) BANDY
(— AWAY) BLOW
(— CONTEMPTUOUSLY) SLIGHT
(— HEAD) CAVE GECK BRANK
(— IN BLANKET) CANVASS
(— OFF) SWAP SWOP
(— OF HORSE'S HEAD) CHACK
(— OF THE HEAD) HEEZE
(— ON WAVES) SURGE
(— THE LIMBS ABOUT) SPRAWL
(— TO AND FRO) WALK
(— TOGETHER CONFUSEDLY)
SCRAMBLE
(— WITH THE HORNS) DOSS HIKE
TOSSING SURGING
(— OF BULLFIGHTER) COGIDA
TOSTAO TESTON
TOT ADD DRAM
TOTAL ADD SUM TAB TOT DEAD
MERE TALE COUNT GROSS MOUNT
SLUMP SUMMA UTTER WHOLE
ENTIRE GLOBAL OMNIUM SUMMED
TOTTLE EMBRACE FOOTING
GENERAL PERFECT ABSOLUTE

COMPLETE ENTIRETY SURMOUNT
TEETOTAL
(REACH THE — OF) RUNTO
(PREF.) HOL(O)
TOTALED KAPUT WRECKED
DEMOLISHED
TOTALITY ALL BODY HEAP BEING
ALLNESS ECOLOGY ETERNITY
HUMANITY INTEGRAL INTERVAL
OMNITUDE SUMTOTAL
TOTALLY COLD GOOD QUITE
WHOLLY
TOTE ADD LUG LOAD PACK CARRY
BURDEN CONVEY
TOTEM HUACA
**TO THE LIGHTHOUSE (AUTHOR
OF —)** WOOLF
(CHARACTER IN —) LILY PRUE JAMES
MCNAB ANDREW BANKES RAMSAY
BRISCOE CAMILLA CHARLES
TANSLEY WILLIAM CARMICHAEL
TOTTER TOT REEL ROCK TOIT WALT
SHAKE WAVER COGGLE DADDLE
DODDER DOTTER FALTER HOTTER
JOGGLE STAVER SWERVE TITTER
TOTTLE WAMBLE WANGLE WAPPER
BRANDLE FRIBBLE STAGGER
TREMBLE WHITHER TITUBATE
VACILLATE
(PREF.) LABE
TOTTERING LURCH SHAKY GROGGY
CRAMBLY PALSIED RICKETY TOTTERY
TITUBANT WAMBLING
TOU (SON OF —) HAMATH
TOUCAN TOCO TUCANA ARACARI
TOUCH GET RAP TAG TIG TIP ABUT
BILL DASH FEEL HAND KISS KNEE
MEET PALP PEAL PLAY RAKE RINE
SCAM TACT TAKE FRAUD GLISK
GRAZE GROPE SPICE TAINT TASTE
TATTO TINGE TRAIT TREAT AFFECT
ATTAIN CARESS FINGER GLANCE
HANDLE REGARD SCRUFF SMUTCH
STRAIN TACTUS TWITCH ATTAINT
ATTINGE CONTACT FEELING PALPATE
SOUPCON TACTION FLOURISH
TINCTURE
(— A KEY) STRIKE
(— BRIEFLY) GLANCE
(— CARESSINGLY) FLATTER
(— CLOSELY) IMPINGE
(— DEEPLY) PIERCE
(— FOREHEAD —) KNUCKLE
(— GENTLY) DAB TAT TICK BRUSH
(— LIGHTLY) GRAZE SCUFF SKIFF
(— OF BRUSH) HAND
(— OF COLOR) EYE
(— OF PAINT) GLOB
(— OF PEN) STROKE
(— OF PLEASURE) GLISK
(— ON) PERSTRINGE
(— RIGHTLY) NICK
(— UP) TATT

(DELICATE —) STROKE
(FINISHING —) HOODER COPECTONE
(PAINTING —) ACCENT
(SLIGHT —) SKIFF SMATCH
(SPIRITUALISTIC —) RAPPORT
(PREF.) TAC TACTO TANGO THIGMO
THIXO
(SUFF.) APHIA
(HAVING A — OF) ISH ISTIC
TOUCHDOWN ROUGE
(MAKE A —) LAND
TOUCHED FEY DOTTY
TOUCHING ABOUT LIBANT TENDER
AGAINST CONTACT TANGENT
ADJACENT PATHETIC POIGNANT
AFFECTING CONTINUOUS
(— LIGHTLY) LAMBENT
(— THE MIND) PUNGENT
TOUCHSTONE TEST TOUCH LYDITE
BASANITE STANDARD
TOUCHWOOD FUNK MONK PUNK
SPUNK PUNKWOOD
TOUCHY HUFFY MIFFY SNAKY TESTY
FEISTY KITTLE SNAKEY SNUFFY
SPUNKY TENDER TETCHY GROUCHY
NERVOUS PEEVISH PEPPERY
STROPPY TEMPERY PETULANT
TICKLISH
TOUGH RUM BHOY HARD TAUT WIRY
BULLY BUTCH CLUNG HARDY STIFF
STOUT WITHY BALLSY KNOTTY
SINEWY STARCH STRONG HICKORY
BULLYBOY LEATHERY UNTENDER
ROUGHNECK TENACIOUS
(NOT —) TENDER
TOUGHEN TAW ANNEAL ENDURE
HARDEN TEMPER
(— METAL) PLANISH
TOUGHENED CLUNG
TOUGHIE LULU
TOUGHNESS TUCK FIBER FIBRE
STRENGTH TENACITY
TOUPEE RUG DOILY SCALP POSTICHE
TOPPIECE
TOUR GIRO TURN SWING TOWER
TURUS JUNKET SAFARI JOURNEY
INVASION PROGRESS TOURETTE
(— OF DUTY) HERD STATION
(CANARY —) GLUCK GLUCKE
TOURACO LORY LOURIE TURAKOO
TOURBILLON KARRUSEL
TOUR DE FORCE STUNT
TOURIST TOURER TRIPPER VISITANT
RUBBERNECK HOLIDAYMAKER
TOURMALINE SHORL SCHORL
DRAVITE ACHROITE SIBERITE
TOURNAMENT TILT JERID JEREED
JOUSTS TOURNEY BONSPIEL
CAROUSEL
TOURNEUR DEALER
TOURNEY PLAY
TOURNIQUET GARROT STANCH
TWISTER STANCHER TORCULAR

TOUSLE MUSS SOOL SOWL RUMPLE
　　TOOZLE
TOUSLED TAUTED TOWZIE
　　TUMBLED UNKEMPT
TOUT SPIV BRUIT PLIER BARKER
　　STEERER TIPSTER
TOW CRIB HAUL PULL HURDS STUPE
　　TRACK TRACT CODILLA CORDELLE
　　(KIND OF —) SKI
TOWAGE TRACKAGE
TOWAI BIRCH KAMAHI
TOWARD AD INTO TORT ANENT
　　ANENST AGAINST FORNENT
　　ADVERSUS GAINWARD
　　(— CENTER) CENTRAD
　　(— CENTER OF EARTH) DOWN
　　(— INTERIOR) INBY INBYE
　　(— ONE SIDE) ASLANT
　　(— THE END) SF
　　(— THE HEAD) ANTERIOR
　　(— THE MOUTH) ORAD
　　(— THE REAR) ABACK DORSAD
　　BACKWARD
　　(— THE RIGHT) DEXTRAD
　　(— THE SIDE) LATERAD
　　(— THE STERN) AFTER
　　(PREF.) AC AD AF AG AL AP AS AT IL
　　IM IN INTRO IR OB PROS
　　(SUFF.) AD
　　(GOING —) PETAL
TOWEL CLOUT WIPER DIAPER
　　LAVABO RUBBER
　　(WORD ON —) HIS HERS
TOWER TOR PEEL PIKE REAR RISE
　　SOAR SPUR TOUR BABEL BROCH
　　HEAVE MINAR MOUNT PYLON SIKAR
　　SPIRE STUPA TEXAS ASCEND ASPIRE
　　BELFRY CASTLE CHULPA DOKHMA
　　DONJON GOPURA ROLLER RONDEL
　　SPRING TURRET BASTIDE CHULLPA
　　DERRICK GIRALDA LANTERN
　　MIRADOR NURAGHE SHIKARA
　　SIKHARA STEEPLE TALAYOT
　　TORREON TOURNEL TRACKER
　　TURRION BARBICAN BASTILLE
　　CLOGHEAD DOMINEER RONDELLE
　　SCRUBBER TOURELLE TOWERLET
　　PEPPERBOX
　　(— CONTAINING COKE) SCRUBBER
　　(— FOR SENTINEL) GUERITE
　　(— OF FORT) SPUR
　　(— OF MOSQUE) MINARET
　　(— OF SILENCE) DAKHMA
　　(— ON SUMMIT) PIKE
　　(— OVER) DROWN BESTRIDE
　　(ATTACHED —) DETAIL
　　(BELL —) CARILLON CAMPANILE
　　(BIBLICAL — SITE) EDAR
　　(CONNING —) SAIL
　　(FRACTIONATING —) STILL
　　(KIND OF —) MARTELLO
　　(PYRAMIDAL —) SIKAR VIMANA
　　SHIKARA SIKHARA

(SIEGE —) BRATTICE
(SIGNAL —) BANTAYAN
(WIND —) BADGIR
(PREF.) PYRGO TURRI
TOWERING EMINENT SUPERNAL
　　AMBITIOUS
TOWERMAN LEVERMAN
TOWER MUSTARD CRUCIFER
TOWHEE JOREE CHEWINK
　　CHEEWINK
TOWING TRACKAGE
TOWLINE CORDELLE
TOWN BY BYE HAM WON BURG
　　CAMP CITY STAD TOON WENE WICK
　　BAYAN BORGO BOURH BRUGH
　　BURGH DERBY MACHI PLACE PLECK
　　SIEGE STAND STEAD VILLE CIUDAD
　　HAMMON ORANGE PUEBLO STAPLE
　　BASTIDE BOROUGH CHESTER
　　OPPIDUM QUIVIRA TOWNLET
　　BOOMTOWN BOURGADE ENCEINTE
　　HOMETOWN TOWNSHIP
　　(DESOLATED —) GUBAT
　　(DULL —) PODUNK
　　(FORTIFIED —) BURG BURGH
　　ENCEINTE
　　(KIND OF —) ONEHORSE
　　(MILITARY —) CANTONMENT
　　(MUSHROOM —) CAMP
　　(MYTHICAL —) QUIVIRA
　　(SMALL —) SHTETL SHTETEL
　　(UNFORTIFIED —) BOURGADE
　　(UNIMPORTANT —) PODUNK
　　(WALLED —) CHESTER
　　(PL.) PARGANA
　　(SUFF.) GRAD
TOWN CRIER BELLMAN
TOWN HALL HALL CABILDO
　　RATHAUS TOLBOOTH
　　STADHOUSE
TOWNSHIP DEME DORP VILL BAYAN
　　TREEN BOROUGH
TOWNSMAN CAD CIT DUDE SNOB
　　TOWNY TOWNEE BURGHER CITIZEN
　　COCKNEY OPPIDAN
　　(PL.) BURGWARE
TOWROPE TOW CABLET GUNLINE
　　TOWLINE CORDELLE
TOXALBUMIN ROBIN PHALLIN
TOXEMIA BLACKLEG ECLAMPSIA
TOXIC VENOMOUS POISONOUS
TOXIN BOTULIN EXOTOXIN
TOY ARK DIE GAY TOP COCK DOLL
　　FOOL MOVE PLAY YOYO BLOCK
　　CORAL DALLY FLIRT HAPPY KNACK
　　LAKIN PLAID SPORT TRICK WALLY
　　BAUBLE DANDLE DIDDLE DOODLE
　　FADDLE FINGER FIZGIG GEWGAW
　　LAKING PRETTY PUPPET RATTLE
　　SUCKER BLOWOUT CRICKET DREIDEL
　　PLAYOCK TANGRAM TRINKET
　　TUMBLER WHIZZER GIMCRACK
　　KICKSHAW PINWHEEL SKIPJACK

SQUAWKER SQUEAKER TEETOTUM
WINDMILL ZOETROPE
(— AMOROUSLY) MIRD
(— RACER) SLOTCAR
(— WITH) PADDLE
(— WITH FINGERS) PADDLE
(FLYING —) PIGEON
(MUSICAL —) OCARINA
(OPTICAL —) STROBOSCOPE
THAUMATROPE
(SOFT —) GONK
(TOUGH —) GIJOE
TOYING DALLIANCE
TOYON TOLLON CHAMISO
TRABEA TOGA
TRACE RUN TUG WAD CAST ECHO
HINT LICK MARK RACK SCAN SHOW
SIGN STEP TANG TINT TROD BRING
GHOST GLEAM GLIFF GRAIN PRINT
RELIC SHADE SPICE SPOOR STAMP
STEAD THEAT TINGE TOUCH TRACK
TRACT TRAIL TRAIN TRESS DERIVE
ENGRAM HARBOR LACING RESENT
SHADOW SKETCH SMUTCH STRAIN
STREAK SWATHE COCKEYE GLIMPSE
KENNING MENTION REMNANT
SOUPCON SURMISE SYMPTOM
THOUGHT UMBRAGE VESTIGE
WHISPER DESCRIBE ENGRAMME
FOOTSTEP SKERRICK TINCTURE
WAINROPE SIMULACRUM
(— A BEE) COURSE
(— A CURVE) SWEEP
(— A DESIGN) CALK
(— MATHEMATICALLY) GENERATE
(— OF A HARE) FARE
(— ON CHART) PRICK
(— THE COURSE OF) DEDUCE
(HARNESS —) TUG THEAT TREAT
(HAVE A —) SMACK
(MEMORY —) ENGRAM ENGRAMME
(SLIGHT —) GHOST STAIN SMATCH
SPARKLE
(SLIGHTEST —) SCINTIL
(PL.) FEUTE
(SUFF.) (HAVING A —) ISH ISTIC
TRACER SEEKER OUTLINER
SEARCHER
TRACERY FANWORK FROSTING
TRAILERY
TRACHEA ARTERY WINDPIPE
(— OF CRANE) TRUMP
TRACHEID HYDROID
TRACHYANDESITE ARSOITE
VULSINITE
TRACHYTE PIPERNO
TRACING BAROGRAM POLYGRAM
TRAILING
TRACK DOG PUG RAT RUT TAN WAD
WAY CLEW CLUE DRAW FARE FOIL
FOOT HUNT LANE MARK PAGE PATH
PIST RACE RACK RAIK RAIL ROAD
SHOE SLOT SPUR TROD VENT BLOCK

CHUTE DRIFT FEUTE HOUND LODGE
PISTE PLANE SLIDE SPACE SPOOR
STEAD SWATH TRACE TRACT TRADE
TRAIL TRAIN TREAD BEARER COURSE
GROOVE HARBOR LADDER RETURN
RUNWAY SIDING SLEUTH STRAIN
STREAM SWATHE CHANNEL FOILING
FOOTING PATHWAY TANGENT
TRAFFIC VESTIGE BACKBONE
FOOTSTEP GUIDEWAY TRANSFER
TRECKPOT TREKPATH WAGONWAY
(— ALONG CREST) RIDGEWAY
(— BY SMELL) SCENT
(— FOR ROPE) CHANNEL
(— GAME) DRAW
(— OF BLOOD) PERSUE
(— OF DEER) SLOT STRAIN
(— OF GAME IN GRASS) FOILING
(— OF HARE) FILE
(— OF SHIP) WAKE
(— OF WOUNDED BEAST) PERSUE
(— ON PRINTING PRESS) BANK
BEARER
(BEATEN —) PISTE
(BRANCH —) SIDELINE
(CYCLING —) VELODROME
(RACING —) SPEEDWAY
(RAILROAD —) LEAD SPUR STUB
SIDING TANGENT APPROACH
BACKBONE
(RUNNING —) FLAT CINDERS
(SHORT BRANCH —) RETURN
(SIDE —) LIE HOLE
(SKATER'S —) FLAT
(SLIPPERY —) SLIDE
(TEMPORARY —) SHOOFLY
(WINDING —) SERPENTINE
(WORM —) NEREITE
(PREF.) ICHN(O)
TRACKER PUGGI PUGGY TRAILER
TRAILMAN
TRACKLESS INVIOUS PATHLESS
TRACKMAN SPIKER
TRACT AREA BEAT DUAR FLAT ZONE
CAMPO CLIME COAST DRIVE ESSAY
FIELD GRABE HORST PATCH SWEEP
TRACK BARONY BUNDLE EXTENT
PARCEL REGION ENCLAVE EURIPUS
QUARTER ROYALTY TERRAIN
TRACTUS BROCHURE CAMPAGNA
CAMPAIGN CINGULUM DISTRICT
FARMHOLD FORESTRY PAMPHLET
PROVINCE TOWNSITE TREATISE
(— KEPT IN NATURAL STATE) PARK
(— OF BARREN LAND) BARREN
DERELICT
(— OF BRAIN FIBERS) PEDUNCLE
(— OF GRASSLAND) PRAIRIE
(— OF LAND) CRU DOAB DUAB DUAR
GORE MARK BLOCK CHASE CLAIM
EJIDO FRITH GRANT LAINE SCOPE
SWELL TALUK EIGHTY ESTATE
FOREST GARDEN ISLAND POLDER

STRATH AIRPORT QUILLET RESERVE
TERRAIN BOUNDARY CLEARING
DERELICT FARMHOLD INTERVAL
SCABLAND SLASHING
(— OF MUDDY GROUND) SLOB
(— OF OPEN UPLAND) DOWN
DOWNS
(— OF UNCOVERED ICE) GLADE
(— OF WASTE LAND) HEATH
(BOGGY —) RUNN MORASS
(CLAYEY —) TAKYR
(CLEARED —) ILLW WOM JOOM
(DRY —) RINGANG
(— TREELESS —) STEPPE
(GENITAL —) REARING
(IRREGULAR —) GORE
(OPEN —) VEGA SLASH
(SANDY —) DEN DENE LANDE
(SHRUBBY —) MONTE
(SWAMPY —) FLOW BAYGALL
(UNOCCUPIED AND UNCULTIVATED
—) DESERT
(WATERLESS —) THIRST
TRACTABLE EASY SOFT TAME
BUXOM TAWIE DOCILE GENTLE
TOWARD DUCTILE FLEXILE PLIABLE
AMENABLE FLEXIBLE GUIDABLE
OBEDIENT TOWARDLY YIELDING
MALLEABLE
TRACTARIANISM PUSEYISM
TRACTION DRAFT DRAUGHT
TRACTOR CAT MULE DRAGON
BOBTAIL CRAWLER PEDRAIL
AGRIMOTOR
(TRAILER —) RIG
TRADE CHAP CHOP COUP DEAL SELL
SWAP CHEAP CRAFT GRAFT PRICE
TREAD TROKE TRUCK BAKERY
BARTER CHANGE EMPLOY HANDLE
METIER MISTER NIFFER OCCUPY
SCORCE SCORSE BARGAIN CALLING
CHAFFER FACULTY MYSTERY
SCIENCE BUSINESS CABOTAGE
EXCHANGE PLUMBING
MERCHANDISE
(OLD-CLOTHES —) FRIPPERY
(PETTY —) DICKER
(SUBSIDIARY —) SIDELINE
(SUFF.) ERY
TRADEMARK CHOP LOGO MARK
BRAND COUPON
TRADER SART BANYA PLIER BALIJA
BANIAN BANYAN CHETTY DEALER
MONGER NEPMAN TROKER
CHAPMAN MARWARI SANGLEY
TRUCKER ASTORIAN CHANDLER
KURVEYOR MERCHANT OPERATOR
(HORSE —) JOCKEY
(INEXPERIENCED —) LAMB
TRADESMAN CIT BAKAL COOPER
EGGLER SELLER TENSOR ARTISAN
FRUITER GOLADAR OCCUPIER
UPHOLDER

TRADESWOMAN WINSTER
TRADING CABOTAGE
(COASTAL —) CABOTAGE
TRADITION CABAL STORY SUNNA
CABALA SMRITI SUNNAH THREAP
HALACHA HALAKAH HEREDITY
HERITAGE TRANSFER
NISI LEGEND
TRADITIONAL CLASSIC POMPIER
TRADUCE ILL SLUR ABUSE DEFAME
MALIGN REVILE VILIFY ASPERSE
DETRACT SCANDAL SLANDER
TRAFFIC COUP DEAL MANG MART
MONG BROKE TRADE BARTER
PALTER TRAVEL CHAFFER DEALING
PASSAGE BUSINESS CHAFFERY
COMMERCE EXCHANGE NAVIGATION
(— CONE) PYLON
(— IN SACRED THINGS) SIMONY
(— IN SLAVES) MAGONIZE
(— JAM) GRIDLOCK
(DRIVE RUDELY IN —) CUTIN
(ILLEGAL —) CONTRABAND
TRAFFICKER COUPER DEALER
TRAGACANTH GUM
TRAGEDY BUSKIN TRAGIC TROIADES
TRAGIC DIRE DREADFUL THESPIAN
TRAGICOMEDY DRAME
TRAGOPAN MONAL
TRAGUS EARLET
TRAIL PAD PUG DRAG FOIL HARL
HUNT NECK PATH PIST SIGN SLOT
BLAZE CRAWL DRAIL PISTE ROUTE
SPOOR STOCK SWEEP TRACE TRADE
TRAIN COMING DAGGLE FOLLOW
RUNWAY SHADOW SLEUTH STRAIN
TAIGLE TRAPES DRAGGLE TRACHLE
TRAFFIC OUTTRAIL STRIGGLE
TRAILERY
(— ALONG) STREEL TRAPES
(— BY SMELL) SCENT
(— DOWN) FALL
(— OF A FISH) LOOM
(— OF AIRCRAFT) CONTRAIL
(— OF STAG) ABATURE
(— OUT) STREAM
(— THROUGH MUD) DAGGLE
(DESCENDING —) BAHADA BAJADA
(JOGGING —) PARCOURSE
(MOUNTAIN —) CLIMB
(SKI —) PISTE
(WAGON —) RUDLOFF
(WATER —) WAKE
TRAILBLAZER HARBINGER
TRAILER SEMI COACH BOXCAR
CARAVAN FLATBED FROGGER
GONDOLA ARTMOBILE
TRAILING (— ON GROUND)
PROSTRATE
TRAIN SET DRAG GAIT SECT TILL TIRE
TURN ZULU BEARD BREED COACH
DRESS DRILL ENTER FOCUS LOCAL
RANGE TRACE TRACT TRADE TRAIL

TRYNE CONVOY DIRECT GENTLE
GROUND INFORM MANURE NUZZLE
RAPIDE REPAIR SCHOOL SEASON
STRING SUBWAY AFFAITE BRIGADE
CARAVAN EDUCATE FREIGHT
GEARING LIMITED PEDDLER RATTLER
RETINUE SHUTTLE VARNISH CIVILIZE
DISCIPLE ELECTRIC EQUIPAGE
EXERCISE HIGHBALL INSTRUCT
MANIFEST REHEARSE
(— AN ANIMAL) BREAK
(— FINE) GAUNT
(— FOR CONTEST) POINT
(— FOR FIGHTING) SPAR
(— OF ANIMALS) COFFLE
(— OF ATTENDANTS) CORTEGE
(— OF COMET) TAIL
(— OF CONSEQUENCES)
CONSECUTION
(— OF EXPLOSIVE) FUSE
(— OF FANCY) REVERY REVERIE
(— OF FEATHERS) TAIL
(— OF GOWN) SACK
(— OF MINING CARS) JAG RUN TRIP
(CAMEL —) KAFILA
(FUNERAL —) CONVOY
(PACK —) CONDUCTA
(RAILROAD —) DRAG HOOK LOCAL
PICKUP EXPRESS FREIGHT LIMITED
RATTLER
TRAINED GOOD MADE ADEPT BROKE
BROKEN
TRAINEE BOOT CADET INTERN
TRAINER FEEDER JINETE LANISTA
TRAINING DRILL THEAT ASCESIS
ASKESIS CULTURE NURTURE PAIDEIA
BREEDING
(— IN HUMANITIES) CIVILITY
(— OF HORSE) DRESSAGE
(EARLY —) TIROCINIUM
(MANUAL —) SLOID SLOYD
(RELIGIOUS —) SADHANA
TRAIPSE GAD WALK TRAMP SASHAY
WANDER
TRAIT ITEM LEAD MARK VEIN ANGLE
CHARM KNACK TRACT TRICK
AMENITY ELEMENT HALLMARK
JAPANISM
(CHARACTERISTIC —) TRICK
(CULTURE —) SURVIVAL
(FOREIGN —) EXOTISM
(GOOD —) THEW
(UNDESIRABLE —) DEMON DAEMON
(WELL-DEFINED —) STREAK
(PL.) CORNERS
TRAITOR RAT JUDAS RUSTY
NITHING WARLOCK APOSTATE
ISCARIOT PRODITOR QUISLING
SQUEALER TRADITOR TREACHER
TRAITOROUS FALSE FELON
APOSTATE RENEGADE
TRAJECTORY SPORABOLA
TRA-LA-LA TRALIRA

TRAM TUB DRAM TRAMCAR
TRAMMEL TRANVIA
(COAL —) TIP
(SET OF —S) JOURNEY
TRAMCAR TRAM DUMMY PICKUP
TRAMMEL TRAM HAMPER STIFLE
COTTEREL
TRAMMER PUTTER
TRAMONTANE ALIEN FOREIGN
OVERBERG
TRAMP BO BUM PAD BOOM HAKE
HIKE HOBO HUMP PUNK SLOG SWAG
VAMP WALK YEGG BIMBO BURLY
CAIRD CLAMP JAVEL PIKER ROGUE ·
SHACK STIFF STRAG TRAIK TRAIL
TRASH TROMP TROUT BAGMAN
GAYCAT JOCKER PICARO STODGE
STRAMP STROLL TINKER TRANCE
TRAPES TRUANT TRUDGE DRUMMER ·
FLOATER RUFFLER SWAGGER
SWAGMAN TRAIPSE TRAMPLE
TROUNCE TROWANE VAGRANT
YEGGMAN CLOCHARD FOOTSLOG
GANGEREL STROLLER TRAVELER
VAGABOND SUNDOWNER
(— ABOUT) WAG
(LONG —) HUMP
(PL.) MONKERY
TRAMPING MONKERY
TRAMPLE HOX JAM PUG FARE FOIL
FULL HOOF CHAMP POACH SCAUT
SPURN STOMP TRAMP TRASH TREAD
DEFOIL DEFOUL PADDLE SAVAGE
STOACH STRAMP WADDLE OPPRESS
OVERRUN SCAMBLE FORTREAD
OVERRIDE
(— IN MUD) POACH
TRANCE RAPTUS AMENTIA ECSTASY
SAMADHI CATALEPSY
TRANQUIL CALM COOL EASY LOWN
MILD SOFT EQUAL QUIET STILL
GENTLE PACATE PIPING SERENE
CALMATO EQUABLE PACIFIC
RESTFUL PEACEFUL
TRANQUILIZE CALM LULL QUIET
STILL BECALM PACIFY SERENE
SETTLE SOFTEN SOOTHE APPEASE
COMPOSE
TRANQUILIZER VALIUM DIAZEPAM
TRANQUILIZING ATARAXIC
SOOTHING
TRANQUILLITY KEF LEE EASE REST
PEACE QUIET SATTVA SERENE
HARMONY ATARAXIA QUIETAGE
QUIETISM QUIETUDE SERENITY
COMPOSURE
TRANQUILLIZER LIBRIUM
RESERPINE
TRANS ANTI
TRANSACT DO PASS AGITATE
CONDUCT PERFORM
TRANSACTION DEAL DEED GAGE
GAGER ACTION AFFAIR FIDDLE

MARGIN SPREAD BARGAIN
MOHABAT PASSAGE CONTRACT
KNOCKOUT OPERATION
PROCEEDING
(— AT LOWER PRICE) DOWNTICK
(GAMBLING —) FLUTTER
(STOCK —) STRADDLE
(PL.) ACTA BUSINESS
TRANSCEND PASS SOAR EXCEED
OVERTOP SURPASS
TRANSCENDENTAL ACOSMIC
TRANSCENDING EXQUISITE
(PREF.) SUPRA
TRANSCRIBE COPY BRAILLE
DESCRIBE EXSCRIBE
TRANSCRIBED CANNED
TRANSCRIBER COPIER COPYIST
TRANSCRIPT COPY SCORE TENOR
DOUBLE APOGRAPH EXSCRIPT
TRANSCRIPTION
(PL.) PAZAND PAZEND
TRANSEPT PLAGE PORCH
TRANSFER CALL CEDE DEED FLIT
GIVE JUMP PASS SALE SELL TURN
ALIEN CABLE CARRY CROSS DROGH
REFER REMIT SHIFT ASSIGN ATTORN
CHANGE DECANT DELATE DONATE
REMOVE SWITCH CESSION CONNECT
CONSIGN DELIVER DEVOLVE
DISPONE MIGRATE TRADUCE
ALIENATE ANTEDATE CROCKING
DELEGATE DELIVERY DONATION
EXCHANGE TRANSACT TRANSUME
VIREMENT NEGOTIATE
(— A RECORDING) OVERDUB
(— DYE) EXHAUST
(— HEAT) CONVECT
(— HOMAGE) ATTORN
(— MOLTEN GLASS) LADE
(— OF ENERGY) FLOW
(— OF PROPERTY) DEED GIFT GRANT
DISPOSAL
(— PIGMENT) FLUSH
(— WITH POWDER) POUNCE
(DECORATIVE —) DECAL
(TEMPORARY —) SECONDMENT
TRANSFERENCE DEMISE EMOTION
REMOVAL DELATION DISPOSAL
TRANSFER
(— OF TRIBUTARY) CAPTURE
TRANSFIGURE DEIFY CLARIFY
TRANSFIX FIX DART STAB PITCH
STAKE STICK SKEWER THRILL
BESTICK
TRANSFORM TURN SHIFT TOUCH
CHANGE STRIKE CONVERT FASHION
PERMUTE RECYCLE CATALYZE
DISGUISE HETERIZE
(— ENERGY) ABSORB
(KIND OF —) FOURIER LAPLACE
TRANSFORMATION CHANGE
HAIRWORK
(— IN ATOM) REACTION

TRANSFORMER SET DIMMER
JIGGER TEASER TOROID VARIAC
BALANCE BOOSTER HEDGEHOG
TRANSFUSE ENDUE INDUE
TRANSGRESS ERR SIN BREAK
OFFEND OVERGO DIGRESS DISOBEY
VIOLATE INFRINGE OVERPASS
OVERSLIP OVERSTEP TRESPASS
TRANSGRESSION SIN SLIP CRIME
FAULT SCAPE BREACH DELICT
ESCAPE MISDEED OFFENSE
DELICTUM OVERLOUP TRESPASS
TRANSGRESSOR SINNER
OFFENDER
TRANSIENCE FUGACITY
TRANSIENT FLEET BUBBLE FLIGHTY
PASSING FLEETING FUGITIVE
MOMENTARY
TRANSIENTLY HOVERLY
TRANSISTOR FET MOSFET
TRANSIT BINOCLE PASSAGE
TRANSEPT
TRANSITION CUT JUMP LEAP
SEGUE SHIFT FERMENT PASSAGE
TRANSITIVE ACTIVE
TRANSITORINESS CADUCITY
TRANSITORY FLEET CADUCE
FLYING BRITTLE PASSANT PASSING
SLIDING VOLATIC WHILEND
CADUCOUS FLEETING FLITTING
TEMPORAL VOLATILE MOMENTARY
TRANSKEI (CAPITAL OF —)
UMTATA
(TOWN OF —) BUTTERWORTH
TRANSLATE PUT DRAW MAKE TURN
WEND RENDER CONVERT ENGLISH
EXPOUND TRADUCE CONSTRUE
INTERPRET
TRANSLATION CAB KEY CRIB PONY
STEP TROT GLOSS HORSE TARGUM
UNSEEN BICYCLE CABBAGE ENGLISH
THARGUM TRADUCT VERSION
SUBTITLE VERBATIM
(— OF BIBLE) PESHITO
(— OF THE CLASSICS) JACK
(BIBLICAL —) PESHITO PESHITTA
PESHITTO
(LOAN —) CALQUE
TRANSLATOR TURNER
TRANSLUCENT CLEAR LUCID
LIMPID LUCENT HYALINE
(PREF.) HYAL(O)
TRANSMIGRATION SAMARA
SAMSARA SANSARA
TRANSMISSION CHAIN DRIVE
ENTAIL DESCENT GEARBOX
PASSAGE SENDING TRANSFER
CONDUCTION CONVECTION
(— OF DISEASE) CONTAGION
(— OF ESTATE) ENTAIL
(— OF SOUND) AUDIO
(— TO OFFSPRING) HEREDITY
(SUFF.) PHORESIS

TRANSMIT AIR BEAM EMIT SEND
CARRY CONVEY DEMISE DERIVE
ENTAIL EXPORT IMPACT IMPART
RENDER CONDUCT CONSIGN
FORWARD TRADUCE TRADUCT
TRAJECT BEQUEATH DESCRIBE
PROPAGATE
(PREF.) DIAGO

TRANSMITTER TUBA SLAVE SPARK
BEACON JAMMER PINGER SENDER
VEHICLE RADIATOR

TRANSMITTING ALIVE

TRANSMUTE CHEMIC CHEMICK
ENNOBLE PERMUTE EXCHANGE
TRANSMUE TRANSUME

TRANSOM PATIBLE TRAVERSE

TRANSPARENCY SLIDE
(— OF DIAMOND) WATER

TRANSPARENT THIN CLEAR FILMY
LUCID BRIGHT LIMPID LUCENT
CRYSTAL FRAGILE HYALINE HYALOID
TIFFANY DIOPTRIC LUCULENT
LUMINOUS LUSTROUS PELLUCID
(IMPERFECTLY —) TRANSLUCENT
(PREF.) DIAPHAN(O) HYAL(O)

TRANSPIRE HAPPEN

TRANSPLANT SPOT SHIFT DEPLANT

TRANSPORT DAK JOY ROB BEAR
BOAT BUSS DAWK DRAY HAUL PASS
PORT RAPE RAPT RIDE SEND SHIP
BLISS CANOE CARRY DROGH FERRY
FLUTE GILLY BANISH BARREL
CONVEY DEPORT GALLOP KURVEY
WAFTER ECSTASY EXPRESS
FRAUGHT ONERARY RAPTURE
TRADUCE TROOPER CABOTAGE
CARRIAGE DAYDREAM ENRAVISH
PALANDER
(— BY PACKHORSE) JAG
(— FOR CRIME) LAG
(— LOGS) BOB
(— ORE) SLUSH
(PREF.) PEREIO

TRANSPORTATION AIR DAK FARE
AIRLIFT BOATAGE FREIGHT MINIVAN
TRAJECT TRANSPORT
(AIRPORT —) LIMO

TRANSPORTED RAPT
(— BY GLACIER) ERRATIC

TRANSPOSE ADJOINT CONVERT
REVERSE

TRANSPOSITION SHIFT ANSWER
ANAGRAM

TRANSUBSTANTIATION METUSIA
(BELIEVER IN —) CAPERNAITE

TRANSUDE SEEP

TRANSVAAL DAISY GERBERA

TRANSVAALER TAKHAAR

TRANSVERSE CROSS FACING
THWART OBLIQUE

TRANSVERSELY ATHWART

TRANSVESTISM EONISM

TRANSVESTITE BERDACHE

TRAP COY GET GIN PIT SET FALL GIRN
GRIN HOOK LACE LIME NAIL PUTT
TIPE TOIL WAIT WEEL BRAKE BRIKE
CATCH LEASH PLANT POUND SNARE
SPELL STALE SWICK SWIKE TRAIN
COBWEB CRUIVE EELPOT ENGINE
KEDDAH POCKET QUILEZ SNATCH
STAYER WILLOW FLYTRAP PITFALL
PITFOLD PUTCHEN PUTCHER
RATTRAP SETTING SPRINGE
TRAMMEL BIRDLIME COALHOLE
DEADFALL DOWNFALL TRAPROCK
(— FOR BIRDS) SCRAPE
(— FOR LARGE GAME) HOPO
(— FOR LOBSTER) POT
(— FOR RABBITS, MICE, ETC) TIPE
TYPE
(— FOR RATS) CLAM
(— FOR SALMON) PUTT
(— FOR SMALL ANIMALS) HATCH
(— FOR THE FEET) CALTROPS
(— IN POKER) SANDBAG
(— IN THEATER) SCRUTO
(— INTO SERVICE) CRIMP
(— OF SCAFFOLD) DROP
(FISH —) FYKE KILL LEAP WEEL WEIR
CREEL WILLY CORRAL CRUIVE
WILLOW
(LOBSTER —) POT
(MOTH —) GYPLURE
(RABBIT —) GATENET
(SAND —) BUNKER

TRAPDOOR DROP SLOT TRAP
SCRUTO VAMPIRE TRAPFALL

TRAPPED CORNERED

TRAPPER WIRER VOYAGEUR

TRAPPINGS GEAR JHOOL ARMORY
TOGGERY BARDINGS EQUIPAGE
HOUSINGS CAPARISON

TRAPSHOOTING SKEET

TRASH ROT BOSH DREK GEAR GOOK
JUNK PELF RAFF TOSH TRAG CLART
DRECK DROSS DRUSH SPANK STUFF
SWASH THROW TRADE TROKE
WASTE WRACK BUSHWA CULTCH
KELTER KITSCH LITTER PADDLE
PALTRY RAMMEL REFUSE RUBBLE
SCULCH TROUSE BAGGAGE
BEGGARY FULLAGE GARBAGE
PEDLARY RUBBISH TOSHERY
TRAFFIC BLATHERY CLAPTRAP
FLUMMERY MUCKMENT PEDDLERY
SKITTLES SMACHRIE TRASHERY
TRUMPERY

TRASHY CHEAP FLASH TOSHY TRIPY
PALTRY SHODDY SLUSHY BAGGAGE
RUBBISH RIFFRAFF RUBBISHY
SIXPENNY TRUMPERY

TRAUMA WOUND INJURY STRESS

TRAVAIL PAIN TASK TOIL AGONY
LABOR TORMENT

TRAVEL GO BAT BUS FLY GIG WAG
FARE GANG HIKE PASS PATH RIVE

TOTE TRIP VAMP WEND COVER KNOCK SLOPE THROW TRACK CRUISE TRANCE VOYAGE EXPRESS JOURNEY TRAVAIL TRUNDLE WAYFARE PROGRESS TRAVERSE
(— **ACROSS SNOW**) MUSH
(— **AIMLESSLY**) SAUNTER
(— **ALONG GROUND**) TAXI
(— **AROUND**) TURN COAST CIRCLE GIRDLE COMPASS
(— **AT GOOD SPEED**) CRACK
(— **AT HIGH SPEED**) HELL BARREL SCORCH
(— **AT RANDOM**) DRIFT
(— **AT SPEED OF**) DO
(— **BACK AND FORTH**) SHUNT COMMUTE
(— **BY AIRCRAFT**) AIR FLY AIRPLANE
(— **BY OX WAGON**) TREK
(— **FAST**) STREAK
(— **IN A VEHICLE**) TOOL
(— **IN STATE**) PROGRESS
(— **IN WATER**) SWIM
(— **ON FOOT**) HIKE SHANK KNAPSACK PERAMBULATE PEREGRINATE
(— **ON WATER**) SAIL
(— **OVER**) TRANCE TRAVERSE
(— **SPEEDILY**) VROOM
(— **THROUGH**) GO
(— **THROUGH AIR**) GLIDE
(— **THROUGH WOODS**) BUSHWACK
(— **WITHOUT EQUIPMENT**) SIWASH
(**DAY'S —**) JORNADA JOURNAL JOURNEY
TRAVELER GOER CRAWL FARER GUEST HORSE BAGMAN GANGER KILROY POSTER SAILOR VIATOR CRUISER DRUMMER FOOTMAN HOWADJI LEEFANG PILGRIM SWAGGIE TRAILER TREKKER TRIPPER WAYGOER ARGONAUT EXPLORER MAGELLAN OUTRIDER VOYAGEUR WAYFARER PASSENGER
(**COMMERCIAL —**) BAGMAN SALESMAN
(**COMPANY OF —S**) CARAVAN
TRAVELER'S JOY HAGROPE BINDWITH CLEMATIS
TRAVELING ERRANT PEREGRINE
TRAVELING SALESMAN RIDER DRUMMER
TRAVELOGUE
(— **TECHNIQUE**) VOICEOVER
TRAVERSE DO GO SEE BURN DENY KNEE LIFT MAKE PASS SPAN WALK COAST COVER CROSS SHEAR SWEEP THIRL TRACE TRACK CIRCLE COURSE DENIAL OVERGO PERCUR TRAVEL VOYAGE WANDER CHANNEL JOURNEY MEASURE OVERRUN PARADOS PERVADE DESCRIBE NAVIGATE OVERPASS OVERWEND SCRAMBLE UNTHREAD PERAMBULATE
TRAVERTINE ONYX TOPHUS ONYCHITE
TRAVESTY EXODE FARCE PARODY SATIRE CHARADE EXODIUM TRAVEST BURLESQUE
TRAVIATA, LA (**CHARACTER IN —**) FLORA VALERY ALFREDO BERVOIX DOUPHOL GERMONT GIORGIO VIOLETTA
(**COMPOSER OF —**) VERDI
TRAVOIS DRAY TRAVOY ALLIGATOR
TRAWL SEINE BOULTER DRAGNET STOWNET TRAWLNET TROTLINE
TRAWLER PAREJA BRAGOZZO
TRAY HOD CASE TILL TRUG BATEA BOARD FLOAT SCALE SLICE SUSAN GALLEY MONKEY SALVER SERVER SERVET VOIDER WAITER BALANCE CABARET COASTER CONSOLE SHALLOW DEJEUNER
(— **FOR CRUMBS**) VOIDER
(— **FOR DRYING FISH**) FLAKE
(— **FOR MATCH SPLINTS**) CAUL MONKEY
(— **FOR SHELLFISH**) FLOAT
(— **FOR TYPE**) GALLEY
(— **TO CATCH OVERFLOW**) SAFE
(**CIRCULAR —**) ROUNDEL
TREACHEROUS FOUL CATTY DIRTY FALSE PUNIC SNAKY SWACK FELINE FICKLE HOLLOW ROTTEN YELLOW SNAKISH FRAUDFUL IMPOSING PLOTTING SLIDDERY
TREACHERY GUILE SWICK TRAIN DECEIT FELONY PERFIDY TREASON UNTRUTH DASTARDY DISTRUST TRAHISON TRAITORY
TREACLE DIBS CLAGGUM THERIAC
TREAD FIT PAD BEAT FOOT PATH POST RUNG STEP VOLT CLAMP TRACK TRADE DEFOIL DEFOUL PADDLE CRAWLER FEATHER FOOTING RETREAD TREADER FOOTSTEP
(— **CLUMSILY**) CLUMP BALTER
(— **DOWN SHOE HEEL**) CAM
(— **HEAVILY**) SPURN TRAMPLE
(— **OF FOWL'S EGG**) GRANDO
(— **ON**) FOIL
(— **TO MUSIC**) FOOT
(— **WARILY**) PUSSYFOOT
(**TIRE —**) COVER
TREADLE PEDAL CHALAZA
TREASON SEDITION TREACHERY
TREASURE POSE ROON HOARD PRIZE STORE TROVE VALUE BURSAR COFFER FINDAL GERSUM WEALTH ASTHORE FINANCE THESAUR WARISON GARRISON TREASURY VALUABLE

(— STATE) MONTANA
(— TROVE) STASH
(LITTLE —) STOREEN
(PL.) CIMELIA
TREASURE BOX HANAPER
TREASURED DEAR CHARY
PRECIOUS VALUABLE
TREASURE ISLAND (AUTHOR OF
—) STEVENSON
(CHARACTER IN —) BEN JIM PEW
GUNN JOHN BONES HANDS ISRAEL
SILVER HAWKINS LIVESEY SMOLLETT
TRELAWNEY
TREASURER FISC BOWSER BURSAR
FISCAL GABBAI BOUCHER HOARDER
SPENDER BHANDARI COFFERER
HAZNADAR PROVISOR QUAESTOR
RECEIVER
TREASURY FISC FISK KIST CHEST
HOARD PURSE COFFER CORBAN
FISCAL FISCUS BOWSERY BURSARY
CHAMBER CHECKER CHEQUER
HORDARY AERARIUM THESAURY
TREASURE STOREHOUSE
(PAPAL —) CAMERA
TREAT RUN USE DEAL DOSE HOCK
LEAD PLAY BEANO BESEE COVER
DIGHT GUIDE LEECH SERVE SETUP
SHOUT TRACT TRAIT WRITE DEMEAN
DOCTOR GOVERN HANDLE LIQUOR
PADDLE REGALO CONDUCT ENTREAT
GARNISH ACTIVATE AIRBRUSH
(— A HIDE) DRUM
(— AS EQUAL) EVEN
(— BADLY) ILLGUIDE
(— BY MELTING) RENDER
(— CARELESSLY) BANG BANDY
(— CLOUDS) SEED
(— CONFIDENTIALLY) HUSH
(— CRUELLY) CRUCIFY
(— DAINTILY) PAMPER
(— DIABOLICALLY) BEDEVIL
(— DISCOURTEOUSLY) DISGRACE
(— FIBERS) GILL
(— FLOUR) AGENIZE
(— FONDLY) DANDLE
(— FUR) CARROT
(— GENTLY) FAVOR
(— HAIR) CONK
(— HARSHLY) STICK
(— ILLNESS) POMSTER
(— IMPROPERLY) MISUSE
(— IMPUDENTLY) NOSE
(— INADEQUATELY) SCANT
(— LIGHTLY) SCRUFF
(— LOVINGLY) COAX
(— MALICIOUSLY) SPITE
(— MASH) LAUTER
(— MERCIFULLY) SPARE
(— OF) DISCOURSE
(— OF DRINKS) SETUP
(— ROUGHLY) BANG MUMBLE
GRABBLE MALTREAT

(— SILK TO RUSTLE) SCROOP
(— SLIGHTINGLY) LIGHTLY
(— STEEL) HARVEY
(— UNFAIRLY) DO OHAFT STICK
(— UNSKILLFULLY) FOOZLE
(— VIOLENTLY) STRONGARM
(— WITH ABUSE) OUTRAGE
(— WITH ACID) SOUR
(— WITH CARE) CODDLE
(— WITH CONSIDERATION) RESPECT
(— WITH CONTEMPT) HUFF SNUB
BLURT FLIRT FLOCK FLOUT FLAUNT
BAUCHLE
(— WITH HEAT) FOMENT
(— WITH HONOR) RESPECT
(— WITH INATTENTION) FORGET
(— WITH INDULGENCE) FONDLE
(— WITH INJUSTICE) OPPRESS
(— WITH NEGLECT) PIGEONHOLE
(— WITH PARTIALITY) ACCEPT
(— WITH PRIDE) TRAMPLE
(— WITH RESPECT) HONOR
(— WITH RIDICULE) SCOUT
(— WITH RUDENESS) FRUMP
(— WITH TAR) BLACK
(— WITH TENDERNESS) CODDLE
(NEW YEAR'S EVE —) HAGMENA
HOGMANAY
TREATISE AGAMA DONET FAUNA
FLORA LIBEL SILVA SUMMA SYLVA
TRACT TREAT BOTANY POETRY
POMONA SERTUM SYSTEM
ALGEBRA ANATOMY BIOLOGY
COMMENT DIETARY GEOLOGY
GRAMMAR HISTORY PANDECT
PHYSICS PINETUM POETICS
ZOOLOGY ALMAGEST BROCHURE
CALCULUS DIDACTIC ECTHESIS
EXERCISE GENETICS GEOMANCY
GEOMETRY GERMANIA HORNBOOK
LAPIDARY MONUMENT PANTHEON
PASTORAL PRACTICE SITOLOGY
SPECULUM TRACTATE MONOGRAPH
(SUFF.) ICS LOGER LOGIA(N)
LOGIC(AL) LOGIST LOGUE LOGY
OLOGY
TREATMENT CURE WORK TREAT
USAGE ANIMUS DETAIL FACIAL
QUARTER BEHAVIOR DEMEANOR
ENTREATY
(— BY MASSAGE) SEANCE
(— BY MUD BATHS) PELOTHERAPY
(— FOR FURS) SECRETAGE
(— FOR WOOLLENS) SPONGING
(— OF DISEASE) ALLOPATHY
(BAD —) MISUSAGE
(COLD —) FREEZE
(COMPASSIONATE —) MERCY
(CONTEMPTUOUS —) SPURN
(CRUEL —) SEVERITY
(DIRE —) DOLE
(HARMFUL —) ABUSE
(HARSH —) SHAFT WHATFOR

(INHUMAN —) CRUELTY
(LUXURIOUS —) DELICACY
(SEVERE —) ROUGH
(PREF.) (MEDICAL —) IATR(O)
(SUFF.) PRAXIS
(MEDICAL —) IATRIA IATRIC(S)
IATRIST IATRY
TREATY MISE ACCORD CARTEL
CONCORD ENTENTE LOCARNO
ALLIANCE ASSIENTO PROTOCOL
TREATISE CONCORDAT
TREBLE TRIPLE DESCANT MINIKIN
SOPRANO TRIPLUM
TREBUCHET DONDINE DONDAINE
TREE TI ACH ADY AMA APA ARN ASH
BAY BEL BEN BUR DAK DAR EBO ELM
FIG FIR GUM HAW KOA KOU LIN NIM
OAK SAJ SAL TAL TUI ULE YEW ACLE
AGBA AKEE AMLA ANAM ANAN
ANDA ARAR ASAK ASOK ATIS ATLE
ATTA AULU AUSU BAEL BAKU BITO
BOGO BOOM BREA BURI BURR CADE
COLA CRAB DATE DHAK DILO DITA
DOON EBOE IPIL JACK KINO KOKO
LIME MABI MORA NEEM OHIA OMBU
PALA PINE POLE POON SADR SORB
SUPA TALA TAWA TCHE TEAK TEIL
TITI TOON TREW TUNG TUNO UPAS
VERA WOOD YATE YAYA AALII ABETO
ABURA ACANA ACAPU ACOMA
AFARA AGATI AGOHO AKEKI ALAMO
ALANI ALDER ALGUM ALISO ALMON
ALMUG AMAGA AMAPA AMBAK
ANABO ANJAN APPLE ARACA ARBOR
ARECA ARJAN ARJUN ARTAR ASOKA
ASPEN ATLEE BABUL BALAO BALSA
BALTA BANAK BEECH BEHEN BETIS
BIRCH BONGO BOREE BOSSE BUMBO
CACAO CARAP CAROB CEBIL CEDAR
CEIBO DADAP DHAVA DHAWA DILLY
DRYAD DURIO ELDER GABUN GAIAC
GENIP GINEP GINKO HAZEL ICICA
IXORA JAMBO JIQUE JIQUI KAPOR
KAPUR KEENA KOKAN KOKIO
KOKUM KONGU KUSAM LANSA
LARCH LARIX LEHUA LEMON LICCA
LIMBA LINDE LINER LINGO MAHOE
MAHUA MAMIE MAPLE MAQUI
NARRA NIEPA NURSE OADAL OSAGE
OSIER PACAY PAPAW PECAN PIPER
RAULI ROBLE ROHAN ROWAN SALAI
SAMAN SASSY SCRAG SIMAL SIRIS
SISSU STICK SUMAC TABOG TARFA
TENIO TERAP TIKUR TIMBO TINGI
TOONA TUART ULMUS UMIRI URUCA
URUCU UVITO WAHOO YACAL YACCA
YULAN ZAMAN ACAJOU AHKROT
AKEAKE ALAGAO ALERCE ALERSE
ALFAJE ALMOND ALUPAG AMAMAU
AMBASH AMUGIS AMUYON ANAGAP
ANAGUA ANAQUA ANGICO ANILAO
ARALIA ARANGA ARBUTE AUSUBO
AZALEA BABOEN BACURY BAHERA

BAKULA BALSAM BANABA BANAGO
BANANA BANCAL BANIAN BANYAN
BARBAS BATAAN BIRIBA BOMBAX
BONDUC BONETE BOTONG BRAUNA
BUCARE BUSTIC CALABA CAMARA
CANELA CANELO CAPUMO CARAPA
CASSIA CATIVO CAUCHO CEDRON
CHALTA CHERRY CHICHA CHINAR
CHOGAK CITRON COBOLA COCUYO
CUMBER DATURA DHAMAN DHAURA
DHAURI DRIMYS DURIAN ELCAJA
EMBLIC EMBUIA FEIJOA FILLER
FUSTIC GABOON GINKGO GUAIAC
GURJAN GURJUN IDESIA IDIGBO
ILIAHI ILLIPE ILLUPI JAGUEY JUJUBE
KAMALA KEMPAS KINDAL KITTUL
LANSAT LANSEH LAUREL LIGNUM
LINDEN LITCHI LOCUST LONGAN
MAFURA MALLET MAYTEN MEDLAR
MILKER MIMOSA ORANGE PANAMA
PAWPAW PIQUIA POPLAR RAMBEH
ROHUNA RUNNEL SABICU SABINO
SANDAN SANTOL SAPELE SAPOTA
SAPOTE SATINE SAWYER SERAYA
SINTOC SISSOO SOUARI STYRAX
SUMACH SUNDRI TALUTO TAMANU
TARATA TEETEE TIKOOR TIMBER
TINGUY TOATOA TOTARA TUPELO
URUCUM URUSHI UVALHA WABAYO
WABOOM WAHAHE WALNUT
WAMARA WAMPEE WANDOO
WATTLE YACHAN YAGHAN YAMBAN
ZAMANG ACHIOTE ACHUETE
AILANTO AKEPIRO AMBATCH
AMBOINA AMUGUIS AMUYONG
ANABONG ANNATTO ANONANG
APITONG APRICOT ARARIBA
ARAROBA ARBORET ARBUTUS
AROEIRA ASSAGAI AVOCADO
AVODIRE BANILAD BANKSIA
BECUIBA BENZOIN BILLIAN BOLLING
BUBINGA BUCKEYE BUISSON
CADAMBA CAJAPUT CAJUPUT
CANELLA CARAIPE CASTANA
CATALPA CAUTIVO CERILLO
CHAMPAC CHECHEM CHECKER
CHENGAL COCULLO CONIFER
CURUPAY CYPRESS DEADMAN
DESCENT DETERMA DHAMNOO
EPACRID FRUITER GONDANG
GRIBBLE GUMIHAN HICKORY
HOLLONG HOPBUSH HORMIGO
KAMASSI KAMBALA KICKXIA
KITTOOL KOKOONA KOOMBAR
KUMQUAT LOGWOOD MADRONA
MANJACK MARGOSA NAARTJE
PARAIBA PEREIRA PIMENTO
PULASAN PYRAMID RATWOOD
REDWOOD SERINGA SERVICE
SHITTAH SPINDLE STOPPER SUNDARI
SURETTE TANGELO TANGHIN
TARAIRI TARATAH TARWOOD
TINDALO TREELET TWISTER

URUNDAY VETERAN WALAHEE
WALLABA WEENONG WONGSHY
WONGSKY YAMANAI YOHIMBE
YOHIMBI ZELKOVA ACEITUNA
ALGAROBA ALLSPICE ALMACIGA
ALMANDER ALMENDRO ALOEWOOD
AMARILLO ARAGUANE ARBOLOCO
ARBUSCLE AVELLANO BAKUPARI
BASSWOOD BAYBERRY BELLWOOD
BINDOREE BITANHOL BLACKBOX
BOARWOOD BORRACHA BREADNUT
CABREUVA CAMELLIA CAMUNING
CARAGANA CARAUNDA CHAMPACA
CHESTNUT CHINCONA CHINOTTO
CINNAMON COCOPLUM COPALCHE
COUMAROU CRABWOOD
CUCUMBOL DEADFALL DOMINANT
DOTTEREL DOVEWOOD DRACAENA
DRUMWOOD ETABALLI FIREFALL
FORESTER GAMDEBOO GEELHOUT
GENISARO GUACACOA GUAYROTO
HALAPEPE HARDTACK HARDWOOD
HOLDOVER HORNBEAM HOROPITO
IRONWOOD ISHPINGO ITCHWOOD
JELOTONG JELUTONG KAJUGARU
KINGWOOD KNOBWOOD LACEBARK
LEADWOOD LORDWOOD
MAHOGANY MANDARIN MILKWOOD
MOKIHANA OITICICA OLEASTER
ONEBERRY PEDIGREE PICHURIM
PINKWOOD RAMBUTAN RASAMALA
SANDARAC SANDWOOD SAPUCAIA
SASSWOOD SEBESTEN SHAGBARK
SHAVINGS SILKWOOD SLOGWOOD
SOAPBARK STANDARD SUCUPIRA
SWEETSOP SYCAMORE TAMARACK
TAMARIND TANEKAHA TREELING
TURMERIC ZAPOTERO PERSIMMON
PISTACHIO SASSAFRAS SATINWOOD
SANDALWOOD
(— CUT BACK) DOTARD POLLARD
(— FURNISHING SUPPORT TO VINE)
HUSBAND
(— IN STREAM) SAWYER
(— LEFT IN CUTTING) HOLDOVER
(— OF HEAVEN) AILANTO AILANTHUS
(— ON WALL) RIDER
(— OVER 2 FT. DIAMETER) VETERAN
(—S IN FOREST) STAND
(— SYMBOLIZING UNIVERSE)
YGDRASIL
(— WITH BRANCHES TRIMMED) LOP
LOPSTICK
(AROMATIC —) CLUSIA LABIATE
(AUSTRALIAN —) ASH GUM TOON
BELAH BELAR BOREE BUNDY BUNYA
GIDIA HAZEL KARRI NONDA PENDA
SALLY WILGA BAOBAB DRIMYS
GIDGEE GIMLET GYMPIE JARRAH
KOWHAI MARARA PEROBA SALLEE
DOGWOOD GEEBUNG PEEBEEN
BEEFWOOD CARABEEN COOLABAH
FLINDOSA GRAVILEA IRONBARK

LACEBARK QUANDONG ROSEBUSH
SANDSTAY SOAPWOOD TILESEED
(BIG —) SEQUOIA
(BORNEO —) BILIAN
(BURMESE —) PADOUK
(CEYLON —) HORA
(CITRUS —) SHADDOCK
(CLOTHES —) COSTUMER
(CLUMP OF —S) TOLL TUMP STELL
(CONTORTED —) SAXAUL
(CUBAN —) JIQUE JIQUI GUACACOA
(CURSED —) WARYTREE
(DEAD —) RUNT SNAG RAMPIKE
(DEAD —S) DRIKI
(DECAYED —) DOTTEREL
(DWARF —) SCRUB ARBUSCLE
(EVERGREEN —) FIR YEW PINE SUGI
TAWA ABIES ATHEL CAROB CEDAR
CLOVE HOLLY LARCH LEMON OLIVE
THUJA BALSAM BIBIRU COIGUE
COIHUE KANAGI KAPUKA LOQUAT
ORANGE SPRUCE ARDISIA BEBEERU
BILIMBI CONIFER HEMLOCK JUNIPER
MADRONA MADROÑO EUCALYPT
EUONYMUS SAPODILLA
SANDORICUM
(FAMILY —) STEMMA DESCENT
LINEAGE PEDIGREE
(FRUIT —) CORDON
(GENEALOGICAL —) ARBOR JESSE
(GROWTH OF —S) SYLVAGE
(GUM —) KARI KINO BABUL BALTA
BUMBO ICICA KARRI KIKAR GIMLET
MALLET STORAX TEWART WANDOO
GOMMIER COOLIBAH
(HAWAIIAN —) KOA LEHUA ILIAHI
(INFERNAL —) ZAQQUM
(JAPANESE —) KAYA KIAKI KEYAKI
KADSURA KATSURA SATSUMA
ZELKOVA
(MANDARIN —) SATSUMA
(MEXICAN —) ULE AMAPA DRAGO
EBANO SERON CAPULI CATENA
CHILTE CAPULIN COPALCHE
(MYTHICAL —) TUBA
(NEW ZEALAND —) AKE KARO KAWA
MIRO PUKA RATA RIMU TAWA TORU
WHAU HINAU KAORI KAURI MAIRE
MANGI MAPAU MATAI TOWAI
AKEAKE KAMAHI KANUKA KAPUKA
KARAKA KARAMU KAWAKA KONINI
MANUKA PURIRI TARATA TITOKI
TOATOA TOTARA WAIHWE AKEPIRO
MANGEAO PUKATEA TARAIRI
TARWOOD KAWAKAWA KOHEKOHE
MAKOMAKO
(ORNAMENTAL —) KABIKI
LABURNUM POINCIANA
(PHILIPPINES —) DAO IBA TUA TUI ATLE
BOGO DITA IFIL IPIL AGOHO AGOJO
ALMON AMAGA ANABO BAYOG
BAYOK BETIS DANLI GUIJO LAUAN
LIGAS TABOG YACAL ALAGAO ALUPAG

AMUYON ANAGAP ANUBIN ARANGA
BANUYO BATAAN BATETE BATINO
BOTONG DUNGON KATMON LANETE
MABOLO MARANG MOLAVE SAGING
TALUTO AMUGUIS AMUYONG
ANABONG ANOBING ANONANG
APITONG BINUKAU CAMAGON
DANGLIN MANCONO MAYAPIS
TINDALO ALMACIGA BITANHOL
KALIPAYA KALUMPIT LUMBAYAO
MACAASIM MALAPAHO TANGUILE
(POISONOUS —) GUAO UPAS LIGAS
TANGHIN TANQUEN MANCHINEEL
(POLYNESIAN —) MACUDA
(SACRED —) CHAMPAC CHAMPAK
(SALT —) ATLE
(SANDARAC —) ARAR
(SHADE —) ELM DILLY GUAMA
HEVEA CATALPA HALESIA INKWOOD
JOEWOOD SYCAMORE
(SHOWY —) ASAK ASOK ASOKA
(SMALL —) AKE BOX TCHE ALDER
CUMAY DWARF HENNA NGAIO
SERON AKEAKE BLOLLY CHANAR
JOJOBA KOWHAI ARBORET
INKWOOD JOEWOOD KADAMBA
STADDLE TREELET EMAJAGUA
HARDTACK HUISACHE OLEASTER
SNOWBELL SOURWOOD TREELING
(SPINY —) LIME AROMA AROMO
HONEY BOOGUM BUCARE BUMELIA
CATECHU COLORIN LAVANGA
COCKSPUR
(STANDING —) FILLER
(STUNTED —) SCRAB SCRUB
SCRUNT
(THORNY —) BEL BAEL BREA LEMON
AMBACH SAMOHU AMBATCH
(TIMBER —) ASH DAR ENG FIR SAL
ACLE ANDA BAKU COCO CUYA EKKI
IPIL PELU PINE TALA TEAK YANG
ACAPU ALMON AMAPA AMATE
AMBAY ANJAN ARACA ARGAN
BANAK BIRCH CAROB CEDAR COCOA
CULLA EBONY ERIZO FOTUI HALDU
ICICA IROKO KAURI KHAYA KIAKI
KOKAN MANIU MAPLE MVULE
NARRA ROBLE TIMBO ALERCE
ALUPAG BABOEN BACURY BANABA
BANCAL CARBON CHUPON CORTEZ
DAGAME DEGAME DUKUMA ESPAVE
FREIJO GAMARI GUMHAR IMBUIA
JACANA LEBBEK MUERMO PADAUK
SANDAN SATINE SISSOO AMUGUIS
AROEIRA BECUIBA BILLIAN CARAIPI
CYPRESS ESPAVEL GATEADO
GOMAVEL GUARABU GUAYABI
HARPULA HOLLONG KOOMBAR
LAPACHO REDWOOD AMARILLO
BOARWOOD CABREUVA CARACOLI
COCOBOLO CRABWOOD DONCELLA
GUATAMBU GUAYACAN MAHOGANY
SLOGWOOD SUCUPIRA

(TRAINED —) ESPALIER
(TROPICAL —) CYP AKEE AULU DALI
DIKA EBOE EKKI GUAO INGA MABA
MAHO MAJO PALM SHEA ACKEE
BALSA BONGO COUMA DALLI FOTUI
GUAMA GUARA ICICA ILAMA JIGUA
MARIA NEPAL NJAVE POOLI TARFA
ANUBIN BAKULA BALATA BANANA
CASHEW CEDRON CHUPON GENIPA
HACKIA ITAUBA LEBBEK LECYTH
MAMMEE OBECHE PERSEA
ANGELIN ANNATTO CAULOTE
COPAIBA DATTOCK EHRETIA
EUGENIA GATEADO GUACIMO
LAPACHO MAJAGUA MOMBINI
SANDBOX SOURSOP SURETTE
BEEFWOOD CALABASH CAMUNING
CORKWOOD FUNTUMIA MUSKWOOD
PATASHTE SWEETSOP TAMARIND
MONKEYPOD MANGOSTEEN
PRINCEWOOD
(UNARMED —) ALBIZZIA
(VARNISH —) DOON THEETSEE
(XEROPHYTIC —) SAXAUL
(YOUNG —) RUNNEL SPRING TILLER
SAPLING SEEDLING SPRINGER
(PL.) BLUFF RINDS SILVA OVERSTORY
(PREF.) ARBORI DENDR(O)
(SUFF.) DENDRON
TREE CREEPER TOMTIT
TREE CYPRESS GILIA
TREE DUCK FIDDLER YAGUAZA
TREE EAR FUNGUS
TREE FROG FERREIRO
TREE MOSS USNEA
TREENAIL NOG GUTTA MOOTER
TRUNNEL
TREE PEONY MOUTAN
TREE SHREW TANA BANXRING
BANGSRING
TREE SNAKE BOOMSLANG
TREE TOAD HYLA HYLID ANURAN
TREE TOMATO TAMARILLO
TREETOP LAP LOP
TREFOIL CANCH LOTUS CLAVER
CROWTOE BEDSTRAW SAINFOIN
TICKSEED
TREHALOSE MYCOSE
TRELLIS TRAIL PERGOLA TARLIES
ESPALIER
TREMATODE FLUKE MARITA
STRIGEID
TREMBLE DARE DIRL RESE BEVER
QUAKE SHAKE SLOWS WIVER
AGRISE DIDDER DINGLE DITHER
DODDER FALTER HOTTER HOTTLE
NITHER QUAVER QUIVER SHIMMY
THRILL TITTER TOTTER TREMOR
TRYMLE WABBLE WOBBLE WUTHER
FLICKER SHUDDER STAGGER
TWIDDLE WHITHER THRIMBLE
(PL.) TIRE TIRES
(PREF.) TREMELLI TROMO

TREMBLER BUZZER HAMMER
VIBRATOR
TREMBLING BEVER SHAKY DITHER
TREMOR TREPID AQUIVER DODDERY
PALSIED QUAKING QUAVERY
QUIVERY TREMBLY TWITTER
TREMBLY WOOZY
TREMENDOUS BIG AWFUL GIANT
GREAT LARGE HOWLING TEARING
ENORMOUS HORRIBLE TERRIBLE
TERRIFIC MONSTROUS
TREMOLO HURRY TRILLO
TREMOR RIGOR SHAKE DINDLE
QUIVER THRILL SHUDDER TREMBLE
TREMULOUS ASPEN QUAKY SHAKY
PALSIED SHIVERY TREMBLY
SHIMMERY TINGLING
TRENCH GAW SAP FOSS GRIP GURT
LINE MOAT RILL SICK SIKE TAJO TRIG
BOYAU CHASE DITCH DRAIN DRILL
FLOAT FOSSE GRAFF GRAFT GRAVE
GROOP SEUCH TRINK COFFER
FURROW GULLET GUTTER SHEUGH
ACEQUIA CUNETTE CUVETTE
OPENCUT SLIDDER ENCROACH
LOCKSPIT PARALLEL SPREADER
THOROUGH TRESPASS
(— BELOW FOREST FIRE) GUTTER
(— FOR BURYING POTATOES) CAMP
(— FOR DRAIN TILES) CHASE
(— FORMED BY BANKING
VEGETABLES) GRAVE
(— ON HILLSIDE) SLIDDER
(ARTIFICIAL —) LEAT
(IRRIGATION —) FLOAT SUGSLOOT
(PREF.) BOTHR(O) BOTHRI(O)
TRENCHANT ACID KEEN EDGED
SHARP TUANT INCISIVE
TRENCHER PLATTER ROUNDEL
TRENCHERMAN EATER
TREND BEND BIAS HAND TONE TURN
BULGE CURVE DRIFT SENSE SLANT
SWING TENOR SQUINT STRIKE
CURRENT DOWNSIDE MOVEMENT
TENDENCY
(LOWERING PRICE —) EASE
TRENDY HIP MOD NOW POP CHIC
GROOVY
TREPANG BALATE SWALLO
SWALLOW TITFISH TEATFISH
TREPIDATION FEAR ALARM DISMAY
TRESPASS DEBT GILUT POACH
BREACH FURTUM INVADE INTRUDE
OFFENSE ENCROACH ENTRENCH
INFRINGE INTRENCH OVERLOUP
TRESS CURL LOCK TAIL BRAID
SWITCH RINGLET WIMPLER
TRES-TINE TRAY ROYAL
TRESTLE MARE HORSE INRUN
CHEVALET SAWHORSE
TREVALLY TURRUM
TREWS TROUSERS
TRIACETATE ACETIN EUROBIN

TRIAD MAJOR TRIAS TRINE TRIUNE
TERNARY TERNION TRILOGY
TRINARY TRINITY TRIMURTI
TIRATNA
TRIAL SAY SHY TRY BOUT DOOM FIRE
HACK OYER STAB TEST TURN ASSAY
CROSS ESSAY GRIEF ISSUE POINT
PROOF TASTE TOUCH WHACK
ASSIZE EFFORT EQUITY TRINAL
APPROOF ATTEMPT CALVARY
DISGUST HEARING PROVING
SCRATCH CRUCIBLE EXERCISE
JUDGMENT QUAESTIO TENTAMEN
PROLUSION
(— BY BATTLE) WAGER
(— BY ORDEAL) ORDALIUM
(— FOR HOUNDS) DERBY
(— OF SPEED) DASH
(— OF STRENGTH) CRUNCH
(— ROUND) HEAT
(AUTHOR OF —) KAFKA
(CHARACTER IN —) LENI JOSEPH
ADVOCATE BURSTNER TITORELLI
(EXPERIMENTAL —) TENTAMEN
(RACING —) PREP
(SEVERE —) ORDEAL CRUCIBLE
(PREF.) PEIRA
TRIANGLE APEX CYMBAL OXYGON
TRIGON PYRAMID SCALENE TRINITY
TRIQUET DINGDONG ISOSCELE
(SPHERICAL —) PENDENTIVE
TRIANGULAR HEATER CUNEATE
HASTATE
(— AREA) QUIRK
(— CLOTH) GORE
(— INSET) GODET
(PREF.) TRIGON(O)
TRIBAL GENTILE GENTLIC TRIBULAR
TRIBE (ALSO SEE NATIVE AND
PEOPLE) AO GI ATI AUS BOH EVE
EWE GOG KHA KIN KRA ROD SUK
YAO ADAI AKAN AKHA AKIM AKKA
BAYA BONI CLAN DAGO GUHA PURU
QUNG RACE RAVI REKI SAHO SEID
SHIK SHOR SIOL SOGA SUKU SUSU
TOBA TURI TUSH UBII VEPS VILI VIRA
YANA AEQUI ANGKA APTAL ARAWA
BASSI BATAK BESSI BONGO BROOD
CHANG CINEL DADJO DEDAN DIERI
FIRCA GIBBI HORDE HOUSE ICENI
KAJAR KANDH KEDAR KHOND KIWAI
KONGO KOTAR KREPI LANGO
MAGOG MARSI MBUBA MENDE
MENDI MOSSI MUTER NANDI PHYLE
PONDO QUADI SERER SOTIK STAMM
SUEVI TAIPI TAULI TCAWI TEKKE
TELEI TUATH VEPSE VOLOF WAKHI
WARRI WASHO WAYAO YOMUD
ADIGHE AGAWAM AMHARA ANAMIM
ANTEVA APAYAO ARAINS BANYAI
BASOGA BUDUMA BUSAOS CHAMPA
CHAWIA CHORAI DOROBO FAMILY
HERULI KARLUK KEREWA KHAMTI

KONYAK KORANA LOBALE MANGAR
MOLALA NATION NERVII PAHARI
PHYLON POKOMO RAMNES SHAGIA
SICULI SIMEON SUKUMA TAINUI
TAMOYO TCHIAM TELEUT THUSHI
TUSHIN TYPEES VENETI WABENA
WABUMA WAGOMA WAGUHA
WAHEHE WARORI WASOGA WAVIRA
ZARAMO ZEGUHA ZENAGA
ABABDEH ABANTES AIAWONG
AKWAPIM AMAKOSA ANOMURA
ANTAIVA ARVERNI BAGIRMI
BAKATAN BAKONGO BAKUNDA
BAMRARA BASONGO CABINDA
CHAOUIA CHAUWIA CHONTAL
CHUKCHI COLLERY DADAYAG
DADSCHO ILLANUN JAZYGES
KABINDA KABONGA KHOKANI
KOLDAJI KONIAGA KOREISH
KUBACHI KURUMBA LLANERO
NAIADES PALAUNG PARISII PIMENTO
RAURACI SAMBALA SAMBARA
SEKHWAN SENONES SEQUANI
SHAMMAR SHERANI SHERPAS
SHUKRIA SII IRAN SUIONES SUKKIIM
TAKELMA TARKANI TURKANA
VIDDHAL WAGWENO WAICURI
WAMBUGU WAREGGA WASANGO
ZONGORA AMAFINGO ANDOROBO
ASHANGOS ASSHURIM AWABAKAL
BARKINJI BATETELA BOANRURA
CHERUSCI CHITRALI GEZRITES
JICAQUES KUKURUKU LANDUMAN
NEBAIOTH ORUNCHUN PALLIYAN
PHASIRON PUPULUCA PURUPURU
RAHANWIN SAKALAVA SHINWARI
SINGSING SINTSINK TCHUKCHI
TENGGRIS USTARANA WANGATTA
WAPOGORO WAPOKOMO
(— OF ISRAEL) DAN GAD ASHER
  REUBEN EPHRAIM IOSACHAR
  MANAOSEH
(CHINESE —S) HU
(PRIVILEGED —) MAGHZEN
  MAKHZAN
(SEA GYPSY —) SELUNG
(PREF.) PHYL(O)
(SUFF.) INI
TRIBROMOETHANOL AVERTIN
TRIBULATION AGONY CROSS
  MISERY SORROW DISTRESS
TRIBUNAL BAR FEME ROTA VEHM
  BENCH COURT FEHME FORUM
  JUNTA VEHME MAJLIS ACUERDO
  ESGUARD MEJLISS RIGSRET
  AREOPAGY KANGAROO
TRIBUNE BEMA VELUTUS
TRIBUTARY ARM BOGAN BRANCH
  FEEDER TYBURN AFFLUENT
  ANABRANCH
TRIBUTE AID FEE TAX CAIN GELT
  KUDO LEVY PORT RENT SCAT CANON
  GAVEL HANSE MAILL SALVO SCATT

CHAUTH HERIOT HIDAGE HOMAGE
IMPOST CARATCH CHEVAGE CHILFRY
OVATION PENSION SYNODAL
TREWAGE AUXILIUM BRENNAGE
HEREGELD PESHKASH ROMESCOT
ROMESHOT
(FEUDAL —) HERIOT
TRICE GIRD BLINK THROW INSTANT
TRICHECHUS MANATUS
TRICHINA NEMATODE
TRICHINIZED MEASLY
TRICHION CRINION
TRICHOME SCALE
TRICHOMONIASIS CANKER
  ABORTION
TRICK DO BAM BOB COG CON CUN
  DAP DOR FOB FOX FUB FUN GIN
  GUM JIG JOB PAW RIG BILK BITE
  BORE CHAW CHIP DIDO DIRT DUPE
  FAKE FIRK FLAM FLUM FOOL GAFF
  GAME GAUD GECK GULL HAVE HOAX
  HOSE IAPE JEST JINK JOUK JUNT
  LOCK LURK PASS PAWK PRAT PULL
  RORT RUSE SELL SKIT SLUR TURN
  WILE WIPE WOOL ANTIC BLEAR
  BLINK CATCH CHEAT CONNU CRAFT
  CREEK CROOK CULLY CURVE DODGE
  DORRE ELUDE FEINT FETCH FOURB
  FRAUD GLEEK GRIFT GUILE KNACK
  PAVIE PLANT PRANK SHIFT SHINE
  SKITE SLICK STUNT TRAIN TRUFF
  TWIST WHEEL WREST WRINK BAFFLE
  BANTER BEGUNK BEJAPE BLENCH
  BROGUE CAUTEL CHOUSE CRADDY
  DECEIT DELUDE DOUBLE EUCHRE
  FOURBE HOCKET HUMBUG II LUDE
  JOCKEY JUGGLE MANNER PLISKY
  POLICY SCONCE SHAVIE SPRING
  TREPAN VAGARY WHEEZE WINNER
  CANTRIP CHICANE CONCEIT FICELLE
  FINESSE FORWARD GUILERY
  KNAVERY MARLOCK PAGEANT
  SHUFFLE SLEIGHT WHIZZER ARTIFICE
  CHALDESE CLAPTRAP CLOWNADE
  CONTOISE CROTCHET DELUSION
  DOUBLING FLAGARIE FLIMFLAM
  GILENYIE INTRIGUE JEOPARDY
  PRACTICE PRANCOME PRESTIGE
  QUENTISE SLAMPAMP TRAVERSE
  TRICKING BAMBOOZLE STRATAGEM
(— OUT) FARD FANGLE FINIFY
(BEGUILING —) WILE
(CARD —) CLUB HEART SPADE STICH
  DIAMOND WEAVING
(FRAUDULENT —) RIG TOP
(JUGGLING —) FOIST
(KIND OF —) ODD
(KNAVISH —) DOGTRICK
(LOVE —) AMORETTO
(MEAN —) TOUCH
(MONKEY —) SINGERIE
(OLD —) CONNU
(PETTY —S) CRANS

(SIX —S) BOOK
(SMART —) LIRIPIPE LIRIPOOP
(STUPID —) SHINE
(VEXING —) CHAW
(WRESTLING —) CHIP CLICK FAULX
  FORWARD
(PL.) DAGS
TRICKER TRUMPER
TRICKERY DOLE GAFF SHAM TRAP
  TRAY WILE COVIN FRAUD HOCUS
  SHARK TRAIN CAUTEL COVINE
  DECEIT JAPERY JUGGLE TREGET
  DODGERY FALLACY GULLERY
  JOUKERY KNAVERY PAWKERY
  SLEIGHT ARTIFICE CHEATING
  COZENAGE JOOKERIE JUGGLERY
  PRACTICE TRICKING TRUMPERY
  SHENANIGAN SHENANIGANS
TRICKILY FOXILY
TRICKINESS PAWKERY
TRICKISH KNAVISH FRAUDFUL
TRICKLE DRIB DRIP DRILL STILL TRILL
  DISTIL DRIVEL GUTTER SICKER
  SIGGER STRAIN ZIGGER DISTILL
  DRIBBLE DRIZZLE DROPPLE TRINTLE
TRICKLET RILL
TRICKSTER GULL SHAM RASCAL
  TRAPAN SLICKER TRICKER SLEEVEEN
  TRAMPOSO TREGETOUR
TRICKSY ELFISH QUIRKSEY
TRICKY SLY DEEP BRAID DODGY FIKIE
  GAUDY ROWDY SNIDE ARTFUL
  CATCHY LUBRIC QUIRKY SHIFTY
  SMARTY TWISTY DEVIOUS SLANTER
  TRICKLE WINDING FLIMFLAM
  JUGGLING LUBRICAL SHIFTUL
  SKITTISH SLIDDERY SLIPPERY
  TORTUOUS TRICKING
TRICLINIC ANORTHIC
TRICOT JERSEY
TRICYCLE VELO CYCLE TRIKE WHEEL
  TANDEM TRICAR RANTOON
  ROADSTER SOCIABLE
TRIDENT SPEAR VAJRA TRISUL
  TRISULA
TRIED TESTED PROBATE WEIGHED
  RELIABLE
TRIFECTA TRIPLE
TRIFLE ACE BOB DAB FIG HAW PIN
  SOU TOY BEAN COOT DOIT FICO
  FOOL HAIR HOOT JAUK MESS MOCK
  MOTE PLAY RUSE WHIT DALLY FLIRT
  FLUKE GLAIK ITEMY NIFLE PLACK
  POINT SCRAT SPORT TRICK TRUFF
  BAWBEE BREATH DABBLE DANDLE
  DAWDLE DELUDE DIBBLE DOODAD
  DOODLE FADDLE FESCUE FIDDLE
  FOOTER FOOTLE FRIVOL GEWGAW
  MONKEY NIDDLE NIGGLE NIGNAY
  PADDLE PALTER PETTLE PICKLE
  PIDDLE PIGGLE PINGLE POTTER
  PUTTER STIVER TIFFLE VANITY
  WANTON FEATHER FLAMFEW

FRIBBLE NOTHING QUIDDLE
THOUGHT TRANEEN TRINKET
TRIVIAL WHIFFLE COQUETTE
FALDERAL FLIMFLAM FOLDEROL
GIMCRACK KICKSHAW MOLEHILL
NIFFNAFF NIHILITY NUGAMENT
RIGMAREE TRANTLUM BAGATELLE
(— WITH) JANK DANDLE DELUDE
  NIGGLE
(ATTRACTIVE —) CONCEIT
(LITERARY —) TOY
(MERE —) SONG STRAW
(MEREST —) FIG
(SHOWY —) WALLY
(PL.) NUGAE TRIVIA GIBLETS
  FEWTRILS NONSENSE
TRIFLER DOODLE PLAYER WANTON
  FLANEUR FOOTLER FRIBBLE
  NUGATOR PINGLER TWIDDLER
  WHIFFLER
TRIFLES
(PREF.) NUGI
TRIFLING AIRY FOND IDLE FUNNY
  INANE LIGHT PETTY POTTY SILLY
  SMALL FADDLE FLIMSY FUTILE
  LEVITY LIMUTE LITTLE PALTRY
  SIMPLE SLIGHT STRAWY TOYISH
  FOOLISH FRIBBLE ITEMING NOMINAL
  PUERILE TRIVIAL TWATTLE
  COQUETRY FIDDLING FLIMFLAM
  FRIPPERY IMMOMENT NONSENSE
  NUGATORY PIDDLING SNIPPING
  FRIBBLING WHIFFLERY NEGLIGIBLE
  TOMFOOLERY
TRIFOLIUM CLOVER TREFOIL
TRIG NEAT SNOD TRIM CHIPPER
TRIGGER CAUSE VERGE TRICKER
TRIGGERFISH COCUYO TURBOT
  OLDWIFE BALISTID FILEFISH
  OLDWENCH
TRIGON TRINE SABBEKA SACKBUT
  SAMBUCA TRIGONON
TRIGONOMETRY SPHERICS
(— FUNCTION) SINE COSINE
TRILBY (AUTHOR OF —) DUMAURIER
  (CHARACTER IN —) ALICE GECKO
  SANDY TAFFY BILLEE TRILBY
  OFERRALL SVENGALI
TRILL BURR FLAP ROLL SHAKE
  QUAVER THRILL TRILLO WARBLE
  ROULADE TRILLET
  (BEGINNINNG OF A —) RIBATTUTA
TRILLED HIRRIENT
TRILLION
(PREF.) TERA TREG(A)
TRILLIONTH
(PREF.) PICO
TRILLIUM SARA TRUE SARAH
  TRUMP BENJAMIN TRUELOVE
TRILOBITE EODISCID
TRIM AX AXE CUT DUB GIM LIP LOP
  MOW NET BARB BEAD BUTT CLIP
  CROP DEFT DINK FEAT FUSS GASH

GIMP HACK JIMP LACE NEAT PICK
SNAG SNOD SNUG SPUR STOW
TACK TOSH TRIG BRAID BRUSH
CLEAN COPSE DRESS FITTY GENTY
HEDGE KEMPT KNIFE NATTY PREEN
PRIME PRUNE PURGE SAUCY SHAVE
SHEAR SHRAG SHRIP SLEEK SMART
SMIRK SPRIG STUMP TIGHT TRICK
VERGE BARBER DAPPER DONSIE
DOUBLE FETTLE PICKED REFORM
SHROUD SOIGNE SPRUCE SVELTE
SWITCH TRIMLY CHIPPER FEATHER
FLOUNCE SCISSOR MANICURE
ORNAMENT TRIMMING SHIPSHAPE
(— A BOAT) SIT
(— ENDS OF HAIR) SHIRL
(— HEDGE) DUB
(— HIDES) ROUND
(— MEAT) CONDITION
(— SAIL) FILL
(— SEAMS) FETTLE
(— SHOE) FOX
(— TREES) PRIME SWAMP
(— WITH EMBROIDERY) GIMP
PANEL
(FURNITURE —) SKIRT
TRIMLY SMARTLY SPRUCELY
TRIMMED PEEKABOO
TRIMMER FINER BRIDLE TACKER
VOLANT ROUNDER SMOCKER
SCRATTER
TRIMMING COQ FUR GIMP LACE
BRAID CHAPE COQUE FRILL GUARD
INKLE JABOT ROBIN RUCHE ERMINE
LACING OSPREY PURFLE ROBING
BEADING CASCADE FALBALA
FURRING GALLOON MARABOU
PUFFING ROULEAU BRAIDING
EAVESING FALDERAL FOLDEROL
FROSTING FROUFROU FURBELOW
JEWELING PAILLETTE PEARLING
PICKADIL PASTRON SOUTACHE
PAILLETTE SPAGHETTI STRAPPING
(— OF KNOTTED THREAD) MACRAME
MACRAMI
(FEATHER —) MARABOU MARABOUT
(PLEATED —) RUCHE
(PL.) LOP FLOTS SHORTS FIXINGS
LOPPING BRAIDING FRILLIES
TRIMURTI TRINITY
TRINE TRENE TRIGON
TRINIDAD-TOBAGO
(CAPITAL OF —) PORTOFSPAIN
(POINT OF —) GALERA
(RIVER OF —) ORTOIRE
(TOWN OF —) TOCO ARIMA COUVA
LABREA MORUGA SIPARIA
TRINITARIAN MATHURIN
TRINITROTOLUENE TNT TOLITE
TRITON
TRINITY TRIAD TRIAS TRINE TRIUNE
GODHEAD TERNARY TRIMURTI
TRINUNITY

TRINKET TOY DIDO GAUD MERE
BIJOU HEART KNACK TAHLI BAUBLE
CHARME DEVICE DOODAD GEWGAW
BIBELOT TRANGAM TRANKUM
GIMCRACK KICKSHAW TRANTLUM
TRINKLET WHIMWHAM TCHOTCHKE
(PL.) TRINKUMS
TRINKETRY KNAVERY
TRIO GLEEK TERCET TERZET TRIUNE
TERZETTO
(THREE —S) NONET
(TWO —S) SEXTET
TRIOLEFIN TRIENE
TRIONYX AMYDA
TRIOPAS (DAUGHTER OF —)
IPHIMEDIA
(FATHER OF —) NEPTUNE
(MOTHER OF —) CANACE
(SON OF —) ERYSICHTHON
TRIOPS APUS
TRIP HOP JAG JET JOG TIP BOUT CHIP
FOOT GAIT GATE KILT LINK RAKE
SKIP TOUR TROT TURN BROAD
DANCE DRIVE HITCH JAUNT SALLY
CRUISE ERRAND FLIGHT HEGIRA
OFFEND OUTING RAMBLE SAFARI
SASHAY VOYAGE JOURNEY MISSTEP
SAILING SETDOWN STUMBLE
TRIPPER CAMPAIGN PERIPLUS
(— ALONG) CHIP LINK
(— BY DOG TEAM) MUSH
(— INTO COUNTRY) CAMPAIGN
(— IN WRESTLING) CHIP CLICK
(— UP) SUPPLANT
(HUNTING —) SHOOT
(KIND OF —) EGO
(MAKE A QUICK —) NIP
(PART OF —) LEG
(PLEASURE —) JUNKET
(SHORT —) HOP
TRIPE GOO PAUNCH ROLPENS
TRILLIBUB CODSWALLOP
TRIPLE TRINE TREBLE TERNARY
TRIFOLD TRIPLEX THRIBBLE TRIFECTA
TRIPLE BOND
(SUFF.)
(CONTAINING —) OLIC
TRIPLET TRIN CODON BRELAN
PARIAL TERCET TRIOLF TRIPLE
TERZINA TRIOLET HEMIOLIA
TRILLING TRIPLING TRISTICH
(— OF BASES) CODON
TRIPLETAIL SAMA CHOBIE FLASHER
GROUPER
TRIPLICITY TRIGON
TRIPOD CAT TRIP SPIDER TEAPOY
TRIPOS TRIVET TRESTLE
TRIPODY HEMIEPES
TRIPOLI SILEX TRIPEL
TRIPPER DECKMAN
TRIPTOLEMUS (FATHER OF —)
CELEUS
(MOTHER OF —) METANIRA

TRISHAW CYCLO PEDICAB
TRISMUS LOCKJAW TETANUS
TRISTAN UND ISOLDE
  (CHARACTER IN —) MARK MELOT
  ISOLDE TRISTAN BRANGANE
  KURWENAL
  (COMPOSER OF —) WAGNER
TRISTE SAD
TRISTRAM SHANDY (AUTHOR OF
  —) STERNE
  (CHARACTER IN —) SLOP TOBY TRIM
  BOBBY SHANDY WADMAN WALTER
  YORICK SUSANNAH TRISTRAM
TRITE FADE HACK WORN BANAL
  CONNU CORNY HOARY MUSTY STALE
  TIRED VAPID BEATEN COMMON
  MODERN HACKNEY PERCOCT TRIVIAL
  BROMIDIC SHOPWORN
TRITENESS BATHOS
TRITERPENOID CERIN
TRITON EFT NEWT TRUMPET
  (FATHER OF —) NEPTUNE
  (MOTHER OF —) AMPHITRITE
TRITURATE POUND POWDER
TRITURATION TRIPSIS
TRITURUS MOLGE
TRIUMPH WIN CROW PALM INSULT
  PREVAIL VICTORY CONQUEST
  (— OVER) SCALP
TRIUMPHANT VICTOR EXULTANT
  JUBILANT
TRIUMPHING OVANT
TRIUNGULIN CRAWLER
TRIVET SPIDER TRIPOD TRESTLE
  TRIPPER BRANDISE
TRIVIAL BALD JERK NICE VAIN
  BANAL LEGER LIGHT PETTY SILLY
  SMALL TIDDY FIDFAD FOOTLE
  PALTRY SLIGHT TOYISH COMICAL
  PIPERLY PUERILE SHALLOW TIDDLEY
  DOGGEREL FEATHERY FOOTLING
  GIMCRACK PIDDLING PILULOUS
  TRIFLING TRINKETY
  (NOT —) SOLID EARNEST
TRIVIALITY FOLLY FROTH NIGNAY
  TRIFLE INANITY IDLENESS
  NONSENSE NUGACITY
TROCHANTER SCAPULA
TROCHE ROTULA TABLET CACHUNDE
  PASTILLE
TROCHEE CHOREE CHOREUS
  TROCHEUS
TROCHLEA PULLEY
TROCTOLITE GABBRO
TRODDEN TRADED
  (MUCH —) BEATEN
TROGLODYTIC SPELEAN
TROGON QUEZAL QUETZAL
  TOCORORO
TROILUS (BELOVED OF —) CRESSIDA
  (FATHER OF —) PRIAM
  (MOTHER OF —) HECUBA
  (SLAYER OF —) ACHILLES

TROILUS AND CRESSIDA
  (AUTHOR OF —) SHAKESPEARE
  (CHARACTER IN —) AJAX HELEN
  PARIS PRIAM AENEAS HECTOR
  NESTOR ANTENOR CALCHAS
  HELENUS TROILUS ULYSSES
  ACHILLES CRESSIDA DIOMEDES
  MENELAUS PANDARUS
  AGAMEMNON ALEXANDER
  CASSANDRA DEIPHOBUS
  PATROCLUS THERSITES
  ANDROMACHE MARGARELON
TROJAN PARIS TROIC DARDAN
  HECTOR ANTENOR
  (PL.) TEUCRI
TROLL DROW HARL SPIN TROW
  ANGLE HARLE MOOCH TRAWL
  TROLLOL
  (— WITH LIVE BAIT) ROVE
TROLLER MOOCHER
TROLLEY CORF BOGEY BOGIE DOLLY
  TRUCK CRADLE PANTOGRAPH
  (OFF ONE'S —) BATS CRAZY
TROLLOP CUT DOXY BITCH DOXIE
  TROLL TRULL DOLLOP
TROMBONE BONE TRAM BUSINE
  POSAUNE SACKBUT SLIPHORN
  (PART OF —) BOW CUP KEY RIM
  BELL CROOK FLARE SHANK SLIDE
  BUMPER FLANGE BALANCER
  MOUTHPIECE
TRONA URAO
TROOP FARE GANG GING ROUT
  TURM ROUTE SOLAK STAND TURMA
  WERED CORNET RISALA ROUGHT
  SCHOOL THREAT TICHEL TROUPE
  COMPANY COMITIVA
  (— OF ARMED MEN) CREW
  (— OF FOXES) SKULK
  (— OF WORSHIPPERS) THIASUS
  (—S ATTACHED TO SOVEREIGN)
  GUARDS
  (—S IN BATTLE ARRAY) SHELTRON
  (—S ON WING OF ARMY) ALARES
  (ASSAULTING —S) WAVE
  (BOMBAY —S) DUCKS
  (CAVALRY —) CORNET
  (GIRL SCOUT —) SHIP
  (LIGHT-ARMED —S) PSILOI
  (MOUNTAIN —) ALPINI
  (MOUNTAIN —S) ALPINI
  (SCOTTISH —S) JOCKS
  (PL.) GIS PARADE
TROOPER BARGIR REITER RUTTER
  BARGEER
  (INDIAN —) SOWAR
TROPARION HIRMOS HEIRMOS
  TROPARY KATABASIS
TROPE IMAGE EVOVAE SIMILE
TROPHONEMA VILLUS
TROPHONIUS (BROTHER OF —)
  AGAMEDES
  (FATHER OF —) APOLLO ERGINUS

TROPHOZOITE CEPHALIN
SPORADIN
TROPHY BAG EMMY HUGO PALM
PRIZE SCALP REWARD LAURELS
(WRITING —) HUGO
TROPIC SOLAR TROPHIC
TROPINE HYOSCINE
TROS (FATHER OF —) ERICTHONIUS
ERICHTHONIUS
(MOTHER OF —) CALLIRRHOE
(SON OF —) ILUS GANYMEDE
ASSARACUS
TROT JOG SPUD TRIG FADGE HURRY
PIAFFE
(KIND OF —) TURKEY
TROTH CERTY TROGS TRUTH CERTIE
TROTTER DRIVER CRUBEEN
SPANKER
TROUBADOR BARD MINSTREL
SORDELLO
TROUBLE ADO AIL DIK HOE ILL IRK
MAI MAR VEX WOE BEAT BUSY CAIN
CARK EARN FASH FIKE GRAM JEEL
MASH MOIL PAIN PINE ROUT SORE
STIR TEEN TINE TRAY UNRO WORK
ANNOY BESET CROSS DROVE DUTCH
GRIEF HAUNT LABOR ROWEL SMITE
SPITE STEER STURT SUSSY THRIE
TWEAK WHILE WORRY BARRAT
BOTHER BURBLE CADDLE CUMBER
DITHER EFFORT GRIEVE GRUDGE
HARASS HATTER KIAUGH MOLEST
POTHER RATTLE RUBBER SORROW
SQUALI TAKING THREAT UNCASE
UNROLL WORRIT AFFLICT AGITATE
ANXIETY CHAGRIN CONCERN
DISEASE DISTURB DRUBBLE
EMBROIL FASHERY INFLICT PERTURB
PILIKIA SCRUPLE SPUTTER THOUGHT
TRACHLE TRAVAIL TRIBBLE TURMOIL
BUSINESS DARKNESS DISORDER
DISQUIET DISTRESS NOISANCE
VEXATION WANDRETH
(— ONE'S SELF) PASS
(EXPRESSION OF —) UHOH
(PL.) CHAGRINS
TROUBLED DRUBLY DRUMLY
GRUMLY QUEASY CAREFUL FRETFUL
HAUNTED AGITATED HARASSED
TROUBLESHOOTER FIXER
TROUBLESOME DIK ILL SAD BUSY
HARD FIKIE PESKY ROWDY SPINY
TIGHT PLAGUY SHREWD STICKY
THORNY UNEASY BRICKLE HARMFUL
ONEROUS PESTFUL PLAGUEY
TEWSOME ANNOYING FASHIOUS
SPITEFUL UNTOWARD PLAGUESOME
TROUBLESOMENESS BOTHER
TROUBLING CHRONIC
TROU-DE-LOUP TRAPHOLE
TROUGH BOX CUP HOD RUN TOM
BACK BOSH BUNK COVE DAIL DALE
DISH DORR SHOE SINK TRAY TROW

VALE BAKIE CHUTE DITCH LAVER
SHOOT SHUTE SLIDE SPOUT STRIP
ALVEUS BACKET BUDDLE GUTTER
HARBOR HOPPER LAVABO MANGER
RUNNER SALTER SINKER SLUICE
STRAKE TROGUE VALLEY WALLOW
CHENEAU CONDUIT LAUNDER
RIFFLER TRENDLE TROFFER
LAVATORY PENSTOCK
(— FOR ASHES) BAKIE
(— FOR COOLING INGOTS) BOSH
(— FOR KNEADING) HUTCH
(— FOR PAPER PULP) RIFFLER
(— FOR WASHING ORE) TOM HUTCH
STRIP BUDDLE STRAKE
(— IN MONASTERY) LAVABO
(— OF A WAVE) SULK
(— OF CIDER MILL) CHASE
(— OF ROCK) SYNCLINE
(— OF THE SEA) ALVEUS
(ANNULAR —) CUP
(BAKER'S —) HUTCH
(EAVES —) CANAL CHENEAU
(GLACIAL —) DORR
(ORE —) TYE
(SHEEP-DIPPING —) DUP
(WOODEN —) TRUG BAKIF TROGUE
(PREF.) BOTHR(O) BOTHRI(O) PYEL(O)
(SUFF.) SCAPH
TROUNCE MOP FLOG MOPUP
THUMP TRAMP WHOMP COURSE
CUDGEL DEFEAT CANVASS
SHELLAC
TROUNCING LACING WARMING
TROUPE BALLET SERVANTS
CUADRILLA
TROUPIAL ORIOLE
TROUSER STROSSER
TROUSERING CASINET
TROUSERS BAGS BELLS CORDS
DUCKS JEANS KICKS PANTS SLOPS
TONGS TREWS BRAIES CHINOS
DENIMS FLARES SHORTS SKILTS
SLACKS WHITES BOTTOMS BRACCAE
BROGUES CUTOFFS KERSEYS
NANKINS SHALWAR SLIVERS
STRIDES BLOOMERS BREECHES
FLANNELS KICKSEYS MOLESKIN
NANKEENS OVERALLS SHINTYAN
PANTALOONS INDESCRIBABLES
(— CUT AT KNEE) CUTOFFS
(— WITH CREASELESS LEGS)
STOVEPIPE
TROUT CHAR KELT PEAL POGY
BROOK BROWN CHARR LAKER
LUNGE SCURF SEWEN SEWIN SHARD
SQUET SQUIT TRUFF FINNOC KIPPER
MYKISS QUASKY SALTER TAIMEN
TRUCHA TULADI BOREGAT BROOKIE
BROWNIE COASTER HERLING
OQUASSA POUNDER RAINBOW
SQUETEE SUNAPEE AUREOLUS
BODIERON GILLAROO HARDHEAD

KAMLOOPS SAIBLING SALMONID
SISCOWET
(SMALL —) SCURLING SKIRLING
(YOUNG —) WHITLING
TROUVERE BLONDEL
TROVATORE, IL (CHARACTER IN —)
INEZ RUIZ DILUNA AZUCENA
LEONORA MANRICO FERRANDO
(COMPOSER OF —) VERDI
TROVE (TREASURE —) STASH
TROW DROW TRUE FAITH BELIEF
COVENANT
TROWEL HAWK LEAF PIPE DARBY
DERBY FLOAT TAPER TREWEL
(HEARTSHAPED —) HEART DOGTAIL
(MOLDER'S —) ILUS TAPER
(PLASTERER'S —) FLOAT
TROY ILION TROIA TROJA
(FOUNDER OF —) ILUS TROS
(INHABITANT OF —) ILIAN
TROYENS, LES (CHARACTER IN —)
ANNA DIDO IOPAS PRIAM AENEAS
HECTOR NARBAL ASCANIUS
PANTHEUS CASSANDRA
CHOROEBUS
(COMPOSER OF —) BERLIOZ
TRUANT HOOKY TRONE TROUT
MICHER MEECHER TRIVANT
VAGRANT
TRUCE PAX BARLEY TREAGUE
INDUCIAE
TRUCK DAN UTE BUNK CORF DRAB
DRAG DUCK DUMP GUNK RACK
WYNN BOGIE BUGGY DILLY DOLLY
GILLY LORRY TROKE BARTER
BUMMER CAMION DIESEL DROGUE
DRUGGE DUMPER JITNEY PICKUP
SLOVEN TIPPER TURTLE CARAVAN
FOURGON GONDOLA SKIDDER
SLEEPER TROLLEY TRUCKLE
TRUNDLE DELIVERY HAULAWAY
TRANSFER
(COAL —) DAN
(FIRE —) PUMPER
(KIND OF —) PANEL
(LOGGING —) BUNK BUMMER
(MINING —) CORF SKIP BARNEY
(PART OF —) DECK HOOD STEP TANK
TIRE GUARD LIGHT STAKE WHEEL
BUMPER GRILLE MIRROR AIRHORN
CARRIER EXHAUST MUDFLAP
BULKHEAD HEADLIGHT TAILLIGHT
COMPRESSOR WINDSHIELD
(TIMBER —) DRUG WYNN
TRUCKING (— RIG) SEMI
TRUCKLE FAWN TOADY SLAVER
TRUCKLING SERVILE
TRUCULENCE BRAG
TRUCULENT MEAN CRUEL HARSH
FIERCE SAVAGE SCATHING
TRUDGE JOG PAD HAKE PLOD STOG
JAUNT TRACE TRAIK TRAMP TRASH
STODGE TAIGLE TRAIPSE

TRUE SO GOOD JUST LEAL PURE
REAL VERY VRAI PLUMB RIGHT
SOOTH SOUND VERAY ACTUAL
FIDELE LAWFUL DEVOTED GENUINE
GERMANE PRECISE SINCERE
STAUNCH FAITHFUL RELIABLE
RIGHTFUL SOOTHFUL UNERRING
(— TO THE FACT) LITERAL
(NECESSARILY —) APODICTIC
APODEICTIC
(NOT —) INEXACT
(QUESTIONABLY —) ALLEGED
(SEEMINGLY —) PLAUSIBLE
(PREF.) ALETHO ETYMO EU ORTH(O)
VERI
TRUFFLE TRUB TRUFF EARTHNUT
TRUISM SOOTH
TRULL DELL BLOWZE CALLET
TRULY YEA AWAT EVEN FEGS IWIS
JUST QUITE SOOTH SYKER TIGHT
ATWEEL DINKUM INDEED SIMPLY
VERILY INSOOTH SOOTHLY
VERAMENT WITTERLY
TRUMP DIS DIX LOW PAM LILY RUFF
BASTA BASTO DEECE TROMBE
MANILLA MATADOR TRIUMPH
SPADILLE
(NOT —S) LAY
(2ND HIGHEST —) MANILLE
TRUMPERY MOCKADO RUBBISH
GIMCRACK PEDDLERY
TRUMPET BEME LURE TUBA SHELL
TRUMP BOZINE BUCCIN CORNET
KERANA LITUUS TROMBA TULNIC
ALCHEMY BUCCINA CLARINO
CLARION KERRANA SALPINX
NARSINGA SLUGHORN SOURDINE
WATERCUP
(— OF DAFFODIL) CORONA
(— OF FLOWER) CORONA
(AUSTRALIAN —) DIDGERIDOO
DIDJERIDOO
(CONCH —) SHELL
(RAM'S HORN —) SHOFAR
SHOPHAR
(PREF.) SALPING(O)
(SUFF.) SALPINX
TRUMPET BELL CODON PAVILON
TRUMPET CALL DIAN DIANA
SENNET
TRUMPET CREEPER TECOMA
COWHAGE CREEPER FOXGLOVE
HELLVINE
TRUMPETER MOKI AGAMI TRUMP
TOOTER JACAMIN TUBICEN
YAKAMIK
TRUMPETER FISH MOKI MOKIHI
TRUMPETER PERCH MADO
TRUMPETS WATERCUP
TRUMPET-SHAPED BUCCINAL
TRUMPETWOOD IMBAUBA
TRUNCATED ABRUPT STUBBED
TRUNKED

TRUNCHEON BATON BILLY WARDER
SPONTON PARTISAN SPONTOON
TRUNDLE HURL RUNG TRILL TROLL
RUNDLE TRUCKLE WALLOWER
TRUNK ROX BODY BOLE BOOT BULK
KIST LICH RUNT STAM STEM STUD
CABER PETER SHAFT STICK STOCK
TORSO ARIGUE BARREL CAUDEX
COFFER LOCKER CARCASS
CORSAGE STOWAGE TRUNCUS
SARATOGA
   (ARTERIAL —) AORTA
   (DEAD TREE —) RUNT
   (ELEPHANT'S —) SNOUT
   (FOSSIL —) CYCAD
   (SMALL —) HATBOX
   (SPLIT —) PUNCHEON
   (SWIM —S) JAMS
   (TREE —) BOLE BUTT STICK RICKER
   (TREE — OVER 8 INCHES IN
   DIAMETER) MAST
   (TRIMMED TREE —) LOG
   (WORSHIPPED TREE —S) IRMINSUL
   (PREF.) CORM(O) PROBOSCI(DI)
TRUNKFISH CHAPIN BOXFISH
COWFISH
TRUSS TIE BIND GIRD SPAN WARREN
DORLACH
   (— OF STRAW) WAP
   (— UP) KILT
TRUST AFFY HOPE LITE POOL RELY
REST TICK TREW TROW FAITH FRIST
GROUP TRUTH BELIEF CARTEL
CHARGE CORNER CREDIT DEPEND
FIANCE LIPPEN OFFICE TICKET
BELIEVE ENTRUST COMBINE
CONFIDE CREANCE CRIANCE
JAWBONE SECRECY VENTURE
AFFIANCE COMMENDA CREDENCE
MONOPOLY RELIANCE
   (KIND OF) TOTTEN
   (PLACE IN —) ESCROW
TRUSTED FIDUCIAL
TRUSTEE CURATOR FEOFFEE
SINDICO VISITOR ASSIGNEE
MUTWALLI
TRUSTWORTHINESS HONOR
TRUST CREDIT HONESTY CREDENCE
AXIOPISTY
TRUSTWORTHY SAFE SURE TRIG
SOOTH SOUND SYKER TRIED
HONEST SECRET SECURE SICKER
STABLE TRUSTY COCKSURE
CREDIBLE FIDUCIAL RELIABLE
TRUSTFUL
TRUSTY TRIG FECKFUL STAUNCH
FAITHFUL RELIABLE
TRUTH TAO UNA SOOTH TROTH
WHITE SATTVA VERITY LOWDOWN
REALITY VERITAS VERACITY VERIDITY
VERIMENT
   (—TABLE) MATRIX
   (FUNDAMENTAL —) PRINCIPLE

   (IDEAL —) CHRIST DHARMA
   (IN —) CERTES
   (RELATING TO —) ALETHIC
   (SELF-EVIDENT —) TRUISM
   (ULTIMATE —) LIGHT SUNYATA
TRUTH AND JUSTICE (AUTHOR OF
—) TAMMSAARE
   (CHARACTER IN —) MARI PAAS
KARIN TIINA ANDRES INDREK
TRUTHFUL TRUE VERY SOOTH
HONEST VERIDIC
TRUTHFULLY GOSPELLY
TRUTHFULNESS HONESTY
VERACITY SINCERITY
TRY GO SAY SHY TAX BASH BURL
FAND HACK PASS PENK PRFE SEEK
SLAP STAB TEST TIRL TURN AFOND
ASSAY CRACK ESSAY ETTLE FLING
GROPE JUDGE OFFER PROVE SENSE
SOUND TASTE TEMPT TOUCH
WHACK WHIRL APPOSE ASSAIL
FRAIST GRIEVE STRIVE AFFLICT
AFFORCE APPROVE ATTEMPT
DISCUSS ESPROVE IMITATE
STAGGER ENDEAVOR STRUGGLE
   (— DESPERATELY) AGONIZE
   (— FOR GOAL) SHOT
   (— HARD) STRIVE
   (— OUT) SAMPLE AUDITION
   (— TO ATTAIN) AFFECT
   (CASUAL —) FLING
   (QUICK —) SLAP
TRYING NASTY ARDUOUS CRUCIAL
GRUELING
TRYSAIL SPENCER
TSAR SALTAN (CHARACTER IN —)
GUIDON SALTAN MILITRISA
POVARIKHA TKACHIKHA
   (COMPOSER OF —)
RIMSKYKORSAKOV
TSAR'S BRIDE, THE (CHARACTER
IN —) IVAN LYKOV MARFA LYUBASHA
GRYANZNOY
   (COMPOSER OF —)
RIMSKYKORSAKOV
TSETSE FLY KIVU GANDI DIPTERAN
GLOSSINA
T-SHAPED TAU
TSILTADEN CHILION
TSUBO BU
TSWANA CHUANA SECHUANA
TUAREG IMOHAGH IMOSHAGH
TUATARA GUANA GUANO IGUANA
HATTERIA
TUB FAT HOD KID KIT SOE SOW TUN
VAT BACK BOWK COOL CORF COWL
GAWN KNOP MEAL SCOW TYND
TYNE BOWIE ESHIN KEEVE KIVER
SKEEL STAND BUCKET KELLER
KILLER KIMNEL TROUGH TURNEL
BATHTUB BREAKER SALTFAT
TANKARD TRUNDLE KOOLIMAN
LAVATORY

(— FOR ALEWIVES) HOD
(— FOR AMALGAMATING ORES) TINA
(— FOR BREAD) BARGE
(— OF BUTTER) COOL
(— OF HOGWASH) SWILLTUB
(— USED AS DIPPER) HANDY PIGGIN
(— WITH SLOPING SIDES) SHAUL
(BREWER'S —) BACK KEEVE
(KIND OF —) HOT
(LAUNDRY —) WASHTRAY
(MESS —) KID KIT
(MINING —) CORF
(PICKLING —) SALTFAT
(TANNING —) LEACH
(WATER —) DAN JAILER
(WOODEN —) KIT SOE KIMNEL
TRINDLE
TUBA BASS HELICON BOMBARDON
TUBE TAG BEAK BODY BOOT CANE
CASE CAST CORE CURL DRUM DUCT
HORN HOSE PIPE REED WORM
BATON CANAL CORER CROOK CRYPT
DRAIN GLAND HEART LINER QUILL
SIGHT SKELP SLIDE SPILE SPOUT
THECA THIEF TRUMP TUBAL VALVE
AUDION BARREL CALCAR CANNEL
CANNON COLUMN CORNET DEWCAP
FILTER GULLET HEADER NOZZLE
OCTODE SLEEVE SUCKER SYRINX
THROAT TRIODE TUBING TUBULE
TUNNEL UPTAKE VESSEL BLOWGUN
CHIMNEY CONDUIT CUVETTE
DROPPER FERRULE FISTULA
HOUSING OOBLAST OVIDUCT
QUILLET ROSTRUM SALPINX
SHALLOT SNORTER SNUFFER
SOXHLET STOPPLE THIMBLE
TUBULUS VENTURI ADJUTAGE
BOMBILLA CORNICLE DIATREME
DRAWTUBE FAIRLEAD GRADUATE
ORTHICON OVARIOLE PENSTOCK
PIPESTEM SAUCISSE SIPHONET
SLEEVING URCEOLUS ZOOECIUM
(— AT BASE OF PETAL) CALCAR
(— CARRYING BASSOON
MOUTHPIECE) CROOK
(— COVERING TRACE CHAIN) PIPING
(— FOR DEPOSITING CONCRETE)
TREMIE
(— FOR DRINKING MATE) BOMBILLA
(— FOR LINING WELL) WELLRING
(— FOR OBOE REED) STAPLE
(— FOR STIFFENING STRING) TAG
(— FOR TRANSFERRING LIQUID)
SIPHON SYPHON
(— FOR WINDING THREAD) COP
(— FROM SHIP'S PUMP) DALE
(— IN ENGINE CYLINDER) LINER
(— OF BALLOON) APPENDIX
(— OF GUN) BORE BARREL
(— OF RETORT) BEAK ROSTRUM
(— OF SPIRIT LEVEL) BUBBLE

(— OF TOBACCO) CIGARET
(— TO LINE A VENT) BOUCHE
(— TWISTED IN COILS) WORM
(— USED IN WHALING) LULL
(AMPLIFIER —) STAGE
(BONE —) SNUFFER
(BOOB —) TV TELLY
(CAMERA —) VIDICON ORTHICON
(DISCHARGE —) TORUS
(DISTILLING —) TOWER
(ELECTRO —) BULB
(ELECTRODE —) AUDION PENTODE
(ELECTRON —) DIODE DRIVER TRIODE
TETRODE KENOTRON KLYSTRON
PLIOTRON TRINISCOPE
(ELECTRONIC INDICATOR —) NIXIE
(FIREWORKS —) LEADER
(GLANDULAR —) CRYPT
(GLASS —) SIGHT MATRASS
(GLASSBLOWER'S —) BLOWPIPE
(HONEY —) NECTARY SIPHONET
(INDICATOR —) NIXIE
(KIND OF —) PITOT
(KNITTED —) STOCKING
(LABORATORY —) PIPETTE
(PAPER —) LEADER PASTILLE
(PASTRY —) CORNET
(POLLEN —) SPERMARY
(PRIMING —) AUGET
(RECTIFIER —) IGNITRON
(SILK — OF SPIDER) SPIGOT
(SPEAKING —) BLOWER GOSPORT
(SUCKING —) STRAW
(SURGICAL —) CANNULA
(THERMOMETER —) STEM
(VACUUM —) DIODE KEYER
HEXODE HEPTODE DYNATRON
MAGNETRON
(PREF.) FISTULI SIPHON(O) SOLEN(O)
SYRING(O)
TUBELET CIRCLET
TUBER ANU OCA SET ANYU BULB
CLOG COCO ROOT SEED SETT YAMP
COCCO SALEP JICAMA PIGNUT
POTATO WAPATA WINDER YAUTIA
EARTHNUT MURRNONG
(DRIED —S) SALEP
TUBERCLE PEARL NODULE STEMMA
CUSPULE VERRUCA
TUBERCULAR PHTHISIC
TUBERCULOSIS CON LUPUS
CLYERS DECLINE PHTHISIS
SCROFULA
TUBING HOSE TUBAGE
TUBMAN DUCKER
TUBULAR PIPY PIPED TUBATE
QUILLED CANNULAR
(NOT —) FARCTATE
(PREF.) SOLEN(O)
TUBULE TRACHEA TUBULET
TUBULUS CISTERNA
TUCANO BETOYAN

TUCK TOKE STUFF TRUSS FLANGE
(— **AWAY**) KEEP SAVE STOW
(— **IN**) TRUSS TROUSS
(— **UP**) FAKE KILT
TUCKER CORDER KILTER PLEATER
(— **OUT**) TIRE
TUESDAY (SECOND — AFTER
EASTER) HOCKDAY HOKEDAY
TUFA TOPHUS
TUFF TRASS PEPERINO PORODITE
SANTORIN
TUFT COP EAR FAG FOB NOB SOP
TOP COMA DOWN KNOB KNOP
MOCK TAIT TATE TUFF TUSK TUZZ
WISP BEARD BUNCH CREST FLOCK
STUPA THRUM WHISK CATKIN
CIRRUS DOLLOP PAPPUS PENCIL
TASSEL TUFFET CIRRHUS FEATHER
FLOCCUS HOBNAIL PANACHE
SCOPULA TOPKNOT TOPPING
TUSSOCK AIGRETTE FLOCCULE
ARBUSCULE
(— **OF BRISTLES**) BIRSE
(**OF CLOTH**) BURR
(— **OF DIRTY WOOL**) DAG
(— **OF DOWN**) FRIEZE
(— **OF FEATHERS**) EAR HORN HULU
EGRET
(— **OF FILAMENTS**) BYSSUS
(— **OF FLOWERS**) TRUSS
(— **OF GRASS**) FAG SOP MOCK
HASSOCK TUSSOCK
(— **OF HAIR**) TOP COMA TUZZ BRUSH
SWITCH COWLICK FEATHER FLOCCUS
SCOPULA TOPKNOT IMPERIAL
KNOWLES
(— **OF HAIR ON HORSE'S HOOF**)
FETLOCK
(— **OF HAY**) COP
(— **OF MALE TURKEY**) BEARD
(— **OF WOOL**) FOB TUSK TUZZ FLOCK
(— **ON BIRD'S HEAD**) COP CUCK
EGRET
(— **ON BONNET**) TOORIE
(— **ON CHIN**) GOATEE
(— **ON PINEAPPLE**) CROWN
(— **ON SEED PLANT**) PAPPUS
(— **ON SPIDER'S FEET**) SCOPULA
(—**S OF ROPE YARN**) THRUM
(**VASCULAR** —) GLOMUS
(**PREF.**) LOPH(O) LOPHI(O)
TUFTED COMOSE TAPPET TAPPIT
CRISTATE
TUG LUG PUG RUG TIT TOG CHUG
DRAG HALE HAUL PULL TOIL TUCK
CHUFF HITCH PLUCK SHRUG TRACE
JIGGER RUGGLE TOWBOAT
TUGBOAT
TUGBOAT TOW TUG TOWBOAT
TRACKER
TUI POE TUA KOKO TUWI POEBIRD
TUITION CUSTODY

TULIP LILY LILIUM BIZARRE BREEDER
PICOTEE TURNSOLE
TULIP TREE POPLAR BASSWOOD
CUCUMBER
TULIPWOOD AUBURN
TULLE ILLUSION
TULWAR SABER
TUMATAKURU IRISHMAN
MATAGORY
TUMBLE TOP COUP WALT LATCH
SPILL THROW TIFLE TRACE COTTON
GROVEL PURLER TIFFLE TOPPLE
WALTER WAMBLE WELTER STUMBLE
WHEMMEL
(— **OVER**) TIPPLE WALLOP
TUMBLE-DOWN RUINOUS
TUMBLER NUT CLICK GLASS LEVER
WIPER ROLLER ACROBAT DRUMMER
TIPPLER TOPPLER VOLTIGEUR
TUMID TURGID BLOATED BULGING
FUSTIAN TURGENT INFLATED
TUMOROUS
TUMOR PAP WEN BEAL PIAN WART
AMPER BOTCH GUMMA MYOMA
NEVUS PHYMA SWELL TALPA
AMBURY ANBURY EPULIS GLIOMA
GYROMA INCOME KELOID LIPOMA
MYXOMA NUROMA RISING WARBLE
ADENOMA ANGIOMA CYSTOMA
DERMOID DESMOID FIBROID
FIBRUMA LUTEOMA MYELOMA
NEUROMA OSTEOMA OSTEOME
SARCOMA TESTUDO THYMOMA
ULCINGUS ATHEROMA BLASTOMA
CHLOROMA CHORDOMA CHORIOMA
EMBRYOMA GANGLION GLANDULE
HEMATOMA LIPPOUMA HOLDFAST
LYMPHOMA MELANOMA MELICERA
NEOPLASM ODONTOMA PHLEGMON
PLASMOMA PSAMMOMA SCIRRHUS
SEMINOMA TERATOID TERATOMA
WINDGALL CHALAZION PAPILLOMA
(— **OF EYELID**) GRANDO
(— **ON HORSE'S LEGS**) JARDE
(**KIND OF** —) GLOMUS
(**PUSTULAR** —) BLAIN
(**SKIN** —) OUCH
(**STUDY OF** —**S**) ONCOLOGY
(**PREF.**) CARCIN(O) GANGLI(O)
GANGLO MYOM(O) ONCO SCIRRH(O)
(**SUFF.**) CELE COELE COELUS OMA
ONCUS SCIRRHUS
TUMULT DIN COIL FARE FLAW FRAY
FUSS HURL MUSS REEL RIOT ROUT
VISE BRAWL BROIL HURLY HURRY
LURRY NOISE ROUST STOOR STOUR
WHIRL AFFRAY BUSTLE CLAMOR
DIRDUM EMFUTE FRACAS HUBBUB
MUTINY PUDDER RABBLE RIPPET
RUMAGE RUFFLE SHINDY STEERY
UPROAR UPSTIR BLUSTER BOBBERY
BRATTLE FACTION FERMENT

GARBOIL TEMPEST TURMOIL DISORDER SEDITION STIRRING STRAMASH COMMOTION PANDEMONIUM

TUMULTUOUS HIGH LOUD RUDE NOISY ROUGH STORMY FURIOUS HURRIED LAWLESS RIOTOUS VIOLENT AGITATED CONFUSED DRAWLING HURTLING

TUMULUS LOW MOTE TUMP MOUND BARROW BURIAN COTERELL

TUN CASK HAAB
(ONE-THIRD —) TERTIAN
(20 —S) KATUN

TUNA AHI ATUN TUNNY BLUEFIN PELAMYD ALBACORE KAWAKAWA
(KIND OF —) SKIPJACK

TUNE AIR ARIA DUMP FADO LEED LILT NOTE PORT RANT SONG CHARM CHORD DITTY DRANT POINT ATTUNE GROUND MAGGOT STRAIN STRING TEMPER GUAJIRA HALLING MEASURE MELISMA SONANCE ANGLAISE FANDANGO GUARACHA HABANERA QUICKSTEP
(— A HARP) WREST
(— AN INSTRUMENT) STRING
(DANCE —) FURIANT ANGLAISE GALLIARD
(FOLK —) FADO
(HILLBILLY —) HOEDOWN
(IN —) ONKEY
(LIGHT —) TOY
(LITTLE —) CATCH
(LIVELY —) LILT SPRING HORNPIPE
(MELANCHOLY —) DUMP
(SACRED —) CHORAL CHORALE
(TRADITIONAL —) TONE

TUNEBO TAME GUACICO

TUNEFUL TUNY CHANTANT TUNESOME

TUNEFULNESS MELODY

TUNGST-
(PREF.) WOLFRAM

TUNGSTEN W WOLFRAM SCHEELIN

TUNGUS EVENK LAMUT

TUNIC COAT JAMA JUPE VEST AODAI COTTE FROCK GIPON GIPPO JAMAH JUPON PALLA ACHKAN BLIAUT CAMISE CHITON CYCLAS FECKET HARDIE KABAYA KIRTLE TABARD ARISARD BLEAUNT CAMISIA DASHIKI PALTOCK SURCOAT TUNICLE COLOBIUM DAISHIKI GANDOURA SUBTUNIC SUBUCULA SUKKENYE
(— OF MAIL) HAUBERK
(AFRICAN —) DASHIKI DAISHIKI
(HOODED FUR —) SOVIK

TUNICATE SALP SALPA SALPID ASCIDIAN TUNICARY UROCHORD

TUNICLE SACCOS

TUNING ANESIS

TUNING FORK EVEL EVIL FORK TUNER DIAPASE DIAPASON MODULANT

TUNING HAMMER KEY

TUNNEL ADIT BORE CAVE CURL PUKA SINK TUBE DRIFT DRIVE KAREZ STALL BURROW PIERCE
(— IN ROCK) SYRINX
(— INTO AN IGLOO) TOSSUT
(IRRIGATION —) QANAT
(KIND OF —) CARPAL
(PROPOSED —) CHUNNEL

TUNNY TUNA ALBACORE SCOMBRID
(YOUNG —) PELAMYD

TUP TIP TRIP MONKEY BLISSOM

TUR
(BROTHER OF —) IRAJ SALM
(FATHER OF —) FARIDUN
(MOTHER OF —) SHAHRINAZ

TURACO LORY

TURANDOT (CHARACTER IN —) LIU CALAF TURANDOT
(COMPOSER OF —) PUCCINI

TURBAN PAT MOAB PATA SASH TUFT LUNGI MITER MITRE PAGRI PATTI TOWEL TUFFE MANDIL WRAPPER KAFFIYEH PUGGAREE SEERBAND TOLIPANE TULIPANT TURBANTO

TURBELLARIA APROCTA

TURBELLARIAN FLATWORM

TURBID FAT RILY DROVY GUMLY MUDDY RILEY ROILY DRUMLY GRUMLY QUALLY FECULENT LUTULENT

TURBIDITY RILE

TURBOT BRET BRILL WHIFF FLATFISH

TURBULENCE CAT FURY UPROAR FERMENT RIOTING
(— IN WATER) BULLER

TURBULENT GURL HIGH LOUD RUDE WILD ROILY ROUGH WROTH

RUGGED STORMY UNRULY YEASTY FURIOUS RABBISH RACKETY TROUBLE VIOLENT MUTINOUS SCAMBLING BOISTEROUS

TURCO IN ITALIA, IL (CHARACTER IN —) DAMELEC GERONIO FIORILLA PROSDOCIMO
(COMPOSER OF —) ROSSINI

TURDUS MERULA

TUREEN DISH TERRINE

TURF SOD VAG CESS DELF FAIL FALE FEAL FLAG FLAT FLAW PONE SUNK DELFT SCRAW SPINE SWARD TRUFF FLAUGHT SHIRREL SODDING GREENSWARD
(— CUT BY GOLF STROKE) DIVOT
(— FOR LINING PARAPET) GAZON
(DRIED — FOR FUEL) VAG
(PARED —) REAT
(ROUGH —) GOR
(SMALL PIECE OF —) TAB
(SMOOTH —) FAIRWAY
(THIN LAYER OF —) FLAW

TURF SPADE SLANE

TURGID ERECT TUMID BLOATED INFLATED PLETHORIC

TURGIDNESS TYMPANY

TURK TURCO TURKO SELJUK CORSAIR OSMANLI OTTOMAN TURQUET KONARIOT

TURKANA ELKUMA

TURKEY BUST FLOP STAG STEG BUSTARD CRECIER ERECTOR FAILURE GOBBLER ALDERMAN
(BRUSH —) VULTURN TALEGALLA
(FLOCK OF —S) RAFTER
(KIND OF —) COLD
(MALE —) TOM
(YOUNG —) POULI

TURKEY
CAPE: INCE BAFRA ANAMUR HINZIR KARATAS KEREMPE
CAPITAL: ANKARA
COIN: LIRA PARA AKCHA ASPER ATTUN REBIA AKCHEH SEQUIN ZEQUIN ALTILIK BESHLIK PATAQUE PIASTER MEDJIDIE ZECCHINO
DISTRICT: PERA BEYOGLU CILICIA
GULF: COS ANTALYA
LAKE: TUZ VAN EGRIDIR BEYSEHIR
MEASURE: DRA OKA OKE PIK DRAA HATT KHAT KILE ZIRA ALMUD BERRI DONUM KILEH ZIRAI ARSHIN CHINIK DJERIB FORTIN HALEBI PARMAK NOCKTAT
MOUNTAIN: AK ALA KARA HASAN HINIS HONAZ MURAT MURIT ARARAT BINGOL BOLGAR SUPHAN ERCIYAS KARACALI
PROVINCE: MUS VAN AGRI BOLU ICEL KARS ORDU HIZE SERT URFA USAK

AYDIN BURSA IZMIR SIIRT ANGORA EYALET
REGION: ANATOLIA
RIVER: DICLE FIRAT GEDIZ HALYS IRMAK KIZIL MESTA SARUS SEIHUN SEYHAN SEYLAN TIGRIS SAKARYA MAEANDER
SEAPORT: ENOS IZMIR MERSIN SAMSUN TRABZON ISTANBUL
TOWN: URFA ADANA BURSA IZMIR IZNIK KONYA MANAS SIIRT SIVAS AINTAB EDESSA EDIRNE ELAZIG MARASH SAMSUN ERZURUM KAYSERI SCUTARI USKUDAR ISTANBUL STAMBOUL
WEIGHT: OKA OKE DRAM KILE ROTL ARTAL ARTEL CEQUI CHEKE KERAT MAUND OBOLU RATEL BATMAN DIRHEM KANTAR MISKAL DRACHMA QUINTAL YUSDRUM

TURKEY BUZZARD AURA BROMVOEL BROMVOGEL GALLINAZO

TURKEY-COCK STAG

TURKEY OAK CERRIS

TURKI KAZAK QAZAQ KAZAKH

TURKISH TURK TURCIC OSMANLI OTTOMAN

TURKISH DELIGHT LOUKOUM

TURKMENISTAN
(ALSO SEE RUSSIA)
CAPITAL: ASHKHABAD
COIN: RUBLE
DESERT: KARAKUM KARAKUMY
MOUNTAIN RANGE: KOPETDAG KHANOPETDAG KUGITANGTAU
NAME: TURKMEN TURKMENIA
OASIS: MURGAB TEDZHEN AMUDARYA KOPETDAG
RIVER: OXUS ATREK MURGAB TEDZHEN AMUDARYA
SEA: CASPIAN
TOWN: MARY MERV NEBITDAG CHARDZHOU KRASNOVODSK
TRIBE: TEKKE YOMUT ERSARI

TURKOMAN SEID ERSAR

TURK'S CAP LILY MARTAGON

TURMERIC REA ANGO HALDI OLENA HULDEE AZAFRAN CURCUMA

TURMIT TURNIP

TURMOIL ADO DIN COIL DUST MOIL TOIL TOSS BURLE HURLY HURRY STROW TOUSE WHIRL HASSLE JABBLE POTHER ROMAGE UPROAR WELTER CLUTTER EMOTION FERMENT GARBOIL HURLING MAKADOO RUMMAGE TEMPEST DISPEACE DISQUIET

TURN GO BOW CUT GEE JAR RUN TON WIN AIRT BEND BOUT BOWL

CALE CAST CHAR CHOP COCK EDDY
GIRO HACK HEAD HINT HURL JAMB
KINK PULL PURL QUIP ROLL ROVE
SLEW TIRL TOUR VEER VERT VICE
WAFT WELT WIND AIRTH ANGLE
BLANK CHARE CRANK CRASH CREEK
CRICK CROOK ELBOW FEEZE GLINT
PIVOT PLUCK PRICK QUIRK SHIFT
SPELL SWING SWIRL TARVE TERVE
TREND TRILL TROLL TWINE TWIST
VERSE VOLTI WHEEL WREST ATTURN
BOUGHT CIRCLE COURSE DEPEND
DIRECT DOUBLE GRUPPO GYRATE
INDENT INTEND INTURN POSSET
QUEEVE RESORT RETURN ROTATE
SPIRAL STRAIN SWIVEL TOURNE
TURKEN VOLUME VOLUTE WIMPLE
CONVERT CRANKLE CRINKLE
DEFLECT DISTURB FLEXION FLEXURE
FLOUNCE INCLINE INFLECT PASSADE
REVERSE REVOLVE SERPENT
SINUATE TWINGLE TWISTER
VERSATE WREATHE CLINAMEN
DOUBLING FLECTION TOURNURE
TRAVERSE VOLUTION
(— ABOUT) SLEW SLUE SLOUGH
WINDLASS
(— AGAINST) CROSS
(— AROUND) GYRE WELT WEND
RATCH BEWEND SPHERE
(— ASIDE) ERR WRY DAFF SKEW
WARD ABHOR AVERT BLENK DETER
EVADE FENCE GLENT SHEER WAIVE
BLENCH DEPART DETURN DIVERT
SWERVE SWITCH CRINKLE DECLINE
DEFLECT DEVIATE DIGRESS DIVERGE
PERVERT SCRITHE
(— AT DRINKING) TIRL
(— ATTENTION) ADVERT ADDRESS
(— AWAY) DOFF AVERT CHARE HIELD
REPEL AVERSE DESERT DETURN
DIVERT REVOLT ABANDON DECLINE
REVERSE OVERTURN WITHTURN
(— AWRY) CONTORT
(— BACK) KEP ABORT FLIPE FLYPE
RETORT RETURN REVERT REFLECT
UNTWIST RENVERSE
(— BACK ON) RUMP
(— BROWN) AUGUST
(— BY TOSSING) FLAP
(— CARD FACE UP) BURN
(— DOWN) DIP DENY VETO
(— DOWNWARDS) SLOPE
(— FOR BETTER) CRISIS
(— FOR INFORMATION) REFER
(— IN ARCHERY) HIELD
(— IN CROQUET) BISK BISQUE
(— IN ROPE) NIP RIDER
(— INSIDE OUT) EVERT FLYPE INVERT
(— INTO ICE) CONGEAL
(— INTO STEEL) ACIERATE
(— INTO VINEGAR) ACETIFY
(— INTO WOOD) LIGNIFY

(— LEAVES OF BOOK) LEAF TOSS
(— LEFT) HAW PORT
(— OF AFFAIRS) GO JOB KICK
(— OF CABLE) BITTER
(— OF DUTY) TOUR SHIFT TRICK
(— OF EVENTS) WENT
(— OF EXPRESSION) CONCETTO
(— OFF) SHUNT DIVERT
(— OF FANCY) GUST
(— OF MIND) FREAK
(— OF STRING) WAP
(— OF TIDE) PINCH
(— OF WIT) FLIRT
(— OF YARN) MOUSING
(— ON) HIT AROUSE
(— ONE'S BACK) TERGIVERSATE
(— ON LATHE) THROW
(— OUT) GO USH BEAR FALL FARE
OUST SORT TAKE CHIVE FUDGE
LOOSE OUTPUT SUCCEED
(— OUT TO BE) PROVE EXFLECT
(— OUTWARD) EVERT SPLAY
(— OVER) CANT FLAP FLIP KEEL
VETTE VOLVE CLINCH DESIGN
AGITATE CAPSIZE OVERSET
(— PAGES) LEAF
(— POINT OF) ABATE
(— RAPIDLY) SPIN TIRL GIDDY
(— RIGHT) GEE HAP HUP
(— SAIL YARD) BRACE
(— SIDEWAYS) TRAVERSE
(— SKIS) STEM
(— SOUR) FOX BLINK PRILL BLEEZE
CHANGE SOUREN
(— SUDDENLY) FLOP SLUE
(— THE BALANCE) PREPONDERATE
(— TO BUY DRINKS) SHOUT
(— TO DUST) MOULDER
(— TO NEAR SIDE) HAW
(— TO OFF SIDE) GEE
(— TO ONE SIDE) CORNER GOGGLE
(— TO STONE) LAPIDIFY
(— TO THE LEFT) HAW PORT WIND
WYND
(— TOWARD WIND) LUFF
(— TO WINDWARD) STAY
(— UP) FACE HAPPEN
(— UP NOSE) FLIRT SNURL
(— UPSIDE DOWN) CANT COUP
WHELM INVERT QUELME WHELVE
WHEMMLE
(— VESSEL IN CIRCLE) CHAPEL
(— WHEELS) CRAMP
(— YELLOW) FIRE
(BALLET —) PIROUETTE
(COMPLETE —) LAP
(DOWNWARD —) SLIDE
(ECCENTRIC —) CRANKUM
(FORTUNATE —) BREAK
(GOOD —) BOON SERVICE
(HALF —) CARACOLE
(IN —) AROUND
(INWARD —) INTROVERT

(SERIES OF —S) CHICANE
(SERIES OF TIGHT —S) MILLRACE
(SHARP —) TWO DOUBLE WRENCH
ZIGZAG HAIRPIN
(SKI —) SWING CHRISTIE TELEMARK
(SUDDEN —) CURL
(TAKE —S) ROTATE
(PL.) ALLEGRO
(PREF.) STREPHO STREPSI STREPT(O)
TREPO TROP(IDO)(O) VERSI
VERTEBR(I)(O) VERTI
(SUFF.) TROPAL TROPE TROPIA
TROPIC TROPY

TURNBUCKLE TURNEL TURNBOUT
TURNCOAT RAT APOSTATE
RENEGADE RENEGADO RENEGATE
TURNED SOUR VERSED COCKEYED
INFLEXED
(— ABOUT) CONVERSE
(— AWAY) FROWARD
(— AWRY) TORTIVE
(— BACK) EVOLUTE RETRORSE
(— DOWNWARD) ABASED DEFLEXED
(— EDGEWISE) BLIND
(— INWARD) VARUS
(— OUTWARD) SPLAY EXTRORSE
(— TOWARD) ANODIC
(— TOWARD ONE SIDE) AWRY
(— UP) ACOCK URVED RETROUSSE
(— WRONG WAY) AWK
(PREF.) STREPSI

TURNER SLICE BODGER SLIDER
TWIRLER
TURNING HEAD WIND TWIST VOLTA
WRINK DETOUR ROTARY FLEXION
FLEXURE VERSION VOLVENT
FLECTION STREPSIS WHEELERY
ACESCENCE
(— ASIDE) APOTROPAIC
(— BACK) RETORTION REFLECTION
(— FREELY) VERSATILE
(— OF EYE) CAST
(— SOUR) ACESCENT
(— SUNWISE) EUTROPIC
EUTROPOUS
(— TO LEFT) SINISTRAL LAEOTROPIC
(— TO RIGHT) DEXTRO
(— TOWARD STEM) ADVERSE
(— UP) OCCURRENT
(METAL —S) SWARF
(PL.) SCULL
(PREF.) STROPH(O) TROPIDO TROPO
(SUFF.) TROPAL TROPE TROPIA
TROPIC(AL) TROPISM TROPOUS
TROPY

TURNIP BAGA NAPE NEEP RAPE
NAVEW SWEDE RAPEYE TURMUT
CRUCIFER RUTABAGA
(KIND OF —) SWEDISH
(PL.) KRAUT RAPPINI
(PREF.) NAPI
TURNIP-SHAPED NAPIFORM
RAPACEUS

TURNIX QUAIL HEMIPOD ORTYGAN
HEMIPODE
TURNKEY SCREW JAILER LOCKSMAN
TURN OF THE SCREW (AUTHOR
OF —) JAMES
(CHARACTER IN —) FLORA MILES
PETER QUINT JESSEL
TURNOUT RIG TEAM SETOUT
EQUIPAGE TRANSFER
TURNOVER PIE PASTY BRIDIE
BRAMBLE CALZONE EMPANADA
FLAPJACK
(PL.) PIROJKI PIROSHKI
TURNPIN TAMPION
TURNSOLE HELIO
TURNSPIT HASTLER
TURNSTILE TIRL STILE MOULINE
TURNGATE TURNPIKE TOURNIQUET
TURNSTONE PLOVER REDLEG
CHICARIC CREDDOCK
TURNTABLE DECK RACER ROTARY
NONSYNC PLAYBACK
TURNUS (FATHER OF —) DAUNUS
(MOTHER OF —) VENILIA
(SLAYER OF —) AENEAS
TURPENTINE THUS TURPS SCRAPE
THINNER OLEORESIN
(BORDEAUX —) GALIPOT
TURPENTINE TREE PEEBEEN
TURPITUDE EVIL FEDITY
TURQUOISE TURKEY TURKIS
CALAITE CALLAIS
TURRET ROUND BELFRY CUPOLA
GARRET GAZEBO LOUVER TOURET
BARMKIN GUERITE MIRADOR
MONITOR BARBETTE BARTIZAN
GUNHOUSE PINNACLE TURRICLE
BELVEDERE PEPPERBOX
(CORNER —) ROUND
TURTLE EMYD ARRAU CARET CAREY
TORUP COODLE COOTER JURARA
RIDLEY SLIDER THURGI TURKLE
CRAWLER CREEPER EMYDIAN
JUNIATA LOGHEAD SNAPPER
TORTUGA CHELONID FLAPJACK
HAWKBILL MATAMATA SHAGTAIL
STINKPOT TERRAPIN TORTOISE
THALASSIAN
(— HAVING COMMERCIAL SHELL)
CHICKEN
(OLD —) MOSSBACK
(PART OF —) EAR BEAK CLAW SHELL
SHIELD CARAPACE PLASTRON
(SEA —) RIDLEY
TURTLEHEAD BALMONY CHELONE
CODHEAD
TUSCAN BROWN MECCA
MOHAWK
TUSCANY COLCOTHAR
TUSK GAM CUSK HORN TUSH IVORY
TOOTH ELEPHANT
(— OF WILD BOAR) RAZOR
(ELEPHANT'S —) SCRIVELLO

TUSSLE TUG SCRAP BICKER TASSEL
TOUSLE WARSLE TUILYIE
TUSSOCK HASSOCK
TUT HOOT TOOT HOOTS
TUTELAGE TUTELE YEMSEL
NURTURE TEACHING
TUTELARY GENIUS
TUTOR DON ABBE TUTE COACH
TRACH DOCENT FEEDER GROUND
MASTER MENTOR PEDANT SCHOOL
GRINDER TEACHER CRANSIER
CREANCER GOVERNOR PANGLOSS
PUPILIZE PRECEPTOR REPETITEUR
SCHOOLMASTER
TUTTI RIPIENO
TUTU TOOT TUPAKIHI
TUVALU (CAPITAL OF —) FUNAFUTI
(FORMER NAME OF —)
ELLICEISLANDS LAGOONISLANDS
(ISLAND OF —) NANUMEA
NUKUFETAU NUKULAILAI
TUXEDO TUX SOFA TUCK
TVASHTRI (DAUGHTER OF —)
SARANYU
TWADDLE ROT BOSH TOSH FUDGE
HAVER BABBLE DRIVEL FOOTLE
PIFFLE TOOTLE FADAISE TWATTLE
NONSENSE SLIPSLOP TOMMYROT
TWANA COLCINE
TWANG TANG PLUCK PLUNK
SNUFFLE TWANGLE TWANKLE
TWANGY NASAL
TWAYBLADE DUFOIL TWIFOIL
(PL.) LISTERA
TWEAK FEAK TWIG
TWEED PATTU PATTOO
TWEEZERS TIT TWIRK TWINGE
TWITCH MULLETS PINCERS PINCETTE
VOLSELLA
TWELFTH TWALT DOZENTH
(— OF INCH) SECOND
(— OF LIGHT PERIOD) INCH
(— PART) UNĊIA
TWELFTH DAY EPIPHANY
TWELFTH NIGHT
(AUTHOR OF —) SHAKESPEARE
(CHARACTER IN —) TOBY BELCH
CURIO FESTE MARIA VIOLA ANDREW
FABIAN OLIVIA ORSINO ANTONIO
MALVOLIO AGUECHEEK SEBASTIAN
VALENTINE
TWELVE TWAL DOZEN DICKER
DODECADE
(PREF.) DODEC(A) DUODECIM
TWELVEMONTH TOWMONT
TWELVER IMAMI
TWELVE-TONE SERIAL
TWELVE-TONE-ROW SET
TWENTIETH VIGESIMAL
VINGTIEME
TWENTY KAPH CORGE KAPPA SCORE
COOREE
(PREF.) ICOS(A) VIGINTI

TWENTY-FIVE QUARTERN
TWENTY-FOURTH CARAT
TWENTY-ONE PONTOON VANJOHN
BLACKJACK
**20,000 LEAGUES UNDER THE
SEA (AUTHOR OF —)** VERNE
(CHARACTER IN —) NED LAND NEMO
PIERRE ARONNAX CONSEIL
TWERP DRIP NERD TWIT DRONGO
SHNOOK
TWICE BIS DOPPIO
(— A DAY) BID
(— IN TIME) AGAIN
(PREF.) BI BIS DI DIS
TWICE-BORN REGENERATE
TWIDDLE TWEEDLE TWITTER
(— FEET) CUT
(— THE FEET) CUT
TWIG COW CHAT RICE RISP SLIP
WAND YARD BIRCH BRIAR BRIER
SHRAG SHRED SPRAY SPRIG STICK
TWIST VIRGA WAVER WITHE BALEYS
BROWSE FESCUE GREAVE SALLOW
SPRING SWITCH WATTLE WICKER
SCOLLOP TWIGLET ANAPHYTE
(— FOR SNUFF) DIP
(— GROWING FROM STUMP) WAVER
(— IN BIRD SNARE) SNEEK
(—S FOR BURNING) CHATWOOD
(—S FOR WATTLING) FRITLES
(—S MADE INTO BROOM) BESOM
(— WORN AT SACRIFICES)
INARCULUM
(BARE —) COW
(BROKEN —S) BRUSH
(CUT —) SARMENT
(DRIED —) CHAD
(LITTLE —) SURCLE
(THATCHING —) SCOLLOP
(WILLOW —) SALLOW ANAPHYTE
(SUFF.) CLEMA
TWIGGED VIRGATE
TWIGGY SPRAYEY
TWILIGHT EVE DIMPS DUMPS
GLOAM TWALE DIMMET DIMMIT
UGHTEN DUCKISH COCKSHUT
EVENFALL EVENGLOW EVENTIDE
GLOAMING GRISPING CREPUSCLE
(— OF THE GODS) RAGNAROK
(DARKER PART OF —) DUSK
(MORNING —) DAWN
TWILL WALE CHINO CADDIS RUSSEL
CADDICE DUNGAREE
TWILLED CORDED
TWIN DUAL GEMEL SOSIE DIDYMUS
JUMELLE SIAMESE TWINDLE
DIDYMATE DIDYMOID DIDYMOUS
PARASITE TWINLING
(PL.) GEMEL COUPLET
(PREF.) DIDYM(O) GEMINI
(SUFF.) DIDYMUS
TWINE MAT COIL DUNE LACE PIRL
WIND WRAP TWIRL TWIST ENLACE

INFOLD INTORT ANAMITE ENTWINE
SKEENYIE
(HANK OF —) RAN
(PITCHED —) WHIPPING
(PREF.) PLEC(O)
TWINEBUSH PINBUSH
TWINFLOWER LINNAEA
TWINGE ACHE GIRD PANG PULL
SHOOT TOUCH TWANG STOUND
(— OF CONSCIENCE) SCRUPLE
(— OF PAIN) GLISK
TWINING VOLUBLE AMPLECTANT
TWINKLE WINK BLINK TWEER TWINK
TWIRE BICKER SECOND SIMPER
WINKLE SPARKLE
TWINKLE-TOED AGILE
TWINKLING TRICE MOMENT
TWINKLY
TWINLEAF HELMETPOD
TWIRL SPIN TIRL DRILL QUERL TRILL
TWIRK TWIST WHIRL TRUNDLE
TWIDDLE TWIZZLE
(— OF BAGPIPE) WARBLER
TWIST DOB CUE MAT PLY WIN WIP
CAST COIL CURL DRAW HURL KICK
KINK PIRL RICK SKEW SLEW SLUB
SLUE TURN WARP WIND WISP WORK
CHINK CRANK CRICK CRINK CROOK
CURVE FEEZE GNARL KINCH PLAIT
QUIRK QUIRL REEVE SCREW SKELL
SNAKE SNIRL SNURL SPIRE SWIRL
THRAW THROW TWEAK TWIND
TWINE TWIRE TWIRL WINCE WITHE
WREST WRICK BOUGHT DETORT
EXTORT HANKLE INTORT QUEEVE
SLOUGH SPRAIN SQUIRL SQUIRM
STRAND TWEEZE WAMBLE WARPLE
WASHIN WICKER WIMBLE WRABBE
WRITHE CHIGNON CONTORT
CHANKLE CRINKLE CROOKLE
CRUMPLE DISTORT ENTWINE
ENTWIST FLOUNCE GIMMICK
SQUINCH TORTURE TWISTER
TWISTLE TWIZZLE WREATHE
WRIGGLE CLINAMEN CONVOLUTE
ENTANGLE FOREHARD FORETURN
SPRINKLE SQUIGGLE VOLUTION
(— A ROPE) DALLY
(— AWAY) WAIVE
(— BACK) RETORT
(— FORCIBLY) WRING
(— IN A ROPE) GRIND SQUIRM
(— IN GRAIN OF A BOW) BOUGHT
(— IN ONE'S NATURE) KINK
(— OF FACE) STITCH
(— OF HAY) HAYBRAND
(— OF PAPER) SPILL
(— OF PEN IN WRITING) QUIRK
(— OF SPEECH) CRANK
(— OF THE MOUTH) DRAD
(— OF TOBACCO) ROLL PIGTAIL
(— OF YARNS) FORETURN
(— OUT OF SHAPE) BUCKLE

CONTORT
(SHARPLY) FEAK
(— TOGETHER) CABLE RADDLE
(CAUSE TO —) TORQUE
(DOUBLE —) ESS
(PREF.) SPIR(I)(O) STREMMATO
STREPHO STREPSI STREPT(O) TORSO
TORTI
TWISTED CAM KAM WRY AWRY
TORT KINKY SCREW TORSE WELKT
WRONG ATWIST GAUCHE HURLED
KNOTTY SCREWY SKEWED SWIRLY
THRAWN THROWN TURKEN TWISTY
WARPED WRITHE CRISPED CROOKED
GNARLED KNOTTED SCREWED
TORQUED TORTILE TORTIVE
WHELKED WREATHY COCKEYED
IMPLICIT INTORTED INVOLVED
NONPLANE THRAWART WREATHEN
(PREF.) PLEC(O) PLECT(O) STREPSI
STREPT(O)
TWISTING DALLY KNECK AJOINT
TWIRLY WIGWAG ENTRAIL TWIDDLY
SQUIGGLY STREPSIS TORTUOUS
(PREF.) STROPH(O)
TWIT TIT CHECK TAUNT TEASE
ETWITE NEEDLE TWITTER RIDICULE
TWITCH TIC TIT FEAK FIRK JERK
JUMP PIRN TWIG WINK YANK PLUCK
START THRIP TWEAK TWICK TWIRK
QUATCH QUETCH QUITCH TWINGE
TWITCHEL VELLICATE
TWITCHING TIC JERKS PALMUS
WORKING SACCADIC
TWITTER TWIT CHIRM CHIRP GARRE
TWINK JARGON WARBLE CHIPPER
CHIRRUP CHITTER QUITTER TWITTLE
WHITTER
TWO TWA BOTH TWAY TWIN TWAIN
BINARY COUPLE DOUBLE
(— LINES) LONGWAYS
(— OF A KIND) BRACE
(IN —) ATWO
(US —) UNC
(PREF.) BI BIS DUO DY(O) TWI
(— EACH) BINI
(IN —) DICH(O)
(MORE THAN —) MULTI
TWO-COLORED BICHROME
(PREF.) DICHRO(O)
TWO-DIMENSIONAL FLAT PLANAR
TWO-DOOR COUPE ROADSTER
TWO-FACED FALSE
DOUBLEDEALING JANUS JANIFORM
(PREF.) JANI
TWO-FIFTEEN PM TIME
TWOFOLD DUAL BINAL DUPLE
BACKED BIFOLD DOUBLE DUPLEX
DIGONAL DIPLOID TWIFOLD
DIDYMATE DIDYMOID DIDYMOUS
DIPLASIC TWEYFOLD BIFARIOUS
(PREF.) DI DIPHY DIPL(O)
TWO-FOOTED BIPED

TWO-FORKED BIFURCAL
TWO GENTLEMEN OF VERONA
(AUTHOR OF —) SHAKESPEARE
(CHARACTER IN —) JULIA MILAN
SPEED LAUNCE SILVIA THURIO
ANTONIO LUCETTA PROTEUS
EGLAMOUR PANTHINO VALENTINE
TWO-HANDED BIMANAL
BIMANOUS
TWO-HEADED
(PREF.) DICRANO JANI
TWO-HORNED BICORN BICORNED
TWOPENCE TUPPENCE
TWO-POINTER BASKET
TWOS POT DEUCE
TWO-UP SWY
**TWO WIDOWS, THE (CHARACTER
IN —)** ANEZKA MUMLAL KAROLINA
LADISLAV
(COMPOSER OF —) SMETANA
TWO-WINGED
(PREF.) DIPTER(O)
TYCHICUS (COMPANION OF —) PAUL
TYCOON SHOGUN TAIKUN
TYDEUS (FATHER OF —) EONEUS
OENEUS
(MOTHER OF —) PERIBOEA
(SON OF —) DIOMEDES
TYKE KIDDIE
TYMPANUM DRUM TYMPAN
EARDRUM EPIPHRAGM
TYNDAREUS (BROTHER OF —)
ICARIUS
(DAUGHTER OF —) PHILOPOE
TIMANDRA CLYTEMNESTRA
(FATHER OF —) OEBALUS PERIERES
(MOTHER OF —) BATIA
GORGOPHONE
(WIFE OF —) LEDA
TYPE CUT ILK CAST KIND MAKE
MOLD NORM SORT TAKE BOGUS
BROOD IMAGE MOULD PRINT STAMP
EMBLEM KICKER KIDNEY LETTER
NATURE SHADOW STRIPE SYMBOL
TAKING TIMBER BATARDE FASHION
PARABLE ANTETYPE EXEMPLAR
(— BLOCK) QUAD
(— OF EXCELLENCE) PARAGON
(— PLACED BOTTOM UP) TURN
(— SET UP) MATTER
(ASSORTMENT OF —) FONT
(DANCE —) LASYA
(DISARRANGED —) PI PIE
(GERMAN —) FRAKTUR
(HEAVY-FACED —) IONIC
(HIGHEST —) PINK
(IDEAL —) CHRIST
(INVERTED —) TURN
(OPPOSITE —) ANTITYPE
(ORIGINAL —) PROTOTYPE
(PART OF —) BACK BALL BODY FACE
FOOT NICK SIZE STEM BEARD BELLY
BEVEL SERIF SHANK GROOVE

COUNTER ASCENDER CROSSBAR
SHOULDER DESCENDER
(PHYSICAL —) HABIT
(RACIAL —) DEHWAR
(REMARKABLE —) SPECIMEN
(REPRESENTATIVE —) GENIUS
(SET —) STICK
(SIZE OF —) (SEE SIZE) PICA POINT
DIAMOND ENGLISH
(STYLE OF —) AGATE CANON DORIC
ELITE GOUDY GREEK IONIC KABEL
ROMAN BODONI CASLON CICERO
GOTHIC HEBREW ITALIC JENSON
MODERN BOOKMAN BREVIER
CENTURY ELZEVIR EMERALD
FULLFACE GARAMOND
(PREF.) MORPH(O)
TYPEBAR
(PL.) BASKET
TYPEE (AUTHOR OF —) MELVILLE
(CHARACTER IN —) TOM TOBY
MARNOO MEHEVI FAYAWAY
KORYKORY
TYPEFACE FACE FRAKTUR
BOLDFACE SANSERIF
TYPEHOLDER PALLET
TYPESETTER MONO
TYPESETTING FAT PHAT
TYPEWRITER MILL TYPER TYPIST
PORTABLE
(PART OF —) BAR KEY BAIL KNOB
LOOP STOP GUIDE LEVER PLATE
SCALE SHIFT HOLDER MARGIN
PLATEN RETURN ROLLER SPACER
CONTROL RELEASE SUPPORT
CARRIAGE KEYBOARD REGULATOR
BACKSPACER
TYPHON (FATHER OF —) TARTARUS
(MOTHER OF —) TERRA
TYPHOON WIND CYCLONE TUFFOON
TYPICAL FAIR TYPAL TYPIC USUAL
AVERAGE CLASSIC PATTERN
PERFECT REGULAR
(PREF.) EU
(SUFF. — OF) ISH ISTIC
TYPIFY TYPE IMAGE SHADOW
ADUMBRATE EPITOMIZE PERSONIFY
REPRESENT SYMBOLIZE
(— BEFOREHAND) FORESHADOW
TYPIFYING GENERIC
TYR ER EAR TIU TYRR
(BROTHER OF —) THOR
(FATHER OF —) ODIN
TYRANNICAL LORDLY SLAVISH
ABSOLUTE DESPOTIC OPPRESSIVE
TYRANNIZE OPPRESS DOMINEER
OVERLORD
TYRANNOUS ABSOLUTE
TYRANNY ROD DESPOTISM
TYRANT ANARCH DESPOT NIMROD
FUEHRER PHARAOH PHALARIS
TYRANT FLYCATCHER PEWEE
TYRE (SITE OF —) SUR

TYRO HAM BABE COLT PUPIL NOVICE
RABBIT TYRONE BEGINNER
NEOPHYTE
(FATHER OF —) SALMONEUS
(HUSBAND OF —) CRETHEUS
(MOTHER OF —) ALCIDICE
(SON OF —) AESON NELEUS PELIAS
PHERES AMYTHAON

TYRRHENIAN ETRUSCAN
TYRRHENUS (BROTHER OF —)
LYDUD TARCHON
(FATHER OF —) ATYS HERCULES
TELEPHUS
(MOTHER OF —) HIERA OMPHALE
CALLITHEA
TYTO ALUCO STRIX

U UNCLE UNION
(PREF.) (— SHAPED) HY(O)
UDDER BAG DUG TID EWER ELDER
SUMEN VESSEL
UFO (STUDY OF —S) UFOLOGY

UGANDA
AIRPORT: ENTEBBE
CAPITAL: KAMPALA
COLLEGE: MAKERERE
FORMER CAPITAL: ENTEBBE
LAKE: KYOGA ALBERT EDWARD
GEORGE VICTORIA
LANGUAGE: ATESO GANDA LUGANDA
SWAHILI
MOUNTAIN: ELGON MARGHERITA
MOUNTAIN RANGE: RUWENZORI
NATIVE: ATESO BANTU LANGO
ACHOLI ANKOLE BAGISU BAKIGA
BASOGA BATORO BAGANDA
BUNYORO LUGBARA NILOTIC
SUDANIC
PLATEAU: ANKOLE
PROVINCE: BUGANDA
RIVER: ASWA KAFU PAGER KATONGA
SEAPORT: MOMBASA
TOWN: ARUA JINJA MBALE KITGUM
MOROTO TORORO ENTEBBE
MOMBASA
WATERFALL: KABALEGA

UGH OOF YECH YUCK YECCH
UGLY FOUL AWFUL OUGLE SNIVY
UNKED CRANKY DREEPY GORGON
GROTTY HOMELY LAIDLY ORNERY
CRABBED GRIZZLY HIDEOUS
HOUGHLY VICIOUS GRUESOME
UGLISOME UNLOVELY
MONSTROUS
UGLY-TEMPERED SNARLISH
UGNI BLANC TREBBIANO
UIGHUR JAGATAI
UINTAITE ASPHALT GILSONITE
UITOTAN KAIMO WITOTAN
UKASE ORDER
UKE JARANA

UKRAINE
(ALSO SEE RUSSIA)
BAY: KALAMIT KARKINIT
CANAL: CRIMEAN
CAPITAL: KIEV
COIN: KARBOVANET
GULF: TAGANROG TAHANROH
LAKE: KIEV KANIV LENIN DNIEPER
SVITYAZ DNIESTER KAKHOVKA
MARSH: PRIPET PRYPYAT

MOUNTAIN: KAMULA HOVERLYA
ROMANKOSH MOHYLABELMAK
MOHYLAMECHETNA
MOUNTAIN RANGE: CRIMEAN
KARPATY CARPATHIAN
PENINSULA: KERCH CRIMEAN
RIVER: BUG BUH STRY TYSA DESNA
INHUL SLUCH TISZA DNIPRO
DONETS PRIPET SALHYR ZBRUCH
DNIEPER DNISTER PRYPYAT TETERIV
VORSKLA DNIESTER
SEA: AZOV BLACK
TOWN: KIEV LVIV LVOV KYYIV ODESSA
DONETSK KHARKIV KHARKOV
KRYVVYRIH CHERNOBYL KRIVOYROG
ZAPOROZHYE ZAPORIZHZHYA
DNIPROPETROVSK

UKRAINIAN RUSSNIAK
UKULELE UKE TAROPATCH
ULAM (FATHER OF —) ESHEK
ULCER FRET KYLE SORE WOLF
BOTCH ISSUE RUPIA ULCUS APHTHA
MORMAL TETTER BEDSORE
CHANCRE EGILOPS ENCAUMA
FISTULA AEGILOPS FONTANEL
FOSSETTE ULCUSCLE
(ARTIFICIAL —) ISSUE
(PREF.) CHANCRI HELC(O)
ULCERATING EXEDENT
ULCERATION NOMA CANKER
CARIES BEDSORE HELCOSIS
ULCEROUS HELCOID
ULEX LING
ULEXITE TIZA
ULLIKUMMI (FATHER OF —)
KUMARBI
ULNA CUBIT CUBITAL CUBITUS
ULTIMATE IT NTH DIRE LAST FINAL
ULTIME SUPREME ABSOLUTE
EVENTUAL FARTHEST ULTIMITY
ULTIMATELY FINALLY
ULTIMO PAST
ULTRA EXTREME FANATIC FORWARD
(NE PLUS —) IDEAL
ULTRACONSERVATISM TORYISM
ULTRACONSERVATIVE WHITE
ULTRAFASHIONABLE RITZY
SWELL SWAGGER
ULTRAMONTANISM CURIALISM
ULTRASOUND SONOGRAPHY
ULUA PAPIO PAPIOPIO
ULULATE HOWL
ULYSSES (AUTHOR OF —) JOYCE
(CHARACTER IN —) BUCK RUDY
BLOOM BREEN MOLLY BLAZES
BOYLAN COFFEY GERTIE HAINES

MARION DEDALUS LEOPOLD
PUREFOY STEPHEN MULLIGAN
MACDOWELL
(FATHER OF —) LAERTES
(MOTHER OF —) ANTICLEA
(SLAYER OF —) TELEGONUS
(SON OF —) TELEMACHUS
(WIFE OF —) PENELOPE
UMBEL RAY AXIS RADIUS SERTULE
UMBELLA SERTULUM UMBELLET
UMBELLIFERONE CUMARIN
COUMARIN
UMBER OMER OMBER PARTRIDGE
UMBILICUS NAVEL
(PREF.) OMPHAL(O)
UMBO BEAK UMBONULE
UMBONES NATES
UMBRA DOGFISH MUDFISH
NUCLEUS UMBRINE
UMBRAGE PIQUE SNUFF OFFENSE
UMBRELLA BELL GAMP MUSH
DUMPY BROLLY CHATTA PAYONG
PILEUS CHATTAH GINGHAM
ROUNDEL FITTIBOL KITTYSOL
MUSHROOM TYRASOLE
BUMBERSHOOT
(PART OF —) CAP RIB ROD TIP GORE
JOINT SPRING SHAFT BULLET HANDLE
RUNNER SPRING CLOSURE FERRULE
STRETCHER
UMBRELLA BIRD COTINGA
COTINGID
UMBRELLA BUSH MILJEE
UMBRELLA PALM KENTIA
UMBRELLA PLANT SEDGE
GLUMAL
UMBRELLA TREE WAHOO
ELKWOOD MAGNOLIA
UMBRETTE UMBRE HOMBRE
UMBRET CICONIID
UMBRIAN IGUVINE
UMBURANA ROBLE
UMLAUT MUTATION METAPHONY
UMPIRE REF UMP JUDGE TRIER
ARBITER DAYSMAN ODDSMAN
REFEREE OVERSMAN STICKLER
BIRLIEMAN BYRLAWMAN
UNABASHED BROWLESS
UNABBREVIATED FULL
UNABLE UNHABILE POWERLESS
UNACCENTED GRAVE LIGHT
ATONIC
UNACCEPTABLE DREADFUL
UNACCOMPANIED BARE SOLO
ALONE SECCO SINGLE
UNACCOUNTABLE STRANGE
UNACCUSTOMED UNUSED
STRANGE INSOLITE WONTLESS
UNACQUAINTED STRANGE
UNCOUTH
UNADORNED DRY BALD PLAIN
SECCO STARK RUSTIC SEVERE
SIMPLE AUSTERE LITERAL INORNATE

UNADULTERATED NET FRANK
HONEST VIRGIN GENUINE SINCERE
ABSOLUTE
UNADVANTAGEOUSLY ILL
UNAFFECTED EASY REAL PLAIN
HOMELY NATIVE RUSTIC SIMPLE
ARTLESS BUCOLIC SINCERE
SEMPLICE
UNAFRAID BOLD BRAVE DEFIANT
UNAGGRESSIVE AMIABLE
UNALERT SUPINE
UNALLOYED DEEP SOLID VIRGIN
GENUINE
UNALTERABLE IMMUTABLE
UNAMBIGUOUS EXPLICIT
UNANIMATED FLAT VAPID INSIPID
UNANIMITY ATTACK CONSENT
UNANIMOUS SOLID WHOLE
UNANIME UNIVOCAL
UNAPPROACHABLE STATELY
UNARMED BARE INERM UNBARBED
(PREF.) ANOPL(O)
UNASPIRATED LENE
UNASSAILABLE SECURE
UNASSUMED NATURAL
UNASSUMING SHY HUMBLE
MODEST SIMPLE NATURAL RETIRING
UNATTACHED FREE LOOSE SINGLE
UNATTENDED SINGLE
UNATTRACTIVE BLAH UGLY PLAIN
WORSE HOMELY FRUMPISH UNLIKELY
UNAVAILING VAIN FUTILE
BOOTLESS GAINLESS NUGATORY
UNAVOIDABLE SHUNLESS
NECESSARY
UNAVOWED SECRET
UNAWARE UNWARE WITLESS
HEEDLESS INNOCENT UNBEWARE
WARELESS OBLIVIOUS
UNAWARES ABACK SHORT
UNBALANCED ALOP HITE DOTTY
NUTTY FRUITY UNEVEN FANATIC
DERANGED LOPSIDED PIXILATED
MOONSTRUCK
UNBAR UNSLOT
UNBARRED UNSTOKEN
UNBEARDED CALLOW
UNBECOMING RUDE INEPT PLAIN
INDIGN UNMEET BENEATH
IMPROPER INDECENT UNSEEMLY
UNWORTHY
UNBEFITTING BENEATH
UNBELIEF UNFAITH
UNBELIEVABLE HOT THIN
UNBELIEVER PAGAN GIAOUR
ATHEIST DOUBTER INFIDEL SCOFFER
SKEPTIC
UNBELIEVING MISCREANT
UNBEND REST THAW FRESE RELAX
UNTIE EXTEND DISBEND UNCROOK
UNBENDING RIGID STARK STERN
STIFF THARF CATONIAN OBDURATE
RAMRODDY RESOLUTE

UNBIASED FAIR JUST DETACHED
UNBIND FREE UNDO UNTIE UNGIRD
UNDRESS
UNBLAMABLE INNOCENT
UNBLEACHED BLAE BLAY ECRU
BEIGE BROWN
UNBLEMISHED FAIR PURE SOUND
WHITE ENTIRE SPOTLESS
UNBLOCK REDD
UNBLOODY INCRUENT
UNBOLT OPEN UNBAR UNPIN
UNBOSOM OPEN
UNBOUGHT UNCOFT
UNBOUND FREE LOOSE
UNBOUNDED HUGE
UNBRANDED SLICK NATIVE
UNBROKEN DEAD FLAT FERAL
FLUSH SHEER SOLID SOUND
SINGLE CERRERO REGULAR
UNRACED STRAIGHT UNBACKED
WAKELESS
UNBUILD DESTROY
UNBUILT UNBIGGED
UNBURDEN EMPTY UNLOAD
UNSHIP
UNBURNISHED WHITE MATTED
UNCALLED (— FOR) GRATUITOUS
UNCANNY EERY UNCO EERIE SCARY
UNCOW UNKID WEIRD WISHT
CREEPY SPOOKY UNCOUTH
ELDRITCH POKERISH
UNCASTRATED INTACT
UNCAUGHT UNHENT
UNCEASING ENDLESS ETERNAL
EASELESS MINUTELY
UNCEREMONIOUS CURT BLUFF
BLUNT SHORT ABRUPT CASUAL
FAMILIAR INFORMAL
UNCERTAIN WAW DARK HAZY WILD
FLUKY SHADY SHAKY WAUGH
CASUAL CLOUDY CRANKY FITFUL
FLUKEY GLEAMY QUEASY CASALTY
CHANCEY COMICAL DUBIOUS
TRICKSY VAGRANT VARIOUS
WILSOME CATCHING DELICATE
FLICKERY FUGITIVE HOVERING
INSECURE SLIPPERY TECHNOUS
TICKLISH
UNCERTAINTY MIST WERE DEMUR
DOUBT MAYBE BAFFLE BALANCE
DUBIETY CASUALTY MISTRUST
SUSPENSE UNSURETY SKEPTICISM
UNCHALLENGED ACCEPTED
UNCHANGEABLE FAST STABLE
DURABLE ETERNAL
UNCHANGING STATIC ETERNAL
UNIFORM CONSTANT STATICAL
UNCHASTE LEWD BAWDY FRAIL
LIGHT LOOSE IMPURE WANTON
FORLAIN HAGGARD SCARLET
IMMODEST
UNCHASTITY BAWDRY STUPRUM
ADULTERY

UNCHECKED LIBERAL RAMPANT
REINLESS
UNCIFORM HAMATUM
UNCINARIA NECATOR
UNCIVIL RUDE BLUFF ROUGH RUSTY
SURLY COARSE CRUSTY RUGGED
UNFEEL IMPOLITE
UNCIVILIZED RUDE WILD MYALL
INCULT SAVAGE UNCIVIL BARBARIC
IGNORANT SYLVATIC
UNCLAD LOOSE UNDRESSED
UNCLE EME OOM TIO YEME BUNKS
NUNKY NUNCLE
UNCLEAN FOUL TREF VILE BLACK
TARRY TERFA TREFA COMMON
FILTHY IMMUND IMPURE DEFILED
UNCLEANLINESS
(PREF.) MYS(O)
UNCLEANNESS DIRT FOULNESS
UNCLEAR DIM HAZY SHAGGY
UNCLEARLY DIMLY
UNCLENCH UNDOUBLE
**UNCLE TOM'S CABIN (AUTHOR OF
—)** STOWE
(CHARACTER IN —) EVA TOM BIRD
CASSY CHLOE ELIZA HALEY HARRY
LOKER MARKS SIMON TOPSY
GEORGE HARRIS LEGREE RACHEL
SHELBY SIMEON OPHELIA STCLAIR
EMMELINE HALLIDAY
UNCLOSE OPE OPEN UNHASP
DISCLOSE
UNCLOTHE TIRL SPOIL UNRIG
DEVEST DESPOIL
UNCLOTHED STARKERS
UNCLOUDED CLEAR SERENE
UNCOIL UNLINK
UNCOLORED FAIR
UNCOMBED TOUSLED UNKAMED
UNTEWED
UNCOMBINED FREE FRANK
LOOSE
UNCOMELY INDECENT
UNCOMFORTABLE HOT EVIL POOR
HARSH UNKET UNKID QUEASY
STICKY UNFELE
UNCOMMON MUCH NICE RARE
SELD UNCO BYOUS FORBY UNCOW
VAUDY DAINTY FORBYE SCARCE
SPECIAL STRANGE UNUSUAL
SINGULAR UNWONTED
UNCOMMONLY UNCO BYOUS
EXTRA JOLLY UNCOW UNCOLY
UNCOMMONNESS SCARCITY
UNCOMMUNICATIVE DUMB
SILENT PRIVATE RESERVED
UNCOMPLICATED RURAL HONEST
SIMPLE
UNCOMPOUNDED SIMPLEX
UNCOMPROMISING ACID FIRM
GRIM RIGID STERN STOUT ULTRA
SEVERE STRICT STRONG EXTREME
HARDSHELL BRASSBOUND

UNCONCEALED BARE OPEN OVERT OUVERT APPARENT
UNCONCERN APATHY EASINESS
UNCONCERNED COOL EASY BLAND BLASE CASUAL CARELESS
UNCONCERNEDLY LIGHTLY
UNCONDITIONAL FREE FRANK UTTER SIMPLE ABSOLUTE EXPLICIT TERMLESS
UNCONDITIONED POSITIVE
UNCONFINED LAX FREE LOOSE
UNCONGENIAL HATEFUL INGRATE KINDLESS
UNCONNECTED GAPPY REMOTE DETACHED
UNCONQUERED INVICT INVICTED
UNCONSCIOUS OUT COLD BRUTE ASLEEP BLOTTO CUCKOO TORPID UNAWARE WITLESS COMATOSE IGNORANT SENSELESS INSENSIBLE
UNCONSIDERED WILD
UNCONSTRAINED EASY FREE UNNET SIMPLE FAMILIAR
UNCONTROLLABLE WILD
UNCONTROLLED FREE MADCAP LIBERAL ABSOLUTE UNBITTED
UNCONVENTIONAL FLAKY GYPSY LOOSE CASUAL FLAKEY DEVIOUS ODDBALL OFFBEAT BOHEMIAN INFORMAL
(— IN STYLE) MOD
UNCONVINCING LAME THIN FALSE FISHY FEEBLE
UNCOOKED RAW
UNCOOL UNHIP
UNCOOPERATIVE
(TO BE —) STONEWALL
UNCOUNTABLE SUMLESS
UNCOUPLE CUT UNDOCK DISLINK
UNCOUTH RUDE CRUDE DORIC GURLY ROUGH UNKED UNKID GOTHIC JUNGLY QUAINT RENISH AWKWARD BOORISH CUBBISH HIRSUTE LOUTISH AGRESTIC UNGAINLY YOKELISH
(— PERSON) TUG
UNCOVER BARE DOFF HUNT ROOT ROUT TIRL TIRR BREAK STRIP TIRVE UNLAP UNLID UNWRY DETECT EXHUME RAKEUP SEARCH UNBARE UNCASE UNHALE UNVEIL UNDRAPE UNEARTH DISCLOSE DISCOVER UNMANTLE UNMUFFLE
UNCOVERED BARE OVERT
(PREF.) GYMN(O)
UNCTION CHRISM OINTMENT
UNCTIOUS SMUG
UNCTUOUS FAT OILY SALVY SLEEK SOAPY SUAVE GREASY SMARMY COURTLY PINGUID OLEAGINOUS
UNCULTIVATED RAW BRUT FERAL DESERT FALLOW INCULT SAVAGE SLOVEN WILDERN

UNCULTURED RUDE INCULT ARTLESS
UNCUT RASPED
UNDAMAGED WHOLE
UNDARKENED CLEAR
UNDAUNTED BOLD BRAVE MANLY SPARTAN FEARLESS INTREPID
UNDE WAVY UNDEE
UNDECAYED GREEN
UNDECEIVE DISABUSE
UNDECIDED MOOT DUBIOUS PENDING DOUBTFUL WAVERING
UNDECIDEDLY HUMDRUM
UNDECLARED SECRET
UNDEFENDED UNKEPT
UNDEFILED PURE CHASTE INTACT VIRGIN
UNDEFINED OBSCURE
UNDELIVERABLE DEAD
UNDEMONSTRATIVE COLD ASEPTIC LACONIC RESERVED
UNDENIABLE BRUTAL
UNDENIABLY INDEED
UNDEPENDABLE CASUAL FLUFFY
UNDER SUB BAJO BELOW INFRA NEATH SOTTO ANEATH ANUNDER BENEATH
(— ORDERS) SUPPOSED
(— THE WORD) IV
(— THE YEAR) SA
(— THIS TITLE) HT
(— THIS WORD) SV SHV
(— WAY) AFOOT
(PREF.) HYPO SUB
UNDERBODICE JUMP BASQUINE CAMISOLE
UNDERBRUSH FILTH COVERT GARSIL MAQUIS RAMMEL ABATURE
UNDERBURNED SOFT SAMEL
UNDERBUTLER WASHPOT
UNDERCARRIAGE BOGY BOGEY BOGIE
UNDERCLAY THILL WARRANT
UNDERCLOTHES LININGS
UNDERCLOTHING LINEN SHORTS UNDIES LININGS LINGERIE BALBRIGGAN
UNDERCOAT PILE ALPACA SURFACER
(WOOL OF — OF MUSK-OX) QIVIUT
UNDERCOVER SECRET
UNDERCRUST ABAISSE
UNDERCURRENT UNDERLAY UNDERRUN UNDERSET
UNDERCUT JAD HOLE LAME POOL SUMP KIRVE NOTCH
UNDERDOG DAVID
UNDERDONE RARE REAR
UNDERDRAWERS FLANNELS
UNDERDRESS SLIP
UNDERESTIMATE DISPRIZE MINIMIZE
UNDERFLEECE PASHM

UNDERFRAME SOLE
UNDERGARMENT BAND SLIP
  CYMAR SIMAR SKIRT SMOCK TUNIC
  WAIST BANIAN BANYAN BODICE
  CAMISE CILICE CORSET GIRDLE
  STAMIN CHEMISE DOUBLET
  DRAWERS STAMMEL TALLITH
  BLOOMERS KNICKERS
  (WOMAN'S —) PANTIHOSE
  (WOMEN'S —) LINGERIE
  (PL.) SMALLS FLANNELS FLIMSIES
  SNUGGIES
UNDERGO PASS SERVE ENDURE
  SUFFER SUSTAIN
  (— GLADLY) WELCOME
UNDERGOER
  (SUFF.) EE
UNDERGRADUATE MAN TASSEL
  SERVITOR
  (CAMBRIDGE —) SUBSIZAR
  (TITLED —) TUFT
UNDERGROWTH RUSH COVER
  RAMMEL SPRING BUSHWOOD
UNDERHAND SLY DERN SHADY
  BYHAND SECRET CROOKED
  OBLIQUE INVOLVED SINISTER
  SNEAKING
UNDERHANDED DERN DIRTY
  FUNNY FILTHY SECRET SINISTER
UNDERHANDEDLY DIRTY
UNDERIVED ORIGINAL
UNDER JAW
  (PREF.) GENYO
UNDERLAYER SLASHING
UNDERLIE SUBTEND
UNDERLING MENIAL SEQUEL
  UNDERER HENCHMAN INFERIOR
UNDERLYING COVERT IMPLICIT
UNDERMINE SAP CAVE HOLE POOL
  ERODE KNIFE WEAKEN FOSSICK
  FOUNDER SUBVERT ENFEEBLE
  SUPPLANT
UNDERMINED ROTTEN
UNDERNEATH BELOW BENEATH
  UNNEATH
  (PREF.) INTRA
UNDERNSONG TIERCE
UNDERPANTS BRIEFS BLOOMERS
  KNICKERS
UNDERPART BELLY
UNDERPASS DIVE SUBWAY
UNDERPINNING GAM
UNDERRATE DECRY DISCOUNT
  EXTENUATE
UNDERRUN BOTTOM
UNDERSACRISTAN CUSTOS
UNDERSHIRT VEST SHIFT SHIRT
  CAMISA JERSEY LINDER SEMMIT
  SINGLET WRAPPER
UNDERSHRUB HEATH PINKEYE
  SEEPWEED SUBSHRUB SAGEBRUSH
  SANTOLINA

UNDERSIDE BOTTOM BREAST
  (— OF CLOUD) BASE
  (— OF FINGER) BALL
  (— OF FLOOR) CEILING
  (— OF STAIRCASE) SOFFIT
  (PREF.) (ON THE —) INFERO
UNDERSIZED DEENY SCRUB STUNT
UNDERSKIRT QUILT CRINOLINE
  PETTICOAT
UNDERSONG FABURDEN
UNDERSTAND CAN CON DIG GET
  KEN SEE GAUM HAVE MAKE READ
  TAKE TWIG BRAIN ENTER GRASP
  REACH SAVVY SEIZE SENSE SKILL
  SPELL ACCEPT COTTON FIGURE
  FOLLOW INTAKE INTEND SUBAUD
  UPTAKE CONCEIT DISCERN
  COMPRISE CONCEIVE CONSTRUE
  CONTRIVE FORSTAND PERCEIVE
  PERSTAND UNDERNIM
  (— PROFOUNDLY) GROK
UNDERSTANDABLE PLAIN
UNDERSTANDING KEN WIT GAUM
  HEAD BRAIN CLASP HEART INWIT
  SENSE SKILL ACCORD INTENT
  NOTION REASON TREATY UPTAKE
  COMPACT CONCEIT CONCEPT
  ENTENTE INSIGHT MEANING
  WITNESS DAYLIGHT PREHENSION
  (— WORDS) ISEE
  (HARMONIOUS —) SYMPATHY
  (IMPERFECT —) DARKNESS
  (INSTINCTIVE —) FREEMASONRY
  (WORDS OF —) ISEE
  (PREF.) NOEMA
UNDERSTATEMENT LITOTES
  MEIOSIS
UNDERSTOOD LUCID SUPPOSED
  (— ONLY BY SPECIALLY INITIATED)
  ESOTERIC
  (EASILY —) EASY CLEAR EXTANT
  (NOT —) DARKSOME
UNDERSTUDY DOUBLE
UNDERSURFACE SOLE
  (— OF BRILLIANT) PAVILION
UNDERTAKE GO TRY DARE FANG
  FOND GRANT OFFER ASSUME
  INCEPT PLEDGE SETOUT ATTEMPT
  EMBRACE EMPRISE PRETEND
  UNDERFO CONTRACT PRESTATE
  (— RESPONSIBILITY) ACCEPT
  ANSWER
UNDERTAKER UPHOLDER
  MORTICIAN
UNDERTAKING JOB AVAL TASK
  CAUTIO EFFORT SCHEME VOYAGE
  ATTEMPT CALLING PROJECT
  VENTURE COVENANT
  (— IN CARDS) EMPRISE
  (HAZARDOUS —) EMPRISE
  (UNPROFITABLE —) FOLLY
UNDERTEACHER USHER

UNDERTONE INKLING SUBTONE
UNDERTOW SEAPOOSE
UNDER TWO FLAGS (AUTHOR OF —) OUIDA
(CHARACTER IN —) RAKE CECIL AMAGUE BERTIE CORONA BERKELEY CIGARETTE GUENEVERE ROYALLIEU CHATEAUROY ROCKINGHAM
UNDERVALUE DECRY DISABLE DISPRIZE DISVALUE MISPRISE MISPRIZE
UNDERVEST BODICE SEMMIT SINGLET
UNDERWAIST CAMISOLE
UNDERWATER
(— DEVICE) OTTER PARAVANE
UNDERWEAR BRIEFS SHORTS SKIVVY UNDIES DESSOUS HEAVIES LONGIES LINGERIE PRETTIES SCANTIES
(MEN'S —) SKIVVIES
(PL.) SMALLS
UNDERWING CATOCALA
UNDERWOOD FRITH BOSCAGE COPPICE
UNDERWORLD DUAT DEWAT HADES ORCUS SHEOL MICTLAN XIBALBA GANGLAND
UNDERWRITE SIGN INSURE ENDORSE
UNDERWRITER INSURER
UNDESERVED INDIGN
UNDETERMINED UNSET DUBIOUS PENDENT AORISTIC DOUBTFUL INFINITE
UNDEVELOPED CRUDE MORON LATENT SLOVEN GERMING IMMATURE JUVENILE
(SEXUALLY —) NEUTER
UNDEVIATINGLY SMACK
UNDIFFERENCED ENTIRE
UNDIFFERENTIATED GLOBAL AMERISTIC
UNDIGESTED CRUDE
UNDIGNIFIED DOGGREL DOGGEREL
UNDILUTED MERE NEAT PURE NAKED SHEER SHORT STRONG STRAIGHT
UNDIMINISHED ENTIRE
UNDIMMED CLEAR
UNDINE NIX
(CHARACTER IN —) HUGO VEIT TOBIAS UNDINE BERTHALDA KUHLEBORN
(COMPOSER OF —) LORTZING
UNDISCIPLINED WANTON COLTISH
UNDISCLOSED HIDDEN SEALED
UNDISCRIMINATING GROSS
UNDISGUISED BALD NAKED PLAIN
UNDISMAYED ONFLEMED
UNDISPUTED LIQUID

UNDISTINGUISHED GROSS COMMON UNNOBLE FAMELESS NAMELESS NOTELESS
UNDISTORTED CLEAR
UNDISTURBED CALM SOUND SERENE VIRGIN TRANQUIL
UNDIVIDED WHOLE ENTIRE SINGLE
UNDO DUP COOK POOP SLIP FORDO SPEED UNPAY DEFEAT DIDDLE FOREDO UNBIND UNKNIT UNLOCK UNMAKE UNTUCK UNWORK DEFEISE DESTROY NULLIFY UNRAVEL UNRIVET UNTWIRL UNWEAVE UNWREST DECIPHER DISSOLVE DISTRUSS UNFASTEN
UNDOER ACHAN
UNDOGMATIC AGNOSTIC
UNDOING DEFEAT DOWNFALL
(PREF.) DE DIS
UNDOMESTICATED WILD FERAL FERINE
UNDOUBTEDLY SURELY FRANKLY
UNDRESS MOB DOFF FLAY PEEL TIRR STRIP UNRAY UNRIG DEVEST DIVEST UNBUSK UNCASE UNLACE UNRIND UNROBE UNTIRE DISCASE UNARRAY UNREADY UNSPOIL UNTRUSS NEGLIGEE UNATTIRE DESHABILLE DISHABILLE
UNDRESSED UNDIGHT
UNDUE EXTREME
UNDULATE SWAY WAVE WAVY FLOAT SWING BILLOW GYROSE KELTER RIPPLE UNDATE UNDOSE FLICKER UNDATED
UNDULATING SURGING FLEXUOUS INDENTED
UNDULATION FOLD ROLL WAVE CRIMP TEETER WAVING CRIMPING
UNDULATORY WAVY
UNDUTIFULNESS IMPIETY
UNDYED CORAH
UNDYING IMMORTAL
UNEARTH DIG MOOT DIGUP EXPOSE UNCOVER DISCOVER
UNEARTHLY EERY EERIE WEIRD AWESOME UNCANNY UNGODLY
UNEASINESS ENVY GENE FIDGET NETTLE SORROW UNEASE AILMENT ANXIETY DISEASE MISEASE TROUBLE DISQUIET DISTASTE
UNEASY ANTSY ONEDGE SICKLY FIDGETY INQUIET NERVOUS RESTIVE UNQUIET WORRIED RESTLESS
UNEDUCATED RUDE SIMPLE IGNORANT
UNEMBELLISHED DRY PROSE STARK AUSTERE
UNEMOTIONAL DRY COLD COOL STOIC STONY STOICAL
UNEMOTIONALLY EVENLY

UNEMPLOYED IDLE ORRA VOID
IDLED ORROW OTIANT OTIOSE
VACANT IDLESET LEISURE UNBUSIED
UNEMPLOYMENT IDLENESS
UNENCUMBERED VACANT
EXPEDITE
UNENDING ABYSMAL AGELONG
CHRONIC ENDLESS UNDYING
TERMLESS TIMELESS
UNENJOYABLE JOYLESS
UNENLIGHTENED MISTY HEATHEN
IGNORANT
UNENTHUSIASTIC COLD
UNEQUAL IMPAR DISPAR UNEGAL
UNEVEN INEQUAL INFERIOR
(— TO STRAIN) FEEBLE
(PREF.) ANIS(O) IMPARI INEQUI
UNEQUALED UNIQUE NONESUCH
UNEQUIVOCAL DIRECT SQUARE
PERFECT DEFINITE DISTINCT
EXPLICIT RESOUNDING
UNERRING DEAD TRUE DEADLY
INERRANT
UNERRINGLY CLEAN
UNEVEN RUDE EROSE GOBBY
HAGGY JAGGY MEALY ROUGH
HOBBLY PLATTY RAGGED RUGGED
SPOTTY TWITTY UNFAIR UNLIKE
BLOTCHY DIURNAL ERRATIC
HOTTERY INEQUAL SCALENE
STREAKY UNEQUAL HUMMOCKY
SCRAGGED SCRATCHY SNAGGLED
ACCIDENTED
(— IN COLOR) CLOUDY
UNEVENLY AWRY
UNEVENNESS BUMP WAVE FRAZE
ANOMALY WRINKLE ACCIDENT
ASPERITY
UNEVENTFUL STILL UNDATED
UNEXCITED LEVEL
UNEXCITING DEAD DULL TAME
BORING PROSAIC
UNEXPECTED EERY EERIE ABRUPT
SUDDEN UNWARY INOPINE
UNLOOKED
UNEXPECTEDLY UNWARES
UNAWARES
UNEXPIRED ALIVE
UNEXPLAINED HIDDEN
UNEXPOSED RAW
UNEXTINGUISHED LIT LEFTON
UNFADABLE FAST
UNFADED FRESH BRIGHT
UNFAILING SURE DEADLY INFALLID
UNERRING
UNFAIR FOUL CROOK WRONG
BIASED SHABBY UNEVEN UNJUST
DEVIOUS PARTIAL SLANTER
UNEQUAL UNSEEMLY WRONGFUL
UNFAIRLY HARDLY
UNFAIRNESS CROSS INEQUITY
UNFAITHFUL INFIDEL TRAITOR
DISLOYAL RECREANT

UNFALTERING SURE TRUE STEADY
UNERRING
UNFAMILIAR NEW FREMD HEATHER
STRANGE UNKNOWN
UNFASTEN FREE OPEN UNDO
LOOSE UNPIN UNBIND UNHASP
UNLIME UNLINK UNLOCK UNMAKE
UNTINE UNDIGHT UNHITCH
UNSTECK UNTRUSS
UNFATHOMABLE ABYSMAL
ABYSSAL PROFOUND
UNFATHOMED COSMIC
UNFAVORABLE BAD ILL FOUL HARD
POOR CRONK SHREWD UNFAIR
UNKIND ADVERSE AWKWARD
FROWARD HOSTILE UNHAPPY
BACKWARD CONTRARY INIMICAL
SINISTER UNKINDLY
(PREF.) DYS
UNFAVORABLY BADLY CROSS
UNFEATHERED SQUAB
UNFEELING COLD DULL HARD
CRASS CRUEL HARSH ROCKY STERN
STONY BRUTAL LEADEN MARBLE
STOLID CALLOUS OBDURATE
UNFEELINGLY HARSHLY
UNFEELINGNESS APATHY
UNFEIGNED OPEN TRUE HEARTY
CORDIAL NATURAL SINCERE
UNFERMENTED AZYMOUS
UNFERTILE BARREN
UNFETTERED FREE UNGYVED
UNFILLED BLANK EMPTY VACANT
VACUOUS
UNFINISHED RAW GRAY GREY
CRUDE KACHA ROUGH KUTCHA
RAGGED KACHCHA STICKIT
IMMATURE INCHOATE
UNFIRED GREEN
UNFIRM UNFAST
UNFIT BAD SICK UNAPT WISHT
WRONG COMMON FAULTY NOUGHT
UNTIDY DISABLE UNFITTY IMPROPER
UNFITTEN UNLIKELY UNLIKING
UNFITTING UNMEETLY
UNFIXED AFLOAT
UNFLAPPABLE CALM SURE STOIC
SECURE ASSURED
UNFLEDGED SQUAB CALLOW
UNFLINCHING LEVEL STAUNCH
UNFOLD OPEN BREAK BURST SOLVE
UNLAP UNTIE DEPLOY EVOLVE
EXPAND EXPLAT FLOWER SPREAD
UNFURL UNPLAT UNROLL UNTUCK
BLOSSOM DEVELOP DISPLAY
DIVULGE EXPLAIN UNPLAIT UNRAVEL
UNWEAVE UNDOUBLE UNPLIGHT
UNFOLDED OPEN EVOLUTE
EXPANDED
UNFOLDING DISPLAY
(— OF EVENTS) ACTION
(— TO VIEW) BURST
UNFORCED EASY GLIB WILLING

UNFORESEEN CASUAL SUDDEN IMPREVU UNAWARE

UNFORGIVING STERN

UNFORMED CALLOW INFORM

UNFORTUNATE ILL EVIL POOR DONCY TOUGH WEARY SHREWD HAPLESS UNHAPPY UNLUCKY LUCKLESS UNTOWARD WANHAPPY WRETCHED

UNFREQUENTED LONE EMPTY UNCOUTH SOLITARY

UNFRIENDLY ILL COLD FOUL CHILL BITTER CHILLY FIERCE FROSTY UNSOME HOSTILE INGRATE STRANGE INIMICAL

UNFROCK DEFROCK DEGRADE DISFROCK UNPRIEST

UNFRUITFUL BLUNT ADDLED BARREN EFFETE WASTED STERILE USELESS INFECUND

UNFULFILLMENT BREACH

UNFURL BREAK SPREAD UNFOLD DEVELOP OUTROOL

UNFURNISHED BARE VACANT

UNGAINLY LANKY SPLAY WEEDY CLUMSY UNGAIN AWKWARD BOORISH NUNTING UNHEPPEN UNLICKED UNWIELDY

UNGENEROUS MEAN SHABBY STINGY GRUDGING

UNGENIAL CHILLY

UNGIRDED DISCINCT

UNGLUED UPSET

UNGODLINESS ATHEISM IMPIETY

UNGODLY SINFUL WICKED GODLESS IMPIOUS PROFANE

UNGOVERNABLE WILD UNRULY FROWARD IMPOTENT

UNGRACEFUL HARD CLUMSY ANGULAR AWKWARD HALTING UNTOWARD

UNGRACEFULLY HARSHLY

UNGRACIOUS GRUFF UNFEEL UNFELE CHURLISH SNAPPISH

UNGRATEFUL UNKIND INGRATE

UNGROOMED UNDRESSED

UNGUARDED OPEN STIFF

UNGUENT SALVE CEROMA CHRISM PIMENT POMADE SMEGMA POMATUM UNCTION OINTMENT (PREF.) MYRO

UNGULATE HOG PIG DEER HORSE TAKIN TAPIR HOOFED AMBLYPOD ELEPHANT RHINOCEROS

UNGUMMED BRIGHT

UNHALLOWED IMPURE UNHOLY PROFANE

UNHAMPERED FREE DIRECT EXPEDITE

UNHAPPINESS MISERY SORROW ILLFARE SADNESS UNBLISS

UNHAPPY SAD POOR TEARY DISMAL UNLUCKY UNLUSTY WANSOME

DEJECTED DOWNBEAT DOWNGONE WOBEGONE WRETCHED

UNHARMED SAFE UNSHENT

UNHARNESS UNGEAR OUTSHUT OUTSPAN UNHORSE UNTACKLE

UNHEALED GREEN

UNHEALTHY BAD MORBID QUEASY SICKLY UNHALE NAUGHTY PECCANT EPINOSIC MALADIVE

UNHEATED COLD

UNHEEDED IGNORED UNTENTED

UNHEEDING DEAF CARELESS

UNHESITATING READY UNPOISED

UNHIDDEN OVERT

UNHITCH OUTSPAN

UNHOLY IMPURE WICKED IMPIOUS PROFANE

UNHORSE PURL THROW UNCOLT DISMOUNT UNSADDLE

UNHURRIED EASY SLOW SOFT SOBER

UNHURT SAFE HARMLESS HURTLESS UNHARMED

UNIAT MALKITE MELCHITE

UNICORN LIN REEM KILIN LICORN LICORNE NARWHAL HOWITZER

UNICORN FISH LIJA UNIE

UNICORN PLANT MARTINOE

UNICUM UNION

UNIDENTIFIED FACELESS INCOGNITO

UNIFICATION SYSTEM ENSEMBLE

UNIFIED GLOBAL

UNIFIER UMBRELLA

UNIFORM KIT DEAD EVEN FLAT JUST LIKE SAME SELF SUIT ALIKE BLUES CLOTH KHAKI SOLID SUITY GLOBAL GREENS LIVERY SINGLE STEADY EQUABLE REGULAR SIMILAR SUNTANS CONSTANT EQUIFORM EQUIPAGE MEASURED STANDARD UNIVOCAL
(— IN COLOR) SELF
(— IN HUE) FLAT
(LEATHER —) BUFF
(NOT —) MOTLEY RAGTAG SQUALLY UNKEMPT
(PRISONER'S —) STRIPES
(PREF.) IS ISO

UNIFORMITY ONENESS EQUALITY EVENNESS MONOTONY SAMENESS
(— OF MOTION) INSISTURE

UNIFORMLY EVENLY EQUALLY

UNIFY MERGE UNITE CEMENT COMPACT UNITIZE COALESCE

UNILATERAL SECUND

UNIMAGINATIVE DULL SODDEN STUPID LIMITED LITERAL PROSAIC UNIDEAL PEDANTIC PEDESTRIAN

UNIMPAIRED FRESH SOUND ENTIRE INTACT
(— BY) DEVOID

UNIMPASSIONED SOBER WHOLE
STEADY
UNIMPEDED FREE EXPEDITE
UNIMPORTANT VAIN LIGHT PETTY
SMALL CASUAL SIMPLE TRIVIAL
IMMOMENT PEDDLING PIDDLING
TRINKETY JERKWATER MINISCULE
SMALLTIME INSIGNIFICANT
UNINFLECTED APTOTIC
UNINFORMED GREEN UNTOLD
IGNORANT
UNINHABITED WILD EMPTY DESERT
VACANT DESOLATE WASTEFUL
UNINHIBITED LARGE
UNINJURED WHOLE INTACT
SINCERE
UNINSPIRED HACK STODGY
POMPIER DRYASDUST
UNINSPIRING TAME
UNINSTRUCTED NAIVE IGNORANT
UNINTELLIGENT DUMB OBTUSE
OPAQUE STUPID ASININE FOOLISH
VACUOUS WITLESS
UNINTELLIGIBLE BLIND MISTY
OPAQUE MYSTICAL
UNINTENTIONAL UNMEANT
UNINTERESTING DRY ARID COLD
DRAB DREE DULL FADE FLAT TAME
DREAR SANDY STALE BORING
DREICH JEJUNE INSIPID BROMIDIC
FRUMPISH
UNINTERMITTENT ITHAND
UNINTERRUPTED SMOOTH
STEADY ENDLESS ETERNAL
STRAIGHT
UNINTERRUPTEDLY AWAY
UNINVITED
(ENTER —) CRASH
UNIO MUSSEL
UNION SUM ZYG BLOC DUAD JOIN
ALLOY GROUP JOINT NONOP UNITY
ENOSIS FUSION GREMIO TAWHID
VEREIN COMPACT CONCERT
CONTACT MEETING ONENESS
SOCIETY ADHESION ALLIANCE
COHESION ESPOUSAL JOINTURE
JUNCTION JUNCTURE SODALITY
SYSTASIS TRIALISM VINCULUM
ZOLLVEREIN
(— OF TWO SETS) CUP
(— OF TWO VOWELS) CRASIS
(MARITAL —) BED
(POLITICAL —) ANSCHLUSS
(SEXUAL —) COPULA COUPLING
(TURKISH —) JETTRU
(PREF.) ZYG(O)(OTO)
(SEXUAL —) GAMO
(SUFF.) APSIS GAM(AE)(IST)(OUS)(Y)
GAMETE
UNIONIST REFUGEE
UNIONIZE ALLY
**UNION OF SOVIET SOCIALIST
REPUBLICS** (SEE RUSSIA)

UNIQUE ODD RARE SOLE UNIC
ALONE UNION SINGLE SULLEN
UNICUM ALONELY SOLEYNE SPECIAL
STRANGE ISOLATED SINGULAR
UNIQUENESS SOLITUDE
UNISON FIRST CONCORD
HOMOPHONY
UNIT (ALSO SEE MEASURE AND
WEIGHT)
(ALSO SEE MEASURE) ACE ONE
ATOM BARN KLAN FLOOR HUMIT
MONAD NEPER ADDRESS DIOPTER
ELEMENT ENERGID KLAVERN
(— IN COUNTING FISH) MEASE
(— IN EARTHWORK) FLOAT FLOOR
(— OF ABSORPTION) SABIN
(— OF ACCELERATION) GAL MILLIGAL
(— OF ACOUSTICAL ABSORPTION)
SABIN
(— OF ACTION) EPISODE
(— OF ANGULAR MEASURE)
CENTRAD
(— OF ARCHEOLOGICAL
CLASSIFICATION) ASPECT
(— OF AREA) DEKAR DECARE DEKARE
(— OF BINARY DIGITS) BYTE
GIGABYTE
(— OF BRIGHTNESS) NIT STILB
LAMBERT
(— OF CAPACITANCE) JAR FARAD
(— OF CAPACITY) COR LAST PIPE
ARDAB ARDEB TIERCE AMPHORA
(— OF CARDS) TRICK
(— OF COMIC STRIP) BOX
(— OF CONDUCTANCE) SIEMENS
(— OF COUNTING) POINT
(— OF CURRENT) AMPERE
(— OF DATA TRANSMISSION SPEED)
BAUD
(— OF DESIGN) LARME
(— OF DISTANCE) DAY VERST
MORGAN PARSEC MEGAPARSEC
(— OF ELASTANCE) DARAF
(— OF ELECTRICAL RESISTANCE)
ABOHM
(— OF ELECTRIC CAPACITY) FARAD
(— OF ELECTRIC CONDUCTANCE)
MHO
(— OF ELECTRIC FORCE) VOLT
KILOVOLT STATVOLT
(— OF ELECTRIC INDUCTANCE)
HENRY
(— OF ELECTRIC INTENSITY) AMPERE
OERSTED
(— OF ELECTRICITY) ES COULOMB
(— OF ELECTRIC RELUCTANCE) REL
STATOHM
(— OF ELECTRIC RESISTANCE)
BEGOHM
(— OF ENERGY) ERG RAD QUAD
JOULE ATOMERG QUANTUM
(— OF FINENESS) CARAT KARAT
(— OF FLOORING) SQUARE

(— OF FLOW) CUSEC
(— OF FLUIDITY) RHE
(— OF FLUX DENSITY) GAUSS
(— OF FORCE) G DYNE STAPP NEWTON STHENE POUNDAL
(— OF FREQUENCY) HERTZ FRESNEL GIGAHERTZ MEGAHERTZ
(— OF GEOLOGIC TIME) AEON
(— OF GOVERNMENT) DEME LAND KREIS GEMEINDE
(— OF HEAT) BTU THERM CALORIE
(— OF ILLUMINANCE) LUX NIT PHOT MICROLUX
(— OF ILLUMINATION) PHOT
(— OF INFORMATION) NIT GIGABIT
(— OF INSTRUCTION) FRAME
(— OF INSULATION) TOG
(— OF INTERSTELLAR SPACE) PARSEC
(— OF JET PROPULSION) JATO
(— OF LAND AREA) ARE SULUNG
(— OF LANGUAGE) SYLLABLE
(— OF LENGTH) FERMI STADE MICRON MICROMETER
(— OF LIGHT) LUMEN
(— OF LIGHT INTENSITY) PYR PHOTON
(— OF LOUDNESS) PHON SONE DECIBEL
(— OF LUMINOUS INTENSITY) CANDELA
(— OF MACHINERY) STAND
(— OF MAGNETIC FLUX) GAUSS WEBER
(— OF MAGNETIC FLUX DENSITY) TESLA
(— OF MAGNETIC FORCE) KAPP GILBERT
(— OF MAGNETIC INTENSITY) GAMMA OERSTED MAGNETON
(— OF MAGNIFICATION) DIAMETER
(— OF MASS) AMU SLUG CRITH DALTON AVOGRAM
(— OF MEANING) SEMANTEME
(— OF MEASURE) KILOBASE
(— OF MEMORY) BIT MNEMON
(— OF METRICAL QUANTITY) MATRA
(— OF MOMENT) DEBYE
(— OF MOMENTUM) BOLE
(— OF NARCOTIC) JOLT
(— OF NYLON FINENESS) DENIER
(— OF ONE INCH) BUTTON
(— OF PAIN INTENSITY) DOL
(— OF PERMEABILITY) DARCY
(— OF PIPE) FOURBLE
(— OF POWER) WATT DYNAM GIGAWATT KILOWATT PONCELET TERAWATT
(— OF PRESSURE) BAR TORR BARAD BARIE BARYE GWELY OSMOL OSMOLE PASCAL KILOBAR MEGABAR CENTIBAR MICROBAR MILLIBAR
(— OF PRESSWORK) TOKEN

(— OF RADIATION) RAD REM REP GRAY LANGLEY
(— OF RADIOACTIVITY) CURIE
(— OF RESISTANCE) OHM
(— OF ROCKET) STAGE
(— OF SATURATION) SATRON
(— OF SOCIETY) CLAN HORDE CHAPTER
(— OF SOUND) SONE
(— OF SPACE AND CIRCULATION) MILLINE
(— OF SPEECH) WORD
(— OF SPEED) BAUD KNOT
(— OF STOCK) SHARE
(— OF STRUCTURE) MICELLE
(— OF TEMPERATURE) KELVIN
(— OF THICKNESS) POINT
(— OF TIME) AEON BEAT SVEDBERG
(— OF TRADING) CONTRACT
(— OF TRANSMISSION SPEED) BAUD
(— OF USEFULNESS) UTIL
(— OF VELOCITY) VELO
(— OF VERSE METER) FOOT
(— OF VISCOSITY) POISE STOKE SECONDS
(— OF WAVELENGTH) ANGSTROM
(— OF WEIGHT) SSU TON GERA GRAM CARAT CATTY GERAH GRAIN LIANG OUNCE POUND RATTI STEIN ARROBA GRAMME RUTTEE
(— OF WIRE MEASUREMENT) MIL
(— OF WORK) ERG CROP HOUR ERGON JOULE KILERG DINAMODE
(— OF YARN) LEA
(— OF YARN SIZE) CUT
(— OF 100 MEN) CENTURY
(— OF 20) CONGE
(ADMINISTRATIVE —) BLOCK HSIEN
AGENCY BUREAU CIRCLE DISTRICT
(ARBITRARY —) OLFACTY
(ARCHERY —) END
(ARMY —) LEGION BRIGADE COMPANY MAHALLA
(ARTILLERY —) BATTERY
(ATOMIC MASS —) DALTON
(AVAILABLE AS —) MARRIED
(BOWLING —) ALLEY
(BOY SCOUT —) SHIP
(BUILDER'S —) SQUARE
(CIGAR-MANUFACTURING —) BUCKEYE
(COLLECTIVE —) COMMUNE
(COMBAT —) ARMAMENT
(DISCRETE —) FRACTION
(EDUCATIONAL —) COURSE
(ELECTROMAGNETIC —) ABFARAD ABHENRY MAXWELL ABAMPERE
(FUNDAMENTAL —) BASE
(GRAMMATICAL —) JUNCTION
(HARMONIC —) CELL
(HOUSING —) HUTMENT
(HYPOTHETICAL —) ID IDANT MICELLE

(INDIVIDUALLY OWNED LIVING —)
CONDO
(LIFE —) BIOPHORE
(LIVING —) BIONT BIOGEN
(LOGARITHMIC —) BEL
(LOGGING —) CHANCE
(METRIC —) DEKAR DECARE DEKARE
(MILITARY —) ARMY GOUM CORPS
GROUP LANCE SQUAD BRIGADE
PLATOON SECTION COMMANDO
DIVISION REGIMENT SQUADRON
(NAZI —) FEHME
(ORGANIZATIONAL —) CELL ACTIVITY
(PHOTOMETRIC —) VIOLLE
(POLITICAL —) POLITY SOVIET
MUNICIPALITY
(RADIOACTIVE DISINTEGRATION —)
RUTHERFORD
(RHYTHMIC —) BASIS COLON
(SELF-PERPETUATING —) BIOSOME
(SHIPPING —) CARLOAD
(SOCIAL —) SEPT GROUP KRAAL
SOCIUS
(STORAGE —) BUFFER
(TELEGRAPHIC —) BAUD
(TEMPERATURE —) KELVIN
(TERRITORIAL —) STAKE STATE
COMMOT CANTRED CANTREF
KINGDOM
(THERMAL —) THERM CALORY
CALORIE
(TRIBAL —) TOWNSHIP
(VOTING —) CENTURY
(SUFF.) MONAS ON
UNITARIAN ARIAN SOCINIAN
UNITE ADD MIX ONE OOP PAN SAM
SEW UNE UNY ALLY BAND BIND
CLUB COAK FUSE HASP JOIN KNIT
KNOT LINK SAMM SEAM SOUD UNIT
WELD BANDY CLOSE GRADE GRAFT
INONE JACOB JOINT MARRY MERGE
NITCH UNIFY WHOLE ATTACH
CEMENT CONCUR COUPLE EMBODY
ENTIRE GATHER LAUREL LEAGUE
SOLDER SPLICE STRIKE SUTURE
ACCRETE AMALGAM CLUSTER
COALITE COMBINE CONJOIN
CONNECT CONSORT JACOBUS
SIAMESE ALLIGATE ANCYLOSE
ANKYLOSE ASSEMBLE COALESCE
COMPOUND CONCRETE CONSPIRE
COPULATE FEDERATE LAMINATE
COLLIGATE
(— ACCURATELY) LAP
(— BY INTERWEAVING) PLEACH
SPLICE
(— BY THREADS) SEW STITCH
(— CLOSELY) FAY YOT WELD CEMENT
COTTON
(— FOR INTRIGUE) CABAL
(— HOSE) COLLECT
(— IN MARRIAGE) WED SACRE SACRI
SPLICE SPOUSE

(— METALS) WELD SWEAT
(— TIMBERS) SCARF
(PREF.) GAMETO GAMO
UNITED ONE TIED ADDED ASONE
ATONE FUSED JOINT ALLIED
CONNATE ENDLESS UNIONED
COMBINED CONCRETE CONJOINT
CONJUNCT FEDERATE COADUNATE
(PREF.) GAM(ETO)(O)
UNITED ARAB EMIRATES
(CAPITAL OF —) ABUDHABI
(FORMER NAME OF —)
TRUCIALOMAN TRUCIALCOAST
TRUCIALSTATES
(MONEY OF —) DIRHAM
(MOUNTAINS OF —) HAJAR
(STATE OF —) AJMAN DUBAI
SHARJAH FUJAIRAH
(TOWN OF —) DUBAI JEBEL BURAIMI
SHARJAH
UNITED KINGDOM (SEE ENGLAND)
UNITED STATES (ALSO SEE
SPECIFIC STATES)

UNITED STATES

LAKE: ERIE MEAD SALT HURON TAHOE
CRATER ONTARIO MICHIGAN
SUPERIOR CHAMPLAIN
OKEECHOBEE
MOUNTAIN: BEAR BONA SILL GREEN
OZARK ROCKY UINTA WHITE
ANTERO ELBERT SHASTA SIERRA
BELFORD FORAKER HARVARD
MASSIVE RAINIER SANFORD
WASATCH WHITNEY CATSKILL
MCKINLEY WRANGELL BLACKBURN
ADIRONDACK BITTERROOT
APPALACHIAN
PRESIDENT: ABE CAL DDE FDR IKE JFK
LBJ BUSH FORD POLK TAFT ADAMS
GRANT HARRY HAYES JIMMY NIXON
TEDDY TYLER ARTHUR CARTER
HOOVER MONROE PIERCE REAGAN
TAYLOR TRUMAN WILSON CLINTON
HARDING JACKSON JOHNSON
KENNEDY LINCOLN MADISON
BUCHANAN COOLIDGE FILLMORE
GARFIELD HARRISON MCKINLEY
VANBUREN JEFFERSON ROOSEVELT
EISENHOWER WASHINGTON
VICE PRESIDENT: BURR BUSH FORD
KING ADAMS AGNEW DAWES
GERRY NIXON TYLER ARTHUR
COLFAX CURTIS DALLAS GARNER
HAMLIN HOBART MORTON TRUMAN
WILSON BARKLEY CALHOUN
CLINTON JOHNSON MONDALE
SHERMAN WALLACE WHEELER
COOLIDGE FILLMORE HUMPHREY
MARSHALL TOMPKINS VANBUREN
FAIRBANKS HENDRICKS JEFFERSON
ROOSEVELT STEVENSON
ROCKEFELLER BRECKINRIDGE

WATERFALL: TWIN AKAKA SEVEN
NARADA RIBBON FFATHER PALOUSE
PASSAIC SLUISKIN YOSEMITE
BRIDALVEIL YELLOWSTONE

UNITING SUTURE
UNITS (SUFF.)
(HAVING TIME —) SEMIC
UNITY UNION SYSTEM ONENESS
UNITUDE IDENTITY SODALITY
SYMPATHY TOTALITY
(— OF SPIRIT AND NATURE)
ABSOLUTE
UNIVALENT MONATOMIC
UNIVERSAL ALL LOCAL QUALE
TOTAL WHOLE WORLD COMMON
GLOBAL PUBLIC VERSAL GENERAL
GENERIC CATHOLIC ECUMENIC
PANDEMIC
(TRANSCENDENT —) IDEA
UNIVERSALITY ALLNESS
OMNITUDE
UNIVERSE ALL LOKA MASS OLAM
WORLD COSMOS SYSTEM CREATURE
EXEMPLAR
(SIDEREAL —) SPACE
(PREF.) COSM(O) COSMETO COSMICO
UNIVERSITY STUDY CAMPUS
SCHOOL ACADEMY COLLEGE
MADRASA STUDIUM VARSITY
MADRASAH REDBRICK
(OF BRITISH —S) REDBRICK
(RELATING TO BRITISH —) OXBRIDGE
REDBRICK PLATEGLASS
UNJUST HARD UNFAIR WANTON
WICKED UNEQUAL UNRICHT
UNRIGHT WRONGFUL
UNJUSTIFIED INVALID
UNJUSTLY UNDULY FALSELY
UNKEELED RATITE
UNKEMPT ROUGH SEEDY FROWZY
MOTLEY RAGTAG RUGGED SHAGGY
INCOMPT RAFFISH RUFFLED
SCRUFFY SHAGRAG TOUSLED
DRAGGLED SCRAGGLY SLIPSHOD
STRUBBLY UNCOMBED SHAMBOLIC
UNKIND BAD ILL MEAN VILE CRUEL
HARSH STERN SEVERE UNMEEK
UNKINDNESS DISFAVOR
UNKNOWABLE SEALED
UNKNOWN IGN UNCO UNKET
UNKID IGNOTE MUNKAR SEALED
SECRET UNWARE UNWIST FARAWAY
OBSCURE UNCOUTH UNHEARD
IGNORANT UNAWARES UNKENNED
UNWITTING
UNLADEN LEAR LEER
UNLATCH UNSNECK
UNLAWFUL ILLEGAL ILLICIT
NONLICET UNLEEFUL UNLEISUM
UNLEARNED LEWD GROSS PLAIN
BOOKLESS IGNORANT UNLEARED
UNLEAVENED AZYMOUS

UNLESS BUT NIF LESS LEST NISI
SAVE BINNA NOBUT LESSEN ONLESS
WITHOUT
(— BEFORE) NIPR NIPRI
(— OTHERWISE NOTED) NAN
UNLETTERED LEWD BORREL
IGNORANT
UNLIGHTED BLIND LAMPLESS
UNLIKE DIFFORM DISLIKE DIVERSE
DIFFERENT DISSIMILAR
(MOST —) OTHEREST
UNLIKELY REMOTE DUBIOUS
(MOST —) LAST
UNLIMITED VAST SOVRAN
ABSOLUTE UNTERMED
(— IN POWER) ALMIGHTY
UNLINED SINGLE
UNLOAD TIP DROP DUMP HOVEL
DECANT STRIKE UNLADE UNSHIP
UNSTOW DELIVER DEPLETE
DETRUCK DISLOAD UNTRUSS
DISCHARGE
UNLOCK UNMAKE RESERATE
UNLOUKEN
UNLOOSE OUTWIND UNRIVET
UNLUCKY BAD FAY ILL EVIL FOUL
DONSY DISMAL DONSIF HOODOO
WICKED HAPLESS INFAUST
UNHAPPY SINISTER UNCHANCY
UNTOWARD MISCHANCY
WANCHANCY
(— THING) AMBSACE
UNMAN UNDO CRUSH UNNERVE
UNMANAGEABLE ROID DONSY
RANDY WANTON RESTIVE CHURLISH
STAFFISH CAMSTAIRY REFRACTORY
UNMANLY SOFT EPICENE MANLESS
UNLUSTY
UNMANNERLY RUDE BOORISH
UNCIVIL IMPOLITE UNGENTLE
MISLEARED
UNMARKED MAVERICK NOTELESS
UNMARRIED ONE LONE SOLE OLEPI
YOUNG ONLEPY SINGLE
UNMASK EXPOSE UNFACE DISMASK
UNCLOAK
UNMASKING EXPOSURE
UNMEASURED UNMEET MODELESS
UNMELODIOUS SCRANNEL
UNMERCHANTABLE SALABLE
SALEABLE
UNMERCIFUL CRUEL PITILESS
RUTHLESS
UNMETHODICAL CURSORY
UNMINDFUL SLOWFUL CARELESS
HEEDLESS MINDLESS
UNMISTAKABLE FLAT OPEN
BROAD CLEAR FRANK PLAIN PATENT
DECIDED EXPRESS APPARENT
DECISIVE MANIFEST UNIVOCAL
UNMISTAKABLY SIGNALLY
UNMITIGATED PURE GROSS RUDDY
ARRANT DAMNED SOVRAN PERFECT

PUREDEE REGULAR ABSOLUTE
OUTRIGHT
UNMIX EXSOLVE
UNMIXED NET DEEP MERE NEAT
PURE SELF SOLE BLANK SHEER
UTTER IMMIXT SIMPLE STRAIGHT
UNMODIFIED BRUTE STRAIGHT
UNMOLESTED SACKLESS
UNMOVED CALM COOL FIRM STONY
TIGHT IMMOTE SERENE ADAMANT
IMMOVED
UNMOVING INERT IMMOBILE
IMMOTIVE
UNMUSICAL NOTELESS
SCABROUS
UNNATURAL EERY EERIE STIFF
CLAMMY CREEPY FORCED UNKIND
STRANGE UNCANNY VIOLENT
ABNORMAL ABSONANT FARCICAL
KINDLESS STRAINED UNKINDLY
MONSTROUS
UNNECESSARY USELESS
NEEDLESS SUPERFLUOUS
UNNEEDED WASTE
UNNERVE UNMAN RATTLE UNMAKE
WEAKEN ENERVATE PARALYZE
UNNERVED SHOOK
UNNILPENTIUM HAHNIUM
UNNILQUADIUM RUTHERFORDIUM
UNNOTICED SILENT
UNOBJECTIONABLE VENIAL
UNOBSERVANT HEEDLESS
UNOBSTRUCTED FAIR FREE OPEN
PATENT THROUGH APPARENT
UNOBTRUSIVE SHY QUIET
MODEST SEDATE DISCREET
RETIRING
UNOCCUPIED IDLE VOID BLANK
EMPTY WASTE OTIOSE VACANT
LEISURE UNSEATED WASTEFUL
UNORGANIZED ACOSMIC
INCHOATE
UNORTHODOX HERETIC
UNOSTENTATIOUS SHY QUIET
LENTEN MODEST
UNPACK UNFARDLE
UNPAID DUE UNQUIT UNWAGED
HONORARY WAGELESS
OUTSTANDING
UNPAIRED IMPAR AZYGOUS
UNPALATABLE SOD HARD BITTER
BRACKISH
UNPARALLELED ALONE UNIQUE
EPOCHAL PEERLESS SINGULAR
UNPEERED
UNPERTURBED BLAND STILL
UNPLEASANT BAD ACID EVIL HARD
NICE SOUR UGLY VILE AWFUL CRUDE
GRIMY GUMMY HAIRY HARSH
MUCKY NASTY ROUGH TOUGH
YUCKY YUKKY BRUTAL CRIMPY
RANCID STICKY THRAWN UNFELE
UNGAIN UNLIEF BEASTLY BILIOUS

GHASTLY INGRATE SPINOUS
UNLUSTY UNQUEME UNSONCY
CHISELLY DREADFUL HORRIBLE
INDECENT SCABROUS UNLOVELY
TRAUMATIC ABOMINABLE
(ANNOYINGLY —) CREEPY
(PREF.) CAC(O) CACH
UNPLEASANTLY QUEER HARDLY
UNWINLY
UNPLEASANTNESS ILLNESS
UNPLOWED LEA
UNPOETICAL MUSELESS
UNPOLISHED ILL RUDE BLIND
CRUDE ROUGH COARSE INCULT
RUGGED RUSTIC SAVAGE SHAGGY
UPLAND INCOMPT UNKEMPT
AGRESTIC
UNPOPULARITY ENVY
UNPRACTICED RAW FRESH
UNTRADED
UNPREDICTABILITY CHAOS
UNPREDICTABLE DICEY CHANCY
CRANKY ERRATIC
UNPREJUDICED FAIR
UNPREMEDITATED CASUAL
UNPREPARED TARDY
UNPREPOSSESSING SEEDY
UNPRETENDING LOWLY HOMELY
HUMBLE
UNPRETENTIOUS HOMY HOMEY
PLAIN SOBER COMMON HOMELY
HUMBLE MODEST SIMPLE DISCREET
HOMESPUN
UNPRINCIPLED LEWD LIMMER
UNPRODUCTIVE DRY SHY ARID
DEAD DEAF LEAN POOR VAIN YELD
YELL ADDLE DUSTY WASTE BARREN
GEASON SAPLESS STERILE
WOODSERE
UNPRODUCTIVENESS BORASCO
BORASQUE BORRASCA
UNPROFESSIONAL LAY BUSH
LAICAL JACKLEG
UNPROFITABLE BAD DRY DEAD
LEAN SECK VAIN BARREN BOOTLESS
GAINLESS UNGAINLY
UNPROGRESSIVE SLOW
DORMANT BACKWARD
UNPROMISING BLUE DUBIOUS
UNPRONOUNCED MUTE
UNPROPITIOUS ILL EVIL FOUL
THRAW MALIGN SULLEN ADVERSE
AVERTED INFAUST OMINOUS
THRAWART
UNPROTECTED NAKED EXPOSED
HELPLESS
UNPROVOKED WANTON
UNPUBLISHED INED INEDITED
UNQUALIFIED NET BARE FULL
MERE PURE VERY BLACK PLUMP
SHEER UNFIT DIRECT ENTIRE
UNABLE CLOTTED PLENARY IMPLICIT
INHABILE POSITIVE

UNQUESTIONABLE ASSURED
CERTAIN DECIDED ABSOLUTE
ELUSIVE DISTINCT
UNQUESTIONED CLEAR
UNQUESTIONING IMPLICIT
UNRAVEL REDD UNDO BREAK
ENODE FEAZE RAVEL RETEX
SOLVE EVOLVE TIFFLE UNFOLD
UNKNIT UNLACE ENODATE
RESOLVE
UNRAVELLING DISCOVERY
DENOUEMENT
UNREAL VAIN AERIAL GOTHIC
CHIMERIC FANCIED SHADOWY
AERIFORM CHIMERIC FARCICAL
ILLUSORY NOTIONAL SCENICAL
VISIONAL
(PREF.) PSEUD(O)
UNREALISTIC CHIMERIC
UNREALIZED BEHIND
UNREASONABLE ABSURD FANATIC
ABSONANT
UNREASONABLENESS ALOGY
INSANITY
UNREASONABLY SINFULLY
UNREASONING BRUTE RABID
UNRECOGNIZED UNSUNG CRYPTIC
UNWITTED
UNRECOVERABLE DEAD
UNRECTIFIED IMPURE
UNREDEEMED CHEAP
UNREFINED RAW DARK LOUD
BRUTE CRUDE DORIC GROSS
COARSE COMMON EARTHY JUNGLY
VULGAR BOORISH UNCOUTH
UNKEMPT DREADFUL SWAINISH
UNREFLECTING GLIB VACANT
UNREGENERACY ADAM
UNREGENERATE NATURAL
UNREGENERATELY MANLY
UNREHEARSED IMPROMPTU
UNRELATED FREMD STRAY UNAKIN
UNTOLD EXTREME FRAMMIT
POSITIVE
UNRELAXED UNSLAKED
UNRELAXING TONIC
UNRELENTING GRIM HARD IRON
CRUEL STERN BRASSY SEVERE
RIGOROUS
UNRELIABLE FISHY SHADY FICKLE
GREASY UNSAFE CASALTY STREAKY
WILDCAT FECKLESS GLIBBERY
SLIPPERY TICKLISH
UNRELIEVED DEAD BRUTE ABJECT
EXQUISITE
UNREMITTING BUSY FAST HARD
DOGGED
UNREMUNERATIVE HONORARY
UNRESERVED FREE CLEAN FRANK
ROUND COMMON UNCLOSE
EXPLICIT
UNRESERVEDNESS FREEDOM
UNRESISTING BUXOM

UNRESPONSIVE DEAD DUMB
BARREN SILENT STUBBORN
UNREST ANOMY ANOMIE MOTION
AILMENT DISREST WANREST
DISQUIET CHEMISTRY PSYCHOSIS
UNRESTRAINED LAX MAD FREE
WILD BROAD FANTI FRANK LARGE
LOOSE FACILE FANTEE LAVISH
UNTIED WANTON FLYAWAY
RAMPANT RIOTOUS BARBARIC
FAMILIAR FREEHAND LAXATIVE
PINDARIC ABANDONED LIBERTINE
UNRESTRAINT LICENSE IMMUNITY
UNRESTRICTED FREE GLOBAL
SOVRAN UNZONED ABSOLUTE
UNRETURNED UNYOLDEN
UNREVEALED UNTOLD
UNRHYMED BLANK
UNRIG STRIP
UNRIGHTEOUSNESS ADHARMA
UNRIPE RAW CRUDE GREEN CALLOW
UNCURED IMMATURE
UNROBE DISROBE UNDRESS
DISARRAY
UNROLL EVOLVE UNCURL DEVELOP
OUTROLL TRINDLE UNTREND
UNROOF TIRL TIRR TIRVE DISROOF
UNRUFFLE SMOOTH SOOTHE
MOLLIFY
UNRUFFLED CALM COOL EASY
EVEN QUIET SOBER STILL ASLEEP
PLACID SEDATE SERENE SMOOTH
DECOROUS
UNRULY HIGH RAMP ROYT TOUGH
HAUNTY WANTON LAWLESS
RAMMAGE ROPABLE UNRULED
VICIOUS WANRULY WAYWARD
INDOCILE MUTINOUS CAMSTAIRY
TURBULENT REFRACTORY
OBSTREPEROUS RAMBUNCTIOUS
UNSADDLE OUTSPAN UNPANEL
UNSADDLED BAREBACKED
UNSAFE HOT OUT FISHY EXPOSED
INSECURE PERILOUS
UNSANCTIFIED PROFANE
UNSATISFACTORY BAD ILL EVIL
POOR CROOK LOUSY SHREWD
WRETCHED
(— PRODUCT) LEMON
UNSATISFYING DUSTY HOLLOW
UNSATURATED
(PREF.) EN
UNSAVORY WERSH INSIPID
WEARISH
UNSAY WITHDRAW
UNSCHOLARLY BOOKLESS
UNSCRUPULOUS SKIN CROOK
BRAZEN DEVIOUS JACKLEG
DEXTROUS RASCALLY
UNSEASONABLE LAT UNRIPE
UNTIDY UNCHANCY UNTIMELY
UNSEASONED RAW GREEN
UNSEAT ADDRESS DISSEAT

UNSEEING BLIND GAZELESS
UNSEEMLY HOIDEN UNFAIR
IMPROPER INDECENT SEEMLESS
UNMEETLY UNWORTHY
UNSEEN SECRET UNEYED CRYPTIC
VIEWLESS INVISIBLE
UNSELFISH (ABSURDLY —)
QUIXOTIC
UNSERRIED LOOSE
UNSETTLE JAR TURN UNFIX UNSET
UPSET COMMOVE DERANGE
DISTURB STAGGER UNHINGE
UNQUEME DISORDER DISQUIET
DISTRACT
UNSETTLED MOOT LIGHT SHAKY
UNSAD VAGUE BROKEN FICKLE
QUEASY VAGOUS DUBIOUS
NOMADIC SHUTTLE UNSTAID
RESTLESS UNSTABLE VAGABOND
UNSETTLING NASTY
UNSHAKABLE DOGGED ADAMANT
IRONCLAD
UNSHAKEN FIRM STEADY
UNMOVED UNSHOOK CONSTANT
RESOLUTE
UNSHAPELY DEFORMED
UNMACKLY
UNSHARED SOLE
UNSHEATHE DISCASE
UNSHEATHED BARE
UNSHELTERED BLEAK
UNSHOD BAREFOOT SHOELESS
DISCALCED
UNSHORN UNPOLLED
UNSIGHTLY UGLY AWFUL MESSY
HOMELY INDECENT
UNSKILLED JAY PUNY GREEN
PUISNE UNGAIN UNSEEN STRANGE
FECKLESS
UNSKILLFUL ILL EVIL RUDE
ARTLESS AWKWARD UNFEATY
BUNGLING TINKERLY UNHEPPEN
UNSMILING GLUM AUSTERE
UNSOCIABLE SULLEN FAROUCHE
INSOCIAL
UNSOILED CLEAN
UNSOPHISTICATE SQUARE
UNSOPHISTICATED JAY DEWY
NAIF PURE FRANK GREEN NAIVE
SILLY CALLOW SIMPLE BUCOLIC
NATURAL VERDANT HOMEBRED
HOMESPUN INNOCENT PROVINCIAL
UNSOUND BAD ILL EVIL SICK ADDLE
BARMY CRAZY CRONK DICKY DOTTY
DOZED SANDY SHAKY WONKY
ABSURD FAULTY FLAWED HOLLOW
INFIRM INSANE ROTTEN UNHALE
INVALID RICKETY UNWHOLE
UNSOUNDNESS CRACK INSANITY
UNSPARING ROUND SEVERE
DRASTIC RIGOROUS RUTHLESS
SCATHING SLASHING
UNSPIRITUAL CARNAL

UNSPOILED RACY UNSHENT
PRISTINE
UNSPOKEN TACIT SILENT
UNSPORTSMANLIKE DIRTY
UNSPOTTED CLEAR SPOTLESS
UNSPUN RAW
UNSTABLE FLUX BATTY LOOSE
SANDY SHAKY BROTEL CHOPPY
FICKLE FITFUL FLITTY LABILE LUBRIC
ROTTEN SHIFTY TICKLE UNFIRM
WANKLE WANKLY ASTATIC DWAIBLE
DWAIBLY DWEEBLE RICKETY SLIDDER
SLIDDRY VOLUBLE FEVERISH
FIRMLESS FUGITIVE INSECURE
LUBRICAL REMUABLE SKITTISH
SLIPPERY TICKLISH TOTTLISH
VARIABLE
(MENTALLY —) BRAINISH
UNSTEADILY GROGGILY
UNSTEADINESS FALTER
UNSTEADY WALT CRANK CRONK
DOTTY FLUKY LIGHT NERVY SLACK
TIPPY TIPSY TOTTY UNSAD WALTY
WONKY COGGLY FICKLE FLICKY
FLUFFY GROGGY JIGGLY JOGGLY
SWIMMY TOTTIE WAFFLY WAGGLY
WAMBLY WANKLE WEEWAW
WEEWOW DODDERY GLAIKIT
JIGGETY QUAVERY QUEACHY
TITTUPY TOTTERY WAYWARD
SKITTISH STAGGERY TICKLISH
TITUBANT UNSTABLE VARIABLE
VERSATILE
UNSTINTED LAVISH ENDLESS
UNSTOPPABLE SUREFIRE
UNSTRESS SLACK
UNSTRESSED SHORT
UNSTRING DISSOLVE
UNSTUDIED GLIB CASUAL
CARELESS GLANCING
UNSUBDUED VIRGIN UNBOWED
UNSUBSTANTIAL TOY AIRY LIMP
THIN WINDY AERIAL BUBBLE CHAFFY
FLIMSY SLEAZY SLEEZY SLIGHT
UNREAL FOLIOUS FRAGILE INSOLID
SHADOWY TENUOUS FILIGREE
FINESPUN FOOTLESS GIMCRACK
VAPOROUS PASTEBOARD
UNSUCCESSFUL BAD MANQUE
UNSPED STICKIT UNHAPPY
ABORTIVE
UNSUITABLE INEPT UNAPT UNDUE
UNFIT UNKIND UNMETE UNCOMELY
UNGAINLY UNLIKELY INELIGIBLE
MALAPROPOS INCONVENIENT
UNSUITABLENESS IMPOLICY
UNSUITED BAD
UNSULLIED FAIR PURE CLEAR
VIRGIN INNOCENT SPOTLESS
VIRGINAL
UNSUPPLIED HELPLESS
UNSUPPORTED BLIND NAKED
BACKWARD STAYLESS

UNSURE TIMID INFIRM DOUBTFUL
INSECURE UNSICKER
UNSURPASSED CHAMPION
UNSUSPECTING INNOCENT
UNSWEET UNSOOT
UNSWEETENED BRUT
UNSWERVING FIXED FLUSH LOYAL
DIRECT STEADY STRICT STURDY
STAUNCH
UNSWERVINGLY HEADLONG
UNSYMMETRICAL LOPSIDED
UNSYMPATHETIC DRY HARD
STONY FROZEN GLASSY HOSTILE
KINDLESS
UNTAINTED FREE GOOD PURE
INNOCENT
UNTAMED WILD FERAL RAMAGE
SAVAGE HAGGARD RAMMISH
WARRAGAL
UNTANGLE FREE SLEAVE UNLACE
UNTARNISHED PURE
UNTAUGHT WASTE UNLERED
IGNORANT
UNTHINKABLE PUERILE
UNTHINKING GLIB BRUTE CASUAL
FECKLESS HEEDLESS VISCERAL
UNTHINKINGLY STUPID
UNTIDINESS JAKES LITTER
UNTIDY DOWDY GAUMY MESSY
ROOKY BUNTING DRAGGLY LITTERY
RUMMAGY SCRUFFY UNSIDED
DRAGGLED SLOVENLY STRUBBLY
UNHEPPEN SHAMBOLIC
UNTIE UNDO UNBIND UNLASH
UNLATCH UNTRUSS UNTWINE
UNFASTEN
UNTIL AD OR TO GIN HENT INTO
UNTO FORTO TWEEN WHILE WHILES
WHILST PENDING
(— THEN) BEFORE
UNTILLED INCULT UNEARED
UNTIMELY UNTIDY IMMATURE
PREVIOUS TIMELESS
(— ARRIVAL) LATECOMER
UNTIRING BUSY SEDULOUS
TIRELESS
UNTITLED (— MEN) AUMAGA
UNTO TILL
UNTOLD VAST UNQUOD
UNTOUCHABLE DOM HARIJAN
CHANDALA
(PL.) PANCHAMA
UNTOUCHED FREE INTACT PRISTINE
(PREF.) INTEGRI
UNTOWARD ILL UNRULY FROWARD
WAYWARD
UNTRAINED RAW RUDE GREEN
HAGGARD
UNTRAMMELED FREE
UNTRIED MAIDEN UNSOUGHT
UNTRIMMED UNTEWED
UNTRODDEN PATHLESS UNFOOTED
UNTROUBLED CHEERY

UNTRUE FLAM FALSE LEASE WRONG
UNFAST DISLOYAL MENDACIOUS
(PREF.) PSEUD(O)
UNTRUSTWORTHINESS FALSITY
UNTRUSTWORTHY PUNIC SHAKY
LIMBER TRICKY UNSURE SLIDDERY
SLIPPERY
UNTRUTH LIE FABLE LEASE SKLENT
FALSITY UNTROTH MENDACITY
UNTRUTHFUL SLANTER
UNTUNABLE ABSONANT
UNTUTORED NATURAL IGNORANT
PRIMITIVE
UNTWILLED PLAIN
UNTWINE FRESE UNTWIST
UNTWIST FAG FFAZE UNLAY
UNSPIN UNTWIRL
UNTWISTED SLEIDED
UNUSABLE WASTE INUTILE
UNUSED IDLE FRESH RUSTY WASTE
INURED MAIDEN VACANT DERELICT
INITIATE UNWONTED
UNUSUAL ODD EERY RARE SELD
TALL CRAZY EERIE FORBY NOVEL
UTTER WEIRD EXEMPT FORBYE
SCREWY SINGLE UNIQUE STRANGE
ABNORMAL DISTINCT ESPECIAL
INSOLENT KNOCKOUT SELCOUTH
SINGULAR SPANKING UNCOMMON
UNTRADED UNWONTED
PRODIGIOUS
(PREF.) ANOM(O)
UNUSUALLY EXTRA
UNVARIED SAMELY
UNVARNISHED EVERYDAY
UNVARYING FLAT SAME FRANK
LEVEL STABLE UNIFORM
UNVEIL REVEAL UNCOVER
UNCROWN UNDRAPE UNSCREEN
UNWIMPLE
UNVENTILATED CLOSE
UNVERSED STRANGE
UNWANTED STRAY TRAMP FAULTY
UNWARRANTED UNDUE
UNWARY RASH UNAWARE
CARELESS HEEDLESS WARELESS
UNWASHED SOAPLESS
UNWASTEFUL FRUGAL
UNWAVERING FIRM CLEAN LEVEL
SOLID GLASSY STABLE EXPRESS
STAUNCH
UNWAVERINGLY FAST
UNWEAKENED CLEAR
UNWELL BAD ILL EVIL PUNK SICK
BADLY CROOK SEEDY AILING CHIPPY
WICKED COMICAL
UNWHOLESOME ILL EVIL SICK
CAGMAG IMPURE MORBID SICKLY
CORRUPT NOISOME NOXIOUS
UNCLEAN DISEASED EPINOSIC
UNWIELDY BULKY CLUMSY UNRIDE
AWKWARD HULKING CUMBROUS
UNGAINLY

UNWILLING CHARY LOATH SWEER
WERSE AVERSE ESCHEW BACKWARD
GRUDGING
(— TO GO FORWARD) RESTIVE
UNWILLINGLY MAUGER MAUGRE
UNWILLINGNESS GRUDGE
NOLITION
UNWIND UNCLEW UNREEL UNREAVE
UNTWINE
UNWISE FALSE INANE SILLY SIMPLE
FOOLISH WITLESS
UNWITTING UNWIST WEETLESS
UNWOMANLY MANKIND
UNWORLDLY WEIRD ASTRAL
SPIRITUAL
UNWORRIED DOWNBEAT
UNWORTHY BASE INDIGN BENEATH
UNDIGNE WANWORDY
UNWOUNDED COLD
UNWREATHE UNPLAT
UNWRINKLED BRANT BRENT
UNWROUGHT RAW LIVE RUDE
UNYIELDING PAT SET ACID DEAF
DOUR FAST FIRM GRIM HARD RIGID
STARK STEEL STIFF STITH STONY
TOUGH FLINTY FROZEN GLASSY
KNOBBY MARBLE STEELY STURDY
ADAMANT AUSTERE COSTIVE
FROWARD CHURLISH OBDURATE
OBEDIENT STUBBORN ROCKRIBBED
PERTINACIOUS
UNYOKE LOWSE UNTEAM OUTSHUT
OUTSPAN
UNYOKED
(PREF.) AZYGO
UP ON ONE OOP ABOUT ASTIR
DORMY NORTH DORMIE
(— AND ABOUT) AFOOT
(— TO) TIL INTO UNTIL
(— TO THE TIME) UNTIL
(— YONDER) UPBY UPBYE
(FARTHER —) ABOVE
(HIGH —) ALOFT
(PREF.) ANA ANO SUR
UPANISHAD ISHA KATHA
UPAS DITA ANTIAR CHETTIK
UPBEAT ARSIS AUFTAKT ANACRUSIS
UP-BOW POUSSE
UPBRAID CHEW RAIL SNUB TUCK
TWIT ABUSE ROUSE SCOLD TAUNT
UPBRAY EMBRAID REPROVE
DISGRACE OUTBRAID
UPCARD STARTER
UPCOMING NEXT FUTURE
UPFOLD SADDLE ANTICLINE
UPHEAVAL BOIL STORM UPLIFT
RUMMAGE UPTHROW
UPHILL UPBANK UPWITH
UPHOLD AID TOM ABET BACK
FAVOR AFFIRM ASSERT DEFEND
SOOTHE BOLSTER SUPPORT
SUSTAIN CHAMPION MAINTAIN
PRESERVE

UPHOLDER DEFENDER ERASTIAN
FEUDALIST
UPHOLDING BEHIND
UPHOLSTER SQUAB
UPHOLSTERER TAPISER UPHOLDER
UPKEEP MAINTENANCE
UPLAND DOWN DOWNS MAUKA
COTEAU FASTLAND
(PL.) BRAES DOWNS
UPLAND PLOVER QUAILY HILLBIRD
PAPABOTE
UPLIFT TOSS BOOST ERECT TOWER
UPTHRUST
UPLIFTED ERECT EXALTEE
UPON ON PON SUR INTO OVER
ABOVE AGAINST
(— THAT) THEREAT
(PREF.) EP EPH EPI OB
UPPER OVER VAMP SKIVE VAMPEY
SUPERIOR
(PL.) FINISH
(PREF.) ANO HYPER SUPERO
(SITUATED ON — SIDE) SUPRA
UPPER CRUST GRATIN
UPPERCUT BOLO
UPPER HURONIAN LAWSON
UPPERMOST UMEST UPMOST
OVEREST BUNEMOST OVERMOST
UPPER VOLTA FASO BURKINA
UPRAISED SUBLIME
UPRIGHT FAIR GOOD HARR JUST
PROP STUD TIDY TRUE ANEND
CHEEK ERECT GUIDE JELLY MORAL
ONEND RIGHT ROMAN SETUP STALE
STALK STILE ARRECT DIRECT ENTIRE
HONEST SQUARE FRIZZEN HOUSING
JANNOCK PITPROP SINCERE
GOALPOST INNOCENT RIGHTFUL
STANDARD STANDING STRAIGHT
VERTICAL VIRTUOUS
(NOT —) ATILT BEVEL
(PL.) STUDDING
(PREF.) ORTH(O)
UPRIGHTNESS HONOR TRUTH
APLOMB EQUITY HONESTY PROBITY
JUSTNESS SINCERITY
UPRISING RIOT EMEUTE MUTINY
PUTSCH REVOLT TUMULT UPRISE
UPRISAL REBELLION
UPROAR DIN RUT CAIN FLAW
GILD HELL MOIL RIOT ROUT BABEL
BURLE CHANG FUROR HOOHA
HURLY RUMOR STOUN STOUR
CLAMOR DIRDUM EMEUTE FRACAS
HABBLE HUBBLE HUBBUB RACKET
RANDAN RATTLE RIPPET RUCKUS
RUMBLE RUMPUS SHINDY STEVEN
STOUND TUMULT CATOUSE
FERMENT GARBOIL GAUSTER
ORATION OUTROAR RUCTION
STASHIE TURMOIL BALLYHOO
BROUHAHA SCOUTHER STIRRING
STRAMASH TINTAMAR CHARIVARI

SHEMOZZLE HULLABALOO
PANDEMONIUM
UPROARIOUS FURIOUS ROUTOUS
ROWDYDOWDY
UPROOT GRUB HACK LOUK MORE
UNROUT UNPLANT DISPLANT
ROOTWALT SUPPLANT
UPROOTED LUMPEN
UPSET ILL TIP TOP TUP CAVE COUP
COWP FUSS JUMP PURL ROCK TILT
TURN WELT EVERT FREAK KNOCK
ROUSE SHAKE SKAIL SKELL SPILL
WHELM BOTHER DISMAY QUELME
TICKED TIPPLE TOPPLE UPCAST
WALTER CAPSIZE DERANGE DISTURB
FRAZZLE HAYWIRE INASTEW
OVERSET PERVERT REVERSE
SLATTER SUBVERT TEMPEST
TURMOIL UNGLUED CAPSIZAL
DISTRAIT OVERTILT OVERTURN
STREAKED SUPPLANT TURNOVER
OVERTHROW
(EASILY —) FUGGY FLAPPABLE
UPSHOT ISSUE SHORT UPSET
EFFECT SEQUEL UPPING OUTCOME
UPSHOOT UPSTROKE
UPSIDE-DOWN CRAZY REVERSE
OVERHAND UPSEDOUN
UPSILON
(PREF.) YPSILI
UPSTAIRS ABOVE
UPSTANDING GRADELY
UPSTART KIP QUAT SNIP SNOB
SQUIRT UPSKIP DAITEEN PARVENU
ARRIVIST MUSHROOM SKIPJACK
UPSPRING
UPTICK RISE INCREASE
UPTIGHT TENSE
UP-TO-DATE AGOGO WITHIT MOD
MODERN TRENDY ABREAST
TODAYISH
UPWARD ALOFT UPLONG UPWAYS
UPWITH SKYWARD UPALONG
UPWARDS
(PREF.) ANO
UPWARD-MOVING ANABATIC
URAEUS ASP
URAMIL MUREXAN
URANUS OURANOS HERSCHEL
(WIFE OF —) GAEA
URAO TRONA
URARTAEAN KHALDIAN
URARTU VAN
URATE LITHATE
URBAN TOWN URBIC URBANE
BURGHAL OPPIDAN
URBANE CIVIL SUAVE POLITE SVELTE
AMIABLE GRACIOUS
URBANITY COMITY SUAVITY
COURTESY ELEGANCE
URCHIN IMP TYKE WAIF ELFIN GAMIN
SCAMP KEELIE NIPPER HURCHEON
(PREF.) (SEA —) ECHIN(O)

URD MUNGO
URDEE MATELEY
URDU REKHTA REKHTI MOORISH
URDUR (SISTER OF —) SKULD
VERTHANDI
URGE ART DUN EGG HIE PLY PUT SIC
SUE TAR YEN BROD COAX CRAM
EDGE FIRK GOAD ITCH MOVE PING
POKE PROD PUSH SICK SPUR WHIP
CROWD DRIVE EGGON FILIP FORCE
HOOSH IMPEL LABOR PRESS PRICK
SPANK TREAT COMPEL DEHORT
DESIRE ENGAGE EXCITE FILLIP
HARDEN HOICKS HUSTLE INCITE
INDUCE INVITE MOTION PROMPT
PROPEL STRAIN THREAP THREAT
ANIMATE COMMOVE ENFORCE
INSTANT OPPRESS PERSIST SOLICIT
SUGGEST URGENCY ADMONISH
INSTANCE PERSUADE
(— IMPORTUNATELY) DUN PRESS
(— ON) EGG ERT HAG SOOL WHIG
ALARM CHIRK CROWD DRIVE FILIP
HASTE HURRY IMPEL ROWEL YOICK
ALARUM FILLIP HARDEN HASTEN
INCITE
(— ON A HORSE) HUP CRAM
CHUCK
(— OUT) EXTRUDE
(— STRONGLY) EXHORT SOLICIT
(— WITH VEHEMENCE) DING
(VITAL —) LIBIDO
URGENCY NEED PRESS STRESS
COGENCE COGENCY URGENCE
EXIGENCY INSTANCE INSTANCY
PRESSURE
URGENT HOT DIRE LOUD RASH
ACUTE HASTY STRONG BURNING
CLAMANT EXIGENT INSTANT
URGEFUL CRITICAL PRESSING
PRESSIVE NECESSITOUS
URGING QUEST
URI (SON OF —) GEBER BEZALEEL
URIAH (WIFE OF —) BATHSHEBA
URIAL SHA OORIAL
URIEL (DAUGHTER OF —) MAACHAH
(FATHER OF —) TAHATH
URIJAH (FATHER OF —) SHEMAIAH
URINAL DUCK PISSOIR SANITARY
URINATE WET LEAK EMPTY STALE
PIDDLE EVACUATE MICTURATE
URINATION MICTION NOCTURIA
URINE MIG SIG LAGE LANT WASH
STALE WATER NETTING EMICTION
(— USED AS COSMETIC) LOTIUM
(PREF.) UR(O) URIC(O) URIN(I)(O)
(SUFF.) URIA URIC
URN JAR EWER KIST URNA VASE
CAPANNA
(— FOR MAKING TEA) KITCHEN
SAMOVAR
(— IN KENO) GOOSE
(BURIAL —) OSSUARY

(CINERARY —) DINOS DEINOS
(STONE —) STEEN
URN-SHAPED URCEOLAR
UROCHORDA ASCIDIA TUNICATA
UROPYGIUM RUMP
UROSTYLE COCCYX
URSA MAJOR OKNARI CHARIOT
WAGONER WAGGONER
URSA MINOR CYNOSURE
URSINE ARCTOID
URTICARIA HIVES UREDO CNIDOSIS
URTICASTRUM LAPORTEA
URUBU ZOPILOTE

URUGUAY

CAPITAL: MONTEVIDEO
DEPARTMENT: ROCHA SALTO FLORES
RIVERA ARTIGAS COLONIA
DURAZNO FLORIDA SORIANO
ESTUARY: PLATA
LAKE: MERIN MIRIM DIFUNTOS
MEASURE: VARA LEGUA CUADRA
SUERTE
RIVER: MALO MIRIM NEGRO ULIMAR
CUAREIM QUEGUAY YAGUARON
CEBOLLATI
TOWN: MELO AIGUA MINAS PANDO
ROCHA SALTO VERAS RIVERA
DURAZNO FLORIDA MERCEDES
PAYSANDU
WEIGHT: QUINTAL

URUGUAYAN ORIENTAL
URUS TUR URE AUROCHS
US HIS HIZ HUZ
U.S.A. (AUTHOR OF —) DOSPASSOS
(CHARACTER IN —) ANN BEN JOE
MAC MARY WARD DELLA FAINY
JANEY MARGO TRENT FRENCH
MAISIE SAVAGE STAPLE STRANG
CHARLEY COMPTON DOWLING
ELEANOR EVELINE RICHARD SPENCER
ANDERSON GERTRUDE HUTCHINS
MCCREARY STODDARD WILLIAMS
ANNABELLE MOOREHOUSE
USABLE FIT UTIBLE SERVABLE
USAGE USE ASAL FORM WONE
HABIT HAUNT SUNNA USURE
CUSTOM MANNER FASHION
HALACHA HALAKAH USATION
PRACTICE
(BAD —) ABUSAGE
(EVIL- —) MISUSE
(HARD —) GRIEF
(ILL —) ABUSE
(LEGAL —) PRACTIC
(RELIGIOUS —) RITUS
(PL.) CEREMONY
(PREF.) NOM(O)
(SUFF.) NOMY
USE URE BOOT CALL DUTY HAVE
NAIT NOTE USUS WISE APPLY AVAIL
GUIDE HABIT SPEND STEAD TREAT

USAGE WASTE BEHOOF EMPLOY
FINISH HANDLE OCCUPY USANCE
ACCOUNT ADHIBIT ENTREAT
IMPROVE PURPOSE SERVICE UTILITY
ACCUSTOM EXERCISE FUNCTION
PRACTICE
(— AS WONTED) ADOPT
(— DILIGENTLY) PLY
(— EXPERIMENTALLY) TRY
(— FIGURE OF SPEECH) TROPE
(— FOR FIRST TIME) FLESH
(— IMPROPERLY) ABUSE
(— INDISCRIMINATELY) HACK
(— OF MORE WORDS THAN
NECESSARY) PLEONASM
(— OF NEW WORD) NEOLOGY
(— OF SUBTERFUGE) CHICANE
(— OSTENTATIOUSLY) SPORT
(— SELFISHLY) HOG
(— SPARINGLY) TAPE SPARE
MANAGE
(— UP) EAT TIRE WEAR SHOOT
SPEND ABSORB DEVOUR EXPEND
GUZZLE PERUSE CONSUME
EXHAUST OVERWEAR
(— WASTEFULLY) SPILL
(— WITH FULL COMMAND) WIELD
(EFFICIENT —) ECONOMY
(EXCESSIVE — OF FACE AND HANDS)
ABHINAYA
(FIRST —) HANSEL HANDSEL
(FOR TEMPORARY —) JURY
(FRUGAL —) SPARE
(GENERAL —) CURRENCY
(GET EXCLUSIVE — OF) SEWUP
(LITURGICAL —) RITE
(MUCH IN —) GREAT
(UNRESTRICTED —) FREEDOM
(WRONG —) ABUSE
(PREF.) USU
USED WONT
(— CONTINUOUSLY) HOT
(— IN FLIGHT) VOLAR
(— UP) ALL BEAT SHOT SPENT
FOREWORN
(CONVENTIONALLY —) STOCK
(MUCH —) GREAT HACKNEY
USEFUL GAIN GOOD UTILE UTIBLE
HELPFUL THRIFTY BEHOVELY
UTENSILE BEHOVEFUL
(— FOR LONG TIME) HARD
(SUFF.) CHRESIS CHRESTIC CHRESTO
USEFULNESS USE AVAIL VALUE
WORTH PROFIT MILEAGE UTILITY
USELESS IDLE LEWD VAIN VOID
WIDE EMPTY WASTE DOLESS
GROTTY NOUGHT OTIOSE SCREWY
TRASHY INUTILE STERILE VAINFUL
BOOTLESS FOOTLESS FOOTLING
WASTEFUL WORTHLESS INEFFECTIVE
USELESSNESS FUTILITY IDLENESS
USER USUS
(SUFF.) STER STRESS

USH SEAT
USHARTI SHAWABTI
USHER BOW USH SEAT SHOW CRIER
ESCORT HERALD ISCHAR SEATER
VERGER CHOBDAR HUISHER
JANITOR MARSHAL STEWARD
USSR (SEE RUSSIA)
USUAL RIFE NOMIC COMMON
FAMOUS NORMAL SOLEMN VULGAR
WONTED AVERAGE GENERAL
NATURAL REGULAR TYPICAL
USITATE EVERYDAY FREQUENT
HABITUAL ORDINARY ORTHODOX
ACCUSTOMED
(NOT —) EXTRAORDINARY
USURER SHARK GAVELER
HARPAGON
USURP ASSUME INVADE PRESUME
ACCROACH ARROGATE
USURY GAVEL OCKER USURE
USANCE GOMBEEN

UTAH

CAPITAL: SALTLAKECITY
COLLEGE: WEBER
COUNTY: IRON JUAB CACHE PIUTE
CARBON SEVIER TOOELE UINTAH
SANPETE
EARLY NAME: DESERET
INDIAN: UTE
LAKE: SALT SWAN SEVIER
MOTTO: INDUSTRY
MOUNTAIN: LENA LION WAAS KINGS
PEALE TRAIL FRISCO NAVAJO
SWASEY GRANITE GRIFFIN
HAWKINS PENNELL LINNAEUS
MOUNTAIN RANGE: CEDAR HENRY
HOGUP UINTA WAHWAH TERRACE
WASATCH CONFUSION
NATIONAL PARK: ZION
NICKNAME: MORMON BEEHIVE
RIVER: UINTA WEBER JORDAN SEVIER
STATE BIRD: SEAGULL
STATE FLOWER: SEGOLILY
STATE TREE: SPRUCE
TOWN: LOA MOAB OREM DELTA
HEBER KANAB LOGAN MAGNA
MANTI NEPHI OGDEN PRICE PROVO
KEARNS TOOELE VERNAL BRIGHAM
BOUNTIFUL COALVILLE

UTENSIL (ALSO SEE IMPLEMENT
AND TOOL) HOD BOAT IRON MOLD
PECK STEW BAKER FRIER FRYER
GRILL KNIFE MOULD RICER SCOOP
SHEET SHELL SIEVE SLICE ULLER
BEATER BEETLE BREWER COOKER
DABBER FUNNEL GRATER GRILLE
KETTLE LINGEL MASKER POPPER
PUSHER SHAKER SIFTER BRAZIER
BROILER DUSTPAN FLIPPER GLUFPOT
MUDDLER SCUMMER SKIMMER
STEAMER STIRRER TOASTER

CALABASH GRIDIRON SAUCEPAN
SAUCEPOT SHREDDER SPOUCHER
STRAINER
(— FOR COVERING FIRE) CURFEW
(COOKING —) WOK
(LITURGICAL —) ASTERISK
(SHIP-SHAPED —) NEF
(PL.) BATTERY COOKWARE
IRONWARE
UTERUS WOMB BELLY METRA
MATRIX BEARING
(EXAMINATION OF —) FETOSCOPY
(PREF.) METR(O)
UTHAI (FATHER OF —) BIGVAI
AMMIHUD
UTHER (WIFE OF —) IGRAINE
UTILITARIAN USEFUL ECONOMIC
UTILITY USE AVAIL USAGE PROFIT
BENEFIT SERVICE
UTILIZE USE EMPLOY ENLIST
CONSUME EXPLOIT HARNESS
HUSBAND
UTILIZING
(SUFF.) IC(AL)
UTMOST END NTH BEST LAST MOST
FINAL EXTREME OUTMOST
SUPREME DAMNDEST POSSIBLE
UTTEREST
UTOPIA ZION
UTOPIAN IDEAL
UTOPIANISM FUTURISM
UTRAQUIST CALIXTIN
UTRICULUS ALVEUO
UTTER ASK OUT SAY BARK BLOW
BOOM DEAD DRIB EMIT FAIR GASP
GIVE HURL MAIN MOOT MOVE PASS
PURE RANK SEND TELL VENT VERY
BLACK COUGH CRUDE FETCH FRAME
FRANK GROSS ISSUE MOUTH PLAIN
RAISE SHEER SLING SOUND SPEAK
SPELL STARK THICK TOTAL VOICE
ACCENT ARRANT BROACH DAMNED
DIRECT ENTIRE INTONE PARLEY
PROFER PROPER TONGUE BLUSTER
BREATHE DELIVER ENOUNCE
EXCLAIM EXPRESS OUTMOST
OUTTELL PERFECT PHONATE
PROLATE UPBRAID ABSOLUTE
BLINKING COMPLETE CRASHING
INTONATE PRONOUNCE BLITHERING
PEREMPTORY
(— ABRUPTLY) BLURT
(— AFFECTEDLY) KNAP MINCE
(— ARGUMENTS) BLAZE
(— CASUALLY) DROP
(— EXPLOSIVELY) BOLT
(— FALSEHOODS) FABLE
(— FOOLISHLY) BLABBER
(— GLIBLY) SCREED
(— HALTINGLY) BLUBBER
(— HURRIEDLY) CHOP
(— INADVERTENTLY) SLIP
(— INDISTINCTLY) CHEW

(— IN HARSH VOICE) GRIT GRATE
(— LOUD CRY) BRAY BLARE
(— LOUDLY) CRY BLAT CALL HALLO HALLOO HULLOO PRABBLE
(— LOW SOUNDS) MURMUR WHISPER
(— MEANINGLESS SOUNDS) BABBLE
(— RAPIDLY) FIRE CHATTER
(— RAUCOUSLY) BLAT
(— REPETITIVELY) CHIME
(— RHETORICALLY) DECLAIM
(— RUTTING CALL OF THE ELK) BUGLE
(— SOLEMNLY) SWEAR
(— STUPIDLY) BLUNDER
(— SUDDENLY) CRACK
(— UNCTUOUSLY) DROOL
(— VIGOROUSLY) FLING
(— WITH EFFORT) HEAVE
UTTERANCE CRY GAB CALL OSSE BLURT DITTY PAROL VOICE ACCENT ACTION BREATH CHORUS DRIVEL GIBBER ORACLE PAROLE TONGUE EXPRESS INKLING LALLING STATUTE DELIVERY FOOTNOTE HOMESPUN JUDGMENT LOCUTION SYLLABIC
(— FROM A DIVINITY) ORACLE
(— OF JESUS) AGRAPHON
(— OF LOVE) ENDEARMENT
(— OF PRAISE) MAGNIFICAT
(— OF VOCAL SOUNDS) PHONESIS
(CONDEMNATORY —) INFAMY
(DEFECTIVE —) STAMMER
(ECSTATIC —) RHAPSODY
(EMPTY —) NOTHING
(FACETIOUS —) PLEASANTRY
(FAINT —) INKLING
(FLUENT —) OUTPOURING
(FOOLISH —) DRIVEL
(FOOLISH —S) GUFF
(GUSHING —) EFFUSION
(HABITUAL —) SONG
(IMPULSIVE —) BLURT
(INDISTINCT —) BUMBLE BUMMLE MUTTER
(INSIPID —) INANITY
(INSPIRED —) PROPHECY
(MALICIOUS —) SLANDER
(MOMENTOUS —) MOUTHFUL
(OFFENSIVE —) AFFRONT
(PROPHETIC —) OSSE
(PUBLIC —) AIR OUTGIVING
(SHORT —) DITTY
(SOLEMN —) EFFATE EFFATUM
(TRADITIONAL —) AGRAPHON
(UNVARIED —) MONOTONE
(VAPID —) CUCKOO
(VIOLENT —) INVECTIVE

(WISE —) ORACLE
(PL.) BYRONICS
UTTERED ORAL SPOKEN
(BOLDLY —) OUTSPOKEN
(INDISTINCTLY —) INARTICULATE
UTTERLY DOG BONE DEAD BLACK OUTLY PLUMB PROOF HOLLOW MERELY BLANKLY OUTERLY SHEERLY PROPERLY
UTU (FATHER OF —) NANNA
UVULA CION UVULE PLECTRUM STAPHYLE
(PREF.) CION(O) STAPHYL(O)
UVULARIA OAKESIA
UZ (FATHER OF —) ARAM NAHOR DISHAN
(GRANDFATHER OF —) SEIR SHEM
UZAI (SON OF —) PALAL
UZAL (FATHER OF —) JOKTAN
UZBEK JAGATAI

UZZAH (BROTHER OF —) AHIO
(FATHER OF —) ABINADAB
UZZI (FATHER OF —) BANI BELA TOLA BUKKI
(SON OF —) ZERAHIAH
UZZIAH (FATHER OF —) AMAZIAH
(SON OF —) ATHAIAH JEHONATHAN
UZZIEL (FATHER OF —) ISHI KOHATH HARHAIAH
(SON OF —) ZITHRI MISHAEL ELIZAPHAN

V

V VEE FIVE VICTOR
  (INVERTED —) CARET
VACANCY HOLE WANT VACUIT
  VACUITY VACATION
  (— IN ENERGY BAND) HOLE
VACANT IDLE OPEN VOID BLANK
  EMPTY FISHY INANE WASTE DEVOID
  HOLLOW DORMANT UNFILLED
  (BECOME —) FALL
  (PREF.) VACUO
VACATE QUIT TOLL VOID AVOID
  EMPTY WAIVE VACANT ABANDON
  RESCIND ABROGATE EVACUATE
VACATION OUT HOLS REST LEAVE
  OUTING RECESS HOLIDAY NONTERM
  VACANCY
  (SUMMER —) LONG
VACCFINE (KIND OF —) SALK
VACCINE LYMPH BACTERIN
  BIOLOGIC
  (KIND OF —) ORAL
VACCINIA COWPOX
VACILLATE HALT SWAG WAVE
  WAVER DACKER DITHER HALPER
  SEESAW TEETER WABBLE WAFFLE
  WOBBLE SHAFFLE STICKLE SWITHER
  WHIFFLE HESITATE
VACILLATING INFIRM MOBILE
  HALTING
VACILLATION SEESAW WAVERING
VACUITY BLOW VACANCY
  FONTANEL NOTHINGNESS
  (MENTAL —) INANITY
VACUOLE GUTTA
VACUOUS DULL BLANK EMPTY
  SILLY VACANT
VACUUM GAPE VOID HOOVER
  VACANCY VACUITY VACATION
VACUUM TUBE
  (SUFF.) TRON
VAGABOND BUM VAG HOBO KERN
  JAVEL ROGUE SHACK STIFF BRIBER
  CANTER HARLOT JOCKEY PICARA
  PICARO RODNEY RUNNER TAGRAG
  TRUANT WAFFIE COASTER ERRATIC
  FAITOUR GADLING GANGREL
  OUTCAST SCOURER SKELDER
  SWAGMAN SWINGER TINKLER
  TRUCKER VAGRANT VAURIEN
  WASTREL BOHEMIAN BRODYAGA
  CURSITOR CUSTROUN FUGITIVE
  GLASSMAN PALLIARD RAPPAREE
  RUNABOUT RUNAGATE WHIPJACK
VAGARY WHIM FANCY FREAK VAGUE
  CAPRICE CONCEIT CRANKUM
  FLAGARIE VAGRANCY
  (PL.) HUMORS

VAGINA
  (PREF.) COLP(O) ELYTR(O)
VAGINATE SHEATHED
VAGRANCY MOPERY ROGUING
  NOMADISM
VAGRANT BUM HOBO WAFF WAIF
  CAIRD PIKER PIKEY ROGUE SKELB
  STRAG TRAMP VAGUE ARRANT
  CASUAL SHAKER SHULER TINKER
  TRUANT VAGROM VAGUER WAFFIE
  DEVIOUS DRIFTER ERRATIC FLOATER
  GANGREL ROGUISH SKILDER
  SWAGMAN TINKLER TRAMPER
  TROGGER BRODYAGA PLANETIC
  STROLLER VAGABOND SHACKLING
  (PL.) FLOTSAM
VAGUE LAX DARK HAZY FOGGY
  FUZZY GROSS LOOSE MISTY MUDDY
  WOOZY CLOUDY DREAMY MYSTIC
  SHAGGY BLURRED EVASIVE
  OBSCURE SHADOWY UNFIXED
  CONFUSED INFINITE NEBULOUS
  NUBILOUS
VAGUELY DIMLY DARKLY DUMBLY
  DREAMILY
VAIN MAD IDLE NULL PUFF VOID
  WANE COCKY EMPTY FLORY PROUD
  SAUCY VOGIE WASTE FLIMSY
  FUTILE HOLLOW OTIOSE VAUNTY
  BIGGITY CARRIED TRIVIAL USELESS
  VAINFUL BOOTLESS CONCEITY
  NUGATORY PEACOCKY VAPOROUS
  WASTEFUL
  (NOT —) SOLID
VAINGLORY POMP RUFF GLORY
  VANITY ELATION
VAINLY IDLY TOOMLY
VAIR POTENT
VAISRAVANA BISHAMON
VAISYA BAIS BICE
VAJEZATHA (FATHER OF —)
  HAMAN
VAJRA DORJE
**VAKULA THE SMITH (CHARACTER
  IN —)** CHUB DEVIL OXANA PANAS
  VAKULA SOLOKHA
  (COMPOSER OF —) TCHAIKOVSKY
VAL LACE
VALANCE PAND PELMET FRONTLET
  PALMETTE
VALE DALE DEAN DELL BACHE BATCH
  ENNIS DINGLE
VALEDICTORY FAREWELL
VALENCE ADICITY ATOMISM
VALENTINE (SISTER OF —)
  GRETCHEN
  (SLAYER OF —) FAUST

VALERIAN HELIO BENNET SUMBUL ALLHEAL CUTHEAL SETWALL CETEWALE

VALERIC PENTOIC

VALET MAN ANDREW JEEVES SIRDAR TARTAR WALLIE CRISPIN TIREMAN

VALIANT SAD BOLD BRAG PREU PROW WILD BRAVE LUSTY ORPED PROUD STOUT WIGHT FIERCE HEROIC DOUGHTY GAILLARD GALLIARD INTREPID STALWART VIRTUOUS
(SON OF PRINCE —) ARN
(WIFE OF PRINCE —) ALETA

VALID FAIR GOOD JUST LEGAL SOUND COGENT LAWFUL BINDING ETERNAL WEIGHTY FORCIBLE VAILABLE VALIDOUS VALUABLE
(PREF.) RATI

VALIDATE FIRM SEAL VALID AFFIRM CONFIRM

VALIDATION PROOF

VALIDITY FORCE VIGOR STRENGTH

VALISE BAG GRIP MAIL DORLACH SATCHEL VALLIES SUITCASE

VALKYRIE BRYNHILD SHIELDMAY

VALLECULA VALLEY

VALLEY DIB GUT COMB COOM COVE DALE DELL DENE GILL HOLE HOPE HOWE HOYA PARK VALE WADI WADY ATRIO BACHE BREAK CHASM COMBE COOMB DHOON GHYLL GLACK GOYAL GOYLE HEUGH SLACK SLADE SWALE TEMPE YUNGA BOLSON BOTTOM CANADA CLOUGH COULEE DINGLE HOLLOW LAAGTE LEEGTE RINCON STRATH AIJALON BLOWOUT GEHENNA VAALITE
(— BETWEEN CONES OF VOLCANO) ATRIO
(— IN OCEAN) DEEP
(— IN THESSALY) TEMPE
(— ON MOON'S SURFACE) RILL CLEFT RILLE
(— ON MT BLANC) NANT
(BROAD —) STRATH
(CIRCULAR —) RINCON
(DEEP —) CANON GRIKE CANYON
(DROWNED —) RIA VIA
(FLAT-FLOORED DESERT —) BOLSON
(GRASSY MOUNTAIN —) HOLE
(LOWEST PART OF —) SOLE
(MINIATURE —) GULLY GULLEY
(NARROW —) DEAN DENE GLEN GLACK GOYLE GRIFF KLOOF CLOUGH
(RIFT —) GRABEN
(RIVER —) WATER
(SECLUDED —) GLEN DÍNGLE
(TRENCHLIKE —) COULEE

VALOR ARETE MERIT VALUE BOUNTY VALOUR BRAVERY COURAGE HEROISM PROWESS STOMACH CHIVALRY VALIANCY

VALOROUS BOLD BRAVE VIRTUOUS

VALUABLE DEAR COSTLY PRIZED WORTHY EMINENT WEALTHY PRECIOUS PRIZABLE SINGULAR

VALUATION PRIZE VALOR VALUE ESTEEM EXTENT ESTIMATE TAXATION

VALUE SET COST FECK FOOT HOLD RATE TELL AVAIL CARAT CHEAP COUNT FORCE PRICE PRIZE STAMP STENT STOCK VALOR WORTH ASSESS ASSIZE EQUITY ESTEEM EXTENT FIGURE HIDAGE MATTER MOMENT PRAISE REGARD VALURE VALUTA VIRTUE ACCOUNT ADVANCE APPRIZE CAPITAL CHERISH COMPUTE PRETIUM RESPECT VALENCY WERGILD ESTIMATE EVALUATE GOODWILL SPLENDOR TREASURE VALIDITY VALLIDOM
(— HIGHLY) PRIZE ENDEAR
(— OF ANGLE) EPOCH
(— OF COW) SET
(— OF STOCKS) OMNIUM
(— OF TIMBER) STUMPAGE
(— WRONGLY) MISRATE
(ABSOLUTE —) MODULUS
(AESTHETIC —) AMENITY
(ANNUAL —) RENTAL
(ESTABLISHED —) PAR
(GOOD —) SNIP
(HIGH —) ESTEEM
(LOWEST —) MINIMUM
(MATHEMATICAL —) EXTREMUM
(MIDDLE —) MEDIAN
(NEGATIVE —) DISVALUE
(OF NO —) IMMOMENT
(SOUND —) POWER
(STUDY OF —) AXIOLOGY
(TESTED —) ASSAY
(PREF.) AXIO TIMO

VALUED DEAR

VALUELESS BAFF STRAWY NAUGHTY

VALVE TAP COCK DISC DISK GATE ORAL STOP CHOKE CLACK MIXER VALVA WAFER BINODE BOTTLE CUTOUT DAMPER KICKER PALLET POPPET POTLID SCUTUM SLUICE SUCKER VENTIL WASHER CLICKET DRAWOFF PETCOCK REDUCER SCALLOP SCOLLOP SHUTOFF VALVULA VALVULE DRAWGATE EPITHECA EPIVALVE STOPCOCK THROTTLE
(— OF BARNACLE) SCUTUM
(— OF MUSICAL INSTRUMENT) PISTON VENTIL
(— OF PUMP BOX) FANG
(ANATOMICAL —) TRICUSPID
(ELECTRODE —) TRIODE

(THERMIONIC —) TUBE
(THIN —) WAFER
(TRIPLE —) KICKER
(PREF.) THYRE(O) THYRO
(SUFF.) THYRIS
VAMBRACE BRACELET
VAMOOSE SCAT SCRAM CHEESE
DECAMP SKIDDOO
VAMPIRE LAMIA ALUKAH
VAN WAN FORE LEAD SAIL FRONT
TRUCK VAUNT WAGON VAWARD
CARAVAN FOURGON FOREWARD
KHALDIAN
(LUGGAGE —) FREIGHTCAR
(TAKE THE —) LEAD
VANADATE UVANITE TURANITE
VANDAL HUN HUNLIKE SARACEN
HOOLIGAN
VANDALIZE MAR TRASH DAMAGE
DEFACE RAVAGE
VANE FAN TEE WEB COCK TAIL WING
FAINE BUCKET TARGET DOGVANE
FLIGHTER VEXILLUM
(— OF ARROW) FEATHER
(— OF CONVEYOR BELT) FLIGHT
(— OF FEATHER) WEB FLUE
VEXILLUM
(— OF SURVEYING STAFF)
TRANSOM
(— OF WINDMILL) FAN FANE TAIL
FAINE
(COOLING — IN BREWING) FLIGHTER
VANESSA PYRAMEIS
VANGUARD LEAD FORLORN
VANIAH
(FATHER OF —) BANI
VANILLA PLAIN ORDINARY
VANISH DIE FLY DROP FADE FI FE
MELT PASS SANT WEDE WEND
CLEAR FLEET SAUNT SLIDE EXHALE
EVANISH SCATTER CONQUEST
DISSOLVE EVANESCE
(— BY DEGREES) DRILL
VANISHED LAPSED EXTINCT
VANITY ABEL POMP VAIN FOLLY
PRIDE EGOISM CONCEIT FEATHER
FOPPERY INANITY SANDUST
IDLENESS IDLESHIP PRETENSION
VANITY FAIR (AUTHOR OF —)
THACKERAY
(CHARACTER IN —) JOS PITT BECKY
SHARP AMELIA DOBBIN GEORGE
JOSEPH RAWDON SEDLEY STEYNE
CRAWLEY OSBORNE WILLIAM
VANNER SLIMER
VANNIC KHALDIAN
VANQUISH GET WIN BEAT LICK MILL
CREAM PASTE UTTER EXPUGN
MASTER OUTRAY SUBDUE THRASH
CONQUER OVERWIN SHELLAC
SMOTHER CONQUEST OVERCOME
SURMOUNT VENKISEN
VANQUISHED CRAVEN

VANUATU (CAPITAL OF —) VILA
(FORMER NAME OF —)
NEWHEBRIDES
(ISLAND OF —) EPI EFATE MALEKULA
PENTECOST ESPIRITUSANTO
(MONEY OF —) VATU
(VOLCANO OF —) TANNA AMBRYN
LOPEVI
VAPID DRY DULL FADE FLAT STALE
TRITE JEJUNE INSIPID WATERISH
VAPOR FOG FUME REEK ROKE STEW
BOAST BRUME EWDER HUMOR
SMOKE STEAM STIFE BREATH
VAPOUR EXHAUST HALITUS
(FROZEN —) SNOW
(HOT —) LUNT
(NOXIOUS —) DAMP
(PETROL —) JUICE
(PL.) BRUME
(PREF.) ATM(O) ATMID(O) MANO
PNEUMAT(O) TYPH(O)
VAPORIZATION BURNUP BOILOFF
VAPORIZE DRIVE FLASH STEAM
AERATE AERIFY VAPORATE
VAPOROUS FUMY FUMID HUMID
FUMISH FUMOSE STEAMY VOLATILE
VARANGIAN VARIAG WARING
(PL.) ROS
VARGUENO DESK
VARIABILITY HETERISM
VARIABLE FLUX FREE CHOPPY
FICKLE FITFUL KITTLE WRAIST
CEPHEID FACIENT FLUXILE MUTABLE
ROLLING STREAKY UNEQUAL
VARIANT VARIOUS ARGUMENT
FLOATING FLEXIBLE SHIFTING
SKITTISH UNSTABLE VEERABLE
(EXCEEDINGLY —) PROTEAN
(MATHEMATICAL —) FUNCTION
(RANDOM —) STATISTIC
VARIANCE ODDS DISCORD DISPUTE
DISCREPANCY
(ANALYSIS OF —) ANOVA
VARIANT STATE VERSION
(— IN WHEAT) SPELTOID
(POSITIONAL —) ALLOPHONE
(SOUND —) ALTERNANT
(PL.) DIAPHONE
VARIATION REX TURN ERROR
ROGUE SHADE CHANGE DOUBLE
JITTER SWITCH CYCLING DESCANT
EXTREME SHADING VARIETY
WINDING DIVISION DYNAMICS
HETERISM MUTATION
(— IN AIR PRESSURE) ROBBING
(— IN CURRENT) SURGE
(— IN FREQUENCY) SWINGING
(— IN SPEED) HUNTING
(— OF COLOR) ABRASH
(— OF PUPIL OF EYE) HIPPUS
(— OF SHOE) SPRING
(— OF VOWELS) ABLAUT
(ALLOWABLE —) LEEWAY

(BALLET —) ATTITUDE
(TOPOGRAPHICAL —) BREAK
(PL.) PIBROCH
VARICOCELE RAMEX
VARIED SORTY DAEDAL SEVERAL
VARIANT VARIOUS MANIFOLD
VARIED BUNTING PRUSIANO
VARIEGATE DROP FRET FLECK
FREAK SHOOT AUMAIL DAPPLE
STRIPE VARIFY CHECKER
VARIEGATED FAW PIED SHOT JASPE
LYART PANED SHELD DAEDAL
MARLED MENALD MOSAIC MOTLEY
SKEWED VEINED BROCKED BROCKIT
CHECKED CLOUDED DAPPLED
FREAKED FRETTED PECKLED
SPARKED VARIOUS DISCOLOR
FRECKLED OVERSHOT PANACHED
SKEWBALD
(— AS GLASS BEADS) AGGRI AGGRY
(NOT —) UNBROKEN
(PREF.) POECIL(O)
VARIEGATION COLOR
VARIETY BREW FORM KIND MODE
SORT BRAND BREED CLASS COLOR
SPICE CHANGE FLAVOR NATURE
STIRPS STRAIN STRIPE SPECIES
VARIENS
(— OF COLOR) SHADE
(PERMANENT —) STIRPS
VARIOLA HORSEPOX SMALLPOX
VARIOUS MANY SERE DIVERS
SUNDER SUNDRY VARIED DIVERSE
SEVERAL VARIANT MANIFOLD
MULTIPLE
(PREF.) PARTI POECIL(O) POEKIL(O)
VARISCITE UTAHITE
VARIX
(PREF.) CIRS(O)
VARLET BOY CAD LAD GIPPO JIPPO
PAVISER COISTREL VARLETTO
VARNISH DOPE JAPAN LACKER
MEDIUM PUNDUM FIXATIF LACQUER
VEHICLE VERMEIL FIXATIVE
OVERGILD THEETSEE
(— INGREDIENT) ALOE COPAL ROSIN
MASTIC
VARY HUNT ALTER BREAK DRIFT
SHIFT SPORT CHANGE DIFFER
RECEDE VARIFY CHECKER DEVIATE
DISSENT DIVERGE VARIATE
DISAGREE OSCILLATE
(— PITCH) MODULATE
VARYING CURRENT
VASE PYX URN OLLA VASA VASO
ASKOS CYLIX DINOS DIOTA KYLIX
PYXIS BASKET BOWPOT COTULA
COTYLA CRATER DEINOS DOLIUM
FILLER HYDRIA KALPIS KOTYLE
KRATER LEKANE SITULA AMPHORA
AMPULLA CANOPUS PATELLA
POTICHE PSYKTER SCYPHUS

SKYPHOS STAMNOS URCEOLE
BOUGHPOT LECYTHUS LEKYTHOS
MURRHINE PROCHOOS
(— FOR PERFUME) CONCH
(— ON PEDESTAL) TAZZA
(—S UNDER THEATER SEATS) SCHEA
(PREF.) POTICHO VAS(I)(O) VASCUL(I)
(O)
VASHNI (FATHER OF —) SAMUEL
VASHTI (HUSBAND OF —)
AHASUERUS
VASODILATOR KELLIN KHELLIN
MINOXIDIL
VASSAL MAN WER BOND LEUD SERF
CEILE LIEGE SLAVE CLIENT GENEAT
SACOPE BONDMAN FEEDMAN
FEODARY HOMAGER RUDIGER
SAMURAI SERVANT SUBJECT
VAVASOR PALATINE
(PL.) MANRED
VASSALAGE MANRENT
VAST HUGE BROAD ENORM GREAT
LARGE STOUR VASTY COSMIC
IMMANE MIGHTY UNTOLD ABYSMAL
IMMENSE OCEANIC VASTITY
ENORMOUS INFINITE MOUNTAIN
SPACIOUS
VASTNESS IMMANE GRANDEUR
WIDENESS
VAT ARK BAC DIP FAT PIT TAP TUN
BACK BECK COOM FATE GAAL GAIL
GYLE KEEL KIER TINE APRON COOMB
FETTE FLOAT KEEVE KIEVE ROUND
STAND STEEP KIMNEL MOTHER
BLUNGER DRAINER GRAINER
KEELVAT STEEPER PRESSFAT
(— USED IN MEASURING SLIPS) ARK
(BLEACHING —) KEIR KIER
(BREWER'S —) BACK FLOAT KEEVE
UNION CUMMING
(CHEESE —) CHESSEL CHESSET
CHESSART
(COOLING —) KELDER
(DYER'S —) JIG LEAD DYEBECK
(EVAPORATING —) APRON GRAINER
(FERMENTING —) TUN COMB COOM
GYLE KEEL COOMB FLOAT
(TANNER'S —) TAP HANGER SPENDER
(TEXTILE —) KIER
(WINE —) LAKE CUVEE
(PREF.) PYEL(O)
VATICAN CITY (BASILICA OF —)
STPETERS
(WALL OF —) LEONINE
VAU DIGAMMA
VAUDEVILLE ZARZUELA
VAULT BOUT COPE JUMP LEAP PEND
SKIP TOMB VOLT WOWT AZURE
CROFT CRYPT EMBOW VOLTO CELLAR
CUPOLA FORNIX SHROUD CONCAVE
DUNGEON TESTUDO VALTAGE
CATACOMB LEAPFROG MONUMENT

(— IN CEILING) LACUNAR
(— OF HEAVEN) WELKIN
(— OF SKY) CONVEX ZENITH
CONCAVE
(PART OF —) PENDENTIVE
VAULTED CONCAVE CRYPTED
EMBOWED
VAULTER VOLTIGEUR
VAULTING POMADA POMMADO
VAUNT GAB BRAG BOAST ROOSE
VOUST AVAUNT INSULT BLUSTER
GLORIFY FLOURISH
(— ONESELF) WIND
VAUNTMURE MANURE
VCR (— BUTTON) RESET
VEAL VEAU SLINK FRICANDO
(— SCALLOPS) SALTIMBOCCA
(LIKE —) VITULINE
(PIECE OF —) PAILLARD
(SCALLOPS OF —) SALTIMBOCCA
(SLICES OF —) SCALLOPINI
VECTOR I K PHASOR GRADIENT
VEDA SHASTER
VEDDOID PANYAN
VEDIC (— PRINCIPLE) RTA RITA
VEER CUT DIP FLY YAW CAST CHOP
SLEW SLUE SWAY TACK WYRE FETCH
SHIFT SWOOP BROACH CHANGE
SLOUGH SWERVE TUMBLE BOXHAUL
DEVIATE WHIFFLE
VEERING DRIFT CHOPPY
VEGA (CONSTELLATION OF —) LYRA
VEGETABLE PEA YAM BEAN BEET
CORN KALE LEEK OKRA CHARD
GRASS ONION SABZI SALAD VEGIE
CARROT CELERY LEGUME LENTIL
POTATO RADISH SQUASH TOMATO
TOPEPO TURNIP VEGGIE BLOATER
CABBAGE CELTUCE LETTUCE
PARSNIP PEASCOD RHUBARB
SPINACH VEGETAL BROCCOLI
EGGPLANT RUTABAGA
(— MATTER) SUDD
(—S FOR MARKET) TRUCK
(EARLY —) PRIMEUR
(EARLY —S) HASTINGS
(GARDEN — S) SASS SAUCE
(HYBRID —) GARLION
(RAW —S) CRUDITES
(PL.) CRUDITES
(PREF.) PHYT(I)(O)
VEGETARIAN VEGAN VEGIE
VEGGIE
VEGETATION HERB COVER GREEN
SCRUB GROWTH HERBAGE
COVERAGE PLANTAGE PLEUSTON
SMELLAGE
(DECOMPOSED —) STAPLE
(SCRUB —) BRUSH
(UNWANTED —) FILTH
(PREF.) PHYT(I)(O)
VEGETATIVE ASEXUAL PLANTAL

VEHEMENCE FURY GLOW HEAT
RAGE WARMTH STRENGTH
VIOLENCE
VEHEMENT HOT HIGH KEEN LOUD
ANGRY EAGER FIERY HEFTY YEDER
ARDENT BITTER FERVID FIERCE
FLASHY HEARTY HEATED RAGING
STRONG ANIMOSE ANIMOUS
FURIOSO INTENSE JEALOUS
VIOLENT
VEHEMENTLY AMAIN PELLMELL
VEHICLE BUS CAB CAR FLY VAN
ARBA AUTO CART DUKE FLAT GOER
JEEP LIMO SLED TAXI TEAM WAIN
ARABA BRAKE BREAK BUGGY CARRY
DILLY FLAIL GUIDE HANSA NODDY
ROVER STAGE WAGON BLADER
CAMPER CHARET CISIUM DIESEL
HEARSE JITNEY MEDIUM RANDEM
SLEDGE SLEIGH SURREY TRISHA
TROIKA CARRIER CHARIOT CRUISER
HOTSHOT ICEBOAT KIBITKA
MACHINE MINIBUS OMNIBUS
PEDICAB PEDRAIL SHEBANG
SHUTTLE SPEEDER SPRAYER
STEAMER STEERER TARTANA
TAXICAB TRAVOIS TRISHAW
TURNOUT UTILITY AUTORAIL
AUTOSLED CARRIAGE CHARETTE
CYCLECAR DEADHEAD DELIVERY
ELECTRIC FILMOGEN SHOWCASE
SOCIABLE UNICYCLE AEROTRAIN
SPACESHIP LOCOMOBILE
MOTORCYCLE SNOWMOBILE
SPACECRAFT
(— DRAWN BY BULLOCK) EKKA
(— FOR COLORS) MEGILP
(— FOR HAULING) TRACTOR
(— FOR SAND USE) DUNEBUGGY
(— IN FINE CONDITION) CREAMPUFF
(— ON RUNNERS) SLED CARRO
SLEDGE SLEIGH ICEBOAT AUTOSLED
(— ON SINGLE RAIL) AEROTRAIN
(— PULLED BY MAN) BROUETTE
RICKSHAW
(— RUNNING ON RAILS) LORRY
TRAIN
(— WITH RUNNERS) SKIBOB
(— WITH 3 HORSES ABREAST)
TROIKA
(— WITH 3 HORSES BEHIND EACH
OTHER) RANDEM
(AIR-CUSHION —) HOVERCRAFT
(AIRPORT —) SKYLOUNGE
(AMMUNITION —) CAISSON
(AMPHIBIOUS —) BUFFALO
(ARCTIC —) SNOCAT
(AWKWARD —) ARK
(CHILD'S —) PRAM WALKER
SCOOTER STROLLER
(COVERED —) SEDAN LANDAU
CARAVAN KIBITKA

(DRAG-RACING —) RAIL
(EARTH-MOVING —) SCOOP
(KIND OF —) LAUNCH
(LITTLE —) HINAYANA
(LUMBERING —) TUG TODE
(MILITARY —) WEASEL AMTRACK
(MOON —) LEM
(MOTOR —) WHEELS
(OBSOLETE —) CRATE
(ONE-WHEELED —) BARROW
(OPERATE MOTOR —) VROOM
(POOR-QUALITY —) DOG
SHANDRYPAN
(RIVER —) HOVERCRAFT
(RUDE —) KIBITKA
(RUSSIAN —) TARANTAS TARANTASS
(SATELLITE —) SLV
(SLEDGE-LIKE —) GAMBO
(SNOW —) SKIBOB
(SPACE —) LEM LANDER
(THREE-WHEELED —) PEDICAB
(WHEELLESS —) DRAY
(2-WHEELED —) GIG CART SULKY
TONGA CISIUM JINGLE LIMBER
BICYCLE CALECHE CROYDON
RICKSHAW
(PL.) PARK
(SUFF.) MOBILE
VEIL WRY FALL FILM HIDE MASK
WRAP COVER GLOSS RUMAL SCARF
SCENE SHADE VELUM VIMPA VOLET
WREIL BUMBLE CHRISM FAILLE
SHADOW SHROUD VEILER WEEPER
WIMPLE CORTINA CURTAIN
ENDOTYS PARANJA VEILING
CALYPTRA ENDOTHYS HEADRAIL
KALYPTRA MAHARMAH MANTILLA
TELEBLEM
(— IN CHURCH) AER ENDOTYS
ENDOTHYS
(— OF MUSLIM WOMEN) YASHMAK
(— ON FUNGI) CORTINA
(— OVER HELMET) LAMBREQUIN
(BIRTH —) CAUL
(DOUBLE —) YASHMAK
(HUMERAL —) SUDARY
(WIDOW'S —) WEEPER
VEILED COVERT LATENT VELATED
SHROUDED
VEILING PURDAH GOSSAMER
VEIN BAR LOB RIB CAVA LODE MOOD
RAKE REEF VENA AMPER CLOUD
COMES COSTA LEDGE MEDIA NERVE
RIDER SCRIN VARIX LEADER MEDIAL
STRAIN STREAK VENULA VENULE
AXILLAR AZYGOUS CUBITAL
DROPPER JUGULAR NERVURE
PRECAVA PRESTER SAPHENA
VEINLET AXILLARY EMULGENT
PREMEDIA PROFUNDA SUBCOSTA
(— IN MARBLE) CLOUD
(— OF LEAF) RIB COSTA MIDRIB
(— OF MINERAL) STREAK STRINGER

(— OF ORE) LODE ROKE BUNCH
LEDGE RIDER SCRIN LEADER STRING
DROPPER UNDERSET
(— OF WING) CUBIT RADIUS CUBITAL
CUBITUS SUBCOSTA SUBCOSTAL
(—S OF LEAF) SKELETON
(GRANITIC —) ELVAN
(QUARTZ —) SADDLE
(VARICOSE —) AMPER
(PREF.) CIRS(O) PHLEB(O) PYL(E)(O)
VENI VENO
(SWOLLEN —) CIRS(O)
VEINED MARBLED NERVOSE
VELA SAILS
VELAR PALATAL GUTTURAL
VELD BUSHVELD SOURVELD
VELELLA SALLYMAN
VELLEITY DESIRE WOULDING
VELLINCH FLINCHER
VELLUM ORIHON
VELOCIPEDE HOBBY STEED TRICAR
BICYCLE DICYCLE RANTOON
SPEEDER DRAISINE TRICYCLE
VELOCITY DRIFT CELERITY RAPIDITY
STRENGTH
(— OF FLOW) CURRENT
(— OF 1 FOOT PER SECOND) VELO
VELOUR SOLEIL
VELOUTE POULETTE
VELUM VEIL VELAMEN VELARIUM
VELVET PILE PANNE YUZEN BIRODO
VELURE FRAYING VELLUTE
VELVETEEN TRIPE
VELVET GRASS FOG
VELVETLEAF DAGGA PAREIRA
VENAL CORRUPT SALABLE BRIBABLE
HIRELING SALEABLE VENDIBLE
VEND HAWK SELL UTTER MARKET
PEDDLE
VENDA (CAPITAL OF —)
THOHOYANDOU
(TOWN OF —) SIBASA MAKWARELA
VENDIBLE VENAL SALABLE
SALEABLE
VENDITION SALE
VENDOR FAKER SELLER VENDER
ALIENOR BUTCHER HUSTLER
PITCHER PURLMAN VIANDER
PITCHMAN SAUCEMAN VENDITOR
VENEER BURL BURR JAPAN SHOOK
OVERLAY SKILLET
VENEERER DUSTER
VENERABLE OLD AGED HOAR SAGE
AWFUL HOARY AUGUST SACRED
VETUST ANCIENT VENERAL VINTAGE
(PREF.) SEBASTO
VENERATE FEAR DREAD HALLOW
REVERE VENERE RESPECT WORSHIP
VENERATED HOLY SACRED
HALLOWED
VENERATION AWE CULT DULIA
CULTISM RESPECT DEVOTION
VENESECTION PHLEBOTOMY

VENETIAN RED SIENA SIERRA
VENETIAN SUMAC SCOTINO

VENEZUELA
CAPITAL: CARACAS
COIN: REAL MEDIO FUERTE BOLIVAR
   CENTIMO MOROCOTA
GULF: PARIA
MEASURE: GALON MILLA FANEGA
   ESTADEL
MOUNTAIN: PAVA YAVI DUIDA ICUTU
   CONCHA CUNEVA PARIMA IMUTACA
   MASAITI RORAIMA
NATIVE: CARIB TIMOTE GUARAUNO
RIVER: META APURE CAURA ARAUCA
   CARONI CUYUNI GUANARE
   ORINOCO ORITUCO PARAGUA
   SUAPURE VICHADA GUAVIARE
   VENTUARI
STATE: LARA APURE SUCRE ZULIA
   ARAGUA FALCON MERIDA BOLIVAR
   COJEDES GUARICO MONAGAS
   TACHIRA YARACUY CARABOBO
   TRUJILLO
TOWN: AROA CORO ATURES CUMANA
   MERIDA BARINAS CABELLO
   GUAWARE MARACAY MATURIN
   CARUPANO TACUPITA VALENCIA
WATERFALL: ANGEL CUQUENAN
WEIGHT: BAG LIBRA

VENGEANCE WRACK WREAK
   WRECK AVENGE UITION WANION
   ALASTOR REVENGE VINDICT
   REQUITAL VINDICTA
VENICE
   (ISLAND NEAR —) LIDO
VENILIA
   (HUSBAND OF —) DAUNUS
   (SISTER OF —) AMATA
   (SON OF —) TURNUS
VENISON BILTONG
VENOM GALL ATTER VIRUS POISON
   SWELTER CROTALIN CROTALUS
VENOMOUS TOXIC ATTERN DEADLY
   SNAKEY VENOMY BANEFUL
   NOXIOUS SMITTLE SNAKISH
   POISONED VIPERINE VIPEROUS
   VIRULENT POISONOUS
VENT EMIT HOLE REEK BELCH DRAIN
   FROTH ISSUE TEWEL OUTAGE
   OUTLET CHIMNEY EXPRESS
   OPENING ORIFICE OUTCAST
   OUTFALL OUTTAKE RELEASE
   VENTAGE APERTURE BREATHER
   DIATREME FONTANEL MOFFETTE
   SESPERAL SPIRACLE SUSPIRAL
   VENTHOLE VOMITORY
   (— IN EARTH'S CRUST) VOLCANO
   (VOLCANIC —) BOCCA DIATREME
   SOLFATARA
VENTILATE AIR WIND AERATE
   EXPRESS

VENTILATED (BADLY —) STUFFY
VENTILATION AERAGE AIRING
VENTILATOR BADGIR LOUVER
   FEMERELL
VENTING GUST
VENTRAL BELLY HEMAL STERNAL
   ANTERIOR INFERIOR
   (PREF.) (— AREA) GASTER(O)
   GASTR(I)(O)
VENTRICLE HEART TRICORN
   DIACOELE
   (SUFF.) CELE COELE COELUS
VENTURE HAB RUN SET CAST DARE
   JUMP KITE LUCK MINT REST RISK
   WAGE ETTLE FLIER FLYER FROST
   RISCO SALLY STAKE TEMPT WAGER
   CHANCE DANGER HAZARD SASHAY
   FLUTTER IMPERIL JEOPARD PRESUME
   PRETEND ENDANGER GETPENNY
   (— AT DICE) THROW
   (— TO SAY) DARESAY
   (RISKY —) CRAPSHOOT
VENTURESOME BOLD RASH RISKY
   DARING PARLOUS TEMEROUS
VENTURESOMELY CHANCILY
VENUS LOVE VESPER LUCIFER
   HESPERUS PHOSPHOR
   (FATHER OF —) JUPITER
   (HUSBAND OF —) VULCAN
   (MOTHER OF —) DIONE
   (SON OF —) AMOR CUPID AENEAS
VENUSIAN VENEREAN
VERACIOUS TRUE VERY TRUTHY
   SINCERE VERIDIC FAITHFUL
   TRUTHFUL
VERACITY HSIN TROTH TRUTH
   VERITY FIDELITY
VERANDA PYAL LANAI PORCH
   STOEP STOOP PIAZZA BALCONY
   GALERIE GALLERY
VERB RHEMA ACTIVE NOMINAL
   PASSIVE DEPONENT VOLITIVE
   INCEPTIVE INCHOATIVE INDICATIVE
   INFINITIVE
   (AUXILIARY —) BE DO CAN MAY
   HAVE MUST WILL SHALL
   (KIND OF —) ACTIVE PASSIVE
   PRETERIT TRANSITIVE
   (LINKING —) COPULA
VERBAL ORAL WORDY
VERBATIM DIRECT VERBAL LITERAL
   DIRECTLY
VERBENA ALOYSIA VERVAIN
VERBENALIN CORNIN
VERBIAGE TALK JABBER
VERBOSE WINDY WORDY PROLIX
   VERBAL DIFFUSE WORDISH
   (NOT —) LEAN
VERBOSITY MACROLOGY
VERDANT BOSKY GREEN VIRID
VERDICT WORD VARDI ASSIZE
   FINDING OPINION DECISION
   JUDGMENT VEREDICT

VERDIGRIS AERUGO CANKER VERDET
VERDIN GOLDTIT
VERDURE GREENTH GREENERY
VIRIDITY
(PREF.) CHLO
VERGE RIM TOP EDGE WAND YARD
BRINK POINT TOUCH BORDER
TRENCH TRIGGER THRESHOLD
VERGER WANDSMAN
VERGILIAN MARONIAN MARONIST
VERIFICATION AUDIT AVERRAL
CHECKUP AVERMENT
VERIFY AVER TRUE AUDIT CHECK
PROVE ATTEST RATIFY COLLATE
CONFIRM CONTROL JUSTIFY
SUPPORT CONSTATE
VERILY YEA AMEN FAITH PARDY
CERTES INDEED PARDIE FAITHLY
VERITABLE REAL TRUE VERY
ACTUAL HONEST PROPER GENUINE
VERIMENT
VERITY TROTH TRUTH REALISM
VERIDITY
VERJUICE VARGE
VERMICELLI FEDELINI
VERMICULE VAALITE
VERMICULITE KERRITE MACONITE
VERMIFUGE KOSIN HARMAL
HARMEL KAMALA KAMELA KOOSIN
COWHAGE HELONIAS PINKROOT
WORMWOOD
VERMILION RED GOYA MINIUM
MINIATE PAPRIKA PIMENTO VERMEIL
ZINOBER CARMETTA CINNABAR
TOREADOR
VERMIN FILTH CARRION VARMINT
VERMIS WORM

VERMONT

CAPITAL: MONTPELIER
COLLEGE: BENNINGTON MIDDLEBURY
COUNTY: ESSEX ORANGE ADDISON
ORLEANS WINDSOR LAMOILLE
LAKE: CASPIAN DUNMORE SEYMOUR
CHAMPLAIN
MOUNTAIN: BROMLEY HOGBACK
ASCUTNEY PROSPECT MANSFIELD
MOUNTAIN RANGE: GREEN TACONIC
NICKNAME: GREENMOUNTAIN
PRESIDENT: ARTHUR COOLIDGE
RIVER: SAXTONS LAMOILLE
NULHEGAN POULTNEY WINOOSKI
STATE BIRD: THRUSH
STATE FLOWER: CLOVER
STATE TREE: MAPLE
TOWN: BARRE STOWE CHELSEA
GRAFTON NEWFANE RUTLAND
BENNINGTON BURLINGTON
UNIVERSITY: NORWICH

VERMOUTH CINZANO CHAMBERY
VERNACULAR LINGO COMMON
JARGON PATOIS ROMAIC TONGUE
VULGAR CHALDEE DIALECT TRIVIAL
SCOTTISH
VERNALIZE IAROVIZE JAROVIZE
YAROVIZE
VERNE (— CAPTAIN) NEMO
VERNIER NONIUS
VERONICA HEBE SUDARIUM
VERNICLE BROOKLIME
VERRUCOSE WARTY WARTED
VERSANT SLOPE
VERSATILE HANDY FICKLE MOBILE
FLEXILE
VERSE FIT EPIC LINE POSE RANN
RICH RIME SONG BLANK IONIC
METER METRE RHYME STAVE STICH ·
TANKA ADONIC ALCAIC BURDEN
CHIAVE CYWYDD DIPODY HEROIC
JINGLE PANTUN SCAZON STANZA
VERSET ANAPEST DICOLON
DOGGREL ELEGIAC PAEONIC
PANTOUM PENNILL SAPPHIC SAVITRI
SOTADIC STICHOS TRIPODY TROILUS
CHOLIAMB DACTYLIC DINGDONG
DOGGEREL GLYCONIC LEONINES
PRIAPEAN RESPONSE SENTENCE
SINGSONG TERETISM TRIMETER
VERSICLE MACARONIC
(— FORM) VIRELAY KYRIELLE
(— OF FOUR MEASURES)
TETRAMETER
(— OF 14 LINES) SONNET
(— OF 2 FEET) DIPODY DIMETER
(— OF 6 FEET) CHOLIAMB SENARIAN
SENARIUS
(— WITH LIMPING MOVEMENT)
SCAZON
(DEVOTIONAL —) ANTIPHON
OFFERTORY
(HINDU —) SLOKA
(JAPANESE —) HAIKU TANKA HAIKAI
(KOREAN — FORM) SIJO
(LINKED —) RENGA
(MEDIEVAL —) SIRVENTE
(NONSENSE —) AMPHIGORY
(NONSENSE —S) AMPHIGORY
(UNMELODIOUS —) TERETISM
(PL.) TRIPOS PINDARICS
GALLIAMBICS HUDIBRASTICS
VERSED SEEN WITTY BESEEN
TRADED STUDIED FREQUENT
OVERSEEN SCIENCED
(WELL —) SKILLFUL
VERSICLE VERSE VERSET STICHOS
SUFFRAGE
VERSIFIER BARD POET RHYMER
VERSER METERER
VERSIFY METER
VERSION DRAM MODEL DRAUGHT
EDITION READING TURNING
REDACTION
(SHORT —) BRIEF
(SIMPLIFIED —) KEY
(TRANSLATED —) CONSTRUE

VERSO REVERSE
VERT VERD POMMÉ VENUS PRASINE
  SINOPLE GREENHEW
VERTEBRA AXIS RACK ATLAS
  DORSAL LUMBAR SACRAL ACANTHA
  CENTRUM CERVICAL METAMERE
  PROATLAS RACKBONE SPONDYLE
  (PREF.) ASTRAGAL(O) SPONDYL(O)
  (SUFF.) SPONDYLI SPONDYLUS
VERTEBRATA CRANIATA CRANIOTA
VERTEBRATE CRANIATE SAUROPSID
VERTEX APEX COPE NODE POLE
  CROWN PITCH SUMMIT VERTICAL
VERTICAL APEAK ERECT PLUMB
  SHEER WHIRL ORTHAL UPRIGHT
  COLUMNAR SHEERING STRAIGHT
  (PREF.) ORTH(O)
VERTICALLY PLUMP ENDLONG
  SHEERLY DIRECTLY PALEWISE
VERTICIL WHORL
VERTIGINOUS DIZZY
VERTIGO DINUS TIEGO MEGRIM
  MIRLIGO SWIMMING WHIRLING
VERUMONTANUM COLLICLE
VERVAIN GERVAO FROGFOOT
  IRONWEED
VERVE PEP BRIO DARE DASH ELAN
  GUSTO BOUNCE ENERGY PANACHE
  VITALITY VIVACITY
VERY SO ALL BIG DOG GAY GEY MUY
  TOO BRAW DEAD FELL FULL JUST
  MAIN MUCH PURE RARE REAL SAME
  SEHR SELF SUCH TRES UNCO WELL
  ASSAI AWFUL BLAME BULLY CRAZY
  DOOMS JOLLY MOLTO PESKY RIGHT
  SOWAN SUPER SWITH UNCOW
  VERRA BITTER BLAMED DAMNED
  DEUCED FREELY GAINLY LIVING
  MAINLY MASTER MIGHTY NATION
  POISON PROPER SORELY STRONG
  TARNAL THRICE VERRAY WONDER
  AWFULLY BOILING GALLOWS
  GREATLY PARLOUS PASSING
  PRECISE SOPPING STRANGE
  DEUCEDLY DREADFUL ENORMOUS
  FAMOUSLY POWERFUL PRECIOUS
  SPANKING SWINGING WHACKING
  ABSOLUTELY
  (PREF.) ERI MALLO
VESICANT LEWISITE MESEREUM
VESICA PISCIS MANDORLA
VESICATORY BLISTER
VESICLE BLEB CYST APTHA BULLA
  BURSE FLOAT APHTHA AMPULLA
  BLADDER BLISTER HYDATID
  OTOCYST POMPHUS UTRICLE
  VACUOLE AEROCYST CISTERNA
  MIDBRAIN VESICULA PHAGOSOME
  (SUFF.) YDATIS
VESICULAR BULLOSE BULLOUS
VESPERAL TOWEL
VESPERS LYCHNIC PLACEBO
  EVENSONG

VESSEL (ALSO SEE BOAT AND SHIP)
  GO CAN CAT COG CUP FAT GUM HOY
  KEG NEF PIG POT TUB VAS VAT VIA
  BARK BOAT BODY BOMB BOOT BOSS
  BOWL BRIG BUSH BUSS CASK CELL
  COWL DISH DRIP DUCT GAWN GRAB
  HORN HULK JACK JUNK KOFF LOTA
  PINK PINT POST PROW SAIL SHIP
  SNOW TING YAWL AMULA BAKIE
  BARGE BASIN BIDET BIKIE BOCAL
  BOYER CADUS CANNE CHURN
  COGUE CRACK CRAER CRAFT CRARE
  CRUET CRUSE DANDY DIOTA DUBBA
  FLASK GLOBE GUIDE JUBBE KETCH
  LADLE LAKER LAVER LINER PIECE
  PYKAR SCOOP SMACK STEAM STILL
  XEBEC YANKY ZABRA BANKER
  BARQUE BARREL BILALO BOILER
  BOTTLE BOUTRE BUCKET BURNER
  CAIQUE CANNER CAPPIE CHARGE
  CODMAN COFFIN CONCHA COOLER
  COPPER CRATER CRAYER CRUISE
  CUTTER DECKER DEINOS DOGGER
  DUBBAH ELUTOR FESSEL FIRKIN
  FLAGON HOLCAD HOOKER JAGGER
  KERNOS KETTLE KRATER LANCHA
  LATEEN LEKANE LORCHA MASLIN
  MONKEY MULLER PACKET PANKIN
  PATERA PICARD PITHOS POURIE
  ROLLER SALTER SATTIE SEALER
  SERVER SETTEE SHIBAR SITULA
  SMOKER TARTAN TENDER TOPMAN
  VESICA WHALER BAGGALA BALLOON
  BALLOON BLICKEY BLICKIE CARAVEL
  CARRIER CISTERN CLIPPER CORSAIR
  COUGNAR CRAGGAN CRESSET
  CRISSET CRUISER CUVETTE DRIFTER
  DRINKER DROGHER FELUCCA
  FLYBOAT FRIGATE GABBARD
  GABBART GAIASSA GALASSA
  GUNBOAT ORANGER PATAMAR
  PINNACE POACHER POLACRE
  PSYKTER REDUCER SALTFAT
  SCALDER SEEDLIP SETTLER SPARGER
  SPOUTER STEAMER STEEPER
  TRACHEA TRENDLE UTENSIL
  BELANDER BENITIER BILANDER
  BILLYBOY BIRDBATH BLEACHER
  BUGGALOW CORVETTE CRUCIBLE
  CRUISKEN CUCURBIT DECANTER
  DIGESTER DUTCHMAN EFFERENT
  EMISSARY FIREBOAT FLESHPOT
  GALLIPOT GALLIVAT GAROOKUH
  GAYDIANG HELLSHIP HONEYPOT
  INKSTAND INRIGGER IRONCLAD
  IRONSIDE KEELBOAT LATEENER
  LAVATORY MONOHULL NITRATOR
  PICAROON SCHOONER SMUGGLER
  SPITTOON WATERPOT BARKENTINE
  STIRRUPCUP
  (— CUT FROM BLOCK OF WOOD)
  BAMBOOS
  (— FOR COAL) GEORDIE

(— FOR DYE) TOBY
(— FOR FEEDING ANIMALS) TROUGH
(— FOR HEATING LIQUIDS) ETNA
(— FOR HOLY WATER) FAT FONT
STOCK STOOP STOUP AMPULLA
BENITIER CHRISMATORY
(— FOR HYPODERMIC USE) AMPUL
AMPULE AMPOULE
(— FOR LIQUID WASTE) DRIP
(— FOR MEASURING ORE) HOPPET
(— FOR MOLTEN METAL) LADLE
(— FOR ORE WASHINGS) LOOL
(— FOR PERFUMES) CENSER
(— FOR PORRIDGE) BICKER
(— FOR SOLDIER'S FOOD) MESSTIN
(— FOR SUGAR) SUCRIER
(— FOR WINE SAMPLING) TASTER
(— HOLDING CONDIMENTS) CRUET
CASTER
(— IN MINE) CORB
(— MADE OF HOLLOW LOG) GUM
(— OF BARK) COOLAMAN
COOLAMON COOLIMAN
(— OF HORN) BUGLE
(— ON TRIPOD) HOLMOS
(— ROWED BY OARS) CATUR GALLEY
(— STATIONED IN ENGLISH
CHANNEL) GROPER
(— USED IN MAKING GLAZE) HILLER
(ABANDONED —) DERELICT
(ARMORED —) CRUISER IRONCLAD
IRONSIDE
(BAILING —) SCOOP
(BAPTISMAL —) FONT
(BARGELIKE —) PANGARA
(BLOOD —) AORTA ARTERY BLEEDER
EFFERENT
(BREWER'S —) ROUND
(CANDLEMAKING —) JACK
(CHEMIST'S —) BATH FLASK STILL
BEAKER RETORT
(CHINESE —) JUNK SAMPAN
(CIRCULAR —) KIT
(CLUMSY —) CRAY CRARE HAGBOAT
(COASTING —) DHOW DONI GRAB
PONTIN SHEBAR SHIBAR TRADER
COASTER GRIBANE MISTICO
BILLYBOY HOVELLER
(CODFISHING —) BANKER CODMAN
(COOKING —) MARMITE
(DECORATIVE —) AIGUIERE
(DISTILLING —) BODY STILL RETORT
MATRASS CUCURBIT
(DRINKING —) CAP CUP TIN BOOT
PECE FOUNT GLASS GOURD JORUM
KOVAH POKAL SCALE BICKER CAPPIE
CHOPIN COOPER COOTIE DIPPER
DUBBER FIRLOT GOBLET KITTIE
KOVSHI QUAICH QUAIGH RABBIT
RUMKIN BIBERON CANAKIN CANIKIN
GALLIOT SCYPHUS SKINKER
SKYPHOS TANKARD CANNIKIN
CYLINDER

(DUTCH —) KOFF YANKY HOOKER
SCHUIT SCHUYT
(EARTHEN —) PIG OLLA BAYAN
PANKIN TINAGE CRAGGAN
(ELECTROPLATING —) TROUGH
(EUCHARISTIC —) AMA PYX AMULA
PYXIS FLAGON COLUMBA CHRISMAL
CIBORIUM MONSTRANCE
(GLASS —) VERRE UNDINE
BALLOON
(HERRING-FISHING —) BUSS
(HOLLOW METALLIC —) BELL
(INVERTED —) BELL
(LADLING —) GAUN
(LARGE-NECKED —) JORDAN
(LATEEN-RIGGED —) DHOW LATEEN
LATEENER
(LEATHER —) BOOT JACK OLPE
GIRBA DUBBER
(LEVANTINE —) JERM SAIC
(LONG-NECKED —) GOGLET GUGLET
(LYMPHATIC —) LACTEAL
(MALAYAN —) PROA COUGNAR
(MELTING —) GRISSET
(OPEN —) LOOM
(PERFORATED —) LEACH
(PINECONE-SHAPED —) THYRSE
(PORTUGUESE —) MULET
(RARE —) SNOW
(SEED —) POD BUTTON BIVALVE
(SERVING —) ARGYLE ARGYLL
SERVER
(SHALLOW —) KIVER SKEEL BEDPAN
PANCHION
(SMALL —) CAG HOY VIAL PHIAL
VEDET JIGGER LIEPOT PICARD
TINLET YETLIN FLIVVER VEDETTE
YETLING GALLIPOT
(TOP-HEAVY —) CRANK
(TURKISH —) MAHONE
(WHALING —) WHALER SPOUTER
(WICKER —) POT
(WINE —) AMA AMULA TINAGE
(WOODEN —) COG KIT BOSS BAKIE
KIVER BICKER CAPPIE COOTIE
DUDDIE FIRKIN STOUND
(PL.) CRAFT WAFTAGE
(PREF.) ANGI(O) ARTERI VAS(I)(O)
VASCUL(I)(O)
(HOLLOW —) CYT(O)
(SUFF.) ANGE ANGIUM
VEST GARB GOWN ROBE GILET
ACCRUE ATTACH FECKET INVEST
JACKET JELICK JERKIN LINDER
WESKIT ENFEOFF CLOTHING
(— IN) STATE
VESTA WAX
(FATHER OF —) SATURN
(MOTHER OF —) RHEA
(SISTER OF—) JUNO CERES
VESTED BESTEAD DONATIVE
VESTIBULE HALL ENTRY FOYER
PORCH ATRIUM EXEDRA EPINAOS

NARTHEX PASSAGE PRONAOS TAMNOUR ANTEROOM VESTIARY

VESTIGE TAG DREG MARK RACK SIGN PRINT RELIC SPARK TRACE TRACK TRACT UMBRA SHADOW MENTION LEFTOVER RUDIMENT TINCTURE

VESTIGIAL REDUCED OBSOLETE

VESTING ADITIO

VESTITURE TIRE RAIMENT TUNICLE

VESTMENT ALB CAP ALBE COPE PALL VEST AMICE COTTA EPHOD FANON RABAT RASON STOLE RHASON ROCHET SACCOS SAKKOS VAKASS MANIPLE ORARION PALLIUM PILLION PLUVIAL TUNICLE VESTURE CHASUBLE DALMATIC PHRYGIUM RATIONAL SCAPULAR SURPLICE VESTIARY

(PL.) GARB GEAR DRESS CLOTHING

VESTRY SACRISTY VESTIARY

VESTURE COAT

VESUVIANITE EGERAN CYPRINE IDOCRASE VESUVIAN XANTHITE

VETCH DAL ERS AKRA LUCK TARE TINE ERVIL FITCH AXSEED FECCHE THETCH ARVEJON TINETARE TINEWEED

VETERAN VET CHAUVIN EMERITUS HARDENED SEASONED WARHORSE

VETERINARIAN VET LEECH FARRIER

VETERINARY VET FARRIERY

VETIVER BEN KHUS CUSCUS KUSKUS KHASGHAS KHUSKHUS

VETO NIX KILL DISALLOW NEGATIVE

VEUGLAIRE FOWLER

VEX FRY IRE NOY TEW CARK CHAW FASH FAZE FRET FYKE GALL HALE HUMP ITCH RILE ROIL RUCK TEEN TOUT YOKE ANGER ANNOY CHAFE FRUMP GRAME GRILL GRIND GRIPE HARRY SCALD SPITE STURT TARRY TEASE WORRY WRACK WRATH YEARN BOTHER BURDEN CORSIE COTTER CUMBER GRIEVE GRUDGE HARASS HARROW INFEST NETTLE OFFEND PLAGUE POTHER RUFFLE THREAT WORRIT AFFLICT BEDEVIL CHAGRIN DESPITE PERPLEX PROVOKE TORMENT TROUBLE ACERBATE BEPESTER BULLYRAG EXERCISE IRRITATE MACERATE

VEXATION VEX CHAW FASH MOIL TEEN TRAY CHAFE CROSS ERROR GRIEF HARRY PIQUE SPITE STEAM THORN WORRY BOTHER REPINE CHAGRIN DISGUST NOISANCE SORENESS

VEXATIOUS MEAN SORE TEEN NASTY PESKY ACHING FIERCE SHREWD THORNY VEXFUL IRKSOME PEEVISH PRICKLY TARSOME ANNOYING CUMBROUS FRAMPOLD

PHRAMPEL UNTOWARD VEXATORY WEARIFUL PESTILENT

VEXATIOUSLY PLAGUY

VEXED DIK MAD RILY SORE TEEN WAXY WILD WRAW ANGRY NARKY RAGGY ROILY MIFFED MUFFED SHIRTY SNUFFY FRABOUS GRIEVED IRKSOME OUTDONE

(EASILY —) CROSS

VEXILLUM WEB VEXIL BANNER STANDARD

VEXING CHRONIC TECHING WAYWARD ANNOYING NETTLING TEACHING

V-GOUGE VEINER

VIABLE VITAL HEALTHY

VIAL AMPUL CRUET PHIAL AMPULE CASTER CASTOR AMPOULE

(— OF AMYL NITRITE) POPPER

VIANDS CATE DIET FOOD CHEER VIANDRY VICTUALS

VIBRANT RINGY BRAWLING RESONANT SONOROUS VIGOROUS

VIBRATE JAR WAG BEAT CAST DIRL PLAY ROCK TIRL WHIR PULSE QUAKE SWING THIRL THROB TRILL WAVER DINDLE HOTTER JUDDER QUAVER QUIVER SHIMMY SHIVER THRILL TINGLE WARBLE CHATTER FLUTTER LIBRATE STAGGER TREMBLE TWIDDLE EVIBRATE FLICHTER RESONATE UNDULATE

(— ABNORMALLY) SHIMMY

VIBRATING PLANGENT

(— OF AIRPLANE) BUFFET

VIBRATION BUZZ DIRL FLIP TIRL VIBE KARMA SWING TRILL DINDLE JUDDER QUAVER QUIVER THRILL TREMOR DANCING FLUTTER TEMBLOR DIADROME FREMITUS VIBRANCY OSCILLATION

(— OF SAW) CUPPING

(RATTLING —) JAR

VIBRATIONS KARMA

VIBRATO TRILL WHINE TREMOLO

VIBRATOR TREMBLER

VIBRISSA HAIR FEELER SMELLER

VIBURNUM MAE MAY SNOWBALL ARROWWOOD SHEEPBERRY

VICAR PROXY DEPUTY STALLAR ALTARIST STALLARY

VICAR OF CHRIST POPE

VICAR OF WAKEFIELD (AUTHOR OF —) GOLDSMITH

(CHARACTER IN —) MOSES GEORGE OLIVIA SOPHIA WILMOT DEBORAH ARABELLA BURCHELL PRIMROSE THORNHILL

VICE SIN EVIL CRIME FAULT TAINT ULCER DEFECT DEPUTY BUGGERY OFFENSE INIQUITY

VICE-GERENT EPHOR

VICE-PRESIDENT CROUPIER

VICE PRESIDENT VEEP
VICE-PRESIDENT CROUPIER
(— OF SANHEDRIN) ABBETDIN
VICEREGENT VICAR SUBPRIOR
VICEROY EARL VALI NABOB NAWAB
NAZIM SUBAH EXARCH KEHAYA
PROREX PROVES SATRAP WARDEN
PROVOST TSUNGTU SUBAHDAR
VICIA FABA
VICINAGE AREA
VICINITY HERE SHADOW ENVIRONS
(— OF MINE SHAFT) COLLAR
(NEAR —) SUBURBS
VICIOUS BAD ILL EVIL LAZY LEWD
MEAN UGLY VILE ROWDY TOUGH
SINFUL STRONG VITIAL WICKED
CORRUPT IMMORAL NAUGHTY
SKAITHY DEPRAVED DEVILISH
FRATCHED INFAMOUS THEWLESS
MONSTROUS NEFARIOUS
VICIOUSNESS VICE
VICISSITUDE CHANGE MUTATION
(— OF FORTUNE) WEATHER
VICTIM BUTT DUPE GOAT GULL PREY
PATHIC QUARRY CASUALTY
(INTENDED —) CHUMP
(PERPETUAL —) NEBBISH
(SACRIFICIAL —) HOST MERIAH
(SCAM —) PATSY
(SUITABLE —) MARK
(UNFORTUNATE —) BASTARD
VICTIMIZATION RIDE
VICTIMIZE HOAX BUNCO BUNKO
COZEN
VICTOR COCK CAPTOR MASTER
WINNER BANGSTER
VICTORFISH AKU
VICTORIA (FATHER OF —) PALLAS
(MOTHER OF —) STYX
VICTORIA LAKE PUCE
VICTORIAN GENTEEL
VICTORIOUS FIRST VICTOR
WINNING
VICTORY WIN PALM SIEG PRICE
BETTER SUBDUE VICTOR MASTERY
SACKING TRIUMPH WINNING
CONQUEST DECISION WALKOVER
(AUTHOR OF —) CONRAD
(CHARACTER IN —) AXEL LENA
WANG HEYST JONES PEDRO MARTIN
RICARDO DAVIDSON MORRISON
SCHOMBERG
(EASY —) BREEZE
(ONE-SIDED —) BLOWOUT
(OVERWHELMING —) SWEEP
VICTUAL BIT VITE VITTLE
(BROKEN —S) SCRAN
(PL.) KAI BITE CHOW FOOD GRUB
PROG SAND VIVERS PROVENDER
PROVISIONS
VICTUALER PURVEYOR
VIDELICET NAMELY SCILICET

VIDEO RECORDING
(— GAME) ATARI
(COMPUTER — DEVICE) MONITOR
VIDEODISC RECORDING
VIDEOTAPE (— RECORDER) VCR
VIDEOTEX VIEWDATA
(— SYSTEM) VIEWDATA
VIE ENVY JOSTLE STRIVE COMPARE
COMPETE CONTEND CONTEST
EMULATE
VIETNAM (SEE NORTH VIETNAM
AND SOUTH VIETNAM)

VIETNAM
CAPITAL: HANOI
COIN: XU XU DONG DONG
COMMUNIST PARTY: VIETCONG
GULF: TONKIN TONKING
MEASURE: GANG PHAN THON
MOUNTAIN: LINH YANGSIN FANSIPAN
PEOPLE: HOA MAN MEO TAY CHAM KINH NUNG THAI MALAY MUONG
PORT: DANANG HONGAI SAIGON BENTHUY HONGGAI QUINHON HAIPHONG NHATRANG HOCHIMINHCITY
REGION: ANNAM COCHIN TONKIN
RIVER: BO CA DA LO MA CHU GAM KOK XAM CHAY BLACK CLEAR NHIHA MEKONG XONGCA DONGHAI PANLONG
TOWN: HUE VINH HOIAN DANANG BACNINH BIENHOA CAOBANG DONGHOI NAMDINH QUINHON SONGCAU TAYNINH THANHOA VIETTRI HAIPHONG PHANRANG QUANGTRI
WEIGHT: CAN YET UYEN

VIETNAMESE ANNAMESE
VIEW EYE KEN FACE GLOM MAKE
VISE ADVEW AVIEW BLUSH CATCH
MOUTH SCAPE SCENE SIGHT VISTA
VIZZY ADVICE ADVISE ASPECT
DEVICE GLANCE REGARD SURVEY
ALOGISM CONCEIT FEELING
GLIMPSE KENNING LOOKOUT
OFFLOOK OPINION RESPECT
SCENERY SURVIEW THOUGHT
AIRSCAPE CONSPECT EYESIGHT
OFFSCAPE PROSPECT SEASCAPE
SENTENCE SENTIMENT
(— ATTENTIVELY) GAZE
(— CLOSELY) INSPECT
(— FROM AFAR) DESCRY
(— FROM ANGLE) SLANT
(— OF MAN) DUALISM
(— WITH SURPRISE) ADMIRE
(BACKWARD —) RETROSPECT
RETROSPECTION
(BRIEF —) SNAPSHOT
(CATCH MOMENTARY —) GLANCE
(COMPREHENSIVE —) PANORAMA

(DEPRESSING —) PESSIMISM
(EXPRESS A —) OPINE
(GENERAL —) LANDSKIP
(OPEN —) LIGHT
(PHYSICAL —) INSIGHT
(PUBLIC —) OPEN
(SATISFYING —) EYEFUL
(SECOND —) DEUTEROSCOPY
(SECTIONAL — OF BODY) CATSCAN
(SUFF.) ORAMA SCOPE SCOPIC
SCOPUS SCOPY
VIEWDATA VIDEOTEX
VIEWER (TELEVISION —) GOGGLER
VIEWING
(SUFF.) SCOPE SCOPIC SCOPUS
SCOPY
VIEWPOINT SIGHT LAXISM
STANDPOINT
VIGIL WAKE WATCH WAKING
AGRYPNIA
VIGILANCE WATCH JEALOUSY
VIGILANT AGOG WARE WARY ALERT
AWAKE AWARE CHARY SHARP
JEALOUS LIDLESS WAKEFUL
CAUTIOUS WATCHFUL
VIGODA ABE
VIGOR GO PEP SAP VIM VIR VIS BIRR
DASH EDGE ELAN LUST PITH SEVE
SNAP SOUL TUCK ARDOR DRIVE
FLUSH FORCE GREEN JUICE NERVE
OOMPH POWER PUNCH VERVE
ENERGY ESPRIT FOISON GINGER
SPRAWL SPRING STARCH STINGO
VIGOUR VIRTUS FREEDOM
SMEDDUM STAMINA STHENIA
FLOURISH STRENGTH TONICITY
VITALITY
(— OF THOUGHT) FLAME
(FULL OF —) LIFESOME
(MENTAL —) DOCITY SPIRIT
(RENEWED —) REST
VIGOROUS YEP ABLE CANT FRIM
HALE LIVE RUDE SPRY YEPE ALIVE
CRANK EAGER FRACK FRANK HEFTY
JUICY LUSTY NIPPY PEPPY PITHY
PROUD SASSY SOLID STARK STIFF
STOUT TOUGH VIVID FLORID
GOLDEN HEARTY LIVELY MANFUL
POTENT PRETTY RAUCLE ROBUST
RUGGED SINEWY SQUARE STRONG
STURDY BUCKISH CHIPPER CORDIAL
DRASTIC FECKFUL FURIOUS
HEALTHY LUSTFUL NERVOSE
NERVOUS VALIANT VIBRANT
ZEALOUS ATHLETIC BOUNCING
CHOPPING FORCEFUL MUSCULAR
SLAMBANG SLASHING STUBBORN
VEHEMENT VIGOROSO YOUTHFUL
TRENCHANT
(NOT —) GENTEEL
VIGOROUSLY DOWN FELL HARD
VERN AMAIN CRANK SNELL TIGHT
VERNE HARDLY SNELLY FRESHLY

SMARTLY STOUTLY WIGHTLY
HEARTILY
VIGOROUSNESS ENERGY
FREEDOM
VIKING DANE WIKING NORSEMAN
VIKRAMADITYA BIKRAM
VILE BAD BASE CLAM FOUL RANK
CHEAP MUCKY POCKY RUSTY SLIMY
WILLE ABJECT CRUSTY DRAFTY
DRASTY FILTHY LECHER NOUGHT
ODIOUS PALTRY SORDID TURPID
UNKIND BEASTLY BENEATH CAITIFF
CORRUPT DEBASED HATEFUL
IGNOBLE SCABBED SLAVISH VICIOUS
BASEBORN DEPRAVED UNKINDLY
(OPENLY —) SCANDALOUS
VILENESS FEDITY VILITY TURPITUDE
VILIFICATION SLANDER REPROACH
VILIFY ILL VILE ABUSE LIBEL SMEAR
STAIN SULLY DEFAME DEFILE
MALIGN REVILE SLIGHT ASPERSE
BLACKEN DEBAUCH DETRACT
SLANDER TRADUCE REPROACH
STRUMPET
VILIPEND SLUR BELITTLE
VILL HAM TOWN TOWNSHIP
VILLA ALDEA DACHA LODGE CHALET
DATCHA QUINTA TRIANON
VILLAGE BY AUL BYE GAV HAM KOM
PAH REW BOMA BURG DORP HOME
MURA TOWN VILL WICK ALDEA
BOURG CASAL PLACE THORP VICUS
ALDEIA BARRIO BUSTEE CAUTLE
GOTHAM HAMLET HAMMON
MOUZAH PETTAH PUEBLO AMBALAM
BOROUGH CAMPODY CASERIO
CLACHAN ENDSHIP MAABARA
MISSION OUTPORT BEREWICK
BOURGADE CAMPOODY CRANFORD
TOLDERIA VILLACHE VILLAGET
VILLAKIN
(— IN WHICH BARLEY IS GROWN)
BEREWICK
(— OUTSIDE OF FORT) PETTAH
(AFRICAN —) STAD KRAAL
(ARABIAN —) DOUAR
(ARGENTINE —) TOLDERIA
(FRENCH —) BASTIDE
(IMAGINARY —) CRANFORD
(INDIAN —) CASTLE PUEBLO
CAMPODY CAMPOODY
(JAPANESE —) MURA BUSTI
BUSTEE
(JAVANESE —) DESSA
(JEWISH —) SHTETL SHTETEL
(MALAY —) CAMPONG KAMPONG
(MAORI —) KAIK KAIKA KAINGA
(MEXICAN —) EJIDO
(NEWFOUNDLAND —) OUTPORT
(NEW ZEALAND FORTIFIED —) PA PAH
(RUSSIAN —) MIR STANITSA
STANITZA
(TENT —) DUAR DOUAR DOWAR

VILLAIN IAGO LOUT SERF BADDY
BRAVO CHURL DEMON DEVIL FAGIN
FELON HEAVY KNAVE ROGUE SCAMP
SHREW VIPER BADDIE VILIACO
SCELERAT SCOUNDREL
VILLAINOUS BAD EVIL GALLUS
GALLOWS KNAVISH RAFFISH VILEYNS
FLAGRANT RASCALLY MISCREANT
VILLAINY CRIME KNAVERY
VILLEIN SERF CHURL BORDAR
COTTER VILLAR BONDMAN
TOWNMAN VILLAIN COTARIUS
VILLI (HAVING —) ZONARY
VILLOUS SHAGGY
VIM ZIP GIMP ZING FORCE OOMPH
VIGOR ENERGY GINGER SPIRIT
STARCH VINEGAR RAZZMATAZZ
VINA BEN BIN BINA
VINCENTIAN LAZARIST
VINDICATE FREE CLEAR RIGHT
SALVE WREAK ACQUIT ASSERT
AVENGE EXCUSE UPHOLD ABSOLVE
DERAIGN JUSTIFY PROPUGN
REVENGE SUSTAIN DARRAIGN
MAINTAIN
VINDICATION BEHALF APOLOGY
DEFENSE THEODICY
COMPURGATION SATISFACTION
JUSTIFICATION
VINDICATOR VINDEX ASSERTER
DEFENDER
VINDICTIVE HOSTILE PUNITIVE
SPITEFUL VENGEFUL
VINE AKA FIG HOP IVY IYO BINE CARO
GOGO ODAL SOMA TINE AKEBI
BUAZE BWAZI CAAPI CACUR GUACO
KAIWI KUDZU LIANA LIANE MAILE
PALAY PRIVY TACSO TIMBO TRAIL
TWINE WITHE WONGA BEJUCO
CISSUS COBAEA COWAGE DERRIS
DODDER ECANDA GERKIN IPOMEA
JICAMA LABLAB PIKAKE RUNNER
TURURI TWINER ULLUCO WINDER
APRICOT BIGROOT BONESET
BRAMBLE CALAMUS CATVINE
CERIMAN CLIMBER COWHAGE
COWITCH CUPSEED EPACRID
GHERKIN IPOMOEA LAVANGA
PAREIRA PUMPKIN TRAILER VINELET
YANGTAO ATRAGENE BINDWEED
BOXTHORN CLEMATIS COMEBACK
CUCUMBER CUCURBIT DECUMARY
DOLICHOS EARDROPS EARTHPEA
EVONYMUS GULANCHA HEARTPEA
HEMPWEED MUSCATEL REDWITHE
TINETARE TINEWEED TRAILERY
TRAILING TREEBINE VINIFERA
WINETREE WISTARIA WISTERIA
OLOLIUQUI
(PREF.) AMPEL(O) VITI
VINEGAR VIM EISEL ESILL ACETUM
ALEGAR ASCILL SOURING BEEREGAR
VINAIGRE

(— AND HONEY) OXYMEL
(PREF.) ACET(O)
VINEGAR EEL EELWORM
VINEGARY ACETOSE ACETOUS
VINEGROWER VINITOR
VINEYARD CRU CLOS COTE VINER
VINERY WINEYARD
VINGT-ET-UN MACAO MACCO
VINOUS WINY
VINTAGE OLD VINT WINE CUVEE
ARCHAIC CLASSIC VENDAGE
OUTMODED
VIOL GUE GIGA LIRA TURR GIGUE
GUDOK TARAU VOYAL VOYOL
CHELYS FIDDLE VIELLE VIOLET
MINIKIN QUINTON SARINDA
SULTANA VIHUELA VIOLONE
BARBITON BASSETTE SERINGHI
VIOLETTE
VIOLA ALTO QUINT TENOR TENORE
VIOLET
(BROTHER OF —) SEBASTIAN
(HUSBAND OF —) ORSINO
VIOLA BASTARDA BARITONE
BARYTONE
VIOLA DA BRACCIO QUINT
VIOLA DA GAMBA GAMBA
VIOLA D'AMORE VIOLET
VIOLATE ERR SIN FLAW ABUSE
BREAK CRACK FORCE FRACT HARRY
LOOSE VIOLE WRONG BREACH
BROACH DEFILE INVADE OFFEND
RAVISH DEBAUCH DISOBEY FALSIFY
INFRACT OUTRAGE POLLUTE
PROFANE VITIATE DEFLOWER
DISHONOR FORSWEAR FRACTURE
INFRINGE MISTREAT STUPRATE
SURPRISE TEMERATE TRESPASS
VIOLENCE
VIOLATED FRACTED INFRACT
VIOLATION SIN DEBT ABUSE CRIME
ERROR FAULT SALLY BREACH INJURY
MISCONDUCT
(HOCKEY —) STICKS
(TRIVIAL —) MOPERY
VIOLATOR WRONGER
VIOLENCE FURY NEED RAGE RUFF
BRUNT FORCE RIGOR STORM BENSIL
ESTURE HUBRIS RANDOM RAPINE
STOUSH STRESS BENSAIL BENSALL
OUTRAGE FEROCITY SEVERITY
SORENESS ROUGHHOUSE
(DEPICTING —) SNUFF
(LETHAL —) DEATH
(OF DEPICTION OF —) SNUFF
VIOLENT BIG HOT TEZ DERF HARD
HIGH MAIN RANK RUDE WILD WOOD
ACUTE FIERY HEADY HEAVY HEFTY
RABID SHARP SMART STARK STERN
STIFF STOOR STOUR STOUT WROTH
BROTHE FIERCE HEARTY MANIAC
MIGHTY SAVAGE SEVERE STORMY
STRONG STURDY SUDDEN CRIMSON

DRASTIC FURIOUS HOTSPUR
RAMMISH RAMPANT RAPEFUL
RUFFIAN TEARING VIOLOUS
WILSOME CHURLISH DIABOLIC
FLAGRANT FORCEFUL IMPOTENT
MANIACAL PERACUTE RIGOROUS
SEETHING SLAMBANG STALWART
VEHEMENT

VIOLENTLY HARD AMAIN HOTLY
HARDLY SORELY HOPPING SOUNDLY

VIOLET CANON GRAPE MAUVE VIOLA
BLAVER CANYON DAHLIA DAMSON
EVEQUE JOHNNY HOOKERS LOBELIA
OPHELIA PRELATE PRIMULA
PUREAYN CLEMATIS DAMEWORT
FINELEAF IANTHINE ROOSTERS
WISTERIA
(KIND OF,—) AFRICAN
(PREF.) IO

VIOLIN GUE KIT ALTO GIGA AMATI
CROWD CRWTH GEIGE GIGUE REBAB
REBEC STRAD TARAU VIOLA CATGUT
CHORUS CROUTH FIDDLE FITHEL
REBECK TAILLE VIOLON CATLING
CHROTTA CREMONA THEYAOU
VIOLAND VIOLINO GUARNERI
KEMANCHA VIOLOTTA
(PART OF —) NUT PEG TOP FROG
HEAD HEEL HOLE NECK BELLY TABLE
BRIDGE BUTTON PEGBOX SCROLL
STRING PURFLING SOUNDBOARD
FINGERBOARD

VIPER ASP HARU ADDER ASPIC
ATHER URUTU WYVER ASPIDE
DABOIA DABOYA JESSUR KATUKA
KUPPER HAGWORM HOGNOSE
MAMUDII VIPERID AMMODYTE
CERASTES JARARACA VIPERINE
BUSHMASTER
(KIND OF —) PIT

VIPER'S BUGLOSS BLUEWEED

VIRAGO NAG RANDY SHREW
AMAZON BELDAM CALLET BELDAME
TRIMMER VIRAGIN RIXATRIX

VIREO REDEYE GRASSET TEACHER
GREENLET PREACHER

VIRGATE YOKE VERGE YARDLAND
(HALF —) MANTAL

VIRGILIAN MARONIAN

VIRGIN NEW LIVE MAID PURE FRESH
CHASTE MAIDEN VESTAL INITIAL
PUCELLE DOROTHEA PARAMOUR
(— OF PARADISE) HURI HOURI
(PREF.) PARTHEN(O)

VIRGINAL CHERRY INTACT
SYMPHONY TRIANGLE

VIRGINIA
CAPITAL: RICHMOND
COLLEGE: AVERETT HOLLINS
MADISON RADFORD LONGWOOD
COUNTY: LEE BATH PAGE WISE BLAND
CRAIG FLOYD SMYTH SURRY WYTHE
AMELIA LOUISA ACCOMAC HENRICO
PATRICK PULASKI ROANOKE
CULPEPER FLUVANNA TAZEWELL
INDIAN: SAPONI TUTELO MONACAN
MANAHOAC MEHERRIN NOTTAWAY
POWHATAN
LAKE: KERR SMITH
MOUNTAIN: CEDAR ELLIOT ROGERS
BALDKNOB
MOUNTAIN RANGE: CLINCH
ALLEGHENY BLUERIDGE
NICKNAME: OLDDOMINION
MOTHEROFSTATES
MOTHEROFPRESIDENTS
PRESIDENT: TYLER MONROE TAYLOR
WILSON MADISON HARRISON
JEFFERSON WASHINGTON
RIVER: DAN JAMES POTOMAC
RAPIDAN
STATE BIRD: CARDINAL
STATE FLOWER: DOGWOOD
STATE TREE: DOGWOOD
TOWN: GALAX LURAY SALEM MARION
BEDFORD BRISTOL EMPORIA
NORFOLK PULASKI ROANOKE
CULPEPER DANVILLE HOPEWELL
MANASSAS STAUNTON TAZEWELL

VIRGINIA COWSLIP LUNGWORT

VIRGINIA CREEPER CREEPER
WOODBIND WOODBINE

VIRGINIA KNOTWEED JUMPSEED

VIRGINIAN BEAGLE COOHEE
CAVALIER TUCKAHOE
(AUTHOR OF —) WISTER
(CHARACTER IN —) WOOD HENRY
MOLLY STEVE SHORTY TRAMPAS

VIRGINIANS
(AUTHOR OF —) THACKERAY
(CHARACTER IN —) THEO WILL
FANNY HARRY HETTY MARIA MILES
ESMOND GEORGE RACHEL LAMBERT
MOUNTAIN BERNSTEIN
CASTLEWOOD WARRINGTON
WASHINGTON

VIRGINIA SNAKEROOT SANGREL
SNAGREL

VIRGINIA STICKSEED SOLDIERS

VIRGINIA WATERLEAF SHAWNY

VIRGINIA WILLOW ITEA

VIRGINITY HONOR CHERRY
CHASTITY PUCELAGE

VIRGIN MARY DESPOINA
THEOTOCOS

VIRGIN'S-BOWER LOVE HONESTY
CLEMATIS MOONWORT

VIRGIN SOIL (AUTHOR OF —)
TURGENEV
(CHARACTER IN —) KOLYA PAHKLIN
SOLOMIN MARIANNA MASHURIN
SIPYAGIN MARKELOFF VALENTINA
NEZHDANOFF OSTRODUMOFF

VIRGO (STAR IN —) SPICA

VIRGULE SLANT VIRGULA
DIAGONAL
VIRIDIAN EMERAUDE
VIRILE MALE MACHO MANLY
(AGGRESSIVELY —) MACHO
VIRILITY LUST GREEN MANHEAD
MANHOOD
VIROLOGIST (FAMOUS —) SABIN
VIRTUAL IMPLICIT PRACTICAL
VIRTUALLY BUT NEARLY MORALLY
VIRTUE JEN HSIN THEW ARETE FAITH
GRACE POWER VALOR VERTU
WORTH BOUNTY DHARMA FOISON
CHARISM CHARITY JUSTICE PROBITY
QUALITY CHARISMA CHASTITY
EFFICACY GOODNESS MORALITY
PARAMITA PROPERTY
(CONFUCIAN —) LI
(PL.) CIVISM
(PREF.) ARETO
VIRTUOSO ACE EXPERT SAVANT
ESTHETE LAPIDARY
VIRTUOUS GOOD PURE BRAVE CIVIL
MORAL PIOUS CHASTE HONEST
MODEST GODDARD SAINTED
SINCERE UPRIGHT VIRTUAL
STRAIGHT
VIRULENCE VIRUS RANCOR
RANCOUR
VIRULENT RANK ACRID RABID
DEADLY MALIGN VIROSE NOXIOUS
VIRIFIC WASPISH VENOMOUS
(LESS THAN —) MITIS
VIRUS PARVO VENOM POISON
PATHOGEN SPECIFIC
(AIDS —) HIV
(PRESENCE OF —) VIREMIA
VIS PEIKTHA
VISAGE FACE PHIZ CHEER IMAGE
VISOR ASPECT FASHION
VISCERA GUTS HASLET INSIDE
UMBLES GARBAGE GIBLETS
HASSLET INMEATS INNARDS
INSIDES NUMBLES ENTRAILS
HARIGALS
(PREF.) SPLANCHNO
VISCERAL GUT
VISCID SLAB WAXY GOOEY GLAIRY
STICKY LENTOUS STRINGY VISCOUS
MOTHERED
VISCIDITY LENTOR
VISCOSITY BODY ROPINESS
(— UNIT) POISE
VISCOUS LIMY ROPY SIZY SLAB
GOBBY GUMMY MUCIC ROPEY
SLIMY STIFF TARRY SIRUPY SLABBY
SMEARY SNOTTY STICKY THONGY
VISCID LENTOUS SQUISHY VISCOSE
MUCULENT
VISE GEE CHAP JACK SHOP VICE
CHEEK CLAMP CRAMP WINCH
(PART OF —) JAW BASE BOLT ANVIL
SCREW SLIDE HANDLE SWIVEL

VISHNU RAMA VASU KALKI KRISHNA
BALARAMA BHAGAVAT
(AVATAR OF —) KALKI KURMA
BUDDHA MATSYA VAMANA VARAHA
KRISHNA NARASINHA
PARASHURAMA RAMACHANDRA
(BREAST JEWEL OF —) KAUSTUBHA
(BREASTMARK OF —) SHRIVATSA
(VEHICLE OF —) GARUDA
(WIFE OF —) SHRI LAKSHMI
(WRIST JEWEL OF —) SYAMANTAKA
VISIBLE OUT FAIR SEEN CLEAR
GROSS EXTANT SIGHTY EVIDENT
GLARING OBVIOUS OPTICAL SIGHTLY
APPARENT DIOPTRIC EXPLICIT
EXTERNAL MANIFEST PROSPECT
(BARELY —) DARK
(SCARCELY —) DIM
(PREF.) DELO PHANER(O) PHANTA
PHANTASMO PHANTO
VISION EYE RAY DREAM FANCY
SIGHT FANTAD SEEING SWEVEN
AISLING SHOWING SPECTER
SPECTRE EYESIGHT PHOTOPIA
PROSPECT SPECULATION
(— IN BRIGHT LIGHT) PHOTOPIA
(— IN DIM LIGHT) SCOTOPIA
(— PROBLEM) REDOUT
(BLURRED —) SWIMMING
(DEFECTIVE —) ANOPIA
(DOUBLE —) DIPLOPIA
(FALSE —) PARABLEPSY
PARABLEPSIS
(FANCIED —) PHANTASM
(IMAGINARY —) SHADOW
(IMPERFECT —) CALIGO DARKNESS
(MENTAL —) VISTA
(MULTIPLE —) POLYOPIA
(PREF.) OPTI(CO) OPTO VISUO
(RANGE OF —) METROPIA
(SUFF.) OPSIA OPSIS OPSY OPTIC
OPTICON
(— DEVIATION) TROPIA
VISIONARY FEY AERY AIRY WILD
BIGOT IDEAL VIEWY ASTRAL INSANE
SHANDY UNREAL DREAMER
FANTAST LAPUTAN UTOPIAN
ACADEMIC DELUSIVE FANCIFUL
FINESPUN IDEALIST NOTIONAL
PHANTAST QUIXOTIC ROMANTIC
UTOPIAST VISIONER
VISIT DO GAM SEE VIS CALL CHAT
STAY APPLY HAUNT TRYST VIZZY
COSHER RESORT RETURN CEILIDH
CEILIDHE FREQUENT INVASION
(— BETWEEN WHALERS) GAM
(— PERSISTENTLY) INFEST
(— PROFESSIONALLY) ATTEND
(— RELATIVES) COUSIN
(— UNEXPECTEDLY) POPIN DROPIN
(— WRETCHED NEIGHBORHOODS)
SLUM
(CEREMONIAL —) SELAMLIK

VISITATION SENE VISIT SENDING
VISITING ACTIVE SOCIAL
VISITOR GUEST LAKER CALLER
VISITANT
(MEALTIME —) SCAMBLER
(PL.) COMPANY
VISOR BILL SIGHT UMBER UMBRE
VIZOR BEAVER MESAIL UMBRIL
VIZARD EYESHADE UMBRIERE
VISTA VIEW SCENE OUTLOOK
PERSPECTIVE
VISUAL OPTIC OCULAR SCOPIC
VISORY VISIBLE
VISUALIZE SEE FANCY IDEATE
SYMBOL IMAGINE PICTURE
CONCEIVE ENVISAGE
VITAL KEY LIVE BASIC CHIEF FRESH
SAPPY LIVELY MOVING VIABLE
ZOETIC ANIMATE CAPITAL CORDIAL
EXIGENT NEEDFUL ESSENTIAL
VITALITY SAP VIM LIFE COLOR
GUSTO JUICE OOMPH PULSE PUNCH
BIOSIS BREATH ENERGY FOISON
HEALTH MARROW PAZAZZ PIZAZZ
STARCH PIZZAZZ VIVENCY
STRENGTH
(DEFICIENT —) ASTHENIA
(LACKING —) STUFFY TURNIPY
VITALIZE ACTIVATE ENERGIZE
VITAMIN BIOTIN CITRIN NIACIN
ADERMIN ANEURIN CHOLINE
RETINOL THIAMIN TORULIN
ADVITANT INOSITOL NUTRAMIN
ORYZANIN VITAMINE
VITAMIN A RETINOL
VITELLINE YOLKY
VITIATE BEAT BLEND SPOIL TAINT
CANCEL DEBASE POISON CORRUPT
DEBAUCH DEPRAVE
VITIATED PICAL CORRUPT
(PREF.) CAC(O) CACH
(SUFF.) CACE
VITICULTURIST VIGNERON
VITREOUS GLASSY GLAIZIE
VITREAN VITROUS
VITRIFY GLAZE
VITRIOL BLUEJACK COPPERAS
(PL.) SORY
VITRIOLIC SHARP BITING BITTER
CAUSTIC MORDANT SCATHING
VITRIOS GLASSWARE
VITTLES CHOW
VITUPERATE RAIL ABUSE CURSE
SCOLD SLANG BERATE REVILE
VITUPERATION ABUSE VITUPER
VITUPERATIVE ABUSIVE REVILING
SHAMEFUL
VIVACE VIVO LEBHAFT
VIVACIOUS GAY AIRY PERT BRISK
CRISP MERRY SUNNY BRIGHT
LIVELY LIVING SPARKY VIVACE
ANIMATE JOCULAR ANIMATED
SPIRITED SPORTIVE FLAMBOYANT

VIVACITY BRIO FIRE LIFE ZEAL
ARDOR VERVE VIGOR ESPRIT GAIETY
GAYETY SPIRIT SPRAWL SPARKLE
VIVARIUM STEW VIVARY STEWPOND
VIVAT HOCH
VIVERRINE CIVET GENET FOUSSA
MUSANG LINSANG FALANAKA
MONGOOSE SURICATE
VIVIANO (BROTHER OF —) MALAGIGI
ALDIGIERI
(SISTER OF —) BRADAMANTE
VIVID DEEP HARD KEEN LIVE RICH
VIVE BRISK FRESH GREEN LURID
QUICK RUDDY SHARP GARISH
LIVELY LIVING STRONG VISUAL
EIDETIC FLAMING FREAKED
GLARING GLOWING GRAPHIC
INTENSE PEPPERY VIOLENT
COLORFUL DISTINCT DRAMATIC
SLASHING STRIKING VIGOROUS
PICTURESQUE
(NOT —) PALE
VIVIDNESS COLOR EMPHASIS
VIVIFY LIFE FOMENT ANIMATE
QUICKEN SPARKLE
VIVIPARUS PALUDINA
VIXEN BARD FURY RANDY SCOLD
SHREW VIRAGO SHARP TRIMMER
VIZIER WAZIR ATABEG ATABEK VISIER
VLACH WALLACH
V-MAIL AIRGRAPH
VOCABULARY CANT LEXIS SLANG
JARGON DICTION LEXICON
POCHISMO WORDBOOK
(FAULTY —) CACOLOGY
(UNDERWORLD —) ARGOT
(PREF.) LEXICO
VOCAL GLIB ORAL VOWEL FLUENT
TONGUED VOCULAR ELOQUENT
VOCALIST BOPPER SINGER BOPPIST
BOPSTER SONGSTER VOCALLER
VOCALIZE MOUTH ORATE INTONE
PHONATE
VOCATION CALL HOBBY METIER
CALLING SCIENCE
VOCATIONAL BANAUSIC
VOCIFERATION CLAMOR OUTCRY
VOCIFEROUS LOUD NOISY
BAWLING BLATANT BRAWLING
STRIDENT
VODKA SAMOGON SAMOGONKA
VOGUE CUT FAD TON CHIC MODE
RAGE TURN STYLE CUSTOM
FASHION RECLAME PRACTICE
VOGUL MANSI
VOICE SAY VOX EMIT GIVE HARP PIPE
TONE TURN WISH FROTH LEDEN
RAISE RUMOR SOUND UTTER ACTIVE
ASSERT CHOICE STEVEN TAISCH
THROAT TONGUE EXPRESS OPINION
SONORIZE DIATHESIS
(— PRAISE) SLAVER
(ARTIFICIAL —) FALSETTO

(BELLOWING —) FOGHORN
(FIFTH —) QUINTUS
(HOARSE —) FOGHORN
(LOWEST —) BASS BASSO
(MIDDLE —) MOTETUS
(OF LYRIC AND DRAMATIC —) SPINTO
(PRINCIPAL —) CANTUS
(PUBLIC —) CRY
(SINGING —) ALTO BASS TENOR
BREAST SPINTO SOPRANO
BARITONE FALSETTO
(SUBDUED —) UNDERBREATH
(TENOR —) TAILLE
(UPPER —) DESCANT DISCANT
(PREF.) PHON(O) PHTHONGO VOCI
(LOUD —) STENTORIOUS
(SUFF.) PHON(E)(IA)(Y)
VOICED SOFT WEAK TONIC MEDIAL
SONANT VIBRANT PHTHONGAL
VOICELESS MUM DUMB HARD
MUTE SURD SHARP ATONIC FLATED
SILENT ANAUDIA APHONIC SPIRATE
APHONOUS BREATHED NOTELESS
VOID NO BAD FREE KORE LEAR LEER
MUTE NULL PASS TOOM ABYSS
AVOID BLANK EGEST EJECT EMPTY
INEPT LAPSE PURGE SLICE SPACE
WASTE DEVOID HOLLOW VACANT
VACUUM CONCAVE INVALID
VACANCY VACUITY EVACUATE
INDIGENT NONBEING
(— OF FEELING) BLATE
(— OF SENSE) INANE
(— OF SUBSTANCE) JEJUNE
VOIDED FALSE CLECHE CLECHY
CLECHEE
VOILE NINON ETAMINE
VOLATILE LIGHT FIGENT LIVELY
VOLAGE BUOYANT DARTING ELASTIC
FLIGHTY FLYAWAY GASEOUS
FUGITIVE SKITTISH VAPOROSE
VAPOROUS FUGACIOUS
(PREF.) PTENO
VOLATILITY LEVITY
VOLCANIC ROCK TRASS
VOLCANO APO DOME ETNA ASKJA
PELEE SHASTA VULCAN FURNACE
RUMBLER VULCANO FUMAROLE
KRAKATOA SPITFIRE VESUVIUS
(MUD —) SALSE SALINELLE
VOLE CRABER CRICETID CAMPAGNOL
VOLITATION FLIGHT VOLATION
VOLITION WILL CHOICE INTENT
VOLENCY VELLEITY
VOLLEY TIRE CROWD DRIFT VOLEE
FLIGHT BARRAGE PLATOON
BLIZZARD
VOLPLANE GLIDE
VOLPONE (AUTHOR OF —) JONSON
(CHARACTER IN —) CELIA MOSCA
BONARIO CORVINO VOLPONE
VOLTORE POLITICK CORBACCIO
PEREGRINE

VOLSUNG WAELS
VOLT VOLTA REPOLON
(— AMPERE UNIT) VAR
VOLTAGE KICKBACK
VOLTAIC GUR GALVANIC
VOLTE-FACE BACKFLIP
VOLUBILITY FLUENCY
VOLUBLE GLIB WORDY FLUENT
VOLUME MO PEN BAND BOOK BULK
CODE SIZE TOME CODEX SPACE
CUBAGE CONTENT DIURNAL
MENAION VOLUMEN CAPACITY
CUBATURE SOLIDITY STRENGTH
(— OF SOUND) STRESS
(— OF WORT) LENGTH
(PATTERN —) DUMMY
VOLUMINOUS FULL AMPLE BULKY
LARGE BOUFFANT
VOLUMNIA (SON OF —)
CORIOLANUS
VOLUNTARILY WILLES WILLICHE
VOLUNTARY FREE WILLY SORTIE
WILFUL PRELUDE SORTITA WILLFUL
WILLING ELECTIVE FREEWILL
HONORARY OPTIONAL POSTLUDE
UNFORCED
VOLUNTEER OFFER ENLIST
PROFFER FENCIBLE STRANGER
(— SERVING AS OFFICER)
REFORMADO
(— STATE) TENNESSEE
VOLUPTUARY SYBARITE
VOLUPTUOUS ADIN BUXOM
LUXIVE LYDIAN SULTRY WANTON
SENSUAL DELICATE LUSCIOUS
SENSUOUS
VOLUPTUOUSNESS DELICE
LUXURY
VOLUTE TURN HELIX SCROLL
VOLUTA CILLERY VOLUTION
VOLUTION COIL TWIST WHORL
VERTICIL
VOLVA CUP WRAPPER
VOMIT CAT PUT BALK BARF BOCK
BOKE CACK CAST PICK PUKE SICK
SPEW SPUE VOME WOOM BRAKE
EVOME HEAVE RALPH REACH RETCH
SHOOT POSSET REJECT VOMITO
CASCADE CASTING REGORGE
DISGORGE PARBREAK SICKNESS
VOMITING
VOMITING BOKE EMESIS
PYEMESIS
(PREF.) EMET(O)
VOMITUS SPEW SPUE
VOODOO HEX OBI CHARM OBEAH
HOODOO SORCERER
(— DESIGN) VERVER
(— PRIEST) BOCOR BOKOR
(— SPELL) MOJO
VOODOOISM VODUN WANGA
VODUN
VOPHSI (SON OF —) NAHBI

VORACIOUS GORB GREEDY
BULIMIC ESURINE GLUTTON
THROATY EDACIOUS ESURIENT
RAVENING RAVENOUS
VORACITY BULIMIA EDACITY
VORTEX APEX EDDY GYRE SWIRL
WHIRL
VOTARESS NUN
VOTARY PALMER ZEALOT DEVOTEE
SECTARY ADHERENT DEVOTARY
FOLLOWER
VOTE AYE CON NAY PRO ELECT
FAGOT GRACE VOICE BALLOT DIVIDE
FAGGOT TONGUE APPROVE
PLUMPER SUFFRAGE
(— AGAINST) NAY KNIFE NEGATIVE
(— APPROVAL) CONFIRM
(— FOR) AY AYE PRO SUPPORT
(— ILLEGALLY) REPEAT
(— OF ASSENT) PLACET
(AFFIRMATIVE —) YEA YES
(INFORMAL —) STRAW
(KIND OF —) WRITEIN
VOTER BOLTER POLLER CHOOSER
ELECTOR FLOATER ASSENTOR
(KIND OF —) CROSSOVER
VOTING POLL
(— FIRST) PREROGATIVE
VOTIVE VOWED
VOTYAK UDMURT
VOUCH ABLE ASSURE ATTEST
AVOUCH ENDORSE ACCREDIT
VOUCHER CHIT CHALAN COUPON
POLICY TICKET WARRANT
VOUCHSAFE GIVE SEND DEIGN
GRANT VOUCH BETEEM PLEASE
WITSAFE
VOUSSOIR QUOIN WEDGE
KEYSTONE SPRINGER
VOW LAY VUM AVOW OATH SNUM
VOTE SWEAR VOUCH BEHEST
PLEDGE BEHIGHT PROMISE PROTEST
(MARRIAGE —) IDO
(PRFF.) EUCHO
VOWEL SHWA WIDE GLIDE SCHWA
VOCOID AUGMENT PALATAL
GEMINATE ORINASAL
(— POINT) SERE
(— SOUND) LONGA
(BACK —) VELAR
(CHANGE OF —) UMLAUT

(GLIDE —) MURMUR
(GROUP OF 2 —S) BROAD DIGRAM
DIGRAPH
(PREFIXED —) AUGMENT
(SHORT —) MATRA
VOYAGE SAIL TRIP VIAGE COURSE
CRUISE FLIGHT TRAVEL CARAVAN
JOURNEY PASSAGE SAILING
STEAMER PERIPLUS SHIPPING
VOYAGING SEA NAVIGANT
VOYEUR PEEPER
VULCAN MULCIBER
(WORKSHOP OF —) AETNA
VULCANITE EBONITE
VULCANIZATION BURNING
VULCANIZE BURN CURE METALIZE
VULCANIZER CEMENTER
VULGAR LOW LEWD LOUD RUDE
BANAL CHEAP FLASH GROSS SLANG
SLIMY TOUGH COARSE COMMON
PORTER RABBLE VULGUS WOOLEN
XRATED BLATANT BOORISH
GENERAL KNAVISH LOWBRED
MOBBISH OBSCENE POPULAR
PROFANE RAFFISH SECULAR
TABLOID VILLAIN WOOLLEN
BANAUSIC CHURLISH MECHANIC
PANDEMIC PLEBEIAN PORTERLY
POTHOUSE SOUTERLY
VULGARIAN CAD SLOB TIGER
KEELIE RAFFISH
VULGARITY RAUNCH SHODDY
FOULNESS HARLOTRY
VULGARIZE PLEBIFY PROFANE
VULGARIZED DEGRADED
VULGARLY CHEAPLY
VULNERABILITY GAP EXPOSURE
VULNERABLE NAKED LIABLE
EXPOSED PREGNABLE
VULPINE SLY FOXY CRAFTY
ALOPECOID
VULTURE AURA GEIR PAPA AREND
GRAAP GRAPE GRIPE SWIPE URUBU
CONDOR CORBIE FALCON GRIPHE
RAPTOR SNATCH TORGOS GRIFFIN
GRIFFON GRYPHON NEKHEBT
AASVOGEL DIRTBIRD GEREAGLE
NEKHEBET ZOPILOTE GALLINAZO
VULVA DOCK PUDENDUM
(PREF.) EPISIO
VUM SNUM

W

W WAW WHISKEY WILLIAM
WA VU KAWA LAWA
WABBLE COCKLE COGGLE HOBBLE
WAGGLE WARBLE WAUBLE WOBBLE
WABBLY COGGLE WAGGLY WOBBLY
WABBY LOON WHABBY
WABRON WAYBERRY
WACKY CRAZY FLAKY WACKO
WIGGY FLAKEY INSANE MENTAL
ERRATIC OFFBEAT
WAD BAT BET BOB PAD COLF LINE
POKE SWAB SWOB WISP WAGER
PLEDGE SCOURER GRAPHITE
WADDING BOMBAST
WADDLE WAG DAIDLE HODDLE
PODDLE TODDLE WALLOP WIDDLE
WAUCHLE
WADDY PEG STICK COWBOY
RUSTLER WHADDIE
WADE FORD WYDE SLOSH PLODGE
PLOUTER PLUTTER
(— IN MUD) LAIR
WADI OUED WASH GULLY RAVINE
WADSET PAWN PLEDGE MORTGAGE
WAFER HOST ABRET OBLEY CACHET
GAUFRE LAVASH MATZOH OFLETE
POPADAM FLATBROD PARTICLE
WAFF WAG FLAP GUST ODOR PUFF
WAVE WHIFF PALTRY FLUTTER
GLIMPSE WINNOW LORBORN
WAFFENSCHMEID, DER
(CHARACTER IN —) GEORG MARIE
CONRAD LIEBENAU STADINGER
(COMPOSER OF —) LORTZING
WAFFIE VAGRANT VAGABOND
WAFFLE GOFER WAFER WAVER
GAUFRE BLATHER
WAFT PUFF WING WHEFT WHIFF
BECKON WINNOW
WAG LUG NOD WIG WIT WOG CARD
CHAP FLAG WAFF WALK DROLL
JOKER ROGUE SHAKE TROLL FARCER
JESTER NICKUM WADDLE WAGGLE
WAGWIT WIGWAG FARCEUR
HUMORIST SLYBOOTS
WAGE FEE PAY WAR HIRE LEVY FIGHT
WADGE WEDGE EMPLOY ENGAGE
PACKET STIPEND OVERTIME
(— BATTLE) STRIKE
WAGER GO BET LAY PUT SET VIE
WED GAGE HOLD PAWN TOSS WOID
BOUND PRIZE RAISE REVIE SPORT
STAKE STOOP WADGE DEPONE
GAMBLE IMPONE LEVANT WEDFEE
STOATER QUINELLA
WAGES FEE PAY UTU GAGE HIRE
MEED STIP GAGES TUNCA REWARD
SALARY PENSION SERVICE STIPEND
GRATUITY LABORAGE PAYCHECK
REQUITAL
WAGGERY JEST ROGUERY
DROLLERY
WAGGISH ARCH DROLL JOKEY
JOCOSE JESTING JOCULAR
PARLOUS ROGUISH WAGSOME
HUMOROUS SPORTIVE
WAGGLE WAG WIGGLE WOBBLE
WOGGLE
WAGON CAR FLY VAN CART CHAR
DRAG DRAY PLOW RACK TEAM
TRAM WAIN WANE BUGGY DILLY
JERKY RULLY TRUCK CAMION
ROLLEY SPIDER TELEGA CAISSON
CHARIOT COASTER FOURGON
SHELVER TUMBREL TUMBRIL
DEMOCRAT LANDSHIP RUNABOUT
WHITETOP
(— WITHOUT SPRINGS) JERKY
TELEGA
(BAGGAGE —) FOURGON
(COVERED —) VAN CARAVAN
TARTANA LANDSHIP CONESTOGA
(KIND OF —) PADDY
(LUMBER —) GILLY
(MINING —) TRAM HUTCH RULLY
ROLLEY
(ROUNDUP —) HOODLUM
(RUSSIAN —) TELEGA KIBITKA
(SCREENED —) ARABA
(STATION —) MICROBUS SUBURBAN
(TEA —) SERVER
WAGONER AURIGA TREKKER
WAINMAN
WAGONETTE BREAK
WAGONLOAD FODDER FOTHER
WAGONMAN FOOTMAN
WAGTAIL MOLLY OATEAR WAGGIE
WASHER MOTACIL WATERIE
SEEDBIRD WASHDISH WASHTAIL
WAHINE WIFE WOMAN FEMALE
VAHINE FEMININE MISTRESS
WAHOO ONO PETO BASSWOOD
EUONYMUS GUARAPUCU
WAIF WEFT STRAY FEEBLE PALTRY
STRAFE CURRENT IGNOBLE WASTREL
WAIL CRY WOW BAWL GURL HOWL
KEEN MOAN RAME YARM CROON
MOURN ULULU LAMENT PLAINT
YAMMER EJULATE PLANGOR
ULULATE ULLAGONE
WAILING WO WOE LAMENT ULULANT
WAIN CART WAGON WEYNE CHARIOT
WAINSCOT CEIL CARDIGAN
WAINSCOTING CEILING PANELING

WAIST JOSIE BASQUE BLOUSE
BODICE HALTER MIDDLE TAILLE
CORSAGE PIERROT
WAISTCOAT VEST BENJY GILET
FECKET JERKIN VESKIT WESKIT
SINGLET CAMISOLE
WAISTER TROUNCER
WAIT BIDE HOLD KEEP LITE PARK
STAY TEND WHET ABIDE ABODE
DEFER HOVER LURCH TARRY WATCH
ATTEND DEPEND EXPECT HARKEN
LAYOUT LINGER
(— A WHILE) TAIHOA
(— FOR) KEEP ABIDE AWAIT ATTEND
EXPECT
(— ON) HOP SEE SERVE INTEND
LACKEY
(— TABLE) HASH SERVE
WAITER MOZO CARHOP COMMIS
DRAWER FLUNKY GARCON HASHER
KIDNEY SALVER TENDER THOMAS
DAPIFER FLUNKEY KELLNER PANNIER
PICCOLO SERVITOR KITMUDGAR
(APPRENTICE —) COMMIS
(WING —) SOMMELIER
WAITING DORMANT
WAITING ROOM LOBBY ANTEROOM
WAITRESS NIPPY HASHER
MOUSMEF PHYLLIS
WAIVE ABEY DEFER EVADE FORGO
ABANDON DECLINE FORSAKE
POSTPONE RENOUNCE RELINQUISH
WAKA CANOE
WAKE WAK CROW NECK PLAY STIR
ALERT HEVEL ROUSE TANGI TRAIL
VIGIL WATCH AROUSE AWAKEN
EXCITE FEATHER
WAKEFUL ALERT WACKER RESTLESS
VIGILANT WALKRIFE WATCHFUL
WAKEFULNESS VIGIL WATCH
INSOMNIA
WAKE-ROBIN ARUM SARA SARAH
TRILLIUM
WAKF WAQF VAKUF VACOUF
WALACHIAN RUMAN VLACH
ROMANESE
WALAHEE ALAHEE
WALAPAI HUALPAI
WALDENSIAN LEONIST PATARIN
VAUDOIS SABOTIER
WALE RIB BEND PICK WEAL WELT
RIDGE WHELP CHOICE HARPIN
STROKE
(PL.) BEND HARPINS
WALES CYMRU CAMBRIA
(PREF.) CAMBRO

WALES

BAY: SWANSEA CARDIGAN TREMADOC
CAPITAL: CARDIFF
COUNTY: FLINT RADNOR DENBIGH
ANGLESEY CARDIGAN MONMOUTH
PEMBROKE
ISLAND: MONA ANGLESEY HOLYHEAD
LAKE: BALA VYRNWY
LANGUAGE: CYMRAEG
MEASURE: COVER CANTRED CANTREF
LESTRAD LISTRED CRANNOCK
MOUNTAIN: SNOWDON
MOUNTAIN RANGE: BERWYN
CAMBRIAN
PEOPLE: CYMRY KYMRY WELSH
PORT: CARDIFF
RIVER: DEE USK WYE TAFF TEME
TOWY TEIFI SEVERN VYRNWY
TOWN: MOLD RHYL ROSS FLINT
TOWYN AMLWCH BANGOR BRECON
RUTHIN CARDIFF NEWPORT
RHONDDA SWANSEA HEREFORD
HOLYHEAD PEMBROKE BRECKNOCK
WATERFALL: CAIN RHAIADR

WALK GO JET MOG FOOT GAIT GANG
HIKE HOOF LAMP PACE PAUT REEL
STEP TROD ALLEE ALLEY ARBOR
LEAVE MARCH PORCH SHANK SLOPE
SPACE STALK TRACE TRACK TRADE
TRAMP TREAD TROOP ATTEND
AVENUE BEHAVE BOUNCE BRIDGE
BROGUE DANDER PASEAR SASHAY
STROKE TODDLE TRAVEL TRUDGE
BALTEUS BERCEAU CRAMBLE
FOOTING GALLERY SHUFFLE
STRETCH TRACHLE TRAIPSE
TURNOUT AMBULATE ARBORWAY
FLAGGING ESPLANADE NAVIGATE
TRAVERSE PROMENADE
PEREGRINATE
(— ABOUT) GLOSH
(— AFFECTEDLY) PRINK
(— AIMLESSLY) PAUP POAP
(— ARROGANTLY) STRUT STRIDE
(— ARROGANTLY —) WALTZ
(— AWKWARDLY) STAUP SHAMBLE
(— BEFORE) PREAMBLE
(— BEHIND BATTLEMENTS) ALURE
(— BRISKLY) LEG SKELP
(— CARELESSLY) JAYWALK
(— CAUTIOUSLY) STALK
(— CLUMSILY) JOLL STUMP LOPPET
(— FOR CATTLE) GANG
(— FOR EXAMINING ENGINE)
GALLERY
(— FOR EXERCISE) HIKE GRIND
(— HEAVILY) PLOD CLOMP CLUMP
STUMP TRAMP LAMPER PLODGE
(— IDLY) DANDER POTTER SAUNTER
(— IN AFFECTED MANNER) MINCE
(— IN SUPERIOR MANNER)
SWAGGER
(— LAME) LIMP HIRPLE HOBBLE
CRIPPLE
(— LEISURELY) AMBLE DANDER
STROLL
(— ON) BEAT TREAD
(— OUT) FLOUNCE

(— **PRIMLY**) MINCE
(— **RAPIDLY**) LAMP LINK STAVE
(— **SHAKILY**) DOTTER
(— **SLOWLY**) JET LAG
(— **SMARTLY**) LINK
(— **STEADILY**) SNOVE SNOOVE
(— **THROUGH WATER**) WADE
(— **UNSTEADILY**) REEL DADDLE
FALTER STAVER STAGGER STUMBLE
(— **WAVERINGLY**) SHEVEL WARPLE
(— **WITH DIFFICULTY**) CRAMBLE
CRAMMEL LOUTHER
(— **WITH JERK**) HIRCH
(— **WITH LOFTY GAIT**) JET
(— **WITH LOOSE GAIT**) GANGLE
(— **WITH OSTENTATION**) PRANCE
(— **WITHOUT LIFTING FEET**) SCUFF
(— **WITH SHUFFLE**) COONJINE
(— **WITH STRIDES**) STAG
(— **WITH TREES**) XYST XYSTUS
ALAMEDA
(**BACKSTAGE** —) BRIDGE
(**COOL** —) FRESCADE
(**COVERED** —) PAWN PORCH
CLOISTER
(**FOLIAGE-COVERED** —) BERCEAU
(**HARD** —) STRAM SWINGE
(**LIMPING** —) GIMP
(**LONG** —) STRAM
(**POMPOUS** —) STRUT
(**PUBLIC** —) XYST XYSTUS ALAMEDA
(**RAISED** —) GALLERY
(**SHADED** —) MALL ARBOR XYSTUS
(**SHORT** —) TURN
(**TEDIOUS** —) TRAIL
(**TREE-PLANTED** —) XYST XYSTUS
(**PL.**) BALTEI
(**PREF.**) AMBULO GRADIO GRADO
WALKER GOER FOOTER FULLER
GANGER FOOTMAN TODDLER
PEDESTRIAN
(**PL.**) FEET
WALKING HOTFOOT PASSANT
AMBULANT GRADIENT TRIPPING
(— **IN SLEEP**) SOMNABULISM
(**PREF.**) BASI BASO
(**SUFF.**) BAT(ES)(IC) GRADE
WALKING STICK BAT CANE GIBBY
KEBBY STICK WADDY KEBBIE
PHASMID SPECTER ASHPLANT
GIBSTAFF WOODHORSE
WALKOUT STRIKE
WALKURE, DIE
(**CHARACTER IN** —) MIME WOTAN
FRICKA HUNDING SIEGMUND
SIEGLINDE BRUNNHILDE
(**COMPOSER OF** —) WAGNER
WALKWAY CATWALK SKYWALK
SIDEWALK
WALL WA DAM FIN MUR WAW BAIL
BELT CELL CORE CRIB CURB DICK
DIKE DRUM DYKE FACE HEAD MURE
PACK SKIN SPUR WING WOGE ATTIC

BOARD CHEEK CRUST DIGUE EMURE
FENCE HEDGE MEURE MURAL PIRCA
SHOJI WOGHE WOUGH BAFFLE
BAILEY BATTER CUTOFF DOKHMA
IMMURE LEADER PARIES PARPEN
PRETIL REBOTE RIPRAP SCREEN
SEPTUM SHIELD VALLUM CHEMISE
CURTAIN ENCLOSE MIZRACH
PARAPET PERPEND PLUTEUS
REREDOS TAMBOUR FIREBACK
SPANDREL TRAVERSE
(— **ABOVE FACADE**) ATTIC
(— **AROUND**) IMMURE
(— **BEHIND ALTAR**) REREDOS
(— **BETWEEN TWO OPENINGS**) PIER
(— **CARRYING CUPOLA**) DRUM
(— **CARRYING ROOF**) BAHUT
(— **CROSSING RAMPART**) SPUR
(— **HANGING**) DRAPERY
(— **IN**) MURE ENTOMB IMMURE
IMPRISON
(— **IN HOCKEY RINK**) BOARD
(— **IN ROMAN ARENA**) SPINA
(— **IN TRUCK**) HEADER
(— **OF BLAST FURNACE**) DAM
INWALL FIREBACK
(— **OF CASTLE**) BARMKIN
(— **OF CLAY**) COTTLE
(— **OF HOOF**) CRUST
(— **OF MINE**) FACE
(— **OF MOUTH**) CHEEK
(— **OF TENT**) KANAT CANAUT
(**BODY** —) MANTLE
(**CIRCULAR** —) CASHEL
(**CORE** —) HEARTING
(**CURVED** —) SWEEP
(**DIVIDING** —) SEPTUM
(**END** — **OF BUILDING**) GABLE
(**FISH** —) LEADER
(**HIGHEST PART OF** —) CRAPWA
(**INNER SLOPE OF** —) BATTER
(**KIND OF** —) TROMBE
(**LOG** —) CRIB
(**LOW** —) BAHUT PODIUM PLUTEUS
(**LOWER PART OF** —) DADO
(**OUTER** — **OF CASTLE**) BAIL BAILEY
(**PEAT** —) COP
(**PUDDLE** —) HEARTING
(**RETAINING** —) CRIB PILING
BULKHEAD
(**SCARPED** —) GHAT
(**SEA** —) GROIN
(**SECONDARY** —) CHEMISE
(**SOMETHING ATTACHED TO** —)
PINUP
(**SUSTAINING** —) RIPRAP
(**THINNED PART OF** —) ALLEGE
(**VENTRAL** —) STERNUM
(**WING** —) AILERON
(**PL.**) PERICARP
(**PREF.**) MURI PARIETO TICHO
(**SUFF.**)
(**COAT OF SPORE** —) SPORIUM

WALLABA APA
WALLADY WURRUP BRUSHER
TOOLACH WURRUNG BOONGARY
KANGAROO PADMELON WHIPTAIL
WALLACHIAN RUMAN
WALLAROO EURO
WALLBOARD GOBO
WALLET JAG JAGG MAIL POKE
BOGET BOUGE BULCH BULGE SCRIP
BUDGET READER SACKET ALFARGA
AI FORJA LEATHER BILLFOLD
NOTECASE POCHETTE
(PREF.) PERO
WALLEYE WHALL SAUGER
LEUCOMA WATCHEYE EXOTROPIA
WALLEYED PIKE DORE DORY JACK
PERCID SALMON WALLEYE PICKEREL
WALLFLOWER CUBA CHEIR GILLY
JACKS KEIRI GELOFER WARRIOR
GILLIVER
WALL HAWKWEED LUNGWORT
WALLOP TAN BEAT BEEN PLOP SLUG
SOCK PASTE POUND VALOP GALLOP
IMPACT WALLOW FLUTTER TROUNCE
FLOUNDER LAMBASTE
WALLOW FADE LAIR ROLL SOIL
SLOSH WALWE GROVEL MUDDLE
WALTER WELTER WITHER SLUDDER
SWELTER FLOUNDER KOMMETJE
VOLUTATE
WALLOWISH FLAT WELSH INSIPID
WALLPAPER GROUND SCENIC
HANGING TENTURE TAPESTRY
WALL PEPPER SEDUM STONECROP
WALL PLATE PAN RASEN
WALL RUE TENTWORT
WALL STREET
(— ORDER) BUY HOLD SELL
WALL-TO-WALL UBIQUITOUS
WALLY TOY FINE SPOIL PAMPER
ROBUST STRONG STURDY SPLENDID
VIGOROUS
WALLY, LA (CHARACTER IN —)
WALLY GELLNER HAGENBACH
(COMPOSER OF —) CATALANI
WALNUT ACAPU NOGAL TRYMA
AKHROT BANNUT HEARTNUT
(BRAZILIAN —) EMBOYA IMBUIA
(PL.) JUGLANS
WALNUT BROWN TAFFY
WALNUT SHELL BOLSTER
WALPI HUALPI
WALRUS MORSE WALTRON
PELAGIAN PINNIPED ROSMARINE
WALT CRANK UNSTEADY
WALTZ LUG CARRY MARCH VALSE
BOSTON BREEZE FLOUNCE
WAMARA CLUBWOOD IRONWOOD
PANOCOCO
WAMBLE ROLL SPIN WAMEL
NAUSEA REVOLVE
WAMBLY FAINT SHAKY
WAME WEM WAMB WYME BELLY

WAMPUM PEAG BEADS DOUGH
FADME HAWOK MONEY PAAGE
SEWAN FATHOM SEAWAN ROANOKE
WAMUS JACKET WAMPUS WARMUS
WAN DIM HAW ASHY FADE PALE PALY
SICK ASHEN BLAKE FAINT WHITE
FEEBLE PALLID SALLOW GHASTLY
LANGUID
WANAPUM SOKULK
WAND ROD VARE YARD BATON STAFF
STICK VERGE VIRGA FERULA THYRSE
WATTLE RHABDOS THYRSUS
CADUCEUS
(JESTER'S —) BAUBLE
(PREF.) RHABD(O)
WANDER BAT BUM ERR GAD WAG
HAAK HAIK MAZE MUCK RAKE
RAVE ROAM ROIL ROLL ROVE WALK
WILL WORE DAVER DRIFT GLAIK
KNOCK RANGE ROGUE SHACK
SLOSH STRAY TAVER TRAIK VAGUE
WAIVE WAVER CANDER CRUISE
DANDER DAUNER FORAGE LOITER
MITHER MOIDER MUCKER PALMER
PERUSE RAMBLE RANGLE STRAKE
STROLL SWERVE WILDER MEANDER
TRAFFIC TRAIPSE VAGRATE VANDYKE
ABERRATE CUTICULA SQUANDER
STRAGGLE STRAVAGE STRAVAIG
(— ABOUT) DIVAGATE
(— ABSTRACTEDLY) MOON
(— AIMLESSLY) SWAN SLOSH TRACE
MEANDER
(— AS A VAGABOND) SHACK
(— AS A VAGRANT) LOITER
(— AT RANDOM) SQUANDER
(— ERRATICALLY) SWASH
(— FROM DIRECT COURSE)
STRAGGLE
(— FROM PLACE TO PLACE) WAG
(— IDLY) HAKE LOUT MAUNDER
SHACKLE
(— IN DELIRIUM) DWALE DWALL
(— IN MIND) DAVER DANDER DELIRE
(— LEISURELY) RUMMEL
(— RESTLESSLY) FEEK
WANDERER HOBO WAIF ROVER
TRAMP VAGUE RANGER DRIFTER
PILGRIM RAMBLER VAGRANT
FUGITIVE RUNAGATE TRAVELER
VAGABOND
(AUTHOR OF —) FOURNIER
(CHARACTER IN —) FRANTZ GALAIS
MILLIE SEUREL YVONNE AUGUSTIN
BLONDEAU FRANCOIS MEAULNES
VALENTINE CHARPENTIER
WANDERING GAD ROAM WAFF
ERROR STRAY VAGUE ARRANT
ASTRAY ERRANT MOBILE ROVING
VAGANT VAGOUS DEVIOUS
NOMADIC ODYSSEY VAGANCY
VAGRANT WINDING ABERRANT
FLOATING FUGITIVE PELASGIC

PLANETAL PLANETIC RAMBLING
RESTLESS TRAILING VAGABOND
WINDRING ITINERANT MIGRATORY
PEREGRINE
(PREF.) PLAN(O) VAGO
(SUFF.) PLANIA

WANDERING JEW (AUTHOR OF —)
SUE
(CHARACTER IN —) ROSE HARDY
RODIN SIMON DJALMA SAMUEL
BAUDOIN GABRIEL JACQUES
ADRIENNE AGRICOLA AIGRIGNY
DAGOBERT FRANCOIS HERODIAS
RENNEPONT CARDOVILLE

WANDFLOWER GALAX SPARAXIS

WANDOROBO WAASI

WAND-SHAPED VIRGATE

WANE GO EBB SET WELK WILK
ABATE DECAY UNWAX WANZE
REPINE DECLINE DWINDLE
DECREASE
(— OF MOON) WADDLE

WANGA CHARM SPELL OUANGA
WONGAH SORCERY

WANGLE FAKE SHAKE WIGGLE
FINAGLE

WANIGAN ARK CHEST COFFER
WANGUN

WANT HURT LACK LIKE MISS NEED
OONT PINE VOID WANE WONT
CRAVE FAULT FORGO BESOIN
CHOOSE DEARTH DEFECT DESIRE
MISTER PENURY PLIGHT ABSENCE
BEGGARY BLEMISH BORASCA
DEFAULT MISEASE NEEDHAM
POVERTY REQUIRE VACANCY
MISCHIEF WANTROKE
(— EXCEEDINGLY) DIE ACHE
(— OF APPETITE) ANOREXY
ANOREXIA
(— OF CONTROL) ACRASY
(— OF ENERGY) ATONY
(— OF FEELING) APATHY
(— OF GOOD SENSE) FOLLY
(— OF LIBERTY) RESTRAINT
(— OF PROPER CARE) NEGLIGENCE
(— OF REST) UNRO
(— OF SPIRIT) FOZINESS
POLTROONERY
(— OF SUCCESS) FAILURE
(— OF VARIETY) MONOPOLY
(— OF VIGOR) DELICACY

WANTAGE ULLAGE

WANTING LACK VOID WANE ALACK
MINUS ABSENT LACKING MISSING
INDIGENT
(— ORIGINALITY) BANAL

WANTON JAY NAG RIG DAFT GOLE
IDLE LEWD NICE RAGE SKIT CADGY
DALLY LIGHT SAUCY GIGLET GIGLOT
HARLOT HAUNTY LACHES LUBRIC
RAKISH RIGSBY TICKLE TOYING
TOYISH UNRULY COLTISH FULSOME

GIGGISH HAGGARD IMMORAL
KITTOCK LUSTFUL PAPHIAN RIGGISH
RIOTOUS SMICKER WAYWARD
FLAGRANT LUSCIOUS MISTRESS
PETULANT PLAYSOME RUMBELOW
SKITTISH SLIPPERY SPITEFUL
SPORTIVE UNCHASTE

WANTONNESS FOLLY PRIDE SPORT
RAGERY SUCCUDRY SURQUIDY

WAP BIND BLOW WHOP WRAP BLAST
FIGHT KNOCK STORM TRUSS
BUNDLE STRIKE

WAPITI ELK ALCE DEER LOSH LUSH
STAG MARAL MOOSE CERVID
WAMPOOSE

WAR WIN CAMP FEUD MART FIGHT
SWORD WORSE WORST BATTLE
CONTEND CRUSADE CONFLICT
GUERILLA OVERCOME
(OPPONENT OF —) DOVE PEACENIK
(RELIGIOUS —) JEHAD JIHAD
(PREF.) BELLI MACHO POLEMO

WAR AND PEACE (AUTHOR OF —)
TOLSTOY
(CHARACTER IN —) LISE ELLEN
MARYA ANDREY PIERRE ROSTOV
ANATOLE BEZUHOV KURAGIN
KUTUZOV NATASHA NIKOLAY
VASSILY NAPOLEON BOLKONSKY
NIKOLUSHKA

WARBLE SING CAROL CHANT CHIRL
CHIRM SHAKE TRILL YODEL JARGON
RALISH RELISH WARNEL WORMIL
DESCANT VIBRATE WOURNIL

WARBLE FLY OXFLY BOTFLY GADFLY
OESTRID OESTRIAN

WARBLER CUT KIT CHAT SMEU
WREN FITTE PEGGY CANARY
EYSOGE REELER SMEUTH SYLVIA
TITIEN CREEPER CROMBEC FANTAIL
HAYBIRD HAYSUCK PITBIRD REDPOLL
SYLVIID TROCHIL BEAMBIRD
BLACKCAP FAUVETTE MALURINE
MOCKBIRD OVENBIRD PINCPINC
REDSTART REEDBIRD RIRORIRO
TROCHILUS CHIFFCHAFF

WAR CLUB MAR MER MERE MERAI
MARREE

WAR CRY ALALA BANZAI SLOGAN

WARD CARE GUARD MAHAL VICUS
WAIRD WATCH ALUMNA BARRIO
CALPUL DEFEND ROWENA KEEPING
NATUARY PROTEGE CALPOLLI
CONTRADA
(— OFF) FEND WEAR WERE AVERT
AWARD FENCE PARRY REPEL
STAVE SHIELD BUCKLER EXPIATE
FORFEND
(— OF WORKHOUSE) SPIKE
(HOSPITAL —) ICU

WARDAGE WARTH

WARDEN ALCADE DIZDAR PORTER
RANGER REGENT ROLAND WARNER

ALCAIDE HOGMACE LEATMAN
ROWLAND BEARWARD CLAVIGER
(AUTHOR OF —) TROLLOPE
(CHARACTER IN —) TOM BOLD JOHN
SUSAN FINNEY TOWERS ABRAHAM
ELEANOR GRANTLY HARDING
SEPTIMUS HAPHAZARD QUIVERFUL
THEOPHILUS

WARDER PORTER GUARDER HEIMDAL
TURNKEY WATCHMAN BEEFEATER

WARDROBE KAS CLOSET VESTRY
ALMIRAH ARMOIRE VESTUARY

WARE CLOTH GOODS SPEND FABRICS
SEAWEED SQUANDER
(CERAMIC —) SPODE BENNINGTON
(CLOISONNE —) SHIPPO
(ENAMELED —) BILSTON COALPORT
(GILT —) ORMOLU
(INFERIOR —S) SLUM
(JAPANESE —) IMARI YAYOI
(JAPANESE CERAMIC —) SETO BIZEN
KARATSU
(KIND OF —) RAKU SETO TING BIZEN
CHIEN SANDA YAYOI KUTANI
MINTON KARATSU WHIELDON
(KIND OF JAPANESE POTTERY —)
SANDA
(MAJOLICA —) DERUTA
(PORCELAIN —) CHINA IMARI BERLIN
(UNGLAZED —) BISQUE
(PL.) TROKE CHAFFER TROGGIN

WAREHOUSE GOLA HONG ETAPE
GOLAH STORE BODEGA I UNDUK
GODOWN STAITH ALMACEN
FUNDUCK SPICERY STOWAGE
ENTREPOT MAGAZINE SERAGLIO

WARFARE WAR ARMS IRON ARMOR
BATTLE PSYWAR MILITIA CONFLICT
(CHEMICAL — AGENT) SARIN
(NONAGGRESSIVE —) SITZKRIEG
(PETTY —) GUERILLA GUERRILLA
(PSYCHOLOGICAL —) PSYWAR
(SUFF.) MACHIA MACHY

WARHEAD MIRV

WAR-HORSE CHARGER COURSER
DESTRER TROOPER DESTRIER

WARILY TIPTOE GINGERLY

WARINESS CAUTEL CAUTION
DISTRUST WARESHIP WARIMENT

WARKLOOM TOOL WARKLUME

WARLIKE WARLY MARTIAL CAVALIER
FIGHTING MILITARY BELLICOSE
(NOT —) IMBELLIC

WARLOCK IMP WITCH SPRITE
WARLOW WIZARD CONJUROR
SORCERER

WARLORD TUCHUN

WARM HOT LEW LOO RUG BASK
BEEK KEEN LEWD MILD CALID CHAFE
EAGER FRESH MALMY MUNGY
SLACK TEPID TOAST ACHAFE
ARDENT BIRSLE DEVOUT DIGEST
FOSTER GENIAL HEARTY HEATED
RIZZLE TENDER TOASTY CHERISH
CLEMENT CORDIAL GLOWING
THERMAL ZEALOUS FRIENDLY
PRESSING SANGUINE
(— UP) SCORE
(MODERATELY —) LEW SLACK TEPID
(PREF.) CAL(E)(I)(ORI)

WARMHEARTED KIND TENDER
FRIENDLY GENEROUS

WARMING FOVENT

WARMOUTH BIGMOUTH FLATFISH
SACALAIT

WARMTH GLOW HEAT LIFE ZEAL
ARDOR LEWTH ENERGY FERVOR
ARDENCY PASSION CALIDITY
FERVENCY
(— OF ADDRESS) UNCTION
(— OF MANNER) EMPRESSEMENT
(INNER —) JUICE

WARN REDE WARD WERN ALERT
AREAD DETER WEIRD ADVERT
ADVISE EXHORT INFORM CAUTION
COMMAND COUNSEL GARNISH
PREVISE ADMONISH THREATEN
(— OFF) FORBID

WARNING AHEM ITEM ALARM
CHECK KNELL BEACON CAVEAT
LESSON NOTICE OFFICE SAMPLE
SIGNAL TIPOFF AVISION CALLING
CAUTION EXAMPLE GRIFFIN JIGGERS
MEMENTO PRESAGE PRESAGE
SUMMONS DOCUMENT GARDYLOO
MONITION PREMONITION
(— OF DISASTER) DIRE
(— ON CHART) VIGIA
(— SIGNAL) RED REDFLAG REDLIGHT
(AIR-RAID —) ALERT
(ARCHERY —) FAST
(DANGER —) VIGIA

WARP CUP WEB BIAS CANE CAST
LIFT WARF WERP WIND ANGLE
CHAIN CHOKE CRAWL CROOK GEYZE
KEDGE PORRY THRAW TWINE WEAVE
BUCKLE CHEESE DEFORM WASHIN
DEFLECT DISTORT SKELLER
(— IN WEAVING) CRAM
(PREF.) HIST(O)

WARPED WRY BUCKLED GNARLED
HOUSING

WARPER BALLER

WARPING BOW PANDATION

WARRAGAL WILD DINGO HORSE
OUTLAW

WARRANT ABLE EARN WARN AMRIT
BERAT FIANT PRESS SANAD VOUCH
AMRITA ASSERT BRANCH BREVET
CAPIAS COUPON DOCKET ENSURE
INSURE PARDON PERMIT PLEVIN
POLICY POTENT SUNNUD TICKET
UPHOLD WARDOG BEHIGHT CAPTION
DESERVE JUSTIFY PRECEPT PROMISE
GUARANTY MITTIMUS
(CUSTOMS —) TRANSIRE

WARRANTED VALID
WARRANT OFFICER BOSN BOSUN
BOATSWAIN
WARRAU GUARANO
WARREN SLUM CONYGER WARRANT
WARRIOR TOA WER EARL HERO
KEMP RINK WEER BERNE FREIK
FREKE HAGEN LLUDD SEPAD SINGH
THANE THEGN OSSIAN WARMAN
WEAPON FIGHTER SOLDIER
STARKAD WARWOLF ZERBINO
CHAMPION RODOMONT SHARDANA
STARKATH SWORDMAN WARFARER
(— CLASS) MAGANI
(— OF NOBLE RANK) EARL
(AMERICAN INDIAN —) BRAVE
SANNUP
(BOASTFUL —) RODOMONT
(BRYTHONIC —) LLUDD
(BURGUNDIAN —) HAGEN
(FEMALE —) AMAZON SHIELDMAY
(GREEK —) AJAX
(IRISH —) FENIAN
(KAFFIR —S) IMPI
(MUSLIM —) GAZI GHAZI
(NOTED —) THANE THEGN
(SCANDINAVIAN —) BERSERK
(SCOTTISH —) ZERBINO
(TROJAN —) AGENOR
(VALIANT —) TOA
(VIRGIN —) CAMILLA
(PL.) IMPI CHIVALRY GAMMADIM
WARSHIP GUIDE RAZEE WAFTER
CRUISER MONITOR SULTANA
SULTANE CORVETTE
(— OF OLD) RAM
WART RAT WRAT AMBURY ANBURY
SYCOMA PUSTULE VERRUCA
VERRUGA EPIDERMA PAPILLOMA
(POTATO —) CANKER
(PREF.) VERRUCI
WART HOG EMGALLA
WARTLIKE PYRENOID
WART SNAKE XENODERM
WARTY MURICATE MURICATED
PAPILLOSE
WARY SHY CAGY WISE AWARE
CAGEY CANNY DOWNY HOOLY
LEERY TENDER CAREFUL GUARDED
PRUDENT WAREFUL CAUTIOUS
SKITTISH VIGILANT WATCHFUL
WAS VAS WIS WUZ WYS PAST
WISSHE
(— ABLE) COULD
(— NOT) NAS
(I —) CHWAS
WASH DO BOG FEN LAG LAP NET
TUB BEER BUCK EDDY HOSE HUSH
LAVE SILT SUDS WADI BATHE CLEAN
CLEAR DOLLY DRAFF ERODE MARSH
RINSE SCRUB SLOSH SOUSE SWILL
BUDDLE CRADLE DOLLIE LOTION
PURIFY SLOOSH SLUICE SOZZLE

STREAM ALLUVIO CLEANSE
LAUNDER SHAMPOO ALLUVIUM
EYEWATER LAVAMENT LAVATORY
(— A GAS) SCRUB
(— AWAY) GULL
(— BY TREADING IN WATER) TRAMP
(— DOWN) SIND SOOGEE
(— EDGE) LIP
(— FOR GOLD) PAN
(— GIVEN TO SWINE) DRAFF
(— GRAVEL) ROCK
(— HAIR) SHAMPOO
(— IN LYE) BUCK
(— LIGHTLY) RINSE
(— OFF) DETERGE
(— ORE) TYE HUTCH BUDDLE CRADLE
STRAKE
(— OUT) SIND ELUTE FLUSH LAVAGE
(— ROUGHLY) SLUSH
(— THOROUGHLY) SCOUR
(— THROAT) GARGLE
(— VIGOROUSLY) SLOSH
(— WITH BROOM) TYE
(— WITH COSMETIC) SURFLE
SURPHUL
(DRY —) ARROYA ARROYO
WASHBASIN LAVER LAVABO
LAVATORY ALJOFAINA
WASHCLOTH FLANNEL
WASHED ABLUTED
(— UP) SHOT THROUGH
WASHED-OUT ANEMIC ANAEMIC
WASHER BUR BURR DRUM ROVE
CLOUT BUTTON RONDEL SOURER
GROMMET LEATHER RACCOON
COTTEREL LAVENDER RONDELLE
SCRUBBER
WASHERMAN DHOBI DHOBIE
LAVANDERO
WASHERWOMAN LAUNDER
WASHING LAG BATH LAVAGE
SLOOSH LAUNDRY ABLUTION
LAVAMENT LAVATION
(PL.) ELUATE
WASHING MACHINE DASHWHEEL

WASHINGTON
CAPITAL: OLYMPIA
COLLEGE: GONZAGA WHITMAN
EVERGREEN WHITWORTH
COUNTY: ASOTIN KITSAP SKAGIT
YAKIMA CLALLAM KITTITAS
DAM: COULEE
INDIAN: HOH LUMMI MAKAH TWANA
SAMISH SKAGIT YAKIMA CHINOOK
CLALLAM COWLITZ SANPOIL
CHIMAKUM OKANAGON
LAKE: SOAP MOSES CHELAN OZETTE
CUSHMAN QUINAULT
MOUNTAIN: JACK TUNK ADAMS
LEMEI LOGAN MOSES SLOAN
QUARTZ SIMCOE STUART OLYMPUS
RAINIER SHUKSAN

MOUNTAIN RANGE: KETTLE CASCADE
OLYMPIC
NICKNAME: CHINOOK EVERGREEN
RIVER: SNAKE YAKIMA COLUMBIA
SOUND: PUGET
STATE BIRD: GOLDFINCH
STATE TREE: HEMLOCK
TOWN: OMAK PASCO TACOMA
YAKIMA EPHRATA EVERETT
OTHELLO SEATTLE SPOKANE
LONGVIEW

WASHOUT FLOP STUMOR FAILURE
WASHROOM BASEMENT LAVATORY
WASHSTAND COMMODE
WASHTUB FLASKET
WASHY SOFT WEAK LOOSE MOIST
FEEBLE PALLID WATERY DILUTED
SHILPIT
WASP MASON SPHEX WHAMP
WOPSE BEMBEX DAUBER DIGGER
HORNET TIPHIA TREMEX VESPID
CYNIPID DRYINID EUMENID MASARID
SCOLIID SERPHID SIRICID SPHECID
STINGER ACULEATE MUTILLID
POMPILID
(KIND OF —) MASON
WASPISH TART TESTY FRETFUL
PEEVISH CHOLERIC SNAPPISH
WASSAIL DRINK TOAST PLEDGE
CAROUSE REVELRY CAROUSAL
WASTE EAT FUD GOB TED BURN
GNAW JUNK LOSS PASS PEAK ROSS
SACK TEAR TINE WEAR WILD DROSS
EXILE HAVOC SCRAP SLOOM SLOTH
SLOUM SPILL TABID THRUM BANGLE
BEZZLE COMMON DEBRIS DESERT
DEVOUR DIDDLE DRAFFY DRIVEL
ELAPSE EXPEND FOREST GARBLE
GOUSTY LAVISH MOLDER MUDDLE
PADDLE PERISH RAVAGE REFUSE
SCATHE SPILTH WESTEN CONNACH
CONSUME EXHAUST FRITTER
GARBAGE MULLOCK RUBBISH
SLATTER CONFOUND DEMOLISH
SLATTERN SQUANDER
(— AWAY) BATE MELT DECAY DWINE
SWAIN SWEAL TRAIK WANZE TABEFY
WINDLE DWINDLE FORPINE MISLIKE
DISSOLVE EMACIATE FORSPEND
MACERATE
(— GRADUALLY) WEAR ABSUME
(— IN DRUNKENNESS) SOT
(— IN RIOT) BEZZLE
(— OF INK) INKSHED
(— OF SILK COCOONS) KNUB
(— TIME) FOOL FRIG IDLE DALLY
DEFER DRILL DAWDLE DIDDLE
FOOTER FOOTLE LOITER DRINGLE
FOOSTER GAUSTER
(COAL —) SLUDGE
(COTTON —) FLUKE SLASHER
SPOOLER

(FOOD —) SLOP
(LIQUID —) DRIPPING EFFLUENT
(MINING —) GOB GOAF
(RADIOACTIVE —) RADWASTE
(WOOL —) FUD MUNGO GARNETT
(YARN —) THRUM EYEBROW
WASTEBASKET HELL HELLBOX
WASTED IDLE FORWORN RAVAGED
DECREPIT
WASTEFUL LAVISH PROFUSE
DESOLATE PRODIGAL SPENDFUL
WASTEFULNESS WAIT UNTHRIFT
WASTELAND MOOR HEATH
CURAGH DESERT CURRACH
WASTER THIEF LEISTER WASTREL
PRODIGAL
WASTING FRET DECAY LIGHT
AWASTE ATROPHY CACHEXY
EXEDENT MISLIKE PREYING TABIFIC
CACHEXIA PHTHISIS SYNTEXIS
TABESCENCE CONSUMPTION
(— AWAY) TABES MARASMUS
SYNTECTIC TABEFACTION
(PREF.) PHTHISIO TABE TABI TABO
(PROGRESSIVE —) TABO
WASTREL WAIF LOSEL REFUSE
WASTER ROUNDER VAGABOND
STROYGOOD
WATCH EYE FOB NIT SEE SPY TAB
DIAL EGEY GLIM GLOM HACK HEED
KEEP LOOK MARK MIND PIPE TOUT
TWIG VACH WAIK WAKE WARD YARD
CLOCK GUARD SCOUT OPIAL SUPER
TIMER VERGE VIGIL VIRGE WAKEN
WHEEL BEHOLD DEFEND DIACLE
FOLLOW HUNTER PERDUE SENTRY
SHADOW TICKER TICTIC TURNIP
WAKING YEMING ORSERVE OVERSEE
ROSKOPF STRIKER THIMBLE
TOMPION HOROLOGE MEDITATE
SENTINEL SPECTATE TICKTICK
STEMWINDER
(— FOR) TENT ABIDE AWAIT
(— OF ARMY) BIVOUAC
(— ON THE SLY) FOX
(— OVER) HOLD KEEP TEND TENT
GUARD ATTEND OVERLOOK
(— OVER DEAD) LIKEWAKE
LYKEWALK
(— PEOPLE EATING) GROAK
(— QUIETLY) HINT
(— THAT STRIKES) STRIKER
REPEATER
(— UNIT) LIGNE
(— WITH HINGED COVER) HUNTER
(ALARM —) TATLER TATTLER
(CLOSE —) SCRUTINY
(NAUTICAL —) HACK DOGWATCH
(NIGHT —) LICHWAKE LYKEWAKE
(PART OF —) BOW FOB CASE DIAL
FACE HAND STEM BEZEL COVER
CROWN FRAME CHAPTER CRYSTAL
DISPLAY NUMERAL SHOULDER

(SUFF.) SCOPE SCOPIC SCOPUS SCOPY

WATCHBAND WRISTER WRISTLET

WATCH CHAIN GUARD SLANG

WATCH CRYSTAL LUNET LUNETTE

WATCHDOG CUR GARM GARMR MATIN BANDOG KRATIM CERBERUS

WATCHER VEIL ARGUS WAKER VIEWER WAITER MUSAHAR SPOTTER WATCHMAN

WATCHFUL IRA ALERT AWARE CANNY CHARY ERECT TENTY WAKER TENTIE WACKER ANXIOUS GUARDED JEALOUS LIDLESS WAKEFUL VIGILANT WAKERIFE WAUKRIFE OBSERVANT

WATCHFULNESS OUTLOOK JEALOUSY

WATCH GLASS CRYSTAL LUNETTE

WATCHING VIGIL CUSTODY CONSERVATION

WATCHMAN FLAG MINA WAIT GUARD SCOUT VIGIL WATCH ASKARI BANTAY GHAFIR SENTRY SERENO SHOMER TOOTER WAITER WARDEN WARDER BELLMAN CHARLEY GUARDER TALLIAR WAKEMAN CHOKIDAR SENTINEL
(NIGHT —) SERENO CHARLIE

WATCHTOWER WARD BEACON GARRET MIZPAH SENTRY ATALAYA LOOKOUT MIRADOR BARBICAN SENTINEL SPECCHIE

WATCHWORD CRY MAXIM ALERTA ENSIGN PAROLE SIGNAL NAYWORD PASSWORD

WATCH WORKS MOVEABLE

WATER EAU TJI AGUA AQUA BATH BRIM BROO BURN LAGE LAKE POND POOL TIDE WAVE ABYSS BILGE FLUME LOUGH LYMPH RIVER TABBY TEARS TUBIG BALLOW BAREGE CAMLET CONGEE CONJEE PAWNEE PHLEGM SALIVA STREAM VADOSE WATHER AQUATIC CRYSTAL JAVELLE IRRIGATE SNOWMELT
(— AFTER BOILING RICE) CONGEE CONJEE
(— AS REFUGE FOR GAME) SOIL
(— AT THE MOUTH) DROOL
(— BY CALENDERING) TABBY
(— FOR BREWING) BURN
(— IN SOIL) HOLARD
(— IN WEIR) LASHER
(— REDDISH WITH IRON) RIDDAM
(— RUNNING AGAINST MAIN CURRENT) EDDY
(— SPIRIT) KELPIE
(— SURROUNDED BY ICE) WAKE
(— TRAIL) WAKE
(— UNDER PRESSURE) HUSH
(ARCH OF —) CURL
(BAPTISMAL —) LAVER

(BARLEY —) PTISAN
(BOTTOM — OF SEA) ABYSS
(BOUNDARY —) SHARD
(BUBBLING —) SPRUDEL
(DEEP —) BALLOW
(DIRTY —) SAUR PUDDLE
(FAST-MOVING —) SOUP
(FEN —) SUDS
(FROZEN —) ICE FROST
(FROZEN FLAVORED — ON A STICK) POPSICLE
(HARD —) ICE
(HOLY —) HYSSOP
(HOT —) SOUP
(LIVING —) RASA
(MINERAL —) VICHY SELTER SELTZER APOLLINARIS
(OPEN —) POLYNYA
(QUININE —) TONIC
(RED —) RESP RIDDAM
(ROUGH —) SEA
(RUNNING —) SEA
(SALT —) BRACK BRINE SEAWATER
(SOAPY —) SUDS GRAITH
(SPLASH OF —) FLASH
(STILL —) KELD LOGIN
(SULPHUR —) BAREGE
(SURFACE OF —) RYME
(SWEETENED —) AMRIT AMRITA
(WASHING —) LAVATION
(WHITE — AFTER WAVE) SOUP
(PL.) APSU
(PREF.) AQUA AQUEO AQUI AQUO HIDRO HYDAT(O) HYDR(O)
(GO THROUGH —) SILLO
(STAGNANT —) TELMAT(O)
(SUFF.) LIMNION YDATIS

WATER ARUM DRAGON

WATER BAG CHAGUL MATARA MUSSUK

WATER BATH BAINMARIE

WATERBIRD ALCATRAS

WATER BOA ANACONDA

WATER BOTTLE CARAFE

WATERBRAIN GID

WATERBUCK COB CHUZWI DEFASSA WATERDOE

WATER BUFFALO KERBAU CARABAO
(WILD —) ARNA

WATER CARRIER BHISTI AGUADOR BHEESTY

WATER CART DILLY

WATER CASK WINGER

WATER CHESTNUT LING CALTROP SALIGOT SINGHARA

WATER CHINQUAPIN BONNET NELUMBO WANKAPIN YONCOPIN RATTLENUT

WATER CLOCK GHURRY CLEPSYDRA

WATER CLOSET PETTY PRIVY STOOL SANITARY NECESSARY

WATER COCK KORA
WATERCOLOR GRAPHIC
WATERCOURSE
(ALSO SEE STREAM AND RIVER) RUN
URN AGOS DIKE DYKE GOTE HAHR
KHOR LADE LEAT REAN WADI WADY
YORA AUWAI BAYOU BROOK CANAL
CANEL COWAL DITCH DRAIN RHINE
ARROYO CANNEL COURSE FURROW
GUTTER KENNEL NULLAH CHANNEL
TRINKET
WATERCRAFT SAILER
WATERCRESS EKER KERS CARSE
KERSE BILDERS NOSESMART
WATER DIVINER DOWSER
WATER DOG OTTER WATERRUG
WATER DRINKER HYDROPOT
WATERED MOIRE TABBY
WATERFALL LIN LYN FALL FOSS
LINN SALT CHUTE FORCE SAULT
SHOOT SPOUT LASHER CASCADE
CATADUPE CATARACT OVERFALL
(FROZEN —) ICEFALL
WATER FENNEL EDGEWEED
WATER FERN PILLWORT
WATER FLEA CYCLOPS DAPHNID
WATERFOWL WADER SWIMMER
WATERFRONT PRAYA
WATERGALL WINDDOG WINDGALL
JELLYFISH
WATER GATE SLUICE
WATER GERMANDER SCORDIUM
WATER HEMLOCK CICUTA
COWBANE DEATHIN JELLICA
WATER HEN GALLINULE
WATER HOG BUSHPIG CAPYBARA
WATER HOLE DUB CHARCO TINAJA
ALBERCA
WATER ICE SHERBET
WATERINESS AQUEITY AQUOSITY
WATERING EPIPHORA RIGATION
WATER JUG GAMLA GOMLAH
GOOLAH
WATERLEAF SHAWNY NEMOPHILA
WATERLESS
(PREF.) ANHYDR(O)
WATER LETTUCE QUIAPO
WATER LILY DUCK LOTOS LOTUS
WOCAS WOKAS BOBBIN CANDOCK
NELUMBO CAMALOTE NENUPHAR
WATERLOGGED SOGGY SODDEN
SWAMPY EDEMATOUS SATURATED
WATERMAN MERMAN QUENCH
OARSMAN
WATERMARK CROWN TIDEMARK
WATERMARKED LAID
WATERMELON PEPO GOURD
MELON TSAMA CITRUL SANDIA
ANGURIA MILLION CUCURBIT
PEPONIDA PEPONIUM SKIPJACK
WATER MOCCASIN CONGO
WATER NEWT ASK TRITON
WATER OPOSSUM YAPOK YAPOCK

WATER OUZEL PIET OOZEL OWZEL
DIPPER DUCKER
WATER PARSNIP SKIRRET
WATER PEPPER LAKEWEED
WATER PIMPERNEL BROOKWEED
WATER PLANT LIMU AQUATIC
WATER PLANTAIN ALISMA
THRUMWORT
WATERPOT FONTAL
WATERPROOF RAINCOAT
(— MATERIAL) KERATOL
WATER RAIL RUNNER BILCOCK
MOORHEN OARCOCK
WATER RAT VOLE CRABER
MUSKRAT WATERRUG
WATER SCORPION NEPID
WATERSHED BROW DIVIDE DIVORT
SNOWSHED
WATER SHIELD FANWORT
DEERFOOD FROGLEAF
WATERSKIN MASHAK MATARA
MUSSUK MUSSACK MUSSICK
WATER SOLDIER PONDWORT
WATER SPIRIT ARIEL KELPY KELPIE
UNDINE
WATERSPOUT RONE CANAL SPATE
SPOUT VORTEX PRESTER TWISTER
CATARACT GARGOYLE
WATER SPRITE KELPY KELPIE
WATER STRIDER SKATER SKIMMER
SKIPPER SKETCHER
WATER THRUSH KICKUP WAGTAIL
WATER TIGER DYTISCID
WATERTIGHT THEAT THEET TIGHT
STANCH THIGHT STAUNCH
WATER WALLY BATAMOTE
WATERWAY GUT CASH DOCK HOLE
LODE DITCH INLET ARTERY SEAWAY
CULVERT FAIRWAY HIGHWAY
IGARAPE
(ARTIFICIAL —) LEAD CANAL
(DUTCH —) ZEE
(PL.) SCUPPERS
WATERWHEEL NORIA SAKIA
SAGEER SAKIEH DANAIDE SAKIYEH
TYMPANUM
WATERY WET LASH PALE SICK THIN
WHEY BOGGY MOIST SAMMY
WASHY BLASHY FLASHY LIQUID
PALLID SEROSE SEROUS SWASHY
AQUATIC AQUEOUS CHOROUS
HYDROUS PHLEGMY SANIOUS
HUMOROUS HYDATOID ICHOROUS
SKINKING
WATT (ONE BILLION —S) GIGAWATT
WATTLE GILL JOWL PLAT SALY TWIG
WAND BOREE COOBA FRITH MULGA
SALLY SALWE STAVE STICK HURDLE
JEWING JOLLOP LAPPET SALLOW
BLUEBUSH CARUNCLE
WATTLEBIRD IAO MOHO MINER
MANUAO MAOMAO GILLBIRD
WATTLE CROW KOKAKO

WAVE FAN FLY JAW SEA WAW BECK FLAG FLAP GUST LUMP PERM SUFF SULK SWAY WAFF WAFT WAWE YTHE BLESS CRIMP FLASH FLOAT FLOTE PULSE SHAKE SURGE SWELL SWING BILLOW COMBER FLAUNT MARCEL RIPPLE ROLLER WAFFLE WINNOW BREAKER BRIMMER CRIMPLE DECUMAN FEATHER FLICKER FLUTTER TSUNAMI WHIFFLE ARTEFACT BRANDISH FLOURISH GRAYBACK UNDULATE UNIPULSE WHISTLER WHITECAP
(— ABOUT) WAMPISH
(— OF EXCITATION) IMPULSE
(— OF FLAG) DOT DASH
(— OF SHIP) BONE
(ARCH OF —) CURL
(BRAIN —) DELTA
(ELECTRIC —) STRAY CARRIER
(ELECTROMAGNETIC —) ALFVEN
(HAIR —) MARCEL PERMANENT
(LARGE —) HEAVY
(LITTLE —) RIPPLE
(RIDE A —) BODYSURF
(SOLITARY —) SOLITON
(SPIN —) MAGNON
(TIDAL —) AEGIR EAGER EAGRE
(PL.) SURF
(PREF.) CUMA CYM(I)(O) CYMATO KYM(I)(O) KYMATO ONDA ONDO UNDI

WAVER HALT REEL SWAG SWAY VARY CHECK DAKER DOUBT FLOAT SWALE SWING WIVER DACKER DAIKER DITHER FALTER MAMMER QUIVER SWERVE TEETER TOTTER WABBLE WAFFLE WOBBLE BALANCE FLICKER FLITTER FLUTTER STAGGER SWITHER VIBRATE HESITATE VACILLATE

WAVERING WAW WAVY WEAK WAUCH WAUGH FICKLE GROGGY UNSURE WAVERY WIGGLY DUBIOUS LAMBENT SHUTTLE DOUBTFUL FLEXUOSE FLEXUOUS FLICKERY HOVERING WAVEROUS PENDULOUS

WAVERLEY (AUTHOR OF —) SCOTT
(CHARACTER IN —) EVAN LEAN ROSE VOHR ALICE COSMO DAVIE FLORA DONALD FERGUS STUART CHARLES EVERARD MACIVOR GARDINER PEMBROKE WAVERLEY GELLATLEY MACCOMBICH BRADWARDINE

WAVINESS CRIMP

WAVING UNDE WAFT AWAVE OUNDY UNDEE WAFTURE FLOURISH
(— OF WEAPON) FLOURISH

WAVY ONDE ONDE UNDY CRISP MOIRE SNAKY UNDEE CRIMPY FLECKY REPAND SNAKEY UNDATE WIGGLY BUCKLED CRINKLY CURVING ENDATED ROLLING SINUATE

UNDULAR ENRIDGED FLEXUOUS ONDOYANT SQUIGGLY UNDULATE
(PEOPLE WITH — HAIR) VEDDOID

WAWL HOWL WAIL WOWL SQUALL

WAX WOX CERE CODE GROW RAGE WACE WOXE SCALE BECOME CAPPING CERESIN KLISTER CARNAUBA CERESINE CEROXYLE COCCERIN EPILATOR INCREASE
(— FAINT) APPAL
(— FROM INSECT) PELA
(— IN HONEYCOMB) CAPPING
(— STRONG) PREVAIL
(CHINESE —) PELA
(COBBLER'S —) CODE
(EAR —) CERUMEN
(KIND OF —) MONTAN PINSANG
(POLISH WITH —) SIMONIZE
(SKI —) KLISTER
(PREF.) CER(I)(O) KERO

WAXBILL ASTRILD REDBILL

WAXEN WAX PALLID CEREOUS

WAXER GLAZER WAXMAN

WAXFLOWER EPIPHYTE

WAXING CRESCIVE

WAX LIGHT TAPER CANDLE

WAX MYRTLE ARRAYAN

WAX PALM CARNAUBA

WAX PLANT HOYA

WAXWING WAXBIRD RECOLLET SILKTAIL

WAXY ANGRY VEXED CEREOUS PLIABLE YIELDING

WAY LAW PAD RUE TAO VIA WON WYE FARE FORE FORM GAIT GANG GATE KIND LANE LARK PACE PATH PAWK RAKE ROAD SORT TOBY WISE ALLEY CHANT FORTH GOING GUISE HABIT MOYEN ROUTE SHEAR STEPS STYLE TRACT TRADE ACCESS AVENUE CAREER CHEMIN COURSE MANNER METHOD PHASIS STREET TRAJET CHANNEL FASHION HIGHWAY PASSAGE SKIDWAY APPROACH CONTRADA DISTRICT FOOTPATH THOROUGH VICINITY LAUNCHING
(— OF DEPARTURE) EXIT
(— OF ESCAPE) BOLTHOLE
(— OF LIFE) LARK TRACE HEDONISM
(— OF LOOKING) SLANT
(— OF SPEAKING) AMBAGE
(— OF THINKING) DIET
(— OF WALKING) JET
(— ON OR OFF) RAMP
(— OUT) IT RAD EXIT SALVO RADICAL
(— THROUGH MINEFIELD) BREACH
(BY ANOTHER —) ALIA
(CLEVER —) KNACK
(COVERED —) CORRIDOR
(DEVIOUS —) ROUNDABOUT
(EVERY —) ROUND
(IN ANY —) SOEVER

(INDIRECT —) AMBAGES
(LONG —) FAR
(MAJOR —) STEM
(NARROW —) DRANG
(ODD —S) JIMJAMS
(PLANK —) BRIDGE
(RAISED —) BANQUETTE
(ROUNDABOUT —) DETOUR CIRCUIT
(ROUNDABOUT —S) AMBAGES
(SETTLED —) BIAS
(SIDE —) BRANCH
(SLOPING —) RAMP
(UNDEVIATING —) GROOVE
(PL.) DAPS
(PREF.) HODO ODO VIA
(SUFF.) ODE OID WISE
WAYBILL CHALAN WILLIE CHALLAN
WAYFARER SHULER VIATOR PILGRIM
SHUILER TRAVELER PASSENGER
WAYFARING TREE WHITTEN
COTTONER VIBURNUM
WAYLAY BELAY BESET BLOCK BRACE
AMBUSH FORLAY FORSET FORELAY
OBSTRUCT SURPRISE
WAYLAYER WAIT
WAYMARK AHU
WAY OF ALL FLESH (AUTHOR OF
—) BUTLER
(CHARACTER IN —) JOHN ELIZA
ELLEN MARIA PRYER ALLABY
ALTHEA ERNEST GEORGE JOSEPH
OVERTON SKINNER MAITLAND
PONTIFEX THEOBALD CHARLOTTE
CHRISTINA
WAY OF THE WORLD (AUTHOR OF
—) CONGREVE
(CHARACTER IN —) FOIBLE FAINALL
MARWOOD ROWLAND WILFULL
WITWOOD MIRABELL WAITWELL
WISHFORT MILLAMANT
WAYSIDE HEDGE
WAYWARD PEEVISH PERVERSE
LOUPTHEDYKE
WEAK DIM LEW COOL DOWY FOND
LAME NESH NICE PALE PUNY SELI
SELY SOFT THIN WASH WAUF WOKE
BAUCH BAUGH CRIMP DICKY FAINT
FLASH FRAIL JERKY LIGHT NAISH
REEDY ROCKY SEELY SHAKY SILLY
SLACK STANK WASHY WAUGH
WEARY WERSH YOUNG CADUKE
DEBILE DILUTE DOTISH EFFETE
FEEBLE FLABBY FLAGGY FLIMSY
FOIBLE GROGGY INFIRM LIMBER
LITTLE MARCID SEMMIT SICKLY
SINGLE SWASHY TENDER UNSURE
UNWISE WAIRCH WATERY BRICKLE
DWAIBLY DWEEBLF FLACCID
FOOLISH FRAGILE INSIPID INVALID
LANGUID PIMPING PUERILE
REGULAR RICKETY SAUGHEN
SHALLOW SHILPIT SLENDER SPINDLY
TOTTERY UNHARDY UNLUSTY

WEARISH ASTHENIC CHILDISH
DECREPIT DEFINITE FECKLESS
FEMININE FLAGGING GRIPLESS
HELPLESS IMBECILE IMPOTENT
LADYLIKE LANGUENT PHTHISIC
RESOLUTE RUSHLIKE SACKLESS
SCRANNEL THEWLESS UNMIGHTY
UNWIELDY SPINELESS
(— FROM FATIGUE) TANGLE
(— FROM HUNGER) LEER
(— IN RESOLUTION) FRAIL
(MENTALLY —) TOTTY
(PREF.) ASTHEN(O) LEPT(O)
WEAKEN GO LAG SAP DAMP FAIL
HURT MELT PALL SINK THIN ABATE
ALLAY BLUNT BREAK CRAZE DELAY
QUAIL SHAKE SPEND WATER APPALL
ATTRIT DEACON DEADEN DEFANG
DEFEAT DEJECT DENUDE DILUTE
FALTER IMPAIR INFIRM LABEFY
LESSEN PERISH REBATE REDUCE
SICKEN SOFTEN CORRODE CORRUPT
CRIPPLE DECLINE DEPRESS DISABLE
MOLLIFY QUALIFY RESOLVE
THREADY UNBRACE UNNERVE
CASTRATE DIMINISH EMBEZZLE
ENERVATE ENFEEBLE ETIOLATE
INFRINGE LABEFACT UNSTRENG
WEAKENED GROGGY ANODYNE
INVALID SHOTTEN DECREPIT
LABEFACT STRAINED
WEAKENING CHRONIC FAILURE
FLAGGING
WEAKEST RECKLING
WEAKFISH DRUM TROUT ACOUPA
SALMON CORBINA CORVINA
DRUMMER SQUETEE TOTOABA
TOTUAVA BLUEFISH CHICKWIT
WEAKLING TOY WRIG DUGON
PULER SLINK SOFTIE DILLING
RECKLING SOFTLING
WEAKLY FEEBLY FEMALE SIMPLY
WEAK-MINDED DAFT DOTY DOTED
FOOLISH
WEAKNESS ATONY CRACK CRAZE
FAULT FOLLY TOUCH ATONIA DEFECT
FOIBLE ACRATIA FAILING FISSURE
FRAILTY LANGUOR ASTHENIA
DEBILITY DELICACY FONDNESS
(— OF DIGESTION) APEPSY
APEPSIA
(— OF MIND) FOLLY
(— OF VOICE) PHONASTHENIA
(CARNAL —) FLESH
(SUFF.) (— FOR) ITIS
WEAL WHEAL RICHES STRIPE
WEALTH WELFARE
WEALTH WAD WON DHAN GEAR
GOLD GOOD MUCK WONE MEANS
THING WORTH GRAITH MAMMON
POCKET PURPLE RICHES TALENT
CASHBOX FORTUNE RICHDOM
WARISON WELFARE CATALLUM

OPULENCE OPULENCY PROPERTY
TREASURE WARRISON MONEYBAGS
(— OF NATION) STOCK
(PATRON OF —) YAKSHA
(PREF.) APHNO PLUT(O)

WEALTHY FAT BEIN BIEN FULL OOFY
RICH WELI AMPLE PURSY TINNY
LOADED OOFIER COUTHIE MONEYED
PURSIVE ABUNDANT AFFLUENT
(— CLASS) PLUTOCRACY

WEAN CHILD SPAIN SPANE WAYNE
INFANT ESTRANGE

WEANING ABLACTATION

WEAPON (ALSO SEE SPECIFIC TYPE
OF WEAPON) ARM BOW GUN BILL
BOLA BOLO CLUB COSH DART EDGE
EPEE FALX FOIL IRON MACE NUKE
PATU PIKE TOOL WIWI ADAGA
ARROW BILLY CAKRA DEATH FLAIL
KNIFE LANCE ONCIN ORGUE SHARP
SPEAR SQUID STEEL SWORD VOUGE
WAPIN CANNON CHAKRA DAGGER
GLAIVE MACANA TOMBOC ARCHERY
BAZOOKA FIREARM GISARME
HALBERD HARPOON HURLBAT
JAVELIN LIANGLE POUNAMU
SHOTGUN SLASHER STICKER
STUNGUN TICKLER WHIFFLE
ARBALEST BLOWBACK BLUDGEON
CROSSBOW FAUCHARD HEDGEHOG
LEEANGLE NUNCHAKU PARTISAN
TOMAHAWK TROMBASH
(CELTIC —) PALSTAFF
(DEADLY —) DEATH
(LINE OF —S) RIDGE
(NUCLEAR —) NUKE
(PREHISTORIC —) CELT
(PL.) WAR TACKLE ARCHERY
WEAPONRY
(PREF.) ARMI HOPL(O)

WEAPONRY ARMS

WEAR KIT BEAR FRAY FRET GROW
HAVE PASS CHAFE GUARD SPEND
VOGUE WEARY ABRADE BATTER
BECOME HAVEON BETHUMB
CONSUME DEFENSE DEGRADE
FASHION FATIGUE FRAZZLE PROCEED
WEATHER PROGRESS
(— AND TEAR) GAFF SLITE GRUELING
(— AN OPENING) BREACH
(— AWAY) EAT FADE FRET GALL
GNAW GULL PINE ERODE GULLY
SCOUR SPEND ABRADE CORRADE
CORRODE CONTRIVE
(— CLOTHES) DRESS
(— DOWN) BRAY GRIND ABRADE
ABRASE GRAVEL
(— FURROWS) GUTTER
(— IN PUBLIC) SPORT
(— OFF) FADE FRAY ABRADE
(— OUT) DO BURN COOK FLOG FRAY
JADE MUSH TIRE TUCK BREAK SLAVE
SLITE SPEND TRASH BUGGER

HATTER MAGGLE PERUSE EXHAUST
FORWEAR FORWORK HACKNEY
INVALID SHACHLE OVERFRET
OVERWEAR
(— SHIP) CAST
(— SHOES OUT OF SHAPE) SHACHLE
SHACKLE
(— TIGHT CORSETS) LACE
(WINTER —) EARMUFF

WEARIED AWEARY FORGONE
FATIGUED WEARIFUL

WEARINESS TIRE FATIGUE
BRAINFAG SICKNESS VEXATION

WEARING DECAY SCUFF BURNING
CLOTHES ABRASION GARMENTS
GRINDING

WEARISOME DRY DULL HARD
SLOW WEARY BORING MORTAL
PROLIX SODDEN IRKSOME
TEDIOUS SAWDUSTY TIRESOME
TOILSOME

WEARISOMENESS TEDIUM

WEARY FAG IRK SAD BEAT BOEG
BORE CLOY MOIL PALL POOP PUNY
SADE TIRE TIRY WEAK WORE WORN
BORED BREAK CURSE SPENT
ABRADE BETOIL HARASS PLAGUE
POOPED SICKLY SQUEAL TUCKER
EXHAUST FATIGUE IRKSOME
SWINKED FATIGATE FORCHASE
GRIEVOUS TIRESOME WRETCHED
FORJASKIT
(— OUT) RAMFEEZLE
(BE —) SAG
(BECOME —) JADE

WEARY WILLIE TRAMP

WEASAND WISEN GULLET THROAT
WIZZEN TRACHEA WINDPIPE

WEASEL CANE VAIR VARE WARE
HULDA HURON SNEAK STOAT TAIRA
TAYRA ERMINE FERRET HULDAH
VERMIN ARCTOID VORMELA
FUTTERET MUISHOND MUSTELIN
WHITRACK
(— OUT OF) EVADE
(— RELATIVE) ZORIL
(PREF.) GALEO

WEASEL CAT LINSANG

WEATHER SKY DIRT RAIN TIME
COLLA STORM WINDWARD
(— CONDITION) WHITEOUT
(— LINE) FRONT
(FAIR —) SHINE
(HOT AND HUMID —) SIZZARD
(INCLEMENT —) SEASON
(INTERVAL OF FAIR —) SLATCH
(OPEN —) FRESH
(OUT OF THE —) ALEE
(UNDER THE —) SEEDY
(VIOLENT —) ELEMENTS
(PREF.) EUDIO METEOR(O)

WEATHERBEATEN GNARLED
SEAGOING

WEATHERCOCK COCK FANE VANE
FAINE FANACLE
WEATHERGLASS BAROMETER
WEAVE CANE HABI HUCK JOIN LACE
LENO LOOM REED ROCK SPIN WALE
WARP WIND WOOF DOBBY DRAPE
PLAIT TWINE UNITE BROCHE
DAMASK DEVISE DIAPER DOBBIE
FABRIC CANILLE ENTWINE FASHION
INDRAPE SATINET SHUTTLE
VANDYKE DIAGONAL DUCHESSE
OVERSHOT
(— PATTERNS INTO) BROCADE
(BASKET —) BARLEYCORN
(CARPET —) FLOSSA
(HERRINGBONE —) SUMAK SOUMAK
SHEMAKA
(LATTICE —) TEE
(OPEN —) LENO BAREGE
(RUG —) RYA
WEAVER KORI TANTI WEBBE
DRAWBOY WEBSTER WOBSTER
PENELOPE TAPESTER
WEAVERBIRD NUN BAYA MAYA
TAHA FINCH MUNIA VIDUA WEBBE
BISHOP CANARY OXBIRD WHIDAH
WHYDAH BENGALI AMADAVAT
AVADAVAT CARDINAL MANNIKIN
WEAVING TANIKO TEXTURE
WEBBING
(— MAIDEN) ARACHNE
(— OF WORDS) CONTEXT
(— TOGETHER) PLEXURE
WEAZEN WIZEN SHRINK WIZENED
WEB PLY WOB CAUL FELT MAZE TENT
TOIL VANE WARP WEFT SKEIN SNARE
THROW TWIST FLEECE TISSUE
ENSNARE FEATHER LAYETTE
TEXTURE SNOWSHOE VEXILLUM
(— IN EYE) HAW
(CRANK —) THROW
(PREF.) HIST(O) HISTI(O) HYPHO
WEBBED RINGED PALMATE
WEBBING MAT WEB PALAMA
WEB-FOOTED PALMATE PALAMATE
PALMIPED
WEB SPINNER EMBIID WEBWORM
WED GET BEWED BRIDE HITCH
MARRY STAKE WAGER ENGAGE
PLEDGE SPOUSE ESPOUSE
WEDLOCK
WEDDING BRIDAL SPLICE NUPTIAL
WEDLOCK ESPOUSAL MARRIAGE
(— WORDS) IDO
WEDGE KEY COIN FROE FROW GLUT
HORN KYLE PLUG SHIM STOB TRIG
TRIP WAGE CHOCK CHUCK CLEAT
COIGN HACEK HORSE QUINE QUOIN
SCOTE SLICE THROW COTTER
CUNEUS QUINET SCOTCH EMBOLUS
QUINNET SCHOCHE VOUSSOIR
(— BETWEEN TWO FEATHERS) KEY
(— IN) JAM JAMB

(— OF OATMEAL) FARL FARLE
(— TO PREVENT MOTION) CHOCK
(CURVED —) CAM
(WOODEN —) COW GLUT JACK
(PREF.) CUNEI CUNEO EMBOL(O)
SPHEN(O)
WEDGER SPRINGER
WEDGE-SHAPED CUNEAL SPHENIC
CUNEATED SPHENOID
(PREF.) CUNEO SPHEN(O)
WEDLOCK WIFE SPOUSAL
MARRIAGE SPOUSAGE
WEDNESDAY MIDWEEK
WEE TINY EARLY SMALL TEENY
YOUNG LITTLE ITSYBITSY
WEED BUR HOE BURR CHOP CULL
DOCK FORB LOUK SHIM SIDA TARE
WEID CIGAR DRANK DRAWK DRESS
DROKE FLESH BLINKS CASUAL
COCKLE DARNEL JIMSON KNAWEL
RIPGUT SARCLE SPURGE SPURRY
STROIL ASHWORT BUGLOSS
COHITRE CUCKOLD EGILOPS
GARMENT GOSMORE HOGWORT
RAGWEED RAGWORT RIBWORT
SANDBUR TOBACCO VERVAIN
VERVINE CHADLOCK COCKSPUR
COWWHEAT PIRIPIRI PLANTAIN
PURSLANE TOADFLAX ALFILERIA
MARIJUANA NIPPLEWORT
(— KILLER) PARAQUAT HERBICIDE
(— OUT) ROGUE
(MEXICAN —) BIRDEYE
(ROADSIDE —) PLANTAGO
(STINGING —) NETTLE
(TROUBLESOME —) KEX TITTER
(WATER —) ANACHARIS
(PL.) FILTH WRACK DISMAL SPRING
WEEDAGE TRUMPERY
WEEDER SARCLER
WEEDY FOUL LANKY
WEEK OOK WOK OULK WOKE SENNET
STANZA HEBDOMAD SENNIGHT
(TWO —S) FORTNIGHT
WEEKDAY FERIA WARDAY
WEEKLY AWEEK HEBDOMADAL
HEBDOMADARY
WEEL LEAP POOL TRAP RIGHT
WHIRLPOOL
WEEN MEAN VENE WEND FANCY
GUESS EXPECT BELIEVE IMAGINE
SUPPOSE CONCEIVE
WEENY TINY SMALL WEESHY
WEEP CRY ORP SOB BAWL BEND GIVE
LEAK OOZE PIPE TEAR WAIL GREET
BEWAIL BEWEEP BOOHOO BUBBLE
LAMENT SHOWER BLUBBER
LAPWING SQUINNY COMPLAIN
WEEPER GREETER MOURNER
CAPUCHIN
(PL.) FLENTES
WEEPING WOP GREET MILCH RAINY
BOOHOO LAMENT OOZING PIPING

BLUBBER MAUDLIN TEARFUL
DRIPPING LACRIMAL MADIDANS
PLORATION
WEEPING SINEW GANGLION
WEEVER JUGULAR STINGBULL
WEEVIL MAX BOUD POPE WHULE
PICUDO WEEBLE BILLBUG BRUCHUS
VAQUITA CURCULIO WOODWORM
(PLUM —) TURK
WEFT WEB PICK WOOF BLAST FABRIC
FILLING
WEIGH GO SIT HEFT PEIS TARE TELL
COUNT HEAVE HOIST PEIZE POISE
RAISE SCALE BURDEN PONDER
ANALYZE BALANCE DEPRESS
LIBRATE CONSIDER EVALUATE
MEDITATE MILITATE
(— DOWN) LADE SWAY SWEE BESET
HEAVY PEISE CADDLE CHARGE
CUMBER PESTER DEPRESS FREIGHT
INGRATE OPPRESS OVERLAY
ENCUMBER
(— UPON) SIT GRIEVE
WEIGHER BOXMAN PEISER SCALER
WEIGHING METAGE
(— MACHINE) TRON SCALE TRONE
WEIGHT
(ALSO SEE MEASURE AND UNIT) BOB
FEN FOB KIN MAN NET OKE RAM SER
SIR TOM TUP ABAS ATOM BEEF
CLOG DROP GRAM HEFT IRON KITE
LEAD LOAD MACE MEAL NAIL ONUS
PEIS POND PORT ROTL SEAM SEER
SINK WAIT ABBAS CLOVE CRITH
GARCE LIVRE MAUND PEASE PEISE
PICUL POISE POIZE PRESS RIDER
SCALE STAMP AUNCEL BURDEN
CHARGE DIRHEM HAMMER IMPORT
MOMENT MONKEY PASSIR PONDER
PONDUS SINKER STRESS BALLAST
DOLPHIN GRAVITY MILLIER PAYLOAD
PLATINE PLUMMET POSIURE
CHALDRON DEMIMARK DUMBBELL
ENCUMBER FARASULA LISPOUND
PRESSURE PRESTIGE QUINCUNX
STANDARD STRENGTH
(— AFTER TARE DEDUCTION)
SUTTLE
(— CARRIED BY HORSE) IMPOST
(— CLOTH) FLOCK
(— FOR HURLING) HAMMER
(— FOR LEAD) FOTHER FOTMAL
(— FOR PRECIOUS STONE) CARAT
(— FOR WOOL) TOD SARPLER
(— FOR WOOL, CHEESE, ETC.) CLOVE
(— OF BROADSIDE) GUNPOWER
(— OF COAL) KEEL
(— OF COFFEE) MAT
(— OF EMPTY VEHICLE) TARE
(— OF HYDROGEN) CRITH
(— OF METAL) JOURNEY
(— OF ONE 10TH TAEL) MACE
(— OF ONE 100TH TAEL) FEN

(— OF PENDULUM) BOB
(— OF PILE DRIVER) TUP
(— OF RAW SILK) PARI
(— OF SILK OR RAYON) DRAMMAGE
(— OF 100 LBS.) CENTAL CENTENA
CENTNER
(— OF 1000 LIVRES) MILLIER
(— OF 20 OR 21 LBS.) SCORE
(— OF 40 BUSHELS) WEY
(— OF 5 UNCIAE) QUINCUNX
(— ON MINE SWEEPER) KITE
(— ON STEELYARD) PEA
(— ON WATCH CHAIN) FOB
(— TO BEND HOT METAL) DUMPER
(— TO DETECT FALSE COINS) PASSIR
(— TO HINDER MOTION) CLOG
(— WHICH VESSEL CAN CARRY)
TONNAGE
(ABYSSINIAN —) FARASULA
(BOXER'S —) FLY HEAVY LIGHT
BANTAM MIDDLE WELTER FEATHER
(CARAT —) SILIQUA
(CLOCK —) PEISE
(COUNTERFEIT —) SLANG
(FALSE —) SLANG
(GREATLY VARYING —) MAN
MAUND
(HEAVY —) MONKEY
(LIGHT —) SUTTLE
(METRIC —) TONNE
(MONEYER'S —) DROIT
(ORIENTAL —) TAEL CATTY
(SASHCORD —) MOUSE
(SHUFFLEBOARD —) SHIP
(SMALL —) MITE GERAH RIDER
(SPLINE —) DOLPHIN
(UNIT OF —) SER VIS WEY GERA
LAST ROTL SEER LIANG LIBRA LINGO
MINAL PECUL PERIT PIKOL KANTAR
LINGOE MISKAL POCKET LISPUND
PRICKLE QUINTAL ZOLOTNIK
(PREF.) BAR(I)(O)(Y) PONDERO
(SUFF.) BAR(IC)
WEIGHTED BIAS LOADED
WEIGHTER FULLER
WEIGHTLESSNESS MICROGRAVITY
WEIGHT-PRODUCING GRAVIFIC
WEIGHTY GRAVE GREAT HEAVY
HEFTY MASSY SOLID VALID COGENT
SOLEMN EARNEST MASSIVE
ONEROUS PEISANT PESANTE
SERIOUS TELLING GRIEVOUS
MATERIAL POWERFUL PREGNANT
PORTENTOUS SIGNIFICANT
WEIR DAM PEN CRIB KEEP LEAP STOP
CAULD DOACH GARTH GORCE
HATCH HEDGE SASSE STANK
LASHER BURROCK MILLPOND
WEIRD ODD EERY UNCO UNKO EERIE
SPACY UNCOW UNKID CREEPY
SPACEY ELDRICH ELRITCH UNCANNY
UNUSUAL WIZARDLY SPACEDOUT
(— SISTERS) FATES

WEIRDO NUT GEEK KOOK CREEP DINGBAT ECCENTRIC
WEITSPEKAN YUROK
WEKA RAIL WOODHEN RAILBIRD
WELCOME SEE FAIN GOOD HAIL ADOPT ALOHA CHEER GREET RESET TREAT ACCOIL INVITE SALUTE ACCLAIM ACCUEIL EMBRACE GRATIFY BIENVENU GREETING HAEREMAI PLEASANT ACCEPTABLE
WELCOMING HOMEY
WELD SHUT WELL SWAGE UNITE WOALD ACACIA
WELDED SHOT
WELDING FUSION SHUTTING
WELFARE SEL GOOD HALE HEAL SELE WEALTH BENISON BLESSING COMMONWEAL
  (PUBLIC —) STATE
WELKIN SKY HEAVENS WALKENE
WELL AIN EYE GAY PIT WEL BENE FINE FLOW GOOD PANT PUIT PURE RITE SAFE SINK WINK AWEEL BOOLY BOWLY GREAT MUSHA OILER QUELL WALLY WISHA ATWEEL BUCKET CENOTE ENOUGH FAIRLY GASSER NICELY OFFSET PUMPER TUNNEL FALLWAY GRADELY HEALTHY WILDCAT BOREHOLE FOUNTAIN GRAITHLY POSTHOLE WATERPIT WEALSOME
  (— AND STRONG) BUNKUM
  (— IN GLACIER) MOULIN
  (— THROUGH FLOORS OF WAREHOUSE) FALLWAY
  (— UP) WALL WALM DIGHT
  (AS —) TOO ALSO
  (FAIRLY —) MIDDLING
  (NONPRODUCTIVE —) DUSTER
  (NOT —) DONNY SOBER INVALID
  (OIL —) OILER GASSER GUSHER SPOUTER WILDCAT STRIPPER
  (RECTANGULAR —) BOOLY BOWLY
  (REMARKABLY—) RARELY
  (SACRED — AT MECCA) ZEMZEM
  (TOLERABLY —) GAYLIES GEYLIES
  (VERY —) BRAWLY CLEVER
  (PREF.) BENE EU
WELL-BALANCED SOBER
WELL-BEHAVED DECOROUS GOOD NICE MODEST MANNERED
WELL-BEING HEAL SKIN WEAL HEALTH WEALTH COMFORT EUCRASY WELFARE EUCRASIA PROSPERITY
WELLBORN GENTLE EUGENIC
WELL-BRED GENTIL POLITE GENTEEL REFINED CULTURED LADYLIKE
WELL-BUILT TIGHT
WELL CASING STEANING
WELL-CHOSEN CHOICE
WELL-CONDITIONED SONSY

WELL-CONSIDERED THRIFTY
WELL CURB PUTEAL
WELL-DEFINED STRICT
WELL-DISPOSED SIB FAIN GOOD VAIN
WELL DONE SHABASH
WELL-DRESSED BRAW GASH SMART BRAWLY
WELL-FED BLOWSY BLOWZY CHUBBY GAWCEY GAWSIE
WELL-FINISHED SOIGNE
WELL-FORMED TIGHT DECENT PROPER SEEMLY SHAPELY
WELL-FOUNDED VALID FIRM GOOD JUST SOUND WORTHY
WELL-GROOMED SMUG CRISP SOIGNE SOIGNEE
WELL-GROUNDED JUST VALID
WELL-GROWN THRODDY
WELL-HUSBANDED THRIFTY
WELL-INFORMED KNOWING PERFECT
WELL-INTENTIONED AMIABLE
WELL-KEPT SMUG POLITE
WELL-KNIT WIRY
WELL-KNOWN BREEM BREME BEATEN FAMOUS KENNED PUBLIC FAMILIAR PROMINENT
WELL-LIKED FANCIED POPULAR
WELL MADE CLEVER FEATOUS
WELL-MANNERED GENTILE POLITE COURTEOUS
WELL-NIGH WELLY ALMOST NEARLY WELLMOST
WELL-ORDERED
  (PREF.) COSM(ETO)(ICO)(O)
WELL-ORGANIZED SNOD
WELL-PLEASED FAIN VAIN
WELL-PROPORTIONED SUING TRETIS HANDSOME
WELL-READ STUDIED LITERARY
WELL-ROUNDED CHUBBY
WELL-SHAPED CLEANCUT CLEVER FEATOUS
WELL-TILLED NOT NOTT
WELL-TO-DO ABLE BEIN BIEN EASY WARM PODDED
WELL-TRODDEN TRITE
WELL-WISHER FRIEND FAVORER
WELS WALLER SHEATFISH
WELSH (ALSO SEE WALES) CYMRY FUDGE TAFFY CYMRIC KYMRIC CAMBRIAN
WELSHER SHICER QUITTER
WELSHMAN CELT KELT TAFFY BRYTHON CAMBRIAN
WELSH ONION CIBOL CIBOULE CHESBOLL
WELT WALE RIDGE STRIP WHELP WELTING BANDELET TURNOVER
  (SHOE —S) WATTIS
WELTANSCHAUUNG FAITH IDEOLOGY

WELTER REEL RIOT TOSS WILT
GROVEL TUMBLE WALLOW WRITHE
SMOTHER STAGGER SWELTER
(— OF SOUNDS) DIN
WELWITSCHIA TUMBOA
WEM FLAW SCAR SPOT STAIN
WEN CYST WYNN CLIER CLYER TALPA
TUMOR GOITER
WENCH DELL DILL DOXY DRAB GILL
GIRL JADE MAID MOLL PRIM TRUG
BIMBO GOUGE KITTY MADAM
QUEAN TRULL WHORE AUDREY
BLOUSE BLOWEN BLOWZE DRAZEL
JILLET KITTIE MOTHER POPLET
WOTLINK POPLOLLY
(CLUMSY —) MODER MODDER
MOTHER MAUTHER
WENCHER DRABBER STRIKER
WEND BOW END SORB VEND STEER
BETAKE DEPART DIRECT TRAVEL
PROCEED SORBIAN LUSATIAN
(— ONE'S WAY) MARK
WENT GODE LANE ROAD YEDE ALLEY
PASSAGE
(— ABOUT) WOLK
WENTLETRAP SCALA
WENZEL JACK
WERE (— IT NOT) SAVE
WEREWOLF TURNSKIN VERSIPEL
WERTHER (BELOVED OF —) LOTTE
WEST STY BEWEST PONENT
OCCIDENT
WESTERN PONENT SCAEAN
HESPERIC SANDWICH
(PREF.) HESPER(O)
WESTERN SAMOA (CAPITAL OF —)
APIA
(ISLAND OF —) UPOLU MANONO
SAVAII APOLIMA
(MONEY OF —) TALA
WEST HIGHLAND KYLOE

WEST INDIES
ISLAND: CAT CUBA LONG ABACO
EXUMA HAITI NEVIS PELEE TURKS
ANDROS BAHAMA CAICOS CAYMAN
INAGUA TOBAGO VIRGIN ACKLINS
ANTIGUA BONAIRE CROOKED
CURACAO GRENADA JAMAICA
LEEWARD STKITTS STLUCIA
TORTOLA ANGUILLA BARBADOS
DOMINICA STTHOMAS TRINIDAD
WINDWARD ELEUTHERA
MARGARITA MAYAGUANA
STVINCENT GUADELOUPE
HISPANIOLA MARTINIQUE
MONTSERRAT PUERTORICO
NATION: BARBADOS

WEST VIRGINIA
CAPITAL: CHARLESTON
COLLEGE: SALEM BETHANY CONCORD
MARSHALL BLUEFIELD
COUNTY: CLAY WIRT BOONE HARDY
MINGO ROANE TUCKER UPSHUR
BARBOUR KANAWHA
INDIAN: MONETON
LAKE: LYNN
NICKNAME: MOUNTAIN
RIVER: ELK OHIO KANAWHA POTOMAC
GUYANDOT
STATE BIRD: CARDINAL
STATE FLOWER: RHODODENDRON
STATE TREE: MAPLE
TOWN: ELKINS KEYSER RIPLEY
VIENNA WESTON BECKLEY
GRAFTON SPENCER WEIRTON
FAIRMONT WHEELING

WESTWARD WESSEL OCCASIVE
WESTLINS
WESTWARD HO (AUTHOR OF —)
KINGSLEY
(CHARACTER IN —) YEO JOHN LUCY
ROSE AMYAS FRANK LEIGH DESOTO
GUZMAN EUSTACE OXENHAM
RICHARD GRENVILE SALTERNE
AYACANORA
WET DEW DIP SOP WAT ASOP DAMP
DANK LASH MOIL SLOW SOAK SOFT
UVID BATHE DABBY DROOK DRUNK
HUMID JUICE JUICY LEACH MADID
MOIST MOOTH RAINY SLAKE SNAPY
SOBBY SOPPY SPEWY STEEP TIGHT
WEAKY CLASHY DABBLE DAGGLE
DAMPEN HUMECT IMBRUE JARBLE
LABBER MADEFY MARSHY MOISTY
QUASHY SHOWER SLABBY SOBBED
SPONGY SPOUTY SWASHY WATERY
ARROUSE BLUBBER DRABBLE
FLOTTER MOISTEN SLOPPED
SOBBING SPEWING SPRINGY
IRRIGATE SATURATE SLATTERY
SLOBBERY SLOTTERY WATERISH
(— AND STORMY) FOUL
(— LIGHTLY) SPRINKLE
(— THOROUGHLY) SOUSE DRENCH
(DRIPPING —) ASOP
(SLIGHTLY —) DEWY
(SOFTLY —) SQUASHY
(VERY —) SOPPY
(PREF.) HYGR(O) UDO
WETHER PUR RAM HAMEL DINMAN
DINMONT
WETNESS DANK
WETTING SOUCE SOUSE SOWSE
MOILING
WHACK DAD LAM TRY BANG BELT
BIFF DEAL HACK SWAK TIME CLONK
DRIVE SHARE STATE SWACK
WHANG CHANCE DEFEAT STROKE
THWACK BARGAIN LAMBACK
PORTION
WHACKING VERY WHALING
WHOPPING EXTREMELY

WHALE SEI CETE HUEL HULL LASH ORCA WALL KOOIA POGGY SCRAG SPERM STUNT BALEEN BELUGA BLOWER FINNER GIBBAR KILLER THRASH BOWHEAD DOLPHIN FINBACK FINFISH GIBBERT GRAMPUS MARSOON RIPSACK RORQUAL SPOUTER ZIPHIAN BALAENID CACHALOT CETACEAN DOEGLING GREYBACK HARDHEAD HUMPBACK JUBARTES MUTILATE PHYSETER THRASHER ZIPHIOID
(— BUTCHER) LEMMER
(— REFUSE) GURRY
(FINBACK —) GRASO
(HERD OF —S) GAM
(KIND OF —) SEI MINKE KILLER
(NEWBORN —) SUCKER
(SCHOOL OF —S) GAM POD
(SMALL —) MINKE
(YOUNG —) CUB
(PREF.) BALAENI BALAENO CET(O)
WHALEBONE BALEEN
WHALER HEADER BUSHMAN SPOUTER SWAGMAN WHACKER WHOPPER CETICIDE
WHALESKIN MUKTUK
WHAMMY HEX
WHANG BEAT BLOW FLOG CHUNK THONG WHACK THRASH RAWHIDE
WHARF KEY POW DOCK GARE PIER QUAY SLIP BERTH JETTY LEVEE STADE STAITH STRAND LANDING PANTALAN STELLING
WHARVE WARVE WHIRL WHORL
WHAT FAT HOT HOW WET WHO HOOT HOTE WHEN STUFF WHICH MATTER PARTLY
WHATA FUTTAH FUTTER
WHAT EVERY WOMAN KNOWS
(AUTHOR OF —) BARRIE
(CHARACTER IN —) JOHN ALICK DAVID JAMES SHAND SYBIL WYLIE BRIERE MAGGIE CHARLES VENABLES TENTERDEN
WHATNOT OMNIUM ETAGERE
WHAT PRICE GLORY (AUTHOR OF —) ANDERSON
(CHARACTER IN —) FLAGG QUIRT CHARMAINE
WHATSIT GIZMO WHATSIS THINGAMAJIG
WHAT'S-ITS-NAME TIMENOGUY
WHATSOEVER MORTAL
WHEAL HIVE HUEL WALE WELT URTICA POMPHUS
WHEAT BLE WIT CORN CONES EMMER FULTZ GRAIN SPELT SPICA TRIGO BULGUR DURGUL CEREAL KANRED STAPLE TURKEY EINKORN FORMITY FRUMETY KUBANKA MARQUIS POLLARD FRUMENTY SPELTOID

(— BOILED IN MILK) FURMITY FRUMENTY
(— MEASURE) TRUG
(BEARDED —) RIVETS
(CRACKED —) GROATS
(GRANULATED —) SUJI SUJEE
(HARD —) DURUM
(PARCHED —) BULGUR
(PREF.) TRITICO
WHEATCAKE PURI
WHEATEAR CHACK ARLING WITTOL CHACKER ORTOLAN SNORTER WITTALL CHICKELL SAXICOLA
WHEATGRASS BLUESTEM
WHEATLIKE VULGARE
WHEEDLE COG CANT CLAW COAX CARNY FLUFF GLOSE GLOZE INGLE JOLLY BANTER CAJOLE CUITER FLEECH GLAVER RADDLE SMOOGE WHILLY BLARNEY CUITTLE PALAVER SMOODGE TWEEDLE BLANDISH COLLOGUE SCROUNGE
WHEEDLING BUTTERY COMETHER
WHEEL BOB BUR COG FAN NUT ORB BEAD BUFF GEAR HELM HURL PURL ROLL ROTA RULL STAR TIRL WYLE ATHEY FLIER FLUFF FLYER IDLER NORIA REWET RHOMB ROWEL SWING TRUCK BILOBE CASTER CASTOR CIRCLE DRIVEN DRIVER FANNER HORRAL JAGGER KURUMA LEADER PINION ROLLER ROTATE RUNDLE RUNNER TRACER BALANCE BICYCLE CHUKKER GUDGEON LANTERN PEDRAIL PRICKER REVOLVE STEPNEY TRAILER TRILOBE TRINDLE TROCHUS TRUCKLE TRUNDLE UNILOBE WILDCAT CARACOLE FOLLOWER ODOMETER SPROCKET
(— A SKIN) FLUFF
(— CHARGED WITH DIAMOND DUST) SLITTER
(— CONTROLLING RUDDER) HELM
(— FOR EXECUTIONS) RAT
(— IN KNITTING MACHINE) BUR BURR
(— IN TIMEPIECE) BALANCE
(— OF DAY AND NIGHT) RHOMB
(— OF LIFE) ZOETROPE
(BUCKET —) LIFTER
(DIAMOND —) SKIVE
(GEAR —) DRIVEN HELICAL
(GRINDING —) SHELL
(GROOVED —) PULLEY SHEAVE SHIVER
(INTERRUPTER —) TICKER TIKKER
(LOCOMOTIVE —) DRIVER
(METAL —) FILET FILLET
(MILL —) PIRN
(PAIR OF LOGGING —S) CATYDID KATYDID
(POINTED —) TRACER
(POLISHING —) BOB BUFF SKAIF SKEIF BUFFER SCAIFE
(POTTER'S —) LATHE THROW

(PULLEY —) TRUCKLE
(ROAD-MEASURING —) AMBULATOR
(SPARE —) STEPNEY
(SPINNING —) TURN CHARKA
CHARKHA
(SPUR —) ROWEL
(TANK —) BOGY BOGEY BOGIE
(TOOTHED —) GEAR PINION
ROULETTE
(TURBINE —) ROTOR
(TWO PAIRS OF —S) CUTS CUTTS
(VANED —) FLIER FLYER
(WATER —) NORIA SAKIA SAKIEH
SAKIYEH TYMPANUM
(PL.) KATYDID
(PREF.) CYCL(O) ROTA ROTATO ROTI
ROTO TROCH(I)(LEI)(O)
(SUFF.) TROCH(A)(AL)(OUS)(US)
WHEELBARROW GURRY BARROW
CARRIAGE
(PART OF —) BED LEG GRIP TIRE
TRAY BRACE FRAME WHEEL HANDLE
BRACKET SUPPORT
WHEELER POLER PUSHER
WHEEL-SHAPED ROTATE TROCHAL
ROTIFORM
WHEELWORK MOTION
(— IN A CLOCK) MOVEMENT
WHEELWRIGHT WHEELER
WOODMAN WHEELMAN
WHEEZE JOKE HOOSE HOOZE TRICK
COGHLE
WHELK FILK GRUB WELT BUCKIE
MAGGOT PAPULE PIMPLE WINKLE
PUSTULE
WHELP CUB PUP SON CHIT FAWN
PUPPY YELPER KITLING SPROCKET
WHEMMEL UPSET FUMMEL
FUMMLE WHAMBLE OVERTURN
WHEN AS BUT FAN FRO GIN THO
WON THAN THEN THOA TILL SINCE
UNTIL ENOUGH ALTHOUGH
WHENEVER ONCE
WHERE AS FAR FUR FAUR FEAR
FERRE PLACE QUAIR THERE WHITHER
LOCATION
(— ABOVE MENTIONED) US
WHEREFORE WHY CAUSE FORWHY
REASON
WHERENESS UBIETY
WHEREVER THERE
WHEREWITHAL MEANS MONEY
RESOURCES
WHERRET BOX CUFF SLAP HURRY
TEASE WORRY TROUBLE WHIRRICK
WHERRY BARGE ROWBOAT WHIRREY
WHET WET GOAD HONE TIME TURN
GRIND POINT RIFLE ROUSE SLITE
WHILE AROUSE EXCITE INCITE
STROKE QUICKEN SHARPEN
APERITIF EXACUATE
WHETHER IF GIF GIN WHAR WHERE
EITHER

WHETSTONE BUR RIP RUB BUHR
BURR SLIP STONE RUBBER STRAIK
SHARPER WASHITA WHITTLE
OILSTONE RUBSTONE STRICKLE
WHEY PALE QUAY WHIG SERUM
THRUST WATERY
(PREF.) ORO
WHIBA UEBA
WHICH AS THE WHO THAT QUILK
WHILK
(— SEE) QV QQV
WHICKER NEIGH WHINNY WIGHER
WHIDAH BIRD VEUVE WEAVER
WHYDAH REDBILL
WHIFF FAN GUF BLOW GUFF GUST
HINT PUFF TIFT WAFT WIFT FLUFF
QUIFF SMOKE EXHALE MAGRIM
MEGRIM WHIFFET
WHIFFLE BLOW FIFE SWAY FLICKER
FLUTTER
WHIFFLETREE HEELTREE
SWINGLEBAR
WHIG JOG QUIG WHEY
WHIGMALEERIE FANCY
WHILE AS BIT GAM THO YET FILE
FYLE TIDE TILL WHEN WHET WOLE
FILIE PIECE SPACE STEAD STOUN
THROW UNTIL STOUND WHENAS
WHILOM BEGUILE TROUBLE
EXERTION OCCASION SOLONGAS
(— AWAY) AMUSE FLEET DIVERT
BEGUILE DECEIVE
(LITTLE —) AWEE DRASS WHILEY
WHILEEN WHILOCK
WHILES UNTIL SOMETIMES
WHILLY GULL CAJOLE WHEEDLE
WHILOM ERST
WHILST TILL UNTIL
WHIM BEE FAD GIG GIN TOY FIKE
FLAM KINK CRANK FANCY FLISK
FOLLY FREAK HUMOR MEINY QUIRK
THRUM FEGARY FITTEN MAGGOT
MEGRIM SPLEEN VAGARY WHIMSY
BOUTADE CAPRICE CONCEIT
WRINKLE CROTCHET
WHIMBREL JACK SPOW SPOWE
CURLEW MAYBIRD MAYFOWL
TITTEREL
WHIMPER GIRN MEWL PULE WAIL
WEAK BLEAT WHINE SIMPER
WHINGE YAMMER GRIZZLE SNIFFLE
SNUFFLE WHINDLE WHINNEL
WHITTER WHINNOCK
WHIMSICAL FAIRY FANCY BAROCK
COCKLE FLISKY NOTION QUAINT
BAROQUE BIZARRE GIGGISH
PUCKISH TOYSOME BIZZARRO
FANCIFUL FREAKISH HUMOROUS
NOTIONAL SINGULAR VAPOROUS
CROTCHETY FANTASTIC PIXILATED
FANTASTICAL
WHIMSY WHIM FREAK VAGARY
CAPRICE WHIMWHAM

WHIN FUN UI FX FURZE WHINCOW
WOODWAX
WHINCHAT TICK UTICK WHEATEAR
WHINE WOW GIRN GOWL MEWL
PULE TIRM TOOT YARM YIRN BLEAT
CROON MEECH QUINE TWINE
WHAUP WHEWT PEENGE SNIVEL
TREBLE WHINGE WINNEL YAMMER
WHIMPER WHINDLE
WHINING QUERULOUS
WHINNY HINNY NEIGH PLAIN
SNICKER WHICKER
WHINSTONE TRAP WHIN SCURDY
WHINYARD SWORD HANGER
POCHARD WHINGER SHOVELER
WHIP CAT EEL FAN GAD ROD TAW
BEAT CAST COIL DICK DUST FIRK
FLOG FOAM GOAD HIDE JEHU JERK
LASH LICK LOUK PLET TAWS URGE
WHUP ABUSE AZOTE BASTE BIRCH
CRACK FLAIL FLICK FLISK IMPEL
KNOUT LEASH PLETE QUILT ROMAL
SLASH STRAP SWEPE SWING SWISH
TAWSE THONG THUMP AROUSE
BREECH CHABUK DEFEAT FEAGUE
INCITE LAINER LARRUP LICKER
MAIDEN NETTLE PIZZLE QUIPPE
SCUTCH SNATCH SWINGE SWITCH
THRASH TICKLE CHABOUK CHICOTE
COWHIDE COWSKIN CURBASH
KURBASH LAMBAST LAYOVER
NAGAIKA RAWHIDE SCOURGE
SHINGLE SJAMBOK SLASHER
TICKLER CHAWBUCK COACHMAN
CONFOUND FLAGELLA KOURBASH
PEPPERER BLACKSNAKE
(— EGGS) CAST
(— HANDLE) CROP
(— IN PIANO ACTION) WIPPEN
(— WITH 3 LASHES) PLET PLETE
(FURIOUS —) JEHU
(HORSE —) WAND CHABOUK
(JOCKEY'S —) BAT
(RIDING —) CROP DICK QUIRT
(RUSSIAN —) KNOUT
(PREF.) FLAGELLI MASTIG(O)
(SUFF.) MASTIX
WHIPLASH THONG COSAQUE
CRACKER
WHIPPED BEATEN BROKEN
DEFEATED FOUETTEE CHANTILLY
WHIPPER TICKLER THIONGMAN
THRASHER THREAPER
WHIPPER-IN PRICKER
WHIPPERSNAPPER SQUIRT
WHIFFET WHIPSTER JACKANAPES
WHIPPING LICK TOCO TOKO HIDING
CLANKER FANNING SERVING
BIRCHING BROWSING SKELPING
WHIPPING POST FORK PILLAR
WHIP SCORPION GRAMPUS
PHRYNID PEDIPALP WHIPTAIL
WHIPSOCKET SNEAD

WHIPSTITCH HEM SEC SEAM
MINUTE INSTANT OVERCAST
WHIR BIRR ZIZZ WHIRRY
WHIRL BIRL EDDY FURL GYRE HURL
PURL REEL RUSH SPIN TIRL DRILL
GIDDY SKIRL SQUIR SWIRL THIRL
THROW TWIRL TWIST WALTZ WHORL
BUSTLE CIRCLE GYRATE HURTLE
SWINGE VORTEX WHORLE WINDLE
WIRBLE MIZMAZE REVOLVE
TRUNDLE TURMOIL VERTICIL
(— ABOUT) DOZE GURGE
(— IN THE AIR) WARP
(— OF ACTIVITY) MERRYGOROUND
WHIRLIGIG GIG TOY SPIN TURN
WHEEL FIZGIG FISHGIG
WHIRLING GIDDY WHEELY STROBIC
GYRATION GYRATORY VORTICAL
PIROUETTE
(PREF.) STROBO
WHIRLPOOL EDDY GULF SUCK
WEEL WELL WIEL GORCE GOURD
GURGE BULLER GORGES SWELTH
VORTEX GURGLET SWALLOW
SWILKIE SUCKHOLE MAELSTROM
(PREF.) DINO
WHIRLWIND OE DEVIL VORTEX
PRESTER TORNADO TOURBILLON
TOURBILLION
WHIRLYBIRD CHOPPER
WHISHT HUSH SILENCE
WHISK ZIP FISK TUFT WHID WHIP
WISP CAURI FLICK FLISK HURRY
SPEED SWISH CHAURI CHOWRY
SWITCH COWTAIL WHISKEN
(— OFF) TROUNCE
WHISKER HAIRLINE VIBRISSA
(PL.) BEARD ZIFFS WEEPER GALWAYS
VIBRISSA MOUSTACHE SIDEBURNS
WHISKY RYE BOND CORN CIDER
IRISH USQUE POTEEN REDEYE
SCOTCH BOURBON BLOCKADE
BUSTHEAD CREATURE POPSKULL
USQUABAE MOONSHINE
TANGLEFOOT USQUEBAUGH
MOUNTAINDEW
(GLASS OF —) RUBDOWN
(RAW —) DRUDGE
WHISPER BUZZ HARK HINT ROUN
RUNE ROUND RUMOR TRACE TUTEL
BREATH BREEZE HARKEN MURMUR
SUSURR TITTLE WHISHT HEARKEN
SUSURRUS
WHIST MORT VINT QUIET BOSTON
SILENT WHEESHT
WHISTLE BLOW CALL PIPE WHEW
FLUTE QUILL WHAUP WHEEP WHUTE
BUMMER DUZZER CUCKOO FUSSLE
HOOTER SIFFLE SISTLE SQUEAL
WARBLE YELPER CATCALL TWEEDLE
BIRDCALL
(— FEEBLY) WHEEDLE WHEEPLE
WHISTLE FLUTE SIFFLOT

WHISTLER PIPER MARMOT ROARER
FLUTIST LAPWING SIFFLEUR
WHISTLING PIPY PIPEY ROARING
SIFFLET RHONCHUS SUSSURANT
WHIT BIT JOT RAP ATOM DOIT HATE
HOOT IOTA QUAT QUIT AUGHT
BODLE GROAT POINT QUITE SPECK
CIVITE PARTICLE TWOPENNY
WHITE CUT WAN BAWN FITE HOAR
LILY PALE QUAT QUIT ASHEN BLOND
HAOLE HOARY LABAN LINEN SNOWY
ALBINO ARGENT BLANCH BRIGHT
BUCKRA CANDID CIVITE ERMINE
SILVER WINTRY CANDENT LEUCOUS
NIVEOUS WHITTLE FAVORITE
INNOCENT LACTEOUS
(— AND SMOOTH) IVORINE
(— OF EGG) GLAIR ALBUMEN
(— PERSON) OFAY
(POOR —) YAHOO CRACKER
(SHADE OF —) IVORY
(PREF.) ALB(I)(O) CALI CALLI LEUC(O)
LEUK(O)
WHITE ALDER CLETHRA
WHITE ANT ANAY NASUTE
TERMITE
WHITEBAIT SMELT ICEFISH
SALANGID SALMONID
WHITEBEAM ARIA SERVICE
MULBERRY
WHITEBOY PET LEVELER
WHITE BRYONY COWBIND
MANDRAKE
WHITE CEDAR JUNIPER
WHITE CLOVER LADINO
SHAMROCK
WHITE COMPANY (AUTHOR OF —)
DOYLE
(CHARACTER IN —) JOHN MAUDE
NIGEL HORDLE LORING SAMKIN
ALLEYNE AYLWARD EDRICSON
WHITEFACE HEREFORD
WHITEFISH BLOAT CISCO PILOT
POWAN BELUGA CHIVEY POLLAN
TULIPI VENDIS BLOATER BOWBACK
GWYNIAD LAVARET VENDACE
BLACKFIN GREYBACK HUMPBACK
MENOMINI SALMONID SCHNABEL
TULLIBEE
WHITEFLY HOMOPTER MEALYWING
WHITE FRIAR CARMELITE
WHITE GUM TUART
WHITEHEAD MILIUM
WHITE-HEADED GOLDEN FAVORED
FORTUNATE
WHITE HEATH BRIAR BRIER
WHITE HELLEBORE ITCHREED
ITCHWEED
WHITE IPECAC ITOUBOU
WHITE LEAD CERUSE
WHITE MAPAN PIRIPIRI
WHITE MUSTARD KEDLOCK
SINAPIS CRUCIFER

WHITEN CAM CAUM SCURF ALBIFY
BLANCH BLANCO BLEACH BLENCH
DEALBATE EMBLANCH ETIOLATE
PIPECLAY
WHITENED DEALBATE
WHITENESS IVORY ALBEDO
ARGENT CANDOR PURITY CANITIES
PALENESS
WHITE OAK ROBLE
WHITE POPLAR ABELE ABELTREE
WHITE SNAKEROOT STEVIA
POOLWORT RICHWEED WHITETOP
WHITE STURGEON BELUGA
WHITETHROAT JACK MUFF MUFTY
MUGGY PEGGY EYSOGE MILLER
MUFFET WHISKY WINNEL HAYSUCK
WHEYBIRD
WHITEWALL TIRE
WHITEWASH LIME GLASS BLANCH
PARGET STIFLE CHICAGO LIMEWASH
PALLIATE
WHITEWEED DAISY
WHITE WHALE BELUGA
WHITHER GUST HURL RUSH WHIZ
HURRY SHAKE WHERE FLURRY
BLUSTER WHERETO
WHITING BARB HAKE CORBINA
CORVINA MERLING KINGFISH
MOONFISH
WHITING-POUT BIB KLEG BLENS
WHITISH BAWN PALE DILUTE
SUBALBID
WHITLOW FELON AGNAIL ANCOME
FETLOW BREEDER PANARIS
BREDSORE RUNROUND PANARITIUM
PARONYCHIA
WHITLOW GRASS DRABA
NAILWORT SHADBLOW
WHITRACK WEASEL FUTTERET
WHITTRET
WHITSUNDAY TERM
WHITSUNTIDE PINXTER PINGSTER
PINKSTER
WHITTLE CUT PARE CARVE KNIFE
STEEL TWITE EXCITE MANTLE
THWITE BLANKET
WHIZ ACE BUZZ DEAL GIRL PIRR QUIZ
SING WHIR ZIZZ BRAIN SOUGH
WHISH WHIZZ WIZARD BARGAIN
SWITHER WHIDDER WHINNER
(— KID) BRAIN GENIUS EINSTEIN
(COMPUTER —) HACKER
WHIZ-BANG EXPERT NOTABLE
WHO AS HOW THE WHA WHAT
WHICH
WHOA WO WAY WHO STOP
WHOEVER WHATSO EVERWHO
WHOLE ALL HOW SUM BODY COOL
EVEN HALE HALF HOLY HULL BLOCK
GREAT GROSS HAILL SOLID SOUND
TOTAL TOTUM TUTTA UNCUT
CORPSE ENTIRE HEALED INTACT
VERSAL GENERAL INFRACT INTEGER

PERFECT SINCERE SOLIDUM
UNITARY COMPLETE ENSEMBLE
ENTIRETY GLOBULAR INTEGRAL
LIVELONG OUTRIGHT UNBROKEN
(— OF ANY ORGANISM) SOMA
(— OF REALITY) ABSOLUTE
(ORGANIC —) SYSTEM
(ORGANIZED —) GESTALT
CONFIGURATION
(PREF.) ALL HOL(O) INTEGRI PAN TOTI
TOTO
WHOLEHEARTED HEARTY SINCERE
ZESTFUL COMPLETE IMPLICIT
WHOLESALE MASSIVE SWEEPING
WHOLESALER JOBBER EXPORTER
WHOLESOME GOOD CLEAN SOUND
SWEET BENIGN SAVORY HEALTHY
PRUDENT CURATIVE HALESOME
HEALSOME HOMELIKE REMEDIAL
SALUTARY HEALTHFUL
WHOLE-SOULED SINCERE
WHOLLY ALL FAIR FLAT HALE ONLY
BLACK CLEAR FULLY QUITE STARK
ALGATE BODILY FLATLY HOLLOW
PURELY SOLELY ALGATES ROUNDLY
SOLIDLY TOTALLY DIRECTLY
ENTIRELY
(PREF.) TOTI
WHOMP CREAM
WHOOP BOOM HOOP HOOT BOOST
RAISE SHOUT EXCITE HALLOO
HOOPOE
WHOOPING COUGH KINKHOST
CHINCOUGH PERTUSSIS
WHOP TAN WAP BEAT THUD THUMP
STRIKE THRASH
WHOPPER LIE TALE SIZER BOUNCER
CRUMPER SLAPPER SNAPPER
SWAPPER SWINGER SCROUGER
STRAPPER WALLOPER
WHOPPING VERY LARGE BANGING
RAPPING WAPPING WHALING
SWINGING THUMPING WHACKING
WALLOPING
WHORE DRAB JILT FILTH QUAIL
WENCH HARLOT PUTAIN DEBAUCH
PINNACE STRUMPET SUCCUBUS
PROSTITUTE
WHOREMONGER HOLOUR
WHORL TURN CYCLE SPIRE SWIRL
WHIRL THWORL VOLUTE WHARVE
WREATH ANNULUS CALYCLE
CALYCULE GYRATION VERTICIL
VOLUTION
(PREF.) SPONDYL(O) VERTICILL(I)
WHORLED (NOT —) ACYCLIC
WHORTLEBERRY HOT HURT
FRAWN HOOTE FRAGHAN BILBERRY
COWBERRY
WHY HOW OUI ENIGMA FORWHY
HOWCOME
WICK BAD EVIL FARM TOWN ANGLE
CREEK DAIRY MATCH QUICK SEAVE

SNAST CORNER LIVING WICKED
VILLAGE FARMSTEAD
(— CLOGGED WITH TALLOW)
ROUGHIE
(LONG WAXED —) TAPER
WICKED BAD SAD DARK EVIL FAST
FOUL IRON LAZY LEWD MEAN PIKY
VILE BLACK CURST FELON SHREW
SORRY WRONG WROTH CURSED
GUILTY LITHER LUTHER NEFAST
PERDIT PITCHY SEVERE SHREWD
SINFUL UNHOLY UNJUST UNLEAD
UNLEDE UNWELL CAITIFF DARKSUM
GODLESS HEINOUS HELLISH
IMMORAL NAUGHTY NINETED
NOXIOUS PRAVOUS PROFANE
ROGUISH UNGODLY UNSEELY
UNSOUND UNWREST VICIOUS
VILLAIN ACCURSED CRIMINAL
DARKSOME DEPRAVED DEVILISH
DIABOLIC ENORMOUS FELONOUS
FIENDISH FLAGRANT MESCHANT
OBDURATE PERVERSE TERRIBLE
UNKINDLY ABANDONED NEFARIOUS
PERNICIOUS
(— ITEM) CANDLE
(PREF.) PONERO
WICKEDNESS ILL SIN EVIL HARM
VICE CRIME FOLLY GUILT BELIAL
FELONY NOUGHT UNGOOD ATHEISM
DEVILRY ILLNESS PRAVITY
DARKNESS DEVILTRY INIQUITY
MISCHIEF SATANISM WANGRACE
WICKER SALE
WICKERWORK WEB WEEL
TWIGGEN BASKETRY
WICKET GATE HOOP HATCH PITCH
STUMP GUICHET
(FALLING OF —S) ROT
WICKETKEEPER STUMP STUMPER
WICKFORD POINT (AUTHOR OF —)
MARQUAND
(CHARACTER IN —) JIM JOE BERG
MARY ALLEN AVERY BELLA BRILL
HARRY STOWE ARCHIE CALDER
HOWARD WRIGHT GIFFORD
SOUTHBY LEIGHTON PATRICIA
CLOTHILDE
WICKIUP HUT WAKIUP SHELTER
WIDDRIM FIT FURY
WIDDY NOOSE WIDOW WITHY HALTER
WIDE FAR LAX DEEP ROOM SIDE
AMPLE BROAD LARGE ROOMY
SHARP SLACK WRONG ASTRAY
ROOMWARD SPACEFUL SPACIOUS
(— OF) BESIDE
(— OF THE MARK) AWRY WILD
ABROAD
(LONG AND —) SIDE
(PREF.) EURY LATI
WIDE-AWAKE FLY FOXY KEEN LIVE
ALERT FLASH LEERY CADDIE SLIPPY
KNOWING WAKEFUL WATCHFUL

WIDELY FAR BROAD ABROAD
GREATLY LARGELY
WIDEN FLAN REAM DILATE EXPAND
EXTEND FLANCH FLANGE FUNNEL
BROADEN
WIDENESS WIDTH BREADTH
WIDESPREAD RIFE DIFFUSE
GENERAL POPULAR PROLATE
REGNANT CATHOLIC EXTENDED
PANDEMIC SWEEPING EXTENSIVE
WIDGEON SMEE WHIM GOOSE
WHEWER ZUISIN POACHER POTCHER
BALDPATE BLUEBILL WHISTLER
WIDGET PART
WIDOW VID BALO DAME SKAT BLIND
KITTY VEUVE WEEDA WIDDY
MATRON RELICT TERCER DOWAGER
EMPRESS BARONESS DOWERESS
(PL.) VIDUAGE
WIDOWED VIDUOUS
WIDOWHOOD VIDUAGE VIDUITY
WIDTH GAPE SIDE RANGE SCOPE
BREADTH OPENING FRONTAGE
FULLNESS LARGEOUR LATITUDE
WIDENESS
(— OF CUT) KERF
(— OF HORSESHOE) COVER
(— OF PALM) HAND
(— OF PAPER) FILL
(— OF PULLEY) FACE
(— OF SHIP) BEAM
(— OF SHIP'S BAND) STRAKE
(— OF TYPE) SET
(— OF WEB) DECKLE
WIELD PLY RUN BEAR WALT WIND
APPLY EXERT SWING VELDE EMPLOY
GOVERN HANDLE MANAGE STRAIN
CONTROL
WIELDER (— OF AUTHORITY)
GAULEITER
(— OF POWER) POTENCY
WIENER FRANK HOTDOG
FRANKFURTER
WIFE UX FEM HEN MRS RIB WYF
BABY BIBI DAME DORA ENID FEME
FERE FRAU FROW JAEL LADY MAKE
MAMA MATE RANI UXOR DIRCE
DONNA DUTCH FEMME LUCKY
MAMMA MATCH MUJER SQUAW
WOMAN ELMIRE EMILIA ESPOSA
GAMMER KEEPER MATRON MISSIS
MISSUS MULIER SPOUSE VENDER
WAHINE BEDMATE DIONYZA
EMPRESS PARTNER WEDLOCK
DEIANIRA DEIDAMIA ERIPHYLE
HELPMATE HELPMEET MISTRESS
PECULIAR
(— OF COTTER) COTQUEAN
(— OF KNIGHT OR BARONET)
DAME
(— OF MOHAMMEDAN) KHADIJA
(AFFIANCED —) FUTURE
(INDIAN'S —) WEBB

(OLD —) GAMMER
(SPEND TIME WITHOUT —) BACHIT
(PL.) PUNALUA
(PREF.) UXOR(I)
WIFTY DITSY DIZZY GIDDY INANE
SILLY
WIG BOB JIZ RUG TIE FRIZ GIZZ JANE
JIZZ LOCK TETE TOUR BUSBY
CAXON FLASH JASEY MAJOR SCALP
SCOLD ADONIS BRUTUS FROWZE
MERKIN PERUKE REBUKE TOUPEE
TOUPET COMBING RAMILIE SCRATCH
SHEITEL SPENCER BOBJEROM
CHEDREUX CHEWELER DALMAHOY
NIGHTCAP PERUKERY POSTICHE
ROGERIAN VALLANCY
(— WITH ROUGHLY CROPPED HAIR)
BRUTUS
(BUSHY —) BUSBY
(GRAY —) GRIZZLE
(WORSTED —) JASEY
(18TH CENTURY —) ADONIS GEORGE
WIGGLE JET HOTCH JIGGLE WABBLE
WANGLE
WIGGLER PUPA LARVA WRYER
WIGGY WACKO WACKY
WIGHT MAN SWIFT STRONG VALIANT
CREATURE STALWART
WIGLET TOUPEE
WIGMAKER WIGGER PERUKER
PERUKIER
WIGWAG SIGNAL
WIGWAM TIPI LODGE TEPEE
WEEKWAM WICKIUP
WIKENO NIKENO HEILTSUK
WILD APE MAD REE SHY FAST RUDE
SCAR WOWF CRAZY FANTI FELON
FERAL GIDDY MYALL RANDY RANTY
ROUGH ROYET SKEER WASTE
DESERT FANTEE FERINE FIERCE
LAVISH MADCAP NATIVE RAMAGE
RANDOM RENISH SAVAGE SHANDY
STORMY UNRULY BERSERK
BREACHY ERRATIC FRANTIC
GALLOUS GALLOWS HAGGARD
HOWLING MADDING NATURAL
OUTWARD RIOTOUS SKADDLE
SKEERED WILDING ABERRANT
AGRESTAL BARBARIC CHIMERIC
DESOLATE FAROUCHE FRENETIC
HALUCKET HELLICAT RECKLESS
UNTILLED WARRAGAL WILLYARD
BOISTEROUS
(— CARD) FREAK
(PREF.) AGRIO
WILD ASS GOUR KIANG KULAN
COTULA KOULAN ONAGER QUAGGA
CHIGETAI
WILD BALSAM APPLE CREEPER
WILD BEE KARBI
WILD BOAR APER SUID TUSKER
SOUNDER SUIDIAN WILRONE
SANGLIER

WILD BUFFALO ARNA ARNEE
WILD BUSH BEAN PHASEMY
WILD CABBAGE YELLOWS
WILD CARDAMOM RUEWORT KNOBWOOD
WILD CARROT DILL ELTROT FIDDLE BIRDNEST HILLTROT
WILDCAT CAT BALU EYRA CHATI CHAUS MANUL TIGER MARGAY SERVAL WAGATI COLOCOLA JAGUARONDI JAGUARUNDI
WILD CELERY ACHE ECHE EELGRASS SMALLAGE
WILD CHERRY GEAN MERRY MAZZARD
WILD CHERVIL KECK COWWEED HONEWORT MILKWEED
WILD CYCLAMEN SOWBREAD
WILD DOG ADJAG DHOLE DINGO GUARA AGUARA AGOUARA CIMARRON WARRAGAL
WILD DUCK (AUTHOR OF —) IBSEN
(CHARACTER IN —) GINA EKDAL SORBY WERLE HANSEN HEDVIG GREGERS HJALMAR RELLING
WILDEBEEST GNU
WILDERNESS BUSH WILD WASTE DESERT FOREST WESTERN SOLITUDE
WILD-EYED HAGGARD RADICAL
WILDFOWL VOLATILE
WILD GARLIC MOLY
WILD GERANIUM ALUMROOT DOVEFOOT FLUXWEED
WILD GOAT TUR IBEX TAHR EVECK PASAN MAZAME MARKHOR AEGAGRUS MARKHOOR
WILD HORSE BRUMBY KUMRAH TARPAN BRUMBIE WARRAGAL WARRIGAL
WILD HYACINTH CUCKOO CROWTOE GREGGLE BRODIAEA CROWFOOT
WILD INDIGO SHOOFLY BAPTISIA TUMBLEWEED
WILD LETTUCE FIREWEED
WILD MAN SAVAGE WOODMAN WOODSMAN
WILD MANGOSTEEN SANTOL
WILD MARJORAM ORGAN ORGAMY ORGANY ORIGAN OREGANO ORGAMENT
WILD MULBERRY YAWWEED
WILD MUSTARD RUNCH CHARLOCK
WILDNESS FERITY HEYDAY HEYDEY FEROCITY SAVAGERY SAVAGISM
WILD OAT DRANK DRAWK DROKE HAVER HEVER EGILOPS
WILD ONION UMBEL UMBELLA
WILD OX BUF YAK ANOA BUFF REEM UNICORN
WILD PARSLEY ELTROT HILLTROT

WILD PEAR DOGBERRY
WILD PLUM SLOE ISLAY
WILD POTATO MANROOT WAPATOO
WILD RADISH RUNCH
WILD RICE MANOMIN
WILD SAGE EYESEED
WILD SARSAPARILLA SHOTBUSH
WILDSCHUTZ, DER (CHARACTER IN —) BACULUS NANETTE EBERBACH FREIMANN GRETCHEN KRONTHAL
(COMPOSER OF —) LORTZING
WILD SERVICE TREE SORB SORBUS
WILD SHEEP SHA AUDAD URIAL AOUDAD ARGALI BHARAL NAYAUR BIGHORN MOUFLON
WILD SWAN ELK
WILD THYME HILLWORT SERPOLET
WILD TOBACCO GAGROOT SOURBUSH MARIJUANA SALVADORA
WILD TURNIP NAVEW
WILD VANILLA LIATRIS
WILE ART PAUK PAWK RUSE FRAUD GUILE TRICK ALLURE BLENCH DECEIT ENGINE ENTICE BEGUILE ARTIFICE TRICKERY
WILGA WILLOW
WILL EGO MAY ULL WAY FATE LIST TEST WISH LEAVE OUGHT SHALL WORST ANIMUS CHOICE CHOOSE DESIRE DEVICE DEVISE LEGATE LIKING QUETHE SCRIPT CODICIL PASSION WILWORD AMBITION APPETITE BEQUEATH PLEASING PLEASURE VOLITION
(— NOT) WONT WINNA WONNA WUNNA WONNOT
(— NOT TO DO) NOLITION
(— OF DEITY) DECREE
(— OF GOD) LAW
(— OF LEGISLATURE) ACT
(— TO LIVE) TANGHA
(FREE —) ACCORD
(GOOD —) GREE
(I —) CHILL
(ILL —) ARR ENVY HEST VENOM ANIMUS ENMITY HATRED UNTHANK AMBITION
(KIND OF —) LIVING
(SUFF.) (CONDITION OF —) THYMIA
(STATE OF —) BOULIA BULIA BULIC
WILLET TATLER TATTLER
WILLFUL HEADY WILLY FEISTY UNRULY HAGGARD WAYWARD WILSOME CAMSTRARY
WILLFULLY WOLDES SCIENTER
WILLIAM TELL (AUTHOR OF —) SCHILLER
(CHARACTER IN —) JOHN TELL FURST HENRY ARNOLD BERTHA ULRICH WALTER WERNER GESSLER WILLIAM MATHILDE BAUMGARTEN
(COMPOSER OF —) ROSSINI

WILLIES JUMPS CREEPS
WILLING BAIN FAIN FREE GAME
GLAD LIEF RATH PRONE READY
MINDED TOWARD CONTENT
OBLIGING UNFORCED
(— TO FORGIVE) PACABLE PLACABLE
WILLINGLY LIEF SOON FREELY
GLADLY LIEFLY FRANKLY READILY
(MORE —) RATHER
WILLINGNESS HEART FREEDOM
FAINNESS
(— TO FIGHT) DEFIANCE
WILLIWAW STORM WOOLLY
TEMPEST
WILLOW DULY ITEA SALE WYLW
OSIER SALEW SALIX SAUGH WIDDY
WITHY WOODY DUSTER SALLOW
TEASER TWILLY WITHEN WUDDIE
(— FOR THATCHING) SPRAYS
(— IN TEXTILES) WOLF
(NATIVE —) COOBA COOBAH
(SIMPLE —) WHIPPER
(PREF.) (— TWIG) LYGO
WILLOWER DULER DUSTER TEASER
WILLIER
WILLOW HERB WICOPY EPILOBE
FIRETOP PIGWEED ROSEBAY
BURNWEED FIREWEED
WILLOW WARBLER SMEU
SMEUTH MUDDLER TROCHIL
OVENBIRD
WILLOW WREN PEGGY
WILLOWY SUPPLE SLIPPER DELICATE
WILLY-NILLY PERFORCE
WILSON'S PLOVER COLLIER
WILSON'S SNIPE JACK SHADBIRD
WILSON'S TERN MEDRICK
WILSON'S THRUSH VEERY
WILT EBB SAG DROP FADE FLAG
WELK DROOP SUCCUMB COLLAPSE
WILTED EMARCID
WILY SLY FOXY CANNY SLICK ARTFUL
ASTUTE CLEVER CRAFTY QUAINT
SHREWD STALKY SUBTLE TRICKY
CUNNING POLITIC VERSUTE
WINDING SERPENTINE
WIMBLE BORE AUGER BRISK ACTIVE
GIMLET LIVELY NIMBLE WIBBLE
WUMMEL
WIMP NERD
WIMPLE BEND WIND CURVE TWIST
GORGET RIPPLE MEANDER
WIMLUNGE
WIN BAG COP HIT DRAW GAIN HAVE
LAND LICK FORCE SCORE ATTACH
CLINCH OBTAIN ACHIEVE ACQUIRE
CONQUER DESERVE HARVEST
POSSESS TRIUMPH DECISION
OVERCOME STRAIGHT
(— AGAINST) BREAK SCOOP
(— AT CHESS) MATE CHECKMATE
(— AWAY) STEAL DEBAUCH
(— BACK) RECOVER

(— BY GUILE) GET POT BEAR CARRY
RAISE TRAIN GATHER CAPTURE
INVEIGLE PROMERIT
(— EASILY) ROMP
(— EVERY MATCH) SWEEP
(— NARROWLY) SQUEEZE
(— OVER) DEFEAT DISARM NOBBLE
(— OVERWHELMINGLY) SWEEP
(— SKILLFULLY) SNARE
(WRESTLING —) PIN
WINCE KICK CHECK QUECH CRINGE
FLINCH QUATCH QUINCH QUITCH
RECOIL SHRINK
WINCH CRAB JACK REEL WINK GIPSY
WINZE ROLLER WHIMSY WINDLE
CATHEAD TRAVELER VARIABLE
WINDLASS
WIND AIR COP LAP BALL BIRR BISE
BIZE COIL CONE CURL EAST FIST
FLAW FOHN GALE GUST KINK PUFF
PUNO ROLL WEST WRAP BATCH
BLAST BLORE CRANK CREEK CROOK
FOEHN QUILL SPOOL STORM TRADE
TREND TWINE TWIST WEAVE WITHE
BOTTOM BOUGHT BREEZE BUSTER
CAURUS COLLAR KECKLE SHAMAL
SPIRAL SPIRIT SQUALL WAMPLE
WESTER ZEPHYR BREATHE CRANKLE
CRINKLE CYCLONE ENTWINE
EQUINOX ETESIAN GREGALE
INVOLVE MEANDER MISTRAL
SERPENT SINUATE TEMPEST
TWINGLE TWISTER WEATHER
WHIRLER WINDILL ARGESTES
DOWNWARD EASTERLY FAVONIUS
(— ABEAM) LASK
(— ABOUT) WIRE SNAKE
(— AFTER DYEING) BATCH
(— DOWN) RELAX UNWIND
(— FROM THE ANDES) ZONDA
PAMPERO
(— IN AND OUT) INDENT WINGLE
(— MAGNETS) COMPOUND
(— OF ARGENTINA) ZONDA
PAMPERO
(— OF CUBA) BAYAMO
(— OF HAWAII) KONA
(— OF OREGON AND WASHINGTON)
CHINOOK
(— OF TUNISIA) CHILE CHILI CHILLI
(— ROPE) WORM WOOLD
(—S OF CHILE AND PERU) SURES
(— THREAD OR YARN) QUILL CHEESE
(— TO PREVENT CHAFING) KECKLE
(— WOOL) TREND
(— YARN) BEAM SERVE WINDLE
(ADRIATIC —) BORA
(BREAKING —) FIST
(BROKEN —) HEAVES
(COLD —) BISE BIZE BORA SARSAR
BLIZZARD
(COOLING —) IMBAT
(DEAD —) NOSER

(DESERT —) SAMUM GIBLEH SAMIEL SIMOOM SIMOON KHAMSIN SIROCCO SCIROCCO
(DRYING —) TRADE
(EASTERLY —) LEVANT LEVANTER
(FIERCE —) BUSTER
(GUST OF —) FLAN FLAW
(HAWAIIAN WINTER —) KONA
(HEAD —) NOSER MUZZLE
(HIGH —) RIG
(HOT —) CHILI GIBLEH SAMIEL SOLANO CHAMSIN KHAMSIN SIROCCO SCIROCCO
(LIGHT GENTLE —) BREEZE
(MOUNTAIN —) PUNA
(NORTH —) BISE AQUILO BOREAS AQUILON MISTRAL
(NORTHEAST —) BURAN GREGALE
(NORTHWEST —) CAURUS MAESTRO ARGESTES
(OF —) EOLIAN VENTAL AEOLIAN
(PERIODICAL —) ETESIAN MONSOON
(PERSIAN GULF —) SHAMAL SHARKI SHIMAL
(PERUVIAN —) PUNA PUNO
(ROARING —) BLORE
(SEVERE —) SNIFTER
(SOUTH —) NOTUS AUSTER
(SOUTHEAST —) EURUS SOLANO
(SOUTHEASTERLY —) SHARKI SHURGEE
(SOUTHWEST —) CHINOOK LIBECCIO
(STRONG —) BIRR
(VIOLENT —) BUSTER SQUALL SNORTER
(WARM —) FOHN FOEHN CHINOOK SANTANA
(WEST —) ZEPHYR FAVONIUS ZEPHYRUS
(WHISTLING —) SARSAR
(PREF.) ANEM(O) AURO VENTI VENTO
(SOUTH —) AUSTRO
WINDAGE DRIFT
WIND-BORNE EOLIC EOLIAN AEOLIAN
WINDER REEL WINCH DRUMMER PLUGGER SKEINER SPOOLER TENDRIL
WINDFALL VAIL GRAVY MANNA CADUAC FALLING BLOWDOWN BUCKSHEE
WINDGALL PUFF WINDDOG
WINDING LINK MAZY CRANK LACET SPIRE CREEKY DETOUR GYRATE SCREWY SPIRAL TWISTY WANLAS CRANKLE CRINKLE DEVIOUS MEANDER SINUATE SINUOSE SINUOUS SNAKING WRIGGLY WRINKLE SINUATED TORTUOUS MEANDERING
(PL.) AMBAGES RADDLINGS
WINDING-SHEET SHROUD SUDARY CEREMENT

WINDING STAIR COCKLE COCLEA WINDER COCHLEA
WIND INSTRUMENT
(PREF.) AEOLO
WINDLASS CRAB REEL WINK FEARN WINCH STOWCE STOWSE TACKLE TURNEL WINDAS WINDLE TWISTER WILDCAT ARTIFICE DRAWBEAM MANEUVER
WINDMILL JUMBO MOTOR COPTER PINWHEEL
(— ARM) VANE
(— BAR) UPLONG
(— SAIL) AWE EIE EIGHE FLIER FLYER SWEEP SWIFT
(PART OF —) BAR CAP FAN AXLE CORD HEEL LINE SAIL WHIP BLADE ROTOR STOCK SWEEP TOWER FANTAIL HELMATH CANNISTER WINDOHAFT
WINDOW BAY EYE LOOP ROSE SASH SLIT SLOT CHAFF GLAZE GRILL INLET LIGHT OGIVE SIGHT THURL AWNING DORMER GRILLE LANCET PEEPER ROSACE SPLITE THURLE WICKET BALCONE COUPLET DORMANT FENSTER GUICHET LUTHERN MIRADOR ORIFICE TRANSOM VENTANA WINDOCK WINNOCK CASEMENT FANLIGHT FENESTER FENESTRA JALOUSIE VENETIAN
(— IN ROOF) SKYLIGHT
(— OF TWO LIGHTS) COUPLET
(BAY —) ORIEL MIRADOR
(BLANK —) ORB
(BLIND —) ORB
(CHURCH —) LYCHNOSCOPE
(CRESCENT-SHAPED —) LUNETTE
(DORMER —) OXEYE DORMANT LUCARNE LUTHERN
(HIGH NARROW —) LANCET
(OVAL —) OXEYE
(PART OF —) BEAD JAMB LOCK PANE RAIL SASH STOP YOKE APRON FRAME SKIRT STILE STOOL STRIP CASING MUNTIN BRICKMOLD WINDOWPANE COUNTERWEIGHT
(POINTED —) OGIVE
(ROUND —) OXEYE OCULUS ROUNDEL
(SEMICIRCULAR —) FANLIGHT
(SMALL LOW —) MEZZANINE
(TICKET —) GRILLE GUICHET
(TWIN —) AJIMEZ
(PL.) STORMS
WINDOW DRESSING TRIM FRONT FACADE
WINDOW FRAME SASH REVEAL
WINDOW OYSTER COPIS
WINDOWPANE LIGHT LOZEN QUIRK LOZENGE TATTERSALL
WINDOWSILL SOLE

WINDPIPE HALS ARBER ARBOR
ERBER HALSE WIZEN ARTERY
GUGGLE STROUP WEEZLE KEACORN
TRACHEA WEASAND THRAPPLE
THROPPLE THROTTLE
(PREF.) BRONCH(I)(IO)(O) TRACHE(O)
TRACHO TRACHY
WINDROW BANK HEAP RIDGE
SWATH SWATHE
WINDSOR CHAIR FANBACK
WINDSTORM BLOW BURA THUD
BURAN BOURRAN
(HAWAIIAN —) KONA
WINDWARD ALOOF WEATHER
AWEATHER
(— SIDE) KOOLAU
WINDY BLOWY EMPTY GASSY
GUSTY HUFFY PROUD STARK SWALE
FLIMSY STORMY WONDIE BREATHY
FEARFUL GUSTFUL NERVOUS
VENTOSE VIOLENT BOISTEROUS
(— CITY) CHICAGO
WINE CUP VIN BOIS BUAL CUIT CUTE
DEAL PALM PORT RAPE ROSE ROSY
TENT TYRE VINO CAPRI GRAPE
KRAMA LUNEL MEDOC PETER PLONK
PORTO RIOJA SCIAN SHRAB SOAVE
TINTO TOKAY VINUM WHITE BAROLO
BARSAC CORTON COUTET GRAVES
KIJAFA LISBON MASDEU PIMENT
ROCHET SAUMUR SHIRAZ SOLERA
TIVOLI ALICANT AMBONNA
BACCHUS BANYULS BARBERA
BASTARD CATAWBA CHACOLI
CHATEAU DEZALEY FALERNO
MARSALA MISSION MOSELLE
ORVIETO PALERMO PIGMENT
RHENISH ROSOLIO SERCIAL SILLERY
VERNAGE VIDONIA VINTAGE
APERITIF BORDEAUX BURGUNDY
CHARNECO DELAWARE LACHRYMA
LIBATION MALVASIA MARSALLA
MOUNTAIN RIESLING ROCHELLE
RULANDER RUMBOOZE SPARKLER
BARDOLINO LAMBRUSCO ZINFANDEL
(— AND PUNCH) GLOGG
(— BOILED WITH HONEY) MULSE
(— CHEST) TANTALUS
(— FROM VINEGAR) ESILL
(— MIXED WITH WATER) KRASIS
(— OF EXCELLENT QUALITY) VINTAGE
(— OF SACRAMENT) BLOOD
(— SELLER) ABKAR BISTRO WINARE
(— SERVING) VOIDEE
(AROMATIZED —) DUBONNET
(BANANA —) MARAMBA
(BULK —) CUVEE
(CONSECRATED —) CUP
(DRY WHITE —) SANCERRE
(FIRST-GROWTH —) LAFITE LAFITTE
(FRANCONIAN —) STEIN LEISTEN
(GREEK —) RUMNEY RETSINA
RESINATA

(HEATED —) WHITEPOT
(INFERIOR —) PLONK
(JAPANESE —) SAKI
(KIND OF —) JUG POP BLUSH
(LIGHT —) BUAL CAPRI BAROLO
CANARY
(MULLED —) NEGUS WASSAIL
GLUHWEIN
(NEW —) MUST
(NEW — BOILED DOWN) CUIT CUTE
(PALM —) SAGWIRE
(RED —) ZIN GAMAY MACON TINTA
BAROLO BEAUNE CLARET MERLOT
CHIANTI HOLLOCK POMMARD
ALICANTE BURGUNDY CABERNET
FLORENCE BARDOLINO ZINFANDEL
(REVIVED —) STUM
(RHINE —) HOCK SYLVANER
(SPANISH —) SACK TENT DULCE
RIOJA OPORTO SHERRY ALICANT
ALIKANT BASTARD TARRAGONA
(STILL —) PONTAC PONTACQ
(SWEET —) TYRE DULCE MULSE
CANARY BASTARD MALMSEY
CHARNECO MUSCATEL
(TENT —) TINTO
(TOKAY —) ESSENCE
(TUSCAN —) VERDEA CHIANTI
FLORENCE
(WHITE —) HOCK SACK CAPRI CASEL
FORST BARSAC MALAGA BROMIAN
CATAWBA CHABLIS CONTHEY
LANGOON ANGELICA BUCELLAS
MUSCADET RIESLING SANCERRE
SAUTERNE VERMOUTH MEURSAULT
VERDICCHIO
(WHITE — APERITIF) KIR
(PL.) PALUS
(PREF.) ENO OEN(O) OINO VINI VINO
WINEBERRY MAKO MAKOMAKO
WINEGLASS FLUTE
WINEGROWER WINER VIGNERON
WINESBURG OHIO
(AUTHOR OF —) ANDERSON
(CHARACTER IN —) JOHN KATE WING
DAVID HARDY HELEN JESSE REEFY
SWIFT WHITE CURTIS GEORGE
LOUISE BENTLEY HARTMAN
WILLARD TRUNNION ELIZABETH
BIDDLEBAUM
WINESHOP BISTRO BODEGA
WINE-VAULT SHADE
WING ALA ARM ELL FAN FLY OAR RIB
VAN AILE FORE JAMB SAIL TAIL
ALULA ANNEX BLOCK FLANK JAMBE
PINNA POINT SHEAR VOLET BRANCH
FLETCH FLIGHT HALTER PENNON
PINION POISER DEMIVOL ELYTRON
ELYTRUM AEROFOIL BALANCER
DISPATCH TORMENTOR
(— OF ARMY) HORN
(— OF BUILDING) ELL JAMB JAMBE
ALETTE ALLETTE FLANKER

(— OF SHELL) AURICLE
(— OF THEATER) COULISSE
TORMENTOR
(— OF TRIPTYCH) VOLET
(—S DISPLAYED) VOL
(BASTARD —) ALULA
(BIRD'S —) FLAG
(FLY'S —S) HALTERES
(KIND OF —) DELIA SINGLE
(PL.) PENS FEATHERS
(PREF.) ALI PTER(O) PTERIDO
PTERYG(O) PTERYLO PTIL(O)
(SUFF.) PTERA PTERIS PTEROUS
PTERUS PTERYX
WING CASE SHEATH ELYTRON
(BEETLE'S —) SHARD
WINGDING GALA
WINGED AILE ALATE LOFTY RAPID
SWIFT ALATED PENNED PENNATE
ELEVATED
(PREF.) PTENO
(SUFF.) PTENE
WINGED DISK FEROHER
WINGED ELM WAHOO
WING-FOOTED FLEET SWIFT
ALIPED
WINGLESS APTERAL
WING-LIKE ALARY ALIFORM
PTEROID PTERGOID
WING SHELL STROMB ELYTRON
STROMBUS
WINGS OF THE DOVE (AUTHOR
OF —) JAMES
(CHARACTER IN —) CROY KATE MARK
MILLY MERTON THEALE DENSHER
WINGTIP SHOE
WINK BAT NAP PINK BLINK DEATH
FLASH PRINK SLEEP TWINK CONNIVE
FLICKER INSTANT NICTATE SPARKLE
TWINKLE NICTITATE
WINKER EYE BLINKER EYELASH
WINKING BLINK
WINKLE PERIWIG TWINKLE
WINNER PLACER VICTOR FACEMAN
BANGSTER
(EASY —) SHOOIN
(NOT A —) ALSORAN
(SURE —) SNIP
WINNIE-THE-POOH (AUTHOR OF
) MILNE
(CHARACTER IN —) ROO KANGA
ROBIN EEYORE PIGLET RABBIT
HEFFALUMP CHRISTOPHER
WINNING GAIN SWEET PROFIT
GAINING VICTORY WINSOME
CHARMING
(— OF ALL TRICKS) CAPOT
SCHWARZ
(PL.) WIN VELVET
WINNOW FAN WIM CHAR SIFT WIND
DIGHT SIEVE DELETE REMOVE
SELECT WINDER SEPARATE
WINNOWER VAN WINDER DIGHTER

WINSOME GAY BUXOM SWEET
CHARMING CHEERFUL PLEASANT
WINTER BISE SNOW YEAR HIEMS
HIVER DECEMBER HIBERNATE
(— AILMENT) STREP
(— OVER) HOG
WINTERBERRY PRINOS
HOOPWOOD
WINTERBLOOM AZALEA
WINTERGREEN JINKS CHINKS
PYROLA DRUNKER BOXBERRY
DRUNKARD EYEBERRY GAYWINGS
IVYBERRY LIMONIUM RATSBANE
SHINLEAF TEABERRY PINEDROPS
PIPSISSEWA
WINTERLIKE BRUMAL
WINTERSET (AUTHOR OF —)
ANDERSON
(CHARACTER IN —) MIO CARR GARTH
GAUNT TROCK ESDRAS SHADOW
ROMAGNA MIRIAMNE BARTOLOMEO
WINTER'S TALE (AUTHOR OF —)
SHAKESPEARE
(CHARACTER IN —) DION MOPSA
DORCAS EMILIA CAMILLO LEONTES
PAULINA PERDITA FLORIZEL
HERMIONE ANTIGONUS AUTOLYCUS
CLEOMENES MAMILLIUS POLIXENES
ARCHIDAMUS
WINTRY AGED COLD WHITE BOREAL
HIEMAL STORMY BRUMOUS
CHILLING HIBERNAL
WINTUN COPEHAN
WINY VINOUS DRUNKEN
WINZE CURSE RAISE OPENING
PASSAGEWAY
WIPE BEAT BLOW DRUB DUST GIBE
DICHT DIGHT SWIPE CANCEL
SPONGE SPUNGE STRIKE ABOLISH
CLEANSE ABSTERGE SQUEEGEE
(— BEAK OF HAWK) FEAK
(— NOSE) SNITE
(— OFF) SCUFF
(— OUT) ERASE SCRUB SWEEP
EFFACE DESTROY
(— UP) SWAB SWOB
WIPEOUT MASSACRE
WIPER DUSTER TRIPPET
WIPING TERSION
(— OF INK ON PLATE) RETROUSSAGE
(— OUT) EXTINCTION
WIRE GUY TAP BINE CORE DENT
DRAG FILE FUSE PURL BRACE CABLE
OUTER RISER SNAKE SWEEP TAPER
BRIDGE FESCUE FINGER HEATER
JUMPER NEEDLE STAPLE STOLON
STRAND DROPPER HAYWIRE
LAMETTA LASHING PRICKER SHIFTER
SNUFFER FILAMENT LIGATURE
PALISADE PULLDOWN STRINGER
TELEGRAM
(— BETWEEN TWO VESSELS) SWEEP
(— FASTENED TO TEETH) BRACES

(— FOR CUTTING CLAY) SLING
(— FOR SUSTAINING HAIR)
PALISADE
(— HOLDING SPOOL) SPIT
(— IN BLASTING CAP) BRIDGE
(— IN CATHETER) STYLET
(— IN WEAVING LOOM) DENT
(— OF GOLD,SILVER OR BRASS)
LAMETTA
(—S BOUND TOGETHER) SELVAGE
(— TO ADJUST WICK) SNUFFER
(— TO CLOSE A BREAK) JUMPER
(— TO REMOVE TUMORS) LIGATURE
(— USED AS POINTER) FESCUE
(— USED IN SPLICING CABLES)
TAPER
(ENAMELED —) LITZ
(FENCE —) DROPPER
(FRAYED —) JAGGER
(GOLD —) KINSEN
(LOOPED —) OESE
(PALLET —) PULLDOWN
(PRIMING —) PICKER EPINGLETTE
(SURGICAL —) STYLET
(TWISTED —) HEALD HEADLE
HEDDLE
(VENT —) PRICKER
(4 —S TWISTED TOGETHER) QUAD
WIRE CUTTER SECATEUR
WIREDRAW WREST OUTWIT
DEFRAUD DISTORT ELONGATE
WIREGLASS FLUTE
WIRE GRASS POA
WIRELESS RADIO
WIRE ROPE JACKSTAY
WIRETAP BUG
(REMOVE —) DEBUG
(REMOVE — DEVICE) DEBUG
WIREWORM ELATER ELATERID
MILLIPEDE
WIRY THIN HARDY STIFF WITHY
FEEBLE KNOTTY SINEWY STRINGY
THREADY
WIS KNOW THINK SURELY SUPPOSE

WISCONSIN

CAPITAL: MADISON
COLLEGE: RIPON BELOIT ALVERNO
CARROLL VITERBO CARTHAGE
COUNTY: DOOR VILAS JUNEAU
CALUMET SHAWANO WAUSHARA
INDIAN: FOX SAUK KICKAPOO
WINNEBAGO
LAKE: POYGAN MENDOTA WISSOTA
WINNEBAGO
MOUNTAIN: TIMSHILL SUGARBUSH
NATIVE: BADGER
NICKNAME: BADGER
RIVER: FOX BLACK STCROIX
CHIPPEWA MENOMINEE
STATE BIRD: ROBIN
STATE FLOWER: VIOLET
STATE TREE: MAPLE

TOWN: ANTIGO BELOIT RACINE
WAUSAU ASHLAND BARABOO
KENOSHA MADISON OSHKOSH
PORTAGE SHAWANO LACROSSE
SUPERIOR WAUKESHA

WISDOM WIT LORE SABE SABBY
SAVEY SENSE SOPHY ADVICE
GNOSIS HOKMAH POLICY SATTVA
SOPHIA WISURE CUNNING MINERVA
SAGESSE SLEIGHT AFTERWIT
JUDGMENT PRUDENCE SAPIENCE
(DIVINE —) WORD THEOMAGY
(ESOTERIC —) GNOSIS
(SUPREME —) PRAJNA
(UNIVERSAL —) PANSOPHY
(PREF.) SOPH(O) SOPHI(O)
(SUFF.) SOPH(ER)(IC)(IST)(Y)
WISE HEP SLY DEEP GASH GOOD
KIND SAGE SANE SEND TURN
CANNY FRESH GUIDE SMART SOUND
WITTY ADVISE CRAFTY DIRECT
QUAINT WITFUL WITTER ANCIENT
ERUDITE GNOSTIC KNOWING
LEARNED POLITIC PRUDENT SAPIENT
THRIVEN PERSUADE PROFOUND
SENSIBLE SPACIOUS
(— GUY) SAGE SOLON
(— MAN) MAGI SAGE MAGUS
AMAUTA ORACLE
(— ONE) OWL
(PREF.) SOPH(O) SOPHI(O)
(SUFF.) SOPH(ER)(IC)(IST)(Y)
WISEACRE SAGE DUNCE GOTHAM
SOLONIST WISEHEAD WISELING
WISECRACK JOKE QUIP
WISE CRACK GASSER
WISENT BISON AUROCH UROCHS
BONASUS
WISH CARE GIVE GOAL HOPE LIST
LUST MIND VOTE WANT WILL
BOSOM COVET CRAVE DREAM
HEART TASTE VOICE DESIRE UTINAM
FAREWELL GODSPEED PLEASURE
(— OTHERWISE) REGRET
(DEATH —) DESTRUDO
(EARNEST —) VOW
(SLIGHT —) VELLEITY
WISHBONE FURCULA FOURCHET
FURCULUM MERRYTHOUGHT
WISHFUL EAGER HOPEFUL LONGING
ALLURING
WISHING ANXIOUS DESIROUS
WISHY-WASHY PALE THIN WEAK
BLAND VAPID FEEBLE DILUTED
INSIPID SLIPSLOP
WISKET BASKET WHISKET
WISP TATE WUSP SCRAP SHRED
SKIFF SKIFT TWIST RUMPLE
CRUMPLE MASSAGE
(— OF HAY) RISP
(— OF STRAW) WAP WASE DOSSIL
(— OF THATCH) TIPPET

WISPY FRAIL NEBULOUS

WISTERIA FUJI KRAUNHIA

WISTFUL INTENT PENSIVE WISHFUL
MOURNFUL YEARNING

WISTITI WISTIT MARMOSET

WIT VAT VYT WAG KNOW NOUS SALT
BRAIN HUMOR IRONY SENSE THINK
WHITE WOTTE ACUMEN ESPRIT
POLICY SANITY SATIRE WISDOM
CONCEIT CUNNING PICADOR
SARCASM SUPPOSE THINKER
WITWORM BADINAGE REPARTEE
(BITING —) DICACITY
(TO —) NAMELY SCILICET
(PL.) SCONCE BUTTONS

WITCH ALP ANI HAG HEG HEX
MARE SAGA TRAT WYCH BRUJA
BUTCH GRERE HEXER LAMIA SIBYL
WEIRD WIGHT ASUANG CARLEY
CARLIN CUMMER DOWDEN DUESSA
HECATE KIMMER PILWIZ WIZARD
AGANICE CANIDIA CARLINE
HAGGARD HELLCAT SYCORAX
BABAJAGA CAROLINE ERICHTHO
SORCERER SPAEWIFE VERSIERA
WALKYRIE
(HOME OF —) ENDOR
(MEETING OF —S) ESBAT
(PL.) COVEN

WITCHCRAFT CHARM GOETY
OBEAH WICCA CUNNING HEXEREI
MYALISM SORCERY BRUJERIA
DEVILTRY PISHOGUE WIZARDRY

WITCH DOCTOR BOCOR BOKOR
GOOFER GUFFER

WITCHERY CHARM SPELL SORCERY
SORTIARY

WITCHES'-BROOM STAGHEAD

WITCHGRASS COUCH PANIC
PANICLE

WITCH HAZEL FOTHERGILLA

WITE WAT BLAME FAULT WAYTE
CENSURE REPROACH HAMESOKEN

WITH BY CUM MID MIT WUD AVEC
CHEZ DOWN AMONG ANENT WIGHT
AGAINST
(— HAND ON HIP) AKIMBO
(— REGARD TO) ABOUT
(— SPEED) TIVY
(PREF.) CO COL COM CON COR META
SYM SYN

WITHDRAW GO COY DROP TAKE
AVOID DEMIT FREAK LOOSE REVEL
SHIFT START UNSAY CHANGE
DECEDE DESERT DETACH DETRAY
DEVOID EFFACE FLINCH MINISH
RECALL RECANT RECEDE RETIRE
REVOKE ROGATE SECEDE SHRINK
SINGLE SYPHON ABSCOND
CONCEAL DESCEND DETRACT
FORSAKE INVEIGH RETRACT
RETREAT SCRATCH SCUTTLE
SECLUDE SUBDUCE SUBDUCT

TURNOFF UNSCREW SEPARATE
SUBTRACT SEGREGATE
SEQUESTER
(— ATTENTION) PRESCIND
(— FROM) VAIK ABANDON
(— FROM COMPETITION) SCRATCH
(— FROM POKER POT) DROP
(— FROM REALITY) FREAK
(— FROM USE) MOTHBALL
(— SUPPORT) ABANDON
(— TEMPORARILY) STOPOUT
(— WITHIN) INVAGINATE

WITHDRAWAL DRAIN FLIGHT
HIDING OFFLAP RETIRE SHRINK
ABSENCE DUNKIRK PULLOUT
REGRESS RETIRAL RETREAT
SCUTTLE RECESSION REVULSION
RETRACTION
(— FROM WORLDLY THINGS)
ABSTRACTION
(— OF BUILDING FACE) SETBACK
(— OF PROMISE) BACKWORD
(— OF SUIT) RETRAXIT

WITHDRAWN SHY ASOCIAL
INGROWN SECLUSE DISTRAIT
ISOLATED SECLUDED RECESSIVE
ABSTRACTED

WITHE HANK ROPE TIER TWIG WITHY
WATTLE WICKER CRINGLE

WITHER BURN DAZE FADE MIFF PINE
RUST SEAR STUN WARP WELK WELT
BLAST CLING DAVER DECAY QUAIL
WIZEN COTTER GIZZEN SHRINK
WALLOW WELTER WILTER WINDER
AREFACT DECLINE FORWELK
SENESCE SHRIVEL LANGUISH
PARALYZE

WITHERED DRY ARID SEAR SERE
CORKY SCRAM MARCID BLASTED
UNGREEN WEARISH WIZENED
AUTUMNAL

WITHERING SCATHING

WITHHELD DEFERRED SUSPENSE

WITHHOLD CURB DENY HIDE KEEP
STOP CHECK SCANT ABSENT
DEPORT DETAIN REFUSE RETAIN
ABSTAIN BOYCOTT DEFORCE
FORBEAR OUTHOLD REPRESS
RESERVE SUSPEND RESTRAIN
SUBTRACT
(— CONSENT) DECLINE

WITHHOLDING DETAINER
(— OF DUES) CHECKOFF
(CONDITIONAL —) SUSPENSION

WITHIN IN ON BEN BIN INBY INLY
INTRA ABOARD HEREIN INSIDE
INWITH INDOORS ENCLOSED
INCLUDED INWARDLY
(PREF.) END(O) ENT(O) ESO IL IM IN
INFRA INTER INTRA INTRO
(ARISING —) IDIO

WITHOUT EX BUT OUT SEN BOUT
FREE OHNE SANS SINE MINUS

SENZA FAILING OUTSIDE WANTING
INNOCENT OUTDOORS
(— **ACCENT**) ENCLITIC
(— **ACTION**) DEEDLESS
(— **A FLANGE**) BALD
(— **A MATE**) ODD
(— **BEGINNING OR END**) ETERNAL
(— **BLEMISH**) CHOICE
(— **BRIGHTNESS**) LACKLUSTER
(— **CONTENTS**) INANE
(— **DELAY**) AWAY FOOTHOT
SUMMARY
(— **DELIBERATION**) HEADLONG
(— **EFFECT**) EMPTY INSIGNIFICANT
(— **EMOTION**) DRYLY DULLY
(— **END**) ENTERNAL
(— **EXCEPTION**) ALWAYS
(— **FEET**) APOD
(— **FUNDS**) CLEAN
(— **HORNS**) ACEROUS
(— **INTEREST**) BARREN
(— **LIFE**) DULL AZOIC INANIMATE
(— **LIGHT**) APHOTIC
(— **LIMITS OF DURATION**) AGELESS
(— **MONEY**) IMPECUNIOUS
(— **ORDER**) ANYHOW
(— **PAYMENT**) FREE
(— **POWER**) ADRIFT
(— **PROFIT**) FRUITLESS
(— **QUALIFICATION**) FLAT
(— **QUESTION**) EASILY SECURELY
(— **REALITY**) AIRY
(— **REASON**) BLINDLY
(— **REMEDY**) BOOTLESS
(— **ROADS**) INVIOUS
(— **RULE OR LAW**) ANARCHIC
(— **SADDLES**) ASELLATE
(— **SALT**) FRESH
(— **SHAME**) BROWLESS
(— **SIN**) IMPECCANT
(— **STRENGTH**) MEAGER MEAGRE
(— **TEETH, TONGUE OR CLAWS**)
MORNE
(— **THORNS**) INERM
(— **WINGS**) APTEROUS
(PREF.) A ECT(O) LIPO
(— **GOVERNMENT**) ANARCH(O)
(SUFF.) LESS
WITHSTAND BIDE DEFY TAKE ABIDE
OPPOSE OPPUGN RESIST CONTAIN
CONTEST FORBEAR SUSTAIN
CONFRONT WITHSTAY
WITHY WIRY AGILE OSIER WOODY
WILLOW WOODIE WINDING
WITLESS MAD GROSS INANE SILLY
INSANE STUPID FATUOUS FOOLISH
UNWITTY HEEDLESS SLAPHAPPY
WITLOOF ENDIVE CHICORY
WITNESS SEE TAKE TEST PROOF
ATTEST BEHOLD MARTYR RECORD
TESTIS TESTOR CURATOR TESTATE
TESTIFY EVIDENCE RECORDER
SUFFRAGE

(FALSE —) JUROR
(PL.) SECTA
(PREF.) TESTI
WITNESS-BOX STAND
WITOTO HUITOTE
WITTICISM WIT JEER JEST JOKE
QUIP SALLY SLENT WHEEZE
WITTING NEWS TIDINGS
WITTINGLY SCIENTER
WITTOL FOOL CUCKOLD WITTALL
WITTY GASH WILY WISE DROLL LEPID
PAWKY SHARP SMART CLEVER
FACETE JOCOSE JOCULAR KNOWING
CONCEITY HUMOROUS
(NOT —) INFICETE
WIVERN DRAGON WYVERN
WIZARD MAGE SEER SHIZ FIEND
WITCH DOCTOR EXPERT PELLAR
WARLOW CHARMED MAGICAL
SPAEMAN WARLOCK WISEMAN
CONJUROR MAGICIAN SORCERER
TROLLMAN WITCHMAN ARCHIMAGE
(PL.) GOETAE
WIZARDRY SORCERY
WIZEN DRY WITHER SHRIVEL
WIZENED SERE GIZZEN WEAZEN
WOAD DYE NIL ODE ANIL KERS NILL
OADE CRESS ANILLA INDICO INDIGO
PASTEL
(PREF.) ISAT(O)
WOADWAXEN ALLELUIA ALLELUJA
WOBBLE COCKLE COGGLE HOBBLE
QUAVER SHIMMY TEETER TITTER
TOTTER WABBLE WIGGLE TREMBLE
NUTATION
(KIND OF —) CHANDLER
WOBBLY LOOSE SHAKY COGGLY
DRUNKEN DOUBTFUL
WODEN ODIN ALLFATHER
WOE WA WEI BALE DULE PAIN
PINE WAWE GRIEF MISERY SORROW
TROUBLE WILLAWA CALAMITY
DISTRESS WELLADAY WELLAWAY
WOEBEGONE WAFF UNHAPPY
DEJECTED DESOLATE DOWNCAST
WOEFUL MEAN DISMAL PALTRY
RUEFUL DIREFUL DOLEFUL RUTHFUL
DOLOROUS PITIABLE WRETCHED
WOLF GLUT LOBO CANID FREKI
YABBI CHANCO COYOTE FAMINE
FENRIR ISGRIN KABERU LOAFER
MASHER SIGRIM THOOID POVERTY
ISENGRIM
(FOX —) ZORRO
(KIND OF —) LONE
(PREF.) LUPI LYC(O) VULPI
WOLFBERRY BUCKBUSH
WOLFHOUND ALAN BORZOI PSOVIE
WOLFISH LUPINE RAVENOUS
WOLFLIKE THOOID
WOLFRAMITE CAL TUNGSTEN
WOLFSBANE ACONITE DOGBANE
FOXBANE

WOLF SPIDER HUNT JAGER HUNTER JAEGER JAYHAWK LYCOSID TARANTULA

WOLVERINE PIG GLUT GORB MIKER GLOTUM HELLUO GLUTTON GUTLING LURCHER MOOCHER RAVENER SWILLER CARCAJOU DRAFFMAN GOURMAND GULLYGUT
(— STATE) MICHIGAN

WOMAN BIM BIT DAM EVE HEN HER JUG MEG SHE TEG TIT BABE BABY BINT BOSS CONY DAME FAIR FEME FLAG FROW JADE JANE LADY MAMA MARY MORT PERI SLUT WIFE BIDDY BIMBO BLADE BROAD CHINA DONAH FEMME FRAIL JATNI LUBRA LUCKY MAMMA MUJER QUEAN SKIRT SMOCK SQUAW TAGGE TOOTS TWIST UMMAN VROUW BURDIE CALICO CARLIN CUMMER FEMALE GIMMER HEIFER KIMMER LUCKIE MANESS MULIER SISTER TOMATO VIRAGO WAHINE CARLING CHANGAR DISTAFF PARTLET PINNACE PLACKET QUAEDAM MISTRESS PETTICOAT
(— DESERTED BY HUSBAND) AGUNAH
(— OF CONSEQUENCE) HERSELF
(— OF LOW CASTE) DASI
(— OF MEXICAN DESCENT) CHICANA
(— OF RANK) DOMINA
(— OF UNSTEADY CHARACTER) FLAP CALLET
(— OF WEALTH) FORTUNE
(— WHO ACTS AS ADVISER) EGERIA
(— WITH ONE CHILD) UNIPARA
(— WITH 3 CHILDREN) TRIPARA
(ABORIGINAL —) GIN LUBRA
(ABUSIVE —) FISHWIFE
(ALLURING —) DISH
(ATHENIAN — OF HIGH RANK) GERARA GERAERA
(ATTRACTIVE —) FOX DOLLY SHEBA DOLLIE LOOKER CHARMER
(AUSTRALIAN —) BINT
(AWKWARD —) ROIL
(BEAUTIFUL —) HURI PERI BELLE HOURI SIREN SPARK CHERUB EYEFUL MUSIDORA
(BIG COURAGEOUS —) VIRAGO
(BLESSED —) BEATA
(BOISTEROUS —) HOYDEN
(BOLD —) RAMP
(CLEANING —) CHAR
(COARSE —) BEAST RUDAS BLOWZE RULLION
(COOLIE —) CHANGAR
(COY —) HAGGARD
(CREMATED —) SATI SUTTEE
(DEAR —) PEAT
(DIRTY —) SLUT SLATTERN
(DISSOLUTE —) SLAG

(DUTCH OR GERMAN —) FRAU FROW FROKIN FRAULEIN
(ENGAGED —) BONDAGER
(ENTICING —) SIREN
(EVIL OLD —) HAG HELLHAG
(EXCITED —) MAENAD
(FASCINATING —) SIREN
(FASHIONABLE —) MILADY GALLANT ELEGANTE
(FAT —) BOSS FUSTILUGS
(FINE —) SCREAMER
(FIRST —) EMBLA PANDORA
(FLIGHTY —) GILLET JILLET FLIPFLOP
(FLIRTING —) CHIPPY FIZGIG
(FOOLISH —) TAWPIF
(FORWARD —) STRAP
(FOUL-MOUTHED —) RUDAS
(FRENCH HOLY —) STE SAINTE
(FRENZIED —) MAENAD
(GAUDY —) JAY
(GENTLE —) DOVE
(GOSSIP —) HAIK HAKE BIDDY TABBY
(GOSSIPY, TALKATIVE —) YENTA
(GROSS —) SOW
(GYPSY —) ROMI ROMNI GITANA
(ILL-TEMPERED —) VIXEN CATAMARAN
(IMMODEST —) TOMBOY
(IMMORAL —) RIG GITCH FLAPPER HARLOTRY
(IMPUDENT —) YANKIE
(INDIAN —) SQUAW WENCH KLOOCH BUCKEEN
(INSPIRED —) PHOEBAD
(ITALIAN —) DONNA
(LASCIVIOUS —) GIGLET
(LEARNED —) PUNDITA CLERGESS
(LEWD —) REP SLUT BITCH HUSSY HUZZY MALKIN BROTHEL CYPRIAN
(LOOSE —) BAG BIM KIT MOB TIB DRAB FLAP BIMBO TROLL GILLOT HARLOT LIMMER BAGGAGE COCOTTE FRANION TROLLOP
(LOUD-SPOKEN —) RANDY
(LOW OR WORTHLESS —) JADE JURR BUNTER SLINGDUST
(MARRIED — OF LOWLY STATION) GOODY
(MASCULINE —) AMAZON RULLION COTQUEAN
(MEEK —) GRIZEL
(MUSLIM —) BEGUM
(MYTHOLOGICAL —) HEROINE
(NON-JEWISH —) SHIKSA
(ODD-LOOKING —) JUDY
(OLD —) GIB HEN BABA TROT CRONE FAGOT FRUMP LUCKY TROUT BELDAM CARLIN GAMMER GEEZER GRANNY LUCKIE CARLINE GRANDAM HARRIDAN CAILLEACH
(OLD SHRIVELED —) FAGOT FAGGOT
(OVERGROWN —) FUSTILUGS

(PAINTED —) PICT
(PEDANTIC —) BLUE
(PERT —) CHIT
(PERVERSE —) JADE
(PORTUGUESE —) SENHORA
(PREGNANT —) GRAVIDA
(PRIGGISH —) PRUDE
(RAPACIOUS —) HARPY
(RAW-BONED —) RANDLETREE
(RICH OLD —) DOWAGER
(RUDE —) SCOLD
(RUSTIC —) JOAN
(SCOLDING —) RANDY SHREW
COTQUEAN RIXATRIX
(SHAMELESS —) JEZEBEL
(SHORT OR STUMPY —) CUTTY
(SHOWY —) ANONYMA
(SHREWISH —) JADE HARPY SKELLAT
(SLATTERNLY —) DRAB FLEABAG
SLAMKIN
(SLENDER GRACEFUL —) SYLPH
(SLIPSHOD —) MAUX CLATCH
TROLLIMOG
(SLOVENLY —) BAG DAW SOW SLUT
BESOM TAWPY TROLL TROLLOP
SLATTERN
(SPANISH —) DONA GITANA
(SPANISH-INDIAN —) CHOLA
(SPITEFUL —) CAT FURY BITCH
(SQUAT —) TRUB
(SQUEAMISH —) COCKNEY
(STAID —) MATRON
(STATELY —) JUNO
(STORMY VIOLENT —) FURY
(TRACTABLE —) SHEEP
(UGLY —) HAG GORGON
(UNATTRACTIVE —) SCRUBBER
(UNCHASTE —) JILT
(UNMARRIED —) DAME GIRL
SPINSTER MADEMOISELLE
(VIOLENT —) FURY
(VIXENISH —) HARRIDAN
(WANTON —) MINX TRUB QUEAN
PARNEL
(WICKED —) JEZEBEL
(WISE —) VOLVA ALRUNA ALRUNE
(WITHERED —) CRONE
(YOUNG —) BIT BIRD BURD CHIT
DAME DELL DOLL GIRL LASS PUSS
BEAST CHICK FILLY FLUFF TOAST
DAMSEL HEIFER PIGEON SHEILA
SUBDEB BAGGAGE CHICKEN
DAMOZEL FLAPPER WINKLOT
DAUGHTER GRISETTE
(PREF.) FEMINO GYN(AE)(AECO)(AEO)
(ANDRO)(E)(EO)(O)
(SUFF.) GYN(E)(IST)(OUS)
WOMAN HATER MISOGYNIST
WOMANHOOD MULIEBRITY
WOMAN IN WHITE (AUTHOR OF —)
COLLINS
(CHARACTER IN —) ANNE FOSCO
GLYDE LAURA PESCA MARIAN
WALTER FAIRLIE HALCOMBE
PERCIVAL CATHERICK HARTRIGHT
WOMANISH FEMALE FEMININE
LADYLIKE PETTICOAT
WOMANIZER ROUE
WOMANKIND WOMEN CALICO
MUSLIN FEMINIE
WOMAN'S TONGUE LEBBEK
WOMB BELLY CRADLE UTERUS
VENTER
(PREF.) COLP(O) HYSTER(O) METRO
UTER(O) VULVI VULVO
(SUFF.) COLPOS METRA METRIUM
WOMBAT KOALA BADGER DIDELPH
VOMBATID
WOMEN DISTAFF
(— OF EARLY CHURCH) SETTERS
AGAPETAE
WON CITY LIVE ROOM ABIDE DWELL
REGION
WONDER AWE MUSE SELI SIGN
TROW UNCO UNKO VERY FARLY
FERLY SELLE SELLY UNCOW ADMIRE
MARVEL MIRATE MAGNALE MIRABLE
MIRACLE PORTENT PRODIGY
STRANGE UNCOUTH AMERVEIL
SELCOUTH SURPRISE
(SMALL —) GEM
(PL.) MIRABILIA
(PREF.) TERAT(O) THAUMA(TO)
THAUMO
WONDERFUL KEEN NEAT SELI
FERLY GRAND GREAT SWELL
WAKON GEASON MIGHTY AMAZING
EPATANT GALLANT MIRABLE MIRIFIC
STRANGE FRABJOUS GLORIOUS
MIRABLE TERRIFIC WONDROUS
WONDERFULLY AMAZING
WONDER-WORKER THEURGIC
THEURGIST
WONDER-WORKING MIRIFIC
WONG FIELD GROVE PLAIN MEADOW
WONKY AWRY SHAKY WRONG
UNSTEADY
WONT APT USE FAIN USED VAIN
HABIT USAGE CUSTOM INCLINED
WONTED TAME USUAL HAUNTED
WOO SUE LOVE SEEK SUIT WALE
COURT SPARK SPOON ASSAIL
SPLUNT SUITOR ADDRESS
WOOD
(ALSO SEE TREE AND TIMBER) HAG
KIP BOIS BOSK BOWL EKKI HOLT
HYLE KIRI MASS MOCK PALO SHAW
SUPA TREE WOLE ALDER CAHUY
CHARK CROWD EDDER FLOUR
GROVE HURST HYRST KOKRA RESAK
SHOLA STICK STUFF WEALD
ALMOND ANGILI AUSUBO BRAZIL
EKHIMI FOREST ITAUBA JARANA
LUMBER PALING SPINNY TIMBER
APITONG AVODIRE BOSCAGE
BOSKAGE COPPICE DADDOCK

DUDGEON HAYBOTE SATINAY
VENESIA BAGTIKAN CRANTARA
FIREBOOT CALAMANDER
(— BURNT AS PERFUME) AGALLOCH
(— FOR CARPENTRY) STUFF
(— FOR OARS) ASH
(— FOR REPAIRING HEDGE) TINING
HAYBOTE
(— OF SMALL EXTENT) GROVE
(OF THE VERA) VENESIA
(— ON RAFTER) FUR
(— ROTATED ON STRING) ROMBOS
RHOMBOS
(— USEFUL FOR TINDER) PUNK
SPONK TOUCHWOOD
(— YIELDING PERFUME) LINALOA
(BABUL —) SUNT
(BLACK —) EBONY
(CONE-SHAPED PIECE OF —) ACORN
(DARK RED —) RATA
(DEAD —) RAMMEL
(DENSIFIED —) STAYPAK
(ELASTIC —) SYCAMORE
(FIR —) DEAL
(FLAT ROUND PIECE OF —)
TRENCHER
(FLEXIBLE —) EDDER
(FOSSIL —) PINITE PEUCITES
(FRAGRANT —) CEDAR
SANDALWOOD
(FUEL —) ESTOVERS
(HARD —) ASH DAO ELM SAL BAKU
IPIL KARI LANA POON ANJAN EBONY
GIDYA KARRI KOKRA MAPLE MAZER
ZANTE BANUYO CAMARA FREIJO
GIDGEE KEMPAS SABICU SAPELE
WALNUT CURUPAY DATTOCK
HICKORY GUAIACUM IRONBARK
MAHOGANY
(HEAVY —) DAO EBON EBONY
CHENGAL GUAYABI SUCUPIRA
(LIGHT —) POON BALSA HEMLOCK
(LIMBA —) KORINA
(LOGGED —) CHIP
(LOST —) CHIPPAGE
(LUSTROUS —) LEZA BOARWOOD
(MATCHBOX —) SKILLET
(MOTTLED —) AMBOINA
CALAMBOUR
(NARROW BAR OF —) SLAT
(NUMBER 1 —) DRIVER
(NUMBER 2 —) BRASSIE
(NUMBER 3 —) SPOON
(NUMBER 4 —) CLEEK
(OILY —) BATETE
(OLIVE —) COLLIE
(PETRIFIED —) LITHOXYL ROCKWOOD
(PINE —) DEAL
(PINKISH —) BOSSE
(POINTED PIECE OF —) TRIPPET
(REDDISH —) KOA KARI KARRI
ARANGA BANABA CHERRY DUNGON
SATINE KAMBALA

(REDDISH-YELLOW —) GUYO
(ROTTEN —) DADDOCK
(SANDARAC —) ALERCE
(SMALL —) SHAW
(SOFT —) KIRI GABUN GABOON
ELKWOOD AGALLOCH ALBURNUM
GUATAMBU
(SPONGY —) PUNK
(SQUARE LOG OF —) NOG
(STICK OF —) BILLET
(STRIP OF —) LATH STAVE BATTEN
REEPER REGLET SPLINE SPLINT
SPLINTER
(WATER-RESISTING —) AMUGIS
(YELLOWISH —) HALDU FUSTIC
IDIGBO KADAMBA KAMASSI
GUATAMBU
(PREF.) HYL(O) LIGN(I)(O) XYL(O)
(SUFF.) XYLON XYLUM
WOOD ALCOHOL METHANOL
WOOD ANEMONE CYME EMONY
BOWBELLA SNOWDROP
WOODBARK SABLE BLONDINE
WOODBINE BIND WIDBIN EGLATERE
WOODCARVER BODGER
WOODCHUCK CHUG CHUCK
MONAX MARMOT SUSLIK WEJACK
MOONACK GROUNDHOG
WOODCOCK QUIS PEWEE PEWIT
SNIPE SNITE SHRUPS BECASSE
SIMPLETON
WOODCUT BLOCK
WOODCUTTER AXEMAN LOGGER
WOODMAN WOODSMAN
WOOD DUCK SQUEALER
BRANCHER
WOODED BOSKY TREEY HYLEAN
SYLVAN FORESTED NEMOROUS
WOODEN DRY DULL STIFF TREEN
CLUMSY STICKY STOLID TIMBER
AWKWARD DEADPAN TIMBERN
LIFELESS
WOOD GUM XYLAN
WOOD HEN WEKA
WOODHEWER PICUCULE
WOOD HOOPOE WHOOP WHOOPE
IRRISOR DUNGBIRD PICARIAN
WOOD HYACINTH SCILLA
CROWTOE GREGGLE HAREBELL
WOOD IBIS STORK GANNET JABIRU
IRONHEAD
WOODLAND DESERT MIOMBO
SPRING BOSCAGE
(WASTE —) WEALD
WOOD LOUSE SLATER SOWBUG
PILLBUG MILLIPED
WOODPECKER AWL CHAB JYNX
KATE PEEK ECCLE HECCO HEWEL
ICKLE PICUS SPEKT HECKLE NICKER
NICKLE PECKER PIANET PICULE
SPRITE TAPPER YAFFLE YUCKER
YUKKEL CLIMBER CREEPER FLICKER
HEWHOLE HICKWAY LOGCOCK

REDHEAD SAPSUCK SNAPPER
SPEIGHT WHETILE WITWALL
WRYNECK DIRTBIRD HICKWALL
PICARIAN PICUCULE POPINJAY
RAINBIRD RAINFOWL WALLHICK
SAPSUCKER
(LIKE A —) PICIFORM
(PREF.) PICI
WOOD-PIGEON CULVER CUSHAT
ZOOZOO RINGDOVE
WOOD PIGEON CUSHAT ZOOZOO
WOODPILE STRAN STRAND
WOODRICK
WOOD ROBIN MIRO TOMTIT
WOODRUFF HAIROF MUGGET
MUGWET WOODROW HAIRHOOF
WOODS BOSK BUSH BOSQUE
(PREF.) NEMO SILVI SYLVI
WOODSMAN BUSHY SILVAN
SYLVAN BUSHMAN BUSHWACK
WOOD SORREL OCA COCKOO
HEARTS LUJULA OXALIS TREFOIL
ALLELUIA ALLELUJA SHAMROCK
STABWORT
WOOD SPIRIT METHANOL
WOOD SUGAR XYLOSE
WOOD THRUSH MAYBIRD
WOODTURNER BODGER
WOODWIND OBOE FLUTE BASSOON
PIBGORN PICCOLO CLARINET
WOODWORK CEILING
WOODWORKER JOINER TURNER
MILLMAN
WOODWORM GRIBBLE
(PREF.) TERMITO
WOODY BOSKY WITHY FRITHY
STICKY SYLVAN XYLOID LIGNOSE
LIGNEOUS
WOOER BEAU LOVER WOWER
SUITOR COURTER WOOSTER
COURTIER PARAMOUR
WOOF WEFT WOUGH FILLING
TEXTURE
WOOING SUIT WOHLAC
WOOL OO COT DAG HOG VOL WOW
BEAT BLUE FRIB PILE PULU ROCK
FADGE LAINE MUNGO STUFF TIPPY
ALPACA ARGALI BOTANY BREECH
FLEECE GREASE JACKET JERSEY
KERSEY LUSTER SLIVER WETHER
COMBING HASLOCK KASHMIR
MORLING STUBBLE WIGGING
CASHMERE CLOTHING COMEBACK
MORTLING PICKLOCK TOMENTUM
(— AS IT COMES FROM SHEEP)
GREASE
(— FROM DEAD SHEEP) MORLING
MORTLING
(— FROM LEOMINSTER) ORE
(— FROM RAGS) EXTRACT
(— OF UNDERCOAT OF MUSK-OX)
QIVIUT
(— ON SHEEP'S LEG) GARE BREECH
(— ON SHEEP'S THROAT) HASLOCK
(— WEIGHT) TOD
(COARSE —) ABB SHAG BRAID
COWTAIL
(COTTON —) CADDIS CADDICE
(DUNGY BIT OF —) FRIB
(FINE —) MERINO
(FINE GRADE OF —) PICKLOCK
SPINNERS
(GREASY —) TIPPY
(INFERIOR GRADE OF —) HEAD
(KNOT OF —) NOIL
(LAMB'S —) WASSAIL
(LOCK OF —) FLOCK STAPLE
(LONG —) BLUE
(LOW GRADE OF —) LIVERY
(MATTED —) DAG KET SHAG
(PULLED —) SLIPE
(RECLAIMED —) MUNGO SHODDY
(REFUSE —) COT COTT FLOCK
PINION
(ROLL OF —) CARDING
(RUSSIAN —) DONSKY
(SMALL PIECE OF —) TATE
(SPUN —) YARN
(WOUND —) TREND
(PREF.) ERIO LAN(I)(O) MALLO
(SUFF.) LAN
WOOLCLOTH HODDEN
WOOLEN (ALSO SEE FABRIC) CADDIS
CAMLET SUCLAT CADDICE
PASHMINA
(PL.) LAINAGE
WOOL FAT LANOLIN
WOOLLY SHEEP WOOZY LANATE
LANOSE COTTONY FLOCCOSE
PERONATE
WOOLLY BEAR WOUBIT
WOOLLY CROTON HOGWORT
WOOLY
(PREF.) DASI DASY ULO
WOOZY SICK DRUNK TIGHT VAGUE
BLURRY WOOLLY
WORD GIG MOT EZEL GULE HAIT
NEWS RAFF TERM VERB WHID WHUD
ADNEX CHEEP COUCH DERRY DILLY
FITCH GLOSS HAPAX HOKEY HYNDE
LEMMA MAXIM ORDER PAROL
RHEMA RUMOR SPELL ACCENT
ADVERB AVOWAL BREATH COPULA
ETYMON KIBBER LATIVE ONEYER
PAROLE PLEDGE QUATCH REMARK
REPORT SAYING ACCOUNT ADJUNCT
BICCHED COMMAND COMMENT
DICTION DUCDAME GENTILE GITTITH
HOMONYM INCIPIT MESSAGE
PALABRA PARONYM PRAYFUL
PRENZIE PROMISE PROVERB
SYNONYM VOCABLE ACROSTIC
CATCHCRY CHEVILLE COMPOUND
ENCLITIC EQUIVOKE FRABJOUS
FRINGENT IDEOGRAM ILLATIVE
LATINISM SYLLABLE SYNTAGMA

NEOLOGISM PALINDROME
PARTICIPLE MONOSYLLABLE
(— AS CALL TO DUCK) DILLY
(— EXPRESSING COMMAND)
JUSSIVE
(— FORMED FROM VOWELS)
EUOUAE
(— FROM INITIAL LETTERS)
ACRONYM
(— IN A PUZZLE) LIGHT
(— MISPRONOUNCED) BEARD
(— OF ADDRESS) SIR
(— OF CONCLUSION) AMEN EXPLICIT
(— OF GOD) LOGOS
(— OF HONOR) PAROLE
(— OF MOUTH) FIDELITY
(— OF OPPOSITE MEANING)
ANTONYM
(— OF RESPECT) SIR
(— OF SECONDARY RANK) ADNEX
(— OF SEVERAL MEANINGS)
POLYSEME
(— OF UNCERTAIN MEANING)
FRINGENT
(— OF UNKNOWN MEANING) KIBBER
ONEYER PRAYFUL PRENZIE
(— REPRESENTED BY SIGN)
GRAMMALOGUE
(— SEGMENT) SYLLABLE
(—S IN LOW TONE) ASIDE
(—S OF GREETING) SALUTATION
(—S OF OPERA) LIBRETTO
(—'S SIGNIFYING UNDERSTANDING)
ISEE
(BIBLICAL — OF DOUBTFUL
MEANING) EZEL HITCH GITTITH
(BIG —) MOUTHFUL
(CALL —) JINGO
(CHARACTERIZING —) EPITHET
(CODE —) DOG FOX JIG ABLE EASY
ECHO GOLF ITEM KING BRAVO DELTA
HOTEL INDIA SUGAR GEORGE
CHARLIE EUPHEMISM
(DISCOURAGING —) TSK
(EMPTY —S) WAFFLE
(FINE —S) DICK
(GATHERING —) SLOGAN
(HARSH —) MISWORD
(HONEYED —S) MANNA
(HYPHENATED —) SOLID
(IDENTIFYING —) LABEL
(LAST — OF SPEECH) CUE
(MAGIC —) ABRACADABRA
(MEANINGLESS —) DERRY
(MEANINGLESS —S) NOISE
(METAPHORICAL —) KENNING
(MNEMONIC —) VIBGYOR
(MYSTIC —) ABRAXAS
(NEW —) NEOLOGISM
(NONSENSE —) RAFF RAFFE
FRABJOUS RUNCIBLE
(ORIGINAL —) STEM
(PARTING —) ENVOI

(PUT INTO —S) LIMN
(QUOTED —) CITATION
(RECURRING —) REPETEND
(REDUNDANT —) CHEVILLE
(ROOT —) ETYMON PRIMITIVE
(SIGNAL —) NAYWORD SECURITY
(SIGNIFICANT —) ACCENT
(SINGLE —) PHRASE
(SMOOTH —S) SOAP
(SOURCE —) ETYMON
(SPREAD THE —) TELL
(TEST —) SHIBBOLETH
(THIEVES' SLANG —) TWAG WHID
(UNEXPLAINED —) DUCDAME
(UTTERED —S) SPEECH
(WAY WITH —S) TACT
(PL.) LIP TALK LYRIC SPEECH
LANGUAGE DISCOURSE
(PREF.) LEXI LEXICO LOG(O)
ONOMATO RHEMATO VERBI VERBO
(SUFF.) EPY LEXIA ONYM
WORD-BLINDNESS ALEXIA
DYSLEXIA ALEXIA
WORDBOOK LEXICON SPELLER
LIBRETTO
WORDINESS VERBIAGE
WORDING LEGEND DICTION
PHRASING
WORDLESS DUMB TACIT SILENT
TACITURN
WORDMAKING RHEMATIC
WORDPLAY EQUIVOKE
WORD PROCESSING (— DISPLAY)
WYSIWYG
WORDS TEXT
WORDY PROLIX VERBAL DIFFUSE
VERBOSE WORDISH REDUNDANT
WORK DO GO ACT FAG JOB DIKE
DYKE FEND FRET NOTE OPUS TASK
TEND TOIL ERGON GRAFT GRIND
KARMA KNEAD LABOR PRESS YAKKA
ARBEIT BEAVER BONNET EFFECT
HUSTLE OEUVRE REDUIT RESULT
STRIVE THRIFT CALLING EXECUTE
EXPLOIT FERMENT HEXAPLA
LOUSTER MISSION OPERATE OPIFICE
OPUSCLE OUVRAGE OVERAGE
PICHERY PURSUIT TRAVAIL
ADVOCACY AGENTING BUSINESS
CAPONIER DEMILUNE DRUDGERY
ENDEAVOR FUNCTION INDUSTRY
LABORAGE OPUSCULE PARERGON
RETRENCH EXECUTION
(— ACROSS GRAIN) THURM
(— ACTIVELY) LOUSTER
(— AGAINST) KNIFE ATTACK COMBAT
(— AIMLESSLY) FIDDLE
(— AS MUSICIAN) GIG
(— AS REPORTER) HEEL
(— BEYOND ONE'S POWERS)
OVERDO
(— BY THE PIECE) TUT
(— CARELESSLY) RABBLE

(— DILIGENTLY) PEG PLUG STRIKE
BELABOR
(— DOGGEDLY) SLOG
(— DONE) WRIHTE
(— FOR) LABOR SERVE BESWINK
(— FREE) START
(— HARD) TEW MOIL SLOG SWOT
BULLOCK LEATHER
(— HIDES) BEAM
(— IMPERFECTLY) MALFUNCTION
(— INEFFECTUALLY) PINGLE
(— INSIDUOUSLY) WORM
(— INTO A MASS) KNEAD
(— INTO SHAPE) REDACT
(— LAND) FLOAT
(— LEISURELY) DAKER DAIKER
(— OCCASIONALLY) SMOOT SMOUT
(— OF ACKNOWLEDGED
EXCELLENCE) CLASSIC
(— OF ART) GEM CRAFT ANTIQUE
CAPRICE CREATION EPIPHANY
EXERCISE MANDORLA
(— OF FICTION) SHOCKER
(— OF HISTORY) STORY
(— OF MENIAL KIND) DRUDGE
(— ONE'S WAY) WISE
(— OUT) BLOCK FUDGE SOLVE TRAIN
DESIGN EVOLVE
(— OUT A PROBLEM) PSYCH PSYCHE
(— OUT IN ADVANCE) FOREPLOT
(— OVER) DIGEST
(— PAID FOR IN ADVANCE) HORSE
(— PART-TIME) TEMP
(— PART TIME) TEMP
(— PERSISTENTLY) HAMMER
(— RESEMBLING PATCHWORK)
CENTO
(— SLIPSHOD) MULLOCK
(— STEADILY) PLY
(— SYSTEM) FLEXTIME FLEXITIME
(— TO EXHAUSTION) FAG
(— TOGETHER) COACT
(— TO WINDWARD) CLAW
(— TRIFLINGLY) PIDDLE
(— UNDER ANOTHER NAME)
ALLONYM
(— UNFAIRLY OR CRUELLY) HORSE
(— UP) MENG MING MENGE SPUNK
SUBACT
(— UPON) TILL LABOR
(— UPWARD) HIKE
(— VIGOROUSLY) BEND
(— WITHOUT FINISHING) SCABBLE
SCAPPLE
(ALLEGORICAL —) BESTIARY
(ANONYMOUS —) ADESPOTA
(BUNGLED —) BOTCH
(CANVAS —) POINT
(CARELESS —) SLAPDASH
(CESSATION OF —) SITIN SITDOWN
(CHASED —) CISELURE
(CLEANING —) CHAR
(CLUMSY —) BOTCH

(COMPLETED —) TRAVAIL
(CONTRACT —) GYPPO
(DAMASCENE —) KOFTGARI
(DAY'S —) DARG DARGUE
(DECORATIVE —) FLOCKING
MARQUETRY
(DIVINE —) THEURGY
(DOING LEGAL —) PROBONO
(DULL —) DRUDGERY
(EMBOSSED —) CELATURE
(FRAUDULENT —) JERRY
(HAND —) CAMAY
(HARD —) TEW MOIL MUCK SWOT
TWIG YERK SWEAT EFFORT MOIDER
LEATHER SLAVERY SLOGGING
(INFERIOR —) KITSCH SLOPWORK
(INLAY —) INTARSIA
(JOINER —) FINISH
(LITERARY —) STUDY CHASER
SEQUEL SERIAL CLASSIC DIPTYCH
PREQUEL PRODUCTION
(LITTLE —) OPUSCLE OPUSCULE
(LURID —) BLOOD
(MANUAL —) FATIGUE
(METAL —) NIELLO
(MINOR —) OPUSCULE OPUSCULUM
(MOSAIC —) EMBLEM
(ORGANIZED ABSENCE FROM —)
SICKOUT
(ORNAMENTAL —) BEADWORK
FILIGREE LEAFWORK
(PIECE OF —) JOB
(REFERENCE —) BIBLE SOURCE
(SACRED —) HIERURGY
(SCHOLASTIC —) SUMMA
(SKILLED MECHANICAL —) SLOJD
SLOYD
(SLOVENLY —) SLAISTER
(SOCIAL —) ALMONING
(USELESS —) BOONDOGGLE
(WOMAN'S —) DISTAFF
(PL.) CANON PLANT STODGE
FACTORY BUSINESS
(PREF.) ERG(O) ERGAT(O) OPERA
(EMBOSSED —) TOREUMATO
(SUFF.) ERGATE ERGY
WORKABLE YOUNG PLIANT VIABLE
FEASIBLE
(EASILY —) SWEET
WORKADAY HUMDRUM PROSAIC
ORDINARY
WORKBASKET CABA CABAS
CALATHUS
WORKBENCH SIEGE DONKEY
TEMPLATE
WORKED INWROUGHT
(— OUT) DEAD
(— UP) ANGRY EXCITED
WORKER
(ALSO SEE WORKMAN AND
LABORER) AGER CARL DOER HAND
HIND ICER SCAB AXMAN BOXER
BUTTY DEMAS DRIER EDGER ENDER

FILER FIRER FIXER FLYER FOXER
GLUER GORER HOLER INKER JERRY
LINER LURER MAXIM MINIM NURSE
PROLE TAPER TOWER ASHMAN
BACKER BAILER BALLER BANDER
BEADER BENDER BINDER BINMAN
BLADER BLOWER BOILER BONDER
BOOKER BOSHER BRACER BUFFER
BUMPER BURNER BURRER CAPPER
CARMAN CASTER CASUAL CHASER
COMBER COOKER DAYMAN DIPPER
DOCKER DOGGER DOTTER DUMPER
ETCHER FACTOR FAGGER FANMAN
FASHER FEEDER FELLER FILLER
FITTER FLAKER FLAMER FLUTER
FLUXER FOILER FOLDER FORCER
FORMER FRAMER GASSER GOFFER
GRADER GUMMER GUTTER HASHER
HEADER HEELER HELPER HEMMER
HOLDER HOOKER HOOPER HOPPER
HUNKIE INKMAN JOGGER JOINER
LEAFER LEASER LEGGER NOILER
PUGGER READER REEDER SCORER
SEAMAN SEAMER SHAKER SKIVER
SLAKER SLICER SLIDER SLOPER
STAVER STAYER TOILER TOPPER
BUILDER CREATOR EMPLOYE
FIELDER LABORER OUVRIER
(— IN LEATHER) BEAMER CHUMAR
JACKER BLACKER CHUCKLER
(— IN METALS) SMITH FLAPPER
(ADDITIONAL —) EXTRA
(AGRICULTURAL —) ARKIE KISAN
(AIRCRAFT —) BOOTMAN
(ANT —) MAXIM ERGATES REPLETE
(ASBESTOS —) COBBER
(AUTO —) DISKER
(BAKERY —) BRAKER COOLER
DIVIDER BENCHMAN SPREADER
(BLUE-COLLAR —) STIFF
(BREWERY —) HOPPER STEEPER
STILLMAN
(BRICK —) DAUBER CROWDER
(CANNERY —) SLIMER SCALDER
SHEDMAN
(CLOCK —) STAKER
(CLUMSY —) BODGE BODGER
(COAL —) SUMPER GEORDIE
SPRAGGER
(COMPULSIVE —) WORKAHOLIC
(CONSTRUCTION —) HARDHAT
(DOCK —) BUNGS HOLDMAN
SHENANGO
(DOMESTIC —) HELP
(FARM —) HODGE
(FELLOW —) CONFRERE
(FOREIGN —) GASTARBEITER
(FOUNDRY —) FLOGGER SNAGGER
(GARMENT —) FACER SLEEVER
ASSORTER INSEAMER
(GUN —) BLUER
(HARD —) SLOGGER
(HAT —) CURLER BRIMMER

(HIDE —) HEFTER COLORER
(HOSPITAL —) ALMONER
(HOTEL —) SCRUB
(ICEHOUSE —) AIRMAN
(JEWELRY —) ARBORER
(LIMITED-TIME —) TEMP
(LOGGING —) SNIPER SKIDDER
(MATTRESS —) BEATER
(MIGRATORY —) HOBO OKIE
(MILL —) BILLER SPOUTER
(MINE —) BYEMAN FOOTER GOPHER
LANDER DROPPER FACEMAN
SLEDGER SWAMPER DRIFTMAN
(NONUNION CONSTRUCTION —S)
LUMP
(OIL WELL —) ROUGHNECK
(ORCHARD —) SMUDGER
(PACKINGHOUSE —) COOK
(PAPERMILL —) SIZER SIZEMAN
(PIANO —) BELLYMAN
(PLODDING —) GRUBBER
(POTTERY —) CASER BATTER BEDDER
FETTLER JOLLIER JUSTLER
(PRINTING —) FLY FLYBOY
(PUERTO RICAN —) GIBARO JIBARO
(QUARRY —) BREAKER
(RAILROAD —) JERRY HERDER
BRAKEMAN
(SAWMILL —) BOLTER SETTER
BOATMAN DECKMAN CHAINMAN
(SHOE —) CASER PACKER ARCHER
FUDGER HEELER OHALKER
BOTTOMER
(SKILLED —) ARTISTE
(SLAUGHTERHOUSE —) FATTER
SHOVER SINGER SLIMER CHEEKER
CHOPPER KNOCKER LIMEMAN
SCALPER SCRIBER STICKER
SNATCHER
(SOCIAL —) ALMONER
(TANNERY —) GATER STONER
CROPPER CURRIER DELIMER
BEAMSMAN SEASONER
(TEXTILE —) DOFFER DOUPER
DRAWER GIGGER LAPPER LEASER
SINGER CREELER DOUBLER
JACKMAN KETTLER SKEINER
SPINNER SHUTTLER SOFTENER
SPLITTER TEASELER
(THEATER —) FLYMAN STAGEMAN
(TOBACCO —) BULKER SIFTER
STEMMER SCRAPMAN SPRIGGER
STICKMAN STRIPPER
(UNSKILLED —) HELPER DILUTEE
GREENER
(USELESS —) TOOL
(WHITE-COLLAR —) EFFENDI
(YARN —) SOURER CHAINER
(PL.) LABOR
(PREF.) ERG(O) ERGAT(O)
(SUFF.) ERGAT(E) URGE URGIC URGY
WORKHORSE AVER AIVER TRESTLE
SAWHORSE

WORKHOUSE UNION FACTORY
WORKSHOP

WORKING PLAY GOING OPENCUT
FUNCTION LABORAGE OPENCAST
OPENWORK OPERATIC OPERATIVE
(— ALONE) HATTING
(— HARD) HOPPING
(— IN THE MIND) MOTION
(— OF MINE) GWAG CROSSCUT
(— ON) PRACTICE
(— TOGETHER) SYNERGIC
SYNERGETIC
(DISUSED —) WASTE
(MINE —S) SPLIT
(NOT —) DUFF

WORKMAN (ALSO SEE WORKER
AND LABORER) BOSS HAND MATE
ROTO CAGER CONER EXTRA FINER
FLINT FLUER FROCK LAYER MAJOR
MIXER POLER TONER TRIER TUBER
BEAMER BLOUSE BOOMER BOWLER
BUCKER BUMMER COATER DIPPER
DRIVER FORKER GAGGER HANGER
LASTER LATHER MASTER NIPPER
OILMAN PUFFER RUNNER SAMMER
SCORER SHAKER SKIVER SLICER
SLIDER SOAKER SPIKER STAGER
STAVER TAPPER TARRER TEEMER
TILTER TIPMAN TIPPER TOPMAN
WARMER WASHER WETTER WRIGHT
ARTISAN DRUMMER HOTSHOT
LUDDITE SHOPMAN
(CHIEF —) BOSS
(CLUMSY —) BUNGLER COBBLER
(FELLOW —) BULLY BUTTY
(ITINERANT —) HOBO
(PROFICIENT —) DEACON
(SKILLED —) PRUDHOMME
(UNSKILLFUL —) HUNKY BUTCHER
(PL.) VOLK

WORKMANLIKE DEFT ADEPT
SKILLFUL

WORKMANSHIP HAND FABRIC
FACTURE OVERAGE ARTIFICE
ARTISANRY

WORKROOM DEN STUDY ATELIER

WORKS HACIENDA
(— OF CLOCK) WATCH
(SALT —) SALINA

WORKSHOP LAB SHED SHOP FORGE
LODGE SMIDDY SMITHY ATELIER
BOTTEGA HOSPITAL OFFICINA
PLUMBERY SKINNERY

WORKTABLE BENCH

WORLD ORB LOKA VALE WARD
EARTH MONDE WADRU WARDE
CAREER PUBLIC KINGDOM MONDIAL
CREATION CREATURE UNIVERSE
(— OF BOXING) FISTIANA
(— OF DARKNESS) SHEOL
(— OF DOGS) DOGDOM
(— OF FASHION) STYLEDOM
SWELLDOM

(— OF GODS) DEVALOKA
(— OF THE DEAD) DEEP
(— OF WOMEN) FEMINIE
(ACADEMIC —) CAMPUS
(EXTERNAL —) NONEGO
(GREAT —) MACROCOSM
(LITTLE —) MICROCOSM
(LOWER —) ORCUS
(PRIVATE —) AUTOCOSM
(THE —) FOLD
(THIRD —) SOUTH
(TWO-DIMENSIONAL —) FLATLAND
(PREF.) COSM(O) MUNDI
(SUFF.) COSM

WORLDLINESS MAMMON

WORLDLING DIVES

WORLDLY LAY WARLY CARNAL
EARTHY MUNDAL EARTHEN EARTHLY
FLESHLY MUNDANE PROFANE
SECULAR SENSUAL TERRENE
(NOT —) INTERIOR

WORLD'S ILLUSION (AUTHOR OF
—) WASSERMANN
(CHARACTER IN —) EVA LAY IVAN
VOSS CYRIL DENIS KAREN SOREL
BECKER AMADEUS BERNARD
CRAMMON CHRISTIAN
ENGELSCHALL WAHNSCHAFFE

WORLD-WEARY JADED BLASE

WORLDWIDE GLOBAL ECUMENIC
GLOBULAR PLANETAL PLANETARY
(PREF.) GLOBO

WORLD-WISE KNOWING
PRUDENT

WORM BOB EEL ESS LOA MAD
LURG NAIS NEMA ARTER CADEW
FLUKE LYTTA PIPER SCREW SNAKE
DRAGON NEREID NEREIS PALMER
PALOLO SHAMIR SYLLID SYLLIS
TEREDO VERMIS WRETCH ANNELID
ASCARID CARBORA ENOPLAN
SABELLA SAGITTA SERPENT
SERPULA SETARID SHUFFLE
SPIONID TAGTAIL TRICLAD
WRIGGLE BRANDLIN CEPHALOB
CERCARIA CHETOPOD GILTTAIL
HELMINTH LEODICID MEASURER
NEMATODE POLYCLAD STRONGYL
TRICHINA VERMICLE NEMERTEAN
TOOTHACHE SCHISTOSOME
POGONOPHORAN
(— IN HAWKS) FILANDER
(— OF DOG'S TONGUE) LYTTA
(— USED FOR BAIT) TAGTAIL
(AQUATIC —) TUBIFEX
(BLOODSUCKING —) LEECH
(CADDIS —) CADEW PIPER CADBAIT
(FLUKE —) PLAICE
(MARINE —) RAGWORM
(MEASURING —) LOOPER
(MUD —) IPO LOA
(SHIP —) BROMA COBRA
(PL.) APODA ENTOZOA

(PREF.) HELMINTH(O) LUMBRICI
SCOLEC(I)(O) VERMI
(SUFF.) SCOLEX

WORM-EATEN PITTED DECAYED
VERMOULU WERMETHE
WORMER JAG
WORMHOLE PIQURE
WORMLIKE VERMIAN
WORMSEED EPAZOTE AMBROSIA
WORMWOOD MOXA ABSINTH
CUDWEED MUGWORT ABSINTHE
COMPOSIT MINGWORT SANTONICA
WORMY EARTHY
WORN SEAR SERE USED PASSE TRITE
MAGGED MIZPAH SHABBY ATTRITE
CONTRITE
(— NEXT TO SKIN) INTIMATE
(— OUT) SHOT BANAL JADED SEELY
SPENT STALE STANK BEATEN BEDRID
BLEARY EFFETE EPUISE SCREWY
SHABBY CRIPPLE FORWORN
DECREPID FOUGHTEN HARASSED
OBSOLETE STRICKEN
(— SMOOTH) BEATEN
WORRICOW DEVIL BUGABOO
BUGBEAR HOBGOBLIN
WORRIED TOEY UNEASY ANXIOUS
FRETTED STREAKED CONCERNED
WORRIT VEX WORRY DISTRESS
WORRY DOG HOE HOW HOX LUG
NAG RUX TEW VEX BAIT BITE CARE
CARK FAZE FIKE FRAB FRET FUSS
HARE MOIL SOOL STEW ANNOY
CHEVY CHOKE DEAVE FEEZE GALLY
HARRY HURRY LURRY PHASE SCALD
SHAKE TEASE TOUSE TOWSE
BOTHER CADDLE CHIVVY COTTER
CUMBER FERRET FIDGET GALLOW
HARASS HATTER HECTOR INFEST
KIAUGH MOIDER PESTER PINGLE
PLAGUE POTHER ANXIETY CHAGRIN
HATCHEL TROUBLE TURMOIL
WHERRET FASHERIE STRANGLE
WORRYING ANXIOUS
WORSE VER WAR SEAMY
WORSEN DESCEND
WORSHIP GOD CULT HERY PUJA
RANK ADORE DULIA HONOR NAMAZ
WURTH YAJNA CREDIT PRAISE
REPUTE REVERE BAALISM ELOHISM
ICONISM IDOLISM IDOLIZE IMAGERY
OBSERVE BLESSING HIERURGY
VENERATE IDOLATRIZE
(— OF ALL GODS) PANTHEISM
(— OF HOST OF HEAVEN) SABAISM
(— OF IMAGES) ICONOLATRY
(— OF SELF) AUTOLATRY
(— OF SHAKESPEARE) BARDOLATRY
(ANCESTOR —) SCIOTHEISM
(DEVIL —) DIABOLISM
(FALSE —) SUPERSTITION
(FORMAL —) EYESERVICE
(FORM OF —) RITUAL

(HERO —) ADULATION
(HIGHEST KIND OF —) LATRIA
(INFERIOR KIND OF —) DULIA
(INSINCERE —) LIPSERVICE
(SERPENT —) OPHISM
(STAR —) SABAISM
(PREF.) LITURGIO THRESKI
(SUFF.) LATER LATRIA LATROUS
LATRY
WORSHIPER ISIAC BHAKTA PRAISER
IDOLATER
(— OF STARS) AKKUM SABIAN
(FIRE —) PARSI GHEBER GUEBER
PARSEE
(SERPENT —) SETHIAN SETHITE
WORSHIPFUL GOOD PROUD
NOTABLE REVERENT
WORST ACE GET BEST LAST OUTDO
SHEND WREST DEFEAT
(SOMETHING THAT IS THE —) PIT
PITS
(PREF.) KAKISTO
WORSTED GARN JERRY SERGE
CUBICA VESSES WHIPCORD
WORT GAIL GYLE SWAT PLANT
LENGTH TUTSAN FILLING KRAUSEN
POTHERB
(FERMENTED —) FEED WASH
(UNFERMENTED —) GROUT
WORTH FECK MEED CARAT MERIT
PRICE VALOR VALUE BECOME
BOUNTY DESERT ESTEEM REGARD
RICHES VALENT VIRTUE WEALTH
DIGNITY PRETIUM VALIANT WORSHIP
SPLENDOR TREASURE VALIDITY
VALLIDOM
(NET —) CAPITAL
(OF LITTLE —) SHLOCK SCHLOCK
(PREF.) AXIO TIMO
WORTHINESS DESERT WORSHIP
WORTHLESS BAD BUM LOW WAF
BAFF BALD BARE BASE EVIL IDLE
LEWD ORRA PUNK RACA SLIM VAIN
VILE WAFF BLANK BLOWN DUSTY
FLASH FOUTY LOSEL LOUSY PUTID
SLINK SORRY STRAW WASHY ABJECT
CHAFFY CHEESY CRUMMY DRAFFY
DRASTY DROSSY HOLLOW LIMMER
LITHER LUTHER MEASLY NAUGHT
PALTRY RASCAL ROTTEN SCREWY
TRASHY WOODEN BAGGAGE
FUSTIAN MAUVAIS NAUGHTY
NOTHING PIPERLY RAFFISH RUBBISH
SCABBED SHILPIT USELESS
FECKLESS HARLOTRY MAUVAISE
NUGATORY PRECIOUS RASCALLY
RUBBISHY SIXPENNY TRUMPERY
VAGABOND WANWORDY WRETCHED
NOACCOUNT STRAMINEOUS
(— THING) AMBSACE
WORTHLESSNESS BELIAL
UNTHRIFT
WORTHWHILE TANTI

WORTHY BIG DEAR FAIR GOOD HOLY
TIDY AUGHT CANNY DIGNE EXALT
HONOR JELLY NOBLE PIOUS GENTLE
CONDIGN GRADELY PAREGAL
THRIFTY ELIGIBLE VALUABLE
WAUREGAN
(— OF BELIEF) CREDIBLE
(— OF DEVOTION) HOLY
(— OF PRAISE) LAUDABLE
(VERY —) SUPERIOR
(SUFF.) ABLE IBLE
WOULD WAD WID WANT WISH
COULD SHOULD
(— NOT) NOLD WADNA WADDENT
(I —) CHUD CHOLD
WOULD-BE MANQUE
WOUND ARR CUT HEW PIP WIN BITE
CALK CLAW DUNT FAKE FOIN GALL
GORE HARM HURT MAIM PAIN PINK
RASE RAZE RIST SCAR SKAG SORE
STAB TEAR VULN WING BLESS
BROKE GANCH GRIEF KNIFE KNOCK
SHOOT STICK STING SUGAT THIRL
TOUCH BREACH BRUISE CREASE
ENTAME GRIEVE HARROW INJURE
LAUNCH LESION MARTYR OFFEND
PIERCE PLAGUE SCOTCH TRAUMA
AFFLICT ATTAINT BATTERY BLIGHTY
DIACOPE GUNSHOT SCRATCH
DISTRESS FLANKARD FLEABITE
INCISION LACERATE SPURGALL
VULNERATE
(— FROM BOAR'S TUSK) GANCH
GAUNCH
(— FROM BULL'S HORN) CORNADA
(— FROM RUBBING) GALL
(— IN DEER'S SIDE) FLANKARD
(— MADE BY THRUST) FOIN
(— ON FOOT) FIKE
(— ON HORSE'S ANKLE) CREPANCE
(— ON HORSE'S FOOT) CREPANCE
(— PRIDE) PIQUE
(— WITH POINTED WEAPON) STAB
SWORD
(DEEP —) DIACOPE
(MINUTE —) PRICK SCART
(TRIFLING —) FLEABITE
(PL.) NOUNS
(PREF.) HELC(O) TRAUMAT(O) VULNI
WOUNDED HURT WUND VULNED
WINGED VULNOSE STRICKEN
WOUNDWORT BETONY ALLHEAL
HERCULES
WOU-WOU WAWA WAWAH CAMPER
GIBBON
WOVEN BROCHE BROWDEN
DAMASSE
(— FULL WIDTH) SEAMLESS
(— WIDE) BROAD
(— WITH RIB) SOLEIL
WOW AWE HIT MEW BARK GOSH
HOWL RAVE WAIL GOLLY WHINE
SUCCESS

WOZZECK (CHARACTER IN —) MARIE
ANDRES WOZZECK
(COMPOSER OF —) BERG
WRACK KELP RACK RUIN VAREC
CUTWEED DESTROY DOWNFALL
EELGRASS WRECKAGE
WRAITH WAFT FETCH GHOST SPOOK
DOUBLE SHADOW SWARTH SPECTRE
WRANGLE RAG YED CAMP MOIL
SPAR TIFT ARGLE ARGUE BRAWL
CHIDE DAFER FLITE JOWER PLEAD
STRUT ARGUFY BICKER CAFFLE
CAMPLE CANGLE DACKER FRAPLE
FRATCH HAGGLE HASSLE JANGLE
RAGGLE THREAP BRABBLE BRANGLE
DISPUTE PICKEER QUARREL
SCRAFFLE SQUABBLE TIRRWIRR
WRANGLER CAMPER COWBOY
GRATER HAFTER WRAGER DEBATER
HAGGLER DEFENDER OPPONENT
WRANGLING JANGLE
WRAP HAP LAP LOT WAP BIND FURL
ROLL WHIP AMICE CLASP CLOAK
LAMBA MANTA NUBIA SERVE SHAWL
TWINE WOOLD AFGHAN BURLAP
CLOTHE COCOON COOLER DOLMAN
EMBALE MOIDER MUFFLE PATTOO
SACQUE SARAPE SWATHE SWATHE
WIMPLE WRIXLE ENVELOP INVOLVE
SWADDLE UMBELAP BARRACAN
(— CABLE) KECKLE
(— CLOSE) SNUGGLE
(— DEAD BODY) CERE
(— ONESELF) HUDDLE
(— UP) HAP MAIL CINCH ENROL
IMPLY
(— UP HEAD) MOB MOP MOBLE
(— WIRE AROUND FISHING LINE)
GANGE
(— WITH BANDAGE) SWATHE
(HEAD —) NUBIA SNOOD
(PL.) SECRECY RESTRAINT
WRAPPER APRON COVER MOTTO
PILCH SHAWL SMOCK COUPON
FARDEL JACKET ENVELOP OVERALL
SARPLER COVERING MAHARMAH
WOOLPACK
(— FOR BOOK) JACKET
(— FOR CUTLET) PAPILLOTE
(— WORN IN EGYPT) GALABIA
GALABEAH
(COOKING —) PAPILLOTE
WRAPPING WAP PACK GELILAH
LAPPING COVERING MANTLING
(— FOR DEAD) CEREMENT
(— MATERIAL) SARAN
(— OF HEBREW SCROLL) GELILAH
(— OF ROPE) SERVICE
WRASSE COOK BALLAN COMBER
CONNER CUNNER LABRID HOGFISH
PIGFISH SEAWIFE CORKWING
DONCELLA JANIZARY LADYFISH
SENORITA

WRATH IRE FURY GRIM ANGER
WROTH CHOLER FELONY PASSION
VIOLENCE
WRATHFUL IRY EVIL HIGH ANGRY
IRATE WROTH IREFUL RAGING
FURIOUS JEALOUS CHOLERIC
WREAK CAUSE AVENGE EXPEND
GRATIFY INDULGE INFLICT REVENGE
(— DESTRUCTION) ESTREPE
WREATH LEI ORLE PLAY CROWN
GREEN LAURE LORRE OLIVE TORSE
WHORL WRASE ANADEM CRANTS
CREASE LAUREL POTONG TORTIL
CHAPLET CORONAL CORONET
CROWNAL DOLPHIN FESTOON
GARLAND WRINKLE KELYPHYTE
(SPIRAL —) VOLUTION
WREATHE BIND WIND CRISP TWINE
TWIST WRING INTORT WRITHE
CONTORT ENTWINE INTWIST
INVOLVE
WREATHED SPIRY TORTILE TORTIVE
WRITHED INTORTED TORTILLE
WRECK CRAB HULK RUIN BLAST
CRACK CREAM PRANG SHOOT
SMASH TRASH WRACK DEFACE
DESPOIL DESTROY FOUNDER
GODSEND SHATTER TORPEDO
DEMOLISH SABOTAGE SHAMBLES
(— COMPLETELY) TOTAL
(HUMAN —) DERELICT
WRECKAGE WRACK FINDAL
FLOTSAM GODSEND WAVESON
SHAMBLES
WRECKED NOUGHT
WRECKERS, THE
(CHARACTER IN —) AVIS MARK
PASCOE THRIZA
(COMPOSER OF —) SMYTH
WREN GIRL STAG TOPE CUTTY
JENNY KITTY PEGGY SALLY STAID
TYDIE SCUTTY TIDIFE TIDLEY TINTIE
TOMTIT WRANNY BLUECAP
REGULUS MALURINE WRANNOCK
(BUSH —) RIFLEBIRD
WRENCH KEY PIN RUG PULL RACK
RICK RUGG TEAR YERK CRICK CRINK
FORCE THRAW THROW TWIST WRAMP
WREST BEDKEY SPRAIN STRAIN
TWEEZE DISTORT SPANNER SPANULE
SQUINCH TORTURE TWISTLE
WREST REAR REND EXACT FORCE
TWIST ARREST EXTORT WRENCH
WRITHE ABSTORT WIREDRAW
(— AWAY) STRIP DESPOIL
WRESTLE PRAY RASSLE SQUIRM
TUSSLE WRAXLE WRITHE GRAPPLE
SCUFFLE THRIMBLE THRUMBLE
WRESTLER MATMAN WELTER
CLICKER MATSTER GRAPPLER
(KIND OF —) SUMO
WRESTLING SUMO SAMBO
PALESTRA WRAXLING

(— TECHNIQUE) GLIMA
(KIND OF —) WRIST
(STYLE OF —) SAMBO
WRETCH DOG MIX FILE WARY MISER
SLAVE THING BUGGER PERSON
SQUALL BRETHEL CAITIFF CAMOOCH
CHINCHE CULLION GLUTTON
HILDING SCROYLE BEZONIAN
CREATURE MESCHANT POLTROON
RECREANT SCULLION
WRETCHED EVIL FOUL LORN MEAN
POOR DAWNY DEENY GAUNT SORRY
WISHT WOFUL YEMER ABJECT
CAITIF DISMAL MEAGER PALTRY
RASCAL SHABBY SICKLY SORDID
UNLEAD UNLEDE WOEFUL ABYSMAL
BENEATH FORLORN OUTWORN
PITIFUL SQUALID UNSEELY
MESCHANT MISERABLE
(— PERSON OR ANIMAL) MISERY
WRIGGLE EEL REG RIG FRIG LASH
WIND WRIG SLIDE WRELE WRING
SQUIRM WAMBLE WANGLE WARPLE
WIDDLE WIMPLE WINTLE WRITHE
EYEBROW SNIGGLE TWIDDLE
TWINGLE WRABILL WRESTLE
SCRIGGLE SQUIGGLE
WRIGGLING EELY SCRIGGLE
SQUIGGLY
WRIGGLY SNAKY SNAKISH
SQUIRMING
WRING RACK DRAIN EXACT SCREW
TWIST WREST EXTORT OPPRESS
SQUEEZE TORMENT TORTURE
(— THE NECK) SCRAG
WRINGER RUNG WRUNG SQUEEZER
WRINKLE RUT DRAW FOLD FURL
HINT KNIT LIRK RUCK RUGA SEAM
BREAK CRIMP CRISP DELVE FAULT
FRILL REEVE RIVEL SNIRL BUCKLE
COCKLE CRAVAT CREASE FURROW
METHOD PUCKER RIMPLE RUMPLE
RUNKLE SCRIMP WREATH BLEMISH
CRANKLE CRINKLE CRUMPLE
CRUNKLE FROUNCE FRUMPLE
CONTRACT IRRUGATE RUGOSITY
(— OF FLESH) CRAVAT
(— REMOVER) IRON IRONER
(PREF.) RUTI RUTID(O)
WRINKLED CRUMP PURFLY RUGATE
RUGGED RUGOSE RUGOUS SEAMED
COCKLED CREASED ROUCHED
SAVOYED CRUMPLED FURROWED
PUCKERED WRITHLED WRIZZLED
WRINKLING KNIT KNOT FROWN
WRIST CARPUS SHACKLE
(PREF.) CARP(O)
WRISTER MUFFETEE
WRISTLET STRAP WRISTER
MUFFETEE
WRISTWATCH BAGUET BAGUETTE
WRIT AIEL CAPE MISE PONE TOLT
ALIAS BREVE BRIEF ERROR RECTO

UTRUM BRIEVE CAPIAS ELEGIT
EXTENT PLAINT VENIRE ACCOUNT
DEDIMUS DETINUE EXIGENT LATITAT
PLURIES PRECEPT PROCESS
SUMMONS WARRANT CESSAVIT
COSINAGE DETAINER DOCUMENT
FORMEDON MANDAMUS MITTIMUS
NOVERINT PRAECIPE QUOMINUS
REPLEVIN SISERARY SUBPOENA
TESTATUM WARRANTY
(— FOR SUMMONING EXTRA
JURORS) TALES
(LEGAL —) CERT
WRITE INK PEN BACK BOOK DITE
DRAW READ SELL CLERK DRAFT
STYLE AUTHOR ENFACE INDITE
SCRIBE SCRIVE ADDRESS COMPILE
COMPOSE DICTATE EMPAPER
EXARATE SCREEVE BIOGRAPH
INSCRIBE
(— ADDRESS) BACK
(— BENEATH) SUBSCRIBE
(— BETWEEN) INTERSCRIBE
(— BRIEFLY) JOT
(— CARELESSLY) DASH SCRAWL
SCRIBBLE
(— DOWN) SIGN BREVE DENOTE
RECORD AMORTIZE DESCRIBE
(— FOR ANOTHER) GHOSTWRITE
(— FURTHER) ADD
(— HASTILY) SCRATCH SCRIBBLE
SQUIGGLE
(— IN A LARGE HAND) ENGROSS
(— IN LARGE CHARACTERS) TEXT
(— IN SHORTHAND) STENOGRAPH
(— LETTER) CORRESPOND
EPISTOLIZE
(— MUSIC) NOTATE COMPOSE
(— ON FRONT OF BILL) ENFACE
(— PASTORAL POEMS) PHILLIS
(— POMPOUSLY) FUSTIANIZE
(— WHAT IS NOT TRUE) FABLE
(SUFF.) GRAPH(ER)(IA)(IC)(Y)
WRITER (ALSO SEE AUTHOR) PEN
BARD HACK PUFF ALVAR GHOST
ODIST SQUIB AUTHOR FATHER
GLOZER HEROIC LAWYER LETTER
MUNSHI NOTARY PENMAN PRABHU
PROSER PURVOE SCRIBE TRAGIC
YEOMAN ADAPTER ADSMITH
ANALYST DIARIST ELOHIST ESSAYER
GLOSSER GNOMIST HYMNIST
IAMBIST JUVENAL LAUDIST
MUNCHEE PENSTER PROPHET
PROSAIC REVUIST SCRIVER STYLIST
SUMMIST TEXTMAN AUGUSTAN
BLURBIST COMEDIAN COMPOSER
DECADENT DECADIST DIDACTIC
EMBOSSER EPISTLER ESSAYIST
FABLEIST FABULIST GROMATIC
HUMORIST IDYLLIST MONODIST
MOONSHEE NOVELIST PARODIST
PENWOMAN PREFACER PRESSMAN

PROSAIST PROSEMAN PSALMIST
REVIEWER SATIRIST SCRIPTER
VERSEMAN HISTORIAN LEGENDARY
LEGENDIST PROSATEUR LIBRETTIST
TRACTARIAN PAMPHLETEER
(— OF BURLESQUE) GABBER
(FAST —) STENO
(FREE-LANCE —) CREEPER
(HACK —) PENSTER
(INCOMPETENT —) BOTCHER
(JESUIT —) BOLLANDIST
(OBITUARY —) NECROGRAPHER
(OBSCENE —) RIBALD
(PROVERB —) PAROEMIOGRAPHER
(SACRED —) HAGIOLOGIST
HAGIOGRAPHER
(SATIRICAL —) SILLOGRAPH
(SPEECH —) LOGOGRAPHER
WRITHE WRY WIND THROW TWIRL
TWIST WRING SQUIRM TERVEE
WAMBLE WRABBE WRENCH
AGONIZE WRESTLE WRIGGLE WRINGLE
CONVOLVE
WRITHING EELY WRING WRITHY
WRITING BOOK DITE FAIT PAGE
POEM KANJI LIBEL SCROW CADJAN
GOSSIP LEGEND LETTER PAGINE
SCRIPT SCRITE SCRIVE UNCIAL
ARTICLE AUTONYM DIPLOMA
ESCRIPT SCREEVE APOCRYPH
CONTRACT DOCUMENT GRAVAMEN
HARANGUE KAKEMONO LETTRURE
LIPOGRAM PAMPHLET SCRIBING
SONNETRY SMALLHAND
JOURNALISM SCRIVENING
(— FOR ANOTHER) ALLOGRAPH
(— OF LITTLE VALUE) STUFF
SCRIBBLE
(— ON PAPER SCROLL) MAKIMONO
(— ON SILK) KAKEMONO
(— ON WAX) CEROGRAPH
(—S OF VIRGIL) POETICA
(— UNDER SEAL) BOND
(BAWDY —) SCULDUDDRY
SCULDUDDERY SKULDUDDERY
(BIBLICAL —) MENE
(BITTER —) DIATRIBE
(CARELESS —) SCRAWL
(CRAMPED —) NIGGLE
(CURSIVE —) JOINHAND
(EASY —) GOSSIP
(FORMAL —) RECORD
(HINDU —) VEDA
(HUMOROUS —S) FACETIAE
(ILLUMINATED —) FRACTUR
(IN THIS —) HERETO
(IRREGULAR —) SCRAWL
(MUSICAL —) GIMEL GYMEL
(NORSE —) EDDA
(OBSCENE —) BALDERDASH
(PRETENTIOUS —) FUSTIAN
(SACRED —) ARANYAKA BRAHMANA
SCRIPTURE

(SATIRICAL —) PASQUINADE
(SECRET —) SCYTALE
(SHORT —) SCRIP
(SHORTHAND —) PHONOGRAPHY
(SPY —) CODE
(STUPID —) PABLUM PABULUM
(STYLE OF —) ACADEMESE
(SWIFT —) SHORTHAND
(SYLLABIC —) KANA
(VAPID —) WASH
(VERBOSE —) TOOTLE
(VOLUMINOUS —) POLYGRAPHY
(WITTY —S) FACETIAE
(WORTHLESS —) TRIPE
(PL.) LEGENDA ARANYAKA
POSTHUMA
(PREF.) GRAMO GRAPHI GRAPHO
(SUFF.) GRAM GRAPH(ER)(IA)(IC)(Y)

WRITING CASE STANDISH
ECRUTOIRE

WRITTEN KETIB KETHIB KTHIBH
GRAPHIC LITERAL
(— ABOVE) SS
(— AFTER) ADSCRIPT
(— HASTILY) STRAY
(SO —) SIC
(PREF.) GRAPTO

WROCLAW BRESLAU

WRONG BAD CAR ILL MIS OUT WET
AWRY HARM HURT SORE SOUR TORT
WITE AGATE AGLEE AGLEY AMISS
CRIME DUTCH FALSE GLEED GRIEF
MALUM UNFIT WATHE WOUGH
AGUILT ASTRAY BLOOEY FAULTY
INJURE INJURY NOUGHT OFFEND
SARAAD SINFUL UNTRUE WICKED
WONDER ABUSION ABUSIVE
DAMNIFY DEFRAUD IMMORAL
INJURIA MISBEDE NAUGHTY
UNRIGHT VIOLATE AGGRIEVE
COCKEYED MISTAKEN PERVERSE
UNLEEFUL
(CIVIL —) TORT
(IMAGINARY —) WINDMILL
(SHOCKINGLY —) MONSTROUS
(PREF.) MIS

WRONGDOER ACTOR SINNER
FAULTER MISDOER OFFENDER

WRONGDOING MISS CRIME FAULT
DEFAULT MISCONDUCT
MALFEASANCE

WRONGFUL UNFAIR UNJUST
TORTIOUS TORTUOUS UNLAWFUL

WRONGHEADED WRY PERVERSE

WRONGLY AMISS BADLY FALSE
NOUGHT UNRICHT UNRIGHT
OVERWART

WROTH ANGRY IRATE IREFUL

WROUGHT BEATEN CARVEN
FORMED SHAPED VROCHT CREATED
HAMMERED
(ELABORATELY —) LABORED

WRY ASKEW AVERT TWIST WRING
WRONG IRONIC WRITHE DEFLECT
DISTORT TWISTED WRITHEN
SATURNINE

WRYNECK IYNX JYNX SLAB WEET
LOXIA PEABIRD WEETBIRD
TORTICOLLIS

WUTHERING HEIGHTS (AUTHOR
OF) BRONTE
(CHARACTER IN —) DEAN EDGAR
ELLEN JOSEPH LINTON ZILLAH
FRANCES HARETON HINDLEY
EARNSHAW ISABELLA LOCKWOOD
CATHERINE HEATHCLIFF

WYCH ELM WITCH WITCHEN

WYLIECOAT WALYCOAT
NIGHTGOWN PETTICOAT

WYND HAW ALLEY CLOSE

WYOMING

CAPITAL: CHEYENNE
COUNTY: TETON UINTA GOSHEN
BIGHORN LARAMIE NIOBRARA
INDIAN: ARAPAHO
LAKE: JACKSON
MOUNTAIN: ELK CLOUD GANNET
HOBACK FREMONT ATLANTIC
SHERIDAN
MOUNTAIN RANGE: TETON ABSARO
BIGHORN LARAMIE RATTLESNAKE
NICKNAME: EQUALITY
RIVER: GREEN SNAKE PLATTE
POWDER BIGHORN
STATE BIRD: MEADOWLARK
STATE FLOWER: PAINTBRUSH
STATE TREE: COTTONWOOD
TOWN: CODY LUSK CASPER BUFFALO
LARAMIE RAWLINS WORLAND
GREYBULL KEMMERER SHERIDAN
SUNDANCE

X

X EX XRAY ERROR MISTAKE
XANADU (SACRED RIVER OF —) ALPH
XANTHIC YELLOW
XANTHIPPE NAG SHREW
  (HUSBAND OF —) SOCRATES
XANTHIPPUS
  (SON OF —) PERICLES
XEBEC SHIP CHEBEC CHEBECK
  SHABEQUE
XENIUM GIFT DAINTY DELICACY
XERES JEREZ SHERRY
XERIC DRY
XHOSA KAFIR KAFFIR
  (PL.) AMAKOSA AMAXOSA
XIPHARES (FATHER OF —)
  MITHRIDATE
XIPHISTERNUM XIFOID

XIPHOSURUS LIMULUS
X-RAY UROGRAM
XUREL SCAD SAUREL
XUTHUS (ADOPTED SON OF —) ION
  (BROTHER OF —) DORUS AEOLUS
  (FATHER OF —) HELLEN
  (MOTHER OF —) ORSEIS
  (SON OF —) ION DURUS ACHAEUS
  (WIFE OF —) CREUSA
XYLEM WOOD HADROM HADROME
  XYLOGEN
XYLOID WOODY LIGNEOUS
XYLOPHONE REGAL SARON
  BALAFO GAMBANG GAMELAN
  MARIMBA BALAPHON GAMELANG
  GIGELIRA STICCADO
XYSTUS WALK XYST PORTICO
  TERRACE

Y

Y WY YA WYE YOD YOKE YANKEE
(**CONNECTION**) SIAMESE
(**— COORDINATE**) SINE
(**PREF.**) (**LETTER —**) YPSILI
YABBER TALK JABBER LANGUAGE
YABBY CRAWLIE
YACARE CAIMAN CAYMAN JACARE
YACHT SAIL SCOW BRUTE YATCH
DINGHY SONDER YEAGHE CRUISER
KEELBOAT
YAFF YAP BARK YELP
YAFFLE ARMFUL YAFFIL
YAHOO BRUTE CLOWN ROWDY
BUMPKIN
YAHWEH GOD JAVE YHWH JAHVAH
YAHWIST JEHOVIST
YAK GAB GAG GAS JOKE YUCK
LAUGH BULBUL SARLAK SARLYK
YAMMER CHATTER
YAKALA JAGA
YAKKA WORK LABOR
YAKUT SAKHA
YAM HOI UBE UBI UVE JAMD LIMA
RAIL TUGUI IGNAME INAMIA INHAME
POTATO BONIATA
(**TARO —**) KOKO
YAMA (**FATHER OF —**) VIVASVANT
(**SISTER OF —**) YAMI
YAM BEAN KAMAG JICAMA WAYAKA
SINCAMAS
YAMEN COURT YAMUN OFFICE
YAMEO LLAMEO
YAMMER CRY WAIL SCOLD WHINE
YEARN YOMER GRUMBLE WHIMPER
YAMP YAMPA SQUAWROOT
YANAN NOZI
YANG HONK GURJUN
YANK FLOG JERK SLAP HOICK SNAKE
BUFFET
YAP BARK YAWP YELP MOUTH SCOLD
WAFFLE BUMPKIN CHATTER
KYOODLE
YAPOK YAPOCK OPOSSUM OYAPOCK
YAQUI YAKI HIAQUI
YARD HAW HOF YED CREW CROW
DUMP FOLD SKID SPAR TILT COURT
GARTH PATIO STICK CANCHA
HOPPET LOANIN CURTAIN GARSTON
KNACKERY OUTGARTH
(**— OF SAWMILL**) DUMP
(**— WHERE COWS ARE MILKED**)
LOANIN LOANING
(**FINAL —**) FELL
(**GRASSY —**) GARSTON
(**PAVED —**) CAUSEY
(**POULTRY —**) BARTON

(**SAIL —**) RAE
(**1-16TH OF A —**) NAIL
(**1-3RD OF CUBIC —**) CARTLOAD
(**20 —S**) SCORE
(**5 AND A HALF —S**) ROD
YARD GRASS ELEUSINE
MANGRASS
YARDLAND VERGE VIRGATE
YARDMASTER DINGER
YARDSTICK YAIRD METRIC
MEASURE METWAND METEWAND
STANDARD CRITERION
YARE YAR AYRE YORE BRISK READY
LIVELY NIMBLE PROMPT
YARETA LLARETA
YARM WAIL NOISE OUTCRY SHRIEK
YARN ABB END FOX CORD GARN
GIMP PIRN SILK SLIP WEFT WHIP
DYNEL FLOSS GRAIN INKLE LUREX
PITCH SPIEL ALASKA ANGORA
BERLIN BROACH CADDIS COTTON
CREWEL CUFFER DACRON ESTRON
FLORET FRIEZE MERINO MOTTLE
PEELER RATINE SAXONY SINGLE
STRAND TASLAN THREAD VINYON
WOOLEN ZEPHYR ACETATE CADDICE
FILLING GENAPPE INGRAIN
MELANGE RACKING SCHAPPE
VIGOGNE WORSTED ASBESTOS
BOURETTE CHENILLE FORTISAN
METALLIC ROUNDING SPINNING
WHEELING ORGANZINE VIGOUREUX
(**— FOR WARP**) ABB
(**— FROM FLOSS SILK**) FLORET
(**— MEASURE**) LEA
(**— SIZE**) TYPP
(**BALL OF —**) CLEW CLUE
(**BITS OF ROPE —**) THRUMS
(**BUNDLE OF —**) PAD
(**CONICAL MASS OF —**) COP
(**ELASTIC —**) LASTEX
(**EXAGGERATED —**) STRETCHER
(**FINE SOFT —**) ZEPHYR KASHMIR
CASHMERE
(**LINEN —**) SPINEL
(**ROLL OF —**) PRICK CHEESE
(**ROPE —S**) SOOGEE
(**SILK —**) TRAM
(**SMALL PIECE OF SPUN —**) RABAND
ROBBIN ROPEBAND
(**UNEVEN —**) BOUCLE
(**PL.**) FOX MENDINGS
YARRAN GIDYA MYALL GIDGEA
GIDGEE
YARROW ALLHEAL CAMMOCK
MAUDLIN MILFOIL PELLITORY

YASHIRO SHA
YASHMAK VEIL ASMACK YAKMAK
YATAGHAN SABER ATAGHAN SIMITAR
YATTER CHATTER PRATTLE
YAUD MARE YADE
YAUPON ASSI HOLLY YUPON CASINA CASSINE
YAUTIA COCO TARO TANIA COCKER TANIER MALANGA
YAW GAPE YAWN LURCH SHEER BROACH SWERVE
YAWL HOWL DANDY MIZZEN SCREAM SCHOKKER
YAWN GAP GALP GANE GANT GAPE YANE ABYSM CHAUM CAVITY TEDIUM DULLNESS OSCITATE
YAWNING HIANT CHASMA GAPING OSCITANT
YAWP BAWL GAPE RANT YELP STARE SQUAWK YAMMER COMPLAIN
YAWS PIAN TUBBA TUBBOE
YAWWEED RHUBARB
YAYA COPA
YEA YA YES YOY YIGH TRULY ASSENT REALLY VERILY
YEAN EAN LAMB
YEANLING KID LAMB EANLING
YEAR EAR SUN AYRE HAAB TIME ANNEE ANNUS VAGUE WINTER ZODIAC TOWMOND TZOLKIN BIRTHDAY
(— OF EMANCIPATION) JUBILEE
(ACADEMIC —) SESSION
(IN THIS —) HA
(LAST —) FERNYEAR
(MANY —S) AGE
(MAYAN —) TUN HAAB
(ONE BILLION —S) AEON
(SABBATICAL —) JUBILE JUBILEE
(1000 —S) MILLENARY MILLENNIUM
(4320 MILLION —S) KALPA
(PL.) SEASONS
(SUFF.) ENNIAL ENNIUM
YEARBOOK ANNUAL SERIAL ANNUARY
YEARLING COLT HORNOTINE
(AUTHOR OF —) RAWLINGS
(CHARACTER IN —) LEM ORA JODY HUTTO PENNY TWINK BAXTER NELLIE OLIVER WILSON GINRIGHT FORRESTER WEATHERBY FODDERWING
YEARLY ANNUAL SOLEMN
YEARN HO YEN ACHE BURN EARN GAPE HONE IRNE LONG PANT PINE SIGH CRAVE GREEN GRIEN ASPIRE CURDLE GRIEVE HANKER YAMMER
YEARNING EROS DESIRE HANKER RENNET CRAVING EARNFUL HOMESICK
YEAST BEE EST BARM BEES EAST KOJI SOTS FROTH SPUME LEAVEN

NEWING RISING SIZING TORULA FERMENT SIZZING EMPTINGS
(FILM —) FLOR
YEASTY LIGHT FROTHY TRIVIAL RESTLESS
YEGG ROBBER BURGLAR
YELL CRY CALL GOWL HOWL ROAR YARM YAUP YOWL YOWT GOLLY SHOUT TIGER BELLOW GOLLAR HOLLER SCREAM YAMMER YELLOCH SCRONACH SKELLOCH
YELLOW (ALSO SEE COLOR) OR GULL AMBER BLAKE BLOND FAVEL FLAVE JAUNE PALEW SHELL YELWE ALMOND BANANA FLAVID MELINE MIMOSA NUGGET OXGALL BISCUIT JASMINE JONQUIL LEGHORN LUTEOUS MEXICAN MUSTARD NANKEEN OATMEAL POPCORN SAFFRON TILLEUL WHEATEN YUCATAN AUREOLIN GENERALL ICTEROID LUMINOUS MARIGOLD ORPIMENT PRIMROSE
(— AS BUTTER) BLAKE
(— ORANGE) SAFFRON
(BROWNISH —) FULVID FULVOUS
(DINGY —) LURID
(GOLDEN —) FLAVID
(GREENISH —) ACACIA
(INDIAN —) PURI PURREE
(LEMON —) GENERALL
(PALE —) EGGSHELL
(PREF.) CHLOR(O) CHRYS(O) FLAV(I) (O) OCHRO XANTH(O) XANTIN(O)
YELLOW ALDER SAGEROSE
YELLOW BEDSTRAW CRUDWORT CURDWORT FLEAWEED
YELLOW BUGLE IVA IVE IVY
YELLOW CLINTONIA DOGBERRY
YELLOW-DOG MEAN CONTEMPTIBLE
YELLOW FEVER VOMITO
YELLOW FOXTAIL STICKERS
YELLOW GENTIAN FELWORT
YELLOW GREEN PISTACHE
YELLOWHAMMER SKYT YITE AMMER GOWDY SKITE GLADDY GOLDIE VERDIN YORLIN FLICKER GLADEYE YELDRIN YOLDRING
(— STATE) ALABAMA
YELLOW IRIS SEDGE LEVERS DAGGERS
YELLOWISH SALLOW ICTERINE SAFFRONY
(— GREEN) GLAUCOUS
(— RED) FALLOW
(PREF.) LUTEO
YELLOW JACKET VESPA VESPID
YELLOW JASMINE WOODBINE
YELLOWLEGS KILLCU TATLER WINTER YELPER TATTLER
YELLOW MACKEREL CREVALLE
YELLOWNESS FLAVEDO

YELLOW POND LILY DUCK CLOTE
  CLOTS NUPHAR
YELLOW POPLAR TULIPWOOD
YELLOW PRICKLE RUBIA
YELLOW RATTLE RATEL
  COCKSCOMB LOUSEWORT
YELLOW TOADFLAX RAMSTEAD
YELLOW WAGTAIL OATEAR
YELLOW WATER LILY KELP
  WOKAS
YELLOWWOOD FUSTIC FUSTOC
  GOPHER MANGWE VIRGILIA
YELP CRY YAP YIP BAFF BARK KIYI
  WAFF YAFF YAUP YAWP BOAST
  YAMPH AVOCET SQUEAL YAFFLE
  YELLOW
YELPING CRY

YEMEN

ANCIENT KINGDOM: SABA SHEBA
CAPITAL: SANA SANAA
COIN: RIAL RIYAL BUQSHA
MUSLIM SECT: SHIA SUNNI
OFFICIAL NAME:
  YEMENARABREPUBLIC
PEOPLE: ZAIDI SHAFAI
PORT: MOKA MOCHA
REGION: TIHAMA
RULER: IMAM
TOWN: MOKA DAMAR MOCHA TAIZZ
  HODEIDA

YEN EYES ITCH LONG URGE YEARN
  DESIRE SUCKER CRAVING LONGING
YENTA GOSSIP TALKER BUSYBODY
YEOMAN CHURL CLERK WRITER
  GOODMAN GUIDMAN GRAYCOAT
  RETAINER BEEFEATER
YERBA SANTA TARBUSH
YERK BEAT GOAD HURL JERK KICK
  STAB YARK THUMP EXCITE THRASH
  LASHING
YES AY DA IS JA OC SI YA AYE ISS YAS
  YAW YEA YEP YIS YUH YUS YEAH
  JOKOL TRULY
YESTERDAY HIER YESTER
  YESTREEN
  (OF —) PRIDIAN
YET AND BUT YIT EVEN STILL ALGATE
  HOWEER THOUGH FINALLY
  HOWEVER HITHERTO
  (AS —) SOFAR UPTONOW
YETI BIGFOOT SNOWMAN
  SASQUATCH
YETT GATE
YEUK EWK YUK ITCH YUCK ITCHING
YEW YO HEW UGH YOE YOW VIEW
  TAXUS TOPIARY CHINWOOD
YEX YOLK
YIDDISH JEWISH
YIELD GO BOW CUT ILD PAN PLY
  BEAR BEND CAST CEDE CESS COME
  CROP DRAG DUCK EMIT FOLD GIVE

HEAR HELD LOUT QUIT SELL VAIL
WAGE AGREE ALLOW AMAIN AVALE
AWALE BRING BUDGE CARRY CAUSE
DEFER GRANT HEALD HIELD LEAVE
OFFER SLAKE STOOP ACCEDE
AFFORD BOUNTY BUCKLE COMPLY
CONFER FOLLOW IMPART OUTPUT
RELENT RENDER RETURN SUBMIT
SUPPLY SWERVE UNGIVE UPGIVE
ABANDON ANALYZE BEARING
CONCEDE DELIVER FURNISH
HARVEST KNUCKLE OUTTURN
PRODUCE PROVIDE REDOUND
RUCKSEY SUCCUMB BEGRUDGE
FRUITAGE OVERGIVE PICKINGS
UNDERLIE RELINQUISH
  (— FRUIT) ADDLE GRAIN
  (— GRASS) GRAZE
  (— OF FIELD) BURDEN
  (— OF MINE) BONANZA
  (— ON BOND) BASIS
  (— TO) INDULGE
  (— TO TEMPTATION) FALL
  (— UP) LET FORLET FORLEIT
  (— WELL) HIT BLEED
  (MINERAL —) PROSPECT
  (SUFF.) FER(ENCE)(ENT)(OUS)
YIELDED
  (SUFF.) GENETIC
YIELDING ABLE MEEK NESH SOFT
  TALL WAXY NAISH WAXEN BONAIR
  CAVING FACILE FEEBLE FLABBY
  LIMBER LITHER OUTPUT PLIANT
  QUAGGY SUPPLE BEARING CESSION
  FINGENT FLACCID DEDITION
  LADYLIKE RECREANT COMPLIANT
  COMPLIANCE SUBMISSIVE
  (— IRREGULARLY) BUNCHY
  (— OF HORSE) FLEXION
  (— STAGE) SEAR
  (— TO IMPULSES) ABANDON
  (— TO INFLUENCE) PLIABLE
  (— UNDERFOOT) SINKY
YIN SHANG
YIRMILIK METALLIK
YODEL SONG JODEL WARBLE
  REFRAIN
YODH IOD JOD
YOGA JOG
  (— POSITION) ASANA
YOGI JOGI FAKIR FAKEER
YOKE BOW YOK BAIL CROW DRAG
  FORK HOOP PAIR POKE SOLE TEAM
  BANGY FURCA SHEBA SPANG
  BANGHY COUPLE INSPAN DRAGBAR
  HARNESS OPPRESS ADJUGATE
  (— BAR) SKEY
  (— TO HOLD DRILL) CROW
  (— TO RAISE CANNON) BAIL
  (PREF.) ZYG(O)(OTO)
  (SUFF.) ZYGOMATIC ZYGOSIS
  ZYGOTE
YOKED (NOT —) AZYGOUS

YOKEFELLOW MATE FELLOW PARTNER YOKEMATE

YOKEL YOB BOOR CLUB JAKE JOCK LOUT YAHOO YOBBO FARMER JOSKIN BUMPKIN HAYSEED HOODLUM WAYBACK ABDERITE CHAWBACON

YOKING BOUT CONTEST MUGGING

YOKO ONO

YOLANTA (CHARACTER IN —) RENE ROBERT YOLANTA VAUDEMONT **(COMPOSER OF —)** TCHAIKOVSKY

YOLDRING YOWLEY

YOLK CENTER YELLOW ESSENCE LATEBRA VITELLUS PARABLAST **(HAVING A —)** LECITHAL **(PREF.)** LECITH(O) VITELLI VITELLO **(SUFF.)** LECITHAL

YON YONDER THITHER BACKWARD

YONDER THAT THERE THOSE THITHER

YORE PAST YARE YEARS **(OF —)** OLDEN

YORKER TICE

YORKSHIREMAN TIKE TYKE LEAROYD

YORUBA NAGO

YOU DU HE IT OW TA TU WE YA YO ONE OWE SHE SIE TOI YOW YUH THOU VOUS YOUSE YOURSELF

YOU CAN'T GO HOME AGAIN (AUTHOR OF —) WOLFE **(CHARACTER IN —)** ELSE JACK LLOYD ESTHER GEORGE KOHLER MCHARG WEBBER EDWARDS FOXHALL

YOU NEVER CAN TELL (AUTHOR OF —) SHAW **(CHARACTER IN —)** BOON BOHUM DOLLY GLORIA PHILIP CLANDON MCCOMAS WILLIAM GRAMPTON VALENTINE

YOUNG FRY JUV BIRD CALF DROP BIRTH BROOD FETUS FRUIT GREEN SMALL UNOLD JUNIOR KINDLE JUVENAL IMMATURE YEANLING YOUTHFUL **(— OF ANY ANIMAL)** FRY BABY CALF FOAL JOEY LAMB TOTO **(— OF BEAST)** SLINK **(— OF BIRD)** CHICK **(— OF CAMEL)** COLT **(— OF DOG)** WHELP **(— OF FISH)** FRY **(— OF SEA TROUT)** HERLING **(VERY —)** SUCKING NEPHIONIC SHIRTTAIL **(PREF.)** FETI FETO FOETI FOETO **(SUFF.) (— ONE)** LING **(MODE OF HATCHING —)** PAEDES

YOUNGER KID LESS PUNEE JUNIOR PUISNE OFFSPRING

YOUNGEST (— OF BROOD) WALLYDRAG

YOUNGSTER KID BIRD COLT CHILD MINOR YOUTH BUTTON SHAVER URCHIN YONKER YOUNKER SPALPEEN

YOUNKER DUPE CHILD KNIGHT NOVICE SQUIRE YUNKER

YOUR OR YO THY YAR YER OURE OWRE SEIN VOTRE YOURN

YOURSELF ITSELF HERSELF HIMSELF ONESELF

YOUTH BOY BUD IMP LAD CHAP COLT PAGE TEEN BAHUR CHABO GROOM HYLAS POULT PRIME SPRIG SWAIN WHELP BOCHUR BURSCH EPHEBE HOYDEN INFANT JUVENT KOUROS MASTER NONAGE SPRING SQUIRT YONKER CALLANT EPHEBOS GOSSOON JUVENAL PUBERTY SAPLING YOUDITH YOUNGTH ENDYMION JUVENILE SPRINGAL **(— WHO SERVES LIQUORS)** GANYMEDE **(AWKWARD —)** HOBBLEDEHOY **(DELINQUENT —)** BODGIE **(GODDESS OF —)** HEBE **(IMPUDENT —)** SQUIRT **(INEXPERIENCED —)** GUNSEL GREENHORN **(NON-JEWISH —)** SHEGETZ **(PERT —)** PRINCOX **(RUDE —)** HOYDEN **(RUSSIAN — ORGANIZATION)** KOMSOMOL **(SILLY —)** CALF SLENDER **(WELLBORN —)** CHILD **(WORLD'S —)** PRIME **(PREF.)** HEBE

YOUTHFUL RATH FRESH GREEN YOUNG BOYISH GOLDEN JUNIOR MAIDEN NEANIC VERNAL VIRGIN YOUTHY LADDISH PUERILE YOUNGLY IMMATURE JUVENILE SPRINGAL VIGOROUS

YOUTHFULNESS JEUNESSE

YOWL GOWL HOWL WAIL YELL YELP

YO-YO FLUCTUATE VACILLATE

YUAN DOLLAR

YUAPIN YARURA

YUCATAN (— PEOPLE) MAYA MAYAS

YUCATEC MAYA

YUCCA LILY PITA YUCA AGAVE DATIL IZOTE PALMA JOSHUA LILIAL LILIUM PALMITO SOAPWEED

YUCKY ICKY DIRTY NASTY SLIMY DISGUSTING

YUGA KALI

YUGOSLAVIA
CAPITAL: BEOGRAD BELGRADE
COIN: PARA DINAR
FORMER REPUBLIC: BOSNIA CROATIA SLOVENIA
GULF: KOTOR

LAKE: OHRID PRESPA SCUTARI
MEASURE: RIF AKOV RALO DONUM KHVAT LANAZ STOPA MOTYKA PALAZE RALICO
MOUNTAIN: DURMITOR
MOUNTAIN RANGE: DINARIC
PORT: KOTOR NOVISAD BELGRADE
REPUBLIC: SERBIA MONTENEGRO
RIVER: DRIM IBAR SAVA DRINA RASKA TISZA DANUBE MORAVA VARDAR
TOWN: NIS BUDVA USKUB BITOLJ PRILEP TETOVO CATTARO NOVISAD PRIZREN SKOPLJE MONASTIR SUBOTICA
WEIGHT: OKA OKE DRAMM TOVAR WAGON SATLIJK

YUKON TERRITORY (CAPITAL OF —) WHITEHORSE
(LAKE OF —) KLUANE
(MOUNTAIN OF —) LOGAN
(MOUNTAIN RANGE OF —) OGILVIE STIKINE MACKENZIE
(RIVER OF —) PEEL LEWES LIARD PELLY WHITE KLONDIKE PORCUPINE
(TOWN OF —) ELSA MAYO BARLOW DAWSON
YULE NOEL CHRISTMAS
YUMA CUCHAN
YUMAN PATAYAN
YUNX WRYNECK
YURT TENT

Z

Z ZAD ZED ZEE ZETA ZULU IZARD ZEBRA IZZARD
  (SHAPED LIKE A —) OPENBAND
ZAAVAN (FATHER OF —) EZER
ZABAD (FATHER OF —) NEBO ZATTU NATHAN
  (MOTHER OF —) SHIMEATH
ZABAGLIONE SABAYON
ZABBAI (SON OF —) BARUCH
ZABBUD (FATHER OF —) BIGVAI
ZABDI (FATHER OF —) ASAPH ZERAH
ZABDIEL (SON OF —) JASHOBEAM
ZABUD (FATHER OF —) NATHAN
ZACCUR (FATHER OF —) IMRI ASAPH JAAZIAH
  (SON OF —) HANAN SHAMMUA
ZACHARIAH (DAUGHTER OF —) ABIJAH
  (FATHER OF —) JEROBOAM
ZACHARIAS (FATHER OF —) BARACHIAS
  (SON OF —) JOHN
  (WIFE OF —) ELISABETH
ZACHER (FATHER OF —) JEHIEL
  (MOTHER OF —) MAACHAH
ZADOK (DAUGHTER OF —) JERUSHAH
  (FATHER OF —) BAANA IMMER AHITUB MERAIOTH
ZAFFER SMALT SAFFIOR ZAPHARA
ZAGREUS (FATHER OF —) JUPITER
  (MOTHER OF —) PROSERPINE
ZAHAM (FATHER OF —) REHOBOAM
  (MOTHER OF —) ABIHAIL

ZAIRE
BOMU UELE
ALTERNATE NAME: CONGO
CAPITAL: KINSHASA
COIN: SENGI LIKUTA MAKUTA
COINS: MAKUTA
LAKE: KIVU MWERU
LANGUAGE: KIKONGO LINGALA SWAHILI TSHILUBA
MONEY: ZAIRE
MOUNTAIN RANGE: MITUMBA VIRUNGA RUWENZORI
PROVINCE: KIVU KASAI SHABA EQUATOR KATANGA BANDUNDU EQUATEUR ORIENTAL
RIVER: RUKI UELE CONGO DENGU IBINA KASAI LINDI LIKATI LOMAMI LUKUGA UBANGI ARUWIMI LUALABA LULONGA

TOWN: BAYA BOMA LEBO AKETI BUKAVU KAMINA KIKWIT MATADI BUTEMBO KANANGA KOLWEZI BAKWANGA YANGAMBI KISANGANI

ZALAPH (SON OF —) HANUN

ZAMBIA
CAPITAL: LUSAKA
COIN: NGWEE KWACHA
FALLS: VICTORIA
LAKE: MWERU BANGWEULU TANGANYIKA
LANGUAGE: LOZI BEMBA TONGA LUVALE NYANJA AFRIKAANS
MOUNTAIN RANGE: MUCHINGA
RIVER: KAFUE LUANGWA LUAPULA ZAMBEZI
TOWN: KITWE NDOLA LUAPULA LUANSHYA MUFULIRA
WATERFALL: VICTORIA

ZAMBO CHINO SAMBO CAFUSO CURIBOCA
ZAMIA BANGA CICAD CYCAD COONTIE
ZAMINDAR MALIK
ZAMOUSE GAMOUS
ZAMPOGNA BAGPIPE PANPIPE
ZANDER ZANT PERCID SANDER SANDRA
ZANTHOXYLUM FAGARA
ZANY NUT FOOL CRAZY TOADY SAWNEY BUFFOON IDIOTIC CLOWNISH SCREWBALL
ZANZIBAR (SEE TANZANIA)
ZAP ZIP ZONK MICROWAVE
ZAPARO IQUITO
ZAPATERO LIMA BOXWOOD CERILLO
ZARA (FATHER OF —) JUDAH
ZARAH KAZOO
ZARPANIT (HUSBAND OF —) MERODACH
ZAZA (FATHER OF —) JONATHAN
ZEAL FIRE MOOD ARDOR FLAME HEART FERVOR WARMTH DEVOTION GOODWILL JEALOUSY
  (MORBID —) ZELOTYPIA
  (WITH —) DINGDONG
  (PREF.) ZELO
ZEALOT BIGOT VOTARY VOTEEN ZELANT DEVOTEE FANATIC CANANEAN SERAPHIC SICARIUS VOTARESS VOTARIST
ZEALOUS HOT AVID HIGH ARDENT FERVID STRING CORDIAL DEVOTED

EARNEST EMULOUS FERVENT
FORWARD JEALOUS PUSHFUL
VIGOROUS PERFERVID RELIGIOUS
(— ABOUT BEAUTY) ESTHETIC
ZEALOUSLY FAST INNERLY
HEARTILY
ZEBADIAH (FATHER OF —) ASAHEL
ISHMAEL JEROHAM MICHAEL
MESHELEMIAH
ZEBAH (SLAYER OF —) GIDEON
ZEBEDEE (SON OF —) JOHN JAMES
(WIFE OF —) SALOME
ZEBINA (FATHER OF —) NEBO
ZEBRA DAUW EQUID HORSE
QUAGGA SOLIPED
ZEBRA FISH DANIO
ZEBRAWOOD ARAROBA ZINGANA
ZEBU BRAMIN BRAGMAN BRAHMIN
(HYBRID OF — AND CATTLE)
CATTABU
(HYBRID OF — AND YAK) ZOBO
ZEBUDAH (HUSBAND OF —) JOSIAH
(SON OF —) JEHOIAKIM
ZEBULUN (FATHER OF —) JACOB
(SON OF —) ELON
ZECCHINO SEQUIN
ZECHARIAH (DAUGHTER OF —) ABI
ABIJAH
(FATHER OF —) IDDO BEBAI HOSAH
JEHIEL PASHUR ISSHIAH PHAROSH
JEHOIADA JONATHAN BERECHIAH
JEBERECHIAH JEHOSHAPHAT
MESHELEMIAH
(SON OF —) JAHAZIEL
ZEDEKIAH (BROTHER OF —)
JEHOAHAZ
(FATHER OF —) JOSIAH HANANIAH
MAASEIAH CHENAANAH
(MOTHER OF —) HAMUTAL
ZEDOARY SETWALL
ZELOPHEHAD (FATHER OF—)
HEPHER
ZELUS (FATHER OF —) PALLAS
(MOTHER OF —) STYX
(SISTER OF —) NIKE
ZEMIRA (FATHER OF —) BECHER
ZEN (— PARADOX) KOAN
(— QUESTIONS) MONDO
ZENANA HAREM HARIM SERAGLIO
ZEND AVESTAN
ZENICK SURICATE
ZENITH ACME PEAK HIGHT PITCH
HEIGHT SUMMIT VERTEX
ZENOBIA (HUSBAND OF —)
ODENATHUS
ZEOLITE ANALCIME ANALCITE
STILBITE GMELINITE NATROLITE
PHACOLITE
ZEPHANIAH (FATHER OF —)
MAASEIAH
(SON OF —) JOSIAH
ZEPHO (FATHER OF —) ELIPHAZ

ZEPHON (FATHER OF —) GAD
ZEPHYR FINE SOFT BERLIN BREEZE
ZEPHYRUS FAVONIUS
(FATHER OF —) AEOLUS ASTRAEUS
(MOTHER OF —) EOS
(SON OF —) CARPOS
(WIFE OF —) CHLORIS
ZEPPELIN ZEP ZEPP AIRSHIP
ZERAH (FATHER OF —) IDDO REUEL
SIMEON
ZERBINETTE (FATHER OF —)
ARGANTE
ZERBINO (BELOVED OF —) ISABELLA
(COMPANION OF —) ORLANDO
(SISTER OF —) GINEVRA
(SLAYER OF —) MANDRICARDO
ZERESH (HUSBAND OF —) HAMAN
ZERETH (FATHER OF —) ASHUR
(MOTHER OF —) HELAH
ZERI (FATHER OF —) JEDUTHUN
ZERO OH NIL NUL BLOB DUCK NULL
AUGHT CLOSE EMPTY OUGHT TRAIN
ZILCH ABSENT CIPHER NAUGHT
LACKING NOTHING NULLITY
SCRATCH NINETEEN
(EQUAL TO —) NILPOTENT
(HAVING — AS LIMIT) NULL
(HAVING VARIABLES EQUAL TO —)
TRIVIAL
ZERUAH (FATHER OF —) NEBAT
(SON OF —) JEROBOAM
ZERUIAH (SON OF —) JOAB ASAHEL
ABISHAI
ZEST EDGE ELAN JASM LIFE GUSTO
SPICE FLAVOR RELISH STINGO
MUSTARD PIQUANCY
ZESTFUL RACY SPICY BREEZY
(— QUALITY) ZAP
ZESTY ZINGY
ZETES (BROTHER OF —) CALAIS
(FATHER OF —) BOREAS
(MOTHER OF —) ORITHYIA
ZETHAM (FATHER OF —) LAADAN
ZETHUS (BROTHER OF —) AMPHION
(FATHER OF —) JUPITER
(MOTHER OF —) ANTIOPE
ZEUS ZAN SOTER ALASTOR CRONION
KRONION POLIEUS CRONIDES
(BROTHER OF —) HADES POSEIDON
(FATHER OF —) CRONUS KRONOS
(MOTHER OF —) RHEA
(SISTER OF —) HERA HESTIA
DEMETER
(SON OF —) ARES ARCAS ARGUS
AEACUS AGACUS APOLLO HERMES
TITYUS PERSEUS DARDANUS
DIONYSUS HERCULES TANTALUS
(WIFE OF —) HERA JUNO METIS
THEMIS EURYNOME
(PREF.) ZENO
ZEUXIS UNDERLAY
ZHIVAGO YURI

ZIBEON (SON OF —) ANAH
ZIBIA (FATHER OF —) SHAHARAIM
(MOTHER OF —) HODESH
ZIBIAH (SON OF —) JOASH
ZICHRI (FATHER OF —) ASAPH IZHAR
(SON OF —) JOEL AMASIAH ELIEZER
ELISHAPHAT
ZIGZAG BOYAU CRANK BROKEN
INDENT SLALOM CRANKLE
CHEVRONY FLEXUOSE TRAVERSE
(PREF.) ZYZZO
ZILCH NIL ZAP ZIP ZERO ZING
NOTHING
ZILIANTE (BROTHER OF —) ORRIGILLE
(FATHER OF —) MONODANTE
(SISTER OF —) BRANDIMARTE
ZILPAH (SON OF —) GAD ASHER
ZIMARRA CYMAR SIMAR CASSOCK
ZIMB FLY ZEBUB

ZIMBABWE
CAPITAL: HARARE SALISBURY
DIVISION: RHODESIA
LANGUAGE: ILA BANTU SHONA
NDEBELE
PEOPLE: BANTU MASHOMA
MATABELE BALOKWAKWA
RIVER: SABI GWAII LUNDI LIMPOPO
SANYATI ZAMBEZI
TOWN: GWELO UMTALI BULAWAYO
WATERFALL: VICTORIA

ZIMMAH (FATHER OF —) SHIMEI
ZIMRAN (MOTHER OF —) KETURAH
ZIMRI (FATHER OF —) SALU ZERAH
ZINA (FATHER OF —) SHIMEI
ZINC FAR SPELT ZINCUM SPELTER
TUTENAG EXCLUDER
(— SALT) ZIRAM
(KIND OF —) MOSSY
ZING PEP VIM ZAP ZIP DASH SNAP
ENERGY SPIRIT RAZZMATAZZ
ZINGEL PERCID
ZINGER MOT
ZINGY ZESTY
ZINKE CORNET
ZINNIA CRASSINA
ZION SION ISRAEL UTOPIA
ZIONIST IRGUNIST
ZIP NIL VIM ZAP DASH NADA SEAL
SNAP ZERO ZING FORCE OOMPH
WHISK ZILCH BUTTON ENERGY
STINGO NOTHING
ZIPHAH (FATHER OF —) JEHALELEEL
ZIPHION (FATHER OF —) GAD
ZIPPER FASTENER
(PART OF —) TAB FACE PULL STOP
TAPE CHAIN SLIDE TOOTH
ZIPPOR (SON OF —) BALAK
ZIPPORAH (FATHER OF —) REUEL
JETHRO
(HUSBAND OF —) MOSES
(SON OF —) ELIEZER GERSHOM

ZIPPY ZAPPY
ZIRCON JARGON AZORITE MALACON
HYACINTH STARLITE
ZITHER KIN QIN CANON CANUN
GUSLI KANOON CITHARA GITERNE
GITTERN AUTOHARP GALEMPONG
(JAPANESE —) KOTO
ZITHER HARP KOTO
ZIZA (FATHER OF —) SHIPHI
REHOBOAM
(MOTHER OF —) MAACHAH
ZIZITH SISITH FRINGES TASSELS
TSITSITH
ZO DZO ZOH ZOBO
ZOARITE BIMMELER
ZOBEBAH (FATHER OF —) COZ
ZOBO ZO DZO ZOH ZOBU
ZODIAC GIRDLE BALDRIC BAWDRICK
SIGNIFIER
(SECTION OF —) TRIGON
(SIGN OF —) LEO RAM BULL CRAB
FISH GOAT LION ARIES LIBRA SCALE
TWINS VIRGO ARCHER CANCER
GEMINI PISCES TAURUS SCORPIO
AQUARIUS CAPRICORN
ZOHAR (FATHER OF —) SIMEON
(SON OF —) EPHRON
ZOHETH (FATHER OF —) ISHI
ZOISITE THULITE
ZONA ZOSTER
ZONE BED AREA BAND BEAM BELT
HALO PLAGE TRACT CIRCLE REGION
ZODIAC CLIMATE HORIZON
ZONULET CINCTURE CINGULUM
FRONTIER HABENULA HISTOGEN
STRINGER
(— OF CONFLICT) FRONT
(— OF FLAME) MANTLE
(— OF MINERALS) CORONA
(— OF VENUS) CEST CESTUS
(ABYSSAL —) BASSALIA
(PALEONTOLOGIC —S) ASSISE
(SAFETY —) ISLET ISLAND REFUGE
(STRATOGRAPHIC —) HEMERA
(WELDING —) ROOT
ZONK WASTE
ZONKED GONZO
ZOO (KIND OF —) PETTING
ZOOECIUM AUTOPORE
ZOOID PERSON SIPHON BRYOZOAN
HYDRANTH POLYPIDE ZOOTHOME
ZOOLOGIST AMERICAN DEAN GILL
ADAMS ALLEN BAIRD BAKER BIRGE
CLARK GOULD GUYER MORSE SHULL
BINNEY BROOKS BUTLER CASTLE
ELLIOT FISHER GARMAN HOLMES
KOFOID MORGAN NEWMAN OLIVER
PARKER RIDDLE STILES WILDER
WILSON AGASSIZ ANDREWS
BARTSCH BIGELOW FERNALD
KELLOGG MCCLUNG NUTTING
VERRILL WHITMAN CRAMPTON
GRINNELL HORNADAY KIRTLAND

MELANDER SHELFORD COCKERELL
DAVENPORT SANDERSON
PETRUNKEVITCH
AUSTRIAN FRISCH
BELGIAN BENEDEN
CANADIAN ANDERSON
DANISH STEENSTRUP
ENGLISH BUSK GRAY OWEN ELTON
FLOWER GROGAN LISTER MORGAN
MORRIS MURRAY NEWTON PARKER
BEDDARD DURRELL GUNTHER
HASWELL MEDAWAR POULTON
YARRELL GOODRICH MACBRIDE
MITCHELL
FRENCH CUVIER DELAGE PERRIER
DUJARDIN BLAINVILLE
VALENCIENNES
GERMAN VOGT BREHM BRONN
CARUS CLAUS DOHRN BOVERI
FRISCH LEYDIG MOBIUS MULLER
GRZIMEK HAECKEL HERTWIG
SIEBOLD SPEMANN BUTSCHLI
GUENTHER BECHSTEIN LEUCKHART
SCHAUDINN BLUMENBACH
GOLDSCHMIDT REICHENBACH
LICHTENSTEIN
ITALIAN GRASSI
NORWEGIAN SARS NANSEN
RUSSIAN PANDER KOVALEVSKI
METCHNIKOFF
SWEDISH LOVEN
ZOOM ZAP SPEED

ZOOPHYTE CORAL SPONGE
HYDROID
ZOOSPORE MONAD SWARMER
ZOOCARP
ZOPHAH (FATHER OF —) HELEM
HOTHAM
ZOPHAI (FATHER OF —) ELKANAH
ZORIL SKUNK POWCAT CHINCHE
POLECAT MUISHOND
ZOROASTRIAN GABAR PARSI
GUEBRE PARSEE
ZOROASTRIANISM MAZDAISM
ZOUAVE ZUZU SCALER ZOUZOU
ZOUNDS OONS WAUNS ZOONS
ZUAR (SON OF —) NETHANEEL
ZUCCHETTO CALOTTE SOLIDEO
SKULLCAP
ZUCCHINI COURGETTE
ZULU CAR TRAIN LUGGER MATABELE
ZUNI CIBOLAN SHALAKO
ZUR (FATHER OF —) JEHIEL
(SON OF —) COZBI
ZURIEL (FATHER OF —) ABIHAIL
ZWINGLIAN TIGURINE
ZYGOMATIC JUGAL
ZYGOSPORE COPULA
ZYGOTE OOCYST OOSPERM
OOSPORE SPORONT OOKINETE
ZYME YEAST ZYMIN ENZYME
FERMENT
ZYMOGEN PEPSINOGEN
ZYRIAN KOMI SYRYAN